THE CHARLTON STANDARD CA

HOCKEY CARDS

NINTH EDITION

published under agreement by

P. M. Fiocca, Publisher
ST. CATHARINES, ONTARIO

W. K. Cross, Publisher
TORONTO, ONTARIO ❖ BIRMINGHAM, MICHIGAN

Canadian Cataloguing in Publication Data

Main entry under title:
The Charlton standard catalogue of hockey cards

Annual.
4th ed.(1993) -
Prepared for Charlton International Inc.
Continues: Charlton hockey card price guide, ISSN 1183-3033
ISSN 1188-7737
ISBN 0-88968-201-1 (9th ed.)

1. Hockey cards - Prices - Periodicals. I. Charlton International Inc.

GV847.C5 769'.497962'0294 C93-030455-1

Printed in Canada
in the Province of Ontario

Editorial Office
103 Lakeshore Road, Suite 202
St. Catharines, Ontario L2N 2T6
Tel: (905) 646-7744 1-800-408-0352
Fax: (905) 646-0995
Website: www.trajan.com
E-mail: office@trajan.com

The Charlton Press

Editorial Office
2040 Yonge Street, Suite 208
Toronto, Ontario M4S 1Z9
Tel: (416) 488-1418 1-800-442-6042
Fax: (416) 488-4656 1-800-442-1542
Website: www.charltonpress.com
E-mail: chpress@charltonpress.com

EDITORIAL

Project Editor	Richard Scott	Production Co-ordinator	Jan Coles
Associate Editors	Baron Bedesky, Lisa Scott	Production Team	Cheryl Venneri
Advertising Sales	Paul Starrs		Mary-Anne Leftley
Publisher	Paul M. Fiocca		Sylvie Tremblay
			Jim Szeplaki

ACKNOWLEDGEMENTS

The Charlton Press and Trajan Publishing Corporation wish to thank all of those who have in the past helped and assisted with The Charlton Standard Catalogue of Hockey Cards.

COLLECTOR CONTRIBUTORS TO THE 9TH EDITION

Ken Creppin, Jukka Vesteren, Steve Rimbault, John Mele, Robert and Ceka Butt, Evan and Brian Owen, John Eadie, Dave Sainsbury, Michel Dubois, Steven Singer, John Wessel, John Doolittle, Angelo Savelli, Selby Colson, Steve Panet, George Gray, Bob Boin, Mark Lee, Eric Beamish, Peter Semerak, George Bridgman, Ronald Villeneuve, Bill Fougere, Terry Brunt, Jari Laakso, Dave and Ron Gibara, Dave Bullis, Bruce Morrison, Darcy Alyea, Joe and Travis Daley, Rob Noyes, Marcel Lavalée, Joe Culligan, Joe Herries, Scott Dean, Rick Plett, Larry Fleming, Len Pottie, Derek Creppin, Ralph Slate, André Archambault, Brad Lightfoot, Bob Blaine, Jim Macie, Jerry Davis, Walter Zakrevsky, Terry Doney, Ross Frizzell, Richard Scarpino, Claude Forget, Aubrey Ferguson, John Wayne Roman, Ken Dool, Tim Melburn, Justin Santoro, Garry Macks

INSTITUTIONAL CONTRIBUTORS

Mike Monson, Pacific Trading Cards; **Melissa Rosen and Kevin Crux,** Topps Chewing Gum; **Jeff Morris,** Pinnacle Brands; **Doug Drotman,** Donruss Trading Cards; **Steve Ryan,** Upper Deck Company; **Rich Bradley, Doug Drotman,** Fleer/SkyBox; **Dan Graham,** Slapshot Images; **Peter Carlson, Antonio Piacente,** Sport FX; **David Sirianni,** Universal Coins; **Dino Fazio**, PHPA; **Carol Carney,** OHL; **Michael Merhab, Nick Pedota,** NHLPA.

CONTRIBUTING RETAIL DEALERS

Joseph E. Filion, Cartomania; **Andrew Kossman**, Action Coin & Card; **Harvey Goldfarb,** A.J. Cards; **Léandre Normand,** Promodium; **Mike & Mary Drandzyk**, Kitchener Coin Shop; **Hans-Lee Tan**, Game Breakers; **Rami Jaber**, Coin de la Carte Sportive; **Brad Norris-Jones**, MVP Sports; **David Chu,** Toronto Sportscards; **Bruce Romaniuk,** Triple C Auctions; **Gary Gagen,** Let's Collect; **John Brenner,** Lookin' For Heroes; **George Kumagai,** Major Leagues; **Frank Leardi,** Frank Leardi Sports Cards**;** **Andre Yip-Hoi,** Time-Out Sports Cards; **Jason Martin,** Martin's Sports Cards; **Bruce Lounsbury,** Bozley's Cards & Collectables; **Doug Scott,** Maple Leaf Cards & Videos; **Daniel May,** The Sports Connection, **Kevin Lawr**, Niagara Sports Cards, **Al Willard,** AJW Sports Cards

CORRECTIONS

The publisher welcomes information, for future editions, from interested collectors, manufacturers and retail dealers concerning any aspect of the listings in this book.

New material deadline for tenth edition is August 15, 1999.

1962 TOPPS
BOBBY HULL
#33
NM 7
05011325
BOBBY HULL
CHICAGO BLACK HAWKS FORWARD
GORDIE HOWE
#8
EX-MT 6
02024273
Gordie Howe Right Wing
DETROIT RED WINGS
1963-64
#55
PARKHURST
CSA140758
GORDIE HOWE
9-MINT

TABLE OF CONTENTS

CHAPTER THREE - NHL TEAM SETS

CHAPTER FOUR- WHA TEAM SETS

CHAPTER FIVE- MINOR LEAGUE TEAM SETS

CHAPTER SIX- JUNIOR/COLLEGE TEAM SETS

CHAPTER SEVEN
ALPHABETICAL PLAYER INDEX

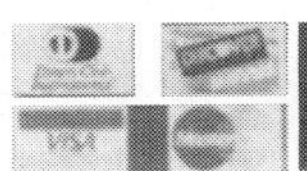

THE
SPORTS
CONNECTION
INC.

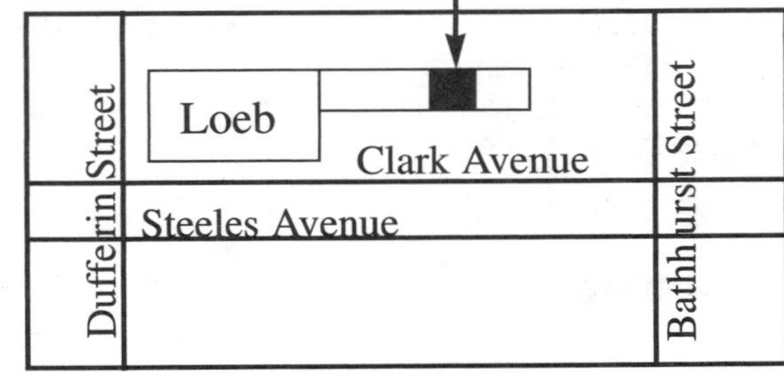
The Sports Connection, Unit #19
Loeb
Clark Avenue
Steeles Avenue
Dufferin Street
Bathhurst Street

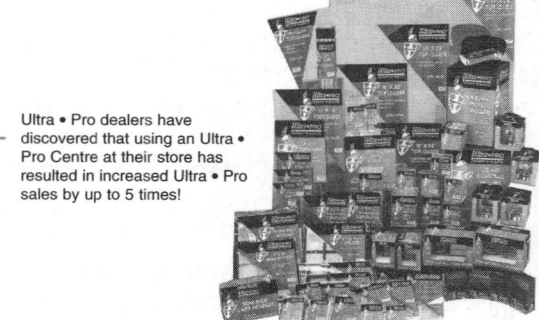

INTRODUCTION

By Richard Scott

Welcome to the ninth edition of the *Charlton Standard Catalogue of Hockey Cards*. In this book, you will find set checklists and price listings for every known hockey set since 1879.

This book is organized into seven chapters. The first chapter from the last edition has been split into two chapters: one for vintage issues (pre World War II) and one for modern issues (post World War II). All sets are listed in chronological order in these two chapters. The only exception is the three groups of BeeHive photos that were released from 1934 through 1967: these popular photos are listed at the beginning of chapter two.

Within each year, sets are listed alphabetically by brand name. Brand names used in this book, primarily with issues from the modern era, are usually found on the card front. Minor, junior and European league sets are also listed chronologically in these two chapters. National team sets are also listed in chapters one and two. Unless otherwise noted, chapter two cards from 1980 forward are all the standard 2-1/2" by 3-1/2" size.

Each check box on the left-hand side of a column represents a single card. Two or more check boxes for one card line denotes parallel versions exist. The number of boxes represents the number of different cards. This rule applies throughout the book.

The only sets not listed in these first two chapters are the team issued or team specific sets. Chapter three covers National Hockey League team sets, chapter four covers World Hockey Association and other international team sets, chapter five covers minor league team sets and chapter six covers junior and college team sets.

Chapters three through six are all organized alphabetically by team and then chronologically by date of issue. Prices are given for complete sets, the most expensive singles and the least expensive singles. Prices are also given for panel or cut-out versions.

All prices in chapters one through six represent average retail values from the past year and are listed in Canadian dollars. Prices are specific to different grading conditions.

The last chapter is an alphabetical index to chapters one through six. Any player card can be cross-referenced using this section. Cards are listed alphabetically by brand instead of chronologically by date of issue. Topps cards from 1968-69 through 1991-92 are listed with O-Pee-Chee cards from the same era. Chapter one and two cards are always listed first, followed by chapter three, four, five, and six cards.

This chapter can even help you identify the brand or year of any card. It can also help you keep track of a player's full list of cards.

Collectors can use the table of contents at the front of the book as well as the alphabetical table of contents found in the appendix. The appendix also has a glossary of terms and abbreviations.

PRICING FOR THE 9TH EDITION

Every set in this book has been carefully monitored over the last year for price changes. The majority of these price movements are followed every month in *Canadian Sportscard Collector.* As mentioned earlier, prices in this book reflect retail selling values from the past year. With that said, it is very important to remember that not all cards are sold at "guide" value: cards are often sold above or below guide values.

Many hobbyists continue to be attracted to new cards. With more than 30 mainstream hockey sets released in 1997-98, there were more new cards than any other given year. With the stream of new releases flowing in every month, many middle-dollar cards from the present decade were discounted to make room for the latest series. Dealers were most willing to sell off mainstream singles and inserts at reduced prices and these trends have been reflected in the ninth edition.

Rookie cards have been especially popular over the last 12 months. While many of the NHL's new superstars only have rookie cards in supply-plenty sets such as 1990-91 Score and 1991-92 Upper Deck, some exciting future stars from the past two seasons do have rookie cards in much more sought after sets. Some of the more exciting rookie cards this past season included Sergei Samsonov's 1994-95 SP card and Alexei Morozov's 1994-95 Select card. With both of these cards, it is important to note that it was the rookie card and not any parallel issues that was being tracked down by collectors. For this reason, you will see that prices for some rookie cards have increased while the price for their tougher parallel issue (if any) has stayed the same or decreased.

Despite all the attention paid to new cards, there remains a good deal of activity in vintage and older cards. The most important criteria in pricing older cards is the grade. High grade cards, whether Excellent-Mint, Near Mint or Mint, always command much higher prices than lower grade cards. Collectors and dealers should always take care in grading their cards when it comes to pricing these older issues. Professionally graded cards, especially those in high grades, are almost always sold at a premium.

The final note on pricing for the ninth edition has to do with retired players. While none of these players are still active to command greater or weaker demands vis-a-vis their peers, a few significant events and milestones that took place over the last year did bring renewed attention to some of these players and their cards. The most significant of these events was the unveiling of *The Hockey News*' 50 greatest NHL players of all-time. The list ranked NHL players from all eras against each other and sparked a great deal of discussion amongst hockey fans and collectors alike. Other significant events and milestones from the past year included the World Hockey Association's 25th anniversary and the creation of the Maurice Richard Trophy for each season's NHL goal scoring champion starting in 1998-99.

HISTORY OF THE HOCKEY CARD

By Baron Bedesky

Manufactured in Canada long before the arrival of baseball and football cards, the first hockey card sets were distributed in cigarette packages during the 1910-13 era. Only three C sets were produced before World War I, with cards measuring 1-1/2" X 2-1/2". The backs of these cards list the player's team membership history.

The first set issued for the 1910-11 season, titled Hockey Series, featured coloured portraits of the leading players. The Hockey Players series of the 1911-12 season is the easiest of the earlier sets to complete and featured players from the Québec, Ottawa, Renfrew, Wanderers, and Montréal teams. The scarce 1912-13 Hockey Series issue featured black and white portraits of players from eastern and western Canadian teams.

After World War I, only one more cigarette set was issued, during the 1924-25 season by Champ's Cigarettes of Hamilton, Ontario. The sepia-toned set featured players from the six NHL teams.

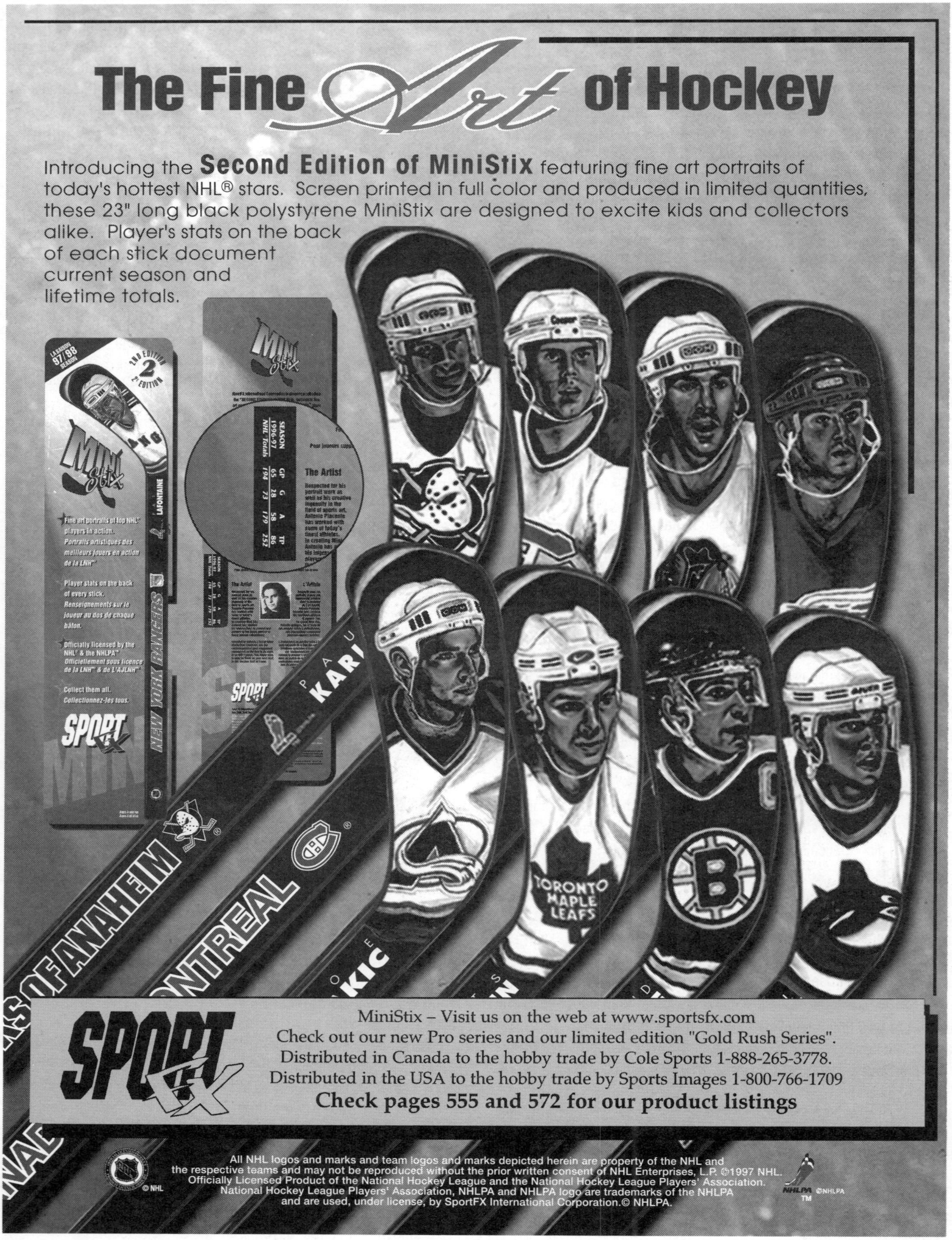

Several food and candy manufacturers produced hockey sets during the 1920s. Paulin's Candy, Maple Crispette, Crescent, Holland Creameries and La Patrie are among those known to have issued sets. The backs of the cards contain information on promotional gift offers that were available by returning a complete card set to the company. On receiving the completed sets, the companies would stamp or punch the cards and return them along with the gift. For this reason, mint condition cards of these sets are very difficult to find. The sets of the 1920s are particularly scarce because their distribution was regional.

Four gum manufacturers Canadian Chewing Gum, Hamilton Chewing Gum, O-Pee-Chee Co., and World Wide Chewing Gum Co. appeared on the scene during the 1933-34 season. O-Pee-Chee outskated its rivals by producing cards with a variety of background colours and more attractive designs, and was the only chewing gum company to issue cards up to the 1940-41 season when production stopped because of World War II.

Hockey cards didn't appear again until the 1951-52 season. A number of food companies joined the popular game with brief promotional appearances. Of these, three of the common household names were York Peanut Butter, Shirriff Desserts and Post Cereal.

Parkhurst Products of Toronto, Ontario, was the major unchallenged issuer for the first three seasons starting in 1951. O-Pee-Chee of London, Ontario, and Topps of Brooklyn, New York, entered the picture during the 1954-55 season.

Topps and O-Pee-Chee missed the next two years, then started up again during the 1957-58 season. The Parkhurst issues lacked originality and had more regional distribution. In contrast, Topps and O-Pee-Chee distributed issues across the nation, featuring more colourful cards and more player information. By the end of the 1963-64 season, Parkhurst was forced to take an extended leave of absence from the arena.

After affiliating in 1968, the Topps/O-Pee-Chee alliance became the dominant North American supplier of hockey cards, with O-Pee-Chee supplying Canada and Topps supplying the United States. The relationship lasted through the 1994-95 season when O-Pee-Chee announced it was discontinuing production and distribution of hockey cards, leaving the responsibilities solely with Topps. After the 1995-96 season, Topps announced they had not reached a new agreement with the NHL and NHLPA to produce cards. It was the end of an era.

Collectors, however, had no reason to worry about new cards. Since the 1990-91 season, a number of new companies have thrown their hats into the ring. Whereas hobbyists were accustomed to one or two different hockey card products being available every year, no fewer than four different manufacturers became involved: OPC/Topps, Pro Set, Score and Upper Deck. These companies were joined by Fleer in 1991-92, and Donruss in 1993-94. Even the Parkhurst name was revived as those who still held rights to the company name reached an agreement with Upper Deck to print and distribute new Parkhurst product. After tremendous success initially, Pro Set was the first of the new players to bow out, releasing their final set in 1992-93 after only three years. The company filed for bankruptcy a few months later.

Upper Deck enjoyed a great deal of financial and critical success and their products quickly became an annual favourite of collectors. Score eventually evolved into Pinnacle Brands, and enhanced their share of the market by purchasing Donruss and releasing hockey cards under both brand names by the mid-1990s.

After a popular five-year run, the Parkhurst name was again retired after the 1995-96 season. Fleer stopped producing cards after 1996-97 and was effectively replaced by Pacific Trading Cards for the 1997-98 season.

Perhaps the most significant changes made by the manufacturers in the 1990s include the tremendous popularity of insert and parallel cards, and the fact that each manufacturer received a license to produce several different brands of hockey card. Whereas Topps or O-Pee-Chee produced only one set per year from the 1950s through the 1980s, card companies in the 1990s obtained licenses permitting them to produce as many as seven sets each per season. The result has seen well over 30 different hockey card products hit the market annually over the past few years.

Insert cards and parallel versions of regular sets, which are basically harder to find cards with lower print runs, have successfully been used to market products and generate sales as collectors buy more unopened product than they normally would in hopes of finding the scarcer cards.

Then along came the inserts. After a couple of years, single cards from regular sets disappeared from tables and showcases to make room for more expensive and more profitable "power" cards. Brand new hand-collated sets or singles almost became an afterthought or even a nuisance as people bought pack after pack, or box after box, in a quest for a Refractor, an Artist's Proof, a Press Proof or Electric Ice card.

No matter how hard you try to keep the hobby and business of card collecting in a positive light, there are some unpleasant aspects and issues that must be confronted from time to time. One of them is something commonly referred to as searching.

Hard core hobbyists know exactly what searching is. Casual collectors, especially youngsters, or even adults relatively new to the business may not be as aware. Everyone should familiarize themselves with the topic because whether they are aware of it or not, it can directly affect collectors.

Every collector loves to open packs and boxes of cards. It is a task steeped in tradition. There is a reason why nearly every card product is packaged and distributed in this manner. While some collectors claim buying unopened product is a bad investment and that hobbyists may be better off buying factory sets or hand-collated sets, looking at your pre-assembled set is not as appealing as the thrill of opening packs and trying to put your own set together.

There is a lottery aspect of opening packs. Most card manufacturers have gone out of their way to promote scarce and valuable insert or redemption cards available within the packs. With a little luck, a collector will buy a few packs and pull out an insert card worth anywhere from five dollars to hundreds or even *thousands* of dollars. On the surface, it is a great idea to help boost sales and put smiles on collectors faces. Along the way though, a monster has been created.

Many people have taken to examining packs or boxes of cards in an effort to figure out which packs contain the more valuable inserts. In the old days, this used to be a simple process. All you had to do was hold a wax-pack near a light and you were able to see the top or bottom card right through the thin wax paper. Others took things a step further and carefully opened a pack, removing any valuable cards and replacing them with commons, before carefully gluing and re-sealing the pack.

The card manufacturers responded with what they refer to as tamper-proof foil-packaging. When there is a will there is a way, however, and all the fancy foil, plastic, and mylar packaging has not been enough to stop some people from carefully opening packs at one end and re-crimping the pack after the search is complete. Unsuspecting buyers will not even be aware the packs they purchased have no good cards or inserts in them. Not many experienced collectors carefully scrutinize packs looking for signs of tampering. It is even more difficult for casual collectors to stay on their toes.

There are other methods of searching. Perhaps they are not as flagrantly immoral as opening packs and removing any good cards, but these methods still cross an ethical line.

Cards, packs, boxes and cases are usually assembled and collated mechanically. Contrary to popular belief, this does not ensure random distribution. Just about anyone will be able to figure out patterns of card and insert distribution after opening just a few boxes. An experienced person will open a case and know exactly which box has the most valuable inserts. Other boxes will be opened and an individual will know exactly which packages contain the most desirable cards.

Others go so far as to use weigh-scales and micrometers in an attempt to determine the contents of a pack. An insert card printed on thicker stock or on heavier foil-stock can be located quickly.

Before any collectors get too discouraged and figure they will never get another valuable card out of a wax package again, there are a few steps you can take to ensure you are not victimized.

Getting to know your dealer is the strongest piece of advice people in the industry will offer. Education is key.

If someone is selling boxes or packs for too cheap, beware. Chances are high that the product has been picked over.

It is also generally a good idea to make sure any wax boxes purchased are still wrapped in the clear plastic with the manufacturer's logo printed on it.

As the novelty of chasing inserts wears off or becomes too expensive, many collectors have moved on to the less confusing older card issues or even memorabilia and autographs.

Some hobbyists have avoided the insert craze altogether, but many others have been unable to resist temptation and sales have increased accordingly.

A number of other smaller manufacturers also dipped in and out of the market in the 1990s, covering a myriad of themes from the NHL Entry Draft to World Junior tournaments, members of the Hall of Fame to league All-Stars.

There remains tremendous popularity among collectors with these smaller-scale releases. They are commonly referred to as food issues or oddball cards. With the tremendous amount of product on the market, hobbyists have been forced to narrow their scope and many seem content to collect in order to put together collections from their local grocery store or fast food restaurant.

Despite a number of changes, there are more different ways than ever to collect hockey cards.

BUYING AND SELLING CARDS

Several avenues are available as sources for buying, selling, or trading individual cards and sets.

Naturally, like any business person, you want to sell your cards for the highest possible price and purchase them at the lowest possible price. Using this price guide as a reference, you will have to shop around to become familiar with pricing differences among the various sources. The sports card market is not as liquid as the stock market and a certain degree of patience is necessary to sell your cards at what you think is a fair price.

It's a good idea to keep abreast of the changing market by regularly reading the several monthly sports card periodicals available. These publications are very useful in keeping up-to-date on pricing fluctuations, collectors' personal advertisements and the dates and locations of shows, auctions, and conventions. *Canadian Sportscard Collector* is the only Canadian national publication available that can provide you with all of this information on a monthly basis.

Shows and conventions offer you the best opportunity to shop around and meet a wide range of dealers and collectors assembled under one roof. Not only do you have a huge selection of older cards to choose from, but you may also buy unopened product by the single pack or by the box.

Whether you are at the Sportscard Expo, or any other show for that matter, to spend $20 or $20,000, it is best to plan your approach. How you approach the show depends largely on what you are looking for and how much you want to spend.

Traditionally, early in a show is pivotal for the serious collector. If you are looking for pre-war vintage items, this is when you will likely do business. If you wait until the weekend, the good stuff is picked over.

Early is also a good time to browse. The crowd is usually small enough that you can get a good look at the different items each dealer has. You may find items you never knew existed. If you are at a large show, it will take a while to get a good look at what everybody has. Don't be afraid to bring a notebook and write down some of the good items you find. It will be the only way to remember where you saw them.

You may also find a corporate presence at a show. The earlier you visit the booths, the more likely you are to get good promo cards. Also, the corporate people are not as busy early on as they are later. You, as a collector, could get the opportunity to talk to some of the inside people at your favourite card companies.

It's also not a bad idea to make note of the show's autograph guests, so you can time your visit to the event around any autograph guests you want to meet.

If you are looking for new product, it may pay to buy these items later in the show. Soon enough, dealer price wars are well underway. Though you may get a better deal if you wait until the last minute, product is more plentiful earlier on.

The best deals in wax are found with products over a year old. Many dealers may be trying to clear out inventory, and you will find more $5 to $20 boxes of cards than you will know what to do with.

If you like cheap wax and cheap hand collated sets, later in a show can be a gold mine. Dealers are preparing to pack up from the show. They are tired, and may want to take back as little as possible. Complete sets can be found for as little as two to five dollars. There may not be a great investment potential in the purchase, but who cares? They are fun sets and they were cheap.

If you have certain sets or boxes you are looking for, be sure to make a want list and jot down prices as you make your first round of the show. Again, we can't tell you how important lists and role books can be in doing a big show. If you are filling in holes in old sets, lists are a given, and you may want to try a time when you know the crowd has thinned out. To fill a want list, you will need to take time to look for what you need. It can be hard in a crowd.

You may wish to maximize your profit by selling your cards on your own. You may advertise in a local newspaper or sports periodical or rent a booth space at a card show if you have a large collection to sell. But before you set out, take into consideration the time you must invest, advertising costs, miscellaneous expenses, your sales ability, and your knowledge of card collecting. These factors will all dictate your success.

For the collector who enjoys assembling a collection slowly, piece by piece, foil packs are usually available at your local convenience store.

If you are in a hurry to make a transaction, or you don't want the hassle of selling your cards yourself, you may choose a dealer as a source. Dealers are in touch with an extensive network of collectors and suppliers and are more knowledgeable at identifying potential buyers for your cards or locating the owners of elusive cards. You must be fully aware, however, that a dealer has to cover expenses and his primary reason for setting up shop is to make a profit. Dealers will pay anywhere from 10 per cent to 75 per cent of the book value depending on demand (measured as the time it takes the dealer to sell the item). You may also arrange for a dealer to accept your cards on consignment. This assures you that he will attempt to obtain the highest possible price, since he will charge a percentage of the sale price as his fee.

Direct mail is another source for obtaining cards. If you choose this route, it would be wise to start off buying small quantities of cards until you become accustomed with the quality of cards purchased unseen. This also gives you a chance to build up a rapport and trust with a mail-order dealer before engaging in larger purchases.

CARD CARE

In order to ensure the continued appreciation in value of your cards, you must keep card handling to a minimum. It is highly recommended that you obtain suitable storage containers to preserve the condition of your delicate cards. Items such as sleeves, boxes and binder sheets are commercially available in specific sizes in which to safely store your prized collectibles.

Card sleeves are handy for displaying single cards. Sleeves are made of various materials, ranging from pliable polypropylene and polyethylene, to a stiffer mylar, to hard acrylic and Plexiglass.

Specially designed cardboard boxes enable you to store hundreds of cards and also facilitate transportation or storage. Try to use boxes with flat bottoms since boxes with bottom flaps can damage your cards. Since some cardboard boxes may contain an element of acid, you may wish to insert your cards into individual sleeves before placing them in boxes. As an added precaution, take care not to place your valuable cards at either end of the box.

Plastic three-ring binder sheets with pockets are a popular means of holding and displaying cards. Make certain that the pockets will hold your cards snugly but not tightly, as some sheets are designed to hold a specific size of card. Sheets made of polyvinyl chloride (PVC) are less flexible and more transparent, but contain certain oils which may, after long periods of time, damage your cards. PVC may be detected by its customary vinyl odour, whereas polypropylene and polyethylene are odourless.

Needless to say, mint condition cards do not have foreign substances applied to them. Adding glue, tape, protective coating, or writing, removing tabs, applying elastic bands to stacks of cards or using photograph corners to store cards in a scrap album are all taboo.

Extreme environmental conditions will, in time, adversely affect the condition of your cards. Prolonged direct sunlight will remove the gloss from cards and fade their colours. High humidity or extreme changes in humidity will result in gradual deterioration and warping, while excessive heat will increase the rate of decomposition.

It's not necessary to handle cards with gloves or tongs, just be aware of the adverse affects of mishandling and take a realistic approach to preserving the condition of your cards.

CARD GRADING

Grading any collectable item is always a subjective decision, but grading is the most important characteristic the collector must understand, for condition determines the price category.

THE CONDITION OF THE CARD MUST BE DETERMINED BEFORE A CARD CAN BE PRICED

The main criteria for judging the condition of a card are centering, corner wear, creases, alterations, and surface wear.

CENTERING

A card in mint condition must have perfect centering from top to bottom and from left to right. A card's centering is refered to in percentages: perfectly centred is 50/50, slightly off-centred may be 45/55 and badly off-centred may be 30/70 or 20/80.

CORNER WEAR

A card in mint condition must have four perfect corners. A card with corner wear may have slightly frayed, dented or rounded corners.

PRINTING DEFECTS

A card in mint condition must have no printing defects. A card with printing defects may have poor quality, missing gloss or foil, a wrong back or an out of focus picture.

SURFACE WEAR

A card in mint condition must have no surface wear. A card with surface wear may have been exposed to creasing, wax or gum stains, ink marks, water drops, discolouration or mishandling.

CONDITION GUIDE

Mint (MT): A card that is in perfect condition. The card must look as though it just came out of the pack and must have no printing defects. The card must have perfect centering, no corner wear and no surface wear.

Near Mint (NRMT): A card with only one minor defect. The card may be slightly off-centred, have slight corner or surface wear or have printer's lines or spots.

Excellent-Mint (EX-MT): A card with two or three minor defects. The card may be slightly off-centred, have slight corner or surface wear or have printer's lines or spots.

Excellent (EX): A card with only a few minor defects. The card may be slightly more off-centred, have rougher corner and surface wear including slight creasing or have more printer's lines and spots.

Very Good (VG): A card with one major defect or several minor defects. The card may be off-centred, have rough or rounded corners, have surface wear and slight creasing, have printer's lines and defects and shows signs of being well handled.

Good (G): A card with two or three major defects as well as minor defects. The card is off-centred, has considerable corner and surface wear, may have printer's lines or defects and shows signs of being over-handled.

Fair (F): A card with a few major defects as well as minor defects. The card is off-centred, has even greater corner and surface wear, may have printer's lines or defects and shows signs of heavy mishandling.

Interac

VISA

1999 is the Year of The Great One!

'99 is #99 Wayne Gretzky's year and Upper Deck will feature Year of The Great One *all-Gretzky inserts in all of our 1999 NHL® products! From Autographed Gretzky Double Game Jersey Cards to sequentially numbered Gretzky inserts to unique Autographed inserts, look for Upper Deck products with the special, commemorative Year of The Great One logo to find the most collectable Gretzky cards ever produced! The Greatest Player. The Greatest Card Company. It's the Year of The Great One.*

Look for special *Year of The Great One* insert cards in every 1999 product including:

Upper Deck
UD Choice
SPx
Black Diamond
SP Authentic
Ionix
Upper Deck Series Two

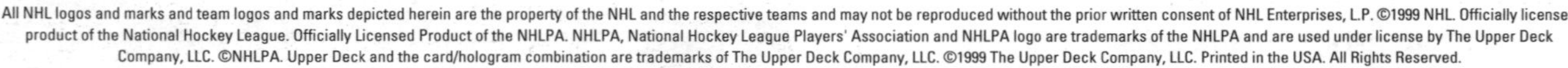

COUNTERFEIT CARDS

The following pages contain information that outlines the differences you must look for to distinguish counterfeit from authentic cards. Study these points carefully. They will be extremely helpful when you enter the market to either buy or sell cards.

PARKHURST 1951 - 52 CARD #18
MAURICE "ROCKET" RICHARD AND TERRY SAWCHUK

This is a very good job of counterfeiting. The photographic detail is very good but the colours are not as strong as the genuine cards and the paper on which they are printed is thicker. The edges look like they have just been cut but the corners have been artifically rounded to make the cards look old.

There are even small printer's marks, very much like those on the originals. Look for small creases which have been photographically produced.

Note: Due to the high price of this set, collectors are warned to be very careful. It is believed that counterfeits exist for every card in this set.

O-PEE-CHEE 1979 - 80 CARD #18
WAYNE GRETZKY

FACE: "C" on the original card face has clear, sharp, wide lettering. The counterfeit has small fuzzy lettering. Under magnification each letter on the reproduction will have jagged outlines.

On the original, Gretzky's skate laces show individual lace strands while the reproduction shows a blurr with no definition of the individual strands.

The colours on the counterfeit are more subdued and the border is a powder blue, versus a sky blue border on the original.

BACK: The skate on the original is sky blue. The counterfeit has a turquoise coloured skate. Also the skate outline on the original has a brown/black border, while the reproduction has only a brown border.

The "WH" of "WHA" is joined on the counterfeit and separate on the original. Some of the reproductions have "reprint" stamped over the O-Pee-Chee copyright notice.

O-PEE-CHEE 1980 - 81 CARD #140
RAY BOURQUE

FACE: The face of the counterfeit card has poor flesh tones and the face of the player is paler than the original. The forgery also has less detail in both the photograph and the type. This gives the card an overall fuzzy appearance. The counterfeit appears to have been printed on card stock that is lighter in colour than that of the original.

BACK: The edge of the puck containing the number of the player is fuzzy and is lighter on the forgery than on the original. Since the counterfeit has been printed on card stock of a lighter colour, unprinted surfaces appear white rather than the darker shade found in the authentic card. The green ink on the back of the copy is much lighter than the darker green found on the original. The yellow areas of the counterfeit are much more of an intense yellow than those areas of the authentic cards.

O-PEE-CHEE 1980 - 81 CARD #289
MARK MESSIER

FACE: The face of the counterfeit card has poor flesh tones and the face of the player is paler than the original. The forgery also has less detail in both the photograph and the type. This gives the card an overall fuzzy appearance. The counterfeit appears to have been printed on card stock that is lighter in colour than that of the original.

BACK: The edge of the puck containing the number of the player is fuzzy and is lighter on the forgery than on the original. Since the counterfeit has been printed on card stock of a lighter colour, unprinted surfaces appear white rather than the darker shade found in the authentic card. The green ink on the back of the copy is much lighter than the darker green found on the original. The yellow areas of the counterfeit are much more of an intense yellow than those areas of the authentic cards.

O-PEE-CHEE 1981 - 82 CARD #111
PAUL COFFEY

FACE: The counterfeit card actually features sharper photographic detail than the original. Borders are cut more sharply and are whiter than those of the authentic cards. This counterfeit, like that of the OPC counterfeit 1980-81 cards, seems to have been printed with slightly more yellow. The yellow word "OILERS" on the face is slightly more intense than on the authentic card.

BACK: The counterfeit, again, seems to have been printed on card stock that is whiter than that of the authentic issue. Unprinted surfaces appear much whiter than those of original cards. The blue on the back of the copy is more of a royal blue and is darker than on the original. There is a white or knock-out box at the bottom of the card that is sharply bordered on the authentic card. The border on the counterfeit is fuzzy.

O-PEE-CHEE 1985 - 86 CARD #9
MARIO LEMIEUX

FACE: This counterfeit is again trimmed more sharply than the authentic issue and has a more yellowish tint. The photograph is fuzzy and there is a bluish tint to the background behind Lemieux that does not exist on the original. The photo on the counterfeit has less detail and the type and artwork are blurred.

BACK: The red border on the original card is a less intense colour. On the counterfeit the red is more of a deep red wine colour and the area containing the player's statistics is more of an orange than the pink colour of the original. The screen used on the back of the counterfeit is much more apparent than on the authentic issue. All unprinted areas appear white on the counterfeit instead of the light grey-brown of the authentic card.

O-PEE-CHEE 1988 - 89 CARD #66
BRETT HULL

FACE: On the original, the push pin that holds the player's nameplate has a small yellow dot on it. This was caused by a small particle of dust during contacting of the final film and is therefore on all cards. The counterfeit cards do not have this yellow dot. On the face of the original and copy there is a series of black dots under the player's nameplate, intended to look like

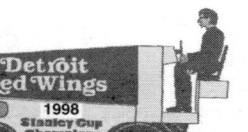

a shadow. These black dots run into the top part of the player's picture. On the original the dots remain solid and roundish in shape, whereas the dots become greyish and fuzzy in appearance on the fake reproduction. This is visible to the naked eye, but becomes much more obvious using a magnifying glass. To the left of Hull's ear on the light coloured area of the original is a mesh effect caused by the lithographic dots starting to align with one another in the reproduction process. This does not occur on the forgery.

BACK: On the back of the card, the type on the original is clear, even and consistent. On the fake the type is ragged and sometimes broken. For instance, in the playoff record area the *C* and the second *r* in *Career* have broken type. This is not the case on the original. Magnification is required to detect the difference.

DURHAM REGIONAL POLICE 1989 - 90 CARD #31
ERIC LINDROS – FIRST COUNTERFEIT

FACE: The face of the counterfeit card, from the ice surface to the card top, has a greenish tinge throughout the background. This is clear when comparing any parts of the background that were white on the original (for example, the boards, the back drop on the stands and the ice in the foreground) with the fake.

As with all photo reproductions, clarity is lost when not using the original art. The facial expression, sweater folds, the red sweater stripe and the edges of the printing surface are all soft and lack sharp detail on the forgery. On the authentic card, the name "OSHAWA GENERALS" is clear and crisp. The type has fewer screen dots than on the copy.

BACK: Another characteristic of photo reproduction is shrinkage and overall loss of detail. When a counterfeit is produced from an original, you can expect a 5 per cent loss of all detail across the newly reproduced card.

DURHAM REGIONAL POLICE 1989 - 90 CARD #31
ERIC LINDROS – SECOND COUNTERFEIT

FACE: Unlike the first counterfeit card, the second does not have the obvious green tinge. However, the detail on the counterfeit is not sharp and the type and the Oshawa Generals' logo in the upper right corner are slightly blurred. The border of the card and the words "OSHAWA GENERALS" at the bottom are browner than the authentic card and screen dots are more in evidence.

The flesh tones on the counterfeit are deeper, because more yellow and red is used. In the counterfeit there is a small green dot just below the word *Centre* at the top of the card. This would seem to indicate that the card was counterfeited from the card found second from the left and two down on the original sheet, as this card also has this green dot. (See photo of sheet above.)

BACK: The detail of the type on this counterfeit has been improved. The logos of the National Sports Centre, the Durham Regional Police, the Lions Club and Magill Business Forms are as sharp as those on the authentic card. However, the overall finish of the counterfeit has a slightly less glossy appearance than the authentic issue.

CHAPTER ONE

VINTAGE ISSUES 1879 TO 1941

1879 - 1905 ANONYMOUS ADVERTISING CARDS

ACC: HD-5
Card Size: 2 13/16" x 4 7/16"
1884 Card Size: 2 13/16" x 4 5/16"
1906 Card Size: 2 3/4" x 4 1/4"
Face: Colourised print, white cardstock
Back: Left blank for addition of advertisement
Imprint: None

	No.	Scene	VG	EX	EX-NRMT
□	4	Eishockey (1879)	65.00	125.00	250.00
□		Le jeu du Hockey (1884)	65.00	125.00	250.00
□		Margarine Belgica (1906)	65.00	125.00	250.00
□		Chocolat Meurisse (1906)	65.00	125.00	250.00

1879 - 1882 BUFFORD LITHO

1879 - 1882 ISSUE

Produced by Bufford Litho of Boston, Massachusetts as "stock cards". The cards were overprinted for various advertisers. The number of cards in the set is unknown. Only two cards are known to involve hockey or can be considered to contain hockey related scenes. Other cards in this series portray other sports or non-sport subjects.

ACC: H-820
Card Size: 2 11/16" x 4 1/2"
Face: Pastel colourised print, beige border, cardstock
Back: Left blank for addition of advertisement
Imprint: Bufford Boston

	No.	Scene	VG	EX	EX-NRMT
□	431	Hockey on the Ice	70.00	140.00	275.00
□	434	Race for the Cup	25.00	50.00	100.00

1880 ISSUE

ACC: HD-5
Card Size: 2 11/16" x 4 5/16"
Face: Multi-colourised print, white cardstock
Back: Left blank for addition of advertisement
Imprint: Bufford

	No.	Scene	VG	EX	EX-NRMT
□	903	Child with field hockey stick and ball	33.00	65.00	125.00

1880 - 1939 ANONYMOUS POSTCARDS

1880 ISSUE

ACC: HD-5
Card Size: 3 1/2" x 5 3/8"
Face: Colourised print, white border, cardstock
Back: Postcard format
Imprint: None

	Scene	VG	EX	EX-NRMT
□	Three children playing ice hockey	25.00	50.00	100.00

1900 ISSUE

Card Size: 3 3/8" x 5 5/16"
Face: Black and white photo, white border, cardstock
Back: Postcard format
Imprint: Imp. Émile Pécaud & Cie, Paris.

	Scene	VG	EX	EX-NRMT
□	Les sports. Le hockey sur la glace	6.00	12.00	25.00

1902 ISSUE

Card Size: 3 3/8" x 5 1/2"
Face: Colourised print, red text, white border, card stock
Back: Postcard format
Imprint: Brefkort

	Scene	VG	EX	EX-NRMT
□	Stockholm Idrottsparken	12.00	25.00	50.00

1908 ISSUE

Card Size: 3 1/2" x 5 7/16"
Face: Black and white, white cardstock
Back: Postcard format
Imprint: Vougs & Cie., Editeurs, Genäve, Suiss

	Scene	VG	EX	EX-NRMT
□	Les Sports d'Hiver a Luchon	6.00	12.00	25.00

1909 ISSUE

Card Size: 3 9/16" x 5 7/16"
Face: Blue pastel colourised print, white border, cardstock
Back: Postcard format
Imprint: None

	Scene	VG	EX	EX-NRMT
□	Hockey	6.00	12.00	25.00

1917 ISSUE

Card Size: 3 1/2" x 5 1/2"
Face: Colourized print, white cardstock
Back: Postcard format
Imprint: None

	Scene	VG	EX	EX-NRMT
□	Playing hockey with square pucks	6.00	12.00	25.00

1920 ISSUE

Card Size: 3 1/2" x 5 3/8"
Face: Colourized drawing, white border, card stock
Back: Postcard format
Imprint: Brefkort

	Scene	VG	EX	EX-NRMT
□	Gelukkig Nieuujaar	12.00	25.00	50.00

1924 ISSUE

Card Size: 3 1/2" x 5 7/16"
Face: Black and white photo, white border, cardstock
Back: Postcard format
Imprint: Made in France

	No.	Scene	VG	EX	EX-NRMT
□	74	Chamonix. Match de Hockey	12.00	25.00	50.00

1925 ISSUE

Card Size: 3 9/16" x 5 9/16"
Face: Colourized print, white cardstock
Back: Postcard format
Imprint: Ve proséch Hospodárské pomoci

	Scene	VG	EX	EX-NRMT
□	Caricature of Goalie	10.00	20.00	40.00

1925 ISSUE

Card Size: 3 1/2" x 5 3/8"
Face: Colourized drawing, white border, cardstock
Back: Postcard format
Imprint: Verlag A. Ruegg & Cie., Éditeurs, Zürich

	No.	Scene	VG	EX	EX-NRMT
□	490	Cartoon depiction of hockey game	6.00	12.00	25.00

1880 ANONYMOUS STOCK CARDS

Unlike other trade cards, the face of this card depicts a generic oriental scene, while the back of the card advertises the "Great Match Game of Polo" between the Ice Polo Cottage City Club and the Providence Club. Ice hockey in the latter part of the 1800's in the U.S.A. was called ice polo.

ACC: HD-2e
Card Size: 2 1/2" x 4"
Face: Pastel blue colourised print, beige cardstock
Back: Blue print on beige cardstock
Imprint: None

	Scene	VG	EX	EX-NRMT
□	Ice Polo Cottage City vs Providence	20.00	40.00	75.00

1888 ATLANTIC AND PACIFIC TRADE CARD

This set of advertising trade cards was printed by Bufford Litho in 1888 to promote A & P's Thea-Nectar tea. The reverse may be found with a different advertisement.

ACC: H-820
Card Size: 3 3/8" x 5 1/8"
Face: Six colour, yellow border print
Back: Black and white
Imprint: Bufford

	No.	Scene	VG	EX	EX-NRMT
□	517	Hockey	75.00	125.00	250.00

1890 F. MAYER BOOT AND SHOE CO.

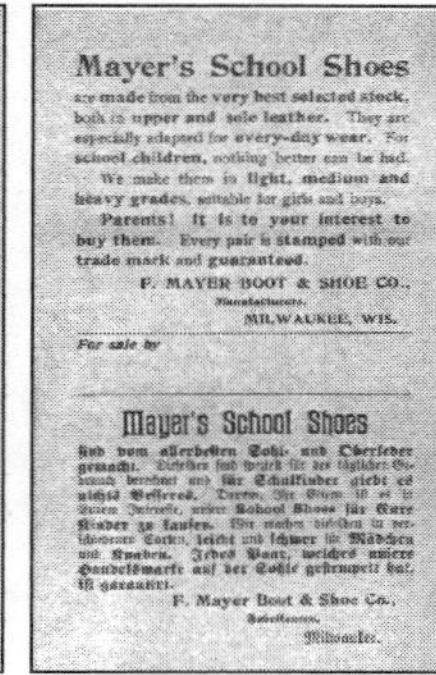

Mayer's School Shoes

are made from the very best selected stock, both in upper and sole leather. They are especially adapted for every-day wear. For school children, nothing better can be had.

We make them in light, medium and heavy grades, suitable for girls and boys.

Parents! It is to your interest to buy them. Every pair is stamped with our trade mark and guaranteed.

F. MAYER BOOT & SHOE CO., Manufacturers, MILWAUKEE, WIS.

For sale by

Mayer's School Shoes

sind vom allerbesten Sohl- und Oberleder gemacht. Dieselben sind speziell für den täglichen Gebrauch berechnet und für Schulkinder giebt es nichts Besseres. Darum, Ihr Eltern, ist es in Ihrem Interesse, unsere School Shoes für Eure Kinder zu kaufen. Wir machen dieselben in verschiedenen Sorten, leicht und schwer für Mädchen und Knaben. Jedes Paar, welches unsere Handelsmarke auf der Sohle gestempelt hat, ist garantirt.

F. Mayer Boot & Shoe Co., Fabrikanten, Milwaukee.

Printed circa 1890 by Forbes Litho for the F. Mayer Boot & Shoe Co., this advertising card was used to promote their line of children's shoes. Two of the children are shown with hockey sticks. A variation of this card by an anonymous lithographer is known to exist.

ACC: HP-3h
Card Size: 3 1/4" x 5 1/2"
Face: Colourised print on white stock
Back: Black and white on card stock
Imprint: Forbes, New York, Boston, Chicago

	Scene	VG	EX	EX-NRMT
☐	Children on Ice	35.00	65.00	125.00

1896 WARWICK BRO'S. & RUTTER

Card Size: 5 9/16" x 3 5/8"
Face: Black and white photo on card stock
Back: Brown and white
Imprint: Warwick Bro's & Rutter, Limited, Publishers, Toronto

No.	Team	VG	EX	EX-NRMT
☐ 3247	New Liskeard's Hockey Team	50.00	100.00	200.00

1900 GOTTMANN AND KRETCHMER

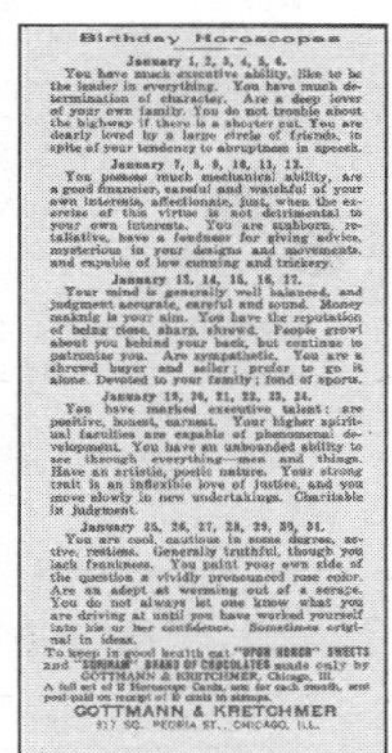

Birthday Horoscopes

January 1, 2, 3, 4, 5, 6.
You have much executive ability, like to be the leader in everything. You have much determination of character. Are a deep lover of your own family. You do not trouble about the highway if there is a shorter cut. You are dearly loved by a large circle of friends, in spite of your tendency to abruptness in speech.

January 7, 8, 9, 10, 11, 12.
You possess much mechanical ability, are a good financier, careful and watchful of your own interests, affectionate, just, when the exercise of this virtue is not detrimental to your own interests. You are stubborn, retaliative, have a fondness for giving advice, mysterious in your designs and movements, and capable of low cunning and trickery.

January 13, 14, 15, 16, 17.
Your mind is generally well balanced, and judgment accurate, careful and sound. Money making is your aim. You have the reputation of being close, sharp, shrewd. People growl about you behind your back, but continue to patronize you. Are sympathetic. You are a shrewd buyer and seller; prefer to go it alone. Devoted to your family; fond of sports.

January 19, 20, 21, 22, 23, 24.
You have marked executive talent; are positive, honest, earnest. Your higher spiritual faculties are capable of phenomenal development. You have an unbounded ability to see through everything—men and things. Have an artistic, poetic nature. Your strong trait is an inflexible love of justice, and you move slowly in new undertakings. Charitable in judgment.

January 25, 26, 27, 28, 29, 30, 31.
You are cool, cautious in some degree, active, restless. Generally truthful, though you lack frankness. You paint your own side of the question a vividly pronounced rose color. Are an adept at worming out of a scrape. You do not always let one know what you are driving at until you have worked yourself into his or her confidence. Sometimes original in ideas.

To keep in good health eat "UPON HONOR" SWEETS and "SURINAM" BRAND OF CHOCOLATES made only by GOTTMANN & KRETCHMER, Chicago, Ill.
A full set of 12 Horoscope Cards, one for each month, sent post-paid on receipt of 10 cents in stamps.

GOTTMANN & KRETCHMER
317 SO. PEORIA ST., CHICAGO, ILL.

This set was issued by the candy manufacturer Gottmann & Kretchmer of Chicago, possibly with "Upon Honor" sweets or "Surinam" chocolates. The 12-card set, one for each month of the year, could be obtained by mailing in 10¢ in stamps. The printer is unknown.

ACC.: HD-8f
Card Size: 2 1/2" x 5 1/8"
Face: Colourised print on card stock
Back: Blue and white
Imprint: GOTTMANN & KRETCHMER, 317 SO. PEORIA ST., CHICAGO, ILL.

No.	Month	VG	EX	EX-NRMT
☐ 1	January	25.00	50.00	100.00

1902 HAMILTON KINGS CARDS

Issued as a redeemable premium. Each card is issued on different coloured card stock. Artwork portrays ladies engaged in various sporting activities.

ACC: T-7
Card Size: 5 15/16" x 8"
Face: Black and blue with white print on beige stock
Back: Blank
Imprint: TURKISH TROPHIES COPYRIGHT, 1902, BY S. ANARGYROS

No.	Scene	VG	EX	EX-NRMT
☐ 6	Hockey	90.00	175.00	350.00

1902 RAPHAEL TUCK AND SONS

There is also a version with "ice-crystal" glued to the card surface area below the players.

Card Size: 3 9/16" x 5 1/2"
Face: Multi-coloured photo, white border, card stock
Back: Postcard format
Imprint: Raphael Tuck & Sons' "Oilette" Printed in England

No.	Team	VG	EX	EX-NRMT
☐ ☐ 2624	Hockey	20.00	40.00	75.00

1905 - 06 MONTRÉAL IMPORT CO.

1905 ISSUE

Card Size: 3 5/8" x 5 7/16"
Face: Colourised cartoon drawing, white border, card stock
Back: Postcard format
Imprint: Montréal Import Co., Montréal

No.	Team	VG	EX	EX-NRMT
☐ 308	"Hockey is a Winter game, very healthful & full of exercise"	10.00	20.00	40.00

1906 ISSUE

ACC: PC-745
Card Size: 3 1/2" x 5 3/8"
Face: Black and white photo, red text, card stock
Back: Postcard format
Imprint: Montréal Import Co., Montréal.

No.	Team	VG	EX	EX-NRMT
☐ 261	Montréal McGill Hockey Team	30.00	60.00	120.00

1905 NATIONAL ART CO.

Card Size: 3 1/2" x 5 3/8"
Face: Coloured litho, card stock
Back: Postcard format
Imprint: Montreal Import Co., Montreal; Copyright by Archie Gunn

No.	Team	VG	EX	EX-NRMT
☐ 39	Female skater with hockey stick	8.00	15.00	30.00

1905 - 06 VELVO

Card Size: 3 1/4" X 5 3/8"
Face: Black and white, card stock
Back: Postcard format
Imprint: Velvo

	Team	VG	EX	EX-NRMT
☐	Grand 'Mere Hockey Club, Intermediate Champions 1905-1906, Eastern Canada League	50.00	100.00	200.00

1907 MONTRÉAL IMPORT CO. CANADIAN SPORTS SERIES ISSUE

ACC: PC-745
Card Size: 3 3/8" x 5 7/16"
Face: Black and white photo, white border, card stock
Back: Postcard format
Imprint: None

	Team	VG	EX	EX-NRMT
☐	Hockey Match	20.00	40.00	75.00

1907 - 08 NORTHERN HARDWARE CO.

Card Size: 5 1/2" x 3 11/16"
Face: Black and white photo on white card stock
Back: Black and white
Imprint: None

	Team	VG	EX	EX-NRMT
☐	Northern Hdw. Co. Hockey Team, Duluth, 1907-1908	25.00	50.00	100.00

1908 AMERICAN TOBACCO COMPANY SMALL/LARGE FLANNELS

The A.T.C. flannels portray players from the sports of baseball, basketball, fencing, football, hockey, hurdles, rowing, shotput, swimming, tennis and track. Each college is portrayed in every sport.

The imprint varies with each cigarette brand and there may be more than the three listed here.

There are 27 colleges with eleven flannels each. Flannels from other colleges exists.

SMALL FLANNELS

ACC: B-33
Size: 3 1/8" x 5 3/8" with fringe
Material: Flannel
Face: Colour print on flannel
Back: Factory stamp in magenta may be present
Imprint:

1. **Factory No. 2163, 3rd Dist. N.Y.**
2. **Factory No. 30, 2nd Dist., N.Y**
3. **Egyptienne Luxury**

College	VG	EX	EX-NRMT
Hockey Flannels:	**35.00**	**65.00**	**125.00**

☐	Amherst	☐	Army
☐	Brown	☐	Chicago
☐	Colgate	☐	Colorado
☐	Columbia	☐	Cornell
☐	Dartmouth	☐	Harvard
☐	Johns Hopkins	☐	Knox
☐	Navy	☐	Oregon
☐	Pennsylvania	☐	Princeton
☐	Rutgers	☐	St. Louis
☐	Stanford	☐	Syracuse
☐	Trinity	☐	Tufts
☐	Utah	☐	Vermont
☐	Williams	☐	Wisconsin
☐	Yale		

LARGE FLANNELS

ACC: B-16-1 and B-16-2 are design variations
Size: 5 1/2" x 8 1/2"
Material: Flannel
Face: Colour print on flannel
Back: Factory stamp may be present
Imprint: None

College	VG	EX	EX-NRMT
Hockey Flannels:	**40.00**	**75.00**	**150.00**

B-16-1 LETTERS IN CORNERS

☐	Baker	☐	Barea
☐	California	☐	Colorado
☐	Illinois	☐	Kentucky
☐	Iowa	☐	Marquette
☐	Missouri	☐	Navy
☐	Notre Dame	☐	Oregon
☐	Princeton	☐	Purdue
☐	South California	☐	Tennessee
☐	Texas	☐	West Point
☐	Yale		

B-16-2 CONVENTIONAL BORDERS

☐	California	☐	Chicago (Shield in centre)
☐	Chicago (C in centre of circle)	☐	Colorado (1870)
☐	Colorado (1876)	☐	Columbia
☐	Cornell	☐	Harvard
☐	Illinois	☐	Johns Hopkins
☐	Michigan	☐	Minnesota
☐	Northwestern College	☐	Ohio
☐	Pennsylvania	☐	Princeton
☐	St. Louis	☐	Syracuse
☐	Stanford Junior	☐	Texas
☐	Wisconsin	☐	Yale

Note: Known hockey flannel is Oregon

1909 - 10 MURAD COLLEGES CARDS

There are six series of 25 cards each. The first two series exist in a 2nd edition with minor graphics changes. A few unfinished errors without printing are known. The cigarette packer number is hand-stamped on the back.

ACC: T-51
Card Size: 2 1/8" x 2 11/16"
Face: Colour print on white card stock
Back: Black and white
Imprint: Murad Cigarettes S. Anargyros, New York. A Corporation Factory No. 7, 3rd Dist. N.Y.

College	VG	EX	EX-NRMT
Hockey Card Price:	**12.50**	**25.00**	**50.00**

☐	Adelphi	☐	Adrian
☐	Albright	☐	Alleghany
☐	Alfred	☐	Alma
☐	Amherst	☐	Amity
☐	Antiosh	☐	Armour
☐	Baker	☐	Bates
☐	Berea	☐	Bethany
☐	Blackburn	☐	Boston College
☐	Barton University	☐	Bowdoin
☐	Brooklyn Poly	☐	Brown
☐	Bucknell	☐	Buchtel
☐	C.C.N.Y.	☐	C.U.A.
☐	C.U. Kentucky	☐	California
☐	Canisius	☐	Carthage
☐	Case	☐	Cedarville
☐	Central College	☐	Chattanooga
☐	Chicago	☐	Cincinatti
☐	Clark	☐	Clarkson
☐	Coe	☐	Colgate
☐	Colorado	☐	Columbia
☐	Cornell	☐	Cotner
☐	Dartmouth	☐	Davidson
☐	Denison	☐	Denver
☐	DePauw	☐	Dickinson
☐	Drake	☐	Fordham
☐	Franklin	☐	Furman
☐	Geneva	☐	Georgetown
☐	George Washington	☐	Greer
☐	Grove City	☐	Guilford
☐	Gustavas Adolphus	☐	Hamilton
☐	Hampden Sidney	☐	Hampton
☐	Harvard	☐	Hastings
☐	Haverford	☐	Heidelberg
☐	Hendrix	☐	Hiram
☐	Hiwassww	☐	Hobart
☐	Holy Cross	☐	Huron
☐	Illinois	☐	Illinois College
☐	Indiana	☐	Iowa
☐	Johns Hopkins	☐	Juniata
☐	K.W.C.	☐	Kansas
☐	Kenyon	☐	Knox
☐	Lafayette	☐	Lawrence
☐	Lebanon	☐	Lehigh
☐	Lenox	☐	Lombard
☐	Louisiana or L.S.U.	☐	Loyola
☐	Luther	☐	McGill
☐	Marietta	☐	Marquette
☐	Massachusetts Tech	☐	Michigan Agri.
☐	Michigan	☐	Millsaps
☐	Minnesota	☐	Missouri
☐	Montana	☐	Mt. Union
☐	N.Y.U.	☐	Navy
☐	North Dakota	☐	North Western College
☐	North Western University	☐	Notre Dame
☐	O.S.U.	☐	O.W.U.
☐	Occidental	☐	Ohio
☐	Oklahoma	☐	Pennsylvania College
☐	Penn. State	☐	Pennsylvania
☐	Pratt	☐	Princeton
☐	Purdue	☐	Rensselaer
☐	Rochester	☐	Rutgers
☐	S.U. Kentucky	☐	St. Lawrence
☐	St. Louis	☐	South Carolina
☐	Stanford	☐	Stephens
☐	Swarthmore	☐	Syracuse
☐	Tennessee	☐	Texas
☐	Toronto	☐	Trinity
☐	Tufts	☐	Vanderbilt
☐	Vermont	☐	Virginia
☐	W. & J.	☐	W.V.U.
☐	Washington and Lee	☐	Wesleyan
☐	Western R.U.	☐	West Point
☐	Whitman	☐	Williams
☐	Wisconsin	☐	Worchester P.I.
☐	Xavier	☐	Yale

1909 - 10 MURAD COLLEGE SILKS

This silk set closely parallels the T-51 card set with a few exceptions.

ACC: S-25
Card Size: 3 1/2" x 1 3/4"
Face: Colour print on silk
Back: Blank
Imprint: EGYPTIENNE LUXURY

College	VG	EX	EX-NRMT
Hockey Card Price:	**12.50**	**25.00**	**50.00**

☐	Adelphi	☐	Adrian
☐	Albright	☐	Alleghany
☐	Alfred	☐	Alma
☐	Amherst	☐	Antiosh
☐	Armour	☐	Baker
☐	Bates	☐	Berea
☐	Bethany	☐	Blackburn
☐	Boston College	☐	Barton University
☐	Bowdoin	☐	Brooklyn Poly
☐	Brown	☐	Bucknell
☐	Buchtel	☐	C.C.N.Y.
☐	C.U.A.	☐	C.U. Kentucky
☐	California	☐	Canisius
☐	Carthage	☐	Case
☐	Cedarville	☐	Chattanooga
☐	Chicago	☐	Cincinatti
☐	Clark	☐	Clarkson
☐	Colgate	☐	Colorado
☐	Columbia	☐	Cornell
☐	Cotner	☐	Dartmouth
☐	Davidson	☐	Denison
☐	Denver	☐	DePauw
☐	Dickinson	☐	Drake
☐	Fordham	☐	Franklin
☐	Geneva	☐	Georgetown
☐	George Washington	☐	Greer
☐	Grove City	☐	Guilford
☐	Gustavas Adolphus	☐	Hamilton
☐	Hampden Sidney	☐	Hampton
☐	Harvard	☐	Haverford
☐	Heidelberg	☐	Hendrix
☐	Hiram	☐	Hiwassww
☐	Hobart	☐	Holy Cross
☐	Huron	☐	Illinois
☐	Illinois College	☐	Indiana
☐	Iowa	☐	Johns Hopkins
☐	Juniata	☐	K.W.C.
☐	Kenyon	☐	Knox
☐	Lafayette	☐	Lawrence
☐	Lebanon	☐	Lehigh
☐	Lombard	☐	Louisiana or L.S.U.
☐	Loyola	☐	Luther
☐	McGill	☐	Marietta
☐	Marquette	☐	Massachusetts Tech
☐	Michigan Agri.	☐	Michigan

☐ Millsaps	☐ Minnesota
☐ Missouri	☐ Montana
☐ Mt. Union	☐ N.Y.U.
☐ Navy	☐ North Dakota
☐ North Western College	☐ North Western U.
☐ Notre Dame	☐ O.S.U.
☐ O.W.U.	☐ Occidental
☐ Ohio	☐ Oklahoma
☐ Pennsylvania College	☐ Penn. State
☐ Pennsylvania	☐ Pratt
☐ Princeton	☐ Purdue
☐ Rensselaer	☐ Rochester
☐ Rutgers	☐ S.U. Kentucky
☐ St. Lawrence	☐ St. Louis
☐ South Carolina	☐ Stanford
☐ Stephens	☐ Swarthmore
☐ Syracuse	☐ Tennessee
☐ Texas	☐ Toronto
☐ Trinity	☐ Tufts
☐ Vanderbilt	☐ Vermont
☐ Virginia	☐ W. & J.
☐ W.V.U.	☐ Washington and Lee
☐ Wesleyan	☐ Western R.U.
☐ West Point	☐ Whitman
☐ Williams	☐ Wisconsin
☐ Worchester P.I.	☐ Xavier
☐ Yale	

1910 - 11 IMPERIAL TOBACCO "C56"

All these cards are considered rookie cards. Cards are numbered on the upper left corner. The player's name and team appear on the bottom border. The name of the series, Hockey Series, appears on the back with a picture of two inverted crossed hockey sticks with a puck below them.

ACC No.: C56

Card Size: 1 1/2" x 2 1/2"
Face: Four colour; Name, Number, Team
Back: Black on card stock; Name, Resume
Imprint: None

Complete Set (36 cards):	**5,500.00**	**7,000.00**	**11,000.00**
No. Player	**VG**	**EX**	**EX-NRMT**
☐ 1 Frank Patrick, Ren., RC	300.00	450.00	850.00
☐ 2 Percy Lesueur (G), Ott., RC	200.00	300.00	400.00
☐ 3 Gordon Roberts, Ott., RC	150.00	225.00	300.00
☐ 4 Barney Holden, Sha., RC	90.00	135.00	180.00
☐ 5 Frank Glass, Mtl.W, RC	90.00	135.00	180.00
☐ 6 Edgar Dey, Hab., RC	90.00	135.00	180.00
☐ 7 Marty Walsh, Cob., RC	150.00	225.00	300.00
☐ 8 Art Ross, Hab., RC	500.00	750.00	1000.00
☐ 9 Angus Campbell, Cob., RC	145.00	215.00	285.00
☐ 10 Harry Hyland, Mtl.W, RC	165.00	245.00	325.00
☐ 11 Herb Clarke, Cob., RC	90.00	135.00	180.00
☐ 12 Art Ross, Hab., RC	500.00	750.00	1000.00
☐ 13 Ed Decarie, Mtl. Can., RC	90.00	135.00	180.00
☐ 14 Tommy Dunderdale, Sha., RC	190.00	285.00	375.00
☐ 15 Fred (Cyclone) Taylor, Ren., RC	500.00	750.00	1000.00
☐ 16 Joe Cattarinich (G), Mtl.C, RC	125.00	190.00	250.00
☐ 17 Bruce Stuart, Ott., RC	165.00	245.00	325.00
☐ 18 Nick Bawlf, Hab., RC	90.00	135.00	180.00
☐ 19 J. Jones, Cob. (G), RC	125.00	190.00	250.00
☐ 20 Ernest Russell, Mtl.W, RC	190.00	285.00	375.00
☐ 21 Jack Laviolette, Mtl.C, RC	165.00	245.00	325.00
☐ 22 Riley Hern (G), Mtl.W, RC	165.00	245.00	325.00
☐ 23 Didier Pitre, Mtl.C, RC	165.00	245.00	325.00
☐ 24 George Poulin, Mtl.C, RC	90.00	135.00	180.00
☐ 25 Art Bernier, Mtl.C, RC	90.00	135.00	180.00
☐ 26 Lester Patrick, Ren., RC	400.00	600.00	800.00
☐ 27 Fred Lake, Ott., RC	90.00	135.00	180.00
☐ 28 Paddy Moran (G), Hab., RC	225.00	340.00	450.00
☐ 29 C. Toms, Cob., RC, LC	90.00	135.00	180.00
☐ 30 Ernie Johnson, Mtl.W, RC	225.00	340.00	450.00
☐ 31 Horace Gaul, Hab., RC, LC	90.00	135.00	180.00
☐ 32 Harold McNamara, Cob., RC, LC	90.00	135.00	180.00
☐ 33 Jack Marshall, Mtl.W, RC	150.00	225.00	300.00
☐ 34 Bruce Ridpath, Ott., RC	90.00	135.00	180.00
☐ 35 Jack Marshall, Sha., RC	150.00	225.00	300.00
☐ 36 Edouard Lalonde, Ren., RC	450.00	675.00	1150.00

1910 - 11 IMPERIAL TOBACCO POSTCARDS

Printed in England by BAT for Imperial Tobacco of Canada, this postcard size hockey card was issued in tin boxes containing 50 Sweet Caporal "Flats" cigarettes. The photographs of this set were used as the basis to generate the drawings for the 1911-12 regular issue.

Card Size: 2 7/8" x 4 5/8"
Face: Black and white on card stock; Name, Team, Number
Back: Blank
Imprint: Printed in Britain.

No. Player	**VG**	**EX**	**EX-NRMT**
☐ 1 Paddy Moran (G), Québec	350.00	550.00	900.00
☐ 2 Joe Hall, Québec	325.00	465.00	600.00
☐ 3 Barney Holden, Québec	160.00	230.00	300.00
☐ 4 Joe Malone, Québec	550.00	775.00	1,000.00
☐ 5 Ed Oatman, Québec	160.00	230.00	300.00
☐ 6 Tommy Dunderdale, Québec	325.00	465.00	600.00
☐ 7 Ken Mallen, Québec	160.00	230.00	300.00
☐ 8 Jack McDonald, Québec	160.00	230.00	300.00
☐ 9 Fred Lake, Ottawa	160.00	230.00	300.00
☐ 10 Albert Kerr, Ottawa	160.00	230.00	300.00
☐ 11 Marty Walsh, Ottawa	265.00	370.00	475.00
☐ 12 Hamby Shore, Ottawa	160.00	230.00	300.00
☐ 13 Alex Currie, Ottawa	160.00	230.00	300.00
☐ 14 Bruce Ridpath, Ottawa	160.00	230.00	300.00
☐ 15 Bruce Stuart, Ottawa	265.00	370.00	475.00
☐ 16 Percy Lesueur (G), Ottawa	325.00	465.00	600.00
☐ 17 Jack Darragh, Ottawa	265.00	370.00	475.00
☐ 18 Steve Vair, Renfew	160.00	230.00	300.00
☐ 19 Don Smith, Renfew	160.00	230.00	300.00
☐ 20 Fred (Cyclone) Taylor, Renfew	650.00	950.00	1250.00
☐ 21 Bert Lindsay (G), Renfew	160.00	230.00	300.00
☐ 22 Larry Gilmour, Renfew	265.00	370.00	475.00
☐ 23 Bobby Rowe, Renfew	160.00	230.00	300.00
☐ 24 Sprague Cleghorn, Renfew	400.00	575.00	750.00
☐ 25 Odie Cleghorn, Renfew	250.00	350.00	450.00
☐ 26 Skene Ronan, Renfew	160.00	230.00	300.00
☐ 27 Walter Smaill, Mt. W.	325.00	465.00	600.00
☐ 28 Ernie Johnson, Mt. W.	270.00	385.00	500.00
☐ 29 Jack Marshall, Mt. W.	265.00	370.00	475.00
☐ 30 Harry Hyland, Mt. W.	265.00	370.00	475.00
☐ 31 Art Ross, Mt. W.	850.00	1225.00	1600.00
☐ 32 Riley Hern (G), Mt. W.	265.00	370.00	475.00
☐ 33 Gordon Roberts, Mt. W.	265.00	370.00	475.00
☐ 34 Frank Glass, Mt. W.	160.00	230.00	300.00
☐ 35 Ernest Russell, Mt. W.	275.00	390.00	500.00
☐ 36 James Gardiner, Mt. W.	265.00	370.00	475.00
☐ 37 Art Bernier, Mtl.	160.00	230.00	300.00
☐ 38 Georges Vézina (G), Mtl.	3200.00	4600.00	6000.00
☐ 39 Henri Dellaire, Mtl.	160.00	230.00	300.00
☐ 40 R. Power, Mtl.	160.00	230.00	300.00
☐ 41 Didier Pitre, Mtl.	265.00	370.00	475.00
☐ 42 Edouard Lalonde, Mtl.	850.00	1225.00	1600.00
☐ 43 Eugene Payan, Mtl.	160.00	230.00	300.00
☐ 44 George Poulin, Mtl.	160.00	230.00	300.00
☐ 45 Jack Laviolette, Mtl.	350.00	550.00	900.00

1910 - 15 IMPERIAL TOBACCO CANADIAN SILKS

These small silks are a multi-subject, multi-sport, multi-colour issue. There are two different hockey silks in this issue and both are known to have several colour variations.

ACC: SC-12
Size: 1 3/4" x 3 1/8"
Face: Multi-coloured prints
Back: Blank
Material: Silk
Imprint: None.

Name	**VG**	**EX**	**EX-NRMT**
☐ Green sticks and lettering, orange puck and bow, black background	10.00	20.00	35.00

1910 - 11 MURAD PICTURE COUPONS

These coupons were packed, one per box in "Murad" cigarettes. Fifteen coupons could be exchanges for one lithographed picture of the College series.

ACC: T-6
Card Size: 2 5/8" x 3 3/34"
Face: Pink and blue; Redemption offer
Back: Pink and blue; Checklist of College Premiums offer
Imprint: S. Anargyros A Corporation.

No. Name	**VG**	**EX**	**EX-NRMT**
☐ 1 Picture Coupon	10.00	20.00	35.00

1910 - 11 MURAD COLLEGE PREMIUM CARDS

Issued as a premium in exchange for 15 picture coupons from Murad Cigarettes. Each college portrays a different sports scene. This series exists with a 2nd edition with minor graphics changes.

ACC: T-6
Card Size: 8" x 5"
Face: Colour print on white card stock
Back: Black and white
Imprint: "Murad" Picture Dept. Drawer S. Jersey City, N.J. This offer expires June 30th, 1911.

College	**VG**	**EX**	**EX-NRMT**
Hockey Singles:	**100.00**	**200.00**	**400.00**

☐ Amherst College (hammer)	☐ Brown University (discus)
☐ Columbia (shot)	☐ Cornell (rowing)
☐ College of the City of N.Y. (pole)	☐ Dartmouth College (unknown)
☐ Fordham University (baseball)	☐ Harvard (football)
☐ New York University (unknown)	☐ Penn.State College (unknown)
☐ Princeton (hammer)	☐ Rochester (hockey)
☐ Swarthmore College (unknown)	☐ Syracuse College (long jump)
☐ Texas University (rowing)	☐ University of California (track)
☐ University of Illinois (unknown)	☐ U. of Michigan (football)
☐ Univeristy of Missouri (unknown)	☐ U. of Pennsylvania (unknown)
☐ University of Kansas (hammer)	☐ U. of Denver (unknown)
☐ Washington & Jefferson	☐ Williams College (unknown)
☐ Yale (rowing)	

1911 STEDMAN BROS. LTD.

Card Size: 3 9/16" x 5 1/2"
Face: Colourized print, card stock
Back: Postcard format
Imprint: Stedman Bros. Ltd., Brantford, Canada. Made in Germany

	Team	VG	EX	EX-NRMT
☐	A popular Cdn. winter sport	20.00	40.00	75.00

1911 - 12 IMPERIAL TOBACCO "C55"

Players in the 1911-12 set are exact duplicates of those on the 1910-11 postcard issue. The player photos appear to form the models for the drawings used on this set. The colour portrait is framed by two hockey sticks. Both the front and back of the card are numbered.

ACC No.: C55

Card Size: 1 1/2" x 2 1/2"
Face: Four colour; Name, Number
Back: Black on card stock; Name, Team, Number, Resume
Imprint: None

	No.	Player	VG	EX	EX-NRMT
		Complete Set (45 cards):	**6,000.00**	**9,000.00**	**12,000.00**
☐	1	Paddy Moran (G), Québec	200.00	300.00	550.00
☐	**2**	**Joe Hall, Québec, RC**	**165.00**	**250.00**	**325.00**
☐	3	Barney Holden, Québec	85.00	130.00	170.00
☐	**4**	**Joe Malone, Québec, RC**	**325.00**	**485.00**	**650.00**
☐	**5**	**Ed Oatman, Québec, RC**	**85.00**	**130.00**	**170.00**
☐	6	Tommy Dunderdale, Québec	170.00	255.00	340.00
☐	**7**	**Ken Mallen, Québec, RC, LC**	**85.00**	**130.00**	**170.00**
☐	**8**	**Jack McDonald, Québec, RC**	**85.00**	**130.00**	**170.00**
☐	9	Fred Lake, Ottawa	85.00	130.00	170.00
☐	**10**	**Albert Kerr, Ottawa, RC**	**85.00**	**130.00**	**170.00**
☐	11	Marty Walsh, Ottawa	140.00	210.00	275.00
☐	**12**	**Hamby Shore, Ottawa, RC**	**85.00**	**130.00**	**170.00**
☐	**13**	**Alex Currie, Ottawa, RC**	**85.00**	**130.00**	**170.00**
☐	14	Bruce Ridpath, Ottawa	85.00	130.00	170.00
☐	15	Bruce Stuart, Ottawa, LC	140.00	210.00	275.00
☐	16	Percy Lesueur (G), Ottawa	165.00	245.00	325.00
☐	**17**	**Jack Darragh, Ottawa, RC**	**140.00**	**210.00**	**275.00**
☐	**18**	**Steve Vair, Renfrew, RC**	**85.00**	**130.00**	**170.00**
☐	**19**	**Don Smith, Renfrew, RC**	**85.00**	**130.00**	**170.00**
☐	20	Fred (Cyclone) Taylor, Renfrew	375.00	565.00	750.00
☐	**21**	**Bert Lindsay (G), Renfrew, RC**	**115.00**	**175.00**	**225.00**
☐	**22**	**Larry Gilmour, Renfrew, RC, LC**	**140.00**	**210.00**	**275.00**
☐	**23**	**Bobby Rowe, Renfrew, RC**	**85.00**	**130.00**	**170.00**
☐	**24**	**S. Cleghorn, Renfrew, RC**	**215.00**	**320.00**	**425.00**
☐	**25**	**Odie Cleghorn, Renfrew, RC**	**125.00**	**190.00**	**250.00**
☐	**26**	**Skene Ronan, Renfrew, RC**	**85.00**	**130.00**	**170.00**
☐	**27A**	**Walter Smaill, Mtl.W., RC, (w Stick)**	**175.00**	**265.00**	**350.00**
☐	**27B**	**Walter Smaill, Mtl.W., RC, (w/o Stick)**	**175.00**	**265.00**	**350.00**
☐	28	Ernie Johnson, Mtl.W.	150.00	225.00	300.00
☐	29	Jack Marshall, Mtl.W.	140.00	210.00	275.00
☐	30	Harry Hyland, Mtl.W.	140.00	210.00	275.00
☐	31	Art Ross, Mtl.W.	450.00	675.00	900.00
☐	32	Riley Hern (G), Mtl.W.	140.00	210.00	275.00
☐	33	Gordon Roberts, Mtl.W.	140.00	210.00	275.00
☐	34	Frank Glass, Mtl.W.	85.00	130.00	170.00
☐	35	Ernest Russell, Mtl.W.	150.00	225.00	300.00
☐	**36**	**James Gardiner, Mtl.W., RC**	**140.00**	**210.00**	**275.00**
☐	37	Art Bernier, Mtl.	85.00	130.00	170.00
☐	38	Georges Vézina (G), Mtl.	2,000.00	3,000.00	4,000.00
☐	39	Henri Dellaire, Mtl.	85.00	130.00	170.00
☐	**40**	**R. Power, Mtl., RC, LC**	**85.00**	**130.00**	**170.00**
☐	41	Didier Pitre, Mtl.	140.00	210.00	275.00
☐	42	Edouard Lalonde, Mtl.	450.00	675.00	900.00
☐	**43**	**Eugene Payan, Mtl., RC**	**85.00**	**130.00**	**170.00**
☐	44	George Poulin, Mtl.	85.00	130.00	170.00
☐	45	Jack Laviolette, Mtl.	200.00	300.00	550.00

1912 - 13 IMPERIAL TOBACCO "C57"

The card number is found on the back to the right of the phrase, "Series of 50". The same crossed hockey sticks and puck design over the series' name "Hockey Series", is found on the C56 series, suggesting that the same producer issued the C56 and C57 issues.

ACC No.: C57

Card Size: 1 1/2" x 2 1/2"
Face: Black and white; Name, Team
Back: Black on card stock; Name, Team, Number, Resume
Imprint: None

	No.	Player	VG	EX	EX-NRMT
		Complete Set (50 cards):	**10,000.00**	**14,000.00**	**18,000.00**
☐	1	Georges Vézina (G), Mtl.C	1,500.00	2,250.00	4,000.00
☐	**2**	**Harry Broadbent, Ott., RC**	**240.00**	**360.00**	**475.00**
☐	**3**	**Clint Benedict (G), Ott, RC**	**325.00**	**465.00**	**600.00**
☐	**4**	**A. Atchinson, NE, RC, LC**	**160.00**	**230.00**	**300.00**
☐	5	Tommy Dunderdale, Que.B	235.00	345.00	450.00
☐	6	Art Bernier, Mtl.W	160.00	230.00	300.00
☐	7	Henri Dellaire, Mtl.C	160.00	230.00	300.00
☐	8	George Poulin, Mtl.C	160.00	230.00	300.00
☐	9	Eugene Payan, Mtl.C, LC	160.00	230.00	300.00
☐	10	Steve Vair, Ren., LC	160.00	230.00	300.00
☐	11	Bobby Rowe, Ren., LC	160.00	230.00	300.00
☐	12	Don Smith, Ren., LC	160.00	230.00	300.00
☐	13	Bert Lindsay (G), Ren.	175.00	265.00	350.00
☐	14	Skene Ronan, Ott., LC	160.00	230.00	300.00
☐	15	Sprague Cleghorn, Ren.	275.00	400.00	525.00
☐	16	Joe Hall, Que.B, LC	260.00	370.00	475.00
☐	17	Jack McDonald, Que.B, LC	160.00	230.00	300.00
☐	18	Paddy Moran (G), Que.B	235.00	345.00	450.00
☐	19	Harry Hyland, Mtl.W	225.00	325.00	425.00
☐	20	Art Ross, Mtl.W	650.00	975.00	1,300.00
☐	21	Frank Glass, Mtl.W	160.00	230.00	300.00
☐	22	Walter Smaill, Mtl.W, LC	160.00	230.00	300.00
☐	23	Gordon Roberts, Mtl.W, LC	225.00	325.00	425.00
☐	24	James Gardiner, Mtl.W	225.00	325.00	425.00
☐	25	Ernie Johnson, Mtl.W	225.00	325.00	425.00
☐	26	Ernest Russell, Mtl.W	225.00	325.00	425.00
☐	27	Percy Lesueur (G), Ott., LC	235.00	445.00	450.00
☐	28	Bruce Ridpath, Ott., LC	160.00	230.00	300.00
☐	29	Jack Darragh, Ott.	225.00	325.00	425.00
☐	30	Hamby Shore, Ott., LC	160.00	230.00	300.00
☐	31	Fred Lake, Ott., LC	160.00	230.00	300.00
☐	32	Alex Currie, Ott., LC	160.00	230.00	300.00
☐	33	Albert Kerr, Ott., LC	160.00	230.00	300.00
☐	**34**	**Eddie Gerard, NE, RC**	**225.00**	**325.00**	**425.00**
☐	**35**	**Carl Kendall, RC**	**160.00**	**230.00**	**300.00**
☐	**36**	**Jack Fournier, RC**	**160.00**	**230.00**	**300.00**
☐	**37**	**Goldie Prodgers, Vic., RC**	**160.00**	**230.00**	**300.00**
☐	**38**	**Jack Marks, Que., RC**	**160.00**	**230.00**	**300.00**
☐	**39**	**G. Broughton (G), Mtl. W, RC, LC**	**175.00**	**265.00**	**350.00**
☐	**40**	**Arthur Boyce (G), Mtl.W, RC, LC**	**175.00**	**265.00**	**350.00**
☐	41	Lester Patrick	425.00	615.00	800.00
☐	**42**	**Joe Dennison, RC**	**160.00**	**230.00**	**300.00**
☐	43	Fred (Cyclone) Taylor	550.00	775.00	1,000.00
☐	44	Edouard Lalonde, Mtl.C	575.00	840.00	1,100.00
☐	45	Didier Pitre, Mtl.C	225.00	325.00	425.00
☐	46	Jack Laviolette, Mtl.C	225.00	325.00	425.00
☐	47	Ed Oatman, Vic.	160.00	230.00	300.00
☐	48	Joe Malone, Que.B	400.00	575.00	750.00
☐	49	Marty Walsh, Ott., LC	225.00	325.00	425.00
☐	50	Odie Cleghorn, Mtl.C	150.00	225.00	450.00

1912 - 13 CALUMET HOCKEY CLUB OF LAURIUM

Card Size: 5 5/16" x 3 9/16"
Face: Black and white photo on card stock
Back: Sepia and white
Imprint: AZO

	Team	VG	EX	EX-NRMT
☐	Calumet Hockey Club of Laurium 1912-13 Northwestern Intermediate Hockey Champions	25.00	50.00	100.00

1912 - 13 A. R. CLARKE AND CO. LTD.

Card Size: 5 9/16" x 3 7/16"
Face: Black and white photo on card stock
Back: Sepia and white
Imprint: AZO

	Team	VG	EX	EX-NRMT
☐	Champions Riverdale Manufacturers' Hockey League, 1912-13	25.00	50.00	100.00

1912 - 13 RICHMOND STRAIGHT CUT CIGARETTES

Silks without sports subjects are valued considerably lower.

Acc: S-23
Size: 3 15/16" x 5 1/2"
Face: Multi-coloured print on white silk
Back: Blank
Material: Silk
Imprint: RICHMOND STRAIGHT CUT CIGARETTES, Factory No. 25, 2nd Dist. Va.

Hockey Singles: 75.00 125.00 250.00

	College		College
			VG / EX / EX-NRMT
☐	Amherst	☐	Annapolis
☐	Arkansas	☐	Brown
☐	C.C.N.Y.	☐	California
☐	Carlisle	☐	Chicago
☐	Colorado	☐	Columbia
☐	Cornell	☐	Dartmouth
☐	Drake	☐	Georgetown
☐	Harvard	☐	Illinois
☐	Iowa	☐	Johns-Hopkins
☐	Kansas	☐	Kentucky
☐	Lafayette	☐	Lehigh
☐	Louisiana	☐	M..I.T.
☐	Michigan	☐	Minnesota
☐	Missouri	☐	Nebraska
☐	Northwestern	☐	Notre Dame
☐	Oberlin	☐	Pennsylvania

☐	Princeton	☐	Purdue
☐	Rochester	☐	Rutgers
☐	Syracuse	☐	Tennessee
☐	Texas	☐	Trinity
☐	Tuffs	☐	Tulane
☐	Vanderbilt	☐	Virginia
☐	Wesleyan	☐	Williams
☐	Wisconsin	☐	West Point
☐	West Virginia	☐	Yale

Note: The only known hockey issue is Trinity College.

1912 - 15 MURAD LARGE & SMALL SILKS

Issued as a redeemable premium. These silks are found with or without an impressed floral design and paper backing sheet. The back is blank and there are 25 colleges as listed below. Each is found in the same ten designs: baseball pitcher, baseball batter, football, golf, hammer throwing, ice hockey, hurdles, rowing, running and putting the shot. Each size was issued with and without an impressed floral design which appears over the entire silk surface.

Large Size: 5" x 7"/ Small Size: 3 1/2" x 5 1/2"
Face: Colour print on white silk
Back: Blank or may come with paper backing sheet
Material: Silk
ACC: S-21 Large; S-22 Small
Imprint: Large Factory No. 7 3rd Dist. N.Y.
Small MURAD CIGARETTES, Factory No. 7 3rd Dist. N.Y.

Large Hockey Set (25 silks):	**750.00**	**1,500.00**	**3,000.00**
Small Hockey Set (25 silks):	**450.00**	**900.00**	**1,800.00**
Common Silk:		**150.00**	**100.00**
		Large	**Small**

	College		
☐☐	Annapolis	☐☐	Brown
☐☐	California	☐☐	Chicago
☐☐	Colorado	☐☐	Columbia
☐☐	Cornell	☐☐	Dartmouth
☐☐	Georgetown	☐☐	Harvard
☐☐	Illinois	☐☐	Michigan
☐☐	Minnesota	☐☐	Missouri
☐☐	Ohio	☐☐	Pennsylvania
☐☐	Princeton	☐☐	Purdue
☐☐	Stanford	☐☐	Texas
☐☐	Syracuse	☐☐	West Point
☐☐	Wisconsin	☐☐	Virginia
☐☐	Yale		

1914 IMPERIAL TOBACCO WINTER CARDS

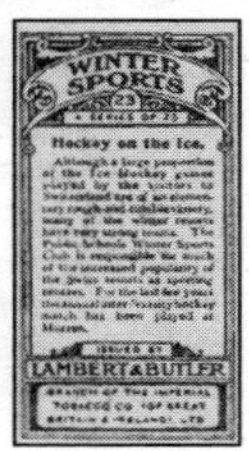

A 25-card set sells at $200 in EX-NRMT. Only the one hockey card is listed below.

Card Size: 1 3/8" x 2 5/8"
Face: Coloured litho, white border; Title
Back: Green on white card stock; Name, number
Imprint: LAMBERT & BUTLER

No.	Scene	VG	EX	EX-NRMT
☐ 23	Hockey on the Ice	7.50	15.00	30.00

1916 ANONYMOUS "CHRISTMAS THOUGHT"

Card Size: 3 1/2" x 5 3/8"
Face: Embossed colourised litho, white border, card stock
Back: Postcard format
Imprint: None

No.	Team	VG	EX	EX-NRMT
☐ C-216	"A Christmas Thought From a Friend" (Two boys play ice-hockey, sprig of holly below)	4.25	8.50	15.00

1919 ANONYMOUS

Card Size: 3 7/16" x 5 3/16"
Face: Black and white cameo photos, white border, card stock
Back: Postcard format
Imprint: None

	Team	VG	EX	EX-NRMT
☐	Victoria Rivers Hockey Club	32.00	65.00	125.00
☐	Victoria Rivers team photo at train station;	45.00	90.00	175.00

1919 VANCOUVER MILLIONAIRES

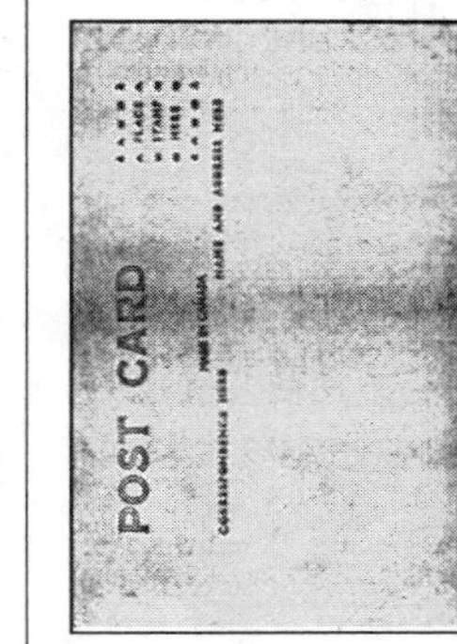

These postcards are unnumbered and listed below in alphabetical order.

Card Size: 3 1/3" x 5 1/2"
Face: Black and white
Back: Black on card stock; Postcard notation
Imprint: None

Complete Set (18 cards):		**1,200.00**	**1,600.00**	**2,00.00**
	Player	**VG**	**EX**	**EX-NRMT**
☐	Lloyd Cook	60.00	80.00	100.00
☐	Art Duncan	60.00	80.00	100.00
☐	Smokey Harris	60.00	80.00	100.00
☐	Alex Irvin	60.00	80.00	100.00
☐	Hughie Lehman (G)	90.00	120.00	150.00
☐	Duncan (Mickey) MacKay	60.00	80.00	100.00
☐	Barney Stanley	150.00	200.00	250.00
☐	Fred (Cyclone) Taylor	250.00	325.00	400.00
☐	C. Uksila	60.00	80.00	100.00

	Caricatures	VG	EX	EX-NRMT
☐	Lloyd Cook	60.00	80.00	100.00
☐	Art Duncan	60.00	80.00	100.00
☐	Smokey Harris	60.00	80.00	100.00
☐	Alex Irvin	60.00	80.00	100.00
☐	Hughie Lehman (G)	90.00	120.00	150.00
☐	Duncan (Mickey) MacKay	60.00	80.00	100.00
☐	Barney Stanley	150.00	200.00	250.00
☐	Fred (Cyclone) Taylor	250.00	325.00	400.00
☐	C. Uksila	60.00	80.00	100.00

1923 NICOLAS SARONY AND CO.

There are 15 cards in this set. Small and large sets are known to exist.

Card Size: 2 1/2" x 3"
Face: Black and white photo, white border, card stock
Back: Postcard format
Imprint: Nicolas Sarony & Co. New Bond Street London. W.
Complete Set (15 cards)

No.	Scene	VG	EX	EX-NRMT
☐ 14	Roman Soldiers Playing Hockey	15.00	20.00	50.00

1923 - 24 CRESCENT ICE CREAM SELKIRKS HOCKEY CLUB

Card number 6 is unknown.
Card Size: 1 9/16" x 2 3/8"
Face: Black and white photo
Back: Black on card stock; Number, Premium offer
Imprint: None

No.	Player	VG	EX	EX-NRMT
	Complete Set (14 cards):	**600.00**	**900.00**	**1200.00**
☐ 1	Cliff O'Meara	50.00	75.00	125.00
☐ 2	Leo Benard	50.00	75.00	100.00
☐ 3	Pete Speirs	50.00	75.00	100.00
☐ 4	Howard Brandow	50.00	75.00	100.00
☐ 5	George Clark	50.00	75.00	100.00
☐ 7	Cecil Browne	50.00	75.00	100.00
☐ 8	Jack Connelly	50.00	75.00	100.00
☐ 9	Chuck Gardner (G)	140.00	210.00	275.00
☐ 10	Ward Turvey	50.00	75.00	100.00
☐ 11	Connie Johanneson	50.00	75.00	100.00
☐ 12	Frank Woodall	50.00	75.00	100.00
☐ 13	Harold McMunn	50.00	75.00	100.00
☐ 14	Connie Neil	50.00	75.00	125.00

1923 - 24 PAULINS CANDY

"Spunk" Sparrow

These cards were issued in Western Canada and feature players from the Western Canadian Hockey League. A prize for was awarded for any one who could complete a 90-card set: either a hockey stick or a box of chocolates.

ACC No.: V128

Card Size: 1 3/8" x 2 3/4"
Face: B&W photo, white border; Name
Back: Black on card stock; Number, Premium offer
Imprint: None

No.	Player	VG	EX	EX-NRMT
	Complete Set (70 cards):	**4,500.00**	**7,000.00**	**9,000.00**
	Common Player:	**65.00**	**100.00**	**130.00**
☐ 1	Bill Borland	80.00	125.00	250.00
☐ 2	Pete Speirs	65.00	100.00	130.00
☐ 3	Jack Hughes	65.00	100.00	130.00
☐ 4	Errol Gillis	65.00	100.00	130.00
☐ 5	Cecil Browne	65.00	100.00	130.00
☐ 6	W. Roberts	65.00	100.00	130.00
☐ 7	Howard Brandow	65.00	100.00	130.00
☐ 8	Fred Comfort	65.00	100.00	130.00
☐ 9	Cliff O'Meara	65.00	100.00	130.00
☐ 10	Leo Benard	65.00	100.00	130.00
☐ 11	Lloyd Harvey	65.00	100.00	130.00
☐ 12	Bobby Connors	65.00	100.00	130.00
☐ 13	Daddy Dalman	65.00	100.00	130.00
☐ 14	Dub Mackie	65.00	100.00	130.00
☐ 15	Lorne Chabot (G)	165.00	250.00	325.00
☐ 16	Phat Wilson	100.00	150.00	200.00
☐ 17	Wilf L'Heureux	65.00	100.00	130.00
☐ 18	Danny Cox	90.00	135.00	175.00
☐ 19	Bill Brydge	90.00	135.00	175.00
☐ 20	Alex Gray	65.00	100.00	130.00
☐ 21	Albert Pudas	65.00	100.00	130.00
☐ 22	Dick Irvine	250.00	375.00	500.00
☐ 23	Puss Traub	65.00	100.00	130.00
☐ 24	Red McCusker (G)	75.00	115.00	150.00
☐ 25	Jack Asseltine	65.00	100.00	130.00
☐ 26	Duke Dutkowski	75.00	115.00	150.00
☐ 27	Charlie McVeigh	90.00	135.00	175.00
☐ 28	George Hay	175.00	265.00	350.00
☐ 29	Amby Moran	65.00	100.00	130.00
☐ 30	Barney Stanley	165.00	250.00	325.00
☐ 31	Art Gagne	75.00	135.00	150.00
☐ 32	Louis Berlinquette	90.00	135.00	175.00
☐ 33	P.C. Stevens	65.00	100.00	130.00
☐ 34	W.D. Elmer	65.00	100.00	130.00
☐ 35	Bill Cook	275.00	425.00	550.00
☐ 36	Leo Reise	90.00	135.00	175.00
☐ 37	Curly Headley	75.00	135.00	150.00
☐ 38	Edouard (Newsy) Lalonde	300.00	450.00	600.00
☐ 39	George Hainsworth (G)	290.00	135.00	575.00
☐ 40	Laurie Scott	65.00	100.00	130.00
☐ 41	Joe Simpson	190.00	275.00	375.00
☐ 42	Bob Trapp	65.00	100.00	130.00
☐ 43	Joe McCormick	65.00	100.00	130.00
☐ 44	Ty Arbour	75.00	115.00	150.00
☐ 45	Duke Keats	65.00	100.00	130.00
☐ 46	Hal Winlker	65.00	100.00	130.00
☐ 47	Johnny Sheppard	90.00	135.00	175.00
☐ 48	Crutchy Morrison	65.00	100.00	130.00
☐ 49	Spunk Sparrow	65.00	100.00	130.00
☐ 50	Percy McGregor	65.00	100.00	130.00
☐ 51	Harry Tuckwell	65.00	100.00	130.00
☐ 52	Chubby Scott	65.00	100.00	130.00
☐ 53	Scotty Fraser	65.00	100.00	130.00
☐ 54	Bob Davis	65.00	100.00	130.00
☐ 55	Clucker White	65.00	100.00	130.00
☐ 56	Bob Armstrong	65.00	100.00	130.00
☐ 57	Doc Langtry	65.00	100.00	130.00
☐ 58	Darb Sommers	65.00	100.00	130.00
☐ 59	Frank Hacquoil	65.00	100.00	130.00
☐ 60	Stan Evans	65.00	100.00	130.00
☐ 61	Ed Oatman	65.00	100.00	130.00
☐ 62	Red Dutton	190.00	275.00	375.00
☐ 63	Herb Gardiner	165.00	250.00	325.00
☐ 64	Bernie Morris	65.00	100.00	130.00
☐ 65	Bobbie Benson	65.00	100.00	130.00
☐ 66	Ernie Anderson	65.00	100.00	130.00
☐ 67	Cully Wilson	75.00	135.00	150.00
☐ 68	Charlie Reid (G)	65.00	100.00	130.00
☐ 69	Harry Oliver	225.00	335.00	450.00
☐ 70	Rusty Crawford	90.00	135.00	300.00

1923 WILLARD'S CHOCOLATES

52
DUNC. MUNRO
CAPTAIN OF CANADIAN OLYMPIC HOCKEY TEAM

This 56-card multi-sport set features only four hockey players. The set was made in the United States and inserted in Willard's Sports Nut Bar. It is uncertain whether a Canadian version was produced.

ACC No.: V122

Photograph Size: 1 3/8" x 3 7/8"
Face: Black and white; Name, Number
Back: Blank
Imprint: None

No.	Player	VG	EX	EX-NRMT
☐ 43	Harry Watson, Cdn.	140.00	210.00	275.00
☐ 45	Ernie Collett (G), Cdn.	75.00	115.00	150.00
☐ 47	Hooley Smith, Cdn.	150.00	225.00	300.00
☐ 52	Dunc Munro, Cdn.	100.00	150.00	200.00

1923 - 24 WILLIAM PATERSON V145-1

10. GEORGES VEZINA
CANADIENS MONTREAL
National Hockey League

This set is very similar to the subsequent V145-2 set except for its sepia (dark brown) colour and size. The name of the player and team appear on the bottom border along with National Hockey League. Card 25 (Bert Corbeau) is extremely rare and not included in the set price.

ACC No.: V145-1

Card Size: 2" x 3 1/4"
Face: Sepia; Name, Team, Number, League
Back: Blank
Imprint: None

No.	Player	VG	EX	EX-NRMT
	Complete Set (40 cards):	**8,000.00**	**12,000.00**	**16,000.00**
☐ 1	Eddie Gerard, Ottawa, LC	150.00	225.00	450.00
☐ **2**	**Frank Nighbor, Ottawa, RC**	**300.00**	**450.00**	**600.00**
☐ **3**	**Francis (King) Clancy, Ott., RC**	**1,200.00**	**1,800.00**	**2,400.00**
☐ 4	Jack Darragh, Ottawa, LC	175.00	265.00	350.00
☐ **5**	**Harry Helman, Ottawa, RC, LC**	**100.00**	**150.00**	**200.00**
☐ **6**	**George Boucher, Ottawa, RC**	**175.00**	**265.00**	**350.00**
☐ 7	Clint Benedict (G), Ottawa	240.00	360.00	475.00
☐ **8**	**Lionel Hitchman, Ottawa, RC**	**140.00**	**210.00**	**275.00**
☐ 9	Harry Broadbent, Ottawa	190.00	285.00	375.00
☐ **10**	**Cy Denneny, Ottawa, RC**	**250.00**	**375.00**	**500.00**
☐ 11	Sprague Cleghorn, Mtl.	215.00	325.00	425.00
☐ **12**	**Sylvio Mantha, Mtl., RC**	**190.00**	**285.00**	**375.00**
☐ 13	Joe Malone, Mtl.	265.00	400.00	525.00
☐ **14**	**Aurèle Joliat, Mtl., RC**	**900.00**	**1,350.00**	**1,800.00**
☐ **15**	**Howie Morenz, Mtl., RC**	**2,750.00**	**4,000.00**	**5,500.00**
☐ **16**	**Billy Boucher, Mtl., RC**	**100.00**	**150.00**	**200.00**
☐ **17**	**Billy Couture, Mtl., RC**	**100.00**	**150.00**	**200.00**
☐ 18	Odie Cleghorn, Mtl.	125.00	185.00	250.00
☐ 19	Georges Vézina (G), Mtl.	900.00	1,350.00	1,800.00
☐ **20**	**Amos Arbour, Tor., RC**	**100.00**	**150.00**	**200.00**
☐ **21**	**Lloyd Andrews, Tor., RC**	**100.00**	**150.00**	**200.00**
☐ **22**	**Billy Stuart, Tor., RC**	**100.00**	**150.00**	**200.00**
☐ **23**	**Cecil (Babe) Dye, Tor., RC**	**240.00**	**360.00**	**475.00**
☐ **24**	**Jack J. Adams, Tor., RC**	**240.00**	**360.00**	**475.00**
☐ **25**	**Bert Corbeau, Tor., RC**		**Extremely Rare**	
☐ **26**	**Reg Noble, Tor., RC**	**175.00**	**265.00**	**350.00**
☐ **27**	**Stan Jackson, Tor., RC**	**100.00**	**150.00**	**200.00**
☐ **28**	**John Roach (G), Tor., RC**	**140.00**	**210.00**	**275.00**
☐ **29**	**Vernon Forbes (G), Ham., RC**	**100.00**	**150.00**	**200.00**
☐ **30**	**Wilf (Shorty) Green, Ham., RC**	**175.00**	**265.00**	**350.00**
☐ **31**	**Redvers (Red) Green, Ham., RC**	**100.00**	**150.00**	**200.00**
☐ 32	Goldie Prodgers, Ham.	100.00	150.00	200.00
☐ **33**	**Leo Reise, Sr., Ham., RC**	**100.00**	**150.00**	**200.00**
☐ **34**	**Ken Randall, Ham., RC**	**100.00**	**150.00**	**200.00**
☐ **35**	**Billy Burch, Ham, RC**	**175.00**	**265.00**	**350.00**
☐ **36**	**Jesse Spring, Ham, RC**	**100.00**	**150.00**	**200.00**
☐ **37**	**Edmond Bouchard, Ham, RC**	**100.00**	**150.00**	**200.00**
☐ **38**	**Mickey Roach, Ham, RC**	**100.00**	**150.00**	**200.00**
☐ **39**	**Charles Fraser, Ham, RC**	**100.00**	**150.00**	**200.00**
☐ **40**	**Corbett Denneny, Ham, RC**	**150.00**	**225.00**	**425.00**

1924 - 25 CHAMP'S CIGARETTE CARDS

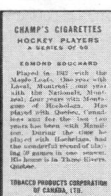

TIGERS
EDMOND BOUCHARD
CHAMP'S CIGARETTES
HOCKEY PLAYERS
A SERIES OF 60
EDMOND BOUCHARD
TOBACCO PRODUCTS CORPORATION OF CANADA, LTD.
HAMILTON, ONT.

The sepia-toned cards contain a short player biography in English on the back.

ACC No.: C144

Card Size: 1 1/2" x 2 1/2"
Face: Sepia; Name
Back: Black on white card stock; Name, Resume
Imprint: TOBACCO PRODUCTS CORPORATION OF CANADA, LTD.

	Player	VG	EX	EX-NRMT
	Complete Set (60 cards):	**8,500.00**	**13,000.00**	**17,000.00**
	Common Player:	**115.00**	**170.00**	**225.00**
☐	**Carson Cooper, Bos., RC**	**115.00**	**170.00**	**225.00**
☐	**Hec Fowler (G), Bos., RC**	**115.00**	**170.00**	**225.00**
☐	**Curley Headley, Bos., RC**	**115.00**	**170.00**	**225.00**
☐	**James Herberts, Bos., RC**	**115.00**	**170.00**	**225.00**
☐	**Herb Mitchell, Bos., RC**	**115.00**	**170.00**	**225.00**
☐	**George Redding, Bos., RC**	**115.00**	**170.00**	**225.00**
☐	**Werner Schnarr, Bos., RC**	**115.00**	**170.00**	**225.00**
☐	**Alfred Skinner, Bos., RC**	**115.00**	**170.00**	**225.00**
☐	Edmond Bouchard, Ham.	115.00	170.00	225.00
☐	Billy Burch, Ham.	175.00	265.00	350.00
☐	Vernon Forbes (.), Ham.	115.00	170.00	225.00
☐	Redvers (Red) Green, Ham.	115.00	170.00	225.00
☐	Wilf (Shorty) Green, Ham.	175.00	265.00	350.00
☐	**Charlie Langlois, Ham., RC**	**115.00**	**170.00**	**225.00**
☐	**Alex McKinnon, Ham., RC**	**115.00**	**170.00**	**225.00**
☐	Goldie Prodgers, Ham.	115.00	170.00	225.00
☐	Ken Randall, Ham.	115.00	170.00	225.00
☐	Mickey Roach, Ham.	115.00	170.00	225.00
☐	Jesse Spring, Ham.	115.00	170.00	225.00
☐	Billy Boucher, Mtl.	115.00	170.00	225.00
☐	Odie Cleghorn, Mtl.	135.00	250.00	265.00
☐	Sprague Cleghorn, Mtl.	215.00	320.00	425.00
☐	Billy Couture, Mtl.	115.00	170.00	225.00
☐	Aurèle Joliat, Mtl.	800.00	1,200.00	1,600.00
☐	Sylvio Mantha, Mtl.	190.00	285.00	375.00

	Player	VG	EX	EX-NRMT
☐	Howie Morenz, Mtl.	1,700.00	2,500.00	3,400.00
☐	Georges Vézina (G), Mtl.	850.00	1,250.00	1,700.00
☐	Clint Benedict (G), Mtl. M., LC	225.00	340.00	450.00
☐	Louis Berlinquette, Mtl. M, RC	115.00	170.00	225.00
☐	Harry Broadbent, Mtl. M, LC	200.00	300.00	400.00
☐	Jim Cain, Mtl. M, RC	115.00	170.00	225.00
☐	George Carroll, Mtl. M, RC	115.00	170.00	225.00
☐	Chuck Dinsmore, Mtl. M, RC	115.00	170.00	225.00
☐	Fred Lowrey, Mtl. M, RC	115.00	170.00	225.00
☐	Dunc Munro, Mtl. M, RC	115.00	170.00	225.00
☐	Gerry Munro, Mtl. M, RC	115.00	170.00	225.00
☐	Sam Rothschild, Mtl. M, RC	115.00	170.00	225.00
☐	Ganton Scott, Mtl. M, RC	115.00	170.00	225.00
☐	Robert Boucher, Ott., RC, LC	115.00	170.00	225.00
☐	Spiff (Earl) Campbell, Ott., RC, LC	115.00	170.00	225.00
☐	Francis (King) Clancy, Ott.	850.00	1,275.00	1,700.00
☐	Alex Connell (G), Ott., RC	215.00	320.00	425.00
☐	Cy Denneny, Ott., LC	240.00	360.00	475.00
☐	Frank Finnigan, Ott., RC	165.00	245.00	325.00
☐	Lionel Hitchman, Ott.	135.00	200.00	265.00
☐	Frank Nighbor, Ott., LC	250.00	375.00	500.00
☐	Hooley Smith, Ott., RC	240.00	360.00	475.00
☐	Jack Adams, Tor.	250.00	375.00	500.00
☐	Lloyd Andrews, Tor.	115.00	170.00	225.00
☐	Bert Corbeau, Tor.	115.00	170.00	225.00
☐	Hap Day, Tor., RC	250.00	375.00	500.00
☐	Babe Dye, Tor.	215.00	320.00	425.00
☐	Albert Holway, Tor., RC	115.00	170.00	225.00
☐	Stan Jackson, Tor., RC	115.00	170.00	225.00
☐	Bert McCaffrey, Tor., RC	115.00	170.00	225.00
☐	Reg Noble, Tor.	190.00	285.00	375.00
☐	Mickey O'Leary, Tor., RC	115.00	170.00	225.00
☐	John Roach (G), Tor.	135.00	200.00	265.00
☐	Chris Speyers, Tor., RC	115.00	170.00	225.00
☐	The Stanley Cup	275.00	415.00	550.00

1924 - 25 MAPLE CRISPETTE

These black and white cards are numbered in the lower right corner and show the player's name in the opposite corner. The backs contain promotional information. Card No. 15, Sprague Cleghorn, is not included in the set price.

ACC No.: V130

Card Size: 1 3/8" x 2 3/8"
Face: Black and white; Name, Number
Back: Black on card stock; Promotional Offer
Imprint: MAPLE CRISPETTE CO, LIMITED
Complete Set (30 cards): 5,000.00 7,400.00 9,800.00

No.	Player	VG	EX	EX-NRMT
☐ 1	Dunc Munro, Mtl. M., RC	135.00	200.00	400.00
☐ 2	Clint Benedict (G), Mtl. M., LC	225.00	340.00	450.00
☐ 3	Hec Fowler (G), Bos., RC	115.00	170.00	225.00
☐ 4	Fern Headley, Bos., RC	115.00	170.00	225.00
☐ 5	Alf Skinner, Bos., RC	115.00	170.00	225.00
☐ 6	Lloyd Cook, Bos., RC	115.00	170.00	225.00
☐ 7	Smokey Harris, Bos., RC	115.00	170.00	225.00
☐ 8	James Herberts, Bos., RC	115.00	170.00	225.00
☐ 9	Carson Cooper, Bos., RC	115.00	170.00	225.00
☐ 10	Redvers (Red) Green, Ham.	115.00	170.00	225.00
☐ 11	Billy Boucher, Mtl.	115.00	170.00	225.00
☐ 12	Howie Morenz, Mtl.	1,600.00	2,400.00	3,200.00
☐ 13	Georges Vézina (G), Mtl.	800.00	1,200.00	1,600.00
☐ 14	Aurèle Joliat, Mtl.	800.00	1,200.00	1,600.00
☐ 15	Sprague Cleghorn, Mtl.		Extremely Rare	
☐ 16	Jim Cain, Mtl. M., RC	115.00	170.00	225.00
☐ 17	Chuck Dinsmore, Mtl. M., RC	115.00	170.00	225.00
☐ 18	Harry Broadbent, Mtl. M., LC	200.00	300.00	400.00
☐ 19	Sam Rothschild, Mtl. M., RC	115.00	170.00	225.00
☐ 20	George Carroll, Mtl. M., RC	115.00	170.00	225.00
☐ 21	Billy Burch, Ham.	175.00	265.00	350.00
☐ 22	Wilf (Shorty) Green, Ham.	175.00	265.00	350.00
☐ 23	Mickey Roach, Ham.	115.00	170.00	225.00
☐ 24	Ken Randall, Ham.	115.00	170.00	225.00
☐ 25	Vernon Forbes (G), Ham.	125.00	190.00	250.00
☐ 26	Charlie Langlois, Ham., RC	115.00	170.00	225.00
☐ 27	Edouard Lalonde, Mtl.	400.00	600.00	800.00
☐ 28	Fred Lowrey, Mtl. M., RC	115.00	170.00	225.00
☐ 29	Ganton Scott, Mtl. M., RC	115.00	170.00	225.00
☐ 30	Louis Berlinquette, Mtl. M., RC	135.00	200.00	400.00

1924 - 25 CRESCENT ICE CREAM SELKIRKS HOCKEY CLUB

These are Sepia cards. Cecil Browne's card is short printed and not included in the set price.

Card Size: 1 9/16" x 2 3/8"
Face: Black and white photo, white border; Team, Name, Position
Back: Black on card stock; Number, Premium offer
Imprint: None
Complete Set (14 cards): 700.00 1,000.00 1,400.00

No.	Player	VG	EX	EX-NRMT
☐ 1	Howard Brandow	50.00	75.00	125.00
☐ 2	Jack Hughes	50.00	75.00	100.00
☐ 3	Tony Baril	50.00	75.00	100.00
☐ 4	Bill Bowman	50.00	75.00	100.00
☐ 5	W. Roberts	50.00	75.00	100.00
☐ 6	Cecil Browne	300.00	450.00	600.00
☐ 7	Errol Gillis	50.00	75.00	100.00
☐ 8	Selkirks Team	115.00	179.00	225.00
☐ 9	Fred Comfort	50.00	75.00	100.00
☐ 10	Cliff O'Meara	50.00	75.00	100.00
☐ 11	Leo Benard	50.00	75.00	100.00
☐ 12	Pete Speirs	50.00	75.00	100.00
☐ 13	Peter Meurer	50.00	75.00	100.00
☐ 14	Billy Borland	50.00	75.00	125.00

1924 - 25 CRESENT ICE CREAM FALCON TIGERS HOCKEY CLUB

Card number 6 is unknown.

Card Size: 1 9/16" x 2 3/8"
Face: Black and white photo, white border; Team, Name, Position
Back: Black on card stock; Number, Premium offer
Imprint: None
Complete Set (14 cards): 1,500.00 2,200.00 3,000.00

No.	Player	VG	EX	EX-NRMT
☐ 1	Bill Cockburn	150.00	225.00	400.00
☐ 2	Wally Byron	150.00	225.00	300.00
☐ 3	Wally Fridfinson	150.00	225.00	300.00
☐ 4	Murray Murdoch	150.00	225.00	300.00
☐ 5	Oliver Redpath	150.00	225.00	300.00
☐ 7	Ward McVey	150.00	225.00	300.00
☐ 8	Tote Mitchell	150.00	225.00	300.00
☐ 9	Lorne Carrol	150.00	225.00	300.00
☐ 10	Tony Wise	150.00	225.00	300.00
☐ 11	Johnny Myres	150.00	225.00	300.00
☐ 12	Gordon McKenzie	150.00	225.00	300.00
☐ 13	Harry Neil	150.00	225.00	300.00
☐ 14	Blake Watson	150.00	225.00	400.00

1924 -25 HOLLAND CREAMERIES WESTERN HOCKEY

Card Size:1 1/2" x 2 7/8"
Face: Black and white photo, white border; Name, Position, Number
Back: Black on card stock; Premium offer
Imprint: None
Complete Set (10 cards): 750.00 1,100.00 1,500.00

No.	Player	VG	EX	EX-NRMT
☐ 1	W. Fridfinnson	75.00	110.00	175.00
☐ 2	Harold McMunn	75.00	110.00	150.00
☐ 3	Art. Somers	75.00	110.00	150.00
☐ 4	Frank Woodall	75.00	110.00	150.00
☐ 5	Frank Fredrickson	125.00	185.00	250.00
☐ 6	R.J. Benson	75.00	110.00	150.00
☐ 7	Harry Neil	75.00	110.00	150.00
☐ 8	Wally Byron	75.00	110.00	150.00
☐ 9	Connie Neil	300.00	450.00	600.00
☐ 10	J. Austman	75.00	110.00	175.00

1924 - 25 WILLIAM PATERSON V145-2

The cards are slightly smaller than the otherwise very similar V145-1 series and have a greenish black tone. Card no.3, Francis Clancy, is the only card numbered the same as in the V145-1 series.

ACC No.: V145-2

Card Size: 1 1/16" x 3 1/4"
Face: Green, Black and white; Name, Team, Number, League
Back: Blank
Imprint: None
Complete Set (60 cards): 8,000.00 12,000.00 16,000.00
Common Player: 95.00 135.00 190.00

No.	Player	VG	EX	EX-NRMT
☐ 1	Joe Ironstone (G), Ott., RC, LC	115.00	175.00	335.00
☐ 2	George Boucher, Ott., LC	125.00	190.00	250.00
☐ 3	Francis (King) Clancy, Ott.	850.00	1,275.00	1,700.00
☐ 4	Lionel Hitchman, Ott.	120.00	180.00	235.00
☐ 5	Hooley Smith, Ott., RC	225.00	340.00	450.00
☐ 6	Frank Nighbor, Ott., LC	225.00	335.00	450.00
☐ 7	Cy Denneny, Ott., LC, Err (Dennenay)	225.00	340.00	450.00
☐ 8	Spiff Campbell, Ott., RC, LC	95.00	135.00	190.00
☐ 9	Frank Finnigan, Ott., RC	125.00	190.00	250.00
☐ 10	Alex Connell (G), Ott., RC	200.00	300.00	400.00
☐ 11	Vernon Forbes (G), Ham.	95.00	145.00	190.00
☐ 12	Ken Randall, Ham.	95.00	145.00	190.00
☐ 13	Billy Burch, Ham.	165.00	250.00	325.00
☐ 14	Wilf (Shorty) Green, Ham.	165.00	250.00	325.00
☐ 15	Redvers (Red) Green, Ham.	95.00	145.00	190.00
☐ 16	Alex McKinnon, Ham., RC	95.00	145.00	190.00
☐ 17	Charlie Langlois, Ham., RC	95.00	145.00	190.00
☐ 18	Mickey Roach, Ham.	95.00	145.00	190.00
☐ 19	Edmond Bouchard, Ham.	95.00	145.00	190.00
☐ 20	Jesse Spring, Error, Ham.	95.00	145.00	190.00
☐ 21	Carson Cooper, Bos., RC	95.00	145.00	190.00
☐ 22	Smokey Harris, Bos., RC	95.00	145.00	190.00
☐ 23	Fern Headley, Bos., RC	95.00	145.00	190.00
☐ 24	Bill Cook, Bos., RC	275.00	415.00	550.00
☐ 25	James Herberts, Bos., RC	95.00	145.00	190.00
☐ 26	Werner Schnarr, Bos., RC	95.00	145.00	190.00
☐ 27	Alf Skinner, Bos., RC	95.00	145.00	190.00
☐ 28	George Redding, Bos., RC	95.00	145.00	190.00
☐ 29	Herb Mitchell, Bos., RC	95.00	145.00	190.00
☐ 30	Hec Fowler (G), Bos., RC	115.00	170.00	225.00
☐ 31	Billy Stuart, Bos.	95.00	145.00	190.00
☐ 32	Clint Benedict (G), Mtl. M., LC	200.00	300.00	400.00
☐ 33	Gerry Munro, Mtl. M., RC	95.00	145.00	190.00
☐ 34	Dunc Munro, Mtl. M., RC	95.00	145.00	190.00
☐ 35	Jim Cain, Mtl. M	95.00	145.00	190.00
☐ 36	Fred Lowrey, Mtl. M., RC	95.00	145.00	190.00
☐ 37	Sam Rothschild,, Mtl. M. RC	95.00	145.00	190.00
☐ 38	Ganton Scott, Mtl. M., RC	95.00	145.00	190.00
☐ 39	Harry Broadbent, Mtl. M, LC	190.00	285.00	375.00
☐ 40	Chuck Dinsmore, Mtl. M., RC	95.00	145.00	190.00
☐ 41	Louis Berlinquette, Mtl. M., RC	95.00	145.00	190.00
☐ 42	George Carroll, Mtl. M., RC	95.00	145.00	190.00
☐ 43	Georges Vézina (G), Mtl.	700.00	1,050.00	1,400.00
☐ 44	Billy Couture, Mtl.	95.00	145.00	190.00
☐ 45	Odie Cleghorn, Mtl.	125.00	190.00	250.00
☐ 46	Billy Boucher, Mtl.	95.00	145.00	190.00
☐ 47	Howie Morenz, Mtl.	1,500.00	2,250.00	3,000.00
☐ 48	Aurèle Joliat, Mtl.	700.00	1,050.00	1,400.00
☐ 49	Sprague Cleghorn, Mtl.	200.00	300.00	400.00
☐ 50	Billy Mantha, Mtl., RC	95.00	145.00	190.00
☐ 51	Reg Noble, Tor. S.P.	175.00	265.00	350.00
☐ 52	John Roach (G), Tor. S.P.	125.00	190.00	250.00
☐ 53	Jack Adams, Tor. S.P.	225.00	340.00	450.00
☐ 54	Babe Dye, Tor. S.P.	200.00	300.00	400.00
☐ 55	Reg Reid, Tor. S.P., RC	95.00	145.00	190.00
☐ 56	Albert Holway, Tor. S.P,. RC	95.00	145.00	190.00
☐ 57	Bert McCaffery, Tor. S.P., RC	95.00	145.00	190.00
☐ 58	Bert Corbeau, Tor. S.P.	125.00	185.00	250.00
☐ 59	Lloyd Andrews, Tor. S.P.	95.00	145.00	190.00
☐ 60	Stan Jackson, Tor. S.P.	110.00	165.00	300.00

1925 - 27 ANONYMOUS ISSUE

It has become evident that more than two different anonymous sets were issued during this time period. Previously designated as "with borders" and "without borders", additional cards have surfaced with numbers that do not correspond to prior checklists. Until further information is available, all these cards will be grouped together. Cards without borders are designated with an "NB".

Card Size: 1 3/8" x 2 3/8"
Face: Black and white photo, white border or borderless; Name
Back: Black on card stock; Premium offer, Bilingual
Imprint: None

	No.	Player	VG	EX	EX-NRMT
		Common Player:	**110.00**	**165.00**	**200.00**
☐	1	Billy Boucher, Mtl.	200.00	300.00	550.00
☐	1	George Hainsworth, Mtl.	550.00	775.00	1,000.00
☐	2	Billy Boucher, Mtl.	285.00	395.00	500.00
☐	2	Billy Coutu, Mtl.	225.00	315.00	400.00
☐	3	Sylvio Mantha, Mtl.	285.00	395.00	500.00
☐	3	Georges Vézina (G), Mtl.	800.00	1,150.00	1,500.00
☐	4	Sylvio Mantha, Mtl.	300.00	425.00	550.00
☐	4	Roland Paulhus, Mtl.	110.00	155.00	200.00
☐	4	Roland Paulhus, Mtl.	110.00	155.00	200.00
☐	5	Alphonse Lacroix (G), Mtl.	110.00	155.00	200.00
☐	6	Albert Leduc, Mtl., Error	50.00	100.00	200.00
☐	7	W. Larochelle, Mtl., Error (Victor)	140.00	195.00	250.00
☐	7	Wildor Larochelle (NB), Mtl..	140.00	195.00	250.00
☐	8	Aurèle Joliat, Mtl.	700.00	1,000.00	1,300.00
☐	9	Howie Morenz, Mtl.	2,700.00	3,600.00	4,500.00
☐	10	Hector Lepiné, Mtl.	110.00	155.00	200.00
☐	11	Alphonse Lacroix (G), Mtl.	110.00	155.00	200.00
☐	11	Amby Moran (G), Mtl.	110.00	155.00	200.00
☐	12	Art Gagné, Mtl.	125.00	190.00	250.00
☐	12	Herb Rheaume (NB) (G), Mtl.	110.00	155.00	200.00
☐	13	Pit Lépine, Mtl.	250.00	350.00	450.00
☐	14	Bill Holmes, Mtl.	110.00	155.00	200.00
☐	15	Leo Dandurand, Director, Mtl.	285.00	395.00	500.00
☐	16	Alex Connell (G), Ott.	325.00	465.00	600.00
☐	16	Frank Nighbor, Ott.	325.00	465.00	600.00
☐	17	Francis (King) Clancy, Ott.	1,000.00	1,400.00	1,800.00
☐	17	Cy Denneny, Ott.	285.00	395.00	500.00
☐	18	Francis (King) Clancy, (NB), Ott.	1,000.00	1,400.00	1,800.00
☐	19	Billy Boucher, Ott.	140.00	195.00	250.00
☐	**19**	**Hec Kilrea, Ott., RC**	**110.00**	**155.00**	**200.00**
☐	**20**	**Hec Kilrea, Ott., RC**	**110.00**	**155.00**	**200.00**
☐	21	Hooley Smith, Ott.	325.00	415.00	600.00
☐	**22**	**Alex Smith, Ott., RC**	**140.00**	**195.00**	**250.00**
☐	22	Alex Smith (NB), Ott.	140.00	195.00	250.00
☐	25	Ed Gorman, Ott.	110.00	155.00	200.00
☐	31	Sprague Cleghorn, Bos.	325.00	465.00	600.00
☐	31	Carson Cooper, Bos.	110.00	155.00	200.00
☐	32	Carson Cooper, Bos.	110.00	155.00	200.00
☐	36	Hugo Harrington, Bos.	110.00	155.00	200.00
☐	38	Herb Mitchell, Bos.	110.00	155.00	200.00
☐	39	Herb Mitchell (NB), Bos.	110.00	155.00	200.00
☐	39	Charles Stewart (G), Bos.	110.00	155.00	200.00
☐	40	Red Stuart, Bos.	110.00	155.00	200.00
☐	41	Lloyd Cook, Bos.	110.00	155.00	200.00
☐	41	Sprague Cleghorn (NB), Bos. (Mtl.)	285.00	395.00	500.00
☐	42	Billy Coutu, Mtl.	225.00	315.00	400.00
☐	42	Billy Coutu, Mtl.	100.00	200.00	400.00
☐	91	Dutch Cain (NB), Bos. (Bos.)	135.00	190.00	250.00
☐	46	Odie Cleghorn, Pgh. P.	150.00	215.00	275.00
☐	46	Odie Cleghorn (NB), Pgh. P.	150.00	215.00	275.00
☐	46	Odie Cleghorn (NB), Mtl.	150.00	215.00	275.00
☐	47	Louis Berlinquette, Pgh. P. (Tor.)	110.00	155.00	200.00
☐	47	Roy Worters, Pgh. P.	450.00	625.00	800.00
☐	48	Hib (Hibbert) Milks, Pgh. P.	110.00	155.00	200.00
☐	52	Hib (Hibbert) Milks (NB), Pgh. P.	110.00	155.00	200.00
☐	57	Odie Cleghorn, Pgh. P.	150.00	215.00	275.00
☐	61	Pete Bellefeuille, Tor.S.P.	200.00	275.00	350.00
☐	76	Charlie Langlois, NY Am.	65.00	125.00	250.00
☐	77	Jake Forbes (G), NY Am.	100.00	200.00	400.00
☐	79	Billy Burch, NY Am.	75.00	150.00	300.00
☐	82	Joe Simpson, NY Am.	75.00	150.00	300.00
☐	62	Gerry Munro, Mtl. M.	110.00	155.00	200.00
☐	64	Bert Corbeau, Mtl. M.	135.00	195.00	250.00
☐	76	Charlie Langlois, Mtl. M.	110.00	155.00	200.00
☐	77	Jake Forbes, Mtl. M.	110.00	155.00	200.00
☐	79	Billie Burch, Mtl. M.	225.00	315.00	400.00
☐	82	Joe Simpson, Mtl. M.	225.00	315.00	400.00
☐	91	Dutch Cain, Mtl. M.	135.00	195.00	250.00
☐	91	Dunc Munro, Mtl. M.	150.00	215.00	275.00
☐	92	Dunc Munro (NB), Mtl. M.	150.00	215.00	275.00
☐	**92**	**Nels Stewart, Mtl. M., RC**	**425.00**	**615.00**	**800.00**
☐	95	Clint Benedict (G), Mtl. M.	350.00	500.00	650.00
☐	96	Reg Noble, Mtl. M.	215.00	295.00	375.00
☐	97	Nels Stewart, Mtl. M.	425.00	615.00	800.00
☐	100	Sam Rothschild, Mtl. M., Err (Rotchild)	110.00	155.00	200.00
☐	121	Harry Holmes (G), Det. C.	225.00	315.00	400.00
☐	127	Clem Loughlin, Det. C.	110.00	155.00	200.00
☐	129	Johnny Sheppard, Det. C.	110.00	155.00	200.00
☐	136	Gord Fraser, Chi.	110.00	155.00	200.00
☐	138	Dick Irvin, Chi.	350.00	500.00	650.00

1925 DOMINION CHOCOLATES

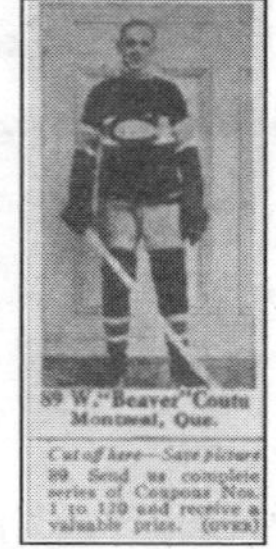

This 120-card multi-sport set features only 32 hockey cards. A 120-card set sells at $9,000.

Card Size: 1 1/4" x 2 7/8"
Face: Black and white, white border; Number, Name
Back: Black on card stock; Name, Resume
Imprint: Dominion Chocolate Co., Limited 72 Duchess Street, Toronto, Canada

	No.	Player	VG	EX	EX-NRMT
☐	13	Granite Club, Olympic Champs	115.00	170.00	225.00
☐	28	North Toronto, O.H.A.	90.00	135.00	175.00
☐	35	Peterborough, O.H.A.	90.00	135.00	175.00
☐	49	Owen Sound Jrs., O.H.A.	90.00	135.00	175.00
☐	55	E.J. Collett, Granite	70.00	100.00	140.00
☐	56	Hughie J. Fox, Granite	70.00	100.00	140.00
☐	57	Dunc Munro, Granite	85.00	125.00	165.00
☐	58	M. Rutherford, Granite	70.00	100.00	140.00
☐	59	Beattie Ramsay, Granite	70.00	100.00	140.00
☐	60	Bert McCaffery, Tor.	70.00	100.00	140.00
☐	61	Soo Greyhounds	90.00	135.00	175.00
☐	68	J.P. Aggatts	70.00	100.00	140.00
☐	69	Hooley Smith, Granite, Err (Hooly)	150.00	225.00	300.00
☐	70	J. Cameron (G), Granite	70.00	100.00	140.00
☐	81	William Fraser, Nova Scotia	70.00	100.00	140.00
☐	82	Vernon Forbes (G), Hamilton	70.00	100.00	140.00
☐	83	Wilf (Shorty) Green, Hamilton	135.00	200.00	265.00
☐	84	Redvers (Red) Green, Hamilton	70.00	100.00	140.00
☐	86	Jack Langtry	70.00	100.00	140.00
☐	89	Billy Coutu, Mtl.C	70.00	100.00	140.00
☐	92	J. Hughes	70.00	100.00	140.00
☐	95	Edouard Lalonde	240.00	360.00	475.00
☐	101	Bill Brydge, Port Arthur	70.00	100.00	140.00
☐	103	Cecil Browne, Selkirk	70.00	100.00	140.00
☐	106	J.C. "Red" Porter, Tor.	70.00	100.00	140.00
☐	112	North Bay Hockey Team	90.00	135.00	175.00
☐	113	Ross Somerville, Tor. Univ.	70.00	100.00	140.00
☐	114	Harry Watson, Granite	150.00	225.00	300.00
☐	117	Odie Cleghorn, Error (Ogie)	90.00	135.00	175.00
☐	118	Lionel Conacher, Tor.	300.00	450.00	600.00
☐	119	Aurèle Joliat, Mtl.	425.00	640.00	850.00
☐	120	Georges Vézina (G), Mtl.	500.00	750.00	1,300.00

1925 FSM WINTERSPORT ISSUE

Card Size: 2 7/16" x 4 1/16"
Face: Multi-coloured print, yellow border, playing card stock
Back: Blue and brown playing card
Imprint: FSM

	No.	Scene	VG	EX	EX-NRMT
☐	XII,4	Eis-Hockey	50.00	100.00	200.00

1926 DOMINION CHOCOLATES

Issued by Dominion Chocolates c1926 this 60-card set features Canadian athletes from several different sports. This set had a premium tab along the bottom of the card. There were two series of this set, both of which are identical except the second set was printed on a lighter weight stock. Only the eleven hockey cards are listed and priced here.

Photograph Size: 1 1/16" x 2 3/8"
Face: Black and white photo, white border; Name, Number, Promotional offer
Back: Black and white; Name, Number, Resume
Imprint: Dominion Chocolate Co., Limited

	No.	Player	VG	EX	EX-NRMT
☐	11	Alex Gray, Toronto	75.00	115.00	150.00
☐	12	Duncan B. Munro, Toronto	100.00	150.00	200.00
☐	17	Gerald Green, Toronto	75.00	115.00	150.00
☐	18	Ernie Williams, Toronto	75.00	115.00	150.00
☐	23	Douglas Young, Toronto	75.00	115.00	150.00
☐	24	A. Gauthier, Toronto	75.00	115.00	150.00
☐	25	Don Cameron, Québec	75.00	115.00	150.00
☐	26	George Clarke	75.00	115.00	150.00
☐	27	"Steve" Rice, Toronto	75.00	115.00	150.00
☐	28	"Ken" Doraty, Regina	125.00	185.00	250.00
☐	29	"Bud" Fisher (G), Toronto	75.00	115.00	150.00

1927 - 32 LA PRESSE

This set was issued by the French Canadian newspaper in Montréal.

Photograph Size: 10" x 16 1/2"
Face: Four colour; Name
Back: Newspaper
Imprint: None

Player \ Date Issued	VG	EX	EX-NRMT
1927 - 28 ISSUE			
☐ Howie Morenz, Mtl.C., December 10	215.00	325.00	425.00
☐ Aurèle Joliat, Mtl.C., December 17	170.00	250.00	335.00
☐ Sylvio Mantha, Mtl.C., December 24	70.00	100.00	140.00
☐ Pit Lépine, Mtl.C., December 31	45.00	65.00	85.00
☐ George Hainsworth (G), Mtl.C., Jan. 7	80.00	120.00	160.00
☐ Art Gagné, Mtl.C., January 14	45.00	65.00	85.00
☐ Herb Gardiner, Mtl.C., January 21	65.00	95.00	125.00
☐ Albert Leduc, Mtl.C., January 28	45.00	65.00	85.00
☐ Wildor Larochelle, Mtl.C., February 4	45.00	65.00	85.00
☐ Léonard Gaudreault, Mtl.C., Feb. 11	45.00	65.00	85.00
☐ Gizzy Hart, Mtl.C., February 18	45.00	65.00	85.00
☐ Charles Langlois, Mtl.C., February 25	45.00	65.00	85.00
☐ Georges Vézina (G), Mtl.C., March 3	200.00	300.00	400.00
☐ Cattarinich/ Hart/ Dandurand, Letourmeau, Mtl.C., March 31	65.00	95.00	125.00
☐ Eddie Shore, Bos., April 7	175.00	250.00	350.00
☐ Lionel Conacher, NYA, April 14	95.00	140.00	185.00
☐ Red Porter, Tor. Grad., April 21	45.00	65.00	85.00
☐ George Patterson, Mtl.C., April 28	45.00	65.00	85.00
1928 - 29 ISSUE			
☐ Martin Burke, Mtl.C., December 15	45.00	65.00	85.00
☐ Nels Stewart, Mtl.M., December 22	85.00	130.00	170.00
☐ Babe Siebert, Mtl.M., January 5	70.00	100.00	140.00
☐ Happy Day, Tor., January 12	65.00	95.00	130.00
☐ Clint Benedict (G), Mtl.M., January 19	80.00	120.00	160.00
☐ Red Dutton, Mtl.M., January 26	65.00	100.00	130.00
☐ Jimmy Ward, Mtl.M., February 2	45.00	65.00	85.00
☐ Bill Phillips, Mtl.M., February 9	45.00	65.00	85.00
☐ Frank Boucher, NYR, February 16	75.00	115.00	150.00
☐ Lucien Brunet, Local League, Feb. 23	45.00	65.00	85.00
☐ George Boucher, Ott., March 2	65.00	95.00	130.00
☐ Armand Mondou, Mtl. C., March 16	45.00	65.00	85.00
☐ Bun Cook, NYR, March 23	70.00	100.00	140.00
☐ Georges Mantha, Mtl.C., April 6	45.00	65.00	85.00
1929 - 30 ISSUE			
☐ Gordon Fraser, Mtl.C., November 30	45.00	65.00	85.00
☐ Bert McCaffrey, Mtl.C., December 7	45.00	65.00	85.00
☐ Hec Kilrea, Ott., December 28	45.00	65.00	85.00
☐ Andy Blair, Tor., January 4	45.00	65.00	85.00
☐ Francis (King) Clancy, Ott., Jan. 11	125.00	185.00	250.00
☐ John Ross Roach (G), Tor., Jan. 18	60.00	90.00	115.00
☐ Leo Bourgeault, NYR, January 25	45.00	65.00	85.00
☐ Raymond Belanger, Club, Champtre, Feb. 1	45.00	65.00	85.00
☐ Lionel Hitchman, Bos., February 8	50.00	75.00	100.00
☐ Joe Primeau, Tor., February 15	75.00	115.00	150.00
☐ Dutch Gainor, Bos., February 22	45.00	65.00	85.00
☐ Tiny Thompson (G), Bos., March 1	80.00	120.00	160.00
☐ Gus Rivers, Mtl.C., March 8	45.00	65.00	85.00
☐ Hooley Smith, Mtl.C., March 29	65.00	100.00	130.00
☐ Flat Walsh, Mtl.M., April 5	45.00	65.00	85.00
☐ Montréal Canadiens Team, April 26	70.00	100.00	140.00
1930 - 31 ISSUE			
☐ Earl Miller, Chi., December 13	45.00	65.00	85.00
☐ Johnny Gagnon, Mtl.C., December 20	45.00	65.00	85.00
☐ Art Sommers, Chi., December 27	45.00	65.00	85.00
☐ Johnny Gottselig, Chi., January 3	50.00	75.00	100.00
☐ Johnny Gallagher, Mtl.M., January 17	45.00	65.00	85.00
☐ Earl Roche, Mtl.M., January 24	45.00	65.00	85.00
☐ Jack McVicar, Mtl.M., January 31	45.00	65.00	85.00
☐ Dave Kerr (G), Mtl.M., February 7	60.00	90.00	120.00
☐ Desse Roche, Mtl.M., February 14	45.00	65.00	85.00
☐ Paul Hayes, Mtl.M., February 21	45.00	65.00	85.00
☐ Al Huggins, Mtl.M., February 28	45.00	65.00	85.00
☐ Red Horner, Tor., March 7	65.00	100.00	130.00
☐ Harvey Jackson, Tor., March 21	75.00	115.00	150.00
☐ Charlie Conacher, Tor., March 28	80.00	120.00	160.00
☐ Ralph Saint Germain, McGill, April 4	45.00	65.00	85.00
☐ Ebbie Goodfellow, Falcons, April 11	65.00	100.00	130.00
1931 - 32 ISSUE			
☐ Normie Himes, NYA, December 19	45.00	65.00	85.00
☐ Rosario (Lolo) Couture, Chi., Dec. 26	45.00	65.00	85.00
☐ George Owen, Bos., January 2	45.00	65.00	85.00
☐ Chuck Gardiner (G), Chi., January 9	65.00	100.00	130.00
☐ Tommy Cook, Chi., January 16	45.00	65.00	85.00
☐ Frank Finnigan, March 12	55.00	80.00	110.00
☐ William Cockburn, Win., March 19	45.00	65.00	85.00
☐ Arthur Alexandre, Mtl., April 16	45.00	65.00	85.00
1938 - 39 ISSUE			
☐ Montreal Team, February 11	70.00	100.00	140.00
1945 - 46 ISSUE			
☐ Maurice Richard, Mtl.C., February 16	130.00	200.00	260.00

1927 IMPERIAL TOBACCO WORLD OF SPORT

There are 50 cards in this set. There is only one hockey card in the set..

Card Size: 1 7/16" x 2 5/8"
Face: Black and white, white border; Title
Back: Black on white card stock; Title, number,
Imprint: LAMBERT & BUTLER

No.	Scene	VG	EX	EX-NRMT
☐ 9	Montreal Victorias			

1927 - 28 MONTREAL CANADIENS LA PATRIE

Photo Size: 8 1/2" x 11"
Sponsor: La Patrie

		VG	EX	EX-NRMT
Complete Set (21 photos):		**900.00**	**1350.00**	**1800.00**
☐ 1	Sylvio Mantha	70.00	100.00	135.00
☐ 2	Art Gagné	25.00	35.00	50.00
☐ 3	Leo Lafrance	25.00	35.00	50.00
☐ 4	Aurèle Joliat	150.00	225.00	300.00
☐ 5	Pit Lepine	40.00	60.00	75.00
☐ 6	Gizzy Hart	25.00	35.00	50.00
☐ 7	Wildor Larochelle	25.00	35.00	50.00
☐ 8	George Hainsworth (G)	75.00	115.00	150.00
☐ 9	Herb Gardiner	50.00	75.00	100.00
☐ 10	Albert LeDuc	40.00	60.00	75.00
☐ 11	Marty Burke	40.00	60.00	75.00
☐ 12	Charlie Langlois	25.00	35.00	50.00
☐ 13	Leo Gaudreault	45.00	70.00	90.00
☐ 14	Howie Morenz	215.00	320.00	425.00
☐ 15	Cecil M. Hart	45.00	70.00	90.00
☐ 16	Leo Dandurand	40.00	60.00	75.00
☐ 17	Edouard Lalonde	75.00	115.00	150.00
☐ 18	Didier Pitre	40.00	60.00	75.00
☐ 19	Jack Laviolette	50.00	75.00	100.00
☐ 20	George Patterson	25.00	35.00	50.00
☐ 21	Georges Vézina (G)	190.00	285.00	375.00

1928 SALEM ZIGARETTENFABRIK WORLD IN PICTURES

Card Size: 1 9/16" x 2 1/4"
Face: Colourized print, white border, card stock
Back: Black and white; Name, Number, Title, German text
Imprint: SALEM ZIGARETTENFABRIK DRESDEN

No.	Scene	VG	EX	EX-NRMT
☐ 2	Kanadas Eishockey - Mannschaft (Canada's Ice Hockey Tournament)	40.00	80.00	150.00

1928 - 29 PAULINS CANDY

Issued in Western Canada during 1928 and 1929, this extremely scarce set has two unknown cards (numbers 9 and 20). Card numbers 51, 53, 72, 75, 82, 84, 85, 86 and 90 depict players from the Calgary Jimmies who have not been identified.

Card Size: 1 3/8" x 2 5/8"
Face: Black and white photo, white border; Name
Back: Black on card stock; Number, Premium offer
Imprint: None

No.	Player	VG	EX	EX-NRMT
Complete Set (90 cards):		**900.00**	**2,250.00**	**4,500.00**
Common Team (1 to 40):		**65.00**	**95.00**	**125.00**
Common Player (41 to 90):		**65.00**	**95.00**	**125.00**
☐ 1	U. of Manitoba Girls Team	65.00	95.00	175.00
☐ 2	Elgin Hockey Team	65.00	95.00	125.00
☐ 3	Brandon Schools Boy Champions	65.00	95.00	125.00
☐ 4	Port Arthur Hockey Team	65.00	95.00	125.00
☐ 5	Enderby Hockey Team	65.00	95.00	125.00
☐ 6	Humbolt H.S. Hockey Team	65.00	95.00	125.00
☐ 7	Regina Collecgiate Hockey Team	65.00	95.00	125.00
☐ 8	Weyburn Beavers	65.00	95.00	125.00
☐ 9	Moose Jaw College Jr. Team	65.00	95.00	125.00
☐ 10	M.A.C. Junior Hockey	65.00	95.00	125.00
☐ 11	Vermilion Agricultural School	65.00	95.00	125.00
☐ 12	Rovers, Cranbrook	65.00	95.00	125.00
☐ 13	Empire School, Moose Jaw	65.00	95.00	125.00
☐ 14	Arts Senior Hockey	65.00	95.00	125.00
☐ 15	Juvenile Varsity Hockey	65.00	95.00	125.00
☐ 16	St. Peter's College Hockey	65.00	95.00	125.00
☐ 17	Arts Girls Hockey Team	65.00	95.00	125.00
☐ 18	Swan River Hockey Team	65.00	95.00	125.00
☐ 19	UMSU Junior Hockey Team	65.00	95.00	125.00
☐ 20	Champion College Hockey Team	65.00	95.00	125.00
☐ 21	Drinkwater Hockey Team	65.00	95.00	125.00
☐ 22	Elks Hockey Team, Biggar, Sask.	65.00	95.00	125.00
☐ 23	South Calgary High School	65.00	95.00	125.00
☐ 24	Meota Hockey	65.00	95.00	125.00
☐ 25	Chartered Accountants	65.00	95.00	125.00
☐ 26	Nutana Collegiate Hockey Team	65.00	95.00	125.00
☐ 27	MacLeod Hockey Team	65.00	95.00	125.00
☐ 28	Arts Junior Hockey	65.00	95.00	125.00
☐ 29	Fort William Juniors	65.00	95.00	125.00
☐ 30	Swan Lake Hockey Team	65.00	95.00	125.00
☐ 31	Dauphin Hockey Team	65.00	95.00	125.00
☐ 32	Mount Royal Hockey Team	65.00	95.00	125.00
☐ 33	Port Arthur W. End Junior Hockey	65.00	95.00	125.00
☐ 34	Hanna Hockey Club	65.00	95.00	125.00
☐ 35	Vermilion Junior Hockey	65.00	95.00	125.00

	No.	Player	VG	EX	EX-NRMT
☐	36	Smithers Hockey Team	65.00	95.00	125.00
☐	37	Lloydminster High School	65.00	95.00	125.00
☐	38	Winnipeg Rangers	65.00	95.00	125.00
☐	39	Delisle Intermediate Hockey	65.00	95.00	125.00
☐	40	Moose Jaw College Senior Hockey	65.00	95.00	125.00
☐	41	Art Bonneyman	65.00	95.00	125.00
☐	42	Jimmy Graham	65.00	95.00	125.00
☐	43	Pat O'Hunter	65.00	95.00	125.00
☐	44	Leo Moret	65.00	95.00	125.00
☐	45	Blondie McLennen	65.00	95.00	125.00
☐	46	Red Beattie	65.00	95.00	125.00
☐	47	Frank Peters	65.00	95.00	125.00
☐	48	Lloyd McIntyre	65.00	95.00	125.00
☐	49	Art Somers	65.00	95.00	125.00
☐	50	Ikey Morrison	65.00	95.00	125.00
☐	51	Calgary Jimmies	65.00	95.00	125.00
☐	52	Don Cummings	65.00	95.00	125.00
☐	53	Calgary Jimmies	65.00	95.00	125.00
☐	54	P. Gerlitz	65.00	95.00	125.00
☐	55	A. Kay	65.00	95.00	125.00
☐	56	Paul Runge	65.00	95.00	125.00
☐	57	J. Gerlitz	65.00	95.00	125.00
☐	58	H. Gerlitz	65.00	95.00	125.00
☐	59	C. Biles	65.00	95.00	125.00
☐	60	Jimmy Evans	65.00	95.00	125.00
☐	61	Ira Stuart	65.00	95.00	125.00
☐	62	Berg Irving	65.00	95.00	125.00
☐	63	Cecil Browne	65.00	95.00	125.00
☐	64	Nick Wasnie	65.00	95.00	125.00
☐	65	Gordon Teal	65.00	95.00	125.00
☐	66	Jack Hughes	65.00	95.00	125.00
☐	67	D. Yeatman	65.00	95.00	125.00
☐	68	Connie Johanneson	65.00	95.00	125.00
☐	69	S. Walters	65.00	95.00	125.00
☐	70	Harold McMunn	65.00	95.00	125.00
☐	71	Smokey Harris	65.00	95.00	125.00
☐	72	Calgary Jimmies	65.00	95.00	125.00
☐	73	Burney Morris	65.00	95.00	125.00
☐	74	J. Fowler	65.00	95.00	125.00
☐	75	Calgary Jimmies	65.00	95.00	125.00
☐	76	Pete Speirs	65.00	95.00	125.00
☐	77	Bill Borland	65.00	95.00	125.00
☐	78	Cliff O'Meara	65.00	95.00	125.00
☐	79	F. Porteous	65.00	95.00	125.00
☐	80	W. Brooks	65.00	95.00	125.00
☐	81	Everett McGowan	65.00	95.00	125.00
☐	82	Calgary Jimmies	65.00	95.00	125.00
☐	83	George Dame	65.00	95.00	125.00
☐	84	Calgary Jimmies	65.00	95.00	125.00
☐	85	Calgary Jimmies	65.00	95.00	125.00
☐	86	Calgary Jimmies	65.00	95.00	125.00
☐	87	Heck Fowler	65.00	95.00	125.00
☐	88	Jimmy Hoyle	65.00	95.00	125.00
☐	89	Chuck Gardiner (G)	140.00	210.00	275.00
☐	90	Calgary Jimmies	65.00	95.00	175.00

1929 IMPERIAL TOBACCO SPORTS AND GAMES IN MANY LANDS

Card Size: 2 1/2" x 3"
Face: Black and white photo, white border, card stock
Back: Postcard format
Imprint: W. A. & A. C. CHURCHMAN

	No.	Scene	VG	EX	EX-NRMT
☐	3	Ice-Hockey, Canada	10.00	20.00	40.00

A. & B.C. CHEWING GUM

This multi-sport set features only five hockey players.

Card Size: 1 13/16" x 3"
Face: Black and white photo, white border, card stock; Name, Number, Team
Back: Blank
Imprint: Present by A. & B. C. CHEWING GUM LTD.

	No.	Player	VG	EX	EX-NRMT
☐	37	Sonny Rost, Wembley Lions	7.50	15.00	30.00
☐	39	Ray Gariepy, Goalie, Wembley Lions	7.50	15.00	30.00
☐	40	George Beach, Wembley Lions	7.50	15.00	30.00
☐	41	Lefty Wilmot, Wembley Lions	7.50	15.00	30.00
☐	76	Tony Licari, Harringay	7.50	15.00	30.00

1930 CAMPBELL'S SOUP AD CARD

I'm always sure
To be a winner
When I've had Campbell's
For my dinner

ACC: HP-2g
Card Size: 2 3/16" x 6 3/4"
Face: Multi-colour die-cut print on white cardstock
Back: Black print on white cardstock
Imprint: Litho. in Canada

	Scene	VG	EX	EX-NRMT
☐	"I'm always sure to be a winner..."	35.00	65.00	125.00

1932 - 36 CCM PHOTOS

This series of photos was issued over a four year period promoting CCM skates. Different border designs were utilized depending on the type of photo. For group photos the decorative border may be wine red, blue or grey. For the individual photos the single line border was green. The photos were available from CCM on a mail order basis with the collector receiving the current photos with matching coloured borders.

Photograph Size: Individual: 8 1/4" x 10 1/2"
Group: 11 1/4" x 8 7/8"
Face: Black and white with coloured border; Name, Team
Back: Blank
Imprint: C.C.M. SKATES CHAMPIONS EVERYWHERE
Complete Set No.: 1933-34 10; 1934-35 10; 1935-36 7
Common Set Price: Unknown

	Team	VG	EX	EX-NRMT
	1932-33 GREY BORDERS			
☐	New York Rangers	50.00	75.00	100.00
☐	Toronto Maple Leafs	60.00	90.00	120.00
☐	Allan Cup: Moncton	30.00	40.00	55.00
☐	Memorial Cup: Newmarket	30.00	40.00	55.00
	1933-34 BROWN BORDERS			
☐	Boston Bruins	50.00	75.00	100.00
☐	Chicago Blackhawks	70.00	100.00	140.00
☐	Detroit Red Wings	50.00	75.00	100.00
☐	Montréal Canadiens	65.00	95.00	125.00
☐	Montréal Maroons	55.00	85.00	110.00
☐	New York Americans	50.00	75.00	100.00
☐	New York Rangers	50.00	75.00	100.00
☐	Toronto Maple Leafs	60.00	90.00	120.00
☐	1934 All-Star Game	100.00	150.00	200.00
☐	Allan Cup: Moncton	30.00	40.00	55.00
☐	Cam-Am: Providence	30.00	40.00	55.00
☐	Memorial Cup: St. Mike's	30.00	40.00	55.00
	1934-35 GREEN BORDERS			
☐	Boston Bruins	50.00	75.00	100.00
☐	Montréal Marrons	55.00	85.00	110.00
☐	Toronto Maple Leafs	55.00	85.00	110.00
☐	Allan Cup: Halifax	30.00	40.00	55.00
☐	Cam-Am: Boston Cubs	30.00	40.00	55.00
☐	Memorial Cup: Winnipeg	30.00	40.00	55.00
☐	AW: Frank Boucher (HOF)	65.00	90.00	115.00
☐	AW: Lorne Chabot	45.00	70.00	90.00
☐	AW: Charlie Conacher	60.00	90.00	120.00
☐	Foster Hewitt (HOF)	45.00	70.00	90.00
	1935-36 BLUE BORDERS			
☐	Allan Cup: Kimberley	30.00	40.00	55.00
☐	Can-Am: Philadelphia	30.00	40.00	55.00
☐	Int'l League: Detroit	30.00	40.00	55.00
☐	Memorial Cup: W. Toronto	30.00	40.00	55.00

1932 SANELLA MARGARINE OLYMPIC ISSUE

Card Size: 2 3/4" x 4 1/8"
Face: Colour litho, white border
Back: Black and white, German text
Imprint: "Sanella" Postfach 125, Berlin C2

	Scene	VG	EX	EX-NRMT
☐	Team Canada	50.00	100.00	200.00

1932 REEMSTMA OLYMPIC ISSUE

Reemstma of Altona and Hamburg, Germany produced these German-language issues from 1928-42. Special albums were issued. The following albums contained hockey: 1924 Paris Olympics; 1928 Amsterdam Olympics; 1932 Los Angeles Olympics; 1936 Berlin Olympics.

SMALL SIZE

Card Size: 3 1/8" x 4 11/16"
Face: Black and white photo, white border
Back: Black and white, Name, Number, German text
Imprint: Weitere Werke in Vorbereitung

	No.	Scene	VG	EX	EX-NRMT
☐	188	Germany vs. Poland	25.00	50.00	100.00

LARGE SIZE

Card Size: 4 3/4" x 6 11/16"
Face: Colourized print, white border
Back: Black and white, German text
Imprint: Weitere Werke in Vorbereitung

	No.	Scene	VG	EX	EX-NRMT
☐	191	Canada vs. U.S.A.	90.00	175.00	350.00

1932 - 33 TORONTO MAPLE LEAFS O'KEEFE COASTERS

We have no pricing information on the final two coasters (19-20).
Coaster Diametre: 3"
Sponsor: O'Keefe

No.	Player	VG	EX	EX-NRMT
☐ 1	Lorne Chabot (G)	170.00	250.00	335.00
☐ 2	Red Horner	150.00	225.00	300.00
☐ 3	Alex Levinsky	95.00	140.00	185.00
☐ 4	Hap Day	170.00	250.00	335.00
☐ 5	Andy Blair	90.00	140.00	185.00
☐ 6	Ace Bailey	200.00	300.00	400.00
☐ 7	King Clancy	375.00	565.00	750.00
☐ 8	Baldy Cotton	95.00	140.00	185.00
☐ 9	Charlie Conacher	250.00	375.00	500.00
☐ 10	Joe Primeau	190.00	285.00	375.00
☐ 11	Harvey Jackson	225.00	340.00	450.00
☐ 12	Frank Finnagan	150.00	225.00	300.00
☐ 13	Bill Thomas			very rare
☐ 14	Bob Gracie	95.00	140.00	185.00
☐ 15	Ken Doraty			very rare
☐ 16	Harry Darragh	95.00	140.00	185.00
☐ 17	Ben Grant	95.00	140.00	185.00
☐ 18	Fred Robertson	95.00	140.00	185.00
☐ 19	Conn Smythe			
☐ 20	Dick Irvin			

1933 GOUDEY SPORT KINGS

This 48-card set features 18 different sports. Listed and priced here are the hockey cards from the set.

Card Size: 2 3/8" x 2 7/8"
Face: Four colour, white bordered
Back: Black on white card stock
Imprint: Printed in Canada

No.	Player	VG	EX	EX-NRMT
☐ 19	Eddie Shore	450.00	675.00	900.00
☐ 24	Howie Morenz	550.00	825.00	1,100.00
☐ 29	Ace Bailey	300.00	450.00	600.00
☐ 30	Ivan (Ching) Johnson	240.00	360.00	475.00

1933 - 34 CANADIAN CHEWING GUM

The black and white pictures are framed in a red border. A premium tab attached to the bottom of the card displays a large single letter in the middle. The back information is written in both French and English. Cards with the tabs removed are worth 50% less.

ACC.No.: V252

Card Size: 2 1/2" x 3 1/4"
Face: Black and white in red frame, white border; Name, "Letter" and premium offer
Back: Black on card stock; Name, Team, Resume, Bilingual
Imprint: CANADIAN CHEWING GUM SALES LTD. DEPT. A-1, 14 DICKENS ST., TORONTO, ONT.

	VG	EX	EX-NRMT
Complete Set (50 cards):	5,500.00	8,000.00	11,000.00
Common Player:	75.00	115.00	150.00

Player	VG	EX	EX-NRMT
☐ Clarence Abel, Chi., RC	150.00	225.00	300.00
☐ Larry Aurie, Det., RC	115.00	170.00	225.00
☐ Ace Bailey, Tor., RC	265.00	400.00	525.00
☐ Helge Bostrom, Chi., RC	75.00	115.00	150.00
☐ Bill Brydge, NYA, RC	75.00	115.00	150.00
☐ Glenn Brydson, Mtl.M, RC	75.00	115.00	150.00
☐ Marty Burke, Mtl.C, RC	75.00	115.00	150.00
☐ Gerry Carson, Mtl.C, RC	75.00	115.00	150.00
☐ Lorne Chabot (G), Mtl.C, RC	150.00	225.00	300.00
☐ Francis (King) Clancy, Tor.	550.00	825.00	1,100.00
☐ Dit Clapper, Bos., RC	215.00	320.00	425.00
☐ Charlie Conacher, Tor., RC	425.00	640.00	850.00
☐ Lionel Conacher, Chi., RC	275.00	415.00	550.00
☐ Alex Connell (G), Ott. LC	165.00	245.00	325.00
☐ Bun Cook, NYR, RC	175.00	265.00	350.00
☐ Danny Cox, Ott., RC, LC	75.00	115.00	150.00
☐ Hap Day, Tor.	165.00	245.00	325.00
☐ Cecil Dillon, NYR, RC	100.00	150.00	200.00
☐ Lorne Duguid, Mtl.M, RC	75.00	115.00	150.00
☐ Duke Dutkowski, NYA, RC	75.00	115.00	150.00
☐ Red Dutton, NYA, RC	175.00	265.00	350.00
☐ Hap Emms, Det., RC	90.00	135.00	175.00
☐ Frank Finnigan, Ott., LC	100.00	150.00	200.00
☐ Chuck Gardiner (G), Chi., RC	175.00	265.00	350.00
☐ Ebbie Goodfellow, Det., RC	165.00	245.00	325.00
☐ Johnny Gottselig, Chi., RC	90.00	135.00	175.00
☐ Bob Gracie, Bos., RC	75.00	115.00	150.00
☐ Geo. Hainsworth (G), Tor., RC	200.00	300.00	400.00
☐ Ott Heller, NYR, RC	75.00	115.00	150.00
☐ Normie Himes, NYA, RC	75.00	115.00	150.00
☐ Red Horner, Tor., RC	165.00	245.00	325.00
☐ Harvey Jackson, Tor., RC	215.00	320.00	425.00
☐ Walt Jackson, NYA, RC	75.00	115.00	150.00
☐ Aurèle Joliat, Mtl.C	450.00	675.00	900.00
☐ Dave Kerr (G), Mtl.M, RC	125.00	190.00	250.00
☐ Pit Lepine, Mtl.C, RC	75.00	115.00	150.00
☐ Georges Mantha, Mtl.C, RC	75.00	115.00	150.00
☐ Howie Morenz, Mtl.C	1,100.00	1,650.00	2,200.00
☐ Murray Murdoch, NYR, RC	75.00	115.00	150.00
☐ Baldy Northcott, Mtl.M, RC	100.00	150.00	200.00
☐ John Roach (G), Det.	125.00	190.00	250.00
☐ Johnny Sheppard, Bos., RC	75.00	115.00	150.00
☐ Babe Siebert, NYR, RC	190.00	280.00	375.00
☐ Alex Smith, Bos.	75.00	115.00	150.00
☐ John Sorrell, Det., RC	75.00	115.00	150.00
☐ Nels Stewart, Bos.,	350.00	525.00	700.00
☐ Dave Trottier, Mtl.M, RC	75.00	115.00	150.00
☐ Bill Touhey, Ott., RC, LC	75.00	115.00	150.00
☐ Jimmy Ward, Mtl.M, RC	75.00	115.00	150.00
☐ Nick Wasnie, Mtl.C, RC	75.00	115.00	150.00

1933 - 34 HAMILTON GUM

The pictures are black and white and could appear with one of four background colours of beige, blue, green or orange. This skip-numbered set contains 21 cards with the backs written in French and English. It is doubtful that missing numbers exist.

ACC.No.: V288

Card Size: 2 3/8" x 3"
Face: Black and white photo on coloured background; Name
Background colours: Blue, Lime green, Beige or Orange
Back: Black on card stock; Name, Number, Team, Position, Bilingual
Imprint: HAMILTON CHEWING GUM, LTD.

No.	Player	VG	EX	EX-NRMT
	Complete Set (21 cards):	3,600.00	5,400.00	7,200.00
☐ 1	Nick Wasnie, Mtl.C, RC	90.00	135.00	250.00
☐ 2	Joe Primeau, Tor., RC	215.00	320.00	425.00
☐ 3	Marty Burke, Mtl.C, RC	75.00	115.00	150.00
☐ 7	Bill Thoms, Tor., RC	95.00	140.00	185.00
☐ 8	Howie Morenz, Mtl.C	1,100.00	1,650.00	2,200.00
☐ 9	Andy Blair, Tor., RC	75.00	115.00	150.00
☐ 11	Ace Bailey, Tor., RC	265.00	400.00	525.00
☐ 14	Wildor Larochelle, Mtl.C, RC	75.00	115.00	150.00
☐ 17	Francis (King) Clancy, Tor.	550.00	825.00	1,100.00
☐ 18	Sylvio Mantha, Mtl.C	175.00	265.00	350.00
☐ 21	Red Horner, Tor., RC	165.00	245.00	325.00
☐ 23	Pit Lépine, Mtl.C, RC	75.00	115.00	150.00
☐ 27	Aurèle Joliat, Mtl.C	450.00	675.00	900.00
☐ 29	Harvey Jackson, Tor., RC	215.00	320.00	425.00
☐ 30	Lorne Chabot (G), Mtl.C., RC	150.00	225.00	300.00
☐ 33	Hap Day, Tor.	165.00	245.00	325.00
☐ 36	Alex Levinsky, Tor., RC	75.00	115.00	150.00
☐ 39	Baldy Cotton, Tor., RC	90.00	135.00	180.00
☐ 42	Ebbie Goodfellow, Det., RC	165.00	245.00	325.00
☐ 44	Larry Aurie, Det., RC	115.00	175.00	225.00
☐ 49	Charlie Conacher, Tor., RC	400.00	700.00	1,000.00

1933 - 34 O-PEE-CHEE SERIES "A"

ACC No.: V304A
Card Size: 2 5/16" x 3 9/16"
Face: Black and white photo on coloured background; Name
Background colours: Blue, Green, Red or Orange
Back: Black on card stock; Name, Number, Resume, Bilingual
Imprint: None

No.	Player	VG	EX	EX-NRMT
	Complete Set (48 cards):	5,500.00	8,250.00	11,000.00
☐ 1	Danny Cox, Ott., RC, LC	100.00	150.00	275.00
☐ 2	Joe Lamb, Bos., RC	70.00	100.00	140.00
☐ 3	Eddie Shore, Bos., RC	750.00	1,100.00	1,500.00
☐ 4	Ken Doraty, Tor., RC	85.00	125.00	165.00
☐ 5	Lionel Hitchman, Bos., LC	90.00	135.00	175.00
☐ 6	Nels Stewart, Bos., RC	325.00	500.00	650.00
☐ 7	Walter Galbraith, Ott., RC, LC	70.00	100.00	140.00
☐ 8	Dit Clapper, Bos., RC	200.00	300.00	400.00
☐ 9	Harry Oliver, Bos., RC	150.00	225.00	300.00
☐ 10	Red Horner, Tor., RC	150.00	225.00	300.00
☐ 11	Alex Levinsky, Tor., RC	70.00	100.00	140.00
☐ 12	Joe Primeau, Tor., RC	200.00	300.00	400.00
☐ 13	Ace Bailey, Tor., RC	250.00	375.00	500.00
☐ 14	George Patterson, NYA, RC	70.00	100.00	140.00
☐ 15	George Hainsworth (G), Tor., RC	190.00	285.00	375.00

No.	Player	VG	EX	EX-NRMT
☐ 16	Ott Heller, NYR, RC	70.00	100.00	140.00
☐ 17	Art Somers, NYR, RC	70.00	100.00	140.00
☐ 18	Lorne Chabot (G), Mtl.C, RC	140.00	210.00	275.00
☐ 19	Johnny Gagnon, Mtl.C, RC	70.00	100.00	140.00
☐ 20	Alfred Lepine, Mtl.C, RC	70.00	100.00	140.00
☐ 21	Wildor Larochelle, Mtl.C, RC	70.00	100.00	140.00
☐ 22	Georges Mantha, Mtl.C, RC	70.00	100.00	140.00
☐ 23	Howie Morenz, Mtl.C	1,000.00	1,500.00	2,000.00
☐ 24	Syd Howe, Ott., RC	190.00	285.00	375.00
☐ 25	Frank Finnigan, Ott., LC	95.00	145.00	190.00
☐ 26	Bill Touhey, Ott., RC, LC	70.00	100.00	140.00
☐ 27	Cooney Weiland, Ott., RC	165.00	245.00	325.00
☐ 28	Leo Bourgeault, Ott., RC, LC	70.00	100.00	140.00
☐ 29	Normie Himes, NYA, RC	70.00	100.00	140.00
☐ 30	Johnny Sheppard, Bos., RC	70.00	100.00	140.00
☐ 31	Francis (King) Clancy, Tor.	500.00	750.00	1,000.00
☐ 32	Hap Day, Tor.	140.00	210.00	275.00
☐ 33	Harvey Jackson, Tor., RC	200.00	300.00	400.00
☐ 34	Charlie Conacher, Tor., RC	425.00	640.00	850.00
☐ 35	Baldy Cotton, Tor., RC	85.00	125.00	165.00
☐ 36	Butch Keeling, NYR, RC	70.00	100.00	140.00
☐ 37	Murray Murdoch, NYR, RC	70.00	100.00	140.00
☐ 38	Bill Cook, NYR	200.00	300.00	400.00
☐ 39	Ivan (Ching) Johnson, NYR, RC	240.00	360.00	475.00
☐ 40	Hap Emms, Det.RW, RC	85.00	125.00	165.00
☐ 41	Bert McInenly, Det.F, RC	70.00	100.00	140.00
☐ 42	John Sorrell, Det.F, RC	70.00	100.00	140.00
☐ 43	Bill Phillips, NYA, RC	70.00	100.00	140.00
☐ 44	Charley McVeigh, NYA, RC	70.00	100.00	140.00
☐ 45	Roy Worters (G), NYA, RC	225.00	340.00	450.00
☐ 46	Albert Leduc, Mtl.C, RC	70.00	100.00	140.00
☐ 47	Nick Wasnie, Mtl.C, RC	70.00	100.00	140.00
☐ 48	Armand Mondou, Mtl.C, RC	100.00	150.00	275.00

1933 - 34 O-PEE-CHEE SERIES "B"

A Hockey Star Picture Album was issued to hold the 72 cards of Series A and B. Each page was cut to hold six cards. An album in VG condition sells for $150.

ACC No.: V304B
Card Size: 2 5/16" x 2 7/16"
Face: Black and white with either red, orange, turquoise or green background; Name.
Back: Black on card stock; Name, Number, Resume, Bilingual
Imprint: None

Complete Set (24 cards):		2,000.00	3,000.00	4,000.00
No.	Player	VG	EX	EX-NRMT
☐ 49	Babe Siebert, NYR	175.00	265.00	450.00
☐ 50	Aurèle Joliat, Mtl.C	425.00	640.00	850.00
☐ 51	Larry Aurie, Det., RC, Err (Laurie)	120.00	175.00	235.00
☐ 52	Ebbie Goodfellow, Det.	150.00	225.00	300.00
☐ 53	John Roach (G), Det.	125.00	190.00	250.00
☐ 54	Bill Beveridge (G), Ott., RC	85.00	125.00	165.00
☐ 55	Earle Robinson, Mtl.M, RC	70.00	100.00	140.00
☐ 56	Jimmy Ward, Mtl.M	70.00	100.00	140.00
☐ 57	Archie Wilcox, Mtl.M, RC	70.00	100.00	140.00
☐ 58	Lorne Duguid, Mtl.M	70.00	100.00	140.00
☐ 59	Dave Kerr (G), Mtl.M	125.00	190.00	250.00
☐ 60	Baldy Northcott, Mtl.M	95.00	145.00	190.00
☐ 61	Cy Wentworth, Mtl.M, RC	70.00	100.00	140.00
☐ 62	Dave Trottier, Mtl.M	70.00	100.00	140.00
☐ 63	Wally Kilrea, Mtl.M, RC	70.00	100.00	140.00
☐ 64	Glenn Brydson, Mtl.M	70.00	100.00	140.00
☐ 65	Vernon Ayers, Mtl.M, RC	70.00	100.00	140.00
☐ 66	Robert Gracie, Bos.	70.00	100.00	140.00
☐ 67	Vic Ripley, Bos., RC	70.00	100.00	140.00
☐ 68	Tiny Thompson (G), Bos., RC	200.00	300.00	400.00
☐ 69	Hooley Smith, Mtl.M	70.00	100.00	140.00
☐ 70	Andy Blair, Tor.	70.00	100.00	140.00
☐ 71	Cecil Dillon, NYR	110.00	165.00	215.00
☐ 72	Fred (Bun) Cook, NYR	160.00	240.00	425.00

1933 - 34 "V129"

These sepia-toned cards are numbered on the back along with a short biography in French and English. Card 39 (Harry Oliver) is extremely rare and was believed to have been held back by the issuer.

ACC.No.: V129

Card Size: 1 5/8" x 2 7/8"
Face: Brown on white card stock, white border; Name
Back: Number, Name, Resume, Bilingual
Imprint: None

Complete Set (50 cards):		7,500.00	11,000.00	15,000.00
No.	Player	VG	EX	EX-NRMT
☐ 1	Red Horner, Tor., RC	200.00	300.00	550.00
☐ 2	Hap Day, Tor.	215.00	320.00	425.00
☐ 3	Ace Bailey, Tor, RC	325.00	440.00	650.00
☐ 4	Buzz Boll,, Tor RC	100.00	150.00	200.00
☐ 5	Charlie Conacher, Tor, RC	550.00	825.00	1,100.00
☐ 6	Harvey Jackson, Tor, RC	275.00	415.00	550.00
☐ 7	Joe Primeau, Tor, RC	250.00	375.00	500.00
☐ 8	Francis (King) Clancy, Tor.	700.00	10,000.00	1,400.00
☐ 9	Alex Levinsky, Tor, RC	100.00	150.00	200.00
☐ 10	Bill Thoms, Tor, RC	140.00	210.00	275.00
☐ 11	Andy Blair, Tor, RC	100.00	150.00	200.00
☐ 12	Baldy Cotton, Tor, RC	120.00	180.00	235.00
☐ 13	George Hainsworth (G), Tor.	275.00	415.00	550.00
☐ 14	Ken Doraty, Tor, RC	120.00	180.00	235.00
☐ 15	Fred Robertson, Bos., RC	100.00	150.00	200.00
☐ 16	Charlie Sands, Bos., RC	100.00	150.00	200.00
☐ 17	Hec Kilrea, Bos.	100.00	150.00	200.00
☐ 18	John Roach (G), Bos.	175.00	265.00	350.00
☐ 19	Larry Aurie, Bos., RC	150.00	225.00	300.00
☐ 20	Ebbie Goodfellow, Bos., RC	215.00	320.00	425.00
☐ 21	Normie Himes, NYA., RC	100.00	150.00	200.00
☐ 22	Bill Brydge, NYA., RC	100.00	150.00	200.00
☐ 23	Red Dutton, NYA.	215.00	320.00	425.00
☐ 24	Cooney Weiland, Ott., RC	225.00	340.00	450.00
☐ 25	Bill Beveridge (G), Ott., RC	125.00	180.00	235.00
☐ 26	Frank Finnigan, Ott., LC	135.00	200.00	265.00
☐ 27	Albert Leduc, Mtl., RC	100.00	150.00	200.00
☐ 28	Babe Siebert, NYR., RC, Err (Seibert)	240.00	360.00	475.00
☐ 29	Murray Murdoch, NYR.	100.00	150.00	200.00
☐ 30	Butch Keeling, NYR., RC	100.00	150.00	200.00
☐ 31	Bill Cook, NYR.	275.00	415.00	550.00
☐ 32	Cecil Dillon, NYR., RC	140.00	210.00	275.00
☐ 33	Ivan (Ching) Johnson, NYR., RC	275.00	415.00	550.00
☐ 34	Ott Heller, NYR., RC	100.00	150.00	200.00
☐ 35	Red Beatty, Bos., Error (Beatty)	100.00	150.00	200.00
☐ 36	Dit Clapper, Bos., RC	275.00	415.00	550.00
☐ 37	Eddie Shore, Bos., RC	1,100.00	1,650.00	2,200.00
☐ 38	Marty Barry, Bos., RC	215.00	320.00	425.00
☐ 39	Harry Oliver, Bos.		Extremely Rare	
☐ 40	Bob Gracie, Bos., RC	100.00	150.00	200.00
☐ 41	Howie Morenz, Mtl.	1,400.00	2,000.00	2,800.00
☐ 42	Pit Lepine, Mtl., RC	100.00	150.00	200.00
☐ 43	Johnny Gagnon, Mtl., RC	100.00	150.00	200.00
☐ 44	Armand Mondou, Mtl., RC	100.00	150.00	200.00
☐ 45	Lorne Chabot (G), Mtl.	200.00	300.00	400.00
☐ 46	Bun Cook, NYR., RC	215.00	320.00	425.00
☐ 47	Alex Smith	100.00	150.00	200.00
☐ 48	Danny Cox, Ott., RC, LC	100.00	150.00	200.00
☐ 49	Baldy Northcott, Mtl.M, RC	140.00	210.00	275.00
☐ 50	Paul Thompson, NY, RC	175.00	265.00	500.00

1933 - 34 WORLD WIDE GUM ICE KINGS

The photos are black and white with the player's face tinted with flesh tones. The player's name is shown on the front of the card. Player biographies appear on the back in either French and English or English only.

ACC.No.: V357

Card Size: 2 3/8" x 2 7/8"
Face: Brown on card stock; Name
Back: Green, Name, Number, Resume, English or Bilingual
Imprint: ICE KINGS, World Wide Gum Co., Ltd. Montréal, Printed in Canada

Complete Set (72 cards):		8,000.00	12,000.00	16,000.00
Common Player (1-48):		75.00	115.00	150.00
Common Player (49-72):		100.00	150.00	200.00
No.	Player	VG	EX	EX-NRMT
☐ 1	Dit Clapper, Bos., RC	200.00	400.00	600.00
☐ 2	Bill Brydge, NYA, RC	75.00	115.00	150.00
☐ 3	Aurèle Joliat, Mtl.	450.00	675.00	900.00
☐ 4	Andy Blair, Tor., RC	75.00	115.00	150.00
☐ 5	Earl Robinson, Mtl.M, RC	75.00	115.00	150.00
☐ 6	Paul Haynes, Mtl.M, RC	75.00	115.00	150.00
☐ 7	Ron Martin, NYA., RC	75.00	115.00	150.00
☐ 8	Babe Siebert, NYR., RC, Err(Seibert)	190.00	285.00	375.00
☐ 9	Archie Wilcox, Mtl.M, RC	75.00	115.00	150.00
☐ 10	Hap Day, Tor.	150.00	225.00	300.00
☐ 11	Roy Worters (G), NYA., RC	240.00	360.00	475.00
☐ 12	Nels Stewart, Bos., RC	350.00	525.00	700.00
☐ 13	Francis (King) Clancy, Tor.	550.00	825.00	1,100.00
☐ 14	Marty Burke, Mtl., RC	75.00	115.00	150.00
☐ 15	Cecil Dillon, NYR., RC	100.00	150.00	200.00
☐ 16	Red Horner, Tor., RC	165.00	245.00	325.00
☐ 17	Armand Mondou, Mtl., RC	75.00	115.00	150.00
☐ 18	Paul Raymond, Mtl., RC	75.00	115.00	150.00
☐ 19	Dave Kerr (G), Mtl.M, RC	125.00	185.00	250.00
☐ 20	Butch Keeling, NYR., RC	75.00	115.00	150.00
☐ 21	Johnny Gagnon, Mtl., RC	75.00	115.00	150.00
☐ 22	Ace Bailey, Tor., RC	265.00	395.00	525.00
☐ 23	Harry Oliver, Bos.	165.00	245.00	325.00
☐ 24	Gerry Carson, Mtl., RC	75.00	115.00	150.00
☐ 25	Red Dutton, NYA.	175.00	265.00	350.00
☐ 26	Georges Mantha, Mtl., RC	75.00	115.00	150.00
☐ 27	Marty Barry, Bos., RC	165.00	245.00	325.00
☐ 28	Wildor Larochelle, Mtl., RC	75.00	115.00	150.00
☐ 29	Red Beattie, Bos.	75.00	115.00	150.00
☐ 30	Bill Cook, NYR.	225.00	335.00	450.00
☐ 31	Hooley Smith, Mtl.M	150.00	225.00	300.00
☐ 32	Art Chapman, Bos., RC	75.00	115.00	150.00
☐ 33	Baldy Cotton, Tor., RC	90.00	135.00	180.00
☐ 34	Lionel Hitchman, Bos., LC	100.00	150.00	200.00
☐ 35	George Patterson, NYA., RC	75.00	115.00	150.00
☐ 36	Howie Morenz, Mtl.	1,100.00	1,650.00	2,200.00
☐ 37	Jimmy Ward, Mtl.M, RC	75.00	45.00	150.00
☐ 38	Charley McVeigh, NYA., RC	75.00	45.00	150.00
☐ 39	Glenn Brydson, Mtl.M, RC, Error	75.00	45.00	150.00
☐ 40	Joe Primeau, Tor., RC	215.00	320.00	425.00
☐ 41	Joe Lamb, Bos., RC	75.00	115.00	150.00
☐ 42	Sylvio Mantha, Mtl.	175.00	265.00	350.00
☐ 43	Cy Wentworth, Mtl.M, RC	100.00	150.00	200.00
☐ 44	Normie Himes, NYA., RC	75.00	115.00	150.00
☐ 45	Doug Brennan, NYR., RC	75.00	115.00	150.00
☐ 46	Pit Lepine, Mtl., RC	75.00	115.00	150.00
☐ 47	Alex Levinsky, Tor., RC	75.00	115.00	150.00
☐ 48	Baldy Northcott, Mtl.M, RC	125.00	185.00	250.00
☐ 49	Ken Doraty, NYA., RC	115.00	175.00	225.00
☐ 50	Bill Thoms, Tor., RC	125.00	185.00	250.00
☐ 51	Vern Ayers, Mtl.M, RC	100.00	150.00	200.00
☐ 52	Lorne Duguid, Mtl.M, RC	100.00	150.00	200.00
☐ 53	Wally Kilrea, Mtl.M, RC	100.00	150.00	200.00
☐ 54	Vic Ripley, Bos., RC	100.00	150.00	200.00
☐ 55	Hap Emms, Det., RC	125.00	185.00	250.00
☐ 56	Duke Dutkowski, NYR., RC	100.00	150.00	200.00
☐ 57	Tiny Thompson (G), Bos., RC	275.00	415.00	550.00
☐ 58	Charlie Sands, Tor., RC	100.00	150.00	200.00
☐ 59	Larry Aurie, Det., RC	150.00	225.00	300.00
☐ 60	Bill Beveridge (G), Ott., RC	125.00	185.00	250.00
☐ 61	Bill MacKenzie, Mtl.C., RC	100.00	150.00	200.00

No.	Player	VG	EX	EX-NRMT
☐ **62**	**Earl Roche, Ott., RC**	**100.00**	**150.00**	**200.00**
☐ **63**	**Bob Gracie, Bos., RC**	**100.00**	**150.00**	**200.00**
☐ 64	Hec Kilrea, Det.	100.00	150.00	200.00
☐ **65**	**Cooney Weiland, Ott., RC**	**250.00**	**375.00**	**450.00**
☐ **66**	**Fred (Bun) Cook, NYR., RC**	**175.00**	**265.00**	**350.00**
☐ 67	John Roach (G), Det.	190.00	280.00	375.00
☐ 68	Murray Murdock, NYR.	100.00	150.00	200.00
☐ 69	Danny Cox, Ott., R.C., LC	100.00	150.00	200.00
☐ **70**	**Desse Roche, Mtl.M, RC, LC**	**100.00**	**150.00**	**200.00**
☐ 71	Lorne Chabot (G), Mtl.	200.00	300.00	400.00
☐ **72**	**Syd Howe, Ott., RC**	**200.00**	**300.00**	**600.00**

1933 - 34 ICE KINGS PREMIUM

The following six cards are write-in offers from the Ice Kings wrappers.

Card Size: 7" x 9"
Face: Black and white; Name
Back: Blank
Imprint: None
Redemption Set (6 cards): 1750.00 2600.00 3500.00

No.	Player	VG	EX	EX-NRMT
☐ 1	Francis (King) Clancy, Tor.	600.00	900.00	1,200.00
☐ 2	Hap Day, Tor.	125.00	185.00	250.00
☐ 3	Aurèle Joliat, Mtl.C	500.00	750.00	1,000.00
☐ 4	Howie Morenz, Mtl.C	1,250.00	1,850.00	2,500.00
☐ 5	Al Shields, Ott.	100.00	150.00	200.00
☐ 6	Hooley Smith, Mtl.M	125.00	185.00	250.00

1933 - 35 DIAMOND MATCH SILVER SERIES

This first issue has a silver finish with green and black stripes running vertically on the left side of the cover. The book cover has a player's portrait with the back giving the player's resume. The back cover is black on green

Card Size: 1 1/16" x 4 1/2"
Face: Black and white with various two colour borders; Name; Team; Picture
Back: Black and white; Black script on light sketched hockey scene on thick card stock
Imprint: THE DIAMOND MATCH CO. N.Y.C.
Complete Set (60 cards): 1000.00 1,500.00 2,000.00
Common Player: 15.00 22.00 30.00

	Player	VG	EX	EX-NRMT
☐	Clarence Abel, Chi.	15.00	22.00	30.00
☐	Marty Barry, Bos.	20.00	30.00	40.00
☐	Jack Beattie, Bos.	15.00	22.00	30.00
☐	Frank Boucher, NYR	25.00	35.00	50.00
☐	Doug Brennan, NYR	15.00	22.00	30.00
☐	Bill Brydge, NYR	15.00	22.00	30.00
☐	Eddie Burke, NYR	15.00	22.00	30.00
☐	Marty Burke, Mtl.	15.00	22.00	30.00
☐	Gerry Carson, Mtl.	15.00	22.00	30.00
☐	Lorne Chabot (G), Mtl.	25.00	35.00	50.00
☐	Art Chapman, Bos.	15.00	22.00	30.00
☐	Dit Clapper, Bos.	30.00	45.00	60.00
☐	Lional Conacher, Chi.	28.00	40.00	55.00
☐	Hugh (Red) Conn, NYA	15.00	22.00	30.00
☐	Bill Cook, NYR	30.00	45.00	60.00
☐	Fred (Bun) Cook, NYR	25.00	35.00	50.00
☐	Tom Cook, Chi.	15.00	22.00	30.00
☐	Rosario (Lolo) Couture, Chi.	15.00	22.00	30.00
☐	Bob Davie, Bos.	15.00	22.00	30.00
☐	Cecil Dillon, NYR	15.00	22.00	30.00
☐	Duke Dutkowski, NYA	15.00	22.00	30.00
☐	Red Dutton, NYA	25.00	35.00	50.00
☐	Johnny Gagnon, Mtl.	15.00	22.00	30.00
☐	Chuck Gardiner (G), Chi.	30.00	45.00	60.00
☐	John Gottselig, Chi.	15.00	22.00	30.00
☐	Bob Gracie, Bos.	15.00	22.00	30.00
☐	Lloyd Gross, NYA	15.00	22.00	30.00
☐	Otto Heller, NYR	15.00	22.00	30.00
☐	Normie Himes, NYA	15.00	22.00	30.00
☐	Lional Hitchman, Bos.	25.00	35.00	50.00
☐	Walter (Red) Jackson, NYA	15.00	22.00	30.00
☐	Roger Jenkins, Chi.	15.00	22.00	30.00
☐	Aurèle Joliat, Mtl.	50.00	75.00	100.00
☐	Butch (Melville) Keeling, Chi.	15.00	22.00	30.00
☐	William Kendall, Chi.	15.00	22.00	30.00
☐	Lloyd Klein, NYA	15.00	22.00	30.00
☐	Joe Lamb, Bos.	15.00	22.00	30.00
☐	Wildor Larochelle, Mtl.	15.00	22.00	30.00
☐	Pit Lépine, Mtl.	15.00	22.00	30.00
☐	Jack Leswick, Chi.	15.00	22.00	30.00
☐	Georges Mantha, Mtl.	20.00	30.00	40.00
☐	Sylvio Mantha, Mtl.	25.00	35.00	50.00
☐	Mush March, Chi.	15.00	22.00	30.00
☐	Ron Martin, NYA	15.00	22.00	30.00
☐	Charley McVeigh, NYA	15.00	22.00	30.00
☐	Howie Morenz, Mtl.	250.00	375.00	500.00
☐	John Murray Murdoch, NYR	15.00	22.00	30.00
☐	Harry Oliver, Bos.	25.00	35.00	50.00
☐	George Patterson, NYA	15.00	22.00	30.00
☐	Hal Picketts, NYA	15.00	22.00	30.00
☐	Vic Ripley, Bos.	15.00	22.00	30.00
☐	Doc Romnes, Chi.	15.00	22.00	30.00
☐	Johnny Sheppard, Bos.	15.00	22.00	30.00
☐	Eddie Shore, Bos.	100.00	150.00	200.00
☐	Art Somers, NYR	15.00	22.00	30.00
☐	Chris Speyers, NYA	15.00	22.00	30.00
☐	Nels Stewart, Bos.	30.00	45.00	60.00
☐	Tiny Thompson (G), Bos.	30.00	45.00	60.00
☐	Louis Trudel, Chi.	15.00	22.00	30.00
☐	Roy Worters (G), NYA	30.00	45.00	60.00

1934 - 35 SWEET CAPORAL PHOTO

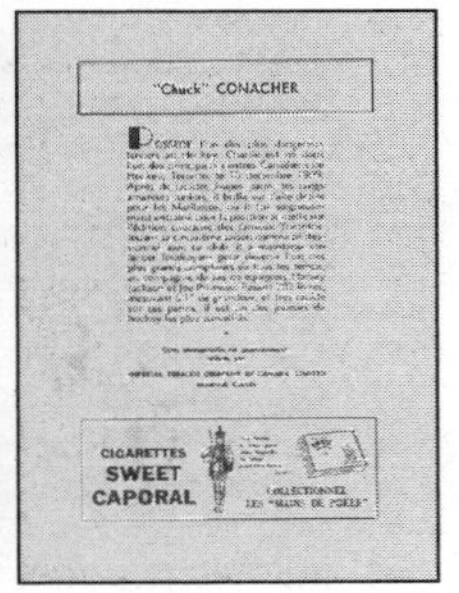

These photos were inserts in the Montréal Forum game programs. A photo was inserted in the home game programs of the Canadiens and the Maroons.

Photo Size: 6 7/8" x 9 1/2"
Face: Four colour
Back: Black on white card stock; Name, Resume, French Text
Imprint: IMPERIAL TOBACCO COMPANY OF CANADA, LIMITED
Complete Set (48 cards): 4,250.00 5,500.00 6,500.00

	Player	VG	EX	EX-NRMT
☐	Eddie Shore, Bos.	425.00	540.00	600.00
☐	Babe Siebert, Bos	135.00	165.00	200.00
☐	Nels Stewart, Bos	235.00	290.00	350.00
☐	Tiny Thompson (G), Bos	150.00	190.00	225.00
☐	Lorne Chabot (G), Chi.	90.00	110.00	135.00
☐	Mush March, Chi.	80.00	100.00	125.00
☐	Howie Morenz, Chi.	525.00	675.00	800.00
☐	Larry Aurie, Det.	80.00	100.00	125.00
☐	Ebbie Goodfellow, Det.	115.00	145.00	175.00
☐	Herbie Lewis, Det.	65.00	85.00	100.00
☐	Ralph Weiland, Det.	135.00	165.00	200.00
☐	Gerry Carson, Error (Jerry), Mtl.	65.00	85.00	100.00
☐	Nels Crutchfield, Mtl.	65.00	85.00	100.00
☐	Wilf Cude (G), Mtl.	80.00	100.00	125.00
☐	Roger Jenkins, Mtl.	65.00	85.00	100.00
☐	Aurèle Joliat, Mtl.	365.00	450.00	550.00
☐	Joe Lamb, Mtl.	65.00	85.00	100.00
☐	Wildor Larochelle, Mtl., Error (Victor)	65.00	85.00	100.00
☐	Pit Lépine, Mtl.	65.00	85.00	100.00
☐	Georges Mantha, Mtl.	65.00	85.00	100.00
☐	Sylvio Mantha, Mtl.	115.00	145.00	175.00
☐	Jack McGill, Mtl.	65.00	85.00	100.00
☐	Armand Mondou, Mtl.	65.00	85.00	100.00
☐	Paul Raymond, Mtl.	65.00	85.00	100.00
☐	Jack Riley, Mtl.	65.00	85.00	100.00
☐	Russ Blinco, Mtl. M.	65.00	85.00	100.00
☐	Herbert Cain, Mtl. M.	80.00	100.00	125.00
☐	Lionel Conacher, Mtl. M.	185.00	235.00	285.00
☐	Alex Connell (G), Mtl. M.	115.00	145.00	175.00
☐	Stewart Evans, Mtl. M.	65.00	85.00	100.00
☐	Dutch Gainor, Mtl. M.	65.00	85.00	100.00
☐	Paul Haynes, Mtl. M.	65.00	85.00	100.00
☐	Gus Marker, Mtl. M.	65.00	85.00	100.00
☐	Baldy Northcott, Mtl. M.	80.00	100.00	125.00
☐	Earle Robinson, Mtl. M.	65.00	85.00	100.00
☐	Hooley Smith, Mtl. M.	115.00	150.00	185.00
☐	Dave Trottier, Mtl. M.	65.00	85.00	100.00
☐	Jimmy Ward, Mtl. M.	65.00	85.00	100.00
☐	Cy Wentworth, Mtl. M.	80.00	100.00	125.00
☐	Bill Cook, NYR.	165.00	210.00	250.00
☐	Fred (Bun) Cook, NYR.	115.00	150.00	185.00
☐	Ivan (Ching) Johnson, NYR.	115.00	150.00	185.00
☐	Dave Kerr (G), NYR.	90.00	115.00	140.00
☐	Francis (King) Clancy, Tor.	365.00	450.00	550.00
☐	Charlie Conacher, Tor.	325.00	415.00	500.00
☐	Red Horner, Tor.	115.00	145.00	175.00
☐	Harvey Jackson, Tor.	150.00	190.00	225.00
☐	Joe Primeau, Tor.	165.00	210.00	250.00

1935 J. A. PATTREIOUEX LTD. SPORTING EVENTS AND STARS

This 96-card set features only two hockey cards.

Card Size: 2" x 3"
Face: Black and white photo, white border; Title
Back: Black on white card stock; Name, Number, Resume
Imprint: SENIOR SERVICE, JUNIOR MEMBER, ILLINGWORTH

No.	Player	VG	EX	EX-NRMT
☐ 31	Ice Skating - Ice Hockey	10.00	20.00	40.00
☐ 89	G. A. Johnson, Manchester	10.00	20.00	40.00

1935 TORONTO CONVENTION AND TOURIST ASSOCIATION

Card Size: 3 1/2" x 5 3/8"
Face: Colourised print, white border, card stock
Back: Postcard format
Imprint: Toronto Convention and Tourist Assn.

No.	Team	VG	EX	EX-NRMT
☐ 35	Maple Leaf Hockey Club Arena, Toronto, Ontario.	12.50	25.00	50.00

1935 - 36 AMALGAMATED PRESS CHAMPION MAGAZINE

These postcards were issued as inserts in a magazine published in Great Britain and distributed in Canada during 1935 and 1936. Paper storage pouches were available from the magazine.

Postcard Size: 4" x 6"
Face: Sepia
Back: Postcard back
Imprint: None
Complete Set (10 postcards): 1,100.00 1,650.00 2,200.00

	Player	VG	EX	EX-NRMT
☐	Marty Barry, Bos.	75.00	115.00	150.00
☐	Francis (King) Clancy, Tor.	300.00	450.00	600.00
☐	Charlie Conacher, Tor.	225.00	340.00	450.00
☐	Fred (Bun) Cook, NYR.	125.00	185.00	250.00
☐	Bill Cook, NYR.	150.00	225.00	300.00
☐	Aurèle Joliat, Mtl.	250.00	375.00	500.00
☐	Reg Kelly, Tor.	75.00	115.00	150.00
☐	Mush March, Chi.	75.00	115.00	150.00
☐	Sweeney Schriner, NYA.	125.00	185.00	250.00
☐	Hooley Smith, Mtl.	125.00	185.00	250.00

1935 - 36 AMALGATED PRESS TRIUMPH MAGAZINE

These postcards were issued as inserts in a magazine published in Great Britain and distributed in Canada during 1935 and 1936. Paper storage pouches were available from the magazine.

Postcard Size: 4" x 6"
Face: Sepia
Back: Postcard back
Imprint: None

	Player	VG	EX	EX-NRMT
Complete Set (10 postcards):		**800.00**	**1,200.00**	**1,600.00**
□	Lionel Conacher, Mtl.	200.00	300.00	400.00
□	Harvey Jackson, Tor.	150.00	225.00	300.00
□	Ivan (Ching) Johnson, NYR.	125.00	185.00	250.00
□	Herbie Lewis, Det.	75.00	115.00	150.00
□	Sylvio Mantha, Mtl.	100.00	150.00	200.00
□	Nick Metz, Tor.	75.00	115.00	150.00
□	Baldy Northcott, Mtl.M	75.00	115.00	150.00
□	Eddie Shore, Bos.	300.00	450.00	600.00
□	Paul Thomson, Chi.	75.00	115.00	150.00
□	Roy Worters (G), NYA.	125.00	185.00	250.00

1935 - 36 O-PEE-CHEE SERIES "C"

This series shows the player's surname on the face of the card and may or may not show the initial of the player's first name.

ACC No.: V304C
Card Size: 2 3/8" x 2 7/8"
Face: Black and white colour background, green, orange, yellow, pink, borderless; Name
Back: Black on card stock; Name, Resume, Bilingual
Imprint: None

No.	Player	VG	EX	EX-NRMT
Complete Set (24 cards):		**1,700.00**	**2,500.00**	**3,300.00**
□ **73**	**Wilf Cude (G), Mtl.C, RC**	**100.00**	**150.00**	**300.00**
□ **74**	**Jack McGill, Mtl.C, RC**	**70.00**	**100.00**	**140.00**
□ **75**	**Russ Blinco, Mtl.M, RC**	**70.00**	**100.00**	**140.00**
□ 76	Hooley Smith, Mtl.M	140.00	210.00	275.00
□ **77**	**Herbert Cain, Mtl.M, RC**	**90.00**	**135.00**	**175.00**
□ **78**	**Gus Marker, Mtl.M, RC**	**70.00**	**100.00**	**140.00**
□ **79**	**Lynn Patrick, NYR, RC**	**200.00**	**300.00**	**400.00**
□ 80	Johnny Gottselig, Chi.	90.00	135.00	175.00
□ 81	Marty Barry, Det.	150.00	225.00	300.00
□ 82	Sylvio Mantha, Mtl.C	140.00	210.00	275.00
□ **83**	**Bill Hollett, Tor., RC**	**70.00**	**100.00**	**140.00**
□ **84**	**Nick Metz, Tor., RC**	**90.00**	**135.00**	**175.00**
□ 85	Bill Thoms, Tor.	90.00	135.00	175.00
□ 86	Hec Kilrea, Det.	70.00	100.00	140.00
□ **87**	**Reg Kelly, Tor., RC**	**70.00**	**100.00**	**140.00**
□ **88**	**Art Jackson, Tor., RC**	**70.00**	**100.00**	**140.00**
□ **89**	**Al Shields, Mtl.M, RC**	**70.00**	**100.00**	**140.00**
□ 90	Buzz Boll, Tor.	70.00	100.00	140.00
□ **91**	**Jean Pusie, Mtl.C, RC**	**70.00**	**100.00**	**140.00**
□ **92**	**Roger Jenkins, Bos., RC, Err (Rogers)**	**70.00**	**100.00**	**140.00**
□ **93**	**Art Coulter, Chi., RC**	**150.00**	**225.00**	**300.00**
□ 94	Art Chapman, NYA	90.00	135.00	175.00
□ 95	Paul Haynes, Mtl.C	70.00	100.00	140.00
□ **96**	**Leroy Goldsworthy, Mtl.C, RC**	**90.00**	**135.00**	**250.00**

1935 - 40 CANADA STARCH CROWN BRAND

With the success of the Bee Hive promotion, Canada Starch was prompted into action. They soon joined the write-in redemption coupon game. The photos issued by Canada Starch are all Rice or Rice Copyrighted from the Rice Studios of Montréal.

Photo Size: 4 1/2" x 7 3/4"
Player Photos with mat: 6 3/4" x 8 3/4"
Team Photos: 9 1/2" x 4 3/4"
Team Photos with mat: 10 3/4" x 6 1/2"
Also: 7 3/4" x 5", with mat: 8 3/4" x 6 1/2"
Face: Black and white on sepia; Facsimile autograph, Number, Write-in premium redeemable with proof of purchase.
Back: Blank
Imprint: None

No.	Player	EX	EX-NRMT
Complete Set (68 photos):		**2,300.00**	**4,500.00**
Common Player:		**25.00**	**50.00**
□ 49	Montréal Maroons 1936-37	40.00	75.00
□ 50	Montréal Les Canadiens 1936-37	40.00	75.00
□ 51	Baldy Northcott, Mtl. M.	30.00	60.00
□ 52	Dave Trottier, Mtl. M.	25.00	50.00
□ 53	Russ Blinco, Mtl. M.	25.00	50.00
□ 54	Earle Robinson, Mtl. M.	25.00	50.00
□ 55	Bob Gracie, Mtl. M.	25.00	50.00
□ 56	Gus Marker, Mtl. M.	25.00	50.00
□ 57	Howie Morenz, Mtl. M.	115.00	225.00
□ 58	Johnny Gagnon, Mtl. M.	25.00	50.00
□ 59	Wilf Cude (G), Mtl. M.	30.00	60.00
□ 60	Georges Mantha, Mtl. M.	25.00	50.00
□ 61	Paul Haynes, Mtl. M.	25.00	50.00
□ 62	Marty Barry, Det.	35.00	70.00
□ 63	Pete Kelly, Det.	25.00	50.00
□ 64	Dave Kerr (G)	35.00	65.00
□ 65	Roy Worters (G)	40.00	80.00
□ 66	Ace Bailey, Tor.	60.00	120.00
□ 67	Art Lesieur	25.00	50.00
□ 68	Frank Boucher, NYR.	40.00	75.00
□ 69	Marty Burke, Chi.	25.00	50.00
□ 70	Alex Levinsky	25.00	50.00
□ 71	The Maple Leaf Team of "Father Levesque's Pewee Hockey Club"	150.00	300.00
□ 72	Six Stars of "Father Levesque's PeeWee Hockey Club	150.00	300.00
□ 76	The "Canadien" team of "Father Levesque's Pewee Hockey Club"	150.00	300.00
□ 77	Stewart Evans, Mtl. M.	25.00	50.00
□ 78	Herbert Cain	30.00	60.00
□ 79	Carl Voss, Mtl. M.	40.00	75.00
□ 80	Roger Jenkins	25.00	50.00
□ 81	Jack McGill	25.00	50.00
□ 82	Mush March	30.00	60.00
□ 106	Montréal Maroons 1937-38	50.00	100.00
□ 107	Montréal Les Canadiens 1937-38	50.00	100.00
□ 108	Toe Blake	60.00	120.00
□ 109	Joffre Desilets	30.00	60.00
□ 110	Babe Siebert	50.00	100.00
□ 111	Francis (King) Clancy	350.00	700.00
□ 112	Aurèle Joliat, Error	115.00	225.00
□ 113	Walt Buswell	30.00	60.00
□ 114	Bill MacKenzie	30.00	60.00
□ 115	Pit Lépine	30.00	60.00
□ 116	Red Goupille	30.00	60.00
□ 117	Rod Lorraine	30.00	60.00
□ 118	Polly Drouin	30.00	60.00
□ 119	Cy Wentworth	35.00	70.00
□ 120	Al Shields	30.00	60.00
□ 121	Jimmy Ward	30.00	60.00
□ 122	Bill Beveridge (G)	35.00	70.00
□ 123	Gerry Shannon	30.00	60.00
□ 124	Des Smith	30.00	60.00
□ 125	Armand Mondou	30.00	60.00
□ 151	Montréal Les Canadiens 1938-39	70.00	135.00
□ 152	Herbert Cain	40.00	80.00
□ 153	Bob Gracie	35.00	70.00
□ 154	Jimmy Ward	35.00	70.00
□ 155	Stewart Evans	35.00	70.00
□ 156	Louis Trudel	35.00	70.00
□ 157	Cy Wentworth	45.00	85.00
□ 195	Marty Barry	50.00	100.00
□ 196	Earl Robinson	35.00	70.00
□ 197	Ray Getliffe	35.00	70.00
□ 198	Charlie Sands	40.00	80.00
□ 199	Claude Bourque (G)	35.00	70.00
□ 200	Douglas Young	35.00	70.00
□ 201	Montréal Les Canadiens 1939-40	70.00	135.00
□	1936 - 37 Montréal Maroons	50.00	100.00
□	1935 - 36 Montréal Canadiens	50.00	100.00
□	1936 Canadian Olympic Team	45.00	90.00

1936 REEMSTMA OLYMPIC ISSUE

GROUP 53, 54

Card Size: 2 3/4" x 4 1/8"
Face: Black and white, white border
Back: Black and white, German text
Imprint: Weitere Werke sind in Vorboreitung

No.	Scene	VG	EX	EX-NRMT
□ 36	Team Great Britain	25.00	50.00	100.00
□ 32	USA vs. Germany	50.00	100.00	200.00
□ 38	Gustav Jaenecke	25.00	50.00	100.00
□ 39	Teiji Homna	25.00	50.00	100.00

1936 - 37 O-PEE-CHEE SERIES "D"

The cards in the fourth series are die-cut, allowing the cards to be folded so they could stand on end. The cards are black and white with a drawing of a mock game in the background. These cards show only the player's surname on the face of the card. This is the most valuable set of the series because the cards are very difficult to find unpopped.

ACC No.: V304D
Card Size: 2 3/8" x 3"
Face: Die Cut, Black and white; Name
Back: Black on white card stock; Number, Resume, Bilingual
Imprint: None

No.	Player	VG	EX	EX-NRMT
Complete Set (36 cards):		**7,200.00**	**9,800.00**	**12,500.00**
□ **97**	**Turk Broda (G), Tor., RC**	**450.00**	**675.00**	**1,300.00**
□ **98**	**Sweeney Schriner, NYA, RC**	**275.00**	**375.00**	**475.00**
□ 99	Jack Shill, Tor., RC, LC	110.00	155.00	200.00
□ **100**	**Bob Davidson, Tor., RC**	**150.00**	**200.00**	**250.00**
□ **101**	**Syl Apps, Sr., Tor., RC**	**425.00**	**590.00**	**750.00**
□ 102	Lionel Conacher, Mtl.M	325.00	465.00	600.00
□ **103**	**Jimmy Fowler, Tor., RC**	**110.00**	**155.00**	**200.00**
□ **104**	**Allan Murray, NYA, RC**	**110.00**	**155.00**	**200.00**
□ **105**	**Neil Colville, NYR, RC**	**275.00**	**375.00**	**475.00**
□ **106**	**Paul Runge, Mtl.M, RC**	**110.00**	**155.00**	**200.00**
□ **107**	**Mike Karakas (G), Chi. RC**	**150.00**	**200.00**	**250.00**
□ **108**	**John Gallagher, NYA, RC1**	**110.00**	**155.00**	**200.00**
□ **109**	**Alex Shibicky, NYR, RC**	**110.00**	**155.00**	**200.00**
□ 110	Herbert Cain, Mtl.M	150.00	200.00	250.00
□ 111	Bill MacKenzie, Mtl.C	110.00	155.00	200.00
□ **112**	**Hal Jackson, Chi., RC, LC**	**110.00**	**155.00**	**200.00**
□ **113**	**Art Wiebe, Chi., RC, Err (Weibe)**	**110.00**	**155.00**	**200.00**

No.	Player	VG	EX	EX-NRMT
☐ **114**	**Joffre Desilets, Mtl.C., RC**	**110.00**	**155.00**	**200.00**
☐ 115	Earle Robinson, Mtl.M	110.00	155.00	200.00
☐ 116	Cy Wentworth, Mtl.M	150.00	215.00	275.00
☐ 117	Ebbie Goodfellow, Det.	235.00	330.00	425.00
☐ 118	Eddie Shore, Bos.	1,000.00	1,400.00	1,800.00
☐ 119	Buzz Boll, Tor.	110.00	155.00	200.00
☐ 120	Wilf Cude (G), Mtl.C	150.00	200.00	250.00
☐ 121	Howie Morenz, Mtl.C	1,400.00	2,000.00	2,600.00
☐ 122	Red Horner, Tor.	235.00	330.00	425.00
☐ 123	Charlie Conacher, Tor.	550.00	775.00	1,000.00
☐ 124	Harvey Jackson, Tor.	300.00	425.00	550.00
☐ 125	Francis (King) Clancy, Tor., LC	650.00	925.00	1,200.00
☐ 126	Dave Trottier, Mtl.M	110.00	155.00	200.00
☐ 127	Russ Blinco, Mtl.M	110.00	155.00	200.00
☐ 128	Lynn Patrick, NYR	285.00	395.00	500.00
☐ 129	Aurèle Joliat, Mtl.C	600.00	850.00	1,100.00
☐ 130	Baldy Northcott, Mtl.M	150.00	215.00	275.00
☐ 131	Larry Aurie, Det.	175.00	235.00	300.00
☐ 132	Hooley Smith, Mtl.M	200.00	300.00	550.00

1936 - 37 WORLD WIDE GUM

The greenish-gray cards show the card number and player's name in a box under the picture. The card number and player information appear on the back in both French and English.

ACC No.: V356

Card Size: 2 3/8" x 2 7/8"
Face: Green-grey, white border; Number
Back: Black and white; Number, Resume, Bilingual, Name
Imprint: Printed in Canada / Imprimé au Canada

		VG	EX	EX-NRMT
Complete Set (135 cards):		**14,000.00**	**20,000.00**	**28,000.00**
Common Player:		**90.00**	**135.00**	**175.00**
No.	**Player**	**VG**	**EX**	**EX-NRMT**
☐ 1	Charlie Conacher, Tor.	450.00	675.00	1,200.00
☐ 2	Jimmy Ward, Mtl.M	90.00	135.00	175.00
☐ 3	Babe Siebert, Mtl.C	215.00	320.00	425.00
☐ 4	Marty Barry, Det.	190.00	285.00	375.00
☐ 5	Eddie Shore, Bos.	750.00	1,100.00	1,500.00
☐ 6	Paul Thompson, Chi.	140.00	210.00	275.00
☐ 7	Roy Worters (G), NYA.	240.00	360.00	475.00
☐ 8	Red Horner, Tor.	200.00	300.00	400.00
☐ 9	Wilf Cude (G), Mtl.	115.00	170.00	225.00
☐ 10	Lionel Conacher, Mtl.M	265.00	395.00	525.00
☐ 11	Ebbie Goodfellow, Det.	200.00	300.00	400.00
☐ 12	Tiny Thompson (G), Bos.	215.00	320.00	425.00
☐ **13**	**Mush March, Chi., RC**	**125.00**	**190.00**	**250.00**
☐ 14	Red Dutton, NYA.	200.00	300.00	400.00
☐ 15	Butch Keeling, NYR.	90.00	135.00	175.00
☐ 16	Frank Boucher, NYR.	200.00	300.00	400.00
☐ 17	Tommy Gorman, Mgr., Mtl.M	90.00	135.00	175.00
☐ 18	Howie Morenz, NYR.	1,200.00	1,800.00	2,400.00
☐ 19	Cy Wentworth, Mtl.M	115.00	170.00	225.00
☐ 20	Hooley Smith, Bos.	190.00	285.00	375.00
☐ 21	Ivan (Ching) Johnson, NYR.	225.00	340.00	450.00
☐ 22	Baldy Northcott	125.00	190.00	250.00
☐ 23	Syl Apps, Sr., Tor.	400.00	600.00	800.00
☐ 24	Hec Kilrea, Tor.	90.00	135.00	175.00
☐ 25	John Sorrell, Det.	90.00	135.00	175.00
☐ **26**	**Lorne Carr, NYA., RC**	**100.00**	**150.00**	**200.00**
☐ 27	Charlie Sands, Bos.	90.00	135.00	175.00
☐ 28	Nick Metz, Tor.	100.00	150.00	200.00
☐ 29	Francis (King) Clancy, Tor., LC	500.00	750.00	1,000.00
☐ 30	Russ Blinco, Mtl.M	90.00	135.00	175.00
☐ 31	Pete Martin, RC, LC	90.00	135.00	175.00
☐ **32**	**Walt Buswell, Mtl.C, RC**	**90.00**	**135.00**	**175.00**
☐ 33	Paul Haynes, Mtl.C	90.00	135.00	175.00
☐ 34	Wildor Larochelle, Chi,	90.00	135.00	175.00
☐ 35	Baldy Cotton, Tor.	115.00	170.00	225.00
☐ 36	Dit Clapper, Bos.	225.00	340.00	450.00
☐ 37	Joe Lamb, NYA.	90.00	135.00	175.00
☐ 38	Bob Gracie, Mtl.M	90.00	135.00	175.00
☐ 39	Jack Shill, Tor., LC	90.00	135.00	175.00
☐ 40	Buzz Boll, Tor.	90.00	135.00	175.00
☐ 41	John Gallagher, NYA.	90.00	135.00	175.00
☐ 42	Art Chapman, NYA.	100.00	150.00	200.00
☐ **43**	**Tom Cook, Chi., RC**	**90.00**	**135.00**	**175.00**
☐ 44	Bill MacKenzie, Mtl.C	90.00	135.00	175.00
☐ 45	Georges Mantha, Mtl.	90.00	135.00	175.00
☐ 46	Herbert Cain, Mtl.M	120.00	180.00	235.00
☐ 47	Mud Bruneteau, Det.	110.00	165.00	215.00
☐ 48	Bob Davidson, Tor.	100.00	150.00	200.00
☐ **49**	**Douglas Young, Det., RC**	**90.00**	**135.00**	**175.00**
☐ **50**	**Polly Drouin, Mtl., RC**	**90.00**	**135.00**	**175.00**
☐ 51	Harvey Jackson, Tor.	250.00	375.00	500.00
☐ 52	Hap Day, Tor.	190.00	285.00	375.00
☐ 53	Dave Kerr (G)	150.00	225.00	300.00
☐ 54	Allan Murray, NYA.	90.00	135.00	175.00
☐ 55	Johnny Gottselig, Chi.	120.00	180.00	235.00
☐ 56	Andy Blair, Chi.	90.00	135.00	175.00
☐ 57	Lynn Patrick, NYR.	225.00	340.00	450.00
☐ **58**	**Sweeney Schriner, NYA., RC**	**200.00**	**300.00**	**400.00**
☐ 59	Hap Emms, NYA.	115.00	170.00	225.00
☐ 60	Al Shields, NYA.	90.00	135.00	175.00
☐ 61	Alex Levinsky, Tor.	90.00	135.00	175.00
☐ 62	Bill Hollett, Bos.	90.00	135.00	175.00
☐ 63	Peggy O'Neil, Bos.	90.00	135.00	175.00
☐ 64	Herbie Lewis, Det.	200.00	300.00	400.00
☐ 65	Aurèle Joliat, Mtl.	500.00	750.00	1,000.00
☐ **66**	**Carl Voss, Mtl.M, RC**	**165.00**	**245.00**	**325.00**
☐ **67**	**Stewart Evans, Mtl.M, RC**	**90.00**	**135.00**	**175.00**
☐ 68	Fred (Bun) Cook, Bos.	190.00	285.00	375.00
☐ 69	Cooney Weiland, Bos.	190.00	285.00	375.00
☐ 70	Dave Trottier, Mtl.M	90.00	135.00	175.00
☐ 71	Louis Trudel, Chi.	90.00	135.00	175.00
☐ 72	Marty Burke, Chi.	90.00	135.00	175.00
☐ 73	Leroy Goldsworthy, Bos.	90.00	135.00	175.00
☐ 74	Norman Smith (G), Det.	100.00	150.00	200.00
☐ 75	Syd Howe, Det.	200.00	300.00	400.00
☐ 76	Gord Pettinger, Det.	90.00	135.00	175.00
☐ 77	Jack McGill, Mtl.	90.00	135.00	175.00
☐ 78	Pit Lepine, Mtl.	90.00	135.00	175.00
☐ 79	Sammy McManus, Bos.	90.00	135.00	175.00
☐ 80	Phil Watson, NYR.	125.00	190.00	250.00
☐ 81	Paul Runge, Mtl.M	90.00	135.00	175.00
☐ 82	Bill Beveridge (G), Mtl.M	115.00	170.00	225.00
☐ 83	Johnny Gagnon, Mtl.C	90.00	135.00	175.00
☐ 84	Bucko McDonald, Det.	90.00	135.00	175.00
☐ 85	Earle Robinson, Mtl.M	90.00	135.00	175.00
☐ 86	Reg (Regis) Kelly, Tor.	90.00	135.00	175.00
☐ 87	Ott Heller, NYR.	90.00	135.00	175.00
☐ 88	Murray Murdock, NYR.	90.00	135.00	175.00
☐ 89	Mac Colville, NYR.	90.00	135.00	175.00
☐ 90	Alex Shibicky, NYR.	90.00	135.00	175.00
☐ 91	Neil Colville, NYR.	200.00	300.00	400.00
☐ 92	Normie Himes, NYA.	90.00	135.00	175.00
☐ 93	Charley McVeigh, NYA.	90.00	135.00	175.00
☐ 94	Lester Patrick, Coach, NYR.	240.00	360.00	475.00
☐ 95	Conn Smythe, Mgr. Tor.	275.00	415.00	550.00
☐ 96	Art Ross, Coach, Bos.	225.00	340.00	450.00
☐ 97	Cecil M. Hart, Coach, Mtl.	165.00	250.00	325.00
☐ 98	Dutch Gainor, Mtl.M	90.00	135.00	175.00
☐ 99	Jack J. Adams, Coach, Det.	200.00	300.00	400.00
☐ 100	Howie Morenz, Jr., Mascot, Mtl.C	250.00	375.00	500.00
☐ **101**	**Buster Mundy, RC, LC**	**90.00**	**135.00**	**175.00**
☐ **102**	**Johnny Wing, RC, LC**	**90.00**	**135.00**	**175.00**
☐ 103	Maurice Croghan, Mtl.M	90.00	135.00	175.00
☐ **104**	**Pete Jotkus, RC, LC**	**90.00**	**135.00**	**175.00**
☐ **105**	**Doug MacQuisten, RC, LC**	**90.00**	**135.00**	**175.00**
☐ **106**	**Lester Brennan, RC LC**	**90.00**	**135.00**	**175.00**
☐ **107**	**Jack O'Connell, RC, LC**	**90.00**	**135.00**	**175.00**
☐ **108**	**Ray Malenfant, RC, LC**	**90.00**	**135.00**	**175.00**
☐ **109**	**Ken Murray, Mtl.R, RC**	**90.00**	**135.00**	**175.00**
☐ **110**	**Frank Stangle, RC, LC**	**90.00**	**135.00**	**175.00**
☐ **111**	**Dave Neville, RC, LC**	**90.00**	**135.00**	**175.00**
☐ **112**	**Claude Burke, RC, LC**	**90.00**	**135.00**	**175.00**
☐ **113**	**Herman Murray, RC, LC**	**90.00**	**135.00**	**175.00**
☐ **114**	**Buddy O'Connor, RC, LC**	**200.00**	**300.00**	**400.00**
☐ **115**	**Albert Perreault, RC, LC**	**90.00**	**135.00**	**175.00**
☐ **116**	**Johnny Taugher, RC, LC**	**90.00**	**135.00**	**175.00**
☐ **117**	**Rene Boudreau, RC, LC**	**90.00**	**135.00**	**175.00**
☐ **118**	**Kenny McKinnon (G), Que.A, RC**	**90.00**	**135.00**	**175.00**
☐ **119**	**Alex Bolduc, RC, LC**	**90.00**	**135.00**	**175.00**
☐ **120**	**Jimmy Keiller, RC, LC**	**90.00**	**135.00**	**175.00**
☐ **121**	**Lloyd McIntyre, RC, LC**	**90.00**	**135.00**	**175.00**
☐ **122**	**Emile Fortin, RC, LC**	**90.00**	**135.00**	**175.00**
☐ **123**	**Mike Karakas, RC, LC**	**110.00**	**170.00**	**215.00**
☐ 124	Art Wiebe, Chi.	90.00	135.00	175.00
☐ **125**	**Louis Denis, RC, LC**	**90.00**	**135.00**	**175.00**
☐ **126**	**Stan Pratt, RC, LC**	**90.00**	**135.00**	**175.00**
☐ **127**	**Jules Cholette, RC ,LC**	**90.00**	**135.00**	**175.00**
☐ **128**	**Jimmy Muir, RC, LC**	**90.00**	**135.00**	**175.00**
☐ **129**	**Pete Morin, RC, LC**	**90.00**	**135.00**	**175.00**
☐ **130**	**Jimmy Heffernan, RC, LC**	**90.00**	**135.00**	**175.00**
☐ **131**	**Morris Bastien, RC, LC**	**90.00**	**135.00**	**175.00**
☐ **132**	**Tuffy Griffiths, RC, LC**	**90.00**	**135.00**	**175.00**
☐ **133**	**John Mahaffy, RC, LC**	**90.00**	**135.00**	**175.00**
☐ **134**	**Truman Donnelly, RC, LC**	**90.00**	**135.00**	**175.00**
☐ **135**	**Bill Stewart , RC, LC**	**110.00**	**160.00**	**325.00**

1936 - 39 DIAMOND MATCH TAN ISSUE

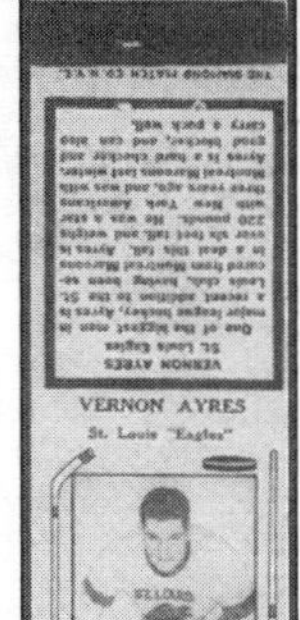

The design of the book was modified with the cover being redesigned and its colour changing to tan. This basic desing continued until the end of the issue in 1939. The issue can be broken down into six different types issued over the years from 1934 to 1939.

TYPE I

At the top of the resume (back) is the player's name and the name of the team or the player's position. The imprint "The Diamond Match Co. NYC." is on one line. Joe Starke's match book is considered very rare.

Card Size: 1 1/16" x 4 1/2"
Face: Black and white photograph on tan coloured template with cream coloured border
Back: Black print on thick, tan coloured card stock
Imprint: THE DIAMOND MATCH COMPANY, N.Y.C.

		VG	EX	EX-NRMT
Complete Set (70 cards):		**750.00**	**1,150.00**	**1,500.00**
Common Player:		**10.00**	**15.00**	**20.00**
	Player	**VG**	**EX**	**EX-NRMT**
☐	Andy Aitkenhead (G), NYR	10.00	15.00	20.00
☐	Vern Ayres, St.L Eagles	10.00	15.00	20.00
☐	Bill Beveridge (G), St. Louis Eagles	12.00	18.00	25.00
☐	Ralph Bowman, St. Louis Eagles	10.00	15.00	20.00
☐	Bill Brydge, NYA.	10.00	15.00	20.00
☐	Glenn Brydson, St. Louis Eagles	10.00	15.00	20.00
☐	Eddie Burke, NYA.	10.00	15.00	20.00
☐	Marty Burke, Chi.	10.00	15.00	20.00
☐	Lorne Carr, NYA.	10.00	15.00	20.00
☐	Gerry Carson, Mtl.	10.00	15.00	20.00
☐	Lorne Chabot (G), Chi.	20.00	30.00	40.00
☐	Art Chapman, NYA.	10.00	15.00	20.00
☐	Hugh (Red) Conn, NYA.	10.00	15.00	20.00
☐	Bert Connolly, NYR.	10.00	15.00	20.00
☐	Bun (Fred) Cook, NYR.	20.00	30.00	40.00
☐	Tom Cook, Chi.	10.00	15.00	20.00
☐	Art Coulter, Chi.	10.00	15.00	20.00
☐	Rosario (Lolo) Couture, Chi.	10.00	15.00	20.00
☐	Bill Cowley, St. Louis Eagles	20.00	30.00	40.00
☐	Wilf Cude (G), Mtl.	12.00	18.00	25.00
☐	Red Dutton, NYA.	20.00	30.00	40.00
☐	Frank Finnigan, St. Louis Eagles	15.00	22.00	30.00
☐	Irvin Frew, St. Louis Eagles	10.00	15.00	20.00
☐	Leroy Goldsworthy, Chi.	10.00	15.00	20.00
☐	Johnny Gottselig, Chi.	10.00	15.00	20.00
☐	Bob Gracie, NYA.	10.00	15.00	20.00
☐	Otto Heller, NYR.	10.00	15.00	20.00
☐	Normie Himes, NYA.	10.00	15.00	20.00
☐	Syd Howe, St. Louis Eagles	20.00	30.00	40.00
☐	Roger Jenkins, Mtl.	10.00	15.00	20.00
☐	Ivan (Ching) Johnson, NYR.	25.00	35.00	50.00
☐	Aurèle Joliat, Mtl.	40.00	55.00	75.00
☐	Max Kaminsky, St. Louis Eagles	10.00	15.00	20.00
☐	Butch (Melville) Keeling, Chi.	10.00	15.00	20.00
☐	William Kendall, Chi.	10.00	15.00	20.00
☐	Lloyd Klein, NYA.	10.00	15.00	20.00
☐	Joe Lamb, Mtl.	10.00	15.00	20.00
☐	Wildor Larochelle, Mtl.	10.00	15.00	20.00
☐	Pit Lépine, Mtl.	10.00	15.00	20.00
☐	Norman Locking, Chi.	10.00	15.00	20.00
☐	Georges Mantha, Mtl.	15.00	22.00	30.00
☐	Sylvio Mantha, Mtl.	20.00	30.00	40.00
☐	Mush March, Chi.	10.00	15.00	20.00
☐	Charley Mason, NYR.	10.00	15.00	20.00
☐	Donnie McFayden, Chi.	10.00	15.00	20.00
☐	Jack McGill, Mtl.	10.00	15.00	20.00
☐	Charley McVeigh, NYA.	10.00	15.00	20.00
☐	Armand Mondou, Mtl.	10.00	15.00	20.00

Howie Morenz, Chi.	175.00	265.00	350.00
John Murray Murdoch, NYR.	10.00	15.00	20.00
Allan Murray, NYA.	10.00	15.00	20.00
Harry Oliver, NYA.	20.00	30.00	40.00
Jean Pusie, Bos.	10.00	15.00	20.00
Paul Raymond, Mtl.	10.00	15.00	20.00
Jack Riley, Mtl.	10.00	15.00	20.00
Vic Ripley, St. Louis Eagles	10.00	15.00	20.00
Desse Roche, St. Louis Eagles	10.00	15.00	20.00
Earl Roche, St. Louis Eagles	10.00	15.00	20.00
Doc Romnes, Chi.	10.00	15.00	20.00
Sweeney Schriner, NYA.	20.00	30.00	40.00
Earl Seibert, NYR.	20.00	30.00	40.00
Gerry Shannon, St. Louis Eagles	10.00	15.00	20.00
Alex Smith, NYA.	10.00	15.00	20.00
Joe Starke, Chi.			very rare
Nels Stewart, Bos.	25.00	35.00	50.00
Paul Thompson, Chi.	10.00	15.00	20.00
Louis Trudel, Chi.	10.00	15.00	20.00
Carl Voss, St. Louis Eagles	15.00	22.00	30.00
Art Wiebe, Chi.	10.00	15.00	20.00
Roy Worters (G), NYA.	25.00	35.00	50.00

TYPE 2

The team name, or team position has been removed from the top of the resumé. The imprint is still on one line as in Type 1.

These match books have the same colours, and design and are the same size as the Type 1 Diamond Match books.

Irving Jaffes and Harold Starr's matchbooks are considered very rare.

Complete Set (65 cards):	750.00	1,150.00	1,500.00
Common Player:	10.00	15.00	20.00
Player	VG	EX	EX-NRMT
Tom Anderson, NYA.	10.00	15.00	20.00
Vern Ayres, NYR.	10.00	15.00	20.00
Frank Boucher, NYR.	20.00	30.00	40.00
Frank Boucher, NYR.	20.00	30.00	40.00
Bill Brydge, NYA.	10.00	15.00	20.00
Marty Burke, Mtl.	10.00	15.00	20.00
Lorne Carr, NYA.	10.00	15.00	20.00
Lorne Chabot (G), NYA.	20.00	30.00	40.00
Art Chapman, NYA.	10.00	15.00	20.00
Bert Connolly, NYR.	10.00	15.00	20.00
Bill Cook, NYR.	25.00	35.00	50.00
Bill Cook, NYR.	25.00	35.00	50.00
Bun (Fred) Cook, NYR.	20.00	30.00	40.00
Tom Cook, Chi.	10.00	15.00	20.00
Art Coulter, Chi.	10.00	15.00	20.00
Rosario (Lolo) Couture, Mtl.	10.00	15.00	20.00
Wilf Cude (G), Mtl.	12.00	18.00	25.00
Cecil Dillon, NYR.	10.00	15.00	20.00
Cecil Dillon, NYR.	10.00	15.00	20.00
Red Dutton, NYA.	20.00	30.00	40.00
Hap Emms, NYA.	10.00	15.00	20.00
Irvin Frew, Mtl.	10.00	15.00	20.00
Johnny Gagnon, Mtl.	10.00	15.00	20.00
Leroy Goldsworthy, Mtl.	10.00	15.00	20.00
Johnny Gottselig, Chi.	10.00	15.00	20.00
William Paul Haynes, Mtl.	10.00	15.00	20.00
Otto Heller, NYR.	10.00	15.00	20.00
Irving Jaffes			very rare
Joe Jerwa, NYA.	10.00	15.00	20.00
Ivan (Ching) Johnson, NYR.	25.00	35.00	50.00
Aurèle Joliat, Mtl.	40.00	55.00	75.00
Butch (Melville) Keeling, NYR.	10.00	15.00	20.00
William Kendall, Chi.	10.00	15.00	20.00
Dave Kerr (G), NYR.	15.00	22.00	30.00
Lloyd Klein, NYA.	10.00	15.00	20.00
Wildor Larochelle, Mtl.	10.00	15.00	20.00
Pit Lepine, Mtl.	10.00	15.00	20.00
Art Lesieur, Mtl.	10.00	15.00	20.00
Alex Levinsky, NYR.	10.00	15.00	20.00
Alex Levinsky, NYR.	10.00	15.00	20.00
Norman Locking, Chi.	10.00	15.00	20.00
George Mantha, Mtl.	15.00	22.00	30.00
Sylvio Mantha, Mtl.	20.00	30.00	40.00
Mush March, Chi.	10.00	15.00	20.00
Charley Mason, NYR.	10.00	15.00	20.00
Donnie McFaydon, Chi.	10.00	15.00	20.00
Jack McGill, Mtl.	10.00	15.00	20.00
Armand Mondou, Mtl.	10.00	15.00	20.00
Howie Morenz, Chi.	175.00	265.00	350.00
John Murray Murdoch, NYR.	10.00	15.00	20.00
Allan Murray, NYA.	10.00	15.00	20.00
Harry Oliver, NYA.	20.00	30.00	40.00
Adelard Ouellette, Chi.	10.00	15.00	20.00
Lynn Patrick, NYR.	25.00	35.00	50.00
Lynn Patrick, NYR.	25.00	50.00	100.00
Paul Runge, Mtl.	10.00	15.00	20.00
Sweeney Schriner, NYA.	20.00	30.00	40.00
Art Somers, NYR.	10.00	15.00	20.00
Harold Starr, NYR.			very rare
Nels Stewart, NYA.	25.00	35.00	50.00
Paul Thompson, Chi.	10.00	15.00	20.00
Louis Trudel, Chi.	10.00	15.00	20.00
Carl Voss, NYA.	15.00	22.00	30.00
Art Wiebe, Chi.	10.00	15.00	20.00
Roy Worters (G), NYA.	25.00	35.00	50.00

TYPE 3

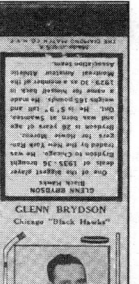

The imprint is now on two lines and reads "Made in the U.S.A./ Diamond Match Co. N.Y.C."

These match books have the same colours, and design and are the same size as the Type 1 Diamond Match books.

Harold Starr's matchbook is considered very rare.

Complete Set (60 cards):	700.00	1,00.00	1,400.00
Common Player:	10.00	15.00	20.00
Player	VG	EX	EX-NRMT
Tom Anderson, NYA.	10.00	15.00	20.00
Vern Ayres, NYR.	10.00	15.00	20.00
Frank Boucher, NYR.	20.00	30.00	40.00
Bill Brydge, NYA.	10.00	15.00	20.00
Marty Burke, Chi.	10.00	15.00	20.00
Walt Buswell, Mtl.	10.00	15.00	20.00
Lorne Carr, NYA.	10.00	15.00	20.00
Lorne Chabot (G), NYA.	20.00	30.00	40.00
Art Chapman, NYA.	10.00	15.00	20.00
Bert Connolly, NYR.	10.00	15.00	20.00
Bill Cook, NYR.	25.00	35.00	50.00
Bun (Fred) Cook, NYR.	20.00	30.00	40.00
Tom Cook, Chi.	10.00	15.00	20.00
Art Coulter, Chi.	10.00	15.00	20.00
Rosario (Lolo) Couture, Mtl.	10.00	15.00	20.00
Wilf Cude (G), Mtl.	12.00	18.00	25.00
Cecil Dillon, NYR.	10.00	15.00	20.00
Red Dutton, NYA.	20.00	30.00	40.00
Hap Emms, NYA.	10.00	15.00	20.00
Irvin Frew, Mtl.	10.00	15.00	20.00
Johnny Gagnon, Mtl.	10.00	15.00	20.00
Leroy Goldsworthy, Mtl.	10.00	15.00	20.00
Johnny Gottselig, Chi.	10.00	15.00	20.00
Paul Haynes, Mtl.	10.00	15.00	20.00
Otto Heller, NYR.	10.00	15.00	20.00
Joe Jerwa, NYA.	10.00	15.00	20.00
Ivan (Ching) Johnson, NYR.	25.00	35.00	50.00
Aurèle Joliat, Mtl.	40.00	55.00	75.00
Mike Karakas (G), Chi.	12.00	18.00	25.00
Butch (Melville) Keeling, NYR.	10.00	15.00	20.00
Dave Kerr (G), NYR.	15.00	22.00	30.00
Lloyd Klein, NYA.	10.00	15.00	20.00
Wildoer Larochelle, Mtl.	10.00	15.00	20.00
Pit Lepine, Mtl.	10.00	15.00	20.00
Art Lesieur, Mtl.	10.00	15.00	20.00
Alex Levinsky, Chi.	10.00	15.00	20.00
Norman Locking, Chi.	10.00	15.00	20.00
Georges Mantha, Mtl.	15.00	22.00	30.00
Sylvio Mantha, Mtl.	20.00	30.00	40.00
Mush March, Chi.	10.00	15.00	20.00
Charlie Mason, NYR.	10.00	15.00	20.00
Charlie Mason, NYR.	10.00	15.00	20.00
Donnie McFayden, Chi.	10.00	15.00	20.00
Jack McGill, Mtl.	10.00	15.00	20.00
Armand Mondou, Mtl.	10.00	15.00	20.00
Howie Morenz, Chi.	175.00	265.00	350.00
John Murray Murdoch, NYR.	10.00	15.00	20.00
Allan Murray, NYA.	10.00	15.00	20.00
Harry Oliver, NYA.	20.00	30.00	40.00
Adelard Ouellette, Chi.	10.00	15.00	20.00
Lynn Patrick, NYR.	25.00	35.00	50.00
Paul Runge, Mtl.	10.00	15.00	20.00
Sweeney Schriner, NYA.	20.00	30.00	40.00
Harold Starr, NYR.			very rare
Nels Stewart, NYA	25.00	35.00	50.00
Paul Thompson, Chi.	10.00	15.00	20.00
Louis Trudel, Chi.	10.00	15.00	20.00
Carl Voss, NYA.	15.00	22.00	30.00
Art Wiebe, Chi.	10.00	15.00	20.00
Roy Worters (G), NYA.	25.00	35.00	50.00

Matchbooks in groups 4 through 6 are all Chicago Blackhawks' players.

TYPE 4

The imprint is again on two lines and reads "Made in the U.S.A./ Diamond Match Co. N.Y.C." The team name reappears below the player's name but above the resume on the back of the book.

These match books have the same colours, and design and are the same size as the Type 1 Diamond Match books.

Complete Set (15 cards):	120.00	185.00	235.00
Player	VG	EX	EX-NRMT
Andy Blair, Chi.	10.00	15.00	20.00
Glenn Brydson, Chi.	10.00	15.00	20.00
Marty Burke, Chi.	10.00	15.00	20.00
Tom Cook, Chi.	10.00	15.00	20.00
Johnny Gottselig, Chi.	10.00	15.00	20.00
Hal Jackson, Chi.	10.00	15.00	20.00
Mike Karakas (G), Chi.	12.00	18.00	25.00
Wildor Larochelle, Chi.	10.00	15.00	20.00
Alex Levinsky, Chi.	10.00	15.00	20.00
Clem Loughlin, Chi.	10.00	15.00	20.00
Mush March, Chi.	10.00	15.00	20.00
Earl Seibert, Chi.	20.00	30.00	40.00
Paul Thompson, Chi.	10.00	15.00	20.00
Louis Trudel, Chi.	10.00	15.00	20.00
Art Wiebe, Chi.	10.00	15.00	20.00

TYPE 5

The imprint is again on two lines and reads "Made in the U.S.A./ Diamond Match Co. N.Y.C." On the back, above the resumé, the team name again disappears as does the "Chicago" of the Chicago Blackhawks on the front cover. The tan background colour covers the complete book with the striker pad being overlaid on the tan.

These match books have the same colours, and design and are the same size as the Type 1 Diamond Match books.

Complete Set (14 cards):		120.00	185.00	235.00
No.	Player	VG	EX	EX-NRMT
	Glenn Brydson, Chi.	10.00	15.00	20.00
	Marty Burke, Chi.	10.00	15.00	20.00
	Tom Cook, Chi.	10.00	15.00	20.00
	Cully Dahlstrom, Chi.	10.00	15.00	20.00
	Johnny Gottselig, Chi.	10.00	15.00	20.00
	Vic Heyliger, Chi.	10.00	15.00	20.00
	Mike Karakas (G), Chi.	12.00	18.00	25.00
	Alex Levinsky, Chi.	10.00	15.00	20.00

	Player	VG	EX	EX-NRMT
☐	Mush March, Chi.	10.00	15.00	20.00
☐	Earl Seibert, Chi.	20.00	30.00	40.00
☐	Bill Stewart, Manager, Chi.	10.00	15.00	20.00
☐	Paul Thompson, Chi.	10.00	15.00	20.00
☐	Louis Trudel, Chi.	10.00	15.00	20.00
☐	Art Wiebe, Chi.	10.00	15.00	20.00

TYPE 6

The imprint is again on two lines and reads "Made in the U.S.A./ Diamond Match Co. N.Y.C."

This variety differs from Type 5 only in the background colour on which the striker is overlaid. This area is a dark brown or black giving the appearance that the tip is black instead of tan.These match books have the same colours, and design and are the same size as the Type 1 Diamond Match books.

Complete Set Price (14 cards):		120.00	185.00	235.00
	Player	VG	EX	EX-NRMT
☐	Glenn Brydson, Chi.	10.00	15.00	20.00
☐	Marty Burke, Chi.	10.00	15.00	20.00
☐	Tom Cook, Chi.	10.00	15.00	20.00
☐	Cully Dahlstrom, Chi.	10.00	15.00	20.00
☐	Johnny Gottselig, Chi.	10.00	15.00	20.00
☐	Vic Heyliger, Chi.	10.00	15.00	20.00
☐	Mike Karakas (G), Chi.	12.00	18.00	25.00
☐	Alex Levinsky, Chi.	10.00	15.00	20.00
☐	Mush March, Chi.	10.00	15.00	20.00
☐	Earl Seibert, Chi.	20.00	30.00	40.00
☐	Bill Stewart, Manager, Chi.	10.00	15.00	20.00
☐	Paul Thompson, Chi.	10.00	15.00	20.00
☐	Louis Trudel, Chi.	10.00	15.00	20.00
☐	Art Wiebe, Chi.	10.00	15.00	20.00

1937 W.D. & H.O. WILLS LTD. BRITISH SPORTING PERSONALITIES

This 48-card set features only two hockey cards.

Card Size: 2" x 3"

Face: Black and white photo, white border; Name

Back: Black on white card stock; Name, Number, Resume

Imprint: IMPERIAL TOBACCO CO. (OF GREAT BRITAIN & IRELAND), LTD.

	No.	Scene	VG	EX	EX-NRMT
☐	36	L. Bates, Wembley Lions	10.00	20.00	40.00
☐	37	Joe Beaton, Richmond Hawks	10.00	20.00	40.00

1937 - 38 O-PEE-CHEE SERIES "E"

Cards can be found with either purple or blue borders.

ACC No.: V304E

Card Size: 2 3/8" x 3 7/8"

Face: Black and white, white border, blue or purple frame

Back: Black on card stock; Name, Team, Bilingual, Resume, Number

Imprint: None

Complete Set (48 cards):			3,300.00	4,800.00	6,500.00
	No.	Player	VG	EX	EX-NRMT
☐	133	Turk Broda (G), Tor.	225.00	340.00	600.00
☐	134	Red Horner, Tor.	125.00	190.00	250.00
☐	135	Jimmy Fowler, Tor.	60.00	90.00	115.00
☐	136	Bob Davidson, Tor.	65.00	100.00	130.00
☐	**137**	**Reg Hamilton, Tor., RC**	**60.00**	**90.00**	**115.00**
☐	138	Charlie Conacher, Tor.	300.00	450.00	600.00
☐	139	Harvey Jackson, Tor.	140.00	210.00	275.00
☐	140	Buzz Boll, Tor.	60.00	90.00	115.00
☐	141	Syl Apps, Sr., Tor.	200.00	300.00	400.00
☐	**142**	**Gordie Drillon, Tor., RC**	**225.00**	**135.00**	**175.00**
☐	143	Bill Thoms, Tor.	90.00	140.00	185.00
☐	144	Nick Metz, Tor.	70.00	100.00	140.00
☐	145	Reg Kelly, Tor.	60.00	90.00	115.00
☐	**146**	**Murray Armstrong, Tor., RC**	**60.00**	**90.00**	**115.00**
☐	**147**	**Murph Chamberlain, Tor., RC**	**60.00**	**90.00**	**115.00**
☐	**148**	**Des Smith, Mtl. M., RC**	**60.00**	**90.00**	**115.00**
☐	149	Wilf Cude (G), Mtl.	70.00	100.00	140.00
☐	150	Babe Siebert	125.00	190.00	250.00
☐	151	Bill MacKenzie, Mtl., Err (McKenzie)	60.00	90.00	115.00
☐	152	Aurèle Joliat, Mtl.	300.00	450.00	600.00
☐	153	Georges Mantha, Mtl.	60.00	90.00	115.00
☐	154	Johnny Gagnon, Mtl.	60.00	90.00	115.00
☐	155	Paul Haynes, Mtl.	60.00	90.00	115.00
☐	156	Joffre Desilets, Mtl.	60.00	90.00	115.00
☐	**157**	**George Brown,, Mtl. RC**	**60.00**	**90.00**	**115.00**
☐	158	Polly Drouin, Mtl.	60.00	90.00	115.00
☐	159	Pit Lépine, Mtl.	60.00	90.00	115.00
☐	**160**	**Toe Blake, Mtl., RC**	**450.00**	**675.00**	**900.00**
☐	161	Bill Beveridge (G), Mtl. M., LC	70.00	100.00	140.00
☐	162	Al Shields, Mtl. M	60.00	90.00	115.00
☐	163	Cy Wentworth, Mtl. M	65.00	100.00	130.00
☐	164	Stewart Evans, Mtl. M	60.00	90.00	115.00
☐	165	Earle Robinson, Mtl. M, LC	60.00	90.00	115.00
☐	166	Baldy Northcott, Mtl. M, LC	90.00	135.00	175.00
☐	167	Paul Runge, Mtl. M	60.00	90.00	115.00
☐	168	Dave Trottier, Mtl. M	60.00	90.00	115.00
☐	169	Russ Blinco, Mtl. M	60.00	90.00	115.00
☐	170	Jimmy Ward, Mtl. M	60.00	90.00	115.00
☐	171	Bob Gracie, Mtl. M	60.00	90.00	115.00
☐	172	Herbert Cain, Mtl. M	85.00	125.00	165.00
☐	173	Gus Marker, Mtl. M	60.00	90.00	115.00
☐	174	Walt Buswell, Mtl.	60.00	90.00	115.00
☐	175	Carl Voss, Mtl. M	100.00	150.00	200.00
☐	**176**	**Rod Lorraine, Mtl., RC, Err (Lorrain)**	**60.00**	**90.00**	**115.00**
☐	177	Armand Mondou, Mtl.	60.00	90.00	115.00
☐	**178**	**Red Goupille, Mtl., RC**	**60.00**	**90.00**	**115.00**
☐	**179**	**Gerry Shannon, Mtl., RC, Err (Jerry)**	**60.00**	**90.00**	**115.00**
☐	180	Tom Cook, Mtl.	100.00	150.00	275.00

1938 - 39 BRIGHTON TIGERS ISSUE

Card Size: 3 3/16" x 5 3/8"

Face: Black and white, white border, cardstock

Back: Postcard format

Imprint: Defoe Photographic Service, Brighton.

	Scene	VG	EX	EX-NRMT
☐	Joffre Seguin	12.00	25.00	50.00

1938 - 39 BOSTON BRUINS MAGAZINE PHOTOS

We have little information on this set and its sponsor. More singles exist.

Photo Size: 8" x 10"

	Player	VG	EX	EX-NRMT
☐	Red Beattie			
☐	Walter Gailbraith			
☐	Lionel Hitchman			
☐	Joseph Lamb			
☐	Harry Oliver			
☐	Art Ross			
☐	Eddie Shore			
☐	Nels Stewart			
☐	Tiny Thompson (G)			

1938 - 39 QUAKER OATS

Photo Size: 6 1/4" x 7 1/2"

Face: Black and white on card stock

Back: Blank

Imprint: None

Complete Set (30 cards):		700.00	1,000.00	1,400.00
	Player	VG	EX	NRMT
☐	Toe Blake, Mtl.	90.00	135.00	175.00
☐	Walt Buswell, Mtl.	25.00	35.00	50.00
☐	Herbert Cain, Mtl.	30.00	45.00	60.00
☐	Wilf Cude (G), Mtl.	30.00	45.00	60.00
☐	Polly Drouin, Mtl.	25.00	35.00	50.00
☐	Stewart Evans, Mtl.	25.00	35.00	50.00
☐	Johnny Gagnon, Mtl.	25.00	35.00	50.00
☐	Bob Gracie, Mtl.	25.00	35.00	50.00
☐	Paul Haynes, Mtl.	25.00	35.00	50.00
☐	Rod Lorrain, Mtl.	25.00	35.00	50.00
☐	Georges Mantha, Mtl.	25.00	35.00	50.00
☐	Babe Siebert, Mtl.	40.00	60.00	80.00
☐	Jimmy Ward, Mtl.	25.00	35.00	50.00
☐	Cy Wentworth, Mtl.	30.00	45.00	60.00
☐	Syl Apps, Sr., Tor.	55.00	85.00	110.00
☐	Buzz Boll, Tor.	25.00	35.00	50.00
☐	Turk Broda (G), Tor.	70.00	100.00	135.00
☐	Murph Chamberlain, Tor.	25.00	35.00	50.00
☐	Bob Davidson, Tor.	30.00	45.00	60.00
☐	Gordie Drillon, Tor.	40.00	60.00	80.00
☐	Jimmy Fowler, Tor.	25.00	35.00	50.00
☐	Reg Hamilton, Tor.	25.00	35.00	50.00
☐	Red Horner, Tor.	40.00	55.00	75.00
☐	Harvey Jackson, Tor.	45.00	65.00	90.00
☐	Bingo Kampman, Tor.	25.00	35.00	50.00
☐	Reg Kelly, Tor.	25.00	35.00	50.00
☐	Nick Metz, Tor.	30.00	45.00	60.00
☐	George Parsons, Tor.	25.00	35.00	50.00
☐	Bill Thoms, Tor.	30.00	45.00	60.00
☐	Foster Hewitt	50.00	75.00	100.00

1939 - 40 O-PEE-CHEE

These black and white cards have blank backs and are larger than the previous issues of the '30s. The player's name, team and position are shown beneath the photo with the card number to the right.

ACC No.: V301-1

Card Size: 5" x 7"

Face: Black and white; Name, Number, Team, Position
Back: Blank
Imprint: LITHOGRAPHED IN CANADA

	VG	EX	EX-NRMT
Complete Set (100 cards):	**3,000.00**	**5,000.00**	**7,000.00**
Common Player:	**25.00**	**45.00**	**60.00**

No.	Player	VG	EX	EX-NRMT
☐ 1	Reg Hamilton, Tor.	25.00	45.00	100.00
☐ 2	Turk Broda (G), Tor.	125.00	190.00	275.00
☐ 3	**Bingo Kampman, Tor., RC**	**25.00**	**45.00**	**60.00**
☐ 4	Gordie Drillon, Tor.	50.00	75.00	125.00
☐ 5	Bob Davidson, Tor.	25.00	55.00	70.00
☐ 6	Syl Apps, Sr., Tor.	75.00	115.00	185.00
☐ 7	**Pete Langelle, Tor., RC**	**25.00**	**45.00**	**60.00**
☐ 8	**Don Metz,, Tor. RC**	**25.00**	**45.00**	**60.00**
☐ 9	Reg Kelly, Tor.	25.00	45.00	60.00
☐ 10	Red Horner, Tor.	50.00	75.00	125.00
☐ 11	**W. Stanowski,, Tor. RC, Err (Stanowsky)**	**35.00**	**55.00**	**75.00**
☐ 12	Murph Chamberlain, Tor.	25.00	45.00	60.00
☐ 13	Bucko McDonald, Tor.	25.00	45.00	60.00
☐ 14	Sweeny Schriner, Tor.	60.00	90.00	140.00
☐ 15	**Billy Taylor, Tor., RC**	**35.00**	**60.00**	**80.00**
☐ 16	Gus Marker, Tor.	25.00	45.00	60.00
☐ 17	Hooley Smith, NYA., LC	50.00	75.00	125.00
☐ 18	Art Chapman, NYA.	25.00	55.00	70.00
☐ 19	Murray Armstrong, NYA.	25.00	45.00	60.00
☐ 20	Harvey Jackson, NYA.	65.00	100.00	160.00
☐ 21	Buzz Boll, NYA.	25.00	45.00	60.00
☐ 22	Red Goupille, Mtl.	25.00	45.00	60.00
☐ 23	Rod Lorraine, Mtl.	25.00	45.00	60.00
☐ 24	Polly Drouin, Mtl.	25.00	45.00	60.00
☐ 25	Johnny Gagnon, Mtl.	25.00	45.00	60.00
☐ 26	Georges Mantha, Mtl.	25.00	45.00	60.00
☐ 27	Armand Mondou, Mtl.	25.00	45.00	60.00
☐ 28	**Claude Bourque (G), Mtl., RC**	**25.00**	**45.00**	**60.00**
☐ 29	**Ray Getliffe, Mtl., RC**	**25.00**	**45.00**	**60.00**
☐ 30	Cy Wentworth, Mtl.	35.00	55.00	75.00
☐ 31	Paul Haynes, Mtl.	25.00	45.00	60.00
☐ 32	Walt Buswell, Mtl.	25.00	45.00	60.00
☐ 33	Ott Heller, NYR.	25.00	45.00	60.00
☐ 34	Art Coulter, NYR.	45.00	70.00	115.00
☐ 35	**Clint Smith, NYR., RC**	**50.00**	**75.00**	**130.00**
☐ 36	Lynn Patrick, NYR.	50.00	75.00	125.00
☐ 37	Dave Kerr (G), NYR.	40.00	60.00	100.00
☐ 38	**Murray Patrick, NYR., RC**	**25.00**	**45.00**	**60.00**
☐ 39	Neil Colville, NYR.	50.00	75.00	130.00
☐ 40	**Jack Portland, Bos., RC**	**25.00**	**45.00**	**60.00**
☐ 41	Bill Hollett, Bos.	25.00	45.00	60.00
☐ 42	Herbert Cain, Bos.	40.00	60.00	90.00
☐ 43	**Mud Bruneteau, Det., RC**	**35.00**	**55.00**	**75.00**
☐ 44	Joffre Desilets, Chi.	25.00	45.00	60.00
☐ 45	Mush March, Chi.	35.00	55.00	75.00
☐ 46	**C. Dahlstrom, Chi., RC, Err. (Dalhstrom)**	**25.00**	**45.00**	**60.00**
☐ 47	Mike Karakas (G), Chi.	25.00	55.00	70.00
☐ 48	Bill Thoms, Chi.	40.00	60.00	85.00
☐ 49	Art Wiebe, Chi.	25.00	15.00	60.00
☐ 50	Johnny Gottselig, Chi.	35.00	55.00	75.00
☐ 51	Nick Metz, Tor.	25.00	55.00	70.00
☐ 52	**Jack Church, Tor., RC**	**25.00**	**45.00**	**60.00**
☐ 53	**Red Heron, Tor., RC**	**25.00**	**45.00**	**60.00**
☐ 54	**Hank Goldup, Tor., RC**	**25.00**	**45.00**	**60.00**
☐ 55	Jimmy Fowler, Tor.	25.00	45.00	60.00
☐ 56	Charlie Sands, Mtl.	25.00	45.00	60.00
☐ 57	Marty Barry, Mtl.	45.00	80.00	125.00
☐ 58	**Doug Young, Mtl., RC**	**25.00**	**45.00**	**60.00**
☐ 59	Charlie Conacher, NYA.	95.00	145.00	235.00
☐ 60	John Sorrell, NYA.	25.00	45.00	60.00
☐ 61	**Tom Anderson, NYA., RC**	**25.00**	**55.00**	**70.00**
☐ 62	Lorne Carr, NYA.	35.00	60.00	80.00
☐ 63	**Earl Robertson (G), NYA., RC, LC**	**25.00**	**45.00**	**60.00**
☐ 64	**Wilf Field, NYA., RC**	**25.00**	**45.00**	**60.00**
☐ 65	**Jimmy Orlando, Det., RC**	**25.00**	**45.00**	**60.00**
☐ 66	Ebbie Goodfellow, Det.	45.00	80.00	120.00
☐ 67	**Jack Keating, Det., RC**	**25.00**	**45.00**	**60.00**
☐ 68	**Sid Abel, Det., RC**	**120.00**	**180.00**	**300.00**
☐ 69	**Gus Giesebrecht, Det., RC**	**25.00**	**45.00**	**60.00**
☐ 70	**Don Deacon, Det., RC**	**25.00**	**45.00**	**60.00**
☐ 71	Hec Kilrea, Det.	25.00	45.00	60.00
☐ 72	Syd Howe, Det., LC	50.00	75.00	125.00
☐ 73	**Eddie Wares, Det., RC**	**25.00**	**45.00**	**60.00**
☐ 74	**Carl Liscombe, Det., RC**	**25.00**	**45.00**	**60.00**
☐ 75	Tiny Thompson (G), Det.	60.00	90.00	150.00
☐ 76	Earl Seibert, Chi.	60.00	90.00	150.00
☐ 77	Des Smith, Chi.	25.00	45.00	60.00
☐ 78	**Les Cunningham, Chi., RC**	**25.00**	**45.00**	**60.00**
☐ 79	**George Allen, Chi., RC**	**25.00**	**45.00**	**60.00**
☐ 80	**Bill Carse, Chi., RC**	**25.00**	**45.00**	**60.00**
☐ 81	Bill MacKenzie, Chi.	25.00	45.00	60.00
☐ 82	**Ab DeMarco, Chi., RC, LC**	**25.00**	**45.00**	**60.00**
☐ 83	**Phil Watson, Chi. , RC**	**40.00**	**60.00**	**90.00**
☐ 84	**Alf Pike, NYR., RC**	**25.00**	**45.00**	**60.00**
☐ 85	**Babe Pratt, NYR., RC**	**60.00**	**90.00**	**150.00**
☐ 86	**Bryan Hextall, Sr., NYR., RC**	**75.00**	**115.00**	**185.00**
☐ 87	**Kilby MacDonald, NYR., RC**	**25.00**	**45.00**	**60.00**
☐ 88	Alex Shibicky, NYR.	25.00	45.00	60.00
☐ 89	**Dutch Hiller, NYR., RC**	**25.00**	**55.00**	**70.00**
☐ 90	**Mac Colville, NYR., RC**	**25.00**	**45.00**	**60.00**
☐ 91	**Roy Conacher, Bos., RC**	**40.00**	**60.00**	**100.00**
☐ 92	Cooney Weiland, Bos., LC	50.00	75.00	125.00
☐ 93	Art Jackson	25.00	45.00	60.00
☐ 94	**Woodie Dumart, Bos., RC**	**60.00**	**90.00**	**150.00**
☐ 95	Dit Clapper, Bos.	70.00	110.00	175.00
☐ 96	**Mel Hill, Bos., RC**	**25.00**	**45.00**	**60.00**
☐ 97	**Frank Brimsek (G), Bos., RC**	**140.00**	**210.00**	**350.00**
☐ 98	**Bill Cowley, Bos., RC**	**140.00**	**210.00**	**350.00**
☐ 99	**Bobby Bauer, Bos., RC**	**45.00**	**70.00**	**115.00**
☐ 100	Eddie Shore, Bos.	185.00	280.00	550.00

1940 - 41 O-PEE-CHEE

This set continues the sequential numbering from the V301-1 issue and follows the same format except for the sepia-toned photos.

ACC No.: V301-2
Card Size: 5" x 7"
Face: Sepia; Name, Cream border; Team, Position, Number
Back: Blank
Imprint: LITHOGRAPHED IN CANADA

	VG	EX	EX-NRMT
Complete Set (50 cards):	**2,000.00**	**3,000.00**	**4,800.00**
Common Player (101 to 125):	**30.00**	**50.00**	**65.00**
Common Player (126 to 150):	**45.00**	**70.00**	**110.00**

No.	Player	VG	EX	EX-NRMT
☐ 101	Toe Blake, Mtl.	100.00	150.00	275.00
☐ 102	Charlie Sands, LC	30.00	50.00	65.00
☐ 103	Wally Stanowski, Tor., LC	35.00	55.00	75.00
☐ 104	**Jack E. Adams, Mtl.C, RC**	**30.00**	**50.00**	**65.00**
☐ 105	**Johnny Mowers (G), RC, LC**	**30.00**	**50.00**	**65.00**
☐ 106	**John Quilty, RC, LC**	**30.00**	**50.00**	**65.00**
☐ 107	Billy Taylor, Tor., LC	35.00	55.00	75.00
☐ 108	Turk Broda (G), Tor.	100.00	150.00	250.00
☐ 109	Bingo Kampman, Tor.	30.00	50.00	65.00
☐ 110	Gordie Drillon, LC	50.00	75.00	120.00
☐ 111	Don Metz, Tor.	30.00	50.00	65.00
☐ 112	Paul Haynes	30.00	50.00	65.00
☐ 113	Gus Marker, Tor.	30.00	50.00	65.00
☐ 114	**Alex Singbush, Mtl.C, RC**	**30.00**	**50.00**	**65.00**
☐ 115	**Alex Motter, RC**	**30.00**	**50.00**	**65.00**
☐ 116	**Ken Reardon, Mtl.C, RC**	**60.00**	**90.00**	**150.00**
☐ 117	Pete Langelle, Tor.	30.00	50.00	65.00
☐ 118	Syl Apps., Tor.	65.00	100.00	160.00
☐ 119	Reg Hamilton, Tor.	30.00	50.00	65.00
☐ 120	Red Goupille, Mtl.C	30.00	50.00	65.00
☐ 121	**Joe Benoît, RC**	**30.00**	**50.00**	**65.00**
☐ 122	Sweeny Schriner, Tor.	50.00	75.00	120.00
☐ 123	**Joe Carveth, Det., RC**	**35.00**	**55.00**	**75.00**
☐ 124	**Jack Stewart, RC**	**60.00**	**90.00**	**150.00**
☐ 125	**Elmer Lach, Mtl.C, RC**	**120.00**	**180.00**	**300.00**
☐ 126	**Jack Schewchuk, RC**	**45.00**	**70.00**	**110.00**
☐ 127	**Norman Larson, RC**	**45.00**	**70.00**	**110.00**
☐ 128	**Don Grosso, RC**	**45.00**	**70.00**	**110.00**
☐ 129	**Les Douglas, Det., RC**	**45.00**	**70.00**	**110.00**
☐ 130	Turk Broda (G), Tor.	140.00	210.00	350.00
☐ 131	**Max Bentley,Chi., RC**	**140.00**	**210.00**	**350.00**
☐ 132	**Milt Schmidt, Bos., RC**	**180.00**	**270.00**	**450.00**
☐ 133	Nick Metz, Tor.	50.00	75.00	120.00
☐ 134	**John Crawford, Bos., RC**	**50.00**	**75.00**	**120.00**
☐ 135	**Bill Benson, RC**	**45.00**	**70.00**	**110.00**
☐ 136	Lynn Patrick, NYR	70.00	110.00	175.00
☐ 137	Cully Dahlstrom, Chi.	45.00	70.00	110.00
☐ 138	Mud Bruneteau, Det.	50.00	75.00	120.00
☐ 139	Dave Kerr (G), LC	55.00	85.00	135.00
☐ 140	Red Heron	45.00	70.00	110.00
☐ 141	Nick Metz, Tor.	55.00	80.00	120.00
☐ 142	Ott Heller, NYR	45.00	70.00	110.00
☐ 143	**Philip Hergesheimer, RC**	**45.00**	**70.00**	**110.00**
☐ 144	**Tony DeMeres, RC**	**45.00**	**70.00**	**110.00**
☐ 145	**Arch Wilder, Det., RC**	**45.00**	**70.00**	**110.00**
☐ 146	Syl Apps, Sr., Tor.	100.00	150.00	250.00
☐ 147	Ray Getliffe	50.00	75.00	110.00
☐ 148	**Lex Chisholm, Tor., RC**	**50.00**	**75.00**	**110.00**
☐ 149	**Eddie Wiseman, RC**	**50.00**	**75.00**	**110.00**
☐ 150	**Paul Goodman (G), Chi., RC**	**50.00**	**75.00**	**140.00**

CHAPTER TWO

MODERN ISSUES 1942 TO 1998

ST. LAWRENCE STARCH COMPANY

BEE HIVE PHOTOS

GROUP I - 1934-1943

The first group has three main varieties of player names printed on the photos as follows:

1. Facsimile Autograph
2. Block Autorgraph
3. Script Autograph

One or two other name styles exist but their use is minimal and cannot be used as an identifying feature.

Photo Size: 4 1/4" x 6 3/4"
Mat Size: 5 1/2" x 8"
Face: Black and white
Mat: Red, blue or beige
Back: Blank except for the trophy photos that are dated

	Player	EX	NRMT
	BOSTON BRUINS		
□	Bobby Bauer	10.00	16.00
□	Red Beattie	12.00	20.00
□	Yank Boyd	75.00	125.00
□	Frank Brimsek (G)	15.00	25.00
□	Dit Clapper	12.00	20.00
□	Roy Conacher	10.00	16.00
□	Fred (Bun) Cook	12.00	20.00
□	Cowboy Cowley	12.00	20.00
□	Johnny Crawford (#19)	10.00	16.00
□	Woody Dumart	15.00	25.00
□	Don Gallinger	85.00	140.00
□	Ray Getliffe	10.00	16.00
□	Bep Guidolin	50.00	80.00
□	Red Hamill	18.00	28.00
□	Melvin Hill	12.00	20.00
□	Alex Motter	20.00	30.00
□	Peggy O'Neill	12.00	20.00
□	Charles Sands	12.00	20.00
□	Jack Schmidt	110.00	175.00
□	Milt Schmidt	12.00	20.00
□	Jack Shewchuk	12.00	20.00
□	Eddie Shore	30.00	50.00
□	Tiny Thompson (G)	20.00	30.00
□	Cooney Weiland	12.00	20.00
	CHICAGO BLACKHAWKS		
□	George Allen	20.00	30.00
□	Doug Bentley	18.00	28.00
□	Max Bentley, Error (Doug Bentley)	18.00	28.00
□	Glenn Brydson	65.00	110.00
□	Marty Burke	15.00	25.00
□	Bill Carse	10.00	16.00
□	Bob Carse	10.00	16.00
□	Lorne Chabot (G)	22.00	35.00
□	Johnny Chad	22.00	35.00
□	Les Cunningham	18.00	28.00
□	Cully Dahlstrom	12.00	20.00
□	Goldy Goldsworthy	18.00	28.00
□	Paul Goodman (G)	22.00	35.00
□	Johnnie Gottselig	15.00	25.00
□	Phil Hergesheimer	12.00	20.00
□	Wingy Johnston	100.00	165.00
□	Alex Kaleta	20.00	30.00
□	Michael Karakas (G)	13.00	22.00
□	Alex Levinsky	22.00	35.00
□	Sam LoPresti (G)	30.00	50.00
□	Dave Mackay	650.00	850.00
□	Mush March	12.00	20.00
□	John Mariucci	28.00	45.00
□	Joe Matte	85.00	140.00
□	Red Mitchell	90.00	145.00
□	Pete Palangio	50.00	80.00
□	Joe Papike	65.00	110.00
□	Fido Purpur	85.00	140.00
□	Doc Romnes	28.00	45.00
□	Earl Seibert	12.00	20.00
□	Paul Thompson	15.00	25.00
□	Louis Trudel	22.00	35.00
□	Audley Tuten	90.00	150.00
□	Art Wiebe	12.00	20.00
	DETROIT RED WINGS		
□	Sid Abel	15.00	25.00
□	Larry Aurie	10.00	16.00
□	Martin J. Barry	12.00	20.00
□	Ralph Bowman	13.00	22.00
□	Adam Brown	65.00	110.00
□	Conny Brown	50.00	80.00
□	Jerry Brown	575.00	750.00
□	Modere Bruneteau	10.00	16.00
□	Eddie Bush	190.00	245.00
□	Joe Carveth	10.00	16.00
□	Les Douglas	25.00	40.00
□	Gus Geisebrecht	10.00	16.00
□	Eb Goodfellow	12.00	20.00
□	Don Grosso	10.00	16.00
□	Sydney H. Howe	13.00	22.00
□	Bill Jennings	45.00	75.00
□	Jack Keating	15.00	25.00
□	Pete Kelly	13.00	22.00
□	Hec Kilrea	10.00	16.00
□	Ken Kilrea	12.00	20.00
□	Wally Kilrea	10.00	16.00
□	Herbert A. Lewis	12.00	20.00
□	Carl Liscombe	10.00	16.00
□	Doug McCaig	60.00	100.00
□	Wilfred McDonald (On ice)	75.00	125.00
□	Wilfred McDonald (Dressing. Rm.)	75.00	125.00
□	Pat McReavy (G)	45.00	75.00
□	Johnny Mowers	13.00	22.00
□	Jimmy Orlando	10.00	16.00
□	Gordon Pettinger	15.00	25.00
□	Johnny Sherf	22.00	35.00
□	Norman E. Smith (G)	20.00	30.00
□	Johnnie Sorrell	18.00	28.00
□	Jack Stewart	18.00	28.00
□	Carl Voss	55.00	85.00
□	Eddie Wares	12.00	20.00
□	Archie Wilder	12.00	20.00
□	Douglas Young	15.00	25.00
	MONTRÉAL CANADIENS		
□	Jack Adams	13.00	22.00
□	Marty Barry	500.00	650.00
□	Joe Benoît	11.00	18.00
□	Paul Bibeault (G)	30.00	50.00
□	Toe Blake	20.00	30.00
□	Emile Bouchard	25.00	40.00
□	Claude Bourque	25.00	40.00
□	George Allan Brown	65.00	110.00
□	Walter Buswell	25.00	40.00
□	Murph Chamberlain	28.00	45.00
□	Wilf Cude (G)	22.00	35.00
□	Bunny Dame	30.00	50.00
□	Tony Demers	11.00	18.00
□	Joffre Desilets	11.00	18.00
□	Gordon Drillon	750.00	1,000.00
□	Polly Drouin	12.00	20.00
□	Johnny Gagnon	10.00	16.00
□	Bert Gardiner (G)	15.00	25.00
□	Ray Getliffe	40.00	70.00
□	Cliff Goupille	12.00	20.00
□	Tony Graboski	11.00	18.00
□	Paul Haynes	10.00	16.00
□	Gerry Heffernan	80.00	130.00
□	Roger Jenkins	40.00	65.00
□	Aurèle Joliat	25.00	40.00
□	Elmer Lach (On ice)	22.00	35.00
□	Léo Lamoureaux	75.00	125.00
□	Pit Lépine	10.00	16.00
□	Rod Lorraine	18.00	28.00
□	Georges Mantha	10.00	16.00
□	Sylvio Mantha	12.00	20.00
□	Armand Mondou	10.00	16.00
□	Howie Morenz	550.00	700.00
□	Pete Morin	85.00	135.00
□	Buddy O'Connor	90.00	150.00
□	Jack Portland	10.00	16.00
□	John Quilty	13.00	22.00
□	Ken Reardon	25.00	40.00
□	Terry Reardon	70.00	115.00
□	Maurice Richard (On Ice)	375.00	500.00
□	Earle Robinson	425.00	550.00
□	Charlie Sands	40.00	65.00
□	Babe Siebert	20.00	30.00
□	Alex Singbush	40.00	70.00
□	Bill Summerhill	90.00	150.00
	Louis Trudel	40.00	70.00
□	Cy Wentworth	Very Rare	
□	Doug Young	45.00	75.00
	MONTRÉAL MAROONS		
□	Bill Beveridge (G)	35.00	55.00
□	Russ Blinco	28.00	45.00
□	Herb Cain	22.00	35.00
□	Jerry Carson	110.00	175.00
□	Alex Connell (G)	40.00	70.00
□	Tommy Cook	22.00	35.00
□	Stew Evans	25.00	40.00
□	Bob Gracie	25.00	40.00
□	Max Kaminsky	175.00	225.00
□	Bill MacKenzie	70.00	120.00
□	Gus Marker	190.00	250.00
□	Baldy Northcott	28.00	45.00
□	Earle Robinson	22.00	35.00
□	Paul Runge	100.00	165.00
□	Jerry Shannon	100.00	165.00
□	Des Smith	22.00	35.00
□	Hooley Smith	22.00	35.00
□	Dave Trottier	55.00	90.00
□	Jimmy Ward	25.00	40.00
□	Cy Wentworth	25.00	40.00
	NEW YORK AMERICANS		
□	Squee Allen	35.00	55.00
□	Tommy Anderson	20.00	30.00
□	Bill Benson	30.00	50.00
□	Lorne Carr	22.00	35.00
□	Art Chapman	20.00	30.00
□	Red Dutton	28.00	45.00
□	Pat Egan	25.00	40.00
□	Hap Emms	40.00	70.00
□	Wilf Field	20.00	30.00
□	Johnny Gallagher	20.00	30.00
□	Joe Jerwa	35.00	55.00
□	Dede Klein	50.00	80.00
□	Joe Krol	1,200.00	1,600.00
□	Joe Lamb	55.00	85.00
□	Norm Larson, Err (Ralph Wycherly)	30.00	50.00
□	Hazen McAndrew	1,350.00	1,800.00
□	Ken Mosdell	350.00	475.00
□	Al Murray	20.00	30.00
□	Johnny O'Flaherty	40.00	70.00
□	Charlie Rayner (G)	150.00	200.00
□	Earl Robertson (G)	28.00	45.00
□	Dave Schriner	22.00	35.00
□	Allen Shields	60.00	100.00
□	Pete Slobodian	40.00	65.00
□	Nels Stewart	35.00	55.00
□	Alfred Thurier	70.00	120.00
□	Harry Watson	195.00	260.00
□	Eddie Wiseman	20.00	30.00
□	Roy Worters	40.00	70.00
□	Ralph Wycherly, Err. (Norm Larson)	40.00	70.00
	NEW YORK RANGERS		
□	Frank Boucher	22.00	35.00
□	Norman Burns	60.00	95.00
□	Mac Colville	11.00	18.00
□	Neil Colville	12.00	20.00
□	Bill Cook	15.00	25.00
□	Joe Cooper	10.00	16.00
□	Art Coulter	12.00	20.00
□	Gord Davidson	40.00	65.00
□	Cecil Dillon	10.00	16.00
□	Jim Franks	100.00	165.00
□	Red Garrett	75.00	130.00
□	Eberhardt Heller	10.00	16.00
□	Jim Henry (G) (Vertical)	75.00	125.00

ST. LAWRENCE STARCH COMPANY BEE HIVE PHOTOS

PLANT OF
ST. LAWRENCE STARCH COMPANY LIMITED
PORT CREDIT. ONT.

The photos were produced by the St. Lawrence Starch Company of Port Credit, Ontario. They were obtained by sending complete labels from St. Lawrence Starch products to the company. The name Bee Hive became associated with the photos because the majority of labels submitted were from Bee Hive Corn Syrup. Collectors were allowed to select the photo of their choice from player lists published each year. Because of this, photos of the favourite players are easier to find. Photos of the less popular players are the hardest to find and are valued higher due to their scarcity. The issuing of these player lists, however, still did not guarantee photo distribution. Some player's names appeared on the lists, but their actual photos remain unconfirmed.

The mat colours the photos were mounted on vary and may be beige, red, or blue. All photographs are unnumbered and are listed alphabetically by team and then by player name. In some cases a number of photographic variations of the same player exist. These variations are included in the listings with brief descriptions indicating the major identifying feature.

The photos are divided into three groups according to their autographs. The information below will help the collector identify the different groups and assign photos to the right era. Over the years, the method used to print the player's name on the photo varied. The groupings below are not 100% fool proof but will prove extremely helpful to collectors.

BEE HIVE VARIATIONS

One of the interesting aspects of the Bee Hive series is the many variations that exist and it seems that more are found each year. We have divided the variations into four major categories. Many of the players have more than one photo issued. Variations of the BeeHive photos were also offered in the form of dress pins and tie clips. The photo was reduced in size and usually cropped around the player's head or upper body. The portrait was then enclosed under a clear plastic shield and included as part of the pin or clip. These are considerably more scarce than the photos and may have only been available to the public for a short period of time. A complete checklist for these does not exist though several dozen different examples have surfaced. We are looking for further information.

UNIFORM VARIATIONS
- "A" on sweater
- Away, light uniform
- Home, dark uniform
- "C" on sweater
- HELMET
- No helmet
- Number on sleeve
- No number on sleeve
- Plain sleeve

PHOTOGRAPH VARIATIONS
- White background
- Light background
- Dark background
- White border around photo
- Action shot
- Posed on ice
- Posed in dressing room
- Portrait pose
- Full length pose
- Horizontal photo
- Vertical photo
- Negative reversed
- Bee Hive promotion

NAME VARIATIONS
- White script
- Black script
- Name away from skate
- Name near skate
- Name overlaps stick
- Name overlaps skate
- Name printed diagonally
- Name parallel to bottom

STICK VARIATIONS
- Blade of stick visible
- Blade of stick not visible

1934 TO 1943 GROUP I

Facsimile Autograph

Block Letter Autograph

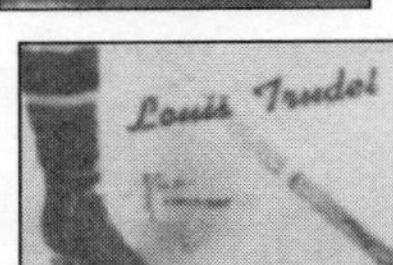

Script Letter Autograph
White Type (upper)
Black Type (lower)

1944 TO 1963 GROUP II

1944 - 1945
Facsimile Autograph

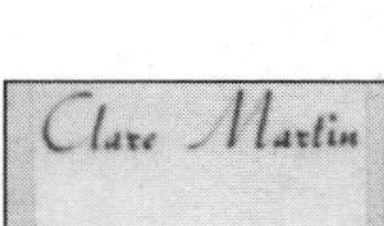

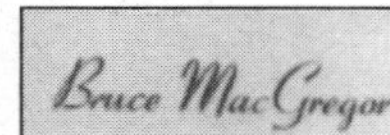

Script Letter Autograph
Thin Type / Thick Type

UNIFORM VARIATIONS

HELMET

NUMBER ON SLEEVE

AWAY, LIGHT UNIFORM

NO HELMET

NO NUMBER ON SLEEVE

HOME, DARK UNIFORM

PHOTOGRAPH VARIATIONS

Action shot

Posed on ice

Posed in dressing room

NAME VARIATIONS AND STICK VARIATIONS

Name overlaps stick

Blade of stick visible

Blade of stick not visible

	Player	EX	NRMT
☐	Jim Henry (G) (Horizontal)	40.00	70.00
☐	Bryan Hextall	15.00	25.00
☐	Dutch Hiller	10.00	16.00
☐	Ivan W. Johnson	13.00	22.00
☐	Bill Juzda	12.00	20.00
☐	Melville Keeling	11.00	18.00
☐	David A. Kerr (G)	13.00	22.00
☐	Bobby Kirk	55.00	85.00
☐	Bob Kirkpatrick	55.00	85.00
☐	Kilby MacDonald	10.00	16.00
☐	Larry Molyneaux	18.00	28.00
☐	John Murray Murdoch	15.00	25.00
☐	Vic Myles	100.00	165.00
☐	Lynn Patrick	13.00	22.00
☐	Murray Patrick	10.00	16.00
☐	Alf. Pike	10.00	16.00
☐	Babe Pratt	15.00	25.00
☐	Alex Shibicky	10.00	16.00
☐	Clint Smith	13.00	22.00
☐	Norman Tustin	65.00	110.00
☐	Grant Warwick	13.00	22.00
☐	Phil Watson	10.00	16.00

TORONTO MAPLE LEAFS

	Player	EX	NRMT
☐	Syl Apps (On ice)	13.00	22.00
☐	Murray Armstrong	10.00	16.00
☐	Andy Blair	10.00	16.00
☐	Buzz Boll	10.00	16.00
☐	George Boothman	125.00	200.00
☐	Turk Broda (G)	15.00	25.00
☐	Lorne Carr	40.00	70.00
☐	Murph Chamberlain	10.00	16.00
☐	Lex Chisholm	11.00	18.00
☐	Jack Church	10.00	16.00
☐	King Clancy	25.00	40.00
☐	Charlie Conacher	18.00	28.00
☐	Robert Copp	35.00	55.00
☐	Harold Cotton	10.00	16.00
☐	Bob Davidson	10.00	16.00
☐	Happy Day	12.00	20.00
☐	Ernie Dickens	100.00	165.00
☐	Gord Drillon	12.00	20.00
☐	Frank Finnigan	15.00	25.00
☐	Jack Forsey	115.00	185.00
☐	Jimmie Fowler	10.00	16.00
☐	Bob Goldham	150.00	200.00
☐	Hank Goldup	10.00	16.00
☐	George Hainsworth (G)	28.00	45.00
☐	Reg Hamilton	10.00	16.00
☐	Red Heron	10.00	16.00
☐	Melvin Hill	190.00	250.00
☐	William Hollett	10.00	16.00
☐	Red Horner	10.00	20.00
☐	Art Jackson	10.00	16.00
☐	Harvey Jackson	13.00	22.00
☐	Rudolph Kampman	10.00	16.00
☐	Reg Kelly	10.00	16.00
☐	Bill Kendall	45.00	75.00
☐	Hec Kilrea	35.00	55.00
☐	Pete Langelle	12.00	20.00
☐	Bucko McDonald	12.00	20.00
☐	Normie Mann	11.00	18.00
☐	Normie Mann (Script over stick)	115.00	185.00
☐	Gus Marker	10.00	16.00
☐	Johnny McCreedy	25.00	40.00
☐	Jack McLean	60.00	100.00
☐	Don Metz	10.00	16.00
☐	Nick Metz	10.00	16.00
☐	George Parsons	13.00	22.00
☐	Norman "Bud" Poile	115.00	185.00
☐	Walter "Babe" Pratt	210.00	275.00
☐	Joe Primeau	15.00	25.00
☐	Doc Romnes	30.00	50.00
☐	Dave Schriner	22.00	35.00
☐	Jack Shill	15.00	25.00
☐	Walter Stanowsky	10.00	16.00
☐	Phil Stein (G)	22.00	35.00
☐	Gaye Stewart (Home)	275.00	350.00
☐	Gaye Stewart (Away)	150.00	225.00
☐	Billy Taylor	10.00	16.00
☐	Rhys Thompson	375.00	500.00
☐	Bill Thoms	10.00	16.00
☐	1944-45 Team Picture	210.00	275.00

MISCELLANEOUS

	Player	EX	NRMT
☐	1937 Winnipeg Monarchs	110.00	175.00
☐	Foster Hewitt	55.00	90.00
☐	Wes McKnight	65.00	110.00

TROPHIES DATED ON BACK

	Trophy	EX	NRMT
☐	Allan Cup	45.00	75.00
☐	Byng Trophy	45.00	75.00
☐	Calder Trophy	45.00	75.00
☐	Hart Trophy	45.00	75.00
☐	Memorial Cup	55.00	85.00
☐	Prince of Wales Trophy	175.00	225.00
☐	Stanley Cup	60.00	95.00
☐	Georges Vezina	45.00	75.00

Trophy Not Dated/Blank Back

	Trophy	EX	NRMT
☐	Allan Cup	90.00	150.00
☐	Byng Trophy	90.00	150.00
☐	Calder Trophy	90.00	150.00
☐	Hart Trophy	90.00	150.00
☐	Memorial Cup	110.00	175.00
☐	Prince of Wales Trophy Stanley Cup	250.00	325.00
☐	(Horizontal Script) Stanley Cup	115.00	185.00
☐	(Diagonal Script)	210.00	275.00
☐	George Vezina Trophy	90.00	150.00

GROUP II - 1945-1964

Photographs were updated starting with the Toronto Maple Leafs team of 1944-45. These photos were issued with the player's facsimile autograph. A team photo of the 1944-45 Stanley Cup champions was also issued. After 1945 the Maple Leaf photos were issued with a new large-size script for the players' names which is now characteristic of Group II. New photos with the new script were gradually added year by year until 1948, when the complete series was available. In some cases, although a player's name may appear on the company photo list, proof of actual photo distribution remains unconfirmed.

Photo Size: 4 1/4" x 6 3/4"
Mat Size: 5 1/2" x 8"
Face: Black and white
Mat: Red, blue or beige
Back: Blank

BOSTON BRUINS

	Player	EX	NRMT
☐	Bob Armstrong	5.00	8.50
☐	Pete Babando	30.00	50.00
☐	Ray Barry	30.00	50.00
☐	Gus Bodnar	50.00	85.00
☐	Leo Boivin	7.00	12.00
☐	Frank Brimsek (White Background)	18.00	30.00
☐	Johnny Bucyk	8.00	13.00
☐	Charlie Burns	5.00	8.50
☐	Jack Caffery	30.00	55.00
☐	Real Chevrefils	5.00	8.50
☐	Wayne Connelly	12.00	20.00
☐	Wayne Connelly (Script over skate)	40.00	70.00
☐	Murray Costello	15.00	25.00
☐	Johnny Crawford (#6)	13.00	22.00
☐	Dave Creighton (White background)	7.00	12.00
☐	Dave Creighton (Dark background)	40.00	70.00
☐	Norm DeFelice	Very Rare	
☐	Woody Dumart	10.00	16.00
☐	Pat Eagan	22.00	35.00
☐	Lorne Ferguson	7.00	12.00
☐	Fernie Flaman	9.00	15.00
☐	Fern Flaman	6.00	10.00
☐	Bruce Gamble (G)	6.00	10.00
☐	Cal Gardner	9.00	15.00
☐	Ray Gariepy	11.00	18.00
☐	Jack Gelineau (G)	11.00	18.00
☐	Jean-Guy Gendron	5.00	8.50
☐	Warren Godfrey (A on jersey)	9.00	15.00
☐	Warren Godfrey (#25, W under skate)	35.00	60.00
☐	Warren Godfrey (#25, W left of skate)	70.00	120.00
☐	Ed Harrison	5.00	8.50
☐	Don Head (G)	6.00	10.00
☐	Andy Hebenton	12.00	20.00
☐	Murray Henderson	9.00	15.00
☐	Jim Henry (G)	20.00	30.00
☐	Larry Hillman	25.00	40.00
☐	Pete Horeck	9.00	15.00
☐	Rudy Horvath	5.00	8.50
☐	Tom Johnson	7.00	12.00
☐	Ed Johnston (G)	9.00	15.00
☐	Joe Klukay	115.00	185.00
☐	Ed Kryznowski	9.00	15.00
☐	Orland Kurtenbach	22.00	35.00
☐	Léo Labine	5.00	8.50
☐	Hal Laycoe	5.00	8.50
☐	Harry Lumley (G)	11.00	18.00
☐	Pentti Lund	Very Rare	
☐	Fleming Mackell	5.00	8.50
☐	Phil Maloney	11.00	18.00
☐	Frank Martin	11.00	18.00
☐	Jack McIntyre	9.00	15.00
☐	Don McKenney	5.00	8.50
☐	Richard Meissner	5.00	8.50
☐	Doug Mohns	5.00	8.50
☐	Murray Oliver	5.00	8.50
☐	Willy O'Ree	9.00	15.00
☐	John Peirson	8.00	13.00
☐	Johnny Peirson	65.00	110.00
☐	C. Pennington (Script away from skate)	12.00	20.00
☐	C. Pennington (Script near skate)	60.00	95.00
☐	Bob Perreault (G)	15.00	25.00
☐	Bob Perreault (G) (Script overlaps skate)	60.00	100.00
☐	Jim Peters	9.00	15.00
☐	Dean Prentice	7.00	12.00
☐	Andre Pronovost	5.00	8.50
☐	Bill Quackenbush	8.00	13.00
☐	Larry Regan	28.00	45.00
☐	Earl Reibel	28.00	45.00
☐	Paul Ronty	7.00	12.00
☐	Ed Sandford	5.00	8.50
☐	Terry Sawchuk	80.00	135.00
☐	Don Simmons (G)	6.00	10.00
☐	Don Simmons (G), Err.(Norm Defelice)	135.00	225.00
☐	Ken Smith	8.00	13.00
☐	P. Stapleton (Script away from skate)	12.00	20.00
☐	P. Stapleton (Script near skate)	55.00	85.00
☐	Vic Stasiuk	5.00	8.50
☐	George Sullivan	13.00	22.00
☐	Jerry Toppazzini	5.00	8.50
☐	Zellio Toppazzini	9.00	15.00
☐	Grant Warwick	18.00	28.00
☐	Tom Williams	5.00	8.50

CHICAGO BLACKHAWKS

	Player	EX	NRMT
☐	Al Arbour	8.00	13.00
☐	Pete Babando	11.00	18.00
☐	Earl Balfour	5.00	8.50
☐	Murray Balfour	5.00	8.50
☐	Jim Bedard	11.00	18.00
☐	Doug Bentley	12.00	20.00
☐	Gus Bodnar	7.00	12.00
☐	Frank Brimsek (G)	28.00	45.00
☐	Adam Brown	15.00	25.00
☐	Hank Ciesla	22.00	35.00
☐	Jim Conacher	7.00	12.00
☐	Pete Conacher	5.00	8.50
☐	Roy Conacher	5.00	8.50
☐	Joe Conn	30.00	50.00
☐	Murray Costello	55.00	85.00
☐	Gerry Couture	11.00	18.00
☐	Al Dewsbury	7.00	12.00
☐	Ernie Dickens	7.00	12.00
☐	Jack Evans	5.00	8.50
☐	Reg Fleming	5.00	8.50
☐	Lee Fogolin	7.00	12.00
☐	Bill Gadsby	7.00	12.00
☐	George Gee	7.00	12.00
☐	Bob Goldham	12.00	20.00
☐	Bep Guidolin	7.00	12.00
☐	Glenn Hall (G)	9.00	15.00
☐	Murray Hall	20.00	30.00
☐	Red Hamill	18.00	28.00
☐	Bill Hay	5.00	8.50

	Player		
☐	Jim Henry (G)	25.00	40.00
☐	Wayne Hillman	15.00	25.00
☐	Bronco Horvath	8.00	13.00
☐	Fred Hucul	12.00	20.00
☐	Bobby Hull (#16)	20.00	30.00
☐	Bobby Hull (#9)	150.00	200.00
☐	Lou Jankowski	20.00	30.00
☐	Forbes Kennedy	40.00	65.00
☐	Ted Lindsay	11.00	18.00
☐	Eddie Litzenberger	6.00	10.00
☐	Harry Lumley (G)	28.00	45.00
☐	Len Lunde	35.00	60.00
☐	Len Lunde (Script over stick)	12.00	20.00
☐	Pat Lundy	9.00	15.00
☐	Al MacNeil (Script over stick and skate)	30.00	50.00
☐	Al MacNeil (Script over stick)	11.00	18.00
☐	Chico Maki	9.00	15.00
☐	Chico Maki (Script over stick)	60.00	100.00
☐	Doug McCaig	15.00	25.00
☐	Ab McDonald	5.00	8.50
☐	Jim McFadden	25.00	40.00
☐	Jerry Melnyk	5.00	8.50
☐	Stan Mikita	9.00	15.00
☐	Gus Mortson	5.00	8.50
☐	Bill Mosienko	9.00	15.00
☐	Ron Murphy	5.00	8.50
☐	Ralph Nattrass	13.00	22.00
☐	Eric Nesterenko	5.00	8.50
☐	Bert Olmstead	12.00	20.00
☐	Jim Peters	28.00	45.00
☐	Pierre Pilote	7.00	12.00
☐	Metro Prystai	7.00	12.00
☐	Clare Raglan	18.00	28.00
☐	Al Rollins (G) (Vertical)	70.00	120.00
☐	Al Rollins (G) (Horizontal)	25.00	40.00
☐	Tod Sloan	5.00	8.50
☐	Dollard St. Laurent	5.00	8.50
☐	Gaye Stewart	12.00	20.00
☐	Jack Stewart	20.00	30.00
☐	Bob Turner	35.00	55.00
☐	Bob Turner (Script over stick)	15.00	25.00
☐	Elmer Vasko	5.00	8.50
☐	Ken Wharram	5.00	8.50
☐	Larry Wilson	11.00	18.00
☐	Howie Young	11.00	18.00

DETROIT RED WINGS

	Player		
☐	Syd Abel (C on jersey)	11.00	18.00
☐	Al Arbour	25.00	40.00
☐	Pete Babando	12.00	20.00
☐	Doug Barkley (Partial Blade)	35.00	55.00
☐	Doug Barkley (No Blade)	9.00	15.00
☐	Hank Bassen (G)	6.00	10.00
☐	Steve Black	15.00	25.00
☐	Marcel Bonin	9.00	15.00
☐	John Bucyk	40.00	70.00
☐	Jim Conacher	80.00	135.00
☐	Jerry Couture	7.00	12.00
☐	Billy Dea	13.00	22.00
☐	Alex Delvecchio	7.00	12.00
☐	Bill Delvecchio	9.00	15.00
☐	Bill Dineen	5.00	8.50
☐	Jim Enio	35.00	60.00
☐	Alex Faulkner	12.00	20.00
☐	Lee Fogolin	9.00	15.00
☐	Val Fonteyne	5.00	8.50
☐	Bill Gadsby (Name Low)	7.00	12.00
☐	Bill Gadsby (Name High)	13.00	22.00
☐	Fern Gauthier (As Jerry Couture)	250.00	325.00
☐	Fern Gauthier	22.00	35.00
☐	George Gee	9.00	15.00
☐	Fred Glover	5.00	8.50
☐	Howie Glover	5.00	8.50
☐	Warren Godfrey	5.00	8.50
☐	Peter Goegan	5.00	8.50
☐	Bob Goldham	8.00	13.00
☐	Glenn Hall (G)	45.00	75.00
☐	Larry Hillman	35.00	60.00
☐	Pete Horeck	28.00	40.00
☐	Gordie Howe (Home jersey)	20.00	30.00
☐	Gordie Howe (Away jersey)	30.00	50.00
☐	Ron Ingram	15.00	25.00
☐	Larry Jeffrey	20.00	30.00
☐	Allan Johnson	5.00	8.50
☐	Red Kelly	7.00	12.00
☐	Forbes Kennedy	5.00	8.50
☐	Léo Labine	5.00	8.50
☐	Tony Leswick	6.00	10.00
☐	Ted Lindsay	8.00	13.00
☐	Ed Litzenberger	18.00	28.00
☐	Harry Lumley (G)	12.00	20.00
☐	Len Lunde	5.00	8.50
☐	Parker MacDonald	5.00	8.50
☐	Bruce MacGregor	5.00	8.50
☐	Clare Martin	12.00	20.00
☐	Jimmy McFadden	11.00	18.00
☐	Max McNab	12.00	20.00
☐	Gerry Melnyk	5.00	8.50
☐	Don Morrison	15.00	25.00
☐	Rod Morrison	28.00	45.00
☐	Gerry Odrowski	5.00	8.50
☐	Murray Oliver	7.00	12.00
☐	Martin Pavelich	5.00	8.50
☐	Jimmy Peters	30.00	50.00
☐	Bud Poile	60.00	100.00
☐	Andre Pronovost	7.00	12.00
☐	Marcel Pronovost	6.00	10.00
☐	Metro Prystai	5.00	8.50
☐	Bill Quackenbush (A)	35.00	60.00
☐	Earl Reibel	5.00	8.50
☐	Leo Reise	5.00	8.50
☐	Terry Sawchuk (G) (Blade)	12.00	20.00
☐	Terry Sawchuk (G) (No blade)	28.00	45.00
☐	Glen Skov	5.00	8.50
☐	Floyd Smith	7.00	12.00
☐	Vic Stasiuk (Home jersey with blade)	15.00	25.00
☐	Vic Stasiuk (Home jersey/No blade)	30.00	50.00
☐	Vic Stasiuk (Away jersey)	5.00	8.50
☐	Gaye Stewart	18.00	28.00
☐	Jack Stewart	22.00	35.00
☐	Norm Ullman	7.00	12.00
☐	Johnny Wilson	5.00	8.50
☐	Ben Woit	5.00	8.50
☐	Howie Young	9.00	15.00
☐	Larry Zeidel	15.00	25.00

MONTRÉAL CANADIENS

	Player		
☐	Ralph Backstrom	5.00	8.50
☐	Dave Balon	5.00	8.50
☐	Jean Béliveau	12.00	20.00
☐	Red Berenson (White Script)	20.00	30.00
☐	Red Berenson (Black Script)	225.00	300.00
☐	Marcel Bonin	5.00	8.50
☐	Emile (Butch) Bouchard	7.00	12.00
☐	Tod Campeau	50.00	80.00
☐	Joe Carveth	9.00	15.00
☐	Murph Chamberlain	30.00	50.00
☐	Doc Couture	35.00	55.00
☐	Floyd Curry	5.00	8.50
☐	Ian Cushenan	7.00	12.00
☐	Lorne Davis	7.00	12.00
☐	Eddie Dorohoy	12.00	20.00
☐	Gilles Dubé	35.00	55.00
☐	Bill Durnan (G)	22.00	35.00
☐	Norman Dussault	13.00	22.00
☐	John Ferguson	7.00	12.00
☐	Bobby Fillion	9.00	15.00
☐	Lou Fontinato	5.00	8.50
☐	Dick Gamble	9.00	15.00
☐	Bernard Geoffrion	8.00	13.00
☐	Phil Goyette	5.00	8.50
☐	Léo Gravelle	13.00	22.00
☐	John Hanna	40.00	70.00
☐	Glen Harmon	8.00	13.00
☐	Terry Harper	5.00	8.50
☐	Doug Harvey	8.00	13.00
☐	Bill Hicke	5.00	8.50
☐	Charlie Hodge (G) (Black Script)	8.00	13.00
☐	Charlie Hodge (G) (White Script)	45.00	75.00
☐	Tom Johnson	7.00	12.00
☐	Vern Kaiser	25.00	40.00
☐	Frank King	25.00	40.00
☐	Elmer Lach (White background)	7.00	12.00
☐	Albert Langlois	5.00	8.50
☐	Jacques Laperriere	7.00	12.00
☐	Hal Laycoe	7.00	12.00
☐	Jack Leclair	5.00	8.50
☐	Roger Leger	9.00	15.00
☐	Eddie Litzenberger	20.00	30.00
☐	Ross Lowe	25.00	40.00
☐	Al MacNeil	6.00	10.00
☐	Bud MacPherson	5.00	8.50
☐	Cesare Maniago (G)	9.00	15.00
☐	Don Marshall	5.00	8.50
☐	Paul Masnick	5.00	8.50
☐	Eddie Mazur	9.00	15.00
☐	John McCormack	7.00	12.00
☐	Alvin McDonald	5.00	8.50
☐	Callum McKay	7.00	12.00
☐	Gerry McNeil (G)	9.00	15.00
☐	Paul Meger	9.00	15.00
☐	Dick Moore	7.00	12.00
☐	Ken Mosdell	8.00	13.00
☐	Bert Olmstead	7.00	12.00
☐	Gerry Plamondon	11.00	18.00
☐	Jacques Plante (G)	18.00	28.00
☐	André Pronovost	5.00	8.50
☐	Claude Provost	5.00	8.50
☐	Kenny Reardon	18.00	28.00
☐	Billy Reay	5.00	8.50
☐	Pocket Richard	11.00	18.00
☐	Maurice Richard (White background)	22.00	35.00
☐	Rip Riopelle	22.00	35.00
☐	George Robertson	60.00	100.00
☐	Bob Rousseau	5.00	8.50
☐	Dollard St. Laurent	5.00	8.50
☐	Jean Guy Talbot	5.00	8.50
☐	Gilles Tremblay (Dark background)	5.00	8.50
☐	Gilles Tremblay (Light background)	210.00	275.00
☐	J.C. Tremblay (Dark background)	5.00	8.50
☐	J.C. Tremblay (Light background)	225.00	300.00
☐	Bob Turner	5.00	8.50
☐	Grant Warwick	20.00	30.00
☐	Gump Worsley (G)	9.00	15.00

NEW YORK RANGERS

	Player		
☐	Clint Albright	9.00	15.00
☐	Dave Balon (Name High)	12.00	20.00
☐	Dave Balon (Name Low)	7.00	12.00
☐	Andy Bathgate (Home jersey)	7.00	12.00
☐	Andy Bathgate (Away jersey)	11.00	18.00
☐	Max Bentley	35.00	55.00
☐	Johnny Bower (G)	40.00	70.00
☐	Hy Buller	9.00	15.00
☐	Larry Cahan (Home jersey)	7.00	12.00
☐	Larry Cahan (Away, Script over both skates)	12.00	20.00
☐	Larry Cahan (Away, Script over right skate)	90.00	150.00
☐	Bob Chrystal	18.00	28.00
☐	Brian Cullen	5.00	8.50
☐	Ian Cushenan	5.00	8.50
☐	Billy Dea	20.00	30.00
☐	Frank Eddolls	5.00	8.50
☐	Pat Egan	22.00	35.00
☐	Jack Evans (Name parallel)	5.00	8.50
☐	Jack Evans (Name diagonal)	28.00	45.00
☐	Duncan Fisher	9.00	15.00
☐	Lou Fontinato	5.00	8.50
☐	Bill Gadsby	6.00	10.00
☐	Guy Gendron	5.00	8.50
☐	Rod Gilbert	8.00	13.00
☐	Howie Glover	30.00	45.00
☐	Jack Gordon	Very Rare	
☐	Phil Goyette	5.00	8.50
☐	Aldo Guidolin	22.00	35.00
☐	Vic Hadfield	6.00	10.00
☐	Ted Hampson	5.00	8.50
☐	Doug Harvey	8.00	13.00
☐	Andy Hebenton	6.00	10.00
☐	Camille Henry	5.00	8.50
☐	Wally Hergesheimer	5.00	8.50
☐	Ike Hildebrand	15.00	25.00
☐	Bronco Horvath	9.00	15.00
☐	Harry Howell	6.00	10.00
☐	Earl Ingarfield (Name Near Stick)	11.00	18.00
☐	Earl Ingarfield (Name Away From Stick)	5.00	8.50
☐	Bing Juckes	15.00	25.00
☐	Alex Kaleta	7.00	12.00
☐	Steve Kraftcheck	20.00	30.00
☐	Ed Kullman	7.00	12.00
☐	Gus Kyle	6.00	10.00
☐	Gordon Labossière	30.00	50.00
☐	Albert Langlois	5.00	8.50
☐	Edgar Laprade	7.00	12.00
☐	Tony Leswick	5.00	8.50
☐	Danny Lewicki	5.00	8.50
☐	Pentti Lund	8.00	13.00
☐	Don Marshall	12.00	20.00
☐	Jack McCartan (G)	7.00	12.00

	Player	EX	NRMT
☐	Bill McDonagh	9.00	15.00
☐	Don McKenney	9.00	15.00
☐	Jack McLeod	9.00	15.00
☐	Nick Mickoski	5.00	8.50
☐	Bill Moe	8.00	13.00
☐	Ron Murphy	5.00	8.50
☐	Buddy O'Connor	8.00	13.00
☐	Marcel Paille (G)	55.00	90.00
☐	Jacques Plante (G)	50.00	85.00
☐	Bud Poile	18.00	28.00
☐	Larry Popein	5.00	8.50
☐	Dean Prentice (Home)	5.00	8.50
☐	Dean Prentice (Away, Name High)	8.00	13.00
☐	Dean Prentice (Away, Name Low)	13.00	22.00
☐	Don Raleigh	7.00	12.00
☐	Jean Ratelle	25.00	40.00
☐	Jean Ratelle, Err. (John)	50.00	80.00
☐	Charlie Rayner (G)	18.00	28.00
☐	Leo Reise	7.00	12.00
☐	Paul Ronty	7.00	12.00
☐	Ken Schinkel	5.00	8.50
☐	Eddie Shack	12.00	20.00
☐	Fred Shero	15.00	25.00
☐	Reggie Sinclair	18.00	28.00
☐	Ed Slowinski	7.00	12.00
☐	Allan Stanley	7.00	12.00
☐	Wally Stanowski	8.00	13.00
☐	Red Sullivan	5.00	8.50
☐	Gump Worsley	9.00	15.00

TORONTO MAPLE LEAFS

	Player	EX	NRMT
☐	Garry Aldcorn	9.00	15.00
☐	Syl Apps (Posed near boards)	95.00	150.00
☐	Al Arbour	5.00	8.50
☐	George Armstrong	7.00	11.00
☐	George Armstrong (Cap., Dark background)	12.00	20.00
☐	George Armstrong (Cap., Light background)	175.00	250.00
☐	Bob Bailey	22.00	35.00
☐	Earl Balfour	11.00	18.00
☐	Bill Barilko	15.00	25.00
☐	Andy Bathgate	35.00	60.00
☐	Bob Baun	5.00	8.50
☐	Max Bentley	18.00	28.00
☐	Jack Bionda	75.00	125.00
☐	Garth Boesch	7.00	12.00
☐	Leo Boivin	8.00	13.00
☐	Hugh Bolton	5.00	8.50
☐	Johnny Bower (G)	11.00	18.00
☐	Carl Brewer	5.00	8.50
☐	Turk Broda (G)	11.00	18.00
☐	Larry Cahan	9.00	15.00
☐	Ray Ceresino	35.00	60.00
☐	Ed Chadwick (G)	6.00	10.00
☐	Pete Conacher	50.00	85.00
☐	Les Costello	25.00	40.00
☐	Dave Creighton	11.00	18.00
☐	Barry Cullen	11.00	18.00
☐	Barry Cullen, Err. (Brian Cullen)	35.00	60.00
☐	Brian Cullen	5.00	8.50
☐	Bob Dawes	18.00	28.00
☐	Kent Douglas	5.00	8.50
☐	Dick Duff	5.00	8.50
☐	Garry Edmundson	5.00	8.50
☐	Gerry Ehman	5.00	8.50
☐	Bill Ezinicki	8.00	13.00
☐	Fern Flaman	35.00	55.00
☐	Cal Gardner	9.00	15.00
☐	Ted Hampson	6.00	10.00
☐	Gord Hannigan	9.00	15.00
☐	Billy Harris	5.00	8.50
☐	Bob Hassard	35.00	60.00
☐	Larry Hillman	5.00	8.50
☐	Tim Horton	11.00	18.00
☐	Bronco Horvath	9.00	15.00
☐	Ron Hurst	85.00	140.00
☐	Gerry James	22.00	35.00
☐	Bill Juzda	9.00	15.00
☐	Red Kelly	7.00	12.00
☐	Red Kelly (Wearing helmet)	22.00	35.00
☐	Ted Kennedy	8.00	13.00
☐	Dave Keon	9.00	15.00
☐	Joe Klukay	5.00	8.50
☐	Steve Kraftcheck	15.00	25.00
☐	Danny Lewicki	11.00	18.00
☐	Ed Litzenberger	5.00	8.50
☐	Harry Lumley (G)	12.00	20.00
☐	Vic Lynn	7.00	12.00
☐	Fleming McKell	7.00	12.00
☐	John MacMillan	5.00	8.50
☐	Al MacNeil	9.00	15.00
☐	Frank Mahovlich	11.00	18.00
☐	Phil Maloney	90.00	150.00
☐	Cesare Maniago (G)	8.00	13.00
☐	Frank Mathers	20.00	30.00
☐	Johnny McCormack	40.00	65.00
☐	Parker McDonald	15.00	25.00
☐	Don McKenney	20.00	30.00
☐	Howie Meeker	7.00	12.00
☐	Don Metz - Older photo	225.00	300.00
☐	Nick Metz - Older photo	175.00	250.00
☐	Rudy Migay	5.00	8.50
☐	Jim Mikol	5.00	8.50
☐	Jim Morrison	5.00	8.50
☐	Gus Mortson	5.00	8.50
☐	Eric Nesterenko	7.00	13.00
☐	Bob Nevin	5.00	8.50
☐	Mike Nykoluk	25.00	40.00
☐	Bert Olmstead	7.00	12.00
☐	Bob Pulford	7.00	12.00
☐	Marc Reaume	9.00	15.00
☐	Larry Regan	5.00	8.50
☐	Dave Reid	100.00	160.00
☐	Al Rollins (G)	20.00	30.00
☐	Eddie Shack(Dark background)	9.00	15.00
☐	Eddie Shack (Light background)	225.00	300.00
☐	Don Simmons (G)	7.00	12.00
☐	Tod Sloan	5.00	8.50
☐	Sid Smith	5.00	8.50
☐	Bob Solinger	35.00	60.00
☐	Allan Stanley, Err.(Alan)	8.00	13.00
☐	Allan Stanley	12.00	20.00
☐	Wally Stanowski	250.00	325.00
☐	Ron Stewart	5.00	8.50
☐	Harry Taylor	25.00	40.00
☐	Jim Thomson	5.00	8.50
☐	Ray Timgren	6.00	10.00
☐	Harry Watson	5.00	8.50
☐	John Wilson	5.00	8.50
☐	1962-63 Team Picture	425.00	550.00

TROPHIES - FOUR WHITE BORDERS

	Player	EX	NRMT
☐	Byng Trophy	285.00	375.00
☐	Calder Memorial Trophy	285.00	375.00
☐	Hart Trophy	285.00	375.00
☐	James Norris Trophy	285.00	375.00
☐	Prince of Wales Trophy	285.00	375.00
☐	Art Ross Trophy	285.00	375.00
☐	Stanley Cup	285.00	375.00
☐	Georges Vezina Trophy	285.00	375.00

TROPHIES - BOTTOM WHITE BORDER

	Player	EX	NRMT
☐	Byng Trophy	80.00	130.00
☐	Calder Memorial Trophy	80.00	130.00
☐	Hart Trophy	80.00	130.00
☐	James Norris Trophy	80.00	130.00
☐	Prince of Wales Trophy	80.00	130.00
☐	Art Ross Trophy	80.00	130.00
☐	Stanley Cup	80.00	130.00
☐	Vezina Trophy	80.00	130.00

WOODGRAIN BORDER SERIES - 1964-1967

These unnumbered black and white photographs feature a wood grain border. They were issued between 1964 and 1967. The players' names appear inscribed in a nameplate at the bottom centre of the border. They were not numbered and are listed alphabetically by team and then alphabetically within the team. As with all Bee Hive groups, it is not known if the listings are complete.

Photo Size: 5 1/2" x 8"

Face: Black and white, wood grain border on paper stock

Back: Blank

	Player	EX	NRMT
	BOSTON BRUINS		
☐	Murray Balfour	18.00	28.00
☐	Leo Boivin	9.00	15.00
☐	Johnny Bucyk	9.00	15.00
☐	Wayne Connelly	100.00	160.00
☐	Bob Dillabough	7.00	12.00
☐	Gary Dornhoefer	7.00	12.00
☐	Reg Fleming	7.00	12.00
☐	Guy Gendron	70.00	120.00
☐	Warren Godfrey	250.00	325.00
☐	Ted Green	7.00	12.00
☐	Andy Hebenton	100.00	160.00
☐	Tom Johnson	9.00	15.00
☐	Ed Johnston (G)	9.00	15.00
☐	Forbes Kennedy	7.00	12.00
☐	Orland Kurtenbach	25.00	40.00
☐	Bob Leiter	7.00	12.00
☐	Parker MacDonald	7.00	12.00
☐	Bob McCord	7.00	12.00
☐	Ab McDonald	7.00	12.00
☐	Murray Oliver	7.00	12.00
☐	Bernard Parent (G)	40.00	65.00
☐	Cliff Pennington	180.00	235.00
☐	Bob Perreault (G)	250.00	325.00
☐	Dean Prentice	7.00	12.00
☐	Ron Schock, Err. (Shock)	7.00	12.00
☐	Pat Stapleton	30.00	50.00
☐	Ron Stewart	9.00	15.00
☐	Ed Westfall	7.00	12.00
☐	Tom Williams	7.00	12.00
	CHICAGO BLACKHAWKS		
☐	Lou Angotti	7.00	12.00
☐	Wally Boyer	7.00	12.00
☐	Dennis DeJordy (G)	9.00	15.00
☐	Dave Dryden (G)	9.00	15.00
☐	Phil Esposito (With blade)	22.00	35.00
☐	Phil Esposito (Blade Cropped)	11.00	18.00
☐	Glenn Hall (G), Err. (Glen)	12.00	20.00
☐	Murray Hall	210.00	275.00
☐	Bill Hay	7.00	12.00
☐	Camille Henry	11.00	18.00
☐	Wayne Hillman	85.00	140.00
☐	Ken Hodge	7.00	12.00
☐	Bobby Hull (Home)	190.00	250.00
☐	Bobby Hull (Home, Neg. reversed)	575.00	750.00
☐	Bobby Hull (Away jersey with blade)	13.00	22.00
☐	Bobby Hull (Away jersey, No blade)	13.00	22.00
☐	Bobby Hull (Promotion picture)	13.00	22.00
☐	Bobby Hull (Home jersey, Portrait)	575.00	750.00
☐	Dennis Hull	7.00	12.00
☐	Doug Jarrett	7.00	12.00
☐	Len Lunde	7.00	12.00
☐	Al MacNeil	7.00	12.00
☐	Chico Maki (Full length pose)	60.00	95.00
☐	Chico Maki (Portrait)	7.00	12.00
☐	Johnny McKenzie	7.00	12.00
☐	Stan Mikita	11.00	18.00
☐	Doug Mohns	7.00	12.00
☐	Eric Nesterenko (Dark Background)	7.00	12.00
☐	Eric Nesterenko (Light Background)	190.00	250.00
☐	Pierre Pilote (Home jersey)	190.00	250.00
☐	Pierre Pilote (Away jersey)	9.00	15.00
☐	Matt Ravlich	7.00	12.00
☐	Fred Stanfield	80.00	135.00
☐	Fred Stanfield (Neg. reversed)	100.00	170.00
☐	Pat Stapleton	7.00	12.00
☐	Bob Turner	225.00	300.00
☐	Ed Van Impe	7.00	12.00
☐	Elmer Vasko	7.00	12.00
☐	Ken Wharram	7.00	12.00
	DETROIT RED WINGS		
☐	Doug Barkley	7.00	12.00
☐	Hank Bassen (G)	9.00	15.00
☐	Andy Bathgate	9.00	15.00
☐	Gary Bergman	7.00	12.00
☐	Leo Boivin	9.00	15.00

- ☐ Roger Crozier (G) 9.00 15.00
- ☐ Alex Delvecchio (Home) 11.00 18.00
- ☐ Alex Delvecchio (Away) 225.00 300.00
- ☐ Alex Faulkner 285.00 375.00
- ☐ Val Fonteyne 7.00 12.00
- ☐ Bill Gadsby 9.00 15.00
- ☐ Warren Godfrey 18.00 28.00
- ☐ Pete Goegan 18.00 28.00
- ☐ Murray Hall 7.00 12.00
- ☐ Ted Hampson 7.00 12.00
- ☐ Billy Harris 18.00 28.00
- ☐ Paul Henderson 9.00 15.00
- ☐ Gordie Howe 22.00 35.00
- ☐ Gordie Howe (C on jersey) 210.00 275.00
- ☐ Ron Ingram 250.00 325.00
- ☐ Larry Jeffrey (Home) 50.00 80.00
- ☐ Larry Jeffrey (Away) 40.00 70.00
- ☐ Eddie Joyal 15.00 25.00
- ☐ Eddie Joyal (Negative reversed) 150.00 200.00
- ☐ Albert Langlois 7.00 12.00
- ☐ Ted Lindsay 9.00 15.00
- ☐ Parker MacDonald 7.00 12.00
- ☐ Bruce MacGregor (Home jersey) 7.00 12.00
- ☐ Bruce MacGregor (Away jersey) 50.00 85.00
- ☐ Pete Mahovlich 7.00 12.00
- ☐ Bert Marshall 7.00 12.00
- ☐ Pit Martin 7.00 12.00
- ☐ Ab McDonald 7.00 12.00
- ☐ Ron Murphy 7.00 12.00
- ☐ Dean Prentice 7.00 12.00
- ☐ Andre Pronovost 11.00 18.00
- ☐ Floyd Smith (Away jersey) 100.00 170.00
- ☐ Floyd Smith (Home jersey) 7.00 12.00
- ☐ Floyd Smith (Home jersey, Neg. reversed) 190.00 250.00
- ☐ Norm Ullman 9.00 15.00
- ☐ Bob Wall 7.00 12.00

MONTRÉAL CANADIENS

- ☐ Ralph Backstrom 7.00 12.00
- ☐ Dave Balon 7.00 12.00
- ☐ Jean Béliveau 13.00 22.00
- ☐ Red Berenson 7.00 12.00
- ☐ Yvan Cournoyer 9.00 15.00
- ☐ Dick Duff 7.00 12.00
- ☐ John Ferguson 7.00 12.00
- ☐ John Hanna 115.00 185.00
- ☐ Terry Harper (Dark background) 7.00 12.00
- ☐ Terry Harper (Light background) 210.00 275.00
- ☐ Ted Harris 7.00 12.00
- ☐ Bill Hicke 7.00 12.00
- ☐ Charlie Hodge (G) 9.00 15.00
- ☐ Jacques Laperriere 9.00 15.00
- ☐ Claude Larose 7.00 12.00
- ☐ Claude Larose (Neg. reversed) 300.00 400.00
- ☐ Claude Provost 7.00 12.00
- ☐ Henri Richard 13.00 22.00
- ☐ Maurice Richard 35.00 55.00
- ☐ Jim Roberts 7.00 12.00
- ☐ Bobby Rousseau 7.00 12.00
- ☐ Jean Guy Talbot 7.00 12.00
- ☐ Gilles Tremblay (#21) 7.00 12.00
- ☐ Gilles Tremblay (#24) 65.00 110.00
- ☐ J. C. Tremblay 7.00 12.00
- ☐ Gump Worsley (G) 11.00 18.00

NEW YORK RANGERS

- ☐ Lou Angotti 7.00 12.00
- ☐ Arnie Brown 7.00 12.00
- ☐ Larry Cahan 300.00 400.00
- ☐ Reg Fleming 7.00 12.00
- ☐ Bernie Geoffrion (G) 9.00 15.00
- ☐ Ed Giacomin 11.00 18.00
- ☐ Rod Gilbert 9.00 15.00
- ☐ Phil Goyette 7.00 12.00
- ☐ Vic Hadfield 7.00 12.00
- ☐ Camille Henry 90.00 150.00
- ☐ Bill Hicke 7.00 12.00
- ☐ Wayne Hillman 7.00 12.00
- ☐ Harry Howell 9.00 15.00
- ☐ Earl Ingarfield 7.00 12.00
- ☐ Orland Kurtenbach 7.00 12.00
- ☐ Gordon Labossière 80.00 130.00
- ☐ Al MacNeil 7.00 12.00
- ☐ Cesare Maniago (G) 9.00 15.00
- ☐ Don Marshall 7.00 12.00
- ☐ Jim Neilson 7.00 12.00
- ☐ Bob Nevin 7.00 12.00
- ☐ Marcel Paille 28.00 45.00
- ☐ Jacques Plante (G) 50.00 85.00
- ☐ Jean Ratelle 15.00 25.00
- ☐ Rod Seiling 7.00 12.00

TORONTO MAPLE LEAFS

- ☐ George Armstrong 9.00 15.00
- ☐ Andy Bathgate (A) 9.00 15.00
- ☐ Bobby Baun (No number) 9.00 15.00
- ☐ Bobby Baun (#21) 70.00 120.00
- ☐ Johnny Bower (G) (No number) 18.00 28.00
- ☐ Johnny Bower (G) (#1) 90.00 150.00
- ☐ Wally Boyer 20.00 30.00
- ☐ John Brenneman 7.00 12.00
- ☐ Carl Brewer 13.00 22.00
- ☐ Turk Broda (G) 18.00 28.00
- ☐ Brian Conacher 7.00 12.00
- ☐ Kent Douglas 7.00 12.00
- ☐ Ron Ellis 7.00 12.00
- ☐ Bruce Gamble (G) 9.00 15.00
- ☐ Billy Harris (No number) 150.00 200.00
- ☐ Billy Harris (#15) 50.00 80.00
- ☐ Larry Hillman 13.00 22.00
- ☐ Tim Horton (No number) 13.00 22.00
- ☐ Tim Horton (#7) 70.00 120.00
- ☐ Bronco Horvath 110.00 175.00
- ☐ Larry Jeffrey 18.00 28.00
- ☐ Eddie Joyal 28.00 45.00
- ☐ Red Kelly 9.00 15.00
- ☐ Ted Kennedy (C) 11.00 18.00
- ☐ Dave Keon (No number) 13.00 22.00
- ☐ Dave Keon (#14) 80.00 130.00
- ☐ Orland Kurtenbach 11.00 18.00
- ☐ Ed Litzenberger 22.00 35.00
- ☐ Frank Mahovlich (No number) 13.00 22.00
- ☐ Frank Mahovlich (#27) 100.00 165.00
- ☐ Don McKenney (Larger image) 11.00 18.00
- ☐ Don McKenney (Smaller image) 60.00 100.00
- ☐ Dickie Moore 9.00 15.00
- ☐ Jim Pappin 9.00 15.00
- ☐ Marcel Pronovost (Blade) 7.00 13.00
- ☐ Marcel Pronovost (No Blade) 13.00 22.00
- ☐ Bob Pulford (No number) 11.00 18.00
- ☐ Bob Pulford (#20) 65.00 110.00
- ☐ Terry Sawchuk (G) 18.00 28.00
- ☐ Brit Selby 7.00 12.00
- ☐ Eddie Shack 11.00 18.00
- ☐ Don Simmons (G) 15.00 25.00
- ☐ Allan Stanley 9.00 15.00
- ☐ Peter Stemkowski 7.00 12.00
- ☐ Ron Stewart (No number) 40.00 65.00
- ☐ Ron Stewart (#12) 110.00 175.00
- ☐ Mike Walton 25.00 40.00

TROPHIES AND MISC.

- ☐ Bernie Geoffrion (Québec coach) 35.00 55.00
- ☐ Byng trophy 85.00 140.00
- ☐ Calder Memorial Trophy 85.00 140.00
- ☐ Hart Trophy 85.00 140.00
- ☐ Prince of Wales Trophy 85.00 140.00
- ☐ J. Norris Memorial Trophy 85.00 140.00
- ☐ Art Ross Trophy 85.00 140.00
- ☐ Stanley Cup 85.00 140.00
- ☐ Vezina Trophy 85.00 140.00

1943 - 47 PARADE SPORTIVE PHOTOS

Issued on semi-glossy paper stock, these items were available at a nominal cost from three radio stations that aired the Parade Sportive show during the 1943 to 1947 era. Most photos are black and white but blue, brown, green and red tints have been seen. Sizes vary from 4 3/4" x 8 3/8" to 6 3/4" x 10". Variations of the same poses are plentiful. Different sizes, tints, script, etc., exist. No variation of a specific pose is scarce or valuable. Other athletes and sports were included but this listing is limited to hockey. It is possible that three different sets, one for each of the three radio stations, exist.

Photo Size: 4 3/4" x 8 3/8" to 6 3/4" x 10"
Face: Black and white; Name, Facsimile autograph
Back: Blank
Imprint: PHOTO, PARADE SPORTIVE

Common Player: 3.50 7.00

Player — EX — NRMT

BOSTON BRUINS

- ☐ Bauer/Schmidt/Dumart 9.00 18.00
- ☐ Frankie Brimsek (G) 7.50 15.00
- ☐ Bill Cowley 6.50 13.00
- ☐ Armand Gaudreault 3.50 7.00
- ☐ Jean Gladu 3.50 7.00
- ☐ Jean Gladu 3.50 7.00

CHICAGO BLACKHAWKS

- ☐ Mike Karakas (G) 4.50 9.00
- ☐ B. Mosienko/M. Bentley/D. Bentley; 9.00 18.00

DETROIT RED WINGS

- ☐ Eddie Bruneteau 3.50 7.00
- ☐ Modere Bruneteau 3.50 7.00
- ☐ Harry Lumley 9.00 18.00

NEW YORK RANGERS

- ☐ Edgar Laprade 5.00 10.00
- ☐ Phil Watson 4.50 9.00

TORONTO MAPLE LEAFS

- ☐ Baz Bastien (G) 4.50 9.00
- ☐ Turk Broda (G) 9.00 18.00
- ☐ Gaye Stewart 3.50 7.00

MINORS

- ☐ Lionel Bouvrette (G) 3.50 7.00
- ☐ Denys Casavant 3.50 7.00
- ☐ Connie Dion (G) 3.50 7.00
- ☐ Jim Henry 5.00 10.00
- ☐ Ernie Laforce 3.50 7.00
- ☐ Jean Marois (G) 3.50 7.00
- ☐ Gerry McNeil (G) 6.00 12.00
- ☐ Robert Pepin 3.50 7.00
- ☐ Gerry Plamondon 3.50 7.00

MONTRÉAL CANADIENS

- ☐ 1943 - 44 Team Photo 9.00 18.00
- ☐ 1944 - 45 Team Photo 9.00 18.00
- ☐ 1945 - 46 Team Photo 9.00 18.00
- ☐ 1946 - 47 Team Photo 9.00 18.00
- ☐ George Allen 3.50 7.00
- ☐ Joe Benoît 3.50 7.00
- ☐ Paul Bibeault (G) 4.50 9.00
- ☐ Toe Blake 6.50 13.00
- ☐ Emile (Butch) Bouchard 5.00 10.00
- ☐ Jean-Claude Campeau 3.50 7.00
- ☐ Bob Carse 3.50 7.00
- ☐ Joe Carveth 3.50 7.00
- ☐ Murph Chamberlain 3.50 7.00
- ☐ Floyd Curry 3.50 7.00
- ☐ Tony Demers 3.50 7.00
- ☐ Bill Durnan (G), 7.50 15.00
- ☐ Norm Dussault 3.50 7.00
- ☐ Frank Eddolls 3.50 7.00
- ☐ Bob Fillion 3.50 7.00
- ☐ Johnny Gagnon 3.50 7.00
- ☐ Gagnon/Joliat/Howie Morenz 15.00 30.00
- ☐ Fern Gauthier 3.50 7.00
- ☐ Gauthier/O'Connor/Hiller 7.50 15.00
- ☐ Léo Gravelle 3.50 7.00
- ☐ Glen Harmon 3.50 7.00
- ☐ Doug Harvey 7.50 15.00
- ☐ Heffernan/O'Connor/Morin 7.50 15.00
- ☐ Dutch Hiller 3.50 7.00
- ☐ Rosairo Joanette 3.50 7.00
- ☐ Elmer Lach 7.50 15.00
- ☐ Léo Lamoreaux 3.50 7.00
- ☐ Bouchard/Lamoureux/Durnan 7.50 15.00
- ☐ Hal Laycoe 3.50 7.00
- ☐ Roger Legér 3.50 7.00
- ☐ Jacques Locas 3.50 7.00
- ☐ Fern Majeau 3.50 7.00
- ☐ Georges Mantha 3.50 7.00
- ☐ Mike McMahon 3.50 7.00
- ☐ Kenny Mosdell 3.50 7.00
- ☐ Buddy O'Connor 6.50 13.00
- ☐ Jim Peters 3.50 7.00
- ☐ John Quilty 3.50 7.00

	Player	EX	NRMT
☐	Paul Raymond	3.50	7.00
☐	Ken Reardon	5.00	10.00
☐	Billy Reay	4.50	9.00
☐	Maurice Richard,	30.00	60.00
☐	Howard Riopellie	3.50	7.00

1945 - 54 QUAKER OATS PHOTOS

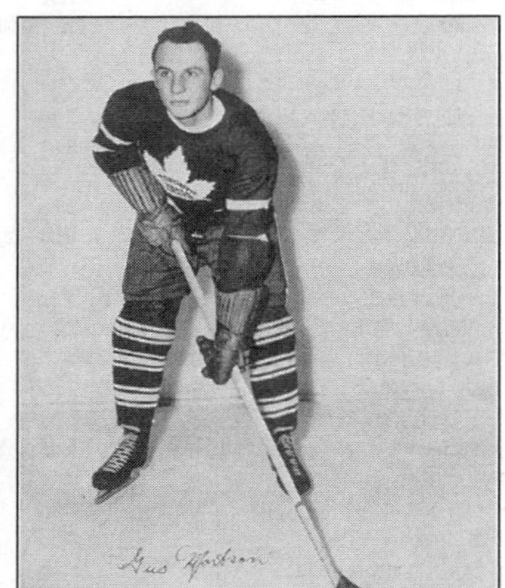

Photo Size: 8" x 10"
Face: Black and whtie photo, white border; Facsimile autograph
Back: Blank
Imprint: None
Complete Set: (202 photos): 3000.00 5000.00
Common Player: 7.00 12.00

No.	Player	EX	NRMT
☐ 1	George Allen, Mtl.	7.00	12.00
☐ 2	Jean Béliveau, Mtl.	80.00	135.00
☐ 3	Joe Benoît, Mtl. (black & white)	7.00	12.00
☐ 3	Joe Benoît, Mtl. (blue tint)	20.00	35.00
☐ 4	Toe Blake, Mtl., autograph above skates	75.00	125.00
☐ 4	Toe Blake, Mtl., autograph below skates	12.00	20.00
☐ 4	Toe Blake,, Mtl. Retouched Photo	18.00	30.00
☐ 5	Emile (Butch) Bouchard, Mtl., Still, Skates Visible	9.00	15.00
☐ 5	Emile (Butch) Bouchard, Mtl., Still, Skates Cropped	9.00	15.00
☐ 5	Emile (Butch) Bouchard, Mtl., Action	9.00	15.00
☐ 6	Tod Campeau, Mtl.	20.00	35.00
☐ 7	Bob Carse, Mtl.	12.00	20.00
☐ 8	Joe Carveth, Mtl.	12.00	20.00
☐ 9	Murph Chamberlain, Mtl., Still, Blue tint	28.00	45.00
☐ 9	Murph Chamberlain, Mtl., Still, Side View	12.00	20.00
☐ 9	Murph Chamberlain, Mtl., Still, Side View, Skates Cropped	12.00	20.00
☐ 10	Gerry Couture, Mtl.	18.00	30.00
☐ 11	Floyd Curry, Mtl., Still	50.00	80.00
☐ 11	Floyd Curry, Mtl., Action	7.00	12.00
☐ 12	Eddie Dorohoy, Mtl.	12.00	20.00
☐ 13	Bill Durnan (G), Mtl., Still, stick cropped	13.00	22.00
☐ 13	Bill Durnan (G), Mtl., Action	20.00	35.00
☐ 13	Bill Durnan (G), Mtl., Still, blue tint	65.00	115.00
☐ 13	Bill Durnan (G), Mtl., Still, handle touches border		
☐ 14	Norm Dussault, Mtl., Portrait	7.00	12.00
☐ 14	Norm Dussault, Mtl., Action	12.00	20.00
☐ 15	Frank Eddolls, Mtl.	7.00	12.00
☐ 16	Bob Fillion, Mtl., Still On Ice	18.00	30.00
☐ 16	Bob Fillion, Mtl., As A) Larger Image	12.00	20.00
☐ 16	Bob Fillion, Mtl., As A) Background Airbrushed	12.00	20.00
☐ 16	Bob Fillion, Mtl., Action	7.00	12.00
☐ 17	Dick Gamble, Mtl.	12.00	20.00
☐ 18	Bernie Geoffrion, Mtl.	15.00	25.00
☐ 19	Léo Gravelle, Mtl., Still, home uniform	7.00	12.00
☐ 19	Léo Gravelle, Mtl., Still, away uniform	20.00	35.00
☐ 19	Léo Gravelle, Mtl., Action	7.00	12.00
☐ 20	Glen Harmon, Mtl., Still, with Puck	12.00	20.00
☐ 20	Glen Harmon, Mtl., Still, no Puck	7.00	12.00
☐ 20	Glen Harmon, Mtl., Action	10.00	18.00
☐ 21	Doug Harvey, Mtl., Still	13.00	22.00
☐ 21	Doug Harvey, Mtl., Action	18.00	30.00
☐ 22	Dutch Hiller, Mtl.	12.00	20.00
☐ 23	Bert Hirschfeld, Mtl.	12.00	20.00
☐ 24	Tom Johnson, Mtl.	12.00	20.00
☐ 25	Vern Kaiser, Mtl.	12.00	20.00
☐ 26	Elmer Lach, Mtl., Still, stick Cropped	10.00	18.00
☐ 26	Elmer Lach, Mtl., Still, stick in Corner	10.00	18.00
☐ 26	Elmer Lach, Mtl., Still, stick near Corner	40.00	65.00
☐ 26	Elmer Lach, Mtl., Action	15.00	25.00
☐ 27	Leo Lamoureux, Mtl., Still-entire Blade	10.00	18.00
☐ 27	Leo Lamoureux, Mtl., Still-blade Cropped	7.00	12.00
☐ 28	Hal Laycoe, Mtl., Action	12.00	20.00
☐ 28	Hal Laycoe, Mtl., Portrait	75.00	125.00
☐ 29	Roger Léger, Mtl., Still, light Background	7.00	12.00
☐ 29	Roger Léger, Mtl., Still, dark Background	7.00	12.00
☐ 29	Roger Lége, Mtl.r, Action	20.00	35.00
☐ 30	Jacques Locas, Mtl.	7.00	12.00
☐ 31	Ross Lowe, Mtl.	10.00	18.00
☐ 32	Calum MacKay, Mtl.	7.00	12.00
☐ 33	Murdo MacKay, Mtl.	7.00	12.00
☐ 34	Paul Masnick, Mtl.	7.00	12.00
☐ 35	John McCormack, Mtl., Horizontal	28.00	45.00
☐ 35	John McCormack, Mtl., Vertical	35.00	60.00
☐ 36	Mike McMahon, Mtl.	40.00	65.00
☐ 37	Gerry McNeil (G), Mtl.	18.00	30.00
☐ 38	Jim McPherson, Mtl.	12.00	20.00
☐ 39	Paul Meger, Mtl.	12.00	20.00
☐ 40	Dickie Moore, Mtl.	18.00	28.00
☐ 41	Kenny Mosdell, Mtl., Still, small Image	12.00	20.00
☐ 41	Kenny Mosdell, Mtl., Still, large Image	15.00	25.00
☐ 41	Kenny Mosdell, Mtl., Still, large Image, auto cropped	15.00	25.00
☐ 41	Kenny Mosdell, Mtl., Action	12.00	20.00
☐ 42	Buddy O'Connor, Mtl., Still, With Blade	20.00	35.00
☐ 42	Buddy O'Connor, Mtl., Still, Blade Cropped	7.00	12.00
☐ 43	Bert Olmstead, Mtl.	12.00	20.00
☐ 44	Jim Peters, Mtl., Still, stick touching border	7.00	12.00
☐ 44	Jim Peters, Mtl., Still, stick away from border	7.00	12.00
☐ 44	Jim Peters, Mtl., Still, small image	7.00	12.00
☐ 45	Gerry Plamondon, Mtl.	7.00	12.00
☐ 46	John Quilty, Mtl.	15.00	25.00
☐ 47	Ken Reardon, Mtl., Still, Small Image	15.00	25.00
☐ 47	Ken Reardon, Mtl., Stil, Large Image	12.00	20.00
☐ 47	Ken Reardon, Mtl., Still, Large higher Image	15.00	25.00
☐ 47	Ken Reardon, Mtl., Action	12.00	20.00
☐ 48	Billy Reay, Mtl., Still, Blade On Border	7.00	12.00
☐ 48	Billy Reay, Mtl., Stil, Blade Away From Border	7.00	12.00
☐ 48	Billy Reay, Mtl., Action	9.00	15.00
☐ 48	Billy Reay, Mtl., small image	30.00	50.00
☐ 49	Maurice Richard, Mtl., Still	60.00	100.00
☐ 49	Maurice Richard, Mtl., full autograph	28.00	45.00
☐ 49	Maurice Richard, Mtl., autograph cropped	25.00	40.00
☐ 49	Maurice Richard, Mtl., Action	18.00	30.00
☐ 50	Howard Riopelle, Mtl., Still	7.00	12.00
☐ 50	Howard Riopelle, Mtl., Action	7.00	12.00
☐ 51	George Robertson, Mtl.	20.00	35.00
☐ 52	Dollard St. Laurent, Mtl.	35.00	60.00
☐ 53	Grant Warwick, Mtl.	60.00	100.00
☐ 54	1947-48-49 Team Picture, Tor.	55.00	90.00
☐ 55	Syl Apps, Sr., Tor., Still Auto. C.J.S. Apps	18.00	30.00
☐ 55	Syl Apps, Sr., Tor., Still Auto. Syl Apps	12.00	20.00
☐ 55	Syl Apps, Sr., Tor., With Stanley Cup	65.00	110.00
☐ 56	George Armstrong, Tor.	12.00	20.00
☐ 57	Doug Baldwin, Tor.	50.00	80.00
☐ 58	Bill Barilko, Tor., Home Uniform	20.00	35.00
☐ 58	Bill Barilko, Tor., Home, higher image	20.00	35.00
☐ 58	Bill Barilko, Tor., Away Uniform	20.00	35.00
☐ 59	Baz Bastien (G), Tor.	80.00	135.00
☐ 60	Gordie Bell (G), Tor.	80.00	135.00
☐ 61	Max Bentley, Tor., Home Uniform	12.00	20.00
☐ 61	Max Bentley, Tor., Away Uniform	12.00	20.00
☐ 61	Max Bentley, Tor., In Front Of Locker	180.00	300.00
☐ 62	Gus Bodnar, Tor.	18.00	28.00
☐ 63	Garth Boesch, Tor., Home Closed "B" In Auto	9.00	15.00
☐ 63	Garth Boesch, Tor., Home Open "B" In Auto	9.00	15.00
☐ 63	Garth Boesch, Tor., Away	28.00	45.00
☐ 64	Leo Boivin, Tor.	18.00	30.00
☐ 65	Hugh Bolton, Tor.	7.00	12.00
☐ 66	Turk Broda (G), Tor., Splits Auto. W.E. Broda	20.00	35.00
☐ 66	Turk Broda (G), Tor., Splits Auto. Turk Broda	20.00	35.00
☐ 66	Turk Broda (G), Tor., Action	20.00	35.00
☐ 67	Lorne Carr, Tor.	15.00	25.00
☐ 68	Les Costello, Tor.	15.00	25.00
☐ 69	Bob Davidson, Tor.	15.00	25.00
☐ 70	Bill Ezinicki, Tor., Still Auto. William Ezinicki	10.00	18.00
☐ 70	Bill Ezinicki, Tor., As A) Larger Image	7.00	12.00
☐ 70	Bill Ezinicki, Tor., Still Auto. Bill Ezinicki	7.00	12.00
☐ 70	Bill Ezinicki, Tor., Action	10.00	18.00
☐ 71	Fern Flaman, Tor.	12.00	20.00
☐ 72	Cal Gardner, Tor., Home Uniform	7.00	12.00
☐ 72	Cal Gardner, Tor., Away Uniform	7.00	12.00
☐ 73	Bob Goldham, Tor., Sweeping "G" Auto.	7.00	12.00
☐ 73	Bob Goldham, Tor., Normal "G" Auto.	7.00	12.00
☐ 73	Bob Goldham, Tor., blade cropped	15.00	25.00
☐ 74	Gord Hannigan, Tor.	15.00	25.00
☐ 75	Bob Hassard, Tor.	25.00	40.00
☐ 76	Mel Hill, Tor.	35.00	60.00
☐ 77	Tim Horton, Tor.	40.00	70.00
☐ 78	Bill Juzda, Tor., Home Uniform	7.00	12.00
☐ 78	Bill Juzda, Tor., Away Uniform	7.00	12.00
☐ 79	Ted Kennedy, Tor., Home blade cropped	25.00	40.00
☐ 79	Ted Kennedy, Tor., Home blade touching border	18.00	30.00
☐ 79	Ted Kennedy, Tor., "C" On Uniform	12.00	20.00
☐ 79	Ted Kennedy, Tor., With Stanley Cup	75.00	125.00
☐ 79	Ted Kennedy, Tor., Away Uniform	12.00	20.00
☐ 80	Joe Klukay, Tor., Home Uniform	7.00	12.00
☐ 80	Joe Klukay, Tor., Away Uniform	7.00	12.00
☐ 81	Danny Lewicki, Tor.	10.00	18.00
☐ 82	Harry Lumley (G), Tor.	30.00	50.00
☐ 83	Vic Lynn, Tor., Home small image	9.00	15.00
☐ 83	Vic Lynn, Tor., Home large image	15.00	25.00
☐ 83	Vic Lynn, Tor., Away Uniform	9.00	15.00
☐ 84	Fleming Mackell, Tor., Home Uniform	7.00	12.00
☐ 84	Fleming Mackell, Tor., Away Uniform	7.00	12.00
☐ 85	Phil Maloney, Tor.	35.00	55.00
☐ 86	Frank Mathers, Tor.	22.00	35.00
☐ 87	Frank McCool (G), Tor.	80.00	135.00
☐ 88	John McCormack, Tor.	15.00	25.00
☐ 89	Howie Meeker, Tor., Home Uniform	9.00	15.00
☐ 89	Howie Meeker, Tor., As A) Larger Image	9.00	15.00
☐ 89	Howie Meeker, Tor., Away Uniform	12.00	20.00
☐ 90	Don Metz, Tor., Still small image	7.00	12.00
☐ 90	Don Metz, Tor., Still large image	10.00	18.00
☐ 90	Don Metz, Tor., blue tint	30.00	50.00
☐ 91	Nick Metz, Tor., Still large image	10.00	18.00
☐ 91	Nick Metz, Tor., As A) Stick Retouched	10.00	18.00
☐ 91	Nick Metz, Tor., blue tint	15.00	25.00
☐ 92	Rudy Migay, Tor.	25.00	40.00
☐ 93	Elwyn Morris, Tor.	30.00	50.00
☐ 94	Jim Morrison, Tor.	7.00	12.00
☐ 95	Gus Mortson, Tor., Home Uniform	7.00	12.00
☐ 95	Gus Mortson, Tor., Away Uniform	7.00	12.00
☐ 96	Eric Nesterenko, Tor.	35.00	55.00
☐ 97	Bud Poile, Tor.	15.00	25.00
☐ 98	Babe Pratt, Tor.	50.00	85.00
☐ 99	Al Rollins (G), Tor.	15.00	25.00
☐ 100	Sweeny Schriner, Tor.	28.00	45.00
☐ 101	Tod Sloan, Tor., Home Uniform	18.00	30.00
☐ 101	Tod Sloan, Tor., Away Uniform	7.00	12.00
☐ 102	Sid Smith, Tor., Home Uniform	10.00	18.00
☐ 102	Sid Smith, Tor., Away Uniform	7.00	12.00
☐ 103	Bob Solinger, Tor.	18.00	30.00
☐ 104	Wally Stanowski, Tor., Full Blade	20.00	35.00
☐ 104	Wally Stanowski, Tor., Blade Cropped	13.00	22.00
☐ 105	Gaye Stewart, Tor., black & white	7.00	12.00
☐ 105	Gaye Stewart, Tor., blue tint	35.00	60.00
☐ 106	Ron Stewart, Tor.	35.00	60.00
☐ 107	Harry Taylor, Tor.	7.00	12.00
☐ 108	W.J. Taylor, Tor.	25.00	40.00
☐ 109	Cy Thomas, Tor.	18.00	30.00
☐ 110	Jim Thomson, Tor., Home blade cropped	15.00	25.00
☐ 110	Jim Thomson, Tor., Home blade touching border	7.00	12.00
☐ 110	Jim Thomson, Tor., Away Uniform	7.00	12.00
☐ 110	Jim Thomson, Tor., blue tint	25.00	40.00
☐ 111	Ray Timgren, Tor., Home Uniform	7.00	12.00
☐ 111	Ray Timgren, Tor., Away Uniform	7.00	12.00
☐ 112	Harry Watson, Tor., Home Uniform	12.00	20.00
☐ 112	Harry Watson, Tor., Higher Image	12.00	20.00
☐ 112	Harry Watson, Tor., Away Uniform	12.00	20.00
☐ 113	Gardner, Watson, Meeker Attack McNeil	140.00	235.00
☐ 114	Gardner Coming In On Harvey	140.00	235.00
☐ 115	Juzda And Rollins Stop Curry	140.00	235.00
☐ 116	McNeil Saves On Gardner	140.00	235.00

1948-52 EXHIBITS

These oversized black and white cards feature a full-bleed design on heavy cardboard stock. The player's name is imprinted near the bottom.

Card Size: 3 1/4" x 5 1/4"
Face: Black and white photo, Name
Back: Blank
Imprint: None
Complete Set (65 cards):
Common Player:

	Player	VG	EX	EX-NRMT
☐	Reggie Abbott, Mtl.			
☐	Sid Abel, Det.			
☐	Bill Barilko, Tor.			
☐	Jean Béliveau, Mtl.			
☐	Jean Béliveau, Québec			
☐	Doug Bentley, Chi.			
☐	Max Bentley, Chi.			
☐	Toe Blake, Mtl.			
☐	Butch Bouchard, Mtl.			
☐	Turk Broda (G), Tor.			
☐	Roy Conacher, Chi.			
☐	Floyd Curry, Tor.			
☐	Bob Fillion, Mtl.			
☐	Dick Gamble, Mtl.			
☐	Cal Gardner, Tor.			
☐	Jack Gelineau, Bos.			
☐	Bernie Geoffrion, Mtl.			
☐	Doug Harvey, Mtl.			
☐	Gordie Howe, Det.			
☐	Tom Johnson, Mtl.			
☐	Bill Juzda, Tor.			
☐	Ted Kennedy, Tor.			
☐	Joe Klukay, Tor.			
☐	Elmer Lach, Mtl.			
☐	Hal Laycoe, Mtl.			
☐	Ted Lindsay, Det.			
☐	Jacques Locas, Mtl.			
☐	Harry Lumley (G), Det.			
☐	Fleming Mackell, Tor.			
☐	Bud McPherson, Mtl			
☐	Paul Maznick, Mtl			
☐	Gerry McNeil (G), Mtl.			
☐	Howie Meeker, Tor.			
☐	Paul Meger, Mtl.			
☐	Dickie Moore, Mtl.			
☐	Gus Mortson, Tor.			
☐	Ken Mosdell, Mtl.			
☐	Bert Olmstead, Mtl			
☐	Chuck Rayner, NYR			
☐	Ken Reardon, Mtl			
☐	Billy Reay, Mtl			
☐	Maurice Richard, Mtl			
☐	Maurice Richard, Mtl. (stairs in background)			
☐	Al Rollins (G), Tor.			
☐	Paul Ronty, Bos.			
☐	Sid Smith, Tor.			
☐	Tod Sloan, Tor.			
☐	Dollard St. Laurent, Mtl.			
☐	Jim Thomson, Tor.			
☐	Ray Timgren, Tor.			
☐	Grant Warwick, Mtl.			
☐	Bos.vs. Mtl.			
☐	Chi. vs. Montreal			
☐	Chi. vs. Mtl. (Bernie Geoffrion)			
☐	Chi. vs. Mtl.: Montréal scores			
☐	Det. vs. NYR. (Gordie Howe)			
☐	Det. vs. Mtl.			
☐	Det. vs. Mtl.: (Terry Sawchuk)			
☐	Det. vs. Mtl.			
☐	Mtl. vs. Bos.			
☐	Mtl. vs. Tor. (Maurice Richard)			
☐	NYR. vs. Mtl. (Maurice Richard)			
☐	NYR. vs. Mtl.			
☐	NYR. vs. Mtl. (M.Richard/ E.Lach/ C.Rayner)			
☐	Tor. vs. Mtl.			

1948 - 59 W. PATTERSON LONG FELLOWS

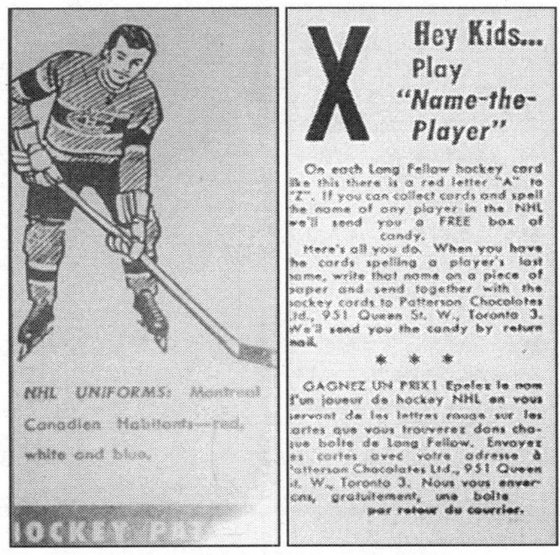

A free box of chocolates was awarded to anyone who could spell the name of an NHL player using the letters on these cards. According to the card back, there is a card for each letter in the alphabet.

ACC No.: V19
Card Size: 1 3/4" x 3 9/16"
Face: Blue sketch and hockey tip, red letter
Back: Blue on white card stock, initial, redemption offer, bilingual
Imprint: none

	No.	Player	EX	EX-NRMT
☐	C	Flip shot	12.00	25.00
☐	D	Face-off	12.00	25.00
☐	G	Goal crease	12.00	25.00
☐	H	Back-checking	12.00	25.00
☐	I	Break away	12.00	25.00
☐	K	Blocking	12.00	25.00
☐	L	Cutting the angle	12.00	25.00
☐	M	Stadium in NHL	12.00	25.00
☐	N	Tip-in	12.00	25.00
☐	P	Slapshot	12.00	25.00
☐	R	NHL Uniforms, Chi.	20.00	50.00
☐	T	NHL Uniforms, NYR.	20.00	50.00
☐	W	NHL Uniforms, Tor.	20.00	50.00
☐	X	NHL Uniforms, Mtl.	20.00	50.00
☐	Y	Memorial Cup	20.00	40.00

1949 CARRERAS LTD. CIGARETTES

There are 50-cards in this multi-sport set.

Card Size: 1 1/2" x 2 11/16"
There are 50 cards in this set
Face: Blue photo, white border; Name, Series
Back: Blank
Imprint: TURF CIGARETTES

	No.	Scene	VG	EX	EX-NRMT
☐	37	Duke Campbell	10.00	20.00	40.00
☐	44	Les Anning, Wembley Lions	10.00	20.00	40.00

1951 BERK ROSS

1951 HIT PARADE OF CHAMPIONS

This is an all-sport set of 72 cards. The cards were issued in panels of two cards and numbered in four series of subsets, one to eighteen, two to eighteen, etc. The centering of this set is poor.

Card Size: 2 1/16" x 2 1/2"
Face: Four colour, white border
Back: Black on card stock; Name, Number, Position, Team
Imprint: Berk Ross Inc. New York, N.Y.

	No.	Player	EX	NRMT
☐		Sid Abel, Det.	60.00	115.00
☐		Jack Stewart, Det.	45.00	85.00
☐	1-17	Bill Durnan (G), Mtl.	65.00	125.00
☐	1-18	Bill Quackenbush, Bos.	45.00	85.00
☐		Bill Quackenbush and Bill Durnan (G)	60.00	125.00

1951 - 52 BAS DU FLEUVE

DENIS BRODEUR – Rivière-du-Loup
Né à Montréal, P.Q., le 12 octobre 1930
Gardien de Buts
No. 2

Complete Set (58 cards): 350.00 750.00
Common Player: 7.00 16.00

	No.	Player	EX	NRMT
☐	1	Gordon Poirier	9.00	25.00
☐	2	Denis Brodeur	20.00	45.00
☐	3	Conrad Poitras	7.00	16.00
☐	4	Clement Tremblay	7.00	16.00
☐	5	Raymond Leduc	7.00	16.00
☐	6	Jacques Armstrong	7.00	16.00
☐	7	Joe Schmidt	7.00	16.00
☐	8	Gilles Laroche	7.00	16.00
☐	9	Frank Pearce	7.00	16.00
☐	10	Wayne Stephenson	7.00	16.00
☐	11	Guy Lapointe	7.00	16.00
☐	12	Guy Delisle	7.00	16.00
☐	13	Ossie Carnegie	7.00	16.00
☐	14	Gilbert Girouard	7.00	16.00
☐	15	Jean-Paul Vandal	7.00	16.00
☐	16	Guy Lalonde	7.00	16.00
☐	17	Roland Bilodeau	7.00	16.00
☐	18	Gaetan Laliberté	7.00	16.00
☐	19	Maurice Benoît	7.00	16.00
☐	20	Thomas McDougall	7.00	16.00
☐	21	Roger Guay	7.00	16.00
☐	22	Bob Brault	7.00	16.00
☐	23	Edouard Theberge	7.00	16.00

No.	Player	EX	NRMT
24	Paul Lessard	7.00	16.00
25	Lucien Gilbert	7.00	16.00
26	Réal Lafrenière	7.00	16.00
27	Rénald Limoges	7.00	16.00
28	Roger Ste. Marie	7.00	16.00
29	Arthur Leyte	7.00	16.00
30	Magella Laforest	7.00	16.00
31	Bill Leblanc	7.00	16.00
32	Pius Gaudet	7.00	16.00
33	Jean-Roch Bellavance	7.00	16.00
34	Gérard Lachance	7.00	16.00
35	Marcel St. Pierre	7.00	16.00
36	Pierre Brillant	7.00	16.00
37	Paul Provost	7.00	16.00
38	Maurice Lamirande	7.00	16.00
39	Roger Hayfield	7.00	16.00
40	Normand Bellavance	7.00	16.00
41	Marcel Houde	7.00	16.00
42	Dan Janelle	7.00	16.00
43	Roland Rossignol	7.00	16.00
44	Roger Gagné	7.00	16.00
45	Jacques Monette	7.00	16.00
46	Bernie Bernaquez	7.00	16.00
47	Paul Gagnon	7.00	16.00
48	Jean-Marie Fillion	7.00	16.00
49	Bert Scullion	7.00	16.00
50	Don Bellringer	7.00	16.00
51	Frank Cote	7.00	16.00
52	Eddy Bolan	7.00	16.00
53	Maurice Parr	7.00	16.00
54	Many McIntyre	7.00	16.00
55	Roger Jodoin	7.00	16.00
56	Mario Senecal	7.00	16.00
57	Denis Fillion	7.00	16.00
58	Marcel Fillion	9.00	25.00

1951 - 52 LAC ST. JEAN

Card Size: 1 3/4" x 2 1/2"
Face: Green tint and white; Name, Number
Back: Blank
Imprint: None

Complete Set (59 cards):		**300.00**	**650.00**
Common Player:		**7.50**	**15.00**
No.	**Player**	**EX**	**NRMT**
1	Eddy Daoust, Jonquière	7.50	15.00
2	Guy Gareau, Jonquière	7.50	15.00
3	Gilles Desrosiers, Jonquière	7.50	15.00
4	Robert Desbiens, Jonquière	7.50	15.00
5	James Hayes, Jonquière	7.50	15.00
6	Paul Gagnon, Jonquière	7.50	15.00
7	Gerry Perreault, Jonquière	7.50	15.00
8	Marcel Dufour, Jonquière	7.50	15.00
9	Armand Bourdon, Jonquière	7.50	15.00
10	Jean-Marc Pichette, Jonquière	7.50	15.00
11	Gerry Gagnon, Jonquière	7.50	15.00
12	Jules Racette, Jonquière	7.50	15.00
13	Real Marcotte, Jonquière	7.50	15.00
14	Gerry Theberge, Jonquière	7.50	15.00
15	Rene Harvey, Jonquière	7.50	15.00
16	Joseph Lacoursiere, Dolbeau	7.50	15.00
17	Fernand Benaquez, Dolbeau	7.50	15.00
18	Andre Boisvert, Dolbeau	7.50	15.00
19	Claude Chretien, Dolbeau	7.50	15.00
20	Nobert Clark, Dolbeau	7.50	15.00
21	Sylvio Lambert, Dolbeau	7.50	15.00
22	Lucien Roy, Dolbeau	7.50	15.00
23	Gerard Audet, Dolbeau	7.50	15.00
24	Jacques Lalancette, Dolbeau	7.50	15.00
25	Maurice St. Jean, Dolbeau	7.50	15.00
26	Camille Lupien, Dolbeau	7.50	15.00
27	Rodrigue Pelchat, Dolbeau	7.50	15.00
28	Conrad L'Heureux, Dolbeau	7.50	15.00
29	Paul Tremblay, Dolbeau	7.50	15.00
30	Robert Vincent, Dolbeau	7.50	15.00
31	Charles Lamirande, Alma	7.50	15.00
32	Léon Gaudreault, Alma	7.50	15.00
33	Maurice Thiffault, Alma	7.50	15.00
34	Marc-Aurele Tremblay, Alma	7.50	15.00
35	René Pronovost, Alma	7.50	15.00
36	Victor Corbin, Alma	7.50	15.00
37	Tiny Tamminen, Alma	7.50	15.00
38	Guildor Levesque, Alma	7.50	15.00
39	Gaston Lamirande, Alma	7.50	15.00
40	Guy Gervais, Alma	7.50	15.00
41	Rayner Makila, Alma	7.50	15.00
42	Jules Tremblay, Alma	7.50	15.00
43	Roland Girard, Alma	7.50	15.00
44	Germain Bergeron, Alma	7.50	15.00
45	Paul Duchesne, Pt. Alfred	7.50	15.00
46	Roger Beaudoin, Pt. Alfred	7.50	15.00
47	Georges Archibal, Pt. Alfred	7.50	15.00
48	Claude Basque, Pt. Alfred	7.50	15.00
49	Roger Sarda, Pt. Alfred	7.50	15.00
50	Edgar Gendron, Pt. Alfred	7.50	15.00
51	Gaston Labossiere, Pt. Alfred	7.50	15.00
52	Roland Clantara, Pt. Alfred	7.50	15.00
53	Florian Gravel, Pt. Alfred	7.50	15.00
54	Jean-Guy Thompson, Pt. Alfred	7.50	15.00
55	Yvan Fortin, Pt. Alfred	7.50	15.00
56	Yves Laporte, Pt. Alfred	7.50	15.00
57	Claude Germain, Pt. Alfred	7.50	15.00
58	Gerry Brunet, Pt. Alfred	7.50	15.00
59	Maurice Courteau, Pt. Alfred	7.50	15.00

1951 - 52 LAVAL DAIRY QHL

RAY FREDERICKS — Ottawa
Né — 31 juillet 1929 — Fort-Frances
Gardien de Buts
No 104

These cards were issued in the province of Québec and Ottawa region. They are scarce.

Card Size: 1 3/4" x 2 1/2"
Face: Black and white photo, white border; Name, Position, Number, French
Back: Blank
Imprint: None

Complete Set (109 cards):		**750.00**	**1,600.00**
Common Player:		**6.00**	**13.00**
No.	**Player**	**EX**	**NRMT**
AS DE QUEBEC			
1	Jean Béliveau, Québec	225.00	500.00
2	Jean Marois (G), Québec	6.00	13.00
3	Joe Crozier, Québec	12.00	20.00
4	Jack Gelineau (G), Québec	6.00	13.00
5	Murdo McKay, Québec	6.00	13.00
6	Arthur Leyte, Québec	6.00	13.00
7	W. Leblanc, Québec	6.00	13.00
8	Robert Hayes, Québec	6.00	13.00
9	Yogi Kraiger, Québec	6.00	13.00
10	Frank King, Quebec	6.00	13.00
11	Ludger Tremblay, Quebec	6.00	13.00
12	Jackie Leclair, Quebec	12.00	20.00
13	Martial Pruneau, Quebec	6.00	13.00
14	Armand Gaudreault, Quebec	6.00	13.00
15	Marcel Bonin, Quebec	20.00	30.00
16	Herbie Carnegie, Quebec	12.00	20.00
17	Claude Robert, Quebec	6.00	13.00
18	Phil Renaud, Quebec	6.00	13.00
19	Roland Hebert, Chicoutimi	6.00	13.00
20	Donat Deschesne, Chicoutimi	6.00	13.00
21	Jacques Gagnon, Chicoutimi	6.00	13.00
22	Normand Dussault, Chicoutimi	6.00	13.00
23	Stan Smrke, Chicoutimi	11.00	18.00
24	Louis Smrke, Chicoutimi	6.00	13.00
25	Floyd Crawford, Chicoutimi	6.00	13.00
26	Germain Leger, Chicoutimi	6.00	13.00
27	Delphis Franche, Chicoutimi	6.00	13.00
28	Dick Wray, Chicoutimi	6.00	13.00
29	Guildor Levesque, Chicoutimi	6.00	13.00
30	Georges Roy, Chicoutimi	6.00	13.00
31	J.P. Lamirande, Chicoutimi	6.00	13.00
32	Gerard Glaude, Chicoutimi	6.00	13.00
33	Marcel Pelletier, Chicoutimi	6.00	13.00
34	Pete Tkachuck, Chicoutimi	6.00	13.00
35	Sherman White, Chicoutimi	6.00	13.00
36	Jimmy Moore, Chicoutimi	6.00	13.00
37	Punch Imlach, Québec	50.00	85.00
38	Alex Sandalax, Sherbrooke	6.00	13.00
39	William Kyle, Sherbrooke	6.00	13.00
40	Kenneth Biggs, Sherbrooke	6.00	13.00
41	Peter Wright, Sherbrooke	6.00	13.00
42	René Pépin, Sherbrooke	6.00	13.00
43	Jean-Claude (Tod) Campeau, Sherbrooke	11.00	18.00
44	John Smith, Sherbrooke	6.00	13.00
45	Thomas McDougall, Sherbrooke	6.00	13.00
46	Jos Lépine, Sherbrooke	6.00	13.00
47	Guy Labrie, Sherbrooke	6.00	13.00
48	Roger Bessette, Sherbrooke	6.00	13.00
49	Yvan Dugre, Sherbrooke	6.00	13.00
50	James Planche, Sherbrooke	6.00	13.00
51	Nils Tremblay, Sherbrooke	6.00	13.00
52	Bill MacDonagh, Shawinigan Falls	6.00	13.00
53	Georges Ouellet, Shawinigan Falls	6.00	13.00
54	Billy Arcand, Shawinigan Falls	6.00	13.00
55	Johnny Mahaffy, Shawinigan Falls	6.00	13.00
56	Bucky Buchanan, Shawinigan Falls	6.00	13.00
57	Al Miller (G), Shawinigan Falls	6.00	13.00
58	Don Penniston, Shawinigan Falls	6.00	13.00
59	Spike Laliberte, Shawinigan Falls	6.00	13.00
60	Ernie Oakley, Shawinigan Falls	6.00	13.00
61	Jack Bownass, Shawinigan Falls	11.00	18.00
62	Ted Hodgson, Shawinigan Falls	6.00	13.00
63	Lyall Wiseman, Shawinigan Falls	6.00	13.00
64	Erwin Grosse, Shawinigan Falls	6.00	13.00
65	Mel Read, Shawinigan Falls	6.00	13.00
66	Lloyd Henchberger, Shawinigan Falls	6.00	13.00
67	Jack Taylor, Shawinigan Falls	6.00	13.00
68	Marcel Bessette, Valleyfield	6.00	13.00
69	Jack Schmidt, Valleyfield	6.00	13.00
70	Paul Saindon, Valleyfield	6.00	13.00
71	J.P. Bisaillon, Valleyfield	6.00	13.00
72	Eddie Redmond, Valleyfield	6.00	13.00
73	Larry Kwong, Valleyfield	11.00	18.00
74	Andre Corriveau, Valleyfield	10.00	16.00
75	Kitoute Joanette, Valleyfield	6.00	13.00
76	Toe Blake, Valleyfield	65.00	110.00
77	Georges Bougie, Valleyfield	6.00	13.00
78	Jack Irvine, Valleyfield	6.00	13.00
79	Paul Larivée, Valleyfield	6.00	13.00
80	Paul Leclerc, Valleyfield	6.00	13.00
81	Bertrand Bourassa, Valleyfield	6.00	13.00
82	Jacques Deslauriers, Valleyfield	6.00	13.00
83	Bingo Ernst, Valleyfield	6.00	13.00
84	Gaston Gervais, Valleyfield	6.00	13.00
85	Gerry Plamondon, Royal de Montréal	11.00	18.00
86	Glen Harmon, Royal de Montréal	12.00	20.00
87	Bob Friday, Royal de Montréal	6.00	13.00
88	Rolland Rousseau, Royal de Montréal	6.00	13.00
89	Billy Goold, Royal de Montréal	6.00	13.00
90	Lloyd Finkbeiner, Royal de Montréal	6.00	13.00
91	Clifford Malone, Royal de Montréal	6.00	13.00
92	Jacques Plante (G), Royal de Montréal	275.00	425.00
93	Gerard Desaulniers, Royal de Montréal	6.00	13.00
94	Arthur Rose, Royal de Montréal	6.00	13.00
95	Jacques Locas, Royal de Montréal	6.00	13.00
96	Walter Clune, Royal de Montréal	6.00	13.00
97	Louis Denis, Royal de Montréal	6.00	13.00
98	Fernand Perreault, Royal de Montréal	6.00	13.00
99	Douglas McNeil, Royal de Montréal	6.00	13.00
100	Les Douglas, Royal de Montréal	10.00	16.00
101	Howard Riopelle, Ottawa	10.00	16.00
102	Vic Grigg, Ottawa	6.00	13.00
103	Bobby Roberts, Ottawa	6.00	13.00
104	Legs Fraser, Ottawa	6.00	13.00
105	Butch Stahan, Ottawa	6.00	13.00
106	Fritz Frazer, Ottawa	6.00	13.00
107	Bill Robinson, Ottawa	6.00	13.00
108	Eddie Emberg, Ottawa	6.00	13.00
109	Leo Gravelle, Ottawa	6.00	28.00

1951 - 52 PARKHURST

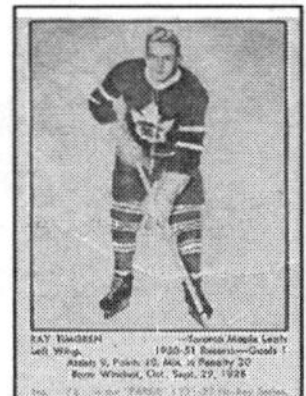

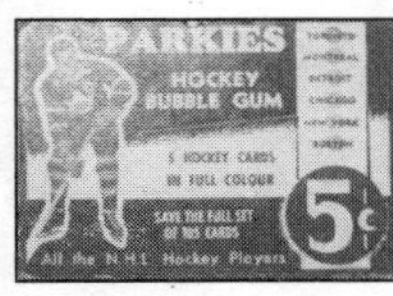

This is the first set of modern cards. This set is almost impossible to find in the higher grades. Mint cards do command a premium. Aging causes discolouration (browning) of the cards. This is a natural process with the card stock and cannot be easily stopped or reversed.

Card Size: 1 3/4" x 2 1/2"
Face: Four colour, Number, Resume
Back: Blank
Imprint: None

		EX	NRMT
Complete Set (105 cards):		8,500.00	14,000.00
Common Player:		35.00	55.00

No.	Player	EX	NRMT
☐ 1	Elmer Lach, Mtl.	250.00	500.00
☐ 2	Paul Meger, Mtl., RC	35.00	55.00
☐ 3	Emile (Butch) Bouchard, Mtl.	60.00	100.00
☐ 4	Maurice Richard, RC, Mtl.	1,300.00	2,200.00
☐ 5	Bert Olmstead, RC, Mtl.	60.00	100.00
☐ 6	Bud MacPherson, RC, Mtl.	35.00	55.00
☐ 7	Tom Johnson, RC, Mtl.	60.00	100.00
☐ 8	Paul Masnick, RC, Mtl.	35.00	55.00
☐ 9	Calum MacKay, RC, Mtl.	35.00	55.00
☐ 10	Doug Harvey, RC, Mtl.	350.00	550.00
☐ 11	Kenny Mosdell, RC, Mtl.	35.00	55.00
☐ 12	Floyd Curry, RC, Mtl.	35.00	55.00
☐ 13	Billy Reay, RC, Mtl.	45.00	70.00
☐ 14	Bernie Geoffrion, RC, Mtl.	350.00	550.00
☐ 15	Gerry McNeil (G), RC, Mtl.	135.00	225.00
☐ 16	Dick Gamble, RC, Mtl.	35.00	55.00
☐ 17	Gerald Couture, RC, Mtl.	35.00	55.00
☐ 18	Ross Lowe, RC, LC, Mtl.	35.00	55.00
☐ 19	Jim Henry (G), RC, Bos.	55.00	95.00
☐ 20	Vic Lynn, RC, LC, Bos.	35.00	55.00
☐ 21	Walter Kyle, RC, LC, Bos.	35.00	55.00
☐ 22	Ed Sandford, RC, Bos.	35.00	55.00
☐ 23	John Henderson, RC, LC, Bos.	35.00	55.00
☐ 24	Robert Fisher, RC, LC, Bos.	35.00	55.00
☐ 25	Hal Laycoe, RC, Bos.	35.00	55.00
☐ 26	Bill Quackenbush, RC, Bos.	60.00	100.00
☐ 27	George Sullivan, RC, Bos.	35.00	55.00
☐ 28	Woody Dumart, Bos.	50.00	80.00
☐ 29	Milt Schmidt, Bos.	80.00	130.00
☐ 30	Adam Brown, RC, LC, Bos.	35.00	55.00
☐ 31	Pentti Lund, RC, Bos.	35.00	55.00
☐ 32	Ray Barry, RC, LC, Bos.	35.00	55.00
☐ 33	Ed. Kryznowski, RC, Err. (Kryzanowski), Bos.	35.00	55.00
☐ 34	Johnny Peirson, RC, Bos.	35.00	55.00
☐ 35	Lorne Ferguson, RC, Bos.	35.00	55.00
☐ 36	Clare Raglan, RC, Bos.	35.00	55.00
☐ 37	Bill Gadsby, RC, Chi.	60.00	100.00
☐ 38	Al Dewsbury, RC, Chi.	35.00	55.00
☐ 39	George Martin, RC, LC, Chi.	35.00	55.00
☐ 40	Gus Bodnar, RC, Chi.	35.00	55.00
☐ 41	Jim Peters, Chi.	35.00	55.00
☐ 42	Bep Guidolin, RC, LC, Chi.	35.00	55.00
☐ 43	George Gee, RC, Chi.	35.00	55.00
☐ 44	Jim McFadden, RC, Chi.	50.00	75.00
☐ 45	Fred Hucul, RC, Chi.	35.00	55.00
☐ 46	Lidio Fogolin, RC, Chi.	35.00	55.00
☐ 47	Harry Lumley (G), RC, Chi.	100.00	160.00
☐ 48	Doug Bentley, RC, LC, Chi.	60.00	100.00
☐ 49	Bill Mosienko, RC, Chi.	60.00	100.00
☐ 50	Roy Conacher, LC, Chi.	40.00	65.00
☐ 51	Pete Babando, RC, Chi.	35.00	55.00
☐ 52	The Winning Goal (Bill Barilko, Tor.), Chi.	325.00	525.00
☐ 53	Jack Stewart, LC, Chi.	45.00	70.00
☐ 54	Marty Pavelich, RC, Chi.	35.00	55.00
☐ 55	Red Kelly, RC, Det., Chi.	190.00	300.00
☐ 56	Ted Lindsay, RC, Det., Chi.	190.00	300.00
☐ 57	Glen Skov, RC, Det., Chi.	35.00	55.00
☐ 58	Benny Woit, RC, Det., Chi.	35.00	55.00
☐ 59	Tony Leswick, RC, Det.	35.00	55.00
☐ 60	Fred Glover, RC, Det.	35.00	55.00
☐ 61	Terry Sawchuk (G), RC, Det.	750.00	1,200.00
☐ 62	Vic Stasiuk, RC, Det.	45.00	70.00
☐ 63	Alex Delvecchio, RC, Det.	190.00	300.00
☐ 64	Sid Abel, LC, Det.	60.00	100.00
☐ 65	Metro Prystai, RC, Det.	35.00	55.00
☐ 66	Gordie Howe, RC, Det.	2,500.00	4,000.00
☐ 67	Bob Goldham, RC, Det.	45.00	70.00
☐ 68	Marcel Pronovost, RC, Det.	60.00	100.00
☐ 69	Leo Reise, Det.	35.00	55.00
☐ 70	Harry Watson, RC, Tor.	50.00	80.00
☐ 71	Danny Lewicki, RC, Tor.	35.00	55.00
☐ 72	Howie Meeker, RC, Tor.	85.00	135.00
☐ 73	Gus Mortson, RC, Tor.	35.00	55.00
☐ 74	Joe Klukay, RC, Tor.	35.00	55.00
☐ 75	Turk Broda (G), Tor.	150.00	250.00
☐ 76	Al Rollins (G), RC, Tor.	55.00	95.00
☐ 77	Bill Juzda, RC, LC, Tor.	35.00	55.00
☐ 78	Ray Timgren, RC, Tor.	35.00	55.00
☐ 79	Hugh Bolton, RC, Tor.	35.00	55.00
☐ 80	Fern Flaman, RC, Tor.	60.00	100.00
☐ 81	Max Bentley, Tor.	60.00	100.00
☐ 82	Jim Thomson, RC, Tor.	35.00	55.00
☐ 83	Fleming Mackell, Tor.	35.00	55.00
☐ 84	Sid Smith, RC, Tor.	45.00	70.00
☐ 85	Cal Gardner, RC, Tor.	35.00	55.00
☐ 86	Ted Kennedy, RC, Tor.	115.00	185.00
☐ 87	Tod Sloan, RC, Tor.	35.00	55.00
☐ 88	Bob Solinger, RC, Tor.	35.00	55.00
☐ 89	Frank Eddolls, RC, LC, Tor.	35.00	55.00
☐ 90	Jack Evans, RC, NYR.	35.00	55.00
☐ 91	Hyman Buller, RC, NYR.	35.00	55.00
☐ 92	Stephen Kraftcheck, RC, NYR.	35.00	55.00
☐ 93	Don Raleigh, RC, NYR.	35.00	55.00
☐ 94	Allan Stanley, RC, NYR.	100.00	160.00
☐ 95	Paul Ronty, RC, NYR.	35.00	55.00
☐ 96	Edgar LaPrade, RC, NYR.	50.00	80.00
☐ 97	Nick Mickoski, RC, NYR.	35.00	55.00
☐ 98	Jackie McLeod, RC, NYR.	35.00	55.00
☐ 99	Gaye Stewart, RC, NYR.	35.00	55.00
☐ 100	Wally Hergesheimer, RC, NYR.	35.00	55.00
☐ 101	Eddie Kullman, NYR., RC	35.00	55.00
☐ 102	Eddie Slowinski, RC, NYR.	35.00	55.00
☐ 103	Reg Sinclair, RC, NYR.	35.00	55.00
☐ 104	Chuck Rayner (G), RC, NYR.	65.00	110.00
☐ 105	Jim Conacher, RC, NYR.	110.00	215.00

1951 - 54 LA PATRIE

Prices are for photos with three stripes down right side intact.

Card Size: 11" x 15 1/2"
Face: Four colour
Back: Newspaper
Imprint: None

		EX	NRMT
Complete Set (44 photos):		1,100.00	1,800.00

No.	Player / Date Issued	EX	NRMT
1951 - 52 ISSUES			
☐ 1	Maurice Richard, Mtl., December 2	120.00	200.00
☐ 2	Emile (Butch) Bouchard, Mtl., December 9	50.00	75.00
☐ 3	Elmer Lach, Mtl., December 16	60.00	25.00
☐ 4	Gerry McNeil, Mtl., December 23	50.00	75.00
☐ 5	Bernie Geoffrion, Mtl., December 31	80.00	125.00
☐ 6	Doug Harvey, Mtl., January 6	80.00	125.00
☐ 7	Jean Béliveau, Québec Aces, January 15	90.00	150.00
☐ 8	Kenny Mosdell, Mtl., January 20	50.00	75.00
☐ 9	Dick Gamble, Mtl., January 27	30.00	50.00
☐ 10	Paul Meger, February 3	30.00	50.00
☐ 11	Billy Reay, Mtl., February 10	35.00	60.00
☐ 12	Floyd Curry, Mtl., February 17	35.00	60.00
☐ 13	Dollard St. Laurent, Mtl., February 24	35.00	60.00
☐ 14	Jean Guy Talbot, Trois Rivières, March 2	30.00	50.00
☐ 15	Dickie Moore, Mtl., March 9	60.00	100.00
☐ 16	Bert Olmstead, Mtl., March 16	50.00	75.00
☐ 17	André Corriveau, Valleyfield, March 23	25.00	40.00
☐ 18	Marcel Pelletier, Les Saguénéens, March 30	25.00	40.00
☐ 19	Tom Johnson, Mtl., April 8	50.00	75.00
☐ 20	Bud MacPherson, Mtl., April 13	25.00	40.00
☐ 21	John McCormack, Mtl., April 20	30.00	50.00
1952 - 53 ISSUES			
☐ 22	Roger Léger, RHC, January 11	30.00	50.00
☐ 23	Henri Richard, Mtl., January 18	80.00	125.00
☐ 24	Camille Henry, Québec Cit., January 25	30.00	50.00
☐ 25	Jean Paul Lamirande, Les Saguénéens, Feb. 1	20.00	30.00
☐ 26	Eddie Litzenberger, RHC, February 8	30.00	50.00
☐ 27	Skippy Burchell, RHC, February 15	25.00	40.00
☐ 28	Herbie Carnegie, Québec Aces, March 1	25.00	40.00
☐ 29	Jean Marois, Québec Aces, March 8	25.00	40.00
☐ 30	Don Raleigh, NYR, March 15	30.00	50.00
☐ 31	Wally Hergesheimer, NYR, March 22	30.00	50.00
☐ 32	Tod Campeau, Sherbrooke Saints, March 29	25.00	40.00
☐ 33	Guy Rousseau, Jr. Canadiens, April 5	20.00	30.00
1953 - 54 ISSUES			
☐ 34	Sherman White, Les Saguénéens, November 29	20.00	30.00
☐ 35	Claude Provost, Mtl., December 13	25.00	40.00
☐ 36	Gaetan Dessureault, Mtl., December 20	20.00	30.00
☐ 37	Del Topoll, Frontenac Que., December 27	20.00	30.00
☐ 38	Claude Pronovost, RHC, January 3	25.00	40.00
☐ 39	Herve Lalonde, Trois Rivières, January 10	20.00	30.00
☐ 40	Guy Rousseau, Frontenac Que., January 17	20.00	30.00
☐ 41	Jean Guy Gendron, Trois Rivières,January 24	25.00	40.00
☐ 42	Claude Dufour, Trois Rivières,January 31	20.00	30.00
☐ 43	Jacques Marcotte, Frontenac Que., February 7	20.00	30.00
☐ 44	Calum Mackay, Mtl., February 14	30.00	50.00

1952 ROYAL DESSERTS

The complete set of this issue features hockey, baseball and basketball players, soldiers, aeroplanes and movie stars. Cards were obtained by cutting the backs from Royal Desserts packages. Many of these cards, as a result, will have rough edges. An album with eight clear envelopes for displaying the cards could be obtained by mail from Royal Desserts.

Card Size: 2 5/8" x 3 1/4"
Face: Four colour, red border at top, white border at bottom; Name, Number, Resume, Facsimile autograph
Back: Blank
Imprint: None

		EX	NRMT
Royal Desserts Set (8 packages):		3,500.00	5,500.00
Album:			150.00

No.	Player	EX	NRMT
☐ 1	Tony Leswick, Det.	140.00	225.00
☐ 2	Chuck Rayner (G), NYR	300.00	500.00
☐ 3	Edgar Laprade, NYR	200.00	325.00
☐ 4	Sid Abel, Det.	335.00	550.00
☐ 5	Ted Lindsay, Det.	400.00	650.00
☐ 6	Leo Reise, Det.	140.00	225.00
☐ 7	Red Kelly, Det.	365.00	600.00
☐ 8	Gordie Howe, Det.	2,500.00	4,000.00

1952 - 53 ANONYMOUS OHL

Card Size: 2" x 3"
Face: Blue tint photo, white border
Back: Black on card stock; Name, Team, Position, Resume, Number
Imprint: None

		EX	NRMT
Complete Set (182 cards):		1,800.00	2,600.00
Common Player:		9.00	15.00

No.	Player	EX	NRMT
☐ 1	Dennis Riggin, Windsor	9.00	25.00
☐ 2	Joe Zorica, Windsor	9.00	15.00
☐ 3	Larry Hillman, Windsor	22.00	35.00
☐ 4	Edward Reid, Windsor	9.00	15.00
☐ 5	Al Arbour, Windsor	55.00	90.00
☐ 6	Marlin McAlendin, Windsor	9.00	15.00
☐ 7	Ross Graham, Windsor	9.00	15.00
☐ 8	Cumming Burton, Windsor	9.00	15.00
☐ 9	Ed Palamar, Windsor	9.00	15.00
☐ 10	Elmer Skov, Windsor	9.00	15.00
☐ 11	Eddie Louttit, Windsor	9.00	15.00
☐ 12	Gerry Price, Windsor	9.00	15.00
☐ 13	Lou Dietrich, Windsor	9.00	15.00
☐ 14	Gaston Marcotte, Windsor	9.00	15.00
☐ 15	Bob Brown, Windsor	9.00	15.00
☐ 16	Archie Burton, Windsor	9.00	15.00
☐ 17	Marven Edwards (G), St. Catharines	15.00	25.00
☐ 18	Norman Defelice (G), St. Catharines	13.00	22.00

☐ 19	Pete Kamula, St. Catharines	9.00	15.00
☐ 20	Charles Marshall, St. Catharines	9.00	15.00
☐ 21	Alex Leslie, St. Catharines	9.00	15.00
☐ 22	Minpy Roberts, St. Catharines	9.00	15.00
☐ 23	Danny Poliziani, St. Catharines	9.00	15.00
☐ 24	Allen Kellog, St. Catharines	9.00	15.00
☐ 25	Brian Cullen, St. Catharines	18.00	28.00
☐ 26	Ken Schinkel, St. Catharines	20.00	30.00
☐ 27	W. Hass, St. Catharines	9.00	15.00
☐ 28	Don Nash, St. Catharines	9.00	15.00
☐ 29	Robert Maxwell, St. Catharines	9.00	15.00
☐ 30	Eddie Mateka, St. Catharines	9.00	15.00
☐ 31	Joe Kastelic, St. Catharines	9.00	15.00
☐ 32	Hank Ciesla, St. Catharines	12.00	20.00
☐ 33	Hugh Barlow, St. Catharines	9.00	15.00
☐ 34	Claude Roy (G), St. Catharines	9.00	15.00
☐ 35	Jean-Guy Gamache, Trois-Rivières	9.00	15.00
☐ 36	Leon Michelin, Trois-Rivières	9.00	15.00
☐ 37	Gerard Bergeron, Trois-Rivières	9.00	15.00
☐ 38	Herve Lalonde, Trois-Rivières	9.00	15.00
☐ 39	J.M. Cossette, Trois-Rivières	9.00	15.00
☐ 40	Jean-Guy Gendron, Trois-Rivières	22.00	35.00
☐ 41	Camille Bedard, Trois-Rivières	9.00	15.00
☐ 42	Alfred Soucy, Trois-Rivières	9.00	15.00
☐ 43	Jean Leclerc, Trois-Rivières	9.00	15.00
☐ 44	Raymond St. Cyr, Trois-Rivières	9.00	15.00
☐ 45	Lester Lahaye, Trois-Rivières	9.00	15.00
☐ 46	Yvan Houle, Trois-Rivières	9.00	15.00
☐ 47	Louis Desrosiers, Trois-Rivières	9.00	15.00
☐ 48	Douglas Lessor, Guelph	9.00	15.00
☐ 49	Irvin Scott, Guelph	9.00	15.00
☐ 50	Danny Blair, Guelph	9.00	15.00
☐ 51	Jim Connelly, Guelph	9.00	15.00
☐ 52	William Chalmers, Guelph	9.00	15.00
☐ 53	Frank Bettiol, Guelph	9.00	15.00
☐ 54	James Holmes, Guelph	9.00	15.00
☐ 55	Birley Dimme, Guelph	9.00	15.00
☐ 56	Donald Beattie, Guelph	9.00	15.00
☐ 57	Terrance Chattington, Guelph	9.00	15.00
☐ 58	Bruce Wallace, Guelph	9.00	15.00
☐ 59	William McCreary, Guelph	15.00	25.00
☐ 60	Fred Brady, Guelph	9.00	15.00
☐ 61	Ronald Murphy, Guelph	22.00	35.00
☐ 62	Lavi Purola, Guelph	9.00	15.00
☐ 63	George Whyte, Guelph	9.00	15.00
☐ 64	Marcel Paille (G), Citadels	20.00	30.00
☐ 65	Maurice Collins, Citadels	9.00	15.00
☐ 66	Gerard Houle, Citadels	9.00	15.00
☐ 67	Gilles Laperrière, Citadels	9.00	15.00
☐ 68	Robert Chevalier, Citadels	9.00	15.00
☐ 69	Bertrand Lepage, Citadels	9.00	15.00
☐ 70	Michel Labadie, Citadels	9.00	15.00
☐ 71	Gabriel Alain, Citadels	9.00	15.00
☐ 72	Jean-Jacques Pichette, Citadels	9.00	15.00
☐ 73	Camille Henry, Citadels	28.00	45.00
☐ 74	Jean-Guy Gignac, Citadels	9.00	15.00
☐ 75	Leo Amadio, Citadels	9.00	15.00
☐ 76	Gilles Thibault, Citadels	9.00	15.00
☐ 77	Gaston Pelletier, Citadels	9.00	15.00
☐ 78	Adolph Kukulowicz, Citadels	9.00	15.00
☐ 79	Roland Leclerc, Citadels	9.00	15.00
☐ 80	Phil Watson, Citadels	25.00	40.00
☐ 81	Raymond Cyr, Citadels	9.00	15.00
☐ 82	Jacques Marcotte, Citadels	9.00	15.00
☐ 83	Floyd Hillman, Oshawa	9.00	15.00
☐ 84	Bob Attersley, Oshawa	9.00	15.00
☐ 85	Harry Sinden, Oshawa	50.00	75.00
☐ 86	Stan Parker, Err. (Owhaha), Oshawa	9.00	15.00
☐ 87	Bob Mader, Oshawa	9.00	15.00
☐ 88	Roger Maisonneuve, Oshawa	9.00	15.00
☐ 89	Phil Chapman, Oshawa	9.00	15.00
☐ 90	Don McIntosh, Oshawa	9.00	15.00
☐ 91	Jack Armstrong, Oshawa	9.00	15.00
☐ 92	Carlo Montemurro, Oshawa	9.00	15.00
☐ 93	Ken Courtney (G), Oshawa	9.00	15.00
☐ 94	Bill Stewart, Oshawa	9.00	15.00
☐ 95	Gerald Casey, Oshawa	9.00	15.00
☐ 96	Fred Etcher, Oshawa	9.00	15.00
☐ 97	Orrin Carver, Barrie	9.00	15.00
☐ 98	Ralph Willis, Barrie	9.00	15.00
☐ 99	Kenneth Robertson, Barrie	9.00	15.00
☐ 100	Don Cherry, Barrie	170.00	275.00
☐ 101	Fred Pletsch, Barrie	9.00	15.00
☐ 102	Larry Thibault, Barrie	9.00	15.00
☐ 103	James Robertson, Barrie	9.00	15.00
☐ 104	Orval Tessier, Barrie	13.00	22.00
☐ 105	Jack Higgins, Barrie	9.00	15.00
☐ 106	Robert White, Barrie	9.00	15.00
☐ 107	Doug Mohns, Barrie	35.00	55.00
☐ 108	William Sexton, Barrie	9.00	15.00
☐ 109	John Martan, Barrie	9.00	15.00
☐ 110	Tony Poeta, Barrie	9.00	15.00
☐ 111	Don McKenney, Barrie	25.00	40.00
☐ 112	Bill Harrington, Barrie	9.00	15.00
☐ 113	Allen Peal, Barrie	9.00	15.00
☐ 114	John Ford, Kitchener	9.00	15.00
☐ 115	Ken Collins, Kitchener	9.00	15.00
☐ 116	Marc Boileau, Kitchener	9.00	15.00
☐ 117	Doug Vaughan, Kitchener	9.00	15.00
☐ 118	Gilles Boisvert, Kitchener	9.00	15.00
☐ 119	Buddy Horne, Kitchener	9.00	15.00
☐ 120	Graham Joyce, Kitchener	9.00	15.00
☐ 121	Gary Collins, Kitchener	9.00	15.00
☐ 122	Roy Greenan, Kitchener	9.00	15.00
☐ 123	Beryl Klynck, Kitchener	9.00	15.00
☐ 124	Grieg Hicks, Kitchener	9.00	15.00
☐ 125	Jack Novak, Kitchener	9.00	15.00
☐ 126	Ken Tennant, Kitchener	9.00	15.00
☐ 127	Glen Cressman, Kitchener	9.00	15.00
☐ 128	Curly Davies, Coach / Manager, Kitchener	9.00	15.00
☐ 129	Charlie Hodge (G), Canadien Jr.	50.00	75.00
☐ 130	Bob McCord, Canadien Jr.	13.00	22.00
☐ 131	Gordie Hollingworth, Canadien Jr.	9.00	15.00
☐ 132	Ronald Pilon, Canadien Jr.	9.00	15.00
☐ 133	Brian MacKay, Canadien Jr.	9.00	15.00
☐ 134	Yvon Chasle, Canadien Jr.	9.00	15.00
☐ 135	Denis Boucher, Canadien Jr.	12.00	20.00
☐ 136	Claude Boileau, Canadien Jr.	9.00	15.00
☐ 137	Claude Vinet, Canadien Jr.	9.00	15.00
☐ 138	Claude Provost, Canadien Jr.	35.00	55.00
☐ 139	Henri Richard, Canadien Jr.	190.00	300.00
☐ 140	Les Lilley, Canadien Jr.	9.00	15.00
☐ 141	Phil Goyette, Canadien Jr.	28.00	45.00
☐ 142	Guy Rousseau, Canadien Jr.	9.00	15.00
☐ 143	Paul Knox, St. Michael's	9.00	15.00
☐ 144	Bill Lee, St. Michael's	9.00	15.00
☐ 145	Ted Topazzini, St. Michael's	9.00	15.00
☐ 146	Marc Reaume, St. Michael's	13.00	22.00
☐ 147	Bill Dineen, St. Michael's	22.00	35.00
☐ 148	Ed Plata, St. Michael's	9.00	15.00
☐ 149	Noel Price, St. Michael's	18.00	28.00
☐ 150	Mike Ratchford, St. Michael's	9.00	15.00
☐ 151	Jim Logan, St. Michael's	9.00	15.00
☐ 152	Art Clune, St. Michael's	9.00	15.00
☐ 153	Jerry MacNamara, St. Michael's	12.00	20.00
☐ 154	Jack Caffery, St. Michael's	13.00	22.00
☐ 155	Less Duff, St. Michael's	9.00	15.00
☐ 156	Murray Costello, St. Michael's	12.00	20.00
☐ 157	Ed. Chadwick (G), St. Michael's	30.00	50.00
☐ 158	Mike Desilets, Royal	9.00	15.00
☐ 159	Ross Watson, Royal	9.00	15.00
☐ 160	Roger Landry, Royal	9.00	15.00
☐ 161	Terry O'Connor, Royal	9.00	15.00
☐ 162	Ovila Gagnon, Royal	9.00	15.00
☐ 163	Dave Broadbelt, Royal	9.00	15.00
☐ 164	Sandy Monrisson, Royal	9.00	15.00
☐ 165	John MacGillvray, Royal	9.00	15.00
☐ 166	Claude Beaupre, Royal	9.00	15.00
☐ 167	Eddie Eustache, Royal	9.00	15.00
☐ 168	Stan Rodek, Royal	9.00	15.00
☐ 169	Maurice Mantha, Galt	9.00	15.00
☐ 170	Hector Lalonde, Galt	9.00	15.00
☐ 171	Bob Wilson, Galt	9.00	15.00
☐ 172	Frank Bonello, Galt	9.00	15.00
☐ 173	Peter Kowalchuck, Galt	9.00	15.00
☐ 174	Les Binkley (G), Galt	22.00	35.00
☐ 175	John Muckler, Galt	30.00	50.00
☐ 176	Ken Wharram, Galt	28.00	45.00
☐ 177	John Sleaver, Galt	9.00	15.00
☐ 178	Ralph Markarian, Galt	9.00	15.00
☐ 179	Ken McMeekin, Galt	9.00	15.00
☐ 180	Ron Boomer, Galt	9.00	15.00
☐ 181	Kenneth Crawford, Galt	9.00	15.00
☐ 182	Jim McBurney, Galt	9.00	25.00

1952 - 53 BAS DU FLEUVE

Imprint:

Complete Set (65 cards):	**325.00**	**700.00**
Common Player:	**6.00**	**15.00**

No.	Player	EX	NRMT
☐ 1	Roger Gagner	8.00	22.00
☐ 2	Martial Pruneau	6.00	15.00
☐ 3	Fernand Gladu	6.00	15.00
☐ 4	Joseph Lacoursière	6.00	15.00
☐ 5	Maurice Lamirande	6.00	15.00
☐ 6	Denis Smith	6.00	15.00
☐ 7	Real Jacques	6.00	15.00
☐ 8	Roland Landry	6.00	15.00
☐ 9	Dan Janelle	6.00	15.00
☐ 10	Pete Gaudette	6.00	15.00
☐ 11	Normand Bellavance	6.00	15.00
☐ 12	Roger Hayfield	6.00	15.00
☐ 13	Bill Leblanc	6.00	15.00
☐ 14	Victor Corbin	6.00	15.00
☐ 15	Gerard Lachance	6.00	15.00
☐ 16	Guy Labrie	6.00	15.00
☐ 17	Denis Brodeur	18.00	40.00
☐ 18	Gerard Paquin	6.00	15.00
☐ 19	Irene St. Hilaire	6.00	15.00
☐ 20	Guy Gervais	6.00	15.00
☐ 21	Marcel Benoît	6.00	15.00
☐ 22	Roger Dumas	6.00	15.00
☐ 23	Gaston Gervais	6.00	15.00
☐ 24	Maurice St. Jean	6.00	15.00
☐ 25	Frank Pearce	6.00	15.00
☐ 26	Fernand Bernaquez	6.00	15.00
☐ 27	Henri-Paul Gagnon	6.00	15.00
☐ 28	Jean-Jacques Pichette	6.00	15.00
☐ 29	Jim Hayes	6.00	15.00
☐ 30	Fernand Rancourt	6.00	15.00
☐ 31	Nils Tremblay	6.00	15.00
☐ 32	Clement Tremblay	6.00	15.00
☐ 33	Jacques Lalancette	6.00	15.00
☐ 34	Marcel Fillion	6.00	15.00
☐ 35	Jacques Monette	6.00	15.00
☐ 36	Frank Côté	6.00	15.00
☐ 37	Bernie Lemonde	6.00	15.00
☐ 38	Guildor Lévesque	6.00	15.00
☐ 39	Hector Legris	6.00	15.00
☐ 40	Jacques Gagnon	6.00	15.00
☐ 41	Donat Deschesnes	6.00	15.00
☐ 42	Bertrand LePage	6.00	15.00
☐ 43	Paul Lavoie	6.00	15.00
☐ 44	Denis Fillion	6.00	15.00
☐ 45	Floyd Crawford	6.00	15.00
☐ 46	Paul Duchesne	6.00	15.00
☐ 47	Rene Pronovost	6.00	15.00
☐ 48	Roger Jodoin	6.00	15.00
☐ 49	Mario Senecal	6.00	15.00
☐ 50	Garry Plamondon	10.00	22.00
☐ 51	Marcel Paille	18.00	40.00
☐ 52	Rene Pepin	6.00	15.00
☐ 53	Gilles Desrosiers	6.00	15.00
☐ 54	Edgard Gendron	6.00	15.00
☐ 55	Ronald Limoges	6.00	15.00
☐ 56	Roland Bilodeau	6.00	15.00
☐ 57	Leon Bouchard	6.00	15.00
☐ 58	Bob Leger	6.00	15.00
☐ 59	Conrad L'Heureux	6.00	15.00
☐ 60	Raymond Leduc	6.00	15.00
☐ 61	Bob Brault	6.00	15.00
☐ 62	Roger Ste. Marie	6.00	15.00
☐ 63	Real Lafreniere	6.00	15.00
☐ 64	Lucien Gilbert	6.00	15.00
☐ 65	Louis Desrosiers	7.00	20.00

1952 - 53 LAVAL DAIRY QHL UPDATE

These cards are believed to have been issued during the 1952-53 season as a subset to include new players and trades that took place between the teams. Short prints are marked with an asterisk(∗).

Card Size: 1 3/4" x 2 1/2"
Face: Black and white photo, white border; Name, Resume, Number, French
Back: Blank
Imprint: None

		EX	NRMT
Complete Set (66 cards):		**550.00**	**1,200.00**
Common Player:		**7.00**	**16.00**
No.	**Player**	**EX**	**NRMT**
☐ 4	Jack Gelineau, As de Québec (*)	12.00	30.00
☐ 7	Al Miller, As de Québec	7.00	16.00
☐ 8	Walter Pawlyshyn, As de Québec	7.00	16.00
☐ 9	Yogi Kraiger, As de Québec (*)	12.00	30.00
☐ 10	Al Baccari, As de Québec	7.00	16.00
☐ 12	Denis Smith, As de Québec	7.00	16.00
☐ 13	Pierre Brillant, As de Québec	7.00	16.00
☐ 14	Frank Mario, As de Québec	7.00	16.00
☐ 15	Danny Nixon, As de Québec	7.00	16.00
☐ 25	Leon Bouchard, As de Québec	7.00	16.00
☐ 26	Pete Taillefer, Chicoutimi	7.00	16.00
☐ 29	Bucky Buchanen, Chicoutimi	7.00	16.00
☐ 36	Marius Groleau, Chicoutimi	7.00	16.00
☐ 38	Fernand Perreault, Chicoutimi	7.00	16.00
☐ 39	Robert Drainville, Sherbrooke	7.00	16.00
☐ 40	Ronnie Matthews, Sherbrooke	7.00	16.00
☐ 44	Roger Roberge, Sherbrooke	7.00	16.00
☐ 46	Pete Wywrot, Sherbrooke	7.00	16.00
☐ 50	Gilles Dubé, Sherbrooke	7.00	16.00
☐ 51	Nils Tremblay, Sherbrooke (*)	12.00	30.00
☐ 52	Bob Pepin, Sherbrooke	7.00	16.00
☐ 53	Dewar Thompson, Sherbrooke	7.00	16.00
☐ 55	Irene St. Hilaire, Sherbrooke	7.00	16.00
☐ 56	Martial Pruneau, Sherbrooke	7.00	16.00
☐ 57	Jacques Locas, Sherbrooke	7.00	16.00
☐ 59	Nelson Podolsky, Shawinigan-Falls	7.00	16.00
☐ 60	Bert Giesebrecht, Shawinigan-Falls	7.00	16.00
☐ 61	Steve Brklacich, Shawinigan-Falls	7.00	16.00
☐ 65	Jack Hamilton, Shawinigan-Falls	7.00	16.00
☐ 66	Dave Gatherum, Shawinigan-Falls	7.00	16.00
☐ 67	Jean-Marie Plante, Shawinigan-Falls	7.00	16.00
☐ 68	Gordie Haworth, Valleyfield	7.00	16.00
☐ 69	Jack Schmidt, Valleyfield (*)	12.00	30.00
☐ 70	Bruce Cline, Valleyfield	10.00	22.00
☐ 72	Phil Vitale, Valleyfield	7.00	16.00
☐ 81	Carl Smelle, Valleyfield	7.00	16.00
☐ 84	Tom Smelle, Valleyfield	7.00	16.00
☐ 85	Gerry Plamondon, Royals	7.00	22.00
☐ 86	Glen Harmon, Royals	11.00	25.00
☐ 89	Frank Bathgate, Shawinigan-Falls	7.00	16.00
☐ 90	Bernie Lemonde, Shawinigan-Falls	7.00	16.00
☐ 92	Jacques Plante (G), Royals	225.00	500.00
☐ 93	Gerard Desaulniers, Royals	7.00	16.00
☐ 94	Jean-Claude. Lebrun, Shawinigan-Falls	7.00	16.00
☐ 95	Bob Leger, Shawinigan-Falls	7.00	22.00
☐ 96	Walter Clune, Royals	7.00	16.00
☐ 97	Louis Denis, Royals	7.00	16.00
☐ 98	Jackie Leclair, Ottawa	11.00	25.00
☐ 99	John Arundel, Ottawa	7.00	16.00
☐ 100	Leslie Douglas, Ottawa	7.00	16.00
☐ 103	Bobby Robertson, Ottawa	7.00	16.00
☐ 104	Ray Fredericks (G), Ottawa	7.00	16.00
☐ 106	Emil Dagenais, Ottawa	7.00	16.00
☐ 108	Al Kuntz, Ottawa	7.00	16.00
☐ 110	Red Johnson, Ottawa	7.00	16.00
☐ 111	John O'Flaherty, Ottawa	7.00	16.00
☐ 112	Jack Giesebrecht, Ottawa	7.00	16.00
☐ 113	Bill Richardson, Ottawa	7.00	16.00
☐ 114	Bep Guidolin, Ottawa	15.00	35.00
☐ 115	Roger Bedard, Shawinigan	7.00	16.00
☐ 116	Renald Lacroix, Valleyfield	7.00	16.00
☐ 117	Gordie Hudson, Québec	7.00	16.00
☐ 118	Dick Wray, Shawinigan	7.00	16.00
☐ 119	Ronnie Hurst, Ottawa	10.00	22.00
☐ 120	Eddie Joss, Shawinigan	7.00	16.00
☐ 121	Lyall Wiseman, Québec	7.00	25.00

1952 - 53 PARKHURST

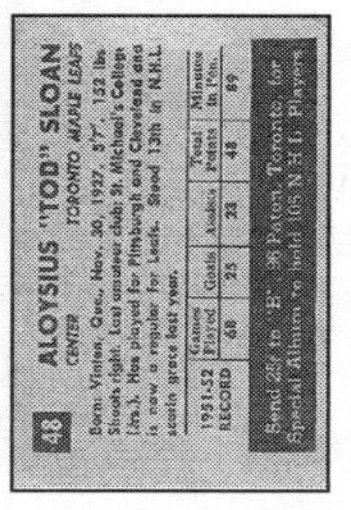

This set is almost impossible to find in the high grade. Mint cards do command a premium. As with the first year of issue this set does not age well and centering is a problem.

Card Size: 1 15/16" x 2 15/16"
Face: Four colour, white border, Signature
Back: Black on card stock, Number
Imprint: None

		EX	NRMT
Complete Set (105 cards):		**5,000.00**	**8,500.00**
Common Player:		**25.00**	**40.00**
Album:		**60.00**	**120.00**
No.	**Player**	**EX**	**NRMT**
☐ 1	Maurice Richard, Mtl.	850.00	1,700.00
☐ 2	Billy Reay, Mtl., LC	25.00	40.00
☐ 3	Bernie Geoffrion, Mtl., Err. (Gioffrion)	150.00	250.00
☐ 4	Paul Meger, Mtl.	25.00	40.00
☐ 5	Dick Gamble, Mtl.	25.00	40.00
☐ 6	Elmer Lach, Mtl.	60.00	95.00
☐ 7	Floyd Curry, Mtl.	25.00	40.00
☐ 8	Kenny Mosdell, Mtl.	25.00	40.00
☐ 9	Tom Johnson, Mtl.	35.00	60.00
☐ **10**	**Dickie Moore, Mtl, RC**	**190.00**	**300.00**
☐ 11	Bud MacPherson, Mtl.	25.00	40.00
☐ 12	Gerry McNeil (G), Mtl.	60.00	95.00
☐ 13	Emile (Butch) Bouchard, Mtl.	35.00	55.00
☐ 14	Doug Harvey, Mtl.	135.00	225.00
☐ **15**	**John McCormack, Mtl., RC**	**25.00**	**40.00**
☐ 16	Pete Babando, Chi., LC	25.00	40.00
☐ 17	Al Dewsbury, Chi.	25.00	40.00
☐ 18	Eddie Kullman, NYR.	25.00	40.00
☐ 19	Eddie Slowinski, NYR.	25.00	40.00
☐ 20	Wally Hergesheimer, NYR.	25.00	40.00
☐ 21	Allan Stanley, NYR.	55.00	90.00
☐ 22	Chuck Rayner (G), NYR.	40.00	65.00
☐ 23	Stephen Kraftcheck, NYR.	25.00	40.00
☐ 24	Paul Ronty, NYR.	25.00	40.00
☐ 25	Gaye Stewart, NYR., LC	25.00	40.00
☐ 26	Fred Hucul, Chi.	25.00	40.00
☐ 27	Bill Mosienko, Chi.	35.00	60.00
☐ **28**	**Jim Morrison, Tor., RC**	**25.00**	**40.00**
☐ 29	Ed. Kryznowski, Chi., LC, Err. (Krysanowski)	25.00	40.00
☐ 30	Cal Gardner, Chi.	25.00	40.00
☐ 31	Al Rollins (G), Chi.	40.00	65.00
☐ **32**	**Enio Sclisizzi , Chi., RC, LC**	**25.00**	**40.00**
☐ **33**	**Pete Conacher, Chi., RC**	**25.00**	**40.00**
☐ **34**	**Leo Boivin, Tor., RC**	**50.00**	**80.00**
☐ 35	Jim Peters, Chi.	25.00	40.00
☐ 36	George Gee, Chi.	25.00	40.00
☐ 37	Gus Bodnar, Chi.	25.00	40.00
☐ 38	Jim McFadden, Chi.	25.00	40.00
☐ 39	Gus Mortson, Chi.	25.00	40.00
☐ 40	Fred Glover, Chi., LC	25.00	40.00
☐ 41	Gerry Couture, Chi.	25.00	40.00
☐ 42	Howie Meeker, Tor., LC	50.00	75.00
☐ 43	Jim Thomson, Tor.	25.00	40.00
☐ 44	Ted Kennedy, Tor.	60.00	100.00
☐ 45	Sid Smith, Tor.	30.00	50.00
☐ 46	Harry Watson, Tor.	35.00	55.00
☐ 47	Fern Flaman, Tor.	35.00	55.00
☐ 48	Tod Sloan, Tor.	25.00	40.00
☐ 49	Leo Reise, NYR.	25.00	40.00
☐ 50	Bob Solinger, Tor.	25.00	40.00
☐ **51**	**George Armstrong, Tor., RC**	**135.00**	**225.00**
☐ **52**	**Dollard St. Laurent, Mtl., RC**	**25.00**	**40.00**
☐ 53	Alex Delvecchio, Det.	90.00	150.00
☐ **54**	**Gordon Hannigan, Tor., RC**	**25.00**	**40.00**
☐ 55	Lidio Fogolin, Chi.	25.00	40.00
☐ 56	Bill Gadsby, Chi.	35.00	60.00
☐ **57**	**Herb Dickenson, NYR., RC, LC**	**25.00**	**40.00**
☐ **58**	**Tim Horton, Tor., RC**	**500.00**	**825.00**
☐ 59	Harry Lumley (G), Tor.	50.00	80.00
☐ 60	Metro Prystai, Det.	25.00	40.00
☐ 61	Marcel Pronovost, Det.	35.00	55.00
☐ 62	Benny Woit, Det.	25.00	40.00
☐ 63	Glen Skov, Det.	25.00	40.00
☐ 64	Bob Goldham, Det.	30.00	50.00
☐ 65	Tony Leswick, Det.	25.00	40.00
☐ 66	Marty Pavelich, Det.	25.00	40.00
☐ 67	Red Kelly, Det.	100.00	160.00
☐ 68	Bill Quackenbush, Bos.	35.00	55.00
☐ 69	Ed Sandford, Bos.	25.00	40.00
☐ 70	Milt Schmidt, Bos.	50.00	80.00
☐ 71	Hal Laycoe, Bos.	25.00	40.00
☐ 72	Woody Dumart, Bos.	35.00	55.00
☐ **73**	**Zellio Toppazzini, Bos., RC, LC**	**25.00**	**40.00**
☐ 74	Jim Henry (G), Bos.	35.00	60.00
☐ 75	Joe Klukay, Bos.	25.00	40.00
☐ **76**	**Dave Creighton, Bos., RC**	**30.00**	**50.00**
☐ **77**	**Jack McIntyre, Bos., RC**	**25.00**	**40.00**
☐ 78	Johnny Peirson, Bos.	25.00	40.00
☐ 79	George Sullivan, Bos.	25.00	40.00
☐ **80**	**Real Chevrefils, Bos., RC**	**25.00**	**40.00**
☐ **81**	**Léo Labine, Bos., RC**	**25.00**	**40.00**
☐ 82	Fleming Mackell, Bos.	25.00	40.00
☐ 83	Pentti Lund, Bos. LC	25.00	40.00
☐ **84**	**Bob Armstrong, Bos., RC**	**25.00**	**40.00**
☐ **85**	**Warren Godfrey, Bos., RC**	**25.00**	**40.00**
☐ 86	Terry Sawchuk (G), Det.	375.00	625.00
☐ 87	Ted Lindsay, Det.	100.00	160.00
☐ 88	Gordie Howe, Det.	800.00	1,300.00
☐ **89**	**Johnny Wilson, Det., RC**	**25.00**	**40.00**
☐ 90	Vic Stasiuk, Det.	30.00	50.00
☐ **91**	**Larry Zeidel, Det., RC**	**25.00**	**40.00**
☐ **92**	**Larry Wilson, Det., RC**	**25.00**	**40.00**
☐ 93	Bert Olmstead, Mtl.	35.00	60.00
☐ **94**	**Ron Stewart, Tor., RC**	**35.00**	**55.00**
☐ 95	Max Bentley, Tor.	35.00	55.00
☐ **96**	**Rudy Migay, Tor., RC**	**25.00**	**40.00**
☐ **97**	**Jack Stoddard, NYR., RC**	**25.00**	**40.00**
☐ 98	Hyman Buller, NYR.	25.00	40.00
☐ 99	Don Raleigh, NYR.	25.00	40.00
☐ 100	Edgar Laprade, NYR.	35.00	55.00
☐ 101	Nick Mickoski, NYR.	25.00	40.00
☐ 102	Jackie McLeod, NYR., LC	25.00	40.00
☐ 103	Jim Conacher, NYR., LC	25.00	40.00
☐ 104	Reg Sinclair, Det., LC	25.00	40.00
☐ **105**	**Bob Hassard, Tor., RC**	**50.00**	**100.00**

1952 - 53 ST. LAWRENCE SALES

Card Size: 1 3/4" x 2 3/4"
Face: Black and white photo, borderless
Back: Black on card stock; Name, Number, Resume, French
Imprint: None

		EX	NRMT
Complete Set (107 cards):		**1,000.00**	**1,600.00**
Common Player:		**9.00**	**15.00**
No.	**Player**	**EX**	**NRMT**
☐ 1	Jacques Plante (G), Royals	150.00	325.00
☐ 2	Glenn Harmon, Royals	9.00	25.00
☐ 3	Jimmy Moore, Royals	9.00	15.00
☐ 4	Gerry Desaulniers, Royals	9.00	15.00
☐ 5	Les Douglas, Royals	12.00	20.00
☐ 6	Fred Burchell, Royals	9.00	15.00
☐ 7	Eddie Litzenberger, Royals	28.00	45.00
☐ 8	Rollie Rousseau, Royals	9.00	15.00
☐ 9	Roger Leger, Royals	9.00	15.00
☐ 10	Phil Samis, Royals	9.00	15.00
☐ 11	Paul Masnick, Royals	9.00	15.00
☐ 12	Walter Clune, Royals	9.00	15.00
☐ 13	Louis Denis, Royals	9.00	15.00
☐ 14	Gerry Plamondon, Royals	12.00	20.00
☐ 15	Cliff Malone, Royals	9.00	15.00

☐ 16	Pete Morin, Royals	9.00	15.00
☐ 17	Jackie Schmidt, Valleyfield	11.00	18.00
☐ 17	Aldo Guidolin, Valleyfield	15.00	25.00
☐ 18	Paul Leclerc, Valleyfield	9.00	15.00
☐ 19	Larry Kwong, Valleyfield	9.00	15.00
☐ 20	Rosario Joanette, Valleyfield	9.00	15.00
☐ 21	Tom Smelle, Valleyfield	9.00	15.00
☐ 22	Gordie Haworth, Valleyfield	9.00	15.00
☐ 23	Bruce Cline, Valleyfield	9.00	15.00
☐ 24	Andre Corriveau, Valleyfield	9.00	15.00
☐ 25	Jacques Deslauriers, Valleyfield	9.00	15.00
☐ 26	Bingo Ernst, Valleyfield	9.00	15.00
☐ 27	Jacques Chartrand, Valleyfield	9.00	15.00
☐ 28	Phil Vitale, Valleyfield	9.00	15.00
☐ 29	Renald Lacroix, Valleyfield	9.00	15.00
☐ 30	J.P. Bisaillon, Valleyfield	9.00	15.00
☐ 31	Jack Irvine, Valleyfield	9.00	15.00
☐ 32	Georges Bougie, Valleyfield	9.00	15.00
☐ 33	Paul Larivee, Valleyfield	9.00	15.00
☐ 34	Carl Smelle, Valleyfield	9.00	15.00
☐ 35	Walter Pawlyschyn, Québec	9.00	15.00
☐ 36	Jean Marois, Québec	9.00	15.00
☐ 37	Jack Gelineau, Québec	9.00	15.00
☐ 38	Danny Nixon, Québec	9.00	15.00
☐ 39	Jean Béliveau, Québec	170.00	275.00
☐ 40	Phil Renaud, Québec	9.00	15.00
☐ 41	Leon Bouchard, Québec	9.00	15.00
☐ 42	Dennis Smith, Québec	9.00	15.00
☐ 43	Jos Crozier, Québec	12.00	20.00
☐ 44	Al Bacari, Québec	9.00	15.00
☐ 45	Murdo MacKay, Québec	9.00	15.00
☐ 46	Gordie Hudson, Québec	9.00	15.00
☐ 47	Claude Robert, Québec	9.00	15.00
☐ 48	Yogi Kraiger, Québec	9.00	15.00
☐ 49	Ludger Tremblay, Québec	9.00	15.00
☐ 50	Pierre Brillant, Québec	9.00	15.00
☐ 51	Frank Mario, Québec	9.00	15.00
☐ 52	Cooper Leyth, Québec	9.00	15.00
☐ 53	Herbie Carnegie, Québec	12.00	20.00
☐ 54	Punch Imlach, Québec	40.00	65.00
☐ 55	Howard Riopelle, Ottawa	9.00	15.00
☐ 56	Ken Laufman, Ottawa	9.00	15.00
☐ 57	Jackie Leclair, Ottawa	15.00	25.00
☐ 58	Bill Robinson, Ottawa	9.00	15.00
☐ 59	George Ford, Ottawa	9.00	15.00
☐ 60	Bill Johnson, Ottawa	9.00	15.00
☐ 61	Leo Gravelle, Ottawa	9.00	15.00
☐ 62	Jack Giesbrecht, Ottawa	9.00	15.00
☐ 63	John Arundel, Ottawa	9.00	15.00
☐ 64	Vic Gregg, Ottawa	9.00	15.00
☐ 65	Bep Guidolin, Ottawa	15.00	25.00
☐ 66	Al Kuntz, Ottawa	9.00	15.00
☐ 67	Emile Dagenais, Ottawa	9.00	15.00
☐ 68	Bill Richardson, Ottawa	9.00	15.00
☐ 69	Bob Robertson, Ottawa	9.00	15.00
☐ 70	Ray Fredericks, Ottawa	9.00	15.00
☐ 71	James O'Flaherty, Ottawa	9.00	15.00
☐ 72	Butch Stahan, Ottawa	9.00	15.00
☐ 73	Roger Roberge, Sherbrooke	9.00	15.00
☐ 74	Guy Labrie, Sherbrooke	9.00	15.00
☐ 75	Gilles Dubé, Sherbrooke	9.00	15.00
☐ 76	Pete Wywrot, Sherbrooke	9.00	15.00
☐ 77	Tod Campeau, Sherbrooke	12.00	20.00
☐ 78	Roger Bessette, Sherbrooke	9.00	15.00
☐ 79	Martial Pruneau, Sherbrooke	9.00	15.00
☐ 80	Nils Tremblay, Sherbrooke	9.00	15.00
☐ 81	Jacques Locas, Sherbrooke	9.00	15.00
☐ 82	René Pépin, Sherbrooke	9.00	15.00
☐ 83	Bob Pepin, Sherbrooke	9.00	15.00
☐ 84	Tom McDougal, Sherbrooke	9.00	15.00
☐ 85	Pete Wright, Sherbrooke	9.00	15.00
☐ 86	Ronnie Mathews, Sherbrooke	9.00	15.00
☐ 87	Irene St. Hilaire, Sherbrooke	9.00	15.00
☐ 88	Dewar Thompson, Sherbrooke	9.00	15.00
☐ 89	Bob Dainville, Sherbrooke	9.00	15.00
☐ 90	Marcel Pelletier, Chicoutimi	9.00	15.00
☐ 91	Delphis Franche, Chicoutimi	9.00	15.00
☐ 92	Georges Roy, Chicoutimi	9.00	15.00
☐ 93	Andy McCallum, Chicoutimi	9.00	15.00
☐ 94	Lou Smrke, Chicoutimi	9.00	15.00
☐ 95	J.P. Lamirande, Chicoutimi	9.00	15.00
☐ 96	Normand Dussault, Chicoutimi	9.00	15.00
☐ 97	Stan Smrke, Chicoutimi	12.00	20.00
☐ 98	Jack Bownass, Chicoutimi	12.00	20.00
☐ 99	Billy Arcand, Shawinigan-Falls	9.00	15.00
☐ 100	Lyall Wiseman, Shawinigan-Falls	9.00	15.00
☐ 101	Jack Hamilton, Shawinigan-Falls	9.00	15.00
☐ 102	Bob Leger, Shawinigan-Falls	9.00	15.00
☐ 103	Larry Regan, Shawinigan-Falls	20.00	30.00
☐ 104	Erwin Grosse, Shawinigan-Falls	9.00	15.00
☐ 105	Roger Bedard, Shawinigan-Falls	9.00	15.00
☐ 106	Ted Hodgson, Shawinigan-Falls	9.00	15.00
☐ 107	Dave Gatherum, Shawinigan-Falls	9.00	25.00

1953 - 54 PARKHURST

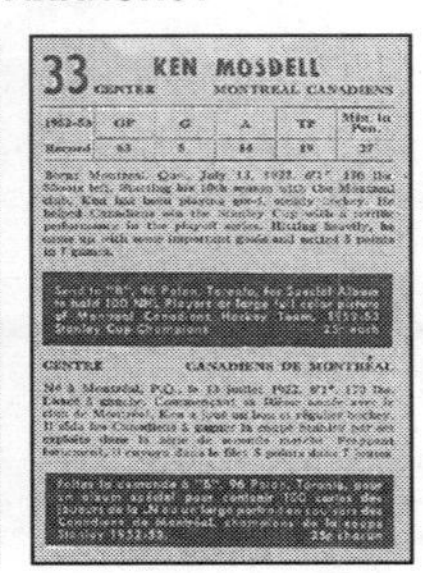

The card stock used for this set ages very poorly, the white face portion turning an uneven light brown across the card face. Beware of cards that do not have this discolouration. It would be unnatural for it not to appear. Parkies NHL Hockey Albums were available for this set.

Mint condition cards do command a premium.

Card Size: 2 1/2" x 3 5/8"
Face: Four colour, white border
Back: Black on card stock, Number, Resume, Bilingual
Imprint: Printed In Canada

Complete Set (100 cards):	**3,500.00**	**5,800.00**
Common Player:	**20.00**	**30.00**
Album:	**50.00**	**100.00**

No.	Player	EX	NRMT
☐ 1	Harry Lumley (G), Tor.	150.00	300.00
☐ 2	Sid Smith, Tor.	25.00	40.00
☐ 3	Gord Hannigan, Tor.	20.00	30.00
☐ 4	Bob Hassard, Tor., LC	20.00	30.00
☐ 5	Tod Sloan, Tor.	20.00	30.00
☐ 6	Leo Boivin, Tor.	28.00	45.00
☐ 7	Ted Kennedy, Tor.	50.00	75.00
☐ 8	Jim Thomson, Tor.	20.00	30.00
☐ 9	Ron Stewart, Tor.	20.00	30.00
☐ **10**	**Eric Nesterenko , Tor., RC**	**28.00**	**45.00**
☐ 11	George Armstrong, Tor.	75.00	120.00
☐ 12	Harry Watson, Tor.	25.00	40.00
☐ 13	Tim Horton, Tor.	225.00	350.00
☐ 14	Fern Flaman, Tor.	28.00	45.00
☐ 15	Jim Morrison, Tor.	20.00	30.00
☐ 16	Bob Solinger, Tor., LC	20.00	30.00
☐ 17	Rudy Migay, Tor.	20.00	30.00
☐ 18	Dick Gamble, Mtl.	20.00	30.00
☐ 19	Bert Olmstead, Mtl.	28.00	45.00
☐ **20**	**Eddie Mazur, Mtl., RC**	**20.00**	**30.00**
☐ 21	Paul Meger, Mtl.	20.00	30.00
☐ 22	Bud MacPherson, Mtl.	20.00	30.00
☐ 23	Dollard St. Laurent, Mtl.	20.00	30.00
☐ 24	Maurice Richard, Mtl.	360.00	600.00
☐ 25	Gerry McNeil (G), Mtl.	45.00	70.00
☐ 26	Doug Harvey, Mtl.	110.00	170.00
☐ **27**	**Jean Béliveau, Mtl., RC**	**550.00**	**900.00**
☐ 28	Dickie Moore, Mtl.	85.00	140.00
☐ 29	Bernie Geoffrion, Mtl.	110.00	175.00
☐ 30	Lach & Richard, Mtl.	150.00	250.00
☐ 31	Elmer Lach, Mtl., LC	35.00	60.00
☐ 32	Emile (Butch) Bouchard, Mtl.	28.00	45.00
☐ 33	Kenny Mosdell, Mtl.	20.00	30.00
☐ 34	John McCormack, Mtl.	20.00	30.00
☐ 35	Floyd Curry, Mtl.	20.00	30.00
☐ **36**	**Earl Reibel, Mtl., RC, Det.**	**20.00**	**30.00**
☐ 37	Al Arbour, Mtl., Err (Bill Dineen)	35.00	60.00
☐ 38	Bill Dineen, Mtl., Err. (Al Arbour)	65.00	110.00
☐ 39	Vic Stasiuk, Mtl.	25.00	40.00
☐ 40	Red Kelly, Mtl.	60.00	100.00
☐ 41	Marcel Pronovost, Mtl.	28.00	45.00
☐ 42	Metro Prystai, Mtl.	20.00	30.00
☐ 43	Tony Leswick, Mtl.	20.00	30.00
☐ 44	Marty Pavelich, Mtl.	20.00	30.00
☐ 45	Benny Woit, Mtl.	20.00	30.00
☐ 46	Terry Sawchuk (G), Mtl.	240.00	400.00
☐ 47	Alex Delvecchio, Mtl.	60.00	100.00
☐ 48	Glen Skov, Mtl.	20.00	30.00
☐ 49	Bob Goldham, Mtl.	25.00	40.00
☐ 50	Gordie Howe, Mtl.	465.00	750.00
☐ 51	Johnny Wilson, Mtl.	20.00	30.00
☐ 52	Ted Lindsay, Mtl.	60.00	100.00
☐ **53**	**Gump Worsley (G), NYR., RC**	**285.00**	**450.00**
☐ 54	Jack Evans, NYR.	20.00	30.00
☐ 55	Max Bentley, NYR., LC	28.00	45.00
☐ **56**	**Andy Bathgate, NYR., RC**	**90.00**	**150.00**
☐ **57**	**Harry Howell, NYR., RC**	**90.00**	**150.00**
☐ 58	Hyman Buller, NYR., LC	20.00	30.00
☐ 59	Chuck Rayner (G), NYR., LC	30.00	50.00
☐ 60	Jack Stoddard, NYR., LC	20.00	30.00
☐ 61	Eddie Kullman, NYR., LC	20.00	30.00
☐ 62	Nick Mickoski, NYR.	20.00	30.00
☐ 63	Paul Ronty, NYR.	20.00	30.00
☐ 64	Allan Stanley, NYR.	40.00	65.00
☐ 65	Leo Reise, NYR.	20.00	30.00
☐ **66**	**Aldo Guidolin, NYR., RC, LC**	**20.00**	**30.00**
☐ 67	Wally Hergesheimer, NYR.	20.00	30.00
☐ 68	Don Raleigh, NYR.	20.00	30.00
☐ 69	Jim Peters, Chi., LC	20.00	30.00
☐ 70	Pete Conacher, Chi.	20.00	30.00
☐ 71	Fred Hucul, Chi., LC	20.00	30.00
☐ 72	Lidio Fogolin, Chi.	20.00	30.00
☐ 73	Larry Zeidel, Chi.	20.00	30.00
☐ 74	Larry Wilson, Chi.	20.00	30.00
☐ 75	Gus Bodnar, Chi.	20.00	30.00
☐ 76	Bill Gadsby, Chi.	28.00	45.00
☐ 77	Jim McFadden, Chi., LC	20.00	30.00
☐ 78	Al Dewsbury, Chi.	20.00	30.00
☐ 79	Clare Raglan, Chi., LC	20.00	30.00
☐ 80	Bill Mosienko, Chi.	30.00	50.00
☐ 81	Gus Mortson, Chi.	20.00	30.00
☐ 82	Al Rollins (G), Chi.	28.00	45.00
☐ 83	George Gee, Chi.	20.00	30.00
☐ 84	Gerald Couture, Chi., LC	20.00	30.00
☐ 85	Dave Creighton, Bos.	20.00	30.00
☐ 86	Jim Henry (G), Bos.	28.00	45.00
☐ 87	Hal Laycoe, Bos.	20.00	30.00
☐ 88	Johnny Peirson, Bos., Err. (Pierson)	20.00	30.00
☐ 89	Real Chevrefils, Bos.	20.00	30.00
☐ 90	Ed Sandford, Bos.	20.00	30.00
☐ 91	Fleming Mackell, Bos. (W/ biography on back)	20.00	30.00
☐ 91	Fleming Mackell, Bos. (W/O biography on back)	20.00	30.00
☐ 92	Milt Schmidt, Bos.	35.00	60.00
☐ 93	Léo Labine, Bos.	20.00	30.00
☐ 94	Joe Klukay, Bos.	20.00	30.00
☐ 95	Warren Godfrey, Bos.	20.00	30.00
☐ 96	Woody Dumart, Bos., LC	28.00	45.00
☐ **97**	**Frank Martin, Bos., RC**	**20.00**	**30.00**
☐ **98**	**Jerry Toppazzini, Bos., RC**	**25.00**	**40.00**
☐ 99	Cal Gardner, Bos.	20.00	30.00
☐ 100	Bill Quackenbush, Bos.	50.00	100.00

1954 - 55 PARKHURST

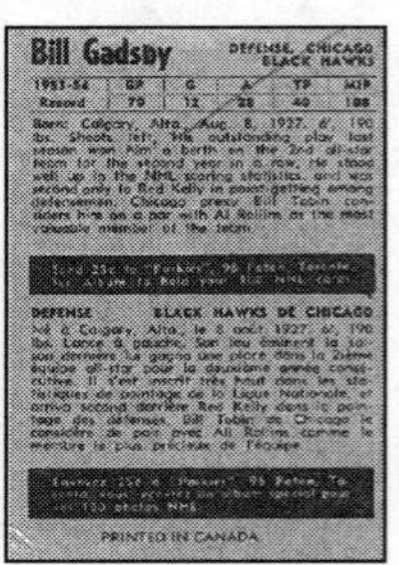

"Lucky Premium" card back versions parallel 1 - 88. Pricing for both versions is the same. Mint condition cards do command a premium.

Card Size: 2 1/2" x 3 5/8"
Face: Four colour, white border, Number, Signature
Back: Black on card stock, Resume, Bilingual
Imprint: Printed In Canada

Complete Set (100 cards):	**3,300.00**	**5,400.00**
Common Player:	**15.00**	**25.00**
Album:	**50.00**	**100.00**

No.	Player	EX	NRMT
☐☐ 1	Gerry McNeil (G), Mtl.	55.00	110.00
☐☐ 2	Dickie Moore, Mtl.	55.00	85.00

	No.	Player	EX	NRMT
☐☐	3	Jean Béliveau, Mtl.	270.00	425.00
☐☐	4	Eddie Mazur, Mtl., LC	15.00	25.00
☐☐	5	Bert Olmstead, Mtl.	25.00	40.00
☐☐	6	Emile (Butch) Bouchard, Mtl.	22.00	35.00
☐☐	7	Maurice Richard, Mtl.	300.00	500.00
☐☐	8	Bernie Geoffrion, Mtl.	75.00	125.00
☐☐	9	John McCormack, Mtl., LC	15.00	25.00
☐☐	10	Tom Johnson, Mtl.	25.00	40.00
☐☐	11	Calum MacKay, Mtl.	15.00	25.00
☐☐	12	Kenny Mosdell, Mtl.	15.00	25.00
☐☐	13	Paul Masnick, Mtl., LC	15.00	25.00
☐☐	14	Doug Harvey, Mtl.	75.00	120.00
☐☐	15	Floyd Curry, Mtl.	15.00	25.00
☐☐	16	Harry Lumley (G), Tor.	35.00	55.00
☐☐	17	Harry Watson, Tor., LC	20.00	30.00
☐☐	18	Jim Morrison, Tor.	15.00	25.00
☐☐	19	Eric Nesterenko, Tor.	15.00	25.00
☐☐	20	Fernie Flaman, Tor.	22.00	35.00
☐☐	21	Rudy Migay, Tor.	15.00	25.00
☐☐	22	Sid Smith, Tor.	15.00	25.00
☐☐	23	Ron Stewart, Tor.	15.00	25.00
☐☐	24	George Armstrong, Tor.	50.00	75.00
☐☐	**25**	**Earl Balfour, Tor., RC**	**15.00**	**25.00**
☐☐	26	Leo Boivin, Tor.	20.00	30.00
☐☐	27	Gord Hannigan, Tor., LC	15.00	25.00
☐☐	**28**	**Bob Bailey, Tor., RC**	**15.00**	**25.00**
☐☐	29	Ted Kennedy, Tor.	35.00	55.00
☐☐	30	Tod Sloan, Tor.	15.00	25.00
☐☐	31	Tim Horton, Tor.	160.00	265.00
☐☐	32	Jim Thomson, Tor., Err. (Thompson)	15.00	25.00
☐☐	33	Terry Sawchuk (G), Det.	190.00	300.00
☐☐	34	Marcel Pronovost, Det.	25.00	40.00
☐☐	35	Metro Prystai, Det., LC	15.00	25.00
☐☐	36	Alex Delvecchio, Det.	50.00	75.00
☐☐	37	Earl Reibel, Det.	15.00	25.00
☐☐	38	Benny Woit, Det., LC	15.00	25.00
☐☐	39	Bob Goldham, Det., LC	20.00	30.00
☐☐	40	Glen Skov, Det.	15.00	25.00
☐☐	41	Gordie Howe, Det.	425.00	700.00
☐☐	42	Red Kelly, Det.	50.00	75.00
☐☐	43	Marty Pavelich, Det., LC	15.00	25.00
☐☐	44	Johnny Wilson, Det.	15.00	25.00
☐☐	45	Tony Leswick, Det., LC	15.00	25.00
☐☐	46	Ted Lindsay, Det.	50.00	75.00
☐☐	**47**	**Keith Allen, Det., RC, LC**	**22.00**	**35.00**
☐☐	**48**	**Bill Dineen, Det., RC**	**20.00**	**30.00**
☐☐	49	Jim Henry (G), Bos., LC	22.00	35.00
☐☐	50	Fleming Mackell, Bos.	15.00	25.00
☐☐	51	Bill Quackenbush, Bos., LC	22.00	35.00
☐☐	52	Hal Laycoe, Bos., LC	15.00	25.00
☐☐	53	Cal Gardner, Bos., LC	15.00	25.00
☐☐	54	Joe Klukay, Bos.	15.00	25.00
☐☐	55	Bob Armstrong, Bos.	15.00	25.00
☐☐	56	Warren Godfrey, Bos.	15.00	25.00
☐☐	**57**	**Doug Mohns, Bos., RC**	**25.00**	**40.00**
☐☐	58	Dave Creighton, Bos.	15.00	25.00
☐☐	59	Milt Schmidt, Bos., LC	25.00	40.00
☐☐	60	Johnny Peirson, Bos., LC	15.00	25.00
☐☐	61	Léo Labine, Bos.	15.00	25.00
☐☐	62	Gus Bodnar, Bos., LC	15.00	25.00
☐☐	63	Real Chevrefils, Bos.	15.00	25.00
☐☐	64	Ed Sandford, Bos., LC	15.00	25.00
☐☐	**65**	**Johnny Bower (G), NYR., RC, Err. (Bowers)**	**240.00**	**400.00**
☐☐	66	Paul Ronty, NYR., LC	15.00	25.00
☐☐	67	Leo Reise, NYR., LC	15.00	25.00
☐☐	68	Don Raleigh, NYR., LC	15.00	25.00
☐☐	**69**	**Bob Chrystal, NYR., RC, LC**	**15.00**	**25.00**
☐☐	70	Harry Howell, NYR.	50.00	75.00
☐☐	71	Wally Hergesheimer, NYR.	15.00	25.00
☐☐	72	Jack Evans, NYR.	15.00	25.00
☐☐	**73**	**Camille Henry, NYR., RC**	**25.00**	**40.00**
☐☐	**74**	**Dean Prentice, NYR., RC**	**20.00**	**40.00**
☐☐	75	Nick Mickoski, NYR.	15.00	25.00
☐☐	**76**	**Ron Murphy, NYR., RC**	**20.00**	**30.00**
☐☐	77	Al Rollins (G), Chi., LC	22.00	35.00
☐☐	78	Al Dewsbury, Chi., LC	15.00	25.00
☐☐	**79**	**Lou Jankowski, Chi., RC, LC**	**15.00**	**25.00**
☐☐	80	George Gee, Chi., LC	15.00	25.00
☐☐	81	Gus Mortson, Chi.	15.00	25.00
☐☐	**82**	**Fred Saskamoose, Chi., RC, LC**	**22.00**	**35.00**
☐☐	**83**	**Ike Hildebrand, Chi., RC, LC**	**15.00**	**25.00**
☐☐	84	Lidio Fogolin, Chi., LC	15.00	25.00
☐☐	85	Larry Wilson, Chi., LC	15.00	25.00
☐☐	86	Pete Conacher, Chi.	15.00	25.00
☐☐	87	Bill Gadsby, Chi.	25.00	40.00
☐☐	88	Jack McIntyre, Chi.	15.00	25.00
☐	89	Busher Curry Goes Up-And-Over	20.00	30.00
☐	90	Delvecchio Finds Leaf Defense Hard to Crack	25.00	40.00
☐	91	The Battle of the All-Stars	25.00	40.00
☐	92	Lum Stops Howe With Help of Stewart's Stick	75.00	125.00
☐	93	Netminder's Nightmare	20.00	30.00
☐	94	Meger Goes Down And Under	20.00	30.00
☐	95	Harvey Takes a Nose-Dive	35.00	60.00
☐	96	Terry Boots Out Teeder's Blast	60.00	100.00
☐	97	Dutch Reibel Tests Habs' Rookie "Mr. Zero"	75.00	125.00
☐	98	Plante Protects Against Slippery Sloan	75.00	125.00
☐	99	Placid Plante Foils Tireless Teeder	75.00	125.00
☐	100	Sawchuk Stops Boom Boom	95.00	185.00

1954 - 55 TOPPS

The bottom border, which is printed in blue, scuffs easily. This compounds the problem of finding NRMT to mint cards. Mint condition cards do command premium. The first issue of Topps was not bilingual.

Card Size: 2 5/8" x 3 3/4"
Face: Four colour, blue and red border along bottom, Team logo
Back: Red and blue on card stock; Number, Resume, Hockey tip
Imprint: T.C.G. printed in U.S.A.

Complete Set (60 cards):			**3,800.00**	**5,800.00**
Common Player:			**28.00**	**45.00**
	No	**Player**	**EX**	**NRMT**
☐	1	Dick Gamble, Chi., LC	75.00	160.00
☐	**2**	**Bob Chrystal, NYR. RC, LC**	**22.50**	**45.00**
☐	3	Harry Howell, NYR.	80.00	125.00
☐	4	Johnny Wilson, Det.	22.50	45.00
☐	5	Red Kelly, Det.	100.00	160.00
☐	6	Real Chevrefils, Bos.	22.50	45.00
☐	7	Bob Armstrong, Bos.	22.50	45.00
☐	8	Gordie Howe, Det.	1,500.00	2,400.00
☐	9	Benny Woit, Det., LC	22.50	45.00
☐	10	Gump Worsley (G), NYR.	160.00	260.00
☐	11	Andy Bathgate, NYR.	80.00	125.00
☐	**12**	**Bucky Hollingworth, Chi., RC, LC**	**22.50**	**45.00**
☐	13	Ray Timgren, Chi., LC	22.50	45.00
☐	14	Jack Evans, NYR.	22.50	45.00
☐	15	Paul Ronty, NYR., LC	22.50	45.00
☐	16	Glen Skov, Det.	22.50	45.00
☐	17	Gus Mortson, Chi.	22.50	45.00
☐	**18**	**Doug Mohns, Bos., RC**	**50.00**	**85.00**
☐	19	Léo Labine, Bos.	22.50	45.00
☐	20	Bill Gadsby, Chi.	50.00	75.00
☐	21	Jerry Toppazzini, Chi.	22.50	45.00
☐	22	Wally Hergesheimer, NYR.	22.50	45.00
☐	23	Danny Lewicki, NYR.	22.50	45.00
☐	24	Metro Prystai, Chi., LC	22.50	45.00
☐	25	Fern Flaman, Bos.	40.00	65.00
☐	26	Al Rollins (G), Chi., LC	40.00	65.00
☐	27	Marcel Pronovost, Det.	40.00	70.00
☐	**28**	**Lou Jankowski, Chi., RC, LC**	**22.50**	**45.00**
☐	29	Nick Mickoski, NYR.	22.50	45.00
☐	30	Frank Martin, Chi., LC	22.50	45.00
☐	31	Lorne Ferguson, Bos.	22.50	45.00
☐	**32**	**Camille Henry, NYR., RC**	**40.00**	**65.00**
☐	33	Pete Conacher, Chi.	22.50	45.00
☐	34	Marty Pavelich, Det., LC	22.50	45.00
☐	**35**	**Don McKenney, Bos., RC**	**35.00**	**65.00**
☐	36	Fleming Mackell, Bos.	22.50	45.00
☐	37	Jim Henry (G), Bos., LC	40.00	65.00
☐	38	Hal Laycoe, Bos., LC	22.50	45.00
☐	39	Alex Delvecchio, Det.	100.00	160.00
☐	40	Larry Wilson, Chi., LC	22.50	45.00
☐	41	Allan Stanley, NYR.	55.00	90.00
☐	**42**	**Red Sullivan, Chi., RC**	**22.50**	**45.00**
☐	43	Jack McIntyre, Chi.	22.50	45.00
☐	**44**	**Ivan Irwin, NYR., RC, LC**	**22.50**	**45.00**
☐	45	Tony Leswick, Det., LC	22.50	45.00
☐	46	Bob Goldham, Det., LC	35.00	60.00
☐	47	Cal Gardner, Bos., LC	22.50	45.00
☐	48	Ed Sandford, Bos., LC	22.50	45.00
☐	49	Bill Quackenbush, Bos., LC	40.00	70.00
☐	50	Warren Godfrey, Bos.	22.50	45.00
☐	51	Ted Lindsay, Det.	95.00	150.00
☐	52	Earl Reibel, Det.	22.50	45.00
☐	53	Don Raleigh, NYR., LC	22.50	45.00
☐	54	Bill Mosienko, Chi., LC	50.00	75.00
☐	**55**	**Larry Popein, NYR., RC**	**22.50**	**45.00**
☐	56	Edgar Laprade, NYR., LC	35.00	60.00
☐	57	Bill Dineen, Det.	22.50	45.00
☐	58	Terry Sawchuk (G), Det.	550.00	850.00
☐	**59**	**Marcel Bonin, Det., RC**	**22.50**	**45.00**
☐	60	Milt Schmidt, Bos., LC	110.00	240.00

1954 - 67 TORONTO STAR WEEKEND MAGAZINE PHOTOS

These photos appeared in the Star Weekend Magazine between 1954 and 1967 to help boost sales. No photos appeared during 1964-65. Note - Pictures within intact magazines valued at about 50% more.

Card Size: 5 1/2" x 6 1/2"
Face: Four colour
Back: Newsprint
Imprint: None
Complete Set:

Common Photo:			**7.00**	**12.00**
Vol.	**No.**	**Player**	**EX**	**NRMT**
1954 ISSUES				
☐ V4	n2	Gordie Howe, Det.	30.00	50.00
☐ V4	n3	Maurice Richard, Mtl.		
☐ V4	n4	Ted Kennedy, Tor.	12.00	20.00
☐ V4	n5	Red Kelly. Det.		
☐ V4	n6	Elmer Lach, Mtl.	12.00	20.00
☐ V4	n7	Gus Mortson, Chi.	7.00	12.00
☐ V4	n8	Ted Lindsay, Det.	12.00	20.00
☐ V4	n9	Milt Schmidt, Bos.	12.00	20.00
☐ V4	n10	Ed Sandford, Bos.	7.00	12.00
☐ V4	n11	Wally Hergesheimer, NYR.	7.00	12.00
☐ V4	n13	Butch Bouchard, Mtl.		
1955 ISSUES				
☐ V5	n2	Harry Lumley (G), Tor.	12.00	20.00
☐ V5	n3	Fleming Mackell, Bos.	7.00	12.00
☐ V5	n4	Bernie Geoffrion, Mtl.	15.00	25.00
☐ V5	n5	Danny Lewicki, NYR.	7.00	12.00
☐ V5	n6	Harry Watson, Chi.	9.00	15.00
☐ V5	n7	Ken Mosdel, Mtl.	7.00	12.00
☐ V5	n8	Earl Reibel, Det.	7.00	12.00
☐ V5	n9	Bill Quackenbush, Bos.	9.00	15.00
☐ V5	n10	Bill Gadsby, NYR.	9.00	15.00
☐ V5	n11	Jimmy Thomson, Tor.	7.00	12.00
1958 - 59 ISSUES				
☐ V6		Dickie Moore, Mtl.	11.00	18.00
☐ V6		Glenn Hall (G), Chi.	20.00	30.00
☐ V6		Frank Mahovlich, Tor.	20.00	30.00
☐ V6		Henri Richard, Mtl.	13.00	22.00
☐ V6		Camille Henry, NYR.	7.00	12.00
☐ V6		Marcel Pronovost , Det.	9.00	15.00
☐ V6		Eddie Litzenberger, Chi.	7.00	12.00
☐ V6		Bob Pulford, Tor.	9.00	15.00
☐ V6		Andy Bathgate, NYR.	9.00	15.00
☐ V6		Fern Flaman, Bos.	9.00	15.00
☐ V6		Doug Harvey, Mtl.	15.00	25.00

No.	Player	EX	NRMT
☐ V6	Vic Stasiuk, Bos.	7.00	12.00
☐ V6	Alex Delvecchio, Det.	11.00	18.00
1959 - 60 ISSUES			
☐ V7	Tom Johnson, Mtl.	9.00	15.00
☐ V7	Dick Duff , Tor.	7.00	12.00
☐ V7	Norm Ullman, Det.	11.00	18.00
☐ V7	Jacques Plante (G), Mtl.	25.00	40.00
☐ V7	Bobby Hull, Chi.	22.00	35.00
☐ V7	Bronco Horvath, Bos.	7.00	12.00
☐ V7	Andy Hebenton, NYR.	7.00	12.00
☐ V7	Leo Boivin, Bos.	9.00	15.00
☐ V7	Terry Sawchuk (G), Det.	25.00	40.00
☐ V7	Billy Harris, Tor.	7.00	12.00
☐ V7	Tod Sloan, Chi.	7.00	12.00
☐ V7	Ralph Backstrom, Mtl.	7.00	12.00
☐ V7	Red Sullivan, NYR.	7.00	12.00
☐ V7	Carl Brewer, Tor.	7.00	12.00
1960 - 61 ISSUES			
☐ V8	Gordie Howe, Det.	30.00	50.00
☐ V8	Jean Béliveau, Mtl.	20.00	30.00
☐ V8	George Armstrong, Tor.	11.00	18.00
☐ V8	Billy Hay, Chi.	7.00	12.00
☐ V8	Lou Fontinato, NYR.	7.00	12.00
☐ V8	Jerry Toppazzini, Bos.	7.00	12.00
☐ V8	Bernie Geoffrion, Mtl.	15.00	25.00
☐ V8	Red Kelly, Tor.	12.00	20.00
☐ V8	John Bucyk, Bos.	11.00	18.00
☐ V8	Dean Prentice, NYR.	7.00	12.00
☐ V8	Pierre Pilote, Chi.	9.00	15.00
☐ V8	Ron Stewart, Tor.	7.00	12.00
☐ V8	Don Marshall, Mtl.	7.00	12.00
1961 - 62 ISSUES			
☐ V9	Claude Provost, Mtl.	7.00	12.00
☐ V9	Elmer Vasko, Chi.	7.00	12.00
☐ V9	Dave Keon, Tor.	13.00	22.00
☐ V9	Warren Godfrey, Det.	7.00	12.00
☐ V9	Gump Worsley (G), NYR.	18.00	28.00
☐ V9	Doug Mohns, Bos.	7.00	12.00
☐ V9	Marcel Bonin, Mtl.	7.00	12.00
☐ V9	Alan Stanley, Tor.	9.00	15.00
☐ V9	Johnny Bower (G), Tor.	15.00	25.00
☐ V9	Stan Mikita, Chi.	20.00	30.00
☐ V9	Don McKenney, Bos.	7.00	12.00
☐ V9	Doug Harvey, NYR.	15.00	25.00
☐ V9	Jean Guy Talbot, Mtl.	7.00	12.00
1962 - 63 ISSUES			
☐ V10	Frank Mahovlich, Tor.	20.00	30.00
☐ V10	Gilles Tremblay, Mtl.	7.00	12.00
☐ V10	Ab McDonald, Chi.	7.00	12.00
☐ V10	Alex Delvecchio, Det.	11.00	18.00
☐ V10	Earl Ingarfield, NYR.	7.00	12.00
☐ V10	Tim Horton, Tor.	20.00	30.00
☐ V10	Glen Hall (G), Chi.	20.00	30.00
☐ V10	Murray Oliver, Bos.	7.00	12.00
☐ V10	Marcel Pronovost, Det.	9.00	15.00
☐ V10	Henri Richard, Mtl.	13.00	22.00
☐ V10	Andy Bathgate, NYR.	9.00	15.00
1963 - 64 ISSUES			
☐ V11	Bobby Rousseau, Mtl.	7.00	12.00
☐ V11	Bob Pulford, Tor.	9.00	15.00
☐ V11	Parker MacDonald, Det.	7.00	12.00
☐ V11	Jacques Plante (G), NYR.	25.00	40.00
☐ V11	Kenny Wharram, Chi.	7.00	12.00
☐ V11	Tom Williams, Bos.	7.00	12.00
☐ V11	Gordie Howe, Det..	30.00	50.00
☐ V11	Dave Balon, Mtl.	7.00	12.00
☐ V11	Phil Goyette, NYR.	7.00	12.00
☐ V11	Carl Brewer, Tor.	7.00	12.00
☐ V11	Terry Sawchuk (G), Det.	25.00	40.00
☐ V11	Bobby Hull, Chi.	22.00	35.00
☐ V11	John Ferguson, Mtl.	7.00	12.00

1965 - 66 ALL STAR TEAM

The All Star Team was issued over three editions of the Weekend Magazine by using back to back photos on both sides of one page.

No.	Player	EX	NRMT
☐	Glenn Hall (G), Chi. / Jacques Laperrière, Mtl.	20.00	25.00
☐	Pierre Pilote, Chi. / Gordie Howe, Det.	30.00	50.00
☐	Stan Mikita, Chi. / Bobby Hull, Chi.	25.00	40.00

1966 - 67 ISSUE

No.	Player	EX	NRMT
☐ 101	Frank Mahovlich, Tor.	20.00	30.00
☐ 102	Bobby Rousseau, Mtl.	7.00	12.00
☐ 103	Pat Stapleton, Chi	7.00	12.00
☐ 104	Roger Crozier (G), Det.	9.00	15.00
☐ 105	Don Marshall, NYR.	7.00	12.00
☐ 106	Terry Sawchuk (G), Tor.	25.00	40.00
☐ 107	Jean Béliveau, Mtl.	20.00	30.00
☐ 108	Doug Mohns, Chi.	7.00	12.00
☐ 109	Bob Nevin, NYR.	7.00	12.00
☐ 110	Pit Martin, Bos.	7.00	12.00
☐ 111	Allan Stanley, Tor.	9.00	15.00
☐ 112	Harry Howell, NYR.	9.00	15.00

1966 - 67 ALL-STAR TEAM

No.	Player	EX	NRMT
☐ 101	Ed Giacomin/Ken Wharram	20.00	30.00
☐ 102	Harry Howell/Pierre Pilote	7.00	12.00
☐ 103	Bobby Hull/Stan Mikita	7.00	12.00

1955 - 56 NABISCO

This set is not complete. We would appreciate hearing from anyone who could supply further information.

ACC: FC-26-3
Coin Size: 1 15/16" x 2 7/8"
Face: Four colour print; Number
Back: Black and white; Name, Number, Resume, Bilingual
Imprint: The Canadian Shredded Wheat Company Ltd., Niagara Falls, Ont.
Complete Set (70 coins):

No.	Player	EX	NRMT
☐ 62	Ted Reeve, Stick Handling	12.00	20.00

1955 - 56 PARKHURST

This set features Oldtime Great cards Nos.21-32 and 55-66. The Oldtime Great subset contains the first and last card of Bill Durnan (#63). The Parkhurst/Quaker Oats issue of 1955-56 is his only appearance on a card. As with all strong coloured borders the bottom red border marks easily. Mint cards do commonad a premium.

Card Size: 2 1/2" x 3 9/16"
Face: Four colour, red borber along bottom, Team logo, Number
Back: Red on card stock; Resume, Hockey trivia, Bilingual
Imprint: Printed In Canada

Complete Set (79 cards):		**3,000.00**	**5,000.00**
Common Player:		**15.00**	**25.00**
No.	**Player**	**EX**	**NRMT**
☐ 1	Harry Lumley (G), Tor., LC	190.00	375.00
☐ 2	Sid Smith, Tor.	15.00	25.00
☐ 3	Tim Horton, Tor.	150.00	250.00
☐ 4	George Armstrong, Tor.	50.00	75.00
☐ 5	Ron Stewart, Tor.	15.00	25.00
☐ 6	Joe Klukay, Tor., LC	15.00	25.00
☐ **7**	**Marc Reaume, Tor., RC**	**15.00**	**25.00**
☐ 8	Jim Morrison, Tor.	15.00	25.00
☐ **9**	**Parker MacDonald, Tor., RC**	**15.00**	**25.00**
☐ 10	Tod Sloan, Tor.	15.00	25.00
☐ 11	Jim Thomson, Tor.	15.00	25.00
☐ 12	Rudy Migay, Tor.	15.00	25.00
☐ **13**	**Brian Cullen, Tor., RC**	**15.00**	**25.00**
☐ 14	Hugh Bolton, Tor.	15.00	25.00
☐ 15	Eric Nesterenko, Tor.	15.00	25.00
☐ **16**	**Larry Cahan, Tor., RC**	**15.00**	**25.00**
☐ **17**	**Willie Marshall, Tor., RC**	**15.00**	**25.00**
☐ **18**	**Dick Duff, Tor., RC**	**50.00**	**75.00**
☐ **19**	**Jack Caffery, Tor., RC**	**15.00**	**25.00**
☐ **20**	**Billy Harris, Tor., RC**	**25.00**	**40.00**
☐ 21	Lorne Chabot (G), Tor.	22.00	35.00
☐ 22	Harvey Jackson, Tor.	35.00	45.00
☐ 23	Turk Broda (G), Tor.	50.00	80.00
☐ 24	Joe Primeau, Tor.	25.00	40.00
☐ 25	Gordie Drillon, Tor.	22.00	35.00
☐ 26	Charlie Conacher, Tor.	35.00	40.00
☐ 27	Sweeney Schriner, Tor.	22.00	35.00
☐ 28	Syl Apps Sr., Tor.	25.00	40.00
☐ 29	Ted Kennedy, Tor.	28.00	45.00
☐ 30	Ace Bailey, Tor.	35.00	55.00
☐ 31	Babe Pratt, Tor.	25.00	40.00
☐ 32	Harold Cotton, Tor.	22.00	35.00
☐ 33	Francis (King) Clancy, Tor., Coach	45.00	70.00
☐ 34	Hap Day, Tor., Manager	22.00	35.00
☐ **35**	**Don Marshall, Mtl., RC**	**28.00**	**45.00**
☐ **36**	**Jackie LeClair, Mtl., RC, LC**	**15.00**	**25.00**
☐ 37	Maurice Richard, Mtl.	285.00	450.00
☐ 38	Dickie Moore, Mtl.	55.00	85.00
☐ 39	Kenny Mosdell, Mtl., LC	15.00	25.00
☐ 40	Floyd Curry, Mtl.	15.00	25.00
☐ 41	Calum MacKay, Mtl., LC	15.00	25.00
☐ 42	Bert Olmstead, Mtl.	25.00	40.00
☐ 43	Bernie Geoffrion, Mtl.	75.00	125.00
☐ 44	Jean Béliveau, Mtl.	200.00	325.00
☐ 45	Doug Harvey, Mtl.	70.00	115.00
☐ 46	Emile (Butch) Bouchard, Mtl., LC	25.00	40.00
☐ 47	Bud MacPherson, Mtl., LC	15.00	25.00
☐ 48	Dollard St. Laurent, Mtl.	15.00	25.00
☐ 49	Tom Johnson, Mtl.	25.00	40.00
☐ **50**	**Jacques Plante (G), Mtl., RC**	**600.00**	**1,000.00**
☐ 51	Paul Meger, Mtl., LC	15.00	25.00
☐ 52	Gerry McNeil (G), Mtl., LC	30.00	50.00
☐ **53**	**Jean-Guy Talbot, Mtl., RC**	**25.00**	**40.00**
☐ **54**	**Bob Turner, Mtl., RC**	**15.00**	**25.00**
☐ 55	Edouard Lalonde, Mtl.	35.00	55.00
☐ 56	Georges Vézina (G), Mtl.	60.00	100.00
☐ 57	Howie Morenz, Mtl.	65.00	110.00
☐ 58	Aurèle Joliat, Mtl.	35.00	55.00
☐ 59	George Hainsworth (G), Mtl.	40.00	65.00
☐ 60	Sylvio Mantha, Mtl.	25.00	40.00
☐ 61	Albert Leduc, Mtl.	22.00	35.00
☐ 62	Babe Siebert, Mtl., Err. (Seibert)	25.00	40.00
☐ 63	Bill Durnan (G), Mtl.	40.00	65.00
☐ 64	Ken Reardon, Mtl.	28.00	45.00
☐ 65	Johnny Gagnon, Mtl.	22.00	35.00
☐ 66	Billy Reay, Mtl.	22.00	35.00
☐ 67	Toe Blake, Coach, Mtl.	35.00	55.00
☐ 68	Frank Selke, Manager, Mtl.	25.00	40.00
☐ 69	Hugh Beats Hodge	25.00	40.00
☐ 70	Lum Stops Boom-Boom	40.00	65.00
☐ 71	Plante Is Protected	55.00	90.00
☐ 72	Rocket Roars Through	60.00	100.00
☐ 73	Richard Tests Lumley	60.00	100.00
☐ 74	Béliveau Bats Puck	50.00	75.00
☐ 75	Leaf Speedster Attack	55.00	90.00
☐ 76	Curry Scores Agains	25.00	40.00
☐ 77	Jammed On The Boards	60.00	95.00
☐ 78	The Montréal Forum	165.00	275.00
☐ 79	Maple Leaf Gardens	145.00	290.00

Note: Parkhurst did not issue a 1956-57 set of cards.

1955 - 56 QUAKER OATS

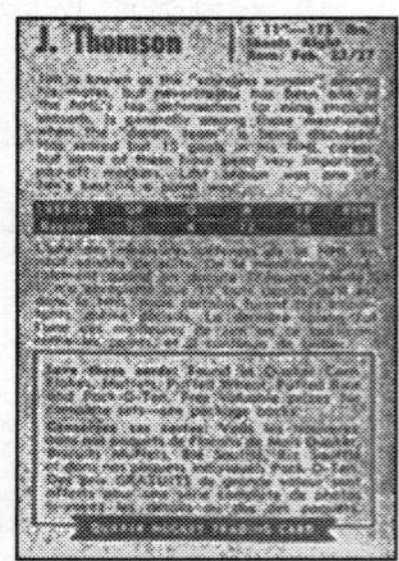

Quaker Oats issued a set virtually identical to the Parkhurst set of the same year. The only difference is the distinctive green backs. A Quaker Oats advertisement is in place of the Did You Know tip on the back of the card. The green-backs are rare. As with all strong coloured borders the bottom red border marks easily. Mint cards do command a premium. Short prints are marked with an asterisk (*)

Card Size: 2 1/2" x 3 9/16"
Face: Four colour, red border along bottom, Team logo, Number
Back: Green on card stock; Resume, Hockey trivia, Bilingual
Imprint: Quaker Hockey Trading Card.

Complete Set (79 cards):			**Unknown**
Common Player:		**50.00**	**100.00**
No.	**Player**	**EX**	**EX-NRMT**
☐ 1	Harry Lumley (G), Tor., LC (*)		Very Rare
☐ 2	Sid Smith, Tor.	50.00	100.00
☐ 3	Tim Horton, Tor.	225.00	450.00
☐ 4	George Armstrong, Tor.	100.00	200.00

☐ 5	Ron Stewart, Tor.	50.00	100.00
☐ 6	Joe Klukay, Tor., LC	50.00	100.00
☐ **7**	**Marc Reaume, Tor., RC**	**50.00**	**100.00**
☐ 8	Jim Morrison, Tor.	50.00	100.00
☐ **9**	**Parker MacDonald, Tor., RC**	**50.00**	**100.00**
☐ 10	Tod Sloan, Tor.	50.00	100.00
☐ 11	Jim Thomson, Tor.	50.00	100.00
☐ 12	Rudy Migay, Tor.	50.00	100.00
☐ **13**	**Brian Cullen, Tor., RC**	**50.00**	**100.00**
☐ 14	Hugh Bolton, Tor.	50.00	100.00
☐ 15	Eric Nesterenko, Tor.	50.00	100.00
☐ **16**	**Larry Cahan, Tor., RC**	**50.00**	**100.00**
☐ **17**	**Willie Marshall, Tor., RC**	**50.00**	**100.00**
☐ **18**	**Dick Duff, Tor., RC**	**100.00**	**200.00**
☐ **19**	**Jack Caffery, Tor., RC**	**50.00**	**100.00**
☐ **20**	**Billy Harris, Tor., RC**	**80.00**	**160.00**
☐ 21	Lorne Chabot (G), Tor.	90.00	175.00
☐ 22	Harvey Jackson, Tor.	100.00	200.00
☐ 23	Turk Broda (G), Tor.	200.00	400.00
☐ 24	Joe Primeau, Tor.	150.00	300.00
☐ 25	Gordie Drillon, Tor.	90.00	175.00
☐ 26	Charlie Conacher, Tor.	100.00	200.00
☐ 27	Sweeny Schriner, Tor.	90.00	175.00
☐ 28	Syl Apps, Sr., Tor.	100.00	200.00
☐ 29	Ted Kennedy, Tor.	150.00	300.00
☐ 30	Ace Bailey, Tor.	150.00	300.00
☐ 31	Babe Pratt, Tor.	90.00	175.00
☐ 32	Baldy Cotton, Tor.	90.00	175.00
☐ 33	Francis (King) Clancy, Coach, Tor. (*)	200.00	400.00
☐ 34	Hap Day, Manager, Tor.	90.00	175.00
☐ **35**	**Don Marshall, Mtl., RC**	**90.00**	**175.00**
☐ **36**	**Jackie Leclair, Mtl., RC, LC**	**50.00**	**100.00**
☐ 37	Maurice Richard, Mtl. (*)	1,000.00	2,000.00
☐ 38	Dickie Moore, Mtl.	85.00	175.00
☐ 39	Kenny Mosdell, Mtl., LC	50.00	100.00
☐ 40	Floyd Curry, Mtl.	50.00	100.00
☐ 41	Calum MacKay, Mtl., LC	50.00	100.00
☐ 42	Bert Olmstead, Mtl.	90.00	175.00
☐ 43	Bernie Geoffrion, Mtl.	265.00	525.00
☐ 44	Jean Béliveau, Mtl.	500.00	1,000.00
☐ 45	Doug Harvey, Mtl.	125.00	250.00
☐ 46	Emile (Butch) Bouchard, Mtl., LC	50.00	100.00
☐ 47	Bud MacPherson, Mtl., LC	50.00	100.00
☐ 48	Dollard St. Laurent, Mtl.	50.00	100.00
☐ 49	Tom Johnson, Mtl.	90.00	175.00
☐ **50**	**Jacques Plante (G), Mtl., RC**	**1,750.00**	**3,500.00**
☐ 51	Paul Meger, Mtl.	50.00	100.00
☐ 52	Gerry McNeil (G), Mtl., LC	100.00	200.00
☐ **53**	**Jean-Guy Talbot, Mtl., RC**	**90.00**	**175.00**
☐ **54**	**Bob Turner, Mtl., RC**	**50.00**	**100.00**
☐ 55	Edouard Lalonde, Mtl.	85.00	175.00
☐ 56	Georges Vézina (G), Mtl.	250.00	500.00
☐ 57	Howie Morenz, Mtl.	250.00	500.00
☐ 58	Aurèle Joliat, Mtl.	150.00	300.00
☐ 59	George Hainsworth (G), Mtl.	100.00	200.00
☐ 60	Sylvio Mantha, Mtl.	100.00	200.00
☐ 61	Albert Leduc, Mtl.	90.00	175.00
☐ 62	Babe Siebert, Mtl., Err. (Seibert)	100.00	200.00
☐ **63**	**Bill Durnan (G), Mtl., RC, LC**	**225.00**	**350.00**
☐ 64	Ken Reardon, Mtl.	100.00	200.00
☐ 65	Johnny Gagnon, Mtl.	100.00	200.00
☐ 66	Billy Reay, Mtl.	100.00	200.00
☐ 67	Toe Blake, Coach, Mtl.	125.00	250.00
☐ 68	Frank Selke, Manager, Mtl.	125.00	250.00
☐ 69	Hugh Beats Hodge	75.00	150.00
☐ 70	Lum Stops Boom-Boom	125.00	250.00
☐ 71	Plante Is Protected	200.00	400.00
☐ 72	Rocket Roars Through	200.00	400.00
☐ 73	Richard Tests Lumley	200.00	400.00
☐ 74	Béliveau Bats Puck	150.00	300.00
☐ 75	Leaf Speedster Attack	125.00	250.00
☐ 76	Curry Scores Again	75.00	150.00
☐ 77	Jammed On The Boards	125.00	250.00
☐ 78	The Montréal Forum	400.00	800.00
☐ 79	Maple Leaf Gardens	500.00	1,000.00

1956 ADVENTURE GUM

This 100-card multi-sport set features one hockey photo.

ACC: R-749
Card Size: 2 1/2" x 3/12"
Face: Four colour print
Back: Blue and grey; Name, Number, Resume
Imprint: Printed in U.S.A. Gum Products Inc 1956

No.	Player	EX	NRMT
☐ 63	Hockey's Hardy Perennials Gordie Howe, Chuck Raynor	90.00	150.00

1955 - 66 TORONTO STAR PHOTOS

We have little information on this series. Other photos may exist.

Face: Four colour, white border; Name
Back: Newsprint
Imprint: None
Common Photo: 7.00 12.00

No.	Players / Date Issued	EX	NRMT
1954 - 55 PHOTOS			
☐ 1	Toronto Team photo, Mar. 26, 1955	15.00	25.00
☐ 2	Team photos, Montréal Canadiens / Detroit Red Wings, April 2, 1955 (double page)	20.00	30.00
1955 - 56 PHOTOS			
☐ 3	Toronyo Team photo, Dec. 10, 1955	15.00	25.00
☐ 4	Kitchener-Waterloo Olympic Team, Feb. 25, 1956	9.00	15.00
☐ 5	Chi. Team photo, March 10, 1956	15.00	25.00
☐ 6	NYR. Team photo, March 24, 1956	15.00	25.00
☐ 7	Mtl. Team photo, Jan. 5, 1957	15.00	25.00
1957 - 58 PHOTOS			
☐ 8	E. Chadwick (G); T. Horton, Tor. Nov. 2	20.00	30.00
☐ 9	S. Smith; B. Pulford, Tor., Nov. 9	9.00	15.00
☐ 10	D. Duff; J. Morrison, Tor., Nov. 16	7.00	12.00
☐ 11	G. Mortson; J. Thompson, Chi., Nov. 23	7.00	12.00
☐ 12	T. Lindsay; E. Nesterenko, Chi., Nov. 30	12.00	20.00
☐ 13	Toronto Maple Leafs Team Photo, Dec. 7	15.00	25.00
☐ 15	M. Richard; H. Richard, Mtl., Dec. 14	30.00	50.00
☐ 16	B. Geoffrion; D. Harvey, Mtl., Dec. 21	20.00	30.00
☐ 17	A. Hebenton; L. Worsley (G), NYR., Dec. 28	18.00	28.00
☐ 18	Montréal Canadiens Team Photo, Jan. 4	15.00	25.00
☐ 19	F. Flaman; D. Simmons (G), Bos., Jan. 11	11.00	18.00
☐ 20	B. Gadsby; C. Henry, NYR., Jan. 18	9.00	15.00
☐ 21	D. McKenney; R. Chevrefils, Bos., Jan. 25	7.00	12.00
☐ 22	G. Howe; R. Kelly, Det., Feb. 1	30.00	50.00
☐ 23	Detroit Red Wings Team Photo, Feb. 8	15.00	25.00
☐ 24	J. Plante; J. Béliveau, Mtl., Feb. 15	30.00	50.00
☐ 25	New York Rangers Team Photo, Feb. 22	15.00	25.00
☐ 26	Whitby Dunlops Team Photo, Mar. 1	9.00	15.00
☐ 27	A. Delvecchio; T. Sawchuk (G), Det., Mar. 8	30.00	50.00
☐ 28	G. Armstrong; B. Cullen, Tor., Mar. 15	9.00	15.00
☐ 29	R. Stewart; F. Mahovlich, Mar. 22	20.00	30.00
1958 - 59 STARS OF THE WORLD'S FASTEST GAME			
☐ 30	G. Armstrong/B. Olmstead/F. Mahovlich/Nov. 29	22.00	35.00
☐ 31	D. Duff/B. Harris/R. Stewart/Dec. 6	7.00	12.00
☐ 32	G. Howe/N. Ullman/A. Delvecchio/Dec. 13	35.00	60.00
☐ 33	Montréal Canadiens Team Photo, Dec. 20	15.00	25.00
☐ 34	K. Wharram/D. Lewicki/T. Lindsay/Dec. 27	12.00	20.00
☐ 35	H. Richard/M. Richard/Jan. 3	30.00	50.00
☐ 36	E. Litzenberger/T. Sloan/L. Ferguson/Jan. 10	7.00	12.00
☐ 37	Boston Bruins Team Photo, Jan. 17	15.00	25.00
☐ 38	Minor Hockey Picture of Boys on Ice, Jan. 24	7.00	12.00
☐ 39	D. Moore/J. Béliveau/A. McDonald/Jan. 31	20.00	30.00
☐ 40	New York Rangers Team Photo, Feb. 7	15.00	25.00
☐ 41	F. Flaman/D. Simmons (G)/J. Morrison/Feb. 14	11.00	18.00
☐ 42	Detroit Red WIngs Team Photo, Feb. 21	15.00	25.00
☐ 43	A. Bathgate/L. Popein/D. Prentice/Feb. 28	9.00	15.00
☐ 44	Toronto Maple Leafs Team Photo, Mar. 7	15.00	25.00
☐ 45	Belleville McFarlands Cdn Hky Champ., Mar. 14	13.00	22.00
☐ 46	J. G. Talbot/T. Johnston/B. Turner/Mar. 21	9.00	15.00
1959 - 60 STARS OF THE WORLD'S FASTEST GAME			
☐ 47	Harry Lumley (G), Bos., Dec. 15	12.00	20.00
☐ 48	Bert Olmstead, Tor., Dec. 26	9.00	15.00
☐ 49	Henri Richard, Mtl., Jan. 2	13.00	22.00
☐ 50	Gordie Howe, Det., Jan. 9	30.00	50.00
☐ 51	Johnny Bower (G), Tor., Jan. 16	15.00	25.00
☐ 52	Red Sullivan, NYR., Jan. 23	7.00	12.00
☐ 53	Tod Sloan, Chi., Jan. 30	7.00	12.00
☐ 54	Bob Armstrong, Bos., Feb. 6	7.00	12.00
☐ 55	Jacques Plante (G), Mtl., Feb. 13	25.00	40.00
☐ 56	Tom Johnson, Mtl., Feb. 20	9.00	15.00
☐ 57	Glenn Hall (G), Chi., Feb. 27	20.00	30.00
☐ 58	Bill Gadsby, NYR., Mar. 5	9.00	15.00
1960-61 STARS OF THE WORLD'S FASTEST GAME			
☐ 59	Bobby Hull, Chi., Dec. 10	22.00	35.00
☐ 60	Frank Mahovlich, Tor, Dec. 17	20.00	30.00
☐ 61	Terry Sawchuk (G) Det., Dec. 24	25.00	40.00
☐ 62	Elmer Vasko, Chi., Jan. 7	7.00	12.00
☐ 63	Andy Bathgate, NYR., Jan. 14	9.00	15.00
☐ 64	Ralph Backstrom, Mtl., Jan. 28	7.00	12.00
☐ 65	Fern Flaman, Bos., Feb. 4	9.00	15.00
☐ 66	Allan Stanley, Tor., Feb. 11	9.00	15.00
☐ 67	Gump Worsley (G), NYR., Feb. 18	18.00	28.00
☐ 68	Not issued		
☐ 69	Marcel Pronovost, Det., Mar. 4	9.00	15.00
☐ 70	Don Marshall, Mtl., Mar. 11	7.00	12.00
1961 - 62 N.H.L. STARS IN ACTION			
☐ 71	Elmer Vasko, Chi., Jan. 6	7.00	12.00
☐ 72	Gump Worsley (G), NYR., Jan. 13	18.00	28.00
☐ 73	Don McKenney, Bos., Jan. 20	7.00	12.00
☐ 74	Eddie Shack, Tor., Jan. 27	12.00	20.00
☐ 75	Claude Provost, Mtl., Feb. 3	7.00	12.00
☐ 76	Gordie Howe, Det., Feb. 10	30.00	50.00
☐ 77	Glenn Hall (G), Chi., Feb. 17	20.00	30.00
☐ 78	Doug Harvey, NYR., Feb. 24	15.00	25.00
☐ 79	Jacques Plante (G), Mtl., Mar. 3	25.00	40.00
☐ 80	Carl Brewer, Tor., Mar. 10	7.00	12.00
☐ 81	Dave Keon, Tor., Mar. 17	13.00	22.00
☐ 82	Bill Gadsby, NYR., Mar. 24	9.00	15.00
1962 - 63 STARS OF THE WORLD'S FASTEST GAME			
☐ 83	Ron Stewart, Tor., Dec. 8	7.00	12.00
☐ 84	Bob Perreault (G), Bos., Dec. 15, (2 pages)	9.00	15.00
☐ 85	Dean Prentice, NYR., Dec. 22	7.00	12.00
☐ 86	Terry Sawchuk (G) Det., Dec. 29, (2 Pages)	25.00	40.00
☐ 87	Bobby Hull, Chi., Dec. 29	22.00	35.00
☐ 88	Louie Fontinato, Mtl., Jan. 5, (2 Pages.)	7.00	12.00
☐ 89	Frank Mahovlich, Tor., Jan. 12	20.00	30.00
☐ 90	Bill Hay, Chi., Jan. 19	7.00	12.00
☐ 91	Charlie Burns, Bos., Jan. 26	7.00	12.00
☐ 92	Rod Gilbert, NYR., Feb. 2	11.00	18.00
☐ 93	Henri Richard, Mtl., Feb. 9	13.00	22.00
☐ 94	Camille Henry, NYR., Feb. 16	7.00	12.00
☐ 95	Leo Boivin, Bos., Feb. 23	9.00	15.00
☐ 96	Dickie Moore, Mtl., Mar. 2	11.00	18.00
☐ 97	Parker MacDonald, Det., Mar. 9	7.00	12.00
☐ 98	Kenny Wharram, Chi., Mar. 16	7.00	12.00
☐ 99	Kent Douglas, Tor., Mar. 23	7.00	12.00
1963 - 64 STARS OF THE WORLD'S FASTEST GAME			
☐ 100	John Bucyk, Bos., Dec. 7	11.00	18.00
☐ 101	Bob Pulford, Tor., Dec. 14	9.00	15.00
☐ 102	Stan Mikita, Chi., Dec. 21	20.00	30.00
☐ 103	Henri Richard, Mtl., Dec. 28	13.00	22.00
☐ 104	Bobby Hull, Chi., Jan. 4	22.00	35.00
☐ 105	Bobby Rousseau, Mtl., Jan. 11	7.00	12.00
☐ 106	Tim Horton, Tor., Jan. 18	20.00	30.00
☐ 107	Andy Bathgate, NYR., Jan. 25	9.00	15.00
☐ 108	Bob Baun, Tor., Feb. 1	7.00	12.00
☐ 109	Glenn Hall (G), Chi., Feb. 8	20.00	30.00
☐ 110	Alan Stanley, Tor., Feb. 15	9.00	15.00
☐ 111	Vic Hadfield, NYR., Feb. 22	9.00	15.00
☐ 112	Kenny Wharram, Chi., Feb. 29	7.00	12.00
☐ 113	Gordie Howe, Det., Mar. 7	30.00	50.00
☐ 114	Charlie Hodge (G), Mtl., Mar. 14	9.00	15.00
☐ 115	Marcel Pronovost, Det., Mar. 21	9.00	15.00
☐ 116	George Armstrong, Tor., Mar. 28	11.00	18.00
☐ 117	Jean Béliveau, Mtl., Apr. 4	20.00	30.00
1964 - 65 STARS OF THE WORLD'S FASTEST GAME			
☐ 118	Stan Mikita, Chi., Dec. 5	20.00	30.00
☐ 119	Bobby Hull, Chi., Dec. 12	22.00	35.00
☐ 120	Tim Horton, Tor., Dec. 19	20.00	30.00
☐ 121	Jean Béliveau, Mtl., Dec. 26	20.00	30.00
☐ 122	Bob Pulford, Tor., Jan. 2	9.00	15.00
☐ 123	Dean Prentice, NYR., Jan. 9	7.00	12.00
☐ 124	Ron Ellis, Tor., Jan. 16	7.00	12.00
☐ 125	Rod Gilbert, NYR., Jan. 23	11.00	18.00
☐ 126	Jacques Laperrière, Mtl., Jan. 30	11.00	18.00

☐ 127	Terry Sawchuk (G), Tor., Feb. 6	25.00	40.00
☐ 128	February 13, Not Issue		
☐ 129	Charlie Hodge (G), Mtl., Feb. 20	9.00	15.00
☐ 130	Vic Hadfield, NYR., Feb. 27	7.00	12.00
☐ 131	Frank Mahovlich, Tor., Mar. 6	20.00	30.00
☐ 132	Glenn Hall (G), Chi., Mar. 13	20.00	30.00
☐ 133	Ken Wharram, Chi., Mar. 20	7.00	12.00
☐ 134	Norm Ullman, Det., Mar. 27	11.00	18.00

1965 - 66 HOCKEY'S HOTTEST

☐ 135	Marcel Pronovost, Tor., Dec. 18	9.00	15.00
☐ 136	Henri Richard, Mtl., Dec. 25	13.00	22.00
☐ 137	Norm Ullman, Det., Jan. 1	11.00	18.00
☐ 138	Frank Mahovlich, Tor., Jan. 8	20.00	30.00
☐ 139	Ed Giacomin (G), NYR., Jan. 15	20.00	30.00
☐ 140	Jean Béliveau, Mtl., Jan. 22	20.00	30.00
☐ 141	Doug Mohns, Chi., Jan. 29	7.00	12.00
☐ 142	Eddie Shack, Tor., Feb. 5	12.00	20.00
☐ 143	Claude Provost, Mtl., Feb. 12	7.00	12.00
☐ 144	Ted Green, Bos., Feb. 19	7.00	12.00
☐ 145	Tim Horton, Tor., Feb. 26	20.00	30.00
☐ 146	Jacques Lapierrère, Mtl., Mar. 5	9.00	15.00
☐ 147	Bill Hay, Chi., Mar. 12	7.00	12.00
☐ 148	Dave Keon, Tor., Mar. 19	13.00	22.00
☐ 149	J. C. Tremblay, Mtl., Mar. 26	9.00	15.00
☐ 150	Bob Baun, Tor., Apr. 2	7.00	12.00

1957 - 58 PARKHURST

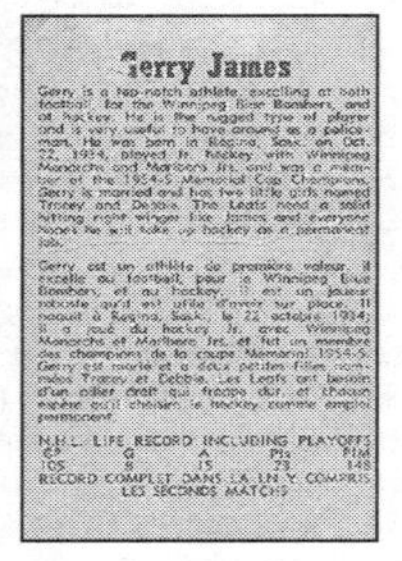

The NHL Album offer no longer appeared on the Parkhurst cards. Mint condition cards do command a premium.

Card Size: 2 7/16" x 3 5/8"
Face: Four colour, white border, Number, Team logo
Back: Blue on card stock, Resume, Bilingual
Imprint: None

Complete Set (50 cards):		**2,200.00**	**3,400.00**
Common Player:		**15.00**	**25.00**
No.	**Player**	**EX**	**NRMT**
☐ 1	Doug Harvey, Mtl. (*)	115.00	225.00
☐ 2	Bernie Geoffrion, Mtl. (*)	80.00	130.00
☐ 3	Jean Béliveau, Mtl. (*)	200.00	325.00
☐ **4**	**Henri Richard, RC, Mtl. (*)**	**400.00**	**650.00**
☐ 5	Maurice Richard, Mtl. (*)	300.00	475.00
☐ 6	Tom Johnson, Mtl.	22.00	35.00
☐ **7**	**André Pronovost, Mtl., RC**	**15.00**	**25.00**
☐ 8	Don Marshall, Mtl.	22.00	35.00
☐ 9	Jean-Guy Talbot, Mtl.	15.00	25.00
☐ 10	Dollard St. Lauren, Mtl.t	15.00	25.00
☐ **11**	**Phil Goyette, Mtl., RC**	**25.00**	**40.00**
☐ **12**	**Claude Provost, Mtl., RC**	**28.00**	**45.00**
☐ 13	Bob Turner, Mtl.	15.00	25.00
☐ 14	Dickie Moore, Mtl.	40.00	65.00
☐ 15	Jacques Plante (G), Mtl.	285.00	450.00
☐ 16	Toe Blake, Coach, Mtl.	28.00	45.00
☐ **17**	**Charlie Hodge (G), Mtl., RC**	**60.00**	**100.00**
☐ 18	Marcel Bonin, Mtl.	15.00	25.00
☐ 19	Bert Olmstead, Mtl.	22.00	35.00
☐ 20	Floyd Curry, Mtl., LC	15.00	25.00
☐ 21	Canadiens on Guard	25.00	40.00
☐ 22	Barry Cullen Scores	20.00	30.00
☐ 23	Puck and Sticks High	28.00	45.00
☐ 24	Geoffrion Sidesteps Chadwick	30.00	50.00
☐ 25	Olmstead Beats Chadwick	35.00	55.00
☐ 1	George Armstrong, Tor. (*)	50.00	80.00
☐ **2**	**Ed Chadwick (G), Tor., RC (*)**	**75.00**	**125.00**
☐ 3	Dick Duff, Tor. (*)	28.00	45.00
☐ **4**	**Bob Pulford, Tor., RC (*)**	**60.00**	**100.00**
☐ 5	Tod Sloan, Tor. (*)	25.00	40.00
☐ 6	Rudy Migay, Tor., LC	15.00	25.00
☐ 7	Ron Stewart, Tor.	15.00	25.00
☐ **8**	**Gerry James, Tor., RC**	**22.00**	**35.00**
☐ 9	Brian Cullen, Tor.	15.00	25.00
☐ 10	Sid Smith, Tor., LC	15.00	25.00
☐ 11	Jim Morrison, Tor.	15.00	25.00
☐ 12	Marc Reaume, Tor.	15.00	25.00
☐ 13	Hugh Bolton, Tor., LC	15.00	25.00
☐ 14	Pete Conacher, Tor., LC	15.00	25.00
☐ 15	Billy Harris, Tor.	15.00	25.00
☐ **16**	**Mike Nykoluk, Tor., RC, LC**	**15.00**	**25.00**
☐ **17**	**Frank Mahovlich, Tor., RC**	**350.00**	**550.00**
☐ **18**	**Kenny Girard, Tor., RC, LC**	**15.00**	**25.00**
☐ **19**	**Al MacNeil, Tor., RC, Err. (McNeil)**	**15.00**	**25.00**
☐ **20**	**Bob Baun, Tor., RC**	**60.00**	**95.00**
☐ **21**	**Barry Cullen, Tor., RC**	**15.00**	**25.00**
☐ 22	Tim Horton, Tor.	135.00	225.00
☐ **23**	**Gary Collins, Tor., RC, LC**	**15.00**	**25.00**
☐ **24**	**Gary Aldcorn, Tor., RC**	**15.00**	**25.00**
☐ 25	Billy Reay, Coach, Tor.	25.00	45.00

1957 - 58 TOPPS

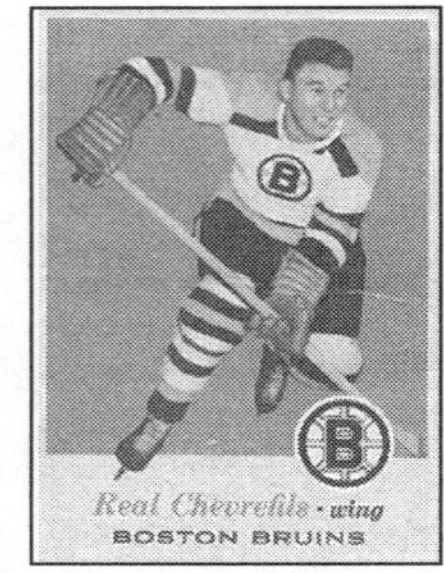

The quality of the card stock continued to create problems with card appearance. A loss of gloss from the card surface occurs as the card ages. Mint condition cards do command a premium.

Card Size: 2 1/2" x 3 1/2"
Face: Four colour, white border, Team logo
Back: Red and blue on card stock, Hockey trivia, Number, Resume, Bilingual
Imprint: T.C.G. PRINTED IN U.S.A.

Complete Set (66 cards):		**1,600.00**	**2,600.00**
Common Player:		**12.00**	**20.00**
No.	**Player**	**EX**	**NRMT**
☐ 1	Real Chevrefils, Bos., LC	22.00	50.00
☐ **2**	**Jack Bionda, Bos., RC, LC**	**12.00**	**20.00**
☐ 3	Bob Armstrong, Bos.	12.00	20.00
☐ 4	Fern Flaman, Bos.	18.00	30.00
☐ 5	Jerry Toppazzini, Bos.	12.00	20.00
☐ **6**	**Larry Regan, Bos., RC**	**12.00**	**20.00**
☐ **7**	**Bronco Horvath, Bos., RC**	**15.00**	**25.00**
☐ 8	Jack Caffery, Bos., LC	12.00	20.00
☐ 9	Léo Labine, Bos.	12.00	20.00
☐ **10**	**John Bucyk, Bos., RC**	**150.00**	**225.00**
☐ 11	Vic Stasiuk, Bos.	12.00	20.00
☐ 12	Doug Mohns, Bos.	15.00	25.00
☐ 13	Don McKenney, Bos.	15.00	25.00
☐ **14**	**Don Simmons (G), Bos., RC**	**20.00**	**30.00**
☐ 15	Allan Stanley, Bos.	25.00	40.00
☐ 16	Fleming Mackell, Bos.	12.00	20.00
☐ **17**	**Larry Hillman, Bos., RC**	**15.00**	**25.00**
☐ 18	Léo Boivin, Bos.	15.00	25.00
☐ 19	Bob Bailey, Chi., LC	12.00	20.00
☐ **20**	**Glenn Hall (G), Chi., RC**	**275.00**	**425.00**
☐ 21	Ted Lindsay, Chi.	35.00	55.00
☐ **22**	**Pierre Pilote, Chi., RC**	**100.00**	**150.00**
☐ 23	Jim Thomson, Chi., LC	12.00	20.00
☐ 24	Eric Nesterenko, Chi.	15.00	25.00
☐ 25	Gus Mortson, Chi.	12.00	20.00
☐ **26**	**Ed Litzenberger, Chi., RC**	**15.00**	**25.00**
☐ **27**	**Elmer Vasko, Chi., RC**	**22.00**	**35.00**
☐ 28	Jack McIntyre, Chi.	12.00	20.00
☐ 29	Ron Murphy, Chi.	12.00	20.00
☐ 30	Glen Skov, Chi.	12.00	20.00
☐ **31**	**Hec Lalande, Chi., RC, LC**	**12.00**	**20.00**
☐ 32	Nick Mickoski, Chi.	12.00	20.00
☐ 33	Wally Hergesheimer, Chi., LC	12.00	20.00
☐ 34	Alex Delvecchio, Det.	35.00	55.00
☐ 35	Terry Sawchuk (G), Det., Err. (Sawchuck)	130.00	215.00
☐ **36**	**Guyle Fielder, Det., RC, LC**	**15.00**	**25.00**
☐ **37**	**Tom McCarthy, Det., RC, LC**	**12.00**	**20.00**
☐ 38	Al Arbour, Det.	30.00	50.00
☐ **39**	**Billy Dea, Det., RC**	**12.00**	**20.00**
☐ 40	Lorne Ferguson, Det.	12.00	20.00
☐ 41	Warren Godfrey, Det.	12.00	20.00
☐ 42	Gordie Howe, Det.	335.00	550.00
☐ 43	Marcel Pronovost, Det.	15.00	25.00
☐ **44**	**Billy McNeill, Det., RC**	**15.00**	**25.00**
☐ 45	Earl Reibel, Det.	12.00	20.00
☐ **46**	**Norm Ullman, Det., RC**	**130.00**	**215.00**
☐ 47	Johnny Wilson, Det.	12.00	20.00
☐ 48	Red Kelly, Det.	35.00	55.00
☐ 49	Bill Dineen, Det., LC	12.00	20.00
☐ **50**	**Forbes Kennedy, Det., RC**	**15.00**	**25.00**
☐ 51	Harry Howell, NYR.	28.00	45.00
☐ **52**	**Jean-Guy Gendron, NYR., RC**	**15.00**	**25.00**
☐ 53	Gump Worsley (G), NYR.	80.00	130.00
☐ 54	Larry Popein, NYR.	12.00	20.00
☐ 55	Jack Evans, NYR.	12.00	20.00
☐ 56	Red Sullivan, NYR.	12.00	20.00
☐ **57**	**Gerry Foley, NYR., RC, LC**	**12.00**	**20.00**
☐ **58**	**Andy Hebenton, NYR., RC**	**12.00**	**20.00**
☐ 59	Larry Cahan, NYR.	12.00	20.00
☐ 60	Andy Bathgate, NYR.	28.00	45.00
☐ 61	Danny Lewicki, NYR.	12.00	20.00
☐ 62	Dean Prentice, NYR.	15.00	25.00
☐ 63	Camille Henry, NYR.	15.00	25.00
☐ **64**	**Louie Fontinato, NYR., RC**	**22.00**	**35.00**
☐ 65	Bill Gadsby, NYR.	22.00	35.00
☐ 66	Dave Creighton, NYR.	22.00	50.00

1958 - 59 PARKHURST

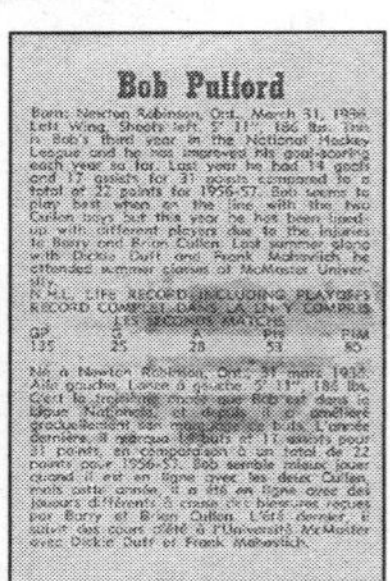

Mint condition cards do command a premium.

Card Size: 2 7/16" x 3 5/8"
Face: Four colour, white border, Team logo, Number, Position
Back: Black on card stock, Resume, Bilingual
Imprint: None

Complete Set (50 cards):		**1,400.00**	**2,400.00**
Common Player:		**12.00**	**25.00**
No.	**Player**	**EX**	**NRMT**
☐ 1	Pulford Comes Close	40.00	75.00
☐ 2	Henri Richard, Mtl.	150.00	250.00
☐ 3	André Pronovost, Mtl.	12.00	25.00
☐ 4	Billy Harris, Tor.	12.00	25.00
☐ **5**	**Al Langlois, Mtl., RC**	**12.00**	**25.00**
☐ **6**	**Noel Price, Tor., RC**	**12.00**	**25.00**
☐ 7	Armstrong Breaks Through	22.00	35.00
☐ 8	Dickie Moore, Mtl.	30.00	50.00
☐ 9	Toe Blake, Coach, Mtl.	22.00	35.00
☐ 10	Tom Johnson, Mtl.	20.00	30.00
☐ 11	An Object of Interest	40.00	65.00
☐ 12	Ed Chadwick (G), Tor.	25.00	40.00
☐ **13**	**Bob Nevin, Tor., RC**	**22.00**	**35.00**
☐ 14	Ron Stewart, Tor.	12.00	25.00
☐ 15	Bob Baun, Tor.	25.00	40.00
☐ **16**	**Ralph Backstrom, Mtl., RC**	**28.00**	**45.00**
☐ 17	Charlie Hodge (G), Mtl.	28.00	45.00
☐ 18	Gary Aldcorn, Tor.	12.00	25.00
☐ 19	Willie Marshall, Tor., LC	12.00	25.00
☐ 20	Marc Reaume, Tor	12.00	25.00
☐ 21	All Eyes on The Puck	40.00	65.00
☐ 22	Jacques Plante (G), Mtl.	200.00	325.00
☐ 23	Allan Stanley, Tor., Err. (Alan/Allen)	22.00	35.00
☐ **24**	**Ian Cushenan, Mtl., RC**	**12.00**	**25.00**
☐ 25	Billy Reay, Coach, Tor.	12.00	25.00
☐ 26	Plante Catches a Shot	40.00	65.00
☐ 27	Bert Olmstead, Tor.	20.00	30.00
☐ 28	Bernie Geoffrion, Mtl.	55.00	90.00
☐ 29	Dick Duff, Tor.	12.00	25.00
☐ **30**	**Ab McDonald, Mtl., RC**	**12.00**	**25.00**
☐ 31	Barry Cullen, Tor.	12.00	25.00

No.	Player	EX	NRMT
☐ 32	Marcel Bonin, Mtl.	12.00	25.00
☐ 33	Frank Mahovlich, Tor.	140.00	235.00
☐ 34	Jean Béliveau, Mtl.	115.00	185.00
☐ 35	Canadiens on Guard	40.00	65.00
☐ 36	Barry Cullen Shoots	12.00	25.00
☐ 37	Stephen Kraftcheck, Tor.	12.00	25.00
☐ 38	Maurice Richard, Mtl.	240.00	375.00
☐ 39	Action Around the Net	40.00	65.00
☐ 40	Bob Turner, Mtl.	12.00	25.00
☐ 41	Jean-Guy Talbot, Mtl.	12.00	25.00
☐ 42	Tim Horton, Tor.	100.00	160.00
☐ 43	Claude Provost, Mtl.	12.00	25.00
☐ 44	Don Marshall, Mtl.	12.00	25.00
☐ 45	Bob Pulford, Tor.	25.00	40.00
☐ 46	Johnny Bower (G), Tor., Err. (Bowers)	110.00	175.00
☐ 47	Phil Goyette, Mtl.	12.00	25.00
☐ 48	George Armstrong, Tor.	28.00	45.00
☐ 49	Doug Harvey, Mtl.	50.00	80.00
☐ 50	Brian Cullen, Tor.	22.00	45.00

1958 - 59 TOPPS

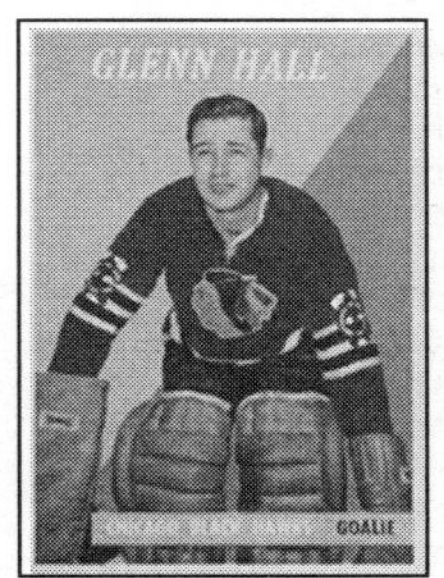

Many cards in this series are off-centre.

Card Size: 2 1/2" x 3 1/2"
Face: Four colour, white border
Back: Black and green on card stock, Number, Resume, Bilingual
Imprint: T.C.G. PRINTED IN U.S.A.

Complete Set (66 cards):		**3,600.00**	**5,800.00**
Common Player:		**12.00**	**20.00**
No.	**Player**	**EX**	**NRMT**
☐ 1	Bob Armstrong, Bos.	20.00	45.00
☐ 2	Terry Sawchuk (G), Det.	135.00	225.00
☐ 3	Glen Skov, Chi.	12.00	20.00
☐ 4	Léo Labine, Bos.	12.00	20.00
☐ 5	Dollard St. Laurent, Chi.	12.00	20.00
☐ 6	Danny Lewicki, Chi., LC	12.00	20.00
☐ **7**	**John Hanna, NYR., RC**	**12.00**	**20.00**
☐ 8	Gordie Howe, Det., Err. (Gordy)	375.00	600.00
☐ 9	Vic Stasiuk, Bos.	12.00	20.00
☐ 10	Larry Regan, Bos.	12.00	20.00
☐ 11	Forbes Kennedy, Det.	12.00	20.00
☐ 12	Elmer Vasko, Chi.	12.00	20.00
☐ 13	Glenn Hall (G), Chi.	120.00	190.00
☐ **14**	**Kenny Wharram, Chi., RC**	**20.00**	**30.00**
☐ **15**	**Len Lunde, Det., RC**	**12.00**	**20.00**
☐ 16	Ed Litzenberger, Chi.	15.00	25.00
☐ **17**	**Norm Johnson, Bos., RC, LC**	**12.00**	**20.00**
☐ **18**	**Earl Ingarfield, NYR., RC**	**15.00**	**25.00**
☐ **19**	**Les Colwill, NYR., RC, LC**	**12.00**	**20.00**
☐ 20	Leo Boivin, Bos.	15.00	25.00
☐ 21	Andy Bathgate, NYR.	12.00	40.00
☐ 22	Johnny Wilson, Det.	12.00	20.00
☐ 23	Larry Cahan, NYR.	12.00	20.00
☐ 24	Marcel Pronovost, Det.	15.00	25.00
☐ 25	Larry Hillman, Bos.	12.00	20.00
☐ **26**	**Jim Bartlett, NYR., RC**	**12.00**	**20.00**
☐ 27	Nick Mickoski, Det.	12.00	20.00
☐ 28	Larry Popein, NYR.	12.00	20.00
☐ 29	Fleming Mackell, Bos.	12.00	20.00
☐ **30**	**Eddie Shack, NYR., RC**	**175.00**	**275.00**
☐ 31	Jack Evans, Chi.	12.00	20.00
☐ 32	Dean Prentice, NYR.	12.00	20.00
☐ **33**	**Claude Laforge, Det., RC**	**12.00**	**20.00**
☐ 34	Bill Gadsby, NYR.	20.00	30.00
☐ 35	Bronco Horvath, Bos.	12.00	20.00
☐ 36	Pierre Pilote, Chi.	50.00	75.00
☐ 37	Earl Balfour, Chi.	12.00	20.00
☐ 38	Gus Mortson, Det., LC	12.00	20.00
☐ 39	Gump Worsley (G), NYR.	60.00	95.00
☐ 40	John Bucyk, Bos.	70.00	110.00
☐ 41	Louie Fontinato, NYR.	12.00	20.00
☐ 42	Tod Sloan, Chi.	12.00	20.00
☐ **43**	**Charlie Burns, Det., RC**	**15.00**	**25.00**
☐ 44	Don Simmons (G), Bos.	15.00	25.00
☐ 45	Jerry Toppazzini, Bos., Err. (Toppazini)	12.00	20.00
☐ 46	Andy Hebenton, NYR.	12.00	20.00
☐ **47**	**Peter Goegan, Det., RC, Err. (Geogan)**	**12.50**	**20.00**
☐ 48	George Sullivan, NYR.	12.00	20.00
☐ **49**	**Hank Ciesla, NYR., RC**	**12.00**	**20.00**
☐ 50	Doug Mohns, Bos.	15.00	25.00
☐ 51	Jean-Guy Gendron, Bos.	12.00	20.00
☐ 52	Alex Delvecchio, Det.	30.00	50.00
☐ 53	Eric Nesterenko, Chi.	15.00	25.00
☐ 54	Camille Henry, NYR.	12.00	20.00
☐ 55	Lorne Ferguson, Chi., LC	12.00	20.00
☐ 56	Fern Flaman, Bos.	20.00	30.00
☐ 57	Earl Reibel, Bos., LC	12.00	20.00
☐ 58	Warren Godfrey, Det.	12.00	20.00
☐ 59	Ron Murphy, Chi.	12.00	20.00
☐ 60	Harry Howell, NYR.	25.00	40.00
☐ 61	Red Kelly, Det.	30.00	45.00
☐ 62	Don McKenney, Bos.	12.00	20.00
☐ 63	Ted Lindsay, Chi.	30.00	45.00
☐ 64	Al Arbour, Chi.	22.00	35.00
☐ 65	Norm Ullman, Det.	75.00	120.00
☐ **66**	**Bobby Hull, Chi., RC**	**1,500.00**	**3,200.00**

1959 - 60 PARKHURST

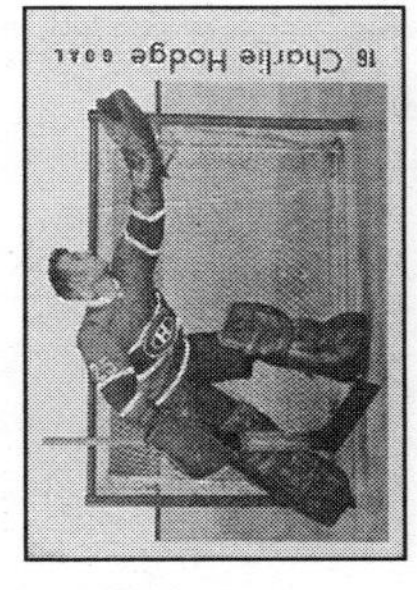

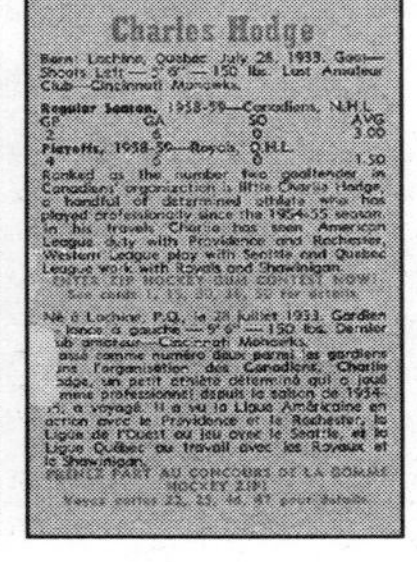

Card Size: 2 7/16" x 3 5/8"
Face: Four colour, white border, Team logo, Mixed Formats, Number
Back: Two colour, red and black on card stock; Resume, Bilingual
Imprint: None

Complete Set (50 cards):		**1,000.00**	**1,700.00**
Common Player:		**13.00**	**22.00**
No.	**Player**	**EX**	**NRMT**
☐ 1	Canadiens on Guard	45.00	90.00
☐ 2	Maurice Richard, Mtl.	200.00	325.00
☐ **3**	**Carl Brewer, Tor., RC**	**35.00**	**55.00**
☐ 4	Phil Goyette, Mtl.	13.00	22.00
☐ 5	Ed Chadwick (G), Tor., LC	20.00	30.00
☐ 6	Jean Béliveau, Mtl.	85.00	140.00
☐ 7	George Armstrong, Tor.	22.00	35.00
☐ 8	Doug Harvey, Mtl.	50.00	75.00
☐ 9	Billy Harris, Tor.	13.00	22.00
☐ 10	Tom Johnson, Mtl.	18.00	28.00
☐ 11	Marc Reaume, Tor.	13.00	22.00
☐ 12	Marcel Bonin, Mtl.	13.00	22.00
☐ 13	Johnny Wilson, Tor.	13.00	22.00
☐ 14	Dickie Moore, Mtl.	25.00	40.00
☐ 15	Punch Imlach, Tor., Manager & Coach	28.00	45.00
☐ 16	Charlie Hodge (G), Mtl.	18.00	28.00
☐ 17	Larry Regan, Tor.	13.00	22.00
☐ 18	Claude Provost, Mtl.	13.00	22.00
☐ **19**	**Gerry Ehman, Tor., RC**	**13.00**	**22.00**
☐ 20	Ab McDonald, Mtl.	13.00	22.00
☐ 21	Bob Baun, Tor.	22.00	35.00
☐ 22	Ken Reardon, Mtl., Vice President	18.00	28.00
☐ 23	Tim Horton, Tor.	75.00	125.00
☐ 24	Frank Mahovlich, Tor.	90.00	145.00
☐ 25	Bower In Action	30.00	50.00
☐ 26	Ron Stewart, Tor.	13.00	22.00
☐ 27	Toe Blake, Coach, Mtl.	20.00	30.00
☐ 28	Bob Pulford, Tor.	20.00	30.00
☐ 29	Ralph Backstrom, Mtl.	13.00	22.00
☐ 30	Action Around the Net	18.00	28.00
☐ **31**	**Bill Hicke, Mtl., RC**	**13.00**	**22.00**
☐ 32	Johnny Bower (G), Tor.	65.00	110.00
☐ 33	Bernie Geoffrion, Mtl.	50.00	75.00
☐ **34**	**Ted Hampson, Tor., RC**	**13.00**	**22.00**
☐ 35	André Pronovost, Mtl.	13.00	22.00
☐ 36	Stafford Smythe, Chairman, Tor.	13.00	22.00
☐ 37	Don Marshall, Mtl.	13.00	22.00
☐ 38	Dick Duff, Tor.	13.00	22.00
☐ 39	Henri Richard, Mtl.	75.00	125.00
☐ 40	Bert Olmstead, Tor.	18.00	28.00
☐ 41	Jacques Plante (G), Mtl.	160.00	265.00
☐ 42	Noel Price, Tor.	13.00	22.00
☐ 43	Bob Turner, Mtl.	13.00	22.00
☐ 44	Allan Stanley, Tor.	20.00	30.00
☐ 45	Al Langlois, Mtl.	13.00	22.00
☐ 46	Officials Intervene	13.00	22.00
☐ 47	Frank Selke, Mtl., Managing Director	18.00	28.00
☐ **48**	**Gary Edmundson, Tor., RC**	**13.00**	**22.00**
☐ 49	Jean-Guy Talbot, Mtl.	13.00	22.00
☐ 50	Francis (King) Clancy, AGM, Tor.	45.00	85.00

1959 - 60 TOPPS

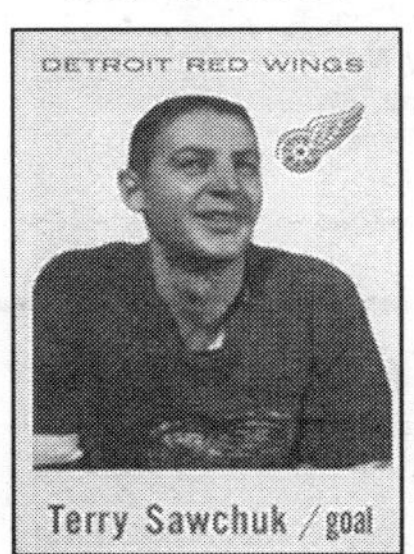

The 59-60 series is perhaps Topps worst effort at centering. Well centered NRMT and mint cards are very scarce and have high price premiums.

Card Size: 2 1/2" x 3 1/2"
Face: Four colour, white border, Team logo
Back: Two colour, red and black on card stock, Number, Resume, Hockey trivia, Bilingual
Imprint: T.C.G. PRINTED IN U.S.A.

Complete Set (66 cards):		**1,600.00**	**2,600.00**
Common Player:		**10.00**	**18.00**
No.	**Player**	**EX**	**NRMT**
☐ 1	Eric Nesterenko, Chi.	20.00	45.00
☐ 2	Pierre Pilote, Chi.	30.00	50.00
☐ 3	Elmer Vasko, Chi.	15.00	25.00
☐ 4	Peter Goegan, Det.	12.00	20.00
☐ 5	Louie Fontinato, NYR.	12.00	20.00
☐ 6	Ted Lindsay, Chi.	25.00	40.00
☐ 7	Léo Labine, Bos.	12.00	20.00
☐ 8	Alex Delvecchio, Det., Err. (Wing)	25.00	40.00
☐ 9	Don McKenney, Bos., Err. (Mckenny)	12.00	20.00
☐ 10	Earl Ingarfield, NYR.	12.00	20.00
☐ 11	Don Simmons (G), Bos.	15.00	25.00
☐ 12	Glen Skov, Chi., LC	12.00	20.00
☐ 13	Tod Sloan, Chi.	12.00	20.00
☐ 14	Vic Stasiuk, Bos.	12.00	20.00
☐ 15	Gump Worsley (G), NYR.	50.00	80.00
☐ 16	Andy Hebenton, NYR.	12.00	20.00
☐ 17	Dean Prentice, NYR.	12.00	20.00
☐ 18	Oops! Pardon My Stick! Strickly Accidental!	10.00	18.00
☐ 19	Fleming Mackell, Bos., LC	12.00	20.00
☐ 20	Harry Howell, NYR.	22.00	35.00
☐ 21	Larry Popein, NYR., LC	12.00	20.00
☐ 22	Len Lunde, Det.	12.00	20.00
☐ 23	John Bucyk, Bos.	50.00	75.00
☐ 24	Jean-Guy Gendron, Bos.	12.00	20.00
☐ 25	Barry Cullen, Det., Err. (Brian's resumé)	12.00	20.00
☐ 26	Leo Boivin, Bos.	15.00	25.00
☐ 27	Warren Godfrey, Det.	12.00	20.00
☐ 28	Hall / Henry (Action)	25.00	40.00
☐ 29	Fern Flaman, Bos.	15.00	25.00
☐ 30	Jack Evans, Chi.	12.00	20.00
☐ 31	John Hanna, NYR., LC	12.00	20.00
☐ 32	Glenn Hall (G), Chi.	70.00	110.00
☐ **33**	**Murray Balfour, Chi., RC**	**15.00**	**25.00**
☐ 34	Andy Bathgate, NYR.	22.00	35.00
☐ 35	Al Arbour, Chi.	20.00	30.00
☐ 36	Jim Morrison, Det.	12.00	20.00
☐ 37	Nick Mickoski, Bos., LC	12.00	20.00
☐ 38	Jerry Toppazzini, Bos.	12.00	20.00
☐ 39	Bob Armstrong, Bos.	12.00	20.00

No.	Player	EX	NRMT
☐ 40	Charlie Burns, Bos., Err. (Charley)	12.00	20.00
☐ 41	Billy McNeill, Det.	12.00	20.00
☐ 42	Terry Sawchuk (G), Det.	110.00	170.00
☐ 43	Dollard St. Laurent, Chi.	12.00	20.00
☐ 44	Marcel Pronovost, Det.	15.00	25.00
☐ 45	Norm Ullman, Det.	50.00	75.00
☐ 46	Camille Henry, NYR.	12.00	20.00
☐ 47	Bobby Hull, Chi., Err. (Center)	400.00	650.00
☐ 48	Howe / Evans (Action)	75.00	120.00
☐ **49**	**Lou Marcon, Det., RC, LC**	**12.00**	**20.00**
☐ 50	Earl Balfour, Chi.	12.00	20.00
☐ 51	Jim Bartlett, NYR., LC	12.00	20.00
☐ 52	Forbes Kennedy, Det.	12.00	20.00
☐ 53	Mickoski / Hanna (Action)	10.00	18.00
☐ 54	N. Johnson / Worsley (Action)	22.00	35.00
☐ 55	Brian Cullen, NYR., LC	12.00	20.00
☐ 56	Bronco Horvath, Bos.	12.00	20.00
☐ 57	Eddie Shack, NYR.	70.00	110.00
☐ 58	Doug Mohns, Bos.	15.00	25.00
☐ 59	George Sullivan. NYR.	12.00	20.00
☐ 60	Pilote / Mackell (Action)	10.00	18.00
☐ 61	Ed Litzenberger, Chi.	12.00	20.00
☐ 62	Bill Gadsby, NYR.	20.00	30.00
☐ 63	Gordie Howe, Det.	300.00	500.00
☐ 64	Claude LaForge, Det.	12.00	20.00
☐ 65	Red Kelly, Det.	22.00	35.00
☐ 66	Ron Murphy, Chi.	20.00	45.00

1960 - 61 PARKHURST

Card Size: 2 7/16" x 3 5/8"
Face: Four colour, white border, black and yellow banner; Number
Back: Resume, Bilingual
Toronto: Red on card stock with blue overprint logo
Detroit and Montréal: Blue on card stock with red overprint logo
Imprint: None

Complete Set (61 cards):		**1,400.00**	**2,300.00**
Common Player:		**12.00**	**20.00**
No.	**Player**	**EX**	**NRMT**
☐ 1	Tim Horton, Tor.	100.00	200.00
☐ 2	Frank Mahovlich, Tor.	75.00	125.00
☐ 3	Johnny Bower (G), Tor.	55.00	85.00
☐ 4	Bert Olmstead, Tor.	15.00	25.00
☐ 5	Gary Edmundson, Tor., LC	12.00	20.00
☐ 6	Ron Stewart, Tor.	12.00	20.00
☐ 7	Gerry James, Tor., LC	12.00	20.00
☐ 8	Gerry Ehman, Tor.	12.00	20.00
☐ 9	Red Kelly, Tor.	22.00	35.00
☐ 10	Dave Creighton, Tor., LC	12.00	20.00
☐ 11	Bob Baun, Tor.	12.00	20.00
☐ 12	Dick Duff, Tor.	12.00	20.00
☐ 13	Larry Regan, Tor., LC	12.00	20.00
☐ 14	Johnny Wilson, Tor., LC	12.00	20.00
☐ 15	Billy Harris, Tor.	12.00	20.00
☐ 16	Allan Stanley, Tor.	20.00	30.00
☐ 17	George Armstrong, Tor.	20.00	30.00
☐ 18	Carl Brewer, Tor.	12.00	20.00
☐ 19	Bob Pulford, Tor.	20.00	30.00
☐ 20	Gordie Howe, Det.	240.00	375.00
☐ **21**	**Val Fonteyne, Det., RC**	**12.00**	**20.00**
☐ **22**	**Murray Oliver, Det., RC**	**20.00**	**30.00**
☐ 23	Sid Abel, Coach, Det.	15.00	25.00
☐ 24	Jack McIntyre, Det., LC	12.00	20.00
☐ 25	Marc Reaume, Det.	12.00	20.00
☐ 26	Norm Ullman, Det.	35.00	55.00
☐ **27**	**Brian S. Smith, Det., RC, LC**	**12.00**	**20.00**
☐ **28**	**Gerry Melnyk, Det., RC, Err. (Jerry)**	**12.00**	**20.00**
☐ 29	Marcel Pronovost, Det.	15.00	25.00
☐ 30	Warren Godfrey, Det.	12.00	20.00
☐ 31	Terry Sawchuk (G), Det.	100.00	160.00
☐ 32	Barry Cullen, Det., LC	12.00	20.00
☐ 33	Gary Aldcorn, Det., LC	12.00	20.00
☐ 34	Peter Goegan, Det.	12.00	20.00
☐ 35	Len Lunde, Det.	12.00	20.00
☐ 36	Alex Delvecchio, Det.	22.00	35.00
☐ **37**	**John McKenzie, Det., RC**	**22.00**	**35.00**
☐ 38	Dickie Moore, Mtl.	22.00	35.00
☐ 39	Al Langlois, Mtl.	12.00	20.00
☐ 40	Bill Hicke, Mtl.	12.00	20.00
☐ 41	Ralph Backstrom, Mtl.	12.00	20.00
☐ 42	Don Marshall, Mtl.	12.00	20.00
☐ 43	Bob Turner, Mtl.	12.00	20.00
☐ 44	Tom Johnson, Mtl.	15.00	25.00
☐ 45	Maurice Richard, Mtl., LC	165.00	275.00
☐ 46	Bernie Geoffrion, Mtl.	40.00	65.00
☐ 47	Henri Richard, Mtl.	60.00	95.00
☐ 48	Doug Harvey, Mtl.	35.00	60.00
☐ 49	Jean Béliveau, Mtl.	65.00	110.00
☐ 50	Phil Goyette, Mtl.	12.00	20.00
☐ 51	Marcel Bonin, Mtl.	12.00	20.00
☐ 52	Jean-Guy Talbot, Mtl.	12.00	20.00
☐ 53	Jacques Plante (G), Mtl.	120.00	200.00
☐ 54	Claude Provost, Mtl.	12.00	20.00
☐ 55	André Pronovost, Mtl.	12.00	20.00
☐ 56	Bill Hicke / Ralph Backstrom / Ab McDonald	15.00	25.00
☐ 57	Don Marshall / Henri Richard / Dickie Moore	35.00	55.00
☐ 58	Claude Provost / Phil Goyette / André Pronovost	15.00	25.00
☐ 59	Bernie Geoffrion / Jean Béliveau / Don Marshall	55.00	90.00
☐ 60	Ab McDonald, Mtl.	12.00	20.00
☐ 61	Jim Morrison, Det.	65.00	130.00

1960 - 1961 SHIRRIFF COINS

This is the first year of issue for Shirriff Foods. These hockey coins were used as premiums in Shirriff's desserts. There is a clear plastic crystal on each coin. The paper was loose under the crystal.

Cap Diameter: 1 9/16"
Face: Four colour; Name, Number
Back: "SAVE 120 'HOCKEY COINS' COLLECTIONNEZ LES 120 PIÈCES DE HOCKEY"
Imprint: Shirriff Lushus Jelly & Puddings Pat. Pend.

Complete Set (120 coins):		**325.00**	**550.00**
Common Player:		**2.50**	**4.25**
No.	**Player**	**EX**	**NRMT**
☐ 1	Johnny Bower (G), Tor.	9.00	15.00
☐ 2	Dick Duff, Tor.	2.50	4.25
☐ 3	Carl Brewer, Tor.	2.50	4.25
☐ 4	Red Kelly, Tor.	6.50	11.00
☐ 5	Tim Horton, Tor.	11.00	18.00
☐ 6	Allan Stanley, Tor.	3.50	6.00
☐ 7	Bob Baun, Tor.	2.50	4.25
☐ 8	Billy Harris, Tor.	2.50	4.25
☐ 9	George Armstrong, Tor.	5.50	9.00
☐ 10	Ron Stewart, Tor.	2.50	4.25
☐ 11	Bert Olmstead, Tor.	3.50	6.00
☐ 12	Frank Mahovlich, Tor.	11.00	18.00
☐ 13	Bob Pulford, Tor.	4.50	7.50
☐ 14	Garry Edmundson, Tor.	2.50	4.25
☐ 15	Johnny Wilson, Tor.	2.50	4.25
☐ 16	Larry Regan, Tor.	2.50	4.25
☐ 17	Gerry James, Tor.	2.50	4.25
☐ 18	Rudy Migay, Tor.	2.50	4.25
☐ 19	Gerry Ehman, Tor.	2.50	4.25
☐ 20	Punch Imlach, Coach, Tor.	3.50	6.00
☐ 21	Jacques Plante (G), Mtl.	15.00	25.00
☐ 22	Dickie Moore, Mtl.	6.50	11.00
☐ 23	Don Marshall, Mtl.	2.50	4.25
☐ 24	Al Langlois, Mtl.	2.50	4.25
☐ 25	Tom Johnson, Mtl.	3.50	6.00
☐ 26	Doug Harvey, Mtl.	8.50	14.00
☐ 27	Phil Goyette, Mtl.	2.50	4.25
☐ 28	Bernie Geoffrion, Mtl.	9.00	15.00
☐ 29	Marcel Bonin, Mtl.	2.50	4.25
☐ 30	Jean Béliveau, Mtl.	15.00	25.00
☐ 31	Ralph Backstrom, Mtl.	2.50	4.25
☐ 32	André Pronovost, Mtl.	2.50	4.25
☐ 33	Claude Provost, Mtl.	2.50	4.25
☐ 34	Henri Richard, Mtl.	8.50	14.00
☐ 35	Jean-Guy Talbot, Mtl.	2.50	4.25
☐ 36	J.C. Tremblay, Mtl.	3.00	5.00
☐ 37	Bob Turner, Mtl.	2.50	4.25
☐ 38	Bill Hicke, Mtl.	2.50	4.25
☐ 39	Charlie Hodge (G), Mtl.	3.50	6.00
☐ 40	Toe Blake, Coach, Mtl.	4.50	7.50
☐ 41	Terry Sawchuk (G), Det.	15.00	25.00
☐ 42	Gordie Howe, Det.	35.00	60.00
☐ 43	John McKenzie, Det.	2.50	4.25
☐ 44	Alex Delvecchio, Det.	8.00	13.00
☐ 45	Norm Ullman, Det.	6.50	11.00
☐ 46	Jack McIntyre, Det.	2.50	4.25
☐ 47	Barry Cullen, Det.	2.50	4.25
☐ 48	Val Fonteyne, Det.	2.50	4.25
☐ 49	Warren Godfrey, Det.	2.50	4.25
☐ 50	Peter Goegan, Det.	2.50	4.25
☐ 51	Gerry Melnyk, Det., Err. (Jerry)	2.50	4.25
☐ 52	Marc Reaume, Det.	2.50	4.25
☐ 53	Gary Aldcorn, Det.	2.50	4.25
☐ 54	Len Lunde, Det.	2.50	4.25
☐ 55	Murray Oliver, Det.	2.50	4.25
☐ 56	Marcel Pronovost, Det.	3.50	6.00
☐ 57	Howie Glover, Det.	2.50	4.25
☐ 58	Gerry Odrowski, Det.	2.50	4.25
☐ 59	Parker MacDonald, Det.	2.50	4.25
☐ 60	Sid Abel, Coach, Det.	3.50	6.00
☐ 61	Glenn Hall (G), Chi.	11.00	18.00
☐ 62	Ed Litzenberger, Chi.	2.50	4.25
☐ 63	Bobby Hull, Chi.	25.00	40.00
☐ 64	Tod Sloan, Chi.	2.50	4.25
☐ 65	Murray Balfour, Chi.	2.50	4.25
☐ 66	Pierre Pilote, Chi.	3.50	6.00
☐ 67	Al Arbour, Chi.	3.50	6.00
☐ 68	Earl Balfour, Chi.	2.50	4.25
☐ 69	Eric Nesterenko, Chi.	2.50	4.25
☐ 70	Kenny Wharram, Chi.	2.50	4.25
☐ 71	Stan Mikita, Chi.	12.00	20.00
☐ 72	Ab McDonald, Chi.	2.50	4.25
☐ 73	Elmer Vasko, Chi.	2.50	4.25
☐ 74	Dollard St. Laurent, Chi.	2.50	4.25
☐ 75	Ron Murphy, Chi.	2.50	4.25
☐ 76	Jack Evans, Chi.	2.50	4.25
☐ 77	Billy Hay, Chi.	2.50	4.25
☐ 78	Reggie Fleming, Chi.	2.50	4.25
☐ 79	Cecil Hoekstra, Chi.	2.50	4.25
☐ 80	Tommy Ivan, Coach, Chi.	2.50	4.25
☐ 81	Jack McCartan (G), NYR.	3.00	5.00
☐ 82	Red Sullivan, NYR.	2.50	4.25
☐ 83	Camille Henry, NYR.	2.50	4.25
☐ 84	Larry Popein, NYR.	2.50	4.25
☐ 85	John Hanna, NYR.	2.50	4.25
☐ 86	Harry Howell, NYR.	3.50	6.00
☐ 87	Eddie Shack, NYR.	5.50	9.00
☐ 88	Irv Spencer, NYR.	2.50	4.25
☐ 89	Andy Bathgate, NYR.	5.50	9.00
☐ 90	Bill Gadsby, NYR.	3.50	6.00
☐ 91	Andy Hebenton, NYR.	2.50	4.25
☐ 92	Earl Ingarfield, NYR.	2.50	4.25
☐ 93	Don Johns, NYR.	2.50	4.25
☐ 94	Dave Balon, NYR.	2.50	4.25
☐ 95	Jim Morrison, NYR.	2.50	4.25
☐ 96	Ken Schinkel, NYR.	2.50	4.25
☐ 97	Louie Fontinato, NYR.	2.50	4.25
☐ 98	Ted Hampson, NYR.	2.50	4.25
☐ 99	Brian Cullen, NYR.	2.50	4.25
☐ 100	Alf Pike, Coach, NYR.	2.50	4.25
☐ 101	Don Simmons (G), Bos.	3.00	5.00
☐ 102	Fern Flaman, Bos.	3.50	6.00
☐ 103	Vic Stasiuk, Bos.	2.50	4.25
☐ 104	John Bucyk, Bos.	8.00	13.00
☐ 105	Bronco Horvath, Bos.	2.50	4.25
☐ 106	Doug Mohns, Bos.	7.00	12.00
☐ 107	Leo Boivin, Bos.	3.50	6.00
☐ 108	Don McKenney, Bos.	2.50	4.25
☐ 109	John-Guy Gendron, Bos.	2.50	4.25
☐ 110	Jerry Toppazzini, Bos.	2.50	4.25
☐ 111	Dick Meissner, Bos.	2.50	4.25
☐ 112	Aut Erickson, Bos.	2.50	4.25
☐ 113	Jim Bartlett, Bos.	2.50	4.25
☐ 114	Orval Tessier, Bos.	2.50	4.25

No.	Player	EX	NRMT
☐ 115	Billy Carter, Bos.	2.50	4.25
☐ 116	Dallas Smith, Bos.	2.50	4.25
☐ 117	Léo Labine, Bos.	2.50	4.25
☐ 118	Bob Armstrong, Bos.	2.50	4.25
☐ 119	Bruce Gamble (G), Bos.	3.00	5.00
☐ 120	Milt Schmidt, Coach, Bos.	7.00	12.00

1960 - 61 TOPPS

The set includes All-Time Great cards as well as players from Boston, Chicago and New York.

Card Size: 2 1/2" x 3 1/2"
Face: Four colour, white border
Back: Orange on card stock, Number, Resume, Quiz, Bilingual
Imprint: T.C.G. PRINTED IN U.S.A.

		EX	NRMT
Complete Set (66 cards):		**1,600.00**	**2,600.00**
Common Player:		**10.00**	**17.00**
No.	**Player**	**EX**	**NRMT**
☐ 1	Lester Patrick, All-Time Great	35.00	75.00
☐ 2	Paddy Moran (G), All-Time Great	15.00	25.00
☐ 3	Joe Malone, All-Time Great	25.00	40.00
☐ 4	Ernest (Moose) Johnson, All-Time Great	13.00	22.00
☐ 5	Nels Stewart, All-Time Great	20.00	30.00
☐ **6**	**Billy Hay, Chi., RC**	**10.00**	**17.00**
☐ 7	Eddie Shack, NYR.	50.00	80.00
☐ 8	Cy Denneny, All-Time Great	13.00	22.00
☐ 9	Jim Morrison, NYR.	10.00	17.00
☐ 10	Bill Cook, All-Time Great	13.00	22.00
☐ 11	John Bucyk, Bos.	35.00	55.00
☐ 12	Murray Balfour, Chi.	10.00	17.00
☐ 13	Léo Labine, Bos.	10.00	17.00
☐ **14**	**Stan Mikita, Chi., RC**	**300.00**	**500.00**
☐ 15	George Hay, All-Time Great	13.00	22.00
☐ 16	Red Dutton, All-Time Great	13.00	22.00
☐ 17	Richard (Dickie) Boon, All-Time Great	13.00	22.00
☐ 18	George Sullivan, NYR.	10.00	17.00
☐ 19	Georges Vézina (G), All-Time Great	40.00	65.00
☐ 20	Eddie Shore, All-Time Great	40.00	65.00
☐ 21	Ed Litzenberger, Chi.	10.00	17.00
☐ 22	Bill Gadsby, NYR.	13.00	22.00
☐ 23	Elmer Vasko, Chi.	10.00	17.00
☐ 24	Charlie Burns, Bos.	10.00	17.00
☐ 25	Glenn Hall (G), Chi.	60.00	100.00
☐ 26	Dit Clapper, All-Time Great	15.00	25.00
☐ 27	Art Ross, All-Time Great	30.00	45.00
☐ 28	Jerry Toppazzini, Bos.	10.00	17.00
☐ 29	Frank Boucher, All-Time Great	13.00	22.00
☐ 30	Jack Evans, Chi.	10.00	17.00
☐ 31	Jean Guy Gendron, Bos.	10.00	17.00
☐ 32	Chuck Gardiner (G), All-Time Great	20.00	30.00
☐ 33	Ab McDonald, Chi.	10.00	17.00
☐ 34	F. Frederickson, All-Time Great, Err. (Fredrickson)	13.00	22.00
☐ 35	Frank Nighbor, All-Time Great	20.00	30.00
☐ 36	Gump Worsley (G), NYR.	40.00	65.00
☐ 37	Dean Prentice, NYR.	10.00	17.00
☐ 38	Hugh Lehman (G), All-Time Great	13.00	22.00
☐ **39**	**Jack McCartan (G), NYR., RC, LC**	**20.00**	**30.00**
☐ 40	Don McKenney, Bos., Err. (Mckenny)	10.00	17.00
☐ 41	Ron Murphy, Chi.	10.00	17.00
☐ 42	Andy Hebenton, NYR.	10.00	17.00
☐ 43	Don Simmons (G), Bos.	13.00	22.00
☐ 44	Herb Gardiner, All-Time Great	13.00	22.00
☐ 45	Andy Bathgate, NYR.	18.00	28.00
☐ 46	Fred (Cyclone) Taylor, All-Time Great	30.00	45.00
☐ 47	Francis (King) Clancy, All-Time Great	30.00	50.00
☐ 48	Edouard (Newsy) Lalonde, All-Time Great	25.00	40.00
☐ 49	Harry Howell, NYR.	18.00	28.00
☐ **50**	**Ken Schinkel, NYR., RC**	**10.00**	**17.00**
☐ 51	Tod Sloan, Chi., LC	10.00	17.00
☐ 52	Doug Mohns, Bos.	10.00	17.00
☐ 53	Camille Henry, NYR.	10.00	17.00
☐ 54	Bronco Horvath, Bos.	10.00	17.00
☐ 55	Tiny Thompson (G), All-Time Great	25.00	40.00
☐ 56	Bob Armstrong, Bos.	10.00	17.00
☐ 57	Fern Flaman, Bos., LC	13.00	22.00
☐ 58	Bobby Hull, Chi.	285.00	450.00
☐ 59	Howie Morenz, All-Time Great	40.00	70.00
☐ 60	Dick Irvin, All-Time Great	22.00	35.00
☐ 61	Louie Fontinato, NYR., LC	10.00	17.00
☐ 62	Leo Boivin, Bos.	13.00	22.00
☐ 63	Francis (Moose) Goheen, All-Time Great	13.00	22.00
☐ 64	Al Arbour, Chi.	18.00	28.00
☐ 65	Pierre Pilote, Chi.	22.00	35.00
☐ 66	Vic Stasiuk, Bos.	20.00	45.00

1960 - 61 WONDER BREAD WRAPPER ISSUE

Single cards of this set came enclosed in plastic at the end of loaves of Wonder Bread. There were two cards per loaf. There was a premium offered whereby customers could send in 25¢ and five cards to Wonder Sports Club for a black and white 5" x 7" photo of the player. This photo was printed on a heavier weight stock than the cards enclosed with the bread.

Card Size: 2 3/4" x 2 3/4"
Face: Red and black
Back: Blank
Imprint: None

		EX	NRMT
Complete Set (4 cards):		**275.00**	**450.00**
No.	**Player**	**EX**	**NRMT**
☐ 1	Gordie Howe, Det.	170.00	275.00
☐ 2	Bobby Hull, Chi.	80.00	135.00
☐ 3	Dave Keon, Tor.	35.00	60.00
☐ 4	Maurice Richard, Mtl.	125.00	200.00

PREMIUM PHOTOS

These photos were available from Wonder Bread by sending 25¢ and five end wrappers to Wonder Sports Club in exchange for a black and white 5" x 7" photo of the player. This photo was printed on a heavier weight stock than the cards enclosed with the bread.

Card Size: 5" x 7"
Face: Black and white glossy on card stock
Back: Blank
Imprint: None

		EX	NRMT
Complete Set (4 cards):		**350.00**	**600.00**
No.	**Player**	**EX**	**NRMT**
☐ 1	Gordie Howe, Det.	200.00	325.00
☐ 2	Bobby Hull, Chi.	110.00	175.00
☐ 3	Dave Keon, Tor.	45.00	75.00
☐ 4	Maurice Richard, Mtl.	150.00	250.00

1960 - 61 YORK PEANUT BUTTER

PREMIUMS

These unnumbered photographs feature players of the Montréal Canadiens and the Toronto Maple Leafs. Players' names are presented in alphabetical order by team. The black and white cards show no indication of the issuer.

Photo Size: 5" x 7"
Face: Black and white; Facsimile autograph
Back: Blank
Imprint: None

		EX	NRMT
Complete Set (37 cards):		**1,500.00**	**2,500.00**
	Player	**EX**	**NRMT**
MONTRÉAL CANADIENS			
☐	Ralph Backstrom	35.00	60.00
☐	Jean Béliveau	120.00	200.00
☐	Marcel Bonin	35.00	60.00
☐	Jean-Guy Gendron	35.00	60.00
☐	Bernie Geoffrion	80.00	130.00
☐	Phil Goyette	35.00	60.00
☐	Doug Harvey	70.00	120.00
☐	Bill Hicke	35.00	60.00
☐	Charlie Hodge (G)	50.00	75.00
☐	Tom Johnson	55.00	85.00
☐	Al Langlois	35.00	60.00
☐	Don Marshall	35.00	60.00
☐	Dickie Moore	60.00	95.00
☐	Jacques Plante (G)	120.00	200.00
☐	Claude Provost	50.00	75.00
☐	Henri Richard	70.00	120.00
☐	Jean-Guy Talbot	35.00	60.00
☐	Gilles Tremblay	35.00	60.00
☐	Bob Turner	35.00	60.00
TORONTO MAPLE LEAFS			
☐	George Armstrong	60.00	95.00
☐	Bob Baun	50.00	75.00
☐	Johnny Bower (G)	80.00	130.00
☐	Carl Brewer	35.00	60.00
☐	Dick Duff	50.00	75.00
☐	Billy Harris	35.00	60.00
☐	Larry Hillman	35.00	60.00
☐	Tim Horton	90.00	145.00
☐	Red Kelly	60.00	100.00
☐	Dave Keon	80.00	130.00
☐	Frank Mahovlich	90.00	145.00
☐	Bob Nevin	35.00	60.00
☐	Bert Olmstead	55.00	85.00
☐	Bob Pulford	55.00	90.00
☐	Larry Regan	35.00	60.00
☐	Eddie Shack	60.00	100.00
☐	Allan Stanley	55.00	85.00
☐	Ron Stewart	35.00	60.00

1960 - 61 PEANUT BUTTER GLASSES

This set may be incomplete. We would appreciate hearing from anyone who could supply further information. Some of the glasses may have been short-printed and are tougher to find.

Imprint:
Glass Height:
Detroit (red) 4 3/4"
Montréal (red) 4 3/4"
Toronto (blue) 4 1/2"

	Player	EX	NRMT
DETROIT			
☐	Alex Delvecchio	90.00	150.00
☐	Gordie Howe	200.00	300.00
☐	Terry Sawchuk (G)	200.00	300.00
MONTRÉAL			
☐	Jean Béliveau	60.00	100.00
☐	Marcel Bonin	30.00	50.00
☐	Bernie Geoffrion	60.00	100.00
☐	Doug Harvey	75.00	125.00
☐	Tom Johnson	30.00	50.00
☐	Albert Langlois	30.00	50.00
☐	Don Marshall	30.00	50.00
☐	Dickie Moore	55.00	90.00
☐	Jacques Plante (G)	200.00	300.00
☐	Henri Richard	50.00	75.00
☐	Gilles Tremblay	30.00	50.00
TORONTO			
☐	George Armstrong	50.00	90.00
☐	Johnny Bower (G)	75.00	125.00
☐	Carl Brewer	30.00	50.00
☐	Dick Duff	30.00	50.00
☐	Tim Horton	90.00	150.00
☐	Red Kelly	50.00	90.00
☐	Dave Keon	65.00	110.00
☐	Frank Mahovlich	90.00	150.00
☐	Bert Olmstead	50.00	75.00
☐	Allan Stanley	50.00	75.00

1961 - 62 PARKHURST

Card Size: 2 7/16" x 3 5/8"
Face: Four colour, white border, Team logo, Number
Back: Black on card stock, Resume, Cartoon quiz
Imprint: None

		EX	NRMT
Complete Set (51 cards):		**1,100.00**	**1,800.00**
Common Player:		**12.00**	**20.00**
No.	**Player**	**EX**	**NRMT**
☐ 1	Tim Horton, Tor.	90.00	175.00
☐ 2	Frank Mahovlich, Tor.	60.00	100.00
☐ 3	Johnny Bower (G), Tor.	50.00	75.00
☐ 4	Bert Olmstead, Tor.	13.00	22.00
☐ **5**	**Dave Keon, Tor., RC**	**165.00**	**275.00**
☐ 6	Ron Stewart, Tor.	12.00	20.00
☐ 7	Eddie Shack, Tor.	50.00	80.00
☐ 8	Bob Pulford, Tor.	15.00	25.00
☐ 9	Red Kelly, Tor.	20.00	30.00
☐ 10	Bob Nevin, Tor.	12.00	20.00
☐ 11	Bob Baun, Tor.	12.00	20.00
☐ 12	Dick Duff, Tor.	12.00	20.00
☐ **13**	**Larry Keenan, Tor., RC**	**12.00**	**20.00**
☐ 14	Larry Hillman, Tor.	12.00	20.00
☐ 15	Billy Harris, Tor.	12.00	20.00
☐ 16	Allan Stanley, Tor.	15.00	25.00
☐ 17	George Armstrong, Tor.	18.00	28.00
☐ 18	Carl Brewer, Tor.	12.00	20.00
☐ **19**	**Howie Glover, Det., RC**	**12.00**	**20.00**
☐ 20	Gordie Howe, Det.	200.00	325.00
☐ 21	Val Fonteyne, Det.	12.00	20.00
☐ **22**	**Al Johnson, Det., RC, LC**	**12.00**	**20.00**
☐ 23	Peter Goegan, Det.	12.00	20.00
☐ 24	Len Lunde, Det.	12.00	20.00
☐ 25	Alex Delvecchio, Det.	20.00	30.00
☐ 26	Norm Ullman, Det.	30.00	50.00
☐ 27	Bill Gadsby, Det.	13.00	22.00
☐ 28	Ed Litzenberger, Det.	12.00	20.00
☐ 29	Marcel Pronovost, Det.	13.00	22.00
☐ 30	Warren Godfrey, Det.	12.00	20.00
☐ 31	Terry Sawchuk (G), Det.	90.00	145.00
☐ 32	Vic Stasiuk, Det.	12.00	20.00
☐ 33	Léo Labine, Det.	12.00	20.00
☐ 34	John McKenzie, Det.	13.00	22.00
☐ 35	Bernie Geoffrion, Mtl.	35.00	60.00
☐ 36	Dickie Moore, Mtl.	18.00	28.00
☐ 37	Al Langlois, Mtl.	12.00	20.00
☐ 38	Bill Hicke, Mtl.	12.00	20.00
☐ 39	Ralph Backstrom, Mtl.	12.00	20.00
☐ 40	Don Marshall, Mtl.	12.00	20.00
☐ 41	Bob Turner, Mtl.	12.00	20.00
☐ 42	Tom Johnson, Mtl.	13.00	22.00
☐ 43	Henri Richard, Mtl.	55.00	90.00
☐ **44**	**Wayne Connelly, Mtl., RC, Err. (Connolly)**	**12.00**	**20.00**
☐ 45	Jean Béliveau, Mtl.	60.00	100.00
☐ 46	Phil Goyette, Mtl.	12.00	20.00
☐ 47	Marcel Bonin, Mtl.	12.00	20.00
☐ 48	Jean-Guy Talbot, Mtl.	12.00	20.00
☐ 49	Jacques Plante (G), Mtl.	90.00	150.00
☐ 50	Claude Provost, Mtl.	12.00	20.00
☐ 51	André Pronovost, Mtl.	30.00	50.00

1961 - 62 SHIRRIFF / SALADA COINS

The hockey coins for the 1961-62 season were produced for both Shirriff and Salada. The only difference is the maker's name. Team shield holders were abailable for this issue. Prices are identical for both versions.

Cap Diameter 1 7/8"
Face: Four colour; Name, Number, Year
Back: "SAVE 120 'HOCKEY COINS' COLLECTIONNEZ LEZ 120 PIÈCES DE HOCKEY"
Imprint: Shirriff Lushus Jelly & Puddings Pat. Pend.

		EX	NRMT
Complete Set (120 coins):		**275.00**	**450.00**
Common Player:		**2.00**	**3.50**
Boston Bruins Team Shield (Brown)		**50.00**	**75.00**
Chicago Blackhawks Team Shield (Yellow)		**50.00**	**75.00**
Toronto Maple Leafs Team Shield (Light Blue)		**50.00**	**75.00**
Detroit Red Wings Team Shield (Red)		**25.00**	**50.00**
New York Rangers Team Shield (Dark Blue)		**25.00**	**50.00**
Montréal CanadiensTeam Shield (White)		**25.00**	**75.00**
No.	**Player**	**EX**	**NRMT**
☐☐ 1	Cliff Pennington, Bos.	2.00	3.50
☐☐ 2	Dallas Smith, Bos.	2.00	3.50
☐☐ 3	André Pronovost, Bos.	2.00	3.50
☐☐ 4	Charlie Burns, Bos.	2.00	3.50
☐☐ 5	Leo Boivin, Bos.	3.50	5.50
☐☐ 6	Don McKenney, Bos.	2.00	3.50
☐☐ 7	John Bucyk, Bos.	6.00	10.00
☐☐ 8	Murray Oliver, Bos.	2.00	3.50
☐☐ 9	Jerry Toppazzini, Bos.	2.00	3.50
☐☐ 10	Doug Mohns, Bos.	2.00	3.50
☐☐ 11	Don Head (G), Bos.	2.50	4.00
☐☐ 12	Bob Armstrong, Bos.	2.00	3.50
☐☐ 13	Pat Stapleton, Bos.	2.75	4.50
☐☐ 14	Orland Kurtenbach, Bos.	2.00	3.50
☐☐ 15	Dick Meissner, Bos.	2.00	3.50
☐☐ 16	Ted Green, Bos.	2.75	4.50
☐☐ 17	Tom Williams, Bos.	2.00	3.50
☐☐ 18	Aut Erickson, Bos.	2.00	3.50
☐☐ 19	Phil Watson, Coach, Bos.	2.00	3.50
☐☐ 20	Ed Chadwick (G), Bos.	2.50	4.00
☐☐ 21	Wayne Hillman, Chi.	12.00	20.00
☐☐ 22	Stan Mikita, Chi.	8.00	13.00
☐☐ 23	Eric Nesterenko, Chi.	2.00	3.50
☐☐ 24	Reggie Fleming, Chi.	2.00	3.50
☐☐ 25	Bobby Hull, Chi.	15.00	25.00
☐☐ 26	Elmer Vasko, Chi.	2.00	3.50
☐☐ 27	Pierre Pilote, Chi.	3.25	5.50
☐☐ 28	Chico Maki, Chi.	2.00	3.50
☐☐ 29	Glenn Hall (G), Chi.	9.00	15.00
☐☐ 30	Murray Balfour, Chi.	2.00	3.50
☐☐ 31	Bronco Horvath, Chi.	2.00	3.50
☐☐ 32	Kenny Wharram, Chi.	2.00	3.50
☐☐ 33	Ab McDonald, Chi.	2.00	3.50
☐☐ 34	Billy Hay, Chi.	2.00	3.50
☐☐ 35	Dollard St. Laurent, Chi.	2.00	3.50
☐☐ 36	Ron Murphy, Chi.	2.00	3.50
☐☐ 37	Bob Turner, Chi.	2.00	3.50
☐☐ 38	Gerry Melnyk, Chi., Error (Jerry)	2.00	3.50
☐☐ 39	Jack Evans, Chi.	2.00	3.50
☐☐ 40	Rudy Pilous, Coach, Chi.	3.50	6.00
☐☐ 41	Johnny Bower (G), Tor.	8.00	13.00
☐☐ 42	Allan Stanley, Tor.	3.25	5.50
☐☐ 43	Frank Mahovlich, Tor.	9.00	15.00
☐☐ 44	Tim Horton, Tor.	9.00	15.00
☐☐ 45	Carl Brewer, Tor.	2.00	3.50
☐☐ 46	Bob Pulford, Tor.	4.00	6.50
☐☐ 47	Bob Nevin, Tor.	2.00	3.50
☐☐ 48	Eddie Shack, Tor.	4.50	7.00
☐☐ 49	Red Kelly, Tor.	5.50	9.00
☐☐ 50	Bob Baun, Tor.	2.00	3.50
☐☐ 51	George Armstrong, Tor.	4.50	7.00
☐☐ 52	Bert Olmstead, Tor.	3.25	5.50
☐☐ 53	Dick Duff, Tor.	2.00	3.50
☐☐ 54	Billy Harris, Tor.	2.00	3.50
☐☐ 55	Larry Keenan, Tor.	2.00	3.50
☐☐ 56	John MacMillan, Tor.	2.00	3.50
☐☐ 57	Punch Imlach, Coach, Tor.	3.25	5.50
☐☐ 58	Dave Keon, Tor.	7.50	12.00
☐☐ 59	Larry Hillman, Tor.	2.00	3.50
☐☐ 60	Al Arbour, Tor.	3.25	5.50
☐☐ 61	Sid Abel, Coach, Det.	3.00	5.00
☐☐ 62	Warren Godfrey, Det.	2.00	3.50
☐☐ 63	Vic Stasiuk, Det.	2.00	3.50
☐☐ 64	Léo Labine, Det.	2.00	3.50
☐☐ 65	Howie Glover, Det.	2.00	3.50
☐☐ 66	Gordie Howe, Det.	25.00	40.00
☐☐ 67	Val Fonteyne, Det.	2.00	3.50
☐☐ 68	Marcel Pronovost, Det.	3.25	5.50
☐☐ 69	Parker MacDonald, Det.	2.00	3.50
☐☐ 70	Alex Delvecchio, Det.	6.00	10.00
☐☐ 71	Ed Litzenberger, Det.	2.00	3.50
☐☐ 72	Al Johnson, Det.	2.00	3.50
☐☐ 73	Bruce MacGregor, Det.	2.00	3.50
☐☐ 74	Howie Young, Det.	2.00	3.50
☐☐ 75	Peter Goegan, Det.	2.00	3.50
☐☐ 76	Norm Ullman, Det.	5.50	9.00
☐☐ 77	Terry Sawchuk (G), Det.	12.00	20.00
☐☐ 78	Gerry Odrowski, Det.	2.00	3.50
☐☐ 79	Bill Gadsby, Det.	3.25	5.50
☐☐ 80	Hank Bassen (G), Det.	2.50	4.00
☐☐ 81	Doug Harvey, NYR., Coach	6.50	11.00
☐☐ 82	Earl Ingarfield, NYR.	2.00	3.50
☐☐ 83	Pat Hannigan, NYR.	2.00	3.50
☐☐ 84	Dean Prentice, NYR.	2.00	3.50
☐☐ 85	Gump Worsley (G), NYR.	8.50	14.00
☐☐ 86	Irv Spencer, NYR.	2.00	3.50
☐☐ 87	Camille Henry, NYR.	2.00	3.50
☐☐ 88	Andy Bathgate, NYR.	4.50	7.50
☐☐ 89	Harry Howell, NYR.	3.25	5.50
☐☐ 90	Andy Hebenton, NYR.	2.00	3.50
☐☐ 91	Red Sullivan, NYR.	2.00	3.50
☐☐ 92	Ted Hampson, NYR.	2.00	3.50
☐☐ 93	Jean-Guy Gendron, NYR.	2.00	3.50
☐☐ 94	Al Langlois, NYR.	2.00	3.50
☐☐ 95	Larry Cahan, NYR.	2.00	3.50
☐☐ 96	Bob Cunningham, NYR.	2.00	3.50
☐☐ 97	Vic Hadfield, NYR.	2.75	4.50
☐☐ 98	Jean Ratelle, NYR.	7.00	12.00
☐☐ 99	Ken Schinkel, NYR.	2.00	3.50
☐☐ 100	Johnny Wilson, NYR.	2.00	3.50
☐☐ 101	Toe Blake, Mtl., Coach	4.00	6.50
☐☐ 102	Jean Béliveau, Mtl.	12.00	20.00
☐☐ 103	Don Marshall, Mtl.	2.00	3.50
☐☐ 104	Bernie Geoffrion, Mtl.	8.00	13.00
☐☐ 105	Claude Provost, Mtl.	2.00	3.50
☐☐ 106	Tom Johnson, Mtl.	3.25	5.50
☐☐ 107	Dickie Moore, Mtl.	5.00	8.50
☐☐ 108	Bill Hicke, Mtl.	2.00	3.50
☐☐ 109	Jean-Guy Talbot, Mtl.	2.00	3.50
☐☐ 110	Henri Richard, Mtl.	6.50	11.00
☐☐ 111	Louie Fontinato, Mtl.	2.00	3.50
☐☐ 112	Gilles Tremblay, Mtl.	2.00	3.50
☐☐ 113	Jacques Plante (G), Mtl.	12.00	20.00
☐☐ 114	Ralph Backstrom, Mtl.	2.00	3.50
☐☐ 115	Marcel Bonin, Mtl.	2.00	3.50
☐☐ 116	Phil Goyette, Mtl.	2.00	3.50
☐☐ 117	Bobby Rousseau, Mtl.	2.00	3.50
☐☐ 118	J.C. Tremblay, Mtl.	2.50	4.00
☐☐ 119	Al MacNeil, Mtl.	2.00	3.50
☐☐ 120	Jean Gauthier, Mtl.	2.00	3.50

1961 - 62 TOPPS

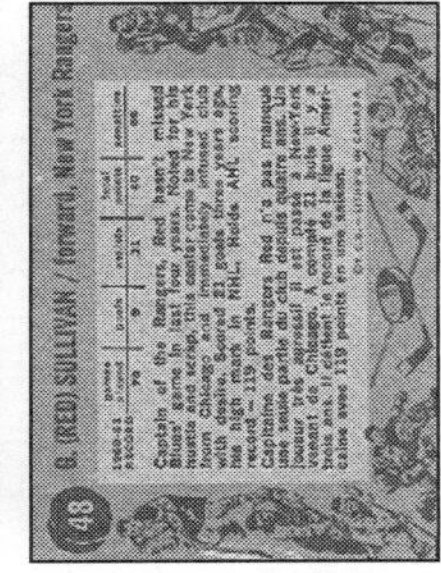

Card Size: 2 1/2" x 3 1/2"
Face: Four colour, white border
Back: Orange and black on card stock; Number, Resume, Bilingual
Imprint: T.C.G. LITHO'D IN CANADA

		EX	NRMT
Complete Set (66 cards):		**1,300.00**	**2,100.00**
Common Player:		**9.00**	**15.00**

No.	Player	EX	NRMT
☐ 1	Phil Watson, Bos., Coach	15.00	35.00
☐ **2**	**Ted Green, Bos., RC**	**25.00**	**40.00**
☐ 3	Earl Balfour, Bos., LC	9.00	15.00
☐ **4**	**Dallas Smith, Bos., RC**	**20.00**	**30.00**
☐ 5	André Pronovost, Bos.	9.00	15.00
☐ **6**	**Dick Meissner, Bos., RC**	**9.00**	**15.00**
☐ 7	Leo Boivin, Bos.	12.00	20.00
☐ 8	John Bucyk, Bos.	30.00	45.00
☐ 9	Jerry Toppazzini, Bos.	9.00	15.00
☐ 10	Doug Mohns, Bos.	9.00	15.00
☐ 11	Charlie Burns, Bos.	9.00	15.00
☐ 12	Don McKenney, Bos.	9.00	15.00
☐ 13	Bob Armstrong, Bos., LC	9.00	15.00
☐ 14	Murray Oliver, Bos.	9.00	15.00
☐ **15**	**Orland Kurtenbach, Bos., RC**	**12.00**	**20.00**
☐ **16**	**Terry Gray, Bos., RC**	**9.00**	**15.00**
☐ **17**	**Don Head (G), Bos., RC, LC**	**12.00**	**20.00**
☐ **18**	**Pat Stapleton, Bos., RC**	**20.00**	**30.00**
☐ **19**	**Cliff Pennington, Bos., RC**	**9.00**	**15.00**
☐ 20	1961 Boston Bruins	35.00	55.00
☐ 21	Balfour / Flaman (Action)	9.00	15.00
☐ 22	Bathgate / Hall (Action)	22.00	32.00
☐ 23	Rudy Pilous, Coach, Chi.	15.00	25.00
☐ 24	Pierre Pilote, Chi.	18.00	28.00
☐ 25	Elmer Vasko, Chi.	9.00	15.00
☐ **26**	**Reggie Fleming, Chi., RC**	**9.00**	**15.00**
☐ 27	Ab McDonald, Chi.	9.00	15.00
☐ 28	Eric Nesterenko, Chi.	9.00	15.00
☐ 29	Bobby Hull, Chi.	200.00	350.00
☐ 30	Kenny Wharram, Chi.	9.00	15.00
☐ 31	Dollard St.Laurent, Chi.	9.00	15.00
☐ 32	Glenn Hall (G), Chi.	40.00	70.00
☐ 33	Murray Balfour, Chi.	9.00	15.00
☐ 34	Ron Murphy, Chi.	9.00	15.00
☐ 35	Red Hay, Chi.	9.00	15.00
☐ 36	Stan Mikita, Chi.	135.00	225.00
☐ **37**	**Denis DeJordy (G), Chi., RC**	**22.00**	**35.00**
☐ **38**	**Wayne Hillman, Chi., RC**	**9.00**	**15.00**
☐ **39**	**Rino Robazza, Chi., RC, LC**	**9.00**	**15.00**
☐ 40	Bronco Horvath, Chi.	9.00	15.00
☐ 41	Bob Turner, Chi.	9.00	15.00
☐ 42	1961 Chicago Blackhawks	35.00	55.00
☐ 43	Wharran (Action)	9.00	15.00
☐ 44	D.St.Laurent / Hall (Action)	20.00	30.00
☐ 45	Doug Harvey, NYR.	30.00	45.00
☐ 46	Al Langlois, NYR.	9.00	15.00
☐ **47**	**Irv Spencer, NYR., RC**	**9.00**	**15.00**
☐ 48	Red Sullivan, NYR.	9.00	15.00
☐ 49	Earl Ingarfield, NYR.	9.00	15.00
☐ 50	Gump Worsley (G), NYR.	30.00	50.00
☐ 51	Harry Howell, NYR.	15.00	25.00
☐ 52	Larry Cahan, NYR.	9.00	15.00
☐ 53	Andy Bathgate, NYR.	15.00	25.00
☐ 54	Dean Prentice, NYR.	9.00	15.00
☐ 55	Andy Hebenton, NYR.	9.00	15.00
☐ 56	Camille Henry, NYR.	9.00	15.00
☐ 57	Jean Guy Gendron, NYR.	9.00	15.00
☐ **58**	**Pat Hannigan, NYR., RC**	**9.00**	**15.00**
☐ 59	Ted Hampson, NYR.	9.00	15.00
☐ **60**	**Jean Ratelle, NYR., RC**	**90.00**	**150.00**
☐ **61**	**Al LeBrun, NYR., RC**	**9.00**	**15.00**
☐ **62**	**Rod Gilbert, NYR., RC**	**90.00**	**150.00**
☐ 63	1961 New York Rangers	35.00	55.00
☐ 64	Meissner / Worsley (Action)	20.00	30.00
☐ 65	Worsley (Action)	20.00	30.00
☐ 66	Checklist (1 - 66)	200.00	425.00

STAMPS

Issued in pairs in 1961-62, these "stamp" inserts are extremely difficult to find in NRMT.

Stamp Size: 1 3/8" x 1 7/8"
Face: Blue and white; Name, Team, Position
Back: Blank (Gum)
Imprint: None

	Player	EX	NRMT
Insert Set (52 stamps):		**950.00**	**1,600.00**
BOSTON BRUINS			
☐	Leo Boivin	13.00	22.00
☐	John Bucyk	30.00	50.00
☐	Charlie Burns	13.00	22.00
☐	Don McKenney	13.00	22.00
☐	Doug Mohns	13.00	22.00
☐	Murray Oliver	13.00	22.00
☐	André Pronovost	13.00	22.00
☐	Dallas Smith	20.00	30.00
NEW YORK RANGERS			
☐	Andy Bathgate	13.00	22.00
☐	Doug Harvey	30.00	50.00
☐	Andy Hebenton	13.00	22.00
☐	Camille Henry	13.00	22.00
☐	Harry Howell	13.00	22.00
☐	Al Langlois	13.00	22.00
☐	Dean Prentice	13.00	22.00
☐	Gump Worsley (G)	35.00	55.00
CHICAGO BLACKHAWKS			
☐	Murray Balfour	13.00	22.00
☐	Jack Evans	13.00	22.00
☐	Glenn Hall (G)	45.00	75.00
☐	Billy Hay	13.00	22.00
☐	Bronco Horvath	13.00	22.00
☐	Bobby Hull	135.00	225.00
☐	Stan Mikita	75.00	120.00
☐	Ron Murphy	13.00	22.00
☐	Pierre Pilote	13.00	22.00
☐	Elmer Vasko	13.00	22.00
ALL TIME GREATS			
☐	Richard Boon	15.00	25.00
☐	Frank Boucher	15.00	25.00
☐	Francis (King) Clancy	28.00	45.00
☐	Dit Clapper	18.00	30.00
☐	Spague Cleghorn	13.00	22.00
☐	Alex Connell (G)	13.00	22.00
☐	Bill Cook	13.00	22.00
☐	Cy Denneny	15.00	25.00
☐	Frank Frederickson	13.00	22.00
☐	Chuck Gardiner (G)	15.00	25.00
☐	Herb Gardiner	10.00	20.00
☐	Eddie Gerard	10.00	20.00
☐	Frank (Moose) Goheen	10.00	20.00
☐	George Hay	15.00	25.00
☐	Dick Irvin	25.00	40.00
☐	Ernest (Moose) Johnson	13.00	22.00
☐	Edouard (Newsy) Lalonde	18.00	30.00
☐	Hugh Lehman	13.00	22.00
☐	Joe Malone	35.00	55.00
☐	Paddy Moran (G)	18.00	30.00
☐	Howie Morenz	60.00	100.00
☐	Frank Nighbor	13.00	22.00
☐	Art Ross	35.00	55.00
☐	Nels Stewart	25.00	40.00
☐	Fred (Cyclone) Taylor	35.00	55.00
☐	Georges Vézina (G)	55.00	90.00

1961 - 62 YORK PEANUT BUTTER YELLOW BACKS

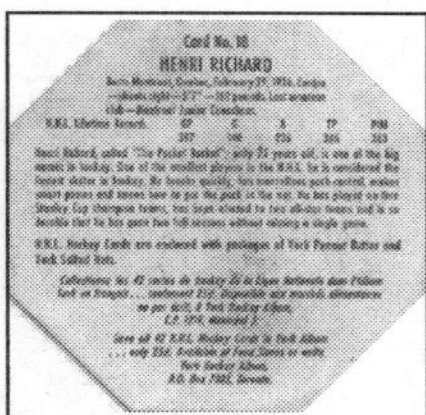

Card Size: 2 1/2" x 2 1/2"
Face: Four colour, coloured background (yellow, green, red and pale blue)
Back: Black on yellow card stock; Number, Name, Resume, Album offer, Bilingual
Imprint: None

		EX	NRMT
Complete Set (42 cards):		**350.00**	**600.00**
Common Player:		**7.00**	**12.00**
Album:		**25.00**	**50.00**

No.	Player	EX	NRMT
☐ 1	Bob Baun, Tor.	11.00	22.00
☐ 2	Dick Duff, Tor.	7.00	12.00
☐ 3	Frank Mahovlich, Tor.	22.00	35.00
☐ 4	Gilles Tremblay, Mtl.	7.00	12.00
☐ 5	Dickie Moore, Mtl.	13.00	22.00
☐ 6	Don Marshall, Mtl.	7.00	12.00
☐ 7	Tim Horton, Tor.	22.00	35.00
☐ 8	Johnny Bower (G), Tor.	18.00	28.00
☐ 9	Allan Stanley, Tor.	12.00	20.00
☐ 10	Jean Béliveau, Mtl.	28.00	45.00
☐ 11	Tom Johnson, Mtl.	12.00	20.00
☐ 12	Jean-Guy Talbot, Mtl.	7.00	12.00
☐ 13	Carl Brewer, Tor.	7.00	12.00
☐ 14	Bob Pulford, Tor.	13.00	22.00
☐ 15	Billy Harris, Tor.	7.00	12.00
☐ 16	Bill Hicke, Mtl.	7.00	12.00
☐ 17	Claude Provost, Mtl.	9.00	15.00
☐ 18	Henri Richard, Mtl.	18.00	28.00
☐ 19	Bert Olmstead, Tor.	12.00	20.00
☐ 20	Ron Stewart, Tor.	7.00	12.00
☐ 21	Red Kelly, Tor.	15.00	25.00
☐ 22	Toe Blake, Coach, Mtl.	13.00	22.00
☐ 23	Jacques Plante (G), Mtl.	30.00	50.00
☐ 24	Ralph Backstrom, Mtl.	7.00	12.00
☐ 25	Eddie Shack, Tor.	13.00	22.00
☐ 26	Bob Nevin, Tor.	7.00	12.00
☐ 27	Dave Keon, Tor.	18.00	28.00
☐ 28	Bernie Geoffrion, Mtl.	18.00	28.00
☐ 29	Marcel Bonin, Mtl.	7.00	12.00
☐ 30	Phil Goyette, Mtl.	7.00	12.00
☐ 31	Larry Hillman, Tor.	7.00	12.00
☐ 32	Larry Keenan, Tor.	7.00	12.00
☐ 33	Al Arbour, Tor.	12.00	20.00
☐ 34	J.C. Tremblay, Mtl.	9.00	15.00
☐ 35	Bobby Rousseau, Mtl.	7.00	12.00
☐ 36	Al MacNeil, Mtl.	7.00	12.00
☐ 37	George Armstrong, Tor.	13.00	22.00
☐ 38	Punch Imlach, Manager & Coach, Tor.	12.00	20.00
☐ 39	Francis (King) Clancy, Tor.	15.00	25.00
☐ 40	Louie Fontinato, Mtl.	7.00	12.00
☐ 41	Césare Maniago (G), Mtl.	7.00	12.00
☐ 42	Jean Gauthier, Mtl.	8.00	16.00

1962 CERAMIC HOCKEY TILES

These ceramic tiles are sqare in shape and white in colour. A full-colour painted drawing of each player is featured on the front. The backs are covered with a sheet of cork which, when removed, reveals the year of issue. These tiles were manufactured, at least in part, in Hamilton, Ontario. Surviving packaging also indicates the tiles came from England. It has been reported that this series was never issued, possibly because of licensing difficulties. Other singles may exist.

Tile Size: 3 1/4" x 5 1/4"
Face: Colour artist rendering of player, Name of player
Back: Blank
Imprint: H.M. Cowan
Common Player:

	Player	VG	EX	EX-NRMT
☐	Al Arbour, Tor.			
☐	George Armstrong, Tor.			
☐	Ralph Backstrom, Mtl.			
☐	Murray Balfour, Chi.			
☐	Dave Balon, NYR.			
☐	Doug Barkley, Det.			
☐	Andy Bathgate, NYR.			
☐	Bobby Baun, Tor.			
☐	Red Berenson, Mtl.			
☐	Leo Boivin, Bos.			
☐	Johnny Bower (G), Tor.			
☐	Carl Brewer, Tor.			
☐	Johnny Bucyk, Bos.			
☐	Charlie Burns, Bos.			
☐	Larry Cahan, NYR.			
☐	Wayne Connelly, Bos.			
☐	Alex Delvecchio, Det.			
☐	Jack Evans, Chi.			
☐	Alex Faulkner, Det.			
☐	Reggie Fleming, Chi.			
☐	Val Fonteyne, Det.			
☐	Lou Fontinato, Mtl.			
☐	Bill Gadsby, Det.			
☐	Jean Gauthier, Mtl.			
☐	Guy Gendron, Bos.			
☐	Bernie Geoffrion, Mtl.			
☐	Warren Godfrey, Bos.			
☐	Phil Goyette, Mtl.			
☐	Ted Green, Bos.			
☐	Vic Hadfield, NYR.			
☐	Glenn Hall (G), Chi.			
☐	Ted Hampson, NYR.			
☐	Billy Harris, Tor.			
☐	Doug Harvey, NYR.			
☐	Bill Hay, Chi.			
☐	Andy Hebenton, NYR.			
☐	Bill Hicke, Mtl.			
☐	Wayne Hicks, Bos.			
☐	Wayne Hillman, Chi.			
☐	Tim Horton, Tor.			
☐	Bronco Horvath, NYR.			
☐	Gordie Howe, Det.			
☐	Harry Howell, NYR.			
☐	Bobby Hull, Chi.			
☐	Punch Imlach, Tor.			
☐	Earl Ingarfield, NYR.			
☐	Tom Johnson, Mtl.			
☐	Red Kelly, Tor.			
☐	Dave Keon, Tor.			
☐	Al Langlois, NYR.			
☐	Eddie Litzenberger, Tor.			
☐	Len Lunde, Chi.			
☐	Parker MacDonald, Det.			
☐	Bruce MacGregor, Det.			
☐	John MacMillan, Tor.			
☐	Al MacNeil, Chi.			
☐	Frank Mahovlich, Tor.			
☐	Chico Maki, Chi.			
☐	Césare Maniago (G), Mtl.			
☐	Don Marshall, Mtl.			
☐	Ab McDonald, Chi.			
☐	Don McKenney, Bos.			
☐	Stan Mikita, Chi.			
☐	Doug Mohns, Bos.			
☐	Dickie Moore, Mtl.			
☐	Ron Murphy, Chi.			
☐	Eric Nesterenko, Chi.			
☐	Bob Nevin, Tor.			
☐	Murray Oliver, Bos.			
☐	Muzz Patrick, Bos.			
☐	Cliff Pennington, Bos.			
☐	Bob Perreault (G), Bos.			
☐	Pierre Pilote, Chi.			
☐	Jacques Plante (G), Mtl.			
☐	Dean Prentice, NYR.			
☐	Andre Pronovost, Bos.			
☐	Marcel Pronovost, Det.			
☐	Claude Provost, Mtl.			
☐	Bob Pulford, Tor.			
☐	Jean Ratelle, NYR.			
☐	Henri Richard, Mtl.			
☐	Dennis Riggin (G), Det.			
☐	Bobby Rousseau, Mtl.			
☐	Terry Sawchuk (G), Det.			
☐	Eddie Shack, Tor.			
☐	Floyd Smith, Det.			
☐	Irv Spencer, Bos.			
☐	Allan Stanley, Tor.			
☐	Pat Stapleton, Bos.			
☐	Vic Stasiuk, Det.			
☐	Ron Stewart, Tor.			
☐	Jean Guy Talbot, Mtl.			
☐	Jerry Toppazini, Bos.			
☐	Gilles Tremblay, Mtl.			
☐	J.C. Tremblay, Mtl.			
☐	Bob Turner, Chi.			
☐	Norm Ullman, Det.			
☐	Elmer Vasko, Chi.			
☐	Ken Wharram, Chi.			
☐	Tommy Williams, Bos.			
☐	Gump Worsley (G), NYR.			
☐	Howie Young, Det.			

1962 - 63 EL PRODUCTO DISKS

Issued in a strip of six, these unnumbered disks are listed as they appear in the strip. There is a 50% premium for intact strips.

Disk Diameter 3"
Face: Four colour, white border
Back: Black on white card stock; Name, Position, Resume, Bilingual
Imprint: None

	Player	EX	NRMT
Complete Set (6 cards):		**120.00**	**200.00**
Common Player:		**20.00**	**30.00**
☐	Jean Béliveau, Mtl.	40.00	60.00
☐	Gordie Howe, Det.	60.00	90.00
☐	Dave Keon, Tor.	22.00	35.00
☐	Glenn Hall (G), Chi.	25.00	40.00
☐	Henri Richard, Mtl.	22.00	35.00
☐	Frank Mahovlich, Tor.	25.00	40.00

1962 - 63 PARKHURST

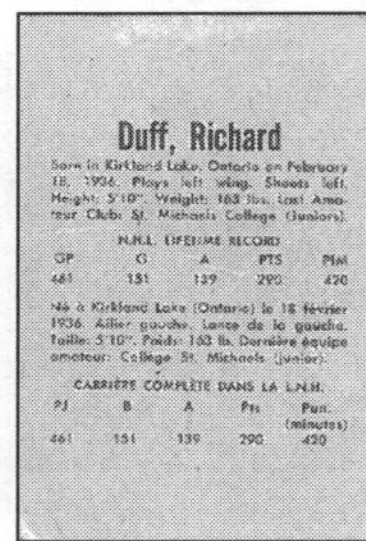

Card Size: 2 7/16" x 3 5/8"
Face: Four colour, white border, Signature, Number
Back: Black on card stock, Resume, Bilingual
Imprint: None

No.	Player	EX	NRMT
Complete Set (55 cards):		**1,300.00**	**2,100.00**
Common Player:		**10.00**	**17.00**
☐ 1	Billy Harris, Tor.	20.00	40.00
☐ 2	Dick Duff, Tor.	10.00	17.00
☐ 3	Bob Baun, Tor.	10.00	17.00
☐ 4	Frank Mahovlich, Tor.	55.00	90.00
☐ 5	Red Kelly, Tor.	18.00	28.00
☐ 6	Ron Stewart, Tor.	10.00	17.00
☐ 7	Tim Horton, Tor.	60.00	100.00
☐ 8	Carl Brewer, Tor.	10.00	17.00
☐ 9	Allan Stanley, Tor.	13.00	22.00
☐ 10	Bob Nevin, Tor.	10.00	17.00
☐ 11	Bob Pulford, Tor.	13.00	22.00
☐ 12	Ed Litzenberger, Tor.	10.00	17.00
☐ 13	George Armstrong, Tor.	13.00	22.00
☐ 14	Eddie Shack, Tor.	40.00	65.00
☐ 15	Dave Keon, Tor.	70.00	115.00
☐ 16	Johnny Bower (G), Tor.	35.00	55.00
☐ 17	Larry Hillman, Tor.	10.00	17.00
☐ 18	Frank Mahovlich, Tor.	55.00	90.00
☐ **19**	**Hank Bassen (G), Det., RC**	**12.00**	**20.00**
☐ **20**	**Gerry Odrowski, Det., RC**	**10.00**	**17.00**
☐ 21	Norm Ullman, Det.	25.00	40.00
☐ 22	Vic Stasiuk, Det.	10.00	17.00
☐ **23**	**Bruce MacGregor, Det., RC**	**10.00**	**17.00**
☐ 24	Claude Laforge, Det., LC	10.00	17.00
☐ 25	Bill Gadsby, Det.	12.00	20.00
☐ 26	Léo Labine, Det., LC	10.00	17.00
☐ 27	Val Fonteyne, Det.	10.00	17.00
☐ 28	Howie Glover, Det., LC	10.00	17.00
☐ **29**	**Marc Boileau, Det., RC, LC**	**10.00**	**17.00**
☐ 30	Gordie Howe, Det.	190.00	300.00
☐ 31	Gordie Howe, Det.	190.00	300.00
☐ 32	Alex Delvecchio, Det.	18.00	28.00
☐ 33	Marcel Pronovost, Det.	12.00	20.00
☐ 34	Sid Abel, Coach, Det.	12.00	20.00
☐ 35	Len Lunde, Det.	10.00	17.00
☐ 36	Warren Godfrey, Det., LC	10.00	17.00
☐ 37	Phil Goyette, Mtl.	10.00	17.00
☐ 38	Henri Richard, Mtl.	50.00	80.00
☐ 39	Jean Béliveau, Mtl.	55.00	90.00
☐ 40	Bill Hicke, Mtl.	10.00	17.00
☐ 41	Claude Provost, Mtl.	10.00	17.00
☐ 42	Dickie Moore, Mtl., LC	13.00	22.00
☐ 43	Don Marshall, Mtl.	10.00	17.00
☐ 44	Ralph Backstrom, Mtl.	10.00	17.00
☐ 45	Marcel Bonin, Mtl., LC	10.00	17.00
☐ **46**	**Gilles Tremblay, Mtl., RC**	**20.00**	**30.00**
☐ **47**	**Bobby Rousseau, Mtl., RC**	**18.00**	**28.00**
☐ 48	Bernie Geoffrion, Mtl.	35.00	55.00
☐ 49	Jacques Plante (G), Mtl.	85.00	140.00
☐ 50	Tom Johnson, Mtl.	12.00	20.00
☐ 51	Jean-Guy Talbot, Mtl.	10.00	17.00
☐ 52	Louie Fontinato, Mtl., LC	10.00	17.00
☐ 53	Bernie Geoffrion, Mtl.	35.00	55.00
☐ **54**	**J.C. Tremblay, Mtl., RC**	**50.00**	**75.00**
☐	Tally Card (Checklist)	285.00	450.00
☐	Zip Card	120.00	200.00

1962 - 63 SHIRRIFF COINS

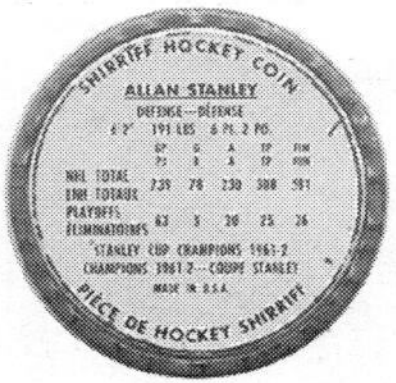

The 1962-63 issue of hockey coins are metal, unlike those of the previous years which were plastic. Coins are hard to find unscratched and well centered.

Cap Diameter 1 1/2"
Face: Four colour; Name, Number
Back: Black on tin; Name, Resume, Bilingual
Imprint: SHIRRIFF HOCKEY COIN PIECE DE HOCKEY SHIRRIFF MADE IN U.S.A.

	No.	Player	EX	NRMT
Complete Set (60 coins):			**250.00**	**400.00**
Common Player:			**3.00**	**5.50**
☐	1	Johnny Bower (G), Tor.	8.50	14.00
☐	2	Allan Stanley, Tor.	4.50	7.00
☐	3	Frank Mahovlich, Tor.	11.00	18.00
☐	4	Tim Horton, Tor.	11.00	18.00
☐	5	Carl Brewer, Tor.	3.00	5.50
☐	6	Bob Pulford, Tor.	5.00	8.50
☐	7	Bob Nevin, Tor.	3.00	5.50
☐	8	Eddie Shack, Tor.	6.00	10.00
☐	9	Red Kelly, Tor.	6.00	10.00
☐	10	George Armstrong, Tor.	5.00	8.50
☐	11	Bert Olmstead, Tor.	4.50	7.00
☐	12	Dick Duff, Tor.	3.00	5.50
☐	13	Billy Harris, Tor.	3.00	5.50
☐	14	John MacMillan, Tor.	3.00	5.50
☐	15	Punch Imlach, Coach, Tor.	4.50	7.50
☐	16	Dave Keon, Tor.	8.00	13.00
☐	17	Larry Hillman, Tor.	3.00	5.50
☐	18	Ed Litzenberger, Tor.	3.00	5.50
☐	19	Bob Baun, Tor.	3.00	5.50
☐	20	Al Arbour, Tor.	4.50	7.00
☐	21	Ron Stewart, Tor.	3.00	5.50
☐	22	Don Simmons (G), Tor.	3.50	6.00
☐	23	Louie Fontinato, Mtl.	3.00	5.50
☐	24	Gilles Tremblay, Mtl.	3.00	5.50
☐	25	Jacques Plante (G), Mtl.	15.00	25.00
☐	26	Ralph Backstrom, Mtl.	3.00	5.50
☐	27	Marcel Bonin, Mtl.	3.00	5.50
☐	28	Phil Goyette, Mtl.	3.00	5.50
☐	29	Bobby Rousseau, Mtl.	3.00	5.50
☐	30	J.C. Tremblay, Mtl.	3.50	6.00
☐	31	Toe Blake, Coach, Mtl.	5.00	8.00
☐	32	Jean Béliveau, Mtl.	15.00	25.00
☐	33	Don Marshall, Mtl.	3.00	5.50
☐	34	Bernie Geoffrion, Mtl.	9.00	15.00
☐	35	Claude Provost, Mtl.	3.00	5.50
☐	36	Tom Johnson, Mtl.	4.50	7.00
☐	37	Dickie Moore, Mtl.	6.00	10.00
☐	38	Bill Hicke, Mtl.	3.00	6.00
☐	39	Jean-Guy Talbot, Mtl.	3.00	5.50
☐	40	Al MacNeil, Mtl.	3.00	5.50
☐	41	Henri Richard, Mtl.	8.00	13.00
☐	42	Red Berenson, Mtl.	3.00	5.50
☐	43	AS: Jacques Plante (G)	11.00	18.00
☐	44	AS: Jean-Guy Talbot	3.00	5.50
☐	45	AS: Doug Harvey	6.50	11.00
☐	46	AS: Stan Mikita	8.50	14.00
☐	47	AS: Bobby Hull	18.00	28.00
☐	48	AS: Andy Bathgate	5.00	8.50
☐	49	AS: Glenn Hall (G)	9.00	15.00
☐	50	AS: Pierre Pilote	4.50	7.00
☐	51	AS: Carl Brewer	3.00	5.50
☐	52	AS: Dave Keon	5.50	9.00
☐	53	AS: Frank Mahovlich	8.50	14.00
☐	54	AS: Gordie Howe	30.00	50.00
☐	55	AW: Dave Keon, Tor.	6.00	10.00
☐	56	AW: Bobby Rousseau, Mtl.	3.00	5.50
☐	57	AW: Bobby Hull, Chi.	20.00	30.00
☐	58	AW: Jacques Plante (G), Mtl.	12.00	20.00
☐	59	AW: Jacques Plante (G), Mtl.	12.00	20.00
☐	60	AW: Doug Harvey, NYR	8.00	13.00

1962 - 63 TOPPS

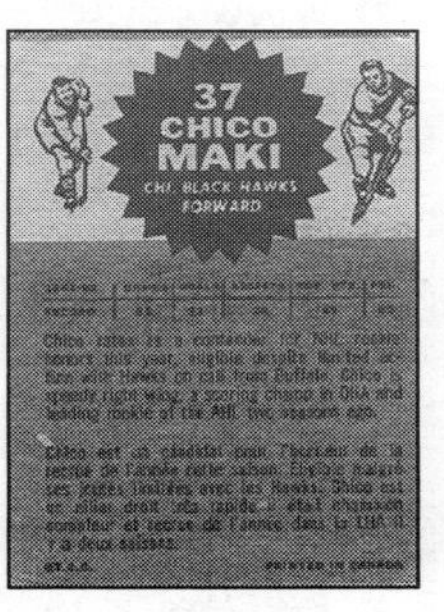

The blue borders that chip easily have made mint cards of this set difficult to locate.

Card Size: 2 1/2" x 3 1/2"
Face: Four colour, blue border, Team logo, Position
Back: Black and blue on card stock, Number, Resume, Bilingual
Imprint: PRINTED IN CANADA T.C.G.

	No.	Player	EX	NRMT
Complete Set (66 cards):			**1,000.00**	**1,700.00**
Common Player:			**9.00**	**15.00**
☐	1	Phil Watson, Coach, Bos.	12.00	30.00
☐	**2**	**Robert (Miche) Perreault (G), Bos., RC, LC**	**12.00**	**20.00**
☐	**3**	**Bruce Gamble (G), Bos., RC**	**12.00**	**20.00**
☐	4	Warren Godfrey, Bos., LC	9.00	15.00
☐	5	Leo Boivin, Bos.	12.00	20.00
☐	6	Doug Mohns, Bos.	9.00	15.00
☐	7	Ted Green, Bos.	9.00	15.00
☐	8	Pat Stapleton, Bos.	9.00	15.00
☐	9	Dallas Smith, Bos.	9.00	15.00
☐	10	Don McKenney, Bos.	9.00	15.00
☐	11	John Bucyk, Bos.	25.00	40.00
☐	12	Murray Oliver, Bos.	9.00	15.00
☐	13	Jerry Toppazzini, Bos.	9.00	15.00
☐	14	Cliff Pennington, Bos., LC	9.00	15.00
☐	15	Charlie Burns, Bos.	9.00	15.00
☐	16	Jean-Guy Gendron, Bos.	9.00	15.00
☐	17	Irv Spencer, Bos., LC	9.00	15.00
☐	18	Wayne Connelly, Bos.	9.00	15.00
☐	19	André Pronovost, Bos.	9.00	15.00
☐	20	Terry Gray, Bos.	9.00	15.00
☐	**21**	**Tom Williams, Bos., RC**	**9.00**	**15.00**
☐	22	Boston Bruins	30.00	50.00
☐	23	Rudy Pilous, Coach, Chi.	12.00	20.00
☐	24	Glenn Hall (G), Chi.	40.00	65.00
☐	25	Denis DeJordy (G), Chi.	12.00	20.00
☐	26	Jack Evans, Chi., LC	9.00	15.00
☐	27	Elmer Vasko, Chi.	9.00	15.00
☐	28	Pierre Pilote, Chi.	18.00	28.00
☐	29	Bob Turner, Chi.	9.00	15.00
☐	30	Dollard St. Laurent, Chi., LC	9.00	15.00
☐	31	Wayne Hillman, Chi.	9.00	15.00
☐	32	Al MacNeil, Chi.	9.00	15.00
☐	33	Bobby Hull, Chi.	200.00	350.00
☐	34	Stan Mikita, Chi.	100.00	160.00
☐	35	Red Hay, Chi.	9.00	15.00
☐	36	Murray Balfour, Chi.	9.00	15.00
☐	**37**	**Chico Maki, Chi., RC**	**15.00**	**25.00**
☐	38	Ab McDonald, Chi., Error (MacDonald)	9.00	15.00
☐	39	Kenny Wharram, Chi.	9.00	15.00
☐	40	Ron Murphy, Chi.	9.00	15.00
☐	41	Eric Nesterenko, Chi.	9.00	15.00
☐	42	Reggie Fleming, Chi.	9.00	15.00
☐	**43**	**Murray Hall, Chi., RC**	**9.00**	**15.00**
☐	44	Chicago Blackhawks	30.00	50.00
☐	45	Gump Worsley (G), NYR.	30.00	45.00
☐	46	Harry Howell, NYR.	15.00	25.00
☐	47	Al Langlois, NYR.	9.00	15.00
☐	48	Larry Cahan, NYR.	9.00	15.00
☐	**49**	**Jim Neilson, NYR., RC**	**15.00**	**25.00**
☐	50	Al LeBrun, NYR., LC	9.00	15.00
☐	51	Earl Ingarfield, NYR.	9.00	15.00
☐	52	Andy Bathgate, NYR.	15.00	25.00
☐	53	Dean Prentice, NYR.	9.00	15.00
☐	54	Andy Hebenton, NYR.	9.00	15.00
☐	55	Ted Hampson, NYR.	9.00	15.00
☐	**56**	**Dave Balon, NYR., RC**	**9.00**	**15.00**
☐	57	Bert Olmstead, NYR., LC	12.00	20.00
☐	58	Jean Ratelle, NYR.	35.00	60.00
☐	59	Rod Gilbert, NYR.	35.00	60.00
☐	**60**	**Vic Hadfield, NYR., RC**	**30.00**	**45.00**
☐	61	Frank Paice, Trainer, NYR.	9.00	15.00
☐	62	Camille Henry, NYR.	9.00	15.00
☐	63	Bronco Horvath, NYR., LC	9.00	15.00
☐	64	Pat Hannigan, NYR., LC, Error (Hanningan)	9.00	15.00
☐	65	New York Rangers	30.00	50.00
☐	66	Checklist (1 - 66)	150.00	325.00

HOCKEY DOLLARS

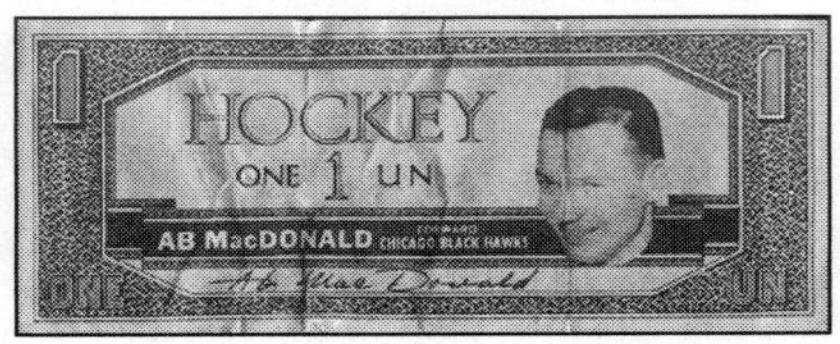

Unnumbered bucks came folded, one per pack.

Dollar Size: 4 1/8" x 1 3/4"
Face: Green on paper stock; Name, Team, Facsimile autograph
Back: Patterned green

	Player	EX	NRMT
Insert Set (24 dollars):		**700.00**	**1,200.00**
BOSTON BRUINS			
☐	Leo Boivin	30.00	45.00
☐	John Bucyk	40.00	65.00
☐	Warren Godfrey	13.00	22.00
☐	Ted Green	22.00	35.00
☐	Don McKenney	22.00	35.00
☐	Doug Mohns	22.00	35.00
☐	Murray Oliver	13.00	22.00
☐	Jerry Toppazzini	13.00	22.00
CHICAGO BLACKHAWKS			
☐	Reggie Fleming	13.00	22.00
☐	Glenn Hall (G)	50.00	80.00
☐	Billy Hay	22.00	35.00
☐	Bobby Hull	150.00	250.00
☐	Ab McDonald, Error (MacDonald)	13.00	22.00
☐	Stan Mikita	70.00	120.00
☐	Pierre Pilote	35.00	60.00
☐	Elmer Vasko	13.00	22.00
NEW YORK RANGERS			
☐	Dave Balon	13.00	22.00
☐	Andy Bathgate	35.00	55.00
☐	Andy Hebenton	13.00	22.00
☐	Harry Howell	25.00	40.00
☐	Earl Ingarfield	22.00	35.00
☐	Al Langlois	22.00	35.00
☐	Dean Prentice	22.00	35.00
☐	Gump Worsley (G)	40.00	70.00

1962 - 63 YORK PEANUT BUTTER IRON-ON TRANSFERS

These iron-on transfers were inserted into jars of peanut butter and packages of salted peanuts. There were twelve players from each of the Toronto, Montréal and Detroit teams.

Card Size: 2 3/16" x 4 5/16"
Face: Blue wording on transfer, team colour; Instructions, Bilingual
Back: Blank
Imprint: None

	No.	Player	EX	NRMT
Complete Set (36 transfers):			**1,500.00**	**2,500.00**
☐	1	Johnny Bower (G), Tor.	50.00	85.00
☐	2	Jacques Plante (G), Mtl.	85.00	140.00
☐	3	Tim Horton, Tor.	65.00	110.00

No.	Player	EX	NRMT
4	Jean-Guy Talbot, Mtl.	25.00	40.00
5	Carl Brewer, Tor.	25.00	40.00
6	J.C. Tremblay, Mtl.	30.00	40.00
7	Dick Duff, Mtl.	25.00	40.00
8	Jean Béliveau, Mtl.	75.00	125.00
9	Dave Keon, Tor.	45.00	75.00
10	Henri Richard, Mtl.	50.00	85.00
11	Frank Mahovlich, Tor.	50.00	85.00
12	Bernie Geoffrion, Mtl.	50.00	80.00
13	Kent Douglas, Tor.	25.00	40.00
14	Claude Provost, Mtl.	30.00	50.00
15	Bob Pulford, Tor.	35.00	60.00
16	Ralph Backstrom, Mtl.	25.00	40.00
17	George Armstrong, Tor.	40.00	70.00
18	Bobby Rousseau, Mtl.	25.00	40.00
19	Gordie Howe, Det.	150.00	250.00
20	Red Kelly,Tor.	45.00	75.00
21	Alex Delvecchio, Det.	45.00	75.00
22	Dickie Moore, Mtl.	40.00	70.00
23	Marcel Pronovost, Mtl.	35.00	55.00
24	Doug Barkley, Det.	25.00	40.00
25	Terry Sawchuk (G), Det.	85.00	140.00
26	Billy Harris, Tor.	25.00	40.00
27	Parker MacDonald, Det.	25.00	40.00
28	Don Marshall, Mtl.	25.00	40.00
29	Norm Ullman, Tor.	50.00	75.00
30	André Pronovost, Mtl.	25.00	40.00
30	Vic Stasiuk, Det.	25.00	40.00
31	Bill Gadsby, Det.	35.00	55.00
32	Eddie Shack, Tor.	45.00	75.00
33	Larry Jeffrey, Det.	25.00	40.00
34	Gilles Trembley, Mtl.	25.00	40.00
35	Howie Young, Det.	25.00	40.00
36	Bruce MacGregor, Det.	25.00	50.00

1963 - 64 PARKHURST

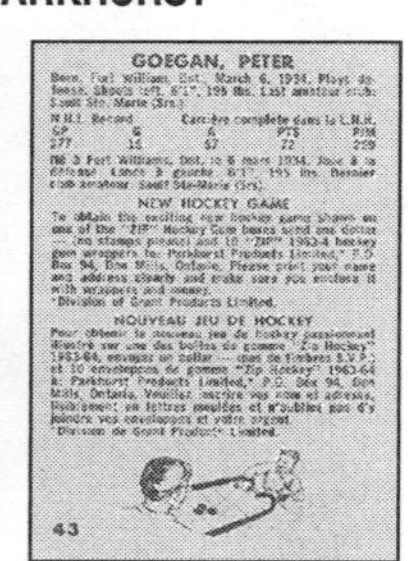

Card Size: 2 7/16" x 3 5/8"
Face: Four colour, white border, mixed backgrounds
Back: Black on card stock, Resume, Number, Bilingual
Imprint: None

Complete Set (99 cards):		**1,600.00**	**2,600.00**
Common Player:		**10.00**	**16.00**
No.	**Player**	**EX**	**NRMT**
1	Allan Stanley, Tor.	25.00	50.00
2	Don Simmons (G), Tor.	12.00	20.00
3	Red Kelly, Tor.	18.00	28.00
4	Dick Duff, Tor.	10.00	16.00
5	Johnny Bower (G), Tor.	30.00	50.00
6	Ed Litzenberger, Tor., LC	10.00	16.00
7	**Kent Douglas, Tor., RC**	**10.00**	**16.00**
8	Carl Brewer, Tor.	10.00	16.00
9	Eddie Shack, Tor.	35.00	60.00
10	Bob Nevin, Tor.	10.00	16.00
11	Billy Harris, Tor.	10.00	16.00
12	Bob Pulford, Tor.	12.00	20.00
13	George Armstrong, Tor.	13.00	22.00
14	Ron Stewart, Tor.	10.00	16.00
15	**John MacMillan, Tor., RC, LC**	**10.00**	**16.00**
16	Tim Horton, Tor.	60.00	100.00
17	Frank Mahovlich, Tor.	60.00	95.00
18	Bob Baun, Tor.	10.00	16.00
19	Punch Imlach, G.M. & Coach, Tor.	13.00	22.00
20	Francis (King) Clancy, A.G.M., Tor.	18.00	28.00
21	Gilles Tremblay, Mtl.	10.00	16.00
22	Jean-Guy Talbot, Mtl.	10.00	16.00
23	Henri Richard, Mtl.	50.00	75.00
24	Ralph Backstrom, Mtl.	10.00	16.00
25	Bill Hicke, Mtl.	10.00	16.00
26	**Red Berenson, Mtl., RC**	**28.00**	**45.00**
27	**Jacques Laperrière, Mtl., RC**	**35.00**	**55.00**
28	**Jean Gauthier, Mtl., RC, LC**	**10.00**	**16.00**
29	Bernie Geoffrion, Mtl.	30.00	50.00
30	Jean Béliveau, Mtl.	50.00	85.00
31	J.C. Tremblay, Mtl.	13.00	22.00
32	**Terry Harper, Mtl., RC**	**20.00**	**30.00**
33	**John Ferguson Sr., Mtl., RC**	**50.00**	**80.00**
34	Toe Blake, Coach, Mtl.	13.00	22.00
35	Bobby Rousseau, Mtl.	10.00	16.00
36	Claude Provost, Mtl.	10.00	16.00
37	Marc Réaume, Mtl.	10.00	16.00
38	Dave Balon, Mtl.	10.00	16.00
39	Gump Worsley (G), Mtl.	30.00	50.00
40	**Césare Maniago (G), Mtl., RC**	**30.00**	**50.00**
41	Bruce MacGregor, Det.	10.00	16.00
42	**Alex Faulkner, Det., RC, LC**	**35.00**	**60.00**
43	Peter Goegan, Det., LC	10.00	16.00
44	Parker MacDonald, Det.	10.00	16.00
45	André Pronovost, Det., LC	10.00	16.00
46	Marcel Pronovost, Det.	12.00	20.00
47	**Bob Dillabough, Det., RC**	**10.00**	**16.00**
48	**Larry Jeffrey, Det., RC**	**10.00**	**16.00**
49	Ian Cushenan, Det., LC	10.00	16.00
50	Alex Delvecchio, Det.	18.00	28.00
51	Hank Ciesla, Det., LC	10.00	16.00
52	Norm Ullman, Det.	25.00	40.00
53	Terry Sawchuk (G), Det.	85.00	140.00
54	**Ron Ingram, Det., RC, LC**	**10.00**	**16.00**
55	Gordie Howe, Det.	270.00	425.00
56	Billy McNeill, Det., LC	10.00	16.00
57	**Floyd Smith, Det., RC**	**12.00**	**20.00**
58	Vic Stasiuk, Det., LC	10.00	16.00
59	Bill Gadsby, Det.	12.00	20.00
60	**Doug Barkley, Det., RC**	**10.00**	**16.00**
61	Allan Stanley, Tor.	13.00	22.00
62	Don Simmons (G), Tor.	12.00	20.00
63	Red Kelly, Tor.	18.00	28.00
64	Dick Duff, Tor.	10.00	16.00
65	Johnny Bower (G), Tor.	30.00	50.00
66	Ed Litzenberger, Tor., LC	10.00	16.00
67	**Kent Douglas, Tor., RC**	**10.00**	**16.00**
68	Carl Brewer, Tor.	10.00	16.00
69	Eddie Shack, Tor.	35.00	60.00
70	Bob Nevin, Tor.	10.00	16.00
71	Billy Harris, Tor.	10.00	16.00
72	Bob Pulford, Tor.	12.00	22.00
73	George Armstrong, Tor.	13.00	22.00
74	Ron Stewart, Tor.	10.00	16.00
75	Dave Keon, Tor.	55.00	85.00
76	Tim Horton, Tor.	60.00	100.00
77	Frank Mahovlich, Tor.	60.00	95.00
78	Bob Baun, Tor.	10.00	16.00
79	Punch Imlach, G.M. & Coach, Tor.	13.00	22.00
80	Gilles Tremblay, Mtl.	10.00	16.00
81	Jean-Guy Talbot, Mtl.	10.00	16.00
82	Henri Richard, Mtl.	50.00	75.00
83	Ralph Backstrom, Mtl.	10.00	16.00
84	Bill Hicke, Mtl.	10.00	16.00
85	**Red Berenson, Mtl., RC**	**28.00**	**45.00**
86	**Jacques Laperrière, Mtl., RC**	**35.00**	**55.00**
87	**Jean Gauthier, Mtl., RC, LC**	**10.00**	**16.00**
88	Bernie Geoffrion, Mtl.	30.00	50.00
89	Jean Béliveau, Mtl.	50.00	85.00
90	J.C. Tremblay, Mtl.	13.00	22.00
91	**Terry Harper, Mtl., RC**	**20.00**	**30.00**
92	**John Ferguson, Mtl., RC**	**50.00**	**80.00**
93	Toe Blake, Coach, Mtl.	13.00	22.00
94	Bobby Rousseau, Mtl.	10.00	16.00
95	Claude Provost, Mtl.	10.00	16.00
96	Marc Reaume, Mtl.	10.00	16.00
97	Dave Balon, Mtl.	10.00	16.00
98	Gump Worsley (G), Mtl.	30.00	50.00
99	**Césare Maniago (G), Mtl., RC**	**85.00**	**165.00**

1963 - 64 TOPPS

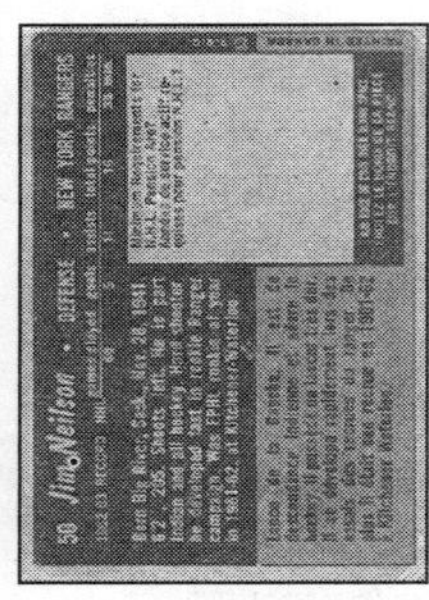

Card Size: 2 1/2" x 3 1/2"
Face: Four colour, black and white action photo at right side
Back: Blue on card stock, Number, Resume, Hockey trivia, Bilingual
Imprint: T.C.G. PRINTED IN CANADA

Complete Set (66 cards):		**800.00**	**1,300.00**
Common Player:		**8.00**	**14.00**
No.	**Player**	**EX**	**NRMT**
1	Milt Schmidt, Coach, Bos.	12.00	30.00
2	**Ed Johnston (G), Bos., RC**	**30.00**	**50.00**
3	Doug Mohns, Bos.	8.00	14.00
4	Tom Johnson, Bos.	11.00	18.00
5	Leo Boivin, Bos.	11.00	18.00
6	**Bob McCord, Bos., RC**	**8.00**	**14.00**
7	Ted Green, Bos.	8.00	14.00
8	**Ed Westfall, Bos., RC**	**20.00**	**30.00**
9	Charlie Burns, Bos.	8.00	14.00
10	Murray Oliver, Bos.	8.00	14.00
11	John Bucyk, Bos.	22.00	35.00
12	Tom Williams, Bos.	8.00	14.00
13	Dean Prentice, Bos.	8.00	14.00
14	**Bobby Leiter, Bos., RC**	**8.00**	**14.00**
15	Andy Hebenton, Bos., LC	8.00	14.00
16	Jean-Guy Gendron, Bos.	8.00	14.00
17	**Wayne Rivers, Bos., RC**	**9.00**	**14.00**
18	Jerry Toppazzini, Bos., LC	8.00	14.00
19	Forbes Kennedy, Bos.	8.00	14.00
20	Orland Kurtenbach, Bos.	8.00	14.00
21	Boston Bruins Team Picture	30.00	45.00
22	Billy Reay, Coach, Chi.	8.00	14.00
23	Glenn Hall (G), Chi.	35.00	55.00
24	Denis DeJordy (G), Chi.	11.00	18.00
25	Pierre Pilote, Chi.	15.00	25.00
26	Elmer Vasko, Chi.	8.00	14.00
27	Wayne Hillman, Chi.	8.00	14.00
28	Al MacNeil, Chi.	8.00	14.00
29	**Howie Young, Chi., RC**	**11.00**	**18.00**
30	**Ed Van Impe, Chi., RC**	**11.00**	**18.00**
31	Reggie Fleming, Chi.	8.00	14.00
32	Bob Turner, Chi., LC	8.00	14.00
33	Bobby Hull, Chi.	185.00	300.00
34	Red Hay, Chi.	8.00	14.00
35	Murray Balfour, Chi.	8.00	14.00
36	Stan Mikita, Chi.	65.00	110.00
37	Ab McDonald, Chi., Error (MacDonald)	8.00	14.00
38	Kenny Wharram, Chi.	8.00	14.00
39	Eric Nesterenko, Chi.	8.00	14.00
40	Ron Murphy, Chi.	8.00	14.00
41	Chico Maki, Chi.	8.00	14.00
42	John McKenzie, Chi.	8.00	14.00
43	Chicago Blackhawks, Team Picture	30.00	45.00
44	Red Sullivan, NYR.	8.00	40.00
45	Jacques Plante (G), NYR.	80.00	125.00
46	**Gilles Villemure (G), NYR., RC**	**20.00**	**30.00**
47	Doug Harvey, NYR., LC	22.00	35.00
48	Harry Howell, NYR.	12.00	20.00
49	Al Langlois, NYR.	8.00	14.00
50	Jim Neilson, NYR.	8.00	14.00
51	Larry Cahan, NYR.	8.00	14.00
52	Andy Bathgate, NYR.	12.00	20.00
53	Don McKenney, NYR.	8.00	14.00
54	Vic Hadfield, NYR.	11.00	18.00
55	Earl Ingarfield, NYR.	8.00	14.00
56	Camille Henry, NYR.	8.00	14.00
57	Rod Gilbert, NYR.	25.00	40.00
58	Phil Goyette, NYR.	8.00	14.00
59	Don Marshall, NYR.	8.00	14.00
60	Dick Meissner, NYR., LC	8.00	14.00
61	Val Fonteyne, NYR.	8.00	14.00

	No.	Player	EX	NRMT
☐	62	Ken Schinkel, NYR.	8.00	14.00
☐	63	Jean Ratelle, NYR.	25.00	40.00
☐	**64**	**Don Johns, NYR., RC, LC**	**8.00**	**14.00**
☐	65	New York Rangers, Team Picture	30.00	45.00
☐	66	Checklist (1 - 66)	135.00	275.00

1963 - 64 TORONTO STARS IN ACTION

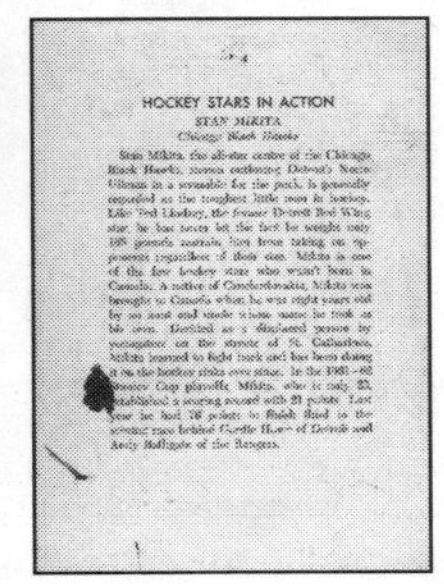
HOCKEY STARS IN ACTION
STAN MIKITA
Chicago Black Hawks

These photos are unnumbered and are listed below alphabetically by team and then by player within the team.

Card Size: 4 3/4" x 6 11/16"
Face: Four colour, white border
Back: Black on paper stock; Name, Team, Player history
Imprint: None
Complete Set (42 cards): 250.00 375.00

	Player	EX	NRMT
☐	Léo Boivin, Bos. (XCX: Andy Hebenton)	4.50	9.00
☐	John Bucyk, Bos. (XCX: Johnny Bower)	6.00	12.00
☐	Jean-Guy Gendron, Bos.	3.00	6.00
☐	Glenn Hall (G), Chi.	7.50	15.00
☐	Billy Hay, Chi.	3.00	6.00
☐	Bobby Hull, Chi.	18.00	35.00
☐	Stan Mikita, Chi.	7.50	15.00
☐	Eric Nesterenko, Chi.	3.00	6.00
☐	Elmer Vasko, Chi.	3.00	6.00
☐	Ken Wharram, Chi. (XCX: Tom Johnson)	3.00	6.00
☐	Alex Delvecchio, Det., Error (Alec)	6.00	12.00
☐	Bill Gadsby, Det.	4.50	9.00
☐	Gordie Howe, Det.	30.00	55.00
☐	Parker MacDonald, Det.	3.00	6.00
☐	Marcel Pronovost, Det., Error (Provost), (XCX: D. Duff)	4.50	9.00
☐	Terry Sawchuk (G), Det.	12.00	25.00
☐	Norm Ullman, Det.	6.00	12.00
☐	Jean Béliveau, Mtl.	11.00	22.00
☐	Bernie Geoffrion, Mtl.	9.00	18.00
☐	Dickie Moore, Mtl. (XCX: Jean-Guy Talbot)	6.00	12.00
☐	Claude Provost, Mtl.	3.00	6.00
☐	Henri Richard, Mtl.	7.50	15.00
☐	Jean-Guy Talbot, Mtl.	3.00	6.00
☐	Gilles Tremblay, Mtl.	3.00	6.00
☐	J.C. Tremblay, Mtl.	3.00	6.00
☐	Andy Bathgate, NYR.	5.00	10.00
☐	Doug Harvey, NYR. (XCX: Floyd Smith)	7.50	15.00
☐	Camille Henry, NYR.	3.00	6.00
☐	George Armstrong, Tor. (XCX: Bobby Hull)	6.00	12.00
☐	Bob Baun, Tor.	3.00	6.00
☐	John Bower (G), Tor.	7.50	15.00
☐	Carl Brewer, Tor. (XCX: Bob Beckett)	3.00	6.00
☐	Kent Douglas, Tor.	3.00	6.00
☐	Dick Duff, Tor.	3.00	6.00
☐	Tim Horton, Tor. (XCX: Parker MacDonald)	9.00	18.00
☐	Red Kelly, Tor.	6.00	12.00
☐	Dave Keon, Tor.	6.00	12.00
☐	Frank Mahovlich, Tor.	9.00	18.00
☐	Bob Pulford, Tor.	5.00	10.00
☐	Eddie Shack, Tor.	6.00	12.00
☐	Allan Stanley, Tor.	4.50	9.00
☐	Ron Stewart, Tor.	3.00	6.00

1963 - 64 YORK PEANUT BUTTER WHITE BACKS

This 54-card set was issued in York Peanut Butter and York Salted Nuts.

Card Size: 2 1/2" x 2 1/2"
Face: Four colour
Back: White card stock; Number, Name, Resume, Bilingual
Imprint: None
Complete Set (54 cards): 500.00 800.00
Common Player: 6.00 10.00
Album: 25.00 50.00

	No.	Player	EX	NRMT
☐	1	Tim Horton, Tor.	18.00	35.00
☐	2	Johnny Bower (G), Tor.	15.00	25.00
☐	3	Ron Stewart, Tor.	6.00	10.00
☐	4	Eddie Shack, Tor.	13.00	22.00
☐	5	Frank Mahovlich, Tor.	22.00	35.00
☐	6	Dave Keon, Tor.	15.00	25.00
☐	7	Bob Baun, Tor.	8.50	14.00
☐	8	Bob Nevin, Tor.	6.00	10.00
☐	9	Dick Duff, Tor.	6.00	10.00
☐	10	Billy Harris, Tor.	6.00	10.00
☐	11	Larry Hillman, Tor.	6.00	10.00
☐	12	Red Kelly, Tor.	13.00	22.00
☐	13	Kent Douglas, Tor.	6.00	10.00
☐	14	Allan Stanley, Tor.	11.00	18.00
☐	15	Don Simmons (G), Tor.	7.00	12.00
☐	16	George Armstrong, Tor.	13.00	22.00
☐	17	Carl Brewer, Tor.	6.00	10.00
☐	18	Bob Pulford, Tor.	12.00	20.00
☐	19	Henri Richard, Mtl.	18.00	28.00
☐	20	Bernie Geoffrion, Mtl.	18.00	28.00
☐	21	Gilles Tremblay, Mtl.	6.00	10.00
☐	22	Gump Worsley (G), Mtl.	18.00	28.00
☐	23	Jean-Guy Talbot, Mtl.	6.00	10.00
☐	24	J. C. Tremblay, Mtl.	8.50	14.00
☐	25	Bobby Rousseau, Mtl.	6.00	10.00
☐	26	Jean Béliveau, Mtl.	28.00	45.00
☐	27	Ralph Backstrom, Mtl.	6.00	10.00
☐	28	Claude Provost, Mtl.	9.00	15.00
☐	29	Jean Gauthier, Mtl.	6.00	10.00
☐	30	Bill Hicke, Mtl.	6.00	10.00
☐	31	Terry Harper, Mtl.	6.00	10.00
☐	32	Marc Réaume, Mtl.	6.00	10.00
☐	33	Dave Balon, Mtl.	6.00	10.00
☐	34	Jacques Laperrière, Mtl.	13.00	22.00
☐	35	John Ferguson, Mtl.	9.00	15.00
☐	36	Red Berenson, Mtl.	6.00	10.00
☐	37	Terry Sawchuk (G), Det.	30.00	50.00
☐	38	Marcel Pronovost, Det.	11.00	18.00
☐	39	Bill Gadsby, Det.	11.00	18.00
☐	40	Parker MacDonald, Det.	6.00	10.00
☐	41	Larry Jeffrey, Det.	6.00	10.00
☐	42	Floyd Smith, Det.	6.00	10.00
☐	43	André Pronovost, Det.	6.00	10.00
☐	44	Art Stratton, Det.	6.00	10.00
☐	45	Gordie Howe, Det.	75.00	125.00
☐	46	Doug Barkley, Det.	6.00	10.00
☐	47	Norm Ullman, Det.	13.00	22.00
☐	48	Eddie Joyal, Det.	6.00	10.00
☐	49	Alex Faulkner, Det.	6.00	10.00
☐	50	Alex Delvecchio, Det.	15.00	25.00
☐	51	Bruce MacGregor, Det.	6.00	10.00
☐	52	Ted Hampson, Det.	6.00	10.00
☐	53	Peter Goegan, Det.	6.00	10.00
☐	54	Ron Ingram, Det.	7.50	15.00

1963 - 65 CHEX PHOTOS

There were two printings of this set. One is believed to have been issued in 1963/64 and the other in 1964/65. The colouring between the two printings varies slightly, with the second printing having more of a reddish tint. The cards are unnumbered. The cards are listed below alphabetically by team and then by player.

Card Size: 5 1/16" x 7"
Face: Four colour, white border, Name
Back: Blank
Imprint: None
Complete Set (59 cards): 1,100.00 1,800.00
Common Player: 12.00 20.00

	Player	EX	NRMT
CHICAGO BLACKHAWKS			
☐	Denis DeJordy	110.00	175.00
☐	Phil Esposito	65.00	110.00
☐	Glenn Hall (G)	45.00	70.00
☐	Billy Hay	12.00	20.00
☐	Wayne Hillman	12.00	20.00
☐	Bobby Hull	75.00	130.00
☐	Chico Maki	12.00	20.00
☐	Stan Mikita	35.00	60.00
☐	Pierre Pilote	22.00	35.00
☐	Elmer Vasko	12.00	20.00
☐	Ken Wharram	12.00	20.00
DETROIT RED WINGS			
☐	Alex Delvecchio	28.00	45.00
☐	Bill Gadsby	22.00	35.00
☐	Paul Henderson	22.00	35.00
☐	Gordie Howe	115.00	185.00
☐	Parker MacDonald	12.00	20.00
☐	Bruce MacGregor	12.00	20.00
☐	Pit Martin	12.00	20.00
☐	Marcel Pronovost	22.00	35.00
☐	Norm Ullman	28.00	45.00
MONTRÉAL CANADIENS			
☐	Ralph Backstrom	12.00	20.00
☐	Dave Balon	12.00	20.00
☐	Jean Béliveau, Front View	55.00	90.00
☐	Jean Béliveau, Side View	55.00	90.00
☐	Red Berenson	12.00	20.00
☐	Toe Blake, Coach	25.00	40.00
☐	John Ferguson	15.00	25.00
☐	Jean Gauthier	12.00	20.00
☐	Bernie Geoffrion	35.00	55.00
☐	Terry Harper	12.00	20.00
☐	Bill Hicke	12.00	20.00
☐	Charlie Hodge (G)	18.00	28.00
☐	Jacques Laperrière	28.00	45.00
☐	Claude Provost	15.00	25.00
☐	Marc Reaume	12.00	20.00
☐	Henri Richard	30.00	50.00
☐	Bobby Rousseau	12.00	20.00
☐	Bobby Rousseau (Bob Rousseau on card)	55.00	90.00
☐	Jean Guy Talbot	12.00	20.00
☐	Gilles Tremblay	12.00	20.00
☐	J.C. Tremblay	15.00	25.00
☐	Gump Worsley (G)	35.00	60.00
TORONTO MAPLE LEAFS			
☐	George Armstrong	25.00	40.00
☐	Bob Baun	15.00	25.00
☐	Johnny Bower (G)	30.00	50.00
☐	Kent Douglas	12.00	20.00
☐	Dick Duff	15.00	25.00
☐	Billy Harris	12.00	20.00
☐	Tim Horton	50.00	80.00

	Player	EX	NRMT
☐	Punch Imlach, Coach	22.00	35.00
☐	Red Kelly	25.00	40.00
☐	Dave Keon	28.00	45.00
☐	Ed Litzenberger	12.00	20.00
☐	John MacMillan	12.00	20.00
☐	Frank Mahovlich	45.00	75.00
☐	Bob Nevin	12.00	20.00
☐	Bob Pulford	25.00	40.00
☐	Eddie Shack	28.00	45.00
☐	Don Simmons (G)	15.00	25.00
☐	Allan Stanley	22.00	35.00
☐	Ron Stewart	12.00	20.00

1964 - 65 COCA-COLA / SPRITE CAPS

These caps were issued by both Coke and Sprite. The Sprite caps are more difficult to find and will command two and a half times the value of the Coke caps. The caps are unnumbered except for a jersey number and are arranged here alphabetically by team and then by player. The prices are listed for the Coke caps

Cap Diameter: 1 1/8"
Face: Player's image; Jersey number
Back: Plain
Imprint: None

		EX	NRMT
Complete Set (108 caps):		**350.00**	**600.00**
Common Player:		**3.00**	**5.00**
Display Plastic Rink:		**150.00**	**300.00**

	Player	EX	NRMT
BOSTON BRUINS			
☐☐	Murray Balfour	3.00	5.00
☐☐	Léo Boivin	5.00	8.50
☐☐	John Bucyk	7.00	12.00
☐☐	Gary Dornhoefer	3.00	5.00
☐☐	Reggie Fleming	3.00	5.00
☐☐	Ted Green	3.00	5.00
☐☐	Tom Johnson	5.00	8.50
☐☐	Eddie Johnston (G)	4.00	7.00
☐☐	Forbes Kennedy	3.00	5.00
☐☐	Orland Kurtenbach	3.00	5.00
☐☐	Bobby Leiter	3.00	5.00
☐☐	Bob McCord	3.00	5.00
☐☐	Ab McDonald	3.00	5.00
☐☐	Murray Oliver	3.00	5.00
☐☐	Dean Prentice	3.00	5.00
☐☐	Ron Schock	3.00	5.00
☐☐	Ed Westfall	3.00	5.00
☐☐	Tom Williams	3.00	5.00
CHICAGO BLACKHAWKS			
☐☐	John Brenneman	3.00	5.00
☐☐	Denis DeJordy (G)	4.00	7.00
☐☐	Phil Esposito	18.00	28.00
☐☐	Glenn Hall (G)	13.00	22.00
☐☐	Billy Hay	3.00	5.00
☐☐	Wayne Hillman	3.00	5.00
☐☐	Bobby Hull	22.00	35.00
☐☐	Al MacNeil	3.00	5.00
☐☐	Chico Maki	3.00	5.00
☐☐	John McKenzie	3.00	5.00
☐☐	Stan Mikita	9.00	15.00
☐☐	Doug Mohns	3.00	5.00
☐☐	Eric Nesterenko	3.00	5.00
☐☐	Pierre Pilote	5.00	8.50
☐☐	Doug Robinson	3.00	5.00
☐☐	Fred Stanfield	3.00	5.00
☐☐	Elmer Vasko	3.00	5.00
☐☐	Kenny Wharram	3.00	5.00
DETROIT RED WINGS			
☐☐	Doug Barkley	3.00	5.00
☐☐	Gary Bergman	3.00	5.00
☐☐	Roger Crozier (G)	5.00	8.50
☐☐	Alex Delvecchio # 10	7.00	12.00
☐☐	Bill Gadsby	5.00	8.50
☐☐	Paul Henderson	5.00	8.50
☐☐	Gordie Howe #9	28.00	45.00
☐☐	Larry Jeffrey	3.00	5.00
☐☐	Eddie Joyal	3.00	5.00
☐☐	Al Langlois	3.00	5.00
☐☐	Ted Lindsay	7.00	12.00
☐☐	Parker MacDonald	3.00	5.00
☐☐	Bruce MacGregor	3.00	5.00
☐☐	Pit Martin	3.00	5.00
☐☐	Ron Murphy	3.00	5.00
☐☐	Marcel Pronovost	5.00	8.50
☐☐	Floyd Smith	3.00	5.00
☐☐	Norm Ullman	7.00	12.00
MONTRÉAL CANADIENS			
☐☐	Ralph Backstrom	3.00	5.00
☐☐	Dave Balon	3.00	5.00
☐☐	Jean Béliveau	15.00	25.00
☐☐	Yvan Cournoyer	10.00	18.00
☐☐	John Ferguson	4.00	7.00
☐☐	Terry Harper	3.00	5.00
☐☐	Ted Harris	3.00	5.00
☐☐	Bill Hicke	3.00	5.00
☐☐	Charlie Hodge (G)	5.00	8.00
☐☐	Jacques Laperrière	5.00	8.50
☐☐	Claude Larose	3.00	5.00
☐☐	Claude Provost	3.00	5.00
☐☐	Henri Richard	9.00	15.00
☐☐	Jim Roberts	3.00	5.00
☐☐	Bobby Rousseau	4.00	7.00
☐☐	Jean-Guy Talbot	3.00	5.00
☐☐	Gilles Tremblay	3.00	5.00
☐☐	J.C. Tremblay	4.00	7.00
NEW YORK RANGERS			
☐☐	Lou Angotti	3.00	5.00
☐☐	Arnie Brown	3.00	5.00
☐☐	Dick Duff	3.00	5.00
☐☐	Val Fonteyne	4.00	7.00
☐☐	Rod Gilbert	7.00	12.00
☐☐	Phil Goyette	3.00	5.00
☐☐	Vic Hadfield	4.00	7.00
☐☐	Camille Henry	3.00	5.00
☐☐	Harry Howell	5.00	8.50
☐☐	Earl Ingarfield	3.00	5.00
☐☐	Don Johns	3.00	5.00
☐☐	Don Marshall	3.00	5.00
☐☐	Jim Mikol	3.00	5.00
☐☐	Jim Neilson	3.00	5.00
☐☐	Bob Nevin	3.00	5.00
☐☐	Marcel Paille (G)	4.00	7.00
☐☐	Jacques Plante (G)	15.00	25.00
☐☐	Rod Seiling	3.00	5.00
TORONTO MAPLE LEAFS			
☐☐	George Armstrong	6.00	10.00
☐☐	Andy Bathgate, #9	6.00	10.00
☐☐	Bob Baun	4.00	7.00
☐☐	Johnny Bower (G)	10.00	18.00
☐☐	Carl Brewer	3.00	5.00
☐☐	Kent Douglas	3.00	5.00
☐☐	Ron Ellis	4.00	7.00
☐☐	Tim Horton	13.00	22.00
☐☐	Red Kelly	6.50	11.00
☐☐	Dave Keon	9.00	15.00
☐☐	Frank Mahovlich	13.00	22.00
☐☐	Don McKenney	3.00	5.00
☐☐	Dickie Moore	6.50	11.00
☐☐	Bob Pulford	6.00	10.00
☐☐	Terry Sawchuk (G)	15.00	25.00
☐☐	Eddie Shack	5.50	9.00
☐☐	Allan Stanley	5.00	8.50
☐☐	Ron Stewart	3.00	5.00

1964 - 65 TOPPS

This issue features players from all six NHL teams. The card is larger than previous years and some of the higher numbers in the second series were short-printed (*).

Card Size: 2 1/2" x 4 11/16"
Face: Four colour, white border, Position
Back: Black and red on card stock, Number, Resume, Cartoon, Bilingual
Imprint: T.C.G. PRINTED IN CANADA

		EX	NRMT
Complete Set (110 cards):		**5,000.00**	**8,000.00**
Common Player (1 - 55):		**13.00**	**22.00**
Common Player (56 - 110):		**35.00**	**55.00**

	No.	Player	EX	NRMT
☐	**1**	**Pit Martin, Det., RC**	**35.00**	**80.00**
☐	2	Gilles Tremblay, Mtl.	13.00	22.00
☐	3	Terry Harper, Mtl.	13.00	22.00
☐	4	John Ferguson, Mtl.	25.00	40.00
☐	5	Elmer Vasko, Chi.	13.00	22.00
☐	6	Terry Sawchuk (G), Tor.	75.00	120.00
☐	7	Billy Hay, Chi.	13.00	22.00
☐	**8**	**Gary Bergman, Det., RC**	**20.00**	**30.00**
☐	9	Doug Barkley, Det.	13.00	22.00
☐	10	Bob McCord, Bos.	13.00	22.00
☐	11	Parker MacDonald, Det.	13.00	22.00
☐	12	Glenn Hall (G), Chi.	50.00	80.00
☐	13	Al Langlois, Det.	13.00	22.00
☐	14	Camille Henry, NYR.	13.00	22.00
☐	15	Norm Ullman, Det.	25.00	40.00
☐	16	Ab McDonald, Bos.	13.00	22.00
☐	17	Charlie Hodge (G), Mtl.	20.00	30.00
☐	18	Orland Kurtenbach, Bos.	13.00	22.00
☐	19	Dean Prentice, Bos.	13.00	22.00
☐	20	Bobby Hull, Chi.	225.00	350.00
☐	21	Ed Johnston (G), Bos.	20.00	30.00
☐	22	Denis DeJordy (G), Chi.	20.00	30.00
☐	23	Claude Provost, Mtl.	13.00	22.00
☐	24	Rod Gilbert, NYR.	30.00	50.00
☐	25	Doug Mohns, Chi.	13.00	22.00
☐	26	Al MacNeil, Chi.	13.00	22.00
☐	27	Billy Harris, Tor.	13.00	22.00
☐	28	Kenny Wharram, Chi.	13.00	22.00
☐	29	Red Sullivan, NYR., LC	13.00	22.00
☐	30	John McKenzie, Chi.	13.00	22.00
☐	31	Stan Mikita, Chi.	70.00	120.00
☐	32	Ted Green, Bos.	13.00	22.00
☐	33	Jean Béliveau, Mtl.	90.00	150.00
☐	**34**	**Arnie Brown, NYR., RC**	**13.00**	**22.00**
☐	35	Reggie Fleming, Bos.	13.00	22.00
☐	**36**	**Jim Mikol, NYR., RC, LC**	**13.00**	**22.00**
☐	37	Dave Balon, Mtl.	13.00	22.00
☐	38	Billy Reay, Coach, Chi.	13.00	22.00
☐	39	Marcel Pronovost, Det.	20.00	30.00
☐	40	Johnny Bower (G), Tor.	35.00	55.00
☐	41	Wayne Hillman, Chi.	13.00	22.00
☐	42	Floyd Smith, Det.	13.00	22.00
☐	43	Toe Blake, Coach, Mtl.	22.00	35.00
☐	44	Red Kelly, Tor.	22.00	35.00
☐	45	Punch Imlach, Coach, Tor.	20.00	30.00
☐	46	Dick Duff, NYR.	13.00	22.00
☐	**47**	**Roger Crozier (G), Det., RC**	**50.00**	**80.00**
☐	48	Henri Richard, Mtl.	55.00	85.00
☐	49	Larry Jeffrey, Det.	13.00	22.00
☐	50	Leo Boivin, Bos.	20.00	30.00
☐	51	Ed Westfall, Bos.	13.00	22.00

☐	52	Jean-Guy Talbot, Mtl.	13.00	22.00
☐	53	Jacques Laperrière, Mtl.	22.00	35.00
☐	54	Checklist 1 (1 - 54)	200.00	350.00
☐	55	Checklist 2 (55 - 110)	315.00	525.00
☐	56	Ron Murphy, Det.	50.00	80.00
☐	57	Bob Baun, Tor.	40.00	65.00
☐	58	Tom Williams, Bos., (*)	130.00	215.00
☐	59	Pierre Pilote, Chi., (*)	140.00	325.00
☐	60	Bob Pulford, Tor.	40.00	65.00
☐	61	Red Berenson, Mtl.	35.00	55.00
☐	62	Vic Hadfield, NYR.	35.00	55.00
☐	63	Bobby Leiter, Bos.	35.00	55.00
☐	**64**	**Jim Pappin, Tor., RC**	**40.00**	**65.00**
☐	65	Earl Ingarfield, NYR.	35.00	55.00
☐	**66**	**Lou Angotti, NYR., RC**	**35.00**	**55.00**
☐	**67**	**Rod Seiling, NYR., RC**	**35.00**	**55.00**
☐	68	Jacques Plante (G), NYR.	120.00	200.00
☐	69	George Armstrong, Tor.	50.00	80.00
☐	70	Milt Schmidt, Coach, Bos.	40.00	65.00
☐	71	Eddie Shack, Tor.	75.00	125.00
☐	**72**	**Gary Dornhoefer, Bos., RC, (*)**	**165.00**	**265.00**
☐	73	Chico Maki, Chi., (*)	130.00	215.00
☐	74	Gilles Villemure (G), NYR., (*)	165.00	265.00
☐	75	Carl Brewer, Tor.	35.00	55.00
☐	76	Bruce MacGregor, Det.	35.00	55.00
☐	77	Bob Nevin, NYR.	35.00	55.00
☐	78	Ralph Backstrom, Mtl.	35.00	55.00
☐	79	Murray Oliver, Bos.	35.00	55.00
☐	80	Bobby Rousseau, Mtl., (*)	130.00	215.00
☐	81	Don McKenney, Tor.	35.00	55.00
☐	82	Ted Lindsay, Det., LC	55.00	90.00
☐	83	Harry Howell, NYR.	45.00	75.00
☐	**84**	**Doug Robinson, Chi., RC**	**35.00**	**55.00**
☐	85	Frank Mahovlich, Tor.	110.00	165.00
☐	86	Andy Bathgate, Tor.	45.00	75.00
☐	87	Phil Goyette, NYR.	35.00	55.00
☐	88	J.C. Tremblay, Mtl.	40.00	65.00
☐	89	Gordie Howe, Det.	350.00	550.00
☐	90	Murray Balfour, Bos., LC	35.00	55.00
☐	91	Eric Nesterenko, Chi., (*)	130.00	215.00
☐	**92**	**Marcel Paille (G), NYR., RC, LC (*)**	**220.00**	**375.00**
☐	93	Sid Abel, Coach, Det.	35.00	55.00
☐	94	Dave Keon, Tor.	65.00	110.00
☐	95	Alex Delvecchio, Det.	55.00	90.00
☐	96	Bill Gadsby, Det.	40.00	65.00
☐	97	Don Marshall, NYR.	35.00	55.00
☐	98	Bill Hicke, Mtl., (*)	130.00	215.00
☐	99	Ron Stewart, Tor.	35.00	55.00
☐	100	John Bucyk, Bos.	60.00	100.00
☐	101	Tom Johnson, Bos.	40.00	65.00
☐	102	Tim Horton, Tor.	110.00	165.00
☐	103	Jim Neilson, NYR.	35.00	55.00
☐	104	Allan Stanley, Tor.	30.00	65.00
☐	105	AS: Tim Horton, Tor., (*)	235.00	400.00
☐	106	AS: Stan Mikita, Chi., (*)	210.00	360.00
☐	107	AS: Bobby Hull, Chi.	150.00	250.00
☐	108	AS: Kenny Wharram, Chi.	35.00	55.00
☐	109	AS: Pierre Pilote, Chi.	50.00	80.00
☐	110	AS: Glenn Hall (G), Chi.	75.00	175.00

1964 - 65 TORONTO STAR

CANADIENS' JEAN BELIVEAU
IS WELL COVERED IN GAME AGAINST MAPLE LEAFS. RED KELLY (HELMET) AND TIM HORTON PIN BELIVEAU IN BATTLE ALONG THE BOARDS. AT SIX-FOOT-FOUR AND 210 LBS., BELIVEAU IS ONE OF LEAGUE'S BIGGEST PLAYERS.

Card Size: 4 1/8"x 5 1/8"
Face: Four colour, white strip at bottom on paper stock; Name, Jersey number, Team, Play-by-play action
Back: Blank
Imprint: None

		EX	NRMT
Complete Set (48 cards):		**250.00**	**375.00**
Common Player:		**3.00**	**6.00**
Album:		**25.00**	**50.00**

	No.	Player	EX	NRMT
☐	1	Léo Boivin, Bos.	4.50	9.00
☐	2	Ted Green, Bos.	3.00	6.00
☐	3	Tom Johnson, Bos.	4.50	9.00
☐	4	Forbes Kennedy, Bos.	3.00	6.00
☐	5	Orland Kurtenbach, Bos.	3.00	6.00
☐	6	Wayne Rivers, Bos.	3.00	6.00
☐	7	Glenn Hall (G), Chi.	7.50	15.00
☐	8	Billy Hay, Chi.	3.00	6.00
☐	9	Wayne Hillman, Chi.	3.00	6.00
☐	10	Bobby Hull, Chi.	18.00	35.00
☐	11	Al MacNeil, Chi.	3.00	6.00
☐	12	Chico Maki, Chi.	3.00	6.00
☐	13	John McKenzie, Chi.	3.00	6.00
☐	14	Stan Mikita, Chi.	7.50	15.00
☐	15	Pierre Pilote, Chi.	4.50	9.00
☐	16	Elmer Vasko, Chi.	3.00	6.00
☐	17	Alex Delvecchio, Det.	6.00	12.00
☐	18	Paul Henderson, Det.	5.00	10.00
☐	19	Gordie Howe, Det.	30.00	55.00
☐	20	Larry Jeffrey, Det.	3.00	6.00
☐	21	Parker MacDonald, Det.	3.00	6.00
☐	22	Marcel Pronovost, Det., Error (Provost)	4.50	9.00
☐	23	Floyd Smith, Det.	3.00	6.00
☐	24	Norm Ullman, Det.	6.00	12.00
☐	25	Dave Balon, Mtl.	3.00	6.00
☐	26	Jean Béliveau, Mtl.	11.00	22.00
☐	27	Red Berenson, Mtl.	3.00	6.00
☐	28	Charlie Hodge (G), Mtl.	4.50	9.00
☐	29	Jacques Laperrière, Mtl.	6.00	12.00
☐	30	Claude Provost, Mtl.	3.00	6.00
☐	31	Henri Richard, Mtl.	7.50	15.00
☐	32	J.C. Tremblay, Mtl.	3.00	6.00
☐	33	Rod Gilbert, NYR.	6.00	12.00
☐	34	Harry Howell, NYR.	4.50	9.00
☐	35	Jim Neilson, NYR.	3.00	6.00
☐	36	Jacques Plante (G), NYR.	10.00	20.00
☐	37	Andy Bathgate, Tor.	5.00	10.00
☐	38	Bob Baun, Tor.	3.00	6.00
☐	39	Carl Brewer, Tor.	3.00	6.00
☐	40	Billy Harris, Tor.	3.00	6.00
☐	41	Tim Horton, Tor.	9.00	18.00
☐	42	Dave Keon, Tor.	6.00	12.00
☐	43	Frank Mahovlich, Tor.	9.00	18.00
☐	44	Don McKenney, Tor.	3.00	6.00
☐	45	Jim Pappin, Tor.	3.00	6.00
☐	46	Bob Pulford, Tor.	5.00	10.00
☐	47	Allan Stanley, Tor.	4.50	9.00
☐	48	Ron Stewart, Tor.	3.00	6.00

1964 - 67 EATON'S GORDIE HOWE

SPORTS ADVISER

These cards were issued by Eaton's between 1964 and 1967 as promotional cards for their Truline Sports Equipment. During the summer months Howe toured Canada appearing at the Eaton stores to promote this line of equipment.

Card Size: 3 1/2" x 5 1/2"
Face: Four colour, white border
Back: Blue and black on white card stock; Facsimile autograph
Imprint: EATON'S

	No.	Player	EX	NRMT
Complete Set (3 cards):			**85.00**	**125.00**
☐	1	1964-65 All-Star Uniform	30.00	50.00
☐	2	1965-66 Action Pose	30.00	50.00
☐	3	1966-67 Standing Pose	30.00	50.00

1965 - 66 COCA-COLA

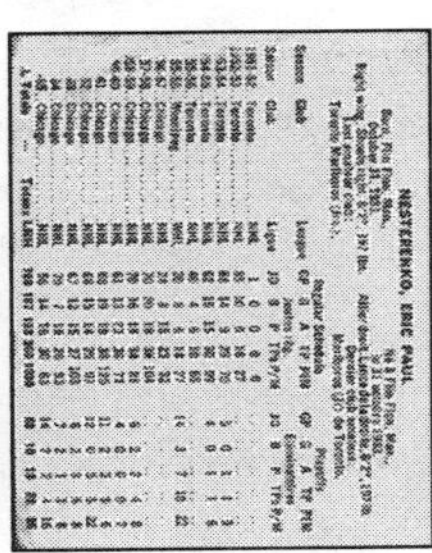

Card Size: 2 3/4" x 3 1/2"
Face: Black and white; Name, Resume
Back: Black and white; Name, Bilingual
Imprint: None

		EX	NRMT
Complete Set Unperforated:		**500.00**	**800.00**
Complete Set (108 cards):		**250.00**	**400.00**
Boston Bruins Unperforated Team Set		**60.00**	**100.00**
Chicago Blackhawks Unperforated Team Set		**120.00**	**200.00**
Detroit Red Wings Unperforated Team Set		**90.00**	**150.00**
Montréal Canadiens Unperforated Team Set		**80.00**	**130.00**
New York Rangers Unperforated Team Set		**55.00**	**90.00**
Toronto Maple Leafs Unperforated Team Set		**100.00**	**175.00**
Common Player:		**1.50**	**2.50**
Album:		**65.00**	**125.00**

	Player	EX	NRMT
BOSTON BRUINS			
☐	Barry Ashbee	3.00	5.00
☐	Don Awrey	1.50	2.50
☐	Léo Boivin	3.25	5.50
☐	John Bucyk	5.00	8.00
☐	Gerry Cheevers (G)	15.00	25.00
☐	Bob Dillabough	1.50	2.50
☐	Reggie Fleming	1.50	2.50
☐	Ted Green	1.50	2.50
☐	Forbes Kennedy	1.50	2.50
☐	Al Langlois	1.50	2.50
☐	Parker MacDonald	1.50	2.50
☐	Murray Oliver	1.50	2.50
☐	Bernie Parent (G)	18.00	28.00
☐	Dean Prentice	1.50	2.50
☐	Ron Stewart	1.50	2.50
☐	Ed Westfall	1.50	2.50
☐	Tom Williams	1.50	2.50
☐	Bob Woytowich	1.50	2.50
CHICAGO BLACKHAWKS			
☐	Dave Dryden (G)	2.50	4.00
☐	Phil Esposito	25.00	40.00
☐	Glenn Hall (G)	10.00	18.00
☐	Billy Hay	1.50	2.50
☐	Ken Hodge	2.50	4.00
☐	Bobby Hull	28.00	45.00
☐	Dennis Hull	3.00	5.00
☐	Doug Jarrett	1.50	2.50
☐	Al MacNeil	1.50	2.50
☐	Chico Maki	1.50	2.50
☐	John McKenzie	1.50	2.50
☐	Stan Mikita	9.00	15.00
☐	Doug Mohns	1.50	2.50
☐	Eric Nesterenko	1.50	2.50
☐	Pierre Pilote	3.25	5.50
☐	Matt Ravlich	1.50	2.50
☐	Fred Stanfield	1.50	2.50
☐	Elmer Vasko	1.50	2.50
☐	Kenny Wharram	1.50	2.50
DETROIT RED WINGS			
☐	Hank Bassen (G)	1.50	2.50
☐	Doug Barkley	1.50	2.50
☐	Gary Bergman	1.50	2.50
☐	Roger Crozier (G)	4.00	6.50
☐	Alex Delvecchio	6.00	10.00
☐	Val Fonteyne	1.50	2.50
☐	Bill Gadsby	3.25	5.50
☐	Warren Godfrey	1.50	2.50
☐	Billy Harris	1.50	2.50
☐	Paul Henderson	3.50	6.00
☐	Gordie Howe	40.00	65.00
☐	Bruce MacGregor	1.50	2.50
☐	Bert Marshall	1.50	2.50

	Player	EX	NRMT
☐	Ab McDonald	1.50	2.50
☐	Ron Murphy	1.50	2.50
☐	Floyd Smith	1.50	2.50
☐	Norm Ullman	5.50	9.00
MONTRÉAL CANADIENS			
☐	Ralph Backstrom	1.50	2.50
☐	Jean Béliveau	15.00	25.00
☐	Yvan Cournoyer	8.50	14.00
☐	Dick Duff	1.50	2.50
☐	John Ferguson	1.50	2.50
☐	Terry Harper	1.50	2.50
☐	Ted Harris	1.50	2.50
☐	Charlie Hodge (G)	2.50	4.00
☐	Jacques Laperrière	3.25	5.50
☐	Claude Larose	1.50	2.50
☐	Garry Peters	1.50	2.50
☐	Claude Provost	1.50	2.50
☐	Henri Richard	8.00	13.00
☐	Jim Roberts	1.50	2.50
☐	Bobby Rousseau	1.50	2.50
☐	Don Simmons (G)	2.50	4.00
☐	Jean-Guy Talbot	1.50	2.50
☐	Gilles Tremblay	1.50	2.50
☐	J.C. Tremblay	1.50	2.50
☐	Gump Worsley (G)	10.00	16.00
NEW YORK RANGERS			
☐	Arnie Brown	1.50	2.50
☐	Ed Giacomin (G)	15.00	25.00
☐	Rod Gilbert	5.00	8.00
☐	Phil Goyette	1.50	2.50
☐	Vic Hadfield	2.50	4.00
☐	Bill Hicke	1.50	2.50
☐	Wayne Hillman	1.50	2.50
☐	Harry Howell	3.25	5.50
☐	Earl Ingarfield	1.50	2.50
☐	Don Marshall	1.50	2.50
☐	Mike McMahon	1.50	2.50
☐	Jim Neilson	1.50	2.50
☐	Bob Nevin	1.50	2.50
☐	Jean Ratelle	5.00	8.00
☐	Doug Robinson	1.50	2.50
TORONTO MAPLE LEAFS			
☐	George Armstrong	3.50	6.00
☐	Andy Bathgate	3.50	6.00
☐	Bob Baun	1.50	2.50
☐	Johnny Bower (G)	8.50	14.00
☐	Kent Douglas	1.50	2.50
☐	Ron Ellis	1.50	2.50
☐	Tim Horton	12.00	20.00
☐	Red Kelly	4.50	7.50
☐	Dave Keon	7.00	12.00
☐	Orland Kurtenbach	1.50	2.50
☐	Frank Mahovlich	12.00	20.00
☐	Bob Pulford	3.50	6.00
☐	Marcel Pronovost	3.25	5.50
☐	Terry Sawchuk (G)	18.00	28.00
☐	Brit Selby	1.50	2.50
☐	Eddie Shack	4.00	7.00
☐	Allan Stanley	3.25	5.50
☐	Pete Stemkowski	1.50	2.50
☐	Mike Walton	1.50	2.50

COKE HOW TO PLAY BOOKLETS

This is a 32-page instructional booklet called "How to Play".

Booklet Size: 4 5/16" x 3 15/16"
Face: Four colour, blue background, black lettering
Back: Black on blue background
Imprint: None

	EX	NRMT
Complete English Set (4 cards):	**80.00**	**135.00**
Complete French Set (4 cards):	**120.00**	**200.00**

No.	Player	EX	NRMT
ENGLISH ISSUE			
☐ A	Johnny Bower, Tor. (Goal)	40.00	60.00
☐ B	David Keon, Tor. (Forward)	28.00	45.00
☐ C	Jacques Laperrière, Mtl. (Defense)	15.00	25.00
☐ D	Henri Richard, Mtl. (Foward)	28.00	45.00
FRENCH ISSUE			
☐ W	Johnny Bower, Tor. (Goal)	50.00	80.00
☐ X	David Keon, Tor. (Forward)	40.00	70.00
☐ Y	Jacques Laperrière, Mtl. (Defense)	22.00	35.00
☐ Z	Henri Richard, Mtl. (Forward)	40.00	70.00

1965 - 66 HELLAS

A set of 160 cards issued by the chewing gum factory Hellas (Leaf) for the Finnish Nationals League. We have no pricing information on this set.

Card Size: 2 1/8" x 3 1/8"
Imprint:
Face: Four colour, white border

No.	Player
☐ 1	Lasse Kiili, Turun Palloseura
☐ 2	Ilkka Mesikammen, Turun Palloseura
☐ 3	Jorma Laapas, Turun Palloseura
☐ 4	Esko Reijonen, Turun Palloseura
☐ 5	Juhani IsoEskeli, Turun Palloseura
☐ 6	Pertti Nieminen, Turun Palloseura
☐ 7	Kari Aro, Turun Palloseura
☐ 8	Juhani Wahlsten, Turun Palloseura
☐ 9	Rauno Heinonen, Turun Palloseura
☐ 10	Kalevi Leppanen, Turun Palloseura
☐ 11	Pertti Karelius, Turun Palloseura
☐ 12	Pekka Olkkonen, Turun Palloseura
☐ 13	Kari Sillanpaa, Turun Palloseura
☐ 14	Jarmo Rantanen, Turun Palloseura
☐ 15	Heikki Heimo, Turun Palloseura
☐ 16	Jorma Valtonen, Turun Palloseura
☐ 17	Risto Kaitala, Rauman Lukko
☐ 18	Kalevi Virkku, Rauman Lukko
☐ 19	Helkko Stenvall, Rauman Lukko
☐ 20	Teppo Rastio, Rauman Lukko
☐ 21	Seppo Vainio, Rauman Lukko
☐ 22	Pentti Jokinen, Rauman Lukko
☐ 23	Matti Keinonen, Rauman Lukko
☐ 24	Matti Koivunen, Rauman Lukko
☐ 25	Esa Isaksson, Rauman Lukko
☐ 26	Juhani Jylha, Rauman Lukko
☐ 27	Pentti Rautalin, Rauman Lukko
☐ 28	Simo Sainio, Rauman Lukko
☐ 29	Hannu Torma, Rauman Lukko
☐ 30	Olli Malmivuori, Rauman Lukko
☐ 31	Matti Saurio, Rauman Lukko
☐ 32	Mikko Erholm, Rauman Lukko
☐ 33	Anto Virtanen, Porin Karhut
☐ 34	Juha Rantasila, Porin Karhut
☐ 35	Jaakko Honkanen, Porin Karhut
☐ 36	Antti Heikkila, Porin Karhut
☐ 37	Lasse Heikkila, Porin Karhut
☐ 38	VeliPekka Ketola, Porin Karhut
☐ 39	Keijo Koistinen, Porin Karhut
☐ 40	Mikko Myllyniemi, Porin Karhut
☐ 41	Matti Salmi, Porin Karhut
☐ 42	Tuomo Pirskanen, Porin Karhut
☐ 43	Matti Jansson, Porin Karhut
☐ 44	Erkki Saine, Porin Karhut
☐ 45	Erkki Harju, Porin Karhut
☐ 46	Kaj Matalamaki, Porin Karhut
☐ 47	Seppo Nystrom, Porin Karhut
☐ 48	Timo Jussila, Porin Karhut
☐ 49	Jorma Rikala, HJK
☐ 50	Tapio Raunio, HJK
☐ 51	Pekka Korjakoff, HJK
☐ 52	Jorma Borgstrom, HJK
☐ 53	Jorma Kyntola, HJK
☐ 54	Jyrki Malmio, HJK
☐ 55	Aarno Hiekkaranta, HJK
☐ 56	Kalevi Salo, HJK
☐ 57	Martti Kuokkanen, HJK
☐ 58	Seppo Ikola, HJK
☐ 59	Hannu Kyllastinen, HJK
☐ 60	Pentti Katainen, HJK
☐ 61	Harri Linnonmaa, HJK
☐ 62	Kyosti Wall, HJK
☐ 63	Kari Kinnunen, HJK
☐ 64	Martti Kallionpaa, HJK
☐ 65	Pekka Kuusisto, RU38 Pori
☐ 66	Johannes Karttunen, RU38 Pori
☐ 67	Heikki Veravainen, RU38 Pori
☐ 68	Pentti Riitahaara, RU38 Pori
☐ 69	Lauri Lehtonen, RU38 Pori
☐ 70	Matti Harju, RU38 Pori
☐ 71	Pertti Kontto, RU38 Pori
☐ 72	Timo Makela, RU38 Pori
☐ 73	Tapio Rautalammi, RU38 Pori
☐ 74	Kimmo Kivela, RU38 Pori
☐ 75	Raimo Maattanen, RU38 Pori
☐ 76	Kari Rajala, RU38 Pori
☐ 77	Tapani Suominen, RU38 Pori
☐ 78	Heimo Tervo, RU38 Pori
☐ 79	Raimo Kilpio, RU38 Pori
☐ 80	Matti Lampainen, RU38 Pori
☐ 81	Raimo Helppolainen, Saimaan
☐ 82	Esko Nenonen, Saimaan
☐ 83	Lalli Partinen, Saimaan
☐ 84	Leo Haakana, Saimaan
☐ 85	Hannu Lemander, Saimaan
☐ 86	Leevi Ryhanen, Saimaan
☐ 87	Yrjo Hakala, Saimaan
☐ 88	Pauli Hyvari, Saimaan
☐ 89	Jorma Hietanen, Saimaan
☐ 90	Juhani Pyyhtia, Saimaan
☐ 91	Timo Vaatamoinen, Saimaan
☐ 92	Heikki Juselius, Saimaan
☐ 93	Pentti Hyvari, Saimaan
☐ 94	Antti Ravi, Saimaan
☐ 95	Markku Eiskonen, Saimaan
☐ 96	Martti Sinkkonen, Saimaan
☐ 97	Tapio Majaniemi, Tampereen
☐ 98	Matti Reunamaki, Tampereen
☐ 99	Rauno Heinonen, Tampereen
☐ 100	Rauno Lehtio, Tampereen
☐ 101	Risto Lehtio, Tampereen
☐ 102	Juhani Tammi, Tampereen
☐ 103	Matti Kautto, Tampereen
☐ 104	Pekka Lehtolainen, Tampereen
☐ 105	Markku Pulli, Tampereen
☐ 106	Eero Holopainen, Tampereen
☐ 107	Aaro Nurminen, Tampereen
☐ 108	Kalevi Pulli, Tampereen
☐ 109	Jorma Suokko, Tampereen
☐ 110	Erkki Suokko, Tampereen
☐ 111	Heino Pulli, Tampereen
☐ 112	Seppo Nikkila, Tampereen
☐ 113	Pentti Pynnonen, Ilves
☐ 114	Lasse Oksanen, Ilves
☐ 115	Olli Wirzenius, Ilves
☐ 116	Pentti Uotila, Ilves
☐ 117	Jaakko Jaskari, Ilves
☐ 118	Markku Hakanen, Ilves
☐ 119	Ilkka Halme, Ilves
☐ 120	Pekka Alfors, Ilves
☐ 121	Tauno Niemi, Ilves
☐ 122	Erkan Nasib, Ilves
☐ 123	Veikko Ukkonen, Ilves
☐ 124	Jarmo Wasama, Ilves
☐ 125	Juhani Lahtinen, Ilves
☐ 126	Jorma Peltonen, Ilves
☐ 127	Kari Palooja, Ilves
☐ 128	Reijo Hakanen, Ilves
☐ 129	Esko Kaonpaa, HIFK
☐ 130	Kimmo Heino, HIFK
☐ 131	Jaakko Siren, HIFK
☐ 132	Seppo Naukkarinen, HIFK
☐ 133	Rainer Kolehmainen, HIFK
☐ 134	Henrik Granholm, HIFK
☐ 135	Erkki Partanen, HIFK
☐ 136	Heikki Jarn, HIFK

- ☐ 137 Jerry Sullivan, HIFK
- ☐ 138 Jaakko Marttinen, HIFK
- ☐ 139 Ulf Lindholm, HIFK
- ☐ 140 Pentti Lindegren, HIFK
- ☐ 141 Pentti Kotkas, HIFK
- ☐ 142 Pekka Perttula, HIFK
- ☐ 143 Esko Rekomaa, HIFK
- ☐ 144 Christer Thun, HIFK
- ☐ 145 Matti Kaski, Tappara
- ☐ 146 Pekka Marjamaki, Tappara
- ☐ 147 Antti Virtanen, Tappara
- ☐ 148 Matti Peltonen, Tappara
- ☐ 149 Reijo Ojanen, Tappara
- ☐ 150 Timo Ahlqvist, Tappara
- ☐ 151 Seppo Makinen, Tappara
- ☐ 152 Jouni Seistamo, Tappara
- ☐ 153 Harri Harvala, Tappara
- ☐ 154 Kari Makinen, Tappara
- ☐ 155 Heikki Koskimies, Tappara
- ☐ 156 Timo Jussila, Tappara
- ☐ 157 Pertti Ansakorpi, Tappara
- ☐ 158 Hannu Elo, Tappara
- ☐ 159 Mikko Holopainen, Tappara
- ☐ 160 Kalevi Numminen, Tappara

1965 - 66 TOPPS

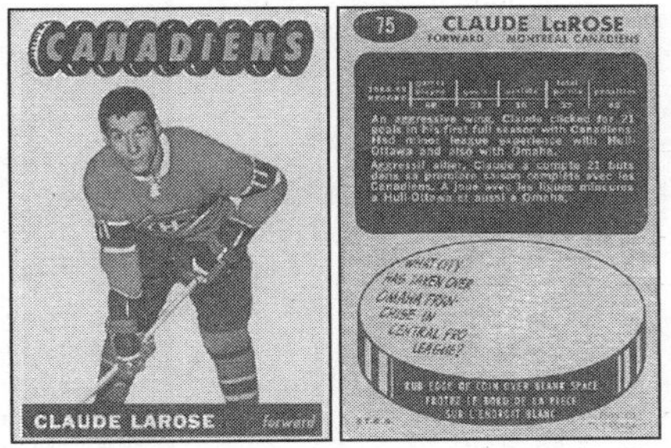

Card nos. 122-128 are difficult to find and are not even listed on the checklist card No. 121.

Card Size: 2 1/2" x 3 1/2"

Face: Four colour, white border Team Cards - Two colour, black and white photograph

Back: Black on card stock; Number, Resume, Hockey trivia, Bilingual

Imprint: T.C.G. PRINTED IN CANADA

		EX	NRMT
Complete Set (128 cards):		**2,200.00**	**3,500.00**
Common Player:		**6.50**	**11.00**
No.	**Player**	**EX**	**NRMT**
☐ 1	Toe Blake, Mtl., Coach	12.00	30.00
☐ 2	Gump Worsley (G), Mtl.	22.00	35.00
☐ 3	Jacques Laperrière, Mtl.	12.00	20.00
☐ 4	Jean-Guy Talbot, Mtl.	6.50	11.00
☐ **5**	**Ted Harris, Mtl., RC**	**6.50**	**11.00**
☐ 6	Jean Béliveau, Mtl.	35.00	60.00
☐ 7	Dick Duff, Mtl.	6.50	11.00
☐ 8	Claude Provost, Mtl.	6.50	11.00
☐ 9	Red Berenson, Mtl.	6.50	11.00
☐ 10	John Ferguson, Mtl.	6.50	11.00
☐ 11	Punch Imlach, Coach, Tor.	9.00	15.00
☐ 12	Terry Sawchuk (G), Tor.	55.00	85.00
☐ 13	Bob Baun, Tor.	9.00	15.00
☐ 14	Kent Douglas, Tor.	6.50	11.00
☐ 15	Red Kelly, Tor.	12.00	20.00
☐ 16	Jim Pappin, Tor.	6.50	11.00
☐ 17	Dave Keon, Tor.	30.00	50.00
☐ 18	Bob Pulford, Tor.	9.00	15.00
☐ 19	George Armstrong, Tor.	11.00	18.00
☐ 20	Orland Kurtenbach, Tor.	6.50	11.00
☐ **21**	**Ed Giacomin (G), NYR., RC**	**95.00**	**150.00**
☐ 22	Harry Howell, NYR.	9.00	15.00
☐ 23	Rod Seiling, NYR.	6.50	11.00
☐ **24**	**Mike McMahon, NYR., RC**	**6.50**	**11.00**
☐ 25	Jean Ratelle, NYR.	20.00	30.00
☐ 26	Doug Robinson, NYR.	6.50	11.00
☐ 27	Vic Hadfield, NYR.	6.50	11.00
☐ **28**	**Garry Peters, NYR., RC, Error (Gary)**	**6.50**	**11.00**
☐ 29	Don Marshall, NYR.	6.50	11.00
☐ 30	Bill Hicke, NYR.	6.50	11.00
☐ **31**	**Gerry Cheevers (G), Bos., RC**	**95.00**	**150.00**
☐ 32	Léo Boivin, Bos.	9.00	15.00
☐ 33	Al Langlois, Bos., LC	6.50	11.00
☐ 34	Murray Oliver, Bos.	6.50	11.00
☐ 35	Tom Williams, Bos.	6.50	11.00
☐ **36**	**Ron Schock, Bos., RC**	**6.50**	**11.00**
☐ 37	Ed Westfall, Bos.	6.50	11.00
☐ 38	Gary Dornhoefer, Bos.	6.50	11.00
☐ 39	Bob Dillabough, Bos.	6.50	11.00
☐ **40**	**Poul Popiel, Bos., RC, Error (Paul)**	**6.50**	**11.00**
☐ 41	Sid Abel, Coach, Det.	9.00	15.00
☐ 42	Roger Crozier (G), Det.	12.00	20.00
☐ 43	Doug Barkley, Det., LC	6.50	11.00
☐ 44	Bill Gadsby, Det., LC	9.00	15.00
☐ **45**	**Bryan Watson, Det., RC**	**12.00**	**20.00**
☐ 46	Bob McCord, Det.	6.50	11.00
☐ 47	Alex Delvecchio, Det.	12.00	20.00
☐ 48	Andy Bathgate, Det.	9.00	15.00
☐ 49	Norm Ullman, Det.	13.00	22.00
☐ 50	Ab McDonald, Det.	6.50	11.00
☐ **51**	**Paul Henderson, Det., RC**	**35.00**	**60.00**
☐ 52	Pit Martin, Det.	6.50	11.00
☐ 53	Billy Harris, Det.	6.50	11.00
☐ 54	Billy Reay, Coach, Chi.	6.50	11.00
☐ 55	Glenn Hall (G), Chi.	25.00	40.00
☐ 56	Pierre Pilote, Chi.	9.00	15.00
☐ 57	Al MacNeil, Chi.	6.50	11.00
☐ 58	Camille Henry, Chi.	6.50	11.00
☐ 59	Bobby Hull, Chi.	115.00	180.00
☐ 60	Stan Mikita, Chi.	55.00	85.00
☐ 61	Kenny Wharram, Chi.	6.50	11.00
☐ 62	Billy Hay, Chi., LC	6.50	11.00
☐ **63**	**Fred Stanfield, Chi., RC**	**6.50**	**11.00**
☐ **64**	**Dennis Hull, Chi., RC**	**20.00**	**30.00**
☐ **65**	**Ken Hodge, Chi., RC**	**20.00**	**30.00**
☐ 66	Checklist (1 - 66)	180.00	300.00
☐ 67	Charlie Hodge (G), Mtl.	9.00	15.00
☐ 68	Terry Harper, Mtl.	6.50	11.00
☐ 69	J.C. Tremblay, Mtl.	6.50	11.00
☐ 70	Bobby Rousseau, Mtl.	6.50	11.00
☐ 71	Henri Richard, Mtl.	25.00	40.00
☐ 72	Dave Balon, Mtl.	6.50	11.00
☐ 73	Ralph Backstrom, Mtl.	6.50	11.00
☐ **74**	**Jim Roberts, Mtl., RC**	**6.50**	**11.00**
☐ **75**	**Claude Larose, Mtl., RC**	**6.50**	**11.00**
☐ **76**	**Yvan Cournoyer, Mtl., RC, Error (Yvon)**	**80.00**	**130.00**
☐ 77	Johnny Bower (G), Tor.	15.00	25.00
☐ 78	Carl Brewer, Tor.	6.50	11.00
☐ 79	Tim Horton, Tor.	35.00	55.00
☐ 80	Marcel Pronovost, Tor.	9.00	15.00
☐ 81	Frank Mahovlich, Tor.	30.00	50.00
☐ **82**	**Ron Ellis, Tor., RC**	**20.00**	**30.00**
☐ 83	Larry Jeffrey, Tor.	6.50	11.00
☐ **84**	**Pete Stemkowski, Tor., RC**	**6.50**	**11.00**
☐ **85**	**Eddie Joyal, Tor., RC**	**6.50**	**11.00**
☐ **86**	**Mike Walton, Tor., RC**	**6.50**	**11.00**
☐ 87	Red Sullivan, NYR., LC	6.50	11.00
☐ 88	Don Simmons (G), NYR., LC	9.00	15.00
☐ 89	Jim Neilson, NYR.	6.50	11.00
☐ 90	Arnie Brown, NYR.	6.50	11.00
☐ 91	Rod Gilbert, NYR.	20.00	30.00
☐ 92	Phil Goyette, NYR.	6.50	11.00
☐ 93	Bob Nevin, NYR.	6.50	11.00
☐ 94	John McKenzie, NYR.	6.50	11.00
☐ **95**	**Ted Taylor, NYR., RC**	**6.50**	**11.00**
☐ 96	Milt Schmidt, Coach, Bos.	7.00	12.00
☐ 97	Ed Johnston (G), Bos.	9.00	15.00
☐ 98	Ted Green, Bos.	6.50	11.00
☐ **99**	**Don Awrey, Bos., RC**	**6.50**	**11.00**
☐ **100**	**Bob Woytowich, Bos., RC**	**6.50**	**11.00**
☐ 101	John Bucyk, Bos.	15.00	25.00
☐ 102	Dean Prentice, Bos.	6.50	11.00
☐ 103	Ron Stewart, Bos.	6.50	11.00
☐ 104	Reggie Fleming, Bos.	6.50	11.00
☐ 105	Parker MacDonald, Bos.	6.50	11.00
☐ 106	Hank Bassen (G), Det.	9.00	11.00
☐ 107	Gary Bergman, Det.	6.50	11.00
☐ 108	Gordie Howe, Det.	100.00	160.00
☐ 109	Floyd Smith, Det.	6.50	11.00
☐ 110	Bruce MacGregor, Det.	6.50	11.00
☐ 111	Ron Murphy, Det.	6.50	11.00
☐ 112	Don McKenney, Det., LC	6.50	11.00
☐ 113	Denis DeJordy (G), Chi.	6.00	11.00
☐ 114	Elmer Vasko, Chi.	6.50	11.00
☐ **115**	**Matt Ravlich, Chi., RC**	**6.50**	**11.00**
☐ **116**	**Phil Esposito, Chi., RC**	**210.00**	**350.00**
☐ 117	Chico Maki, Chi.	6.50	11.00
☐ 118	Doug Mohns, Chi.	6.50	11.00
☐ 119	Eric Nesterenko, Chi.	6.50	11.00
☐ 120	Pat Stapleton, Chi.	6.50	11.00
☐ 121	Checklist (67 - 128)	180.00	300.00
☐ 122	Gordie Howe, (600 Goals)	250.00	425.00
☐ 123	Toronto Maple Leafs	60.00	100.00
☐ 124	Chicago Blackhawks	55.00	90.00
☐ 125	Detroit Red Wings	55.00	90.00
☐ 126	Montréal Canadiens	60.00	100.00
☐ 127	New York Rangers	55.00	90.00
☐ 128	Boston Bruins	110.00	240.00

1966 - 67 CHAMPION

A set of 220 cards issued by the chewing gum factory Champion for the Finnish National League. We have no pricing information on this set.

Card Size: 2 1/8" x 3 1/8"

No.	Player
☐ 1	Jukka Haapala, Rauman Lukko
☐ 2	Simo Saimo, Rauman Lukko
☐ 3	Hannu Torma, Rauman Lukko
☐ 4	Jukka Savunen, Rauman Lukko
☐ 5	Tenho Lotila, Rauman Lukko
☐ 6	Tapani Koskimaki, Rauman Lukko
☐ 7	Matti Saurio, Rauman Lukko
☐ 8	Risto Kaitala, Rauman Lukko
☐ 9	Raimo Tiainen, Rauman Lukko
☐ 10	Esa Isaksson, Rauman Lukko
☐ 11	Pentti Rautalin, Rauman Lukko
☐ 12	Helkko Stenvall, Rauman Lukko
☐ 13	Teppo Rastio, Rauman Lukko
☐ 14	Jorma Vehmanen, Rauman Lukko
☐ 15	Raimo Kilpio, RU38 Pori
☐ 16	Veikko Ukkonen, RU38 Pori
☐ 17	Lauri Lehtonen, RU38 Pori
☐ 18	Heikki Veravainen, RU38 Pori
☐ 19	Pentti Riitahaara, RU38 Pori
☐ 20	Pekka Kuusisto, RU38 Pori
☐ 21	Tapio Rautalammi, RU38 Pori
☐ 22	Raimo Tuli, RU38 Pori
☐ 23	Matti Paivinen, RU38 Pori
☐ 24	Matti Harju, RU38 Pori
☐ 25	Kari Sillanpaa, RU38 Pori
☐ 26	Matti Keinonen, RU38 Pori
☐ 27	Pekka Lahti, RU38 Pori
☐ 28	Johannes Karttunen, RU38 Pori
☐ 29	Sakari Isomaki, RU38 Pori
☐ 30	Samu Leikko, RU38 Pori
☐ 31	Tapani Suominen, RU38 Pori
☐ 32	Esa Vesslin, Porin Karhut
☐ 33	Pekka Jalava, Porin Karhut
☐ 34	Pertti Makela, Porin Karhut
☐ 35	Juha Rantasila, Porin Karhut
☐ 36	Jukka Haanpaa, Porin Karhut
☐ 37	Teuvo Helenius, Porin Karhut
☐ 38	Anto Virtanen, Porin Karhut
☐ 39	Kimmo Nokikuru, Porin Karhut
☐ 40	Jaakko Honkanen, Porin Karhut
☐ 41	Seppo Nystrom, Porin Karhut
☐ 42	Tuomo Pirskainen, Porin Karhut
☐ 43	Matti Jansson, Porin Karhut
☐ 44	Alpo Suhonen, Porin Karhut
☐ 45	Matti Varpela, Porin Karhut
☐ 46	Kaj Matalamaki, Porin Karhut
☐ 47	Antti Heikkila, Porin Karhut
☐ 48	Jaakko Jaskari, Porin Karhut
☐ 49	Jouko Ojansuu, Porin Karhut
☐ 50	Mikko Myllyniemi, Porin Karhut
☐ 51	VeliPekka Ketola, Porin Karhut
☐ 52	Matti Salmi, Porin Karhut

☐ 53 Pentti Vihanto, Turun Taverit
☐ 54 Hannu Luojola, Turun Taverit
☐ 55 Seppo Parikka, Turun Taverit
☐ 56 Martti Salonen, Turun Taverit
☐ 57 Risto Forss, Turun Taverit
☐ 58 Hannu Niittoaho, Turun Taverit
☐ 59 Kari Johansson, Turun Taverit
☐ 60 Henry Leppa, Turun Taverit
☐ 61 Jarmo Rantanen, Turun Taverit
☐ 62 Kari Torkkel, Turun Taverit
☐ 63 Seppo Vikstrom, Turun Taverit
☐ 64 Veijo Saarinen, Turun Taverit
☐ 65 Pekka Lahtela, Turun Taverit
☐ 66 Risto Vainio, Turun Taverit
☐ 67 Reijo Paksal, Turun Taverit
☐ 68 Erkan Nasib, Turun Taverit
☐ 69 Matti Breilin, Turun Taverit
☐ 70 Voitto Soini, Turun Taverit
☐ 71 Urpo Ylonen, Turun Taverit
☐ 72 Rauno Heinonen, Turun Palloseura
☐ 73 Heikki Heino, Turun Palloseura
☐ 74 Lasse Kiili, Turun Palloseura
☐ 75 Ilkka Mesikammen, Turun Palloseura
☐ 76 Timo Nummelin, Turun Palloseura
☐ 77 Pertti Kuismanen, Turun Palloseura
☐ 78 Juhani Wahlsten, Turun Palloseura
☐ 79 Rauli Ottila, Turun Palloseura
☐ 80 Pertti Karelius, Turun Palloseura
☐ 81 Teuvo Andelmin, Turun Palloseura
☐ 82 Kari Varjanen, Turun Palloseura
☐ 83 Kalevi Leppanen, Turun Palloseura
☐ 84 Juhani IsoEskeli, Turun Palloseura
☐ 85 Hannu Koivunen, Turun Palloseura
☐ 86 Yrjo Hakala, Saimaan
☐ 87 Kari Ruontimo, Saimaan
☐ 88 Raimo Lohko, Saimaan
☐ 89 Markku Eiskonen, Saimaan
☐ 90 Hannu Lemander, Saimaan
☐ 91 Timo Vaatamoinen, Saimaan
☐ 92 Pekka Moisio, Saimaan
☐ 93 Martti Makia, Saimaan
☐ 94 Risto Heinvirta, Saimaan
☐ 95 Taisto Jahma, Saimaan
☐ 96 Veikko Makia, Saimaan
☐ 97 Raimo Helppolainen, Saimaan
☐ 98 Lalli Partinen, Saimaan
☐ 99 Keijo Sinkkonen, Saimaan
☐ 100 Antti Ravi, Saimaan
☐ 101 Martti Sinkkonen, Saimaan
☐ 102 Heikki Juselius, Saimaan
☐ 103 Timo Rantala, Lahden Reipas
☐ 104 Heikki Mikkola, Lahden Reipas
☐ 105 Jaakko Siren, Lahden Reipas
☐ 106 Matti Korhonen, Lahden Reipas
☐ 107 Erkki Mononen, Lahden Reipas
☐ 108 Pertti Valkonen, Lahden Reipas
☐ 109 Ilpo Koskela, Lahden Reipas
☐ 110 Bengt Wilenius, Lahden Reipas
☐ 111 Hannu Lindberg, Lahden Reipas
☐ 112 Kristen Bertell, Lahden Reipas
☐ 113 Veikko Kuusisto, Lahden Reipas
☐ 114 Tapio Majaniemi, Lahden Reipas
☐ 115 Leo Vankka, Lahden Reipas
☐ 116 Pentti Harju, Lahden Reipas
☐ 117 Ari Myllymaki, Lahden Reipas
☐ 118 Matti Koskinen, Lahden Reipas
☐ 119 Pentti Andersson, Lahden Reipas
☐ 120 Pertti Heikkinen, Lahden Reipas
☐ 121 Pekka Peltoniemi, Lahden Reipas
☐ 122 Jouko Jarvinen, Lahden Reipas
☐ 123 Matti Vartiainen, Lahden Reipas
☐ 124 Esko Reijonen, Sapko
☐ 125 Erkki Rasanen, Sapko
☐ 126 Timo Viskari, Sapko
☐ 127 Raimo Turkulainen, Sapko
☐ 128 Paavo Tirkkonen, Sapko
☐ 129 Orvo Paatero, Sapko
☐ 130 Juhani Leirivaara, Sapko
☐ 131 Jyrki Turunen, Sapko
☐ 132 Timo Tuomainen, Sapko
☐ 133 Pentti Karkkainen, Sapko
☐ 134 Jussi Piuhola, Sapko
☐ 135 Pentti Pihlapuro, Sapko
☐ 136 Pentti Pennanen, Sapko
☐ 137 Esa Viskari, Sapko
☐ 138 Timo Luostarinen, Sapko
☐ 139 Seppo Iivonen, Sapko
☐ 140 Risto Alho, Sapko
☐ 141 Esko Kiuru, Sapko
☐ 142 Jaakko Hovinheimo, Sapko
☐ 143 Jaakko Koikkalainen, Sapko
☐ 144 Juhani Sodervik, Sapko
☐ 145 Seppo Makinen, Tappara
☐ 146 Teuvo Peltola, Tappara
☐ 147 Antti Alenius, Tappara
☐ 148 Kalevi Numminen, Tappara
☐ 149 Esko Kaonpaa, Tappara
☐ 150 Lauri Salomaa, Tappara
☐ 151 Risto Pirttiaho, Tappara
☐ 152 Antti Leppanen, Tappara
☐ 153 Kari Makinen, Tappara
☐ 154 Jorma Oksala, Tappara
☐ 155 Pekka Marjamaki, Tappara
☐ 156 Jouni Seistamo, Tappara
☐ 157 Pertti Ansakorpi, Tappara
☐ 158 Erkki Jarkko, Tappara
☐ 159 Juhani Peltola, Tappara
☐ 160 Erkki Mannikko, Tappara
☐ 161 Keijo Mannisto, Tappara
☐ 162 Matti Peltonen, Tappara
☐ 163 Hannu Heikkonen, Tappara
☐ 164 Pentti Hyytiainen, Tappara
☐ 165 Antti Virtanen, Tappara
☐ 166 Seppo Nurmi, Tampereen
☐ 167 Matti Reunamaki, Tampereen
☐ 168 Mikko Raikkonen, Tampereen
☐ 169 Esko Rantanen, Tampereen
☐ 170 Eero Holopainen, Tampereen
☐ 171 Juhani Ruohonen, Tampereen
☐ 172 Veikko Savolainen, Tampereen
☐ 173 Heikki Sivonen, Tampereen
☐ 174 Markku Pulli, Tampereen
☐ 175 Pekka Uitus, Tampereen
☐ 176 Heikki Keinonen, Tampereen
☐ 177 Jorma Saarikorpi, Tampereen
☐ 178 Rauno Lehtio, Tampereen
☐ 179 Kalevi Toivonen, Tampereen
☐ 180 Jorma Vilen, Tampereen
☐ 181 Pentti Kuusinen, Tampereen
☐ 182 Olavi Haapalainen, Tampereen
☐ 183 Seppo Nikkila, Tampereen
☐ 184 Jorma Suokko, Tampereen
☐ 185 Heino Pulli, Tampereen
☐ 186 Risto Lehtio, Tampereen
☐ 187 Pekka Lehtolainen, Tampereen
☐ 188 Timo Hirsimaki, Ilves
☐ 189 Kari Palooja, Ilves
☐ 190 Pekka Leimu, Ilves
☐ 191 Ali Saadetin, Ilves
☐ 192 Erkki Jarvinen, Ilves
☐ 193 Markku Hakanen, Ilves
☐ 194 Jorma Kallio, Ilves
☐ 195 Vaino Kolkka, Ilves
☐ 196 Timo Saari, Ilves
☐ 197 Jorma Peltonen, Ilves
☐ 198 Pentti Pynnonen, Ilves
☐ 199 Pentti Uotila, Ilves
☐ 200 Timo Lahtinen, Ilves
☐ 201 Juhani Lahtinen, Ilves
☐ 202 Reijo Hakanen, Ilves
☐ 203 Lasse Oksanen, Ilves
☐ 204 Juhani Aromaki, Ilves
☐ 205 Jukka Alkula, Hermes Kokkola
☐ 206 Pekka Olkkonen, Hermes Kokkola
☐ 207 Tapani Salo, Hermes Kokkola
☐ 208 Vesa Kartsalo, Hermes Kokkola
☐ 209 Antti Komsi, Hermes Kokkola
☐ 210 Asko Sallamaa, Hermes Kokkola
☐ 211 Juhani Tarkiainen, Hermes Kokkola
☐ 212 Antero Hakala, Hermes Kokkola
☐ 213 Ulf Slotte, Hermes Kokkola
☐ 214 Raimo Savolainen, Hermes Kokkola
☐ 215 Matias Savolainen, Hermes Kokkola
☐ 216 Risto Savolainen, Hermes Kokkola
☐ 217 Keijo Makinen, Hermes Kokkola
☐ 218 Tapio Makinen, Hermes Kokkola
☐ 219 Ossi Peltoniemi, Hermes Kokkola
☐ 220 Matti Valikangas, Hermes Kokkola

1966 - 67 POST HOCKEY TIPS

LARGE SIZE

Issued on the backs of Post cereal boxes, these cards are unnumbered and have blank backs. Two different photos of each player were issued.

Card Size: 6" x 9 1/4"
Face: Four colour; Name, Facsimile signature, Hockey tip, Bilingual
Back: Blank
Imprint: None

Complete Set (18 cards):		150.00	250.00
No.	Player	EX	NRMT
☐ 1	AS: Glenn Hall (G), Chi.	15.00	25.00
☐ 2	AS: Tim Horton, Tor.	15.00	25.00
☐ 3	AS: Gordie Howe, Det.	25.00	40.00
☐ 4	AS: Harry Howell, NYR.	9.00	15.00
☐ 5	AS: Dave Keon, Tor.	12.00	20.00
☐ 6	AS: Frank Mahovlich, Tor.	15.00	25.00
☐ 7	AS: Stan Mikita, Chi.	13.00	22.00
☐ 8	AS: Bob Nevin, NYR	6.00	10.00
☐ 9	AS: Murray Oliver, Bos.	6.00	10.00
☐ 10	AS: Pierre Pilote, Chi.	9.00	15.00
☐ 11	AS: Bob Pulford, Tor.	11.00	18.00
☐ 12	AS: Norm Ullman, Det.	11.00	18.00
☐ 13	Jacques Laperrière, Mtl.	9.00	15.00
☐ 14	Henri Richard, Mtl.	12.00	20.00
☐ 15	Bobby Rousseau, Mtl.	6.00	10.00
☐ 16	Gilles Tremblay, Mtl.	6.00	10.00
☐ 17	J.C. Tremblay, Mtl.	7.00	12.00
☐ 18	Gump Worsley (G), Mtl.	13.00	22.00

SMALL SIZE

Card Size: 2 5/8" x 2 5/8"
Face: Four colour
Back: Blank
Imprint: None

Complete Set (9 cards):		60.00	100.00
No.	Player	EX	NRMT
☐ 1	AS: Glenn Hall (G), Chi.	11.00	18.00
☐ 2	AS: Gordie Howe, Det.	20.00	30.00
☐ 3	AS: Dave Keon, Tor.	8.00	13.00
☐ 4	AS: Frank Mahovlich, Tor.	11.00	18.00
☐ 5	AS: Bob Nevin, NYR.	5.00	7.50
☐ 6	AS: Bob Pulford, Tor.	7.00	12.00
☐ 7	Bobby Rousseau, Mtl.	5.00	7.50
☐ 8	J.C. Tremblay, Mtl.	5.00	7.50
☐ 9	Gump Worsley (G), Mtl.	9.00	15.00

1966 - 67 TOPPS

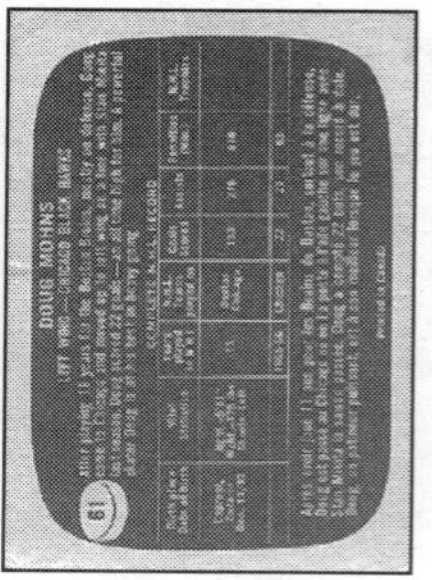

The unique format of this issue simulates a television screen with a wood grain border. The key card in this issue is Bobby Orr's rookie card. The card backs summarize the player's entire NHL record. The wood grain border printed to the card edge makes these cards difficult to obtain in mint.

Card Size: 2 1/2" x 3 1/2"
Face: Four colour, wood grain border, Position
Back: Black on card stock, Number, Resume, Bilingual
Imprint: Printed in Canada

Complete Set (132 cards):		**3,600.00**	**5,200.00**
Common Player:		**6.50**	**11.00**
No.	**Player**	**EX**	**NRMT**
☐ 1	Toe Blake, Coach, Mtl.	12.00	30.00
☐ 2	Gump Worsley (G), Mtl.	20.00	30.00
☐ 3	Jean-Guy Talbot, Mtl.	6.50	11.00
☐ 4	Gilles Tremblay, Mtl.	6.50	11.00
☐ 5	J.C. Tremblay, Mtl.	6.50	11.00
☐ 6	Jim Roberts, Mtl.	6.50	11.00
☐ 7	Bobby Rousseau, Mtl.	6.50	11.00
☐ 8	Henri Richard, Mtl.	20.00	30.00
☐ 9	Claude Provost, Mtl.	6.50	11.00
☐ 10	Claude Larose, Mtl.	6.50	11.00
☐ 11	Punch Imlach, Coach, Tor.	9.00	15.00
☐ 12	Johnny Bower (G), Tor.	15.00	25.00
☐ 13	Terry Sawchuk (G), Tor.	40.00	70.00
☐ 14	Mike Walton, Tor.	6.50	11.00
☐ 15	Pete Stemkowski, Tor.	6.50	11.00
☐ 16	Allan Stanley, Tor.	9.00	15.00
☐ 17	Eddie Shack, Tor.	22.00	35.00
☐ **18**	**Brit Selby, Tor., RC**	**6.50**	**11.00**
☐ 19	Bob Pulford, Tor.	9.00	15.00
☐ 20	Marcel Pronovost, Tor.	9.00	15.00
☐ 21	Emile Francis, Coach, NYR.	20.00	30.00
☐ 22	Rod Seiling, NYR.	6.50	11.00
☐ 23	Ed Giacomin (G), NYR.	35.00	60.00
☐ 24	Don Marshall, NYR.	6.50	11.00
☐ 25	Orland Kurtenbach, NYR.	6.50	11.00
☐ 26	Rod Gilbert, NYR.	18.00	28.00
☐ 27	Bob Nevin, NYR.	6.50	11.00
☐ 28	Phil Goyette, NYR.	6.50	11.00
☐ 29	Jean Ratelle, NYR.	18.00	28.00
☐ 30	Earl Ingarfield, NYR.	6.50	11.00
☐ 31	Harry Sinden, Coach, Bos.	30.00	45.00
☐ 32	Ed Westfall, Bos.	6.50	11.00
☐ **33**	**Joe Watson, Bos., RC**	**6.50**	**11.00**
☐ 34	Bob Woytowich, Bos.	6.50	11.00
☐ **35**	**Bobby Orr, Bos., RC**	**1,700.00**	**2,700.00**
☐ **36**	**Gilles Marotte, Bos., RC**	**6.50**	**11.00**
☐ 37	Ted Green, Bos.	6.50	11.00
☐ 38	Tom Williams, Bos.	6.50	11.00
☐ 39	John Bucyk, Bos.	13.00	22.00
☐ 40	Wayne Connelly, Bos.	6.50	11.00
☐ 41	Pit Martin, Bos.	6.50	11.00
☐ 42	Sid Abel, Coach, Det.	9.00	15.00
☐ 43	Roger Crozier (G), Det.	12.00	20.00
☐ 44	Andy Bathgate, Det.	9.00	15.00
☐ 45	Dean Prentice, Det.	6.50	11.00
☐ 46	Paul Henderson, Det.	12.00	20.00
☐ 47	Gary Bergman, Det.	6.50	11.00
☐ 48	Bryan Watson, Det.	6.50	11.00
☐ **49**	**Bob Wall, Det., RC**	**6.50**	**11.00**
☐ 50	Leo Boivin, Det.	9.00	15.00
☐ **51**	**Bert Marshall, Det., RC**	**6.50**	**11.00**
☐ 52	Norm Ullman, Det.	12.00	20.00
☐ 53	Billy Reay, Coach, Chi.	6.50	11.00
☐ 54	Glenn Hall (G), Chi.	22.00	35.00
☐ **55**	**Wally Boyer, Chi., RC**	**6.50**	**11.00**
☐ 56	Fred Stanfield, Chi.	6.50	11.00
☐ 57	Pat Stapleton, Chi.	6.50	11.00
☐ 58	Matt Ravlich, Chi.	6.50	11.00
☐ 59	Pierre Pilote, Chi.	9.00	15.00
☐ 60	Eric Nesterenko, Chi.	6.50	11.00
☐ 61	Doug Mohns, Chi.	6.50	11.00
☐ 62	Stan Mikita, Chi.	40.00	70.00
☐ 63	Phil Esposito, Chi.	85.00	140.00
☐ 64	Bobby Hull, Scoring Leader	55.00	90.00
☐ 65	AW: Hodge & Worsley	22.00	35.00
☐ 66	Checklist 1 (1 - 66)	180.00	300.00
☐ 67	Jacques Laperrière, Mtl.	12.00	20.00
☐ 68	Terry Harper, Mtl.	6.50	11.00
☐ 69	Ted Harris, Mtl.	6.50	11.00
☐ 70	John Ferguson, Mtl.	6.50	11.00
☐ 71	Dick Duff, Mtl.	6.50	11.00
☐ 72	Yvan Cournoyer, Mtl.	35.00	60.00
☐ 73	Jean Béliveau, Mtl.	35.00	60.00
☐ 74	Dave Balon, Mtl.	6.50	11.00
☐ 75	Ralph Backstrom, Mtl.	6.50	11.00
☐ 76	Jim Pappin, Tor.	6.50	11.00
☐ 77	Frank Mahovlich, Tor.	25.00	40.00
☐ 78	Dave Keon, Tor.	22.00	35.00
☐ 79	Red Kelly, Tor., LC	12.00	20.00
☐ 80	Tim Horton, Tor.	25.00	40.00
☐ 81	Ron Ellis, Tor.	6.50	11.00
☐ 82	Kent Douglas, Tor.	6.50	11.00
☐ 83	Bob Baun, Tor.	6.50	11.00
☐ 84	George Armstrong, Tor.	9.00	15.00
☐ 85	Bernie Geoffrion, NYR.	22.00	35.00
☐ 86	Vic Hadfield, NYR.	6.50	11.00
☐ 87	Wayne Hillman, NYR.	6.50	11.00
☐ 88	Jim Neilson, NYR.	6.50	11.00
☐ 89	Al MacNeil, NYR., LC	6.50	11.00
☐ 90	Arnie Brown, NYR.	6.50	11.00
☐ 91	Harry Howell, NYR.	9.00	15.00
☐ 92	Red Berenson, NYR.	6.50	11.00
☐ 93	Reggie Fleming, NYR.	6.50	11.00
☐ 94	Ron Stewart, Bos.	6.50	11.00
☐ 95	Murray Oliver, Bos.	6.50	11.00
☐ 96	Ron Murphy, Bos.	6.50	11.00
☐ 97	John McKenzie, Bos.	6.50	11.00
☐ 98	Bob Dillabough, Bos.	6.50	11.00
☐ 99	Ed Johnston (G), Bos.	9.00	15.00
☐ 100	Ron Schock, Bos.	6.50	11.00
☐ 101	Dallas Smith, Bos.	6.50	11.00
☐ 102	Alex Delvecchio, Det.	12.00	20.00
☐ **103**	**Pete Mahovlich, Det., RC**	**25.00**	**40.00**
☐ 104	Bruce MacGregor, Det.	6.50	11.00
☐ 105	Murray Hall, Det.	6.50	11.00
☐ 106	Floyd Smith, Det.	6.50	11.00
☐ 107	Hank Bassen (G), Det., LC	9.00	15.00
☐ 108	Val Fonteyne, Det.	6.50	11.00
☐ 109	Gordie Howe, Det.	150.00	235.00
☐ 110	Chico Maki, Chi.	6.50	11.00
☐ **111**	**Doug Jarrett, Chi., RC**	**6.50**	**11.00**
☐ 112	Bobby Hull, Chi.	100.00	170.00
☐ 113	Dennis Hull, Chi.	9.00	15.00
☐ 114	Ken Hodge, Chi.	6.50	11.00
☐ 115	Denis DeJordy (G), Chi.	9.00	15.00
☐ 116	Lou Angotti, Chi.	6.50	11.00
☐ 117	Kenny Wharram, Chi.	6.50	11.00
☐ 118	Montréal Canadiens	20.00	30.00
☐ 119	Detroit Red Wings	20.00	30.00
☐ 120	Checklist 2 (67 - 132)	180.00	300.00
☐ 121	AS: Gordie Howe, Det.	75.00	125.00
☐ 122	AS: Jacques Laperrière, Mtl.	7.00	12.00
☐ 123	AS: Pierre Pilote, Chi.	7.00	12.00
☐ 124	AS: Stan Mikita, Chi.	22.00	35.00
☐ 125	AS: Bobby Hull, Chi. (/b: G. Howe)	55.00	90.00
☐ 126	AS: Glenn Hall (G), Chi.	12.00	20.00
☐ 127	AS: Jean Béliveau, Mtl.	20.00	30.00
☐ 128	AS: Allan Stanley, Tor.	9.00	15.00
☐ 129	AS: Pat Stapleton, Chi.	6.50	11.00
☐ 130	AS: Gump Worsley (G), Mtl. (/b: B. Orr)	10.00	18.00
☐ 131	AS: Frank Mahovlich, Mtl.	9.00	18.00
☐ 132	AS: Bobby Rousseau, Mtl.	12.00	30.00

1966 - 67 TOPPS USA TEST SET

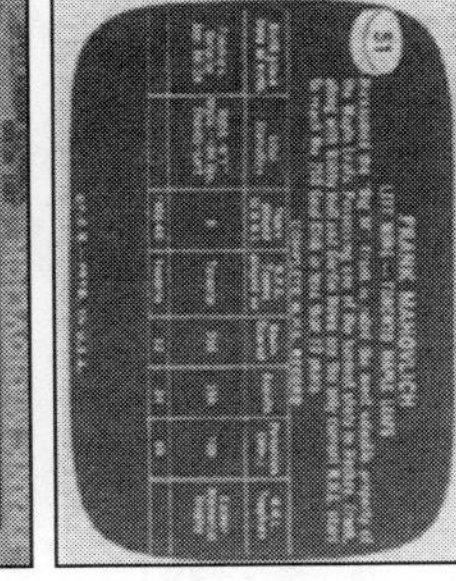

Thought to be a market test, this issue is very rare because of its limited distribution. The card format is very similar to that of the regular 1966-67 Topps series, except the card backs are printed in English only. The wood grain border, which simulates a television screen, is a lighter shade than the regular issue. The prices below are indications only since so few cards trade hands. Three uncut sheets of this issue are known to exist.

Card Size: 2 1/2" x 3 1/2"
Face: Four colour, wood grain border, Position
Back: Black on card stock, Number, Resume
Imprint: T.C.G.

Complete Set (66 cards):		**6,750.00**	**13,500.00**
Common Player:		**30.00**	**50.00**
No.	**Player**	**EX**	**NRMT**
☐ 1	Dennis Hull, Chi.	40.00	100.00
☐ 2	Gump Worsley (G), Mtl.	90.00	150.00
☐ 3	Dallas Smith, Bos.	30.00	50.00
☐ 4	Gilles Tremblay, Mtl.	30.00	50.00
☐ 5	J.C. Tremblay, Mtl.	30.00	50.00
☐ 6	Ralph Backstrom, Mtl.	30.00	50.00
☐ 7	Bobby Rousseau, Mtl.	30.00	50.00
☐ 8	Henri Richard, Mtl.	40.00	150.00
☐ 9	Claude Provost, Mtl.	30.00	50.00
☐ 10	Red Berenson, NYR.	30.00	50.00
☐ 11	Punch Imlach, Coach, Tor.	45.00	75.00
☐ 12	Johnny Bower (G), Tor.	75.00	125.00
☐ 13	Yvan Cournoyer, Mtl.	180.00	300.00
☐ 14	Mike Walton. Tor.	30.00	50.00
☐ 15	Pete Stemkowski, Tor.	30.00	50.00
☐ 16	Allan Stanley, Tor.	45.00	75.00
☐ 17	George Armstrong, Tor.	45.00	75.00
☐ 18	Harry Howell, NYR.	45.00	75.00
☐ 19	Vic Hadfield, NYR.	30.00	50.00
☐ 20	Marcel Pronovost, Tor.	45.00	75.00
☐ 21	Pete Mahovlich, Det.	125.00	200.00
☐ 22	Rod Seiling, NYR.	30.00	50.00
☐ 23	Gordie Howe, Det.	650.00	1,100.00
☐ 24	Don Marshall, NYR.	30.00	50.00
☐ 25	Orland Kurtenbach, NYR.	30.00	50.00
☐ 26	Rod Gilbert, NYR	85.00	140.00
☐ 27	Bob Nevin, NYR.	30.00	50.00
☐ 28	Phil Goyette, NYR.	30.00	50.00
☐ 29	Jean Ratelle, NYR.	85.00	140.00
☐ 30	Dave Keon, Tor.	110.00	175.00
☐ 31	Jean Béliveau, Mtl.	185.00	300.00
☐ 32	Ed Westfall, Bos.	30.00	50.00
☐ 33	Ron Murphy, Bos.	30.00	50.00
☐ 34	Wayne Hillman, NYR.	30.00	50.00
☐ 35	Bobby Orr, Bos.	7,000.00	12,000.00
☐ 36	Bernie Geoffrion, NYR.	110.00	175.00
☐ 37	Ted Green, Bos.	30.00	50.00
☐ 38	Tom Williams, Bos.	30.00	50.00
☐ 39	John Bucyk, Bos.	65.00	110.00
☐ 40	Bobby Hull, Bos.	500.00	850.00
☐ 41	Ted Harris, Mtl.	30.00	50.00
☐ 42	Red Kelly, Tor., LC	60.00	100.00
☐ 43	Roger Crozier (G), Det.	60.00	100.00
☐ 44	Kenny Wharram, Chi.	30.00	50.00
☐ 45	Dean Prentice, Det.	30.00	50.00
☐ 46	Paul Henderson, Det.	60.00	100.00
☐ 47	Gary Bergman, Det.	30.00	50.00
☐ 48	Arnie Brown, NYR.	30.00	50.00
☐ 49	Jim Pappin, Tor.	30.00	50.00
☐ 50	Denis DeJordy (G), Chi.	45.00	75.00
☐ 51	Frank Mahovlich, Mtl.	125.00	200.00
☐ 52	Norm Ullman, Det.	60.00	100.00
☐ 53	Chico Maki, Chi.	30.00	50.00
☐ 54	Reggie Fleming, NYR.	30.00	50.00
☐ 55	Jim Neilson, NYR.	30.00	50.00
☐ 56	Bruce MacGregor, Det.	30.00	50.00
☐ 57	Pat Stapleton, Chi.	30.00	50.00
☐ 58	Matt Ravlich, Chi.	30.00	50.00
☐ 59	Pierre Pilote, Chi.	45.00	75.00
☐ 60	Eric Nesterenko, Chi.	30.00	50.00
☐ 61	Doug Mohns, Chi.	30.00	50.00
☐ 62	Stan Mikita, Chi.	225.00	350.00
☐ 63	Alex Delvecchio, Det.	60.00	100.00
☐ 64	Ed Johnston (G), Bos.	45.00	75.00
☐ 65	John Ferguson, Sr., Mtl.	30.00	75.00
☐ 66	John McKenzie, Bos.	40.00	100.00

1967 - 68 POST

Issued on the backs of Post cereal boxes, these cards are unnumbered and have blank backs. Two different photos of each player were issued.

Card Size: 6 1/8" x 7 1/8"
Face: Four colour, Borderless; Facsimile autograph
Back: Blank
Imprint: None

	Complete Set (12 cards):	**150.00**	**250.00**
	Player	**EX**	**NRMT**
☐	Gordie Howe, Det. with net	25.00	40.00
☐	Gordie Howe, Det. without net	25.00	40.00
☐	Harry Howell, NYR, Passing	9.00	15.00
☐	Harry Howell, NYR Blocking Shot	9.00	15.00
☐	Jacques Laperrière, Mtl. with net	9.00	15.00
☐	Jacques Laperrière, Mtl. without net	9.00	15.00
☐	Stan Mikita, Chi.	13.00	22.00
☐	Stan Mikita, Chi.	13.00	22.00
☐	Bobby Orr, Bos., Still	30.00	50.00
☐	Bobby Orr, Bos., Action	30.00	50.00
☐	Henri Richard, Mtl., Puck in skates	12.00	20.00
☐	Henri Richard, Mtl.	12.00	20.00

1967 - 68 POST CEREAL FLIP BOOKS

Each "Hockey Tips" book shows one Maple Leafs' player and one Canadiens' player.

Book Size: 1 1/4" x 2 3/4"
Imprint:

	Complete Set (12):		**150.00**	**250.00**
	No.	**Player**	**EX**	**NRMT**
☐	1	Johnny Bower (G)/ Gump Worsley (G)	18.00	30.00
☐	2	Johnny Bower (G)/ Rogatien Vachon	18.00	30.00
☐	3	Tim Horton/ Gilles Tremblay, Err. (J.C.)	15.00	25.00
☐	4	Marcel Pronovost/ Jacques Laperriére	12.00	20.00
☐	5	Frank Mahovlich/ Henri Richard	25.00	40.00
☐	6	Dave Keon/ Dick Duff	18.00	38.00
☐	7	Jim Pappin/ Jean Béliveau	25.00	40.00
☐	8	Ron Ellis/ Jean Béliveau	25.00	40.00
☐	9	George Armstrong/ Gilles Tremblay	12.00	20.00
☐	10	Pete Stemkowski/ J.C. Tremblay	9.00	15.00
☐	11	Bob Pulford/ Ralph Backstrom	12.00	20.00
☐	12	Larry Hillman/ Bobby Rousseau	9.00	15.00

1967 - 68 TOPPS

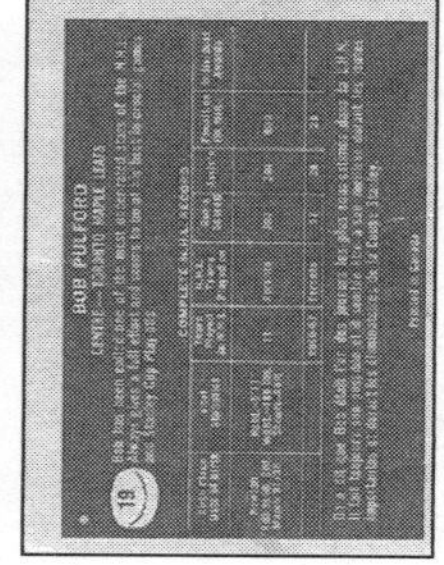

Card Size: 2 1/2" x 3 1/2"
Face: Four colour, white border, Position
Back: Black on card stock, Number, Resume, Bilingual
Imprint: Printed in Canada

	Complete Set (132 cards):	**2,200.00**	**3,400.00**
	Common Player:	**6.00**	**10.00**
No.	**Player**	**EX**	**NRMT**
☐ 1	Gump Worsley (G), Mtl.	25.00	55.00
☐ 2	Dick Duff, Mtl.	6.00	10.00
☐ **3**	**Jacques Lemaire, Mtl., RC**	**50.00**	**80.00**
☐ 4	Claude Larose, Mtl.	6.00	10.00
☐ 5	Gilles Tremblay, Mtl.	6.00	10.00
☐ 6	Terry Harper, Mtl.	6.00	10.00
☐ 7	Jacques Laperrière, Mtl.	9.00	15.00
☐ **8**	**Garry Monahan, Mtl., RC**	**6.00**	**10.00**
☐ **9**	**Carol Vadnais, Mtl., RC**	**7.50**	**13.00**
☐ 10	Ted Harris, Mtl.	6.00	10.00
☐ 11	Dave Keon, Tor.	12.00	20.00
☐ 12	Pete Stemkowski, Tor.	6.00	10.00
☐ 13	Allan Stanley, Tor.	7.50	10.00
☐ 14	Ron Ellis, Tor.	6.00	10.00
☐ 15	Mike Walton, Tor.	6.00	10.00
☐ 16	Tim Horton, Tor.	25.00	40.00
☐ **17**	**Brian Conacher, Tor., RC**	**6.00**	**10.00**
☐ 18	Bruce Gamble (G), Tor.	7.50	13.00
☐ 19	Bob Pulford, Tor.	7.50	13.00
☐ **20**	**Duane Rupp, Tor., RC**	**6.00**	**10.00**
☐ 21	Larry Jeffrey, NYR.	6.00	10.00
☐ 22	Wayne Hillman, NYR.	6.00	10.00
☐ 23	Don Marshall, NYR.	6.00	10.00
☐ 24	Red Berenson, NYR.	6.00	10.00
☐ 25	Phil Goyette, NYR.	6.00	10.00
☐ 26	Camille Henry, NYR.	6.00	10.00
☐ 27	Rod Seiling, NYR.	6.00	10.00
☐ 28	Bob Nevin, NYR.	6.00	10.00
☐ 29	Bernie Geoffrion, NYR., LC	18.00	28.00
☐ 30	Reggie Fleming, NYR.	6.00	10.00
☐ 31	Jean Ratelle, NYR.	13.00	22.00
☐ 32	Phil Esposito, Bos.	55.00	95.00
☐ **33**	**Derek Sanderson, Bos., RC**	**60.00**	**100.00**
☐ 34	Eddie Shack, Bos.	15.00	25.00
☐ **35**	**Ross Lonsberry, Bos., RC**	**6.00**	**10.00**
☐ 36	Fred Stanfield, Bos.	6.00	10.00
☐ 37	Don Awrey, Bos., Error (Skip Krake)	6.00	10.00
☐ **38**	**Glen Sather, Bos., RC**	**25.00**	**40.00**
☐ 39	John McKenzie, Bos.	6.00	10.00
☐ 40	Tom Williams, Bos.	6.00	10.00
☐ 41	Dallas Smith, Bos.	6.00	10.00
☐ 42	John Bucyk, Bos.	12.00	20.00
☐ 43	Gordie Howe, Det.	110.00	175.00
☐ **44**	**Gary Jarrett, Det., RC**	**6.00**	**10.00**
☐ 45	Bert Marshall, Det.	6.00	10.00
☐ 46	Dean Prentice, Det.	6.00	10.00
☐ 47	Gary Bergman, Det.	6.00	10.00
☐ 48	Roger Crozier (G), Det.	7.50	13.00
☐ 49	Howie Young, Det.	6.00	10.00
☐ **50**	**Doug Roberts, Det., RC**	**6.00**	**10.00**
☐ 51	Alex Delvecchio, Det.	11.00	18.00
☐ 52	Floyd Smith, Det.	6.00	10.00
☐ **53**	**Doug Shelton, Chi., RC, LC**	**6.00**	**10.00**
☐ **54**	**Gerry Goyer, Chi., RC, LC**	**6.00**	**10.00**
☐ **55**	**Wayne Maki, Chi., RC**	**6.00**	**10.00**
☐ 56	Dennis Hull, Chi.	6.00	10.00
☐ **57**	**Dave Dryden (G), Chi., RC**	**12.00**	**20.00**
☐ **58**	**Paul Terbenche, Chi., RC**	**5.00**	**10.00**
☐ 59	Gilles Marotte, Chi.	6.00	10.00
☐ 60	Eric Nesterenko, Chi.	6.00	10.00
☐ 61	Pat Stapleton, Chi.	6.00	10.00
☐ 62	Pierre Pilote, Chi.	7.50	13.00
☐ 63	Doug Mohns, Chi.	6.00	10.00
☐ 64	AW: Stan Mikita, Chi.	20.00	30.00
☐ 65	AW: Hall & DeJordy, Chi.	15.00	25.00
☐ 66	Checklist 1 (1 - 66)	175.00	275.00
☐ 67	Ralph Backstrom, Mtl.	6.00	10.00
☐ 68	Bobby Rousseau, Mtl.	6.00	10.00
☐ 69	John Ferguson, Mtl.	6.00	10.00
☐ 70	Yvan Cournoyer, Mtl.	22.00	35.00
☐ 71	Claude Provost, Mtl.	6.00	10.00
☐ 72	Henri Richard, Mtl.	15.00	25.00
☐ 73	J.C. Tremblay, Mtl.	6.00	10.00
☐ 74	Jean Béliveau, Mtl.	25.00	45.00
☐ **75**	**Rogatien Vachon (G), Mtl., RC**	**55.00**	**95.00**
☐ 76	Johnny Bower (G), Tor.	13.00	22.00
☐ **77**	**Wayne Carleton, Tor., RC**	**6.00**	**10.00**
☐ 78	Jim Pappin, Tor.	6.00	10.00
☐ 79	Frank Mahovlich, Tor.	25.00	35.00
☐ 80	Larry Hillman, Tor.	6.00	10.00
☐ 81	Marcel Pronovost, Tor.	7.50	13.00
☐ 82	Murray Oliver, Tor.	6.00	10.00
☐ 83	George Armstrong, Tor.	7.50	13.00
☐ 84	Harry Howell, NYR.	7.50	13.00
☐ 85	Ed Giacomin (G), NYR.	25.00	45.00
☐ 86	Gilles Villemure (G), NYR.	7.50	13.00
☐ 87	Orland Kurtenbach, NYR.	6.00	10.00
☐ 88	Vic Hadfield, NYR.	6.00	10.00
☐ 89	Arnie Brown, NYR.	6.00	10.00
☐ 90	Rod Gilbert, NYR.	13.00	22.00
☐ 91	Jim Neilson, NYR.	6.00	10.00
☐ 92	Bobby Orr, Bos.	435.00	725.00
☐ 93	Skip Krake, Bos., Error (Don Awrey)	6.00	10.00
☐ 94	Ted Green, Bos.	6.00	10.00
☐ 95	Ed Westfall, Bos.	6.00	10.00
☐ 96	Ed Johnston (G), Bos.	7.50	13.00
☐ **97**	**Gary Doak, Bos., RC**	**6.00**	**10.00**
☐ 98	Ken Hodge, Bos.	6.00	10.00
☐ 99	Gerry Cheevers (G), Bos.	35.00	55.00
☐ 100	Ron Murphy, Bos.	6.00	10.00
☐ 101	Norm Ullman, Det.	11.00	18.00
☐ 102	Bruce MacGregor, Det.	6.00	10.00
☐ 103	Paul Henderson, Det.	7.50	13.00
☐ 104	Jean Guy Talbot, Det.	6.00	10.00
☐ **105**	**Bart Crashley, Det., RC**	**6.00**	**10.00**
☐ **106**	**Roy Edwards (G), Det., RC**	**7.50**	**13.00**
☐ **107**	**Jim Watson, Det., RC**	**6.00**	**10.00**
☐ 108	Ted Hampson, Det.	6.00	10.00
☐ **109**	**Bill Orban, Chi., RC, LC**	**6.00**	**10.00**
☐ **110**	**Jeff Powis, Chi., RC, LC**	**6.00**	**10.00**
☐ 111	Chico Maki, Chi.	6.00	10.00
☐ 112	Doug Jarrett, Chi.	6.00	10.00
☐ 113	Bobby Hull, Chi.	80.00	130.00
☐ 114	Stan Mikita, Chi.	35.00	60.00
☐ 115	Denis DeJordy (G), Chi.	7.50	13.00
☐ 116	Pit Martin, Chi.	6.00	10.00
☐ 117	Kenny Wharram, Chi.	6.00	10.00
☐ 118	AW: Bobby Orr, Bos.	210.00	325.00
☐ 119	AW: Harry Howell, NYR.	7.00	12.00
☐ 120	Checklist 2 (67 - 132)	210.00	325.00
☐ 121	AS: Harry Howell, NYR.	7.00	12.00
☐ 122	AS: Pierre Pilote, Chi.	7.00	12.00
☐ 123	AS: Ed Giacomin (G), NYR.	15.00	25.00
☐ 124	AS: Bobby Hull, Chi.	50.00	80.00
☐ 125	AS: Kenny Wharram, Chi.	6.00	10.00
☐ 126	AS: Stan Mikita, Chi.	20.00	30.00
☐ 127	AS: Tim Horton, Tor.	12.00	20.00
☐ 128	AS: Bobby Orr, Bos.	210.00	325.00
☐ 129	AS: Glenn Hall (G), Chi.	15.00	25.00
☐ 130	AS: Don Marshall, NYR.	6.00	10.00
☐ 131	AS: Gordie Howe, Det.	70.00	115.00
☐ 132	AS: Norm Ullman, Det.	10.00	25.00

1967 - 68 YORK ACTION PHOTOS

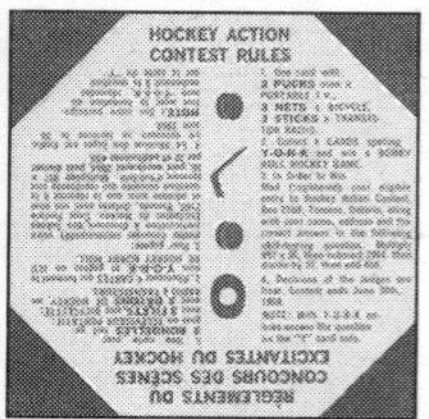

This set was issued in York Peanut Butter. Each card displays two or three players in action. The first twelve cards are unnumbered.

Card Size: 2 7/8" x 2 7/8"
Face: Four colour, white border; Number (13-36) or unnumbered, Name, Jersey Number
Back: Black on white card stock; Contest rules
Imprint: Weekend Magazine Photo

	Complete Set (36 cards):	**350.00**	**550.00**
	Common Player:	**7.50**	**13.00**
	Player	**EX**	**NRMT**
☐	B. Conacher/A. Stanley/L. Rochefort	9.00	15.00
☐	T. Harper/G. Worsley (G)/M. Walton	11.00	18.00
☐	T. Horton/G. Armstrong/J. Béliveau	22.00	35.00
☐	D. Keon/G. Armstrong/C. Provost	13.00	22.00
☐	J. Laperrière/R. Vachon (G)/B. Pulford	13.00	22.00
☐	B. Pulford/B. Conacher/C. Provost	11.00	18.00
☐	B. Pulford/J. Pappin/T. Harper	9.00	15.00
☐	P. Stemkowski/J. Pappin/T. Harris	7.50	13.00

	No.	Player	EX	NRMT
☐		J.C. Tremblay/R. Vachon (G)/P. Stemkowski	9.00	15.00
☐		R. Vachon (G)/R. Backstrom/B. Pulford	11.00	18.00
☐		R. Vachon (G)/J. Laperrière/M. Walton	11.00	18.00
☐		M. Walton/P. Stemkowski/J.C. Tremblay	7.50	13.00
☐	13	D. Keon/M. Walton/J.C. Tremblay	11.00	18.00
☐	14	P. Stemkowski/R. Backstrom	7.50	13.00
☐	15	R. Vachon (G)/B. Pulford	11.00	18.00
☐	16	J. Bower (G)/R. Ellis/J. Ferguson, Sr.	11.00	18.00
☐	17	R. Ellis/G. Worsley (G)	11.00	18.00
☐	18	G. Worsley (G)/J. Laperrière/F. Mahovlich	22.00	35.00
☐	19	J.C. Tremblay/D. Keon	11.00	18.00
☐	20	C. Provost/F. Mahovlich	13.00	22.00
☐	21	J. Ferguson, Sr./T. Horton	13.00	22.00
☐	22	G. Worsley (G)/R. Ellis	11.00	18.00
☐	23	J. Bower (G)/M. Walton/J. Béliveau	18.00	28.00
☐	24	J.C. Tremblay/G. Worsley (G)/B. Pulford	15.00	25.00
☐	25	T. Horton/J. Bower (G)/J. Béliveau	25.00	40.00
☐	26	A. Stanley/J. Bower (G)/D. Duff	15.00	25.00
☐	27	R. Backstrom/J. Bower	11.00	18.00
☐	28	Y. Cournoyer/J. Béliveau/F. Mahovlich	30.00	50.00
☐	29	J. Bower (G)/L. Hillman/Y. Cournoyer	15.00	25.00
☐	30	J. Bower/Y. Cournoyer	15.00	25.00
☐	31	T. Horton/R. Vachon (G)	15.00	25.00
☐	32	J. Pappin/B. Pulford/R. Vachon	11.00	18.00
☐	33	T. Harper/B. . Rousseau/M. Pronovost	9.00	15.00
☐	34	J. Bower (G)/M. Pronovost/R. Backstrom	12.00	20.00
☐	35	F. Mahovlich/G. Worsley (G)	18.00	28.00
☐	36	C. Provost/J. Bower (G)	12.00	20.00

1968 - 69 BAUER SKATES

Photograph Size: 8" x 10"
Face: Four colour, white border
Back: Blank
Imprint: None

	No.	Player	EX	NRMT
		Complete Set (22 photos):	**225.00**	**450.00**
☐	1	Andy Bathgate, Pgh.	15.00	30.00
☐	2	Gary Bergman, Det.	10.00	20.00
☐	3	Charlie Burns, Pgh.	10.00	20.00
☐	4	Ray Cullen, Min.	10.00	20.00
☐	5	Gary Dornhoefer, Pha.	10.00	20.00
☐	6	Kent Douglas, Tor.	10.00	20.00
☐	7	Tim Ecclestone, Stl.	10.00	20.00
☐	8	Bill Flett, L.A.	10.00	20.00
☐	9	Ed Giacomin (G), NYR.	25.00	50.00
☐	10	Ted Harris, Mtl.	10.00	20.00
☐	11	Paul Henderson, Tor.	15.00	30.00
☐	12	Ken Hodge, Bos.	10.00	20.00
☐	13	Harry Howell, NYR	15.00	30.00
☐	14	Earl Ingarfield, Pgh.	10.00	20.00
☐	15	Gilles Marotte, Chi.	10.00	20.00
☐	16	Mike McMahon, Min.	10.00	20.00
☐	17	Doug Mohns, Chi.	10.00	20.00
☐	18	Bobby Orr, Bos.	65.00	125.00
☐	19	Claude Provost, Mtl.	10.00	20.00
☐	20	Gary Sabourin, Stl.	10.00	20.00
☐	21	Brian Smith, Det.	10.00	20.00
☐	22	Bob Woytowich, Min.	10.00	20.00

1968 - 69 O-PEE-CHEE

Centering was a problem with this set. Well centered cards command a price premium over the normal issue either in NRMT or mint. Card number 193 is found numbered or unnumbered.

Face: Four colour, white border, Team logo, Position
Back: Black and red on grey card stock, Resume, Number, Cartoon, Bilingual
Imprint: T.C.G.

	No.	Player	EX	NRMT
		Complete Set (216 cards):	**1,250.00**	**2,500.00**
		Common Player:	**3.00**	**6.00**
☐	1	Doug Harvey, Stl., LC	18.00	50.00
☐	2	Bobby Orr, Bos.	200.00	400.00
☐	3	Don Awrey, Bos., Error (Skip Krake)	3.00	6.00
☐	4	Ted Green, Bos.	3.00	6.00
☐	5	John Bucyk, Bos.	6.50	13.00
☐	6	Derek Sanderson, Bos.	20.00	40.00
☐	7	Phil Esposito, Bos.	28.00	55.00
☐	8	Ken Hodge, Bos.	3.00	6.00
☐	9	John McKenzie, Bos.	3.00	6.00
☐	10	Fred Stanfield, Bos.	3.00	6.00
☐	11	Tom Williams, Bos.	3.00	6.00
☐	12	Denis DeJordy (G), Chi.	4.00	7.50
☐	13	Doug Jarrett, Chi.	3.00	6.00
☐	14	Gilles Marotte, Chi.	3.00	6.00
☐	15	Pat Stapleton, Chi.	3.00	6.00
☐	16	Bobby Hull, Chi.	55.00	110.00
☐	17	Chico Maki, Chi.	3.00	6.00
☐	18	Pit Martin, Chi.	3.00	6.00
☐	19	Doug Mohns, Chi.	3.00	6.00
☐	20	John Ferguson, Mtl.	4.00	7.50
☐	21	Jim Pappin, Chi.	3.00	6.00
☐	22	Kenny Wharram, Chi.	3.00	6.00
☐	23	Roger Crozier (G), Det.	4.00	7.50
☐	24	Bob Baun, Det.	3.00	6.00
☐	25	Gary Bergman, Det.	3.00	6.00
☐	26	Kent Douglas, Det., LC	3.00	6.00
☐	**27**	**Ron Harris, Det., RC**	**3.00**	**6.00**
☐	28	Alex Delvecchio, Det.	6.50	13.00
☐	29	Gordie Howe, Det.	70.00	135.00
☐	30	Bruce MacGregor, Det.	3.00	6.00
☐	31	Frank Mahovlich, Det.	10.00	20.00
☐	32	Dean Prentice, Det.	3.00	6.00
☐	33	Pete Stemkowski, Det.	3.00	6.00
☐	34	Terry Sawchuk (G), Det.	25.00	50.00
☐	35	Larry Cahan, L.A.	3.00	6.00
☐	**36**	**Real Lemieux, L.A., RC**	**3.00**	**6.00**
☐	**37**	**Bill White, L.A., RC**	**4.00**	**7.50**
☐	**38**	**Gord Labossiere, L.A., RC**	**3.00**	**6.00**
☐	**39**	**Ted Irvine, L.A., RC**	**3.00**	**6.00**
☐	40	Eddie Joyal, L.A.	3.00	6.00
☐	**41**	**Dale Rolfe, L.A., RC**	**3.00**	**6.00**
☐	**42**	**Lowell MacDonald, L.A., RC**	**3.00**	**6.00**
☐	43	Skip Krake, L.A., Error (Don Awrey)	3.00	6.00
☐	44	Terry Gray, L.A., LC	3.00	6.00
☐	45	Césare Maniago (G), Min.	4.00	7.50
☐	46	Mike McMahon, Min.	3.00	6.00
☐	47	Wayne Hillman, Min.	3.00	6.00
☐	48	Larry Hillman, Mtl.	3.00	6.00
☐	49	Bob Woytowich, Min.	3.00	6.00
☐	50	Wayne Connelly, Min.	3.00	6.00
☐	51	Claude Larose, Min.	3.00	6.00
☐	**52**	**Danny Grant, Min., RC**	**5.00**	**10.00**
☐	**53**	**Andre Boudrias, Min., RC**	**3.00**	**6.00**
☐	**54**	**Ray Cullen, Min., RC**	**3.00**	**6.00**
☐	55	Parker MacDonald, Min., Error, (/b: Jacques) LC	3.00	6.00
☐	56	Lorne Worsley (G), Mtl.	10.00	20.00
☐	57	Terry Harper, Mtl.	3.00	6.00
☐	58	Jacques Laperrière, Mtl.	5.00	10.00
☐	59	J.C. Tremblay, Mtl.	4.00	7.50
☐	60	Ralph Backstrom, Mtl.	3.00	6.00
☐	61	Checklist I	115.00	225.00
☐	62	Yvan Cournoyer, Mtl.	10.00	20.00
☐	63	Jacques Lemaire, Mtl.	13.00	26.00
☐	**64**	**Mickey Redmond, Mtl., RC**	**18.00**	**35.00**
☐	65	Bobby Rousseau, Mtl.	3.00	6.00
☐	66	Gilles Tremblay, Mtl.	3.00	6.00
☐	67	Ed Giacomin (G), NYR.	13.00	25.00
☐	68	Arnie Brown, NYR.	3.00	6.00
☐	69	Harry Howell, NYR.	5.00	10.00
☐	**70**	**Al Hamilton, NYR., RC**	**4.00**	**7.50**
☐	71	Rod Seiling, NYR.	3.00	6.00
☐	72	Rod Gilbert, NYR.	6.50	13.00
☐	73	Phil Goyette, NYR.	3.00	6.00
☐	74	Larry Jeffrey, NYR.	3.00	6.00
☐	75	Don Marshall, NYR.	3.00	6.00
☐	76	Bob Nevin, NYR.	3.00	6.00
☐	77	Jean Ratelle, NYR.	6.50	13.00
☐	78	Charlie Hodge (G), Oak.	4.00	7.50
☐	79	Bert Marshall, Oak.	3.00	6.00
☐	80	Billy Harris, Oak., LC	3.00	6.00
☐	81	Carol Vadnais, Oak.	3.00	6.00
☐	82	Howie Young, Chi., LC	3.00	6.00
☐	**83**	**John Brenneman, Oak., RC, LC**	**3.00**	**6.00**
☐	84	Gerry Ehman, Oak.	3.00	6.00
☐	85	Ted Hampson, Oak.	3.00	6.00
☐	86	Bill Hicke, Oak.	3.00	6.00
☐	87	Gary Jarrett, Oak.	3.00	6.00
☐	88	Doug Roberts, Oak.	3.00	6.00
☐	**89**	**Bernie Parent (G), Pha., RC**	**65.00**	**130.00**
☐	90	Joe Watson, Pha.	3.00	6.00
☐	91	Ed Van Impe, Pha.	3.00	6.00
☐	92	Larry Zeidel, Pha., LC	3.00	6.00
☐	**93**	**John Miszuk, Pha., RC**	**3.00**	**6.00**
☐	94	Gary Dornhoefer, Pha.	3.00	6.00
☐	**95**	**Leon Rochefort, Pha., RC**	**3.00**	**6.00**
☐	96	Brit Selby, Pha.	3.00	6.00
☐	97	Forbes Kennedy, Pha., LC	3.00	6.00
☐	**98**	**Ed Hoekstra, Pha., RC, LC**	**3.00**	**6.00**
☐	99	Garry Peters, Pha.	3.00	6.00
☐	**100**	**Les Binkley (G), Pgh., RC**	**7.50**	**15.00**
☐	101	Leo Boivin, Pgh.	5.00	10.00
☐	102	Earl Ingarfield, Pgh.	3.00	6.00
☐	103	Lou Angotti, Pgh.	3.00	6.00
☐	104	Andy Bathgate, Pgh.	5.00	10.00
☐	105	Wally Boyer, Pgh.	3.00	6.00
☐	106	Ken Schinkel, Pgh.	3.00	6.00
☐	107	Ab McDonald, Stl.	3.00	6.00
☐	108	Charlie Burns, Pgh.	3.00	6.00
☐	109	Val Fonteyne, Pgh.	3.00	6.00
☐	110	Noel Price, Pgh.	3.00	6.00
☐	111	Glenn Hall (G), Stl.	10.00	20.00
☐	**112**	**Bob Plager, Stl., RC**	**6.50**	**13.00**
☐	113	Jim Roberts, Stl.	3.00	6.00
☐	114	Red Berenson, Stl.	3.00	6.00
☐	115	Larry Keenan, Stl.	3.00	6.00
☐	116	Camille Henry, Stl.	3.00	6.00
☐	**117**	**Gary Sabourin, Stl., RC**	**3.00**	**6.00**
☐	118	Ron Schock, Stl.	3.00	6.00
☐	**119**	**Gary Veneruzzo, Stl., RC**	**3.00**	**6.00**
☐	120	Gerry Melnyk, Stl., LC	3.00	6.00
☐	121	Checklist II	120.00	235.00
☐	122	Johnny Bower (G), Tor.	8.00	16.00
☐	123	Tim Horton, Tor.	14.00	28.00
☐	124	Pierre Pilote, Tor., LC	5.00	10.00
☐	125	Marcel Pronovost, Tor., LC	5.00	10.00
☐	126	Ron Ellis, Tor.	3.00	6.00
☐	127	Paul Henderson, Tor.	5.00	10.00
☐	128	Al Arbour, Stl.	5.00	10.00
☐	129	Bob Pulford, Tor.	5.00	10.00
☐	130	Floyd Smith, Tor.	3.00	6.00
☐	131	Norm Ullman, Tor.	6.50	13.00
☐	132	Mike Walton, Tor.	3.00	6.00
☐	133	Eddie Johnston (G), Bos.	4.00	7.50
☐	134	Glen Sather, Bos.	7.00	14.00
☐	135	Ed Westfall, Bos.	3.00	6.00
☐	136	Dallas Smith, Bos.	3.00	6.00
☐	137	Eddie Shack, Bos.	9.00	18.00
☐	138	Gary Doak, Bos.	3.00	6.00
☐	139	Ron Murphy, Bos.	3.00	6.00
☐	140	Gerry Cheevers (G), Bos.	14.00	28.00
☐	**141**	**Bob Falkenberg, Det., RC**	**3.00**	**6.00**
☐	**142**	**Garry Unger, Det., RC**	**11.00**	**22.00**
☐	143	Pete Mahovlich, Det.	3.00	6.00
☐	144	Roy Edwards (G), Det.	4.00	7.50
☐	**145**	**Gary Bauman (G), Min., RC, LC**	**4.00**	**7.50**
☐	146	Bob McCord, Min.	3.00	6.00
☐	147	Elmer Vasko, Min., LC	3.00	6.00
☐	**148**	**Bill Goldsworthy, Min., RC**	**7.50**	**15.00**
☐	**149**	**Jean-Paul Parise, Min., RC**	**4.00**	**7.50**
☐	150	Dave Dryden (G), Chi.	4.00	7.50
☐	151	Howie Young, Chi., LC	3.00	6.00
☐	152	Matt Ravlich, Chi.	3.00	6.00
☐	153	Dennis Hull, Chi.	3.00	6.00
☐	154	Eric Nesterenko, Chi.	3.00	6.00
☐	155	Stan Mikita, Chi.	20.00	40.00
☐	156	Bob Wall, L.A.	3.00	6.00
☐	**157**	**Dave Amadio, L.A., RC**	**3.00**	**6.00**
☐	**158**	**Howie Hughes, L.A., RC**	**3.00**	**6.00**
☐	**159**	**Bill Flett, L.A., RC**	**4.00**	**7.50**
☐	160	Doug Robinson, L.A., LC	3.00	6.00
☐	161	Dick Duff, Min.	3.00	6.00
☐	162	Ted Harris, Mtl.	3.00	6.00
☐	163	Claude Provost, Mtl.	3.00	6.00
☐	164	Rogatien Vachon (G), Mtl.	25.00	45.00
☐	165	Henri Richard, Mtl.	10.00	20.00
☐	166	Jean Béliveau, Mtl.	15.00	30.00

No.	Player	EX	NRMT
167	Reggie Fleming, NYR.	3.00	6.00
168	Ron Stewart, NYR.	3.00	6.00
169	Dave Balon, NYR.	3.00	6.00
170	Orland Kurtenbach, NYR.	3.00	6.00
171	Vic Hadfield, NYR.	3.00	6.00
172	Jim Neilson, NYR.	3.00	6.00
173	Bryan Watson, Oak.	3.00	6.00
174	**George Swarbrick, Oak., RC**	**3.00**	**6.00**
175	**Joe Szura, Oak., RC**	**3.00**	**6.00**
176	**Gary Smith (G), Oak., RC**	**8.00**	**16.00**
177	**Barclay Plager, St., RC, Error (Bob Player)**	**7.00**	**14.00**
178	**Tim Ecclestone, Stl., RC**	**3.00**	**6.00**
179	Jean Guy Talbot, Stl.	3.00	6.00
180	Ab McDonald, Stl.	3.00	6.00
181	Jacques Plante (G), Stl.	30.00	60.00
182	**Bill E. McCreary, Stl., RC**	**3.00**	**6.00**
183	Allan Stanley, Pha., LC, Error (/b: Alan)	5.00	10.00
184	**Andre Lacroix, Pha., RC**	**5.00**	**10.00**
185	Jean Guy Gendron, Pha.	3.00	6.00
186	**Jim Johnson, Pha., RC**	**3.00**	**6.00**
187	**Simon Nolet, Pha., RC**	**3.00**	**6.00**
188	**Joe Daley (G), Pgh., RC**	**6.50**	**13.00**
189	**John Arbour, Pgh., RC**	**3.00**	**6.00**
190	Billy Dea, Pgh.	3.00	6.00
191	Bob Dillabough, Pgh.	3.00	6.00
192	Bob Woytowich, Pgh.	3.00	6.00
193	**Keith McCreary, Pgh., RC, Error (no #)**	**3.00**	**6.00**
193	**Keith McCreary, Pgh., RC, Corrected**	**3.00**	**6.00**
194	Murray Oliver, Tor.	3.00	6.00
195	**Larry Mickey, Tor., RC**	**3.00**	**6.00**
196	**Bill Sutherland, Tor., RC**	**3.00**	**6.00**
197	Bruce Gamble (G), Tor.	4.00	7.50
198	Dave Keon, Tor.	7.00	14.00
199	AS: Gump Worsley (G), Mtl.	6.00	12.00
200	AS: Bobby Orr, Bos.	100.00	200.00
201	AS: Tim Horton, Tor.	7.50	15.00
202	AS: Stan Mikita, Chi.	13.00	25.00
203	AS: Gordie Howe, Det.	40.00	75.00
204	AS: Bobby Hull, Chi.	35.00	65.00
205	AS: Ed Giacomin (G), NYR.	9.00	15.00
206	AS: J.C. Tremblay, Mtl.	3.00	6.00
207	AS: Jim Neilson, NYR.	3.00	6.00
208	AS: Phil Esposito, Bos.	20.00	30.00
209	AS: Rod Gilbert, NYR.	4.00	8.00
210	AS: John Bucyk, Bos.	4.00	8.00
211	AW: Stan Mikita, Chi.	13.00	25.00
212	AW: Worsley & Vachon (G)	6.00	12.00
213	AW: Derek Sanderson, Bos.	18.00	35.00
214	AW: Bobby Orr, Bos.	100.00	200.00
215	AW: Glenn Hall, Chi.	6.00	12.00
216	AW: Claude Provost, Mtl.	7.00	20.00

O-PEE-CHEE PUCK STICKERS

Push out — Moisten Back
Press Firmly to Flat Surface
Poussez pour sortir—Humectez l'endos
Collez fermement sur une surface plate
GLEN HALL
GOAL
ST. LOUIS
No. 13 of 21

Insert Set (21 stickers + 1 card): 190.00 375.00

No.	Player	EX	NRMT
1	Stan Mikita, Chi.	9.00	18.00
2	Frank Mahovlich, Det.	9.00	18.00
3	Bobby Hull, Chi.	25.00	45.00
4	Bobby Orr, Bos.	45.00	85.00
5	Phil Esposito, Bos.	10.00	20.00
6	Gump Worsley (G), Mtl.	9.00	18.00
7	Jean Béliveau, Mtl.	15.00	30.00
8	Elmer Vasko, Min.	3.00	6.00
9	Rod Gilbert, NYR.	5.00	10.00
10	Roger Crozier (G), Det.	4.00	8.00
11	Lou Angotti, Pgh.	3.00	6.00
12	Charlie Hodge (G), Oak.	4.00	8.00
13	Glenn Hall (G), Stl., Error (Glen)	9.00	18.00
14	Doug Harvey, Stl.	7.50	15.00
15	Jacques Plante (G), Stl.	14.00	28.00
16	Allan Stanley, Pha.	5.00	10.00
17	Johnny Bower (G), Tor.	6.00	12.00
18	Tim Horton, Tor.	13.00	25.00
19	Dave Keon, Tor.	6.00	12.00
20	Terry Sawchuk (G), Det.	14.00	28.00
21	Henri Richard, Mtl.	7.50	15.00
	Gordie Howe, Det. 700th Goal	50.00	95.00

1968 - 69 POST MARBLES

A white plastic rink-shaped game board was available. The Montréal and Toronto team logos and the Post logo was dispalyed on the rink, and the wording was bilingual. There were perforations on the rink and in the penalty box to hold the marbles.

Marble Diameter: 3/4"
Face: Four colour; Name
Back: Team colours
Imprint: None
Complete Set (30 cards): 150.00 285.00
Rink (30" x 18"): 100.00 200.00

No.	Player	EX	NRMT
1	Ralph Backstrom, Mtl.	5.00	10.00
2	Jean Béliveau, Mtl.	18.00	35.00
3	Yvan Cournoyer, Mtl.	9.00	18.00
4	John Ferguson, Mtl.	5.00	10.00
5	Terry Harper, Mtl.	5.00	10.00
6	Ted Harris, Mtl.	5.00	10.00
7	Jacques Laperrière, Mtl.	6.50	13.00
8	Jacques Lemaire, Mtl.	9.00	18.00
9	Henri Richard, Mtl.	9.00	18.00
10	Bobby Rousseau, Mtl.	5.00	10.00
11	Serge Savard, Mtl.	7.50	15.00
12	Gilles Tremblay, Mtl.	5.00	10.00
13	J.C. Tremblay, Mtl.	6.00	12.00
14	Rogatien Vachon (G), Mtl.	7.00	14.00
15	Gump Worsley (G), Mtl.	11.00	22.00
16	Johnny Bower (G), Tor.	10.00	20.00
17	Wayne Carleton, Tor.	5.00	10.00
18	Ron Ellis, Tor.	5.00	10.00
19	Bruce Gamble (G), Tor.	6.00	12.00
20	Paul Henderson, Tor.	7.50	15.00
21	Tim Horton, Tor.	14.00	28.00
22	Dave Keon, Tor.	9.00	18.00
23	Murray Oliver, Tor.	5.00	10.00
24	Mike Pelyk, Tor.	5.00	10.00
25	Pierre Pilote, Tor.	6.50	13.00
26	Marcel Pronovost, Tor.	6.50	13.00
27	Bob Pulford, Tor.	7.50	15.00
28	Floyd Smith, Tor.	5.00	10.00
29	Norm Ullman, Tor.	7.50	15.00
30	Mike Walton, Tor.	5.00	10.00

1968 - 69 SHIRRIFF COINS

The numbering on this set is a little different than the previous coins. The coins are numbered within the teams. Some coins were short-issued and are marked with an asterisk (*).

Cap Diametre: 1 3/8"
Face: Four colour; Name, Number
Back: Team colours
Imprint: Save hockey coins / collectionez les pièces de hockey
Complete Set (176 coins): 4,000.00 6,500.00
Common Player: (Original Six) 4.00 6.50

No.	Player	EX	NRMT
	BOSTON BRUINS		
1	Eddie Shack	9.00	15.00
2	Ed Westfall	4.00	6.50
3	Don Awrey	4.00	6.50
4	Gerry Cheevers (G)	15.00	25.00
5	Bobby Orr	110.00	175.00
6	John Bucyk	11.00	18.00
7	Derek Sanderson	11.00	18.00
8	Phil Esposito	22.00	35.00
9	Fred Stanfield	4.00	6.50
10	Ken Hodge	4.00	6.50
11	John McKenzie	4.00	6.50
12	Ted Green	4.00	6.50
13	Dallas Smith (*)	75.00	125.00
14	Gary Doak (*)	75.00	125.00
15	Glen Sather (*)	85.00	140.00
16	Tom Williams (*)	75.00	125.00
	CHICAGO BLACKHAWKS		
1	Bobby Hull	40.00	65.00
2	Pat Stapleton	4.00	6.50
3	Wayne Maki	4.00	6.50
4	Denis DeJordy (G)	5.00	8.00
5	Kenny Wharram	4.00	6.50
6	Pit Martin	4.00	6.50
7	Chico Maki	4.00	6.50
8	Doug Mohns	4.00	6.50
9	Stan Mikita	15.00	25.00
10	Doug Jarrett	4.00	6.50
11	Dennis Hull Small Portrait	110.00	175.00
11	Dennis Hull Large Portrait	22.00	35.00
12	Matt Ravlich	4.00	6.50
13	Dave Dryden (G) (*)	75.00	125.00
14	Eric Nesterenko (*)	75.00	125.00
15	Gilles Marotte (*)	75.00	125.00
16	Jim Pappin (*)	75.00	125.00
	DETROIT RED WINGS		
1	Gary Bergman	4.00	6.50
2	Roger Crozier (G)	7.00	12.00
3	Pete Mahovlich	4.00	6.50
4	Alex Delvecchio	12.00	20.00
5	Dean Prentice	4.00	6.50
6	Kent Douglas	4.00	6.50
7	Roy Edwards (G)	5.00	8.00
8	Bruce MacGregor	4.00	6.50
9	Garry Unger	6.00	10.00
10	Pete Stemkowski,	4.00	6.50
11	Gordie Howe	80.00	130.00
12	Frank Mahovlich	20.00	30.00
13	Bob Baun (*)	80.00	135.00
14	Brian Conacher (*)	80.00	135.00
15	Jimmy Watson (*)	70.00	120.00
16	Nick Libett (*)	70.00	120.00
	LOS ANGELES KINGS		
1	Real Lemieux	4.00	6.50
2	Ted Irvine	4.00	6.50
3	Bob Wall	4.00	6.50
4	Bill White	4.00	6.50
5	Gord Labossiere	4.00	6.50
6	Eddie Joyal	4.00	6.50
7	Lowell MacDonald	4.00	6.50
8	Bill Flett	4.00	6.50
9	Wayne Rutledge (G)	5.00	8.00
10	Dave Amadio	4.00	6.50
11	Skip Krake (*)	55.00	85.00
12	Doug Robinson (*)	55.00	85.00
	MINNESOTA NORTH STARS		
1	Wayne Connelly	4.00	6.50
2	Bob Woytowich	4.00	6.50
3	Andre Boudrias	4.00	6.50
4	Bill Goldsworthy	4.00	6.50
5	Cesare Maniago (G)	5.00	8.00
6	Milan Marcetta	4.00	6.50
7	Bill Collins	35.00	60.00
7	Claude Larose	90.00	150.00
8	Parker MacDonald	4.00	6.50
9	Ray Cullen	4.00	6.50
10	Mike McMahon	4.00	6.50
11	Bob McCord (*)	55.00	90.00
12	Larry Hillman (*)	55.00	90.00
	MONTRÉAL CANADIENS		
1	Gump Worsley (G)	15.00	25.00
2	Rogatien Vachon (G)	9.00	15.00
3	Ted Harris	4.00	6.50
4	Jacques Laperrière	9.00	15.00

☐ 5	J.C. Tremblay	6.00	10.00
☐ 6	Jean Béliveau	35.00	55.00
☐ 7	Gilles Tremblay	4.00	6.50
☐ 8	Ralph Backstrom	4.00	6.50
☐ 9	Bobby Rousseau	4.00	6.50
☐ 10	John Ferguson	6.00	10.00
☐ 11	Dick Duff	4.00	6.50
☐ 12	Terry Harper	4.00	6.50
☐ 13	Yvan Cournoyer	13.00	22.00
☐ 14	Jacques Lemaire	13.00	22.00
☐ 15	Henri Richard	12.00	20.00
☐ 16	Claude Provost (*)	100.00	165.00
☐ 17	Serge Savard (*)	135.00	225.00
☐ 18	Mickey Redmond (*)	120.00	200.00
NEW YORK RANGERS			
☐ 1	Rod Seiling	4.00	6.50
☐ 2	Jean Ratelle	12.00	20.00
☐ 3	Ed Giacomin (G)	15.00	25.00
☐ 4	Reggie Fleming	4.00	6.50
☐ 5	Phil Goyette	4.00	6.50
☐ 6	Arnie Brown	4.00	6.50
☐ 7	Don Marshall	4.00	6.50
☐ 8	Orland Kurtenbach	4.00	6.50
☐ 9	Bob Nevin	4.00	6.50
☐ 10	Rod Gilbert	12.00	20.00
☐ 11	Harry Howell	9.00	15.00
☐ 12	Jim Neilson	4.00	6.50
☐ 13	Vic Hadfield (*)	115.00	185.00
☐ 14	Larry Jeffrey (*)	350.00	600.00
☐ 15	Dave Balon (*)	90.00	150.00
☐ 16	Ron Stewart (*)	90.00	150.00
OAKLAND SEALS			
☐ 1	Gerry Ehman	4.00	6.50
☐ 2	John Brenneman	4.00	6.50
☐ 3	Ted Hampson	4.00	6.50
☐ 4	Billy Harris	4.00	6.50
☐ 5	George Swarbrick	35.00	60.00
☐ 5	Carol Vadnais, SP	425.00	700.00
☐ 6	Gary Smith (G)	5.00	8.00
☐ 7	Charlie Hodge (G)	6.00	10.00
☐ 8	Bert Marshall	4.00	6.50
☐ 9	Bill Hicke	4.00	6.50
☐ 10	Tracy Pratt	4.00	6.50
☐ 11	Gary Jarrett (*)	425.00	700.00
☐ 12	Howie Young (*)	500.00	800.00
PHILADELPHIA FLYERS			
☐ 1	Bernie Parent (G)	20.00	30.00
☐ 2	John Miszuk	4.00	6.50
☐ 3	Ed Hoekstra	35.00	60.00
☐ 3	Allan Stanley	100.00	170.00
☐ 4	Gary Dornhoefer	6.00	10.00
☐ 5	Doug Favell (G)	5.00	8.00
☐ 6	Andre Lacroix	4.00	6.50
☐ 7	Brit Selby	4.00	6.50
☐ 8	Don Blackburn	4.00	6.50
☐ 9	Leon Rochefort	4.00	6.50
☐ 10	Forbes Kennedy	4.00	6.50
☐ 11	Claude Laforge (*)	70.00	120.00
☐ 12	Pat Hannigan (*)	70.00	120.00
PITTSBURGH PENGUINS			
☐ 1	Ken Schinkel	4.00	6.50
☐ 2	Earl Ingarfield	4.00	6.50
☐ 3	Val Fonteyne	4.00	6.50
☐ 4	Noel Price	4.00	6.50
☐ 5	Andy Bathgate	9.00	15.00
☐ 6	Les Binkley (G)	5.00	8.00
☐ 7	Leo Boivin	9.00	15.00
☐ 8	Paul Andrea	4.00	6.50
☐ 9	Dunc McCallum	4.00	6.50
☐ 10	Keith McCreary	4.00	6.50
☐ 11	Lou Angotti (*)	60.00	100.00
☐ 12	Wally Boyer (*)	60.00	100.00
ST. LOUIS BLUES			
☐ 1	Ron Schock	4.00	6.50
☐ 2	Bob Plager	6.00	10.00
☐ 3	Al Arbour	9.00	15.00
☐ 4	Red Berenson	4.00	6.50
☐ 5	Glenn Hall (G)	20.00	30.00
☐ 6	Jim Roberts	4.00	6.50
☐ 7	Noel Picard	4.00	6.50
☐ 8	Barclay Plager	6.00	10.00
☐ 9	Larry Keenan	4.00	6.50
☐ 10	Terry Crisp	7.00	12.00
☐ 11	Gary Sabourin (*)	70.00	120.00
☐ 12	Ab McDonald (*)	70.00	120.00
TORONTO MAPLE LEAFS			
☐ 1	George Armstrong	9.00	15.00
☐ 2	Wayne Carleton	4.00	6.50
☐ 3	Paul Henderson	9.00	15.00
☐ 4	Bob Pulford	9.00	15.00
☐ 5	Mike Walton	4.00	6.50
☐ 6	Johnny Bower (G)	13.00	22.00
☐ 7	Ron Ellis	4.00	6.50
☐ 8	Mike Pelyk	4.00	6.50
☐ 9	Murray Oliver	4.00	6.50
☐ 10	Norm Ullman	11.00	18.00
☐ 11	Dave Keon	13.00	22.00
☐ 12	Floyd Smith	4.00	6.50
☐ 13	Marcel Pronovost	9.00	15.00
☐ 14	Tim Horton	20.00	30.00
☐ 15	Bruce Gamble (G)	6.00	10.00
☐ 16	Jim McKenny (*)	70.00	120.00
☐ 17	Mike Byers (*)	70.00	120.00
☐ 18	Pierre Pilote (*)	85.00	140.00

1968 - 69 TOPPS

Topps did not issue bilingual backs this year. They did, however, plug the sport with the caption "Watch NHL Hockey on CBS Network".

Card Size: 2 1/2" x 3 1/2"

Face: Four colour, white border, Team logo, Position

Back: Red and blue on card stock, Number, Resume, Hockey facts

Imprint: T.C.G.

Complete Set (132 cards):		**375.00**	**750.00**
Common Player:		**1.75**	**3.50**
No.	**Player**	**EX**	**NRMT**
☐ 1	Gerry Cheevers (G), Bos.	10.00	30.00
☐ 2	Bobby Orr, Bos.	125.00	250.00
☐ 3	Don Awrey, Bos., Error (Skip Krake)	1.75	3.50
☐ 4	Ted Green, Bos.	1.75	3.50
☐ 5	John Bucyk, Bos.	4.50	8.50
☐ 6	Derek Sanderson, Bos.	13.00	25.00
☐ 7	Phil Esposito, Bos.	20.00	40.00
☐ 8	Ken Hodge, Bos.	1.75	3.50
☐ 9	John McKenzie, Bos.	1.75	3.50
☐ 10	Fred Stanfield, Bos.	1.75	3.50
☐ 11	Tom Williams, Bos.	1.75	3.50
☐ 12	Denis DeJordy (G), Chi.	2.50	5.00
☐ 13	Doug Jarrett, Chi.	1.75	3.50
☐ 14	Gilles Marotte, Chi.	1.75	3.50
☐ 15	Pat Stapleton, Chi.	1.75	3.50
☐ 16	Bobby Hull, Chi.	35.00	70.00
☐ 17	Chico Maki, Chi.	1.75	3.50
☐ 18	Pit Martin, Chi.	1.75	3.50
☐ 19	Doug Mohns, Chi.	1.75	3.50
☐ 20	Stan Mikita, Chi.	11.00	22.00
☐ 21	Jim Pappin, Chi.	1.75	3.50
☐ 22	Kenny Wharram, Chi.	1.75	3.50
☐ 23	Roger Crozier (G), Det.	2.50	5.00
☐ 24	Bob Baun, Det.	1.75	3.50
☐ 25	Gary Bergman, Det.	1.75	3.50
☐ 26	Kent Douglas, Det., LC	1.75	3.50
☐ **27**	**Ron Harris, Det., RC**	**1.75**	**3.50**
☐ 28	Alex Delvecchio, Det.	4.50	8.50
☐ 29	Gordie Howe, Det.	50.00	100.00
☐ 30	Bruce MacGregor, Det.	1.75	3.50
☐ 31	Frank Mahovlich, Det.	7.00	14.00
☐ 32	Dean Prentice, Det.	1.75	3.50
☐ 33	Pete Stemkowski, Det.	1.75	3.50
☐ 34	Terry Sawchuk (G), L.A.	20.00	40.00
☐ 35	Larry Cahan, L.A.	1.75	3.50
☐ **36**	**Real Lemieux, L.A., RC**	**1.75**	**3.50**
☐ **37**	**Bill White, L.A., RC**	**2.50**	**5.00**
☐ **38**	**Gord Labossiere,, L.A. RC**	**1.75**	**3.50**
☐ **39**	**Ted Irvine,, L.A. RC**	**1.75**	**3.50**
☐ 40	Eddie Joyal, L.A.	1.75	3.50
☐ **41**	**Dale Rolfe, L.A., RC**	**1.75**	**3.50**
☐ **42**	**Lowell MacDonald, L.A., RC**	**1.75**	**3.50**
☐ 43	Skip Krake, L.A., Error (Don Awrey)	1.75	3.50
☐ 44	Terry Gray, L.A., LC	1.75	3.50
☐ 45	Césare Maniago (G), Min.	2.50	5.00
☐ 46	Mike McMahon, Min.	1.75	3.50
☐ 47	Wayne Hillman, Min.	1.75	3.50
☐ 48	Larry Hillman, Min.	1.75	3.50
☐ 49	Bob Woytowich, Min.	1.75	3.50
☐ 50	Wayne Connelly, Min.	1.75	3.50
☐ 51	Claude Larose, Min.	1.75	3.50
☐ **52**	**Danny Grant, Min., RC**	**2.50**	**5.00**
☐ **53**	**Andre Boudrias, Min., RC**	**1.75**	**3.50**
☐ **54**	**Ray Cullen, Min., RC**	**1.75**	**3.50**
☐ 55	Parker MacDonald, Min., LC	1.75	3.50
☐ 56	Gump Worsley (G), Mtl.	6.50	13.00
☐ 57	Terry Harper, Mtl.	1.75	3.50
☐ 58	Jacques Laperrière, Mtl.	2.50	5.00
☐ 59	J.C. Tremblay, Mtl.	1.75	3.50
☐ 60	Ralph Backstrom, Mtl.	1.75	3.50
☐ 61	Jean Béliveau, Mtl.	10.00	20.00
☐ 62	Yvan Cournoyer, Mtl.	6.50	13.00
☐ 63	Jacques Lemaire, Mtl.	8.00	16.00
☐ 64	Henri Richard, Mtl.	6.00	12.00
☐ 65	Bobby Rousseau, Mtl.	1.75	3.50
☐ 66	Gilles Tremblay, Mtl.	1.75	3.50
☐ 67	Ed Giacomin (G), NYR.	8.00	16.00
☐ 68	Arnie Brown, NYR.	1.75	3.50
☐ 69	Harry Howell, NYR.	2.50	5.00
☐ 70	Jim Neilson, NYR.	1.75	3.50
☐ 71	Rod Seiling, NYR.	1.75	3.50
☐ 72	Rod Gilbert, NYR.	4.50	9.00
☐ 73	Phil Goyette, NYR.	1.75	3.50
☐ 74	Vic Hadfield, NYR.	1.75	3.50
☐ 75	Don Marshall, NYR.	1.75	3.50
☐ 76	Bob Nevin, NYR.	1.75	3.50
☐ 77	Jean Ratelle, NYR.	4.50	9.00
☐ 78	Charlie Hodge (G), Oak.	2.50	5.00
☐ 79	Bert Marshall, Oak.	1.75	3.50
☐ 80	Billy Harris, Oak., LC	1.75	3.50
☐ 81	Carol Vadnais, Oak.	1.75	3.50
☐ 82	Howie Young, Oak., LC	1.75	3.50
☐ **83**	**John Brenneman, Oak., RC, LC**	**1.75**	**3.50**
☐ 84	Gerry Ehman, Oak.	1.75	3.50
☐ 85	Ted Hampson, Oak.	1.75	3.50
☐ 86	Bill Hicke, Oak.	1.75	3.50
☐ 87	Gary Jarrett, Oak.	1.75	3.50
☐ 88	Doug Roberts, Oak.	1.75	3.50
☐ **89**	**Bernie Parent (G), Pha., RC**	**45.00**	**90.00**
☐ 90	Joe Watson, Pha.	1.75	3.50
☐ 91	Ed Van Impe, Pha.	1.75	3.50
☐ 92	Larry Zeidel, Pha., LC	1.75	3.50
☐ **93**	**John Miszuk, Pha., RC**	**1.75**	**3.50**
☐ 94	Gary Dornhoefer, Pha.	1.75	3.50
☐ **95**	**Leon Rochefort, Pha., RC**	**1.75**	**3.50**
☐ 96	Brit Selby, Pha.	1.75	3.50
☐ 97	Forbes Kennedy, Pha., LC	1.75	3.50
☐ **98**	**Ed Hoekstra, Pha., RC, LC**	**1.75**	**3.50**
☐ 99	Garry Peters, Pha.	1.75	3.50
☐ **100**	**Les Binkley (G), Pgh., RC**	**5.00**	**10.00**
☐ 101	Léo Boivin, Pgh.	2.50	5.00
☐ 102	Earl Ingarfield, Pgh.	1.75	3.50
☐ 103	Lou Angotti, Pgh.	1.75	3.50
☐ 104	Andy Bathgate, Pgh.	2.50	5.00
☐ 105	Wally Boyer, Pgh.	1.75	3.50
☐ 106	Ken Schinkel, Pgh.	1.75	3.50
☐ 107	Ab McDonald, Pgh.	1.75	3.50
☐ 108	Charlie Burns, Pgh.	1.75	3.50
☐ 109	Val Fonteyne, Pgh.	1.75	3.50
☐ 110	Noel Price, Pgh.	1.75	3.50
☐ 111	Glenn Hall (G), Stl.	7.00	14.00
☐ **112**	**Bob Plager, Stl., RC**	**4.50**	**8.50**
☐ 113	Jim Roberts, Stl.	1.75	3.50
☐ 114	Red Berenson, Stl.	1.75	3.50
☐ 115	Larry Keenan, Stl.	1.75	3.50
☐ 116	Camille Henry, Stl.	1.75	3.50
☐ **117**	**Gary Sabourin, Stl., RC**	**1.75**	**3.50**
☐ 118	Ron Schock, Stl.	1.75	3.50
☐ **119**	**Gary Veneruzzo, Stl., RC**	**1.75**	**3.50**
☐ 120	Gerry Melnyk, Stl., LC	1.75	3.50
☐ 121	Checklist (1 - 132)	60.00	115.00
☐ 122	Johnny Bower (G), Tor.	5.00	10.00
☐ 123	Tim Horton, Tor.	8.00	16.00
☐ 124	Pierre Pilote, Tor., LC	2.50	5.00
☐ 125	Marcel Pronovost, Tor., LC	2.50	5.00
☐ 126	Ron Ellis, Tor.	1.75	3.50
☐ 127	Paul Henderson, Tor.	2.50	5.00

No.	Player	EX	NRMT
☐ 128	Dave Keon, Tor.	4.50	8.50
☐ 129	Bob Pulford, Tor.	2.50	5.00
☐ 130	Floyd Smith, Tor.	1.75	3.50
☐ 131	Norm Ullman, Tor.	4.50	8.50
☐ 132	Mike Walton, Tor.	3.00	8.50

1969 - 70 O-PEE-CHEE

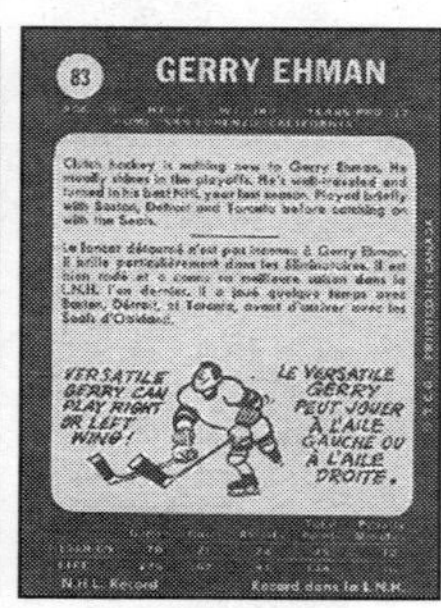

The backs were printed in navy blue ink resulting in the possible image transfer to the face of the card below if cards have been stored in stacks. This transferring of images on the face results in loss of value.

The backs of card nos. 206, 208, 209, 210, 212, 213, 218, 225, 226, 230 and 231 form a picture puzzle of Bobby Orr. The backs of card nos. 205, 207, 211, 214, 215, 216, 217, 220, 221, 222, 223, 224, 227, 228 and 229 form a picture puzzle of Phil Exposito.

Card Size: 2 1/2" x 3 1/2"
Face: Four colour, white border, Team logo
Back: Blue and yellow on card stock, Resume, Number, Hockey trivia, Bilingual
Imprint: T.C.G.

Complete Set (231 cards):		**950.00**	**1,900.00**
Common Player:		**2.75**	**5.50**
No.	**Player**	**EX**	**NRMT**
☐ 1	Gump Worsley (G), Mtl.	12.00	35.00
☐ 2	Ted Harris, Mtl.	2.75	5.50
☐ 3	Jacques Laperrière, Mtl.	4.00	8.00
☐ **4**	**Serge Savard, Mtl., RC**	**20.00**	**40.00**
☐ 5	J. C. Tremblay, Mtl.	2.75	5.50
☐ 6	Yvan Cournoyer, Mtl.	7.50	15.00
☐ 7	John Ferguson, Mtl.	2.75	5.50
☐ 8	Jacques Lemaire, Mtl.	7.50	15.00
☐ 9	Bobby Rousseau, Mtl.	2.75	5.50
☐ 10	Jean Béliveau, Mtl.	13.00	26.00
☐ 11	Dick Duff, Mtl.	2.75	5.50
☐ 12	Glenn Hall (G), Stl.	7.50	15.00
☐ 13	Bob Plager, Stl.	2.75	5.50
☐ **14**	**Ron C. Anderson, Stl., RC**	**2.75**	**5.50**
☐ 15	Jean-Guy Talbot, Stl.	2.75	5.50
☐ 16	Andre Boudrias, Stl.	2.75	5.50
☐ 17	Camille Henry, Stl., LC	2.75	5.50
☐ 18	Ab McDonald, Stl.	2.75	5.50
☐ 19	Gary Sabourin, Stl.	2.75	5.50
☐ 20	Red Berenson, Stl.	2.75	5.50
☐ 21	Phil Goyette, Stl.	2.75	5.50
☐ 22	Gerry Cheevers (G), Bos.	10.00	20.00
☐ 23	Ted Green, Bos.	2.75	5.50
☐ 24	Bobby Orr, Bos.	115.00	225.00
☐ 25	Dallas Smith, Bos.	2.75	5.50
☐ 26	John Bucyk, Bos.	5.00	10.00
☐ 27	Ken Hodge, Bos.	2.75	5.50
☐ 28	John McKenzie, Bos.	2.75	5.50
☐ 29	Ed Westfall, Bos.	2.75	5.50
☐ 30	Phil Esposito, Bos.	20.00	40.00
☐ 31	Checklist 2 (133 - 231)	90.00	175.00
☐ 32	Fred Stanfield, Bos.	2.75	5.50
☐ 33	Ed Giacomin (G), NYR.	10.00	20.00
☐ 34	Arnie Brown, NYR.	2.75	5.50
☐ 35	Jim Neilson, NYR.	2.75	5.50
☐ 36	Rod Seiling, NYR.	2.75	5.50
☐ 37	Rod Gilbert, NYR.	5.00	10.00
☐ 38	Vic Hadfield, NYR.	2.75	5.50
☐ 39	Don Marshall, NYR.	2.75	5.50
☐ 40	Bob Nevin, NYR.	2.75	5.50
☐ 41	Ron Stewart, NYR.	2.75	5.50
☐ 42	Jean Ratelle, NYR.	5.00	10.00
☐ **43**	**Walt Tkaczuk, NYR., RC**	**4.50**	**9.00**
☐ 44	Bruce Gamble (G), Tor.	3.50	7.00
☐ **45**	**Jim Dorey, Tor., RC**	**2.75**	**5.50**
☐ 46	Ron Ellis, Tor.	2.75	5.50
☐ 47	Paul Henderson, Tor.	4.00	8.00
☐ 48	Brit Selby, Tor.	2.75	5.50
☐ 49	Floyd Smith, Tor.	2.75	5.50
☐ 50	Mike Walton, Tor.	2.75	5.50
☐ 51	Dave Keon, Tor.	5.00	10.00
☐ 52	Murray Oliver, Tor.	2.75	5.50
☐ 53	Bob Pulford, Tor.	4.00	8.00
☐ 54	Norm Ullman, Tor.	5.00	10.00
☐ 55	Roger Crozier (G), Det.	4.00	8.00
☐ 56	Roy Edwards (G), Det.	3.50	7.00
☐ 57	Bob Baun, Det.	2.75	5.50
☐ 58	Gary Bergman, Det.	2.75	5.50
☐ 59	Carl Brewer, Det.	2.75	5.50
☐ 60	Wayne Connelly, Det.	2.75	5.50
☐ 61	Gordie Howe, Det.	55.00	110.00
☐ 62	Frank Mahovlich, Det.	9.00	18.00
☐ 63	Bruce MacGregor, Det.	2.75	5.50
☐ 64	Ron Harris, Det.	2.75	5.50
☐ 65	Pete Stemkowski, Det.	2.75	5.50
☐ 66	Denis DeJordy (G), Chi.	3.50	7.00
☐ 67	Doug Jarrett, Chi.	2.75	5.50
☐ 68	Gilles Marotte, Chi.	2.75	5.50
☐ 69	Pat Stapleton, Chi.	2.75	5.50
☐ 70	Bobby Hull, Chi.	40.00	80.00
☐ 71	Dennis Hull, Chi.	2.75	5.50
☐ 72	Doug Mohns, Chi.	2.75	5.50
☐ **73**	**Howie Menard, Chi., RC**	**2.75**	**5.50**
☐ 74	Kenny Wharram, Chi., LC	2.75	5.50
☐ 75	Pit Martin, Chi.	2.75	5.50
☐ 76	Stan Mikita, Chi.	15.00	30.00
☐ 77	Charlie Hodge (G), Cal.	3.50	7.00
☐ 78	Gary Smith (G), Cal.	3.50	7.00
☐ 79	Harry Howell, Cal.	4.00	8.00
☐ 80	Bert Marshall, Cal.	2.75	5.50
☐ 81	Doug Roberts, Cal.	2.75	5.50
☐ 82	Carol Vadnais, Cal.	2.75	5.50
☐ 83	Gerry Ehman, Cal.	2.75	5.50
☐ **84**	**Brian Perry, Cal., RC, LC**	**2.75**	**5.50**
☐ 85	Gary Jarrett, Cal.	2.75	5.50
☐ 86	Ted Hampson, Cal.	2.75	5.50
☐ 87	Earl Ingarfield, Cal.	2.75	5.50
☐ **88**	**Doug Favell (G), Pha, RC**	**7.50**	**15.00**
☐ 89	Bernie Parent (G), Pha.	28.00	55.00
☐ 90	Larry Hillman, Pha.	2.75	5.50
☐ 91	Wayne Hillman, Pha.	2.75	5.50
☐ 92	Ed Van Impe, Pha.	2.75	5.50
☐ 93	Joe Watson, Pha.	2.75	5.50
☐ 94	Gary Dornhoefer, Pha.	2.75	5.50
☐ 95	Reggie Fleming, Pha.	2.75	5.50
☐ **96**	**Ralph MacSweyn, Pha., RC, LC**	**2.75**	**5.50**
☐ 97	Jim Johnson, Pha.	2.75	5.50
☐ 98	Andre Lacroix, Pha.	2.75	5.50
☐ **99**	**Gerry Desjardins (G), L.A., RC**	**7.00**	**14.00**
☐ 100	Dale Rolfe, L.A.	2.75	5.50
☐ 101	Bill White, L.A.	2.75	5.50
☐ 102	Bill Flett, L.A.	2.75	5.50
☐ 103	Ted Irvine, L.A.	2.75	5.50
☐ 104	Ross Lonsberry, L.A.	2.75	5.50
☐ 105	Leon Rochefort, L.A.	2.75	5.50
☐ **106**	**Brian Campbell**, L.A., **RC**	**2.75**	**5.50**
☐ **107**	**Dennis Hextall**, L.A., **RC**	**2.75**	**5.50**
☐ 108	Eddie Joyal, L.A.	2.75	5.50
☐ 109	Gord Labossiere, L.A.	2.75	5.50
☐ 110	Les Binkley (G), Pgh.	3.50	7.00
☐ **111**	**Tracy Pratt, Pgh., RC**	**2.75**	**5.50**
☐ 112	Bryan Watson, Pgh.	2.75	5.50
☐ **113**	**Bob Blackburn, Pgh., RC, LC**	**2.75**	**5.50**
☐ 114	Keith McCreary, Pgh.	2.75	5.50
☐ 115	Dean Prentice, Pgh.	2.75	5.50
☐ 116	Glen Sather, Pgh.	3.50	7.00
☐ 117	Ken Schinkel, Pgh.	2.75	5.50
☐ 118	Wally Boyer, Pgh.	2.75	5.50
☐ 119	Val Fonteyne, Pgh.	2.75	5.50
☐ 120	Ron Schock, Pgh.	2.75	5.50
☐ 121	Césare Maniago (G), Min.	3.50	7.00
☐ 122	Leo Boivin, Min.	4.00	8.00
☐ 123	Bob McCord, Min.	2.75	5.50
☐ 124	John Miszuk, Min.	2.75	5.50
☐ 125	Danny Grant, Min.	2.75	5.50
☐ **126**	**Bill Collins, Min., RC**	**2.75**	**5.50**
☐ 127	J. P. Parise, Min.	2.75	5.50
☐ 128	Tom Williams, Min.	2.75	5.50
☐ 129	Charlie Burns, Min.	2.75	5.50
☐ 130	Ray Cullen, Min.	2.75	5.50
☐ **131**	**Danny O'Shea, Min., RC**	**2.75**	**5.50**
☐ 132	Checklist 1 (1 - 132)	120.00	235.00
☐ 133	Jim Pappin, Chi.	2.75	5.50
☐ 134	Lou Angotti, Chi.	2.75	5.50
☐ **135**	**Terry Caffery, Chi., RC, LC**	**2.75**	**5.50**
☐ 136	Eric Nesterenko, Chi.	2.75	5.50
☐ 137	Chico Maki, Chi.	2.75	5.50
☐ **138**	**Tony Esposito (G), Chi., RC**	**90.00**	**180.00**
☐ 139	Eddie Shack, L.A.	7.00	14.00
☐ 140	Bob Wall, L.A.	2.75	5.50
☐ **141**	**Skip Krake, L.A., RC**	**2.75**	**5.50**
☐ 142	Howie Hughes, L.A., LC	2.75	5.50
☐ **143**	**Jimmy Peters, L.A., RC**	**2.75**	**5.50**
☐ **144**	**Brent Hughes, L.A., RC**	**2.75**	**5.50**
☐ 145	Bill Hicke, Cal.	2.75	5.50
☐ **146**	**Norm Ferguson, Cal., RC**	**2.75**	**5.50**
☐ **147**	**Dick Mattiussi, Cal., RC**	**2.75**	**5.50**
☐ **148**	**Mike Laughton, Cal., RC**	**2.75**	**5.50**
☐ **149**	**Gene Ubriaco, Cal., RC, LC**	**2.75**	**5.50**
☐ 150	Bob Dillabough, Cal., LC	2.75	5.50
☐ 151	Bob Woytowich, Pgh.	2.75	5.50
☐ 152	Joe Daley (G), Pgh.	3.50	7.00
☐ 153	Duane Rupp, Pgh.	2.75	5.50
☐ **154**	**Bryan Hextall, Jr., Pgh., RC**	**2.75**	**5.50**
☐ **155**	**Jean Pronovost, Pgh., RC**	**4.50**	**9.00**
☐ 156	Jim Morrison, Pgh.	2.75	5.50
☐ 157	Alex Delvecchio, Det.	5.50	11.00
☐ 158	Poul Popiel, Det.	2.75	5.50
☐ 159	Garry Unger, Det.	4.50	9.00
☐ 160	Garry Monahan, Det.	2.75	5.50
☐ 161	Matt Ravlich, Det.	2.75	5.50
☐ **162**	**Nick Libett, Det., RC, Error (Libbett)**	**2.75**	**5.50**
☐ 163	Henri Richard, Mtl.	7.50	15.00
☐ 164	Terry Harper, Mtl.	2.75	5.50
☐ 165	Rogatien Vachon (G), Mtl.	10.00	20.00
☐ 166	Ralph Backstrom, Mtl.	2.75	5.50
☐ 167	Claude Provost, Mtl.	2.75	5.50
☐ 168	Gilles Tremblay, Mtl., LC	2.75	5.50
☐ 169	Jean-Guy Gendron, Pha.	2.75	5.50
☐ **170**	**Earl Heiskala, Pha., RC**	**2.75**	**5.50**
☐ 171	Garry Peters, Pha.	2.75	5.50
☐ 172	Bill Sutherland, Pha.	2.75	5.50
☐ **173**	**Dick Cherry, Pha., RC, LC**	**2.75**	**5.50**
☐ 174	Jim Roberts, Stl.	2.75	5.50
☐ **175**	**Noel Picard, Stl., RC**	**2.75**	**5.50**
☐ **176**	**Barclay Plager, Stl., RC**	**3.50**	**7.00**
☐ **177**	**Frank St. Marseille, Stl., RC**	**2.75**	**5.50**
☐ 178	Al Arbour, Stl., LC	4.00	8.00
☐ 179	Tim Ecclestone, Stl.	2.75	5.50
☐ 180	Jacques Plante (G), Stl.	25.00	50.00
☐ 181	Billy McCreary, Stl., LC	2.75	5.50
☐ 182	Tim Horton, Tor.	11.00	22.00
☐ **183**	**Rick Ley, Tor., RC**	**3.50**	**7.00**
☐ 184	Wayne Carleton, Tor.	2.75	5.50
☐ **185**	**Marv Edwards (G), Tor., RC, LC**	**3.50**	**7.00**
☐ **186**	**Pat Quinn, Tor., RC**	**10.00**	**20.00**
☐ 187	Johnny Bower (G), Tor., LC	6.00	12.00
☐ 188	Orland Kurtenbach, NYR.	2.75	5.50
☐ 189	Terry Sawchuk (G), NYR., LC	25.00	50.00
☐ 190	Real Lemieux, NYR.	2.75	5.50
☐ 191	Dave Balon, NYR.	2.75	5.50
☐ 192	Al Hamilton, NYR.	2.75	5.50
☐ 193	Gordie Howe, Error (no#)	90.00	175.00
☐ 193	Gordie Howe, Corrected	90.00	175.00
☐ 194	Claude Larose, Min.	2.75	5.50
☐ 195	Bill Goldsworthy, Min	2.75	5.50
☐ **196**	**Bob Barlow, Min, RC**	**2.75**	**5.50**
☐ **197**	**Ken Broderick (G), Min, RC**	**3.50**	**7.00**
☐ **198**	**Lou Nanne, Min, RC**	**4.00**	**8.00**
☐ **199**	**Tom Polonic, Min, RC, LC**	**2.75**	**5.50**
☐ 200	Eddie Johnston (G), Bos.	3.50	7.00
☐ 201	Derek Sanderson, Bos.	11.00	22.00
☐ 202	Gary Doak, Bos.	2.75	5.50
☐ 203	Don Awrey, Bos.	2.75	5.50
☐ 204	Ron Murphy, Bos., LC	2.75	5.50
☐ 205	AW: Phil Esposito, Bos., Error (#214)	13.00	25.00
☐ 205	AW: Phil Esposito, Bos., Corrected	13.00	25.00
☐ 206	AW: Alex Delvecchio	3.00	6.00
☐ 207	AW: J. Plante, G. Hall, Stl.	28.00	55.00
☐ 208	J. Plante, G. Hall, Stl.Danny Grant, Min.	3.50	7.00
☐ 209	AW: Bobby Orr, Bos.	45.00	85.00
☐ 210	AW: Serge Savard, Mtl.	6.00	12.00
☐ 211	AS: Glenn Hall (G), Stl.	5.00	10.00
☐ 212	AS: Bobby Orr, Bos.	45.00	85.00
☐ 213	AS: Tim Horton, Tor.	6.50	13.00
☐ 214	AS: Phil Esposito, Bos.	13.00	25.00

No.	Player	EX	NRMT
☐ 215	AS: Gordie Howe, Det.	30.00	60.00
☐ 216	AS: Bobby Hull, Chi.	25.00	45.00
☐ 217	AS: Ed Giacomin (G), NYR.	6.00	12.00
☐ 218	AS: Ted Green, Bos.	2.75	5.50
☐ 219	AS: Ted Harris, Mtl.	2.75	5.50
☐ 220	AS: Jean Béliveau, Mtl.	7.50	15.00
☐ 221	AS: Yvan Cournoyer, Mtl.	4.50	9.00
☐ 222	AS: Frank Mahovlich, Det.	5.00	10.00
☐ 223	The Art Ross Trophy	4.00	8.00
☐ 224	The Hart Memorial Trophy	4.00	8.00
☐ 225	The Lady Byng Trophy	4.00	8.00
☐ 226	The Vezina Trophy	4.50	9.00
☐ 227	The Calder Memorial Trophy	4.00	8.00
☐ 228	The James Norris Memorial Trophy	4.00	8.00
☐ 229	The Conn Smythe Trophy	4.00	8.00
☐ 230	The Prince of Wales Trophy	4.00	8.00
☐ 231	The Stanley Cup	35.00	70.00

O-PEE-CHEE STAMPS

The stamps were included as inserts with the regular first series set of the same year and were intended to be applied to the backs of the respective cards in that set. The Card numbers are 6, 10, 12, 20, 24, 27, 30, 33, 37, 42, 51, 54, 61, 62, 70, 76, 82, 86, 89, 98, 99, 108, 110, 114, 125, 130. However, applying the stamps will decrease the value of both items and is discouraged among collectors. The stamps are unnumbered and are listed in alphabetical order.

Stamp Size: 2 1/2" x 1 1/4"

Insert Set (18 stamps): 90.00 175.00

	Player	EX	NRMT
☐	Jean Béliveau, Mtl.	7.50	15.00
☐	Red Berenson, Stl.	1.50	3.00
☐	Les Binkley (G), Pgh.	2.50	5.00
☐	Yvan Cournoyer, Mtl.	4.00	8.00
☐	Ray Cullen, Min.	1.50	3.00
☐	Gerry Desjardins (G), L.A.	2.50	5.00
☐	Phil Esposito, Bos.	6.00	12.00
☐	Ed Giacomin (G), NYR.	4.00	8.00
☐	Rod Gilbert, NYR.	3.50	7.00
☐	Danny Grant, Min.	1.50	3.00
☐	Glenn Hall (G), Stl.	6.00	12.00
☐	Ted Hampson, Cgy.	1.50	3.00
☐	Ken Hodge Bos.	1.50	3.00
☐	Gordie Howe, Det.	18.00	35.00
☐	Bobby Hull, Chi.	11.00	22.00
☐	Eddie Joyal, L.A.	1.50	3.00
☐	Dave Keon, Tor.	4.00	8.00
☐	André Lacroix, Pha.	1.50	3.00
☐	Frank Mahovlich, Det.	6.00	12.00
☐	Keith McCreary, Pgh.	1.50	3.00
☐	Stan Mikita, Chi.	5.00	10.00
☐	Bobby Orr, Bos.	25.00	50.00
☐	Bernie Parent (G), Pha.	5.00	10.00
☐	Jean Ratelle, NYR.	3.50	7.00
☐	Norm Ullman, Tor.	3.50	7.00
☐	Carol Vadnais, Cgy.	1.50	3.00

O-PEE-CHEE MINI CARDS

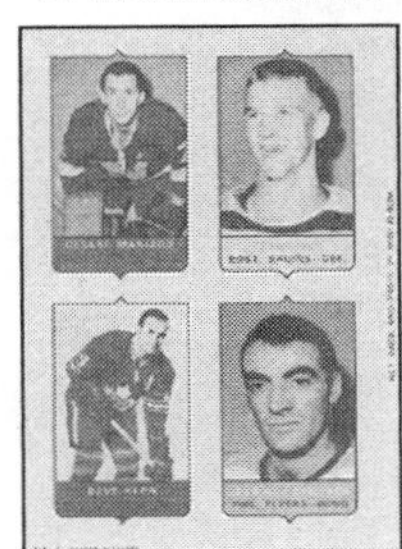

These standard size cards have four stickers each measuring 1" x 1 1/2".

Series 2 Insert Set (18 cards): 425.00 850.00

	Player	EX	NRMT
☐	Bob Baun, Det./ Ken Schinkel, Pgh.; Tim Horton, Tor./ Bernie Parent (G), Pha.	35.00	70.00
☐	Les Binkley (G), Pgh./ Ken Hodge, Bos./ Reggie Fleming, Pha./ Jacques Laperrière, Mtl.	18.00	35.00
☐	Yvan Cournoyer, Mtl./ Jim Neilson, NYR./ Gary Sabourin, Stl./ John Miszuk, Min.	20.00	40.00
☐	Bruce Gamble (G), Tor./ Carol Vadnais, Oak./ Frank Mahovlich, Det./ Larry Hillman, Pha.	25.00	45.00
☐	Ed Giacomin (G), NYR./ Jean Béliveau, Mtl./ Eddie Joyal, L.A./ Léo Boivin, Min.	40.00	80.00
☐	Phil Goyette, Stl./ Doug Jarrett, Chi./ Ted Green, Bos./ Bill Hicke, Oak.	18.00	35.00
☐	Ted Hampson, Oak./ Carl Brewer, Det., Denis DeJordy (G), Chi./ Leon Rochefort, L.A.	18.00	35.00
☐	Charlie Hodge (G), Oak./ Pat Quinn, Tor./ Derek Sanderson, Bos./ Duane Rupp, Pgh.	20.00	40.00
☐	Earl Ingarfield, Oak./ Jim Roberts, Stl./ Gump Worsley (G), Mtl./ Bobby Hull, Chi.	50.00	100.00
☐	Andre Lacroix, Pha./ Bob Wall, L.A./ Serge Savard, Mtl./ Roger Crozier (G), Det.	18.00	35.00
☐	César Maniago (G), Mtl./ Bobby Orr, Bos./ Dave Keon, Tor./ Jean-Guy Gendron, Pha.	100.00	200.00
☐	Keith McCreary, Pgh./ Claude Larose, Min./ Rod Gilbert, NYR./ Gerry Cheevers (G), Bos.	28.00	55.00
☐	Stan Mikita, Chi./ Al Arbour, Stl./ Rod Seiling, NYR./ Ron Schock, Pgh.	25.00	50.00
☐	Doug Mohns, Chi./ Bob Woytowich, Pgh./ Gordie Howe, Det./ Gerry Desjardins (G), L.A.	75.00	150.00
☐	Bob Nevin, NYR./ Jacques Plante (G), Stl./ Mike Walton, Tor./ Ray Cullen, Min.	30.00	60.00
☐	Bob Pulford, Tor./ Henri Richard, Mtl./ Red Berenson, Stl./ Eddie Shack, L.A.	35.00	65.00
☐	Pat Stapleton, Chi./ Danny Grant, Min./ Bert Marshall, Oak./ Jean Ratelle, NYR.	20.00	40.00
☐	Ed Van Impe, Pha./ Dale Rolfe, L.A./ Alex Delvecchio, Det./ Phil Esposito, Bos.	40.00	75.00

MINI-CARD ALBUMS

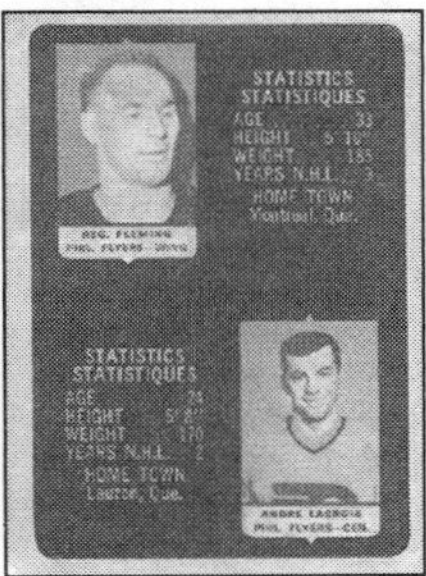

Booklet Size: 2 3/8" x 3 1/2"

Series 2 Insert Set (12 albums): 40.00 75.00

	Player	EX	NRMT
☐	Boston Bruins	4.50	9.00
☐	Chicago Blackhawks	4.50	9.00
☐	Detroit Red Wings	4.50	9.00
☐	Los Angeles Kings	4.50	9.00
☐	Minnesota North Stars	4.50	9.00
☐	Montréal Canadiens	4.50	9.00
☐	New York Rangers	4.50	9.00
☐	Oakland Seals	4.50	9.00
☐	Philadelphia Flyers	4.50	9.00
☐	Pittsburgh Penguins	4.50	9.00
☐	St. Louis Blues	4.50	9.00
☐	Toronto Maple Leafs	4.50	8.50

1969 - 70 WORLD CHAMPIONSHIP MÄSTAR SERIES

Card Size: 2 3/8" x 3 5/16"

Face: Four colour

Back: Blank

Imprint: Mästar Serien

No.	Player	EX	NRMT
☐ 1	Vladimir Dzurila (G), CSR.	2.50	5.00
☐ 2	Jozef Golonka	.50	1.00
☐ 3	Jiri Holik	.50	1.00
☐ 4	Vaclav Nedomansky, CSR.	1.50	3.00
☐ 5	Vaclav Nedomansky, CSR.	1.50	3.00
☐ 6	Jaroslav Holik	.50	1.00
☐ 7	Jozef Golonka	.50	1.00
☐ 8	Vaclav Nedomansky, CSR.	1.50	3.00
☐ 9	Vladimir Bednar	.50	1.00
☐ 10	Jan Havel	.50	1.00
☐ 11	Jan Hrbaty	.50	1.00
☐ 12	Jan Suchy	.50	1.00
☐ 13	Lasse Oksane	.50	1.00
☐ 14	Urpo Ylonen	.50	1.00
☐ 15	Michael Curran	.50	1.00
☐ 16	Gary Begg	.50	1.00
☐ 17	Carl Lackey, USA.	.50	1.00
☐ 18	Terry O'Malley	.50	1.00
☐ 19	Gary Gamuicci	.50	1.00
☐ 20	Seppo Lindstrom	.50	1.00
☐ 21	U.S.S.R. Nationals	.75	1.50
☐ 22	Victor Pujkov, USSR	.50	1.00
☐ 23	Alexander Ragulin, USSR	.75	1.50
☐ 24	Gerry Pinder	.75	1.50
☐ 25	Fran Huck	.50	1.00
☐ 26	Ken Dryden (G), Cdn.	50.00	100.00
☐ 27	Viktor Zinger, USSR	.50	1.00
☐ 28	Vladimir Petrov, USSR	2.50	5.00
☐ 29	I.Romishevsky/ V. Zinger	.50	1.00
☐ 30	Valeri Kharlamov, USSR	6.00	12.00
☐ 31	Alexander Ragulin, USSR	.75	1.50
☐ 32	Ab DeMarco	.75	1.50
☐ 33	Morris Mott	.50	1.00
☐ 34	Fran Huck	.50	1.00
☐ 35	Vyacheslav Starsinov	.50	1.00
☐ 36	L.G. Nilsson/ R.Bourbonnais	.50	1.00
☐ 37	Stig-Goran Johansson, Swe. (xcx:K.Dryden)	4.00	7.50
☐ 38	Leif Holmqvist, Swe.	.75	1.50
☐ 39	Hakan Nygren, Swe.	.50	1.00
☐ 40	Tord Lundström, Swe.	.50	1.00
☐ 41	Ulf Sterner, Swe.	.50	1.00
☐ 42	Lars-Eik Sjoberg, Swe.	.50	1.00
☐ 43	Kjell-Rune Milton, Swe.	.50	1.00
☐ 44	Leif Holmqvist, Swe.	.50	1.00
☐ 45	Stefan Karlsson, Swe.	.50	1.00
☐ 46	Lennart Svedberg, Swe.	.50	1.00
☐ 47	Tord Lundström, Swe.	.50	1.00
☐ 48	Ulf Sterner, Swe.	.50	1.00
☐ 49	Tord Lundström, Swe.	.50	1.00
☐ 50	Lennart Svedberg, Swe.	.50	1.00

1969 - 70 SOVIET STARS POSTCARDS

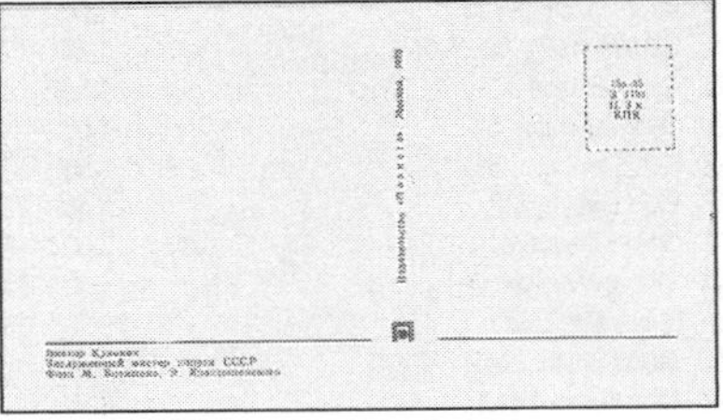

Card Size: 3 1/2" x 6"

Face: Four colour

Back: Russian text

Imprint:

	Player	EX	NRMT
Complete Set (26 cards and folder):		**75.00**	**150.00**
☐	Victor Zinger (G)	3.50	7.00
☐	Vitaly Davydov	2.50	5.00
☐	Vladimir Lutchenko	2.50	5.00
☐	Victor Kuzkin	2.50	5.00
☐	Alexander Ragulin	7.50	15.00
☐	Igor Romishevsky	2.50	5.00
☐	Boris Mikhailov	10.00	20.00
☐	Vyacheslav Starshinov	2.50	5.00
☐	Evgeny Zimin	2.50	5.00
☐	Alexander Maltsev	5.00	10.00
☐	Anatoli Firsov	2.50	5.00
☐	Evgeny Paladiev	2.50	5.00
☐	Alexander Yakushev	10.00	20.00
☐	Vladimir Petrov	5.00	10.00
☐	Valery Kharlamov	13.00	25.00
☐	Vladimir Vikulov	2.50	5.00
☐	Vladimir Yursinov	2.50	5.00
☐	Victor Pushkov	2.50	5.00
☐	A. Czepnishev	2.50	5.00
☐	A. Tapasov	2.50	5.00
☐	U.S.S.R. vs. Sweden	4.00	8.00
☐	U.S.S.R. vs. Sweden	4.00	8.00
☐	U.S.S.R. vs. Sweden	4.00	8.00
☐	U.S.S.R. vs. Finland, Sweden	4.00	8.00
☐	U.S.S.R. vs. Canada, Sweden	7.50	15.00
☐	Team Photo	7.50	15.00

1969 - 70 TOPPS

Card Size: 2 1/2" x 3 1/2"
Face: Four colour, white border, Team logo, Position
Back: Yellow and blue on card stock, Number, Resume, Hockey trivia / stamps
Imprint: T.C.G.

No.	Player	EX	NRMT
Complete Set (132 cards):		**300.00**	**575.00**
Common Player:		**1.50**	**3.00**
☐ 1	Gump Worsley (G), Mtl.	7.50	22.00
☐ 2	Ted Harris, Mtl.	1.50	3.00
☐ 3	Jacques Laperrière, Mtl.	2.50	5.00
☐ **4**	**Serge Savard, Mtl., RC**	**13.00**	**25.00**
☐ 5	J.C. Tremblay, Mtl.	1.50	3.00
☐ 6	Yvan Cournoyer, Mtl.	5.00	10.00
☐ 7	John Ferguson, Mtl.	1.50	3.00
☐ 8	Jacques Lemaire, Mtl.	5.00	10.00
☐ 9	Bobby Rousseau, Mtl.	1.50	3.00
☐ 10	Jean Béliveau, Mtl.	9.00	18.00
☐ 11	Henri Richard, Mtl.	4.50	8.50
☐ 12	Glenn Hall (G), Stl.	5.50	11.00
☐ 13	Bob Plager, Stl.	1.50	3.00
☐ 14	Jim Roberts, Stl.	1.50	3.00
☐ 15	Jean-Guy Talbot, Stl.	1.50	3.00
☐ 16	Andre Boudrias, Stl.	1.50	3.00
☐ 17	Camille Henry, Stl., LC	1.50	3.00
☐ 18	Ab McDonald, Stl.	1.50	3.00
☐ 19	Gary Sabourin, Stl.	1.50	3.00
☐ 20	Red Berenson, Stl.	1.50	3.00
☐ 21	Phil Goyette, Stl.	1.50	3.00
☐ 22	Gerry Cheevers (G), Bos.	7.00	14.00
☐ 23	Ted Green, Bos.	1.50	3.00
☐ 24	Bobby Orr, Bos.	75.00	150.00
☐ 25	Dallas Smith, Bos.	1.50	3.00
☐ 26	John Bucyk, Bos.	3.50	7.00
☐ 27	Ken Hodge, Bos.	1.50	3.00
☐ 28	John McKenzie, Bos.	1.50	3.00
☐ 29	Ed Westfall, Bos.	1.50	3.00
☐ 30	Phil Esposito, Bos.	14.00	28.00
☐ 31	Derek Sanderson, Bos.	7.00	14.00
☐ 32	Fred Stanfield, Bos.	1.50	3.00
☐ 33	Ed Giacomin (G), NYR.	7.00	14.00
☐ 34	Arnie Brown, NYR.	1.50	3.00
☐ 35	Jim Neilson, NYR.	1.50	3.00
☐ 36	Rod Seiling, NYR.	1.50	3.00
☐ 37	Rod Gilbert, NYR.	3.50	7.00
☐ 38	Vic Hadfield, NYR.	1.50	3.00
☐ 39	Don Marshall, NYR.	1.50	3.00
☐ 40	Bob Nevin, NYR.	1.50	3.00
☐ 41	Ron Stewart, NYR.	1.50	3.00
☐ 42	Jean Ratelle, NYR.	3.50	7.00
☐ **43**	**Walt Tkaczuk, NYR., RC**	**3.25**	**6.50**
☐ 44	Bruce Gamble (G), Tor.	2.50	5.00
☐ 45	Tim Horton, Tor.	6.50	13.00
☐ 46	Ron Ellis, Tor.	1.50	3.00
☐ 47	Paul Henderson, Tor.	2.50	5.00
☐ 48	Brit Selby, Tor.	1.50	3.00
☐ 49	Floyd Smith, Tor.	1.50	3.00
☐ 50	Mike Walton, Tor.	1.50	3.00
☐ 51	Dave Keon, Tor.	3.50	7.00
☐ 52	Murray Oliver, Tor.	1.00	3.00
☐ 53	Bob Pulford, Tor.	2.50	5.00
☐ 54	Norm Ullman, Tor.	3.50	7.00
☐ 55	Roger Crozier (G), Det.	2.50	5.00
☐ 56	Roy Edwards (G), Det.	2.50	5.00
☐ 57	Bob Baun, Det.	1.50	3.00
☐ 58	Gary Bergman, Det.	1.50	3.00
☐ 59	Carl Brewer, Det.	1.50	3.00
☐ 60	Wayne Connelly, Det.	1.50	3.00
☐ 61	Gordie Howe, Det.	35.00	65.00
☐ 62	Frank Mahovlich, Det.	6.00	12.00
☐ 63	Bruce MacGregor, Det.	1.50	3.00
☐ 64	Alex Delvecchio, Det.	3.50	7.00
☐ 65	Pete Stemkowski, Det.	1.50	3.00
☐ 66	Denis DeJordy (G), Chi.	2.50	5.00
☐ 67	Doug Jarrett, Chi.	1.50	3.00
☐ 68	Gilles Marotte, Chi.	1.50	3.00
☐ 69	Pat Stapleton, Chi.	1.50	3.00
☐ 70	Bobby Hull, Chi.	25.00	50.00
☐ 71	Dennis Hull, Chi.	1.50	3.00
☐ 72	Doug Mohns, Chi.	1.50	3.00
☐ 73	Jim Pappin, Chi.	1.50	3.00
☐ 74	Kenny Wharram, Chi., LC	1.50	3.00
☐ 75	Pit Martin, Chi.	1.50	3.00
☐ 76	Stan Mikita, Chi.	9.00	18.00
☐ 77	Charlie Hodge (G), Oak.	2.50	5.00
☐ 78	Gary Smith (G), Oak.	2.50	5.00
☐ 79	Harry Howell, Oak.	2.50	5.00
☐ 80	Bert Marshall, Oak.	1.50	3.00
☐ 81	Doug Roberts, Oak.	1.50	3.00
☐ 82	Carol Vadnais, Oak.	1.50	3.00
☐ 83	Gerry Ehman, Oak.	1.50	3.00
☐ 84	Bill Hicke, Oak.	1.50	3.00
☐ 85	Gary Jarrett, Oak.	1.50	3.00
☐ 86	Ted Hampson, Oak.	1.50	3.00
☐ 87	Earl Ingarfield, Oak.	1.50	3.00
☐ **88**	**Doug Favell (G), Pha., RC**	**4.50**	**8.50**
☐ 89	Bernie Parent (G), Pha.	20.00	35.00
☐ 90	Larry Hillman, Pha.	1.50	3.00
☐ 91	Wayne Hillman, Pha.	1.50	3.00
☐ 92	Ed Van Impe, Pha.	1.50	3.00
☐ 93	Joe Watson, Pha.	1.50	3.00
☐ 94	Gary Dornhoefer, Pha.	1.50	3.00
☐ 95	Reggie Fleming, Pha.	1.50	3.00
☐ 96	Jean Guy Gendron, Pha.	1.50	3.00
☐ 97	Jim Johnson, Pha.	1.50	3.00
☐ 98	André Lacroix, Pha.	1.50	3.00
☐ **99**	**Gerry Desjardins (G), L.A., RC**	**4.00**	**8.00**
☐ 100	Dale Rolfe, L.A.	1.50	3.00
☐ 101	Bill White, L.A.	1.50	3.00
☐ 102	Bill Flett, L.A.	1.50	3.00
☐ 103	Ted Irvine, L.A.	1.50	3.00
☐ 104	Ross Lonsberry, L.A.	1.50	3.00
☐ 105	Leon Rochefort, L.A.	1.50	3.00
☐ 106	Eddie Shack, L.A.	4.00	7.50
☐ **107**	**Dennis Hextall, L.A., RC**	**1.50**	**3.00**
☐ 108	Eddie Joyal, L.A.	1.50	3.00
☐ 109	Gord Labossiere, L.A.	1.50	3.00
☐ 110	Les Binkley (G), Pgh.	2.50	5.00
☐ **111**	**Tracy Pratt, Pgh., RC**	**1.50**	**3.00**
☐ 112	Bryan Watson, Pgh.	1.50	3.00
☐ 113	Bob Woytowich, Pgh.	1.50	3.00
☐ 114	Keith McCreary, Pgh.	1.50	3.00
☐ 115	Dean Prentice, Pgh.	1.50	3.00
☐ 116	Glen Sather, Pgh.	2.50	5.00
☐ 117	Ken Schinkel, Pgh.	1.50	3.00
☐ 118	Wally Boyer, Pgh.	1.50	3.00
☐ 119	Val Fonteyne, Pgh.	1.50	3.00
☐ 120	Ron Schock, Pgh.	1.50	3.00
☐ 121	Césare Maniago (G), Min.	2.50	5.00
☐ 122	Leo Boivin, Min.	2.50	5.00
☐ 123	Bob McCord, Min.	1.50	3.00
☐ 124	John Miszuk, Min.	1.50	3.00
☐ 125	Danny Grant, Min.	1.50	3.00
☐ 126	Claude Larose, Min.	1.50	3.00
☐ 127	Jean Paul Parise, Min.	1.50	3.00
☐ 128	Tom Williams, Min.	1.50	3.00
☐ 129	Charlie Burns, Min.	1.50	3.00
☐ 130	Ray Cullen, Min.	1.50	3.00
☐ **131**	**Danny O'Shea, Min., RC**	**1.50**	**3.00**
☐ 132	Checklist (1 - 132)	45.00	90.00

1970 - 71 COLGATE STAMPS

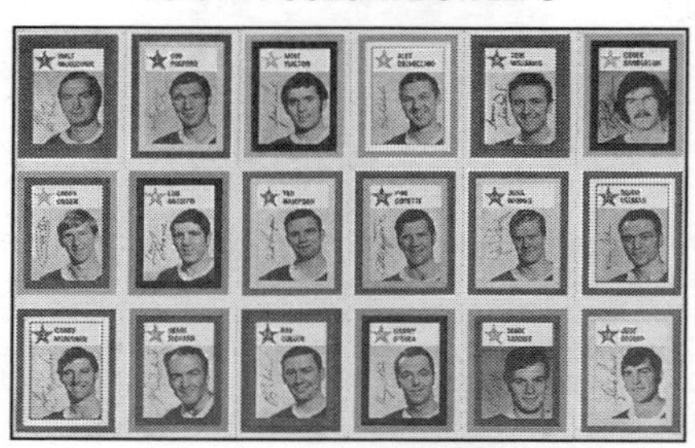

Sheets of 31 stamps were offered as premiums with various size tubes of toothpaste.

Stamp Size: 1" x 1 1/4"
Face: Four colour, whtie border; Name, Number, Facsimile autograph
Back: Blank
Imprint: None

No.	Player	EX	NRMT
Complete Set (93 stamps):		**50.00**	**100.00**
Common Player:		**.50**	**1.00**
☐ 1	Walt McKechnie, Min.	.50	1.00
☐ 2	Bob Pulford, L.A.	1.00	2.00
☐ 3	Mike Walton, Tor.	.50	1.00
☐ 4	Alex Delvecchio, Det.	1.50	3.00
☐ 5	Tom Williams, Min.	.50	1.00
☐ 6	Derek Sanderson, Bos.	1.50	3.00
☐ 7	Garry Unger, Det.	.50	1.00
☐ 8	Lou Angotti, Chi.	.50	1.00
☐ 9	Ted Hampson, Cgy.	.50	1.00
☐ 10	Phil Goyette, Buf.	.50	1.00
☐ 11	Juha Widing, L.A.	.50	1.00
☐ 12	Norm Ullman, Tor.	1.50	3.00
☐ 13	Garry Monahan, Tor.	.50	1.00
☐ 14	Henri Richard, Mtl.	2.00	4.00
☐ 15	Ray Cullen, Van.	.50	1.00
☐ 16	Danny O'Shea, Chi.	.50	1.00
☐ 17	Marc Tardif, Mtl.	.50	1.00
☐ 18	Jude Drouin, Min.	.50	1.00
☐ 19	Charlie Burns, Min.	.50	1.00
☐ 20	Gerry Meehan, Buf.	.50	1.00
☐ 21	Ralph Backstrom, Mtl.	.50	1.00
☐ 22	Frank St. Marseille, Stl.	.50	1.00
☐ 23	Orland Kurtenbach, Van.	.50	1.00
☐ 24	Red Berenson, Stl.	.50	1.00
☐ 25	Jean Ratelle, NYI.	1.75	3.50
☐ 26	Syl Apps, Pgh.	.50	1.00
☐ 27	Don Marshall, Buf.	.50	1.00
☐ 28	Gilbert Perreault, Buf.	5.00	10.00
☐ 29	André Lacroix, Pha.	.50	1.00
☐ 30	Jacques Lemaire, Mtl.	1.75	3.50
☐ 31	Pit Martin, Chi.	.50	1.00
☐ 32	Dennis Hull, Chi.	.50	1.00
☐ 33	Dave Balon, NYI.	.50	1.00
☐ 34	Keith McCreary, Pgh.	.50	1.00
☐ 35	Bobby Rousseau, Min.	.50	1.00
☐ 36	Danny Grant, Min.	.50	1.00
☐ 37	Brit Selby, Stl.	.50	1.00
☐ 38	Bob Nevin, NYI.	.50	1.00
☐ 39	Rosaire Paiement, Van.	.50	1.00
☐ 40	Gary Dornhoefer, Pha.	.50	1.00
☐ 41	Eddie Shack, L.A.	1.00	2.00

	No.	Player	EX	NRMT
☐	42	Ron Schock, Pgh.	.50	1.00
☐	43	Jim Pappin, Chi.	.50	1.00
☐	44	Mickey Redmond, Mtl.	1.00	2.00
☐	45	Vic Hadfield, NYI.	.50	1.00
☐	46	John Bucyk, Bos.	1.50	3.00
☐	47	Gordie Howe, Det.	15.00	30.00
☐	48	Ron C. Anderson, Buf.	.50	1.00
☐	49	Gary Jarrett, Cal.	.50	1.00
☐	50	Jean Pronovost, Pgh.	.50	1.00
☐	51	Simon Nolet, Pha.	.50	1.00
☐	52	Bill Goldsworthy, Min.	.50	1.00
☐	53	Rod Gilbert, NYI.	1.75	3.50
☐	54	Ron Ellis, Tor.	.50	1.00
☐	55	Mike Byers, L.A.	.50	1.00
☐	56	Norm Ferguson, Cal.	.50	1.00
☐	57	Gary Sabourin, Stl.	.50	1.00
☐	58	Tim Ecclestone, Stl.	.50	1.00
☐	59	John McKenzie, Bos.	.50	1.00
☐	60	Yvan Cournoyer, Mtl.	1.75	3.50
☐	61	Ken Schinkel, Pgh.	.50	1.00
☐	62	Ken Hodge., Bos.	.50	1.00
☐	63	Césare Maniago (G), Min.	.75	1.50
☐	64	J.C. Tremblay, Mtl.	.75	1.50
☐	65	Gilles Marotte, L.A.	.50	1.00
☐	66	Bob Baun, Tor.	.50	1.00
☐	67	Gerry Desjardins (G), Chi.	.75	1.50
☐	68	Charlie Hodge (G), Van.	.75	1.50
☐	69	Matt Ravlich, L.A.	.50	1.00
☐	70	Ed Giacomin (G), NYI.	2.00	4.00
☐	71	Gerry Cheevers (G), Bos.	2.00	4.00
☐	72	Pat Quinn, Van.	1.00	2.00
☐	73	Gary Bergman, Det.	.50	1.00
☐	74	Serge Savard, Mtl.	1.00	2.00
☐	75	Les Binkley (G), Pgh.	.75	1.50
☐	76	Arnie Brown, NYI.	.50	1.00
☐	77	Pat Stapleton, Chi.	.50	1.00
☐	78	Ed Van Impe, Pha.	.50	1.00
☐	79	Jim Dorey, Tor.	.50	1.00
☐	80	Dave Dryden (G), Buf.	.75	1.50
☐	81	Dale Tallon, Van.	.50	1.00
☐	82	Bruce Gamble (G), Tor.	.75	1.50
☐	83	Roger Crozier (G), Buf.	.75	1.50
☐	84	Denis DeJordy (G), L.A.	.75	1.50
☐	85	Rogatien Vachon (G), Mtl.	1.00	2.00
☐	86	Carol Vadnais, Cal.	.50	1.00
☐	87	Bobby Orr, Bos.	20.00	40.00
☐	88	Noel Picard, Stl.	.50	1.00
☐	89	Gilles Villemure (G), NYI.	.75	1.50
☐	90	Gary Smith (G), Cal.	.75	1.50
☐	91	Doug Favell (G), Pha.	.75	1.50
☐	92	Ernie Wakely (G), Stl.	.75	1.50
☐	93	Bernie Parent (G), Pha.	2.50	5.00

1970 - 71 DAD'S COOKIES

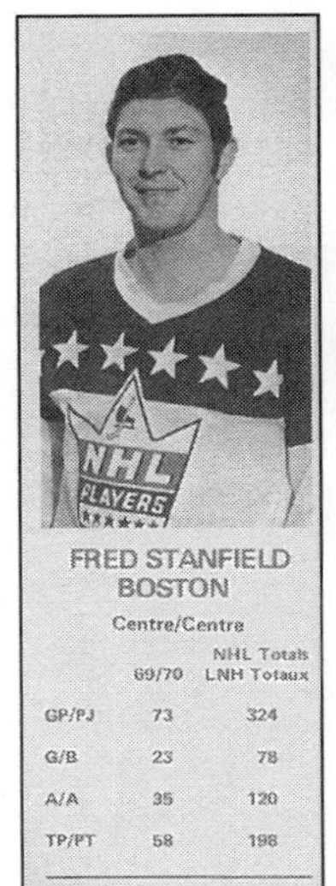

FRED STANFIELD
BOSTON
Centre/Centre
NHL Totals
69/70 LNH Totaux
GP/PJ 73 324
G/B 23 78
A/A 35 120
TP/PT 58 198

N.H.L. Players Association trading cards available in specially marked packages of Dad's cookies and in "Hat-Trick", a milk chocolate cookie bar. Collect all 144 trading cards.

Cartes à échanger de l'Association des joueurs de la LNH dans les emballages spécialement marqués des biscuits Dad's et dans ceux de "Hat-Trick" LNH, barre-biscuit au chocolat au lait. Collectionnez tout les 144 cartes.

SPECIAL OFFER
OFFRE SPECIALE

Get your official N.H.L. Players Association decal. Send 6 "Hat-Trick" wrappers and 10¢ with your name and address to Hat Trick, P.O. Box 216, Scarborough, Ont. (Please Print). Allow 2 weeks for delivery. Offer expires September 30, 1971.

Demandez votre décalcomanie officielle de l'Association des joueurs de la LNH. Envoyez 6 emballages de "Hat-Trick" et 10¢ et vos nom et adresse à l'adresse suivante : Hat Trick, P.O. Box 216, Scarborough, Ont. (écrire en lettres moulées). Compter un délai de livraison d'au moins 2 semaines. Cette offre prend fin le 30 septembre 1971.

©1969 N.H.L. Players Association

Card Size: 1 7/8" x 5 3/8"
Face: Four colour; Name, Team, Resume
Back: Black on card stock; Promotional offer, Bilingual
Imprint: 1969 N.H.L. PLAYERS ASSOCIATION

		EX	NRMT
Complete Set (144 cards):		95.00	185.00
Common Player:		.50	1.00
	Player	**EX**	**NRMT**
BOSTON BRUINS			
☐	Don Awrey	.50	1.00
☐	John Bucyk	1.75	3.50
☐	Gerry Cheevers (G)	2.75	5.50
☐	Phil Esposito	4.00	8.00
☐	Ted Green	.50	1.00
☐	Ken Hodge	.50	1.00
☐	Eddie Johnston	.75	1.50
☐	John McKenzie	.50	1.00
☐	Bobby Orr	25.00	45.00
☐	Derek Sanderson	1.75	3.50
☐	Fred Stanfield	.50	1.00
BUFFALO SABRES			
☐	Roger Crozier (G)	.75	1.50
☐	Dick Duff	.50	1.00
☐	Reggie Fleming	.50	1.00
☐	Phil Goyette	.50	1.00
☐	Al Hamilton	.50	1.00
☐	Skip Krake	.50	1.00
☐	Don Marshall	.50	1.00
☐	Mike McMahon	.50	1.00
☐	Gilbert Perreault	5.00	10.00
☐	Tracy Pratt	.50	1.00
☐	Eddie Shack	1.75	3.50
☐	Floyd Smith	.50	1.00
CALIFORNIA GOLDEN SEALS			
☐	Gerry Ehman	.50	1.00
☐	Norm Ferguson	.50	1.00
☐	Ted Hampson	.50	1.00
☐	Bill Hicke	.50	1.00
☐	Harry Howell	1.25	2.50
☐	Earl Ingarfield.	.50	1.00
☐	Gary Jarrett	.50	1.00
☐	Bert Marshall	.50	1.00
☐	Wayne Muloin	.50	1.00
☐	Carol Vadnais	.50	1.00
CHICAGO BLACKHAWKS			
☐	Lou Angotti	.50	1.00
☐	Tony Esposito (G)	4.50	8.50
☐	Bobby Hull	11.00	22.00
☐	Dennis Hull	.50	1.00
☐	Doug Jarrett	.50	1.00
☐	Keith Magnuson	.50	1.00
☐	Chico Maki	.50	1.00
☐	Pit Martin	.50	1.00
☐	Stan Mikita	3.25	6.50
☐	Doug Mohns	.50	1.00
☐	Pat Stapleton	.50	1.00
DETROIT RED WINGS			
☐	Gary Bergman	.50	1.00
☐	Wayne Connelly	.50	1.00
☐	Alex Delvecchio	1.75	3.50
☐	Roy Edwards (G)	.75	1.50
☐	Gordie Howe	18.00	35.00
☐	Bruce MacGregor	.50	1.00
☐	Frank Mahovlich	4.00	7.50
☐	Dale Rolfe	.50	1.00
☐	Garry Unger	.50	1.00
☐	Tom Webster	.50	1.00
LOS ANGELES KINGS			
☐	Larry Cahan	.50	1.00
☐	Denis DeJordy (G)	.75	1.50
☐	Bill Flett	.50	1.00
☐	Gilles Marotte	.50	1.00
☐	Larry Mickey	.50	1.00
☐	Bob Pulford	1.50	3.00
☐	Matt Ravlich	.50	1.00
☐	Juha Widing	.50	1.00
MINNESOTA NORTH STARS			
☐	Charlie Burns	.50	1.00
☐	Bill Goldsworthy	.50	1.00
☐	Danny Grant	.50	1.00
☐	Ted Harris	.50	1.00
☐	Murray Oliver	.50	1.00
☐	Danny O'Shea	.50	1.00
☐	Jean Paul Parise	.50	1.00
☐	Bobby Rousseau	.50	1.00
☐	Tom Williams	.50	1.00
☐	Gump Worsley (G)	3.25	6.50
MONTRÉAL CANADIENS			
☐	Jean Béliveau	5.00	10.00
☐	Yvan Cournoyer	2.25	4.50
☐	John Ferguson	.50	1.00
☐	Terry Harper	.50	1.00
☐	Jacques Laperrière	1.25	2.50
☐	Jacques Lemaire	2.50	5.00
☐	Mickey Redmond	1.25	2.25
☐	Henri Richard	3.00	6.00
☐	Serge Savard	1.50	3.00
☐	J.C. Tremblay	.50	1.00
☐	Rogatien Vachon (G)	1.25	2.50
NEW YORK RANGERS			
☐	Arnie Brown	.50	1.00
☐	Ed Giacomin (G)	2.75	5.50
☐	Rod Gilbert	1.75	3.50
☐	Vic Hadfield	.50	1.00
☐	Jim Neilson	.50	1.00
☐	Bob Nevin	.50	1.00
☐	Brad Park	3.00	6.00
☐	Jean Ratelle	1.75	3.50
☐	Rod Seiling	.50	1.00
☐	Walt Tkaczuk	.50	1.00
PHILADELPHIA FLYERS			
☐	Bobby Clarke	5.50	11.00
☐	Gary Dornhoefer	.50	1.00
☐	Doug Favell (G)	.75	1.50
☐	Jean-Guy Gendron	.50	1.00
☐	Larry Hillman	.50	1.00
☐	Wayne Hillman	.50	1.00
☐	André Lacroix	.75	1.50
☐	Bernie Parent (G)	4.00	7.50
☐	Ed Van Impe	.50	1.00
☐	Joe Watson	.50	1.00
PITTSBURGH PENGUINS			
☐	Les Binkley (G)	.75	1.50
☐	Wally Boyer	.50	1.00
☐	Bryan Hextall	.50	1.00
☐	Keith McCreary	.50	1.00
☐	Dean Prentice	.50	1.00
☐	Jean Pronovost	.50	1.00
☐	Glen Sather	1.75	3.25
☐	Ken Schinkel	.50	1.00
☐	Bryan Watson	.50	1.00
☐	Bob Woytowich	.50	1.00
ST. LOUIS BLUES			
☐	Red Berenson	.50	1.00
☐	Tim Ecclestone	.50	1.00
☐	Ab McDonald	.50	1.00
☐	Noel Picard	.50	1.00
☐	Barclay Plager	.50	1.00
☐	Jim Roberts	.50	1.00
☐	Gary Sabourin	.50	1.00
☐	Brit Selby	.50	1.00
☐	Frank St. Marseille	.50	1.00
☐	Bob Wall	.50	1.00
TORONTO MAPLE LEAFS			
☐	Bob Baun	.50	1.00
☐	Ron Ellis	.50	1.00
☐	Bruce Gamble (G)	.75	1.50
☐	Paul Henderson	1.00	2.00
☐	Dave Keon	2.25	4.50
☐	Rick Ley	.50	1.00
☐	Jim McKenny	.50	1.00
☐	Mike Pelyk	.50	1.00
☐	Jacques Plante (G)	6.00	12.00
☐	Norm Ullman	2.00	4.00
☐	Mike Walton	.50	1.00
VANCOUVER CANUCKS			
☐	André Boudrias	.50	1.00
☐	Ray Cullen	.50	1.00
☐	Bob Dillabough	.50	1.00
☐	Gary Doak	.50	1.00
☐	Charlie Hodge (G)	.75	1.50
☐	Orland Kurtenbach	.50	1.00
☐	Rosaire Paiement	.50	1.00
☐	Pat Quinn	.50	1.00
☐	Dale Tallon	.50	1.00
☐	Jim Wiste	.50	1.00

1970 - 71 EDDIE SARGENT STICKERS

Sticker Size: 1 7/8" x 2 1/2"
Face: Four colour, white border; Name, Team, Number
Back: Blank
Imprint: 1971 NHLPA PRINTED IN USA

	EX	NRMT
Complete Set (224 stickers):	275.00	550.00
Common Player:	.50	1.00
Album:		100.00

No.	Player	EX	NRMT
☐ 1	Bobby Orr, Bos.	45.00	90.00
☐ 2	Don Awrey, Bos.	.50	1.00
☐ 3	Derek Sanderson, Bos.	2.00	4.00
☐ 4	Ted Green, Bos.	.50	1.00
☐ 5	Ed. Johnston (G), Bos.	.75	1.50
☐ 6	Wayne Carleton, Bos.	.50	1.00
☐ 7	Ed. Westfall, Bos.	.50	1.00
☐ 8	John Bucyk, Bos.	3.00	6.00
☐ 9	John McKenzie, Bos.	.50	1.00
☐ 10	Ken Hodge, Bos.	.50	1.00
☐ 11	Rick Smith, Bos.	.50	1.00
☐ 12	Fred Stanfield, Bos.	.50	1.00
☐ 13	Garnet Bailey, Bos.	.50	1.00
☐ 14	Phil Esposito, Bos.	7.50	15.00
☐ 15	Gerry Cheevers (G), Bos.	4.00	7.50
☐ 16	Dallas Smith, Bos.	.50	1.00
☐ 17	Joe Daley (G), Buf.	.75	1.50
☐ 18	Ron Anderson, Buf.	.50	1.00
☐ 19	Tracy Pratt, Buf.	.50	1.00
☐ 20	Gerry Meehan, Buf.	.50	1.00
☐ 21	Reg Fleming, Buf.	.50	1.00
☐ 22	Allan Hamilton, Buf.	.50	1.00
☐ 23	Gilbert Perreault, Buf.	5.00	10.00
☐ 24	Skip Krake, Buf.	.50	1.00
☐ 25	Kevin O'Shea, Buf.	.50	1.00
☐ 26	Roger Crozier (G), Buf.	.75	1.50
☐ 27	Bill Inglis, Buf.	.50	1.00
☐ 28	Mike McMahon, Buf.	.50	1.00
☐ 29	Cliff Shmautz, Buf.	.50	1.00
☐ 30	Floyd Smith, Buf.	.50	1.00
☐ 31	Randy Wyrozub, Buf.	.50	1.00
☐ 32	Jim Watson, Buf.	.50	1.00
☐ 33	Tony Esposito (G), Chi.	6.00	12.00
☐ 34	Doug Jarrett, Chi.	.50	1.00
☐ 35	Keith Magnuson, Chi.	.50	1.00
☐ 36	Dennis Hull, Chi.	.50	1.00
☐ 37	Cliff Koroll, Chi.	.50	1.00
☐ 38	Eric Nesterenko, Chi.	.50	1.00
☐ 39	Pit Martin, Chi.	.50	1.00
☐ 40	Lou Angotti, Chi.	.50	1.00
☐ 41	Jim Pappin, Chi.	.50	1.00
☐ 42	Gerry Pinder, Chi.	.50	1.00
☐ 43	Bobby Hull, Chi.	13.00	25.00
☐ 44	Pat Stapleton, Chi.	.50	1.00
☐ 45	Gerry Desjardins (G), Chi.	.75	1.50
☐ 46	Chico Maki, Chi.	.50	1.00
☐ 47	Doug Mohns, Chi.	.50	1.00
☐ 48	Stan Mikita, Chi.	4.50	9.00
☐ 49	Gary Bergman, Det.	.50	1.00
☐ 50	Pete Stemkowski, Det.	.50	1.00
☐ 51	Bruce MacGregor, Det.	.50	1.00
☐ 52	Ron Harris, Det.	.50	1.00
☐ 53	Billy Dea, Det.	.50	1.00
☐ 54	Wayne Connelly, Det.	.50	1.00
☐ 55	Dale Rolfe, Det.	.50	1.00
☐ 56	Gordie Howe, Det.	35.00	65.00
☐ 57	Tom Webster, Det.	.50	1.00
☐ 58	Al Karlander, Det.	.50	1.00
☐ 59	Alex Delvecchio, Det.	2.50	5.00
☐ 60	Nick Libett, Det.	.50	1.00
☐ 61	Garry Unger, Det.	.50	1.00
☐ 62	Roy Edwards (G), Det.	.75	1.50
☐ 63	Frank Mahovlich, Det.	5.00	10.00
☐ 64	Bob Baun, Det.	.50	1.00
☐ 65	Dick Duff, L.A.	.50	1.00
☐ 66	Ross Lonsberry, L.A.	.50	1.00
☐ 67	Ed Joyal, L.A.	.50	1.00
☐ 68	Dale Hoganson, L.A.	.50	1.00
☐ 69	Ed Shack, L.A.	2.50	5.00
☐ 70	Réal Lemieux, L.A.	.50	1.00
☐ 71	Matt Ravlich, L.A.	.50	1.00
☐ 72	Bob Pulford, L.A.	2.00	4.00
☐ 73	Denis Dejordy (G), L.A.	.75	1.50
☐ 74	Larry Mickey, L.A.	.50	1.00
☐ 75	Bill Flett, L.A.	.50	1.00
☐ 76	Juha Widing, L.A.	.50	1.00
☐ 77	Jim Peters, L.A.	.50	1.00
☐ 78	Gilles Marotte, L.A.	.50	1.00
☐ 79	Larry Cahan, L.A.	.50	1.00
☐ 80	Howie Hughes, L.A.	.50	1.00
☐ 81	Césare Maniago (G), Min.	.75	1.50
☐ 82	Ted Harris, Min.	.50	1.00
☐ 83	Tom Williams, Min.	.50	1.00
☐ 84	Gump Worsley (G), Min.	4.00	8.00
☐ 85	Tom Reid, Min.	.50	1.00
☐ 86	Murray Oliver, Min.	.50	1.00
☐ 87	Charlie Burns, Min.	.50	1.00
☐ 88	Jude Drouin, Min.	.50	1.00
☐ 89	Walt McKechnie, Min.	.50	1.00
☐ 90	Danny O'Shea, Min.	.50	1.00
☐ 91	Barry Gibbs, Min.	.50	1.00
☐ 92	Danny Grant, Min.	.50	1.00
☐ 93	Bob Barlow, Min.	.50	1.00
☐ 94	Jean Paul Parise, Min.	.50	1.00
☐ 95	Bill Goldsworthy, Min.	.50	1.00
☐ 96	Bob Rousseau, Min.	.50	1.00
☐ 97	Jacques Laperrière, Mtl.	2.00	4.00
☐ 98	Henri Richard, Mtl.	3.25	6.50
☐ 99	J.C. Tremblay, Mtl.	.75	1.50
☐ 100	Rogatien Vachon (G), Mtl.	2.50	5.00
☐ 101	Claude Larose, Mtl.	.50	1.00
☐ 102	Peter Mahovlich, Mtl.	.50	1.00
☐ 103	Jacques Lemaire, Mtl.	3.50	7.00
☐ 104	Bill Collins, Mtl.	.50	1.00
☐ 105	Guy Lapointe, Mtl.	2.00	4.00
☐ 106	Mickey Redmond, Mtl.	1.00	2.00
☐ 107	Larry Pleau, Mtl.	.50	1.00
☐ 108	Jean Béliveau, Mtl.	9.00	18.00
☐ 109	Yvan Cournoyer, Mtl.	3.50	7.00
☐ 110	Serge Savard, Mtl.	2.00	4.00
☐ 111	Terry Harper, Mtl.	.50	1.00
☐ 112	Phil Myre (G), Mtl.	.75	1.50
☐ 113	Syl Apps, NYR.	.50	1.00
☐ 114	Ted Irvine, NYR.	.50	1.00
☐ 115	Ed Giacomin (G), NYR.	3.50	7.00
☐ 116	Arnie Brown, NYR.	.50	1.00
☐ 117	Walt Tkaczuk, NYR.	1.00	2.00
☐ 118	Jean Ratelle, NYR.	2.50	5.00
☐ 119	Dave Balon, NYR.	.50	1.00
☐ 120	Ron Stewart, NYR.	.50	1.00
☐ 121	Jim Neilson, NYR.	.50	1.00
☐ 122	Rod Gilbert, NYR.	2.50	5.00
☐ 123	Bill Fairbairn, NYR.	.50	1.00
☐ 124	Brad Park, NYR.	4.00	8.00
☐ 125	Tim Horton, NYR.	4.00	8.00
☐ 126	Vic Hadfield, NYR.	.50	1.00
☐ 127	Bob Nevin, NYR.	.50	1.00
☐ 128	Rod Seiling, NYR.	.50	1.00
☐ 129	Gary Smith (G), Cal.	.75	1.50
☐ 130	Carol Vadnais, Cal.	.50	1.00
☐ 131	Bert Marshall, Cal.	.50	1.00
☐ 132	Earl Ingarfield, Cal.	.50	1.00
☐ 133	Dennis Hextall, Cal.	.50	1.00
☐ 134	Harry Howell, Cal.	2.00	4.00
☐ 135	Wayne Muloin, Cal.	.50	1.00
☐ 136	Mike Laughton, Cal.	.50	1.00
☐ 137	Ted Hampson, Cal.	.50	1.00
☐ 138	Doug Roberts, Cal.	.50	1.00
☐ 139	Dick Mattiussi, Cal.	.50	1.00
☐ 140	Gary Jarrett, Cal.	.50	1.00
☐ 141	Gary Croteau, Cal.	.50	1.00
☐ 142	Norm Ferguson, Cal.	.50	1.00
☐ 143	Bill Hicke, Cal.	.50	1.00
☐ 144	Gerry Ehman, Cal.	.50	1.00
☐ 145	Ralph MacSweyn, Pha.	.50	1.00
☐ 146	Bernie Parent (G), Pha.	4.00	8.00
☐ 147	Brent Hughes, Pha.	.50	1.00
☐ 148	Bob Clarke, Pha.	6.00	12.00
☐ 149	Gary Dornhoefer, Pha.	.50	1.00
☐ 150	Simon Nolet, Pha.	.50	1.00
☐ 151	Garry Peters, Pha.	.50	1.00
☐ 152	Doug Favell (G), Pha.	.75	1.50
☐ 153	Jim Johnson, Pha.	.50	1.00
☐ 154	André Lacroix, Pha.	.50	1.00
☐ 155	Larry Hale, Pha.	.50	1.00
☐ 156	Joe Watson, Pha.	.50	1.00
☐ 157	Jean-Guy Gendron, Pha.	.50	1.00
☐ 158	Larry Hillman, Pha.	.50	1.00
☐ 159	Ed Van Impe, Pha.	.50	1.00
☐ 160	Wayne Hillman, Pha.	.50	1.00
☐ 161	Al Smith (G), Pgh.	.75	1.50
☐ 162	Jean Pronovost, Pgh.	1.00	2.00
☐ 163	Bob Woytowich, Pgh.	.50	1.00
☐ 164	Bryan Watson, Pgh.	.50	1.00
☐ 165	Dean Prentice, Pgh.	.50	1.00
☐ 166	Duane Rupp, Pgh.	.50	1.00
☐ 167	Glen Sather, Pgh.	1.50	3.00
☐ 168	Keith McCreary, Pgh.	.50	1.00
☐ 169	Jim Morrison, Pgh.	.50	1.00
☐ 170	Ron Schock, Pgh.	.50	1.00
☐ 171	Wally Boyer, Pgh.	.50	1.00
☐ 172	Nick Harbaruk, Pgh.	.50	1.00
☐ 173	Andy Bathgate, Pgh.	2.00	4.00
☐ 174	Ken Schinkel, Pgh.	.50	1.00
☐ 175	Les Binkley (G), Pgh.	.75	1.50
☐ 176	Val Fonteyne, Pgh.	.50	1.00
☐ 177	Red Berenson, Stl.	.50	1.00
☐ 178	Ab McDonald, Stl.	.50	1.00
☐ 179	Jim Roberts, Stl.	.50	1.00
☐ 180	Frank St. Marseille, Stl.	.50	1.00
☐ 181	Ernie Wakely (G), Stl.	.75	1.50
☐ 182	Terry Crisp, Stl.	1.00	2.00
☐ 183	Bob Plager, Stl.	.50	1.00
☐ 184	Barclay Plager, Stl.	.50	1.00
☐ 185	Christian Bordeleau, Stl.	.50	1.00
☐ 186	Gary Sabourin, Stl.	.50	1.00
☐ 187	Bill Plager, Stl.	.50	1.00
☐ 188	Tim Ecclestone, Stl.	.50	1.00
☐ 189	Jean-Guy Talbot, Stl.	.50	1.00
☐ 190	Noel Picard, Stl.	.50	1.00
☐ 191	Bob Wall, Stl.	.50	1.00
☐ 192	Jim Lorentz, Stl.	.50	1.00
☐ 193	Bruce Gamble (G), Tor.	.75	1.50
☐ 194	Jim Harrison, Tor.	.50	1.00
☐ 195	Paul Henderson, Tor.	1.00	2.00
☐ 196	Brian Glennie, Tor.	.50	1.00
☐ 197	Jim Dorey, Tor.	.50	1.00
☐ 198	Rick Ley, Tor.	.50	1.00
☐ 199	Jacques Plante (G), Tor.	10.00	20.00
☐ 200	Ron Ellis, Tor.	1.00	2.00
☐ 201	Jim McKenny, Tor.	.50	1.00
☐ 202	Brit Selby, Tor.	.50	1.00
☐ 203	Mike Pelyk, Tor.	.50	1.00
☐ 204	Norm Ullman, Tor.	3.00	6.00
☐ 205	Bill MacMillan, Tor.	.50	1.00
☐ 206	Mike Walton, Tor.	.50	1.00
☐ 207	Garry Monahan, Tor.	.50	1.00
☐ 208	Dave Keon, Tor.	3.00	6.00
☐ 209	Pat Quinn, Van.	1.00	2.00
☐ 210	Wayne Maki, Van.	.50	1.00
☐ 211	Charlie Hodge (G), Van.	.75	1.50
☐ 212	Orland Kurtenbach, Van.	.50	1.00
☐ 213	Poul Popiel, Van.	.50	1.00
☐ 214	Danny Johnson, Van.	.50	1.00
☐ 215	Dale Tallon, Van.	.50	1.00
☐ 216	Ray Cullen, Van.	.50	1.00
☐ 217	Bob Dillabough, Van.	.50	1.00
☐ 218	Gary Doak, Van.	.50	1.00
☐ 219	André Boudrias, Van.	.50	1.00
☐ 220	Rosaire Paiement, Van.	.50	1.00
☐ 221	Darryl Sly, Van.	.50	1.00
☐ 222	George Gardner (G), Van.	.75	1.50
☐ 223	Jim Wiste, Van.	.50	1.00
☐ 224	Murray Hall, Van.	.50	1.00

1970 - 71 ESSO POWER PLAYERS

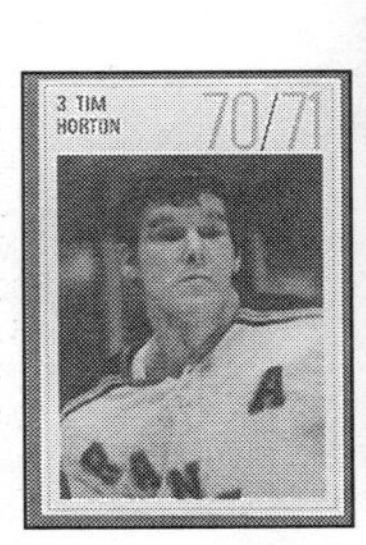

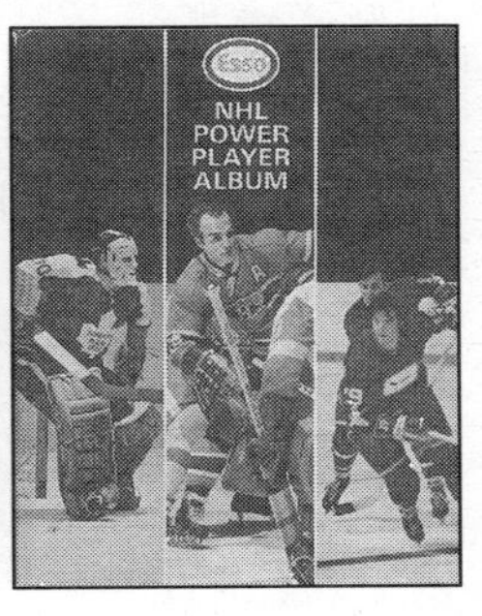

Sticker Size: 1 1/2" x 2 1/8"
Face: Four colour, white border; Player's name and jersey number
Back: Blank
Imprint: None

	EX	NRMT
Complete Set (252 cards):	**70.00**	**135.00**
Common Player:	**.25**	**.50**
Album: Hard Cover	**30.00**	**60.00**
Album: Soft Cover	**18.00**	**35.00**
Vinyl Wallet:		**5.00**

	Player	EX	NRMT
	BOSTON BRUINS		
☐	Don Awrey	.25	.50
☐	Garnet Bailey	.25	.50
☐	John Bucyk	1.00	2.00
☐	Wayne Carleton	.25	.50
☐	Wayne Cashman	.25	.50
☐	Gerry Cheevers (G)	1.25	2.50
☐	Phil Esposito	2.25	4.50
☐	Ted Green	.25	.50
☐	Ken Hodge	.25	.50
☐	Eddie Johnston (G)	.50	1.00
☐	Don Marcotte	.25	.50
☐	John McKenzie	.25	.50
☐	Bobby Orr	9.00	18.00
☐	Derek Sanderson	1.00	1.75
☐	Dallas Smith	.25	.50
☐	Rick Smith	.25	.50
☐	Fred Stanfield	.25	.50
☐	Ed Westfall	.25	.50
	BUFFALO SABRES		
☐	Paul Andrea	.25	.50
☐	Ron C. Anderson	.25	.50
☐	Steve Atkinson	.25	.50
☐	Doug Barrie	.25	.50
☐	Roger Crozier (G)	.50	1.00
☐	Reggie Fleming	.25	.50
☐	Phil Goyette	.25	.50
☐	Al Hamilton	.25	.50
☐	Larry Keenan	.25	.50
☐	Skip Krake	.25	.50
☐	Don Marshall	.25	.50
☐	Gerry Meehan	.25	.50
☐	Gilbert Perreault	1.75	3.50
☐	Tracy Pratt	.25	.50
☐	Cliff Schmautz	.25	.50
☐	Eddie Shack	1.00	1.75
☐	Floyd Smith	.25	.50
☐	Jimmy Watson	.25	.50
	CALIFORNIA GOLDEN SEALS		
☐	Gary Croteau	.25	.50
☐	Gerry Ehman	.25	.50
☐	Tony Featherstone	.25	.50
☐	Ted Hampson	.25	.50
☐	Joe Hardy	.25	.50
☐	Dennis Hextall	.25	.50
☐	Bill Hicke	.25	.50
☐	Ernie Hicke	.25	.50
☐	Harry Howell	.75	1.50
☐	Earl Ingarfield	.25	.50
☐	Gary Jarrett	.25	.50
☐	Dick Mattiussi	.25	.50
☐	Wayne Muloin	.25	.50
☐	Doug Roberts	.25	.50
☐	Gary Smith (G)	.50	1.00
☐	Bob Sneddon (G)	.50	1.00
☐	Ron Stackhouse	.25	.50
☐	Carol Vadnais	.25	.50
	CHICAGO BLACKHAWKS		
☐	Lou Angotti	.25	.50
☐	Bryan Campbell	.25	.50
☐	Gerry Desjardins (G)	.250	1.00
☐	Tony Esposito (G)	2.25	4.50
☐	Bobby Hull	5.00	10.00
☐	Dennis Hull	.25	.50
☐	Doug Jarrett	.25	.50
☐	Cliff Koroll	.25	.50
☐	Keith Magnuson, Err. (Magnusson)	.25	.50
☐	Chico Maki	.25	.50
☐	Pit Martin	.25	.50
☐	Stan Mikita	1.50	3.00
☐	Doug Mohns	.25	.50
☐	Eric Nesterenko	.25	.50
☐	Jim Pappin	.25	.50
☐	Gerry Pinder	.25	.50
☐	Pat Stapleton	.25	.50
☐	Bill White	.25	.50
	DETROIT RED WINGS		
☐	Gary Bergman	.25	.50
☐	Larry Brown	.25	.50
☐	Wayne Connelly	.25	.50
☐	Billy Dea	.25	.50
☐	Alex Delvecchio	1.00	2.00
☐	Roy Edwards (G)	.50	1.00
☐	Ron Harris	.25	.50
☐	Gordie Howe	7.50	15.00
☐	Al Karlander	.25	.50
☐	Serge Lajeunesse	.25	.50
☐	Nick Libett	.25	.50
☐	Don Luce	.25	.50
☐	Bruce MacGregor	.25	.50
☐	Frank Mahovlich	1.75	3.50
☐	Dale Rolfe	.25	.50
☐	Jim Rutherford (G)	.50	1.00
☐	Garry Unger	.25	.50
☐	Tom Webster	.25	.50
	LOS ANGELES KINGS		
☐	Bob Berry	.25	.50
☐	Mike Byers	.25	.50
☐	Larry Cahan	.25	.50
☐	Paul Curtis	.25	.50
☐	Denis DeJordy (G)	.50	1.00
☐	Bill Flett	.25	.50
☐	Dale Hoganson	.25	.50
☐	Eddie Joyal	.25	.50
☐	Gord Labossiere	.25	.50
☐	Ross Lonsberry	.25	.50
☐	Gilles Marotte	.25	.50
☐	Larry Mickey	.25	.50
☐	Jack Norris (G)	.50	1.00
☐	Noel Price	.25	.50
☐	Bob Pulford	.75	1.50
☐	Matt Ravlich	.25	.50
☐	Doug Robinson	.25	.50
☐	Juha Widing	.25	.50
	MINNESOTA NORTH STARS		
☐	Fred Barrett	.25	.50
☐	Charlie Burns	.25	.50
☐	Barry Gibbs	.25	.50
☐	Bill Goldsworthy	.25	.50
☐	Danny Grant	.25	.50
☐	Ted Harris	.25	.50
☐	Fred (Buster) Harvey	.25	.50
☐	Danny Lawson	.25	.50
☐	Césare Maniago (G)	.50	1.00
☐	Walt McKechnie	.25	.50
☐	Lou Nanne	.25	.50
☐	Murray Oliver	.25	.50
☐	Danny O'Shea	.25	.50
☐	Jean Paul Parise	.25	.50
☐	Tom Reid	.25	.50
☐	Bobby Rousseau	.25	.50
☐	Tom Williams	.25	.50
☐	Gump Worsley (G)	1.75	3.25
	MONTRÉAL CANADIENS		
☐	Jean Béliveau	3.50	7.00
☐	Bill Collins	.25	.50
☐	Yvan Cournoyer	1.25	2.25
☐	John Ferguson	.25	.50
☐	Terry Harper	.25	.50
☐	Fran Huck	.25	.50
☐	Guy Lapointe	.75	1.50
☐	Jacques Laperrière	.75	1.50
☐	Claude Larose	.25	.50
☐	Jacques Lemaire	1.25	2.50
☐	Pete Mahovlich	.25	.50
☐	Phil Myre (G)	.50	1.00
☐	Mickey Redmond	.50	1.00
☐	Henri Richard	1.25	2.25
☐	Serge Savard	1.00	1.75
☐	Marc Tardif	.25	.50
☐	J.C. Tremblay	.25	.50
☐	Rogatien Vachon (G)	1.00	2.00
	NEW YORK RANGERS		
☐	Dave Balon	.25	.50
☐	Arnie Brown	.25	.50
☐	Jack Egers	.25	.50
☐	Bill Fairbairn	.25	.50
☐	Ed Giacomin (G)	1.25	2.50
☐	Rod Gilbert	1.00	2.00
☐	Vic Hadfield	.25	.50
☐	Tim Horton	1.75	3.50
☐	Ted Irvine	.25	.50
☐	Jim Neilson	.25	.50
☐	Bob Nevin	.25	.50
☐	Brad Park	1.75	3.50
☐	Jean Ratelle	1.00	2.00
☐	Rod Seiling	.25	.50
☐	Pete Stemkowski	.25	.50
☐	Ron Stewart	.25	.50
☐	Walt Tkaczuk	.25	.50
☐	Gilles Villemure (G)	.50	1.00
	PHILADELPHIA FLYERS		
☐	Barry Ashbee	.25	.50
☐	Serge Bernier	.25	.50
☐	Bobby Clarke	2.00	4.00
☐	Gary Dornhoefer	.25	.50
☐	Doug Favell (G)	.50	1.00
☐	Jean-Guy Gendron	.25	.50
☐	Larry Hale	.25	.50
☐	Earl Heiskala	.25	.50
☐	Larry Hillman	.25	.50
☐	Wayne Hillman	.25	.50
☐	Jim Johnson	.25	.50
☐	Bob Kelly	.25	.50
☐	André Lacroix	.50	1.00
☐	Lew Morrison	.25	.50
☐	Bernie Parent (G)	1.25	2.50
☐	Garry Peters	.25	.50
☐	Ed Van Impe	.25	.50
☐	Joe Watson	.25	.50
	PITTSBURGH PENGUINS		
☐	Andy Bathgate	1.00	1.75
☐	Les Binkley (G)	.50	1.00
☐	Bob Blackburn	.25	.50
☐	Wally Boyer	.25	.50
☐	Nick Harbaruk	.25	.50
☐	Bryan Hextall	.25	.50
☐	Dunc McCallum	.25	.50
☐	Keith McCreary	.25	.50
☐	Jim Morrison	.25	.50
☐	Dean Prentice	.25	.50
☐	Jean Pronovost	.25	.50
☐	Duane Rupp	.25	.50
☐	Glen Sather	.50	1.00
☐	Ken Schinkel	.25	.50
☐	Ron Schock	.25	.50
☐	Al Smith (G)	.50	1.00
☐	Bryan Watson	.25	.50
☐	Bob Woytowich	.25	.50
	ST. LOUIS BLUES		
☐	Red Berenson	.25	.50
☐	Chris Bordeleau	.25	.50
☐	Terry Crisp	.50	1.00
☐	Tim Ecclestone	.25	.50
☐	Glenn Hall (G)	1.75	3.50
☐	Jim Lorentz	.25	.50
☐	Bill E. McCreary	.25	.50
☐	Ab McDonald	.25	.50
☐	George Morrison	.25	.50
☐	Noel Picard	.25	.50
☐	Bob Plager	.25	.50
☐	Barclay Plager	.25	.50
☐	Jim Roberts	.25	.50
☐	Gary Sabourin	.25	.50
☐	Brit Selby	.25	.50

	Player		
☐	Frank St. Marseille	.25	.50
☐	Bob Wall	.25	.50
☐	Ernie Wakely (G)	.50	1.00
TORONTO MAPLE LEAFS			
☐	Bob Baun	.25	.50
☐	Jim Dorey	.25	.50
☐	Ron Ellis	.25	.50
☐	Bruce Gamble (G)	.50	1.00
☐	Brian Glennie	.25	.50
☐	Paul Henderson	1.50	3.00
☐	Jim Harrison	.25	.50
☐	Dave Keon	1.50	1.00
☐	Rick Ley	.25	.50
☐	Billy MacMillan	.25	.50
☐	Jim McKenny	.25	.50
☐	Garry Monahan	.25	.50
☐	Mike Pelyk	.25	.50
☐	Jacques Plante (G)	2.00	4.00
☐	Darryl Sittler	2.00	4.00
☐	Guy Trottier	.25	.50
☐	Norm Ullman	1.00	2.00
☐	Mike Walton	.25	.50
VANCOUVER CANUCKS			
☐	André Boudrias	.25	.50
☐	Mike Corrigan	.25	.50
☐	Ray Cullen	.25	.50
☐	Gary Doak	.25	.50
☐	Murray Hall	.25	.50
☐	Charlie Hodge (G)	.50	1.00
☐	Danny Johnson	.25	.50
☐	Orland Kurtenbach	.25	.50
☐	Len Lunde	.25	.50
☐	Wayne Maki	.25	.50
☐	Rosaire Paiement	.25	.50
☐	Poul Popiel	.25	.50
☐	Pat Quinn	.50	1.00
☐	Marc Reaume	.25	.50
☐	Darryl Sly	.25	.50
☐	Dale Tallon	.25	.50
☐	Barry Wilkins	.25	.50
☐	Dunc Wilson (G)	.50	1.00

1970 - 71 KUVAJULKAISUT

A set of 384 cards plus a collecting album for the 1971 World Championships and the Finnish National and Junior Leagues. We have no pricing information on this set.

Card Size: 1 7/8" x 2 1/2"

Imprint:

No. Player

☐ 1 Vitali Davydov, USSR
☐ 2 Anatoli Firsov, USSR
☐ 3 Valeri Kharlamov, USSR
☐ 4 Alexander Yakushev, USSR
☐ 5 Viktor Konovalenko, USSR
☐ 6 Vladimir Lutchenko, USSR
☐ 7 Aleksandr Maltsev, USSR
☐ 8 Boris Mikhailov, USSR
☐ 9 Jevgeni Mishakov, USSR
☐ 10 Valeri Nikitin, USSR
☐ 11 Vladimir Petrov, USSR
☐ 12 Evgeni Paladiev, USSR
☐ 13 Viktor Polupanov, USSR
☐ 14 Alexandr Ragulin, USSR
☐ 15 Igor Romishevski, USSR
☐ 16 Vladimir Shadrin, USSR
☐ 17 Vyatjeslav Starsinov, USSR
☐ 18 Vladislav Tretiak (G), USSR
☐ 19 Valeri Vasiliev, USSR
☐ 20 Vladimir Vikulov, USSR
☐ 21 Tommy Abrahamsson, Swe.
☐ 22 Gunnar Backman, Swe.
☐ 23 Arne Carlsson, Swe.
☐ 24 Anders Hagstrom, Swe.
☐ 25 Anders Hedberg, Swe.
☐ 26 Leif Holmqvist, Swe.
☐ 27 Nils Johansson, Swe.
☐ 28 StigGoran Johansson, Swe.
☐ 29 Stefan Karlsson, Swe.
☐ 30 Hans Lindberg, Swe.
☐ 31 Tord Lundstrom, Swe.
☐ 32 Kjell-Rune Milton, Swe.
☐ 33 Lars-Goran Nilsson, Swe.
☐ 34 Anders Nordin, Swe.
☐ 35 Roger Olsson, Swe.
☐ 36 Bjorn Palmqvist, Swe.
☐ 37 Lars-Erik Sjoberg, Swe.
☐ 38 Ulf Sterner, Swe.
☐ 39 Lennart Svedberg, Swe.
☐ 40 Hakan Wickberg, Swe.
☐ 41 Vladimir Bednar, CSR.
☐ 42 Josef Cerny, CSR.
☐ 43 Vladimir Dzurilla, CSR.
☐ 44 Richard Farda, CSR.
☐ 45 Julius Haas, CSR.
☐ 46 Ivan Hlinka, CSR.
☐ 47 Jaroslav Holik, CSR.
☐ 48 Jiri Holik, CSR.
☐ 49 Josef Horesovsky, CSR.
☐ 50 Jan Hrbaty, CSR.
☐ 51 Jiri Kochta, CSR.
☐ 52 Miroslav Lacky, CSR.
☐ 53 Oldrich Machac, CSR.
☐ 54 Vladislav Martinec, CSR.
☐ 55 Vaclav Nedomansky, CSR.
☐ 56 Frantisek Pospisil, CSR.
☐ 57 Stanislav Pryl, CSR.
☐ 58 Frantisek Sevcik, CSR.
☐ 59 Jan Suchy, CSR.
☐ 60 Lubomir Ujvary, CSR.
☐ 61 Matti Keinonen, Fin.
☐ 62 VeliPekka Ketola, Fin.
☐ 63 Vaino Kolkka, Fin.
☐ 64 Ilpo Koskela, Fin.
☐ 65 Pekka Leimu, Fin.
☐ 66 Seppo Lindstrom, Fin.
☐ 67 Harri Linnonmaa, Fin.
☐ 68 Pekka Marjamaki, Fin.
☐ 69 Lauri Mononen, Fin.
☐ 70 Matti Murto, Fin.
☐ 71 Lasse Oksanen, Fin.
☐ 72 Lalli Partinen, Fin.
☐ 73 Esa Peltonen, Fin.
☐ 74 Jorma Peltonen, Fin.
☐ 75 Juha Rantasila, Fin.
☐ 76 Heikki Riihiranta, Fin.
☐ 77 Juhani Tamminen, Fin.
☐ 78 Jorma Valtonen, Fin.
☐ 79 Jorma Vehmanen, Fin.
☐ 80 Urpo Ylonen, Fin.
☐ 81 Rolf Bielas, DDR.
☐ 82 Frank Braun, DDR.
☐ 83 Dieter Dewitz, DDR.
☐ 84 Lothar Fuchs, DDR.
☐ 85 Bernd Hiller, DDR.
☐ 86 Klaus Hirche, DDR.
☐ 87 Reinhard Karger, DDR.
☐ 88 Bernd Karrenbauer, DDR.
☐ 89 Hartmut Nickel, DDR.
☐ 90 Rudiger Noack, DDR.
☐ 91 Helmut Novy, DDR.
☐ 92 Rainer Patschinski, DDR.
☐ 93 Dietmar Peters, DDR.
☐ 94 Wolfgang Plotka, DDR.
☐ 95 Peter Prusa, DDR.
☐ 96 Dieter Purschel, DDR.
☐ 97 Wilfried Rohrbach, DDR.
☐ 98 Dieter Rohl, DDR.
☐ 99 Peter Slapke, DDR.
☐ 100 Joachim Ziesche, DDR.
☐ 101 Juhani Bostrom, HIFK
☐ 102 Henrik Granholm, HIFK
☐ 103 Matti Harju, HIFK
☐ 104 Kimmo Heino, HIFK
☐ 105 Esa Isaksson, HIFK
☐ 106 Juhani Jylha, HIFK
☐ 107 Heikki Jarn, HIFK
☐ 108 Mauri Kaukokari, HIFK
☐ 109 Vaino Kolkka, HIFK
☐ 110 Harri Linnonmaa, HIFK
☐ 111 Matti Murto, HIFK
☐ 112 Lalli Partinen, HIFK
☐ 113 Juha Rantasila, HIFK
☐ 114 Heikki Riihiranta, HIFK
☐ 115 Jorma Rikala, HIFK
☐ 116 Jorma Thusberg, HIFK
☐ 117 Matti Vaisanen, HIFK
☐ 118 Sakari Ahlberg, Ilves
☐ 119 Jorma Aro, Ilves
☐ 120 Esko Eriksson, Ilves
☐ 121 Markku Hakanen, Ilves
☐ 122 Matti Hakanen, Ilves
☐ 123 Reijo Hakanen, Ilves
☐ 124 Pentti Hartin, Ilves
☐ 125 Timo Hirsimaki, Ilves
☐ 126 Jorma Kallio, Ilves
☐ 127 Pekka Kuusisto, Ilves
☐ 128 Juhani Lahtinen, Ilves
☐ 129 Timo Lahtinen, Ilves
☐ 130 Pekka Leimu, Ilves
☐ 131 Jukka Mattila, Ilves
☐ 132 Esko Makinen, Ilves
☐ 133 Lasse Oksanen, Ilves
☐ 134 Kari Palooja, Ilves
☐ 135 Jorma Peltonen, Ilves
☐ 136 Ali Saadetdin, Ilves
☐ 137 Timo Saari, Ilves
☐ 138 Heikki Hurme, Turun Toverit
☐ 139 Matti Jakonen, Turun Toverit
☐ 140 Kari Johansson, Turun Toverit
☐ 141 Keijo Jarvinen, Turun Toverit
☐ 142 Reijo Leppanen, Turun Toverit
☐ 143 Seppo Lindstrom, Turun Toverit
☐ 144 Hannu Luojola, Turun Toverit
☐ 145 Hannu Niittoaho, Turun Toverit
☐ 146 Reijo Paksal, Turun Toverit
☐ 147 Seppo Parikka, Turun Toverit
☐ 148 Jarmo Rantanen, Turun Toverit
☐ 149 Martti Salonen, Turun Toverit
☐ 150 Voitto Soini, Turun Toverit
☐ 151 Kari Torkkel, Turun Toverit
☐ 152 Risto Vainio, Turun Toverit
☐ 153 Pentti Vihanto, Turun Toverit
☐ 154 Urpo Ylonen, Turun Toverit
☐ 155 Rauno Heinonen, Turun Palloseura
☐ 156 Lauri Jamsen, Turun Palloseura
☐ 157 Lasse Kiili, Turun Palloseura
☐ 158 Hannu Koivunen, Turun Palloseura
☐ 159 Jarmo Koivunen, Turun Palloseura
☐ 160 Pertti Kuismanen, Turun Palloseura
☐ 161 Pekka Lahtela, Turun Palloseura
☐ 162 Harry Luoto, Turun Palloseura
☐ 163 Jaakko Marttinen, Turun Palloseura
☐ 164 Timo Nummelin, Turun Palloseura
☐ 165 Rauli Ottila, Turun Palloseura
☐ 166 Matti Rautee, Turun Palloseura
☐ 167 Pekka Rautee, Turun Palloseura
☐ 168 Jouni Samuli, Turun Palloseura
☐ 169 Rauli Tammelin, Turun Palloseura
☐ 170 Juhani Tamminen, Turun Palloseura
☐ 171 Kari Varjanne, Turun Palloseura
☐ 172 Pertti Ahokas, Jokerit
☐ 173 Pertti Hiirros, Jokerit
☐ 174 Eero Holopainen, Jokerit
☐ 175 VeliPekka Ketola, Jokerit
☐ 176 Kari Kinnunen, Jokerit
☐ 177 Ilpo Koskela, Jokerit
☐ 178 Osmo Kuusisto, Jokerit
☐ 179 Timo Kyntola, Jokerit
☐ 180 Henry Leppa, Jokerit
☐ 181 Erkki Mononen, Jokerit
☐ 182 Lauri Mononen, Jokerit
☐ 183 Pertti Nurmi, Jokerit
☐ 184 Antti Perttula, Jokerit
☐ 185 Seppo Peraoja, Jokerit
☐ 186 Timo Relas, Jokerit
☐ 187 Alpo Suhonen, Jokerit
☐ 188 Timo Turunen, Jokerit
☐ 189 Tapio Flinck, Assat

☐ 190 Jaakko Honkanen, Assat
☐ 191 Antti Heikkila, Assat
☐ 192 Matti Jansson, Assat
☐ 193 Esa Kari, Assat
☐ 194 Raimo Kilpio, Assat
☐ 195 Tapio Koskinen, Assat
☐ 196 Kaj Matalamaki, Assat
☐ 197 Ilkka Mesikammen, Assat
☐ 198 Pertti Makela, Assat
☐ 199 Jaakko Nurminen, Assat
☐ 200 Pekka Rautakallio, Assat
☐ 201 Tapio Rautalammi, Assat
☐ 202 Markku Riihimaki, Assat
☐ 203 Matti Salmi, Assat
☐ 204 KariPekka Toivonen, Assat
☐ 205 Jorma Valtonen, Assat
☐ 206 Anto Virtanen, Assat
☐ 207 Erkki Vakiparta, Assat
☐ 208 Pertti Ansakorpi, Tappara
☐ 209 Pertti Koivulahti, Tappara
☐ 210 Ilpo Kuisma, Tappara
☐ 211 Harri Lappalainen, Tappara
☐ 212 Pekka Marjamaki, Tappara
☐ 213 Mikko Mynttinen, Tappara
☐ 214 Kari Makinen, Tappara
☐ 215 Pekka Makinen, Tappara
☐ 216 Seppo Makinen, Tappara
☐ 217 Keijo Mannisto, Tappara
☐ 218 Jorma Oksala, Tappara
☐ 219 Matti Peltonen, Tappara
☐ 220 Tuomo Rautiainen, Tappara
☐ 221 Lauri Salomaa, Tappara
☐ 222 Risto Seesvuori, Tappara
☐ 223 Jorma Siitarinen, Tappara
☐ 224 Teemu Sistonen, Tappara
☐ 225 Lasse Aaltonen, Rauman Lukko
☐ 226 Mikko Erholm, Rauman Lukko
☐ 227 Jukka Haapala, Rauman Lukko
☐ 228 Veikko Ihalainen, Rauman Lukko
☐ 229 Matti Keinonen, Rauman Lukko
☐ 230 Tapani Koskimaki, Rauman Lukko
☐ 231 Arto Laine, Rauman Lukko
☐ 232 Hannu Lunden, Rauman Lukko
☐ 233 Pentti Rautalin, Rauman Lukko
☐ 234 Paavo Riekkinen, Rauman Lukko
☐ 235 Kai Rosvall, Rauman Lukko
☐ 236 Matti Saurio, Rauman Lukko
☐ 237 Jukka Savunen, Rauman Lukko
☐ 238 Hannu Siivonen, Rauman Lukko
☐ 239 Helkko Stenvall, Rauman Lukko
☐ 240 Jorma Vehmanen, Rauman Lukko
☐ 241 Hannu Haapalainen, Tampereen
☐ 242 Timo Jarvinen, Tampereen
☐ 243 Heikki Keinonen, Tampereen
☐ 244 Heimo Keinonen, Tampereen
☐ 245 Rauno Lehtio, Tampereen
☐ 246 Tapio Nummela, Tampereen
☐ 247 Seppo Nurmi, Tampereen
☐ 248 Markku Pulli, Tampereen
☐ 249 Esko Rantanen, Tampereen
☐ 250 Juhani Ruohonen, Tampereen
☐ 251 Mikko Raikkonen, Tampereen
☐ 252 Jorma Saarikorpi, Tampereen
☐ 253 Veikko Savolainen, Tampereen
☐ 254 Leo Seppanen, Tampereen
☐ 255 Pertti Sihvonen, Tampereen
☐ 256 Pekka Uitus, Tampereen
☐ 257 Jorma Vilen, Tampereen
☐ 258 Tapio Virhimo, Tampereen
☐ 259 Jaakko Koikkalainen, Sapko
☐ 260 Jorma Muikku, Sapko
☐ 261 Ossi Oksala, Sapko
☐ 262 Pekka Parikka, Sapko
☐ 263 Pentti Pennanen, Sapko
☐ 264 Jussi Piuhola, Sapko
☐ 265 Seppo Repo, Sapko
☐ 266 Erkki Rasanen, Sapko
☐ 267 Juhani Sodervik, Sapko
☐ 268 Heikki Tirkkonen, Sapko
☐ 269 Paavo Tirkkonen, Sapko
☐ 270 Timo Tuomainen, Sapko
☐ 271 Raimo Turkulainen, Sapko
☐ 272 Jyrki Turunen, Sapko
☐ 273 Martti Turunen, Sapko
☐ 274 Timo Viskari, Sapko
☐ 275 Antero Vaatamoinen, Sapko
☐ 276 Juhani Aaltonen, HJK.
☐ 277 Matti Ahvenharju, HJK.
☐ 278 Hannu Auvinen, HJK.
☐ 279 Jorma Borgstrom, HJK.
☐ 280 Seppo Laakkio, HJK.
☐ 281 Jarmo Laukkanen, HJK.
☐ 282 Hannu Lindberg, HJK.
☐ 283 Reijo Myyrylainen, HJK.
☐ 284 Raimo Maattanen, HJK.
☐ 285 Esa Peltonen, HJK.
☐ 286 Keijo Puhakka, HJK.
☐ 287 Antti Ravi, HJK.
☐ 288 Erkki Suni, HJK.
☐ 289 Henrik Wahl, HJK.
☐ 290 Stig Wetzell, HJK.
☐ 291 Olli Viilma, HJK.
☐ 292 Esa Willberg, HJK.
☐ 293 Kauko Fomin, Kiekko 67
☐ 294 Risto Forss, Kiekko 67
☐ 295 Rauno Karlsson, Kiekko 67
☐ 296 Jarmo Kiprusoff, Kiekko 67
☐ 297 Matti Koivunen, Kiekko 67
☐ 298 Timo Kokkonen, Kiekko 67
☐ 299 Timo Lehtonen, Kiekko 67
☐ 300 Kalevi Leppanen, Kiekko 67
☐ 301 Hans Martin, Kiekko 67
☐ 302 Timo Nurminen, Kiekko 67
☐ 303 Jari Rosberg, Kiekko 67
☐ 304 Veijo Saarinen, Kiekko 67
☐ 305 Simo Suoknuuti, Kiekko 67
☐ 306 Veikko Suominen, Kiekko 67
☐ 307 Seppo Wikstrom, Kiekko 67
☐ 308 JuhaPekka Aho, Ilves Jrs.
☐ 309 Seppo Aro, Ilves Jrs.
☐ 310 Kari Jokinen, Ilves Jrs.
☐ 311 Pekka Karhunen, Ilves Jrs.
☐ 312 Pertti Kettunen, Ilves Jrs.
☐ 313 Lauri Kosonen, Ilves Jrs.
☐ 314 Jyrki Kahonen, Ilves Jrs.
☐ 315 Marko Lepaus, Ilves Jrs.
☐ 316 Matti Lisko, Ilves Jrs.
☐ 317 Marko Niemi, Ilves Jrs.
☐ 318 Hannu Pohja, Ilves Jrs.
☐ 319 Jarmo Ronkainen, Ilves Jrs.
☐ 320 Mikko Silvasti, Ilves Jrs.
☐ 321 Jari Suokas, Ilves Jrs.
☐ 322 Kimmo Turunen, Ilves Jrs.
☐ 323 Jari Viitala, Ilves Jrs.
☐ 324 Mikko Vilonen, Ilves Jrs.
☐ 325 Jaakko Virtanen, Ilves Jrs.
☐ 326 Jarmo Viteli, Ilves Jrs.
☐ 327 Kari Anttila, Assat Pori Jrs.
☐ 328 Harri Hiltunen, Assat Pori Jrs.
☐ 329 Arto Javanainen, Assat Pori Jrs.
☐ 330 Tapio Jylhasaari, Assat Pori Jrs.
☐ 331 Jorma Korkeamaki, Assat Pori Jrs.
☐ 332 Kari Koskinen, Assat Pori Jrs.
☐ 333 Martti Lunden, Assat Pori Jrs.
☐ 334 Petri Niskanen, Assat Pori Jrs.
☐ 335 Jari Nystrom, Assat Pori Jrs.
☐ 336 Ari Peltola, Assat Pori Jrs.
☐ 337 Jari Peltonen, Assat Pori Jrs.
☐ 338 Petri Salminen, Assat Pori Jrs.
☐ 339 Juha Salo, Assat Pori Jrs.
☐ 340 Esa Salosensaari, Assat Pori Jrs.
☐ 341 Rauli Siimes, Assat Pori Jrs.
☐ 342 Esa Suvanto, Assat Pori Jrs.
☐ 343 Jukka Tuli, Assat Pori Jrs.
☐ 344 Jukka Virtanen, Assat Pori Jrs.
☐ 345 Pertti Vaisanen, Assat Pori Jrs.
☐ 346 Timo Hyrsky, Turun P. Jrs.
☐ 347 Jorma Jokinen, Turun P. Jrs.
☐ 338 Jari Kokkola, Turun P. Jrs.
☐ 349 Pentti Kuosmanen, Turun P. Jrs.
☐ 350 Pekka Laukkanen, Turun P. Jrs.
☐ 351 Tom Lund, Turun P. Jrs.
☐ 352 Jouni Niemela, Turun P. Jrs.
☐ 353 Kari Rantanen, Turun P. Jrs.
☐ 354 Pekka Reimola, Turun P. Jrs.
☐ 355 Teijo Salminen, Turun P. Jrs.
☐ 356 VeliMatti Tammi, Turun P. Jrs.
☐ 357 Juha Tamminen, Turun P. Jrs.
☐ 358 Risto Vaihinen, Turun P. Jrs.
☐ 359 Antti Vanne, Turun P. Jrs.
☐ 360 Ari Vanne, Turun P. Jrs.
☐ 361 Hannu Vehmanen, Turun P. Jrs.
☐ 362 Heikki Virta, Turun P. Jrs.
☐ 363 Hannu Virtanen, Turun P. Jrs.
☐ 364 Jyrki Valimaki, Turun P. Jrs.
☐ 365 Pekka Anttila, Oulun Jrs.
☐ 366 Jouni Honkanen, Oulun Jrs.
☐ 367 Kari Jalonen, Oulun Jrs.
☐ 368 Ari Kaikkonen, Oulun Jrs.
☐ 369 Timo Kajula, Oulun Jrs.
☐ 370 Jorma Kinnunen, Oulun Jrs.
☐ 371 Esa Kontio, Oulun Jrs.
☐ 372 Tapio Kuiri, Oulun Jrs.
☐ 373 Pekka Kyllonen, Oulun Jrs.
☐ 374 Ari Mustaniemi, Oulun Jrs.
☐ 375 Jukka Pajala, Oulun Jrs.
☐ 376 Pentti Perhomaa, Oulun Jrs.
☐ 377 Reijo Raatesalmi, Oulun Jrs.
☐ 378 Markku Ruotsalainen, Oulun Jrs.
☐ 379 Reijo Ruotsalainen, Oulun Jrs.
☐ 380 Jarmo Tauriainen, Oulun Jrs.
☐ 381 Ari Timosaari, Oulun Jrs.
☐ 382 Pekka Tuomisto, Oulun Jrs.
☐ 383 Timo Vahanen, Oulun Jrs.
☐ 384 Sakari Valiharju, Oulun Jrs.

1970 - 71 O-PEE-CHEE

Card Size: 2 1/2" x 3 1/2"
Face: Four colour, white border, Position
Back: Green and black on card stock; Number, Resume, Player sketch, Bilingual
Imprint: © OPEECHEE

	Complete Set (264 cards):	**950.00**	**1,900.00**
	Common Player:	**2.50**	**5.00**
No.	**Player**	**EX**	**NRMT**
☐ 1	Gerry Cheevers (G), Bos.	10.00	30.00
☐ 2	John Bucyk, Bos.	4.00	8.00
☐ 3	Bobby Orr, Bos.	85.00	165.00
☐ 4	Don Awrey, Bos.	2.50	5.00
☐ 5	Fred Stanfield, Bos.	2.50	5.00
☐ 6	John McKenzie, Bos.	2.50	5.00
☐ 7	**Wayne Cashman, Bos., RC**	**7.50**	**15.00**
☐ 8	Ken Hodge, Bos.	2.50	5.00
☐ 9	Wayne Carleton, Bos.	2.50	5.00
☐ 10	**Garnet Bailey, Bos., RC**	**2.50**	**5.00**
☐ 11	Phil Esposito, Bos.	15.00	30.00
☐ 12	Lou Angotti, Chi.	2.50	5.00
☐ 13	Jim Pappin, Chi.	2.50	5.00
☐ 14	Dennis Hull, Chi.	2.50	5.00
☐ 15	Bobby Hull, Chi.	28.00	55.00
☐ 16	Doug Mohns, Chi.	2.50	5.00
☐ 17	Pat Stapleton, Chi.	2.50	5.00
☐ 18	Pit Martin, Chi.	2.50	5.00
☐ 19	Eric Nesterenko, Chi.	2.50	5.00
☐ 20	Stan Mikita, Chi.	13.00	25.00
☐ 21	Roy Edwards (G), Det.	3.50	7.00
☐ 22	Frank Mahovlich, Det.	7.50	15.00
☐ 23	Ron Harris, Det.	2.50	5.00
☐ 24	Checklist	75.00	150.00
☐ 25	Pete Stemkowski, Det.	2.50	5.00
☐ 26	Garry Unger, Det.	2.50	5.00
☐ 27	Bruce MacGregor, Det.	2.50	5.00
☐ 28	Larry Jeffrey, Det., LC	2.50	5.00
☐ 29	Gordie Howe, Det.	50.00	95.00
☐ 30	Billy Dea, Det., LC	2.50	5.00
☐ 31	Denis DeJordy (G), L.A.	3.50	7.00
☐ 32	Matt Ravlich, L.A., LC	2.50	5.00
☐ 33	Dave Amadio, L.A., LC	2.50	5.00

No.	Player		
☐ 34	Gilles Marotte, L.A.	2.50	5.00
☐ 35	Eddie Shack, L.A.	6.00	12.00
☐ 36	Bob Pulford, L.A.	3.50	7.00
☐ 37	Ross Lonsberry, L.A.	2.50	5.00
☐ 38	Gord Labossiere, L.A.	2.50	5.00
☐ 39	Eddie Joyal, L.A.	2.50	5.00
☐ 40	Gump Worsley (G), Min.	7.00	14.00
☐ 41	Bob McCord, Min., LC	2.50	5.00
☐ 42	Leo Boivin, Min., LC	3.50	7.00
☐ **43**	**Tom Reid, Min., RC**	**2.50**	**5.00**
☐ 44	Charlie Burns, Min.	2.50	5.00
☐ 45	Bob Barlow, Min., LC	2.50	5.00
☐ 46	Bill Goldsworthy, Min.	2.50	5.00
☐ 47	Danny Grant, Min.	2.50	5.00
☐ **48**	**Norm Beaudin, Min., RC**	**2.50**	**5.00**
☐ 49	Rogatien Vachon (G), Mtl.	6.50	13.00
☐ 50	Yvan Cournoyer, Mtl.	6.00	12.00
☐ 51	Serge Savard, Mtl.	6.00	12.00
☐ 52	Jacques Laperrière, Mtl.	3.50	7.00
☐ 53	Terry Harper, Mtl.	2.50	5.00
☐ 54	Ralph Backstrom, Mtl.	2.50	5.00
☐ 55	Jean Béliveau, Mtl., LC	10.00	20.00
☐ 56	Claude Larose, Mtl.	2.50	5.00
☐ 57	Jacques Lemaire, Mtl.	5.00	10.00
☐ 58	Pete Mahovlich, Mtl.	2.50	5.00
☐ 59	Tim Horton, NYR.	9.00	18.00
☐ 60	Bob Nevin, NYR.	2.50	5.00
☐ 61	Dave Balon, NYR.	2.50	5.00
☐ 62	Vic Hadfield, NYR.	2.50	5.00
☐ 63	Rod Gilbert, NYR.	4.00	8.00
☐ 64	Ron Stewart, NYR.	2.50	5.00
☐ 65	Ted Irvine, NYR.	2.50	5.00
☐ 66	Arnie Brown, NYR.	2.50	5.00
☐ **67**	**Brad Park, NYR., RC**	**30.00**	**60.00**
☐ 68	Ed Giacomin (G), NYR.	7.00	14.00
☐ 69	Gary Smith (G), Cal.	3.50	7.00
☐ 70	Carol Vadnais, Cal.	2.50	5.00
☐ 71	Doug Roberts, Cal.	2.50	5.00
☐ 72	Harry Howell, Cal.	3.50	7.00
☐ 73	Joe Szura, Cal.	2.50	5.00
☐ 74	Mike Laughton, Cal., LC	2.50	5.00
☐ 75	Gary Jarrett, Cal.	2.50	5.00
☐ 76	Bill Hicke, Cal.	2.50	5.00
☐ **77**	**Paul Andrea, Pha., RC, LC**	**2.50**	**5.00**
☐ 78	Bernie Parent (G), Pha.	18.00	35.00
☐ 79	Joe Watson, Pha.	2.50	5.00
☐ 80	Ed Van Impe, Pha.	2.50	5.00
☐ 81	Larry Hillman, Pha.	2.50	5.00
☐ 82	George Swarbrick, Pha., LC	2.50	5.00
☐ 83	Bill Sutherland, Stl.	2.50	5.00
☐ 84	André Lacroix, Pgh.	2.50	5.00
☐ 85	Gary Dornhoefer, Pgh.	2.50	5.00
☐ 86	Jean Guy Gendron, Pgh.	2.50	5.00
☐ **87**	**Al Smith (G), Pgh., RC**	**3.50**	**7.00**
☐ 88	Bob Woytowich, Pgh.	2.50	5.00
☐ 89	Duane Rupp, Pgh.	2.50	5.00
☐ 90	Jim Morrison, Pgh., LC	2.50	5.00
☐ 91	Ron Schock, Pgh.	2.50	5.00
☐ 92	Ken Schinkel, Pgh.	2.50	5.00
☐ 93	Keith McCreary, Pgh.	2.50	5.00
☐ 94	Bryan Hextall, Pgh.	2.50	5.00
☐ **95**	**Wayne Hicks, Jr., Pgh., RC, LC**	**2.50**	**5.00**
☐ 96	Gary Sabourin, Stl.	2.50	5.00
☐ **97**	**Ernie Wakely (G), Stl., RC**	**3.50**	**7.00**
☐ 98	Bob Wall, Stl.	2.50	5.00
☐ 99	Barclay Plage, Stl.r	2.50	5.00
☐ 100	Jean-Guy Talbot, Stl., LC	2.50	5.00
☐ 101	Gary Veneruzzo, Stl.	2.50	5.00
☐ 102	Tim Ecclestone, Stl.	2.50	5.00
☐ 103	Red Berenson, Stl.	2.50	5.00
☐ 104	Larry Keenan, Stl., LC	2.50	5.00
☐ 105	Bruce Gamble (G), Tor.	3.50	7.00
☐ 106	Jim Dorey, Tor.	2.50	5.00
☐ **107**	**Mike Pelyk, Tor., RC**	**2.50**	**5.00**
☐ 108	Rick Ley, Tor.	2.50	5.00
☐ 109	Mike Walton, Tor.	2.50	5.00
☐ 110	Norm Ullman, Tor.	4.00	8.00
☐ 111	Brit Selby, Stl. (Traded to)	3.50	7.00
☐ 111	Brit Selby, Stl. (No Trade)	20.00	40.00
☐ 112	Garry Monahan, Tor.	2.50	5.00
☐ 113	George Armstrong, Tor., LC	3.50	7.00
☐ 114	Gary Doak, Van.	2.50	5.00
☐ **115**	**Darryl Sly, Van., RC, LC**	**2.50**	**5.00**
☐ 116	Wayne Maki, Van.	2.50	5.00
☐ 117	Orland Kurtenbach, Van.	2.50	5.00
☐ 118	Murray Hall, Van.	2.50	5.00
☐ 119	Marc Reaume, Van., LC	2.50	5.00
☐ 120	Pat Quinn, Van.	3.50	7.00
☐ 121	Andre Boudrias, Van.	2.50	5.00
☐ 122	Poul Popiel, Van.	2.50	5.00
☐ 123	Paul Terbenche, Buf.	2.50	5.00
☐ 124	Howie Menard, Buf., LC	2.50	5.00
☐ **125**	**Gerry Meehan, Buf., RC**	**3.50**	**7.00**
☐ 126	Skip Krake, Buf., LC	2.50	5.00
☐ 127	Phil Goyette, Buf.	2.50	5.00
☐ 128	Reggie Fleming, Buf.	2.50	5.00
☐ 129	Don Marshall, Buf.	2.50	5.00
☐ **130**	**Bill Inglis, Buf., RC, LC**	**2.50**	**5.00**
☐ **131**	**Gilbert Perreault, Buf., RC**	**45.00**	**90.00**
☐ 132	Checklist 2	75.00	150.00
☐ 133	Eddie Johnston (G), Bos.	3.50	7.00
☐ 134	Ted Green, Bos.	2.50	5.00
☐ **135**	**Rick Smith, Bos., RC**	**2.50**	**5.00**
☐ 136	Derek Sanderson, Bos.	7.00	14.00
☐ 137	Dallas Smith, Bos.	2.50	5.00
☐ **138**	**Don Marcotte, Bos., RC**	**2.50**	**5.00**
☐ 139	Ed Westfall, Bos.	2.50	5.00
☐ 140	Floyd Smith, Buf.	2.50	5.00
☐ **141**	**Randy Wyrozub, Buf., RC, LC**	**2.50**	**5.00**
☐ **142**	**Cliff Schmautz, Buf., RC, LC**	**2.50**	**5.00**
☐ 143	Mike McMahon, Buf.	2.50	5.00
☐ 144	Jim Watson, Buf.	2.50	5.00
☐ 145	Roger Crozier (G), Buf.	3.50	7.00
☐ 146	Tracy Pratt, Buf.	2.50	5.00
☐ **147**	**Cliff Koroll, Chi., RC**	**2.50**	**5.00**
☐ **148**	**Gerry Pinder, Chi., RC**	**2.50**	**5.00**
☐ 149	Chico Maki, Chi.	2.50	5.00
☐ 150	Doug Jarretti, Chi.	2.50	5.00
☐ **151**	**Keith Magnusoni, Chi., RC**	**4.50**	**9.00**
☐ 152	Gerry Desjardins (G), Chi.	3.50	7.00
☐ 153	Tony Esposito (G), Chi.	35.00	65.00
☐ 154	Gary Bergman, Det.	2.50	5.00
☐ **155**	**Tom Webster, Det., RC**	**3.50**	**7.00**
☐ 156	Dale Rolfe, Det.	2.50	5.00
☐ 157	Alex Delvecchio, Det.	4.00	8.00
☐ 158	Nick Libett, Det.	2.50	5.00
☐ 159	Wayne Connelly, Det.	2.50	5.00
☐ **160**	**Mike Byers, L.A., RC**	**2.50**	**5.00**
☐ 161	Bill Flett, L.A.	2.50	5.00
☐ 162	Larry Mickey, L.A.	2.50	5.00
☐ 163	Noel Price, L.A.	2.50	5.00
☐ 164	Larry Cahan, L.A.	2.50	5.00
☐ **165**	**Jack Norris (G), L.A., RC**	**3.50**	**7.00**
☐ 166	Ted Harris, Min.	2.50	5.00
☐ 167	Murray Oliver, Min.	2.50	5.00
☐ 168	J.P. Parise, Min.	2.50	5.00
☐ 169	Tom Williams, Min.	2.50	5.00
☐ 170	Bobby Rousseau, Min.	2.50	5.00
☐ **171**	**Jude Drouin, Min., RC**	**2.50**	**5.00**
☐ **172**	**Walt McKechnie, Min., RC**	**2.50**	**5.00**
☐ 173	Césare Maniago (G), Min.	3.50	7.00
☐ **174**	**Réjean Houle, Mtl., RC**	**6.00**	**12.00**
☐ 175	Mickey Redmond, Mtl.	4.50	8.50
☐ 176	Henri Richard, Mtl.	6.00	12.00
☐ **177**	**Guy Lapointe, Mtl., RC**	**13.00**	**25.00**
☐ 178	J.C. Tremblay, Mtl.	2.50	5.00
☐ **179**	**Marc Tardif, Mtl., RC**	**3.50**	**7.00**
☐ 180	Walt Tkaczuk, NYR.	2.50	5.00
☐ 181	Jean Ratelle, NYR.	4.00	8.00
☐ 182	Pete Stemkowski, NYR.	2.50	5.00
☐ 183	Gilles Villemure (G), NYR.	3.50	7.00
☐ 184	Rod Seiling, NYR.	2.50	5.00
☐ 185	Jim Neilson, NYR.	2.50	5.00
☐ 186	Dennis Hextall, Cal.	2.50	5.00
☐ 187	Gerry Ehman, Cal., LC	2.50	5.00
☐ 188	Bert Marshall, Cal.	2.50	5.00
☐ **189**	**Gary Croteau, Cal., RC**	**2.50**	**5.00**
☐ 190	Ted Hampson, Cal.	2.50	5.00
☐ 191	Earl Ingarfield, Cal., LC	2.50	5.00
☐ 192	Dick Mattiussi, Cal., LC	2.50	5.00
☐ 193	Earl Heiskala, Pha., LC	2.50	5.00
☐ 194	Simon Nolet, Pha.	2.50	5.00
☐ **195**	**Bobby Clarke, Pha., RC**	**70.00**	**140.00**
☐ 196	Garry Peters, Pha., LC	2.50	5.00
☐ **197**	**Lew Morrison, Pha., RC**	**2.50**	**5.00**
☐ 198	Wayne Hillman, Pha.	2.50	5.00
☐ 199	Doug Favell (G), Pha.	3.50	7.00
☐ 200	Les Binkley (G), Pgh.	3.50	7.00
☐ 201	Dean Prentice, Pgh.	2.50	5.00
☐ 202	Jean Pronovost, Pgh.	2.50	5.00
☐ 203	Wally Boyer, Pgh.	2.50	5.00
☐ 204	Bryan Watson, Pgh.	2.50	5.00
☐ 205	Glen Sather, Pgh.	3.50	7.00
☐ 206	Lowell MacDonald, Pgh.	2.50	5.00
☐ 207	Andy Bathgate, Pgh., LC	3.50	7.00
☐ 208	Val Fonteyne, Pgh.	2.50	5.00
☐ **209**	**Jim Lorentz, Stl., RC**	**2.50**	**5.00**
☐ 210	Glenn Hall (G), Stl., LC	6.50	13.00
☐ 211	Bob Plager, Stl.	2.50	5.00
☐ 212	Noel Picard, Stl.	2.50	5.00
☐ 213	Jim Roberts, Stl.	2.50	5.00
☐ 214	Frank St. Marseille, Stl.	2.50	5.00
☐ 215	Ab McDonald, Stl.	2.50	5.00
☐ **216**	**Brian Glennie, Tor., RC**	**2.50**	**5.00**
☐ 217	Paul Henderson, Tor.	3.50	7.00
☐ **218**	**Darryl Sittler, Tor., RC**	**65.00**	**125.00**
☐ 219	Dave Keon, Tor.	4.00	8.00
☐ **220**	**Jim Harrison, Tor., RC**	**2.50**	**5.00**
☐ 221	Ron Ellis, Tor.	2.50	5.00
☐ 222	Jacques Plante (G), Tor.	18.00	35.00
☐ 223	Bob Baun, Tor.	2.50	5.00
☐ **224**	**George Gardner (G), Van., RC**	**3.50**	**7.00**
☐ **225**	**Dale Tallon, Van., RC**	**2.50**	**5.00**
☐ **226**	**Rosaire Paiement, Van., RC**	**2.50**	**5.00**
☐ **227**	**Mike Corrigan, Van., RC**	**2.50**	**5.00**
☐ 228	Ray Cullen, Van., LC	2.50	5.00
☐ 229	Charlie Hodge (G), Van., LC	3.50	7.00
☐ 230	Len Lunde, Van., LC	2.50	5.00
☐ 231	Terry Sawchuk (G)	35.00	65.00
☐ 232	Boston Bruins Team: Stanley Cup Champions	8.00	16.00
☐ 233	Esposito Line: Hodge, Esposito, Cashman	13.00	26.00
☐ 234	AS: Tony Esposito (G), Chi.	15.00	30.00
☐ 235	AS: Bobby Hull, Chi.	14.00	28.00
☐ 236	AS: Bobby Orr, Bos.	35.00	70.00
☐ 237	AS: Phil Esposito, Bos.	7.50	15.00
☐ 238	AS: Gordie Howe, Det.	25.00	45.00
☐ 239	AS: Brad Park, NYR.	12.00	24.00
☐ 240	AS: Stan Mikita, Chi.	6.50	13.00
☐ 241	AS: John McKenzie, Bos.	2.50	5.00
☐ 242	AS: Frank Mahovlich, Det.	3.75	7.50
☐ 243	AS: Carl Brewer, Det.	2.50	5.00
☐ 244	AS: Ed Giacomin (G), NYR.	4.50	9.00
☐ 245	AS: J. Laperrière, Mtl., Err. (Perreault Rookie)	3.50	7.00
☐ 245	Jacques Laperrière, Mtl.	3.50	7.00
☐ 246	AW: Bobby Orr	35.00	70.00
☐ 247	AW: Tony Esposito	15.00	30.00
☐ 248	AW: Bobby Orr, Err. (no overprint)	35.00	70.00
☐ 248	AW: Bobby Orr, Corrected	35.00	70.00
☐ 249	AW: Bobby Orr	35.00	70.00
☐ 250	AW: Tony Esposito	15.00	30.00
☐ 251	AW: Phil Goyette	3.50	7.00
☐ 252	AW: Bobby Orr	35.00	70.00
☐ 253	AW: Pit Martin	3.50	7.00
☐ 254	The Stanley Cup	10.00	20.00
☐ 255	The Prince of Wales Trophy	3.50	7.00
☐ 256	The Conn Smythe Trophy	3.50	7.00
☐ 257	The James Norris Memorial Trophy	3.50	7.00
☐ 258	The Calder Memorial Trophy	3.50	7.00
☐ 259	The Vezina Trophy	3.50	7.00
☐ 260	The Lady Byng Trophy	3.50	7.00
☐ 261	The Hart Memorial Trophy	3.50	7.00
☐ 262	The Art Ross Trophy	3.50	7.00
☐ 263	The Clarence S. Campbell Bowl	3.50	7.00
☐ 264	John Ferguson, LC	6.00	15.00

O-PEE-CHEE DECKLE EDGE PHOTOS

These inserts have black and white photos.

Card Size: 2 1/4" x 3 1/4"

Insert Set (48 cards): 175.00 350.00

No.	Player	EX	NRMT
☐ 1	Pat Quinn, Van.	4.00	7.50
☐ 2	Eddie Shack, L.A.	4.00	7.50
☐ 3	Eddie Joyal, L.A.	2.00	4.00
☐ 4	Bobby Orr, Bos.	40.00	80.00
☐ 5	Derek Sanderson, Bos.	4.00	7.50
☐ 6	Phil Esposito, Bos.	10.00	20.00
☐ 7	Fred Stanfield, Bos.	2.00	4.00
☐ 8	Bob Woytowich, Pgh.	2.00	4.00
☐ 9	Ron Schock, Pgh.	2.00	4.00
☐ 10	Les Binkley (G), Pgh.	3.00	6.00
☐ 11	Roger Crozier (G), Buf.	4.00	7.50
☐ 12	Reggie Fleming, Buf.	2.00	4.00
☐ 13	Charlie Burns, Min.	2.00	4.00
☐ 14	Bobby Rousseau, Min.	2.00	4.00
☐ 15	Leo Boivin, Min.	4.00	7.50
☐ 16	Garry Unger, Det.	3.00	6.00
☐ 17	Frank Mahovlich, Det.	7.50	15.00
☐ 18	Gordie Howe, Det.	35.00	65.00
☐ 19	Jacques Lemaire, Mtl.	6.00	12.00
☐ 20	Jacques Laperrière, Mtl.	4.00	7.50
☐ 21	Jean Béliveau, Mtl.	11.00	22.00
☐ 22	Rogatien Vachon (G), Mtl.	4.00	7.50
☐ 23	Yvan Cournoyer, Mtl.	5.00	10.00
☐ 24	Henri Richard, Mtl.	5.00	10.00
☐ 25	Red Berenson, Stl.	2.00	4.00
☐ 26	Frank St. Marseille, Stl.	2.00	4.00
☐ 27	Glenn Hall (G), Stl.	7.50	15.00
☐ 28	Gary Sabourin, Stl.	2.00	4.00
☐ 29	Doug Mohns, Chi.	2.00	4.00
☐ 30	Bobby Hull, Chi.	18.00	35.00
☐ 31	Ray Cullen, Van.	2.00	4.00
☐ 32	Tony Esposito (G), Chi.	10.00	20.00
☐ 33	Gary Dornhoefer, Pha.	2.00	4.00
☐ 34	Ed Van Impe, Pha.	2.00	4.00
☐ 35	Doug Favell (G), Pha.	3.00	6.00
☐ 36	Carol Vadnais, Cgy.	2.00	4.00
☐ 37	Harry Howell, Cgy.	4.00	7.50
☐ 38	Bill Hicke, Cgy.	2.00	4.00
☐ 39	Rod Gilbert, NYR.	4.50	8.50
☐ 40	Jean Ratelle, NYR.	4.50	8.50
☐ 41	Walt Tkaczuk, NYR.	2.00	4.00
☐ 42	Ed Giacomin (G), NYR.	5.00	10.00
☐ 43	Brad Park, NYR.	6.00	12.00
☐ 44	Bruce Gamble (G), Tor.	3.00	6.00
☐ 45	Orland Kurtenbach, Van.	2.00	4.00
☐ 46	Ron Ellis, Tor.	2.00	4.00
☐ 47	Dave Keon, Tor.	4.50	8.50
☐ 48	Norm Ullman, Tor.	4.50	8.50

O-PEE-CHEE STICKER STAMPS

Insert Set (33 stickers):	165.00	325.00
Player	EX	NRMT
☐ Jean Béliveau	13.00	25.00
☐ Red Berenson	2.50	5.00
☐ Wayne Carleton	2.50	5.00
☐ Tim Ecclestone	2.50	5.00
☐ Ron Ellis	2.50	5.00
☐ Phil Esposito	11.00	22.00
☐ Tony Esposito (G)	11.00	22.00
☐ Bill Flett	2.50	5.00
☐ Ed Giacomin (G)	6.00	12.00
☐ Rod Gilbert	5.00	10.00
☐ Danny Grant	2.50	5.00
☐ Bill Hicke	2.50	5.00
☐ Gordie Howe	40.00	75.00
☐ Bobby Hull	20.00	40.00
☐ Earl Ingarfield	2.50	5.00
☐ Eddie Joyal	2.50	5.00
☐ Dave Keon	5.00	10.00
☐ André Lacroix	2.50	5.00
☐ Jacques Laperrière	4.00	7.50
☐ Jacques Lemaire	7.00	14.00
☐ Frank Mahovlich	9.00	18.00
☐ Keith McCreary	2.50	5.00
☐ Stan Mikita	8.00	16.00
☐ Bobby Orr	45.00	90.00
☐ Jean Paul Parise	2.50	5.00
☐ Jean Ratelle	5.00	10.00
☐ Derek Sanderson	4.00	7.50
☐ Frank St. Marseille	2.50	5.00
☐ Ron Schock	2.50	5.00
☐ Garry Unger	4.00	7.50
☐ Carol Vadnais	2.50	5.00
☐ Ed Van Impe	2.50	5.00
☐ Bob Woytowich	2.50	5.00

1970-71 POST SHOOTERS

These flat plastic hockey-player shaped figures were pulled from cereal boxes and were intended for use as part of a game. Each figure came with a sheet of stickers meant to be applied to the figure. The player was pictured in his NHLPA uniform and came with a red-shoulder or blue-shoulder version.

Figurine Height: 4 1/2"
Face: Colour caricature, Name
Back: Blank
Imprint:
Complete Set: (16 cards)

Player	VG	EX	EX-NRMT
☐ Johnny Bucyk, Bos.			
☐ Ron Ellis, Tor.			
☐ Ed Giacomin (G), NYR			
☐ Paul Henderson, Tor.			
☐ Ken Hodge, Bos.			
☐ Dennis Hull, Chi.			
☐ Orland Kurtenbach, Van.			
☐ Jacques Laperriere, Mtl.			
☐ Jacques Lemaire, Mtl.			
☐ Frank Mahovlich, Mtl.			
☐ Peter Mahovlich, Mtl.			
☐ Bobby Orr, Bos.			
☐ Jacques Plante (G), Tor.			
☐ Jean Ratelle, NYR			
☐ Dale Tallon, Van.			
☐ J.C. Tremblay, Mtl.			

1970 - 71 SOVIET STARS POSTCARDS

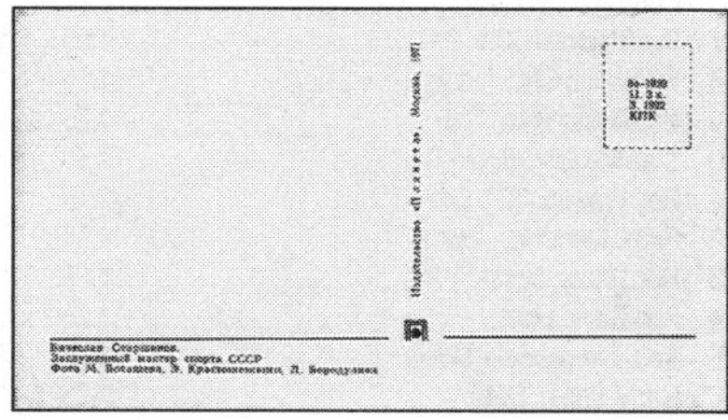

Card Size: 3 1/2" x 5 3/4"
Face: Four colour
Back: Russian text
Imprint:

Complete Set (27 cards and folder):	100.00	200.00
Player	EX	NRMT
☐ Victor Konovalenko (G)	3.50	7.00
☐ Valery Davydov	2.50	5.00
☐ Vladimir Lutchenko	2.50	5.00
☐ Valeri Nikitin	2.50	5.00
☐ Alexander Ragulin	6.00	12.00
☐ Igor Romishevsky	2.50	5.00
☐ Evgeny Paladiev	2.50	5.00
☐ Vyacheslav Starshinov	2.50	5.00
☐ Viktor Polupanov	2.50	5.00
☐ Alexander Maltsev	4.00	8.00
☐ Anatoli Firsov	2.50	5.00
☐ Evgeny Mishakov	2.50	5.00
☐ Boris Mikhailov	7.50	15.00
☐ Valery Vasiliev	5.00	10.00
☐ Alexander Yakushev	7.50	15.00
☐ Vladimir Petrov	4.00	8.00
☐ Valery Kharlamov	10.00	20.00
☐ Vladimir Vikulov	2.50	5.00
☐ Vladimir Shadrin	2.50	5.00
☐ Vladislav Tretiak (G)	30.00	60.00
☐ A. Czepnishev	2.50	5.00
☐ A. Tapasov	2.50	5.00
☐ Team Photo	6.00	12.00
☐ U.S.S.R. vs. C.S.S.R.	4.00	8.00
☐ U.S.S.R. vs. Finland	4.00	8.00
☐ Team Photo	7.50	15.00
☐ Airport shot	4.00	8.00

1970 - 71 TOPPS

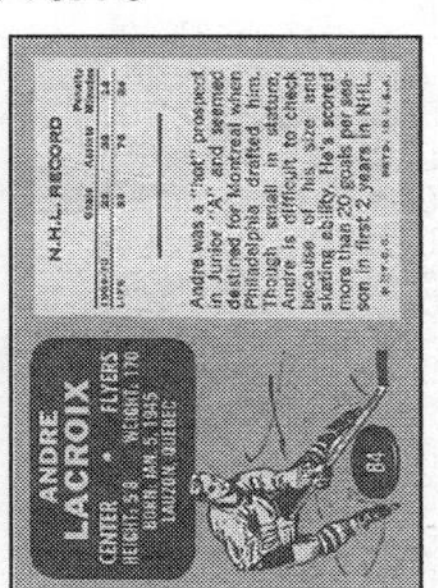

Card Size: 2 1/2" x 3 1/2"
Face: Four colour, white border, Position
Back: Black and green on card stock, Number, Resume
Imprint: * T.C.G.

Complete Set (132 cards):		250.00	500.00
Common Player:		1.25	2.25
No.	Player	EX	NRMT
☐ 1	Gerry Cheevers (G), Bos.	7.50	22.00

□ 2	John Bucyk, Bos.	2.50	5.00
□ 3	Bobby Orr, Bos.	50.00	100.00
□ 4	Don Awrey, Bos.	1.25	2.25
□ 5	Fred Stanfield, Bos.	1.25	2.25
□ 6	John McKenzie, Bos.	1.25	2.25
□ 7	**Wayne Cashman, Bos., RC**	**5.50**	**11.00**
□ 8	Ken Hodge, Bos.	1.25	2.25
□ 9	Wayne Carleton, Bos.	1.25	2.25
□ 10	**Garnet Bailey, Bos., RC**	**1.25**	**2.25**
□ 11	Phil Esposito, Bos.	12.00	24.00
□ 12	Lou Angotti, Chi.	1.25	2.25
□ 13	Jim Pappin, Chi.	1.25	2.25
□ 14	Dennis Hull, Chi.	1.25	2.25
□ 15	Bobby Hull, Chi.	20.00	40.00
□ 16	Doug Mohns, Chi.	1.25	2.25
□ 17	Pat Stapleton, Chi.	1.25	2.25
□ 18	Pit Martin, Chi.	1.25	2.25
□ 19	Eric Nesterenko, Chi.	1.25	2.25
□ 20	Stan Mikita, Chi.	7.50	15.00
□ 21	Roy Edwards (G), Det.	1.75	3.50
□ 22	Frank Mahovlich, Det.	4.50	9.00
□ 23	Ron Harris, Det.	1.25	2.25
□ 24	Bob Baun, Buf.	1.25	2.25
□ 25	Pete Stemkowski, Det.	1.25	2.25
□ 26	Garry Unger, Det.	1.75	3.50
□ 27	Bruce MacGregor, Det.	1.25	2.25
□ 28	Larry Jeffrey, Det., LC	1.25	2.25
□ 29	Gordie Howe, Det.	35.00	65.00
□ 30	Billy Dea, Det., LC	1.25	2.25
□ 31	Denis DeJordy (G), L.A.	1.75	3.50
□ 32	Matt Ravlich, L.A., LC	1.25	2.25
□ 33	Dave Amadio, L.A., LC	1.25	2.25
□ 34	Gilles Marotte, L.A.	1.25	2.25
□ 35	Eddie Shack, L.A.	3.50	7.00
□ 36	Bob Pulford, L.A.	1.75	3.50
□ 37	Ross Lonsberry, L.A.	1.25	2.25
□ 38	Gord Labossiere, L.A.	1.25	2.25
□ 39	Eddie Joyal, L.A.	1.25	2.25
□ 40	Gump Worsley (G), Min.	4.00	8.00
□ 41	Bob McCord, Min., LC	1.25	2.25
□ 42	Leo Boivin, Min., LC	1.75	3.50
□ 43	**Tom Reid, Min., RC**	**1.25**	**2.25**
□ 44	Charlie Burns, Min.	1.25	2.25
□ 45	Bob Barlow, Min., LC	1.25	2.25
□ 46	Bill Goldsworthy, Min.	1.25	2.25
□ 47	Danny Grant, Min.	1.25	2.25
□ 48	Norm Beaudin, Min., RC	1.25	2.25
□ 49	Rogatien Vachon (G), Mtl.	4.00	7.50
□ 50	Yvan Cournoyer, Mtl.	3.50	7.00
□ 51	Serge Savard, Mtl.	4.50	8.50
□ 52	Jacques Laperrière, Mtl.	1.75	3.50
□ 53	Terry Harper, Mtl.	1.25	2.25
□ 54	Ralph Backstrom, Mtl.	1.25	2.25
□ 55	Jean Béliveau, Mtl., LC	7.50	15.00
□ 56	Claude Larose, Mtl., Err. (LaRose)	1.25	2.25
□ 57	Jacques Lemaire, Mtl.	4.00	7.50
□ 58	Pete Mahovlich, Mtl.	1.25	2.25
□ 59	Tim Horton, NYR.	6.00	12.00
□ 60	Bob Nevin, NYR.	1.25	2.25
□ 61	Dave Balon, NYR.	1.25	2.25
□ 62	Vic Hadfield, NYR.	1.25	2.25
□ 63	Rod Gilbert, NYR.	2.75	5.50
□ 64	Ron Stewart, NYR.	1.25	2.25
□ 65	Ted Irvine, NYR.	1.25	2.25
□ 66	Arnie Brown, NYR.	1.25	2.25
□ 67	**Brad Park, NYR., RC**	**15.00**	**30.00**
□ 68	Ed Giacomin (G), NYR.	4.50	9.00
□ 69	Gary Smith (G), Cal.	1.75	3.50
□ 70	Carol Vadnais, Cal.	1.25	2.25
□ 71	Doug Roberts, Cal.	1.25	2.25
□ 72	Harry Howell, Cal.	1.75	3.50
□ 73	Joe Szura, Cal.	1.25	2.25
□ 74	Mike Laughton, Cal., LC	1.25	2.25
□ 75	Gary Jarrett, Cal.	1.25	2.25
□ 76	Bill Hicke, Cal.	1.25	2.25
□ 77	**Paul Andrea, Buf., RC, LC**	**1.25**	**2.25**
□ 78	Bernie Parent (G), Pha.	10.00	20.00
□ 79	Joe Watson, Pha.	1.25	2.25
□ 80	Ed Van Impe, Pha.	1.25	2.25
□ 81	Larry Hillman, Pha.	1.25	2.25
□ 82	George Swarbrick, Pha., LC	1.25	2.25
□ 83	Bill Sutherland, Stl.	1.25	2.25
□ 84	Andre Lacroix, Pha.	1.25	2.25
□ 85	Gary Dornhoefer, Pha.	1.25	2.25
□ 86	Jean-Guy Gendron, Pha.	1.25	2.25
□ 87	**Al Smith (G), Pgh., RC**	**1.75**	**3.50**
□ 88	Bob Woytowich, Pgh.	1.25	2.25
□ 89	Duane Rupp, Pgh.	1.25	2.25
□ 90	Jim Morrison, Pgh., LC	1.25	2.25
□ 91	Ron Schock, Pgh.	1.25	2.25
□ 92	Ken Schinkel, Pgh.	1.25	2.25
□ 93	Keith McCreary, Pgh.	1.25	2.25
□ 94	Bryan Hextall, Pgh.	1.25	2.25
□ 95	**Wayne Hicks, Jr., Pgh., RC, LC**	**1.25**	**2.25**
□ 96	Gary Sabourin, Stl.	1.25	2.25
□ 97	**Ernie Wakely (G), Stl., RC**	**1.75**	**3.50**
□ 98	Bob Wall, Stl.	1.25	2.25
□ 99	Barclay Plager, Stl.	1.25	2.25
□ 100	Jean-Guy Talbot, Stl., LC	1.25	2.25
□ 101	Gary Veneruzzo, Stl.	1.25	2.25
□ 102	Tim Ecclestone, Stl.	1.25	2.25
□ 103	Red Berenson, Stl.	1.25	2.25
□ 104	Larry Keenan, Stl., LC	1.25	2.25
□ 105	Bruce Gamble (G), Tor.	1.75	3.50
□ 106	Jim Dorey, Tor.	1.25	2.25
□ 107	**Mike Pelyk, Tor., RC**	**1.25**	**2.25**
□ 108	Rick Ley, Tor.	1.25	2.25
□ 109	Mike Walton, Tor.	1.25	2.25
□ 110	Norm Ullman, Tor.	2.50	5.00
□ 111	Brit Selby, Stl.	1.25	2.25
□ 112	Garry Monahan, Tor.	1.25	2.25
□ 113	George Armstrong,Tor., LC	1.75	3.50
□ 114	Gary Doak, Van.	1.25	2.25
□ 115	**Darryl Sly, Van., RC, LC**	**1.25**	**2.25**
□ 116	Wayne Maki, Van.	1.25	2.25
□ 117	Orland Kurtenbach, Van.	1.25	2.25
□ 118	Murray Hall, Van.	1.25	2.25
□ 119	Marc Reaume, Van., LC	1.25	2.25
□ 120	Pat Quinn, Van.	1.75	3.50
□ 121	Andre Boudrias, Van.	1.25	2.25
□ 122	Poul Popiel, Buf., Err. (Paul)	1.25	2.25
□ 123	Paul Terbenche, Buf.	1.25	2.25
□ 124	Howie Menard, Buf., LC	1.25	2.25
□ 125	**Gerry Meehan, Buf., RC**	**1.75**	**3.50**
□ 126	Skip Krake, Buf., LC	1.25	2.25
□ 127	Phil Goyette, Buf.	1.25	2.25
□ 128	Reggie Fleming, Buf.	1.25	2.25
□ 129	Don Marshall, Buf.	1.25	2.25
□ 130	**Bill Inglis, Buf., RC, LC**	**1.25**	**2.25**
□ 131	**Gilbert Perreault, Buf., RC**	**30.00**	**60.00**
□ 132	Checklist (1 - 132)	50.00	100.00

DECKLE EDGE

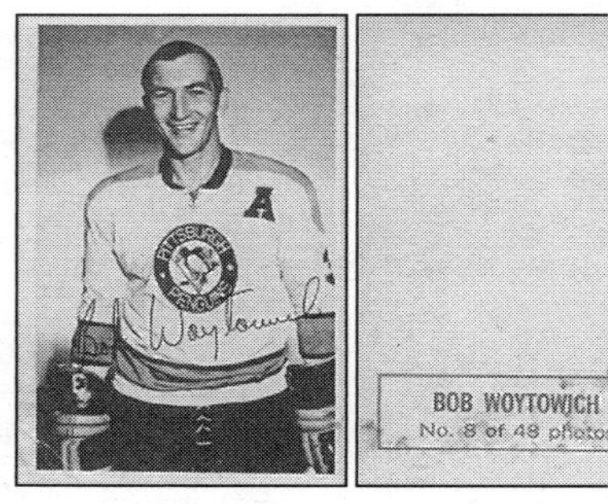

These inserts have black and white photos.

Insert Set (48 cards):		175.00	350.00
No.	Player	EX	NRMT
□ 1	Pat Quinn, Van.	2.50	7.50
□ 2	Eddie Shack, L.A.	4.00	7.50
□ 3	Eddie Joyal, L.A.	2.00	4.00
□ 4	Bobby Orr, Bos.	40.00	80.00
□ 5	Derek Sanderson, Bos.	4.00	7.50
□ 6	Phil Esposito, Bos.	10.00	20.00
□ 7	Fred Stanfield, Bos.	2.00	4.00
□ 8	Bob Woytowich, Pgh.	2.00	4.00
□ 9	Ron Schock, Pgh.	2.00	4.00
□ 10	Les Binkley (G), Pgh.	3.00	6.00
□ 11	Roger Crozier (G), Buf.	4.00	7.50
□ 12	Reggie Fleming, Buf.	2.00	4.00
□ 13	Charlie Burns, Min.	2.00	4.00
□ 14	Bobby Rousseau, Min..	2.00	4.00
□ 15	Léo Boivin, Min.	4.00	7.50
□ 16	Garry Unger, Det.	3.00	6.00
□ 17	Frank Mahovlich, Det.	7.50	15.00
□ 18	Gordie Howe, Det.	35.00	65.00
□ 19	Jacques Lemaire, Mtl.	6.00	12.00
□ 20	Jacques Laperrière, Mtl.	4.00	7.50
□ 21	Jean Béliveau, Mtl.	11.00	22.00
□ 22	Rogatien Vachon (G), Mtl.	4.00	7.50
□ 23	Yvan Cournoyer, Mtl.	5.00	10.00
□ 24	Henri Richard, Mtl.	5.00	10.00
□ 25	Red Berenson, Stl.	2.00	4.00
□ 26	Frank St. Marseille, Stl.	2.00	4.00
□ 27	Glenn Hall (G), Stl.	7.50	15.00
□ 28	Gary Sabourin, Stl.	2.00	4.00
□ 29	Doug Mohns, Chi.	2.00	4.00
□ 30	Bobby Hull, Chi.	20.00	35.00
□ 31	Ray Cullen, Van.	2.00	4.00
□ 32	Tony Esposito (G), Chi.	10.00	20.00
□ 33	Gary Dornhoefer, Pha.	2.00	4.00
□ 34	Ed Van Impe, Pha.	2.00	4.00
□ 35	Doug Favell (G), Pha., Error	3.00	6.00
□ 36	Carol Vadnais, Cal.	2.00	4.00
□ 37	Harry Howell, Cal.	4.00	7.50
□ 38	Bill Hicke, Cal.	2.00	4.00
□ 39	Rod Gilbert, NYR.	4.50	8.50
□ 40	Jean Ratelle, NYR.	4.50	8.50
□ 41	Walt Tkaczuk, NYR.	2.00	4.00
□ 42	Ed Giacomin (G), NYR.	5.00	10.00
□ 43	Brad Park, NYR.	6.00	12.00
□ 44	Bruce Gamble (G), Tor.	3.00	6.00
□ 45	Orland Kurtenbach, Van.	2.00	4.00
□ 46	Ron Ellis, Tor.	2.00	4.00
□ 47	Dave Keon, Tor.	4.50	8.50
□ 48	Norm Ullman, Tor.	4.50	8.50

TOPPS STICKER STAMPS

Insert Set (33 stickers):		165.00	325.00
	Player	EX	NRMT
□	Jean Béliveau, Mtl.	13.00	25.00
□	Red Berenson, Stl.	2.50	5.00
□	Wayne Carleton, Bos.	2.50	5.00
□	Tim Ecclestone, Stl.	2.50	5.00
□	Ron Ellis, Tor.	2.50	5.00
□	Phil Esposito, Bos.	11.00	22.00
□	Tony Esposito (G), Chi.	11.00	22.00
□	Bill Flett, L.A.	2.50	5.00
□	Ed Giacomin (G), NYR.	6.00	12.00
□	Rod Gilbert, NYR.	5.00	10.00
□	Danny Grant, Min.	2.50	5.00
□	Bill Hicke, Oak.	2.50	5.00
□	Gordie Howe, Det.	40.00	75.00
□	Bobby Hull, Chi.	20.00	40.00
□	Earl Ingarfield, Oak.	2.50	5.00
□	Eddie Joyal, L.A.	2.50	5.00
□	Dave Keon, Tor.	5.00	10.00
□	André Lacroix, Pha.	2.50	5.00
□	Jacques Laperrière, Mtl.	4.00	7.50
□	Jacques Lemaire, Mtl.	7.00	14.00
□	Frank Mahovlich, Det.	9.00	18.00
□	Keith McCreary, Pgh.	2.50	5.00
□	Stan Mikita, Chi.	8.00	16.00
□	Bobby Orr, Bos.	45.00	90.00
□	Jean Paul Parise, Min.	2.50	5.00
□	Jean Ratelle, NYR.	5.00	10.00
□	Frank St. Marseille, Stl.	2.50	5.00
□	Derek Sanderson, Bos.	4.00	7.50
□	Ron Schock, Pgh.	2.50	5.00
□	Garry Unger, Det.	4.00	7.50
□	Carol Vadnais, Oak.	2.50	5.00
□	Ed Van Impe, Pha.	2.50	5.00
□	Bob Woytowich, Pgh.	2.50	5.00

1971 KELLOGG'S IRON ON TRANSFERS

Transfer Size: 8 1/2" x 6 1/2"
Face: Four colour caricature on light paper stock
Back: Blank
Imprint: None

No.	Player	EX	NRMT
Complete Set (6 transfers):		**150.00**	**300.00**
☐ 1	Ron Ellis. Tor.	18.00	35.00
☐ 2	Phil Esposito, Bos.	40.00	80.00
☐ 3	Rod Gilbert, NYR.	25.00	50.00
☐ 4	Bobby Hull, Chi.	55.00	110.00
☐ 5	Frank Mahovlich, Tor.	35.00	65.00
☐ 6	Stan Mikita, Chi.	30.00	60.00

1971 - 72 BAZOOKA PANELS

Issued in twelve panels of three cards each, one panel was included on the bottom of each Bazooka Bubble Gum box. The designs are identical to 1971-72 O-Pee-Chee and Topps regular issues.

Card Size: 2 1/2" x 3 1/2"
Face: Four colour, white border; Number, Team logo, Position
Back: Blank
Imprint: None

No.	Player	EX	NRMT
Complete Set (36 cards):		**1,500.00**	**3,000.00**
Common Player:		**20.00**	**40.00**
Panel 1 - 3:		**300.00**	**500.00**
Panel 4 - 6:		**500.00**	**1,000.00**
Panel 7 - 9:		**175.00**	**350.00**
Panel 10 - 12:		**175.00**	**350.00**
Panel 13- 15:		**125.00**	**250.00**
Panel 16 - 18:		**125.00**	**250.00**
Panel 19 - 21:		**90.00**	**175.00**
Panel 22 - 24:		**40.00**	**175.00**
Panel 25 - 26:		**90.00**	**175.00**
Panel 28 - 30:		**250.00**	**500.00**
Panel 31 - 33:		**90.00**	**125.00**
Panel 34 - 36:		**1,000.00**	**2,000.00**
☐ 1	Phil Esposito, Bos.	125.00	250.00
☐ 2	Frank Mahovlich, Mtl.	40.00	175.00
☐ 3	Ed Van Impe, Pha.	20.00	40.00
☐ 4	Bobby Hull, Chi.	250.00	500.00
☐ 5	Henri Richard, Mtl.	65.00	125.00
☐ 6	Gilbert Perreault, Buf.	40.00	175.00
☐ 7	Alex Delvecchio, Det.	45.00	90.00
☐ 8	Denis DeJordy (G), L.A.	25.00	50.00
☐ 9	Ted Harris, Min.	20.00	40.00
☐ 10	Gilles Villemure (G), NYR.	25.00	50.00
☐ 11	Dave Keon, Tor.	65.00	125.00
☐ 12	Derek Sanderson, Bos.	40.00	75.00
☐ 13	Orland Kurtenbach, Van.	20.00	40.00
☐ 14	Bob Nevin, Min.	20.00	40.00
☐ 15	Yvan Cournoyer, Mtl.	65.00	125.00
☐ 16	André Boudrias, Van.	20.00	40.00
☐ 17	Frank St. Marseille, Stl.	20.00	40.00
☐ 18	Norm Ullman, Tor.	45.00	90.00
☐ 19	Garry Unger, Stl.	25.00	50.00
☐ 20	Pierre Bouchard, Mtl.	20.00	40.00
☐ 21	Roy Edwards (G), L.A.	25.00	50.00
☐ 22	Ralph Backstrom, L.A.	20.00	40.00
☐ 23	Guy Trottier, Tor.	20.00	40.00
☐ 24	Serge Bernier, Pha.	20.00	40.00
☐ 25	Bert Marshall, Cal.	20.00	40.00
☐ 26	Wayne Hillman, Pha.	20.00	40.00
☐ 27	Tim Ecclestone, Det.	20.00	40.00
☐ 28	Walt McKechnie, Cal.	20.00	40.00
☐ 29	Tony Esposito (G), Chi.	125.00	250.00
☐ 30	Rod Gilbert, NYR.	45.00	90.00
☐ 31	Walt Tkaczuk, NYR.	20.00	40.00
☐ 32	Roger Crozier (G), Det.	25.00	50.00
☐ 33	Ken Schinkel, Pgh.	20.00	40.00
☐ 34	Ron Ellis, Tor.	20.00	40.00
☐ 35	Stan Mikita, Chi.	90.00	125.00
☐ 36	Bobby Orr, Bos.	700.00	1,400.00

1971 - 72 COLGATE HOCKEY HEADS

Short prints are marked with an asterick.

Head Size: 1 1/4" Height
Head: Moulded beige plastic; Name on back
Imprint: None

	Player	EX	NRMT
Complete Set (16 heads):		**85.00**	**170.00**
☐	Yvan Cournoyer, Mtl.	4.25	8.50
☐	Marcel Dionne, Det.	10.00	20.00
☐	Ken Dryden (G), Mtl.	9.00	18.00
☐	Paul Henderson, Tor.	3.00	6.00
☐	Guy Lafleur, Mtl.	9.00	18.00
☐	Frank Mahovlich, Mtl.	7.50	15.00
☐	Richard Martin, Buf. (*)	13.00	25.00
☐	Bobby Orr, Bos.	15.00	30.00
☐	Brad Park, NYI. (*)	18.00	35.00
☐	Jacques Plante (G), Tor.	6.50	13.00
☐	Jean Ratelle, NYI.	3.50	7.00
☐	Derek Sanderson, Bos.	4.50	9.00
☐	Dale Tallon, Van.	2.00	4.00
☐	Walter Tkaczuk, NYI.	2.00	4.00
☐	Norn Ullman, Tor., Error (Ullmann)	9.00	18.00
☐	Norm Ullman, Tor., Corrected	7.50	15.00
☐	Garry Unger, Stl.	2.00	4.00

1971 - 72 EDDIE SARGENT STICKERS

These stickers were issued in a 7 3/4" x 9 3/4" sheet with 14 players and 2 series stickers per sheet. Each sheet contains one player from each of the 14 teams in the NHL during that season.

Sticker Size: 1 7/8" x 2 1/2"
Face: Four colour, white border; Name, Team, Number
Back: Blank
Imprint: 1971 NHLPA PRINTED IN USA

No.	Player	EX	NRMT
Complete Set (224 cards):		**215.00**	**425.00**
Common Player:		**.35**	**.75**
Album:			**100.00**
☐ 1	Fred Stanfield, Bos.	.35	.75
☐ 2	Ed Westfall, Bos.	.35	.75
☐ 3	John McKenzie, Bos.	.35	.75
☐ 4	Derek Sanderson, Bos.	1.75	3.25
☐ 5	Rick Smith, Bos.	.35	.75
☐ 6	Ted Green, Bos.	.35	.75
☐ 7	Phil Esposito, Bos.	6.00	12.00
☐ 8	Ken Hodge, Bos.	.35	.75
☐ 9	John Bucyk, Bos.	2.50	5.00
☐ 10	Bobby Orr, Bos.	35.00	70.00
☐ 11	Dallas Smith, Bos.	.35	.75
☐ 12	Mike Walton, Bos.	.35	.75
☐ 13	Don Awrey, Bos.	.35	.75
☐ 14	Wayne Cashman, Bos.	.35	.75
☐ 15	Ed Johnston (G), Bos.	.60	1.25
☐ 16	Gerry Cheevers (G), Bos.	2.75	5.50
☐ 17	Gerry Meehan, Buf.	.35	.75
☐ 18	Ron C. Anderson, Buf.	.35	.75
☐ 19	Gilbert Perreault, Buf.	3.25	6.50
☐ 20	Eddie Shack, Buf.	2.00	4.00
☐ 21	Jim Watson, Buf.	.35	.75
☐ 22	Kevin O'Shea, Buf.	.35	.75
☐ 23	Al Hamilton, Buf.	.35	.75
☐ 24	Dick Duff, Buf.	.35	.75
☐ 25	Tracy Pratt, Buf.	.35	.75
☐ 26	Don Luce, Buf.	.35	.75
☐ 27	Roger Crozier (G), Buf.	.60	1.25
☐ 28	Doug Barrie, Buf.	.35	.75
☐ 29	Mike Robitaille, Buf.	.35	.75
☐ 30	Phil Goyette, Buf.	.35	.75
☐ 31	Larry Keenan, Buf.	.35	.75
☐ 32	Dave Dryden (G), Buf.	.60	1.25
☐ 33	Stan Mikita, Chi.	3.50	7.00
☐ 34	Bobby Hull, Chi.	13.00	25.00
☐ 35	Cliff Koroll, Chi.	.35	.75
☐ 36	Chico Maki, Chi.	.35	.75
☐ 37	Danny O'Shea, Chi.	.35	.75
☐ 38	Lou Angotti, Chi.	.35	.75
☐ 39	André Lacroix, Chi.	.35	.75
☐ 40	Jim Pappin, Chi.	.35	.75
☐ 41	Doug Jarrett, Chi.	.35	.75
☐ 42	Pit Martin, Chi.	.35	.75
☐ 43	Gary Smith (G), Chi.	.60	1.25
☐ 44	Tony Esposito (G), Chi.	6.00	12.00
☐ 45	Pat Stapleton, Chi.	.35	.75
☐ 46	Dennis Hull, Chi.	.35	.75
☐ 47	Bill White, Chi.	.35	.75
☐ 48	Keith Magnasun, Chi.	.35	.75
☐ 49	Bill Collins, Det.	.35	.75
☐ 50	Bob Wall, Det.	.35	.75
☐ 51	Red Berenson, Det.	.35	.75
☐ 52	Mickey Redmond, Det.	.60	1.25
☐ 53	Nick Libett, Det.	.35	.75
☐ 54	Gary Bergman, Det.	.35	.75
☐ 55	Alex Delvecchio, Det.	2.00	4.00
☐ 56	Tim Ecclestone, Det.	.35	.75
☐ 57	Arnie Brown, Det.	.35	.75
☐ 58	Ron Harris, Det.	.35	.75
☐ 59	Ab McDonald, Det.	.35	.75
☐ 60	Guy Charron, Det.	.35	.75
☐ 61	Al Smith (G), Det.	.60	1.25
☐ 62	Joe Daley (G), Det.	.60	1.25
☐ 63	Leon Rochefort, Det.	.35	.75
☐ 64	Ron Stackhouse, Det.	.35	.75
☐ 65	Juha Widing, L.A.	.35	.75
☐ 66	Bob Pulford, L.A.	1.50	3.00
☐ 67	Bill Flett, L.A.	.35	.75
☐ 68	Rogatien Vachon (G), L.A.	1.75	3.50
☐ 69	Ross Lonsberry, L.A.	.35	.75
☐ 70	Gilles Marotte, L.A.	.35	.75
☐ 71	Harry Howell, L.A.	1.50	3.00
☐ 72	Réal Lemieux, L.A.	.35	.75
☐ 73	Butch Goring, L.A.	.35	.75
☐ 74	Ed Joyal, L.A.	.35	.75
☐ 75	Larry Hillman, L.A.	.35	.75
☐ 76	Lucien Grenier, L.A.	.35	.75
☐ 77	Paul Curtis, L.A.	.35	.75
☐ 78	Jim Stanfield, L.A.	.35	.75
☐ 79	Ralph Backstrom, L.A.	.35	.75
☐ 80	Mike Byers, L.A.	.35	.75
☐ 81	Tom Reid, Min.	.35	.75
☐ 82	Jude Drouin, Min.	.35	.75
☐ 83	Jean Paul Parise, Min.	.35	.75
☐ 84	Doug Mohns, Min.	.35	.75
☐ 85	Danny Grant, Min.	.35	.75
☐ 86	Bill Goldsworthy, Min.	.35	.75
☐ 87	Charlie Burns, Min.	.35	.75
☐ 88	Murray Oliver, Min.	.35	.75
☐ 89	Dean Prentice, Min.	.35	.75
☐ 90	Bob Nevin, Min.	.35	.75
☐ 91	Ted Harris, Min.	.35	.75
☐ 92	Césare Maniago (G), Min.	.60	1.25
☐ 93	Lou Nanne, Min.	.35	.75
☐ 94	Ted Hampson, Min.	.35	.75
☐ 95	Barry Gibbs, Min.	.35	.75
☐ 96	Gump Worsley (G), Min.	3.25	6.50
☐ 97	J. C. Tremblay, Mtl.	.35	.75
☐ 98	Guy Lapointe, Mtl.	1.50	3.00
☐ 99	Peter Mahovlich, Mtl.	.35	.75
☐ 100	Larry Pleau, Mtl.	.35	.75
☐ 101	Phil Myre (G), Mtl.	.60	1.25
☐ 102	Yvan Cournoyer, Mtl.	2.75	5.50
☐ 103	Henri Richard, Mtl.	2.50	5.00
☐ 104	Frank Mahovlich, Mtl.	4.00	7.00
☐ 105	Jacques Lemaire, Mtl.	2.50	5.00
☐ 106	Claude Larose, Mtl.	.35	.75
☐ 107	Terry Harper, Mtl.	.35	.75

☐ 108	Jacques Laperrière, Mtl.	1.50	3.00
☐ 109	Phil Roberto, Mtl.	.35	.75
☐ 110	Serge Savard, Mtl.	1.75	3.50
☐ 111	Pierre Bouchard, Mtl.	.35	.75
☐ 112	Marc Tardif, Mtl.	.35	.75
☐ 113	Rod Gilbert, NYR.	2.00	4.00
☐ 114	Jean Ratelle, NYR.	2.00	4.00
☐ 115	Peter Stemkowski, NYR.	.35	.75
☐ 116	Brad Park, NYR.	3.00	6.00
☐ 117	Bobby Rousseau, NYR.	.35	.75
☐ 118	Dale Rolfe, NYR.	.35	.75
☐ 119	Rod Seiling, NYR.	.35	.75
☐ 120	Walt Tkachuk, NYR.	.35	.75
☐ 121	Vic Hadfield, NYR.	.35	.75
☐ 122	Jim Neilson, NYR.	.35	.75
☐ 123	Bill Fairbairn, NYR.	.35	.75
☐ 124	Bruce MacGregor, NYR.	.35	.75
☐ 125	Dave Balon, NYR.	.35	.75
☐ 126	Ted Irvine, NYR.	.35	.75
☐ 127	Gilles Villemure (G), NYR.	.60	1.25
☐ 128	Ed Giacomin (G), NYR.	2.75	5.50
☐ 129	Walt McKechnie, Cal.	.35	.75
☐ 130	Tommy Williams, Cal.	.35	.75
☐ 131	Wayne Carleton, Cal.	.35	.75
☐ 132	Gerry Pinder, Cal.	.35	.75
☐ 133	Gary Croteau, Cal.	.35	.75
☐ 134	Bert Marshall, Cal.	.35	.75
☐ 135	Tom Webster, Cal.	.35	.75
☐ 136	Norm Ferguson, Cal.	.35	.75
☐ 137	Carol Vadnais, Cal.	.35	.75
☐ 138	Gary Jarrett, Cal.	.35	.75
☐ 139	Ernest Hicke, Cal.	.35	.75
☐ 140	Paul Shmyr, Cal.	.35	.75
☐ 141	Marshall Johnston, Cal.	.35	.75
☐ 142	Don O'Donoghue, Cal.	.35	.75
☐ 143	Joey Johnston, Cal.	.35	.75
☐ 144	Dick Redmond, Cal.	.35	.75
☐ 145	Jim Johnson, Pha.	.35	.75
☐ 146	Wayne Hillman, Pha.	.35	.75
☐ 147	Brent Hughes, Pha.	.35	.75
☐ 148	Simon Nolet, Pha.	.35	.75
☐ 149	Larry Mickey, Pha.	.35	.75
☐ 150	Ed Van Impe, Pha.	.35	.75
☐ 151	Gary Dornhoffer, Pha.	.35	.75
☐ 152	Bob Clarke, Pha.	4.00	8.00
☐ 153	Jean-Guy Gendron, Pha.	.35	.75
☐ 154	Larry Hale, Pha.	.35	.75
☐ 155	Serge Bernier, Pha.	.35	.75
☐ 156	Doug Favel (G), Pha.	.60	1.25
☐ 157	Bob Kelly, Pha.	.35	.75
☐ 158	Joe Watson, Pha.	.35	.75
☐ 159	Larry Brown, Pha.	.35	.75
☐ 160	Bruce Gamble (G), Pha.	.60	1.25
☐ 161	Syl Apps, Pgh.	.35	.75
☐ 162	Ken Schinkel, Pgh.	.35	.75
☐ 163	Val Fonteyne, Pgh.	.35	.75
☐ 164	Bryan Watson, Pgh.	.35	.75
☐ 165	Bob Woytowich, Pgh.	.35	.75
☐ 166	Les Binkley (G), Pgh.	.60	1.25
☐ 167	Roy Edwards (G), Pgh.	.60	1.25
☐ 168	Jean Pronovost, Pgh.	.35	.75
☐ 169	Tim Horton, Pgh.	3.50	7.00
☐ 170	Ron Schock, Pgh.	.35	.75
☐ 171	Nick Harbaruk, Pgh.	.35	.75
☐ 172	Greg Polis, Pgh.	.35	.75
☐ 173	Bryan Hextall, Pgh.	.35	.75
☐ 174	Keith McCreary, Pgh.	.35	.75
☐ 175	Bill Hicke, Pgh.	.35	.75
☐ 176	Jim Rutherford (G), Pgh.	.60	1.25
☐ 177	Gary Sabourin, Stl.	.35	.75
☐ 178	Garry Unger, Stl.	.35	.75
☐ 179	Terry Crisp, Stl.	.60	1.25
☐ 180	Noel Picard, Stl.	.35	.75
☐ 181	Jim Roberts, Stl.	.35	.75
☐ 182	Barclay Plager, Stl.	.35	.75
☐ 183	Brit Selby, Stl.	.35	.75
☐ 184	Frank St. Marseille, Stl.	.35	.75
☐ 185	Ernie Wakley (G), Stl.	.60	1.25
☐ 186	Wayne Connelly, Stl.	.35	.75
☐ 187	Christain Bordeleau, Stl.	.35	.75
☐ 188	Bill Sutherland, Stl.	.35	.75
☐ 189	Bob Plager, Stl.	.35	.75
☐ 190	Bill Plager, Stl.	.35	.75
☐ 191	George Morrison, Stl.	.35	.75
☐ 192	Jim Lorentz, Stl.	.35	.75
☐ 193	Norm Ullman, Tor.	2.50	5.00
☐ 194	Jim McKenny, Tor.	.35	.75
☐ 195	Rick Ley, Tor.	.35	.75
☐ 196	Bob Baun, Tor.	.35	.75
☐ 197	Mike Pelyk, Tor.	.35	.75
☐ 198	Bill MacMillan, Tor.	.35	.75
☐ 199	Garry Monahan, Tor.	.35	.75
☐ 200	Paul Henderson, Tor.	.75	1.50
☐ 201	Jim Dorey, Tor.	.35	.75
☐ 202	Jim Harrison, Tor.	.35	.75
☐ 203	Ron Ellis, Tor.	.35	.75
☐ 204	Darryl Sittler, Tor.	3.50	7.00
☐ 205	Bernie Parent. (G), Tor.	2.75	5.50
☐ 206	Dave Keon, Tor.	2.50	5.00
☐ 207	Brad Selwood, Tor.	.35	.75
☐ 208	Don Marshall, Tor.	.35	.75
☐ 209	Dale Tallon, Van.	.35	.75
☐ 210	Danny Johnson, Van.	.35	.75
☐ 211	Murray Hall, Van.	.35	.75
☐ 212	Poul Popiel, Van.	.35	.75
☐ 213	George Gardner (G), Van.	.60	1.25
☐ 214	Gary Doak, Van.	.35	.75
☐ 215	Andre Boudrais, Van.	.35	.75
☐ 216	Orland Kurtenbach, Van.	.35	.75
☐ 217	Wayne Maki, Van.	.35	.75
☐ 218	Rosaire Paiement, Van.	.35	.75
☐ 219	Pat Quinn, Van.	.75	1.50
☐ 220	Fred Speck, Van.	.35	.75
☐ 221	Barry Wilkins, Van.	.35	.75
☐ 222	Dunc Wilson (G), Van.	.60	1.25
☐ 223	Ted Taylor, Van.	.35	.75
☐ 224	Mike Corrigan, Van.	.35	.75

1971 - 72 FRITO-LAY

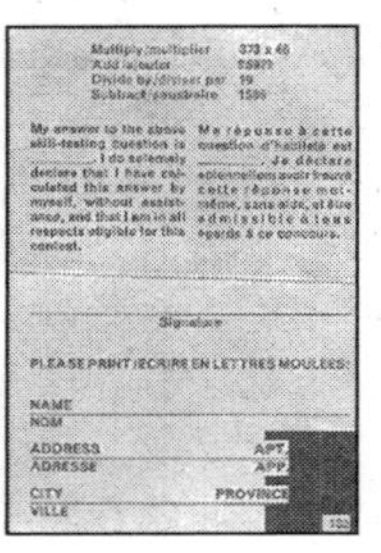

These paper cards were folded once.
Card Size: 2" x 3"
Face: Four colour
Back: Blue text
Imprint: None

	Complete Set (10 cards):	**50.00**	**100.00**
	Player	**EX**	**NRMT**
☐	Bobby Baun, Tor.	3.75	7.50
☐	Yvan Cournoyer, Mtl.	6.50	13.00
☐	Ken Dryden, Mtl.	15.00	30.00
☐	Ron Ellis, Tor.	3.00	6.00
☐	Paul Henderson, Tor.	4.50	9.00
☐	Frank Mahovlich, Mtl.	7.50	15.00
☐	Jacques Plante, (G), Tor.	10.00	20.00
☐	Henri Richard, Mtl.	6.00	12.00
☐	J. C. Tremblay, Mtl.	3.75	7.50
☐	Norm Ullman, Tor.	5.50	11.00

1971 - 72 O-PEE-CHEE

Card Size: 2 1/2" x 3 1/2"
Face: Four colour, white border, Team logo, Position
Back: Green and black on card stock, Number, Resume; Hockey trivia, Bilingual
Imprint: © O.P.C.

	Complete Set (264 cards):	**1,100.00**	**2,100.00**
	Common Player:	**2.25**	**4.50**
No.	**Player**	**EX**	**NRMT**
☐ 1	Poul Popiel, Van.	3.00	9.00
☐ **2**	**Pierre Bouchard, Mtl., RC**	**2.25**	**4.50**
☐ 3	Don Awrey, Bos.	2.25	4.50
☐ **4**	**Paul Curtis, L.A., RC**	**2.25**	**4.50**
☐ **5**	**Guy Trottier, Tor., RC**	**2.25**	**4.50**
☐ **6**	**Paul Shmyr, CA, RC**	**2.25**	**4.50**
☐ 7	Fred Stanfield, Bos.	2.25	4.50
☐ **8**	**Mike Robitaille, Buf., RC**	**2.25**	**4.50**
☐ 9	Vic Hadfield, NYR.	2.25	4.50
☐ 10	Jim Harrison, Tor.	2.25	4.50
☐ 11	Bill White, Chi.	2.25	4.50
☐ 12	Andre Boudrias, Van.	2.25	4.50
☐ 13	Gary Sabourin, Stl.	2.25	4.50
☐ 14	Arnie Brown, Det.	2.25	4.50
☐ 15	Yvan Cournoyer, Mtl.	4.50	9.00
☐ 16	Bryan Hextall, Pgh.	2.25	4.50
☐ 17	Gary Croteau, Cal.	2.25	4.50
☐ 18	Gilles Villemure (G), NYR.	3.00	6.00
☐ **19**	**Serge Bernier, Pha., RC**	**2.25**	**4.50**
☐ 20	Phil Esposito, Bos.	13.00	25.00
☐ 21	Tom Reid, Min.	2.25	4.50
☐ **22**	**Doug Barrie, Buf., RC**	**2.25**	**4.50**
☐ 23	Eddie Joyal, L.A.	2.25	4.50
☐ **24**	**Dunc Wilson (G), Van., RC**	**3.00**	**6.00**
☐ 25	Pat Stapleton, Chi.	2.25	4.50
☐ 26	Garry Unger, Stl., Err. (Gary)	2.25	4.50
☐ 27	Al Smith (G), Det.	3.00	6.00
☐ 28	Bob Woytowich, Pgh.	2.25	4.50
☐ 29	Marc Tardif, Mtl., Err. (Tardiff)	2.25	4.50
☐ 30	Norm Ullman, Tor.	3.50	7.00
☐ 31	Tom Williams, Cal.	2.25	4.50
☐ 32	Ted Harris, Min.	2.25	4.50
☐ 33	Andre Lacroix, Pha.	2.25	4.50
☐ 34	Mike Byers, L.A., LC	2.25	4.50
☐ 35	John Bucyk, Bos	3.50	7.00
☐ 36	Roger Crozier (G), Buf.	3.00	6.00
☐ 37	Alex Delvecchio, Det.	3.50	7.00
☐ 38	Frank St. Marseille, Stl.	2.25	4.50
☐ 39	Pit Martin, Chi.	2.25	4.50
☐ 40	Brad Park, NYR.	10.00	20.00
☐ **41**	**Greg Polis, Pgh., RC**	**2.25**	**4.50**
☐ 42	Orland Kurtenbach, Van.	2.25	4.50
☐ **43**	**Jim McKenny, Tor., RC**	**2.25**	**4.50**
☐ 44	Bob Nevin, Min.	2.25	4.50
☐ **45**	**Ken Dryden (G), Mtl., RC**	**190.00**	**375.00**
☐ 46	Carol Vadnais, Cal.	2.25	4.50
☐ 47	Bill Flett, L.A.	2.25	4.50
☐ 48	Jim Johnson, Pha., LC	2.25	4.50
☐ 49	Al Hamilton, Buf.	2.25	4.50
☐ 50	Bobby Hull, Chi.	25.00	50.00
☐ **51**	**Chris Bordeleau, Stl., RC**	**2.25**	**4.50**
☐ 52	Tim Ecclestone, Det.	2.25	4.50
☐ 53	Rod Seiling, NYR.	2.25	4.50
☐ 54	Gerry Cheevers (G), Bos.	5.50	11.00
☐ 55	Bill Goldsworthy, Min.	2.25	4.50
☐ 56	Ron Schock, Pgh.	2.25	4.50
☐ 57	Jim Dorey, Tor.	2.25	4.50
☐ 58	Wayne Maki, Van.	2.25	4.50
☐ 59	Terry Harper, Mtl.	2.25	4.50

- ☐ 60 Gilbert Perreault, Buf. 18.00 35.00
- ☐ **61 Ernie Hicke, Cal., RC 2.25 4.50**
- ☐ 62 Wayne Hillman, Pha. 2.25 4.50
- ☐ 63 Denis DeJordy (G), L.A. 3.00 6.00
- ☐ 64 Ken Schinkel, Pgh. 2.25 4.50
- ☐ 65 Derek Sanderson, Bos. 5.00 10.00
- ☐ 66 Barclay Plager, Stl. 2.25 4.50
- ☐ 67 Paul Henderson, Tor. 3.00 6.00
- ☐ 68 Jude Drouin, Min. 2.25 4.50
- ☐ 69 Keith Magnuson, Chi. 2.25 4.50
- ☐ 70 Ron Harris, Det. 2.25 4.50
- ☐ 71 Jacques Lemaire, Mtl. 4.00 8.00
- ☐ 72 Doug Favell (G), Pha. 3.00 6.00
- ☐ 73 Bert Marshall, Cal. 2.25 4.50
- ☐ 74 Ted Irvine, NYR. 2.25 4.50
- ☐ 75 Walt Tkaczuk, NYR. 2.25 4.50
- ☐ **76 Bob Berry, L.A., RC 3.00 6.00**
- ☐ **77 Syl Apps, Jr., Pgh., RC 2.25 4.50**
- ☐ 78 Tom Webster, Det. 2.25 4.50
- ☐ 79 Danny Grant, Min. 2.25 4.50
- ☐ 80 Dave Keon, Tor. 3.25 6.50
- ☐ 81 Ernie Wakely (G), Stl. 3.00 6.00
- ☐ 82 John McKenzie, Bos. 2.25 4.50
- ☐ **83 Ron Stackhouse, Cal., RC 2.25 4.50**
- ☐ 84 Pete Mahovlich, Mtl. 2.25 4.50
- ☐ 85 Dennis Hull, Chi. 2.25 4.50
- ☐ **86 Juha Widing, L.A., RC 2.25 4.50**
- ☐ 87 Gary Doak, Van. 2.25 4.50
- ☐ 88 Phil Goyette, Buf., LC 2.25 4.50
- ☐ 89 Lew Morrison, Pha. 2.25 4.50
- ☐ **90 Ab DeMarco, NYR., RC 2.25 4.50**
- ☐ 91 Red Berenson, Det. 2.25 4.50
- ☐ 92 Mike Pelyk, Tor. 2.25 4.50
- ☐ 93 Gary Jarrett, Cal. 2.25 4.50
- ☐ 94 Bob Pulford, L.A., LC 3.00 6.00
- ☐ **95 Danny Johnson, Van., RC, LC 2.25 4.50**
- ☐ 96 Eddie Shack, Buf. 4.25 8.50
- ☐ 97 Jean Ratelle, NYR. 3.50 7.00
- ☐ 98 Jim Pappin, Chi. 2.25 4.50
- ☐ 99 Roy Edwards (G), Pgh. 3.00 6.00
- ☐ 100 Bobby Orr, Bos. 50.00 100.00
- ☐ 101 Ted Hampson, Min., LC 2.25 4.50
- ☐ 102 Mickey Redmond, Det. 3.25 6.50
- ☐ 103 Bob Plager, Stl. 2.25 4.50
- ☐ **104 Barry Ashbee, Pha., RC 2.25 4.50**
- ☐ 105 Frank Mahovlich, Mtl. 5.50 11.00
- ☐ **106 Dick Redmond, Cal., RC 2.25 4.50**
- ☐ 107 Tracy Pratt, Buf. 2.25 4.50
- ☐ 108 Ralph Backstrom, L.A. 2.25 4.50
- ☐ 109 Murray Hall, Van. 2.25 4.50
- ☐ 110 Tony Esposito (G), Chi. 25.00 50.00
- ☐ 111 Checklist 1 (1 - 132) 350.00 700.00
- ☐ 112 Jim Neilson, NYR. 2.25 4.50
- ☐ 113 Ron Ellis, Tor. 2.25 4.50
- ☐ 114 Bobby Clarke, Pha. 30.00 60.00
- ☐ 115 Ken Hodge, Bos. 2.25 4.50
- ☐ 116 Jim Roberts, Stl. 2.25 4.50
- ☐ 117 Césare Maniago (G), Min. 3.00 6.00
- ☐ 118 Jean Pronovost, Pgh. 2.25 4.50
- ☐ 119 Gary Bergman, Det. 2.25 4.50
- ☐ 120 Henri Richard, Mtl. 4.25 8.50
- ☐ 121 Ross Lonsberry, L.A. 2.25 4.50
- ☐ 122 Pat Quinn, Van. 3.00 6.00
- ☐ 123 Rod Gilbert, NYR. 3.50 7.00
- ☐ 124 Walt McKechnie, Cal. 2.25 4.50
- ☐ 125 Stan Mikita, Chi. 9.00 18.00
- ☐ 126 Ed Van Impe, Pha. 2.25 4.50
- ☐ **127 Terry Crisp, Stl., RC 7.00 14.00**
- ☐ **128 Fred Barrett, Min., RC 2.25 4.50**
- ☐ 129 Wayne Cashman, Bos. 2.25 4.50
- ☐ 130 J. C. Tremblay, Mtl. 2.25 4.50
- ☐ 131 Bernie Parent (G), Tor. 11.00 22.00
- ☐ 132 Bryan Watson, Pgh. 2.25 4.50
- ☐ **133 Marcel Dionne, Det., RC 60.00 120.00**
- ☐ 134 Ab McDonald, Det. 2.25 4.50
- ☐ 135 Leon Rochefort, Det. 2.25 4.50
- ☐ **136 Serge Lajeunesse, Det., RC, LC 2.25 4.50**
- ☐ 137 Joe Daley (G), Det. 3.00 6.00
- ☐ 138 Brian Conacher, Det., LC 2.25 4.50
- ☐ 139 Bill Collins, Det. 2.25 4.50
- ☐ 140 Nick Libett, Det. 2.25 4.50
- ☐ 141 Bill Sutherland, Det., LC 2.25 4.50
- ☐ 142 Bill Hicke, Det. 2.25 4.50
- ☐ 143 Serge Savard, Mtl. 3.50 7.00
- ☐ 144 Jacques Laperrière, Mtl. 3.00 6.00
- ☐ 145 Guy Lapointe, Mtl. 4.00 7.50
- ☐ 146 Claude Larose, Mtl., Err. (La Rose) 2.25 4.50
- ☐ 147 Réjean Houle, Mtl. 3.00 6.00
- ☐ **148 Guy Lafleur, Mtl., RC, Err. (LaFleur) 140.00 275.00**
- ☐ **149 Dale Hoganson, Mtl., RC 2.25 4.50**
- ☐ **150 Al McDonough, L.A., RC 2.25 4.50**
- ☐ 151 Gilles Marotte, L.A. 2.25 4.50
- ☐ **152 Butch Goring, L.A., RC 6.50 13.00**
- ☐ 153 Harry Howell, L.A. 3.00 6.00
- ☐ 154 Real Lemieux, L.A. 2.25 4.50
- ☐ **155 Gary Edwards (G), L.A., RC 3.00 6.00**
- ☐ 156 Rogatien Vachon (G), L.A. 4.25 8.50
- ☐ 157 Mike Corrigan, L.A. 2.25 4.50
- ☐ 158 Floyd Smith, Buf. 2.25 4.50
- ☐ 159 Dave Dryden (G), Buf. 3.00 6.00
- ☐ 160 Gerry Meehan, Buf. 2.25 4.50
- ☐ **161 Rick Martin, Buf., RC 10.00 20.00**
- ☐ **162 Steve Atkinson, Buf., RC 2.25 4.50**
- ☐ 163 Ron C. Anderson, Buf. 2.25 4.50
- ☐ 164 Dick Duff, Buf., LC 2.25 4.50
- ☐ 165 Jim Watson, Buf., LC 2.25 4.50
- ☐ **166 Don Luce, Buf., RC 2.25 4.50**
- ☐ 167 Larry Mickey, Buf., LC 2.25 4.50
- ☐ 168 Larry Hillman, Buf. 2.25 4.50
- ☐ 169 Ed Westfall, Bos. 2.25 4.50
- ☐ 170 Dallas Smith, Bos. 2.25 4.50
- ☐ 171 Mike Walton, Bos. 2.25 4.50
- ☐ 172 Eddie Johnston (G), Bos. 3.00 6.00
- ☐ 173 Ted Green, Bos. 2.25 4.50
- ☐ 174 Rick Smith, Bos. 2.25 4.50
- ☐ **175 Reggie Leach, Bos., RC 7.00 14.00**
- ☐ 176 Don Marcotte, Bos. 2.25 4.50
- ☐ **177 Bobby Sheehan, Cal., RC 2.25 4.50**
- ☐ 178 Wayne Carleton, Cal. 2.25 4.50
- ☐ 179 Norm Ferguson, Cal. 2.25 4.50
- ☐ **180 Don O'Donoghue, Cal., RC, LC 2.25 4.50**
- ☐ **181 Gary Kurt (G), Cal., RC 3.00 6.00**
- ☐ **182 Joey Johnston, Cal., RC 2.25 4.50**
- ☐ **183 Stan Gilbertson, Cal., RC 2.25 4.50**
- ☐ **184 Craig Patrick, Cal., RC 6.00 12.00**
- ☐ 185 Gerry Pinder, Cal. 2.25 4.50
- ☐ 186 Tim Horton, Pgh. 6.50 13.00
- ☐ **187 Darryl Edestrand, Pgh., RC 2.25 4.50**
- ☐ 188 Keith McCreary, Pgh. 2.25 4.50
- ☐ 189 Val Fonteyne, Pgh. 2.25 4.50
- ☐ **190 Sheldon Kannegiesser, Pgh., RC 2.25 4.50**
- ☐ **191 Nick Harbaruk, Pgh., RC 2.25 4.50**
- ☐ 192 Les Binkley (G), Pgh. 3.00 6.00
- ☐ 193 Darryl Sittler, Tor. 25.00 50.00
- ☐ 194 Rick Ley, Tor. 2.25 4.50
- ☐ 195 Jacques Plante (G), Tor. 15.00 30.00
- ☐ 196 Bobby Baun, Tor. 2.25 4.50
- ☐ 197 Brian Glennie, Tor. 2.25 4.50
- ☐ **198 Brian Spencer, Tor., RC 3.25 6.50**
- ☐ 199 Don Marshall, Tor., LC 2.25 4.50
- ☐ **200 Denis Dupère, Tor., RC 2.25 4.50**
- ☐ 201 Bruce Gamble (G), Pha., LC 3.00 6.00
- ☐ 202 Gary Dornhoefer, Pha. 2.25 4.50
- ☐ **203 Bob Kelly, Pha., RC 2.25 4.50**
- ☐ 204 Jean-Guy Gendron, Pha. 2.25 4.50
- ☐ 205 Brent Hughes, Pha. 2.25 4.50
- ☐ 206 Simon Nolet, Pha. 2.25 4.50
- ☐ **207 Rick MacLeish,, Pha. RC 9.00 18.00**
- ☐ 208 Doug Jarrett, Chi. 2.25 4.50
- ☐ 209 Cliff Koroll, Chi. 2.25 4.50
- ☐ 210 Chico Maki, Chi. 2.25 4.50
- ☐ 211 Danny O'Shea, Chi. 2.25 4.50
- ☐ 212 Lou Angotti, Chi. 2.25 4.50
- ☐ 213 Eric Nesterenko, Chi., LC 2.25 4.50
- ☐ 214 Bryan Campbell, Chi. 2.25 4.50
- ☐ **215 Bill Fairbairn, NYR., RC 2.25 4.50**
- ☐ 216 Bruce MacGregor, NYR. 2.25 4.50
- ☐ 217 Pete Stemkowski, NYR. 2.25 4.50
- ☐ 218 Bobby Rousseau, NYR. 2.25 4.50
- ☐ 219 Dale Rolfe, NYR. 2.25 4.50
- ☐ 220 Ed Giacomin (G), NYR. 5.50 11.00
- ☐ 221 Glen Sather, NYR. 3.00 6.00
- ☐ 222 Carl Brewer, Stl., LC 2.25 4.50
- ☐ **223 George Morrison, Stl., RC 2.25 4.50**
- ☐ 224 Noel Picard, Stl. 2.25 4.50
- ☐ **225 Pete McDuffe (G), Stl., RC, Err. (Defence) 3.00 6.00**
- ☐ 226 Brit Selby, Stl., LC 2.25 4.50
- ☐ 227 Jim Lorentz, Stl. 2.25 4.50
- ☐ **228 Phil Roberto, Stl., RC 2.25 4.50**
- ☐ 229 Dave Balon, Van. 2.25 4.50
- ☐ **230 Barry Wilkins, Van., RC 2.25 4.50**
- ☐ **231 Dennis Kearns, Van., RC 2.25 4.50**
- ☐ **232 Jocelyn Guevremont, Van., RC 2.25 4.50**
- ☐ 233 Rosaire Paiement, Van. 2.25 4.50
- ☐ 234 Dale Tallon, Van. 2.25 4.50
- ☐ 235 George Gardner (G), Van., LC 3.00 6.00
- ☐ 236 Ron Stewart, Van., LC 2.25 4.50
- ☐ 237 Wayne Connelly, Van. 2.25 4.50
- ☐ 238 Charlie Burns, Min. 2.25 4.50
- ☐ 239 Murray Oliver, Min. 2.25 4.50
- ☐ 240 Lou Nanne, Min. 2.25 4.50
- ☐ 241 Gump Worsley (G), Min. 5.50 11.00
- ☐ 242 Doug Mohns, Min. 2.25 4.50
- ☐ 243 J. P. Parise, Min. 2.25 4.50
- ☐ 244 Dennis Hextall, Min. 2.25 4.50
- ☐ 245 AW: Bobby Orr, Bos. 35.00 65.00
- ☐ 246 AW: Gilbert Perreault, Buf. 10.00 20.00
- ☐ 247 AW: Phil Esposito, Bos. 7.50 15.00
- ☐ 248 AW: E. Giacomin/ G. Villemure, NYR. 4.00 8.00
- ☐ 249 AW: John Bucyk Bos. 3.00 6.00
- ☐ 250 AS: Ed Giacomin (G), NYR. 3.25 6.50
- ☐ 251 AS: Bobby Orr, Bos. 35.00 65.00
- ☐ 252 AS: J. C. Tremblay, Mtl. 2.25 4.50
- ☐ 253 AS: Phil Esposito, Bos. 7.50 15.00
- ☐ 254 AS: Ken Hodge, Sr., Bos. 2.25 4.50
- ☐ 255 AS: John Bucyk, Bos. 3.00 6.00
- ☐ 256 AS: Jacques Plante (G), Tor., Err. (63 shutouts) 4.00 8.00
- ☐ 257 AS: Brad Park, NYR. 6.00 12.00
- ☐ 258 AS: Pat Stapleton, Chi. 9.00 18.00
- ☐ 259 AS: Dave Keon, Tor. 3.00 6.00
- ☐ 260 AS: Yvan Cournoyer, Mtl. 3.00 6.00
- ☐ 261 AS: Bobby Hull, Chi. 15.00 30.00
- ☐ 262 Gordie Howe, Mr. Hockey 50.00 100.00
- ☐ 263 Jean Béliveau, Le Gros Bill 30.00 60.00
- ☐ 264 Checklist 2 (133 - 264) 75.00 225.00

O-PEE-CHEE BOOKLETS

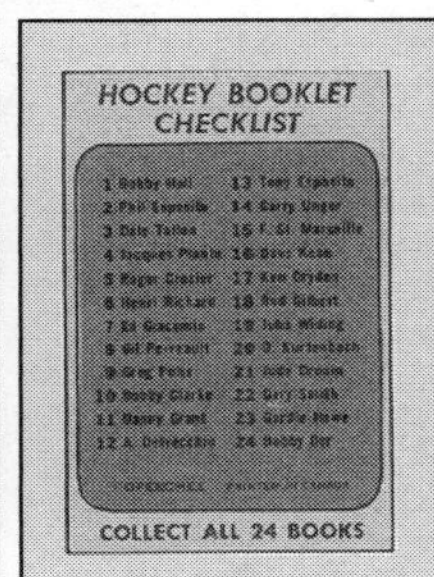

These eight-page comic style booklets were issued as inserts with the regular 1971-72 O-Pee-Chee set. The back cover is a checklist. The inside story is a brief history of the player.

Insert Set (24 booklets): 70.00 140.00

No.	Player	EX	NRMT
☐ 1	Bobby Hull, Chi.	6.00	18.00
☐ 2	Phil Esposito, Bos.	4.50	8.50
☐ 3	Dale Tallon, Van.	1.50	3.00
☐ 4	Jacques Plante (G), Tor.	6.00	12.00
☐ 5	Roger Crozier (G), Buf.	2.50	5.00
☐ 6	Henri Richard, Mtl.	4.00	8.00
☐ 7	Ed Giacomin (G), NYR.	4.00	8.00
☐ 8	Gilbert Perreault, Buf.	4.00	8.00
☐ 9	Greg Polis, Pgh.	1.50	3.00
☐ 10	Bobby Clarke, Pha.	4.00	8.00
☐ 11	Danny Grant, Min.	1.50	3.00
☐ 12	Alex Delvecchio, Det.	2.50	5.00
☐ 13	Tony Esposito (G), Chi.	4.50	8.50
☐ 14	Garry Unger, Stl.	2.50	5.00
☐ 15	Frank St. Marseille, Stl.	1.50	3.00
☐ 16	Dave Keon, Tor.	3.25	6.50
☐ 17	Ken Dryden (G), Mtl.	11.00	22.00
☐ 18	Rod Gilbert, NYR.	3.25	6.50
☐ 19	Juha Widing, L.A.	1.50	3.00
☐ 20	Orland Kurtenbach, Van.	1.50	3.00
☐ 21	Jude Drouin, Min.	1.50	3.00
☐ 22	Gary Smith (G), Cal.	2.50	5.00
☐ 23	Gordie Howe, Det.	14.00	28.00
☐ 24	Bobby Orr, Bos.	20.00	35.00

1971 - 72 O-PEE-CHEE POSTERS

Posters are numbered _ of 24. Most posters have the player's facsimile autograph. The numbered posters were issued on their own, without cards, packaged folded with two to a wax pack.

Poster Size: 9 15/16" x 17 7/8"
Face: Four colour on coated newsprint; Bilingual
Back: Blank
Imprint: O.P.C.

		EX	NRMT
Complete Set (24 posters):		**400.00**	**800.00**
Common Player:		**9.00**	**18.00**
No.	**Player**	**EX**	**NRMT**
☐ 1	Bobby Orr, Bos.	65.00	175.00
☐ 2	Bob Pulford, L.A.	13.00	25.00
☐ 3	Dave Keon, Tor.	18.00	35.00
☐ 4	Yvan Cournoyer, Mtl.	18.00	35.00
☐ 5	Dale Tallon, Van.	9.00	18.00
☐ 6	Richard Martin, Buf.	11.00	22.00
☐ 7	Rod Gilbert, NYR.	15.00	30.00
☐ 8	Tony Esposito (G), Chi.	25.00	50.00
☐ 9	Bobby Hull, Chi.	35.00	70.00
☐ 10	Red Berenson, Det.	9.00	18.00
☐ 11	Norm Ullman, Tor.	15.00	30.00
☐ 12	Orland Kurtenbach, Van.	9.00	18.00
☐ 13	Guy Lafleur, Mtl.	45.00	90.00
☐ 14	Gilbert Perreault, Buf.	25.00	45.00
☐ 15	Jacques Plante (G), Tor.	28.00	55.00
☐ 16	Bruce Gamble (G), Pha.	11.00	22.00
☐ 17	Walt McKechnie, Cal.	9.00	18.00
☐ 18	Tim Horton, Pgh.	25.00	45.00
☐ 19	Jean Ratelle, NYR.	15.00	30.00
☐ 20	Garry Unger, Stl.	9.00	18.00
☐ 21	Phil Esposito, Bos.	20.00	40.00
☐ 22	Ken Dryden (G), Mtl.	50.00	100.00
☐ 23	Gump Worsley (G), Min.	20.00	40.00
☐ 24	Club de Hockey Canadien 1970-71	25.00	50.00

1971 - 72 PRO STAR PROMOTIONS

We have little information on this set. This set may have been released in a different year. Other singles may exist.

Card Size: 3 1/2" x 5 7/16"
Imprint:

	Players	EX	NRMT
☐	Bos./NYR.: R. Gilbert/ P. Esposito	10.00	20.00
☐	Bos./NYR.: B. Rousseau/ Rod Serling/ B. Orr	25.00	50.00
☐	Bos./Tor.: B. Orr/ J. Mckenney/ etc.	25.00	50.00
☐	Bos./Mtl.: Y. Cournoyer/ F. Mahovlich/ B. Orr	25.00	50.00
☐	Bos./Min.: J. Bucyk/ etc.	7.50	15.00
☐	Mtl./Bos.: B. Orr/ D. Marcotte/ K. Dryden	30.00	60.00
☐	Mtl./NYR.: R. Seiling/ F. Mahovlich	15.00	30.00
☐	Mtl./Det.: G. Bergman/ K. Dryden	20.00	40.00
☐	Mtl./Min.: K. Dryden/ J. Roberts/ etc.	20.00	40.00
☐	Mtl./Det.: S. Savard/ K. Dryden/ etc.	25.00	45.00
☐	Mtl./Min.: Y. Cournoyer/ etc.	10.00	20.00
☐	Mtl./NYR.: G. Lapointe/ E. Giacomin/ etc.	10.00	20.00
☐	Mtl./NYR.: R. Seiling/ E. Giacomin/ Y. Cournoyer	10.00	20.00
☐	Mtl./NYR.: J. Neilson/ H. Richard/ G. Villeneuve	7.50	15.00
☐	Mtl./NYR.: P. Mahovlich/ E. Giacomin/ etc.	7.50	15.00
☐	Mtl./NYR.:	7.50	15.00
☐	NYR./Chi.:	7.50	15.00
☐	Van./Atl.:	7.50	15.00
☐	Van./Atl.:	7.50	15.00
☐	Van./Atl.:	7.50	15.00
☐	Van./Mtl.:	7.50	15.00
☐	Van./Mtl.:	7.50	15.00

1971 - 72 SOVIET STARS POSTCARDS

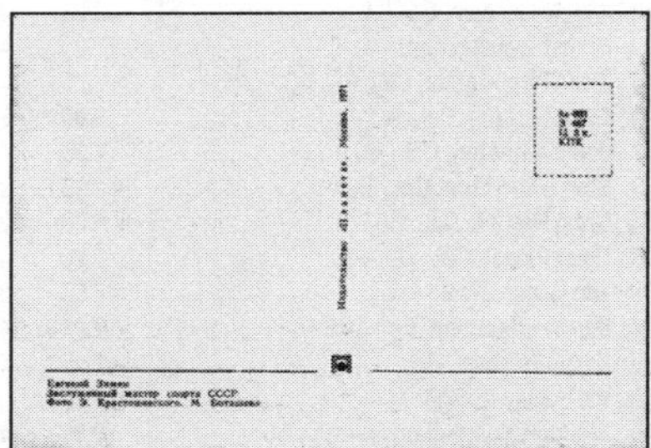

Postcard Size: 4 1/8" x 5 3/4"
Front: Four colour
Back: Russian text
Imprint:

	Player	EX	NRMT
Complete Set (25 cards and folder):		**75.00**	**150.00**
	Player	**EX**	**NRMT**
☐	Victor Konovalenko (G)	3.50	7.00
☐	Valery Davydov	2.50	5.00
☐	Vladimir Lutchenko	2.50	5.00
☐	Viktor Kuzkin	2.50	5.00
☐	Alexander Ragulin	5.00	10.00
☐	Igor Romishevsky	2.50	5.00
☐	Gennady Tsycakov	2.50	5.00
☐	Vyacheslav Starshinov	2.50	5.00
☐	Evgney Zimin	2.50	5.00
☐	Alexander Maltsev	4.00	8.00
☐	Anatoli Firsov	2.50	5.00
☐	Evgeny Mishakov	2.50	5.00
☐	Boris Mikhailov	6.00	12.00
☐	Yuri Liapkin	2.50	5.00
☐	Alexander Martiniuk	2.50	5.00
☐	Vladimir Petrov	4.00	8.00
☐	Valery Kharlamov	7.50	15.00
☐	Vladimir Vikulov	2.50	5.00
☐	Vladimir Shadrin	2.50	5.00
☐	Vladislav Tretiak (G)	15.00	30.00
☐	Team Photo	6.00	12.00
☐	A. Czepnishev	2.50	5.00
☐	A. Tapasov	2.50	5.00
☐	U.S.S.R. vs. Finland	4.00	8.00
☐	U.S.S.R. in action	4.00	8.00

1971 - 72 TOPPS

Card Size: 2 1/2" x 3 1/2"
Face: Four colour, white border, Team logo, Position
Back: Yellow and green on card stock, Number, Resume, Hockey trivia
Imprint: T.C.G.

		EX	NRMT
Topps Set (176 cards):		**200.00**	**400.00**
Common Player:		**.75**	**1.50**
No.	**Player**	**EX**	**NRMT**
☐ 1	LL: P. Esposito/J. Bucyk/B. Hull	8.50	25.00
☐ 2	LL: B. Orr/P. Esposito/J. Bucyk	9.00	18.00
☐ 3	LL: P. Esposito/B. Orr/J. Bucyk	9.00	18.00
☐ 4	LL: T. Esposito/E. Johnston/G. Cheevers/E. Giacomin	6.50	13.00
☐ 5	LL: E. Giacomin/T. Esposito/C. Maniago	4.50	8.50
☐ 6	LL: J. Plante/E. Giacomin/T. Esposito	8.00	16.00
☐ 7	Fred Stanfield, Bos.	.75	1.50
☐ **8**	**Mike Robitaille, Buf., RC**	**.75**	**1.50**
☐ 9	Vic Hadfield, NYR.	.75	1.50
☐ 10	Jacques Plante (G), Tor.	10.00	20.00
☐ 11	Bill White, Chi.	.75	1.50
☐ 12	Andre Boudrias, Van.	.75	1.50
☐ 13	Jim Lorentz, Stl.	.75	1.50
☐ 14	Arnie Brown, Det.	.75	1.50
☐ 15	Yvan Cournoyer, Mtl.	2.75	5.50
☐ 16	Bryan Hextall, Jr., Pgh.	.75	1.50
☐ 17	Gary Croteau, Cal.	.75	1.50
☐ 18	Gilles Villemure (G), NYR.	1.25	2.50
☐ **19**	**Serge Bernier, Pha., RC**	**.75**	**1.50**
☐ 20	Phil Esposito, Bos.	9.00	18.00
☐ 21	Charlie Burns, Min.	.75	1.50
☐ **22**	**Doug Barrie, Buf., RC**	**.75**	**1.50**
☐ 23	Eddie Joyal, L.A.	.75	1.50
☐ 24	Rosaire Paiement, Van.	.75	1.50
☐ 25	Pat Stapleton, Chi.	.75	1.50
☐ 26	Garry Unger,Stl.	1.25	2.50
☐ 27	Al Smith (G), Det.	1.25	2.50
☐ 28	Bob Woytowich, Pgh.	.75	1.50
☐ 29	Marc Tardif, Mtl.	.75	1.50
☐ 30	Norm Ullman, Tor.	2.25	4.50
☐ 31	Tom Williams, Cal.	.75	1.50
☐ 32	Ted Harris, Min.	.75	1.50
☐ 33	André Lacroix, Pha.	.75	1.50
☐ 34	Mike Byers, L.A., LC	.75	1.50
☐ 35	John Bucyk, Bos.	2.25	4.50
☐ 36	Roger Crozier (G), Buf.	1.75	3.50
☐ 37	Alex Delvecchio, Det.	2.50	5.00
☐ 38	Frank St. Marseille,Stl.	.75	1.50
☐ 39	Pit Martin, Chi.	.75	1.50
☐ 40	Brad Park, NYR.	7.00	14.00
☐ **41**	**Greg Polis, Pgh., RC**	**.75**	**1.50**
☐ 42	Orland Kurtenbach, Van.	.75	1.50
☐ **43**	**Jim McKenny, Tor., RC**	**.75**	**1.50**
☐ 44	Bob Nevin, Min.	.75	1.50
☐ **45**	**Ken Dryden (G), Mtl., RC**	**80.00**	**160.00**
☐ 46	Carol Vadnais, Cal.	.75	1.50
☐ 47	Bill Flett, L.A.	.75	1.50
☐ 48	Jim Johnson, Pha., LC	.75	1.50
☐ 49	Allan Hamilton, Buf.	.75	1.50
☐ 50	Bobby Hull, Chi.	15.00	30.00
☐ **51**	**Chris Bordeleau, Stl., RC**	**.75**	**1.50**
☐ 52	Tim Ecclestone, Det.	.75	1.50
☐ 53	Rod Seiling, NYR.	.75	1.50
☐ 54	Gerry Cheevers (G), Bos.	3.25	6.50
☐ 55	Bill Goldsworthy, Min.	.75	1.50
☐ 56	Ron Schock, Pgh.	.75	1.50
☐ 57	Jim Dorey, Tor.	.75	1.50
☐ 58	Wayne Maki, Van.	.75	1.50
☐ 59	Terry Harper, Mtl.	.75	1.50

☐ 60	Gilbert Perreault, Buf.	11.00	22.00
☐ **61**	**Ernie Hicke, Cal., RC**	**.75**	**1.50**
☐ 62	Wayne Hillman, Pha.	.75	1.50
☐ 63	Denis DeJordy (G), L.A.	1.25	2.50
☐ 64	Ken Schinkel, Pgh.	.75	1.50
☐ 65	Derek Sanderson, Bos.	3.00	6.00
☐ 66	Barclay Plager,Stl.	.75	1.50
☐ 67	Paul Henderson, Tor.	1.25	2.50
☐ 68	Jude Drouin, Min.	.75	1.50
☐ 69	Keith Magnuson, Chi.	.75	1.50
☐ 70	Gordie Howe, Det.	35.00	65.00
☐ 71	Jacques Lemaire, Mtl.	2.75	5.50
☐ 72	Doug Favell (G), Pha.	1.25	2.50
☐ 73	Bert Marshall, Cal.	.75	1.50
☐ 74	Gerry Meehan, Buf.	.75	1.50
☐ 75	Walt Tkaczuk, NYR.	.75	1.50
☐ **76**	**Bob Berry, L.A., RC**	**1.25**	**2.50**
☐ **77**	**Syl Apps, Pgh., RC**	**.75**	**1.50**
☐ 78	Tom Webster, Det.	.75	1.50
☐ 79	Danny Grant, Min.	.75	1.50
☐ 80	Dave Keon, Tor.	2.25	4.50
☐ 81	Ernie Wakely (G),Stl.	1.25	2.50
☐ 82	John McKenzie, Bos.	.75	1.50
☐ 83	Doug Roberts, Cal.	.75	1.50
☐ 84	Peter Mahovlich, Mtl.	.75	1.50
☐ 85	Dennis Hull, Chi.	.75	1.50
☐ **86**	**Juha Widing, L.A., RC**	**.75**	**1.50**
☐ 87	Gary Doak, Van.	.75	1.50
☐ 88	Phil Goyette, Buf., LC	.75	1.50
☐ 89	Gary Dornhoefer, Pha.	.75	1.50
☐ 90	Ed Giacomin (G), NYR.	3.25	6.50
☐ 91	Red Berenson, Det.	.75	1.50
☐ 92	Mike Pelyk, Tor.	.75	1.50
☐ 93	Gary Jarrett, Cal.	.75	1.50
☐ 94	Bob Pulford, L.A., LC	1.75	3.50
☐ 95	Dale Tallon, Van.	.75	1.50
☐ 96	Eddie Shack, Buf.	2.75	5.50
☐ 97	Jean Ratelle, NYR.	2.50	5.00
☐ 98	Jim Pappin, Chi.	.75	1.50
☐ 99	Roy Edwards (G), Pgh.	1.25	2.50
☐ 100	Bobby Orr, Bos.	30.00	55.00
☐ 101	Ted Hampson, Min., LC	.75	1.50
☐ 102	Mickey Redmond, Det.	2.25	4.50
☐ 103	Bob Plager,Stl.	.75	1.50
☐ 104	Bruce Gamble (G), Pha., LC	1.25	2.50
☐ 105	Frank Mahovlich, Mtl.	3.50	7.00
☐ **106**	**Tony Featherstone, Cal., RC**	**.75**	**1.50**
☐ 107	Tracy Pratt, Buf.	.75	1.50
☐ 108	Ralph Backstrom., L.A.	.75	1.50
☐ 109	Murray Hall, Van.	.75	1.50
☐ 110	Tony Esposito (G), Chi.	14.00	28.00
☐ 111	Checklist (1 - 132)	40.00	80.00
☐ 112	Jim Neilson, NYR.	.75	1.50
☐ 113	Ron Ellis, Tor.	.75	1.50
☐ 114	Bobby Clarke, Pha.	20.00	40.00
☐ 115	Ken Hodge, Bos.	.75	1.50
☐ 116	Jim Roberts,Stl.	.75	1.50
☐ 117	Césare Maniago (G), Min.	1.25	2.50
☐ 118	Jean Pronovost, Pgh.	1.25	2.50
☐ 119	Gary Bergman, Det.	.75	1.50
☐ 120	Henri Richard, Mtl.	3.00	6.00
☐ 121	Ross Lonsberry, L.A.	.75	1.50
☐ 122	Pat Quinn, Van.	1.25	2.50
☐ 123	Rod Gilbert, NYR.	2.50	5.00
☐ 124	Gary Smith (G), Cal.	1.25	2.50
☐ 125	Stan Mikita, Chi.	6.00	12.00
☐ 126	Ed Van Impe, Pha.	.75	1.50
☐ 127	Wayne Connelly,Stl.	.75	1.50
☐ 128	Dennis Hextall, Min.	.75	1.50
☐ 129	Wayne Cashman, Bos.	1.25	2.50
☐ 130	J.C. Tremblay, Mtl.	.75	1.50
☐ 131	Bernie Parent (G), Tor.	6.50	13.00
☐ **132**	**Dunc McCallum, Pgh., RC, LC**	**2.25**	**6.50**

BOOKLETS

These eight-page comic-style booklets were issued as inserts with the regular 1971-72 Topps set. Six inside pages tell the story of the player listed on the cover. The back cover is a checklist.

Insert Set (24 booklets): **70.00** **140.00**

No.	Player	EX	NRMT
☐ 1	Bobby Hull, Chi.	6.00	18.00
☐ 2	Phil Esposito, Bos.	4.50	8.50
☐ 3	Dale Tallon, Van.	1.50	3.00
☐ 4	Jacques Plante (G), Tor.	6.00	12.00
☐ 5	Roger Crozier (G), Buf.	2.50	5.00
☐ 6	Henri Richard, Mtl.	4.00	8.00
☐ 7	Ed Giacomin (G), NYR.	4.00	8.00
☐ 8	Gilbert Perreault, Buf.	4.00	8.00
☐ 9	Greg Polis, Pgh.	1.50	3.00
☐ 10	Bobby Clarke, Pha.	4.00	8.00
☐ 11	Danny Grant, Min.	1.50	3.00
☐ 12	Alex Delvecchio, Det.	2.50	5.00
☐ 13	Tony Esposito (G), Chi.	4.50	8.50
☐ 14	Garry Unger, Stl.	2.50	5.00
☐ 15	Frank St. Marseille, Stl.	1.50	3.00
☐ 16	Dave Keon, Tor.	3.25	6.50
☐ 17	Ken Dryden (G), Mtl.	11.00	22.00
☐ 18	Rod Gilbert, NYR.	3.25	6.50
☐ 19	Juha Widing, L.A.	1.50	3.00
☐ 20	Orland Kurtenbach, Van.	1.50	3.00
☐ 21	Jude Drouin, Min.	1.50	3.00
☐ 22	Gary Smith (G), Cal.	2.50	5.00
☐ 23	Gordie Howe, Det.	14.00	28.00
☐ 24	Bobby Orr, Bos.	20.00	35.00

1971 - 72 TORONTO SUN PHOTOS

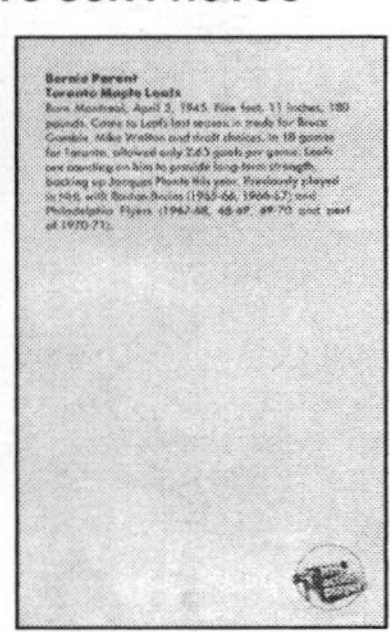

This series was also issued in the Vancouver area with the Columbian logo replacing the Sun logo, and in Moncton, NB, with Les Etoiles, De la LNH en Action Presentees Le Progrès l'évangéline.

Card Size: 5 1/4" x 7"
Face: Four colour, cream border; Name, Facsimile autograph, Team
Back: Black on beige paper stock; Name, Team, Resumé, Logo
Imprint: THE TORONTO SUN; COLUMBIAN; LES ETOILES

Complete Set (294 photos):		**200.00**	**400.00**
Common Player:		**.50**	**1.00**
Album:		**20.00**	**40.00**
	Player	**EX**	**NRMT**
TITLE CARD			
☐☐☐	Scott Young	1.00	2.00
BOSTON BRUINS			
☐☐☐	Bruins Team Crest	1.00	2.00
☐☐☐	Don Awrey	.50	1.00
☐☐☐	Garnet Bailey	.50	1.00
☐☐☐	Ivan Boldirev	.50	1.00
☐☐☐	John Bucyk	2.00	4.00
☐☐☐	Wayne Cashman	.50	1.00
☐☐☐	Gerry Cheevers (G)	2.50	5.00
☐☐☐	Phil Esposito	4.50	9.00
☐☐☐	Ted Green	.50	1.00
☐☐☐	Ken Hodge	.50	1.00
☐☐☐	Eddie Johnston (G)	1.00	2.00
☐☐☐	Reggie Leach	.50	1.00
☐☐☐	Don Marcotte	.50	1.00
☐☐☐	John McKenzie	.50	1.00
☐☐☐	Bobby Orr	25.00	45.00
☐☐☐	Derek Sanderson	1.75	3.50
☐☐☐	Dallas Smith	.50	1.00
☐☐☐	Rick Smith	.50	1.00
☐☐☐	Fred Stanfield	.50	1.00
☐☐☐	Mike Walton	.50	1.00
☐☐☐	Ed Westfall	.50	1.00
BUFFALO SABRES			
☐☐☐	Sabres Team Crest	1.00	2.00
☐☐☐	Doug Barrie	.50	1.00
☐☐☐	Roger Crozier (G)	1.00	2.00
☐☐☐	Dave Dryden (G)	1.00	2.00
☐☐☐	Dick Duff	.50	1.00
☐☐☐	Phil Goyette	.50	1.00
☐☐☐	Al Hamilton	.50	1.00
☐☐☐	Larry Keenan	.50	1.00
☐☐☐	Danny Lawson	.50	1.00
☐☐☐	Don Luce	.50	1.00
☐☐☐	Richard Martin	1.25	2.50
☐☐☐	Ray McKay	.50	1.00
☐☐☐	Gerry Meehan	.50	1.00
☐☐☐	Kevin O'Shea	.50	1.00
☐☐☐	Gilbert Perreault	4.00	8.00
☐☐☐	Tracy Pratt	.50	1.00
☐☐☐	Mike Robitaille	.50	1.00
☐☐☐	Eddie Shack	1.75	3.50
☐☐☐	Jimmy Watson	.50	1.00
☐☐☐	Rod Zaine	.50	1.00
CALIFORNIA GOLDEN SEALS			
☐☐☐	California Team Crest	1.00	2.00
☐☐☐	Wayne Carleton	.50	1.00
☐☐☐	Lyle Carter (G)	1.00	2.00
☐☐☐	Gary Croteau	.50	1.00
☐☐☐	Norm Ferguson	.50	1.00
☐☐☐	Stan Gilbertson	.50	1.00
☐☐☐	Ernie Hicke	.50	1.00
☐☐☐	Gary Jarrett	.50	1.00
☐☐☐	Joey Johnston	.50	1.00
☐☐☐	Marshall Johnston	.50	1.00
☐☐☐	Bert Marshall	.50	1.00
☐☐☐	Walt McKechnie	.50	1.00
☐☐☐	Don O'Donoghue	.50	1.00
☐☐☐	Gerry Pinder	.50	1.00
☐☐☐	Dick Redmond	.50	1.00
☐☐☐	Bobby Sheehan	.50	1.00
☐☐☐	Paul Shmyr	.50	1.00
☐☐☐	Ron Stackhouse	.50	1.00
☐☐☐	Carol Vadnais	.50	1.00
☐☐☐	Tom Williams	.50	1.00
CHICAGO BLACKHAWKS			
☐☐☐	Chicago Team Crest	1.00	2.00
☐☐☐	Lou Angotti	.50	1.00
☐☐☐	Bryan Campbell	.50	1.00
☐☐☐	Tony Esposito (G)	4.50	9.00
☐☐☐	Bobby Hull	13.00	25.00
☐☐☐	Dennis Hull	.50	1.00
☐☐☐	Doug Jarrett	.50	1.00
☐☐☐	Jerry Korab	.50	1.00
☐☐☐	Cliff Koroll	.50	1.00
☐☐☐	Daryl Maggs	.50	1.00
☐☐☐	Keith Magnuson	.50	1.00
☐☐☐	Chico Maki	.50	1.00
☐☐☐	Dan Maloney	.50	1.00
☐☐☐	Pit Martin	.50	1.00
☐☐☐	Stan Mikita	3.25	6.50
☐☐☐	Eric Nesterenko	.50	1.00
☐☐☐	Danny O'Shea	.50	1.00
☐☐☐	Jim Pappin	.50	1.00
☐☐☐	Gary Smith (G)	1.00	2.00
☐☐☐	Pat Stapleton	.50	1.00
☐☐☐	Bill White	.50	1.00
DETROIT RED WINGS			
☐☐☐	Detroit Team Crest	1.00	2.00
☐☐☐	Red Berenson	.50	1.00
☐☐☐	Gary Bergman	.50	1.00
☐☐☐	Arnie Brown	.50	1.00
☐☐☐	Guy Charron	.50	1.00
☐☐☐	Bill Collins	.50	1.00
☐☐☐	Brian Conacher	.50	1.00
☐☐☐	Joe Daley (G)	1.00	2.00
☐☐☐	Alex Delvecchio	2.00	4.00
☐☐☐	Marcel Dionne	4.50	8.50
☐☐☐	Tim Ecclestone	.50	1.00
☐☐☐	Ron Harris	.50	1.00
☐☐☐	Gerry Hart	.50	1.00
☐☐☐	Gordie Howe	18.00	35.00
☐☐☐	Al Karlander	.50	1.00
☐☐☐	Nick Libett	.50	1.00
☐☐☐	Ab McDonald	.50	1.00
☐☐☐	Jim Niekamp	.50	1.00
☐☐☐	Mickey Redmond	1.00	2.00
☐☐☐	Leon Rochefort	.50	1.00
☐☐☐	Al Smith (G)	1.00	2.00
LOS ANGELES KINGS			
☐☐☐	Kings Team Crest	1.00	2.00
☐☐☐	Ralph Backstrom	.50	1.00
☐☐☐	Robert Perry	.50	1.00
☐☐☐	Mike Byers	.50	1.00
☐☐☐	Larry Cahan	.50	1.00
☐☐☐	Paul Curtis	.50	1.00
☐☐☐	Denis DeJordy (G)	1.00	2.00
☐☐☐	Gary Edwards (G)	1.00	2.00

	Player		
□ □□	Bill Flett	.50	1.00
□ □□	Butch Goring	.50	1.00
□ □□	Lucien Grenier	.50	1.00
□ □□	Larry Hillman	.50	1.00
□ □□	Dale Hoganson	.50	1.00
□ □□	Harry Howell	1.25	2.50
□ □□	Eddie Joyal	.50	1.00
□ □□	Real Lemieux	.50	1.00
□ □□	Ross Lonsberry	.50	1.00
□ □□	Al McDonough	.50	1.00
□ □□	Jean Potvin	.50	1.00
□ □□	Bob Pulford	1.50	3.00
□ □□	Juha Widing	.50	1.00

MINNESOTA NORTH STARS

	Player		
□ □□	Minnesota Team Crest	1.00	2.00
□ □□	Fred Barrett	.50	1.00
□ □□	Charlie Burns	.50	1.00
□ □□	Jude Drouin	.50	1.00
□ □□	Barry Gibbs	.50	1.00
□ □□	Gilles Gilbert (G)	1.00	2.00
□ □□	Bill Goldsworthy	.50	1.00
□ □□	Danny Grant	.50	1.00
□ □□	Ted Hampson	.50	1.00
□ □□	Ted Harris	.50	1.00
□ □□	Buster (Fred) Harvey	.50	1.00
□ □□	Césare Maniago (G)	1.00	2.00
□ □□	Doug Mohns	.50	1.00
□ □□	Lou Nanne	.50	1.00
□ □□	Bob Nevin	.50	1.00
□ □□	Dennis O'Brien	.50	1.00
□ □□	Murray Oliver	.50	1.00
□ □□	Jean Paul Parise	.50	1.00
□ □□	Dean Prentice	.50	1.00
□ □□	Tom Reid	.50	1.00
□ □□	Gump Worsley (G)	3.25	6.50

MONTRÉAL CANADIENS

	Player		
□ □□	Montréal Team Crest	1.00	2.00
□ □□	Pierre Bouchard	.50	1.00
□ □□	Yvan Cournoyer	2.25	4.50
□ □□	Ken Dryden (G)	10.00	20.00
□ □□	Terry Harper	.50	1.00
□ □□	Réjean Houle	1.00	2.00
□ □□	Guy Lafleur	10.00	20.00
□ □□	Jacques Laperrière	1.25	2.50
□ □□	Guy Lapointe	1.50	3.00
□ □□	Claude Larose	.50	1.00
□ □□	Jacques Lemaire	2.50	5.00
□ □□	Frank Mahovlich	4.00	7.50
□ □□	Pete Mahovlich	.50	1.00
□ □□	Phil Myre (G)	1.00	2.00
□ □□	Larry Pleau	.50	1.00
□ □□	Henri Richard	2.75	5.50
□ □□	Phil Roberto	.50	1.00
□ □□	Serge Savard	1.50	3.00
□ □□	Marc Tardif	.50	1.00
□ □□	J.C. Tremblay	.50	1.00
□ □□	Rogatien Vachon (G)	1.25	2.50

NEW YORK RANGERS

	Player		
□ □□	Rangers Team Crest	1.00	2.00
□ □□	Dave Balon	.50	1.00
□ □□	Ab DeMarco	.50	1.00
□ □□	Jack Egers	.50	1.00
□ □□	Bill Fairbairn	.50	1.00
□ □□	Ed Giacomin (G)	2.50	5.00
□ □□	Rod Gilbert	2.00	4.00
□ □□	Vic Hadfield	.50	1.00
□ □□	Ted Irvine	.50	1.00
□ □□	Bruce MacGregor	.50	1.00
□ □□	Jim Neilson	.50	1.00
□ □□	Brad Park	2.75	5.50
□ □□	Jean Ratelle	2.00	4.00
□ □□	Dale Rolfe	.50	1.00
□ □□	Bobby Rousseau	.50	1.00
□ □□	Glen Sather	1.50	3.00
□ □□	Rod Seiling	.50	1.00
□ □□	Pete Stemkowski	.50	1.00
□ □□	Walt Tkaczuk	.50	1.00
□ □□	Gilles Villemure (G)	1.00	2.00

PHILADELPHIA FLYERS

	Player		
□ □□	Flyers Team Crest	1.00	2.00
□ □□	Barry Ashbee	.50	1.00
□ □□	Serge Bernier	.50	1.00
□ □□	Larry Brown	.50	1.00
□ □□	Bobby Clarke	5.00	10.00
□ □□	Gary Dornhoefer	.50	1.00
□ □□	Doug Favell (G)	1.00	2.00
□ □□	Bruce Gamble (G)	1.00	2.00
□ □□	Jean-Guy Gendron	.50	1.00
□ □□	Larry Hale	.50	1.00
□ □□	Wayne Hillman	.50	1.00
□ □□	Brent Hughes	.50	1.00
□ □□	Jim Johnson	.50	1.00
□ □□	Bob Kelly	.50	1.00
□ □□	Andre Lacroix	1.00	2.00
□ □□	Bill Lesuk	.50	1.00
□ □□	Rick MacLeish	1.00	2.00
□ □□	Larry Mickey	.50	1.00
□ □□	Simon Nolet	.50	1.00
□ □□	Pierre Plante	.50	1.00
□ □□	Ed Van Impe	.50	1.00
□ □□	Joe Watson	.50	1.00

PITTSBURGH PENGUINS

	Player		
□ □□	Penguins Team Crest	1.00	2.00
□ □□	Syl Apps	.50	1.00
□ □□	Les Binkley (G)	1.00	2.00
□ □□	Wally Boyer	.50	1.00
□ □□	Darryl Edestrand	.50	1.00
□ □□	Roy Edwards (G)	1.00	2.00
□ □□	Nick Harbaruk	.50	1.00
□ □□	Bryan Hextall	.50	1.00
□ □□	Bill Hicke	.50	1.00
□ □□	Tim Horton	4.50	8.50
□ □□	Sheldon Kannegiesser	.50	1.00
□ □□	Bobby Leiter	.50	1.00
□ □□	Keith McCreary	.50	1.00
□ □□	Joe Noris	.50	1.00
□ □□	Greg Polis	.50	1.00
□ □□	Jean Pronovost	.50	1.00
□ □□	Rene Robert	.50	1.00
□ □□	Duane Rupp	.50	1.00
□ □□	Ken Schinkel	.50	1.00
□ □□	Ron Schock	.50	1.00
□ □□	Bryan Watson	.50	1.00
□ □□	Bob Woytowich	.50	1.00

ST. LOUIS BLUES

	Player		
□ □□	Blues Team Crest	1.00	2.00
□ □□	Al Arbour	1.00	2.00
□ □□	John Arbour	.50	1.00
□ □□	Chris Bordeleau	.50	1.00
□ □□	Carl Brewer	.50	1.00
□ □□	Gene Carr	.50	1.00
□ □□	Wayne Connelly	.50	1.00
□ □□	Terry Crisp	1.00	2.00
□ □□	Jim Lorentz	.50	1.00
□ □□	Pete McDuffe (G)	1.00	2.00
□ □□	George Morrison	.50	1.00
□ □□	Michel Parizeau	.50	1.00
□ □□	Noel Picard	.50	1.00
□ □□	Barclay Plager	1.00	2.00
□ □□	Bob Plager	.50	1.00
□ □□	Jim Roberts	.50	1.00
□ □□	Gary Sabourin	.50	1.00
□ □□	Jim Shires	.50	1.00
□ □□	Frank St. Marseille	.50	1.00
□ □□	Bill Sutherland	.50	1.00
□ □□	Garry Unger	1.00	2.00
□ □□	Ernie Wakely (G)	1.00	2.00

TORONTO MAPLE LEAFS

	Player		
□ □□	Toronto Team Crest	1.00	2.00
□ □□	Bob Baun	.50	1.00
□ □□	Jim Dorey	.50	1.00
□ □□	Denis Dupère	.50	1.00
□ □□	Ron Ellis	.50	1.00
□ □□	Brian Glennie	.50	1.00
□ □□	Jim Harrison	.50	1.00
□ □□	Paul Henderson	1.25	2.50
□ □□	Dave Keon	2.25	4.50
□ □□	Rick Ley	.50	1.00
□ □□	Billy MacMillan	.50	1.00
□ □□	Don Marshall	.50	1.00
□ □□	Jim McKenny	.50	1.00
□ □□	Garry Monahan	.50	1.00
□ □□	Bernie Parent (G)	3.50	7.00
□ □□	Mike Pelyk	.50	1.00
□ □□	Jacques Plante (G)	6.00	12.00
□ □□	Brad Selwood	.50	1.00
□ □□	Darryl Sittler	4.50	9.00
□ □□	Brian Spencer	.50	1.00
□ □□	Guy Trottier	.50	1.00
□ □□	Norm Ullman	2.00	4.00

VANCOUVER CANUCKS

	Player		
□ □□	Canucks Team Crest	1.00	2.00
□ □□	André Boudrias	.50	1.00
□ □□	George Gardner (G)	1.00	2.00
□ □□	Jocelyn Guevremont	.50	1.00
□ □□	Murray Hall	.50	1.00
□ □□	Danny Johnson	.50	1.00
□ □□	Dennis Kearns	.50	1.00
□ □□	Orland Kurtenbach	.50	1.00
□ □□	Bobby Lalonde	.50	1.00
□ □□	Wayne Maki	.50	1.00
□ □□	Rosaire Paiement	.50	1.00
□ □□	Poul Popeil	.50	1.00
□ □□	Pat Quinn	1.00	2.00
□ □□	John Schella	.50	1.00
□ □□	Bobby Schmautz	.50	1.00
□ □□	Fred Speck	.50	1.00
□ □□	Dale Tallon	.50	1.00
□ □□	Ron Ward	.50	1.00
□ □□	Barry Wilkins	.50	1.00
□ □□	Dunc Wilson (G)	1.00	2.00

1971 - 72 WILLIAMS FINNISH

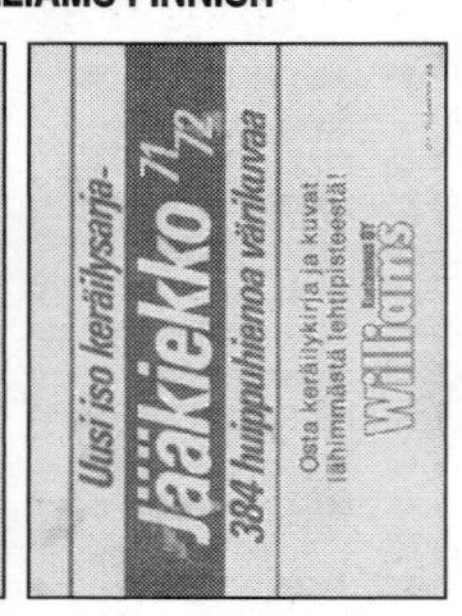

A set of 384 cards plus a collecting album for the World Championships and the Finnish National and Junior League. We have no pricing information on this set.

Card Size: 1 7/8" x 2 9/16"
Imprint:
Face: Four Colour
Back: Red Finnish text

	No.	Player
□	1	Vitaly Davydov, USSR
□	2	Anatoli Firsov, USSR
□	3	Valeri Kharlamov, USSR
□	4	Viktor Konovalenko (G), USSR
□	5	Viktor Kuzkin, USSR
□	6	Yuri Liapkin, USSR
□	7	Vladimir Lutchenko, USSR
□	8	Alexander Maltsev, USSR
□	9	Alexander Martiniuk, USSR
□	10	Boris Mikhailov, USSR
□	11	Evgeni Mishakov, USSR
□	12	Vladimir Petrov, USSR
□	13	Alexander Ragulin, USSR
□	14	Igor Romishevski, USSR
□	15	Vladimir Shadrin, USSR
□	16	Viatjeslav Starshinov, USSR
□	17	Vladislav Tretiak (G), USSR
□	18	Gennady Tsicankov, USSR
□	19	Vladimir Vikulov, USSR
□	20	Evgeni Zimin, USSR
□	21	Bedrich Brunschk, CSR.
□	22	Jiri Bubla, CSR.
□	23	Josef Cerny, CSR.
□	24	Richard Farda, CSR.
□	25	Jan Havel, CSR.
□	26	Ivan Hlinka, CSR.
□	27	Jiri Holecek, CSR.
□	28	Jiri Holik, CSR.
□	29	Josef Horesovsky, CSR.
□	30	Jiri Kochta, CSR.
□	31	Oldrich Machac, CSR.
□	32	Vladimir Martinec, CSR.
□	33	Vaclav Nedomansky, CSR.
□	34	Eduard Novak, CSR.
□	35	Frantisek Panchartek, CSR.
□	36	Frantisek Pospisil, CSR.
□	37	Marcel Sakac, CSR.
□	38	Bohuslav Stastny, CSR.

- ☐ 39 Jan Suchy, CSR.
- ☐ 40 Christer Abrahamsson, Swe.
- ☐ 41 Thommy Abrahamsson, Swe.
- ☐ 42 Thommie Bergman, Swe.
- ☐ 43 Arne Carlsson, Swe.
- ☐ 44 Inge Hammarstrom, Swe.
- ☐ 45 Anders Hedberg, Swe.
- ☐ 46 Leif Holmqvist, Swe.
- ☐ 47 StigGoran Johansson, Swe.
- ☐ 48 Stefan Karlsson, Swe.
- ☐ 49 Hans Lindberg, Swe.
- ☐ 50 Tord Lundstrom, Swe.
- ☐ 51 William Lofqvist, Swe.
- ☐ 52 Kjell-Rune Milton, Swe.
- ☐ 53 LarsGoran Nilsson, Swe.
- ☐ 54 Bert-Ola Nordlander, Swe.
- ☐ 55 Hakan Nygren, Swe.
- ☐ 56 Bjorn Palmqvist, Swe.
- ☐ 57 Hakan Pettersson, Swe.
- ☐ 58 Ulf Sterner, Swe.
- ☐ 59 Lennart Svedberg, Swe.
- ☐ 60 Hakan Wickberg, Swe.
- ☐ 61 Esa Isaksson, Fin.
- ☐ 62 Heikki Jarn, Fin.
- ☐ 63 Veli-Pekka Ketola, Fin.
- ☐ 64 Ilpo Koskela, Fin.
- ☐ 65 Seppo Lindstrom, Fin.
- ☐ 66 Harri Linnonmaa, Fin.
- ☐ 67 Hannu Luojola, Fin.
- ☐ 68 Pekka Marjamaki, Fin.
- ☐ 69 Erkki Mononen, Fin.
- ☐ 70 Lauri Mononen, Fin.
- ☐ 71 Matti Murto, Fin.
- ☐ 72 Lasse Oksanen, Fin.
- ☐ 73 Esa Peltonen, Fin.
- ☐ 74 Seppo Repo, Fin.
- ☐ 75 Tommi Salmelainen, Fin.
- ☐ 76 Juhani Tamminen, Fin.
- ☐ 77 Jorma Valtonen, Fin.
- ☐ 78 Jorma Vehmanen, Fin.
- ☐ 79 Urpo Ylonen, Fin.
- ☐ 80 Jouko Oystila, Fin.
- ☐ 81 Tapio Flinck, Assat Pori
- ☐ 82 Antti Heikkila, Assat Pori
- ☐ 83 Reijo Heinonen, Assat Pori
- ☐ 84 Jaakko Honkanen, Assat Pori
- ☐ 85 Veli-Pekka Ketola, Assat Pori
- ☐ 86 Raimo Kilpio, Assat Pori
- ☐ 87 Tapio Koskinen, Assat Pori
- ☐ 88 Kaj Matalamaki, Assat Pori
- ☐ 89 Pertti Makela, Assat Pori
- ☐ 90 Pekka Rautakallio, Assat Pori
- ☐ 91 Markku Riihimaki, Assat Pori
- ☐ 92 Matti Salmi, Assat Pori
- ☐ 93 Jorma Valtonen, Assat Pori
- ☐ 94 Anto Virtanen, Assat Pori
- ☐ 95 Erkki Vakiparta, Assat Pori
- ☐ 96 Pertti Ahokas, Jokerit
- ☐ 97 Pertti Arvaja, Jokerit
- ☐ 98 Olli Hietanen, Jokerit
- ☐ 99 Pentti Hiiros, Jokerit
- ☐ 100 Eero Holopainen, Jokerit
- ☐ 101 Kari Kinnunen, Jokerit
- ☐ 102 Ilpo Koskela, Jokerit
- ☐ 103 Timo Kyntola, Jokerit
- ☐ 104 Henry Leppa, Jokerit
- ☐ 105 Erkki Mononen, Jokerit
- ☐ 106 Pertti Nurmi, Jokerit
- ☐ 107 Timo Relas, Jokerit
- ☐ 108 Timo Sutinen, Jokerit
- ☐ 109 Timo Turunen, Jokerit
- ☐ 110 Jouko Oystila, Jokerit
- ☐ 111 Juhani Bostrom, HIFK
- ☐ 112 Kimmo Heino, HIFK
- ☐ 113 Esa Isaksson, HIFK
- ☐ 114 Juhani Jylha, HIFK
- ☐ 115 Heikki Jarn, HIFK
- ☐ 116 Mauri Kaukokari, HIFK
- ☐ 117 Vaino Kolkka, HIFK
- ☐ 118 Harri Linnonmaa, HIFK
- ☐ 119 Jaakko Marttinen, HIFK
- ☐ 120 Matti Murto, HIFK
- ☐ 121 Lalli Partinen, HIFK
- ☐ 122 Juha Rantasila, HIFK
- ☐ 123 Heikki Riihiranta, HIFK
- ☐ 124 Jorma Rikala, HIFK
- ☐ 125 Tommi Salmelainen, HIFK
- ☐ 126 Jorma Thusberg, HIFK
- ☐ 127 Matti Vaisanen, HIFK
- ☐ 128 Jukka Alkula, Tappara
- ☐ 129 Pertti Ansakorpi, Tappara
- ☐ 130 Keijo Jarvinen, Tappara
- ☐ 131 Pertti Koivulahti, Tappara
- ☐ 132 Ilpo Kuisma, Tappara
- ☐ 133 Vesa Lehtoranta, Tappara
- ☐ 134 Antti Leppanen, Tappara
- ☐ 135 Pekka Marjamaki, Tappara
- ☐ 136 Mikko Mynttinen, Tappara
- ☐ 137 Pekka Makinen, Tappara
- ☐ 138 Seppo Makinen, Tappara
- ☐ 139 Keijo Mannisto, Tappara
- ☐ 140 Antti Perttula, Tappara
- ☐ 141 Tuomo Rautiainen, Tappara
- ☐ 142 Juhani Saarelainen, Tappara
- ☐ 143 Jorma Saarikorpi, Tappara
- ☐ 144 Risto Seesvuori, Tappara
- ☐ 145 Jorma Siitarinen, Tappara
- ☐ 146 Raimo Suoniemi, Tappara
- ☐ 147 Juhani Aaltonen, HJK.
- ☐ 148 Matti Ahvenharju, HJK.
- ☐ 149 Hannu Auvinen, HJK.
- ☐ 150 Jorma Borgstrom, HJK.
- ☐ 151 Martti Immonen, HJK.
- ☐ 152 Matti Keinonen, HJK.
- ☐ 153 Seppo Laakkio, HJK.
- ☐ 154 Timo Lahtinen, HJK.
- ☐ 155 Esa Peltonen, HJK.
- ☐ 156 Keijo Puhakka, HJK.
- ☐ 157 Antti Ravi, HJK.
- ☐ 158 Timo Saari, HJK.
- ☐ 159 Esa Siren, HJK.
- ☐ 160 Erkki Suni, HJK.
- ☐ 161 Seppo Suoraniemi, HJK.
- ☐ 162 Juhani Tamminen, HJK.
- ☐ 163 Jorma Vehmanen, HJK.
- ☐ 164 Stig Wetzell, HJK.
- ☐ 165 Olli Viilma, HJK.
- ☐ 166 Leo Aikas, HJK.
- ☐ 167 Sakari Ahlberg, Ilves
- ☐ 168 Seppo Ahokainen, Ilves
- ☐ 169 Jorma Aro, Ilves
- ☐ 170 Esko Eriksson, Ilves
- ☐ 171 Markku Hakanen, Ilves
- ☐ 172 Matti Hakanen, Ilves
- ☐ 173 Reijo Hakanen, Ilves
- ☐ 174 Martti Helle, Ilves
- ☐ 175 Timo Hirsimaki, Ilves
- ☐ 176 Jorma Kallio, Ilves
- ☐ 177 Esko Kaonpaa, Ilves
- ☐ 178 Pentti Koskela, Ilves
- ☐ 179 Pekka Kuusisto, Ilves
- ☐ 180 Pekka Leimu, Ilves
- ☐ 181 Jukka Mattila, Ilves
- ☐ 182 Lasse Oksanen, Ilves
- ☐ 183 Kari Palooja, Ilves
- ☐ 184 Jorma Peltonen, Ilves
- ☐ 185 Tuomo Sillman, Ilves
- ☐ 186 Jaakko Siren, Ilves
- ☐ 187 Veikko Suominen, Ilves
- ☐ 188 Matti Jakonen, Turun Toverit
- ☐ 189 Kari Johansson, Turun Toverit
- ☐ 190 Arto Kaunonen, Turun Toverit
- ☐ 191 Timo Kokkonen, Turun Toverit
- ☐ 192 Reijo Leppanen, Turun Toverit
- ☐ 193 Seppo Lindstrom, Turun Toverit
- ☐ 194 Hannu Luojola, Turun Toverit
- ☐ 195 Hannu Niittoaho, Turun Toverit
- ☐ 196 Reijo Paksal, Turun Toverit
- ☐ 197 Seppo Parikka, Turun Toverit
- ☐ 198 Jarmo Rantanen, Turun Toverit
- ☐ 199 Veijo Saarinen, Turun Toverit
- ☐ 200 Martti Salonen, Turun Toverit
- ☐ 201 Voitto Soini, Turun Toverit
- ☐ 202 Kari Torkkel, Turun Toverit
- ☐ 203 Risto Vainio, Turun Toverit
- ☐ 204 Pentti Vihanto, Turun Toverit
- ☐ 205 Seppo Wikstrom, Turun Toverit
- ☐ 206 Urpo Ylonen, Turun Toverit
- ☐ 207 Hannu Haapalainen, Koovee
- ☐ 208 JukkaPekka Jarvenpaa, Koovee
- ☐ 209 Timo Jarvinen, Koovee
- ☐ 210 Heikki Keinonen, Koovee
- ☐ 211 Heimo Keinonen, Koovee
- ☐ 212 Rauno Lehtio, Koovee
- ☐ 213 Markku Moisio, Koovee
- ☐ 214 Seppo Nurmi, Koovee
- ☐ 215 Esko Rantanen, Koovee
- ☐ 216 Juhani Ruohonen, Koovee
- ☐ 217 Mikko Raikkonen, Koovee
- ☐ 218 Lauri Salomaa, Koovee
- ☐ 219 Veikko Savolainen, Koovee
- ☐ 220 Leo Seppanen, Koovee
- ☐ 221 Pekka Uitus, Koovee
- ☐ 222 Jorma Vilen, Koovee
- ☐ 223 Tapio Virhimo, Koovee
- ☐ 224 Kauko Fomin, Turun Palloseura
- ☐ 225 Heikki Hurme, Turun Palloseura
- ☐ 226 Eero Juntunen, Turun Palloseura
- ☐ 227 Lauri Jamsen, Turun Palloseura
- ☐ 228 Lasse Kiili, Turun Palloseura
- ☐ 229 Hannu Koivunen, Turun Palloseura
- ☐ 230 Jarmo Koivunen, Turun Palloseura
- ☐ 231 Pekka Lahtela, Turun Palloseura
- ☐ 232 Ilkka Mesikammen, Turun Palloseura
- ☐ 233 Timo Nummelin, Turun Palloseura
- ☐ 234 Rauli Ottila, Turun Palloseura
- ☐ 235 Matti Rautee, Turun Palloseura
- ☐ 236 Pekka Rautee, Turun Palloseura
- ☐ 237 Jari Rosberg, Turun Palloseura
- ☐ 238 Jouni Samuli, Turun Palloseura
- ☐ 239 Harry Silver, Turun Palloseura
- ☐ 240 Rauli Tammelin, Turun Palloseura
- ☐ 241 Bengt Wilenius, Turun Palloseura
- ☐ 242 Mikko Erholm, Rauman Lukko
- ☐ 243 Veikko Ihalainen, Rauman Lukko
- ☐ 244 Heikki Kauhanen, Rauman Lukko
- ☐ 245 Tapani Koskimaki, Rauman Lukko
- ☐ 246 Antti Laine, Rauman Lukko
- ☐ 247 Arto Laine, Rauman Lukko
- ☐ 248 Timo Lehtorinne, Rauman Lukko
- ☐ 249 Hannu Lunden, Rauman Lukko
- ☐ 250 Teppo Rastio, Rauman Lukko
- ☐ 251 Pentti Rautalin, Rauman Lukko
- ☐ 252 Kai Rosvall, Rauman Lukko
- ☐ 253 Ilkka Saarikko, Rauman Lukko
- ☐ 254 Jari Sarronlahti, Rauman Lukko
- ☐ 255 Matti Saurio, Rauman Lukko
- ☐ 256 Hannu Siivonen, Rauman Lukko
- ☐ 257 Erkki Sundelin, Rauman Lukko
- ☐ 258 Simo Suoknuuti, Rauman Lukko
- ☐ 259 Martti Haapala, Joensuun
- ☐ 260 Yrjo Hakulinen, Joensuun
- ☐ 261 Pentti Hirvonen, Joensuun
- ☐ 262 Antero Honkanen, Joensuun
- ☐ 263 Pekka Lavikainen, Joensuun
- ☐ 264 Pentti Lavikainen, Joensuun
- ☐ 265 Pertti Martikainen, Joensuun
- ☐ 266 Pentti Matikainen, Joensuun
- ☐ 267 Seppo Nevalainen, Joensuun
- ☐ 268 Tapio Pohtinen, Joensuun
- ☐ 269 Kari Puustinen, Joensuun
- ☐ 270 Markku Rouhiainen, Joensuun
- ☐ 271 Jarmo Sahlman, Joensuun
- ☐ 272 Seppo Saros, Joensuun
- ☐ 273 Juha Silvennoinen, Joensuun
- ☐ 274 Unto Turpeinen, Joensuun
- ☐ 275 Kari Viitalahti, Joensuun
- ☐ 276 Erkki Airaksinen, Karhukissat
- ☐ 277 Kauko Alkunen, Karhukissat
- ☐ 278 Jarmo Gummerus, Karhukissat
- ☐ 279 Bjorn Herbert, Karhukissat
- ☐ 280 Jarmo Jaakkola, Karhukissat
- ☐ 281 Hannu Kapanen, Karhukissat
- ☐ 282 Matti Koskinen, Karhukissat
- ☐ 283 Martti Kuokkanen, Karhukissat
- ☐ 284 Juhani Laine, Karhukissat
- ☐ 285 Heikki Leppik, Karhukissat
- ☐ 286 Juhani Langstrom, Karhukissat
- ☐ 287 Osmo Lotjonen, Karhukissat
- ☐ 288 Lauri Mononen, Karhukissat
- ☐ 289 Christer Nordblad, Karhukissat
- ☐ 290 Juha Poikolainen, Karhukissat
- ☐ 291 Kimmo Rantanen, Karhukissat
- ☐ 292 Seppo Repo, Karhukissat
- ☐ 293 Ilpo Ruokosalmi, Karhukissat

☐ 294 Arto Siissala, Karhukissat
☐ 295 Bo Sjostedt, Karhukissat
☐ 296 Pentti Viitanen, Karhukissat
☐ 297 Pekka Arbelius, Oulun Jrs.
☐ 298 Olli Enqvist, Oulun Jrs.
☐ 299 Hannu Hiltunen, Oulun Jrs.
☐ 300 Paavo Holopainen, Oulun Jrs.
☐ 301 Juha Huikari, Oulun Jrs.
☐ 302 Ari Jalonen, Oulun Jrs.
☐ 303 Kari Jalonen, Oulun Jrs.
☐ 304 Ari Kaikkonen, Oulun Jrs.
☐ 305 Ari Kalmokoski, Oulun Jrs.
☐ 306 Arto Lehtinen, Oulun Jrs.
☐ 307 Markku Narhi, Oulun Jrs.
☐ 308 Ilkka Okkonen, Oulun Jrs.
☐ 309 Matti Perhonmaa, Oulun Jrs.
☐ 310 JuhaPekka Porvari, Oulun Jrs.
☐ 311 Arto Ruotanen, Oulun Jrs.
☐ 312 Reijo Ruotsalainen, Oulun Jrs.
☐ 313 Matti Ruutti, Oulun Jrs.
☐ 314 Pertti Raisanen, Oulun Jrs.
☐ 315 Ari Timosaari, Oulun Jrs.
☐ 316 Janne Oro, Oulun Jrs.
☐ 317 Anssi Eronen, Sapko Jrs.
☐ 318 Seppo Hirvonen, Sapko Jrs.
☐ 319 Jari Hannu Hamalainen, Sapko Jrs.
☐ 320 Jari Pekka Hamalainen, Sapko Jrs.
☐ 321 Timo Harkonen, Sapko Jrs.
☐ 322 Jouko Ikonen, Sapko Jrs.
☐ 323 Lasse Kaiponen, Sapko Jrs.
☐ 324 Jyri Kemppinen, Sapko Jrs.
☐ 325 Jouni Kostiainen, Sapko Jrs.
☐ 326 Kai Kulhoranta, Sapko Jrs.
☐ 327 Olli Lemola, Sapko Jrs.
☐ 328 Jari Lopponen, Sapko Jrs.
☐ 329 Pasi Makkonen, Sapko Jrs.
☐ 330 Vesa Massinen, Sapko Jrs.
☐ 331 Timo Minkkila, Sapko Jrs.
☐ 332 Petri Pellinen, Sapko Jrs.
☐ 333 Juha Rasanen, Sapko Jrs.
☐ 334 Pasi Sallinen, Sapko Jrs.
☐ 335 Kauko Tamminen, Sapko Jrs.
☐ 336 Olli Teijonmaa, Sapko Jrs.
☐ 337 Ismo Tolvanen, Sapko Jrs.
☐ 338 Timo Vaahtoluoto, Sapko Jrs.
☐ 339 Kari Heikkila, Ilves, Jrs.
☐ 340 Pekka Helander, Ilves, Jrs.
☐ 341 Jari Hirsimaki, Ilves, Jrs.
☐ 342 Jari Huotari, Ilves, Jrs.
☐ 343 Ilkka Huura, Ilves, Jrs.
☐ 344 Tero Juojarvi, Ilves, Jrs.
☐ 345 Jari Jarvinen, Ilves, Jrs.
☐ 346 Mika Laine, Ilves, Jrs.
☐ 347 Marko Lepaus, Ilves, Jrs.
☐ 338 Pertti Lundberg, Ilves, Jrs.
☐ 349 Tino Minetti, Ilves, Jrs.
☐ 350 Jarmo Partanen, Ilves, Jrs.
☐ 351 OlliPekka Perala, Ilves, Jrs.
☐ 352 Ari Ruuska, Ilves, Jrs.
☐ 353 Kai Saario, Ilves, Jrs.
☐ 354 OlliPekka Turunen, Ilves, Jrs.
☐ 355 VeliMatti Uusimaa, Ilves, Jrs.
☐ 356 Mauri Viita, Ilves, Jrs.
☐ 357 Timo Virtanen, Ilves, Jrs.
☐ 358 Jarmo Viteli, Ilves, Jrs.
☐ 359 Petri Viteli, Ilves, Jrs.
☐ 360 Ari Havukainen, Rauman Jrs.
☐ 361 Ismo Heinonen, Rauman Jrs.
☐ 362 Riku Hoyden, Rauman Jrs.
☐ 363 Jari Jokinen, Rauman Jrs.
☐ 364 Timo Joutsenvuori, Rauman Jrs.
☐ 365 Jyrki Jantti, Rauman Jrs.
☐ 366 Kimmo Jantti, Rauman Jrs.
☐ 367 Toni Ketola, Rauman Jrs.
☐ 368 Juha Korhonen, Rauman Jrs.
☐ 369 Ari Laine, Rauman Jrs.
☐ 370 Kari Lainio, Rauman Jrs.
☐ 371 Juha Makinen, Rauman Jrs.
☐ 372 Reima Numminen, Rauman Jrs.
☐ 373 Mika Pirila, Rauman Jrs.
☐ 374 Kai Pulli, Rauman Jrs.
☐ 375 Tero Tommila, Rauman Jrs.
☐ 376 Harri Tuohimaa, Rauman Jrs.
☐ 377 Pasi Tuohimaa, Rauman Jrs.
☐ 378 Ari Veijalainen, Rauman Jrs.
☐ 379 Jean Béliveau, Mtl.
☐ 380 Phil Esposito, Bos.
☐ 381 Tony Esposito (G), Chi.
☐ 382 Gordie Howe, Det.
☐ 383 Bobby Hull, Chi.
☐ 384 Bobby Orr, Bos.

1972 HELLAS MM-JENKKI

A set of 99 cards plus a collecting album issued by Hellas (Leaf) for the 1972 World Championships. We have no pricing information on this set.

Card Size: 2 1/8" x 3 1/8"
Front: Four colour
Imprint:
Complete Set (99 cards):

No. Player

☐ 1 Seppo Ahokainen, Fin.
☐ 2 VeliPekka Ketola, Fin.
☐ 3 Henry Leppa, Fin.
☐ 4 Harri Linnonmaa, Fin.
☐ 5 Pekka Marjamaki, Fin.
☐ 6 Lauri Mononen, Fin.
☐ 7 Matti Murto, Fin.
☐ 8 Timo Nummelin, Fin.
☐ 9 Lasse Oksanen, Fin.
☐ 10 Esa Peltonen, Fin.
☐ 11 Pekka Rautakallio, Fin.
☐ 12 Seppo Repo, Fin.
☐ 13 Heikki Riihiranta, Fin.
☐ 14 Tommi Salmelainen, Fin.
☐ 15 Leo Seppanen, Fin.
☐ 16 Juhani Tamminen, Fin.
☐ 17 Timo Turunen, Fin.
☐ 18 Pertti Valkeapaa, Fin.
☐ 19 Jorma Valtonen, Fin.
☐ 20 Jouko Oystila, Fin.
☐ 21 Timo Saari, Fin.
☐ 22 Seppo Suoraniemi, Fin.
☐ 23 Leif Holmqvist, Swe.
☐ 24 Thommy Abrahamsson, Swe.
☐ 25 Thommie Bergman, Swe.
☐ 26 Stig Ostling, Swe.
☐ 27 Lars Sjoberg, Swe.
☐ 28 Carl Sundquist, Swe.
☐ 29 Bjorn Johansson, Swe.
☐ 30 Tord Lundstrom, Swe.
☐ 31 StigGoran Johansson, Swe.
☐ 32 Stefan Karlsson, Swe.
☐ 33 LarsGoran Nilsson, Swe.
☐ 34 Stig Larsson, Swe.
☐ 35 Mats Lindh, Swe.
☐ 36 Bjorn Palmqvist, Swe.
☐ 37 Inge Hammarstrom, Swe.
☐ 38 Anders Hedberg, Swe.
☐ 39 Kurt Larsson, Swe.
☐ 40 Hakan Pettersson, Swe.
☐ 41 Hakan Wickberg, Swe.
☐ 42 Borje Salming, Swe.
☐ 43 Franz Funk, BRD.
☐ 44 Otto Schneitberger, BRD.
☐ 45 Josef Volk, BRD.
☐ 46 Rudolph Thanner, BRD.
☐ 47 Paul Langner, BRD.
☐ 48 Harald Kadow, BRD.
☐ 49 Anton Pohl, BRD.
☐ 50 KarlHeine Egger, BRD.
☐ 51 Lorenz Funk, BRD.
☐ 52 Alois Schloder, BRD.
☐ 53 Gustav Hanig, BRD.
☐ 54 Philip Reiner, BRD.
☐ 55 Bernd Kuhn, BRD.
☐ 56 Johann Eimansberger, BRD.
☐ 57 Rainer Makatsch, BRD.
☐ 58 Michael Eibl, BRD.
☐ 59 Hans Schichtl, BRD.
☐ 60 Anton Hoffher, BRD.
☐ 61 Vladimir Sepovalov, USSR
☐ 62 Aleksandr Gusev, USSR
☐ 63 Vladimir Lutchenko, USSR
☐ 64 Viktor Kuzkin, USSR
☐ 65 Aleksandr Ragulin, USSR
☐ 66 Igor Romishevski, USSR
☐ 67 Gennadi Tsigankov, USSR
☐ 68 Valeri Vasiliev, USSR
☐ 69 Yuri Blinov, USSR
☐ 70 Alexander Maltsev, USSR
☐ 71 Evgeny Mishakov, USSR
☐ 72 Boris Mikhailov, USSR
☐ 73 Vjatseslav Anisin, USSR
☐ 74 Alexander Yakhailov, USSR
☐ 75 Vladimir Petrov, USSR
☐ 76 Valeri Kharlamov, USSR
☐ 77 Vladimir Vikulov, USSR
☐ 78 Vladimir Shadrin, USSR
☐ 79 Vladislav Tretiak (G), USSR
☐ 80 Vladimir Dzurilla, CSR.
☐ 81 Jiri Holecek, CSR.
☐ 82 Josef Horesovsky, CSR.
☐ 83 Oldrich Machac, CSR.
☐ 84 Jaroslav Holik, CSR.
☐ 85 Rudolf Tajhnar, CSR.
☐ 86 Frantisek Pospisil, CSR.
☐ 87 Jiri Kochta, CSR.
☐ 88 Jan Klapac, CSR.
☐ 89 Vladimir Martinec, CSR.
☐ 90 Richard Farda, CSR.
☐ 91 Bohuslav Stastny, CSR.
☐ 92 Vaclav Nedomansky, CSR.
☐ 93 Julius Haas, CSR.
☐ 94 Josef Palecek, CSR.
☐ 95 Jiri Bubla, CSR.
☐ 96 Milan Kuzela, CSR.
☐ 97 Vladimir Bednar, CSR.
☐ 98 Jiri Holik, CSR.
☐ 99 Ivan Hlinka, CSR.

1972 PANDA MM - TORONTO

A set of 112 cards issued by the chocolate factory Panda for the 1972 World Championships and the Finnish National League. We have no pricing information on this set.

Card Size: 2 1/8" x 3 1/8"
Imprint:
Face: Four colour

Player

HIFK Helsinki

☐ Juhani Bostrom
☐ Gary Engberg
☐ Kimmo Heino
☐ Mauri Kaukokari
☐ Vaino Kolkka
☐ Harri Linnonmaa
☐ Jaakko Marttinen
☐ Matti Murto
☐ Lalli Partinen
☐ Juha Rantasila
☐ Heikki Riihiranta
☐ Jorma Rikala
☐ Tommi Salmelainen
☐ Jorma Thusberg
☐ Jorma Virtanen
☐ Matti Vaisanen

ILVES Tampere
- ☐ Sakari Ahlberg
- ☐ Jorma Aro
- ☐ Esko Eriksson
- ☐ Markku Hakanen
- ☐ Matti Hakanen
- ☐ Reijo Hakanen
- ☐ Timo Hirsimaki
- ☐ Jorma Kallio
- ☐ Esko Kaonpaa
- ☐ Pentti Koskela
- ☐ Pekka Kuusisto
- ☐ Pekka Leimu
- ☐ Lasse Oksanen
- ☐ Kari Palooja
- ☐ Jorma Peltonen
- ☐ Veikko Suominen

ASSAT Pori
- ☐ Tapio Flinck
- ☐ Pentti Hakamaki
- ☐ Antti Heikkila
- ☐ Reijo Heinonen
- ☐ Jaakko Honkanen
- ☐ VeliPekka Ketola
- ☐ Raimo Kilpio
- ☐ Tapio Koskinen
- ☐ Kaj Matalamaki
- ☐ Pekka Rautakallio
- ☐ Matti Salmi
- ☐ KariPekka Toivonen
- ☐ Jorma Valtonen
- ☐ Anto Virtanen
- ☐ Erkki Vakiparta

USSR
- ☐ Vitaly Davydov
- ☐ Anatoli Firsov
- ☐ Valery Kharlamov
- ☐ Victor Konovalenko (G)
- ☐ Victor Kuzkin
- ☐ Yuri Liapkin
- ☐ Vladimir Lutchenko
- ☐ Alexander Maltsev
- ☐ Alexander Martiniuk
- ☐ Boris Mikhailov
- ☐ Alexander Ragulin
- ☐ Igor Romishevskyi
- ☐ Vladimir Shadrin
- ☐ Viacheslav Starshinov
- ☐ Vladislav Tretiak (G)
- ☐ Evgenyi Zimin

SWEDEN
- ☐ Christer Abrahamsson
- ☐ Tommy Abrahamsson
- ☐ Arne Carlsson
- ☐ Inge Hammarstrom
- ☐ Leif Holmqvist
- ☐ StigGoran Johansson
- ☐ Stefan Karlsson
- ☐ Hans Lindberg
- ☐ Tord Lundstrom
- ☐ LarsGoran Nilsson
- ☐ BertOla Nordlander
- ☐ Hakan Nygren
- ☐ Bjorn Palmqvist
- ☐ Ulf Sterner
- ☐ Lennart Svedberg
- ☐ Hakan Wickberg

CZECHOSLOVAKIA
- ☐ Josef Cerny
- ☐ Richard Farda
- ☐ Ivan Hlinka
- ☐ Jiri Holecek
- ☐ Jiri Holik
- ☐ Josef Horesovsky
- ☐ Milan Kuzela
- ☐ Oldrich Machac
- ☐ Vladimir Martinec
- ☐ Vladimir Nadrachal
- ☐ Vaclav Nedomansky
- ☐ Frantisek Panchartek
- ☐ Frantisek Pospisil
- ☐ Marcel Sakac
- ☐ Bohuslav Stastny
- ☐ Rudolf Tajcnar

FINLAND
- ☐ Esa Isaksson
- ☐ Heikki Jarn
- ☐ VeliPekka Ketola
- ☐ Ilpo Koskela
- ☐ Seppo Lindstrom
- ☐ Harri Linnonmaa
- ☐ Pekka Marjamaki
- ☐ Erkki Mononen
- ☐ Lauri Mononen
- ☐ Matti Murto
- ☐ Lasse Oksanen
- ☐ Esa Peltonen
- ☐ Seppo Repo
- ☐ Tommi Salmelainen
- ☐ Jorma Valtonen
- ☐ Urpo Ylonen
- ☐ Jouko Oystila

1972 SCOTIA BANK POSTCARD ISSUE

Postcard Size: 5 13/16" x 3 15/16"
Face: Four colour
Back: Red and blue on white card stock
Imprint: Scotia Bank

	Player	EX	NRMT
☐	Team Canada	6.00	12.00

1972 SEMIC STICKERS

A set of 233 cards issued by Semic Press into both Finland (JÅÅKIEKKO/OLYMPIA-MM72) and Sweden (ISHOCKEY/OS-VM72).
Sticker Size: 1 7/8" x 2 9/16"
Face: Four colour
Back: Black text
Imprint: Sweden - printed in Italy
Imprint: Finland - Painettu Italiassa

		EX	NRMT
Complete Set (233 cards):		225.00	450.00
Common Player:		.35	.75

	No.	Player	EX	NRMT
☐☐	1	Viktor Konovalenko (G), USSR	.35	.75
☐☐	2	Vitali Davydov, USSR	.35	.75
☐☐	3	Vladimir Lutchenko, USSR	.35	.75
☐☐	4	Viktor Kuzkin, USSR	.35	.75
☐☐	5	Aleksandr Ragulin, USSR	1.25	2.50
☐☐	6	Igor Romishevski, USSR	.35	.75
☐☐	7	Gennadi Tsycankov, USSR	.35	.75
☐☐	8	Vjatsjeslav Starsinov, USSR	.35	.75
☐☐	9	Jevgeni Zimin, USSR	.35	.75
☐☐	10	Alexander Maltsev, USSR	2.00	4.00
☐☐	11	Anatoli Firsov, USSR	1.00	2.00
☐☐	12	Evgeny Mishakov, USSR	.35	.75
☐☐	13	Boris Mikhailov, USSR	2.50	5.00
☐☐	14	Yuri Liapkin, USSR	.35	.75
☐☐	15	Alexander Martiniuk, USSR	.35	.75
☐☐	16	Vladimir Petrov, USSR	1.50	3.00
☐☐	17	Valeri Harlamov, USSR	5.00	10.00
☐☐	18	Vladimir Vikulov, USSR	.35	.75
☐☐	19	Vladimir Shadrin, USSR	.35	.75
☐☐	20	Vladislav Tretiak (G), USSR	11.00	22.00
☐☐	21	Marcel Sakac, CSR.	.35	.75
☐☐	22	Jiri Holecek, CSR.	1.00	2.00
☐☐	23	Josef Horesovsky, CSR.	.35	.75
☐☐	24	Oldrich Machac, CSR.	.35	.75
☐☐	25	Rudolf Tajcnar, CSR.	.35	.75
☐☐	26	Frantisek Panchartek, CSR.	.35	.75
☐☐	27	Frantisek Pospisil, CSR.	.35	.75
☐☐	28	Jiri Kochta, CSR.	.35	.75
☐☐	29	Jan Havel, CSR.	.35	.75
☐☐	30	Vladimir Martinec, CSR.	.35	.75
☐☐	31	Richard Farda, CSR.	.35	.75
☐☐	32	Bohuslav Stastny, CSR.	.35	.75
☐☐	33	Vaclav Nedomansky, CSR.	1.25	2.50
☐☐	34	Josef Cerny, CSR.	.35	.75
☐☐	35	Bedrich Brunchlik, CSR.	.35	.75
☐☐	36	Jan Suchy, CSR.	.35	.75
☐☐	37	Eduard Novak, CSR.	.35	.75
☐☐	38	Jiri Bubla, CSR.	1.00	2.00
☐☐	39	Jiri Holik, CSR.	.35	.75
☐☐	40	Ivan Hlinka, CSR.	1.00	2.00
☐☐	41	Vladimir Bednar, CSR.	.35	.75
☐☐	42	Leif Holmqqvist, Swe.	.35	.75
☐☐	43	Christer Abrahamsson, Swe.	1.00	2.00
☐☐	44	Christer Andersson, Swe.	.35	.75
☐☐	45	Lars-Erik Sjöjberg, Swe.	1.25	2.50
☐☐	46	Lennart Svedberg, Swe.	.35	.75
☐☐	47	Stig-Göran Johansson, Swe.	.35	.75
☐☐	48	Bert-Ola Nordlander, Swe.	.35	.75
☐☐	49	Thommy Abrahamsson, Swe.	1.00	2.00
☐☐	50	Arne Carlsson, Swe.	.35	.75
☐☐	51	Stefan Karlsson, Swe.	.35	.75
☐☐	52	Håkan Wickberg, Swe.	.35	.75
☐☐	53	Håkan Nygren, Swe.	.35	.75
☐☐	54	Lars-Göran Nilsson, Swe.	.35	.75
☐☐	55	Thommie Bergman, Swe.	1.50	3.00
☐☐	56	Ulf Sterner, Swe.	.35	.75
☐☐	57	Hans Lindberg, Swe.	.35	.75
☐☐	58	Tord Lundström, Swe.	.35	.75
☐☐	60	Björn Palmqvist, Swe.	.35	.75
☐☐	61	Inge Hammarström, Swe.	2.00	4.00
☐☐	62	Kjell-Rune Milton, Swe.	.35	.75
☐☐	63	Kjell Brus, Swe.	.35	.75
☐☐	64	Kenneth Ekman, Swe.	.35	.75
☐☐	65	Bengt-Göran Karlsson, Swe.	.35	.75
☐☐	66	Håkan Pettersson, Swe.	.35	.75
☐☐	67	Dan Labraaten, Swe.	1.00	2.00
☐☐	68	Dan Söderström, Swe.	.35	.75
☐☐	69	Anders Hedberg, Swe.	4.00	8.00
☐☐	70	Ake Söderberg, Swe.	.35	.75
☐☐	71	Urpo Ylönen, Fin.	.35	.75
☐☐	72	Ilpo Koskela, Fin.	.35	.75
☐☐	73	Seppo Lindström, Fin.	.35	.75
☐☐	74	Hannu Luojola, Fin.	.35	.75
☐☐	75	Pekka Marjamåki, Fin.	.35	.75
☐☐	76	Jouko Öystilå, Fin.	.35	.75
☐☐	77	Heikki Jårn, Fin.	.35	.75
☐☐	78	Esa Isaksson, Fin.	.35	.75
☐☐	79	Veli-Pekka Ketola, Fin.	1.25	2.50
☐☐	80	Harri Linnonmtaa, Fin.	.35	.75
☐☐	81	Erkki Mononen, Fin.	.35	.75
☐☐	82	Lauri Mononen, Fin.	.35	.75
☐☐	83	Matti Murto, Fin.	.35	.75
☐☐	84	Lasse Oksanen, Fin.	.35	.75
☐☐	85	Esa Peltonen, Fin.	.35	.75
☐☐	86	Seppo Repo, Fin.	.35	.75
☐☐	87	Tommi Salmelainen, Fin.	.35	.75
☐☐	88	Juhani Tamminen, Fin.	.35	.75
☐☐	89	Jorma Vehmanen, Fin.	.35	.75
☐☐	90	Jorma Valtonen, Fin.	.35	.75
☐☐	91	Matti Keinonen, Fin.	.35	.75
☐☐	92	Juha Rantasila, Fin.	.35	.75
☐☐	93	Toni Kehle, BRD.	.35	.75
☐☐	94	Josef Schramm, BRD.	.35	.75
☐☐	95	Waiter Stadler, BRD.	.35	.75
☐☐	96	Josef Völk, BRD.	.35	.75
☐☐	97	Hans Schichtl, BRD.	.35	.75
☐☐	98	Erwin Riedmeier, BRD.	.35	.75
☐☐	99	Werner Modes, BRD.	.35	.75
☐☐	100	Johan Eimansberger, BRD.	.35	.75
☐☐	101	Heinz Egger, BRD.	.35	.75

	No.	Player	EX	NRMT
☐☐	102	Lorentz Funk, BRD.	.35	.75
☐☐	103	Klaus Ego, BRD.	.35	.75
☐☐	104	Anton Hofherr, BRD.	.35	.75
☐☐	105	Otto Schneitberger, BRD.	.35	.75
☐☐	106	Heinz Weisenbach, BRD.	.35	.75
☐☐	107	Alois Schloder, BRD.	.35	.75
☐☐	108	Gustav Hanig, BRD.	.35	.75
☐☐	109	Rainer Philipp, BRD.	.35	.75
☐☐	110	Bernd Kuhn, BRD.	.35	.75
☐☐	111	Paul Langner, BRD.	.35	.75
☐☐	112	Franz Hofherr, BRD.	.35	.75
☐☐	113	Reinhold Bauer, BRD.	.35	.75
☐☐	114	Johann Rotkirch, BRD.	.35	.75
☐☐	115	Walter Köberle, BRD.	.35	.75
☐☐	116	Rainer Makatsch, BRD.	.35	.75
☐☐	117	Carl Wetzel, USA.	.35	.75
☐☐	118	Mike Curran, USA.	.35	.75
☐☐	119	Jim McElmury, USA.	.75	1.50
☐☐	120	Bruce Riutta, USA.	.35	.75
☐☐	121	Tom Mellor, USA.	.35	.75
☐☐	122	Don Ross, USA.	.35	.75
☐☐	123	Gary Gambucci, USA.	.35	.75
☐☐	124	Keith Christiansen, USA.	.35	.75
☐☐	125	Len Lilyholm, USA.	.35	.75
☐☐	126	Henry Boucha, USA.	1.00	2.00
☐☐	127	Craig Falkman, USA.	.35	.75
☐☐	128	Tim Sheehy, USA.	.35	.75
☐☐	129	Kevin Ahearn, USA.	1.75	3.50
☐☐	130	Craig Patrick, USA.	.35	.75
☐☐	131	Pete Fichuk, USA.	.35	.75
☐☐	132	George Konik, USA.	.35	.75
☐☐	133	Dick McGlynn, USA.	.35	.75
☐☐	134	Dick Toomey, USA.	.35	.75
☐☐	135	Paul Schilling, USA.	.35	.75
☐☐	136	Bob Lindberg, USA.	.35	.75
☐☐	137	Dick Tomasoni, USA.	.35	.75
☐☐	138	Nando Mathieu, Sui.	.35	.75
☐☐	139	Francis Reinhard, Sui.	.35	.75
☐☐	140	Gaston Furrer, Sui.	.35	.75
☐☐	141	Bruno Wittwer, Sui.	.35	.75
☐☐	142	Andre Berra, Sui.	.35	.75
☐☐	143	Hens Keller, Sui.	.35	.75
☐☐	144	Peter Luthi, Sui.	.35	.75
☐☐	145	Peter Aeschlimann, Sui.	.35	.75
☐☐	146	Werner Kuenzi, Sui.	.35	.75
☐☐	147	Tony Neininger, Sui.	.35	.75
☐☐	148	Jacques Pousaz, Sui.	.35	.75
☐☐	149	Roger Chappot, Sui.	.35	.75
☐☐	150	Charly Henzen, Sui.	.35	.75
☐☐	151	Paul Probst, Sui.	.35	.75
☐☐	152	Guy Duboi, Sui.	.35	.75
☐☐	153	Rene Sgualdo, Sui.	.35	.75
☐☐	154	Rene Hueguenin, Sui.	.35	.75
☐☐	155	Gaston Pelletier, Sui.	.35	.75
☐☐	156	Beat Kaufmann, Sui.	.35	.75
☐☐	157	Alfio Molina, Sui.	.35	.75
☐☐	158	Gerald Rigolet, Sui.	.35	.75
☐☐	159	Harald Jones, Sui.	.35	.75
☐☐	160	Gilbert Mathieu, Sui.	.35	.75
☐☐	161	Michel Turler, Sui.	.35	.75
☐☐	162	Reto Taillens , Sui.	.35	.75
☐☐	163	Norm Ullman	1.50	3.00
☐☐	164	Dave Keon	2.50	5.00
☐☐	165	Roger Crozier (G)	1.25	2.50
☐☐	166	Ron Ellis	.75	1.50
☐☐	167	Paul Henderson	1.25	2.50
☐☐	168	Jim Dorey	.75	1.50
☐☐	169	Jacques Plante (G)	10.00	20.00
☐☐	171	Gary Smith (G)	1.25	2.50
☐☐	172	Dennis Hextall	.75	1.50
☐☐	173	Norm Ferguson	.75	1.50
☐☐	174	Simon Nolet	.75	1.50
☐☐	175	Bernie Parent (G)	5.00	10.00
☐☐	176	Ted Hampson	.75	1.50
☐☐	177	Earl Ingarfield	.75	1.50
☐☐	178	Larry Hillman	.75	1.50
☐☐	179	Gary Dornhoefer	.75	1.50
☐☐	180	Gary Croteau	.75	1.50
☐☐	181	Carol Vadnais	.75	1.50
☐☐	182	Jim Roberts	.75	1.50
☐☐	183	Red Berenson	.75	1.50
☐☐	184	Phil Esposito	5.00	10.00
☐☐	185	John McKenzie	.75	1.50
☐☐	186	Barclay Plager	.75	1.50
☐☐	187	Glenn Hall (G)	7.50	15.00
☐☐	188	Gerry Cheevers (G)	4.00	8.00
☐☐	189	Jim McKenny	.75	1.50
☐☐	190	Gordie Howe	25.00	45.00
☐☐	191	Garry Unger	.75	1.50
☐☐	192	Roy Edwards (G)	1.25	2.50
☐☐	193	Alex Delvecchio	2.00	4.00
☐☐	194	Brad Park	2.50	5.00
☐☐	195	Frank Mahovlich	4.00	8.00
☐☐	196	Phil Goyette	.75	1.50
☐☐	197	Don Marshall	.75	1.50
☐☐	198	Henri Richard	2.50	5.00
☐☐	199	Claude Larose	.75	1.50
☐☐	200	Bobby Rousseau	.75	1.50
☐☐	201	Lorne Worsley (G)	4.00	8.00
☐☐	202	Gilles Marotte	.75	1.50
☐☐	203	Bob Pulford	1.50	3.00
☐☐	204	Yvan Cournoyer	2.50	5.00
☐☐	205	Eddie Joyal	.75	1.50
☐☐	206	Ross Lonsberry	.75	1.50
☐☐	207	Jean Béliveau	7.50	15.00
☐☐	208	Jacques Lemaire	2.50	5.00
☐☐	209	Orland Kurtenbach	.75	1.50
☐☐	210	André Boudrias	.75	1.50
☐☐	211	Jim Nielson	.75	1.50
☐☐	212	Walt Tkaczuk	.75	1.50
☐☐	213	Ed Giacomin (G)	4.00	8.00
☐☐	214	Jean Ratelle	2.00	4.00
☐☐	215	Les Binkley (G)	1.25	2.50
☐☐	216	Jean Pronovost	.75	1.50
☐☐	217	Bryan Watson	.75	1.50
☐☐	218	Dean Prentice	.75	1.50
☐☐	219	Jean-Paul Parise	.75	1.50
☐☐	220	Bill Goldworthy	.75	1.50
☐☐	221	Wayne Maki	.75	1.50
☐☐	222	Dale Tallon	.75	1.50
☐☐	223	Bobby Orr	30.00	60.00
☐☐	224	Pit Martin	.75	1.50
☐☐	225	Jacques Laperrière	1.50	3.00
☐☐	226	Bill Flett	.75	1.50
☐☐	227	Stan Mikita	4.00	8.00
☐☐	228	Bobby Hull	13.00	25.00
☐☐	229	Larry Pleau	.75	1.50
☐☐	230	Keith Magnuson	.75	1.50
☐☐	231	Tony Esposito (G)	5.00	10.00
☐☐	232	Rogatien Vachon (G)	1.50	3.00
☐☐	233	Mickey Redmond	1.25	2.50

1972 TOWERS INSTRUCTION BOOKLETS

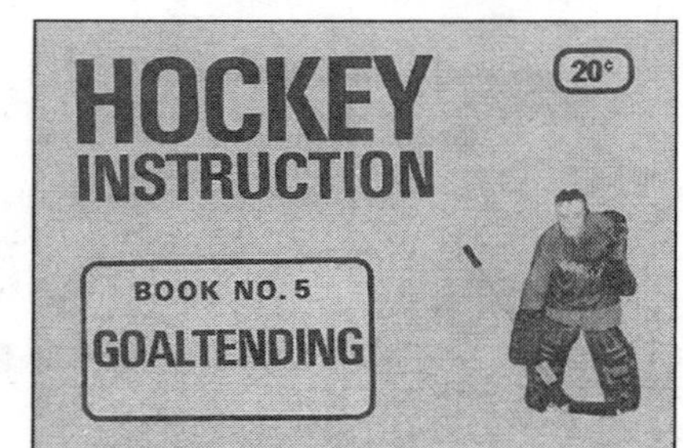

Booklet Size: 5" x 7"
Face: Four colour; Number
Back: Black on newsprint
Imprint: Copyright 1972 Photo Pix Productions,Toronto.

	No.	Player	EX	NRMT
		Complete Set (6 booklets):	**20.00**	**40.00**
☐	1	Skating Skills	5.00	10.00
☐	2	Puck Control	5.00	10.00
☐	3	Shooting	5.00	10.00
☐	4	Checking	5.00	10.00
☐	5	Goaltending	5.00	10.00
☐	6	Team Play	5.00	10.00

1972 - 73 EDDIE SARGENT STICKERS

Issued one sheet per NHL team, the 16 stamp sheets had 14 players plus two series number stickers. Two different covered albums were available.

Sticker Size: 1 7/8" x 2 1/2"
Face: Four colour, white border; Name, Team, Number
Back: Blank
Imprint: 1972 NATIONAL HOCKEY LEAGUE PLAYERS' ASSOCIATION, SPORTS ALBUM INC., EDDIE SARGENT PROMOTIONS LTD

	No.	Player	EX	NRMT
		Complete Set (224 cards):	**125.00**	**250.00**
		Common Player:	**.25**	**.50**
		Album: (Henderson)	**25.00**	**50.00**
		Album: (Orr)	**50.00**	**100.00**
☐	1	Lucien Grenier, Atl.	.25	.50
☐	2	Phil Myre (G), Atl.	.25	.50
☐	3	Ernie Hicke, Atl.	.35	.75
☐	4	Keith McCreary, Atl.	.25	.50
☐	5	Billy MacMillan, Atl.	.25	.50
☐	6	Pat Quinn, Atl.	.35	.75
☐	7	Bill Plager, Atl.	.25	.50
☐	8	Noel Price, Atl.	.25	.50
☐	9	Bobby Leiter, Atl.	.25	.50
☐	10	Randy Manery, Atl.	.25	.50
☐	11	Bob Paradise, Atl.	.25	.50
☐	12	Larry Romanchych, Atl.	.25	.50
☐	13	Lew Morrison, Atl.	.25	.50
☐	14	Dan Bouchard (G), Atl.	.50	1.00
☐	15	Fred Stanfield, Bos.	.25	.50
☐	16	John Bucyk, Bos.	1.50	3.00
☐	17	Bobby Orr, Bos.	15.00	30.00
☐	18	Wayne Cashman, Bos.	.25	.50
☐	19	Dallas Smith, Bos.	.25	.50
☐	20	Eddie Johnston (G), Bos.	.35	.75
☐	21	Phil Esposito, Bos.	3.00	6.00
☐	22	Ken Hodge, Sr., Bos.	.25	.50
☐	23	Don Awrey, Bos.	.25	.50
☐	24	Mike Walton, Bos.	.25	.50
☐	25	Carol Vadnais, Bos.	.25	.50
☐	26	Doug Roberts, Bos.	.25	.50
☐	27	Don Marcotte, Bos.	.25	.50
☐	28	Garnet Bailey, Bos.	.25	.50
☐	29	Gerry Meehan, Buf.	.25	.50
☐	30	Tracy Pratt, Buf.	.25	.50
☐	31	Gilbert Perreault, Buf.	2.25	4.50
☐	32	Roger Crozier (G), Buf.	.35	.75
☐	33	Don Luce, Buf.	.25	.50
☐	34	Dave Dryden (G), Buf.	.35	.75
☐	35	Richard Martin, Buf.	.50	1.00
☐	36	Jim Lorentz, Buf.	.25	.50
☐	37	Tim Horton, Buf.	2.25	4.50
☐	38	Craig Ramsey, Buf.	.35	.75
☐	39	Larry Hillman, Buf.	.25	.50
☐	40	Steve Atkinson, Buf.	.25	.50
☐	41	Jim Schoenfeld, Buf.	.60	1.25
☐	42	René Robert, Buf.	.25	.50
☐	43	Walt McKechnie, Cal.	.25	.50
☐	44	Marshall Johnston, Cal.	.25	.50
☐	45	Joey Johnston, Cal.	.25	.50
☐	46	Dick Redmond, Cal.	.25	.50
☐	47	Bert Marshall, Cal.	.25	.50
☐	48	Gary Croteau, Cal.	.25	.50
☐	49	Marv Edwards (G), Cal.	.35	.75
☐	50	Gilles Meloche (G), Cal.	.50	1.00
☐	51	Ivan Boldirev, Cal.	.25	.50
☐	52	Stan Gilbertson, Cal.	.25	.50
☐	53	Pete Laframboise, Cal.	.25	.50
☐	54	Reggie Leach, Cal.	.25	.50
☐	55	Craig Patrick, Cal.	.25	.50
☐	56	Bob Stewart, Cal.	.25	.50
☐	57	Keith Magnuson, Chi.	.25	.50
☐	58	Doug Jarrett., Chi.	.25	.50

☐ 59 Cliff Koroll, Chi. .25 .50
☐ 60 Chico Maki, Chi. .25 .50
☐ 61 Gary Smith (G), Chi. .35 .75
☐ 62 Bill White, Chi. .25 .50
☐ 63 Stan Mikita, Chi. 2.75 5.50
☐ 64 Jim Pappin, Chi. .25 .50
☐ 65 Lou Angotti, Chi. .25 .50
☐ 66 Tony Esposito (G), Chi. 2.75 5.50
☐ 67 Dennis Hull, Chi. .25 .50
☐ 68 Pit Martin, Chi. .25 .50
☐ 69 Pat Stapleton, Chi. .25 .50
☐ 70 Dan Maloney, Chi. .25 .50
☐ 71 Bill Collins, Det. .25 .50
☐ 72 Arnie Brown, Det. .25 .50
☐ 73 Red Berenson, Det. .25 .50
☐ 74 Mickey Redmond, Det. .35 .75
☐ 75 Nick Libett, Det. .25 .50
☐ 76 Alex Delvecchio, Det. 1.25 2.50
☐ 77 Ron Stackhouse, Det. .25 .50
☐ 78 Tim Ecclestone, Det. .25 .50
☐ 79 Gary Bergman, Det. .25 .50
☐ 80 Guy Charron, Det. .25 .50
☐ 81 Leon Rochefort, Det. .25 .50
☐ 82 Larry Johnston, Det. .25 .50
☐ 83 Andy Brown (G), Det. .35 .75
☐ 84 Henry Boucha, Det. .25 .50
☐ 85 Paul Curtis, L.A. .25 .50
☐ 86 Jim Stanfield, L.A. .25 .50
☐ 87 Rogatien Vachon (G), L.A. .75 1.50
☐ 88 Ralph Backstrom, L.A. .25 .50
☐ 89 Gilles Marotte, L.A. .25 .50
☐ 90 Harry Howell, L.A. .75 1.50
☐ 91 Réal Lemieux, L.A. .25 .50
☐ 92 Butch Goring, L.A. .25 .50
☐ 93 Juha Widing, L.A. .25 .50
☐ 94 Mike Corrigan, L.A. .25 .50
☐ 95 Larry Brown, L.A. .25 .50
☐ 96 Terry Harper, L.A. .25 .50
☐ 97 Serge Bernier, L.A. .25 .50
☐ 98 Bob Berry, L.A. .25 .50
☐ 99 Tom Reid, Min. .25 .50
☐ 100 Jude Drouin, Min. .25 .50
☐ 101 Jean Paul Parise, Min. .25 .50
☐ 102 Doug Mohns, Min. .25 .50
☐ 103 Danny Grant, Min. .25 .50
☐ 104 Bill Goldsworthy, Min. .25 .50
☐ 105 Gump Worsley (G), Min. 2.00 4.00
☐ 106 Charlie Burns, Min. .25 .50
☐ 107 Murray Oliver, Min. .25 .50
☐ 108 Barry Gibbs, Min. .25 .50
☐ 109 Ted Harris, Min. .25 .50
☐ 110 Césare Maniago (G), Min. .35 .75
☐ 111 Lou Nanne, Min. .25 .50
☐ 112 Bob Nevin, Min. .25 .50
☐ 113 Guy Lapointe, Mtl. .50 1.00
☐ 114 Pete Mahovlich, Mtl. .25 .50
☐ 115 Jacques Lemaire, Mtl. 1.50 3.00
☐ 116 Pierre Bouchard, Mtl. .25 .50
☐ 117 Yvan Cournoyer, Mtl. 1.75 3.25
☐ 118 Marc Tardif, Mtl. .25 .50
☐ 119 Henri Richard, Mtl. 1.75 3.50
☐ 120 Frank Mahovlich, Mtl. 2.50 5.00
☐ 121 Jacques Laperrière, Mtl. .75 1.50
☐ 122 Claude Larose, Mtl. .25 .50
☐ 123 Serge Savard, Mtl. .75 1.50
☐ 124 Ken Dryden (G), Mtl. 9.00 18.00
☐ 125 Réjean Houle, Mtl. .35 .75
☐ 126 Jim Roberts, Mtl. .25 .50
☐ 127 Ed Westfall, NYI. .25 .50
☐ 128 Terry Crisp, NYI. .25 .50
☐ 129 Gerry Desjardins (G), NYI. .35 .75
☐ 130 Denis DeJordy (G), NYI., Error (Dennis) .35 .75
☐ 131 Billy Harris, NYI. .25 .50
☐ 132 Brian Spencer, NYI. .25 .50
☐ 133 Germain Gagnon, NYI. .25 .50
☐ 134 Dave Hudson, NYI. .25 .50
☐ 135 Lorne Henning, NYI. .25 .50
☐ 136 Brian Marchinko, NYI. .25 .50
☐ 137 Tom Miller, NYI. .25 .50
☐ 138 Gerry Hart, NYI. .25 .50
☐ 139 Bryan Lefley, NYI. .25 .50
☐ 140 Jim Mair, NYI. .25 .50
☐ 141 Rod Gilbert, NYR. 1.25 2.50
☐ 142 Jean Ratelle, NYR. 1.25 2.50
☐ 143 Pete Stemkowski, NYR. .25 .50
☐ 144 Brad Park, NYR. 1.75 3.50
☐ 145 Bobby Rousseau, NYR. .25 .50
☐ 146 Dale Rolfe, NYR. .25 .50
☐ 147 Ed Giacomin (G), NYR. 1.75 3.25
☐ 148 Rod Seiling, NYR. .25 .50
☐ 149 Walt Tkaczuk, NYR. .25 .50
☐ 150 Bill Fairbairn, NYR. .25 .50
☐ 151 Vic Hadfield, NYR. .25 .50
☐ 152 Ted Irvine, NYR. .25 .50
☐ 153 Bruce MacGregor, NYR. .25 .50
☐ 154 Jim Neilson, NYR. .25 .50
☐ 155 Brent Hughes, Pha. .25 .50
☐ 156 Wayne Hillman, Pha. .25 .50
☐ 157 Doug Favell (G), Pha. .35 .75
☐ 158 Simon Nolet, Pha. .25 .50
☐ 159 Joe Watson, Pha. .25 .50
☐ 160 Ed Van Impe, Pha. .25 .50
☐ 161 Gary Dornhoefer, Pha. .25 .50
☐ 162 Bobby Clarke, Pha. 3.00 6.00
☐ 163 Bob Kelly, Pha. .25 .50
☐ 164 Bill Flett, Pha. .25 .50
☐ 165 Rick Foley, Pha. .25 .50
☐ 166 Ross Lonsberry, Pha. .25 .50
☐ 167 Rick MacLeish, Pha. .35 .75
☐ 168 Bill Clement, Pha. .25 .50
☐ 169 Syl Apps, Jr., Pgh. .25 .50
☐ 170 Ken Schinkel, Pgh. .25 .50
☐ 171 Nick Harbaruk, Pgh. .25 .50
☐ 172 Bryan Watson, Pgh. .25 .50
☐ 173 Bryan Hextall, Jr., Pgh. .25 .50
☐ 174 Roy Edwards (G), Pgh. .35 .75
☐ 175 Jim Rutherford (G), Pgh. .35 .75
☐ 176 Jean Pronovost, Pgh. .25 .50
☐ 177 Rick Kessell, Pgh. .25 .50
☐ 178 Greg Polis, Pgh. .25 .50
☐ 179 Ron Schock, Pgh. .25 .50
☐ 180 Duane Rupp, Pgh. .25 .50
☐ 181 Darryl Edestrand, Pgh. .25 .50
☐ 182 Dave Burrows, Pgh. .25 .50
☐ 183 Gary Sabourin, Stl. .25 .50
☐ 184 Garry Unger, Stl. .20 .40
☐ 185 Noel Picard, Stl. .25 .50
☐ 186 Bob Plager, Stl. .25 .50
☐ 187 Barclay Plager, Stl. .25 .50
☐ 188 Frank St. Marseille, Stl. .25 .50
☐ 189 Danny O'Shea, Stl. .25 .50
☐ 190 Kevin O'Shea, Stl. .25 .50
☐ 191 Wayne Stephenson (G), Stl. .35 .75
☐ 192 Chris Evans, Stl. .25 .50
☐ 193 Jacques Caron (G), Stl. .35 .75
☐ 194 André Dupont, Stl. .25 .50
☐ 195 Mike Murphy, Stl. .25 .50
☐ 196 Jack Egers, Stl. .25 .50
☐ 197 Norm Ullman, Tor. 1.50 3.00
☐ 198 Jim McKenny, Tor. .25 .50
☐ 199 Bob Baun, Tor. .25 .50
☐ 200 Mike Pelyk, Tor. .25 .50
☐ 201 Ron Ellis, Tor. .25 .50
☐ 202 Garry Monahan, Tor. .25 .50
☐ 203 Paul Henderson, Tor. 1.00 2.00
☐ 204 Darryl Sittler, Tor. 2.25 4.50
☐ 205 Brian Glennie, Tor. .25 .50
☐ 206 Dave Keon, Tor. 1.50 3.00
☐ 207 Jacques Plante (G), Tor. 2.75 5.50
☐ 208 Pierre Jarry, Tor. .25 .50
☐ 209 Rick Kehoe, Tor. .50 1.00
☐ 210 Denis Dupère, Tor. .25 .50
☐ 211 Dale Tallon, Van. .25 .50
☐ 212 Murray Hall, Van. .25 .50
☐ 213 Dunc Wilson (G), Van. .35 .75
☐ 214 André Boudrias, Van. .25 .50
☐ 215 Orland Kurtenbach, Van. .25 .50
☐ 216 Wayne Maki, Van. .25 .50
☐ 217 Barry Wilkins, Van. .25 .50
☐ 218 Richard Lemieux, Van. .25 .50
☐ 219 Bobby Schmautz, Van. .25 .50
☐ 220 Dave Balon, Van. .25 .50
☐ 221 Bobby Lalonde, Van. .25 .50
☐ 222 Jocelyn Guevremont, Van. .25 .50
☐ 223 Gregg Boddy, Van. .25 .50
☐ 224 Dennis Kearns, Van. .25 .50

1972 - 73 LETRASET ACTION TRANSFERS

Issued in booklet form, the action transfers could be used on any part of the action rink illustrated in the booklet.

Transfer Size: 4 7/8" x 2 3/8"
Face: Four colour
Back: Blank
Imprint: GK 121/ Patented. Printed in England by Letraset Ltd.

			EX	NRMT
Complete Set (24 transfers):			**175.00**	**350.00**
Common Sheet:			**5.00**	**10.00**
	No.	**Player**	**EX**	**NRMT**
☐	1	Rogatien Vachon (G)/David Keon/Gilles Marotte	9.00	18.00
☐	2	Ken Dryden (G)/Chiko Maki/Jacques Laperrière	20.00	40.00
☐	3	Gary Dornhoefer/Roger Crozier (G)/Tracy Pratt	5.00	10.00
☐	4	Walt Tkaczuk/Gump Worsley (G)/Vic Hadfield	10.00	20.00
☐	5	Dallas Smith/Bobby Orr/Walt McKechnie	25.00	50.00
☐	6	Ab MacDonald/Gary Sabourin/Garry Unger	5.00	10.00
☐	7	Jim Rutherford/Orland Kurtenbach/Bob Woytowich	5.00	10.00
☐	8	Gerry Cheevers (G)/Frank Mahovlich/Don Awrey	18.00	35.00
☐	9	Tim Ecclestone/Bob Baun/Jacques Plante (G)	15.00	30.00
☐	10	Stan Mikita/Ed Giacomin (G)/Jim Pappin	15.00	30.00
☐	11	Doug Favell (G)/Danny Grant/Ed Van Impe	5.00	10.00
☐	12	Ernie Wakley/Barclay Plager/Gary Croteau	5.00	10.00
☐	13	Bryan Hextall/Tony Esposito (G)/Pat Stapleton	13.00	25.00
☐	14	Jean Ratelle/Rod Gilbert/Jim Roberts	10.00	20.00
☐	15	Jacques Lemaire/Henri Richard/Yvan Cournoyer	15.00	30.00
☐	16	George Gardiner/Dennis Hull/Lou Angotti	5.00	10.00
☐	17	Ed Johnston/Norm Ullman/Bobby Orr	30.00	60.00
☐	18	Gilles Meloche/Wayne Carleton/Dick Redmond	5.00	10.00
☐	19	Al Smith/Gary Bergman/Stan Gilbertson	5.00	10.00
☐	20	Dunc Wilson (G)/Brad Park/Dale Tallon	7.50	15.00
☐	21	Jude Drouin/Doug Favell (G)/Barry Ashbee	5.00	10.00
☐	22	Ron Ellis/Ken Dryden (G)/Paul Henderson	20.00	40.00
☐	23	Gary Edwards (G)/Jean Pronovost/Ron Schock	5.00	10.00
☐	24	Césare Maniago (G)/Chris Bordeleau/Ted Harris	5.00	10.00

1972 - 73 O-PEE-CHEE

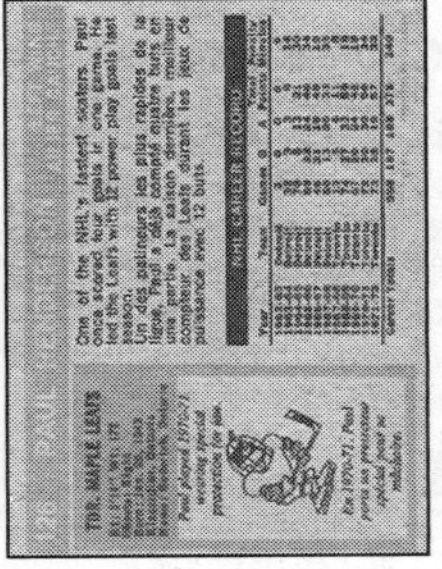

Card number 208 was not issued.

Card Size: 2 1/2" x 3 1/2"
Face: Four colour, beige border, Team logo
Back: Orange and black on card stock; Number, Resume, Hockey trivia, Bilingual
Imprint: © O.P.C.

	EX	NRMT
Complete Set (341 cards):	**800.00**	**1,600.00**
Common (1 - 110):	**1.25**	**2.25**
Common (210 - 289):	**2.50**	**5.00**
Common (290 - 341):	**5.50**	**11.00**

No.	Player	EX	NRMT
☐ 1	John Bucyk, Bos.	3.50	10.00
☐ **2**	**René Robert, Buf., RC**	**3.00**	**6.00**
☐ 3	Gary Croteau, Cal.	1.25	2.25
☐ 4	Pat Stapleton, Chi.	1.25	2.25
☐ 5	Ron Harris, Atl.	1.25	2.25
☐ 6	Checklist 1(1 - 110)	35.00	65.00
☐ 7	1971 - 72 NHL Playoffs: Game 1 at Boston	1.75	3.50
☐ 8	Marcel Dionne, Det.	18.00	35.00
☐ 9	Bob Berry, L.A.	1.25	2.25
☐ 10	Lou Nanne, Min.	1.25	2.25
☐ 11	Marc Tardif, Mtl.	1.25	2.25
☐ 12	Jean Ratelle, NYR.	2.50	5.00
☐ **13**	**Craig Cameron, NYI., RC**	**1.25**	**2.25**
☐ 14	Bobby Clarke, Pha.	20.00	40.00
☐ **15**	**Jim Rutherford (G), Pgh., RC**	**5.50**	**11.00**
☐ **16**	**André Dupont, Stl., RC**	**1.25**	**2.25**
☐ 17	Mike Pelyk, Tor.	1.25	2.25
☐ 18	Dunc Wilson (G), Van.	1.75	3.50
☐ 19	Checklist, Error	30.00	60.00
☐ 20	1971 - 72 NHL Playoffs: Game 2 at Boston	1.75	3.50
☐ 21	Dallas Smith, Bos.	1.25	2.25
☐ 22	Gerry Meehan, Buf.	1.25	2.25
☐ 23	Rick Smith, Cal., Err. (GP=265)	1.25	2.25
☐ 24	Pit Martin, Chi.	1.25	2.25
☐ 25	Keith McCreary, Atl.	1.25	2.25
☐ 26	Alex Delvecchio, Det.	2.75	5.50
☐ 27	Gilles Marotte, L.A.	1.25	2.25
☐ 28	Gump Worsley (G), Min.	3.25	6.50
☐ 29	Yvan Cournoyer, Mtl.	3.00	6.00
☐ 30	1971 - 72 NHL Playoffs: Game 3 at New York	1.75	3.50
☐ 31	Vic Hadfield, NYR.	1.25	2.25
☐ **32**	**Tom Miller, NYI., RC**	**1.25**	**2.25**
☐ 33	Ed Van Impe, Pha.	1.25	2.25
☐ 34	Greg Polis, Pgh.	1.25	2.25
☐ 35	Barclay Plager, Stl.	1.25	2.25
☐ 36	Ron Ellis, Tor.	1.25	2.25
☐ 37	Jocelyn Guevremont, Van.	1.25	2.25
☐ 38	1971 - 72 NHL Playoffs: Game 4 at New York	1.75	3.50
☐ 39	Carol Vadnais, Bos.	1.25	2.25
☐ 40	Steve Atkinson, Buf.	1.25	2.25
☐ **41**	**Ivan Boldirev, Cal., RC**	**1.75**	**3.50**
☐ 42	Jim Pappin, Chi.	1.25	2.25
☐ **43**	**Phil Myre (G), Atl., RC**	**4.00**	**7.50**
☐ 44	Yvan Cournoyer (Action)	2.00	4.00
☐ 45	Nick Libett, Det.	1.25	2.25
☐ 46	Juha Widing, L.A.	1.25	2.25
☐ 47	Jude Drouin, Min.	1.25	2.25
☐ 48	Jean Ratelle (Action), Err. (Defence)	3.00	6.00
☐ 48	Jean Ratelle(Action), Corrected	2.00	4.00
☐ 49	Ken Hodge, Sr., Bos.	1.25	2.25
☐ 50	Roger Crozier (G), Buf.	1.75	3.50
☐ 51	Reggie Leach, Cal.	2.00	4.00
☐ 52	Dennis Hull, Chi.	1.25	2.25
☐ **53**	**Larry Hale, Atl., RC, LC**	**1.25**	**2.25**
☐ 54	1971 - 72 NHL Playoffs: Game 5 at Boston	1.75	3.50
☐ 55	Tim Ecclestone, Det.	1.25	2.25
☐ 56	Butch Goring, L.A.	2.00	4.00
☐ 57	Danny Grant, Min.	1.25	2.25
☐ 58	Bobby Orr (Action)	20.00	40.00
☐ 59	Guy Lafleur, Mtl.	30.00	60.00
☐ 60	Jim Neilson, NYR.	1.25	2.25
☐ 61	Brian Spencer, NYI.	1.25	2.25
☐ 62	Joe Watson, Pha.	1.25	2.25
☐ 63	1971 - 72 NHL Playoffs: Game 6 at New York	1.75	3.50
☐ 64	Jean Pronovost, Pgh.	1.25	2.25
☐ 65	Frank St. Marseille, Stl.	1.25	2.25
☐ 66	Bob Baun, Tor., LC	1.25	2.25
☐ 67	Poul Popiel, Van.	1.25	2.25
☐ 68	Wayne Cashman, Bos.	1.25	2.25
☐ 69	Tracy Pratt, Buf.	1.25	2.25
☐ 70	Stan Gilbertson, Cal.	1.25	2.25
☐ 71	Keith Magnuson, Chi.	1.25	2.25
☐ 72	Ernie Hicke, Atl.	1.25	2.25
☐ 73	Gary Doak, Det.	1.25	2.25
☐ 74	Mike Corrigan, L.A.	1.25	2.25
☐ 75	Doug Mohns, Min.	1.25	2.25
☐ 76	Phil Esposito (Action)	4.50	9.00
☐ 77	Jacques Lemaire, Mtl.	3.00	6.00
☐ 78	Pete Stemkowski, NYR.	1.25	2.25
☐ **79**	**Bill Mikkelson, NYI., RC**	**1.25**	**2.25**
☐ **80**	**Rick Foley, Pha., RC, LC**	**1.25**	**2.25**
☐ 81	Ron Schock, Pgh.	1.25	2.25
☐ 82	Phil Roberto, Stl.	1.25	2.25
☐ 83	Jim McKenny, Tor.	1.25	2.25
☐ 84	Wayne Maki, Van., LC	1.25	2.25
☐ 85	Brad Park (Action), Err. (Centre)	3.25	6.00
☐ 85B	Brad Park (Action), Corrected	2.00	4.00
☐ 86	Guy Lapointe, Mtl.	2.00	4.00
☐ 87	Bill Fairbairn, NYR.	1.25	2.25
☐ 88	Terry Crisp, NYI.	2.00	4.00
☐ 89	Doug Favell (G), Pha.	1.75	3.50
☐ 90	Bryan Watson, Pgh.	1.25	2.25
☐ 91	Gary Sabourin, Stl.	1.25	2.25
☐ 92	Jacques Plante (G), Tor.	13.00	25.00
☐ 93	André Boudrias, Van.	1.25	2.25
☐ 94	Mike Walton, Bos.	1.25	2.25
☐ 95	Don Luce, Buf.	1.25	2.25
☐ 96	Joey Johnston, Cal.	1.25	2.25
☐ 97	Doug Jarrett, Chi.	1.25	2.25
☐ **98**	**Billy MacMillan, Atl., RC**	**1.25**	**2.25**
☐ 99	Mickey Redmond, Det.	1.75	3.50
☐ 100	Rogatien Vachon (G), L.A., Err. (Ragatien)	3.00	6.00
☐ **101**	**Barry Gibbs, Min., RC**	**1.25**	**2.25**
☐ 102	Frank Mahovlich, Mtl.	3.00	6.00
☐ 103	Bruce MacGregor, NYR.	1.25	2.25
☐ 104	Ed Westfall, NYI.	1.25	2.25
☐ 105	Rick MacLeish, Pha.	3.00	6.00
☐ 106	Nick Harbaruk, Pgh.	1.25	2.25
☐ **107**	**Jack Egers, Stl., RC**	**1.25**	**2.25**
☐ 108	Dave Keon, Tor.	2.50	5.00
☐ 109	Barry Wilkins, Van.	1.25	2.25
☐ 110	Walt Tkaczuk (Action)	1.25	2.25
☐ 111	Phil Esposito, Bos.	9.00	18.00
☐ **112**	**Gilles Meloche (G), Cal., RC**	**6.00**	**12.00**
☐ 113	Gary Edwards (G), L.A.	1.75	3.50
☐ 114	Brad Park, NYR.	7.00	14.00
☐ 115	Syl Apps, Pgh.	1.25	2.25
☐ 116	Jim Lorentz, Buf.	1.25	2.25
☐ 117	Gary Smith (G), Chi.	1.75	3.50
☐ 118	Ted Harris, Min.	1.25	2.25
☐ 119	Gerry Desjardins (G), NYI.	1.75	3.50
☐ 120	Garry Unger, Stl.	1.25	2.25
☐ 121	Dale Tallon, Van.	1.25	2.25
☐ **122**	**William Plager, Atl., RC, LC**	**1.25**	**2.25**
☐ 123	Red Berenson, Det.	1.25	2.25
☐ 124	Pete Mahovlich, Mtl.	1.25	2.25
☐ 125	Simon Nolet, Pha.	1.25	2.25
☐ 126	Paul Henderson, Tor.	1.75	3.50
☐ 127	Hart Memorial Trophy: Bobby Orr, Bos.	2.00	4.00
☐ 128	NHL Action: Montréal Vs. Toronto	2.50	5.00
☐ 129	Bobby Orr, Bos.	40.00	75.00
☐ 130	Bert Marshall, Cal.	1.25	2.25
☐ 131	Ralph Backstrom, L.A.	1.25	2.25
☐ 132	Gilles Villemure (G), NYR.	1.75	3.50
☐ **133**	**Dave Burrows, Pgh., RC**	**1.25**	**2.25**
☐ 134	Calder Trophy: Ken Dryden, Mtl.	2.00	4.00
☐ 135	NHL Action: Boston vs. Toronto	1.25	2.25
☐ 136	Gilbert Perreault, Buf.	9.00	18.00
☐ 137	Tony Esposito (G), Chi.	13.00	25.00
☐ 138	Césare Maniago (G), Min.	1.75	3.50
☐ **139**	**Gerry Hart, NYI., RC**	**1.25**	**2.25**
☐ **140**	**Jacques Caron (G), Stl., RC, LC**	**1.75**	**3.50**
☐ 141	Orland Kurtenbach, Van.	1.25	2.25
☐ 142	James Norris Trophy: Bobby Orr, Bos.	2.00	4.00
☐ 143	Lew Morrison, Atl.	1.25	2.25
☐ 144	Arnie Brown, NYI.	1.25	2.25
☐ 145	Ken Dryden (G), Mtl.	35.00	65.00
☐ 146	Gary Dornhoefer, Pha.	1.25	2.25
☐ 147	Norm Ullman, Tor.	2.00	4.00
☐ 148	Art Ross Trophy: Phil Esposito, Bos.	2.00	4.00
☐ 149	NHL Action: Vancouver vs. Toronto	1.25	2.25
☐ 150	Fred Stanfield, Bos.	1.25	2.25
☐ 151	Dick Redmond, Cal.	1.25	2.25
☐ 152	Serge Bernier, L.A.	1.25	2.25
☐ 153	Rod Gilbert, NYR.	2.50	5.00
☐ 154	Duane Rupp, Pgh.	1.25	2.25
☐ 155	Vezina Trophy: T. Esposito, G. Smith, Chi.	2.00	4.00
☐ 156	NHL Action: Chicago vs. Toronto	2.75	5.50
☐ 157	Rick Martin, Buf.	3.25	6.50
☐ 158	Bill White, Chi.	1.25	2.25
☐ 159	Bill Goldsworthy, Min.	1.25	2.25
☐ **160**	**Jack Lynch, Pgh., RC**	**1.25**	**2.25**
☐ 161	Bob Plager, Stl.	1.25	2.25
☐ 162	Dave Balon, Van., LC, Err. (Ballon)	1.25	2.25
☐ 163	Noel Price, Atl.	1.25	2.25
☐ 164	Gary Bergman, Det.	1.25	2.25
☐ 165	Pierre Bouchard, Mtl.	1.25	2.25
☐ 166	Ross Lonsberry, Pha.	1.25	2.25
☐ 167	Denis Dupère, Tor.	1.25	2.25
☐ 168	Lady Byng Trophy: Jean Ratelle, NYR.	2.00	4.00
☐ 169	NHL Action: Boston vs. Toronto	1.25	2.25
☐ 170	Don Awrey, Bos.	1.25	2.25
☐ **171**	**Marshall Johnston, Cal., RC**	**1.25**	**2.25**
☐ 172	Terry Harper, L.A.	1.25	2.25
☐ 173	Ed Giacomin (G), NYR.	4.00	7.50
☐ 174	Bryan Hextall, Pgh.	1.25	2.25
☐ 175	Conn Smythe Trophy: Bobby Orr, Bos.	2.00	4.00
☐ 176	Larry Hillman, Buf., LC	1.25	2.25
☐ 177	Stan Mikita, Chi.	5.50	11.00
☐ 178	Charlie Burns, Min., LC	1.25	2.25
☐ **179**	**Brian Marchinko, NYI., RC, LC**	**1.25**	**2.25**
☐ 180	Noel Picard, Stl., LC	1.25	2.25
☐ **181**	**Bobby Schmautz, Van., RC**	**1.25**	**2.25**
☐ 182	NHL Action: Buffalo vs. Toronto	1.25	2.25
☐ 183	Pat Quinn, Atl.	1.25	2.25
☐ 184	Denis DeJordy (G), Det., LC,	1.75	3.50
☐ 185	Serge Savard, Mtl.	2.00	4.00
☐ 186	NHL Action: Pittsburgh vs. Toronto	1.25	2.25
☐ 187	Bill Flett, Pha.	1.25	2.25
☐ 188	Darryl Sittler, Tor.	15.00	30.00
☐ 189	NHL Action: Minnesota vs. Toronto	2.00	4.00
☐ 190	Checklist	45.00	85.00
☐ 191	Garnet Bailey, Bos.	1.25	2.25
☐ 192	Walt McKechnie, Cal.	1.25	2.25
☐ 193	Harry Howell, L.A., LC	1.25	2.25
☐ 194	Rod Seiling, NYR.	1.25	2.25
☐ 195	Darryl Edestrand, Pgh.	1.25	2.25
☐ 196	NHL Action: Chicago vs. Toronto	6.00	12.00
☐ 197	Tim Horton, Buf.	5.00	10.00
☐ 198	Chico Maki, Chi.	1.25	2.25
☐ 199	J. P. Parise, Min.	1.25	2.25
☐ **200**	**Germaine Gagnon, NYI., RC**	**1.25**	**2.25**
☐ 201	Danny O'Shea, Stl., LC	1.25	2.25
☐ **202**	**Richard Lemieux, Van., RC**	**1.00**	**2.00**
☐ **203**	**Dan Bouchard (G), Atl., RC**	**5.00**	**10.00**
☐ 204	Léon Rochefort, Det.	1.25	2.25
☐ 205	Jacques Laperrière, Mtl.	1.25	2.25
☐ 206	Barry Ashbee, Pha., LC	1.25	2.25
☐ 207	Garry Monahan, Tor.	1.25	2.25
☐ 209	NHL Action: Toronto vs. Chicago	1.25	2.25
☐ 210	Réjean Houle, Mtl.	4.00	7.50
☐ **211**	**Dave Hudson, NYI., RC**	**2.50**	**5.00**
☐ 212	Ted Irvine, NYR.	2.50	5.00
☐ **213**	**Don Saleski, Pha., RC**	**2.50**	**5.00**
☐ 214	Lowell MacDonald, Pgh.	2.50	5.00
☐ **215**	**Mike Murphy, Stl., RC**	**4.00**	**7.50**
☐ 216	Brian Glennie, Tor.	2.50	5.00
☐ **217**	**Bobby Lalonde, Van., RC**	**2.50**	**5.00**
☐ **218**	**Bobby Leiter, Atl., RC**	**2.50**	**5.00**
☐ 219	Don Marcotte, Bos.	2.50	5.00
☐ **220**	**Jim Schoenfeld, Buf., RC**	**8.00**	**16.00**
☐ 221	Craig Patrick, Cal.	4.00	7.50
☐ 222	Cliff Koroll, Chi.	2.50	5.00
☐ **223**	**Guy Charron, Det., RC**	**2.50**	**5.00**
☐ 224	Jimmy Peters, L.A.	2.50	5.00
☐ 225	Dennis Hextall, Min.	2.50	5.00
☐ 226	AS: Tony Esposito (G), Chi.	7.50	15.00
☐ 227	AS: B. Orr, Bos./ B. Park, NYR.	25.00	50.00
☐ 228	AS: Bobby Hull, Chi.	18.00	35.00
☐ 229	AS: Rod Gilbert, NYR.	4.00	7.50
☐ 230	AS: Phil Esposito, Bos.	6.00	12.00
☐ 231	Claude Larose, Mtl., LC, Err. (La Rose)	2.50	5.00
☐ **232**	**Jim Mair, NYI., RC, LC**	**2.50**	**5.00**
☐ 233	Bobby Rousseau, NYR.	2.50	5.00
☐ 234	Brent Hughes, Stl.	2.50	5.00
☐ 235	Al McDonough, Pgh.	2.50	5.00
☐ **236**	**Chris Evans, Stl., RC**	**2.50**	**5.00**
☐ **237**	**Pierre Jarry, Tor., RC**	**2.50**	**5.00**
☐ **238**	**Don Tannahill, Van., RC**	**2.50**	**5.00**
☐ **239**	**Rey Comeau, Atl., RC**	**2.50**	**5.00**
☐ **240**	**Gregg Sheppard, Bos., RC, Err. (Greg)**	**2.50**	**5.00**
☐ 241	Dave Dryden (G), Buf.	4.00	7.50
☐ **242**	**Ed McAneeley, Cal., RC**	**2.50**	**5.00**
☐ 243	Lou Angotti, Chi.	2.50	5.00
☐ **244**	**Len Fontaine, Det., RC, LC**	**2.50**	**5.00**
☐ **245**	**Bill Lesuk, L.A., RC**	**2.50**	**5.00**
☐ 246	Fred (Buster) Harvey, Min.	2.50	5.00
☐ 247	AS: Ken Dryden (G), Mtl.	18.00	35.00
☐ 248	AS: Bill White, Chi.	2.50	5.00
☐ 249	AS: Pat Stapleton, Chi.	2.50	5.00
☐ 250	AS: V. Hadfield/ J. Ratelle/ Y. Cournoyer	4.50	8.50
☐ 251	Henri Richard, Mtl.	4.50	8.50
☐ **252**	**Bryan Lefley, NYI., RC**	**2.50**	**5.00**
☐ 253	Stanley Cup Trophy: Boston Bruins	6.50	13.00

No.	Player	EX	NRMT
☐ **254**	**Steve Vickers, NYR., RC**	**4.50**	**8.50**
☐ 255	Wayne Hillman, Pha., LC	2.50	5.00
☐ 256	Ken Schinkel, Pgh., LC, Err. (Shinkel)	2.50	5.00
☐ **257**	**Kevin O'Shea, Stl., RC, LC**	**2.50**	**5.00**
☐ **258**	**Ron Low, Tor. (G), RC**	**8.00**	**16.00**
☐ **259**	**Don Lever, Van., RC**	**4.00**	**7.50**
☐ **260**	**Randy Manery, Atl., RC**	**2.50**	**5.00**
☐ 261	Eddie Johnston (G), Bos.	4.00	7.50
☐ **262**	**Craig Ramsay, Buf., RC**	**4.00**	**7.50**
☐ **263**	**Pete Laframboise, Cal., RC**	**2.50**	**5.00**
☐ **264**	**Dan Maloney, Chi., RC**	**4.00**	**7.50**
☐ 265	Bill Collins, Det.	2.50	5.00
☐ 266	Paul Curtis, L.A., LC	2.50	5.00
☐ 267	Bob Nevin, Min.	2.50	5.00
☐ 268	LL: B. Watson/K. Magnuson/G. Dornhoefer	4.00	7.50
☐ 269	Jim Roberts, Mtl.	2.50	5.00
☐ **270**	**Brian Lavender, NYI., RC, LC**	**2.50**	**5.00**
☐ 271	Dale Rolfe, NYR.	2.50	5.00
☐ 272	Goals Ldrs: P. Esposito/V. Hadfield/ B. Hull	13.00	25.00
☐ **273**	**Michel Belhumeur (G), Pha., RC**	**4.00**	**7.50**
☐ 274	Eddie Shack, Pgh.	4.00	7.50
☐ **275**	**Wayne Stephenson (G), Stl., RC**	**4.00**	**7.50**
☐ 276	Stanley Cup Champions: Boston Bruins	4.50	8.50
☐ **277**	**Rick Kehoe, Tor., RC**	**4.50**	**8.50**
☐ **278**	**Gerry O'Flaherty, Van., RC, Err. (Jerry)**	**2.50**	**5.00**
☐ **279**	**Jacques Richard, Atl., RC**	**2.50**	**5.00**
☐ 280	Scoring Ldrs: P. Esposito/ B. Orr/ J. Ratelle	18.00	35.00
☐ **281**	**Nick Beverley, Bos., RC**	**2.50**	**5.00**
☐ **282**	**Larry Carriere, Buf., RC**	**2.50**	**5.00**
☐ 283	Assist Ldrs: B. Orr/ P. Esposito/ J. Ratelle	18.00	35.00
☐ 284	Rick Smith, Cal.	2.50	5.00
☐ **285**	**Jerry Korab, Chi., RC**	**2.50**	**5.00**
☐ 286	LL:T. Esposito/G. Villemure/G. Worsley	7.00	14.00
☐ 287	Ron Stackhouse, Det.	2.50	5.00
☐ **288**	**Barry Long, L.A., RC**	**2.50**	**5.00**
☐ 289	Dean Prentice, Min., LC	2.50	5.00
☐ 290	Norm Beaudin, Winnipeg	5.50	11.00
☐ **291**	**Mike Amodeo,Ottawa, RC**	**5.50**	**11.00**
☐ 292	Jim Harrison, Alberta.	5.50	11.00
☐ 293	J. C. Tremblay, Québec	7.50	15.00
☐ 294	Murray Hall, Houston, LC	5.50	11.00
☐ 295	Bart Crashley, Los Angeles, LC	5.50	11.00
☐ 296	Wayne Connelly, Minnesota	5.50	11.00
☐ 297	Bobby Sheehan, New York	5.50	11.00
☐ **298**	**Ron C. Anderson, Chicago, RC**	**5.50**	**11.00**
☐ 299	Chris Bordeleau, Winnipeg	5.50	11.00
☐ 300	Les Binkley (G), Ottawa, LC	7.50	15.00
☐ **301**	**Ron Walters, Alberta, RC, LC**	**5.50**	**11.00**
☐ 302	Jean-Guy Gendron, Quebec, LC	5.50	11.00
☐ 303	Gord Labossiere, Houston	5.50	11.00
☐ 304	Gerry Odrowski, Los Angeles	5.50	11.00
☐ 305	Mike McMahon, Minnesota, LC	5.50	11.00
☐ 306	Gary Kurt (G), New York	7.50	15.00
☐ 307	Larry Cahan, Chicago, LC	5.50	11.00
☐ 308	Wally Boyer, Winnipeg, LC	5.50	11.00
☐ **309**	**Bob Charlebois, Ottawa, RC, LC**	**5.50**	**11.00**
☐ 310	Bob Falkenberg, Alberta, LC	5.50	11.00
☐ **311**	**Jean Payette, Quebec, RC, LC**	**5.50**	**11.00**
☐ 312	Ted Taylor, Houston, LC	5.50	11.00
☐ 313	Joe Szura, Los Angeles, LC	5.50	11.00
☐ 314	George Morrison, Minnesota, LC	5.50	11.00
☐ 315	Wayne Rivers, New York	5.50	11.00
☐ 316	Reggie Fleming, Chicago, LC	5.50	11.00
☐ **317**	**Larry Hornung, Winnipeg, RC, LC**	**5.50**	**11.00**
☐ **318**	**Ron Climie, Ottawa, RC**	**5.50**	**11.00**
☐ 319	Val Fonteyne, Alberta, LC	5.50	11.00
☐ **320**	**Michel Archambault, Quebec, RC, LC**	**5.50**	**11.00**
☐ 321	Ab McDonald, Winnipeg, LC	5.50	11.00
☐ **322**	**Bob Leduc, Ottawa, RC, LC**	**5.50**	**11.00**
☐ 323	Bob Wall, Alberta, LC	5.50	11.00
☐ **324**	**Alain Caron, Quebec, RC, LC**	**5.50**	**11.00**
☐ 325	Bob Woytowich, Winnipeg	5.50	11.00
☐ 326	Guy Trottier, Ottawa, LC	5.50	11.00
☐ 327	Bill Hicke, Alberta, LC	5.50	11.00
☐ **328**	**Guy Dufour, Quebec, RC, LC**	**5.50**	**11.00**
☐ **329**	**Wayne Rutledge, Houston (G), RC**	**7.50**	**15.00**
☐ 330	Gary Veneruzzo, Los Angeles	5.50	11.00
☐ **331**	**Fred Speck, Minnesota, RC, LC**	**5.50**	**11.00**
☐ **332**	**Ron Ward, New York, RC**	**5.50**	**11.00**
☐ 333	Rosaire Paiement, Chicago	5.50	11.00
☐ 334	Checklist 3, Err. (210 - 341)	50.00	100.00
☐ 334	Checklist 3, Corrected	40.00	80.00
☐ **335**	**Michel Parizeau, Quebec, RC**	**5.50**	**11.00**
☐ 336	Bobby Hull,Winnipeg	35.00	65.00
☐ 337	Wayne Carleton, Ottawa, Err. (Carlton)	5.50	11.00
☐ 338	John McKenzie, Philadelphia	5.50	11.00
☐ 339	Jim Dorey, New England	5.50	11.00
☐ 340	Gerry Cheevers (G), Cleveland	20.00	40.00
☐ 341	Gerry Pinder, Cleveland	10.00	30.00

O-PEE-CHEE PLAYER CREST

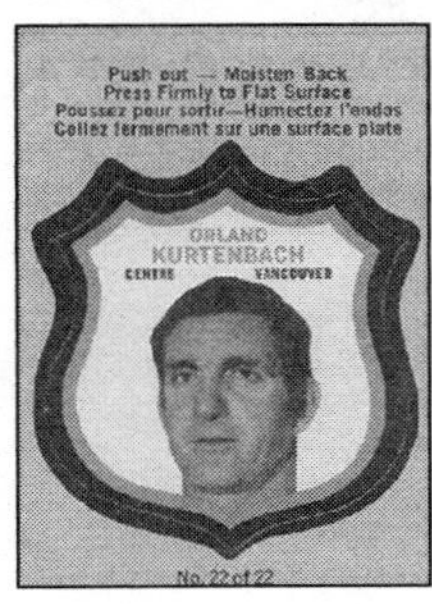

Series 1 Insert Set (22 stickers):		65.00	125.00
No.	Player	EX	NRMT
☐ 1	Pat Quinn, Atl.	2.00	4.00
☐ 2	Phil Esposito, Bos.	6.00	12.00
☐ 3	Bobby Orr, Bos.	25.00	50.00
☐ 4	Richard Martin, Buf.	3.00	6.00
☐ 5	Stan Mikita, Chi.	5.00	10.00
☐ 6	Bill White, Chi.	2.00	4.00
☐ 7	Red Berenson, Det.	2.00	4.00
☐ 8	Gary Bergman, Det.	2.00	4.00
☐ 9	Gary Edwards (G), L.A.	3.00	6.00
☐ 10	Bill Goldsworthy, Min.	2.00	4.00
☐ 11	Jacques Laperrière, Mtl.	4.00	8.00
☐ 12	Ken Dryden (G), Mtl.	14.00	28.00
☐ 13	Ed Westfall, NYI.	2.00	4.00
☐ 14	Walt Tkaczuk, NYR.	2.00	4.00
☐ 15	Brad Park, NYR.	5.00	10.00
☐ 16	Doug Favell (G), Pha.	3.00	6.00
☐ 17	Eddie Shack, Pgh.	3.00	6.00
☐ 18	Jacques Caron (G), Stl.	3.00	6.00
☐ 19	Paul Henderson, Tor.	3.00	6.00
☐ 20	Jim Harrison, AIO	2.00	4.00
☐ 21	Dale Tallon, Van.	2.00	4.00
☐ 22	Orland Kurtenbach, Van.	2.00	4.00

TEAM CANADA

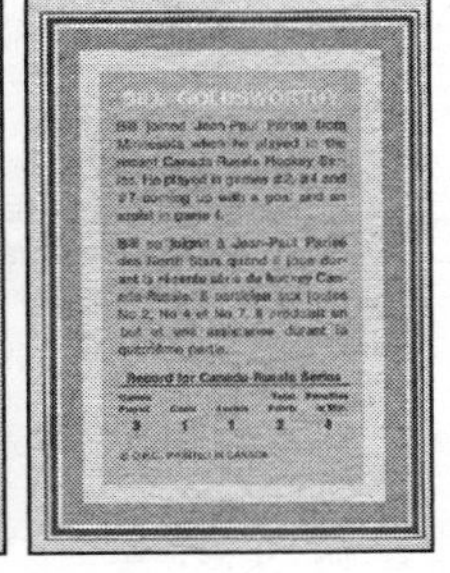

This unnumbered set features the 28 Team Canada members who played an eight game series against the Russian team in the fall of 1972. This set was an insert issued with the regular O-Pee-Chee second series issue of the same year.

Series 2 Insert Set (28 cards):		100.00	200.00
	Player	EX	NRMT
☐	Don Awrey	2.25	4.50
☐	Red Berenson	2.25	4.50
☐	Gary Bergman	2.25	4.50
☐	Wayne Cashman	3.00	6.00
☐	Bobby Clarke	7.50	15.00
☐	Yvan Cournoyer	6.00	12.00
☐	Ken Dryden (G)	15.00	30.00
☐	Ron Ellis	2.25	4.50
☐	Phil Esposito	10.00	20.00
☐	Tony Esposito (G)	9.00	18.00
☐	Rod Gilbert	4.50	9.00
☐	Bill Goldsworthy	2.25	4.50
☐	Vic Hadfield	2.25	4.50
☐	Paul Henderson	9.00	18.00
☐	Dennis Hull	2.25	4.50
☐	Guy Lapointe	4.00	7.50
☐	Frank Mahovlich	7.50	15.00
☐	Pete Mahovlich	2.25	4.50
☐	Stan Mikita	7.00	14.00
☐	Jean Paul Parise	2.25	4.50
☐	Brad Park	6.00	12.00
☐	Gilbert Perreault	6.00	12.00
☐	Jean Ratelle	4.50	9.00
☐	Mickey Redmond	2.25	4.50
☐	Serge Savard	4.00	7.50
☐	Rod Seiling	2.25	4.50
☐	Pat Stapleton	2.25	4.50
☐	Bill White	2.25	4.50

O-PEE-CHEE TEAM EMBLEMS

These stickers differ from the 1973-74 stickers in that they do not have the application instructions on the face of the sticker.

Series 3 Insert Set (30 stickers):		85.00	170.00
	Team	EX	NRMT
☐	NHL Logo	2.00	4.00
☐	Atlanta Flames	4.00	8.00
☐	Boston Bruins	2.00	4.00
☐	Buffalo Sabres	2.00	4.00
☐	California Golden Seals	2.00	4.00
☐	Chicago Blackhawks	2.00	4.00
☐	Detroit Red Wings	2.00	4.00
☐	Los Angeles Kings	2.00	4.00
☐	Minnesota North Stars	2.00	4.00
☐	Montréal Canadiens	2.00	4.00
☐	New York Islanders	4.00	8.00
☐	New York Rangers	2.00	4.00
☐	Philadelphia Flyers	2.00	4.00
☐	Pittsburgh Penguins	2.00	4.00
☐	St. Louis Blues	2.00	4.00
☐	Toronto Maple Leafs	2.00	4.00
☐	Vancouver Canucks	2.00	4.00
☐	WHA Logo	6.50	13.00
☐	Chicago Cougars	6.50	13.00
☐	Cleveland Crusaders	6.50	13.00
☐	Edmonton Oilers	6.50	13.00
☐	Houston Aeros	6.50	13.00
☐	Los Angeles Sharks	6.50	13.00
☐	Minnesota Fighting Saints	6.50	13.00
☐	New England Whalers	6.50	13.00
☐	New York Raiders	6.50	13.00
☐	Ottawa Nationals	6.50	13.00
☐	Philadelphia Blazers	6.50	13.00
☐	Québec Nordiques	6.50	13.00
☐	Winnipeg Jets	6.50	13.00

1972 - 73 7 - ELEVEN WHA CUPS

We have little information on these cups.

	Player
☐	Norm Beaudin, Winnipeg
☐	Christian Bordeleau, Winnipeg
☐	Carl Brewer, Toronto
☐	Wayne Carleton, Toronto
☐	Gerry Cheevers (G), Cleveland
☐	Wayne Connelly, Minnesota
☐	Jean-Guy Gendron, Québec
☐	Ted Green, New England
☐	Al Hamilton, Alberta
☐	Jim Harrison, Alberta
☐	Bobby Hull, Winnipeg
☐	André Lacroix, New York
☐	Danny Lawson, Vancouver
☐	John McKenzie, Vancouver
☐	Jim McLeod, Chicago
☐	Jack Norris, Alberta
☐	John Schella, Houston
☐	Jean-Claude Tremblay, Québec
☐	Ron Ward, Vancouver
☐	Jim Watson, Los Angeles

1972 - 73 POST ACTION TRANSFERS

These transfers are numbered PR 146 - 1 of 12.

Booklet Size: 4 7/8" x 3"
Face: Four colour; Number, Post logo, Bilingual
Back: Four colour on blue background; Two players, Name, Resume, Bilingual
Imprint: 1972 Letraset (Industrial) Limited, London S.E. 1 England. General Foods Ltd. / Phase III Promotions Ltd.
Transfer Size: 4 7/8" x 2 5/8"
Face: Four colour; Four transfers per sheet
Back: Transfer instructions, Bilingual
Imprint: PR146 PATENTED PRINTED IN ENGLAND BY LETRASET

Complete Set Price in Packages:	**300.00**	**500.00**
Complete Set (12 cards):	**150.00**	**250.00**

No.	Player	EX	NRMT
☐ 1	Defense: G. Unger/B. Orr	50.00	75.00
☐ 2	In the Corner: R. Berenson/D. Tallon	12.00	20.00
☐ 3	Face off: G. Dornhoefer/W. Cashman	12.00	20.00
☐ 4	Power save: J. McKenny/E. Giacomin (G)	20.00	30.00
☐ 5	Power play goal: P. Quinn/K. Magnuson	12.00	20.00
☐ 6	Break away: P. Shmyr/R. Seiling	12.00	20.00
☐ 8	Rebound: S. Apps Jr./S. Savard	15.00	25.00
☐ 9	Wrist shot: G. Worsley (G)/G. Bergman	20.00	30.00
☐ 10	Last minute: R. Crozier (G)/E. Westfall	15.00	25.00
☐ 11	Goalmouth scramble: D. Hull/O. Kurtenbach	12.00	20.00
☐ 12	Chest save: R. Vachon (G)/Y. Cournoyer	22.00	35.00

1972 - 73 TOPPS

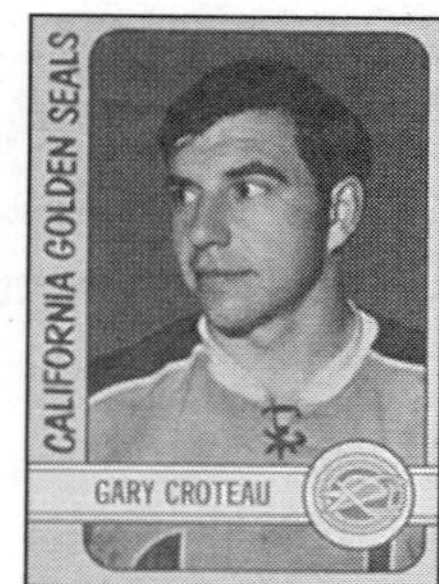

Card Size: 2 1/2" x 3 1/2"
Face: Four colour, beige border, Team logo
Back: Orange and black on card stock, Number, Resume, Trivia
Imprint: TCG PRTD.

Complete Set (198 cards):	**200.00**	**375.00**
Common Player:	**.65**	**1.25**

No.	Team	EX	NRMT
☐ 1	Boston Bruins	2.00	6.00
☐ 2	Game 1 at Boston	1.00	2.00
☐ 3	Game 2 at Boston	1.00	2.00
☐ 4	Game 3 at New York	1.00	2.00
☐ 5	Game 4 at New York	1.00	2.00
☐ 6	Game 5 at Boston	1.00	2.00
☐ 7	Game 6 at New York	1.00	2.00
☐ 8	Stanley Cup Trophy	2.50	5.00
☐ 9	Ed Van Impe, Pha.	.65	1.25
☐ 10	Yvan Cournoyer, Mtl.	1.75	3.25
☐ 11	Syl Apps, Jr., Pgh.	.65	1.25
☐ **12**	**Bill Plager, Stl. (Atl.), RC, LC**	**.65**	**1.25**
☐ 13	Ed Johnston (G), Bos.	1.00	2.00
☐ 14	Walt Tkaczuk, NYR.	.65	1.25
☐ 15	Dale Tallon, Van.	.65	1.25
☐ 16	Gerry Meehan, Buf.	.65	1.25
☐ 17	Reggie Leach, Cal.	.65	1.25
☐ 18	Marcel Dionne, Det.	9.00	18.00
☐ **19**	**André Dupont, NYI. (Stl.), RC**	**.65**	**1.25**
☐ 20	Tony Esposito (G), Chi.	8.00	16.00
☐ 21	Bob Berry, L.A.	.65	1.25
☐ **22**	**Craig Cameron, NYI, RC**	**.65**	**1.25**
☐ 23	Ted Harris, Min.	.65	1.25
☐ 24	Jacques Plante (G), Tor.	7.00	14.00
☐ 25	Jacques Lemaire, Mtl.	1.50	3.00
☐ 26	Simon Nolet, Pha.	.65	1.25
☐ 27	Keith McCreary, Pgh. (Atl.)	.65	1.25
☐ 28	Duane Rupp, Pgh.	.65	1.25
☐ 29	Wayne Cashman, Bos.	1.00	2.00
☐ 30	Brad Park, NYR.	4.00	8.00
☐ 31	Roger Crozier (G), Buf.	1.25	2.50
☐ 32	Wayne Maki, Van., LC	.65	1.25
☐ 33	Tim Ecclestone, Det.	.65	1.25
☐ 34	Rick Smith, Cal.	.65	1.25
☐ 35	Garry Unger, Stl	.65	1.25
☐ 36	Serge Bernier, L.A.	.65	1.25
☐ 37	Brian Glennie, Tor.	.65	1.25
☐ 38	Gerry Desjardins (G), Cal. (NYI.)	1.00	2.50
☐ 39	Danny Grant, Min.	.65	1.25
☐ 40	Bill White, Chi.	.65	1.25
☐ 41	Gary Dornhoefer, Pha.	.65	1.25
☐ 42	Pete Mahovlich, Mtl.	.65	1.25
☐ 43	Greg Polis, Pgh.	.65	1.25
☐ **44**	**Larry Hale, Pha. (Atl.), RC, LC**	**.65**	**1.25**
☐ 45	Dallas Smith, Bos.	.65	1.25
☐ 46	Orland Kurtenbach, Van.	.65	1.25
☐ 47	Steve Atkinson, Buf.	.65	1.25
☐ 48	Joey Johnston, Cal.	.65	1.25
☐ 49	Gary Bergman, Det.	.65	1.25
☐ 50	Jean Ratelle, NYR.	1.50	3.00
☐ 51	Rogatien Vachon (G), L.A.	1.75	3.25
☐ 52	Phil Roberto, Mtl. (Stl.)	.65	1.25
☐ 53	Brian Spencer, Tor. (NYI.)	.65	1.25
☐ 54	Jim McKenny, Tor.	.65	1.25
☐ 55	Gump Worsley (G), Min.	2.25	4.50
☐ 56	Stan Mikita, Chi.	3.25	6.50
☐ 57	Guy Lapointe, Mtl.	1.25	2.50
☐ 58	Lew Morrison, Pha. (Atl.)	.65	1.25
☐ 59	Ron Schock, Pgh.	.65	1.25
☐ 60	John Bucyk, Bos.	1.75	3.50
☐ 61	LL: P. Esposito/ V. Hadfield/ B. Hull	6.00	12.00
☐ 62	LL: B. Orr/ P. Esposito/ J. Ratelle	8.00	16.00
☐ 63	LL: P. Esposito/ B. Orr/ J. Ratelle	8.00	16.00
☐ 64	LL: T. Esposito/ G. Villemure/ G. Worsley	4.50	8.50
☐ 65	LL: B. Watson/ K. Magnuson/ G. Dornhoefer	1.00	2.00
☐ 66	Jim Neilson, NYR.	.65	1.25
☐ 67	Nick Libett, Det.	.65	1.25
☐ 68	Jim Lorentz, Stl. (Buf.)	.65	1.25
☐ **69**	**Gilles Meloche (G), Cal., RC**	**3.75**	**7.50**
☐ 70	Pat Stapleton, Chi.	.65	1.25
☐ 71	Frank St. Marseille, Stl.	.65	1.25
☐ 72	Butch Goring, L.A.	1.50	3.00
☐ 73	Paul Henderson, Tor.	1.00	2.00
☐ 74	Doug Favell (G), Pha.	1.00	2.00
☐ 75	Jocelyn Guevremont, Van.	.65	1.25
☐ **76**	**Tom Miller, Buf. (NYI.), RC**	**.65**	**1.25**
☐ **77**	**Billy MacMillan, Tor. (Atl.), RC**	**.65**	**1.25**
☐ 78	Doug Mohns, Min.	.65	1.25
☐ 79	Guy Lafleur, Mtl.	15.00	30.00
☐ 80	Rod Gilbert, NYR.	1.50	3.00
☐ 81	Gary Doak, Det.	.65	1.25
☐ **82**	**Dave Burrows, Pgh., RC**	**.65**	**1.25**
☐ 83	Gary Croteau, Cal.	.65	1.25
☐ 84	Tracy Pratt, Buf.	.65	1.25
☐ 85	Carol Vadnais, Cal. (Bos.)	.65	1.25
☐ **86**	**Jacques Caron (G), Stl., RC, LC**	**1.00**	**2.00**
☐ 87	Keith Magnuson, Chi.	.65	1.25
☐ 88	Dave Keon, Tor.	1.50	3.00
☐ 89	Mike Corrigan, Van. (L.A.)	.65	1.25
☐ 90	Bobby Clarke, Pha.	10.00	20.00
☐ 91	Dunc Wilson (G), Van.	1.00	2.00
☐ **92**	**Gerry Hart, Det. (NYI.), RC**	**.65**	**1.25**
☐ 93	Lou Nanne, Min.	.65	1.25
☐ 94	Checklist (1-176)	20.00	40.00
☐ 95	Red Berenson, Det.	.65	1.25
☐ 96	Bob Plager, Stl.	.65	1.25
☐ **97**	**Jim Rutherford (G), Det. (Pgh.), RC**	**3.25**	**6.50**
☐ **98**	**Rick Foley, Pha., RC, LC**	**.65**	**1.25**
☐ 99	Pit Martin, Chi.	.65	1.25
☐ 100	Bobby Orr, Bos.	20.00	40.00
☐ 101	Stan Gilbertson, Cal.	.65	1.25
☐ 102	Barry Wilkins, Van.	.65	1.25
☐ 103	Terry Crisp, Stl. (NYI.)	.65	1.25
☐ 104	Césare Maniago (G), Min.	1.00	2.00
☐ 105	Marc Tardif, Mtl.	.65	1.25
☐ 106	Don Luce, Buf.	.65	1.25
☐ 107	Mike Pelyk, Tor.	.65	1.25
☐ 108	Juha Widing, L.A.	.65	1.25
☐ **109**	**Phil Myre (G), Mtl. (Atl.), RC**	**2.00**	**4.00**
☐ 110	Vic Hadfield, NYR.	.65	1.25
☐ 111	Arnie Brown, Det.	.65	1.25
☐ 112	Ross Lonsberry, Pha.	.65	1.25
☐ 113	Dick Redmond, Cal.	.65	1.25
☐ 114	Gary Smith (G), Chi.	1.00	2.00
☐ 115	Bill Goldsworthy, Min.	.65	1.25
☐ 116	Bryan Watson, Pgh.	.65	1.25
☐ 117	Dave Balon, Van., LC	.65	1.25
☐ **118**	**Bill Mikkelson, L.A. (NYI.), RC**	**.65**	**1.25**
☐ 119	Terry Harper, Mtl.	.65	1.25
☐ 120	Gilbert Perreault, Buf.	4.50	8.50
☐ 121	Tony Esposito (G), Chi.	4.00	8.00
☐ 122	Bobby Orr, Bos.	10.00	20.00
☐ 123	Brad Park, NYR.	2.00	4.00
☐ 124	Phil Esposito, Bos.	3.00	6.00
☐ 125	Rod Gilbert, NYR.	1.50	3.00
☐ 126	Bobby Hull, Chi.	10.00	20.00
☐ 127	Ken Dryden (G), Mtl.	7.50	15.00
☐ 128	Bill White, Chi.	.65	1.25
☐ 129	Pat Stapleton, Chi.	.65	1.25
☐ 130	Jean Ratelle, NYR.	1.25	2.50
☐ 131	Yvan Cournoyer, Mtl.	1.25	2.50
☐ 132	Vic Hadfield, NYR.	.65	1.25
☐ 133	Ralph Backstrom, L.A.	.65	1.25
☐ 134	Bob Baun, Tor.	.65	1.25
☐ 135	Fred Stanfield, Bos.	.65	1.25
☐ 136	Barclay Plager, Stl.	.65	1.25
☐ 137	Gilles Villemure (G), NYR.	1.00	2.00
☐ 138	Ron Harris, Det. (Atl.)	.65	1.25
☐ 139	Bill Flett, Pha.	.65	1.25
☐ 140	Frank Mahovlich, Mtl.	3.00	6.00
☐ 141	Alex Delvecchio, Det.	1.50	3.00
☐ 142	Poul Popiel, Van.	.65	1.25
☐ 143	Jean Pronovost, Pgh.	.65	1.25
☐ 144	Denis DeJordy (G), L.A. (NYI.), LC	1.00	2.00
☐ 145	Rick Martin, Buf.	2.00	4.00
☐ **146**	**Ivan Boldirev, Cal., RC**	**1.00**	**2.00**
☐ **147**	**Jack Egers, Stl., RC**	**.65**	**1.25**
☐ 148	Jim Pappin, Chi.	.65	1.25
☐ 149	Rod Seiling, NYR.	.65	1.25
☐ 150	Phil Esposito, Bos.	6.00	12.00
☐ 151	Gary Edwards (G), L.A.	1.00	2.00
☐ 152	Ron Ellis, Tor.	.65	1.25
☐ 153	Jude Drouin, Min.	.65	1.25
☐ 154	Ernie Hicke, Cal. (Atl.)	.65	1.25
☐ 155	Mickey Redmond, Det.	1.00	2.00
☐ 156	Joe Watson, Pha.	.65	1.25
☐ 157	Bryan Hextall, Jr., Pgh.	.65	1.25
☐ 158	Andre Boudrias, Van.	.65	1.25
☐ 159	Ed Westfall, NYI	.65	1.25
☐ 160	Ken Dryden (G), Mtl.	25.00	45.00
☐ **161**	**Rene Robert, Pgh. (Buf.), RC**	**1.75**	**3.25**
☐ 162	Bert Marshall, Cal.	.65	1.25
☐ 163	Gary Sabourin, Stl.	.65	1.25
☐ 164	Dennis Hull, Chi.	.65	1.25
☐ 165	Ed Giacomin (G), NYR.	1.75	3.50
☐ 166	Ken Hodge, Bos.	.65	1.25
☐ 167	Gilles Marotte, L.A.	.65	1.25
☐ 168	Norm Ullman, Tor.	1.25	2.50
☐ **169**	**Barry Gibbs, Min., RC**	**.65**	**1.25**
☐ 170	The Art Ross Trophy: Phil Esposito	1.25	2.50
☐ 171	The Hart Memorial Trophy: Bobby Orr	1.50	3.00
☐ 172	The James Norris Memorial Trophy: Bobby Or	1.50	3.00
☐ 173	The Vezina Trophy: Tony Esposito, Gary Smith	1.25	2.50
☐ 174	The Calder Memorial Trophy: Ken Dryden	1.50	3.00
☐ 175	The Lady Byng Memorial Trophy: Jean Ratelle	1.25	2.50
☐ 176	The Conn Smythe Trophy: Bobby Orr	1.50	4.50

1972 - 73 WILLIAMS FINNISH

A set of 360 cards plus a collecting album for the World Championships and the Finnish National and Junior League. We have no pricing information on this set.

Card Size: 1 7/8" x 2 1/4"

Imprint:

No. Player

- ☐ 1 Vladimir Bednar, CSR.
- ☐ 2 Jiri Bubla, CSR.
- ☐ 3 Vladimir Dzurilla, CSR.
- ☐ 4 Richard Farda, CSR.
- ☐ 5 Julius Haas, CSR.
- ☐ 6 Ivan Hlinka, CSR.
- ☐ 7 Jiri Holecek, CSR.
- ☐ 8 Jaroslav Holik, CSR.
- ☐ 9 Jiri Holik, CSR.
- ☐ 10 Josef Horesovsky, CSR.
- ☐ 11 Jan Klapac, CSR.
- ☐ 12 Jiri Kochta, CSR.
- ☐ 13 Milan Kuzela, CSR.
- ☐ 14 Oldrich Machac, CSR.
- ☐ 15 Vladimir Martinec, CSR.
- ☐ 16 Vaclav Nedomansky, CSR.
- ☐ 17 Josef Palecek, CSR.
- ☐ 18 Frantisek Pospisil, CSR.
- ☐ 19 Bohuslav Stastny, CSR.
- ☐ 20 Rudolf Tajcnar, CSR.
- ☐ 21 Vyatcheslav Anisin, USSR
- ☐ 22 Yuri Blinov, USSR
- ☐ 23 Alexander Gusev, USSR
- ☐ 24 Valeri Kharlamov, USSR
- ☐ 25 Alexander Yakushev, USSR
- ☐ 26 Viktor Kuzkin, USSR
- ☐ 27 Vladimir Lutshenko, USSR
- ☐ 28 Alexander Maltsev, USSR
- ☐ 29 Boris Mikhailov, USSR
- ☐ 30 Evgeny Mishakov, USSR
- ☐ 31 Vladimir Petrov, USSR
- ☐ 32 Alexander Ragulin, USSR
- ☐ 33 Igor Romishevski, USSR
- ☐ 34 Vladimir Shadrin, USSR
- ☐ 35 Vladimir Shepovalov, USSR
- ☐ 36 Vjatsjeslav Soloduhin, USSR
- ☐ 37 Vladimir Tretiak, USSR
- ☐ 38 Gennady Tsicankov, USSR
- ☐ 39 Valeri Vasiliev, USSR
- ☐ 40 Vladimir Vikulov, USSR
- ☐ 41 Christer Abrahamsson, Swe.
- ☐ 42 Thommy Abrahamsson, Swe.
- ☐ 43 Thommie Bergman, Swe.
- ☐ 44 Inge Hammarstrom, Swe.
- ☐ 45 Anders Hedberg, Swe.
- ☐ 46 Leif Holmqvist, Swe.
- ☐ 47 Bjorn Johansson, Swe.
- ☐ 48 StigGoran Johansson, Swe.
- ☐ 49 Stefan Karlsson, Swe.
- ☐ 50 Stig Larsson, Swe.
- ☐ 51 Mats Lind, Swe.
- ☐ 52 Tord Lundstrom, Swe.
- ☐ 53 LarsGoran Nilsson, Swe.
- ☐ 54 Bjorn Palmqvist, Swe.
- ☐ 55 Hakan Pettersson, Swe.
- ☐ 56 Borje Salming, Swe.
- ☐ 57 LarsErik Sjoberg, Swe.
- ☐ 58 Carl Sundqvist, Swe.
- ☐ 59 Hakan Wickberg, Swe.
- ☐ 60 Stig Ostling, Swe.
- ☐ 61 Seppo Ahokainen, Fin.
- ☐ 62 Matti Keinonen, Fin.
- ☐ 63 VeliPekka Ketola, Fin.
- ☐ 64 Harri Linnonmaa, Fin.
- ☐ 65 Pekka Marjamaki, Fin.
- ☐ 66 Lauri Mononen, Fin.
- ☐ 67 Matti Murto, Fin.
- ☐ 68 Timo Nummelin, Fin.
- ☐ 69 Lasse Oksanen, Fin.
- ☐ 70 Esa Peltonen, Fin.
- ☐ 71 Juha Rantasila, Fin.
- ☐ 72 Pekka Rautakallio, Fin.
- ☐ 73 Seppo Repo, Fin.
- ☐ 74 Heikki Riihiranta, Fin.
- ☐ 75 Juhani Tamminen, Fin.
- ☐ 76 Timo Turunen, Fin.
- ☐ 77 Pertti Valkeapaa, Fin.
- ☐ 78 Jorma Valtonen, Fin.
- ☐ 79 Stig Wetzell, Fin.
- ☐ 80 Jouko Oystila, Fin.
- ☐ 81 Juhani Bostrom, HIFK
- ☐ 82 Kimmo Heino, HIFK
- ☐ 83 Pentti Karlsson, HIFK
- ☐ 84 Mauri Kaukokari, HIFK
- ☐ 85 Jarmo Koivunen, HIFK
- ☐ 86 Heikki Kojola, HIFK
- ☐ 87 Vaino Kolkka, HIFK
- ☐ 88 Harri Linnonmaa, HIFK
- ☐ 89 Jaakko Marttinen, HIFK
- ☐ 90 Matti Murto, HIFK
- ☐ 91 Lalli Partinen, HIFK
- ☐ 92 Juha Rantasila, HIFK
- ☐ 93 Heikki Riihiranta, HIFK
- ☐ 94 Jorma Rikala, HIFK
- ☐ 95 Henry Saleva, HIFK
- ☐ 96 Tommi Salmelainen, HIFK
- ☐ 97 Jorma Thusberg, HIFK
- ☐ 98 Jorma Virtanen, HIFK
- ☐ 99 Matti Vaisanen, HIFK
- ☐ 100 Juhani Aaltonen, HJK
- ☐ 101 Jorma Immonen, HJK
- ☐ 102 Martti Immonen, HJK
- ☐ 103 Heikki Jarn, HJK
- ☐ 104 Matti Keinonen, HJK
- ☐ 105 Seppo Laakkio, HJK
- ☐ 106 Timo Lahtinen, HJK
- ☐ 107 Esa Peltonen, HJK
- ☐ 108 Keijo Puhakka, HJK
- ☐ 109 Seppo Railio, HJK
- ☐ 110 Antti Ravi, HJK
- ☐ 111 Timo Saari, HJK
- ☐ 112 Esa Siren, HJK
- ☐ 113 Seppo Suoraniemi, HJK
- ☐ 114 Juhani Tamminen, HJK
- ☐ 115 Jorma Vehmanen, HJK
- ☐ 116 Stig Wetzell, HJK
- ☐ 117 Leo Aikas, HJK
- ☐ 118 Sakari Ahlberg, Ilves
- ☐ 119 Seppo Ahokainen, Ilves
- ☐ 120 Jorma Aro, Ilves
- ☐ 121 Esko Eriksson, Ilves
- ☐ 122 Markku Hakanen, Ilves
- ☐ 123 Timo Hirsimaki, Ilves
- ☐ 124 Jorma Kallio, Ilves
- ☐ 125 Esko Kaonpaa, Ilves
- ☐ 126 Pentti Koskela, Ilves
- ☐ 127 Pekka Kuusisto, Ilves
- ☐ 128 Pekka Leimu, Ilves
- ☐ 129 Len Lunde, Ilves
- ☐ 130 Jukka Mattila, Ilves
- ☐ 131 Lasse Oksanen, Ilves
- ☐ 132 Hannu Palmu, Ilves
- ☐ 133 Kari Palooja, Ilves
- ☐ 134 Jorma Peltonen, Ilves
- ☐ 135 Tuomo Sillman, Ilves
- ☐ 136 Veikko Suominen, Ilves
- ☐ 137 Pertti Ahokas, Jokerit
- ☐ 138 Pertti Arvaja, Jokerit
- ☐ 139 Christer Bergenheim, Jokerit
- ☐ 140 Jorma Borgstrom, Jokerit
- ☐ 141 Olli Hietanen, Jokerit
- ☐ 142 Pentti Hiiros, Jokerit
- ☐ 143 Eero Holopainen, Jokerit
- ☐ 144 Kari Kinnunen, Jokerit
- ☐ 145 Keijo Koivunen, Jokerit
- ☐ 146 Ilpo Koskela, Jokerit
- ☐ 147 Timo Kyntola, Jokerit
- ☐ 148 Henry Leppa, Jokerit
- ☐ 149 Erkki Mononen, Jokerit
- ☐ 150 Pertti Nurmi, Jokerit
- ☐ 151 Tero Raty, Jokerit
- ☐ 152 Timo Sutinen, Jokerit
- ☐ 153 Timo Turunen, Jokerit
- ☐ 154 Jouko Oystila, Jokerit
- ☐ 155 Hannu Haapalainen, Koovee
- ☐ 156 Olavi Haapalainen, Koovee
- ☐ 157 JukkaPekka Jarvenpaa, Koovee
- ☐ 158 Heimo Keinonen, Koovee
- ☐ 159 Markku Moisio, Koovee
- ☐ 160 Heikki Nurmi, Koovee
- ☐ 161 Seppo Nurmi, Koovee
- ☐ 162 Oiva Oijennus, Koovee
- ☐ 163 Reino Pulkkinen, Koovee
- ☐ 164 Esko Rantanen, Koovee
- ☐ 165 Juhani Ruohonen, Koovee
- ☐ 166 Mikko Raikkonen, Koovee
- ☐ 167 Lauri Salomaa, Koovee
- ☐ 168 Leo Seppanen, Koovee
- ☐ 169 Pekka Uitus, Koovee
- ☐ 170 Jorma Vilen, Koovee
- ☐ 171 Tapio Virhimo, Koovee
- ☐ 172 Leo Haakana, Saipa
- ☐ 173 Seppo Hyvonen, Saipa
- ☐ 174 Heikki Juselius, Saipa
- ☐ 175 Hannu Lemander, Saipa
- ☐ 176 Kyosti Lahde, Saipa
- ☐ 177 Ari Mikkola, Saipa
- ☐ 178 Martti Makia, Saipa
- ☐ 179 Martti Narinen, Saipa
- ☐ 180 Pekka Nieminen, Saipa
- ☐ 181 Teijo Rasanen, Saipa
- ☐ 182 Timo Sartiala, Saipa
- ☐ 183 Pekka Sartjarvi, Saipa
- ☐ 184 Keijo Sinkkonen, Saipa
- ☐ 185 Martti Sinkkonen, Saipa
- ☐ 186 Arto Summanen, Saipa
- ☐ 187 Erkki Suni, Saipa
- ☐ 188 Seppo Urpalainen, Saipa
- ☐ 189 Matti Vaatamoinen, Saipa
- ☐ 190 Timo Vaatamoinen, Saipa
- ☐ 191 Jukka Alkula, Tappara
- ☐ 192 Pertti Ansakorpi, Tappara
- ☐ 193 Keijo Jarvinen, Tappara
- ☐ 194 Pertti Koivulahti, Tappara
- ☐ 195 Ilpo Kuisma, Tappara
- ☐ 196 Vesa Lehtoranta, Tappara
- ☐ 197 Antti Leppanen, Tappara
- ☐ 198 Pekka Marjamaki, Tappara
- ☐ 199 Mikko Mynttinen, Tappara
- ☐ 200 Pekka Makinen, Tappara
- ☐ 201 Seppo Makinen, Tappara
- ☐ 202 Antti Perttula, Tappara
- ☐ 203 Tuomo Rautiainen, Tappara
- ☐ 204 Jorma Saarikorpi, Tappara
- ☐ 205 Jorma Siitarinen, Tappara
- ☐ 206 Raimo Suoniemi, Tappara
- ☐ 207 Pertti Valkeapaa, Tappara
- ☐ 208 Kari Horkko, Turun Palloseura
- ☐ 209 Eero Juntunen, Turun Palloseura
- ☐ 210 Lauri Jamsen, Turun Palloseura
- ☐ 211 Kari Kauppila, Turun Palloseura
- ☐ 212 Lasse Kiili, Turun Palloseura
- ☐ 213 Olli Kokkonen, Turun Palloseura
- ☐ 214 Pekka Lahtela, Turun Palloseura
- ☐ 215 Robert Lamoureux, Turun Palloseura
- ☐ 216 Ilkka Mesikammen, Turun Palloseura
- ☐ 217 Timo Nummelin, Turun Palloseura
- ☐ 218 Rauli Ottila, Turun Palloseura
- ☐ 219 Matti Rautee, Turun Palloseura
- ☐ 220 Pekka Rautee, Turun Palloseura
- ☐ 221 Jari Rosberg, Turun Palloseura
- ☐ 222 Jouni Samuli, Turun Palloseura
- ☐ 223 Harri Silver, Turun Palloseura
- ☐ 224 Rauli Tammelin, Turun Palloseura
- ☐ 225 Bengt Wilenius, Turun Palloseura
- ☐ 226 Pertti Hasanen, Turun Toverit
- ☐ 227 Kari Johansson, Turun Toverit
- ☐ 228 Arto Kaunonen, Turun Toverit
- ☐ 229 Timo Kokkonen, Turun Toverit
- ☐ 230 Reijo Leppanen, Turun Toverit
- ☐ 231 Seppo Lindstrom, Turun Toverit
- ☐ 232 Hannu Luojola, Turun Toverit
- ☐ 233 Hannu Niittoaho, Turun Toverit
- ☐ 234 Reijo Paksal, Turun Toverit
- ☐ 235 Seppo Parikka, Turun Toverit
- ☐ 236 Jarmo Rantanen, Turun Toverit

☐ 237 Kari Salonen, Turun Toverit
☐ 238 Tapani Sura, Turun Toverit
☐ 239 Kari Torkkel, Turun Toverit
☐ 240 Risto Vainio, Turun Toverit
☐ 241 Pentti Vihanto, Turun Toverit
☐ 242 Seppo Wikstrom, Turun Toverit
☐ 243 Urpo Ylonen, Turun Toverit
☐ 244 Tapio Flinck, Assat Pori
☐ 245 Antti Heikkila, Assat Pori
☐ 246 Reijo Heinonen, Assat Pori
☐ 247 Jaakko Honkanen, Assat Pori
☐ 248 VeliPekka Ketola, Assat Pori
☐ 249 Raimo Kilpio, Assat Pori
☐ 250 Tapio Koskinen, Assat Pori
☐ 251 Jarkko Levonen, Assat Pori
☐ 252 Kaj Matalamaki, Assat Pori
☐ 253 Pertti Makela, Assat Pori
☐ 254 Hannu Pulkkinen, Assat Pori
☐ 255 Pekka Rautakallio, Assat Pori
☐ 256 Markku Riihimaki, Assat Pori
☐ 257 Matti Salmi, Assat Pori
☐ 258 Jorma Valtonen, Assat Pori
☐ 259 Anto Virtanen, Assat Pori
☐ 260 Erkki Vakiparta, Assat Pori
☐ 261 Martti Jarkko, Tappara Jrs.
☐ 262 Torsti Jarvenpaa, Tappara Jrs.
☐ 263 Tapio Kallio, Tappara Jrs.
☐ 264 Jussi Kiansten, Tappara Jrs.
☐ 265 Kimmo Korpela, Tappara Jrs.
☐ 266 Jarmo Kuisma, Tappara Jrs.
☐ 267 Antero Lehtonen, Tappara Jrs.
☐ 268 Mikko Leinonen, Tappara Jrs.
☐ 269 Tuomas Leinonen, Tappara Jrs.
☐ 270 Lasse Litma, Tappara Jrs.
☐ 271 Seppo Makinen, Tappara Jrs.
☐ 272 Heikki Niemi, Tappara Jrs.
☐ 273 Reijo Narvanen, Tappara Jrs.
☐ 274 Kalevi Paakkonen, Tappara Jrs.
☐ 275 Reijo Rossi, Tappara Jrs.
☐ 276 Seppo Sevon, Tappara Jrs.
☐ 277 Jorma Siren, Tappara Jrs.
☐ 278 Risto Sirkkola, Tappara Jrs.
☐ 279 Risto Hevonkorpi, Koovee Jrs.
☐ 280 Veijo Hukkanen, Koovee Jrs.
☐ 281 Timo Hytti, Koovee Jrs.
☐ 282 Kalle Impola, Koovee Jrs.
☐ 283 Pertti Jarvenpaa, Koovee Jrs.
☐ 284 Rauno Jarvinen, Koovee Jrs.
☐ 285 Antti Kaivola, Koovee Jrs.
☐ 286 Jorma Karvonen, Koovee Jrs.
☐ 287 Pekka Karvonen, Koovee Jrs.
☐ 288 Seppo Kettunen, Koovee Jrs.
☐ 289 Kari Niemi, Koovee Jrs.
☐ 290 Timo Niiniviita, Koovee Jrs.
☐ 291 Jari Nurminen, Koovee Jrs.
☐ 292 Pentti Poussu, Koovee Jrs.
☐ 293 Matti Rautiainen, Koovee Jrs.
☐ 294 Vesa Ronkainen, Koovee Jrs.
☐ 295 Mauri Salminen, Koovee Jrs.
☐ 296 Kari Silius, Koovee Jrs.
☐ 297 Kimmo Turtiainen, Koovee Jrs.
☐ 298 Juha Wikman, Koovee Jrs.
☐ 299 JuhaPekka Aho, Ilves Jrs.
☐ 300 Matti Estola, Ilves Jrs.
☐ 301 Markku Heinonen, Ilves Jrs.
☐ 302 Mauri Heinonen, Ilves Jrs.
☐ 303 Jukka Hirsimaki, Ilves Jrs.
☐ 304 Jarmo Huhtala, Ilves Jrs.
☐ 305 Harri Huotari, Ilves Jrs.
☐ 306 Kari Jarvinen, Ilves Jrs.
☐ 307 Jari Kaarela, Ilves Jrs.
☐ 308 Kai Lehto, Ilves Jrs.
☐ 309 Jari Leppanen, Ilves Jrs.
☐ 310 Jarmo Lilius, Ilves Jrs.
☐ 311 Markus Mattsson, Ilves Jrs.
☐ 312 Jari Niinimaki, Ilves Jrs.
☐ 313 Hannu Oksanenx, Ilves Jrs.
☐ 314 Sakari Pehu, Ilves Jrs.
☐ 315 Mika Rajala, Ilves Jrs.
☐ 316 Risto Siltanen, Ilves Jrs.
☐ 317 Jarmo Siro, Ilves Jrs.
☐ 318 Jukka Siro, Ilves Jrs.
☐ 319 Jari Uusikartano, Ilves Jrs.
☐ 320 Seppo Vartiainen, Ilves Jrs.
☐ 321 Mika Weissman, Ilves Jrs.
☐ 322 Seppo Aro, Ilves Jrs.
☐ 323 Jari Huotari, Ilves Jrs.
☐ 324 Ilkka Huura, Ilves Jrs.
☐ 325 Jari Hytti, Ilves Jrs.
☐ 326 Jarmo Jamalainen, Ilves Jrs.
☐ 327 Jari Jokinen, Ilves Jrs.
☐ 328 Tero Juojarvi, Ilves Jrs.
☐ 329 Jari Jarvinen, Ilves Jrs.
☐ 330 Lauri Kosonen, Ilves Jrs.
☐ 331 Aki Laakso, Ilves Jrs.
☐ 332 Ismo Laine, Ilves Jrs.
☐ 333 Matti Lisko, Ilves Jrs.
☐ 334 Dale Lunde, Ilves Jrs.
☐ 335 Markku Pirkkalaniem, Ilves Jrs.i
☐ 336 Rauno Saarnio, Ilves Jrs.
☐ 337 Jukka Silander, Ilves Jrs.
☐ 338 OlliPekka Turunen, Ilves Jrs.
☐ 339 Mauri Unkila, Ilves Jrs.
☐ 340 Jarmo Viteli, Ilves Jrs.
☐ 341 Jukka Ahonen, Ilves Jrs.
☐ 342 Jari Hallila, Ilves Jrs.
☐ 343 Jari Helle, Ilves Jrs.
☐ 344 Jari Hirsimaki, Ilves Jrs.
☐ 345 Petri Jokinen, Ilves Jrs.
☐ 346 Kari Jarvinen, Ilves Jrs.
☐ 347 Arto Laine, Ilves Jrs.
☐ 348 Ari Leinonen, Ilves Jrs.
☐ 349 Jukka Oksanen, Ilves Jrs.
☐ 350 Sten Pakarinen, Ilves Jrs.
☐ 351 Jyrki Seppa, Ilves Jrs.
☐ 352 Jari Simola, Ilves Jrs.
☐ 353 Olli Sarkilahti, Ilves Jrs.
☐ 354 KariPekka Tarko, Ilves Jrs.
☐ 355 Timo Toivonen, Ilves Jrs.
☐ 356 VeliMatti Uusimaa, Ilves Jrs.
☐ 357 Risto Viljanen, Ilves Jrs.
☐ 358 Timo Virtanen, Ilves Jrs.
☐ 359 Teppo Valimaki, Ilves Jrs.
☐ 360 Juha Yrjola, Ilves Jrs.

1972 - 84 DIMANCHE / DERNIÈRE PHOTOS

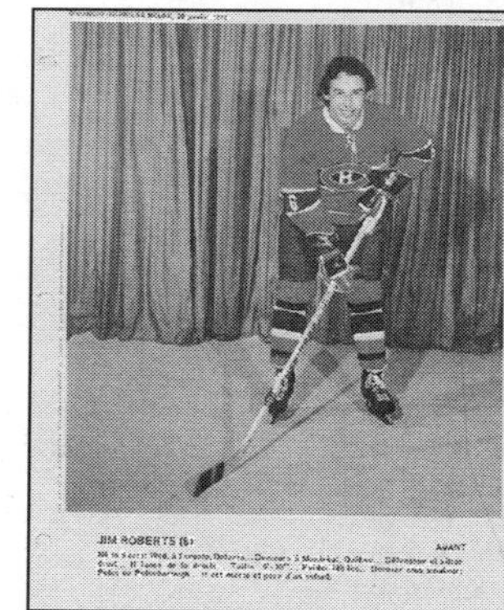

These photos were inserted in Dernière magazine. Three holes were punched on the left side to allow for storage in a binder. This set of photographs included hockey, baseball, football and soccer players, as well as those in wrestling, boxing, car racing and golf. Only the hockey photos are listed here.

Stamp Size: 8" x 10"
Face: Four colour, white border; Name, Jersey Number, Position, Resume, French
Back: Blank
Imprint: DERNIERE PHOTOS

	Common Player:	**1.50**	**3.00**
No.	**Player / Date Issued**	**EX**	**NRMT**
1972 - 73 ISSUE			
☐ 15OCT	Ken Dryden (G)	10.00	20.00
☐ 22OCT	Frank Mahovlich	5.00	10.00
☐ 29OCT	Guy Lapointe	3.00	6.00
☐ 5NOV	Serge Savard	3.00	6.00
☐ 12NOV	Jacques Lemaire	3.50	7.00
☐ 19NOV	Pierre Bouchard	1.50	3.00
☐ 26 NOV	Henri Richard	3.50	7.00
☐ 3DEC	Guy Lafleur	6.00	12.00
☐ 10DEC	Jacques Laperrière	3.00	6.00
☐ 17DEC	Marc Tardif	1.50	3.00
☐ 24DEC	Scotty Bowman, Coach	2.50	5.00
☐ 31DEC	Pete Mahovlich	1.50	3.00
☐ 7JAN	Michel Plasse (G)	2.50	5.00
☐ 14JAN	Chuck Lefley	1.50	3.00
☐ 21JAN	Claude Larose	1.50	3.00
☐ 28JAN	Jim Roberts	1.50	3.00
☐ 4FEB	Bob Murdoch	1.50	3.00
☐ 11FEB	Chuck Arnason	1.50	3.00
☐ 18FEB	Murray Wilson	1.50	3.00
☐ 25FEB	Wayne Thomas (G)	2.50	5.00
☐ 4MAR	Dale Hoganson	1.50	3.00
☐ 11MAR	Larry Robinson	4.00	8.00
☐ 18MAR	Rejean Houle	2.50	5.00
☐ 25MAR	Steve Shutt	3.50	7.00
☐ 1APR	Yvan Cournoyer	3.50	7.00
☐ 8APR	Jean Béliveau	6.00	12.00
1973 - 74 ISSUE			
☐ 18NOV	Henri Richard	3.50	7.00
☐ 25NOV	Guy Lapointe	3.00	6.00
☐ 2DEC	Chuck Lefley	1.50	3.00
☐ 9DEC	Yvan Cournoyer	3.50	7.00
☐ 16DEC	Guy Lafleur	6.00	12.00
☐ 23DEC	Pierre Bouchard	1.50	3.00
☐ 30DEC	Wayne Thomas (G)	2.50	5.00
☐ 6JAN	Jacques Laperrière	3.00	6.00
☐ 13JAN	Serge Savard	3.00	6.00
☐ 20JAN	Frank Mahovlich	5.00	10.00
☐ 27JAN	Claude Larose	1.50	3.00
☐ 3FEB	Michel Plasse (G)	2.50	5.00
☐ 10FEB	Michel Larocque (G)	2.50	5.00
☐ 17FEB	Pete Mahovlich	1.50	3.00
☐ 24FEB	Steve Shutt	2.50	5.00
☐ 3MAR	Jim Roberts	1.50	3.00
☐ 10MAR	Bob Gainey	3.50	7.00
☐ 17MAR	Murray Wilson	1.50	3.00
☐ 24MAR	Larry Robinson	4.00	8.00
☐ 31MAR	Yvon Lambert	1.50	3.00
☐ 7APR	Jacques Lemaire	3.50	7.00
1977 - 78 ISSUE			
☐ 13MAR	Réal Cloutier	1.50	3.00
☐ 20MAR	Rogatien Vachon (G)	3.00	6.00
☐ 27MAR	Bernard Parent (G)	5.00	10.00
☐ 3APR	Réal Cloutier	1.50	3.00
☐ 10APR	Jean-Claude Tremblay	1.50	3.00
☐ 17APR	Serge Bernier	1.50	3.00
☐ 24APR	Denis Potvin	4.00	8.00
☐ 1JAN	Robert Picard	1.50	3.00
☐ 8JAN	Lucien Deblois	1.50	3.00
☐ 15JAN	Michael Bossy	5.00	10.00
☐ 22JAN	Jean Savard	1.50	3.00
☐ 29JAN	Jere Gillis	1.50	3.00
☐ 5FEB	Maurice Richard	7.50	15.00
☐ 12FEB	Toe Blake, Coach	4.00	8.00
☐ 19FEB	Elmer Lach	5.00	10.00
☐ 26FEB	Jean Béliveau	6.00	12.00
☐ 5MAR	Floyd Curry	1.50	3.00
☐ 12MAR	Emile Bouchard	3.00	6.00
☐ 19MAR	Tom Johnson	3.00	6.00
☐ 26MAR	Bernard Geoffrion	5.00	10.00
☐ 2APR	Henri Richard	3.50	7.00
☐ 9APR	Dickie Moore	3.50	7.00
☐ 16APR	Claude Provost	1.50	3.00
☐ 23APR	Jean-Guy Talbot	1.50	3.00
☐ 30APR	Jacques Plante (G)	7.50	15.00
1978 - 79 ISSUE			
☐ 10DEC	Jean-Claude Tremblay	1.50	3.00
☐ 17DEC	Nordique Player	1.50	3.00
☐ 24DEC	Danny Geoffrion	1.50	3.00
☐ 31DEC	Paul Baxter	1.50	3.00
☐ 7JAN	Normand Dubé	1.50	3.00
☐ 14JAN	Jim Corsi (G)	2.50	5.00
☐ 21JAN	Jim Dorey, January 21	1.50	3.00
☐ 28JAN	Marc Tardiff	1.50	3.00
☐ 4FEB	Bob Fitchner	1.50	3.00
☐ 11FEB	Alain Côté	1.50	3.00
☐ 18FEB	Richard David	1.50	3.00
☐ 25FEB	Jacques Demers, Coach	2.50	5.00
☐ 4MAR	François Lacombe	1.50	3.00
☐ 11MAR	Réal Cloutier	1.50	3.00
☐ 18MAR	Curt Brackenbury	1.50	3.00
☐ 25MAR	Richard Brodeur (G)	2.50	5.00
☐ 1APR	Dale Hoganson	1.50	3.00
☐ 8APR	Wally Weir	1.50	3.00
☐ 15APR	Serge Bernier	1.50	3.00
☐ 2APR	Gary Larivière	1.50	3.00
☐ 29APR	Paul Baxter	1.50	3.00

1979 - 80 ISSUE

☐	2DEC	Jean Ratelle	3.50	7.00
☐	9DEC	Guy Chouinard	1.50	3.00
☐	16DEC	Ray Bourque	6.00	12.00
☐	23DEC	Robert Picard	1.50	3.00
☐	30DEC	Carol Vadnais	1.50	3.00
☐	6JAN	Marcel Dionne	5.00	10.00
☐	13JAN	Anders Hedberg	1.50	3.00
☐	20JAN	Bobby Hul	9.00	18.00
☐	27JAN	Wilf Paiement	1.50	3.00
☐	3FEB	Guy Charron	1.50	3.00
☐	10FEB	Phil Myre (G)	2.50	5.00
☐	17FEB	René Robert	1.50	3.00
☐	24FEB	Bobby Clarke	5.00	10.00
☐	2MAR	J.P. Bordeleau	1.50	3.00
☐	9MAR	André Dupont	1.50	3.00
☐	16MAR	Brad Park	3.50	7.00
☐	23MAR	Pierre Bouchard	1.50	3.00
☐	30MAR	Borje Salming	3.50	7.00
☐	6APR	Dale McCourt	1.50	3.00
☐	13APR	Daniel Bouchard (G)	2.50	5.00

1980 - 81 ISSUE

☐	30NOV	Serge Savard	3.00	6.00
☐	7DEC	Yvon Lambert	1.50	3.00
☐	14DEC	Bob Gainey	3.50	7.00
☐	21DEC	Réjean Houle	2.50	5.00
☐	28DEC	Claude Ruel, Coach	1.50	3.00
☐	4JAN	Doug Jarvis	1.50	3.00
☐	11JAN	Michel Larocque (G)	2.50	5.00
☐	18JAN	Pierre Larouche	1.50	3.00
☐	25JAN	Larry Robinson	4.00	8.00
☐	1FEB	Mario Tremblay	2.50	5.00
☐	8FEB	Guy Lapointe	3.00	6.00
☐	15FEB	Gaston Gingras	1.50	3.00
☐	22FEB	Richard / Bossy	7.50	15.00
☐	1MAR	Brian Engblom	1.50	3.00
☐	8MAR	Doug Risebrough	1.50	3.00
☐	15MAR	Rod Langway	3.00	6.00
☐	22MAR	Guy Lafleur	6.00	12.00
☐	29MAR	Steve Shutt	3.50	7.00
☐	5APR	Mark Napier	1.50	3.00
☐	12APR	Richard Sevigny (G)	2.50	5.00
☐	119APR	Chris Nilan	1.50	3.00
☐	26APR	Pierre Mondou	1.50	3.00
☐	3MAY	Keith Acton	1.50	3.00
☐	10MAY	Denis Herron (G)	2.50	5.00

1981 - 82 ISSUE

☐	8NOV	Marc Tardif	1.50	3.00
☐	15NOV	Michel Bergeron	1.50	3.00
☐	22NOV	Daniel Bouchard (G)	2.50	5.00
☐	29NOV	Jacques Richard	1.50	3.00
☐	6DEC	Marian Stastny	1.50	3.00
☐	13DEC	Michel Goulet	3.50	7.00
☐	20DEC	André Dupont	1.50	3.00
☐	27DEC	Robbie Ftorek	1.50	3.00
☐	3JAN	Michel Plasse (G)	2.50	5.00
☐	10JAN	Pierre Lacroix	1.50	3.00
☐	17JAN	Dale Hoganson	1.50	3.00
☐	24JAN	Mario Marois	1.50	3.00
☐	31JAN	Normand Rochefort	1.50	3.00
☐	7FEB	Anton Stastny	2.50	5.00
☐	14FEB	Dale Hunter	2.50	5.00
☐	21FEB	Dave Pichette	1.50	3.00
☐	28FEB	Pierre Aubry	1.50	3.00
☐	7MAR	Réal Cloutier	1.50	3.00
☐	14MAR	Alain Côte	1.50	3.00
☐	21MAR	Wally Weir	1.50	3.00
☐	28MAR	Peter Stastny	4.00	8.00
☐	4APR	Miroslav Frycer	1.50	3.00
☐	11APR	Wayne Gretzky	15.00	30.00

1982 - 83 ISSUE

☐	14NOV	Ray Bourque	5.00	10.00
☐	21NOV	Denis Savard	4.00	8.00
☐	28NOV	Serge Savard	3.00	6.00
☐	5DEC	Bryan Trottier	5.00	10.00
☐	12DEC	Wilf Paiement	1.50	3.00
☐	19DEC	Michael Bossy	5.00	10.00
☐	26DEC	Ron Duguay	1.50	3.00
☐	2JAN	Bobby Clarke	5.00	10.00
☐	9JAN	Mike Rogers	1.50	3.00
☐	16JAN	Darryl Sittler	5.00	10.00
☐	23JAN	Carol Vadnais	1.50	3.00
☐	30JAN	Mark Howe	3.00	6.00
☐	6FEB	Vladislav Tretiak (G)	10.00	20.00
☐	13FEB	Pierre Larouche	2.50	5.00
☐	20FEB	Gilbert Perreault	4.00	8.00
☐	27FEB	Gaston Gingras	1.50	3.00
☐	6MAR	Richard Brodeur (G)	2.50	5.00
☐	13MAR	Dale Hawerchuk	4.00	8.00
☐	20MAR	Pat LaFontaine	10.00	20.00
☐	27MAR	Brian Engblom	1.50	3.00
☐	3APR	Dan Daoust	1.50	3.00
☐	10APR	Doug Risebrough	1.50	3.00
☐	17APR	Rod Langway	3.00	6.00
☐	24APR	Doug Jarvis	1.50	3.00

1983 - 84 ISSUE

☐	20NOV	Superstar	1.50	3.00
☐	27NOV	Rick Wamsley (G)	2.50	5.00
☐	4DEC	Larry Robinson	4.00	8.00
☐	11DEC	Guy Lafleur	6.00	12.00
☐	18DEC	Mario Tremblay	2.50	5.00
☐	25DEC	Mats Naslund	1.50	3.00
☐	1JAN	Chris Nilan	5.00	10.00
☐	8JAN	Les Canadiens	10.00	20.00
☐	15JAN	Marcel Dionne	5.00	10.00
☐	22JAN	Pierre Mondou	1.50	3.00
☐	29JAN	Steve Shutt	3.50	7.00
☐	5FEB	Bill Root	1.50	3.00

DATES UNKNOWN

☐		Marcel Dionne	5.00	10.00
☐		Real Cloutier	1.50	3.00
☐		Pierre Larouche	2.50	5.00
☐		Richard Martin	2.50	5.00
☐		Gilbert Perreault	4.00	8.00
☐		Jean Pronovost	1.50	3.00
☐		Dan Bouchard	2.50	5.00
☐		Christian Bordeleau	2.00	4.00

1973 - 74 MAC'S MILK

These disks show caricatures of various players.

Disk Diameter: 3"

Face: Four colour, red, purple, green, blue or black border; Name

Back: Blank

Imprint: NHLPA

	Player	EX	NRMT
	Complete Set (30 disks):	**70.00**	**140.00**
☐	Gary Bergman, Det.	1.50	3.00
☐	John Bucyk, Bos.	3.50	7.00
☐	Wayne Cashman, Bos.	1.50	3.00
☐	Bobby Clarke, Phi.	5.00	10.00
☐	Yvan Cournoyer, Mtl.	4.00	8.00
☐	Ron Ellis, Tor.	1.50	3.00
☐	Rod Gilbert, NYR.	3.50	7.00
☐	Brian Glennie, Tor.	1.50	3.00
☐	Paul Henderson, Tor.	2.50	5.00
☐	Eddie Johnston (G), Tor.	2.50	5.00
☐	Rick Kehoe, Tor.	1.50	3.00
☐	Orland Kurtenbach, Van.	1.50	3.00
☐	Guy Lapointe, Mtl.	3.00	6.00
☐	Jacques Lemaire, Mtl.	4.00	8.00
☐	Frank Mahovlich, Mtl.	6.00	12.00
☐	Pete Mahovlich, Mtl.	1.50	3.00
☐	Richard Martin, Buf.	2.50	5.00
☐	Jim McKenny, Tor.	1.50	3.00
☐	Bobby Orr, Bos.	18.00	35.00
☐	Jean Paul Parise, Min.	1.50	3.00
☐	Brad Park, NYR.	3.50	7.00
☐	Jacques Plante (G), Tor.	9.00	18.00
☐	Jean Ratelle, NYR	3.50	7.00
☐	Mickey Redmond, Det.	2.50	5.00
☐	Serge Savard, Mtl.	3.00	6.00
☐	Darryl Sittler, Tor.	5.00	10.00
☐	Pat Stapleton, Chi.	1.50	3.00
☐	Dale Tallon, Chi.	1.50	3.00

☐	Norm Ullman, Tor.	3.50	7.00
☐	Bill White, Chi.	1.50	3.00

1973 - 74 NABISCO SUGAR DADDY PRO FACES

This 25 sticker set features players from four different sports. Other singles exist. A 18" x 24" Wall Poster was also available.

Card Size: 1 1/16" x 2 3/4"

Face: Four colour

Back: Black and white

Imprint: Nabisco Confections, Inc.

	No.	Player	EX	NRMT
☐	11	Phil Esposito	7.50	15.00
☐	12	Dennis Hull	4.00	7.50
☐	13	Reg Fleming	2.50	5.00
☐	14	Garry Unger	2.50	5.00
☐	15	Derek Sanderson	4.50	8.50
☐	16	Jerry Korab	2.50	5.00
☐	22	Mickey Redmond	4.00	7.50

1973 - 74 O-PEE-CHEE

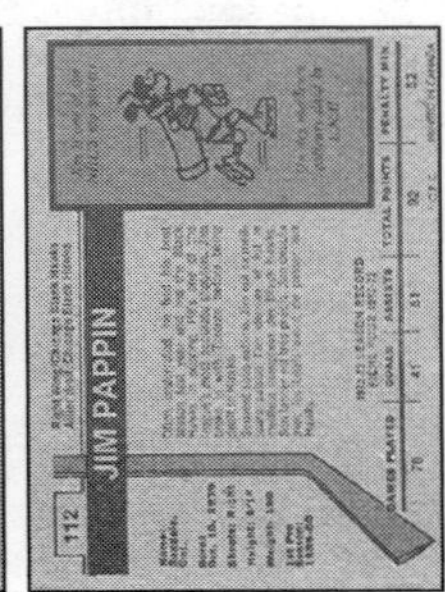

This set was produced from two different card stocks; one light beige and the other grey. Cards 1 to 132 have a red border while cards 133 to 264 were printed with a green border. These full colour borders mark easily, making mint cards difficult to find. The set price listed below is for a set with mixed card stocks. A set printed on uniform card stock would command a premium over this price.

Card Size: 2 1/2" x 3 1/2"

Face: Four colour, red or green border, Position

Back: Dark and light brown on light beige or grey card stock, Number, Resume, Hockey trivia, Bilingual

Imprint: © O.P.C.

	No.	Player	EX	NRMT
		Complete Set (264 cards):	**265.00**	**525.00**
		Common Player:	**.75**	**1.50**
☐	1	Alex Delvecchio, Det., LC	2.50	7.50
☐	2	Gilles Meloche, Cal. (G)	1.25	2.50
☐	3	Phil Roberto, Stl.	.75	1.50
☐	4	Orland Kurtenbach, Van., LC	.75	1.50
☐	5	Gilles Marotte, L.A.	.75	1.50
☐	6	Stan Mikita, Chi.	5.00	10.00
☐	7	Paul Henderson, Tor.	1.25	2.50
☐	8	Gregg Sheppard, Bos., Err. (Greg)	.75	1.50
☐	9	Rod Seiling, NYR.	.75	1.50
☐	10	Red Berenson, Det.	.75	1.50
☐	11	Jean Pronovost, Pgh.	.75	1.50
☐	12	Dick Redmond, Chi.	.75	1.50
☐	13	Keith McCreary, Atl.	.75	1.50
☐	14	Bryan Watson, Pgh.	.75	1.50
☐	15	Garry Unger, Stl.	.75	1.50
☐	**16**	**Neil Komadoski, L.A., RC**	**.75**	**1.50**
☐	17	Marcel Dionne, Det.	11.00	22.00
☐	18	Ernie Hicke, NYI.	.75	1.50
☐	19	André Boudrias, Van.	.75	1.50
☐	20	AS: Bill Flett, Pha.	1.25	2.50
☐	21	Marshall Johnston, Cal., LC	.75	1.50

☐ 22	Gerry Meehan, Buf.	.75	1.50
☐ 23	Eddie Johnston (G), Tor.	1.25	2.50
☐ 24	Serge Savard, Mtl.	1.75	3.50
☐ 25	Walt Tkaczuk, NYR.	.75	1.50
☐ 26	Ken Hodge, Bos.	.75	1.50
☐ 27	Norm Ullman, Tor.	1.75	3.50
☐ 28	Cliff Koroll, Chi.	.75	1.50
☐ 29	Rey Comeau, Alt.	.75	1.50
☐ 30	AS: Bobby Orr, Bos.	35.00	65.00
☐ 31	Wayne Stephenson (G), Stl.	1.25	2.50
☐ 32	Dan Maloney, L.A.	.75	1.50
☐ **33**	**Henry Boucha, Det., RC**	**.75**	**1.50**
☐ 34	Gerry Hart, NYI.	.75	1.50
☐ 35	Bobby Schmautz, Van.	.75	1.50
☐ 36	Ross Lonsberry, Pha.	.75	1.50
☐ 37	Ted McAneeley, Cal.	.75	1.50
☐ 38	Don Luce, Buf.	.75	1.50
☐ 39	Jim McKenny, Tor.	.75	1.50
☐ 40	Jacques Laperrière, Mtl.	1.75	3.50
☐ 41	Bill Fairbairn, NYR.	.75	1.50
☐ 42	Craig Cameron, NYI.	.75	1.50
☐ 43	Bryan Hextall, Jr., Pgh.	.75	1.50
☐ **44**	**Chuck Lefley, Mtl., RC**	**.75**	**1.50**
☐ 45	Dan Bouchard (G), Atl.	1.25	2.00
☐ 46	J. P. Parise, Min.	.75	1.50
☐ 47	Barclay Plager, Stl.	.75	1.50
☐ 48	Mike Corrigan, L.A.	.75	1.50
☐ 49	Nick Libett, Det.	.75	1.50
☐ 50	AS: Bobby Clarke, Pha.	14.00	28.00
☐ 51	Bert Marshall, NYI.	.75	1.50
☐ 52	Craig Patrick, Cal.	1.25	2.50
☐ 53	Richard Lemieux, Van.	.75	1.50
☐ 54	Tracy Pratt, Buf.	.75	1.50
☐ 55	Ron Ellis, Tor.	.75	1.50
☐ 56	Jacques Lemaire, Mtl.	2.50	5.00
☐ 57	Steve Vickers, NYR.	.75	1.50
☐ 58	Carol Vadnais, Bos.	.75	1.50
☐ 59	Jim Rutherford (G), Pgh.	1.25	2.50
☐ 60	Rick Kehoe, Tor.	.75	1.50
☐ 61	Pat Quinn, Atl.	.75	1.50
☐ 62	Bill Goldsworthy, Min.	.75	1.50
☐ 63	Dave Dryden (G), Buf.	1.25	2.50
☐ 64	Rogatien Vachon (G), L.A.	3.00	6.00
☐ 65	Gary Bergman, Det.	.75	1.50
☐ 66	Bernie Parent (G), Pha.	5.00	10.00
☐ 67	Ed Westfall, NYI.	.75	1.50
☐ 68	Ivan Boldirev, Cal.	.75	1.50
☐ 69	Don Tannahill, Van., LC	.75	1.50
☐ 70	Gilbert Perreault, Buf.	7.50	15.00
☐ 71	Mike Pelyk, Tor.	.75	1.50
☐ 72	Guy Lafleur, Mtl.	18.00	35.00
☐ 73	Pit Martin, Chi.	.75	1.50
☐ **74**	**Gilles Gilbert (G), Bos., RC**	**3.50**	**7.00**
☐ 75	Jim Lorentz, Buf.	.75	1.50
☐ 76	Syl Apps, Jr., Pgh.	.75	1.50
☐ 77	Phil Myre (G), Atl.	1.25	2.50
☐ 78	AS: Bill White, Chi.	1.25	2.50
☐ 79	Jack Egers, Stl.	.75	1.50
☐ 80	Terry Harper, L.A.	.75	1.50
☐ **81**	**Bill Barber, Pha., RC**	**11.00**	**22.00**
☐ 82	Roy Edwards (G), Det., LC	1.25	2.50
☐ 83	Brian Spencer, NYI.	.75	1.50
☐ 84	Reggie Leach, Cal.	.75	1.50
☐ 85	Wayne Cashman, Bos.	.75	1.50
☐ 86	Jim Schoenfeld, Buf.	2.25	4.50
☐ 87	Henri Richard, Mtl.	3.00	6.00
☐ **88**	**Dennis O'Brien, Min., RC**	**.75**	**1.50**
☐ 89	Al McDonough, Pgh.	.75	1.50
☐ 90	AS: Tony Esposito (G), Chi.	9.00	18.00
☐ 91	Joe Watson, Pha.	.75	1.50
☐ 92	Atlanta Flames	2.75	5.50
☐ 93	Boston Bruins	2.75	5.50
☐ 94	Buffalo Sabres	2.75	5.50
☐ 95	California Golden Seals	2.75	5.50
☐ 96	Chicago Blackhawks	2.75	5.50
☐ 97	Detroit Red Wings	2.75	5.50
☐ 98	Los Angeles Kings	2.75	5.50
☐ 99	Minnesota North Stars	2.75	5.50
☐ 100	Montréal Canadiens	2.75	5.50
☐ 101	New York Islanders	2.75	5.50
☐ 102	New York Rangers	2.75	5.50
☐ 103	Philadelphia Flyers	2.75	5.50
☐ 104	Pittsburgh Penguins	2.75	5.50
☐ 105	St. Louis Blues	2.75	5.50
☐ 106	Toronto Maple Leafs	2.75	5.50
☐ 107	Vancouver Canucks	2.75	5.50
☐ 108	Vic Hadfield, NYR.	.75	1.50
☐ 109	Tom Reid, Min.	.75	1.50
☐ **110**	**Hilliard Graves, Cal., RC**	**.75**	**1.50**
☐ 111	Don Lever, Van.	.75	1.50
☐ 112	Jim Pappin, Chi.	.75	1.50
☐ 113	André Dupont, Pha.	.75	1.50
☐ 114	AS: Guy Lapointe, Mtl.	1.25	2.50
☐ 115	Dennis Hextall, Min.	.75	1.50
☐ 116	Checklist 1 (1 - 132)	30.00	55.00
☐ 117	Bobby Leiter, Atl.	.75	1.50
☐ 118	Ab DeMarco, Stl.	.75	1.50
☐ 119	Gilles Villemure (G), NYR.	1.25	2.50
☐ 120	AS: Phil Esposito, Bos.	5.00	10.00
☐ 121	Mike Robitaille, Buf.	.75	1.50
☐ 122	Réal Lemieux, L.A., LC	.75	1.50
☐ 123	Jim Neilson, NYR.	.75	1.50
☐ **124**	**Steve Durbano, Stl., RC**	**.75**	**1.50**
☐ 125	Jude Drouin, Min.	.75	1.50
☐ 126	Gary Smith (G), Van.	1.25	2.50
☐ 127	Césare Maniago (G), Min.	1.25	2.50
☐ 128	Lowell MacDonald, Pgh.	.75	1.50
☐ 129	Checklist, Error	30.00	55.00
☐ **130**	**Billy Harris, NYI., RC**	**.75**	**1.50**
☐ 131	Randy Manery, Atl.	.75	1.50
☐ 132	Darryl Sittler, Tor.	11.00	22.00
☐ 133	LL: P. Esposito, Bos./ R. MacLeish, Pha.	2.50	5.00
☐ 134	LL: P. Esposito, Bos./ B. Clarke, Pha.	4.50	9.00
☐ 135	LL: P. Esposito, Bos./ B. Clarke, Pha.	4.50	9.00
☐ 136	LL: K. Dryden, Mtl./ T. Esposito,Chi.	7.50	15.00
☐ 137	LL:J. Schoenfeld, Buf./ D. Schultz, Pha.	1.25	2.50
☐ 138	LL: P. Esposito, Bos./ R. MacLeish, Pha.	2.50	5.00
☐ 139	René Robert, Buf.	.75	1.50
☐ 140	Dave Burrows, Pgh.	.75	1.50
☐ 141	Jean Ratelle, NYR.	1.75	3.50
☐ **142**	**Billy Smith (G), NYI., RC**	**20.00**	**40.00**
☐ 143	Jocelyn Guevremont, Van.	.75	1.50
☐ 144	Tim Ecclestone, Tor.	.75	1.50
☐ 145	AS: Frank Mahovlich, Mtl.	4.00	7.50
☐ 146	Rick MacLeish, Pha.	.75	1.50
☐ 147	John Bucyk, Bos.	1.75	3.50
☐ 148	Bob Plager, Stl.	.75	1.50
☐ **149**	**Curt Bennett, Atl., RC**	**.75**	**1.50**
☐ 150	Dave Keon, Tor.	1.75	3.50
☐ 151	Keith Magnuson, Chi.	.75	1.50
☐ 152	Walt McKechnie, Cal.	.75	1.50
☐ 153	Roger Crozier (G), Buf.	1.25	2.50
☐ 154	Ted Harris, Det., LC	.75	1.50
☐ 155	Butch Goring, L.A.	.75	1.50
☐ 156	Rod Gilbert, NYR.	1.75	3.50
☐ 157	Yvan Cournoyer, Mtl.	2.50	5.00
☐ 158	Doug Favell (G), Tor.	1.25	2.50
☐ 159	Juha Widing, L.A.	.75	1.50
☐ 160	Ed Giacomin (G), NYR.	2.75	5.50
☐ 161	Germaine Gagnon, NYI.	.75	1.50
☐ 162	Dennis Kearns, Van.	.75	1.50
☐ 163	Bill Collins, Det.	.75	1.50
☐ 164	Pete Mahovlich, Mtl.	.75	1.50
☐ 165	Brad Park, NYR.	4.00	8.00
☐ **166**	**Dave Schultz, Pha., RC**	**7.50**	**15.00**
☐ 167	Dallas Smith, Bos.	.75	1.50
☐ 168	Gary Sabourin, Stl.	.75	1.50
☐ 169	Jacques Richard, Atl.	.75	1.50
☐ 170	Brian Glennie, Tor.	.75	1.50
☐ 171	AS: Dennis Hull, Chi.	1.25	2.50
☐ 172	Joey Johnston, Cal.	.75	1.50
☐ 173	Rick Martin, Buf.	1.25	2.50
☐ 174	AS: Barry Gibbs, Min.	1.25	2.50
☐ 175	Bob Berry, L.A.	.75	1.50
☐ 176	Greg Polis, Pgh.	.75	1.50
☐ 177	Dale Rolfe, NYR.	.75	1.50
☐ 178	Gerry Desjardins (G), NYI.	1.25	2.50
☐ 179	Bobby Lalonde, Van.	.75	1.50
☐ 180	AS: Mickey Redmond, Det.	1.25	2.50
☐ 181	Jim Roberts, Mtl.	.75	1.50
☐ 182	Gary Dornhoefer, Pha.	.75	1.50
☐ 183	Derek Sanderson, Bos.	3.25	6.50
☐ 184	Brent Hughes, Det.	.75	1.50
☐ **185**	**Larry Romanchych, Atl., RC**	**.75**	**1.50**
☐ 186	Pierre Jarry, Det.	.75	1.50
☐ 187	Doug Jarrett, Chi.	.75	1.50
☐ **188**	**Bob Stewart, Cal., RC**	**.75**	**1.50**
☐ 189	Tim Horton, Buf., LC	4.50	8.50
☐ 190	Fred (Buster) Harvey, Min.	.75	1.50
☐ 191	Canadiens vs. Sabres	1.25	2.50
☐ 192	Flyers vs. North Stars	1.25	2.50
☐ 193	Blackhawks vs. Blues	1.25	2.50
☐ 194	Rangers vs. Bruins	1.25	2.50
☐ 195	Canadiens vs. Flyers	1.25	2.50
☐ 196	Blackhawks vs. Rangers	1.25	2.50
☐ 197	Canadiens vs Blackhawks	1.75	3.50
☐ 198	Stanley Cup Champs: Montréal Canadiens	2.50	5.00
☐ 199	Gary Edwards (G), L.A.	1.25	2.50
☐ 200	Ron Schock, Pgh.	.75	1.50
☐ 201	Bruce MacGregor, NYR.	.75	1.50
☐ **202**	**Bob Nystrom, NYI., RC**	**4.00**	**7.50**
☐ 203	Jerry Korab, Van.	.75	1.50
☐ **204**	**Thommie Bergman, Det., RC**	**.75**	**1.50**
☐ 205	Bill Lesuk, L.A.	.75	1.50
☐ 206	Ed Van Impe, Pha.	.75	1.50
☐ 207	Doug Roberts, Det.	.75	1.50
☐ 208	Chris Evans, Stl.	.75	1.50
☐ **209**	**Lynn Powis, Chi., RC**	**.75**	**1.50**
☐ 210	Denis Dupère, Tor.	.75	1.50
☐ 211	Dale Tallon, Chi.	.75	1.50
☐ 212	Stan Gilbertson, Cal.	.75	1.50
☐ 213	Craig Ramsay, Buf.	.75	1.50
☐ 214	Danny Grant, Min.	.75	1.50
☐ **215**	**Doug Volmar, L.A., RC, LC**	**.75**	**1.50**
☐ 216	Darryl Edestrand, Bos.	.75	1.50
☐ 217	Pete Stemkowski, NYR.	.75	1.50
☐ **218**	**Lorne Henning, NYI., RC**	**.75**	**1.50**
☐ **219**	**Bryan McSheffrey, Van., RC, LC**	**.75**	**1.50**
☐ 220	Guy Charron, Det.	.75	1.50
☐ **221**	**Wayne Thomas (G), Mtl., RC**	**3.25**	**6.50**
☐ 222	Simon Nolet, Pha.	.75	1.50
☐ **223**	**Fred O'Donnell, Bos., RC, LC**	**.75**	**1.50**
☐ 224	Lou Angotti, Stl.	.75	1.50
☐ 225	Arnie Brown, Atl., LC	.75	1.50
☐ 226	Garry Monahan, Tor.	.75	1.50
☐ 227	Chico Maki, Chi.	.75	1.50
☐ 228	Gary Croteau, Cal.	.75	1.50
☐ 229	Paul Terbenche, Buf.	.75	1.50
☐ 230	Gump Worsley (G), Min., LC	2.75	5.50
☐ 231	Jimmy Peters, L.A., LC	.75	1.50
☐ 232	Jack Lynch, Pgh.	.75	1.50
☐ 233	Bobby Rousseau, NYR.	.75	1.50
☐ 234	Dave Hudson, NYI.	.75	1.50
☐ **235**	**Gregg Boddy, Van., RC, Err. (Greg)**	**.75**	**1.50**
☐ 236	Ron Stackhouse, Det.	.75	1.50
☐ **237**	**Larry Robinson, Mtl., RC**	**35.00**	**65.00**
☐ **238**	**Bobby Taylor (G), Pha., RC, LC**	**1.25**	**2.50**
☐ 239	Nick Beverley, Pgh.	.75	1.50
☐ 240	Don Awrey, Stl.	.75	1.50
☐ 241	Doug Mohns, Atl.	.75	1.50
☐ 242	Eddie Shack, Tor., LC	1.25	2.50
☐ **243**	**Phil Russell, Chi., RC**	**1.25**	**2.50**
☐ 244	Pete Laframboise, Cal.	.75	1.50
☐ 245	Steve Atkinson, Buf.	.75	1.50
☐ 246	Lou Nanne, Min.	.75	1.50
☐ **247**	**Yvon Labre, Pgh., RC**	**.75**	**1.50**
☐ 248	Ted Irvine, NYR.	.75	1.50
☐ 249	Tom Miller, NYI., LC	.75	1.50
☐ 250	Gerry O'Flaherty, Van.	.75	1.50
☐ **251**	**Larry Johnston, Det., RC**	**.75**	**1.50**
☐ **252**	**Michel Plasse (G), Mtl., RC**	**2.25**	**4.50**
☐ 253	Bob Kelly, Pha.	.75	1.50
☐ **254**	**Terry O'Reilly, Bos., RC**	**6.50**	**13.00**
☐ **255**	**Pierre Plante, Stl., RC**	**.75**	**1.50**
☐ 256	Noel Price, Atl.	.75	1.50
☐ 257	Dunc Wilson (G), Tor.	1.25	2.50
☐ **258**	**J. P. Bordeleau, Chi., RC**	**.75**	**1.50**
☐ **259**	**Terry Murray, Cal., RC**	**1.25**	**2.50**
☐ 260	Larry Carriere, Buf.	.75	1.50
☐ 261	Pierre Bouchard, Mtl.	.75	1.50
☐ 262	Frank St. Marseille, L.A.	.75	1.50
☐ 263	Checklist	28.00	55.00
☐ 264	Fred Barrett, Min.	1.50	4.50

O-PEE-CHEE TEAM LOGO

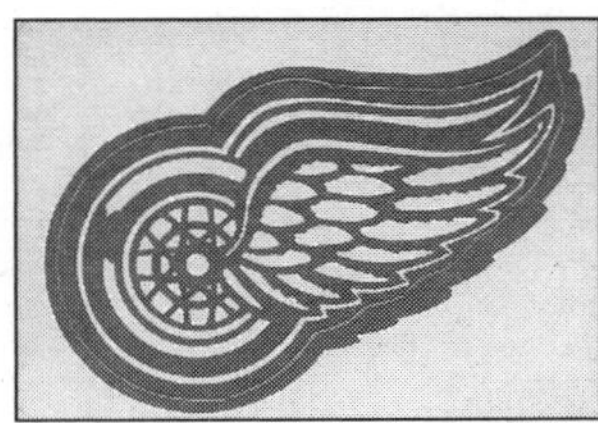

Team logo stickers were inserted one per pack with the regular set of the same year. The 1973-74 stickers have application instructions on the face distinguishing them from the 1972-73 Team Logo Stickers.

Insert Set (17 cards):		**25.00**	**45.00**
No.	**Player**	**EX**	**NRMT**
☐ 1	NHL Logo	2.00	4.00
☐ 2	Atlanta Flames	2.00	4.00
☐ 3	Boston Bruins	2.00	4.00
☐ 4	Buffalo Sabres	2.00	4.00
☐ 5	California Golden Seals	2.00	4.00
☐ 6	Chicago Blackhawks	2.00	4.00
☐ 7	Detroit Red Wings	2.00	4.00
☐ 8	Los Angeles Kings	2.00	4.00
☐ 9	Minnesota North Stars	2.00	4.00
☐ 10	Montréal Canadiens	2.00	4.00
☐ 11	New York Islanders	2.00	4.00
☐ 12	New York Rangers	2.00	4.00
☐ 13	Philadelphia Flyers	2.00	4.00
☐ 14	Pittsburgh Penguins	2.00	4.00
☐ 15	Saint Louis Blues	2.00	4.00
☐ 16	Toronto Maple Leafs	2.00	4.00
☐ 17	Vancouver Canucks	2.00	4.00

O-PEE-CHEE TEAM RINGS

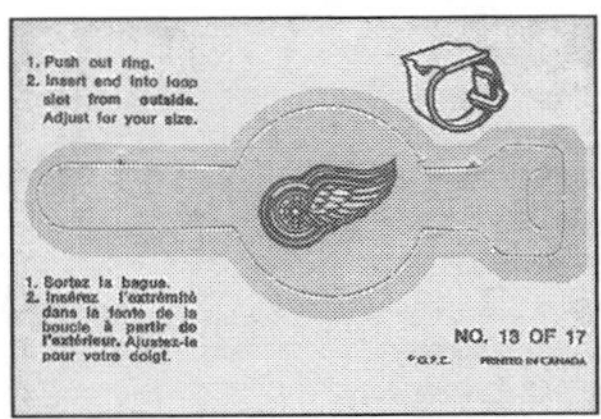

Cards are numbered _ of 17. Numbered cards contain a punch-out ring with assembly instructions.
Imprint: O.P.C. PRINTED IN CANADA

Insert Set (17 cards):		**30.00**	**60.00**
No.	**Player**	**EX**	**NRMT**
☐ 1	Vancouver Canucks	2.50	5.00
☐ 2	Montréal Canadiens	2.50	5.00
☐ 3	Toronto Maple Leafs	2.50	5.00
☐ 4	NHL Logo	2.50	5.00
☐ 5	Minnesota North Stars	2.50	5.00
☐ 6	New York Rangers	2.50	5.00
☐ 7	California Golden Seals	2.50	5.00
☐ 8	Pittsburgh Penguins	2.50	5.00
☐ 9	Philadelphia Flyers	2.50	5.00
☐ 10	Chicago Blackhawks	2.50	5.00
☐ 11	Boston Bruins	2.50	5.00
☐ 12	Los Angeles Kings	2.50	5.00
☐ 13	Detroit Red Wings	2.50	5.00
☐ 14	St. Louis Blues	2.25	4.50
☐ 15	Buffalo Sabres	2.25	4.50
☐ 16	Atlanta Flames	2.25	4.50
☐ 17	New York Islanders	2.25	4.50

1973 - 74 OPC WHA POSTERS

Poster Size: 7 1/2" x 12 1/2"
Face: Four colour, white border; Team logo or WHA logo, Name, Position, Numbered _ of 20, Bilingual
Back: Blank
Imprint: O.P.C.

Complete Set (20 posters):		**45.00**	**85.00**
No.	**Player**	**EX**	**NRMT**
☐ 1	Al Smith (G), New England	2.25	4.50
☐ 2	J.C. Tremblay, Québec	2.00	4.00
☐ 3	Guy Dufour, Québec	1.25	2.50
☐ 4	Pat Stapleton, Chicago	1.25	2.50
☐ 5	Rosaire Paiement, Chicago	1.25	2.50
☐ 6	Gerry Cheevers (G), Cleveland	4.50	8.50
☐ 7	Gerry Pinder, Cleveland	1.25	2.50
☐ 8	Wayne Carleton, Toronto	1.25	2.50
☐ 9	Bob LeDuc, Toronto	1.25	2.50
☐ 10	André Lacroix, New Jersey	1.25	2.50
☐ 11	Jim Harrison, Edmonton	1.25	2.50
☐ 12	Ron Climie, Edmonton	1.25	2.50
☐ 13	Gordie Howe, Houston	15.00	30.00
☐ 14	The Howe Family: Marty,Gordie and Mark	11.00	22.00
☐ 15	Mike Walton, Minnesota	1.25	2.50
☐ 16	Bobby Hull, Winnipeg	10.00	20.00
☐ 17	Chris Bordeleau, Winnipeg	1.25	2.50
☐ 18	Claude St. Sauveur, Vancouver	1.25	2.50
☐ 19	Bryan Campbell, Vancouver, Err. (Brian)	1.25	2.50
☐ 20	Marc Tardif, Los Angeles	2.25	4.50

1973 - 74 QUAKER OATS WORLD HOCKEY ASSOCIATION

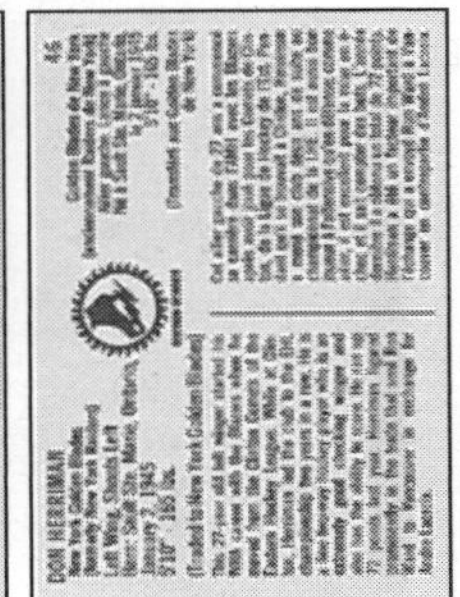

These cards were issued as panels of five cards in Quaker Oats products.
Card Size: 2 1/4" x 3 1/4"
Face: Four colour, white border; Name, TeamBack: Black and blue on white card stock; Name, Team, Position, Team logo, Number, Resume, Bilingual
Imprint: None

Complete Set (50 Cards):		**125.00**	**250.00**
Panel 1 (1 - 5):		**20.00**	**35.00**
Panel 2 (6 - 10):		**30.00**	**60.00**
Panel 3 (11 - 15):		**15.00**	**30.00**
Panel 4 (16 - 20):		**10.00**	**35.00**
Panel 5 (21 - 25):		**20.00**	**35.00**
Panel 6 (26 - 30):		**25.00**	**40.00**
Panel 7 (31 - 35):		**15.00**	**30.00**
Panel 8 (36 - 40):		**15.00**	**30.00**
Panel 9 (41 - 45):		**20.00**	**35.00**
Panel 10 (46 - 50):		**60.00**	**115.00**
Common Player:		**2.25**	**4.50**
No.	**Player**	**EX**	**NRMT**
☐ 1	Jim Wiste, Cleveland	3.50	7.00
☐ 2	Al Smith (G), New England	3.50	7.00
☐ 3	Rosaire Paiement, Calgary	2.25	4.50
☐ 4	Ted Hampson, Minnesota	2.25	4.50
☐ 5	Gavin Kirk, Toronto	2.25	4.50
☐ 6	Andre Lacroix, New York	3.25	6.50
☐ 7	John Schella, Houston	2.25	4.50
☐ 8	Gerry Cheevers (G), Cleveland	11.00	22.00
☐ 9	Norm Beaudin, Winnipeg	2.25	4.50
☐ 10	Jim Harrison, Alberta	2.25	4.50
☐ 11	Gerry Pinder, Cleveland	2.25	4.50
☐ 12	Bob Sicinski, Calgary	2.25	4.50
☐ 13	Bryan Campbell, Vancouver	2.25	4.50
☐ 14	Murray Hall, Houston	2.25	4.50
☐ 15	Chris Bordeleau, Winnipeg	2.25	4.50
☐ 16	Al Hamilton, Alberta	3.00	6.00
☐ 17	Jim McLeod (G), Chicago (New York)	2.25	4.50
☐ 18	Larry Pleau, New England	2.25	4.50
☐ 19	Larry Lund, Houston	2.25	4.50
☐ 20	Bobby Sheehan, New York	2.25	4.50
☐ 21	Jan Popiel, Calgary	2.25	4.50
☐ 22	Andre Gaudette, Québec	2.25	4.50
☐ 23	Bob Charlebois, New England	2.25	4.50
☐ 24	Gene Peacosh, New York	2.25	4.50
☐ 25	Rick Ley, New England	4.00	8.00
☐ 26	Larry Hornung, Winnipeg	2.25	4.50
☐ 27	Gary Jarrett, Cleveland	2.25	4.50
☐ 28	Ted Taylor, Houston	2.25	4.50
☐ 29	Pete Donnelly (G), New York (Vancouver)	3.00	6.00
☐ 30	J.C. Tremblay, Québec	3.50	7.00
☐ 31	Jim Cardiff, Vancouver	2.25	4.50
☐ 32	Gary Veneruzzo, Los Angeles	2.25	4.50
☐ 33	John French, New England	2.25	4.50
☐ 34	Ron Ward, New York (Vancouver)	2.25	4.50
☐ 35	Wayne Connelly, Minnesota	2.25	4.50
☐ 36	Ron Buchanan, Cleveland	2.25	4.50
☐ 37	Ken Block, New York	2.25	4.50
☐ 38	Alain Caron, Québec	2.25	4.50
☐ 39	Brit Selby, New England (Toronto)	2.25	4.50
☐ 40	Guy Trottier, Toronto	2.25	4.50
☐ 41	Ernie Wakely (G), Winnipeg	3.50	7.00
☐ 42	J.P. LeBlanc, Los Angeles	2.25	4.50
☐ 43	Michel Parizeau, Quebec	2.25	4.50
☐ 44	Wayne Rivers, New York	2.25	4.50
☐ 45	Reggie Fleming, Calgary	2.25	4.50
☐ 46	Don Herriman, Vancouver (New York)	2.25	4.50
☐ 47	Jim Dorey, New England	2.25	4.50
☐ 48	Danny Lawson, Vancouver	2.25	4.50
☐ 49	Dick Paradise, Minnesota	2.25	4.50
☐ 50	Bobby Hull, Winnipeg	25.00	65.00

1973 - 74 SOVIET CHAMPIONS POSTCARDS

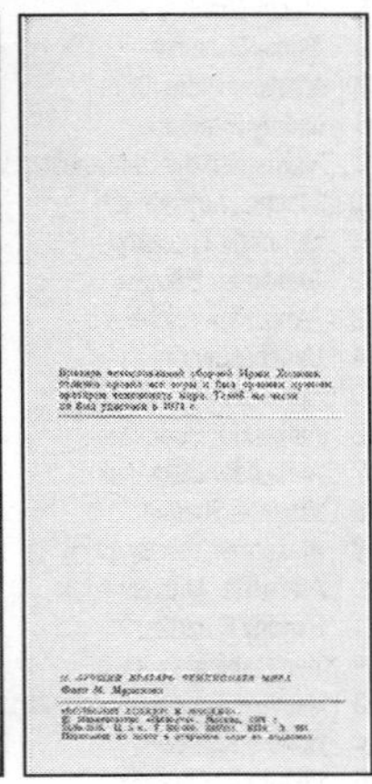

Card Size: 8 1/2" x 3 1/2"

Face: Four colour
Back: Black and white, Russian text
Imprint:

Complete Set (17 cards and folder):		**75.00**	**150.00**
No.	**Player**	**EX**	**NRMT**
☐ 1	World Champions	6.00	12.00
☐ 2	U.S.S.R. Champions/ Goalie Mask	6.00	12.00
☐ 3	Sweden/ Boris Mikhailov vs. Sweden	6.00	12.00
☐ 4	USSR vs. CSSR/ CSSR	4.00	8.00
☐ 5	USSR vs. Finland/ USSR vs. Sweden	4.00	8.00
☐ 6	USSR vs. CSSR/ Tretiak and USSR	7.50	15.00
☐ 7	USSR/ Alexander Yakushev	6.00	12.00
☐ 8	A.Ragulin vs. Sweden/ Sweden vs. USSR	4.00	8.00
☐ 9	Sweden/ Alexander Yakushev/ USSR	6.00	12.00
☐ 10	A.Yakushev/ G.Tsycankov and A.Ragulin	6.00	12.00
☐ 11	V.Tretiak/ V.Petrov/ USSR	7.50	15.00
☐ 12	V.Kharlamov and USSR/ CSSR (G)	6.00	12.00
☐ 13	V.Treitiak and V.Vasiliev/ USSR	7.50	15.00
☐ 14	V.Kharlamov and B.Mikhailov/ B.Mikhailov	6.00	12.00
☐ 15	B.Mikhailov, V.Tretiak and USSR/ USSR flag	7.50	15.00
☐ 16	V.Tretiak and USSR/ World Champions	7.50	15.00
☐ 17	Autographed Sticks/ European Champions	4.00	8.00

1973 - 74 SOVIET STARS POSTCARDS

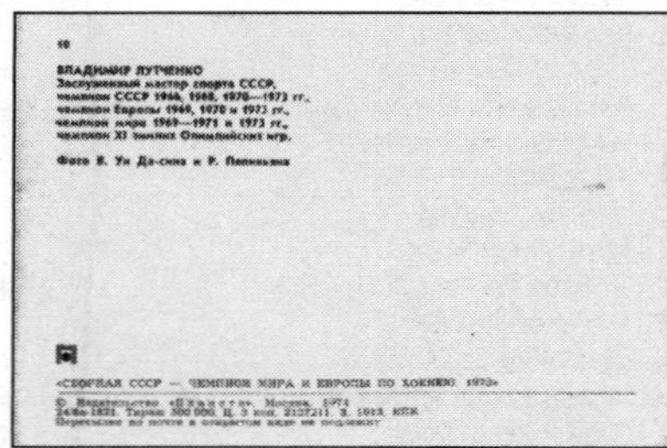

Card Size: 5 3/4" x 4 1/6"
Face: Four colour
Back: Black and white, Russian text
Imprint:

Complete Set (25 cards and folder):		**65.00**	**125.00**
No.	**Player**	**EX**	**NRMT**
☐ 1	Team Photo	5.00	10.00
☐ 2	Vladislav Tretiak (G)	13.00	25.00
☐ 3	Alexander Sidelnikov	2.50	5.00
☐ 4	Alexander Gusov	2.50	5.00
☐ 5	Valery Vasiliev	2.50	5.00
☐ 6	Boris Mikhailov	5.00	10.00
☐ 7	Vladimir Petrov	4.00	8.00
☐ 8	Valery Kharlamov	6.00	12.00
☐ 9	V. Kharlamov/ B. Mikhailov/ V. Petrov	7.50	15.00
☐ 10	Vladimir Lutchenko	2.50	5.00
☐ 11	Gennedy Tsycakov	2.50	5.00
☐ 12	Alexander Regulin	4.00	8.00
☐ 13	Alexander Volchkov	2.50	5.00
☐ 14	Vyacheslav Anisin	2.50	5.00
☐ 15	Yuri Lebedev	2.50	5.00
☐ 16	Alexander Bodunov	2.50	5.00
☐ 17	Alexander Martyniuk	2.50	5.00
☐ 18	Vladimir Shadrin	2.50	5.00
☐ 19	Alexander Yakushev	7.50	15.00
☐ 20	Alexander Maltsev	4.00	8.00
☐ 21	Evgeny Paladiev	2.50	5.00
☐ 22	Yuri Liapkin	2.50	5.00
☐ 23	Vsevold Bobrov, Boris Kulagin	2.50	5.00
☐ 24	Boris Mikhailov	5.00	10.00
☐ 25	Viktor Kuzkin and opponent	2.50	5.00

1973 - 74 TOPPS

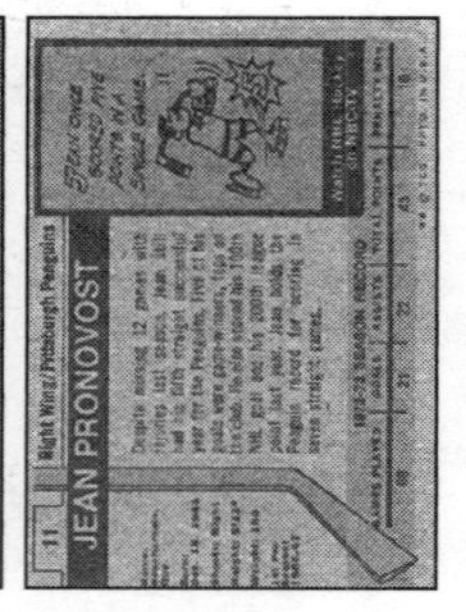

The team cards show team and player records on the back. Blue, green, red and yellow were used as border colours in this issue. Sets with identical borders command price premiums.

Card Size: 2 1/2" x 3 1/2"
Face: Four colour, red, green, yellow and blue borders, Position
Back: Brown and orange on card stock, Number, Resume, Hockey Trivia
Imprint: TCG

Complete Set (198 cards):		**125.00**	**250.00**
Common Player:		**.35**	**.75**
No.	**Player**	**EX**	**NRMT**
☐ 1	LL: P. Esposito/ R. MacLeish	2.50	7.50
☐ 2	LL: P. Esposito/ B. Clarke	3.25	6.50
☐ 3	LL: P. Esposito/ B. Clarke	3.25	6.50
☐ 4	LL: K. Dryden/ T. Esposito	5.00	10.00
☐ 5	LL:J. Schoenfeld/ D. Schultz	1.00	1.75
☐ 6	LL:P. Esposito/ R. MacLeish	2.00	4.00
☐ 7	Paul Henderson, Tor.	.65	1.25
☐ 8	Gregg Sheppard, Bos., Err. (Greg)	.35	.75
☐ 9	Rod Seiling, NYR.	.35	.75
☐ 10	Ken Dryden (G), Mtl.,	30.00	60.00
☐ 11	Jean Pronovost, Pgh.	.35	.75
☐ 12	Dick Redmond, Chi.	.35	.75
☐ 13	Keith McCreary, Atl.	.35	.75
☐ 14	Ted Harris, Min., LC	.35	.75
☐ 15	Garry Unger,Stl.	.35	.75
☐ **16**	**Neil Komadoski, L.A., RC**	**.35**	**.75**
☐ 17	Marcel Dionne, Det.	7.50	15.00
☐ 18	Ernie Hicke, NYI	.35	.75
☐ 19	André Boudrias, Van.	.35	.75
☐ 20	AS: Bill Flett, Pha	.35	.75
☐ 21	Marshall Johnston, Cal., LC	.35	.75
☐ 22	Gerry Meehan, Buf.	.35	.75
☐ 23	Ed Johnston (G), Tor.	.65	1.25
☐ 24	Serge Savard, Mtl.	1.00	1.75
☐ 25	Walt Tkaczuk, NYR.	.35	.75
☐ 26	John Bucyk, Bos.	1.00	1.25
☐ 27	Dave Burrows, Pgh.	.35	.75
☐ 28	Cliff Koroll, Chi.	.35	.75
☐ 29	Rey Comeau, Atl.	.35	.75
☐ 30	AS: Barry Gibbs, Min.	.35	.75
☐ 31	Wayne Stephenson (G),Stl.	.65	1.25
☐ 32	Dan Maloney, L.A.	.35	.75
☐ **33**	**Henry Boucha, Det., RC**	**.35**	**.75**
☐ 34	Gerry Hart, NYI.	.35	.75
☐ 35	Bobby Schmautz, Van.	.35	.75
☐ 36	Ross Lonsberry, Pha.	.35	.75
☐ 37	Ted McAneeley, Cal.	.35	.75
☐ 38	Don Luce, Buf.	.35	.75
☐ 39	Jim McKenny, Tor.	.35	.75
☐ 40	AS: Frank Mahovlich, Mtl.	2.50	5.00
☐ 41	Bill Fairbairn, NYR.	.35	.75
☐ 42	Dallas Smith, Bos.	.35	.75
☐ 43	Bryan Hextall, Pgh.	.35	.75
☐ 44	Keith Magnuson, Chi.	.35	.75
☐ 45	Dan Bouchard (G), Atl.	.65	1.25
☐ 46	Jean Paul Parise, Min.	.35	.75
☐ 47	Barclay Plager,Stl.	.35	.75
☐ 48	Mike Corrigan, L.A.	.35	.75
☐ 49	Nick Libett, Det.	.35	.75
☐ 50	AS: Bobby Clarke, Pha.	6.50	13.00
☐ 51	Bert Marshall, NYI.	.35	.75
☐ 52	Craig Patrick, Cal.	.35	.75
☐ 53	Richard Lemieux, Van.	.35	.75
☐ 54	Tracy Pratt, Buf.	.35	.75
☐ 55	Ron Ellis, Tor.	.35	.75
☐ 56	Jacques Lemaire, Mtl.	1.25	2.50
☐ 57	Steve Vickers, NYR.	.35	.75
☐ 58	Carol Vadnais, Bos.	.35	.75
☐ 59	Jim Rutherford (G), Pgh.	.65	1.25
☐ 60	AS: Dennis Hull, Chi.	.35	.75
☐ 61	Pat Quinn,Stl.	.35	.75
☐ 62	Bill Goldsworthy, Min.	.35	.75
☐ **63**	**Frank Huck,Stl., RC**	**.35**	**.75**
☐ 64	Rogatien Vachon (G), L.A.	1.50	2.75
☐ 65	Gary Bergman, Det.	.35	.75
☐ 66	Bernie Parent (G), Pha.	3.50	7.00
☐ 67	Ed Westfall, NYI	.35	.75
☐ 68	Ivan Boldirev, Cal.	.35	.75
☐ 69	Don Tannahill, Van., LC	.35	.75
☐ 70	Gilbert Perreault, Buf.	4.00	8.00
☐ 71	Mike Pelyk, Tor.	.35	.75
☐ 72	Guy Lafleur, Mtl.	9.00	18.00
☐ 73	Jean Ratelle, NYR.	1.00	1.75
☐ **74**	**Gilles Gilbert (G), Bos., RC**	**1.75**	**3.50**
☐ 75	Greg Polis, Pgh.	.35	.75
☐ 76	Doug Jarrett, Chi.	.35	.75
☐ 77	Phil Myre (G), Atl.	.65	1.25
☐ 78	Buster Harvey, Min.	.35	.75
☐ 79	Jack Egers,Stl.	.35	.75
☐ 80	Terry Harper, L.A.	.35	.75
☐ **81**	**Bill Barber, Pha., RC**	**7.50**	**15.00**
☐ 82	Roy Edwards (G), Det., LC	.65	1.25
☐ 83	Brian Spencer, NYI	.35	.75
☐ 84	Reggie Leach, Cal.	.35	.75
☐ 85	Dave Keon, Tor.	1.00	1.75
☐ 86	Jim Schoenfeld, Buf.	1.50	2.75
☐ 87	Henri Richard, Mtl.	1.25	2.50
☐ 88	Rod Gilbert, NYR.	1.00	1.75
☐ 89	Don Marcotte, Bos.	.35	.75
☐ 90	AS: Tony Esposito (G), Chi.	4.50	9.00
☐ 91	Joe Watson, Pha.	.35	.75
☐ 92	Atlanta Flames	1.25	2.50
☐ 93	Boston Bruins	1.25	2.50
☐ 94	Buffalo Sabres	1.25	2.50
☐ 95	California Golden Seals	1.25	2.50
☐ 96	Chicago Blackhawks	1.25	2.50
☐ 97	Detroit Red Wings	1.25	2.50
☐ 98	Los Angeles Kings	1.25	2.50
☐ 99	Minnesota North Stars	1.25	2.50
☐ 100	Montréal Canadiens	1.25	2.50
☐ 101	New York Islanders	1.25	2.50
☐ 102	New York Rangers	1.25	2.50
☐ 103	Philadelphia Flyers	1.25	2.50
☐ 104	Pittsburgh Penguins	1.25	2.50
☐ 105	St. Louis Blues	1.25	2.50
☐ 106	Toronto Maple Leafs	1.25	2.50
☐ 107	Vancouver Canucks	1.25	2.50
☐ 108	Roger Crozier (G), Buf.	1.00	1.75
☐ 109	Tom Reid, Min.	.35	.75
☐ **110**	**Hilliard Graves, Cal., RC**	**.35**	**.75**
☐ 111	Don Lever, Van.	.35	.75
☐ 112	Jim Pappin, Chi.	.35	.75
☐ 113	Ron Schock, Pgh.	.35	.75
☐ 114	Gerry Desjardins (G), NYI	.65	1.25
☐ 115	Yvan Cournoyer, Mtl.	1.25	2.50
☐ 116	Checklist (1 - 198)	14.00	28.00
☐ 117	Bobby Leiter, Atl.	.35	.75
☐ 118	Ab DeMarco,Stl.	.35	.75
☐ 119	Doug Favell (G), Tor.	.65	1.25
☐ 120	AS: Phil Esposito, Bos.	4.50	8.50
☐ 121	Mike Robitaille, Buf.	.35	.75
☐ 122	Réal Lemieux, L.A., LC	.35	.75
☐ 123	Jim Neilson, NYR.	.35	.75
☐ 124	Tim Ecclestone, Det.	.35	.75
☐ 125	Jude Drouin, Min.	.35	.75
☐ 126	Gary Smith (G), Van.	.65	1.25
☐ 127	Walt McKechnie, Cal.	.35	.75
☐ 128	Lowell MacDonald, Pgh.	.35	.75
☐ 129	Dale Tallon, Chi.	.35	.75
☐ **130**	**Billy Harris, NYI, RC**	**.35**	**.75**
☐ 131	Randy Manery, Atl.	.35	.75
☐ 132	Darryl Sittler, Tor.	4.00	7.50
☐ 133	Ken Hodge, Bos.	.35	.75
☐ 134	Bob Plager,Stl.	.35	.75
☐ 135	Rick MacLeish, Pha.	1.50	3.00
☐ 136	Dennis Hextall, Min.	.35	.75
☐ 137	Jacques Laperrière, Mtl.	1.00	1.75
☐ 138	Butch Goring, L.A.	.50	1.00
☐ 139	René Robert, Buf.	.35	.75
☐ 140	Ed Giacomin (G), NYR.	1.75	3.25
☐ 141	Alex Delvecchio, Det., LC	1.25	2.25

☐ 142	Jocelyn Guevremont, Van.	.35	.75
☐ 143	Joey Johnston, Cal.	.35	.75
☐ 144	Bryan Watson, Pgh.	.35	.75
☐ 145	Stan Mikita, Chi.	3.50	7.00
☐ 146	Césare Maniago (G), Min.	.65	1.25
☐ 147	Craig Cameron, NYI.	.35	.75
☐ 148	Norm Ullman,Tor.	1.00	1.75
☐ 149	**Dave Schultz, Pha., RC**	**5.00**	**10.00**
☐ 150	AS: Bobby Orr, Bos.	18.00	35.00
☐ 151	Phil Roberto, Stl.	.35	.75
☐ 152	**Curt Bennett, Atl., RC**	**.35**	**.75**
☐ 153	Gilles Villemure (G), NYR.	.65	1.25
☐ 154	**Chuck Lefley, Mtl., RC**	**.35**	**.75**
☐ 155	Rick Martin, Buf.	1.00	1.75
☐ 156	Juha Widing, L.A.	.35	.75
☐ 157	Orland Kurtenbach, Van., LC	.35	.75
☐ 158	Bill Collins, Det.	.35	.75
☐ 159	**Bob Stewart, Ca.l, RC**	**.35**	**.75**
☐ 160	Syl Apps, Pgh.	.35	.75
☐ 161	Danny Grant, Min.	.35	.75
☐ 162	**Billy Smith (G), NYI., RC**	**14.00**	**28.00**
☐ 163	Brian Glennie, Tor.	.35	.75
☐ 164	Pit Martin, Chi.	.35	.75
☐ 165	Brad Park, NYR.	2.50	5.00
☐ 166	Wayne Cashman, Bos.	.65	1.25
☐ 167	Gary Dornhoefer, Pha.	.35	.75
☐ 168	**Steve Durbano, Stl., RC**	**1.00**	**1.75**
☐ 169	Jacques Richard, Atl.	.35	.75
☐ 170	AS: Guy Lapointe, Mtl.	.50	1.00
☐ 171	Jim Lorentz, Buf.	.35	.75
☐ 172	Bob Berry, L.A.	.35	.75
☐ 173	Dennis Kearns, Van.	.35	.75
☐ 174	Red Berenson, Det.	.35	.75
☐ 175	Gilles Meloche (G), Cal.	.65	1.25
☐ 176	Al McDonough, Pgh.	.35	.75
☐ 177	**Dennis O'Brien, Min., RC**	**.35**	**.75**
☐ 178	Germaine Gagnon, NYI.	.35	.75
☐ 179	Rick Kehoe, Tor.	.35	.75
☐ 180	AS: Bill White, Chi.	.35	.75
☐ 181	Vic Hadfield, NYR	.35	.75
☐ 182	Derek Sanderson, Bos.	1.75	3.50
☐ 183	André Dupont, Pha.	.35	.75
☐ 184	Gary Sabourin, Stl.	.35	.75
☐ 185	**Larry Romanchych, Atl., RC**	**.35**	**.75**
☐ 186	Pete Mahovlich, Mtl.	.35	.75
☐ 187	Dave Dryden (G), Buf.	.65	1.25
☐ 188	Gilles Marotte, L.A.	.35	.75
☐ 189	Bobby Lalonde, Van.	.35	.75
☐ 190	AS: Mickey Redmond, Det.	.65	1.25
☐ 191	Playoffs: Canadiens vs. Sabres	1.00	2.00
☐ 192	Playoffs: Flyers vs. North Stars	1.00	2.00
☐ 193	Playoffs: Blackhawks vs. Blues	1.00	2.00
☐ 194	Playoffs: Rangers vs. Bruins	1.00	2.00
☐ 195	Playoffs: Canadiens vs. Flyers	1.00	2.00
☐ 196	Playoffs: Blackhawks vs. Rangers	1.00	2.00
☐ 197	Playoffs: Canadiens vs. Blackhawks	1.00	2.00
☐ 198	Stanley Cup Champions : Montréal Canadiens	2.00	4.00

1973 - 74 WILLIAMS FINNISH STICKERS

A set of 324 stickers plus a collecting album for the World Championships and the Finnish National League. We have no pricing information on this set.

Card Size: 1 1/2" x 1 7/8"

Imprint:

No. Player

☐ 1 Vyatsjeslav Anisin, USSR
☐ 2 Alexander Bodunov, USSR
☐ 3 Alexander Gusev, USSR
☐ 4 Valeri Kharlamov, USSR
☐ 5 Alexander Yakushev, USSR
☐ 6 Juri Lebedev, USSR
☐ 7 Yuri Liapkin, USSR
☐ 8 Vladimir Lutchenko, USSR
☐ 9 Alexander Maltsev, USSR
☐ 10 Alexander Martiniuk, USSR
☐ 11 Boris Mikhailov, USSR
☐ 12 Evgeni Paladiev, USSR
☐ 13 Vladimir Petrov, USSR
☐ 14 Alexander Ragulin, USSR
☐ 15 Vladimir Shadrin, USSR
☐ 16 Alexander Sidelnikov, USSR
☐ 17 Vladislav Tretiak (G), USSR
☐ 18 Gennadi Bycankov, USSR
☐ 19 Valeri Vasiliev, USSR
☐ 20 Vladimir Vikulov, USSR
☐ 21 Alexander Volchkov, USSR
☐ 22 Christer Abrahamsson, Swe.
☐ 23 Thommy Abrahamsson, Swe.
☐ 24 Roland Bond, Swe.
☐ 25 Arne Carlsson, Swe.
☐ 26 Inge Hammarstrom, Swe.
☐ 27 Anders Hedberg, Swe.
☐ 28 Bjorn Johansson, Swe.
☐ 29 Stefan Karlsson, Swe.
☐ 30 Curt Larsson, Swe.
☐ 31 Tord Lundstrom, Swe.
☐ 32 William Lofqvist, Swe.
☐ 33 Ulf Nilsson, Swe.
☐ 34 Borje Salming, Swe.
☐ 35 LarsErik Sjoberg, Swe.
☐ 36 Ulf Sterner, Swe.
☐ 37 KarlJohan Sundqvist, Swe.
☐ 38 Dan Soderstrom, Swe.
☐ 39 Hakan Wickberg, Swe.
☐ 40 KjellArne Wicktsrom, Swe.
☐ 41 Dick Yderstrom, Swe.
☐ 42 Mats Ahlberg, Swe.
☐ 43 Peter Adamik, CSR.
☐ 44 Jiri Bubla, CSR.
☐ 45 Jiri Crha, CSR.
☐ 46 Richard Farda, CSR.
☐ 47 Ivan Hlinka, CSR.
☐ 48 Jiri Holecek, CSR.
☐ 49 Jaroslav Holik, CSR.
☐ 50 Jiri Holik, CSR.
☐ 51 Josef Horesovsky, CSR.
☐ 52 Jan Klapac, CSR.
☐ 53 Jiri Kochta, CSR.
☐ 54 Milan Kuzela, CSR.
☐ 55 Oldrich Machac, CSR.
☐ 56 Vladimir Martinec, CSR.
☐ 57 Vaclav Nedomansky, CSR.
☐ 58 Jiri Novak, CSR.
☐ 59 Josef Palecek, CSR.
☐ 60 Frantisek Pospisil, CSR.
☐ 61 Bohuslav Stastny, CSR.
☐ 62 Karel Vohralik, CSR.
☐ 63 Seppo Ahokainen, Fin.
☐ 64 Matti Keinonen, Fin.
☐ 65 Veli-Pekka Ketola, Fin.
☐ 66 Ilpo Koskela, Fin.
☐ 67 Ilpo Kuisma, Fin.
☐ 68 Pekka Kuusisto, Fin.
☐ 69 Henry Leppa, Fin.
☐ 70 Antti Leppanen, Fin.
☐ 71 Seppo Lindstrom, Fin.
☐ 72 Lauri Mononen, Fin.
☐ 73 Timo Nummelin, Fin.
☐ 74 Lalli Partinen, Fin.
☐ 75 Esa Peltonen, Fin.
☐ 76 Pekka Rautakallio, Fin.
☐ 77 Seppo Repo, Fin.
☐ 78 Heikki Riihiranta, Fin.
☐ 79 Timo Sutinen, Fin.
☐ 80 Juhani Tamminen, Fin.
☐ 81 Timo Turunen, Fin.
☐ 82 Jorma Valtonen, Fin.
☐ 83 Jorma Vehmanen, Fin.
☐ 84 Jouko Oystila, Fin.
☐ 85 Josef Batkiewicz, Pol.
☐ 86 Krzysztof Bialynicki, Pol.
☐ 87 Stefan Chowaniec, Pol.
☐ 88 Ludwik Czachovski, Pol.
☐ 89 Andrzej Czczepaniec, Pol.
☐ 90 Stanislav Fryzlewicz, Pol.
☐ 91 Robert Goralczyk, Pol.
☐ 92 Mieczyslaw Jaskiersk, Pol.i
☐ 93 Tadeusz Kacik, Pol.
☐ 94 Adam Kopczynski, Pol.
☐ 95 Valery Kosyl, Pol.
☐ 96 Tadeusz Obloj, Pol.
☐ 97 Jerzy Potz, Pol.
☐ 98 Andrzej Slowakiewicz, Pol.
☐ 99 Josef Slowakiewicz, Pol.
☐ 100 Jan Szeja, Pol.
☐ 101 Leszek Tokarz, Pol.
☐ 102 Wieslav Tokarz, Pol.
☐ 103 Henryk Vojtynek, Pol.
☐ 104 Walenty Zietara, Pol.
☐ 105 Pertti Arvaja, Jokerit
☐ 106 Olli J. Hietanen, Jokerit
☐ 107 Olli T. Hietanen, Jokerit
☐ 108 Pentti Hiiros, Jokerit
☐ 109 Eero Holopainen, Jokerit
☐ 110 Kari Kinnunen, Jokerit
☐ 111 Ilpo Koskela, Jokerit
☐ 112 Timo Kyntola, Jokerit
☐ 113 Henry Leppa, Jokerit
☐ 114 Jan Lindberg, Jokerit
☐ 115 Lauri Mononen, Jokerit
☐ 116 Mika Rajala, Jokerit
☐ 117 Pertti Nurmi, Jokerit
☐ 118 Jyrki Seivo, Jokerit
☐ 119 Jorma Siitarinen, Jokerit
☐ 120 Seppo Suoraniemi, Jokerit
☐ 121 Timo Sutinen, Jokerit
☐ 122 Timo Turunen, Jokerit
☐ 123 Jorma Valtonen, Jokerit
☐ 124 Seppo Vartiainen, Jokerit
☐ 125 Jouko Oystila, Jokerit
☐ 126 Juhani Bostrom, HIFK
☐ 127 Matti Hagman, HIFK
☐ 128 Kimmo Heino, HIFK
☐ 129 Jorma Immonen, HIFK
☐ 130 Pentti Karlsson, HIFK
☐ 131 Mauri Kaukokari, HIFK
☐ 132 Jarmo Koivunen, HIFK
☐ 133 Vaino Kolkka, HIFK
☐ 134 Harri Linnonmaa, HIFK
☐ 135 Jaakko Marttinen, HIFK
☐ 136 Matti Murto, HIFK
☐ 137 Lalli Partinen, HIFK
☐ 138 Esa Peltonen, HIFK
☐ 139 Juha Rantasila, HIFK
☐ 140 Heikki Riihiranta, HIFK
☐ 141 Jorma Rikala, HIFK
☐ 142 Tommi Salmelainen, HIFK
☐ 143 Henry Saleva, HIFK
☐ 144 Juhani Tamminen, HIFK
☐ 145 Jorma Thusberg, HIFK
☐ 146 Jorma Virtanen, HIFK
☐ 147 Matti Vaisanen, HIFK
☐ 148 Stig Wetzell, HIFK
☐ 149 Jukka Alkula, Tappara
☐ 150 Pertti Ansakorpi, Tappara
☐ 151 Hannu Haapalainen, Tappara
☐ 152 Martti Jarkko, Tappara
☐ 153 Keijo Jarvinen, Tappara
☐ 154 Pertti Koivulahti, Tappara
☐ 155 Ilpo Kuisma, Tappara
☐ 156 Antero Lehtonen, Tappara
☐ 157 Antti Leppanen, Tappara
☐ 158 Lasse Litma, Tappara
☐ 159 Pekka Marjamaki, Tappara
☐ 160 Mikko Mynttinen, Tappara
☐ 161 Pekka Makinen, Tappara
☐ 162 Seppo I. Makinen, Tappara
☐ 163 Seppo S. Makinen, Tappara
☐ 164 Keijo Mannisto, Tappara
☐ 165 Antti Perttula, Tappara
☐ 166 Tuomo Rautiainen, Tappara
☐ 167 Jorma Saarikorpi, Tappara
☐ 168 Juha Silvennoinen, Tappara
☐ 169 Jorma Siren, Tappara
☐ 170 Raimo Suoniemi, Tappara
☐ 171 Pertti Valkeapaa, Tappara
☐ 172 Sakari Ahlberg, Ilves
☐ 173 Seppo Ahokainen, Ilves
☐ 174 Jorma Aro, Ilves
☐ 175 Esko Eriksson, Ilves
☐ 176 Markku Hakanen, Ilves
☐ 177 Reijo Hakanen, Ilves

☐ 178 Martti Helle, Ilves
☐ 179 Erkki Jarvinen, Ilves
☐ 180 Jorma Kallio, Ilves
☐ 181 Erkki Kesalainen, Ilves
☐ 182 Pekka Kuusisto, Ilves
☐ 183 Pekka Leimu, Ilves
☐ 184 Jukka Mattila, Ilves
☐ 185 Esko Makinen, Ilves
☐ 186 Lasse Oksanen, Ilves
☐ 187 Kari Palooja, Ilves
☐ 188 Jorma Peltonen, Ilves
☐ 189 Pekka Rampa, Ilves
☐ 190 Heikki Salminen, Ilves
☐ 191 Tuomo Sillman, Ilves
☐ 192 Veikko Suominen, Ilves
☐ 193 Tapio Virhimo, Ilves
☐ 194 Juhani Aaltonen, HJK
☐ 195 Bjorn Herbert, HJK
☐ 196 Hannu Kapanen, HJK
☐ 197 Matti Keinonen, HJK
☐ 198 Lasse Kiili, HJK
☐ 199 Matti Koskinen, HJK
☐ 200 Martti Kuokkanen, HJK
☐ 201 Urpo Kuukauppi, HJK
☐ 202 Seppo Laakkio, HJK
☐ 203 Timo Lahtinen, HJK
☐ 204 Juhani Laine, HJK
☐ 205 Heikki Leppik, HJK
☐ 206 Osmo Lotjonen, HJK
☐ 207 Kyosti Majava, HJK
☐ 208 Keijo Puhakka, HJK
☐ 209 Antti Ravi, HJK
☐ 210 Seppo Repo, HJK
☐ 211 Timo Saari, HJK
☐ 212 Arto Siissala, HJK
☐ 213 Jorma Vehmanen, HJK
☐ 214 Pentti Viitanen, HJK
☐ 215 Leo Aikas, HJK
☐ 216 Raine Heinonen, Koovee
☐ 217 Vladimir Jursinov, Koovee
☐ 218 JukkaPekka Jarvenpaa, Koovee
☐ 219 Pertti Jarvenpaa, Koovee
☐ 220 Heimo Keinonen, Koovee
☐ 221 Seppo Kettunen, Koovee
☐ 222 Veikko Kirveskoski, Koovee
☐ 223 Reijo Laksola, Koovee
☐ 224 Raimo Majapuro, Koovee
☐ 225 Markku Moisio, Koovee
☐ 226 Heikki Nurmi, Koovee
☐ 227 Seppo Nurmi, Koovee
☐ 228 Oiva Oijennus, Koovee
☐ 229 Esko Rantanen, Koovee
☐ 230 Matti Rautiainen, Koovee
☐ 231 Juhani Ruohonen, Koovee
☐ 232 Mikko Raikkonen, Koovee
☐ 233 Lauri Salomaa, Koovee
☐ 234 Veikko Savolainen, Koovee
☐ 235 Leo Seppanen, Koovee
☐ 236 Veikko Seppanen, Koovee
☐ 237 Pekka Uitus, Koovee
☐ 238 Kari Viitalahti, Koovee
☐ 239 Jorma Vilen, Koovee
☐ 240 Asko Ahonen, Assat Pori
☐ 241 Tapio Flinck, Assat Pori
☐ 242 Matti Hakanen, Assat Pori
☐ 243 Antti Heikkila, Assat Pori
☐ 244 Reijo Heinonen, Assat Pori
☐ 245 Jaakko Honkanen, Assat Pori
☐ 246 Jari Kaski, Assat Pori
☐ 247 VeliPekka Ketola, Assat Pori
☐ 248 Raimo Kilpio, Assat Pori
☐ 249 Tapio Koskinen, Assat Pori
☐ 250 Jarkko Levonen, Assat Pori
☐ 251 Kaj Matalamaki, Assat Pori
☐ 252 Pertti Makela, Assat Pori
☐ 253 Jaakko Niemi, Assat Pori
☐ 254 Hannu Pulkkinen, Assat Pori
☐ 255 Pekka Rautakallio, Assat Pori
☐ 256 Markku Riihimaki, Assat Pori
☐ 257 Anto Virtanen, Assat Pori
☐ 258 Erkki Vakiparta, Assat Pori
☐ 259 Pertti Hasanen, Turun Toverit
☐ 260 Rainer Holmroos, Turun Toverit
☐ 261 Kari Johansson, Turun Toverit
☐ 262 Arto Kaunonen, Turun Toverit
☐ 263 Timo Kokkonen, Turun Toverit
☐ 264 Reijo Leppanen, Turun Toverit
☐ 265 Seppo Lindstrom, Turun Toverit
☐ 266 Hannu Luojola, Turun Toverit
☐ 267 Hannu Niittoaho, Turun Toverit
☐ 268 Reijo Paksal, Turun Toverit
☐ 269 Seppo Parikka, Turun Toverit
☐ 270 Jarmo Rantanen, Turun Toverit
☐ 271 Kari Hyokki, Turun Toverit
☐ 272 Kari Salonen, Turun Toverit
☐ 273 Tapani Sura, Turun Toverit
☐ 274 Kari Torkkel, Turun Toverit
☐ 275 Risto Vainio, Turun Toverit
☐ 276 Pentti Vihanto, Turun Toverit
☐ 277 Urpo Ylonen, Turun Toverit
☐ 278 Lars Ellfolk, Turun Palloseura
☐ 279 Kari Horkko, Turun Palloseura
☐ 280 Hannu Jortikka, Turun Palloseura
☐ 281 Eero Juntunen, Turun Palloseura
☐ 282 Lauri Jamsen, Turun Palloseura
☐ 283 Jari Kapanen, Turun Palloseura
☐ 284 Kari Kauppila, Turun Palloseura
☐ 285 Matti Kauppila, Turun Palloseura
☐ 286 Jukka Koskilahti, Turun Palloseura
☐ 287 Jukka Koivu, Turun Palloseura
☐ 288 Ilkka Laaksonen, Turun Palloseura
☐ 289 Robert Lamoureux, Turun Palloseura
☐ 290 Hannu Lunden, Turun Palloseura
☐ 291 Ilkka Mesikammen, Turun Palloseura
☐ 292 Timo Nummelin, Turun Palloseura
☐ 293 Timo Nurminen, Turun Palloseura
☐ 294 Rauli Ottila, Turun Palloseura
☐ 295 Matti Rautee, Turun Palloseura
☐ 296 Pekka Rautee, Turun Palloseura
☐ 297 Jari Rosberg, Turun Palloseura
☐ 298 Tarmo Saarni, Turun Palloseura
☐ 299 Asko Salminen, Turun Palloseura
☐ 300 Jouni Samuli, Turun Palloseura
☐ 301 Rauli Tammelin, Turun Palloseura
☐ 302 Veijo Wahlsten, Turun Palloseura
☐ 303 Bengt Wilenius, Turun Palloseura
☐ 304 Denis Bavaudin, Rauman Lukko
☐ 305 Mikko Erholm, Rauman Lukko
☐ 306 Matti Forss, Rauman Lukko
☐ 307 Esa Hakkarainen, Rauman Lukko
☐ 308 Veikko Ihalainen, Rauman Lukko
☐ 309 Esa Isaksson, Rauman Lukko
☐ 310 Juhani Jylha, Rauman Lukko
☐ 311 Heikki Kauhanen, Rauman Lukko
☐ 312 Jari Laiho, Rauman Lukko
☐ 313 Arto Laine, Rauman Lukko
☐ 314 Jouni Peltonen, Rauman Lukko
☐ 315 Jouni Rinne, Rauman Lukko
☐ 316 Kai Rosvall, Rauman Lukko
☐ 317 Seppo Santala, Rauman Lukko
☐ 318 Jari Sarronlahti, Rauman Lukko
☐ 319 Matti Saurio, Rauman Lukko
☐ 320 Ari Sjoman, Rauman Lukko
☐ 321 Erkki Sundelin, Rauman Lukko
☐ 322 Ismo Villa, Rauman Lukko
☐ 323 Mikko Ylaja, Rauman Lukko
☐ 324 Veijo Ylonen, Rauman Lukko

1974 HELLAS MM - JENKKI

A set of 120 cards plus a collecting album issued by Hellas (Leaf) for the World Championships. We have no pricing information on this set.
Card Size: 2 1/8" x 3 1/8"
Imprint:

	No.	Player
☐	1	Sakari Ahlberg, Fin.
☐	2	Seppo Ahokainen, Fin.
☐	3	Jukka Alkula, Fin.
☐	4	Jorma Aro, Fin.
☐	5	Hannu Haapalainen, Fin.
☐	6	VeliPekka Ketola, Fin.
☐	7	Tapio Koskinen, Fin.
☐	8	Henry Leppa, Fin.
☐	9	Antti Leppanen, Fin.
☐	10	Reijo Leppanen, Fin.
☐	11	Pekka Marjamaki, Fin.
☐	12	Matti Murto, Fin.
☐	13	Esa Peltonen, Fin.
☐	14	Pekka Rautakallio, Fin.
☐	15	Leo Seppanen, Fin.
☐	16	Juha Silvennoinen, Fin.
☐	17	Raimo Suoniemi, Fin.
☐	18	Seppo Suoraniemi, Fin.
☐	19	Timo Sutinen, Fin.
☐	20	Juhani Tamminen, Fin.
☐	21	Pertti Valkeapaa, Fin.
☐	22	Christer Abrahamsson, Swe.
☐	23	Thommie Bergman, Swe.
☐	24	Roland Bond, Swe.
☐	25	Anders Hedberg, Swe.
☐	26	Bjorn Johansson, Swe.
☐	27	Stefan Karlsson, Swe.
☐	28	Mats Lind, Swe.
☐	29	Tord Lundstrom, Swe.
☐	30	William Lofqvist, Swe.
☐	31	Ulf Nilsson, Swe.
☐	32	Bjorn Palmqvist, Swe.
☐	33	Hakan Pettersson, Swe.
☐	34	LarsErik Sjoberg, Swe.
☐	35	Ulf Sterner, Swe.
☐	36	KarlJohan Sundqvist, Swe.
☐	37	Hakan Wickberg, Swe.
☐	38	KjellArne Wickstrom, Swe.
☐	39	Dick Yderstrom, Swe.
☐	40	Mats Ahlberg, Swe.
☐	41	Stig Ostling, Swe.
☐	42	Vjatseslav Anisin, USSR
☐	43	Aleksandr Bodunov, USSR
☐	44	Aleksandr Gusev, USSR
☐	45	Valeri Kharlamov, USSR
☐	46	Alexander Yakushev, USSR
☐	47	Yuri Liapkin, USSR
☐	48	Vladimir Lutshenko, USSR
☐	49	Alexander Maltsev, USSR
☐	50	Alexander Martiniuk, USSR
☐	51	Boris Mikhailov, USSR
☐	52	Evgeny Paladiev, USSR
☐	53	Vladimir Petrov, USSR
☐	54	Alexander Ragulin, USSR
☐	55	Vladimir Shadrin, USSR
☐	56	Alexander Sidelnikov, USSR
☐	57	Vladimir Tretiak, USSR
☐	58	Gennadi Tsicankov, USSR
☐	59	Valeri Vasiliev, USSR
☐	60	Vladimir Vikulov, USSR
☐	61	Alexander Voltshkov, USSR
☐	62	Julij Blinov, USSR
☐	63	Vladimir Sepovalov, USSR
☐	64	Josef Horesovsky, CSR.
☐	65	Peter Adamik, CSR.
☐	66	Vladimir Bednar, CSR.
☐	67	Jiri Bubla, CSR.
☐	68	Richard Farda, CSR.
☐	69	Julius Haas, CSR.
☐	70	Ivan Hlinka, CSR.
☐	71	Jiri Holecek, CSR.
☐	72	Jaroslav Holik, CSR.
☐	73	Jiri Holik, CSR.
☐	74	Jan Klapac, CSR.
☐	75	Jiri Kochta, CSR.
☐	76	Milan Kuzela, CSR.
☐	77	Oldrich Machac, CSR.
☐	78	Vladimir Martinec, CSR.
☐	79	Vaclav Nedomansky, CSR.
☐	80	Josef Palecek, CSR.
☐	81	Frantisek Pospisil, CSR.
☐	82	Bohuslav Stastny, CSR.
☐	83	Rudolf Tajcnar, CSR.
☐	84	Karel Vohralik, CSR.

	No.	Player
☐	85	Jerzy Potz, Pol.
☐	86	Andrzej Slowakiewicz, Pol.
☐	87	Josef Slowakiewicz, Pol.
☐	88	Leszek Tokarz, Pol.
☐	89	Wieslav Tokarz, Pol.
☐	90	Henryk Vojtynek, Pol.
☐	91	Walenty Zietara, Pol.
☐	92	Josef Batkiewicz, Pol.
☐	93	Stefan Chowaniec, Pol.
☐	94	Ludvik Czachovski, Pol.
☐	95	Andrzej Czczepaniec, Pol.
☐	96	Robert Goralczyk, Pol.
☐	97	Mieczyslaw Jaskierski, Pol.
☐	98	Tadeusz Kacik, Pol.
☐	99	Adam Kopczynski, Pol.
☐	100	Valery Kosyl, Pol.
☐	101	Tadeusz Obloj, Pol.
☐	102	Joachim Stasche, DDR.
☐	103	Roland Peters, DDR.
☐	104	Dietmar Peters, DDR.
☐	105	Bernd Karrenbauer, DDR.
☐	106	Peter Prusa, DDR.
☐	107	Rainer Patschinski, DDR.
☐	108	Hartmut Nickel, DDR.
☐	109	Dieter Dewitz, DDR.
☐	110	Harald Felber, DDR.
☐	111	Joachim Hurbanek, DDR.
☐	112	Wolfgang Fischer, DDR.
☐	113	Frank Braun, DDR.
☐	114	Dieter Huscfo, DDR.
☐	115	Ruediger Hoack, DDR.
☐	116	Dieter Simon, DDR.
☐	117	Hartwig Schur, DDR.
☐	118	Jochen Philip, DDR.
☐	119	Rolf Bielas, DDR.
☐	120	Peter Slapke, DDR.

1974 HOWIE MEEKER STOP ACTION PHOTOS

Little is known about how these were distributed or how many were issued. A youngster is shown in a sequence of photos performing the exercise on the card front. Hoiwe Meeker is pictured on the back with an explanation of the drill.

Card Size: 3 1/2" x 5 1/2"

Face: Black and white photos, Bilingual title, Facsimile Meeker signature in blue ink, white border

Back: Title and explanation of drill, photo of Howie Meeker

Imprint: Copyright 1974 © All rights reserved Downie Advertising Limited

	Player	EX	EX-NRMT
☐	Kick Three Times		
☐	Russian Exercise		
☐	Skating Hips Down		

1974 SCOTIA BANK GO CANADA POSTCARD

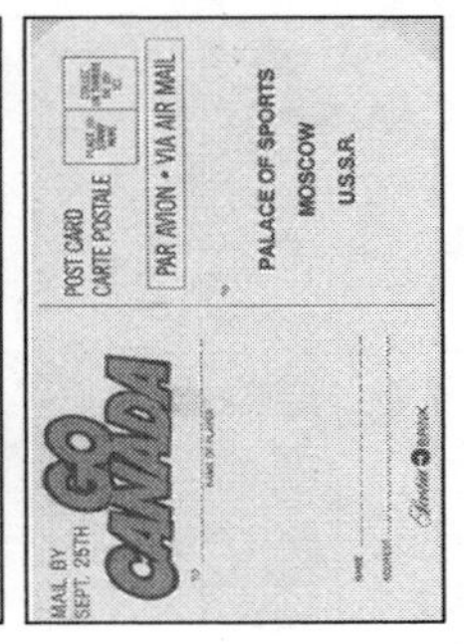

Postcard Size: 3 1/2" x 5 3/4"

Face: Four colour, white border

Back: Red and black on card stock

Imprint: Scotia Bank

	Player	EX	NRMT
☐	Team Canada	5.00	10.00

1974 SEMIC STICKERS

Sticker Size:

Imprint:

		EX	NRMT
Complete Set (100 cards):		**50.00**	**100.00**
Common Player:		**.35**	**.75**

	No.	Player	EX	NRMT
☐	1	Christer Abrahamsson, Swe.	1.00	2.00
☐	2	William Löfqvist, Swe.	.35	.75
☐	3	Arne Carlsson, Swe.	.35	.75
☐	4	Lars-Erik Sjöberg, Swe.	1.25	2.50
☐	5	Björn Johansson, Swe.	.35	.75
☐	6	Thommy Abrahamsson, Swe.	1.00	2.00
☐	7	Karl-Johan Sundqvist, Swe.	.35	.75
☐	8	Ulf Nilsson, Swe.	3.50	7.00
☐	9	Håkan Wickberg, Swe.	.35	.75
☐	10	Dan Söderström, Swe.	.35	.75
☐	11	Mats Åhlberg, Swe.	.35	.75
☐	12	Anders Hedberg, Swe.	3.00	6.00
☐	13	Dick Yderström, Swe.	.35	.75
☐	14	Stefan Karlssonn, Swe.	.35	.75
☐	15	Roland Bond, Swe.	.35	.75
☐	16	Kjell-Rune Milton, Swe.	.35	.75
☐	17	Willy Lindström, Swe.	2.00	4.00
☐	18	Mats Waltin, Swe.	.35	.75
☐	19	Lars-Göran Nilsson, Swe.	.35	.75
☐	20	Björn Palmqvist, Swe.	.35	.75
☐	21	Stig-Göran Johansson, Swe.	.35	.75
☐	22	Bo Berggren, Swe.	.35	.75
☐	23	Dan Labraaten, Swe.	1.00	2.00
☐	24	Curt Larsson, Swe.	.35	.75
☐	25	Mats Lindh, Swe.	.35	.75
☐	26	Vladislav Tretiak, USSR	7.50	15.00
☐	27	Alexander Ragulin, USSR	1.25	2.50
☐	28	Vladimir Lutchenko, USSR	.35	.75
☐	29	Gennadij Tsycankov, USSR	.35	.75
☐	30	Alexander Gusev, USSR	.35	.75
☐	31	Evgeny Poladiev, USSR	.35	.75
☐	32	Yuri Liapkin, USSR	.35	.75
☐	33	Boris Mikhailov, USSR	2.00	4.00
☐	34	Valeri Kharlamov, USSR	4.50	9.00
☐	35	Vladimir Petrov, USSR	1.50	3.00
☐	36	Alexander Maltsev, USSR	2.00	4.00
☐	37	Vladimir Sjadrin, USSR	.35	.75
☐	38	Alexander Yakushev, USSR	3.50	7.00
☐	39	Alexander Martiniuk, USSR	.35	.75
☐	40	Yuri Lebedev, USSR	.35	.75
☐	41	Alexander Bodunov, USSR	.35	.75
☐	42	Anatoli Firsov, USSR	1.00	2.00
☐	43	Vitali Davydov, USSR	.35	.75
☐	44	Vjateslav Starsjinov, USSR	.35	.75
☐	45	Viktor Kuzkin, USSR	.35	.75
☐	46	Igor Romitjevskij, USSR	.35	.75
☐	47	Evgeny Zimin, USSR	.35	.75
☐	48	Evgeny Mishakov, USSR	.35	.75
☐	49	Vladimir Vikulov, USSR	.35	.75
☐	50	Viktor Konovalenko, USSR	.35	.75
☐	51	Jiri Holecek, CSR.	1.00	2.00
☐	52	Frantisek Pospjsil, CSR.	.35	.75
☐	53	Jiri Bubla, CSR.	1.00	2.00
☐	54	Josef Horesovs, CSR.	.35	.75
☐	55	Oldrich Machac, CSR.	.35	.75
☐	56	Vladimir Martinec, CSR.	.35	.75
☐	57	Vaclav Nedomansky, CSR.	1.00	2.00
☐	58	Jiri Kochta, CSR.	.35	.75
☐	59	Milan Novy, CSR.	1.50	3.00
☐	60	Jaroslav Holik, CSR.	.35	.75
☐	61	Jiri Holik, CSR.	.35	.75
☐	62	Jiri Klapac, CSR.	.35	.75
☐	63	Richard Farda, CSR.	.35	.75
☐	64	Bohuslav Stastny, CSR.	.35	.75
☐	65	Jiri Novak, CSR.	.35	.75
☐	66	Ivan Hlinka, CSR.	1.00	2.00
☐	67	Jan Suchy, CSR.	.35	.75
☐	68	Vladimir Bednar, CSR.	.35	.75
☐	69	Rudolf Tajcnar, CSR.	.35	.75
☐	70	Josef Cerny, CSR.	.35	.75
☐	71	Jan Haveln, CSR.	.35	.75
☐	72	Marcel Sakac, CSR.	.35	.75
☐	73	Frantisek Pancharek, CSR.	.35	.75
☐	74	Bedrich Brunchk, CSR.	.35	.75
☐	75	Edvard Novak, CSR.	.35	.75
☐	76	Jorma Valtonen, Fin.	.35	.75
☐	77	Seppo Lindström, Fin.	.35	.75
☐	78	Pekka Marjamäki, Fin.	.35	.75
☐	79	Pekka Rautakallio, Fin.	1.00	2.00
☐	80	Heikki Riihiranta, Fin.	1.00	2.00
☐	81	Seppo Suoraniemi, Fin.	.35	.75
☐	82	Jouko Öystiiä, Fin.	.35	.75
☐	83	Veli-Pekka Ketola, Fin.	1.25	2.50
☐	84	Henry Leppä, Fin.	.35	.75
☐	85	Harri Linnonmaa, Fin.	.35	.75
☐	86	Matti Murto, Fin.	.35	.75
☐	87	Lasse Oksanen, Fin.	.35	.75
☐	88	Esa Peltonen, Fin.	.35	.75
☐	89	Seppo Repo, Fin.	.35	.75
☐	90	Raimo Suoniemi, Fin.	.35	.75
☐	91	Time Sutinen, Fin.	.35	.75
☐	92	Juhani Tamminen, Fin.	.35	.75
☐	93	Leo Seppanen, Fin.	.35	.75
☐	94	Hannu Haapalainen, Fin.	.35	.75
☐	95	Pertti Valkeapää, Fin.	.35	.75
☐	96	Sakari Ahlberg, Fin.	.35	.75
☐	97	Antti Leppänen, Fin.	.35	.75
☐	98	Kalevi Numminen, Fin.	.35	.75
☐	99	Lauri Mononen, Fin.	.35	.75
☐	100	Ilpo Koskela , Fin.	.35	.75

1974 - 75 LIPTON SOUP

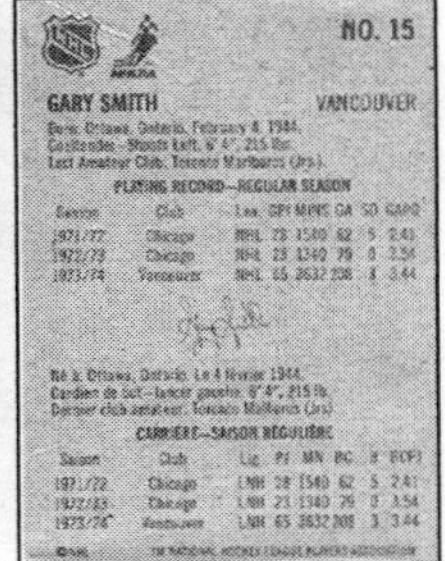

This set was issued as two cards per back panel of Lipton Soup packages.

Note - a 50% premium applies to cards in 2-card panels.

Card Size: 2 1/4" x 3 3/8"

Face: Four colour, white border; Name, Team

Back: Black on buff card stock; name, Number, Team, Resume, Bilingual, Facsimile signature
Imprint: NHL TM NATIONAL HOCKEY LEAGUE PLAYERS ASSOCIATION

Complete Set (51 cards):		**300.00**
Common Player:		**3.50**

	No.	Player	NRMT-MT
☐	1	Norm Ullman, Tor.	12.00
☐	2	Gilbert Perreault, Buf.	13.00
☐	3	Darryl Sittler, Tor.	13.00
☐	4	Jean Paul Parise, Min.	3.50
☐	5	Garry Unger, Stl.	3.50
☐	6	Ron Ellis, Tor.	3.50
☐	7	Rogatien Vachon (G), L.A.	8.00
☐	8	Bobby Orr, Bos.	65.00
☐	9	Wayne Cashman, Bos.	3.50
☐	10	Brad Park, NYR.	10.00
☐	11	Serge Savard, Mtl.	8.50
☐	12	Walt Tkaczuk, NYR.	3.50
☐	13	Yvan Cournoyer, Mtl.	10.00
☐	14	André Boudrias, Van.	3.50
☐	15	Gary Smith (G), Van.	5.00
☐	16	Guy Lapointe, Mtl.	8.50
☐	17	Dennis Hull, Chi.	3.50
☐	18	Bernie Parent (G), Pha.	13.00
☐	19	Ken Dryden (G), Mtl.	40.00
☐	20	Rick MacLeish, Pha.	5.00
☐	21	Bobby Clarke, Pha.	14.00
☐	22	Dale Tallon, Chi.	3.50
☐	23	Jim McKenny, Tor.	3.50
☐	24	René Robert, Buf.	3.50
☐	25	Red Berenson, Det.	3.50
☐	26	Ed Giacomin (G), NYR.	13.00
☐	27	Césare Maniago (G), Min.	5.00
☐	28	Ken Hodge., Bos.	3.50
☐	29	Gregg Sheppard, Bos.	3.50
☐	30	Dave Schultz, Pha.	8.00
☐	31	Bill Barber, Pha.	12.00
☐	32	Henry Boucha, Det.	3.50
☐	33	Richard Martin, Buf.	6.00
☐	34	Steve Vickers, NYR.	3.50
☐	35	Billy Harris, NYI.	3.50
☐	36	Jim Pappin, Chi., Err. (Papin)	3.50
☐	37	Pit Martin, Chi.	3.50
☐	38	Jacques Lemaire, Mtl.	11.00
☐	39	Pete Mahovlich, Mtl.	3.50
☐	40	Rod Gilbert, NYR.	10.00
☐	41	Borje Salming, Tor., Horizontal picture	12.00
☐	41	Borje Salming, Tor., Vertical picture	12.00
☐	42	Pete Stemkowski, NYR.	3.50
☐	43	Ron Schock, Pgh.	3.50
☐	44	Dan Bouchard (G), Atl.	5.00
☐	45	Tony Esposito (G), Chi.	15.00
☐	46	Craig Patrick, Cgy.	3.50
☐	47	Ed Westfall, NYI.	3.50
☐	48	Jocelyn Guevremont, Van.	3.50
☐	49	Syl Apps, Pgh.	3.50
☐	50	Dave Keon, Tor.	12.00

1974 - 75 LOBLAWS NHL ACTION PLAYERS

Stamp Size: 1 11/16" x 2 1/4"
Face: Four colour, white border; Jersey number, Name, Position, Team
Back: 1. Black print on paper stock
2. Black with white print on paper stock; Loblaws logo
3. Blank
Imprint: Printed in U.S.A. or Printed in Canada

Complete Set (324 stamps):		**250.00**
Common Player:		**.50**
Album:		**35.00**

	Player	NRMT-MT
ATLANTA FLAMES		
☐	Curt Bennett	.50
☐	Dan Bouchard (G)	1.00
☐	Arnie Brown	.50
☐	Jerry Byers	.50
☐	Rey Comeau	.50
☐	Fred (Buster) Harvey	.50
☐	Bobby Leiter	.50
☐	Jean Lemieux	.50
☐	Tom Lysiak	.50
☐	Randy Manery	.50
☐	Keith McCreary	.50
☐	Bob Murray	.50
☐	Phil Myre (G)	1.00
☐	Noel Price	.50
☐	Pat Quinn	1.00
☐	Jacques Richard	.50
☐	Larry Romanchych	.50
☐	Eric Vail	.50
BOSTON BRUINS		
☐	Ross Brooks (G)	1.00
☐	John Bucyk	1.75
☐	Wayne Cashman	.50
☐	Darryl Edestrand	.50
☐	Phil Esposito	4.00
☐	Dave Forbes	.50
☐	Gilles Gilbert (G)	1.00
☐	Ken Hodge	.50
☐	Don Marcotte	.50
☐	Walt McKechnie	.50
☐	Terry O'Reilly	.50
☐	Bobby Orr	22.00
☐	André Savard	.50
☐	Bobby Schmautz	.50
☐	Gregg Sheppard	.50
☐	Al Sims	.50
☐	Dallas Smith	.50
☐	Carol Vadnais	.50
BUFFALO SABRES		
☐	Gary Bromley (G)	1.00
☐	Larry Carrière	.50
☐	Roger Crozier (G)	1.00
☐	Rick Dudley	.50
☐	Lee Fogolin	.50
☐	Norm Gratton	.50
☐	Jerry Korab	.50
☐	Jim Lorentz	.50
☐	Don Luce	.50
☐	Richard Martin	1.00
☐	Gerry Meehan	.50
☐	Larry Mickey	.50
☐	Gilbert Perreault	3.50
☐	Craig Ramsay	.50
☐	René Robert	.50
☐	Mike Robitaille	.50
☐	Jim Schoenfeld	.50
☐	Brian Spencer	.50
CALIFORNIA GOLDEN SEALS		
☐	Bruce Affleck	.50
☐	Mike Christie	.50
☐	Len Frig	.50
☐	Stan Gilbertson	.50
☐	Rick Hampton	.50
☐	David Hrechkosy	.50
☐	Ron Huston	.50
☐	Joseph Johnston	.50
☐	Wayne King	.50
☐	Al MacAdam	.50
☐	Ted McAneely	.50
☐	Gilles Meloche (G)	1.00
☐	Jim Neilson	.50
☐	Larry Patey	.50
☐	Craig Patrick	1.00
☐	Bob Stewart	.50
☐	Stan Weir	.50
☐	Larry Wright	.50
CHICAGO BLACKHAWKS		
☐	Ivan Boldirev	.50
☐	J.P. Bordeleau	.50
☐	Tony Esposito (G)	3.25
☐	Germain Gagnon	.50
☐	Dennis Hull	.50
☐	Doug Jarrett	.50
☐	Cliff Koroll	.50
☐	Keith Magnuson	.50
☐	Chico Maki	.50
☐	John Marks	.50
☐	Pit Martin	.50
☐	Stan Mikita	3.50
☐	Jim Pappin	.50
☐	Dick Redmond	.50
☐	Darcy Rota	.50
☐	Phil Russell	.50
☐	Dale Tallon	.50
☐	Bill White	.50
DETROIT RED WINGS		
☐	Red Berenson	.50
☐	Thommie Bergman	.50
☐	Guy Charron	.50
☐	Marcel Dionne	4.00
☐	Danny Grant	.50
☐	Doug Grant (G)	.50
☐	Jean Hamel	.50
☐	Bill Hogaboam	.50
☐	Pierre Jarry	.50
☐	Nick Libett	.50
☐	Bill Lochead	.50
☐	Jack Lynch	.50
☐	Hank Nowak	.50
☐	Nelson Pyatt	.50
☐	Mickey Redmond	1.00
☐	Doug Roberts	.50
☐	Jim Rutherford (G)	1.00
☐	Bryan Watson	.50
KANSAS CITY SCOUTS		
☐	Robin Burns	.50
☐	Gary Coalter	.50
☐	Gary Croteau	.50
☐	Chris Evans	.50
☐	Ed Gilbert	.50
☐	Doug Horbul	.50
☐	Dave Hudson	.50
☐	Brent Hughes	.50
☐	Bryan Lefley	.50
☐	Richard Lemieux	.50
☐	Pete McDuffe (G)	1.00
☐	Simon Nolet	.50
☐	Dennis Patterson	.50
☐	Michel Plasse (G)	1.00
☐	Lynn Powis	.50
☐	Randy Rota	.50
☐	Ted Snell	.50
☐	John Wright	.50
LOS ANGELES KINGS		
☐	Bob Berry	.50
☐	Gene Carr	.50
☐	Mike Corrigan	.50
☐	Gary Edwards (G)	1.00
☐	Butch Goring	.50
☐	Terry Harper	.50
☐	Dave Hutchison	.50
☐	Sheldon Kannegiesser	.50
☐	Neil Komadoski	.50
☐	Don Kozak	.50
☐	Dan Maloney	.50
☐	Bob Murdoch	.50
☐	Mike Murphy	1.00
☐	Bob Nevin	.50
☐	Frank St. Marseille	.50
☐	Rogatien Vachon (G)	1.75
☐	Juha Widing	.50
☐	Tom Williams	.50
MINNESOTA NORTH STARS		
☐	Chris Ahrens	.50
☐	Fred Barrett	.50
☐	Gary Bergman	.50
☐	Henry Boucha	.50
☐	Jude Drouin	.50
☐	Blake Dunlop	.50
☐	Barry Gibbs	.50
☐	Bill Goldsworthy	.50
☐	Dennis Hextall	.50
☐	Césare Maniago (G)	1.00

	Player	
☐	Don Martineau	.50
☐	Lou Nanne	.50
☐	Dennis O'Brien	.50
☐	Murray Oliver	.50
☐	Jean Paul Parise	.50
☐	Tom Reid	.50
☐	Fern Rivard (G)	1.00
☐	Fred Stanfield	.50

MONTRÉAL CANADIENS

	Player	
☐	Pierre Bouchard	.50
☐	Yvan Cournoyer	2.50
☐	Ken Dryden (G)	18.00
☐	Guy Lafleur	9.00
☐	Yvon Lambert	.50
☐	Jacques Laperrière	1.50
☐	Guy Lapointe	1.50
☐	Michel Larocque (G)	1.00
☐	Claude Larose	.50
☐	Chuck Lefley	.50
☐	Jacques Lemaire	2.00
☐	Pete Mahovlich	.50
☐	Henri Richard	2.00
☐	Jim Roberts	.50
☐	Larry Robinson	4.50
☐	Serge Savard	1.50
☐	Steve Shutt	2.75
☐	Murray Wilson	.50

NEW YORK ISLANDERS

	Player	
☐	Craig Cameron	.50
☐	Clark Gillies	.50
☐	Billy Harris	.50
☐	Gerry Hart	.50
☐	Lorne Henning	.50
☐	Ernie Hicke	.50
☐	Garry Howatt	.50
☐	Dave Lewis	.50
☐	Billy MacMillan	.50
☐	Bert Marshall	.50
☐	Bob Nystrom	.50
☐	Denis Potvin	8.00
☐	Jean Potvin	.50
☐	Glenn Resch (G)	2.50
☐	Doug Rombough	.50
☐	Billy Smith (G)	3.50
☐	Ralph Stewart	.50
☐	Ed Westfall	.50

NEW YORK RANGERS

	Player	
☐	Jerry Butler	.50
☐	Bill Fairbairn	.50
☐	Ed Giacomin (G)	2.25
☐	Rod Gilbert	1.75
☐	Ron Harris	.50
☐	Ted Irvine	.50
☐	Gilles Marotte	.50
☐	Brad Park	2.75
☐	Greg Polis	.50
☐	Jean Ratelle	1.75
☐	Dale Rolfe	.50
☐	Bobby Rousseau	.50
☐	Derek Sanderson	2.00
☐	Rod Seiling	.50
☐	Pete Stemkowski	.50
☐	Walt Tkaczuk	.50
☐	Steve Vickers	.50
☐	Gilles Villemure (G)	1.00

PHILADELPHIA FLYERS

	Player	
☐	Bill Barber	2.25
☐	Tom Bladon	.50
☐	Bobby Clarke	5.00
☐	Bill Clement	.50
☐	Terry Crisp	.50
☐	Gary Dornhoefer	.50
☐	André Dupont	.50
☐	Bob Kelly	.50
☐	Orest Kindrachuk	.50
☐	Reggie Leach	.50
☐	Ross Lonsberry	.50
☐	Rick MacLeish	1.00
☐	Bernie Parent (G)	3.25
☐	Don Saleski	.50
☐	Dave Schultz	1.00
☐	Ed Van Impe	.50
☐	Jimmy Watson	.50
☐	Joe Watson	.50

PITTSBURGH PENGUINS

	Player	
☐	Syl Apps	.50
☐	Chuck Arnason	.50
☐	Wayne Bianchin	.50
☐	Dave Burrows	.50
☐	Nelson Debenedet	.50
☐	Ab DeMarco	.50
☐	Steve Durbano	.50
☐	Vic Hadfield	.50
☐	Denis Herron	1.00
☐	Bob Johnson (G)	1.00
☐	Rick Kehoe	.50
☐	Bob Kelly	.50
☐	Bobby Lalonde	.50
☐	Lowell MacDonald	.50
☐	Bob Paradise	.50
☐	Jean Pronovost	.50
☐	Ron Schock	.50
☐	Ron Stackhouse	.50

ST. LOUIS BLUES

	Player	
☐	Don Awrey	.50
☐	Ace Bailey	.50
☐	Bill Collins	.50
☐	John Davidson (G)	2.00
☐	Dave Gardner	.50
☐	Bob Gassoff	.50
☐	Larry Giroux	.50
☐	Eddie Johnston (G)	1.00
☐	Wayne Merrick	.50
☐	Brian Ogilvie	.50
☐	Barclay Plager	.50
☐	Bob Plager	.50
☐	Pierre Plante	.50
☐	Phil Roberto	.50
☐	Larry Sacharuk	.50
☐	Floyd Thomson	.50
☐	Garry Unger	.50
☐	Rick Wilson	.50

TORONTO MAPLE LEAFS

	Player	
☐	Willie Brossart	.50
☐	Tim Ecclestone	.50
☐	Ron Ellis	.50
☐	Doug Favell (G)	1.00
☐	Bill Flett	.50
☐	Brian Glennie	.50
☐	Inge Hammarstrom	.50
☐	Dave Keon	2.00
☐	Lanny McDonald	5.00
☐	Jim McKenny	.50
☐	Bob Neely	.50
☐	Gary Sabourin	.50
☐	Borje Salming	3.00
☐	Darryl Sittler	4.00
☐	Errol Thompson	.50
☐	Ian Turnbull	.50
☐	Norm Ullman	1.75
☐	Dunc Wilson (G)	1.00

VANCOUVER CANUCKS

	Player	
☐	Gregg Boddy	.50
☐	Paulin Bordeleau	.50
☐	André Boudrias	.50
☐	Bob Dailey	.50
☐	Dave Dunn	.50
☐	John Gould	.50
☐	Jocelyn Guevremont	.50
☐	Dennis Kearns	.50
☐	Don Lever	.50
☐	Ken Lockett (G)	1.00
☐	Bryan McSheffrey	.50
☐	Chris Oddleifson	.50
☐	Gerry O'Flaherty	.50
☐	Tracy Pratt	.50
☐	Gary Smith (G)	1.00
☐	Dennis Ververgaert	.50
☐	Jim Wiley	.50
☐	Barry Wilkins	.50

WASHINGTON CAPITALS

	Player	
☐	Ron H. Anderson	.50
☐	Steve Atkinson	.50
☐	Mike Bloom	.50
☐	Gord Brooks	.50
☐	Bob Collyard	.50
☐	Jack Egers	.50
☐	Lawrence Fullan	.50
☐	Bob Gryp	.50
☐	Jim Hrycuik	.50
☐	Greg Joly	.50
☐	Dave Kryskow	.50
☐	Peter Laframboise	.50
☐	Ron Low (G)	1.00
☐	Joe Lundrigan	.50
☐	Mike Marson	.50
☐	Bill Mikkelson	.50
☐	Doug Mohns	.50
☐	Lew Morrison	.50

LOBLAWS UPDATE

Update Set (45 stickers):

	Player
☐	Barry Gibbs, Atl.
☐	Hank Nowak, Buf.
☐	Jocelyn Guevremont, Buf.
☐	Fred Stanfield, Buf.
☐	Bryan McSheffrey, Buf.
☐	Dave Gardner, Cal.
☐	Morris Mott, Cal.
☐	Gary Simmons, Cal.
☐	Dave Kryskow, Det.
☐	Ted Snell, Det.
☐	Gary Bergman, Det.
☐	Phil Roberto, Det.
☐	Walt McKechnie, Det.
☐	Guy Charron, K.C.
☐	Denis Herron, K.C.
☐	J.G. Lagace, K.C.
☐	Doug Rombough, Min.
☐	Ernie Hicke, Min.
☐	Craig Cameron, Min.
☐	John Flesch, Min.
☐	Norm Gratton, Min.
☐	Don Awrey, Mtl.
☐	Wayne Thomas, Mtl.
☐	J.P. Parise, NYI.
☐	Jude Drouin, NYI.
☐	Dave Fortier, NYI.
☐	Rick Middleton, NYR.
☐	Barry Wilkins, Pgh.
☐	Lew Morrison, Pgh.
☐	Michel Plasse, Pgh.
☐	Craig Patrick, Stl.
☐	Chris Evans, Stl.
☐	Chuck Lefley, Stl.
☐	Claude Larose, Stl.
☐	Red Berenson, Stl.
☐	Dave Dunn, Tor.
☐	Rod Seiling, Tor.
☐	George Ferguson, Tor.
☐	Gerry Meehan, Van.
☐	Mike Robitaille, Van.
☐	Ab DeMarco, Van.
☐	Garry Monahan, Van.
☐	Jack Lynch, Wsh.
☐	Ron Lalonde, Wsh.
☐	Willie Brossart, Wsh.

1974 - 75 NABISCO SUGAR DADDY ALL-STARS

This 25 sticker set features players from four different sports. Other hockey singles exist. A 10" x 15" Wall Poster was also available.

Card Size: 1 1/16" x 2 3/4"

Face: Four colour

Back: Black and white

Imprint: Nabisco confections, Inc.

	No.	Player	NRMT-MT
☐	11	Phil Esposito	15.00
☐	13	Brad Park	10.00
☐	14	Tom Lysiak	5.00
☐	15	Bernie Parent (G)	12.00
☐	16	Mickey Redmond	7.50
☐	22	Don Awrey	5.00

1974 - 75 O-PEE-CHEE

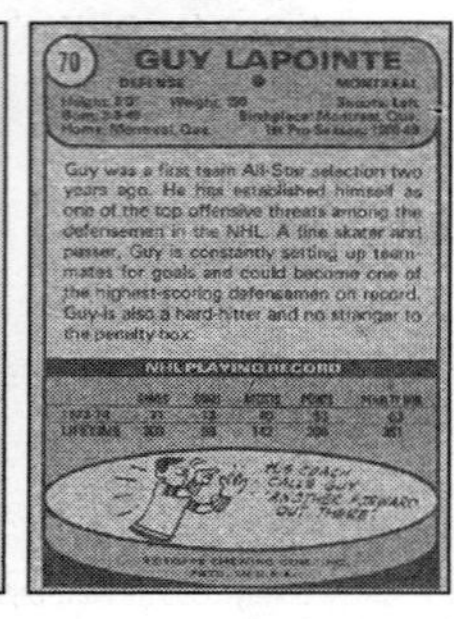

Card Size: 2 1/2" x 3 1/2"
Face: Four colour, white border, Team logo
Back: Two colour, brown and blue on card stock, Number, Resume, Hockey trivia, Bilingual
Imprint: O.P.C.

Complete Set (396 cards):			**500.00**
Common Player:			**1.25**
	No.	**Player**	**NRMT-MT**
☐	1	LL: P. Esposito/ B. Goldsworthy	7.50
☐	2	LL: B. Orr/ D. Hextall	10.00
☐	3	LL: P. Esposito/ B. Clarke	7.50
☐	4	LL: D. Favel (G) / B. Parent (G)	3.00
☐	5	LL: B. Watson/ D. Schultz	2.00
☐	6	LL: M. Redmond/ R. MacLeish	2.00
☐	**7**	**Gary Bromley (G), Buf., RC**	**2.00**
☐	8	Bill Barber, Pha.	10.00
☐	9	Emile Francis, Coach, NYR.	2.00
☐	10	Gilles Gilbert (G), Bos.	2.00
☐	**11**	**John Davidson (G), Stl., RC**	**18.00**
☐	12	Ron Ellis, Tor.	1.25
☐	13	Syl Apps, Pgh.	1.25
☐	14	TL: J. Richard/ T. Lysiak/ K. McCreary	2.50
☐	15	Dan Bouchard (G), Atl.	3.00
☐	16	Ivan Boldirev, Chi.	1.25
☐	**17**	**Gary Coalter, K.C., RC**	**1.25**
☐	18	Bob Berry, L.A.	1.25
☐	19	Red Berenson, Det.	1.25
☐	20	Stan Mikita, Chi.	9.00
☐	21	Fred Shero, Coach, Pha.	4.50
☐	22	Gary Smith (G), Van.	2.00
☐	23	Bill Mikkelson, Wsh.	1.25
☐	24	Jacques Lemaire, Mtl., Err. (Buf.)	4.00
☐	25	Gilbert Perreault, Buf.	10.00
☐	26	Césare Maniago (G), Min.	2.00
☐	27	Bobby Schmautz, Bos.	1.25
☐	28	TL: P. Esposito/ B. Orr/ J. Bucyk	15.00
☐	29	Steve Vickers, NYR.	1.25
☐	30	Lowell MacDonald, Pgh.	1.25
☐	31	Fred Stanfield, Min.	1.25
☐	32	Ed Westfall, NYI.	1.25
☐	33	Curt Bennett, Atl.	1.25
☐	34	Bep Guidolin, Coach, K.C.	1.25
☐	35	Cliff Koroll, Chi.	1.25
☐	36	Gary Croteau, K.C.	1.25
☐	37	Mike Corrigan, L.A.	1.25
☐	38	Henry Boucha, Det.	1.25
☐	39	Ron Low (G), Wsh.	2.00
☐	40	Darryl Sittler, Tor.	13.00
☐	41	Tracy Pratt, Van.	1.25
☐	42	TL: R. Martin/ R. Robert,	2.50
☐	43	Larry Carrière, Buf.	1.25
☐	44	Gary Dornhoefer, Pha.	1.25
☐	**45**	**Denis Herron (G), Pgh., RC**	**5.00**
☐	46	Doug Favell (G), Tor.	2.00
☐	**47**	**Dave Gardner, Stl., RC**	**1.25**
☐	**48**	**Morris Mott, Cal., RC, LC**	**1.25**
☐	49	Marc Boileau, Coach, Pgh.	1.25
☐	50	Brad Park, NYR.	6.00
☐	51	Bobby Leiter, Atl.	1.25
☐	52	Tom Reid, Min.	1.25
☐	53	Serge Savard, Mtl.	3.00
☐	54	Checklist 1	45.00
☐	55	Terry Harper, L.A.	1.25
☐	56	TL: J. Johnston/ W. McKechnie	2.50
☐	57	Guy Charron, Det.	1.25
☐	58	Pit Martin, Chi.	1.25
☐	59	Chris Evans, K.C.	1.25
☐	60	Bernie Parent (G), Pha.	7.00
☐	61	Jim Lorentz, Buf.	1.25
☐	**62**	**Dave Kryskow, Wsh., RC**	**1.25**
☐	63	Lou Angotti, Stl., LC	1.25
☐	64	Bill Flett, Tor.	1.25
☐	65	Vic Hadfield, Pgh.	1.25
☐	**66**	**Wayne Merrick, Stl., RC**	**1.25**
☐	67	André Dupont, Pha.	1.25
☐	**68**	**Tom Lysiak, Atl., RC**	**2.00**
☐	69	TL: J. Pappin/ S. Mikita/ J. P. Bordeleau	2.50
☐	70	Guy Lapointe, Mtl.	3.00
☐	71	Gerry O'Flaherty, Van.	1.25
☐	72	Marcel Dionne, Det.	15.00
☐	**73**	**Butch Deadmarsh, K.C., RC**	**1.25**
☐	74	Butch Goring, L.A.	1.25
☐	75	Keith Magnuson, Chi.	1.25
☐	76	Red Kelly, Coach, Tor.	2.50
☐	77	Pete Stemkowski, NYR.	1.25
☐	78	Jim Roberts, Mtl.	1.25
☐	79	Don Luce, Buf.	1.25
☐	80	Don Awrey, Stl.	1.25
☐	81	Rick Kehoe, Tor.	1.25
☐	82	Billy Smith (G), NYI.	15.00
☐	83	J. P. Parise, Min.	1.25
☐	84	TL: M. Redmond/ M. Dionne/ B. Hogaboom	2.50
☐	85	Ed Van Impe, Pha.	1.25
☐	86	Randy Manery, Atl.	1.25
☐	87	Barclay Plager, Stl.	1.25
☐	**88**	**Inge Hammarstrom, Tor., RC**	**1.25**
☐	89	Ab DeMarco, Pgh.	1.25
☐	90	Bill White, Chi.	1.25
☐	91	Al Arbour, Coach, NYI.	2.50
☐	92	Bob Stewart, Cal.	1.25
☐	93	Jack Egers, Wsh.	1.25
☐	94	Don Lever, Van.	1.25
☐	95	Reggie Leach, Pha.	1.25
☐	96	Dennis O'Brien, Min.	1.25
☐	97	Pete Mahovlich, Mtl.	1.25
☐	98	TL: B. Goring/ F. St, Marseille/ D. Kozak	2.50
☐	99	Gerry Meehan, Buf.	1.25
☐	100	Bobby Orr, Bos.	45.00
☐	**101**	**Jean Potvin, NYI., RC**	**1.25**
☐	102	Rod Seiling, NYR.	1.25
☐	103	Keith McCreary, Atl., LC	1.25
☐	104	Phil Maloney, Coach, Van.	1.25
☐	105	Denis Dupère, Wsh.	1.25
☐	106	Steve Durbano, Pgh.	1.25
☐	107	Bob Plager, Stl., Err. (Barclay Plager)	1.25
☐	**108**	**Chris Oddleifson, Van., RC**	**1.25**
☐	109	Jim Neilson, Cal.	1.25
☐	110	Jean Pronovost, Pgh.	1.25
☐	**111**	**Don Kozak, L.A., RC**	**1.25**
☐	112	TL: B. Goldsworthy/ D. Hextall/ D. Grant	6.00
☐	113	Jim Pappin, Chi.	1.25
☐	114	Richard Lemieux, K.C.	1.25
☐	115	Dennis Hextall, Min.	1.25
☐	**116**	**Bill Hogaboam, Det., RC**	**1.25**
☐	117	TL: D. Ververgaert/ B. Schmautz/ A. Boudrias/D. Tannahill	2.50
☐	118	Jim Anderson, Coach, Wsh.	1.25
☐	119	Walt Tkaczuk, NYR.	1.25
☐	120	Mickey Redmond, Det.	2.50
☐	121	Jim Schoenfeld, Buf.	1.25
☐	122	Jocelyn Guevremont, Van.	1.25
☐	123	Bob Nystrom, NYI.	2.50
☐	124	TL: Y. Cournoyer/ F. Mahovlich/ C. Larose	3.50
☐	125	Lew Morrison, Wsh.	1.25
☐	126	Terry Murray, Cal., LC	1.25
☐	127	AS: Rick Martin, Buf.	2.00
☐	128	AS: Ken Hodge, Sr., Bos.	1.25
☐	129	AS: Phil Esposito, Bos.	5.00
☐	130	AS: Bobby Orr, Bos.	24.00
☐	131	AS: Brad Park, NYR.	3.50
☐	132	AS: Gilles Gilbert (G) Bos.	2.00
☐	133	AS: Lowell MacDonald, Pgh.	1.25
☐	134	AS: Bill Goldsworthy, Min.	1.25
☐	135	AS: Bobby Clarke, Pha.	9.00
☐	136	AS: Bill White, Chi.	1.25
☐	137	AS: Dave Burrows, Pgh.	1.25
☐	138	AS: Bernie Parent (G) Pha.	4.00
☐	139	Jacques Richard, Atl.	1.25
☐	140	Yvan Cournoyer, Mtl.	4.25
☐	141	TL: R. Gilbert/ B. Park	3.75
☐	142	René Robert, Buf.	1.25
☐	**143**	**J. Bob Kelly, Pgh., RC**	**1.25**
☐	144	Ross Lonsberry, Pha.	1.25
☐	145	Jean Ratelle, NYR.	3.00
☐	146	Dallas Smith, Bos.	1.25
☐	147	Bernie Geoffrion, Coach, Atl.	4.25
☐	148	Ted McAneeley, Cal., LC	1.25
☐	149	Pierre Plante, Stl.	1.25
☐	150	Dennis Hull, Chi.	1.25
☐	151	Dave Keon, Tor.	3.00
☐	**152**	**Dave Dunn, Van., RC**	**1.25**
☐	153	Michel Belhumeur (G), Wsh.	2.00
☐	154	TL: B. Clarke/ D. Schultz	4.00
☐	155	Ken Dryden (G), Mtl.	35.00
☐	**156**	**John Wright, K.C., RC, LC**	**1.25**
☐	157	Larry Romanchych, Atl.	1.25
☐	**158**	**Ralph Stewart, NYI., RC**	**1.25**
☐	159	Mike Robitaille, Buf.	1.25
☐	160	Ed Giacomin (G), NYR.	3.00
☐	161	Don Cherry, Coach, Bos.	35.00
☐	162	Checklist 2 (133 - 264)	45.00
☐	163	Rick MacLeish, Pha.	2.00
☐	164	Greg Polis, Stl.	1.25
☐	165	Carol Vadnais, Bos.	1.25
☐	166	Pete Laframboise, Wsh.	1.25
☐	167	Ron Schock, Pgh.	1.25
☐	**168**	**Lanny McDonald, Tor., RC**	**30.00**
☐	169	Kansas City Scouts Emblem : Entered NHL, 1974	2.50
☐	170	Tony Esposito (G), Chi.	12.00
☐	171	Pierre Jarry, Det.	1.25
☐	172	Dan Maloney, L.A.	1.25
☐	173	Pete McDuffe (G), K.C.	2.00
☐	174	Danny Grant, Min.	1.25
☐	**175**	**John Stewart, Cal., RC, LC**	**1.25**
☐	176	Floyd Smith, Buf., LC	1.25
☐	177	Bert Marshall, NYI.	1.25
☐	178	Chuck Lefley, Mtl., Err. (Pierre Bouchard)	1.25
☐	179	Gilles Villemure (G), NYR.	2.00
☐	**180**	**Borje Salming, Tor., RC**	**30.00**
☐	181	Doug Mohns, Wsh., LC	1.25
☐	182	Barry Wilkins, Van.	1.25
☐	183	TL: L. MacDonald/ Syl Apps	2.50
☐	184	Gregg Sheppard, Bos.	1.25
☐	185	Joey Johnston, Cal.	1.25
☐	186	Dick Redmond, Chi.	1.25
☐	187	Simon Nolet, K.C.	1.25
☐	188	Ron Stackhouse, Pgh.	1.25
☐	189	Marshall Johnston, Coach, Cal.	1.25
☐	190	Rick Martin, Buf.	2.00
☐	191	André Boudrias, Van.	1.25
☐	192	Steve Atkinson, Wsh., LC	1.25
☐	193	Nick Libett, Det.	1.25
☐	194	Bob J. Murdoch, L.A., RC	1.25
☐	195	Denis Potvin, NYI., RC	45.00
☐	196	Dave Schultz, Pha.	4.25
☐	197	TL: G. Unger/ P. Plante	2.50
☐	198	Jim McKenny, Tor.	1.25
☐	199	Gerry Hart, NYI.	1.25
☐	200	Phil Esposito, Bos.	10.00
☐	201	Rod Gilbert, NYR.	3.00
☐	202	Jacques Laperrière, Mtl., LC	2.50
☐	203	Barry Gibbs, Min.	1.25
☐	204	Billy Reay, Coach, Chi.	1.25
☐	205	Gilles Meloche (G), Cal.	2.00
☐	206	Wayne Cashman, Bos.	1.25
☐	**207**	**Dennis Ververgaert, Van., RC**	**1.25**
☐	208	Phil Roberto, Stl.	1.25
☐	209	Playoffs: Flyers vs. Flames	2.50
☐	210	Playoffs: Rangers vs. Canadiens	2.50
☐	211	Playoffs: Bruins vs. Maple Leafs	2.50
☐	212	Playoffs: Blackhawks vs. Kings	2.50
☐	213	Playoffs: Flyers vs. Rangers	2.50
☐	214	Playoffs: Blackhawks vs. Bruins	2.50
☐	215	Playoffs: Flyers vs. Bruins	3.00
☐	216	Stanley Cup Champions: Philadelphia Flyers	3.00
☐	217	Joe Watson, Pha.	1.25
☐	218	Wayne Stephenson (G), Stl.	2.00
☐	219	TL: D. Sittler/ N. Ullman/ P. Henderson/ D. Dupère	3.00
☐	220	Bill Goldsworthy, Min.	1.25
☐	221	Don Marcotte, Bos.	1.25
☐	222	Alex Delvecchio, Coach, Det.	2.50
☐	223	Stan Gilbertson, Cal.	1.25
☐	224	Mike Murphy, L.A.	1.25
☐	225	Jim Rutherford (G), Det.	2.00
☐	226	Phil Russell, Chi.	1.25
☐	227	Lynn Powis, K.C.	1.25
☐	228	Billy Harris, NYI.	1.25
☐	229	Bob Pulford, Coach, L.A.	2.50

	No.	Player	Price
☐	230	Ken Hodge, Bos.	1.25
☐	231	Bill Fairbairn, NYR.	1.25
☐	232	Guy Lafleur, Mtl.	30.00
☐	233	TL: B. Harris/ R. Stewart/ D. Potvin/ R. Stewart	4.00
☐	234	Fred Barrett, Min.	1.25
☐	235	Rogatien Vachon (G), L.A.	4.00
☐	236	Norm Ullman, Tor.	3.00
☐	237	Garry Unger, Stl.	1.25
☐	238	Jackie Gordon, Coach, Min.	1.25
☐	239	John Bucyk, Bos.	3.00
☐	**240**	**Bob Dailey, Van., RC**	**1.25**
☐	241	Dave Burrows, Pgh.	1.25
☐	**242**	**Len Frig, Cal., RC**	**1.25**
☐	243	AW: Henri Richard, Mtl.	2.00
☐	244	AW: Phil Esposito, Bos.	5.00
☐	245	AW: John Bucyk, Bos.	2.00
☐	246	AW: Phil Esposito, Bos.	5.00
☐	247	AW: Boston Bruins	2.00
☐	248	AW: Bobby Orr, Bos.	24.00
☐	249	AW: Bernie Parent (G), Pha.	4.00
☐	250	AW: Philadelphia Flyers	3.00
☐	251	AW: Bernie Parent (G), Pha.	4.00
☐	252	AW: Denis Potvin, NYI.	13.00
☐	253	AW: Philadelphia Flyers	2.50
☐	254	Pierre Bouchard, Mtl.	1.25
☐	255	Jude Drouin, Min.	1.25
☐	256	Washington Capitals Emblem: Entered NHL, 1974	2.50
☐	257	Michel Plasse (G), K.C.	2.00
☐	258	Juha Widing, L.A.	1.25
☐	259	Bryan Watson, Det.	1.25
☐	260	Bobby Clarke, Pha.	15.00
☐	261	Scotty Bowman, Coach, Mtl.	30.00
☐	262	Craig Patrick, Cal.	1.25
☐	263	Craig Cameron, NYI.	1.25
☐	264	Ted Irvine, NYR.	1.25
☐	265	Eddie Johnston (G), Stl.	2.00
☐	**266**	**Dave Forbes, Bos., RC**	**1.25**
☐	267	Detroit Red Wings Checklist	6.00
☐	**268**	**Rick Dudley, Buf., RC**	**2.00**
☐	**269**	**Darcy Rota, Chi., RC**	**1.25**
☐	270	Phil Myre (G), Atl.	2.00
☐	**271**	**Larry Brown, L.A., RC**	**1.25**
☐	**272**	**Bob Neely, Tor., RC**	**1.25**
☐	**273**	**Jerry Byers, Atl., RC, LC**	**1.25**
☐	274	Pittsburgh Penguins Checklist	6.00
☐	**275**	**Glenn Goldup, Mtl., RC, Err. (Glen)**	**1.25**
☐	276	Ron Harris, NYR., LC	1.25
☐	**277**	**Joe Lundrigan, Wsh., RC, LC**	**1.25**
☐	**278**	**Mike Christie, Cal., RC**	**1.25**
☐	**279**	**Doug Rombough, NYI., RC**	**1.25**
☐	280	Larry Robinson, Mtl.	25.00
☐	281	St. Louis Blues Checklist	6.00
☐	**282**	**John Marks, Chi., RC**	**1.25**
☐	283	Don Saleski, Pha.	1.25
☐	**284**	**Rick Wilson, Stl., RC**	**1.25**
☐	**285**	**André Savard, Bos., RC**	**1.25**
☐	286	Pat Quinn, Atl.	1.25
☐	287	Los Angeles Kings Checklist	6.00
☐	**288**	**Norm Gratton, Buf., RC**	**1.25**
☐	**289**	**Ian Turnbull, Tor., RC**	**2.00**
☐	290	Derek Sanderson, NYR.	5.00
☐	291	Murray Oliver, Min.	1.25
☐	**292**	**Wilf Paiement, K.C., RC, Err. (Paiemont)**	**2.50**
☐	**293**	**Nelson Debenedet, Pgh., RC, LC**	**1.25**
☐	**294**	**Greg Joly, Wsh., RC**	**1.25**
☐	295	Terry O'Reilly, Bos.	3.00
☐	296	Rey Comeau, Atl.	1.25
☐	**297**	**Michel Larocque (G), Mtl., RC**	**6.50**
☐	**298**	**Floyd Thomson, Stl., RC, Err. (Thompson)**	**1.25**
☐	**299**	**Jean-Guy Lagace, Pgh., RC**	**1.25**
☐	300	Philadelphia Flyers Checklist	6.00
☐	**301**	**Al MacAdam, Cal., RC**	**2.00**
☐	**302**	**George Ferguson, Tor., RC**	**1.25**
☐	**303**	**Jimmy Watson, Pha., RC**	**1.25**
☐	**304**	**Rick Middleton, NYR., RC**	**18.00**
☐	305	Craig Ramsay, Buf.	1.25
☐	306	Hilliard Graves, Atl.	1.25
☐	307	New York Islanders Checklist	6.00
☐	**308**	**Blake Dunlop, Min., RC**	**1.25**
☐	309	J. P. Bordeleau, Chi.	1.25
☐	310	Brian Glennie, Tor.	1.25
☐	311	Checklist 3 (265 - 396)	45.00
☐	312	Doug Roberts, Det., LC	1.25
☐	313	Darryl Edestrand, Bos.	1.25
☐	**314**	**Ron H. Anderson, Wsh., RC, LC**	**1.25**
☐	315	Chicago Blackhawks Checklist	6.00
☐	**316**	**Steve Shutt, Mtl., RC**	**22.00**
☐	**317**	**Doug Horbul, K.C., RC, LC**	**1.25**
☐	**318**	**Bill Lochead, Det., RC**	**1.25**
☐	319	Fred (Buster) Harvey, Atl.	1.25
☐	**320**	**Gene Carr, L.A., RC**	**1.25**
☐	321	Henri Richard, Mtl., LC	3.75
☐	322	Vancouver Canucks Checklist	6.00
☐	323	Tim Ecclestone, Tor.	1.25
☐	**324**	**Dave Lewis, NYI., RC**	**4.00**
☐	325	Lou Nanne, Min.	1.25
☐	326	Bobby Rousseau, NYR., LC	1.25
☐	327	Dunc Wilson (G), Tor.	2.00
☐	328	Brian Spencer, Buf.	1.25
☐	**329**	**Rick Hampton, Cal., RC**	**1.25**
☐	330	Montréal Canadiens Checklist	6.00
☐	331	Jack Lynch, Det.	1.25
☐	332	Garnet Bailey, Stl.	1.25
☐	**333**	**Al Sims, Bos., RC**	**2.00**
☐	**334**	**Orest Kindrachuk, Pha., RC**	**1.25**
☐	335	Dave Hudson, K.C.	1.25
☐	**336**	**Bob Murray, Atl., RC**	**1.25**
☐	337	Buffalo Sabres Checklist	6.00
☐	338	Sheldon Kannegiesser, L.A.	1.25
☐	339	Billy MacMillan, NYI.	1.25
☐	**340**	**Paulin Bordeleau, Van., RC**	**1.25**
☐	341	Dale Rolfe, NYR., LC	1.25
☐	**342**	**Yvon Lambert, Mtl., RC**	**2.00**
☐	**343**	**Bob Paradise, Pgh., RC**	**1.25**
☐	344	Germain Gagnon, Chi.	1.25
☐	345	Yvon Labre, Wsh.	1.25
☐	**346**	**Chris Ahrens, Min., RC**	**1.25**
☐	**347**	**Doug Grant (G), Det., RC**	**2.00**
☐	**348**	**Blaine Stoughton, Tor., RC**	**4.00**
☐	349	Gregg Boddy, Van., Err. (Greg)	1.25
☐	350	Boston Bruins Checklist	6.00
☐	351	Doug Jarrett, Chi.	1.25
☐	352	Terry Crisp, Pha.	1.25
☐	**353**	**Glenn Resch (G), NYI., RC, Err. (Glen)**	**18.00**
☐	354	Jerry Korab, Buf.	1.25
☐	**355**	**Stan Weir, Cal., RC**	**1.25**
☐	356	Noel Price, Atl.	1.25
☐	**357**	**Bill Clement, Pha., RC**	**10.00**
☐	358	Neil Komadoski, L.A.	1.25
☐	**359**	**Murray Wilson, Mtl., RC**	**1.25**
☐	360	Dale Tallon, Chi., Err. (Talon)	1.25
☐	361	Gary Doak, Bos.	1.25
☐	**362**	**Randy Rota, K.C., RC**	**1.25**
☐	363	Minnesota North Stars Checklist	6.00
☐	364	Bill Collins, Stl., LC	1.25
☐	365	Thommie Bergman, Det., Err, (Tommie)	1.25
☐	366	Dennis Kearns, Van.	1.25
☐	367	Lorne Henning, NYI.	1.25
☐	368	Gary Sabourin, Tor.	1.25
☐	**369**	**Mike Bloom, Wsh., RC**	**1.25**
☐	370	New York Rangers Checklist	6.00
☐	**371**	**Gary Simmons (G), Cal., RC**	**3.50**
☐	**372**	**Dwight Bialowas, Atl., RC**	**1.25**
☐	373	Gilles Marotte, NYR.	1.25
☐	374	Frank St. Marseille, L.A.	1.25
☐	**375**	**Garry Howatt, NYI., RC**	**1.25**
☐	**376**	**Ross Brooks (G), Bos., RC, LC**	**2.00**
☐	377	Atlanta Flames Checklist	6.00
☐	378	Bob Nevin, L.A.	1.25
☐	**379**	**Lyle Moffat, Tor., RC**	**1.25**
☐	380	Bob Kelly, Pha.	1.25
☐	**381**	**John Gould, Van., RC**	**1.25**
☐	**382**	**Dave Fortier, NYI., RC**	**1.25**
☐	**383**	**Jean Hamel, Det., RC**	**1.25**
☐	**384**	**Bert Wilson, NYR., RC**	**1.25**
☐	**385**	**Chuck Arnason, Pgh., RC**	**1.25**
☐	**386**	**Bruce Cowick, Wsh., RC, LC**	**1.25**
☐	387	Ernie Hicke, NYI.	1.25
☐	**388**	**Bob Gainey, Mtl., RC**	**28.00**
☐	**389**	**Vic Venasky, L.A., RC**	**1.25**
☐	390	Toronto Maple Leafs Checklist	6.00
☐	**391**	**Eric Vail, Atl., RC**	**1.25**
☐	392	Bobby Lalonde, Van.	1.25
☐	**393**	**Jerry Butler, NYR., RC**	**1.25**
☐	**394**	**Tommy Williams, L.A., RC**	**1.25**
☐	395	Chico Maki, Chi., LC	1.25
☐	**396**	**Tom Bladon, Pha., RC**	**6.00**

1974 - 75 O-PEE-CHEE WORLD HOCKEY ASSOCIATION

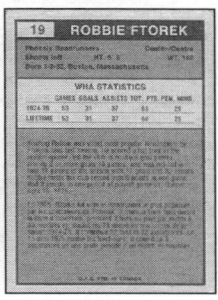

Card Size: 2 1/2" x 3 1/2"
Face: Four colour, white border, Position
Back: Two colour, brown and blue on card stock, Number, Resume, Hockey trivia, Bilingual
Imprint: O.P.C.

Complete Set (66 cards):		**230.00**
Common Player:		**3.50**

	No.	Player	NRMT-MT
☐	1	The Howes: Gordie, Mark, Marty, Houston	100.00
☐	2	Bruce MacGregor, Edmonton	3.50
☐	**3**	**Wayne Dillon, Toronto, RC**	**3.50**
☐	**4**	**Ulf Nilsson, Winnipeg, RC**	**13.00**
☐	5	Serge Bernier, Québec	3.50
☐	6	Bryan Campbell, Vancouver	3.50
☐	7	Rosaire Paiement, Chicago	3.50
☐	8	Tom Webster, New England	3.50
☐	9	Gerry Pinder, Cleveland	3.50
☐	10	Mike Walton, Minnesota	3.50
☐	11	Norm Beaudin, Winnipeg, LC	3.50
☐	**12**	**Bob Whitlock, Indianapolis, RC**	**3.50**
☐	13	Wayne Rivers, San Diego	3.50
☐	14	Gerry Odrowski, Phoenix, LC	3.50
☐	15	Ron Climie, Edmonton	3.50
☐	**16**	**Tom Simpson, Toronto, RC**	**3.50**
☐	**17**	**Anders Hedberg, Winnipeg, RC**	**13.00**
☐	18	J. C. Tremblay, Québec,	5.00
☐	19	Mike Pelyk, Vancouver	3.50
☐	20	Dave Dryden (G), Chicago	5.00
☐	21	Ron Ward, Cleveland.	3.50
☐	**22**	**Larry Lund, Houston, RC**	**3.50**
☐	**23**	**Ron Buchanan, Edmonton, RC**	**3.50**
☐	**24**	**Pat Hickey, Toronto, RC**	**3.50**
☐	**25**	**Danny Lawson, Vancouver, RC**	**3.50**
☐	**26**	**Bobby Guindon, Québec, RC, LC**	**3.50**
☐	**27**	**Gene Peacosh, San Diego, RC**	**3.50**
☐	28	Fran Huck, Minnesota	3.50
☐	29	Al Hamilton, Edmonton	5.00
☐	30	Gerry Cheevers (G), Cleveland	20.00
☐	**31**	**Heikki Riihiranta, Winnipeg, RC**	**3.50**
☐	**32**	**Don Burgess, Vancouver, RC**	**3.50**
☐	**33**	**John French, New England, RC**	**3.50**
☐	34	Jim Wiste, Indianapolis, RC, LC	3.50
☐	35	Pat Stapleton, Chicago, LC	5.00
☐	**36**	**J. P. LeBlanc, Michigan, RC**	**3.50**
☐	**37**	**Mike Antonovich, Minnesota, RC**	**3.50**
☐	38	Joe Daley (G), Winnipeg	5.00
☐	**39**	**Ross Perkins, Edmonton, RC, LC**	**3.50**
☐	40	Frank Mahovlich, Toronto	15.00
☐	41	Réjean Houle, Québec	5.00
☐	**42**	**Ron Chipperfield, Vancouver, RC**	**3.50**
☐	43	Marc Tardif, Michigan	5.00
☐	**44**	**Murray Keogan, Phoenix, RC, LC**	**3.50**
☐	45	Wayne Carleton, New England	3.50
☐	**46**	**André Gaudette, Québec, RC, LC**	**3.50**
☐	47	Ralph Backstrom, Chicago	3.50
☐	**48**	**Don McLeod (G), Vancouver, RC**	**5.00**
☐	**49**	**Vaclav Nedomansky, Toronto, RC**	**5.00**
☐	50	Bobby Hull, Winnipeg	50.00
☐	**51**	**Rusty Patenaude, Edmonton, RC**	**3.50**
☐	52	Michel Parizeau, Québec, LC	3.50
☐	53	Checklist (1- 66)	45.00
☐	54	Wayne Connelly, Minnesota	3.50
☐	55	Gary Veneruzzo, Michigan	3.50
☐	**56**	**Dennis Sobchuk, Phoenix, RC**	**3.50**
☐	57	Paul Henderson, Toronto	7.50
☐	**58**	**Andy Brown (G), Indianapolis, RC, LC**	**5.00**

No.	Player	
59	Poul Popiel, Houston	3.50
60	André Lacroix, San Diego	5.00
61	Gary Jarrett, Cleveland	3.50
62	**Claude St. Sauveur, Vancouver, RC**	**3.50**
63	**Réal Cloutier, Québec, RC**	**3.50**
64	Jacques Plante (G), Edmonton	55.00
65	**Gilles Gratton (G), Toronto, RC**	**10.00**
66	**Lars-Erik Sjoberg, Winnipeg, RC**	**10.00**

1974 - 75 SOVIET STARS POSTCARDS

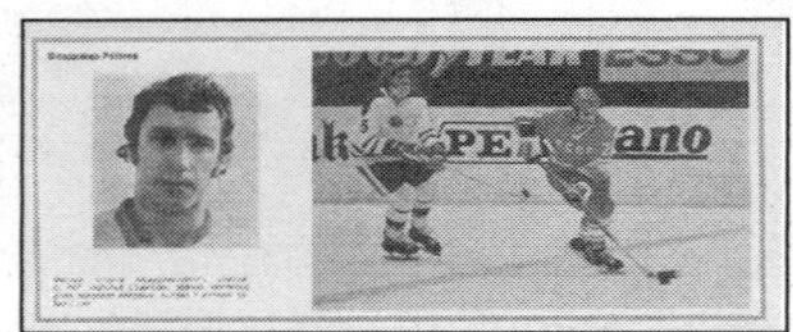

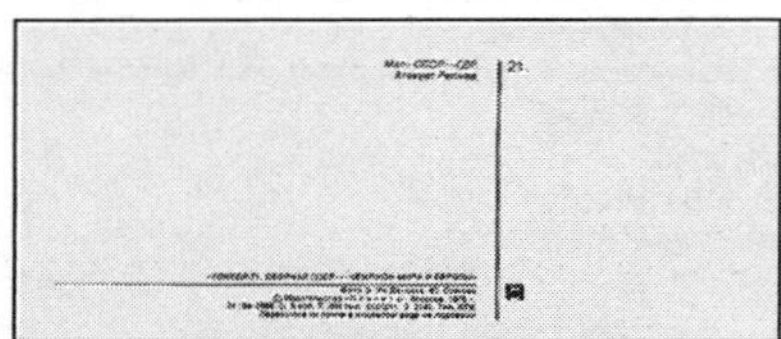

Card Size: 8 1/4" x 3 1/2"
Face: Four colour
Back: Black and white, Russian text.
Imprint:
Complete Set (25 cards and folder): 125.00

No.	Player	NRMT-MT
1	U.S.S.R.	8.00
2	Vladislav Tretiak (G)	20.00
3	Alexander Sidelnikov	5.00
4	Alexander Gusev	5.00
5	Valery Vasiliev	5.00
6	Vladimir Lutchenko	5.00
7	Yuri Liapkin	5.00
8	Gennady Tsycankov	5.00
9	Yuri Shatalov	5.00
10	Viktor Kuzkin	5.00
11	Boris Mikhailov	8.00
12	Vladimir Petrov	8.00
13	Valery Kharlamov	10.00
14	Alexander Maltsev	8.00
15	Vladimir Shadrin	5.00
16	Alexander Yakushev	12.00
17	Yuri Lebedev	5.00
18	Vyacheslav Anisin	5.00
19	Alexander Bodunov	5.00
20	Sergei Kapustin	5.00
21	Vladimir Repnev	5.00
22	Vsevold Bobrov	5.00
23	Boris Kulagin	5.00
24	Boris Mikhailov	8.00
25	U.S.S.R.	8.00

1974 - 75 TOPPS

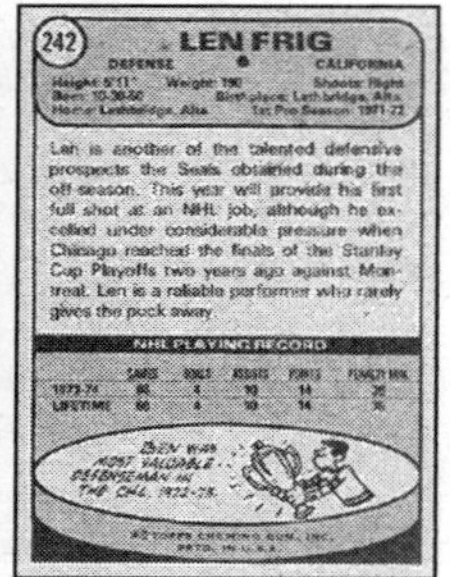

Card Size: 2 1/2" x 3 1/2"
Face: Four colour, white border, Team logo
Back: Brown and blue on card stock, Number, Resume, Hockey trivia
Imprint: TOPPS CHEWING GUM, INC.
Complete Set (264 cards): 260.00
Common Player: .60

No.	Player	MINT
1	LL: P. Esposito/B. Goldsworthy	4.50
2	LL: B. Orr/D. Hextall	7.00
3	LL: P. Esposito/B. Clarke	5.50
4	LL: D. Favell/B. Parent	1.50
5	LL: B. Watson/D. Schultz	1.00
6	LL: M. Redmond/R. MacLeish	1.00
7	**Gary Bromley (G), Buf., RC**	**1.00**
8	Bill Barber, Pha.	6.50
9	Emile Francis, Coach, NYR.	1.50
10	Gilles Gilbert (G), Bos.	1.00
11	**John Davidson (G), Stl., RC**	**10.00**
12	Ron Ellis, Tor.	.60
13	Syl Apps, Pgh.	.60
14	TL: J. Richard/T. Lysiak/K. McCreary	1.00
15	Dan Bouchard (G), Atl.	1.00
16	Ivan Boldirev, Chi.	.60
17	**Gary Coalter, K.C., RC**	**.60**
18	Bob Berry, L.A.	.60
19	Red Berenson, Det.	.60
20	Stan Mikita, Chi.	5.50
21	Fred Shero, Coach, Pha.	3.25
22	Gary Smith (G), Van.	1.00
23	Bill Mikkelson, Wpg.	.60
24	Jacques Lemaire, Mtl., Err. (Sabres)	2.50
25	Gilbert Perreault, Buf.	5.50
26	Césare Maniago (G), Min.	1.00
27	Bobby Schmautz, Bos.	.60
28	TL: P. Esposito/B. Orr/J. Bucyk	10.00
29	Steve Vickers, NYR.	.60
30	Lowell MacDonald, Pgh.	.60
31	Fred Stanfield, Min.	.60
32	Ed Westfall, NYI.	.60
33	Curt Bennett, Atl.	.60
34	Bep Guidolin, Coach, K.C.	.60
35	Cliff Koroll, Chi.	.60
36	Gary Croteau, K.C.	.60
37	Mike Corrigan, L.A.	.60
38	Henry Boucha, Det.	.60
39	Ron Low (G), Wpg.	1.00
40	Darryl Sittler, Tor.	7.00
41	Tracy Pratt, Van.	.60
42	TL: R. Martin/R. Robert	1.00
43	Larry Carrière, Buf.	.60
44	Gary Dornhoefer, Pha., Error	.60
45	**Denis Herron (G), Ppg., RC**	**3.00**
46	Doug Favell (G), Tor.	.60
47	**Dave Gardner, Stl., RC**	**.60**
48	**Morris Mott, Cal., RC, LC**	**.60**
49	Marc Boileau, Coach, Pgh.	.60
50	Brad Park, NYR.	4.00
51	Bobby Leiter, Atl.	.60
52	Tom Reid, Min.	.60
53	Serge Savard, Mtl.	1.50
54	Checklist 1 (1 - 132)	18.00
55	Terry Harper, L.A.	.60
56	TL: J. Johnston/W. McKechnie	.60
57	Guy Charron, Det.	.60
58	Pit Martin, Chi.	.60
59	Chris Evans, K.C.	.60
60	Bernie Parent (G), Pha.	4.00
61	Jim Lorentz, Buf.	.60
62	**Dave Kryskow, Wsh., RC**	**.60**
63	Lou Angotti, Stl., LC	.60
64	Bill Flett, Tor.	.60
65	Vic Hadfield, Pgh.	.60
66	**Wayne Merrick, Stl., RC**	**.60**
67	André Dupont, Pha.	.60
68	**Tom Lysiak, Atl., RC**	**1.00**
69	TL: J. Pappin/S. Mikita/J. P. Bordelaeau	1.50
70	Guy Lapointe, Mtl.	1.50
71	Gerry O'Flaherty, Van.	.60
72	Marcel Dionne, Det.	9.00
73	**Butch Deadmarsh, K.C., RC**	**.60**
74	Butch Goring, L.A.	.60
75	Keith Magnuson, Chi.	.60
76	Red Kelly, Coach, Tor.	1.50
77	Pete Stemkowski, NYR.	.60
78	Jim Roberts, Mtl.	.60
79	Don Luce, Buf.	.60
80	Don Awrey, Stl.	.60
81	Rick Kehoe, Tor.	.60
82	Billy Smith (G), NYI.	9.00
83	J. P. Parise, Min.	.60
84	TL: M. Redmond/M. Dionne/B. Hogaboam	2.00
85	Ed Van Impe, Pha.	.60
86	Randy Manery, Atl.	.60
87	Barclay Plager, Stl.	.60
88	**Inge Hammarstrom, Tor., RC**	**.60**
89	Ab DeMarco, Pgh.	.60
90	Bill White, Chi.	.60
91	Al Arbour, Coach, NYI.	1.50
92	Bob Stewart, Cal.	.60
93	Jack Egers, Wpg.	.60
94	Don Lever, Van.	.60
95	Reggie Leach, Pha.	.60
96	Dennis O'Brien, Min.	.60
97	Pete Mahovlich, Mtl.	.60
98	TL: B. Goring/F. St. Marseille/D. Kozak	1.00
99	Gerry Meehan, Buf.	.60
100	Bobby Orr, Bos.	30.00
101	**Jean Potvin, NYI., RC**	**.60**
102	Rod Seiling, NYR.	.60
103	Keith McCreary, Atl., LC	.60
104	Phil Maloney, Coach, Van.	.60
105	Denis Dupère, Wpg.	.60
106	Steve Durbano, Pgh.	.60
107	Bob Plager, Stl., Err. (Barclay Plager)	.60
108	**Chris Oddleifson, Van., RC**	**.60**
109	Jim Neilson, Cal.	.60
110	Jean Pronovost, Pgh.	.60
111	**Don Kozak, L.A., RC**	**.60**
112	TL: B. Goldsworthy/D. Hextall/D. Grant	1.00
113	Jim Pappin, Chi.	.60
114	Richard Lemieux, K.C.	.60
115	Dennis Hextall, Min.	.60
116	**Bill Hogaboam, Det., RC**	**.60**
117	TL: D. Ververgaert/B. Schmautz/A. Boudrias/D. Tannahill	1.00
118	Jim Anderson, Coach, Wpg.	.60
119	Walt Tkaczuk, NYR.	.60
120	Mickey Redmond, Det.	1.25
121	Jim Schoenfeld, Buf.	.60
122	Jocelyn Guevremont, Van.	.60
123	Bob Nystrom, NYI.	.60
124	TL: Y. Cournoyer/F. Mahovlich/C. Larose	2.75
125	Lew Morrison, Wpg.	.60
126	Terry Murray, Cal., LC	.60
127	AS: Rick Martin, Buf.	1.00
128	AS: Ken Hodge, Bos.	.60
129	AS: Phil Esposito, Bos.	3.00
130	AS: Bobby Orr, Bos.	15.00
131	AS: Brad Park, NYR.	2.00
132	AS: Gilles Gilbert (G), Bos.	1.00
133	AS: Lowell MacDonald, Pgh.	.60
134	AS: Bill Goldsworthy, Min.	.60
135	AS: Bobby Clarke, Pha.	6.00
136	AS: Bill White, Chi.	.60
137	AS: Dave Burrows, Pgh.	.60
138	AS: Bernie Parent (G), Pha.	2.50
139	Jacques Richard, Atl.	.60
140	Yvan Cournoyer, Mtl.	3.00
141	TL: R. Gilbert/B. Park	2.25
142	René Robert, Buf.	.60
143	**J. Bob Kelly, Ppg., RC**	**.60**
144	Ross Lonsberry, Pha.	.60
145	Jean Ratelle, NYR.	2.00
146	Dallas Smith, Bos.	.60
147	Bernie Geoffrion, Coach, Atl.	3.00
148	Ted McAneeley, Cal., LC	.60
149	Pierre Plante, Stl.	.60
150	Dennis Hull, Chi.	.60
151	Dave Keon, Tor.	2.00
152	**Dave Dunn, Van., RC**	**.60**
153	Michel Belhumeur (G), Wpg.	1.00
154	TL: B. Clarke/D. Schultz	3.00
155	Ken Dryden (G), Mtl.	25.00
156	**John Wright, K.C., RC, LC**	**.60**
157	Larry Romanchych, Atl.	.60
158	**Ralph Stewart, NYI., RC**	**.60**
159	Mike Robitaille, Buf.	.60
160	Ed Giacomin (G), NYR.	2.00
161	Don Cherry, Coach, Bos.	20.00
162	Checklist 2 (133 - 264)	18.00
163	Rick MacLeish, Pha.	1.00
164	Greg Polis, Stl.	.60
165	Carol Vadnais, Bos.	.60
166	Pete Laframboise, Wpg.	.60
167	Ron Schock, Pgh.	.60
168	**Lanny McDonald, Tor., RC**	**15.00**
169	Kansas City Scouts Emblem Entered NHL, 1974	1.50

	No.	Player	NRMT-MT
☐	170	Tony Esposito (G), Chi.	6.50
☐	171	Pierre Jarry, Det.	.60
☐	172	Dan Maloney, L.A.	.60
☐	173	Pete McDuffe (G), K.C.	1.00
☐	174	Danny Grant, Min.	.60
☐	**175**	**John Stewart, Cal., RC, LC**	**.60**
☐	176	Floyd Smith, Buf., LC	.60
☐	177	Bert Marshall, NYI.	.60
☐	178	Chuck Lefley, Mtl., Err. (Pierre Bouchard)	.60
☐	179	Gilles Villemure (G), NYR.	1.00
☐	**180**	**Borje Salming, Tor., RC**	**15.00**
☐	181	Doug Mohns, Wsh., LC	.60
☐	182	Barry Wilkins, Van.	.60
☐	183	TL: L. MacDonald/S. Apps	1.00
☐	184	Gregg Sheppard, Bos.	.60
☐	185	Joey Johnston, Cal.	.60
☐	186	Dick Redmond, Chi.	.60
☐	187	Simon Nolet, K.C.	.60
☐	188	Ron Stackhouse, Pgh.	.60
☐	189	Marshall Johnston, Coach, Cal.	.60
☐	190	Rick Martin, Buf.	1.00
☐	191	André Boudrias, Van.	.60
☐	192	Steve Atkinson, Wsh., LC	.60
☐	193	Nick Libett, Det.	.60
☐	**194**	**Bob J. Murdoch, L.A., RC**	**.60**
☐	**195**	**Denis Potvin, NYI., RC**	**28.00**
☐	196	Dave Schultz, Pha.	3.00
☐	197	TL: G. Unger/P. Plante	1.00
☐	198	Jim McKenny, Tor.	.60
☐	199	Gerry Hart, NYI.	.60
☐	200	Phil Esposito, Bos.	5.50
☐	201	Rod Gilbert, NYR.	2.00
☐	202	Jacques Laperrière, Mtl., LC	.60
☐	203	Barry Gibbs, Min.	.60
☐	204	Billy Reay, Coach, Chi.	.60
☐	205	Gilles Meloche (G), Cal.	1.00
☐	206	Wayne Cashman, Bos.	.60
☐	**207**	**Dennis Ververgaert, Van., RC**	**.60**
☐	208	Phil Roberto, Stl.	.60
☐	209	Playoffs: Flyers vs. Flames	1.00
☐	210	Playoffs: Rangers vs. Canadiens	1.00
☐	211	Playoffs: Bruins vs. Maple Leafs	1.00
☐	212	Playoffs: Blackhawks vs. Kings	1.00
☐	213	Playoffs: Flyers vs. Rangers	1.00
☐	214	Playoffs: Blackhawks vs. Bruins	1.00
☐	215	Playoffs: Flyers vs. Bruins	1.50
☐	216	Stanley Cup Champions: Philadelphia Flyers	2.00
☐	217	Joe Watson, Pha.	.60
☐	218	Wayne Stephenson (G), Stl.	1.00
☐	219	TL: D. Sittler/N. Ullman/P. Henderson & D. Dupère	2.00
☐	220	Bill Goldsworthy, Min.	.60
☐	221	Don Marcotte, Bos.	.60
☐	222	Alex Delvecchio, Coach, Det.	1.50
☐	223	Stan Gilbertson, Cal.	.60
☐	224	Mike Murphy, L.A.	1.00
☐	225	Jim Rutherford (G), Det.	1.00
☐	226	Phil Russell, Chi.	.60
☐	227	Lynn Powis, K.C.	.60
☐	228	Billy Harris, NYI.	.60
☐	229	Bob Pulford, Coach, L.A.	1.50
☐	230	Ken Hodge, Bos.	.60
☐	231	Bill Fairbairn, NYR.	.60
☐	232	Guy Lafleur, Mtl.	20.00
☐	233	TL: B. Harris/R. Stewart/D. Potvin/R. Steward	3.00
☐	234	Fred Barrett, Min.	.60
☐	235	Rogatien Vachon (G), L.A.	2.75
☐	236	Norm Ullman, Tor.	2.00
☐	237	Garry Unger, Stl.	.60
☐	238	Jackie Gordon, Coach, Min.	.60
☐	239	John Bucyk, Bos.	2.00
☐	**240**	**Bob Dailey, Van., RC**	**.60**
☐	241	Dave Burrows, Pgh.	.60
☐	**242**	**Len Frig, Cal., RC**	**.60**
☐	243	AW: Henri Richard, Canadiens	1.50
☐	244	AW: Phil Esposito, Bruins	3.00
☐	245	AW: John Bucyk, Bruins	1.50
☐	246	AW: Phil Esposito, Bruins	3.00
☐	247	AW: Boston Bruins	1.00
☐	248	AW: Bobby Orr, Bruins	15.00
☐	249	AW: Bernie Parent (G), Flyers	2.50
☐	250	Stanley Cup, 1973-74 Winner: Philadelphia Flyers	2.00
☐	251	AW: Bernie Parent (G),Flyers	2.50
☐	252	AW: Denis Potvin, Islanders	9.00
☐	253	AW: Philadelphia Flyers	1.50
☐	254	Pierre Bouchard, Mtl.	.60
☐	255	Jude Drouin, Min.	.60
☐	256	Washington Capitals Entered NHL, 1974	.60
☐	257	Michel Plasse (G), K.C.	1.80
☐	258	Juha Widing, L.A.	.60
☐	259	Bryan Watson, Det.	.60
☐	260	Bobby Clarke, Pha.	10.00
☐	261	Scotty Bowman, Coach, Mtl.	20.00
☐	262	Craig Patrick, Cal.	1.00
☐	263	Craig Cameron, NYI.	.60
☐	264	Ted Irvine, NYR.	2.00

1975 - 76 HOCKEY HEROES STAND UPS

Card Size: 13 1/2" x 7 1/2 or 15 1/2" x 8 3/4"
Face:
Back:
Imprint:
Complete Set (31 cards): **225.00**

	Player	NRMT-MT
☐	Bill Barber, Pha.	10.00
☐	Gerry Cheevers (G), Bos.	15.00
☐	Bobby Clarke, Pha.	15.00
☐	Yvan Cournoyer, Mtl.	12.00
☐	Billy Harris, NYI.	5.00
☐	Gerry Hart, NYI.	5.00
☐	Guy Lafleur, Mtl.	20.00
☐	Reggie Leach, Pha.	5.00
☐	Jacques Lemaire, Mtl.	12.00
☐	Rick MacLeish, Pha.	5.00
☐	Peter Mahovlich, Mtl.	5.00
☐	Lanny McDonald, Tor.	10.00
☐	Terry O'Reilly, Bos.	5.00
☐	Bobby Orr, Bos.	50.00
☐	Bernie Parent (G), Pha.	15.00
☐	Brad Park, Bos.	10.00
☐	Denis Potvin, NYI.	12.00
☐	Jean Ratelle, Bos.	10.00
☐	Glenn Resch (G), NYI.	7.00
☐	Doug Riseborough, Mtl.	5.00
☐	Larry Robinson, Mtl.	12.00
☐	Borje Salming, Tor.	10.00
☐	André Savard, Bos.	5.00
☐	Dave Schultz, Pha.	10.00
☐	Gregg Sheppard, Bos.	5.00
☐	Darryl Sittler, Tor.	12.00
☐	Wayne Thomas (G), Tor.	7.00
☐	Errol Thompson, Tor.	5.00
☐	Bryan Trottier, NYI.	15.00
☐	Ed Westfall, NYI.	5.00
☐	Dave Williams, Tor.	10.00

1975 - 76 O-PEE-CHEE

The face of cards 1-330 are for the most part identical to those issued by Topps for this year. Checklist card number 395 was not issued, but two different checklist cards, both numbered 267, were produced. Team photo cards (81-90) have a checklist of players included on the back.

Card Size: 2 1/2" x 3 1/2"
Face: Four colour, white border, Position
Back: Two colour, brown on card stock, Number, Resume, Hockey trivia, Bilingual
Imprint: O.P.C.
Complete Set (396 cards): **350.00**
Common Player: **1.00**

	No.	Player	NRMT-MT
☐	1	Playoffs: Philadelphia vs. Buffalo	3.50
☐	2	Playoffs: Philadelphia vs. N.Y. Islanders	2.00
☐	3	Playoffs: Buffalo vs. Montréal	2.00
☐	4	Playoffs: N.Y. Islanders vs. Pittsburgh	2.00
☐	5	Playoffs: Montréal vs. Vancouver	2.00
☐	6	Playoffs: Buffalo vs. Chicago	2.00
☐	7	Playoffs: Philadelphia vs. Toronto	2.00
☐	8	Curt Bennett, Atl.	1.00
☐	9	John Bucyk, Bos.	3.00
☐	10	Gilbert Perreault, Buf.	7.50
☐	11	Darryl Edestrand, Bos.	1.00
☐	12	Ivan Boldirev, Chi.	1.00
☐	13	Nick Libett, Det.	1.00
☐	**14**	**Jim McElmury, K.C., RC**	**1.00**
☐	15	Frank St. Marseille, L.A.	1.00
☐	16	Blake Dunlop, Min.	1.00
☐	17	Yvon Lambert, Mtl.	1.00
☐	18	Gerry Hart, NYI.	1.00
☐	19	Steve Vickers, NYR.	1.00
☐	20	Rick MacLeish, Pha.	1.00
☐	21	Bob Paradise, Pgh.	1.00
☐	22	Red Berenson, Stl.	1.00
☐	23	Lanny McDonald, Tor.	10.00
☐	24	Mike Robitaille, Van.	1.00
☐	25	Ron Low (G), Wsh.	2.00
☐	26	Bryan Hextall, Det.	1.00
☐	27	Carol Vadnais, Bos.	1.00
☐	28	Jim Lorentz, Buf.	1.00
☐	29	Gary Simmons (G), Cal.	2.00
☐	30	Stan Mikita, Chi.	6.00
☐	31	Bryan Watson, Det.	1.00
☐	32	Guy Charron, K.C.	1.00
☐	33	Bob J. Murdoch, L.A.	1.00
☐	34	Norm Gratton, Min., LC	1.00
☐	35	Ken Dryden (G), Mtl.	28.00
☐	36	Jean Potvin, NYI.	1.00
☐	37	Rick Middleton, NYR.	5.50
☐	38	Ed Van Impe, Pha.	1.00
☐	39	Rick Kehoe, Pgh.	1.00
☐	40	Garry Unger, Stl.	1.00
☐	41	Ian Turnbull, Tor.	1.00
☐	42	Dennis Ververgaert, Van.	1.00
☐	**43**	**Mike Marson, Wsh., RC, LC**	**1.00**
☐	44	Randy Manery, Atl.	1.00
☐	45	Gilles Gilbert (G), Bos.	2.00
☐	46	René Robert, Buf.	1.00
☐	47	Bob Stewart, Cal.	1.00
☐	48	Pit Martin, Chi.	1.00
☐	49	Danny Grant, Det.	1.00
☐	50	Pete Mahovlich, Mtl.	1.00
☐	**51**	**Dennis Patterson, K.C., RC, LC**	**1.00**
☐	52	Mike Murphy, L.A.	1.00
☐	53	Dennis O'Brien, Min.	1.00
☐	54	Garry Howatt, NYI.	1.00
☐	55	Ed Giacomin (G), NYR. (Det.)	3.00
☐	56	André Dupont, Pha.	1.00
☐	57	Chuck Arnason, Pgh.	1.00
☐	**58**	**Bob Gassoff, Stl., RC**	**1.00**
☐	59	Ron Ellis, Tor.	1.00
☐	60	André Boudrias, Van.	1.00
☐	61	Yvon Labre, Wsh.	1.00
☐	62	Hilliard Graves, Atl.	1.00
☐	63	Wayne Cashman, Bos.	1.00
☐	**64**	**Danny Gare, Buf., RC**	**3.50**
☐	65	Rick Hampton, Cal.	1.00
☐	66	Darcy Rota, Chi.	1.00
☐	67	Bill Hogaboam, Det.	1.00
☐	68	Denis Herron (G), K.C.	2.00
☐	69	Sheldon Kannegiesser, L.A.	1.00
☐	70	Yvan Cournoyer, Mtl., Err. (Yvon)	3.50
☐	71	Ernie Hicke, Min.	1.00
☐	72	Bert Marshall, NYI.	1.00
☐	73	Derek Sanderson, NYR. (Stl.)	4.00
☐	74	Tom Bladon, Pha.	1.00
☐	75	Ron Schock, Pgh.	1.00
☐	**76**	**Larry Sacharuk, Stl., RC, LC, (NYR.)**	**1.00**
☐	77	George Ferguson, Tor.	1.00
☐	78	Ab DeMarco, Van.	1.00
☐	79	Tom Williams, Wsh., LC	1.00
☐	80	Phil Roberto, Det.	1.00
☐	81	Boston Bruins	5.00
☐	82	California Golden Seals	5.00
☐	83	Buffalo Sabres	5.00
☐	84	Chicago Blackhawks	5.00
☐	85	Atlanta Flames	5.00
☐	86	Los Angeles Kings	5.00
☐	87	Detroit Red Wings	5.00
☐	88	Kansas City Scouts	5.00

	No.	Card	Price
☐	89	Minnesota North Stars	5.00
☐	90	Montréal Canadiens	5.00
☐	91	Toronto Maple Leafs	5.00
☐	92	New York Islanders	5.00
☐	93	Pittsburgh Penguins	5.00
☐	94	New York Rangers	5.00
☐	95	Philadelphia Flyers	5.00
☐	96	St. Louis Blues	5.00
☐	97	Vancouver Canucks	5.00
☐	98	Washington Capitals	5.00
☐	99	Checklist 1 (1 - 110)	22.00
☐	100	Bobby Orr, Bos.	45.00
☐	101	Germain Gagnon, Chi., LC, (K.C.)	1.00
☐	102	Phil Russell, Chi.	1.00
☐	103	Bill Lochead, Det.	1.00
☐	**104**	**Robin Burns, K.C., RC, LC**	**1.00**
☐	105	Gary Edwards (G), L.A.	2.00
☐	106	Dwight Bialowas, Min.	1.00
☐	107	Doug Risebrough, Mtl., Error (Bob Gainey)	3.50
☐	108	Dave Lewis, NYI.	1.50
☐	109	Bill Fairbairn, NYR.	1.00
☐	110	Ross Lonsberry, Pha.	1.00
☐	111	Ron Stackhouse, Pgh.	1.00
☐	112	Claude Larose, Stl.	1.00
☐	113	Don Luce, Buf.	1.00
☐	**114**	**Errol Thompson, Tor., RC**	**2.00**
☐	115	Gary Smith (G), Van.	2.00
☐	116	Jack Lynch, Wsh.	1.00
☐	117	Jacques Richard, Atl. (Buf.)	1.00
☐	118	Dallas Smith, Bos.	1.00
☐	119	Dave Gardner, Cal.	1.00
☐	120	Mickey Redmond, Det.	1.00
☐	121	John Marks, Chi.	1.00
☐	122	Dave Hudson, K.C.	1.00
☐	123	Bob Nevin, L.A.	1.00
☐	124	Fred Barrett, Min.	1.00
☐	125	Gerry Desjardins (G), Buf.	2.00
☐	126	Guy Lafleur, Mtl., Error (defence)	25.00
☐	127	J. P. Parise, NYI.	1.00
☐	128	Walt Tkaczuk, NYR.	1.00
☐	129	Gary Dornhoefer, Pha.	1.00
☐	130	Syl Apps, Pgh.	1.00
☐	131	Bob Plager, Stl.	1.00
☐	132	Stan Weir, Tor.	1.00
☐	133	Tracy Pratt, Van.	1.00
☐	134	Jack Egers, Wsh., LC	1.00
☐	135	Eric Vail, Atl.	1.00
☐	136	Al Sims, Bos.	1.00
☐	**137**	**Larry Patey, Cal., RC**	**1.00**
☐	138	Jim Schoenfeld, Buf.	1.00
☐	139	Cliff Koroll, Chi.	1.00
☐	140	Marcel Dionne, L.A.	10.00
☐	141	Jean-Guy Lagacé, K.C., LC	1.00
☐	142	Juha Widing, L.A.	1.00
☐	143	Lou Nanne, Min.	1.00
☐	144	Serge Savard, Mtl.	2.50
☐	145	Glenn Resch (G), NYI.	5.00
☐	**146**	**Ronald Greschner, NYR., RC**	**3.25**
☐	147	Dave Schultz, Pha.	2.00
☐	148	Barry Wilkins, Pgh.	1.00
☐	149	Floyd Thomson, Stl.	1.00
☐	150	Darryl Sittler, Tor.	10.00
☐	151	Paulin Bordeleau, Van.	1.00
☐	**152**	**Ron Lalonde, Wsh., RC**	**1.00**
☐	153	Larry Romanchych, Atl.	1.00
☐	154	Larry Carrière, Buf. (Atl.)	1.00
☐	155	André Savard, Bos.	1.00
☐	**156**	**Dave Hrechkosy, Cal., RC**	**1.00**
☐	157	Bill White, Chi.	1.00
☐	158	Dave Kryskow, Atl., LC	1.00
☐	159	Denis Dupere, K.C.	1.00
☐	160	Rogatien Vachon (G), L.A.	3.75
☐	161	Doug Rombough, Min., LC	1.00
☐	162	Murray Wilson, Mtl.	1.00
☐	**163**	**Bob Bourne, NYI., RC**	**2.00**
☐	164	Gilles Marotte, NYR.	1.00
☐	165	Vic Hadfield, Pgh.	1.00
☐	166	Reggie Leach, Pha.	1.00
☐	167	Jerry Butler, Stl.	1.00
☐	168	Inge Hammarstrom, Tor.	1.00
☐	169	Chris Oddleifson, Van.	1.00
☐	170	Greg Joly, Wsh.	1.00
☐	171	Checklist 2 (111 - 220)	22.00
☐	172	Pat Quinn, Atl.	2.00
☐	173	Dave Forbes, Bos.	1.00
☐	174	Len Frig, Cal.	1.00
☐	175	Rick Martin, Buf.	1.00
☐	176	Keith Magnuson, Chi.	1.00
☐	177	Dan Maloney, Det.	1.00
☐	178	Craig Patrick, K.C.	1.00
☐	179	Tommy Williams, L.A.	1.00
☐	180	Bill Goldsworthy, Min.	1.00
☐	181	Steve Shutt, Mtl.	7.00
☐	182	Ralph Stewart, NYI.	1.00
☐	183	John Davidson (G), NYR.	4.00
☐	184	Bob Kelly, Pha.	1.00
☐	185	Eddie Johnston (G), Stl.	2.00
☐	186	Dave Burrows, Pgh.	1.00
☐	187	Dave Dunn, Tor., LC	1.00
☐	188	Dennis Kearns, Van.	1.00
☐	189	Bill Clement, Wsh.	3.00
☐	190	Gilles Meloche (G), Cal.	2.00
☐	191	Bobby Leiter, Atl., LC	1.00
☐	192	Jerry Korab, Buf.	1.00
☐	193	Joey Johnston, Chi.	1.00
☐	194	Walt McKechnie, Det.	1.00
☐	195	Wilf Paiement, K.C.	1.00
☐	196	Bob Berry, L.A.	1.00
☐	**197**	**Dean Talafous, Min., RC**	**1.00**
☐	198	Guy Lapointe, Mtl.	2.50
☐	**199**	**Clark Gillies, NYI., RC**	**7.50**
☐	200	Phil Esposito, "Traded" Bos.	7.50
☐	200	Phil Esposito, "Not Traded", Bos.	7.50
☐	201	Greg Polis, NYR.	1.00
☐	202	Jimmy Watson, Pha.	1.00
☐	**203**	**Gord McRae (G), Tor., RC**	**2.00**
☐	204	Lowell MacDonald, Pgh.	1.00
☐	205	Barclay Plager, Stl., LC	1.00
☐	206	Don Lever, Van.	1.00
☐	207	Bill Mikkelson, Wsh., LC	1.00
☐	208	LL: P. Esposit/ G. Lafleur/ R. Martin	6.00
☐	209	LL: B. Orr/ B. Clarke/ P. Mahovlich	9.00
☐	210	LL: B. Orr/ P. Esposito/ M. Dionne	12.00
☐	211	LL: D. Schultz/ A. Dupont/ P. Russell	1.50
☐	212	LL: P. Esposito/ R. Martin/ D. Grant	4.00
☐	213	LL: B. Parent (G)/ R. Vachon (G)/ K. Dryden (G)	12.00
☐	214	Barry Gibbs, Atl.	1.00
☐	215	Ken Hodge, Sr., Bos.	1.00
☐	216	Jocelyn Guevremont, Buf.	1.00
☐	**217**	**Warren Williams, Cal., RC, LC**	**1.00**
☐	218	Dick Redmond, Chi.	1.00
☐	219	Jim Rutherford (G), Det.	2.00
☐	220	Simon Nolet, K.C.	1.00
☐	221	Butch Goring, L.A.	1.00
☐	222	Glen Sather, Min.	1.00
☐	**223**	**Mario Tremblay, Mtl., RC, Err. (wrong photo)**	**8.00**
☐	224	Jude Drouin, NYI.	1.00
☐	225	Rod Gilbert, NYR.	3.00
☐	226	Bill Barber, Phi	6.00
☐	**227**	**Gary Inness (G), Pgh., RC**	**2.00**
☐	228	Wayne Merrick, Stl.	1.00
☐	229	Rod Seiling, Tor.	1.00
☐	230	Tom Lysiak, Atl.	1.00
☐	231	Bob Dailey, Van.	1.00
☐	232	Michel Belhumeur (G), Wsh.	2.00
☐	**233**	**Bill Hajt, Buf., RC**	**2.00**
☐	234	Jim Pappin, Cal., LC	1.00
☐	235	Gregg Sheppard, Bos.	1.00
☐	236	Gary Bergman, Det.	1.00
☐	237	Randy Rota, K.C.	1.00
☐	238	Neil Komadoski, L.A.	1.00
☐	239	Craig Cameron, Min.	1.00
☐	240	Tony Esposito (G), Chi.	8.00
☐	241	Larry Robinson, Mtl.	15.00
☐	242	Billy Harris, NYI.	1.00
☐	243	Jean Ratelle, NYR.	3.00
☐	244	Ted Irvine, Stl., Err. (Ted Harris)	1.00
☐	245	Bob Neely, Tor.	1.00
☐	246	Bobby Lalonde, Van.	1.00
☐	**247**	**Ron Jones, Wsh., RC, LC**	**1.00**
☐	248	Rey Comeau, Atl.	1.00
☐	249	Michel Plasse (G), Pgh.	2.00
☐	250	Bobby Clarke, Pha.	12.00
☐	251	Bobby Schmautz, Bos.	1.00
☐	**252**	**Peter McNab, Buf., RC**	**3.25**
☐	253	Al MacAdam, Cal.	1.00
☐	254	Dennis Hull, Chi.	1.00
☐	255	Terry Harper, Det.	1.00
☐	256	Pete McDuffe (G), K.C., L.C, (Det.)	2.00
☐	257	Jean Hamel, Det.	1.00
☐	258	Jacques Lemaire, Mtl.	3.00
☐	259	Bob Nystrom, NYI.	1.00
☐	260	Brad Park, "Traded", NYR.	4.25
☐	260	Brad Park, "Not Traded", NYR.	4.25
☐	261	Césare Maniago (G), Min.	2.00
☐	262	Don Saleski, Pha.	1.00
☐	263	J. Bob Kelly, Pgh.	1.00
☐	**264**	**Bob Hess, Stl., RC**	**1.00**
☐	265	Blaine Stoughton, Tor.	1.00
☐	266	John Gould, Van.	1.00
☐	267	Checklist 3 (221-330)	30.00
☐	267	Checklist 4 (331-396), Error (should be 395)	30.00
☐	268	Dan Bouchard (G), Atl.	2.00
☐	269	Don Marcotte, Bos.	1.00
☐	270	Jim Neilson, Cal.	1.00
☐	271	Craig Ramsay, Buf.	1.00
☐	**272**	**Grant Mulvey, Chi., RC**	**1.00**
☐	**273**	**Larry Giroux, Det., RC, LC**	**1.00**
☐	274	Richard Lemieux, K.C. (Atl.)	1.00
☐	275	Denis Potvin, NYI.	15.00
☐	276	Don Kozak, L.A.	1.00
☐	277	Tom Reid, Min.	1.00
☐	278	Bob Gainey, Mtl.	8.50
☐	279	Nick Beverley, NYR.	1.00
☐	280	Jean Pronovost, Pgh.	1.00
☐	281	Joe Watson, Pha.	1.00
☐	282	Chuck Lefley, Stl.	1.00
☐	283	Borje Salming, Tor.	7.00
☐	284	Garnet Bailey, Wsh.	1.00
☐	285	Gregg Boddy, Van., LC	1.00
☐	286	AS: Bobby Clarke, Pha.	7.00
☐	287	AS: Denis Potvin, NYI.	9.00
☐	288	AS: Bobby Orr, Bos.	20.00
☐	289	AS: Rick Martin, Buf.	1.00
☐	290	AS: Guy Lafleur, Mtl.	12.00
☐	291	AS: Bernie Parent (G), Pha.	3.00
☐	292	AS: Phil Esposito, Bos.	4.50
☐	293	AS: Guy Lapointe, Mtl.	1.00
☐	294	AS: Borje Salming, Tor.	4.00
☐	295	AS: Steve Vickers, NYR.	1.00
☐	296	AS: René Robert, Buf.	1.00
☐	297	AS: Rogatien Vachon (G), L.A.	2.25
☐	298	Fred (Buster) Harvey, Atl., (K.C.)	1.00
☐	299	Gary Sabourin, Cal.	1.00
☐	300	Bernie Parent (G), Pha.	5.50
☐	301	Terry O'Reilly, Bos.	1.00
☐	302	Ed Westfall, NYI.	1.00
☐	303	Pete Stemkowski, NYR.	1.00
☐	304	Pierre Bouchard, Mtl.	1.00
☐	**305**	**Pierre Larouche, Pgh., RC**	**6.50**
☐	**306**	**Lee Fogolin, Buf., RC**	**1.00**
☐	307	Gerry O'Flaherty, Van.	1.00
☐	308	Phil Myre (G), Atl.	2.00
☐	309	Pierre Plante, Stl.	1.00
☐	310	Dennis Hextall, Min.	1.00
☐	311	Jim McKenny, Tor.	1.00
☐	312	Vic Venasky, L.A.	1.00
☐	313	TL: E. Vail/ T. Lysiak/	2.00
☐	314	TL: P. Esposito/ B. Orr	10.00
☐	315	TL: R. Martin/ R. Robert	2.00
☐	316	TL: D. Hrechkosy/ L. Patey/ S. Weir,	2.00
☐	317	TL: S. Mikita/ J. Pappin	3.00
☐	318	TL: D. Grant/ M. Dionne	2.00
☐	319	TL: S. Nolet/ W. Paiement/ G. Charron	2.00
☐	320	TL: B. Nevin/ /J. Widing/ B. Berry	2.00
☐	321	TL: B. Goldsworthy/ D. Hextall	2.00
☐	322	TL: G. Lafleur/ P. Mahovlich	4.00
☐	323	TL: B. Nystrom/ D. Potvin/ C. Gilles	2.50
☐	324	TL: S. Vickers/ R. Gilbert/ J. Ratelle	2.00
☐	325	TL: R. Leach/ B. Clarke	3.00
☐	326	TL: J. Pronovost/ R. Schock	2.00
☐	327	TL: G. Unger/ L. Sacharuk	2.00
☐	328	TL: D. Sittler	3.00
☐	329	TL: D. Leve/ A. Boudria	2.00
☐	330	TL: T. Williams/ G. Bailey/ T. Williams	2.00
☐	331	Noel Price, Atl., LC, (Retired)	1.00
☐	332	Fred Stanfield, Buf.	1.00
☐	333	Doug Jarrett, Chi., LC, (NYR.)	1.00
☐	334	Gary Coalter, K.C., LC	1.00
☐	335	Murray Oliver, Min., LC, (Retired)	1.00
☐	336	Dave Fortier, NYI.	1.00
☐	337	Terry Crisp, Pha., LC	1.00
☐	338	Bert Wilson, Stl.	1.00
☐	**339**	**John Grisdale, Van., RC**	**1.00**
☐	340	Ken Broderick (G), Bos.	2.00

341	**Frank Spring, Cal., RC, LC**	**1.00**
342	**Mike Korney, Det., RC, LC**	**1.00**
343	Gene Carr, L.A.	1.00
344	Don Awrey, Mtl.	1.00
345	Pat Hickey, NYR.	1.00
346	**Colin Campbell, Pgh., RC**	**2.50**
347	Wayne Thomas (G), Tor.	2.00
348	**Bob Gryp, Wsh., RC, LC**	**1.00**
349	Bill Flett, Atl.	1.00
350	Roger Crozier (G), Buf., LC	2.00
351	Dale Tallon, Chi.	1.00
352	Larry Johnston, K.C., LC	1.00
353	**John Flesch, Min., RC, LC**	**1.00**
354	Lorne Henning, NYI.	1.00
355	Wayne Stephenson (G), Pha.	2.00
356	Rick Wilson, Stl.	1.00
357	Garry Monahan, Van.	1.00
358	Gary Doak, Bos.	1.00
359	Pierre Jarry, Det.	1.00
359	Pierre Jarry, Det., (Min.)	1.00
360	**George Pesut, Cal., RC, LC**	**1.00**
361	Mike Corrigan, L.A.	1.00
362	Michel Larocque (G), Mtl.	2.00
363	Wayne Dillon, NYR.	1.00
364	Pete Laframboise, Pgh., LC	1.00
365	Brian Glennie, Tor.	1.00
366	Mike Christie, Cal.	1.00
367	**Jean Lemieux, Atl., RC**	**1.00**
368	Gary Bromley (G), Buf.	2.00
369	J.P. Bordeleau, Chi.	1.00
370	**Ed Gilbert, K.C., RC**	**1.00**
371	Chris Ahrens, Min., LC	1.00
372	Billy Smith (G), NYI.	9.00
373	**Larry Goodenough, Pha., RC**	**1.00**
374	Leon Rochefort, Van., LC	1.00
375	**Doug Gibson, Bos., RC, LC**	**1.00**
376	Mike Bloom, Det.	1.00
377	Larry Brown, L.A.	1.00
378	Jim Roberts, Mtl.	1.00
379	Gilles Villemure (G), NYR., (Chi.)	2.00
380	**Dennis Owchar, Pgh., RC**	**1.00**
381	Doug Favell (G), Tor.	2.00
382	Stan Gilbertson, Wsh., Err. (Denis Dupère)	1.00
383	**Ed Kea, Atl., RC**	**1.00**
384	Brian Spencer, Buf.	1.00
385	**Mike Veisor (G), Chi., RC**	**2.00**
386	Bob Murray, Van.	1.00
387	**André St. Laurent, NYI., RC**	**1.00**
388	**Rick Chartraw, Mtl., RC**	**1.00**
389	Orest Kindrachuk, Pha.	1.00
390	**Dave Hutchison, L.A., RC**	**1.00**
391	Glenn Goldup, Mtl.	1.00
392	**Jerry Holland, NYR., RC**	**1.00**
393	**Peter Sturgeon, Bos., RC, LC**	**1.00**
394	**Alain Daigle, Chi., RC**	**1.00**
396	**Harold Snepsts, Van., RC**	**24.00**

1975 - 76 O-PEE-CHEE WORLD HOCKEY ASSOCIATION

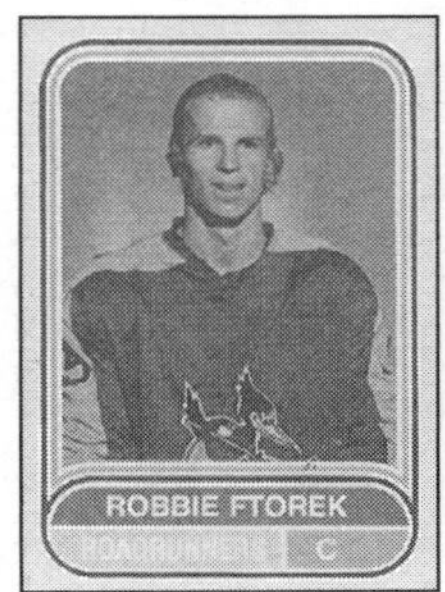

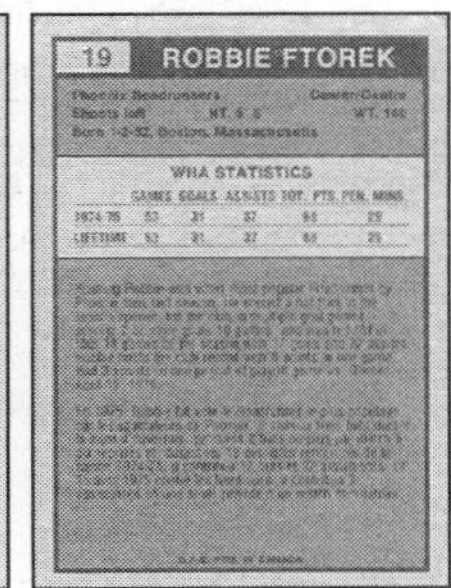

Card Size: 2 1/2" x 3 1/2"
Front: Four colour, white border, position
Back: Black and brown on card stock, Number, Resume, Bilingual
Imprint: O.P.C.
Complete Set (132 cards): 550.00
Common Player: 4.50

No.	Player	NRMT-MT
1	Bobby Hull, Winnipeg	75.00
2	Dale Hoganson (G), Québec	4.50
3	**Serge Aubry, Cincinnati, RC, LC, Err. (Aubrey)**	**4.50**
4	Ron Chipperfield, Calgary	4.50
5	Paul Shmyr, Cleveland	4.50
6	**Perry Miller, Winnipeg, RC**	**4.50**
7	**Mark Howe, Houston, RC**	**50.00**
8	**Mike Rogers, Edmonton, RC**	**8.50**
9	**Byron Baltimore, Ottawa, RC, LC, Err. (Bryon)**	**4.50**
10	André Lacroix, San Diego	6.00
11	Nick Harbaruk, Indianapolis, LC	4.50
12	**John Garrett (G), Minnesota, RC**	**13.00**
13	**Lou Nistico, Toronto, RC, LC**	**4.50**
14	Rick Ley, New England	4.50
15	**Veli-Pekka Ketola, Winnipeg, RC.**	**6.00**
16	Réal Cloutier, Québec	4.50
17	**Pierre Guite, Cincinnati, RC**	**4.50**
18	Duane Rupp, Calgary, LC	4.50
19	**Robbie Ftorek, Phoenix, RC**	**7.50**
20	Gerry Cheevers (G), Cleveland	20.00
21	**John Schella, Houston, RC**	**4.50**
22	Bruce MacGregor, Edmonton, LC	4.50
23	Ralph Backstrom, Ottawa	4.50
24	Gene Peacosh, San Diego	4.50
25	**Pierre Roy, Québec, RC, LC**	**4.50**
26	Mike Walton, Minnesota	4.50
27	Vaclav Nedomansky, Toronto	4.50
28	**Christer Abrahamsson (G), New England, RC**	**4.50**
29	Thommie Bergman, Winnipeg	4.50
30	Marc Tardif, Québec	6.00
31	Bryan Campbell, Cincinnati	4.50
32	Don McLeod (G), Calgary	6.00
33	Al McDonough, Cleveland	4.50
34	Jacques Plante (G), Edmonton LC	55.00
35	**André Hinse, Houston, RC, LC**	**4.50**
36	Eddie Joyal, Edmonton, LC	4.50
37	**Ken Baird, Edmonton, RC**	**4.50**
38	Wayne Rivers, San Diego, LC	4.50
39	Ron Buchanan, Indianapolis, LC	4.50
40	Anders Hedberg, Winnipeg	6.00
41	Rick Smith, Minnesota	4.50
42	Paul Henderson, Toronto	6.00
43	Wayne Carleton, New England, LC	4.50
44	**Richard Brodeur (G), Québec, RC**	**18.00**
45	**John Hughes, Cincinnati, RC**	**4.50**
46	**Larry Israelson, Calgary, RC, LC**	**4.50**
47	Jim Harrison, Cleveland	4.50
48	**Cam Connor, Phoenix, RC**	**4.50**
49	Al Hamilton, Edmonton	4.50
50	**Ron Grahame (G), Houston, RC**	**6.00**
51	**Frank Rochon, Ottawa, RC, LC**	**4.50**
52	Ron Climie, New England, LC	4.50
53	**Murray Heatley, Indianapolis, RC, LC**	**4.50**
54	John Arbour, Ottawa, LC	4.50
55	**Jim Shaw, Toronto (G), RC, LC**	**6.00**
56	**Larry Pleau, New England, RC**	**4.50**
57	Ted Green, Winnipeg	4.50
58	Rick Dudley, Cincinnati	4.50
59	Butch Deadmarsh, Calgary	4.50
60	Serge Bernier, Québec	4.50
61	AS: Ron Grahame (G), Houston	6.00
62	AS: J. C. Tremblay, Québec	6.00
63	AS: Kevin Morrison, San Diego	4.50
64	AS: André Lacroix, San Diego	4.50
65	AS: Bobby Hull, Winnipeg	28.00
66	AS: Gordie Howe, Houston	35.00
67	AS: Gerry Cheevers (G), Cleveland	10.00
68	AS: Poul Popiel, Houston	4.50
69	AS: Barry Long, Edmonton	4.50
70	AS: Serge Bernier, Québec	4.50
71	AS: Marc Tardif, Québec	6.00
72	AS: Anders Hedberg, Winnipeg	6.00
73	Ron Ward, Cleveland	4.50
74	**Michel Cormier, Phoenix, RC, LC**	**4.50**
75	**Marty Howe, Houston, RC**	**7.50**
76	Rusty Patenaude, Edmonton	4.50
77	John McKenzie, Minnesota	4.50
78	**Mark Napier, Toronto, RC**	**6.00**
79	Henry Boucha, Minnesota	4.50
80	**Kevin Morrison, San Diego, RC**	**4.50**
81	Tom Simpson, Toronto, LC	4.50
82	**Brad Selwood, New England, RC, LC**	**4.50**
83	Ulf Nilsson, Winnipeg	6.00
84	Réjean Houle, Québec	6.00
85	**Normand Lapointe, Cle., RC, LC, Ere. (LaPoint)**	**4.50**
86	Danny Lawson, Calgary	4.50
87	Gary Jarrett, Cle., LC, Err. (Garry)	4.50
88	**Al McLeod, Phoenix, RC**	**6.00**
89	Gord Labossierre, Houston, LC, Err. (Labossiere)	4.50
90	Barry Long, Edmonton	4.50
91	**Rick Morris, Ottawa, RC, LC**	**4.50**
92	Norm Ferguson, San Diego	4.50
93	Bob Whitlock, Indianapolis, LC	4.50
94	Jim Dorey, Toronto	4.50
95	Tom Webster, New England	4.50
96	**Gordie Gallant, Québec, RC, LC**	**4.50**
97	Dave Keon, Minnesota	7.50
98	**Ron Plumb, Cincinnati, RC**	**4.50**
99	**Rick Jodzio, Calgary, RC**	**4.50**
100	Gordie Howe, Houston	65.00
101	Joe Daley (G), Winnipeg	6.00
102	**Wayne Muloin, Cleveland, RC, LC**	**4.50**
103	**Gavin Kirk, Toronto, RC**	**4.50**
104	Dave Dryden (G), Edmonton	6.00
105	**Bob Liddington, Ottawa, RC, LC**	**4.50**
106	Rosaire Paiement, New England	4.50
107	**John Sheridan, Indianapolis, RC, LC**	**4.50**
108	**Nick Fotiu, New England, RC**	**9.00**
109	Lars-Erik Sjoberg, Win., Err. (Sjoverg)	4.50
110	Frank Mahovlich, Toronto	15.00
111	Mike Antonovich, Minnesota	4.50
112	Paul Terbenche, Calgary, LC	4.50
113	**Rich LeDuc, Cleveland, RC**	**4.50**
114	Jack Norris (G), Phoenix, LC	6.00
115	Dennis Sobchuk, Cincinnati	4.50
116	Chris Bordeleau, Québec	4.50
117	Doug Barrie, Edmonton	4.50
118	**Hugh Harris, Calgary, RC**	**4.50**
119	**Cam Newton (G), Ottawa, RC, LC**	**6.00**
120	Poul Popiel, Houston	4.50
121	Fran Huck, Minnesota, LC	4.50
122	Tony Featherstone, Toronto, LC	4.50
123	Bob Woytowich, Indianapolis, LC	4.50
124	Claude St. Sauveur, Calgary, (Atl.)	4.50
125	Heikki Riihiranta, Winnipeg	4.50
126	Gary Kurt (G), Phoenix	6.00
127	**Thommy Abrahamsson, New England, RC**	**4.50**
128	**Danny Gruen, Cleveland, RC, LC**	**4.50**
129	**Jacques Locas, Cincinnati, RC, LC**	**4.50**
130	J.C. Tremblay, Québec	6.00
131	Checklist (1 - 132)	55.00
132	Ernie Wakely (G), San Diego	8.00

1975 - 76 POPSICLE

Card Size: 2 1/2" x 3 1/2"
Face: Four colour; Team name, history and logo
Back: Team resume, Bilingual
Imprint: None
Complete Set (18 cards): 35.00
Common Team: 3.00

Atlanta Flames	Boston Bruins
Buffalo Sabres	California Golden Seals
Chicago Blackhawks	Detroit Red Wings
Kansas City Scouts	Los Angeles Kings
Minnesota North Stars	Montréal Canadiens
New York Islanders	New York Rangers
Philadelphia Flyers	Pittsburgh Penguins
St. Louis Blues	Toronto Maple Leafs
Vancouver Canucks	Washington Capitals

1975 - 76 TOPPS

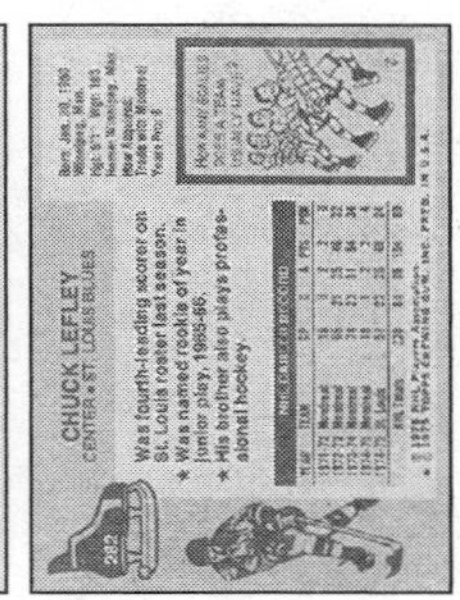

The fronts of cards 1-330 are almost identical to those issued by O-Pee-Chee the same year. Team photo cards (81-90) have a checklist of players on the reverse side.

Card Size: 2 1/2" x 3 1/2"
Face: Four colour, white border, Position
Back: Brown and black on card stock; Number, Resume, Hockey trivia
Imprint: © 1975 TOPPS CHEWING GUM, INC.

Complete Set (330 cards): **200.00**
Common Player: **.50**

No.	Teams	NRMT-MT
1	Playoffs: Philadelphia vs. Buffalo	2.25
2	Playoffs: Philadelphia vs. NY Islanders	1.00
3	Playoffs: Buffalo vs. Montréal	1.00
4	Playoffs: NY Islanders vs. Pittsburgh	1.00
5	Playoffs: Montréal vs. Vancouver	1.00
6	Playoffs: Buffalo vs. Chicago	1.00
7	Playoffs: Philadelphia vs. Toronto	1.00
8	Curt Bennett, Atl.	.50
9	John Bucyk, Bos.	1.75
10	Gilbert Perreault, Buf.	4.25
11	Darryl Edestrand, Bos.	.50
12	Ivan Boldirev, Chi.	.50
13	Nick Libett, Det.	.50
14	**Jim McElmury, K.C., RC**	**.50**
15	Frank St. Marseille, L.A.	.50
16	Blake Dunlop, Min.	.50
17	Yvon Lambert, Mtl.	.50
18	Gerry Hart, NYI.	.50
19	Steve Vickers, NYR.	.50
20	Rick MacLeish, Pha.	.50
21	Bob Paradise, Pgh.	.50
22	Red Berenson, Stl.	.50
23	Lanny McDonald, Tor.	7.00
24	Mike Robitaille, Van.	.50
25	Ron Low (G), Wsh.	1.00
26	Bryan Hextall, Det.	.50
27	Carol Vadnais, Bos.	.50
28	Jim Lorentz, Buf.	.50
29	Gary Simmons (G), Cal.	1.00
30	Stan Mikita, Chi.	4.25
31	Bryan Watson, Det.	.50
32	Guy Charron, K.C.	.50
33	Bob J. Murdoch, L.A.	.50
34	Norm Gratton, Min., LC	.50
35	Ken Dryden (G), Mtl.	20.00
36	Jean Potvin, NYI.	.50
37	Rick Middleton, NYR.	3.25
38	Ed Van Impe, Pha.	.50
39	Rick Kehoe, Pgh.	.50
40	Garry Unger, Stl.	.50
41	Ian Turnbull, Tor.	.50
42	Dennis Ververgaert, Van.	.50
43	**Mike Marson, Wsh., RC, LC**	**.50**
44	Randy Manery, Atl.	.50
45	Gilles Gilbert (G), Bos.	1.00
46	René Robert, Buf.	.50
47	Bob Stewart, Cal.	.50
48	Pit Martin, Chi.	.50
49	Danny Grant, Det.	.50
50	Pete Mahovlich, Mtl.	.50
51	**Dennis Patterson, K.C., RC, LC**	**.50**
52	Mike Murphy, L.A.	.50
53	Dennis O'Brien, Min.	.50
54	Garry Howatt, NYI.	.50
55	Ed Giacomin (G), NYR.	1.75
56	André Dupont, Pha.	.50
57	Chuck Arnason, Pgh.	.50
58	**Bob Gassoff, Stl., RC**	**.50**
59	Ron Ellis, Tor.	.50
60	André Boudrias, Van.	.50
61	Yvon Labre, Wsh.	.50
62	Hilliard Graves, Atl.	.50
63	Wayne Cashman, Bos.	.50
64	**Danny Gare, Buf., RC**	**2.50**
65	Rick Hampton, Cal.	.50
66	Darcy Rota, Chi.	.50
67	Bill Hogaboam, Det.	.50
68	Denis Herron (G), K.C.	1.00
69	Sheldon Kannegiesser, L.A.	.50
70	Yvan Cournoyer, Mtl., Err. (Yvon)	2.25
71	Ernie Hicke, Min.	.50
72	Bert Marshall, NYI.	.50
73	Derek Sanderson, NYR.	2.75
74	Tom Bladon, Pha.	.50
75	Ron Schock, Pgh.	.50
76	**Larry Sacharuk, Stl., RC, LC**	.50
77	George Ferguson, Tor.	.50
78	Ab DeMarco, Van.	.50
79	Tom Williams, Wsh., LC	.50
80	Phil Roberto, Det.	.50
81	Boston Bruins	3.00
82	California Golden Seals	3.00
83	Buffalo Sabres	3.00
84	Chicago Blackhawks	3.00
85	Atlanta Flames	3.00
86	Los Angeles Kings	3.00
87	Detroit Red Wings	3.00
88	Kansas City Scouts, Error	3.00
89	Minnesota North Stars	3.00
90	Montréal Canadiens	3.00
91	Toronto Maple Leafs	3.00
92	New York Islanders	3.00
93	Pittsburgh Penguins	3.00
94	New York Rangers	3.00
95	Philadelphia Flyers	3.00
96	St. Louis Blues	3.00
97	Vancouver Canucks	3.00
98	Washington Capitals	3.00
99	Checklist 1 (1 - 110)	15.00
100	Bobby Orr, Bos.	28.00
101	Germaine Gagnon, Chi., LC, Err. (Germain)	.50
102	Phil Russell, Chi.	.50
103	Bill Lochead, Det.	.50
104	**Robin Burns, K.C., RC, LC**	**.50**
105	Gary Edwards (G), L.A.	1.00
106	Dwight Bialowas, Min.	.50
107	Doug Risebrough, Mtl., Err. (Bob Gainey)	2.50
108	Dave Lewis, NYI.	.75
109	Bill Fairbairn, NYR.	.50
110	Ross Lonsberry, Pha.	.50
111	Ron Stackhouse. Pgh.	.50
112	Claude Larose, Stl.	.50
113	Don Luce, Buf.	.50
114	**Errol Thompson, Tor., RC**	**1.00**
115	Gary Smith (G), Van.	1.00
116	Jack Lynch, Wsh.	.50
117	Jacques Richard, Atl.	.50
118	Dallas Smith, Bos.	.50
119	Dave Gardner, Cal.	.50
120	Mickey Redmond, Det.	1.25
121	John Marks, Chi.	.50
122	Dave Hudson, K.C.	.50
123	Bob Nevin, L.A.	.50
124	Fred Barrett, Min.	.50
125	Gerry Desjardins (G), Buf.	1.00
126	Guy Lafleur, Mtl., Err. (defence)	15.00
127	J. P. Parise, NYI.	.50
128	Walt Tkaczuk, NYR.	.50
129	Gary Dornhoefer, Pha.	.50
130	Syl Apps, Pgh.	.50
131	Bob Plager, Stl.	.50
132	Stan Weir, Tor.	.50
133	Tracy Pratt, Van.	.50
134	Jack Egers, Wsh., LC	.50
135	Eric Vail, Atl.	.50
136	Al Sims, Bos.	.50
137	**Larry Patey, Cal., RC**	**.50**
138	Jim Schoenfeld, Buf.	.50
139	Cliff Koroll, Chi.	.50
140	Marcel Dionne, L.A.	7.00
141	Jean-Guy Lagacé, K.C., LC	.50
142	Juha Widing, L.A.	.50
143	Lou Nanne, Min.	.50
144	Serge Savard, Mtl.	1.25
145	Glenn Resch (G), NYI.	3.25
146	**Ronald Greschner, NYR., RC**	**2.25**
147	Dave Schultz, Pha.	.50
148	Barry Wilkins, Pgh.	.50
149	Floyd Thomson, Stl.	.50
150	Darryl Sittler, Tor.	5.00
151	Paulin Bordeleau, Van.	.50
152	**Ron Lalonde, Wsh., RC**	**.50**
153	Larry Romanchych, Atl.	.50
154	Larry Carrière, Buf.	.50
155	André Savard, Bos.	.50
156	**Dave Hrechkosy, Cal., RC**	**.50**
157	Bill White, Chi.	.50
158	Dave Kryskow, Atl., LC	.50
159	Denis Dupere, K.C.	.50
160	Rogatien Vachon (G), L.A.	2.50
161	Doug Rombough, Min., LC	.50
162	Murray Wilson, Mtl.	.50
163	**Bob Bourne, NYI., RC**	**1.50**
164	Gilles Marotte, NYR.	.50
165	Vic Hadfield, Pgh., LC	.50
166	Reggie Leach, Pha.	.50
167	Jerry Butler, Stl.	.50
168	Inge Hammarstrom, Tor.	.50
169	Chris Oddleifson, Van.	.50
170	Greg Joly, Wsh.	.50
171	Checklist 2 (111 - 220)	15.00
172	Pat Quinn, Atl.	.50
173	Dave Forbes, Bos.	.50
174	Len Frig, Cal.	.50
175	Rick Martin, Buf.	.50
176	Keith Magnuson, Chi.	.50
177	Dan Maloney, Det.	.50
178	Craig Patrick, K.C.	1.00
179	Tommy Williams, L.A.	.50
180	Bill Goldsworthy, Min.	.50
181	Steve Shutt, Mtl.	4.25
182	Ralph Stewart, NYI.	.50
183	John Davidson (G), NYR.	2.75
184	Bob Kelly, Pha.	.50
185	Ed Johnston (G), Stl.	1.00
186	Dave Burrows, Pgh.	.50
187	Dave Dunn, Tor., LC	.50
188	Dennis Kearns, Van.	.50
189	Bill Clement, Wsh.	.50
190	Gilles Meloche (G), Cal.	1.00
191	Bobby Leiter, Atl., LC	.50
192	Jerry Korab, Buf.	.50
193	Joey Johnston, Chi.	.50
194	Walt McKechnie, Det.	.50
195	Wilf Paiement, K.C.	.50
196	Bob Berry, L.A.	.50
197	**Dean Talafous, Min., RC**	**.50**
198	Guy Lapointe, Mtl.	1.25
199	**Clark Gillies, NYI., RC**	**5.00**
200	Phil Esposito, Bos.	4.25
201	Greg Polis, NYR.	.50
202	Jimmy Watson, Pha.	.50
203	**Gord McRae (G), Tor., RC**	**1.00**
204	Lowell MacDonald, Pgh.	.50
205	Barclay Plager, Stl., LC	.50
206	Don Lever, Van.	.50
207	Bill Mikkelson, Wsh., LC	.50
208	LL: P. Esposito/G. Lafleur/R. Martin	4.25
209	LL: B. Orr/B. Clarke/P. Mahovlich	5.50
210	LL: B. Orr/P. Esposito/M. Dionne	7.50
211	LL: D. Schultz/A. Dupont/P. Russel	1.00
212	LL: P. Esposito/R. Martin/D. Grant	2.25
213	LL: B. Parent/R. Vachon/K. Dryden	7.50
214	Barry Gibbs, Alt.	.50
215	Ken Hodge, Bos.	.50
216	Jocelyn Guevremont, Buf.	.50
217	**Warren Williams, Cal., RC, LC**	**.50**
218	Dick Redmond, Chi.	.50
219	Jim Rutherford (G), Det.	1.00
220	Simon Nolet, K.C.	.50
221	Butch Goring, L.A.	.50
222	Glen Sather, Min.	1.25
223	**Mario Tremblay, Mtl., RC**	**4.00**
224	Jude Drouin, NYI.	.50
225	Rod Gilbert, NYR.	1.75
226	Bill Barber, Pha.	3.75
227	**Gary Inness (G), Pgh., RC**	**1.00**
228	Wayne Merrick, Stl..	.50
229	Rod Seiling, Tor.	.50
230	Tom Lysiak, Atl.	.50
231	Bob Dailey, Van.	.50
232	Michel Belhumeur (G), Wsh.	1.00
233	**Bill Hajt, Buf., RC**	**1.00**
234	Jim Pappin, Cal., LC	.50
235	Gregg Sheppard, Bos.	.50
236	Gary Bergman, Det.	.50
237	Randy Rota, K.C.	.50
238	Neil Komadoski, L.A.	.50
239	Craig Cameron, Min.	.50
240	Tony Esposito (G), Chi.	4.50
241	Larry Robinson, Mtl.	8.50
242	Billy Harris, NYI.	.50
243	Jean Ratelle, NYR.	1.75
244	Ted Irvine, Stl., Err. (Ted Harris)	.50
245	Bob Neely, Tor.	.50
246	Bobby Lalonde, Van.	.50

	No.	Player	Price
☐	**247**	**Ron Jones, Wsh., RC, LC**	**.50**
☐	248	Rey Comeau, Atl.	.50
☐	249	Michel Plasse (G), Pgh.	1.00
☐	250	Bobby Clarke, Pha.	7.50
☐	251	Bobby Schmautz, Bos.	.50
☐	**252**	**Peter McNab, Buf., RC**	**2.25**
☐	253	Al MacAdam, Cal.	.50
☐	254	Dennis Hull, Chi.	.50
☐	255	Terry Harper, Det.	.50
☐	256	Peter McDuffe (G), K.C., LC	1.00
☐	257	Jean Hamel, Det.	.50
☐	258	Jacques Lemaire, Mtl.	1.75
☐	259	Bob Nystrom, NYI.	.50
☐	260	Brad Park, NYR.	2.50
☐	261	Césare Maniago (G), Min.	1.00
☐	262	Don Saleski, Pha.	.50
☐	263	J. Bob Kelly, Pgh.	.50
☐	**264**	**Bob Hess, Stl., RC**	**.50**
☐	265	Blaine Stoughton, Tor.	.50
☐	266	John Gould, Van.	.50
☐	267	Checklist 3 (221 - 330)	15.00
☐	268	Dan Bouchard (G), Atl.	1.00
☐	269	Don Marcotte, Bos.	.50
☐	270	Jim Neilson, Cal.	.50
☐	271	Craig Ramsay, Buf.	.50
☐	**272**	**Grant Mulvey, Chi., RC**	**.50**
☐	**273**	**Larry Giroux, Det., RC, LC**	**.50**
☐	274	Richard Lemieux, K.C.	.50
☐	275	Denis Potvin, NYI.	10.00
☐	276	Don Kozak, L.A.	.50
☐	277	Tom Reid, Min.	.50
☐	278	Bob Gainey, Mtl.	5.00
☐	279	Nick Beverley, NYR.	.50
☐	280	Jean Pronovost, Pgh.	.50
☐	281	Joe Watson, Pha.	.50
☐	282	Chuck Lefley, Stl.	.50
☐	283	Borje Salming, Tor.	4.50
☐	284	Garnet Bailey, Wsh.	.50
☐	285	Gregg Boddy, Van., LC	.50
☐	286	AS: Bobby Clarke, Pha.	4.50
☐	287	AS: Denis Potvin, NYI.	6.00
☐	288	AS: Bobby Orr, Bos.	15.00
☐	289	AS: Rick Martin, Buf.	1.00
☐	290	AS: Guy Lafleur, Mtl.	7.50
☐	291	AS: Bernie Parent (G), Pha.	2.00
☐	292	AS: Phil Esposito, Bos.	2.50
☐	293	AS: Guy Lapointe, Mtl.	1.00
☐	294	AS: Borje Salming, Tor.	2.50
☐	295	AS: Steve Vickers, NYR.	.50
☐	296	AS: René Robert, Buf.	.50
☐	297	AS: Rogatien Vachon (G), L.A.	1.5
☐	298	Buster Harvey, Atl.	.50
☐	299	Gary Sabourin, Cal.	.50
☐	300	Bernie Parent (G), Pha.	3.25
☐	301	Terry O'Reilly, Bos.	.50
☐	302	Ed Westfall, NYI.	.50
☐	303	Pete Stemkowski, NYR.	.50
☐	304	Pierre Bouchard, Mtl.	.50
☐	**305**	**Pierre Larouche, Pgh., RC**	**4.25**
☐	**306**	**Lee Fogolin, Buf., RC**	**.50**
☐	307	Gerry O'Flaherty, Van.	.50
☐	308	Phil Myre (G), Atl.	1.00
☐	309	Pierre Plante, Stl.	.50
☐	310	Dennis Hextall, Min.	.50
☐	311	Jim McKenny, Tor.	.50
☐	312	Vic Venasky, L.A.	.50
☐	313	TL: E. Vail/T. Lysiak	1.00
☐	314	TL: P. Esposito/B. Orr	7.50
☐	315	TL: R. Martin/R. Robert,	1.00
☐	316	TL: D. Hrechkosy/L. Patey/S. Weir	1.00
☐	317	TL: S. Mikita/J. Pappin	1.50
☐	318	TL: D. Grant/M. Dionne	1.50
☐	319	TL: S. Nolet/W. Paiement/G. Charron	1.00
☐	320	TL: B. Nevin/J. Widing/B. Berry	1.00
☐	321	TL: B. Goldsworthy/D. Hextall	1.00
☐	322	TL: G. Lafleur/P. Mahovlich	2.25
☐	323	TL: B. Nystrom/D. Potvin/C. Gilles	1.50
☐	324	TL: R. Gilbert/J. Ratelle/S. Vickers	1.75
☐	325	TL: R. Leach/. Clarke	2.00
☐	326	TL: J. Pronovost/R. Schock	1.00
☐	327	TL: G. Unger/Sacharuk	1.00
☐	328	TL: D. Sittler	2.00
☐	329	TL: D. Lever/A. Boudrias	1.00
☐	330	TL: T. Williams/G. Bailey	1.00

1976 - 77 O-PEE-CHEE

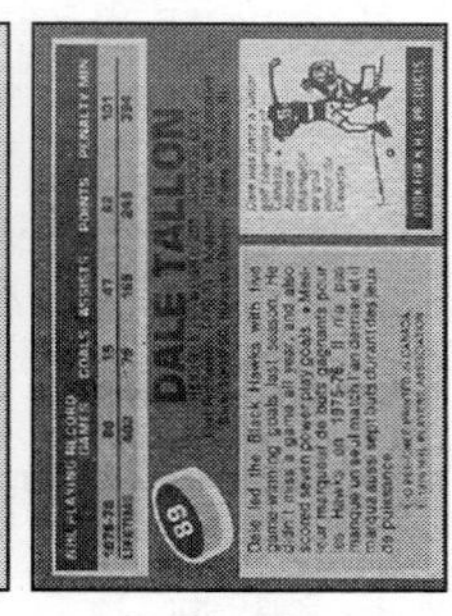

The card faces are similar to the Topps set for the same year. Team cards (132-149) have a checklist on the back for all players in the set. The set features four record breaking cards Nos. 65-68.

Card Size: 2 1/2" x 3 1/2"
Face: Four colour, white border, Team logo, Position
Back: Blue and green on card stock, Number, Resume, Hockey trivia, Bilingual
Imprint: © O-PEE-CHEE
Complete Set (396 cards): 210.00
Common Player: .75

	No.	Player	NRMT-MT
☐	1	LL: R. Leach/ G. Lafleur/ P. Larouche	5.00
☐	2	LL: B. Clarke/ P. Mahovlich/ G. Lafleur/G. Perreault/ J. Ratelle	4.50
☐	3	LL: G. Lafleur/ B. Clarke/ G. Perrault	4.50
☐	4	LL: S. Durbano/ B. Watson/ D. Schultz	.75
☐	5	LL: P. Esposito/ G. Lafleur/ R. Martin/P. Larouche/ D. Potvin	4.50
☐	6	LL: K. Dryden (G)/ G. Resch (G)/ M. Larocque (G)	5.00
☐	7	Gary Doak, Bos.	.75
☐	8	Jacques Richard, Buf.	.75
☐	9	Wayne Dillon, NYR.	.75
☐	10	Bernie Parent (G), Pha.	4.00
☐	11	Ed Westfall, NYI.	.75
☐	12	Dick Redmond, Chi.	.75
☐	13	Bryan Hextall, Min., LC	.75
☐	14	Jean Pronovost, Pgh.	.75
☐	15	Pete Mahovlich, Mtl.	1.00
☐	16	Danny Grant, Det.	.75
☐	17	Phil Myre (G), Atl.	1.50
☐	18	Wayne Merrick, Cle.	.75
☐	19	Steve Durbano, Col., LC	.75
☐	20	Derek Sanderson, Stl.	3.00
☐	21	Mike Murphy, L.A.	.75
☐	22	AS: Borje Salming, Tor	4.00
☐	23	Mike Walton, Van.	.75
☐	24	Randy Manery, Atl.	.75
☐	25	Ken Hodge, NYR.	.75
☐	**26**	**Mel Bridgman, Pha., RC**	**2.25**
☐	27	Jerry Korab, Buf.	.75
☐	28	Gilles Gratton (G), NYR.	1.50
☐	29	André St. Laurent, NYI.	.75
☐	30	Yvan Cournoyer, Mtl.	2.75
☐	31	Phil Russell, Chi.	.75
☐	32	Dennis Hextall, Det.	.75
☐	33	Lowell MacDonald, Pgh.	.75
☐	34	Dennis O'Brien, Min.	.75
☐	35	Gerry Meehan, Wsh.	.75
☐	36	Gilles Meloche (G), Cal., (Cle).	1.50
☐	37	Wilf Paiement, K.C., (Col.)	.75
☐	**38**	**Bob MacMillan, Stl., RC**	**.75**
☐	39	Ian Turnbull, Tor.	.75
☐	40	Rogatien Vachon (G), L.A.	1.50
☐	41	Nick Beverley, NYR.	.75
☐	42	René Robert, Buf.	.75
☐	43	André Savard, Buf.	.75
☐	44	Bob Gainey, Mtl.	4.25
☐	45	Joe Watson, Pha.	.75
☐	46	Billy Smith (G), NYI.	6.50
☐	47	Darcy Rota, Chi.	.75
☐	**48**	**Rick Lapointe, Det., RC**	**.75**
☐	49	Pierre Jarry, Min.	.75
☐	50	Syl Appš, Pgh.	.75
☐	51	Eric Vail, Atl.	.75
☐	52	Greg Joly, Wsh.	.75
☐	53	Don Lever, Van.	.75
☐	**54**	**Bob L. Murdoch, Cal., RC, (Cle.)**	**.75**
☐	55	Denis Herron (G), K.C., (Pgh.)	1.50
☐	56	Mike Bloom, Det.	.75

	No.	Player	Price
☐	57	Bill Fairbairn, NYR.	.75
☐	58	Fred Stanfield, Buf.	.75
☐	59	Steve Shutt, Mtl.	4.00
☐	60	AS: Brad Park, Bos	3.25
☐	61	Gilles Villemure (G), Chi., LC	1.50
☐	62	Bert Marshall, NYI.	.75
☐	63	Chuck Lefley, Stl.	.75
☐	64	Simon Nolet, Col., LC	.75
☐	65	Most Goals, Playoffs: Reggie Leach, Pha.,	1.50
☐	66	Most Points, Game: Darryl Sittler, Tor.,	2.00
☐	67	Most Points, Season, Rookie: Bryan Trottier, NYI.,	10.00
☐	68	Most Consecutive Games, Lifetime: Garry Unger, Stl.,	1.50
☐	69	Ron Low (G), Wsh.	1.50
☐	70	AS: Bobby Clarke, Pha.	8.50
☐	**71**	**Michel Bergeron, Det., RC**	**2.00**
☐	72	Ron Stackhouse, Pgh.	.75
☐	73	Bill Hogaboam, Min.	.75
☐	74	Bob J. Murdoch, L.A.	.75
☐	75	Steve Vickers, NYR.	.75
☐	76	Pit Martin, Chi.	.75
☐	77	Gerry Hart, NYI.	.75
☐	78	Craig Ramsay, Buf.	1.00
☐	79	Michel Larocque (G), Mtl.	1.50
☐	80	Jean Ratelle, Bos.	2.00
☐	81	Don Saleski, Pha.	.75
☐	82	Bill Clement, Atl.	.75
☐	83	Dave Burrows, Pgh.	.75
☐	84	Wayne Thomas (G), Tor.	1.50
☐	85	John Gould, Van.	.75
☐	**86**	**Dennis Maruk, Cal., RC, (Cle.)**	**3.50**
☐	87	Ernie Hicke, Min.	.75
☐	88	Jim Rutherford (G), Det.	1.50
☐	89	Dale Tallon, Chi.	.75
☐	90	Rod Gilbert, NYR.	2.00
☐	91	Marcel Dionne, L.A.	9.00
☐	92	Chuck Arnason, Col.	.75
☐	93	Jean Potvin, NYI.	.75
☐	94	Don Luce, Buf.	.75
☐	95	John Bucyk, Bos.	2.00
☐	96	Larry Goodenough, Pha.	.75
☐	97	Mario Tremblay, Mtl.	2.00
☐	**98**	**Nelson Pyatt, Wsh., RC, (Col.)**	**.75**
☐	99	Brian Glennie, Tor.	.75
☐	100	Tony Esposito (G), Chi.	5.50
☐	101	Dan Maloney, Det.	.75
☐	102	Dunc Wilson (G), Pgh.	1.50
☐	103	Dean Talafous, Min.	.75
☐	**104**	**Ed Staniowski (G), Stl., RC**	**1.50**
☐	105	Dallas Smith, Bos., LC	.75
☐	106	Jude Drouin, NYI.	.75
☐	107	Pat Hickey, NYR.	.75
☐	108	Jocelyn Guevremont, Buf.	.75
☐	**109**	**Doug Risebrough, Mtl., RC**	**2.00**
☐	110	AS: Reggie Leach, Pha.	1.00
☐	111	Dan Bouchard (G), Atl.	1.50
☐	112	Chris Oddleifson, Van.	.75
☐	113	Rick Hampton, Cal., (Cle.)	.75
☐	114	John Marks, Chi.	.75
☐	**115**	**Bryan Trottier, NYI., RC**	**50.00**
☐	116	Checklist 1 (1 - 132)	15.00
☐	117	Greg Polis, NYR.	.75
☐	118	Peter McNab, Bos.	.75
☐	119	Jim Roberts, Mtl.	.75
☐	120	Gerry Cheevers (G), Bos.	4.00
☐	121	Rick MacLeish, Pha.	.75
☐	122	Bill Lochead, Det.	.75
☐	123	Tom Reid, Min.	.75
☐	124	Rick Kehoe, Pgh.	1.00
☐	125	Keith Magnuson, Chi.	.75
☐	126	Clark Gillies, NYI.	2.00
☐	127	Rick Middleton, Bos.	3.25
☐	128	Bill Hajt, Buf.	.75
☐	129	Jacques Lemaire, Mtl.	2.00
☐	130	Terry O'Reilly, Bos.	.75
☐	131	André Dupont, Pha.	.75
☐	132	Atlanta Flames	4.00
☐	133	Bruins, Adams Division	4.00
☐	134	Sabres, Adams Division	4.00
☐	135	Seals, Adams Division, (Cleveland)	4.00
☐	136	Blackhawks, Smythe Division	4.00
☐	137	Red Wings, Norris Division	4.00
☐	138	Scouts, Smythe Division, (Colorado)	4.00
☐	139	Kings, Norris Division	4.00
☐	140	North Stars, Smythe Division	4.00
☐	141	Canadiens, Norris Division	4.00

No.	Card	Price
142	Islanders, Patrick Division	4.00
143	Rangers, Patrick Division	4.00
144	Flyers, Patrick Division	4.00
145	Penguins, Norris Division	4.00
146	Blues, Smythe Division	4.00
147	Maple Leafs, Adams Division	4.00
148	Canucks, Smythe Division	4.00
149	Capitals, Norris Division	4.00
150	Dave Schultz, Pha. (L.A.)	.75
151	Larry Robinson, Mtl.	9.00
152	Al Smith (G), Buf.	1.50
153	Bob Nystrom, NYI.	.75
154	Ron Greschner, NYR.	1.00
155	Gregg Sheppard, Bos.	.75
156	Alain Daigle, Chi.	.75
157	Ed Van Impe, Pgh., LC	.75
158	**Tim Young, Min., RC**	**1.50**
159	Bryan Lefley, Col.	.75
160	Ed Giacomin (G), Det.	2.00
161	Yvon Labre, Wsh.	.75
162	Jim Lorentz, Buf.	.75
163	AS: Guy Lafleur, Mtl.	20.00
164	Tom Bladon, Pha.	.75
165	Wayne Cashman, Bos.	.75
166	Pete Stemkowski, NYR.	.75
167	Grant Mulvey, Chi.	.75
168	**Yves Belanger (G), Stl., RC**	**1.50**
169	Bill Goldsworthy, Min.	.75
170	AS: Denis Potvin, NYI.	10.00
171	Nick Libett, Det.	.75
172	Michel Plasse (G), Col.	1.50
173	Lou Nanne, Min.	.75
174	Tom Lysiak, Atl.	.75
175	Dennis Ververgaert, Van.	.75
176	Gary Simmons (G), Cle.	1.50
177	Pierre Bouchard, Mtl.	1.00
178	AS: Bill Barber, Pha.	3.25
179	Darryl Edestrand, Bos.	.75
180	AS: Gilbert Perreault, Buf.	4.00
181	**Dave Maloney, NYR., RC**	**2.00**
182	J. P. Parise, NYI.	.75
183	Jim Harrison, Chi.	.75
184	**Pete LoPresti (G), Min., RC**	**1.50**
185	Don Kozak, L.A.	.75
186	Guy Charron, K.C. (Wsh.)	.75
187	Stan Gilbertson, Pgh.	.75
188	**Bill Nyrop, Mtl., RC**	**.75**
189	Bobby Schmautz, Bos.	.75
190	Wayne Stephenson (G), Pha.	1.50
191	Brian Spencer, Buf.	.75
192	Gilles Marotte, NYR. (Stl.), LC	.75
193	Lorne Henning, NYI.	.75
194	Bob Neely, Tor.	.75
195	Dennis Hull, Chi.	1.00
196	Walt McKechnie, Det.	.75
197	**Curt Ridley (G), Van., RC**	**1.50**
198	Dwight Bialowas, Min.	.75
199	Pierre Larouche, Pgh.	2.00
200	AS: Ken Dryden (G), Mtl.	25.00
201	Ross Lonsberry, Pha.	.75
202	Curt Bennett, Atl.	.75
203	**Hartland Monahan, Wsh., RC**	**.75**
204	John Davidson (G), NYR.	2.00
205	Serge Savard, Mtl.	1.50
206	Garry Howatt, NYI.	.75
207	Darryl Sittler, Tor.	6.00
208	J. P. Bordeleau, Chi.	.75
209	Henry Boucha, K.C. (Col.), LC	.75
210	AS: Rick Martin, Buf.	1.00
211	Vic Venasky, L.A.	.75
212	Fred (Buster) Harvey, Det.	.75
213	Bobby Orr, Chi.	35.00
214	French Connection: Martin/ Perreault/ Robert, Buf.	4.00
215	LCB Line: Barber/ Clarke/ Leach, Pha.	5.00
216	Long Island Lightning Co.:Gillies/ Trottier/ Harris, NYI.	6.50
217	Checking Line: Gainey/ Jarvis/ Roberts, Mtl.	1.50
218	Bicentennial Line:MacDonald/ Apps/ Pronovost, Pgh.	1.50
219	Bob Kelly, Pha.	.75
220	Walt Tkaczuk, NYR.	.75
221	Dave Lewis, NYI.	1.00
222	Danny Gare, Buf.	1.00
223	AS: Guy Lapointe, Mtl.	1.50
224	**Hank Nowak, Bos., RC, LC**	**.75**
225	Stan Mikita, Chi.	5.00
226	Vic Hadfield, Pgh., LC	.75
227	**Bernie Wolfe (G), Wsh., RC**	**1.50**
228	Bryan Watson, Det.	.75
229	Ralph Stewart, NYI. (Van.)	.75
230	Gerry Desjardins (G), Buf.	1.50
231	**John Bednarski, NYR., RC, LC**	**.75**
232	Yvon Lambert, Mtl.	.75
233	Orest Kindrachuk, Pha.	.75
234	Don Marcotte, Bos.	.75
235	Bill White, Chi., LC	.75
236	Red Berenson, Stl.	.75
237	Al MacAdam, Cal. (Cle.)	.75
238	**Rick Blight, Van., RC**	**.75**
239	Butch Goring, L.A.	1.00
240	Césare Maniago (G), Van.	1.50
241	Jim Schoenfeld, Buf.	.75
242	Cliff Koroll, Chi.	.75
243	**Scott Garland, Tor., RC**	**.75**
244	Rick Chartraw, Mtl.	.75
245	Phil Esposito, NYR.	5.00
246	Dave Forbes, Bos.	.75
247	Jimmy Watson, Pha.	.75
248	Ron Schock, Pgh.	.75
249	Fred Barrett, Min.	.75
250	AS: Glenn Resch (G)	2.00
251	Ivan Boldirev, Chi.	.75
252	Billy Harris, NYI.	.75
253	Lee Fogolin, Buf.	.75
254	Murray Wilson, Mtl.	.75
255	Gilles Gilbert (G), Bos.	1.50
256	Gary Dornhoefer, Pha.	.75
257	Carol Vadnais, NYR.	.75
258	Checklist 2 (133 - 264)	15.00
259	Errol Thompson, Tor.	.75
260	Garry Unger, Stl.	1.00
261	J. Bob Kelly, Pgh.	.75
262	Terry Harper, Det.	.75
263	Blake Dunlop, Min.	.75
264	'75-76 Stanley Cup Champions: Canadiens	2.00
265	**Richard Mulhern, Atl., RC**	**.75**
266	Gary Sabourin, Cle., LC	.75
267	**Bill McKenzie (G), Col., RC, Err. (KcKenzie)**	**1.50**
268	Mike Corrigan, Pgh.	.75
269	Rick Smith, Stl.	.75
270	Stan Weir, Tor.	.75
271	**Ron Sedlbauer, Van., RC**	**.75**
272	Jean Lemieux, Wsh., LC	.75
273	Hilliard Graves, Atl.	.75
274	Dave Gardner, Cle.	.75
275	Tracy Pratt, Col., LC	.75
276	Frank St. Marseille, L.A., LC	.75
277	Bob Hess, Stl.	.75
278	Bobby Lalonde, Van.	.75
279	**Tony White, Wsh., RC**	**.75**
280	Rod Seiling, Stl.	.75
281	Larry Romanchych, Atl., LC	.75
282	**Ralph Klassen, Cle., RC**	**.75**
283	Gary Croteau, Col.	.75
284	Neil Komadoski, L.A.	.75
285	Eddie Johnston (G), Stl.	1.50
286	George Ferguson, Tor.	.75
287	Gerry O'Flaherty, Van.	.75
288	Jack Lynch, Wsh.	.75
289	Pat Quinn, Atl., LC	1.50
290	Gene Carr, L.A.	.75
291	Bob Stewart, Cle.	.75
292	Doug Favell (G), Col.	1.50
293	Rick Wilson, Det.	.75
294	**Jack Valiquette, Tor., RC**	**.75**
295	Garry Monahan, Van.	.75
296	Michel Belhumeur (G), Atl., LC	1.50
297	Larry Carrière, Atl.	.75
298	**Fred Ahern, Cle., RC**	**.75**
299	Dave Hudson, Col.	.75
300	Bob Berry, L.A.	.75
301	Bob Gassoff, Stl., LC	.75
302	Jim McKenny, Tor.	.75
303	**Gord Smith, Wsh., RC**	**.75**
304	Garnet Bailey, Wsh.	.75
305	**Bruce Affleck, Stl., RC**	**.75**
306	**Doug Halward, Bos., RC**	**.75**
307	Lew Morrison, Pgh.	.75
308	**Bob Sauvé (G), Buf., RC**	**3.50**
309	Bob Murray, Chi.	.75
310	Claude Larose, Stl.	.75
311	Don Awrey, Pgh.	.75
312	Billy MacMillan, NYI., LC	.75
313	**Doug Jarvis, Mtl., RC**	**3.75**
314	Dennis Owchar, Pgh.	.75
315	Jerry Holland, NYR., LC	.75
316	**Guy Chouinard, Atl., RC**	**.75**
317	Gary Smith (G), Min.	1.50
318	**Pat Price, NYI., RC**	**.75**
319	Tommy Williams, L.A.	.75
320	Larry Patey, Stl.	.75
321	**Claire Alexander, Tor., RC, LC**	**.75**
322	**Larry Bolonchuk, Wsh., RC**	**.75**
323	**Bob Sirois, Wsh., RC**	**.75**
324	**Joe Zanussi, Bos., RC, LC**	**.75**
325	Joey Johnston, Chi., LC	.75
326	J. P. LeBlanc, Det., Err. (LaBlanc)	.75
327	Craig Cameron, Min., LC	.75
328	Dave Fortier, Van., LC	.75
329	Ed Gilbert, Pgh., LC	.75
330	**John Van Boxmeer, Mtl., RC**	**.75**
331	Gary Inness (G), Pha.	1.50
332	Bill Flett, Atl.	.75
333	Mike Christie, Cle.	.75
334	Denis Dupere, Col.	.75
335	Sheldon Kannegiesser, L.A.	.75
336	Jerry Butler, Stl.	.75
337	Gord McRae (G), Tor., LC	1.50
338	Dennis Kearns, Van.	.75
339	Ron Lalonde, Wsh.	.75
340	Jean Hamel, Det.	.75
341	Barry Gibbs, Atl.	.75
342	Mike Pelyk, Tor., LC	.75
343	Rey Comeau, Atl.	.75
344	Jim Neilson, Cle.	.75
345	Phil Roberto, Col., LC	.75
346	Dave Hutchison, L.A.	.75
347	Ted Irvine, Stl., LC	.75
348	Lanny McDonald, Tor., Err. (MacDonald)	5.50
349	**Jim Moxey, Cle., RC, LC**	**.75**
350	Bob Dailey, Van.	.75
351	Tim Ecclestone, Atl.	.75
352	Len Frig, Cle.	.75
353	Randy Rota, Col., LC	.75
354	Juha Widing, L.A.	.75
355	Larry Brown, L.A.	.75
356	Floyd Thomson, Stl.	.75
357	**Richard Nantais, Min., RC, LC**	**.75**
358	Inge Hammarstrom, Tor.	.75
359	Mike Robitaille, Van., LC	.75
360	Réjean Houle, Mtl.	1.00
361	Ed Kea, Atl.	.75
362	**Bob Girard, Cle., RC**	**.75**
363	Bob Murray, Van.	.75
364	Dave Hrechkosy, Stl., LC	.75
365	Gary Edwards (G), L.A.	1.50
366	Harold Snepsts, Van.	3.75
367	**Pat Boutette, Tor., RC**	**.75**
368	Bob Paradise, Wsh.	.75
369	Bob Plager, Stl., LC	.75
370	**Tim Jacobs, Cle., RC, LC**	**.75**
371	Pierre Plante, Stl.	.75
372	Colin Campbell, Col.	1.00
373	**David Williams, Tor., RC**	**20.00**
374	Ab DeMarco, L.A.	.75
375	**Mike Lampman, Wsh., RC**	**.75**
376	**Mark Heaslip, NYR., RC**	**.75**
377	Checklist 3 (265 - 396)	15.00
378	Bert Wilson, L.A.	.75
379	TL: C. Bennett/ T. Lysiak/ P. Quinn/ C. St. Sauveur	1.50
380	TL: D. Gare/ G. Perreault/ R. Martin	2.00
381	TL: J. Bucyk/ J. Ratelle/ T. O'Reilly,	2.00
382	TL: P. Martin/ D. Tallon/ P. Russell/ C. Koroll	1.50
383	TL: W. Merrick/ A. MacAdam/ R. Hampton/ M. Christie/ B. Murdoch	1.50
384	TL: G. Charron/ S. Durbano	1.50
385	TL: M. Bergeron/ W. McKechnie/ B. Watson	1.50
386	TL: M. Dionne/ D. Hutchison/ M. Corrigan	2.00
387	TL: B. Hogaboam/ T. Young/ D. O'Brien	1.50
388	TL: G. Lafleur/ P. Mahovlich/ D. Risebrough	2.00
389	TL: Gilles/ D. Potvin/ G. Howatt,	2.00
390	TL: R. Gilbert/ S. Vickers/ C. Vadnais/ P. Esposito	2.00
391	TL: R. Leach/ B. Clarke/ D. Schultz/ B. Barber	2.00
392	TL: P. Larouche/ S. Apps/ R. Shock	1.50
393	TL: C. Lefley/ G. Unger/ B. Gassoff	1.50
394	TL: E. Thompson/ D. Sittle/ D. Williams	2.00
395	TL: D. Ververgaer/ C. Oddleifson/ D. Kearns/H. Snepsts	1.50
396	TL: N. Pyatt/ G. Meehan/ Y. Labre/ T. White	1.50

1976 - 77 O-PEE-CHEE WORLD HOCKEY ASSOCIATION

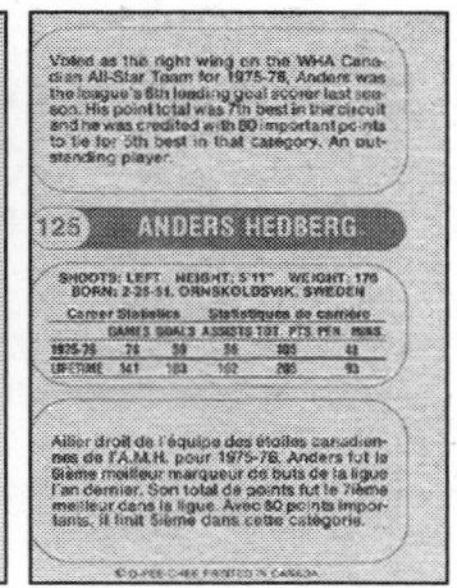

Card Size: 2 1/2" x 3 1/2"
Face: Four colour, white border, Team logo, Position
Back: Blue and brown on card stock; Number, Resume, Bilingual
Imprint: © O-PEE-CHEE
Complete Set (132 cards): 210.00
Common Player: 2.00

	No.	Player	NRMT-MT
☐	1	LL: M. Tardif/ R. Cloutier/ V. Nedomansky	6.00
☐	2	LL: J.C. Tremblay/M. Tardif/ U. Nilsson	3.00
☐	3	LL: M. Tardif/ B. Hull/ R. Cloutie/ U. Nilsson	8.50
☐	4	LL: C. Brackenbury/ G. Gallant	2.00
☐	5	LL: M. Tardif/ B. Hull/ U. Nilsson	8.50
☐	6	LL: M. Dion(G)/J. Daley (G)/W. Rutledge (G)	3.50
☐	7	Barry Long, Winnipeg	2.00
☐	8	Danny Lawson, Calgary, LC	2.00
☐	9	Ulf Nilsson, Winnipeg	3.50
☐	10	Kevin Morrison, San Diego, LC	2.00
☐	11	Gerry Pinder, Minnesota, LC	2.00
☐	12	Richard Brodeur (G), Québec	6.50
☐	13	Robbie Ftorek, Phoenix	3.50
☐	14	Tom Webster, New England	2.00
☐	15	Marty Howe, Houston	3.50
☐	16	Bryan Campbell, Edmonton	2.50
☐	17	Rick Dudley, Cincinnati	2.50
☐	**18**	**Jim Turkiewicz, Birmingham, RC, LC**	**2.50**
☐	19	Rusty Patenaude, Edmonton, LC	2.50
☐	20	Joe Daley (G), Winnipeg	3.50
☐	21	Gary Veneruzzo, San Diego, LC	2.50
☐	22	Chris Evans, Calgary, LC	2.50
☐	23	Mike Antonovich, Minnesota	2.50
☐	24	Jim Dorey, Québec, LC	2.50
☐	**25**	**John Gray, Houston, RC, LC**	**2.50**
☐	26	Larry Pleau, New England, LC	2.50
☐	27	Poul Popiel, Houston	2.50
☐	**28**	**René Leclerc, Indianapolis, RC, LC**	**2.50**
☐	29	Dennis Sobchuk, Cincinnati	2.50
☐	30	Lars-Erik Sjoberg, Winnipeg	2.50
☐	**31**	**Wayne Wood (G), Birmingham, RC**	**3.50**
☐	32	Ron Chipperfield, Calgary	2.50
☐	**33**	**Tim Sheehy, Edmonton, RC, LC**	**2.50**
☐	34	Brent Hughes, San Diego, LC	2.50
☐	35	Ron Ward, Minnesota, LC	2.50
☐	**36**	**Ron Huston, Phoenix, RC, LC**	**2.50**
☐	37	Rosaire Paiement, Indianapolis	2.50
☐	**38**	**Terry Ruskowski, Houston, RC**	**5.00**
☐	39	Hugh Harris, Indianapolis, LC	2.50
☐	40	J. C.Tremblay, Québec	3.50
☐	41	Rich LeDuc, Cincinnati	2.50
☐	**42**	**Peter Sullivan, Winnipeg, RC**	**2.50**
☐	**43**	**Jerry Rollins, Phoenix, RC, LC**	**2.50**
☐	44	Ken Broderick (G), Edmonton	3.50
☐	**45**	**Pete Driscoll, Calgary, RC, LC**	**2.50**
☐	**46**	**Joe Noris, San Diego, RC**	**2.50**
☐	47	Al McLeod, Houston, LC	2.50
☐	**48**	**Bruce Landon (G), New England, RC, LC**	**3.50**
☐	49	Chris Bordeleau, Québec, LC	2.50
☐	50	Gordie Howe, Houston	45.00
☐	51	Thommie Bergman, Winnipeg	2.50
☐	52	Dave Keon, Minnesota	5.50
☐	53	Butch Deadmarsh, Minnesota, LC	2.50
☐	**54**	**Bryan Maxwell, Cincinnati, RC**	**2.50**
☐	55	John Garrett (G), Birmingham	3.50
☐	56	Glen Sather, Edmonton, LC	3.50
☐	57	John Miszuk, Calgary, LC	2.50
☐	58	Heikki Riihiranta, Winnipeg, LC	2.50
☐	**59**	**Richard Grenier, Québec, RC, LC**	**2.50**
☐	60	Gene Peacosh, Indianapolis, LC	2.50
☐	61	AS: Joe Daley (G), Winnipeg	3.50
☐	62	AS: J. C. Tremblay, Québec	2.50
☐	63	AS: Lars-Erik Sjoberg, Winnipeg	2.50
☐	64	AS: Vaclav Nedomansky, Toronto	2.50
☐	65	AS: Bobby Hull, Winnipeg	20.00
☐	66	AS: Anders Hedberg, Winnipeg	3.50
☐	67	AS: Christer Abrahamsson, New England (G)	3.50
☐	68	AS: Kevin Morrison, San Diego, LC	2.50
☐	69	AS: Paul Shmyr, Cleveland	2.50
☐	70	André Lacroix, San Diego	2.50
☐	71	AS: Gene Peacosh, San Diego	2.50
☐	72	AS: Gordie Howe, Houston	25.00
☐	73	Bob Nevin, Edmonton, LC	2.50
☐	74	Richard Lemieux, Calgary, LC	2.50
☐	**75**	**Mike Ford, Calgary, RC, LC**	**2.50**
☐	76	Real Cloutier, Québec	2.50
☐	77	Al McDonough, Minnesota, LC	2.50
☐	**78**	**Del Hall, Phoenix, RC, LC**	**2.50**
☐	79	Thommy Abrahamsson, New England, LC	2.50
☐	80	André Lacroix, San Diego	3.50
☐	**81**	**Frank Hughes, Phoenix, RC, LC**	**2.50**
☐	**82**	**Reg Thomas, Indianapolis, RC**	**2.50**
☐	**83**	**Dave Inkpen, Cincinnati, RC**	**2.50**
☐	84	Paul Henderson, Birmingham	3.50
☐	85	Dave Dryden (G), Edmonton	3.50
☐	86	Lynn Powis, Calgary, LC	2.50
☐	87	André Boudrias, Québec, LC	2.50
☐	88	Veli-Pekka Ketola, Winnipeg, LC	2.50
☐	89	Cam Connor, Houston	2.50
☐	90	Claude St. Sauver, Calgary	2.50
☐	**91**	**Garry Swain, New England, RC, LC**	**2.50**
☐	92	Ernie Wakely, San Diego (G), LC	3.50
☐	**93**	**Blair MacDonald, Indianapolis, RC**	**2.50**
☐	94	Ron Plumb, Cincinnati	2.50
☐	95	Mark Howe, Houston	13.00
☐	**96**	**Peter Marrin, Birmingham, RC**	**2.50**
☐	97	Al Hamilton, Edmonton	2.50
☐	98	Paulin Bordeleau, Québec	2.50
☐	99	Gavin Kirk, LC	2.50
☐	100	Bobby Hull, Winnipeg	40.00
☐	101	Rick Ley, New England	3.50
☐	102	Gary Kurt (G), Phoenix, LC	3.50
☐	103	John McKenzie, Minnesota	2.50
☐	**104**	**Al Karlander, Indianapolis, RC, LC**	**2.50**
☐	105	John French, San Diego, LC	2.50
☐	106	John Hughes, Cincinnati, LC	2.50
☐	107	Ron Grahame (G), Houston	3.50
☐	108	Mark Napier, Birmingham	3.50
☐	109	Serge Bernier, Québec	2.50
☐	110	Christer Abrahamsson (G), New England, LC	3.50
☐	111	Frank Mahovlich, Birmingham	6.50
☐	112	Ted Green, Winnipeg, LC	2.50
☐	113	Rick Jodzio, Calgary, LC	2.50
☐	**114**	**Michel Dion (G), Indianapolis, RC**	**5.00**
☐	**115**	**Rich Preston, Houston, RC**	**2.50**
☐	**116**	**Pekka Rautakallio, Phoenix, RC**	**2.50**
☐	117	Checklist (1 - 132)	30.00
☐	118	Marc Tardif, Québec	3.50
☐	119	Doug Barrie, Edmonton, LC	2.50
☐	120	Vaclav Nedomansky, Birmingham	2.50
☐	121	Bill Lesuk, Winnipeg	2.50
☐	122	Wayne Connelly, Calgary, LC	2.50
☐	123	Pierre Guite, Cincinnati, LC	2.50
☐	124	Ralph Backstrom, New England, LC	2.50
☐	125	Anders Hedberg, Winnipeg	3.50
☐	126	Norm Ullman, Edmonton, LC	4.50
☐	**127**	**Steve Sutherland, Québec, RC, LC**	**2.50**
☐	128	John Schella, Houston, LC	2.50
☐	129	Don McLeod (G), Calgary	3.50
☐	130	Canadian O'Keefe Finals: Winnipeg Wins	3.50
☐	131	U.S. Finals: Houston wins	3.50
☐	132	World Trophy Finals: Winnipeg wins Trophy	9.00

1976 - 77 POPSICLE

Card Size: 2 1/2" x 3 1/2"
Face: Four colour; Name, Team, Team and NHL logos
Back: Black and white; Team history
Imprint: Printed in U.S.A.
Complete (18 cards): 35.00
Common Team: 3.00

☐ Atlanta Flames	☐ Boston Bruins
☐ Buffalo Sabres	☐ Cleveland Barons Seals
☐ Chicago Blackhawks	☐ Detroit Red Wings
☐ Colorado Rockies	☐ Los Angeles Kings
☐ Minnesota North Stars	☐ Montréal Canadiens
☐ New York Islanders	☐ New York Rangers
☐ Philadelphia Flyers	☐ Pittsburgh Penguins
☐ St. Louis Blues	☐ Toronto Maple Leafs
☐ Vancouver Canucks	☐ Washington Capitals

1976 - 77 TOPPS

The card faces are very similar to the O-Pee-Chee set for the same year. The only exceptions are Nos. 102, 159, 183, and 243. Team cards 132 to 149 have a checklist on the back for all players in the set. The set features four record breaking cards 65 to 68.

Card Size: 2 1/2" x 3 1/2"
Face: Four colour, white border, Team logo, Position
Back: Green and blue on card stock, Number, Resume, Hockey trivia
Imprint: © 1976 TOPPS CHEWING GUM, INC.
Complete Set (264 cards): 145.00
Common Player: .35

	No.	Player	NRMT-MT
☐	1	LL: R. Leach/G. Lafleur/P. Larouche	3.25
☐	2	LL: B. Clarke/P. Mahovlich/G. Lafleur/G. Perreault/J. Ratelle	3.00
☐	3	LL: G. Lafleur/B. Clarke/G. Perreault	3.00
☐	4	LL: Steve Durbano/Bryan Watson/Dave Schultz	.75
☐	5	LL: P. Esposito/G. Lafleur/R. Martin/P. Larouche/D. Potvin	3.00
☐	6	LL: K. Dryden/G. Resch/M. Larocque	3.25
☐	7	Gary Doak, Bos.	.35
☐	8	Jacques Richard, Buf.	.35
☐	9	Wayne Dillon, NYR.	.35
☐	10	Bernie Parent (G), Pha.	2.75
☐	11	Ed Westfall, NYI.	.35
☐	12	Dick Redmond, Chi.	.35
☐	13	Bryan Hextall, Min., LC	.35
☐	14	Jean Pronovost, Pgh.	.35
☐	15	Pete Mahovlich, Mtl.	.50
☐	16	Danny Grant, Det.	.35
☐	17	Phil Myre (G), Atl.	.75
☐	18	Wayne Merrick, Cal.	.35
☐	19	Steve Durbano, K.C., LC	.35
☐	20	Derek Sanderson, Stl.	2.00
☐	21	Mike Murphy, L.A.	.35
☐	22	Borje Salming, Tor.	2.25
☐	23	Mike Walton, Van.	.35
☐	24	Randy Manery, Atl.	.35
☐	25	Ken Hodge, Sr., NYR.	.35
☐	**26**	**Mel Bridgman, Pha., RC**	**1.50**
☐	27	Jerry Korab, Buf.	.35
☐	28	Gilles Gratton (G), NYR.	.75
☐	29	André St. Laurent, NYI.	.35
☐	30	Yvan Cournoyer, Mtl.	1.75
☐	31	Phil Russell, Chi.	.35
☐	32	Dennis Hextall, Det.	.35
☐	33	Lowell MacDonald, Pgh.	.35
☐	34	Dennis O'Brien, Min.	.35
☐	35	Gerry Meehan, Wsh.	.35
☐	36	Gilles Meloche (G), Cal.	.75
☐	37	Wilf Paiement, K.C.	.35
☐	**38**	**Bob MacMillan, Stl., RC**	**.35**
☐	39	Ian Turnbull, Tor.	.35
☐	40	Rogatien Vachon (G), L.A.	1.00
☐	41	Nick Beverley, NYR.	.35
☐	42	René Robert, Buf.	.35
☐	43	André Savard, Buf.	.35
☐	44	Bob Gainey, Mtl.	3.00
☐	45	Joe Watson, Pha.	.35
☐	46	Billy Smith (G), NYI.	3.50
☐	47	Darcy Rota, Chi.	.35

	No.	Player	Price
☐	**48**	**Rick Lapointe, Det., RC**	**.35**
☐	49	Pierre Jarry, Min.	.35
☐	50	Syl Apps, Pgh.	.35
☐	51	Eric Vail, Atl.	.35
☐	52	Greg Joly, Wsh.	.35
☐	53	Don Lever, Van.	.35
☐	**54**	**Bob L. Murdoch, Cal., RC**	**.35**
☐	55	Denis Herron (G), K.C.	.75
☐	56	Mike Bloom, Det.	.35
☐	57	Bill Fairbairn, NYR.	.35
☐	58	Fred Stanfield, Buf.	.35
☐	59	Steve Shutt, Mtl.	2.50
☐	60	Brad Park, Bos.,	2.00
☐	61	AS: Gilles Villemure (G), Chi., LC	.75
☐	62	AS: Bert Marshall, NYI.	.35
☐	63	AS: Chuck Lefley, Stl.	.35
☐	64	AS: Simon Nolet, Pgh., LC	.35
☐	65	Most Goals, Playoffs: Reggie Leach, Pha.	.35
☐	66	Most Points, Game: Darryl Sittler, Tor.	2.00
☐	67	Most Points, Season, Rookie: Bryan Trottier, NYI.	6.50
☐	68	Most Consecutive Games, Lifetime: Garry Unger, Stl.	.35
☐	69	Ron Low (G), Wsh.	.75
☐	70	AS: Bobby Clarke, Pha.	5.50
☐	**71**	**Michel Bergeron, Det., RC**	**.75**
☐	72	Ron Stackhouse, Pgh.	.35
☐	73	Bill Hogaboam, Min.	.35
☐	74	Bob J. Murdoch, L.A.	.35
☐	75	Steve Vickers, NYR.	.35
☐	76	Pit Martin, Chi.	.35
☐	77	Gerry Hfd., NYI.	.35
☐	78	Craig Ramsay, Buf.	.50
☐	79	Michel Larocque (G), Mtl.	.75
☐	80	Jean Ratelle, Bos.	1.25
☐	81	Don Saleski, Pha.	.35
☐	82	Bill Clement, Atl.	.35
☐	83	Dave Burrows, Pgh.	.35
☐	84	Wayne Thomas (G), Tor.	.75
☐	85	John Gould, Van.	.35
☐	**86**	**Dennis Maruk, Cal., RC**	**2.50**
☐	87	Ernie Hicke, Min.	.35
☐	88	Jim Rutherford (G), Det.	.75
☐	89	Dale Tallon, Chi.	.35
☐	90	Rod Gilbert, NYR.	1.25
☐	91	Marcel Dionne, L.A.	5.50
☐	92	Chuck Arnason, K.C.	.35
☐	93	Jean Potvin, NYI.	.35
☐	94	Don Luce, Buf.	.35
☐	95	John Bucyk, Bos.	1.25
☐	96	Larry Goodenough, Pha.	.35
☐	97	Mario Tremblay, Mtl.	.35
☐	**98**	**Nelson Pyatt, Wsh., RC**	**.35**
☐	99	Brian Glennie, Tor.	.35
☐	100	Tony Esposito (G), Chi.	3.00
☐	101	Dan Maloney, Det.	.35
☐	102	Barry Wilkins, Pgh., LC	.35
☐	103	Dean Talafous, Min.	.35
☐	**104**	**Ed Staniowski (G), Stl., RC**	**.75**
☐	105	Dallas Smith, Bos., LC	.35
☐	106	Jude Drouin, NYI.	.35
☐	107	Pat Hickey, NYR.	.35
☐	108	Jocelyn Guevremont, Buf.	.35
☐	**109**	**Doug Risebrough, Mtl., RC**	**.75**
☐	110	Reggie Leach, Pha.	.50
☐	111	Dan Bouchard (G), Atl.	.75
☐	112	Chris Oddleifson, Van.	.35
☐	113	Rick Hampton, Cal.	.35
☐	114	John Marks, Chi.	.35
☐	**115**	**Bryan Trottier, NYI., RC**	**35.00**
☐	116	Checklist 1 (1 - 132)	9.00
☐	117	Greg Polis, NYR.	.35
☐	118	Peter McNab, Bos.	.35
☐	119	Jim Roberts, Mtl.	.35
☐	120	Gerry Cheevers (G), Bos.	2.75
☐	121	Rick MacLeish, Pha.	.35
☐	122	Bill Lochead, Det.	.35
☐	123	Tom Reid, Min.	.35
☐	124	Rick Kehoe, Pgh.	.50
☐	125	Keith Magnuson, Chi.	.35
☐	126	Clark Gillies, NYI.	1.25
☐	127	Rick Middleton, Bos.	2.25
☐	128	Bill Hajt, Buf.	.35
☐	129	Jacques Lemaire, Mtl.	1.25
☐	130	Terry O'Reilly, Bos.	.35
☐	131	André Dupont, Pha.	.35
☐	132	CL: Flames, Patrick Division	2.25
☐	133	CL: Bruins, Adams Division	2.25
☐	134	CL: Sabres, Adams Division	2.25
☐	135	CL: Seals, Adams Division	2.25
☐	136	CL: Blackhawks, Smythe Division	2.25
☐	137	CL: Red Wings, Norris Division	2.25
☐	138	CL: Scouts, Smythe Division	2.25
☐	139	CL: Kings, Norris Division	2.25
☐	140	CL: North Stars, Smythe Division	2.25
☐	141	CL: Canadiens, Norris Division	2.25
☐	142	CL: Islanders, Patrick Division	2.25
☐	143	CL: Rangers, Patrick Division	2.25
☐	144	CL: Flyers, Patrick Division	2.25
☐	145	CL: Penguins, Norris Division	2.25
☐	146	CL: Blues, Smythe Division	2.25
☐	147	CL: Maple Leafs, Adams Division	2.25
☐	148	CL: Canucks, Smythe Division	2.25
☐	149	CL: Capitals, Norris Division	2.25
☐	150	Dave Schultz, Pha.	.35
☐	151	Larry Robinson, Mtl.	5.00
☐	152	Al Smith (G), Buf.	.75
☐	153	Bob Nystrom, NYI.	.50
☐	154	Ron Greschner, NYR.	.75
☐	155	Gregg Sheppard, Bos.	.35
☐	156	Alain Daigle, Chi.	.35
☐	157	Ed Van Impe, Pgh., LC	.35
☐	**158**	**Tim Young, Min., RC**	**.75**
☐	159	Gary Bergman, K.C., LC	.35
☐	160	Ed Giacomin (G), Det.	1.25
☐	161	Yvon Labre, Wsh.	.35
☐	162	Jim Lorentz, Buf.	.35
☐	163	Guy Lafleur, Mtl.,	12.00
☐	164	Tom Bladon, Pha.	.35
☐	165	Wayne Cashman, Bos.	.35
☐	166	Pete Stemkowski, NYR.	.35
☐	167	Grant Mulvey, Chi.	.35
☐	**168**	**Yves Belanger (G), Stl., RC**	**.75**
☐	169	Bill Goldsworthy, Min.	.35
☐	170	Denis Potvin, NYI..	6.00
☐	171	Nick Libett, Det.	.35
☐	172	Michel Plasse (G), Pgh.	.75
☐	173	Lou Nanne, Min.	.35
☐	174	Tom Lysiak, Atl.	.35
☐	175	Dennis Ververgaert, Van.	.35
☐	176	Gary Simmons (G), Cal.	.75
☐	177	Pierre Bouchard, Mtl.	.50
☐	178	Bill Barber, Pha.	2.00
☐	179	Darryl Edestrand, Bos.	.35
☐	180	Gilbert Perreault, Buf.,	2.75
☐	**181**	**Dave Maloney, NYR., RC**	**.75**
☐	182	J. P. Parise, NYI.	.35
☐	183	Bobby Sheehan, Chi.	.35
☐	**184**	**Pete LoPresti (G), Min., RC**	**.75**
☐	185	Don Kozak, L.A.	.35
☐	186	Guy Charron, K.C.	.35
☐	187	Stan Gilbertson, Pgh.	.35
☐	**188**	**Bill Nyrop, Mtl., RC**	**.35**
☐	189	Bobby Schmautz, Bos.	.35
☐	190	Wayne Stephenson (G), Pha.	.75
☐	191	Brian Spencer, Buf.	.35
☐	192	Gilles Marotte, NYR., LC	.35
☐	193	Lorne Henning, NYI.	.35
☐	194	Bob Neely, Tor.	.35
☐	195	Dennis Hull, Chi.	.50
☐	196	Walt McKechnie, Det.	.35
☐	**197**	**Curt Ridley (G), Van., RC**	**.75**
☐	198	Dwight Bialowas, Min.	.35
☐	199	Pierre Larouche, Pgh.	1.25
☐	200	Ken Dryden (G), Mtl.,	15.00
☐	201	Ross Lonsberry, Pha.	.35
☐	202	Curt Bennett, Atl.	.35
☐	**203**	**Hartland Monahan, Wsh., RC**	**.35**
☐	204	John Davidson (G), NYR.	1.25
☐	205	Serge Savard, Mtl.	1.00
☐	206	Garry Howatt, NYI.	.35
☐	207	Darryl Sittler, Tor.	3.75
☐	208	J.P. Bordeleau, Chi.	.35
☐	209	Henry Boucha, K.C.	.35
☐	210	Rick Martin, Buf.	.50
☐	211	Vic Venasky, L.A.	.35
☐	212	Fred (Buster) Harvey, Det.	.35
☐	213	Bobby Orr, Bos.	25.00
☐	214	French Connection: Martin/ Perreault/ Robert, Buf.	2.75
☐	215	LCB Line: Barber/ Clarke/ Leach, Pha.	3.00
☐	216	Long Island Lightning Co.: Gillies/ Trottier/ Harris, NYI.	4.00
☐	217	Checking Line: Gainey/ Jarvis/ Roberts, Mtl.	1.00
☐	218	Bicentennial Line: MacDonald/ Apps/ Pronovost, Pgh.	.75
☐	219	Bob Kelly, Pha.	.35
☐	220	Walt Tkaczuk, NYR.	.35
☐	221	Dave Lewis, NYI.	.50
☐	222	Danny Gare, Buf.	.50
☐	223	Guy Lapointe, Mtl.	1.00
☐	**224**	**Hank Nowak, Bos., RC, LC**	**.35**
☐	225	Stan Mikita, Chi.	3.25
☐	226	Vic Hadfield, Pgh., LC	.35
☐	**227**	**Bernie Wolfe (G), Wsh., RC**	**.75**
☐	228	Bryan Watson, Det.	.35
☐	229	Ralph Stewart, NYI.	.35
☐	230	Gerry Desjardins (G), Buf.	.75
☐	**231**	**John Bednarski, NYR., RC, LC**	**.35**
☐	232	Yvon Lambert, Mtl.	.35
☐	233	Orest Kindrachuk, Pha.	.35
☐	234	Don Marcotte, Bos.	.35
☐	235	Bill White, Chi., LC	.35
☐	236	Red Berenson, Stl.	.35
☐	237	Al MacAdam, Cal.	.35
☐	**238**	**Rick Blight, Van., RC**	**.35**
☐	239	Butch Goring, L.A.	.50
☐	240	Césare Maniago (G), Min.	.75
☐	241	Jim Schoenfeld, Buf.	.35
☐	242	Cliff Koroll, Chi.	.35
☐	243	Mickey Redmond, Det., LC	.75
☐	244	Rick Chartraw, Mtl.	.35
☐	245	Phil Esposito, NYR.	3.25
☐	246	Dave Forbes, Bos.	.35
☐	247	Jimmy Watson, Pha.	.35
☐	248	Ron Schock, Pgh.	.35
☐	249	Fred Barrett, Min.	.35
☐	250	Glenn Resch (G), NYI.,	1.25
☐	251	Ivan Boldirev, Chi.	.35
☐	252	Billy Harris, NYI.	.35
☐	253	Lee Fogolin, Buf	.35
☐	254	Murray Wilson, Mtl.	.35
☐	255	Gilles Gilbert (G), Bos.	.75
☐	256	Gary Dornhoefer, Pha.	.35
☐	257	Carol Vadnais, NYR.	.35
☐	258	Checklist 2 (133 - 264)	9.00
☐	259	Errol Thompson, Tor.	.35
☐	260	Garry Unger, Stl.	.50
☐	261	J. Bob Kelly, Pgh.	.35
☐	262	Terry Harper, Det.	.35
☐	263	Blake Dunlop, Min.	.35
☐	264	'75-76 Stanley Cup Champions: Canadiens	2.50

TOPPS GLOSSY INSERT SET

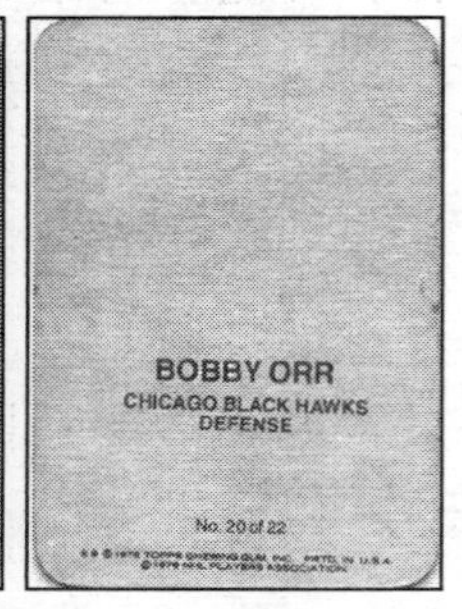

BOBBY ORR
CHICAGO BLACK HAWKS
DEFENSE
No. 20 of 22

This 22-card insert set was randomly inserted in the 1976-77 regular issue wax packs. The cards are numbered _ of 22.

Card Size: 2 1/4" x 3 1/4"
Face: Four colour, borderless; Facsimile autograph
Back: Blue on card stock; Name, Team, Position, Number
Insert Set (22 cards): 85.00

	No.	Player	NRMT-MT
☐	1	Bobby Clarke, Pha.	4.50
☐	2	Brad Park, Bos.	3.50
☐	3	Tony Esposito (G), Chi.	5.00
☐	4	Marcel Dionne, L.A.	5.00
☐	5	Ken Dryden (G), Mtl.	15.00
☐	6	Glenn Resch (G), NYI.	2.50
☐	7	Phil Esposito, NYR.	6.00
☐	8	Darryl Sittler, Tor.	5.00
☐	9	Gilbert Perreault, Buf.	4.00
☐	10	Denis Potvin, NYI.	5.00
☐	11	Guy Lafleur, Mtl.	12.00
☐	12	Bill Barber, Pha.	3.50
☐	13	Syl Apps, Jr., Pgh.	1.50
☐	14	John Bucyk, Bos.	3.50

	No.	Player	Price
☐	15	Bryan Trottier, NYI.	10.00
☐	16	Dennis Hull, Chi.	1.50
☐	17	Guy Lapointe, Mtl.	3.00
☐	18	Rod Gilbert, NYR.	3.50
☐	19	Richard Martin, Buf.	1.50
☐	20	Bobby Orr, Chi.	30.00
☐	21	Reggie Leach, Pha.	1.50
☐	22	Jean Ratelle, NYR.	3.50

1977 - 78 COCA-COLA MINIS

Card Size: 1 3/8" x 1 3/8"
Face: Four colour; Name, Team
Back: Resume
Imprint: THE COCA-COLA COMPANY
Complete Set (30 Cards): 125.00

	Player	NRMT-MT
☐	Syl Apps, Pgh.	2.50
☐	Dave Burrows, Pgh.	2.50
☐	Bobby Clarke, Pha.	8.50
☐	Yvan Cournoyer, Mtl.	6.00
☐	John Davidson (G), NYR.	5.00
☐	Marcel Dionne, L.A.	7.50
☐	Doug Favell (G)	4.00
☐	Rod Gilbert, NYR.	6.00
☐	Brian Glennie, Tor.	2.50
☐	Butch Goring, L.A.	2.50
☐	Lorne Henning, NYI.	2.50
☐	Cliff Koroll, Chi.	2.50
☐	Guy Lapointe, Mtl.	5.00
☐	Dave Maloney, NYR.	2.50
☐	Pit Martin, Chi.	2.50
☐	Lou Nanne, Min.	2.50
☐	Bobby Orr, Chi.	50.00
☐	Brad Park, Bos.	6.00
☐	Craig Ramsay, Buf.	2.50
☐	Larry Robinson, Mtl.	7.50
☐	Jim Rutherford (G), Det.	4.00
☐	Don Saleski, Pha.	2.50
☐	Steve Shutt, Mtl.	6.00
☐	Darryl Sittler, Tor.	7.50
☐	Billy Smith (G), NYI.	7.50
☐	Bob Stewart, Cle.	2.50
☐	Rogatien Vachon (G), L.A.	5.00
☐	Jimmy Watson, Pha.	2.50
☐	Joe Watson, Pha.	2.50
☐	Ed Westfall, NYI.	2.50

1977 - 78 O-PEE-CHEE

Cards 322-339 show the team emblem on the front and player records on the back. The set features all-star and record breaking players.

Card Size: 2 1/2" x 3 1/2"
Face: Four colour, white border, Team logo, Position
Back: Brown and blue on card stock, Number, Resume, Hockey trivia, Bilingual
Imprint: © 1977 O-PEE-CHEE
Complete Set (396 cards): 165.00
Common Player: .50

	No.	Player	NRMT-MT
☐	1	LL: S. Shutt/ G. Lafleur/ M. Dionne	5.00
☐	2	LL: G. Lafleur/ M. Dionne/ L. Robinson/B. Salming/T. Young	3.00
☐	3	LL: G. Lafleur/ M. Dionne/ S. Shutt	3.75
☐	4	LL: D. Williams/ D. Polonich/ B. Gassoff	1.00
☐	5	LL: L. McDonald/ P. Esposito/ T. Williams	2.00
☐	6	LL: M. Larocque (G)/ K. Dryden (G)/ G. Resch (G)	3.25
☐	7	LL: G. Perreault/ S, Shutt/ G. Lafleur/ R. MacLeish/P. McNab	3.75
☐	8	LL: K. Dryden(G)/ R. Vachon (G) / B. Parent (G)/D. Wilson (G)	5.00
☐	9	Brian Spencer, Buf., (Pgh)	.50
☐	10	AS: Denis Potvin	6.00
☐	11	Nick Fotiu, NYR.	.50
☐	12	Bob Murray, Chi.	.75
☐	13	Pete LoPresti (G), Min.	1.00
☐	14	J. Bob Kelly, Pgh., (Chi.)	.50
☐	15	Rick MacLeish, Pha.	.75
☐	16	Terry Harper, Det.	.50
☐	**17**	**Willi Plett, Atl., RC**	**2.00**
☐	18	Peter McNab, Bos.	.50
☐	19	Wayne Thomas (G), Tor. (NYR.)	1.00
☐	20	Pierre Bouchard, Mtl.	.50
☐	21	Dennis Maruk, Cle.	.50
☐	22	Mike Murphy, L.A.	.50
☐	23	Césare Maniago (G), Van., LC	1.00
☐	**24**	**Paul Gardner, Col., RC**	**.50**
☐	25	Rod Gilbert, NYR., LC	1.50
☐	26	Orest Kindrachuk, Pha.	.50
☐	27	Bill Hajt, Buf.	.50
☐	28	John Davidson (G), NYR.	1.50
☐	29	J. P. Parise, NYI.	.50
☐	30	AS: Larry Robinson	6.50
☐	31	Yvon Labre, Wsh.	.50
☐	32	Walt McKechnie, Det. (Wsh.)	.50
☐	33	Rick Kehoe, Pgh.	.75
☐	**34**	**Randy Holt, Chi., RC**	**.50**
☐	35	Garry Unger, Stl.	.75
☐	36	Lou Nanne, Min., LC	.50
☐	37	Dan Bouchard (G), Atl.	1.00
☐	38	Darryl Sittler, Tor.	4.25
☐	39	Bob L. Murdoch, Cle.	.50
☐	40	Jean Ratelle, Bos.	1.50
☐	41	Dave Maloney, NYR.	.50
☐	42	Danny Gare, Buf.	.75
☐	43	Jimmy Watson, Pha.	.50
☐	44	Tommy Williams, L.A.	.50
☐	45	Serge Savard, Mtl.	1.50
☐	46	Derek Sanderson, Van., LC	.50
☐	47	John Marks, Chi.	.50
☐	**48**	**Al Cameron, Det., RC**	**.50**
☐	49	Dean Talafous, Min.	.50
☐	50	Glenn Resch (G), NYI.	1.00
☐	51	Ron Schock, Pgh. (Buf.)	.50
☐	52	Gary Croteau, Col.	.50
☐	53	Gerry Meehan, Wsh.	.50
☐	54	Ed Staniowski (G), Stl.	1.00
☐	55	Phil Esposito, NYR.	4.50
☐	56	Dennis Ververgaert, Van.	.50
☐	57	Rick Wilson, Det., LC	.50
☐	58	Jim Lorentz, Buf.	.50
☐	59	Bobby Schmautz, Bos.	.50
☐	60	AS: Guy Lapointe	1.50
☐	61	Ivan Boldirev, Chi.	.50
☐	62	Bob Nystrom, NYI.	.75
☐	63	Rick Hampton, Cle.	.50
☐	64	Jack Valiquette, Tor.	.50
☐	65	Bernie Parent (G), Pha.	2.75
☐	66	Dave Burrows, Pgh.	.50
☐	67	Butch Goring, L.A.	.75
☐	68	Checklist 1 (1 - 132)	12.00
☐	69	Murray Wilson, Mtl., LC	.50
☐	70	Ed Giacomin (G), Det., LC	1.50
☐	71	CL: Atlanta Flames	1.50
☐	72	CL: Boston Bruins	1.50
☐	73	CL: Buffalo Sabres	1.50
☐	74	CL: Chicago Blackhawks	1.50
☐	75	CL: Cleveland Barons	1.50
☐	76	CL: Colorado Rockies	1.50
☐	77	CL: Detroit Red Wings	1.50
☐	78	CL: Los Angeles Kings	1.50
☐	79	CL: Minnesota North Stars	1.50
☐	80	CL: Montréal Canadiens	1.50
☐	81	CL: New York Islanders	1.50
☐	82	CL: New York Rangers	1.50
☐	83	CL: Philadelphia Flyers	1.50
☐	84	CL: Pittsburgh Penguins	1.50
☐	85	CL: St. Louis Blues	1.50
☐	86	CL: Toronto Maple Leafs	1.50
☐	87	CL: Vancouver Canucks	1.50
☐	88	CL: Washington Capitals	1.50
☐	89	Keith Magnuson, Chi.	.50
☐	90	Walt Tkaczuk, NYR.	.50
☐	91	Bill Nyrop, Mtl.	.50
☐	92	Michel Plasse (G), Col.	1.00
☐	93	Bob Bourne, NYI.	.50
☐	94	Lee Fogolin, Buf.	.50
☐	95	Gregg Sheppard, Bos.	.50
☐	96	Hartland Monahan, Wsh. (L.A.)	.50
☐	97	Curt Bennett, Atl.	.50
☐	98	Bob Dailey, Pha.	.50
☐	99	Bill Goldsworthy, NYR., LC	.50
☐	100	AS: Ken Dryden, Mtl. (G)	20.00
☐	101	Grant Mulvey, Chi.	.50
☐	102	Pierre Larouche, Pgh.	.50
☐	103	Nick Libett, Det.	.50
☐	104	Rick Smith, Bos.	.50
☐	105	Bryan Trottier, NYI.	20.00
☐	106	Pierre Jarry, Min., LC	.50
☐	107	Red Berenson, Stl.	.50
☐	108	Jim Schoenfeld, Buf.	.575
☐	109	Gilles Meloche (G), Cle.	1.00
☐	110	AS: Lanny McDonald	3.50
☐	111	Don Lever, Van.	.50
☐	112	Greg Polis, NYR.	.50
☐	**113**	**Gary Sargent, L.A., RC**	**.50**
☐	**114**	**Earl Anderson, Bos., RC, LC**	**50**
☐	115	Bobby Clarke, Pha.	6.00
☐	116	Dave Lewis, NYI.	.75
☐	117	Darcy Rota, Chi.	.50
☐	118	André Savard, Buf.	.50
☐	119	Denis Herron (G), Pgh.	1.00
☐	120	AS: Steve Shutt, Mtl.	2.50
☐	121	Mel Bridgman, Pha.	.50
☐	122	Fred (Buster) Harvey, Det., LC	.50
☐	**123**	**Rolie Eriksson, Min., RC**	**.50**
☐	124	Dale Tallon, Chi.	.50
☐	125	Gilles Gilbert (G), Bos.	1.00
☐	126	Billy Harris, NYI.	.50
☐	127	Tom Lysiak, Atl.	.50
☐	128	Jerry Korab, Buf.	.50
☐	129	Bob Gainey, Mtl.	3.00
☐	130	Wilf Paiement, Col.	.50
☐	131	Tom Bladon, Pha.	.50
☐	132	Ernie Hicke, Min. (L.A.), LC	.50
☐	133	J. P. LeBlanc, Det., LC	.50
☐	**134**	**Mike Milbury, Bos., RC**	**6.00**
☐	135	Pit Martin, Chi. (Van.)	.50
☐	136	Steve Vickers, NYR.	.50
☐	137	Don Awrey, Pgh. (NYR.)	.50
☐	138	Bernie Wolfe (G), Wsh.	1.00
☐	139	Doug Jarvis, Mtl.	1.50
☐	140	AS: Borje Salming	2.50
☐	141	Bob MacMillan, Stl.	.50
☐	142	Wayne Stephenson (G), Pha.	1.00
☐	143	Dave Forbes, Bos. (Wsh.)	.50
☐	144	Jean Potvin, NYI.	.50
☐	145	Guy Charron, Wsh.	.50
☐	146	Cliff Koroll, Chi.	.50
☐	147	Danny Grant, Det.	.50
☐	148	Bill Hogaboam, Min.	.50
☐	149	Al MacAdam, Cle.	.50
☐	150	Gerry Desjardins (G), Buf., LC	1.00
☐	151	Yvon Lambert, Mtl.	.50
☐	152	Rick Lapointe, Pha.	.50
☐	153	Ed Westfall, NYI.	.50
☐	154	Carol Vadnais, NYR.	.50
☐	155	John Bucyk, Bos., LC	1.50
☐	156	J. P. Bordeleau, Chi.	.50
☐	157	Ron Stackhouse, Pgh.	.50
☐	**158**	**Glen Sharpley, Min., RC**	**.50**
☐	159	Michel Bergeron, Det. (NYI.)	.50
☐	160	AS: Rogatien Vachon (G)	1.50
☐	161	Fred Stanfield, Buf.	.50
☐	162	Gerry Hart, NYI.	.50
☐	163	Mario Tremblay, Mtl.	1.00
☐	164	André Dupont, Pha.	.50
☐	165	Don Marcotte, Bos.	.50
☐	166	Wayne Dillon, NYR.	.50
☐	167	Claude Larose, Stl., LC	.50
☐	168	Eric Vail, Atl.	.50
☐	**169**	**Tom Edur, Col., RC**	**.50**
☐	170	Tony Esposito (G), Chi.	3.75
☐	171	André St. Laurent, NYI., (Det.)	.50
☐	172	Dan Maloney, Det.	.50
☐	173	Dennis O'Brien, Min.	.50
☐	**174**	**Blair Chapman, Pgh., RC**	**.50**
☐	175	Dennis Kearns, Van.	.50
☐	176	Wayne Merrick, Cle.	.50
☐	177	Michel Larocque (G), Mtl.	1.00
☐	178	Bob Kelly, Pha.	.50

	No.	Player	Price
☐	**179**	**Dave Farrish, NYR., RC**	**.50**
☐	180	AS: Rick Martin, Buf.	.75
☐	181	Gary Doak, Bos.	.50
☐	182	Jude Drouin, NYI.	.50
☐	**183**	**Barry Dean, Col. (Pha.), RC**	**.50**
☐	184	Gary Smith (G), Min. (Wsh.)	1.00
☐	185	Reggie Leach, Pha.	.75
☐	186	Ian Turnbull, Tor.	.50
☐	187	Vic Venasky, L.A.	.50
☐	**188**	**Wayne Bianchin, Pgh., RC**	**.50**
☐	189	Doug Risebrough, Mtl.	.50
☐	190	Brad Park, Bos.	2.50
☐	191	Craig Ramsay, Buf.	.75
☐	192	Ken Hodge, NYR., LC	.50
☐	193	Phil Myre (G), Atl.	1.00
☐	194	Garry Howatt, NYI.	.50
☐	195	Stan Mikita, Chi.	4.25
☐	196	Garnet Bailey, Wsh., LC	.50
☐	197	Dennis Hextall, Det.	.50
☐	198	Nick Beverley, Min.	.50
☐	199	Larry Patey, Stl.	.50
☐	200	AS: Guy Lafleur, Mtl.	16.00
☐	**201**	**Don Edwards (G), Buf., RC**	**4.00**
☐	202	Gary Dornhoefer, Pha., LC	.50
☐	203	Bob Paradise, Pgh.	.50
☐	**204**	**Alex Pirus, Min., RC, LC**	**.50**
☐	205	Pete Mahovlich, Mtl.	.75
☐	206	Bert Marshall, NYI.	.50
☐	207	Gilles Gratton (G), NYR., LC	1.00
☐	208	Alain Daigle, Chi.	.50
☐	209	Chris Oddleifson, Van.	.50
☐	210	AS: Gilbert Perreault, Buf.	3.00
☐	**211**	**Mike Palmateer (G), Tor., RC**	**10.00**
☐	212	Bill Lochead, Det.	.50
☐	213	Dick Redmond, Chi., (Stl.)	.50
☐	214	RB: Guy Lafleur, Mtl.	3.00
☐	215	RB: Ian Turnbull, Tor.	1.00
☐	216	RB: Guy Lafleur, Mtl.	3.00
☐	217	RB: Steve Shutt, Mtl.	1.50
☐	218	RB: Guy Lafleur, Mtl.	3.00
☐	219	Lorne Henning, NYI.	.50
☐	220	Terry O'Reilly, Bos.	.50
☐	221	Pat Hickey, NYR.	.50
☐	222	René Robert, Buf.	.50
☐	223	Tim Young, Min.	.50
☐	224	Dunc Wilson (G), Pgh., LC	1.00
☐	225	Dennis Hull, Chi., LC	.75
☐	226	Rod Seiling, Stl.	.50
☐	227	Bill Barber, Pha.	1.50
☐	**228**	**Dennis Polonich, Det., RC**	**.50**
☐	229	Billy Smith (G), NYI.	3.25
☐	230	Yvan Cournoyer, Mtl.	1.50
☐	231	Don Luce, Buf.	.50
☐	**232**	**Mike McEwen, NYR., RC**	**.50**
☐	233	Don Saleski, Pha.	.50
☐	234	Wayne Cashman, Bos.	.50
☐	235	Phil Russell, Chi.	.50
☐	236	Mike Corrigan, Pgh., LC	.50
☐	237	Guy Chouinard, Atl.	.50
☐	**238**	**Steve Jensen, Min., RC**	**.50**
☐	239	Jim Rutherford (G), Det.	1.00
☐	240	AS: Marcel Dionne, L.A.	6.50
☐	241	Réjean Houle, Mtl.	.75
☐	242	Jocelyn Guevremont, Buf.	.50
☐	243	Jim Harrison, Chi., LC	.50
☐	**244**	**Don Murdoch, NYR., RC**	**1.00**
☐	**245**	**Richard Green, Wsh., RC**	**1.00**
☐	246	Rick Middleton, Bos.	1.50
☐	247	Joe Watson, Pha.	.50
☐	248	Syl Apps, Pgh., (L.A.)	.50
☐	249	Checklist 2 (133 - 264)	12.00
☐	250	Clark Gillies, NYI.	.75
☐	251	Bobby Orr, Chi., LC	25.00
☐	252	Nelson Pyatt, Col.	.50
☐	**253**	**Gary McAdam, Buf., RC**	**.50**
☐	254	Jacques Lemaire, Mtl.	1.50
☐	255	Bob Girard, Cle.	.50
☐	256	Ron Greschner, NYR.	.50
☐	257	Ross Lonsberry, Pha.	.50
☐	258	Dave Gardner, Cle.	.50
☐	259	Rick Blight, Van.	.50
☐	260	Gerry Cheevers (G), Bos.	2.75
☐	261	Jean Pronovost, Pgh.	.50
☐	262	Playoffs: Canadiens Skate Past Islanders	1.00
☐	263	Playoffs: Bruins Advance to Finals	1.00
☐	264	Playoffs: Canadiens Win 20th Stanley Cup	1.50
☐	**265**	**Rick Bowness, Atl. (Det)., RC**	**1.00**
☐	266	George Ferguson, Tor.	.50
☐	**267**	**Mike Kitchen, Col., RC**	**.50**
☐	268	Bob Berry, L.A., LC	.50
☐	**269**	**Greg Smith, Cle., RC**	**.50**
☐	**270**	**Stan Jonathan, Bos., RC**	**2.50**
☐	271	Dwight Bialowas, Min., LC	.50
☐	272	Pete Stemkowski, (L.A.)	.50
☐	273	Greg Joly, Det.	.50
☐	**274**	**Ken Houston, Atl., RC**	**.50**
☐	275	Brian Glennie, Tor.	.50
☐	276	Eddie Johnston (G), Stl., LC	1.00
☐	277	John Grisdale, Van.	.50
☐	278	Craig Patrick, Wsh., LC	.50
☐	**279**	**Ken Breitenbach, Buf., RC, LC**	**.50**
☐	280	Fred Ahern, Cal. (Cle.),	.50
☐	281	Jim Roberts, Mtl. (Stl.), LC	.50
☐	**282**	**Harvey Bennett, Pha., RC**	**.50**
☐	283	Ab DeMarco, L.A. (Atl.), LC	.50
☐	284	Pat Boutette, Tor.	.50
☐	285	Bob Plager, Stl.	.50
☐	286	Hilliard Graves, Van.	.50
☐	**287**	**Gordie Lane, Wsh., RC**	**.50**
☐	**288**	**Ron Andruff, Col., RC**	**.50**
☐	289	Larry Brown, L.A.	.50
☐	**290**	**Mike Fidler, Cle., RC**	**.50**
☐	291	Fred Barrett, Min.	.50
☐	292	Bill Clement, Atl.	.50
☐	293	Errol Thompson, Tor.	.50
☐	294	Doug Grant (G), Stl.	1.00
☐	295	Harold Snepsts, Van.	.75
☐	**296**	**Rick Bragnalo, Wsh., RC**	**.50**
☐	297	Bryan Lefley, Col.	.50
☐	298	Gene Carr, L.A. (Pgh.)	.50
☐	299	Bob Stewart, Cle.	.50
☐	300	Lew Morrison, Pgh., LC	.50
☐	301	Ed Kea, Atl.	.50
☐	302	Scott Garland, Tor.	.50
☐	303	Bill Fairbairn, NYR. (Stl.)	.50
☐	304	Larry Carrière, Van.	.50
☐	305	Ron Low (G), Wsh. (Det.)	1.00
☐	306	Tom Reid, Min., LC	.50
☐	**307**	**Paul Holmgren, Pha., RC**	**2.75**
☐	308	Pat Price, NYI.	.50
☐	**309**	**Kirk Bowman, Chi., RC**	**.50**
☐	**310**	**Bobby Simpson, Atl., RC**	**.50**
☐	311	Ron Ellis, Tor.	.50
☐	312	Rick Bourbonnais, Stl., Err. (Bernie Federko)	.50
☐	313	Bobby Lalonde, (Atl.)	.50
☐	314	Tony White, Wsh., LC	.50
☐	315	John Van Boxmeer, Col.	.50
☐	316	Don Kozak, L.A.	.50
☐	317	Jim Neilson, NYR. (Cle.), LC	.50
☐	**318**	**Terry Martin, Buf., RC**	**.50**
☐	319	Barry Gibbs, Atl.	.50
☐	320	Inge Hammarstrom, Tor. (Stl.)	.50
☐	321	Darryl Edestrand, Bos.	.50
☐	322	Atlanta Flames	3.00
☐	323	Boston Bruins	3.00
☐	324	Buffalo Sabres	3.00
☐	325	Chicago Blackhawks	3.00
☐	326	Cleveland Barons	3.00
☐	327	Colorado Rockies	3.00
☐	328	Detroit Red Wings	3.00
☐	329	Los Angeles Kings	3.00
☐	330	Minnesota North Stars	3.00
☐	331	Montréal Canadiens	3.00
☐	332	New York Islanders	3.00
☐	333	New York Rangers	3.00
☐	334	Philadelphia Flyers	3.00
☐	335	Pittsburgh Penguins	3.00
☐	336	St. Louis Blues	3.00
☐	337	Toronto Maple Leafs	3.00
☐	338	Vancouver Canucks	3.00
☐	339	Washington Capitals	3.00
☐	340	Chuck Lefley, Stl.	.50
☐	341	Garry Monahan, Van.	.50
☐	342	Bryan Watson, Wsh.	.50
☐	343	Dave Hudson, Col.	.50
☐	344	Neil Komadoski, L.A.	.50
☐	345	Gary Edwards (G), L.A. (Cle.)	1.00
☐	346	Rey Comeau, Atl.	.50
☐	347	Bob Neely, Tor., LC	.50
☐	348	Jean Hamel, Det.	.50
☐	349	Jerry Butler, (Tor.)	.50
☐	350	Mike Walton, Van.	.50
☐	351	Bob Sirois, Wsh.	.50
☐	352	Jim McElmury, Col., LC	.50
☐	353	Dave Schultz, (Pgh.)	.50
☐	**354**	**Doug Palazzari, Stl., RC, LC**	**.50**
☐	**355**	**Dave Shand, Atl., RC**	**.50**
☐	356	Stan Weir, Tor.	.50
☐	357	Mike Christie, Cle.	.50
☐	358	Floyd Thomson, Stl., LC	.50
☐	359	Larry Goodenough, Pha. (Van.)	.50
☐	**360**	**Bill Riley, Wsh., RC**	**.60**
☐	**361**	**Doug Hicks, Min., RC**	**.50**
☐	**362**	**Dan Newman, NYR., RC**	**.50**
☐	363	Rick Chartraw, Mtl.	.50
☐	364	Tim Ecclestone, Atl., LC	.50
☐	**365**	**Don Ashby, Tor., RC**	**.50**
☐	366	Jacques Richard, Buf.	.50
☐	367	Yves Belanger (G), Stl.	1.00
☐	368	Ron Sedlbauer, Van.	.50
☐	369	Jack Lynch, Wsh., LC, Err. (Bill Collins)	.50
☐	370	Doug Favell (G), Col.	1.00
☐	371	Bob Murdoch, L.A.	.50
☐	372	Ralph Klassen, Cle.	.50
☐	373	Richard Mulhern, Atl.	.50
☐	374	Jim McKenny, Tor., LC	.50
☐	375	Mike Bloom, Det., LC	.50
☐	376	Bruce Affleck, Stl.	.50
☐	377	Gerry O'Flaherty, Van.	.50
☐	378	Ron Lalonde, Wsh.	.50
☐	379	Chuck Arnason, Col.	.50
☐	380	Dave Hutchison, L.A.	.50
☐	381	Checklist 3 (265 - 396)	12.00
☐	382	John Gould, Atl.	.50
☐	383	Dave Williams, Tor.	4.00
☐	384	Len Frig, Cle. (Stl.), LC.	.50
☐	385	Pierre Plante, Stl. (Chi.)	.50
☐	386	Ralph Stewart, Van., LC	.50
☐	387	Gord Smith, Wsh.	.50
☐	388	Denis Dupère, Col.	.50
☐	389	Randy Manery, Atl. (L.A.)	.50
☐	390	Lowell MacDonald, Pgh., LC	.50
☐	391	Dennis Owchar, Pgh.	.50
☐	392	Jimmy Roberts, Min., RC	.50
☐	393	Mike Veisor (G), Chi.	1.00
☐	394	Bob Hess, Stl.	.50
☐	395	Curt Ridley (G), Van.	1.00
☐	396	Mike Lampman, Wsh., LC	.60

GLOSSY PHOTOS

The glossy colour photos come with square or rounded corners. Photos are numbered _ of 22.

Photo Size: 2 1/2" x 3 1/2"
Face: Four colour, borderless; Player's facsimile autograph
Back: Dark blue on card stock; Name, Team, Position, Number
Imprint: 1977 O-PEE-CHEE
Insert Set (22 cards): 18.00

	No.	Player	NRMT-MT
☐	1	Wayne Cashman, Bos.	.50
☐	2	Gerry Cheevers (G), Bos.	1.50
☐	3	Bobby Clarke, Pha.	2.00
☐	4	Marcel Dionne, L.A.	1.50
☐	5	Ken Dryden (G), Mtl.	4.50
☐	6	Clark Gillies, NYI.	.50
☐	7	Guy Lafleur, Mtl.	4.00
☐	8	Reggie Leach, Pha.	.50
☐	9	Rick MacLeish, Pha.	.50
☐	10	Dave Maloney, NYR.	.50
☐	11	Richard Martin, Buf.	.50
☐	12	Don Murdoch, NYR.	.50
☐	13	Brad Park, Bos.	1.00
☐	14	Gilbert Perreault, Buf.	1.25
☐	15	Denis Potvin, NYI.	2.00
☐	16	Jean Ratelle, Bos.	1.00
☐	17	Glenn Resch (G), NYI.	.75
☐	18	Larry Robinson, Mtl.	1.00
☐	19	Steve Shutt, Mtl.	1.25
☐	20	Darryl Sittler, Tor.	2.00
☐	21	Rogatien Vachon (G), L.A.	1.00
☐	22	Tim Young, Min.	.50

1977 - 78 O-PEE-CHEE WORLD HOCKEY ASSOCIATION

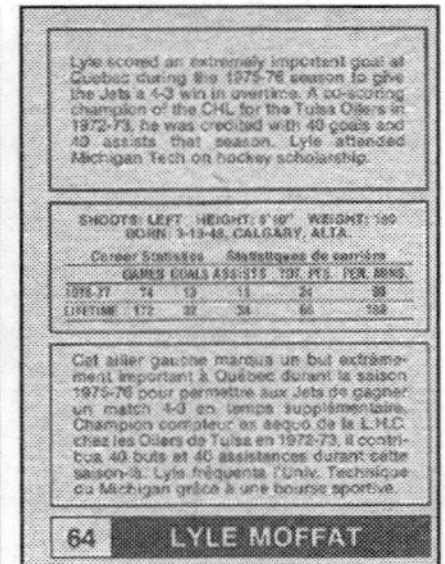

This was the final set produced by O-Pee-Chee for the World Hockey Association. Card number 1 recognizes Gordie Howe's 1,000th career goal.

Card Size: 2 1/2" x 3 1/2"
Face: Four colour, white border; Team logo, Position
Back: Blue and brown on card stock, Number, Resume, Bilingual
Imprint: © 1977 O-PEE-CHEE

Complete Set (66 cards):			**90.00**
Common Player:			**1.00**
	No.	**Player**	**NRMT-MT**
☐	1	Gordie Howe, New England	45.00
☐	**2**	**Jean Bernier, Québec, RC, LC**	**1.00**
☐	3	Anders Hedberg, Winnipeg	2.00
☐	4	Ken Broderick (G), Québec, LC	2.00
☐	5	Joe Noris, Birmingham, LC	1.00
☐	6	Blaine Stoughton, Cleveland	1.00
☐	7	Claude St. Sauveur, Indianapolis, LC	1.00
☐	8	Réal Cloutier, Québec	1.00
☐	9	Joe Daley (G), Winnipeg, LC	2.00
☐	10	Ron Chipperfield, Edmonton	1.00
☐	11	Wayne Rutledge (G), Houston, LC	2.00
☐	12	Mark Napier, Birmingham	2.00
☐	13	Rich LeDuc, Cincinnati	1.00
☐	14	Don McLeod (G), Québec, LC	2.00
☐	15	Ulf Nilsson, Winnipeg	2.00
☐	16	Blair MacDonald, Edmonton	1.00
☐	17	Mike Rogers, New England	1.00
☐	18	Gary Inness (G), Indianapolis	2.00
☐	19	Larry Lund, Houston, LC	1.00
☐	20	Marc Tardif, Québec	1.00
☐	21	Lars-Erik Sjoberg, Winnipeg	1.00
☐	22	Bryan Campbell, Edmonton, LC	1.00
☐	23	John Garrett (G), Birmingham.	2.00
☐	24	Ron Plumb, Cincinnati	1.00
☐	25	Mark Howe, New England	7.50
☐	**26**	**Garry Lariviere, Québec, RC**	**1.00**
☐	27	Peter Sullivan, Winnipeg	1.00
☐	28	Dave Dryden (G), Edmonton	2.00
☐	29	Reg Thomas, Indianapolis, LC	1.00
☐	30	André Lacroix, Houston	2.00
☐	31	Paul Henderson, Birmingham, LC	3.50
☐	32	Paulin Bordeleau, Québec, LC	1.00
☐	33	Juha Widing, Edmonton, LC	1.00
☐	34	Mike Antonovich, New England	1.00
☐	35	Robbie Ftorek, Cincinnati	2.00
☐	36	Rosaire Paiement, Indianapolis, LC,	1.00
☐	37	Terry Ruskowski, Houston	1.00
☐	38	Richard Brodeur (G), Québec	5.00
☐	**39**	**Willy Lindstrom, Winnipeg, RC**	**2.00**
☐	40	Al Hamilton, Edmonton	1.00
☐	41	John McKenzie, New England, LC	1.00
☐	42	Wayne Wood (G), Birmingham, LC	2.00
☐	43	Claude Larose, Cincinnati, LC	1.00
☐	44	J. C. Tremblay, Québec, LC	2.00
☐	45	Gary Bromley (G), Winnipeg	2.00
☐	46	Ken Baird, Edmonton, LC	1.00
☐	47	Bobby Sheehan, Indianapolis	1.00
☐	**48**	**Don Larway, Houston, RC, LC**	**1.00**
☐	49	Al Smith (G), New England	2.00
☐	50	Bobby Hull, Winnipeg.	25.00
☐	51	Peter Marrin, Birmingham, LC	1.00
☐	52	Norm Ferguson, Edmonton, LC	1.00
☐	53	Dennis Sobchuk, Cincinnati, LC	1.00
☐	**54**	**Norm Dubé, Québec, RC, LC**	**1.00**
☐	55	Tom Webster, New England, LC	1.00
☐	**56**	**Jim Park (G), Indianapolis, RC, LC**	**2.00**
☐	**57**	**Dan Labraaten, Winnipeg, RC**	**1.00**
☐	58	Checklist (1 - 66)	15.00
☐	59	Paul Shmyr, Edmonton	1.00
☐	60	Serge Bernier, Québec	1.00
☐	61	Frank Mahovlich, Birmingham, LC	5.50
☐	62	Michel Dion (G), Cincinnati,	2.00
☐	63	Poul Popiel, Houston, LC	1.00
☐	64	Lyle Moffat, Winnipeg	1.00
☐	65	Marty Howe, New England	2.00
☐	66	Don Burgess, Indianapolis, LC	3.50

1977 - 78 TOPPS

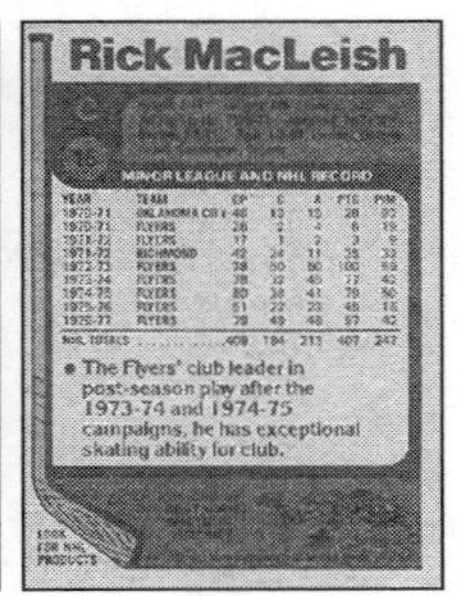

Only cards 203 and 255 show different players than the O-Pee-Chee set of the same year.

Card Size: 2 1/2" x 3 1/2"
Face: Four colour, white border, Team logo, Position
Back: Brown and blue on card stock, Number, Resume, Hockey trivia
Imprint: © 1977 TOPPS CHEWING GUM, INC.

Complete Set (264 cards):			**100.00**
Common Player:			**.30**
	No.	**Player**	**NRMT-MT**
☐	1	LL: S. Shutt/G. Lafleur/M. Dionne	3.50
☐	2	LL: G. Lafleur/M. Dionne/L. Robinson/B. Salming/T. Young	2.00
☐	3	LL: G. Lafleur/M. Dionne/S. Shutt	2.50
☐	4	LL: D. Williams/D. Polonich/B. Gassoff	1.00
☐	5	LL: L. McDonald/P. Esposito/T. Williams	1.50
☐	6	LL: M. Larocque/K. Dryden/G. Resch	2.00
☐	7	LL: G. Perreault/S. Shutt/G. Lafleur/R. MacLeish/P. McNab	2.25
☐	8	LL: K. Dryden/R. Vachon/B. Parent/D. Wilson	3.50
☐	9	Brian Spencer, Buf.	.30
☐	10	Denis Potvin, NYI..	3.75
☐	11	Nick Fotiu, NYR.	.30
☐	12	Bob Murray, Chi.	.50
☐	13	Pete LoPresti (G), Min.	.60
☐	14	J. Bob Kelly, Pgh.	.30
☐	15	Rick MacLeish, Pha.	.50
☐	16	Terry Harper, Det.	.30
☐	**17**	**Willi Plett, Atl., RC**	**1.25**
☐	18	Peter McNab, Bos.	.30
☐	19	Wayne Thomas (G), Tor.	.60
☐	20	Pierre Bouchard, Mtl.	.30
☐	21	Dennis Maruk, Cle.	.60
☐	22	Mike Murphy, L.A.	.30
☐	23	Césare Maniago (G), Van., LC	.60
☐	**24**	**Paul Gardner, Col., RC**	**.30**
☐	25	Rod Gilbert, NYR., LC	1.00
☐	26	Orest Kindrachuk, Pha.	.30
☐	27	Bill Hajt, Buf.	.30
☐	28	John Davidson (G), NYR.	.75
☐	29	J. P. Parise, NYI.	.30
☐	30	Larry Robinson, Mtl.,	4.00
☐	31	Yvon Labre, Wsh.	.30
☐	32	Walt McKechnie, Det.	.30
☐	33	Rick Kehoe, Pgh.	.50
☐	**34**	**Randy Holt, Chi., RC**	**.30**
☐	35	Garry Unger, Stl.	.50
☐	36	Lou Nanne, Min., LC	.30
☐	37	Dan Bouchard (G), Atl.	.60
☐	38	Darryl Sittler, Tor.	2.50
☐	39	Bob L. Murdoch, Cle.	.30
☐	40	Jean Ratelle, Bos.	1.00
☐	41	Dave Maloney, NYR.	.30
☐	42	Danny Gare, Buf.	.50
☐	43	Jimmy Watson, Pha.	.30
☐	44	Tommy Williams, L.A.	.30
☐	45	Serge Savard, Mtl.	.75
☐	46	Derek Sanderson, Van., LC	1.00
☐	47	John Marks, Chi.	.30
☐	**48**	**Al Cameron, Det., RC**	**.30**
☐	49	Dean Talafous, Min.	.30
☐	50	Glenn Resch (G), NYI.	.60
☐	51	Ron Schock, Pgh.	.30
☐	52	Gary Croteau, Col.	.30
☐	53	Gerry Meehan, Wsh.	.30
☐	54	Ed Staniowski (G), Stl.	.60
☐	55	Phil Esposito, NYR.	3.00
☐	56	Dennis Ververgaert, Van.	.30
☐	57	Rick Wilson, Det., LC	.30
☐	58	Jim Lorentz, Buf.	.30
☐	59	Bobby Schmautz, Bos.	.30
☐	60	Guy Lapointe, Mtl.	.75
☐	61	Ivan Boldirev, Chi.	.30
☐	62	Bob Nystrom, NYI.	.50
☐	63	Rick Hampton, Cle.	.30
☐	64	Jack Valiquette, Tor.	.30
☐	65	Bernie Parent (G), Pha.	2.25
☐	66	Dave Burrows, Pgh.	.30
☐	67	Butch Goring, L.A.	.50
☐	68	Checklist 1 (1 - 132)	6.50
☐	69	Murray Wilson, Mtl., LC	.30
☐	70	Ed Giacomin (G), Det., LC	1.00
☐	71	CL: Atlanta Flames	1.00
☐	72	CL: Boston Bruins	1.00
☐	73	CL: Buffalo Sabres	1.00
☐	74	CL: Chicago Blackhawks	1.00
☐	75	CL: Cleveland Barons	1.00
☐	76	CL: Colorado Rockies	1.00
☐	77	CL: Detroit Red Wings	1.00
☐	78	CL: Los Angeles Kings	1.00
☐	79	CL: Minnesota North Stars	1.00
☐	80	CL: Montréal Canadiens	1.00
☐	81	CL: New York Islanders	1.00
☐	82	CL: New York Rangers	1.00
☐	83	CL: Philadelphia Flyers	1.00
☐	84	CL: Pittsburgh Penguins	1.00
☐	85	CL: St. Louis Blues	1.00
☐	86	CL: Toronto Maple Leafs	1.00
☐	87	CL: Vancouver Canucks	1.00
☐	88	CL: Washington Capitals	1.00
☐	89	Keith Magnuson, Chi.	.30
☐	90	Walt Tkaczuk, NYR.	.30
☐	91	Bill Nyrop, Mtl.	.30
☐	92	Michel Plasse (G), Col.	.60
☐	93	Bob Bourne, NYI.	.30
☐	94	Lee Fogolin, Buf.	.30
☐	95	Gregg Sheppard, Bos.	.30
☐	96	Hartland Monahan, Wsh.	.30
☐	97	Curt Bennett, Atl.	.30
☐	98	Bob Dailey, Pha.	.30
☐	99	Bill Goldsworthy, NYR., LC	.30
☐	100	Ken Dryden (G), Mtl.	12.00
☐	101	Grant Mulvey, Chi.	.30
☐	102	Pierre Larouche, Pgh.	.30
☐	103	Nick Libett, Det.	.30
☐	104	Rick Smith, Bos.	.30
☐	105	Bryan Trottier, NYI.	12.00
☐	106	Pierre Jarry, Min., LC	.30
☐	107	Red Berenson, Stl.	.30
☐	108	Jim Schoenfeld, Buf.	.50
☐	109	Gilles Meloche (G), Cle.	.60
☐	110	AS: Lanny McDonald, Tor.	2.25
☐	111	Don Lever, Van.	.30
☐	112	Greg Polis, NYR.	.30
☐	**113**	**Gary Sargent, L.A., RC**	**.50**
☐	**114**	**Earl Anderson, Bos., RC, LC**	**.30**
☐	115	Bobby Clarke, Pha.	3.75
☐	116	Dave Lewis, NYI.	.50
☐	117	Darcy Rota, Chi.	.30
☐	118	André Savard, Buf.	.30
☐	119	Denis Herron (G), Pgh.	.60
☐	120	AS: Steve Shutt, Mtl.	1.75
☐	121	Mel Bridgman, Pha.	.30
☐	122	Buster Harvey, Det., LC	.30
☐	**123**	**Rolie Eriksson, Min., RC**	**.30**
☐	124	Dale Tallon, Chi.	.30
☐	125	Gilles Gilbert (G), Bos.	.60
☐	126	Billy Harris, NYI.	.30
☐	127	Tom Lysiak, Atl.	.30
☐	128	Jerry Korab, Buf.	.30
☐	129	Bob Gainey, Mtl.	2.00
☐	130	Wilf Paiement, Col.	.30
☐	131	Tom Bladon, Pha., Error (Bob Dailey)	.30

	No.	Player	Price
☐	131	Tom Bladon, Pha., Corrected	.30
☐	132	Ernie Hicke, Min., LC	.30
☐	133	J. P. LeBlanc, Det.. LC	.30
☐	**134**	**Mike Milbury, Bos., RC**	**3.50**
☐	135	Pit Martin, Chi.	.30
☐	136	Steve Vickers, NYR.	.30
☐	137	Don Awrey, Pgh.	.30
☐	138	Bernie Wolfe (G), Wsh., Error (MacAdam)	2.00
☐	138	Bernie Wolfe (G), Wsh., Corrected	.30
☐	139	Doug Jarvis, Mtl.	.50
☐	140	AS: Borje Salming, Tor.	1.50
☐	141	Bob MacMillan, Stl.	.30
☐	142	Wayne Stephenson (G), Pha.	.60
☐	143	Dave Forbes, Bos.	.30
☐	144	Jean Potvin, NYI.	.30
☐	145	Guy Charron, Wsh.	.30
☐	146	Cliff Koroll, Chi.	.30
☐	147	Danny Grant, Det.	.30
☐	148	Bill Hogaboam, Min., Error (Bergeron)	.30
☐	149	Al MacAdam, Cle., Error (Wolfe)	2.00
☐	149	Al MacAdam, Cle., Corrected	.30
☐	150	Gerry Desjardins (G), Buf., LC	.60
☐	151	Yvon Lambert, Mtl.	.30
☐	152	Rick Lapointe, Pha., Without mustache	.30
☐	152	Rick Lapointe, Pha., With mustache	.30
☐	153	Ed Westfall, NYI.	.30
☐	154	Carol Vadnais, NYR.	.30
☐	155	John Bucyk, Bos., LC	1.00
☐	156	J. P. Bordeleau, Chi.	.30
☐	157	Ron Stackhouse, Pgh.	.30
☐	**158**	**Glen Sharpley, Min., RC**	**.30**
☐	159	Michel Bergeron, Det.	.30
☐	160	Rogatien Vachon (G), L.A.	.75
☐	161	Fred Stanfield, Buf.	.30
☐	162	Gerry Hart, NYI.	.30
☐	163	Mario Tremblay, Mtl.	.30
☐	164	André Dupont, Pha.	.30
☐	165	Don Marcotte, Bos.	.30
☐	166	Wayne Dillon, NYR.	.30
☐	167	Claude Larose, Stl., LC	.30
☐	168	Eric Vail, Atl.	.30
☐	**169**	**Tom Edur, Col., RC**	**.30**
☐	170	Tony Esposito (G), Chi.	2.25
☐	171	André St. Laurent, NYI.	.30
☐	172	Dan Maloney, Det.	.30
☐	173	Dennis O'Brien, Min.	.30
☐	**174**	**Blair Chapman, Pgh., RC**	**.30**
☐	175	Dennis Kearns, Van.	.30
☐	176	Wayne Merrick, Cle.	.30
☐	177	Michel Larocque (G), Mtl.	.60
☐	178	Bob Kelly, Pha.	.30
☐	**179**	**Dave Farrish, NYR., RC**	**.30**
☐	180	Rick Martin, Buf.	.50
☐	181	Gary Doak, Bos.	.30
☐	182	Jude Drouin, NYI.	.30
☐	**183**	**Barry Dean, Col., RC**	**.30**
☐	184	Gary Smith (G), Min.	.60
☐	185	Reggie Leach, Pha.	.50
☐	186	Ian Turnbull, Tor.	.30
☐	187	Vic Venasky, L.A.	.30
☐	**188**	**Wayne Bianchin, Pgh., RC**	**.30**
☐	189	Doug Risebrough, Mtl.	.30
☐	190	Brad Park, Bos.	1.75
☐	191	Craig Ramsay, Buf.	.50
☐	192	Ken Hodge, NYR., LC	.30
☐	193	Phil Myre (G), Atl.	.60
☐	194	Garry Howatt, NYI.	.30
☐	195	Stan Mikita, Chi.	2.75
☐	196	Garnet Bailey, Wsh., LC	.30
☐	197	Dennis Hextall, Det.	.30
☐	198	Nick Beverley, Min.	.30
☐	199	Larry Patey, Stl.	.30
☐	200	Guy Lafleur, Mtl.	9.00
☐	**201**	**Don Edwards (G), Buf., RC**	**2.50**
☐	202	Gary Dornhoefer, Pha., LC	.30
☐	203	Stan Gilbertson, Pgh., LC	.30
☐	**204**	**Alex Pirus, Min., RC, LC**	**.30**
☐	205	Peter Mahovlich, Mtl.	.50
☐	206	Bert Marshall, NYI.	.30
☐	207	Gilles Gratton (G), NYR., LC	.60
☐	208	Alain Daigle, Chi.	.30
☐	209	Chris Oddleifson, Van.	.30
☐	210	Gilbert Perreault, Buf.	2.00
☐	**211**	**Mike Palmateer (G), Tor., RC**	**5.50**
☐	212	Bill Lochead, Det.	.30
☐	213	Dick Redmond, Chi.	.30
☐	214	RB: Guy Lafleur, Mtl.	2.00
☐	215	RB: Ian Turnbull, Tor.	1.00
☐	216	RB: Guy Lafleur, Mtl.	2.00
☐	217	RB: Steve Shutt, Mtl.	1.00
☐	218	RB: Guy Lafleur, Mtl.	2.00
☐	219	Lorne Henning, NYI.	.30
☐	220	Terry O'Reilly, Bos.	.30
☐	221	Pat Hickey, NYR.	.30
☐	222	René Robert, Buf.	.30
☐	223	Tim Young, Min.	.30
☐	224	Dunc Wilson (G), Pgh., LC	.60
☐	225	Dennis Hull, Chi., LC	.50
☐	226	Rod Seiling, Stl.	.30
☐	227	Bill Barber, Pha.	1.00
☐	**228**	**Dennis Polonich, Det., RC**	**.30**
☐	229	Billy Smith (G), NYI.	2.25
☐	230	Yvan Cournoyer, Mtl.	1.00
☐	231	Don Luce, Buf.	.30
☐	**232**	**Mike McEwen, NYR., RC**	**.30**
☐	233	Don Saleski, Pha.	.30
☐	234	Wayne Cashman, Bos.	.30
☐	235	Phil Russell, Chi.	.30
☐	236	Mike Corrigan, Pgh., LC	.30
☐	237	Guy Chouinard, Atl.	.30
☐	**238**	**Steve Jensen, Min., RC**	**.30**
☐	239	Jim Rutherford (G), Det.	.60
☐	240	AS: Marcel Dionne, L.A.	4.25
☐	241	Réjean Houle, Mtl.	.50
☐	242	Jocelyn Guevremont, Buf.	.30
☐	243	Jim Harrison, Chi., LC	.30
☐	**244**	**Don Murdoch, NYR., RC**	**.30**
☐	**245**	**Richard Green, Wsh., RC**	**.30**
☐	246	Rick Middleton, Bos.	1.00
☐	247	Joe Watson, Pha.	.30
☐	248	Syl Apps, Pgh.	.30
☐	249	Checklist 2 (133 - 264)	6.50
☐	250	Clark Gillies, NYI.	.50
☐	251	Bobby Orr, Chi., LC	20.00
☐	252	Nelson Pyatt, Col.	.30
☐	**253**	**Gary McAdam, Buf., RC**	**.30**
☐	254	Jacques Lemaire, Mtl.	1.00
☐	255	Bill Fairbairn, Min.	.30
☐	256	Ronald Greschner, NYR.	.30
☐	257	Ross Lonsberry, Pha.	.30
☐	258	Dave Gardner, Cle.	.30
☐	259	Rick Blight, Van.	.30
☐	260	Gerry Cheevers (G), Bos.	1.75
☐	261	Jean Pronovost, Pgh.	.30
☐	262	Semi-finals: Canadiens Skate Past Islanders	1.00
☐	263	Semi-finals: Bruins Advance to Finals	1.00
☐	264	Finals: Canadiens Win 20th Stanley Cup	2.00

TOPPS GLOSSY PHOTOS

These glossy colour photos come with square or rounded corners. The two varieties appear to have been issued in equal quantities and there is no price differential. The only difference between the O-Pee-Chee and the Topps inserts is the imprint. These photos are numbered _ of 22.

Photo Size: Square Corners: 2 1/2" x 3 1/2"
Round Corners: 2 1/4" x 3 1/4"
Face: Four colour, borderless; Facsimile autograph
Back: Blue on card stock; Name, Team, Position, Number
Insert Set (22 cards): **18.00**

	No.	Player	NRMT-MT
☐	1	Wayne Cashman, Bos.	.50
☐	2	Gerry Cheevers (G), Bos.	1.50
☐	3	Bobby Clarke, Pha.	2.00
☐	4	Marcel Dionne, L.A.	1.50
☐	5	Ken Dryden (G), Mtl.	4.50
☐	6	Clark Gillies, NYI.	.50
☐	7	Guy Lafleur, Mtl.	4.00
☐	8	Reggie Leach, Pha.	.50
☐	9	Rick MacLeish, Pha.	.50
☐	10	Dave Maloney, NYR.	.50
☐	11	Richard Martin, Buf.	.50
☐	12	Don Murdoch, NYR.	.50
☐	13	Brad Park, Bos.	1.00
☐	14	Gilbert Perreault, Buf.	1.25
☐	15	Denis Potvin, NYI.	2.00
☐	16	Jean Ratelle, Bos.	.75
☐	17	Glenn Resch (G), NYI.	1.00
☐	18	Larry Robinson, Mtl.	1.00
☐	19	Steve Shutt, Mtl.	1.25
☐	20	Darryl Sittler, Tor.	2.00
☐	21	Rogatien Vachon (G), L.A.	1.00
☐	22	Tim Young, Min.	.50

1977 - 79 SPORTSCASTER CARDS

This set is made up of 150 different sports with 2,184 cards in all. Listed here are the hockey cards only.

Card Size: 4 3/4" x 6 1/4"
Face: Four colour, top blue border; Name
Back: Black on white card stock; Name, Resume
Imprint:
Complete Hockey Set (65 cards): **850.00**
Common Player: **6.00**

	No.	Player	NRMT-MT
☐	01-02	Bobby Orr	40.00
☐	02-06	Gordie Howe	35.00
☐	02-13	Yvan Cournoyer ("The Stanley Cup")	12.00
☐	03-19	Phil Esposito, Bos. ("Sibling Rivalry")	20.00
☐	05-09	U.S.A. vs. C.S.S.R.	6.00
☐	05-20	Bobby Hull	25.00
☐	06-07	Gump Worsley (G), Min.	12.00
☐	07-08	Team U.S.S.R. '76	10.00
☐	07-17	Brad Park, NYR.	10.00
☐	10-14	Jean Béliveau	20.00
☐	11-19	Bob Hodges ("Hat Trick")	6.00
☐	12-15	U.S.S.R. vs. C.S.S.R. (XCX-V.Petrov)	8.00
☐	12-22	Stan Mikita	12.00
☐	17-09	Denis Potvin	12.00
☐	14-23	Ken Dryden (G)	30.00
☐	15-13	Yvan Cournoyer	12.00
☐	18-23	Garry Unger	6.00
☐	19-15	Canada vs. C.S.S.R.	10.00
☐	21-12	Fussen WGE ("The Equipment")	6.00
☐	27-24	National Hockey League	6.00
☐	29-08	Phil Esposito, NYR. ("The Power Play")	15.00
☐	31-03	Bobby Clarke ("Penalty Killing")	15.00
☐	33-03	Rod Gilbert ("Lines In The Ice")	6.00
☐	35-03	The Spengler Cup (U.S.S.R. vs. C.S.S.R.)	6.00
☐	38-07	Guy Lafleur, Mtl.	20.00
☐	40-24	Rangers vs. Blues (XCX-Ed Giacomin)	8.00
☐	43-04	Major and Minor Penalties	6.00
☐	43-06	Rogatien Vachon (G)	8.00
☐	44-03	Jaroslav Jirik	6.00
☐	44-20	Gerry Cheevers (G)	12.00
☐	45-13	Steve Shutt	10.00
☐	46-14	In The Corners	6.00
☐	46-21	Bryan Trottier	15.00
☐	47-16	B.Trottier/ C.Gillies/ M.Bossy	20.00
☐	47-18	Darryl Sittler	15.00
☐	50-03	Bobby Hull ("Sticks")	25.00
☐	50-04	Facemasks	8.00
☐	51-01	Czechoslovakia 1977	6.00
☐	51-18	Guy Lafleur, Mtl.	20.00
☐	55-14	Jiri Holik/ Jaroslav Holik	6.00
☐	55-23	Bobby Hull, Winnipeg	25.00
☐	56-06	Montréal Forum	8.00
☐	60-12	Bobby Clarke	15.00
☐	61-03	Ed Giacomin (G) ("Lingo")	10.00
☐	62-17	Lester Patrick	10.00
☐	63-09	The Howe Family	35.00
☐	64-16	Pete Stemkowski ("Sudden Death")	6.00
☐	67-21	Bill Chadwick	6.00
☐	70-06	Hall of Fame	6.00
☐	71-12	A.Hedberg/ U. Nilsson	8.00
☐	73-01	U.S.S.R. vs. NHL	10.00
☐	73-11	Czechoslovakia 1976	6.00
☐	74-17	Team U.S.S.R.	10.00
☐	74-24	Vaclav Nedomansky	6.00
☐	76-03	NCAA Hockey Champions	6.00
☐	77-01	Wayne Gretzky	450.00
☐	77-24	NHL Expansions - Oilers, Whalers	6.00
☐	78-04	Réal Cloutier	6.00
☐	80-18	John Davidson (G)	10.00

No.	Player	NRMT-MT
81-19	Jacques Lemaire	10.00
82-05	Scotty Bowman	10.00
82-23	Dave Dryden (G)	8.00
102-14	V. Kharlamov/ V.Petrov/ B. Mikhailov	15.00
103-08	Alexander Volchkov	10.00

FINNISH - SPORTSCASTER

Complete Hockey Set (130 cards): 1,000.00

Common Player: 4.00

No.	Player	NRMT-MT
UK-327	Suomen jääkiekkoilu	4.00
02-27	Tsekkoslovakia	4.00
02-39	Stanley Cup	6.00
03-71	Olympiakiekkoilu 1960	4.00
04-83	Bobby Orr	40.00
05-105	Phil and Tony Esposito	20.00
05-115	Tappara 1976-77	4.00
07-152	Soviet Union 1976	10.00
07-168	Gordie Howe	35.00
08-181	Bobby Hull	25.00
12-279	MM-kilpailut I	4.00
14-335	Finnish maajoukkue	4.00
16-364	A. Leppänen, J. Valtonen	4.00
17-397	Veli-Pekka Ketola	6.00
19-436	Pekka Marrjamäki	4.00
19-447	MM-kilpailut II	4.00
20-469	Vaclav Nedomansky	6.00
21-492	Pelaajien varusteet	4.00
23-532	Hat Trick	4.00
26-673	Kharlamov, Petrov, Mikhailov	15.00
29-692	Brad Park	10.00
31-736	National Hockey League	6.00
32-747	Matti Hagman	6.00
33-775	Porin Ässät	4.00
33-785	Jean Beliveau	20.00
36-845	Lalli Partinen	4.00
37-869	Phil Esposito	15.00
38-891	Bobby Clarke	15.00
38-895	Guy Lafleur	20.00
40-937	Matti Keinonen	4.00
40-945	Stanley Cup	6.00
41-961	Matti Murto	4.00
42-1008	Viivoja jäässä	4.00
43-1009	HIFK	4.00
43-1031	C. and T. Abrahamsson	6.00
45-1057	Lasse Oksanen	4.00
45-1069	Jaroslav Jirik	4.00
45-1075	Ilves Tampere	4.00
46-1084	Juhani Tamminen	4.00
47-1106	Pekka Rautakallio	6.00
47-1113	Helmut Balderis	8.00
47-1125	Liiga-TPS	4.00
48-1145	Ken Dryden	30.00
48-1152	Timo Nummelin	4.00
49-1174	Gerry Cheevers	12.00
49-1175	Esa Peltonen	4.00
49-1197	Bryan Trottier	15.00
50-1178	Steve Shutt	12.00
50-1188	Izvestija-turnaus	4.00
50-1190	"Lämäri"	4.00
50-1197	Rogie Vachon	8.00
50-1199	Teppo Rastio	4.00
51-1201	Markus Mattson	6.00
51-1212	Pienet and isot rangaistukset	4.00
51-1214	Jokerit Helsinki	4.00
51-1218	Jiri and Jaroslav Holik	4.00
51-1224	Stan Mikita	12.00
52-1230	Nurkkapeli	4.00
52-1232	Garry Unger	8.00
52-1235	Oulun Kärpät	4.00
52-1243	Ilpo Koskela	4.00
53-1265	Darryl Sittler	15.00
54-1273	Antero Lehtonen	4.00
54-1290	Trio Grande	20.00
56-1324	Denis Potvin	12.00
57-1356	Guy Lafleur	20.00
57-1358	Bobby Hull	25.00
57-1364	Kasvosuojukset	4.00
58-1381	Bobby Hull	25.00
58-1392	Yvan Cournoyer	12.00
66-1566	Montreal Forum	4.00
68-1623	Pete Stemkowski	4.00
69-1649	Bobby Clarke	15.00
70-1663	Börje Salming	10.00
70-1670	Howen perhe	4.00
71-1686	Alexander Yakushev	10.00
71-1699	Soviet Union 1978-79	10.00
72-1705	Jukka Porvari	4.00
72-1716	Lester Patrick	8.00
73-1730	Kanadan jääkiekkomuseo	4.00
74-1758	Eddie Giacomin	10.00
74-1760	Seppo Repo	4.00
75-1796	Risto Siltanen	6.00
75-1800	Kalevi Numminen	4.00
76-1801	Pertti Koivulahti	4.00
76-1821	Mikko Leinonen	4.00
77-1848	Jari Kurri	15.00
78-1849	Tapio Levo	6.00
78-1861	Vladislav Tretiak (G)	30.00
78-1872	Kiekkoreipas	4.00
79-1973	KooVee	4.00
79-1896	Rauman Lukko	4.00
80-1911	A. Hedberg, U. Nilsson	8.00
80-1918	Olympiakisat	4.00
81-1922	NHL and Soviet Union	10.00
81-1931	Tsekkoslovakia 1976-1977	4.00
82-1949	Hannu Haapalainen	4.00
82-1955	Markku and Yrjö Hakulinen	4.00
83-1970	Reijo Leppänen	4.00
83-1982	Seppo Lindström	4.00
83-1983	Jiri Holecek	6.00
84-2006	Kanada	10.00
84-2015	Aleksandr Yakushev	10.00
84-2016	Lasse Litma	4.00
85-2017	Seppo Suoraniemi	4.00
85-2024	Dave Dryden	8.00
85-2035	Jacques Lemaire	10.00
86-2041	Reijo Ruotsalainen	6.00
86-2064	Hannu Koskinen	4.00
87-2072	Jouni Rinne	4.00
87-2075	Nuorten MM-kisat	4.00
88-2103	Helsingin IFK	4.00
89-2127	Wayne Gretzky	450.00
90-2139	Real Cloutier	6.00
90-2148	Antero Kivelä	4.00
90-2150	Markku Kiimalainen	4.00
90-2152	Jarmo Mäkitalo	4.00
90-2160	NHL and WHA	6.00
90-2162	Scotty Bowman	10.00
90-2165	Ismo Villa	4.00
90-2169	Timo Susi	4.00
103-2455	Ivan Hlinka	6.00
105-2513	Soviet Union 1979	6.00
107-2559	Jorma Valtonen	4.00
108-2573	Henry Leppä	4.00
108-2579	Ruotsi	4.00
108-2583	Suomen jäähallit	4.00
108-2587	Saimaan Pallo	4.00

1978 - 79 O-PEE-CHEE

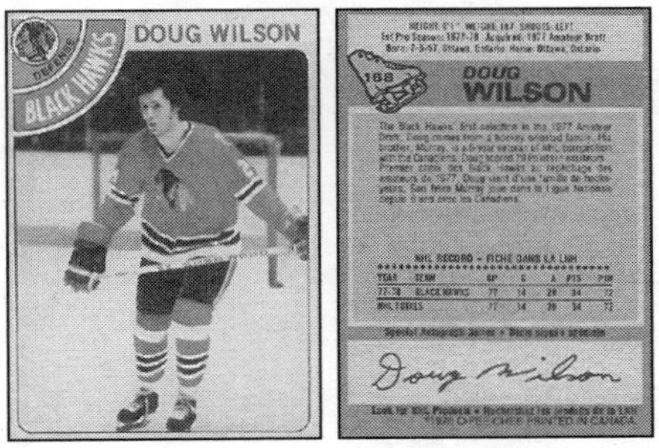

Card number 300 commemorates the early retirement of Bobby Orr. Poor centering and poor cutting thoughout this set place a premium on well centered cards.

Card Size: 2 1/2" x 3 1/2"

Face: Four colour, white border, Team Logo, Position

Back: Two colour, brown and green on card stock, Number, Resume, Player's autograph, Bilingual

Imprint: © 1978 O-PEE-CHEE

Complete Set (396 cards): 175.00

Common Player: .35

No.	Player	NRMT-MT
1	HL: Mike Bossy, NYI.	10.00
2	HL: Phil Esposito, NYR.	1.50
3	HL: Guy Lafleur, Mtl.	2.25
4	HL: Darryl Sittler, Tor.	1.50
5	HL: Garry Unger, Stl.	.75
6	Gary Edwards (G), Min.	.75
7	Rick Blight, Van.	.35
8	Larry Patey, Stl.	.35
9	Craig Ramsay, Buf.	.50
10	Bryan Trottier, NYI.	10.00
11	Don Murdoch, NYR.	.35
12	Phil Russell, Chi.	.35
13	Doug Jarvis, Mtl.	.50
14	Gene Carr, Atl., LC	.35
15	Bernie Parent (G), Pha., LC	2.50
16	Perry Miller, Det.	.35
17	**Kent-Erik Andersson, Min., RC**	**.35**
18	Gregg Sheppard, Pgh.	.35
19	Dennis Owchar, Col., LC	.35
20	Rogatien Vachon (G), L.A., (Det.)	1.00
21	Dan Maloney, Tor.	.35
22	Guy Charron, Wsh.	.35
23	Dick Redmond, Bos.	.35
24	Checklist 1 (1 - 132)	7.50
25	Anders Hedberg, NYR.	.35
26	Mel Bridgman, Pha.	.35
27	Lee Fogolin, Buf.	.35
28	Gilles Meloche (G), Min.	.75
29	Garry Howatt, NYI.	.35
30	Darryl Sittler, Tor.	3.00
31	Curt Bennett, Stl.	.35
32	André St. Laurent, Det.	.35
33	Blair Chapman, Pgh.	.35
34	Keith Magnuson, Chi., LC	.35
35	Pierre Larouche, Mtl.	.35
36	Michel Plasse (G), Col.	.75
37	Gary Sargent, Min.	.35
38	Mike Walton, Stl.	.35
39	**Robert Picard, Wsh., RC**	**.35**
40	Terry O'Reilly, Bos.	.75
41	Dave Farrish, NYR.	.35
42	Gary McAdam, Buf.	.35
43	Joe Watson, Pha. (Col.), LC	.35
44	Yves Belanger (G), Atl., LC	.35
45	Steve Jensen, Min. (L.A.)	.35
46	Bob Stewart, Stl.	.35
47	Darcy Rota, Chi.	.35
48	Dennis Hextall, Det.	.35
49	Bert Marshall, NYI., LC	.35
50	Ken Dryden (G), Mtl.	15.00
51	Pete Mahovlich, Pgh.	.50
52	Dennis Ververgaert, Van.	.35
53	Inge Hammarstrom, Stl., LC	.35
54	Doug Favell (G), Col.	.75
55	Steve Vickers, NYR.	.35
56	Syl Apps, Jr., L.A.	.35
57	Errol Thompson, Det.	.35
58	Don Luce, Buf.	.35
59	Mike Milbury, Bos.	.35
60	Yvan Cournoyer, Mtl., LC	1.50
61	Kirk Bowman, Chi., LC	.35
62	Billy Smith (G), NYI.	2.25
63	LL: G. Lafleur/ M. Bossy/ S. Shutt	5.00
64	LL: B. Trottier/ G. Lafleur/ D. Sittler	3.50
65	LL: G. Lafleur/ B. Trottie/ D. Sittler	3.50
66	LL: D. Schultz/ D. Williams/ D. Polonich	.75
67	LL: M. Bossy/ P. Esposito/ S. Shutt,	4.50
68	LL: K. Dryden (G)/ B. Parent (G)/ G. Gilbert (G)	4.25
69	LL: G. Lafleur/ B. Barber/ D. Sittler/ B. Bourne	3.50
70	LL: B. Parent (G)/ K. Dryden (G)/ D. Edwards (G)/ T. Esposito (G)/ M. Palmateer (G)	6.00
71	Bob Kelly, Pha.	.35
72	Ron Stackhouse, Pgh.	.35
73	Wayne Dillon, NYR.	.35
74	Jim Rutherford (G), Det.	.75
75	Stan Mikita, Chi.	3.00
76	Bob Gainey, Mtl.	2.25
77	Gerry Hart, NYI.	.35
78	Lanny McDonald, Tor.	2.25
79	Brad Park, Bos.	2.00
80	Rick Martin, Buf.	.50
81	Bernie Wolfe (G), Wsh., LC	.75
82	Bob MacMillan, Atl.	.35
83	**Brad Maxwell, Min., RC**	**.35**
84	Mike Fidler, Min.	.35
85	Carol Vadnais, NYR.	.35
86	Don Lever, Van.	.35

	No.	Player	Price
☐	87	Phil Myre (G), Stl.	.75
☐	88	Paul Gardner, Col.	.35
☐	89	Bob Murray, Chi.	.35
☐	90	Guy Lafleur, Mtl.	12.00
☐	91	Bob J. Murdoch, L.A.	.35
☐	92	Ron Ellis, Tor.	.35
☐	93	Jude Drouin, NYI.	.35
☐	94	Jocelyn Guevremont, Buf.	.35
☐	95	Gilles Gilbert (G), Bos.	.75
☐	96	Bob Sirois, Wsh.	.35
☐	97	Tom Lysiak, Atl.	.35
☐	98	André Dupont, Pha.	.35
☐	**99**	**Per-Olov Brasar, Min., RC**	**.35**
☐	100	Phil Esposito, NYR.	4.00
☐	101	J. P. Bordeleau, Chi.	.35
☐	**102**	**Pierre Mondou, Mtl., RC**	**.75**
☐	103	Wayne Bianchin, Pgh.	.35
☐	104	Dennis O'Brien, Bos.	.35
☐	105	Glenn Resch (G), NYI.	.75
☐	106	Dennis Polonich, Det.	.35
☐	**107**	**Kris Manery, Min., RC**	**.35**
☐	108	Bill Hajt, Buf.	.35
☐	**109**	**Jere Gillis, Van., RC**	**.35**
☐	110	Garry Unger, Stl.	.50
☐	111	Nick Beverley, Min. (L.A.), LC	.35
☐	112	Pat Hickey, NYR.	.35
☐	113	Rick Middleton, Bos.	.35
☐	114	Orest Kindrachuk, Pgh.	.35
☐	**115**	**Mike Bossy, NYI., RC**	**55.00**
☐	116	Pierre Bouchard, Mtl. (Retired)	.35
☐	117	Alain Daigle, Chi.	.35
☐	118	Terry Martin, Buf.	.35
☐	119	Tom Edur, Pgh. (Stl.), LC	.35
☐	120	Marcel Dionne, L.A.	4.50
☐	**121**	**Barry Beck, Col., RC**	**1.75**
☐	122	Bill Lochead, Det.	.35
☐	**123**	**Paul Harrison (G), Tor., RC**	**.75**
☐	124	Wayne Cashman, Bos.	.35
☐	125	Rick MacLeish, Pha.	.50
☐	126	Bob Bourne, NYI.	.35
☐	127	Ian Turnbull, Tor.	.35
☐	128	Gerry Meehan, Wsh., LC	.35
☐	129	Eric Vail, Atl.	.35
☐	130	Gilbert Perreault, Buf.	2.25
☐	131	Bob Dailey, Pha.	.35
☐	**132**	**Dale McCourt, Det., RC**	**.75**
☐	**133**	**John Wensink, Bos., RC**	**.35**
☐	134	Bill Nyrop, Mtl., LC	.35
☐	135	Ivan Boldirev, Chi.	.35
☐	**136**	**Lucien Deblois, NYR., RC**	**.35**
☐	137	Brian Spencer, Pgh., LC	.35
☐	138	Tim Young, Min.	.35
☐	139	Ron Sedlbauer, Van.	.35
☐	140	Gerry Cheevers (G), Bos.	2.25
☐	141	Dennis Maruk, Min. (Wsh.)	.35
☐	142	Barry Dean, Pha.	.35
☐	**143**	**Bernie Federko, Stl., RC**	**12.00**
☐	**144**	**Stefan Persson, NYI., RC**	**.35**
☐	145	Wilf Paiement, Col.	.35
☐	146	Dale Tallon, Chi. (Pgh.), LC	.35
☐	147	Yvon Lambert, Mtl.	.35
☐	148	Greg Joly, Det.	.35
☐	149	Dean Talafous, Min. (NYR.)	.35
☐	150	Don Edwards (G), Buf.	.75
☐	151	Butch Goring, L.A.	.50
☐	152	Tom Bladon, Pgh.	.35
☐	153	Bob Nystrom, NYI.	.35
☐	154	Ron Greschner, NYR.	.35
☐	155	Jean Ratelle, Bos.	1.50
☐	**156**	**Russ Anderson, Pgh., RC**	**.35**
☐	157	John Marks, Chi.	.35
☐	158	Michel Larocque (G), Mtl.	.75
☐	**159**	**Paul Woods, Det., RC**	**.35**
☐	160	Mike Palmateer (G), Tor.	1.50
☐	161	Jim Lorentz, Buf. (Retired), LC	.35
☐	162	Dave Lewis, NYI.	.50
☐	163	Harvey Bennett, Min. (Stl.), LC	.35
☐	164	Rick Smith, Bos.	.35
☐	165	Reggie Leach, Pha.	.50
☐	166	Wayne Thomas (G), NYR.	.75
☐	167	Dave Forbes, Wsh., LC	.35
☐	168	Doug Wilson, Chi., RC	10.00
☐	169	Dan Bouchard (G), Atl.	.75
☐	170	Steve Shutt, Mtl.	2.00
☐	**171**	**Mike Kaszycki, NYI., RC**	**.35**
☐	172	Denis Herron (G), Pgh.	.75
☐	173	Rick Bowness, Det. (Stl.)	.35
☐	174	Rick Hampton, Min. (L.A.)	.35
☐	175	Glen Sharpley, Min.	.35
☐	176	Bill Barber, Pha.	1.50
☐	**177**	**Ron Duguay, NYR., RC**	**3.50**
☐	178	Jim Schoenfeld, Buf.	.50
☐	179	Pierre Plante, Chi. (NYR.)	.35
☐	180	Jacques Lemaire, Mtl., LC	1.25
☐	181	Stan Jonathan, Bos.	.35
☐	182	Billy Harris, NYI.	.35
☐	183	Chris Oddleifson, Van.	.35
☐	184	Jean Pronovost, Pgh. (Atl.)	.35
☐	185	Fred Barrett, Min.	.35
☐	186	Ross Lonsberry, Pgh.	.35
☐	187	Mike McEwen, NYR.	.35
☐	188	René Robert, Buf.	.35
☐	189	J. Bob Kelly, Chi.	.35
☐	190	Serge Savard, Mtl.	1.25
☐	191	Dennis Kearns, Van.	.35
☐	192	CL: Atlanta Flames	1.50
☐	193	CL: Boston Bruins	1.50
☐	194	CL: Buffalo Sabres	1.50
☐	195	CL: Chicago Blackhawks	1.50
☐	196	CL: Colorado Rockies	1.50
☐	197	CL: Detroit Red Wings	1.50
☐	198	CL: Los Angeles Kings	1.50
☐	199	CL: Minnesota North Stars	1.50
☐	200	CL: Montréal Canadiens	1.50
☐	201	CL: New York Islanders	1.50
☐	202	CL: New York Rangers	1.50
☐	203	CL: Philadelphia Flyers	1.50
☐	204	CL: Pittsburgh Penguins	1.50
☐	205	CL: St. Louis Blues	1.50
☐	206	CL: Toronto Maple Leafs	1.50
☐	207	CL: Vancouver Canucks	1.50
☐	208	CL: Washington Capitals	1.50
☐	209	Danny Gare, Buf.	.50
☐	210	Larry Robinson, Mtl.	3.00
☐	211	John Davidson (G), NYR.	1.00
☐	212	Peter McNab, Bos.	.35
☐	213	Rick Kehoe, Pgh.	.50
☐	214	Terry Harper, Det., LC	.35
☐	215	Bobby Clarke, Pha.	4.25
☐	216	Bryan Maxwell, Min., Err. (Brad Maxwell)	.35
☐	**217**	**Ted Bulley, Chi., RC**	**.35**
☐	218	Red Berenson, Stl. (Retired), LC	.35
☐	219	Ron Grahame (G), Bos. (L.A.), LC	.75
☐	220	Clark Gillies, NYI.	.35
☐	221	Dave Maloney, NYR.	.35
☐	**222**	**Derek Smith, Buf., RC**	**.35**
☐	223	Wayne Stephenson (G), Pha.	.75
☐	224	John Van Boxmeer, Col.	.35
☐	225	Dave Schultz, Pgh.	.35
☐	**226**	**Reed Larson, Det., RC**	**.75**
☐	227	Réjean Houle, Mtl.	.50
☐	228	Doug Hicks, Chi.	.35
☐	229	Mike Murphy, L.A.	.35
☐	230	Pete LoPresti (G), Min.	.75
☐	231	Jerry Korab, Buf.	.35
☐	232	Ed Westfall, NYI., LC	.35
☐	**233**	**Greg Malone, Pgh., RC**	**.35**
☐	234	Paul Holmgren, Pha.	.35
☐	235	Walt Tkaczuk, NYR.	.35
☐	236	Don Marcotte, Bos.	.35
☐	237	Ron Low (G), Det.	.75
☐	238	Rick Chartraw, Mtl.	.35
☐	239	Cliff Koroll, Chi.	.35
☐	240	Borje Salming, Tor.	1.75
☐	241	Rolie Eriksson, Van.	.35
☐	**242**	**Ric Seiling, Buf., RC**	**.35**
☐	**243**	**Jim Bedard (G), Wsh., RC**	**.75**
☐	**244**	**Peter Lee, Pgh., RC**	**.35**
☐	245	Denis Potvin, NYI.	4.25
☐	246	Greg Polis, NYR.	.35
☐	247	Jimmy Watson, Pha.	.35
☐	248	Bobby Schmautz, Bos.	.35
☐	249	Doug Risebrough, Mtl.	.35
☐	250	Tony Esposito (G), Chi.	2.75
☐	251	Nick Libett, Det.	.35
☐	**252**	**Ron Zanussi, Min., RC**	**.35**
☐	253	André Savard, Buf.	.35
☐	254	Dave Burrows, Tor.	.35
☐	255	Ulf Nilsson, NYR.	.35
☐	256	Richard Mulhern, Atl.	.35
☐	257	Don Saleski, Pha., LC	.35
☐	258	Wayne Merrick, NYI.	.35
☐	259	Checklist 2 (133 - 264)	7.50
☐	260	Guy Lapointe, Mtl.	1.00
☐	261	Grant Mulvey, Chi.	.35
☐	262	Semi-Finals, Canadiens sweep Maple Leafs	.75
☐	263	Semi-Finals, Bruins skate past the Flyers	.75
☐	264	Cup: Larry Robinson, Mtl.	1.25
☐	265	Bob Sauvé (G), Buf.	.75
☐	266	Randy Manery, L.A.	.35
☐	267	Bill Fairbairn, Stl., LC	.35
☐	268	Garry Monahan, Tor., LC	.35
☐	269	Colin Campbell, Pgh.	.50
☐	270	Dan Newman, NYR. (Mtl.), LC	.35
☐	**271**	**Dwight Foster, Bos., RC**	**.35**
☐	272	Larry Carrière, Van. (Buf.), LC	.35
☐	273	Michel Bergeron, NYI. (Wsh.), LC	.35
☐	274	Scott Garland, Tor. (L.A.), LC	.35
☐	275	Bill McKenzie (G), Col., LC	.75
☐	276	Garnet Bailey, Wsh., LC	.35
☐	277	Ed Kea, Atl.	.35
☐	278	Dave Gardner, Cle. (L.A.), LC	.35
☐	279	Bruce Affleck, Stl., LC	.35
☐	**280**	**Bruce Boudreau, Tor., RC**	**.35**
☐	281	Jean Hamel, Det.	.35
☐	**282**	**Kurt Walker, Tor. (L.A.), RC, LC**	**.35**
☐	283	Denis Dupere, Col., LC	.35
☐	284	Gordie Lane, Wsh.	.35
☐	285	Bobby Lalonde, Atl.	.35
☐	286	Pit Martin, Van., LC	.35
☐	287	Jean Potvin, NYI. (Min.)	.35
☐	**288**	**Jimmy Jones, Tor., RC**	**.35**
☐	289	Dave Hutchison, Tor.	.35
☐	290	Pete Stemkowski, L.A., LC	.35
☐	291	Mike Christie, Col.	.35
☐	292	Bill Riley, Wsh.	.35
☐	293	Rey Comeau, Atl. (Col.)	.35
☐	**294**	**Jack McIlhargey, Van., RC**	**.35**
☐	**295**	**Tom Younghans, Min., RC**	**.35**
☐	**296**	**Mario Faubert, Pgh., RC**	**.35**
☐	297	Checklist 3 (265 - 396)	7.50
☐	**298**	**Rob Palmer, L.A., RC**	**.35**
☐	299	Dave Hudson, Col., LC	.35
☐	300	Bobby Orr, Cdn.	45.00
☐	**301**	**Lorne Stamler, Tor., RC, LC**	**.35**
☐	302	Curt Ridley (G), Van., LC	.75
☐	303	Greg Smith, Cle. (Min.)	.35
☐	304	Jerry Butler, Tor.	.35
☐	305	Gary Doak, Bos.	.35
☐	306	Danny Grant, Det. (L.A.), LC	.35
☐	**307**	**Mark Suzor, Col. (Bos.), RC, LC**	**.35**
☐	308	Rick Bragnalo, Wsh., LC	.35
☐	309	John Gould, Atl.	.35
☐	310	Sheldon Kannegiesser, Van., LC	.35
☐	311	Bobby Sheehan, Chi. (Min.), LC	.35
☐	**312**	**Randy Carlyle, Tor. (Pgh.), RC**	**5.50**
☐	313	Lorne Henning, NYI.	.35
☐	314	Tommy Williams, L.A., LC	.35
☐	315	Ron Andruff, Col., LC	.35
☐	316	Bryan Watson, Wsh., LC	.35
☐	317	Willi Plett, Atl.	.35
☐	318	John Grisdale, Van., LC	.35
☐	**319**	**Brian Sutter, Stl., RC**	**7.50**
☐	**320**	**Trevor Johansen, Tor., RC, LC**	**.35**
☐	321	Vic Venasky, L.A.	.35
☐	322	Rick Lapointe, Pha.	.35
☐	**323**	**Ron Delorme, Col., RC**	**.35**
☐	324	Yvon Labre, Wsh.	.35
☐	325	AS: Bryan Trottier, NYI.	6.00
☐	326	AS: Guy Lafleur, Mtl.	6.00
☐	327	AS: Clark Gillies, NYI.	.75
☐	328	AS: Borje Salming, Tor.	1.00
☐	329	AS: Larry Robinson, Mtl.	1.75
☐	330	AS: Ken Dryden (G), Mtl.	9.00
☐	331	AS: Darryl Sittler, Tor.	1.75
☐	332	AS: Terry O'Reilly, Bos.	.75
☐	333	AS: Steve Shutt, Mtl.	1.25
☐	334	AS: Denis Potvin, NYI.	2.50
☐	335	AS: Serge Savard, Mtl.	.75
☐	336	AS: Don Edwards (G), Buf.	.75

Note: cards 325-336 feature a puzzle of Ken Dryden, Larry Robinson and Wayne Cashman

	No.	Player	Price
☐	337	Glenn Goldup, L.A.	.35
☐	338	Mike Kitchen, Col.	.35
☐	339	Bob Girard, Wsh., LC	.35

	No.	Player	Price
☐	340	Guy Chouinard, Atl.	.35
☐	341	Randy Holt, Chi. (Van.)	.35
☐	342	Jimmy Roberts, Min., LC	.35
☐	**343**	**Dave Logan, Chi., RC, LC**	**.35**
☐	344	Walt McKechnie, Tor.	.35
☐	345	Brian Glennie, Tor. (L.A.)	.35
☐	346	Ralph Klassen, Col., LC	.35
☐	347	Gord Smith, Wsh.	.35
☐	348	Ken Houston, Atl.	.35
☐	**349**	**Bob Manno, Van., RC**	**.35**
☐	350	J. P. Parise, NYI. (Min.)	.35
☐	351	Don Ashby, Tor., LC	.35
☐	352	Fred Stanfield, Buf., LC	.35
☐	**353**	**David Taylor, L.A., RC**	**15.00**
☐	354	Nelson Pyatt, Col., LC	.35
☐	**355**	**Blair Stewart, Wsh., RC**	**.35**
☐	356	Dave Shand, Atl.	.35
☐	357	Hilliard Graves, Van.	.35
☐	358	Bob Hess, Stl., LC	.35
☐	359	David Williams, Tor.	2.00
☐	**360**	**Larry Wright, Det., RC, LC**	**.35**
☐	361	Larry Brown, L.A.	.35
☐	362	Gary Croteau, Col.	.35
☐	363	Richard Green, Wsh.	.35
☐	364	Bill Clement, Atl.	.35
☐	365	Gerry O'Flaherty, Van. (Atl.), LC	.35
☐	**366**	**John Baby, Cle. (Min.), RC**	**.35**
☐	367	Nick Fotiu, NYR.	.35
☐	368	Pat Price, NYI.	.35
☐	369	Bert Wilson, L.A., LC	.35
☐	370	Bryan Lefley, Col., LC	.35
☐	371	Ron Lalonde, Wsh., LC	.35
☐	372	Bobby Simpson, Atl., LC	.35
☐	373	Doug Grant (G), Stl., LC	.75
☐	374	Pat Boutette, Tor.	.35
☐	375	Bob Paradise, Pgh., LC	.35
☐	376	Mario Tremblay, Mtl.	.35
☐	377	Darryl Edestrand, Bos. (L.A.)	.35
☐	**378**	**Andy Spruce, Col., RC, LC**	**.35**
☐	**379**	**Jack Brownschidle, Stl., RC**	**.35**
☐	380	Harold Snepsts, Van.	.35
☐	381	Al MacAdam, Cle. (Min.)	.35
☐	382	Neil Komadoski, L.A. (Stl.), LC	.35
☐	383	Don Awrey, NYR. (Col.), LC.	.35
☐	384	Ron Schock, Pgh. (Buf.), LC	.35
☐	385	Gary Simmons (G), L.A., LC	.75
☐	386	Fred Ahern, Col. (Min.), LC	.35
☐	387	Larry Bolonchuk, Wsh., LC	.35
☐	**388**	**Brad Gassoff, Van., RC**	**.35**
☐	389	Chuck Arnason, Col. (Min.), LC	.35
☐	390	Barry Gibbs, (Stl.)	.35
☐	391	Jack Valiquette, Tor. (Col.)	.35
☐	392	Doug Halward, Bos. (L.A.)	.35
☐	393	Hartland Monahan, L.A., LC	.35
☐	394	Rod Seiling, Stl. (Atl.), LC	.35
☐	395	George Ferguson, Tor. (Pgh.)	.35
☐	396	Al Cameron, Det., LC	.35

1978 - 79 SM - LIIGA

A set of 240 cards plus a collecting album for the Finnish National League.
Note - We have no pricing information on this set.
Card Size: 2" x 2 3/8"
Imprint:

	No.	**Player**
☐	1	Hannu Kamppuri, Fin.
☐	2	Pekka Rautakallio, Fin.
☐	3	Timo Nummelin, Fin.
☐	4	Pertti Valkeapaa, Fin.
☐	5	Risto Siltanen, Fin.
☐	6	Hannu Haapalainen, Fin.
☐	7	Markku Kiimalainen, Fin.
☐	8	Tapio Levo, Fin.
☐	9	Lasse Litma, Fin.
☐	10	Reijo Ruotsalainen, Fin.
☐	11	Jukka Porvari, Fin.
☐	12	Matti Rautiainen, Fin.
☐	13	VeliPekka Ketola, Fin.
☐	14	Antero Lehtonen, Fin.
☐	15	Martti Jarkko, Fin.
☐	16	Juhani Tamminen, Fin.
☐	17	Pertti Koivulahti, Fin.
☐	18	Kari Makkonen, Fin.
☐	19	Antero Kivela, Fin.
☐	20	VeliMatti Ruisma, Fin.
☐	21	Stig Wetzell, HIFK
☐	22	Kyosti Majava, HIFK
☐	23	Seppo Pakola, HIFK
☐	24	Reijo Laksola, HIFK
☐	25	Heikki Riihiranta, HIFK
☐	26	Raimo Hirvonen, HIFK
☐	27	Jorma Immonen, HIFK
☐	28	Terry Ball, HIFK
☐	29	Pertti Lehtonen, HIFK
☐	30	Jaakko Marttinen, HIFK
☐	31	Esa Peltonen, HIFK
☐	32	Lauri Mononen, HIFK
☐	33	Tommi Salmelainen, HIFK
☐	34	Hannu Kapanen, HIFK
☐	35	Matti Forss, HIFK
☐	36	Harri Linnonmaa, HIFK
☐	37	Matti Murto, HIFK
☐	38	Juhani Bostrom, HIFK
☐	39	Matti Hagman, HIFK
☐	40	Ilkka Sinisalo, HIFK
☐	41	Tomi Taimio, HIFK
☐	42	Ari Lahteenmaki, HIFK
☐	43	Tapio Virhimo, Ilves
☐	44	Jukka Airaksinen, Ilves
☐	45	Hannu Helander, Ilves
☐	46	Jorma Aro, Ilves
☐	47	Jouko Urvikko, Ilves
☐	48	Hannu Pulkkinen, Ilves
☐	49	Olli Pennanen, Ilves
☐	50	Ari Kankaanpera, Ilves
☐	51	Risto Siltanen, Ilves
☐	52	Jari Jarvinen, Ilves
☐	53	Sakari Ahlberg, Ilves
☐	54	Keijo Kivela, Ilves
☐	55	Lasse Oksanen, Ilves
☐	56	Risto Kankaanpera, Ilves
☐	57	Kari Jarvinen, Ilves
☐	58	Pekka Orimus, Ilves
☐	59	Jarmo Huhtala, Ilves
☐	60	Hannu Oksanen, Ilves
☐	61	Jari Viitala, Ilves
☐	62	Veikko Suominen, Ilves
☐	63	Antti Heikkila, Ilves
☐	64	Seppo Hiitela, Ilves
☐	65	Hannu Kamppuri, Jokerit
☐	66	Patrik Wainio, Jokerit
☐	67	Timo Blomqvist, Jokerit
☐	68	Ilmo Uotila, Jokerit
☐	69	Pertti Savolainen, Jokerit
☐	70	Jussi Lepisto, Jokerit
☐	71	Jorma Piisinen, Jokerit
☐	72	Robert Barnes, Jokerit
☐	73	Ari Makinen, Jokerit
☐	74	David Conte, Jokerit
☐	75	Juha Jyrkkio, Jokerit
☐	76	Jari Kurri, Jokerit
☐	77	Matti Heikkila, Jokerit
☐	78	Henry Leppa, Jokerit
☐	79	Pekka Kaski, Jokerit
☐	80	Jari Kapanen, Jokerit
☐	81	Ari Mikkola, Jokerit
☐	82	Vesa Rajaniemi, Jokerit
☐	83	Ari Blomqvist, Jokerit
☐	84	Erkki Korhonen, Jokerit
☐	85	Rainer Risku, Jokerit
☐	86	Henry Saleva, Jokerit
☐	87	Leo Seppanen, Koovee
☐	88	Rauli Sohlman, Koovee
☐	89	Juhani Ruohonen, Koovee
☐	90	Tuomo Martin, Koovee
☐	91	Reijo Mansikka, Koovee
☐	92	Reino Pulkkinen, Koovee
☐	93	Mauri Kultakuusi, Koovee
☐	94	Kari Saarikko, Koovee
☐	95	Kari Viitalahti, Koovee
☐	96	Barry Salovaara, Koovee
☐	97	Auvo Vaananen, Koovee
☐	98	Pauli Pyykko, Koovee
☐	99	Ari Jortikka, Koovee
☐	100	JukkaPekka Jarvenpaa, Koovee
☐	101	Seppo Sevon, Koovee
☐	102	Pekka Koskela, Koovee
☐	103	Arto Jokinen, Koovee
☐	104	Timo Niinivirta, Koovee
☐	105	Matti Rautiainen, Koovee
☐	106	Pertti Jarvenpaa, Koovee
☐	107	Reima Pullinen, Koovee
☐	108	JukkaPekka Vuorinen, Koovee
☐	109	Petteri Kanerva, Kiekkoreipas
☐	110	Kalevi Rantanen, Kiekkoreipas
☐	111	Jorma Virtanen, Kiekkoreipas
☐	112	Matti Kaario, Kiekkoreipas
☐	113	Frank Neal, Kiekkoreipas
☐	114	Eero Mantere, Kiekkoreipas
☐	115	Harri Nyman, Kiekkoreipas
☐	116	Olli Saarinen, Kiekkoreipas
☐	117	Jari Saarela, Kiekkoreipas
☐	118	Pasi Virta, Kiekkoreipas
☐	119	Dave Chalk, Kiekkoreipas
☐	120	Hannu Koskinen, Kiekkoreipas
☐	121	Harri Toivonen, Kiekkoreipas
☐	122	Jarmo Makitalo, Kiekkoreipas
☐	123	Kari Makitalo, Kiekkoreipas
☐	124	Olavi Niemenranta, Kiekkoreipas
☐	125	Pekka Laine, Kiekkoreipas
☐	126	Markku Hakulinen, Kiekkoreipas
☐	127	Pekka Nissinen, Kiekkoreipas
☐	128	Yrjo Hakulinen, Kiekkoreipas
☐	129	Timo Heino, Kiekkoreipas
☐	130	Hannu Savolainen, Kiekkoreipas
☐	131	Ari Hellgren, Oulun
☐	132	Matti Saikkonen, Oulun
☐	133	Ilpo Kukkola, Oulun
☐	134	Pentti Karlsson, Oulun
☐	135	Pekka Karjala, Oulun
☐	136	Juha Tuohimaa, Oulun
☐	137	Pekka Makinen, Oulun
☐	138	Reijo Ruotsalainen, Oulun
☐	139	Seppo Tenhunen, Oulun
☐	140	Hannu Jalonen, Oulun
☐	141	Jari Virtanen, Oulun
☐	142	Juha Huikuri, Oulun
☐	143	Veikko Torkkeli, Oulun
☐	144	Markku Kiimalainen, Oulun
☐	145	Kalevi Hongisto, Oulun
☐	146	Eero Vartiainen, Oulun
☐	147	Jouko Kamarainen, Oulun
☐	148	Kai Suikkanen, Oulun
☐	149	Ilkka Alatalo, Oulun
☐	150	Markku Perkkio, Oulun
☐	151	Jorma Torkkeli, Oulun
☐	152	Kari Jalonen, Oulun
☐	153	Hannu Siivonen, Rauman Lukko
☐	154	Kari Kaupinsalo, Rauman Lukko
☐	155	Teppo Mattsson, Rauman Lukko
☐	156	Esa Hakkarainen, Rauman Lukko
☐	157	Jouni Peltonen, Rauman Lukko
☐	158	Timo Peltonen, Rauman Lukko
☐	159	Hannu Luojola, Rauman Lukko
☐	160	Tapani Koskimaki, Rauman Lukko
☐	161	Tuomo Jormakka, Rauman Lukko
☐	162	Mika Rajala, Rauman Lukko
☐	163	Pekka Santanen, Rauman Lukko
☐	164	Jorma Vehmanen, Rauman Lukko
☐	165	Olli Tuominen, Rauman Lukko
☐	166	Hannu Kemppainen, Rauman Lukko
☐	167	Ismo Villa, Rauman Lukko
☐	168	Matti Tynkkynen, Rauman Lukko
☐	169	Jouni Rinne, Rauman Lukko
☐	170	Jari Rastio, Rauman Lukko
☐	171	Harri Tuohimaa, Rauman Lukko
☐	172	Jari Laiho, Rauman Lukko
☐	173	Juhani Wallenius, Rauman Lukko
☐	174	Pekka Strander, Rauman Lukko
☐	175	Pertti Hasanen, Tappara
☐	176	Petri Karjalainen, Tappara
☐	177	Jorma Kallio, Tappara
☐	178	Pekka Marjamaki, Tappara

	No.	Player
☐	179	Hannu Haapalainen, Tappara
☐	180	Pertti Valkeapaa, Tappara
☐	181	Lasse Litma, Tappara
☐	182	Jukka Hirsimaki, Tappara
☐	183	Oiva Oijennus, Tappara
☐	184	Jukka Alkula, Tappara
☐	185	Timo Susi, Tappara
☐	186	Jukka Porvari, Tappara
☐	187	Erkki Lehtonen, Tappara
☐	188	Antero Lehtonen, Tappara
☐	189	Juha Silvennoinen, Tappara
☐	190	Pertti Koivulahti, Tappara
☐	191	Keijo Mannisto, Tappara
☐	192	Jorma Sevon, Tappara
☐	193	Martti Jarkko, Tappara
☐	194	Jari Lindgren, Tappara
☐	195	Tapio Kallio, Tappara
☐	196	Tero Kapynen, Tappara
☐	197	Urpo Ylonen, Turun Palloseura
☐	198	Jorma Valtonen, Turun Palloseura
☐	199	Harri Kari, Turun Palloseura
☐	200	Hannu Jortikka, Turun Palloseura
☐	201	Timo Nummelin, Turun Palloseura
☐	202	Seppo Suoraniemi, Turun Palloseura
☐	203	Ilkka Mesikammen, Turun Palloseura
☐	204	Pertti Ahokas, Turun Palloseura
☐	205	Hannu Niittoaho, Turun Palloseura
☐	206	Arto Kaunonen, Turun Palloseura
☐	207	Pekka Rautee, Turun Palloseura
☐	208	Juhani Tamminen, Turun Palloseura
☐	209	Timo Viljanen, Turun Palloseura
☐	210	Kari Kauppila, Turun Palloseura
☐	211	Bengt Wilenius, Turun Palloseura
☐	212	Reijo Leppanen, Turun Palloseura
☐	213	Rauli Tammelin, Turun Palloseura
☐	214	Jukka Koskilahti, Turun Palloseura
☐	215	Markku Haapaniemi, Turun Palloseura
☐	216	Kari Horkko, Turun Palloseura
☐	217	Kalevi Aho, Turun Palloseura
☐	218	Hakan Hjerpe, Turun Palloseura
☐	219	Antero Kivela, Assat Pori
☐	220	Pertti Lehti, Assat Pori
☐	221	Antti Heikkila, Assat Pori
☐	222	Tapio Flinck, Assat Pori
☐	223	Pekka Rautakallio, Assat Pori
☐	224	Jaakko Niemi, Assat Pori
☐	225	Tapio Levo, Assat Pori
☐	226	Jyrki Levonen, Assat Pori
☐	227	Harry Nikander, Assat Pori
☐	228	Arto Javanainen, Assat Pori
☐	229	Pekka Makela, Assat Pori
☐	230	Tapio Koskinen, Assat Pori
☐	231	Pekka Stenfors, Assat Pori
☐	232	Ari Peltola, Assat Pori
☐	233	VeliPekka Ketola, Assat Pori
☐	234	Erkki Vakiparta, Assat Pori
☐	235	Rauli Levonen, Assat Pori
☐	236	Martti Nenonen, Assat Pori
☐	237	Jouni Makitalo, Assat Pori
☐	238	VeliMatti Ruisma, Assat Pori
☐	239	Tauno Makela, Assat Pori
☐	240	Kari Makkonen, Assat Pori

1978 - 79 TOPPS

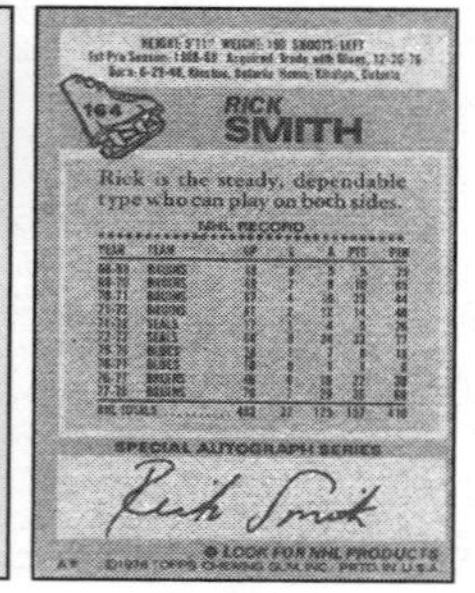

Card Size: 2 1/2" x 3 1/2"
Face: Four colour, white border, Team logo, Position
Back: Orange and green on card stock, Number, Resume, Player's facsimile

Imprint: © 1978 TOPPS CHEWING GUM, INC.
Complete Set (264 cards): 80.00
Common Player: .25

	No.	Player	NRMT-MT
☐	1	Mike Bossy Sets Record for Goals by a Rookie	7.00
☐	2	Phil Esposito Tops Mark with 29th Hat Trick	1.30
☐	3	Guy Lafleur Scores vs. Every Team League	1.50
☐	4	Darryl Sittler Finds Net in 9 Straight Games	.75
☐	5	Garry Unger Plays in 803rd Consecutive Game	.50
☐	6	Gary Edwards (G), Min.	.50
☐	7	Rick Blight, Van.	.25
☐	8	Larry Patey, Stl.	.25
☐	9	Craig Ramsay, Buf.	.35
☐	10	AS: Bryan Trottier, NYI.	6.00
☐	11	Don Murdoch, NYR.	.25
☐	12	Phil Russell, Chi.	.25
☐	13	Doug Jarvis, Mtl.	.35
☐	14	Gene Carr, Pgh., LC	.25
☐	15	Bernie Parent (G), Pha., LC	1.50
☐	16	Perry Miller, Det.	.25
☐	**17**	**Kent-Erik Andersson, Min., RC**	**.25**
☐	18	Gregg Sheppard, Bos.	.25
☐	19	Dennis Owchar, Col., LC	.25
☐	20	Rogatien Vachon (G), L.A.	.60
☐	21	Dan Maloney, Tor.	.25
☐	22	Guy Charron, Wsh.	.25
☐	23	Dick Redmond, Atl.	.25
☐	24	Checklist 1 (1 - 132)	4.00
☐	25	Anders Hedberg, NYR.	.25
☐	26	Mel Bridgman, Pha.	.25
☐	27	Lee Fogolin, Buf.	.25
☐	28	Gilles Meloche (G), Min.	.50
☐	29	Garry Howatt, NYI.	.25
☐	30	AS: Darryl Sittler, Tor.	1.75
☐	31	Curt Bennett, Stl.	.25
☐	32	André St. Laurent, Det.	.25
☐	33	Blair Chapman, Pgh.	.25
☐	34	Keith Magnuson, Chi., LC	.25
☐	35	Pierre Larouche, Mtl.	.25
☐	36	Michel Plasse (G), Col.	.50
☐	37	Gary Sargent, L.A.	.25
☐	38	Mike Walton, Stl.	.25
☐	**39**	**Robert Picard, Wsh., RC**	**.25**
☐	40	AS: Terry O'Reilly, Bos.	.25
☐	41	Dave Farrish, NYR.	.25
☐	42	Gary McAdam, Buf.	.25
☐	43	Joe Watson., Pha., LC	.25
☐	44	Yves Belanger (G), Atl., LC	.50
☐	45	Steve Jensen, Min.	.25
☐	46	Bob Stewart, Min.	.25
☐	47	Darcy Rota, Chi.	.25
☐	48	Dennis Hextall, Det.	.25
☐	49	Bert Marshall, NYI., LC	.25
☐	50	AS: Ken Dryden (G), Mtl.	8.00
☐	51	Pete Mahovlich, Pgh.	.35
☐	52	Dennis Ververgaert, Van.	.25
☐	53	Inge Hammarstrom, Stl., LC	.25
☐	54	Doug Favell (G), Col.	.50
☐	55	Steve Vickers, NYR.	.25
☐	56	Syl Apps, L.A.	.25
☐	57	Errol Thompson, Det.	.25
☐	58	Don Luce, Buf.	.25
☐	59	Mike Milbury, Bos.	.75
☐	60	Yvan Cournoyer, Mtl., LC	.75
☐	61	Kirk Bowman, Chi., LC	.25
☐	62	Billy Smith (G), NYI.	1.25
☐	63	LL: G. Lafleur/M. Bossy/S. Shutt	3.25
☐	64	LL: B. Trottier.G. Lafleur/D.Sittler	2.25
☐	65	LL: G. Lafleur/B. Trottier/D. Sittler	2.25
☐	66	LL: D. Schultz/D. Williams/D. Polonich	.50
☐	67	LL M. Bossy/P. Esposito/S. Shutt	3.00
☐	68	LL: K. Dryden/B. Parent/G. Gilbert	2.50
☐	69	LL: G. Lafleur/B. Barber/D. Sittler/B. Bourne	2.00
☐	70	LL: B. Parent/K. Dryden/D. Edwards/T. Esposito/M. Palmateer	3.50
☐	71	Bob Kelly, Pha.	.25
☐	72	Ron Stackhouse, Pgh.	.25
☐	73	Wayne Dillon, NYR.	.25
☐	74	Jim Rutherford (G), Det.	.50
☐	75	Stan Mikita, Chi.	2.25
☐	76	Bob Gainey, Mtl.	1.50
☐	77	Gerry Hart, NYI.	.25
☐	78	Lanny McDonald, Tor.	1.50
☐	79	Brad Park, Bos.	1.50
☐	80	Rick Martin, Buf.	.35
☐	81	Bernie Wolfe (G), Wsh., LC	.50
☐	82	Bob MacMillan, Atl.	.25
☐	**83**	**Brad Maxwell, Min., RC**	**.25**
☐	84	Mike Fidler, Min.	.25
☐	85	Carol Vadnais, NYR.	.25
☐	86	Don Lever, Van.	.25
☐	87	Phil Myre (G), Stl.	.50
☐	88	Paul Gardner, Col.	.25
☐	89	Bob Murray, Chi.	.25
☐	90	AS: Guy Lafleur, Mtl.	6.00
☐	91	Bob J. Murdoch, L.A.	.25
☐	92	Ron Ellis, Tor.	.25
☐	93	Jude Drouin, NYI.	.25
☐	94	Jocelyn Guevremont, Buf.	.25
☐	95	Gilles Gilbert (G), Bos.	.50
☐	96	Bob Sirois, Wsh.	.25
☐	97	Tom Lysiak, Atl.	.25
☐	98	André Dupont, Pha.	.25
☐	**99**	**Per-Olov Brasar, Min., RC**	**.25**
☐	100	Phil Esposito, NYR.	2.50
☐	101	J. P. Bordeleau, Chi.	.25
☐	**102**	**Pierre Mondou, Mtl., RC**	**.75**
☐	103	Wayne Bianchin, Pgh.	.25
☐	104	Dennis O'Brien, Bos.	.25
☐	105	Glenn Resch (G), NYI.	.50
☐	106	Dennis Polonich, Det.	.25
☐	**107**	**Kris Manery, Min., RC**	**.25**
☐	108	Bill Hajt, Buf.	.25
☐	**109**	**Jere Gillis, Van., RC**	**.25**
☐	110	Garry Unger, Stl.	.35
☐	111	Nick Beverley, Min., LC	.25
☐	112	Pat Hickey, NYR.	.25
☐	113	Rick Middleton, Bos.	.75
☐	114	Orest Kindrachuk, Pgh.	.25
☐	**115**	**Mike Bossy, NYI., RC**	**30.00**
☐	116	Pierre Bouchard, Mtl.	.25
☐	117	Alain Daigle, Chi.	.25
☐	118	Terry Martin, Buf.	.25
☐	119	Tom Edur, Pgh., LC	.25
☐	120	Marcel Dionne, L.A.	3.25
☐	**121**	**Barry Beck, Col., RC**	**1.00**
☐	122	Bill Lochead, Det.	.25
☐	**123**	**Paul Harrison (G), Tor., RC**	**.50**
☐	124	Wayne Cashman, Bos.	.25
☐	125	Rick MacLeish, Pha.	.35
☐	126	Bob Bourne, NYI.	.25
☐	127	Ian Turnbull, Tor.	.25
☐	128	Gerry Meehan, Wsh., LC	.25
☐	129	Eric Vail, Atl.	.25
☐	130	Gilbert Perreault, Buf.	1.50
☐	131	Bob Dailey, Pha.	.25
☐	**132**	**Dale McCourt, Det., RC**	**.75**
☐	**133**	**John Wensink, Bos., RC**	**.25**
☐	134	Bill Nyrop, Mtl., LC	.25
☐	135	Ivan Boldirev, Chi.	.25
☐	**136**	**Lucien DeBlois, NYR.., RC**	**.50**
☐	137	Brian Spencer, Pgh., LC	.25
☐	138	Tim Young, Min.	.25
☐	139	Ron Sedlbauer, Van.	.25
☐	140	Gerry Cheevers (G), Bos.	1.50
☐	141	Dennis Maruk, Min.	.25
☐	142	Barry Dean, Pha.	.25
☐	**143**	**Bernie Federko, Stl., RC**	**7.50**
☐	144	Stefan Persson, NYI., RC	.25
☐	145	Wilf Paiement, Col.	.25
☐	146	Dale Tallon, Chi., LC	.25
☐	147	Yvon Lambert, Mtl.	.25
☐	148	Greg Joly, Det.	.25
☐	149	Dean Talafous, Min.	.25
☐	150	AS: Don Edwards (G), Buf.	.50
☐	151	Butch Goring, L.A.	.35
☐	152	Tom Bladon, Pgh.	.25
☐	153	Bob Nystrom, NYI.	.25
☐	154	Ron Greschner, NYR.	.25
☐	155	Jean Ratelle, Bos.	.75
☐	**156**	**Russ Anderson, Pgh., RC**	**.25**
☐	157	John Marks, Chi.	.25
☐	158	Michel Larocque (G), Mtl.	.50
☐	**159**	**Paul Woods, Det., RC**	**.25**
☐	160	Mike Palmateer (G), Tor.	.75
☐	161	Jim Lorentz, Buf., LC	.25
☐	162	Dave Lewis, NYI.	.35
☐	163	Harvey Bennet, Min., LC	.25
☐	164	Rick Smith, Bos.	.25
☐	165	Reggie Leach, Pha.	.35
☐	166	Wayne Thomas (G), NYR.	.50

	No.	Player	NRMT-MT
☐	167	Dave Forbes, Wsh., LC	.25
☐	**168**	**Doug Wilson, Chi., RC**	**6.50**
☐	169	Dan Bouchard (G), Atl.	.50
☐	170	AS: Steve Shutt, Mtl.	1.25
☐	**171**	**Mike Kaszycki, NYI., RC**	**.25**
☐	172	Denis Herron (G), Pgh.	.50
☐	173	Rick Bowness, Det.	.25
☐	174	Rick Hampton, Min.	.25
☐	175	Glen Sharpley, Min.	.25
☐	176	Bill Barber, Pha.	.75
☐	**177**	**Ron Duguay, NYR., RC**	**2.50**
☐	178	Jim Schoenfeld, Buf.	.35
☐	179	Pierre Plante, Chi.	.25
☐	180	Jacques Lemaire, Mtl., LC	.75
☐	181	Stan Jonathan, Bos.	.25
☐	182	Billy Harris, NYI.	.25
☐	183	Chris Oddleifson, Van.	.25
☐	184	Jean Pronovost, Pgh.	.25
☐	185	Fred Barrett, Min.	.25
☐	186	Ross Lonsberry, Pgh.	.25
☐	187	Mike McEwen, NYR.	.25
☐	188	René Robert, Buf.	.25
☐	189	J. Bob Kelly, Chi.	.25
☐	190	AS: Serge Savard, Mtl.	.75
☐	191	Dennis Kearns, Van.	.25
☐	192	CL: Atlanta Flames	.85
☐	193	CL: Boston Bruins	.85
☐	194	CL: Buffalo Sabres	.85
☐	195	CL: Chicago Blackhawks	.85
☐	196	CL: Colorado Rockies	.85
☐	197	CL: Detroit Red Wings	.85
☐	198	CL: Los Angeles Kings	.85
☐	199	CL: Minnesota North Stars	.85
☐	200	CL: Montréal Canadiens	.85
☐	201	CL: New York Islanders	.85
☐	202	CL: New York Rangers	.85
☐	203	CL: Philadelphia Flyers	.85
☐	204	CL: Pittsburgh Penguins	.85
☐	205	CL: St. Louis Blues	.85
☐	206	CL: Toronto Maple Leafs	.85
☐	207	CL: Vancouver Canucks	.85
☐	208	CL: Washington Capitals	.85
☐	209	Danny Gare, Buf.	.35
☐	210	AS: Larry Robinson, Mtl.	2.00
☐	211	John Davidson (G), NYR.	.75
☐	212	Peter McNab, Bos.	.25
☐	213	Rick Kehoe, Pgh.	.35
☐	214	Terry Harper, Det., LC	.25
☐	215	Bobby Clarke, Pha.	2.50
☐	216	Bryan Maxwell, Min., Err. (Brad Maxwell)	.25
☐	**217**	**Ted Bulley, Chi., RC**	**.25**
☐	218	Red Berenson, Stl., LC	.25
☐	219	Ron Grahame (G), Bos., LC	.50
☐	220	AS: Clark Gillies, NYI.	.25
☐	221	Dave Maloney, NYR.	.25
☐	**222**	**Derek Smith, Buf., RC**	**.25**
☐	223	Wayne Stephenson (G), Pha.	.50
☐	224	John Van Boxmeer, Col.	.25
☐	225	Dave Schultz, Pgh.	.25
☐	**226**	**Reed Larson, Det., RC**	**.50**
☐	227	Réjean Houle, Mtl.	.25
☐	228	Doug Hicks, Chi.	.25
☐	229	Mike Murphy, L.A.	.25
☐	230	Pete LoPresti (G), Min.	.50
☐	231	Jerry Korab, Buf.	.25
☐	232	Ed Westfall, NYI., LC	.25
☐	**233**	**Greg Malone, Pgh., RC**	**.25**
☐	234	Paul Holmgren, Pha.	.25
☐	235	Walt Tkaczuk, NYR.	.25
☐	236	Don Marcotte, Bos.	.25
☐	237	Ron Low (G), Det.	.50
☐	238	Rick Chartraw, Mtl.	.25
☐	239	Cliff Koroll, Chi	.25
☐	240	AS: Borje Salming, Tor.	1.25
☐	241	Roland Eriksson, Min.	.25
☐	**242**	**Ric Seiling, Buf., RC**	**.25**
☐	**243**	**Jim Bedard (G), Wsh., RC**	**.50**
☐	**244**	**Peter Lee, Pgh., RC**	**.25**
☐	245	AS: Denis Potvin, NYI.	2.25
☐	246	Greg Polis, NYR.	.25
☐	247	Jimmy Watson, Pha.	.25
☐	248	Bobby Schmautz, Bos.	.25
☐	249	Doug Risebrough, Mtl.	.25
☐	250	Tony Esposito (G), Chi.	1.75
☐	251	Nick Libett, Det.	.25
☐	**252**	**Ron Zanussi, Min., RC**	**.25**
☐	253	André Savard, Buf.	.25
☐	254	Dave Burrows, Tor.	.25
☐	255	Ulf Nilsson, NYR.	.25
☐	256	Richard Mulhern, Atl.	.25
☐	257	Don Saleski, Pha., LC	.25
☐	258	Wayne Merrick, NYI.	.25
☐	259	Checklist 2 (133 - 264)	4.00
☐	260	Guy Lapointe, Mtl.	.60
☐	261	Grant Mulvey, Chi.	.25
☐	262	Semi-finals Canadiens sweep Maple Leafs.	.35
☐	263	Semi-finals Bruins skate past the Flyers.	.35
☐	264	Finals Canadiens win 3rd straight cup.	1.50

TOPPS TEAM INSERTS

This 22-card sticker insert set features team logos, numbers, sticks, pucks and various words. They were intended as helmet stickers for young hockey players and collectors.

Card Size: 2 1/2" x 3 1/2"
Face: Logo, words and numbers
Back: Blank
Imprint: 1978 TOPPS CHEWING GUM, INC. PRTD IN U.S.A.

Insert Set (22 cards):			**25.00**
Common Team:			**1.50**
	No.	**Team**	**NRMT-MT**
☐	1	Altanta Flames	1.50
☐	2	Boston Bruins/Hockey stick/3	1.50
☐	3	Boston Bruins/Puck/1	1.50
☐	4	Buffalo Sabres	1.50
☐	5	Chicago Blackhawks	1.50
☐	6	Colorado Rockies	1.50
☐	7	Detroit Red Wings	1.50
☐	8	Los Angeles Kings	1.50
☐	9	Minnesota North Stars	1.50
☐	10	Montréal Canadiens/Mask/5	1.50
☐	11	Montréal Canadiens/Puck/0	1.50
☐	12	New York Islanders/Crossed sticks/7	1.50
☐	13	New York Islanders/Hockey Stick/2	1.50
☐	14	New York Rangers/Mask/1	1.50
☐	15	New York Rangers/Crossed Sticks/9	1.50
☐	16	Philadelphia Flyers/Mask/6	1.50
☐	17	Philadelphia Flyers/Crossed Sticks/8	1.50
☐	18	Pittsburgh Penguins	1.50
☐	19	St. Louis Blues	1.50
☐	20	Toronto Maple Leafs	1.50
☐	21	Vancouver Canucks	1.50
☐	22	Washington Capitals	1.50

1979 PANINI STICKERS

Sticker Size: 1 15/16" x 2 11/16"
Face: Four colour, white border; Name, Team
Back: Blue on white stock; Number, English, German, French
Imprint: PRINTED IN ITALY BY EDIZIONI PANINI S.p.a.-MODENA

Complete Set (400 stickers):			**75.00**
Common Player:			**.20**
Album:			**6.00**
	No.	**Player**	**NRMT-MT**
☐	1	Wash-Out	.20
☐	2	Butt-Ending	.20
☐	3	Delayed Calling of Penalty	.20
☐	4	Hooking	.20
☐	5	Charging	.20
☐	6	Misconduct	.20
☐	7	Holding	.20
☐	8	High-Sticking	.20
☐	9	Tripping	.20
☐	10	Cross-Checking	.20
☐	11	Elbowing	.20
☐	12	Off-Side	.20
☐	13	Icing	.20
☐	14	Boarding	.20
☐	15	Kneeing	.20
☐	16	Slashing	.20
☐	17	Roughness	.20
☐	18	Spearing	.20
☐	19	Interference	.20
☐	20	MA 78 PRAHA, Czechoslovakia	.20
☐	21	Czechoslovakia - U.S.S.R. 6-4	.20
☐	22	Czechoslovakia - U.S.S.R. 6-4	.20
☐	23	U.S.S.R. - Czechoslovakia 3-1	.20
☐	24	U.S.S.R. - Czechoslovakia 3-1	.20
☐	25	U.S.S.R. - Czechoslovakia 3-1	.20
☐	26	U.S.S.R. - Czechoslovakia 3-1	.20
☐	27	Canada - Sweden 3-2	.20
☐	28	Canada - Sweden 3-2	.20
☐	29	U.S.S.R. - Canada 5-1	.30
☐	30	U.S.S.R. - Canada 5-1	.30
☐	31	Czechoslovakia - Canada 3-2	.20
☐	32	Czechoslovakia - Canada 3-2	.20
☐	33	U.S.S.R. - Sweden 7-1	.20
☐	34	U.S.S.R. - Sweden 7-1	.20
☐	35	USA - Finland 4-3	.20
☐	36	USA - Finland 4-3	.20
☐	37	Finland - DDR 7-2	.20
☐	38	DDR - BRD 0-0	.20
☐	39	DDR - BRD 0-0	.20
☐	40	Czechoslovakia	.20
☐	41	Poland	.20
☐	42	U.S.S.R.	.20
☐	43	USA	.20
☐	44	Canada	.20
☐	45	Deutschland - BRD	.20
☐	46	Finland	.20
☐	47	Sweden	.20
☐	48	Canada, Team Photo	.20
☐	49	Canada, Team Photo	.20
☐	50	Canada, Team Photo	.20
☐	51	Canada, Team Photo	.20
☐	52	Denis Herron (G), Cdn.	1.00
☐	53	Dan Bouchard (G), Cdn.	1.50
☐	54	Rick Hampton, Cdn.	.50
☐	55	Robert Picard, Cdn.	.50
☐	56	Brad Maxwell, Cdn.	.50
☐	57	David Shand, Cdn.	.50
☐	58	Dennis Kearns, Cdn.	.50
☐	59	Tom Lysiak, Cdn.	1.00
☐	60	Dennis Maruk, Cdn.	1.50
☐	61	Marcel Dionne, Cdn.	5.00
☐	62	Guy Charron, Cdn.	.50
☐	63	Glen Sharpley, Cdn.	.50
☐	64	Jean Pronovost, Cdn.	.50
☐	65	Don Lever, Cdn.	.50
☐	66	Bob MacMillan, Cdn.	.50
☐	67	Wilf Paiement, Cdn.	.50
☐	68	Pat Hickey, Cdn.	.50
☐	69	Mike Murphy, Cdn.	.50
☐	70	Czechoslovakia, Team Photo	.20
☐	71	Czechoslovakia, Team Photo	.20
☐	72	Czechoslovakia, Team Photo	.20
☐	73	Czechoslovakia, Team Photo	.20
☐	74	Jiri Holecek (G), CSR.	.50
☐	75	Jiri Crha (G), CSR.	1.00
☐	76	Jiri Bubla, CSR.	.50
☐	77	Milan Kajkl, CSR.	.20
☐	78	Miroslav Dvorak, CSR.	.20
☐	79	Milan Chalupa, CSR.	.20
☐	80	Frantisek Kaberle, CSR.	.20
☐	81	Jan Zajicek, CSR.	.20

	No.	Player / Card	Price
☐	82	Jiri Novak, CSR.	.20
☐	83	Ivan Hlinka, CSR.	.50
☐	84	Peter Stastny, CSR.	6.00
☐	85	Milan Novy, CSR.	.20
☐	86	Vladimir Martinec, CSR.	.20
☐	87	Jaroslav Pouzar, CSR.	.50
☐	88	Pavel Richter, CSR.	.20
☐	89	Bohuslav Ebermann, CSR.	.20
☐	90	Marian Stastny, CSR.	1.00
☐	91	Frantisek Cernick, CSR.	.20
☐	92	Deutschland - BRD Team Photo	.20
☐	93	Deutschland - BRD Team Photo	.20
☐	94	Deutschland - BRD Team Photo	.20
☐	95	Deutschland - BRD Team Photo	.20
☐	96	Erich Weishaupt (G), BRD.	.20
☐	97	Bernhard Engelbrecht (G), BRD.	.20
☐	98	Ignaz Berndaner, BRD.	.20
☐	99	Robert Murray, BRD.	.20
☐	100	Udo Kiessling, BRD.	.20
☐	101	Klaus Auhuber, BRD.	.20
☐	102	Horst Kretschmer, BRD.	.20
☐	103	Erich Kuhnhackl, BRD.	.20
☐	104	Martin Wild, BRD.	.20
☐	105	Lorenz Funk, BRD.	.20
☐	106	Martin Hinterstocker, BRD.	.20
☐	107	Alois Schloder, BRD.	.20
☐	108	Rainer Philipp, BRD.	.20
☐	109	Hermann Hinterstocker, BRD.	.20
☐	110	Franz Reindl, BRD.	.20
☐	111	Walter Koberle, BRD.	.20
☐	112	Johann Zach, BRD.	.20
☐	113	Marcus Kuhl, BRD.	.20
☐	114	Poland Team Photo	.20
☐	115	Poland Team Photo	.20
☐	116	Poland Team Photo	.20
☐	117	Poland Team Photo	.20
☐	118	Henryk Wojtynek (G), Pol.	.20
☐	119	Tadeusz Slowakiewicz (G), Pol.	.20
☐	120	Henryk Janiszewski, Pol.	.20
☐	121	Henryk Gruth, Pol.	.20
☐	122	Andrzej Slowakiewicz, Pol.	.20
☐	123	Andrzej Iskrzycki, Pol.	.20
☐	124	Jerzy Potz, Pol.	.20
☐	125	Marek Marcinczak, Pol.	.20
☐	126	Jozef Batkiewicz, Pol.	.20
☐	127	Stefan Chowaniec, Pol.	.20
☐	128	Andrzej Malysiak, Pol.	.20
☐	129	Walenty Zietara, Pol.	.20
☐	130	Henryk Pytel, Pol.	.20
☐	131	Mieczyslaw Jaskierski, Pol.	.20
☐	132	Andrzej Zabawa, Pol.	.20
☐	133	Tadeusz Obloj, Pol.	.20
☐	134	Jan Piecko, Pol.	.20
☐	135	Leszek Tokarz, Pol.	.20
☐	136	U.S.S.R. Team Photo	.20
☐	137	U.S.S.R. Team Photo	.20
☐	138	U.S.S.R. Team Photo	.20
☐	139	U.S.S.R. Team Photo	.20
☐	140	Vladislav Tretiak (G), USSR	10.00
☐	141	Viacheslav Fetisov, USSR	5.00
☐	142	Vladimir Lutchenko, USSR	1.00
☐	143	Vasili Pervukhin, USSR	1.00
☐	144	Valery Vasiljev, USSR	2.50
☐	145	Gennady Tsycankov, USSR	1.00
☐	146	Yuri Fedorov, USSR	.50
☐	147	Vladimir Petrov, USSR	2.50
☐	148	Vladimir Golikov, USSR	.50
☐	149	Victor Zhluktov, USSR	.50
☐	150	Boris Mikhailov, USSR	3.00
☐	151	Valery Kharlamov, USSR	6.00
☐	152	Helmut Balderis, USSR	1.50
☐	153	Sergei Kapustin, USSR	.50
☐	154	Alexander Golikov, USSR	.50
☐	155	Alexander Maltsev, USSR	3.00
☐	156	Yuri Lebedev, USSR	.50
☐	157	Sergei Makarov, USSR	6.00
☐	158	Finland Team Photo	.20
☐	159	Finland Team Photo	.20
☐	160	Finland Team Photo	.20
☐	161	Finland Team Photo	.20
☐	162	Urpo Ylonen, Fin.	.20
☐	163	Antero Kivela (G), Fin.	.20
☐	164	Pekka Rautakallio, Fin.	.50
☐	165	Timo Nummelin, Fin.	.20
☐	166	Risto Siltanen, Fin.	.50
☐	167	Pekka Marjamaki, Fin.	.20
☐	168	Tapio Levo, Fin.	.20
☐	169	Lasse Litma, Fin.	.20
☐	170	Esa Peltonen, Fin.	.20
☐	171	Martti Jarkko, Fin.	.20
☐	172	Matti Hagman, Fin.	.20
☐	173	Seppo Repo, Fin.	.20
☐	174	Pertti Koivulahti, Fin.	.20
☐	175	Seppo Ahokainen, Fin.	.20
☐	176	Juhani Tamminen, Fin.	.20
☐	177	Jukko Provari, Fin.	.20
☐	178	Mikko Leinonen, Fin.	.20
☐	179	Matti Rautiainen, Fin.	.20
☐	180	Sweden Team Photo	.20
☐	181	Sweden Team Photo	.20
☐	182	Sweden Team Photo	.20
☐	183	Sweden Team Photo	.20
☐	184	Goran Hogosta, Swe.	.20
☐	185	Hardy Astrom, Swe.	.20
☐	186	Stig Ostling, Swe.	.20
☐	187	Ulf Weinstock, Swe.	.20
☐	188	Mats Waltin, Swe.	.20
☐	189	Stig Salming, Swe.	.20
☐	190	Lars Zetterstrom, Swe.	.20
☐	191	Lars Lindgren, Swe.	.50
☐	192	Leif Holmgren, Swe.	.20
☐	193	Roland Eriksson, Swe.	.20
☐	194	Rolf Edberg, Swe.	.20
☐	195	Per Olov Brasar, Swe.	.50
☐	196	Mats Ahlberg, Swe.	.20
☐	197	Bengt Lundholm, Swe.	.20
☐	198	Lars Gunnar Lundberg, Swe.	.20
☐	199	Nils Olov Olsson, Swe.	.20
☐	200	Kent Erik Andersson, Swe.	.50
☐	201	Thomas Gradin, Swe.	1.00
☐	202	USA Team Photo	.20
☐	203	USA Team Photo	.20
☐	204	USA Team Photo	.20
☐	205	USA Team Photo	.20
☐	206	Peter LoPresti (G), USA.	.20
☐	207	Jim Warden, USA.	.20
☐	208	Dick Lamby, USA.	.20
☐	209	Craig Norwich, USA.	.20
☐	210	Glen Patrick, USA.	.20
☐	211	Patrick Westrum, USA.	.20
☐	212	Don Jackson, USA.	.20
☐	213	Mark Johnson, USA.	1.00
☐	214	Curt Bennett, USA.	.20
☐	215	Dave Debol, USA.	.20
☐	216	Robert Collyard, USA.	.20
☐	217	Mike Fidler, USA.	.20
☐	218	Tom Younghans, USA.	.20
☐	219	Harvey Bennett, USA.	.20
☐	220	Steve Jensen, USA.	.20
☐	221	Jim Warner, USA.	.20
☐	222	Mike Eaves, USA.	.20
☐	223	William Gilligan, USA.	.20
☐	224	HOCKEY 76, Yugoslavia	.20
☐	225	Poland - Romania 8-6	.20
☐	226	Poland - Romania 8-6	.20
☐	227	Poland - Romania 8-6	.20
☐	228	Poland - Romania 8-6	.20
☐	229	Poland - Magyarorszag 7-2	.20
☐	230	Poland - Magyarorszag 7-2	.20
☐	231	Japan - Yugoslavia 6 - 1	.20
☐	232	Japan - Yugoslavia 6-1	.20
☐	233	Italy - Yugoslavia 12-3	.20
☐	234	Italy - Yugoslavia 12-3	.20
☐	235	Romania - Italy 5-5	.20
☐	236	Romania - Italy 5-5	.20
☐	237	Poland	.20
☐	238	Poland	.20
☐	239	Deutschland - DDR	.20
☐	240	Magyarorszag	.20
☐	241	Netherlands	.20
☐	242	Romania	.20
☐	243	Helvetia	.20
☐	244	Japan	.20
☐	245	Norway	.20
☐	246	Austria	.20
☐	247	Deutschland - DDR	.20
☐	248	Deutschland - DDR	.20
☐	249	Roland Herzig/Wolfgang Kraske, DDR.	.20
☐	250	Dieter Simon/Dietmar Peters, DDR.	.20
☐	251	Dieter Frenzel/Joachim Lempio, DDR.	.20
☐	252	Reinhard Frengler/Peter Slapke, DDR.	.20
☐	253	Rainer Patschinski/Rolf Bielas, DDR.	.20
☐	254	Roland Peters/Eckhard Scholz, DDR.	.20
☐	255	Friedhelm Bogelsack/Joachim Stasche, DDR.	.20
☐	256	Helvetia	.20
☐	257	Helvetia	.20
☐	258	Edgar Grubauer/Olivier Anken, Sui.	.20
☐	259	Aldo Zenhausern/Andreas Meyer, Sui.	.20
☐	260	Jakob Kolliker/Jean-Claude Locher, Sui.	.20
☐	261	Georg Mattli/Giovanni Conte, Sui.	.20
☐	262	Renzo Holzer/Roland Dellsperger, Sui.	.20
☐	263	Michael Horisberger/Luca Rossetti, Sui.	.20
☐	264	Jurg Berger/Lorenz Schmid, Sui.	.20
☐	265	Magyarorszag	.20
☐	266	Magyarorszag	.20
☐	267	Janos Balogh/Andras Farkas, Hun.	.20
☐	268	Csaba Kovacs/Janos Hajzer, Hun.	.20
☐	269	Peter Flora/Adam Kereszty, Hun.	.20
☐	270	Antal Palla/Andras Meszoly, Hun.	.20
☐	271	Gaspar Menyhart/Peter Havran, Hun.	.20
☐	272	Janos Poth/Albert Muhr, Hun.	.20
☐	273	Gyorgy Buzas/Gyorgy Pek, Hun.	.20
☐	274	Netherlands	.20
☐	275	Netherlands	.20
☐	276	Harry Van Bilsen/Henk Krikke, Ned.	.20
☐	277	Frank Van Soldt/George Peternousek, Ned.	.20
☐	278	Patrick Kolijn/Klaas Van Den Broek, Ned.	.20
☐	279	Larry Van Wieren/Johan Toren, Ned.	.20
☐	280	Robert Van Onlangs/Jerry Schaffer, Ned.	.20
☐	281	Jan Janssen/John Van Der Griendt, Ned.	.20
☐	282	Jack De Heer/Leo Koopmans, Ned.	.20
☐	283	Japan	.20
☐	284	Japan	.20
☐	285	Takeshi Iwamoto/Minoru Misawa, Jap.	.20
☐	286	Norio Ito/Kazuma Tonozaki, Jap.	.20
☐	287	Hiroshi Hori/Iwao Nakayama, Jap.	.20
☐	288	Yasushin Tanaka/Yoshiaki Kyoya, Jap.	.20
☐	289	Katsutoshi Kawamura/Yoshio Hoshino, Jap.	.20
☐	290	Satoru Misawa/Teruo Sakurai, Jap.	.20
☐	291	Sadaki Honma/Tsutomu Hanzawa, Jap.	.20
☐	292	Norway	.20
☐	293	Norway	.20
☐	294	Tore Walberg/Jorn Goldstein, Nor.	.20
☐	295	Thor Martisen/Rune Molberg, Nor.	.20
☐	296	Nils Nilsen/Jone Erevik, Nor.	.20
☐	297	Sven Lien/Tom Roymark, Nor.	.20
☐	298	Per Erik Eriksen/Roar Ovstedal, Nor.	.20
☐	299	Vidar Johansen/Harry Haraldsen, Nor.	.20
☐	300	Morten Sethereng/Kjell Thorkildsen, Nor.	.20
☐	301	Austria	.20
☐	302	Austria	.20
☐	303	Schilcheri/Prohaska, Aut.	.20
☐	304	Pentti Hyytaienen/Othmar Russ, Aut.	.20
☐	305	Silvester Staribacher/Walter Schneider, Aut.	.20
☐	306	Franz Kotnauer/Herbert Pök, Aut.	.20
☐	307	Alexander Sadjina/Rudolf Konig, Aut.	.20
☐	308	Herbert Mortl/Gerhard Pepeunig, Aut.	.20
☐	309	Werner Schilcher/Herbert Haisza, Aut.	.20
☐	310	Romania	.20
☐	311	Romania	.20
☐	312	Gheorghe Hutan/Valerian Netedu, Rom.	.20
☐	313	Elod Antal/Sandor Gall, Rom.	.20
☐	314	Gheorghe Iustinian/Ion Ionita, Rom.	.20
☐	315	Vasile Hutanu/Alexandru Halauca, Rom.	.20
☐	316	Doru Tureanu/Dimitru Axinte, Rom.	.20
☐	317	Zoltan Nagy/Marian Costea, Rom.	.20
☐	318	Constantin Nistor/Adrian Olenici, Rom.	.20
☐	319	World Championship Ice Hockey 1978	.20
☐	320	Denmark - Netherlands 3-3	.20
☐	321	Denmark - Netherlands 3-3	.20
☐	322	Netherlands - Spain 19-0	.20
☐	323	Netherlands - Spain 19-0	.20
☐	324	Austria - Denmark 7-4	.20
☐	325	Austria - Denmark 7-4	.20
☐	326	Netherlands - Bulgaria 8-0	.20
☐	327	China - Denmark 3-2	.20
☐	328	China - France 8-4	.20
☐	329	Bulgaria	.20
☐	330	France	.20
☐	331	Italy	.20
☐	332	Yugoslavia	.20
☐	333	Belgium	.20
☐	334	China	.20
☐	335	Denmark	.20
☐	336	Spain	.20

☐ 337 Belgium .20
☐ 338 Belgium .20
☐ 339 Pierre Smeets/Guy Lauwers, Bel. .20
☐ 340 Georges Andriaensen/Alain Zwikel, Bel. .20
☐ 341 Christian Cuvelier/Pierre Sarazin, Bel. .20
☐ 342 Philippe Vermeulen/Christian Voskertian, Bel. .20
☐ 343 Bob Verschraegen/Patrick Arnould, Bel. .20
☐ 344 Jozef Lejeune/Pierre Langh, Bel. .20
☐ 345 Bulgaria .20
☐ 346 Bulgaria .20
☐ 347 Atanas Iliev/Dimitar Lazarov, Bul. .20
☐ 348 Gueorgui Iliev/Dimo Krastinov, Bul. .20
☐ 349 Kroum Hristov/Nikolay Petrov, Bul. .20
☐ 350 Ivan Atanasov/Milcho Nenov, Bul. .20
☐ 351 Atanas Todorov/Lubomir Stoilov, Bul. .20
☐ 352 Kiril Guerasimov/Marin Batchvarov, Bul. .20
☐ 353 China .20
☐ 354 China .20
☐ 355 Tsui Ting Wen/Yang Yung Ke, Chi. .20
☐ 356 Cheng Ke/Pien Shao Tang, Chi. .20
☐ 357 Wan Ta Chun/Chang Yung Sheng, Chi. .20
☐ 358 Chen Hsi Kiang/Wei Chang Shun, Chi. .20
☐ 359 Li Cheng Hsin/Liu Te Hsi, Chi. .20
☐ 360 Hsiang Shu Ching/Chen Sheng Wen, Chi. .20
☐ 361 Denmark .20
☐ 362 Denmark .20
☐ 363 Bent Hansen/Per Holten Moller, Den. .20
☐ 364 Richard Andersen/Tommy Pedersen, Den. .20
☐ 365 Kenneth Henriksen/Jesper Hviid, Den. .20
☐ 366 Frits Nielsen/Steen Thomsen, Den. .20
☐ 367 Carsten Nielsen/Egon Kahl, Den. .20
☐ 368 Jens Jensen/Sören Jerding, Den. .20
☐ 369 Spain .20
☐ 370 Spain .20
☐ 371 Sergio Estrada/Josian Lizarraga, Esp. .20
☐ 372 Francisco Gonzalez/Ramon Munitiz, Esp. .20
☐ 373 Alberto Marin/Bievenido Aguado, Esp. .20
☐ 374 Toni Raventos/Ezequiel Encinas, Esp. .20
☐ 375 Antonio Capillas/Jose Sarazibar, Esp. .20
☐ 376 Perico Labayen/Antonio Plaza, Esp. .20
☐ 377 France .20
☐ 378 France .20
☐ 379 Daniel Maric/Pascal Del Monaco, Fra. .20
☐ 380 Robert Oprandi/Bernard Combe, Fra. .20
☐ 381 Allard/Le Blond, Fra. .20
☐ 382 Jean Vassieux/Philippe Rey, Fra. .20
☐ 383 Guy Galiay/Jean Le Blond, Fra. .20
☐ 384 Alain Vinard/Louis Smaniotto, Fra. .20
☐ 385 Italy .20
☐ 386 Italy .20
☐ 387 Giorgio Tigliani/Norbert Gasser, Ita. .20
☐ 388 Kostner/Pasqualotto\, Ita. .20
☐ 389 Renato Lacedelli/Fabio Polloni, Ita. .20
☐ 390 Adolf Insam/Renato De Toni, Ita. .20
☐ 391 Herbert Strohmaier/Fabrizio Kasslatter, Ita. .20
☐ 392 Pat De Marchi/Mario Pugliese, Ita. .20
☐ 393 Yugoslavia .20
☐ 394 Yugoslavia .20
☐ 395 Marjan Zbontar/Ivan Scap, Yug. .20
☐ 396 Bojan Kumar/Tomaz Kosir, Yug. .20
☐ 397 Ignac Kavec/Roman Smolej, Yug. .20
☐ 398 Edvard Hafner/Tomaz Lepsa, Yug. .20
☐ 399 Silvo Poljansek/Saso Kosir, Yug. .20
☐ 400 Petar-Igor Klemenc/Milan Jan, Yug. .20

1979 SOVIET NATIONAL TEAM PHOTO CARD

Card Size: 8 1/4" x 5 7/8"
Face: Four colour; Moscow 1979
Back: Black and white; Sketch of Championship
Imprint: N3 Aatembctbo Anakat Mockba 1980

No.	Player	NRMT-MT
☐ 1	Team Photograph	4.00

1979 - 80 O-PEE-CHEE

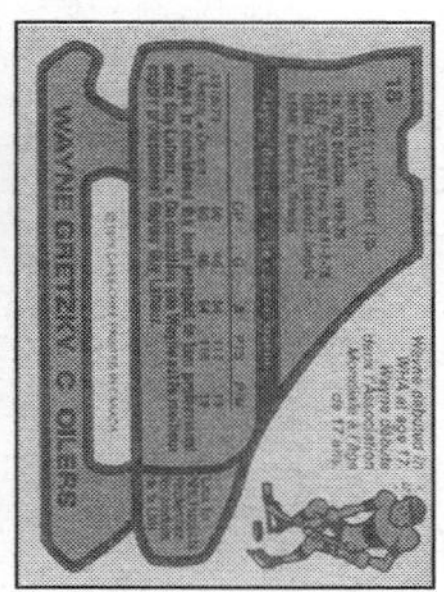

Face: Four colour, blue border, Team logo, Position
Back: Two colour, blue and brown on card stock, Number, Resume, Hockey trivia, Bilingual
Imprint: © 1979 O-PEE-CHEE
Complete Set (396 cards): 1,000.00
Common Player: .75

No.	Player	NRMT-MT
☐ 1	LL: M. Bossy/ M. Dionne/ G.Lafleur	6.00
☐ 2	LL: B. Trottier/ G. Lafleur/ M. Dionne/ B. MacMillan	4.25
☐ 3	LL: B. Trottier/ M. Dionne/ G. Lafleur	4.25
☐ 4	LL: D. Williams/ R. Holt/ D. Schultz,	1.00
☐ 5	LL: M. Bossy/ M. Dionne/ L. McDonald/ P. Gardner	3.25
☐ 6	LL: K. Dryden (G)/ G. Resch (G)/ B. Parent (G)	4.50
☐ 7	LL: G. Lafleur/ M. Bossy/ B. Trottier/ J. Pronovost/ T. Bulley	4.50
☐ 8	LL: K. Dryden (G)/ T. Esposito (G)/ M. Palmateer/ M. Lessard (G)/ B. Parent (G)	6.50
☐ 9	Greg Malone, Pgh.	.75
☐ 10	Rick Middleton, Bos.	1.25
☐ 11	Greg Smith, Min.	.75
☐ 12	René Robert , Buf., (Col.)	.75
☐ 13	Doug Risebrough, Mtl.	1.00
☐ 14	Bob Kelly, Pha.	.75
☐ 15	Walt Tkaczuk, NYR.	.75
☐ 16	John Marks, Chi.	.75
☐ **17**	**Willie Huber, Det., RC**	**.75**
☐ **18**	**Wayne Gretzky, Edm., RC**	**900.00**
☐ 19	Ron Sedlbauer, Van.	.75
☐ 20	AS: Glenn Resch (G), NYI.	1.25
☐ 21	Blair Chapman, Pgh.	.75
☐ 22	Ron Zanussi, Min.	.75
☐ 23	Brad Park, Bos.	1.50
☐ 24	Yvon Lambert, Mtl.	.75
☐ 25	André Savard, Buf.	.75
☐ 26	Jimmy Watson, Pha.	.75
☐ **27**	**Harold Phillipoff, Chi., RC, LC**	**.75**
☐ 28	Dan Bouchard (G), Atl.	1.25
☐ 29	Bob Sirois, Wsh.	.75
☐ 30	Ulf Nilsson, NYR.	.75
☐ 31	Mike Murphy, L.A.	.75
☐ 32	Stefan Persson, NYI.	.75
☐ 33	Garry Unger (Atl.)	1.00
☐ 34	Réjean Houle, Mtl.	1.00
☐ 35	Barry Beck, NYR.	.75
☐ 36	Tim Young, Min.	.75
☐ 37	Rick Dudley, Buf.	.75
☐ 38	Wayne Stephenson (G), Pha., (Wsh.)	1.25
☐ 39	Peter McNab, Bos.	.75
☐ 40	AS: Borje Salming, Tor.	1.50
☐ 41	Tom Lysiak, Chi.	.75
☐ **42**	**Don Maloney, NYR., RC**	**1.25**
☐ 43	Mike Rogers, Hfd.	.75
☐ 44	Dave Lewis, NYI.	1.00
☐ 45	Peter Lee, Pgh.	.75
☐ 46	Marty Howe, Hfd.	.75
☐ 47	Serge Bernier, Que.	.75
☐ 48	Paul Woods, Det.	.75
☐ 49	Bob Sauvé (G), Buf.	1.25
☐ 50	AS: Larry Robinson, Mtl.	2.75
☐ **51**	**Tom Gorence, Pha., RC**	**.75**
☐ 52	Gary Sargent, Min.	.75
☐ **53**	**Thomas Gradin, Van., RC**	**2.50**
☐ 54	Dean Talafous, NYR.	.75
☐ 55	Bob Murray, Chi.	.75
☐ 56	Bob Bourne, NYI.	.75
☐ 57	Larry Patey, Stl.	.75
☐ 58	Ross Lonsberry, Pgh.	.75
☐ 59	Rick Smith, Bos., LC, Error (/b: Kinston)	.75
☐ 60	Guy Chouinard, Atl.	.75
☐ 61	Danny Gare, Buf.	1.00
☐ 62	Jim Bedard (G), Wsh., LC	1.25
☐ 63	Dale McCourt, Det.	.75
☐ **64**	**Steve Payne, Min., RC**	**.75**
☐ **65**	**Pat Hughes, Mtl. (Pgh.), RC**	**.75**
☐ 66	Mike McEwen, NYR. (Col.)	.75
☐ **67**	**Reg Kerr, Chi., RC**	**.75**
☐ 68	Walt McKechnie, Tor.	.75
☐ 69	Michel Plasse (G), Col.	1.25
☐ 70	AS: Denis Potvin, NYI.	2.75
☐ 71	Dave Dryden (G), Edm., LC	1.25
☐ 72	Gary McAdam, Pgh.	.75
☐ 73	André St. Laurent (L.A.)	.75
☐ 74	Jerry Korab, Buf.	.75
☐ 75	Rick MacLeish, Pha.	.75
☐ 76	Dennis Kearns, Van.	.75
☐ 77	Jean Pronovost, Atl.	.75
☐ 78	Ron Greschner, NYR.	.75
☐ 79	Wayne Cashman, Bos.	.75
☐ 80	Tony Esposito (G), Chi.	3.00
☐ 81	CL: Winnipeg Jets	9.00
☐ 82	CL: Edmonton Oilers	15.00
☐ 83	Stanley Cup Finals: Montréal vs. New York Rangers	2.00
☐ 84	Brian Sutter, Stl.	3.00
☐ 85	Gerry Cheevers (G), Bos., LC	2.25
☐ 86	Pat Hickey, NYR., (Col.)	.75
☐ 87	Mike Kaszycki, NYI.	.75
☐ 88	Grant Mulvey, Chi.	.75
☐ 89	Derek Smith, Buf.	.75
☐ 90	Steve Shutt, Mtl.	1.50
☐ 91	Robert Picard, Wsh.	.75
☐ 92	Dan Labraaten, Det.	.75
☐ 93	Glen Sharpley, Min.	.75
☐ 94	Denis Herron (G), Pgh. (Mtl.)	1.25
☐ 95	Reggie Leach, Pha.	1.00
☐ 96	John Van Boxmeer, Col., (Buf.)	.75
☐ 97	Dave Williams, Tor.	1.25
☐ 98	Butch Goring, L.A.	1.00
☐ 99	Don Marcotte, Bos.	.75
☐ 100	AS: Bryan Trottier, NYI.	5.00
☐ 101	AS: Serge Savard, Mtl.	1.25
☐ 102	Cliff Koroll, Chi., LC	.75
☐ 103	Gary Smith (G), Wpg., LC	1.25
☐ 104	Al MacAdam, Min.	.75
☐ 105	Don Edwards (G), Buf.	1.25
☐ 106	Errol Thompson, Det.	.75
☐ 107	André Lacroix, Hfd., LC	.75
☐ 108	Marc Tardif, Que.	.75
☐ 109	Rick Kehoe, Pgh.	1.00
☐ 110	John Davidson (G), NYR.	1.50
☐ **111**	**Behn Wilson, Pha., RC**	**.75**
☐ 112	Doug Jarvis, Mtl.	.75
☐ **113**	**Tom Rowe, Wsh., RC**	**.75**
☐ 114	Mike Milbury, Bos.	1.25
☐ 115	Billy Harris, NYI.	.75
☐ **116**	**Greg Fox, Chi., RC**	**.75**
☐ **117**	**Curt Fraser, Van., RC**	**.75**
☐ 118	J. P. Parise, Min., LC	.75
☐ 119	Ric Seiling, Buf.	.75
☐ 120	Darryl Sittler, Tor.	2.50
☐ 121	Rick Lapointe, Stl.	.75
☐ 122	Jim Rutherford (G), Det.	1.25
☐ 123	Mario Tremblay, Mtl.	.75
☐ 124	Randy Carlyle, Pgh.	1.50
☐ 125	Bobby Clarke, Pha.	2.50
☐ 126	Wayne Thomas (G), NYR., LC	.75
☐ 127	Ivan Boldirev, Atl.	.75
☐ 128	Ted Bulley, Chi.	.75
☐ 129	Dick Redmond, Bos.	.75
☐ 130	AS: Clark Gillies, NYI.	.75
☐ 131	Checklist 1 (1 - 132)	12.00
☐ 132	Vaclav Nedomansky, Det.	.75
☐ 133	Richard Mulhern, L.A.	.75
☐ 134	Dave Schultz, Buf., LC	.75
☐ 135	Guy Lapointe, Mtl.	1.25
☐ 136	Gilles Meloche (G), Min.	1.25
☐ 137	Randy Pierce, Col., Error (Ron Delorme)	.75
☐ 138	Cam Connor, Edm.	.75
☐ 139	George Ferguson, Pgh.	.75
☐ 140	AS: Bill Barber, Pha.	1.50
☐ 141	Terry Ruskowski, Chi., Error (Ruskouski)	.75
☐ **142**	**Wayne Babych, Stl., RC**	**.75**
☐ 143	Phil Russell, Atl.	.75
☐ 144	Bobby Schmautz, Bos., LC	.75

No.	Card	Price
145	Carol Vadnais, NYR.	.75
146	**John Tonelli, NYI., RC**	**7.00**
147	**Peter Marsh, Wpg., RC**	**.75**
148	Thommie Bergman, Det., LC	.75
149	Rick Martin, Buf.	1.00
150	AS: Ken Dryden (G), Mtl., LC	15.00
151	Kris Manery, Min.	.75
152	Guy Charron, Wsh.	.75
153	Lanny McDonald, Tor.	2.00
154	Ron Stackhouse, Pgh.	.75
155	Stan Mikita, Chi., LC	3.00
156	Paul Holmgren, Pha.	.75
157	Perry Miller, Det.	.75
158	Gary Croteau, Col., LC	.75
159	Dave Maloney, NYR.	1.00
160	AS: Marcel Dionne, L.A.	4.00
161	RB: Mike Bossy, NYI.	4.50
162	RB: Don Maloney, NYR.	.75
163	CL: Hartford Whalers	8.00
164	RB: Brad Park, Bos.	1.25
165	RB: Bryan Trottier, NYI.	2.00
166	**Al Hill, Pha., RC**	**.75**
167	Gary Bromley (G), Van.	1.25
168	Don Murdoch, NYR.	.75
169	Wayne Merrick, NYI.	.75
170	Bob Gainey, Mtl.	1.50
171	Jim Schoenfeld, Buf.	1.00
172	Gregg Sheppard, Pgh.	.75
173	**Dan Bolduc, Det., RC, LC**	**.75**
174	Blake Dunlop, Stl.	.75
175	Gordie Howe, Hfd., LC	35.00
176	Richard Brodeur (G), Que. (NYI.)	1.25
177	Tom Younghans, Min.	.75
178	André Dupont, Pha.	.75
179	**Eddie Johnstone, NYR., RC**	**.75**
180	Gilbert Perreault, Buf.	2.00
181	Bob Lorimer, NYI., RC	.75
182	John Wensink, Bos.	.75
183	Lee Fogolin, Edm.	.75
184	**Greg Carroll, Det. (Hfd.)**	**.75**
185	Bobby Hull, Chi. (Wpg.)	28.00
186	Harold Snepsts, Van.	1.00
187	Pete Mahovlich, Pgh. (Det.)	1.00
188	Eric Vail, Atl.	.75
189	Phil Myre (G), Pha.	1.00
190	Wilf Paiement, Col.	.75
191	**Charlie Simmer, L.A., RC**	**5.00**
192	Per-Olov Brasar, Min.	.75
193	Lorne Henning, NYI., LC	.75
194	Don Luce, Buf.	.75
195	Steve Vickers, NYR.	.75
196	**Bob Miller, Bos., RC**	**.75**
197	Mike Palmateer (G), Tor.	1.50
198	Nick Libett , Det. (Pgh.)	.75
199	**Pat Ribble, Chi., RC**	**.75**
200	AS: Guy Lafleur, Mtl.	10.00
201	Mel Bridgman, Pha.	.75
202	**Morris Lukowich, Wpg., RC**	**.75**
203	Don Lever, Van.	.75
204	Tom Bladon, Pgh.	.75
205	Garry Howatt, NYI.	.75
206	**Bobby Smith, Min., RC**	**7.50**
207	Craig Ramsay, Buf.	1.00
208	Ron Duguay, NYR.	1.00
209	Gilles Gilbert (G), Bos.	1.00
210	Bob MacMillan, Atl.	.75
211	Pierre Mondou, Mtl.	.75
212	J. P. Bordeleau, Chi.	.75
213	Reed Larson, Det.	.75
214	Dennis Ververgaert, Pha.	.75
215	Bernie Federko, Stl.	4.50
216	Mark Howe, Hfd.	3.50
217	Bob Nystrom, NYI.	1.00
218	Orest Kindrachuk, Pgh.	.75
219	Mike Fidler, Min.	.75
220	Phil Esposito, NYR.	3.75
221	Bill Hajt, Buf.	.75
222	Mark Napier, Mtl.	.75
223	Dennis Maruk, Wsh.	.75
224	Dennis Polonich, Det.	.75
225	Jean Ratelle, Bos.	1.00
226	Bob Dailey, Pha.	.75
227	Alain Daigle, Chi., LC	.75
228	Ian Turnbull, Tor.	.75
229	Jack Valiquette, Col.	.75
230	AS: Mike Bossy, NYI.	18.00
231	Brad Maxwell, Min.	.75
232	Dave Taylor, L.A.	6.00
233	Pierre Larouche, Mtl.	1.00
234	**Rod Schutt, Pgh., RC**	**.75**
235	Rogatien Vachon (G), Det.	1.50
236	**Ryan Walter, Wsh., RC**	**1.50**
237	Checklist 2 (133 - 264), Error (245 - Bruins)	12.00
238	Terry O'Reilly, Bos.	1.00
239	Réal Cloutier, Que.	.75
240	Anders Hedberg, NYR.	1.25
241	**Ken Linseman, Pha., RC**	**3.50**
242	Billy Smith (G), NYI.	1.50
243	Rick Chartraw, Mtl.	.75
244	CL: Atlanta Flames	3.00
245	CL: Boston Bruins	3.00
246	CL: Buffalo Sabres	3.00
247	CL: Chicago Blackhawks	3.00
248	CL: Colorado Rockies	3.00
249	CL: Detroit Red Wings	3.00
250	CL: Los Angeles Kings	3.00
251	CL: Minnesota North Stars	3.00
252	CL: Montréal Canadiens	3.00
253	CL: New York Islanders	3.00
254	CL: New York Rangers	3.00
255	CL: Philadelphia Flyers	3.00
256	CL: Pittsburgh Penguins	3.00
257	CL: St. Louis Blues	3.00
258	CL: Toronto Maple Leafs	3.00
259	CL: Vancouver Canucks	3.00
260	CL: Washington Capitals	3.00
261	CL: Québec Nordiques	9.00
262	Jean Hamel, Det.	.75
263	Stan Jonathan, Bos.	.75
264	Russ Anderson, Pgh., LC	.75
265	**Gord Roberts, Hfd., RC**	**1.50**
266	Bill Flett, Edm., LC	.75
267	Robbie Ftorek, Que.	1.00
268	Mike Amodeo, Wpg., LC	.75
269	Vic Venasky, L.A.	.75
270	Bob Manno, Van.	.75
271	Dan Maloney, Tor.	.75
272	Al Sims, Hfd.	.75
273	Greg Polis, Wsh., LC	.75
274	Doug Favell (G), Col. (Edm.), LC	1.25
275	Pierre Plante, Que.	.75
276	Bob J. Murdoch, Atl.	.75
277	Lyle Moffat, Wpg., LC	.75
278	Jack Brownschidle, Stl.	.75
279	Dave Keon, Hfd.	1.50
280	Darryl Edestrand, L.A., LC	.75
281	**Greg Millen (G), Pgh., RC**	**5.00**
282	John Gould, Atl. (Buf.)., LC	.75
283	Rich LeDuc, Que.	.75
284	Ron Delorme, Col.	.75
285	Gord Smith, Wpg., LC	.75
286	Nick Fotiu, Hfd.	.75
287	**Kevin McCarthy, Pha. (Van.), RC**	**.75**
288	Jimmy Jones, Tor., LC	.75
289	Pierre Bouchard, Mtl. (Wsh.)	.75
290	Wayne Bianchin, Pgh (Edm.)	.75
291	Garry Larivière, Que.	.75
292	Steve Jensen, L.A.	.75
293	John Garrett (G), Hfd.	1.25
294	Hilliard Graves, Wpg.,LC	.75
295	Bill Clement, Atl.	.75
296	Michel Larocque (G), Mtl.	.75
297	Bob Stewart, Stl., LC	.75
298	**Doug Patey, Wsh. (Edm.), RC, LC**	**.75**
299	Dave Farrish, Que.	.75
300	Al Smith (G), Hfd.	1.25
301	Bill Lochead, Det (NYR.)	.75
302	Dave Hutchison, Tor.	.75
303	Bill Riley, Wsh (Wpg.)., LC	.75
304	Barry Gibbs, Stl. (L.A.)	.75
305	Chris Oddleifson, Van.	.75
306	J. Bob Kelly, Pha. (Edm.), LC, Error (Bob Kelly)	.75
307	**Al Hangsleben, Hfd., RC**	**.75**
308	**Curt Brackenbury, Que., RC**	**.75**
309	Rick Green, Wsh.	.75
310	Ken Houston, Atl.	.75
311	Greg Joly, Det.	.75
312	Bill Lesuk, Wpg., LC	.75
313	**Bill Stewart, Buf., RC, LC**	**.75**
314	Rick Ley, Hfd.	.75
315	**Brett Callighen, Edm., RC**	**.75**
316	Michel Dion (G), Que.	1.25
317	Randy Manery, L.A.	.75
318	Barry Dean, Pha., LC	.75
319	Pat Boutette, Tor.	.75
320	Mark Heaslip, L.A. (Wpg.)	.75
321	Dave Inkpen, Hfd., LC	.75
322	Jere Gillis, Van.	.75
323	Larry Brown, L.A. (Edm.)	.75
324	**Alain Côté, Que., RC**	**1.00**
325	Gordie Lane, Wsh.	.75
326	Bobby Lalonde, Atl. (Bos.)	.75
327	Ed Staniowski (G), Stl.	1.25
328	Ron Plumb, S.D. (Hfd.)	.75
329	Jude Drouin, Wpg.	.75
330	Rick Hampton, Cle. (L.A.), LC	.75
331	Stan Weir, Edm.	.75
332	Blair Stewart, Wsh. (Que.), LC	.75
333	**Mike Polich, Min., RC**	**.75**
334	Jean Potvin, NYI., LC	.75
335	**Jordy Douglas, Hfd., RC**	**.75**
336	**Joel Quenneville, Tor., RC**	**2.00**
337	**Glen Hanlon (G), Van., RC**	**3.00**
338	**Dave Hoyda, Wpg., RC**	**.75**
339	Colin Campbell, Pgh. (Edm.)	1.00
340	**John Smrke, Que., RC, LC**	**.75**
341	Brian Glennie, L.A., LC	.75
342	Don Kozak, Hfd., LC	.75
343	Yvon Labre, Wsh., LC	.75
344	Curt Bennett, Atl., LC	.75
345	Mike Christie, Col.	.75
346	Checklist 3 (265 - 396)	12.00
347	Pat Price, NYI. (Edm.)	.75
348	Ron Low (G), Wsh. (Que.)	1.50
349	Mike Antonovich, Hfd., LC	.75
350	Rolie Eriksson, Min. (Wpg.), LC	.75
351	Bob L. Murdoch (Stl.), LC	.75
352	Rob Palmer, L.A.	.75
353	Brad Gassoff, Van., LC	.75
354	Bruce Boudreau, Tor., LC	.75
355	Al Hamilton, Edm., LC	.75
356	Blaine Stoughton, Hfd.	.75
357	John Baby, Que., LC	.75
358	Gary Inness (G), Wsh., LC	1.25
359	Wayne Dillon, Wpg., LC	.75
360	Darcy Rota, Atl.	.75
361	**Brian Engblom, Mtl., RC**	**.75**
362	Bill Hogaboam, Det., LC	.75
363	Dave Debol, Hfd., RC	.75
364	Pete LoPresti (G), Min. (Edm.), LC	1.25
365	Gerry Hart, Que.	.75
366	Syl Apps, Jr., L.A.	.75
367	Jack McIlhargey, Van., LC	.75
368	Willy Lindstrom, Wpg.	.75
369	**Don Laurence, Atl. (Stl.), RC**	**.75**
370	**Chuck Luksa, Hfd., RC, LC**	**.75**
371	**Dave Semenko, Edm., RC**	**3.50**
372	**Paul Baxter, Que., RC, LC**	**.75**
373	Ron Ellis, Tor.	.75
374	**Leif Svensson, Wsh., RC, LC**	**.75**
375	Dennis O'Brien, Min. (Bos.)	.75
376	Glenn Goldup, L.A.	.75
377	**Terry Richardson (G), Hfd., RC, LC**	**1.25**
378	Peter Sullivan, Wpg.	.75
379	Doug Hicks, Chi. (Edm.)	.75
380	**Jamie Hislop, Que., RC**	**.75**
381	Jocelyn Guevremont, Buf. (NYR.)	.75
382	Willi Plett, Atl.	.75
383	Larry Goodenough, Van., LC	.75
384	**Jim Warner, Hfd., RC, LC**	**.75**
385	Rey Comeau, Col., LC	.75
386	**Barry Melrose, Wpg., RC**	**3.50**
387	**Dave Hunter, Edm., RC**	**.75**
388	**Wally Weir, Que., RC**	**.75**
389	**Mario Lessard (G), L.A.., RC**	**1.25**
390	Ed Kea, Atl. (Stl.)	.75
391	**Bob Stephenson, Hfd., RC, LC**	**.75**
392	Dennis Hextall, Wsh., LC	.75
393	Jerry Butler, Tor.	.75
394	Dave Shand, Atl.	.75
395	Rick Blight, Van.	.75
396	Lars-Erik Sjoberg, Wpg., LC	2.50

1979 - 80 SOVIET STARS

Card Size: 8 1/4" x 5 7/8"
Face: Four colour; Name, Resume
Back: Black and white; Stats, Resume
Imprint: N3 arenbctbo Nnafat Mockba 1979
Complete Set (24 cards with folder): 50.00

	No.	Player	NRMT-MT
☐	1	Title Card: Team Photograph	3.00
☐	2	Victor Tikhonov, Coach	1.50
☐	3	Vladimir Yursinov, Coach	1.50
☐	4	Vladislav Tretiak (G)	10.00
☐	5	Alexander Pashkov (G)	3.00
☐	6	Vladimir Lutchenko	1.50
☐	7	Valeri Vasiliev	1.50
☐	8	Gennady Tsygankov	1.50
☐	9	Yuri Fedorov	1.50
☐	10	Viacheslav Fetisov	6.00
☐	11	Zinetula Bilylatinov	1.50
☐	12	Vasiliy Pervukhin	1.50
☐	13	Boris Mikhailov	3.00
☐	14	Vladimir Petrov	3.00
☐	15	Valeri Kharlamov	5.00
☐	16	Alexander Maltsev	3.00
☐	17	Sergei Kapustin	1.50
☐	18	Yuri Lebedev	1.50
☐	19	Viktor Zluktov	1.50
☐	20	Helmut Balderis	3.00
☐	21	Alexander Golikov	1.50
☐	22	Sergei Makarov	6.00
☐	23	Vladimir Golikov	1.50
☐	24	Closing Ceremonies	1.50

1979 - 80 TOPPS

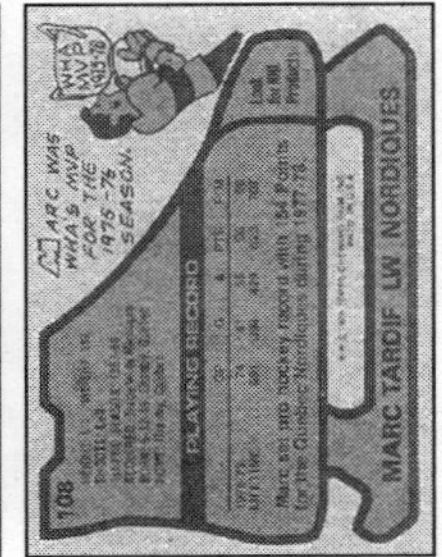

Card Size: 2 1/2" x 3 1/2"
Face: Four colour, blue border, Team logo, Position
Back: Blue and black on card stock; Number, Resume, Hockey trivia
Imprint: © 1979 TOPPS CHEWING GUM, INC.
Complete Set (264 cards): 600.00
Common Player: .50

	No.	Player	NRMT-MT
☐	1	LL: M. Bossy/M. Dionne/G. Lafleur	3.25
☐	2	LL: B. Trottier/G. Lafleur/M. Dionne/B. MacMillan	2.50
☐	3	LL: B. Trottier/M. Dionne/G. Lafleur	2.50
☐	4	LL: D. Williams/R. Holt/D. Schultz	.75
☐	5	LL: M. Bossy/M. Dionne/L. McDonald/P. Gardner	2.50
☐	6	LL: K. Dryden/G. Resch/B. Parent	3.00
☐	7	LL: G. Lafleur/M. Bossy/B. Trottier/Pronovost/JT. Bulley	2.75
☐	8	LL: K. Dryden/T. Esposito/ M. Palmateer/M. Lessard/B. Parent, Error	10.00
☐	8	LL: Corrected, (Palmateer and Lessard reversed)	3.75
☐	9	Greg Malone, Pgh.	.50
☐	10	Rick Middleton, Bos.	.75
☐	11	Greg Smith, Min.	.50
☐	12	Réne Robert, Buf.	.50
☐	13	Doug Risebrough, Mtl.	.50
☐	14	Bob Kelly, Pha.	.50
☐	15	Walt Tkaczuk, NYR.	.50
☐	16	John Marks, Chi.	.50
☐	**17**	**Willie Huber, Det., RC**	**.50**
☐	**18**	**Wayne Gretzky, Edm., RC**	**450.00**
☐	19	Ron Sedlbauer, Van.	.50
☐	20	AS: Glenn Resch (G), NYI.	.75
☐	21	Blair Chapman, Pgh.	.50
☐	22	Ron Zanussi. Min.	.50
☐	23	Brad Park, Bos.	1.00
☐	24	Yvon Lambert, Mtl.	.50
☐	25	André Savard, Buf.	.50
☐	26	Jimmy Watson, Pha.	.50
☐	**27**	**Harold Phillipoff, Chi., RC, LC**	**.50**
☐	28	Dan Bouchard (G), Atl.	.75
☐	29	Bob Sirois, Wsh.	.50
☐	30	Ulf Nilsson, NYR.	.50
☐	31	Mike Murphy, L.A.	.50
☐	32	Stefan Persson, NYI.	.50
☐	33	Garry Unger, Stl.	.60
☐	34	Réjean Houle, Mtl.	.60
☐	35	Barry Beck, Col.	.50
☐	36	Tim Young, Min.	.50
☐	37	Rick Dudley, Buf.	.50
☐	38	Wayne Stephenson (G), Pha.	.75
☐	39	Peter McNab, Bos.	.50
☐	40	AS: Borje Salming, Tor.	1.00
☐	41	Tom Lysiak, Chi.	.50
☐	**42**	**Don Maloney, NYR., RC**	**.75**
☐	43	Mike Rogers, Hfd.	.50
☐	44	Dave Lewis, NYI.	.60
☐	45	Peter Lee, Pgh.	.50
☐	46	Marty Howe, Hfd.	.50
☐	47	Serge Bernier, Que.	.50
☐	48	Paul Woods, Det.	.50
☐	49	Bob Sauvé (G), Buf.	.75
☐	50	AS: Larry Robinson, Mtl.	1.75
☐	**51**	**Tom Gorence, Pha., RC**	**.50**
☐	52	Gary Sargent, Min.	.50
☐	**53**	**Thomas Gradin, Van., RC**	**1.75**
☐	54	Dean Talafous, NYR.	.50
☐	55	Bob Murray, Chi.	.50
☐	56	Bob Bourne, NYI.	.50
☐	57	Larry Patey, Stl.	.50
☐	58	Ross Lonsberry, Pgh.	.50
☐	59	Rick Smith, Bos.	.50
☐	60	Guy Chouinard, Atl.	.50
☐	61	Danny Gare, Buf.	.60
☐	62	Jim Bedard (G), Wsh., LC	.75
☐	63	Dale McCourt, L.A.	.50
☐	**64**	**Steve Payne, Min., RC**	**.50**
☐	**65**	**Pat Hughes, Mtl., RC**	**.50**
☐	66	Mike McEwen, NYR.	.50
☐	**67**	**Reg Kerr, Chi., RC**	**.50**
☐	68	Walt McKechnie, Tor.	.50
☐	69	Michel Plasse (G), Col.	.75
☐	70	AS: Denis Potvin, NYI.	1.50
☐	71	Dave Dryden (G), Edm., LC	.75
☐	72	Gary McAdam, Pgh.	.50
☐	73	André St. Laurent, Det.	.50
☐	74	Jerry Korab, Buf.	.50
☐	75	Rick MacLeish, Pha.	.50
☐	76	Dennis Kearns, Van.	.50
☐	77	Jean Pronovost, Atl.	.50
☐	78	Ron Greschner, NYR..	.50
☐	79	Wayne Cashman, Bos.	.50
☐	80	Tony Esposito (G), Chi.	1.75
☐	81	Semi-finals: Canadiens Squeak Past Bruins	.50
☐	82	Semi-finals: Rangers Upset Islanders in 6	.50
☐	83	Finals: Canadiens Make it 4 Straight Cups	1.50
☐	84	Brian Sutter, Stl.	2.00
☐	85	Gerry Cheevers (G), Bos., LC	1.50
☐	86	Pat Hickey, NYR.	.50
☐	87	Mike Kaszycki, NYI.	.50
☐	88	Grant Mulvey, Chi.	.50
☐	89	Derek Smith, Buf.	.50
☐	90	Steve Shutt, Mtl.	1.00
☐	91	Robert Picard, Wsh.	.50
☐	92	Dan Labraaten, Det.	.50
☐	93	Glen Sharpley, Min.	.50
☐	94	Denis Herron (G), Pgh.	.75
☐	95	Reggie Leach, Pha.	.60
☐	96	John Van Boxmeer, Col.	.50
☐	97	Dave Williams, Tor.	.75
☐	98	Butch Goring, L.A.	.75
☐	99	Don Marcotte, Bos.	.50
☐	100	AS: Bryan Trottier, NYI.	3.50
☐	101	AS: Serge Savard, Mtl.	.75
☐	102	Cliff Koroll, Chi., LC	.50
☐	103	Gary Smith (G), Wpg., LC	.75
☐	104	Al MacAdam, Min.	.50
☐	105	Don Edwards (G), Buf.	.75
☐	106	Errol Thompson, Det.	.50
☐	107	André Lacroix, Hfd., LC	.50
☐	108	Marc Tardif, Que.	.50
☐	109	Rick Kehoe, Pgh.	.60
☐	110	John Davidson (G), NYR.	1.00
☐	**111**	**Behn Wilson, Pha., RC**	**.50**
☐	112	Doug Jarvis, Mtl.	.50
☐	**113**	**Tom Rowe, Wsh., RC**	**.50**
☐	114	Mike Milbury, Bos.	.75
☐	115	Billy Harris, NYI.	.50
☐	**116**	**Greg Fox, Chi., RC**	**.50**
☐	**117**	**Curt Fraser, Van., RC**	**.50**
☐	118	J. P. Parise, Min., LC	.50
☐	119	Ric Seiling, Buf.	.50
☐	120	Darryl Sittler, Tor.	1.50
☐	121	Rick Lapointe, Stl.	.50
☐	122	Jim Rutherford (G), Det.	.85
☐	123	Mario Tremblay, Mtl.	.50
☐	124	Randy Carlyle, Pgh.	1.00
☐	125	Bobby Clarke, Pha.	1.75
☐	126	Wayne Thomas (G), NYR., LC	.50
☐	127	Ivan Boldirev, Atl.	.50
☐	128	Ted Bulley, Chi.	.50
☐	129	Dick Redmond, Bos.	.50
☐	130	AS: Clark Gillies, NYI.	.50
☐	131	Checklist 1 (1 - 132)	6.50
☐	132	Vaclav Nedomansky, Det.	.50
☐	133	Richard Mulhern, L.A.	.50
☐	134	Dave Schultz, Buf., LC	.50
☐	135	Guy Lapointe, Mtl.	.85
☐	136	Gilles Meloche (G), Min.	.75
☐	137	Randy Pierce, Col., Error (Ron Delorme)	.50
☐	138	Cam Connor, Edm.	.50
☐	139	George Ferguson, Pgh.	.50
☐	140	AS: Bill Barber, Pha.	1.00
☐	141	Mike Walton, Chi., LC	.50
☐	**142**	**Wayne Babych, Stl., RC**	**.50**
☐	143	Phil Russell, Atl.	.50
☐	144	Bobby Schmautz, Bos., LC	.50
☐	145	Carol Vadnais, NYR.	.50
☐	**146**	**John Tonelli, NYI., RC**	**5.00**
☐	**147**	**Peter Marsh, Wpg., RC**	**.50**
☐	148	Thommie Bergman, Det., LC	.50
☐	149	Rick Martin, Buf.	.60
☐	150	AS: Ken Dryden (G), Mtl.	8.00
☐	151	Kris Manery, Min.	.50
☐	152	Guy Charron, Wsh.	.50
☐	153	Lanny McDonald, Tor.	1.25
☐	154	Ron Stackhouse, Pgh.	.50
☐	155	Stan Mikita, Chi., LC	2.00
☐	156	Paul Holmgren, Pha.	.50
☐	157	Perry Miller, Det.	.50
☐	158	Gary Croteau, Col., LC	.50
☐	159	Dave Maloney, NYR.	.75
☐	160	AS: Marcel Dionne, L.A.	2.75
☐	161	RB: Mike Bossy, NYI.	3.00
☐	162	RB: Don Maloney, NYR.	.50
☐	163	RB: Ulf Nilsson, NYR.	.50
☐	164	RB: Brad Park, Bos.	.60
☐	165	RB: Bryan Trottier, NYI.	1.25
☐	**166**	**Al Hill, Pha., RC**	**.50**
☐	167	Gary Bromley (G), Van.	.75
☐	168	Don Murdoch, NYR.	.50
☐	169	Wayne Merrick, NYI.	.50
☐	170	Bob Gainey, Mtl.	1.00
☐	171	Jim Schoenfeld, Buf.	.60
☐	172	Gregg Sheppard, Pgh.	.50
☐	**173**	**Dan Bolduc, Det., RC, LC**	**.50**
☐	174	Blake Dunlop, Stl.	.50
☐	175	Gordie Howe, Hfd., LC	25.00
☐	176	Richard Brodeur (G), Que.	.75
☐	177	Tom Younghans, Min.	.50
☐	178	André Dupont, Pha.	.50
☐	**179**	**Eddie Johnstone, NYR., RC**	**.50**
☐	180	Gilbert Perreault, Buf.	1.50
☐	**181**	**Bob Lorimer, NYI., RC**	**.50**
☐	182	John Wensink, Bos.	.50
☐	183	Lee Fogolin, Edm.	.50
☐	**184**	**Greg Carroll, Det., RC, LC**	**.50**
☐	185	Bobby Hull, Chi., LC	20.00
☐	186	Harold Snepsts, Van.	.60
☐	187	Pete Mahovlich, Pgh.	.60
☐	188	Eric Vail, Atl.	.50
☐	189	Phil Myre (G), Pha.	.75
☐	190	Wilf Paiement, Col.	.50
☐	**191**	**Charlie Simmer, L.A., RC**	**3.25**
☐	192	Per-Olov Brasar, Min.	.50
☐	193	Lorne Henning, NYI., LC	.50
☐	194	Don Luce, Buf.	.50
☐	195	Steve Vickers, NYR.	.50

	No.	Player	Value
☐	**196**	**Bob Miller, Bos., RC**	**.50**
☐	197	Mike Palmateer (G), Tor.	1.00
☐	198	Nick Libett, Det., LC	.50
☐	**199**	**Pat Ribble, Chi., RC**	**.50**
☐	200	AS: Guy Lafleur, Mtl.	5.00
☐	201	Mel Bridgman, Pha.	.50
☐	**202**	**Morris Lukowich, Wpg., RC**	**.50**
☐	203	Don Lever, Van.	.50
☐	204	Tom Bladon, Pgh.	.50
☐	205	Garry Howatt, NYI.	.50
☐	**206**	**Bobby Smith, Min., RC**	**5.50**
☐	207	Craig Ramsay, Buf.	.60
☐	208	Ron Duguay, NYR.	.60
☐	209	Gilles Gilbert (G), Bos.	.75
☐	210	Bob MacMillan, Atl.	.50
☐	211	Pierre Mondou, Mtl.	.60
☐	212	J. P. Bordeleau, Chi.	.50
☐	213	Reed Larson, Det.	.50
☐	214	Dennis Ververgaert, Pha.	.50
☐	215	Bernie Federko, Stl.	3.00
☐	216	Mark Howe, Hfd.	2.50
☐	217	Bob Nystrom, NYI.	.60
☐	218	Orest Kindrachuk, Pgh.	.50
☐	219	Mike Fidler, Min.	.50
☐	220	Phil Esposito, NYR.	2.50
☐	221	Bill Hajt, Buf.	.50
☐	222	Mark Napier, Mtl.	.50
☐	223	Dennis Maruk, Wsh.	.50
☐	224	Dennis Polonich, Det.	.50
☐	225	Jean Ratelle, Bos.	.60
☐	226	Bob Dailey, Pha.	.50
☐	227	Alain Daigle, Chi., LC	.50
☐	228	Ian Turnbull, Tor.	.50
☐	229	Jack Valiquette, Col.	.50
☐	230	AS: Mike Bossy, NYI.	10.00
☐	231	Brad Maxwell, Min.	.50
☐	232	David Taylor, L.A.	5.00
☐	233	Pierre Larouche, Mtl.	.60
☐	**234**	**Rod Schutt, Pgh., RC**	**.50**
☐	235	Rogatien Vachon (G), Det.	1.00
☐	**236**	**Ryan Walter, Wsh., RC**	**1.00**
☐	237	Checklist 2 (133 - 264)	6.50
☐	238	Terry O'Reilly, Bos.	.60
☐	239	Réal Cloutier, Que.	.50
☐	240	Anders Hedberg, NYR.	.75
☐	**241**	**Ken Linseman, Pha., RC**	**2.25**
☐	242	Billy Smith (G), NYI.	1.00
☐	243	Rick Chartraw, Mtl.	.50
☐	244	CL: Atlanta Flames	2.25
☐	245	CL: Boston Bruins	2.25
☐	246	CL: Buffalo Sabres	2.25
☐	247	CL: Chicago Blackhawks	2.25
☐	248	CL: Colorado Rockies	2.25
☐	249	CL: Detroit Red Wings	2.25
☐	250	CL: Los Angeles Kings	2.25
☐	251	CL: Minnesota North Stars	2.25
☐	252	CL: Montréal Canadiens	2.25
☐	253	CL: New York Islanders	2.25
☐	254	CL: New York Rangers	2.25
☐	255	CL: Philadelphia Flyers	2.25
☐	256	CL: Pittsburgh Penguins	2.25
☐	257	CL: St. Louis Blues	2.25
☐	258	CL: Toronto Maple Leafs	2.25
☐	259	CL: Vancouver Canucks	2.25
☐	260	CL: Washington Capitals	2.25
☐	261	CL: 1979 - 80 Entries Edmonton Oilers, Hartford Whalers, Winnipeg Jets, Québec Nordiques Logos	15.00
☐	262	Jean Hamel, Det.	.50
☐	263	Stan Jonathan, Bos.	.50
☐	264	Russ Anderson, Pgh., LC	.50

HELMET AND STICK DECALS INSERTS

The one card per pack insert contains one team decal and three assorted decals.

Card Size: 2 1/2" x 3 1/2"
Face: Four colour, white border, Team, Name
Back: Four colour on white card stock; Promotional offer
Insert Set (21 cards): 18.00

	No.	Team	NRMT-MT
☐	1	Atlanta Flames	1.25
☐	2	Boston Bruins	1.25
☐	3	Buffalo Sabres	1.25
☐	4	Chicago Blackhawks	1.25
☐	5	Colorado Rockies	1.25
☐	6	Detroit Red Wings	1.25
☐	7	Edmonton Oilers	1.25
☐	8	Hartford Whalers	1.25
☐	9	Los Angeles Kings	1.25
☐	10	Minnesota North Stars	1.25
☐	11	Montréal Canadiens	1.25
☐	12	New York Islanders	1.25
☐	13	New York Rangers	1.25
☐	14	Philadelphia Flyers	1.25
☐	15	Pittsburgh Penguins	1.25
☐	16	Québec Nordiques	1.25
☐	17	St. Louis Blues	1.25
☐	18	Toronto Maple Leafs	1.25
☐	19	Vancouver Canucks	1.25
☐	20	Washington Capitals	1.25
☐	21	Winnipeg Jets	1.25

1980 U.S.A. OLYMPIC MINI-PICS

These cards feature black and white photography.

Card Size: 1 3/4" x 2 3/4"
Front: Black and white; Name, Position
Back: Black and white; Gold medal winners
Imprint: None
Complete Set (16 cards): 40.00

	No.	Player	NRMT-MT
☐	1	Jim Craig (G)	5.00
☐	2	Mike Eruzione	5.00
☐	3	John Harrington	2.00
☐	4	Mark Johnson	3.50
☐	5	Rob McClanahan	2.00
☐	6	Jack O'Callahan	3.00
☐	7	Phil Verchota	2.00
☐	8	Bob Suter	2.00
☐	9	Eric Strobel	2.00
☐	10	Dave Silk	2.00
☐	11	Mike Ramsey	5.00
☐	12	Mark Pavelich	3.00
☐	13	Steve Christoff	2.00
☐	14	Dave Christian	5.00
☐	15	Herb Brooks, Coach	5.00
☐	16	1980 Game Scores	2.00

1980 U.S.S.R. OLYMPIC MINI-PICS

These cards feature black and white photography.

Card Size: 1 1/2" x 2 5/8"
Imprint: None
Complete Set (10 cards): 30.00

	Player	NRMT-MT
☐	Yuri Fedorov	2.00
☐	Irek Gimayev	2.00
☐	Alexander Golikov	2.00
☐	Sergei Kapustin	2.00
☐	V. Kovin	2.00
☐	Boris Mikhailov	5.00
☐	V. Myshikin (G)	2.00
☐	Vladimir Petrov	5.00
☐	Vladislav Tretiak (G)	12.00
☐	Valeri Vasiliev	2.00

1980 - 81 MALLASJUOMA

A set of 220 cards plus a collecting album issued by the brewery Mallasjuoma for the Finnish National League. We have no pricing information on this set.

Card Size: 2" x 2 5/16"
Label Size: 3" x 3 1/2"
Imprint:

	No.	Player
LABEL "LATKA"		
☐		Jukka Porvari
☐	1	Stig Wetzell, HIFK
☐	2	Seppo Pakola, HIFK
☐	3	Frank Neal, HIFK
☐	4	Heikki Riihiranta, HIFK
☐	5	Esa Peltonen, HIFK
☐	6	Tommi Salmelainen, HIFK
☐	7	Matti Forss, HIFK
☐	8	Olli Ignatius, HIFK
☐	9	Raimo Hirvonen, HIFK
☐	10	Harri Linnonmaa, HIFK
☐	11	Jorma Immonen, HIFK
☐	12	Arto Sirvio, HIFK
☐	13	Matti Murto, HIFK
☐	14	Jari Kapanen, HIFK
☐	15	Ilkka Sinisalo, HIFK
☐	16	Arto Jokinen, HIFK
☐	17	Pertti Lehtonen, HIFK
☐	18	Timo Ukkola, HIFK
☐	19	Rainer Risku, HIFK
☐	20	Ari Lahteenmaki, HIFK
☐	21	Hannu Riihimaki, HIFK
☐	22	Jarmo Vuorinen, HIFK
☐	23	Jukka Airaksinen, Ilves
☐	24	Reijo Laksola, Ilves
☐	25	Jorma Aro, Ilves
☐	26	Jari Jarvinen, Ilves
☐	27	Jouko Urvikko, Ilves
☐	28	Ari Jokinen, Ilves
☐	29	Kari Heikkila, Ilves
☐	30	Auvo Vaananen, Ilves
☐	31	Risto Jalo, Ilves
☐	32	Lasse Oksanen, Ilves
☐	33	Lasse Tasala, Ilves
☐	34	Kari Jarvinen, Ilves
☐	35	Jarmo Lilius, Ilves
☐	36	Jyrki Seppa, Ilves
☐	37	Jorma Huhtala, Ilves
☐	38	Jari Viitala, Ilves
☐	39	Antti Heikkila, Ilves
☐	40	Matti Rautiainen, Ilves
☐	41	Pertti Jarvenpaa, Ilves
☐	42	Seppo Sevon, Ilves
☐	43	Henry Lehvonen, Ilves
☐	44	Tapio Virhimo, Ilves
☐	45	Rauli Sohlman, Jokerit
☐	46	Martti Tuomisto, Jokerit
☐	47	Pekka Rasanen, Jokerit
☐	48	Aarre Kourula, Jokerit
☐	49	Timo Saari, Jokerit
☐	50	Arto Laine, Jokerit
☐	51	Anssi Melametsa, Jokerit
☐	52	VeliPekka Kinnunen, Jokerit
☐	53	Matti Heikkila, Jokerit
☐	54	Tony Arima, Jokerit
☐	55	Ismo Lehkonen, Jokerit
☐	56	Matti Virmanen, Jokerit
☐	57	Sakari Petajaaho, Jokerit
☐	58	Antti Lehto, Jokerit
☐	59	Pasi Mustonen, Jokerit
☐	60	Erkki Korhonen, Jokerit
☐	61	Ilmo Uotila, Jokerit
☐	62	Jussi Lepisto, Jokerit
☐	63	Hannu Nykvist, Jokerit
☐	64	Ari Blomqvist, Jokerit
☐	65	Henry Leppa, Jokerit
☐	66	Ari Makinen, Jokerit
☐	67	Jari Vuorio, Kiekkoreipas
☐	68	Olli Saarinen, Kiekkoreipas
☐	69	Matti Kaario, Kiekkoreipas
☐	70	Timo Blomqvist, Kiekkoreipas
☐	71	Petteri Kanerva, Kiekkoreipas
☐	72	Timo Harkanen, Kiekkoreipas
☐	73	Keijo Koivisto, Kiekkoreipas
☐	74	Eero Mantere, Kiekkoreipas
☐	75	Harri Nyman, Kiekkoreipas
☐	76	Harri Toivanen, Kiekkoreipas
☐	77	Mika Laine, Kiekkoreipas
☐	78	Olavi Niemenranta, Kiekkoreipas
☐	79	Pekka Laine, Kiekkoreipas
☐	80	Harri Haapaniemi, Kiekkoreipas
☐	81	Juha Silvennoinen, Kiekkoreipas
☐	82	Pekka Lumela, Kiekkoreipas

	No.	Player
☐	83	Yrjo Hakulinen, Kiekkoreipas
☐	84	Tom Regnier, Kiekkoreipas
☐	85	Richard Regnier, Kiekkoreipas
☐	86	Jukka Holtari, Kiekkoreipas
☐	87	Timo Heino, Kiekkoreipas
☐	88	Hannu Koskinen, Kiekkoreipas
☐	89	Ari Hellgren, Oulun
☐	90	Arto Ruotanen, Oulun
☐	91	Hannu Jalonen, Oulun
☐	92	Kari Suoraniemi, Oulun
☐	93	Hannu Hiltunen, Oulun
☐	94	Juha Tuohimaa, Oulun
☐	95	Pentti Perhomaa, Oulun
☐	96	Reijo Ruotsalainen, Oulun
☐	97	Seppo Tenhunen, Oulun
☐	98	Kari Jalonen, Oulun
☐	99	Markku Kiimalainen, Oulun
☐	100	Juha Huikari, Oulun
☐	101	Pekka Tuomisto, Oulun
☐	102	Jouni Koutuaniemi, Oulun
☐	103	Veikko Torkkeli, Oulun
☐	104	Jouko Kamarainen, Oulun
☐	105	Kai Suikkanen, Oulun
☐	106	Jorma Torkkeli, Oulun
☐	107	Mikko Leinonen, Oulun
☐	108	Ari Timosaari, Oulun
☐	109	Jarmo Tauriainen, Oulun
☐	110	Pekka Arbelius, Oulun
☐	111	Teppo Mattsson, Rauman Lukko
☐	112	Esa Hakkarainen, Rauman Lukko
☐	113	Jouni Peltonen, Rauman Lukko
☐	114	Jarmo Kuusisto, Rauman Lukko
☐	115	Timo Peltonen, Rauman Lukko
☐	116	Ari-Pekka Strander, Rauman Lukko
☐	117	Jorma Vehmanen, Rauman Lukko
☐	118	Pasi Tuohimaa, Rauman Lukko
☐	119	Olli Tuominen, Rauman Lukko
☐	120	Hannu Kemppainen, Rauman Lukko
☐	121	Ismo Villa, Rauman Lukko
☐	122	Esa Wallin, Rauman Lukko
☐	123	Matti Tynkkynen, Rauman Lukko
☐	124	Jari Rastio, Rauman Lukko
☐	125	Kari Kaupinsalo, Rauman Lukko
☐	126	Lasse Lindberg, Rauman Lukko
☐	127	Olli-Pekka Rajala, Rauman Lukko
☐	128	Harri Tuohimaa, Rauman Lukko
☐	129	Hannu Vierimaa, Rauman Lukko
☐	130	Jari Laiho, Rauman Lukko
☐	131	Juhani Wallenius, Rauman Lukko
☐	132	Jarmo Kaistakari, Rauman Lukko
☐	133	Jukka Peitsoma, Saipa
☐	134	Tuomo Martin, Saipa
☐	135	Keijo Taskula, Saipa
☐	136	Martti Immonen, Saipa
☐	137	Ilkka Kaarna, Saipa
☐	138	Pertti Ahokas, Saipa
☐	139	Ari Lehikoinen, Saipa
☐	140	Jyrki Paakkarinen, Saipa
☐	141	Jouko Kukko, Saipa
☐	142	Harri Poyhia, Saipa
☐	143	Pentti Matikainen, Saipa
☐	144	Juha Sokkanen, Saipa
☐	145	Antero Vaatamoinen, Saipa
☐	146	Pertti Heikkeri, Saipa
☐	147	Esko Heikkeri, Saipa
☐	148	Heikki Malkia, Saipa
☐	149	Tuomo Laukkanen, Saipa
☐	150	Kari Weckstrom, Saipa
☐	151	Seppo Urpalainen, Saipa
☐	152	Kari Saarikko, Saipa
☐	153	Tuomo Jormakka, Saipa
☐	154	Juha Henttonen, Saipa
☐	155	Lasse Schultz, Tappara
☐	156	Mikko Vilonen, Tappara
☐	157	Hannu Helander, Tappara
☐	158	Pertti Valkeapaa, Tappara
☐	159	Lasse Litma, Tappara
☐	160	Timo Jutila, Tappara
☐	161	Oiva Oijennus, Tappara
☐	162	Timo Susi, Tappara
☐	163	Jukka Porvari, Tappara
☐	164	Erkki Lehtonen, Tappara
☐	165	Esa Valioja, Tappara
☐	166	Pertti Koivulahti, Tappara
☐	167	Juha Nurmi, Tappara
☐	168	Hannu Kamppuri, Tappara
☐	169	Petri Karjalainen, Tappara
☐	170	Timo Penttila, Tappara
☐	171	Jari Lindgren, Tappara
☐	172	Seppo Virta, Tappara
☐	173	Jukka Hirsimaki, Tappara
☐	174	Petri Niukkanen, Tappara
☐	175	Seppo Ahokainen, Tappara
☐	176	Antero Lehtonen, Tappara
☐	177	Hannu Jortikka, Turun Palloseura
☐	178	Timo Nummelin, Turun Palloseura
☐	179	Seppo Suoraniemi, Turun Palloseura
☐	180	Pasi Virta, Turun Palloseura
☐	181	Kari Vaihinen, Turun Palloseura
☐	182	Henry Saleva, Turun Palloseura
☐	183	Jari Hytti, Turun Palloseura
☐	184	Kari Kauppila, Turun Palloseura
☐	185	Reijo Leppanen, Turun Palloseura
☐	186	Rauli Tammelin, Turun Palloseura
☐	187	Markku Haapaniemi, Turun Palloseura
☐	188	Kari Horkko, Turun Palloseura
☐	189	Martti Jarkko, Turun Palloseura
☐	190	Juhani Tamminen, Turun Palloseura
☐	191	Kalevi Aho, Turun Palloseura
☐	192	Reima Pullinen, Turun Palloseura
☐	193	Hakan Hjerppe, Turun Palloseura
☐	194	Rauno Sjoroos, Turun Palloseura
☐	195	Hannu Niittoaho, Turun Palloseura
☐	196	Jari Paavola, Turun Palloseura
☐	197	Petteri Lehto, Turun Palloseura
☐	198	Jim Bedard, Turun Palloseura
☐	199	Antero Kivela, Assat Pori
☐	200	Antti Heikkila, Assat Pori
☐	201	Tapio Flinck, Assat Pori
☐	202	Arto Javanainen, Assat Pori
☐	203	Jukka Virtanen, Assat Pori
☐	204	Risto Tuomi, Assat Pori
☐	205	Tapio Koskinen, Assat Pori
☐	206	Juha Jyrkkio, Assat Pori
☐	207	Ari Peltola, Assat Pori
☐	208	Tapio Levo, Assat Pori
☐	209	Veli-Pekka Ketola, Assat Pori
☐	210	Erkki Vakiparta, Assat Pori
☐	211	Simo Ketola, Assat Pori
☐	212	Rauli Levonen, Assat Pori
☐	213	Jari Nystrom, Assat Pori
☐	214	Matti Ruisma, Assat Pori
☐	215	Tauno Makela, Assat Pori
☐	216	Kari Makkonen, Assat Pori
☐	217	Harry Nikander, Assat Pori
☐	218	Pentti Rautakallio, Assat Pori
☐	219	Martti Nenonen, Assat Pori
☐	220	Kari Takko, Assat Pori

1980 - 81 O-PEE-CHEE

Face: Four colour, white border, Position
Back: Green and yellow on card stock, Number, Resume, Hockey trivia, Bilingual
Imprint: © 1980 O-PEE-CHEE
Complete Set (396 cards): 500.00
Common Player: .35

	No.	Player	NRMT-MT
☐	1	RB: Philadelphia Flyers go to 35 games without a loss	1.50
☐	2	RB: Ray Bourque, Bos.	14.00
☐	3	RB: Wayne Gretzky, Edm.	40.00
☐	4	RB: Charlie Simmer, L.A.	.50
☐	5	RB: Billy Smith (G), MYI.	.75
☐	6	Jean Ratelle, Bos., LC	.50
☐	7	Dave Maloney, NYR.	.35
☐	8	Phil Myre (G), Pha., LC	.50
☐	**9**	**Ken Morrow, NYI., RC**	**.75**
☐	10	Guy Lafleur, Mtl.	6.50
☐	**11**	**Bill Derlago, Tor., RC**	**.50**
☐	12	Doug Wilson, Chi.	1.00
☐	13	Craig Ramsay, Buf.	.50
☐	14	Pat Boutette, Hfd.	.35
☐	15	Eric Vail, Cgy.	.35
☐	16	TL: Mike Foligno, Det.	.50
☐	17	Bobby Smith, Min.	2.00
☐	18	Rick Kehoe, Pgh.	.50
☐	19	Joel Quenneville, Col.	.75
☐	20	Marcel Dionne, L.A.	1.75
☐	21	Kevin McCarthy, Van.	.35
☐	**22**	**Jim Craig (G), Bos., RC, LC**	**1.50**
☐	23	Steve Vickers, NYR., LC	.35
☐	24	Ken Linseman, Pha.	.50
☐	25	Mike Bossy, NYI.	10.00
☐	26	Serge Savard, Mtl.	.75
☐	27	TL: Grant Mulvey, Chi.	.50
☐	28	Pat Hickey, Tor.	.35
☐	29	Peter Sullivan, Wpg., LC	.35
☐	30	Blaine Stoughton, Hfd.	.35
☐	**31**	**Mike Liut (G), Stl., RC**	**8.00**
☐	32	Blair MacDonald, Edm.	.35
☐	33	Rick Green, Wsh.	.35
☐	34	Al MacAdam, Min.	.35
☐	35	Robbie Ftorek, Que.	.50
☐	36	Dick Redmond, Bos.	.35
☐	37	Ron Duguay, NYR.	.50
☐	38	TL: Danny Gare, Buf.	.50
☐	**39**	**Brian Propp, Pha., RC**	**6.00**
☐	40	Bryan Trottier, NYI.	3.00
☐	41	Rich Preston, Chi.	.35
☐	42	Pierre Mondou, Mtl.	.35
☐	43	Reed Larson, Det.	.35
☐	44	George Ferguson, Pgh.	.35
☐	45	Guy Chouinard, Cgy.	.35
☐	46	Billy Harris, L.A.	.35
☐	47	Gilles Meloche (G), Min.	.50
☐	48	Blair Chapman, Stl.	.35
☐	49	TL: Mike Gartner, Wsh.	8.50
☐	50	Darryl Sittler, Tor.	1.00
☐	51	Rick Martin, Buf., LC	.35
☐	52	Ivan Boldirev, Van.	.50
☐	**53**	**Craig Norwich, Stl., RC, LC**	**.35**
☐	54	Dennis Polonich, Det., LC	.35
☐	55	Bobby Clarke, Pha.	1.75
☐	56	Terry O'Reilly, Bos.	.50
☐	57	Carol Vadnais, NYR.	.35
☐	58	Bob Gainey, Mtl.	1.00
☐	59	TL: Blaine Stoughton, Hfd.	.50
☐	60	Billy Smith (G), NYI.	1.00
☐	**61**	**Mike O'Connell, Chi., RC**	**.50**
☐	62	Lanny McDonald, Col.	1.00
☐	63	Lee Fogolin, Edm.	.35
☐	**64**	**Rocky Saganiuk, Tor., RC**	**.35**
☐	**65**	**Rolf Edberg, Wsh., RC, LC**	**.35**
☐	66	Paul Shmyr, Min., LC	.35
☐	**67**	**Michel Goulet, Que., RC**	**20.00**
☐	68	Dan Bouchard (G), Cgy.	.50
☐	**69**	**Mark Johnson, Pgh., RC**	**.35**
☐	70	Reggie Leach, Pha.	.50
☐	71	TL: Bernie Federko, Stl.	.50
☐	72	Pete Mahovlich, Det., LC	.50
☐	73	Anders Hedberg, NYR.	.50
☐	74	Brad Park, Bos.	.75
☐	75	Clark Gillies, NYI.	.50
☐	76	Doug Jarvis, Mtl.	.50
☐	77	John Garrett (G), Hfd.	.50
☐	78	Dave Hutchison, Chi., LC	.35
☐	**79**	**John Anderson, Tor., RC**	**.50**
☐	80	Gilbert Perreault, Buf.	1.00
☐	81	AS: Marcel Dionne, L.A.	1.00
☐	82	AS: Guy Lafleur, Mtl.	3.25
☐	83	AS: Charlie Simmer, L.A.	.50
☐	84	AS: Larry Robinson, Mtl.	.65
☐	85	AS: Borje Salming, Tor.	.50
☐	86	AS: Tony Esposito (G), Chi.	1.00
☐	87	AS: Wayne Gretzky, Edm.	60.00
☐	88	AS: Danny Gare, Buf.	.50
☐	89	AS: Steve Shutt, Mtl.	.50
☐	90	AS: Barry Beck, NYR.	.50
☐	91	AS: Mark Howe, Hfd.	.50
☐	92	AS: Don Edwards (G), Buf.	.50

	No.	Player	Price
☐	**93**	**Tom McCarthy, Min., RC**	**.35**
☐	94	TL: P. McNab/R. Middleton, Bos.	.50
☐	95	Mike Palmateer (G), Wsh.	.75
☐	96	Jim Schoenfeld, Buf.	.50
☐	97	Jordy Douglas, Hfd.	.35
☐	**98**	**Keith Brown, Chi., RC**	**.50**
☐	99	Dennis Ververgaert, Pha. (Wsh.)	.35
☐	100	Phil Esposito, NYR., LC	2.00
☐	101	Jack Brownschidle, Stl.	.35
☐	102	Bob Nystrom, NYI.	.50
☐	**103**	**Steve Christoff, Min., RC**	**.35**
☐	104	Rob Palmer, L.A., LC	.35
☐	105	Dave Williams, Van.	.50
☐	106	TL: Kent Nilsson, Cgy.	.50
☐	107	Morris Lukowich, Wpg.	.35
☐	108	Jack Valiquette, Col., LC	.35
☐	**109**	**Richard Dunn, Buf., RC**	**.35**
☐	110	Rogatien Vachon (G), Bos.	.50
☐	111	Mark Napier, Mtl.	.35
☐	112	Gord Roberts, Hfd.	.35
☐	113	Stan Jonathan, Bos.	.35
☐	114	Brett Callighen, Edm.	.35
☐	115	Rick MacLeish, Pha.	.35
☐	116	Ulf Nilsson, NYR.	.35
☐	117	TL: Rick Kehoe, Pgh.	.50
☐	118	Dan Maloney, Tor.	.35
☐	119	Terry Ruskowski, Chi.	.35
☐	120	Denis Potvin, NYI.	1.75
☐	121	Wayne Stephenson (G), Wsh., LC	.50
☐	122	Rich LeDuc, Que., LC	.35
☐	123	Checklist 1 (1 - 132)	9.00
☐	124	Don Lever, Cgy.	.35
☐	125	Jim Rutherford (G), Det., LC	.50
☐	126	Ray Allison, Hfd., RC, LC	.35
☐	**127**	**Mike Ramsey, Buf., RC**	**3.00**
☐	128	TL: Stan Smyl, Van.	.50
☐	**129**	**Al Secord, Bos., RC**	**2.00**
☐	130	Denis Herron (G), Mtl.	.50
☐	131	Bob Dailey, Pha.	.35
☐	132	Dean Talafous, NYR.	.35
☐	133	Ian Turnbull, Tor.	.35
☐	134	Ron Sedlbauer, Chi.	.35
☐	135	Tom Bladon, Pgh. (Edm.)	.35
☐	136	Bernie Federko, Stl.	2.00
☐	137	Dave Taylor, L.A.	3.00
☐	138	Bob Lorimer, NYI.	.35
☐	139	TL: A. MacAdam/S. Payne, Min.	.50
☐	**140**	**Ray Bourque, Bos., RC**	**125.00**
☐	141	Glen Hanlon (G), Van.	.50
☐	142	Willy Lindstrom, Wpg.	.35
☐	143	Mike Rogers, Hfd.	.35
☐	**144**	**Tony McKegney, Buf., RC**	**.50**
☐	145	Behn Wilson, Pha.	.35
☐	146	Lucien DeBlois, Col.	.35
☐	147	Dave Burrows, Tor. (Pgh.)	.35
☐	148	Paul Woods, Det.	.35
☐	149	TL: Phil Esposito, NYR.	1.00
☐	150	Tony Esposito (G), Chi.	2.00
☐	151	Pierre Larouche, Mtl.	.50
☐	152	Brad Maxwell, Min.	.35
☐	153	Stan Weir, Edm.	.35
☐	154	Ryan Walter, Wsh.	.50
☐	155	Dale Hoganson, Que.	.35
☐	**156**	**Anders Kallur, NYI., RC**	**.35**
☐	**157**	**Paul Reinhart, Cgy., RC**	**1.00**
☐	158	Greg Millen (G), Pgh.	.50
☐	159	Ric Seiling, Buf.	.35
☐	160	Mark Howe, Hfd.	1.00
☐	161	LL: D. Gare/ C. Simmer/ B. Stoughton	.50
☐	162	LL: W. Gretzky/ M. Dionne/ G. Lafleur	20.00
☐	163	LL: M. Dionne/ W. Gretzky/ G. Lafleur	20.00
☐	164	LL: J. Mann/ D. Williams/ P. Holmgren	.50
☐	165	LL: C. Simmer/ M. Dionne,/ D. Gare/S. Shutt/ D. Sittler	.50
☐	166	LL: B. Sauvé (G)/ D. Herron (G)/ D. Edwards (G)	.50
☐	167	LL: D. Gare/ P. McNab/ B. Stoughton	.50
☐	168	LL: T. Esposito (G)/G. Cheevers (G)/ B. Sauvé (G)/ R. Vachon (G)	2.25
☐	**169**	**Perry Turnbull, Stl., RC**	**.35**
☐	170	Barry Beck, NYR.	.35
☐	171	TL: Charlie Simmer, L.A.	.50
☐	172	Paul Holmgren, Pha.	.35
☐	173	Willie Huber, Det.	.35
☐	174	Tim Young, Min.	.35
☐	175	Gilles Gilbert (G), Det.	.50
☐	**176**	**Dave Christian, Wpg., RC**	**2.00**
☐	**177**	**Lars Lindgren, Van., RC**	**.35**
☐	178	Réal Cloutier, Que.	.35
☐	**179**	**Laurie Boschman, Tor., RC**	**.50**
☐	180	Steve Shutt, Mtl.	.75
☐	181	Bob Murray, Chi.	.35
☐	182	TL: Wayne Gretzky, Edm.	25.00
☐	183	John Van Boxmeer, Buf.	.35
☐	184	Nick Fotiu, Hfd.	.35
☐	185	Mike McEwen, Col.	.35
☐	186	Greg Malone, Pgh.	.35
☐	**187**	**Mike Foligno, Det., RC**	**3.50**
☐	**188**	**Dave Langevin, NYI., RC**	**.35**
☐	189	Mel Bridgman, Pha.	.35
☐	190	John Davidson (G), NYR.	.35
☐	191	Mike Milbury, Bos.	.35
☐	192	Ron Zanussi, Min.	.35
☐	193	TL: Darryl Sittler, Tor.	.75
☐	194	John Marks, Chi.	.35
☐	**195**	**Mike Gartner, Wsh., RC**	**70.00**
☐	196	Dave Lewis, L.A.	.50
☐	**197**	**Kent Nilsson, Cgy., RC**	**4.00**
☐	198	Rick Ley, Hfd., LC	.35
☐	199	Derek Smith, Buf.	.35
☐	200	Bill Barber, Pha.	.75
☐	201	Guy Lapointe, Mtl.	.75
☐	202	Vaclav Nedomansky, Det.	.35
☐	203	Don Murdoch, Edm., LC	.35
☐	204	TL: Mike Bossy, NYI.	3.00
☐	**205**	**Pierre Hamel, Wpg. (G), RC**	**.35**
☐	**206**	**Mike Eaves, Min., RC**	**.35**
☐	207	Doug Halward, L.A.	.35
☐	**208**	**Stan Smyl, Van., RC**	**.35**
☐	**209**	**Mike Zuke, Stl., RC**	**.35**
☐	210	Borje Salming, Tor.	1.00
☐	211	Walt Tkaczuk, NYR., LC	.35
☐	212	Grant Mulvey, Chi.	.35
☐	**213**	**Rob Ramage, Col., RC**	**2.50**
☐	214	Tom Rowe, Hfd.	.35
☐	215	Don Edwards (G), Buf.	.50
☐	216	TL: G. Lafleur/P Larouche, Mtl.	2.00
☐	217	Dan Labraaten, Det.	.35
☐	218	Glen Sharpley, Min.	.35
☐	219	Stefan Persson, NYI.	.35
☐	220	Peter McNab, Bos.	.35
☐	221	Doug Hicks, Edm.	.35
☐	**222**	**Bengt Gustafsson, Wsh., RC**	**.35**
☐	223	Michel Dion (G), Que.	.50
☐	224	Jimmy Watson, Pha.	.35
☐	225	Wilf Paiement, Tor.	.35
☐	226	Phil Russell, Cgy.	.35
☐	227	TL: Morris Lukowich, Wpg.	.50
☐	228	Ron Stackhouse, Pgh.	.35
☐	229	Ted Bulley, Chi.	.35
☐	230	Larry Robinson, Mtl.	1.00
☐	231	Don Maloney, NYR.	.35
☐	**232**	**Rob McClanahan, Buf., RC**	**.35**
☐	233	Al Sims, Hfd.	.35
☐	234	Errol Thompson, Det., LC	.35
☐	235	Glenn Resch (G), NYI.	.50
☐	236	Bob Miller, Bos., LC	.35
☐	237	Gary Sargent, Min., LC	.35
☐	238	TL: Réal Cloutier, Que.	.50
☐	239	René Robert, Col.	.35
☐	240	Charlie Simmer, L.A.	.75
☐	241	Thomas Gradin, Van.	.50
☐	**242**	**Rick Vaive, Tor., RC**	**2.50**
☐	**243**	**Ron Wilson, Wpg., RC**	**.35**
☐	244	Brian Sutter, Stl.	1.00
☐	245	Dale McCourt, Det.	.35
☐	246	Yvon Lambert, Mtl.	.35
☐	247	Tom Lysiak, Chi.	.35
☐	248	Ron Greschner, NYR.	.35
☐	249	TL: Reggie Leach, Pha.	.50
☐	250	Wayne Gretzky, Edm.	145.00
☐	251	Rick Middleton, Bos.	.50
☐	252	Al Smith (G), Hfd. (Col.)	.50
☐	253	Fred Barrett, Min., LC	.35
☐	254	Butch Goring, NYI.	.50
☐	255	Robert Picard, Tor.	.35
☐	256	Marc Tardif, Que.	.35
☐	257	Checklist 2 (133 - 264)	9.00
☐	258	Barry Long, Det., (Wpg.)	.35
☐	259	TL: René Robert, Col.	.50
☐	260	Danny Gare, Buf.	.50
☐	261	Réjean Houle, Mtl.	.50
☐	262	Cup: Mike Bossy, Gibertl Perreault	.35
☐	263	Semi-Finals: Flyers skate past North Stars	.35
☐	264	Cup: Billy Smith (G)	.65
☐	265	Bobby Lalonde, Atl. (Bos.)	.35
☐	266	Bob Sauvé (G), Buf.	.50
☐	267	Bob MacMillan, Cgy.	.35
☐	268	Greg Fox, Chi.	.35
☐	**269**	**Hardy Astrom, Col. (G), RC, LC**	**.50**
☐	270	Greg Joly, Det.	.35
☐	**271**	**Dave Lumley, Edm., RC**	**.35**
☐	272	Dave Keon, Hfd.	.75
☐	273	Garry Unger, Stl. (L.A.)	.50
☐	274	Steve Payne, Min.	.35
☐	275	Doug Risebrough, Mtl., Error (Serge Savard)	.50
☐	276	Bob Bourne, NYI.	.35
☐	277	Eddie Johnstone, NYR.	.35
☐	278	Peter Lee, Pgh.	.35
☐	**279**	**Pete Peeters (G), Pha., RC**	**6.00**
☐	280	Ron Chipperfield, Edm. (Que.), LC	.35
☐	281	Wayne Babych, Stl.	.35
☐	282	Dave Shand, Atl., (Tor.), LC	.35
☐	283	Jere Gillis, Van. (NYR.)	.35
☐	284	Dennis Maruk, Wsh.	.35
☐	285	Jude Drouin, NYI. (Wpg.), LC	.35
☐	286	Mike Murphy, L.A.	.35
☐	287	Curt Fraser, Van.	.35
☐	288	Gary McAdam, Pgh.	.35
☐	**289**	**Mark Messier, Edm., RC**	**150.00**
☐	290	Vic Venasky, L.A., LC	.35
☐	291	Per-Olov Brasar, Van., LC	.35
☐	292	Orest Kindrachuk, Pgh., LC	.35
☐	293	Dave Hunter, Edm.	.35
☐	294	Steve Jensen, L.A.	.35
☐	295	Chris Oddleifson, Van., LC	.35
☐	**296**	**Larry Playfair, Buf., RC**	**.35**
☐	297	Mario Tremblay, Mtl.	.35
☐	**298**	**Gilles Lupien, Pgh., RC, LC**	**.35**
☐	299	Pat Price, Edm.	.35
☐	300	Jerry Korab, Buf. (L.A.)	.35
☐	301	Darcy Rota, Atl. (Van.)	.35
☐	302	Don Luce, Buf.	.35
☐	303	Ken Houston, Cgy.	.35
☐	304	Brian Engblom, Mtl.	.35
☐	305	John Tonelli, NYI.	1.50
☐	**306**	**Doug Sulliman, NYR., RC**	**.35**
☐	307	Rod Schutt, Pgh.	.35
☐	**308**	**Norm Barnes, Pha., RC, LC**	**.35**
☐	309	Serge Bernier, Que., LC	.35
☐	310	Larry Patey, Stl.	.35
☐	311	Dave Farrish, Que. (Tor.)	.35
☐	312	Harold Snepsts, Van.	.50
☐	313	Bob Sirois, Wsh., LC	.35
☐	314	Peter Marsh, Wpg.	.35
☐	**315**	**Risto Siltanen, Edm., RC**	**.35**
☐	316	André St. Laurent, L.A.	.35
☐	**317**	**Craig Hartsburg, Min., RC**	**3.00**
☐	318	Wayne Cashman, Bos.	.35
☐	**319**	**Lindy Ruff, Buf., RC**	**1.00**
☐	320	Willi Plett, Cgy.	.35
☐	321	Ron Delorme, Col.	.35
☐	**322**	**Gaston Gingras, Mtl., RC**	**.50**
☐	323	Gordie Lane, NYI.	.35
☐	**324**	**Doug Soetaert (G), NYR., RC**	**.50**
☐	325	Gregg Sheppard, Pgh.	.35
☐	**326**	**Mike Busniuk, Pha., RC**	**.35**
☐	327	Jamie Hislop, Que.	.35
☐	328	Ed Staniowski (G), Stl.	.50
☐	329	Ron Ellis, Tor., LC	.50
☐	330	Gary Bromley (G), Van., LC	.50
☐	**331**	**Mark Lofthouse, Wsh., RC, LC**	**.35**
☐	332	Dave Hoyda, Wpg., LC	.35
☐	333	Ron Low (G), Wsh. (Edm.)	.50
☐	334	Barry Gibbs, L.A., LC	.35
☐	335	Gary Edwards (G), Min., LC	.35
☐	336	Don Marcotte, Bos.	.35
☐	337	Bill Hajt, Buf.	.35
☐	**338**	**Brad Marsh, Cgy., RC**	**3.00**
☐	339	J. P. Bordeleau, Chi., LC	.35
☐	**340**	**Randy Pierce, Col., RC, LC**	**.35**
☐	**341**	**Ed Mio, Edm. (G), RC**	**.35**
☐	342	Randy Manery, L.A., LC	.35
☐	343	Tom Younghans, Min.	.35
☐	**344**	**Rod Langway, Mtl., RC**	**7.50**
☐	345	Wayne Merrick, NYI.	.35
☐	**346**	**Steve Baker (G), NYR., RC**	**.50**

	No.	Player	NRMT-MT
☐	347	Pat Hughes, Pgh.	.35
☐	348	Al Hill, Pha., LC	.35
☐	349	Gerry Hart, Que. (Stl.)	.35
☐	350	Richard Mulhern, Bos. (Tor.), LC	.35
☐	351	Jerry Butler, Tor. (Van.)	.35
☐	352	Guy Charron, Wsh., LC	.35
☐	**353**	**Jimmy Mann, Wpg., RC**	**.35**
☐	**354**	**Brad McCrimmon, Bos., RC**	**2.50**
☐	355	Rick Dudley, Buf.	.35
☐	356	Pekka Rautakallio, Cgy.	.35
☐	**357**	**Tim Trimper, Chi., RC**	**.35**
☐	358	Mike Christie, Col., LC	.35
☐	**359**	**John Ogrodnick, Det., RC**	**2.00**
☐	360	Dave Semenko, Edm.	.50
☐	361	Mike Veisor (G), Chi. (Hfd.)	.50
☐	362	Syl Apps, L.A., LC	.35
☐	363	Mike Polich, Min.	.35
☐	364	Rick Chartraw, Mtl., LC	.35
☐	**365**	**Steve Tambellini, NYI., RC**	**.50**
☐	**366**	**Ed Hospodar, NYR., RC**	**.35**
☐	367	Randy Carlyle, Pgh.	.50
☐	368	Tom Gorence Pha.	.35
☐	369	Pierre Plante, Que., LC	.35
☐	370	Blake Dunlop, Pha. (Stl.)	.35
☐	371	Mike Kaszycki, NYI. (Tor.), LC	.35
☐	372	Rick Blight, Van., LC	.35
☐	373	Pierre Bouchard, Wsh., LC	.50
☐	374	Gary Doak, Bos., LC	.35
☐	375	André Savard, Buf.	.35
☐	376	Bill Clement, Cgy.	.35
☐	377	Reg Kerr, Chi.	.35
☐	378	Walt McKechnie, Tor. (Col.)	.35
☐	**379**	**George Lyle, Det., RC**	**.35**
☐	380	Colin Campbell, Edm.	.50
☐	381	Dave Debol, Hfd., LC	.35
☐	382	Glenn Goldup, L.A., LC	.35
☐	383	Kent-Erik Andersson, Min.	.35
☐	**384**	**Tony Currie, Stl., RC**	**.35**
☐	**385**	**Richard Sévigny (G), Mtl., RC**	**.50**
☐	386	Garry Howatt, NYI.	.35
☐	387	Cam Connor, NYR., LC	.35
☐	388	Ross Lonsberry, Pgh.	.35
☐	**389**	**Frank Bathe, Pha., RC, LC**	**.35**
☐	390	John Wensink, Bos. (Que.), LC	.35
☐	391	Paul Harrison (G), Tor., LC	.50
☐	392	Dennis Kearns, Van.	.35
☐	393	Pat Ribble, Atl. (Wsh.)	.35
☐	**394**	**Markus Mattsson (G), Wpg., RC**	**.50**
☐	395	Chuck Lefley, Stl., LC	.35
☐	396	Checklist 3 (265 - 396)	12.00

1980 - 81 O-PEE-CHEE PHOTOS

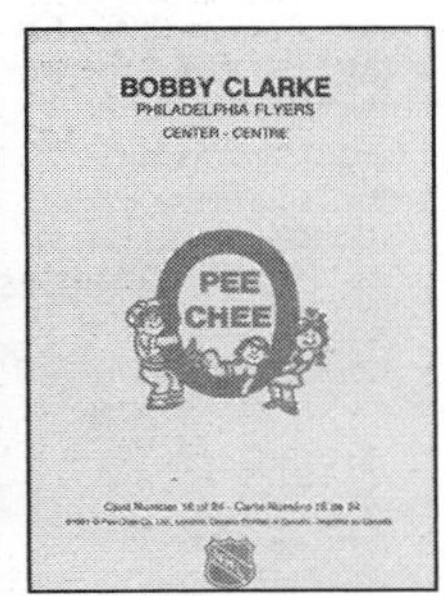

The colour photographs are printed on thick cardboard stock and were distributed unwrapped. Photos are numbered of 24.

Photo Size: 5" x 7"
Face: Four colour, white border; Name
Back: Black and grey on card stock; Name, Team, Position, Number
Imprint: © 1981 O-Pee-Chee Co. Ltd.
Complete Set (24 cards): 40.00

	No.	Player	NRMT-MT
☐	1	Brad Park, Bos.	3.00
☐	2	Gilbert Perreault, Buf.	2.50
☐	3	Kent Nilsson, Cgy.	1.25
☐	4	Tony Esposito (G), Chi.	4.00
☐	5	Lanny McDonald, Col.	3.00
☐	6	Pete Mahovlich, Det.	1.25
☐	7	Wayne Gretzky, Edm.	14.00
☐	8	Marcel Dionne, L.A.	3.50
☐	9	Bob Gainey, Mtl.	3.00
☐	10	Guy Lafleur, Mtl.	6.50
☐	11	Larry Robinson, Mtl.	3.00
☐	12	Mike Bossy, NYI.	5.00
☐	13	Denis Potvin, NYI.	3.00
☐	14	Phil Esposito, NYR.	3.50
☐	15	Anders Hedberg, NYR.	1.25
☐	16	Bobby Clarke, Pha.	3.50
☐	17	Marc Tardif, Que.	1.25
☐	18	Bernie Federko, Stl.	2.00
☐	19	Borje Salming, Tor.	2.75
☐	20	Darryl Sittler, Tor.	3.50
☐	21	Ian Turnbull, Tor.	1.25
☐	22	Glen Hanlon, Van.	2.00
☐	23	Mike Palmateer (G), Wsh.	2.50
☐	24	Morris Lukowich, Wpg.	1.25

1980 - 81 PEPSI CAPS

Cap Diameter: 1 1/8"
Face: Black and white portrait; Name, Team
Back: Pepsi promotional information
Imprint: PEPSI
Complete Set (140 caps): 175.00
Common Player: 1.50
Plastic Display: 65.00

	Player	NRMT-MT
	CALGARY FLAMES	
☐	Dan Bouchard (G)	2.00
☐	Guy Chouinard	1.50
☐	Bill Clement	1.50
☐	Randy Holt	1.50
☐	Ken Houston	1.50
☐	Kevin LaVallée, Error (LaValee)	1.50
☐	Don Lever	1.50
☐	Bob MacMillan	1.50
☐	Bradl Marsh	2.00
☐	Bob Murdoch	1.50
☐	Kent Nilsson	2.00
☐	Jim Peplinski	1.50
☐	Willi Plett	1.50
☐	Pekka Rautakillio	1.50
☐	Paul Reinhart	1.50
☐	Pat Riggin (G)	2.00
☐	Phil Russell	1.50
☐	Brad Smith	1.50
☐	Eric Vail	1.50
☐	Bert Wilson	1.50
	EDMONTON OILERS	
☐	Glenn Anderson	3.50
☐	Curt Brackenbury	1.50
☐	Brett Callighen	1.50
☐	Paul Coffey	9.00
☐	Lee Fogolin	1.50
☐	Matti Hagman	1.50
☐	John Hughes	1.50
☐	Dave Hunter	1.50
☐	Jari Kurri	7.50
☐	Ron Low (G)	2.00
☐	Kevin Lowe	3.00
☐	Dave Lumley	1.50
☐	Blair MacDonald	1.50
☐	Mark Messier	12.00
☐	Ed Mio (G)	2.00
☐	Don Murdoch	1.50
☐	Pat Price	1.50
☐	Dave Semenko	1.50
☐	Risto Siltanen	1.50
☐	Stan Weir	1.50
	MONTRÉAL CANADIENS	
☐	Keith Acton	2.00
☐	Brian Engblom	1.50
☐	Bob Gainey	3.00
☐	Gaston Gingras	1.50
☐	Denis Herron (G)	2.00
☐	Réjean Houle	2.00
☐	Doug Jarvis	2.00
☐	Yvon Lambert	1.50
☐	Rod Langway	3.00
☐	Guy Lapointe	2.50
☐	Pierre Larouche	1.50
☐	Pierre Mondou	1.50
☐	Mark Napier	1.50
☐	Chris Nilan	2.00
☐	Doug Risebrough	2.00
☐	Larry Robinson	3.00
☐	Serge Savard	2.50
☐	Steve Shutt	2.50
☐	Mario Tremblay	2.50
☐	Doug Wickenheiser	1.50
	QUÉBEC NORDIQUES	
☐	Serge Bernier	1.50
☐	Kim Clackson	1.50
☐	Real Cloutier	1.50
☐	André Dupont	1.50
☐	Robbie Ftorek	1.50
☐	Michel Goulet	5.00
☐	Jamie Hislop	1.50
☐	Dale Hoganson	1.50
☐	Dale Hunter	3.00
☐	Pierre Lacroix	1.50
☐	Garry Larivière	1.50
☐	Rich Leduc	1.50
☐	John Paddock	1.50
☐	Michel Plasse (G)	2.00
☐	Jacques Richard	1.50
☐	Anton Stastny	1.50
☐	Peter Stastny	5.00
☐	Marc Tardif	1.50
☐	Wally Weir	1.50
☐	John Wensink	1.50
	TORONTO MAPLE LEAFS	
☐	John Anderson	1.50
☐	Laurie Boschman	1.50
☐	Jiri Crha (G)	2.00
☐	Bill Derlago	1.50
☐	Vitezslav Duris	1.50
☐	Ron Ellis	1.50
☐	Dave Farrish	1.50
☐	Stewart Gavin	1.50
☐	Pat Hickey	1.50
☐	Dan Maloney	1.50
☐	Terry Martin	1.50
☐	Barry Melrose	1.50
☐	Wilf Paiement	1.50
☐	Robert Picard	1.50
☐	Jim Rutherford (G)	2.00
☐	Rocky Saganiuk	1.50
☐	Borje Salming	3.00
☐	Dave Shand	1.50
☐	Ian Turnbull	1.50
☐	Rick Vaive	2.00
	VANCOUVER CANUCKS	
☐	Brent Ashton	1.50
☐	Ivan Boldirev	1.50
☐	Per-Olov Brasar	1.50
☐	Richard Brodeur (G)	2.00
☐	Jerry Butler	1.50
☐	Colin Campbell	2.00
☐	Curt Fraser	1.50
☐	Thomas Gradin	1.50
☐	Dennis Kearns	1.50
☐	Rick Lanz	1.50
☐	Lars Lindgren	1.50
☐	Dave Logan	1.50
☐	Mario Marois	1.50
☐	Kevin McCarthy	1.50
☐	Gerry Minor	1.50
☐	Darcy Rota	1.50
☐	Bobby Schmautz	1.50
☐	Stan Smyl	2.00
☐	Harold Snepsts	2.00
☐	Dave Williams	2.00
	WINNIPEG JETS	
☐	Dave Babych	2.00
☐	Al Cameron	1.50
☐	Scott Campbell	1.50

Player	Price
Dave Christian	1.50
Jude Drouin	1.50
Norm Dupont	1.50
Danny Geoffrion	1.50
Pierre Hamel (G)	2.00
Barry Legge	1.50
Willy Lindstrom	1.50
Barry Long	1.50
Kris Manery	1.50
Jimmy Mann	1.50
Moe Mantha	1.50
Markus Mattsson (G)	2.00
Don Spring	1.50
Doug Smail	1.50
Anders Steen	1.50
Peter Sullivan	1.50
Ron Wilson	1.50

1980 - 81 TOPPS

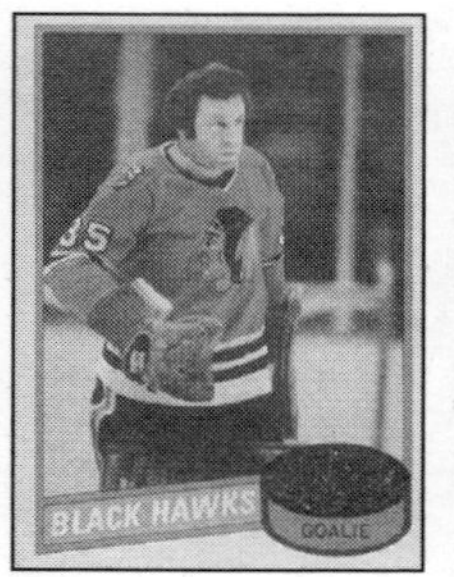

Face: Four colour, white border, Position
Back: Green and yellow on card stock; Number, Resume, Hockey trivia
Imprint: © 1980 TOPPS CHEWING GUM, INC.
Topps Set (264 cards): 300.00
Common Player: .25

No.	Player	NRMT-MT
1	HL: Flyers Extend Streak to 35	1.00
2	HL: Ray Bourque, Bos.	8.00
3	HL: Wayne Gretzky, Edm.	25.00
4	HL: Charlies Simmer, L.A.	.35
5	HL: Billy Smith (G), NYI.	.50
6	Jean Ratelle, Bos., LC	.35
7	Dave Maloney, NYR.	.25
8	Phil Myre (G), Pha., LC	.35
9	**Ken Morrow, NYI., RC**	**.50**
10	Guy Lafleur, Mtl.	4.50
11	**Bill Derlago, Tor., RC**	**.35**
12	Doug Wilson, Chi.	.75
13	Craig Ramsay, Buf.	.35
14	Pat Boutette, Hfd.	.25
15	Eric Vail, Cgy.	.25
16	TL: Mike Foligno, Det.	.35
17	Bobby Smith, Min.	1.50
18	Rick Kehoe, Pgh.	.35
19	Joel Quenneville, Col.	.50
20	Marcel Dionne, L.A.	1.50
21	Kevin McCarthy, Van.	.25
22	**Jim Craig (G), Bos., RC, LC**	**1.50**
23	Steve Vickers, NYR., LC	.25
24	Ken Linseman, Pha.	.35
25	Mike Bossy, NYI.	6.00
26	Serge Savard, Mtl.	.50
27	TL: Grant Mulvey,Chi.	.35
28	Pat Hickey, Tor.	.25
29	Peter Sullivan, Wpg., LC	.25
30	Blaine Stoughton, Hfd.	.25
31	**Mike Liut (G), Stl., RC**	**5.50**
32	Blair MacDonald, Edm.	.25
33	Rick Green, Wsh.	.25
34	Al MacAdam, Min.	.25
35	Robbie Ftorek, Que.	.35
36	Dick Redmond, Bos.	.25
37	Ron Duguay, NYR.	.35
38	TL: Danny Gare, Buf.	.35
39	**Brian Propp, Pha., RC**	**3.75**
40	Bryan Trottier, NYI.	2.00
41	Rich Preston, Chi.	.25
42	Pierre Mondou, Mtl.	.35
43	Reed Larson, Det.	.25
44	George Ferguson, Pgh.	.25
45	Guy Chouinard, Atl.	.25
46	Billy Harris, L.A.	.25
47	Gilles Meloche (G), Min.	.35
48	Blair Chapman, Stl.	.25
49	TL: Mike Gartner, Wsh.	5.50
50	Darryl Sittler, Tor.	.75
51	Rick Martin, Buf., LC	.25
52	Ivan Boldirev, Van.	.25
53	**Craig Norwich, Stl., RC, LC**	**.25**
54	Dennis Polonich, Det., LC	.25
55	Bobby Clarke, Pha.	1.50
56	Terry O'Reilly, Bos.	.35
57	Carol Vadnais, NYR.	.25
58	Bob Gainey, Mtl.	.75
59	TL: Blaine Stoughton, Hfd.	.35
60	Billy Smith (G), NYI.	.75
61	**Mike O'Connell, Chi., RC**	**.35**
62	Lanny McDonald, Col.	.75
63	Lee Fogolin, Edm.	.25
64	**Rocky Saganiuk, Tor., RC**	**.25**
65	**Rolf Edberg, Wsh., RC, LC**	**.25**
66	Paul Shmyr, Min., LC	.25
67	**Michel Goulet, Que., RC**	**12.00**
68	Dan Bouchard (G), Cgy.	.35
69	**Mark Johnson, Pgh., RC**	**.75**
70	Reggie Leach, Pha.	.35
71	TL: Bernie Federko, Stl.	.35
72	Pete Mahovlich, Det., LC	.35
73	Anders Hedberg, NYR.	.35
74	Brad Park, Bos.	.50
75	Clark Gillies, NYI.	.35
76	Doug Jarvis, Mtl.	.35
77	John Garrett (G), Hfd.	.35
78	Dave Hutchison, Chi., LC	.25
79	**John Anderson, Tor., RC**	**.35**
80	Gilbert Perreault, Buf.	.75
81	AS: Marcel Dionne, L.A.	.75
82	AS: Guy Lafleur, Mtl.	1.50
83	AS: Charlie Simmer, L.A.	.35
84	AS: Larry Robinson, Mtl.	.50
85	AS: Borje Salming, Tor.	.35
86	AS: Tony Esposito (G), Chi.	.75
87	AS: Wayne Gretzky, Edm.	35.00
88	AS: Danny Gare, Buf.	.35
89	AS: Steve Shutt, Mtl.	.35
90	AS: Barry Beck, NYR.	.35
91	AS: Mark Howe, Hfd.	.35
92	AS: Don Edwards (G), Buf.	.35
93	**Tom McCarthy, Min., RC**	**.25**
94	TL: P. McNab/R. Middleton, Bos.	.35
95	Mike Palmateer (G), Wsh.	.50
96	Jim Schoenfeld, Buf.	.35
97	Jordy Douglas, Hfd.	.25
98	**Keith Brown, Chi., RC**	**.35**
99	Dennis Ververgaert, Pha.	.25
100	Phil Esposito, NYR., LC	1.75
101	Jack Brownschidle, Stl.	.25
102	Bob Nystrom, NYI.	.35
103	**Steve Christoff, Min., RC**	**.25**
104	Rob Palmer, L.A., LC	.25
105	Dave Williams, Van.	.35
106	TL: Kent Nilsson, Cgy.	.35
107	Morris Lukowich, Wpg.	.25
108	Jack Valiquette, Col., LC	.25
109	**Richard Dunn, Buf., RC**	**.25**
110	Rogatien Vachon (G), Bos.	.35
111	Mark Napier, Mtl.	.25
112	Gord Roberts, Hfd.	.25
113	Stan Jonathan, Bos.	.25
114	Brett Callighen, Edm.	.25
115	Rick MacLeish, Pha.	.25
116	Ulf Nilsson, NYR.	.25
117	TL: Rick Kehoe, Pgh.	.35
118	Dan Maloney, Tor.	.25
119	Terry Ruskowski, Chi.	.25
120	Denis Potvin, NYI.	1.50
121	Wayne Stephenson (G), Wsh., LC	.35
122	Rich LeDuc, Que., LC	.25
123	Checklist 1 (1 - 132)	5.00
124	Don Lever, Cgy.	.25
125	Jim Rutherford (G), Det., LC	.35
126	**Ray Allison, Hfd., RC**	**.25**
127	**Mike Ramsey, Buf., RC**	**2.00**
128	TL: Stan Smyl, Van.	.35
129	**Al Secord, Bos., RC**	**1.50**
130	Denis Herron (G), Mtl.	.35
131	Bob Dailey, Pha.	.25
132	Dean Talafous, NYR.	.25
133	Ian Turnbull, Tor.	.25
134	Ron Sedlbauer, Chi.	.25
135	Tom Bladon, Pgh., LC	.25
136	Bernie Federko, Stl.	1.50
137	Dave Taylor, L.A.	2.50
138	Bob Lorimer, NYI.	.25
139	TL: MacAdam/Payne, Min.	.35
140	**Ray Bourque, Bos., RC**	**80.00**
141	Glen Hanlon (G), Van.	.35
142	Willy Lindstrom, Wpg.	.25
143	Mike Rogers, Hfd.	.25
144	**Tony McKegney, Buf., RC**	**.35**
145	Behn Wilson, Pha.	.25
146	Lucien DeBlois, Col.	.25
147	Dave Burrows, Tor., LC	.25
148	Paul Woods, Det.	.25
149	TL: Phil Esposito, NYR.	.75
150	Tony Esposito (G), Chi.	1.50
151	Pierre Larouche. Mtl.	.35
152	Brad Maxwell, Min.	.25
153	Stan Weir, Edm.	.25
154	Ryan Walter, Wsh.	.35
155	Dale Hoganson, Que.	.25
156	**Anders Kallur, NYI., RC**	**.25**
157	**Paul Reinhart, Cgy., RC**	**75**
158	Greg Millen (G), Pgh.	.35
159	Ric Seiling, Buf.	.25
160	Mark Howe, Hfd.	.75
161	LL: D. Gare/ C. Simmer/ B. Stoughton	.35
162	LL: W. Gretzky/ M. Dionne/ G. Lafleur	15.00
163	LL: M. Dionne/ W. Gretzky/ G. Lafleur	15.00
164	LL: J. Mann/ D. Williams/ P. Holmgren	.35
165	LL: C. Simmer/ M. Dionne/ D. Gare/ S. Shutt/ D. Sittler	.35
166	LL: B. Sauvé (G)/ D. Herron (G)/ D. Edwards (G)	.35
167	LL: D. Gare/ P. McNab/ B. Stoughton	.35
168	LL: T. Esposito(G)/ G. Cheevers (G)/ B. Sauvé (G)/ R. Vachon (G)	1.50
169	**Perry Turnbull, Stl., RC**	**.25**
170	Barry Beck, NYR.	.25
171	TL: Charlie Simmer, L.A.	.35
172	Paul Holmgren, Pha.	.25
173	Willie Huber, Det.	.25
174	Tim Young, Min.	.25
175	Gilles Gilbert (G), Det.	.35
176	**Dave Christian, Wpg., RC**	**1.75**
177	**Lars Lindgren, Van., RC**	**.25**
178	Réal Cloutier, Que.	.25
179	**Laurie Boschman, Tor., RC**	**.35**
180	Steve Shutt, Mtl.	.50
181	Bob Murray, Chi.	.25
182	TL: Wayne Gretzky, Edm.	20.00
183	John Van Boxmeer, Buf.	.25
184	Nick Fotiu, Hfd.	.25
185	Mike McEwen, Col.	.25
186	Greg Malone, Pgh.	.25
187	**Mike Foligno, Det., RC**	**2.50**
188	**Dave Langevin, NYI., RC**	**.25**
189	Mel Bridgman, Pha.	.25
190	John Davidson (G), NYR.	.75
191	Mike Milbury, Bos.	.50
192	Ron Zanussi, Min.	.25
193	TL: Darryl Sittler, Tor.	.50
194	John Marks, Chi.	.25
195	**Mike Gartner, Wsh., RC**	**35.00**
196	Dave Lewis, L.A.	.35
197	**Kent Nilsson, Cgy., RC**	**3.25**
198	Rick Ley, Hfd., LC	.25
199	Derek Smith, Buf.	.25
200	Bill Barber, Pha.	.50
201	Guy Lapointe, Mtl.	.50
202	Vaclav Nedomansky, Det.	.25
203	Don Murdoch, Edm., LC	.25
204	TL: Mike Bossy, NYI.	2.00
205	**Pierre Hamel (G), Wpg., RC**	**.25**
206	**Mike Eaves, Min., RC**	**.25**
207	Doug Halward, L.A.	.25
208	**Stan Smyl, Van., RC**	**.75**
209	**Mike Zuke, Stl., RC**	**.25**
210	Borje Salming, Tor.	.75
211	Walt Tkaczuk, NYR., LC	.25
212	Grant Mulvey, Chi.	.25

	No.	Player	Value
☐	**213**	**Rob Ramage, Col., RC**	**2.00**
☐	214	Tom Rowe, Hfd.	.25
☐	215	Don Edwards (G), Buf.	.35
☐	216	TL: Lafleur/Larouche, Mtl.	1.50
☐	217	Dan Labraaten, Det.	.25
☐	218	Glen Sharpley, Min.	.25
☐	219	Stefan Persson, NYI.	.25
☐	220	Peter McNab, Bos.	.25
☐	221	Doug Hicks, Edm.	.25
☐	**222**	**Bengt Gustafsson, Wsh., RC**	**.25**
☐	223	Michel Dion (G), Que.	.35
☐	224	Jimmy Watson, Pha.	.25
☐	225	Wilf Paiement, Tor.	.25
☐	226	Phil Russell, Cgy.	.25
☐	227	TL: Morris Lukowich, Wpg.	.35
☐	228	Ron Stackhouse, Pgh.	.25
☐	229	Ted Bulley, Chi.	.25
☐	230	Larry Robinson, Mtl.	.75
☐	231	Don Maloney, NYR.	.25
☐	**232**	**Rob McClanahan, Buf., RC**	**.25**
☐	233	Al Sims, Hfd.	.25
☐	234	Errol Thompson, Det., LC	.25
☐	235	Glenn Resch (G), NYI.	.35
☐	236	Bob Miller, Bos., LC	.25
☐	237	Gary Sargent, Min., LC	.25
☐	238	TL: Réal Cloutier, Que.	.35
☐	239	René Robert, Col.	.25
☐	240	Charlie Simmer, L.A.	.50
☐	241	Thomas Gradin, Van.	.35
☐	**242**	**Rick Vaive, Tor., RC**	**1.75**
☐	**243**	**Ron Wilson, Wpg., RC**	**.25**
☐	244	Brian Sutter, Stl.	.75
☐	245	Dale McCourt, Det.	.25
☐	246	Yvon Lambert, Mtl.	.25
☐	247	Tom Lysiak, Chi.	.25
☐	248	Ron Greschner, NYR.	.25
☐	249	TL: Reggie Leach, Pha.	.35
☐	250	Wayne Gretzky, Edm.	120.00
☐	251	Rick Middleton, Bos.	.35
☐	252	Al Smith (G), Hfd., LC	.35
☐	253	Fred Barrett, Min., LC	.25
☐	254	Butch Goring, NYI.	.35
☐	255	Robert Picard, Tor.	.25
☐	256	Marc Tardif, Que.	.25
☐	257	Checklist 2 (133 - 264)	5.00
☐	258	Barry Long, Det.	.25
☐	259	TL: René Robert, Col.	.35
☐	260	Danny Gare, Buf.	.35
☐	261	Réjean Houle, Mtl.	.35
☐	262	Semi-finals: Islanders defeat Sabres in Six	.25
☐	263	Semi-finals: Flyers Skate Past North Stars	.25
☐	264	Stanley Cup Finals: Islanders Win	1.00

TEAM POSTERS

These blank-back photos came folded inside the pack.

Poster Size: 5" x 7"

Complete Set (16 posters): **16.00**

	No.	Team	NRMT-MT
☐	1	New York Islanders	2.00
☐	2	New York Rangers	2.00
☐	3	Philadelphia Flyers	1.50
☐	4	Boston Bruins	2.00
☐	5	Hartford Whalers	3.00
☐	6	Buffalo Sabres	1.50
☐	7	Chicago Blackhawks	1.50
☐	8	Detroit Red Wings	1.50
☐	9	Minnesota North Stars	1.50
☐	10	Toronto Maple Leafs	2.00
☐	11	Montréal Canadiens	2.00
☐	12	Colorado Rockies	1.50
☐	13	Los Angeles Kings	1.50
☐	14	Vancouver Canucks	1.50
☐	15	St. Louis Blues	1.50
☐	16	Washington Captials	1.50

1981 - 82 O-PEE-CHEE

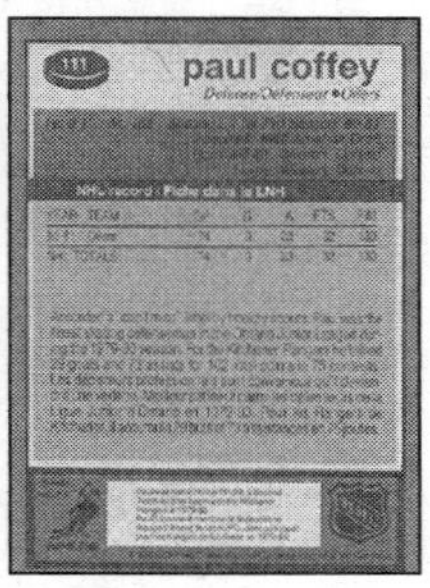

Face: Four colour, white border, Team logo, Position

Back: Blue and black on card stock, Number, Resume, Bilingual

Imprint: © 1981 O-Pee-Chee

Complete Set (396 cards): **400.00**

Common Player: **.35**

	No.	Player	NRMT-MT
☐	1	Ray Bourque, Bos.	45.00
☐	2	Rick Middleton, Bos.	.50
☐	3	Dwight Foster, Bos. (Col.)	.35
☐	**4**	**Steve Kasper, Bos., RC**	**2.00**
☐	5	Peter McNab, Bos.	.35
☐	6	Mike O'Connell, Bos.	.35
☐	7	Terry O'Reilly, Bos.	.50
☐	8	Brad Park, Bos.	.50
☐	9	Dick Redmond, Bos., LC	.35
☐	10	Rogatien Vachon (G), Bos.	.50
☐	11	Wayne Cashman, Bos.	.35
☐	**12**	**Mike Gillis, Bos., RC, LC**	**.35**
☐	13	Stan Jonathan, Bos., LC	.35
☐	14	Don Marcotte, Bos.	.35
☐	15	Brad McCrimmon, Bos.	1.25
☐	16	Mike Milbury, Bos.	.50
☐	17	Super Action: Ray Bourque, Bos.	9.00
☐	18	Super Action: Rick Middleton, Bos.	.50
☐	19	TL: Rick Middleton, Bos.	.50
☐	20	Danny Gare, Buf. (Det.)	.50
☐	21	Don Edwards (G), Buf.	.50
☐	22	Tony McKegney, Buf.	.35
☐	23	Bob Sauvé (G), Buf. (Det.)	.50
☐	24	André Savard, Buf.	.35
☐	25	Derek Smith, Buf. (Det.)	.35
☐	26	John Van Boxmeer, Buf.	.35
☐	27	Super Action: Danny Gare, Buf. (Det.)	.35
☐	28	TL: Danny Gare, Buf.	.35
☐	29	Richard Dunn, Buf.	.35
☐	30	Gilbert Perreault, Buf.	1.00
☐	31	Craig Ramsay, Buf.	.50
☐	32	Ric Seiling, Buf.	.35
☐	33	Guy Chouinard, Cgy.	.35
☐	34	Kent Nilsson, Cgy.	.35
☐	35	Willi Plett, Cgy.	.35
☐	36	Paul Reinhart, Cgy.	.35
☐	**37**	**Pat Riggin (G), Cgy., RC**	**.50**
☐	38	Eric Vail, Cgy. (Det.)	.35
☐	39	Bill Clement, Cgy.	.35
☐	40	Jamie Hislop, Cgy.	.35
☐	41	Randy Holt, Cgy. (Wsh.), LC	.35
☐	42	Dan Labraaten, Cgy., LC	.35
☐	**43**	**Kevin LaVallée, Cgy., RC**	**.35**
☐	**44**	**Réjean Lemelin (G), Cgy., RC**	**6.00**
☐	45	Don Lever, Cgy. (Col.)	.35
☐	46	Bob MacMillan, Cgy. (Col.)	.35
☐	47	Brad Marsh, Cgy. (Pha.)	.35
☐	48	Bob J. Murdoch, Cgy.	.35
☐	**49**	**Jim Peplinski, Cgy., RC**	**2.00**
☐	50	Pekka Rautakallio, Cgy., LC	.35
☐	51	Phil Russell, Cgy.	.35
☐	52	Super Action: Kent Nilsson, Cgy.	.35
☐	53	TL: Kent Nilsson, Cgy.	.35
☐	54	Tony Esposito (G), Chi.	1.00
☐	55	Keith Brown, Chi.	.35
☐	56	Ted Bulley, Chi.	.35
☐	**57**	**Tim Higgins, Chi., RC**	**.35**
☐	58	Reg Kerr, Chi.	.35
☐	59	Tom Lysiak, Chi.	.35
☐	60	Grant Mulvey, Chi.	.35
☐	61	Bob Murray, Chi.	.35
☐	62	Terry Ruskowski, Chi.	.35
☐	**63**	**Denis Savard, Chi., RC**	**20.00**
☐	64	Glen Sharpley, Chi.	.35
☐	**65**	**Darryl Sutter, Chi., RC**	**1.25**
☐	66	Doug Wilson, Chi.	1.00
☐	67	Super Action: Tony Esposito (G), Chi.	.50
☐	**68**	**Murray Bannerman (G), Chi., RC**	**.75**
☐	69	Greg Fox, Chi.	.35
☐	70	John Marks, Chi., LC	.35
☐	71	Peter Marsh, Chi., LC	.35
☐	72	Al Secord, Chi.	.35
☐	73	TL: Tom Lysiak, Chi.	.35
☐	74	Lucien DeBlois, Wpg.	.35
☐	**75**	**Paul Gagné, Col., RC**	**.35**
☐	**76**	**Merlin Malinowski, Col., RC**	**.35**
☐	77	Lanny McDonald, Col. (Cgy.)	.75
☐	78	Joel Quenneville, Col.	.50
☐	79	Rob Ramage, Col.	.50
☐	80	Glenn Resch (G), Col.	.50
☐	81	Steve Tambellini, Col.	.35
☐	82	Ron Delorme, Col. (Van.)	.35
☐	83	Mike Kitchen, Col., LC	.35
☐	**84**	**Yvon Vautour, Col., RC, LC**	**.35**
☐	85	TL: Lanny McDonald, Col.	.50
☐	86	Dale McCourt, Det. (Buf.)	.35
☐	87	Mike Foligno, Det. (Buf.)	.35
☐	88	Gilles Gilbert (G), Det.	.50
☐	89	Willie Huber, Det.	.35
☐	**90**	**Mark Kirton, Det., RC**	**.35**
☐	**91**	**Jim Korn, Det., RC**	**.35**
☐	92	Reed Larson, Det.	.35
☐	93	Gary McAdam, Det. (Cgy.)	.35
☐	94	Vaclav Nedomansky, Det., LC	.35
☐	95	John Ogrodnick, Det.	.50
☐	96	Super Action: Dale McCourt, Det. (Buf.)	.35
☐	97	Jean Hamel, Det. (Que.)	.35
☐	**98**	**Glenn Hicks, Det. (Wpg.), RC, LC**	**.35**
☐	**99**	**Larry Lozinski (G), Det., RC, LC**	**.50**
☐	100	George Lyle, Det. (Hfd.) LC	.35
☐	101	Perry Miller, Det., LC	.35
☐	102	Brad Maxwell, Det. (Min.)	.35
☐	**103**	**Brad Smith, Det., RC, LC**	**.35**
☐	104	Paul Woods, Det.	.35
☐	105	TL: Dale McCourt, Det.	.35
☐	106	Wayne Gretzky, Edm.	70.00
☐	107	Jari Kurri, Edm., RC	40.00
☐	**108**	**Glenn Anderson, Edm., RC**	**8.00**
☐	109	Curt Brackenbury, Edm., LC	.35
☐	110	Brett Callighen, Edm.	.35
☐	**111**	**Paul Coffey, Edm., RC**	**90.00**
☐	112	Lee Fogolin, Edm.	.35
☐	**113**	**Matti Hagman, Edm., RC**	**.35**
☐	114	Doug Hicks, Edm.	.35
☐	115	Dave Hunter, Edm.	.35
☐	116	Garry Larivière, Que., (Edm.)	.35
☐	**117**	**Kevin Lowe, Edm., RC**	**9.00**
☐	118	Mark Messier, Edm.	60.00
☐	119	Ed Mio (G), Edm.	.50
☐	**120**	**Andy Moog (G), Edm., RC**	**30.00**
☐	121	Dave Semenko, Edm.	.35
☐	122	Risto Siltanen, Edm.	.35
☐	123	Garry Unger, Que., (Edm.)	.35
☐	124	Stan Weir, Edm., LC	.35
☐	125	Super Action: Wayne Gretzky, Edm.	30.00
☐	126	TL: Wayne Gretzky, Edm.	12.00
☐	127	Mike Rogers, Hfd. (NYR.)	.35
☐	128	Mark Howe, Hfd.	.75
☐	129	Dave Keon, Hfd., LC	.50
☐	**130**	**Warren Miller, Hfd., RC**	**.35**
☐	131	Al Sims, Hfd. (L.A.), LC	.35
☐	132	Blaine Stoughton, Hfd.	.35
☐	133	Rick MacLeish, Hfd.	.35
☐	134	Greg Millen (G), Hfd.	.50
☐	135	Super Action: Mike Rogers, Hfd.	.35
☐	136	Mike Fidler, Hfd., LC	.35
☐	137	John Garrett (G), Hfd.	.50
☐	**138**	**Donald Nachbauer, Hfd., RC, LC**	**.35**
☐	139	Tom Rowe, Hfd., LC	.35
☐	140	TL: Mike Rogers, Hfd.	.35
☐	141	Marcel Dionne, L.A.	1.75

No.	Card	Price
☐ 142	Charlie Simmer, L.A.	.75
☐ 143	Dave Taylor, L.A.	.75
☐ 144	Billy Harris, L.A. (Tor.)	.35
☐ 145	Jerry Korab, L.A., LC	.35
☐ 146	Mario Lessard (G), L.A.	.35
☐ 147	Don Luce, Tor., LC	.35
☐ **148**	**Larry Murphy, L.A., RC**	**12.00**
☐ 149	Mike Murphy, L.A., LC	.35
☐ 150	Super Action: Marcel Dionne, L.A.	1.00
☐ 151	Super Action: Charlie Simmer, L.A.	.50
☐ 152	Super Action: Dave Taylor, L.A.	.50
☐ **153**	**Jim Fox, L.A., RC**	**.35**
☐ 154	Steve Jensen, L.A., LC	.35
☐ **155**	**Greg Terrion, L.A., RC**	**.35**
☐ 156	TL: Marcel Dionne, L.A.	.75
☐ 157	Bobby Smith, Min.	1.00
☐ 158	Kent-Erik Andersson, Min.	.35
☐ **159**	**Don Beaupré (G), Min., RC**	**6.00**
☐ 160	Steve Christoff, Min.	.35
☐ **161**	**Dino Ciccarelli, Min., RC**	**20.00**
☐ 162	Craig Hartsburg, Min.	.50
☐ 163	Al MacAdam, Min.	.35
☐ 164	Tom McCarthy, Min.	.35
☐ 165	Gilles Meloche (G), Min.	.50
☐ 166	Steve Payne, Min.	.35
☐ 167	Gord Roberts, Min.	.35
☐ 168	Greg Smith, Min. (Det.)	.35
☐ 169	Tim Young, Min.	.35
☐ 170	Super Action: Bobby Smith, Min.	.50
☐ 171	Mike Eaves, Min.	.35
☐ 172	Mike Polich, Min., LC	.35
☐ 173	Tom Younghans, Min. (NYR.) LC	.35
☐ 174	TL: Bobby Smith, Min.	.50
☐ 175	Brian Engblom, Mtl.	.35
☐ 176	Bob Gainey, Mtl.	.75
☐ 177	Guy Lafleur, Mtl.	5.00
☐ 178	Mark Napier, Mtl.	.35
☐ 179	Larry Robinson, Mtl.	1.00
☐ 180	Steve Shutt, Mtl.	.75
☐ **181**	**Keith Acton, Mtl., RC**	**.50**
☐ 182	Gaston Gingras, Mtl.	.35
☐ 183	Réjean Houle, Mtl.	.50
☐ 184	Doug Jarvis, Mtl.	.50
☐ 185	Yvon Lambert, Mtl. (Buf.)	.35
☐ 186	Rod Langway, Mtl.	1.50
☐ 187	Pierre Larouche, Mtl.	.35
☐ 188	Pierre Mondou, Mtl.	.35
☐ 189	Robert Picard, Mtl.	.35
☐ 190	Doug Risebrough, Mtl.	.50
☐ 191	Richard Sévigny (G), Mtl.	.50
☐ 192	Mario Tremblay, Mtl.	.50
☐ **193**	**Doug Wickenheiser, Mtl., RC**	**.50**
☐ 194	Super Action: Bob Gainey, Mtl.	.50
☐ 195	Super Action: Guy Lafleur, Mtl.	2.00
☐ 196	Super Action: Larry Robinson, Mtl.	.50
☐ 197	TL: Steve Shutt, Mtl.	.50
☐ 198	Mike Bossy, NYI.	5.00
☐ 199	Denis Potvin, NYI.	1.50
☐ 200	Bryan Trottier, NYI.	2.50
☐ 201	Bob Bourne, NYI.	.35
☐ 202	Clark Gillies, NYI.	.50
☐ 203	Butch Goring, NYI.	.35
☐ 204	Anders Kallur, NYI.	.35
☐ 205	Ken Morrow, NYI.	.35
☐ 206	Stefan Persson, NYI.	.35
☐ 207	Billy Smith (G), NYI.	.75
☐ 208	Super Action: Mike Bossy, NYI.	2.50
☐ 209	Super Action: Denis Potvin, NYI.	.75
☐ 210	Super Action: Bryan Trottier, NYI.	1.00
☐ **211**	**Duane Sutter, NYI., RC**	**1.25**
☐ 212	Gord Lane, NYI., LC	.35
☐ 213	Dave Langevin, NYI.	.35
☐ 214	Bob Lorimer, NYI. (Col.)	.35
☐ 215	Mike McEwen, Col., (NYI.)	.35
☐ 216	Wayne Merrick, NYI.	.35
☐ 217	Bob Nystrom, NYI.	.35
☐ 218	John Tonelli, NYI.	.75
☐ 219	TL: Mike Bossy, NYI.	2.00
☐ 220	Barry Beck, NYR.	.35
☐ **221**	**Mike Allison, NYR., RC**	**.35**
☐ 222	John Davidson (G), NYR., LC	.50
☐ 223	Ron Duguay, NYR.	.50
☐ 224	Ron Greschner, NYR.	.35
☐ 225	Anders Hedberg, NYR.	.35
☐ 226	Eddie Johnstone, NYR.	.35
☐ 227	Dave Maloney, NYR.	.35
☐ 228	Don Maloney, NYR.	.35
☐ 229	Ulf Nilsson, NYR., LC	.35
☐ 230	Super Action: Barry Beck, NYR.	.35
☐ 231	Steve Baker (G), NYR., LC	.50
☐ 232	Jere Gillis, Van., (NYR.)	.35
☐ 233	Ed Hospodar, NYR., LC	.35
☐ **234**	**Tom Laidlaw, NYR., RC**	**.35**
☐ 235	Dean Talafous, NYR., LC	.35
☐ 236	Carol Vadnais, NYR.	.35
☐ 237	TL: Anders Hedberg, NYR.	.35
☐ 238	Bill Barber, Pha.	.75
☐ 239	Behn Wilson, Pha.	.35
☐ 240	Bobby Clarke, Pha.	1.75
☐ 241	Bob Dailey, Pha., LC	.35
☐ 242	Paul Holmgren, Pha.	.35
☐ 243	Reggie Leach, Pha.	.35
☐ 244	Ken Linseman, Pha.	.35
☐ 245	Pete Peeters (G), Pha.	.75
☐ 246	Brian Propp, Pha.	1.50
☐ 247	Super Action: Bill Barber, Pha.	.50
☐ 248	Mel Bridgman, Cgy., (Pha.)	.35
☐ 249	Mike Busniuk, Pha., LC	.35
☐ 250	Tom Gorence, Pha.	.35
☐ **251**	**Tim Kerr, Pha., RC**	**3.50**
☐ **252**	**Rick St. Croix (G), Pha., RC**	**.50**
☐ 253	TL: Bill Barber, Pha.	.50
☐ 254	Rick Kehoe, Pgh.	.50
☐ 255	Pat Boutette, Pgh.	.35
☐ 256	Randy Carlyle, Pgh.	.50
☐ 257	Paul Gardner, Pgh.	.35
☐ 258	Peter Lee, Pgh., LC	.35
☐ 259	Rod Schutt, Pgh., LC	.35
☐ 260	Super Action: Rick Kehoe, Pgh.	.50
☐ 261	Mario Faubert, Pgh., LC	.35
☐ 262	George Ferguson, Pgh.	.35
☐ 263	Ross Lonsberry, Pgh., LC	.35
☐ 264	Greg Malone, Pgh.	.35
☐ 265	Pat Price, Pgh. (Pgh.)	.35
☐ 266	Ron Stackhouse, Pgh.	.35
☐ 267	TL: Rick Kehoe, Pgh.	.35
☐ 268	Jacques Richard, Que.	.35
☐ **269**	**Peter Stastny, Que., RC**	**20.00**
☐ 270	Dan Bouchard (G), Que.	.50
☐ **271**	**Kim Clackson, Que. (Tor.), RC, LC**	**.35**
☐ 272	Alain Côté, Que.	.35
☐ 273	André Dupont, Que.	.35
☐ 274	Robbie Ftorek, Que.	.50
☐ 275	Michel Goulet, Que.	4.50
☐ 276	Dale Hoganson, Que., LC	.35
☐ **277**	**Dale Hunter, Que., RC**	**10.00**
☐ **278**	**Pierre Lacroix, Que., RC**	**.35**
☐ **279**	**Mario Marois, Que. (Que.), RC**	**.35**
☐ **280**	**Dave Pichette, Que., RC**	**.35**
☐ 281	Michel Plasse (G), Que., LC	.35
☐ **282**	**Anton Stastny, Que., RC**	**.50**
☐ 283	Marc Tardif, Que.	.35
☐ 284	Wally Weir, Que.	.35
☐ 285	Super Action: Jacques Richard, Que.	.35
☐ 286	Super Action: Peter Stastny, Que.	7.00
☐ 287	TL: Peter Stastny, Que.	4.00
☐ 288	Bernie Federko, Stl.	1.00
☐ 289	Mike Liut (G), Stl.	2.25
☐ 290	Wayne Babych, Stl.	.35
☐ 291	Blair Chapman, Stl., LC	.35
☐ 292	Tony Currie, Stl.	.35
☐ 293	Blake Dunlop, Stl.	.35
☐ 294	Ed Kea, Stl., LC	.35
☐ 295	Rick Lapointe, Stl.	.35
☐ **296**	**Jorgen Pettersson, Stl., RC**	**.35**
☐ 297	Brian Sutter, Stl.	.50
☐ 298	Perry Turnbull, Stl.	.35
☐ 299	Mike Zuke, Stl.	.35
☐ 300	Super Action: Bernie Federko, Stl.	.50
☐ 301	Super Action: Mike Liut, Stl.	1.00
☐ 302	Jack Brownschidle, Stl.	.35
☐ 303	Larry Patey, Stl.	.35
☐ 304	TL: Bernie Federko, Stl.	.50
☐ 305	Bill Derlago, Tor.	.35
☐ 306	Wilf Paiement, Tor.	.35
☐ 307	Borje Salming, Tor.	.50
☐ 308	Darryl Sittler, Tor.	.75
☐ 309	Ian Turnbull, Tor. (L.A.), LC	.35
☐ 310	Rick Vaive, Tor.	.50
☐ 311	Super Action: Wilf Paiement, Tor.	.35
☐ 312	Super Action: Darryl Sittler, Tor.	.50
☐ 313	John Anderson, Tor.	.35
☐ 314	Laurie Boschman, Tor.	.35
☐ **315**	**Jiri Crha (G), Tor., RC, LC**	**.50**
☐ **316**	**Vitezslav Duris, Tor., RC, LC**	**.35**
☐ 317	Dave Farrish, Tor.	.35
☐ 318	Pat Hickey, Tor. (NYR.)	.35
☐ 319	Michel Larocque (G), Tor., Mtl., (Tor.)	.50
☐ 320	Dan Maloney, Tor.	.35
☐ 321	Terry Martin, Tor. (Tor.)	.35
☐ 322	René Robert, Tor.	.35
☐ 323	Rocky Saganiuk, Tor.	.35
☐ 324	Ron Sedlbauer, Tor. (Tor.), LC	.35
☐ 325	Ron Zanussi, Tor. (Tor.), LC	.35
☐ 326	TL: Wilf Paiement, Tor.	.35
☐ 327	Thomas Gradin, Van.	.35
☐ 328	Stan Smyl, Van.	.50
☐ 329	Ivan Boldirev, Van.	.35
☐ 330	Per-Olov Brasar, Van., Error (Brent Ashton)	.35
☐ 331	Richard Brodeur (G), Van.	.50
☐ 332	Jerry Butler, Van., LC	.35
☐ 333	Colin Campbell, Van.	.50
☐ 334	Curt Fraser, Van.	.35
☐ 335	Doug Halward, Van.	.35
☐ 336	Glen Hanlon (G), Van.	.50
☐ 337	Dennis Kearns, Van., LC	.35
☐ 338	Rick Lanz, Van., Error (Thomas Gradin)	.35
☐ 339	Pat Ribble, Wsh., LC	.35
☐ 340	Blair MacDonald, Van.	.35
☐ 341	Kevin McCarthy, Van.	.35
☐ **342**	**Gerry Minor, Van., RC**	**.35**
☐ 343	Darcy Rota, Van.	.35
☐ 344	Harold Snepsts, Van.	.50
☐ 345	Dave Williams, Van.	.50
☐ 346	TL: Thomas Gradin, Van.	.35
☐ 347	Mike Gartner, Wsh.	15.00
☐ 348	Rick Green, Wsh.	.35
☐ 349	Bob Kelly, Wsh., LC	.35
☐ 350	Dennis Maruk, Wsh.	.35
☐ 351	Mike Palmateer (G), Wsh.	.50
☐ 352	Ryan Walter, Wsh.	.35
☐ 353	Bengt Gustafsson, Wsh.	.35
☐ 354	Al Hangsleben, Wsh., LC	.35
☐ 355	Jean Pronovost, Wsh., LC	.35
☐ 356	Dennis Ververgaert, Wsh., LC	.35
☐ 357	TL: Dennis Maruk, Wsh.	.35
☐ **358**	**Dave Babych, Wpg., RC**	**1.75**
☐ 359	Dave Christian, Wpg.	.35
☐ 360	Super Action: Dave Christian, Wpg.	.35
☐ 361	Rick Bowness, Wpg., LC	.35
☐ 362	Rick Dudley, Wpg., LC	.35
☐ **363**	**Norm Dupont, Wpg., RC**	**.35**
☐ **364**	**Danny Geoffrion, Wpg., RC, LC**	**.35**
☐ 365	Pierre Hamel (G), Wpg., LC	.35
☐ 366	Dave Hoyda, Wpg., Error (Doug Lecuyer)	.35
☐ **367**	**Doug Lecuyer, Wpg., RC, LC**	**.35**
☐ 368	Willy Lindstrom, Wpg.	.35
☐ 369	Barry Long, Wpg., LC	.35
☐ 370	Morris Lukowich, Wpg.	.35
☐ 371	Kris Manery, Wpg., LC	.35
☐ 372	Jimmy Mann, Wpg., LC	.35
☐ **373**	**Moe Mantha, Wpg., RC**	**.50**
☐ 374	Markus Mattsson (G), Wpg., LC	.50
☐ **375**	**Don Spring, Wpg., RC**	**.35**
☐ 376	Tim Trimper, Wpg.	.35
☐ 377	Ron Wilson, Wpg.	.35
☐ 378	TL: Dave Christian, Wpg.	.35
☐ 379	Checklist 1 (1 - 132)	7.50
☐ 380	Checklist 2 (133 - 264)	7.50
☐ 381	Checklist 3 (265 - 396)	7.50
☐ 382	LL: Mike Bossy, NYI.	2.00
☐ 383	LL: Wayne Gretzky, Edm.	12.00
☐ 384	LL: Wayne Gretzky, Edm.	12.00
☐ 385	LL: Dave Williams, Van.	.50
☐ 386	LL: Mike Bossy, NYI.	2.00
☐ 387	LL: Richard Sévigny, Mtl.	.50
☐ 388	LL: Mike Bossy, NYI.	2.00
☐ 389	LL: Don Edwards/G. Resch	.50
☐ 390	RB: Mike Bossy, NYI.	2.00
☐ 391	RB: Dionne Simmer, Taylor, L.A.	3.50
☐ 392	RB: Wayne Gretzky, Edm.	12.00
☐ 393	RB: Larry Murphy, L.A.	3.50
☐ 394	RB: Mike Palmateer (G), Wsh.	.50
☐ 395	RB: Peter Stastny, Que.	4.00
☐ 396	Bob Manno, Tor.	.50

1981 - 82 O-PEE-CHEE STICKERS

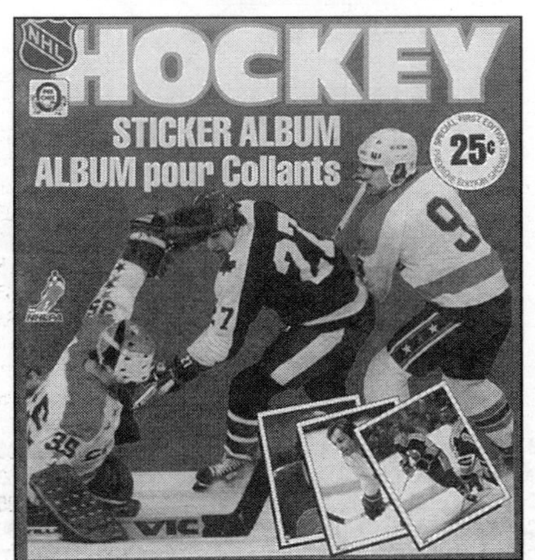

Sticker Size: 2" x 2 1/2"
Face: Four colour; Number
Back: Black and white; Number, Name, Team, Instructions, Bilingual
Imprint: 1981 O-PEE-CHEE CO. LTD.

Complete Set (269 stickers): 60.00
Common Player: .25
Album: 5.00

	No.	Player	NRMT-MT
☐	1	Foil: The Stanley Cup	.35
☐	2	Foil: The Stanley Cup	.35
☐	3	Foil: The Stanley Cup	.35
☐	4	Foil: The Stanley Cup	.35
☐	5	Foil: The Stanley Cup	.35
☐	6	Foil: The Stanley Cup	.35
☐	7	Oilers vs. Islanders	.25
☐	8	Oilers vs. Islanders	.25
☐	9	Oilers vs. Islanders	.25
☐	10	Oilers vs. Islanders	.25

Note: Stickers 7-10 feature B. Trottier, D. Potvin, G. Anderson and M. Hagman

	No.	Player	NRMT-MT
☐	11	Jari Kurri, Edm.	3.00
☐	12	Pat Riggin (G)	.35
☐	13	Flames vs. Flyers	.25
☐	14	Flames vs. Flyers	.25
☐	15	Flames vs. Flyers	.25
☐	16	Flames vs. Flyers	.25

Note: Stickers 13-16 feature Willi Plett and Pete Peeters

	No.	Player	NRMT-MT
☐	17	Stanley Cup Winners 1980/81 N.Y. Islanders	.25
☐	18	Stanley Cup Winners 1980/81 N.Y. Islanders	.25
☐	19	Foil: Conn Smythe, Trophy MVP - Finals	.35
☐	20	Butch Goring, Most Valuable Player	.25
☐	21	North Stars vs. Islanders	.25
☐	22	Steve Payne	.25
☐	23	North Stars vs. Islanders	.25
☐	24	North Stars vs. Islanders	.25
☐	25	North Stars vs. Islanders	.25
☐	26	North Stars vs. Islanders	.25

Note: Stickers 23-26 feature Ken Morrow, Dino Ciccarelli and Dave Langevin.

	No.	Player	NRMT-MT
☐	27	Foil: Prince of Wales Trophy	.35
☐	28	Foil: Prince of Wales Trophy	.35
☐	29	Guy Lafleur, Mtl.	2.00
☐	30	Bob Gainey, Mtl.	.50
☐	31	Larry Robinson, Mtl.	.75
☐	32	Steve Shutt, Mtl.	.50
☐	33	Brian Engblom, Mtl.	.25
☐	34	Doug Jarvis, Mtl.	.25
☐	35	Yvon Lambert, Mtl.	.25
☐	36	Mark Napier, Mtl.	.25
☐	37	Réjean Houle, Mtl.	.35
☐	38	Pierre Larouche, Mtl.	.25
☐	39	Rod Langway, Mtl.	.35
☐	40	Richard Sévigny (G), Mtl.	.35
☐	41	Guy Lafleur, Mtl.	2.00
☐	42	Larry Robinson, Mtl.	.75
☐	43	Bob Gainey, Mtl.	.50
☐	44	Steve Shutt, Mtl.	.50
☐	45	Rick Middleton, Bos.	.35
☐	46	Peter McNab, Bos.	.25
☐	47	Rogatien Vachon (G), Bos.	.35
☐	48	Brad Park, Bos.	.50
☐	49	Ray Bourque, Bos.	3.00
☐	50	Terry O'Reilly, Bos.	.35
☐	51	Steve Kasper, Bos.	.25
☐	52	Dwight Foster, Bos.	.25
☐	53	Danny Gare, Buf.	.35
☐	54	André Savard, Buf.	.25
☐	55	Don Edwards (G), Buf.	.35
☐	56	Bob Sauvé (G), Buf.	.35
☐	57	Tony McKegney, Buf.	.25
☐	58	John Van Boxmeer, Buf.	.25
☐	59	Derek Smith, Buf.	.25
☐	60	Gilbert Perreault, Buf.	.75
☐	61	Mike Rogers, Hfd.	.25
☐	62	Mark Howe, Hfd.	.50
☐	63	Blaine Stoughton, Hfd.	.25
☐	64	Rick Ley, Hfd.	.25
☐	65	Jordy Douglas, Hfd.	.25
☐	66	Al Sims, Hfd.	.25
☐	67	Norm Barnes, Hfd.	.25
☐	68	John Garrett (G), Hfd.	.35
☐	69	Peter Stastny, Que.	1.50
☐	70	Anton Stastny, Que.	.25
☐	71	Jacques Richard, Que.	.25
☐	72	Robbie Ftorek, Que.	.35
☐	73	Dan Bouchard (G), Que.	.35
☐	74	Réal Cloutier, Que.	.25
☐	75	Michel Goulet, Que.	1.50
☐	76	Marc Tardif, Que.	.25
☐	77	Capitals vs. Maple Leafs	.25
☐	78	Capitals vs. Maple Leafs	.25
☐	79	Capitals vs. Maple Leafs	.25
☐	80	Capitals vs. Maple Leafs	.25
☐	81	Paul Mulvey, Wsh.	.25
☐	82	Whalers player	.25
☐	83	Canadiens vs. Capitals	.25
☐	84	Dan Bouchard (G), Que.	.35
☐	85	North Stars vs. Capitals	.25
☐	86	North Stars vs. Capitals	.25

Note: Stickers 85-86 feature Craig Hartsburg and Paul Mulvey

	No.	Player	NRMT-MT
☐	87	Bruins vs. Capitals	.25
☐	88	Bobby Smith, Min.	.50
☐	89	Don Beaupré (G), Min.	.75
☐	90	Al MacAdam, Min.	.25
☐	91	Craig Hartsburg, Min.	.35
☐	92	Steve Payne, Min.	.25
☐	93	Gilles Meloche (G), Min.	.35
☐	94	Tim Young, Min.	.25
☐	95	Tom McCarthy, Min.	.25
☐	96	Wilf Paiement, Tor.	.25
☐	97	Darryl Sittler, Tor.	.50
☐	98	Borje Salming, Tor.	.50
☐	99	Bill Derlago, Tor.	.25
☐	100	Ian Turnbull, Tor.	.25
☐	101	Rick Vaive, Tor.	.50
☐	102	Dan Maloney, Tor.	.25
☐	103	Laurie Boschman, Tor.	.25
☐	104	Pat Hickey, Tor.	.25
☐	105	Michel Larocque (G), Tor.	.35
☐	106	Jiri Crha (G), Tor.	.35
☐	107	John Anderson, Tor.	.25
☐	108	Bill Derlago, Tor.	.25
☐	109	Darryl Sittler, Tor.	.50
☐	110	Wilf Paiement, Tor.	.25
☐	111	Borje Salming, Tor.	.50
☐	112	Denis Savard, Chi.	2.00
☐	113	Tony Esposito (G), Chi.	.75
☐	114	Tom Lysiak, Chi.	.25
☐	115	Keith Brown, Chi.	.35
☐	116	Glen Sharpley, Chi.	.25
☐	117	Terry Ruskowski, Chi.	.25
☐	118	Reg Kerr, Chi.	.25
☐	119	Bob Murray, Chi.	.25
☐	120	Dale McCourt, Det.	.25
☐	121	John Ogrodnick, Det.	.35
☐	122	Mike Foligno, Det.	.25
☐	123	Gilles Gilbert (G), Det.	.35
☐	124	Reed Larson, Det.	.25
☐	125	Vaclav Nedomansky, Det.	.25
☐	126	Willie Huber, Det.	.25
☐	127	Jim Korn, Det.	.25
☐	128	Bernie Federko, Stl.	.50
☐	129	Mike Liut (G), Stl.	.75
☐	130	Wayne Babych, Stl.	.25
☐	131	Blake Dunlop, Stl.	.25
☐	132	Mike Zuke, Stl.	.25
☐	133	Brian Sutter, Stl.	.50
☐	134	Rick Lapointe, Stl.	.25
☐	135	Jorgen Pettersson, Stl.	.25
☐	136	Dave Christian, Wpg.	.25
☐	137	Dave Babych, Wpg.	.50
☐	138	Morris Lukowich, Wpg.	.25
☐	139	Norm Dupont, Wpg.	.25
☐	140	Ron Wilson, Wpg.	.25
☐	141	Danny Geoffrion, Wpg.	.25
☐	142	Barry Long, Wpg.	.25
☐	143	Pierre Hamel (G), Wpg.	.25
☐	144	AS: Foil: Charlie Simmer, L.A.	.35
☐	145	AS: Foil: Mark Howe, Hfd.	.50
☐	146	AS: Foil: Don Beaupré (G), Min.	.75
☐	147	AS: Foil: Marcel Dionne, L.A.	.75
☐	148	AS: Foil: Larry Robinson, Mtl.	.75
☐	149	AS: Foil: Dave Taylor, L.A.	.35
☐	150	AS: Foil: Mike Bossy, NYI.	1.00
☐	151	AS: Foil: Denis Potvin, NYI.	.75
☐	152	AS: Foil: Bryan Trottier, NYI.	.75
☐	153	AS: Foil: Mike Liut (G), Stl.	.75
☐	154	AS: Foil: Rob Ramage, Col.	.35
☐	155	AS: Foil: Bill Barber, Pha.	.35
☐	156	Foil: Campbell Bowl	.35
☐	157	Foil: Campbell Bowl	.35
☐	158	Mike Bossy, NYI.	1.00
☐	159	Denis Potvin, NYI.	.75
☐	160	Bryan Trottier, NYI.	.75
☐	161	Billy Smith (G), NYI.	.50
☐	162	Anders Kallur, NYI.	.25
☐	163	Bob Bourne, NYI.	.25
☐	164	Clark Gillies, NYI.	.25
☐	165	Ken Morrow, NYI.	.25
☐	166	Anders Hedberg, NYR.	.25
☐	167	Ron Greschner, NYR.	.25
☐	168	Barry Beck, NYR.	.25
☐	169	Eddie Johnstone (G), NYR.	.35
☐	170	Don Maloney, NYR.	.25
☐	171	Ron Duguay, NYR.	.35
☐	172	Ulf Nilsson, NYR.	.25
☐	173	Dave Maloney, NYR.	.25
☐	174	Bill Barber, Pha.	.50
☐	175	Behn Wilson, Pha.	.25
☐	176	Ken Linseman, Pha.	.25
☐	177	Pete Peeters (G), Pha.	.35
☐	178	Bobby Clarke, Pha.	1.00
☐	179	Paul Holmgren, Pha.	.25
☐	180	Brian Propp, Pha.	.50
☐	181	Reggie Leach, Pha.	.25
☐	182	Rick Kehoe, Pgh.	.35
☐	183	Randy Carlyle, Pgh.	.35
☐	184	George Ferguson, Pgh.	.25
☐	185	Peter Lee, Pgh.	.25
☐	186	Rod Schutt, Pgh.	.25
☐	187	Paul Gardner, Pgh.	.25
☐	188	Ron Stackhouse, Pgh.	.25
☐	189	Mario Faubert, Pgh.	.25
☐	190	Mike Gartner, Wsh.	2.50
☐	191	Dennis Maruk, Wsh.	.25
☐	192	Ryan Walter, Wsh.	.25
☐	193	Rick Green, Wsh.	.25
☐	194	Mike Palmateer (G), Wsh.	.35
☐	195	Bob Kelly, Wsh.	.25
☐	196	Jean Pronovost, Wsh.	.25
☐	197	Al Hangsleben, Wsh.	.25
☐	198	Flames vs. Capitals	.25
☐	199	Oilers vs. Islanders	.25
☐	200	Oilers vs. Islanders	.25
☐	201	Oilers vs. Islanders	.25
☐	202	Oilers vs. Islanders	.25
☐	203	Rangers vs. Islanders	.25

	No.	Player	Price
☐	204	Rangers vs. Islanders	.25
☐	205	Flyers vs. Capitals	.25
☐	206	Flyers vs. Capitals	.25
☐	207	Rangers vs. Capitals	.25
☐	208	Canadiens (Bob Gainey) vs. Capitals	.35
☐	209	Wayne Gretzky, Edm.	15.00
☐	210	Mark Messier, Edm.	6.50
☐	211	Jari Kurri, Edm.	4.00
☐	212	Brett Callighen, Edm.	.25
☐	213	Matti Hagman, Edm.	.25
☐	214	Risto Siltanen, Edm.	.25
☐	215	Lee Fogolin, Edm.	.25
☐	216	Ed Mio (G), Edm.	.35
☐	217	Glenn Anderson, Edm.	1.50
☐	218	Kent Nilsson, Cgy.	.25
☐	219	Guy Chouinard, Cgy.	.25
☐	220	Eric Vail, Cgy.	.25
☐	221	Pat Riggin (G), Cgy.	.25
☐	222	Willi Plett, Cgy.	.25
☐	223	Pekka Rautakallio, Cgy.	.25
☐	224	Paul Reinhart, Cgy.	.25
☐	225	Brad Marsh, Cgy.	.35
☐	226	Phil Russell, Cgy.	.25
☐	227	Lanny McDonald, Col.	.75
☐	228	Merlin Malinowski, Col.	.25
☐	229	Rob Ramage, Col.	.35
☐	230	Glenn Resch (G), Col.	.35
☐	231	Ron Delorme, Col.	.25
☐	232	Lucien DeBlois, Col.	.25
☐	233	Paul Gagne, Col.	.25
☐	234	Joel Quenneville, Col.	.35
☐	235	Marcel Dionne, L.A.	.75
☐	236	Charlie Simmer, L.A.	.25
☐	237	Dave Taylor, L.A.	.35
☐	238	Mario Lessard (G), L.A.	.35
☐	239	Larry Murphy, L.A.	1.25
☐	240	Jerry Korab, L.A.	.25
☐	241	Mike Murphy, L.A.	.25
☐	242	Billy Harris, L.A.	.25
☐	243	Thomas Gradin, Van.	.25
☐	244	Per-Olov Brasar, Van.	.25
☐	245	Glen Hanlon (G), Van.	.50
☐	246	Chris Oddleifson, Van.	.25
☐	247	Dave Williams, Van.	.35
☐	248	Kevin McCarthy, Van.	.25
☐	249	Dennis Kearns, Van.	.25
☐	250	Harold Snepsts, Van.	.25
☐	251	LL: Foil: Art Ross Trophy, Most Points	.35
☐	252	LL: Art Ross Trophy Winner: Wayne Gretzky, Edm.	8.00
☐	253	LL: Most Goals: Mike Bossy, NYI.	.75
☐	254	LL: Foil: Norris Trophy, Best Defenseman	.35
☐	255	LL: James Norris Trophy Winner: Randy Carlyle, Pgh.	.35
☐	256	LL: Vezina Trophy Winner: Richard Sévigny, Mtl.	.35
☐	257	LL: Foil: Vezina Trophy, Goal Tending - Team	.35
☐	258	LL: Vezina Trophy Winner: Denis Herron, Mtl.	.35
☐	259	LL: Vezina Trophy Winner: Michel Larocque, Mtl.	.35
☐	260	LL: Foil: Lady Byng Trophy, Sportsmanship	.35
☐	261	LL: Lady Byng Trophy Winner: Rick Kehoe, Pgh.	.25
☐	262	LL: Foil: Calder Trophy, Rookie of the Year	.35
☐	263	LL: Calder Trophy Winner: Peter Stastny, Que.	1.00
☐	264	LL: Hart Trophy Winner: Wayne Gretzky, Edm.	8.00
☐	265	LL: Foil: Hart Trophy. Most Valuable Player	.35
☐	266	LL: Charlie Simmer	.35
☐	267	LL: Marcel Dionne	.75
☐	268	LL: Dave Taylor	.35
☐	269	LL: Bob Gainey, Mtl.	.50

1981 - 82 POST STARS IN ACTION

Booklet Size: 2 3/16" x 3 3/16"

Face: Four colour standup, facsimile signature, "Pop-up" instructions, bilingual
Back: Blank
Imprint: General Foods Inc. Megaprint Canada Ltd.
Complete Set (28 booklets): 55.00
Common Player: 1.00
Promo card (Darryl Sittler): 5.00

	No.	Player	NRMT-MT
☐	1	Ray Bourque, Bos.	12.00
☐	2	Gilbert Perreault, Bos.	1.00
☐	3	Denis Savard, Chi.	1.00
☐	4	Dale McCourt, Det.	1.00
☐	5	Bobby Smith, Min.	2.00
☐	6	Mike Bossy, NYI.	6.00
☐	7	Bobby Clarke, Pha.	5.00
☐	8	Randy Carlyle, Pgh.	1.00
☐	9	Mike Palmateer (G), Wsh.	1.00
☐	10	Dave Williams, Van.	1.50
☐	11	Mark Howe, Hfd.	1.00
☐	12	Marcel Dionne, L.A.	1.00
☐	13	Mike Liut (G), Stl.	4.00
☐	14	Barry Beck, NYR.	1.00
☐	15	Mark Messier, Edm.	15.00
☐	16	Larry Robinson, Mtl.	4.00
☐	17	Real Cloutier, Que.	1.00
☐	18	Borje Salming, Tor.	2.00
☐	19	Morris Lukowich, Wpg.	1.00
☐	20	Brett Callighen, Edm.	1.00
☐	21	Rob Ramage, Col.	1.50
☐	22	Wilf Paiement, Tor.	1.00
☐	23	Mario Tremblay, Mtl.	1.00
☐	24	Robbie Ftorek, Que.	1.00
☐	25	Stan Smyl, Van.	1.50
☐	26	Dave Babych, Wpg.	1.50
☐	27	Willi Plett, Cgy.	1.00
☐	28	Kent Nilsson, Cgy.	1.00

1981 - 82 TCMA

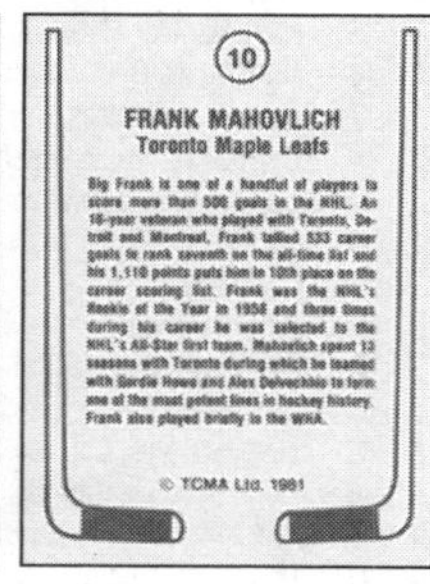

Face: Four colour, white border
Back: Black and white on card stock; Two black hockey sticks on either side of the resume
Imprint: TMCA Ltd. 1981
Complete Set (13 cards): 45.00

	No.	Player	NRMT-MT
☐	1	Norm Ullman, Det.	2.50
☐	2	Gump Worsley (G), NYR.	5.00
☐	3	J.C. Tremblay, Mtl.	1.00
☐	4	Louie Fontinato, NYR.	1.00
☐	5	John Bucyk, Bos.	2.50
☐	6	Harry Howell, NYR.	2.00
☐	7	Henri Richard, Mtl.	5.00
☐	8	Andy Bathgate, NYR.	2.00
☐	9	Bobby Orr, Bos.	25.00
☐	10	Frank Mahovlich, Tor.	5.00
☐	11	Jean Béliveau, Mtl.	8.00
☐	12	Jacques Plante (G), Mtl.	8.00
☐	13	Stan Mikita, Chi.	5.00

1981 - 82 TOPPS

Cards 1 to 66 are double printed.
Front: Four colour, white border; Team logo
Back: Blue and black on card stock; Number, Resume, Hockey trivia
Imprint: © 1981 TOPPS CHEWING GUM, INC.
Complete Set (198 cards): 90.00
Common Player (1-66): .15
Common Player (East 67-132): .20
Common Player (West 67-132): .30

	No.	Player	NRMT-MT
☐	**1**	**Dave Babych, Wpg., RC**	**.85**
☐	2	Bill Barber, Pha.	.25
☐	3	Barry Beck, NYR.	.15
☐	4	Mike Bossy, NYI.	3.00
☐	5	Ray Bourque, Bos.	5.50
☐	6	Guy Chouinard, Cgy.	.15
☐	7	Dave Christian, Wpg.	.15
☐	8	Bill Derlago, Tor.	.15
☐	9	Marcel Dionne, L.A.	1.00
☐	10	Brian Engblom, Mtl.	.15
☐	11	Tony Esposito (G), Chi.	.50
☐	12	Bernie Federko, Stl.	.50
☐	13	Bob Gainey, Mtl.	.35
☐	14	Danny Gare, Buf.	.25
☐	15	Thomas Gradin, Van.	.15
☐	16	Wayne Gretzky, Edm.	15.00
☐	17	Rick Kehoe, Pgh.	.25
☐	**18**	**Jari Kurri, Edm., RC**	**7.50**
☐	19	Guy Lafleur, Mtl.	3.00
☐	20	Mike Liut (G), Stl.	1.00
☐	21	Dale McCourt, Det.	.15
☐	22	Rick Middleton, Bos.	.25
☐	23	Mark Napier, Mtl.	.15
☐	24	Kent Nilsson, Cgy.	.25
☐	25	Wilf Paiement, Tor.	.15
☐	26	Willi Plett, Cgy.	.15
☐	27	Denis Potvin, NYI.	.60
☐	28	Paul Reinhart, Cgy.	.15
☐	29	Jacques Richard, Que.	.15
☐	**30**	**Pat Riggin (G), Cgy., RC**	**.25**
☐	31	Larry Robinson, Mtl.	.50
☐	32	Mike Rogers, Hfd.	.15
☐	33	Borje Salming, Tor.	.25
☐	34	Steve Shutt, Mtl.	.35
☐	35	Charlie Simmer, L.A.	.25
☐	36	Darryl Sittler, Tor.	.35
☐	37	Bobby Smith, Min.	.25
☐	38	Stan Smyl, Van.	.15
☐	**39**	**Peter Stastny, Que., RC**	**4.50**
☐	40	David Taylor, L.A.	.35
☐	41	Bryan Trottier, NYI.	1.50
☐	42	Ian Turnbull, Tor., LC	.15
☐	43	Eric Vail, Cgy.	.15
☐	44	Rick Vaive, Tor.	.25
☐	45	Behn Wilson, Pha.	.15
☐	46	TL: Rick Middleton, Bos.	.25
☐	47	TL: Danny Gare, Buf.	.25
☐	48	TL: Kent Nilsson, Cgy.	.25
☐	49	TL: Tom Lysiak, Chi.	.15
☐	50	TL: Lanny McDonald, Col.	.25
☐	51	TL: Dale McCourt, Det.	.15
☐	52	TL: Wayne Gretzky, Edm.	4.00
☐	53	TL: Mike Rogers, Hfd.	.15
☐	54	TL: Marcel Dionne, L.A.	.35
☐	55	TL: Bobby Smith, Min.	.25
☐	56	TL: Steve Shutt, Mtl.	.25
☐	57	TL: Mike Bossy, NYI.	1.00
☐	58	TL: Anders Hedberg, NYR.	.15

	No.	Player	Price
☐	59	TL: Bill Barber, Pha.	.15
☐	60	TL: Rick Kehoe, Pgh.	.25
☐	61	TL: Peter Stastny, Que.	2.00
☐	62	TL: Bernie Federko, Stl.	.25
☐	63	TL: Wilf Paiement, Tor.	.15
☐	64	TL: Thomas Gradin, Van.	.15
☐	65	TL: Dennis Maruk, Wsh.	.15
☐	66	TL: Dave Christian, Wpg.	.15

EASTERN DISTRIBUTION

	No.	Player	Price
☐	67	Dwight Foster, Bos.	.20
☐	**68**	**Steve Kasper, Bos., RC**	**1.00**
☐	69	Peter McNab, Bos.	.20
☐	70	Mike O'Connell, Bos.	.20
☐	71	Terry O'Reilly, Bos.	.35
☐	72	Brad Park, Bos.	.50
☐	73	Dick Redmond, Bos., LC	.20
☐	74	Rogatien Vachon (G), Bos.	.35
☐	75	Don Edwards (G), Buf.	.20
☐	76	Tony McKegney, Buf.	.20
☐	77	Bob Sauvé (G), Buf.	.35
☐	78	André Savard, Buf.	.20
☐	79	Derek Smith, Buf.	.20
☐	80	John Van Boxmeer, Buf.	.20
☐	81	Pat Boutette, Pgh.	.20
☐	82	Mark Howe, Hfd.	.50
☐	83	Dave Keon, Hfd., LC	.35
☐	**84**	**Warren Miller, Hfd., RC**	**.20**
☐	85	Al Sims, Hfd., LC	.20
☐	86	Blaine Stoughton, Hfd.	.20
☐	87	Bob Bourne, NYI.	.20
☐	88	Clark Gillies, NYI.	.25
☐	89	Butch Goring, NYI.	.25
☐	90	Anders Kallur, NYI.	.20
☐	91	Ken Morrow, NYI.	.20
☐	92	Stefan Persson, NYI.	.20
☐	93	Billy Smith (G), NYI.	.50
☐	**94**	**Mike Allison, NYR., RC**	**.20**
☐	95	John Davidson (G), NYR., LC	.35
☐	96	Ron Duguay, NYR.	.20
☐	97	Ron Greschner, NYR.	.20
☐	98	Anders Hedberg, NYR.	.20
☐	99	Eddie Johnstone, NYR.	.20
☐	100	Dave Maloney, NYR.	.20
☐	101	Don Maloney, NYR.	.20
☐	102	Ulf Nilsson, NYR., LC	.20
☐	103	Bobby Clarke, Pha.	.85
☐	104	Bob Dailey, Pha., LC	.20
☐	105	Paul Holmgren, Pha.	.20
☐	106	Reggie Leach, Pha.	.20
☐	107	Ken Linseman, Pha.	.20
☐	108	Rick MacLeish, Hfd.	.20
☐	109	Pete Peeters (G), Pha,	.35
☐	110	Brian Propp, Pha.	.35
☐	111	Checklist 1 (1 - 132)	1.75
☐	112	Randy Carlyle, Pgh.	.35
☐	113	Paul Gardner, Pgh.	.20
☐	114	Peter Lee, Pgh., LC	.20
☐	115	Greg Millen (G), Hfd.	.35
☐	116	Rod Schutt, Pgh., LC	.20
☐	117	Mike Gartner, Wsh.	6.00
☐	118	Rick Green, Wsh.	.20
☐	119	Bob Kelly, Wsh., LC	.20
☐	120	Dennis Maruk, Wsh.	.20
☐	121	Mike Palmateer (G), Wsh.	.35
☐	122	Ryan Walter, Wsh.	.20
☐	123	Super Action: Bill Barber, Pha.	.35
☐	124	Super Action: Barry Beck, NYR.	.20
☐	125	Super Action: Mike Bossy, NYI.	1.25
☐	126	Super Action: Ray Bourque, Bos.	3.00
☐	127	Super Action: Danny Gare, Buf.	.25
☐	128	Super Action: Rick Kehoe, Pgh.	.35
☐	129	Super Action: Rick Middleton, Bos.	.35
☐	130	Super Action: Denis Potvin, NYI.	.50
☐	131	Super Action: Mike Rogers, Hfd.	.20
☐	132	Super Action: Bryan Trottier, NYI.	.65

WESTERN DISTRIBUTION

	No.	Player	Price
☐	67	Keith Brown, Chi.	.30
☐	68	Ted Bulley, Chi.	.30
☐	**69**	**Tim Higgins, Chi., RC**	**.30**
☐	70	Reg Kerr, Chi.	.30
☐	71	Tom Lysiak, Chi.	.30
☐	72	Grant Mulvey, Chi.	.30
☐	73	Bob Murray, Chi.	.30
☐	74	Terry Ruskowski, Chi.	.30
☐	**75**	**Denis Savard, Chi., RC**	**10.00**
☐	76	Glen Sharpley, Chi.	.30
☐	**77**	**Darryl Sutter, Chi., RC**	**1.00**
☐	78	Doug Wilson, Chi.	.75
☐	79	Lucien DeBlois, Wpg.	.30
☐	**80**	**Paul Gagné, Col., RC**	**.30**
☐	**81**	**Merlin Malinowski, Col., RC**	**.30**
☐	82	Lanny McDonald, Col.	.75
☐	83	Joel Quenneville, Col.	.50
☐	84	Rob Ramage, Col.	.50
☐	85	Glenn Resch (G), Col.	.50
☐	86	Steve Tambellini, Col.	.30
☐	87	Mike Foligno, Det.	.30
☐	88	Gilles Gilbert (G), Det.	.50
☐	89	Willie Huber, Det.	.30
☐	**90**	**Mark Kirton, Det., RC**	**.30**
☐	**91**	**Jim Korn, Det., RC**	**.30**
☐	92	Reed Larson, Det.	.30
☐	93	Gary McAdam, Det.	.30
☐	94	Vaclav Nedomansky, Det., LC	.30
☐	95	John Ogrodnick, Det.	.30
☐	96	Billy Harris, L.A.	.30
☐	97	Jerry Korab, L.A., LC	.30
☐	98	Mario Lessard (G), L.A.	.50
☐	99	Don Luce, Tor., LC	.30
☐	**100**	**Larry Murphy, L.A., RC**	**5.00**
☐	101	Mike Murphy, L.A., LC	.30
☐	102	Kent-Erik Andersson, Min.	.30
☐	**103**	**Don Beaupré (G), Min., RC**	**3.50**
☐	104	Steve Christoff, Min.	.30
☐	**105**	**Dino Ciccarelli, Min., RC**	**12.00**
☐	106	Craig Hartsburg, Min.	.50
☐	107	Al MacAdam, Min.	.30
☐	108	Tom McCarthy, Min.	.30
☐	109	Gilles Meloche (G), Min.	.50
☐	110	Steve Payne, Min.	.30
☐	111	Gord Roberts, Min.	.30
☐	112	Greg Smith, Min.	.30
☐	113	Tim Young, Min.	.30
☐	114	Wayne Babych, Stl.	.30
☐	115	Blair Chapman, Stl., LC	.30
☐	116	Tony Currie, Stl.	.30
☐	117	Blake Dunlop, Stl.	.30
☐	118	Ed Kea, Stl., LC	.30
☐	119	Rick Lapointe, Stl.	.30
☐	120	Checklist 2 (1 - 132)	2.50
☐	**121**	**Jorgen Pettersson, Stl., RC**	**.30**
☐	122	Brian Sutter, Stl.	.50
☐	123	Perry Turnbull, Stl.	.30
☐	124	Mike Zuke, Stl.	.30
☐	125	Super Action: Marcel Dionne, L.A.	.75
☐	126	Super Action: Tony Esposito (G), Chi.	.75
☐	127	Super Action: Bernie Federko, Stl.	.75
☐	128	Super Action: Mike Liut (G), Stl.	.75
☐	129	Super Action: Dale McCourt, Det.	.30
☐	130	Super Action: Charlie Simmer, L.A.	.50
☐	131	Super Action: Bobby Smith, Min.	.50
☐	132	Super Action: Dave Taylor, L.A.	.50

1982 MALLASJUOMA MM

A set of 4 labels of the World Championships. We have no pricing information on this set.

Card Size: 3" x 3 1/2"

Imprint:

	Player
☐	Timo Nummelin
☐	Jukka Porvari
☐	Reijo Ruotsalainen
☐	Ilkka Sinisalo

1982 SEMIC STICKER

Sticker Size: 2 1/8" x 3"

Face: Four colour

Back: Black and white, Swedish text

Imprint: TMCA Ltd. 1981

Complete Set (162 stickers): 45.00

Album: 4.00

	No.	Player	NRMT-MT
☐	1	Peter Lindmark, Swe.	.25
☐	2	Göte Wälitalo, Swe.	.25
☐	3	Gunnar Leidborg, Swe.	.25
☐	4	Göran Lindblom, Swe.	.25
☐	5	Thomas Eriksson, Swe.	.25
☐	6	Mats Waltin, Swe.	.25
☐	7	Jan Eriksson, Swe.	.25
☐	8	Mats Thelin, Swe.	.25
☐	9	Peter Helander, Swe.	.25
☐	10	Tommy Samuelsson, Swe.	.25
☐	11	Bo Ericsson, Swe.	.25
☐	12	Peter Andersson, Swe.	.25
☐	13	Mats Näslund, Swe.	5.00
☐	14	Ulf Isaksson, Swe.	.25
☐	15	Patrik Sundström, Swe.	2.00
☐	16	Peter Sundstrom, Swe.	.50
☐	17	Thomas Rundqvist, Swe.	.25
☐	18	Mats Ulander, Swe.	.25
☐	19	Tommy Mörth, Swe.	.25
☐	20	Ove Olsson, Swe.	.25
☐	21	Rolf Edberg, Swe.	.25
☐	22	Håkan Loob, Swe.	5.00
☐	23	Leif Holmgren, Swe.	.50
☐	24	Jan Erixon, Swe.	1.00
☐	25	Harald Luckner, Swe.	.25
☐	26	Hannu Kamppuri, Fin.	.25
☐	27	Hannu Lassila, Fin.	.25
☐	28	Kari Heikkilå, Fin.	.25
☐	29	Time Nummelin, Fin.	.25
☐	30	Pertti Lehtonen, Fin.	.25
☐	31	Raimo Hirvonen, Fin.	.25
☐	32	Seppo Suoraniemi, Fin.	.25
☐	33	Juha Huikari, Fin.	.25
☐	34	Hannu Helander, Fin.	.25
☐	35	Lasse Litma, Fin.	.25
☐	36	Håkan Hjerpe, Fin.	.25
☐	37	Kari Jalonen, Fin.	.25
☐	38	Arte Javanainen, Fin.	.25
☐	39	Jari Lindgren, Fin.	.25
☐	40	Markku Kiimalainen, Fin.	.25
☐	41	Jarmo Mäkitalo, Fin.	.25
☐	42	Jorma Seven, Fin.	.25
☐	43	Erkki Laine, Fin.	.25
☐	44	Hannu Koskinen, Fin.	.25
☐	45	Reijo Leppänen, Fin.	.25
☐	46	Pekka Arbelius, Fin.	.25
☐	47	Markku Hakulinen, Fin.	.25
☐	48	Time Susi, Fin.	.25
☐	49	Esa Peltonen, Fin.	.25
☐	50	Juhani Tamminen, Fin.	.50
☐	51	Vladislav Tretiak (G), USSR	12.00
☐	52	Vladimir Mishkin, USSR	.25
☐	53	Viacheslav Fetisov, USSR	4.00
☐	54	Sergei Babinov, USSR	.25
☐	55	Vasili Pervuchin, USSR	.25
☐	56	Valeri Vasiliev, USSR	1.00
☐	57	Alexie Kasatonov, USSR	1.00
☐	58	Zinetula Biljaletdinov, USSR	.25
☐	59	Sergei Starikov, USSR	.35
☐	60	Sergei Makarov, USSR	3.00
☐	61	Sergei Sjepelev, USSR	.75

	No.	Player	Price
☐	62	Vladimir Krutov, USSR	1.00
☐	63	Nikolaj Drozdetskij, USSR	.25
☐	64	Viktor Ziluktov, USSR	.25
☐	65	Viktor Sjalimov, USSR	.25
☐	66	Vladimir Golikov, USSR	.25
☐	67	Alexander Maltsev, USSR	2.00
☐	68	Andre Khomutov, USSR	1.50
☐	69	Sergei Svetlov, USSR	.25
☐	70	Helmut Balderis, USSR	1.50
☐	71	Sergei Kapustin, USSR	.25
☐	72	Vladimir Zubkov, USSR	.25
☐	73	Alexander Kozjevnikov, USSR	.25
☐	74	Yuri Lebedev, USSR	.25
☐	75	Nikolai Makarov, USSR	.25
☐	76	Jiri Kralik, CSR.	.25
☐	77	Karel Lang, CSR.	.25
☐	78	Jaromir Sindel, CSR.	.25
☐	79	Miroslav Horava, CSR.	.25
☐	80	Milan Chalupa, CSR.	.25
☐	81	Stanislav Hajdusek, CSR.	.25
☐	82	Arnold Kadlec, CSR.	.25
☐	83	Miroslav Dvorak, CSR.	.25
☐	84	Jan Neliba, CSR.	.25
☐	85	Petr Misek, CSR.	.25
☐	86	Eduard Ulvira, CSR.	.25
☐	87	Milan Novy, CSR.	.50
☐	88	Frantisek Cerny, CSR.	.25
☐	89	Jiri Lala, CSR.	.25
☐	90	Jindrich Kokrment, CSR.	.25
☐	91	Frantisek Cernik, CSR.	.25
☐	92	Darius Rusnak, CSR.	.25
☐	93	Dusan Pasek, CSR.	.25
☐	94	Lubomir Penicka, CSR.	.25
☐	95	Jaroslav Korbela, CSR.	.25
☐	96	Peter Ihnacak, CSR.	.50
☐	97	Jaroslav Hrdina, CSR.	.25
☐	98	Igor Liban, CSR.	.25
☐	99	Peter Slaninan, CSR.	.25
☐	100	Vincent Lukac, CSR.	.25
☐	101	Erich Weishaupt, BRD.	.25
☐	102	Bernhard Engelbrecht, BRD.	.25
☐	103	Robert Murray, BRD.	.25
☐	104	Peter Gailer, BRD.	.25
☐	105	Udo Kiessling, BRD.	.25
☐	106	Harold Kreis, BRD.	.25
☐	107	Joachim Reil, BRD.	.25
☐	108	Harald Krull, BRD.	.25
☐	109	Ulrich Egen, BRD.	.25
☐	110	Marcus Kuhl, BRD.	.25
☐	111	Peter Schiller, BRD.	.25
☐	112	Erich Kuhnhackl, BRD.	.25
☐	113	Holger Meitinger, BRD.	.25
☐	114	Ernst Höfner, BRD.	.25
☐	115	Vladimir Vacatko, BRD.	.25
☐	116	Manfred Wolf, BRD.	.25
☐	117	Johann Mörz, BRD.	.25
☐	118	Franz Reindl, BRD.	.25
☐	119	Helmut Steiger, BRD.	.25
☐	120	Georg Holzmann, BRD.	.25
☐	121	Roy Roedeger, BRD.	.25
☐	122	Jim Corsi, Ita.	.25
☐	123	Nick Santa, Ita.	.25
☐	124	GuidoTenisi, Ita.	.25
☐	125	Erwin Kostner, Ita.	.25
☐	126	Mike Amodeo, Ita.	.25
☐	127	John Bellio, Ita.	.25
☐	128	DaveTomassoni, Ita.	.25
☐	129	Daniel Pupillo, Ita.	.25
☐	130	Giulio Francella, Ita.	.25
☐	131	Fabio Polloni, Ita.	.25
☐	132	Adolf Insam, Ita.	.25
☐	133	Patrick Dell'Jannone, Ita.	.25
☐	134	Rick Bragnalo, Ita.	.25
☐	135	Michael Mair, Ita.	.25
☐	136	Alberto Di Fazio, Ita.	.25
☐	137	Cary Farelli, Ita.	.25
☐	138	Tom Milani, Ita.	.25
☐	139	Martin Pavlu, Ita.	.25
☐	140	Bob De Piero, Ita.	.25
☐	141	Grant Goegan, Ita.	.25
☐	142	Jerry Ciarcia, Ita.	.25
☐	143	Börje Salming	4.00
☐	144	Lars Lindgren	.50
☐	145	Ulf Nilsson	2.00
☐	146	Bengt Gustavsson	.50
☐	147	Kent Nilsson	3.00
☐	148	Thomas Gradin	2.00
☐	149	Lars Molin	.50
☐	150	Thomas Steen, Swe.	2.00
☐	151	Bengt Lundholm	.50
☐	152	Jörgen Pettersson	.50
☐	153	Jukka Porvari	.25
☐	154	Tapio Levo	.25
☐	155	Reijo Ruotsalainen	2.00
☐	156	Matti Hagman	.50
☐	157	Risto Siltanen	.50
☐	158	Ilkka Sinisalo	.50
☐	159	Markus Mattson (G)	.50
☐	160	Mikko Leinonen	.50
☐	161	Pekka Rautakalli	.50
☐	162	Veli-Pekka Ketola	1.00

1982 SKOPBANK

A set of two 8 sticker sheets issued by the Skopbank. The set was issued in Finnish and in Swedish. We have no pricing information on this set.

Size: 2 1/2" x 3 3/4"

Imprint:

	Player		Player
☐	Pekka Arbelius	☐	Ari Hellgren
☐	Raimo Hirvonen	☐	Hannu Kamppuri
☐	Markku Kiimalainen	☐	Pertti Koivulahti
☐	Hannu Koskinen	☐	Mikko Leinonen
☐	Reijo Leppanen	☐	Tapio Levo
☐	Timo Nummelin	☐	Jukka Porvari
☐	Reijo Ruotsalainen	☐	Seppo Suoraniemi
☐	Timo Susi	☐	Juhani Tamminen

1982 VALIO

A set of ice cream labels issued by the Valio dairy company for the 1982 World Championships. We have no pricing information on this set.

Diameter: 2 3/8"

Imprint:

	Player		Player
☐	Kari Eloranta	☐	Jari Kurri
☐	Tapio Levo	☐	Markus Mattsson
☐	Jukka Porvari	☐	Pekka Rautakallio

1982 ? J.D. McCARTHY POSTCARDS

Very little is known about this set. Some of these cards were released as early as the 1960s. Photos are either in black and white or in colour.

Size: 3 1/4" x 5 1/2"

Front: Black and white or colour

Imprint: J.D. McCarthy, 8441 Northfield, Oak Park 37, Michigan

	Player	NRMT-MT
BOSTON BRUINS		
☐	Andy Hebenton	2.00
☐	Willie O'Ree	2.00
CHICAGO BLACKHAWKS		
☐	Bobby Hull (home)	10.00
☐	Bobby Hull (away)	10.00
☐	Dennis Hull	5.00
DETROIT RED WINGS		
☐	Earl Anderson	2.00
☐	Al Arbour	2.00
☐	Garnet Bailey	2.00
☐	Red Berenson	2.00
☐	Gary Bergman	2.00
☐	Thommie Bergman	2.00
☐	Marcel Bonin	2.00
☐	Henry Boucha	2.00
☐	Charlie Burns	2.00
☐	Guy Charron	2.00
☐	Bill Collins	2.00
☐	Barry Cullen	2.00
☐	Alex Delvecchio	5.00
☐	Marcel Dionne	5.00
☐	Val Fonteyne	2.00
☐	Pete Goegan	2.00
☐	Danny Grant	2.00
☐	Doug Grant	2.00
☐	Jean Hamel	2.00
☐	Ted Harris	2.00
☐	Bill Hogaboam	2.00
☐	Brent Hughes	2.00
☐	Pierre Jarry	2.00
☐	Larry Johnston	2.00
☐	Nick Libett	2.00
☐	Bill Lochead	2.00
☐	Jack Lynch	2.00
☐	Tom Mellor	2.00
☐	Gerry Melnyk	2.00
☐	Hank Nowak	2.00
☐	Marcel Pronovost	2.00
☐	Metro Prystai	2.00
☐	Bill Quackenbush	2.00
☐	Doug Roberts	2.00
☐	Jim Rutherford (G)	3.00
☐	Barry Salovaara	2.00
☐	Terry Sawchuk (G)	8.00
☐	Jimmy Skinner	2.00
☐	Ron Stackhouse	2.00
☐	Vic Stasiuk	2.00
☐	Greg Stefan (G)	2.00
☐	Blair Stewart	2.00
☐	Jerry Toppazzini	2.00
☐	Norm Ullman	4.00
☐	Bryan Watson	2.00
☐	Benny Woit	2.00
EDMONTON OILERS		
☐	Wayne Gretzky	25.00

1982 - 83 MCDONALD'S STICKERS

The set was issued only in Québec. It has a 12-page album.

Sticker Size: 1 15/16" x 2 9/16"
Face: Four colour, red border; Name, McDonald's logo
Back: Black on buff card stock; Name, Number, Position, Team, Bilingual
Imprint: 1983 La corporation McDonald's/McDonald's Corporation
Complete Set (36 stickers): 25.00
Album: 5.00

	No.	Player	NRMT-MT
☐	1	Dan Bouchard (G), Que.	.25
☐	2	Richard Brodeur (G), Van.	.25
☐	3	Gilles Meloche (G), Min.	.25
☐	4	Billy Smith (G), NYI.	1.00
☐	5	Rick Wamsley (G), Mtl.	.25
☐	6	Mike Bossy, NYI.	2.00
☐	7	Dino Ciccarelli, Min.	1.00
☐	8	Guy Lafleur, Mtl.	3.00
☐	9	Rick Middleton, Bos.	.25
☐	10	Marian Stastny, Que.	.25
☐	11	Bill Barber, Pha.	.75
☐	12	Bob Gainey, Mtl.	1.00
☐	13	Clark Gillies, NYI.	.25
☐	14	Michel Goulet, Que.	1.00
☐	15	Mark Messier, Edm.	4.00
☐	16	AS: Billy Smith (G), NYI.	1.00
☐	17	AS: Larry Robinson, Mtl.	1.00
☐	18	AS: Denis Potvin, NYI.	1.00
☐	19	AS: Michel Goulet, Que.	1.00
☐	20	AS: Wayne Gretzky, Edm.	8.00
☐	21	AS: Mike Bossy, NYI.	1.50
☐	22	Wayne Gretzky, Edm.	10.00
☐	23	Denis Savard, Chi.	1.00
☐	24	Peter Stastny, Que.	1.00
☐	25	Bryan Trottier, NYI.	1.50
☐	26	Doug Wickenheiser, Mtl.	.25
☐	27	Barry Beck, NYR.	.25
☐	28	Ray Bourque, Bos.	3.50
☐	29	Brian Engblom, Wsh.	.25
☐	30	Craig Hartsburg, Min.	.50
☐	31	Mark Howe, Pha.	.50
☐	32	Rod Langway, Wsh.	.25
☐	33	Denis Potvin, NYI.	1.00
☐	34	Larry Robinson, Mtl.	1.00
☐	35	Normand Rochefort, Que.	.25
☐	36	Doug Wilson, Chi.	.50

1982 - 83 NEILSON'S WAYNE GRETZY

Card Size: 2 1/2" x 3 1/2"
Face: Black and white or Four colour photographs, blue border; Number, Facsimile autograph
Back: Blue and black on grey card stock; Facsimile autograph, Hockey tip, Bilingual
Imprint: Neilson
Complete Set (50 cards): 185.00

	No.	Player	NRMT-MT
☐	1	Discard Broken Stick	8.50
☐	2	Handling the Puck	5.00
☐	3	Offsides	5.00
☐	4	Penalty Shot	5.00
☐	5	Icing the Puck	5.00
☐	6	Taping your Stick	5.00
☐	7	Skates	5.00
☐	8	The Helmet	5.00
☐	9	Selecting Skates	5.00
☐	10	Choosing a Stick (w/G.Howe)	20.00
☐	11	General Equipment Care	5.00
☐	12	The Hook Check (w/M. Dionne)	8.50
☐	13	The Hip Check	5.00
☐	14	Forward Skating (w/M. Gartner)	6.00
☐	15	Stopping	5.00
☐	16	Sharp Turning	5.00
☐	17	Fast Starts	5.00
☐	18	Backward Skating	5.00
☐	19	The Grip	5.00
☐	20	The Wrist Shot	5.00
☐	21	The Back Hand Shot	5.00
☐	22	The Slap Shot	5.00
☐	23	The Flip Shot	5.00
☐	24	Pass Receiving	5.00
☐	25	Faking	5.00
☐	26	Puck Handling	5.00
☐	27	Deflecting Shots	5.00
☐	28	One On One	5.00
☐	29	Keep Your Head Up	5.00
☐	30	Passing to the Slot	5.00
☐	31	Winning Face-Offs w/G. Lafleur/M. Bossy	15.00
☐	32	Forechecking	5.00
☐	33	Body Checking	5.00
☐	34	Breaking Out	5.00
☐	35	The Drop Pass	5.00
☐	36	Backchecking (w/P. Esposito)	12.00
☐	37	Using the Boards	5.00
☐	38	The Power Play	5.00
☐	39	Passing the Puck	5.00
☐	40	Clear the Slot	5.00
☐	41	Leg Lifts	5.00
☐	42	Balance Exercise	5.00
☐	43	Leg Stretches (w/M. Zuke)	5.00
☐	44	Hip and Groin Stretch	5.00
☐	45	Toe Touches (w/M. Messier)	10.00
☐	46	Goalie Warm Up Drill	5.00
☐	47	Leg Exercises	5.00
☐	48	Arm Exercises (w/J. Stackhouse)	5.00
☐	49	Wrist Exercises	5.00
☐	50	Flip Pass	8.50

1982 - 83 O-PEE-CHEE

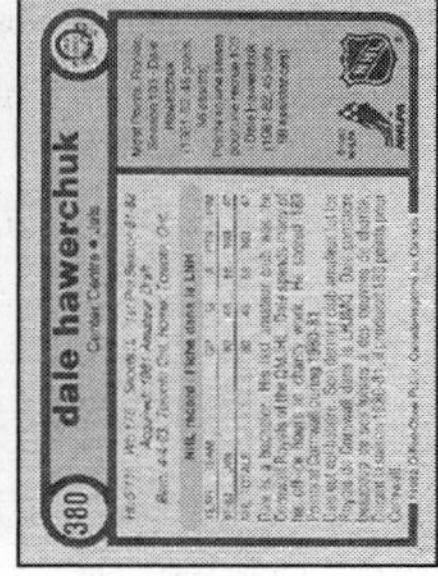

Face: Four colour, white border, Team logo, Position
Back: Purple on card stock, Number, Resume, Bilingual
Imprint: © 1982 O-Pee-Chee
Complete Set (396 cards): 115.00
Common Player: .30

	No.	Player	NRMT-MT
☐	1	Wayne Gretzky, Edm.	15.00
☐	2	Mike Bossy, NYI.	1.50
☐	3	Dale Hawerchuk, Wpg.	5.50
☐	**4**	**Mikko Leinonen, NYR., RC**	**.30**
☐	5	Bryan Trottier, NYI.	.75
☐	6	TL: Rick Middleton, Bos.	.30
☐	7	Ray Bourque, Bos.	12.00
☐	8	Wayne Cashman, Bos., LC	.30
☐	**9**	**Bruce Crowder, Bos., RC**	**.30**
☐	**10**	**Keith Crowder, Bos., RC**	**.30**
☐	**11**	**Tom Fergus, Bos., RC**	**.50**
☐	12	Steve Kasper, Bos.	.30
☐	**13**	**Normand Léveillé, Bos., RC, LC**	**.30**
☐	14	Don Marcotte, Bos., LC	.30
☐	15	Rick Middleton, Bos.	.50
☐	16	Peter McNab, Bos.	.30
☐	17	Mike O'Connell, Bos.	.30
☐	18	Terry O'Reilly, Bos.	.30
☐	19	Brad Park, Bos.	.50
☐	**20**	**Barry Pederson, Bos., RC**	**1.00**
☐	**21**	**Brad Palmer, Bos., RC, LC**	**.30**
☐	22	Pete Peeters (G), Bos.	.50
☐	23	Rogatien Vachon (G), Bos., LC	.50
☐	24	In Action: Ray Bourque, Bos.	4.00
☐	25	TL: Gilbert Perreault, Buf.	.50
☐	26	Mike Foligno, Buf.	.30
☐	27	Yvon Lambert, Buf., LC	.30
☐	28	Dale McCourt, Buf.	.30
☐	29	Tony McKegney, Buf.	.30
☐	30	Gilbert Perreault, Buf.	.75
☐	31	Lindy Ruff, Buf.	.50
☐	32	Mike Ramsey, Buf.	.30
☐	**33**	**J.F. Sauvé, Buf., RC, LC**	**.30**
☐	34	Bob Sauvé (G), Buf.	.50
☐	35	Ric Seiling, Buf.	.30
☐	36	John Van Boxmeer, Buf.	.30
☐	37	In Action: John Van Boxmeer, Buf.	.30
☐	38	TL: Lanny McDonald, Cgy.	.50
☐	39	Mel Bridgman, Cgy.	.30
☐	40	In Action: Mel Bridgman, Cgy.	.30
☐	41	Guy Chouinard, Cgy.	.30
☐	42	Steve Christoff, Cgy.	.30
☐	**43**	**Denis Cyr, Cgy., RC, LC**	**.30**
☐	44	Bill Clement, Cgy., LC	.30
☐	45	Rich Dunn, Cgy.	.30
☐	46	Don Edwards (G), Cgy.	.50
☐	47	Jamie Hislop, Cgy.	.30
☐	**48**	**Steve Konroyd, Cgy., RC**	**.30**
☐	49	Kevin LaVallée, Cgy.	.30
☐	50	Réjean Lemelin (G), Cgy.	.50
☐	51	Lanny McDonald, Cgy.	.50
☐	52	In Action: Lanny McDonald, Cgy.	.50
☐	53	Bob Murdoch, Cgy., LC	.30
☐	54	Kent Nilsson, Cgy.	.30
☐	55	Jim Peplinski, Cgy.	.30
☐	56	Paul Reinhart, Cgy.	.30
☐	57	Doug Risebrough, Cgy.	.30
☐	58	Phil Russell, Cgy.	.30
☐	**59**	**Howard Walker, Cgy., RC, LC**	**.30**
☐	60	TL: Al Secord, Chi.	.30
☐	61	Murray Bannerman (G), Chi.	.50
☐	62	Keith Brown, Chi.	.30
☐	**63**	**Doug Crossman, Chi., RC**	**.50**
☐	64	Tony Esposito (G), Chi.	.85
☐	65	Greg Fox, Chi.	.30
☐	66	Tim Higgins, Chi.	.30
☐	67	Reg Kerr, Chi., LC	.30
☐	68	Tom Lysiak, Chi.	.30
☐	69	Grant Mulvey, Chi., LC	.30
☐	70	Bob Murray, Chi.	.30
☐	71	Rich Preston, Chi.	.30
☐	72	Terry Ruskowski (L.A.), Chi.	.30
☐	73	Denis Savard, Chi.	4.50
☐	74	Al Secord, Chi.	.30
☐	75	Glen Sharpley, Chi., LC	.30
☐	76	Darryl Sutter, Chi.	.50
☐	77	Doug Wilson, Chi.	.75
☐	78	In Action: Doug Wilson, Chi.	.50
☐	79	TL: John Ogrodnick, Det.	.30
☐	**80**	**John Barrett, Det., RC**	**.30**
☐	**81**	**Mike Blaisdell, Det., RC**	**.30**
☐	82	Colin Campbell, Det.	.50
☐	83	Danny Gare, Det.	.50
☐	84	Gilles Gilbert (G), Det., LC	.30
☐	85	Willie Huber, Det.	.30
☐	86	Greg Joly, Det., LC	.30
☐	87	Mark Kirton, Det.	.30
☐	88	Reed Larson, Det.	.30
☐	89	In Action: Reed Larson, Det.	.30
☐	90	Reggie Leach, Det., LC	.30
☐	91	Walt McKechnie, Det., LC	.30
☐	92	John Ogrodnick, Det.	.30
☐	**93**	**Mark Osborne, Det., RC**	**.50**
☐	94	Jim Schoenfeld, Det.	.50

	No.	Player	Price
☐	95	Derek Smith, Det., LC	.30
☐	96	Greg Smith, Det.	.30
☐	97	Eric Vail, Det., LC	.30
☐	98	Paul Woods, Det.	.30
☐	99	TL: Wayne Gretzky, Edm.	6.00
☐	100	Glenn Anderson, Edm.	4.00
☐	101	Paul Coffey, Edm.	18.00
☐	102	In Action: Paul Coffey, Edm.	7.50
☐	103	Brett Callighen, Edm., LC	.30
☐	104	Lee Fogolin, Edm.	.30
☐	**105**	**Grant Fuhr (G), Edm., RC**	**30.00**
☐	106	Wayne Gretzky, Edm.	50.00
☐	107	In Action: Wayne Gretzky, Edm.	20.00
☐	108	Matti Hagman, Edm., LC	.30
☐	109	Pat Hughes, Edm.	.30
☐	110	Dave Hunter, Edm.	.30
☐	111	Jari Kurri, Edm.	8.50
☐	112	Ron Low (G), Edm.	.50
☐	113	Kevin Lowe, Edm.	2.00
☐	114	Dave Lumley, Edm.	.30
☐	115	Ken Linseman, Edm.	.30
☐	116	Garry Larivière, Edm., LC	.30
☐	117	Mark Messier, Edm.	25.00
☐	**118**	**Tom Roulston, Edm., RC**	**.30**
☐	119	Dave Semenko, Edm., LC	.30
☐	120	Garry Unger, Edm., LC	.50
☐	121	Checklist 1(1 - 132)	4.00
☐	122	TL: Blaine Stoughton, Hfd.	.30
☐	**123**	**Ron Francis, Hfd., RC**	**25.00**
☐	**124**	**Chris Kotsopoulos, Hfd., RC**	**.30**
☐	125	Pierre Larouche, Hfd.	.30
☐	126	Greg Millen (G), Hfd.	.50
☐	127	Warren Miller, Hfd., LC	.30
☐	128	Merlin Malinowski, Hfd.	.30
☐	129	Risto Siltanen, Hfd.	.30
☐	130	Blaine Stoughton, Hfd.	.30
☐	131	In Action: Blaine Stoughton, Hfd.	.30
☐	132	Doug Sulliman, Hfd.	.30
☐	**133**	**Blake Wesley, Hfd., RC**	**.30**
☐	134	TL: Steve Tambellini, N.J.	.30
☐	**135**	**Brent Ashton, N.J., RC**	**.30**
☐	**136**	**Aaron Broten, N.J., RC**	**.50**
☐	**137**	**Joe Cirella, N.J., RC**	**.50**
☐	138	Dwight Foster, N.J. (Det.)	.30
☐	139	Paul Gagné, N.J.	.30
☐	140	Garry Howatt, N.J.	.30
☐	141	Don Lever, N.J.	.30
☐	142	Bob Lorimer, N.J.	.30
☐	143	Bob MacMillan, N.J.	.30
☐	**144**	**Rick Meagher, N.J., RC**	**.50**
☐	145	Glenn Resch (G), N.J.	.50
☐	146	In Action: Glenn Resch (G), N.J.	.50
☐	147	Steve Tambellini, N.J., LC	.30
☐	148	Carol Vadnais, N.J., LC	.30
☐	149	TL: Marcel Dionne, L.A.	.65
☐	**150**	**Dan Bonar, L.A., RC, LC**	**.30**
☐	**151**	**Steve Bozek, L.A., RC**	**.30**
☐	152	Marcel Dionne, L.A.	1.50
☐	153	In Action: Marcel Dionne, L.A.	.65
☐	154	Jim Fox, L.A.	.30
☐	**155**	**Mark Hardy, L.A., RC**	**.30**
☐	156	Mario Lessard (G), L.A., LC	.50
☐	157	Dave Lewis, L.A.	.50
☐	158	Larry Murphy, L.A.	4.00
☐	159	Charlie Simmer, L.A.	.50
☐	**160**	**Doug Smith, L.A., RC**	**.30**
☐	161	Dave Taylor, L.A.	.50
☐	162	TL: Dino Ciccarelli, Min.	1.50
☐	163	Don Beaupré (G), Min.	1.25
☐	**164**	**Neal Broten, Min., RC**	**4.50**
☐	165	Dino Ciccarelli, Min.	4.50
☐	**166**	**Curt Giles, Min., RC**	**.30**
☐	167	Craig Hartsburg, Min.	.50
☐	168	Brad Maxwell, Min.	.30
☐	169	Tom McCarthy, Min.	.30
☐	170	Gilles Meloche (G), Min.	.50
☐	171	Al MacAdam, Min.	.30
☐	172	Steve Payne, Min.	.30
☐	173	Willi Plett, Min.	.30
☐	174	Gord Roberts, Min.	.30
☐	175	Bobby Smith, Min.	.50
☐	176	In Action: Bobby Smith, Min.	.50
☐	177	Tim Young, Min.	.30
☐	178	TL: Mark Napier, Mtl.	.30
☐	179	Keith Acton, Mtl.	.30
☐	180	In Action: Keith Acton, Mtl.	.30
☐	181	Bob Gainey, Mtl.	.75
☐	182	Gaston Gingras, Mtl.	.30
☐	183	Rick Green, Mtl.	.30
☐	184	Réjean Houle, Mtl., LC	.30
☐	**185**	**Mark Hunter, Mtl., RC**	**.30**
☐	186	Guy Lafleur, Mtl.	4.50
☐	187	In Action: Guy Lafleur, Mtl.	1.50
☐	188	Pierre Mondou, Mtl.	.30
☐	189	Mark Napier, Mtl.	.30
☐	190	Robert Picard, Mtl.	.30
☐	191	Larry Robinson, Mtl.	.75
☐	192	Steve Shutt, Mtl.	.50
☐	193	Mario Tremblay, Mtl.	.30
☐	194	Ryan Walter, Mtl.	.30
☐	**195**	**Rick Wamsley (G), Mtl., RC**	**1.25**
☐	196	Doug Wickenheiser, Mtl.	.30
☐	197	TL: Mike Bossy, NYI.	1.25
☐	198	Bob Bourne, NYI.	.30
☐	199	Mike Bossy, NYI.	4.00
☐	200	Butch Goring, NYI.	.50
☐	201	Clark Gillies, NYI.	.50
☐	**202**	**Tomas Jonsson, NYI., RC**	**.50**
☐	203	Anders Kallur, NYI., LC	.30
☐	204	Dave Langevin, NYI.	.30
☐	205	Wayne Merrick, NYI., LC	.30
☐	206	Ken Morrow, NYI.	.30
☐	207	Mike McEwen, NYI., LC	.30
☐	208	Bob Nystrom, NYI.	.30
☐	209	Stefan Persson, NYI.	.30
☐	210	Denis Potvin, NYI.	.75
☐	211	Billy Smith (G), NYI.	.75
☐	212	Duane Sutter, NYI.	.50
☐	213	John Tonelli, NYI.	.50
☐	214	Bryan Trottier, NYI.	2.00
☐	215	In Action: Bryan Trottier, NYI.	.75
☐	**216**	**Brent Sutter, NYI., RC**	**2.50**
☐	217	TL: Ron Duguay, NYR.	.30
☐	218	Kent-Erik Andersson, Min. (NYR.), LC	.30
☐	219	Barry Beck, NYR.	.30
☐	220	In Action: Barry Beck, NYR.	.30
☐	221	Ron Duguay, NYR.	.30
☐	222	Nick Fotiu, NYR.	.30
☐	223	Robbie Ftorek, NYR.	.50
☐	224	Ron Greschner, NYR.	.30
☐	225	Anders Hedberg, NYR.	.50
☐	226	Eddie Johnstone, NYR.	.30
☐	227	Tom Laidlaw, NYR.	.30
☐	228	Dave Maloney, NYR.	.30
☐	229	Don Maloney, NYR.	.30
☐	230	Ed Mio (G), NYR.	.50
☐	**231**	**Mark Pavelich, NYR., RC**	**.30**
☐	232	Mike Rogers, NYR.	.30
☐	**233**	**Reijo Ruotsalainen, NYR., RC**	**.50**
☐	**234**	**Steve Weeks (G), NYR., RC**	**.50**
☐	235	LL: Wayne Gretzky, Edm.	6.00
☐	236	LL: Paul Gardner, Pgh.	.30
☐	237	LL: Wayne Gretzky/Michel Goulet	6.00
☐	238	LL: Paul Baxter, Pgh.	.30
☐	239	LL: Denis Herron, Mtl.	.50
☐	240	LL: Wayne Gretzky, Edm.	6.00
☐	241	LL: Denis Herron, Mtl.	.50
☐	242	LL: Wayne Gretzky, Edm.	6.00
☐	243	LL: Wayne Gretzky, Edm.	6.00
☐	244	TL: Bill Barber, Pha.	.50
☐	**245**	**Fred Arthur, Pha., RC, LC**	**.30**
☐	246	Bill Barber, Pha.	.50
☐	247	In Action: Bill Barber, Pha.	.50
☐	248	Bobby Clarke, Pha.	1.50
☐	**249**	**Ron Flockhart, Pha., RC**	**.30**
☐	250	Tom Gorence, Pha., LC	.30
☐	251	Paul Holmgren, Pha.	.30
☐	252	Mark Howe, Pha.	.50
☐	253	Tim Kerr, Pha.	.75
☐	254	Brad Marsh, Pha.	.50
☐	255	Brad McCrimmon, Pha.	1.25
☐	256	Brian Propp, Pha.	.50
☐	257	Darryl Sittler, Pha.	.50
☐	258	Rick St. Croix (G), Pha.	.50
☐	259	Jimmy Watson, Pha., LC	.30
☐	260	Behn Wilson, Pha., LC	.30
☐	261	Checklist 2 (133 - 264)	4.00
☐	262	TL: Mike Bullard, Pgh.	.50
☐	263	Pat Boutette, Pgh.	.30
☐	**264**	**Mike Bullard, Pgh., RC**	**.50**
☐	265	Randy Carlyle, Pgh.	.30
☐	266	In Action: Randy Carlyle, Pgh.	.30
☐	267	Michel Dion (G), Pgh.	.50
☐	268	George Ferguson, Pgh. (Min.)	.30
☐	269	Paul Gardner, Pgh.	.30
☐	270	Denis Herron (G), Pgh.	.50
☐	271	Rick Kehoe, Pgh.	.50
☐	272	Greg Malone, Pgh.	.30
☐	273	Rick MacLeish, Pgh., LC	.30
☐	274	Pat Price, Pgh.	.30
☐	275	Ron Stackhouse, Pgh., LC	.30
☐	276	TL: Peter Stastny, Que.	1.50
☐	**277**	**Pierre Aubry, Que., RC**	**.30**
☐	278	Dan Bouchard (G), Que.	.50
☐	279	Réal Cloutier, Que.	.30
☐	280	In Action: Réal Cloutier, Que.	.30
☐	281	Alain Côté, Que.	.30
☐	282	André Dupont, Que., LC	.30
☐	283	John Garrett (G), Que.	.50
☐	284	Michel Goulet, Que.	2.50
☐	285	Dale Hunter, Que.	2.50
☐	286	Pierre Lacroix, Que., LC	.30
☐	287	Mario Marois, Que.	.30
☐	288	Wilf Paiement, Que.	.30
☐	289	Dave Pichette, Que.	.30
☐	290	Jacques Richard, Que., LC	.30
☐	**291**	**Normand Rochefort, Que., RC**	**.30**
☐	292	Peter Stastny, Que.	4.00
☐	293	In Action: Peter Stastny, Que.	2.00
☐	294	Anton Stastny, Que.	.30
☐	**295**	**Marian Stastny, Que., RC**	**.30**
☐	296	Marc Tardif, Que.	.30
☐	297	Wally Weir, Que.	.30
☐	298	TL: Brian Sutter, Stl.	.50
☐	299	Wayne Babych, Stl.	.30
☐	300	Jack Brownschidle, Stl.	.30
☐	301	Blake Dunlop, Stl.	.30
☐	302	Bernie Federko, Stl.	.50
☐	303	In Action: Bernie Federko, Stl.	.50
☐	304	Pat Hickey, Stl., LC	.30
☐	305	Guy Lapointe, Stl., LC	.50
☐	306	Mike Liut (G), Stl.	.50
☐	**307**	**Joe Mullen, Stl., RC**	**8.00**
☐	308	Larry Patey, Stl.	.30
☐	309	Jorgen Pettersson, Stl.	.30
☐	310	Rob Ramage, Stl.	.50
☐	311	Brian Sutter, Stl.	.50
☐	312	Perry Turnbull, Stl.	.30
☐	313	Mike Zuke, Stl.	.30
☐	314	TL: Rick Vaive, Tor.	.50
☐	315	John Anderson, Tor.	.30
☐	**316**	**Normand Aubin, Tor., RC, LC**	**.30**
☐	**317**	**Jim Benning, Tor., RC**	**.30**
☐	**318**	**Fred Boimistruck, Tor., RC, LC**	**.30**
☐	319	Bill Derlago, Tor.	.30
☐	320	In Action: Bill Derlago, Tor.	.30
☐	**321**	**Miroslav Frycer, Tor., RC**	**.30**
☐	322	Billy Harris, Tor.	.30
☐	323	James Korn, Tor.	.30
☐	324	Michel Larocque (G), Tor., LC	.50
☐	325	Bob Manno, Tor.	.30
☐	326	Dan Maloney, Tor., LC	.30
☐	**327**	**Bob McGill, Tor., RC**	**.30**
☐	328	Barry Melrose, Tor., LC	.30
☐	329	Terry Martin, Tor.	.30
☐	330	René Robert, Tor., LC	.30
☐	331	Rocky Saganiuk, Tor., LC	.30
☐	332	Borje Salming, Tor.	.50
☐	333	Greg Terrion, Tor. (Tor.)	.30
☐	**334**	**Vincent Tremblay (G), Tor., RC, LC**	**.50**
☐	335	Rick Vaive, Tor.	.50
☐	336	In Action: Rick Vaive, Tor.	.50
☐	337	TL: Thomas Gradin, Van.	.30
☐	338	Ivan Boldirev, Van.	.30
☐	339	Richard Brodeur (G), Van.	.50
☐	340	In Action: Richard Brodeur (G), Van.	.50
☐	341	Tony Currie, Van., LC	.30
☐	**342**	**Marc Crawford, Van., RC, LC**	**2.00**
☐	343	Curt Fraser, Van.	.30
☐	344	Thomas Gradin, Van.	.30
☐	345	In Action: Thomas Gradin, Van.	.30
☐	**346**	**Ivan Hlinka, Van., RC, LC, Error (Jiri Bubla)**	**.30**
☐	347	Ron Delorme, Van.	.30
☐	348	Rick Lanz, Van.	.30
☐	349	Lars Lindgren, Van.	.30

	No.	Player	Price
☐	350	Blair MacDonald, Van., LC	.30
☐	351	Kevin McCarthy, Van.	.30
☐	352	Gerry Minor, Van., LC	.30
☐	**353**	**Lars Molin, Van., RC, LC**	**.30**
☐	**354**	**Gary Lupul, Van., RC**	**.30**
☐	355	Darcy Rota, Van.	.30
☐	356	Stan Smyl, Van.	.50
☐	357	Harold Snepsts, Van.	.50
☐	358	Dave Williams, Van.	.50
☐	359	TL: Dennis Maruk, Wsh.	.30
☐	360	Ted Bulley (Wsh.), LC	.30
☐	**361**	**Bob Carpenter, Wsh., RC**	**1.25**
☐	362	Brian Engblom, Wsh.	.30
☐	363	Mike Gartner, Wsh.	8.00
☐	364	Bengt Gustafsson, Wsh.	.30
☐	365	Doug Hicks, Wsh., LC	.30
☐	366	Ken Houston, Wsh.	.30
☐	367	Doug Jarvis, Mtl., (Wsh.)	.50
☐	368	Rod Langway, Mtl., (Wsh.)	.75
☐	369	Dennis Maruk, Wsh.	.30
☐	370	In Action: Dennis Maruk, Wsh.	.30
☐	**371**	**Dave Parro (G), Wsh., RC, LC**	**.30**
☐	372	Pat Riggin (G), Wsh.	.30
☐	**373**	**Chris Valentine, Wsh., RC, LC**	**.30**
☐	374	TL: Dale Hawerchuk, Wpg.	4.00
☐	375	Dave Babych, Wpg.	.50
☐	376	In Action: Dave Babych, Wpg.	.50
☐	377	Dave Christian, Wpg.	.30
☐	378	Norm Dupont, Wpg., LC	.30
☐	379	Lucien DeBlois, Wpg.	.30
☐	**380**	**Dale Hawerchuk, Wpg., RC**	**15.00**
☐	381	In Action: Dale Hawerchuk, Wpg.	6.00
☐	**382**	**Craig Levie, Wpg., RC, LC**	**.30**
☐	383	Morris Lukowich, Wpg.	.30
☐	384	Willy Lindstrom, Wpg.	.30
☐	**385**	**Bengt Lundholm, Wpg., RC**	**.30**
☐	**386**	**Paul MacLean, Wpg., RC**	**.50**
☐	387	Bryan Maxwell, Wpg., LC	.30
☐	**388**	**Doug Smail, Wpg., RC**	**.30**
☐	389	Doug Soetaert (G), Wpg.	.30
☐	390	Serge Savard, Wpg., LC	.50
☐	**391**	**Thomas Steen, Wpg., RC**	**3.50**
☐	392	Don Spring, Wpg.	.30
☐	393	Ed Staniowski (G), Wpg., LC	.30
☐	394	Tim Trimper, Wpg., LC	.30
☐	**395**	**Tim Watters, Wpg., RC**	**.30**
☐	396	Checklist 3 (265 - 396)	5.00

1982 - 83 O-PEE-CHEE / TOPPS STICKERS

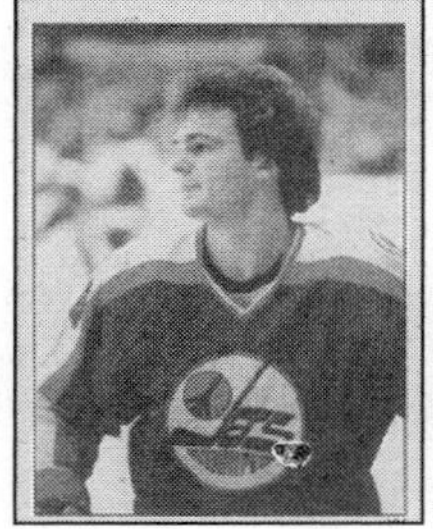

It is believed that some Topps stickers were never issued. Prices for the O-Pee-Chee and Topps stickers are the same.

Sticker Size: 2" x 2 1/2"
Face: Four colour, white border
Back: Black on buff; Number, Name, Team, Bilingual
Imprint:
Complete Set (263 stickers): 50.00
Common Player: .25
Album: (Wayne Gretzky on cover) 6.00

	No.	Player	NRMT-MT
☐☐	1	Conn Smythe Trophy: Mike Bossy, NYI.	.25
☐☐	2	Foil: Conn Smythe Trophy	.25
☐☐	3	1981/82 Stanley Cup Winners: NY Islanders	.25
☐☐	4	1981/82 Stanley Cup Winners: NY Islanders	.25
☐☐	5	Stanley Cup Finals	.25
☐☐	6	Stanley Cup Finals	.25

Note: Stickers 5-6 feature Ken Morrow, Thomas Gradin and Billy Smith

	No.	Player	NRMT-MT
☐☐	7	Richard Brodeur (G)	.35
☐☐	8	Victory	.25
☐☐	9	Curt Fraser, Van.	.25
☐☐	10	Billy Smith (G), NYI.	.35
☐☐	11	Stanley Cup Playoffs	.25
☐☐	12	Stanley Cup Playoffs	.25
☐☐	13	Stanley Cup Playoffs	.25
☐☐	14	Tom Lysiak	.25
☐☐	15	Peter Stastny	.75
☐☐	16	Stanley Cup Playoffs	.25
☐☐	17	Stanley Cup Playoffs	.25
☐☐	18	Butch Goring/Peter Stastny	.35
☐☐	19	Peter Stastny, Que.	.75
☐☐	20	Marian Stastny, Que.	.25
☐☐	21	Marc Tardif, Que.	.25
☐☐	22	Wilf Paiement, Que.	.25
☐☐	23	Réal Cloutier, Que.	.25
☐☐	24	Anton Stastny, Que.	.25
☐☐	25	Michel Goulet, Que.	.75
☐☐	26	Dale Hunter, Que.	.50
☐☐	27	Dan Bouchard (G), Que.	.35
☐☐	28	Guy Lafleur, Mtl.	2.00
☐☐	29	Guy Lafleur (Action), Mtl.	1.00
☐☐	30	Mario Tremblay, Mtl.	.25
☐☐	31	Larry Robinson, Mtl.	.50
☐☐	32	Steve Shutt, Mtl.	.35
☐☐	33	Steve Shutt (Action), Mtl.	.35
☐☐	34	Rod Langway, Mtl.	.35
☐☐	35	Pierre Mondou, Mtl.	.25
☐☐	36	Bob Gainey, Mtl.	.50
☐☐	37	Rick Wamsley (G), Mtl.	.35
☐☐	38	Mark Napier, Mtl.	.25
☐☐	39	Mark Napier (Action), Mtl.	.25
☐☐	40	Doug Jarvis, Mtl.	.35
☐☐	41	Denis Herron (G), Mtl.	.35
☐☐	42	Keith Acton, Mtl.	.25
☐☐	43	Keith Acton (Action), Mtl.	.25
☐☐	44	Foil: Prince of Wales Trophy	.25
☐☐	45	Foil: Prince of Wales Trophy	.25
☐☐	46	Denis Potvin, NYI.	.50
☐☐	47	Bryan Trottier, NYI.	.50
☐☐	48	Bryan Trottier (Action), NYI.	.50
☐☐	49	John Tonelli, NYI.	.35
☐☐	50	Mike Bossy, NYI.	.75
☐☐	51	Mike Bossy (Action), NYI.	.75
☐☐	52	Duane Sutter, NYI.	.35
☐☐	53	Bob Bourne, NYI.	.35
☐☐	54	Clark Gillies, NYI.	.35
☐☐	55	Clark Gillies (Action), NYI.	.35
☐☐	56	Brent Sutter, NYI.	.35
☐☐	57	Anders Kallur, NYI.	.25
☐☐	58	Ken Morrow, NYI.	.25
☐☐	59	Bob Nystrom, NYI.	.35
☐☐	60	Billy Smith (G), NYI.	.50
☐☐	61	Billy Smith (G) (Action), NYI.	.50
☐☐	62	Rick Vaive, Tor.	.35
☐☐	63	Rick Vaive (Action), Tor.	.35
☐☐	64	Jim Benning, Tor.	.25
☐☐	65	Miroslav Frycer, Tor.	.25
☐☐	66	Terry Martin, Tor.	.25
☐☐	67	Bill Derlago, Tor.	.25
☐☐	68	Bill Derlago (Action), Tor.	.25
☐☐	69	Rocky Saganiuk, Tor.	.25
☐☐	70	Vincent Tremblay (G), Tor.	.35
☐☐	71	Bob Manno, Tor.	.25
☐☐	72	Dan Maloney, Tor.	.25
☐☐	73	John Anderson, Tor.	.25
☐☐	74	John Anderson (Action), Tor.	.25
☐☐	75	Borje Salming, Tor.	.35
☐☐	76	Borje Salming (Action), Tor.	.35
☐☐	77	Michel Larocque (G), Tor.	.35
☐☐	78	Rick Middleton, Bos.	.35
☐☐	79	Rick Middleton (Action), Bos.	.35
☐☐	80	Keith Crowder, Bos.	.25
☐☐	81	Steve Kasper, Bos.	.25
☐☐	82	Brad Park, Bos.	.35
☐☐	83	Peter McNab, Bos.	.25
☐☐	84	Peter McNab (Action), Bos.	.25
☐☐	85	Terry O'Reilly, Bos.	.35
☐☐	86	Ray Bourque, Bos.	2.50
☐☐	87	Ray Bourque (Action), Bos.	2.50
☐☐	88	Tom Fergus, Bos.	.25
☐☐	89	Mike O'Connell, Bos.	.25
☐☐	90	Brad McCrimmon, Bos.	.35
☐☐	91	Don Marcotte, Bos.	.25
☐☐	92	Barry Pederson, Bos.	.25
☐☐	93	Barry Pederson (Action), Bos.	.25
☐☐	94	Mark Messier, Edm.	3.00
☐☐	95	Grant Fuhr (G), Edm.	2.00
☐☐	96	Kevin Lowe, Edm.	.35
☐☐	97	Wayne Gretzky, Edm.	8.00
☐☐	98	Wayne Gretzky (Action), Edm.	8.00
☐☐	99	Glenn Anderson, Edm.	.50
☐☐	100	Glenn Anderson (Action), Edm.	.50
☐☐	101	Dave Lumley, Edm.	.25
☐☐	102	Dave Hunter, Edm.	.25
☐☐	103	Matti Hagman, Edm.	.25
☐☐	104	Paul Coffey, Edm.	2.50
☐☐	105	Paul Coffey (Action), Edm.	2.50
☐☐	106	Lee Fogolin, Edm.	.25
☐☐	107	Ron Low (G), Edm.	.35
☐☐	108	Jari Kurri, Edm.	1.00
☐☐	109	Jari Kurri (Action), Edm.	1.00
☐☐	110	Bill Barber, Pha.	.35
☐☐	111	Brian Propp, Pha.	.35
☐☐	112	Ken Linseman, Pha.	.25
☐☐	113	Ron Flockhart, Pha.	.25
☐☐	114	Darryl Sittler, Pha.	.50
☐☐	115	Bobby Clarke, Pha.	.50
☐☐	116	Paul Holmgren, Pha.	.25
☐☐	117	Pete Peeters (G), Pha	.35
☐☐	118	Gilbert Perreault, Buf.	.50
☐☐	119	Dale McCourt, Buf.	.25
☐☐	120	Mike Foligno, Buf.	.25
☐☐	121	John Van Boxmeer, Buf.	.25
☐☐	122	Tony McKegney, Buf.	.25
☐☐	123	Ric Seiling, Buf.	.25
☐☐	124	Don Edwards (G), Buf.	.35
☐☐	125	Yvon Lambert, Buf.	.25
☐☐	126	Blaine Stoughton, Hfd.	.25
☐☐	127	Pierre Larouche, Hfd.	.25
☐☐	128	Doug Sulliman, Hfd.	.25
☐☐	129	Ron Francis, Hfd.	2.50
☐☐	130	Greg Millen (G), Hfd.	.35
☐☐	131	Mark Howe, Hfd.	.35
☐☐	132	Chris Kotsopoulos, Hfd.	.25
☐☐	133	Garry Howatt, Hfd.	.25
☐☐	134	Ron Duguay, NYR.	.25
☐☐	135	Barry Beck, NYR.	.25
☐☐	136	Mike Rogers, NYR.	.25
☐☐	137	Don Maloney, NYR.	.25
☐☐	138	Mark Pavelich, NYR.	.25
☐☐	139	Eddie Johnstone (G), NYR.	.35
☐☐	140	Dave Maloney, NYR.	.25
☐☐	141	Steve Weeks (G), NYR.	.35
☐☐	142	Ed Mio (G), NYR.	.35
☐☐	143	Rick Kehoe, Pgh.	.25
☐☐	144	Randy Carlyle, Pgh.	.35
☐☐	145	Paul Gardner, Pgh.	.25
☐☐	146	Michel Dion (G), Pgh.	.35
☐☐	147	Rick MacLeish, Pgh.	.25
☐☐	148	Pat Boutette, Pgh.	.25
☐☐	149	Mike Bullard, Pgh.	.25
☐☐	150	George Ferguson, Pgh.	.25
☐☐	151	Dennis Maruk, Wsh.	.25
☐☐	152	Ryan Walter, Wsh.	.25
☐☐	153	Mike Gartner, Wsh.	2.00
☐☐	154	Bob Carpenter, Wsh.	.25
☐☐	155	Chris Valentine, Wsh.	.25
☐☐	156	Rick Green, Wsh.	.25
☐☐	157	Bengt Gustafsson, Wsh.	.25
☐☐	158	Dave Parro (G), Wsh.	.25
☐☐	159	AS: Foil: Mark Messier, Edm.	3.00

	No.	Player	Price
☐☐	160	AS: Foil: Paul Coffey, Edm.	2.50
☐☐	161	AS: Foil: Grant Fuhr (G), Edm.	2.00
☐☐	162	AS: Foil: Wayne Gretzky, Edm.	8.00
☐☐	163	AS: Foil: Doug Wilson, Chi.	.35
☐☐	164	AS: Foil: Dave Taylor, L.A.	.35
☐☐	165	AS: Foil: Mike Bossy, NYI.	.75
☐☐	166	AS: Foil: Ray Bourque, Bos.	2.50
☐☐	167	AS: Foil: Peter Stastny, Que.	.75
☐☐	168	AS: Foil: Michel Dion (G), Pgh.	.35
☐☐	169	AS: Foil: Larry Robinson, Mtl.	.50
☐☐	170	AS: Foil: Bill Barber, Pha.	.35
☐☐	171	Denis Savard, Chi.	1.00
☐☐	172	Doug Wilson, Chi.	.35
☐☐	173	Grant Mulvey, Chi.	.25
☐☐	174	Tom Lysiak, Chi.	.25
☐☐	175	Al Secord, Chi.	.25
☐☐	176	Reg Kerr, Chi.	.25
☐☐	177	Tim Higgins, Chi.	.25
☐☐	178	Terry Ruskowski, Chi.	.25
☐☐	179	John Ogrodnick, Det.	.25
☐☐	180	Reed Larson, Det.	.25
☐☐	181	Bob Sauvé (G), Det.	.35
☐☐	182	Mark Osborne, Det.	.25
☐☐	183	Jim Schoenfeld, Det.	.35
☐☐	184	Danny Gare, Det.	.35
☐☐	185	Willie Huber, Det.	.25
☐☐	186	Walt McKechnie, Det.	.25
☐☐	187	Paul Woods, Det.	.25
☐☐	188	Bobby Smith, Min.	.50
☐☐	189	Dino Ciccarelli, Min.	1.00
☐☐	190	Neal Broten, Min.	.75
☐☐	191	Steve Payne, Min.	.25
☐☐	192	Craig Hartsburg, Min.	.35
☐☐	193	Don Beaupré (G), Min.	.35
☐☐	194	Steve Christoff, Min.	.25
☐☐	195	Gilles Meloche (G), Min.	.35
☐☐	196	Mike Liut (G), Stl.	.50
☐☐	197	Bernie Federko, Stl.	.50
☐☐	198	Brian Sutter, Stl.	.50
☐☐	199	Blake Dunlop, Stl.	.25
☐☐	200	Joe Mullen, Stl.	1.00
☐☐	201	Wayne Babych, Stl.	.25
☐☐	202	Jorgen Pettersson, Stl.	.25
☐☐	203	Perry Turnbull, Stl.	.25
☐☐	204	Dale Hawerchuk, Wpg.	2.50
☐☐	205	Morris Lukowich, Wpg.	.25
☐☐	206	Dave Christian, Wpg.	.25
☐☐	207	Dave Babych, Wpg.	.35
☐☐	208	Paul MacLean, Wpg.	.25
☐☐	209	Willy Lindstrom, Wpg.	.25
☐☐	210	Ed Staniowski (G), Wpg.	.35
☐☐	211	Doug Soetaert (G), Wpg.	.35
☐☐	212	Lucien DeBlois, Wpg.	.25
☐☐	213	Mel Bridgman, Cgy.	.25
☐☐	214	Lanny McDonald, Cgy.	.35
☐☐	215	Guy Chouinard, Cgy.	.25
☐☐	216	Jim Peplinski, Cgy.	.25
☐☐	217	Kent Nilsson, Cgy.	.25
☐☐	218	Pekka Rautakallio, Cgy.	.25
☐☐	219	Paul Reinhart, Cgy.	.25
☐☐	220	Kevin LaVallée, Cgy.	.25
☐☐	221	Ken Houston, Cgy.	.25
☐☐	222	Glenn Resch (G), Col.	.35
☐☐	223	Rob Ramage, Col.	.25
☐☐	224	Don Lever, Col.	.25
☐☐	225	Bob MacMillan, Col.	.25
☐☐	226	Steve Tambellini, Col.	.25
☐☐	227	Brent Ashton, Col.	.25
☐☐	228	Bob Lorimer, Col.	.25
☐☐	229	Merlin Malinowski, Col.	.25
☐☐	230	Marcel Dionne, L.A.	.50
☐☐	231	Dave Taylor, L.A.	.35
☐☐	232	Larry Murphy, L.A.	.35
☐☐	233	Steve Bozek, L.A.	.25
☐☐	234	Greg Terrion, L.A.	.25
☐☐	235	Jim Fox, L.A.	.25
☐☐	236	Mario Lessard (G), L.A.	.35
☐☐	237	Charlie Simmer, L.A.	.35
☐☐	238	Foil: Campbell Bowl	.25
☐☐	239	Foil: Campbell Bowl	.25
☐☐	240	Thomas Gradin, Van.	.25
☐☐	241	Ivan Boldirev, Van.	.25
☐☐	242	Stan Smyl, Van.	.35
☐☐	243	Harold Snepsts, Van.	.25
☐☐	244	Curt Fraser, Van.	.25
☐☐	245	Lars Molin, Van.	.25
☐☐	246	Kevin McCarthy, Van.	.25
☐☐	247	Richard Brodeur (G), Van.	.35
☐☐	248	Foil: Calder Trophy	.25
☐☐	249	AW: Dale Hawerchuk, Wpg.	1.00
☐☐	250	Foil: Vezina Trophy	.25
☐☐	251	AW: Billy Smith, NYI.	.35
☐☐	252	AW: Denis Herron/Rick Wamsley, Mtl.	.35
☐☐	253	AW: Steve Kasper, Bos.	.25
☐☐	254	AW: Doug Wilson, Chi.	.35
☐☐	255	Foil: Norris Trophy	.25
☐☐	256	AW: Wayne Gretzky, Edm.	6.00
☐☐	257	AW: Wayne Gretzky	6.00
☐☐	258	AW: Wayne Gretzky	6.00
☐☐	259	AW: Wayne Gretzky	6.00
☐☐	260	Foil: Hart Trophy	.25
☐☐	261	Foil: Art Ross Trophy	.25
☐☐	262	AW: Rick Middleton, Bos.	.25
☐☐	263	Foil: Lady Byng Trophy	.25

1982 - 83 POST

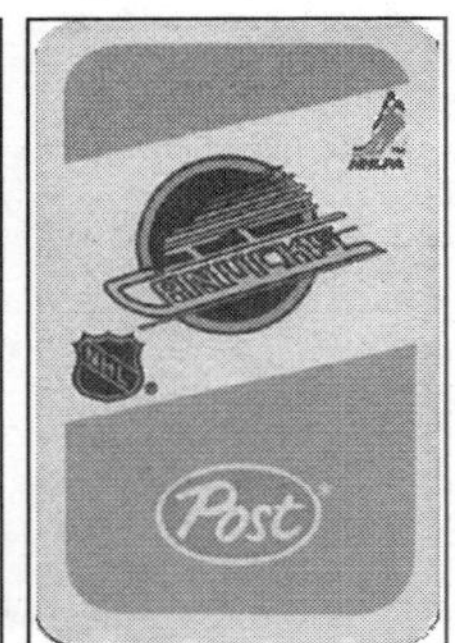

These cards were issued in 16-card strips with Post cereal. Cut-out cards measure 1 5/8" x 2 1/8".

Panel Size: 13 1/4" x 4 1/8"
Face: Four colour, cream border, Player's name and jersey number
Back: Blue, red and white on card stock; Team and sponsor logos
Imprint: None
Complete Set (21 panels): 100.00

	Player	NRMT-MT
☐	Boston Bruins: R. Bourque/ W. Cashman/ B. Crowder/ T. Fergus M. Gillis/ S. Jonathan/ S. Kasper/ B. McCrimmon P. McNab/ L. Melnyk/ R. Middleton/ M. Milbury Mike O'Connell/ T. O'Reilly/ B. Park/ R. Vachon (G)	8.00
☐	Buffalo Sabres: R. Dunn/ D. Edwards (G)/ M. Foligno/ B. Hajt Y. Lambert/ D. McCourt/ T. McKegney/ G. Perreault L. Playfair/ C. Ramsey/ M. Ramsey/ L. Ruff R. Seiling/ J.F. Sauvé/ A. Savard/ J. Van Boxmeer	4.00
☐	Calgary Flames: M. Bridgman/ G. Chouinard/ D. Cyr/ J. Hislop K. Houston/ K. LaValée/ G. McAdam/ L. McDonald B. Murdoch/ K. Nilsson/ J. Peplinski/ W. Plett P. Rautakallio/ P. Reinhart/ P. Riggin (G)/ P. Russell	4.00
☐	Chicago Blackhawks: T. Bulley/ D. Crossman/ T. Esposito (G)/ G. Fox B. Gardner/ T. Higgins/ D. Hutchison/ R. Kerr T. Lysiak/ G. Mulvey/ R. Paterson/ R. Preston T. Ruskowski/ D. Savard/ A. Secord/ D. Wilson	6.00
☐	Colorado Rockies: B. Ashton/ D. Cameron/ J. Cirella/ D. Foster M. Kitchen/ D. Lever/ B. Lorimer/ M. Malinowski B. MacMillan/ K. Maxwell/ J. Micheletti/B. Miller R. Ramage/G. Resch (G)/S. Tambellini/J. Wensink	3.00
☐	Detroit Red Wings: John Barrett/ Mike Blaisdell/ Danny Gare/ Willie Huber Greg Joly/ Mark Kirton/ Reed Larson/ Walt McKechnie V. Nedomansky/ J. Ogrodnick/ M. Osborne/ B. Sauvé (G) J. Schoenfeld/ D. Smith/ G. Smith/ P. Woods	3.00
☐	Edmonton Oilers: G. Anderson/ B. Callighen/ P. Coffey/ L. Fogolin G. Fuhr (G)/ W. Gretzky/ M. Hagman/P. Hughes D. Hunter/ J. Kurri/ G. Larivière/ K. Lowe D. Lumley/ M. Messier/ D. Semenko/ R. Siltanen	25.00
☐	Hartford Whalers: J. Douglas/ R. Francis/ G. Howatt/ M. Howe D. Keon/ C. Kotsopoulos/ P. Larouche/ G. Lyle J. McIlhargey/ G. Millen (G)/ W. Miller/ D. Nachbauer P. Shmyr/ B. Stoughton/ D. Sulliman/ B. Wesley	3.00
☐	Los Angeles Kings: S. Bozek/ R. Chartraw/ M. Dionne/J. Fox M. Hardy/ D. Hopkins/ S. Jensen/J.P. Kelly J. Korab/ M. Lessard (G)/ D. Lewis/ L. Murphy C. Simmer/ D. Smith/ D. Taylor/ J. Wells	4.00
☐	Minnesota North Stars: K. E. Andersson/ F. Barrett/ S. Christoff/ D. Ciccarelli C. Giles/ C. Hartsburg/ B. Maxwell/ A. MacAdam T. McCarthy/ G. Meloche (G)/ B. Palmer/ S. Payne G. Roberts/ G. Sargent/ B. Smith/ T. Young	3.00
☐	Montréal Canadiens: K. Acton/ B. Engblom/ B. Gainey/ M. Hunter Doug Jarvis/ Guy Lafleur/ Rod Langway/ Craig Laughlin P. Mondou/ M. Napier/ R. Picard/ D. Risebrough L. Robinson/ R. Sévigny (G)/ S. Shutt/ M. Tremblay	10.00
☐	New York Islanders: M. Bossy/ B. Bourne/ C. Gillies/ B. Goring A. Kallur/T. Jonsson/ D. Langevin/ M. McEwen W. Merrick/ K. Morrow/ B. Nystrom/ S. Persson D. Potvin/ B. Smith (G)/ J. Tonelli/ B. Trottier	10.00
☐	New York Rangers: M. Allison/ B. Beck/ A. Dore/ R. Duguay N. Fotiu/ R. Ftorek/ R. Greschner/ E. Johnstone T. Laidlaw/ D. Maloney/ D. Maloney/ M. Pavelich/ M. Rogers/ R. Ruotsalainen/ S. Weeks (G)/ S. Vickers	3.00
☐	Philadelphia Flyers F. Arthur/ R. Bailey/ B. Barber/ B. Clarke G. Cochrane/ P. Holmgren/ T. Kerr/ R. Leach K. Linsemam/ B. Marsh/ P. Peeters (G)/ I. Sinisalo D. Sittler/ B. Prop/ Ji. Watson/ B. Wilson	5.00
☐	Pittsburgh Penguins P. Baxter/ P. Boutette/ M. Bullard/ R. Carlyle M. Chorney/ M. Dion (G)/ G. Ferguson/ P. Gardner P. Graham/ R. Kehoe/ P. Lee/ G. Malone P. Price/ D. Shedden/ G. Sheppard/ R. Stackhouse	3.00
☐	Québec Nordiques: R. Cloutier/ A. Côté/ A. Dupont/ J. Garrett (G) J. Gillis/ M. Goulet/ . Hunter/ M. Marois W. Paiement/ J. Richard/ N. Rochefort/ A. Stastny M. Stastny/ P. Stastny/ M. Tardif/ W. Weir	5.00
☐	St. Louis Blues: W. Babych/ B. Baker/ J. Brownschidle/ M. Crombeen B. Dunlop/ B. Federko/ E. Kea/ R. Lapointe G. Lapointe/ M. Liut (G)/ L. Patey/ J. Pavese J. Pettersson/ B. Sutter/ P. Turnbull/ M. Zuke	3.00
☐	Toronto Maple Leafs: J. Anderson/ N. Aubin/ J. Benning/ F. Boimistruck B. Derlago/ M. Frycer/ S. Gavin/ M. Larocque (G) B. Manno/ T. Martin/ B. McGill/ B. Melrose W. Poddubny/ R. Saganiuk/ B. Salming/ R. Vaive	4.00
☐	Vancouver Canucks: I. Boldirev/ R. Brodeur (G)/ M. Crawford/ R. Delorme C. Fraser/ T. Gradin/ D. Halward/ I. Hlinka L. Lindgren/ G. Lupul/ K. McCarthy/ L. Molin D. Rota/ S. Smyl/ H. Snepsts/ D. Williams	3.00
☐	Washington Capitals: B. Carpenter/ G. Currie/ G. Duchesne/ M. Gartner B. Gould/ R. Green/ B. Gustafsson/ D. Hicks R. Holt/ A. Jensen (G)/ D. Maruk/ T. Murray G. Theberge/ C. Valentine/ D. Veitch/ R. Walter	4.00
☐	Winnipeg Jets: S. Arniel/ D. Babych/ D. Christian/ L. DeBlois N. Dupont/ D. Hawerchuk/ W. Lindstrom/ B. Lundholm M. Lukowich/ P. MacLean/ B. Maxwell/ S. Savard D. Spring/ E. Staniowski (G)/ T. Trimper/ T. Watters	4.00

1982 - 83 STATER MINT HOCKEY DOLLARS

Each cupro-nickel coin came with a 3" x 8 3/8" perforated card. Apparently 110,000 coins were produced of Lanny McDonald while only 20,000 coins were produced of the other five Flames. Other singles may exist.

Coin Diameter: 1 1/4"
Face: Player portrait, name
Back Team logo
Imprint: None

	No.	Player	NRMT-MT
☐	1	Mel Bridgman, Cgy.	3.00
☐	2	Don Edwards (G), Cgy.	4.00
☐	3	Lanny McDonald, Cgy.	5.00
☐	4	Kent Nilsson, Cgy.	4.00
☐	5	Jim Peplinski, Cgy.	3.00
☐	6	Paul Reinhart, Cgy.	3.00

1983 CANADIAN JUNIOR TEAM POSTCARDS

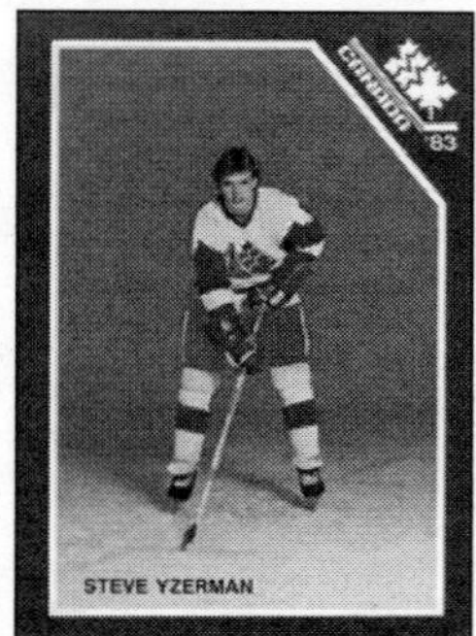

Card Size: 3 9/16" x 5"
Face: Four colour, red border; Name
Back: Blank
Imprint: None
Complete Set (21 cards): 150.00

	Player	NRMT-MT
☐	Title Card	1.00
☐	Dave Andreychuk	10.00
☐	Joe Cirella	2.00
☐	Paul Cyr	1.00
☐	Dale Derkatch	1.00
☐	Mike Eagles	1.00
☐	Pat Flately	3.00
☐	Mario Gosselin (G)	1.50
☐	Gary Leeman	2.00
☐	Mario Lemieux	90.00
☐	Mark Morrison	1.00
☐	James Patrick	3.00
☐	Mike Sands (G)	1.50
☐	Gord Sherven	1.00
☐	Tony Tanti	2.00
☐	Larry Trader	1.00
☐	Sylvain Turgeon	2.00
☐	Pat Verbeek	5.00
☐	Mike Vernon (G)	15.00
☐	Steve Yzerman	50.00
☐	Canada's National Junior Team	5.00

LARGE POSTCARDS

	Player	NRMT-MT
☐	1982 Champions 9 3/4" x 7 3/16"	10.00
☐	1982 Celebration 5" x 7 3/16"	10.00

1983 HOCKEY HALL OF FAME POSTCARDS

These cards were produced by Cartophilium with artwork by Carlton McDiarmid and write-ups by Lefty Reid of the Hockey Hall of Fame. This set consists of 15 subseries of 16 players elected to the Hockey Hall of Fame.

Card Size: 4" x 6"
Face: Four colour, white border; Name
Back: Black on white card stock; Name, Resume, Number, Bilingual
Imprint: HOCKEY HALL OF FAME / C. McDIARMID/CARTOPHILIUM 1983 Printed in Canada/Imprimé au Canada
Complete Set (240 cards): 450.00
Common Player: 1.50

	No.	Player	NRMT-MT
☐	A1	Sid Abel	3.00
☐	A2	Harry Broadbent	3.00
☐	A3	Clarence Campbell	1.50
☐	A4	Neil Colville	1.50
☐	A5	Charlie Conacher	5.00
☐	A6	Red Dutton	1.50
☐	A7	Foster Hewitt	3.00
☐	A8	Fred Hume	1.50
☐	A9	Mickey Ion	1.50
☐	A10	Ernest (Moose) Johnson	1.50
☐	A11	Bill Mosienko	1.50
☐	A12	Maurice Richard	15.00
☐	A13	Russell (Barney) Stanley	1.50
☐	A14	Lord Stanley	1.50
☐	A15	Fred Taylor	3.00
☐	A16	Tiny Thompson (G)	3.00
☐	B1	Donald Bain	1.50
☐	B2	Hobey Baker	1.50
☐	B3	Frank Calder	1.50
☐	B4	Frank Foyston	1.50
☐	B5	James Hendy	1.50
☐	B6	Gordie Howe	18.00
☐	B7	Harry Lumley (G)	3.00
☐	B8	Reg Noble	1.50
☐	B9	Frank Patrick	1.50
☐	B10	Harvey Pulford	1.50
☐	B11	Ken Reardon	1.50
☐	B12	Joe Simpson	1.50
☐	B13	Conn Smythe	1.50
☐	B14	Red Storey	1.50
☐	B15	Lloyd Turner	1.50
☐	B16	Georges Vézina (G)	12.00
☐	C1	Jean Béliveau	12.00
☐	C2	Max Bentley	2.50
☐	C3	Francis Clancy	6.00
☐	C4	Babe Dye	1.50
☐	C5	Ebbie Goodfellow	1.50
☐	C6	Charles Hay	1.50
☐	C7	Percy Lesueur (G)	3.00
☐	C8	Tommy Lockhart	1.50
☐	C9	Jack Marshall	1.50
☐	C10	Lester Patrick	3.00
☐	C11	Bill Quackenbush	1.50
☐	C12	Frank Selke	1.50
☐	C13	Cooper Smeaton	1.50
☐	C14	Hooley Smith	1.50
☐	C15	James T. Sutherland	1.50
☐	C16	Fred Whitcroft	1.50
☐	D1	Charles Adams	1.50
☐	D2	Russell Bowie	1.50
☐	D3	Frank Frederickson	1.50
☐	D4	Billy Gilmour	1.50
☐	D5	Ivan (Ching) Johnson	3.00
☐	D6	Tom Johnson	1.50
☐	D7	Aurel Joliat	7.50
☐	D8	Duke Keats	1.50
☐	D9	Red Kelly	3.00
☐	D10	Frank McGee	1.50
☐	D11	James D. Norris	1.50
☐	D12	Philip Ross	1.50
☐	D13	Terry Sawchuk (G)	12.00
☐	D14	Babe Siebert	1.50
☐	D15	Anatoli V. Tarasov	1.50
☐	D16	Roy Worters (G)	3.00
☐	E1	T. Franklin Ahearn	1.50
☐	E2	Harold Ballard	3.00
☐	E3	Billy Burch	1.50
☐	E4	Bill Chadwick	1.50
☐	E5	Sprague Cleghorn	3.00
☐	E6	Rusty Crawford	1.50
☐	E7	Alex Delvecchio	4.00
☐	E8	George Dudley	1.50
☐	E9	Ted Kennedy	5.00
☐	E10	Edouard Lalonde	4.00
☐	E11	Billy McGimsie	1.50
☐	E12	Frank Nighbor	3.00
☐	E13	Bobby Orr	20.00
☐	E14	Sen. Donat Raymond	1.50
☐	E15	Art Ross	3.00
☐	E16	Jack Walker	1.50
☐	F1	Doug Bentley	3.00
☐	F2	Walter Brown	1.50
☐	F3	Dit Clapper	3.00
☐	F4	Hap Day	1.50
☐	F5	Frank Dilio	1.50
☐	F6	Bobby Hewitson	1.50
☐	F7	Harry Howell	1.50
☐	F8	Paul Loicq	1.50
☐	F9	Sylvio Mantha	1.50
☐	F10	Jacques Plante (G)	12.00
☐	F11	George Richardson	1.50
☐	F12	Nels Stewart	3.00
☐	F13	Hod Stuart	1.50
☐	F14	Harry Trihey	1.50
☐	F15	Marty Walsh	1.50
☐	F16	Arthur Wirtz	1.50
☐	G1	Toe Blake	3.00
☐	G2	Frank Boucher	3.00
☐	G3	Turk Broda (G)	6.00
☐	G4	Harry Cameron	1.50
☐	G5	Leo Dandurand	1.50
☐	G6	Joe Hall	1.50
☐	G7	George Hay	1.50
☐	G8	William A. Hewitt	1.50
☐	G9	Bouse Hutton	1.50
☐	G10	Dick Irvin	1.50
☐	G11	Henri Richard	5.00
☐	G12	John Ross Robertson	1.50
☐	G13	Frank D. Smith	1.50
☐	G14	Allan Stanley	1.50
☐	G15	Norm Ullman	1.50
☐	G16	Harry Watson	1.50
☐	H1	Clint Benedict (G)	3.00
☐	H2	Richard Boon	1.50
☐	H3	Gordie Drillon	3.00
☐	H4	Bill Gadsby	1.50
☐	H5	Rod Gilbert	1.50
☐	H6	Francis (Moose) Goheen	1.50
☐	H7	Tommy Gorman	1.50
☐	H8	Glenn Hall (G)	7.50
☐	H9	Red Horner	1.50
☐	H10	John Kilpatrick	1.50
☐	H11	Robert LeBel	1.50
☐	H12	Howie Morenz	15.00
☐	H13	Fred Scanlan	1.50
☐	H14	Tommy Smith	1.50
☐	H15	Fred C. Waghorne	1.50
☐	H16	Cooney Weiland	1.50
☐	I1	Weston W. Adams	1.50
☐	I2	Montagu Allan	1.50
☐	I3	Frankie Brimsek (G)	4.00
☐	I4	Angus Campbell	1.50
☐	I5	Bill Cook	3.00
☐	I6	Tommy Dunderdale	1.50
☐	I7	Emile Francis	1.50
☐	I8	Chuck Gardiner (G)	3.00
☐	I9	Elmer Lach	1.50
☐	I10	Frank Mahovlich	5.00
☐	I11	Didier Pitre	1.50
☐	I12	Joe Primeau	3.00
☐	I13	Frank Rankin	1.50
☐	I14	Ernie Russell	1.50
☐	I15	W. Thayer Tutt	1.50
☐	I16	Harry Westwick	1.50
☐	J1	Jack J. Adams	1.50
☐	J2	J. Frank Ahearne	1.50
☐	J3	J.P. Bickell	1.50
☐	J4	John Bucyk	3.00
☐	J5	Art Coulter	1.50
☐	J6	Graham Drinkwater	1.50
☐	J7	George Hainsworth (G)	4.00
☐	J8	Tim Horton	6.00
☐	J9	Frederic McLaughlin	1.50
☐	J10	Dickie Moore	3.00
☐	J11	Pierre Pilote	1.50
☐	J12	Claude Robinson	1.50
☐	J13	Sweeny Schriner	1.50
☐	J14	Oliver Seibert	1.50
☐	J15	Albert Smith	1.50
☐	J16	Phat Wilson	1.50
☐	K1	Yvan Cournoyer	3.00
☐	K2	Scotty Davidson	1.50
☐	K3	Cy Denneny	3.00
☐	K4	Bill Durnan (G)	4.00
☐	K5	Wilf (Shorty) Green	1.50
☐	K6	Riley Hern (G)	3.00
☐	K7	Bryan Hextall, Sr.	1.50
☐	K8	Bill Jennings	1.50
☐	K9	Gordon W. Juckes	1.50
☐	K10	Paddy Moran (G)	3.00
☐	K11	James D. Norris	1.50
☐	K12	Harry Oliver	1.50
☐	K13	Sam Pollock	1.50

	No.	Player	Price
☐	K14	Marcel Pronovost	1.50
☐	K15	Jack Ruttan	1.50
☐	K16	Earl Seibert	1.50
☐	L1	Buck Boucher	1.50
☐	L2	George V. Brown	1.50
☐	L3	Arthur F. Farrell	1.50
☐	L4	Herb Gardiner	1.50
☐	L5	Si Griffis	1.50
☐	L6	Harry Holmes (G)	3.00
☐	L7	Harry Hyland	1.50
☐	L8	Tommy Ivan	1.50
☐	L9	Jack Laviolette	1.50
☐	L10	Ted Lindsay	5.00
☐	L11	Francis Nelson	1.50
☐	L12	William Northey	1.50
☐	L13	Babe Pratt	1.50
☐	L14	Chuck Rayner (G)	3.00
☐	L15	Mike Rodden	1.50
☐	L16	Milt Schmidt	3.00
☐	M1	Emile (Butch) Bouchard	1.50
☐	M2	Jack Butterfield	1.50
☐	M3	Joseph Cattarinich (G)	3.00
☐	M4	Alex Connell (G)	3.00
☐	M5	Bill Cowley	2.50
☐	M6	Chaucer Elliott	1.50
☐	M7	Jimmy Gardner	1.50
☐	M8	Bernie Geoffrion	5.00
☐	M9	Tom Hooper	1.50
☐	M10	Syd Howe	1.50
☐	M11	Harvey Jackson	3.00
☐	M12	Al Leader	1.50
☐	M13	Kevin Maxwell	1.50
☐	M14	Blair Russell	1.50
☐	M15	Bill Wirtz	1.50
☐	M16	Gump Worsley (G)	5.00
☐	N1	George Armstrong	3.00
☐	N2	Ace Bailey	4.00
☐	N3	Jack Darragh	1.50
☐	N4	Ken Dryden (G)	12.00
☐	N5	Eddie Gerard	1.50
☐	N6	Jack Gibson	1.50
☐	N7	Hugh Lehman (G)	3.00
☐	N8	Mickey MacKay	1.50
☐	N9	Joe Malone	1.50
☐	N10	Bruce A. Norris	3.00
☐	N11	J.A. O'Brien	1.50
☐	N12	Lynn Patrick	1.50
☐	N13	Tommy Phillips	1.50
☐	N14	Allan W. Pickard	1.50
☐	N15	Jack Stewart	1.50
☐	N16	Frank Udvari	1.50
☐	O1	Syl Apps	3.00
☐	O2	John Ashley	1.50
☐	O3	Marty Barry	1.50
☐	O4	Andy Bathgate	1.50
☐	O5	Johnny Bower (G)	5.00
☐	O6	Frank Buckland	1.50
☐	O7	James Dunn	1.50
☐	O8	Mike Grant	1.50
☐	O9	Doug Harvey	5.00
☐	O10	George McNamara	1.50
☐	O11	Stan Mikita	5.00
☐	O12	Sen. H. de M. Molson	1.50
☐	O13	Gordon Roberts	1.50
☐	O14	Eddie Shore	12.00
☐	O15	Bruce Stuart	1.50
☐	O16	Carl Voss	1.50

1983 AND 1987 HOCKEY HALL OF FAME

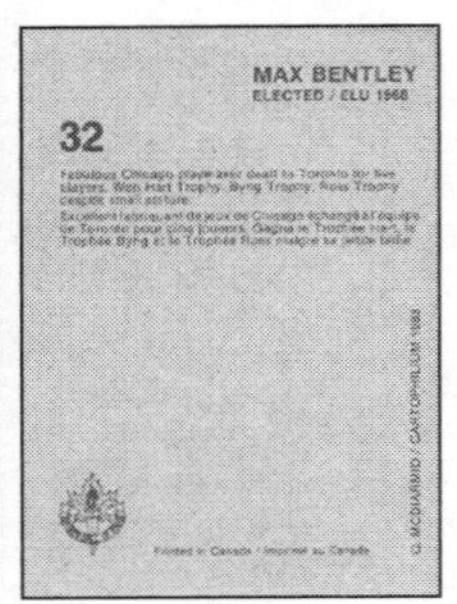

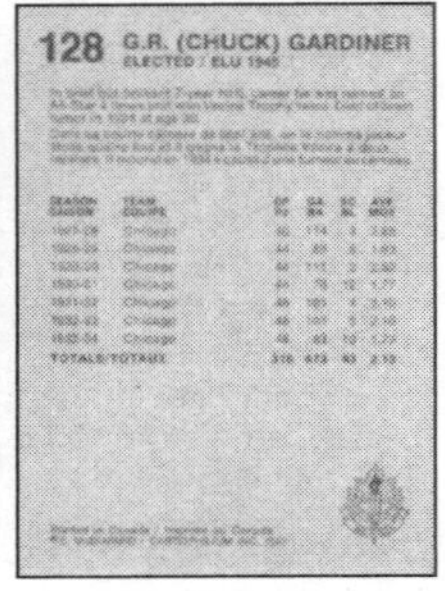

The first series was released in 1983. The second set was released in 1987 and added another 21 cards to include Hall of Fame inductees after 1983. The two sets are distinguished by the copyright year marked on the backs of the cards. The 1987 series also includes career statistics. Colour artwork interpretations were supplied by Carlton McDiarmid. Prices for the 1983 copyright and 1987 copyright are the same.

Card Size: 2 1/2" x 3 1/2"
Face: Four colour
Back: Black and white; Name, Resume, Bilingual
1983 Imprint: C. McDIARMID/CARTOPHILIUM 1983
1987 Imprint: © C. McDIARMID/CARTOPHILIUM INC. 1987

1983 Set (240 cards):	**80.00**
1987 Set (261 cards):	**100.00**
Common Player:	**.75**

	No.	**Player**	**NRMT-MT**
☐ ☐	1	Maurice Richard, Mtl.	7.50
☐ ☐	2	Sid Abel	1.50
☐ ☐	3	Punch Broadbent, OH.	1.50
☐ ☐	4	Clarence Campbell	.75
☐ ☐	5	Neil Colville, NYR.	.75
☐ ☐	6	Charlie Conacher, Tor.	2.50
☐ ☐	7	Red Dutton, NYA.	.75
☐ ☐	8	Foster Hewitt	1.50
☐ ☐	9	Mickey Ion, Referee	.75
☐ ☐	10	Ernest (Moose) Johnson	.75
☐ ☐	11	Bill Mosienko, Chi.	.75
☐ ☐	12	Russell (Barney) Stanley	.75
☐ ☐	13	Lord Stanley	.75
☐ ☐	14	Fred Taylor	1.50
☐ ☐	15	Tiny Thompson (G)	1.50
☐ ☐	16	Gordie Howe, Det.	9.00
☐ ☐	17	Hobey Baker	.75
☐ ☐	18	Frank Calder	.75
☐ ☐	19	Jim Hendy	.75
☐ ☐	20	Frank Foyston, Sea.	.75
☐ ☐	21	Harry Lumley (G)	1.50
☐ ☐	22	Reg Noble, Tor St. Pats.	.75
☐ ☐	23	Frank Patrick, Van.	.75
☐ ☐	24	Harvey Pulford, Ott.	.75
☐ ☐	25	Ken Reardon	.75
☐ ☐	26	Joe Simpson, NYA.	.75
☐ ☐	27	Conn Smythe	.75
☐ ☐	28	Red Storey	.75
☐ ☐	29	Lloyd Turner	.75
☐ ☐	30	Georges Vézina (G), Mtl.	6.00
☐ ☐	31	Jean Béliveau, Mtl.	6.00
☐ ☐	32	Max Bentley, Tor.	1.25
☐ ☐	33	King Clancy, Tor.	3.00
☐ ☐	34	Babe Dye, Tor St. Pats.	.75
☐ ☐	35	Ebbie Goodfellow, Det.	.75
☐ ☐	36	Charles Hay	.75
☐ ☐	37	Percy Lesueur (G)	1.50
☐ ☐	38	Tommy Lockhart	.75
☐ ☐	39	Jack Marshall	.75
☐ ☐	40	Lester Patrick, NYR.	1.50
☐ ☐	41	Frank Selke	.75
☐ ☐	42	Cooper Smeaton	.75
☐ ☐	43	Hooley Smith, Mtl. Maroons	.75
☐ ☐	44	James T. Sutherland	.75
☐ ☐	45	Fred Whitcroft, Kenora	.75
☐ ☐	46	Terry Sawchuk (G)	6.00
☐ ☐	47	Charles Adams, Bos.	.75
☐ ☐	48	Russell Bowie	.75
☐ ☐	49	Frank Frederickson, Error	.75
☐ ☐	50	Billy Gilmour, Ott.	.75
☐ ☐	51	Ching Johnson, NYR.	1.50
☐ ☐	52	Tom Johnson	.75
☐ ☐	53	Aurèle Joliat, Mtl.	4.00
☐ ☐	54	Duke Keats, Chi.	.75
☐ ☐	55	Red Kelly	1.50
☐ ☐	56	Frank McGee	.75
☐ ☐	57	James D. Norris, Det.	.75
☐ ☐	58	Philip Ross, Cup Trustee	.75
☐ ☐	59	Babe Siebert	.75
☐ ☐	60	Roy Worters (G), NYA.	1.50
☐ ☐	61	Bobby Orr, Bos.	10.00
☐ ☐	62	T. Franklin Ahearn	.75
☐ ☐	63	Harold Ballard, Tor.	1.50
☐ ☐	64	Billy Burch	.75
☐ ☐	65	Bill Chadwick	.75
☐ ☐	66	Sprague Cleghorn	1.50
☐ ☐	67	Rusty Crawford	.75
☐ ☐	68	George Dudley, CAHA President	.75
☐ ☐	69	Ted Kennedy	2.50
☐ ☐	70	Edouard Lalonde	2.00
☐ ☐	71	Billy McGimsie	.75
☐ ☐	72	Frank Nighbor, OH.	1.50
☐ ☐	73	Donat Raymond	.75
☐ ☐	74	Art Ross	1.50
☐ ☐	75	Jack Walker, Sea.	.75
☐ ☐	76	Jacques Plante (G)	6.00
☐ ☐	77	Doug Bentley	1.50
☐ ☐	78	Walter Brown	.75
☐ ☐	79	Dit Clapper	1.50
☐ ☐	80	Hap Day	.75
☐ ☐	81	Frank Dilio	.75
☐ ☐	82	Bobby Hewitson	.75
☐ ☐	83	Harry Howell	.75
☐ ☐	84	Sylvio Mantha	.75
☐ ☐	85	George Richardson	.75
☐ ☐	86	Nels Stewart	1.50
☐ ☐	87	Hod Stuart	.75
☐ ☐	88	Harry Trihey	.75
☐ ☐	89	Marty Walsh	.75
☐ ☐	90	Arthur Wirtz, Chi.	.75
☐ ☐	91	Henri Richard	2.50
☐ ☐	92	Toe Blake	1.50
☐ ☐	93	Frank Boucher	1.50
☐ ☐	94	Turk Broda (G)	3.00
☐ ☐	95	Harry Cameron	.75
☐ ☐	96	Leo Dandurand	.75
☐ ☐	97	Joe Hall	.75
☐ ☐	98	George Hay	.75
☐ ☐	99	William A. Hewitt	.75
☐ ☐	100	J.B. Hutton (G), Ott.	.75
☐ ☐	101	Dick Irvin	.75
☐ ☐	102	John Ross Robertson	.75
☐ ☐	103	Frank D. Smith, MTHL Secretary	.75
☐ ☐	104	Norm Ullman	.75
☐ ☐	105	Harry Watson	.75
☐ ☐	106	Howie Morenz	7.50
☐ ☐	107	Clint Benedict (G)	1.50
☐ ☐	108	Richard Boon, Mtl. Wanderers	.75
☐ ☐	109	Gordie Drillon	1.50
☐ ☐	110	Bill Gadsby	.75
☐ ☐	111	Rod Gilbert	.75
☐ ☐	112	Francis (Moose) Goheen	.75
☐ ☐	113	Tommy Gorman	.75
☐ ☐	114	Glenn Hall (G)	4.00
☐ ☐	115	Red Horner	.75
☐ ☐	116	John Kilpatrick, NYR.	.75
☐ ☐	117	Robert LeBel	.75
☐ ☐	118	Fred Scanlan	.75
☐ ☐	119	Fred C. Waghorne	.75
☐ ☐	120	Cooney Weiland	.75
☐ ☐	121	Frank Mahovlich	2.50
☐ ☐	122	Weston W. Adams Sr.	.75
☐ ☐	123	Montagu Allan	.75

	No.	Player	Price
☐☐	124	Frankie Brimsek (G)	2.00
☐☐	125	Angus Campbell	.75
☐☐	126	Bill Cook	1.50
☐☐	127	Tommy Dunderdale	.75
☐☐	128	Chuck Gardiner (G), Chi.	1.50
☐☐	129	Elmer Lach	.75
☐☐	130	Didier Pitre	.75
☐☐	131	Joe Primeau	1.50
☐☐	132	Frank Rankin	.75
☐☐	133	Ernie Russell	.75
☐☐	134	W. Thayer Tutt	.75
☐☐	135	Harry Westwick	.75
☐☐	136	Yvan Cournoyer	1.50
☐☐	137	Scotty Davidson	.75
☐☐	138	Cy Denneny	1.50
☐☐	139	Bill Durnan (G)	2.00
☐☐	140	Wilf (Shorty) Green	.75
☐☐	141	Bryan Hextall, Sr.	.75
☐☐	142	William Jennings	.75
☐☐	143	Gordon W. Juckes	.75
☐☐	144	Paddy Moran (G)	1.50
☐☐	145	James D. Norris	.75
☐☐	146	Harry Oliver	.75
☐☐	147	Sam Pollock	.75
☐☐	148	Marcel Pronovost	.75
☐☐	149	Jack Ruttan	.75
☐☐	150	Earl Seibert	.75
☐☐	151	Ted Lindsay	2.50
☐☐	152	George V. Brown	.75
☐☐	153	Arthur Farrell	.75
☐☐	154	Herb Gardiner	.75
☐☐	155	Si Griffis, Kenora	.75
☐☐	156	Harry Holmes (G)	1.50
☐☐	157	Harry Hyland, Mtl. Wanderers	.75
☐☐	158	Tommy Ivan	.75
☐☐	159	Jack Laviolette	.75
☐☐	160	Francis Nelson, OHA	.75
☐☐	161	William Northey, Mtl. AAA President	.75
☐☐	162	Babe Pratt	.75
☐☐	163	Chuck Rayner (G)	1.50
☐☐	164	Mike Rodden	.75
☐☐	165	Milt Schmidt	1.50
☐☐	166	Bernie Geoffrion	2.50
☐☐	167	Jack Butterfield	.75
☐☐	168	Joseph Cattarinich (G)	1.50
☐☐	169	Alex Connell (G)	1.50
☐☐	170	Bill Cowley	1.25
☐☐	171	Chaucer Elliott	.75
☐☐	172	Jimmy Gardner, Mtl. Wanderers	.75
☐☐	173	Tom Hooper, Kenora	.75
☐☐	174	Syd Howe	.75
☐☐	175	Harvey (Busher) Jackson	1.50
☐☐	176	Al Leader	.75
☐☐	177	Fred Maxwell	.75
☐☐	178	Blair Russell	.75
☐☐	179	Bill Wirtz, Chi.	.75
☐☐	180	Gump Worsley (G)	2.50
☐☐	181	John Bucyk	1.50
☐☐	182	Jack J. Adams	.75
☐☐	183	J. Frank Ahearne, IIHF	.75
☐☐	184	J.P. Bickell	.75
☐☐	185	Art Coulter	.75
☐☐	186	Graham Drinkwater	.75
☐☐	187	George Hainsworth (G)	2.00
☐☐	188	Tim Horton	3.00
☐☐	189	Frederic McLaughlin	.75
☐☐	190	Dickie Moore	1.50
☐☐	191	Pierre Pilote	.75
☐☐	192	Claude Robinson	.75
☐☐	193	Oliver Seibert	.75
☐☐	194	Alf Smith	.75
☐☐	195	Gord (Phat) Wilson	.75
☐☐	196	Ken Dryden (G), Mtl.	6.00
☐☐	197	George Armstrong	1.50
☐☐	198	Ace Bailey	2.00
☐☐	199	Jack Darragh	.75
☐☐	200	Eddie Gerard	.75
☐☐	201	Jack Gibson	.75
☐☐	202	Hugh Lehman (G)	1.50
☐☐	203	Mickey MacKay	.75
☐☐	204	Joe Malone	1.50
☐☐	205	Bruce Norris	.75
☐☐	206	J.A. O'Brien	.75
☐☐	207	Lynn Patrick	.75
☐☐	208	Tom Phillips	.75
☐☐	209	Allan Pickard	.75
☐☐	210	Jack Stewart, Det.	.75
☐☐	211	Johnny Bower (G)	2.50
☐☐	212	Syl Apps, Sr.	1.50
☐☐	213	John Ashley, Referee	.75
☐☐	214	Marty Barry	.75
☐☐	215	Andy Bathgate	.75
☐☐	216	Frank Buckland	.75
☐☐	217	James Dunn	.75
☐☐	218	Mike Grant	.75
☐☐	219	Doug Harvey	2.50
☐☐	220	George McNamara	.75
☐☐	221	Hartland Molson	.75
☐☐	222	Gordon Roberts	.75
☐☐	223	Eddie Shore	6.00
☐☐	224	Bruce Stuart	.75
☐☐	225	Carl Voss	.75
☐☐	226	Stan Mikita, Chi.	2.50
☐☐	227	Donald Bain	.75
☐☐	228	Emile (Butch) Bouchard	.75
☐☐	229	George Boucher	.75
☐☐	230	Alex Delvecchio	2.00
☐☐	231	Emile Francis	.75
☐☐	232	Riley Hern (G)	1.50
☐☐	233	Fred Hume	.75
☐☐	234	Paul Loicq	.75
☐☐	235	Bill Quackenbush	.75
☐☐	236	Sweeny Schriner	.75
☐☐	237	Tommy Smith	.75
☐☐	238	Allan Stanley	.75
☐☐	239	Anatoli Tarasov	.75
☐☐	240	Frank Udvari	.75
☐	241	Harry Sinden	.75
☐	242	Bobby Hull	6.00
☐	243	Punch Imlach, Buf.	.75
☐	244	Phil Esposito	5.00
☐	245	Jacques Lemaire, Mtl.	1.50
☐	246	Bernard Marcel	.75
☐	247	Rudy Pilous, Chi.	.75
☐	248	Bert Olmstead, Mtl.	.75
☐	249	Jean Ratelle, NYR.	.75
☐	250	Gerry Cheevers (G)	2.00
☐	251	Bill Hanley, OHA Secretary Mgr.	.75
☐	252	Léo Boivin, Bos.	.75
☐	253	Jake Milford, Van.	.75
☐	254	John Mariucci	.75
☐	255	Dave Keon, Tor.	2.00
☐	256	Serge Savard	1.50
☐	257	John Ziegler, NHL President	.75
☐	258	Bobby Clarke, Pha.	3.00
☐	259	Ed Giacomin (G), NYR.	1.50
☐	260	Jacques Laperrière, Mtl.	1.50
☐	261	Matt Pavelich, NHL Linesman	.75

1983 - 84 ESSO

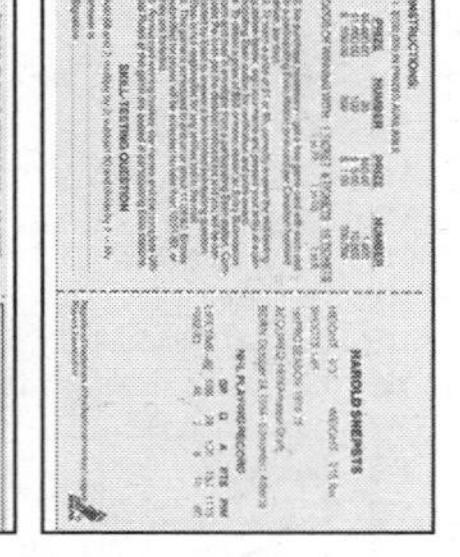

This unnumbered set was issued as part of a lottery game, one in French and one in English. Actual player photographs measure 2" x 3" with statistics on the back. Distributed throughout Canada with the exception of Québec.

Card Size: 2" x 3"
Face: Four colour, white border; Name
Back: Black on white card stock; Name, Resume
Imprint: Registered Trademark of the National Hockey League Players Association
Complete Set (21 cards): 25.00
Common Player: 1.00

	Player	NRMT-MT
☐☐	Glenn Anderson, Edm.	2.00
☐☐	John Anderson, Tor.	1.00
☐☐	Dave Babych, Wpg.	1.00
☐☐	Richard Brodeur (G), Van.	2.00
☐☐	Paul Coffey, Edm.	3.00
☐☐	Bill Derlago, Tor.	1.00
☐☐	Bob Gainey, Mtl.	2.00
☐☐	Michel Goulet, Que.	2.00
☐☐	Dale Hawerchuk, Wpg.	3.00
☐☐	Dale Hunter, Que.	1.00
☐☐	Morris Lukowich, Wpg.	1.00
☐☐	Lanny McDonald, Cgy.	2.00
☐☐	Mark Messier, Edm.	4.50
☐☐	Jim Peplinski, Cgy.	1.00
☐☐	Paul Reinhart, Cgy.	1.00
☐☐	Larry Robinson, Mtl.	2.00
☐☐	Stanl Smyl, Van.	1.00
☐☐	Harold Snepsts, Van.	1.00
☐☐	Marc Tardif, Que.	1.00
☐☐	Mario Tremblay, Mtl.	1.00
☐☐	Rick Vaive, Tor.	1.00

1983 - 84 FUNMATE PUFFY STICKERS

These stickers were issued in cello packs of six stickers each. The 25 different packs are first numbered Series 1 to 21. While last 4 packs are unnumbered. The trophy stickers' panel was never issued.

Sticker Size: Oval 1 3/8" x 1 13/16"
Face: Four colour, wood grain bordèr; Team, Name
Back: Blank
Imprint: None
Complete Set (25 Cello Packs): 50.00
Album: 10.00

	No.	Players	NRMT-MT
☐	1	D. Risebrough/ W. Gretzky/ M. Naslund/ B. Derlago/ R. Brodeur/ D. Babych	10.00
☐	2	G. Anderson/ L. Robinson/ R. Vaive/ S. Smyl/S. Arniel/ D. Edwards	2.00
☐	3	R. Walter/ P. Ihnacak/ T. Gradin/ M. Lukowich/ K. Nilsson/ P. Coffey	3.00
☐	4	J. Anderson/ D. Williams/ B. Mullen/ S. Tambellini/ M. Messier/ G. Lafleur	4.00
☐	5	D. Rota/ D. Hawerchuk/ P. Reinhart/ J. Kurri/ M. Tremblay/ M. Palmateer (G)	2.00
☐	6	P. MacLean/ L. McDonald/ K. Linseman/ S. Shutt// B. Salming/ K. McCarthy	2.00
☐	7	B. Pederson/ M. Foligno/ J. Fox/ D. Lever/ B. Clarke/ G. Malone	2.00
☐	8	G. Perreault/ C. Simmer/ H. Marini/ M. Howe/ R. Kehoe/ J. Schoenfeld	2.00
☐	9	L. Murphy/ P. Russell/ B. Barber/ M. Bullard/ P. Peeters (G)/ J. Van Boxmeer	2.00
☐	10	T. Levo/ D. Sittler/ P. Gardner/ R. Middleton/ R. Cloutier/ B. Nicholls	2.00
☐	11	B. Propp/ M. Dion/ R. Bourque/ D. McCourt/ M. Dionne/ B. MacMillan	3.50
☐	12	R. Carlyle/ T. O'Reilly/ P. Housley/ D. Taylor/ G. Resch (G)/ B. Wilson	2.00
☐	13	T. Esposito (G)/ R. Duguay/ P. Larouche/ N. Broten/ P. Stastny/ B. Dunlop	2.00
☐	14	W. McKechnie/ R. Siltanen/ B. Smith (G)/ A. Stastny/ M. Liut (G)/ D. Wilson	2.00
☐	15	B. Stoughton/ D. Ciccarelli/ M. Goulet/ J. Pettersson/ T. Lysiak/ B. Park	2.00
☐	16	C. Hartsburg/ M. Stastny/ R. Ramage/ A. Secord/ J. Ogrodnick/ G. Millen	2.00
☐	17	T. McKegney/ B. Sutter/ S. Larmer/ D. Gare/ M. Johnson/ B. Bellows	2.00
☐	18	B. Federko/ D. Savard/ R. Larson/ R. Francis/ D. Maruk/ D. Bouchard	2.00
☐	19	M. Bossy/ A. Hedberg/ R. Langway/ B. Smith (G)/ R. Ruotsalainen/ M. Novy	2.00

	No.	Player	NRMT-MT
☐	20	B. Beck/ B. Carpenter/ C. Gillies/ R. McClanahan/ B. Engblom/ D. Potvin	2.00
☐	21	M. Gartner/ J. Tonelli/ W. Huber/ P. Riggin (G)/ B. Trottier/ D. Maloney	2.00
☐		Norris Division: Blackhawks/ Red Wings/ North Stars/ Blues/ Maple Leafs/ NHL	2.00
☐		Patrick Division: Devils/ Islanders/ Rangers/ Flyers/ Penguins/ Capitals	2.00
☐		Adams Division: Bruins/ Sabres/ Whalers/ Canadiens/ Nordiques/ NHL	2.00
☐		Smythe Division: Flames/ Oilers/ Kings/ Canucks/ Jets/ NHL	2.00

1983 - 84 O-PEE-CHEE

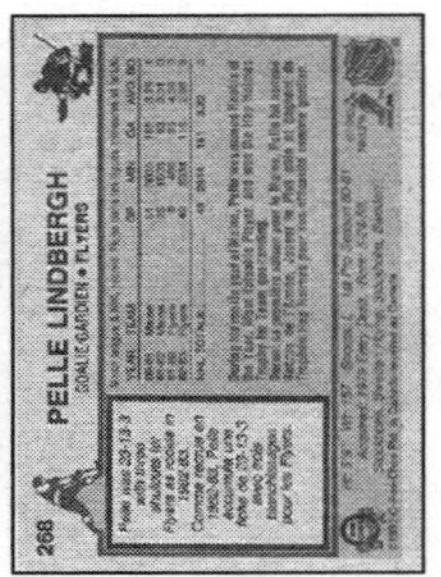

Face: Four colour, white border, Team logo
Back: Green and blue on card stock, Number, Resume, Bilingual
Imprint: © 1983 O-Pee-Chee

Complete Set (396 cards):			**120.00**
Common Player:			**.30**

	No.	Player	NRMT-MT
☐	1	TL: Mike Bossy, NYI.	1.00
☐	2	HL: Denis Potvin, NYI.	.50
☐	3	Mike Bossy, NYI.	3.50
☐	4	Bob Bourne, NYI.	.30
☐	**5**	**Billy Carroll, NYI., RC**	**.30**
☐	6	Clark Gillies, NYI.	.50
☐	7	Butch Goring, NYI.	.50
☐	**8**	**Mats Hallin, NYI., RC, LC**	**.30**
☐	9	Tomas Jonsson, NYI.	.30
☐	10	Gord Lane, NYI., LC	.30
☐	11	Dave Langevin, NYI.	.50
☐	**12**	**Rollie Melanson (G), NYI., RC**	**.35**
☐	13	Ken Morrow, NYI.	.30
☐	14	Bob Nystrom, NYI.	.30
☐	15	Stefan Persson, NYI.	.30
☐	16	Denis Potvin, NYI.	.75
☐	17	Billy Smith (G), NYI.	.75
☐	18	Brent Sutter, NYI.	.50
☐	19	Duane Sutter, NYI.	.50
☐	20	John Tonelli, NYI.	.50
☐	21	Bryan Trottier, NYI.	2.00
☐	22	TL: Wayne Gretzky, Edm.	6.00
☐	23	HL: Messier & Gretzky, Edm.	40.00
☐	24	Glenn Anderson, Edm.	2.00
☐	25	Paul Coffey, Edm.	10.00
☐	26	Lee Fogolin, Edm.	.30
☐	27	Grant Fuhr (G), Edm.	6.00
☐	**28**	**Randy Gregg, Edm., RC**	**.30**
☐	29	Wayne Gretzky, Edm.	35.00
☐	**30**	**Charlie Huddy, Edm., RC**	**1.50**
☐	31	Pat Hughes, Edm.	.30
☐	32	Dave Hunter, Edm.	.30
☐	**33**	**Don Jackson, Edm., RC**	**.30**
☐	34	Jari Kurri, Edm.	6.00
☐	35	Willy Lindstrom, Edm.	.30
☐	36	Ken Linseman, Edm.	.30
☐	37	Kevin Lowe, Edm.	1.25
☐	38	Dave Lumley, Edm.	.30
☐	39	Mark Messier, Edm.	18.00
☐	40	Andy Moog (G), Edm.	5.50
☐	**41**	**Jaroslav Pouzar, Edm., RC**	**.30**
☐	42	Tom Roulston, Edm.	.30
☐	43	TL: Rick Middleton, Bos.	.50
☐	44	HL: Pete Peeters (G), Bos.	.50
☐	45	Ray Bourque, Bos.	10.00
☐	46	Bruce Crowder, Bos., LC	.30
☐	47	Keith Crowder, Bos.	.30
☐	**48**	**Luc Dufour, Bos., RC**	**.30**
☐	49	Tom Fergus, Bos.	.30
☐	50	Steve Kasper, Bos.	.30
☐	**51**	**Gord Kluzak, Bos., RC**	**.30**
☐	**52**	**Mike Krushelnyski, Bos., RC**	**.50**
☐	53	Peter McNab, Bos.	.30
☐	54	Rick Middleton, Bos.	.50
☐	55	Mike Milbury, Bos.	.50
☐	56	Mike O'Connell, Bos.	.30
☐	57	Barry Pederson, Bos.	.30
☐	58	Pete Peeters (G), Bos.	.50
☐	59	Jim Schoenfeld, Bos., LC	.50
☐	60	TL: Tony McKegney, Buf.	.30
☐	61	HL: Bob Sauvé (G), Buf.	.50
☐	62	Réal Cloutier, Buf.	.30
☐	63	Mike Foligno, Buf.	.30
☐	64	Bill Hajt, Buf.	.30
☐	**65**	**Phil Housley, Buf., RC**	**3.75**
☐	66	Dale McCourt, Buf. (Tor.), LC	.30
☐	67	Gilbert Perreault, Buf.	.75
☐	**68**	**Brent Peterson, Buf., RC**	**.30**
☐	69	Craig Ramsay, Buf.	.50
☐	70	Mike Ramsey, Buf.	.30
☐	71	Bob Sauvé (G), Buf.	.50
☐	72	Ric Seiling, Buf.	.30
☐	73	John Van Boxmeer, Buf. (Que), LC	.30
☐	74	TL: Lanny McDonald, Cgy.	.50
☐	75	HL: Lanny McDonald, Cgy.	.50
☐	**76**	**Ed Beers, Cgy., RC**	**.30**
☐	77	Steve Bozek, Cgy.	.30
☐	78	Guy Chouinard, Cgy. (Stl.), LC	.30
☐	79	Mike Eaves, Cgy.	.30
☐	80	Don Edwards (G), Cgy.	.50
☐	**81**	**Kari Eloranta, Cgy., RC**	**.30**
☐	**82**	**Dave Hindmarch, Cgy., RC**	**.30**
☐	83	Jamie Hislop, Cgy., LC	.30
☐	**84**	**Jim Jackson, Cgy., RC**	**.30**
☐	85	Steve Konroyd, Cgy.	.30
☐	86	Réjean Lemelin (G), Cgy.	.50
☐	87	Lanny McDonald, Cgy.	.50
☐	**88**	**Greg Meredith, Cgy., RC, LC**	**.30**
☐	89	Kent Nilsson, Cgy.	.50
☐	90	Jim Peplinski, Cgy.	.30
☐	91	Paul Reinhart, Cgy.	.30
☐	92	Doug Risebrough, Cgy.	.30
☐	93	Steve Tambellini, Cgy.	.30
☐	**94**	**Mickey Volcan, Cgy., RC, LC**	**.30**
☐	95	TL: Al Secord, Chi.	.30
☐	96	HL: Denis Savard, Chi.	1.00
☐	97	Murray Bannerman (G), Chi.	.50
☐	98	Keith Brown, Chi.	.30
☐	99	Tony Esposito (G), Chi., LC	.75
☐	**100**	**Dave Feamster, Chi., RC, LC**	**.30**
☐	101	Greg Fox, Chi.	.30
☐	102	Curt Fraser, Chi.	.30
☐	**103**	**Bill Gardner, Chi., RC**	**.30**
☐	104	Tim Higgins, Chi.	.30
☐	**105**	**Steve Larmer, Chi., RC, Error (Steve Ludzik)**	**15.00**
☐	**106**	**Steve Ludzik, Chi., RC, Error (Steve Larmer)**	**3.25**
☐	107	Tom Lysiak, Chi.	.30
☐	108	Bob Murray, Chi.	.30
☐	**109**	**Rick Paterson, Chi., RC**	**.30**
☐	110	Rich Preston, Chi.	.30
☐	111	Denis Savard, Chi.	2.75
☐	112	Al Secord, Chi.	.30
☐	113	Darryl Sutter, Chi.	.50
☐	114	Doug Wilson, Chi.	.60
☐	115	TL: John Ogrodnick, Det.	.30
☐	116	HL: Corrado Micalef (G), Det.	.50
☐	117	John Barrett, Det.	.30
☐	118	Ivan Boldirev, Det.	.30
☐	119	Colin Campbell, Det.	.50
☐	**120**	**Murray Craven, Det., RC**	**1.00**
☐	121	Ron Duguay, Det.	.30
☐	122	Dwight Foster, Det.	.30
☐	123	Danny Gare, Det.	.50
☐	124	Eddie Johnstone, Det.	.30
☐	125	Reed Larson, Det.	.30
☐	**126**	**Corrado Micalef (G), Det., RC, Error (Carrado)**	**.50**
☐	127	Ed Mio (G), Det.	.50
☐	128	John Ogrodnick, Det.	.30
☐	129	Brad Park, Det.	.50
☐	130	Greg Smith, Det.	.30
☐	**131**	**Ken Solheim, Det. (Min.), RC, LC**	**.30**
☐	132	Bob Manno, Det.	.30
☐	133	Paul Woods	.30
☐	134	Checklist 1 (1 - 132)	4.00
☐	135	TL: Blaine Stoughton, Hfd.	.30
☐	136	HI: Blaine Stoughton, Hfd.	.30
☐	137	Richie Dunn, Hfd.	.30
☐	138	Ron Francis, Hfd.	7.50
☐	139	Marty Howe, Hfd.	.30
☐	140	Mark Johnson, Hfd.	.30
☐	**141**	**Paul Lawless, Hfd., RC, LC**	**.30**
☐	142	Merlin Malinowski, Hfd. (Playing in Europe), LC	.30
☐	143	Greg Millen (G), Hfd.	.50
☐	**144**	**Ray Neufeld, Hfd., RC**	**.30**
☐	145	Joel Quenneville, Hfd.	.50
☐	146	Risto Siltanen, Hfd.	.30
☐	147	Blaine Stoughton, Hfd.	.30
☐	148	Doug Sulliman, Hfd.	.30
☐	**149**	**Bob Sullivan, Hfd., RC, LC**	**.30**
☐	150	TL: Marcel Dionne, L.A.	.50
☐	151	HL: Marcel Dionne, L.A.	.50
☐	152	Marcel Dionne, L.A.	1.25
☐	**153**	**Daryl Evans, L.A., RC, LC**	**.30**
☐	154	Jim Fox, L.A.	.30
☐	155	Mark Hardy, L.A.	.30
☐	**156**	**Gary Laskoski (G), L.A., RC, LC**	**.50**
☐	157	Kevin LaVallée, L.A.	.30
☐	158	Dave Lewis, L.A. (N.J.)	.50
☐	159	Larry Murphy, L.A.	2.00
☐	**160**	**Bernie Nicholls, L.A., RC**	**8.00**
☐	161	Terry Ruskowski, L.A.	.30
☐	162	Charlie Simmer, L.A.	.30
☐	163	Dave Taylor, L.A.	.60
☐	164	TL: Dino Ciccarelli, Min.	1.00
☐	165	HL: Brian Bellows, Min.	1.75
☐	166	Don Beaupré (G), Min.	.50
☐	**167**	**Brian Bellows, Min., RC**	**4.50**
☐	168	Neal Broten, Min.	1.50
☐	169	Steve Christoff, Min. (L.A.)	.30
☐	170	Dino Ciccarelli, Min.	2.50
☐	171	George Ferguson, Min., LC	.30
☐	172	Craig Hartsburg, Min.	.50
☐	173	Al MacAdam, Min.	.30
☐	174	Dennis Maruk, Min.	.30
☐	175	Brad Maxwell, Min.	.30
☐	176	Tom McCarthy, Min.	.30
☐	177	Gilles Meloche (G), Min.	.50
☐	178	Steve Payne, Min.	.30
☐	179	Willi Plett, Min., LC	.30
☐	180	Gord Roberts, Min.	.30
☐	181	Bobby Smith, Min. (Mtl.)	.50
☐	182	TL: Mark Napier, Mtl.	.30
☐	183	HL: Guy Lafleur, Mtl.	1.00
☐	184	Keith Acton, Mtl. (Min.)	.30
☐	**185**	**Guy Carbonneau, Mtl., RC**	**4.50**
☐	**186**	**Gilbert Delorme, Mtl., RC**	**.30**
☐	187	Bob Gainey, Mtl.	.60
☐	188	Rick Green, Mtl.	.30
☐	189	Guy Lafleur, Mtl.	4.00
☐	**190**	**Craig Ludwig, Mtl., RC**	**.60**
☐	191	Pierre Mondou, Mtl.	.30
☐	192	Mark Napier, Mtl. (Min.)	.30
☐	**193**	**Mats Naslund, Mtl., RC, Error (wrong stats)**	**3.50**
☐	**194**	**Chris Nilan, Mtl., RC**	**1.75**
☐	195	Larry Robinson, Mtl.	.60
☐	**196**	**Bill Root, Mtl., RC**	**.30**
☐	197	Richard Sévigny (G), Mtl.	.50
☐	198	Steve Shutt, Mtl.	.50
☐	199	Mario Tremblay, Mtl.	.30
☐	200	Ryan Walter, Mtl.	.30
☐	201	Rick Wamsley (G), Mtl.	.50
☐	202	Doug Wickenheiser, Mtl.	.30
☐	203	AW: Wayne Gretzky	6.00
☐	204	AW: Wayne Gretzky	6.00
☐	205	AW: Mike Bossy	1.00
☐	206	AW: Steve Larmer	3.25
☐	207	AW: Rod Langway	.50
☐	208	AW: Lanny McDonald	.50
☐	209	AW: Pete Peeters	.50
☐	210	RB: Mike Bossy, NYI.	1.00
☐	211	RB: Marcel Dionne, L.A.	.50
☐	212	RB: Wayne Gretzky, Edm.	6.00
☐	213	RB: Pat Hughes, Edm.	.30
☐	214	RB: Rick Middleton, Bos.	.50
☐	215	LL: Wayne Gretzky, Edm.	6.00
☐	216	LL: Wayne Gretzky, Edm.	6.00
☐	217	LL: Wayne Gretzky, Edm.	6.00
☐	218	LL: Brian Propp, Pha.	.30
☐	219	LL: Paul Gardner/ Al Secord	.30

	No.	Player	Price
☐	220	LL: Randy Holt, Wsh.	.30
☐	221	LL: Pete Peeters (G), Bos.	.50
☐	222	LL: Pete Peeters (G), Bos.	.50
☐	223	TL: Steve Tambellini, N.J.	.30
☐	224	HL: Don Lever, N.J.	.30
☐	225	Brent Ashton, N.J. (Min.)	.30
☐	226	Mel Bridgman, N.J.	.30
☐	227	Aaron Broten, N.J.	.30
☐	**228**	**Murray Brumwell, N.J., RC, LC**	**.30**
☐	229	Garry Howatt, N.J., LC	.30
☐	**230**	**Jeff Larmer, N.J., RC**	**.30**
☐	231	Don Lever, N.J.	.30
☐	232	Bob Lorimer, N.J.	.30
☐	233	Ron Low (G), N.J.	.50
☐	234	Bob MacMillan, N.J.	.30
☐	**235**	**Hector Marini, N.J., RC, LC**	**.30**
☐	236	Glenn Resch (G), N.J.	.50
☐	237	Phil Russell, N.J.	.30
☐	238	TL: Mark Pavelich, NYR.	.30
☐	239	HL: Mark Pavelich, NYR.	.30
☐	**240**	**Bill Baker, NYR., RC, LC**	**.30**
☐	241	Barry Beck, NYR.	.30
☐	242	Mike Blaisdell, NYR., LC	.30
☐	243	Nick Fotiu, NYR.	.30
☐	244	Robbie Ftorek, NYR., LC	.50
☐	245	Anders Hedberg, NYR.	.50
☐	246	Willie Huber, NYR.	.30
☐	247	Tom Laidlaw, NYR.	.30
☐	248	Mikko Leinonen, NYR., LC	.30
☐	249	Dave Maloney, NYR.	.30
☐	250	Don Maloney, NYR.	.30
☐	251	Rob McClanahan, NYR.	.30
☐	252	Mark Osborne, NYR.	.30
☐	253	Mark Pavelich, NYR.	.30
☐	254	Mike Rogers, NYR.	.30
☐	255	Reijo Ruotsalainen, NYR.	.30
☐	256	Checklist 2 (133 - 264)	4.00
☐	257	TL: Darryl Sittler, Pha.	.50
☐	258	HL: Darryl Sittler, Pha.	.50
☐	259	Ray Allison, Pha., LC	.30
☐	260	Bill Barber, Pha.	.50
☐	**261**	**Lindsay Carson, Pha., RC, LC**	**.30**
☐	262	Bobby Clarke, Pha., LC	1.25
☐	263	Doug Crossman, Pha.	.30
☐	264	Ron Flockhart, Pha.	.30
☐	**265**	**Bob Froese (G), Pha., RC**	**.60**
☐	266	Paul Holmgren, Pha.	.30
☐	267	Mark Howe, Pha.	.60
☐	**268**	**Pelle Lindbergh (G), Pha., RC**	**12.00**
☐	269	Brad Marsh, Pha.	.30
☐	270	Brad McCrimmon, Pha.	.50
☐	271	Brian Propp, Pha.	.50
☐	272	Darryl Sittler, Pha.	.60
☐	**273**	**Mark Taylor, Pha., RC**	**.30**
☐	274	TL: Rick Kehoe, Pgh.	.30
☐	275	HL: Paul Gardner, Pgh.	.30
☐	276	Pat Boutette, Pgh.	.30
☐	277	Mike Bullard, Pgh.	.30
☐	278	Randy Carlyle, Pgh.	.30
☐	279	Michel Dion (G), Pgh.	.50
☐	280	Paul Gardner, Pgh., LC	.30
☐	**281**	**Dave Hannan, Pgh., RC**	**.50**
☐	282	Rick Kehoe, Pgh.	.50
☐	**283**	**Randy Boyd, Pgh., RC, LC**	**.30**
☐	284	Greg Malone, Pgh. (Hfd.)	.30
☐	**285**	**Doug Shedden, Pgh., RC**	**.30**
☐	286	André St. Laurent, Pgh., LC	.30
☐	287	TL: Michel Goulet, Que.	.75
☐	288	HL: Michel Goulet, Que.	.75
☐	289	Pierre Aubry, Que., LC	.30
☐	290	Dan Bouchard (G), Que.	.50
☐	291	Alain Côté, Que.	.30
☐	292	Michel Goulet, Que.	1.50
☐	293	Dale Hunter, Que.	.75
☐	294	Rick Lapointe, Que., LC	.30
☐	295	Mario Marois, Que.	.30
☐	296	Tony McKegney, Que.	.30
☐	**297**	**Randy Moller, Que., RC**	**.50**
☐	298	Wilf Paiement, Que.	.30
☐	299	Dave Pichette, Que.	.30
☐	300	Normand Rochefort, Que.	.30
☐	**301**	**Louis Sleigher, Que., RC**	**.30**
☐	302	Anton Stastny, Que.	.30
☐	303	Marian Stastny, Que.	.30
☐	304	Peter Stastny, Que.	2.25
☐	305	Marc Tardif, Que., LC	.30
☐	306	Wally Weir, Que., LC	.30
☐	307	Blake Wesley, Que.	.30
☐	308	TL: Brian Sutter, Stl.	.50
☐	309	HL: Mike Liut (G), Stl.	.50
☐	310	Wayne Babych, Stl.	.30
☐	311	Jack Brownschidle, Stl., LC	.30
☐	**312**	**Mike Crombeen, Stl. (Hfd.), RC, LC**	**.30**
☐	**313**	**André Doré, Stl., RC**	**.30**
☐	314	Blake Dunlop, Stl., LC	.30
☐	315	Bernie Federko, Stl.	.60
☐	316	Mike Liut (G), Stl.	.60
☐	317	Joe Mullen, Stl.	3.00
☐	318	Jorgen Pettersson, Stl.	.30
☐	319	Rob Ramage, Stl.	.50
☐	320	Brian Sutter, Stl.	.50
☐	321	Perry Turnbull, Stl.	.30
☐	322	Mike Zuke, Stl. (Hfd.)	.30
☐	323	TL: Rick Vaive, Tor.	.50
☐	324	HL: Rick Vaive, Tor.	.50
☐	325	John Anderson, Tor.	.30
☐	326	Jim Benning, Tor.	.30
☐	327	Bill Derlago, Tor.	.30
☐	**328**	**Dan Daoust, Tor., RC**	**.30**
☐	329	Dave Farrish, Tor.	.30
☐	330	Miroslav Frycer, Tor.	.30
☐	**331**	**Stewart Gavin, Tor., RC**	**.50**
☐	332	Gaston Gingras, Tor.	.30
☐	333	Billy Harris, Tor., LC	.30
☐	**334**	**Peter Ihnacak, Tor., RC, LC**	**.30**
☐	335	Jim Korn, Tor.	.30
☐	336	Terry Martin, Tor.	.30
☐	**337**	**Frank Nigro, Tor., RC, LC**	**.30**
☐	338	Mike Palmateer (G), Tor.	.50
☐	**339**	**Walt Poddubny, Tor., RC**	**.30**
☐	340	Rick St. Croix (G), Tor.	.35
☐	341	Borje Salming, Tor.	.50
☐	342	Greg Terrion, Tor.	.30
☐	343	Rick Vaive, Tor.	.50
☐	344	TL: Darcy Rota, Van.	.30
☐	345	HL: Darcy Rota, Van.	.30
☐	346	Richard Brodeur (G), Van.	.50
☐	**347**	**Jiri Bubla, Van., RC**	**.30**
☐	348	Ron Delorme, Van.	.30
☐	349	John Garrett (G), Van.	.50
☐	350	Thomas Gradin, Van.	.30
☐	351	Doug Halward, Van.	.30
☐	352	Mark Kirton, Van., LC	.30
☐	353	Rick Lanz, Van.	.30
☐	354	Lars Lindgren, Van. (Min.), LC	.30
☐	355	Gary Lupul, Van.	.30
☐	356	Kevin McCarthy, Van.	.30
☐	**357**	**Jim Nill, Van., RC**	**.30**
☐	358	Darcy Rota, Van.	.30
☐	359	Stan Smyl, Van.	.30
☐	360	Harold Snepsts, Van.	.30
☐	**361**	**Patrik Sundstrom, Van., RC**	**.50**
☐	**362**	**Tony Tanti, Van., RC**	**.75**
☐	363	Dave Williams, Van.	.50
☐	364	TL: Mike Gartner, Wsh.	1.50
☐	365	HL: Rod Langway, Wsh.	.50
☐	366	Bob Carpenter, Wsh.	.50
☐	367	Dave Christian, Wsh.	.30
☐	368	Brian Engblom, Wsh. (L.A.)	.30
☐	369	Mike Gartner, Wsh.	5.50
☐	370	Bengt Gustafsson, Wsh.	.30
☐	371	Ken Houston, Wsh. (Min.), LC	.30
☐	372	Doug Jarvis, Wsh.	.30
☐	**373**	**Al Jensen (G), Wsh., RC**	**.50**
☐	374	Rod Langway, Wsh.	.60
☐	**375**	**Craig Laughlin, Wsh., RC**	**.30**
☐	**376**	**Scott Stevens, Wsh., RC**	**13.00**
☐	377	TL: Dale Hawerchuk, Wpg.	1.50
☐	378	HL: Lucien DeBlois, Wpg.	.30
☐	**379**	**Scott Arniel, Wpg., RC**	**.30**
☐	380	Dave Babych, Wpg.	.50
☐	381	Laurie Boschman, Wpg.	.30
☐	382	Wade Campbell, Wpg., LC	.30
☐	383	Lucien DeBlois, Wpg.	.30
☐	**384**	**Murray Eaves, Wpg., RC, LC**	**.30**
☐	385	Dale Hawerchuk, Wpg.	6.00
☐	386	Morris Lukowich, Wpg.	.30
☐	387	Bengt Lundholm, Wpg.	.30
☐	388	Paul Maclean, Wpg.	.30
☐	**389**	**Brian Mullen, Wpg., RC**	**.50**
☐	390	Doug Smail, Wpg.	.30
☐	391	Doug Soetaert (G), Wpg.	.50
☐	392	Don Spring, Wpg., LC	.30
☐	393	Thomas Steen, Wpg.	.50
☐	394	Tim Watters, Wpg.	.30
☐	395	Tim Young, Wpg.	.30
☐	396	Checklist 3 (265 - 396)	5.00

1983 - 84 O-PEE-CHEE / TOPPS STICKERS

An album was issued to hold these stickers.

Sticker Size: 1 15/16" x 2 9/16"

Face: Four colour, white or foil border; Number

Back: Blue on card stock; Name, Number, Bilingual

Imprint:

Complete Set (330 stickers): 50.00

Common Player: .20

Album: 5.00

	No.	Player	NRMT-MT
☐☐	1	Foil: Marcel Dionne, L.A.	.50
☐☐	2	Foil: Guy Lafleur, Mtl.	.75
☐☐	3	Foil: Darryl Sittler, Pha.	.35
☐☐	4	Foil: Gilbert Perreault, Buf.	.35
☐☐	5	Bill Barber, Pha.	.25
☐☐	6	Steve Shutt, Mtl.	.35
☐☐	7	Wayne Gretzky, Edm.	5.00
☐☐	8	Lanny McDonald, Cgy.	.35
☐☐	9	Reggie Leach, Det.	.20
☐☐	10	Mike Bossy, NYI.	.50
☐☐	11	Rick Kehoe, Pgh.	.20
☐☐	12	Bobby Clarke, Pha.	.50
☐☐	13	Butch Goring, NYI.	.20
☐☐	14	Rick Middleton, Bos.	.25
☐☐	15	Foil: Conn Smythe Trophy	.25
☐☐	16	AW:.Billy Smith (G), NYI., MVP	.20
☐☐	17	Lee Fogolin, Edm.	.20
☐☐	18	Stanley Cup Finals	1.00
☐☐	19	Stanley Cup Finals	.20
☐☐	20	Stanley Cup Finals	.20
☐☐	21	Stanley Cup Finals	.20

Stickers 18-21 feature Jari Kurri shooting on Billy Smith.

	No.	Player	NRMT-MT
☐☐	22	Foil: Stanley Cup	.25
☐☐	23	Foil: Stanley Cup	.25
☐☐	24	Foil: Stanley Cup	.25
☐☐	25	Rick Vaive, Tor.	.25
☐☐	26	Rick Vaive, Tor.	.25
☐☐	27	Billy Harris, Tor.	.20
☐☐	28	Dan Daoust, Tor.	.20

	No.	Player	Price
□□	29	Dan Daoust, Tor.	.20
□□	30	John Anderson, Tor.	.20
□□	31	John Anderson, Tor.	.20
□□	32	Peter Ihnacak, Tor.	.20
□□	33	Borje Salming, Tor.	.35
□□	34	Borje Salming, Tor.	.35
□□	35	Bill Derlago, Tor.	.20
□□	36	Rick St. Croix (G), Tor.	.25
□□	37	Greg Terrion, Tor.	.20
□□	38	Miroslav Frycer, Tor.	.20
□□	39	Mike Palmateer (G), Tor.	.25
□□	40	Gaston Gingras, Tor.	.20
□□	41	Pete Peeters (G), Bos.	.25
□□	42	Pete Peeters (G), Bos.	.25
□□	43	Mike Krushelnyski, Bos.	.25
□□	44	Rick Middleton, Bos.	.25
□□	45	Rick Middleton, Bos.	.25
□□	46	Ray Bourque, Bos.	2.00
□□	47	Ray Bourque, Bos.	2.00
□□	48	Brad Park, Bos.	.25
□□	49	Barry Pederson, Bos.	.20
□□	50	Barry Pederson, Bos.	.20
□□	51	Peter McNab, Bos.	.20
□□	52	Mike O'Connell, Bos.	.20
□□	53	Steve Kasper, Bos.	.20
□□	54	Marty Howe, Bos.	.20
□□	55	Tom Fergus, Bos.	.20
□□	56	Keith Crowder, Bos.	.20
□□	57	Steve Shutt, Mtl.	.35
□□	58	Guy Lafleur, Mtl.	1.50
□□	59	Guy Lafleur, Mtl.	1.50
□□	60	Larry Robinson, Mtl.	.35
□□	61	Larry Robinson, Mtl.	.35
□□	62	Ryan Walter, Mtl.	.20
□□	63	Ryan Walter, Mtl.	.20
□□	64	Mark Napier, Mtl.	.20
□□	65	Mark Napier, Mtl.	.20
□□	66	Bob Gainey, Mtl.	.25
□□	67	Doug Wickenheiser, Mtl.	.20
□□	68	Pierre Mondou, Mtl.	.20
□□	69	Mario Tremblay, Mtl.	.25
□□	70	Gilbert Delorme, Mtl.	.20
□□	71	Mats Naslund, Mtl.	.50
□□	72	Rick Wamsley (G), Mtl.	.25
□□	73	Ken Morrow, NYI.	.20
□□	74	John Tonelli, NYI.	.20
□□	75	John Tonelli, NYI.	.20
□□	76	Bryan Trottier, NYI.	.50
□□	77	Bryan Trottier, NYI.	.50
□□	78	Mike Bossy, NYI.	.50
□□	79	Mike Bossy, NYI.	.50
□□	80	Bob Bourne, NYI.	.20
□□	81	Denis Potvin, NYI.	.50
□□	82	Denis Potvin, NYI.	.50
□□	83	Dave Langevin, NYI.	.20
□□	84	Clark Gillies, NYI.	.20
□□	85	Bob Nystrom, NYI.	.20
□□	86	Billy Smith (G), NYI.	.35
□□	87	Tomas Jonsson, NYI.	.20
□□	88	Rollie Melanson (G), NYI.	.20
□□	89	Wayne Gretzky, Edm.	6.00
□□	90	Wayne Gretzky, Edm.	6.00
□□	91	Willy Lindstrom, Edm.	.20
□□	92	Glenn Anderson, Edm.	.50
□□	93	Glenn Anderson, Edm.	.50
□□	94	Paul Coffey, Edm.	1.50
□□	95	Paul Coffey, Edm.	1.50
□□	96	Charlie Huddy, Edm.	.20
□□	97	Mark Messier, Edm.	1.75
□□	98	Mark Messier, Edm.	1.75
□□	99	Andy Moog (G), Edm.	1.25
□□	100	Lee Fogolin, Edm.	.20
□□	101	Kevin Lowe, Edm.	.50
□□	102	Ken Linseman, Edm.	.20
□□	103	Tom Roulston, Edm.	.20
□□	104	Jari Kurri, Edm.	1.00
□□	105	Darryl Sutter, Chi.	.25
□□	106	Denis Savard, Chi.	.75
□□	107	Denis Savard, Chi.	.75
□□	108	Steve Larmer, Chi.	1.50
□□	109	Bob Murray, Chi.	.20
□□	110	Tom Lysiak, Chi.	.20
□□	111	Al Secord, Chi.	.20
□□	112	Doug Wilson, Chi.	.25
□□	113	Murray Bannerman (G), Chi.	.25
□□	114	Gord Roberts, Min.	.20
□□	115	Tom McCarthy, Min.	.20
□□	116	Bobby Smith, Min.	.25
□□	117	Craig Hartsburg, Min.	.25
□□	118	Dino Ciccarelli, Min.	.50
□□	119	Dino Ciccarelli, Min.	.50
□□	120	Neal Broten, Min.	.35
□□	121	Steve Payne, Min.	.20
□□	122	Don Beaupré (G), Min.	.25
□□	123	Jorgen Pettersson, Stl.	.20
□□	124	Perry Turnbull, Stl.	.20
□□	125	Bernie Federko, Stl.	.35
□□	126	Mike Crombeen, Stl.	.20
□□	127	Brian Sutter, Stl.	.35
□□	128	Brian Sutter, Stl.	.35
□□	129	Mike Liut (G), Stl.	.35
□□	130	Rob Ramage, Stl.	.20
□□	131	Blake Dunlop, Stl.	.20
□□	132	Ivan Boldirev, Det.	.20
□□	133	Dwight Foster, Det.	.20
□□	134	Reed Larson, Det.	.20
□□	135	Danny Gare, Det.	.20
□□	136	Jim Schoenfeld, Det.	.25
□□	137	John Ogrodnick, Det.	.20
□□	138	John Ogrodnick, Det.	.20
□□	139	Willie Huber, Det.	.20
□□	140	Greg Smith, Det.	.20
□□	141	Eddy Beers, Cgy.	.20
□□	142	Brian Bellows, Min.	.75
□□	143	Jiri Bubla, Van.	.20
□□	144	Daryl Evans, L.A.	.20
□□	145	Randy Gregg, Edm.	.20
□□	146	Jim Jackson, Cal.	.20
□□	147	Corrado Micalef (G), Det.	.25
□□	148	Brian Mullen, Wpg.	.20
□□	149	Frank Nigro, Tor.	.20
□□	150	Walt Poddubny, Tor.	.20
□□	151	Jaroslav Pouzar, Edm.	.20
□□	152	Patrik Sundstrom, Van.	.20
□□	153	Denis Savard, Chi.	.75
□□	154	Dave Hunter, Edm.	.20
□□	155	Andy Moog (G), Edm.	1.25
□□	156	Al Secord, Chi.	.20
□□	157	Mark Messier, Edm.	1.75
□□	158	Glenn Anderson, Edm.	.50
□□	159	Jaroslav Pouzar, Edm.	.20
□□	160	AS: Al Secord, Chi.	.20
□□	161	AS: Wayne Gretzky, Edm.	6.00
□□	162	AS: Lanny McDonald, Cgy.	.35
□□	163	AS: Dave Babych, Wpg.	.25
□□	164	AS: Murray Bannerman (G), Chi.	.25
□□	165	AS: Doug Wilson, Chi.	.25
□□	166	AS: Michel Goulet, Que.	.50
□□	167	AS: Peter Stastny, Que.	.50
□□	168	AS: Marian Stastny, Que.	.20
□□	169	AS: Denis Potvin, NYI.	.50
□□	170	AS: Pete Peeters (G), Bos.	.25
□□	171	AS: Mark Howe, Pha.	.25
□□	172	Luc Dufour, Bos.	.20
□□	173	Ray Bourque, Bos.	2.00
□□	174	Bob Bourne, NYI.	.20
□□	175	Denis Potvin, NYI.	.50
□□	176	Mike Bossy, NYI.	.50
□□	177	Butch Goring, NYI.	.20
□□	178	Brad Park, Bos.	.25
□□	179	Murray Brumwell, N.J.	.20
□□	180	Guy Carbonneau, Mtl.	.75
□□	181	Lindsay Carson, Pha.	.20
□□	182	Luc Dufour, Bos.	.20
□□	183	Bob Froese (G), Pha.	.25
□□	184	Mats Hallin, NYI.	.20
□□	185	Gord Kluzak, Bos.	.20
□□	186	Jeff Larmer, N.J.	.20
□□	187	Milan Novy, Wsh.	.20
□□	188	Scott Stevens, Wsh.	1.50
□□	189	Bob Sullivan, Hfd.	.20
□□	190	Mark Taylor, Pha.	.20
□□	191	Darryl Sittler, Pha.	.35
□□	192	Ron Flockhart, Pha.	.20
□□	193	Brad McCrimmon, Pha.	.20
□□	194	Bill Barber, Pha.	.35
□□	195	Mark Howe, Pha.	.25
□□	196	Mark Howe, Pha.	.25
□□	197	Pelle Lindbergh (G), Pha.	3.00
□□	198	Bobby Clarke, Pha.	.50
□□	199	Brian Propp, Pha.	.25
□□	200	Ken Houston, Wsh.	.20
□□	201	Rod Langway, Wsh.	.25
□□	202	Al Jensen (G), Wsh.	.25
□□	203	Brian Engblom, Wsh.	.20
□□	204	Dennis Maruk, Wsh.	.20
□□	205	Dennis Maruk, Wsh.	.20
□□	206	Bob Carpenter, Wsh.	.20
□□	207	Mike Gartner, Wsh.	1.50
□□	208	Doug Jarvis, Wsh.	.20
□□	209	Ed Mio (G), NYR.	.25
□□	210	Barry Beck, NYR.	.20
□□	211	Dave Maloney, NYR.	.20
□□	212	Don Maloney, NYR.	.20
□□	213	Mark Pavelich, NYR.	.20
□□	214	Mark Pavelich, NYR.	.20
□□	215	Anders Hedberg, NYR.	.20
□□	216	Reijo Ruotsalaine, NYR.	.25
□□	217	Mike Rogers, NYR.	.20
□□	218	Don Lever, N.J.	.20
□□	219	Steve Tambellini, N.J.	.20
□□	220	Bob MacMillan, N.J.	.20
□□	221	Hector Marini, N.J.	.20
□□	222	Glenn Resch (G), N.J.	.25
□□	223	Glenn Resch (G), N.J.	.25
□□	224	Carol Vadnais, N.J.	.20
□□	225	Joel Quenneville, N.J.	.25
□□	226	Aaron Broten, N.J.	.20
□□	227	Randy Carlyle, Pgh.	.20
□□	228	Doug Shedden, Pgh.	.20
□□	229	Greg Malone, Pgh.	.20
□□	230	Paul Gardner, Pgh.	.20
□□	231	Rick Kehoe, Pgh.	.20
□□	232	Rick Kehoe, Pgh.	.20
□□	233	Pat Boutette, Pgh.	.20
□□	234	Michel Dion (G), Pgh.	.25
□□	235	Mike Bullard, Pgh.	.20
□□	236	Dale McCourt, Buf.	.20
□□	237	Mike Foligno, Buf.	.20
□□	238	Phil Housley, Buf.	.50
□□	239	Tony McKegney, Buf.	.20
□□	240	Gilbert Perreault, Buf.	.35
□□	241	Gilbert Perreault, Buf.	.35
□□	242	Bob Sauvé (G), Buf.	.25
□□	243	Mike Ramsey, Buf.	.20
□□	244	John Van Boxmeer, Buf.	.20
□□	245	Dan Bouchard (G), Que.	.25
□□	246	Réal Cloutier, Que.	.20
□□	247	Marc Tardif, Que.	.20
□□	248	Randy Moller, Que.	.20
□□	249	Michel Goulet, Que.	.50
□□	250	Michel Goulet, Que.	.50
□□	251	Marian Stastny, Que.	.20
□□	252	Anton Stastny, Que.	.20
□□	253	Peter Stastny, Que.	.50
□□	254	Mark Johnson, Hfd.	.20
□□	255	Ron Francis, Hfd.	1.50
□□	256	Doug Sulliman, Hfd.	.20
□□	257	Risto Siltanen, Hfd.	.20
□□	258	Blaine Stoughton, Hfd.	.20
□□	259	Blaine Stoughton, Hfd.	.20
□□	260	Ray Neufeld, Hfd.	.20
□□	261	Pierre Lacroix, Hfd.	.20
□□	262	Greg Millen (G), Hfd.	.20
□□	263	Lanny McDonald, Cgy.	.35
□□	264	Paul Reinhart, Cgy.	.20
□□	265	Mel Bridgman, Cgy.	.20
□□	266	Réjean Lemelin (G), Cgy.	.25
□□	267	Kent Nilsson, Cgy.	.20
□□	268	Kent Nilsson, Cgy.	.20
□□	269	Doug Risebrough, Cgy.	.20
□□	270	Kari Eloranta, Cgy.	.20
□□	271	Phil Russell, Cgy.	.20
□□	272	Darcy Rota, Van.	.20
□□	273	Thomas Gradin, Van	.20
□□	274	Stan Smyl, Van	.25
□□	275	John Garrett (G), Van	.25
□□	276	Richard Brodeur (G), Van	.25
□□	277	Richard Brodeur (G), Van	.25
□□	278	Doug Halward, Van	.20
□□	279	Kevin McCarthy, Van	.20
□□	280	Rick Lanz, Van	.20
□□	281	Morris Lukowich, Wpg.	.20
□□	282	Dale Hawerchuk, Wpg.	1.50
□□	283	Paul MacLean, Wpg.	.20

	#	Player	Price
☐☐	284	Lucien DeBlois, Wpg.	.20
☐☐	285	Dave Babych, Wpg.	.25
☐☐	286	Dave Babych, Wpg.	.25
☐☐	287	Doug Smail, Wpg.	.20
☐☐	288	Doug Soetaert (G), Wpg.	.25
☐☐	289	Thomas Steen, Wpg.	.25
☐☐	290	Charlie Simmer, L.A.	.25
☐☐	291	Terry Ruskowski, L.A.	.20
☐☐	292	Bernie Nicholls, L.A.	.75
☐☐	293	Jim Fox, L.A.	.20
☐☐	294	Marcel Dionne, L.A.	.50
☐☐	295	Marcel Dionne, L.A.	.50
☐☐	296	Gary Laskoski (G), L.A.	.25
☐☐	297	Jerry Korab, L.A.	.20
☐☐	298	Larry Murphy, L.A.	.35
☐☐	299	Foil: Hart Trophy	.25
☐☐	300	Foil: Hart Trophy	.25
☐☐	301	AW: Wayne Gretzky, Edm.	6.00
☐☐	302	AW: Bobby Clarke, Pha.	.50
☐☐	303	AW: Lanny McDonald, Cgy.	.35
☐☐	304	Foil: Lady Byng Trophy	.25
☐☐	305	Foil: Lady Byng Trophy	.25
☐☐	306	AW: Mike Bossy, NYI.	.50
☐☐	307	AW: Wayne Gretzky, Edm.	6.00
☐☐	308	Foil: Art Ross Trophy	.25
☐☐	309	Foil: Art Ross Trophy	.25
☐☐	310	Foil: Calder Trophy	.25
☐☐	311	Foil: Calder Trophy	.25
☐☐	312	AW: Steve Larmer, Chi.	1.50
☐☐	313	AW: Rod Langway, Wsh.	.25
☐☐	314	Foil: Norris Trophy	.25
☐☐	315	Foil: Norris Trophy	.25
☐☐	316	AW: Billy Smith, NYI.	.35
☐☐	317	AW: Rollie Melanson, NYI.	.25
☐☐	318	AW: Pete Peeters, Bos.	.25
☐☐	319	Foil: Vezina Trophy	.25
☐☐	320	Foil: Vezina Trophy	.25
☐☐	321	Foil: Mike Bossy, NYI.	.50
☐☐	322	Foil: Mike Bossy, NYI.	.50
☐☐	323	Foil: Marcel Dionne, Stl.	.50
☐☐	324	Foil: Marcel Dionne, Stl.	.50
☐☐	325	Foil: Wayne Gretzky, Edm.	6.00
☐☐	326	Foil: Wayne Gretzky, Edm.	6.00
☐☐	327	Foil: Pat Hughes, Edm.	.20
☐☐	328	Foil: Pat Hughes, Edm.	.20
☐☐	329	Foil: Rick Middleton, Bos.	.25
☐☐	330	Foil: Rick Middleton, Bos.	.25

1983 - 84 7 - ELEVEN "COKE IS IT" CUPS

We have little information on these cups. Other cups may exist.

Imprint:

	Player
☐	Keith Acton, Mtl.
☐	Glenn Anderson, Edm.
☐	John Anderson, Tor.
☐	Scott Arniel, Wpg.
☐	Dave Babych, Wpg.
☐	Bill Derlago, Tor.
☐	Marcel Dionne, L.A.
☐	Tony Esposito (G), Chi.
☐	Thomas Gradin, Van.
☐	Dale Hawerchuk, Wpg.
☐	Jari Kurri, Edm.
☐	Lanny McDonald, Cgy.
☐	Mark Messier, Edm.
☐	Pierre Mondou, Mtl.
☐	Andy Moog (G), Edm.
☐	Brian Mullen, Wpg.
☐	Bob Murray, Chi.
☐	Kent Nilsson, Cgy.
☐	Mike Palmateer (G), Tor.
☐	Jim Peplinski, Cgy.
☐	Doug Risebrough, Cgy.
☐	Larry Robinson, Mtl.
☐	Borje Salming, Tor.
☐	Richard Sévigny, Mtl.
☐	Steve Shutt, Mtl.
☐	Charlie Simmer, L.A.
☐	Harold Snepts, Van.
☐	Tony Tanti, Van.
☐	Rick Vaive, Tor.
☐	Dave Williams, Van.

1983 - 84 SOUHAITS RENAISSANCE KEY CHAIN CARDS

Cards are listed and priced per team. Each set of seven check-boxes signify that there are seven mini-cards to each team set. The St. Louis Blues were the only team not produced. There is a small hole punch in the top left corner of each card.

Card Size: 1 1/4" x 2 1/8"

Imprint: © 1983 Souhaits Renaissance Inc.

Complete Set (140 cards): 65.00

	Team/Player	NRMT-MT
☐☐☐☐☐☐☐	Boston Bruins: Bruins/ P.Peeters (G); G.Kluzak/ R.Bourque; B.Pederson/ R.Middleton; M.O'Connell/ R.Hillier; M.Krushelnyski/ M.Milbury; T.Fergus/ L.Dufour; B.Crowder/ Title Card	8.00
☐☐☐☐☐☐☐	Buffalo Sabres: Sabres/ J.Cloutier (G); J.Van Boxmeer/ M.Ramsey; P.Housley/ D.McCourt; T.McKegney/ C.Ramsay; G.Perreault/ A.Savard; R.Seiling/ M.Foligno; B.Peterson/ Title Card	5.00
☐☐☐☐☐☐☐	Calgary Flames: Flames/ D.Edwards (G); P.Russell/ R.Dunn; G.Chouinard/ D.Risebrough; L.McDonald/ K.Nilsson; J.Hislop/ K.Eloranta; P.Reinhart/ J.Peplinski; M.Bridgman/ Title Card	5.00
☐☐☐☐☐☐☐	Chicago Blackhawks: Blackhawks/ G.Fox; B.Murray/ T.Lysiak; B.Gardner/ R.Preston; D.Savard/ A.Secord; D.Crossman/ Do.Wilson; Da.Sutter/ S.Larmer; T.Esposito (G)/ Title Card	5.00
☐☐☐☐☐☐☐	Detroit Red Wings: Red Wings/ J.Schoenfeld; C.Campbell/ G.Smith; W.Huber/ W.McKechnie; D.Gare/ D.Foster; M.Blaisdell/ M.Osborne; J.Ogrodnick/ R.Larson; C.Micalef/ Title Card	5.00
☐☐☐☐☐☐☐	Edmonton Oilers: Oilers/ L.Fogolin; G.Anderson/ M.Messier; K.Lowe/ P.Coffey; K.Linseman/ P.Hughes; J.Kurri/ C.Huddy; D.Semenko/ A.Moog (G); W.Gretzky/ Title Card	15.00
☐☐☐☐☐☐☐	Hartford Whalers: Whaler/ M.Volcan; P.Lacroix/ R.Siltanen; R.Francis/ R.Neufeld; C.Kotsopoulos/ M.Renaud; B.Stoughton/ D.Sulliman; B.Sullivan/ P.Larouche; G.Millen (G)/ Title Card	5.00
☐☐☐☐☐☐☐	Los Angeles Kings: Kings/ J.Korab; L.Murphy/ D.Kennedy; M.Murphy/ B.Nicholls; C.Simmer/ D.Evans; M.Dionne/ J.Fox; M.Hardy/ D.Lewis; G.Laskoski (G)/ Title Card	5.00
☐☐☐☐☐☐☐	Minnesota North Stars: North Stars/ C.Giles; F.Barrett/ C.Hartsburg; Brad Maxwell/ T.McCarthy; J.Douglas/ Bob.Smith; D.Ciccarelli/ B.Bellows; W.Plett/ S.Payne; D.Beaupré/ Title Card	5.00
☐☐☐☐☐☐☐	Montréal Canadiens: Canadiens/ R.Green; G.Lafleur/ K.Acton; M.Tremblay/ L.Robinson; S.Shutt/ B.Gainey; D.Wickenheiser/ M.Naslund; G.Delorme/ M.Napier; R.Sévigny (G)/ Title Card	8.00
☐☐☐☐☐☐☐	New Jersey Devils: Devils/ G.Resch (G); B.Lorimer/ J.Quenneville; J.Larmer/ T.Levo; D.Lever/ B.MacMillan; S.Tambellini/ B.Ashton/ R.Meagher/ P.Gagné; M.Kitchen/ TItle Card	5.00
☐☐☐☐☐☐☐	New York Islanders: Islanders/ T.Jonsson; B.Trottier/ Bre.Sutter; M.Bossy/ D.Langevin; D.Potvin/ S.Persson; J.Tonelli/ Bill Smith; C.Gillies/ B.Bourne; B.Goring/ Title Card	8.00
☐☐☐☐☐☐☐	New York Rangers: Rangers/ G.Hanlon (G); B.Beck/ R. McClanahan; R.Duguay/ Do.Maloney; A.Hedberg/ E.Johnstone; Da.Maloney/ M.Rogers; M.Leinonen/ R.Ruotsalainen; M. Pavelich; Title Card	6.00
☐☐☐☐☐☐☐	Philadelphia Flyers: Flyers/ Mark Howe; D.Sittler/ G.Cochrane; I.Sinisalo/ B.Propp; B.Barber/ M.Dvorak; B.Clarke/ P.Holmgren; B.McCrimmon/ R.Flockhart; B.Froese (G)/ Title Card	5.00
☐☐☐☐☐☐☐	Pittsburgh Penguins: Penguins/ P.Lee; M.Dion (G)/D.Hannan; M.Bullard/ R.Carlyle; G.Malone/ D.Shedden; P.Boutette/ M.Chorney; R.Kehoe/ P.Gardner; A.St.Laurent/ Title Card	5.00
☐☐☐☐☐☐☐	Québec Nordiques: Nordiques/ N.Rochefort; R.Cloutier/ P.Aubry; M.Goulet/ M.Stastny; A.Stastny/ R.Moller; B.Wesley/ P.Stastny; W.Paiement/ Dale Hunter; D.Bouchard (G)/ Title Card	5.00
☐☐☐☐☐☐☐	Toronto Maple Leafs: Maple Leafs/ G.Nylund; G.Terrion/ W.Poddubny; J.Anderson/ G.Gingras; M.Frycer/ B.Derlago; B.Salming/ R.Vaive; D.Daoust/ T.Martin; M.Palmateer (G)/ Title Card	6.00
☐☐☐☐☐☐☐	Vancouver Canucks: Canucks/ D.Halward; R.Lanz/ J.Nill; I.Hlinka/ D.Williams; S.Smyl/ D.Rota; T.Gradin/ L.Molin; J.Bubla/ H.Snepsts; R.Brodeur/ Title Card	5.00
☐☐☐☐☐☐☐	Washington Capitals: Capitals/ R.Langway; B.Carpenter/ M.Gartner; G.Currie/ A.Haworth; B.Gustafsson/K.Houston; D.Maruk/ B.Gould; D.Jarvis/ A.Jensen (G); M.Novy/ Title Card	5.00
☐☐☐☐☐☐☐	Winnipeg Jets: Jets/ Bry.Maxwell; D.Hawerchuk/ S.Arniel; M.Lukowich/ D.Christian; P.MacLean/ S.Savard; L.DeBlois/ D.Spring; N.Dupont/ E.Stanowski (G); D.Babych/ Title Card	5.00

1983 - 84 SOVIET STARS

Complete Set (23 cards w/folder): 55.00

	Player	NRMT-MT
☐	Sergei Babinov	2.00
☐	Helmut Balderis	2.00
☐	Zinetula Bilyaletdinov	2.00
☐	Vyacheslav Bykov	5.00
☐	Viacheslav Fetisov	12.00
☐	Irek Gimayev	2.00
☐	Sergei Kapustin	2.00
☐	Alexei Kasatonov	4.00
☐	Andrei Khomutov	4.00
☐	Vladimir Krutov	4.00
☐	Igor Larionov	12.00
☐	Sergei Makarov	8.00
☐	Alexander Maltsev	4.00
☐	Vasili Pervukhin	2.00
☐	Sergei Shepelev	2.00
☐	Alexander Skvorstsov	2.00
☐	Sergei Starikov	2.00
☐	Viktor Tikhonov, Coach	5.00
☐	Vladislav Tretiak (G)	15.00
☐	Mikhail Vasiliev	2.00
☐	Vladimir Yursinov	2.00
☐	Viktor Zhluktov	2.00
☐	Vladimir Zubkov	2.00

1983 - 84 STATER MINT HOCKEY DOLLARS

Each cupro-nickel coin came with a 3" x 8 3/8" perforated card. Other singles may exist.

Coin Diameter: 1 1/4"
Face: Player portrait, name
Back: Team logo
Imprint: none

	No.	Player	NRMT-MT
☐	H1	Lanny McDonald, Cgy.	4.00
☐	H7	Dale Hawerchuk, Wpg.	8.00
☐	H8	Dave Babych, Wpg.	5.00
☐	H9	Morris Lukowich, Wpg.	3.00
☐	H10	Brian Mullen, Wpg.	4.00
☐	H11	Lucien DeBlois, Wpg.	3.00
☐	H12	Brian Hayward (G), Wpg.	4.00
☐	H13	Tim Watters, Wpg.	3.00
☐	H14	Wayne Gretzky, Edm.	15.00
☐	H15	Andy Moog (G), Edm	8.00
☐	H16	Dave Hunter, Edm.	4.00
☐	H17	Ken Linseman, Edm. (*)	25.00
☐	H18	Lee Fogolin, Edm. (*)	25.00
☐	H19	Dave Semenko, Edm.	4.00
☐	H20	Mark Messier, Edm.	10.00

1983 - 84 VACHON

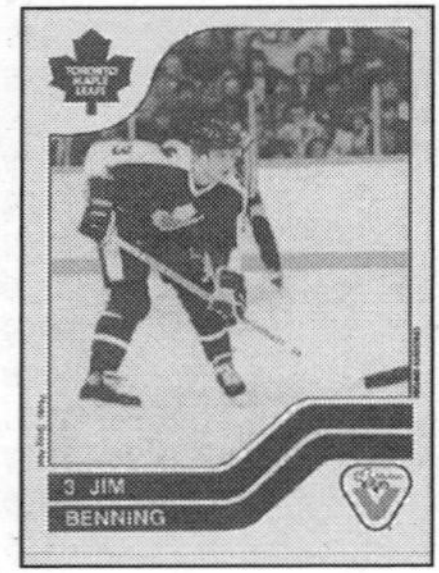

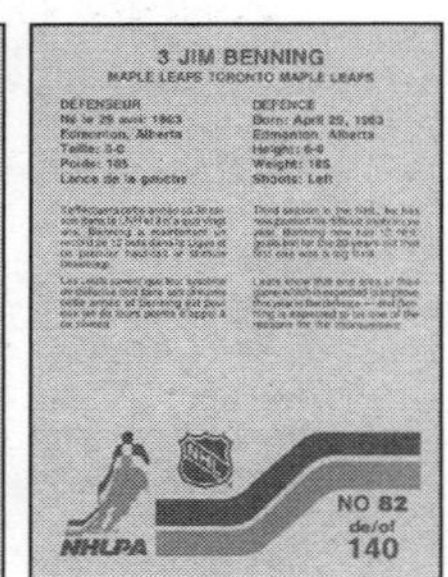

The set was issued as a two-card panel on Vachon Food product packages. The error noted for card no.96 was corrected in the second series issue. Vachon also sold complete sets. Cards are numbered of 140.

Card Size: 2 9/16" x 3 9/16"
Face: Four colour, white border; Name, Number, Team and Sponsor logos
Back: Blue on buff card stock; Name, Number, Team, Resume, Bilingual
Imprint: PROMO MARKETING NHLPA
Complete Set (140 cards): 185.00
Common Player: .75

	No.	Player	NRMT-MT
☐	1	Paul Baxter, Cgy.	.75
☐	2	Eddy Beers, Cgy.	.75
☐	3	Steve Bozek, Cgy.	.75
☐	4	Mike Eaves, Cgy.	.75
☐	5	Don Edwards (G), Cgy.	1.00
☐	6	Kari Eloranta, Cgy.	.75
☐	7	Dave Hindmarch, Cgy.	.75
☐	8	Jamie Hislop, Cgy.	.75
☐	9	Stephen Konroyd, Cgy.	.75
☐	10	Réjean Lemelin (G), Cgy.	.75
☐	11	Hakan Loob, Cgy.	1.50
☐	12	Jamie Macoun, Cgy.	.75
☐	13	Lanny McDonald, Cgy.	2.75
☐	14	Kent Nilsson, Cgy.	.75
☐	15	Colin Patterson, Cgy.	.75
☐	16	Jim Peplinski, Cgy.	.75
☐	17	Paul Reinhart, Cgy.	.75
☐	18	Doug Risebrough, Cgy.	.75
☐	19	Steve Tambellini, Cgy.	.75
☐	20	Mickey Volcan, Cgy.	.75
☐	21	Glenn Anderson, Edm.	2.00
☐	22	Paul Coffey, Edm.	7.50
☐	23	Lee Fogolin, Edm.	.75
☐	24	Grant Fuhr (G), Edm.	6.75
☐	25	Randy Gregg, Edm.	.75
☐	26	Wayne Gretzky, Edm.	45.00
☐	27	Charlie Huddy, Edm.	.75
☐	28	Pat Hughes, Edm.	.75
☐	29	Dave Hunter, Edm.	.75
☐	30	Don Jackson, Edm.	.75
☐	31	Jari Kurri, Edm.	4.00
☐	32	Willy Lindstrom, Edm.	.75
☐	33	Ken Linseman, Edm.	.75
☐	34	Kevin Lowe, Edm.	1.75
☐	35	Dave Lumley, Edm.	.75
☐	36	Mark Messier, Edm.	15.00
☐	37	Andy Moog (G), Edm.	3.25
☐	38	Jaroslav Pouzar, Edm.	.75
☐	39	Tom Roulston, Edm.	.75
☐	40	Dave Semenko, Edm.	.75
☐	41	Guy Carbonneau, Mtl.	2.00
☐	42	Kent Carlson, Mtl.	.75
☐	43	Gilbert Delorme, Mtl.	.75
☐	44	Bob Gainey, Mtl.	2.25
☐	45	Jean Hamel, Mtl.	.75
☐	46	Mark Hunter, Mtl.	.75
☐	47	Guy Lafleur, Mtl.	8.00
☐	48	Craig Ludwig, Mtl.	.75
☐	49	Pierre Mondou, Mtl.	.75
☐	50	Mats Naslund, Mtl.	1.75
☐	51	Chris Nilan, Mtl.	1.50
☐	52	Greg Paslawski, Mtl.	.75
☐	53	Larry Robinson, Mtl.	3.00
☐	54	Richard Sévigny (G), Mtl.	1.00
☐	55	Steve Shutt, Mtl.	2.75
☐	56	Bobby Smith, Mtl.	2.00
☐	57	Mario Tremblay, Mtl.	.75
☐	58	Ryan Walter, Mtl.	.75
☐	59	Rick Wamsley (G), Mtl.	1.00
☐	60	Doug Wickenheiser, Mtl.	.75
☐	61	Bo Berglund, Que.	.75
☐	62	Dan Bouchard (G), Que.	1.00
☐	63	Alain Côté, Que.	.75
☐	64	Brian Ford (G), Que.	1.00
☐	65	Michel Goulet, Que.	2.75
☐	66	Dale Hunter, Que.	1.50
☐	67	Mario Marois, Que.	.75
☐	68	Tony McKegney, Que.	.75
☐	69	Randy Moller, Que.	.75
☐	70	Wilf Paiement, Que.	.75
☐	71	Pat Price, Que.	.75
☐	72	Normand Rochefort, Que.	.75
☐	73	André Savard, Que.	.75
☐	74	Louis Sleigher, Que.	.75
☐	75	Anton Stastny, Que.	1.50
☐	76	Marian Stastny, Que.	.75
☐	77	Peter Stastny, Que.	3.75
☐	78	John Van Boxmeer, Que.	.75
☐	79	Wally Weir, Que.	.75
☐	80	Blake Wesley, Que.	.75
☐	81	John Anderson, Tor.	.75
☐	82	Jim Benning, Tor.	.75
☐	83	Dan Daoust, Tor.	.75
☐	84	Bill Derlago, Tor.	.75
☐	85	Dave Farrish, Tor.	.75
☐	86	Miroslav Frycer, Tor.	.75
☐	87	Stewart Gavin, Tor.	.75
☐	88	Gaston Gingras, Tor.	.75
☐	89	Billy Harris, Tor.	.75
☐	90	Peter Ihnacak, Tor.	.75
☐	91	James Korn, Tor.	.75
☐	92	Terry Martin, Tor.	.75
☐	93	Dale McCourt, Tor.	.75
☐	94	Gary Nylund, Tor.	.75
☐	95	Mike Palmateer (G), Tor.	1.00
☐	96	Walt Poddubny, Tor., Error	10.00
☐	96	Walt Poddubny, Tor., Corrected	2.50
☐	97	Borje Salming, Tor.	2.25
☐	98	Rick St. Croix (G), Tor.	1.00
☐	99	Greg Terrion, Tor.	.75
☐	100	Rick Vaive, Tor.	.75
☐	101	Richard Brodeur (G), Van.	1.00
☐	102	Jiri Bubla, Van.	.75
☐	103	Garth Butcher, Van.	.75
☐	104	Ron Delorme, Van.	.75
☐	105	John Garrett (G), Van.	.75
☐	106	Jere Gillis, Van.	.75
☐	107	Thomas Gradin, Van.	.75
☐	108	Doug Halward, Van.	.75
☐	109	Mark Kirton, Van.	.75
☐	110	Rick Lanz, Van.	.75
☐	111	Gary Lupul, Van.	.75
☐	112	Kevin McCarthy, Van.	.75
☐	113	Lars Molin, Van.	.75
☐	114	James Nill, Van.	.75
☐	115	Darcy Rota, Van.	.75
☐	116	Stan Smyl, Van.	.75
☐	117	Harold Snepsts, Van.	.75
☐	118	Patrik Sundstrom, Van.	.75
☐	119	Tony Tanti, Van.	1.00
☐	120	Dave Williams, Van.	.75
☐	121	Scott Arniel, Wpg.	.75
☐	122	Dave Babych, Wpg.	.75
☐	123	Laurie Boschman, Wpg.	.75
☐	124	Wade Campbell, Wpg.	.75
☐	125	Lucien DeBlois, Wpg.	.75
☐	126	Dale Hawerchuk, Wpg.	5.00
☐	127	Brian Hayward (G), Wpg.	.75
☐	128	James Kyte, Wpg.	.75
☐	129	Morris Lukowich, Wpg.	.75
☐	130	Bengt Lundholm, Wpg.	.75
☐	131	Paul MacLean, Wpg.	.75
☐	132	Moe Mantha, Wpg.	.75
☐	133	Andrew McBain, Wpg.	.75
☐	134	Brian Mullen, Wpg.	.75
☐	135	Robert Picard, Wpg.	.75
☐	136	Doug Smail, Wpg.	.75
☐	137	Doug Soetaert, Wpg.	.75
☐	138	Thomas Steen, Wpg.	.75
☐	139	Tim Watters, Wpg.	.75
☐	140	Tim Young, Wpg.	.75

1984 - 85 ISLANDER NEWS BRYAN TROTTIER

Card Size: 2 1/2" x 3 1/2"
Face: Four colour or black and white photo, pale blue border; Number, Facsimile autograph.
Imprint: ISLANDER NEWS
Complete Set (33 cards): 30.00

	No.	Player	NRMT-MT
☐	1	Using Drugs Puts You In A Permanent Penalty Box	
☐	2	Say No to Drugs!	
☐	3	Don't Drink. Don't Smoke. Don't Play With Drugs...	
☐	4	Don't Let Your Mind Go To Pot	
☐	5	Friends Don't Let Friends Drive Drunk	
☐	6	Enjoy Alternatives To Drugs & Booze	
☐	7	Help Friends Feel Good About Themselves	
☐	8	People Who Are Involved Don't Need Drugs	
☐	9	Think Before You Drink	
☐	10	It's Your Choice. Don't Be A Victim	

☐	11	Drugs...Don't Let This Five Letter Word Ruin Your Life
☐	12	Living With Drugs Can Hurt
☐	13	Alcohol Is The Worst Drug Of All
☐	14	Drugs And School Don't Mix
☐	15	Don't Be Embarrassed If You Have A Problem...Get Help
☐	16	Be A Winner...Don't Play With Drugs
☐	17	Develop Good Habits...Not Drug Habits
☐	18	Alcholol is A Drug Think Don't Drink
☐	19	It May Take Five Years To Cure A Drug Addict
☐	20	Grow Up Tall, Use No Drugs At All
☐	21	Don't Play With Drugs...It's A Losing Game
☐	22	Keep Off The Grass
☐	23	Don't Be A Fool Trying To Act Cool..."Be Straight"
☐	24	Even A Kid Can Become An Alcoholic
☐	25	Drugs...Be Smart...Don't Start
☐	26	You Can't Take Your Best Shot When You're High On Drugs
☐	27	You Don't Need Drugs...You Can Make It On Your Own
☐	28	Drugs Can Cause Genetic Damage
☐	29	Make The Save Of Your Life...Don't Drink
☐	30	Be A Winner...Shut Out Drugs
☐	31	Stopping Is Hard...Don't Start On Drugs
☐	32	Starting With Drugs Can Finish Your Life
☐	33	Real Life Is Fun...Don't Drop Out With Drugs

1984 - 85 KELLOGG'S PLAYER DISCS

These player disks were issued in strips of six disks and the team logos individually. Both came inside a black or orange plastic puck with the NHL crest moulded on the top lid. The pucks in turn can be mounted in a display shield. The disks are arranged in alphabetical order by the first player of each strip. The seventh and eighth panel feature Olympic athletes. An 8-panel set sells for $45.

Disk Diameter: 2 1/16"
Face: Four colour, white border
Back: Black on white card stock; Team logo, Name, Position, Resume, Bilingual, Facsimile autograph
Imprint: None
Complete Set (6 panels): 35.00
Shield: 50.00

	No.	Player	NRMT-MT
☐	1	Paul Coffey, Edm.	8.00
	2	Mario Tremblay, Chi.	
	3	John Anderson, Tor.	
	4	Dale Hawerchuk, Wpg.	
	5	Rick Kehoe, Pgh.	
	6	Barry Beck, NYR.	
☐	7	Bernie Federko, Stl.	7.00
	8	Ron Francis, Hfd.	
	9	Stan Smyl, Van.	
	10	Mike Gartner, Wsh.	
	11	Dave Babych, Wpg.	
	12	Lanny McDonald, Cgy.	
☐	13	Paul Reinhart, Cgy.	9.00
	14	Jari Kurri, Edm.	
	15	Michel Goulet, Que.	
	16	Richard Brodeur (G), Van.	
	17	Mike Bossy, NYI	
	18	Dino Ciccarelli, Min.	
☐	19	Larry Robinson, Mtl.	6.00
	20	Doug Risebrough, Cgy.	
	21	Paul MacLean, Wpg.	
	22	Peter Stastny, Que.	
	23	Marcel Dionne, L.A.	
	24	Reed Larson, Det.	
☐	25	Borje Salming, Tor.	9.00
	26	Kevin Lowe, Edm.	
	27	Guy Lafleur, Mtl.	
	28	Rick Middleton, Bos.	
	29	Gilbert Perreault, Buf.	
	30	The Stanley Cup	
☐	31	Rick Vaive, Tor.	6.00
	32	Glenn Resch (G), N.J.	
	33	Darryl Sittler, Pha.	
	34	Doug Wilson, Chi.	
	35	Dale Hunter, Que.	
	36	Thomas Gradin, Van.	

1984 - 85 KELOWNA WINGS & WHL GRADUATES

Face: Black and white
Back: Black on white card stock
Imprint:
Complete Set (56 cards): 75.00

	No.	Player	NRMT-MT
☐	1	Checklist	2.00
☐	2	Darcy Wakaluk (G)	2.25
☐	3	Stacey Nickel	.75
☐	4	Jeff Sharples	1.50
☐	5	Greg Zuk	.75
☐	6	Daryn Sivertson	.75
☐	7	Randy Cameron	.75
☐	8	Mark Fioretti	.75
☐	9	Ron Viglasi	.75
☐	10	Ian Herbers	.75
☐	11	Mike Wegleitner	.75
☐	12	Terry Zaporzan	.75
☐	13	Dwaine Hutton	.75
☐	14	Rod Williams	.75
☐	15	Jeff Rohlicek	.75
☐	16	Brent Gilchrist	2.50
☐	17	Rocky Dundas	.75
☐	18	Grant Delcourt	.75
☐	19	Cam Laroruk	.75
☐	20	Tony Horacek	1.00
☐	21	Mark Wingerter	.75
☐	22	Mick Vukota	1.00
☐	23	Danny Gare	2.50
☐	24	Rich Sutter	1.25
☐	25	Alfie Turcotte	.75
☐	26	Bryan Trottier	10.00
☐	27	Bill Derlago	1.25
☐	28	Stan Smyl	2.00
☐	29	Brent Sutter	3.00
☐	30	Mel Bridgman	1.50
☐	31	Paul Cyr	1.25
☐	32	Gary Lupul	1.00
☐	33	Ray Neufeld	1.25
☐	34	Brian Propp	3.00
☐	35	Bob Nystrom	2.00
☐	36	Ryan Walter	1.25
☐	37	Russ Courtnall	4.00
☐	38	Larry Playfair	1.00
☐	39	Ron Delorme	1.00
☐	40	Ron Sutter	1.25
☐	41	Bobby Clarke	10.00
☐	42	Bob Bourne	1.25
☐	43	Cam Neely	10.00
☐	44	Murray Craven	2.25
☐	45	Clark Gillies	3.00
☐	46	Ron Flockhart	1.00
☐	47	Harold Snepts	2.50
☐	48	Duane Sutter	1.75
☐	49	Garth Butcher	2.00
☐	50	Bill Hajt	1.00
☐	51	Jim Benning	1.00
☐	52	Ray Allison	1.00
☐	53	Ken Wregget (G)	5.00
☐	54	Phil Russell	1.00
☐	55	Brad McCrimmon	2.50
☐	56	Dan Hodgson	1.00

1984 - 85 O-PEE-CHEE

Face: Four colour, white border; Position
Back: Pink and blue on card stock; Number, Resume, Bilingual
Imprint: © 1984 O-Pee-Chee
Complete Set (396 cards): 230.00
Common Player: .25

	No.	Player	NRMT-MT
☐	1	Ray Bourque, Bos.	8.00
☐	2	Keith Crowder, Bos.	.25
☐	3	Luc Dufour, Bos., LC	.25
☐	4	Tom Fergus, Bos.	.25
☐	**5**	**Doug Keans (G), Bos., RC**	**.35**
☐	6	Gord Kluzak, Bos.	.25
☐	7	Ken Linseman, Bos.	.25
☐	**8**	**Nevin Markwart, Bos., RC**	**.25**
☐	9	Rick Middleton, Bos.	.35
☐	10	Mike Milbury, Bos., LC	.25
☐	11	Jim Nill, Bos.	.25
☐	12	Mike O'Connell, Bos.	.25
☐	13	Terry O'Reilly, Bos., LC	.35
☐	14	Barry Pederson, Bos.	.25
☐	15	Pete Peeters (G), Bos.	.35
☐	**16**	**Dave Silk, Bos., RC, LC**	**.25**
☐	**17**	**Dave Andreychuk, Buf., RC**	**6.00**
☐	**18**	**Tom Barrasso (G), Buf., RC**	**6.00**
☐	19	Réal Cloutier, Buf., LC	.25
☐	20	Mike Foligno, Buf.	.25
☐	21	Bill Hajt, Buf.	.25
☐	**22**	**Gilles Hamel, Buf., RC**	**.25**
☐	23	Phil Housley, Buf.	1.75
☐	24	Gilbert Perreault, Buf.	.75
☐	25	Brent Peterson, Buf.	.25
☐	26	Larry Playfair, Buf.	.25
☐	27	Craig Ramsay, Buf.	.35
☐	28	Mike Ramsey, Buf.	.25
☐	29	Lindy Ruff, Buf.	.35
☐	30	Bob Sauvé (G), Buf.	.35
☐	31	Ric Seiling, Buf.	.25
☐	32	Murray Bannerman (G), Chi.	.35
☐	33	Keith Brown, Chi.	.25
☐	34	Curt Fraser, Chi.	.25
☐	35	Bill Gardner, Chi., LC	.25
☐	36	Jeff Larmer, Chi., LC	.25
☐	37	Steve Larmer, Chi.	3.50
☐	38	Steve Ludzik, Chi., LC	.25
☐	39	Tom Lysiak, Chi.	.25
☐	40	Bob MacMillan, Chi.	.25
☐	41	Bob Murray, Chi.	.25
☐	**42**	**Troy Murray, Chi., RC**	**.50**
☐	**43**	**Jack O'Callahan, Chi., RC**	**.25**
☐	44	Rick Paterson, Chi., LC	.25
☐	45	Denis Savard, Chi.	1.75
☐	46	Alan Secord, Chi.	.25
☐	47	Darryl Sutter, Chi.	.35
☐	48	Doug Wilson, Chi.	.35
☐	49	John Barrett, Det., LC	.25
☐	50	Ivan Boldirev, Det.	.25
☐	51	Colin Campbell, Det., LC	.35
☐	52	Ron Duguay, Det.	.25
☐	53	Dwight Foster, Det.	.25
☐	54	Danny Gare, Det.	.35
☐	55	Eddie Johnstone, Det., LC	.25
☐	**56**	**Kelly Kisio, Det., RC**	**.50**
☐	**57**	**Lane Lambert, Det., RC**	**.25**
☐	58	Reed Larson, Det.	.25
☐	59	Bob Manno, Det.	.25
☐	**60**	**Randy Ladouceur, Det., RC**	**.25**
☐	61	Ed Mio (G), Det., LC	.35
☐	62	John Ogrodnick, Det.	.25
☐	63	Brad Park, Det., LC	.50
☐	64	Greg Smith, Det., LC	.25
☐	**65**	**Greg Stefan (G), Det., RC**	**.35**
☐	66	Paul Woods, Det., LC	.25
☐	**67**	**Steve Yzerman, Det., RC**	**100.00**
☐	**68**	**Bob Crawford, Hfd., RC**	**.25**
☐	69	Rich Dunn, Hfd., LC	.25
☐	70	Ron Francis, Hfd.	4.00
☐	71	Marty Howe, Hfd., LC	.25
☐	72	Mark Johnson, Hfd.	.25
☐	73	Chris Kotsopoulos, Hfd.	.25
☐	74	Greg Malone, Hfd.	.25
☐	75	Greg Millen (G), Hfd.	.35
☐	76	Ray Neufeld, Hfd.	.25
☐	77	Joel Quenneville, Hfd.	.35
☐	78	Risto Siltanen, Hfd.	.25
☐	**79**	**Sylvain Turgeon, Hfd., RC**	**.50**
☐	80	Mike Zuke, Hfd.	.25
☐	81	Steve Christoff, L.A., LC	.25
☐	82	Marcel Dionne, L.A.	.75
☐	83	Brian Engblom, L.A.	.25
☐	84	Jim Fox, L.A.	.25
☐	**85**	**Anders Hakansson, L.A., RC, LC**	**.25**
☐	86	Mark Hardy, L.A.	.25
☐	**87**	**Brian MacLellan, L.A., RC**	**.25**
☐	88	Bernie Nicholls, L.A.	2.50
☐	89	Terry Ruskowski, L.A.	.25

	No.	Player	Price
☐	90	Charlie Simmer, L.A. (Bos.)	.25
☐	91	Doug Smith, L.A.	.25
☐	92	Dave Taylor, L.A.	.35
☐	93	Keith Acton, Min.	.25
☐	94	Don Beaupré (G), Min.	.35
☐	95	Brian Bellows, Min.	1.25
☐	96	Neal Broten, Min.	.35
☐	97	Dino Ciccarelli, Min.	1.25
☐	98	Craig Hartsburg, Min.	.35
☐	**99**	**Tom Hirsch, Min., RC, LC**	**.25**
☐	100	Paul Holmgren, Min., LC	.25
☐	101	Dennis Maruk, Min.	.25
☐	102	Brad Maxwell, Min.	.25
☐	103	Tom McCarthy, Min.	.25
☐	104	Gilles Meloche (G), Min.	.35
☐	105	Mark Napier, Min.	.25
☐	106	Steve Payne, Min.	.25
☐	107	Gord Roberts, Min.	.25
☐	108	Harold Snepsts, Min.	.25
☐	109	Mel Bridgman, N.J.	.25
☐	110	Joe Cirella, N.J.	.25
☐	111	Tim Higgins, N.J.	.25
☐	112	Don Lever, N.J.	.25
☐	113	Dave Lewis, N.J.	.25
☐	114	Bob Lorimer, N.J., LC	.25
☐	115	Ron Low (G), N.J., LC	.35
☐	**116**	**Jan Ludvig, N.J., RC, LC**	**.25**
☐	117	Gary McAdam, N.J., LC	.25
☐	118	Rich Preston, Chi., (N.J.)	.25
☐	119	Glenn Resch (G), N.J.	.35
☐	120	Phil Russell, N.J.	.25
☐	**121**	**Pat Verbeek, N.J., RC**	**7.50**
☐	122	Mike Bossy, NYI.	3.00
☐	123	Bob Bourne, NYI.	.25
☐	**124**	**Patrick Flatley, NYI., RC**	**1.00**
☐	**125**	**Greg Gilbert, NYI., RC**	**.50**
☐	126	Clark Gillies, NYI.	.35
☐	127	Butch Goring, NYI., LC	.35
☐	128	Tomas Jonsson, NYI.	.25
☐	**129**	**Pat LaFontaine, NYI., RC**	**30.00**
☐	130	Rollie Melanson (G), NYI.	.35
☐	131	Ken Morrow, NYI.	.25
☐	132	Bob Nystrom, NYI.	.25
☐	133	Stefan Persson, NYI., LC	.25
☐	134	Denis Potvin, NYI.	.75
☐	135	Billy Smith (G), NYI.	.60
☐	136	Brent Sutter, NYI.	.35
☐	137	Duane Sutter, NYI.	.25
☐	138	John Tonelli, NYI.	.35
☐	139	Bryan Trottier, NYI.	1.50
☐	140	Barry Beck, NYR.	.25
☐	141	Ron Greschner, NYR.	.25
☐	142	Glen Hanlon (G), NYR.	.35
☐	143	Anders Hedberg, NYR., LC	.35
☐	144	Tom Laidlaw, NYR.	.25
☐	145	Pierre Larouche, NYR.	.25
☐	146	Dave Maloney, NYR.	.25
☐	147	Don Maloney, NYR.	.25
☐	148	Mark Osborne, NYR.	.25
☐	149	Larry Patey, NYR., LC	.25
☐	**150**	**James Patrick, NYR., RC**	**1.25**
☐	151	Mark Pavelich, NYR.	.25
☐	152	Mike Rogers, NYR.	.25
☐	153	Reijo Ruotsalainen, NYR.	.25
☐	154	Blaine Stoughton, NYR., LC	.25
☐	**155**	**Peter Sundstrom, NYR., RC, LC**	**.50**
☐	156	Bill Barber, Pha., LC	.35
☐	157	Doug Crossman, Pha.	.25
☐	**158**	**Thomas Eriksson, Pha., RC, LC**	**.25**
☐	159	Bob Froese (G), Pha.	.35
☐	**160**	**Paul Guay, Pha., RC, LC**	**.25**
☐	161	Mark Howe, Pha.	.35
☐	162	Tim Kerr, Pha.	.35
☐	163	Brad Marsh, Pha.	.35
☐	164	Brad McCrimmon, Pha.	.35
☐	**165**	**Dave Poulin, Pha., RC**	**1.50**
☐	166	Brian Propp, Pha.	.35
☐	**167**	**Ilkka Sinisalo, Pha., RC**	**.25**
☐	168	Darryl Sittler, Pha., (Det.), LC	.50
☐	**169**	**Rich Sutter, Pha., RC**	**.50**
☐	**170**	**Ron Sutter, Pha., RC**	**.50**
☐	171	Pat Boutette, Pgh., LC	.25
☐	172	Mike Bullard, Pgh.	.25
☐	173	Michel Dion (G), Pgh., LC	.35
☐	174	Ron Flockhart, Pgh.	.25
☐	175	Greg Fox, Pgh., LC	.25
☐	176	Denis Herron (G), Pgh.	.35
☐	177	Rick Kehoe, Pgh., LC	.25
☐	178	Kevin McCarthy, Pgh., LC	.25
☐	179	Tom Roulston, Pgh., LC	.25
☐	180	Mark Taylor, Pgh., LC	.25
☐	181	Wayne Babych, Stl., (Pgh)	.25
☐	**182**	**Tim Bothwell, Stl., RC**	**.25**
☐	183	Kevin LaVallée, Stl., LC	.25
☐	184	Bernie Federko, Stl.	.35
☐	**185**	**Doug Gilmour, Stl., RC**	**40.00**
☐	**186**	**Terry Johnson, Stl., RC, LC**	**.25**
☐	187	Mike Liut (G), Stl.	.35
☐	188	Joe Mullen, Stl.	1.75
☐	189	Jorgen Pettersson, Stl., LC	.25
☐	190	Rob Ramage, Stl.	.25
☐	**191**	**Dwight Schofield, Stl., RC, LC**	**.25**
☐	192	Brian Sutter, Stl.	.35
☐	193	Doug Wickenheiser, Stl.	.25
☐	194	Bob Carpenter, Wsh.	.35
☐	195	Dave Christian, Wsh.	.25
☐	**196**	**Bob Gould, Wsh., RC**	**.25**
☐	197	Mike Gartner, Wsh.	3.25
☐	198	Bengt Gustafsson, Wsh.	.25
☐	**199**	**Alan Haworth, Wsh., RC**	**.25**
☐	200	Doug Jarvis, Wsh.	.25
☐	201	Al Jensen (G), Wsh.	.35
☐	202	Rod Langway, Wsh.	.35
☐	203	Craig Laughlin, Wsh.	.25
☐	204	Larry Murphy, Wsh.	.75
☐	205	Pat Riggin (G), Wsh.	.35
☐	206	Scott Stevens, Wsh.	3.50
☐	207	AS: Michel Goulet, Que.	.50
☐	208	AS: Wayne Gretzky, Edm.	6.00
☐	209	AS: Mike Bossy, NYI.	.75
☐	210	AS: Rod Langway, Wsh.	.35
☐	211	AS: Ray Bourque, Bos.	3.50
☐	212	AS: Tom Barrasso (G), Buf.	1.75
☐	213	AS: Mark Messier, Edm.	4.00
☐	214	AS: Bryan Trottier, NYI.	.50
☐	215	AS: Jari Kurri, Edm.	2.00
☐	216	AS: Denis Potvin, NYI.	.50
☐	217	AS: Paul Coffey, Edm.	2.50
☐	218	AS: Pat Riggin (G), Wsh.	.35
☐	219	Ed Beers, Cgy.	.25
☐	220	Steve Bozek, Cgy.	.25
☐	221	Mike Eaves, Cgy.	.25
☐	222	Don Edwards (G), Cgy.	.35
☐	223	Kari Eloranta, Cgy., LC	.25
☐	224	Dave Hindmarch, Cgy., LC	.25
☐	225	Jim Jackson, Cgy., LC	.25
☐	226	Steve Konroyd, Cgy.	.25
☐	**227**	**Richard Kromm, Cgy., RC**	**.25**
☐	228	Réjean Lemelin (G), Cgy.	.35
☐	**229**	**Hakan Loob, Cgy., RC**	**3.00**
☐	**230**	**Jamie Macoun, Cgy., RC**	**.50**
☐	231	Lanny McDonald, Cgy.	.50
☐	232	Kent Nilsson, Cgy., LC	.25
☐	233	James Peplinski, Cgy.	.25
☐	**234**	**Dan Quinn, Cgy., RC**	**.35**
☐	235	Paul Reinhart, Cgy.	.25
☐	236	Doug Risebrough, Cgy.	.35
☐	237	Steve Tambellini, Cgy.	.25
☐	238	Glenn Anderson, Edm.	1.50
☐	239	Paul Coffey, Edm.	6.00
☐	240	Lee Fogolin, Edm.	.25
☐	241	Grant Fuhr (G), Edm.	3.75
☐	242	Randy Gregg, Edm.	.25
☐	243	Wayne Gretzky, Edm.	25.00
☐	244	Charlie Huddy, Edm.	.35
☐	245	Pat Hughes, Edm., LC	.25
☐	246	Dave Hunter, Edm.	.25
☐	247	Don Jackson, Edm., LC	.25
☐	248	Mike Krushelnyski, Bos., (Edm.)	.25
☐	249	Jari Kurri, Edm.	4.50
☐	250	Willy Lindstrom, Edm.	.25
☐	251	Kevin Lowe, Edm.	.50
☐	252	Dave Lumley, Edm., (Hfd.), LC	.25
☐	**253**	**Kevin McClelland, Edm., RC**	**.25**
☐	254	Mark Messier, Edm.	10.00
☐	255	Andy Moog (G), Edm.	3.50
☐	256	Jaroslav Pouzar, Edm., LC	.25
☐	257	Guy Carbonneau, Mtl.	1.50
☐	**258**	**John Chabot, Mtl., RC**	**.25**
☐	**259**	**Chris Chelios, Mtl., RC**	**30.00**
☐	260	Lucien DeBlois, Mtl., Error (Deblois)	.25
☐	261	Bob Gainey, Mtl.	.50
☐	262	Rick Green, Mtl.	.25
☐	263	Jean Hamel, Mtl., LC	.25
☐	264	Guy Lafleur, Mtl.	3.50
☐	265	Craig Ludwig, Mtl.	.35
☐	266	Pierre Mondou, Mtl.	.25
☐	267	Mats Naslund, Mtl.	.75
☐	268	Chris Nilan, Mtl.	.25
☐	**269**	**Steve Penney (G), Mtl., RC**	**.35**
☐	270	Larry Robinson, Mtl.	.60
☐	271	Bill Root, Mtl., (Tor.), LC	.25
☐	272	Steve Shutt, Mtl., LC	.35
☐	273	Bobby Smith, Mtl.	.35
☐	274	Mario Tremblay, Mtl.	.35
☐	275	Ryan Walter, Mtl.	.35
☐	**276**	**Bo Berglund, Que., RC, LC**	**.25**
☐	277	Dan Bouchard (G), Que.	.35
☐	278	Alain Côté, Que.	.25
☐	279	André Doré, Que., (NYR.), LC	.25
☐	280	Michel Goulet, Que.	.50
☐	281	Dale Hunter, Que.	.50
☐	282	Mario Marois, Que.	.25
☐	283	Tony McKegney, Que.	.25
☐	284	Randy Moller, Que.	.25
☐	285	Wilf Paiement, Que.	.25
☐	286	Pat Price, Que., LC	.25
☐	287	Normand Rochefort, Que.	.25
☐	288	André Savard, Que., LC	.25
☐	289	Richard Sévigny (G), Que., LC	.25
☐	290	Louis Sleigher, Que., (Bos.), LC	.25
☐	291	Anton Stastny, Que.	.25
☐	292	Marian Stastny, Que., LC	.25
☐	293	Peter Stastny, Que.	1.50
☐	294	Blake Wesley, Que., LC	.25
☐	295	John Anderson, Tor.	.25
☐	296	Jim Benning, Tor.	.25
☐	**297**	**Allan Bester (G), Tor., RC, Error (Alan)**	**.35**
☐	**298**	**Rich Costello, Tor., RC, LC**	**.25**
☐	299	Dan Daoust, Tor.	.25
☐	300	Bill Derlago, Tor.	.25
☐	301	Dave Farrish, Tor., LC	.25
☐	302	Stewart Gavin, Tor.	.25
☐	303	Gaston Gingras, Tor.	.25
☐	304	Jim Korn, Tor.	.25
☐	**305**	**Gary Leeman, Tor., RC**	**.35**
☐	306	Terry Martin, Tor., (Edm.), LC	.25
☐	**307**	**Gary Nylund, Tor., RC**	**.25**
☐	308	Mike Palmateer (G), Tor., LC	.35
☐	309	Walt Poddubny, Tor.	.25
☐	310	Rick St. Croix (G), Tor., LC	.35
☐	311	Borje Salming, Tor.	.35
☐	312	Greg Terrion, Tor.	.25
☐	313	Rick Vaive, Tor.	.35
☐	314	Richard Brodeur (G), Van.	.35
☐	315	Jiri Bubla, Van., LC	.25
☐	316	Ron Delorme, Van., LC	.25
☐	317	John Garrett (G), Van., LC	.35
☐	318	Jere Gillis, Van., LC	.25
☐	319	Thomas Gradin, Van.	.25
☐	320	Doug Halward, Van.	.25
☐	321	Rick Lanz, Van.	.25
☐	**322**	**Moe Lemay, Van., RC**	**.25**
☐	323	Gary Lupul, Van., LC	.25
☐	324	Al MacAdam, Min., (Van.)	.25
☐	325	Rob McClanahan, Van., LC	.25
☐	326	Peter McNab, Van., LC	.25
☐	**327**	**Cam Neely, Van., RC**	**30.00**
☐	328	Darcy Rota, Van., LC	.25
☐	**329**	**Andy Schliebener, Van., RC, LC**	**.25**
☐	330	Stan Smyl, Van.	.25
☐	331	Patrik Sundstrom, Van.	.25
☐	332	Tony Tanti, Van.	.35
☐	333	Scott Arniel, Wpg.	.25
☐	334	Dave Babych, Wpg.	.35
☐	335	Laurie Boschman, Wpg.	.25
☐	336	Wade Campbell, Wpg., LC	.25
☐	337	Randy Carlyle, Wpg.	.35
☐	338	Jordy Douglas, Wpg., LC	.25
☐	339	Dale Hawerchuk, Wpg.	3.50
☐	340	Morris Lukowich, Wpg.	.25
☐	341	Bengt Lundholm, Wpg., LC	.25
☐	342	Paul MacLean, Wpg.	.25
☐	**343**	**Andrew McBain, Wpg., RC**	**.25**
☐	344	Brian Mullen, Wpg.	.25

	No.	Player	Price
☐	345	Robert Picard, Wpg.	.25
☐	346	Doug Smail, Wpg.	.25
☐	347	Doug Soetaert (G), Wpg., (Mtl.), LC	.35
☐	348	Thomas Steen, Wpg.	.25
☐	349	Perry Turnbull, Wpg.	.25
☐	350	Tim Watters, Wpg.	.25
☐	351	Tim Young, Wpg., LC	.25
☐	352	Boston Bruins: Rick Middleton	.25
☐	353	Buffalo Sabres: Dave Andreychuk	2.25
☐	354	Calgary Flames: Ed Beers	.25
☐	355	Chicago Blackhawks: Denis Savard	.75
☐	356	Detroit Red Wings: John Ogrodnick	.25
☐	357	Edmonton Oilers Leader: Wayne Gretzky	6.00
☐	358	Los Angeles Kings Leader: Charlie Simmer	.25
☐	359	Minnesota North Stars: Brian Bellows	.50
☐	360	Montréal Canadiens: Guy Lafleur	1.25
☐	361	New Jersey Devils: Mel Bridgman	.25
☐	362	New York Islanders: Mike Bossy	.75
☐	363	New York Rangers: Pierre Larouche	.25
☐	364	Philadelphia Flyers: Tim Kerr	.25
☐	365	Pittsburgh Penguins: Mike Bullard	.25
☐	366	Québec Nordiques: Michel Goulet	.35
☐	367	St. Louis Blues: B. Federko & J. Mullen	.35
☐	368	Toronto Maple Leafs: Rick Vaive	.25
☐	369	Vancouver Canucks: Tony Tanti	.25
☐	370	Washington Capitals: Mike Gartner	1.50
☐	371	Winnipeg Jets: Paul MacLean	.25
☐	372	Hartford Whalers: Sylvain Turgeon	.25
☐	373	Art Ross Trophy: Wayne Gretzky	6.00
☐	374	Hart Trophy: Wayne Gretzky	6.00
☐	375	Calder Trophy: Tom Barrasso	1.75
☐	376	Lady Byng Trophy: Mike Bossy	1.75
☐	377	Norris Trophy: Rod Langway	.35
☐	378	Masterton Trophy: Brad Park	.35
☐	379	Vezina Trophy: Tom Barrasso	1.75
☐	380	LL: Scoring: Wayne Gretzky, Edm.	6.00
☐	381	LL: Goals: Wayne Gretzky, Edm.	6.00
☐	382	LL: Assists: Wayne Gretzky, Edm.	6.00
☐	383	LL: Power Play Goals: Wayne Gretzky, Edm.	6.00
☐	384	LL: Game Winning Goals: Michel Goulet, Que	.35
☐	385	LL: Rookie Scorer: Steve Yzerman, Det.	15.00
☐	386	LL: Goals Against Average: Pat Riggin, Wsh.	.35
☐	387	LL: Save Percentage: Rollie Melanson, NYI.	.35
☐	388	Wayne Gretzky, Edm.	6.00
☐	389	Denis Potvin, NYI.	.35
☐	390	Brad Park, Det.	.35
☐	391	Michel Goulet, Que.	.35
☐	392	Pat LaFontaine, NYI.	7.00
☐	393	Dale Hawerchuk, Wpg.	1.50
☐	394	Checklist 1 (1 - 132)	3.00
☐	395	Checklist 2 (133 -264)	3.00
☐	396	Checklist 3 (264 - 396)	4.00

1984 - 85 O-PEE-CHEE STICKERS

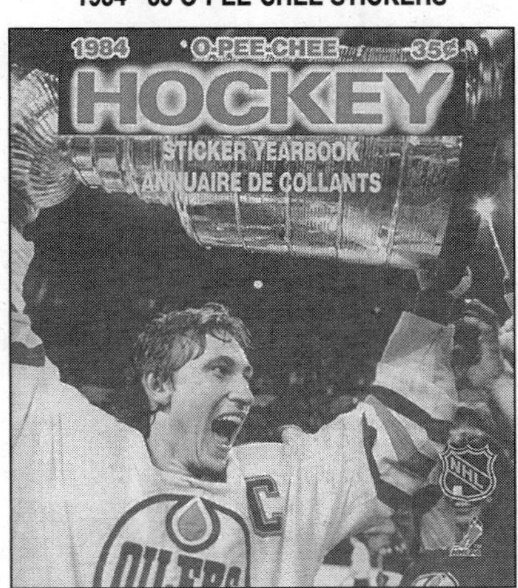

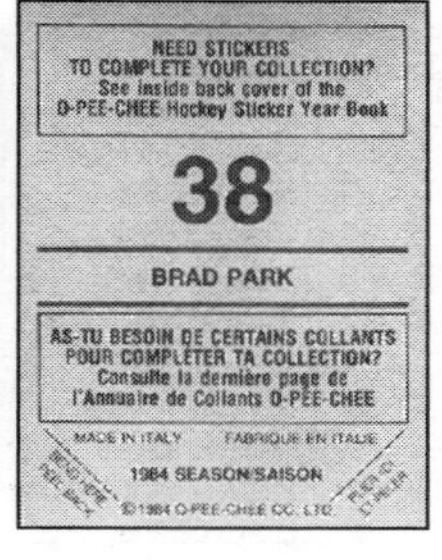

Sticker Size: 1 7/8" x 2 15/16"
Face: Four colour, white on foil border; Number
Back: Black on card stock; Name, Number, Bilingual
Imprint: 1984 O-PEE-CHEE CO. LTD.

Complete Set (270 stickers):	**50.00**
Common Player:	**.20**
Album (Wayne Gretzky):	**5.00**

	No.	Player	NRMT-MT
☐	1	Islanders vs. Oilers	.20
☐	2	Islanders vs. Oilers	.20
☐	3	Islanders vs. Oilers	.20
☐	4	Islanders vs. Oilers	.20
☐	5	Foil: Mark Messier, Edm.	1.50
☐	7	Borje Salming, Tor.	.25
☐	8	Borje Salming, Tor.	.25
☐	9	Dan Daoust, Tor.	.20
☐	10	Dan Daoust, Tor.	.20
☐	11	Rick Vaive, Tor.	.25
☐	12	Rick Vaive, Tor.	.25
☐	13	Dale McCourt, Tor.	.20
☐	14	Bill Derlago, Tor.	.20
☐	15	Gary Nylund, Tor.	.20
☐	16	Gary Nylund, Tor.	.20
☐	17	Jim Korn, Tor.	.20
☐	18	John Anderson, Tor.	.20
☐	19	Greg Terrion, Tor.	.20
☐	20	Allan Bester (G), Tor.	.25
☐	21	Jim Benning, Tor.	.20
☐	22	Mike Palmateer (G), Tor.	.25
☐	24	Denis Savard, Chi.	.50
☐	25	Denis Savard, Chi.	.50
☐	26	Bob Murray, Chi.	.20
☐	27	Doug Wilson, Chi.	.25
☐	28	Keith Brown, Chi.	.20
☐	29	Steve Larmer, Chi.	1.00
☐	30	Darryl Sutter, Chi.	.20
☐	31	Tom Lysiak, Chi.	.20
☐	32	Murray Bannerman (G), Chi.	.25
☐	34	John Ogrodnick, Det.	.20
☐	35	John Ogrodnick, Det.	.20
☐	36	Reed Larson, Det.	.20
☐	37	Steve Yzerman, Det.	15.00
☐	38	Brad Park, Det.	.25
☐	39	Ivan Boldirev, Det.	.20
☐	40	Kelly Kisio, Det.	.20
☐	41	Greg Stefan (G), Det.	.25
☐	42	Ron Duguay, Det.	.20
☐	44	Brian Bellows, Min.	.35
☐	45	Brian Bellows, Min.	.35
☐	46	Neal Broten, Min.	.20
☐	47	Dino Ciccarelli, Min.	.35
☐	48	Dennis Maruk, Min.	.20
☐	49	Steve Payne, Min.	.20
☐	50	Brad Maxwell, Min.	.20
☐	51	Gilles Meloche (G), Min.	.25
☐	52	Tom McCarthy, Min.	.20
☐	54	Bernie Federko, Stl.	.25
☐	55	Bernie Federko, Stl.	.25
☐	56	Brian Sutter, Stl.	.25
☐	57	Mike Liut (G), Stl.	.25
☐	58	Doug Wickenheiser, Stl.	.20
☐	59	Jorgen Pettersson, Stl.	.20
☐	60	Doug Gilmour, Stl.	6.00
☐	61	Joe Mullen, Stl.	.50
☐	62	Rob Ramage, Stl.	.20
☐	68	Glenn Resch (G), N.J.	.35
☐	69	Glenn Resch (G), N.J.	.35
☐	70	Don Lever, N.J.	.20
☐	71	Mel Bridgman, N.J.	.20
☐	72	Bob MacMillan, N.J.	.20
☐	73	Pat Verbeek, N.J.	1.00
☐	74	Joe Cirella, N.J.	.20
☐	75	Phil Russell, N.J.	.20
☐	76	Jan Ludvig, N.J.	.20
☐	78	Denis Potvin, NYI.	.30
☐	79	Denis Potvin, NYI.	.30
☐	80	John Tonelli, NYI.	.20
☐	81	John Tonelli, NYI.	.20
☐	82	Mike Bossy, NYI.	.50
☐	83	Mike Bossy, NYI.	.50
☐	84	Butch Goring, NYI.	.20
☐	85	Bob Nystrom, NYI.	.20
☐	86	Bryan Trottier, NYI.	.35
☐	87	Bryan Trottier, NYI.	.35
☐	88	Brent Sutter, NYI.	.20
☐	89	Bob Bourne, NYI.	.20
☐	90	Greg Gilbert, NYI.	.20
☐	91	Billy Smith (G), NYI.	.25
☐	92	Rolllie Melanson (G), NYI.	.20
☐	93	Ken Morrow, NYI.	.20
☐	95	Don Maloney, NYR.	.20
☐	96	Don Maloney, NYR.	.20
☐	97	Mark Pavelich, NYR.	.20
☐	98	Glen Hanlon (G), NYR.	.25
☐	99	Mike Rogers, NYR.	.20
☐	100	Barry Beck, NYR.	.20
☐	101	Reijo Ruotsalainen, NYR.	.20
☐	102	Anders Hedberg, NYR.	.20
☐	103	Pierre Larouche, NYR.	.20
☐	105	Tim Kerr, Pha.	.25
☐	106	Tim Kerr, Pha.	.25
☐	107	Ron Sutter, Pha.	.25
☐	108	Darryl Sittler, Pha.	.25
☐	109	Mark Howe, Pha.	.25
☐	110	Dave Poulin, Pha.	.25
☐	111	Rich Sutter, Pha.	.25
☐	112	Brian Propp, Pha.	.25
☐	113	Bob Froese (G), Pha.	.25
☐	115	Ron Flockhart, Pgh.	.20
☐	116	Ron Flockhart, Pgh.	.20
☐	117	Rick Kehoe, Pgh.	.20
☐	118	Mike Bullard, Pgh.	.20
☐	119	Kevin McCarthy, Pgh.	.20
☐	120	Doug Shedden, Pgh.	.20
☐	121	Mark Taylor, Pgh.	.20
☐	122	Denis Herron (G), Pgh.	.25
☐	123	Tom Roulston, Pgh.	.20
☐	125	Rod Langway, Wsh.	.25
☐	126	Rod Langway, Wsh.	.25
☐	127	Larry Murphy, Wsh.	.25
☐	128	Al Jensen (G), Wsh.	.25
☐	129	Doug Jarvis, Wsh.	.20
☐	130	Bengt Gustafsson, Wsh.	.20
☐	131	Mike Gartner, Wsh.	1.00
☐	132	Bob Carpenter, Wsh.	.25
☐	133	Dave Christian, Wsh.	.20
☐	134	AS: Foil: Paul Coffey, Edm.	2.00
☐	135	AS: Foil: Murray Bannerman (G), Chi.	.25
☐	136	AS: Foil: Rob Ramage, Stl.	.25
☐	137	AS: Foil: John Ogrodnick, Det.	.25
☐	138	AS: Foil: Wayne Gretzky, Edm.	6.00
☐	139	AS: Foil: Rick Vaive, Tor.	.35
☐	140	AS: Foil: Michel Goulet, Que.	.35
☐	141	AS: Foil: Peter Stastny, Que.	.35
☐	142	AS: Foil: Rick Middleton, Bos.	.20
☐	143	AS: Foil: Ray Bourque, Bos.	2.50
☐	144	AS: Foil: Pete Peeters (G), Bos.	.35
☐	145	AS: Foil: Denis Potvin, NYI.	.50
☐	147	Larry Robinson, Mtl.	.35
☐	148	Larry Robinson, Mtl.	.35
☐	149	Guy Lafleur, Mtl.	1.50
☐	150	Guy Lafleur, Mtl.	1.50
☐	151	Bobby Smith, Mtl.	.25
☐	152	Bobby Smith, Mtl.	.25
☐	153	Bob Gainey, Mtl.	.25
☐	154	Craig Ludwig, Mtl.	.20
☐	155	Mats Naslund, Mtl.	.35
☐	156	Mats Naslund, Mtl.	.35
☐	157	Rick Wamsley (G), Mtl.	.25
☐	158	Jean Hamel, Mtl.	.20
☐	159	Ryan Walter, Mtl.	.20
☐	160	Guy Carbonneau, Mtl.	.35
☐	161	Mario Tremblay, Mtl.	.25
☐	162	Pierre Mondou, Mtl.	.20
☐	164	Peter Stastny, Que.	.50
☐	165	Peter Stastny, Que.	.50

No.	Player	Price
166	Mario Marois, Que.	.20
167	Mario Marois, Que.	.20
168	Michel Goulet, Que.	2.50
169	Michel Goulet, Que.	2.50
170	André Savard, Que.	.20
171	Tony McKegney, Que.	.20
172	Dan Bouchard (G), Que.	.25
173	Dan Bouchard (G), Que.	.25
174	Randy Moller, Que.	.20
175	Wilf Paiement, Que.	.20
176	Normand Rochefort, Que.	.20
177	Marian Stastny, Que.	.20
178	Anton Stastny, Que.	.20
179	Dale Hunter, Que.	.25
181	Rick Middleton, Bos.	.25
182	Rick Middleton, Bos.	.25
183	Ray Bourque, Bos.	2.00
184	Pete Peeters (G), Bos.	.25
185	Mike O'Connell, Bos.	.20
186	Gord Kluzak, Bos.	.20
187	Barry Pederson, Bos.	.20
188	Mike Krushelnyski, Bos.	.20
189	Tom Fergus, Bos.	.20
191	Sylvain Turgeon, Hfd.	.25
192	Sylvain Turgeon, Hfd.	.25
193	Mark Johnson, Hfd.	.20
194	Greg Malone, Hfd.	.20
195	Mike Zuke, Hfd.	.20
196	Ron Francis, Hfd.	1.50
197	Bob Crawford, Hfd.	.20
198	Greg Millen (G), Hfd.	.25
199	Ray Neufeld, Hfd.	.20
201	Gilbert Perreault, Buf.	.35
202	Gilbert Perreault, Buf.	.35
203	Phil Housley, Buf.	.35
204	Phil Housley, Buf.	.35
205	Tom Barrasso (G), Buf.	1.50
206	Tom Barrasso (G), Buf.	1.50
207	Larry Playfair, Buf.	.20
208	Bob Sauvé (G), Buf.	.25
209	Dave Andreychuk, Buf.	1.50
210	Dave Andreychuk, Buf.	1.50
211	Mike Ramsey, Buf.	.20
212	Mike Foligno, Buf.	.20
213	Lindy Ruff, Buf.	.20
214	Bill Hajt, Buf.	.20
215	Craig Ramsay, Buf.	.20
216	Ric Seiling, Buf.	.20
237	Lanny McDonald, Cgy.	.25
238	Lanny McDonald, Cgy.	.25
239	Steve Tambellini, Cgy.	.20
240	Réjean Lemelin (G), Cgy.	.25
241	Doug Risebrough, Cgy.	.20
242	Hakan Loob, Cgy.	.20
243	Eddy Beers, Cgy.	.20
244	Mike Eaves, Cgy.	.20
245	Kent Nilsson, Cgy.	.20
247	Glenn Anderson, Edm.	.50
248	Glenn Anderson, Edm.	.50
249	Jari Kurri, Edm.	1.25
250	Jari Kurri, Edm.	1.25
251	Paul Coffey, Edm.	1.50
252	Paul Coffey, Edm.	1.50
253	Kevin Lowe, Edm.	.25
254	Lee Fogolin, Edm.	.20
255	Wayne Gretzky, Edm.	5.00
256	Wayne Gretzky, Edm.	5.00
257	Randy Gregg, Edm.	.20
258	Charlie Huddy, Edm.	.20
259	Grant Fuhr (G), Edm.	1.00
260	Willy Lindstrom, Edm.	.20
261	Mark Messier, Edm.	2.00
262	Andy Moog (G), Edm.	1.00
264	Marcel Dionne, L.A.	.35
265	Marcel Dionne, L.A.	.35
266	Charlie Simmer, L.A.	.20
267	Dave Taylor, L.A.	.25
268	Jim Fox, L.A.	.20
269	Bernie Nicholls, L.A.	.20
270	Terry Ruskowski, L.A.	.20
271	Brian Engblom, L.A.	.20
272	Mark Hardy, L.A.	.20
274	Tony Tanti, Van.	.25
275	Tony Tanti, Van.	.25
276	Rick Lanz, Van.	.20
277	Richard Brodeur (G), Van.	.25
278	Doug Halward, Van.	.20
279	Patrik Sundstrom, Van.	.20
280	Darcy Rota, Van.	.20
281	Stan Smyl, Van.	.25
282	Thomas Gradin, Van.	.20
284	Dale Hawerchuk, Wpg.	1.25
285	Dale Hawerchuk, Wpg.	1.25
286	Scott Arniel, Wpg.	.20
287	Dave Babych, Wpg.	.25
288	Laurie Boschman, Wpg.	.20
289	Paul MacLean, Wpg.	.20
290	Lucien DeBlois, Wpg.	.20
291	Randy Carlyle, Wpg.	.25
292	Thomas Steen, Wpg.	.20

MULTIPLE STICKERS

No.	Sticker	Price
6/23	Foil: Toronto Maple Leafs/Chicago Blackhawks	.20
33/43	Foil: Detroit Red Wings/Minnesota North Stars	.20
53/67	Foil: St. Louis Blues/New Jersey Devils	.20
63/64	Foil: Wayne Gretzy/Michel Goulet	4.00
65/66	Foil: Pat Riggin (G)/Denis Potvin	.35
77/94	Foil: New York Islanders/New York Rangers	.20
104/114	Foil: Philadelphia Flyers/Pittburgh Penguins	.20
124/146	Foil: Washington Capitals/Montréal Canadiens	.20
163/180	Foil: Québec Nordiques/Boston Bruins	.20
190/200	Foil: Hartford Whalers/Buffalo Sabres	.20
217/224	Foil: Hart Trophy/Selke Trophy	.20
218/223	Foil: Vezina Trophy/Masterton Trophy	.20
219/221	Foil: Jennings Trophy/Art Ross Trophy	.20
220/225	Foil: Calder Trophy/Lady Byng Trophy	.20
222/283	Norris Trophy/ Foil: Norris Trophy Winnipeg	.20
226/227	AW: Wayne Gretzky/Tom Barrasso (G)	4.00
228/229	AW: Tom Barrasso (G)/Wayne Gretzky	4.00
230/231	AW: Rod Langway/Brad Park	.25
232/233	AW: Al Jensen (G)/Pat Riggin (G)	.20
234/235	AW: Doug Jarvis/Mike Bossy	.35
235/246	Foil: Calgary Flames Edmonton Oilers	.20
263/273	Foil: Los Angeles Kings/Vancouver Canucks	.20

1984 - 85 7-ELEVEN DISKS

The disks are listed in alphabetically by team in the order of appearance on the original checklist.

Disk Diameter: 2"
Face: Four colour, coloured border; Alternating photo/team logo, Jersey number, Name, Team logo
Back: Blank
Imprint: None

Complete Set (60 disks): 85.00
Common Player: 1.00

Player	NRMT-MT
Ray Bourque, Bos.	7.00
Rick Middleton, Bos.	1.50
Tom Barrasso (G), Buf.	3.00
Gilbert Perreault, Buf.	2.00
Réjean Lemelin (G), Cgy.	1.00
Lanny McDonald, Cgy.	2.00
Paul Reinhart, Cgy.	1.00
Doug Risebrough, Cgy.	1.00
Denis Savard, Chi.	2.50
Alan Secord, Chi.	1.00
Dave Williams, Det.	1.00
Steve Yzerman, Det.	15.00
Glenn Anderson, Edm.	1.50
Paul Coffey, Edm.	6.00
Wayne Gretzky, Edm	20.00
Charlie Huddy, Edm.	1.00
Pat Hughes, Edm.	1.00
Jari Kurri, Edm.	4.00
Kevin Lowe, Edm.	2.00
Mark Messier, Edm.	8.00
Ron Francis, Hfd.	5.00
Sylvain Turgeon, Hfd.	1.00
Marcel Dionne, L.A.	3.00
Dave Taylor, L.A.	2.00
Brian Bellows, Min.	2.00
Dino Ciccarelli, Min.	2.00
Harold Snepsts, Min.	1.00
Bob Gainey, Mtl.	2.50
Larry Robinson, Mtl.	3.00
Mel Bridgman, N.J.	1.00
Glenn Resch (G), N.J.	1.50
Mike Bossy, NYI.	5.00
Bryan Trottier, NYI.	3.00
Barry Beck, NYR.	1.00
Don Maloney, NYR.	1.00
Tim Kerr, Pha.	1.50
Darryl Sittler, Pha.	1.50
Mike Bullard, Pgh.	1.00
Rick Kehoe, Pgh.	1.00
Michel Goulet, Que.	3.00
Peter Stastny, Que.	3.00
Bernie Federko, Stl.	1.50
Rob Ramage, Stl.	1.00
John Anderson, Tor.	1.00
Bill Derlago, Tor.	1.00
Gary Nylund, Tor.	1.00
Rick Vaive, Tor.	1.50
Richard Brodeur (G), Van.	1.50
Gary Lupul, Van.	1.00
Darcy Rota, Van.	1.00
Stan Smyl, Van.	1.50
Tony Tanti, Van.	1.50
Mike Gartner, Wsh.	4.00
Rod Langway, Wsh.	1.50
Scott Arniel, Wpg.	1.00
Dave Babych, Wpg.	1.50
Laurie Boschman, Wpg.	1.00
Dale Hawerchuk, Wpg.	3.00
Paul MacLean, Wpg.	1.00
Brian Mullen, Wpg.	1.00
Large Disk	**NRMT-MT**
Wayne Gretzky, Edm.	20.00

1984 - 85 TOPPS

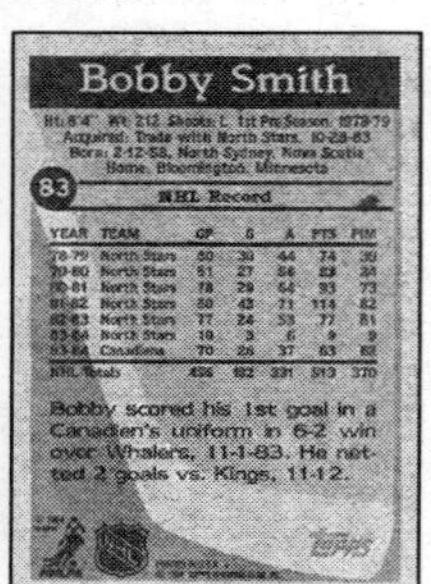

Face: Four colour, white border, Position
Back: Purple and mauve on card stock; Number, Resume
Imprint: © 1984 TOPPS CHEWING GUM, INC.

Complete Set (165 cards): 40.00
Common Player: .10
Single Prints (*): .15

No.	Player	NRMT-MT
1	Ray Bourque, Bos.	2.00
2	Keith Crowder, Bos. (*)	.15
3	Tom Fergus, Bos.	.10
4	**Doug Keans (G), Bos., RC**	**.20**
5	Gord Kluzak, Bos. (*)	.15
6	Mike Krushelnyski, Bos. (*)	.15
7	**Nevin Markwart, Bos., RC**	**.10**
8	Rick Middleton, Bos.	.20
9	Mike O'Connell, Bos.	.10
10	Terry O'Reilly, Bos., LC (*)	.15
11	Barry Pederson, Bos.	.10
12	Pete Peeters (G), Bos.	.20
13	**Dave Andreychuk, Buf., RC (*)**	**4.50**
14	**Tom Barrasso (G), Buf., RC**	**4.00**
15	Réal Cloutier, Buf., LC (*)	.15
16	Mike Foligno, Buf.	.10
17	Bill Hajt, Buf. (*)	.15

	No.	Player	Price
☐	18	Phil Housley, Buf. (*)	1.50
☐	19	Gilbert Perreault, Buf.	.25
☐	20	Larry Playfair, Buf. (*)	.15
☐	21	Craig Ramsay, Buf. (*)	.15
☐	22	Mike Ramsey, Buf. (*)	.15
☐	23	Lindy Ruff, Buf. (*)	.15
☐	24	Ed Beers, Cgy.	.10
☐	25	Réjean Lemelin (G), Cgy. (*)	.30
☐	26	Lanny McDonald, Cgy.	.20
☐	27	Murray Bannerman (G), Chi.	.20
☐	28	Keith Brown, Chi. (*)	.15
☐	29	Curt Fraser, Chi.	.10
☐	30	Steve Larmer, Chi.	1.50
☐	31	Tom Lysiak, Chi.	.10
☐	32	Bob Murray, Chi.	.10
☐	**33**	**Jack O'Callahan, Chi., RC (*)**	**.15**
☐	34	Rich Preston, Chi.	.10
☐	35	Denis Savard, Chi.	.75
☐	36	Darryl Sutter, Chi.	.20
☐	37	Doug Wilson, Chi.	.20
☐	38	Ivan Boldirev, Det.	.10
☐	39	Colin Campbell, Det., LC (*)	.25
☐	40	Ron Duguay, Det. (*)	.15
☐	41	Dwight Foster, Det. (*)	.15
☐	42	Danny Gare, Det. (*)	.15
☐	43	Eddie Johnstone, Det., LC	.10
☐	44	Reed Larson, Det. (*)	.15
☐	45	Ed Mio (G), Det., LC (*)	.25
☐	46	John Ogrodnick, Det.	.10
☐	47	Brad Park, Det., LC	.20
☐	**48**	**Greg Stefan (G), Det., RC (*)**	**.25**
☐	**49**	**Steve Yzerman, Det., RC**	**20.00**
☐	50	Paul Coffey, Edm.	2.50
☐	51	Wayne Gretzky, Edm.	10.00
☐	52	Jari Kurri, Edm.	1.25
☐	**53**	**Bob Crawford, Hfd., RC**	**.10**
☐	54	Ron Francis, Hfd.	2.00
☐	55	Marty Howe, Hfd., LC	.10
☐	56	Mark Johnson, Hfd. (*)	.15
☐	57	Greg Malone, Hfd. (*)	.15
☐	58	Greg Millen (G), Hfd. (*)	.25
☐	59	Ray Neufeld, Hfd.	.10
☐	60	Joel Quenneville, Hfd. (*)	.25
☐	61	Risto Siltanen, Hfd.	.10
☐	**62**	**Sylvain Turgeon, Hfd., RC**	**.35**
☐	63	Mike Zuke, Hfd. (*)	.15
☐	64	Marcel Dionne, L.A.	.35
☐	65	Brian Engblom, L.A. (*)	.15
☐	66	Jim Fox, L.A. (*)	.15
☐	67	Bernie Nicholls, L.A.	1.00
☐	68	Terry Ruskowski, L.A. (*)	.15
☐	69	Charlie Simmer, L.A.	.10
☐	70	Don Beaupré (G), Min.	.20
☐	71	Brian Bellows, Min.	.75
☐	72	Neal Broten, Min. (*)	.35
☐	73	Dino Ciccarelli, Min.	.50
☐	74	Paul Holmgren, Min. (*), LC	.15
☐	75	Al MacAdam, Min. (*)	.15
☐	76	Dennis Maruk, Min.	.10
☐	77	Brad Maxwell, Min. (*)	.15
☐	78	Tom McCarthy, Min. (*)	.15
☐	79	Gilles Meloche (G), Min. (*)	.25
☐	80	Steve Payne, Min.	.10
☐	81	Guy Lafleur, Mtl.	2.50
☐	82	Larry Robinson, Mtl.	.25
☐	83	Bobby Smith, Mtl.	.25
☐	84	Mel Bridgman, N.J.	.10
☐	85	Joe Cirella, N.J.	.10
☐	86	Don Lever, N.J.	.10
☐	87	Dave Lewis, N.J.	.10
☐	**88**	**Jan Ludvig, N.J., RC, LC**	**.10**
☐	89	Glenn Resch (G), N.J.	.20
☐	**90**	**Pat Verbeek, N.J., RC**	**4.00**
☐	91	Mike Bossy, NYI.	2.00
☐	92	Bob Bourne, NYI.	.10
☐	**93**	**Greg Gilbert, NYI., RC**	**.25**
☐	94	Clark Gillies, NYI. (*)	.25
☐	95	Butch Goring, NYI., LC (*)	.25
☐	**96**	**Pat LaFontaine, NYI., RC (*)**	**8.50**
☐	97	Ken Morrow, NYI.	.10
☐	98	Bob Nystrom, NYI. (*)	.15
☐	99	Stefan Persson, NYI., LC (*)	.15
☐	100	Denis Potvin, NYI.	.35
☐	101	Billy Smith (G), NYI. (*)	.35
☐	102	Brent Sutter, NYI. (*)	.35
☐	103	John Tonelli, NYI.	.10
☐	104	Bryan Trottier, NYI.	.35
☐	105	Barry Beck, NYR.	.10
☐	106	Glen Hanlon (G), NYR. (*)	.25
☐	107	Anders Hedberg, NYR., LC (*)	.15
☐	108	Pierre Larouche, NYR. (*)	.15
☐	109	Don Maloney, NYR. (*)	.15
☐	110	Mark Osborne, NYR. (*)	.15
☐	111	Larry Patey, NYR., LC	.10
☐	**112**	**James Patrick, NYR., RC**	**.75**
☐	113	Mark Pavelich, NYR. (*)	.15
☐	114	Mike Rogers, NYR. (*)	.15
☐	115	Reijo Ruotsalainen, NYR. (*)	.15
☐	**116**	**Peter Sundstrom, NYR., RC, LC (*)**	**.15**
☐	117	Rob Froese (G), Pha.	.20
☐	118	Mark Howe, Pha.	.25
☐	119	Tim Kerr, Pha. (*)	.25
☐	**120**	**David Poulin, Pha., RC**	**1.00**
☐	121	Darryl Sittler, Pha., LC (*)	.25
☐	122	Ron Sutter, Pha.	.25
☐	123	Mike Bullard, Pgh. (*)	.15
☐	124	Ron Flockhart, Pgh. (*)	.15
☐	125	Rick Kehoe, Pgh., LC	.10
☐	126	Kevin McCarthy, Pgh., LC (*)	.15
☐	127	Mark Taylor, Pgh., LC	.10
☐	128	Dan Bouchard (G), Que.	.20
☐	129	Michel Goulet, Que.	.35
☐	130	Peter Stastny, Que. (*)	.75
☐	131	Bernie Federko, Stl.	.20
☐	132	Mike Liut (G), Stl.	.20
☐	133	Joe Mullen, Stl. (*)	.75
☐	134	Rob Ramage, Stl.	.20
☐	135	Brian Sutter, Stl.	.25
☐	136	John Anderson, Tor. (*)	.15
☐	137	Dan Daoust, Tor.	.10
☐	138	Rick Vaive, Tor.	.20
☐	139	Darcy Rota, Van., LC (*)	.15
☐	140	Stan Smyl, Van. (*)	.25
☐	141	Tony Tanti, Van.	.20
☐	142	Dave Christian, Wsh. (*)	.15
☐	143	Mike Gartner, Wsh. (*)	1.75
☐	144	Bengt Gustafsson, Wsh. (*)	.15
☐	145	Doug Jarvis, Wsh.	.10
☐	146	Al Jensen (G), Wsh.	.20
☐	147	Rod Langway, Wsh.	.25
☐	148	Pat Riggin (G), Wsh. (*)	.20
☐	149	Scott Stevens, Wsh.	2.50
☐	150	Dave Babych, Wpg.	.20
☐	151	Laurie Boschman, Wpg.	.10
☐	152	Dale Hawerchuk, Wpg.	1.50
☐	153	AS: Michel Goulet, Que.	.25
☐	154	AS: Wayne Gretzky, Edm.	3.50
☐	155	AS: Mike Bossy, NYI.	.25
☐	156	AS: Rod Langway, Wsh.	.20
☐	157	AS: Ray Bourque, Bos.	.75
☐	158	AS: Tom Barrasso (G), Buf.	.75
☐	159	AS: Mark Messier, Edm.	2.50
☐	160	AS: Bryan Trottier, NYI.	.25
☐	161	AS: Jari Kurri, Edm.	.60
☐	162	AS: Denis Potvin, NYI.	.25
☐	163	AS: Paul Coffey, Edm.	.75
☐	164	AS: Pat Riggin (G), Wsh.	.20
☐	165	Checklist (*) (1 - 165)	3.00

1985 - 86 O-PEE-CHEE

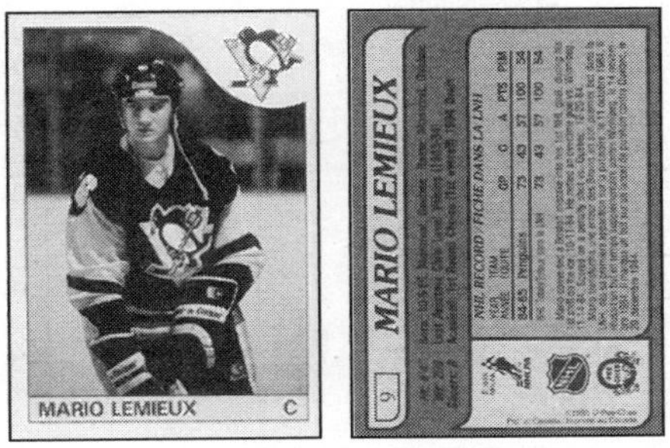

Face: Four colour, white border, Team logo, Position
Back: Rust and blue on card stock, Number, Resume, Bilingual
Imprint: © 1985 O-Pee-Chee
Complete Set (264 cards): 525.00
Common Player: .50

	No.	Player	NRMT-MT
☐	1	Lanny McDonald, Cgy.	.75
☐	2	Mike O'Connell, Bos.	.50
☐	3	Curt Fraser, Chi.	.50
☐	4	Steve Penney (G), Mtl.	.65
☐	5	Brian Engblom, L.A.	.50
☐	6	Ron Sutter, Pha.	.50
☐	7	Joe Mullen, Stl.	1.75
☐	8	Rod Langway, Wsh.	.65
☐	**9**	**Mario Lemieux, Pgh., RC**	**400.00**
☐	10	Dave Babych, Wpg.	.65
☐	11	Bob Nystrom, NYI.	.50
☐	12	Andy Moog (G), Edm.	3.25
☐	13	Dino Ciccarelli, Min.	1.50
☐	14	Dwight Foster, Det., LC	.50
☐	15	James Patrick, NYR.	.50
☐	16	Thomas Gradin, Van., LC	.50
☐	17	Mike Foligno, Buf.	.50
☐	**18**	**Mario Gosselin (G), Que., RC**	**.50**
☐	19	Mike Zuke, Hfd., LC	.50
☐	20	John Anderson, Tor. (Que.)	.50
☐	21	Dave Pichette, N.J., LC	.50
☐	22	Nick Fotiu, NYR., LC	.50
☐	23	Tom Lysiak, Chi., LC	.50
☐	**24**	**Peter Zezel, Pha., RC**	**2.00**
☐	25	Denis Potvin, NYI.	1.00
☐	26	Bob Carpenter, Wsh.	.50
☐	27	Murray Bannerman (G), Chi.	.65
☐	28	Gord Roberts, Min.	.50
☐	29	Steve Yzerman, Det.	40.00
☐	30	Phil Russell, N.J.	.50
☐	31	Peter Stastny, Que.	1.50
☐	32	Craig Ramsay, Buf., LC	.65
☐	33	Terry Ruskowski, Pgh.	.50
☐	**34**	**Kevin Dineen, Hfd., RC**	**3.50**
☐	35	Mark Howe, Pha.	.75
☐	36	Glenn Resch (G), N.J.	.65
☐	37	Danny Gare, Det.	.75
☐	**38**	**Doug Bodger, Pgh., RC**	**.75**
☐	39	Mike Rogers, NYR., LC	.50
☐	40	Ray Bourque, Bos.	6.00
☐	41	John Tonelli, NYI.	.65
☐	42	Mel Bridgman, N.J.	.50
☐	43	Sylvain Turgeon, Hfd.	.50
☐	44	Mark Johnson, Stl.	.50
☐	45	Doug Wilson, Chi.	.65
☐	46	Mike Gartner, Wsh.	3.50
☐	47	Brent Peterson, Buf.	.50
☐	48	Paul Reinhart, Cgy.	.50
☐	49	Mike Krushelnyski, Edm.	.50
☐	50	Brian Bellows, Min.	.65
☐	51	Chris Chelios, Mtl.	12.00
☐	52	Barry Pederson, Bos.	.50
☐	53	Murray Craven, Pha.	.50
☐	54	Pierre Larouche, NYR., LC	.50
☐	55	Reed Larson, Det.	.50
☐	56	Pat Verbeek, N.J.	2.00
☐	57	Randy Carlyle, Wpg.	.50
☐	58	Ray Neufeld, Hfd.	.50
☐	59	Keith Brown, Chi.	.50
☐	60	Bryan Trottier, NYI.	1.00
☐	61	Jim Fox, L.A.	.50
☐	62	Scott Stevens, Wsh.	3.50
☐	63	Phil Housley, Buf.	1.50
☐	64	Rick Middleton, Bos.	.65
☐	65	Steve Payne, Min.	.50
☐	66	Dave Lewis, N.J.	.65
☐	67	Mike Bullard, Pgh.	.50
☐	68	Stan Smyl, Van.	.50
☐	69	Mark Pavelich, NYR., LC	.50
☐	70	John Ogrodnick, Det.	.50
☐	71	Bill Derlago, Tor. (Bos.)	.50
☐	72	Brad Marsh, Pha.	.50
☐	73	Denis Savard, Chi.	1.75
☐	**74**	**Mark Fusco, Hfd., RC, LC**	**.50**
☐	75	Pete Peeters (G), Bos. (Wsh.)	.65
☐	76	Doug Gilmour, Stl.	15.00
☐	77	Mike Ramsey, Buf.	.50
☐	78	Anton Stastny, Que.	.50
☐	79	Steve Kasper, Bos.	.50
☐	**80**	**Bryan Erickson, Wsh., RC**	**.50**
☐	81	Clark Gillies, NYI.	.65
☐	82	Keith Acton, Min.	.50
☐	83	Pat Flatley, NYI.	.50
☐	**84**	**Kirk Muller, N.J., RC**	**6.00**

☐ 85 Paul Coffey, Edm. 6.00
☐ 86 Ed Olczyk, Chi., RC 1.50
☐ 87 Charlie Simmer, Bos. .50
☐ 88 Mike Liut (G), Hfd. .65
☐ 89 Dave Maloney, Buf., LC .50
☐ 90 Marcel Dionne, L.A. 1.00
☐ 91 Tim Kerr, Pha. .65
☐ 92 Ivan Boldirev, Det., LC .50
☐ 93 Ken Morrow, NYI. .50
☐ 94 Don Maloney, NYR. .50
☐ 95 Réjean Lemelin (G), Cgy. .65
☐ 96 Curt Giles, Min. .50
☐ 97 Bob Bourne, NYI. .50
☐ 98 Joe Cirella, N.J. .50
☐ 99 Dave Christian, Wsh. .50
☐ 100 Darryl Sutter, Chi. .65
☐ 101 Kelly Kisio, Det. .50
☐ 102 Mats Naslund, Mtl. .65
☐ 103 Joel Quenneville, Hfd. .65
☐ 104 Bernie Federko, Stl. .65
☐ 105 Tom Barrasso (G), Buf. 2.50
☐ 106 Rick Vaive, Tor. .65
☐ 107 Brent Sutter, NYI. .65
☐ 108 Wayne Babych, Stl. (Que.) .50
☐ 109 Dale Hawerchuk, Wpg. 3.00
☐ 110 Pelle Lindbergh (G), Pha., LC 12.00
☐ 111 Dennis Maruk, Min. .50
☐ 112 Reijo Ruotsalainen, NYR. .50
☐ 113 Tom Fergus, Bos. (Tor.) .50
☐ 114 Bob Murray, Chi. .50
☐ 115 Patrik Sundstrom, Van. .50
☐ 116 Ron Duguay, Det. .50
☐ 117 Alan Haworth, Wsh. .50
☐ 118 Greg Malone, Hfd., LC .50
☐ 119 Bill Hajt, Buf. .50
☐ 120 Wayne Gretzky, Edm. 30.00
☐ 121 Craig Redmond, L.A., RC, LC .50
☐ 122 Kelly Hrudey (G), NYI., RC 6.00
☐ 123 Tomas Sandstrom, NYR., RC 7.00
☐ 124 Neal Broten, Min. .65
☐ 125 Moe Mantha, Pgh. .50
☐ 126 Greg Gilbert, NYI. .50
☐ 127 Bruce Driver, N.J., RC 1.50
☐ 128 Dave Poulin, Pha. .65
☐ 129 Morris Lukowich, Bos., LC .50
☐ 130 Mike Bossy, NYI. 3.00
☐ 131 Larry Playfair, Buf. .50
☐ 132 Steve Larmer, Chi. 3.25
☐ 133 Doug Keans (G), Bos. .65
☐ 134 Bob Manno, Det., LC .50
☐ 135 Brian Sutter, Stl. 1.75
☐ 136 Pat Riggin (G), Wsh. (Bos.), LC .50
☐ 137 Pat LaFontaine, NYI. 9.00
☐ 138 Barry Beck, NYR., LC .50
☐ 139 Rich Preston, N.J. .50
☐ 140 Ron Francis, Hfd. 3.75
☐ 141 Brian Propp, Pha. .50
☐ 142 Don Beaupré (G), Min. .65
☐ 143 Dave Andreychuk, Buf. 3.50
☐ 144 Ed Beers, Cgy. .50
☐ 145 Paul MacLean, Wpg. .50
☐ 146 Troy Murray, Chi. .50
☐ 147 Larry Robinson, Mtl. 1.00
☐ 148 Bernie Nicholls, L.A. 2.00
☐ 149 Glen Hanlon (G), NYR. .65
☐ 150 Michel Goulet, Que. 1.00
☐ 151 Doug Jarvis, Wsh. .50
☐ 152 Warren Young, Pgh. (Det.), RC .50
☐ 153 Tony Tanti, Van. .50
☐ 154 Tomas Jonsson, NYI. .50
☐ 155 Jari Kurri, Edm. 3.25
☐ 156 Tony McKegney, Min. .50
☐ 157 Greg Stefan (G), Det. .65
☐ 158 Brad McCrimmon, Pha. .50
☐ 159 Keith Crowder, Bos. .50
☐ 160 Gilbert Perreault, Buf. .75
☐ 161 Tim Bothwell, Stl. (Hfd.) .50
☐ 162 Bob Crawford, Hfd., LC .50
☐ 163 Paul Gagné, N.J., LC .50
☐ 164 Dan Daoust, Tor. .50
☐ 165 Checklist 1 (1 - 132) 6.00
☐ 166 Tim Bernhardt (G), Tor., RC .65
☐ 167 Gord Kluzak, Bos. .50
☐ 168 Glenn Anderson, Edm. 1.00
☐ 169 Bob Gainey, Mtl. .75
☐ 170 Brent Ashton, Que. .50
☐ 171 Ron Flockhart, Stl. .50
☐ 172 Gary Nylund, Tor. .50
☐ 173 Moe Lemay, Van. .50
☐ 174 Bob Sauvé (G), Chi. .65
☐ 175 Doug Smail, Wpg. .50
☐ 176 Dan Quinn, Cgy. .50
☐ 177 Mark Messier, Edm. 10.00
☐ 178 Jay Wells, L.A., RC .50
☐ 179 Dale Hunter, Que. .75
☐ 180 Richard Brodeur (G), Van. .65
☐ 181 Bobby Smith, Mtl. .50
☐ 182 Ron Greschner, NYR. .50
☐ 183 Don Edwards (G), Tor., LC .65
☐ 184 Hakan Loob, Cgy. .50
☐ 185 David Ellett, Wpg., RC 1.25
☐ 186 Denis Herron (G), Pgh., LC .65
☐ 187 Charlie Huddy, Edm. .50
☐ 188 Ilkka Sinisalo, Pha. .50
☐ 189 Doug Halward, Van. .50
☐ 190 Craig Laughlin, Wsh. .50
☐ 191 Carey Wilson, Cgy., RC .50
☐ 192 Craig Ludwig, Mtl. .50
☐ 193 Bob MacMillan, Chi., LC .50
☐ 194 Mario Marois, Que. .50
☐ 195 Brian Mullen, Wpg. .50
☐ 196 Rob Ramage, Stl. .50
☐ 197 Rick Lanz, Van. .50
☐ 198 Miroslav Frycer, Tor. .50
☐ 199 Randy Gregg, Edm. .50
☐ 200 Corrado Micalef (G), Det., LC .65
☐ 201 Jamie Macoun, Cgy. .50
☐ 202 Bob Brooke, NYR., RC .50
☐ 203 Billy Carroll, Edm., LC .50
☐ 204 Brian MacLellan, L.A. .50
☐ 205 Alain Côté, Que. .50
☐ 206 Thomas Steen, Wpg. .50
☐ 207 Grant Fuhr (G), Edm. 3.50
☐ 208 Rich Sutter, Pha. .50
☐ 209 Al MacAdam, Van., LC .50
☐ 210 Al Iafrate, Tor., RC 5.50
☐ 211 Pierre Mondou, Mtl., LC .50
☐ 212 Randy Hillier, Pgh., RC .50
☐ 213 Mike Eaves, Cgy., LC .50
☐ 214 Dave Taylor, L.A. .50
☐ 215 Robert Picard, Wpg. .50
☐ 216 Randy Ladouceur, Det. .50
☐ 217 Willy Lindstrom, Pgh. .50
☐ 218 Torrie Robertson, Hfd., RC .50
☐ 219 Tom Kurvers, Mtl., RC .50
☐ 220 John Garrett, Van. .65
☐ 221 Greg Millen (G), Stl. .65
☐ 222 Richard Kromm, Cgy. .50
☐ 223 Bob Janecyk (G), L.A., RC .50
☐ 224 Brad Maxwell, Tor. .50
☐ 225 Mike McPhee, Mtl., RC 1.25
☐ 226 Brian Hayward (G), Wpg., RC 2.00
☐ 227 Duane Sutter, NYI. .65
☐ 228 Cam Neely, Van. 12.00
☐ 229 Doug Wickenheiser, Stl. .50
☐ 230 Rollie Melanson (G), Min. .65
☐ 231 Bruce Bell, Stl., RC, LC .50
☐ 232 Harold Snepsts, Det. .50
☐ 233 Guy Carbonneau, Mtl. .65
☐ 234 Doug Sulliman, N.J. .50
☐ 235 Lee Fogolin, Edm. .50
☐ 236 Larry Murphy, Wsh. .75
☐ 237 Al MacInnis, Cgy., RC 25.00
☐ 238 Don Lever, Buf., LC .50
☐ 239 Kevin Lowe, Edm. 1.00
☐ 240 Randy Moller, Que. .50
☐ 241 Doug Lidster, Van., RC .65
☐ 242 Craig Hartsburg, Min. .65
☐ 243 Doug Risebrough, Cgy. .65
☐ 244 John Chabot, Pgh. .50
☐ 245 Mario Tremblay, Mtl. .65
☐ 246 Dan Bouchard (G), Wpg., LC .65
☐ 247 Doug Shedden, Pgh. .50
☐ 248 Borje Salming, Tor. .65
☐ 249 Aaron Broten, N.J. .50
☐ 250 Jim Benning, Tor. .50
☐ 251 Laurie Boschman, Wpg. .50
☐ 252 George McPhee, NYR., RC, LC 1.00
☐ 253 Mark Napier, Edm. .50
☐ 254 Perry Turnbull, Wpg. .50
☐ 255 Warren Skorodenski (G), Chi., RC, LC .65
☐ 256 Checklist 2 (133 - 264) 6.00
☐ 257 LL: Wayne Gretzky, Edm. 7.00
☐ 258 LL: Wayne Gretzky, Edm. 7.00
☐ 259 LL: Wayne Gretzky, Edm. 7.00
☐ 260 LL: Tim Kerr, Pha. .50
☐ 261 LL: Jari Kurri, Edm. 1.25
☐ 262 LL: Mario Lemieux, Pgh. 45.00
☐ 263 LL: Tom Barrasso (G), Buf. .65
☐ 264 LL: Warren Skorodenski (G), Chi. .65

BOX BOTTOMS

These four-card panels were issued on the bottom of O-Pee-Chee and Topps wax-boxes.

Panel Size: 5 1/16" x 7"

Complete Set (16 cards):	**120.00**
Panel A - D:	**10.00**
Panel E - H:	**35.00**
Panel I - L:	**90.00**
Panel M - P:	**4.00**

	No.	Player	NRMT-MT
☐	A	Brian Bellows, Min.	1.00
☐	B	Ray Bourque, Bos.	6.00
☐	C	Bob Carpenter, Wsh.	1.00
☐	D	Chris Chelios, Mtl.	6.00
☐	E	Marcel Dionne, L.A.	2.50
☐	F	Ron Francis, Hfd.	5.00
☐	G	Wayne Gretzky, Edm.	30.00
☐	H	Tim Kerr, Pha.	1.00
☐	I	Mario Lemieux, Pgh.	85.00
☐	J	John Ogrodnick, Det.	1.00
☐	K	Gilbert Perreault, Buf.	2.00
☐	L	Glenn Resch (G), N.J.	1.50
☐	M	Reijo Ruotsalainen, NYR.	1.00
☐	N	Brian Sutter, Stl.	1.00
☐	O	John Tonelli, NYI.	1.00
☐	P	Doug Wilson, Chi.	1.00

STICKER INSERTS

Insert Set (33 stickers):	**18.00**

	No.	Player	NRMT-MT
☐	1	John Ogrodnick, Det.	.35
☐	2	Wayne Gretzky, Edm.	8.00
☐	3	Jari Kurri, Edm.	1.00
☐	4	Paul Coffey, Edm.	1.50
☐	5	Ray Bourque, Bos.	2.00
☐	6	Pelle Lindbergh (G), Pha.	4.00
☐	7	John Tonelli, NYI.	.35
☐	8	Dale Hawerchuk, Wpg.	1.00
☐	9	Mike Bossy, NYI.	1.50
☐	10	Rod Langway, Wsh.	.50
☐	11	Doug Wilson, Chi.	.50
☐	12	Tom Barrasso (G), Buf.	.65
☐	13	Toronto Maple Leafs	.25
☐	14	Buffalo Sabres	.25
☐	15	Detroit Red Wings	.25
☐	16	Pittsburgh Penguins	.25
☐	17	New York Rangers	.25
☐	18	Calgary Flames	.25
☐	19	Winnpeg Jets	.25
☐	20	Québec Nordiques	.25
☐	21	Chicago Blackhawks	.25
☐	22	Los Angeles Kings	.25
☐	23	Montréal Canadiens	.25
☐	24	Vancouver Canucks	.25
☐	25	Hartford Whalers	.25
☐	26	Philadelphia Flyers	.25
☐	27	New Jersey Devils	.25
☐	28	St. Louis Blues	.25
☐	29	Minnesota North Stars	.25
☐	30	Washington Capitals	.25
☐	31	Boston Bruins	.25
☐	32	New York Islanders	.25
☐	33	Edmonton Oilers	.25

1985 - 86 O-PEE-CHEE STICKERS

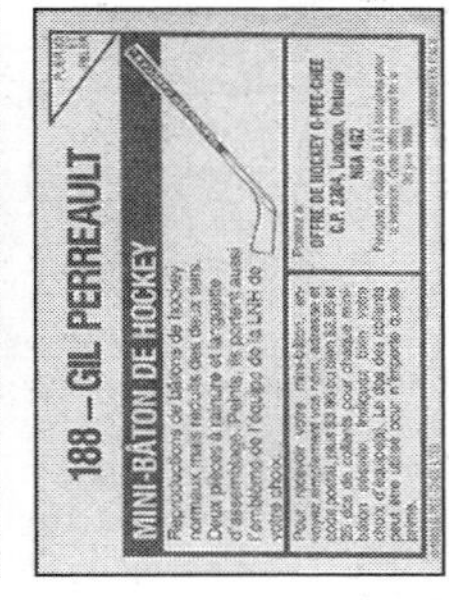

Sticker Size: 2 1/8" x 2 15/16"
Face: Four colour, white border; Number
Back: Blue on stock; Name, Number, Hockey Offer, French and English
Imprint: 1985 O-PEE-CHEE CO. LTD

Complete Set (163 stickers):		**60.00**
Common Player:		**.20**
Album:		**5.00**

No.	Player	NRMT-MT
☐ 1	Stanley Cup Final	.20
☐ 2	Stanley Cup Final	.20
☐ 3	Stanley Cup Final	.20
☐ 4	Stanley Cup Final	.20

Note: Stickers 1-4 feature Mark Messier, Don Jackson and Tim Kerr.

No.	Player	NRMT-MT
☐ 5	Wayne Gretzky, Edm.	6.00
☐ 6	Rick Vaive, Tor.	.25
☐ 7	Bill Derlago, Tor.	.20
☐ 12	Borje Salming, Tor.	.25
☐ 21	Miroslav Frycer, Tor.	.20
☐ 22	Denis Savard, Chi.	.50
☐ 25	Doug Wilson, Chi.	.25
☐ 30	Steve Yzerman, Det.	6.00
☐ 37	John Ogrodnick, Det.	.20
☐ 38	Keith Acton, Min.	.20
☐ 41	Brian Bellows, Min.	.25
☐ 46	Brian Sutter, Stl.	.25
☐ 53	Bernie Federko, Stl.	.25
☐ 57	Mel Bridgman, N.J.	.20
☐ 64	Kirk Muller, N.J.	.20
☐ 65	Bryan Trottier, NYI.	.25
☐ 66	Mike Bossy, NYI.	.50
☐ 71	Brent Sutter, NYI.	.25
☐ 80	John Tonelli, NYI.	.20
☐ 81	Reijo Ruotsalainen, NYR.	.20
☐ 84	Mark Pavelich, NYR.	.20
☐ 89	Dave Poulin, Pha.	.20
☐ 96	Tim Kerr, Pha.	.25
☐ 97	Mario Lemieux, Pgh.	20.00
☐ 100	Warren Young, Pgh.	.20
☐ 105	Rod Langway, Wsh.	.20
☐ 112	Bob Carpenter, Wsh.	.20
☐ 113	Foil-AS: Rod Langway, Wsh.	.50
☐ 114	Foil-AS: Tom Barrasso (G), Buf.	.75
☐ 115	Foil-AS: Ray Bourque, Bos.	3.00
☐ 116	Foil-AS: John Tonelli, NYI.	.25
☐ 117	Foil-AS: Brent Sutter, NYI.	.35
☐ 118	Foil-AS: Mike Bossy, NYI.	.75
☐ 119	Foil-AS: John Ogrodnick, Det.	.25
☐ 120	Foil-AS: Wayne Gretzky, Edm.	9.00
☐ 121	Foil-AS: Jari Kurri, Edm.	1.50
☐ 122	Foil-AS: Doug Wilson, Chi.	.35
☐ 123	Foil-AS: Andy Moog (G), Edm.	1.50
☐ 124	Foil-AS: Paul Coffey, Edm.	2.00
☐ 125	Chris Chelios, Mtl.	2.00
☐ 126	Steve Penney (G), Mtl.	.25
☐ 131	Mats Naslund, Mtl.	.25
☐ 140	Larry Robinson, Mtl.	.25
☐ 141	Michel Goulet, Que.	.35
☐ 142	Bruce Bell, Que.	.20
☐ 147	Anton Stastny, Que.	.20
☐ 156	Peter Stastny, Que.	.35
☐ 157	Ray Bourque, Bos.	2.00
☐ 160	Pete Peeters (G), Bos.	.25
☐ 165	Sylvain Turgeon, Hfd.	.20
☐ 172	Ron Francis, Hfd.	1.00
☐ 173	Phil Housley, Buf.	.25
☐ 174	Mike Foligno, Buf.	.20
☐ 179	Tom Barrasso (G), Buf.	.50
☐ 188	Gilbert Perreault, Buf.	.25
☐ 208	Kent Nilsson, Cgy.	.20
☐ 215	Lanny McDonald, Cgy.	.20
☐ 216	Charlie Huddy, Edm.	.20
☐ 217	Paul Coffey, Edm.	1.50
☐ 222	Wayne Gretzky, Edm.	7.00
☐ 231	Jari Kurri, Edm.	1.25
☐ 232	Bernie Nicholls, L.A.	.50
☐ 235	Marcel Dionne, L.A.	.25
☐ 240	Thomas Gradin, Van.	.20
☐ 247	Stan Smyl, Van.	.20
☐ 248	Dale Hawerchuk, Wpg.	.75
☐ 251	Randy Carlyle, Wpg.	.20

MULTIPLE STICKERS

No.	Player	NRMT-MT
☐ 8/136	Rick St. Croix (G), Tor./Doug Soetaert (G), Mtl.	.25
☐ 9/137	Tim Bernhardt (G), Tor./Mark Hunter, Mtl.	.25
☐ 10/138	John Anderson, Tor./Bob Gainey, Mtl.	.35
☐ 11/139	Dan Daoust, Tor./Petr Svoboda, Mtl.	.25
☐ 13/143	Al Iafrate, Tor./Dan Bouchard (G), Que.	1.50
☐ 14/144	Gary Nylund, Tor./Mario Marois, Que.	.25
☐ 15/145	Bob McGill, Tor./Randy Moller, Que.	.25
☐ 16/146	Jim Benning, Tor./Mario Gosselin (G), Que.	.35
☐ 17/148	Stewart Gavin, Tor./Normand Rochefort, Que.	.25
☐ 18/149	Greg Terrion, Tor./Alain Côté, Que.	.25
☐ 19/150	Peter Ihnacak, Tor./Paul Gillis, Que.	.25
☐ 20/151	Russ Courtnall, Tor./Dale Hunter, Que.	1.00
☐ 23/152	Darryl Sutter, Chi./Wilf Paiement, Que.	.25
☐ 24/153	Curt Fraser, Chi./Brent Ashton, Que.	.25
☐ 26/154	Ed Olczyk, Chi./Brad Maxwell, Que.	.25
☐ 27/155	Murray Bannerman (G), Chi./J.F. Sauvé, Que.	.35
☐ 28/128	Steve Larmer, Chi./Charlie Simmer, Bos.	.75
☐ 29/159	Troy Murray, Chi./Rick Middleton, Bos.	.35
☐ 31/161	Greg Stefan (G), Det./Mike O'Connell, Bos.	.35
☐ 32/162	Ron Duguay, Det./Terry O'Reilly, Bos.	.25
☐ 33/163	Reed Larson, Det./Keith Crowder, Bos.	.25
☐ 34/164	Ivan Boldirev, Det./Tom Fergus, Bos.	.25
☐ 35/166	Danny Gare, Det./Greg Malone, Hfd.	.20
☐ 36/167	Darryl Sittler, Det./Bob Crawford, Hfd.	.35
☐ 39/168	Dino Ciccarelli, Min./Kevin Dineen, Hfd.	.50
☐ 40/169	Neal Broten, Min./Mike Liut (G), Hfd.	.35
☐ 42/170	Steve Payne, Min./Joel Quenneville, Hfd.	.35
☐ 43/171	Gord Roberts, Min./Ray Neufeld, Hfd.	.25
☐ 44/175	Harold Snepsts, Min./Craig Ramsay, Buf.	.25
☐ 45/176	Tony McKegney, Min./Bill Hajt, Buf.	.25
☐ 47/177	Joe Mullen, Stl./Dave Maloney, Buf.	.35
☐ 48/178	Doug Gilmour, Stl./Brent Peterson, Buf.	3.00
☐ 49/180	Tim Bothwell, Stl./Mike Ramsey, Buf.	.25
☐ 50/151	Mark Johnson, Stl./Bob Sauvé (G), Buf.	.35
☐ 51/182	Greg Millen (G), Stl./Ric Seiling, Buf.	.35
☐ 52/183	Doug Wickenheiser, Stl./Paul Cyr, Buf.	.25
☐ 54/197	Foil: Wayne Gretzky, Edm./Vezina Trophy	5.00
☐ 55/203	Foil: Tom Barrasso, Buf./Hart Trophy	.35
☐ 56/204	Foil: Paul Coffey, Edm./Calder Trophy	1.00
☐ 58/184	Phil Russell, N.J./John Tucker, Buf.	.25
☐ 59/185	Dave Lewis, N.J./Gilles Hamel, Buf.	.25
☐ 60/186	Paul Gagne, N.J./Mal Davis, Buf.	.25
☐ 61/187	Glenn Resch (G), N.J./Dave Andreychuk, Buf.	.35
☐ 62/189	Aaron Broten, N.J./Tom Barrasso (G), Buf.	.50
☐ 63/190	Dave Pichette, N.J./Bob Sauvé (G), Buf.	.35
☐ 67/191	Bob Bourne, NYI./Paul Coffey, Edm.	1.00
☐ 68/192	Clark Gillies, NYI./Craig Ramsay, Buf.	.25
☐ 69/193	Bob Nystrom, NYI./Pelle Lindbergh (G), Pha.	1.50
☐ 70/198	Denis Potvin, NYI./Wayne Gretzky, Edm.	6.00
☐ 72/199	Duane Sutter, NYI./Mario Lemieux, Pgh.	10.00
☐ 73/200	Patrick Flatley, NYI./Anders Hedberg, NYR.	.25
☐ 74/201	Pat LaFontaine, NYI./Jari Kurri, Edm.	2.00
☐ 75/202	Greg Gilbert, NYI./Wayne Gretzky, Edm.	5.00
☐ 76/209	Billy Smith (G), NYI./Paul Reinhart, Cgy.	.35
☐ 77/210	Gord Lane, NYI./Réjean Lemelin (G), Cgy.	.35
☐ 78/211	Tomas Jonsson, NYI./Al MacInnis, Cgy.	4.00
☐ 79/212	Kelly Hrudey (G), NYI./Jamie Macoun, Cgy.	.25
☐ 82/213	Barry Beck, NYR./Carey Wilson, Cgy.	.25
☐ 83/214	James Patrick, NYR./Eddy Beers, Cgy.	.25
☐ 85/218	Pierre Larouche, NYR./Lee Fogolin, Edm.	.25
☐ 86/219	Mike Rogers, NYR./Kevin Lowe, Edm.	.35
☐ 87/220	Glen Hanlon (G), NYR./Andy Moog (G), Edm.	1.00
☐ 88/221	John Vanbiesbrouck (G), NYR./Grant Fuhr (G), Edm.	5.00
☐ 90/223	Brian Propp, Pha./Mike Krushelnyski, Edm.	.25
☐ 91/224	Pelle Lindbergh (G), Pha./Billy Carroll, Edm.	1.50
☐ 92/225	Brad McCrimmon, Pha./Randy Gregg, Edm.	.25
☐ 93/226	Mark Howe, Pha./Willy Lindstrom, Edm.	.35
☐ 94/227	Peter Zezel, Pha./Glenn Anderson, Edm.	.35
☐ 95/228	Murray Craven, Pha./Mark Messier, Edm.	1.50
☐ 98/229	Moe Mantha, Pgh./Pat Hughes, Edm.	.25
☐ 99/230	Doug Bodger, Pgh./Kevin McClelland, Edm.	.25
☐ 101/233	John Chabot, Pgh./Brian Engblom, L.A.	.25
☐ 102/234	Doug Shedden, Pgh./Mark Hardy, L.A.	.25
☐ 103/236	Wayne Babych, Pgh./Jim Fox, L.A.	.25
☐ 104/237	Mike Bullard, Pgh./Terry Ruskowski, L.A.	.25
☐ 106/238	Pat Riggin (G), Wsh./Dave Taylor, L.A.	.35
☐ 107/239	Scott Stevens, Wsh./Bob Janecyk (G), L.A.	.50
☐ 108/241	Alan Haworth, Wsh./Patrik Sundstrom, Van.	.25
☐ 109/242	Doug Jarvis, Wsh./Al MacAdam, Van.	.25
☐ 110/243	Dave Christian, Wsh./Doug Halward, Van.	.25
☐ 111/244	Mike Gartner, Wsh./Peter McNab, Van.	.50
☐ 127/245	Chris Nilan, Mtl./Tony Tanti, Van.	.25
☐ 128/246	Ron Flockhart, Mtl./Moe Lemay, Van.	.25
☐ 129/249	Tom Kurvers, Mtl./Dave Babych, Wpg.	.35
☐ 130/250	Craig Ludwig, Mtl./Paul MacLean, Wpg.	.25
☐ 132/252	Bobby Smith, Mtl./Robert Picard, Wpg.	.25
☐ 133/253	Pierre Mondou, Mtl./Thomas Steen, Wpg.	.25
☐ 134/254	Mario Tremblay, Mtl./Laurie Boschman, Wpg.	.25
☐ 135/255	Guy Carbonneau, Mtl./Doug Smail, Wpg.	.25
☐ 194/205	Foil: Jennings Trophy/Masterton Trophy	.25
☐ 195/206	Foil: Norris Trophy/Lady Byng Trophy	.25
☐ 196/207	Foil: Selke Trophy/Art Ross Trophy	.25

1985 - 86 7-ELEVEN CREDIT CARDS

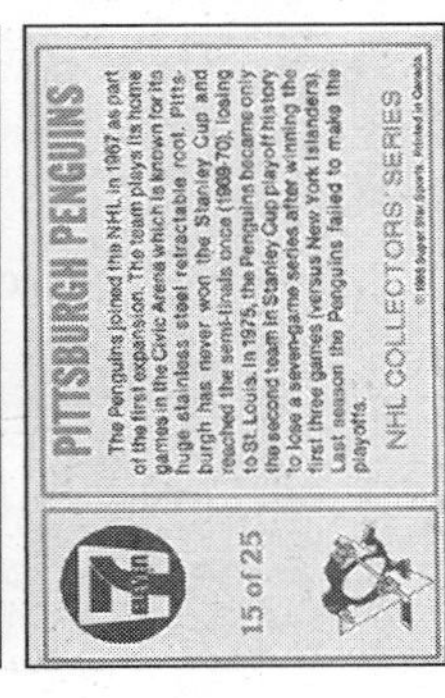

Card Size: 2 1/8" x 3 3/8"
Face: Four colour, black border; Name Position, Jersey number
Back: Blue and red on plastic; Team, Numbered of 25, Resume, Team and sponsor logos
Imprint: 1985 Super Star Sports.

Complete Set (25 cards):		**40.00**
Album:		**5.00**

No.	Player	NRMT-MT
☐ 1	Ray Bourque / Rick Middleton	4.00
☐ 2	Tom Barrasso (G) / Gilbert Perreault	2.00
☐ 3	Paul Reinhart / Lanny McDonald	1.50
☐ 4	Denis Savard / Doug Wilson	2.00
☐ 5	Ron Duguay / Steve Yzerman	10.00
☐ 6	Paul Coffey / Jari Kurri	4.00
☐ 7	Ron Francis / Mike Liut (G)	2.00
☐ 8	Marcel Dionne / Dave Taylor	2.00
☐ 9	Brian Bellows / Dino Ciccarelli	1.50
☐ 10	Larry Robinson / Guy Carbonneau	2.00
☐ 11	Mel Bridgman / Chico Resch (G)	1.00
☐ 12	Mike Bossy / Bryan Trottier	3.50
☐ 13	Reijo Ruotsalainen / Barry Beck	1.00
☐ 14	Tim Kerr / Mark Howe	1.50
☐ 15	Mario Lemieux / Mike Bullard	25.00
☐ 16	Peter Stastny / Michel Goulet	4.00
☐ 17	Rob Ramage / Brian Sutter	1.50
☐ 18	Rick Vaive / Borje Salming	2.00
☐ 19	Patrik Sundstrom / Stan Smyl	1.50
☐ 20	Rod Langway / Mike Gartner	3.00
☐ 21	Dale Hawerchuk / Paul MacLean	3.00
☐ 22	Stanley Cup Winners	1.00
☐ 23	Prince of Wales; Trophy Winners	1.00
☐ 24	Clarence S. Campbell; Bowl Winners	1.00
☐ 25	Title Card: Superstar Collectors' Series	1.00

1985 - 86 TOPPS

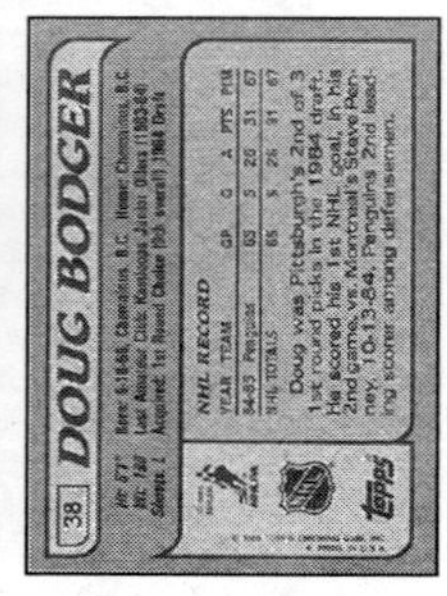

Face: Four colour, white border, Team logo, Name, Position
Back: Red and blue on card stock; Number, Resume
Imprint: © 1985 TOPPS CHEWING GUM, INC.

Complete Set (165 cards):	**280.00**
Common Player:	**.25**
Single Prints (*):	**.35**

	No.	Player	NRMT-MT
☐	1	Lanny McDonald, Cgy.	.60
☐	2	Mike O'Connell, Bos. (*)	.35
☐	3	Curt Fraser, Chi. (*)	.35
☐	4	Steve Penney, Mtl. (G)	.25
☐	5	Brian Engblom, L.A.	.25
☐	6	Ron Sutter, Pha.	.30
☐	7	Joe Mullen, Stl.	1.00
☐	8	Rod Langway, Wsh.	.35
☐	**9**	**Mario Lemieux, Pgh., RC**	**200.00**
☐	10	Dave Babych, Wpg.	.35
☐	11	Bob Nystrom, NYI.	.35
☐	12	Andy Moog (G), Edm. (*)	2.75
☐	13	Dino Ciccarelli, Min.	1.25
☐	14	Dwight Foster, Det., LC (*)	.35
☐	15	James Patrick, NYR. (*)	.35
☐	16	Thomas Gradin, Van., LC (*)	.35
☐	17	Mike Foligno, Buf.	.25
☐	**18**	**Mario Gosselin (G), Que., RC**	**.35**
☐	19	Mike Zuke, Hfd., LC (*)	.35
☐	20	John Anderson, Tor. (*)	.35
☐	21	Dave Pichette, N.J., LC	.25
☐	22	Nick Fotiu, NYR., LC (*)	.35
☐	23	Tom Lysiak, Chi., LC	.25
☐	**24**	**Peter Zezel, Pha., RC**	**1.25**
☐	25	Denis Potvin, NYI.	.75
☐	26	Bob Carpenter, Wsh.	.35
☐	27	Murray Bannerman (G), Chi. (*)	.50
☐	28	Gord Roberts, Min. (*)	.35
☐	29	Steve Yzerman, Det.	20.00
☐	30	Phil Russell, N.J.	.25
☐	31	Peter Stastny, Que.	1.00
☐	32	Craig Ramsay, Buf., LC (*)	.50
☐	33	Terry Ruskowski, L.A. (*)	.35
☐	**34**	**Kevin Dineen, Hfd., RC (*)**	**2.50**
☐	35	Mark Howe, Pha.	.35
☐	36	Glenn Resch, N.J. (G)	.35
☐	37	Danny Gare, Det. (*)	.50
☐	**38**	**Doug Bodger, Pgh., RC**	**.50**
☐	39	Mike Rogers, NYR., LC	.25
☐	40	Ray Bourque, Bos.	3.50
☐	41	John Tonelli, NYI.	.25
☐	42	Mel Bridgman, N.J.	.25
☐	43	Sylvain Turgeon, Hfd. (*)	.35
☐	44	Mark Johnson, Stl.	.25
☐	45	Doug Wilson, Chi.	.35
☐	46	Mike Gartner, Wsh.	2.50
☐	47	Brent Peterson, Buf.	.25
☐	48	Paul Reinhart, Cgy. (*)	.35
☐	49	Mike Krushelnyski, Edm.	.25
☐	50	Brian Bellows, Min.	.50
☐	51	Chris Chelios, Mtl.	6.50
☐	52	Barry Pederson, Bos. (*)	.35
☐	53	Murray Craven, Pha. (*)	.35
☐	54	Pierre Larouche, NYR., LC (*)	.35
☐	55	Reed Larson, Det.	.25
☐	56	Pat Verbeek, N.J. (*)	1.50
☐	57	Randy Carlyle, Wpg.	.25
☐	58	Ray Neufeld, Hfd. (*)	.35
☐	59	Keith Brown, Chi. (*)	.35
☐	60	Bryan Trottier, NYI.	.75
☐	61	Jim Fox, L.A. (*)	.35
☐	62	Scott Stevens, Wsh.	2.25
☐	63	Phil Housley, Buf.	1.00
☐	64	Rick Middleton, Bos.	.35
☐	65	Steve Payne, Min.	.25
☐	66	Dave Lewis, N.J.	.25
☐	67	Mike Bullard, Pgh.	.25
☐	68	Stan Smyl, Van. (*)	.50
☐	69	Mark Pavelich, NYR., LC (*)	.35
☐	70	John Ogrodnick, Det.	.25
☐	71	Bill Derlago, Tor. (*)	.35
☐	72	Brad Marsh, Pha. (*)	.35
☐	73	Denis Savard, Chi.	1.25
☐	**74**	**Mark Fusco, Hfd., RC, LC**	**.25**
☐	75	Pete Peeters (G), Bos.	.35
☐	76	Doug Gilmour, Stl.	10.00
☐	77	Mike Ramsey, Buf.	.25
☐	78	Anton Stastny, Que. (*)	.35
☐	79	Steve Kasper, Bos. (*)	.35
☐	**80**	**Bryan Erickson, Wsh., RC (*)**	**.35**
☐	81	Clark Gillies, NYI.	.25
☐	82	Keith Acton, Min.	.25
☐	83	Patrick Flatley, NYI.	.25
☐	**84**	**Kirk Muller, N.J., RC**	**4.50**
☐	85	Paul Coffey, Edm.	3.50
☐	**86**	**Ed Olczyk, Chi., RC**	**1.00**
☐	87	Charlie Simmer, Bos.	.25
☐	88	Mike Liut (G), Hfd.	.35
☐	89	Dave Maloney, Buf., LC	.25
☐	90	Marcel Dionne, L.A.	.75
☐	91	Tim Kerr, Pha.	.35
☐	92	Ivan Boldirev, Det., LC (*)	.35
☐	93	Ken Morrow, NYI. (*)	.35
☐	94	Don Maloney, NYR. (*)	.35
☐	95	Réjean Lemelin (G), Cgy.	.35
☐	96	Curt Giles, Min.	.25
☐	97	Bob Bourne, NYI.	.25
☐	98	Joe Cirella, N.J.	.25
☐	99	Dave Christian, Wsh. (*)	.35
☐	100	Darryl Sutter, Chi.	.35
☐	101	Kelly Kisio, Det.	.25
☐	102	Mats Naslund, Mtl.	.35
☐	103	Joel Quenneville, Hfd. (*)	.50
☐	104	Bernie Federko, Stl.	.35
☐	105	Tom Barrasso (G), Buf.	1.25
☐	106	Rick Vaive, Tor.	.35
☐	107	Brent Sutter, NYI.	.35
☐	108	Wayne Babych, Pgh.	.25
☐	109	Dale Hawerchuk, Wpg.	1.75
☐	110	Pelle Lindbergh (G), Pha., LC (*)	12.00
☐	111	Dennis Maruk, Min. (*)	.35
☐	112	Reijo Ruotsalainen, NYR. (*)	.35
☐	113	Tom Fergus, Bos. (*)	.35
☐	114	Bob Murray, Chi. (*)	.35
☐	115	Patrik Sundstrom, Van.	.25
☐	116	Ron Duguay, Det. (*)	.35
☐	117	Alan Haworth, Wsh. (*)	.35
☐	118	Greg Malone, Hfd., LC	.25
☐	119	Bill Hajt, Buf.	.25
☐	120	Wayne Gretzky, Edm.	22.00
☐	**121**	**Craig Redmond, L.A., RC, LC**	**.25**
☐	**122**	**Kelly Hrudey (G), NYI., RC**	**4.50**
☐	**123**	**Tomas Sandstrom, NYR., RC**	**4.50**
☐	124	Neal Broten, Min.	.35
☐	125	Moe Mantha, Pgh. (*)	.35
☐	126	Gregory Gilbert, NYI. (*)	.35
☐	**127**	**Bruce Driver, N.J., RC**	**1.00**
☐	128	Dave Poulin, Pha.	.25
☐	129	Morris Lukowich, Bos., LC	.25
☐	130	Mike Bossy, NYI.	2.00
☐	131	Larry Playfair, Buf. (*)	.35
☐	132	Steve Larmer, Chi.	2.00
☐	133	Doug Keans (G), Bos. (*)	.50
☐	134	Bob Manno, Det., LC	.25
☐	135	Brian Sutter, Stl.	.50
☐	136	Pat Riggin (G), Wsh., LC	.35
☐	137	Pat LaFontaine, NYI.	7.00
☐	138	Barry Beck, NYR., LC (*)	.35
☐	139	Rich Preston, N.J. (*)	.35
☐	140	Ron Francis, Hfd.	2.50
☐	141	Brian Propp, Pha. (*)	.35
☐	142	Don Beaupré (G), Min.	.35
☐	143	David Andreychuk, Buf. (*)	3.00
☐	144	Ed Beers, Cgy.	.25
☐	145	Paul MacLean, Wpg.	.25
☐	146	Troy Murray, Chi. (*)	.35
☐	147	Larry Robinson, Mtl.	.75
☐	148	Bernie Nicholls, L.A.	1.50
☐	149	Glen Hanlon (G), NYR. (*)	.50
☐	150	Michel Goulet, Que.	.75
☐	151	Doug Jarvis, Wsh. (*)	.35
☐	**152**	**Warren Young, Pgh., RC**	**.25**
☐	153	Tony Tanti, Van.	.35
☐	154	Tomas Jonsson, NYI. (*)	.35
☐	155	Jari Kurri, Edm.	2.00
☐	156	Tony McKegney, Min.	.25
☐	157	Greg Stefan (G), Det. (*)	.50
☐	158	Brad McCrimmon, Pha. (*)	.35
☐	159	Keith Crowder, Bos. (*)	.35
☐	160	Gilbert Perreault, Buf.	.50
☐	161	Tim Bothwell, Stl. (*)	.35
☐	162	Bob Crawford, Hfd., LC (*)	.35
☐	163	Paul Gagné, N.J., LC (*)	.35
☐	164	Dan Daoust, Tor. (*)	.35
☐	165	Checklist (*)	4.00

STICKER INSERTS

Imprint: 1985 TOPPS CHEWING GUM, INC. PRTD. IN U.S.A. 1985

Insert Set (33 stickers):	**18.00**

	No.	Player	NRMT-MT
☐	1	AS: John Ogrodnick, Det.	.35
☐	2	AS: Wayne Gretzky, Edm.	8.00
☐	3	AS: Jari Kurri, Edm.	1.00
☐	4	AS: Paul Coffey, Edm.	1.50
☐	5	AS: Ray Bourque, Bos.	2.00
☐	6	AS: Pelle Lindbergh (G), Pha.	4.00
☐	7	AS: John Tonelli, NYI.	.35
☐	8	AS: Dale Hawerchuk, Wpg.	1.00
☐	9	AS: Mike Bossy, NYI.	1.50
☐	10	AS: Rod Langway, Wsh.	.50
☐	11	AS: Doug Wilson, Chi.	.50
☐	12	AS: Tom Barrasso (G), Buf.	.65
☐	13	Toronto Maple Leafs	.25
☐	14	Buffalo Sabres	.25
☐	15	Detroit Red Wings	.25
☐	16	Pittsburgh Penguins	.25
☐	17	New York Rangers	.25
☐	18	Calgary Flames	.25
☐	19	Winnpeg Jets	.25
☐	20	Québec Nordiques	.25
☐	21	Chicago Blackhawks	.25
☐	22	Los Angeles Kings	.25
☐	23	Montréal Canadiens	.25
☐	24	Vancouver Canucks	.25
☐	25	Hartford Whalers	.25
☐	26	Philadelphia Flyers	.25
☐	27	New Jersey Devils	.25
☐	28	St. Louis Blues	.25
☐	29	Minnesota North Stars	.25
☐	30	Washington Capitals	.25
☐	31	Boston Bruins	.25
☐	32	New York Islanders	.25
☐	33	Edmonton Oilers	.25

TOPPS BOX BOTTOMS

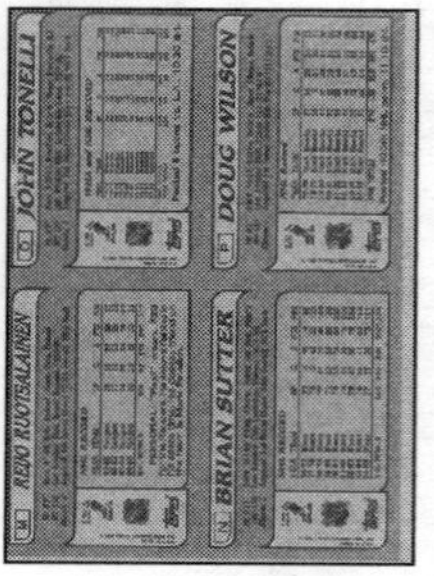

These four-card panels were issued on the bottom of Topps and O-Pee-Chee wax boxes.

Panel Size: 5" x 7"
Imprint:

Complete Set (16 cards):	**100.00**
Panel A - D:	**8.00**
Panel E - H:	**30.00**
Panel I - L:	**80.00**
Panel M - P:	**3.00**

	No.	Player	NRMT-MT
☐	A	Brian Bellows, Min.	.75
☐	B	Ray Bourque, Bos.	5.00

		Player	
☐	C	Bob Carpenter, Wsh.	.75
☐	D	Chris Chelios, Mtl.	5.00
☐	E	Marcel Dionne, L.A.	1.50
☐	F	Ron Francis, Hfd.	4.00
☐	G	Wayne Gretzky, Edm.	25.00
☐	H	Tim Kerr, Pha.	.25
☐	I	Mario Lemieux, Pgh.	75.00
☐	J	John Ogrodnick, Det.	.75
☐	K	Gilbert Perreault, Buf.	1.50
☐	L	Glenn Resch (G), N.J.	.75
☐	M	Reijo Ruotsalainen, NYR.	.75
☐	N	Brian Sutter, Stl.	.75
☐	O	John Tonelli, NYI.	.75
☐	P	Doug Wilson, Chi.	.75

1986 - 87 KRAFT SPORTS / POSTERS

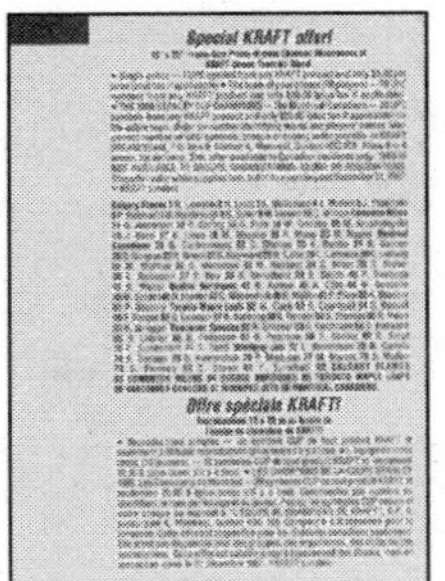

The cards come in two different card stock weights due to the different packaging. Jerry Hersh drew 42 and Carleton McDiarmid drew 30 of the 81 black and white drawings. A set of posters was also available.

Card Size: 2 1/2" x 3 5/16"
Poster Size: 16" x 20"
Face: Black and white; Name, Jersey number, Logos
Back: Black and white; Checklist, Offer
Imprint: KRAFT LIMITED

			Thin	Thick	Poster
Complete Set (81 cards):			70.00	300.00	550.00
Album:					50.00
Common Player:			.75	2.50	4.00
	No.	**Player**	**Thin**	**Thick**	**Poster**
☐☐☐	1	Réjean Lemelin (G), Cgy.	1.00	3.00	5.00
☐☐☐	2	Hakan Loob, Cgy.	.75	2.50	4.00
☐☐☐	3	Lanny McDonald, Cgy.	1.75	6.00	10.00
☐☐☐	4	Joe Mullen, Cgy.	1.00	3.00	5.00
☐☐☐	5	Jim Peplinski, Cgy.	.75	2.50	4.00
☐☐☐	6	Paul Reinhart, Cgy.	.75	2.50	4.00
☐☐☐	7	Doug Risebrough, Cgy.	.75	2.50	4.00
☐☐☐	8	Gary Suter, Cgy.	1.25	4.00	6.00
☐☐☐	9	Mike Vernon (G), Cgy.	5.00	20.00	35.00
☐☐☐	10	Carey Wilson, Cgy.	.75	2.50	4.00
☐☐☐	11	Glenn Anderson, Edm.	1.00	3.00	5.00
☐☐☐	12	Paul Coffey, Edm.	3.50	15.00	25.00
☐☐☐	13	Grant Fuhr (G), Edm.	2.50	9.00	15.00
☐☐☐	14	Wayne Gretzky, Edm.	25.00	100.00	175.00
☐☐☐	15	Mike Krushelnyski, Edm.	.75	2.50	4.00
☐☐☐	16	Jari Kurri, Edm.	2.00	7.00	12.00
☐☐☐	17	Kevin Lowe, Edm.	1.00	3.00	5.00
☐☐☐	18	Mark Messier, Edm.	6.50	30.00	50.00
☐☐☐	19	Andy Moog (G), Edm.	2.00	7.00	12.00
☐☐☐	20	Mark Napier, Edm.	.75	2.50	4.00
☐☐☐	21	Guy Carbonneau, Mtl.	1.00	3.00	5.00
☐☐☐	22	Chris Chelios, Mtl.	3.50	15.00	25.00
☐☐☐	23	Kjell Dahlin, Mtl.	.75	2.50	4.00
☐☐☐	24	Bob Gainey, Mtl.	1.50	5.00	8.00
☐☐☐	25	Gaston Gingras, Mtl.	.75	2.50	4.00
☐☐☐	26	Rick Green, Mtl.	.75	2.50	4.00
☐☐☐	27	Brian Hayward (G), Mtl.	1.00	3.00	5.00
☐☐☐	28	Mike Lalor, Mtl.	.75	2.50	4.00
☐☐☐	29	Claude Lemieux, Mtl.	2.25	8.00	13.00
☐☐☐	30	Craig Ludwig, Mtl.	.75	2.50	4.00
☐☐☐	31	Mike McPhee, Mtl.	.75	2.50	4.00
☐☐☐	32	Sergio Momesso, Mtl.	.75	2.50	4.00
☐☐☐	33	Mats Naslund, Mtl.	1.00	3.00	5.00
☐☐☐	34	Chris Nilan, Mtl.	.75	2.50	4.00
☐☐☐	35	Stéphane Richer, Mtl.	1.25	4.00	6.00
☐☐☐	36	Larry Robinson, Mtl.	1.75	6.00	10.00
☐☐☐	37	Patrick Roy (G), Mtl.	18.00	75.00	135.00
☐☐☐	38	Brian Skrudland, Mtl.	.75	2.50	4.00
☐☐☐	39	Bobby Smith, Mtl.	1.00	3.00	5.00
☐☐☐	40	Petr Svoboda, Mtl.	.75	2.50	4.00
☐☐☐	41	Ryan Walter, Mtl.	.75	2.50	4.00
☐☐☐	42	Brent Ashton, Que.	.75	2.50	4.00
☐☐☐	43	Alain Côté, Que.	.75	2.50	4.00
☐☐☐	44	Mario Gosselin (G), Que.	1.00	3.00	5.00
☐☐☐	45	Michel Goulet, Que.	1.25	4.00	6.00
☐☐☐	46	Dale Hunter, Que.	1.00	3.00	5.00
☐☐☐	47	Clint Malarchuk (G), Que.	1.00	3.00	5.00
☐☐☐	48	Randy Moller, Que.	.75	2.50	4.00
☐☐☐	49	Pat Price, Que.	.75	2.50	4.00
☐☐☐	50	Anton Stastny, Que.	.75	2.50	4.00
☐☐☐	51	Peter Stastny, Que.	1.50	5.00	8.00
☐☐☐	52	Wendel Clark, Tor.	5.00	20.00	35.00
☐☐☐	53	Russ Courtnall, Tor.	1.25	4.00	6.00
☐☐☐	54	Dan Daoust, Tor.	.75	2.50	4.00
☐☐☐	55	Tom Fergus, Tor.	.75	2.50	4.00
☐☐☐	56	Gary Leeman, Tor.	.75	2.50	4.00
☐☐☐	57	Borje Salming, Tor.	1.50	5.00	8.00
☐☐☐	58	Greg Terrion, Tor.	.75	2.50	4.00
☐☐☐	59	Steve Thomas, Tor.	1.25	4.00	6.00
☐☐☐	60	Rick Vaive, Tor.	1.00	3.00	5.00
☐☐☐	61	Ken Wregget (G), Tor.	2.00	7.00	12.00
☐☐☐	62	Richard Brodeur (G), Van.	1.00	3.00	5.00
☐☐☐	63	Glen Cochrane, Van.	.75	2.50	4.00
☐☐☐	64	Doug Halward, Van.	.75	2.50	4.00
☐☐☐	65	Doug Lidster, Van.	.75	2.50	4.00
☐☐☐	66	Barry Pederson, Van.	.75	2.50	4.00
☐☐☐	67	Brent Peterson, Van.	.75	2.50	4.00
☐☐☐	68	Petri Skriko, Van.	.75	2.50	4.00
☐☐☐	69	Stan Smyl, Van., Error (Syml)	1.00	3.00	5.00
☐☐☐	70	Patrik Sundstrom, Van.	.75	2.50	4.00
☐☐☐	71	Tony Tanti, Van.	1.00	3.00	5.00
☐☐☐	72	Laurie Boschman, Wpg.	.75	2.50	4.00
☐☐☐	73	Randy Carlyle, Wpg.	.75	2.50	4.00
☐☐☐	74	Bill Derlago, Wpg.	.75	2.50	4.00
☐☐☐	75	Dale Hawerchuk, Wpg.	1.75	6.00	10.00
☐☐☐	76	Paul MacLean, Wpg.	.75	2.50	4.00
☐☐☐	77	Mario Marois, Wpg.	.75	2.50	4.00
☐☐☐	78	Brian Mullen, Wpg.	.75	2.50	4.00
☐☐☐	79	Steve Penney (G), Wpg.	1.00	3.00	5.00
☐☐☐	80	Thomas Steen, Wpg.	.75	2.50	4.00
☐☐☐	81	Perry Turnbull, Wpg.	.75	2.50	4.00

1986 - 87 O-PEE-CHEE

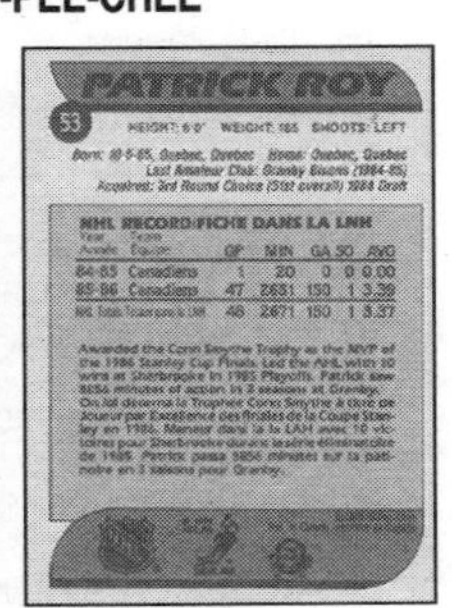

Face: Four colour, white border, Team Logo, Position
Back: Blue and black on card stock, Number, Resume, Bilingual
Imprint: © 1986 O-Pee-Chee

Complete Set (264 cards):			315.00
Common Player:			.35
	No.	**Player**	**NRMT-MT**
☐	1	Ray Bourque, Bos.	5.00
☐	2	Pat LaFontaine, NYI.	6.50
☐	3	Wayne Gretzky, Edm.	28.00
☐	4	Lindy Ruff, Buf.	.35
☐	5	Brad McCrimmon, Pha.	.35
☐	6	Dave Williams, L.A., LC	.35
☐	7	Denis Savard, Chi.	.85
☐	8	Lanny McDonald, Cgy.	.50
☐	**9**	**John Vanbiesbrouck (G), NYR., RC**	**60.00**
☐	**10**	**Greg Adams, N.J., RC**	**2.75**
☐	11	Steve Yzerman, Det.	18.00
☐	12	Craig Hartsburg, Min.	.50
☐	13	John Anderson, Hfd.	.35
☐	14	Bob Bourne, NYI. (L.A.)	.35
☐	**15**	**Kjell Dahlin, Mtl., RC, LC**	**.35**
☐	16	Dave Andreychuk, Buf.	2.00
☐	17	Rob Ramage, Stl.	.35
☐	18	Ron Greschner, NYR.	.35
☐	19	Bruce Driver, N.J.	.35
☐	20	Peter Stastny, Que.	.85
☐	21	Dave Christian, Wsh.	.35
☐	22	Doug Keans (G), Bos.	.50
☐	**23**	**Scott Bjugstad, Min., RC**	**.35**
☐	24	Doug Bodger, Pgh.	.50
☐	25	Troy Murray, Chi.	.35
☐	26	Al Iafrate, Tor.	2.00
☐	27	Kelly Hrudey (G), NYI.	2.00
☐	28	Doug Jarvis, Hfd.	.35
☐	29	Rich Sutter, Van.	.35
☐	30	Marcel Dionne, L.A.	.85
☐	31	Curt Fraser, Chi., LC	.35
☐	32	Doug Lidster, Van.	.35
☐	33	Brian MacLellan, Cgy. (Min.)	.35
☐	34	Barry Pederson, Van.	.35
☐	35	Craig Laughlin, Wsh.	.35
☐	36	Ilkka Sinisalo, Pha.	.35
☐	**37**	**John MacLean, N.J., RC**	**5.00**
☐	38	Brian Mullen, Wpg.	.35
☐	39	Duane Sutter, NYI.	.50
☐	40	Brian Engblom, Buf. (Cgy.), LC	.35
☐	**41**	**Chris Cichocki, Det., RC, LC**	**.35**
☐	42	Gord Roberts, Min.	.35
☐	43	Ron Francis, Hfd.	2.50
☐	44	Joe Mullen, Cgy.	.75
☐	45	Moe Mantha, Pgh.	.35
☐	46	Pat Verbeek, N.J.	1.50
☐	**47**	**Clint Malarchuk (G), Que., RC**	**1.25**
☐	48	Bob Brooke, NYR.	.35
☐	49	Darryl Sutter, Chi., LC	.50
☐	50	Stan Smyl, Van.	.50
☐	51	Greg Stefan (G), Det.	.50
☐	52	Bill Hajt, Buf., LC	.35
☐	**53**	**Patrick Roy (G), Mtl., RC**	**235.00**
☐	54	Gord Kluzak, Bos.	.35
☐	55	Bob Froese (G), Pha.	.50
☐	56	Grant Fuhr (G), Edm.	2.50
☐	57	Mark Hunter, Stl.	.35
☐	**58**	**Dana Murzyn, Hfd., RC**	**.75**
☐	59	Mike Gartner, Wsh.	2.00
☐	60	Dennis Maruk, Min.	.35
☐	61	Rich Preston, N.J. (Chi.)	.35
☐	62	Larry Robinson, Mtl.	.75
☐	63	Dave Taylor, L.A.	.50
☐	64	Bob Murray, Chi.	.35
☐	65	Ken Morrow, NYI.	.35
☐	**66**	**Mike Ridley, NYR., RC**	**2.00**
☐	**67**	**John Tucker, Buf., RC**	**.50**
☐	68	Miroslav Frycer, Tor., LC	.35
☐	69	Danny Gare, Det. (Edm.), LC	.35
☐	**70**	**Randy Burridge, Bos., RC**	**1.00**
☐	71	Dave Poulin, Pha.	.50
☐	72	Brian Sutter, Stl., LC	.50
☐	73	Dave Babych, Hfd.	.50
☐	74	Dale Hawerchuk, Wpg.	1.75
☐	75	Brian Bellows, Min.	.50
☐	**76**	**Dave Pasin, Bos., RC, LC**	**.35**
☐	77	Pete Peeters (G), Wsh.	.50
☐	78	Tomas Jonsson, NYI.	.35
☐	79	Gilbert Perreault, Buf., LC	.60
☐	80	Glenn Anderson, Edm.	1.00
☐	81	Don Maloney, NYR.	.35
☐	82	Ed Olczyk, Chi.	.50
☐	83	Mike Bullard, Pgh	.35
☐	84	Tom Fergus, Tor.	.35
☐	85	Dave Lewis, N.J. (Det.)	.50
☐	86	Brian Propp, Pha.	.50
☐	87	John Ogrodnick, Det.	.35
☐	88	Kevin Dineen, Hfd.	.50
☐	89	Don Beaupré (G), Min.	.50
☐	90	Mike Bossy, NYI.	2.50
☐	91	Tom Barrasso (G), Buf.	1.50
☐	92	Michel Goulet, Que.	.85
☐	93	Doug Gilmour, Stl.	8.00
☐	94	Kirk Muller, N.J.	1.75
☐	**95**	**Larry Melnyk, NYR., RC**	**.35**
☐	96	Bob Gainey, Mtl.	.85
☐	97	Steve Kasper, Bos.	.35
☐	**98**	**Petr Klima, Det., RC**	**1.00**
☐	99	Neal Broten, Min.	.50
☐	100	Al Secord, Chi.	.35
☐	101	Bryan Erickson, L.A.	.35
☐	102	Réjean Lemelin (G), Cgy.	.50
☐	103	Sylvain Turgeon, Hfd.	.35
☐	104	Bob Nystrom, NYI., LC	.35
☐	105	Bernie Federko, Stl.	.75

☐ 106 Doug Wilson, Chi. .75
☐ 107 Alan Haworth, Wsh. .35
☐ 108 Jari Kurri, Edm. 2.25
☐ 109 Ron Sutter, Pha. .35
☐ 110 Reed Larson, Bos. .35
☐ 111 Terry Ruskowski, Pgh. .35
☐ 112 Mark Johnson, N.J. .35
☐ 113 James Patrick, NYR. .35
☐ 114 Paul MacLean, Wpg. .35
☐ 115 Mike Ramsey, Buf. .35
☐ 116 Kelly Kisio, Det. (NYR.) .35
☐ 117 Brent Sutter, NYI. .50
☐ 118 Joel Quenneville, Hfd. .50
☐ 119 Curt Giles, Min. .35
☐ 120 Tony Tanti, Van. .35
☐ 121 Doug Sulliman, N.J. .35
☐ 122 Mario Lemieux, Pgh. 60.00
☐ 123 Mark Howe, Pha. .50
☐ 124 Bob Sauvé (G), Chi. .50
☐ 125 Anton Stastny, Que. .35
☐ 126 Scott Stevens, Wsh. 1.75
☐ 127 Mike Foligno, Buf. .35
☐ 128 Reijo Ruotsalainen, NYR., LC .35
☐ 129 Denis Potvin, NYI. .85
☐ 130 Keith Crowder, Bos. .35
☐ 131 Bob Janecyk (G), L.A., LC .50
☐ 132 John Tonelli, Cgy. .35
☐ 133 Mike Liut (G), Hfd. .35
☐ 134 Tim Kerr, Pha. .50
☐ 135 Al Jensen (G), Wsh., LC .50
☐ 136 Mel Bridgman, N.J. .35
☐ 137 Paul Coffey, Edm. 4.50
☐ 138 Dino Ciccarelli, Min. .85
☐ 139 Steve Larmer, Chi. 1.50
☐ 140 Mike O'Connell, Det. .35
☐ 141 Clark Gillies, NYI. (Buf.) .50
☐ 142 Phil Russell, Buf., LC .35
☐ **143 Dirk Graham, Min., RC 1.50**
☐ 144 Randy Carlyle, Wpg. .35
☐ 145 Charlie Simmer, Bos. .35
☐ 146 Ron Flockhart, Stl. .35
☐ 147 Tom Laidlaw, NYR. .35
☐ **148 Dave Tippett, Hfd., RC .50**
☐ **149 Wendel Clark, Tor., RC 22.00**
☐ 150 Bob Carpenter, Wsh. .35
☐ **151 Bill Watson, Chi., RC, LC .35**
☐ **152 Roberto Romano (G), Pgh., RC, LC .50**
☐ 153 Doug Shedden, Det. .35
☐ 154 Phil Housley, Buf. .75
☐ 155 Bryan Trottier, NYI. .85
☐ 156 Patrik Sundstrom, Van. .35
☐ 157 Rick Middleton, Bos. .50
☐ 158 Glenn Resch (G), Pha., LC .50
☐ 159 Bernie Nicholls, L.A. 1.50
☐ **160 Ray Ferraro, Hfd., RC 4.50**
☐ 161 Mats Naslund, Mtl. .50
☐ 162 Patrick Flatley, NYI. .35
☐ 163 Joe Cirella, N.J. .35
☐ 164 Rod Langway, Wsh. .50
☐ 165 Checklist 1 (1 - 132) 3.50
☐ 166 Carey Wilson, Cgy. .35
☐ 167 Murray Craven, Pha. .35
☐ **168 Paul Gillis, Que., RC .35**
☐ 169 Borje Salming, Tor. .75
☐ 170 Perry Turnbull, Wpg., LC .35
☐ 171 Chris Chelios, Mtl. 5.00
☐ 172 Keith Acton, Min. .35
☐ 173 Al MacInnis, Cgy. 10.00
☐ **174 Russ Courtnall, Tor., RC 5.00**
☐ 175 Brad Marsh, Pha. .35
☐ 176 Guy Carbonneau, Mtl. .50
☐ 177 Ray Neufeld, Wpg. .35
☐ **178 Craig MacTavish, Edm., RC 3.00**
☐ 179 Rick Lanz, Van. .35
☐ 180 Murray Bannerman (G), Chi., LC .50
☐ 181 Brent Ashton, Que. .35
☐ 182 Jim Peplinski, Cgy. .35
☐ 183 Mark Napier, Edm., LC .35
☐ 184 Laurie Boschman, Wpg. .35
☐ 185 Larry Murphy, Wsh. .75
☐ 186 Mark Messier, Edm. 6.00
☐ 187 Risto Siltanen, Que., LC .35
☐ 188 Bobby Smith, Mtl. .50
☐ **189 Gary Suter, Cgy., RC 4.00**
☐ 190 Peter Zezel, Pha. .50
☐ 191 Rick Vaive, Tor. .50
☐ 192 Dale Hunter, Que. .50
☐ 193 Mike Krushelnyski, Edm. .35
☐ 194 Scott Arniel, Wpg. (Buf.) .35
☐ 195 Larry Playfair, L.A. .35
☐ 196 Doug Risebrough, Cgy., LC .50
☐ 197 Kevin Lowe, Edm. .75
☐ 198 Checklist 2 (133 - 264) 3.50
☐ 199 Chris Nilan, Mtl. .35
☐ **200 Paul Cyr, Buf., RC .35**
☐ 201 Ric Seiling, Det., LC .35
☐ 202 Doug Smith, Buf., LC .35
☐ 203 Jamie Macoun, Cgy. .35
☐ 204 Dan Quinn, Cgy. .35
☐ 205 Paul Reinhart, Cgy. .35
☐ 206 Keith Brown, Chi. .35
☐ 207 Jack O'Callahan, Chi., LC .35
☐ **208 Steve Richmond, N.J., RC, LC .35**
☐ 209 Warren Young, Pgh., LC .35
☐ 210 Lee Fogolin, Edm., LC .35
☐ 211 Charlie Huddy, Edm. .35
☐ 212 Andy Moog (G), Edm. 2.00
☐ 213 Wayne Babych, Hfd., LC .35
☐ 214 Torrie Robertson, Hfd. .35
☐ 215 Jim Fox, L.A. .35
☐ **216 Phil Sykes, L.A., RC .35**
☐ 217 Jay Wells, L.A. .35
☐ 218 Dave Langevin, Min., LC .35
☐ 219 Steve Payne, Min., LC .35
☐ 220 Craig Ludwig, Mtl. .35
☐ 221 Mike McPhee, Mtl. .50
☐ 222 Steve Penney (G), Wpg., LC .50
☐ 223 Mario Tremblay, Mtl., LC (Now retired from NHL) .50
☐ 224 Ryan Walter, Mtl. .50
☐ **225 Alain Chevrier (G), N.J., RC .35**
☐ **226 Ullie Hiemer, N.J., RC, LC, Error (Uli) .35**
☐ 227 Tim Higgins, Det., LC .35
☐ 228 Billy Smith (G), NYI. .75
☐ 229 Richard Kromm, NYI., LC .35
☐ 230 Tomas Sandstrom, NYR. 2.25
☐ **231 Jim Johnson, Pgh., RC .50**
☐ 232 Willy Lindstrom, Pgh., LC .35
☐ 233 Alain Côté, Que. .35
☐ 234 Gilbert Delorme, Que. .35
☐ 235 Mario Gosselin (G), Que. .50
☐ **236 David Shaw, Que., RC .50**
☐ **237 Dave Barr, Hfd., RC .35**
☐ 238 Ed Beers, Stl., LC .35
☐ **239 Charlie Bourgeois, Stl., RC, LC .35**
☐ 240 Rick Wamsley (G), Stl.. .50
☐ 241 Dan Daoust, Tor. .35
☐ 242 Brad Maxwell, Van., LC .35
☐ 243 Gary Nylund, Chi. .35
☐ 244 Greg Terrion, Tor. .35
☐ **245 Steve Thomas, Tor., RC 3.00**
☐ 246 Richard Brodeur (G), Van. .50
☐ **247 Joel Otto, RC, Error (Moe Lemay) 2.00**
☐ 248 Doug Halward, Van. .35
☐ 249 Moe Lemay, LC, Error (Joel Otto) .75
☐ 250 Cam Neely, Bos. 8.00
☐ 251 Brent Peterson, Van. .35
☐ **252 Petri Skriko, Van., RC .50**
☐ **253 Greg Adams, Wsh., RC .35**
☐ 254 Bill Derlago, Wpg., LC .35
☐ 255 Brian Hayward (G), Mtl. .50
☐ 256 Doug Smail, Wpg. .35
☐ 257 Thomas Steen, Wpg. .35
☐ 258 LL: Jari Kurri, Edm. 1.50
☐ 259 LL: Wayne Gretzky, Edm. 6.50
☐ 260 LL: Wayne Gretzky, Edm. 6.50
☐ 261 LL: Tim Kerr, Pha. .35
☐ 262 LL: Kjell Dahlin, Mtl. .35
☐ 263 LL: Bob Froese (G), Pha. .50
☐ 264 LL: Bob Froese (G), Pha. .50

OPC BOX BOTTOMS

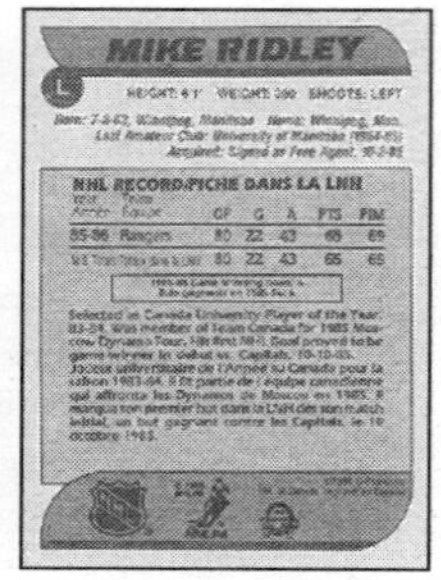

These four-card panels were issued on the bottom of O-Pee-Chee and Topps wax boxes.

Panel Size: 5" x 7"

Complete Set (16 cards):	**50.00**
Panel A - D:	**5.00**
Panel E - H:	**25.00**
Panel I - L:	**30.00**
Panel M - P:	**5.00**

	No.	Player	NRMT-MT
☐	A	Greg Adams, N.J.	1.00
☐	B	Mike Bossy, NYI.	2.00
☐	C	Dave Christian, Wsh.	1.00
☐	D	Mike Foligno, Buf.	1.00
☐	E	Michel Goulet, Que.	1.50
☐	F	Wayne Gretzky, Edm.	22.00
☐	G	Tim Kerr, Pha.	1.00
☐	H	Jari Kurri, Edm.	1.00
☐	I	Mario Lemieux, Pgh.	25.00
☐	J	Lanny McDonald, Cgy.	1.00
☐	K	Bernie Nicholls, L.A.	1.50
☐	L	Mike Ridley, NYR.	1.50
☐	M	Larry Robinson, Mtl.	1.50
☐	N	Denis Savard, Chi.	1.50
☐	O	Brian Sutter, Stl.	1.00
☐	P	Bryan Trottier, NYI.	2.00

1986 - 87 O-PEE-CHEE STICKERS

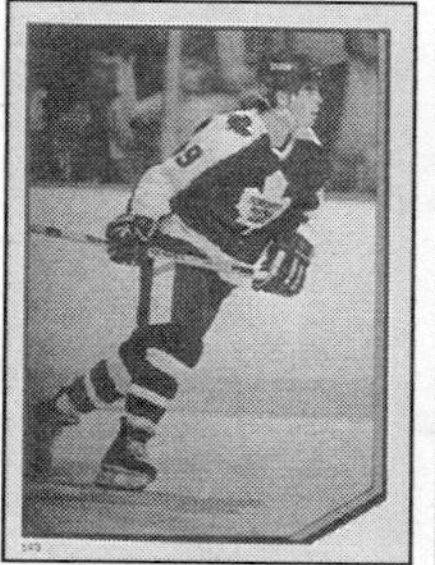

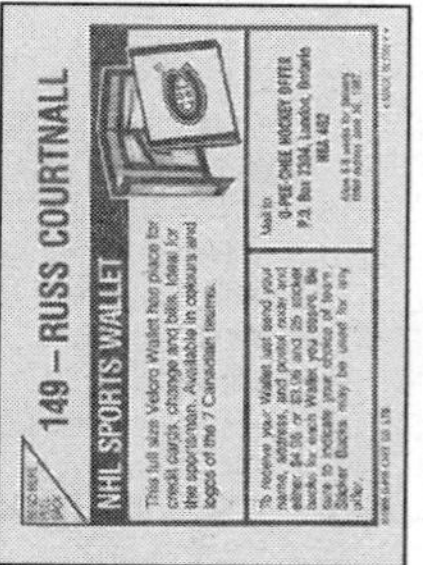

Sticker Size: 2 1/8" x 3" or 1 1/2" x 2 1/8"
Face: Four colour, white border; Number
Back: Black on card stock; Name, Number
Imprint: 1986 O-PEE-CHEE CO. LTD

Complete Set (167 cards): **50.00**
Common Player: **.20**
Album: (Patrick Roy on cover) **5.00**

	No.	Player	NRMT-MT
□	1	Stanley Cup Finals	1.00
□	2	Stanley Cup Finals	1.00
□	3	Stanley Cup Finals	1.00
□	4	Stanley Cup Finals	1.00

Note: Stickers 1-4 feature Patrick Roy, Larry Robinson, Steve Bozek.

	No.	Player	NRMT-MT
□	5	Foil: Patrick Roy (G), Mtl.	12.00
□	8	Larry Robinson, Mtl.	.35
□	11	Mats Naslund, Mtl.	.35
□	12	Bob Gainey, Mtl.	.35
□	13	Bobby Smith, Mtl.	.25
□	18	Kjell Dahlin, Mtl.	.20
□	19	Patrick Roy (G), Mtl.	15.00
□	22	Michel Goulet, Que.	.35
□	25	Brent Ashton, Que.	.20
□	26	Peter Stastny, Que.	.35
□	27	Anton Stastny, Que.	.20
□	32	Dale Hunter, Que.	.25
□	33	Clint Malarchuk (G), Que.	.25
□	34	Ray Bourque, Bos.	2.00
□	37	Keith Crowder, Bos.	.20
□	42	Mike Foligno, Buf.	.20
□	49	Dave Andreychuk, Buf.	.35
□	50	Dave Babych, Hfd.	.25
□	53	Sylvain Turgeon, Hfd.	.20
□	58	Craig Wolanin/Scott Arniel	.20
□	59	Gilles Meloche	.20
□	60	Reijo Ruotsalainen	.20
□	61	Kirk Muller/Bob Janecyk	.25
□	62	Tom Barrasso, etc.	.20
□	63	Joe Cirella, etc.	.20
□	64	Doug Jarvis, etc.	.20
□	65	Kirk Muller, etc.	.20
□	68	Paul Coffey, Edm.	1.50
□	71	Lee Fogolin, Edm.	.20
□	72	Wayne Gretzky, Edm.	6.00
□	73	Jari Kurri, Edm.	1.25
□	78	Glenn Anderson, Edm.	.35
□	79	Mark Messier, Edm.	1.50
□	80	Lanny McDonald, Cgy.	.25
□	83	Réjean Lemelin (G), Cgy.	.25
□	88	Marcel Dionne, L.A.	.35
□	95	Bernie Nicholls, L.A.	.35
□	96	Stan Smyl, Van.	.25
□	99	Tony Tanti, Van.	.20
□	104	Dale Hawerchuk, Wpg.	.50
□	111	Laurie Boschman, Wpg.	.20
□	138	Rick Vaive, Tor.	.25
□	141	Wendel Clark, Tor.	4.00
□	142	Miroslav Frycer, Tor.	.20
□	143	Tom Fergus, Tor.	.20
□	148	Al Iafrate, Tor.	.35
□	149	Russ Courtnall, Tor.	.75
□	150	Denis Savard, Chi.	.35
□	153	Doug Wilson, Chi.	.25
□	158	John Ogrodnick, Det.	.20
□	165	Greg Stefan (G), Det.	.25
□	166	Neal Broten, Min.	.25
□	169	Dino Ciccarelli, Min.	.35
□	174	Bernie Federko, Stl.	.35
□	181	Mark Hunter, Stl.	.20
□	196	Greg Adams, N.J.	.35
□	203	Mel Bridgman, N.J.	.20
□	206	Pat LaFontaine, NYI.	.50
□	209	Denis Potvin, NYI.	.35
□	210	Duane Sutter, NYI.	.25
□	211	Brent Sutter, NYI.	.25
□	216	Bryan Trottier, NYI.	.35
□	217	Mike Bossy, NYI.	.50
□	218	John Vanbiesbrouck (G), NYR.	8.00
□	221	Mike Ridley, NYR.	.50
□	226	Terry Ruskowski, Pgh.	.20
□	233	Mario Lemieux, Pgh.	7.00
□	236	Bob Froese (G), Pha.	.25
□	239	Brian Propp, Pha.	.25
□	240	Tim Kerr, Pha.	.25
□	241	Dave Poulin, Pha.	.25
□	246	Mark Howe, Pha.	.25
□	247	Brad McCrimmon, Pha.	.20
□	248	Dave Christian, Wsh.	.20
□	251	Mike Gartner, Wsh.	.50

MULTIPLE STICKERS

	No.	Player	NRMT-MT
□	6/151	Chris Chelios, Mtl./Darryl Sutter, Chi.	1.00
□	7/152	Guy Carbonneau, Mtl./Bob Sauvé (G), Chi.	.35
□	9/154	Mario Tremblay, Mtl./Troy Murray, Chi.	.35
□	10/155	Tom Kurvers, Mtl./Al Secord, Chi.	.25
□	14/156	Craig Ludwig, Mtl./Ed Olczyk, Chi.	.25
□	15/157	Mike McPhee, Mtl./Steve Larmer, Chi.	.35
□	16/159	Doug Soetaert (G), Mtl./Danny Gare, Det.	.35
□	17/160	Petr Svoboda, Mtl./Mike O'Connell, Det.	.25
□	20/161	Alain Côté, Que./Steve Yzerman, Det.	5.00
□	21/162	Mario Gosselin (G), Que./Petr Klima, Det.	.35
□	23/163	J.F. Sauvé, Que./Kelly Kisio, Det.	.25
□	24/164	Paul Gillis, Que./Doug Shedden, Det.	.25
□	28/167	Gilbert Delorme, Que./Brian Bellows, Min.	.35
□	29/168	Risto Siltanen, Que./Scott Bjugstad, Min.	.25
□	30/170	Robert Picard, Que./Dennis Maruk, Min.	.25
□	31/171	David Shaw, Que./Dirk Graham, Min.	.25
□	35/172	Rick Middleton, Bos./Curt Giles, Min.	.35
□	36/173	Charlie Simmer, Bos./Craig Hartsburg, Min.	.35
□	38/175	Barry Pederson, Bos./Brian Sutter, Stl.	.35
□	39/176	Reed Larson, Bos./Ron Flockhart, Stl.	.25
□	40/177	Steve Kasper, Bos./Doug Gilmour, Stl.	2.00
□	41/178	Pat Riggin (G), Bos./Charlie Bourgeois, Stl.	.35
□	43/179	Gilbert Perreault, Buf./Rick Wamsley (G), Stl.	.35
□	44/180	Mike Ramsey, Buf./Rob Ramage, Stl.	.25
□	45/186	Tom Barrasso (G), Buf./Bob Froese (G), Pha.	.50
□	46/187	Brian Engblom, Buf./Darren Jensen, Pha.	.25
□	47/188	Phil Housley, Buf./Paul Coffey, Edm.	1.00
□	48/189	John Tucker, Buf./Troy Murray, Chi.	.25
□	51/190	Ron Francis, Hfd./John Vanbiesbrouck (G), NYR.	3.00
□	52/191	Mike Liut (G), Hfd./Wayne Gretzky, Edm.	5.00
□	54/192	John Anderson, Hfd./Gary Suter, Cgy.	.25
□	55/193	Joel Quenneville, Hfd./Bob Froese (G), Pha.	.35
□	56/194	Kevin Dineen, Hfd./Mike Bossy, NYI.	.50
□	57/195	Ray Ferraro, Hfd./Wayne Gretzky, Edm.	5.00
□	66/197	Andy Moog (G), Edm./Dave Lewis, N.J.	.75
□	67/198	Grant Fuhr (G), Edm./Joe Cirella, N.J.	.75
□	69/199	Charlie Huddy, Edm./Rich Preston, N.J.	.25
□	70/200	Kevin Lowe, Edm./Mark Johnson, N.J.	.35
□	74/201	Mike Krushelnyski, Edm./Kirk Muller, N.J.	.75
□	75/202	Mark Napier, Edm./Pat Verbeek, N.J.	.35
□	76/204	Craig MacTavish, Edm./Bob Nystrom, NYI.	.35
□	77/205	Kevin McClelland, Edm./Clark Gillies, NYI.	.25
□	81/207	John Tonelli, Cgy./Patrick Flatley, NYI.	.25
□	82/208	Joe Mullen, Cgy./Bob Bourne, NYI.	.25
□	84/212	Jim Peplinski, Cgy./Kelly Hrudey (G), NYI.	.35
□	85/213	Jamie Macoun, Cgy./Billy Smith (G), NYI.	.35
□	86/214	Al MacInnis, Cgy./Tomas Jonsson, NYI.	1.00
□	87/215	Dan Quinn, Cgy./Ken Morrow, NYI.	.25
□	89/219	Jim Fox, L.A./Bob Brooke, NYR.	.25
□	90/220	Dave Taylor, L.A./James Patrick, NYR.	.35
□	91/222	Bob Janecyk (G), L.A./Ron Greschner, NYR.	.35
□	92/223	Jay Wells, L.A./Thomas Laidlaw, NYR.	.25
□	93/224	Bryan Erikson, L.A./Larry Melnyk, NYR.	.25
□	94/225	Dave Williams, L.A./Reijo Ruotsalainen, NYR.	.25
□	97/227	Doug Halward, Van./Willy Lindstrom, Pgh.	.25
□	98/228	Richard Brodeur (G), Van./Mike Bullard, Pgh.	.35
□	100/229	Brent Peterson, Van./Roberto Romano (G), Pgh.	.35
□	101/230	Patrik Sundstrom, Van./John Chabot, Pgh.	.25
□	102/231	Doug Lidster, Van./Moe Mantha, Pgh.	.25
□	103/232	Petri Skriko, Van./Doug Bodger, Pgh.	.25
□	105/234	Bill Derlago, Wpg./Glenn Resch (G), Pha.	.35
□	106/235	Ray Neufeld, Wpg./Brad Marsh, Pha.	.25
□	107/237	Randy Carlyle, Wpg./Doug Crossman, Pha.	.25
□	108/238	Paul MacLean, Wpg./Ilkka Sinisalo, Pha.	.25
□	109/242	Brian Mullen, Wpg./Rich Sutter, Pha.	.25
□	110/243	Thomas Steen, Wpg./Ron Sutter, Pha.	.25
□	112/126	Foil: Paul Coffey, Edm./Kjell Dahlin, Mtl.	1.00
□	113/127	Foil: Michel Goulet, Que./Per-Erik Eklund, Pha.	.50
□	114/128	Foil: John Vanbiesbrouck (G), NYR./Jim Johnson, Pgh.	3.00
□	115/129	Foil: Wayne Gretzky, Edm./Petr Klima, Det.	5.00
□	116/130	Foil: Mark Howe, Pha./Joel Otto, Cgy.	.35
□	117/131	Foil: Mike Bossy, NYI./Mike Ridley, NYR.	.50
□	118/132	Foil: Jari Kurri, Edm./Patrick Roy (G), Mtl.	10.00
□	119/133	Foil: Ray Bourque, Bos./David Shaw, Que.	.25
□	120/134	Foil: Mario Lemieux, Pgh./Gary Suter, Cgy.	5.00
□	121/135	Foil: Grant Fuhr (G), Edm./Steve Thomas, Tor.	.75
□	122/182	Foil: Mats Naslund, Mtl./Bob Froese (G), Pha.	.35
□	123/183	Foil: Larry Robinson, Mtl./Wayne Gretzky, Edm.	5.00
□	124/184	Foil: Chris Cichocki, Det./Mark Howe, Pha.	.35
□	125/185	Foil: Wendel Clark, Tor./Jari Kurri, Edm.	3.00
□	136/244	Borje Salming, Tor./Murray Craven, Pha.	.35
□	137/245	Gary Nylund, Tor./Peter Zezel, Pha.	.25
□	139/249	Don Edwards (G), Tor./Rod Langway, Wsh.	.35
□	140/250	Steve Thomas, Tor./Bob Carpenter, Wsh.	.35
□	144/252	Marian Stastny, Tor./Al Jensen (G), Wsh.	.35
□	145/253	Brad Maxwell, Tor./Craig Laughlin, Wsh.	.25
□	146/254	Dan Daoust, Tor./Scott Stevens, Wsh.	.35
□	147/255	Greg Terrion, Tor./Alan Haworth, Wsh.	.25

1986 - 87 TOPPS

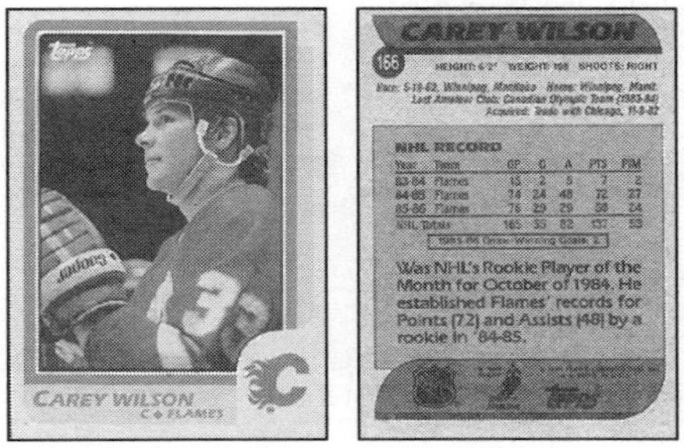

Face: Four colour, white border, Team logo, Position
Back: Blue and black on card stock, Number, Resume, Hockey trivia
Imprint: 1986 TOPPS CHEWING GUM, INC.

Complete Set (198 cards): **160.00**
Common Player: **.25**
Double Prints (**): **.20**

	No.	Player	NRMT-MT
□	1	Ray Bourque, Bos.	3.00
□	2	Pat LaFontaine, NYI. (**)	3.25
□	3	Wayne Gretzky, Edm.	20.00
□	4	Lindy Ruff, Buf.	.25
□	5	Brad McCrimmon, Pha.	.25
□	6	Dave Williams, L.A., LC	.25
□	7	Denis Savard, Chi. (**)	.35
□	8	Lanny McDonald, Cgy.	.35
□	**9**	**John Vanbiesbrouck (G), NYR., RC (**)**	**30.00**
□	**10**	**Greg Adams, N.J., RC**	**1.75**
□	11	Steve Yzerman, Det.	10.00
□	12	Craig Hartsburg, Min.	.35
□	13	John Anderson, Hfd. (**)	.20
□	14	Bob Bourne, NYI. (**)	.20
□	**15**	**Kjell Dahlin, Mtl., RC, LC**	**.25**
□	16	Dave Andreychuk, Buf.	1.25
□	17	Rob Ramage, Stl. (**)	.20
□	18	Ron Greschner, NYR. (**)	.20
□	19	Bruce Driver, N.J.	.25
□	20	Peter Stastny, Que.	.65
□	21	Dave Christian, Wsh.	.25
□	22	Doug Keans (G), Bos.	.35
□	**23**	**Scott Bjugstad, Min., RC**	**.25**
□	24	Doug Bodger, Pgh. (**)	.25
□	25	Troy Murray, Chi. (**)	.20
□	26	Al Iafrate, Tor.	1.50
□	27	Kelly Hrudey (G), NYI.	1.25
□	28	Doug Jarvis, Hfd.	.25
□	29	Rich Sutter, Van.	.25
□	30	Marcel Dionne, L.A.	.65
□	31	Curt Fraser, Chi., LC	.25
□	32	Doug Lidster, Van.	.25
□	33	Brian MacLellan, NYR.	.25
□	34	Barry Pederson, Van.	.25
□	35	Craig Laughlin, Wsh.	.25
□	36	Ilkka Sinisalo, Pha. (**)	.20
□	**37**	**John MacLean, N.J., RC**	**3.50**
□	38	Brian Mullen, Wpg.	.25
□	39	Duane Sutter, NYI. (**)	.25
□	40	Brian Engblom, Buf., LC	.25
□	**41**	**Chris Cichocki, Det., RC, LC**	**.25**
□	42	Gord Roberts, Min.	.25
□	43	Ron Francis, Hfd.	1.75
□	44	Joe Mullen, Cgy.	.50
□	45	Moe Mantha, Pgh. (**)	.20
□	46	Pat Verbeek, N.J.	1.00
□	**47**	**Clint Malarchuk (G), Que., RC**	**.75**
□	48	Bob Brooke, NYR. (**)	.20
□	49	Darryl Sutter, Chi., LC (**)	.25
□	50	Stan Smyl, Van. (**)	.25
□	51	Greg Stefan (G), Det.	.35
□	52	Bill Hajt, Buf., LC (**)	.20
□	**53**	**Patrick Roy (G), Mtl., RC**	**125.00**
□	54	Gord Kluzak, Bos.	.25
□	55	Bob Froese (G), Pha. (**)	.25
□	56	Grant Fuhr (G), Edm.	2.00

	No.	Player	Price
☐	57	Mark Hunter, Stl. (**)	.20
☐	**58**	**Dana Murzyn, Hfd., RC**	**.50**
☐	59	Mike Gartner, Wsh.	1.00
☐	60	Dennis Maruk, Min.	.25
☐	61	Rich Preston, N.J., LC	.25
☐	62	Larry Robinson, Mtl. (**)	.35
☐	63	David Taylor, L.A. (**)	.25
☐	64	Bob Murray, Chi. (**)	.20
☐	65	Ken Morrow, NYI.	.20
☐	**66**	**Mike Ridley, NYR., RC**	**1.25**
☐	**67**	**John Tucker, Buf., RC**	**.20**
☐	68	Miroslav Frycer, Tor., LC	.20
☐	69	Danny Gare, Det., LC	.20
☐	**70**	**Randy Burridge, Bos., RC**	**.75**
☐	71	Dave Poulin, Pha.	.35
☐	72	Brian Sutter, Stl., LC	.35
☐	73	Dave Babych, Hfd.	.35
☐	74	Dale Hawerchuk, Wpg. (**)	1.00
☐	75	Brian Bellows, Min.	.35
☐	**76**	**Dave Pasin, Bos., RC, LC**	**.25**
☐	77	Pete Peeters (G), Wsh. (**)	.25
☐	78	Tomas Jonsson, NYI. (**)	.20
☐	79	Gilbert Perreault, Buf., LC (**)	.50
☐	80	Glenn Anderson, Edm. (**)	.35
☐	81	Don Maloney, NYR.	.25
☐	82	Ed Olczyk, Chi. (**)	.25
☐	83	Mike Bullard, Pgh.	.25
☐	84	Tom Fergus, Tor.	.25
☐	85	Dave Lewis, N.J.	.35
☐	86	Brian Propp, Pha.	.35
☐	87	John Ogrodnick, Det.	.25
☐	88	Kevin Dineen, Hfd. (**)	1.25
☐	89	Don Beaupré (G), Min.	.25
☐	90	Mike Bossy, NYI. (**)	1.50
☐	91	Tom Barrasso (G), Buf. (**)	.75
☐	92	Michel Goulet, Que. (**)	.35
☐	93	Doug Gilmour, Stl.	5.00
☐	94	Kirk Muller, N.J.	1.00
☐	**95**	**Larry Melnyk, NYR., RC (**)**	**.20**
☐	96	Bob Gainey, Mtl. (**)	.35
☐	97	Steve Kasper, Bos.	.25
☐	**98**	**Petr Klima, Det., RC**	**.75**
☐	99	Neal Broten, Min. (**)	.25
☐	100	Al Secord, Chi. (**)	.20
☐	101	Bryan Erickson, L.A. (**)	.20
☐	102	Réjean Lemelin (G), Cgy.	.35
☐	103	Sylvain Turgeon, Hfd.	.25
☐	104	Bob Nystrom, NYI., LC	.25
☐	105	Bernie Federko, Stl.	.50
☐	106	Doug Wilson, Chi. (**)	.35
☐	107	Alan Haworth, Wsh.	.25
☐	108	Jari Kurri, Edm.	1.75
☐	109	Ron Sutter, Pha.	.25
☐	110	Reed Larson, Bos. (**)	.20
☐	111	Terry Ruskowski, Pgh. (**)	.20
☐	112	Mark Johnson, N.J. (**)	.20
☐	113	James Patrick, NYR.	.25
☐	114	Paul MacLean, Wpg.	.25
☐	115	Mike Ramsey, Buf. (**)	.20
☐	116	Kelly Kisio, Det. (**)	.20
☐	117	Brent Sutter, NYI.	.35
☐	118	Joel Quenneville, Hfd.	.35
☐	119	Curt Giles, Min. (**)	.20
☐	120	Tony Tanti, Van. (**)	.20
☐	121	Doug Sulliman, N.J. (**)	.20
☐	122	Mario Lemieux, Pgh.	40.00
☐	123	Mark Howe, Pha. (**)	.25
☐	124	Bob Sauvé (G), Chi.	.25
☐	125	Anton Stastny, Que.	.20
☐	126	Scott Stevens, Wsh. (**)	1.00
☐	127	Mike Foligno, Buf.	.25
☐	128	Reijo Ruotsalainen, NYR., LC (**)	.20
☐	129	Denis Potvin, NYI.	.65
☐	130	Keith Crowder, Bos.	.25
☐	131	Bob Janecyk (G), LA, LC (**)	.25
☐	132	John Tonelli, Cgy.	.25
☐	133	Mike Liut (G), Hfd. (**)	.25
☐	134	Tim Kerr, Pha. (**)	.25
☐	135	Al Jensen (G), Wsh., LC	.35
☐	136	Mel Bridgman, N.J.	.25
☐	137	Paul Coffey, Edm. (**)	1.75
☐	138	Dino Ciccarelli, Min. (**)	.35
☐	139	Steve Larmer, Chi.	1.25
☐	140	Mike O'Connell, Det.	.25
☐	141	Clark Gillies, NYI.	.35
☐	142	Phil Russell, Buf., LC (**)	.20
☐	143	Dirk Graham, Min., RC (**)	1.00
☐	144	Randy Carlyle, Wpg.	.25
☐	145	Charlie Simmer, Bos.	.25
☐	146	Ron Flockhart, Stl. (**)	.20
☐	147	Tom Laidlaw, NYR.	.25
☐	**148**	**Dave Tippett, Hfd., RC**	**.35**
☐	**149**	**Wendel Clark, Tor., RC (**)**	**12.00**
☐	150	Bob Carpenter, Wsh. (**)	.20
☐	**151**	**Bill Watson, Chi., RC, LC**	**.25**
☐	**152**	**Roberto Romano (G), Pgh., RC, LC (**)**	**.25**
☐	153	Doug Shedden, Det.	.25
☐	154	Phil Housley, Buf.	.50
☐	155	Bryan Trottier, NYI.	.65
☐	156	Patrik Sundstrom, Van. (**)	.20
☐	157	Rick Middleton, Bos. (**)	.25
☐	158	Glenn Resch (G), Pha., LC	.35
☐	159	Bernie Nicholls, L.A. (**)	.75
☐	**160**	**Ray Ferraro, Hfd., RC**	**3.00**
☐	161	Mats Naslund, Mtl. (**)	.25
☐	162	Patrick Flatley, NYI. (**)	.20
☐	163	Joe Cirella, N.J.	.25
☐	164	Rod Langway, Wsh. (**)	.25
☐	165	Checklist 1 (1 - 99)	1.75
☐	166	Carey Wilson, Cgy.	.25
☐	167	Murray Craven, Pha.	.25
☐	**168**	**Paul Gillis, Que., RC**	**.25**
☐	169	Borje Salming, Tor.	.50
☐	170	Perry Turnbull, Wpg., LC	.25
☐	171	Chris Chelios, Mtl.	3.00
☐	172	Keith Acton, Min.	.25
☐	173	Al MacInnis, Cgy.	6.50
☐	**174**	**Russ Courtnall, Tor., RC**	**3.75**
☐	175	Brad Marsh, Pha.	.25
☐	176	Guy Carbonneau, Mtl.	.35
☐	177	Ray Neufeld, Wpg.	.25
☐	**178**	**Craig MacTavish, Edm., RC**	**1.75**
☐	179	Rick Lanz, Van.	.25
☐	180	Murray Bannerman (G), Chi., LC	.35
☐	181	Brent Ashton, Que.	.25
☐	182	Jim Peplinski, Cgy.	.25
☐	183	Mark Napier, Edm., LC	.25
☐	184	Laurie Boschman, Wpg.	.25
☐	185	Larry Murphy, Wsh.	.50
☐	186	Mark Messier, Edm.	4.00
☐	187	Risto Siltanen, Que., LC	.25
☐	188	Bobby Smith, Mtl.	.35
☐	**189**	**Gary Suter, Cgy., RC**	**3.00**
☐	190	Peter Zezel, Pha.	.35
☐	191	Rick Vaive, Tor.	.35
☐	192	Dale Hunter, Que.	.35
☐	193	Mike Krushelnyski, Edm.	.25
☐	194	Scott Arniel, Wpg.	.25
☐	195	Larry Playfair, L.A.	.25
☐	196	Doug Risebrough, Cgy., LC	.35
☐	197	Kevin Lowe, Edm.	.50
☐	198	Checklist 2 (100 - 198)	2.25

STICKER INSERTS

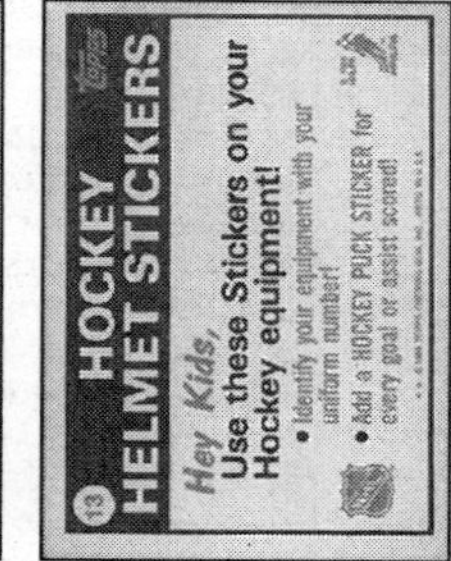

Insert Set (33 stickers): 28.00

	No.	Player	NRMT-MT
☐	1	AS: John Vanbiesbrouck (G), NYR.	10.00
☐	2	AS: Michel Goulet, Que.	.50
☐	3	AS: Wayne Gretzky, Edm.	8.00
☐	4	AS: Mike Bossy, NYI.	2.50
☐	5	AS: Paul Coffey, Edm.	2.50
☐	6	AS: Mark Howe, Pha.	.50
☐	7	AS: Bob Froese (G), Pha.	.50
☐	8	AS: Mats Naslund, Mtl.	.50
☐	9	AS: Mario Lemieux, Pgh.	10.00
☐	10	AS: Jari Kurri, Edm.	1.00
☐	11	AS: Ray Bourque, Bos.	3.00
☐	12	AS: Larry Robinson, Mtl.	.75
☐	13	Toronto Maple Leafs	.25
☐	14	Buffalo Sabres	.25
☐	15	Detroit Red Wings	.25
☐	16	Pittsburgh Penguins	.25
☐	17	New York Rangers	.25
☐	18	Calgary Flames	.25
☐	19	Winnipeg Jets	.25
☐	20	Québec Nordiques	.25
☐	21	Chicago Blackhawks	.25
☐	22	Los Angeles Kings	.25
☐	23	Montréal Canadiens	.25
☐	24	Vancouver Canucks	.25
☐	25	Hartford Whalers	.25
☐	26	Philadelphia Flyers	.25
☐	27	New Jersey Devils	.25
☐	28	St. Louis Blues	.25
☐	29	Minnesota North Stars	.25
☐	30	Washington Capitals	.25
☐	31	Boston Bruins	.25
☐	32	New York Islanders	.25
☐	33	Edmonton Oilers	.25

TOPPS BOX BOTTOMS

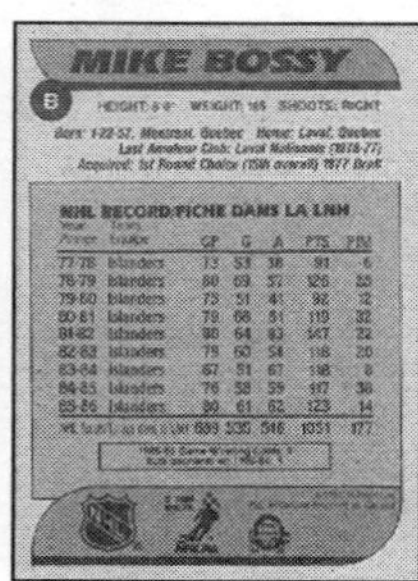

These four card panels were issued on the bottom of Topps and O-Pee-Chee wax boxes.

Panel Size: 5" x 7"

Complete Set (16 cards):	**40.00**
Panel A - D:	**4.00**
Panel E - H:	**20.00**
Panel I - L:	**22.00**
Panel M - P:	**4.00**

	No.	Player	NRMT-MT
☐	A	Greg Adams, N.J.	.75
☐	B	Mike Bossy, NYI.	1.50
☐	C	Dave Christian, Wsh.	.75
☐	D	Mike Foligno, Buf.	.75
☐	E	Michel Goulet, Que.	1.00
☐	F	Wayne Gretzky, Edm.	18.00
☐	G	Tim Kerr, Pha.	.75
☐	H	Jari Kurri, Edm.	2.00
☐	I	Mario Lemieux, Pgh.	20.00
☐	J	Lanny McDonald, Cgy.	.75
☐	K	Bernie Nicholls, L.A.	1.00
☐	L	Mike Ridley, NYR.	1.00
☐	M	Larry Robinson, Mtl.	1.00
☐	N	Denis Savard, Chi.	1.00
☐	O	Brian Sutter, Stl.	.75
☐	P	Bryan Trottier, NYI.	1.50

1987 - 88 O-PEE-CHEE

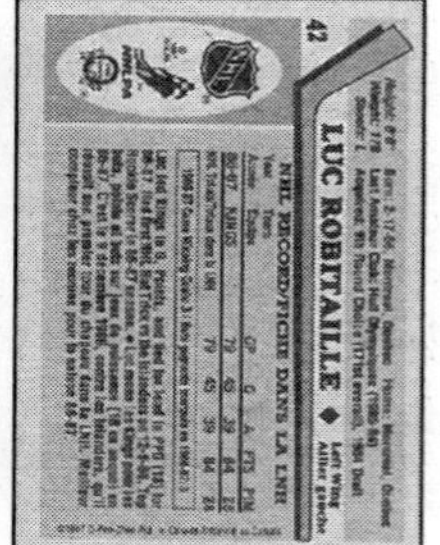

Face: Four colour, white border, Team name, Position
Back: Pink and black on card stock, Number, Resume, Bilingual

Imprint: © 1987 O-Pee-Chee
Complete Set (264 cards): 200.00
Common Player: .20

No.	Player	NRMT-MT
1	Denis Potvin, NYI., LC	.75
2	**Rick Tocchet, Pha., RC**	**10.00**
3	Dave Andreychuk, Buf.	.75
4	Stan Smyl, Van.	.20
5	Dave Babych, Hfd.	.35
6	Pat Verbeek, N.J.	.35
7	**Esa Tikkanen, Edm., RC**	**7.00**
8	Mike Ridley, Wsh.	.35
9	Randy Carlyle, Wpg., Error (Calryle)	.20
10	**Greg Paslawski, Stl., RC**	**.50**
11	Neal Broten, Min.	.35
12	Wendel Clark, Tor.	7.50
13	**Bill Ranford (G), Bos., RC**	**12.00**
14	Doug Wilson, Chi.	.35
15	Mario Lemieux, Pgh.	35.00
16	Mats Naslund, Mtl.	.35
17	Mel Bridgman, Det., LC	.20
18	James Patrick, NYR.	.20
19	Rollie Melanson (G), L.A.	.20
20	Lanny McDonald, Cgy.	.35
21	Peter Stastny, Que.	.50
22	Murray Craven, Pha.	.20
23	**Ulf Samuelsson, Hfd., RC**	**7.00**
24	**Michael Thelven, Bos., RC, LC, Error (Thelvin)**	**.30**
25	Scott Stevens, Wsh.	.35
26	Petr Klima, Det.	.20
27	Brent Sutter, NYI.	.35
28	Tomas Sandstrom, NYR.	.50
29	Tim Bothwell, Stl., LC	.20
30	Bob Carpenter, L.A.	.35
31	Brian MacLellan, Min.	.20
32	John Chabot, Pgh.	.20
33	Phil Housley, Buf.	.20
34	Patrik Sundstrom, Van.	.20
35	Dave Ellett, Wpg.	.20
36	John Vanbiesbrouck (G), NYR.	20.00
37	Dave Lewis, Det., LC	.20
38	Tom McCarthy, Bos., LC	.20
39	Dave Poulin, Pha.	.35
40	Mike Foligno, Buf.	.20
41	Gord Roberts, Min.	.20
42	**Luc Robitaille, L.A., RC**	**20.00**
43	Duane Sutter, NYI.	.35
44	Pete Peeters (G), Wsh.	.35
45	John Anderson, Hfd.	.20
46	Aaron Broten, N.J.	.20
47	Keith Brown, Chi.	.20
48	Bobby Smith, Mtl.	.35
49	Don Maloney, NYR.	.20
50	Mark Hunter, Stl.	.20
51	Moe Mantha, Pgh.	.20
52	Charlie Simmer, Bos.	.20
53	Wayne Gretzky, Edm.	22.00
54	Mark Howe, Pha.	.35
55	Robert Gould, Wsh.	.20
56	Steve Yzerman, Det.	10.00
57	Larry Playfair, L.A., LC	.20
58	Alain Chevrier (G), N.J.	.35
59	Steve Larmer, Chi.	.50
60	Bryan Trottier, NYI.	.50
61	Stewart Gavin, Hfd.	.20
62	Russ Courtnall, Tor.	1.00
63	Mike Ramsey, Buf.	.20
64	Bob Brooke, Min.	.20
65	Rick Wamsley (G), Stl.	.20
66	Ken Morrow, NYI.	.20
67	**Gerard Gallant, Det., RC, Error (Gerald)**	**.35**
68	**Kevin Hatcher, Wsh., RC**	**3.00**
69	Cam Neely, Bos.	3.50
70	Sylvain Turgeon, Hfd.	.20
71	Peter Zezel, Pha.	.35
72	Al MacInnis, Cgy.	4.25
73	Terry Ruskowski, Pgh., LC	.20
74	Troy Murray, Chi.	.20
75	Jim Fox, L.A.	.20
76	Kelly Kisio, NYR.	.20
77	Michel Goulet, Que.	.50
78	Tom Barrasso (G), Buf.	.50
79	Bruce Driver, N.J.	.35
80	**Craig Simpson, Pgh., RC**	**.35**
81	Dino Ciccarelli, Min.	.35
82	Gary Nylund, Chi.	.20
83	Bernie Federko, Stl.	.35
84	John Tonelli, Cgy.	.20
85	Brad McCrimmon, Pha.	.20
86	Dave Tippett, Hfd.	.20
87	Ray Bourque, Bos.	3.50
88	Dave Christian, Wsh.	.20
89	Glen Hanlon (G), Det.	.35
90	**Brian Curran, NYI., RC**	**.20**
91	Paul MacLean, Wpg.	.20
92	**Jimmy Carson, L.A., RC**	**.50**
93	Willie Huber, NYR. (Van.), LC	.20
94	Brian Bellows, Min.	.35
95	Doug Jarvis, Hfd., LC	.20
96	Clark Gillies, Buf.	.20
97	Tony Tanti, Van.	.20
98	**Per-Erik Eklund, Pha., RC**	**.35**
99	Paul Coffey, Edm.	3.00
100	Brent Ashton, Det.	.20
101	Mark Johnson, N.J.	.20
102	**Greg Johnston, Bos., RC, LC**	**.20**
103	Ron Flockhart, Stl., LC	.20
104	Ed Olczyk, Chi. (Tor.)	.35
105	Mike Bossy, NYI., LC	2.00
106	Chris Chelios, Mtl.	3.50
107	Gilles Meloche (G), Pgh.	.35
108	Rod Langway, Wsh.	.35
109	Ray Ferraro, Hfd.	1.25
110	Ron Duguay, NYR., LC	.20
111	Al Secord, Chi. (Tor.)	.20
112	Mark Messier, Edm.	4.50
113	Ron Sutter, Pha.	.20
114	**Darren Veitch, Det., RC**	**.20**
115	Rick Middleton, Bos.	.35
116	Doug Sulliman, N.J.	.20
117	Dennis Maruk, Min., LC	.20
118	Dave Taylor, L.A.	.35
119	Kelly Hrudey (G), NYI.	.50
120	Tom Fergus, Tor.	.20
121	**Christian Ruuttu, Buf., RC**	**.35**
122	**Brian Benning, Stl., RC**	**.20**
123	**Adam Oates, Det., RC**	**25.00**
124	Kevin Dineen, Hfd.	.35
125	Doug Bodger, Pgh.	.35
126	Joe Mullen, Cgy.	.35
127	Denis Savard, Chi.	.50
128	Brad Marsh, Pha.	.20
129	Marcel Dionne, NYR.	.50
130	Bryan Erickson, L.A., LC	.20
131	Reed Larson, Bos.	.20
132	Don Beaupré (G), Min.	.35
133	Larry Murphy, Wsh.	.35
134	John Ogrodnick, Que.	.20
135	Greg Adams, N.J.	.35
136	Patrick Flatley, NYI.	.20
137	Scott Arniel, Buf.	.20
138	Dana Murzyn, Hfd.	.20
139	Greg Adams, Wsh.	.20
140	Bob Sauvé (G), N.J., LC	.35
141	Mike O'Connell, Det.	.20
142	Walt Poddubny, NYR.	.20
143	Paul Reinhart, Cgy.	.20
144	Tim Kerr, Pha.	.35
145	**Brian Lawton, Min., RC**	**.20**
146	**Gino Cavallini , Stl., RC**	**.20**
147	Doug Keans (G), Bos., LC	.35
148	Jari Kurri, Edm.	1.50
149	Dale Hawerchuk, Wpg.	.75
150	**Randy Cunneyworth, Pgh., RC**	**1.00**
151	Jay Wells, L.A.	.20
152	Mike Liut (G), Hfd.	.35
153	Steve Konroyd, NYI.	.20
154	John Tucker, Buf.	.20
155	Rick Vaive, Tor. (Chi.)	.35
156	Bob Murray, Chi.	.20
157	Kirk Muller, N.J.	.75
158	Brian Propp, Pha.	.35
159	Ron Greschner, NYR.	.20
160	Rob Ramage, Stl.	.20
161	Craig Laughlin, Wsh.	.20
162	Steve Kasper, Bos.	.20
163	Patrick Roy (G), Mtl.	50.00
164	**Shawn Burr, Det., RC**	**.50**
165	Craig Hartsburg, Min.	.35
166	**Dean Evason, Hfd., RC**	**.35**
167	Bob Bourne, L.A.	.20
168	Mike Gartner, Wsh.	1.75
169	**Ron Hextall (G), Pha., RC**	**10.00**
170	Joe Cirella, N.J.	.20
171	Dan Quinn, Pgh.	.20
172	Tony McKegney, Stl.	.20
173	Pat LaFontaine, NYI.	2.50
174	**Allen Pedersen, Bos., RC**	**.20**
175	Doug Gilmour, Stl.	5.00
176	Gary Suter, Cgy.	.35
177	Barry Pederson, Van.	.20
178	Grant Fuhr (G), Edm.	2.00
179	**Wayne Presley, Chi., RC**	**.35**
180	Wilf Paiement, Pgh., LC	.20
181	Doug Smail, Wpg.	.20
182	Doug Crossman, Pha.	.20
183	Bernie Nicholls, L.A., Error (Nichols)	.50
184	Dirk Graham, Min., Error (Dick)	.35
185	Anton Stastny, Que.	.20
186	Greg Stefan (G), Det.	.20
187	Ron Francis, Hfd.	2.00
188	Steve Thomas, Tor. (Chi.)	1.00
189	**Kelly Miller, Wsh., RC**	**.50**
190	Tomas Jonsson, NYI.	.20
191	John MacLean, N.J.	.75
192	Larry Robinson, Mtl.	.50
193	Doug Wickenheiser, Stl.	.20
194	Keith Crowder, Bos.	.20
195	Bob Froese (G), NYR., LC	.20
196	Jim Johnson, Pgh.	.20
197	Checklist 1 (1 - 132)	2.50
198	Checklist 2 (133 - 264)	2.50
199	Glenn Anderson, Edm.	.50
200	Kevin Lowe, Edm.	.20
201	Kevin McClelland, Edm.	.20
202	Mike Krushelnyski, Edm.	.20
203	Craig MacTavish, Edm.	.20
204	Andy Moog (G), Edm.	1.75
205	**Marty McSorley, Edm., RC**	**8.00**
206	**Craig Muni, Edm., RC**	**.20**
207	Charlie Huddy, Edm.	.20
208	Hakan Loob, Cgy.	.20
209	Jim Peplinski, Cgy.	.20
210	Mike Bullard, Cgy.	.20
211	Carey Wilson, Cgy.	.20
212	Joel Otto, Cgy.	.35
213	**Neil Sheehy, Cgy., RC**	**.35**
214	Jamie Macoun, Cgy.	.20
215	**Mike Vernon (G), Cgy., RC**	**10.00**
216	Steve Bozek, Cgy.	.20
217	**Daniel Berthiaume (G), Wpg., RC**	**.35**
218	Gilles Hamel, Wpg., LC	.20
219	Tim Watters, Wpg.	.20
220	Mario Marois, Wpg., Error (Marios)	.20
221	Thomas Steen, Wpg.	.20
222	Laurie Boschman, Wpg.	.20
223	**Steve Rooney, Wpg., RC, LC**	**.20**
224	Ron Wilson, Wpg.	.20
225	**Fredrik Olausson, Wpg. RC**	**.20**
226	**Jim Kyte, Wpg., RC**	**.20**
227	**Claude Lemieux, Mtl., RC**	**15.00**
228	Bob Gainey, Mtl.	.35
229	Gaston Gingras, Stl.	.20
230	Brian Hayward (G), Mtl.	.35
231	Ryan Walter, Mtl.	.35
232	Guy Carbonneau, Mtl.	.35
233	**Stéphane Richer, Mtl., RC**	**5.00**
234	Rick Green, Mtl.	.20
235	**Brian Skrudland, Mtl., RC**	**1.75**
236	Allan Bester (G), Tor.	.35
237	Borje Salming, Tor.	.35
238	Al Iafrate, Tor.	.20
239	Rick Lanz, Tor.	.20
240	Gary Leeman, Tor.	.20
241	Greg Terrion, Tor., LC	.20
242	**Ken Wregget (G), Tor., RC**	**5.00**
243	**Vincent Damphousse, Tor., RC**	**15.00**
244	Chris Kotsopoulos, Tor.	.20
245	Dale Hunter, Wsh.	.35
246	Clint Malarchuk (G), Wsh.	.35
247	Paul Gillis, Que.	.20
248	Robert Picard, Que.	.20
249	Doug Shedden, Que.	.20
250	Mario Gosselin (G), Que.	.35
251	Randy Moller, Que.	.20

	No.	Player	NRMT-MT
☐	252	David Shaw, Que.	.20
☐	**253**	**Mike Eagles, Que., RC**	**.35**
☐	254	Alain Côté, Que.	.20
☐	255	Petri Skriko, Van.	.20
☐	256	Doug Lidster, Van.	.20
☐	257	Richard Brodeur (G), Van., LC	.35
☐	258	Rich Sutter, Van.	.20
☐	259	Steve Tambellini, Van.	.20
☐	260	Jim Benning, Van.	.20
☐	**261**	**Dave Richter, Van., RC, LC**	**.20**
☐	**262**	**Michel Petit, Van. (NYR.), RC**	**.50**
☐	263	Brent Peterson, Van., LC	.20
☐	**264**	**Jim Sandlak, Van., RC**	**.20**

O-PEE-CHEE BOX BOTTOMS

These four-card panels were issued on the bottom of O-Pee-Chee and Topps wax boxes.

Panel Size: 5" x 7"

Complete Set (16 cards):	**30.00**
Panel A - D:	**25.00**
Panel E - H:	**6.00**
Panel I - L:	**3.00**
Panel M - P:	**3.50**

	No.	Player	NRMT-MT
☐	A	Wayne Gretzky, Edm.	18.00
☐	B	Tim Kerr, Pha.	.75
☐	C	Steve Yzerman, Det.	8.00
☐	D	Luc Robitaille, L.A.	8.00
☐	E	Doug Gilmour, Stl.	4.00
☐	F	Ray Bourque, Bos.	5.00
☐	G	Joe Mullen, Cgy.	.75
☐	H	Larry Murphy, Wsh.	.75
☐	I	Dale Hawerchuk, Wpg.	1.50
☐	J	Ron Francis, Hfd.	1.50
☐	K	Walt Poddubny, NYR.	.75
☐	L	Mats Naslund, Mtl.	.75
☐	M	Michel Goulet, Que.	1.00
☐	N	Denis Savard, Chi.	1.00
☐	O	Bryan Trottier, NYI.	1.00
☐	P	Russ Courtnall, Tor.	1.00

1987 - 88 O-PEE-CHEE HOCKEY LEADERS

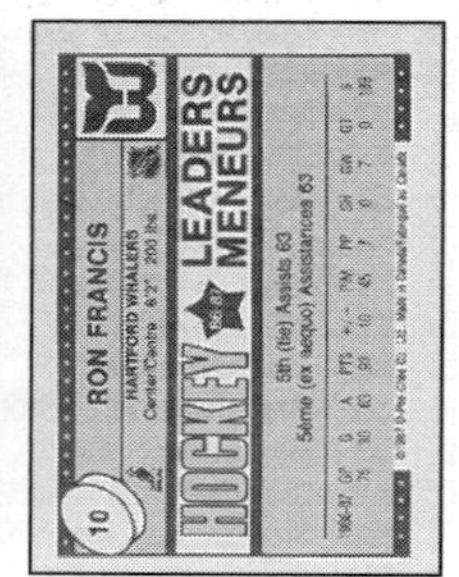

Card Size: 2 1/8" x 3"
Face: Four colour, white border; Name
Back: Two colour, blue and pink on white card stock; Name, Number, Resume, Bilingual
Imprint: © 1987 O-Pee-Chee Co. Ltd.

Complete Set (42 cards):			**20.00**
	No.	**Player**	**NRMT-MT**
☐	1	Glenn Anderson, Edm.	.35
☐	2	Brian Benning, Stl.	.20
☐	3	Daniel Berthiaume (G), Wpg.	.35
☐	4	Ray Bourque, Bos.	2.00
☐	5	Shawn Burr, Det.	.20
☐	6	Jimmy Carson, L.A.	.20
☐	7	Dino Ciccarelli, Min.	.50
☐	8	Paul Coffey, Edm.	1.00
☐	9	Per-Erik Eklund, Pha.	.20
☐	10	Ron Francis, Hfd.	1.00
☐	11	Doug Gilmour, Stl.	1.50
☐	12	Michel Goulet, Que.	.35
☐	13	Wayne Gretzky, Edm.	7.00
☐	14	Glen Hanlon (G), Det.	.35
☐	15	Brian Hayward (G), Mtl.	.35
☐	16	Ron Hextall (G), Pha.	.60
☐	17	Phil Housley, Buf.	.20
☐	18	Mark Howe, Pha.	.35
☐	19	Doug Jarvis, Hfd.	.20
☐	20	Tim Kerr, Pha.	.20
☐	21	Jari Kurri, Edm.	.50
☐	22	Pat LaFontaine, NYI.	.50
☐	23	Mario Lemieux, Pgh.	6.00
☐	24	Mike Liut (G), Hfd.	.35
☐	25	Kevin Lowe, Edm.	.35
☐	26	Al MacInnis, Cgy.	.50
☐	27	Brad McCrimmon, Pha.	.20
☐	28	Mark Messier, Edm.	2.00
☐	29	Joe Mullen, Cgy.	.35
☐	30	Craig Muni, Edm.	.20
☐	31	Larry Murphy, Wsh.	.35
☐	32	Dave Poulin, Pha.	.20
☐	33	Brian Propp, Pha.	.20
☐	34	Paul Reinhart, Cgy.	.20
☐	35	Luc Robitaille, L.A.	1.50
☐	36	Patrick Roy (G), Mtl.	5.00
☐	37	Christian Ruuttu, Buf.	.20
☐	38	Tomas Sandstrom, NYR.	.35
☐	39	Denis Savard, Chi.	.35
☐	40	Petri Skriko, Van.	.20
☐	41	Bryan Trottier, NYI.	.50
☐	42	Checklist (1-42)	.50

1987 - 88 O-PEE-CHEE STICKERS

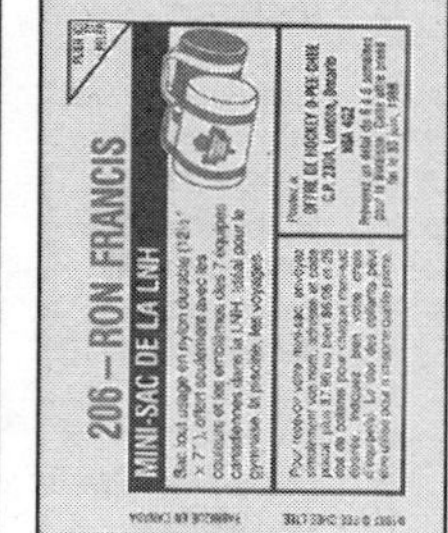

Card Size: 2 1/8" x 3"
Face: Four colour, white border; Name
Back: Two colour, blue and red on white card stock; Name, Number, Promotional offer, Bilingual
Imprint: © 1987 O-Pee-Chee Co. Ltd.

Complete Set (178 stickers):	**35.00**
Common Player:	**.15**
Album:	**5.00**

	No.	Player	NRMT-MT
☐	1	Ron Hextall (G), Pha., M.V.P.	.75
☐	2	Stanley Cup Action	.20
☐	3	Stanley Cup Action	.20
☐	4	Stanley Cup Action	.20
☐	5	Stanley Cup Action	.20

Note: Stickers 2-5 feature Craig MacTavish and Grant Fuhr.

	No.	Player	NRMT-MT
☐	6	Mats Naslund, Mtl.	.25
☐	9	Chris Chelios, Mtl.	1.00
☐	10	Bobby Smith, Mtl.	.25
☐	13	Patrick Roy (G), Mtl.	5.00
☐	16	Larry Robinson, Mtl.	.25
☐	19	Claude Lemieux, Mtl.	1.50
☐	24	Bernie Federko, Stl.	.25
☐	27	Doug Gilmour, Stl.	1.00
☐	32	Walt Poddubny, NYR.	.15
☐	35	Tomas Sandstrom, NYR.	.15
☐	36	Joe Mullen, Cgy.	.25
☐	39	Paul Reinhart, Cgy.	.15
☐	40	Al MacInnis, Cgy.	.50
☐	43	Lanny McDonald, Cgy.	.25
☐	46	Jim Peplinski, Cgy.	.15
☐	49	Gary Suter, Cgy.	.75
☐	54	Craig Hartsburg, Min.	.25
☐	57	Dino Ciccarelli, Min.	.50
☐	62	Aaron Broten, N.J.	.15
☐	65	Kirk Muller, N.J.	.15
☐	66A	Face-off: Jim Sandlak, Van.	.15
☐	66B	Face-off: Steve Kasper, Bos.	.15
☐	67	Ray Bourque/Brian Propp	.50
☐	68	Calgary vs Boston	.15
☐	69	Murray Craven, Pha.	.15
☐	70	Boston Bruins	.15
☐	71	New York Islanders	.15
☐	72	Alain Chevrier (G), N.J.	.15
☐	73	Patrick Roy (G)/Mike Lalor	3.50
☐	78	Denis Savard, Chi.	.35
☐	81	Steve Larmer, Chi.	.50
☐	82	Jari Kurri, Edm.	.75
☐	85	Grant Fuhr (G), Edm.	.50
☐	86	Wayne Gretzky, Edm.	4.00
☐	89	Paul Coffey, Edm.	.75
☐	92	Mark Messier, Edm.	1.00
☐	95	Glenn Anderson, Edm.	.25
☐	100	Mark Howe, Pha.	.25
☐	103	Tim Kerr, Pha.	.15
☐	108	Brent Ashton, Det.	.15
☐	111	Steve Yzerman, Det.	2.50
☐	140	Ray Bourque, Bos.	1.00
☐	143	Cam Neely, Bos.	.75
☐	148	Tom Barrasso (G), Buf.	.25
☐	151	Phil Housley, Buf.	.15
☐	152	Wendel Clark, Tor.	1.00
☐	155	Rick Vaive, Tor.	.15
☐	156	Russ Courtnall, Tor.	.50
☐	159	Tom Fergus, Tor.	.15
☐	162	Allan Bester (G), Tor.	.25
☐	165	Borje Salming, Tor.	.25
☐	170	Mario Lemieux, Pgh.	4.00
☐	173	Dan Quinn, Pgh.	.15
☐	188	Barry Pederson, Van.	.15
☐	191	Doug Lidster, Van.	.15
☐	192	Petri Skriko, Van.	.15
☐	195	Tony Tanti, Van.	.15
☐	198	Stan Smyl, Van.	.15
☐	201	Patrik Sundstrom, Van.	.15
☐	206	Ron Francis, Hfd.	.75
☐	209	Mike Liut (G), Hfd.	.15
☐	214	Bernie Nicholls, L.A.	.15
☐	217	Luc Robitaille, L.A.	3.50
☐	218	John Ogrodnick, Que.	.15
☐	221	Paul Gillis, Que.	.15
☐	222	Peter Stastny, Que.	.35
☐	225	Michel Goulet, Que.	.35
☐	228	Anton Stastny, Que.	.15
☐	231	Mario Gosselin (G), Que.	.25
☐	236	Rod Langway, Wsh.	.15
☐	239	Mike Gartner, Wsh.	.50
☐	244	Mike Bossy, NYI.	.50
☐	247	Denis Potvin, NYI.	.35
☐	252	Paul MacLean, Wpg.	.15
☐	255	Dale Hawerchuk, Wpg.	.35

MULTIPLE STICKERS

	No.	Players	NRMT-MT
☐	7/146	Guy Carbonneau, Mtl./Steve Dykstra, Buf.	.25
☐	8/147	Gaston Gingras, Mtl./Dave Andreychuk, Buf.	.50
☐	11/149	Rick Green, Mtl./Mike Ramsey, Buf.	.20
☐	12/150	Bob Gainey, Mtl./Mike Foligno, Buf.	.25
☐	14/153	Kjell Dahlin, Mtl./Greg Terrion, Tor.	.20
☐	15/154	Chris Nilan, Mtl./Steve Thomas, Tor.	.25
☐	17/157	Ryan Walter, Mtl./Rick Lanz, Tor.	.20
☐	18/158	Petr Svoboda, Mtl./Miroslav Frycer, Tor.	.20
☐	20/160	Rob Ramage, Stl./Al Iafrate, Tor.	.20
☐	21/161	Mark Hunter, Stl./Gary Leeman, Tor.	.20
☐	22/163	Rick Wamsley (G), Stl./Todd Gill, Tor.	.25
☐	23/164	Greg Palawski, Stl./Ken Wregget (G), Tor.	.50
☐	25/166	Ron Flockhart, Stl./Craig Simpson, Pgh.	.20
☐	26/167	Tim Bothwell, Stl./Terry Ruskowski, Pgh.	.20
☐	28/168	Kelly Kisio, NYR./Gilles Meloche (G), Pgh.	.25

	No.	Player	Price
☐	29/169	Don Maloney, NYR./John Chabot, Pgh.	.20
☐	30/171	James Patrick, NYR./Moe Mantha, Pgh.	.20
☐	31/172	Willie Huber, NYR./Jim Johnson, Pgh.	.20
☐	33/178	John Vanbiesbrouck (G), NYR./Ray Bourque, Bos.	2.00
☐	34/179	Marcel Dionne, NYR./Dave Poulin, Pha.	.35
☐	37/180	Mike Bullard, Cgy./Wayne Gretzky, Edm.	3.00
☐	38/181	Neil Sheehy, Cgy./Wayne Gretzky, Edm.	3.00
☐	41/182	Mike Vernon (G), Cgy./Ron Hextall (G), Pha.	2.00
☐	42/183	Joel Otto, Cgy./Doug Jarvis, Hfd.	.20
☐	44/184	Hakan Loob, Cgy./Brian Hayward (G), Mtl.	.25
☐	45/185	Carey Wilson, Cgy./Patrick Roy (G), Mtl.	3.00
☐	47/186	John Tonelli, Cgy./Joe Mullen, Cgy.	.25
☐	48/187	Jamie Macoun, Cgy./Luc Robitaille, L.A.	1.25
☐	50/189	Dennis Maruk, Min./Richard Brodeur (G), Van.	.25
☐	51/190	Don Beaupré (G), Min./Dave Richter, Van.	.25
☐	52/193	Neal Broten, Min./Rich Sutter, Van.	.25
☐	53/194	Brian Bellows, Min./Jim Sandlak, Van.	.20
☐	55/196	Gord Roberts, Min./Michel Petit, Van.	.20
☐	56/197	Steve Payne, Min./Jim Benning, Van.	.20
☐	58199	Pat Verbeek, N.J./Brent Peterson, Van.	.20
☐	59/200	Doug Sulliman, N.J./Garth Butcher, Van.	.20
☐	60/202	Bruce Driver, N.J./Kevin Dineen, Hfd.	.20
☐	61/203	Joe Cirella, N.J./Sylvain Turgeon, Hfd.	.20
☐	63/204	Alain Chevrier (G), N.J./John Anderson, Hfd.	.20
☐	64/205	Mark Johnson, N.J./Ulf Samuelsson, Hfd.	.20
☐	74/207	Al Secord, Chi./Doug Jarvis, Hfd.	.20
☐	75/208	Bob Sauvé (G), Chi./Dave Babych, Hfd.	.20
☐	76/210	Ed Olczyk, Chi./Jimmy Carson, L.A.	.20
☐	77/211	Doug Wilson, Chi./Larry Playfair, L.A.	.20
☐	79/212	Troy Murray, Chi./Jay Wells, L.A.	.20
☐	80/213	Gary Nylund, Chi./Rollie Melanson (G), L.A.	.20
☐	83/215	Esa Tikkanen, Edm./Dave Taylor, L.A.	.50
☐	84/216	Kevin Lowe, Edm./Jim Fox, L.A.	.35
☐	87/219	Charlie Huddy, Edm./Jason Lafrenière, Que.	.20
☐	88/220	Kent Nilsson, Edm./Mike Hough, Que.	.20
☐	90/223	Mike Krushelnyski, Edm./David Shaw, Que.	.20
☐	91/224	Craig MacTavish, Edm./Bill Derlago, Que.	.20
☐	93/226	Andy Moog (G), Edm./Doug Shedden, Que.	.50
☐	94/227	Randy Gregg, Edm./Basil McRae, Que.	.20
☐	96/229	Peter Zezel, Pha./Randy Moller, Que.	.20
☐	97/230	Brian Propp, Pha./Robert Picard, Que.	.20
☐	98/232	Dave Poulin, Pha./Larry Murphy, Wsh.	.20
☐	99/233	Brad McCrimmon, Pha./Scott Stevens, Wsh.	.20
☐	101/234	Ron Hextall (G), Pha./Mike Ridley, Wsh.	1.25
☐	102/235	Ron Sutter, Pha./Dave Christian, Wsh.	.20
☐	104/237	Petr Klima, Det./Bob Gould, Wsh.	.20
☐	105/238	Adam Oates, Det./Bob Mason (G), Wsh.	4.00
☐	106/240	Gerard Gallant, Det./Bryan Trottier, NYI.	.25
☐	107/241	Mike O'Connell, Det./Brent Sutter, NYI.	.25
☐	109/242	Glen Hanlon (G), Det./Kelly Hrudey (G), NYI.	.25
☐	110/243	Harold Snepsts, Det./Pat LaFontaine, NYI.	.75
☐	112/124	Mark Howe, Pha./Brian Benning, Stl.	.25
☐	113/125	Michel Goulet, Que./Shawn Burr, Det.	.25
☐	114/126	Ron Hextall (G), Pha./Jimmy Carson, L.A.	.50
☐	115/127	Wayne Gretzky, Edm./Shayne Corson, Mtl.	3.00
☐	116/128	Ray Bourque, Bos./Vincent Damphousse, Tor.	1.50
☐	117/129	Jari Kurri, Edm./Ron Hextall (G), Pha.	.50
☐	118/130	Dino Ciccarelli, Min./Jason Lafrenière, Que.	.35
☐	119/131	Larry Murphy, Wsh./Ken Leiter, NYI.	.25
☐	120/132	Mario Lemieux, Pha./Allen Pedersen, Bos.	3.00
☐	121/133	Mike Liut (G), Hfd./Luc Robitaille, L.A.	1.25
☐	122/134	Luc Robitaille, L.A./Christian Ruuttu, Buf.	1.25
☐	123/135	Al MacInnis, Cgy./Jim Sandlak, Van.	.25
☐	136/245	Keith Crowder, Bos./Pat Flatley, NYI.	.20
☐	137/246	Charlie Simmer, Bos./Ken Morrow, NYI.	.20
☐	138/248	Rick Middleton, Bos./Randy Carlyle, Wpg.	.25
☐	139/249	Doug Keans (G), Bos./Daniel Berthiaume (G), Wpg.	.35
☐	141/250	Tom McCarthy, Bos./Mario Marois, Wpg.	.20
☐	142/251	Reed Larson, Bos./Dave Ellett, Wpg.	.20
☐	144/253	Christian Ruuttu, Buf./Gilles Hamel, Wpg.	.20
☐	145/254	John Tucker, Buf./Doug Smail, Wpg.	.20
☐	174/176	Wayne Gretzky, Edm./Mark Howe, Pha.	3.00
☐	175/177	Brian Hayward (G), Mtl./Luc Robitaille, L.A.	1.25

1987 - 88 PANINI STICKERS

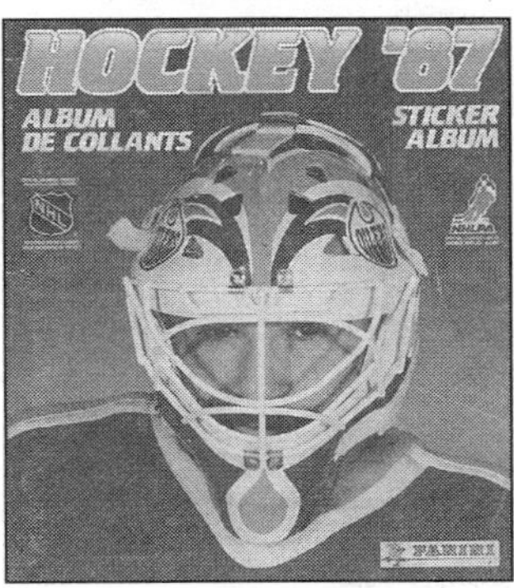

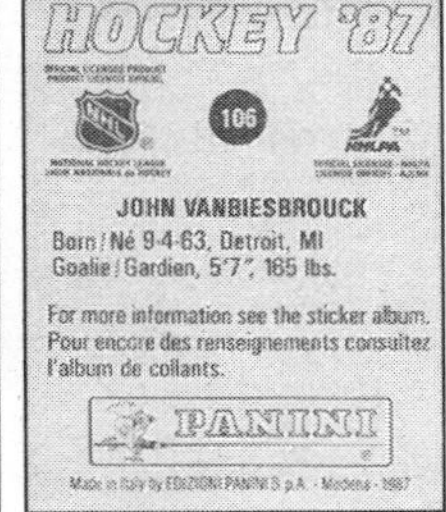

Sticker Size: 2 1/8" x 2 11/6"
Face: Four colour; name, Team, Logo
Back: Black and white; Name, Number, Resume
Imprint: PANINI

Complete Set (396 stickers):		**75.00**
Common Player:		**.20**
Album (Grant Fuhr):		**5.00**

	No.	Player	NRMT-MT
☐	1	Stanley Cup	.20
☐	2	Charlie Simmer (Action), Bos.	.20
☐	3	Boston Bruins Team Logo	.20
☐	4	Doug Keans (G), Bos.	.25
☐	5	Bill Ranford (G), Bos.	2.25
☐	6	Ray Bourque, Bos.	1.00
☐	7	Reed Larson, Bos.	.20
☐	8	Mike Milbury, Bos.	.25
☐	9	Michael Thelven, Bos.	.20
☐	10	Cam Neely, Bos.	1.00
☐	11	Charlie Simmer, Bos.	.20
☐	12	Rick Middleton, Bos.	.25
☐	13	Tom McCarthy, Bos.	.20
☐	14	Keith Crowder, Bos.	.20
☐	15	Steve Kasper, Bos.	.20
☐	16	Ken Linseman, Bos.	.20
☐	17	Dwight Foster, Bos.	.20
☐	18	Jay Miller, Bos.	.20
☐	19	Dave Andreychuk, Buf.	.35
☐	20	Buffalo Sabres Team Logo	.20
☐	21	Jacques Cloutier (G), Buf.	.25
☐	22	Tom Barrasso (G), Buf.	.35
☐	23	Daren Puppa (G), Buf.	.75
☐	24	Phil Housley, Buf.	.35
☐	25	Mike Ramsey, Buf.	.20
☐	26	Bill Hajt, Buf.	.20
☐	27	Dave Andreychuk, Buf.	.75
☐	28	Christian Ruuttu, Buf.	.20
☐	29	Mike Foligno, Buf.	.20
☐	30	John Tucker, Buf.	.20
☐	31	Adam Creighton, Buf.	.20
☐	32	Wilf Paiement, Buf.	.20
☐	33	Paul Cyr, Buf.	.20
☐	34	Clark Gillies, Buf.	.20
☐	35	Lindy Ruff, Buf.	.25
☐	36	Sylvain Turgeon, Hfd.	.35
☐	37	Hartford Whalers Team Logo	.20
☐	38	Mike Liut (G), Hfd.	.25
☐	39	Steve Weeks (G), Hfd.	.25
☐	40	Dave Babych, Hfd.	.25
☐	41	Ulf Samuelsson, Hfd.	.75
☐	42	Dana Murzyn, Hfd.	.20
☐	43	Ron Francis, Hfd.	.75
☐	44	Kevin Dineen, Hfd.	.20
☐	45	John Anderson, Hfd.	.20
☐	46	Ray Ferraro, Hfd.	.20
☐	47	Dean Evason, Hfd.	.20
☐	48	Paul Lawless, Hfd.	.20
☐	49	Stewart Gavin, Hfd.	.20
☐	50	Sylvain Turgeon, Hfd.	.20
☐	51	Dave Tippett, Hfd.	.20
☐	52	Doug Jarvis, Hfd.	.20
☐	53	Bob Gainey, Mtl.	.35
☐	54	Montréal Canadiens Team Logo	.20
☐	55	Brian Hayward (G), Mtl.	.25
☐	56	Patrick Roy (G), Mtl.	6.00
☐	57	Larry Robinson, Mtl.	.50
☐	58	Chris Chelios, Mtl.	1.00
☐	59	Craig Ludwig, Mtl.	.20
☐	60	Rick Green, Mtl.	.20
☐	61	Mats Naslund, Mtl.	.35
☐	62	Bobby Smith, Mtl.	.25
☐	63	Claude Lemieux, Mtl.	1.50
☐	64	Guy Carbonneau, Mtl.	.25
☐	65	Stéphane Richer, Mtl.	1.00
☐	66	Mike McPhee, Mtl.	.20
☐	67	Brian Skrudland, Mtl.	.20
☐	68	Chris Nilan, Mtl.	.20
☐	69	Bob Gainey, Mtl.	.50
☐	70	Kirk Muller, N.J.	.35
☐	71	New Jersey Devils Team Logo	.20
☐	72	Craig Billington (G), N.J.	.25
☐	73	Alain Chevrier (G), N.J.	.25
☐	74	Bruce Driver, N.J.	.20
☐	75	Joe Cirella, N.J.	.20
☐	76	Ken Daneyko, N.J.	.20
☐	77	Craig Wolanin, N.J.	.20
☐	78	Aaron Broten, N.J.	.20
☐	79	Kirk Muller, N.J.	.50
☐	80	John MacLean, N.J.	.25
☐	81	Pat Verbeek, N.J.	.25
☐	82	Doug Sulliman, N.J.	.20
☐	83	Mark Johnson, N.J.	.20
☐	84	Greg Adams, N.J.	.25
☐	85	Claude Loiselle, N.J.	.20
☐	86	Andy Brickley, N.J.	.20
☐	87	New York Islanders "Action Player"	.20
☐	88	New York Islanders Team Logo	.20
☐	89	Billy Smith (G), NYI.	.50
☐	90	Kelly Hrudey (G), NYI.	.35
☐	91	Denis Potvin, NYI.	.50
☐	92	Tomas Jonsson, NYI.	.20
☐	93	Ken Leiter, NYI.	.20
☐	94	Ken Morrow, NYI.	.20
☐	95	Brian Curran, NYI.	.20
☐	96	Bryan Trottier, NYI.	.75
☐	97	Mike Bossy, NYI.	.75
☐	98	Pat LaFontaine, NYI.	1.00
☐	99	Brent Sutter, NYI.	.20
☐	100	Mikko Makelä, NYI.	.20
☐	101	Patrick Flatley, NYI.	.20
☐	102	Duane Sutter, NYI.	.25
☐	103	Richard Kromm, NYI.	.20
☐	104	Ron Greschner, NYR.	.20
☐	105	New York Rangers Team Logo	.20
☐	106	John Vanbiesbrouck (G), NYR.	2.50
☐	107	James Patrick, NYR.	.20
☐	108	Ron Greschner, NYR.	.20
☐	109	Willie Huber, NYR.	.20
☐	110	Curt Giles, NYR.	.20
☐	111	Larry Melnyk, NYR.	.20
☐	112	Walt Poddubny, NYR.	.20
☐	113	Marcel Dionne, NYR.	.50
☐	114	Tomas Sandstrom, NYR.	.35
☐	115	Kelly Kisio, NYR.	.20
☐	116	Pierre Larouche, NYR.	.20
☐	117	Don Maloney, NYR.	.20
☐	118	Tony McKegney, NYR.	.20
☐	119	Ron Duguay, NYR.	.20
☐	120	Jan Erixon, NYR.	.20
☐	121	Brad McCrimmon, Pha.	.20
☐	122	Philadelphia Flyers Team Logo	.20
☐	123	Ron Hextall (G), Pha.	1.75
☐	124	Mark Howe, Pha.	.35
☐	125	Doug Crossman, Pha.	.20
☐	126	Brad McCrimmon, Pha.	.20
☐	127	Brad Marsh, Pha.	.20
☐	128	Tim Kerr, Pha.	.25

	No.	Card	Price
☐	129	Peter Zezel, Pha.	.20
☐	130	Dave Poulin, Pha.	.20
☐	131	Brian Propp, Pha.	.20
☐	132	Per-Erik Eklund, Pha.	.20
☐	133	Murray Craven, Pha.	.20
☐	134	Rick Tocchet, Pha.	1.75
☐	135	Derrick Smith, Pha.	.20
☐	136	Ilkka Sinisalo, Pha.	.20
☐	137	Ron Sutter, Pha.	.20
☐	138	Terry Rustowski, Pgh.	.20
☐	139	Pittsburgh Penguins Team Logo	.20
☐	140	Gilles Meloche (G), Pgh.	.25
☐	141	Doug Bodger, Pgh.	.20
☐	142	Moe Mantha, Pgh.	.20
☐	143	Jim Johnson, Pgh.	.20
☐	144	Rod Buskas, Pgh.	.20
☐	145	Randy Hillier, Pgh.	.20
☐	146	Mario Lemieux, Pgh.	5.00
☐	147	Dan Quinn, Pgh.	.20
☐	148	Randy Cunneyworth, Pgh.	.50
☐	149	Craig Simpson, Pgh.	.20
☐	150	Terry Ruskowski, Pgh.	.20
☐	151	John Chabot, Pgh.	.20
☐	152	Bob Errey, Pgh.	.20
☐	153	Dan Frawley, Pgh.	.20
☐	154	Dave Hannan, Pgh.	.20
☐	155	Dale Hunter, Que.	.35
☐	156	Québec Nordiques Team Logo	.20
☐	157	Mario Gosselin (G), Que.	.25
☐	158	Clint Malarchuk (G), Que.	.25
☐	159	Risto Siltanen, Que.	.20
☐	160	Robert Picard, Que.	.20
☐	161	Normand Rochefort, Que.	.20
☐	162	Randy Moller, Que.	.20
☐	163	Michel Goulet, Que.	.50
☐	164	Peter Stastny, Que.	.50
☐	165	John Ogrodnick, Que.	.20
☐	166	Anton Stastny, Que.	.20
☐	167	Paul Gillis, Que.	.20
☐	168	Dale Hunter, Que.	.35
☐	169	Alain Côté, Que.	.20
☐	170	Mike Eagles, Que.	.20
☐	171	Jason Lafrenière, Que.	.20
☐	172	Greg Smith, Wsh.	.20
☐	173	Washington Capitals Team Logo	.20
☐	174	Pete Peeters (G), Wsh.	.25
☐	175	Bob Mason (G), Wsh.	.25
☐	176	Larry Murphy, Wsh.	.25
☐	177	Scott Stevens, Wsh.	.50
☐	178	Rod Langway, Wsh.	.25
☐	179	Kevin Hatcher, Wsh.	1.25
☐	180	Mike Gartner, Wsh.	.50
☐	181	Mike Ridley, Wsh.	.25
☐	182	Craig Laughlin, Wsh.	.20
☐	183	Gaetan Duchesne, Wsh.	.20
☐	184	Dave Christian, Wsh.	.20
☐	185	Greg Adams, Wsh.	.20
☐	186	Kelly Miller, Wsh.	.20
☐	187	Alan Haworth, Wsh.	.20
☐	188	Lou Franceschetti, Wsh.	.20
☐	189	Stanley Cup	.25
☐	190	Stanley Cup	.25
☐	191	Ron Hextall (G), Pha.	1.00
☐	192	Wayne Gretzky, Edm.	5.00
☐	193	Brian Propp, Phi.	.20
☐	194	Mark Messier, Edm.	1.50
☐	195	Mark Messier Skates Through Flyers Defence During Stanley Cup	1.00
☐	196	Mark Messier Skates Through Flyers Defence During Stanley Cup	1.00
☐	197	Gretzky Hoists The Stanley Cup for the Third Time in Four Years	4.00
☐	198	Gretzky Hoists The Stanley Cup for the Third Time in Four Years	4.00
☐	199	Gretzky Hoists The Stanley Cup for the Third Time in Four Years	4.00
☐	200	Gretzky Hoists The Stanley Cup for the Third Time in Four Years	4.00
☐	201	Hakan Loob, Cgy.	.20
☐	202	Calgary Flames Team Logo	.20
☐	203	Mike Vernon (G), Cgy.	2.50
☐	204	Réjean Lemelin (G), Cgy.	.25
☐	205	Al MacInnis, Cgy.	.75
☐	206	Paul Reinhart, Cgy.	.20
☐	207	Gary Suter, Cgy.	.35
☐	208	Jamie Macoun, Cgy.	.20
☐	209	Neil Sheehy, Cgy.	.20
☐	210	Joe Mullen, Cgy.	.50
☐	211	Carey Wilson, Cgy.	.20
☐	212	Joel Otto, Cgy.	.25
☐	213	Jim Peplinski, Cgy.	.20
☐	214	Hakan Loob, Cgy.	.20
☐	215	Lanny McDonald, Cgy.	.50
☐	216	Tim Hunter, Cgy.	.20
☐	217	Gary Roberts, Cgy.	2.50
☐	218	Murray Bannerman (G), Chi.	.25
☐	219	Chicago Blackhawks Team Logo	.20
☐	220	Bob Sauvé (G), Chi.	.25
☐	221	Murray Bannerman (G), Chi.	.25
☐	222	Doug Wilson, Chi.	.25
☐	223	Rob Murray, Chi.	.20
☐	224	Gary Nylund, Chi.	.20
☐	225	Denis Savard, Chi.	.50
☐	226	Steve Larmer, Chi.	.35
☐	227	Troy Murray, Chi.	.20
☐	228	Wayne Presley, Chi.	.20
☐	229	Al Secord, Chi.	.20
☐	230	Ed Olczyk, Chi.	.20
☐	231	Curt Fraser, Chi.	.20
☐	232	Bill Watson, Chi.	.20
☐	233	Keith Brown, Chi.	.20
☐	234	Darryl Sutter, Chi.	.25
☐	235	Lee Norwood, Det.	.20
☐	236	Detroit Red Wings Team Logo	.20
☐	237	Greg Stefan (G), Det.	.25
☐	238	Glen Hanlon (G), Det.	.25
☐	239	Darren Veitch, Det.	.20
☐	240	Mike O'Connell, Det.	.20
☐	241	Harold Snepsts, Det.	.20
☐	242	Dave Lewis, Det.	.20
☐	243	Steve Yzerman, Det.	3.00
☐	244	Brent Ashton, Det.	.20
☐	245	Gerard Gallant, Det.	.20
☐	246	Petr Klima, Det.	.20
☐	247	Shawn Burr, Det.	.20
☐	248	Adam Oates, Det.	4.00
☐	249	Mel Bridgman, Det.	.20
☐	250	Tim Higgins, Det.	.20
☐	251	Joey Kocur, Det.	.20
☐	252	Mark Messier, Edm.	1.50
☐	253	Edmonton Oilers Team Logo	.20
☐	254	Grant Fuhr (G), Edm.	1.00
☐	255	Andy Moog (G), Edm.	1.00
☐	256	Paul Coffey, Edm.	1.00
☐	257	Kevin Lowe, Edm.	.35
☐	258	Craig Muni, Edm.	.20
☐	259	Steve Smith, Edm.	.20
☐	260	Charlie Huddy, Edm.	.20
☐	261	Wayne Gretzky, Edm.	6.00
☐	262	Jari Kurri, Edm.	.75
☐	263	Mark Messier, Edm.	2.00
☐	264	Esa Tikkanen, Edm.	.50
☐	265	Glenn Anderson, Edm.	.35
☐	266	Mike Krushelnyski, Edm.	.25
☐	267	Craig MacTavish, Edm.	.20
☐	268	Dave Hunter, Edm.	.20
☐	269	Los Angeles Kings "Action Player"	.20
☐	270	Los Angeles Kings Team Logo	.20
☐	271	Rolllie Melanson (G), L.A.	.25
☐	272	Darren Eliot (G), L.A.	.25
☐	273	Grant Ledyard, L.A.	.25
☐	274	Jay Wells, L.A.	.20
☐	275	Mark Hardy, L.A.	.20
☐	276	Dean Kennedy, L.A.	.20
☐	277	Luc Robitaille, L.A.	2.50
☐	278	Bernie Nicholls, L.A.	.50
☐	279	Jimmy Carson, L.A.	.25
☐	280	Dave Taylor, L.A.	.25
☐	281	Jim Fox, L.A.	.20
☐	282	Bryan Erickson, L.A.	.20
☐	283	Dave Williams, L.A.	.20
☐	284	Sean McKenna, L.A.	.20
☐	285	Phil Sykes, L.A.	.20
☐	286	Brian Bellows, Min.	.20
☐	287	Minnesota North Stars Team Logo	.20
☐	288	Kari Takko (G), Min.	.25
☐	289	Don Beaupré (G), Min.	.25
☐	290	Craig Hartsburg, Min.	.25
☐	291	Ron Wilson, Min.	.20
☐	292	Frantisek Musil, Min.	.20
☐	293	Dino Ciccarelli, Min.	.35
☐	294	Brian MacLellan, Min.	.20
☐	295	Dirk Graham, Min.	.20
☐	296	Brian Bellows, Min.	.35
☐	297	Neal Broten, Min.	.25
☐	298	Dennis Maruk, Min.	.20
☐	299	Keith Acton, Min.	.20
☐	300	Brian Lawton, Min.	.20
☐	301	Bob Brooke, Min.	.20
☐	302	Willi Plett, Min.	.20
☐	303	Brian Sutter, Stl.	.25
☐	304	St. Louis Blues Team Logo	.20
☐	305	Rick Wamsley (G), Stl.	.25
☐	306	Rob Ramage, Stl.	.20
☐	307	Ric Nattress, Stl.	.20
☐	308	Bruce Bell, Stl.	.20
☐	309	Charlie Bourgeois, Stl.	.20
☐	310	Jim Pavese, Stl.	.20
☐	311	Doug Gilmour, Stl.	.50
☐	312	Bernie Federko, Stl.	.25
☐	313	Mark Hunter, Stl.	.20
☐	314	Greg Paslawski, Stl.	.20
☐	315	Gino Cavallini, Stl.	.20
☐	316	Rick Meagher, Stl.	.20
☐	317	Ron Flockhart, Stl.	.20
☐	318	Doug Wickenheiser, Stl.	.20
☐	319	Jocelyn Lemieux, Stl.	.20
☐	320	Wendel Clark, Tor.	.25
☐	321	Toronto Maple Leafs Team Logo	.20
☐	322	Ken Wregget (G), Tor.	.50
☐	323	Allan Bester (G), Tor.	.25
☐	324	Todd Gill, Tor.	.25
☐	325	Al Iafrate, Tor.	.35
☐	326	Borje Salming, Tor.	.35
☐	327	Russ Courtnall, Tor.	.25
☐	328	Rick Vaive, Tor.	.25
☐	329	Steve Thomas, Tor.	.25
☐	330	Wendel Clark, Tor.	1.00
☐	331	Gary Leeman, Tor.	.20
☐	332	Tom Fergus, Tor.	.20
☐	333	Vincent Damphousse, Tor.	2.00
☐	334	Peter Ihnacak, Tor.	.20
☐	335	Brad Smith, Tor.	.20
☐	336	Miroslav Ihnacak, Tor.	.20
☐	337	Stan Smyl, Van.	.25
☐	338	Vancouver Canucks Team Logo	.20
☐	339	Frank Caprice (G), Van.	.25
☐	340	Richard Brodeur (G), Van.	.25
☐	341	Doug Lidster, Van.	.20
☐	342	Michel Petit, Van.	.20
☐	343	Garth Butcher, Van.	.20
☐	344	Dave Richter, Van.	.20
☐	345	Tony Tanti, Van.	.20
☐	346	Barry Pederson, Van.	.20
☐	347	Petri Skriko, Van.	.20
☐	348	Patrik Sundstrom, Van.	.20
☐	349	Stan Smyl, Van.	.25
☐	350	Rich Sutter, Van.	.20
☐	351	Steve Tambellini, Van.	.20
☐	352	Jim Sandlak, Van.	.20
☐	353	Dave Lowry, Van.	.25
☐	354	Paul MacLean, Wpg.	.20
☐	355	Winnipeg Jets Team Logo	.20
☐	356	Daniel Berthiaume (G), Wpg.	.25
☐	357	Eldon Reddick (G), Wpg.	.25
☐	358	Dave Ellett, Wpg.	.20
☐	359	Mario Marois, Wpg.	.20
☐	360	Randy Carlyle, Wpg.	.20
☐	361	Fredrick Olausson, Wpg.	.20
☐	362	Jim Kyte, Wpg.	.20
☐	363	Dale Hawerchuk, Wpg.	.50
☐	364	Paul MacLean, Wpg.	.20
☐	365	Thomas Steen, Wpg.	.20
☐	366	Gilles Hamel, Wpg.	.20
☐	367	Doug Smail, Wpg.	.20
☐	368	Laurie Boschman, Wpg.	.20
☐	369	Ray Neufeld, Wpg.	.20
☐	370	Andrew McBain, Wpg.	.20
☐	371	LL: Wayne Gretzky, Edm.	5.00
☐	372	Hart Memorial Trophy	.25
☐	373	LL: Wayne Gretzky, Edm.	5.00
☐	374	Art Ross Trophy	.25
☐	375	LL: William M. Jennings Trophy	.25
☐	376A	LL: Brian Hayward (G), Mtl.	4.50
	376B	LL: Patrick Roy (G), Mtl.	
☐	377	Vezina Trophy	.25
☐	378	LL: Ron Hextall (G), Pha.	.75
☐	379	LL: Luc Robitaille, L.A.	1.25
☐	380	Calder Memorial Trophy	.25
☐	381	LL: Ray Bourque, Bos.	1.00
☐	382	James Norris Memorial Trophy	.25

	No.	Player	NRMT-MT
☐	383	Lady Byng Memorial Trophy	.25
☐	384	LL: Joe Mullen, Cgy.	.35
☐	385	LL: Frank J. Selke Trophy	.25
☐	386	LL: Dave Poulin, Pha.	.25
☐	387	LL: Doug Jarvis, Hfd.	.20
☐	388	Bill Masterton Memorial Trophy	.25
☐	389	LL: Wayne Gretzky, Edm.	5.00
☐	390	Emery Edge Award	.25
☐	391	Philadelphia Flyers Team Photo	.20
☐	392	Philadelphia Flyers Team Photo	.20
☐	393	Prince of Wales Trophy	.20
☐	394	Clarence S. Campbell Bowl	.20
☐	395	Edmonton Oilers Team Photo	.20
☐	396	Edmonton Oilers Team Photo	.20

1987 - 88 PRO-SPORT CELEBRITY WATCHES

This 17-card set is unique. The cards themselves were part of a folder package for quartz watches. As such they are printed on heavy card stock. The card face is one piece of the actual packaging and the card back is another. Card 4 was not issued; there are two cards 17.

Folder Size: 3 3/8" x 6 3/4"
Card Size: 3 11/16" x 6 13/16"
Face: Card face: Four colour, borderless with facimile autograph
Card back: blank
Back: Card back: Four colour, black and white; Name, Jersey number, Resume, Bilingual, Team, NHL and NHLPA logos
Imprint: Celebrity Watch Inc. Montre Célèbrité Inc.

Complete Set (17 watchs): 80.00

	No.	Player	NRMT-MT
☐	CW1	Larry Robinson, Mtl.	5.00
☐	CW2	Guy Carbonneau, Mtl.	4.00
☐	CW3	Chris Chelios, Mtl.	6.00
☐	CW5	Mario Lemieux, Pgh.	20.00
☐	CW6	Mike Bossy, NYI.	6.00
☐	CW7	Dale Hawerchuk, Wpg.	5.00
☐	CW8	Joe Mullen, Cgy.	5.00
☐	CW9	Rick Vaive, Tor.	5.00
☐	CW10	Wendel Clark, Tor.	6.00
☐	CW11	Michel Goulet, Que.	5.00
☐	CW12	Peter Stastny, Que.	5.00
☐	CW13	Mark Messier, Edm.	10.00
☐	CW14	Paul Coffey, Edm.	6.00
☐	CW15	Tony Tanti, Van.	5.00
☐	CW16	Borje Salming, Tor.	5.00
☐	CW17	Chris Nilan, Mtl.	4.00
☐	CW17	Mats Naslund, Mtl.	5.00

1987 - 88 SOVIET STARS

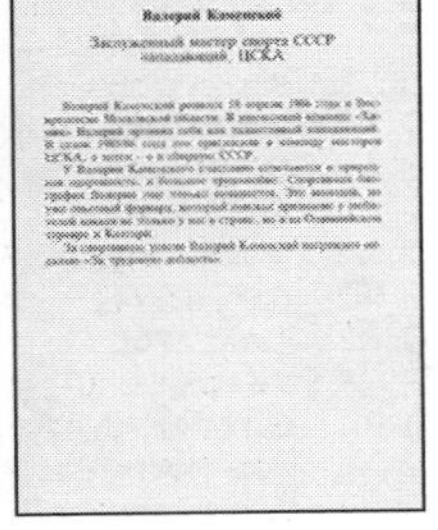

Complete Set (24 cards): 45.00

	Player	NRMT-MT
☐	Sergei Ageikin	1.00
☐	Evgeny Belosheikin	1.00
☐	Zinetula Bilyaletdinov	1.00
☐	Vyacheslav Bykov	3.00
☐	Sergei Fedorov	10.00
☐	Viacheslav Fetisov	8.00
☐	Alexei Gusarov	2.00
☐	Valeri Kamensky	5.00
☐	Yuri Khmylev	2.00
☐	Valeri Kasatonov	2.00
☐	Andrei Khomutov	2.00
☐	Vladimir Konstantinov	5.00
☐	Vladimir Krutov	2.00
☐	Igor Larionov	8.00
☐	Sergei Makarov	5.00
☐	Sergei Mylnikov (G)	1.00
☐	Vasili Pervukhin	1.00
☐	Sergei Starikov	1.00
☐	Igor Stelnov	1.00
☐	Viktor Tikhonov	3.00
☐	Viktor Tjumenev	1.00
☐	Michael Varnakov	1.00
☐	Sergei Yashin	1.00
☐	Vladimir Yursinov	1.00

1987 - 88 TOPPS

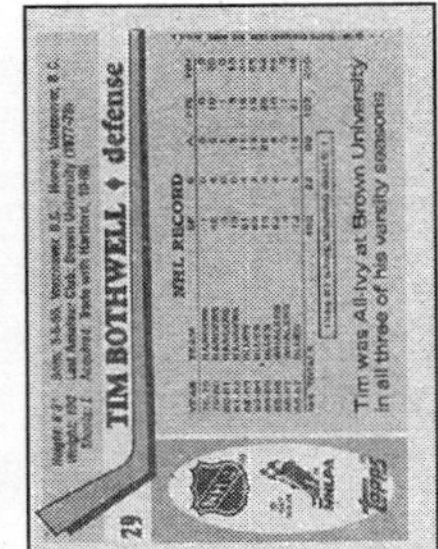

Face: Four colour, white border, Position
Back: Purple and black on card stock, Number, Resume, Hockey trivia
Imprint: © TOPPS CHEWING GUM, INC.

Complete Set (198 cards): 135.00
Common Player: .15
Double Prints (**): .10

	No.	Player	NRMT-MT
☐	1	Denis Potvin, NYI., LC (**)	.50
☐	**2**	**Rick Tocchet, Pha., RC**	**8.00**
☐	3	Dave Andreychuk, Buf.	.75
☐	4	Stan Smyl, Van.	.20
☐	5	Dave Babych, Hfd. (**)	.15
☐	6	Pat Verbeek, N.J.	.25
☐	**7**	**Esa Tikkanen, Edm., RC**	**5.00**
☐	8	Mike Ridley, Wsh.	.25
☐	9	Randy Carlyle, Wpg.	.15
☐	**10**	**Greg Paslawski, Stl., RC**	**.15**
☐	11	Neal Broten, Min.	.20
☐	12	Wendel Clark, Tor. (**)	3.50
☐	**13**	**Bill Ranford (G), Bos., RC (**)**	**6.00**
☐	14	Doug Wilson, Chi.	.20
☐	15	Mario Lemieux, Pgh.	25.00
☐	16	Mats Naslund, Mtl.	.20
☐	17	Mel Bridgman, Det., LC	.15
☐	18	James Patrick, NYR. (**)	.10
☐	19	Rollie Melanson (G), LA	.15
☐	20	Lanny McDonald, Cgy.	.20
☐	21	Peter Stastny, Que.	.25
☐	22	Murray Craven, Pha.	.15
☐	**23**	**Ulf Samuelsson, Hfd., RC (**)**	**3.50**
☐	**24**	**Michael Thelven, Bos., RC, LC (**), Err. (Thelvin)**	**.10**
☐	25	Scott Stevens, Wsh.	.25
☐	26	Petr Klima, Det.	.15
☐	27	Brent Sutter, NYI. (**)	.15
☐	28	Tomas Sandstrom, NYR.	.35
☐	29	Tim Bothwell, Stl., LC	.15
☐	30	Rob Carpenter, L.A. (**)	.10
☐	31	Brian MacLellan, Min. (**)	.10
☐	32	John Chabot, Pgh.	.15
☐	33	Phil Housley, Buf. (**)	.15
☐	34	Patrik Sundstrom, Van. (**)	.10
☐	35	Dave Ellett, Wpg.	.20
☐	36	John Vanbiesbrouck (G), NYR.	12.00
☐	37	Dave Lewis, Det., LC	.15
☐	38	Tom McCarthy, Bos., LC (**)	.10
☐	39	Dave Poulin, Pha.	.20
☐	40	Mike Foligno, Buf.	.15
☐	41	Gord Roberts, Min.	.15
☐	**42**	**Luc Robitaille, L.A., RC**	**15.00**
☐	43	Duane Sutter, NYI.	.20
☐	44	Pete Peeters (G), Wsh.	.20
☐	45	John Anderson, Hfd.	.15
☐	46	Aaron Broten, N.J.	.15
☐	47	Keith Brown, Chi.	.15
☐	48	Bobby Smith, Mtl.	.20
☐	49	Don Maloney, NYR.	.15
☐	50	Mark Hunter, Stl.	.15
☐	51	Moe Mantha, Pgh.	.15
☐	52	Charlie Simmer, Bos.	.15
☐	53	Wayne Gretzky, Edm.	18.00
☐	54	Mark Howe, Pha.	.20
☐	55	Bob Gould, Wsh.	.15
☐	56	Steve Yzerman, Det. (**)	5.00
☐	57	Larry Playfair, L.A., LC	.15
☐	58	Alain Chevrier (G), N.J.	.20
☐	59	Steve Larmer, Chi.	.35
☐	60	Bryan Trottier, NYI.	.35
☐	61	Stewart Gavin, Hfd. (**)	.10
☐	62	Russ Courtnall, Tor. (**)	.50
☐	63	Mike Ramsey, Buf. (**)	.10
☐	64	Bob Brooke, Min.	.15
☐	65	Rick Wamsley (G), Stl. (**)	.15
☐	66	Ken Morrow, NYI.	.15
☐	**67**	**Gerard Gallant, Det., RC, Error (Gerald)**	**.20**
☐	**68**	**Kevin Hatcher, Wsh., RC**	**2.00**
☐	69	Cam Neely, Bos.	2.75
☐	70	Sylvain Turgeon, Hfd. (**)	.10
☐	71	Peter Zezel, Pha.	.15
☐	72	Al MacInnis, Cgy.	2.75
☐	73	Terry Ruskowski, Pgh., LC (**)	.10
☐	74	Troy Murray, Chi.	.15
☐	75	Jim Fox, L.A. (**)	.10
☐	76	Kelly Kisio, NYR.	.15
☐	77	Michel Goulet, Que. (**)	.25
☐	78	Tom Barrasso (G), Buf. (**)	.25
☐	79	Bruce Driver, N.J. (**)	.15
☐	**80**	**Craig Simpson, Pgh., RC (**)**	**.20**
☐	81	Dino Ciccarelli, Min.	.25
☐	82	Gary Nylund, Chi. (**)	.10
☐	83	Bernie Federko, Stl.	.20
☐	84	John Tonelli, Cgy. (**)	.10
☐	85	Brad McCrimmon, Pha. (**)	.10
☐	86	Dave Tippett, Hfd. (**)	.10
☐	87	Ray Bourque, Bos. (**)	1.25
☐	88	Dave Christian, Wsh.	.15
☐	89	Glen Hanlon (G), Det.	.20
☐	**90**	**Brian Curran, NYI., RC**	**.15**
☐	91	Paul MacLean, Wpg.	.15
☐	**92**	**Jimmy Carson, L.A., RC**	**.35**
☐	93	Willie Huber, NYR., LC	.15
☐	94	Brian Bellows, Min	.25
☐	95	Doug Jarvis, Hfd., LC (**)	.10
☐	96	Clark Gillies, Buf.	.15
☐	97	Tony Tanti, Van.	.15
☐	**98**	**Per-Erik Eklund, Pha., RC (**)**	**.20**
☐	99	Paul Coffey, Edm.	1.75
☐	100	Brent Ashton, Det. (**)	.10
☐	101	Mark Johnson, N.J.	.15
☐	**102**	**Greg Johnston, Bos., RC, LC**	**.15**
☐	103	Ron Flockhart, Stl., LC	.15
☐	104	Ed Olczyk, Chi.	.25
☐	105	Mike Bossy, NYI., LC	1.00
☐	106	Chris Chelios, Mtl.	2.00
☐	107	Gilles Meloche (G), Pgh.	.20
☐	108	Rod Langway, Wsh.	.20
☐	109	Ray Ferraro, Hfd. (**)	.65
☐	110	Ron Duguay, NYR., LC (**)	.10
☐	111	Al Secord, Chi. (**)	.10
☐	112	Mark Messier, Edm.	3.25
☐	113	Ron Sutter, Pha.	.15
☐	**114**	**Darren Veitch, Det., RC**	**.15**
☐	115	Rick Middleton, Bos. (**)	.15
☐	116	Doug Sulliman, N.J.	.15
☐	117	Dennis Maruk, Min., LC (**)	.10
☐	118	David Taylor, L.A.	.20

	No.	Player	NRMT-MT
☐	119	Kelly Hrudey (G), NYI.	.35
☐	120	Tom Fergus, Tor.	.15
☐	**121**	**Christian Ruuttu, Buf., RC**	**.20**
☐	**122**	**Brian Benning, Stl., RC**	**.15**
☐	**123**	**Adam Oates, Det., RC**	**18.00**
☐	124	Kevin Dineen, Hfd.	.25
☐	125	Doug Bodger, Pgh. (**)	.15
☐	126	Joe Mullen, Cgy.	.25
☐	127	Denis Savard, Chi.	.35
☐	128	Brad Marsh, Pha.	.15
☐	129	Marcel Dionne, NYR. (**)	.25
☐	130	Bryan Erickson, L.A., LC	.15
☐	131	Reed Larson, Bos. (**)	.10
☐	132	Don Beaupré (G), Min.	.20
☐	133	Larry Murphy, Wsh. (**)	.20
☐	134	John Ogrodnick, Que. (**)	.10
☐	135	Greg Adams, N.J. (**)	.25
☐	136	Patrick Flatley, NYI. (**)	.10
☐	137	Scott Arniel, Buf.	.15
☐	138	Dana Murzyn, Hfd.	.20
☐	139	Greg Adams, Wsh.	.15
☐	140	Bob Sauvé (G), N.J., LC	.20
☐	141	Walt O'Connell, Det.	.15
☐	142	Walt Poddubny, NYR. (**)	.10
☐	143	Paul Reinhart, Cgy.	.15
☐	144	Tim Kerr, Pha. (**)	.10
☐	**145**	**Brian Lawton, Min., RC**	**.15**
☐	**146**	**Gino Cavallini, Stl., RC**	**.15**
☐	147	Doug Keans (G), Bos., LC (**)	.15
☐	148	Jari Kurri, Edm.	.85
☐	149	Dale Hawerchuk, Wpg.	.60
☐	**150**	**Randy Cunneyworth, Pgh., RC**	**.75**
☐	151	Jay Wells, L.A.	.15
☐	152	Mike Liut (G), Hfd. (**)	.15
☐	153	Steve Konroyd, NYI.	.15
☐	154	John Tucker, Buf.	.15
☐	155	Rick Vaive, Tor. (**)	.20
☐	156	Bob Murray, Chi.	.15
☐	157	Kirk Muller, N.J. (**)	.60
☐	158	Brian Propp, Pha.	.15
☐	159	Ron Greschner, NYR.	.15
☐	160	Rob Ramage, Stl.	.20
☐	161	Craig Laughlin, Wsh.	.15
☐	162	Steve Kasper, Bos. (**)	.10
☐	163	Patrick Roy (G), Mtl.	30.00
☐	164	Shawn Burr, Det., RC (**)	.25
☐	165	Craig Hartsburg, Min. (**)	.15
☐	**166**	**Dean Evason, Hfd., RC**	**.25**
☐	167	Bob Bourne, L.A.	.15
☐	168	Mike Gartner, Wsh.	1.25
☐	**169**	**Ron Hextall (G), Pha., RC**	**8.00**
☐	170	Joe Cirella, N.J.	.15
☐	171	Dan Quinn, Pgh. (**)	.10
☐	172	Tony McKegney, Stl.	.15
☐	173	Pat LaFontaine, NYI. (**)	1.25
☐	**174**	**Allen Pedersen, Bos., RC (**)**	**.10**
☐	175	Doug Gilmour, Stl.	3.50
☐	176	Gary Suter, Cgy. (**)	.20
☐	177	Barry Pederson, Van. (**)	.10
☐	178	Grant Fuhr (G), Edm. (**)	1.25
☐	**179**	**Wayne Presley, Chi., RC**	**.20**
☐	180	Wilf Paiement, Pgh., LC	.15
☐	181	Doug Smail, Wpg.	.15
☐	182	Doug Crossman, Pha. (**)	.10
☐	183	Bernie Nicholls, L.A., Error (Nichols)	.35
☐	184	Dirk Graham, Min., Error (Dick)	.20
☐	185	Anton Stastny, Que.	.15
☐	186	Greg Stefan (G), Det.	.20
☐	187	Ron Francis, Hfd.	1.25
☐	188	Steve Thomas, Tor. (**)	.25
☐	**189**	**Kelly Miller, Wsh., RC**	**.35**
☐	190	Tomas Jonsson, NYI.	.15
☐	191	John MacLean, N.J.	.50
☐	192	Larry Robinson, Mtl. (**)	.25
☐	193	Doug Wickenheiser, Stl. (**)	.10
☐	194	Keith Crowder, Bos. (**)	.10
☐	195	Bob Froese (G), NYR., LC	.20
☐	196	Jim Johnson, Pgh.	.15
☐	197	Checklist 1 (1 - 99)	1.25
☐	198	Checklist 2 (100 - 198)	1.50

STICKER INSERTS

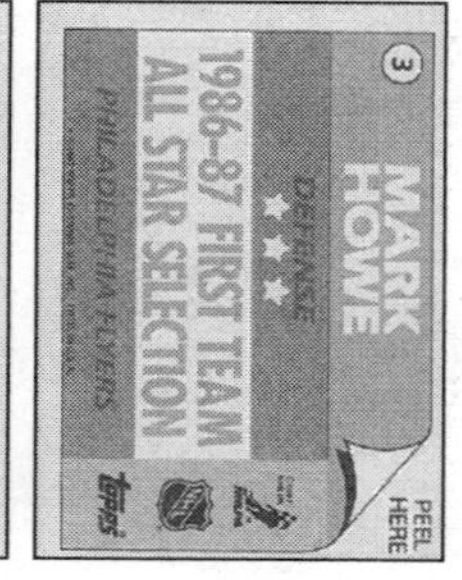

Insert Set (33 stickers): 24.00

	No.	Player	NRMT-MT
☐	1	AS: Ray Bourque, Bos.	2.50
☐	2	AS: Ron Hextall (G)	1.00
☐	3	AS: Mark Howe	.35
☐	4	AS: Jari Kurri, Edm.	1.00
☐	5	AS: Wayne Gretzky, Edm.	7.00
☐	6	AS: Michel Goulet	1.00
☐	7	AS: Larry Murphy	.50
☐	8	AS: Mike Liut (G)	.35
☐	9	AS: Al MacInnis	1.00
☐	10	AS: Tim Kerr	.35
☐	11	AS: Mario Lemieux	7.00
☐	12	AS: Luc Robitaille	1.50
☐	13	Toronto Maple Leafs	.25
☐	14	Buffalo Sabres	.25
☐	15	Detroit Red Wings	.25
☐	16	Pittsburgh Penguins	.25
☐	17	New York Rangers	.25
☐	18	Calgary Flames	.25
☐	19	Winnipeg Jets	.25
☐	20	Québec Nordiques	.25
☐	21	Chicago Blackhawks	.25
☐	22	Los Angeles Kings	.25
☐	23	Montréal Canadiens	.25
☐	24	Vancouver Canucks	.25
☐	25	Hartford Whalers	.25
☐	26	Philadelphia Flyers	.25
☐	27	New Jersey Devils	.25
☐	28	St. Louis Blues	.25
☐	29	Minnesota North Stars	.25
☐	30	Washington Capitals	.25
☐	31	Boston Bruins	.25
☐	32	New York Islanders	.25
☐	33	Edmonton Oilers	.25

TOPPS BOX BOTTOMS

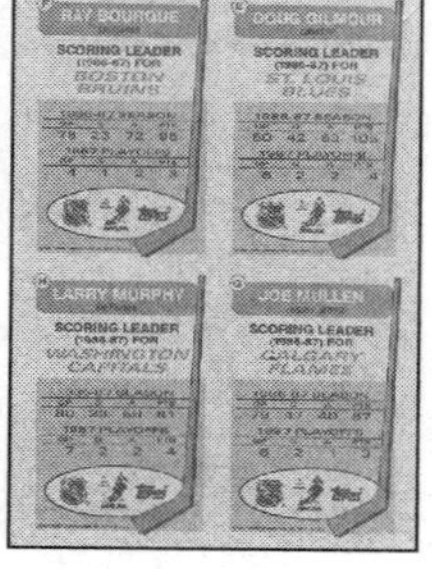

These four-card panels wer issued on bottom of Topps and O-Pee-Chee wax boxes.

Panel Size: 5" x 7"
Complete Set (16 cards): 25.00
Panel A - D: 20.00
Panel E - H: 5.00
Panel I - L: 2.00
Panel M - P: 2.50

	No.	Player	NRMT-MT
☐	A	Wayne Gretzky, Edm.	15.00
☐	B	Tim Kerr, Pha.	.50
☐	C	Steve Yzerman, Det.	6.00
☐	D	Luc Robitaille, L.A.	6.00
☐	E	Doug Gilmour, Stl.	3.00
☐	F	Ray Bourque, Bos.	3.50
☐	G	Joe Mullen, Cgy.	.50
☐	H	Larry Murphy, Wsh.	.50
☐	I	Dale Hawerchuk, Wpg.	1.00
☐	J	Ron Francis, Hfd.	1.00
☐	K	Walt Poddubny, NYR.	.50
☐	L	Mats Naslund, Mtl.	.50
☐	M	Michel Goulet, Que.	.75
☐	N	Denis Savard, Chi.	.75
☐	O	Bryan Trottier, NYI.	.75
☐	P	Russ Courtnall, Tor.	.75

1988 SOVIET NATIONAL TEAM / OLYMPIC GAMES

Card Size: 3 5/8" x 5 5/8"
Face: Black and white photo card
Back: Black and white; Number, Title, Resume
Imprint: Moscow 1985-1988
Complete Set (14 cards): 35.00

	No.	Player	NRMT-MT
☐	1	Sweden vs USR, Corinta 1956	2.50
☐	2	Tregubov, Alexaudsov, Puchkov, Squaw Valley 1960	2.50
☐	3	Statshinov, Konovalenko, Ivanov, Yakushev, Innsbruck 1964	2.50
☐	4	Three Times Olympic Champions Grenoble 1968	2.50
☐	5	A. Firsov, Sapporo 1972	2.50
☐	6	Soviets vs Finland, Innsbruck 1976	2.50
☐	7	Silver Medalist, Lake Placid 1980	2.50
☐	8	Olympic Champions, Sarajevo 1984	2.50
☐	9	Soviet Coaches of Olympic Teams	2.50
☐	10	Captains of Olympic Gold Teams	2.50
☐	11	Three Time Winners of Olympic Gold Medals	2.50
☐	12	Vsevolod Bobrov, Coach, Gold Medalist	2.50
☐	13	Valeri Kharlamov, Twice Gold Medalis	3.00
☐	14	Makarov, Larionov, Krutov, Fetisov, Kasatonov, Calgary 1988	5.00

1988 - 89 ESSO ALL-STAR STICKERS

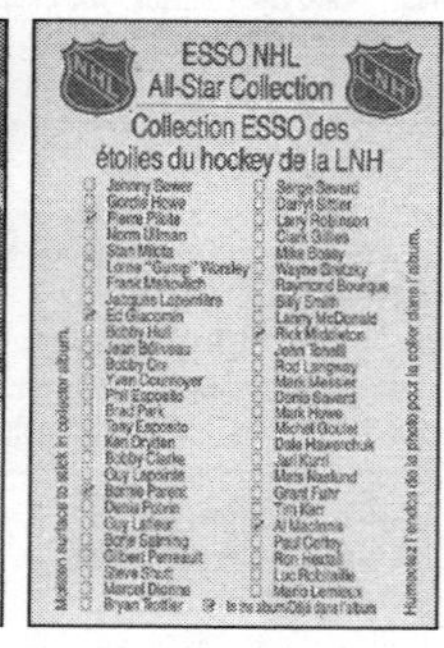

A 32-page album was available in English or French to hold the stickers.

Sticker Size: 2 1/8" x 3 1/4"
Imprint: None
Complete Set (48 stickers): 16.00
Album: (English) 5.00
Album: (French) 5.00

	Player	NRMT-MT
☐	Jean Béliveau, Mtl.	1.25
☐	Mike Bossy, NYI.	.75
☐	Ray Bourque, Bos.	.75
☐	Johnny Bower (G), Tor.	.60
☐	Bobby Clarke, Pha.	.60
☐	Paul Coffey, Pgh.	.75
☐	Yvan Cournoyer, Mtl.	.50
☐	Marcel Dionne, L.A.	.60
☐	Ken Dryden (G), Mtl.	1.25
☐	Phil Esposito, Bos.	.75
☐	Tony Esposito (G),Chi.	.75
☐	Grant Fuhr (G), Edm.	.60
☐	Clark Gillies, NYI.	.25
☐	Michel Goulet, Que.	.25
☐	Wayne Gretzky, Edm.	2.50
☐	Dale Hawerchuk, Wpg.	.25
☐	Ron Hextall (G), Pha.	.50
☐	Gordie Howe, Det.	2.00
☐	Mark Howe, Pha.	.25
☐	Bobby Hull, Chi.	1.50
☐	Tim Kerr, Pha.	.25
☐	Jari Kurri, Edm.	.60
☐	Guy Lafleur, Mtl.	1.25
☐	Rod Langway, Wsh.	.25
☐	Jacques Laperrière, Mtl.	.35
☐	Guy Lapointe, Mtl.	.35

	Player	
☐	Mario Lemieux, Pgh.	2.00
☐	Frank Mahovlich, Mtl.	.75
☐	Lanny McDonald, Cgy.	.50
☐	Mark Messier, Edm.	1.00
☐	Stan Mikita, Chi.	.60
☐	Mats Naslund, Mtl.	.25
☐	Bobby Orr, Bos.	2.50
☐	Brad Park, NYR.	.50
☐	Gilbert Perreault, Buf.	.60
☐	Denis Potvin, NYI.	.50
☐	Larry Robinson, Mtl.	.50
☐	Luc Robitaille, L.A.	.50
☐	Borje Salming, Tor.	.25
☐	Denis Savard, Chi.	.25
☐	Serge Savard, Mtl.	.35
☐	Steve Shutt, Mtl.	.50
☐	Darryl Sittler, Tor.	.75
☐	Billy Smith (G), NYI.	.60
☐	John Tonelli, NYI.	.25
☐	Bryan Trottier, NYI.	.50
☐	Norm Ullman, Tor.	.50
☐	Gump Worsley (G), Mtl.	.75

1988 - 89 FRITO-LAY STICKERS

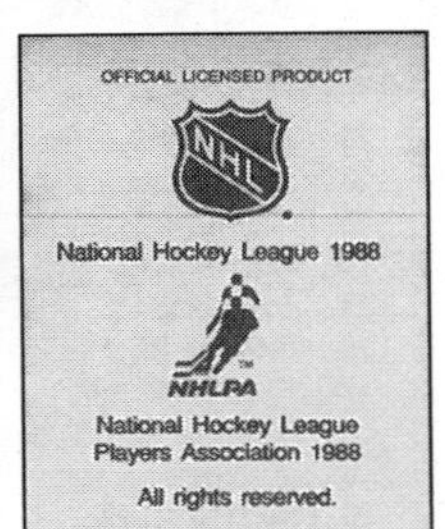

One of 42 different stickers was available in specially marked Frito Lay potato chip bags.

Sticker Size: 1 3/8" x 1 3/4"
Imprint: None
Complete Set (42 stickers): 30.00
Poster: 5.00

	Player	NRMT-MT
☐	Glenn Anderson, Edm.	.25
☐	Tom Barrasso (G), Buf.	.25
☐	Brian Bellows, Min.	.25
☐	Ray Bourque, Bos.	2.00
☐	Neal Broten, Min.	.25
☐	Sean Burke (G), N.J.	.50
☐	Wendel Clark, Tor.	.50
☐	Paul Coffey, Pgh.	1.50
☐	Kevin Dineen, Hfd.	.25
☐	Marcel Dionne, NYR.	.75
☐	Bernie Federko, Stl.	.25
☐	Michael Foligno, Buf.	.25
☐	Ron Francis, Hfd.	.75
☐	Mike Gartner, Wsh.	.75
☐	Doug Gilmour, Stl.	1.00
☐	Michel Goulet, Que.	.75
☐	Dale Hawerchuk, Wpg.	.75
☐	Ron Hextall (G), Pha.	.50
☐	Pat LaFontaine, NYI.	.50
☐	Mario Lemieux, Pgh.	5.00
☐	Al MacInnis, Cgy.	.50
☐	Andrew McBain, Wpg.	.25
☐	Mark Messier, Edm.	2.00
☐	Kirk Muller, N.J.	.50
☐	Troy Murray, Chi.	.25
☐	Mats Naslund, Mtl.	.50
☐	Cam Neely, Bos.	1.00
☐	Bernie Nicholls, L.A.	.25
☐	Joe Nieuwendyk, Cgy.	.50
☐	Ed Olczyk, Tor.	.25
☐	James Patrick, NYR.	.25
☐	Barry Pederson, Van.	.25
☐	Dave Poulin, Pha.	.25
☐	Bob Probert, Det.	.50
☐	Stéphane Richer, Mtl.	.50
☐	Luc Robitaille, L.A.	1.00
☐	Denis Savard, Chi.	.75
☐	Peter Stastny, Que.	.75
☐	Scott Stevens, Wsh.	.25
☐	Tony Tanti, Van.	.25
☐	Bryan Trottier, NYI.	1.00
☐	Steve Yzerman, Det.	3.50

1988 - 89 O-PEE-CHEE

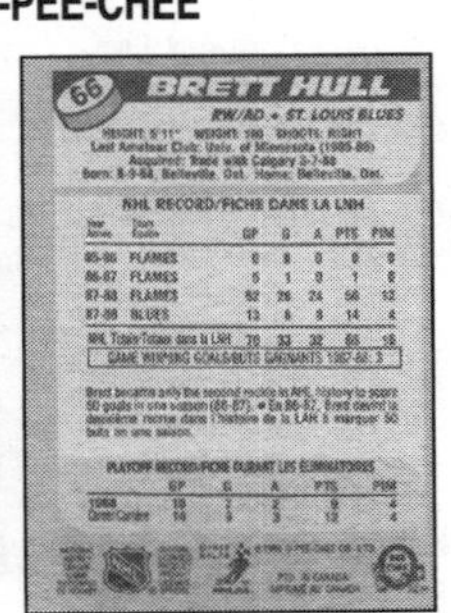

Imprint: © 1988 O-PEE-CHEE CO. LTD.
Complete Set (264 cards): 145.00
Common Player: .20

	No.	Player	NRMT-MT
☐	1	Mario Lemieux, Pgh.	12.00
☐	**2**	**Bob Joyce, Bos., RC**	**.20**
☐	3	Joel Quenneville, Hfd.	.35
☐	4	Tony McKegney, Stl.	.20
☐	5	Stéphane Richer, Mtl.	1.00
☐	6	Mark Howe, Pha.	.35
☐	7	Brent Sutter, NYI.	.35
☐	8	Gilles Meloche (G), Pgh., LC	.35
☐	9	Jimmy Carson, Edm.	.20
☐	10	John MacLean, N.J.	.35
☐	11	Gary Leeman, Tor.	.20
☐	12	Gerard Gallant, Det.	.20
☐	13	Marcel Dionne, NYR., LC	.75
☐	14	Dave Christian, Wsh.	.20
☐	15	Gary Nylund, Chi.	.20
☐	**16**	**Joe Nieuwendyk, Cgy., RC**	**8.00**
☐	17	Billy Smith (G), NYI.	.50
☐	18	Christian Ruuttu, Buf.	.20
☐	19	Randy Cunneyworth, Pgh.	.35
☐	20	Brian Lawton, Min.	.20
☐	**21**	**Scott Mellanby, Pha., RC**	**2.50**
☐	22	Peter Stastny, Que.	.50
☐	23	Gord Kluzak, Bos.	.20
☐	24	Sylvain Turgeon, Hfd.	.20
☐	25	Clint Malarchuk (G), Wsh.	.35
☐	26	Denis Savard, Chi.	.50
☐	27	Craig Simpson, Edm.	.20
☐	28	Petr Klima, Det.	.20
☐	29	Pat Verbeek, N.J.	.35
☐	30	Moe Mantha, Min.	.20
☐	31	Chris Nilan, NYR.	.20
☐	32	Barry Pederson, Van.	.20
☐	33	Randy Burridge, Bos.	.35
☐	34	Ron Hextall (G), Pha.	2.00
☐	35	Gaston Gingras, Stl.	.20
☐	36	Kevin Dineen, Hfd.	.35
☐	37	Tom Laidlaw, L.A.	.20
☐	38	Paul MacLean, Det.	.20
☐	39	John Chabot, Det.	.20
☐	40	Lindy Ruff, Buf.	.20
☐	41	Dan Quinn, Pgh.	.20
☐	42	Don Beaupré (G), Min.	.35
☐	43	Gary Suter, Cgy.	.35
☐	**44**	**Mikko Makelä, NYI., RC**	**.20**
☐	45	Mark Johnson, N.J.	.20
☐	46	Dave Taylor, L.A.	.35
☐	**47**	**Ulf Dahlen, NYR., RC**	**1.50**
☐	**48**	**Jeff Sharples, Det., RC**	**.20**
☐	49	Chris Chelios, Mtl.	2.50
☐	50	Mike Gartner, Wsh.	1.00
☐	**51**	**Darren Pang (G), Chi., RC**	**.35**
☐	52	Ron Francis, Hfd.	1.50
☐	53	Ken Morrow, NYI., LC	.20
☐	54	Michel Goulet, Que.	.50
☐	**55**	**Ray Sheppard, Buf., RC**	**2.50**
☐	56	Doug Gilmour, Stl. (Cgy.)	2.50
☐	57	David Shaw, NYR.	.20
☐	58	Cam Neely, Bos.	1.50
☐	59	Grant Fuhr (G), Edm.	1.50
☐	60	Scott Stevens, Wsh.	.35
☐	61	Bob Brooke, Min.	.20
☐	62	Dave Hunter, Pgh. (Wpg.), LC	.20
☐	**63**	**Alan Kerr, NYI., RC**	**.20**
☐	64	Brad Marsh, Pha. (Tor.)	.20
☐	65	Dale Hawerchuk, Wpg.	.50
☐	**66**	**Brett Hull, Stl., RC**	**50.00**
☐	67	Patrik Sundstrom, N.J.	.20
☐	68	Greg Stefan (G), Det.	.35
☐	69	James Patrick, NYR.	.20
☐	70	Dale Hunter, Wsh.	.35
☐	71	Al Iafrate, Tor.	.35
☐	72	Bob Carpenter, L.A.	.20
☐	73	Ray Bourque, Bos.	2.50
☐	74	John Tucker, Buf.	.20
☐	75	Carey Wilson, Hfd.	.20
☐	76	Joe Mullen, Cgy.	.35
☐	77	Rick Vaive, Chi.	.35
☐	78	Shawn Burr, Det.	.35
☐	79	Murray Craven, Pha.	.20
☐	80	Clark Gillies, Buf., LC	.20
☐	81	Bernie Federko, Stl.	.35
☐	82	Tony Tanti, Van.	.20
☐	83	Greg Gilbert, NYI.	.20
☐	84	Kirk Muller, N.J.	.50
☐	85	Dave Tippett, Hfd.	.20
☐	86	Kevin Hatcher, Wsh.	.50
☐	87	Rick Middleton, Bos., LC	.35
☐	88	Bobby Smith, Mtl.	.35
☐	89	Doug Wilson, Chi.	.35
☐	90	Scott Arniel, Buf.	.20
☐	91	Brian Mullen, NYR.	.20
☐	92	Mike O'Connell, Det.	.20
☐	93	Mark Messier, Edm.	3.00
☐	**94**	**Sean Burke (G), N.J., RC**	**5.00**
☐	95	Brian Bellows, Min.	.35
☐	96	Doug Bodger, Pgh.	.20
☐	97	Bryan Trottier, NYI.	.65
☐	98	Anton Stastny, Que.	.20
☐	99	Checklist 1, Error (1-99)	.75
☐	99	Checklist 1, Corrected (1-132)	.75
☐	100	Dave Poulin, Pha.	.20
☐	101	Bob Bourne, L.A., LC	.20
☐	102	John Vanbiesbrouck (G), NYR.	10.00
☐	103	Allen Pedersen, Bos.	.20
☐	104	Mike Ridley, Wsh.	.35
☐	105	Andrew McBain, Wpg.	.20
☐	106	Troy Murray, Chi.	.20
☐	107	Tom Barrasso (G), Buf.	.35
☐	108	Tomas Jonsson, NYI., LC	.20
☐	**109**	**Rob Brown, Pgh., RC**	**.50**
☐	110	Hakan Loob, Cgy., LC	.20
☐	111	Ilkka Sinisalo, Pha.	.20
☐	**112**	**Dave Archibald, Min., RC**	**.20**
☐	113	Doug Halward, Det., LC	.20
☐	114	Ray Ferraro, Hfd.	.35
☐	**115**	**Doug Brown, N.J., RC**	**.25**
☐	116	Patrick Roy (G), Mtl.	20.00
☐	117	Greg Millen (G), Stl..	.35
☐	118	Ken Linseman, Bos.	.20
☐	119	Phil Housley, Buf.	.35
☐	120	Wayne Gretzky, L.A.	20.00
☐	121	Tomas Sandström, NYR.	.35
☐	**122**	**Brendan Shanahan, N.J., RC**	**70.00**
☐	123	Pat LaFontaine, NYI.	1.50
☐	124	Luc Robitaille, L.A.	4.00
☐	125	Ed Olczyk, Tor.	.20
☐	126	Ron Sutter, Pha.	.20
☐	127	Mike Liut (G), Hfd.	.35
☐	128	Brent Ashton, Wpg.	.20
☐	**129**	**Tony Hrkac, Stl., RC**	**.20**
☐	130	Kelly Miller, Wsh.	.20
☐	131	Alan Haworth, Que.	.20

	No.	Player	NRMT-MT
☐	**132**	**Dave McLlwain, Pgh., RC**	**.35**
☐	133	Mike Ramsey, Buf.	.20
☐	**134**	**Bob Sweeney, Bos., RC**	**.35**
☐	135	Dirk Graham, Chi.	.20
☐	136	Ulf Samuelsson, Hfd.	.75
☐	137	Petri Skriko, Van.	.20
☐	138	Aaron Broten, N.J.	.20
☐	139	Jim Fox, L.A.	.20
☐	**140**	**Randy Wood, NYI., RC**	**.35**
☐	141	Larry Murphy, Wsh.	.35
☐	142	Daniel Berthiaume (G), Wpg.	.35
☐	143	Kelly Kisio, NYR.	.20
☐	144	Neal Broten, Min.	.35
☐	145	Reed Larson, Bos.	.20
☐	146	Peter Zezel, Pha.	.20
☐	147	Jari Kurri, Edm.	1.00
☐	148	Jim Johnson, Pgh.	.20
☐	149	Gino Cavallini, Stl.	.20
☐	150	Glen Hanlon (G), Det.	.35
☐	151	Bengt Gustafsson, Wsh.	.20
☐	152	Mike Bullard, Cgy. (Stl.)	.20
☐	153	John Ogrodnick, NYR.	.20
☐	154	Steve Larmer, Chi.	.50
☐	155	Kelly Hrudey (G), NYI.	.35
☐	156	Mats Naslund, Mtl.	.35
☐	157	Bruce Driver, N.J.	.35
☐	158	Randy Hillier, Pgh.	.20
☐	159	Craig Hartsburg, Min., LC	.35
☐	160	Rollie Melanson (G), L.A., LC	.35
☐	161	Adam Oates, Det.	4.00
☐	162	Greg Adams, Van.	.35
☐	163	Dave Andreychuk, Buf.	.35
☐	164	Dave Babych, Hfd.	.35
☐	**165**	**Brian Noonan, Chi., RC**	**.65**
☐	**166**	**Glen Wesley, Bos., RC**	**.65**
☐	167	Dave Ellett, Wpg.	.35
☐	168	Brian Propp, Pha.	.20
☐	169	Bernie Nicholls, L.A.	.35
☐	170	Walt Poddubny, NYR. (Que.)	.20
☐	171	Steve Konroyd, NYI.	.20
☐	172	Doug Sulliman, N.J. (Pha.)	.20
☐	173	Mario Gosselin (G), Que.	.35
☐	174	Brian Benning, Stl.	.20
☐	175	Dino Ciccarelli, Min.	.35
☐	176	Steve Kasper, Bos.	.20
☐	177	Rick Tocchet, Pha.	2.50
☐	178	Brad McCrimmon, Cgy.	.20
☐	179	Paul Coffey, Pgh.	2.25
☐	180	Pete Peeters (G), Wsh.	.35
☐	**181**	**Bob Probert, Det., RC**	**3.00**
☐	**182**	**Steve Duchesne, L.A., RC**	**3.00**
☐	183	Russ Courtnall, Tor.	.35
☐	184	Mike Foligno, Buf.	.20
☐	185	Wayne Presley, Chi.	.20
☐	186	Réjean Lemelin (G), Bos.	.35
☐	187	Mark Hunter, Stl. (Cgy.)	.20
☐	188	Joe Cirella, N.J.	.20
☐	189	Glenn Anderson, Edm.	.35
☐	190	John Anderson, Hfd.	.20
☐	191	Pat Flatley, NYI.	.20
☐	192	Rod Langway, Wsh.	.35
☐	193	Brian MacLellan, Min	.20
☐	**194**	**Pierre Turgeon, Buf., RC**	**20.00**
☐	195	Brian Hayward (G), Mtl.	.35
☐	196	Steve Yzerman, Det.	8.00
☐	197	Doug Crossman, Pha.	.20
☐	198	Checklist 2, Error (100 - 198)	.75
☐	198	Checklist 2, Corrected (133 - 264)	.75
☐	199	Greg Adams, Wsh. (Edm.)	.20
☐	200	Laurie Boschman, Wpg.	.20
☐	**201**	**Jeff Brown, Que., RC**	**1.00**
☐	**202**	**Garth Butcher, Van., RC**	**.20**
☐	203	Guy Carbonneau, Mtl.	.20
☐	204	Randy Carlyle, Wpg.	.20
☐	205	Alain Côté, Que.	.20
☐	206	Keith Crowder, Bos.	.20
☐	207	Vincent Damphousse, Tor.	3.75
☐	**208**	**Gaetan Duchesne, Que., RC**	**.20**
☐	**209**	**Iain Duncan, Wpg., RC**	**.20**
☐	**210**	**Tommy Albelin, Que., RC**	**.20**
☐	211	Per-Erik Eklund, Pha.	.20
☐	**212**	**Jan Erixon, NYR., RC**	**.20**
☐	**213**	**Paul Fenton, L.A., RC**	**.20**
☐	214	Tom Fergus, Tor.	.20
☐	**215**	**Dave Gagner, Min., RC**	**1.75**
☐	216	Bob Gainey, Mtl., LC	.50
☐	217	Stewart Gavin, Hfd. (Min.)	.20
☐	218	Charlie Huddy, Edm.	.20
☐	**219**	**Jeff Jackson, Que., RC**	**.20**
☐	**220**	**Uwe Krupp, Buf., RC**	**.75**
☐	221	Mike Krushelnyski, Edm. (L.A.)	.20
☐	222	Tom Kurvers, N.J.	.20
☐	**223**	**Jason Lafrenière, Que., RC**	**.20**
☐	224	Lane Lambert, Que.	.20
☐	225	Rick Lanz, Tor.	.20
☐	**226**	**Brad Lauer, NYI., RC**	**.20**
☐	227	Claude Lemieux, Mtl.	2.75
☐	228	Doug Lidster, Van.	.20
☐	229	Kevin Lowe, Edm., Error	.35
☐	230	Craig Ludwig, Mtl.	.20
☐	231	Al MacInnis, Cgy.	1.75
☐	232	Craig MacTavish, Edm.	.20
☐	233	Mario Marois, Wpg., Error (Marios)	.20
☐	234	Lanny McDonald, Cgy.	.35
☐	235	Rick Meagher, Stl.	.20
☐	236	Craig Muni, Edm.	.20
☐	237	Mike McPhee, Mtl.	.20
☐	**238**	**Ric Nattress, Cgy., RC**	**.20**
☐	239	Ray Neufeld, Wpg.,	.20
☐	**240**	**Lee Norwood, Det., RC**	**.20**
☐	241	Mark Osborne, Tor., Error (Osbourne)	.20
☐	242	Joel Otto, Cgy.	.20
☐	243	Jim Peplinski, Cgy.	.20
☐	244	Rob Ramage, Cgy.	.20
☐	**245**	**Luke Richardson, Tor., RC**	**1.00**
☐	246	Larry Robinson, Mtl.	.35
☐	247	Borje Salming, Tor.	.35
☐	**248**	**David Saunders, Van., RC, LC**	**.20**
☐	249	Al Secord, Tor.,	.20
☐	250	Charlie Simmer, Pgh., LC	.20
☐	251	Doug Smail, Wpg.	.20
☐	**252**	**Steve Smith, Edm., RC**	**1.50**
☐	253	Stan Smyl, Van.	.25
☐	254	Thomas Steen, Wpg.	.20
☐	255	Rich Sutter, Van.	.20
☐	**256**	**Petr Svoboda, Mtl., RC**	**1.00**
☐	**257**	**Peter Taglianetti, Wpg., RC**	**.20**
☐	258	Steve Tambellini, Van.	.20
☐	259	Steve Thomas, Chi.	.25
☐	260	Esa Tikkanen, Edm.	2.00
☐	261	Mike Vernon (G), Cgy.	2.00
☐	262	Ryan Walter, Mtl.	.25
☐	263	Doug Wickenheiser, Van. (NYR.)	.20
☐	264	Ken Wregget (G), Tor.	.50

O-PEE-CHEE BOX BOTTOMS

These four-card panels were found on the bottom of O-Pee-Chee and Topps wax boxes.

Panel Size: 5" x 7"

Complete Set (16 cards):	**20.00**
Panel A - D:	**12.00**
Panel E - H:	**2.50**
Panel I - L:	**6.00**
Panel M - P:	**3.50**

	No.	Player	NRMT-MT
☐	A	Ron Francis, Hfd.	1.00
☐	B	Wayne Gretzky, L.A.	10.00
☐	C	Pat LaFontaine, NYI.	1.00
☐	D	Bobby Smith, Mtl.	.75
☐	E	Bernie Federko, Stl.	.75
☐	F	Kirk Muller, N.J.	.75
☐	G	Ed Olczyk, Tor.	.75
☐	H	Denis Savard, Chi.	.75
☐	I	Ray Bourque, Bos.	4.00
☐	J	Murray Craven/Brian Propp, Pha.	.75
☐	K	Dale Hawerchuk, Wpg.	1.00
☐	L	Steve Yzerman, Det.	6.00
☐	M	Dave Andreychuk, Buf.	.75
☐	N	Mike Gartner, Wsh.	1.00
☐	O	Hakan Loob, Cgy.	.75
☐	P	Luc Robitaille, L.A.	2.00

1988 - 89 OPC NHL STARS

Card Size: 2 1/8" x 3"
Face: Four colour, white border; Name
Back: Two colour, pink and purple on white card stock; Name, Number, Resume, Bilingual
Imprint: © 1988 O-PEE-CHEE CO.

Complete Set (46 cards):			**22.00**
	No.	**Player**	**NRMT-MT**
☐	1	Tom Barrasso (G), Buf.	.35
☐	2	Bob Bourne, L.A.	.20
☐	3	Ray Bourque, Bos.	1.50
☐	4	Guy Carbonneau, Mtl.	.35
☐	5	Jimmy Carson, Edm.	.20
☐	6	Paul Coffey, Pgh.	1.00
☐	7	Ulf Dahlen, NYR.	.20
☐	8	Marcel Dionne, NYR.	.50
☐	9	Grant Fuhr (G), Edm.	.50
☐	10	Michel Goulet, Que.	.35
☐	11	Wayne Gretzky, L.A.	6.00
☐	12	Dale Hawerchuk, Wpg.	.35
☐	13	Brian Hayward (G), Mtl.	.35
☐	14	Ron Hextall (G), Pha.	.50
☐	15	Tony Hrkac, Stl.	.20
☐	16	Brett Hull, Stl.	4.00
☐	17	Steve Larmer, Chi.	.35
☐	18	Réjean Lemelin (G), Bos.	.35
☐	19	Mario Lemieux, Pgh.	4.50
☐	20	Mike Liut (G), Hfd.	.35
☐	21	Hakan Loob, Cgy.	.20
☐	22	Al MacInnis, Cgy.	.35
☐	23	Paul MacLean, Wpg.	.20
☐	24	Brad McCrimmon, Cgy.	.20
☐	25	Mark Messier, Edm.	1.50
☐	26	Mats Naslund, Mtl.	.35
☐	27	Cam Neely, Bos.	.60
☐	28	Bernie Nicholls, L.A.	.35
☐	29	Joe Nieuwendyk, Cgy.	.50
☐	30	Pete Peeters (G), Wsh.	.35
☐	31	Stéphane Richer, Mtl.	.50
☐	32	Luc Robitaille, L.A.	.50
☐	33	Patrick Roy (G), Mtl.	4.50
☐	34	Denis Savard, Chi.	.35
☐	35	Ray Sheppard, Buf.	.50
☐	36	Craig Simpson, Edm.	.20
☐	37	Peter Stastny, Que.	.35
☐	38	Greg Stefan (G), Det.	.35
☐	39	Scott Stevens, Wsh.	.35
☐	40	Gary Suter, Cgy.	.35
☐	41	Petr Svoboda, Mtl.	.20
☐	42	John Vanbiesbrouck (G), NYR.	2.50
☐	43	Pat Verbeek, N.J.	.35
☐	44	Mike Vernon (G), Cgy.	.35
☐	45	Carey Wilson, Hfd.	.20
☐	46	Checklist (1-46)	.35

1988 - 89 O-PEE-CHEE STICKERS

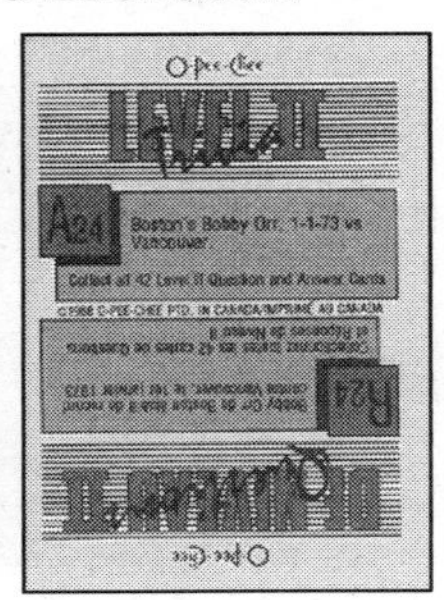

Sticker Size: 2 1/2" x 3 1/2"
Imprint: © 1988 O-PEE-CHEE CO. LTD.
Complete Set (152 stickers): 25.00
Common Player: .15
Album: 5.00

	No.	Player	NRMT-MT
☐	1	Wayne Gretzky, L.A., M.V.P.	3.00
☐	2	Oilers vs Bruins	.15
☐	3	Oilers vs Bruins	.15
☐	4	Oilers vs Bruins	.15
☐	5	Oilers vs Bruins	.15

Note: Stickers 2-5 feature Keith Crowder, Steve Smith and Grant Fuhr.

	No.	Player	NRMT-MT
☐	12	Steve Larmer, Chi.	.15
☐	13	Denis Savard, Chi.	.15
☐	20	Doug Gilmour, Stl.	1.00
☐	21	Bernie Federko, Stl.	.20
☐	22	Cam Neely, Bos.	.50
☐	23	Ray Bourque, Bos.	1.00
☐	30	Keith Crowder/Steve Kasper	.15
☐	31	Canadiens vs Bruins	.15
☐	32	Canadiens vs Bruins	.15

Note: Stickers 31-32 feature Patrick Roy (G)/Bob Sweeney.

	No.	Player	NRMT-MT
☐	33	Blues vs Devils	.15
☐	34	Canadiens vs Bruins	.15
☐	35	Canadiens vs Bruins	.15
☐	36	Canadiens vs Bruins	.15
☐	37	Canadiens vs Bruins	.15

Note: Stickers 34-37 feature Réjean Lemelin, Ray Bourque, Larry Robinson and Bob Sweeney.

	No.	Player	NRMT-MT
☐	38	Brian Skrudland/Ray Bourque	.15
☐	45	Patrick Roy (G), Mtl.	2.50
☐	46	Bobby Smith, Mtl.	.20
☐	49	Stéphane Richer, Mtl.	.20
☐	50	Mats Naslund, Mtl.	.25
☐	51	Chris Chelios, Mtl.	1.00
☐	52	Brian Hayward (G), Mtl.	.20
☐	59	Tony Tanti, Van.	.15
☐	60	Stan Smyl, Van.	.20
☐	63	Doug Lidster, Van.	.15
☐	64	Petri Skriko, Van.	.15
☐	65	Barry Pederson, Van.	.15
☐	66	Greg Adams, Van.	.15
☐	67	Mike Gartner, Wsh.	.50
☐	68	Scott Stevens, Wsh.	.15
☐	75	Kirk Muller, N.J.	.15
☐	76	Aaron Broten, N.J.	.15
☐	89	Gary Suter, Cgy.	.20
☐	90	Joe Nieuwendyk, Cgy.	.50
☐	93	Mike Bullard, Cgy.	.15
☐	94	Hakan Loob, Cgy.	.15
☐	95	Joe Mullen, Cgy.	.50
☐	96	Brad McCrimmon, Cgy.	.15
☐	103	Ron Hextall (G), Pha.	.50
☐	104	Mark Howe, Pha.	.20
☐	111	Pat LaFontaine, NYI.	.50
☐	112	Bryan Trottier, NYI.	.25
☐	143	Dale Hawerchuk, Wpg.	.35
☐	144	Paul MacLean, Wpg.	.15
☐	147	Andrew McBain, Wpg.	.15
☐	148	Randy Carlyle, Wpg.	.15
☐	149	Daniel Berthiaume (G), Wpg.	.25
☐	150	Dave Ellett, Wpg.	.15
☐	157	Luc Robitaille, L.A.	.75
☐	158	Jimmy Carson, L.A.	.15
☐	159	Randy Burridge/Patrick Roy (G)	1.50
☐	160	Nordiques vs Devils	.15
☐	161	Nordiques vs Devils	.15

Note: Stickers 160-161 feature Randy Moller, Claude Loiselle, Paul Gillis, Dave Maley, Clint Malarchuk, and Robert Picard.

	No.	Player	NRMT-MT
☐	162	A. Chevrier/B. MacLellan/G. Mark	.15
☐	163	Oilers vs Devils	.15
☐	164	Oilers vs Devils	.15
☐	165	Oilers vs Devils	.15
☐	166	Oilers vs Devils	.15

Note: Stickers 163-166 feature Grant Fuhr, Kevin Lowe, Craig Muni, Patrik Sundstrom and Doug Sulliman.

	No.	Player	NRMT-MT
☐	167	C. Neely/P. Roy (G)	1.50
☐	174	Borje Salming, Tor.	.25
☐	175	Russ Courtnall, Tor.	.15
☐	178	Gary Leeman, Tor.	.15
☐	179	Al Secord, Tor.	.15
☐	180	Al Iafrate, Tor.	.15
☐	181	Ed Olczyk, Tor.	.15
☐	188	Michel Goulet, Que.	.35
☐	189	Peter Stastny, Que.	.35
☐	192	Jeff Brown, Que.	.35
☐	193	Mario Gosselin (G), Que.	.25
☐	194	Anton Stastny, Que.	.15
☐	195	Alan Haworth, Que.	.15
☐	202	Dino Ciccarelli, Min.	.35
☐	203	Brian Bellows, Min.	.15
☐	214	Brian Hayward/Patrick Roy (G), Mtl.	1.50
☐	223	Grant Fuhr (G), Edm.	.50
☐	224	Wayne Gretzky, Edm.	3.50
☐	227	Jari Kurri, Edm.	.50
☐	228	Craig Simpson, Edm.	.15
☐	229	Glenn Anderson, Edm.	.25
☐	230	Mark Messier, Edm.	1.00
☐	231	Randy Cunneyworth, Pgh.	.25
☐	232	Mario Lemieux, Pgh.	3.00
☐	239	Kelly Kisio, NYR.	.15
☐	240	Walt Poddubny, NYR.	.15
☐	253	Steve Yzerman, Det.	1.50
☐	254	Gerald Gallant, Det.	.15
☐	261	Dave Andreychuk, Buf.	.35
☐	262	Ray Sheppard, Buf.	.15
☐	263	Mike Liut (G), Hfd.	.25
☐	264	Ron Francis, Hfd.	.50

MULTIPLE STICKERS

	No.	Player	NRMT-MT
☐	6/135	Doug Wilson, Chi./Darren Pang (G), Chi.	.25
☐	7/136	Dirk Graham, Chi./Kirk McLean (G), Van.	.75
☐	8/137	Darren Pang (G), Chi./Doug Smail, Wpg.	.25
☐	9/138	Rick Vaive, Chi./Thomas Steen, Wpg.	.20
☐	10/139	Troy Murray, Chi./Laurie Boschman, Wpg.	.20
☐	11/140	Brian Noonan, Chi./Iain Duncan, Wpg.	.25
☐	14/141	Mark Hunter, Stl./Ray Neufeld, Wpg.	.20
☐	15/142	Brian Sutter, Stl./Mario Marois, Wpg.	.20
☐	16/145	Brett Hull, Stl./Jim Kyte, Wpg.	2.50
☐	17/146	Tony McKegney, Stl./Eldon Reddick (G), Wpg.	.25
☐	18/151	Brian Benning, Stl./Rollie Melanson (G), L.A.	.25
☐	19/152	Tony Hrkac, Stl./Steve Duchesne, L.A.	.25
☐	24/153	Réjean Lemelin (G), Bos./Bob Carpenter, L.A.	.25
☐	25/154	Gord Kluzak, Bos./Jim Fox, L.A.	.20
☐	26/155	Rick Middleton, Bos./Dave Taylor, L.A.	.20
☐	27/156	Steve Kasper, Bos./Bernie Nicholls, L.A.	.20
☐	28/168	Bob Sweeney, Bos./Mark Osborne, Tor.	.20
☐	29/169	Randy Burridge, Bos./Dan Daoust, Tor.	.20
☐	39/170	Larry Robinson, Mtl./Tom Fergus, Tor.	.35
☐	40/171	Ryan Walter, Mtl./Vincent Damphousse, Tor.	.50
☐	41/172	Guy Carbonneau, Mtl./Wendel Clark, Tor.	.50
☐	42/173	Bob Gainey, Mtl./Luke Richardson, Tor.	.35
☐	43/176	Claude Lemieux, Mtl./Rick Lanz, Tor.	.20
☐	44/177	Petr Svoboda, Mtl./Ken Wregget (G), Tor.	.25
☐	47/182	Mike McPhee, Mtl./Normand Rochefort, Que.	.20
☐	48/183	Craig Ludwig, Mtl./Lane Lambert, Que.	.20
☐	53/184	Larry Melnyk, Van./Tommy Albelin, Que.	.20
☐	54/185	Garth Butcher, Van./Jason Lafrenière, Que.	.20
☐	55/186	Kirk McLean (G), Van./Alain Côté, Que.	.75
☐	56/187	Doug Wickenheiser, Van./Gaetan Duchesne, Que.	.20
☐	57/190	Rich Sutter, Van./Jeff Jackson, Que.	.20
☐	58/191	Jim Benning, Van./Mike Eagles, Que.	.20
☐	61/196	David Saunders, Van./Don Beaupré (G), Min.	.25
☐	62/197	Steve Tambellini, Van./Brian MacLellan, Min.	.20
☐	69/198	Rod Langway, Wsh./Brian Lawton, Min.	.20
☐	70/199	Dave Christian, Wsh./Craig Hartsburg, Min.	.25
☐	71/200	Larry Murphy, Wsh./Moe Mantha, Min.	.35
☐	72/201	Clint Malarchuk (G), Wsh./Neal Broten, Min.	.20
☐	73/204	Dale Hunter, Wsh./Mario Lemieux, Pgh.	2.00
☐	74/205	Mike Ridley, Wsh./Joe Nieuwendyk, Cgy.	.50
☐	77/206	Bruce Driver, N.J./Brad McCrimmon, Cgy.	.20
☐	78/207	John MacLean, N.J./Pete Peeters (G), Wsh.	.25
☐	79/208	Joe Cirella, N.J./Ray Bourque, Bos.	.50
☐	80/209	Doug Brown, N.J./Guy Carbonneau, Mtl.	.20
☐	81/210	Pat Verbeek, N.J./Mario Lemieux, Pgh.	2.00
☐	82/211	Sean Burke (G), N.J./Mario Lemieux, Pgh.	2.50
☐	83/212	Joel Otto, Cgy./Grant Fuhr (G), Edm.	.50
☐	84/213	Rob Ramage, Cgy./Bob Bourne, L.A.	.20
☐	85/215	Lanny McDonald, Cgy./Mats Naslund, Mtl.	.25
☐	86/216	Mike Vernon (G), Cgy./Joe Nieuwendyk, Cgy.	1.00
☐	87/217	John Tonelli, Cgy./Craig MacTavish, Edm.	.20
☐	88/218	Jim Peplinski, Cgy./Chris Joseph, Edm.	.20
☐	91/219	Ric Nattress, Cgy./Kevin Lowe, Edm.	.25
☐	92/220	Al MacInnis, Cgy./Esa Tikkanen, Edm.	.35
☐	97/221	Brian Propp, Pha./Charlie Huddy, Edm.	.20
☐	98/222	Murray Craven, Pha./Geoff Courtnall, Edm.	.25
☐	99/225	Rick Tocchet, Pha./Steve Smith, Edm.	.20
☐	100/226	Doug Crossman, Pha./Mike Krushelnyski, Edm.	.20
☐	101/233	Brad Marsh, Pha./Paul Coffey, Pgh.	.35
☐	102/234	Peter Zezel, Pha./Doug Bodger, Pgh.	.20
☐	105/235	Brent Sutter, NYI./Dave Hunter, Pgh.	.20
☐	106/236	Alan Kerr, NYI./Dan Quinn, Pgh.	.20
☐	107/237	Randy Wood, NYI./Rob Brown, Pgh.	.20
☐	108/238	Mikko Makelä, NYI./Gilles Meloche (G), Pgh.	.25
☐	109/241	Kelly Hrudey (G), NYI./John Vanbiesbrouck (G), NYR.	1.50
☐	110/242	Steve Konroyd, NYI./Tomas Sandstrom, NYR.	.20
☐	113/243	Gary Suter, Cgy./David Shaw, NYR.	.20
☐	114/244	Luc Robitaille, L.A./Marcel Dionne, NYR.	.50
☐	115/245	Patrick Roy (G), Mtl./Chris Nilan, NYR.	1.50
☐	116/246	Mario Lemieux, Pgh./James Patrick, NYR.	2.00
☐	117/247	Ray Bourque, Bos./Bob Probert, Det.	.50
☐	118/248	Hakan Loob, Cgy./Mike O'Connell, Det.	.20
☐	119/249	Mike Bullard, Cgy./Jeff Sharples, Det.	.20
☐	120/250	Brad McCrimmon, Cgy./Brent Ashton, Det.	.20
☐	121/251	Wayne Gretzky, L.A./Petr Klima, Det.	3.50
☐	122/252	Grant Fuhr (G), Edm./Greg Stefan (G), Det.	.35
☐	123/255	Craig Simpson, Edm./Phil Housley, Buf.	.20
☐	124/256	Mark Howe, Pha./Christian Ruuttu, Buf.	.20
☐	125/257	Joe Nieuwendyk, Cgy./Mike Foligno, Buf.	.75
☐	126/258	Ray Sheppard, Buf./Scott Arniel, Buf.	.50
☐	127/259	Brett Hull, Stl./Tom Barrasso (G), Buf.	2.50
☐	128/260	Ulf Dahlen, NYR./Mike Ramsey, Buf.	.20
☐	129/265	Tony Hrkac, Stl./Ulf Samuelsson, Hfd.	.35
☐	130/266	Bob Sweeney, Bos./Carey Wilson, Hfd.	.20
☐	131/267	Rob Brown, Pgh./Dave Babych, Hfd.	.25
☐	132/268	Iain Duncan, Wpg./Ray Ferraro, Hfd.	.20
☐	133/269	Pierre Turgeon, Buf./Kevin Dineen, Hfd.	2.00
☐	134/270	Calle Johansson, Buf./John Anderson, Hfd.	.20

FUTURE STARS

These "Future Stars" insert cards appear on the back of sticker nos. 53/184, 23, 63, 158, 126/258, 108/238, 123/255, 36, 81/210, 90, 254, 189, 11/140, 134/270, 147, 18/151, 74/205, 161, 68, 69/198, 85/215, 202. After the sticker has been removed you are left with the insert card.

Card Size: 2 1/8" x 3"
Insert Set (22 cards): 13.00

	No.	Player	NRMT-MT
☐	1	Dave Archibald, Min.	.25
☐	2	Doug Brown, N.J.	.25
☐	3	Rob Brown, Pgh.	.25
☐	4	Sean Burke (G), N.J.	.75
☐	5	Ulf Dahlen, NYR.	.25
☐	6	Iain Duncan, Wpg.	.25
☐	7	Glenn Healy (G), L.A.	.50
☐	8	Tony Hrkac, Stl.	.25
☐	9	Brett Hull, Stl.	4.00
☐	10	Craig Janney, Bos.	1.00
☐	11	Calle Johansson, Buf.	.25
☐	12	Brian Leetch, NYR.	3.00
☐	13	Kirk McLean (G), Van.	.75
☐	14	Joe Nieuwendyk, Cgy.	1.00
☐	15	Brian Noonan, Chi. (/b:147)	.50
☐	16	Darren Pang (G), Chi.	.50
☐	17	Jeff Sharples, Det.	.25
☐	18	Ray Sheppard, Buf.	1.00

No.	Player	NRMT-MT
19	Bob Sweeney, Bos.	.25
20	Pierre Turgeon, Buf.	2.25
21	Glen Wesley, Bos.	.50
22	Randy Wood, NYI.	.25

1988 - 89 PANINI STICKERS

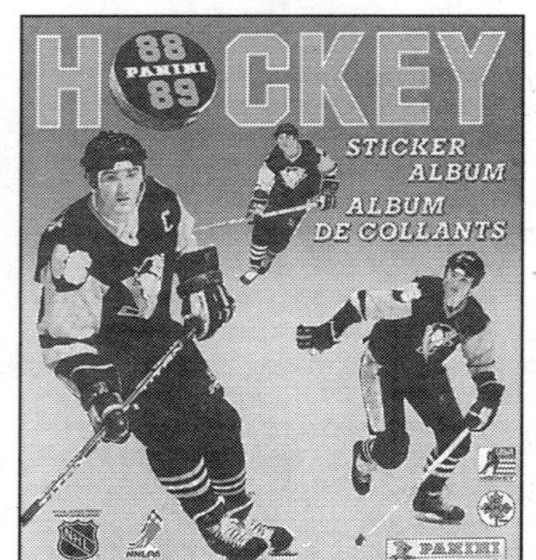

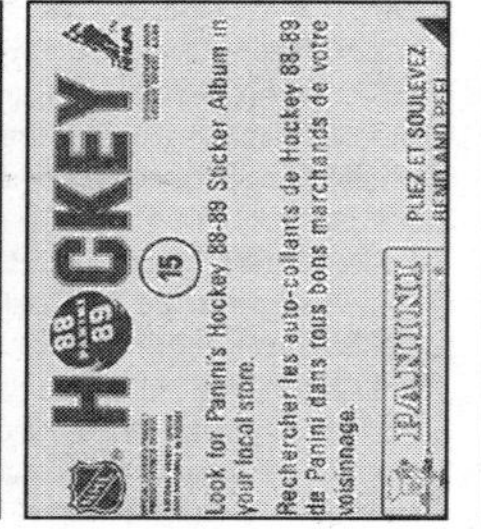

Sticker Size: 2 1/8" x 2 15/16"
Imprint: PANINI
Complete Set (408 stickers): **40.00**
Common Player: **.15**
Album (Mario Lemieux): **10.00**

No.	Player	NRMT-MT
1	Road to the Cup Stanley Cup Draw	.15
2	Calgary Flames Team Logo	.15
3	Calgary Flames Uniform	.15
4	Mike Vernon (G), Cgy.	.50
5	Al MacInnis, Cgy.	.25
6	Brad McCrimmon, Cgy.	.15
7	Gary Suter, Cgy.	.15
8	Mike Bullard, Cgy.	.15
9	Hakan Loob, Cgy.	.15
10	Lanny McDonald, Cgy.	.20
11	Joe Mullen, Cgy.	.25
12	Joe Nieuwendyk, Cgy.	1.00
13	Joel Otto, Cgy.	.15
14	Jim Peplinski, Cgy.	.20
15	Gary Roberts, Cgy.	.50
16	Calgary Flames Team Photo	.15
17	Calgary Flames Team Photo	.15
18	Chicago Blackhawks Team Logo	.15
19	Chicago Blackhawks Uniform	.15
20	Bob Mason (G), Chi.	.20
21	Darren Pang (G), Chi.	.25
22	Rob Murray, Chi.	.15
23	Gary Nylund, Chi.	.15
24	Doug Wilson, Chi.	.15
25	Dirk Graham, Chi.	.15
26	Steve Larmer, Chi.	.25
27	Troy Murray, Chi.	.15
28	Brian Noonan, Chi.	.25
29	Denis Savard, Chi.	.35
30	Steve Thomas, Chi.	.20
31	Rick Vaive, Chi.	.15
32	Chicago Blackhawks Team	.15
33	Chicago Blackhawks Team	.15
34	Detroit Red Wings Team Logo	.15
35	Detroit Red Wings Uniform	.15
36	Glen Hanlon (G), Det.	.20
37	Greg Stefan (G), Det.	.20
38	Jeff Sharples, Det.	.15
39	Darren Veitch, Det.	.15
40	Brent Ashton, Det.	.15
41	Shawn Burr, Det.	.15
42	John Chabot, Det.	.15
43	Gerard Gallant, Det.	.15
44	Petr Klima, Det.	.15
45	Adam Oates, Det.	1.25
46	Bob Probert, Det.	.50
47	Steve Yzerman, Det.	2.00
48	Detroit Red Wings Team Photo	.15
49	Detroit Red Wings Team Photo	.15
50	Edmonton Oilers Team Logo	.15
51	Edmonton Oilers Uniform	.15
52	Grant Fuhr (G), Edm.	.35
53	Charlie Huddy, Edm.	.15
54	Kevin Lowe, Edm.	.20
55	Steve Smith, Edm.	.15
56	Jeff Beukeboom, Edm.	.15
57	Glenn Anderson, Edm.	.20
58	Wayne Gretzky, Edm.	3.50
59	Jari Kurri, Edm.	.25
60	Craig MacTavish, Edm.	.15
61	Mark Messier, Edm.	1.00
62	Craig Simpson, Edm.	.15
63	Esa Tikkanen, Edm.	.25
64	Edmonton Oilers Team Photo	.15
65	Edmonton Oilers Team Photo	.15
66	Los Angeles Kings Team Logo	.15
67	Los Angeles Kings Uniform	.15
68	Glenn Healy (G), L.A.	.50
69	Rollie Melanson (G), L.A.	.20
70	Steve Duchesne, L.A.	.50
71	Thomas Laidlaw, L.A.	.15
72	Jay Wells, L.A.	.15
73	Mike Allison, L.A.	.15
74	Bobby Carpenter, L.A.	.15
75	Jimmy Carson, L.A.	.20
76	Jim Fox, L.A.	.15
77	Bernie Nicholls, L.A.	.35
78	Luc Robitaille, L.A.	.75
79	Dave Taylor, L.A.	.20
80	Los Angeles Kings Team Photo	.15
81	Los Angeles Kings Team Photo	.15
82	Minnesota North Stars Team Logo	.15
83	Minnesota North Stars Uniform	.15
84	Don Beaupré (G), Min.	.20
85	Kari Takko (G), Min.	.20
86	Craig Hartsburg, Min.	.25
87	Frantisek Musil, Min.	.15
88	Dave Archibald, Min.	.15
89	Brian Bellows, Min.	.25
90	Scott Bjugstad, Min.	.15
91	Bob Brooke, Min.	.15
92	Neal Broten, Min.	.25
93	Dino Ciccarelli, Min.	.25
94	Brian Lawton, Min.	.15
95	Brian MacLellan, Min.	.15
96	Minnesota North Stars Team Photo	.15
97	Minnesota North Stars Team Photo	.15
98	St. Louis Blues Team Logo	.15
99	St. Louis Blues Uniform	.15
100	Greg Millen (G), Stl.	.20
101	Brian Benning, Stl.	.15
102	Gord Roberts, Stl.	.15
103	Gino Cavallini, Stl.	.15
104	Bernie Federko, Stl.	.25
105	Doug Gilmour, Stl.	.75
106	Tony Hrkac, Stl.	.15
107	Brett Hull, Stl.	4.50
108	Mark Hunter, Stl.	.15
109	Tony McKegney, Stl.	.15
110	Rick Meagher, Stl.	.15
111	Brian Sutter, Stl.	.25
112	St. Louis Blues Team Photo	.15
113	St. Louis Blues Team Photo	.15
114	Toronto Maple Leafs Team Logo	.15
115	Toronto Maple Leafs Uniform	.15
116	Allan Bester (G), Tor.	.20
117	Ken Wregget (G), Tor.	.35
118	Al Iafrate, Tor.	.15
119	Luke Richardson, Tor.	.15
120	Borje Salming, Tor.	.25
121	Wendel Clark, Tor.	.60
122	Russ Courtnall, Tor.	.20
123	Vincent Damphousse, Tor.	.75
124	Dan Daoust, Tor.	.15
125	Gary Leeman, Tor.	.15
126	Ed Olczyk, Tor.	.15
127	Mark Osborne, Tor.	.15
128	Toronto Maple Leafs Team Photo	.15
129	Toronto Maple Leafs Team Photo	.15
130	Vancouver Canucks Team Logo	.15
131	Vancouver Canucks Uniform	.15
132	Kirk McLean (G), Van.	.60
133	Jim Benning, Van.	.15
134	Garth Butcher, Van.	.15
135	Doug Lidster, Van.	.15
136	Greg Adams, Van.	.20
137	David Bruce, Van.	.15
138	Barry Pederson, Van.	.15
139	Jim Sandlak, Van.	.10
140	Petri Skriko, Van.	.15
141	Stan Smyl, Van.	.20
142	Rich Sutter, Van.	.15
143	Tony Tanti, Van.	.20
144	Vancouver Canucks Team Photo	.15
145	Vancouver Canucks Team Photo	.15
146	Winnipeg Jets Team Logo	.15
147	Winnipeg Jets Uniform	.15
148	Daniel Berthiaume (G), Wpg.	.20
149	Randy Carlyle, Wpg.	.15
150	Dave Ellett, Wpg.	.15
151	Mario Marois, Wpg.	.15
152	Peter Taglianetti, Wpg.	.15
153	Laurie Boschman, Wpg.	.15
154	Iain Duncan, Wpg.	.15
155	Dale Hawerchuk, Wpg.	.35
156	Paul MacLean, Wpg.	.15
157	Andrew McBain, Wpg.	.15
158	Doug Smail, Wpg.	.15
159	Thomas Steen, Wpg.	.15
160	Winnipeg Jets Team Photo	.15
161	Winnipeg Jets Team Photo	.15
162	Prince of Wales Trophy	.15
163	Washington Defeats Flyers	.15
164	Boston Beat Montréal	.15
165	Devils Skate Past the Capitals	.15
166	Bruins Were Victorious Over New Jersey	.15
167	Bruins Were Victorious Over New Jersey	.15
168	Calgary Too Much For Kings	.15
169	Clarence S. Campbell Bowl	.15
170	Edmonton Put Out Flames	3.00
171	Detroit Defeats St. Louis	.15
172	Oilers Overpowered Detroit	.15
173	Oilers Overpowered Detroit	.15
174	Edmonton Celebrate a Victory in Game 1	.15
175	Game 2, Oilers Eyed Another Victory	.15
176	Stanley Cup	.15
177	Stanley Cup	.15
178	Gretzky & Teammates Take a Commanding 3-0 Lead in Boston	.30
179	Gretzky & Teammates Take a Commanding 3-0 Lead in Boston	1.50
180	Gretzky & Teammates Take a Commanding 3-0 Lead in Boston	.30
181	Wayne Gretzky, Edm., M.V.P.	3.00
182	Conn Smythe Trophy	.15
183	Edmonton Oilers Celebrate	.15
184	Edmonton Oilers Celebrate	.15
185	Edmonton Oilers Celebrate	.15
186	Edmonton Oilers Celebrate	.15

Note: cards 183-186 feature Geoff Courtnall.

No.	Player	NRMT-MT
187	Calgary Flames Action	.15
188	Grant Fuhr (G), Edm.	.35
189	New Jersey Devils Action	.15
190	Marcel Dionne	.25
191	Bruins Action	.15
192	Washington Capitals Action	.15
193	Wayne Gretzky	3.00
194	Winnipeg Jets	.15
195	Boston Bruins	.15
196	St. Louis Blues	.15
197	Philadelphia Flyers vs Washington Capitals	.15
198	New York Islanders	.15
199	Calgary Flames	.15
200	Pittsburgh Penguins	.15
201	Boston Bruins Team Logo	.15
202	Boston Bruins Uniform	.15
203	Réjean Lemelin (G), Bos.	.20
204	Ray Bourque, Bos.	.50
205	Gord Kluzak, Bos.	.15
206	Michael Thelven, Bos.	.15
207	Glen Wesley, Bos.	.15
208	Randy Burridge, Bos.	.15

	No.	Player	Value
☐	209	Keith Crowder, Bos.	.15
☐	210	Steve Kasper, Bos.	.15
☐	211	Ken Linseman, Bos.	.15
☐	212	Jay Miller, Bos.	.15
☐	213	Cam Neely, Bos.	.60
☐	214	Bob Sweeney, Bos.	.15
☐	215	Boston Bruins Team Photo	.15
☐	216	Boston Bruins Team Photo	.15
☐	217	Buffalo Sabres Team Logo	.15
☐	218	Buffalo Sabres Uniform	.15
☐	219	Tom Barrasso (G), Buf.	.25
☐	220	Phil Housley, Buf.	.25
☐	221	Calle Johansson, Buf.	.25
☐	222	Mike Ramsey, Buf.	.15
☐	223	Dave Andreychuk, Buf.	.50
☐	224	Scott Arniel, Buf.	.15
☐	225	Adam Creighton, Buf.	.15
☐	226	Mike Foligno, Buf.	.15
☐	227	Christian Ruuttu, Buf.	.15
☐	228	Ray Sheppard, Buf.	1.00
☐	229	John Tucker, Buf.	.15
☐	230	Pierre Turgeon, Buf.	2.00
☐	231	Buffalo Sabres Team Photo	.15
☐	232	Buffalo Sabres Team Photo	.15
☐	233	Hartford Whalers Team Logo	.15
☐	234	Hartford Whalers Uniform	.15
☐	235	Mike Liut (G), Hfd.	.25
☐	236	Dave Babych, Hfd.	.50
☐	237	Sylvain Côté, Hfd.	.15
☐	238	Ulf Samuelsson, Hfd.	.25
☐	239	John Anderson, Hfd.	.15
☐	240	Kevin Dineen, Hfd.	.15
☐	241	Ray Ferraro, Hfd.	.15
☐	242	Ron Francis, Hfd.	.50
☐	243	Paul MacDermid, Hfd.	.15
☐	244	Dave Tippett, Hfd.	.15
☐	245	Sylvain Turgeon, Hfd.	.15
☐	246	Carey Wilson, Hfd.	.15
☐	247	Hartford Whalers Team Photo	.15
☐	248	Hartford Whalers Team Photo	.15
☐	249	Montréal Canadiens Team Logo	.15
☐	250	Montréal Canadiens Uniform	.15
☐	251	Brian Hayward (G), Mtl.	.20
☐	252	Patrick Roy (G), Mtl.	2.50
☐	253	Chris Chelios, Mtl.	.50
☐	254	Craig Ludwig, Mtl.	.15
☐	255	Petr Svoboda, Mtl.	.15
☐	256	Guy Carbonneau, Mtl.	.15
☐	257	Claude Lemieux, Mtl.	.15
☐	258	Mike McPhee, Mtl.	.15
☐	259	Mats Naslund, Mtl.	.20
☐	260	Stéphane Richer, Mtl.	.50
☐	261	Bobby Smith, Mtl.	.10
☐	262	Ryan Walter, Mtl.	.15
☐	263	Montréal Canadiens Team Photo	.15
☐	264	Montréal Canadiens Team Photo	.15
☐	265	New Jersey Devils Team Logo	.15
☐	266	New Jersey Devils Uniform	.15
☐	267	Sean Burke (G), N.J.	.75
☐	268	Joe Cirella, N.J.	.15
☐	269	Bruce Driver, N.J.	.15
☐	270	Craig Wolanin, N.J.	.15
☐	271	Aaron Broten, N.J.	.15
☐	272	Doug Brown, N.J.	.15
☐	273	Claude Loiselle, N.J.	.15
☐	274	John MacLean, N.J.	.20
☐	275	Kirk Muller, N.J.	.25
☐	276	Brendan Shanahan, N.J.	5.00
☐	277	Patrik Sundstrom, N.J.	.15
☐	278	Pat Verbeek, N.J.	.15
☐	279	New Jersey Devils Team Photo	.15
☐	280	New Jersey Devils Team Photo	.15
☐	281	New York Islanders Team Logo	.15
☐	282	New York Islanders Uniform	.15
☐	283	Kelly Hrudey (G), NYI.	.25
☐	284	Steve Konroyd, NYI.	.15
☐	285	Ken Morrow, NYI.	.15
☐	286	Patrick Flatley, NYI.	.15
☐	287	Greg Gilbert, NYI.	.15
☐	288	Alan Kerr, NYI.	.15
☐	289	Derek King, NYI.	.15
☐	290	Pat LaFontaine, NYI.	.60
☐	291	Mikko Makelä, NYI.	.15
☐	292	Brent Sutter, NYI.	.20
☐	293	Bryan Trottier, NYI.	.25
☐	294	Randy Wood, NYI.	.15
☐	295	New York Islanders Team	.15
☐	296	New York Islanders Team	.15
☐	297	New York Rangers Team Logo	.15
☐	298	New York Rangers Uniform	.15
☐	299	Bob Froese (G), NYR.	.20
☐	300	John Vanbiesbrouck (G), NYR.	2.00
☐	301	Brian Leetch, NYR.	2.00
☐	302	Norm Maciver, NYR.	.25
☐	303	James Patrick, NYR.	.15
☐	304	Michel Petit, NYR.	.15
☐	305	Ulf Dahlen, NYR.	.15
☐	306	Jan Erixon, NYR.	.15
☐	307	Kelly Kisio, NYR.	.15
☐	308	Don Maloney, NYR.	.15
☐	309	Walt Poddubny, NYR.	.15
☐	310	Tomas Sandstrom, NYR.	.15
☐	311	New York Rangers Team Photo	.15
☐	312	New York Rangers Team Photo	.15
☐	313	Philadelphia Flyers Team Logo	.15
☐	314	Philadelphia Flyers Uniform	.15
☐	315	Ron Hextall (G), Pha.	.50
☐	316	Mark Howe, Pha.	.25
☐	317	Kerry Huffman, Pha.	.15
☐	318	Kjell Samuelsson, Pha.	.15
☐	319	Dave Brown, Pha.	.15
☐	320	Murray Craven, Pha.	.15
☐	321	Tim Kerr, Pha.	.15
☐	322	Scott Mellanby, Pha.	.15
☐	323	Dave Poulin, Pha.	.15
☐	324	Brian Propp, Pha.	.20
☐	325	Ilkka Sinisalo, Pha.	.15
☐	326	Rick Tocchet, Pha.	.50
☐	327	Philadelphia Flyers Team Photo	.15
☐	328	Philadelphia Flyers Team Photo	.15
☐	329	Pittsburgh Penguins Team Logo	.15
☐	330	Pittsburgh Penguins Uniform	.15
☐	331	Frank Pietrangelo (G), Pgh.	.25
☐	332	Doug Bodger, Pgh.	.15
☐	333	Paul Coffey, Pgh.	.50
☐	334	Jim Johnson, Pgh.	.15
☐	335	Ville Siren, Pgh.	.15
☐	336	Rob Brown, Pgh.	.20
☐	337	Randy Cunneyworth, Pgh.	.20
☐	338	Dan Frawley, Pgh.	.15
☐	339	Dave Hunter, Pgh.	.15
☐	340	Mario Lemieux, Pgh.	3.00
☐	341	Troy Loney, Pgh.	.15
☐	342	Dan Quinn, Pgh.	.15
☐	343	Pittsburgh Penguins Team Photo	.15
☐	344	Pittsburgh Penguins Team Photo	.15
☐	345	Québec Nordiques Team Logo	.15
☐	346	Québec Nordiques Uniform	.15
☐	347	Mario Gosselin (G), Que.	.20
☐	348	Tommy Albelin, Que.	.15
☐	349	Jeff Brown, Que.	.60
☐	350	Steven Finn, Que.	.15
☐	351	Randy Moller, Que.	.15
☐	352	Alain Côté, Que.	.15
☐	353	Gaetan Duchesne, Que.	.15
☐	354	Mike Eagles, Que.	.15
☐	355	Michel Goulet, Que.	.35
☐	356	Lane Lambert, Que.	.15
☐	357	Anton Stastny, Que.	.15
☐	358	Peter Stastny, Que.	.35
☐	359	Québec Nordiques Team Photo	.15
☐	360	Québec Nordiques Team Photo	.15
☐	361	Washington Capitals Team Logo	.15
☐	362	Washington Capitals Uniform	.15
☐	363	Clint Malarchuk (G), Wsh.	.20
☐	364	Pete Peeters (G), Wsh.	.20
☐	365	Kevin Hatcher, Wsh.	.50
☐	366	Rod Langway, Wsh.	.20
☐	367	Larry Murphy, Wsh.	.25
☐	368	Scott Stevens, Wsh.	.25
☐	369	Dave Christian, Wsh.	.15
☐	370	Mike Gartner, Wsh.	.35
☐	371	Bengt Gustafsson, Wsh.	.15
☐	372	Dale Hunter, Wsh.	.25
☐	373	Kelly Miller, Wsh.	.15
☐	374	Mike Ridley, Wsh.	.20
☐	375	Washington Capitals Team Photo	.15
☐	376	Washington Capitals Team Photo	.15
☐	377	Hockey Rink	.15
☐	378	Hockey Rink	.15
☐	379	Cross-checking	.15
☐	380	Elbowing	.15
☐	381	High-sticking	.15
☐	382	Holding	.15
☐	383	Hooking	.15
☐	384	Interference	.15
☐	385	Spearing	.15
☐	386	Tripping	.15
☐	387	Boarding	.15
☐	388	Charging	.15
☐	389	Delayed Calling of Penalty	.15
☐	390	Kneeing	.15
☐	391	Misconduct	.15
☐	392	Roughing	.15
☐	393	Slashing	.15
☐	394	Unsportsmanlike Conduct	.15
☐	395	Wash-out	.15
☐	396	Icing	.15
☐	397	Off-side	.15
☐	398	Wash-out	.15
☐	399	AW: Bob Bourne, Pgh.	.15
☐	400	AW: Mario Lemieux, Pgh.	2.25
☐	401	AW: Mario Lemieux, Pgh.	2.25
☐	402	AW: Brian Hayward/Patrick Roy, Mtl.	1.50
☐	403	AW: Grant Fuhr, Edm.	.25
☐	404	AW: Joe Nieuwendyk, Cgy.	.75
☐	405	AW: Ray Bourque, Bos.	.50
☐	406	AW: Mats Naslund, Mtl.	.20
☐	407	AW: Guy Carbonneau, Mtl.	.15
☐	408	AW: Brad McCrimmon, Cgy.	.15

1988 - 89 PRO CARDS TEAM SETS

These cards have a red border.

Face: Four colour, red border, League logo, Position

Back: Black on white card stock, Resume, Team Logo

Imprint: © 1988 ProCards, Inc.

Complete AHL Set (348 cards):	**100.00**
Complete IHL Set (119 cards):	**65.00**
Common Player:	**.35**

ADIRONDACK RED WINGS - AHL

Team Set (25 cards): 8.00

	Player	NRMT-MT
☐	John Blum	.35
☐	Jeff Brubaker	.35
☐	Dave Casey, Head Trainer	.35
☐	Tim Cheveldae (G)	1.00
☐	Lou Crawford	.35
☐	Bill Dineen, Coach	.35
☐	Peter Dineen	.35
☐	Rob Doyle	.35
☐	Murray Eaves	.35
☐	Brent Fedyk	1.00
☐	Joe Ferras	.35
☐	Mike Gober	.35
☐	Miroslav Ihnacak	.35
☐	Dave Korol	.35
☐	Dale Krentz	.35
☐	Randy McKay	1.00
☐	Glenn Merkosky	.35
☐	John Mokosak	.35
☐	Dean Morton	.35
☐	Rob Nichols	.35
☐	Tim Paris, Assistant Trainer	.35
☐	Mark Reimer (G)	.50
☐	Sam St. Laurent (G)	.50
☐	Daniel Shank	.35
☐	Dennis Smith	.35

BALTIMORE SKIPJACKS - AHL

Team Set (23 cards): 8.00

	Player	NRMT-MT
□	Robin Bawa	.35
□	Tim Bergland	.35
□	Shawn Cronin	.35
□	Frank Dimuzio	.35
□	Dallas Eakins	.50
□	David Farrish	.35
□	Chris Felix	.35
□	Lou Franceschetti	.35
□	Jeff Greenlaw	.35
□	Mark Hatcher	.35
□	Bill Houlder	.50
□	Doug Keans (G)	.50
□	Tyler Larter	.35
□	J.P. Mattingly, Trainer	.35
□	Scott McCrory	.35
□	Mike Millar	.35
□	Rob Murray	.35
□	Terry Murray, G.M./Coach	1.00
□	Mike Richard	.35
□	Steve Seftel	.35
□	Dave Sherrid, Head Trainer	.35
□	Shawn Simpson (G)	.50
□	Rob Whistle	.35

BINGHAMTON WHALERS - AHL

Team Set (24 cards): 8.00

	Player	NRMT-MT
□	Charles Bourgeois	.35
□	Chris Brant	.35
□	Richard Brodeur (G)	1.00
□	Lindsay Carson, Error (Lindsy)	.35
□	Gary Callaghan	.35
□	Brian Chapman	.35
□	Jim Culhane	.35
□	Mark Dumas, Equip. Manager	.35
□	Dallas Gaume	.35
□	Roger Kortko	.35
□	Todd Krygier	1.00
□	Marc Laforge	.35
□	Claude Larose, Coach	.35
□	Mark Lavarre	.35
□	Tom Mitchell, General Manager	.35
□	David O'Brien	.35
□	Mark Reeds	.35
□	Dave Rowbotham	.35
□	Jon Smith, Trainer	.35
□	Larry Trader	.35
□	Allan Tuer	.35
□	Mike Vellucci	.35
□	Kay Whitmore (G)	1.00
□	Terry Yake	1.00

CAPE BRETON OILERS - AHL

Team Set (24 cards): 8.00

	Player	NRMT-MT
□	Marlo Barbe	.35
□	Darren Beals (G)	.35
□	Nicholas Beaulieu	.35
□	Dan Currie	.35
□	Jim Ennis	.35
□	Larry Floyd	.35
□	Mike Glover	.35
□	David Haas	.35
□	John B. Hanna	.35
□	Kim Issel	.35
□	Fabian Joseph	.35
□	Mark Lamb	.50
□	Brad MacGregor	.35
□	Rob MacInnis	.35
□	Don Martin	.35
□	Alan May	.35
□	Jamie Nichols	.35
□	Selmar Odelein	.35
□	Daryl Reaugh (G)	.50
□	Dave Roach (G)	.50
□	Ron Shudra	.35
□	Shaun Van Allen (Black & White)	1.00
□	Mike Ware	.35
□	Jim Wiemer	.35

HALIFAX CITADELS - AHL

Team Set (23 cards): 8.00

	Player	NRMT-MT
□	Joel Baillargeon	.35
□	Gerald Bzdel	.35
□	Doug Carpenter, Coach/G.M.	.35
□	Bobby Dollas	.50
□	Marc Fortier	.35
□	Scott Gordon (G)	.50
□	Dean Hopkins	.35
□	Mike Hough	1.00
□	Claude Julien	.75
□	Darin Kimble	.35
□	Jacques Mailhot	.35
□	Ken McRae	.35
□	Max Middendorf	.35
□	Keith Miller	.35
□	Mike Natyshak	.35
□	Ken Quinney	.35
□	Jean-Marc Richard	.35
□	Jean-Marc Routhier	.35
□	Jaroslav Sevcik	.35
□	Brent Severyn	.50
□	Scott Shaunessy	.35
□	Ladislav Tresel	.35
□	Ron Tugnutt (G)	2.00

HERSHEY BEARS - AHL

Team Set (28 cards): 8.00

	Player	NRMT-MT
□	Don Biggs	.35
□	Brian Bucciarelli, Assistant Trainer	.35
□	J.J. Daigneault	.50
□	Marc D'Amour (G)	.50
□	David Fenyves	.35
□	Mark Freer	.35
□	Darryl Gilmour (G)	.35
□	Jeff Harding	.35
□	Warren Harper	.35
□	Kent Hawley	.35
□	Al Hill	.50
□	Tony Horacek	.35
□	Chris Jensen	.35
□	Craig Kitteringham	.35
□	Mark Lofthouse	.35
□	Frank Mathers, President/G.M.	.35
□	Kevin McCarthy, Assistant Coach	.50
□	Don Nachbaur	.35
□	Gordon Paddock	.35
□	John Paddock, Coach	.50
□	Jocelyn Perrault (G)	.35
□	Bruce Randall	.35
□	Shawn Sabol	.35
□	Glen Seabrooke	.50
□	John Stevens	.35
□	Mike Stothers	.35
□	Dan Stuck, Head Trainer	.35
□	Doug Yingst, Assist.General Manager	.35

MAINE MARINERS - AHL

Team Set (22 cards): 7.00

	Player	NRMT-MT
□	Paul Beraldo	.35
□	John Carter	.35
□	Phil Degaetano	.35
□	Scott Drevitch	.35
□	Joe Flaherty	.35
□	Doug Foerster, Public Relations/Tickets	.35
□	Norm Foster (G)	.50
□	Paul Guay	.35
□	Greg Hawgood	.50
□	Mike Jeffrey (G)	.50
□	Jeff Lamb	.35
□	Jean-Marc Lanthier	.35
□	Darren Lowe	.35
□	Carl Mokosak	.35
□	Mitch Molloy	.35
□	Mike Neill	.35
□	Ray Podloski	.35
□	Stéphane Quintal	1.00
□	Bruce Shoebottom	.35
□	Terry Taillefer (G)	.50
□	Steve Tsujiura	.35
□	Scott Wykoff, Broadcaster/ PR	.35

MONCTON HAWKS - AHL

Team Set (21 cards): 7.00

		Player	NRMT-MT
□	170	Stéphane Beauregard (G)	.50
□	171	Rick Bowness, Coach	1.00
□	172	Sean Clement	.35
□	173	Tom Draper (G)	.50
□	174	Wayne Flemming, Equipment Manager	.35
□	175	Steven Fletcher	.35
□	176	Todd Flichel	.35
□	177	Guy Gosselin	.35
□	178	Gilles Hamel	.35
□	179	Matt Hervey	.35
□	180	Brent Hughes	.35
□	181	Jamie Husgen	.35
□	182	Stuart Kulak	.35
□	183	Guy Larose	.35
□	184	Neil Meadmore	.35
□	185	Len Nielson	.35
□	186	Chris Norton	.35
□	187	Scott Schneider	.35
□	188	Rob Snitzer, Athletic Therapist	.35
□	189	Mike Warus	.35
□	190	Ron Wilson	.50

NEW HAVEN NIGHTHAWKS - AHL

Team Set (32 cards): 10.00

	Player	NRMT-MT
□	Ken Baumgartner	1.00
□	François Breault	.35
□	Mario Chitaroni	.35
□	Sylvain Couturier	.35
□	Rick Dudley, Head Coach	.50
□	John English	.35
□	Mark Fitzpatrick (G)	2.00
□	Eric Germain	.35
□	Dan Gratton	.35
□	Scott Green, Medical Trainer	.35
□	Pat Hickey, Director of Operations	.50
□	Brad Hyatt	.35
□	Paul Kelly	.35
□	Bob Kudelski	1.00
□	Denis Larocque	.35
□	Bob Logan	.35
□	Sal Lombardi, Athletic Trainer	.35
□	Al Loring (G)	.50
□	Hubie McDonough	.35
□	Chris Panek	.35
□	Dave Pasin	.35
□	Joe Paterson	.35
□	Lyle Phair	.35
□	Petr Prajsler	.35
□	Tom Pratt	.35
□	Steve Richmond	.35
□	Phil Sykes	.35
□	Tim Tookey	.35
□	John Tortorella, Assistant Coach	.35
□	Gordie Walker	.35
□	Brian Wilks	.35
□	Darryl Williams	.35

NEWMARKET SAINTS - AHL

Team Set (22 cards): 7.00

	Player	NRMT-MT
□	Tim Armstrong	.35
□	Tim Bernhardt (G)	.50
□	Brian Blad	.35
□	Mike Blaisdell	.35
□	Jack Capuano	.35
□	Marty Dallman	.35
□	Daryl Evans	.35
□	Paul Gagné	.35
□	Alan Hepple	.35
□	Brian Hoard	.35
□	Greg Hotham	.35
□	Wes Jarvis	.35
□	Trevor Jobe	.35
□	Mark Kirton	.35
□	Sean McKenna	.35
□	Jim Ralph (G), Error (stats missing)	.50
□	Jeff Reese (G)	.50
□	Bill Root	.35
□	Darryl Shannon	1.00
□	Doug Shedden	.35
□	Greg Terrion	.35
□	Ken Yaremchuk	.35

ROCHESTER AMERICANS - AHL

Team Set (24 cards): 8.00

	Player	NRMT-MT
☐	Shawn Anderson	.35
☐	Mikael Andersson	.50
☐	John Van Boxmeer, Coach	.50
☐	Paul Brydges	.35
☐	Jeff Capello	.35
☐	Jacques Cloutier (G)	.50
☐	Mike Donnelly	.50
☐	Richie Dunn	.35
☐	Mark Ferner	.35
☐	Jody Gage	.50
☐	François Guay	.35
☐	Jim Hofford	.35
☐	Jim Jackson	.35
☐	Kevin Kerr	.35
☐	Don McSween	.35
☐	Scott Metcalfe	.35
☐	Jeff Parker	.35
☐	Ken Priestlay	.35
☐	Rob Ray	1.00
☐	Steve Smith	.35
☐	Grant Tkachuk	.35
☐	Wayne Van Dorp	.35
☐	Darcy Wakaluk (G)	.75
☐	Mascot The Moose	.35

SHERBROOKE CANADIENS - AHL

Team Set (29 cards): 12.00

	Player	NRMT-MT
☐	Steve Bisson	.35
☐	Bobby Boulanger, Equip. Manager	.35
☐	Benoît Brunet	1.50
☐	Rob Bryden	.35
☐	José Charbonneau	.35
☐	Ron Chyzowski	.35
☐	J.J. Daigneault	.750
☐	Martin Desjardins	.35
☐	Donald Dufresne	.50
☐	Rocky Dundas	.35
☐	Randy Exelby (G)	.50
☐	Luc Gauthier	.35
☐	François Gravel (G)	.50
☐	Jean Hamel, Head Coach	.50
☐	Claude Larose, Assistant Coach	.50
☐	Stéphan Lebeau	.50
☐	Sylvain Lefebvre	2.00
☐	Jocelyn Lemieux	.35
☐	Jyrki Lumme	2.00
☐	Steven Martinson	.35
☐	Jim Nesich	.35
☐	Martin Nicoletti	.35
☐	Jacques Parent, Athletic Therapist	.35
☐	Mark Pederson	.35
☐	Stéphane Richer	.35
☐	Mario Roberge	.35
☐	Serge Roberge	.35
☐	Scott Sandelin	.35
☐	Marc Saumier	.35

SPRINGFIELD INDIANS - AHL

Team Set (25 cards): 10.00

	Player	NRMT-MT
☐	Bill Berg	.35
☐	Bruce Boudreau	.35
☐	Stu Burnie	.35
☐	Shawn Byram	.35
☐	Ralph Calvanese, Equipment Manager	.35
☐	Kerry Clark	.50
☐	Rod Dallman	.35
☐	Rob DiMaio	.75
☐	Shawn Evans	.35
☐	Jeff Finley	.35
☐	Tom Fitzgerald	.50
☐	Jeff Hackett (G)	5.00
☐	Dale Henry	.35
☐	Richard Kromm	.35
☐	Hank Lammens	.35
☐	Duncan MacPherson	.35
☐	George Maneluk (G)	.50
☐	Todd McLellan	.35
☐	Chris Prior	.35
☐	Jim Roberts, Coach	.50
☐	Vern Smith	.35
☐	Mike Stevens	.35
☐	Ed Tyburski, Head Trainer	.35
☐	Mike Walsh	.35
☐	Doug Weiss	.35

UTICA DEVILS - AHL

Team Set (24 cards): 8.00

	Player	NRMT-MT
☐	Robert Bill, Athletic Trainer	.35
☐	Craig Billington (G)	1.50
☐	John Blessman	.35
☐	Neil Brady	.35
☐	Murray Brumwell	.35
☐	Anders Carlsson	.35
☐	Chris Cichocki	.35
☐	Jeff Croop, Head Trainer	.35
☐	Dan Delianedls (G)	.50
☐	Dan Dorion	.35
☐	Jamie Huscroft	.35
☐	Marc Laniel	.35
☐	Tim Lenardon	.35
☐	Jeff Madill	.35
☐	David Marcinyshyn	.35
☐	Tom McVie, Coach	.50
☐	Scott Moon, Trainer's Assistant	.35
☐	Janne Ojanen	.35
☐	Alan Stewart	.35
☐	Chris Terreri (G)	2.00
☐	Kevin Todd	.50
☐	John Walker	.35
☐	Eric Weinrich	1.00
☐	Paul Ysebaert	1.00

INDIANAPOLIS ICE - IHL

Team Set (22 cards): 7.00

	Player	NRMT-MT
☐	Dave Allison	.50
☐	Rick Barkovich	.35
☐	Brad Beck	.35
☐	Geoff Benic	.35
☐	Graham Bonar	.35
☐	Rick Boyd	.35
☐	Scott Clements	.35
☐	Shane Doyle	.35
☐	Ron Handy	.35
☐	Archie Henderson	.35
☐	Paul Houck	.35
☐	Glen Johannesen	.35
☐	Bob Lakso	.35
☐	Jimmy Mann	.35
☐	Darwin McCutcheon	.35
☐	Chris McSorley	.50
☐	Rich Oberlin, Trainer	.35
☐	Alan Perry (G)	.50
☐	Brent Sapergia	.35
☐	Gary Stewart	.35
☐	Randy Taylor	.35
☐	Mark Teevens	.35

KALAMAZOO WINGS - IHL

Team Set (21 cards): 7.00

	Player	NRMT-MT
☐	Andy Akervik	.35
☐	Warren Babe	.35
☐	Darin Baker (G)	.50
☐	Mike Berger	.35
☐	Scott Bjugstad	.35
☐	Larry Dyck (G)	.50
☐	Ken Hodge	.50
☐	Joe Lockwood	.35
☐	Gary McColgan	.35
☐	Scott McCrady	.35
☐	Michael McHugh	.35
☐	Mitch Messier	.35
☐	Jarmo Myllys (G)	.75
☐	D'Arcy Norton	.35
☐	Stéphane Roy	.35
☐	Dave Schofield	.35
☐	Randy Smith	.35
☐	Kirk Tomlinson	.35
☐	Emanuel Viveiros	.35
☐	Neil Wilkinson	.50
☐	Rob Zettler	.50

MUSKEGON LUMBERJACKS - IHL

Team Set (23 cards): 20.00

	Player	NRMT-MT
☐	Brad Aitken	.35
☐	Jock Callander	.35
☐	Todd Charlesworth	.35
☐	Jeff Cooper (G)	.35
☐	Jeff Daniels	.35
☐	Greg Davies	.35
☐	Lee Giffin	.35
☐	Dave Goertz	.35
☐	Steve Gotaas	.35
☐	Scott Gruhl	.35
☐	Doug Hobson	.35
☐	Kevin MacDonald	.35
☐	Pat Mayer	.35
☐	Dave McLlwain	.50
☐	Dave Michayluk	.35
☐	Glenn Mulvenna	.35
☐	Jim Paek	.50
☐	Frank Pietrangelo (G)	.50
☐	Bruce Racine (G)	.50
☐	Mark Recchi	15.00
☐	Troy Vollhoffer	.35
☐	Jeff Waver	.35
☐	Mitch Wilson	.35

PEORIA RIVERMEN - IHL

Team Set (28 cards): 15.00

	Player	NRMT-MT
☐	Tim Bothwell	.50
☐	Kelly Chase	.35
☐	Peter Douris	.35
☐	Toby Ducolon	.35
☐	Greg Eberle, Head Trainer	.35
☐	Glen Featherstone	.35
☐	Wayne Gagne	.35
☐	Scott Harlow	.35
☐	Pat Jablonski (G)	1.00
☐	Dominic Lavoie	.35
☐	Dave Lowry	1.00
☐	Shane MacEachern	.35
☐	Terry MacLean	.35
☐	Darrell May (G)	.50
☐	Brad McCaughey	.35
☐	Ed McMurray, Assistant General Manager	.35
☐	Lyle Odelein	2.00
☐	Scott Paluch	.35
☐	Peoria Rivermen 1988-1989	.35
☐	Skip Probst, General Manager	.35
☐	Sheryl Reeves, Administration	.35
☐	Cliff Ronning	3.00
☐	Darin Smith	.35
☐	Wayne Thomas, Coach	.35
☐	Dave Thomlinson	.35
☐	Charlie Thompson, Sales Manager	.35
☐	Tony Twist	2.00
☐	Jim Vesey	.35

SAGINAW HAWKS - IHL

Team Set (25 cards): 30.00

	Player	NRMT-MT
☐	Ed Belfour (G)	20.00
☐	Bruce Cassidy	.35
☐	Chris Clifford (G)	.50
☐	Mario Doyon	.35
☐	Bill Gardner	.35
☐	Mark Kurzawski	.35
☐	Lonnie Loach	.50
☐	Steve Ludzik	.50
☐	David Mackey	.35
☐	Dale Marquette	.35
☐	Gary Moscaluk	.35
☐	Marty Nanne	.35
☐	Brian Noonan	2.00
☐	Mark Paterson	.35
☐	Kent Paynter	.35
☐	Guy Phillips	.35
☐	John Reid (G)	.35
☐	Mike Rucinski	.35
☐	Warren Rychel	.50
☐	Everett Sanipass	.35
☐	Mike Stapleton	.50
☐	Darryl Sutter, Coach	1.00
☐	Jari Torkki	.35

Player	NRMT-MT
Bill Watson	.35
Sean Williams	.35

1988 - 89 TOPPS

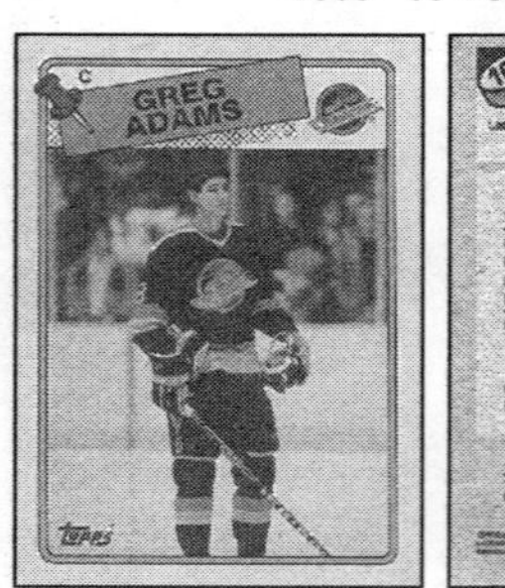

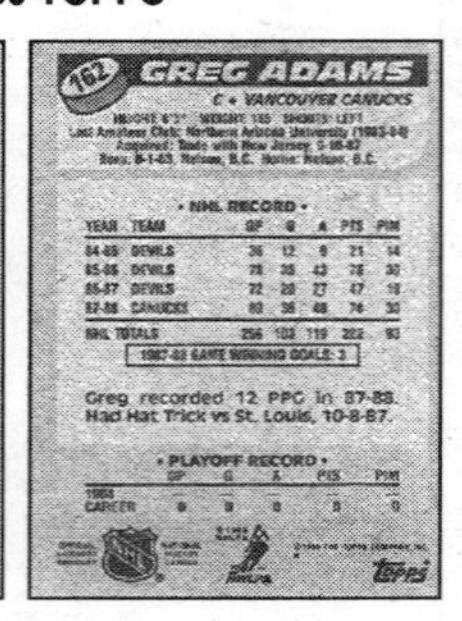

Imprint: © 1988 THE TOPPS COMPANY, INC.

Complete Set (198 cards): **90.00**
Common Player: **.15**
Double Prints (**): **.10**

No.	Player	NRMT-MT
1	Mario Lemieux, Pgh. (**)	6.00
2	**Bob Joyce, Bos., RC (**)**	**.10**
3	Joel Quenneville, Hfd. (**)	.15
4	Tony McKegney, Stl.	.15
5	Stéphane Richer, Mtl. (**)	.50
6	Mark Howe, Pha. (**)	.15
7	Brent Sutter, NYI. (**)	.15
8	Gilles Meloche (G), Pgh., LC (**)	.15
9	Jimmy Carson, Edm. (**)	.10
10	John MacLean, N.J.	.25
11	Gary Leeman, Tor.	.15
12	Gerard Gallant, Det. (**)	.10
13	Marcel Dionne, NYR., LC	.50
14	Dave Christian, Wsh. (**)	.10
15	Gary Nylund, Chi.	.15
16	**Joe Nieuwendyk, Cgy., RC**	**5.00**
17	Billy Smith (G), NYI., LC (**)	.25
18	Christian Ruuttu, Buf.	.15
19	Randy Cunneyworth, Pgh.	.25
20	Brian Lawton, Min.	.15
21	**Scott Mellanby, Pha., RC (**)**	**1.25**
22	Peter Stastny, Que. (**)	.25
23	Gord Kluzak, Bos.	.15
24	Sylvain Turgeon, Hfd.	.15
25	Clint Malarchuk (G), Wsh.	.20
26	Denis Savard, Chi.	.35
27	Craig Simpson, Edm.	.15
28	Petr Klima, Det.	.15
29	Pat Verbeek, N.J.	.20
30	Moe Mantha, Min.	.15
31	Chris Nilan, NYR.	.15
32	Barry Pederson, Van	.15
33	Randy Burridge, Bos.	.15
34	Ron Hextall (G), Pha.	1.50
35	Gaston Gingras, Stl.	.15
36	Kevin Dineen, Hfd.	.20
37	Thomas Laidlaw, L.A.	.15
38	Paul MacLean, Det. (**)	.10
39	John Chabot, Det. (**)	.10
40	Lindy Ruff, Buf.	.15
41	Dan Quinn, Pgh. (**)	.10
42	Don Beaupré (G), Min.	.20
43	Gary Suter, Cgy.	.20
44	**Mikko Makelä, NYI., RC (**)**	**.10**
45	Mark Johnson, N.J. (**)	.10
46	Dave Taylor, L.A. (**)	.20
47	**Ulf Dahlen, NYR., RC**	**1.00**
48	**Jeff Sharples, Det., RC**	**.15**
49	Chris Chelios, Mtl.	1.75
50	Mike Gartner, Wsh. (**)	.50
51	**Darren Pang (G), Chi., RC (**)**	**.20**
52	Ron Francis, Hfd.	1.25
53	Ken Morrow, NYI., LC	.15
54	Michel Goulet, Que.	.35
55	**Ray Sheppard, Buf., RC**	**1.75**
56	Doug Gilmour, Stl.	2.00
57	David Shaw, NYR. (**)	.10
58	Cam Neely, Bos. (**)	1.00
59	Grant Fuhr (G), Edm. (**)	1.00
60	Scott Stevens, Wsh.	.25
61	Bob Brooke, Min.	.15
62	Dave Hunter, Pgh.	.15
63	**Alan Kerr, NYI., RC**	**.15**
64	Brad Marsh, Pha.	.15
65	Dale Hawerchuk, Win. (**)	.25
66	**Brett Hull, Stl., RC (**)**	**25.00**
67	Patrik Sundstrom, N.J. (**)	.10
68	Greg Stefan (G), Det.	.20
69	James Patrick, NYR.	.15
70	Dale Hunter, Wsh. (**)	.10
71	Al Iafrate, Tor.	.20
72	Bob Carpenter, L.A.	.15
73	Ray Bourque, Bos. (**)	1.25
74	John Tucker, Buf. (**)	.10
75	Carey Wilson, Hfd.	.15
76	Joe Mullen, Cgy.	.25
77	Rick Vaive, Chi.	.20
78	Shawn Burr, Det. (**)	.15
79	Murray Craven, Pha.	.15
80	Clark Gillies, Buf., LC	.15
81	Bernie Federko, Stl.	.20
82	Tony Tanti, Van.	.15
83	Greg Gilbert, NYI.	.15
84	Kirk Muller, N.J.	.35
85	Dave Tippett, Hfd.	.15
86	Kevin Hatcher, Wsh. (**)	.25
87	Rick Middleton, Bos., LC (**)	.15
88	Bobby Smith, Mtl.	.20
89	Doug Wilson, Chi. (**)	.15
90	Scott Arniel, Buf.	.15
91	Brian Mullen, NYR.	.15
92	Mike O'Connell, Det. (**)	.15
93	Mark Messier, Edm. (**)	1.50
94	**Sean Burke (G), N.J., RC**	**3.00**
95	Brian Bellows, Min. (**)	.15
96	Doug Bodger, Pgh.	.15
97	Bryan Trottier, NYI.	.50
98	Anton Stastny, Que.	.15
99	Checklist 1 (1 - 99)	.50
100	Dave Poulin, Pha. (**)	.10
101	Bob Bourne, L.A. (**)	.10
102	John Vanbiesbrouck (G), NYR.	5.00
103	Allen Pedersen, Bos.	.15
104	Mike Ridley, Wsh.	.20
105	Andrew McBain, Wpg.	.15
106	Troy Murray, Chi. (**)	.10
107	Tom Barrasso (G), Buf.	.25
108	Tomas Jonsson, NYI., LC	.15
109	**Rob Brown, Pgh., RC**	**.35**
110	Hakan Loob, Cgy., LC (**)	.10
111	Ilkka Sinisalo, Pha. (**)	.10
112	**Dave Archibald, Min., RC**	**.15**
113	Doug Halward, Det., LC	.15
114	Ray Ferraro, Hfd.	.25
115	**Doug Brown, N.J., RC**	**.20**
116	Patrick Roy (G), Mtl. (**)	10.00
117	Greg Millen (G), Stl.	.20
118	Ken Linseman, Bos.	.15
119	Phil Housley, Buf. (**)	.15
120	Wayne Gretzky, L.A.	35.00
121	Tomas Sandstrom, NYR.	.20
122	**Brendan Shanahan, N.J., RC**	**35.00**
123	Pat LaFontaine, NYI.	1.00
124	Luc Robitaille, L.A. (**)	2.00
125	Ed Olczyk, Tor. (**)	.10
126	Ron Sutter, Pha.	.15
127	Mike Liut (G), Hfd.	.25
128	Brent Ashton, Wpg. (**)	.10
129	**Tony Hrkac, Stl., RC**	**.15**
130	Kelly Miller, Wsh.	.15
131	Alan Haworth, Que.	.15
132	**Dave McLlwain, Pgh., RC**	**.20**
133	Mike Ramsey, Buf.	.15
134	**Bob Sweeney, Bos., RC**	**.25**
135	Dirk Graham, Chi. (**)	.10
136	Ulf Samuelsson, Hfd.	.50
137	Petri Skriko, Van.	.15
138	Aaron Broten, N.J. (**)	.10
139	Jim Fox, L.A.	.15
140	**Randy Wood, NYI., RC (**)**	**.15**
141	Larry Murphy, Wsh.	.20
142	Daniel Berthiaume (G), Wpg. (**)	.15
143	Kelly Kisio, NYR.	.15
144	Neal Broten, Min.	.20
145	Reed Larson, Bos.	.15
146	Peter Zezel, Pha. (**)	.10
147	Jari Kurri, Edm.	.75
148	Jim Johnson, Pgh.	.15
149	Gino Cavallini, Stl. (**)	.10
150	Glen Hanlon (G), Det. (**)	.15
151	Bengt Gustafsson, Wsh., LC	.15
152	Mike Bullard, Cgy. (**)	.10
153	John Ogrodnick, NYR.	.15
154	Steve Larmer, Chi.	.35
155	Kelly Hrudey (G), NYI.	.25
156	Mats Naslund, Mtl.	.20
157	Bruce Driver, N.J.	.20
158	Randy Hillier, Pgh.	.15
159	Craig Hartsburg, Min., LC	.20
160	Roland Melanson (G), L.A., LC	.20
161	Adam Oates, Det.	3.00
162	Greg Adams, Van.	.20
163	Dave Andreychuk, Buf.	.25
164	Dave Babych, Hfd.	.20
165	**Brian Noonan, Chi., RC**	**.50**
166	**Glen Wesley, Bos., RC**	**.50**
167	Dave Ellett, Wpg.	.20
168	Brian Propp, Pha.	.15
169	Bernie Nicholls, L.A.	.20
170	Walt Poddubny, NYR.	.15
171	Steve Konroyd, NYI.	.15
172	Doug Sulliman, N.J. (**)	.10
173	Mario Gosselin (G), Que.	.20
174	Brian Benning, Stl.	.15
175	Dino Ciccarelli, Min.	.25
176	Steve Kasper, Bos.	.15
177	Rick Tocchet, Pha.	2.00
178	Brad McCrimmon, Cgy.	.15
179	Paul Coffey, Pgh.	1.50
180	Pete Peeters (G), Wsh.	.20
181	**Bob Probert, Det., RC (**)**	**2.00**
182	**Steve Duchesne, L.A., RC (**)**	**1.75**
183	Russ Courtnall, Tor.	.20
184	Mike Foligno, Buf. (**)	.10
185	Wayne Presley, Chi. (**)	.10
186	Réjean Lemelin (G), Bos.	.20
187	Mark Hunter, Stl.	.15
188	Joe Cirella, N.J.	.15
189	Glenn Anderson, Edm. (**)	.15
190	John Anderson, Hfd.	.15
191	Patrick Flatley, NYI.	.15
192	Rod Langway, Wsh.	.20
193	Brian MacLellan, Min.	.15
194	**Pierre Turgeon, Buf., RC**	**15.00**
195	Brian Hayward (G), Mtl.	.20
196	Steve Yzerman, Det. (**)	4.00
197	Doug Crossman, Pha.	.15
198	Checklist 2 (100 - 198)	.50

STICKER INSERTS

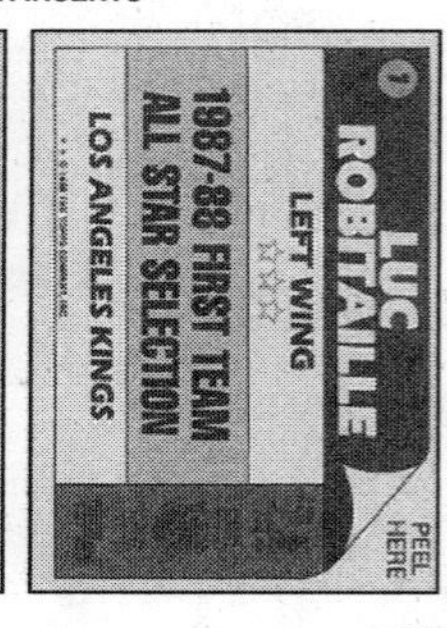

Insert Set (33 stickers): **20.00**

No.	Player	NRMT-MT
1	AS: Luc Robitaille, L.A.	.85
2	AS: Mario Lemieux, Pgh.	4.50
3	AS: Hakan Loob, Cgy.	.35
4	AS: Scott Stevens, Wsh.	.75
5	AS: Ray Bourque, Bos.	1.50
6	AS: Grant Fuhr (G), Edm.	1.00
7	AS: Michel Goulet, Que.	.50
8	AS: Wayne Gretzky, Edm.	6.00
9	AS: Cam Neely, Bos.	1.00
10	AS: Brad McCrimmon, Pha.	.35
11	AS: Gary Suter, Cgy.	.35
12	AS: Patrick Roy (G), Mtl.	4.50
13	Toronto Maple Leafs	.25
14	Buffalo Sabres	.25

	No.	Team	
☐	15	Detroit Red Wings	.25
☐	16	Pittsburgh Penguins	.25
☐	17	New York Rangers	.25
☐	18	Calgary Flames	.25
☐	19	Winnipeg Jets	.25
☐	20	Québec Nordiques	.25
☐	21	Chicago Blackhawks	.25
☐	22	Los Angeles Kings	.25
☐	23	Montréal Canadiens	.25
☐	24	Vancouver Canucks	.25
☐	25	Hartford Whalers	.25
☐	26	Philadelphia Flyers	.25
☐	27	New Jersey Devils	.25
☐	28	St. Louis Blues	.25
☐	29	Minnesota North Stars	.25
☐	30	Washington Capitals	.25
☐	31	Boston Bruins	.25
☐	32	New York Islanders	.25
☐	33	Edmonton Oilers	.25

TOPPS BOX BOTTOMS

These four card panels were found on the bottom of Topps and O-Pee-Chee wax boxes.

Panel Size: 5" x 7"

Complete Set (16 cards): 15.00
Panel A - D: 9.00
Panel E - H: 2.00
Panel I - L: 5.00
Panel M - P: 3.00

	No.	Player	NRMT-MT
☐	A	Ron Francis, Hfd.	.75
☐	B	Wayne Gretzky, L.A.	8.00
☐	C	Pat LaFontaine, NYI.	.75
☐	D	Bobby Smith, Mtl.	.50
☐	E	Bernie Federko, Stl.	.50
☐	F	Kirk Muller, N.J.	.50
☐	G	Ed Olczyk, Tor.	.50
☐	H	Denis Savard, Chi.	.50
☐	I	Ray Bourque, Bos.	3.00
☐	J	Murray Craven, Pha.; Brian Propp, Pha.	.50
☐	K	Dale Hawerchuk, Wpg.	.75
☐	L	Steve Yzerman, Det.	4.50
☐	M	Dave Andreychuk, Buf.	.50
☐	N	Mike Gartner, Wsh.	.75
☐	O	Hakan Loob, Cgy.	.50
☐	P	Luc Robitaille, L.A.	1.50

1989 PELIMIEHEN PASSI

A set of 6 stickers issued by the Finnish Ice Hockey Assosiation. A poster was also issued. We have no pricing information on this set.

Size: 3 1/8" x 3 7/8"

Imprint:

	Player
☐	Kari Eloranta
☐	Jari Kurri
☐	Reijo Ruotsalainen
☐	Christian Ruuttu
☐	Kari Takko
☐	Esa Tikkanen

1989 SEMIC STICKERS

Sticker Size: 2 1/8" x 3"
Face: Four Colour
Imprint:
Complete Set (200 stickers): 60.00
Album: 6.00

	No.	Player	NRMT-MT
☐	1	Sweden	.20
☐	2	Tommy Sandlin	.20
☐	3	Peter Lindmark	.20
☐	4	Rolf Ridderwall	.20
☐	5	Tomas Jonsson	.35
☐	6	Tommy Albelin	.35
☐	7	Mats Kihlström	.20
☐	8	Tommy Samuelsson	.20
☐	9	Anders Eldebrink	.20
☐	10	Fredrik Olausson	.35
☐	11	Peter Andersson	.20
☐	12	Thomas Eriksson	.20
☐	13	Them Eklund	.20
☐	14	Bo Berglund	.20
☐	15	Thomas Steen	.50
☐	16	Ulf Sandström	.20
☐	17	Jonas Bergqvist	.20
☐	18	Thomas Rundqvist	.20
☐	19	Per-Erik Eklund	.50
☐	20	Bengt Gustavsson	.35
☐	21	Patrik Sundström	.35
☐	22	Mikael Johansson	.20
☐	23	Hakan Södergren	.20
☐	24	Kent Nilsson	.50
☐	25	Lars-Gunnar Pettersson	.20
☐	26	Finland	.20
☐	27	Pentii Matikainen	.20
☐	28	Jukka Tammi (G)	.20
☐	29	Sakari Lindfors	.35
☐	30	Reijo Ruotsalainen	.35
☐	31	Kari Eloranta	.20
☐	32	Timo Blomqvist	.20
☐	33	Simo Saarinen	.20
☐	34	Hannu Virta	.20
☐	35	Jouko Narvanmaa	.20
☐	36	Jarmo Kuusisto	.20
☐	37	Kari Suoraniemi	.20
☐	38	Reijo Mikkolainen	.20
☐	39	Raimo Helminen	.20
☐	40	Raimo Summanen	.20
☐	41	Mikko Mäkelä	.20
☐	42	Kari Jalonen	.20
☐	43	Kari Laitinen	.20
☐	44	Petri Skriko	.20
☐	45	Erkki Laine	.20
☐	46	Pauli Järvinen	.20
☐	47	Jukka Vilander	.20
☐	48	Esa Keskinen	.35
☐	49	Ari Vuori	.20
☐	50	Mika Nieminen	.20
☐	51	Canada	.35
☐	52	Dave King	.50
☐	53	Grant Fuhr (G)	1.50
☐	54	Patrick Roy (G)	8.00
☐	55	Ron Hextall (G)	.75
☐	56	Al MacInnis	.50
☐	57	Ray Bourque	3.00
☐	58	Scott Stevens	.50
☐	59	Paul Coffey	2.00
☐	60	Zarley Zalapski	.35
☐	61	James Patrick	.35
☐	62	Kevin Lowe	.50
☐	63	Brad McCrimmon	.35
☐	64	Mario Lemieux	8.00
☐	65	Wayne Gretzky	12.00
☐	66	Denis Savard	.50
☐	67	Dale Hawerchuk	.75
☐	68	Luc Robitaille	.75
☐	69	Mark Messier	3.00
☐	70	Michel Goulet	.75
☐	71	Cam Neely	1.50
☐	72	Steve Yzerman	5.00
☐	73	Bernie Nicholls	.50
☐	74	Joe Nieuwendyk	.50
☐	75	Mike Gartner	1.50
☐	76	Soviet Union	.35
☐	77	Victor Tikhonov	.20
☐	78	Evgeni Belosjejkin	.20
☐	79	Sergei Mylnikov (G)	.20
☐	80	Sergei Golosjumov	.20
☐	81	Alexei Kasatonov	.35
☐	82	Alexei Gusarov	.50
☐	83	Andrei Smirnov	.20
☐	84	Valeri Shiryev	.20
☐	85	Igor Stelnov	.20
☐	86	Vladimir Konstantinov	3.00
☐	87	Viacheslav Fetisov	1.50
☐	88	Sergei Yashin	.20
☐	89	Vladimir Krutov	.50
☐	90	Igor Larionov	1.50
☐	91	Valeri Kamenski	2.00
☐	92	Vyachelsav Bykov	.75
☐	93	Andrei Khomutov	.50
☐	94	Yuri Kmylev	.50
☐	95	Sergei Nemchinov	.50
☐	96	Sergei Makarov	1.00
☐	97	Igor Jesmantoviti	.20
☐	98	Andrei Lomakin	.35
☐	99	Anatoli Semenov	.50
☐	100	Alexander Tiernych	.20
☐	101	Germany	.20
☐	102	Xaver Unsinn	.20
☐	103	Karl Friesen	.20
☐	104	Josef Schlickenrieder	.20
☐	105	Matthias Hoppe	.20
☐	106	Andreas Niederberger	.20
☐	107	Udo Kiessling	.20
☐	108	Uli Hiemer	.20
☐	109	Harold Kreis	.20
☐	110	Manfred Schuster	.20
☐	111	Jörg Hanft	.20
☐	112	Ron Fischer	.20
☐	113	Michael Heidt	.20
☐	114	Dieter Hegen	.20
☐	115	Gerd Truntschka	.20
☐	116	Helmut Steiger	.20
☐	117	Georg Franz	.20
☐	118	Georg Holzmann	.20
☐	119	Peter Obresa	.20
☐	120	Berndt Truntschka	.20
☐	121	Manfred Wolf	.20
☐	122	Roy Roedger	.20
☐	123	Axel Kammerer	.20
☐	124	Peter Draisatl	.20
☐	125	Daniel Held	.20
☐	126	Poland	.20
☐	127	Leszek Lejczyk	.20
☐	128	Jerzy Mruk	.20
☐	129	Andrzei Hanisz	.20
☐	130	Dariusz Wieczorek	.20
☐	131	Jacek Zamojski	.20
☐	132	Marek Cholewa	.20
☐	133	Henryk Gruth	.20
☐	134	Robert SzoDinski	.20
☐	135	Jerzv Potz	.20
☐	136	Andrzei Swiate	.20
☐	137	Ludvik Czapka	.20
☐	138	Piotr Zdunek	.20
☐	139	Jedrzej Kasperczyk	.20
☐	140	Krzysztof Podsiadlo	.20
☐	141	Miroslav Copija	.20
☐	142	Krzysztof Bujar	.20

	No.	Player	NRMT-MT
☐	143	Janusz Adamiec	.20
☐	144	Jasek Solinski	.20
☐	145	Roman Steblecki	.20
☐	146	Adam Fraszkol	.20
☐	147	Leszek Minge	.20
☐	148	Piotr Kwasigroch	.20
☐	149	Ireneusz Pacula	.20
☐	150	MM-kisatunnus	.20
☐	151	USA	.20
☐	152	Art Berglund	.20
☐	153	Tom Barrasso (G)	.50
☐	154	John Vanbiesbrouck (G)	4.00
☐	155	Gary Suter	.35
☐	156	Phil Housley	.35
☐	157	Chris Chelios	2.00
☐	158	Mike Ramsey	.35
☐	159	Rod Langway	.50
☐	160	Mark Howe	.50
☐	161	Brian Leetch	5.00
☐	162	Al Iafrate	.35
☐	163	Jimmy Carson	.35
☐	164	Pat LaFontaine	1.50
☐	165	Neal Broten	.50
☐	166	Dave Christian	.35
☐	167	Brett Hull	4.00
☐	168	Bob Carpenter	.35
☐	169	Ed Olczyk	.35
☐	170	Joe Mullen	.50
☐	171	Bob Brooke	.35
☐	172	Brian Lawton	.35
☐	173	Craig Janney	.50
☐	174	Mark Johnson	.35
☐	175	Chris Nilan	.35
☐	176	Czechoslovakia	.20
☐	177	Pavel Wohl	.20
☐	178	Dominik Hasek	5.00
☐	179	Jaromir Sindel	.20
☐	180	Petr Briza (G)	.35
☐	181	Antonin Stavjana	.20
☐	182	Bedrich Scerban	.20
☐	183	Petr Slanina	.20
☐	184	Frantisek Kucera	.20
☐	185	Jergus Baca	.20
☐	186	Leo Gudas	.20
☐	187	Drahomir Kadlec	.20
☐	188	Mojmir Bozik	.20
☐	189	Petr Vlk	.20
☐	190	Vladimir Ruzicka	.20
☐	191	Otakar Janecky	.20
☐	192	Jan Vodila	.20
☐	193	Jiri Dolezal	.20
☐	194	Rostislav Vlach	.20
☐	195	Jiri Kucera	.20
☐	196	Jiri Sejba	.20
☐	197	Oldrich Valek	.20
☐	198	Jiri Lala	.20
☐	199	Robert Kron	.20
☐	200	Petr Rosol	.20

1989 - 90 ACTION PACKED PROMOS

Face: Four colour, gold border Name, Team
Back: Four colour, gold border; Name, Number, Resume
Imprint: HI-PRO MKTG., INC. Copyright 1990
Complete Set (3 cards): 750.00

	No.	Player	NRMT-MT
☐	1	Wayne Gretzky, L.A.	225.00
☐	2	Mario Lemieux, Pgh.	175.00
☐	3	Steve Yzerman, Det. (*)	350.00

1989 - 90 KRAFT

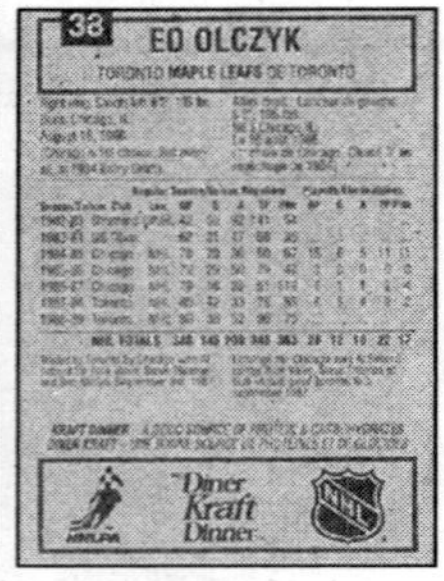

Cards 1 to 51 and 64 were issued on the backs of packages of Kraft Dinner, Rock-O-Rama, Spirals and Egg Noodles. Cards 52 to 63 were issued only in full cases of Kraft Dinner as six panels of two cards. Factory cut cards were also available by mail. Also included in the mail offering was a spiral bound album.

Imprint: KRAFT
Factory Set (including album): 100.00
Complete Set (64 cards): 75.00
Common Player: .50
Album: 30.00

	No.	Player	NRMT-MT
☐	1	Doug Gilmour, Cgy.	2.50
☐	2	Theoren Fleury, Cgy.	2.50
☐	3	Al MacInnis, Cgy.	1.00
☐	4	Sergei Makarov, Cgy.	1.25
☐	5	Joe Nieuwendyk, Cgy.	1.25
☐	6	Joel Otto, Cgy.	.50
☐	7	Colin Patterson, Cgy.	.50
☐	8	Sergei Priakin, Cgy.	.50
☐	9	Paul Ranheim, Cgy.	.50
☐	10	Glenn Anderson, Edm.	.75
☐	11	Grant Fuhr (G), Edm.	1.25
☐	12	Charlie Huddy, Edm.	.50
☐	13	Jari Kurri, Edm.	1.25
☐	14	Kevin Lowe, Edm.	.75
☐	15	Mark Messier, Edm.	3.50
☐	16	Craig Simpson, Edm.	.50
☐	17	Steve Smith, Edm.	.50
☐	18	Esa Tikkanen, Edm.	.50
☐	19	Guy Carbonneau, Mtl.	.75
☐	20	Chris Chelios, Mtl.	1.50
☐	21	Shayne Corson, Mtl.	.50
☐	22	Russ Courtnall, Mtl.	.50
☐	23	Mats Naslund, Mtl.	.75
☐	24	Stéphane Richer, Mtl.	.75
☐	25	Patrick Roy (G), Mtl.	7.50
☐	26	Bobby Smith, Mtl.	.75
☐	27	Petr Svoboda, Mtl.	.50
☐	28	Jeff Brown, Que.	.50
☐	29	Paul Gillis, Que.	.50
☐	30	Michel Goulet, Que.	.75
☐	31	Guy Lafleur, Que.	3.50
☐	32	Joe Sakic, Que.	4.50
☐	33	Peter Stastny, Que.	.75
☐	34	Wendel Clark, Tor.	2.25
☐	35	Vincent Damphousse, Tor.	1.50
☐	36	Gary Leeman, Tor.	.50
☐	37	Daniel Marois, Tor.	.50
☐	38	Ed Olczyk, Tor.	.50
☐	39	Rob Ramage, Tor.	.50
☐	40	Vladimir Krutov, Van.	.50
☐	41	Igor Larionov, Van.	1.50
☐	42	Trevor Linden, Van.	2.00
☐	43	Kirk McLean (G), Van.	1.50
☐	44	Paul Reinhart, Van.	.50
☐	45	Tony Tanti, Van.	.50
☐	46	Brent Ashton, Wpg.	.50
☐	47	Randy Carlyle, Van.	.50
☐	48	Randy Cunneyworth, Van.	.50
☐	49	Dave Ellett, Van.	.50
☐	50	Dale Hawerchuk, Van.	1.25
☐	51	Fredrik Olausson, Van.	.50
☐	52	AS: Ray Bourque	2.50
☐	53	AS: Sean Burke (G)	1.75
☐	54	AS: Paul Coffey	2.50
☐	55	AS: Mario Lemieux	7.50
☐	56	AS: Cam Neely	2.50
☐	57	AS: Rick Tocchet	1.75
☐	58	AS: Steve Duchesne	1.25
☐	59	AS: Wayne Gretzky	8.50
☐	60	AS: Joey Mullen	1.25
☐	61	AS: Gary Suter	1.25
☐	62	AS: Mike Vernon (G)	2.00
☐	63	AS: Steve Yzerman	3.50
☐	64	Checklist	2.00

KRAFT STICKERS

These stickers were issued in packages of Kraft Cheese Slices and were designed to complement the album issued for the regular cards of 1990. Panels of six stickers each, 2 players and 4 team logos were issued. The panels are numbered of 6.

Panel Size: 4 1/2" x 2 3/4"
Imprint: KRAFT
Kraft Stickers Set (6 panels): 20.00

	No.	Player	NRMT-MT
☐	1	Paul Reinhart/ Mike McPhee/ Montréal/ Washington/ Toronto/ Vancouver	1.50
☐	2	Wayne Gretzky/ Rick Tocchet/ Los Angeles/ Minnesota/ Philadelphia/ Québec	10.00
☐	3	Paul Coffey/ Steve Yzerman/ Detroit/ Hartford/ Rangers/ Prince of Wales Conference	6.00
☐	4	Mike Vernon (G)/ Ray Bourque/ Calgary/ St. Louis/ Islanders/ Boston	4.00
☐	5	Jari Kurri/ Mario Lemieux/ Pittsburgh/ Buffalo/ Winnipeg/ NHL	8.00
☐	6	Kevin Lowe/ Sean Burke (G)/ Edmonton/ Chicago/ New Jersey/ Clarence Campbell Conference	2.00

1989 - 90 O-PEE-CHEE

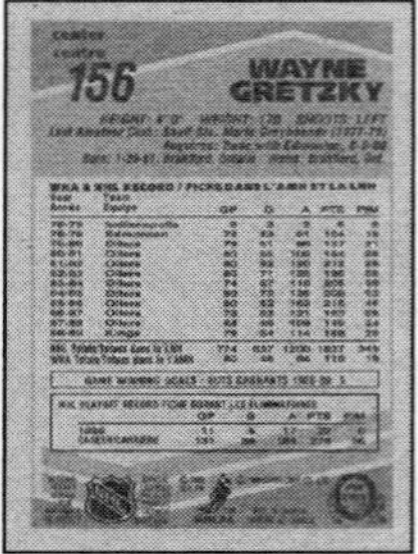

Imprint: © 1989 O-PEE-CHEE CO. LTD.
Complete Set (330 cards): 20.00
Common Player: .10

	No.	Player	NRMT-MT
☐	1	Mario Lemieux, Pgh.	2.00
☐	2	Ulf Dahlen, NYR.	.10
☐	**3**	**Terry Carkner, Pha., RC**	**.10**
☐	4	Tony McKegney, Det.	.10
☐	5	Denis Savard, Chi.	.25
☐	**6**	**Derek King, NYI., RC**	**.10**
☐	7	Lanny McDonald, Cgy., LC	.25
☐	8	John Tonelli, L.A.	.10
☐	9	Tom Kurvers, N.J. (Tor.)	.10
☐	10	Dave Archibald, Min.	.10
☐	**11**	**Peter Sidorkiewicz (G), Hfd., RC**	**.10**
☐	12	Esa Tikkanen, Edm.	.10
☐	13	Dave Barr, Det.	.10
☐	14	Brent Sutter, NYI.	.10
☐	15	Cam Neely, Bos.	.25
☐	**16**	**Calle Johansson, Wsh., RC**	**.10**
☐	17	Patrick Roy (G), Mtl.	2.00
☐	**18**	**Dale DeGray, L.A., RC**	**.10**
☐	**19**	**Phil Bourque, Pgh., RC**	**.10**
☐	20	Kevin Dineen, Hfd.	.10
☐	21	Mike Bullard, Pha.	.10
☐	22	Gary Leeman, Tor.	.10
☐	23	Greg Stefan (G), Det.	.10
☐	24	Brian Mullen, NYR.	.10
☐	25	Pierre Turgeon, Buf.	1.00
☐	**26**	**Bob Rouse, Wsh., RC**	**.10**
☐	27	Peter Zezel, Stl.	.10
☐	28	Jeff Brown, Que.	.10
☐	**29**	**Andy Brickley, Bos., RC**	**.10**
☐	30	Mike Gartner, Min.	.50
☐	31	Darren Pang (G), Chi.	.10
☐	32	Pat Verbeek, Hfd.	.10
☐	33	Petri Skriko, Van.	.10

- ☐ 34 Tom Laidlaw, L.A. .10
- ☐ 35 Randy Wood, NYI. .10
- ☐ 36 Tom Barrasso (G), Pgh. .25
- ☐ 37 John Tucker, Buf. .10
- ☐ 38 Andrew McBain, Pgh. .10
- ☐ 39 David Shaw, NYR. .10
- ☐ 40 Réjean Lemelin (G), Bos. .10
- ☐ 41 Dino Ciccarelli, Wsh. .25
- ☐ 42 Jeff Sharples, Det. .10
- ☐ 43 Jari Kurri, Edm. .25
- ☐ 44 Murray Craven, Pha. .10
- ☐ **45 Cliff Ronning, Stl., RC .50**
- ☐ 46 Dave Babych, Hfd. .10
- ☐ 47 Bernie Nicholls, L.A. .10
- ☐ **48 Jon Casey (G), Min., RC .25**
- ☐ 49 Al MacInnis, Cgy. .25
- ☐ **50 Bob Errey, Pgh., RC .10**
- ☐ 51 Glen Wesley, Bos. .10
- ☐ 52 Dirk Graham, Chi. .10
- ☐ 53 Guy Carbonneau, Mtl. .10
- ☐ 54 Tomas Sandström, NYR. .10
- ☐ 55 Rod Langway, Wsh. .10
- ☐ 56 Patrik Sundstrom, N.J. .10
- ☐ 57 Michel Goulet, Que. .25
- ☐ 58 Dave Taylor, L.A. .10
- ☐ 59 Phil Housley, Buf. .10
- ☐ 60 Pat LaFontaine, NYI. .25
- ☐ **61 Kirk McLean (G), Van., RC 1.00**
- ☐ 62 Ken Linseman, Bos. .10
- ☐ 63 Randy Cunneyworth, Wpg. .10
- ☐ 64 Tony Hrkac, Stl. .10
- ☐ 65 Mark Messier, Edm. 1.00
- ☐ 66 Carey Wilson, NYR. .10
- ☐ **67 Stephen Leach, Wsh., RC .10**
- ☐ 68 Christian Ruuttu, Buf. .10
- ☐ 69 Dave Ellett, Wpg. .10
- ☐ 70 Ray Ferraro, Hfd. .10
- ☐ **71 Colin Patterson, Cal., RC .10**
- ☐ 72 Tim Kerr, Pha. .10
- ☐ 73 Bob Joyce, Bos. .10
- ☐ 74 Doug Gilmour, Cgy. .50
- ☐ 75 Lee Norwood, Det. .10
- ☐ 76 Dale Hunter, Wsh. .10
- ☐ 77 Jim Johnson, Pgh. .10
- ☐ 78 Mike Foligno, Buf. .10
- ☐ 79 Al Iafrate, Tor. .10
- ☐ 80 Rick Tocchet, Pha. .10
- ☐ **81 Greg Hawgood, Bos., RC .10**
- ☐ 82 Steve Thomas, Chi. .10
- ☐ 83 Steve Yzerman, Det. 1.25
- ☐ 84 Mike McPhee, Mtl. .10
- ☐ **85 David Volek, NYI., RC .10**
- ☐ 86 Brian Benning, Stl. .10
- ☐ 87 Neal Broten, Min. .10
- ☐ 88 Luc Robitaille, L.A. .50
- ☐ **89 Trevor Linden, Van., RC 2.00**
- ☐ 90 James Patrick, NYR. .10
- ☐ 91 Brian Lawton, Hfd. .10
- ☐ 92 Sean Burke (G), N.J. .25
- ☐ 93 Scott Stevens, Wsh. .10
- ☐ **94 Pat Elynuik, Wpg., RC .10**
- ☐ 95 Paul Coffey, Pgh. .65
- ☐ 96 Jan Erixon, NYR. .10
- ☐ 97 Mike Liut (G), Hfd. .10
- ☐ 98 Wayne Presley, Chi. .10
- ☐ 99 Craig Simpson, Edm. .10
- ☐ **100 Kjell Samuelsson, Pha., RC .10**
- ☐ 101 Shawn Burr, Det. .10
- ☐ 102 John MacLean, N.J. .10
- ☐ 103 Tom Fergus, Tor. .10
- ☐ 104 Mike Krushelnyski, L.A. .10
- ☐ 105 Gary Nylund, NYI. .10
- ☐ 106 Dave Andreychuk, Buf. .25
- ☐ 107 Bernie Federko, Det. .10
- ☐ 108 Gary Suter, Cgy. .10
- ☐ 109 Dave Gagner, Min. .10
- ☐ 110 Ray Bourque, Bos. .75
- ☐ **111 Geoff Courtnall, Wsh., RC .50**
- ☐ 112 Doug Wilson, Chi. .25
- ☐ **113 Joe Sakic, Que., RC 7.50**
- ☐ 114 John Vanbiesbrouck (G), NYR. 1.25
- ☐ 115 Dave Poulin, Pha. .10
- ☐ 116 Rick Meagher, Stl. .10
- ☐ 117 Kirk Muller, N.J. .10
- ☐ 118 Mats Naslund, Mtl. .10
- ☐ 119 Ray Sheppard, Buf. .20
- ☐ **120 Jeff Norton, NYI., RC .10**
- ☐ 121 Randy Burridge, Bos. .10
- ☐ 122 Dale Hawerchuk, Wpg. .25
- ☐ 123 Steve Duchesne, L.A. .10
- ☐ 124 John Anderson, Hfd., LC .10
- ☐ 125 Rick Vaive, Buf. .10
- ☐ 126 Randy Hillier, Pgh. .10
- ☐ 127 Jimmy Carson, Edm. .10
- ☐ 128 Larry Murphy, Min. .25
- ☐ 129 Paul MacLean, Stl. .10
- ☐ 130 Joe Cirella, Que. .10
- ☐ 131 Kelly Miller, Wsh. .10
- ☐ 132 Alain Chevrier (G), Chi. .10
- ☐ 133 Ed Olczyk, Tor. .10
- ☐ 134 Dave Tippett, Hfd. .10
- ☐ 135 Bob Sweeney, Bos. .10
- ☐ **136 Brian Leetch, NYR., RC 3.00**
- ☐ 137 Greg Millen (G), Stl. .10
- ☐ 138 Joe Nieuwendyk, Cgy. .25
- ☐ 139 Brian Propp, Pha. .10
- ☐ 140 Mike Ramsey, Buf. .10
- ☐ 141 Mike Allison, L.A. .10
- ☐ **142 Shawn Chambers, Min., RC .10**
- ☐ 143 Peter Stastny, Que. .25
- ☐ 144 Glen Hanlon (G), Det. .10
- ☐ **145 John Cullen, Pgh., RC .25**
- ☐ 146 Kevin Hatcher, Wsh. .25
- ☐ 147 Brendan Shanahan, N.J. 2.50
- ☐ 148 Paul Reinhart, Van. .10
- ☐ 149 Bryan Trottier, NYI. .25
- ☐ **150 Dave Manson, Chi., RC .50**
- ☐ **151 Mark Habscheid, Det., RC .10**
- ☐ 152 Dan Quinn, Pgh. .10
- ☐ 153 Stéphane Richer, Mtl. .10
- ☐ 154 Doug Bodger, Buf. .10
- ☐ 155 Ron Hextall (G), Pha. .50
- ☐ 156 Wayne Gretzky, L.A. 2.50
- ☐ **157 Steve Tuttle, Stl., RC .10**
- ☐ 158 Charlie Huddy, Edm. .10
- ☐ 159 Dave Christian, Wsh. .10
- ☐ 160 Andy Moog (G), Bos. .25
- ☐ **161 Tony Granato, NYR., RC .25**
- ☐ **162 Sylvain Côté, Hfd., RC .10**
- ☐ 163 Mike Vernon (G), Cgy. .35
- ☐ **164 Steve Chiasson, Det., RC .10**
- ☐ 165 Mike Ridley, Wsh. .10
- ☐ 166 Kelly Hrudey (G), LA .10
- ☐ 167 Bobby Carpenter, Bos. .10
- ☐ **168 Zarley Zalapski, Pgh., RC .10**
- ☐ **169 Derek Laxdal, Tor., RC .10**
- ☐ 170 Clint Malarchuk (G), Buf. .10
- ☐ 171 Kelly Kisio, NYR. .10
- ☐ 172 Gerard Gallant, Det. .10
- ☐ 173 Ron Sutter, Pha. .10
- ☐ 174 Chris Chelios, Mtl. .75
- ☐ 175 Ron Francis, Hfd. .60
- ☐ 176 Gino Cavallini, Stl. .10
- ☐ 177 Brian Bellows, Min. .10
- ☐ 178 Greg Adams, Van. .10
- ☐ 179 Steve Larmer, Chi. .25
- ☐ 180 Aaron Broten, N.J. .10
- ☐ 181 Brent Ashton, Wpg. .10
- ☐ **182 Gerald Diduck, NYI., RC .10**
- ☐ **183 Paul MacDermid, Hfd., RC .10**
- ☐ 184 Walt Poddubny, N.J. .10
- ☐ 185 Adam Oates, Stl. .60
- ☐ 186 Brett Hull, Stl. 2.00
- ☐ 187 Scott Arniel, Buf. .10
- ☐ 188 Bobby Smith, Mtl. .10
- ☐ 189 Guy Lafleur, NYR. .75
- ☐ **190 Craig Janney, Bos., RC .50**
- ☐ 191 Mark Howe, Pha. .10
- ☐ 192 Grant Fuhr (G), Edm. .50
- ☐ 193 Rob Brown, Pgh. .10
- ☐ 194 Steve Kasper, L.A. .10
- ☐ 195 Pete Peeters (G), Pha. .10
- ☐ 196 Joe Mullen, Cgy. .10
- ☐ 197 Checklist 1 (1 - 110) .10
- ☐ 198 Checklist 2 (111 - 220) .10
- ☐ 199 Keith Crowder, L.A. .10
- ☐ **200 Daren Puppa (G), Buf., RC .50**
- ☐ **201 Benoît Hogue, Buf., RC .20**
- ☐ **202 Gary Roberts, Cgy., RC 1.00**
- ☐ 203 Brad McCrimmon, Cgy. .10
- ☐ 204 Rick Wamsley (G), Cgy. .10
- ☐ 205 Joel Otto, Cgy. .10
- ☐ 206 Jim Peplinski, Cgy. .10
- ☐ 207 Jamie Macoun, Cgy. .10
- ☐ 208 Brian MacLellan, Cgy. .10
- ☐ **209 Scott Young, Hfd., RC .50**
- ☐ 210 Ulf Samuelsson, Hfd. .10
- ☐ 211 Joel Quenneville, Hfd. .10
- ☐ 212 Tim Watters, L.A. .10
- ☐ 213 Curt Giles, Min. .10
- ☐ 214 Stewart Gavin, Min. .10
- ☐ 215 Bob Brooke, Min. .10
- ☐ **216 Basil McRae, Min., RC .10**
- ☐ **217 Frantisek Musil, Min., RC .10**
- ☐ **218 Adam Creighton, Chi., RC .10**
- ☐ 219 Troy Murray, Chi. .10
- ☐ 220 Steve Konroyd, Chi. .10
- ☐ 221 Duane Sutter, Chi. .10
- ☐ **222 Trent Yawney, Chi., RC .10**
- ☐ 223 Mike O'Connell, Det. .10
- ☐ 224 James Nill, Det., LC .10
- ☐ 225 John Chabot, Det. .10
- ☐ 226 Glenn Anderson, Edm. .10
- ☐ 227 Kevin Lowe, Edm. .10
- ☐ 228 Steve Smith, Edm. .10
- ☐ 229 Randy Gregg, Edm. .10
- ☐ 230 Craig MacTavish, Edm. .10
- ☐ 231 Craig Muni, Edm. .10
- ☐ **232 Theoren Fleury, Cal., RC 4.00**
- ☐ 233 Bill Ranford (G), Edm. .50
- ☐ 234 Claude Lemieux, Mtl. .50
- ☐ 235 Larry Robinson, L.A. .35
- ☐ 236 Craig Ludwig, Mtl. .10
- ☐ 237 Brian Hayward (G), Mtl. .10
- ☐ 238 Petr Svoboda, Mtl. .10
- ☐ 239 Russ Courtnall, Mtl. .10
- ☐ 240 Ryan Walter, Mtl. .10
- ☐ 241 Tommy Albelin, N.J. .10
- ☐ 242 Doug Brown, N.J. .10
- ☐ **243 Ken Daneyko, N.J., RC .10**
- ☐ 244 Mark Johnson, N.J. .10
- ☐ **245 Randy Velischek, N.J., RC .10**
- ☐ **246 Brad Dalgarno, NYI., RC .10**
- ☐ 247 Mikko Makela, NYI. .10
- ☐ **248 Shayne Corson, Mtl., RC 1.50**
- ☐ **249 Marc Bergevin, NYI., RC .10**
- ☐ 250 Patrick Flatley, NYI. .10
- ☐ 251 Michel Petit, NYR. (Que.) .10
- ☐ 252 Mark Hardy, NYR. .10
- ☐ 253 Scott Mellanby, Pha. .10
- ☐ 254 Keith Acton, Pha. .10
- ☐ 255 Ken Wregget (G), Pha. .10
- ☐ **256 Gord Dineen, Pgh., RC .10**
- ☐ 257 David Hannan,Pgh. (Tor.) .10
- ☐ 258 Mario Gosselin (G), LA .10
- ☐ 259 Randy Moller,Que. (NYR.) .10
- ☐ 260 Mario Marois, Que. .10
- ☐ 261 Robert Picard, Que. .10
- ☐ **262 Marc Fortier, Que., RC .10**
- ☐ **263 Ron Tugnutt (G), Que., RC .50**
- ☐ **264 Iiro Jarvi, Que., RC .10**
- ☐ 265 Paul Gillis, Que. .10
- ☐ **266 Mike Hough, Que., RC .25**
- ☐ 267 Jim Sandlak, Van. .10
- ☐ 268 Greg Paslawski, Wpg. .10
- ☐ **269 Paul Cavallini, Stl., RC .10**
- ☐ 270 Gaston Gingras, Stl. .10
- ☐ 271 Allan Bester (G), Tor. .10
- ☐ 272 Vincent Damphousse, Tor. .75
- ☐ **273 Daniel Marois, Tor., RC .25**
- ☐ 274 Mark Osborne, Tor., Error .10
- ☐ 275 Craig Laughlin, Tor., LC .10
- ☐ 276 Brad Marsh, Tor. .10
- ☐ 277 Dan Daoust, Tor. .10
- ☐ 278 Borje Salming, Det. .25
- ☐ 279 Chris Kotsopoulos, Det. .10
- ☐ 280 Tony Tanti, Van. .10
- ☐ 281 Barry Pederson, Van. .10
- ☐ 282 Rick Sutter, Van. .10
- ☐ 283 Stan Smyl, Van. .10
- ☐ 284 Doug Lidster, Van. .10
- ☐ 285 Steve Weeks (G), Van. .10
- ☐ 286 Harold Snepsts, Van. .10
- ☐ **287 Brian Bradley, Van., RC .50**
- ☐ 288 Larry Melnyk, Van. .10

No.	Player	NRMT-MT
289	Bob Gould, Wsh. (Bos.)	.10
290	Thomas Steen, Wpg.	.10
291	Randy Carlyle, Wpg.	.10
292	**Hannu Jarvenpaa, Wpg., RC**	**.10**
293	Iain Duncan, Wpg.	.10
294	Doug Smail, Wpg.	.10
295	James Kyte, Pgh.	.10
296	Daniel Berthiaume (G), Wpg.	.10
297	Peter Taglianetti, Wpg.	.10
298	Boston Bruins	.10
299	Buffalo Sabres	.10
300	Calgary Flames	.10
301	Chicago Blackhawks	.10
302	Detroit Red Wings	.10
303	Edmonton Oilers	.10
304	Hartford Whalers	.10
305	Los Angeles Kings	.10
306	Minnesota North Stars	.10
307	Montréal Canadiens	.10
308	New Jersey Devils	.25
309	New York Islanders	.10
310	New York Rangers	.10
311	Philadelphia Flyers	.10
312	Pghtsburgh Penguins	.75
313	Québec Nordiques	.75
314	St. Louis Blues	.10
315	Toronto Maple Leafs	.10
316	Vancouver Canucks	.10
317	Washington Capitals	.10
318	Winnipeg Jets	.10
319	AW: Mario Lemieux, Pgh	1.00
320	AW: Wayne Gretzky, L.A.	1.25
321	AW: Brian Leetch, NYR.	.75
322	AW: Patrick Roy, Mtl.	1.00
323	AW: Chris Chelios, Mtl.	.35
324	AW: Joe Mullen, Cgy.	.10
325	HL: Wayne Gretzky	1.25
326	HL: Brian Leetch, Error (Photo: David Shaw)	.75
327	HL: Mario Lemieux	1.00
328	HL: Esa Tikkanen	.10
329	HL: Stanley Cup Champions: Flames	.10
330	Checklist 3 (221 - 330)	.10

BOX BOTTOMS

These four-card panels were found on the bottom of O-Pee-Chee wax boxes.

Panel Size: 5" x 7"

Complete Set (16 cards):	**12.00**
Panel A - D:	**5.00**
Panel E - H:	**6.00**
Panel I - L:	**4.00**
Panel M - P:	**1.50**

No.	Player	NRMT-MT
A	Mario Lemieux, Pgh.	4.00
B	Mike Ridley, Wsh.	.50
C	Tomas Sandstrom, NYR.	.50
D	Petri Skriko, Van.	.50
E	Wayne Gretzky, L.A.	5.00
F	Brett Hull, Stl.	2.00
G	Tim Kerr, Pha.	.50
H	Mats Naslund, Mtl.	.50
I	Jari Kurri, Edm.	.75
J	Steve Larmer, Chi.	.50
K	Cam Neely, Bos.	.75
L	Steve Yzerman, Det.	3.00
M	Kevin Dineen, Hfd.	.50
N	Dave Gagner, Min.	.50
O	Joe Mullen, Cgy.	.50
P	Pierre Turgeon, Buf.	1.00

1989 - 90 O-PEE-CHEE STICKERS

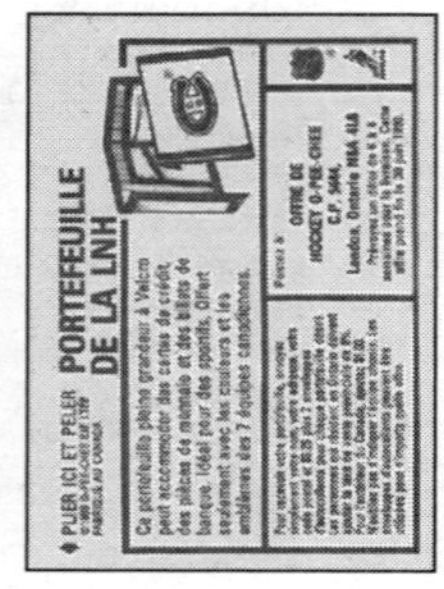

Sticker Size: 2 1/8" x 3"

Imprint: 1989 O-PEE-CHEE CO. LTD.

Complete Set (152 stickers):	**25.00**
Common Player:	**.15**
Album: (Lanny McDonald)	**5.00**

No.	Player	NRMT-MT
1	Calgary Flames vs Montréal Canadiens	.15
2	Calgary Flames vs Montréal Canadiens	.15
3	Calgary Flames vs Montréal Canadiens	.15
4	Calgary Flames vs Montréal Canadiens	.15
5	Al MacInnis, Cgy., MVP	.25
6	Calgary Flames vs Montréal Canadiens	.15
7	Calgary Flames vs Montréal Canadiens	.15
8	Calgary Flames vs Montréal Canadiens	.15
9	Calgary Flames vs Montréal Canadiens	.15
16	Denis Savard, Chi.	.25
17	Steve Larmer, Chi.	.25
22	Brett Hull, Stl.	.50
23	Peter Zezel, Stl.	.15
32	Ray Bourque, Bos.	.50
33	Cam Neely, Bos.	.50
46	Mats Naslund, Mtl.	.20
47	Bobby Smith, Mtl.	3.00
50	Brian Hayward (G), Mtl.	.20
51	Stéphane Richer, Mtl.	.25
56	Chris Chelios, Mtl.	.50
57	Patrick Roy (G), Mtl.	2.00
60	Barry Pederson, Van.	.15
61	Trevor Linden, Van.	.75
64	Kirk McLean (G), Van.	.50
65	Paul Reinhart, Van.	.15
70	Petri Skriko, Van.	.15
71	Tony Tanti, Van.	.15
80	Geoff Courtnall, Wsh.	.15
81	Mike Ridley, Wsh.	.15
86	Sean Burke (G), NJ	.35
87	John MacLean. NJ	.15
90	Joe Mullen, Cgy.	.25
91	Brad McCrimmon, Cgy.	.15
94	Mike Vernon (G), Cgy.	.50
95	Al MacInnis, Cgy.	.15
100	Gary Suter, Cgy.	.15
101	Joe Nieuwendyk, Cgy.	.35
110	Tim Kerr, Pha.	.15
111	Ron Hextall (G), Pha.	.25
118	Bryan Trottier, NYI.	.25
119	Pat LaFontaine, NYI.	.50
120	St. Louis Blues vs Boston Bruins	.15
121	St. Louis Blues vs Boston Bruins	.15
122	New York Rangers vs Boston Bruins	.15
123	New York Rangers vs Boston Bruins	.15
124	Chicago Blackhawks	.15
125	Boston Bruins vs Montréal Canadiens	.15
126	New Jersey Devils vs Boston Bruins	.15
127	Calgary Flames vs New Jersey Devils	.15
128	Montréal Canadiens vs Philadelphia Flyers	.15
129	Philadelphia Flyers vs Edmonton Oilers	.15
130	Vancouver Canucks vs Boston Bruins	.15
131	Vancouver Canucks vs Boston Bruins	.15
132	Minnesota North Stars vs Boston Bruins	.15
133	Minnesota North Stars vs Boston Bruins	.15
134	Dale Hawerchuk, Wpg.	.35
135	Andrew McBain, Wpg.	.15
138	Brent Ashton, Wpg.	.15
139	Dave Ellett, Wpg.	.15
144	Thomas Steen, Wpg.	.15
145	Hannu Jarvenpaa, Wpg.	.15
154	Wayne Gretzky, L.A.	3.00
155	Bernie Nicholls, L.A.	.15
168	Gary Leeman, Tor.	.15
169	Allan Bester (G), Tor.	.15
172	Ed Olczyk, Tor.	.15
173	Tom Fergus, Tor.	.15
178	Al Iafrate, Tor.	.15
179	Vincent Damphousse, Tor.	.35
182	Peter Stastny, Que.	.15
183	Paul Gillis, Que.	.15
186	Michel Goulet, Que.	.25
187	Joe Sakic, Que.	2.00
192	Iiro Jarvi, Que.	.15
193	Jeff Brown, Que.	.15
202	Neal Broten, Min.	.15
203	Dave Gagner, Min.	.15
211	Patrick Roy/Brian Hayward	1.50
217	Craig Simpson, Edm.	.15
218	Glenn Anderson, Edm.	.15
221	Jari Kurri, Edm.	.25
222	Jimmy Carson, Edm.	.15
227	Mark Messier, Edm.	.75
228	Grant Fuhr (G), Edm.	.35
237	Paul Coffey, Pgh.	.50
238	Mario Lemieux, Pgh.	2.25
243	Brian Mullen, NYR.	.15
244	Tomas Sandstrom, NYR.	.15
253	Gerard Gallant, Det.	.15
254	Steve Yzerman, Det.	1.00
261	Phil Housley, Buf.	.15
262	Pierre Turgeon, Buf.	.75
269	Ron Francis, Hfd.	.35
270	Kevin Dineen, Hfd.	.15

MULTIPLE STICKERS

No.	Player	NRMT-MT
10/150	Darren Pang (G), Chi./Steve Duchesne, L.A.	.20
11/151	Troy Murray, Chi./Dave Taylor, L.A.	.20
12/152	Dirk Graham, Chi./Steve Kasper, L.A.	.20
13/153	Dave Manson, Chi./Mike Krushelnyski, L.A.	.20
14/156	Doug Wilson, Chi./Chris Chelios, Mtl.	.50
15/157	Steve Thomas, Chi./Gerard Gallant, Det.	.20
18/158	Paul MacLean, Stl./Mario Lemieux, Pgh.	1.50
19/159	Paul Cavallini, Stl./Al MacInnis, Cgy.	.25
20/160	Cliff Ronning, Stl./Joe Mullen, Cgy.	.20
21/161	Gaston Gingras, Stl./Patrick Roy (G), Mtl.	1.25
24/162	Brian Benning, Stl./Ray Bourque, Bos.	.50
25/163	Tony Hrkac, Stl./Rob Brown, Pgh.	.20
26/164	Ken Linseman, Bos./Geoff Courtnall, Wsh.	.20
27/165	Glen Wesley, Bos./Steve Duchesne, L.A.	.20
28/166	Randy Burridge, Bos./Wayne Gretzky, L.A.	2.50
29/167	Craig Janney, Bos./Mike Vernon (G), Cgy.	.50
30/170	Andy Moog (G), Bos./David Reid, Tor.	.35
31/171	Bob Joyce, Bos./Craig Laughlin, Tor.	.20
34/174	Sean Burke (G), N.J./Mark Osborne, Tor.	.35
35/175	Pat Elynuik, Wpg./Brad Marsh, Tor.	.20
36/176	Tony Granato, NYR./Daniel Marois, Tor.	.20
37/177	Benoît Hogue, Buf./Dan Daoust, Tor.	.20
38/180	Craig Janney, Bos./Chris Kotsopoulos, Tor.	.50
39/181	Brian Leetch, NYR./Derek Laxdal, Tor.	1.00
40/184	Trevor Linden, Van./Jeff Jackson, Que.	.50
41/185	Joe Sakic, Que./Mario Marois, Que.	1.50
42/188	Peter Sidorkiewicz (G), Hfd./Bob Mason (G), Que.	.25
43/189	David Volek, NYI./Marc Fortier, Que.	.20
44/190	Scott Young, Hfd./Robert Picard, Que.	.20
45/191	Zarley Zalapski, Pgh./Steven Finn, Que.	.20
48/194	Guy Carbonneau, Mtl./Gaetan Duchesne, Que.	.20
49/195	Shayne Corson, Mtl./Randy Moller, Que.	.20
52/196	Claude Lemieux, Mtl./Mike Gartner, Min.	.35
53/197	Russ Courtnall, Mtl./Jon Casey (G), Min.	.25
54/198	Petr Svoboda, Mtl./Marc Habscheid, Min.	.20
55/199	Larry Robinson, Mtl./Larry Murphy, Min.	.25
58/200	Bob Gainey, Mtl./Brian Bellows, Min.	.25
59/201	Mike McPhee, Mtl./Dave Archibald, Min.	.20
62/204	Rich Sutter, Van./Vezina Trophy	.20
63/205	Brian Bradley, Van./Jennings Trophy	.20
66/206	Robert Nordmark, Van./Selke Trophy	.20
67/207	Steve Bozek, Van./Masterton Trophy	.20
68/208	Stan Smyl, Van./Mario Lemieux, Pgh.	1.50
69/209	Doug Lidster, Van./Wayne Gretzky, L.A.	2.50
72/210	Garth Butcher, Van./Patrick Roy, Mtl.	1.25
73/212	Larry Melnyk, Van./Chris Chelios, Mtl.	.50
74/213	Kelly Miller, Wsh./Guy Carbonneau, Mtl.	.20
75/214	Dino Ciccarelli, Wsh./Joe Mullen, Cgy.	.25
76/215	Scott Stevens, Wsh./Brian Leetch, NYR.	1.00
77/216	Rod Langway, Wsh./Tim Kerr, Pha.	.25
78/219	Dave Christian, Wsh./Esa Tikkanen, Edm.	.20
79/220	Steve Leach, Wsh./Charlie Huddy, Edm.	.20

	No.	Player	NRMT-MT
□	82/223	Patrik Sundstrom, N.J./Steve Smith, Edm.	.20
□	83/224	Kirk Muller, N.J./Kevin Lowe, Edm.	.25
□	84/225	Tom Kurvers, N.J./Chris Joseph, Edm.	.20
□	85/226	Walt Poddubny, N.J./Craig MacTavish, Edm.	.20
□	88/229	Aaron Broten, N.J./Craig Muni, Edm.	.20
□	89/230	Brendan Shanahan, N.J./Bill Ranford (G), Edm.	1.50
□	92/231	Lanny McDonald, Cgy./John Cullen, Pgh.	.25
□	93/232	Rick Wamsley (G), Cgy./Zarley Zalapski, Pgh.	.25
□	96/233	Joel Otto, Cgy./Bob Errey, Pgh.	.20
□	97/234	Jiri Hrdina, Cgy./Dan Quinn, Pgh.	.20
□	98/235	Gary Roberts, Cgy./Tom Barrasso (G), Pgh.	.50
□	99/236	Jim Peplinski, Cgy./Rob Brown, Pgh.	.20
□	102/239	Colin Patterson, Cgy./Carey Wilson, NYR.	.20
□	103/240	Doug Gilmour, Cgy./Brian Leetch, NYR.	1.50
□	104/241	Mike Bullard, Pha./Tony Granato, NYR.	.20
□	105/242	Per-Erik Eklund, Pha./James Patrick, NYR.	.20
□	106/245	Brian Propp, Pha./Guy Lafleur, NYR.	.35
□	107/246	Ron Sutter, Pha./John Vanbiesbrouck (G), NYR.	1.00
□	108/247	Rick Tocchet, Pha./Bernie Federko, Det.	.25
□	109/248	Mark Howe, Pha./Greg Stefan (G), Det.	.25
□	112/249	Mikko Makela, NYI./Mike O'Connell, Det.	.20
□	113/250	David Volek, NYI./Dave Barr, Det.	.20
□	114/251	Gary Nylund, NYI./Lee Norwood, Det.	.20
□	115/252	Brent Sutter, NYI./Shawn Burr, Det.	.20
□	116/255	Derek King, NYI./Christian Ruuttu, Buf.	.20
□	117/256	Gerald Diduck, NYI./Rick Vaive, Buf.	.20
□	136/257	Iain Duncan, Wpg./Doug Bodger, Buf.	.20
□	137/258	Eldon Reddick (G), Wpg./Dave Andreychuk, Buf.	.25
□	140/259	Jim Kyte, Wpg./Ray Sheppard, Buf.	.35
□	141/260	Doug Smail, Wpg./Mike Foligno, Buf.	.20
□	142/263	Pat Elynuik, Wpg./Ray Ferraro, Hfd.	.20
□	143/264	Randy Carlyle, Wpg./Scott Young, Hfd.	.20
□	146/265	Peter Taglianetti, Wpg./Dave Babych, Hfd.	.20
□	147/266	Laurie Boschman, Wpg./Paul MacDermid, Hfd.	.20
□	148/267	Luc Robitaille, L.A./Mike Liut (G), Hfd.	.35
□	149/268	Kelly Hrudey (G), L.A./Dave Tippett, Hfd.	.20

FUTURE STARS

The Future Stars insert cards appear on the backs of sticker nos. 2, 4, 7, 10/150, 14/156, 18, 21/161, 32, 47, 54/198, 55/199, 60, 61, 63/205, 64, 65, 66/206, 67/207, 72/210, 76/215, 77/216, 88/229, 91, 96/233, 102/239, 107/246, 112/249, 117/256, 146/265, 175/35, 185/41, 187, 184/40, 203. After the sticker has been removed you are left with the insert card.

Card Size: 2 1/2" x 3"

Insert Set (34 cards): 15.00

	No.	Player	NRMT-MT
□	1	Greg Hawgood, Bos.	.25
□	2	Craig Janney, Bos.	.75
□	3	Bob Joyce, Bos.	.25
□	4	Benoît Hogue, Buf.	.25
□	5	Jiri Hrdina, Cgy.	.25
□	6	Peter Sidorkiewicz (G), Hfd.	.25
□	7	Scott Young, Hfd.	.35
□	8	Sean Burke (G), N.J.	.35
□	9	David Volek, NYI.	.25
□	10	Tony Granato, NYR.	.25
□	11	Brian Leetch, NYR.	1.25
□	12	Gord Murphy, Pha.	.25
□	13	John Cullen, Pgh.	.25
□	14	Zarley Zalapski, Pgh.	.25
□	15	Iiro Jarvi, Que.	.25
□	16	Joe Sakic, Que.	1.75
□	17	Vincent Riendeau (G), Stl.	.35
□	18	Daniel Marois, Tor.	.25
□	19	Trevor Linden, Van.	.75
□	20	Pat Elynuik, Wpg.	.25
□	21	Bob Essensa (G), Wpg.	.35
□	22	Checklist (1-34)	.25
□	23	AS: Joe Mullen, Cgy.	.35
□	24	AS: Mario Lemieux, Pgh.	2.25
□	25	AS: Gerard Gallant, Cgy.	.25
□	26	AS: Chris Chelios, Mtl.	.50
□	27	AS: Al MacInnis, Cgy.	.35
□	28	AS: Patrick Roy (G), Mtl.	2.00
□	29	AS: Geoff Courtnall, Wsh.	.25
□	30	AS: Wayne Gretzky, L.A.	3.00
□	31	AS: Rob Brown, Pgh.	.25
□	32	AS: Steve Duchesne, L.A.	.25
□	33	AS: Ray Bourque, Bos.	.75
□	34	AS: Mike Vernon (G), Cgy.	.50

1989 - 90 PANINI STICKERS

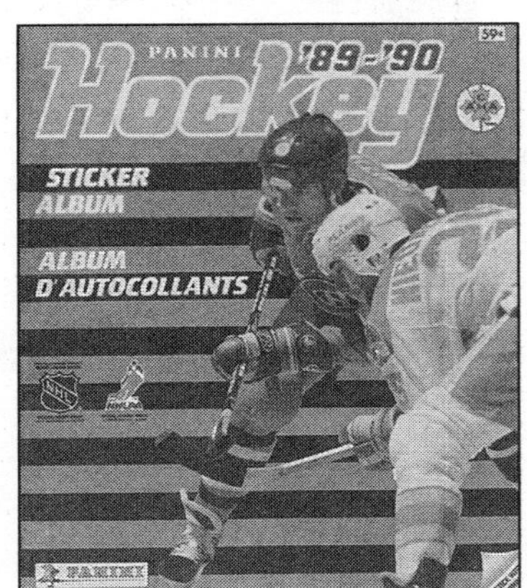

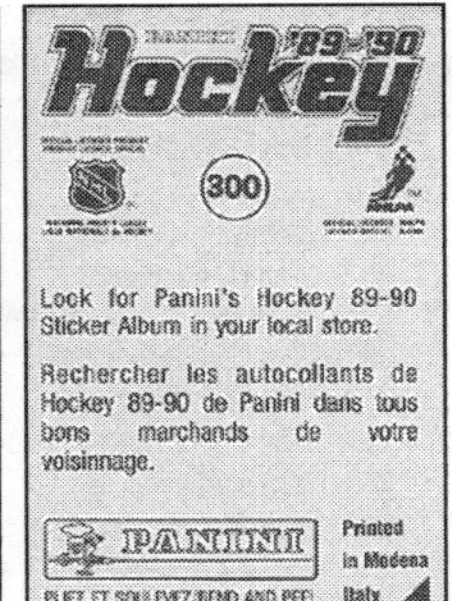

Sticker Size: 1 7/8" x 3"

Imprint: PANINI

Complete Set (384 stickers): 40.00

Common Player: .15

Album: 5.00

	No.	Player	NRMT-MT
□	1	NHL Logo	.15
□	2	Playoff schedule	.15
□	3	Calgary Flames vs Chicago Blackhawks	.15
□	4	Joe Nieuwendyk/ Kirk McLean	.25
□	5	Los Angeles Kings vs Edmonton Oilers	.15
□	6	Calgary Flames vs Chicago Blackhawks	.25
□	7	Calgary Flames vs Chicago Blackhawks	.25

Note: Stickers 6-7 feature Steve Konroyd, Mike Vernon and Hakan Loob.

	No.	Player	NRMT-MT
□	8	Boston Bruins vs Buffalo Sabres	.15
□	9	Montréal Canadiens vs Boston Bruins	.15
□	10	Philadelphia Flyers score	.15
□	11	Montréal Canadiens vs Philadelphia Flyers	.50
□	12	Montréal Canadiens vs Philadelphia Flyers	.15

Note: Stickers 11-12 feature Rick Green, Patrick Roy and Tim Kerr.

	No.	Player	NRMT-MT
□	13	Patrick Roy (G), etc	.50
□	14	Celebration: Montréal Canadiens	.15
□	15	R. Walter/D Gilmour/J. Macoun	.25
□	16	Montréal Canadiens vs Calgary Flames	.50
□	17	Celebration: Calgary Flames	.15
□	18	Calgary Flames vs Montréal Canadiens	.15
□	19	Calgary Flames vs Montréal Canadiens	.50

Note: Stickers 18-19 feature B. MacLellan, P. Roy and C. Ludwig.

	No.	Player	NRMT-MT
□	20	Conn Smythe Trophy: Al MacInnis	.15
□	21	Calgary Flames	.15
□	22	Calgary Flames	.15
□	23	Calgary Flames	.15
□	24	Calgary Flames	.15
□	25	Stanley Cup	.15
□	26	Calgary Flames Logo	.15
□	27	Joe Mullen, Cgy.	.20
□	28	Doug Gilmour, Cgy.	.50
□	29	Joe Nieuwendyk, Cgy.	.35
□	30	Gary Suter, Cgy.	.20
□	31	D. Gilmour/ B. McCrimmon/ R. Ramage, Cgy.	.15
□	32	Al MacInnis, Cgy.	.20
□	33	Brad McCrimmon, Cgy.	.15
□	34	Mike Vernon (G), Cgy.	.35
□	35	Gary Roberts, Cgy.	.35
□	36	Colin Patterson, Cgy.	.15
□	37	Jim Peplinski, Cgy.	.15
□	38	Jamie Macoun, Cgy.	.15
□	39	Lanny McDonald, Cgy.	.25
□	40	Saddledome, Cgy.	.15
□	41	Chicago Blackhawks Logo	.15
□	42	Darren Pang (G), Chi.	.20
□	43	Steve Larmer, Chi.	.25
□	44	Dirk Graham, Chi.	.15
□	45	Doug Wilson, Chi.	.15
□	46	Ed Belfour (G), Chi.	1.50
□	47	Dave Manson, Chi.	.15
□	48	Troy Murray, Chi.	.15
□	49	Denis Savard, Chi.	.35
□	50	Steve Thomas, Chi.	.15
□	51	Adam Creighton, Chi.	.15
□	52	Wayne Presley, Chi.	.15
□	53	Trent Yawney, Chi.	.15
□	54	Alain Chevrier (G), Chi.	.25
□	55	Chicago Stadium	.15
□	56	Detroit Red Wings Logo	.15
□	57	Steve Yzerman, Det.	1.00
□	58	Gerard Gallant, Det.	.15
□	59	Greg Stefan (G), Det.	.15
□	60	Dave Barr, Det.	.15
□	61	G. Hanlon/ M. O'Connell/ G. Gallant/ P. LaFontaine	.15
□	62	Steve Chiasson, Det.	.20
□	63	Shawn Burr, Det.	.15
□	64	Rick Zombo, Det.	.15
□	65	Glen Hanlon (G), Det.	.20
□	66	Jeff Sharples, Det.	.15
□	67	Joey Kocur, Det.	.15
□	68	Lee Norwood, Det.	.15
□	69	Mike O'Connell, Det.	.15
□	70	Joe Louis Arena, Det.	.15
□	71	Edmonton Oilers Logo	.15
□	72	Jimmy Carson, Edm.	.15
□	73	Jari Kurri, Edm.	.25
□	74	Mark Messier, Edm.	.50
□	75	Craig Simpson, Edm.	.15
□	76	Kevin Miller/ Keith Acton, Edm.	.15
□	77	Glenn Anderson, Edm.	.20
□	78	Craig MacTavish, Edm.	.15
□	79	Kevin Lowe, Edm.	.15
□	80	Craig Muni, Edm.	.15
□	81	Bill Ranford (G), Edm.	.50
□	82	Charlie Huddy, Edm.	.15
□	83	Steve Smith, Edm.	.15
□	84	Normand Lacombe, Edm.	.15
□	85	Northlands Coliseum, Edm.	.15
□	86	Los Angeles Kings Logo	.15
□	87	Wayne Gretzky, L.A.	3.00
□	88	Bernie Nicholls, L.A.	.25
□	89	Kelly Hrudey (G), L.A.	.20
□	90	John Tonelli, L.A.	.15
□	91	K. Hrudey/ G. Anderson, L.A.	.15
□	92	Steve Kasper, L.A.	.15
□	93	Steve Duchesne, L.A.	.20
□	94	Mike Krushelnyski, L.A.	.15
□	95	Luc Robitaille, L.A.	.25
□	96	Ron Duguay, L.A.	.15
□	97	Glenn Healy (G), L.A.	.35
□	98	Dave Taylor, L.A.	.15
□	99	Marty McSorley, L.A.	.15
□	100	The Great Western Forum	.15
□	101	Minnesota North Stars Logo	.15
□	102	Kari Takko (G), Min.	.20
□	103	Dave Gagner, Min.	.20
□	104	Mike Gartner, Min.	.25
□	105	Brian Bellows, Min.	.20
□	106	Kari Takko, Min.	.15
□	107	Neal Broten, Min.	.20
□	108	Larry Murphy, Min.	.20
□	109	Basil McRae, Min.	.15
□	110	Perry Berezan, Min.	.15
□	111	Shawn Chambers, Min.	.15
□	112	Curt Giles, Min.	.15
□	113	Stewart Gavin, Min.	.15

	No.	Player	Price
☐	114	Jon Casey (G), Min.	.20
☐	115	Metropolitan Sports Center, Min.	.15
☐	116	St. Louis Blues Logo	.15
☐	117	Brett Hull, Stl.	1.50
☐	118	Peter Zezel, Stl.	.15
☐	119	Tony Hrkac, Stl.	.15
☐	120	Vincent Riendeau (G), Stl.	.20
☐	121	St. Louis Blues vs New York Islanders	.15
☐	122	Cliff Ronning, Stl.	.20
☐	123	Gino Cavallini, Stl.	.15
☐	124	Brian Benning, Stl.	.15
☐	125	Rick Meagher, Stl.	.15
☐	126	Steve Tuttle, Stl.	.15
☐	127	Paul Cavallini, Stl.	.15
☐	128	Tom Tilley, Stl.	.15
☐	129	Greg Millen (G), Stl.	.20
☐	130	St. Louis Arena, Stl.	.15
☐	131	Toronto Maple Leafs Logo	.15
☐	132	Ed Olczyk, Tor.	.15
☐	133	Gary Leeman, Tor.	.15
☐	134	Vincent Damphousse, Tor.	.50
☐	135	Tom Fergus, Tor.	.15
☐	136	Mark Osborne, Tor.	.15
☐	137	Daniel Marois, Tor.	.15
☐	138	Mark Osborne, Tor.	.15
☐	139	Allan Bester (G), Tor.	.20
☐	140	Al Iafrate, Tor.	.20
☐	141	Brad Marsh, Tor.	.15
☐	142	Luke Richardson, Tor.	.15
☐	143	Todd Gill, Tor.	.15
☐	144	Wendel Clark, Tor.	.25
☐	145	Maple Leaf Gardens, Tor.	.15
☐	146	Vancouver Canucks Logo	.15
☐	147	Petri Skriko, Van.	.15
☐	148	Trevor Linden, Van.	.50
☐	149	Tony Tanti, Van.	.15
☐	150	Steve Weeks (G), Van.	.20
☐	151	T. Tanti/ Canucks #21/ M. Makela, Van.	.15
☐	152	Brian Bradley, Van.	.15
☐	153	Barry Pederson, Van.	.15
☐	154	Greg Adams, Van.	.15
☐	155	Kirk McLean (G), Van.	.50
☐	156	Jim Sandlak, Van.	.15
☐	157	Rich Sutter, Van.	.15
☐	158	Garth Butcher, Van.	.15
☐	159	Stan Smyl, Van.	.15
☐	160	Pacific Coliseum, Van.	.15
☐	161	Winnipeg Jets Logo	.15
☐	162	Dale Hawerchuk, Wpg.	.25
☐	163	Thomas Steen, Wpg.	.15
☐	164	Brent Ashton, Wpg.	.15
☐	165	Pat Elynuik, Wpg.	.15
☐	166	R. Carlyle/ P. Flatley, Wpg.	.15
☐	167	Dave Ellett, Wpg.	.15
☐	168	Randy Carlyle, Wpg.	.15
☐	169	Laurie Boschman, Wpg.	.15
☐	170	Iain Duncan, Wpg.	.15
☐	171	Doug Smail, Wpg.	.15
☐	172	Teppo Numminen, Wpg.	.15
☐	173	Bob Essensa (G), Wpg.	.20
☐	174	Peter Taglianetti, Wpg.	.15
☐	175	Winnipeg Arena, Wpg.	.15
☐	176	AS: Steve Duchesne	.20
☐	177	AS: Luc Robitaille	.25
☐	178	AS: Mike Vernon (G)	.35
☐	179	AS: Wayne Gretzky	3.00
☐	180	AS: Kevin Lowe	.15
☐	181	AS: Jari Kurri	.25
☐	182	AS: Cam Neely	.35
☐	183	AS: Paul Coffey	.50
☐	184	AS: Mario Lemieux	2.25
☐	185	AS: Sean Burke (G)	.35
☐	186	AS: Rob Brown	.15
☐	187	AS: Ray Bourque	.50
☐	188	Boston Bruins Logo	.15
☐	189	Greg Hawgood, Bos.	.15
☐	190	Ken Linseman, Bos.	.15
☐	191	Andy Moog (G), Bos.	.25
☐	192	Cam Neely, Bos.	.35
☐	193	Boston Bruins vs Philadelphia Flyers	.15
☐	194	Andy Brickley, Bos.	.15
☐	195	Réjean Lemelin (G), Bos.	.20
☐	196	Bob Carpenter, Bos.	.15
☐	197	Randy Burridge, Bos.	.15
☐	198	Craig Janney, Bos.	.50
☐	199	Bob Joyce, Bos.	.15
☐	200	Glen Wesley, Bos.	.15
☐	201	Ray Bourque, Bos.	.50
☐	202	Boston Garden, Bos.	.15
☐	203	Buffalo Sabres Logo	.15
☐	204	Pierre Turgeon, Buf.	.75
☐	205	Phil Housley, Buf.	.25
☐	206	Rick Vaive, Buf.	.15
☐	207	Christian Ruuttu, Buf.	.15
☐	208	Philadelphia Flyers vs Buffalo Sabres	.15
☐	209	Doug Bodger, Buf.	.15
☐	210	Mike Foligno, Buf.	.15
☐	211	Ray Sheppard, Buf.	.15
☐	212	John Tucker, Buf.	.15
☐	213	Scott Arniel, Buf.	.15
☐	214	Daren Puppa (G), Buf.	.35
☐	215	Dave Andreychuk, Buf.	.35
☐	216	Uwe Krupp, Buf.	.15
☐	217	Memorial Auditorium, Buf.	.15
☐	218	Hartford Whalers Logo	.15
☐	219	Kevin Dineen, Hfd.	.15
☐	220	Peter Sidorkiewicz (G), Hfd.	.20
☐	221	Ron Francis, Hfd.	.35
☐	222	Ray Ferraro, Hfd.	.15
☐	223	Dean Evanson vs. Islanders	.15
☐	224	Scott Young, Hfd.	.15
☐	225	Dave Babych, Hfd.	.15
☐	226	Dave Tippett, Hfd.	.15
☐	227	Paul MacDermid, Hfd.	.15
☐	228	Ulf Samuelsson, Hfd.	.15
☐	229	Sylvain Côté, Hfd.	.15
☐	230	Jody Hull, Hfd.	.15
☐	231	Don Maloney, Hfd.	.15
☐	232	Hartford Civic Center, Hfd.	.15
☐	233	Montréal Canadiens Logo	.15
☐	234	Mats Naslund, Mtl.	.20
☐	235	Patrick Roy (G), Mtl.	2.00
☐	236	Bobby Smith, Mtl.	.15
☐	237	Chris Chelios, Mtl.	.50
☐	238	T. Hunter/ C. Chelios, Mtl.	.25
☐	239	Stéphane Richer, Mtl.	.20
☐	240	Claude Lemieux, Mtl.	.20
☐	241	Guy Carbonneau, Mtl.	.15
☐	242	Shayne Corson, Mtl.	.15
☐	243	Mike McPhee, Mtl.	.15
☐	244	Petr Svoboda, Mtl.	.15
☐	245	Larry Robinson, Mtl.	.20
☐	246	Brian Hayward (G), Mtl.	.20
☐	247	Montréal Forum, Mtl.	.15
☐	248	New Jersey Devils Logo	.15
☐	249	John MacLean, N.J.	.20
☐	250	Patrik Sundstrom, N.J.	.15
☐	251	Kirk Muller, N.J.	.15
☐	252	Tom Kurvers, N.J.	.15
☐	253	Pat Conacher, N.J.	.15
☐	254	Aaron Broten, N.J.	.15
☐	255	Brendan Shanahan, N.J.	1.00
☐	256	Sean Burke (G), N.J.	.35
☐	257	Tommy Albelin, N.J.	.15
☐	258	Ken Daneyko, N.J.	.15
☐	259	Randy Velischek, N.J.	.15
☐	260	Mark Johnson, N.J.	.15
☐	261	Jim Korn, N.J.	.15
☐	262	Brendan Byrne Arena, N.J.	.15
☐	263	New York Islanders Logo	.15
☐	264	Pat LaFontaine, NYI.	.50
☐	265	Mark Fitzpatrick (G), NYI.	.25
☐	266	Brent Sutter, NYI.	.20
☐	267	David Volek, NYI.	.15
☐	268	P. Flatley/ M. Makelä/ L. DeBlois, NYI.	.15
☐	269	Bryan Trottier, NYI.	.25
☐	270	Mikko Makela, NYI.	.15
☐	271	Derek King, NYI.	.15
☐	272	Patrick Flatley, NYI.	.15
☐	273	Jeff Norton, NYI.	.15
☐	274	Gerald Diduck, NYI.	.15
☐	275	Alan Kerr, NYI.	.15
☐	276	Jeff Hackett (G), NYI.	.35
☐	277	Nassau Veterans Memorial Coliseum, NYI.	.15
☐	278	New York Rangers Logo	.15
☐	279	Brian Leetch, NYR.	1.00
☐	280	Carey Wilson, NYR.	.15
☐	281	Tomas Sandström, NYR.	.15
☐	282	John Vanbiesbrouck (G), NYR.	1.00
☐	283	Michel Petit, NYR.	.15
☐	284	Bob Froese (G), NYR.	.20
☐	285	Tony Granato, NYR.	.25
☐	286	Brian Mullen, NYR.	.15
☐	287	Kelly Kisio, NYR.	.15
☐	288	Ulf Dahlen, NYR.	.15
☐	289	James Patrick, NYR.	.15
☐	290	John Ogrodnick, NYR.	.15
☐	291	Michel Petit, NYR.	.15
☐	292	Madison Square Garden, NYR.	.15
☐	293	Philadelphia Flyers Logo	.15
☐	294	Tim Kerr, Pha.	.20
☐	295	Rick Tocchet, Pha.	.25
☐	296	Per-Erik Eklund, Pha.	.15
☐	297	Terry Carkner, Pha.	.15
☐	298	Philadelphia Flyers vs Montréal Canadiens	.15
☐	299	Ron Sutter, Pha.	.15
☐	300	Mark Howe, Pha.	.20
☐	301	Keith Acton, Pha.	.15
☐	302	Ron Hextall (G), Pha.	.35
☐	303	Gord Murphy, Pha.	.15
☐	304	Derrick Smith, Pha.	.15
☐	305	Dave Poulin, Pha.	.15
☐	306	Brian Propp, Pha.	.15
☐	307	The Spectrum, Pha.	.15
☐	308	Pittsburgh Penguins Logo	.15
☐	309	Mario Lemieux, Pgh.	2.25
☐	310	Rob Brown, Pgh.	.15
☐	311	Paul Coffey, Pgh.	.50
☐	312	Tom Barrasso (G), Pgh.	.25
☐	313	T. Barrasso (G)/ Ron Sutter/etc., Pgh.	.15
☐	314	Dan Quinn, Pgh.	.15
☐	315	Bob Errey, Pgh.	.15
☐	316	John Cullen, Pgh.	.25
☐	317	Phil Bourque, Pgh.	.15
☐	318	Zarley Zalapski, Pgh.	.15
☐	319	Troy Loney, Pgh.	.15
☐	320	Jim Johnson, Pgh.	.15
☐	321	Kevin Stevens, Pgh.	.50
☐	322	Civic Arena, Pgh.	.15
☐	323	Québec Nordiques Logo	.15
☐	324	Peter Stastny, Que.	.35
☐	325	Jeff Brown, Que.	.15
☐	326	Michel Goulet, Que.	.35
☐	327	Joe Sakic, Que.	2.50
☐	328	Tim Kerr/ Mario Marois, Que.	.15
☐	329	Iiro Jarvi, Que.	.15
☐	330	Paul Gillis, Que.	.15
☐	331	Randy Moller, Que.	.15
☐	332	Ron Tugnutt (G), Que.	.35
☐	333	Robert Picard, Que.	.15
☐	334	Curtis Leschyshyn, Que.	.15
☐	335	Marc Fortier, Que.	.15
☐	336	Mario Marois, Que.	.15
☐	337	Le Colisée, Que.	.15
☐	338	Washington Capitals Logo	.15
☐	339	Mike Ridley, Wsh.	.15
☐	340	Geoff Courtnall, Wsh.	.25
☐	341	Scott Stevens, Wsh.	.20
☐	342	Dino Ciccarelli, Wsh.	.25
☐	343	Tim Hunter, Wsh.	.15
☐	344	Bob Mason (G), Wsh.	.20
☐	345	Dave Christian, Wsh.	.15
☐	346	Dale Hunter, Wsh.	.20
☐	347	Kevin Hatcher, Wsh.	.15
☐	348	Kelly Miller, Wsh.	.15
☐	349	Steve Leach, Wsh.	.15
☐	350	Rod Langway, Wsh.	.20
☐	351	Bob Rouse, Wsh.	.15
☐	352	Capital Centre, Wsh.	.15
☐	353	Calgary Flames	.15
☐	354	Edmonton Oilers	.15
☐	355	Winnipeg Jets	.15
☐	356	Toronto Maple Leafs	.15
☐	357	Buffalo Sabres	.15
☐	358	Montréal Canadiens	.15
☐	359	Québec Nordiques	.15
☐	360	New Jersey Devils	.15
☐	361	Boston Bruins	.15
☐	362	Hartford Whalers	.15
☐	363	Vancouver Canucks	.15
☐	364	Minnesota North Stars	.15
☐	365	Los Angeles Kings	.15
☐	366	St. Louis Blues	.15
☐	367	Chicago Blackhawks	.15
☐	368	Detroit Red Wings	.15

	No.	Player	NRMT-MT
☐	369	Pittsburgh Penguins	.15
☐	370	Washington Capitals	.15
☐	371	Philadelphia Flyers	.15
☐	372	New York Rangers	.15
☐	373	New York Islanders	.15
☐	374	LL: Wayne Gretzky	3.00
☐	375	LL: Mario Lemieux	2.25
☐	376	LL: Patrick Roy (G)/Brian Hayward (G)	1.50
☐	377	LL: Tim Kerr	.20
☐	378	LL: Brian Leetch	.75
☐	379	LL: Chris Chelios	.50
☐	380	LL: Joe Mullen	.20
☐	381	LL: Guy Carbonneau	.15
☐	382	LL: Bryan Trottier	.25
☐	383	LL: Patrick Roy (G)	2.00
☐	384	LL: Joe Mullen	.20

1989 - 90 PRO CARDS TEAM SETS

These cards have a yellow border.
Imprint: © 1989 ProCards, Inc.
Complete AHL Set (360 cards): **90.00**
Complete IHL Set (208 cards): **60.00**
Common Player: **.35**

NEW HAVEN NIGHTHAWKS - AHL

Team Set (27 cards): **7.00**

	No.	Player	NRMT-MT
☐	1	New Haven Nighthawks Checklist	.35
☐	2	François Breault	.35
☐	3	Paul Kelly	.35
☐	4	Phil Skyes	.35
☐	5	Ron Scott (G)	.50
☐	6	Micah Aivazoff	.35
☐	7	Sylvain Couturier	.35
☐	8	Carl Repp (G)	.50
☐	9	Murray Brumwell	.35
☐	10	Todd Elik	.50
☐	11	Darwin Bozek	.35
☐	12	Eric Germain	.35
☐	13	Scott Young	.35
☐	14	Chris Kontos	.35
☐	15	Scot Bjugstad	.35
☐	16	Eric Ricard	.35
☐	17	Ross Wilson	.35
☐	18	Graham Stanley	.35
☐	19	Chris Panek	.35
☐	20	Nick Fotiu	.50
☐	21	René Chapdelaine	.35
☐	22	Gordie Walker	.35
☐	23	Tim Bothwell	.35
☐	24	Kevin MacDonald	.35
☐	25	Darryl Williams	.35
☐	26	John Van Kessel	.35
☐	27	Paul Brydges	.35

MONCTON HAWKS - AHL

Team Set (25 cards): **8.00**

	No.	Player	NRMT-MT
☐	28	Moncton Hawks Checklist	.35
☐	29	Guy Larose	.35
☐	30	Danton Cole	.35
☐	31	Brent Hughes	.35
☐	32	Larry Bernard	.35
☐	33	Stu Kulak	.35
☐	34	Bob Essensa (G)	.75
☐	35	Luciano Borsato	.35
☐	36	Guy Gosselin	.35
☐	37	Todd Flichel	.35
☐	38	Brian Hunt	.35
☐	39	Neil Meadmore	.35
☐	40	Matt Hervey	.35
☐	41	Dallas Eakins	.50
☐	42	Brad Jones	.35
☐	43	Chris Norton	.35
☐	44	Bryan Marchment	1.00
☐	45	Rick Tabaracci (G)	3.00
☐	46	Grant Richison	.35
☐	47	Brian McReynolds	.35
☐	48	Tony Joseph	.35
☐	49	Dave Farish, Coach/G.M.	.35
☐	50	Rob Snitzer, Trainer	.35
☐	51	Ron Wilson	.50
☐	52	Scott Schneider	.35

MAINE MARINERS - AHL

Team Set (24 cards): **8.00**

	No.	Player	NRMT-MT
☐	53	Maine Mariners Checklist	.35
☐	54	Dave Buda	.35
☐	55	Paul Beraldo	.35
☐	56	Lou Crawford	.35
☐	57	Mark Montanari	.35
☐	58	Don Sweeney	1.00
☐	59	Jeff Sirkka	.35
☐	60	Norm Foster (G)	.50
☐	61	Greg Poss	.35
☐	62	Gord Cruickshank	.35
☐	63	Bruce Shoebottom	.35
☐	64	Mark Ziliotto	.35
☐	65	Ron Hoover	.35
☐	66	Scott Harlow	.35
☐	67	Mike Millar	.35
☐	68	Bob Beers	.35
☐	69	Ray Neufeld	.50
☐	70	Graeme Townshend	.35
☐	71	Billy O'Dwyer	.35
☐	72	Frank Caprice (G)	.50
☐	73	John Blum	.35
☐	74	Jerry Foster, Trainer	.35
☐	75	Bill Sutherland, Assistant Coach/Rick Bowness, Coach	.35
☐	76	Scott Drevitch	.35

BALTIMORE SKIPJACKS - AHL

Team Set (27 cards): **8.00**

	No.	Player	NRMT-MT
☐	77	Baltimore Skipjacks Checklist	.35
☐	78	John Purves	.35
☐	79	Jeff Greenlaw	.35
☐	80	Tim Taylor	.50
☐	81	Alfie Turcotte	.35
☐	82	Dan Redmond, Trainer	.35
☐	83	Chris Felix	.35
☐	84	Bobby Babcock	.35
☐	85	Steve Maltais	.35
☐	86	Mike Richard	.35
☐	87	Skipjacks Team Photo	.35
☐	88	Bob Mason (G)	.50
☐	89	Mark Ferner	.35
☐	90	Steve Seftel	.35
☐	91	Brian Tutt	.35
☐	92	Terry Murray, Coach	.75
☐	93	Jim Hrivnak (G)	.50
☐	94	Tyler Larter	.35
☐	95	Tim Bergland	.35
☐	96	Dennis Smith	.35
☐	97	Steve Hollett	.35
☐	98	Shawn Simpson (G)	.50
☐	99	Robin Bawa	.35
☐	100	John Druce	.50
☐	101	Kent Paynter	.35
☐	102	Alain Côté	.35
☐	103	J.P. Mattingly, Trainer	.35

NEWMARKET SAINTS - AHL

Team Set (25 cards): **8.00**

	No.	Player	NRMT-MT
☐	104	Newmarket Saints Checklist	.35
☐	105	Dean Anderson (G)	.50
☐	106	Wes Jarvis	.35
☐	107	Brian Blad	.35
☐	108	Derek Laxdal	.35
☐	109	Kent Hulst	.35
☐	110	Tim Bernhardt (G)	.50
☐	111	Brian Hoard	.35
☐	112	Bill Root	.35
☐	113	Paul Gardner, Coach	.50
☐	114	Tim Armstrong	.35
☐	115	Sean McKenna	.35
☐	116	Tim Bean	.35
☐	117	Alan Hepple	.35
☐	118	Greg Hotham	.35
☐	119	Scott Pearson	.50
☐	120	Peter Ihnacak	.60
☐	121	John McIntyre	.50
☐	122	Paul Gagné	.35
☐	123	Darren Veitch	.35
☐	124	Mark LaForest (G)	.50
☐	125	Doug Shedden	.35
☐	126	Bobby Reynolds	.35
☐	127	Tie Domi	3.00
☐	128	Ken Hammond	.35

CAPE BRETON OILERS - AHL

Team Set (23 cards): **8.00**

	No.	Player	NRMT-MT
☐	129	Cape Breton Oilers Checklist	.35
☐	130	Wade Campbell	.35
☐	131	Chris Joseph	.50
☐	132	Mario Barbe	.35
☐	133	Mike Greenlay (G)	.50
☐	134	Peter Soberlak	.35
☐	135	Bruce Bell	.35
☐	136	Dan Currie	.35
☐	137	Fabian Joseph	.35
☐	138	Stan Drulia	.35
☐	139	Todd Charlesworth	.35
☐	140	Norm Maciver	1.00
☐	141	David Haas	.35
☐	142	Tim Tisdale	.35
☐	143	Eldon Reddick (G)	.50
☐	144	Alexander Tyjnych (G)	.50
☐	145	Kim Issel	.35
☐	146	Corey Foster	.35
☐	147	Tomas Kapusta	.35
☐	148	Brian Wilks	.35
☐	149	John LeBlanc	.35
☐	150	Ivan Matulik	.35
☐	151	Shaun Van Allen	1.00

HALIFAX CITADELS - AHL

Team Set (27 cards): **8.00**

	No.	Player	NRMT-MT
☐	152	Halifax Citadels Checklist	.35
☐	153	Scott Gordon (G)	.50
☐	154	Trevor Steinburg	.35
☐	155	Miroslav Ihnacak	.35
☐	156	Jamie Baker	.35
☐	157	Robbie Ftorek, Coach	.35
☐	158	Chris McQuaid, Equip. Mgr./Brent Smith, Trainer	.35
☐	159	Mario Brunetta (G)	.50
☐	160	Jean-Marc Routhier	.35
☐	161	David Espe	.35
☐	162	Ken Quinney	.35
☐	163	Mark Vermette	.35
☐	164	Dean Hopkins	.35
☐	165	Claude Julien	.50
☐	166	Claude Lapointe	.50
☐	167	Stéphane Morin	.35
☐	168	Bryan Fogarty	.35
☐	169	Dave Pichette	.50
☐	170	Kevin Kaminski	.35
☐	171	Brent Severyn	.35
☐	172	Max Middendorf	.35
☐	173	Jean-Marc Richard	.35
☐	174	Gerald Bzdel	.35
☐	175	Ladislav Tresl	.35
☐	176	Jaroslav Sevcik	.35
☐	177	Greg Smyth	.35
☐	178	Joel Baillargeon	.35

SHERBROOKE CANADIENS - AHL

Team Set (23 cards): **10.00**

	No.	Player	NRMT-MT
☐	179	Sherbrook Canadiens Checklist	.35
☐	180	André Racicot (G)	.50
☐	181	J.C. Bergeron (G)	.50
☐	182	Jim Nesich	.35
☐	183	Todd Richards	.35

	No.	Player	NRMT-MT
☐	184	François Gravel (G)	.35
☐	185	Lyle Odelein	1.50
☐	186	Benoît Brunet	1.50
☐	187	Mario Roberge	.35
☐	188	Marc Saumier	.35
☐	189	Normand Desjardins	.35
☐	190	Dan Woodley	.35
☐	191	Andrew Cassels	2.00
☐	192	Roy Mitchell	.35
☐	193	Guy Darveau	.35
☐	194	Ed Cristofoli	.35
☐	195	Stéphane Richer	.35
☐	196	Jacques Parent, Athletic Therapist	.35
☐	197	Luc Gauthier	.35
☐	198	John Ferguson	.35
☐	199	Mathieu Schneider	2.50
☐	200	Serge Roberge	.35
☐	201	Jean Hamel, Coach	.35

UTICA DEVILS - AHL

Team Set (27 cards): 8.00

	No.	Player	NRMT-MT
☐	202	Utica Devils Checklist	.35
☐	203	Jason Simon	.35
☐	204	Jeff Madill	.35
☐	205	Kevin Todd	.50
☐	206	Myles O'Connor	.35
☐	207	Jon Morris	.35
☐	208	Bob Hoffmeyer, Associate Coach	.35
☐	209	Paul Ysebaert	1.00
☐	210	Steve Rooney	.35
☐	211	Claude Vilgrain	.35
☐	212	Paul Guay	.35
☐	213	Rollie Melanson (G)	.50
☐	214	Tom McVie, Coach	.50
☐	215	Dave Marcinyshyn	.35
☐	216	Perry Anderson	.35
☐	217	Jamie Huscroft	.35
☐	218	Bob Woods	.35
☐	219	Pat Conacher	1.00
☐	220	Jean-Marc Lanthier	.35
☐	221	Chris Kiene	.35
☐	222	Eric Weinrich	1.00
☐	223	Brian Fitzgerald, Assistant Trainer	.35
☐	224	Craig Billington (G)	1.50
☐	225	Jim Thomson	.35
☐	226	Tim Budy	.35
☐	227	Marc Laniel	.35
☐	228	Robert Bill, Trainer	.35

SPRINGFIELD INDIANS - AHL

Team Set (26 cards): 10.00

	No.	Player	NRMT-MT
☐	229	Springfield Indians Checklist	.35
☐	230	Mike Walsh	.35
☐	231	Dale Henry	.35
☐	232	Bill Berg	.35
☐	233	Hank Lammens	.35
☐	234	Rob DiMaio	.75
☐	235	Shawn Byram	.35
☐	236	Jeff Hackett (G)	3.00
☐	237	Wayne McBean	.35
☐	238	Tim Hanley	.35
☐	239	Tom Fitzgerald	.50
☐	240	Mike Stevens	.35
☐	241	George Maneluk (G)	.50
☐	242	Dean Ewen	.35
☐	243	Dale Kushner	.35
☐	244	Shawn Evans	.35
☐	245	Rod Dallman	.35
☐	246	Mike Kelfer	.35
☐	247	Sean Lebrun	.35
☐	248	Kerry Clark	.50
☐	249	Ed Tyburski, Trainer	.35
☐	250	Derek King	2.00
☐	251	Marc Bergevin	.50
☐	252	Jeff Finley	.35
☐	253	Jim Roberts, Coach	.35
☐	254	Chris Pryor	.35

ROCHESTER AMERICANS - AHL

Team Set (28 cards): 10.00

	No.	Player	NRMT-MT
☐	255	Rochester Americans Checklist	.35
☐	256	Rob Ray	1.00
☐	257	Ken Priestlay	.35
☐	258	Darcy Wakaluk (G)	.75
☐	259	Richie Dunn	.35
☐	260	Ken Sutton	.50
☐	261	Terry Martin, Assistant Coach	.35
☐	262	Scott Metcalfe	.35
☐	263	Joel Savage	.35
☐	264	Brad Miller	.35
☐	265	Donald Audette	3.00
☐	266	John Van Boxmeer, Coach	.50
☐	267	Mascot The Moose	.35
☐	268	Brian Ford (G)	.50
☐	269	Darcy Loewen	.35
☐	270	Bob Halkidis	.35
☐	271	Steve Ludzik	.35
☐	272	Steve Smith	.35
☐	273	François Guay	.35
☐	274	Mike Donnelly	.35
☐	275	Darrin Shannon	1.00
☐	276	Jody Gage	.50
☐	277	Dave Baseggio	.35
☐	278	Bob Corkum	.50
☐	279	Jim Jackson	.35
☐	280	Don McSween	.35
☐	281	Jim Hofford	.35
☐	282	Scott McCrory	.35

BINGHAMTON WHALERS - AHL

Team Set (23 cards): 7.00

	No.	Player	NRMT-MT
☐	283	Binghamton Whalers Checklist	.35
☐	284	Raymond Saumier	.35
☐	285	Mike Berger	.35
☐	286	Corey Beaulieu	.35
☐	287	Doug McKay, Coach	.35
☐	288	Blair Atcheynum	.75
☐	289	Al Tuer	.35
☐	290	Chris Lindberg	.35
☐	291	Daryl Reaugh (G)	.50
☐	292	James Black	.35
☐	293	Vern Smith	.35
☐	294	Todd Krygier	.50
☐	295	Bob Bodak	.35
☐	296	Jon Smith, Trainer	.35
☐	297	Michel Picard	.50
☐	298	Jim Culhane	.35
☐	299	Brian Chapman	.35
☐	300	Jim Ennis	.35
☐	301	Jacques Caron, Goal Coach	.35
☐	302	Jim McKenzie	.35
☐	303	Kay Whitmore (G)	.50
☐	304	Terry Yake	.50
☐	305	Mike Moller	.35

ADIRONDACK RED WINGS - AHL

Team Set (24 cards): 8.00

	No.	Player	NRMT-MT
☐	306	Adirondack Red Wings Checklist	.35
☐	307	Bob Wilkie	.35
☐	308	Chris McRae	.35
☐	309	Chris Kotsopoulos	.50
☐	310	Steve Sumner, Assistant Trainer	.35
☐	311	Timothy Abbott, Assistant Trainer	.35
☐	312	Gordon Kruppke	.35
☐	313	Mike Gober	.35
☐	314	Al Conroy	.35
☐	315	Sam St. Laurent (G)	.50
☐	316	Dave Casey, Trainer	.35
☐	317	Yves Racine	.75
☐	318	Randy McKay	1.00
☐	319	Dale Krentz	.35
☐	320	Sheldon Kennedy	3.00
☐	321	Barry Melrose, Coach	1.00
☐	322	Dennis Holland	.35
☐	323	Glenn Merkosky	.35
☐	324	Murray Eaves	.35
☐	325	Mark Reimer (G)	.50
☐	326	Tim Cheveldae (G)	.75
☐	327	Peter Dineen	.35
☐	328	Dean Morton	.35
☐	329	Derek Mayer	.35

HERSHEY BEARS - AHL

Team Set (31 cards): 9.00

	No.	Player	NRMT-MT
☐	330	Hershey Bears Checklist	.35
☐	331	Don Biggs	.35
☐	332	Scott Sandelin	.35
☐	333	Shaun Sabol	.35
☐	334	Murray Baron	.50
☐	335	David Fenyves	.35
☐	336	Glen Seabrooke	.35
☐	337	Mark Freer	.50
☐	338	Ray Allison	.35
☐	339	Chris Jensen	.35
☐	340	Ross Fitzpatrick	.35
☐	341	Brian Dobbin	.35
☐	342	Darren Rumble	.35
☐	343	Mike Stothers	.35
☐	344	Jiri Latal	.35
☐	345	Don Nachbaur	.35
☐	346	John Stevens	.35
☐	347	Steven Fletcher	.35
☐	348	Kent Hawley	.35
☐	349	Bill Armstrong	.35
☐	350	Bruce Hoffort (G)	.50
☐	351	Gordon Paddock	.35
☐	352	Marc D'Amour (G)	.50
☐	353	Tim Tookey	.35
☐	354	Reid Simpson	.35
☐	355	Mark Bassen	.35
☐	356	Rocky Trottier	.35
☐	357	Harry Bricker, Assistant Trainer	.35
☐	358	Dan Stuck, Head Trainer	.35
☐	359	Al Hill, Assistant Coach	.50
☐	360	Kevin McCarthy, Coach	.50

PEORIA RIVERMAN - IHL

Team Set (23 cards): 30.00

	No.	Player	NRMT-MT
☐	1	Peoria Rivermen Checklist	.35
☐	2	Darwin McPherson	.35
☐	3	Pat Jablonski (G)	1.00
☐	4	Scott Paluch	.35
☐	5	Guy Hebert (G), Error	7.00
☐	6	Richard Pion	.35
☐	7	Curtis Joseph (G)	18.00
☐	8	Robert Dirk	.50
☐	9	Darin Smith	.35
☐	10	Terry MacLean	.35
☐	11	Kevin Miehm	.50
☐	12	Toby Ducolon	.35
☐	13	Mike Wolak	.35
☐	14	Adrien Plavsic	.50
☐	15	Dave Thomlinson	.35
☐	16	Jim Vesey	.35
☐	17	Michel Mongeau	.35
☐	18	Tom Nash, Trainer	.35
☐	19	David O'Brien	.35
☐	20	Dominic Lavoie	.35
☐	21	Keith Osborne	.35
☐	22	Rob Robinson	.35
☐	23	Wayne Thomas, Coach	.35

FLINT SPIRITS - IHL

Team Set (25 cards): 20.00

	No.	Player	NRMT-MT
☐	24	Flint Spirits Checklist	.35
☐	25	Jason Lafrenière	.35
☐	26	Rick Knickle (G)	.50
☐	27	Jerry Tarrant	.35
☐	28	Paul Broten	.50
☐	29	Kevin Miller	.50
☐	30	James Latos	.35
☐	31	Daniel Lacroix	.35
☐	32	Dennis Vial	.75
☐	33	Denis Larocque	.35
☐	34	Mike Golden	.35
☐	35	Mike Hurlbut	.35
☐	36	Scott Brower (G)	.50
☐	37	Lee Giffin	.35
☐	38	Jeff Bloemberg	.35
☐	39	Simon Wheeldon	.35
☐	40	Rob Zamuner	3.00
☐	41	Joe Paterson	.35
☐	42	Barry Chyzowski	.35
☐	43	Peter Laviolette	.35

	No.	Player	NRMT-MT
☐	44	Corey Millen	.50
☐	45	Darren Lowe	.35
☐	46	Peter Florentino	.35
☐	47	Soren True	.35
☐	48	Mike Richter (G)	15.00

INDIANAPOLIS ICE - IHL

Team Set (25 cards): 8.00

	No.	Player	NRMT-MT
☐	49	Indianapolis Ice Checklist	.35
☐	50	Sean Williams	.35
☐	51	Bruce Cassidy	.35
☐	52	Mark Kurzawski	.35
☐	53	Bob Bassen	.75
☐	54	Marty Nanne	.35
☐	55	Jari Torkki	.35
☐	56	Ryan McGill	.35
☐	57	Mike Peluso	1.00
☐	58	Darryl Sutter, Coach	1.00
☐	59	Dan Vincelette	.35
☐	60	Lonnie Loach	.50
☐	61	Mike Rucinski	.35
☐	62	Jim Playfair	.50
☐	63	Everett Sanipass	.35
☐	64	Dale Marquette	.35
☐	65	Gary Moscaluk	.35
☐	66	Mario Doyon	.35
☐	67	Ray Leblanc (G)	.50
☐	68	Mike Eagles	.50
☐	69	Warren Rychel	.50
☐	70	Jim Johannson	.35
☐	71	Cam Russell	.50
☐	72	Michael McNeill	.35
☐	73	Jim Waite (G)	1.00

KALAMAZOO WINGS - IHL

Team Set (25 cards): 8.00

	No.	Player	NRMT-MT
☐	74	Kalamazoo Wings Checklist	.35
☐	75	Kevin Schamehorn	.35
☐	76	Kevin Evans	.35
☐	77	D'Arcy Norton	.35
☐	78	Scott Robinson	.35
☐	79	Larry PePalma	.35
☐	80	Ed Courtenay	.35
☐	81	Rob Zettler	.50
☐	82	Dusan Pasek	.35
☐	83	Gary Emmons	.35
☐	84	Peter Lappin	.35
☐	85	Mario Thyer	.35
☐	86	Mike McHugh	.35
☐	87	Randy Smith	.35
☐	88	Link Gaetz	.50
☐	89	Ken Hodge	.35
☐	90	Pat MacLeod	.35
☐	91	Neil Wilkinson	.50
☐	92	Brett Barnett	.35
☐	93	Larry Dyck (G)	.35
☐	94	Dean Kolstad	.35
☐	95	Jarmo Myllys (G)	.75
☐	96	Paul Jerrard	.35
☐	97	Jean-François Quintin	.50
☐	98	Mitch Messier	.35

PHOENIX ROADRUNNERS - IHL

Team Set (23 cards): 7.00

	No.	Player	NRMT-MT
☐	99	Phoenix Roadrunners Checklist	.35
☐	100	Bryant Perrier	.35
☐	101	Keith Gretzky	1.00
☐	102	Don Martin	.35
☐	103	David Littman (G)	.50
☐	104	Mike Decarle	.35
☐	105	Grant Tkachuk	.35
☐	106	Richard Novak	.35
☐	107	Chris Luongo	.35
☐	108	Bruce Boudreau	.35
☐	109	Nick Beaulieu	.35
☐	110	Jeff Lamb	.35
☐	111	Rob Nichols	.35
☐	112	Gary Unger, Coach	.50
☐	113	Larry Floyd	.35
☐	114	Brent Sapergia	.35
☐	115	Randy Exelby (G)	.50
☐	116	Jim McGeough	.35
☐	117	Tom Karalis	.35
☐	118	Ken Spangler	.35
☐	119	Jacques Mailhot	.35
☐	120	Shawn Dineen, Assistant Coach	.35
☐	121	Dave Korol	.35

FORT WAYNE KOMETS - IHL

Team Set (20 cards): 6.00

	No.	Player	NRMT-MT
☐	122	Fort Wayne Komets Checklist	.35
☐	123	Colin Chin	.35
☐	124	Scott Shaunessy	.35
☐	125	Bob Lakso	.35
☐	126	Duane Joyce	.35
☐	127	Joe Stephan	.35
☐	128	Ron Shudra	.35
☐	129	Bob Fowler	.35
☐	130	Steve Bisson	.35
☐	131	Craig Endean	.35
☐	132	Carl Mokosak	.35
☐	133	Carey Lucyk	.35
☐	134	Craig Channell	.35
☐	135	Frédéric Chabot (G)	.50
☐	136	Brian Hannon	.35
☐	137	Keith Miller	.35
☐	138	Al Sims, Coach	.50
☐	139	Stéphane Beauregard (G)	.50
☐	140	Ron Handy	.35
☐	141	Byron Lomow	.35

MUSKEGON LUMBERJACKS - IHL

Team Set (23 cards): 6.00

	No.	Player	NRMT-MT
☐	142	Muskegon Lumberjacks Checklist	.35
☐	143	Jamie Leach	.35
☐	144	Chris Clifford (G)	.50
☐	145	Dave Capuano	.35
☐	146	Jeff Daniels	.35
☐	147	Dave Goertz	.35
☐	148	Perry Ganchar	.35
☐	149	Mitch Wilson	.35
☐	150	Scott Gruhl	.35
☐	151	Randy Taylor	.35
☐	152	Bruce Racine (G)	.50
☐	153	Dave Michayluk	.35
☐	154	Richard Zemlak	.35
☐	155	Brad Aitken	.35
☐	156	Paul Stanton	.50
☐	157	Darren Stolk	.35
☐	158	Jim Paek	.35
☐	159	Mark Kachowski	.35
☐	160	Dan Frawley	.35
☐	161	Mike Mersch	.35
☐	162	Glenn Mulvenna	.35
☐	163	Phil Russell, Assistant Coach	.50
☐	164	Blair MacDonald, Coach	.35

MILWAUKEE ADMIRALS - IHL

Team Set (25 cards): 8.00

	No.	Player	NRMT-MT
☐	165	Milwaukee Admirals Checklist	.35
☐	166	Shaun Clouston	.35
☐	167	Steve Veilleux	.35
☐	168	Peter George Bakovic	.35
☐	169	Peter Deboer	.35
☐	170	Ernie Vargas	.35
☐	171	Keith Street	.35
☐	172	Rob Murphy	.35
☐	173	David Bruce	.50
☐	174	Shannon Travis	.35
☐	175	Jeff Rohlicek	.35
☐	176	Jay Mazur	.35
☐	177	Kevan Guy	.35
☐	178	Troy Gamble (G)	.50
☐	179	Ronnie Stern	.35
☐	180	Jime Revenberg	.35
☐	181	José Charbonneau	.35
☐	182	Ian Kidd	.35
☐	183	Todd Hawkins	.35
☐	184	Carl Valimont	.35
☐	185	Jim Agnew	.35
☐	186	Curtis Hunt	.35
☐	187	Dean Cook (G)	.50
☐	188	Ron Wilson, Assistant Coach	3.00
☐	189	Ron Lapointe, Coach	.35

SALT LAKE GOLDEN EAGLES - IHL

Team Set (19 cards): 6.00

	No.	Player	NRMT-MT
☐	190	Salt Lake Golden Eagles Checklist	.35
☐	191	Brian Glynn	.35
☐	192	Stéphane Matteau	1.00
☐	193	Rick Barkovich	.35
☐	194	Jeff Wenaas	.35
☐	195	Darryl Olsen	.35
☐	196	Rick Lessard	.35
☐	197	Kevin Grant	.35
☐	198	Rich Chernomaz	.35
☐	199	Stu Grimson	.75
☐	200	Jamie Hislop, Asst. Coach/Bob Francis, Coach	.35
☐	201	Doug Pickell	.35
☐	202	Chris Biotti	.35
☐	203	Tim Sweeney	.50
☐	204	Ken Sabourin	.35
☐	205	Randy Bucyk	.35
☐	206	Wayne Cowley (G)	.50
☐	207	Rick Hayward	.35
☐	208	Marc Bureau	.50

1989 - 90 SEMIC ELITSERIEN STICKERS

Sticker Size: 3" x 2 1/8"
Imprint:
Complete Set (285 stickers): 45.00
Album: 6.00
Common Player: .20

	No.	Player	NRMT-MT
☐	1	AIK	.20
☐	2	Ake Lilljebojorn	.20
☐	3	Thomas Ostlund	.20
☐	4	Mats Thelin	.20
☐	5	Thomas Ahlen	.20
☐	6	Petri Liimatainen	.20
☐	7	Roger Ohman	.20
☐	8	Rikard Franzen	.20
☐	9	Stefan Claesson	.20
☐	10	Tommy Hedlund	.20
☐	11	Stefan Jansson	.20
☐	12	Peter Gradin	.20
☐	13	Thomas Gradin	.35
☐	14	Bo Berglund	.20
☐	15	Heinze Ehlers	.20
☐	16	Robert Burakovsky	.20
☐	17	Alexander Kozjevnikov	.20
☐	18	Peter Hammarstrom	.20
☐	19	Anders Gozzi	.20
☐	20	Thomas Bjuhr	.20
☐	21	Patric Englund	.20
☐	22	O. Nilsson	.20
☐	23	Mats Lindberg	.20
☐	24	Peter Johansson	.20
☐	25	Patric Kjellberg	.20
☐	26	Brynas IF	.20
☐	27	Lars Eriksson	.20
☐	28	Michael Sundlov	.20
☐	29	Per Djoos	.20
☐	30	Tommy Sjodin	.20
☐	31	Nikolai Davydkin	.20
☐	32	Niklas Gallstedt	.20
☐	33	Mikael Lindman	.20
☐	34	Jan-Erik Stormqvist	.20
☐	35	Tommy Melkersson	.20
☐	36	Mikael Enander	.20
☐	37	Anders Huuss	.20
☐	38	Anders Carlsson	.20
☐	39	Willy Lindstrom	.20
☐	40	Kyosti Karjalainen	.20
☐	41	Jan Larsson	.20
☐	42	Patrik Erickson	.20
☐	43	Joakim Persson	.20
☐	44	Johan Brummer	.20
☐	45	Peter Eriksson	.20
☐	46	Peter Gustafsson	.20
☐	47	Thomas Olund	.20
☐	48	Magnus Aberg	.20
☐	49	Djurgardens IF	.20
☐	50	Rolf Ridderwall	.20
☐	51	Tommy Söderström (G)	2.00
☐	52	Thomas Eriksson	.20
☐	53	Arto Blomsten	.20

	No.	Player	Price
☐	54	Orvar Stambert	.20
☐	55	Christian Due-Boje	.20
☐	56	Kenneth Kennholt	.20
☐	57	Mats Wallin	.20
☐	58	Karl-Erik Lilja	.20
☐	59	Marcus Ragnarsson	.50
☐	60	Hakan Sodergren	.20
☐	61	Mikael Johannson	.20
☐	62	Jens Ohling	.20
☐	63	Jan Viktorsson	.20
☐	64	Peter Nilsson	.20
☐	65	Charles Berglund	.20
☐	66	Ken Johansson	.20
☐	67	Johan Garpenlov	.35
☐	68	Ole Andersson	.20
☐	69	Anders Jonsson	.20
☐	70	Bengt Akerblom	.20
☐	71	Ola Josefsson	.20
☐	72	Mats Sundin	15.00
☐	73	Farjestads BK	.20
☐	74	Anders Bergman	.20
☐	75	Jorgen Ryden	.20
☐	76	Tommy Samuelsson	.20
☐	77	Fredrik Olausson	.50
☐	78	Peter Hasselblad	.20
☐	79	Jesper Duus	.20
☐	80	Anders Berglund	.20
☐	81	Mattias Andersson	.20
☐	82	Mattias Olsson	.20
☐	83	Greger Artursson	.20
☐	84	Jacob Karlsson	.20
☐	85	Thomas Rundqvist	.20
☐	86	Staffan Lundh	.20
☐	87	Jan Ingman	.20
☐	88	Kjell Dahlin	.20
☐	89	Bengt Gustafsson	.35
☐	90	Magnus Roupe	.20
☐	91	Hakan Loob	2.00
☐	92	Mikael Holmberg	.20
☐	93	Daniel Rydmark	.20
☐	94	Lars Karlsson	.20
☐	95	Peter Ottosson	.20
☐	96	HV 71	.20
☐	97	Kenneth Johansson	.20
☐	98	Claes Heljemo	.20
☐	99	Lars Ivarsson	.20
☐	100	Arto Routanen	.20
☐	101	Fredrik Stillman	.20
☐	102	Klas Heed	.20
☐	103	Nils-Gunnar Svensson	.20
☐	104	Per Gustafsson	1.00
☐	105	Tommy Fritz	.20
☐	106	Mats Nilsson	.20
☐	107	Hasse Sjoo	.20
☐	108	Mats Loov	.20
☐	109	Ove Thornberg	.20
☐	110	Eddy Ericsson	.20
☐	111	Ivan Avdejev	.20
☐	112	Stefan Persson	.35
☐	113	Rick Erdall	.20
☐	114	Stefan Nilsson	.20
☐	115	Stefan Ornskog	.20
☐	116	Patrik Ross	.20
☐	117	Stefan Falk	.20
☐	118	Claes Roupe	.20
☐	119	Peter Ekelund	.20
☐	120	Leksands IF	.20
☐	121	Peter Aslin	.20
☐	122	O. Sundstrom	.20
☐	123	Jonas Leven	.20
☐	124	Tomas Jonsson	.50
☐	125	Magnus Svensson	.35
☐	126	Ricard Persson	.35
☐	127	Per Lundell	.20
☐	128	Tomas Nord	.20
☐	129	Peter Wallin	.20
☐	130	Orjan Lindmark	.20
☐	131	Henric Bjorkman	.20
☐	132	Anders Pettersson	.20
☐	133	Per-Olaf Carlsson	.20
☐	134	Tomas Forslund	.20
☐	135	Niklas Eriksson	.20
☐	136	Richard Kromm	.20
☐	137	Jarmo Makitalo	.20
☐	138	Peter Lundmark	.20
☐	139	Ronny Reichenberg	.20
☐	140	Cenneth Soderlund	.20
☐	141	Jens Nielsen	.20
☐	142	Marcus Thuresson	.20
☐	143	Anders Broms	.20
☐	144	Joakim Backlund	.20
☐	145	Lulea HF	.20
☐	146	Robert Skoog	.20
☐	147	Tomas Javeblad	.20
☐	148	Lars Modig	.20
☐	149	Jan-Ove Mettavainio	.20
☐	150	Osmo Soutokorva	.20
☐	151	Torbjorn Lindberg	.20
☐	152	Timo Jutila	.20
☐	153	Roger Akerstrom	.20
☐	154	Per Ljusterdang	.20
☐	155	Tomas Lilja	.20
☐	156	Johan Stromvall	.20
☐	157	Lars-Gunnar Pettersson	.20
☐	158	Lars Hurtig	.20
☐	159	Morgan Samuelsson	.20
☐	160	Stefan Nilsson	.20
☐	161	Vesa Kangas	.20
☐	162	Kari Jaako	.20
☐	163	Juha Nurmi	.20
☐	164	Jens Hellgren	.20
☐	165	Tomas Berglund	.20
☐	166	Lars Edstrom	.20
☐	167	Petter Antti	.20
☐	168	MoDo HK	.20
☐	169	Fredrik Andersson	.20
☐	170	Goran Arnmark	.20
☐	171	Timo Blomqvist	.20
☐	172	Hakan Stromqvist	.20
☐	173	Robert Frestadius	.20
☐	174	Lars Jansson	.20
☐	175	Hans Lodin	.20
☐	176	Ove Pettersson	.20
☐	177	Tony Olofsson	.20
☐	178	Jorgen Eriksson	.20
☐	179	Ulf Sandstrom	.20
☐	180	Michael Hjalm	.20
☐	181	Urban Nordin	.20
☐	182	Lars Bystrom	.20
☐	183	Jens Ohman	.20
☐	184	Ulf Odmark	.20
☐	185	Mikael Stahl	.20
☐	186	Per Nilsson	.20
☐	187	Ingmar Strom	.20
☐	188	Kent Lantz	.20
☐	189	Kent Norberg	.20
☐	190	Patrik Soderholm	.20
☐	191	Skelleftea HC	.20
☐	192	Sam Lindstahl	.20
☐	193	Dick Andersson	.20
☐	194	Kari Suoraniemi	.20
☐	195	Robert Larsson	.20
☐	196	Kari Yli-Maenpaa	.20
☐	197	Ola Stenlund	.20
☐	198	Tony Barthelson	.20
☐	199	Lars Marklund	.20
☐	200	Glenn Hedman	.20
☐	201	Dick Burlin	.20
☐	202	Michael Granstedt	.20
☐	203	Pekka Jarvela	.20
☐	204	Hans Hjalmar	.20
☐	205	Mats Lundstrom	.20
☐	206	Martin Pettersson	.20
☐	207	Johnny Forsman	.20
☐	208	Daniel Petteresson	.20
☐	209	Niklas Mannberg	.20
☐	210	Niklas Brannstrom	.20
☐	211	Jan Johansson	.20
☐	212	Jorgen Wannstrom	.20
☐	213	Leif Johansson	.20
☐	214	Par Mikaelsson	.20
☐	215	Fredrik Andersson	.20
☐	216	Sodertalji SK	.20
☐	217	Reino Sundberg	.20
☐	218	Jari Luoma	.20
☐	219	Anders Eldebrink	.20
☐	220	Mats Kilstrom	.20
☐	221	Jonas Heed	.20
☐	222	Hans Pettersson	.20
☐	223	Jan Bergman	.20
☐	224	Thomas Carlsson	.20
☐	225	Stefan Jonsson	.20
☐	226	Thomas Eklund	.20
☐	227	Ola Rosander	.20
☐	228	Bjorn Carlsson	.20
☐	229	Thomas Sjogren	.20
☐	230	Thomas Ljungbergh	.20
☐	231	Stefan Olsson	.20
☐	232	Reine Landsgren	.20
☐	233	Anders Frykbo	.20
☐	234	Conny Jansson	.20
☐	235	Peter larsson	.20
☐	236	Tomas Eriksson	.20
☐	237	Erik Holmberg	.20
☐	238	Patrik Lindh	.20
☐	239	Vasteras IK	.20
☐	240	Mats Ytter (G)	.20
☐	241	Par Hellenberg	.20
☐	242	Jan Eriksson	.20
☐	243	Peter Popovic	.50
☐	244	Tore Lindgren	.20
☐	245	Leif Rohlin	.50
☐	246	Henrik Andersson	.20
☐	247	Nicklas Lidström	4.00
☐	248	Jan Karlsson	.20
☐	249	Peter Jacobsson	.20
☐	250	Patrik Juhlin	.50
☐	251	Goran Sjoberg	.20
☐	252	Fredrik Nilsson	.20
☐	253	Stefan Hellkvist	.20
☐	254	Tomas Strandberg	.20
☐	255	Anders Berglund	.20
☐	256	Claes Lindblom	.20
☐	257	Magnus Wallin	.20
☐	258	Bjorn Akerblom	.20
☐	259	Joakim Lundholm	.20
☐	260	Jorgen Holmberg	.20
☐	261	Ronny Hansen	.20
☐	262	Misjat Fachrutdinov	.20
☐	263	Vastra Frolunda HC	.20
☐	264	Hakan Algotsson	.20
☐	265	Per Lundbergh	.20
☐	266	Jan Karlsson	.20
☐	267	Loacim Esbjors	.20
☐	268	Leif Carlsson	.20
☐	269	Stefan Axelsson	.20
☐	270	Peter Ekroth	.20
☐	271	Jorgen Palm	.20
☐	272	Hakan Nordin	.20
☐	273	Stefan Larsson	.20
☐	274	Mikael Andersson	.35
☐	275	Terho Koskela	.20
☐	276	Patrik Carnback	.35
☐	277	Serge Boisvert	.20
☐	278	Arto Sirvio	.20
☐	279	Peter Berndtsson	.20
☐	280	Jorgen Petterson	.20
☐	281	Niklas Andersson	.25
☐	282	Peter Gustavsson	.20
☐	283	Paul Andersson	.20
☐	284	Mats Graesen	.20
☐	285	Kent Orrgren	.20

1989 - 90 7TH INNING SKETCH OHL

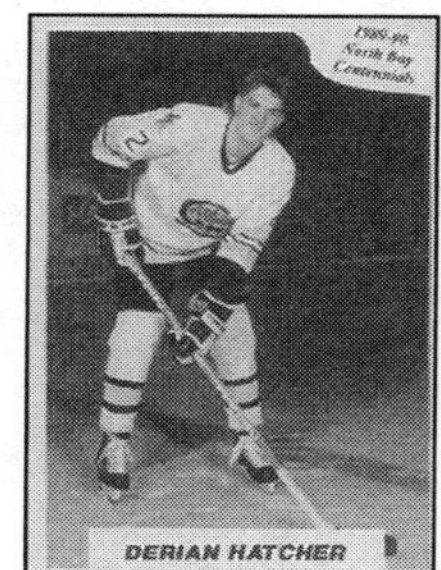

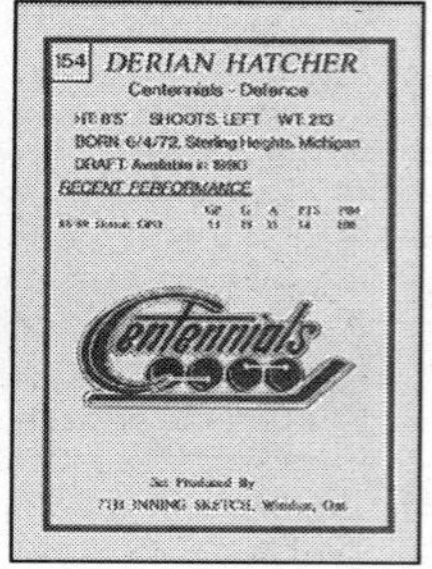

These cards have a yellow border.

Imprint: 7TH INNING SKETCH

Complete Set (200 cards):	**45.00**
Common Player:	**.15**

No.	Player	NRMT-MT
1	Eric Lindros, Oshawa Generals	12.00
2	Jarrod Skalde, Oshawa Generals	.25
3	Joe Busillo, Oshawa Generals	.15
4	Dale Craigwell, Oshawa Generals	.25
5	Clair Cornish, Oshawa Generals	.15
6	Jean-Paul Davis, Oshawa Generals	.15
7	Craig Donaldson, Oshawa Generals	.15
8	Wade Simpson, Oshawa Generals	.15
9	Mike Craig, Oshawa Generals	1.50
10	Mark Deazeley, Oshawa Generals	.15
11	Scott Hollis, Oshawa Generals	.15
12	Brian Grieve, Oshawa Generals	.15
13	Dave Craievich, Oshawa Generals	.15
14	Paul O'Hagan, Oshawa Generals	.15
15	Matt Hoffman, Oshawa Generals	.15
16	Trevor McIvor, Oshawa Generals	.15
17	Cory Banika, Oshawa Generals	.15
18	Kevin Butt (G), Oshawa Generals	.20
19	Iain Fraser, Oshawa Generals	.25
20	Bill Armstrong, Oshawa Generals	.15
21	Scott Luik, Oshawa Generals	.15
22	Brent Grieve, Oshawa Generals	.25
23	Fred Brathwaite (G), Oshawa Generals	.50
24	Paul Holden, London Knights	.15
25	Trevor Dam, London Knights	.15
26	Chris Taylor, London Knights	.15
27	Mark Guy, London Knights	.15
28	Louie DeBrusk, London Knights	.50
29	John Battice, London Knights	.15
30	Chris Crombie, London Knights	.15
31	Sean Basilio (G), London Knights	.20
32	Aaron Nagy, London Knights	.15
33	Greg Ryan, London Knights	.15
34	Steve Martell, London Knights	.15
35	Scott MacKay, London Knights	.15
36	Dennis Purdie, London Knights	.15
37	Steve Boyd, London Knights	.15
38	John Tanner (G), London Knights	.20
39	David Anderson, London Knights	.15
40	Rick Corriveau, London Knights	.15
41	Todd Hlushko, London Knights	.50
42	Doug Synishin, London Knights	.15
43	Dan LeBlanc, London Knights	.15
44	Dave Noseworthy, London Knights	.15
45	Karl Taylor, London Knights	.15
46	Jeff Hogden, London Knights	.15
47	Mike Kelly/Gary Agnew, Asst. Coaches, London Knights	.15
48	Wayne Maxner, Coach, London Knights	.15
49	Brett Seguin, Ottawa 67's	.15
50	Greg Walters, Ottawa 67's	.15
51	Chris Snell, Ottawa 67's	.25
52	Troy Binnie, Ottawa 67's	.15
53	Joni Lehto, Ottawa 67's	.15
54	Steve Kluczkowski, Ottawa 67's	.15
55	Ryan Kuwabara, Ottawa 67's	.15
56	Chris Simon, Ottawa 67's	1.75
57	Jerrett DeFazio, Ottawa 67's	.15
58	Robert Sangster, Ottawa 67's	.15
59	Greg Clancy, Ottawa 67's	.15
60	Peter Ambroziak, Ottawa 67's	.25
61	Jeff Ricciardi, Ottawa 67's	.15
62	John East, Ottawa 67's	.15
63	Joey McTamney, Ottawa 67's	.15
64	Dan Poirier, Ottawa 67's	.15
65	Gairin Smith, Ottawa 67's	.15
66	Wade Gibson, Ottawa 67's	.15
67	Checklist (1 - 88)	.15
68	Andrew Brodie, Ottawa 67's	.15
69	Craig Wilson, Ottawa 67's	.15
70	Peter McGlynn (G), Ottawa 67's	.20
71	George Dourian (G), Ottawa 67's	.20
72	Bob Berg, Belleville Bulls	.15
73	Richard Fatrola, Belleville Bulls	.15
74	Craig Fraser, Belleville Bulls	.15
75	Brent Gretzky, Belleville Bulls	.75
76	Jake Grimes, Belleville Bulls	.15
77	Darren McCarty, Belleville Bulls	2.00
78	Ted Miskolczi, Belleville Bulls	.15
79	Rob Pearson, Belleville Bulls	.35
80	Gordon Pell, Belleville Bulls	.15
81	John Porco, Belleville Bulls	.15
82	Ken Rowbotham, Belleville Bulls	.15
83	Scott Thornton, Belleville Bulls	.50
84	Shawn Way, Belleville Bulls	.15
85	Steve Bancroft, Belleville Bulls	.15
86	Greg Bignell, Belleville Bulls	.15
87	Scott Boston, Belleville Bulls	.15
88	Scott Feasby, Belleville Bulls	.15
89	Derek Morin, Belleville Bulls	.15
90	Sean O'Reilly, Belleville Bulls	.15
91	Jason Skellet, Belleville Bulls	.15
92	Greg Dreveny, Belleville Bulls	.15
93	Jeff Fife, Belleville Bulls	.15
94	Rob Stopar (G), Belleville Bulls	.20
95	Joe Desrosiers, Trainer, Belleville Bulls	.15
96	Danny Flynn, Head Coach, Belleville Bullsh	.15
97	Dr. R.L. Vaughan, Owner, Belleville Bulls	.15
98	Troy Stephens, Peterborough Petes	.15
99	Dan Brown, Peterborough Petes	.15
100	Mike Ricci, Peterborough Petes	1.50
101	Brent Pope, Peterborough Petes	.15
102	Mike Dagenais, Peterborough Petes	.15
103	Scott Campbell, Peterborough Petes	.15
104	Jamie Pegg, Peterborough Petes	.15
105	Joe Hawley, Peterborough Petes	.15
106	Jason Dawe, Peterborough Petes	1.50
107	Paul Mitton, Peterborough Petes	.15
108	Mike Tomlinson, Peterborough Petes	.15
109	David Lorentz, Peterborough Petes	.15
110	Dale McTavish, Peterborough Petes	.15
111	Willie McGarvey, Peterborough Petes	.15
112	Don O'Neill, Peterborough Petes	.15
113	Mark Myles, Peterborough Petes	.15
114	Chris Longo, Peterborough Petes	.15
115	Tom Hopkins, Peterborough Petes	.15
116	Jassen Cullimore, Peterborough Petes	.50
117	Geoff Ingram, Peterborough Petes	.15
118	Twohey/Bovair, Asst. Coaches, Peterborough Petes	.15
119	Doug Searle, Peterborough Petes	.15
120	Bryan Gendron, Peterborough Petes	.15
121	Andrew Verner (G), Peterborough Petes	.25
122	Todd Bojcun (G), Peterborough Petes	.20
123	Dick Todd, Head Coach, Peterborough Petes	.15
124	George Burnett, Head Coach, Peterborough Petes	.15
125	Brad May, Niagara Falls Thunder	1.00
126	David Benn, Niagara Falls Thunder	.15
127	Brian Mueggler, Niagara Falls Thunder	.15
128	Todd Coopman, Niagara Falls Thunder	.15
129	Geoff Rawson, Niagara Falls Thunder	.15
130	Keith Primeau, Niagara Falls Thunder	4.00
131	Mark Lawrence, Niagara Falls Thunder	.25
132	Randy Hall, Asst. Coach/GM, Niagara Falls Thunder	.15
133	Greg Suchan, Niagara Falls Thunder	.15
134	Ken Ruddick, Niagara Falls Thunder	.15
135	Jason Winch, Niagara Falls Thunder	.15
136	Paul Wolanski, Niagara Falls Thunder	.15
137	Dennis Scott, Trainer, Niagara Falls Thunder	.15
138	Steve Udvari (G), Niagara Falls Thunder	.20
139	Roch Belley (G), Niagara Falls Thunder	.20
140	Donald Pancoe, Niagara Falls Thunder	.15
141	Paul Bruneau, Asst. Trainer, Niagara Falls Thunder	.15
142	Paul Laus, Niagara Falls Thunder	.50
143	Mike St. John, Niagara Falls Thunder	.15
144	John Johnson, Niagara Falls Thunder	.15
145	Greg Allen, Niagara Falls Thunder	.15
146	Don McConnell, Niagara Falls Thunder	.15
147	Andy Bezeau, Niagara Falls Thunder	.15
148	Jeff Walker, Niagara Falls Thunder	.15
149	John Spoltore, North Bay Centennials	.15
150	Derek Switzer, North Bay Centennials	.15
151	Tyler Ertel, North Bay Centennials	.15
152	Shawn Antoski, North Bay Centennials	.50
153	Jason Corrigan, North Bay Centennials	.15
154	Derian Hatcher, North Bay Centennials	1.25
155	John Vary, North Bay Centennials	.15
156	Jamie Caruso, North Bay Centennials	.15
157	Trevor Halverson, North Bay Centennials	.15
158	Robert Deschamps, North Bay Centennials	.15
159	Jeff Gardiner, North Bay Centennials	.15
160	Gary Miller, North Bay Centennials	.15
161	Shayne Antoski, North Bay Centennials	.40
162	John Van Kessel, North Bay Centennials	.15
163	Colin Austin, North Bay Centennials	.15
164	Tom Purcell, North Bay Centennials	.15
165	Joel Morin, North Bay Centennials	.15
166	Tim Favot, North Bay Centennials	.15
167	Checklist (89 - 176)	.15
168	Jason Beaton, North Bay Centennials	.15
169	Chris Ottmann, North Bay Centennials	.15
170	Mike Matuszek (G), North Bay Centennials	.20
171	Rob Fournier (G), North Bay Centennials	.20
172	Ron Bertrand (G), North Bay Centennials	.20
173	Bert Templeton, Head Coach/GM, North Bay Centennials	.15
174	Centennials Mascot, Casey Jones, North Bay Centennials	.15
175	Robert Frayn, North Bay Centennials	.15
176	Claude Noel, Asst. Coach, North Bay Centennials	.15
177	AW: Sean Basilio (G), London Knights	.20
178	AW: Chris Longo, Peterborough Petes	.15
179	AW: Cory Keenan, Kitchener Rangers	.15
180	AW: Owen Nolan, Cornwall Royals	3.00
181	AS: Steven Rice, Kitchener Rangers	1.25
182	AS: Shayne Stevenson, Kitchener Rangers	.15
183	AW: Mike Ricci, Peterborough Petes	.75
184	AW: Jason Firth, Kitchener Rangers	.15
185	AW: John Slaney, Cornwall Royals	.25
186	AW: Iain Fraser, Oshawa Generals	.25
187	AW: Steven Rice, Kitchener Rangers	1.25
188	AW: Eric Lindros, Oshawa Generals	6.50
189	AW: Keith Primeau, Niagara Falls	2.50
190	AW: Mike Ricci, Peterborough Petes	.75
191	AS: Mike Torchia (G), Kitchener Rangers	.25
192	AS: Mike Torchia (G), Kitchener Rangers	.25
193	AS: Jarrod Skalde, Oshawa Generals	.15
194	AS: Paul O'Hagan, Oshawa Generals	.15
195	Eric Lindros, Oshawa Generals	6.50
196	AS: Eric Lindros, Oshawa Generals	6.50
197	AS: Jeff Fife, Belleville Bulls (G)	.15
198	AW: Iain Fraser, Oshawa Generals	.25
199	AS: Bill Armstrong, Oshawa Generals	.15
200	Checklist (177 - 200)	.15

1989 - 90 7TH INNING SKETCH MEMORIAL CUP

These cardsw have a blue border.

Imprint: 7TH INNING SKETCH, WINDSOR, ONT.

Complete Set (100 cards): 150.00

Common Player: .50

No.	Player	NRMT-MT
1	Len Barrie, Kamloops Blazers	.50
2	Zac Boyer, Kamloops Blazers	.50
3	David Chyzowski, Kamloops Blazers	.50
4	Shea Esselmont, Kamloops Blazers	.50
5	Todd Esselmont, Kamloops Blazers	.50
6	Phil Huber, Kamloops Blazers	.50
7	Lance Johnson, Kamloops Blazers	.50
8	Paul Kruse, Kamloops Blazers	.75
9	Cal McGowan, Kamloops Blazers	.50
10	Mike Needham, Kamloops Blazers	.75
11	Brian Shantz, Kamloops Blazers	.50
12	Daryl Sydor, Kamloops Blazers	3.00
13	Jeff Watchorn, Kamloops Blazers	.50
14	Jarrett Bousquet, Kamloops Blazers	.50
15	Todd Harris, Kamloops Blazers	.50
16	Dean Malkoc, Kamloops Blazers	.50
17	Joey Mittelsteadt, Kamloops Blazers	.50
18	Scott Niedermayer, Kamloops Blazers	8.00
19	Clayton Young, Kamloops Blazers	.50
20	Trevor Sim, Kamloops Blazers	.50
21	Murray Duval, Kamloops Blazers	.50
22	Steve Yule, Kamloops Blazers	.50
23	Craig Bonner, Kamloops Blazers	.50
24	Dale Masson (G), Kamloops Blazers	.75
25	Corey Hirsch (G), Kamloops Blazers	6.00
26	Joe McDonnell, Coach, Kitchener Rangers	.50
27	Rick Chambers, Trainer, Kitchener Rangers	.50
28	John Finnie (G), Kitchener Rangers	.75
29	Randy Pearce, Kitchener Rangers	.50

	No.	Player	NRMT-MT
☐	30	Mark Montanari, Kitchener Rangers	.50
☐	31	Mike Torchia (G), Kitchener Rangers	.75
☐	32	Jason York, Kitchener Rangers	2.00
☐	33	Jason Firth, Kitchener Rangers	.50
☐	34	Jamie Israel, Kitchener Rangers	.50
☐	35	Richard Borgo, Kitchener Rangers	.50
☐	36	John Uniac, Kitchener Rangers	.50
☐	37	Steve Smith, Kitchener Rangers	.50
☐	38	Steven Rice, Kitchener Rangers	.50
☐	39	Gilbert Dionne, Kitchener Rangers	.50
☐	40	Cory Keenan, Kitchener Rangers	.50
☐	41	Rick Allain, Kitchener Rangers	.50
☐	42	John Copley, Kitchener Rangers	.50
☐	43	Gib Tucker, Kitchener Rangers	.50
☐	44	Chris LiPuma, Kitchener Rangers	.50
☐	45	Brad Barton, Kitchener Rangers	.50
☐	46	Rival Fullum, Kitchener Rangers	.50
☐	47	Joey St. Aubin, Kitchener Rangers	.50
☐	48	Jack Williams, Kitchener Rangers	.50
☐	49	Shayne Stevenson, Kitchener Rangers	.50
☐	50	Pierre Creamer, Coach, Laval Titan	.50
☐	51	Carl Mantha, Laval Titan	.50
☐	52	Julian Cameron (G), Laval Titan	.75
☐	53	Sandy McCarthy, Laval Titan	3.00
☐	54	Gino Odjick, Laval Titan	3.00
☐	55	Eric Raymond (G), Laval Titan	.75
☐	56	Carl Boudreau, Laval Titan	.50
☐	57	Greg MacEachern, Laval Titan	.50
☐	58	Allen Kerr, Laval Titan	.50
☐	59	Patrice Brisebois, Laval Titan	3.00
☐	60	Eric Bissonnette, Laval Titan	.50
☐	61	Martin Lapointe, Laval Titan	3.00
☐	62	Michel Gingras, Laval Titan	.50
☐	63	Sylvain Naud, Laval Titan	.50
☐	64	Patrick Caron, Laval Titan	.50
☐	65	Regis Tremblay, Laval Titan	.50
☐	66	François Pelletier, Laval Titan	.50
☐	67	Jason Brousseau, Laval Titan	.50
☐	68	Eric Dubois, Laval Titan	.50
☐	69	Claude Boivin, Laval Titan	.50
☐	70	Denis Chalifoux, Laval Titan	.50
☐	71	Jim Bermingham, Laval Titan	.50
☐	72	Daniel Arsenault, Laval Titan	.50
☐	73	Normand Demers, Laval Titan	.50
☐	74	Serge Anglehart, Laval Titan	.50
☐	75	Rick Cornacchia, Coach, Oshawa Generals	.50
☐	76	Kevin Butt (G), Oshawa Generals	.75
☐	77	Fred Brathwaite (G), Oshawa Generals	1.00
☐	78	Paul O'Hagan, Oshawa Generals	.50
☐	79	Craig Donaldson, Oshawa Generals	.50
☐	80	Jean-Paul Davis, Oshawa Generals	.50
☐	81	Brian Grieve, Oshawa Generals	.50
☐	82	Bill Armstrong, Oshawa Generals	.50
☐	83	Wade Simpson, Oshawa Generals	.50
☐	84	Dave Craievich, Error, Oshawa Generals	.50
☐	85	Dale Craigwell, Oshawa Generals	.50
☐	86	Joe Busillo, Oshawa Generals	.50
☐	87	Cory Banika, Oshawa Generals	.50
☐	88	Eric Lindros, Oshawa Generals	50.00
☐	89	Iain Fraser, Oshawa Generals	1.00
☐	90	Mike Craig, Oshawa Generals	1.50
☐	91	Jarrod Skalde, Oshawa Generals	.50
☐	92	Brent Grieve, Oshawa Generals	.50
☐	93	Scott Luik, Oshawa Generals	.50
☐	94	Matt Hoffman, Oshawa Generals	.50
☐	95	Trevor McIvor, Oshawa Generals	.50
☐	96	Scott Hollis, Oshawa Generals	.50
☐	97	Mark Deazeley, Oshawa Generals	.50
☐	98	Clair Cornish, Oshawa Generals	.50
☐	99	O.H.L. Champions, Oshawa Generals	.50
☐	100	Checklist	.50

1989 - 90 SOVIET HOCKEY STARS

Card Size: 4 1/8" x 5 5/8"
Face: Four colour, borderless; Facsimile autograph
Back: Black and white; Name, Team, Position, Resume
Imprint: None
Complete Set (24 cards with folder): 30.00

	Player	NRMT-MT
☐	Ilya Byakin	1.00
☐	Viacheslav Bykov	1.50
☐	Alexander Chernik	1.00
☐	Igor Dmitriev, Assistant Coach	1.00
☐	Sergei Fedorov	8.00
☐	Viacheslav Fetisov	3.00
☐	Alexei Gusarov	1.00
☐	Arturs Irbe (G)	2.00
☐	Valeri Kamensky	4.00
☐	Alexsei Kasatonov	1.00
☐	Sviatoslav Khalizov	1.00
☐	Yuri Khmylev	1.00
☐	Andrei Khomutov	1.00
☐	Vladimir Konstantinov	5.00
☐	Vladimir Krutov	1.00
☐	Dmitri Kvartalnov	1.00
☐	Igor Larionov	3.00
☐	Sergei Makarov	2.00
☐	Vladimir Mishkin (G)	1.00
☐	Sergei Mylnikov (G)	1.00
☐	Sergei Nemchinov	1.50
☐	Valeri Shiriaev	1.00
☐	Victor Tikhonov, Head Coach	1.50
☐	Sergei Yashin	1.00

1989 - 90 TOPPS

Imprint: © 1989 THE TOPPS COMPANY, INC.
Topps Set (198 cards): 32.00
Common Player: .15
Double Print (**): .10

	No.	Player	NRMT-MT
☐	1	Mario Lemieux, Pgh.	3.00
☐	2	Ulf Dahlen, NYR.	.15
☐	**3**	**Terry Carkner, Pha., RC**	**.15**
☐	4	Tony McKegney, Det.	.15
☐	5	Denis Savard, Chi.	.15
☐	**6**	**Derek King, NYI., RC, (**)**	**.10**
☐	7	Lanny McDonald, Cgy.	.15
☐	8	John Tonelli, L.A.	.15
☐	9	Tom Kurvers, N.J., (**)	.10
☐	10	Dave Archibald, Min., LC	.15
☐	**11**	**Peter Sidorkiewicz (G), Hfd., RC**	**.15**
☐	12	Esa Tikkanen, Edm.	.15
☐	13	Dave Barr, Det.	.15
☐	14	Brent Sutter, NYI.	.15
☐	15	Cam Neely, Bos.	.30
☐	**16**	**Calle Johansson, Wsh., RC**	**.15**
☐	17	Patrick Roy (G), Mtl., (**)	2.50
☐	**18**	**Dale DeGray, L.A., RC, (**)**	**.10**
☐	19	Phil Bourque, Pgh., RC	.15
☐	20	Kevin Dineen, Hfd.	.15
☐	21	Mike Bullard, Pha.	.15
☐	22	Gary Leeman, Tor.	.15
☐	23	Greg Stefan (G), Det.	.15
☐	24	Brian Mullen, NYR.	.15
☐	25	Pierre Turgeon, Buf., (**)	1.25
☐	**26**	**Bob Rouse, Wsh., RC, (**)**	**.10**
☐	27	Peter Zezel, Stl.	.15
☐	28	Jeff Brown, Que., (**)	.10
☐	**29**	**Andy Brickley, Bos., RC, (**)**	**.10**
☐	30	Mike Gartner, Min.	.75
☐	31	Darren Pang (G), Chi.	.15
☐	32	Patrick Verbeek, Hfd.	.15
☐	33	Petri Skriko, Van.	.15
☐	34	Tom Laidlaw, L.A.	.15
☐	35	Randy Wood, NYI.	.15
☐	36	Tom Barrasso (G), Pgh., (**)	.20
☐	37	John Tucker, Buf.	.15
☐	38	Andrew McBain, Pgh.	.15
☐	39	David Shaw, NYR.	.15
☐	40	Réjean Lemelin (G), Bos.	.15
☐	41	Dino Ciccarelli, Wsh., (**)	.10
☐	42	Jeff Sharples, Det.	.15
☐	43	Jari Kurri, Edm.	.30
☐	44	Murray Craven, Pha.	.15
☐	**45**	**Cliff Ronning, Stl., RC, (**)**	**.65**
☐	46	Dave Babych, Hfd.	.15
☐	47	Bernie Nicholls, L.A., (**)	.10
☐	**48**	**Jon Casey (G), Min., RC**	**.30**
☐	49	Al MacInnis, Cgy.	.30
☐	**50**	**Bob Errey, Pgh., RC, (**)**	**.10**
☐	51	Glen Wesley, Bos.	.15
☐	52	Dirk Graham, Chi.	.15
☐	53	Guy Carbonneau, Mtl.	.15
☐	54	Tomas Sandström, NYR.	.15
☐	55	Rod Langway, Wsh., (**)	.10
☐	56	Patrik Sundstrom, N.J.	.15
☐	57	Michel Goulet, Que.	.15
☐	58	Dave Taylor, L.A.	.15
☐	59	Phil Housley, Buf.	.15
☐	60	Pat LaFontaine, NYI., (**)	.25
☐	**61**	**Kirk McLean (G), Van., RC, (**)**	**1.25**
☐	62	Ken Linseman, Bos.	.15
☐	63	Randy Cunneyworth, Wpg. (Pgh.)	10.00
☐	63	Randy Cunneyworth, Wpg.	.15
☐	64	Tony Hrkac, Stl.	.15
☐	65	Mark Messier, Edm., (**)	1.25
☐	66	Carey Wilson, NYR.	.15
☐	**67**	**Stephen Leach, Wsh., RC**	**.15**
☐	68	Christian Ruuttu, Buf.	.15
☐	69	Dave Ellett, Wpg.	.15
☐	70	Ray Ferraro, Hfd.	.15
☐	**71**	**Colin Patterson, Cgy., RC**	**.15**
☐	72	Tim Kerr, Pha.	.15
☐	73	Bob Joyce, Bos.	.15
☐	74	Doug Gilmour, Cgy., (**)	.65
☐	75	Lee Norwood, Det., (**)	.10
☐	76	Dale Hunter, Wsh.	.15
☐	77	Jim Johnson, Pgh.	.15
☐	78	Mike Foligno, Buf.	.15
☐	79	Al Iafrate, Tor.	.15
☐	80	Rick Tocchet, Pha., (**)	.10
☐	**81**	**Greg Hawgood, Bos., RC, (**)**	**.10**
☐	82	Steve Thomas, Chi.	.15
☐	83	Steve Yzerman, Det., (**)	1.25
☐	84	Mike McPhee, Mtl.	.15
☐	**85**	**David Volek, NYI., RC, (**)**	**.10**
☐	86	Brian Benning, Stl.	.15
☐	87	Neal Broten, Min.	.15
☐	88	Luc Robitaille, L.A., (**)	.65
☐	**89**	**Trevor Linden, Van., RC, (**)**	**4.00**
☐	90	James Patrick, NYR.	.15
☐	91	Brian Lawton, Hfd.	.15
☐	92	Sean Burke (G), N.J., (**)	.10
☐	93	Scott Stevens, Wsh.	.15
☐	**94**	**Pat Elynuik, Wpg., RC, (**)**	**.10**
☐	95	Paul Coffey, Pgh.	1.00
☐	96	Jan Erixon, NYR., (**)	.10
☐	97	Mike Liut (G), Hfd.	.15
☐	98	Wayne Presley, Chi.	.15
☐	99	Craig Simpson, Edm.	.15
☐	**100**	**Kjell Samuelsson, Pha., RC**	**.15**
☐	101	Shawn Burr, Det.	.15
☐	102	John MacLean, N.J.	.15
☐	103	Tom Fergus, Tor.	.15
☐	104	Michael Krushelnyski, L.A.	.15
☐	105	Gary Nylund, NYI.	.15
☐	106	Dave Andreychuk, Buf.	.15
☐	107	Bernie Federko, Det.	.15
☐	108	Gary Suter, Cgy.	.15
☐	109	Dave Gagner, Min., (**)	.10
☐	110	Ray Bourque, Bos.	1.25
☐	**111**	**Geoff Courtnall, Wsh., RC**	**.75**
☐	112	Douglas Wilson, Chi.	.15
☐	**113**	**Joe Sakic, Que., RC**	**20.00**
☐	114	John Vanbiesbrouck (G), NYR.	1.75
☐	115	David Poulin, Pha.	.15
☐	116	RickMeagher, Stl.	.15
☐	117	Kirk Muller, N.J., (**)	.10
☐	118	Mats Naslund, Mtl.	.15
☐	119	Ray Sheppard, Buf.	.30
☐	**120**	**Jeff Norton, NYI., RC**	**.15**
☐	121	Randy Burridge, Bos.	.15
☐	122	Dale Hawerchuk, Wpg., (**)	.25
☐	123	Steve Duchesne, L.A.	.25
☐	124	John Anderson, Hfd., LC	.15
☐	125	Rick Vaive, Buf.	.15
☐	126	Randy Hillier, Pgh.	.15

	No.	Player	Price
☐	127	Jimmy Carson, Edm.	.15
☐	128	Larry Murphy, Min.	.25
☐	129	Paul MacLean, Stl.	.15
☐	130	Joe Cirella, Que.	.15
☐	131	Kelly Miller, Wsh.	.15
☐	132	Alain Chevrier (G), Chi.	.15
☐	133	Ed Olczyk, Tor.	.15
☐	134	Dave Tippett, Hfd.	.15
☐	135	Bob Sweeney, Bos.	.15
☐	**136**	**Brian Leetch, NYR., RC**	**6.50**
☐	137	Greg Millen (G), Stl.	.15
☐	138	Joe Nieuwendyk, Cgy.	.15
☐	139	Brian Propp, Pha.	.15
☐	140	Mike Ramsey, Buf.	.15
☐	141	Mike Allison, L.A.	.15
☐	**142**	**Shawn Chambers, Min., RC**	**.15**
☐	143	Peter Stastny, Que.,(**)	.10
☐	144	Glen Hanlon (G), Det.	.15
☐	**145**	**John Cullen, Pgh., RC**	**.30**
☐	146	Kevin Hatcher, Wsh.	.15
☐	147	Brendan Shanahan, N.J.	3.75
☐	148	Paul Reinhart, Van.	.15
☐	149	Bryan Trottier, NYI.	.30
☐	**150**	**Dave Manson, Chi., RC**	**.75**
☐	**151**	**Marc Habscheid, Det., RC, (**)**	**.10**
☐	152	Dan Quinn, Pgh.	.15
☐	153	Stéphane Richer, Mtl., (**)	.10
☐	154	Doug Bodger, Buf.	.15
☐	155	Ron Hextall (G), Pha.	.75
☐	156	Wayne Gretzky, L.A.	3.75
☐	**157**	**Steve Tuttle, Stl., RC, (**)**	**.10**
☐	158	Charlie Huddy, Edm.	.15
☐	159	Dave Christian, Wsh.	.15
☐	160	Andy Moog (G), Bos.	.30
☐	**161**	**Tony Granato, NYR., RC**	**.30**
☐	**162**	**Sylvain Côté, Hfd., RC**	**.15**
☐	163	Mike Vernon (G), Cgy.	.30
☐	**164**	**Steve Chiasson, Det., RC**	**.15**
☐	165	Mike Ridley, Wsh.	.15
☐	166	Kelly Hrudey (G), LA	.15
☐	167	Bob Carpenter, Bos.	.15
☐	**168**	**Zarley Zalapski, Pgh., RC**	**.15**
☐	**169**	**Derek Laxdal, Tor., RC**	**.15**
☐	170	Clint Malarchuk (G), Buf.	.15
☐	171	Kelly Kisio, NYR.	.15
☐	172	Gerard Gallant, Det.	.15
☐	173	Ron Sutter, Pha.	.15
☐	174	Chris Chelios, Mtl.	1.25
☐	175	Ron Francis, Hfd.	.75
☐	176	Gino Cavallini, Stl.	.15
☐	177	Brian Bellows, Min., (**)	.10
☐	178	Greg Adams, Van.	.15
☐	179	Steve Larmer, Chi.	.15
☐	180	Aaron Broten, N.J.	.15
☐	181	Brent Ashton, Wpg.	.15
☐	**182**	**Gerald Diduck, NYI., RC, (**)**	**.10**
☐	**183**	**Paul MacDermid, Hfd., RC**	**.15**
☐	184	Walt Poddubny, N.J.	.15
☐	185	Adam Oates, Stl.	.75
☐	186	Brett Hull, Stl.	3.00
☐	187	Scott Arniel, Buf.	.15
☐	188	Bobby Smith, Mtl.	.15
☐	189	Guy Lafleur, NYR.	.75
☐	**190**	**Craig Janney, Bos., RC**	**.75**
☐	191	Mark Howe, Pha.	.15
☐	192	Grant Fuhr (G), Edm., (**)	.25
☐	193	Rob Brown, Pgh.	.15
☐	194	Steve Kasper, L.A.	.15
☐	195	Pete Peeters (G), Pha.	.15
☐	196	Joe Mullen, Cgy.	.15
☐	197	Checklist 1 (1 - 99)	.15
☐	198	Checklist 2 (100 - 198)	.15

TOPPS STICKER INSERTS

Sticker Size: 2 1/2" x 3 1/2"
Insert Set (33 stickers): 15.00

	No.	Player	NRMT-MT
☐	1	AS: Chris Chelios, Mtl.	1.25
☐	2	AS: Gerard Gallant, Det. (**)	.15
☐	3	AS: Mario Lemieux, Pgh.	5.00
☐	4	AS: Al MacInnis, Cgy.	.50
☐	5	AS: Joe Mullen, Cgy. (**)	.15
☐	6	AS: Patrick Roy (G), Mtl.	5.00
☐	7	AS: Ray Bourque, Bos.	1.25
☐	8	AS: Rob Brown, Pgh.	.35
☐	9	AS: Geoff Courtnall, Wsh. (**)	.35
☐	10	AS: Steve Duchesne, L.A.	.15
☐	11	AS: Wayne Gretzky, L.A.	5.00
☐	12	AS: Mike Vernon (G), Cgy.	.35
☐	13	Toronto Maple Leafs	.25
☐	14	Buffalo Sabres	.25
☐	15	Detroit Red Wings	.25
☐	16	Pittsburgh Penguins	.25
☐	17	New York Rangers	.25
☐	18	Calgary Flames	.25
☐	19	Winnpeg Jets	.25
☐	20	Québec Nordiques	.25
☐	21	Chicago Blackhawks	.25
☐	22	Los Angeles Kings	.25
☐	23	Montréal Canadiens	.25
☐	24	Vancouver Canucks	.25
☐	25	Hartford Whalers	.25
☐	26	Philadelphia Flyers	.25
☐	27	New Jersey Devils	.25
☐	28	St. Louis Blues	.25
☐	29	Minnesota North Stars	.25
☐	30	Washington Capitals	.25
☐	31	Boston Bruins	.25
☐	32	New York Islanders	.25
☐	33	Edmonton Oilers	.25

TOPPS BOX BOTTOMS

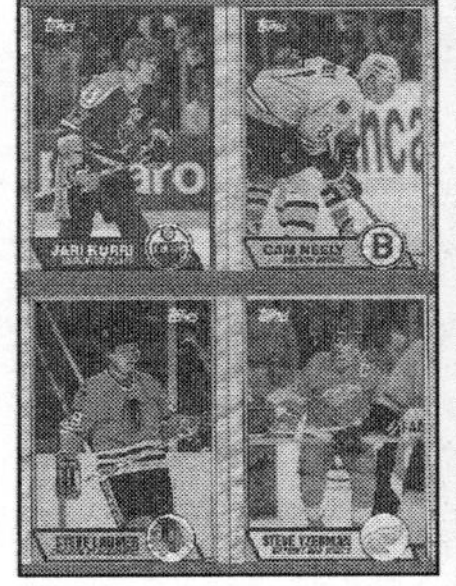

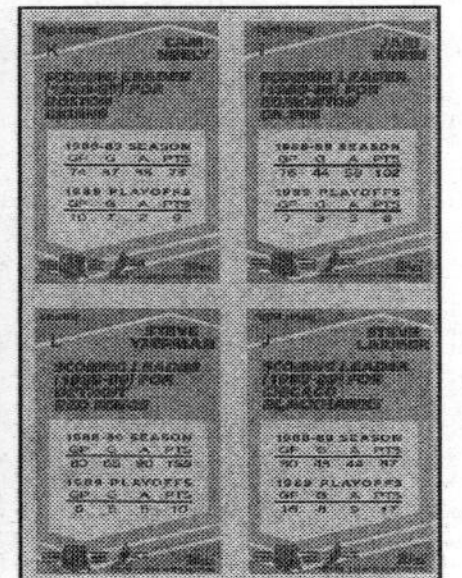

These four-card panels were found on the bottom of Topps wax boxes.
Panel Size: 5" x 7"
Complete Set (16 cards): 10.00
Panel A-D: 4.00
Panel E-H: 5.00
Panel I-L: 3.00
Panel M-P: 1.00

	No.	Player	NRMT-MT
☐	A	Mario Lemieux, Pgh	3.00
☐	B	Mike Ridley, Wsh.	.35
☐	C	Tomas Sandström, NYR.	.35
☐	D	Petri Skriko, Van.	.35
☐	E	Wayne Gretzky, L.A.	5.00
☐	F	Brett Hull, Stl.	1.50
☐	G	Tim Kerr, Pha.	.35
☐	H	Mats Naslund, Mtl.	.35
☐	I	Jari Kurri, Edm.	.50
☐	J	Steve Larmer, Chi.	.35
☐	K	Cam Neely, Bos.	.50
☐	L	Steve Yzerman, Det.	2.00
☐	M	Kevin Dineen, Hfd.	.35
☐	N	Dave Gagner, Min.	.35
☐	O	Joe Mullen, Cgy.	.35
☐	P	Pierre Turgeon, Buf.	.75

1990 - 91 BOWMAN

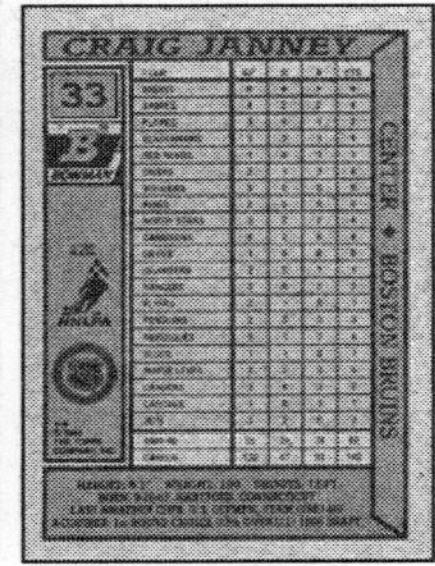

Imprint: © 1990 THE TOPPS COMPANY, INC.

	No.	Player	Regular	Tiffany
Complete Set (264 cards):			**15.00**	**60.00**
Common Player:			**.10**	**.50**
☐☐	**1**	**Jeremy Roenick, Chi., RC**	**1.00**	**10.00**
☐☐	2	Doug Wilson, Chi.	.25	1.50
☐☐	3	Greg Millen (G), Chi.	.10	.50
☐☐	4	Steve Thomas, Chi.	.10	.50
☐☐	5	Steve Larmer, Chi.	.25	1.50
☐☐	6	Denis Savard, Chi.	.25	1.50
☐☐	**7**	**Ed Belfour (G), Chi., RC**	**1.50**	**9.00**
☐☐	8	Dirk Graham, Chi.	.10	.50
☐☐	9	Adam Creighton, Chi.	.10	.50
☐☐	**10**	**Keith Brown, Chi., RC**	**.10**	**.50**
☐☐	**11**	**Jacques Cloutier (G), Chi., RC**	**.10**	**.50**
☐☐	12	Al Secord, Chi., Error (Duane Sutter)	.10	.50
☐☐	13	Troy Murray, Chi.	.10	.50
☐☐	**14**	**Kelly Chase, Stl., RC**	**.10**	**.50**
☐☐	**15**	**Dave Lowry, Stl., RC**	**.10**	**.50**
☐☐	16	Adam Oates, Stl.	.35	2.50
☐☐	**17**	**Sergio Momesso, Stl., RC**	**.10**	**.50**
☐☐	18	Paul MacLean, Stl.	.10	.50
☐☐	19	Peter Zezel, Stl.	.10	.50
☐☐	**20**	**Vincent Riendeau (G), Stl., RC**	**.10**	**.50**
☐☐	**21**	**Dave Thomlinson, Stl., RC**	**.10**	**.50**
☐☐	22	Paul Cavallini, Stl.	.10	.50
☐☐	**23**	**Rod Brind'Amour, Stl., RC**	**.75**	**4.50**
☐☐	24	Brett Hull, Stl.	.50	5.00
☐☐	25	Jeff Brown, Stl.	.10	.50
☐☐	**26**	**Dominic Lavoie, Stl., RC**	**.10**	**.50**
☐☐	27	Andy Brickley, Bos.	.10	.50
☐☐	28	Bob Sweeney, Bos.	.10	.50
☐☐	29	Cam Neely, Bos.	.25	1.50
☐☐	30	Bob Carpenter, Bos.	.10	.50
☐☐	31	Ray Bourque, Bos.	.50	5.00
☐☐	32	Réjean Lemelin (G), Bos.	.10	.50
☐☐	33	Craig Janney, Bos.	.10	.50
☐☐	**34**	**Bob Beers, Bos., RC**	**.10**	**.50**
☐☐	35	Andy Moog (G), Bos.	.25	1.50
☐☐	36	Dave Poulin, Bos.	.10	.50
☐☐	37	Brian Propp, Bos.	.10	.50
☐☐	**38**	**John Byce, Bos., RC**	**.10**	**.50**
☐☐	**39**	**John Carter, Bos., RC**	**.10**	**.50**
☐☐	40	Dave Christian, Bos.	.10	.50
☐☐	41	Shayne Corson, Mtl.	.25	1.50
☐☐	42	Chris Chelios, Mtl.	.35	3.50
☐☐	43	Mike McPhee, Mtl.	.10	.50
☐☐	44	Guy Carbonneau, Mtl.	.10	.50
☐☐	45	Stéphane Richer, Mtl.	.10	.50
☐☐	46	Petr Svoboda, Mtl., Error (Photo: Chris Chelios)	.10	.50
☐☐	47	Russ Courtnall, Mtl.	.10	.50
☐☐	**48**	**Sylvain Lefebvre, Mtl., RC**	**.10**	**.50**
☐☐	49	Brian Skrudland, Mtl.	.10	.50
☐☐	50	Patrick Roy (G), Mtl.	1.50	15.00
☐☐	51	Bobby Smith, Mtl.	.10	.50
☐☐	**52**	**Mathieu Schneider, Mtl., RC**	**.10**	**.50**
☐☐	**53**	**Stéphan Lebeau, Mtl., RC**	**.10**	**.50**
☐☐	54	Petri Skriko, Van.	.10	.50
☐☐	55	Jim Sandlak, Van.	.10	.50

	No.	Player	Regular	Tiffany
□ □	56	Doug Lidster, Van.	.10	.50
□ □	57	Kirk McLean (G), Van.	.25	1.50
□ □	58	Brian Bradley, Van.	.10	.50
□ □	59	Greg Adams, Van.	.10	.50
□ □	60	Paul Reinhart, Van.	.10	.50
□ □	61	Trevor Linden, Van.	.25	1.50
□ □	**62**	**Adrien Plavsic, Van., RC**	**.10**	**.50**
□ □	**63**	**Igor Larionov, Van., RC**	**.25**	**1.50**
□ □	64	Steve Bozek, Van.	.10	.50
□ □	65	Dan Quinn, Van.	.10	.50
□ □	66	Mike Liut (G), Wsh.	.10	.50
□ □	**67**	**Nick Kypreos, Wsh., RC**	**.10**	**.50**
□ □	**68**	**Michal Pivonka, Wsh., RC**	**.10**	**.50**
□ □	69	Dino Ciccarelli, Wsh.	.25	1.50
□ □	70	Kevin Hatcher, Wsh.	.10	.50
□ □	71	Dale Hunter, Wsh.	.10	.50
□ □	72	Don Beaupré (G), Wsh.	.10	.50
□ □	73	Geoff Courtnall, Wsh.	.10	.50
□ □	**74**	**Rob Murray, Wsh., RC**	**.10**	**.50**
□ □	75	Calle Johansson, Wsh.	.10	.50
□ □	76	Kelly Miller, Wsh.	.10	.50
□ □	77	Mike Ridley, Wsh.	.10	.50
□ □	**78**	**Alan May, Wsh., RC**	**.10**	**.50**
□ □	79	Bob Brooke, N.J.	.10	.50
□ □	**80**	**Viacheslav Fetisov, N.J., RC**	**.25**	**1.50**
□ □	81	Sylvain Turgeon, N.J.	.10	.50
□ □	82	Kirk Muller, N.J.	.10	.50
□ □	83	John MacLean, N.J.	.10	.50
□ □	**84**	**Jon Morris, N.J., RC**	**.10**	**.50**
□ □	85	Brendan Shanahan, N.J.	.50	5.00
□ □	86	Peter Stastny, N.J.	.60	6.00
□ □	87	Bruce Driver, N.J.	.10	.50
□ □	**88**	**Neil Brady, N.J., RC**	**.10**	**.50**
□ □	89	Patrik Sundstrom, N.J.	.10	.50
□ □	**90**	**Eric Weinrich, N.J., RC**	**.10**	**.50**
□ □	91	Joe Nieuwendyk, Cgy.	.25	1.50
□ □	**92**	**Sergei Makarov, Cgy., RC**	**.25**	**1.50**
□ □	93	Al MacInnis, Cgy.	.25	1.50
□ □	94	Mike Vernon (G), Cgy.	.25	1.50
□ □	95	Gary Roberts, Cgy.	.25	1.50
□ □	96	Doug Gilmour, Cgy.	.25	2.50
□ □	97	Joe Mullen, Cgy.	.10	.50
□ □	98	Rick Wamsley (G), Cgy.	.10	.50
□ □	99	Joel Otto, Cgy.	.10	.50
□ □	**100**	**Paul Ranheim, Cgy., RC**	**.10**	**.50**
□ □	101	Gary Suter, Cgy.	.10	.50
□ □	102	Theoren Fleury, Cgy.	.25	2.50
□ □	**103**	**Sergei Priakin, Cgy., RC**	**.10**	**.50**
□ □	**104**	**Tony Horacek, Pha., RC**	**.10**	**.50**
□ □	105	Ron Hextall (G), Pha.	.10	.50
□ □	**106**	**Gord Murphy, Pha.. RC**	**.10**	**.50**
□ □	107	Per-Erik Eklund, Pha.	.10	.50
□ □	108	Rick Tocchet, Pha.	.10	.50
□ □	109	Murray Craven, Pha.	.10	.50
□ □	110	Doug Sulliman, Pha.	.10	.50
□ □	111	Kjell Samuelsson, Pha.	.10	.50
□ □	112	Ilkka Sinisalo, Pha.	.10	.50
□ □	113	Keith Acton, Pha.	.10	.50
□ □	114	Mike Bullard, Pha.	.10	.50
□ □	115	Doug Crossman, NYI.	.10	.50
□ □	**116**	**Tom Fitzgerald, NYI., RC**	**.10**	**.50**
□ □	117	Don Maloney, NYI.	.10	.50
□ □	118	Alan Kerr, NYI.	.10	.50
□ □	**119**	**Mark Fitzpatrick (G), NYI., RC**	**.10**	**.50**
□ □	**120**	**Hubie McDonough, NYI., RC**	**.10**	**.50**
□ □	121	Randy Wood, NYI.	.10	.50
□ □	122	Jeff Norton, NYI.	.10	.50
□ □	123	Pat LaFontaine, NYI.	.25	1.50
□ □	124	Patrick Flatley, NYI.	.10	.50
□ □	**125**	**Joe Reekie, NYI., RC**	**.10**	**.50**
□ □	126	Brent Sutter, NYI.	.10	.50
□ □	127	David Volek, NYI.	.10	.50
□ □	**128**	**Shawn Cronin, Wpg., RC**	**.10**	**.50**
□ □	129	Dale Hawerchuk, Wpg.	.25	1.50
□ □	130	Brent Ashton, Wpg.	.10	.50
□ □	**131**	**Bob Essensa (G), Wpg., RC**	**.10**	**.50**
□ □	132	Dave Ellett, Wpg.	.10	.50
□ □	133	Thomas Steen, Wpg.	.10	.50
□ □	134	Doug Smail, Wpg.	.10	.50
□ □	135	Fredrik Olausson, Wpg.	.10	.50
□ □	136	Dave McLlwain, Wpg.	.10	.50
□ □	137	Pat Elynuik, Wpg.	.10	.50
□ □	**138**	**Teppo Numminen, Wpg., RC**	**.10**	**.50**
□ □	139	Paul Fenton, Wpg.	.10	.50
□ □	140	Tony Granato, L.A.	.10	.50
□ □	141	Tomas Sandström, L.A.	.10	.50
□ □	**142**	**Rob Blake, L.A., RC**	**.25**	**1.50**
□ □	143	Wayne Gretzky, L.A.	2.00	20.00
□ □	144	Kelly Hrudey (G), L.A.	.10	.50
□ □	145	MikeKrushelnyski, L.A.	.10	.50
□ □	146	Steve Duchesne, L.A.	.10	.50
□ □	147	Steve Kasper, L.A.	.10	.50
□ □	148	John Tonelli, L.A.	.10	.50
□ □	149	DaveTaylor, L.A.	.10	.50
□ □	150	Larry Robinson, L.A.	.25	1.50
□ □	**151**	**Todd Elik, L.A., RC**	**.10**	**.50**
□ □	152	Luc Robitaille, L.A.	.25	1.50
□ □	153	Al Iafrate, Tor.	.10	.50
□ □	154	Allan Bester (G), Tor.	.10	.50
□ □	155	Gary Leeman, Tor.	.10	.50
□ □	156	Mark Osborne, Tor.	.10	.50
□ □	157	Tom Fergus, Tor.	.10	.50
□ □	158	Brad Marsh, Tor.	.10	.50
□ □	159	Wendel Clark, Tor.	.10	.50
□ □	160	Daniel Marois, Tor.	.10	.50
□ □	161	Ed Olczyk, Tor.	.10	.50
□ □	162	Rob Ramage, Tor.	.10	.50
□ □	163	Vincent Damphousse, Tor.	.25	1.50
□ □	**164**	**Lou Franceschetti, Tor., RC**	**.10**	**.50**
□ □	165	Paul Gillis, Que.	.10	.50
□ □	**166**	**Craig Wolanin, Que., RC**	**.10**	**.50**
□ □	167	Marc Fortier, Que.	.10	.50
□ □	168	Tony McKegney, Que.	.10	.50
□ □	169	Joe Sakic, Que.	.85	8.50
□ □	170	Michel Petit, Que.	.10	.50
□ □	**171**	**Scott Gordon (G), Que., RC**	**.10**	**.50**
□ □	172	Tony Hrkac, Que.	.10	.50
□ □	**173**	**Bryan Fogarty, Que., RC**	**.10**	**.50**
□ □	174	Mike Hough, Que.	.10	.50
□ □	**175**	**Claude Loiselle, Que., RC**	**.10**	**.50**
□ □	176	Ulf Dahlen, Min.	.10	.50
□ □	177	Larry Murphy, Min.	.25	1.50
□ □	178	Neal Broten, Min.	.10	.50
□ □	**179**	**Don Barber, Min., RC**	**.10**	**.50**
□ □	180	Shawn Chambers, Min.	.10	.50
□ □	**181**	**C. Donatelli, Min., RC, Err. (wrong birthday)**	**.10**	**.50**
□ □	182	Brian Bellows, Min.	.10	.50
□ □	183	Jon Casey (G), Min.	.10	.50
□ □	**184**	**Neil Wilkinson, Min., RC**	**.10**	**.50**
□ □	185	Aaron Broten, Min.	.10	.50
□ □	186	Dave Gagner, Min.	.10	.50
□ □	187	Basil McRae, Min.	.10	.50
□ □	**188**	**Mike Modano, Min., RC**	**.50**	**5.00**
□ □	189	Grant Fuhr (G), Edm.	.25	1.50
□ □	**190**	**Martin Gelinas, Edm., RC**	**.10**	**.50**
□ □	191	Jari Kurri, Edm.	.25	1.50
□ □	**192**	**Geoff Smith, Edm., RC**	**.10**	**.50**
□ □	193	Craig MacTavish, Edm.	.10	.50
□ □	194	Esa Tikkanen, Edm.	.10	.50
□ □	195	Glenn Anderson, Edm.	.10	.50
□ □	**196**	**Joe Murphy, Edm., RC**	**.10**	**.50**
□ □	197	Petr Klima, Edm.	.10	.50
□ □	198	Kevin Lowe, Edm.	.10	.50
□ □	199	Mark Messier, Edm.	.50	5.00
□ □	200	Steve Smith, Edm.	.10	.50
□ □	201	Craig Simpson, Edm.	.10	.50
□ □	202	Rob Brown, Pgh.	.10	.50
□ □	**203**	**Wendell Young (G), Pgh., RC**	**.10**	**.50**
□ □	204	Mario Lemieux, Pgh.	1.50	15.00
□ □	205	Phil Bourque, Pgh.	.10	.50
□ □	**206**	**Mark Recchi, Pgh., RC**	**1.00**	**6.00**
□ □	207	Zarley Zalapski, Pgh.	.10	.50
□ □	**208**	**Kevin Stevens, Pgh., RC**	**.25**	**1.50**
□ □	209	Tom Barrasso (G), Pgh.	.25	1.50
□ □	210	John Cullen, Pgh.	.10	.50
□ □	211	Paul Coffey, Pgh.	.25	1.50
□ □	212	Bob Errey, Pgh.	.10	.50
□ □	213	Tony Tanti, Pgh.	.10	.50
□ □	214	Carey Wilson, NYR.	.10	.50
□ □	215	Brian Leetch, NYR., Error (Eetch)	.25	2.50
□ □	215	Brian Leetch, NYR., Corrected	.25	2.50
□ □	**216**	**Darren Turcotte, NYR., RC**	**.10**	**.50**
□ □	217	Brian Mullen, NYR.	.10	.50
□ □	**218**	**Mike Richter (G), NYR., RC**	**1.25**	**7.50**
□ □	**219**	**Troy Mallette, NYR., RC**	**.10**	**.50**
□ □	220	Mike Gartner, NYR.	.25	1.50
□ □	221	Bernie Nicholls, NYR.	.10	.50
□ □	222	John Vanbiesbrouck (G), NYR.	.60	6.00
□ □	223	John Ogrodnick, NYR.	.10	.50
□ □	**224**	**Paul Broten, NYR., RC**	**.10**	**.50**
□ □	225	James Patrick, NYR.	.10	.50
□ □	**226**	**Mark Janssens, NYR., RC**	**.10**	**.50**
□ □	**227**	**Randy McKay, Det., RC**	**.10**	**.50**
□ □	228	Marc Habscheid, Det.	.10	.50
□ □	229	Jimmy Carson, Det.	.10	.50
□ □	**230**	**Yves Racine, Det., RC**	**.10**	**.15**
□ □	231	Dave Barr, Det.	.10	.50
□ □	232	Shawn Burr, Det.	.10	.50
□ □	233	Steve Yzerman, Det.	1.00	10.00
□ □	234	Steve Chiasson, Det.	.10	.50
□ □	**235**	**Daniel Shank, Det., RC**	**.10**	**.50**
□ □	236	John Chabot, Det.	.10	.50
□ □	237	Gerard Gallant, Det.	.10	.50
□ □	238	Bernie Federko, Det.	.10	.50
□ □	239	Phil Housley, Buf.	.10	.50
□ □	**240**	**Alexander Mogilny, Buf., RC**	**1.25**	**7.50**
□ □	241	Pierre Turgeon, Buf.	.25	1.50
□ □	242	Daren Puppa (G), Buf.	.10	.50
□ □	243	Scott Arniel, Buf.	.10	.50
□ □	244	Christian Ruuttu, Buf.	.10	.50
□ □	245	Doug Bodger, Buf.	.10	.50
□ □	246	Dave Andreychuk, Buf.	.10	.50
□ □	247	Mike Foligno, Buf.	.10	.50
□ □	**248**	**Dean Kennedy, Buf., RC**	**.10**	**.50**
□ □	**249**	**Dave Snuggerud, Buf., RC**	**.10**	**.50**
□ □	250	Rick Vaive, Buf.	.10	.50
□ □	**251**	**Todd Krygier, Hfd., RC**	**.10**	**.50**
□ □	**252**	**Adam Burt, Hfd., RC**	**.10**	**.50**
□ □	253	Scott Young, Hfd.	.10	.50
□ □	254	Ron Francis, Hfd.	.25	2.50
□ □	255	Peter Sidorkiewicz (G), Hfd.	.10	.50
□ □	256	Dave Babych, Hfd.	.10	.50
□ □	257	Pat Verbeek, Hfd.	.10	.50
□ □	258	Ray Ferraro, Hfd.	.10	.50
□ □	**259**	**Chris Govedaris, Hfd., RC**	**.10**	**.50**
□ □	**260**	**Brad Shaw, Hfd., RC**	**.10**	**.50**
□ □	261	Kevin Dineen, Hfd.	.10	.50
□ □	262	Dean Evason, Hfd.	.10	.50
□ □	263	Checklist 1 (1 - 132)	.10	.50
□ □	264	Checklist 2 (133 - 264)	.10	.50

BOWMAN HAT TRICKS

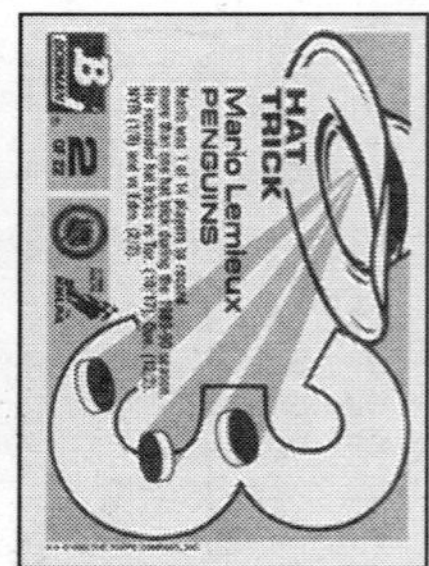

One card was issued in each of the standard wax packs.

Insert Set (22 cards): **8.00** **25.00**

	No.	Player	Regular	Tiffany
□ □	1	Brett Hull, Stl.	1.00	5.00
□ □	2	Mario Lemieux, Pgh.	3.25	15.00
□ □	3	Rob Brown, Pgh.	.25	.50
□ □	4	Mark Messier, Edm.	1.00	5.00
□ □	5	Steve Yzerman, Det.	2.00	10.00
□ □	6	Vincent Damphousse, Tor.	.50	3.00
□ □	7	Kevin Dineen, Hfd.	.25	.50
□ □	8	Mike Gartner, Min., Error (Toronto)	.50	1.50
□ □	9	Pat LaFontaine, NYI.	.50	1.50
□ □	10	Gary Leeman, Tor.	.25	.50
□ □	11	Stéphane Richer, Mtl.	.25	.50
□ □	12	Luc Robitaille, L.A.	.50	1.50
□ □	13	Steve Thomas, Chi.	.25	.50
□ □	14	Rick Tocchet, Pha.	.25	.50
□ □	15	Dino Ciccarelli, Wsh.	.50	1.50
□ □	16	John Druce, Wsh.	.25	.50
□ □	17	Mike Gartner, NYR.	.50	1.50
□ □	18	Tony Granato, L.A.	.25	.50
□ □	19	Jari Kurri, Edm.	.50	1.50
□ □	20	Bernie Nicholls, NYR.	.25	.50
□ □	21	Tomas Sandström, L.A.	.25	.50
□ □	22	Dave Taylor, L.A.	.25	.50

1990 - 91 CANADIAN OLYMPIC TEAM - ALBERTA LOTTERIES

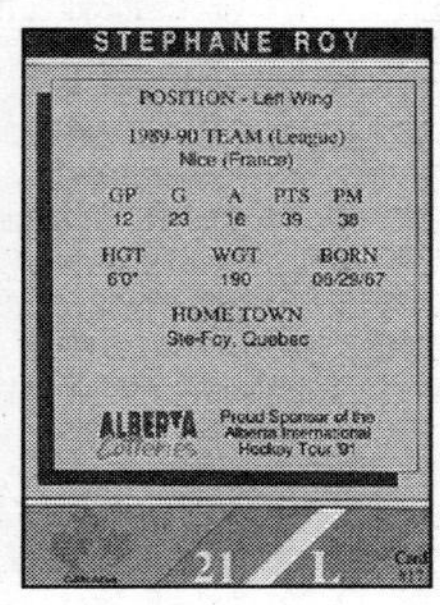

Imprint: ALBERTA LOTTERIES

Complete Set (23 cards): 15.00

	No.	Player	NRMT-MT
☐	1	Craig Billington (G)	.75
☐	2	Doug Dadswell (G)	.25
☐	3	Greg Andrusak	.25
☐	4	Karl Dykhuis	.25
☐	5	Gord Hynes	.75
☐	6	Ken MacArthur	.75
☐	7	Jim Paek	.75
☐	8	Brad Schlegel	.75
☐	9	Dave Archibald	.75
☐	10	Stu Barnes	2.50
☐	11	Brad Bennett	.75
☐	12	Todd Brost	.75
☐	13	José Charbonneau	.75
☐	14	Jason Lafrenière	.75
☐	15	Chris Lindberg	.75
☐	16	Ken Priestlay	.75
☐	17	Stéphane Roy	.75
☐	18	Randy Smith	.75
☐	19	Todd Strueby	.75
☐	20	Vladislav Tretiak	4.00
☐	21	David King	2.00
☐	22	Wayne Fleming	.75
☐	23	Checklist	.75

1990 - 91 JYVASHYVA HOCKEY LIIGA

A set of 12 stickers issued by the biscuit factory JyvasHyva of the Finnish National League team logos. We have no pricing information on this set.

Size: 1 5/8" x 4 1/4"

Imprint:

☐	HIFK Helsinki	☐	Hockeyreipas
☐	HPK Hameenlinna	☐	Ilves Tampere
☐	Jokerit Helsinki	☐	JyPHT
☐	KalPa Kuopio	☐	Lukko Raumo
☐	SaiPa	☐	Tappara Tampere
☐	TPS Turku	☐	Assat Pori

1990 - 91 KRAFT

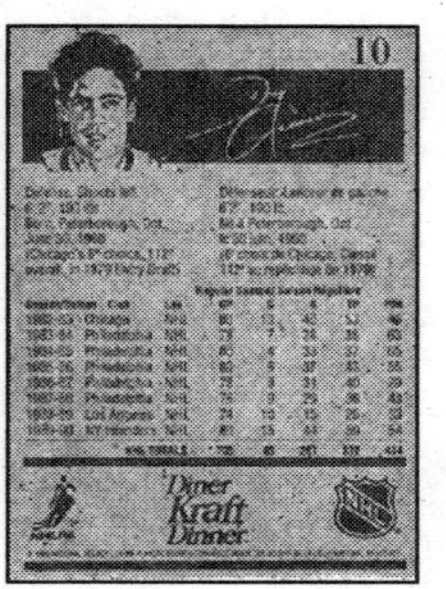

Card Nos. 1 to 64: Red backs on box stock; Issued on Kraft Dinner, Spirals and Noodles boxes. Card Nos. 65 to 91: Red backs on box stock; Issued on Jell-O boxes. Card Nos. 92 to 112: Blue backs on box stock; Issued in Kraft Cheese Singles packages. No stickers were issued in 1990-91. Again factory trimmed cards were available. These will command a price premium of twice the box cut cards.

Card Size: 2 1/2" x 3 1/2"

Imprint: KRAFT

Factory Set (Including album): 125.00

Complete Set (112 cards): 75.00

Common Player: .65

Album: 35.00

	No.	Player	NRMT-MT
☐	1	Dave Babych, Hfd.	.65
☐	2	Brian Bellows, Min.	.65
☐	3	Ray Bourque, Bos.	2.00
☐	4	Sean Burke (G), N.J.	1.00
☐	5	Jimmy Carson, Det.	.65
☐	6	Chris Chelios, Chi.	1.75
☐	7	Dino Ciccarelli, Wsh.	1.00
☐	8	Paul Coffey, Pgh.	1.00
☐	9	Geoff Courtnall, Stl.	.65
☐	10	Doug Crossman, NYI.	.65
☐	11	Kevin Dineen, Hfd.	.65
☐	12	Pat Elynuik, Wpg.	.65
☐	13	Ron Francis, Hfd.	1.50
☐	14	Gerard Gallant, Det.	.65
☐	15	Wayne Gretzky, L.A.	8.00
☐	16	Dale Hawerchuk, Buf.	1.00
☐	17	Ron Hextall (G), Pha.	1.00
☐	18	Phil Housley, Wpg.	.65
☐	19	Mark Howe, Pha.	1.00
☐	20	Brett Hull, Stl.	2.00
☐	21	Al Iafrate, Tor.	.65
☐	22	Guy Lafleur, Que.	2.00
☐	23	Pat LaFontaine, NYI.	1.00
☐	24	Rod Langway, Wsh.	.65
☐	25	Igor Larionov, Van.	1.00
☐	26	Steve Larmer, Chi.	1.00
☐	27	Gary Leeman, Tor.	.65
☐	28	Brian Leetch, NYR.	1.00
☐	29	Mario Lemieux, Pgh.	6.00
☐	30	Trevor Linden, Van.	1.00
☐	31	Mike Liut (G), Wsh.	.65
☐	32	Mark Messier, Edm.	2.00
☐	33	Al MacInnis, Cgy.	1.00
☐	34	Mike Modano, Min.	2.00
☐	35	Andy Moog (G), Bos.	1.00
☐	36	Joe Mullen, Pgh.	.65
☐	37	Kirk Muller, N.J.	.65
☐	38	Petr Nedved, Van.	1.00
☐	39	Cam Neely, Bos.	1.00
☐	40	Bernie Nicholls, NYR.	.65
☐	41	Joe Nieuwendyk, Cgy.	1.00
☐	42	Mats Sundin, Que.	2.00
☐	43	Daren Puppa (G), Buf.	.65
☐	44	Rob Ramage, Tor.	.65
☐	45	Bill Ranford (G), Edm.	1.00
☐	46	Stéphane Richer, Mtl.	.65
☐	47	Larry Robinson, L.A.	1.00
☐	48	Luc Robitaille, L.A.	1.00
☐	49	Patrick Roy (G), Mtl.	6.00
☐	50	Joe Sakic, Que.	3.50
☐	51	Denis Savard, Mtl.	1.00
☐	52	Craig Simpson, Edm.	.65
☐	53	Bobby Smith, Min.	.65
☐	54	Peter Stastny, N.J.	.65
☐	55	Thomas Steen, Wpg.	.65
☐	56	Scott Stevens, Stl.	.65
☐	57	Brent Sutter, NYI.	.65
☐	58	Rick Tocchet, Pha.	.65
☐	59	Pierre Turgeon, Buf.	1.00
☐	60	John Vanbiesbrouck (G), NYR.	2.50
☐	61	Mike Vernon (G), Cgy.	1.00
☐	62	Doug Wilson, Chi.	1.00
☐	63	Steve Yzerman, Det.	4.00
☐	64	Checklist	.65
☐	65	AS: Steve Duchesne, L.A.	.65
☐	66	AS: Brett Hull, Stl.	2.00
☐	67	AS: Wayne Gretzky, L.A.	8.00
☐	68	AS: Jari Kurri, Edm.	1.00
☐	69	AS: Mike Gartner, NYR.	1.00
☐	70	AS: Kirk McLean (G), Van.	1.00
☐	71	AS: Mark Messier, Edm.	2.00
☐	72	AS: Joe Mullen, Pgh.	.65
☐	73	AS: Bernie Nicholls, NYR.	.65
☐	74	AS: Joe Nieuwendyk, Cgy.	1.00
☐	75	AS: Luc Robitaille, L.A.	1.00
☐	76	AS: Mike Vernon (G), Cgy.	1.00
☐	77	AS: Doug Wilson, Chi.	.65
☐	78	AS: Steve Yzerman, Det.	4.00
☐	79	AS: Joe Sakic, Que.	3.50
☐	80	AS: Ray Bourque, Bos.	2.00
☐	81	AS: Chris Chelios, Chi.	1.75
☐	82	AS: Paul Coffey, Pgh.	1.00
☐	83	AS: Ron Francis, Hfd.	1.50
☐	84	AS: Cam Neely, Bos.	1.00
☐	85	AS: Phil Housley, Wpg.	.65
☐	86	AS: Pat LaFontaine, NYI.	1.00
☐	87	AS: Mario Lemieux, Pgh.	6.00
☐	88	AS: Kirk Muller, N.J.	.65
☐	89	AS: Stéphane Richer, Mtl.	.65
☐	90	AS: Patrick Roy (G), Mtl.	6.00
☐	91	AS: Pierre Turgeon, Buf.	1.00
☐	92	Boston Bruins	1.00
☐	93	Buffalo Sabres	1.00
☐	94	Calgary Flames	1.00
☐	95	Chicago Blackhawks	1.00
☐	96	Detroit Red Wings	1.00
☐	97	Edmonton Oilers	1.00
☐	98	Hartford Whalers	1.00
☐	99	Los Angeles Kings	1.00
☐	100	Minnesota North Stars	1.00
☐	101	Montréal Canadiens	1.00
☐	102	New Jersey Devils	1.00
☐	103	New York Islanders	1.00
☐	104	New York Rangers	1.00
☐	105	Philadelphia Flyers	1.00
☐	106	Pittsburgh Penguins	1.00
☐	107	Québec Nordiques	1.00
☐	108	St. Louis Blues	1.00
☐	109	Toronto Maple Leafs	1.00
☐	110	Vancouver Canucks	1.00
☐	111	Washington Capitals	1.00
☐	112	Winnipeg Jets	1.00

1990 - 91 O-PEE-CHEE / TOPPS

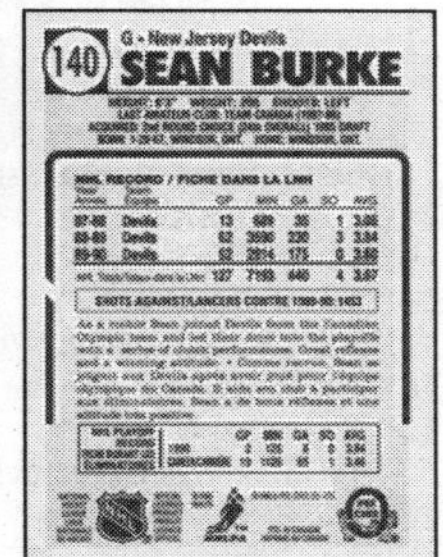

There are up to three versions for this series: a topps and Topps Tiffany card (1 - 396) plus an O-Pee-Chee card (1 - 528). The topps and O-Pee-Chee cards have the same value.

Imprint: © 1990 O-PEE-CHEE CO. LTD.

O-Pee-Chee Set (528 cards): 16.00

Topps Set (396 cards): 100.00 15.00

Common Player: .50 .10

	No.	Player	Tiffany	Reg
☐☐☐	1	Wayne Gretzky, Indianapolis Press	10.00	1.00
☐☐☐	2	Wayne Gretzky, Edmonton Times	10.00	1.00

☐☐☐	3	Wayne Gretzky, Los Angeles News	10.00	1.00
☐☐☐	4	HL: Brett Hull, Stl.	3.50	.35
☐☐☐	5	HL: Jari Kurri, Edm., Error (Jarri)	1.00	.20
☐☐☐	6	HL: Bryan Trottier, NYI.	1.00	.20
☐☐☐	**7**	**Jeremy Roenick, Chi., RC**	**8.00**	**1.00**
☐☐☐	8	Brian Propp, Bos.	.50	.10
☐☐☐	**9**	**J. Hrivnak (G), Wsh., RC**	**.50**	**.10**
☐☐☐	**10**	**Mick Vukota, NYI., RC**	**.50**	**.10**
☐☐☐	11	Tom Kurvers, Tor.	.50	.10
☐☐☐	12	Ulf Dahlen, Min.	.50	.10
☐☐☐	13	Bernie Nicholls, NYR.	.50	.10
☐☐☐	14	Peter Sidorkiewicz (G), Hfd.	.50	.10
☐☐☐	15	Peter Zezel, Stl. (Wsh.)	.50	.10
☐☐☐	**16**	**Mike Hartman, Buf., RC**	**.50**	**.10**
☐☐☐	17	Bernie Nicholls/ Marty McSorley	.50	.10
☐☐☐	18	Jim Sandlak, Van.	.50	.10
☐☐☐	19	Rob Brown, Pgh.	.50	.10
☐☐☐	**20**	**Paul Ranheim, Cal., RC**	**.50**	**.10**
☐☐☐	**21**	**Rick Zombo, Det., RC**	**.50**	**.10**
☐☐☐	22	Paul Gillis, Que.	.50	.10
☐☐☐	23	Brian Hayward (G), Mtl.	.50	.10
☐☐☐	24	Brent Ashton, Wpg.	.50	.10
☐☐☐	**25**	**Mark Lamb, Edm., RC**	**.50**	**.10**
☐☐☐	26	Rick Tocchet, Pha.	.50	.10
☐☐☐	**27**	**Viacheslav Fetisov, N.J., RC**	**1.50**	**.25**
☐☐☐	28	Denis Savard, Chi. (Mtl.)	1.50	.25
☐☐☐	29	Chris Chelios, Mtl. (Chi.)	3.50	.35
☐☐☐	**30**	**Janne Ojanen, N.J., RC**	**.50**	**.10**
☐☐☐	31	Don Maloney, NYI.	.50	.10
☐☐☐	32	Allan Bester (G), Tor.	.50	.10
☐☐☐	**33**	**Geoff Smith, Edm., RC**	**.50**	**.10**
☐☐☐	**34**	**Daniel Shank, Det., RC**	**.50**	**.10**
☐☐☐	**35**	**Mikael Andersson, Hfd., RC**	**.50**	**.10**
☐☐☐	36	Gino Cavallini, Stl.	.50	.10
☐☐☐	**37**	**Rob Murphy, Van., RC**	**.50**	**.10**
☐☐☐	38	TC: Jim Peplinski, Cgy.	.50	.10
☐☐☐	39	Laurie Boschman, Wpg.	.50	.10
☐☐☐	**40**	**Craig Wolanin, Que., RC**	**.50**	**.10**
☐☐☐	41	Phil Bourque, Pgh.	.50	.10
☐☐☐	**42**	**Alexander Mogilny, Buf., RC**	**10.00**	**1.25**
☐☐☐	43	Ray Bourque, Bos.	5.00	.50
☐☐☐	44	Mike Liut (G), Wsh.	.50	.10
☐☐☐	45	Ron Sutter, Pha.	.50	.10
☐☐☐	**46**	**Bob Kudelski, L.A., RC**	**.50**	**.10**
☐☐☐	47	Larry Murphy, Min.	1.50	.25
☐☐☐	**48**	**Darren Turcotte, NYR., RC**	**.50**	**.10**
☐☐☐	**49**	**Paul Ysebaert, N.J., RC**	**.50**	**.10**
☐☐☐	50	Alan Kerr, NYI.	.50	.10
☐☐☐	51	Randy Carlyle, Wpg.	.50	.10
☐☐☐	52	Iiro Jarvi, Que.	.50	.10
☐☐☐	**53**	**Don Barber, Min., RC**	**.50**	**.10**
☐☐☐	54	Carey Wilson, Hfd., Error (Cary)	.50	.10
☐☐☐	**55**	**Joey Kocur, Det., RC**	**.50**	**.10**
☐☐☐	56	Steve Larmer, Chi.	1.50	.25
☐☐☐	57	Paul Cavallini, Stl.	.50	.10
☐☐☐	58	Shayne Corson, Mtl.	1.50	.25
☐☐☐	59	TC: Brian Bradley, Van.	.50	.10
☐☐☐	**60**	**Sergei Makarov, Cgy., RC**	**2.00**	**.25**
☐☐☐	61	Kjell Samuelsson, Pha.	.50	.10
☐☐☐	62	Tony Granato, L.A.	.50	.10
☐☐☐	63	Tom Fergus, Tor.	.50	.10
☐☐☐	**64**	**Martin Gelinas, Edm., RC**	**4.00**	**.50**
☐☐☐	65	Tom Barrasso (G), Pgh.	1.50	.25
☐☐☐	66	Pierre Turgeon, Buf.	1.50	.25
☐☐☐	67	Randy Cunneyworth, Hfd.	.50	.10
☐☐☐	**68**	**Michal Pivonka, Wsh., RC**	**.50**	**.10**
☐☐☐	69	Cam Neely, Bos.	1.50	.25
☐☐☐	70	Brian Bellows, Min.	.50	.10
☐☐☐	71	Pat Elynuik, Wpg.	.50	.10
☐☐☐	72	Doug Crossman, NYI.	.50	.10
☐☐☐	73	Sylvain Turgeon, N.J.	.50	.10
☐☐☐	74	Shawn Burr, Det.	.50	.10
☐☐☐	75	John Vanbiesbrouck (G), NYR.	6.00	.60
☐☐☐	76	Steve Bozek, Van.	.50	.10
☐☐☐	77	Brett Hull, Stl.	5.00	.50
☐☐☐	78	Zarley Zalapski, Pgh.	.50	.10
☐☐☐	79	Wendel Clark, Tor.	1.50	.25
☐☐☐	80	TC: Bruce Hoffort (G), Pha.	.50	.10
☐☐☐	81	Kelly Miller, Wsh.	.50	.10
☐☐☐	**82**	**Mark Pederson, Mtl., RC**	**.50**	**.10**
☐☐☐	83	Adam Creighton, Chi.	.50	.10
☐☐☐	84	Scott Young, Hfd.	.50	.10
☐☐☐	85	Petr Klima, Edm.	.50	.10
☐☐☐	86	Steve Duchesne, L.A.	.50	.10
☐☐☐	87	Joe Nieuwendyk, Cgy.	1.50	.25
☐☐☐	88	Andy Brickley, Bos.	.50	.10
☐☐☐	89	Phil Housley, Buf. (Wpg.)	.50	.10
☐☐☐	90	Neal Broten, Min.	.50	.10
☐☐☐	91	Al Iafrate, Tor.	.50	.10
☐☐☐	92	Steve Thomas, Chi.	.50	.10
☐☐☐	93	Guy Carbonneau, Mtl.	.50	.10
☐☐☐	94	Steve Chiasson, Det.	.50	.10
☐☐☐	**95**	**Mike Tomlak, Hfd., RC**	**.50**	**.10**
☐☐☐	**96**	**Roger Johansson, Cgy., RC**	**.50**	**.10**
☐☐☐	97	Randy Wood, NYI.	.50	.10
☐☐☐	98	Jim Johnson, Pgh.	.50	.10
☐☐☐	99	Bob Sweeney, Bos.	.50	.10
☐☐☐	100	Dino Ciccarelli, Wsh.	1.50	.25
☐☐☐	101	TC: New York Rangers	.50	.10
☐☐☐	102	Mike Ramsey, Buf.	.50	.10
☐☐☐	103	Kelly Hrudey (G), LA	.50	.10
☐☐☐	104	Dave Ellett, Wpg.	.50	.10
☐☐☐	105	Bob Brooke, N.J.	.50	.10
☐☐☐	106	Greg Adams, Van.	.50	.10
☐☐☐	107	Joe Cirella, Que.	.50	.10
☐☐☐	108	Jari Kurri, Edm.	1.50	.25
☐☐☐	109	Pete Peeters (G), Pha.	.50	.10
☐☐☐	110	Paul MacLean, Stl.	.50	.10
☐☐☐	111	Doug Wilson, Chi.	1.50	.25
☐☐☐	112	Pat Verbeek, Hfd.	.50	.10
☐☐☐	**113**	**Bob Beers, Bos., RC**	.50	.10
☐☐☐	114	Mike O'Connell, Det.	.50	.10
☐☐☐	115	Brian Bradley, Van.	.50	.10
☐☐☐	116	Paul Coffey, Pgh.	1.50	.25
☐☐☐	117	Doug Brown, N.J.	.50	.10
☐☐☐	118	Aaron Broten, Min.	.50	.10
☐☐☐	**119**	**Bob Essensa (G), Wpg., RC**	**.50**	**.10**
☐☐☐	120	Wayne Gretzky, L.A.	17.50	1.75
☐☐☐	121	Vincent Damphousse, Tor.	2.50	.35
☐☐☐	122	TC: Paul Gillis, Que.	.50	.10
☐☐☐	123	Mike Foligno, Buf.	.50	.10
☐☐☐	124	Russ Courtnall, Mtl.	.50	.10
☐☐☐	125	Rick Meagher, Stl.	.50	.10
☐☐☐	**126**	**Craig Fisher, Pha., RC**	**.50**	**.10**
☐☐☐	127	Al MacInnis, Cgy.	1.50	.25
☐☐☐	128	Derek King, NYI.	.50	.10
☐☐☐	129	Dale Hunter, Wsh.	.50	.10
☐☐☐	130	Mark Messier, Edm.	5.00	.50
☐☐☐	131	James Patrick, NYR.	.50	.10
☐☐☐	132	Checklist 1 (1 - 132)	.50	.10
☐☐☐	133	TC: Steve Yzerman/ Gerald Gallant, Det.	2.50	.25
☐☐☐	134	Barry Pederson, Pgh.	.50	.10
☐☐☐	135	Gary Leeman, Tor.	.50	.10
☐☐☐	136	Doug Gilmour, Cgy.	2.50	.35
☐☐☐	137	Mike McPhee, Mtl.	.50	.10
☐☐☐	138	Bob Murray, Chi., LC	.50	.10
☐☐☐	139	Bob Carpenter, Bos.	.50	.10
☐☐☐	140	Sean Burke (G), N.J.	1.50	.25
☐☐☐	141	Dale Hawerchuk, Wpg. (Buf.)	1.50	.25
☐☐☐	142	Guy Lafleur, Que.	5.00	.50
☐☐☐	143	Lindy Ruff, NYR.	.50	.10
☐☐☐	144	TC: Hartford Whalers	.50	.10
☐☐☐	145	Glenn Anderson, Edm.	.50	.10
☐☐☐	**146**	**Dave Chyzowski, NYI., RC**	**.50**	**.10**
☐☐☐	147	Kevin Hatcher, Wsh.	.50	.10
☐☐☐	148	Rick Vaive, Buf.	.50	.10
☐☐☐	149	Adam Oates, Stl.	2.50	.35
☐☐☐	150	Garth Butcher, Van.	.50	.10
☐☐☐	151	Basil McRae, Min.	.50	.10
☐☐☐	152	Ilkka Sinisalo, Pha. (Miin.)	.50	.10
☐☐☐	153	Steve Kasper, L.A.	.50	.10
☐☐☐	154	Greg Paslawski, Wpg.	.50	.10
☐☐☐	155	Brad Marsh, Tor.	.50	.10
☐☐☐	156	Esa Tikkanen, Edm.	.50	.10
☐☐☐	157	Tony Tanti, Pgh.	.50	.10
☐☐☐	158	Mario Marois, Que.	.50	.10
☐☐☐	**159**	**Sylvain Lefebvre, Mtl., RC**	**.50**	**.10**
☐☐☐	160	Troy Murray, Chi.	.50	.10
☐☐☐	161	Gary Roberts, Cgy.	1.50	.25
☐☐☐	162	Randy Ladouceur, Hfd.	.50	.10
☐☐☐	163	John Chabot, Det.	.50	.10
☐☐☐	164	Calle Johansson, Wsh.	.50	.10
☐☐☐	165	TC: Boston Bruins	1.00	.20
☐☐☐	166	Jeff Norton, NYI.	.50	.10
☐☐☐	167	Mike Krushelnyski, L.A.	.50	.10
☐☐☐	168	Dave Gagner, Min.	.50	.10
☐☐☐	169	Dave Andreychuk, Buf.	1.50	.25
☐☐☐	**170**	**Dave Capuano, Van., RC**	**.50**	**.10**
☐☐☐	**171**	**Curtis Joseph (G), Stl., RC**	**10.00**	**1.50**
☐☐☐	172	Bruce Driver, N.J.	.50	.10
☐☐☐	173	Scott Mellanby, Pha.	.50	.10
☐☐☐	174	John Ogrodnick, NYR.	.50	.10
☐☐☐	175	Mario Lemieux, Pgh.	15.00	1.50
☐☐☐	176	Mark Fortier, Que.	.50	.10
☐☐☐	**177**	**Vincent Riendeau (G), Stl., RC**	**.50**	**.10**
☐☐☐	178	Mark Johnson, N.J.	.50	.10
☐☐☐	179	Dirk Graham, Chi.	.50	.10
☐☐☐	180	TC: Stéphane Beauregard (G), Wpg.	.50	.10
☐☐☐	**181**	**Robb Stauber, (G), L.A., RC**	**.50**	**.10**
☐☐☐	182	Christian Ruuttu, Buf.	.50	.10
☐☐☐	183	Dave Tippett, Hfd.	.50	.10
☐☐☐	184	Pat LaFontaine, NYI.	1.50	.25
☐☐☐	185	Mark Howe, Pha.	1.50	.25
☐☐☐	186	Stéphane Richer, Mtl.	.50	.10
☐☐☐	187	Jan Erixon, NYR.	.50	.10
☐☐☐	188	Neil Sheehy, Wsh.	.50	.10
☐☐☐	189	Craig MacTavish, Edm.	.50	.10
☐☐☐	190	Randy Burridge, Bos.	.50	.10
☐☐☐	191	Bernie Federko, Det.	.50	.10
☐☐☐	192	Shawn Chambers, Min.	.50	.10
☐☐☐	193	AS: Mark Messier, Edm.	3.50	.35
☐☐☐	194	AS: Luc Robitaille, L.A.	1.50	.20
☐☐☐	195	AS: Brett Hull, Stl.	2.50	.25
☐☐☐	196	AS: Ray Bourque, Bos.	2.50	.25
☐☐☐	197	AS: Al MacInnis, Cgy.	1.00	.20
☐☐☐	198	AS: Patrick Roy (G), Mtl.	7.50	.75
☐☐☐	199	AS: Wayne Gretzky, L.A.	10.00	1.00
☐☐☐	200	AS: Brian Bellows, Min.	.50	.10
☐☐☐	201	AS: Cam Neely, Bos.	1.00	.25
☐☐☐	202	AS: Paul Coffey, Pgh.	1.50	.25
☐☐☐	203	AS: Doug Wilson, Chi.	1.00	.25
☐☐☐	204	AS: Daren Puppa (G), Buf.	.50	.10
☐☐☐	205	Gary Suter, Cgy.	.50	.10
☐☐☐	206	Ed Olczyk, Tor.	.50	.10
☐☐☐	207	Doug Lidster, Van.	.50	.10
☐☐☐	208	John Cullen, Pgh.	.50	.10
☐☐☐	209	Luc Robitaille, L.A.	1.50	.25
☐☐☐	210	Tim Kerr, Pha.	.50	.10
☐☐☐	211	Scott Stevens, Wsh. (Stl.)	1.50	.25
☐☐☐	212	Craig Janney, Bos.	.50	.10
☐☐☐	213	Kevin Dineen, Hfd.	.50	.10
☐☐☐	**214**	**Jimmy Waite, (G), Chi., RC**	**.50**	**.10**
☐☐☐	215	Benoît Hogue, Buf.	.50	.10
☐☐☐	**216**	**Curtis Leschyshyn, Que., RC**	**.50**	**.10**
☐☐☐	217	Brad Lauer, NYI.	.50	.10
☐☐☐	218	Joe Mullen, Cgy. (NYR.)	1.50	.25
☐☐☐	219	Patrick Roy (G), Mtl.	15.00	1.50
☐☐☐	220	TC: St. Louis Blues	.50	.10
☐☐☐	221	Brian Leetch, NYR.	2.50	.35
☐☐☐	222	Steve Yzerman, Det.	10.00	1.00
☐☐☐	**223**	**Stéphane Beauregard (G), Wpg., RC**	**.50**	**.10**
☐☐☐	224	John MacLean, N.J.	.50	.10
☐☐☐	225	Trevor Linden, Van.	1.50	.25
☐☐☐	226	Bill Ranford (G), Edm.	1.50	.25
☐☐☐	227	Mark Osborne, Tor.	.50	.10
☐☐☐	228	Curt Giles, Min.	.50	.10
☐☐☐	229	Mikko Makelä, L.A.	.50	.10
☐☐☐	230	Bob Errey, Pgh.	.50	.10
☐☐☐	231	Jimmy Carson, Det.	.50	.10
☐☐☐	**232**	**Kay Whitmore, (G), Hfd., RC**	**.50**	**.10**
☐☐☐	233	Gary Nylund, NYI.	.50	.10
☐☐☐	**234**	**Jiri Hrdina, Cgy., RC**	**.50**	**.10**
☐☐☐	235	Stephen Leach, Wsh., Err. (Stephan)	.50	.10
☐☐☐	236	Greg Hawgood, Bos	.50	.10
☐☐☐	**237**	**Jocelyn Lemieux, Chi., RC**	**.50**	**.10**
☐☐☐	238	Daren Puppa (G), Buf.	.50	.10
☐☐☐	239	Kelly Kisio, NYR.	.50	.10
☐☐☐	240	Craig Simpson, Edm.	.50	.10
☐☐☐	241	TC: Vincent Damphouse, Tor.	1.00	.20
☐☐☐	242	Fredrik Olausson, Wpg.	.50	.10
☐☐☐	243	Ron Hextall (G), Pha.	1.50	.25
☐☐☐	**244**	**Sergio Momesso, Stl., RC**	**.50**	**.10**
☐☐☐	245	Kirk Muller, N.J.	.50	.10
☐☐☐	246	Petr Svoboda, Mtl.	.50	.10
☐☐☐	247	Daniel Berthiaume (G), Min.	.50	.10
☐☐☐	248	Andrew McBain, Van.	.50	.10
☐☐☐	249	Jeff Jackson, Que.	.50	.10
☐☐☐	**250**	**Randy Gilhen, Pgh., RC**	**.50**	**.10**
☐☐☐	251	TC: Adam Graves, Edm.	.50	.10
☐☐☐	**252**	**Eric Bennet, NYR., RC**	**.50**	**.10**
☐☐☐	253	Don Beaupré (G), Wsh.	.50	.10
☐☐☐	254	Per-Erik Eklund, Pha.	.50	.10
☐☐☐	255	Greg Gilbert, Chi.	.50	.10
☐☐☐	256	Gord Roberts, Stl.	.50	.10
☐☐☐	257	Kirk McLean (G), Van.	1.50	.25

	No.	Player		
☐☐☐	258	Brent Sutter, NYI.	.50	.10
☐☐☐	259	Brendan Shanahan, N.J.	6.00	.60
☐☐☐	**260**	**Todd Krygier, Hfd., RC**	**.50**	**.10**
☐☐☐	261	Larry Robinson, L.A.	1.50	.25
☐☐☐	262	TC: Buffalo Sabres	.50	.10
☐☐☐	263	Dave Christian, Bos.	.50	.10
☐☐☐	264	Checklist 2 (133 - 264)	.50	.10
☐☐☐	265	Jamie Macoun, Cgy.	.50	.10
☐☐☐	266	Glen Hanlon (G), Det.	.50	.10
☐☐☐	267	Daniel Marois, Tor.	.50	.10
☐☐☐	268	Doug Smail, Wpg.	.50	.10
☐☐☐	269	Jon Casey (G), Min.	.50	.10
☐☐☐	270	Brian Skrudland, Mtl.	.50	.10
☐☐☐	271	Michel Petit, Que.	.50	.10
☐☐☐	272	Dan Quinn, Van.	.50	.10
☐☐☐	273	Geoff Courtnall, Wsh. (Stl.)	.50	.10
☐☐☐	274	Mike Bullard, Pha.	.50	.10
☐☐☐	275	Randy Gregg, Edm.	.50	.10
☐☐☐	276	Keith Brown, Chi.	.50	.10
☐☐☐	**277**	**Troy Mallette, NYR., RC**	**.50**	**.10**
☐☐☐	278	Steve Tuttle, Stl.	.50	.10
☐☐☐	**279**	**Brad Shaw, Hfd., RC**	**.50**	**.10**
☐☐☐	**280**	**Mark Recchi, Pgh., RC**	**8.00**	**1.00**
☐☐☐	281	John Tonelli, L.A.	.50	.10
☐☐☐	282	Doug Bodger, Buf.	.50	.10
☐☐☐	283	Thomas Steen, Wpg.	.50	.10
☐☐☐	284	TC: Chris Terreri, N.J.	.50	.10
☐☐☐	285	Lee Norwood, Det.	.50	.10
☐☐☐	286	Brian MacLellan, Cgy.	.50	.10
☐☐☐	287	Bobby Smith, Mtl.	.50	.10
☐☐☐	**288**	**Robert Cimetta, Bos., RC**	**.50**	**.10**
☐☐☐	**289**	**Rob Zettler, Min., RC**	**.50**	**.10**
☐☐☐	**290**	**David Reid, Tor., RC**	**.50**	**.10**
☐☐☐	291	Bryan Trottier, NYI. (Pgh.)	1.50	.25
☐☐☐	292	Brian Mullen, NYR.	.50	.10
☐☐☐	293	Paul Reinhart, Van.	.50	.10
☐☐☐	294	Andy Moog (G), Bos.	1.50	.25
☐☐☐	295	Jeff Brown, Stl.	.50	.10
☐☐☐	296	Ryan Walter, Mtl.	.50	.10
☐☐☐	297	Trent Yawney, Chi.	.50	.10
☐☐☐	**298**	**John Druce, Wsh., RC**	**.50**	**.10**
☐☐☐	299	Dave McLlwain, Wpg.	.50	.10
☐☐☐	300	David Volek, NYI.	.50	.10
☐☐☐	301	Tomas Sandström, L.A.	.50	.10
☐☐☐	**302**	**Gord Murphy, Pha., RC**	**.50**	**.10**
☐☐☐	**303**	**Lou Franceschetti, Tor., RC**	**.50**	**.10**
☐☐☐	304	Dana Murzyn, Cgy.	.50	.10
☐☐☐	305	TC: Minnesota North Stars	.50	.10
☐☐☐	306	Patrik Sundstrom, N.J.	.50	.10
☐☐☐	307	Kevin Lowe, Edm.	.50	.10
☐☐☐	308	Dave Barr, Det.	.50	.10
☐☐☐	**309**	**Wendell Young (G), Pgh., RC**	**.50**	**.10**
☐☐☐	**310**	**Darrin Shannon, Buf., RC**	**.50**	**.10**
☐☐☐	311	Ron Francis, Hfd.	2.50	.35
☐☐☐	**312**	**Stéphane Fiset, (G), Que., RC**	**4.00**	**.50**
☐☐☐	313	Paul Fenton, Wpg.	.50	.10
☐☐☐	314	Dave Taylor, L.A.	.50	.10
☐☐☐	315	TC: Pat LaFontaine/ Alan Kerr, NYI.	1.00	.20
☐☐☐	316	Petri Skriko, Van.	.50	.10
☐☐☐	317	Rob Ramage, Tor.	.50	.10
☐☐☐	318	Murray Craven, Pha.	.50	.10
☐☐☐	319	Gaetan Duchesne, Min.	.50	.10
☐☐☐	320	Brad McCrimmon, Cgy., (Det.)	.50	.10
☐☐☐	321	Grant Fuhr (G), Edm.	1.50	.25
☐☐☐	322	Gerard Gallant, Det.	.50	.10
☐☐☐	323	Tommy Albelin, N.J.	.50	.10
☐☐☐	324	Scott Arniel, Buf. (Wpg.)	.50	.10
☐☐☐	**325**	**Mike Keane, Mtl., RC**	**.50**	**.10**
☐☐☐	326	TC: Doug Smith, Pgh.	.50	.10
☐☐☐	327	Mike Ridley, Wsh.	.50	.10
☐☐☐	328	Dave Babych, Hfd.	.50	.10
☐☐☐	329	Michel Goulet, Chi.	1.50	.25
☐☐☐	**330**	**Mike Richter (G), NYR., RC**	**8.00**	**1.25**
☐☐☐	**331**	**Garry Galley, Bos., RC**	**.50**	**.10**
☐☐☐	**332**	**Rod Brind'Amour, Stl., RC**	**4.00**	**.75**
☐☐☐	333	Tony McKegney, Que.	.50	.10
☐☐☐	334	Peter Stastny, N.J.	.50	.10
☐☐☐	335	Greg Millen (G), Chi.	.50	.10
☐☐☐	336	Ray Ferraro, Hfd.,	.50	.10
☐☐☐	**337**	**Miloslav Horava, NYR., RC**	**.50**	**.10**
☐☐☐	338	Paul MacDermid, Wpg.	.50	.10
☐☐☐	**339**	**Craig Coxe, Van., RC**	**.50**	**.10**
☐☐☐	**340**	**Dave Snuggerud, Buf., RC**	**.50**	**.10**
☐☐☐	**341**	**Mike Lalor, Stl. (Wsh.), RC**	**.50**	**.10**
☐☐☐	342	Marc Habscheid, Det.	.50	.10
☐☐☐	343	Réjean Lemelin (G), Bos.	.50	.10
☐☐☐	344	Charlie Huddy, Edm.	.50	.10
☐☐☐	345	Ken Linseman, Pha.	.50	.10
☐☐☐	346	TC: Montréal Canadiens	.50	.10
☐☐☐	**347**	**Troy Loney, Pgh., RC**	**.50**	**.10**
☐☐☐	**348**	**Mike Modano, Min., RC**	**6.00**	**.75**
☐☐☐	**349**	**Jeff Reese, (G), Tor., RC**	**.50**	**.10**
☐☐☐	350	Patrick Flatley, NYI.	.50	.10
☐☐☐	351	Mike Vernon (G), Cgy.	1.50	.25
☐☐☐	**352**	**Todd Elik, L.A., RC**	**.50**	**.10**
☐☐☐	353	Rod Langway, Wsh.	.50	.10
☐☐☐	354	Moe Mantha, Wpg.	.50	.10
☐☐☐	355	Keith Acton, Pha.	.50	.10
☐☐☐	**356**	**Scott Pearson, Tor., RC**	**.50**	**.10**
☐☐☐	**357**	**Perry Berezan, Min., RC**	**.50**	**.10**
☐☐☐	**358**	**Alexei Kasatonov, N.J., RC**	**.50**	**.10**
☐☐☐	**359**	**Igor Larionov, Van., RC**	**2.00**	**.25**
☐☐☐	**360**	**Kevin Stevens, Pgh., RC**	**4.00**	**.50**
☐☐☐	**361**	**Yves Racine, Det., RC**	**.50**	**.10**
☐☐☐	362	Dave Poulin, Bos.	.50	.10
☐☐☐	363	TC: Chicago Blackhawks	.50	.10
☐☐☐	**364**	**Yvon Corriveau, Hfd., RC**	**.50**	**.10**
☐☐☐	365	Brian Benning, L.A.	.50	.10
☐☐☐	**366**	**Hubie McDonough, NYI., RC**	**.50**	**.10**
☐☐☐	367	Ron Tugnutt (G), Que.	.50	.10
☐☐☐	368	Steve Smith, Edm.	.50	.10
☐☐☐	369	Joel Otto, Cgy.	.50	.10
☐☐☐	**370**	**Dave Lowry, Stl., RC**	**.50**	**.10**
☐☐☐	371	Clint Malarchuk (G), Buf.	.50	.10
☐☐☐	**372**	**Mathieu Schneider, Mtl., RC**	**.50**	**.10**
☐☐☐	373	Mike Gartner, NYR.	1.50	.25
☐☐☐	374	John Tucker, Wsh. (Buf.)	.50	.10
☐☐☐	**375**	**Chris Terreri (G), N.J., RC**	**.50**	**.10**
☐☐☐	376	Dean Evason, Hfd.	.50	.10
☐☐☐	**377**	**Jamie Leach, Pgh., RC**	**.50**	**.10**
☐☐☐	**378**	**Jacques Cloutier (G), Chi., RC**	**.50**	**.10**
☐☐☐	379	Glen Wesley, Bos.	.50	.10
☐☐☐	**380**	**Vladimir Krutov, Van., RC**	**.50**	**.10**
☐☐☐	381	Terry Carkner, Pha.	.50	.10
☐☐☐	**382**	**John McIntyre, Tor., RC**	**.50**	**.10**
☐☐☐	**383**	**Ville Siren, Min., RC**	**.50**	**.10**
☐☐☐	384	Joe Sakic, Que.	7.50	.75
☐☐☐	**385**	**Teppo Numminen, Wpg., RC**	**.50**	**.10**
☐☐☐	386	Theoren Fleury, Cgy.	2.50	.35
☐☐☐	**387**	**Glen Featherstone, Stl., RC**	**.50**	**.10**
☐☐☐	**388**	**Stéphan Lebeau, Mtl., RC**	**.50**	**.10**
☐☐☐	389	Kevin McClelland, Det.	.50	.10
☐☐☐	390	Uwe Krupp, Buf.	.50	.10
☐☐☐	**391**	**Mark Janssens, NYR., RC**	**.50**	**.10**
☐☐☐	392	Marty McSorley, L.A.	.50	.10
☐☐☐	**393**	**Vladimir Ruzicka, Edm., RC**	**.50**	**.10**
☐☐☐	394	TC: Scott Stevens, Wsh.	1.50	.25
☐☐☐	**395**	**Mark Fitzpatrick (G), NYI., RC**	**.50**	**.10**
☐☐☐	396	Checklist 3 (265 - 396)	.50	.10

	No.	Player	OPC
☐	397	Dave Manson, Chi.	.10
☐	398	Bob Gould, Bos.	.10
☐	**399**	**Bill Houlder, Wsh., RC**	**.10**
☐	**400**	**Glenn Healy (G), NYI., RC**	**.10**
☐	**401**	**John Kordic, Tor., RC**	**.10**
☐	402	Stewart Gavin, Min.	.10
☐	403	David Shaw, NYR.	.10
☐	**404**	**Ed Kastelic, Hfd., RC**	**.10**
☐	405	Rich Sutter, Stl.	.10
☐	**406**	**Grant Ledyard, Buf., RC**	**.10**
☐	407	Steve Weeks (G), Van.	.10
☐	408	Randy Hillier, Pgh.	.10
☐	409	Rick Wamsley (G), Cgy.	.10
☐	**410**	**Doug Houda, Det., RC**	**.10**
☐	**411**	**Ken McRae, Que., RC**	**.10**
☐	412	Craig Ludwig, Mtl.	.10
☐	**413**	**Doug Evans, Wpg., RC**	**.10**
☐	**414**	**Ken Baumgartner, NYI., RC**	**.10**
☐	415	Ken Wregget (G), Pha.	.10
☐	**416**	**Eric Weinrich, N.J., RC**	**.10**
☐	417	Mike Allison, L.A.	.10
☐	418	Joel Quenneville, Hfd.	.10
☐	419	Larry Melnyk, Van.	.10
☐	420	Colin Patterson, Cgy.	.10
☐	421	Gerald Diduck, NYI.	.10
☐	**422**	**Brent Gilchrist, Mtl., RC**	**.10**
☐	423	Craig Muni, Edm.	.10
☐	**424**	**Mike Hudson, Chi., RC**	**.10**
☐	**425**	**Eric Desjardins, Mtl., RC**	**.25**
☐	426	Walt Poddubny, N.J.	.10
☐	427	Mike Hough, Que.	.10
☐	428	Luke Richardson, Tor.	.10
☐	**429**	**Joe Murphy, Edm., RC**	**.10**
☐	**430**	**Tim Cheveldae (G), Det., RC**	**.10**
☐	**431**	**Adam Burt, Hfd., RC**	**.10**
☐	**432**	**Kelly Chase, Stl., RC**	**.10**
☐	**433**	**Robert Nordmark, Van., RC**	**.10**
☐	**434**	**Tim Hunter, Cgy., RC**	**.10**
☐	435	Peter Taglianetti, Wpg.	.10
☐	436	Alain Chevrier (G), Pgh.	.10
☐	**437**	**Darin Kimble, Que., RC**	**.10**
☐	**438**	**David Maley, N.J., RC**	**.10**
☐	**439**	**James Wiemer, Bos., RC, LC**	**.10**
☐	**440**	**Nick Kypreos, Wsh., RC**	**.10**
☐	441	Lucien DeBlois, Que.	.10
☐	442	Mario Gosselin (G), LA	.10
☐	**443**	**Neil Wilkinson, Min., RC**	**.10**
☐	**444**	**Mark Kumpel, Wpg., RC**	**.10**
☐	**445**	**Sergei Mylnikov (G), Que., RC, Error (Sergi)**	**.10**
☐	446	Ray Sheppard, Buf. (NYR.)	.10
☐	447	Ron Greschner, NYR.	.10
☐	**448**	**Craig Berube, Pha., RC**	**.10**
☐	449	Dave Hannan, Tor.	.10
☐	450	James Korn, Cgy.	.10
☐	451	Claude Lemieux, Mtl.	.10
☐	**452**	**Eldon Reddick (G), Edm., RC**	**.10**
☐	453	Randy Velischek, N.J.	.10
☐	454	Chris Nilan, NYR. (Bos.)	.10
☐	455	Jim Benning, Van.	.10
☐	456	Wayne Presley, Chi.	.10
☐	**457**	**Jon Morris, N.J., RC**	**.10**
☐	**458**	**Clark Donatelli, Min., RC**	**.10**
☐	459	Ric Nattress, Cgy.	.10
☐	**460**	**Rob Murray, Wsh., RC**	**.10**
☐	461	Tim Watters, L.A.	.10
☐	462	Checklist 4 (397 - 528)	.10
☐	**463**	**Derrick Smith, Pha., RC**	**.10**
☐	**464**	**Lyndon Byers, Bos., RC**	**.10**
☐	**465**	**Jeff Chychrun, Pha., RC**	**.10**
☐	466	Duane Sutter, Chi.	.10
☐	467	AW: Bill Ranford (G)	.25
☐	**468**	**Anatoli Semenov, Dynamo Riga, RC**	**.10**
☐	**469**	**Konstanin Kurashov, Soviet Wings, RC**	**.10**
☐	470	Gord Dineen, Pgh.	.10
☐	**471**	**Jeff Beukeboom, Edm., RC**	**.10**
☐	**472**	**Andrei Lomakin, Dynamo Riga, RC**	**.10**
☐	473	Doug Sulliman, Pha.	.10
☐	**474**	**Alexander Kerch, Dynamo Riga**	**.10**
☐	475	AW: Ray Bourque	.25
☐	476	Keith Crowder, L.A.	.10
☐	**477**	**Oleg Znarok, Dynamo Riga, RC**	**.10**
☐	**478**	**Dimitri Zinovjev, Dynamo Riga, RC**	**.10**
☐	**479**	**Igor Esmantovich, Soviet Wings, RC**	**.10**
☐	**480**	**Adam Graves, Edm., RC**	**.10**
☐	**481**	**Petr Prajsler, L.A., RC**	**.10**
☐	**482**	**Sergei Yashin, Dynamo Riga, RC**	**.10**
☐	**483**	**Jeff Bloemberg, NYR., RC**	**.10**
☐	**484**	**Yuri Strakhov, Soviet Wings, RC**	**.10**
☐	**485**	**Sergei B. Makarov, Soviet Wings, RC**	**.10**
☐	486	AW: R. Lemelin / A. Moog, Bos.	.10
☐	**487**	**Sergei Zaitsev, Soviet Wings, RC**	**.10**
☐	488	AW: Rick Meagher	.10
☐	**489**	**Yuri Kusnetsov, Soviet Wings, RC**	**.10**
☐	**490**	**Tom Chorske, Mtl., RC**	**.10**
☐	**491**	**Igor Akulinin, Dynamo Riga, RC**	**.10**
☐	**492**	**Mikhail Panin, Soviet Wings, RC**	**.10**
☐	**493**	**Sergei Nemchinov, Soviet Wings, RC**	**.10**
☐	**494**	**Vladimir Yurzinov, Coach, Dynamo Riga, RC**	**.10**
☐	495	Gord Kluzak, Bos.	.10
☐	**496**	**Sergei Skosyrev, Dynamo Riga, RC**	**.10**
☐	**497**	**Jeff Parker, Buf., RC, (Wpg.)**	**.10**
☐	**498**	**Tom Tilley, Stl., RC**	**.10**
☐	**499**	**Alexander Smirnov, Dynamo Riga, RC**	**.10**
☐	**500**	**Alexander Lysenko, Soviet Wings, RC**	**.10**
☐	**501**	**Arturs Irbe (G), Dynamo Riga, RC, Error (Artur)**	**.10**
☐	**502**	**Alexei Frolikov, Dynamo Riga, RC**	**.10**
☐	503	AW: Sergei Makarov	.10
☐	**504**	**Nikolai Varjanov, Dynamo Riga, RC**	**.10**
☐	505	Allen Pedersen, Bos.	.10
☐	**506**	**Vladimir Shashov, Dynamo Riga, RC**	**.10**
☐	**507**	**Tim Bergland, Wsh., RC**	**.10**
☐	**508**	**Gennady Lebedev, Soviet Wings, RC**	**.10**
☐	**509**	**Rod Buskas, Pgh, RC**	**.10**
☐	**510**	**Grant Jennings, Hfd., RC**	**.10**
☐	511	Ulf Samuelsson, Hfd.	.10

	No.	Player	NRMT-MT
☐	512	AW: Patrick Roy (G)	.75
☐	513	AW: Brett Hull	.25
☐	**514**	**Dimitri Mironov, Soviet Wings, RC**	**.10**
☐	515	Randy Moller, NYR.	.10
☐	**516**	**Kerry Huffman, Pha., RC**	**.10**
☐	517	Gilbert Delorme, Pgh.	.10
☐	518	Greg C. Adams, Det.	.10
☐	519	AW: Mark Messier	.25
☐	**520**	**Sheldon Kennedy, Det., RC**	**.25**
☐	**521**	**Harijs Vitolinsh, Dynamo Riga, RC**	**.10**
☐	522	AW: Wayne Gretzky	1.00
☐	**523**	**Dmitri Frolov, Dynamo Riga, RC**	**.10**
☐	524	Thomas Laidlaw, L.A.	.10
☐	**525**	**Oleg Bratash, Soviet Wings (G), RC**	**.10**
☐	**526**	**Kris King, NYR., RC**	**.10**
☐	**527**	**Wayne Van Dorp, Chi., RC**	**.10**
☐	**528**	**Chris Dahlquist, Pgh., RC**	**.10**

O-PEE-CHEE - CENTRAL RED ARMY

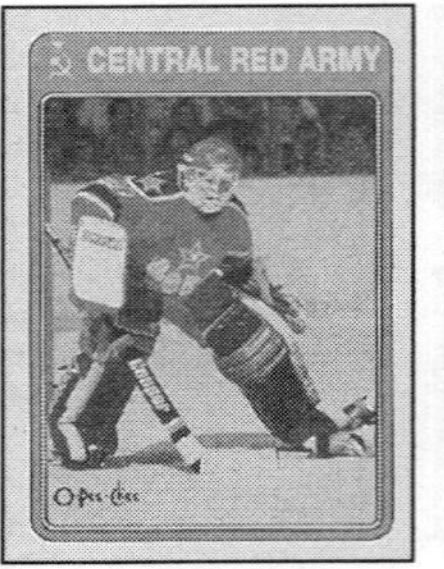

O-Pee-Chee Insert Set (22 cards): 8.00

	No.	Player	NRMT-MT
☐	1R	Ilya Byalsin	.25
☐	2R	Vladimir Malakhov	.50
☐	3R	Andrei Khomutov	.50
☐	4R	Valeri Kamensky	1.50
☐	5R	Dimitri Motkov	.25
☐	6R	Evgeny Shastin	.25
☐	7R	Arturs Irbe (G)	.50
☐	8R	Igor Chibirev	.50
☐	9R	Maxim Mikhailovsky (G)	.25
☐	10R	Vyacheslav Bykov	.50
☐	11R	Super Series A (1976; 1980; 1986)	.25
☐	12R	Super Series B (1989; 1990)	.25
☐	13R	Valeri Shiryev	.25
☐	14R	Igor Maslennikov	.25
☐	15R	Igor Malykhin	.25
☐	16R	Dimitri Khristich	.25
☐	17R	Viktor Tikhonov, Coach	.50
☐	18R	Evgeny Davydov	.25
☐	19R	Sergei Fedorov	4.00
☐	20R	Pavel Kostichkin	.25
☐	21R	Vladimir Konstantinov	1.00
☐	22R	Checklist (1R - 22R)	.25

TOPPS SCORING LEADERS

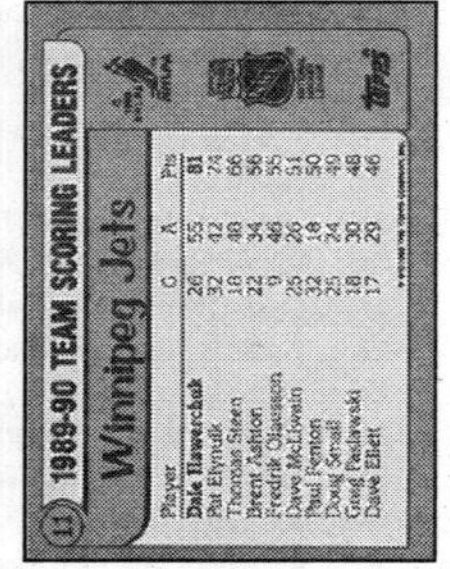

These cards have two versions: the regular inserts and a Tiffany parallel.

Topps Insert Set (21 cards): 10.00 40.00

	No.	Player	Regular	Tiffany
☐☐	1	Steve Larmer, Chi.	.50	.65
☐☐	2	Brett Hull, Stl.	.75	5.00
☐☐	3	Cam Neely, Bos.	.50	1.50
☐☐	4	Stéphane Richer, Mtl.	.25	.65
☐☐	5	Paul Reinhart, Van.	.25	.65
☐☐	6	Dino Ciccarelli, Wsh.	.50	1.50
☐☐	7	Kirk Muller, N.J.	.25	.65
☐☐	8	Joe Nieuwendyk, Cgy.	.50	1.50
☐☐	9	Rick Tocchet, Pha.	.25	.65
☐☐	10	Pat LaFontaine, NYI.	.50	1.50
☐☐	11	Dale Hawerchuk, Wpg.	.50	1.50
☐☐	12	Wayne Gretzky, L.A.	3.00	17.50
☐☐	13	Gary Leeman, Tor.	.25	.65
☐☐	14	Joe Sakic, Que	1.25	8.00
☐☐	15	Brian Bellows, Min.	.25	.65
☐☐	16	Mark Messier, Edm.	.75	5.00
☐☐	17	Mario Lemieux, Pgh.	2.50	15.00
☐☐	18	John Ogrodnick, NYR.	.25	.65
☐☐	19	Steve Yzerman, Det.	1.50	6.00
☐☐	20	Pierre Turgeon, Buf.	.50	1.50
☐☐	21	Ron Francis, Hfd.	.50	2.50

BOX BOTTOMS

These four-card panels were found on the bottom of both O-Pee-Chee and Topps wax boxes.

Panel Size: 5" x 7"

Complete Set (16 cards):	**10.00**
Panel A - D:	**4.00**
Panel E - H:	**4.00**
Panel I - L:	**2.50**
Panel M - P:	**2.00**

	No.	Player	NRMT-MT
☐☐	A	Alexander Mogilny, Buf.	1.00
☐☐	B	Jon Casey (G), Min.	.50
☐☐	C	Paul Coffey, Pgh.	.75
☐☐	D	Wayne Gretzky, L.A.	3.50
☐☐	E	Patrick Roy (G), Mtl.	2.50
☐☐	F	Mike Modano, Min.	1.25
☐☐	G	Mario Lemieux, Pgh.	2.50
☐☐	H	Al MacInnis, Cgy.	.50
☐☐	I	Ray Bourque, Bos.	1.25
☐☐	J	Steve Yzerman, Det.	2.00
☐☐	K	Darren Turcotte, NYR.	.50
☐☐	L	Mike Vernon (G), Cgy.	.75
☐☐	M	Pierre Turgeon, Buf.	.75
☐☐	N	Doug Wilson, Chi.	.50
☐☐	O	Don Beaupré (G), Wsh.	.50
☐☐	P	Sergei Makarov, Cgy.	.50

1990 - 91 O-PEE-CHEE PREMIER

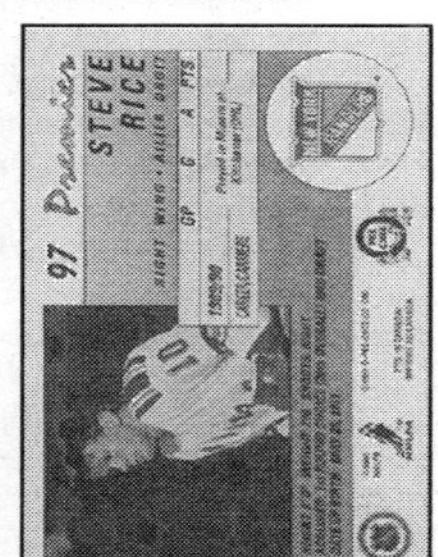

Complete Set (132 cards):	**75.00**
Common Player:	**.25**

	No.	Player	NRMT-MT
☐	1	Scott Arniel, Wpg.	.25
☐	**2**	**Jergus Baca, Hfd., RC**	**.25**
☐	3	Brian Bellows, Min.	.25
☐	**4**	**Jean-Claude Bergeron (G), Mtl., RC**	**.25**
☐	5	Daniel Berthiaume (G), LA	.25
☐	**6**	**Rob Blake, L.A., RC**	**1.50**
☐	**7**	**Peter Bondra, Wsh., RC**	**8.00**
☐	8	Laurie Boschman, N.J.	.25
☐	9	Ray Bourque, Bos.	1.50
☐	10	Aaron Broten, Que. (Tor.)	.25
☐	**11**	**Greg Brown, Buf., RC**	**.25**
☐	12	Jimmy Carson, Det.	.25
☐	13	Chris Chelios, Chi.	1.25
☐	14	Dino Ciccarelli, Wsh.	.50
☐	**15**	**Zdeno Ciger, N.J., RC**	**.25**
☐	16	Paul Coffey, Pgh.	.50
☐	**17**	**Danton Cole, Wpg., RC**	**.25**
☐	18	Geoff Courtnall, Stl.	.25
☐	**19**	**Mike Craig, Min., RC,**	**.25**
☐	20	John Cullen, Pgh.	.25
☐	21	Vincent Damphousse, Tor.	1.00
☐	22	Gerald Diduck, Mtl.	.25
☐	23	Kevin Dineen, Hfd.	.25
☐	**24**	**Per Djoos, Det., RC**	**.25**
☐	**25**	**Tie Domi, NYR., RC**	**2.00**
☐	**26**	**Peter Douris, Bos., RC**	**.25**
☐	**27**	**Rob DiMaio, NYI., RC**	**.25**
☐	28	Pat Elynuik, Wpg.	.25
☐	**29**	**Bob Essensa (G), Wpg., RC**	**.25**
☐	**30**	**Sergei Fedorov, Det., RC**	**15.00**
☐	**31**	**Brent Fedyk, Det, RC**	**.25**
☐	32	Ron Francis, Hfd.	1.00
☐	**33**	**Link Gaetz, Min., RC**	**.25**
☐	**34**	**Troy Gamble. (G), Van, RC**	**.25**
☐	**35**	**Johan Garpenlov, Det., RC**	**.25**
☐	36	Mike Gartner, NYR.	.50
☐	37	Rick Green, Det.	.25
☐	38	Wayne Gretzky, L.A.	6.00
☐	**39**	**Jeff Hackett (G), NYI., RC**	**2.50**
☐	40	Dale Hawerchuk, Buf.	.50
☐	41	Ron Hextall (G), Pha.	.50
☐	**42**	**Bruce Hoffort (G), Pha., RC**	**.25**
☐	**43**	**Bobby Holik, Hfd., RC**	**1.00**
☐	**44**	**Martin Hostak, Pha., RC**	**.25**
☐	45	Phil Housley, Wpg.	.25
☐	**46**	**Jody Hull, NYR., RC**	**.25**
☐	47	Brett Hull, Stl.	1.50
☐	48	Al Iafrate, Tor.	.25
☐	**49**	**Peter Ing (G), Tor., RC**	**.25**
☐	**50**	**Jaromir Jagr, Pgh., RC**	**30.00**
☐	**51**	**Curtis Joseph (G), Stl., RC**	**8.00**
☐	**52**	**Robert Kron, Van., RC**	**.25**
☐	**53**	**Frantisek Kucera, Chi., RC**	**.25**
☐	**54**	**Dale Kushner, Pha., RC**	**.25**
☐	55	Guy Lafleur, Que.	1.50
☐	56	Pat LaFontaine, NYI.	.50
☐	**57**	**Mike Lalor, Wsh., RC**	**.25**
☐	58	Steve Larmer, Chi.	.50
☐	**59**	**Jiri Latal, Pha., RC**	**.25**
☐	**60**	**Jamie Leach, Pgh., RC**	**.25**
☐	61	Brian Leetch, NYR.	1.50
☐	62	Claude Lemieux, N.J.	.25
☐	63	Mario Lemieux, Pgh.	5.00
☐	64	Craig Ludwig, NYI.	.25
☐	65	Al MacInnis, Cgy.	.50
☐	66	Mikko Makela, Buf.	.25
☐	**67**	**David Marcinyshyn, N.J., RC**	**.25**
☐	**68**	**Stéphane Matteau, Cgy., RC**	**.25**
☐	69	Brad McCrimmon, Det.	.25
☐	70	Kirk McLean (G), Van.	.50
☐	71	Mark Messier, Edm.	1.50
☐	72	Kelly Miller, Wsh.	.25
☐	**73**	**Kevin Miller, NYR., RC**	**.25**
☐	**74**	**Mike Modano, Min., RC**	**8.00**
☐	**75**	**Alexander Mogilny, Buf., RC**	**5.00**
☐	76	Andy Moog (G), Bos.	.50
☐	77	Joe Mullen, Pgh.	.25
☐	78	Kirk Muller, N.J.	.25
☐	**79**	**Pat Murray, Pha., RC**	**.25**
☐	**80**	**Jarmo Myllys (G), Min., RC**	**.25**
☐	**81**	**Petr Nedved, Van., RC**	**2.50**
☐	82	Cam Neely, Bos.	.50
☐	83	Bernie Nicholls, NYR.	.25
☐	84	Joe Nieuwendyk, Cgy.	.50
☐	85	Christ Nilan, Bos.	.25
☐	**86**	**Owen Nolan, Que., RC**	**3.50**
☐	87	Brian Noonan, Chi., Error (Dan Vincelette)	.25
☐	88	Adam Oates, Stl.	1.00
☐	**89**	**Greg Parks, NYI., RC**	**.25**
☐	**90**	**Adrien Plavsic, Van., RC**	**.25**
☐	**91**	**Keith Primeau, Det., RC**	**5.00**
☐	92	Brian Propp, Min.	.25
☐	93	Dan Quinn, Van.	.25
☐	94	Bill Ranford (G), Edm.	.50
☐	**95**	**Robert Reichel, Cgy., RC**	**3.00**
☐	**96**	**Mike Ricci, Pha., RC, Error (wrong birthday)**	**1.00**
☐	**97**	**Steven Rice, NYR., RC**	**.25**
☐	98	Stéphane Richer, Mtl.	.25
☐	99	Luc Robitaille, L.A.	.50
☐	**100**	**Jeremy Roenick, Chi., RC**	**5.00**
☐	101	Patrick Roy (G), Mtl.	5.00
☐	102	Joe Sakic, Que.	3.00
☐	103	Denis Savard, Mtl.	.50
☐	**104**	**Anatoli Semenov, Edm., RC**	**.25**
☐	105	Brendan Shanahan, N.J.	2.00
☐	106	Ray Sheppard, NYR.	.25
☐	**107**	**Mike Sillinger, Det., RC**	**.25**
☐	108	Ilkka Sinisalo, Min.	.25
☐	109	Bobby Smith, Min.	.25
☐	**110**	**Paul Stanton, Pgh., RC**	**.25**

	No.	Player	Price
☐	**111**	**Kevin Stevens, Pgh., RC**	.75
☐	112	Scott Stevens, Stl.	.25
☐	**113**	**Allan Stewart, N.J., RC**	.25
☐	**114**	**Mats Sundin, Que., RC**	8.00
☐	115	Brent Sutter, NYI.	.25
☐	**116**	**Tim Sweeney, Cgy., RC**	.25
☐	117	Peter Taglianetti, Min.	.25
☐	**118**	**John Tanner (G), Que., RC**	.25
☐	119	Dave Tippett, Wsh.	.25
☐	120	Rick Tocchet, Pha.	.25
☐	121	Bryan Trottier, Pgh.	.50
☐	122	John Tucker, Buf.	.25
☐	**123**	**Darren Turcotte, NYR., RC**	.25
☐	124	Pierre Turgeon, Buf.	.50
☐	125	Randy Velischek, Que.	.25
☐	126	Mike Vernon (G), Cgy.	.50
☐	**127**	**Wes Walz, Bos., RC**	.25
☐	128	Carey Wilson, Hfd.	.25
☐	129	Doug Wilson, Chi.	50
☐	130	Steve Yzerman, Det.	3.00
☐	131	Peter Zezel, Wsh.	.25
☐	132	Checklist (1 - 132)	.25

1990 - 91 PANINI STICKERS

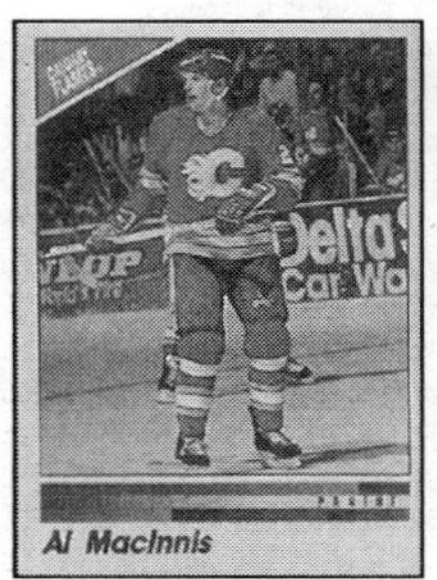

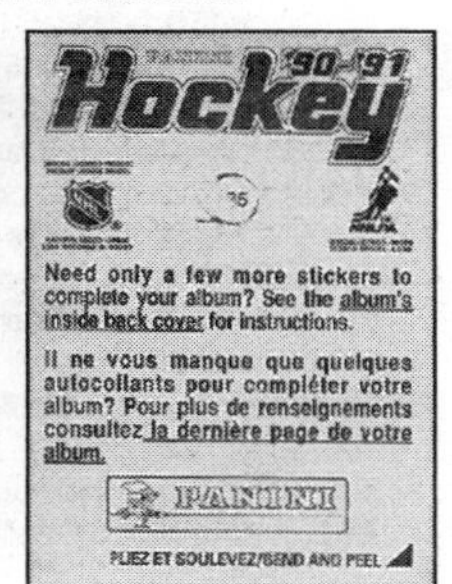

Sticker Size: 2 1/6" x 2 15/16"
Imprint: PANINI

Complete Set (351 stickers):		**20.00**
Common Player:		**.10**
Album (Wayne Gretzky):		**5.00**

	No.	Trophy	NRMT-MT
☐	1	Prince of Wales Conference	.10
☐	2	Clarence Campbell Conference	.10
☐	3	Stanley Cup	.10
☐	4	Dave Poulin, Bos.	.10
☐	5	Brian Propp, Bos.	.10
☐	6	Glen Wesley, Bos.	.10
☐	7	Bob Carpenter, Bos.	.10
☐	8	John Carter, Bos.	.10
☐	9	Cam Neely, Bos.	.25
☐	10	Greg Hawgood, Bos.	.10
☐	11	Andy Moog (G), Bos.	.25
☐	12	Boston Bruins Logo	.10
☐	13	Réjean Lemelin (G), Bos.	.10
☐	14	Craig Janney, Bos.	.10
☐	15	Bob Sweeney, Bos.	.10
☐	16	Andy Brickley, Bos.	.10
☐	17	Ray Bourque, Bos.	.50
☐	18	Dave Christian, Bos.	.10
☐	19	Dave Snuggerud, Buf.	.10
☐	20	Christian Ruuttu, Buf.	.10
☐	21	Phil Housley, Buf.	.10
☐	22	Uwe Krupp, Buf.	.10
☐	23	Rick Vaive, Buf.	.10
☐	24	Mike Ramsey, Buf.	.10
☐	25	Mike Foligno, Buf.	.10
☐	26	Clint Malarchuk (G), Buf.	.10
☐	27	Buffalo Sabres Logo	.10
☐	28	Pierre Turgeon, Buf.	.25
☐	29	Dave Andreychuk, Buf.	.25
☐	30	Scott Arniel, Buf.	.10
☐	31	Daren Puppa (G), Buf.	.10
☐	32	Mike Hartman, Buf.	.10
☐	33	Doug Bodger, Buf.	.10
☐	34	Scott Young, Hfd.	.10
☐	35	Todd Krygier, Hfd.	.10
☐	36	Pat Verbeek, Hfd.	.10
☐	37	Dave Tippett, Hfd.	.10
☐	38	Peter Sidorkiewicz (G), Hfd.	.10
☐	39	Ron Francis, Hfd.	.35
☐	40	Dave Babych, Hfd.	.10
☐	41	Randy Ladouceur, Hfd.	.10
☐	42	Hartford Whalers Logo	.10
☐	43	Kevin Dineen, Hfd.	.10
☐	44	Dean Evason, Hfd.	.10
☐	45	Ray Ferraro, Hfd.	.10
☐	46	Mike Tomlak, Hfd.	.10
☐	47	Mikael Andersson, Hfd.	.10
☐	48	Brad Shaw, Hfd.	.10
☐	49	Chris Chelios, Mtl.	.35
☐	50	Petr Svoboda, Mtl.	.10
☐	51	Patrick Roy (G), Mtl.	1.50
☐	52	Bobby Smith, Mtl.	.10
☐	53	Stéphane Richer, Mtl.	.10
☐	54	Shayne Corson, Mtl.	.25
☐	55	Brian Skrudland, Mtl.	.10
☐	56	Russ Courtnall, Mtl.	.10
☐	57	Montréal Canadiens Logo	.10
☐	58	Guy Carbonneau, Mtl.	.10
☐	59	Sylvain Lefebvre, Mtl.	.10
☐	60	Mathieu Schneider, Mtl.	.10
☐	61	Brian Hayward (G), Mtl.	.10
☐	62	Mats Naslund, Mtl.	.10
☐	63	Mike McPhee, Mtl.	.10
☐	64	Brendan Shanahan, N.J.	.60
☐	65	Patrik Sundstrom, N.J.	.10
☐	66	Mark Johnson, N.J.	.10
☐	67	Doug Brown, N.J.	.10
☐	68	Chris Terreri (G), N.J.	.10
☐	69	Bruce Driver, N.J.	.10
☐	70	Peter Stastny, N.J.	.10
☐	71	Sylvain Turgeon, N.J.	.10
☐	72	New Jersey Devils Logo	.10
☐	73	Kirk Muller, N.J.	.10
☐	74	John MacLean, N.J.	.10
☐	75	Viacheslav Fetisov, N.J.	.25
☐	76	Tommy Albelin, N.J.	.10
☐	77	Sean Burke (G), N.J.	.25
☐	78	Janne Ojanen, N.J.	.10
☐	79	Randy Wood, NYI.	.10
☐	80	Gary Nylund, NYI.	.10
☐	81	Pat LaFontaine, NYI.	.25
☐	82	Patrick Flatley, NYI.	.10
☐	83	Bryan Trottier, NYI.	.25
☐	84	Don Maloney, NYI.	.10
☐	85	Gerald Diduck, NYI.	.10
☐	86	New York Islanders Logo	.10
☐	87	Mark Fitzpatrick (G), NYI.	.10
☐	88	Glenn Healy (G), NYI.	.10
☐	89	Alan Kerr, NYI.	.10
☐	90	Brent Sutter, NYI.	.10
☐	91	Doug Crossman, NYI.	.10
☐	92	Hubie McDonough, NYI.	.10
☐	93	Jeff Norton, NYI.	.10
☐	94	Kelly Kisio, NYR.	.10
☐	95	Brian Leetch, NYR.	.35
☐	96	Brian Mullen, NYR.	.10
☐	97	James Patrick, NYR.	.10
☐	98	Mike Richter (G), NYR.	.35
☐	99	John Ogrodnick, NYR.	.10
☐	100	Troy Mallette, NYR.	.10
☐	101	Mark Janssens, NYR.	.10
☐	102	New York Rangers Logo	.10
☐	103	Mike Gartner, NYR.	.25
☐	104	Jan Erixon, NYR.	.10
☐	105	Carey Wilson, NYR.	.10
☐	106	Bernie Nicholls, NYR.	.10
☐	107	Darren Turcotte, NYR.	.10
☐	108	John Vanbiesbrouck (G), NYR.	.60
☐	109	Ron Sutter, Pha.	.10
☐	110	Kjell Samuelsson, Pha	.10
☐	111	Ken Linseman, Pha	.10
☐	112	Ken Wregget (G), Pha	.10
☐	113	Per-Erik Eklund, Pha	.10
☐	114	Terry Carkner, Pha	.10
☐	115	Gord Murphy, Pha	.10
☐	116	Murray Craven, Pha	.10
☐	117	Philadelphia Flyers Logo	.10
☐	118	Ron Hextall (G), Pha	.25
☐	119	Mike Bullard, Pha	.10
☐	120	Tim Kerr, Pha	.10
☐	121	Rick Tocchet, Pha	.10
☐	122	Mark Howe, Pha.	.25
☐	123	Ilkka Sinisalo, Pha	.10
☐	124	Tony Tanti, Pgh.	.10
☐	125	John Cullen, Pgh.	.10
☐	126	Zarley Zalapski, Pgh.	.10
☐	127	Wendell Young (G), Pgh.	.10
☐	128	Rob Brown, Pgh.	.10
☐	129	Phil Bourque, Pgh.	.10
☐	130	Mark Recchi, Pgh.	.35
☐	131	Kevin Stevens, Pgh.	.10
☐	132	Pittsburgh Penguins Logo	.10
☐	133	Bob Errey, Pgh.	.10
☐	134	Tom Barrasso (G), Pgh.	.25
☐	135	Paul Coffey, Pgh.	.25
☐	136	Mario Lemieux, Pgh.	1.50
☐	137	Randy Hillier, Pgh.	.10
☐	138	Troy Loney, Pgh.	.10
☐	139	Joe Sakic, Que.	.75
☐	140	Lucien DeBlois, Que.	.10
☐	141	Joe Cirella, Que.	.10
☐	142	Ron Tugnutt (G), Que.	.10
☐	143	Paul Gillis, Que.	.10
☐	144	Bryan Fogarty, Que.	.10
☐	145	Guy Lafleur, Que.	.50
☐	146	Tony Hrkac, Que.	.10
☐	147	Québec Nordiques Logo	.10
☐	148	Michel Petit, Que.	.10
☐	149	Tony McKegney, Que.	.10
☐	150	Curtis Leschyshyn, Que.	.10
☐	151	Claude Loiselle, Que.	.10
☐	152	Mario Brunetta (G), Que.	.10
☐	153	Marc Fortier, Que.	.10
☐	154	Michal Pivonka, Wsh.	.10
☐	155	Scott Stevens, Wsh.	.10
☐	156	Kelly Miller, Wsh.	.10
☐	157	John Tucker, Wsh.	.10
☐	158	Don Beaupré (G), Wsh.	.10
☐	159	Geoff Courtnall, Wsh.	.10
☐	160	Alan May, Wsh.	.10
☐	161	Dino Ciccarelli, Wsh.	.25
☐	162	Washington Capitals Logo	.10
☐	163	Mike Ridley, Wsh.	.10
☐	164	Bob Rouse, Wsh.	.10
☐	165	Mike Liut (G), Wsh.	.10
☐	166	Stephen Leach, Wsh.	.10
☐	167	Kevin Hatcher, Wsh.	.10
☐	168	Dale Hunter, Wsh.	.10
☐	169	Prince of Wales Trophy	.10
☐	170	Clarence Campbell Trophy	.10
☐	171	Stanley Cup Championship	.10
☐	172	Doug Gilmour, Cgy.	.35
☐	173	Brad McCrimmon, Cgy.	.10
☐	174	Joe Nieuwendyk, Cgy.	.25
☐	175	Mike Vernon (G), Cgy.	.25
☐	176	Theoren Fleury, Cgy.	.35
☐	177	Gary Suter, Cgy.	.10
☐	178	Jamie Macoun, Cgy.	.10
☐	179	Gary Roberts, Cgy.	.25
☐	180	Calgary Flames Logo	.10
☐	181	Paul Ranheim, Cgy.	.10
☐	182	Jiri Hrdina, Cgy.	.10
☐	183	Joe Mullen, Cgy.	.10
☐	184	Sergei Makarov, Cgy.	.25
☐	185	Al MacInnis, Cgy.	.25
☐	186	Rick Wamsley (G), Cgy.	.10
☐	187	Trent Yawney, Chi.	.10
☐	188	Greg Millen (G), Chi.	.10
☐	189	Doug Wilson, Chi.	.25
☐	190	Jocelyn Lemieux, Chi.	.10
☐	191	Dirk Graham, Chi.	.10
☐	192	Keith Brown, Chi.	.10
☐	193	Adam Creighton, Chi.	.10
☐	194	Steve Larmer, Chi.	.25
☐	195	Chicago Black Hawks Logo	.10
☐	196	Greg Gilbert, Chi.	.10
☐	197	Jacques Cloutier (G), Chi.	.10
☐	198	Denis Savard, Chi.	.25
☐	199	Dave Manson, Chi.	.10
☐	200	Troy Murray, Chi.	.10
☐	201	Jeremy Roenick, Chi.	.35
☐	202	Lee Norwood, Det.	.10
☐	203	Glen Hanlon (G), Det.	.10
☐	204	Marc Habscheid, Det.	.10
☐	205	Gerard Gallant, Det.	.10
☐	206	Rick Zombo, Det.	.10
☐	207	Steve Chiasson, Det.	.10
☐	208	Steve Yzerman, Det.	1.00
☐	209	Bernie Federko, Det.	.10

☐ 210 Detroit Red Wings Logo .10
☐ 211 Joey Kocur, Det. .10
☐ 212 Tim Cheveldae (G), Det. .10
☐ 213 Shawn Burr, Det. .10
☐ 214 Jimmy Carson, Det. .10
☐ 215 Mike O'Connell, Det. .10
☐ 216 John Chabot, Det. .10
☐ 217 Craig Muni, Edm. .10
☐ 218 Bill Ranford (G), Edm. .25
☐ 219 Mark Messier, Edm. .50
☐ 220 Craig MacTavish, Edm. .10
☐ 221 Charlie Huddy, Edm. .10
☐ 222 Jari Kurri, Edm. .25
☐ 223 Esa Tikkanen, Edm. .10
☐ 224 Kevin Lowe, Edm. .10
☐ 225 Edmonton Oilers Logo .10
☐ 226 Steve Smith, Edm. .10
☐ 227 Glenn Anderson, Edm. .10
☐ 228 Petr Klima, Edm. .10
☐ 229 Craig Simpson, Edm. .10
☐ 230 Grant Fuhr (G), Edm. .25
☐ 231 Randy Gregg, Edm. .10
☐ 232 Bob Kudelski, L.A. .10
☐ 233 Luc Robitaille, L.A. .25
☐ 234 Marty McSorley, L.A. .10
☐ 235 John Tonelli, L.A. .10
☐ 236 Dave Taylor, L.A. .10
☐ 237 Mikko Makelä, L.A. .10
☐ 238 Steve Kasper, L.A. .10
☐ 239 Tony Granato, L.A. .10
☐ 240 Los Angeles Kings Logo .10
☐ 241 Steve Duchesne, L.A. .10
☐ 242 Wayne Gretzky, L.A. 2.00
☐ 243 Tomas Sandström, L.A. .10
☐ 244 Larry Robinson, L.A. .25
☐ 245 Mike Krushelnyski, L.A. .10
☐ 246 Kelly Hrudey (G), L.A. .10
☐ 247 Aaron Broten, Min. .10
☐ 248 Dave Gagner, Min. .10
☐ 249 Basil McRae, Min. .10
☐ 250 Curt Giles, Min. .10
☐ 251 Larry Murphy, Min. .25
☐ 252 Shawn Chambers, Min. .10
☐ 253 Mike Modano, Min. .50
☐ 254 Jon Casey (G), Min. .10
☐ 255 Minnesota North Stars Logo .10
☐ 256 Gaetan Duchesne, Min. .10
☐ 257 Brian Bellows, Min. .10
☐ 258 Frantisek Musil, Min. .10
☐ 259 Don Barber, Min. .10
☐ 260 Stewart Gavin, Min. .10
☐ 261 Neal Broten, Min. .10
☐ 262 Brett Hull, Stl. .50
☐ 263 Sergio Momesso, Stl. .10
☐ 264 Peter Zezel, Stl. .10
☐ 265 Gino Cavallini, Stl. .10
☐ 266 Rod Brind'Amour, Stl. .25
☐ 267 Mike Lalor, Stl. .10
☐ 268 Vincent Riendeau (G), Stl. .10
☐ 269 Gord Roberts, Stl. .10
☐ 270 St. Louis Blues Logo, Stl. .10
☐ 271 Paul MacLean, Stl. .10
☐ 272 Curtis Joseph (G), Stl. .60
☐ 273 Rick Meagher, Stl. .10
☐ 274 Jeff Brown, Stl. .10
☐ 275 Adam Oates, Stl. .25
☐ 276 Paul Cavallini, Stl. .10
☐ 277 Brad Marsh, Tor. .10
☐ 278 Mark Osborne, Tor. .10
☐ 279 Gary Leeman, Tor. .10
☐ 280 Rob Ramage, Tor. .10
☐ 281 Jeff Reese (G), Tor. .10
☐ 282 Tom Fergus, Tor. .10
☐ 283 Ed Olczyk, Tor. .10
☐ 284 Daniel Marois, Tor. .10
☐ 285 Toronto Maple Leafs Logo .10
☐ 286 Wendel Clark, Tor. .25
☐ 287 Tom Kurvers, Tor. .10
☐ 288 Gilles Thibaudeau, Tor. .10
☐ 289 Lou Franceschetti, Tor. .10
☐ 290 Al Iafrate, Tor. .10
☐ 291 Vincent Damphousse, Tor. .35
☐ 292 Stan Smyl, Van. .10
☐ 293 Paul Reinhart, Van. .10
☐ 294 Igor Larionov, Van. .25
☐ 295 Doug Lidster, Van. .10
☐ 296 Kirk McLean (G), Van. .25
☐ 297 Andrew McBain, Van. .10
☐ 298 Petri Skriko, Van. .10
☐ 299 Trevor Linden, Van. .25
☐ 300 Vancouver Canucks Logo .10
☐ 301 Steve Bozek, Van. .10
☐ 302 Brian Bradley, Van. .10
☐ 303 Greg Adams, Van. .10
☐ 304 Vladimir Krutov, Van. .10
☐ 305 Dan Quinn, Van. .10
☐ 306 Jim Sandlak, Van. .10
☐ 307 Teppo Numminen, Wpg. .10
☐ 308 Doug Smail, Wpg. .10
☐ 309 Greg Paslawski, Wpg. .10
☐ 310 Dave Ellett, Wpg. .10
☐ 311 Bob Essensa (G), Wpg. .10
☐ 312 Pat Elynuik, Wpg. .10
☐ 313 Paul Fenton, Wpg. .10
☐ 314 Randy Carlyle, Wpg. .10
☐ 315 Winnipeg Jets Logo .10
☐ 316 Thomas Steen, Wpg. .10
☐ 317 Dale Hawerchuk, Wpg. .25
☐ 318 Fredrick Olausson, Wpg. .10
☐ 319 Dave McLlwain, Wpg. .10
☐ 320 Laurie Boschman, Wpg. .10
☐ 321 Brent Ashton, Wpg. .10
☐ 322 AS: Ray Bourque, Bos. .25
☐ 323 AS: Patrick Roy (G), Mtl. 1.00
☐ 324 AS: Paul Coffey, Pgh. .25
☐ 325 AS: Brian Propp, Pha. .10
☐ 326 AS: Mario Lemieux, Pgh. 1.00
☐ 327 AS: Cam Neely, Bos. .25
☐ 328 AS: Al MacInnis, Cgy. .25
☐ 329 AS: Mike Vernon (G), Cgy. .25
☐ 330 AS: Kevin Lowe, Edm. .10
☐ 331 AS: Luc Robitaille, L.A. .25
☐ 332 AS: Wayne Gretzky, L.A. 1.50
☐ 333 AS: Brett Hull, Stl. .25
☐ 334 Sergei Makarov, Cgy. .25
☐ 335 Alexei Kasatonov, Bos. .10
☐ 336 Igor Larionov, Van. .25
☐ 337 Vladamir Krutov, Van. .10
☐ 338 Alexander Mogilny, Buf. .25
☐ 339 Viacheslav Fetisov, N.J. .25
☐ 340 Mike Modano, Min. .25
☐ 341 Mark Recchi, Pgh. .25
☐ 342 Paul Ranheim, Cgy. .10
☐ 343 Rod Brind'Amour, Stl. .25
☐ 344 Brad Shaw, Hfd. .10
☐ 345 Mike Richter (G), NYR. .25
☐ 346 Hart Memorial Trophy .10
☐ 347 Art Ross Trophy .10
☐ 348 Calder Memorial Trophy .10
☐ 349 Lady Byng Memorial Trophy .10
☐ 350 James Norris Memorial Trophy .10
☐ 351 Vezina Trophy .10

1990 - 91 PANINI TEAM STICKER PANELS

Team panels were issued for the seven Canadian NHL teams. Each team bag contained two 16-sticker panels and one poster. Each cut-out sticker measures 2 1/8" x 2 7/8".

Panel Size: 9" x 12"
Imprint: PANINI
Complete Set (7 panels): 50.00

Teams NRMT-MT

☐ Vancouver Canucks (32 stickers plus poster) 8.00
1 J.Agnew/ 2 G.Adams/ 3 S. Bozek/ 4 B. Bradley/
5 G. Butcher/ 6 D.Capuano/ 7 C.Coxe/ 8 T.Gamble/
9 K. Guy/ 10 R.Kron/ 11 I. Larionov/ 12 D. Lidster/
13 T. Linden/ 14 J. Lumme/ 15 A. McBain/ 16 R. Murphy/
17 P. Nedved/ 18 R. Nordmark/ 19 A. Plavsic/ 20 D. Quinn/
21 J. Sandlak/ 22 P. Skriko/ 23 S. Smyl/ 24 R. Stern/
A-B Logo/ C-F Action/ G K. McLean/ H T. Linden

☐ Calgary Flames (32 stickers plus poster) 8.00
1 T. Fleury/ 2 D. Gilmour/ 3 J. Hrdina/ 4 M. Hunter/
5 T. Hunter/ 6 R. Johansson/ 7 Al MacInnis/ 8 B. MacLellan/
9 J. Macoun/ 10 S. Makarov/ 11 S. Matteau/ 12 D. Murzyn/
13 R. Nattress/ 14 J. Nieuwendyk/ 15 J. Otto/ 16 C. Patterson/
17 S. Priakin/ 18 P. Ranheim/ 19 G. Roberts/ 20 K. Sabourin/
21 G. Suter/ 22 T. Sweeney/ 23 M. Vernon/ 24 R. Wamsley/
A-B Logo/ C-F Action/ G J. Otto, R. Johansson/ H G. Suter

☐ Edmonton Oilers (32 stickers plus poster) 8.00
1 G. Anderson/ 2 J. Beukeboom/ 3 D. Brown/ 4 K. Buchberger/
5 M. Gelinas/ 6 A. Graves/ 7 C. Huddy/ 8 C. Joseph/
9 P. Klima/ 10 M. Lamb/ 11 K. Linseman/ 12 K. Lowe/
13 C. MacTavish/ 14 M. Messier/ 15 C. Muni/ 16 J. Murphy/
17 B. Ranford/ 18 E. Reddick/ 19 A. Semenov/ 20 C. Simpson/
21 G. Smith/ 22 S. Smith/ 23 E. Tikkanen/ 24 Action
A-B Logo/ C-F Action/ G M. Messier/ H Action

☐ Winnipeg Jets (32 stickers plus poster) 8.00
1 S. Arniel/ 2. B. Ashton/ 3 S. Beauregard/ 4 R. Carlyle/
5 D. Cole/ 6 S. Cronin/ 7 G. Donnelly/ 8 K. Draper/
9 D. Ellett/ 10 P. Elynuik/ 11 D. Evans/ 12 P. Fenton/
13 P. Housley/ 14 M. Kumpel/ 15 P. MacDermid/ 16 M. Mantha/
17 D. McLlwain/ 18 T. Numminen/ 19 F. Olausson/ 20 G. Paslawski/
21 D. Smail/ 22 T. Steen/ 23 P. Sykes/ 24 R. Tabaracci/
A-B Logo/ C-F Action/ G P. Fenton/ H P. Housley

☐ Toronto Maple Leafs (32 stickers plus poster) 8.00
1 D. Berehowsky/ 2 A. Bester/ 3 W. Clark/ 4 B. Curran/
5 V. Damphousse/ 6 L. Franceschetti/ 7 T. Gill/ 8 D. Hannan/
9 A. Iafrate/ 10 P. Ing/ 11 T. Kurvers/ 12 G. Leeman/
13 K. Maguire/ 14 D. Marois/ 15 B. Marsh/ 16 J. McIntyre/
17 E. Olczyk/ 18 M. Osborne/ 19 S. Pearson/ 20 R. Ramage/
21 J. Reese/ 22 D. Reid/ 23 L. Richardson/ 24 Action/
A-B Logo/ C-F Action/G A.Iafrate,K.Wregget/H G.Leeman,J.Kordic

☐ Montréal Canadiens (32 stickers plus poster) 10.00
1 J.C. Bergeron/ 2 G. Carbonneau/ 3 A. Cassels/ 4 T. Chorske/
5 S. Corson/ 6 R. Courtnall/ 7 J.J. Daigneault/ 8 E. Desjardins/
9 G. Diduck/ 10 D. Dufresne/ 11 T. Ewen/ 12 B. Gilchrist/
13 M. Keane/ 14 S. Lebeau/ 15 S. Lefebvre/ 16 M. McPhee/
17 M. Pederson/ 18 S. Richer/ 19 P. Roy/ 20 D. Savard/
21 M. Schneider/ 22 B. Skrudland/ 23 P. Svoboda/ 24 R. Walter/
A-B Logo/ C-F Action/ G Patrick Roy/ H Action

☐ Québec Nordiques (32 stickers plus poster) 10.00
1 J. Cirella/ 2 D. Doré/ 3 S. Finn/ 4 B. Fogarty/
5 M. Fortier/ 6 P. Gillis/ 7 S. Gordon/ 8 S. Guerard/
9 M. Hough/ 10 T. Hrkac/ 11 D. Kimble/ 12 G. Lafleur/
13 C. Leschyshyn/ 14 C. Loiselle/ 15 T. McKegney/ 16 K. McRae/
17 O. Nolan/ 18 J. Sakic/ 19 E. Sanipass/ 20 M. Sundin/
21 J. Tanner/ 22 R. Tugnutt/ 23 R. Velischek/ 24 C. Wolanin/
A-B Logo/ C-F Action/ G G. Lafleur/ H M. Sundin

1990 - 91 PRO CARDS TEAM SETS

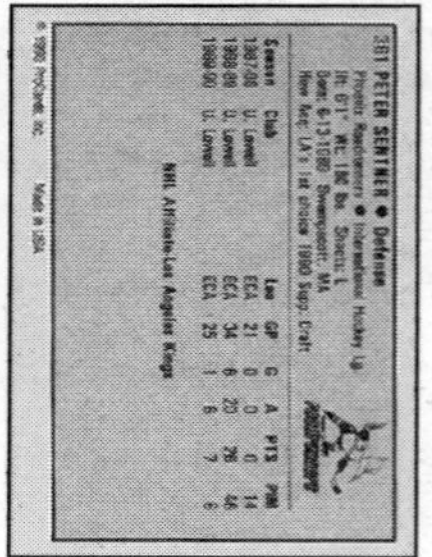

Imprint: © 1990 ProCards, Inc.
Complete Set (629 cards): 120.00
Common Player: .25

BINGHAMTON RANGERS - AHL

Team Set (25 cards): 6.00

	No.	Player	NRMT-MT
☐	1	Rob Zamuner	3.00
☐	2	Todd Charlesworth	.25
☐	3	Bob Bodak	.25
☐	4	Len Hachborn	.25
☐	5	Peter Fiorentino	.25
☐	6	Kord Cernich	.25
☐	7	Daniel Lacroix	.25
☐	8	Joe Paterson	.25
☐	9	Sam St. Laurent (G)	.35
☐	10	Jeff Bloemberg	.25
☐	11	Mike Golden	.25
☐	12	Mike Hurlbut	.25
☐	13	Mark Laforest (G)	.25
☐	14	Chris Cichocki	.25
☐	15	John Paddock, Coach	.50
☐	16	Peter Laviolette	.25
☐	17	Martin Bergeron	.25
☐	18	Rudy Poeschek	.25
☐	19	Eric Germain	.25
☐	20	Al Hill, Assistant Coach	.25
☐	21	Ric Bennett	.25

	No.	Player	NRMT-MT
☐	22	Tie Domi	1.00
☐	23	Ross Fitzpatrick	.25
☐	24	Brian McReyonolds	.25
☐	25	Binghamton Rangers Checklist	.25

HERSHEY BEARS - AHL

Team Set (28 cards): 6.00

	No.	Player	NRMT-MT
☐	26	Mike Eaves, Coach	.25
☐	27	Lance Pitlick	.50
☐	28	Dale Kushner	.25
☐	29	Reid Simpson	.25
☐	30	Craig Fisher	.25
☐	31	Dominic Roussel (G)	1.00
☐	32	David Fenyves	.25
☐	33	Brian Dobbin	.25
☐	34	Darren Rumble	.25
☐	35	Murray Baron	.25
☐	36	Bruce Hoffort (G)	.35
☐	37	Steve Beadle	.25
☐	38	Chris Jensen	.25
☐	39	Mike Stothers	.25
☐	40	Kent Hawley	.25
☐	41	Scott Sandelin	.25
☐	42	Guy Phillips	.25
☐	43	Mark Bassen	.25
☐	44	Steve Scheifele	.25
☐	45	Bill Armstrong	.25
☐	46	Shaun Sabol	.25
☐	47	Mark Freer	.25
☐	48	Claude Boivin	.25
☐	49	Len Barrie	.25
☐	50	Bill Armstrong	.25
☐	51	Tim Tookey	.25
☐	52	Harry Bricker, Assistant Coach	.25
☐	53	Hershey Bears Checklist	.25

FREDERICTON CANADIENS - AHL

Team Set (22 cards): 5.00

	No.	Player	NRMT-MT
☐	54	Alain Côté	.25
☐	55	Luc Gauthier	.25
☐	56	Eric Charron	.25
☐	57	Mario Roberge	.25
☐	58	Tom Sagissor	.25
☐	59	Brent Bobyck	.25
☐	60	John Ferguson	.25
☐	61	Jim Nesich	.25
☐	62	Gilbert Dionne	.35
☐	63	Herbert Hohenberger	.25
☐	64	Dan Woodley	.25
☐	65	Roy Mitchell	.25
☐	66	Fréderic Chabot (G)	.35
☐	67	André Racicot (G)	.35
☐	68	Paul DiPietro	.50
☐	69	Norman Desjardins	.25
☐	70	Martin St. Amour	.25
☐	71	Jessie Belanger	.25
☐	72	Ed Cristofoli	.25
☐	73	Patrick Lebeau	.25
☐	74	Paulin Bordeleau, Coach	.50
☐	75	Fredericton Canadiens Checklist	.25

PEORIA RIVERMEN - IHL

Team Set (24 cards): 8.00

	No.	Player	NRMT-MT
☐	76	Keith Osborne	.25
☐	77	Richard Pion	.25
☐	78	Alain Raymond (G)	.35
☐	79	Rob Robinson	.25
☐	80	Andy Rymsha	.25
☐	81	Randy Skarda	.25
☐	82	Dave Thomlinson	.25
☐	83	Tom Tilley	.25
☐	84	Steve Tuttle	.25
☐	85	Tony Twist	1.00
☐	86	David Bruce	.25
☐	87	Kelly Chase	.25
☐	88	Nelson Emerson	1.00
☐	89	Guy Hebert (G)	3.00
☐	90	Tony Hejna	.25
☐	91	Michel Mongeau	.25
☐	92	David O'Brien	.25
☐	93	Kevin Miehm	.50
☐	94	Darwin McPherson	.25
☐	95	Dominic Lavoie	.25
☐	96	Yves Heroux	.25
☐	97	Pat Jablonski (G)	.75
☐	98	Bob Plager, Coach	.25
☐	99	Peoria Rivermen Checklist	.25

KALAMAZOO WINGS - IHL

Team Set (24 cards): 6.00

	No.	Player	NRMT-MT
☐	99	Jayson More	.25
☐	100	Kevin Evans	.25
☐	101	Warren Babe	.25
☐	102	Mitch Messier	.25
☐	103	John Blue (G)	.35
☐	104	Larry Dyck (G)	.35
☐	105	Duane Joyce	.25
☐	106	Kari Takko (G)	.75
☐	107	Brett Barnett	.25
☐	108	Pat MacLeod	.25
☐	109	Peter Lappin	.25
☐	110	Link Gaetz	.35
☐	111	Larry DePalma	.25
☐	112	Steve Gotaas	.25
☐	113	Mike McHugh	.25
☐	114	Dan Keczmer	.25
☐	115	Jackson Penney	.25
☐	116	Ed Courtenay	.25
☐	117	Jean-François Quintin	.25
☐	118	Scott Robinson	.25
☐	119	Mario Thyer	.25
☐	120	Enrico Ciccone	.50
☐	121	Kevin Constantine, Asst. Coach; John Marks, Coach	.25
☐	122	Kalamazoo Wings Checklist	.25

MAINE MARINERS - AHL

Team Set (23 cards): 5.00

	No.	Player	NRMT-MT
☐	123	Shayne Stevenson	.25
☐	124	Jeff Lazaro	.25
☐	125	Matt Delguidice (G)	.35
☐	126	Ron Hoover	.25
☐	127	John Mokosak	.25
☐	128	John Blum	.25
☐	129	Mike Parson (G)	.35
☐	130	Bruce Shoebottom	.25
☐	131	Dave Donnelly	.25
☐	132	Ralph Barahona	.25
☐	133	Graeme Townshend	.25
☐	134	Ken Hodge	.25
☐	135	Norm Foster (G)	.35
☐	136	Greg Poss	.25
☐	137	Brad James	.25
☐	138	Lou Crawford	.25
☐	139	Rick Allain	.25
☐	140	Bob Beers	.25
☐	141	Ken Hammond	.25
☐	142	Mark Montanari	.25
☐	143	Rick Bowness, Coach	.35
☐	144	Bob Gould, Player/Coach	.25
☐	145	Maine Mariners Checklist	.25

NEWMARKET SAINTS - AHL

Team Set (25 cards): 7.00

	No.	Player	NRMT-MT
☐	146	Mike Stevens	.25
☐	147	Greg Walters	.25
☐	148	Mike Moes	.25
☐	149	Kent Hulst	.25
☐	150	Len Esau	.25
☐	151	Darryl Shannon	.50
☐	152	Bobby Reynolds	.25
☐	153	Derek Langille	.25
☐	154	Jeff Serowik	.25
☐	155	Darren Veitch	.25
☐	156	Joe Sacco	.50
☐	157	Alan Hepple	.25
☐	158	Doug Shedden	.25
☐	159	Steve Bancroft	.25
☐	160	Greg Johnston	.25
☐	161	Trevor Jobe	.25
☐	162	Bill Root	.25
☐	163	Tim Bean	.25
☐	164	Brian Blad	.25
☐	165	Robert Horyna (G)	.35
☐	166	Dean Anderson (G)	.35
☐	167	Damian Rhodes (G)	2.00
☐	168	Mike Millar	.25
☐	169	Mike Jackson	.25
☐	170	Newmarket Saints Checklist	.25

SPRINGFIELD INDIANS - AHL

Team Set (24 cards): 5.00

	No.	Player	NRMT-MT
☐	171	Cal Brown	.25
☐	172	Michel Picard	.35
☐	173	Cam Brauer	.25
☐	174	Jim Burke	.25
☐	175	Jim McKenzie	.25
☐	176	Mike Tomlak	.25
☐	177	Ross McKay (G)	.35
☐	178	Blair Atcheynum	.25
☐	179	Chris Tancill	.25
☐	180	Mark Greig	.25
☐	181	Joe Day	.25
☐	182	Jim Roberts, Coach	.50
☐	183	Emanuel Viveiros	.25
☐	184	Daryl Reaugh (G)	.35
☐	185	Tommie Eriksen	.25
☐	186	Terry Yake	.25
☐	187	Chris Govedaris	.25
☐	188	Chris Bright	.25
☐	189	John Stevens	.25
☐	190	Brian Chapman	.25
☐	191	James Black	.25
☐	192	Scott Daniels	.25
☐	193	Kelly Ens	.25
☐	194	Springfield Indians Checklist	.25

BALTIMORE SKIPJACKS - AHL

Team Set (25 cards): 5.00

	No.	Player	NRMT-MT
☐	195	Ken Lovsin	.25
☐	196	Kent Paynter	.25
☐	197	Jim Mathieson	.25
☐	198	Bob Mendel	.25
☐	199	Reggie Savage	.25
☐	200	Alfie Turcotte	.25
☐	201	Victor Gervais	.25
☐	202	Todd Hlushko	.35
☐	203	Steve Seftel	.25
☐	204	Thomas Sjogren	.25
☐	205	Steve Maltais	.25
☐	206	Bob Joyce	.25
☐	207	Tyler Larter	.25
☐	208	Mark Ferner	.35
☐	209	Bobby Babcock	.25
☐	210	Jeff Greenlaw	.25
☐	211	Tim Taylor	.50
☐	212	John Purves	.25
☐	213	Chris Felix	.25
☐	214	Jiri Vykoukal	.25
☐	215	Shawn Simpson (G)	.35
☐	216	Jim Hrivnak (G)	.35
☐	217	Rob Laird, Coach/General Manager	.25
☐	218	Barry Trotz, Assistant Coach	.25
☐	219	Baltimore Skipjacks Checklist	.25

CAPE BRETON OILERS - AHL

Team Set (23 cards): 5.00

	No.	Player	NRMT-MT
☐	220	David Haas	.25
☐	221	Wade Campbell	.25
☐	222	Dan Currie	.25
☐	223	Shaun Van Allen	.50
☐	224	Norm MacIver	.50
☐	225	Mike Greenlay (G)	.35
☐	226	Peter Soberlak	.25
☐	227	Tim Tisdale	.25
☐	228	Mario Barbe	.25
☐	229	Shjon Podein	.25
☐	230	Trevor Sim	.25
☐	231	Corey Foster	.25
☐	232	Mike Ware	.25
☐	233	Marc LaForge	.25
☐	234	Bruce Bell	.25
☐	235	Tomas Kapusta	.25
☐	236	Alexander Tyjnych (G)	.35
☐	237	Tomas Srsen	.25
☐	238	Collin Bauer	.25
☐	239	François Leroux	.35

No.	Player	NRMT-MT
240	Don MacAdam, Coach	.25
241	Norm Ferguson, Assistant Coach	.25
242	Cape Breton Oilers Checklist	.25

MONCTON HAWKS - AHL

Team Set (24 cards): 5.00

No.	Player	NRMT-MT
243	Tony Joseph	.25
244	Brent Hughes	.35
245	Larry Bernard	.25
246	Simon Wheeldon	.25
247	Todd Filchel	.25
248	Craig Duncanson	.25
249	Iain Duncan	.25
250	Bryan Marchment	.25
251	Matt Hervey	.25
252	Chris Norton	.25
253	Dallas Eakins	.35
254	Peter Hankinson	.25
255	Grant Richison	.25
256	Lee Davidson	.25
257	Denis Larocque	.25
258	Scott Levins	.25
259	Guy Larose	.25
260	Scott Schneider	.25
261	Sergei Kharin	.25
262	Mascot The Hawk	.25
263	Dave Farrish, Coach/General Manager	.25
264	Moncton Hawks Checklist	.25
343	Rick Tabaracci (G)	1.00
344	Mike O'Neill (G)	.35

ROCHESTER AMERICANS - AHL

Team Set (31 cards): 7.00

No.	Player	NRMT-MT
265	Kevin Haller	.35
266	Joel Savage	.25
267	Scott Metcalfe	.25
268	Ian Boyce	.25
269	David Littman (G)	.35
270	Dave Baseggio	.25
271	Ken Sutton	.35
272	Brad Miller	.25
273	Bill Houlder	.25
274	Dan Frawley	.25
275	Scott McCrory	.25
276	Steve Ludzik	.25
277	Rob Ray	.75
278	Darrin Shannon	.75
279	Dale Degray	.25
280	Bob Corkum	.25
281	Grant Tkachuk	.25
282	Kevin Kerr	.25
283	Mitch Molloy	.25
284	Darcy Loewen	.25
285	Jody Gage	.25
286	Jiri Sejba	.25
287	Steve Smith	.25
288	Darcy Wakaluk (G)	.50
289	Donald Audette	2.00
290	Don McSween	.25
291	Francois Guay	.25
292	Terry Martin, Assistant Coach	.25
293	Don Lever, Coach	.25
294	Mascot The Moose	.25
295	Rochester Americans Checklist	.25

SAN DIEGO GULLS - IHL

Team Set (26 cards): 6.00

No.	Player	NRMT-MT
296	Mike O'Connell, Head Coach	.25
297	Paul Marshall	.25
298	Darin Bannister	.25
299	Rob Nichols	.25
300	Charlie Simmer, Player/Asst. Coach	.50
301	Bob Jones	.25
302	Scott Brower (G)	.35
303	Taylor Hall	.25
304	Carl Mokosak	.25
305	Glen Hanlon (G)	1.00
306	Peter Dineen	.25
307	Mike Sullivan	.25
308	Steven Martinson	.25
309	Dave Korol	.25
310	Darren Lowe	.25
311	Mark Reimer (G)	.35
312	Mike Gober	.25
313	Al Tuer	.25
314	Dean Morton	.25
315	Jim McGeough	.25
316	Clark Donatelli	.25
317	Steven Dykstra	.25
318	Brent Sapergia	.25
319	Larry Floyd	.25
320	D'Arcy Norton	.25
321	San Diego Gulls Checklist	.25

MILWAUKEE ADMIRALS - IHL

Team Set (21 cards): 6.00

No.	Player	NRMT-MT
322	Garry Valk	.25
323	Ian Kidd	.25
324	Todd Hawkins	.25
325	Carl Valimont	.25
326	Peter DeBoer	.25
327	Curt Fraser, Assistant Coach	.35
328	David Mackey	.25
329	Jim Benning	.25
330	Peter George Bakovic	.25
331	Steve Weeks (G)	.50
332	Steve Veilleux	.25
333	Shaun Clouston	.25
334	Gino Odjick	1.00
335	Mike Murphy, Coach	.25
336	Cam Brown	.25
337	Patrice Lefebvre	.25
338	Eric Murano	.25
339	Jim Revenberg	.25
340	Don Gibson	.25
341	Steve McKichan (G)	.35
342	Milwaukee Admirals Checklist	.25

PHOENIX ROADRUNNERS - IHL

Team Set (25 cards): 5.00

No.	Player	NRMT-MT
345	Rick Hayward	.25
346	Sean Whyte	.25
347	Petr Prajsler	.25
348	John Van Kessel	.25
349	Mario Gosselin (G)	.35
350	Kyosti Karjalainen	.25
351	Mikael Lindholm	.25
352	David Goverde (G)	.35
353	Graham Stanley	.25
354	Stéphane Richer	.25
355	Brian Lawton	.35
356	Jerome Bechard	.25
357	Jeff Rohlicek	.25
358	Steve Jaques	.25
359	Chris Kontos	.35
360	Sylvain Couturier	.25
361	Peter Sentner	.25
362	Steve Graves	.25
263	Daryn McBride	.25
364	Steve Rooney	.25
365	Mickey Volcan	.25
366	Kevin MacDonald	.25
367	Ralph Backstrom, Coach	.50
368	Gary Unger, Assistant Coach	.50
369	Phoenix Roadrunners Checklist	.25

MUSKEGON LUMBERJACKS - IHL

Team Set (23 cards): 5.00

No.	Player	NRMT-MT
370	Rob Dopson (G)	.35
371	John Callander	.25
372	Chris Clifford (G)	.35
373	Sandy Smith	.25
374	Jim Kyte	.25
375	Mike Needham	.25
376	Mitch Wilson	.25
377	Dave Goertz	.25
378	Mark Kachowski	.25
379	Perry Ganchar	.25
380	Mark Major	.25
381	Joel Gardner	.25
382	Scott Gruhl	.25
383	Todd Nelson	.25
384	Darren Stolk	.25
385	Scott Shaunessy	.25
386	Mike Mersch	.25
387	Glenn Mulvenna	.25
388	Brad Aitken	.25
389	Dave Michayluk	.25
390	Blair MacDonald, Coach	.25
391	Phil Russell, Assistant Coach	.35
392	Muskegon Lumberjacks Checklist	.25

INDIANAPOLIS ICE - IHL

Team Set (22 cards): 20.00

No.	Player	NRMT-MT
393	Sean Williams	.25
394	Ryan McGill	.25
395	Mike Eagles	.35
396	Jim Johannson	.25
397	Marty Nanne	.25
398	JIm Playfair	.25
399	Warren Rychel	.35
400	Cam Russell	.35
401	Jim Waite (G)	.75
402	Mike Stapleton	.25
403	Trevor Dam	.25
404	Tracey Egeland	.25
405	Owen Lessard	.25
406	Jeff Sirkka	.25
407	Mike Dagenais	.25
408	Alex Roberts	.25
409	Dominik Hasek (G)	15.00
410	Martin Desjardins	.25
411	Frantisek Kucera	.35
412	Carl Mokosak	.25
413	Dave McDowall, Coach	.25
414	Indianapolis Ice Checklist	.25

NEW HAVEN NIGHTHAWKS - AHL

Team Set (27 cards): 6.00

No.	Player	NRMT-MT
415	Paul Saundercook	.25
416	Darryl Williams	.25
417	Micah Aivazoff	.25
418	Robb Stauber (G)	.50
419	Tom Martin	.25
420	Billy O'Dwyer	.25
421	Scott Harlow	.25
422	Jim Thomson	.25
423	Jim Pavese	.25
424	Ron Scott (G)	.35
425	Dave Pasin	.25
426	Serge Roy	.25
427	Darryl Gilmour (G)	.35
428	Mike Donnelly	.35
429	René Chapdelaine	.25
430	Brandy Semchuk	.25
431	Paul Holden	.25
432	Bob Berg	.25
433	Ladislav Tresl	.25
434	Eric Ricard	.25
435	Murray Brumwell, Player/Asst. Coach	.25
436	Shawn McCosh	.25
437	Ross Wilson	.25
438	Scott Young	.25
439	David Moylan	.25
440	Marcel Comeau, Coach	.25
441	New Haven Nighthawks Checklist	.25

HALIFAX CITADELS - AHL

Team Set (27 cards): 7.00

No.	Player	NRMT-MT
442	David Espe	.25
443	Mario Doyon	.25
444	Gerald Bzdel	.25
445	Claude Lapointe	.35
446	Dean Hopkins, Asst Coach	.25
447	Clement Jodoin, G.M./Coach	.25
448	Kevin Kaminski	.35
449	Jamie Baker	.75
450	Mark Vermette	.25
451	Iiro Jarvi	.25
452	Kip Miller	.25
453	Greg Smyth	.25
454	Serge Roberge	.25
455	Stéphane Morin	.25
456	Brent Severyn	.25
457	Jean-Marc Richard	.25
458	Ken Quinney	.25

No.	Player	NRMT-MT
☐ 459	Jeff Jackson	.25
☐ 460	Jaroslav Sevcik	.25
☐ 461	Dave Latta	.25
☐ 462	Trevor Stienburg	.25
☐ 463	Miroslav Ihnacak	.25
☐ 464	Jim Sprott	.25
☐ 465	Mike Bishop (G)	.35
☐ 466	Stéphane Fiset (G)	3.00
☐ 467	Scott Gordon (G)	.35
☐ 468	Halifax Citadels Checklist	.25

ADIRONDACK RED WINGS - AHL

Team Set (25 cards): 6.00

No.	Player	NRMT-MT
☐ 469	Gord Kruppke	.25
☐ 470	Glenn Merkosky	.25
☐ 471	Dennis Holland	.25
☐ 472	Chris McRae	.25
☐ 473	Al Conroy	.25
☐ 474	Yves Racine	.35
☐ 475	Jim Nill, Player/Assistant Coach	.35
☐ 476	Barry Melrose, Coach	.75
☐ 477	Bob Wilkie	.25
☐ 478	Guy Dupuis	.25
☐ 479	Doug Houda	.25
☐ 480	Tom Bissett	.25
☐ 481	Bill McDougall	.25
☐ 482	Glen Goodall	.25
☐ 483	Kory Kocur	.25
☐ 484	Chris Luongo	.25
☐ 485	Serge Anglehart	.25
☐ 486	Marc Potvin	.35
☐ 487	Stewart Malgunas	.25
☐ 488	John Chabot	.25
☐ 489	Daniel Shank	.25
☐ 490	Randy Hansch (G)	.35
☐ 491	Dave Gagnon (G)	.35
☐ 492	Scott King (G)	.35
☐ 493	Adirondack Red Wings Checklist	.25

CAPITAL DISTRICT ISLANDERS - AHL

Team Set (21 cards): 6.00

No.	Player	NRMT-MT
☐ 494	Derek Laxdal	.25
☐ 495	Sean Lebrun	.25
☐ 496	Shawn Byram	.25
☐ 497	Wayne Doucet	.25
☐ 498	Rich Kromm	.25
☐ 499	Chris Pryor, Player/Assistant Coach	.25
☐ 500	George Maneluk (G)	.35
☐ 501	Brad Lauer	.25
☐ 502	Wayne McBean	.25
☐ 503	Jeff Finley	.25
☐ 504	Jim Culhane	.25
☐ 505	Paul Cohen (G)	.35
☐ 506	Brent Grieve	.25
☐ 507	Kevin Cheveldayoff	.25
☐ 508	Dennis Vaske	.25
☐ 509	Dave Chyzowski	.35
☐ 510	Travis Green	1.50
☐ 511	Dean Chynoweth	.35
☐ 512	Rob DiMaio	.35
☐ 513	Paul Guay	.25
☐ 514	Capital District Islanders Checklist	.25

ALBANY CHOPPERS - IHL

Team Set (21 cards): 5.00

No.	Player	NRMT-MT
☐ 515	Rick Knickle (G)	.35
☐ 516	Curtis Hunt	.25
☐ 517	Bruce Racine (G)	.35
☐ 518	Yves Heroux	.25
☐ 519	Joe Stefan	.25
☐ 520	Torrie Robertson	.25
☐ 521	Nicholas Beaulieu	.25
☐ 522	Dave Richter	.25
☐ 523	Jeff Waver	.25
☐ 524	Gordon Paddock	.25
☐ 525	Darryl Noren	.25
☐ 526	Byron Lomow	.25
☐ 527	Ivan Matulik	.25
☐ 528	Dan Woodley	.25
☐ 529	Dale Henry	.25
☐ 530	Soren True	.25
☐ 531	Stuart Burnie	.25
☐ 532	Rob MacInnis	.25
☐ 533	Vern Smith	.25
☐ 534	Paul Laus	.50
☐ 535	Albany Choppers Checklist	.25

FORT WAYNE KOMETS - IHL

Team Set (21 cards): 5.00

No.	Player	NRMT-MT
☐ 536	Robin Bawa	.25
☐ 537	Steven Fletcher	.25
☐ 538	Lonnie Loach	.25
☐ 539	Al Sims, Coach	.25
☐ 540	Colin Chin	.25
☐ 541	Bruce Boudreau, Player/Assistant Coach	.25
☐ 542	Bob Lasko	.25
☐ 543	John Anderson	.50
☐ 544	Kevin Kaminski	.25
☐ 545	Bruce Major	.25
☐ 546	Stéphane Brochu	.25
☐ 547	Peter Hankinson	.25
☐ 548	Carey Lucyk	.25
☐ 549	Tom Karalis	.25
☐ 550	Bob Jay	.25
☐ 551	Mike Butters	.25
☐ 552	Brian McKee	.25
☐ 553	Ray LeBlanc (G)	.35
☐ 554	Tom Draper (G)	.35
☐ 555	Steve Laurin (G)	.35
☐ 556	Fort Wayne Komets Checklist	.25

UTICA DEVILS - AHL

Team Set (25 cards): 6.00

No.	Player	NRMT-MT
☐ 557	Sergei Starikov	.35
☐ 558	Claude Vilgrain	.25
☐ 559	Jeff Sharples	.25
☐ 560	Bob Woods	.25
☐ 561	Perry Anderson	.25
☐ 562	Brennan Maley	.25
☐ 563	Mike Posma	.25
☐ 564	Tom McVie, General Manager/Coach	.25
☐ 565	Chris Palmer	.25
☐ 566	Bill Huard	.25
☐ 567	Marc Laniel	.25
☐ 568	Neil Brady	.25
☐ 569	Jason Simon	.25
☐ 570	Kevin Todd	.50
☐ 571	Jeff Madill	.25
☐ 572	Jeff Christian	.25
☐ 573	Todd Copeland	.25
☐ 574	Mike Bodnarchuk	.25
☐ 575	Chris Kiene	.25
☐ 576	Myles O'Connor	.25
☐ 577	Jamie Huscroft	.25
☐ 578	Mark Romaine (G)	.35
☐ 579	Rollie Melanson (G)	.35
☐ 580	Team Photo	.25
☐ 581	Utica Devils Checklist	.25

KANSAS CITY BLADES - IHL

Team Set (21 cards): 5.00

No.	Player	NRMT-MT
☐ 582	Ron Handy	.25
☐ 583	Cam Plante	.25
☐ 584	Lee Giffin	.25
☐ 585	Jim Latos	.25
☐ 586	Stu Kulak	.25
☐ 587	Claude Julien	.35
☐ 588	Rick Barkovich	.25
☐ 589	Randy Exelby (G)	.25
☐ 590	Mark Vichorek	.25
☐ 591	Darin Smith	.25
☐ 592	Mike Kelfer	.25
☐ 593	Andy Akervik	.25
☐ 594	Mike Hiltner	.25
☐ 595	Kevin Sullivan	.25
☐ 596	Troy Frederick	.25
☐ 597	Claudio Scremin	.25
☐ 598	Kurt Semandel	.25
☐ 599	Mike Colman	.25
☐ 600	Jeff Odgers	1.00
☐ 601	Wade Flaherty (G)	.50
☐ 602	Kansas City Blades Checklist	.25

SALT LAKE GOLDEN EAGLES - IHL

Team Set (26 cards): 6.00

No.	Player	NRMT-MT
☐ 603	Marc Bureau	.35
☐ 604	Darryl Olsen	.25
☐ 605	Rick Lessard	.25
☐ 606	Kevin Grant	.25
☐ 607	Rich Chernomaz	.25
☐ 608	Randy Bucyk	.25
☐ 609	Wayne Cowley (G)	.25
☐ 610	Ken Sabourin	.25
☐ 611	Bob Francis, Head Coach	.25
☐ 612	Jamie Hislop, Coach	.35
☐ 613	Kevan Melrose	.25
☐ 614	Scott McCrady	.25
☐ 615	Corey Lyons	.25
☐ 616	Martin Simard	.25
☐ 617	C. J. Young	.25
☐ 618	Mark Osiecki	.25
☐ 619	Bryan Deasley	.25
☐ 620	Kerry Clark	.35
☐ 621	Paul Kruse	.25
☐ 622	Darren Banks	.25
☐ 623	Richard Zemlak	.25
☐ 624	Todd Harkins	.25
☐ 625	Warren Sharples (G)	.35
☐ 626	Andrew McKim	.50
☐ 627	Steve Guenette (G)	.35
☐ 628	Salt Lake Golden Eagles Checklist	.25

1990-91 PRO SET

Imprint: Pro Set NHL & NHLPA 1990

Complete Set (705 cards):	16.00
Common Player:	.05
Promo Card: (Brett Hull, #1)	4.00
Hologram Card: (Stanley Cup, #/5,000)	75.00

No.	Player	NRMT-MT
☐ 1	Ray Bourque, Bos., Error (Borque)	.50
☐ 1	Ray Bourque, Bos., Corrected	.35
☐ 2	Randy Burridge, Bos.	.05
☐ **3**	**Lyndon Byers, Bos., RC**	**.05**
☐ 4	Bobby Carpenter, Bos., Error	.05
☐ **5**	**John Carter, Bos., RC**	**.05**
☐ 6	Dave Christian, Bos., Error	.05
☐ **7**	**Garry Galley, Bos., RC, Error (Gary)**	**.10**
☐ **7**	**Garry Galley, Bos., RC, Corrected**	**.10**
☐ 8	Craig Janney, Bos.	.05
☐ 9	Réjean Lemelin (G), Bos., Error	.05
☐ 10	Andy Moog (G), Bos., Error	.10
☐ 11	Cam Neely, Bos., Error	.15
☐ 12	Allen Pedersen, Bos.	.05
☐ 13	Dave Poulin, Bos., Error	.05
☐ 14	Brian Propp, Bos., Error	.05
☐ 15	Bob Sweeney, Bos.	.05
☐ 16	Glen Wesley, Bos.	.05
☐ 17	Dave Andreychuk, Buf., Error (/b: Amiel)	.10
☐ 17	Dave Andreychuk, Buf., Error (Traded)	.10
☐ 17	Dave Andreychuk, Buf., Corrected	.10
☐ 18	Scott Arniel, Buf., Error (/b: Andreychuk)	.10
☐ 18	Scott Arniel, Buf., Corrected	.10
☐ 19	Doug Bodger, Buf.	.05
☐ 20	Mike Foligno, Buf.	.05
☐ 21	Phil Housley, Buf.	.10
☐ 21	Phil Housley, Buf., Variation (Traded)	.10
☐ **22**	**Dean Kennedy, Buf., RC, Error**	**.05**
☐ 23	Uwe Krupp, Buf.	.05
☐ **24**	**Grant Ledyard, , Buf., RC**	**.05**
☐ 25	Clint Malarchuk (G), Buf., Error	.05

☐ **26 Alexander Mogilny, Buf., RC .50**
☐ 27 Daren Puppa (G), Buf., Error .05
☐ 28 Mike Ramsey, Buf. .05
☐ 29 Christian Ruuttu, Buf., Error .05
☐ **30 Dave Snuggerud, Buf., RC .05**
☐ 31 Pierre Turgeon, Buf. .05
☐ 32 Rick Vaive, Buf., Error .05
☐ 33 Theoren Fleury, Cgy. .20
☐ 34 Doug Gilmour, Cgy. .20
☐ 35 Al MacInnis, Cgy., Error .05
☐ 36 Brian MacLellan, Cgy. .05
☐ 37 Jamie Macoun, Cgy., Error .05
☐ **38 Sergei Makarov, Cgy., RC .20**
☐ 39 Brad McCrimmon, Cgy., Error (Uniform #) (Det.) .10
☐ 39 Brad McCrimmon, Cgy., Corrected (Traded) .10
☐ 40 Joe Mullen, Cgy. .10
☐ 40 Joe Mullen, Cgy., (Traded) .10
☐ 41 Dana Murzyn, Cgy. .05
☐ 42 Joe Nieuwendyk, Cgy., Error (Niewendyk) 1.00
☐ 42 Joe Nieuwendyk, Cgy., Corrected .10
☐ 43 Joel Otto, Cgy. .05
☐ **44 Paul Ranheim, Cgy., RC, Error .05**
☐ 45 Gary Roberts, Cgy. .15
☐ 46 Gary Suter, Cgy. .05
☐ 47 Mike Vernon (G), Cgy. .05
☐ 48 Rick Wamsley (G), Cgy., Error .05
☐ 49 Keith Brown, Chi. .05
☐ 50 Adam Creighton, Chi. .05
☐ 51 Dirk Graham, Chi., Error .05
☐ 52 Steve Konroyd, Chi., Error (White on red) .10
☐ 53 Steve Larmer, Chi., Error .10
☐ 53 Steve Larmer, Chi., Corrected .10
☐ 54 Dave Manson, Chi., Error (Konroyd) .10
☐ 54 Dave Manson, Chi., Corrected .10
☐ 55 Bob McGill, Chi. .05
☐ 56 Greg Millen (G), Chi. .05
☐ 57 Troy Murray, Chi., Error (White on red) .10
☐ 57 Troy Murray, Chi., Corrected .10
☐ **58 Jeremy Roenick, Chi., RC .75**
☐ 59 Denis Savard, Chi. .15
☐ 59 Denis Savard, Chi., (Traded) .15
☐ 60 Al Secord, Chi., Error (/b: Alan) .10
☐ 60 Al Secord, Chi., Corrected .10
☐ 61 Duane Sutter, Chi., Error (RW) .10
☐ 61 Duane Sutter, Chi., (Retired) .10
☐ 62 Steve Thomas, Chi. .05
☐ 63 Doug Wilson, Chi., Error (White on red) .15
☐ 63 Doug Wilson, Chi., Corrected .15
☐ 64 Trent Yawney, Chi. .05
☐ 65 David Barr, Det. .05
☐ 66 Shawn Burr, Det., Error (Without resume) .10
☐ 66 Shawn Burr, Det., Corrected .10
☐ 67 Jimmy Carson, Det. .05
☐ 68 John Chabot, Det. .05
☐ 69 Steve Chiasson, Det. .05
☐ 70 Bernie Federko, Det., Error .05
☐ 71 Gerard Gallant, Det. .05
☐ 72 Glen Hanlon (G), Det. .05
☐ **73 Joey Kocur, Det., RC .05**
☐ 74 Lee Norwood, Det. .05
☐ 75 Mike O'Connell, Det., Error .05
☐ 76 Bob Probert, Det. .05
☐ 77 Torrie Robertson, Det. .05
☐ **78 Daniel Shank, Det., RC .05**
☐ 79 Steve Yzerman, Det. .50
☐ **80 Rick Zombo, Det., RC .05**
☐ 81 Glenn Anderson, Edm. .05
☐ 82 Grant Fuhr (G), Edm. .15
☐ **83 Martin Gelinas, Edm., RC, Error (/b: J. Murphy) .25**
☐ **84 Adam Graves, Edm., RC, Error .25**
☐ 85 Charlie Huddy, Edm., Error .05
☐ 86 Petr Klima, Edm., Error .05
☐ 87 Jari Kurri, Edm. .15
☐ 87 Jari Kurri, Edm., (Milan) .35
☐ **88 Mark Lamb, Edm., RC .35**
☐ 89 Kevin Lowe, Edm., Error .05
☐ 90 Craig MacTavish, Edm. .05
☐ 91 Mark Messier, Edm. .35
☐ 92 Craig Muni, Edm. .05
☐ **93 Joe Murphy, Edm., RC .05**
☐ 94 Bill Ranford (G), Edm. .15
☐ 95 Craig Simpson, Edm., Error .05
☐ 96 Steve Smith, Edm., Error .05
☐ 97 Esa Tikkanen, Edm. .05
☐ **98 Mikael Andersson, Hfd., RC .05**
☐ 99 Dave Babych, Hfd., Error .05
☐ **100 Yvon Corriveau, Hfd., RC, Error .05**
☐ 101 Randy Cunneyworth, Hfd., Error .05
☐ 102 Kevin Dineen, Hfd. .05
☐ 103 Dean Evason, Hfd. .05
☐ 104 Ray Ferraro, Hfd. .05
☐ 105 Ron Francis, Hfd. .20
☐ **106 Grant Jennings, Hfd., RC .05**
☐ **107 Todd Krygier, Hfd., RC .05**
☐ 108 Randy Ladouceur, Hfd. .05
☐ 109 Ulf Samuelsson, Hfd. .05
☐ **110 Brad Shaw, Hfd., RC .05**
☐ 111 Dave Tippett, Hfd., Error .05
☐ 112 Pat Verbeek, Hfd. .05
☐ 113 Scott Young, Hfd. .05
☐ 114 Brian Benning, L.A., Error .05
☐ 115 Steve Duchesne, L.A., Error .05
☐ **116 Todd Elik, L.A., RC .05**
☐ 117 Tony Granato, L.A., Error .05
☐ 118 Wayne Gretzky, L.A. 1.25
☐ 119 Kelly Hrudey (G), L.A. .05
☐ 120 Steve Kasper, L.A. .05
☐ 121 Mike Krushelnyski, L.A., Error (No Pos.) .10
☐ 121 Mike Krushelnyski, L.A., Corrected .10
☐ **122 Bob Kudelski, L.A., RC, Error .05**
☐ 123 Tom Laidlaw, L.A. .05
☐ 124 Marty McSorley, L.A. .05
☐ 125 Larry Robinson, L.A. .15
☐ 126 Luc Robitaille, L.A., Error .15
☐ 127 Tomas Sandström, L.A., Error .10
☐ 128 Dave Taylor, L.A. .05
☐ 129 John Tonelli, L.A., Error (Tonnelli) .10
☐ 129 John Tonelli, L.A., Corrected .10
☐ 130 Brian Bellows, Min., Error (b: Gagner) .10
☐ 130 Brian Bellows, Min., Corrected .10
☐ 131 Aaron Broten, Min., Error .05
☐ 132 Neal Broten, Min. .05
☐ 133 Jon Casey (G), Min., Error .05
☐ 134 Shawn Chambers, Min., Error .05
☐ **135 Shane Churla, Min., RC .05**
☐ 136 Ulf Dahlen, Min., Error .05
☐ 137 Gaetan Duchesne, Min. .05
☐ 138 Dave Gagner, Min. .05
☐ 139 Stewart Gavin, Min. .05
☐ 140 Curt Giles, Min. .05
☐ 141 Basil McRae, Min. .05
☐ **142 Mike Modano, Min., RC .50**
☐ 143 Larry Murphy, Min. .05
☐ **144 Ville Siren, Min., RC .05**
☐ **145 Mark Tinordi, Min., RC .05**
☐ 146 Guy Carbonneau, Mtl., Error .05
☐ 147 Chris Chelios, Mtl. .35
☐ 147 Chris Chelios, Mtl. (Traded) .35
☐ 148 Shayne Corson, Mtl. .05
☐ 149 Russ Courtnall, Mtl., Error .05
☐ 150 Brian Hayward (G), Mtl. .05
☐ **151 Mike Keane, Mtl., RC .05**
☐ **152 Stéphan Lebeau, Mtl., RC .05**
☐ 153 Claude Lemieux, Mtl., Error .05
☐ 154 Craig Ludwig, Mtl. .05
☐ 155 Mike McPhee, Mtl. .05
☐ 156 Stéphane Richer, Mtl. .05
☐ 157 Patrick Roy (G), Mtl. 1.00
☐ **158 Mathieu Schneider, Mtl., RC .05**
☐ 159 Brian Skrudland, Mtl. .05
☐ 160 Bobby Smith, Mtl., Error .05
☐ 161 Petr Svoboda, Mtl. .05
☐ 162 Tommy Albelin, N.J. .05
☐ 163 Doug Brown, N.J., Error .05
☐ 164 Sean Burke (G), N.J. .15
☐ 165 Ken Daneyko, N.J. .05
☐ 166 Bruce Driver, N.J. .05
☐ **167 Viacheslav Fetisov, N.J., RC, Error (Vlacheslav) .25**
☐ **167 Viacheslav Fetisov, N.J., RC, Error (airbrushed "L") .25**
☐ **167 Viacheslav Fetisov, N.J., RC, Corrected .25**
☐ 168 Mark Johnson, N.J. .05
☐ **169 Alexei Kasatonov, N.J., RC, Error .05**
☐ 170 John MacLean, N.J., Error .05
☐ **171 David Maley, N.J., RC, Error (Rev. Negative) .10**
☐ **171 David Maley, N.J., RC, Corrected .10**
☐ 172 Kirk Muller, N.J. .05
☐ **173 Janne Ojanen, N.J., RC .05**
☐ 174 Brendan Shanahan, N.J. .35
☐ 175 Peter Stastny, N.J., Error (Sundstrom) .10
☐ 175 Peter Stastny, N.J., Corrected .10
☐ 176 Patrik Sundstrom, N.J., Error (Stastny) .10
☐ 176 Patrik Sundstrom, N.J., Corrected .10
☐ 177 Sylvain Turgeon, N.J. .05
☐ **178 Ken Baumgartner, NYI., RC .05**
☐ 179 Doug Crossman, NYI., Error .05
☐ 180 Gerald Diduck, NYI. .05
☐ **181 Mark Fitzpatrick (G), NYI., RC .05**
☐ 182 Patrick Flatley, NYI., Error .05
☐ **183 Glenn Healy, NYI., RC (G), Error (Glen) .15**
☐ 184 Alan Kerr, NYI. .05
☐ 185 Derek King, NYI. .05
☐ 186 Pat LaFontaine, NYI. .25
☐ 187 Donald Maloney, NYI. .05
☐ **188 Hubie McDonough, NYI., RC, Error .05**
☐ 189 Jeff Norton, NYI., Error .05
☐ 190 Gary Nylund, NYI. .05
☐ 191 Brent Sutter, NYI. .05
☐ 192 Bryan Trottier, NYI., Error .15
☐ 193 David Volek, NYI., Error .05
☐ 194 Randy Wood, NYI. .05
☐ 195 Jan Erixon, NYR. .05
☐ 196 Mike Gartner, NYR., Error .20
☐ 197 Ron Greschner, NYR. .05
☐ **198 Miloslav Horava, NYR., RC, Error (Miroslav) .10**
☐ **198 Miloslav Horava, NYR., RC, Corrected .10**
☐ **199 Mark Janssens, NYR., RC .05**
☐ 200 Kelly Kisio, NYR. .05
☐ 201 Brian Leetch, NYR. .25
☐ 202 Randy Moller, NYR. .05
☐ 203 Brian Mullen, NYR. .05
☐ 204 Bernie Nicholls, NYR., Error .05
☐ 205 Chris Nilan, NYR. .10
☐ 205 Chris Nilan, NYR. (Traded) .10
☐ 206 John Ogrodnick, NYR. .05
☐ 207 James Patrick, NYR. .05
☐ **208 Darren Turcotte, NYR., RC, Error .05**
☐ **209 John Vanbiesbrouck (G), NYR., Error .50**
☐ 210 Carey Wilson, NYR. .05
☐ 211 Mike Bullard, Pha. .05
☐ 212 Terry Carkner, Pha. .05
☐ **213 Jeff Chychrun, Pha., RC .05**
☐ 214 Murray Craven, Pha. .05
☐ 215 Per-Erik Eklund, Pha., Error .05
☐ 216 Ron Hextall (G), Pha., Error .10
☐ 217 Mark Howe, Pha. .10
☐ 218 Tim Kerr, Pha. .05
☐ 219 Ken Linseman, Pha., Error .05
☐ 220 Scott Mellanby, Pha. .05
☐ **221 Gordon Murphy, Pha., RC .05**
☐ 222 Kjell Samuelsson, Pha., Error .05
☐ 223 Ilkka Sinisalo, Pha. .05
☐ 224 Ron Sutter, Pha. .05
☐ 225 Rick Tocchet, Pha. .05
☐ 226 Ken Wregget (G), Pha. .05
☐ 227 Tom Barrasso (G), Pgh. .10
☐ 228 Phil Bourque, Pgh., Error (Borque) .10
☐ 228 Phil Bourque, Pgh., Corrected .10
☐ 229 Rob Brown, Pgh., Error .05
☐ 230 Alain Chevrier (G), Pgh., Error .05
☐ 231 Paul Coffey, Pgh., Error .20
☐ 232 John Cullen, Pgh. .05
☐ 233 Gord Dineen, Pgh., Error .05
☐ 234 Bob Errey, Pgh. .05
☐ 235 Jim Johnson, Pgh., Error .05
☐ 236 Mario Lemieux, Pgh., Error 1.00
☐ **237 Troy Loney, Pgh., RC .05**
☐ 238 Barry Pederson, Pgh., Error .05
☐ **239 Mark Recchi, Pgh., RC .75**
☐ **240 Kevin Stevens, Pgh., RC, Error .20**
☐ 241 Tony Tanti, Pgh., Error .05
☐ 242 Zarley Zalapski, Pgh., Error .05
☐ 243 Joe Cirella, Que. .05
☐ 244 Lucien DeBlois, Que., Error .05
☐ 245 Marc Fortier, Que., Error (Mark) .10
☐ 245 Marc Fortier, Que., Corrected .10
☐ 246 Paul Gillis, Que. .05
☐ 247 Mike Hough, Que. .05
☐ 248 Tony Hrkac, Que., Error .05
☐ 249 Jeff Jackson, Que. .05
☐ 250 Guy Lafleur, Que. .35
☐ **251 Curtis Leschyshyn, Que., RC .05**
☐ **252 Claude Loiselle, Que., RC .05**
☐ 253 Mario Marois, Que. .05
☐ 254 Tony McKegney, Que., Error .05
☐ **255 Ken McRae, Que., RC .05**

	No.	Card	Price
☐	256	Michel Petit, Que., Error (Wrong uniform #)	.10
☐	256	Michel Petit, Que., Corrected	.10
☐	257	Joe Sakic, Que., Error	.50
☐	258	Ron Tugnutt (G), Que.	.05
☐	**259**	**Rod Brind'Amour, Stl., RC, Error**	**.35**
☐	260	Jeff Brown, Stl., Error	.05
☐	261	Gino Cavallini, Stl., Error	.05
☐	262	Paul Cavallini, Stl.	.05
☐	263	Brett Hull, Stl.	.35
☐	**264**	**Mike Lalor, Stl., RC, Error**	**.05**
☐	**265**	**Dave Lowry, Stl., RC**	**.05**
☐	266	Paul MacLean, Stl.	.05
☐	267	Rick Meagher, Stl.	.05
☐	**268**	**Sergio Momesso, Stl., RC, Error**	**.05**
☐	269	Adam Oates, Stl.	.15
☐	**270**	**Vincent Riendeau (G), Stl., RC**	**.05**
☐	271	Gord Roberts, Stl.	.05
☐	272	Rich Sutter, Stl., Error	.05
☐	273	Steve Tuttle, Stl.	.05
☐	274	Peter Zezel, Stl., Error	.05
☐	275	Allan Bester (G), Tor., Error (Alan)	.10
☐	275	Allan Bester (G), Tor., Corrected	.10
☐	276	Wendel Clark, Tor.	.15
☐	277	Brian Curran, Tor., Error	.05
☐	278	Vincent Damphousse, Tor.	.15
☐	279	Tom Fergus, Tor.	.05
☐	**280**	**Lou Franceschetti, Tor., RC**	**.05**
☐	281	Al Iafrate, Tor.	.05
☐	282	Tom Kurvers, Tor., Error	.05
☐	283	Gary Leeman, Tor.	.05
☐	284	Daniel Marois, Tor.	.05
☐	285	Brad Marsh, Tor.	.05
☐	286	Ed Olczyk, Tor., Error	.05
☐	287	Mark Osborne, Tor.	.05
☐	288	Rob Ramage, Tor.	.05
☐	289	Luke Richardson, Tor.	.05
☐	**290**	**Gilles Thibaudeau, Tor., RC, Error**	**.05**
☐	291	Greg Adams, Van., Error	.05
☐	292	Jim Benning, Van.	.05
☐	293	Steve Bozek, Van.	.05
☐	294	Brian Bradley, Van.	.05
☐	295	Garth Butcher, Van.	.05
☐	**296**	**Vladimir Krutov, Van., RC**	**.05**
☐	**297**	**Igor Larionov, Van., RC, Error**	**.20**
☐	298	Doug Lidster, Van.	.05
☐	299	Trevor Linden, Van.	.20
☐	**300**	**Jyrki Lumme, Van., RC, Error**	**.05**
☐	301	Andrew McBain, Van., Error (/b: Sandlak)	.10
☐	301	Andrew McBain, Van., Corrected	.10
☐	302	Kirk McLean (G),Van., Error	.10
☐	303	Dan Quinn, Van., Error	.05
☐	304	Paul Reinhart, Van., Error	.05
☐	305	Jim Sandlak, Van.	.05
☐	306	Petri Skriko, Van.	.05
☐	307	Don Beaupré (G), Wsh.	.05
☐	308	Dino Ciccarelli, Wsh.	.10
☐	309	Geoff Courtnall, Wsh., Error	.05
☐	**310**	**John Druce, Wsh., RC**	**.05**
☐	311	Kevin Hatcher, Wsh.	.05
☐	312	Dale Hunter, Wsh., Error	.05
☐	313	Calle Johansson, Wsh., Error	.05
☐	314	Rod Langway, Wsh.	.05
☐	315	Stephen Leach, Wsh.	.05
☐	316	Mike Liut (G), Wsh., Error	.05
☐	**317**	**Alan May, Wsh., RC**	**.05**
☐	318	Kelly Miller, Wsh., Error	.05
☐	**319**	**Michal Pivonka, Wsh., RC, Error**	**.05**
☐	320	Mike Ridley, Wsh., Error (/b: point.s.)	.10
☐	320	Mike Ridley, Wsh., Corrected	.10
☐	321	Scott Stevens, Wsh., Error	.05
☐	322	John Tucker, Wsh., Error	.05
☐	323	Brent Ashton, Wpg.	.05
☐	324	Laurie Boschman, Wpg.	.05
☐	325	Randy Carlyle, Wpg.	.05
☐	326	Dave Ellett, Wpg.	.05
☐	327	Pat Elynuik, Wpg.	.05
☐	**328**	**Bob Essensa (G), Wpg., RC**	**.05**
☐	329	Paul Fenton, Wpg., Error	.05
☐	330	Dale Hawerchuk, Wpg.	.10
☐	330	Dale Hawerchuk, Wpg. (Traded)	.10
☐	331	Paul MacDermid, Wpg.	.05
☐	332	Moe Mantha, Wpg.	.05
☐	333	Dave McLlwain, Wpg., Error	.05
☐	**334**	**Teppo Numminen, Wpg., RC**	**.05**
☐	335	Fredrik Olausson (Fred), Wpg.	.10
☐	335	Fredrik Olausson (Fredrik), Wpg.	.10
☐	336	Greg Paslawski, Wpg., Error	.05
☐	337	AS: Al MacInnis, Cgy.	.10
☐	338	AS: Mike Vernon (G), Cgy., Error	.10
☐	339	AS: Kevin Lowe, Edm.	.05
☐	340	AS: Wayne Gretzky, L.A.	.65
☐	341	AS: Luc Robitaille, L.A., Error	.05
☐	342	AS: Brett Hull, Stl.	.20
☐	343	AS: Joe Mullen, Cgy.	.05
☐	344	AS: Joe Nieuwendyk, Cal., Error	.10
☐	345	AS: Steve Larmer, Chi.	.05
☐	346	AS: Doug Wilson, Chi., Error	.10
☐	347	AS: Steve Yzerman, Det.	.35
☐	348	AS: Jari Kurri, Edm.	.25
☐	348	AS: Jari Kurri, Edm.	.25
☐	349	AS: Mark Messier, Edm.	.20
☐	350	AS: Steve Duchesne, L.A., Error	.05
☐	351	AS: Mike Gartner, Min., Error	.20
☐	352	AS: Bernie Nicholls, L.A.	.05
☐	353	AS: Paul Cavallini, Stl.	.05
☐	354	AS: Al Iafrate, Tor.	.05
☐	355	AS: Kirk McLean (G), Van.	.05
☐	356	AS: Thomas Steen, Wpg., Error (Doug Smail)	.05
☐	357	AS: Ray Bourque, Bos.	.20
☐	358	AS: Cam Neely, Bos.	.10
☐	359	AS: Patrick Roy (G), Mtl.	.50
☐	360	AS: Brian Propp, Pha., Error	.05
☐	361	AS: Paul Coffey, Pgh., Error	.20
☐	362	AS: Mario Lemieux, Pgh.	.50
☐	363	AS: Dave Andreychuk, Buf.	.10
☐	364	AS: Phil Housley, Buf.	.05
☐	365	AS: Daren Puppa (G), Buf.	.05
☐	366	AS: Pierre Turgeon, Buf.	.05
☐	367	AS: Ron Francis, Hfd.	.20
☐	368	AS: Chris Chelios, Mtl.	.20
☐	369	AS: Shayne Corson, Mtl., Error	.15
☐	369	AS: Shayne Corson, Mtl., Corrected	.15
☐	370	AS: Stéphane Richer, Mtl.	.05
☐	371	AS: Kirk Muller, N.J.	.05
☐	372	AS: Pat LaFontaine, NYI	.05
☐	373	AS: Brian Leetch, NYR	.20
☐	374	AS: Rick Tocchet, Pha.	.05
☐	375	AS: Joe Sakic, Que.	.35
☐	376	AS: Kevin Hatcher, Wsh.	.05
☐	377	Adams: Bob Murdoch, Coach, Error	.10
☐	378	Byng: Brett Hull, Stl., Error	.10
☐	**379**	**Calder: Sergei Makarov, Cal., RC**	**.05**
☐	380	Clancy: Kevin Lowe, Edm.	.10
☐	381	Hart: Mark Messier, Edm.	.05
☐	382	Jennings: Moog/Lemelin, Bos.	.05
☐	383	Masterton: Gordon Kluzak, Bos., Error	.05
☐	384	Norris: Raymond Bourque, Bos., Error	.10
☐		Patrick: Len Ceglarski, Error (no #)	.10
☐	385	Patrick: Len Ceglarski, Corrected	.10
☐	386	Pearson: Mark Messier, Edm.	.10
☐	387	Presidents' Trophy: Boston Bruins	.05
☐	388	Art Ross: Wayne Gretzky, L.A., Error	.25
☐	389	Selke: Richard Meagher, Stl.	.05
☐	390	Smythe: Bill Ranford (G), Edm.	.05
☐	391	Vezina: Patrick Roy (G), Mtl.	.20
☐	392	Campbell Bowl: Edmonton Oilers	.05
☐	393	Prince of Wales Trophy: Boston Bruins	.05
☐	394	LL: Wayne Gretzky, L.A., Error	.65
☐	395	LL: Brett Hull, Stl., Error	.20
☐	396	LL: Sergei Makarov, Cgy.	.20
☐	397	LL: Mark Messier, Edm.	.20
☐	398	LL: Mike Richter (G), NYR.	.20
☐	399	LL: Patrick Roy (G), Mtl.	.50
☐	400	LL: Darren Turcotte, NYR.	.05
☐	403	Phil Esposito, Bos.	.20
☐	404	Darryl Sittler, Tor.	.20
☐	405	Stan Mikita, Chi.	.20
☐	**401**	**Owen Nolan, Que., RC**	**.25**
☐	**402**	**Petr Nedved, Van., RC**	**.20**
☐	406	Andy Brickley, Bos.	.05
☐	**407**	**Peter Douris, Bos., RC**	**.05**
☐	408	Nevin Markwart, Bos.	.05
☐	409	Chris Nilan, Bos.	.05
☐	**410**	**Stéphane Quintal, Bos., RC**	**.05**
☐	**411**	**Bruce Shoebottom, Bos., RC**	**.05**
☐	**412**	**Don Sweeney, Bos., RC**	**.05**
☐	**413**	**James Wiemer, Bos., RC**	**.05**
☐	**414**	**Mike Hartman, Buf., RC**	**.05**
☐	415	Dale Hawerchuk, Buf.	.15
☐	416	Benoît Hogue, Buf.	.05
☐	**417**	**Bill Houlder (Buf.), RC**	**.05**
☐	418	Mikko Makelä, Buf.	.05
☐	**419**	**Robert Ray, Buf., RC**	**.05**
☐	420	John Tucker, Buf.	.05
☐	**421**	**Jiri Hrdina, Cgy., (Pgh.), RC**	**.05**
☐	422	Mark Hunter, Cgy.	.05
☐	**423**	**Tim Hunter, Cgy., RC**	**.05**
☐	**424**	**Roger Johansson, Cgy, RC**	**.05**
☐	425	Frantisek Musil, (Cgy.)	.05
☐	426	Ric Nattress, Cgy.	.05
☐	427	Chris Chelios, Chi.	.25
☐	**428**	**Jacques Cloutier (G), Chi., RC, Error**	**.05**
☐	429	Greg Gilbert, Chi.	.05
☐	430	Michel Goulet, Chi., Error	.15
☐	**431**	**Mike Hudson, Chi., RC**	**.05**
☐	**432**	**Jocelyn Lemieux, Chi., RC**	**.05**
☐	433	Brian Noonan, Chi.	.05
☐	434	Wayne Presley, Chi.	.05
☐	**435**	**Brent Fedyk, Det., RC**	**.05**
☐	436	Rick Green, Det.	.05
☐	437	Marc Habscheid, Det.	.05
☐	438	Brad McCrimmon, Det.	.05
☐	**439**	**Jeff Beukeboom, Edm., RC**	**.05**
☐	**440**	**Dave Brown, Edm., RC**	**.05**
☐	**441**	**Kelly Buchberger, Edm., RC**	**.05**
☐	442	Greg Hawgood, Edm.	.05
☐	**443**	**Chris Joseph, Edm., RC**	**.05**
☐	444	Ken Linseman, Edm.	.05
☐	**445**	**Eldon Reddick (G), Edm., RC**	**.05**
☐	**446**	**Geoff Smith, Edm., RC**	**.05**
☐	**447**	**Adam Burt, Hfd., RC**	**.05**
☐	448	Sylvain Côté, Hfd.	.05
☐	**449**	**Paul Cyr, Hfd., RC**	**.05**
☐	**450**	**Edward Kastelic, Hfd., RC**	**.05**
☐	451	Peter Sidorkiewicz (G), Hfd.	.05
☐	**452**	**Mike Tomlak, Hfd., RC**	**.05**
☐	453	Carey Wilson, Hfd.	.05
☐	454	Daniel Berthiaume (G), L.A.	.05
☐	455	Scott Bjugstad, L.A.	.05
☐	**456**	**Rod Buskas, L.A., RC**	**.05**
☐	**457**	**John McIntyre Tor., (L.A.), RC**	**.05**
☐	458	Tim Watters, L.A.	.05
☐	**459**	**Perry Berezan, Min., RC**	**.05**
☐	460	Brian Propp, Min.	.05
☐	461	Ilkka Sinisalo, Min.	.05
☐	462	Doug Smail, Wpg., (Min.)	.05
☐	463	Bobby Smith, Min.	.05
☐	464	Chris Dahlquist, Pgh. (Min.)	.05
☐	**465**	**Neil Wilkinson, Min., RC**	**.05**
☐	**466**	**J. J. Daigneault, Mtl., RC**	**.05**
☐	**467**	**Eric Desjardins, Mtl., RC**	**.15**
☐	468	Gerald Diduck, Mtl.	.05
☐	**469**	**Donald Dufresne, Mtl., RC**	**.05**
☐	**470**	**Todd Ewen, Mtl., RC, Error (/b: Desjardins)**	**.10**
☐	**470**	**Todd Ewen, Mtl., RC, Corrected**	**.10**
☐	**471**	**Brent Gilchrist, Mtl., RC**	**.05**
☐	**472**	**Sylvain Lefebvre, Mtl., RC**	**.05**
☐	473	Denis Savard, Mtl.	.15
☐	474	Sylvain Turgeon, N.J. (Mtl.)	.05
☐	475	Ryan Walter, Mtl.	.05
☐	476	Laurie Boschman, N.J.	.05
☐	**477**	**Pat Conacher, N.J., RC**	**.05**
☐	478	Claude Lemieux, N.J.	.05
☐	479	Walt Poddubny, N.J.	.05
☐	**480**	**Allan Stewart, N.J., RC, Error (Alan)**	**.05**
☐	**481**	**Chris Terreri (G), N.J., RC**	**.05**
☐	482	Brad Dalgarno, NYI.	.05
☐	**483**	**Dave Chyzowski, NYI., RC**	**.05**
☐	484	Craig Ludwig, NYI.	.05
☐	**485**	**Wayne McBean, NYI., RC**	**.05**
☐	**486**	**Richard Pilon, NYI., RC**	**.05**
☐	**487**	**Joe Reekie, NYI., RC**	**.05**
☐	**488**	**Mick Vukota, NYI., RC**	**.05**
☐	489	Mark Hardy, NYR.	.05
☐	**490**	**Jody Hull, NYR., RC**	**.05**
☐	**491**	**Kris King, NYR., RC**	**.05**
☐	**492**	**Troy Mallette, NYR., RC**	**.05**
☐	**493**	**Kevin Miller, NYR., RC**	**.05**
☐	494	Normand Rochefort, NYR.	.05
☐	495	David Shaw, NYR.	.05
☐	496	Ray Sheppard, NYR.	.05
☐	497	Keith Acton, Pha.	.05
☐	**498**	**Craig Berube, Pha., RC**	**.05**
☐	**499**	**Tony Horacek, Pha., RC**	**.05**
☐	**500**	**Normand Lacombe, Pha., RC**	**.05**

	No.	Player	Price
☐	**501**	**Jiri Latal, Pha., RC**	**.05**
☐	502	Pete Peeters (G), Pha.	.05
☐	**503**	**Derrick Smith, Pha., RC**	**.05**
☐	**504**	**Jay Caufield, Pgh., RC**	**.05**
☐	505	Peter Taglianetti, Min., (Pgh.)	.05
☐	**506**	**Randy Gilhen, Pgh., RC**	**.05**
☐	507	Randy Hillier, Pgh.	.05
☐	508	Joe Mullen, Pgh.	.10
☐	**509**	**Frank Pietrangelo (G), Pgh., RC**	**.05**
☐	510	Gord Roberts, Pgh.	.05
☐	511	Bryan Trottier, Pgh.	.10
☐	**512**	**Wendell Young (G), Pgh., RC**	**.05**
☐	**513**	**Shawn Anderson, Que., RC**	**.05**
☐	**514**	**Steven Finn, Que., RC**	**.05**
☐	**515**	**Bryan Fogarty, Que., RC**	**.05**
☐	516	Mike Hough, Que., Error	.05
☐	**517**	**Darin Kimble, Que., RC**	**.05**
☐	518	Randy Velischek, Que.	.05
☐	**519**	**Craig Wolanin, Que., RC**	**.05**
☐	**520**	**Bob Bassen, Stl., RC**	**.05**
☐	521	Geoff Courtnall, Stl.	.05
☐	**522**	**Robert Dirk, Stl., RC**	**.05**
☐	**523**	**Glen Featherstone, Stl., RC**	**.05**
☐	524	Mario Marois, Stl.	.05
☐	**525**	**Herb Raglan, Stl., RC**	**.05**
☐	526	Cliff Ronning, Stl.	.05
☐	527	Harold Snepsts, Stl.	.05
☐	528	Scott Stevens, Stl.	.05
☐	529	Ron Wilson, Stl.	.05
☐	530	Aaron Broten, Que., (Tor.)	.05
☐	531	Lucien DeBlois, Tor.	.05
☐	532	Dave Ellett, Tor.	.05
☐	533	Paul Fenton,Tor., Error (Inverted TM)	.10
☐	533	Paul Fenton, Tor., Corrected	.10
☐	**534**	**Todd Gill, Tor., RC**	**.05**
☐	535	Dave Hannan, Tor.	.05
☐	**536**	**John Kordic, Tor., RC**	**.05**
☐	537	Mike Krushelnyski, Tor.	.05
☐	**538**	**Kevin Maguire, Tor., RC**	**.05**
☐	539	Michel Petit, Tor.	.05
☐	**540**	**Jeff Reese (G), Tor., RC**	**.05**
☐	**541**	**David Reid, Tor., RC**	**.05**
☐	542	Doug Shedden, Tor.	.05
☐	**543**	**Dave Capuano, Van., RC**	**.05**
☐	**544**	**Craig Coxe, Van., RC**	**.05**
☐	**545**	**Kevan Guy, Van., RC**	**.05**
☐	**546**	**Rob Murphy, Van., RC**	**.05**
☐	**547**	**Robert Nordmark, Van., RC**	**.05**
☐	548	Stan Smyl, Van.	.05
☐	**549**	**Ron Stern, Van., RC**	**.05**
☐	**550**	**Tim Bergland, Wsh., RC**	**.05**
☐	**551**	**Nick Kypreos, Wsh., RC**	**.05**
☐	**552**	**Mike Lalor, Wsh., RC**	**.05**
☐	**553**	**Rob Murray, Wsh., RC**	**.05**
☐	554	Bob Rouse, Wsh.	.05
☐	555	Dave Tippett, Wsh.	.05
☐	556	Peter Zezel, (Wsh.)	.05
☐	557	Scott Arniel, Wpg.	.05
☐	**558**	**Don Barber, Wpg., RC**	**.05**
☐	**559**	**Shawn Cronin, Wpg., RC**	**.05**
☐	**560**	**Gord Donnelly, Wpg., RC**	**.05**
☐	**561**	**Doug Evans, Wpg., RC**	**.05**
☐	562	Phil Housley, Wpg.	.05
☐	563	Ed Olczyk, Wpg.	.05
☐	564	Mark Osborne, Wpg.	.05
☐	565	Thomas Steen, Wpg.	.05
☐	566	Boston Bruins	.05
☐	567	Buffalo Sabres	.05
☐	568	Calgary Flames	.05
☐	569	Chicago Black Hawks	.05
☐	570	Detroit Red Wings	.05
☐	571	Edmonton Oilers	.05
☐	572	Hartford Whalers	.05
☐	573	Los Angeles Kings, Error	.05
☐	573	Los Angeles Kings, Corrected	.05
☐	574	Minnesota North Stars	.05
☐	575	Montréal Canadiens	.05
☐	576	New Jersey Devils	.05
☐	577	New York Islanders	.05
☐	578	New York Rangers	.05
☐	579	Philadelphia Flyers	.05
☐	580	Pittsburgh Penguins	.05
☐	581	Québec Nordiques	.05
☐	582	St. Louis Blues	.05
☐	583	Toronto Maple Leafs	.05
☐	584	Vancouver Canucks	.05
☐	585	Washington Capitals	.05
☐	586	Winnipeg Jets	.05
☐	**587**	**Kenneth Hodge, Bos., RC**	**.05**
☐	**588**	**Vladimir Ruzicka, Bos., RC**	**.05**
☐	**589**	**Wes Walz, Bos., RC**	**.05**
☐	**590**	**Greg Brown, Buf., RC**	**.05**
☐	**591**	**Brad Miller, Buf., RC**	**.05**
☐	**592**	**Darrin Shannon, Buf., RC**	**.05**
☐	**593**	**Stéphane Matteau, Cgy., RC**	**.05**
☐	**594**	**Sergei Priakin, Cgy., RC**	**.05**
☐	**595**	**Robert Reichel, Cgy., RC**	**.20**
☐	**596**	**Ken Sabourin, Cgy., RC**	**.05**
☐	**597**	**Tim Sweeney, Cgy., RC**	**.05**
☐	**598**	**Ed Belfour (G), Chi., RC, Error (Carmen)**	**1.00**
☐	**599**	**Frantisek Kucera, Chi., RC**	**.05**
☐	**600**	**Mike McNeill, Chi., RC**	**.05**
☐	**601**	**Mike Peluso, Chi., RC**	**.05**
☐	**602**	**Tim Cheveldae (G), Det., RC**	**.05**
☐	**603**	**Per Djoos, Det., RC**	**.05**
☐	**604**	**Sergei Fedorov, Det., RC**	**1.00**
☐	**605**	**Johan Garpenlov, Det., RC**	**.05**
☐	**606**	**Keith Primeau, Det., RC**	**.35**
☐	**607**	**Paul Ysebaert, Det., RC**	**.05**
☐	**608**	**Anatoli Semenov, Edm., RC**	**.05**
☐	**609**	**Bobby Holik, Hfd., RC**	**.15**
☐	**610**	**Kay Whitmore (G), Hfd., RC**	**.05**
☐	**611**	**Rob Blake, L.A., RC**	**.25**
☐	**612**	**François Breault, L.A., RC**	**.05**
☐	**613**	**Mike Craig, Min., RC**	**.05**
☐	**614**	**Jean-Claude Bergeron (G), Mtl., RC**	**.05**
☐	**615**	**Andrew Cassels, Mtl., RC**	**.05**
☐	**616**	**Tom Chorske, Mtl., RC**	**.05**
☐	**617**	**Lyle Odelein, Mtl., RC**	**.05**
☐	**618**	**Mark Pederson, Mtl., RC**	**.05**
☐	**619**	**Zdeno Ciger, N.J., RC**	**.05**
☐	**620**	**Troy Crowder, N.J., RC**	**.05**
☐	**621**	**Jon Morris, N.J., RC**	**.05**
☐	**622**	**Eric Weinrich, N.J., RC**	**.05**
☐	**623**	**David Marcinyshyn, N.J., RC**	**.05**
☐	**624**	**Jeff Hackett (G), NYI., RC**	**.05**
☐	**625**	**Rob DiMaio, NYI., RC**	**.05**
☐	**626**	**Steven Rice, NYR., RC**	**.05**
☐	**627**	**Mike Richter (G), NYR., RC**	**1.00**
☐	**628**	**Dennis Vial, NYR., RC**	**.05**
☐	**629**	**Martin Hostak, Pha. RC**	**.05**
☐	**630**	**Pat Murray, Pha. RC**	**.05**
☐	**631**	**Mike Ricci, Pha. RC**	**.20**
☐	**632**	**Jaromir Jagr, Pgh., RC**	**1.00**
☐	**633**	**Paul Stanton, Pgh., RC**	**.05**
☐	**634**	**Scott Gordon (G), Que., RC, Error (Nordique)**	**.05**
☐	**635**	**Owen Nolan, Que., RC**	**.25**
☐	**636**	**Mats Sundin, Que., RC**	**.50**
☐	**637**	**John Tanner (G), Que., RC**	**.05**
☐	**638**	**Curtis Joseph (G), Stl., RC**	**.50**
☐	**639**	**Peter Ing (G), Tor., RC**	**.05**
☐	**640**	**Scott Thornton, Tor., RC**	**.05**
☐	**641**	**Troy Gamble (G), Van., RC**	**.05**
☐	**642**	**Robert Kron, Van., RC**	**.05**
☐	643	Petr Nedved, Van., RC	.20
☐	**644**	**Adrien Plavsic, Van., RC**	**.05**
☐	**645**	**Peter Bondra, Wsh., RC**	**.50**
☐	**646**	**Jim Hrivnak (G), Wsh., RC**	**.05**
☐	**647**	**Mikhail Tatarinov, Wsh., RC**	**.05**
☐	**648**	**Stéphane Beauregard (G), Wpg., RC, Error**	**.05**
☐	**649**	**Rick Tabaracci (G), Wpg., RC**	**.05**
☐	650	Mike Bossy, NYI	.20
☐	651	Bobby Clarke, Pha.	.20
☐	652	Alex Delvecchio, Det.	.20
☐	653	Marcel Dionne,L.A.	.20
☐	654	Gordie Howe, Hfd.	.50
☐	655	Stan Mikita, Chi.	.20
☐	656	Denis Potvin, NYI	.20
☐	657	Bobby Clarke, Pha.	.20
☐	658	Alex Delvecchio, Det.	.20
☐	659	Tony Esposito (G), Chi.,	.20
☐	660	Gordie Howe, Hfd.	.50
☐	661	Mike Milbury, Coach, Bos.	.10
☐	662	Rick Dudley, Coach, Buf.	.05
☐	663	Doug Risebrough, Coach, Cgy.	.05
☐	664	Bryan Murray, Coach, Det.	.05
☐	665	John Muckler, Coach, Edm.	.05
☐	666	Rick Ley, Coach, Hfd.	.05
☐	667	Tom Webster, Coach, L.A.	.05
☐	668	Bob Gainey, Coach, Min.	.20
☐	669	Pat Burns, Coach, Mtl.	.25
☐	670	John Cunniff, Coach, N.J.	.05
☐	671	Al Arbour, Coach, NYI	.10
☐	672	Roger Neilson, Coach, NYR	.10
☐	673	Paul Holmgren, Coach, Pha.	.05
☐	674	Bob Johnson, Coach, Pgh.	.10
☐	675	Dave Chambers, Coach, Que.	.05
☐	676	Brian Sutter, Coach, Stl.	.05
☐	677	Tom Watt, Coach, Tor.	.05
☐	678	Bob McCammon, Coach, Van.	.05
☐	679	Terry Murray, Coach, Wsh.	.05
☐	680	Bob J. Murdoch, Coach, Wpg.	.05
☐	681	Ron Asselstine, Linesman	.05
☐	682	Wayne Bonney, Linesman	.05
☐	683	Kevin Collins, Linesman	.05
☐	684	Pat Dapuzzo, Linesman	.05
☐	685	Ron Finn, Linesman	.05
☐	686	Kerry Fraser, Referee	.05
☐	687	Gérard Gauthier, Linesman	.05
☐	688	Terry Gregson, Referee	.05
☐	689	Bob Hodges, Linesman	.05
☐	690	Ron Hoggarth, Referee	.05
☐	691	Don Koharski, Referee	.05
☐	692	Dan Marouelli, Referee	.05
☐	693	Dan McCourt, Linesman	.05
☐	694	Bill McCreary, Referee	.05
☐	695	Denis Morel, Referee	.05
☐	696	Jerry Pateman, Linesman	.05
☐	697	Ray Scapinello, Linesman	.05
☐	698	Rob Shick, Referee	.05
☐	699	Paul Stewart, Referee	.05
☐	700	Leon Stickle, Linesman	.05
☐	701	Andy van Hellemond, Referee	.05
☐	702	Mark Vines, Linesman	.05
☐	703	Wayne Gretzky, 2,000th point	.75
☐	704	Edmonton Oilers, Mark Messier	.20
☐	705	The Puck	.05

1990 - 91 PRO SET PLAYER OF THE MONTH

These cards were issued each month to honour the player selected Pro Set Player of the Month. October 1990 and March 1991 player cards were not issued.

Complete Set (4 cards): **28.00**

	No.	Player	NRMT-MT
☐		November 1990: Pete Peeters (G). Pha.	4.00
☐	P1	December 1990: Tom Barrasso (G). Pgh.	4.00
☐	P2	January 1991: Wayne Gretzky, L.A.	20.00
☐	P3	February 1991: Brett Hull, Stl.	5.00

1990 - 91 SCORE

This series has two versions: the American version (English) and the Canadian version (Bilingual). The logo on the back of promo cards is 8mm high as opposed to 6mm high on regular cards.

Imprint: © 1990 SCORE

			USA	Cdn.
Complete Set (440 cards):			**15.00**	**20.00**
Factory Set (445 cards):			**18.00**	**23.00**
Common Player:			**.10**	**.10**
	No.	**Promo**	**USA**	**Cdn.**
☐	1	Wayne Gretzky, L.A., Error (Catches)	25.00	.-
☐	1	Wayne Gretzky, L.A., Corrected	18.00	.-
☐	10	Patrick Roy (G), Mtl.	.-	15.00
☐	40	Gary Leeman, Tor.	.-	2.00
☐	100	Mark Messier, Edm.	.-	6.00
☐	100	Mark Messier, Edm.	.-	6.00
☐	179	Jeremy Roenick, Chi.	3.00	.-
☐	200	Ray Bourque, Bos.	6.00	.-

No.	Player	USA	Cdn.
1	Wayne Gretzky, L.A.	1.50	1.75
2	Mario Lemieux, Pgh.	1.00	1.25
3	Steve Yzerman, Det.	.75	.75
4	Cam Neely, Bos.	.25	.25
5	Al MacInnis, Cgy.	.25	.25
6	Paul Coffey, Pgh.	.25	.25
7	Brian Bellows, Min.	.10	.10
8	Joe Sakic, Que.	.75	.75
9	Bernie Nicholls, NYR.	.10	.10
10	Patrick Roy (G), Mtl.	1.00	1.25
11	**Doug Houda, Det., RC**	**.10**	**.10**
12	David Volek, NYI.	.10	.10
13	Esa Tikkanen, Edm.	.10	.10
14	Thomas Steen, Wpg.	.10	.10
15	Chris Chelios, Mtl.	.35	.35
16	Bobby Carpenter, Bos.	.10	.10
17	Dirk Graham, Chi.	.10	.10
18	Garth Butcher, Van.	.10	.10
19	Patrik Sundstrom, N.J.	.10	.10
20	Rod Langway, Wsh.	.10	.10
21	Scott Young, Hfd.	.10	.10
22	Ulf Dahlen, Min.	.10	.10
23	Mike Ramsey, Buf.	.10	.10
24	Peter Zezel, Stl.	.10	.10
25	Ron Hextall (G), Pha.	.25	.25
26	Steve Duchesne, L.A.	.10	.10
27	Allan Bester (G), Tor.	.10	.10
28	**Everett Sanipass, Que., RC**	**.10**	**.10**
29	Steve Konroyd, Chi.	.10	.10
30	Joe Nieuwendyk, Cgy.	.25	.25
31	Brent Ashton, Wpg.	.10	.10
32	Trevor Linden, Van.	.25	.25
33	Mike Ridley, Wsh.	.10	.10
34	Sean Burke (G), N.J.	.25	.25
35	Pat Verbeek, Hfd.	.10	.10
36	Rob Ramage, Tor.	.10	.10
37	Kelly Kisio, NYR.	.10	.10
38	Craig Muni, Edm., Error (/b: C. Simpson)	.10	.10
38	Craig Muni, Edm.,Corrected	.10	.10
39	Brent Sutter, NYI.	.10	.10
40	Gary Leeman, Tor.	.10	.10
41	Jeff Brown, Stl.	.10	.10
42	Greg Millen (G), Chi.	.10	.10
43	**Alexander Mogilny, Buf., RC**	**1.00**	**1.25**
44	Dale Hunter, Wsh.	.10	.10
45	Randy Moller, NYI.	.10	.10
46	Peter Sidorkiewicz (G), Hfd.	.10	.10
47	Terry Carkner, Pha.	.10	.10
48	Tony Granato. L.A.	.10	.10
49	Shawn Burr, Det.	.10	.10
50	Dale Hawerchuk, Wpg.	.25	.25
51	**Don Sweeney, Bos., RC**	.10	.10
52	Mike Vernon (G), Cgy., Error	.25	.25
53	**Kevin Stevens, Pgh., RC**	**.25**	**.25**
54	**Bryan Fogarty, Que., RC**	.10	.10
55	Dan Quinn, Van.	.10	.10
56	Murray Craven, Pha.	.10	.10
57	Shawn Chambers, Min.	.10	.10
58	Craig Simpson, Edm	.10	.10
59	Doug Crossman, NYI.	.10	.10
60	Daren Puppa (G), Buf.	.10	.10
61	Bobby Smith, Mtl.	.10	.10
62	**Viacheslav Fetisov, N.J., RC**	**.25**	**.25**
63	Gino Cavallini, Stl.	.10	.10
64	Jimmy Carson, Det.	.10	.10
65	David Ellett, Wpg.	.10	.10
66	Steve Thomas, Chi.	.10	.10
67	**Mike Lalor, Stl., RC**	.10	.10
68	Mike Liut (G), Wsh.	.10	.10
69	Tom Laidlaw, L.A.	.10	.10
70	Ron Francis, Hfd.	.35	.35
71	**Sergei Makarov, Cgy., RC**	**.25**	**.25**
72	Randy Burridge, Bos.	.10	.10
73	Doug Lidster, Van.	.10	.10
74	**Mike Richter (G), NYR., RC**	**1.00**	**1.25**
75	Stéphane Richer, Mtl.	.10	.10
76	Randy Hillier, Pgh.	.10	.10
77	Christian Ruuttu, Buf.	.10	.10
78	Marc Fortier, Que.	.10	.10
79	Bill Ranford (G), Edm.	.25	.25
80	Rick Tocchet, Pha.	.10	.10
81	Fredrik Olausson, Wpg.	.10	.10
82	Adam Creighton, Chi.	.10	.10
83	Sylvain Côté, Hfd.	.10	.10
84	Brian Mullen, NYR.	.10	.10
85	Adam Oates, Stl.	.35	.35
86	Gary Nylund, NYI.	.10	.10
87	**Tim Cheveldae (G), Det., RC**	**.10**	**.10**
88	Gary Suter, Cgy.	.10	.10
89	John Tonelli, L.A.	.10	.10
90	Kevin Hatcher, Wsh.	.10	.10
91	Guy Carbonneau, Mtl.	.10	.10
92	**Curtis Leschyshyn, Que., RC**	**.10**	**.10**
93	Kirk McLean (G), Van.	.25	.25
94	Curt Giles, Min.	.10	.10
95	Vincent Damphousse, Tor.	.35	.35
96	Peter Stastny, N.J.	.10	.10
97	Glen Wesley, Bos.	.10	.10
98	David Shaw, NYR.	.10	.10
99	**Brad Shaw, Hfd., RC**	**.10**	**.10**
100	Mark Messier, Edm.	.50	.50
101	**Rick Zombo, Det., RC**	**.10**	**.10**
102	**M. Fitzpatrick (G), NYI, RC, Err. (Catches right)**	**.10**	**.10**
102	**Mark Fitzpatrick (G), NYI, RC, Corrected**	**.10**	**.10**
103	Rick Vaive, Buf.	.10	.10
104	Mark Osborne. Tor.	.10	.10
105	Rob Brown, Pgh.	.10	.10
106	Gary Roberts, Cgy.	.25	.25
107	**Vincent Riendeau (G), Stl., RC**	**.10**	**.10**
108	Dave Gagner, Min.	.10	.10
109	Bruce Driver, N.J.	.10	.10
110	Pierre Turgeon, Buf.	.25	.25
111	Claude Lemieux, Mtl.	.10	.10
112	**Bob Essensa (G), Wpg., RC**	**.10**	**.10**
113	John Ogrodnick, NYR.	.10	.10
114	Glenn Anderson, Edm.	.10	.10
115	Kelly Hrudey (G), L.A.	.10	.10
116	Sylvain Turgeon, N.J.	.10	.10
117	**Gord Murphy, Pha., RC**	**.10**	**.10**
118	Craig Janney, Bos.	.10	.10
119	Randy Wood, NYI.	.10	.10
120	**Mike Modano, Min., RC**	**.75**	**.75**
121	Tom Barrasso (G), Pgh.	.25	.25
122	Daniel Marois, Tor.	.10	.10
123	**Igor Larionov, Van., RC**	**.25**	**.25**
124	Geoff Courtnall, Wsh.	.10	.10
125	Denis Savard, Chi.	.25	.25
126	Ron Tugnutt (G), Que.	.10	.10
127	**Mathieu Schneider, Mtl., RC**	**.10**	**.10**
128	Joel Otto, Cgy.	.10	.10
129	Steve Smith, Edm.	.10	.10
130	Mike Gartner, NYR.	.25	.25
131	**Rod Brind'Amour, Stl., RC**	**.50**	**.50**
132	**Jyrki Lumme, Van., RC**	**.10**	**.10**
133	Mike Foligno, Buf.	.10	.10
134	Ray Ferraro, Hfd.	.10	.10
135	Steve Larmer, Chi.	.25	.25
136	Randy Carlyle, Wpg.	.10	.10
137	Tony Tanti, Pgh.	.10	.10
138	**Jeff Chychrun, Pha., RC**	**.10**	**.10**
139	Gerald Diduck, NYI.	.10	.10
140	Andy Moog (G), Bos.	.25	.25
141	Paul Gillis, Que.	.10	.10
142	Tom Kurvers,Tor.	.10	.10
143	Bob Probert, Det.	.10	.10
144	Neal Broten, Min.	.10	.10
145	Phil Housley, Buf.	.10	.10
146	Brendan Shanahan, N.J.	.50	.50
147	Bob Rouse, Wsh.	.10	.10
148	Russ Courtnall, Mtl.	.10	.10
149	Normand Rochefort, NYR.	.10	.10
150	Luc Robitaille, L.A.	.25	.25
151	**Curtis Joseph (G), Stl., RC**	**1.00**	**1.25**
152	Ulf Samuelsson, Hfd.	.10	.10
153	Ron Sutter, Pha.	.10	.10
154	Petri Skriko, Van.	.10	.10
155	Doug Gilmour, Cgy.	.35	.35
156	Paul Fenton, Wpg.	.10	.10
157	Jeff Norton, NYI.	.10	.10
158	Jari Kurri, Edm.	.25	.25
159	Réjean Lemelin (G), Bos.	.10	.10
160	Kirk Muller, N.J.	.10	.10
161	Keith Brown, Chi.	.10	.10
162	Aaron Broten, Min., Error (D. Archibald)	.10	.10
163	**Adam Graves, Edm., RC**	**.35**	**.35**
164	John Cullen, Pgh.	.10	.10
165	Craig Ludwig, Mtl.	.10	.10
166	Dave Taylor, L.A.	.10	.10
167	**Craig Wolanin, Que., RC**	**.10**	**.10**
168	Kelly Miller, Wsh.	.10	.10
169	Uwe Krupp, Buf.	.10	.10
170	Kevin Lowe, Edm.	.10	.10
171	Wendel Clark, Tor.	.25	.25
172	Dave Babych, Hfd.	.10	.10
173	Paul Reinhart, Van.	.10	.10
174	Patrick Flatley, NYI.	.10	.10
175	John Vanbiesbrouck (G), NYR.	.50	.50
176	**Teppo Numminen, Wpg., RC**	**.10**	**.10**
177	Tim Kerr, Pha.	.10	.10
178	Ken Daneyko, N.J.	.10	.10
179	**Jeremy Roenick, Chi., RC**	**.85**	**1.00**
180	Gerard Gallant, Det.	.10	.10
181	Allen Pedersen, Bos.	.10	.10
182	Jon Casey (G), Min.	.10	.10
183	Tomas Sandström, L.A.	.10	.10
184	Brad McCrimmon, Cgy.	.10	.10
185	Paul Cavallini, Stl.	.10	.10
186	**Mark Recchi, Pgh., RC**	**.85**	**1.00**
187	Michel Petit, Que.	.10	.10
188	Scott Stevens, Wsh.	.10	.10
189	Dave Andreychuk, Buf.	.20	.20
190	John MacLean, N.J.	.10	.10
191	Petr Svoboda, Mtl.	.10	.10
192	Dave Tippett, Hfd.	.10	.10
193	Dave Manson, Chi.	.10	.10
194	James Patrick, NYR.	.10	.10
195	Al Iafrate, Tor.	.10	.10
196	Doug Smail, Wpg.	.10	.10
197	Kjell Samuelsson, Pha.	.10	.10
198	Brian Bradley, Van.	.10	.10
199	Charlie Huddy, Edm.	.10	.10
200	Ray Bourque, Bos.	.50	.50
201	**Joey Kocur, Det., RC**	**.10**	**.10**
202	Jim Johnson, Pgh.	.10	.10
203	Paul MacLean, Stl.	.10	.10
204	Tim Watters, L.A.	.10	.10
205	Pat Elynuik, Wpg.	.10	.10
206	Larry Murphy, Min.	.25	.25
207	**Claude Loiselle, Que., RC**	**.10**	**.10**
208	Joe Mullen, Cgy.	.25	.25
209	**Alexei Kasatonov, N.J., RC**	**.10**	**.10**
210	Ed Olczyk, Tor.	.10	.10
211	Doug Bodger, Buf.	.10	.10
212	Kevin Dineen, Hfd.	.10	.10
213	Shayne Corson, Mtl.	.25	.25
214	Steve Chiasson, Det.	.10	.10
215	Don Beaupré (G), Wsh.	.10	.10
216	Jamie Macoun, Cgy.	.10	.10
217	David Poulin, Bos.	.10	.10
218	Zarley Zalapski, Pgh.	.10	.10
219	Brad Marsh, Tor.	.10	.10
220	Mark Howe, Pha.	.25	.25
221	Michel Goulet, Chi.	.25	.25
222	**Hubie McDonough, NYI., RC**	**.10**	**.10**
223	Frantisek Musil, Min.	.10	.10
224	**Sergio Momesso, Stl., RC**	**.10**	**.10**
225	Brian Leetch, NYR.	.35	.35
226	Theoren Fleury, Cgy.	.35	.35
227	Mike Krushelnyski, L.A.	.10	.10
228	Glen Hanlon (G), Det.	.10	.10
229	Mario Marois, Que.	.10	.10
230	Dino Ciccarelli, Wsh.	.25	.25
231	Dave McLlwain, Wpg., Error (shoots right)	.10	.10
231	Dave McLlwain, Wpg., Corrected	.10	.10
232	Petr Klima, Edm.	.10	.10
233	**Grant Ledyard, Buf., RC**	**.10**	**.10**
234	Phil Bourque, Pgh.	.10	.10
235	Bob Sweeney, Bos.	.10	.10
236	Luke Richardson, Tor.	.10	.10
237	**Todd Krygier, Hfd., RC**	**.10**	**.10**
238	Brian Skrudland, Mtl.	.10	.10
239	**Chris Terreri (G), N.J., RC**	**.10**	**.10**
240	Greg Adams, Van.	.10	.10
241	**Darren Turcotte, NYR., RC**	**.10**	**.10**
242	Scott Mellanby, Pha.	.10	.10
243	Troy Murray, Chi.	.10	.10
244	Stewart Gavin, Min.	.10	.10
245	Gord Roberts, Stl.	.10	.10
246	**John Druce, Wsh., RC**	**.10**	**.10**
247	Steve Kasper, L.A.	.10	.10
248	**Paul Ranheim, Cgy., RC**	**.10**	**10**
249	Greg Paslawski, Wpg.	.10	.10
250	Pat LaFontaine, NYI.	.25	.25
251	Scott Arniel, Buf.	.10	.10

□ □	252	Bernie Federko, Det.	.10	.10
□ □	**253**	**Garry Galley, Bos., RC**	**.10**	**.10**
□ □	254	Carey Wilson, NYR.	.10	.10
□ □	255	Bob Errey, Pgh.	.10	.10
□ □	256	Tony Hrkac, Que.	.10	.10
□ □	257	Andrew McBain, Van.	.10	.10
□ □	258	Craig MacTavish, Edm.	.10	.10
□ □	259	Dean Evason, Hfd., Error (rev. neg.)	.10	.10
□ □	259	Dean Evason, Hfd., Corrected	.10	.10
□ □	260	Larry Robinson, L.A.	.25	.25
□ □	261	Basil McRae, Min.	.10	.10
□ □	**262**	**Stéphan Lebeau, Mtl., RC**	**.10**	**.10**
□ □	263	Ken Wregget (G), Pha.	.10	.10
□ □	264	Greg Gilbert, Chi.	.10	.10
□ □	**265**	**Ken Baumgartner, NYI., RC**	**.10**	**.10**
□ □	**266**	**Lou Franceschetti, Tor., RC**	**.10**	**.10**
□ □	267	Rick Meagher, Stl.	.10	.10
□ □	**268**	**Michal Pivonka, Wsh., RC**	**.10**	**.10**
□ □	269	Brian Propp, Bos.	.10	.10
□ □	270	Bryan Trottier, NYI.	.25	.25
□ □	271	Marty McSorley, L.A.	.10	.10
□ □	272	Jan Erixon, NYR.	.10	.10
□ □	**273**	**Vladimir Krutov, Van., RC**	**.10**	**.10**
□ □	274	Dana Murzyn, Cgy.	.10	.10
□ □	275	Grant Fuhr (G), Edm.	.25	.25
□ □	276	Randy Cunneyworth, Hfd.	.10	.10
□ □	277	John Chabot, Det.	.10	.10
□ □	278	Walt Poddubny, N.J.	.10	.10
□ □	279	Stephen Leach, Wsh.	.10	.10
□ □	280	Doug Wilson, Chi.	.25	.25
□ □	281	Rick Sutter, Stl.	.10	.10
□ □	**282**	**Stéphane Beauregard (G), Wpg., RC, Error**	**.10**	**.10**
□ □	**283**	**John Carter, Bos., RC**	**.10**	**.10**
□ □	**284**	**Don Barber, Min., RC**	**.10**	**.10**
□ □	285	Tom Fergus, Tor.	.10	.10
□ □	286	Ilkka Sinisalo, Pha.	.10	.10
□ □	287	Kevin McClelland, Det.	.10	.10
□ □	**288**	**Troy Mallette, NYR., RC**	**.10**	**.10**
□ □	289	Clint Malarchuk (G), Buf.	.10	.10
□ □	290	Guy Lafleur, Que.	.50	.50
□ □	291	Bob Joyce, Wsh.	.10	.10
□ □	292	Trent Yawney, Chi.	.10	.10
□ □	**293**	**Joe Murphy, Edm., RC**	**.10**	**.10**
□ □	**294**	**Glenn Healy (G), NYI, RC**	**.10**	**.10**
□ □	295	Dave Christian, Bos.	.10	.10
□ □	296	Paul MacDermid, Wpg.	.10	.10
□ □	**297**	**Todd Elik, L.A., RC**	**.10**	**.10**
□ □	**298**	**Wendell Young (G), Pgh, RC**	**.10**	**.10**
□ □	**299**	**Dean Kennedy, Buf., RC**	**.10**	**.10**
□ □	300	Brett Hull, Stl.	.50	.50
□	**301**	**Martin Gelinas, Edm., RC**	**.–**	**.35**
□	301	Keith Acton, Pha.	.10	.–
□	302	Ric Nattress, Cgy.	.–	.10
□	302	Yvon Corriveau, Hfd.	.10	.–
□	303	Jim Sandlak, Van.	.–	.10
□	303	Don Maloney, NYI.	.10	.–
□	304	Brian Hayward (G), Mtl.	.–	.10
□	**304**	**Mark Tinordi, Min., RC**	**.10**	**.–**
□	305	Joe Cirella, Que.	.–	.10
□	**305**	**Bob Kudelski, L.A., RC**	**.10**	**.–**
□	306	Randall Gregg, Edm.	.–	.10
□	306	Brian Benning, L.A.	.10	.–
□	**307**	**Sylvain Lefebvre, Mtl., RC**	**.–**	**.10**
□	307	Alan Kerr, NYI.	.10	.–
□	**308**	**Mark Lamb, Edm., RC**	**.–**	**.10**
□	308	Per-Erik Eklund, Pha.	.10	.–
□	309	Rick Wamsley (G), Cgy.	.–	.10
□	309	Calle Johansson (G), Wsh.	.10	.–
□	310	Moe Mantha, Wpg.	.–	.10
□	**310**	**David Maley, N.J., RC**	**.10**	**.–**
□	311	Tony McKegney, Que.	.–	.10
□	311	Chris Nilan, NYR.	.10	.–
□ □	312	AS: Patrick Roy (G), Mtl.	.65	.65
□ □	313	AS: Ray Bourque, Bos.	.20	.20
□ □	314	AS: Al MacInnis, Cgy.	.20	.20
□ □	315	AS: Mark Messier, Edm.	.20	.20
□ □	316	AS: Luc Robitaille, L.A.	.20	.20
□ □	317	AS: Brett Hull, Stl.	.20	.20
□ □	318	AS: Daren Puppa (G), Buf.	.10	.10
□ □	319	AS: Paul Coffey, Pgh.	.20	.20
□ □	320	AS: Doug Wilson, Chi.	.20	.20
□ □	321	AS: Wayne Gretzky, L.A.	.85	1.00
□ □	322	AS: Brian Bellows, Min.	.10	.10
□ □	323	AS: Cam Neely, Bos.	.20	.20
□ □	324	Bob Essensa (G), Wpg.	.10	.10
□ □	325	Brad Shaw, Hfd.	.10	.10
□ □	326	Geoff Smith, Edm.	.10	.10
□ □	327	Mike Modano, Min.	.25	.25
□ □	328	Rod Brind'Amour, Stl.	.20	.20
□ □	329	Sergei Makarov, Cgy.	.20	.20
□	330	Kip Miller	.10	.–
□	330	Oshawa Generals	.–	.50
□ □	331	Bill Ranford with Cup	.20	.20
□ □	332	Paul Coffey, Pgh.	.20	.20
□ □	333	Mike Gartner, NYR.	.20	.20
□ □	334	Al Iafrate, Tor.	.10	.10
□ □	335	Al MacInnis, Cgy.	.20	.20
□ □	336	Wayne Gretzky, L.A.	.85	1.00
□ □	337	Mario Lemieux, Pgh.	.65	.65
□ □	338	Wayne Gretzky, L.A.	.85	1.00
□ □	339	Steve Yzerman, Det.	.35	.35
□ □	340	Cam Neely, Bos.	.20	.20
□ □	341	Scott Stevens, Wsh.	.10	.10
□ □	342	Esa Tikkanen, Edm.	.10	.10
□ □	343	Jan Erixon, NYR.	.10	.10
□ □	344	Patrick Roy (G), Mtl.	.65	.65
□ □	345	Bill Ranford (G), Edm.	.20	.20
□ □	346	Brett Hull, Stl.	.20	.20
□ □	347	Wayne Gretzky, L.A.	.85	1.00
□ □	348	Jari Kurri, Edm.,	.20	.20
□ □	349	Paul Cavallini, Stl.	.10	.10
□ □	350	Sergei Makarov, Cgy.	.10	.10
□ □	351	Brett Hull, Stl.	.20	.20
□ □	352	Wayne Gretzky, L.A.	.85	1.00
□ □	353	Wayne Gretzky, L.A.	.85	1.00
□ □	354	Patrick Roy (G)/Mike Liut (G)	.50	.50
□ □	355	Gilbert Perreault, Buf.	.25	.25
□ □	356	Bill Barber, Pha.	.25	.25
□ □	357	Fern Flaman, Bos.	.20	.20
□ □	358	Bill Ranford (G), Edm.	.10	.10
□ □	359	Rick Meagher, Stl.	.10	.10
□ □	360	Mark Messier, Edm.	.20	.20
□ □	361	Wayne Gretzky, L.A.	.85	1.00
□ □	362	Sergei Makarov, Cgy.	.10	.10
□ □	363	Ray Bourque, Bos.	.20	.20
□ □	364	Patrick Roy (G), Mtl.	.65	.65
□ □	365	Réjean Lemelin / Andy Moog (G), Bos.	.10	.10
□ □	366	Brett Hull, Stl.	.20	.20
□ □	367	Gord Kluzak, Bos.	.10	.10
□ □	368	Boston Bruins vs. Capitals	.10	.10
□ □	369	Edmonton Oilers vs. Blackhawks	.10	.10
□ □	**370**	**Adam Burt, Hfd., RC**	**.10**	**.10**
□ □	**371**	**Troy Loney, Pgh, RC**	**.10**	**.10**
□ □	**372**	**Dave Chyzowski, NYI., RC**	**.10**	**.10**
□ □	**373**	**Geoff Smith, Edm., RC**	**.10**	**.10**
□ □	374	Stan Smyl, Van.	.10	.10
□ □	375	Gaetan Duchesne, Min.	.10	.10
□ □	376	Bob Murray, Chi., LC	.10	.10
□ □	**377**	**Daniel Shank, Det., RC**	**.10**	**.10**
□ □	378	Tommy Albelin, N.J.	.10	.10
□ □	**379**	**Perry Berezan, Min., RC**	**.10**	**.10**
□ □	380	Ken Linseman, Pha.	.10	.10
□ □	**381**	**Stéphane Matteau, Cgy., RC**	**.10**	**.10**
□ □	**382**	**Mario Thyer, Min., RC**	**.10**	**.10**
□ □	**383**	**Nelson Emerson, Stl., RC**	**.10**	**.10**
□ □	**384**	**Kory Kocur, Det., RC**	**.10**	**.10**
□ □	**385**	**Bob Beers, Bos., RC**	**.10**	**.10**
□ □	**386**	**Jim Hrivnak (G), Wsh., RC**	**.10**	**.10**
□ □	**387**	**Mark Pederson, Mtl., RC**	**.10**	**.10**
□ □	**388**	**Jeff Hackett (G), NYI, RC**	**.25**	**.25**
□ □	**389**	**Eric Weinrich, N.J., RC**	**.10**	**.10**
□ □	**390**	**Steven Rice, NYR., RC**	**.10**	**.10**
□ □	**391**	**Stu Barnes, Wpg., RC**	**.10**	**.10**
□ □	**392**	**Olaf Kolzig (G), Wsh., RC**	**.85**	**1.00**
□ □	**393**	**François Leroux, Edm., RC**	**.10**	**.10**
□ □	**394**	**Adrien Plavsic, Van., RC**	**.10**	**.10**
□ □	**395**	**Michel Mongeau, Stl., RC**	**.10**	**.10**
□ □	**396**	**Rick Corriveau, Stl., RC**	**.10**	**.10**
□ □	**397**	**Wayne Doucet, NYI., RC**	**.10**	**.10**
□ □	**398**	**Mats Sundin, Que., RC**	**1.00**	**1.25**
□ □	**399**	**Murray Baron, Pha., RC**	**.10**	**.10**
□ □	**400**	**Rick Bennett, NYR., RC**	**.10**	**.10**
□ □	**401**	**Jon Morris, N.J., RC**	**.10**	**.10**
□ □	**402**	**Kay Whitmore (G), Hfd., RC**	**.10**	**.10**
□ □	**403**	**Peter Lappin, Min., RC**	**.10**	**.10**
□ □	**404**	**Kris Draper, Wpg. RC**	**.10**	**.10**
□ □	**405**	**Shayne Stevenson, Bos., RC**	**.10**	**.10**
□ □	**406**	**Paul Ysebaert, N.J., RC**	**.10**	**.10**
□ □	**407**	**Jimmy Waite (G), Chi., RC, Err. (catches right)**	**.10**	**.10**
□ □	**407**	**Jimmy Waite (G), Chi., RC, Corrected**	**.10**	**.10**
□ □	**408**	**Cam Russell, Chi., RC**	**.10**	**.10**
□ □	**409**	**Kim Issel, Edm., RC**	**.10**	**.10**
□ □	**410**	**Darrin Shannon, Buf., RC**	**.10**	**.10**
□ □	**411**	**Link Gaetz, Min., RC**	**.10**	**.10**
□ □	**412**	**Craig Fisher, Pha., RC**	**.10**	**.10**
□ □	**413**	**Bruce Hoffort (G), Pha., RC**	**.10**	**.10**
□ □	**414**	**Peter Ing (G), Tor., RC**	**.10**	**.10**
□ □	**415**	**Stéphane Fiset (G), Que., RC**	**.25**	**.25**
□ □	**416**	**Dominic Lavoie, Stl., RC**	**.10**	**.10**
□ □	**417**	**Steve Maltais, Wsh., RC**	**.10**	**.10**
□ □	**418**	**Wes Walz, Bos., RC**	**.10**	**.10**
□ □	**419**	**Terry Yake, Hfd., RC**	**.10**	**.10**
□ □	**420**	**Jamie Leach, Pgh., RC**	**.10**	**.10**
□ □	**421**	**Rob Blake, L.A., RC**	**.25**	**.25**
□ □	**422**	**Andrew Cassels, Mtl., RC**	**.20**	**.20**
□ □	**423**	**Marc Bureau, Cgy., RC**	**.10**	**.10**
□ □	**424**	**Scott Allison, Edm., RC**	**.10**	**.10**
□ □	**425**	**Darryl Sydor, L.A., RC**	**.10**	**.10**
□ □	**426**	**Turner Stevenson, Mtl., RC**	**.10**	**.10**
□ □	**427**	**Brad May, Buf., RC**	**.10**	**.10**
□ □	**428**	**Jaromir Jagr, Pgh., RC**	**2.50**	**3.00**
□ □	**429**	**Shawn Antoski, Van., RC**	**.10**	**.10**
□ □	**430**	**Derian Hatcher, Min., RC**	**.10**	**.10**
□ □	**431**	**Mark Greig, Hfd., RC**	**.10**	**.10**
□ □	**432**	**Scott Scissons, NYI., RC**	**.10**	**.10**
□ □	**433**	**Mike Ricci, Pha., RC**	**.20**	**.20**
□ □	**434**	**Drake Berehowsky, Tor., RC**	**.10**	**.10**
□ □	**435**	**Owen Nolan, Que., RC**	**.50**	**.50**
□ □	**436**	**Keith Primeau, Det., RC**	**.25**	**.25**
□ □	**437**	**Karl Dykhuis, Chi., RC**	**.10**	**.10**
□ □	**438**	**Trevor Kidd (G), Cgy., RC**	**.20**	**.20**
□ □	**439**	**Martin Brodeur (G), N.J., RC**	**4.00**	**5.00**
□ □	**440**	**Eric Lindros, Oshawa Generals, RC**	**12.00**	**16.00**
□ □	B1	Eric Lindros, Oshawa Generals	1.00	1.00
□ □	B2	Eric Lindros, Oshawa Generals	1.00	1.00
□ □	B3	Eric Lindros, Oshawa Generals	1.00	1.00
□ □	B4	Eric Lindros, Oshawa Generals	1.00	1.00
□ □	B5	Eric Lindros, Oshawa Generals	1.00	1.00

HOCKEY'S 100 HOTTEST AND RISING STARS

Score renumbered 100 cards from the 1990 - 91 regular issue set for Publications International, Ltd. They included these cards in Value Pack which also contained a Hottest and Rising Star book.

Imprint:

Complete Set (100 cards): **12.00**

Common Card: **.15**

Album **3.00**

	No.	Player	NRMT-MT
□	1	Wayne Gretzky, L.A.	3.50
□	2	Craig Simpson, Edm.	.15
□	3	Brian Bellows, Min.	.15
□	4	Steve Yzerman, Det	1.50
□	5	Bernie Nicholls, NYR.	.15
□	6	Esa Tikkanen, Edm.	.15
□	7	Joe Sakic, Que.	1.00
□	8	Thomas Steen, Wpg.	.15
□	9	Chris Chelios, Mtl.	.50
□	10	Patrik Sundstrom, N.J.	.15
□	11	Rod Langway, Wsh.	.15
□	12	Scott Young, Hfd.	.15
□	13	Mike Ramsey, Buf.	.15
□	14	Ron Hextall (G), Pha.	.35
□	15	Steve Duchesne, L.A.	.15
□	16	Trevor Linden, Van.	.35
□	17	Sean Burke (G), N.J.	.35
□	18	Pat Verbeek, Hfd.	.15
□	19	Brent Sutter, NYI.	.15
□	20	Gary Leeman, Tor.	.15
□	21	Shawn Burr, Det.	.15
□	22	Dale Hawerchuk, Wpg.	.35
□	23	Mike Vernon (G), Cgy.	.35
□	24	Dan Quinn, Van.	.15
□	25	Patrick Roy (G), Mtl.	2.50
□	26	Daren Puppa (G), Buf.	.15
□	27	Gino Cavallini, Stl.	.15
□	28	Jimmy Carson, Det.	.15
□	29	David Ellett, Wpg.	.15
□	30	Steve Thomas, Chi.	.15
□	31	Jeremy Roenick, Chi.	.75
□	32	Mike Liut (G), Wsh.	.15
□	33	Mark Messier, Edm.	.75
□	34	Mario Lemieux, Pgh.	2.50
□	35	Ray Bourque, Bos.	.75
□	36	Al MacInnis, Cgy.	.35
□	37	Ron Francis, Hfd.	.50

	No.	Player	NRMT-MT
☐	38	Stéphane Richer, Mtl.	.15
☐	39	Bill Ranford (G), Edm.	.35
☐	40	Rick Tocchet, Pha.	.15
☐	41	Adam Oates, Stl.	.50
☐	42	Kevin Hatcher, Wsh.	.15
☐	43	Guy Carbonneau, Mtl.	.15
☐	44	Curtis Leschyshyn, Que.	.15
☐	45	Joe Nieuwendyk, Cgy.	.35
☐	46	Kirk McLean (G), Van.	.35
☐	47	Vincent Damphousse, Tor.	.35
☐	48	Peter Stastny, N.J.	.15
☐	49	Rick Zombo, Det.	.15
☐	50	Mark Fitzpatrick (G), NYI.	.15
☐	51	Rob Brown, Pgh.	.15
☐	52	Dave Gagner, Min.	.15
☐	53	Pierre Turgeon, Buf.	.35
☐	54	Glenn Anderson, Edm.	.15
☐	55	Kelly Hrudey (G), L.A.	.15
☐	56	Gord Murphy, Pha.	.15
☐	57	Glen Wesley, Bos.	.15
☐	58	Craig Janney, Bos.	.15
☐	59	Denis Savard, Chi.	.35
☐	60	Mike Gartner, NYR.	.35
☐	61	Steve Larmer, Chi.	.35
☐	62	Andy Moog (G), Bos.	.35
☐	63	Phil Housley, Buf.	.15
☐	64	Ulf Samuelsson, Hfd.	.15
☐	65	Paul Coffey, Pgh.	.35
☐	66	Luc Robitaille, L.A.	.35
☐	67	Cam Neely, Bos.	.35
☐	68	Doug Wilson, Chi.	.35
☐	69	Doug Gilmour, Cgy.	.50
☐	70	Jeff Norton, NYI.	.15
☐	71	Kirk Muller, N.J.	.15
☐	72	Aaron Broten, Min.	.15
☐	73	John Cullen, Pgh.	.15
☐	74	Craig Ludwig, Mtl.	.15
☐	75	Kevin Lowe, Edm.	.15
☐	76	John Vanbiesbrouck (G), NYR.	1.00
☐	77	Tim Kerr, Pha.	.15
☐	78	Gerard Gallant, Det.	.15
☐	79	Tomas Sandström, L.A.	.15
☐	80	Jon Casey (G), Min.	.15
☐	81	Mark Recchi, Pgh.	1.25
☐	82	Scott Stevens, Wsh.	.15
☐	83	John MacLean, N.J.	.15
☐	84	James Patrick, NYR.	.15
☐	85	Al Iafrate, Tor.	.15
☐	86	Pat Elynuik, Wpg.	.15
☐	87	Dave Andreychuk, Buf.	.35
☐	88	Joe Mullen, Cgy.	.15
☐	89	Ed Olczyk, Tor.	.15
☐	90	Kevin Dineen, Hfd.	.15
☐	91	Shayne Corson, Mtl.	.35
☐	92	Marke Howe, Pha.	.35
☐	93	Brian Leetch, NYR.	.75
☐	94	Dino Ciccarelli, Wsh.	.35
☐	95	Pat LaFontaine, NYI.	.35
☐	96	Guy Lafleur, Que.	.75
☐	97	Mike Modano, Min.	.75
☐	98	Rod Brind'Amour, Stl.	.35
☐	99	Sergei Makarov, Cgy.	.35
☐	100	Brett Hull, Stl.	.75

ROOKIE AND TRADED

Insert Set (110 cards): 12.00
Common Player: .10

	No.	Player	NRMT-MT
☐	1T	Denis Savard, Mtl.	.25
☐	2T	Dale Hawerchuk, Buf.	.25
☐	3T	Phil Housley, Wpg.	.10
☐	4T	Chris Chelios, Chi.	.50
☐	5T	Geoff Courtnall, Stl.	.10
☐	6T	Peter Zezel, Wsh.	.10
☐	7T	Joe Mullen, Pgh.	.10
☐	8T	Craig Ludwig, NYI.	.10
☐	9T	Claude Lemieux, N.J.	.10
☐	10T	Bobby Holik, Hfd.	.10
☐	11T	Peter Ing (G), Tor.	.10
☐	12T	Rod Buskas, L.A.	.10
☐	13T	Tim Sweeney, Cgy.	.10
☐	14T	Don Barber, Wpg.	.10
☐	15T	Ray Ferraro, NYI.	.10
☐	16T	Peter Taglianetti, Min.	.10
☐	17T	Johan Garpenlov, Det.	.10
☐	18T	Kevin Miller, NYR.	.10
☐	19T	Frantisek Musil, Cgy.	.10
☐	**20T**	**Sergei Fedorov, Det., RC**	**4.00**
☐	21T	Aaron Broten, Tor.	.10
☐	22T	Chris Nilan, Bos.	.10
☐	23T	Gerald Diduck, Mtl.	.10
☐	24T	Marc Habscheid, Det.	.10
☐	25T	Glen Featherstone, Stl.	.10
☐	26T	Mikko Makela, Buf.	.10
☐	27T	Paul Stanton, Pgh.	.10
☐	28T	Mark Osborne, Wpg.	.10
☐	29T	Dave Tippett, Wsh.	.10
☐	**30T**	**Robert Reichel, Cgy., RC**	**.35**
☐	31T	Grant Jennings, Hfd.	.10
☐	32T	Troy Gamble (G), Van.	.10
☐	33T	Mark Janssens, NYR.	.10
☐	34T	Brian Propp, Min.	.10
☐	35T	Donald Dufresne, Mtl.	.10
☐	36T	Martin Hostak, Pha.	.10
☐	37T	Brad McCrimmon, Det.	.10
☐	38T	Dave Lowry, Stl.	.10
☐	39T	Anatoli Semenov, Edm.	.10
☐	40T	Scott Stevens, Stl.	.35
☐	41T	Paul Broten, NYR.	.10
☐	42T	Carey Wilson, Hfd.	.10
☐	43T	Troy Crowder, N.J.	.10
☐	44T	Vladimir Ruzicka, Bos.	.10
☐	45T	Rich Pilon, NYI.	.10
☐	46T	John McIntyre, L.A.	.10
☐	47T	Mike Krushelnyski, Tor.	.10
☐	48T	Dave Snuggerud, Buf.	.10
☐	49T	Robert McGill, Chi.	.10
☐	50T	Petr Nedved, Van.	.50
☐	51T	Ed Olczyk, Wpg.	.10
☐	52T	Doug Crossman, Hfd.	.10
☐	53T	Mikhail Tatarinov, Wsh.	.10
☐	54T	Michel Petit, Tor.	.10
☐	55T	Frank Pietrangelo (G), Pgh.	.10
☐	56T	Brian MacLellan, Cgy.	.10
☐	57T	Paul Fenton, Tor.	.10
☐	58T	Eric Desjardins, Mtl.	.35
☐	59T	Mike Craig, Min.	.10
☐	60T	Mike Ricci, Pha.	.35
☐	61T	Harold Snepsts, Stl.	.10
☐	62T	John Byce, Bos.	.10
☐	63T	Laurie Boschman, N.J.	.10
☐	64T	Randy Velischek, Que.	.10
☐	65T	Robert Kron, Van.	.10
☐	66T	Jocelyn Lemieux, Chi.	.10
☐	67T	David Ellett, Tor.	.10
☐	68T	Scott Arniel, Wpg.	.10
☐	69T	Doug Smail, Min.	.10
☐	70T	Jaromir Jagr, Pgh.	5.00
☐	**71T**	**Peter Bondra, Wsh., RC**	**2.00**
☐	72T	Paul Cyr, Hfd.	.10
☐	73T	Daniel Berthiaume (G), L.A.	.10
☐	74T	Lee Norwood, N.J.	.10
☐	75T	Bobby Smith, Min.	.10
☐	76T	Kris King, NYR.	.10
☐	77T	Mark Hunter, Cgy.	.10
☐	78T	Brian Hayward (G), Min.	.10
☐	79T	Greg Hawgood, Edm.	.10
☐	80T	Owen Nolan, Que.	.50
☐	81T	Cliff Ronning, Stl.	.10
☐	82T	Zdeno Ciger, N.J.	.10
☐	83T	Gord Roberts, Pgh.	.10
☐	84T	Rick Green, Det.	.10
☐	85T	Ken Hodge, Bos.	.10
☐	86T	Derek King, NYI.	.10
☐	87T	Brent Gilchrist, Mtl.	.10
☐	88T	Eric Lindros, Can.	6.00
☐	89T	Steve Bozek, Van.	.10
☐	90T	Keith Primeau, Det.	.35
☐	91T	Roger Johansson, Cgy.	.10
☐	92T	Wayne Presley, Chi.	.10
☐	93T	Ilkka Sinisalo, Min.	.10
☐	94T	Mario Marois, Stl.	.10
☐	95T	Ken Linseman, Edm.	.10
☐	96T	Greg Brown, Buf.	.10
☐	97T	Ray Sheppard, NYR.	.10
☐	98T	Mike Lalor, Wsh.	.10
☐	99T	Norman Lacombe, Pha.	.10
☐	100T	Mats Sundin, Que.	2.00
☐	101T	Jergus Baca, Hfd.	.10
☐	102T	Mike Keane, Mtl.	.10
☐	103T	Ed Belfour (G), Chi.	2.00
☐	104T	Mark Hardy, NYR.	.10
☐	105T	Dave Capuano, Van.	.10
☐	106T	Bryan Trottier, Pgh.	.25
☐	107T	Per Olav Djoos, Det.	.10
☐	108T	Sylvain Turgeon, Mtl.	.10
☐	109T	David Reid, Tor.	.10
☐	110T	Wayne Gretzky, L.A.	2.50

1990 - 91 YOUNG SUPERSTARS

Imprint: © 1990 SCORE
Complete Set (40 cards): 8.00

	No.	Player	NRMT-MT
☐	1	Pierre Turgeon, Buf.	.25
☐	2	Brian Leetch, NYR.	.60
☐	3	Daniel Marois, Tor.	.15
☐	4	Peter Sidorkiewicz (G), Hfd.	.15
☐	5	Rob Brown, Pgh.	.15
☐	6	Theoren Fleury, Cgy.	.50
☐	7	Mats Sundin, Que.	.85
☐	8	Glen Wesley, Bos.	.15
☐	9	Sergei Fedorov, Det.	.85
☐	10	Joe Sakic, Que.	1.50
☐	11	Sean Burke (G), N.J.	.25
☐	12	Dave Chyzowski, NYI.	.15
☐	13	Gord Murphy, Pha.	.15
☐	14	Scott Young, Hfd.	.15
☐	15	Curtis Joseph (G), Stl.	1.00
☐	16	Darren Turcotte, NYR.	.15
☐	17	Kevin Stevens, Pgh.	.15
☐	18	Mathieu Schneider, Mtl.	.15
☐	19	Trevor Linden, Van.	.35
☐	20	Mike Modano, Min.	.85
☐	21	Martin Gelinas, Edm.	.25
☐	22	Stéphane Fiset (G), Que.	.25
☐	23	Brendan Shanahan, N.J.	1.00
☐	24	Jeremy Roenick, Chi.	.50
☐	25	John Druce, Wsh.	.15
☐	26	Alexander Mogilny, Buf.	.50
☐	27	Mike Richter (G), NYR..	.50
☐	28	Pat Elynuik, Wpg.	.15
☐	29	Robert Reichel, Cgy.	.25
☐	30	Craig Janney, Bos.	.15
☐	31	Rod Brind'Amour, Stl.	.25
☐	32	Mark Fitzpatrick (G), NYI.	.15
☐	33	Tony Granato, L.A.	.15
☐	34	Bobby Holik, Hfd.	.15
☐	35	Mark Recchi, Pgh.	.25
☐	36	Owen Nolan, Que.	.25
☐	37	Petr Nedved, Van.	.25
☐	38	Keith Primeau, Det.	.25
☐	39	Mike Ricci, Pha.	.15
☐	40	Eric Lindros, Osh. Gen.	4.00

1990 - 91 SEMIC ELISTERIEN STICKERS

Sticker Size: 3" x 2 1/8"
Imprint:
Complete Set (294 stickers): 40.00
Common Player: .20
Album: 6.00

	No.	Player	NRMT-MT
☐	1	MoDo Logo	.20
☐	2	MoDo Photo	.20
☐	3	Fredrik Andersson	.20
☐	4	Goran Arnmark	.20
☐	5	Ari Salo	.20
☐	6	Anders Berglund	.20
☐	7	Lars Jansson	.20
☐	8	Hans Lodin	.20
☐	9	Ove Pettersson	.20
☐	10	Jorgen Eriksson	.20
☐	11	Tony Olofsson	.20
☐	12	Tomas Nanzen	.20
☐	13	Michael Jhalm	.20
☐	14	Erik Holmberg	.20
☐	15	Urban Nordin	.20
☐	16	Kent Lantz	.20
☐	17	Lars Bystrom	.20
☐	18	Jens Ohman	.20
☐	19	Ulf Odmark	.20
☐	20	Mikael Stahl	.20
☐	21	Ingemar Strom	.20
☐	22	Tommy Pettersson	.20
☐	23	Markus Naslund	.50
☐	24	Per Wallin	.20
☐	25	Vastra Frolunda Logo	.20
☐	26	Vastra Frolunda Photo	.20
☐	27	Ake Lilljebjorn	.20
☐	28	Hakan Algotsson	.20
☐	29	Leif Carlsson	.20
☐	30	Jonas Heed	.20
☐	31	Hakan Nordin	.20
☐	32	Joacim Esbjors	.20
☐	33	Stefan Axelsson	.20
☐	34	Stefan Larsson	.20
☐	35	Jorgen Palm	.20
☐	36	Oscar Ackertstrom	.20
☐	37	Patrik Carnback	.20
☐	38	Mats Lundstrom	.20
☐	39	Niklas Andersson	.20
☐	40	Serge Boisvert	.20
☐	41	Arto Sirvio	.20
☐	42	Terho Koskela	.20
☐	43	Kari Jaako	.20
☐	44	Peter Berndtsson	.20
☐	45	Mikael Andersson	.20
☐	46	Per Edlund	.20
☐	47	Jonas Andersson	.20
☐	48	Johan Witehall	.20
☐	49	Sodertalje Logo	.20
☐	50	Sodertalje Photo	.20
☐	51	Reino Sundberg	.20
☐	52	Jari Luom	.20
☐	53	Mats Kilstrom	.20
☐	54	Stefan Jonsson	.20
☐	55	Peter Ekroth	.20
☐	56	Mats Waltin	.20
☐	57	Jan Bergman	.20
☐	58	Hans Pettersson	.20
☐	59	Stefan Nyman	.20
☐	60	Conny Jansson	.20
☐	61	Thomas Eklund	.20
☐	62	Otakar Hascak	.20
☐	63	Morgan Samuelsson	.20
☐	64	Reine Landgren	.20
☐	65	Bjorn Carlsson	.20
☐	66	Ola Andersson	.20
☐	67	Thomas Eriksson	.20
☐	68	Bert-Olav Karlsson	.20
☐	69	Ola Rosander	.20
☐	70	Stefan Olsson	.20
☐	71	Scott Moore	.20
☐	72	Anders Frykbo	.20
☐	73	AIK Logo	.20
☐	74	AIK Photo	.20
☐	75	Thomas Ostlund	.20
☐	76	Sami Lindstahl	.20
☐	77	Borje Salming	2.00
☐	78	Mats Thelin	.20
☐	79	Petter Salsten	.20
☐	80	Petri Liimatainen	.20
☐	81	Rikard Franzen	.20
☐	82	Stefan Claesson	.20
☐	83	Torbjorn Mattsson	.20
☐	84	Daniel Jardemyre	.20
☐	85	Robert Burakovsky	.20
☐	86	Peter Gradin	.20
☐	87	Thomas Bjuhr	.20
☐	88	Heinz Ehlers	.20
☐	89	Tommy Lehmann	.20
☐	90	Peter Hammarstrom	.20
☐	91	Patric Kjellberg	.20
☐	92	Patric Englund	.20
☐	93	Mats Lindberg	.20
☐	94	Peter Johansson	.20
☐	95	Kristian Gahn	.20
☐	96	Niklas Sundblad	.20
☐	97	Erik Andersson	.20
☐	98	HV 71 Logo	.20
☐	99	HV 71 Photo	.20
☐	100	Peter Aslin	.20
☐	101	Kenneth Johansson	.20
☐	102	Arto Ruotanen	.20
☐	103	Fredrik Stillman	.20
☐	104	Lars Ivarsson	.20
☐	105	Klas Heed	.20
☐	106	Per Gustafsson	.75
☐	107	Mathias Svedberg	.20
☐	108	Tommy Fritz	.20
☐	109	Mats Nilsson	.20
☐	110	Peter Eriksson	.20
☐	111	Risto Kurkinen	.20
☐	112	Thomas Ljungbergh	.20
☐	113	Ove Thornberg	.20
☐	114	Mats Loov	.20
☐	115	Eddy Ericsson	.20
☐	116	Stefan Ornskog	.20
☐	117	Patrik Ross	.20
☐	118	Stefan Persson	.20
☐	119	Dennis Strom	.20
☐	120	Peter Ekelund	.20
☐	121	Jonas Jonsson	.20
☐	122	Torbjorn Persson	.20
☐	123	Malmo IF Logo	.20
☐	124	Malmo IF Photo	.20
☐	125	Peter Lindmark	.20
☐	126	Roger Nordström (G)	.20
☐	127	Timo Blomqvist	.20
☐	128	Peter Andersson	.20
☐	129	Mats Lusth	.20
☐	130	Johan Salle	.20
☐	131	Roger Ohman	.20
☐	132	Anders Svensson	.20
☐	133	Peter Imhauser	.20
☐	134	Johan Norgren	.20
☐	135	Raimo Helminen	.20
☐	136	Peter Sundstrom	.20
☐	137	Mats Hallin	.20
☐	138	Matti Pauna	.20
☐	139	Patrik Gustavsson	.20
☐	140	Hakan Ahlund	.20
☐	141	Daniel Rydmark	.20
☐	142	Lennart Hermansson	.20
☐	143	Carl-Erik Larsson	.20
☐	144	Rick Erdall	.20
☐	145	Bo Svanberg	.20
☐	146	Frerik Johansson	.20
☐	147	Jens Hemstrom	.20
☐	149	Vasteras IK Logo	.20
☐	150	Vasteras IK Photo	.20
☐	150	Mats Ytter (G)	.20
☐	151	Par Hellenberg	.20
☐	152	Nicklas Lidström	5.00
☐	153	Leif Rohlin	.35
☐	154	Peter Popovic	.35
☐	155	Jan Karlsson	.20
☐	156	Henrik Andersson	.20
☐	157	Tore Lindgren	.20
☐	158	Peter Jacobsson	.20
☐	159	Pierre Ivarsson	.20
☐	160	Jan Eriksson	.20
☐	161	Goran Sjoberg	.20
☐	162	Mishat Fahrutdinov	.20
☐	163	Anders Berglund	.20
☐	164	Claes Lindblom	.20
☐	165	Jorgen Holmberg	.20
☐	166	Stefan Hellkvist	.20
☐	167	Tomas Strandberg	.20
☐	168	Bjorn Akerblom	.20
☐	169	Ronny Hansen	.20
☐	170	Fredrik Nilsson	.20
☐	171	Patrik Juhlin	.20
☐	172	Henrik Nilsson	.20
☐	173	Brynas IF Logo	.20
☐	174	Brynas IF Photo	.20
☐	175	Michael Sundlov	.20
☐	176	Lars Eriksson	.20
☐	177	Tommy Sjodin	.35
☐	178	Brad Berry	.20
☐	179	Niklas Gallstedt	.20
☐	180	Mikael Lindman	.20
☐	181	Urban Molander	.20
☐	182	Jan-Erik Stormqvist	.20
☐	183	Stefan Klockare	.20
☐	184	Tommy Melkersson	.20
☐	185	Anders Carlsson	.20
☐	186	Patrik Erickson	.20
☐	187	Anders Huuss	.20
☐	188	Jan Larsson	.20
☐	189	Peter Larsson	.20
☐	190	Anders Gozzi	.20
☐	191	Joakim Persson	.20
☐	192	Peter Gustafsson	.20
☐	193	Peter Eriksson	.20
☐	194	Johan Brummer	.20
☐	195	Tomas Olund	.20
☐	196	Kenneth Andersson	.20
☐	197	Leksands IF Logo	.20
☐	198	Leksands IF Photo	.20
☐	199	O. Sundstrom	.20
☐	200	Lars-Erik Lord	.20
☐	201	Jonas Leven	.20
☐	202	Tomas Jonsson	.20
☐	203	Ricard Persson	.20
☐	204	Per Lundell	.20
☐	205	Tomas Nord	.20
☐	206	Mattias Andersson	.20
☐	207	Henric Bjorkman	.20
☐	208	Orjan Lindmark	.20
☐	209	Tomas Forslund	.35
☐	210	Niklas Eriksson	.20
☐	211	Peter Lundmark	.20
☐	212	Per-Olof Carlsson	.20
☐	213	Marcus Thuresson	.20
☐	214	Jens Nielsen	.20
☐	215	Kenneth Soderlund	.20
☐	216	Markus Akerblom	.20
☐	217	Ronny Reichenberg	.20
☐	218	Fredrik Olsson	.20
☐	219	Niklas Hillblom	.20
☐	220	Magnus Gustafsson	.20
☐	221	Fredrik Jax	.20
☐	222	Lulea HF Logo	.20
☐	223	Lulea HF Photo	.20
☐	224	Robert Skoog	.20
☐	225	Tomas Javeblad	.20
☐	226	Timo Jutila	.35
☐	227	Per Ljusterang	.20
☐	228	Lars Modig	.20
☐	229	Torbjorn Lindberg	.20
☐	230	Tomas Lilja	.20
☐	231	Osmo Soutukorva	.20
☐	232	Jan-Ove Mettavainio	.20
☐	233	Roger Akerstrom	.20
☐	234	Johan Stromvall	.20
☐	235	Ulf Sandstrom	.20
☐	236	Lars-Gunnar Pettersson	.20
☐	237	Pauli Jarvinen	.20
☐	238	Lars Hurtig	.20
☐	239	Tomas Berglund	.20
☐	240	Stefan Nilsson	.20
☐	241	Mikael Renberg	4.00
☐	242	Hans Hjalmar	.20
☐	243	Jens Hellgren	.20
☐	244	Lars Edstrom	.20
☐	245	Robert Nordberg	.20
☐	246	Farjestads BK Logo	.20

	No.	Player	Price
☐	247	Farjestads BK Photo	.20
☐	248	Anders Bergman	.20
☐	249	Jorgen Ryden	.20
☐	250	Patrik Haltia	.20
☐	251	Tommy Samuelsson	.20
☐	252	Jim Leavins	.20
☐	253	Peter Hasselblad	.20
☐	254	Jesper Duus	.20
☐	255	Mattis Olsson	.20
☐	256	Greger Artursson	.20
☐	257	Jacob Karlsson	.20
☐	258	Thomas Rhodin	.20
☐	259	Bengt Gustafsson	.35
☐	260	Hakan Loob	.20
☐	261	Thomas Rundqvist	.20
☐	262	Kjell Dahlin	.25
☐	263	Magnus Roupe	.20
☐	264	Jan Ingman	.20
☐	265	Lars Karlsson	.20
☐	266	Mikael Holmberg	.20
☐	267	Staffan Lundh	.20
☐	268	Peter Ottosson	.20
☐	269	Jonas Hoglund	.20
☐	270	Clas Eriksson	.20
☐	271	Djurgardens IF Logo	.20
☐	272	Djurgardens IF Photo	.20
☐	273	Tommy Söderström (G)	.75
☐	274	Joakim Persson	.20
☐	275	Thomas Eriksson	.20
☐	276	Arto Blomsten	.20
☐	277	Kenneth Kennholt	.20
☐	278	Christian Due-Boje	.20
☐	279	Orvar Stambert	.20
☐	280	Per Nygards	.20
☐	281	Marcus Ragnarsson	.50
☐	282	Thomas Johansson	.20
☐	283	Ronnie Pettersson	.20
☐	284	Charles Berglund	.20
☐	285	Jan Viktorsson	.20
☐	286	Jens Ohling	.20
☐	287	Ola Josefsson	.20
☐	288	Peter Nilsson	.20
☐	289	Anders Jonsson	.20
☐	290	Hakan Sodergren	.20
☐	291	Stefan Gustavson	.20
☐	292	Magnus Jansson	.20
☐	293	Mikael Johansson	.20
☐	294	Johan Lindstedt	.20

1990 - 91 7TH INNING SKETCH OHL

Face: Four colour, white border
Back: Four colour, Number, Resume, Position
Imprint: 1991 7th Inning Sketch Printed in Canada
Complete Set (400 cards): 25.00
Common Player: .10
Promo Card (Eric Lindros, #1): 10.00

	No.	Player	NRMT-MT
☐	1	Eric Lindros, Oshawa	5.00
☐	2	Greg Dreveny (G), Belleville, Error	.15
☐	3	TC: Chris Varga, Belleville	.10
☐	4	Richard Fatrola, Belleville, Error	.10
☐	5	Craig Fraser, Belleville	.10
☐	6	Robert Frayn, Belleville	.10
☐	7	Brent Gretzky, Belleville	.50
☐	8	Jake Grimes, Belleville	.10
☐	9	Darren Hurley, Belleville	.10
☐	10	Rick Marshall, Belleville	.10
☐	11	TC: Keli Corpse, Kingston	.10
☐	12	Darren McCarty, Belleville	1.25
☐	13	Derek Morin, Belleville	.10
☐	14	Sean O'Reilly, Belleville	.10
☐	15	Rob Pearson, Oshawa, Error (Belleville Bulls)	.25
☐	15	Rob Pearson, Oshawa, Corrected	.25
☐	16	John Porco, Belleville	.10
☐	17	Ken Rowbotham, Belleville	.10
☐	18	Ken Ruddick, Belleville	.10
☐	19	Jim Sonmez, Belleville	.10
☐	20	Brad Teichmann (G), Belleville	.15
☐	21	Chris Varga, Belleville	.10
☐	22	TC: Jeremy Stevenson, Cornwall	.10
☐	23	Larry Mavety, Coach, Belleville	.10
☐	24	Rival Fullum, Cornwall, Variation	.10
☐	25	Nathan Lafayette, Cornwall, Variation	.50
☐	26	Darren Bell, Cornwall	.10
☐	27	Craig Brocklehurst, Cornwall	.10
☐	28	Shawn Caplice, Cornwall	.10
☐	29	Mike Cavanagh, Cornwall	.10
☐	30	Jason Cirone, Cornwall	.10
☐	31	Chris Clancy, Cornwall	.10
☐	32	Mark DeSantis, Cornwall	.10
☐	33	Rob Dykeman (G), Cornwall	.15
☐	34	Shayne Gaffar, Cornwall	.10
☐	35	Ilpo Kauhanen (G), Cornwall	.15
☐	36	Rob Kinghan, Cornwall	.25
☐	37	Dave Lemay, Cornwall	.10
☐	38	Guy Leveque, Cornwall	.10
☐	39	Matt McGuffin, Cornwall	.10
☐	40	Marcus Middleton, Cornwall	.10
☐	41	Thomas Nemeth, Cornwall	.10
☐	42	Rod Pasma, Cornwall	.10
☐	43	Richard Raymond, Cornwall, Error	.10
☐	44	Jeff Reid, Cornwall	.10
☐	45	Jerry Ribble, Cornwall	.10
☐	46	Jean-Alain Schneider, Cornwall	.10
☐	47	John Slaney, Cornwall	.25
☐	48	Jeremy Stevenson, Cornwall	.10
☐	49	Ryan VandenBussche	.50
☐	50	Marc Crawford, Coach, Cornwall	1.00
☐	51	Tony Bella, Kingston	.10
☐	52	Drake Berehowsky, Kingston, Error	.25
☐	53	Jason Chipman (G), Kingston	.15
☐	54	Tony Cimellaro, Kingston	.10
☐	55	Keli Corpse, Kingston	.10
☐	56	Mike Dawson, Kingston, Error	.10
☐	56	Mike Dawson, Kingston, Corrected	.10
☐	57	Sean Gauthier(G), Kingston	.15
☐	58	Fred Goltz, Kingston, Error	.10
☐	59	Gord Harris, Kingston	.10
☐	60	Tony Iob, Kingston	.10
☐	61	John Bernie, Kingston	.10
☐	62	Dale Junkin, Kingston	.10
☐	63	Nathan Lafayette, Kingston	.50
☐	64	Blake Martin, Kingston	.10
☐	65	Mark McCague, Kingston	.10
☐	66	Bob McKillop, Kingston	.10
☐	67	Justin Morrison, Kingston	.10
☐	68	Bill Robinson, Kingston	.10
☐	69	Joel Sandie, Kingston	.10
☐	70	Kevin King, Kingston	.10
☐	71	Dave Stewart, Kingston	.10
☐	72	Joel Washkurak, Kingston	.10
☐	73	Brock Woods, Kingston	.10
☐	74	Randy Hall, Coach, Kingston	.10
☐	75	John Vary, Kingston, Error	.10
☐	75	John Vary, Kingston, Corrected	.10
☐	76	Peter Ambroziak, Ottawa	.25
☐	77	Troy Binnie, Ottawa	.10
☐	78	Curt Bowen, Ottawa	.25
☐	79	Andrew Brodie, Ottawa	.10
☐	80	TC: Grant Marshall, Ottawa	.10
☐	81	Greg Clancy, Ottawa	.10
☐	82	Jerrett DeFazio, Ottawa	.10
☐	83	Kris Draper, Ottawa	.75
☐	84	Wade Gibson, Ottawa	.10
☐	85	Ryan Kuwabara, Ottawa	.10
☐	86	Joni Lehto, Ottawa	.10
☐	87	Donald MacPherson, Ottawa	.10
☐	88	Grant Marshall, Ottawa	.50
☐	89	Pete McGlynn (G), Ottawa	.15
☐	90	Maurice O'Brien, Ottawa	.10
☐	91	Jeff Ricciardi, Ottawa	.10
☐	92	Brett Seguin, Ottawa	.10
☐	93	Lenny DeVuono, Ottawa, Error	.10
☐	93	Lenny DeVuono, Ottawa, Corrected	.10
☐	94	Gerry Skrypec, Ottawa	.10
☐	95	Chris Snell, Ottawa	.25
☐	96	Jason Snow, Ottawa	.10
☐	97	Sean Spencer (G), Ottawa	.15
☐	98	Brad Spry, Ottawa	.10
☐	99	Matt Stone, Ottawa	.10
☐	100	Brian Kilrea, Coach, Ottawa	.50
☐	101	Kevin Butt (G), Detroit, Error	.15
☐	102	Glen Craig, Detroit	.10
☐	103	Paul Doherty, Detroit	.10
☐	104	Mark Donahue, Detroit	.10
☐	105	Jeff Gardiner, Detroit	.10
☐	106	Trent Gleason, Detroit	.10
☐	107	Troy Gleason, Detroit	.10
☐	108	Mark Lawrence, Detroit	.25
☐	109	Trevor McIvor, Detroit, Error	.10
☐	110	Paul Mitton, Detroit	.10
☐	111	David Myles, Detroit	.10
☐	112	Jeff Nolan, Detroit, Error	.10
☐	113	Rob Papineau, Detroit	.10
☐	114	Pat Peake, Detroit, Error	.50
☐	114	Pat Peake, Detroit, Corrected	.50
☐	115	Chris Phelps, Detroit	.10
☐	116	John Pinches, Detroit	.10
☐	117	Jamie Shea (G), Detroit, Error	.15
☐	117	Jamie Shea (G), Detroit, Corrected	.15
☐	118	Jamie Sheehan, Detroit, Error	.10
☐	118	Jamie Sheehan, Detroit, Corrected	.10
☐	119	John Stios, Detroit, Error	.10
☐	120	Tom Sullivan, Detroit	.10
☐	121	John Wynne, Detroit	.10
☐	122	Robert Thorpe, North Bay, Error	.10
☐	123	David Benn, Detroit	.10
☐	124	Andy Weidenbach, Coach, Detroit, Error	.10
☐	125	TC: Pat Peake, Detroit	.25
☐	126	David Anderson, London	.10
☐	127	Sean Basilio (G), London, Error	.15
☐	128	Brent Brownlee (G), London	.15
☐	129	Rick Corriveau, London	.10
☐	130	Derrick Crane, London	.10
☐	131	Chris Crombie, London	.10
☐	132	Louie DeBrusk, London	.50
☐	133	Mark Guy, London	.10
☐	134	Brett Marietti, London	.10
☐	135	Steve Martell, London	.10
☐	136	Scott McKay, London	.10
☐	137	Aaron Nagy, London	.10
☐	138	Brett Nicol, London	.10
☐	139	Barry Potomski, London	.25
☐	140	Dennis Purdie, London	.10
☐	141	Kelly Reed, London	.10
☐	142	Gregory Ryan, London	.10
☐	143	Brad Smyth, London	.50
☐	144	Nick Stajduhar, London	.25
☐	145	John Tanner (G), London, Error	.15
☐	146	Chris Taylor, London	.25
☐	147	Mark Visheau, London	.10
☐	148	Gary Agnew, Coach, London, Error	.10
☐	149	TC: Mark Visheau, London	.10
☐	150	TC: Jarrett Reid, Sault Ste. Marie	.10
☐	151	David Babcock, Sault Ste. Marie	.10
☐	152	Drew Bannister, Sault Ste. Marie	.50
☐	153	Bob Boughner, Sault Ste. Marie	.10
☐	154	Joe Busillo, Sault Ste. Marie, Error	.10
☐	155	Mike DeCoff, Sault Ste. Marie	.10
☐	156	Jason Denomme, Sault Ste. Marie	.10
☐	157	Adam Foote, Sault Ste. Marie	1.25
☐	158	Kevin Hodson (G), Sault Ste. Marie	.75
☐	159	Shaun Imber, Sault Ste. Marie, Error	.10
☐	160	Ralph Intranuovo, Sault Ste. Marie	.25
☐	161	Kevin King, Sault Ste. Marie	.10
☐	162	Rick Kowalsky, Sault Ste. Marie	.10
☐	163	Chris Kraemer, Sault Ste. Marie, Error	.10
☐	164	Denny Lambert, Sault Ste. Marie	.50
☐	165	Mike Lenarduzzi (G), Sault Ste. Marie	.25
☐	166	Tom MacDonald, Sault Ste. Marie	.10
☐	167	Mark Matier, Sault Ste. Marie	.10
☐	168	David Matsos, Sault Ste. Marie	.10
☐	169	Colin Miller, Sault Ste. Marie	.10
☐	170	Perry Pappas, Sault Ste. Marie	.10
☐	171	Jarret Reid, Sault Ste. Marie	.10
☐	172	Kevin Reid, Sault Ste. Marie	.10
☐	173	Brad Tiley, Sault Ste. Marie, Error	.10
☐	174	TC: Todd Warriner, Windsor	.25

	No.	Player	Nrmt-mt
☐	175	Wade Whitten, Sault Ste. Marie	.10
☐	176	Ted Nolan, Sault Ste. Marie	.50
☐	177	Sean Burns, Windsor	.10
☐	178	Jason Cirone, Windsor, Error	.10
☐	179	John Copley, Windsor	.10
☐	180	Tyler Ertel, Windsor	.10
☐	181	Brian Forestell, Windsor	.10
☐	182	Rival Fullum, Windsor, Error	.10
☐	183	Steve Gibson, Windsor	.10
☐	184	Leonard MacDonald, Windsor	.10
☐	185	Mike Speer, Windsor, Error	.10
☐	186	Kevin MacKay, Windsor	.10
☐	187	Ryan Merritt, Windsor	.10
☐	188	Doug Minor, Windsor	.10
☐	189	Rick Morton, Windsor	.10
☐	190	Sean O'Hagan (G), Windsor	.15
☐	191	Mike Polano, Windsor	.10
☐	192	Cory Stillman, Windsor	.50
☐	193	Jason Stos, Windsor	.10
☐	194	Trevor Walsh, Windsor	.10
☐	195	Todd Warriner, Windsor	.50
☐	196	Jeff Wilson (G), Windsor	.10
☐	197	Jason York, Windsor	.50
☐	198	Jason Zohil, Windsor, Error	.10
☐	199	Steve Smith, Windsor, Error	.10
☐	200	Brad Smith, Coach, Windsor	.10
☐	201	Jeff Bes, Hamilton	.25
☐	202	Ken Blum, Hamilton	.10
☐	203	Sean Brown, Hamilton	.10
☐	204	Darcy Cahill, Hamilton	.10
☐	205	Dale Chokan, Hamilton	.10
☐	206	Chris Code, Hamilton	.10
☐	207	George Dourian (G), Hamilton	.15
☐	208	Todd Gleason, Hamilton	.10
☐	209	TC: Jeff Bes, Hamilton	.10
☐	210	Michael Hartwick, Hamilton	.10
☐	211	Scott Jenkins, Hamilton	.10
☐	212	Rob Leask, Hamilton	.10
☐	213	Gordon Pell, Hamilton	.10
☐	214	Michael Reier, Hamilton	.10
☐	215	Kayle Short, Hamilton	.10
☐	216	Jason Skellett, Hamilton	.10
☐	217	Gairin Smith, Hamilton	.10
☐	218	Jeff Smith, Hamilton	.10
☐	219	Jason Soules, Hamilton	.10
☐	220	Alek Stojanov, Hamilton	.50
☐	221	Dan Tanevski (G), Hamilton	.15
☐	222	Gary Taylor, Hamilton	.10
☐	223	Brent Watson, Hamilton	.10
☐	224	Steve Woods, Hamilton	.10
☐	225	Jay Johnston, Coach, Hamilton, Error	.10
☐	226	Mike Allen, Kitchener	.10
☐	227	Brad Barton, Kitchener	.10
☐	228	Richard Borgo, Kitchener	.10
☐	229	Justin Cullen, Kitchener	.10
☐	230	Len DeVuono, Ottawa, Error	.10
☐	231	Norman Dezainde, Kitchener	.10
☐	232	Jason Firth, Kitchener	.10
☐	233	Derek Gauthier, Kitchener	.10
☐	234	Jamie Israel, Kitchener	.10
☐	235	Chris LiPuma, Kitchener	.25
☐	236	Tony McCabe, Kitchener	.10
☐	237	Paul McCallion, Kitchener, Error	.10
☐	237	Paul McCallion, Kitchener, Corrected	.10
☐	238	Shayne McCosh, Kitchener	.10
☐	239	Rod Saarinen, Kitchener	.10
☐	240	Steve Smith, Kitchener	.10
☐	241	Joey St. Aubin, Kitchener, Error	.10
☐	242	Rob Stopar (G), Kitchener	.15
☐	243	Jason Zohil, Kitchener, Error	.10
☐	244	Mike Torchia (G), Kitchener	.50
☐	245	Gib Tucker, Kitchener	.10
☐	246	John Uniac, Kitchener	.10
☐	247	Jack Williams, Kitchener	.10
☐	248	Joe McDonnell, Coach, Kitchener	.10
☐	249	Steve Rice, Kitchener, Error	.10
☐	250	Mike Polano, Kitchener, Error	.10
☐	251	Greg Allen, Niagara Falls	.10
☐	252	Roch Belley (G), Niagara Falls	.15
☐	253	Andy Bezeau, Niagara Falls	.25
☐	254	Derek Booth, Niagara Falls, Error	.10
☐	255	Kevin Brown, Niagara Falls	.25
☐	256	Mark Cardiff, Niagara Falls	.10
☐	257	Jason Coles, Niagara Falls	.10
☐	258	Todd Coopman, Niagara Falls	.10
☐	259	Richard Girhiny, Niagara Falls	.10
☐	260	Brian Holk, Niagara Falls	.10
☐	261	John Johnson, Niagara Falls	.10
☐	262	Dan Krisko, Niagara Falls	.10
☐	263	Manny Legacé (G), Niagara Falls, Error	.50
☐	264	Brad May, Niagara Falls	.50
☐	265	Don McConnell, Niagara Falls	.10
☐	266	TC: Steve Staios, Niagra Falls	.25
☐	267	Aaron Morrison, Niagara Falls	.10
☐	268	Cory Pageau, Niagara Falls	.10
☐	269	Geoff Rawson, Niagara Falls	.10
☐	270	Todd Simon, Niagara Falls	.25
☐	271	Steve Staios, Niagara Falls	.50
☐	272	Jeff Walker, Niagara Falls	.10
☐	273	Todd Wetzel, Niagara Falls	.25
☐	274	Jason Winch, Niagara Falls	.10
☐	275	Paul Wolanski, Niagara Falls	.10
☐	276	TC: Geordie Maynard, Owen Sound	.10
☐	277	Andrew Brunette, Owen Sound	.10
☐	278	Wyatt Buckland, Owen Sound	.10
☐	279	Jason Buetow, Owen Sound	.10
☐	280	Jason Castellan, Owen Sound	.10
☐	281	Trent Cull, Owen Sound	.25
☐	282	Robert Deschamps, Owen Sound	.10
☐	283	Chris Driscoll, Owen Sound	.10
☐	284	Bryan Drury, Owen Sound	.10
☐	285	Todd Hunter (G), Owen Sound	.15
☐	286	Troy Hutchinson, Owen Sound	.10
☐	287	Kirk Maltby, Owen Sound	.25
☐	288	Geordie Maynard, Owen Sound	.10
☐	289	Kevin McDougall (G), Owen Sound	.15
☐	290	Ted Miskolczi, Owen Sound	.10
☐	291	Steven Parson, Owen Sound	.10
☐	292	Jeff Perry, Owen Sound	.10
☐	293	Grayden Reid, Owen Sound	.10
☐	294	Mike Speer, Owen Sound, Error	.10
☐	295	Mark Strohack, Owen Sound	.10
☐	296	Mark Vilneff, Owen Sound	.10
☐	297	Keith Whitmore, Owen Sound	.10
☐	298	Jim Brown, Owen Sound	.10
☐	299	Len McNamara, Coach, Owen Sound	.10
☐	300	David Branch, Error	.10
☐	301	Shayne Antoski, North Bay	.10
☐	302	Jason Beaton, North Bay	.10
☐	303	Ron Bertrand (G), North Bay	.15
☐	304	Michael Burman, North Bay	.10
☐	305	Jamie Caruso, North Bay, Error	.10
☐	305	Jamie Caruso, North Bay, Corrected	.10
☐	306	Allan Cox, North Bay, Error	.10
☐	307	Tim Favot, North Bay	.10
☐	308	Trevor Halverson, North Bay	.10
☐	309	Derian Hatcher, North Bay	1.00
☐	310	Bill Lang, North Bay	.10
☐	311	Jason MacDonald, North Bay	.25
☐	312	Gary Miller, North Bay	.10
☐	313	Chris Ottmann, North Bay	.10
☐	314	Chad Penney, North Bay	.25
☐	315	Rick Pollard (G), North Bay, Error	.15
☐	316	Bradley Shepard, North Bay	.10
☐	317	John Spoltore, North Bay	.10
☐	318	Derek Switzer, North Bay	.10
☐	319	Karl Taylor, North Bay	.10
☐	320	John Vary, North Bay	.10
☐	321	Kevin White, North Bay,	.10
☐	322	Billy Wright, North Bay	.10
☐	323	Bert Templeton, Coach, North Bay, Error	.10
☐	324	TC: Jason MacDonald, North Bay	.10
☐	325	TC: Mike Côté, Oshawa	.10
☐	326	Jan Benda, Oshawa	.10
☐	327	Fred Brathwaite (G), Oshawa	.50
☐	328	Markus Brunner, Oshawa	.10
☐	329	Trevor Burgess, Oshawa, Error	.10
☐	330	Clair Cornish, Oshawa	.10
☐	331	Mike Cote, Oshawa	.10
☐	332	David Craievich, Oshawa	.10
☐	333	Dale Craigwell, Oshawa	.25
☐	334	Jean-Paul Davis, Oshawa	.10
☐	335	Mark Deazeley, Oshawa	.10
☐	336	Mike Fountain (G), Oshawa	.50
☐	337	Brain Grieve, Oshawa	.10
☐	338	Matt Hoffman, Oshawa, Error	.10
☐	339	Scott Hollis, Oshawa	.10
☐	340	Scott Boston, Belleville	.10
☐	341	Scott Luik, Oshawa	.10
☐	342	Craig Lutes, Oshawa, Error	.10
☐	342	Craig Lutes, Oshawa, Corrected	.10
☐	343	William MacPherson, Oshawa, Error	.10
☐	344	Paul O'Hagan, Oshawa	.10
☐	345	Wade Simpson, Oshawa	.10
☐	346	Jarrod Skalde, Belleville, Error (Generals)	.25
☐	346	Jarrod Skalde, Belleville, Corrected	.25
☐	347	Troy Sweet, Oshawa	.10
☐	348	Jason Weaver, Oshawa, Error (Craig Lutes)	.10
☐	349	Rick Cornacchia, Coach, Oshawa	.10
☐	350	The Trophy, Oshawa, Error	.10
☐	351	Greg Bailey, Peterborough	.10
☐	352	Ryan Black, Peterborough	.10
☐	353	Todd Bojcun, Goalie, Peterborough, Error (Rev. Neg.)	.10
☐	354	Toby Burkitt, Peterborough, Error	.10
☐	355	Scott Campbell, Peterborough	.10
☐	356	Jassen Cullimore, Peterborough	.50
☐	357	Jason Dawe, Peterborough	.75
☐	358	Dan Ferguson, Peterborough	.10
☐	359	Bryan Gendron, Peterborough	.10
☐	360	Michael Harding, Peterborough	.10
☐	361	Joe Hawley, Peterborough	.10
☐	362	TC: Ryan Black, Peterborough	.10
☐	363	Geordie Kinnear, Peterborough	.25
☐	364	Chris Longo, Peterborough, Error	.10
☐	365	Dale McTavish, Peterborough	.10
☐	366	Mark Myles, Peterborough	.10
☐	367	Don O'Neill, Peterborough	.10
☐	368	Jamie Pegg, Peterborough	.10
☐	369	Brent Pope, Peterborough	.10
☐	370	TC: Shayne McCosh, Kitchener	.10
☐	371	Douglas Searle, Peterborough	.10
☐	372	Troy Stephens, Peterborough, Error (/b: Rev. Neg.)	.10
☐	373	Mike Tomlinson, Peterborough	.10
☐	374	Brent Tully, Peterborough	.25
☐	375	Andrew Verner (G), Peterborough	.25
☐	376	Dick Todd, Coach, Peterborough, Error (/b: Rev. Neg.)	.15
☐	377	John Tanner (G), Sudbury, Error	.15
☐	377	John Tanner (G), Sudbury, Corrected	.15
☐	378	Adam Bennett (G), Sudbury	.15
☐	379	Kyle Blacklock (G), Sudbury	.15
☐	380	Terry Chitaroni	.10
☐	381	Brandon Convery, Sudbury	.50
☐	382	J.D. Eaton (G), Sudbury	.10
☐	383	Derek Etches, Sudbury	.10
☐	384	Rod Hinks	.10
☐	385	Bill Kovacs	.10
☐	386	Alain Laforge, Error	.10
☐	387	Jamie Matthews	.10
☐	388	Glen Murray	.50
☐	389	Dean Cull, Error	.10
☐	390	Sean O'Donnell	.50
☐	391	TC: Michael Peca, Sudbury	1.50
☐	392	Michael Peca, Error	2.50
☐	393	Shawn Rivers, Error	.10
☐	394	Dan Ryder (G)	.10
☐	395	Alastair Still	.10
☐	396	Michael Yeo	.10
☐	397	Barry Young	.10
☐	398	Jason Young	.10
☐	399	Ken MacKenzie, Coach	.10
☐	400	Bob Berg, Error	.10

	Description	**Nrmt-mt**
☐	White card stock	4.00
☐	Silver foil card stock	8.00

1990 - 91 7TH INNING SKETCH QMJHL

Face: Four colour, white border, Position
Back: Four colour, Number, Resume, Position

Imprint: 1990 7th Inning Sketch Printed in Canada

Complete Set (268 cards): 25.00

Common Player: .10

	No.	Player	NRMT-MT
☐	1	Patrick Poulin, St-Hyacinthe	.50
☐	2	Steve Lupien (G), Drummondville	.15
☐	3	Pierre Gagnon (G), Drummondville	.15
☐	4	Eric Plante, Drummondville	.10
☐	5	Stéphane Desjardins, Drummondville	.10
☐	6	Peter Valenta, Drummondville	.10
☐	7	Alexandre Legault, Drummondville	.10
☐	8	Patrice Brisebois, Drummondville	.50
☐	9	Martin Charrois, Drummondville	.10
☐	10	Eric Dandenault, Drummondville	.10
☐	11	Claude Jutras, Drummondville	.10
☐	12	David Pekarek, Drummondville	.10
☐	13	Denis Chassé, Drummondville	.25
☐	14	Ian Laperrière, Drummondville	.10
☐	15	Roger Larche, Drummondville	.10
☐	16	Dave Paquet, Drummondville	.10
☐	17	Pascal Lebrasseur, Drummondville	.10
☐	18	Eric Meloche, Drummondville	.10
☐	19	The Face Off, Action, Drummondville	.10
☐	20	Sylvain Rodrigue (G), Chicoutimi	.15
☐	21	Dany Girard, Chicoutimi	.10
☐	22	Eric Rochette, Chicoutimi	.10
☐	23	Steve Gosselin, Chicoutimi	.10
☐	24	Martin Lavallée, Chicoutimi	.10
☐	25	Martin Lapointe, Laval	.50
☐	26	Eric Brulé, Chicoutimi, Error	.10
☐	27	Martin Lacombe, Chicoutimi	.10
☐	28	Patrice Martineau, Chicoutimi	.10
☐	29	Dave Tremblay, Chicoutimi	.10
☐	30	Steve Larouche, Chicoutimi	.50
☐	31	Danny Beauregard, Chicoutimi	.10
☐	32	François Bélanger, Chicoutimi	.10
☐	33	Michel St-Jacques, Chicoutimi	.10
☐	34	Patrick Bisaillon, Chicoutimi	.10
☐	35	Félix Potvin (G), Chicoutimi	4.50
☐	36	Sébastien Parent, Chicoutimi	.10
☐	37	Eric Duchesne, Chicoutimi	.10
☐	38	Gilles Bouchard, Chicoutimi	.10
☐	39	Martin Gagné, Chicoutimi	.10
☐	40	Stéphane Charbonneau, Chicoutimi	.10
☐	41	Martin Beaupré, Chicoutimi	.10
☐	42	Daniel Paradis, Chicoutimi	.10
☐	43	Joe Canale, Coach, Chicoutimi	.10
☐	44	George Vezina Arena, Chicoutimi	.10
☐	45	François Leblanc (G), Laval	.15
☐	46	Martin Chaput, Lava	.10
☐	47	Marc Beaucage, Laval	.10
☐	48	Carl Mantha, Laval	.10
☐	49	Jim Bermingham, Laval	.10
☐	50	Philippe Boucher, Granby	.50
☐	51	Denis Chalifoux, Laval	.10
☐	52	Sylvain Naud, Laval	.10
☐	53	Jean Roberge, Laval	.10
☐	54	Sandy McCarthy, Laval	.75
☐	55	Eric Dubois, Laval	.10
☐	56	Jean Blouin, Laval	.10
☐	57	Jason Brousseau, Laval	.10
☐	58	Pierre Sandke, Laval	.10
☐	59	Benoît Larose, Laval	.10
☐	60	Yannick Fréchette, Laval	.10
☐	61	Pierre Calder, Granby	.10
☐	62	Patrick Grisé, Granby	.10
☐	63	Martin Balleux, Granby	.10
☐	64	Boris Rousson (G), Granby	.15
☐	65	Martin Trudel, Granby	.10
☐	66	Carl Leblanc, Granby	.10
☐	67	Martin Brochu (G), Granby	.15
☐	68	Benoît Therrien, Granby	.10
☐	69	Q.M.J.H.L. Action	.10
☐	70	Pascal Vincent, Laval	.10
☐	71	Christian Tardif, Granby	.10
☐	72	Christian Campeau, Granby	.10
☐	73	Eric Raymond (G), Laval	.15
☐	74	John Kovacs, Laval	.10
☐	75	Steve Arés, Trois Rivières	.10
☐	76	Pascal Dufalt, Granby	.10
☐	77	Greg MacEachern, Laval	.10
☐	78	Rémi Belliveau, Laval	.10
☐	79	Jocelyn Langlois, Granby	.10
☐	80	Carl Ménard, Granby, Error	.10
☐	81	Sébastien Fortier, Granby	.10
☐	82	Jean-François Grégoire, Granby	.10
☐	83	Normand Demers, Granby	.10
☐	84	Nicolas Lefebvre, Trois Rivières	.10
☐	85	Dominic Maltais, Trois Rivières	.10
☐	86	Mario Thérrien, Trois Rivières	.10
☐	87	Daniel Thibault, Trois Rivières	.10
☐	88	Jean-François Labbé (G), Trois Rivières	.50
☐	89	Alain Côté, Trois Rivières	.10
☐	90	Eric Prillo, Trois Rivières	.10
☐	91	Patrick Nadeau, Trois Rivières	.10
☐	92	Claude Poirier, Trois Rivières	.10
☐	93	Stéphane Julien, Trois Rivières	.10
☐	94	Patrice René, Trois Rivières	.10
☐	95	Francis Courturier, Trois Rivières, Error	.10
☐	96	Guy Lefebvre, Trois Rivières	.10
☐	97	Carl Boudreau, Trois Rivières	.10
☐	98	Jacques Parent, Trois Rivières	.10
☐	99	Stéphane Bourget, Shawinigan	.10
☐	100	Yanic Perreault, Trois Rivières	1.50
☐	101	Yvan Bergeron, Shawinigan	.10
☐	102	Jean-François Rivard (G), Beauport	.10
☐	103	Daniel Laflamme, Beauport	.10
☐	104	François Bourdeau, Shawinigan	.10
☐	105	Yvan Charrois, Shawinigan	.10
☐	106	Patrick Genest, Beauport	.10
☐	107	Hervé Lapointe, Beauport	.10
☐	108	Jean-François Jomphe, Shawinigan	.25
☐	109	Marc Tardif, Shawinigan	.10
☐	110	Eric Cardinal, Beauport	.10
☐	111	Denis Cloutier, Beauport	.10
☐	112	Q.M.J.H.L. Action	.10
☐	113	Alain Sanscartier, Coach, Shawinigan	.10
☐	114	Marquis Mathieu, Beauport	.10
☐	115	Stéphane Tartari, Error, Beauport	.10
☐	116	Q.M.J.H.L. Action	.10
☐	117	Q.M.J.H.L. Action	.10
☐	118	Martin Roy, Beauport	.10
☐	119	David Boudreau, Beauport	.10
☐	120	Mario Dumoulin, Beauport	.10
☐	121	Jean-François Picard, Beauport	.10
☐	122	Q.M.J.H.L. Action	.10
☐	123	Q.M.J.H.L. Action	.10
☐	124	Maxime Gagné, Beauport	.10
☐	125	Stéphane Ouellet, St-Jean	.10
☐	126	Steven Paiement, Beauport	.10
☐	127	François Paquette, Hull	.10
☐	128	Eric Cool, Beauport	.10
☐	129	Simon Toupin, Beauport	.10
☐	130	Shane Doiron, Hull	.10
☐	131	Todd Sparks, Hull	.10
☐	132	Bruno Lajeunesse, Beauport	.10
☐	133	Marcel Cousineau (G), Beauport	.50
☐	134	Claude-Charles Sauriol, Hull, Error	.10
☐	135	Eric Bellerose, Hull	.10
☐	136	Q.M.J.H.L. Action	.10
☐	137	Q.M.J.H.L. Action	.10
☐	138	Martin Lepage, Hull	.10
☐	139	Michal Longauer, Hull	.10
☐	140	Frédéric Boivin, Hull	.10
☐	141	Steven Dionl, Hull	.10
☐	142	Q.M.J.H.L. Action	.10
☐	143	Q.M.J.H.L. Action	.10
☐	144	Dan Paolucci, Hull	.10
☐	145	Bruno Villeneuve, Hull	.10
☐	146	Les Draveurs de Trois-Rivières, Error	.10
☐	147	Les Bisons de Granby, Error	.10
☐	148	Stefan Simoes, Hull	.10
☐	149	Joel Blain, Hull	.10
☐	150	Eric Lavigne, Hull	.25
☐	151	Le Titan de Laval	.10
☐	152	Le Laser de St-Hyacinthe	.10
☐	153	Robert Melanson, Hull	.10
☐	154	Brian Rogger, Hull	.10
☐	155	Les Lynx de St-Jean	.10
☐	156	Les Olympiques de Hull, Error	.10
☐	157	Francis Ouellette (G), Hull	.15
☐	158	Q.M.J.H.L. Action	.10
☐	159	Les Saguenéens, Error	.10
☐	160	Les Voltigeurs de Drummondville, Error	.10
☐	161	Le College Français	.10
☐	162	Les Tigres de Victoriaville	.10
☐	163	Q.M.J.H.L. Action	.10
☐	164	Q.M.J.H.L. Action	.10
☐	165	Les Harfangs de Beauport, Error	.10
☐	166	Les Cataractes de Shawinigan	.10
☐	167	Q.M.J.H.L. Action	.10
☐	168	Q.M.J.H.L. Action	.10
☐	169	Pierre Fillion, Trois Rivières	.10
☐	170	Yanick Degrâce (G), Trois Rivières	.15
☐	171	Paul Daigneault, St-Jean	.10
☐	172	Stacy Dallaire, St-Jean	.10
☐	173	Steve Searles, Trois Rivières	.10
☐	174	Todd Gillingham, Trois Rivières	.10
☐	175	Yves Sarault, St-Jean	.25
☐	176	Jason Downey, St-Jean	.10
☐	177	Paul Brousseau, Trois Rivières	.10
☐	178	Raymond Delarosbil, St-Jean	.10
☐	179	Yvan Corbin, St-Jean	.10
☐	180	Gaston Drapeau, Coach, Trois Rivières	.10
☐	181	The Celebration, Trois Rivières	.10
☐	182	Reginald Brézeault, St-Jean	.10
☐	183	Eric Lafrance, St-Jean	.10
☐	184	Martin Lavallée (G), St-Jean	.15
☐	185	Sébastien Lavallière, St-Jean, Error	.10
☐	186	Martin Lefebvre, St-Jean	.10
☐	187	Richard Hamelin, Shawinigan	.10
☐	188	Eric Beauvais, Shawinigan	.10
☐	189	Hughes Mongeon, Shawinigan	.10
☐	190	Alain Côté, Shawinigan	.10
☐	191	Eric Desrochers (G), Shawinigan	.15
☐	192	Eric Joyal, Shawinigan	.10
☐	193	Steve Dontigny, Shawinigan	.10
☐	194	Frédérick Lefebvre, Shawinigan	.10
☐	195	Patrick Hébert, Shawinigan	.10
☐	196	Johnny Lorenzo (G), Shawinigan	.15
☐	197	Sylvain Cormier, Victoriaville	.10
☐	198	Q.M.J.H.L. Action	.10
☐	199	Dave Morissette, Shawinigan	.10
☐	200	Yanick Dupré, Drummondville	.50
☐	201	Eric Marcoux, Shawinigan	.10
☐	202	Bruno Duchame	.10
☐	203	Martin Caron	.10
☐	204	Yves Meunier	.10
☐	205	Eric Bissonette	.10
☐	206	Jason Underhill	.10
☐	207	Dave Bélliveau	.10
☐	208	Steve Lapointe	.10
☐	209	Dean Melanson	.10
☐	210	Trevor Duhaime	.10
☐	211	Jacques Leblanc	.10
☐	212	Norm Paquet	.10
☐	213	Hughes Laliberté	.10
☐	214	Craig Prior	.10
☐	215	Patrick Labrecque	.10
☐	216	Patrick Cloutier	.10
☐	217	Michael Bazinet	.10
☐	218	Christian Proulx	.10
☐	219	Action Card	.10
☐	220	Charles Poulin	.10
☐	221	Christian Larivièrre	.10
☐	222	Martin Brodeur (G)	6.00
☐	223	Yanick Lemay	.10
☐	224	Denis Leblanc	.10
☐	225	François Groleau	.10
☐	226	Pierre Sévigny	.25
☐	227	Pierre Allard	.10
☐	228	Craig Martin	.25
☐	229	Karl Dykhuis	.25
☐	230	Etienne Lavoie	.10
☐	231	Stan Melanson	.10
☐	232	Dominic Rhéaume	.10
☐	233	Mario Nobili	.10
☐	234	Martin Gendron	.10
☐	235	Stéphane Menard	.10
☐	236	David St. Pierre	.10
☐	237	Yan Arsenault	.10
☐	238	Norman Flynn	.10
☐	239	Action Card	.10
☐	240	David Chouinard	.10
☐	241	Robert Guillet	.10
☐	242	Martin Lajeunesse	.10
☐	243	Nichol Cloutier	.10
☐	244	Joel Bouchard	.10
☐	245	Donald Brashear	.50
☐	246	Sébastien Tremblay	.10
☐	247	Dominique Grandmaison	.10
☐	248	Nicolas Lefebvre	.10
☐	249	Joseph Napolitano	.10
☐	250	Marc Savard	.10
☐	251	Alain Gauthier	.10

	No.	Player	Price
☐	252	Patrick Côté	.10
☐	253	Richard Aimonette	.10
☐	254	Martin Laitre	.10
☐	255	Carl Lamonthe	.10
☐	256	Action Card	.10
☐	257	André Durocher	.10
☐	258	Jocelyn Martel	.10
☐	259	Jeanot Ferlard	.10
☐	260	Claude Savoie	.10
☐	262	Denis Beauchamp	.10
☐	263	Jean-François Gagnon	.10
☐	264	André Boulaine	.10
☐	265	Paul-Emile Exantus	.10
☐	266	Danny Nolet	.10
☐	267	Jean Lebreau	.10
☐	268	Claude Barthe	.10

1990 - 91 7TH INNING SKETCH - WHL

Card 120 was not issued.

Imprint:

Complete Set (347 cards): **25.00**

Common Player: **.10**

	No.	Player	NRMT-MT
☐	1	Brent Bilodeau, Seattle	.25
☐	2	Craig Chapman, Seattle	.10
☐	3	Jeff Jubenville, Seattle	.10
☐	4	Al Kinisky, Seattle	.10
☐	5	Kevin Malgunas, Seattle	.10
☐	6	Andy MacIntyre, Seattle	.25
☐	7	Darren McAusland, Seattle	.10
☐	8	Mike Seaton, Seattle	.10
☐	9	Turner Stevenson, Seattle	.75
☐	10	Lindsay Vallis, Seattle	.10
☐	11	Dave Wilkie, Seattle	.50
☐	12	Jesse Wilson, Seattle	.10
☐	13	Dody Wood, Seattle	.50
☐	14	Bradley Zavisha, Seattle	.10
☐	15	Vince Boe, Seattle	.10
☐	16	Scott Davis, Seattle	.10
☐	17	Troy Hyatt, Seattle	.10
☐	18	Trevor Pennock, Seattle	.10
☐	19	Corey Schwab (G), Seattle	1.00
☐	20	Scott Bellefontaine (G), Seattle	.10
☐	21	Travis Kelln, Seattle	.10
☐	22	Peter Anholt, Coach/GM, Seattle	.10
☐	23	Sonny Mignacca (G), Medicine Hat	.10
☐	24	Chris Osgood (G), Medicine Hat	4.00
☐	25	Murray Garbutt, Medicine Hat	.10
☐	26	Kalvin Knibbs, Medicine Hat	.10
☐	27	Jason Krywulak, Medicine Hat	.10
☐	28	Jason Miller, Medicine Hat	.10
☐	29	Rob Niedermayer, Medicine Hat	1.75
☐	30	Clayton Norris, Medicine Hat	.25
☐	31	Jason Prosofsky, Medicine Hat	.10
☐	32	Dana Rieder, Medicine Hat	.10
☐	33	Kevin Riehl, Medicine Hat	.10
☐	34	Tyler Romanchuk, Medicine Hat	.10
☐	35	Dave Shute, Medicine Hat	.10
☐	36	Lorne Toews, Medicine Hat	.10
☐	37	Scott Townsend, Medicine Hat	.10
☐	38	David Cooper, Medicine Hat	.35
☐	39	Jon Duval, Medicine Hat	.10
☐	40	Dan Kordic, Medicine Hat	.25
☐	41	Mike Rathje, Medicine Hat	.50
☐	42	Tim Bothwell, Coach, Medicine Hat	.10
☐	43	Brent Thompson, Medicine Hat	.25
☐	44	Jeff Knight, Medicine Hat	.10
☐	45	Van Burgess, Swift Current	.10
☐	46	Kimbi Daniels, Swift Current	.10
☐	47	Curtis Friesen, Swift Current	.10
☐	48	Todd Holt, Swift Current	.10
☐	49	Blake Knox, Swift Current	.10
☐	50	Trent McCleary, Swift Current	.50
☐	51	Mark McFarlane, Swift Current	.10
☐	52	Eddie Patterson, Swift Current	.10
☐	53	Lloyd Pellitier, Swift Current	.10
☐	54	Geoff Sanderson, Swift Current	2.00
☐	55	Andrew Schneider, Swift Current	.10
☐	56	Tyler Wright, Swift Current	.25
☐	57	Joel Dyck, Swift Current	.10
☐	58	Len MacAusland, Swift Current	.10
☐	59	Evan Marble, Swift Current	.10
☐	60	David Podlubny, Swift Current	.10
☐	61	Kurt Seher, Swift Current	.10
☐	62	Jason Smith, Swift Current	.75
☐	63	Justin Burke (G), Swift Current	.10
☐	64	Kelly Thiessen (G), Swift Current	.10
☐	65	Todd Esselmont, Swift Current	.10
☐	66	Graham James, Coach/GM, Swift Current	.10
☐	67	Chris Herperger, Swift Current	.10
☐	68	Mark McCoy, Swift Current	.10
☐	69	Dean Malkoc, Swift Current	.25
☐	70	Dennis Sproxton (G), Swift Current	.10
☐	71	Centennial Civic Centre, Swift Current	.10
☐	72	Kimbi Daniels, Swift Current, (Special Achievement)	.10
☐	73	Shane Calder, Saskatoon	.10
☐	74	Mark Franks, Saskatoon	.10
☐	75	Greg Leahy, Saskatoon	.10
☐	76	Dean Rambo, Saskatoon	.10
☐	77	Scott Scissons, Saskatoon	.10
☐	78	David Struch, Saskatoon	.25
☐	79	Derek Tibbatts, Saskatoon	.10
☐	80	Shawn Yakimishyn, Saskatoon	.10
☐	81	Trent Coghill, Saskatoon	.10
☐	82	Robert Lelacheur, Saskatoon	.10
☐	83	Richard Matvichuk, Saskatoon	.50
☐	84	Mark Raiter, Saskatoon	.10
☐	85	Trevor Sherban, Saskatoon	.10
☐	86	Mark Wotton, Saskatoon	.25
☐	87	Cam Moon (G), Saskatoon	.10
☐	88	Trevor Robins (G), Saskatoon	.10
☐	89	Jeff Buchanan, Saskatoon	.25
☐	90	Ryan Strain, Saskatoon	.10
☐	91	Tim Cox, Saskatoon	.10
☐	92	Terry Ruskowski, Coach, Saskatoon	.10
☐	93	Saskatchewan Place, Saskatoon	.10
☐	94	Darin Bader, Saskatoon	.10
☐	95	Gaetan Blouin, Saskatoon	.10
☐	96	Rick Kozuback, Coach/GM, Tri-City	.10
☐	97	Jason Bowen, Tri-City	.25
☐	98	Fran Deferenza, Tri-City	.10
☐	99	Terry Degner, Tri-City	.10
☐	100	Devin Derksen, Tri-City	.10
☐	101	Martin Svetlik, Tri-City	.10
☐	102	Jeremy Warring (G), Tri-City	.10
☐	103	Corey Jones (G), Tri-City	.10
☐	104	Dean Tiltgen, Tri-City	.10
☐	105	Ryan Fujita, Tri-City	.10
☐	106	Jeff Fancy, Tri-City	.10
☐	107	Terry Virtue, Tri-City	.10
☐	108	Dennis Pinfold, Tri-City	.10
☐	109	Kyle Reeves, Tri-City	.10
☐	110	Steve McNutt, Tri-City	.10
☐	111	Todd Klassen, Tri-City	.10
☐	112	Darren Hastman, Tri-City	.10
☐	113	Bill Lindsay, Tri-City	.75
☐	114	Brian Sakic, Tri-City	.10
☐	115	Dan Sherstenka, Tri-City	.10
☐	116	Don Blishen (G), Tri-City	.10
☐	117	Jason Marshall, Tri-City	.10
☐	118	Dean Zayonce, Tri-City	.10
☐	119	Brad Loring, Tri-City	.10
☐	121	Darcy Austin (G), Lethbridge	.10
☐	122	Darcy Werenka, Lethbridge	.10
☐	123	Shane Peacock, Lethbridge	.10
☐	124	Bob Hartnell, Lethbridge	.10
☐	125	Brad Zimmer, Lethbridge	.10
☐	126	Allan Egeland, Lethbridge	.25
☐	127	Brad Rubachuk, Lethbridge	.10
☐	128	Jamie Pushor, Lethbridge	.75
☐	129	Jamie McLennan (G), Lethbridge	.50
☐	130	Lance Burns, Lethbridge	.10
☐	131	Ryan Smith, Lethbridge	.10
☐	132	Jason McBain, Lethbridge	.10
☐	133	Duane Maruschak, Lethbridge	.10
☐	134	Kevin St. Jacques, Lethbridge	.10
☐	135	Jason Sorochan, Lethbridge	.10
☐	136	Jason Widmer, Lethbridge	.25
☐	137	Bob Loucks, Coach, Lethbridge	.10
☐	138	Jason Ruff, Lethbridge	.25
☐	139	Pat Pylypuik, Lethbridge	.10
☐	140	Scott Adair, Lethbridge	.10
☐	141	Radek Sip, Lethbridge	.10
☐	142	Russ West, Moose Jaw	.10
☐	143	Scott Thomas, Moose Jaw	.25
☐	144	Kent Staniforth, Moose Jaw	.10
☐	145	Travis Thiessen, Moose Jaw	.25
☐	146	Marc Hussey, Moose Jaw	.10
☐	147	Kevin Masters, Moose Jaw	.10
☐	148	Todd Johnson, Moose Jaw	.10
☐	149	Bob Loucks, Moose Jaw	.10
☐	150	Rob Reimer, Moose Jaw	.10
☐	151	Jeff Petruic, Moose Jaw	.10
☐	152	Chris Schmidt, Moose Jaw	.10
☐	153	Scott Barnstable, Moose Jaw	.10
☐	154	Ian Layton, Moose Jaw	.10
☐	155	Kevin Smyth, Moose Jaw	.25
☐	156	Kim Deck, Moose Jaw	.10
☐	157	Jason White, Moose Jaw	.10
☐	158	Peter Cox, Moose Jaw	.10
☐	159	Jeff Calvert (G), Moose Jaw	.10
☐	160	Paul Dyck, Moose Jaw	.10
☐	161	Derek Kletzel, Moose Jaw	.10
☐	162	Jason Fitzsimmons (G), Moose Jaw	.10
☐	163	Darcy Jerome, Moose Jaw	.10
☐	164	Hal Christiansen, Regina	.10
☐	165	Terry Hollinger, Regina	.25
☐	166	Mike Risdale (G), Regina	.10
☐	167	Jamie Heward, Regina	.10
☐	168	Louis Dumont, Regina	.10
☐	169	Cory Dosdall, Regina	.10
☐	170	Terry Bendera, Regina	.10
☐	171	Jamie Hayden, Regina	.10
☐	172	Kelly Chotowetz, Regina	.10
☐	173	Brad Scott, Regina	.10
☐	174	Jeff Shantz, Regina	.75
☐	175	Kelly Markwart, Regina	.10
☐	176	Gary Pearce, Regina	.10
☐	177	Kerry Biette, Regina	.10
☐	178	Jamie Splett, Regina	.10
☐	179	Frank Kovacs, Regina	.10
☐	180	Greg Pankewicz, Regina	.25
☐	181	Colin Ruck, Regina	.10
☐	182	Brad Tippett, Coach, Regina	.10
☐	183	Dusty Imoo (G), Regina	.10
☐	184	Derek Eberle, Regina	.10
☐	185	Heath Weenk, Regina	.10
☐	186	Mike Sillinger, Regina	.75
☐	187	Erin Thornton, Seattle	.10
☐	188	Mike Chrun, Spokane	.10
☐	189	Pat Falloon, Spokane	1.00
☐	190	Bobby House, Spokane	.25
☐	191	Mike Jickling, Spokane	.10
☐	192	Trevor Tovell, Spokane	.10
☐	193	Steve Junker, Spokane	.25
☐	194	Shane Maitland, Spokane	.10
☐	195	Chris Lafrenière, Spokane	.10
☐	196	Frank Evans, Spokane	.10
☐	197	Jon Klemm, Spokane	.75
☐	198	Shawn Dietrich (G), Spokane	.10
☐	199	Dennis Saharachuk, Spokane	.10
☐	200	Mark Woolf, Spokane	.10
☐	201	Ray Whitney, Spokane	.25
☐	202	Scott Bailey (G), Spokane	.50
☐	203	Mike Ruark, Spokane	.10
☐	204	Brent Thurston, Spokane	.10
☐	205	Dan Faassen, Spokane	.10
☐	206	Kerry Toporowski, Spokane	.10
☐	207	Des Christopher (G), Spokane	.10
☐	208	Geoff Grandberg, Spokane	.10
☐	209	Bryan Maxwell, Coach, Spokane	.10
☐	210	Cam Danyluk, Spokane	.10
☐	211	Bram Vanderkracht, Spokane	.10
☐	212	Calvin Thudium, Spokane	.10
☐	213	Mark Szoke, Spokane	.10
☐	214	Kelly McCrimmon, Coach/GM, Brandon	.10
☐	215	Kevin Robertson, Brandon	.10
☐	216	Brian Purdy, Brandon	.10

☐ 217 Hardy Sauter, Brandon .10
☐ 218 Dwayne Gylywoychuk, Brandon .10
☐ 219 Bart Cote, Brandon .10
☐ 220 Merv Priest, Brandon .10
☐ 221 Jeff Hoad, Brandon .10
☐ 222 Glen Gulutzan, Brandon .10
☐ 223 Johan Skillgard, Brandon .10
☐ 224 Byron Penstock (G), Brandon .10
☐ 225 Mike Vandenberghe, Brandon .10
☐ 226 Trevor Kidd (G), Brandon 2.50
☐ 227 Dan Kopec, Brandon .10
☐ 228 Greg Hutchings, Brandon .10
☐ 229 Chris Constant, Brandon .10
☐ 230 Glen Webster, Brandon .10
☐ 231 Rob Puchniak, Brandon .10
☐ 232 Calvin Flint, Brandon .10
☐ 233 Stuart Scantlebury, Brandon .10
☐ 234 Jason White, Brandon .10
☐ 235 Gary Audette, Brandon .10
☐ 236 Kevin Schmalz, Brandon .10
☐ 237 Dwayne Newman, Victoria .10
☐ 238 Chris Catellier, Victoria .10
☐ 239 Todd Harris, Victoria .10
☐ 240 Mike Shemko, Victoria .10
☐ 241 John Badduke, Victoria .25
☐ 242 Mark Cipriano, Victoria .10
☐ 243 Brad Bagu, Victoria .10
☐ 244 Ross Harris, Victoria .10
☐ 245 Dino Caputo, Victoria .10
☐ 246 Cam Bristow, Victoria .10
☐ 247 Jarret Zukiwsky, Victoria .10
☐ 248 Jason Knox, Victoria .10
☐ 249 Gerry St. Cyr, Victoria .10
☐ 250 Larry Woo, Victoria .10
☐ 251 Jason Peters, Victoria .10
☐ 252 Shane Stangby, Victoria .10
☐ 253 Dave McMillen, Victoria .10
☐ 254 Colin Gregor, Victoria .10
☐ 255 Steve Passmore (G), Victoria .25
☐ 256 Shayne Green, Victoria .10
☐ 257 Kevin Koopman (G), Victoria .10
☐ 258 Lanny Watkins, Victoria .10
☐ 259 Scott Fukami, Victoria .10
☐ 260 Rick Hopper, Coach, Victoria .10
☐ 261 Laurie Billeck, Prince Albert .10
☐ 262 Rob Daum, Coach/GM, Prince Albert .25
☐ 263 Mark Stowe, Prince Albert .10
☐ 264 Curtis Regnier, Prince Albert .10
☐ 265 David Neilson, Prince Albert .10
☐ 266 Brain Pellerin, Prince Albert .10
☐ 267 Dean McAmmond, Prince Albert .75
☐ 268 Darren Van Impe, Prince Albert .10
☐ 269 Troy Neumeier, Prince Albert .10
☐ 270 Mike Langen (G), Prince Albert .10
☐ 271 Dan Kesa, Prince Albert .10
☐ 272 Travis Laycock (G), Prince Albert .10
☐ 273 Scott Allison, Prince Albert .10
☐ 274 Jeff Gorman, Prince Albert .10
☐ 275 Lee J. Leslie, Prince Albert .10
☐ 276 Jason Kwiatkowski, Prince Albert .10
☐ 277 Donevan Hextall, Prince Albert .10
☐ 278 Shane Zulyniak, Prince Albert .10
☐ 279 Darren Perkins, Prince Albert .10
☐ 280 Chad Seibel, Prince Albert .10
☐ 281 Jeff Nelson, Prince Albert .25
☐ 282 Troy Hjertas, Prince Albert .10
☐ 283 Jamie Linden, Prince Albert .10
☐ 284 Zac Boyer, Kamloops .10
☐ 285 Jarret Bousquet, Kamloops .10
☐ 286 Steven Yule, Kamloops .10
☐ 287 Tom Renney, Coach, Kamloops .10
☐ 288 Lance Johnson, Kamloops .25
☐ 289 Scott Niedermayer, Kamloops 1.75
☐ 290 Ryan Harrison, Kamloops .10
☐ 291 Ed Patterson, Kamloops .25
☐ 292 Jeff Watchorn, Kamloops .10
☐ 293 Cal McGowan, Kamloops .10
☐ 294 Dale Masson (G), Kamloops .10
☐ 295 Joey Mittelsteadt, Kamloops .10
☐ 296 Scott Loucks, Kamloops .10
☐ 297 Shea Esselmont, Kamloops .10
☐ 298 Craig Bonner, Kamloops .10
☐ 299 Mike Mathers, Kamloops .10
☐ 300 Fred Hettle, Kamloops .10
☐ 301 Craig Lyons, Kamloops .10
☐ 302 Murray Duval, Kamloops .10
☐ 303 Jamie Barnes, Kamloops .10
☐ 304 Bryan Gourlie, Kamloops .10
☐ 305 Chad Berezniuk, Kamloops .10
☐ 306 Corey Hirsch (G), Kamloops 1.00
☐ 307 Darryl Sydor, Kamloops 1.25
☐ 308 Jarrett Deuling, Kamloops .25
☐ 309 Cory Stock, Kamloops .10
☐ 310 Chris Rowland, Portland .10
☐ 311 Mike Ruark, Portland .10
☐ 312 Steve Konowalchuk, Portland 1.00
☐ 313 Jeff Sebastian, Portland .10
☐ 314 Brandon Smith, Portland .10
☐ 315 Greg Gatto, Portland .10
☐ 316 Brad Harrison, Portland .10
☐ 317 Brantt Myhres, Portland .25
☐ 318 Jamie Black, Portland .10
☐ 319 Colin Foley, Portland .10
☐ 320 Cam Danyluk, Portland .10
☐ 321 Dean Dorchak, Portland .10
☐ 322 Ryan Slemko, Portland .10
☐ 323 Kim Deck, Portland .10
☐ 324 Kelly Harris, Portland .10
☐ 325 Murray Bokenfohr, Portland .10
☐ 326 Dean Intwert (G), Portland .10
☐ 327 Dennis Saharchuk, Portland .10
☐ 328 Shane Seiker, Portland .10
☐ 329 Terry Virtue, Portland .10
☐ 330 Josh Erdman, Portland .10
☐ 331 Layne Roland, Portland .10
☐ 332 Michel Michon, Portland .10
☐ 333 Scott Mydan, Portland .10
☐ 334 CL: Trevor Kidd, Brandon 1.50
☐ 335 CL: Moose Jaw .10
☐ 336 CL: Geoff Sanderson, Swift Current 1.50
☐ 337 CL: Regina .10
☐ 338 CL: Saskatoon .10
☐ 339 CL: Medicine Hat .10
☐ 340 The Goalmouth .10
☐ 341 CL: Portland .10
☐ 342 CL: Kamloops .10
☐ 343 CL: Victoria .10
☐ 344 CL: Brian Sakic, Tri City .25
☐ 345 CL: Pat Falloon, Spokane .50
☐ 346 CL: Brent Bilodeau, Seattle .10
☐ 347 CL: Jason Ruff, Lethbridge .10
☐ 348 CL: Prince Albert .10

No. Description NRMT-MT

☐ White card stock - Christmas 4.00
☐ Silver foil card stock- Christmas 8.00

1990 - 91 7TH INNING SKETCH MEMORIAL CUP

Issued in 1991 as a limited edition, this set was packaged in a display box and numbered of 20,000. An Eric Lindros card was originally projected for this set but was cancelled at the last minute due to the inability to reach an agreement. It is estimated that 1300 sets containing the Lindros card were available at the Memorial Cup Game. Seventeen cards were withdrawn (W/D) from the set.

Imprint: 1990 7th Inning Sketch Printed in Canada
Complete Set (130 cards): 200.00
Common Player: .20

No. Player NRMT-MT

☐ 1 Mike Lenarduzzi (G), S.S. Marie .25
☐ 2 Kevin Hodson (G), S.S. Marie 1.00
☐ 3 OHL Action, S.S. Marie .20
☐ 4 Bob Boughner, S.S. Marie .35
☐ 5 Adam Foote, S.S. Marie 1.00
☐ 6 Brad Tilley, S.S. Marie .20
☐ 7 Brian Goudie, S.S. Marie .20
☐ 8 Wade Whitten, S.S. Marie .20
☐ 9 Jason Denomme, S.S. Marie .20
☐ 10 David Matsos, S.S. Marie .20
☐ 11 Rick Kowalsky, S.S. Marie .20
☐ 12 Jarret Reid, S.S. Marie .20
☐ 13 Perry Pappas, S.S. Marie .20
☐ 14 Tom MacDonald, S.S. Marie .20
☐ 15 Mike DeCoff, S.S. Marie .20
☐ 16 Joe Busillo, S.S. Marie .20
☐ 17 Denny Lambert, S.S. Marie .20
☐ 18 Mark Matier, S.S. Marie .20
☐ 19 Shaun Imber, S.S. Marie .20
☐ 20 Ralph Intranuovo, S.S. Marie .35
☐ 21 Chris Snell, (W/D), S.S. Marie 3.00
☐ 22 Tony Iob, S.S. Marie .20
☐ 23 Colin Miller, S.S. Marie .20
☐ 24 Ted Nolan, Coach, S.S. Marie .50
☐ 25 Sylvain Rodigue (G), Chicoutimi .25
☐ 26 Félix Potvin (G), Chicoutimi 6.00
☐ 27 Martin Lavallée, Chicoutimi .20
☐ 28 Eric Brulé, Chicoutimi .20
☐ 29 Steve Larouche, Chicoutimi .35
☐ 30 Michel St-Jacques, Chicoutimi .20
☐ 31 Patrick Clement, Chicoutimi .20
☐ 32 Patrick Bisailon, Chicoutimi .20
☐ 33 Checklist (62 to 131), Original, (W/D) 3.00
☐ 33 Checklist (62 to 131), Replacement .20
☐ 34 Gilles Bouchard, Chicoutimi .20
☐ 35 Eric Rochette, Chicoutimi .20
☐ 36 Rob Dykeman (G) (W/D), Chicoutimi 3.00
☐ 37 Checklist (1 to 61), Original, (W/D) 3.00
☐ 37 Checklist (1 to 61), Replacement .20
☐ 38 Patrice Martineau, Chicoutimi .20
☐ 39 Danny Beauregard, Chicoutimi .20
☐ 40 François Bélanger, Chicoutimi .20
☐ 41 Sébastien Parent, Chicoutimi .20
☐ 42 Martin Gagné, Chicoutimi .20
☐ 43 Stéphane Charbonneau, Chicoutimi .20
☐ 44 Martin Beaupré, Chicoutimi .20
☐ 45 Daniel Paradis, Chicoutimi .20
☐ 46 Joe Canale, Coach, Chicoutimi .20
☐ 47 OHL Action .20
☐ 48 Jubilation .20
☐ 49 Steve Lupien (G), Drummondville .25
☐ 50 Pierre Gagnon (G), Drummondville .25
☐ 51 Alexandre Legault, Drummondville .20
☐ 52 Martin Charrois, Drummondville .20
☐ 53 Eric Dandenault, Drummondville .20
☐ 54 Denis Chassé, Drummondville .35
☐ 55 Guy Lehoux, Drummondville .20
☐ 56 Ian Laperrière, Drummondville .35
☐ 57 Hugo Proulx, Drummondville .20
☐ 58 Dave Whittom, Drummondville .20
☐ 59 Yanick Dupré, Drummondville .50
☐ 60 Eric Plante, Drummondville .20
☐ 61 Stéphane Desjardins, Drummondville .20
☐ 62 Patrice Brisebois, Drummondville .75
☐ 63 René Corbet, Drummondville .50
☐ 64 Marc Savard, Drummondville .20
☐ 65 Claude Jutras, Drummondville .20
☐ 66 David Pekarek, Drummondville .20
☐ 67 Roger Larche, Drummondville, Error .20
☐ 68 Dave Paquet, Drummondville .20
☐ 69 Eric Meloche, Drummondville .20
☐ 70 CHL Action .20
☐ 71 The Celebration 1.00
☐ 72 MVP: Félix Potvin (G) 6.00
☐ 73 Scott Bailey (G), Spokane .25
☐ 74 Trevor Kidd (G), Spokane 2.00
☐ 75 Chris Lafreniere, Spokane .20
☐ 76 Frank Evans, Spokane .20
☐ 77 Jon Klemm, Spokane .35
☐ 78 Brent Thurston, Spokane .20
☐ 79 Jamie McLennan, Spokane .50
☐ 80 Steve Junker, Spokane .20
☐ 81 Mark Szoke, Spokane .20
☐ 82 Ray Whitney, Spokane .50
☐ 83 Geoff Grandberg, Spokane .20
☐ 84 Cam Danyluk, Spokane .20
☐ 85 Kerry Toporowski, Spokane .20
☐ 86 Trevor Tovell, Spokane .20
☐ 87 Pat Falloon, Spokane 1.25
☐ 88 Bram Vanderkracht, Spokane .20
☐ 89 Mike Jickling, Spokane .20
☐ 90 Murray Garbutt, Spokane .20
☐ 91 Calvin Thudium, Spokane .20
☐ 92 Mark Woolf, Spokane .20
☐ 93 Shane Maitland, Spokane .20
☐ 94 Bart Cote, Spokane .20
☐ 95 Bryan Maxwell, Coach, Spokane .20
☐ 96 Eric Lindros (W/D), Oshawa 60.00
☐ 97 Scott Niedermayer 2.50
☐ 98 Patrick Poulin .35
☐ 99 Brent Bilodeau .20
☐ 100 Pat Falloon .50
☐ 101 Darcy Werenka .20
☐ 102 Martin Lapointe .50
☐ 103 Philippe Bouche .20

	No.	Player	
☐	104	Jeff Nelson	.20
☐	105	René Corbet	.50
☐	106	Pat Peake (W/D)	6.00
☐	107	Steve Staios (W/D)	4.00
☐	108	Richard Matvichuk	.20
☐	109	Dean McAmmond	.20
☐	110	Alex Stojanov (W/D)	3.00
☐	111	Glen Murray (W/D)	4.00
☐	112	Tyler Wright	.20
☐	113	Jason Dawe (W/D)	6.00
☐	114	Nathan Lafayette (W/D)	4.00
☐	115	Yanic Perreault	.50
☐	116	Guy Léveque (W/D)	3.00
☐	117	Darren Van Impe	.20
☐	118	Shayne Antoski (W/D)	3.00
☐	119	Eric Lindros (W/D)	60.00
☐	120	Dennis Perdie (W/D)	3.00
☐	121	Terry Chitaroni (W/D)	3.00
☐	122	Jamie Pushor	.20
☐	123	Chris Osgood	5.00
☐	124	Jamie Matthews (W/D)	3.00
☐	125	Yves Sarault	.20
☐	126	Yanick Dupré	.50
☐	127	Brad Zimmer	.20
☐	128	Copps Coliseum	.20
☐	129	Jason Widmer	.20
☐	130	Marc Savard	.20

1990 - 91 TIM HORTON

These cards were issued to advertise the Sports Collectible Show in Oakville, Ontario, during May 1991.

Imprint: None

	No.	Player	NRMT-MT
☐	1	Tim Horton	3.00

1990 - 91 UPPER DECK

These cards have two versions: an English issue and a French issue.

Imprint: 1990 The Upper Deck Co. Printed in USA

Low Series Set (400 cards):	**30.00**	**40.00**
High Series Set (150 cards):	**35.00**	**55.00**
Promo Card: (Wayne Gretzky, #241)		**30.00**
Promo Card: (Patrick Roy, #241)		**25.00**
Common Player:	**.10**	**.15**

	No.	Player	English	French
☐☐	1	David Volek, NYI.	.10	.15
☐☐	2	Brian Propp, Bos.	.10	.15
☐☐	3	Wendel Clark, Tor.	.25	.35
☐☐	4	Adam Creighton, Chi.	.10	.15
☐☐	5	Mark Osborne, Tor.	.10	.15
☐☐	6	Murray Craven, Pha.	.10	.15
☐☐	7	Doug Crossman, NYI.	.10	.15
☐☐	8	Mario Marois, Que.	.10	.15
☐☐	9	Curt Giles, Min.	.10	.15
☐☐	10	Rick Wamsley (G), Cgy.	.10	.15
☐☐	**11**	**Troy Mallette, NYR.., RC**	**.10**	**.15**
☐☐	12	John Cullen, Pgh.	.10	.15
☐☐	**13**	**Miloslav Horava, NYR.., RC**	**.10**	**.15**
☐☐	**14**	**Kevin Stevens, Pgh., RC**	**.50**	**.65**
☐☐	15	David Shaw, NYR.	.10	.15
☐☐	16	Randy Wood, NYI.	.10	.15
☐☐	17	Peter Zezel, Stl.	.10	.15
☐☐	**18**	**Glenn Healy (G), NYI., RC**	**.60**	**.75**
☐☐	**19**	**Sergio Momesso, Stl, RC**	**.10**	**.15**
☐☐	20	Don Maloney, NYI.	.10	.15
☐☐	21	Craig Muni, Edm.	.10	.15
☐☐	22	Phil Housley, Buf.	.10	.15
☐☐	**23**	**Martin Gelinas, Edm., RC**	**.75**	**1.00**
☐☐	**24**	**Alexander Mogilny, Buf., RC**	**2.00**	**2.50**
☐☐	25	Star-Rookie: John Byce, Bos.	.10	.15
☐☐	26	Joe Nieuwendyk, Cgy.	.25	.35
☐☐	27	Ron Tugnutt (G), Que.	.10	.15
☐☐	**28**	**Don Barber, Min., RC**	**.10**	**.15**
☐☐	29	Gary Roberts, Cgy.	.25	.35
☐☐	30	Basil McRae, Min.	.10	.15
☐☐	31	Phil Bourque, Pgh.	.10	.15
☐☐	**32**	**Mike Richter (G), NYR.., RC**	**2.00**	**2.50**
☐☐	33	Zarley Zalapski, Pgh.	.10	.15
☐☐	34	Bernie Nicholls, NYR.	.10	.15
☐☐	**35**	**Bob Corkum, Buf., RC**	**.10**	**.15**
☐☐	**36**	**Rod Brind'Amour, Stl., RC**	**1.50**	**2.00**
☐☐	**37**	**Mark Fitzpatrick (G), NYI., RC**	**.75**	**1.00**
☐☐	38	Gino Cavallini, Stl.	.10	.15
☐☐	**39**	**Mick Vukota, NYI.., RC**	**.10**	**.15**
☐☐	**40**	**Mike Lalor, Stl., RC**	**.10**	**.15**
☐☐	41	Dave Andreychuk, Buf.	.25	.35
☐☐	42	Bill Ranford (G), Edm.	.25	.35
☐☐	43	Pierre Turgeon, Buf.	.35	.50
☐☐	44	Mark Messier, Edm.	1.00	1.50
☐☐	**45**	**Rob Blake, L.A., RC**	**.50**	**.65**
☐☐	**46**	**Mike Modano, Min., RC**	**2.50**	**3.50**
☐☐	47	Theoren Fleury, Cgy.	.35	.50
☐☐	48	Neal Broten, Min.	.10	.15
☐☐	49	Paul Gillis, Que.	.10	.15
☐☐	50	Doug Bodger, Buf.	.10	.15
☐☐	**51**	**Stéphan Lebeau, Mtl., RC**	**.10**	**.15**
☐☐	52	Larry Robinson, L.A.	.25	.35
☐☐	53	Dale Hawerchuk, Wpg.	.25	.35
☐☐	54	Wayne Gretzky, L.A.	3.00	4.50
☐☐	**55**	**Ed Belfour (G), Chi., RC**	**2.00**	**2.50**
☐☐	56	Steve Yzerman, Det.	1.50	2.00
☐☐	57	Rod Langway, Wsh.	.10	.15
☐☐	58	Bernie Federko, Det.	.10	.15
☐☐	59	Lemieux's Scoring Streak, Pgh.	1.00	1.50
☐☐	60	Doug Lidster, Van.	.10	.15
☐☐	61	Dave Christian, Bos.	.10	.15
☐☐	62	Rob Ramage, Tor.	.10	.15
☐☐	**63**	**Jeremy Roenick, Chi., RC**	**2.00**	**2.50**
☐☐	64	Ray Bourque, Bos.	1.00	1.50
☐☐	65	Star-Rookie: Jon Morris, N.J.	.10	.15
☐☐	66	Sean Burke (G), N.J.	.25	.35
☐☐	67	Ron Francis, Hfd.	.50	.75
☐☐	68	Ron Sutter, Pha.	.10	.15
☐☐	69	Peter Sidorkiewicz (G), Hfd.	.10	.15
☐☐	70	Sylvain Turgeon, N.J.	.10	.15
☐☐	71	David Ellett, Wpg.	.10	.15
☐☐	72	Bobby Smith, Mtl.	.10	.15
☐☐	73	Luc Robitaille, L.A.	.25	.35
☐☐	74	Pat Elynuik, Wpg.	.10	.15
☐☐	**75**	**Jason Soules, Edm., RC**	**.10**	**.15**
☐☐	76	Dino Ciccarelli, Wsh.	.25	.35
☐☐	**77**	**Vladimir Krutov, Van., RC**	**.10**	**.15**
☐☐	78	Lee Norwood, Det.	.10	.15
☐☐	79	Brian Bradley, Van.	.10	.15
☐☐	**80**	**Michal Pivonka, Wsh., RC**	**.20**	**.30**
☐☐	**81**	**Mark LaForest (G), Tor., RC**	**.10**	**.15**
☐☐	82	Trent Yawney, Chi.	.10	.15
☐☐	83	Tom Fergus, Tor.	.10	.15
☐☐	84	Andy Brickley, Bos.	.10	.15
☐☐	85	Dave Manson, Chi.	.10	.15
☐☐	**86**	**Gord Murphy, Pha., RC**	**.10**	**.15**
☐☐	87	Scott Young, Hfd.,	.10	.15
☐☐	88	Tommy Albelin, N.J.	.10	.15
☐☐	89	Ken Wregget (G), Pha.	.10	.15
☐☐	**90**	**Brad Shaw, Hfd., RC**	**.10**	**.15**
☐☐	91	Mario Gosselin (G), L.A.	.10	.15
☐☐	92	Paul Fenton, Wpg.	.10	.15
☐☐	93	Brian Skrudland, Mtl.	.10	.15
☐☐	94	Thomas Steen, Wpg.	.10	.15
☐☐	95	John Tonelli, L.A.	.10	.15
☐☐	96	Steve Chiasson, Det.	.10	.15
☐☐	97	Mike Ridley, Wsh.	.10	.15
☐☐	98	Garth Butcher, Van.	.10	.15
☐☐	**99**	**Daniel Shank, Det., RC**	**.10**	**.15**
☐☐	100	Checklist 1 (1 - 100)	.10	.15
☐☐	101	Jamie Macoun, Cgy.	.10	.15
☐☐	**102**	**Wendell Young (G), Pgh., RC**	**.10**	**.15**
☐☐	103	Laurie Boschman, Wpg.	.10	.15
☐☐	**104**	**Paul Ranheim, Cgy., RC**	**.10**	**.15**
☐☐	105	Doug Smail, Wpg.	.10	.15
☐☐	106	Shawn Chambers, Min.	.10	.15
☐☐	107	Steve Weeks (G), Van.	.10	.15
☐☐	108	Gaetan Duchesne, Min.	.10	.15
☐☐	109	Kevin Hatcher, Wsh.	.10	.15
☐☐	110	Paul Reinhart, Van.	.10	.15
☐☐	111	Shawn Burr, Det.	.10	.15
☐☐	112	Troy Murray, Chi.	.10	.15
☐☐	113	John Chabot, Det.	.10	.15
☐☐	**114**	**Jacques Cloutier (G), Chi., RC**	**.10**	**.15**
☐☐	**115**	**Rick Zombo, Det., RC**	**.10**	**.15**
☐☐	116	Kjell Samuelsson, Pha.	.10	.15
☐☐	117	Tim Watters, L.A.	.10	.15
☐☐	118	Patrick Flatley, NYI.	.10	.15
☐☐	119	Tom Laidlaw, L.A.	.10	.15
☐☐	120	Ilkka Sinisalo, Pha.	.10	.15
☐☐	121	Tom Barrasso (G), Pgh.	.25	.35
☐☐	**122**	**Bob Essensa (G), Wpg., RC**	**.10**	**.15**
☐☐	**123**	**Sergei Makarov, Cgy., RC**	**.35**	**.50**
☐☐	124	Paul Coffey, Pgh.	.25	.35
☐☐	**125**	**Bob Beers, Bos., RC**	**.10**	**.15**
☐☐	126	Brian Bellows, Min.	.10	.15
☐☐	127	Mike Liut (G), Wsh.	.10	.15
☐☐	**128**	**Igor Larionov, Van., RC**	**1.25**	**1.75**
☐☐	129	Craig Simpson, Edm.	.10	.15
☐☐	130	Kelly Miller, Wsh.	.10	.15
☐☐	131	Dirk Graham, Chi.	.10	.15
☐☐	132	Jimmy Carson, Det.	.10	.15
☐☐	133	Michel Goulet, Chi.	.25	.35
☐☐	134	Gerard Gallant, Det.	.10	.15
☐☐	**135**	**Bruce Hoffort (G), Pha., RC**	**.10**	**.15**
☐☐	136	Steve Duchesne, L.A.	.10	.15
☐☐	137	Bryan Trottier, NYI.	.25	.35
☐☐	138	Per-Erik Eklund, Pha.	.10	.15
☐☐	139	Gary Nylund, NYI.	.10	.15
☐☐	140	Steve Kasper, L.A.	.10	.15
☐☐	141	Joel Otto, Cgy.	.10	.15
☐☐	142	Rob Brown, Pgh.	.10	.20
☐☐	143	Al MacInnis, Cgy.	.25	.35
☐☐	144	Mario Lemieux, Pgh.	2.00	3.00
☐☐	**145**	**Peter Eriksson, Edm., RC**	**.10**	**.15**
☐☐	146	Jari Kurri, Edm.	.25	.35
☐☐	147	Petri Skriko, Van.	.10	.15
☐☐	148	Steve Smith, Edm.	.10	.15
☐☐	149	Calle Johansson, Wsh.	.10	.15
☐☐	150	Stewart Gavin, Min.	.10	.15
☐☐	151	Randy Ladouceur, Hfd.	.10	.15
☐☐	**152**	**Vincent Riendeau (G), Stl., RC**	**.10**	**.15**
☐☐	153	Patrick Roy (G), Mtl.	2.00	3.00
☐☐	154	Brett Hull, Stl.	1.50	2.00
☐☐	**155**	**Craig Fisher, Pha., RC**	**.10**	**.15**
☐☐	156	Cam Neely, Bos.	.25	.35
☐☐	157	Al Iafrate, Tor.	.10	.15
☐☐	158	Bob Carpenter, Bos.	.10	.15
☐☐	159	Doug Brown, N.J.	.10	.15
☐☐	160	Tom Kurvers, Tor.	.10	.15
☐☐	161	John MacLean, N.J.	.10	.15
☐☐	162	Guy Lafleur, Que.	1.00	1.50
☐☐	163	Peter Stastny, N.J.	.25	.35
☐☐	164	Joe Sakic, Que.	2.00	3.00
☐☐	**165**	**Robb Stauber (G), L.A., RC**	**.10**	**.15**
☐☐	166	Daren Puppa (G), Buf.	.20	.30
☐☐	167	Esa Tikkanen, Edm.	.10	.15
☐☐	168	Mike Ramsey, Buf.	.10	.15
☐☐	169	Craig MacTavish, Edm.	.10	.15
☐☐	170	Christian Ruuttu, Buf.	.10	.15
☐☐	171	Brian Hayward (G), Mtl.	.10	.15
☐☐	172	Pat Verbeek, Hfd.	.10	.15
☐☐	173	Adam Oates, Stl.	.50	.75
☐☐	174	Chris Chelios, Mtl.	.50	.75
☐☐	**175**	**Curtis Joseph, (G), Stl., RC**	**2.50**	**3.50**
☐☐	**176**	**Viacheslav Fetisov, N.J., RC**	**.65**	**1.00**
☐☐	177	Dave Poulin, Bos.	.10	.15
☐☐	**178**	**Mark Recchi, Pgh., RC**	**1.50**	**2.00**

□ □	179	Daniel Marois, Tor.	.10	.15
□ □	180	Mark Johnson, N.J.	.10	.15
□ □	181	Michel Petit, Que.	.10	.15
□ □	182	Brian Mullen, NYR.	.10	.15
□ □	**183**	**Chris Terreri (G), N.J., RC**	**.20**	**.30**
□ □	184	Tony Hrkac, Que.	.10	.15
□ □	185	James Patrick, NYR.	.10	.15
□ □	186	Craig Ludwig, Mtl.	.10	.15
□ □	187	Uwe Krupp, Buf.	.10	.15
□ □	188	Guy Carbonneau, Mtl.	.10	.15
□ □	**189**	**Dave Snuggerud, Buf., RC**	**.10**	**.15**
□ □	**190**	**Joe Murphy, Edm., RC**	**.10**	**.15**
□ □	191	Jeff Brown, Stl.	.10	.15
□ □	192	Dean Evason, Hfd.	.10	.15
□ □	193	Petr Svoboda, Mtl.	.10	.15
□ □	194	Dave Babych, Hfd.	.10	.15
□ □	195	Steve Tuttle, Stl.	.10	.15
□ □	196	Randy Burridge, Bos.	.10	.15
□ □	197	Tony Tanti, Pgh.	.10	.15
□ □	198	Bob Sweeney, Bos.	.10	.15
□ □	199	Brad Marsh, Tor.	.10	.15
□ □	200	Checklist 2 (101 - 200)	.10	.15
□ □	201	AW: Bill Ranford (G), Edm.	.20	.30
□ □	202	AW: Sergei Makarov, Cgy.	.20	.30
□ □	203	AW: Brett Hull, Stl.	.75	1.25
□ □	204	AW: Ray Bourque, Bos.	.35	.50
□ □	205	AW: Wayne Gretzky, L.A.	1.50	2.25
□ □	206	AW: Mark Messier, Edm.	.50	.75
□ □	207	AW: Patrick Roy, (G), Mtl.	1.00	1.50
□ □	208	AW: Rick Meagher, Stl.	.10	.15
□ □	209	AW: A. Moog/R. Lemelin	.20	.30
□ □	210	Aaron Broten, Min.	.10	.15
□ □	**211**	**John Carter, Bos., RC**	**.10**	**.15**
□ □	212	Marty McSorley, L.A.	.10	.15
□ □	213	Greg Millen (G), Chi.	.10	.15
□ □	214	Dave Taylor, L.A.	.10	.15
□ □	215	Réjean Lemelin (G), Bos.	.10	.15
□ □	216	Dave McLlwain, Wpg.	.10	.15
□ □	217	Don Beaupré (G), Wsh.	.10	.15
□ □	218	Paul MacDermid, Wpg.	.10	.15
□ □	219	Dale Hunter, Wsh.	.10	.15
□ □	220	Brent Ashton, Wpg.	.10	.15
□ □	221	Steve Thomas, Chi.	.10	.15
□ □	222	Ed Olczyk, Tor.	.10	.15
□ □	223	Doug Wilson, Chi.	.25	.35
□ □	224	Vincent Damphousse, Tor.	.35	.50
□ □	**225**	**Rob DiMaio, NYI.., RC**	**.10**	**.15**
□ □	**226**	**Hubie McDonough, NYI.., RC**	**.10**	**.15**
□ □	227	Ron Hextall (G), Pha.	.25	.35
□ □	**228**	**Dave Chyzowski, NYI.., RC, Error**	**.10**	**.15**
□ □	229	Larry Murphy, Min.	.25	.35
□ □	230	Mike Bullard, Pha.	.10	.15
□ □	231	Kelly Hrudey (G), L.A.	.10	.15
□ □	232	Andy Moog (G), Bos.	.25	.35
□ □	**233**	**Todd Elik, L.A., RC**	**.10**	**.15**
□ □	234	Craig Janney, Bos.	.10	.15
□ □	**235**	**Star-Rookie: Peter Lappin, Min., RC**	**.10**	**.15**
□ □	236	Scott Stevens, Wsh.	.10	.15
□ □	237	Fredrik Olausson, Wpg.	.10	.15
□ □	238	Geoff Courtnall, Wsh.	.10	.15
□ □	239	Greg Paslawski, Wpg.	.10	.15
□ □	**240**	**Alan May, Wsh., RC**	**.10**	**.15**
□ □	241	Allan Bester (G), Tor.	.10	.15
□ □	242	Steve Larmer, Chi.	.25	.35
□ □	243	Gary Leeman, Tor.	.10	.15
□ □	244	Denis Savard, Chi.	.25	.35
□ □	**245**	**Eric Weinrich, N.J., RC**	**.10**	**.15**
□ □	246	Pat LaFontaine, NYI.	.25	.35
□ □	247	Tim Kerr, Pha.	.10	.15
□ □	248	Dave Gagner, Min.	.10	.15
□ □	249	Brent Sutter, NYI.	.10	.15
□ □	**250**	**Claude Vilgrain, N.J., RC**	**.10**	**.15**
□ □	251	Tomas Sandström, L.A.	.10	.15
□ □	252	Joe Mullen, Cgy.	.10	.15
□ □	253	Brian Leetch, NYR.	.75	1.25
□ □	254	Mike Vernon (G), Cgy.	.25	.35
□ □	**255**	**Star-Rookie: Daniel Doré, Que., RC**	**.10**	**.15**
□ □	256	Trevor Linden, Van.	.75	1.25
□ □	257	David Barr, Det.	.10	.15
□ □	258	John Ogrodnick, NYR.	.10	.15
□ □	259	Russ Courtnall, Mtl.	.10	.15
□ □	260	Dan Quinn, Van.	.10	.15
□ □	261	Mark Howe, Pha.	.10	.15
□ □	262	Kevin Lowe, Edm.	.10	.15
□ □	263	Rick Tocchet, Pha.	.10	.15
□ □	264	Grant Fuhr (G), Edm.	.25	.35
□ □	**265**	**Andrew Cassels, Mtl., RC**	**.25**	**.35**
□ □	266	Kevin Dineen, Hfd.	.10	.15
□ □	267	Kirk Muller, N.J.	.10	.15
□ □	268	Randy Cunneyworth, Hfd.	.10	.15
□ □	269	Brendan Shanahan, N.J.	1.25	1.75
□ □	270	Dave Tippett, Hfd.	.10	.15
□ □	271	Doug Gilmour, Cgy.	.50	.75
□ □	272	Tony Granato, L.A.	.10	.15
□ □	273	Gary Suter, Cgy.	.10	.15
□ □	**274**	**Darren Turcotte, NYR.., RC**	**.20**	**.30**
□ □	**275**	**Murray Baron, Pha., RC**	**.10**	**.15**
□ □	276	Stéphane Richer, Mtl.	.10	.15
□ □	277	Mike Gartner, NYR.	.35	.50
□ □	278	Kirk McLean (G), Van.	.25	.35
□ □	279	John Vanbiesbrouck (G), NYR..	1.50	2.00
□ □	280	Shayne Corson, Mtl.	.25	.35
□ □	281	Paul Cavallini, Stl.	.10	.15
□ □	282	Petr Klima, Edm.	.10	.15
□ □	283	Ulf Dahlen, Min.	.10	.15
□ □	284	Glenn Anderson, Edm.	.10	.15
□ □	285	Rick Meagher, Stl.	.10	.15
□ □	**286**	**Alexei Kasatonov, N.J., RC**	**.10**	**.15**
□ □	287	Ulf Samuelsson, Hfd.	.10	.15
□ □	288	Patrik Sundstrom, N.J.	.10	.15
□ □	289	Ray Ferraro, Hfd.	.10	.15
□ □	**290**	**Janne Ojanen, N.J., RC**	**.10**	**.15**
□ □	291	Jeff Jackson, Que.	.10	.15
□ □	**292**	**Jiri Hrdina, Cgy., RC**	**.10**	**.15**
□ □	293	Joe Cirella, Que.	.10	.15
□ □	294	Brad McCrimmon, Cgy.	.10	.15
□ □	**295**	**Curtis Leschyshyn, Que., RC**	**.10**	**.15**
□ □	296	Kelly Kisio, NYR.	.10	.15
□ □	**297**	**Jyrki Lumme, Van., RC**	**.10**	**.15**
□ □	**298**	**Mark Janssens, NYR.., RC**	**.10**	**.15**
□ □	299	Stan Smyl, Van.	.10	.15
□ □	300	Checklist 3 (201 - 300)	.10	.15
□ □	301	Québec Nordiques: Joe Sakic	.75	1.00
□ □	302	Vancouver Canucks: Petri Skriko	.10	.15
□ □	303	Detroit Red Wings: Steve Yzerman	.75	1.00
□ □	304	Philadelphia Flyers: Tim Kerr	.10	.15
□ □	305	Pittsburgh Penguins: Mario Lemieux	1.00	1.50
□ □	306	New York Islanders; Pat LaFontaine	.25	.35
□ □	307	Los Angeles Kings: Wayne Gretzky	1.50	2.25
□ □	308	Minnesota North Stars: Brian Bellows	.10	.15
□ □	309	Washington Capitals: Rod Langway	.10	.15
□ □	310	Toronto Maple Leafs : Gary Leeman	.10	.15
□ □	311	New Jersey Devils: Kirk Muller	.10	.15
□ □	312	St. Louis Blues: Brett Hull	.75	1.00
□ □	313	Winnipeg Jets: Thomas Steen	.10	.15
□ □	314	Hartford Whalers: Ron Francis	.25	.35
□ □	315	New York Rangers: Brian Leetch	.35	.50
□ □	316	Chicago Blackhawks: Jeremy Roenick	.50	.65
□ □	317	Montréal Canadiens: Patrick Roy (G)	1.00	1.50
□ □	318	Buffalo Sabres: Pierre Turgeon	.25	.35
□ □	319	Calgary Flames: Al MacInnis	.25	.35
□ □	320	Boston Bruins: Ray Bourque	.25	.35
□ □	321	Edmonton Oilers: Mark Messier	.50	.75
□ □	**322**	**Jody Hull, Hfd., RC**	**.10**	**.15**
□ □	**323**	**Chris Joseph, Edm., RC**	**.20**	**.30**
□ □	**324**	**Adam Burt, Hfd., RC**	**.10**	**.15**
□ □	**325**	**Star-Rookie: Jason Herter, Van., RC**	**.10**	**.15**
□ □	326	Geoff Smith, Edm.	.10	.15
□ □	327	Brad Shaw, Hfd.	.10	.15
□ □	328	Rich Sutter, Stl.	.10	.15
□ □	329	Barry Pederson, Pgh.	.10	.15
□ □	330	Paul MacLean, Stl.	.10	.15
□ □	331	Randy Carlyle, Wpg.	.10	.15
□ □	**332**	**Donald Dufresne, Mtl., RC**	**.10**	**.15**
□ □	**333**	**Brent Hughes, Wpg., RC**	**.10**	**.15**
□ □	**334**	**Mathieu Schneider, Mtl., RC**	**.60**	**.75**
□ □	**335**	**Jason Miller, N.J., RC**	**.10**	**.15**
□ □	336	Sergei Makarov, Cgy.	.20	.30
□ □	337	Bob Essensa (G), Wpg.	.10	.15
□ □	**338**	**Claude Loiselle, Que., RC**	**.10**	**.15**
□ □	339	Wayne Presley, Chi.	.10	.15
□ □	340	Tony McKegney, Que.	.10	.15
□ □	341	Charlie Huddy, Edm.	.10	.15
□ □	342	Greg Adams, Van., Error (I.Larionov)	.10	.15
□ □	**343**	**Mike Tomlak, Hfd., RC**	**.10**	**.15**
□ □	**344**	**Adam Graves, Edm., RC**	**1.25**	**1.75**
□ □	**345**	**Michel Mongeau, Stl., RC**	**.10**	**.15**
□ □	346	Mike Modano, Min.	.50	.65
□ □	347	Rod Brind'Amour, Stl.	.35	.50
□ □	348	Dana Murzyn, Cgy.	.10	.15
□ □	**349**	**Dave Lowry, Stl., RC**	**.20**	**.30**
□ □	350	Star Rookie Checklist	.10	.15
□ □	351	CL: Nolan/Primeau/Nedved/Ricci	.50	.65
□ □	**352**	**Owen Nolan, Que., RC**	**1.50**	**2.00**
□ □	**353**	**Petr Nedved, Van., RC**	**1.25**	**1.75**
□ □	**354**	**Keith Primeau, Det., RC**	**1.25**	**1.75**
□ □	**355**	**Mike Ricci, Pha., RC**	**.60**	**.75**
□ □	**356**	**Jaromir Jagr, Pgh., RC**	**8.00**	**10.00**
□ □	**357**	**Scott Scissons, NYI.., RC**	**.10**	**.15**
□ □	**358**	**Darryl Sydor, L.A., RC**	**.20**	**.30**
□ □	**359**	**Derian Hatcher, Min., RC**	**.50**	**.75**
□ □	**360**	**John Slaney, Wsh., RC**	**.10**	**.15**
□ □	**361**	**Drake Berehowsky, Tor., RC**	**.10**	**.15**
□ □	362	Luke Richardson, Tor.	.10	.15
□ □	363	Lucien DeBlois, Que.	.10	.15
□ □	**364**	**David Reid, Tor., RC**	**.10**	**.15**
□ □	**365**	**Mats Sundin, Que., RC**	**2.50**	**3.00**
□ □	366	Jan Erixon, NYR.	.10	.15
□ □	**367**	**Troy Loney, Pgh., RC**	**.10**	**.15**
□ □	368	Chris Nilan, NYR.	.10	.15
□ □	369	Gord Dineen, Pgh.	.10	.15
□ □	**370**	**Jeff Bloemberg, NYR.., RC**	**.10**	**.15**
□ □	**371**	**John Druce, Wsh., RC**	**.10**	**.15**
□ □	372	Brian MacLellan, Cgy.	.10	.15
□ □	373	Bruce Driver, N.J.	.10	.15
□ □	374	Marc Habscheid, Det.	.10	.15
□ □	**375**	**Paul Ysebaert, N.J., RC**	**.10**	**.15**
□ □	376	Rick Vaive, Buf.	.10	.15
□ □	377	Glen Wesley, Bos.	.10	.15
□ □	378	Mike Foligno, Buf.	.10	.15
□ □	**379**	**Garry Galley, Bos., RC**	**.10**	**.15**
□ □	**380**	**Dean Kennedy, Buf., RC**	**.10**	**.15**
□ □	381	Daniel Berthiaume (G), Min.	.10	.15
□ □	**382**	**Mike Keane, Mtl., RC**	**.25**	**.35**
□ □	383	Frantisek Musil, Min	.10	.15
□ □	384	Mike McPhee, Mtl.	.10	.15
□ □	385	Jon Casey (G), Min.	.10	.15
□ □	386	Jeff Norton, NYI.	.10	.15
□ □	387	John Tucker, Wsh.	.10	.15
□ □	388	Alan Kerr, NYI.	.10	.15
□ □	389	Bob Rouse, Wsh.	.10	.15
□ □	390	Gerald Diduck, NYI.	.10	.15
□ □	391	Greg Hawgood, Bos.	.10	.15
□ □	392	Randy Velischek, N.J.	.10	.15
□ □	**393**	**Tim Cheveldae (G), Det., RC**	**.10**	**.15**
□ □	394	Mike Krushelnyski, L.A.	.10	.15
□ □	395	Glen Hanlon (G), Det.	.10	.15
□ □	**396**	**Lou Franceschetti, Tor., RC**	**.10**	**.15**
□ □	397	Scott Arniel, Buf.	.10	.15
□ □	398	Terry Carkner, Pha.	.10	.15
□ □	399	Clint Malarchuk (G), Buf.	.10	.15
□ □	400	Checklist 4 (301 - 400)	.10	.15
□ □	**401**	**Mikhail Tatarinov, Wsh., RC**	**.10**	**.20**
□ □	402	Benoît Hogue, Buf.	.10	.20
□ □	**403**	**Frank Pietrangelo (G), Pgh., RC**	**.10**	**.20**
□ □	**404**	**Paul Stanton, Pgh., RC**	**.10**	**.20**
□ □	**405**	**Anatoli Semenov, Edm., RC**	**.10**	**.20**
□ □	406	Bobby Smith, Min.	.10	.20
□ □	407	Derek King, NYI.	.10	.20
□ □	**408**	**Jean-Claude Bergeron (G), Mtl., RC**	**.10**	**.20**
□ □	409	Brian Propp, Bos.	.10	.20
□ □	**410**	**Jiri Latal, Pha., RC**	**.10**	**.20**
□ □	**411**	**Joey Kocur, Det., RC**	**.20**	**.40**
□ □	412	Daniel Berthiaume (G), L.A.	.10	.20
□ □	413	David Ellett, Wpg.	.10	.20
□ □	**414**	**Jay Miller, L.A., RC**	**.10**	**.20**
□ □	**415**	**Stéphane Beauregard (G), Wpg., RC**	**.10**	**.20**
□ □	416	Mark Hardy, NYR.	.10	.20
□ □	**417**	**Todd Krygier, Hfd., RC**	**.10**	**.20**
□ □	418	Randy Moller, NYR.	.10	.20
□ □	419	Doug Crossman, Hfd.	.10	.20
□ □	420	Ray Sheppard, NYR.	.25	.50
□ □	**421**	**Sylvain Lefebvre, Mtl., RC**	**.25**	**.50**
□ □	422	Chris Chelios, Chi.	.50	1.00
□ □	423	Joe Mullen, Pgh.	.10	.20
□ □	424	Pete Peeters (G), Pha.	.10	.20
□ □	425	Bryan Trottier, Pgh.	.25	.50
□ □	426	Denis Savard, Mtl.	.25	.50
□ □	427	Ken Daneyko, N.J.	.10	.20
□ □	**428**	**Eric Desjardins, Mtl., RC**	**.75**	**1.25**
□ □	**429**	**Zdeno Ciger, N.J., RC**	**.10**	**.20**
□ □	430	Brad McCrimmon, Det.	.10	.20
□ □	431	Ed Olczyk, Wpg.	.10	.20
□ □	**432**	**Peter Ing (G), Tor., RC**	**.10**	**.20**
□ □	**433**	**Bob Kudelski, L.A., RC**	**.25**	**.35**

	No.	Player		
☐☐	**434**	**Troy Gamble (G), Van., RC**	**.10**	**15**
☐☐	435	Phil Housley, Buf.	.10	.20
☐☐	436	Scott Stevens, Stl.	.25	.50
☐☐	437	Normand Rochefort, NYR.	.10	.20
☐☐	438	Geoff Courtnall, Wsh.	.10	.20
☐☐	**439**	**Ken Baumgartner, NYI.., RC**	**.10**	**.20**
☐☐	**440**	**Kris King, NYR.., RC**	**.25**	**.35**
☐☐	**441**	**Troy Crowder, N.J., RC**	**.10**	**.20**
☐☐	442	Chris Nilan, Bos.	.10	.20
☐☐	443	Dale Hawerchuk, Buf.	.25	.50
☐☐	**444**	**Kevin Miller, NYR.., RC**	**.10**	**.20**
☐☐	445	Keith Acton, Pha.	.10	.20
☐☐	**446**	**Jeff Chychrun, Pha., RC**	**.10**	**.20**
☐☐	447	Claude Lemieux, Mtl.	.10	.20
☐☐	448	Bob Probert, Det.	.20	.30
☐☐	449	Brian Hayward (G), Mtl.	.10	.20
☐☐	**450**	**Craig Berube, Pha., RC**	**.10**	**.20**
☐☐	451	Canadian National Junior Team	.25	.35
☐☐	**452**	**Mike Sillinger, Cdn., RC**	**.25**	**.35**
☐☐	**453**	**Jason Marshall, Cdn., RC**	**.10**	**.20**
☐☐	**454**	**Patrice Brisebois, Cdn., RC**	**.25**	**.35**
☐☐	**455**	**Brad May, Cdn., RC**	**.25**	**.35**
☐☐	**456**	**Pierre Sévigny, Cdn., RC**	**.25**	**.35**
☐☐	**457**	**John Slaney, Cdn., RC**	**.25**	**.35**
☐☐	**458**	**Félix Potvin (G), Cdn., RC**	**8.00**	**12.00**
☐☐	**459**	**Scott Thornton, Cdn., RC**	**.10**	**.20**
☐☐	**460**	**Greg Johnson, Cdn., RC**	**.35**	**.50**
☐☐	**461**	**Scott Niedermayer, Cdn., RC**	**1.50**	**2.25**
☐☐	**462**	**Steven Rice, Cdn., RC**	**.35**	**.50**
☐☐	**463**	**Trevor Kidd (G), Cdn., RC**	**1.50**	**2.25**
☐☐	**464**	**Dale Craigwell, Cdn., RC**	**.10**	**.20**
☐☐	**465**	**Kent Manderville, Cdn., RC**	**.10**	**.20**
☐☐	**466**	**Kris Draper, Cdn., RC**	**.50**	**.65**
☐☐	**467**	**Martin Lapointe, Cdn., RC**	**.50**	**.65**
☐☐	**468**	**Chris Snell, Cdn., RC**	**.10**	**.20**
☐☐	**469**	**Pat Falloon, Cdn., RC**	**.35**	**.50**
☐☐	**470**	**David Harlock, Cdn., RC**	**.10**	**.20**
☐☐	**471**	**Karl Dykhuis, Cdn., RC**	**.25**	**.35**
☐☐	**472**	**Mike Craig, Cdn., RC**	**.25**	**.35**
☐☐	473	Canada's Captains: Draper/ Rice/ Lindros	4.50	6.50
☐☐	474	AS: Brett Hull, Stl.	.75	1.50
☐☐	475	AS: Darren Turcotte, NYR.	.10	.20
☐☐	476	AS: Wayne Gretzky, L.A.	1.50	3.00
☐☐	477	AS: Steve Yzerman, Det.	.75	1.50
☐☐	478	AS: Theoren Fleury, Cgy.	.25	.50
☐☐	479	AS: Pat LaFontaine, NYI.	.25	.50
☐☐	480	AS: Trevor Linden, Van.	.35	.70
☐☐	481	AS: Jeremy Roenick, Chi.	.50	1.00
☐☐	482	AS: Scott Stevens, Stl.	.25	.50
☐☐	483	AS: Adam Oates, Stl.	.25	.50
☐☐	484	AS: Vincent Damphousse, Tor.	.25	.50
☐☐	485	AS: Brian Leetch, NYR.	.35	.75
☐☐	486	AS: Kevin Hatcher, Wsh.	.10	.20
☐☐	487	AS: Mark Recchi, Pgh.	.25	.50
☐☐	488	AS: Rick Tocchet, Pha.	.10	.20
☐☐	489	AS: Ray Bourque, Bos.	.35	.75
☐☐	490	AS: Joe Sakic, Que.	.75	1.50
☐☐	491	AS: Chris Chelios, Mtl.	.25	.50
☐☐	492	AS: John Cullen, Pgh.	.10	.20
☐☐	493	AS: Cam Neely, Bos	.25	.50
☐☐	494	AS: Mark Messier, Edm.	.50	1.00
☐☐	495	AS: Mike Vernon (G), Cgy.	.20	.40
☐☐	496	AS: Patrick Roy, Mtl. (G)	1.00	2.00
☐☐	497	AS: Al MacInnis, Cgy.	.25	.50
☐☐	498	AS: Paul Coffey, Pgh.	.35	.75
☐☐	499	AS: Steve Larmer, Chi.	.20	.40
☐☐	500	Checklist 1 (401 - 500)	.10	.20
☐☐	501	Heroes Checklist	.20	.30
☐☐	502	Red Kelly, Det.	.25	.50
☐☐	503	Eric Nesterenko, Tor.	.25	.50
☐☐	504	Darryl Sittler, Tor.	.25	.50
☐☐	505	Jim Schoenfeld, Buf.	.25	.50
☐☐	506	Serge Savard, Mtl.	.25	.50
☐☐	507	Glenn Resch (G), NYI.	.25	.50
☐☐	508	Lanny McDonald, Tor.	.25	.50
☐☐	509	Bobby Clarke, Pha.	.35	.75
☐☐	510	Phil Esposito, Chi.	.35	.75
☐☐	511	Harry Howell, NYR.	.25	.50
☐☐	512	Rod Gilbert, NYR.	.25	.50
☐☐	513	Pit Martin, Det.	.25	.50
☐☐	514	Jimmy Watson, Pha.	.25	.50
☐☐	515	Denis Potvin, NYI.	.35	.75
☐☐	**516**	**Rob Ray, Buf., RC**	**.20**	**.30**
☐☐	**517**	**Danton Cole, Wpg., RC**	**.10**	**.20**
☐☐	**518**	**Gino Odjick, Van., RC**	**.25**	**.35**
☐☐	519	Donald Audette, Buf., RC	.25	.35
☐☐	**520**	**Rick Tabaracci (G), Pgh., RC**	**.35**	**.50**
☐☐	521	CL: Fedorov/Garpenlov, Det.	1.00	1.50
☐☐	**522**	**Kip Miller, Que., RC**	**.10**	**.20**
☐☐	**523**	**Johan Garpenlov, Det., RC**	**.10**	**.20**
☐☐	**524**	**Stéphane Morin, Que., RC**	**.10**	**.20**
☐☐	**525**	**Sergei Fedorov, Det., RC**	**9.00**	**13.00**
☐☐	**526**	**Pavel Bure, Van., RC**	**15.00**	**22.00**
☐☐	**527**	**Wes Walz, Bos., RC**	**.10**	**.20**
☐☐	**528**	**Robert Kron, Van., RC**	**.10**	**.20**
☐☐	**529**	**Ken Hodge, Bos., RC**	**.10**	**.20**
☐☐	**530**	**Garry Valk, Van., RC**	**.10**	**.20**
☐☐	**531**	**Tim Sweeney, Cgy., RC**	**.10**	**.20**
☐☐	**532**	**Mark Pederson, Mtl., RC**	**.10**	**.20**
☐☐	**533**	**Robert Reichel, Cgy., RC**	**.25**	**.35**
☐☐	**534**	**Bobby Holik, Hfd., RC**	**.50**	**1.00**
☐☐	**535**	**Stéphane Matteau, Cgy., RC**	**.20**	**.30**
☐☐	**536**	**Peter Bondra, Wsh., RC**	**2.00**	**3.00**
☐☐	**537**	**Dimitri Khristich, Wsh., RC**	**.25**	**.35**
☐☐	**538**	**Vladimir Ruzicka, Bos., RC**	**.10**	**.20**
☐☐	539	Al Iafrate, Wsh.	.10	.20
☐☐	**540**	**Rick Bennett, NYR.., RC**	**.10**	**.20**
☐☐	**541**	**Daryl Reaugh (G), Hfd., RC**	**.10**	**.20**
☐☐	**542**	**Martin Hostak, Pha., RC**	**.10**	**.20**
☐☐	**543**	**Kari Takko (G), Edm., RC**	**.10**	**.20**
☐☐	**544**	**Jocelyn Lemieux, Chi., RC**	**.10**	**.20**
☐☐	545	Wayne Gretzky, L.A. (2000 Pts.)	1.50	3.00
☐☐	546	Brett Hull, Stl. (50/50)	.75	1.50
☐☐	**547**	**Neil Wilkinson, Min., RC**	**.10**	**.20**
☐☐	**548**	**Bryan Fogarty, Que., RC**	**.10**	**.20**
☐☐	549	Frank J. Zamboni/Rink Resurfer	.10	.20
☐☐	550	Checklist 2 (501 - 550)	.10	.20

STEREOGRAMS

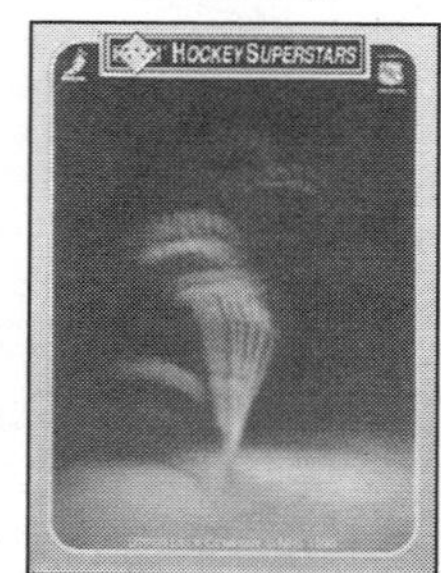

These hologram cards were inserted in both Low Series and High Series packs.

	Player	NRMT-MT
☐	Wayne Gretzky, L.A. (Shooting)	2.00
☐	Wayne Gretzky, L.A. (Stadning)	2.00
☐	Wayne Gretzky, L.A. (Stopping)	2.00
☐	Brett Hull, Stl.,	.75
☐	Mark Messier, Edm.	.75
☐	Steve Yzerman, Det.	1.00
☐	Steve Yzerman, Det.	1.00
☐	Brett Hull, Stl./Mark Messier, Edm.	.50
☐	Mark Messier, Edm./Steve Yzerman, Det.	.50
☐	Steve Yzerman, Det./Brett Hull, Stl.	.50

1990 - 91 UPPER DECK COMMEMORATIVE SHEETS

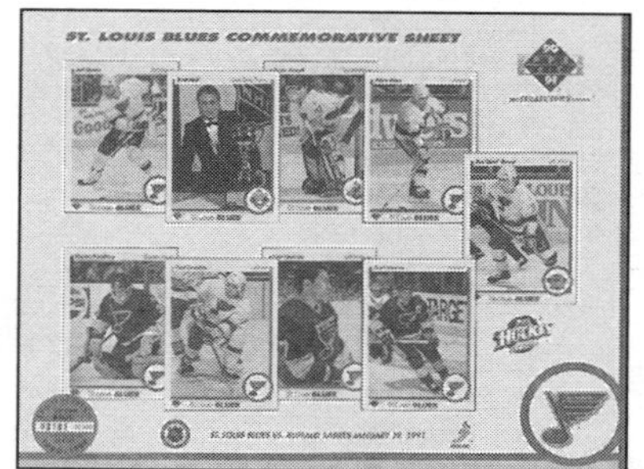

These sheets were issued at home team arenas on the dates printed on the sheet and commemorate a home team game on that date. Complete sets are difficult to obtain.

Card Size: 8 1/2" x 11"

Imprint:

Complete Set (11 cards): 125.00

	No.	Sheet	NRMT-MT
☐	1	Tor. Maple Leafs vs. Det. Red Wings, Nov 17/90	10.00
☐	2	Det. Red Wings vs. Bos. Bruins, Dec 4/90	10.00
☐	3	L.A. Kings vs. Cgy. Flames, Dec 13/90	10.00
☐	4	N.Y. Rangers vs. Hfd. Whalers, Jan. 13/91	10.00
☐	5	N.Y. Rangers vs. Chi. Blackhawks, Jan. 17/91	10.00
☐	6	Chicago Stadium: Campbell Div. All Stars, Jan. 19/91	20.00
☐	7	Chicago Stadium: Wales Div. All Stars, Jan. 19/91	20.00
☐	8	Stl. Blues vs. Buf. Sabres, Jan 29/91	10.00
☐	9	Det. Red Wings vs. Min. North Stars, Feb 16/91	10.00
☐	10	N.Y. Rangers vs. N.Y. Islanders, Feb. 18/91	10.00
☐	11	All-Rookie Team, June 21/91	20.00

1990 - 91 WAYNE GRETZKY CUPS

We have little information on this Wayne Gretzky "Athlete of the Decade" cup set.

Imprint:

Complete Set (5 cups): 25.00

	Player	NRMT-MT
☐	Wayne Gretzky 1981-82	6.00
☐	Wayne Gretzky 1983-84	6.00
☐	Wayne Gretzky 1985-86	6.00
☐	Wayne Gretzky 1987-88	6.00
☐	Wayne Gretzky 1989-90	6.00

1991 C55 REPRINT SET

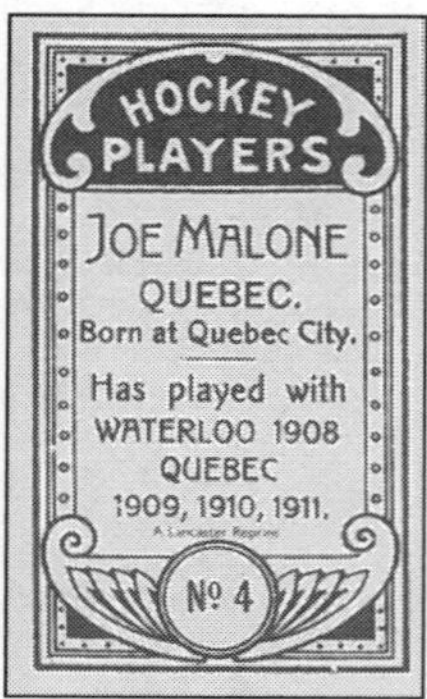

This series was published by Windhill Publishing and was limited to 50,000 copies.

Card Size: 1 1/2" x 2 1/2"

Imprint: None

Complete Set (45 cards): 20.00

Album: 5.00

	No.	Player	NRMT-MT
☐	1	Paddy Moran (G), Québec	1.25
☐	2	Joe Hall, Québec	.85
☐	3	Barney Holden, Québec	.50
☐	4	Joe Malone, Québec	1.50
☐	5	Ed Oatman, Québec	.50
☐	6	Tommy Dunderdale, Québec	.85
☐	7	Ken Mallen, Québec	.50
☐	8	Jack McDonald, Québec	.50
☐	9	Fred Lake, Ott.	.50
☐	10	Albert Ker, Ott.	.50
☐	11	Marty Walsh, Ott.	.75
☐	12	Hamby Shore, Ott.	.50
☐	13	Alex Currie, Ott.	.50
☐	14	Bruce Ridpath, Ott.	.50
☐	15	Bruce Stuart, Ott., LC	.75
☐	16	Percy Lesueur (G), Ott.	.85
☐	17	Jack Darragh, Ott.	.75
☐	18	Steve Vair, Renfrew	.50
☐	19	Don Smith, Renfrew	.50
☐	20	Fred Taylor, Renfrew	2.00
☐	21	Bert Lindsay (G), Renfrew	.50
☐	22	Larry Gilmour, Renfrew	.75
☐	23	Bobby Rowe, Renfrew	.50
☐	24	Sprague Cleghorn, Renfrew	1.50
☐	25	Odie Cleghorn, Renfrew	.75
☐	26	Skein Ronan, Renfrew	.75
☐	27	Walter Smaill, Mtl. W.	.85
☐	28	Ernie Johnson, Mtl. W.	.85

No.	Player	Price
29	Jack Marshall, Mtl. W.	.75
30	Harry Hyland, Mtl. W.	.75
31	Art Ross, Mtl. W.	3.00
32	Riley Hern (G), Mtl. W.	.75
33	Gord Roberts, Mtl. W.	.75
34	Frank Glass, Mtl. W.	.50
35	Ernest Russell, Mtl. W.	.75
36	James Gardiner, Mtl. W.	.75
37	Art Bernier, Mtl.	.50
38	Georges Vézina (G), Mtl.	7.00
39	Henri Dellaire, Mtl.	.50
40	R. Power, Mtl.	.50
41	Didier Pitre, Mtl.	.75
42	Edouard Lalonde, Mtl.	2.50
43	Eugene Payan, Mtl.	.50
44	Georges Poulin, Mtl.	.50
45	Jack Laviolette, Mtl.	1.25

1991 IVAN FIODOROV PRESS SPORT UNITE HEARTS SOVIET TEAM

There are 50,000 sets available.

Imprint:

Complete Set (11 cards): **8.00**

No.	Player	NRMT-MT
1	USSR National Team	.50
2	Sergei Fedorov	2.00
3	Viacheslav Fetisov	1.00
4	Alexei Gusarov	.50
5	Alexei Kasatonov	.50
6	Vladimir Konstantinov	1.00
7	Igor Larionov	1.00
8	Sergei Makarov	1.00
9	Alexander Mogilny	1.50
10	Mikhail Tatarinov	.50
11	Vladislav Tretiak (G)	3.00

1991 PRO SET NHL AWARDS SPECIAL

Cards 1-16 were given out June 5, 1991 at the NHL Awards Banquet in Toronto, while cards 17-23 were given out June 6, 1991 at the Hockey News Sponsor Awards also in Toronto. Cards have the same design as the 1991-92 Pro Set basic set.

Awards Special Set (17 cards): **500.00**

Sponsor Awards Set (8 cards): **100.00**

No.	Player	NRMT-MT
	Title Card: 1990-91 NHL Awards Special	5.00
AC1	Ed Belfour (G), Chi.	25.00
AC2	Mike Richter (G), NYR.	20.00
AC3	Patrick Roy, Mtl.	100.00
AC4	Wayne Gretzky, L.A.	200.00
AC5	Joe Sakic, Que.	65.00
AC6	Brett Hull, Stl.	30.00
AC7	Ray Bourque, Bos.	30.00
AC8	Al MacInnis, Cgy.	8.00
AC9	Luc Robitaille, L.A.	10.00
AC10	Sergei Fedorov, Det.	30.00
AC11	Ken Hodge, Bos.	5.00
AC12	Dirk Graham, Chi.	5.00
AC13	Steve Larmer, Chi.	10.00
AC14	Esa Tikkanen, Edm.	5.00
AC15	Chris Chelios, , Chi.	25.00
AC16	Dave Taylor, L.A.	5.00
	Title Card: 1990-91 NHL Sponsor Awards	5.00
AC17	Kevin Dineen, Hfd.	5.00
AC18	Brett Hull, Stl.	30.00
AC19	Ed Belfour, Chi.	25.00
AC20	Theoren Fleury, Cgy.	15.00
AC21	Marty McSorley, L.A.	5.00
AC22	Mike Ilitch, Owner, Det.	10.00
AC23	Rod Gilbert, NYR.	15.00

1991 SEMIC STICKERS

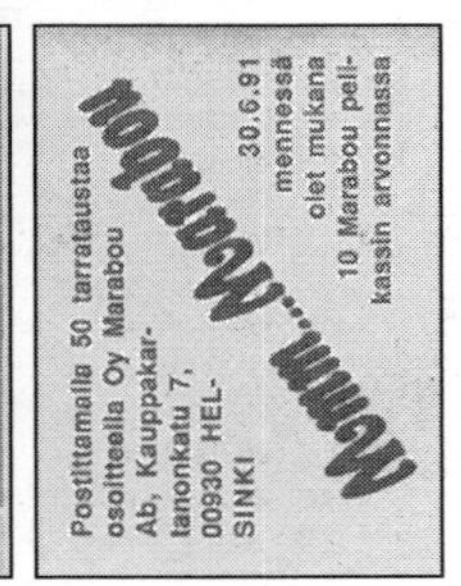

There are three versions of these stickers: Blank backs, "Marabou" backs and "Milky Way" backs. All three versions have the same value.

Imprint: None

Complete Set (250 stickers): **50.00**

Common Player: **.15**

No.	Player	NRMT-MT
1	Finland	.15
2	Markus Ketterer (G)	.15
3	Sakari Lindfors (G)	.15
4	Jukka Tammi (G)	.15
5	Time Jutila	.25
6	Hannu Virta	.15
7	Simo Saarinen	.15
8	Jukka Marttila	.15
9	Ville Siren	.15
10	Pasi Huura	.15
11	Hannu Henriksson	.15
12	Arte Ruotanen	.15
13	Ari Haanpää	.15
14	Pauli Järvinen	.15
15	Teppo Kivelä	.15
16	Risto Kurkinen	.15
17	Mika Nieminen	.15
18	Jari Kurri, Milan	1.00
19	Esa Keskinen	.15
20	Raimo Summanen	.15
21	Teemu Selänne	5.00
22	Jari Torkki	.15
23	Hannu Järvenpää	.15
24	Raimo Helminen	.15
25	Time Peltomaa	.15
26	Sweden	.15
27	Peter Lindmark	.15
28	Rolf Ridderwall	.15
29	Tommy Söderström (G)	1.00
30	Thomas Eriksson	.15
31	Nicklas Lidström, Swe.	2.00
32	Tomas Jonsson	.15
33	Tommy Samuelsson	.15
34	Fredrik Stillman	.15
35	Peter Andersson	.15
36	Peter Andersson, Swe.	.15
37	Kenneth Kennholt	.15
38	Håkan Loob	.25
39	Thomas Rundqvist	.15
40	Håkan Åhlund	.15
41	Jan Viktorsson	.15
42	Charles Berglund	.15
43	Mikael Johansson	.15
44	Robert Burakovsky	.15
45	Bengt Gustafsson	.15
46	Patrik Carnbäck	.15
47	Patrik Erickson	.15
48	Anders Carlsson	.15
49	Mats Naslund	.25
50	Kent Nilsson	.25
51	Canada	.15
52	Patrick Roy (G)	8.00
53	Ed Belfour (G)	1.50
54	Daniel Berthiaume (G)	.25
55	Ray Bourque	2.50
56	Scott Stevens	.25
57	Al MacInnis	.25
58	Paul Coffey	1.00
59	Paul Cavallini, Stl.	.25
60	Zarley Zalapski	.25
61	Steve Duchesne	.25
62	Dave Ellett	.25
63	Mark Messier	2.50
64	Wayne Gretzky	10.00
65	Steve Yzerman, Det.	5.00
66	Pierre Turgeon	.50
67	Bernie Nicholls, NYR.	.25
68	Cam Neely, Bos.	.50
69	Joe Nieuwendyk	.25
70	Luc Robitaille, L.A.	.50
71	Kevin Dineen, Hfd.	.25
72	John Cullen	.25
73	Steve Larmer	.25
74	Mark Recchi	1.00
75	Joe Sakic	4.00
76	Soviet Union	.15
77	Arturs Irbe (G), USSR	.25
78	Alexei Marjin	.15
79	Mikhail Shtalenkov (G)	.25
80	Vladimir Malakhov	.25
81	Vladimir Konstantinov	2.00
82	Igor Kravchuk	.25
83	Ilja Byakin	.15
84	Dimitri Mironov	.15
85	Vladimir Tiurikov	.15
86	Vyacheslav Uvajev	.15
87	Vladimir Fedosov	.15
88	Valeri Kamensky	2.00
89	Pavel Bure	5.00
90	Viatcheslav Butsayev	.15
91	Igor Maslennikov	.15
92	Evgeny Davydov	.15
93	Andrei Kovalev	.15
94	Alexander Semak	.25
95	Alexei Zhamnov	2.00
96	Sergei Nemchinov	.25
97	Viktor Gordiouk	.15
98	Vyacheslav Kozlov, USSR	1.50
99	Andrei Khomutov	.25
100	Vyacheslav Bykov	.25
101	Czechoslovakia	.15
102	Petr Briza (G)	.15
103	Dominik Hasek (G)	5.00
104	Eduard Hartmann (G)	.15
105	Bedrich Scerban	.15
106	Jiri Slegr	.25
107	Josef Reznicek	.15
108	Petr Pavlas	.15
109	Peter Slanina	.15
110	Martin Maskarinec	.15
111	Antonin Stavjana	.15
112	Stanislav Medrik	.15
113	Dusan Pasek	.15
114	Jiri Lala	.15
115	Darius Rusnak	.15
116	Otto Hascak	.15
117	Radek Toupal	.15
118	Pavel Pycha	.15
119	Lubomir Kolnik	.15
120	Libor Dolana	.15
121	Ladislav Lubina	.15
122	Tomas Jelinek	.15
123	Petr Vlk	.15
124	Vladimir Petovka	.15
125	Richard Zemlicka	.15
126	USA	.15
127	John Vanbiesbrouck (G)	3.00
128	Mike Richter (G), NYR..	2.00
129	Chris Terreri (G), N.J.	.25
130	Chris Chelios	1.50
131	Brian Leetch, NYR.	2.00
132	Gary Suter	.25
133	Phil Housley	.25
134	Mark Howe, Pha.	.50
135	Al Iafrate	.25
136	Kevin Hatcher, Wsh.	.25
137	Mathieu Schneider, Mtl.	.25
138	Pat LaFontaine, NYI.	.50
139	Darren Turcotte, NYR.	.25
140	Neal Broten, Min.	.25
141	Mike Modano	2.50
142	Dave Christian	.25
143	Craig Janney	.25

	No.	Player	Value
□□□	144	Brett Hull, Stl.	2.50
□□□	145	Kevin Stevens, Pgh.	.25
□□□	146	Joe Mullen, Pgh.	.25
□□□	147	Tony Granato	.25
□□□	148	Ed Olczyk	.25
□□□	149	Jeremy Roenick, Chi.	1.50
□□□	150	Jimmy Carson	.25
□□□	151	Germany	.15
□□□	152	Helmut De Raaf	.15
□□□	153	Josef Heiss (G)	.15
□□□	154	Karl Friessen	.15
□□□	155	Uli Hiemer	.15
□□□	156	Harold Kreiss	.15
□□□	157	Udo Kiessling	.15
□□□	158	Michael Schmidt	.15
□□□	159	Michael Heidt	.15
□□□	160	Andreas Polorny	.15
□□□	161	Bernd Wagner	.15
□□□	162	Uwe Krupp	.25
□□□	163	Gerd Truntschka	.15
□□□	164	Bernd Truntschka	.15
□□□	165	Thomas Brandl	.15
□□□	166	Peter Draisatl	.15
□□□	167	Andreas Brockmann	.15
□□□	168	Ulrich Liebsch	.15
□□□	169	Ralf Hantschke	.15
□□□	170	Thomas Schinko	.15
□□□	171	Anton Krinner	.15
□□□	172	Thomas Werner	.15
□□□	173	Dieter Hegen	.15
□□□	174	Selmut Steiger	.15
□□□	175	Georg Franz	.15
□□□	176	Switzerland	.15
□□□	177	Renato Tosio (G)	.15
□□□	178	Reto Pavoni	.15
□□□	179	Dino Stecher	.15
□□□	180	Sven Leuenberger	.15
□□□	181	Rick Tschumi	.15
□□□	182	Patrice Brasey	.15
□□□	183	Didier Massy	.15
□□□	184	Sandro Bertaggia	.15
□□□	185	Samuel Palmer	.15
□□□	186	Martin Rauch	.15
□□□	187	Marc Leuenberger	.15
□□□	188	Jörg Eberle	.15
□□□	189	Fredy Luhti	.15
□□□	190	Andy Ton	.15
□□□	191	Raymond Walder	.15
□□□	192	Manuele Celio	.15
□□□	193	Roman Wäger	.15
□□□	194	Felix Hollenstein	.15
□□□	195	Andre Rötheli	.15
□□□	196	Christian Weber	.15
□□□	197	Peter Jaks	.15
□□□	198	Gil Montandon	.15
□□□	199	Oliver Hoffman	.15
□□□	200	Thomas Vrabec	.15
□□□	201	Teppo Numminen	.25
□□□	202	Jyrki Lumme, Van.	.25
□□□	203	Esa Tikkanen	.25
□□□	204	Petri Skriko	.25
□□□	205	Christian Ruuttu	.25
□□□	206	Ilkka Sinisalo	.25
□□□	207	Calle Johansson	.25
□□□	208	Tomas Sandström	.25
□□□	209	Thomas Steen	.25
□□□	210	Per-Erik Eklund	.25
□□□	211	Mats Sundin	2.50
□□□	212	Johan Garpenlöv, Det.	.25
□□□	213	Viacheslav Fetisov, N.J.	.50
□□□	214	Alexei Kasatonov	.25
□□□	215	Michail Tatarinov	.25
□□□	216	Sergei Makarov	.50
□□□	217	Igor Larionov	.50
□□□	218	Alexander Mogilny	2.00
□□□	219	Sergei Fedorov, Det.	4.00
□□□	220	Petr Klima	.25
□□□	221	David Volek	.25
□□□	222	Michal Pivonka	.25
□□□	223	Robert Reichel, Cgy.	.50
□□□	224	Bobby Holik	.50
□□□	225	Jaromir Jagr	6.00
□□□	226	Urpo Ylönen	.15
□□□	227	Ilpo Koskela	.15
□□□	228	Pekka Rautakallio	.15
□□□	229	Lasse Oksanen	.15
□□□	230	Veli-Pekka Ketola	.25
□□□	231	Leif Holmqvist	.15
□□□	232	Lennart Svedberg	.15
□□□	233	Sven Tumba	.15
□□□	234	Ulf Sterner	.15
□□□	235	Anders Hedberg	.25
□□□	236	Ken Dryden	4.00
□□□	237	Bobby Orr	10.00
□□□	238	Gordie Howe	8.00
□□□	239	Bobby Hull	3.00
□□□	240	Phil Esposito, Bos.	1.50
□□□	241	Vladislav Tretiak (G)	4.00
□□□	242	Aleksandr Ragulin	.25
□□□	243	Anatoli Firsov	.25
□□□	244	Valeri Kharlamov	1.50
□□□	245	Alexander Maltsev	.50
□□□	246	Jiri Holecek	.15
□□□	247	Jan Suchy	.15
□□□	248	Josef Golonka	.15
□□□	249	Vaclav Nedomansky	.15
□□□	250	Ivan Hlinka	.15

1991 TEAM CANADA - JL PRODUCTIONS

Card Size: 8" x 10"
Imprint: JL Productions

Complete Set (22 cards):	**50.00**
Album:	**10.00**

	Player	NRMT-MT
□	Bill Ranford (G), Cdn.	4.00
□	Al MacInnis, Cdn.	4.00
□	Scott Stevens, Cdn.	4.00
□	Paul Coffey, Cdn.	4.00
□	Larry Murphy, Cdn.	4.00
□	Eric Desjardins, Cdn.	4.00
□	Mark Tinordi, Cdn.	3.00
□	Steve Smith, Cdn.	3.00
□	Brent Sutter, Cdn.	3.00
□	Dale Hawerchuk, Cdn.	4.00
□	Russ Courtnall, Cdn.	3.00
□	Dirk Graham, Cdn.	3.00
□	Theoren Fleury, Cdn.	4.00
□	Brendan Shanahan, Cdn.	6.00
□	Rick Tocchet, Cdn.	3.00
□	Shayne Corson, Cdn.	4.00
□	Luc Robitaille, Cdn.	4.00
□	Steve Larmer, Cdn.	3.00
□	Eric Lindros, Cdn.	10.00
□	Mark Messier, Cdn.	5.00
□	Wayne Gretzky, Cdn.	15.00
□	Team Canada - Team Photo	5.00

1991 - 92 ACE NOVELTY MVP COLLECTOR PINS

These collector pins were packaged with a 1991-92 ProSet hockey card. Other singles exist.

Imprint: © 1991 Ace Novelty Co. Inc.

	No.	Player
□	71002	Cam Neely, Bos.
□	71080	Sergei Fedorov, Det.

1991 - 92 AIR CANADA SASKATCHEWAN JUNIOR HOCKEY LEAGUE

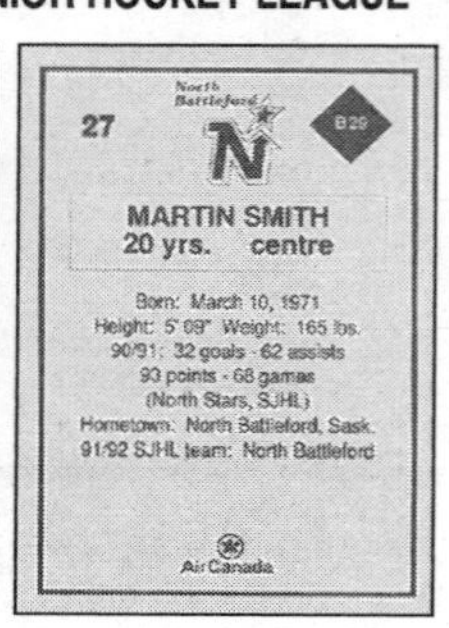

Complete Set (250 cards):	**25.00**
Common Player:	**.15**

	No.	Player	NRMT-MT
□	1	Jeff Kungle, Mft.	.15
□	2	Jay Dunn, Nip.	.15
□	3	Kevin Dickie, Coach, Mft.	.15
□	4	Martin Smith, NB	.15
□	5	Jeff Cole, Hum.	.15
□	6	Trent Hamm, Nip.	.15
□	7	Kent Rogers, Stn.	.15
□	8	Dean Gerard, Mft.	.15
□	9	Jim McLarty, Nip.	.15
□	10	Malcolm Kostuchenko, NB	.15
□	11	Mark Scollan, Mvl.	.15
□	12	Brad Federenko, Mft.	.15
□	13	Rob Beck, FF	.15
□	14	Bryce Bohun, NB	.15
□	15	Kory Karlander, Stn.	.15
□	16	Scott Christison, ND	.15
□	17	Tyler Kuhn, FF	.15
□	18	Corri Moffatt, Mvl.	.15
□	19	Layne Douglas, Min.	.15
□	20	Shane Holunga, Wey.	.15
□	21	Mike Matteucci, Est.	.15
□	22	Bart Vanstaalduinen, ND	.15
□	23	Brad McEwen, Gm/Coach, Mvl.	.15
□	24	Kim Maier, Est.	.15

- ☐ 25 Jamie Ling, ND .15
- ☐ 26 Dean Seymour, Yor. .15
- ☐ 27 Derek Crimin, Min. .15
- ☐ 28 Evan Anderson, Est. .15
- ☐ 29 Craig Matatall, ND .15
- ☐ 30 Keith Murphy, Mvl. .15
- ☐ 31 Jason Feiffer, Wey. .15
- ☐ 32 Michel Cook, Yor. .15
- ☐ 33 Rod Krushel, Mvl. .15
- ☐ 34 Tyler Rice, ND .15
- ☐ 35 Gerald Tallaire, Est. .15
- ☐ 36 Richard Nagy, FF .15
- ☐ 37 Taras Lendzyk, Hum. .15
- ☐ 38 Jeff Knight, Mft. .15
- ☐ 39 Darren Opp, Nip. .15
- ☐ 40 Dwayne Rhinehart, FF .15
- ☐ 41 Minot Americans All-Stars .15
- ☐ 42 Scott Bellefontaine (G), Yor. .25
- ☐ 43 Darren Maloney, Mvl. .15
- ☐ 44 1992 SJHL North Division .15
- ☐ 45 Yorkton Terriers All-Stars .15
- ☐ 46 Melville Millionaires All-Stars .15
- ☐ 47 The 1992 Best All Star Team .15
- ☐ 48 Estevan Bruins All-Stars .15
- ☐ 49 Notre Dame Hounds All-Stars .15
- ☐ 50 Bob Robson, Coach, Est. .15
- ☐ A1 Dean Normand, Hum. .15
- ☐ A2 Dan Meyers, Est. .15
- ☐ A3 Tyson Balog, Wey. .15
- ☐ A4 Tyler McMillan, Wey. .15
- ☐ A5 Jason Selkirk, Stn. .15
- ☐ A6 Bryce Bohun, NB .15
- ☐ A7 Blaire Hornung, Stn. .15
- ☐ A8 Craig McKechnie, Mvl. .15
- ☐ A9 Rejean Stringer, Nip. .25
- ☐ A10 Corri Moffat, Mvl. .15
- ☐ A11 Dion Johnson, Nip. .15
- ☐ A12 Rod Krushel, Mvl. .15
- ☐ A13 Mike Langen (G), Wey. .25
- ☐ A14 Jeff Hassman, Mvl. .15
- ☐ A15 Dean Moore, ND .15
- ☐ A16 Trevor Wathen, Min. .15
- ☐ A17 Curtis Knight, Hum. .15
- ☐ A18 Chris Morgan, Min. .15
- ☐ A19 Trevor Thurston, FF .15
- ☐ A20 Wayne Filipenko, Min. .15
- ☐ A21 Jason Feiffer, Wey. .15
- ☐ A22 Layne Douglas, Min. .15
- ☐ A23 Dave Gardner, Nip. .15
- ☐ A24 Ryan Sandholm, ND .15
- ☐ A25 Corey McKee, Mft. .15
- ☐ A26 Trevor Schmiess, Hum. .15
- ☐ A27 Todd Hollinger (G), Stn. .25
- ☐ A28 Jay Dunn, Nip. .15
- ☐ A29 Jamie Ling, ND .15
- ☐ A30 Todd Small, Stn. .15
- ☐ A31 Barret Kropf, Mft. .15
- ☐ A32 Dean Gerard, Mft. .15
- ☐ A33 Christian Dutil (G), Yor./Aaron Campbell, Mft. .25
- ☐ A34 Tyler Scheidt, Mft.; .15
- ☐ A35 Dean Sideroff, Hum. .15
- ☐ A36 Dan Dufresne, ND .15
- ☐ A37 Cam Yager (G), NB .25
- ☐ A38 Richard Nagy (G), FF .25
- ☐ A39 Aaron Cain, FF .15
- ☐ A40 Rob Beck, FF .15
- ☐ A41 Blair Wagar, Yor. .15
- ☐ A42 Kim Mairer, Est. .15
- ☐ A43 Brent Hoiness, NB .15
- ☐ A44 Troy Edwards, Est. .15
- ☐ A45 Evan Anderson, Est. .15
- ☐ A46 Carlin Nordstrom, NB .15
- ☐ A47 Dean Seymour, Yor. .15
- ☐ A48 Scott Wotton, Yor. .15
- ☐ A49 Curtis Joseph, ND .15
- ☐ B1 Richard Boscher (G), Stn. .25
- ☐ B2 James Schaeffler, Stn. .15
- ☐ B3 Wes Rommel, Nip. .15
- ☐ B4 Corey Thompson, Nip. .15
- ☐ B5 Rob Phillips, Nip. .15
- ☐ B6 Jim McLean, Nip. .15
- ☐ B7 Trevor Warrener, Stn. .15
- ☐ B8 Peter Boake, Wey. .15
- ☐ B9 Kevin Riffel (G), Est. .15
- ☐ B10 Tom Perry, Hum. .15
- ☐ B11 Mark Baird, Hum. .15
- ☐ B12 Stacy Prevost, Yor. .15
- ☐ B13 Taras Lendzyk (G), Hum. .25
- ☐ B14 Shawn Reis (G), Mft. .25
- ☐ B15 Shawn Thompson, Mvl. .15
- ☐ B16 Curtis Kleisinger, ND .15
- ☐ B17 Kent Rogers, Stn. .15
- ☐ B18 Scott Christion (G), ND .25
- ☐ B19 Gerald Tallaire, Est. .15
- ☐ B20 Kelly Hollingshead, Est. .15
- ☐ B21 Mike Savard (G), NB .25
- ☐ B22 Darren Maloney, Mvl. .15
- ☐ B23 Jason Hynd, NB .15
- ☐ B24 Scott Stewart, FF .15
- ☐ B25 Scott Beattie, Mvl. .15
- ☐ B26 Dave McAmmond, FF .15
- ☐ B27 Myles Gibb, NB .15
- ☐ B28 Ryan Bach (G), ND .15
- ☐ B29 Martin Smith, NB .15
- ☐ B30 Leigh Brookbank, Yor. .15
- ☐ B31 Todd Markus, Mft. .15
- ☐ B32 The Boys From PA .15
- ☐ B33 Randy Muise, Wey. .15
- ☐ B34 George Gervais, Est. .15
- ☐ B35 Keith Harris, Wey. .15
- ☐ B36 Jamie Stelmak (G), Mvl. .15
- ☐ B37 Bart Vanstaalduinen, ND .15
- ☐ B38 Scott Murray, Min. .15
- ☐ B39 Danny Galarneau, Yor. .15
- ☐ B40 Keith Murphy, Mvl. .15
- ☐ B41 Jeff Kungle, Mft. .15
- ☐ B42 Michel Cook, Yor. .15
- ☐ B43 Daryl Krauss, Wey. .15
- ☐ B44 Derek Wynne, Min. .15
- ☐ B45 Derek Crimin, Min. .15
- ☐ B46 Jason Brown, FF .15
- ☐ B47 Bruce Matatall, Min. .15
- ☐ B48 Chris Hatch, FF .15
- ☐ B49 Kurtise Souchotte, Mvl. .15
- ☐ B50 Michael Brennan, Hum. .15
- ☐ B51 Orrin Hergott, Hum. .15
- ☐ C1 Craig Matatall, ND .15
- ☐ C2 Brad Prefontaine, Mvl. .15
- ☐ C3 Mike Evans, ND .15
- ☐ C4 Jody Reiter, NB .15
- ☐ C5 Jeremy Mylymok, Mvl. .15
- ☐ C6 Dave Doucet, Mvl. .15
- ☐ C7 Randy Kerr, Mvl. .15
- ☐ C8 Gordon McCann, Mvl. .15
- ☐ C9 Quinn Fair, ND .15
- ☐ C10 Kyle Niemegeers, Est. .15
- ☐ C11 Ryan Smith, NB .15
- ☐ C12 Mike Hillock, Min. .15
- ☐ C13 Vern Anderson, NB .15
- ☐ C14 Trent Hamm, Nip. .15
- ☐ C15 Curtis Folkett, Est. .15
- ☐ C16 Warren Pickford, Nip. .15
- ☐ C17 Craig Volstad (G), Nip. .15
- ☐ C18 Sean Tallaire, Est. .15
- ☐ C19 Jason Yaganiski, Min. .15
- ☐ C20 Jim McLarty, Nip. .15
- ☐ C21 Jamie Byfuglien, Min. .15
- ☐ C22 Terry Metro, Min. .15
- ☐ C23 Todd Kozak, NB .15
- ☐ C24 Jeff Huckle, Stn. .15
- ☐ C25 Darren McLean, Est. .15
- ☐ C26 Bret Mohninger, Stn. .15
- ☐ C27 Tim Slukynsky, Yor. .15
- ☐ C28 Roman Mrhalek, Yor. .15
- ☐ C29 Joel Martinson, Hum. .15
- ☐ C30 Ron Patterson, FF .15
- ☐ C31 Mark Gorgi, Mft. .15
- ☐ C32 Tom Thomson, Stn. .15
- ☐ C33 Greg Wahl, Stn. .15
- ☐ C34 Craig Perrett, Mft. .15
- ☐ C35 Mike Harder, Wey. .15
- ☐ C36 Jeff Cole, Hum. .15
- ☐ C37 Justin Christoffer, Hum. .15
- ☐ C38 Nolan Weir, FF .15
- ☐ C39 Jeff Knight, Mft. .15
- ☐ C40 Lyle Vaughan, Yor. .15
- ☐ C41 Scott Bellefontaine (G), Yor. .15
- ☐ C42 Trevor Mathias, Wey. .15
- ☐ C43 Chris Schinkel (G), Hum. .15
- ☐ C44 Scott Rogers, Mft. .15
- ☐ C45 Shane Holunga, Wey. .15
- ☐ C46 Dwayne Rhinehart, FF .15
- ☐ C47 Eddy Marchant, FF .15
- ☐ C48 Travis Smith, Wey. .15
- C49 Not Issued
- ☐ C50 Mike Hidlebaugh, Nip. .15
- ☐ D1 Darcy Herlick, Wey. .15
- ☐ D2 Joel Appleton, Hum. .15
- ☐ D3 Bobby Standish, Mft. .15
- ☐ D4 Kory Karlander, Stn. .15
- ☐ D5 Brett Kinaschuk, Hum. .15
- ☐ D6 Kevin Messer, Nip. .15
- ☐ D7 Jason Martin, Wey. .15
- ☐ D8 Devin Zimmer, Min. .15
- ☐ D9 David Foster, Hum. .15
- ☐ D10 Bob Schwark, Mft. .15
- ☐ D11 Ted Grayling, Mvl. .15
- ☐ D12 Travis Vantighem, Mvl. .15
- ☐ D13 Darren Houghton, Mvl. .15
- ☐ D14 Wade Welte, Mvl. .15
- ☐ D15 1991 NB All Stars .15
- ☐ D16 Kevin Powell, Min. .15
- ☐ D17 Returning Hounds .15
- ☐ D18 Dennis Budeau, Min. .15
- ☐ D19 Darren Opp, Nip. .15
- ☐ D20 Jeff Greenwood, Nip. .15
- ☐ D21 Mark Daniels, Stn. .15
- ☐ D22 Todd Murphy, Nip. .15
- ☐ D23 Scott Weaver, Min. .15
- ☐ D24 Robby Bear, Yor. .15
- ☐ D25 Nigel Werenka, Yor. .15
- ☐ D26 Sean Timmins, ND .15
- ☐ D27 Ken Melenfant, Stn. .15
- ☐ D28 Greg Taylor, Mft. .15
- ☐ D29 Sheldon Bylsma, Yor. .15
- ☐ D30 Clint Hooge (G), FF .25
- ☐ D31 Bob McIntosh, ND .15
- ☐ D32 Dave Lovsin, ND .15
- ☐ D33 Jeremy Mathies, NB .15
- ☐ D34 Blaine Fomradas, Wey. .15
- ☐ D35 Cory Borys, Wey. .15
- ☐ D36 Brad Purdie, Wey. .15
- ☐ D37 J Sotropa, Stn. .15
- ☐ D38 Duane Vardale, NB .15
- ☐ D39 Jim Nellis, NB .15
- ☐ D40 Brent Sheppard, Hum. .15
- ☐ D41 Cam Bristow, Mft. .15
- ☐ D42 Steven Brent, Est. .15
- ☐ D43 Mike Matteucci, Est. .15
- ☐ D44 Bryan Cossette, Est. .15
- ☐ D45 Tyler Kuhn, FF .15
- ☐ D46 Dave Debusschere, Est. .15
- ☐ D47 Darryl Dickson, FF .15
- ☐ D48 Derek Meikle, FF .15
- ☐ D49 Ex SJHLer: Parris Duffus (G), Mft. .25
- ☐ D50 Future Propect: Lance Wakefield, Weyburn Elks .15
- ☐ D51 Ex SJHLer: Rod Brind'Amour, ND 4.00

1991 - 92 ARENA DRAFT PICKS

These cards have four versions: an English issue, a French issue, a silver-ink autographed and a gold-ink autographed. There are 667 silver autographs (English) and 333 gold autographs (French).

Production: Cases: 9,900; Sets: 198,000

Imprint:

Complete Set (33 cards): 5.00

ARENA DRAFT PICKS

	No.	Player	Reg.	Silver	Gold
□□□□	1	Pat Falloon	.25	8.00	10.00
□□□□	2	Scott Niedermayer	.35	10.00	15.00
□□□□	3	Scott Lachance	.25	8.00	10.00
□□□□	4	Peter Forsberg	2.00	60.00	80.00
□□□□	5	Alek Stojanov	.10	5.00	6.00
□□□□	6	Richard Matvichuk	.10	5.00	6.00
□□□□	7	Patrick Poulin	.10	5.00	6.00
□□□□	8	Martin Lapointe	.25	8.00	10.00
□□□□	9	Tyler Wright	.10	5.00	6.00
□□□□	10	Philippe Boucher	.10	5.00	6.00
□□□□	11	Pat Peake	.25	8.00	10.00
□□□□	12	Markus Naslund	.25	8.00	10.00
□□□□	13	Brent Bilodeau	.10	5.00	6.00
□□□□	14	Glen Murray	.10	5.00	6.00
□□□□	15	Niklas Sundblad	.10	5.00	6.00
□□□□	16	Trevor Halverson	.10	5.00	6.00
□□□□	17	Dean McAmmond	.10	5.00	6.00
□□□□	18	René Corbet	.10	5.00	6.00
□□□□	19	Eric Lavigne	.10	5.00	6.00
□□□□	20	Steve Staios	.10	5.00	6.00
□□□□	21	Jim Campbell	.35	20.00	30.00
□□□□	22	Jassen Cullimore	.10	5.00	6.00
□□□□	23	Jamie Pushor	.10	5.00	6.00
□□□□	24	Donevan Hextall	.10	5.00	6.00
□□□□	25	Andrew Verner (G)	.10	5.00	6.00
□□□□	26	Jason Dawe	.25	8.00	10.00
□□□□	27	Jeff Nelson	.10	5.00	6.00
□□□□	28	Darcy Werenka	.10	5.00	6.00
□□□□	29	François Groleau	.10	5.00	6.00
□□□□	30	Guy Lévêque	.10	5.00	6.00
□□□□	31	Yanic Perreault	.25	10.00	15.00

	No.	Player	Eng.	Bil.
□□	32	S. Lachance/P. Falloon	.25	.25
□□	33	Checklist	.10	.10

	Hologram	NRMT-MT
□	Pat Falloon	2.00

1991-92 AVANT GARDE B.C.J.H.L.

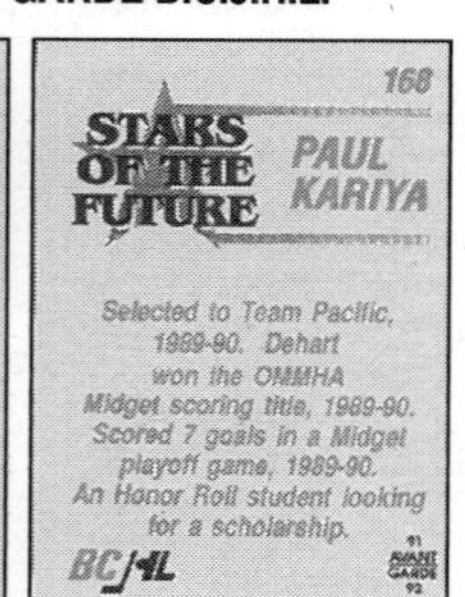

Imprint: 91-92 Avant Garde

Complete Set (170 cards):	**120.00**
Common Player:	**.15**

	No.	Player	NRMT-MT
□	1	Vernon Lakers	.15
□	2	Scott Longstaff	.15
□	3	Rick Crowe	.15
□	4	Sheldon Wolitski	.15
□	5	Kevan Rilcof	.15
□	6	Greg Buchanan	.15
□	7	Vernon Lakers	.15
□	8	Murray Caton	.15
□	9	Adrian Bubola	.15
□	10	Troy Becker	.15
□	11	Shawn Potyok	.15
□	12	John Morabito	.15
□	13	Peter Zurba	.15
□	14	Chad Schraeder	.15
□	15	Shawn Bourgeois	.15
□	16	Michal Sup	.15
□	17	Rick Eremenko	.15
□	18	David Lemanowicz	.15
□	19	Daniel Blasko	.15
□	20	Gary Audette	.15
□	21	Graham Harder	.15
□	22	Ryan Nessman	.15
□	23	Jason Switzer	.15
□	24	Roland Ramoser	.15
□	25	Dusty McLellan	.15
□	26	Dustin Green	.15
□	27	Steve Roberts	.15
□	28	Jason Lowe	.15
□	29	Brad Knight	.15
□	30	Pavel Suchanek	.15
□	31	Ken Crockett	.15
□	32	Adam Smith	.15
□	33	Glen Pullishy	.15
□	34	Mike Zambon	.15
□	35	Scott Chartier	.15
□	36	Donny Hearn	.15
□	37	Jeff Denham	.15
□	38	Jamie Marriott	.15
□	39	Silverio Mirao	.15
□	40	Darren Tymchyshyn	.15
□	41	Mark Basanta	.15
□	42	Trevor Prest	.15
□	43	Jim Lessard	.15
□	44	Jade Kersey	.15
□	45	Geordie Young	.15
□	46	Darren Holmes	.15
□	47	Wade Dayley	.15
□	48	Dan Murphy	.15
□	49	Paul Taylor	.15
□	50	Sjon Wynia	.15
□	51	Ryan Loxam	.15
□	52	Andy Faulkner	.15
□	53	Scott Kowalski	.15
□	54	Mickey McGuire	.15
□	55	Jason Disiewich	.15
□	56	Jim Ingram	.15
□	57	Ryan Keller	.15
□	58	Brian Schiebel	.15
□	59	Shawn York	.15
□	60	Sean Krause	.15
□	61	Casey Hungle	.15
□	62	Chris Jones	.15
□	63	Doug Stewart	.15
□	64	Jason Sirota	.15
□	65	Dave Dunnigan	.15
□	66	Aaron Hoffman	.15
□	67	Jason Timewell	.15
□	68	Pat Meehan	.15
□	69	Mike Leduc	.15
□	70	Brad Koopmans	.15
□	71	Guy Prince	.15
□	72	Dorel Gecse	.15
□	73	Scott Salmond	.15
□	74	Brian Zakall	.15
□	75	Mike Josephson	.15
□	76	Derek Harper	.15
□	77	John Graham	.15
□	78	Dan Morrissey	.15
□	79	Glenn Calder	.15
□	80	Jason Northard	.15
□	81	Chris Kerr	.15
□	82	Bill Muckalt	.15
□	83	Greg Hunt	.15
□	84	Paul Kariya	20.00
□	85	Dean Rowland	.15
□	86	Paul Kariya	20.00
□	87	David Kilduff	.15
□	88	Jeff Tory	.15
□	89	Mike Newman	.15
□	90	Tyler Boucher	.15
□	91	Paul Kariya	20.00
□	92	Phil Valk	.15
□	93	Paul Kariya	20.00
□	94	Bob Lewis	.15
□	95	Steve Williams	.15
□	96	James Pelzer	.15
□	97	Shawn Carter	.15
□	98	Ryan Erasmas	.15
□	99	John Dehart	.15
□	100	David Green	.15
□	101	Derek Gecse	.15
□	102	Brian Barnes	.15
□	103	Jason Given	.15
□	104	Jason Podollan	.50
□	105	Brian Veale	.15
□	106	Rob Tallas (G)	.50
□	107	Bob McBurnie	.15
□	108	Paul McMillan	.15
□	109	Ryan Donovan	.15
□	110	Kevin Robertson	.15
□	111	Milt Mastad	.15
□	112	Kees Roodbol	.15
□	113	Carey Causey	.15
□	114	Patrick O'Flaherty	.15
□	115	Chad Vestergaard	.15
□	116	Tyler Quiring	.15
□	117	Loui Mellios	.15
□	118	Bob Bell	.15
□	119	Rob Tallas, (G)	.50
□	120	Clint MacDonald	.15
□	121	Bart Taylor	.15
□	122	Mark Basanta	.15
□	123	Don McCusker	.15
□	124	Jason Howse	.15
□	125	Mike McKinlay	.15
□	126	Trevor Pennock	.15
□	127	Dean Shmyr	.15
□	128	Chris Kerr	.15
□	129	Erin Thornton	.15
□	130	Dennis Archibald	.15
□	131	Brian McDonald	.15
□	132	Bob Quinnell	.15
□	133	Clint Black	.15
□	134	Jason Peters	.15
□	135	Doug Ast	.15
□	136	Jason Bilous	.15
□	137	Lee Schill	.15
□	138	Jason Sanford	.15
□	139	Jeff Hokanson	.15
□	140	Marc Gagnon	.15
□	141	Gunnar Henrikson	.15
□	142	Jamie Lund	.15
□	143	Jason White	.15
□	144	Jag Bal	.15
□	145	Brad Loring	.15
□	146	Marc Gagnon	.15
□	147	Brian Veale	.15
□	148	Checklist	.15
□	149	Checklist	.15
□	150	The Centennial Cup	.15
□	151	Brian Law	.15
□	152	Al Radke	.15
□	153	Faulkner/Disiewich/Holmes/Hungle/Jones	.15
□	154	Team Photo	.15
□	155	McLellan/Ramoser/Eremenko/Wolitski/Potok/Longstaff	.15
□	156	Hendrikson/Anchikoski/Gagnon/White	.15
□	157	Graham/Dunnigan	.15
□	158	Chartier/Zambon/Taylor/Lowe	.15
□	159	Tory/Boucher/Kilduff/Davidson/Dehart/Burns	.15
□	160	Didmon/Bentham/Marsh/Walsh	.15
□	161	Lipsett/McNeill/Klyn/Edgington	.15
□	162	All-Stars	.15
□	163	Johnson/Meek/Welker/Fitzpatrick/Collins Sofikitas/Hutson/Herman	.15
□	164	John Dehart	.15
□	165	John Craighead	.15
□	166	Mike Josephson	.15
□	167	Wayne Anchikoski	.15
□	168	Paul Kariya	20.00
□	169	Jim Lessard	.15
□	170	Tommy Virkgunen	.15

1991 - 92 BOWMAN

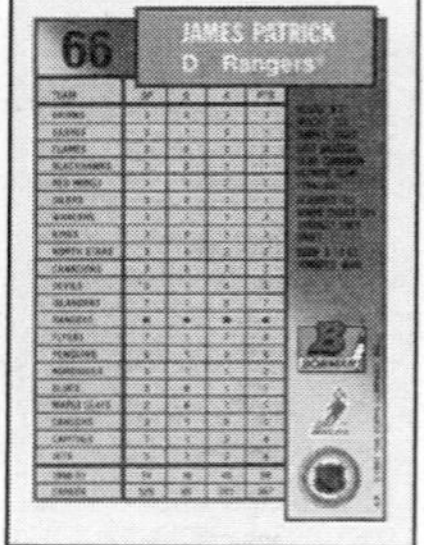

Playoff and Hat Trick subset cards were inserted one card per pack. The promo cards were originally issued as a nine-card sheet with five Topps promo cards.

Imprint: © 1991 THE TOPPS COMPANY, INC.

Complete Set (429 cards):	**15.00**

Common Player: .10

	No.	Promos	NRMT-MT
☐		Ray Bourque, Bos.	2.00
☐		Wayne Gretzky, LA	5.00
☐		Mark Messier, Edm.	2.00
☐		Steve Yzerman, Det.	3.00

	No.	Player	NRMT-MT
☐	1	John Cullen, Hfd.	.10
☐	2	Todd Krygier, Hfd.	.10
☐	3	Kay Whitmore (G), Hfd.	.10
☐	4	Terry Yake, Hfd.	.10
☐	5	Randy Ladouceur, Hfd.	.10
☐	6	Kevin Dineen, Hfd.	.10
☐	7	Jim McKenzie, Hfd.	.10
☐	8	Brad Shaw, Hfd.	.10
☐	9	Mark Hunter, Hfd.	.10
☐	10	Dean Evason, Hfd.	.10
☐	11	Mikael Andersson, Hfd.	.10
☐	12	Pat Verbeek, Hfd.	.10
☐	13	Peter Sidorkiewicz (G), Hfd.	.10
☐	14	Mike Tomlak, Hfd.	.10
☐	15	Zarley Zalapski, Hfd.	.10
☐	16	Rob Brown, Hfd.	.10
☐	17	Sylvain Côté, Hfd.	.10
☐	18	Bobby Holik, Hfd.	.10
☐	19	Daryl Reaugh (G), Hfd.	.10
☐	20	Paul Cyr, Hfd.	.10
☐	21	Doug Bodger, Buf.	.10
☐	22	Dave Andreychuk, Buf.	.25
☐	23	Clint Malarchuk (G), Buf.	.10
☐	24	Darrin Shannon, Buf.	.10
☐	25	Christian Ruuttu, Buf.	.10
☐	26	Uwe Krupp, Buf.	.10
☐	27	Pierre Turgeon, Buf.	.25
☐	**28**	**Kevin Haller, Buf., RC**	**.10**
☐	29	Dave Snuggerud, Buf.	.10
☐	30	Alexander Mogilny, Buf.	.35
☐	31	Dale Hawerchuk, Buf.	.25
☐	32	Mike Ramsey, Buf.	.10
☐	33	Darcy Wakaluk (G), Buf.	.10
☐	34	Tony Tanti, Buf.	.10
☐	35	Jay Wells, Buf.	.10
☐	36	Mikko Makelä, Buf.	.10
☐	37	Daren Puppa (G), Buf.	.10
☐	38	Benoît Hogue, Buf.	.10
☐	39	Rick Vaive, Buf.	.10
☐	40	Grant Ledyard, Buf.	.10
☐	41	Steve Yzerman, Det.	1.00
☐	42	Steve Yzerman, Det.	1.00
☐	43	Shawn Burr, Det.	.10
☐	44	Yves Racine, Det.	.10
☐	45	Johan Garpenlov, Det.	.10
☐	46	Keith Primeau, Det.	.25
☐	47	Tim Cheveldae (G), Det.	.10
☐	48	Brad McCrimmon, Det.	.10
☐	49	David Barr, Det.	.10
☐	50	Sergei Fedorov, Det.	.50
☐	51	Brent Fedyk, Det.	.10
☐	52	Jimmy Carson, Det.	.10
☐	53	Paul Ysebaert, Det.	.10
☐	54	Rick Zombo, Det.	.10
☐	55	Bob Probert, Det.	.10
☐	56	Gerard Gallant, Det.	.10
☐	57	Kevin Miller, Det.	.10
☐	58	Randy Moller, NYR.	.10
☐	59	Kris King, NYR.	.10
☐	**60**	**Corey Millen, NYR.., RC**	**.10**
☐	61	Brian Mullen, NYR. (S.J.)	.10
☐	62	Darren Turcotte, NYR.	.10
☐	63	Ray Sheppard, NYR. (Det.)	.10
☐	64	David Shaw, NYR.	.10
☐	65	Troy Mallette, NYR.	.10
☐	66	James Patrick, NYR.	.10
☐	67	Mark Janssens, NYR.	.10
☐	68	John Vanbiesbrouck (G), NYR..	.60
☐	69	Joey Kocur, NYR.	.10
☐	70	Mike Richter (G), NYR..	.25
☐	71	John Ogrodnick, NYR.	.10
☐	72	Kelly Kisio, NYR. (S.J.)	.10
☐	73	Normand Rochefort, NYR.	.10
☐	74	Mike Gartner, NYR.	.25
☐	75	Brian Leetch, NYR.	.35
☐	76	Bernie Nicholls, NYR.	.10
☐	77	Jan Erixon, NYR.	.10
☐	78	Larry Murphy, Pgh.	.25
☐	79	Joe Mullen, Pgh.	.25
☐	80	Tom Barrasso (G), Pgh.	.25
☐	81	Paul Coffey, Pgh.	.25
☐	82	Jiri Hrdina, Pgh.	.10
☐	83	Mark Recchi, Pgh.	.25
☐	84	Randy Gilhen, Pgh. (L.A.)	.10
☐	85	Bob Errey, Pgh.	.10
☐	86	Scott Young, Pgh.	.10
☐	87	Mario Lemieux, Pgh.	1.25
☐	88	Ulf Samuelsson, Pgh.	.10
☐	89	Frank Pietrangelo (G), Pgh.	.10
☐	90	Ron Francis, Pgh.	.25
☐	91	Paul Stanton, Pgh.	.10
☐	92	Kevin Stevens, Pgh.	.10
☐	93	Bryan Trottier, Pgh.	.25
☐	94	Phil Bourque, Pgh.	.10
☐	95	Jaromir Jagr, Pgh.	1.00
☐	96	Petr Klima, Edm.	.15
☐	97	Adam Graves, Edm.	.10
☐	98	Esa Tikkanen, Edm.	.10
☐	**99**	**Norm Maciver, Edm., RC**	**.10**
☐	100	Craig MacTavish, Edm.	.10
☐	101	Bill Ranford (G), Edm.	.25
☐	102	Martin Gelinas, Edm.	.10
☐	103	Charlie Huddy, Edm. (L.A.)	.10
☐	104	Petr Klima, Edm.	.10
☐	105	Ken Linseman, Edm.	.10
☐	106	Steve Smith, Edm.	.10
☐	107	Craig Simpson, Edm.	.10
☐	108	Chris Joseph, Edm.	.10
☐	109	Joe Murphy, Edm.	.10
☐	110	Jeff Beukeboom, Edm.	.10
☐	111	Grant Fuhr (G), Edm.	.25
☐	112	Geoff Smith, Edm.	.10
☐	113	Anatoli Semenov, Edm.	.10
☐	114	Mark Messier, Edm.	.50
☐	115	Kevin Lowe, Edm.	.10
☐	116	Glenn Anderson, Edm.	.10
☐	117	Bobby Smith, Min.	.10
☐	118	Doug Smail, Min.	.10
☐	119	Jon Casey (G), Min.	.10
☐	120	Gaetan Duchesne, Min.	.10
☐	121	Neal Broten, Min.	.10
☐	122	Brian Hayward (G), Min. (S.J.)	.10
☐	123	Brian Propp, Min.	.10
☐	124	Mark Tinordi, Min.	.10
☐	125	Mike Modano, Min.	.50
☐	126	Marc Bureau, Min.	.10
☐	127	Ulf Dahlen, Min.	.10
☐	128	Chris Dahlquist, Min.	.10
☐	129	Brian Bellows, Min.	.10
☐	130	Mike Craig, Min.	.10
☐	131	Dave Gagner, Min.	.10
☐	132	Brian Glynn, Min.	.10
☐	133	Joe Sakic, Que.	.75
☐	134	Owen Nolan, Que.	.25
☐	135	Everett Sanipass, Que.	.10
☐	**136**	**Jamie Baker, Que., RC**	**.10**
☐	137	Mats Sundin, Que.	.50
☐	138	Craig Wolanin, Que.	.10
☐	139	Kip Miller, Que.	.10
☐	140	Steven Finn, Que.	.10
☐	141	Tony Hrkac, Que. (S.J.)	.10
☐	142	Curtis Leschyshyn, Que.	.10
☐	143	Mike McNeill, Que.	.10
☐	144	Mike Hough, Que.	.10
☐	**145**	**Alexei Gusarov, Que., RC**	**.10**
☐	146	Jacques Cloutier (G), Que.	.10
☐	147	Shawn Anderson, Que.	.10
☐	148	Stéphane Morin, Que.	.10
☐	149	Bryan Fogarty, Que.	.10
☐	150	Scott Pearson, Que.	.10
☐	151	Ron Tugnutt (G), Que.	.10
☐	152	Randy Velischek, Que.	.10
☐	153	Dave Reid, Tor.	.10
☐	154	Rob Ramage, Tor. (Min.)	.10
☐	155	David Hannan, Tor.	.10
☐	156	Wendel Clark, Tor.	.25
☐	157	Peter Ing (G), Tor.	.10
☐	158	Michel Petit, Tor.	.10
☐	159	Brian Bradley, Tor.	.10
☐	160	Rob Cimetta, Tor.	.10
☐	161	Gary Leeman, Tor.	.10
☐	162	Aaron Broten, Tor.	.10
☐	163	David Ellett, Tor.	.10
☐	164	Peter Zezel, Tor.	.10
☐	165	Daniel Marois, Tor.	.10
☐	166	Mike Krushelnyski, Tor.	.10
☐	167	Luke Richardson, Tor.	.10
☐	168	Scott Thornton, Tor.	.10
☐	169	Mike Foligno, Tor.	.10
☐	170	Vincent Damphousse, Tor.	.25
☐	171	Todd Gill, Tor.	.10
☐	172	Kevin Maguire, Tor.	.10
☐	173	Wayne Gretzky, L.A.	1.75
☐	174	Tomas Sandström, L.A.	.15
☐	175	John Tonelli, L.A. (Chi.)	.10
☐	176	Wayne Gretzky, L.A.	1.75
☐	177	Larry Robinson, L.A.	.20
☐	178	Jay Miller, L.A.	.10
☐	179	Tomas Sandström, L.A.	.10
☐	180	John McIntyre, L.A.	.10
☐	**181**	**Brad Jones, L.A., RC**	**.10**
☐	182	Rob Blake, L.A.	.25
☐	183	Kelly Hrudey (G), L.A.	.10
☐	184	Marty McSorley, L.A.	.10
☐	185	Todd Elik, L.A. (Min.)	.10
☐	186	DaveTaylor, L.A.	.10
☐	187	Steve Kasper, L.A. (Pha.)	.10
☐	188	Luc Robitaille, L.A.	.25
☐	189	Bob Kudelski, L.A.	.10
☐	190	Daniel Berthiaume (G), L.A.	.10
☐	191	Steve Duchesne, L.A. (Pha.)	.10
☐	192	Tony Granato, L.A.	.10
☐	193	Bob Essensa (G), Wpg.	.10
☐	194	Phil Sykes, Wpg.	.10
☐	195	Paul MacDermid, Wpg.	.10
☐	196	Dave McLlwain, Wpg.	.10
☐	197	Phil Housley, Wpg.	.10
☐	198	Pat Elynuik, Wpg.	.10
☐	199	Randy Carlyle, Wpg.	.10
☐	200	Thomas Steen, Wpg.	.10
☐	201	Teppo Numminen, Wpg.	.10
☐	202	Danton Cole, Wpg.	.10
☐	203	Doug Evans, Wpg.	.10
☐	204	Ed Olczyk, Wpg.	.10
☐	205	Moe Mantha, Wpg.	.10
☐	206	Scott Arniel, Wpg.	.10
☐	207	Rick Tabaracci (G), Wpg.	.25
☐	**208**	**Bryan Marchment, Wpg. (Chi.), RC**	**.10**
☐	209	Mark Osborne, Wpg.	.10
☐	210	Fredrik Olausson, Wpg.	.10
☐	211	Brent Ashton, Wpg.	.10
☐	212	Ray Ferraro, NYI.	.10
☐	213	Mark Fitzpatrick (G), NYI.	.10
☐	214	Hubie McDonough, NYI.	.10
☐	215	Joe Reekie, NYI.	.10
☐	**216**	**Bill Berg, NYI.., RC**	**.10**
☐	217	Wayne McBean, NYI.	.10
☐	218	Patrick Flatley, NYI.	.10
☐	219	Jeff Hackett (G), NYI. (S.J.)	.25
☐	220	Derek King, NYI.	.10
☐	221	Craig Ludwig, NYI. (Min.)	.10
☐	222	Pat LaFontaine, NYI.	.25
☐	223	David Volek, NYI.	.10
☐	224	Glenn Healy (G), NYI.	.10
☐	225	Jeff Norton, NYI.	.10
☐	226	Brent Sutter, NYI.	.10
☐	227	Randy Wood, NYI.	.10
☐	228	Gary Nylund, NYI.	.10
☐	229	David Chyzowski, NYI.	.10
☐	230	Rick Tocchet, Pha.	.10
☐	231	Ken Wregget (G), Pha.	.10
☐	232	Terry Carkner, Pha.	.10
☐	233	Martin Hostak, Pha.	.10
☐	234	Ron Hextall (G), Pha.	.25
☐	235	Gord Murphy, Pha.	.10
☐	236	Scott Mellanby, Pha. (Edm.)	.10
☐	237	Pete Peeters (G), Pha.	.10
☐	238	Ron Sutter, Pha.	.10
☐	239	Murray Craven, Pha.	.10
☐	240	Kjell Samuelsson, Pha.	.10
☐	241	Per-Erik Eklund, Pha.	.10
☐	242	Mark Pederson, Pha.	.10
☐	243	Murray Baron, Pha.	.10
☐	244	Keith Acton, Pha.	.10
☐	245	Derrick Smith, Pha.	.10
☐	246	Mike Ricci, Pha.	.10
☐	247	Dale Kushner, Pha.	.10
☐	248	Normand Lacombe, Pha.	.10

	No.	Player	Price
☐	249	Hat Trick: Theoren Fleury, Cgy.	.35
☐	250	Hat Trick: Sergei Makarov, Cgy.	.15
☐	251	Paul Ranheim, Cgy.	.10
☐	252	Joe Nieuwendyk, Cgy.	.25
☐	253	Mike Vernon (G), Cgy.	.25
☐	254	Gary Suter, Cgy.	.10
☐	255	Doug Gilmour, Cgy.	.35
☐	256	Paul Fenton, Cgy.	.10
☐	257	Roger Johansson, Cgy.	.10
☐	258	Stéphane Matteau, Cgy.	.10
☐	259	Frantisek Musil, Cgy.	.10
☐	260	Joel Otto, Cgy.	.10
☐	261	Tim Sweeney, Cgy.	.10
☐	262	Al MacInnis, Cgy.	.25
☐	263	Gary Roberts, Cgy.	.25
☐	264	Sergei Makarov, Cgy.	.10
☐	265	Carey Wilson, Cgy.	.10
☐	266	Ric Nattress, Cgy.	.10
☐	267	Robert Reichel, Cgy.	.25
☐	268	Rick Wamsley (G), Cgy.	.10
☐	269	Brian MacLellan, Cgy. (Det.)	.10
☐	270	Theoren Fleury, Cgy.	.35
☐	271	Claude Lemieux, N.J.	.15
☐	272	John MacLean, N.J.	.15
☐	273	Viacheslav Fetisov, N.J.	.25
☐	274	Kirk Muller, N.J.	.10
☐	275	Sean Burke (G), N.J.	.25
☐	276	Alexei Kasatonov, N.J.	.10
☐	277	Claude Lemieux, N.J.	.10
☐	278	Eric Weinrich, N.J.	.10
☐	279	Patrik Sundstrom, N.J,	.10
☐	280	Zdeno Ciger, N.J.	.10
☐	281	Bruce Driver, N.J.	.10
☐	282	Laurie Boschman, N.J.	.10
☐	283	Chris Terreri (G), N.J.	.10
☐	284	Ken Daneyko, N.J.	.10
☐	285	Doug Brown, N.J.	.10
☐	286	Jon Morris, N.J.	.10
☐	287	Peter Stastny, N.J.	.25
☐	288	Brendan Shanahan, N.J. (Stl.)	.60
☐	289	John MacLean, N.J.	.10
☐	290	Mike Liut (G), Wsh.	.10
☐	291	Michal Pivonka, Wsh.	.10
☐	292	Kelly Miller, Wsh.	.10
☐	293	John Druce, Wsh.	.10
☐	294	Calle Johansson, Wsh.	.10
☐	295	Alan May, Wsh.	.10
☐	296	Kevin Hatcher, Wsh.	.10
☐	297	Tim Bergland, Wsh.	.10
☐	298	Mikhail Tatarinov, Wsh., (Que.)	.10
☐	299	Peter Bondra, Wsh.	.35
☐	300	Al Iafrate, Wsh.	.10
☐	301	Nick Kypreos, Wsh.	.10
☐	302	Dino Ciccarelli, Wsh.	.25
☐	303	Dale Hunter, Wsh.	.10
☐	304	Don Beaupré (G), Wsh.	.10
☐	305	Jim Hrivnak (G), Wsh.	.10
☐	306	Stephen Leach, Wsh. (Bos.)	.10
☐	307	Dimitri Khristich, Wsh., Error	.10
☐	308	Mike Ridley, Wsh.	.10
☐	309	Sergio Momesso, Van.	.10
☐	310	Kirk McLean (G), Van.	.20
☐	311	Greg Adams, Van.	.10
☐	312	Adrien Plavsic, Van.	.10
☐	313	Cliff Ronning, Van.	.10
☐	314	Garry Valk, Van.	.10
☐	315	Troy Gamble (G), Van.	.10
☐	316	Gino Odjick, Van.	.10
☐	317	Doug Lidster, Van.	.10
☐	318	Geoff Courtnall, Van.	.10
☐	319	Tom Kurvers, Van. (NYI.)	.10
☐	320	Robert Kron, Van.	.10
☐	321	Jyrki Lumme, Van.	.10
☐	**322**	**Jay Mazur, Van., RC**	**.10**
☐	323	Dave Capuano, Van.	.10
☐	324	Petr Nedved, Van.	.10
☐	325	Steven Bozek, Van.	.10
☐	326	Igor Larionov, Van.	.25
☐	327	Trevor Linden, Van.	.25
☐	328	Shayne Corson, Mtl.	.25
☐	329	Eric Desjardins, Mtl.	.25
☐	330	Stéphane Richer, Mtl.	.10
☐	331	Brian Skrudland, Mtl.	.10
☐	332	Sylvain Lefebvre, Mtl.	.10
☐	333	Stéphan Lebeau, Mtl.	.10
☐	334	Mike Keane, Mtl.	.10
☐	335	Patrick Roy (G), Mtl., Error (Bergeron)	1.00
☐	336	Brent Gilchrist, Mtl.	.10
☐	**337**	**André Racicot (G), Mtl., RC**	**.10**
☐	338	Guy Carbonneau, Mtl.	.10
☐	339	Mike McPhee, Mtl.	.10
☐	340	Andrew Cassels, Mtl.	.10
☐	341	Petr Svoboda, Mtl.	.10
☐	342	Denis Savard, Mtl.	.25
☐	343	Mathieu Schneider, Mtl.	.10
☐	**344**	**John LeClair, Mtl., RC**	**1.50**
☐	345	Tom Chorske, Mtl.	.10
☐	346	Russ Courtnall, Mtl.	.10
☐	347	Ken Hodge, Bos.	.15
☐	348	Cam Neely, Bos.	.25
☐	349	Randy Burridge, Bos. (Wsh.)	.10
☐	350	Glen Wesley, Bos., Error	.10
☐	351	Chris Nilan, Bos.	.10
☐	**352**	**Jeff Lazaro, Bos., RC**	**.10**
☐	353	Wes Walz, Bos.	.10
☐	354	Réjean Lemelin (G), Bos.	.10
☐	355	Craig Janney, Bos.	.10
☐	356	Ray Bourque, Bos.	.50
☐	357	Bob Sweeney, Bos.	.10
☐	358	David Christian, Bos.	.10
☐	359	Dave Poulin, Bos.	.10
☐	360	Garry Galley, Bos.	.10
☐	361	Andy Moog (G), Bos.	.25
☐	362	Ken Hodge, Bos.	.10
☐	363	Jim Wiemer, Bos.	.10
☐	364	Petri Skriko, Bos.	.10
☐	365	Don Sweeney, Bos.	.10
☐	366	Cam Neely, Bos.	.25
☐	367	Brett Hull, Stl.	.50
☐	368	Gino Cavallini, Stl.	.10
☐	369	Scott Stevens, Stl.	.10
☐	370	Rich Sutter, Stl.	.10
☐	371	Glen Featherstone, Stl. (Bos.)	.10
☐	372	Vincent Riendeau (G), Stl.	.10
☐	373	Dave Lowry, Stl.	.10
☐	374	Rod Brind'Amour, Stl.	.25
☐	375	Brett Hull, Stl.	.50
☐	376	Dan Quinn, Stl.	.10
☐	377	Tom Tilley, Stl.	.10
☐	378	Paul Cavallini, Stl.	.10
☐	379	Bob Bassen, Stl.	.10
☐	380	Mario Marois, Stl.	.10
☐	381	Darin Kimble, Stl.	.10
☐	382	Ron Wilson, Stl.	.10
☐	383	Garth Butcher, Stl.	.10
☐	384	Adam Oates, Stl.	.35
☐	385	Jeff Brown, Stl.	.10
☐	386	Jeremy Roenick, Chi.	.35
☐	387	Tony McKegney, Chi.	.10
☐	388	Troy Murray, Chi. (Wpg.)	.10
☐	389	Dave Manson, Chi.	.10
☐	390	Ed Belfour (G), Chi.	.35
☐	391	Steve Thomas, Chi.	.10
☐	392	Michel Goulet, Chi.	.25
☐	393	Trent Yawney, Chi.	.10
☐	394	Adam Creighton, Chi.	.10
☐	395	Steve Larmer, Chi.	.25
☐	396	Jimmy Waite (G), Chi.	.10
☐	397	Dirk Graham, Chi.	.10
☐	398	Chris Chelios, Chi.	.35
☐	399	Mike Hudson, Chi.	.10
☐	400	Doug Wilson, Chi.	.25
☐	401	Greg Gilbert, Chi.	.10
☐	402	Wayne Presley, Chi.	.10
☐	403	Jeremy Roenick, Chi.	.35
☐	404	Frantisek Kucera, Chi.	.10
☐	405	Steve Larmer/Steve Duchesne	.10
☐	406	Adam Oates	.35
☐	407	Grant Fuhr (G)	.25
☐	408	Zdeno Ciger/Ulf Samuelsson	.10
☐	409	John Ogratnick/Kevin Hatcher	.10
☐	410	Randy Burridge	.10
☐	411	André Racicot (G)/Christian Ruuttu	.10
☐	412	D. Murzyn/ T. Granato/T. Kurvers	.10
☐	413	M. Pivonka/ B. Errey/J. Druce	.10
☐	414	Russ Courtnall	.10
☐	415	C. Dahlquist/G. Cavallini/M. Modano	.10
☐	416	D. Taylor/C.MacTavish	.10
☐	417	S. Smith/Marc Bureau	.10
☐	418	Andy Moog (G)/Kevin Stevens	.20
☐	419	T. Barrasso/D.Gagner/U.Samuelsson	.10
☐	420	Neal Broten/Tom Barrasso (G)	.10
☐	421	G. Duchesne/K. Stevens/R. Francis	.10
☐	422	K. Stevens/U. Dahlen	.10
☐	423	T. Barasso/U. Dahlen	.10
☐	424	B. Propp/D. Gagner/T. Barrasso	.10
☐	425	MVP: Mario Lemieux, Pgh.	1.00
☐	426	Checklist I (1 - 108)	.10
☐	427	Checklist II (109 - 216)	.10
☐	428	Checklist III (217 - 324)	.10
☐	429	Checklist IV (325 - 429)	.10

1991 - 92 CANADIAN OLYMPIC TEAM - ALBERTA LOTTERIES

Imprint:

Complete Set (24 cards): 24.00

	Player	NRMT-MT
☐	Dave Archibald	.75
☐	Todd Brost	.75
☐	Sean Burke (G)	3.00
☐	Terry Crisp	1.50
☐	Kevin Dahl	.75
☐	Karl Dykhuis	.75
☐	Wayne Fleming	.75
☐	Curt Giles	.75
☐	Gord Hynes	.75
☐	Fabian Joseph	.75
☐	Joé Juneau	2.00
☐	Trevor Kidd (G)	3.00
☐	Dave King G.M./Coach	2.00
☐	Chris Kontos	.75
☐	Chris Lindberg	.75
☐	Kent Manderville	.75
☐	Adrien Plavsic	.75
☐	Dan Ratushny	.75
☐	Stéphane Roy	.75
☐	Brad Schlegel	.75
☐	Scott Scissons	.75
☐	Randy Smith	.75
☐	Jason Woolley	.75
☐	Title Card	.75

1991 - 92 CLASSIC DRAFT PICKS

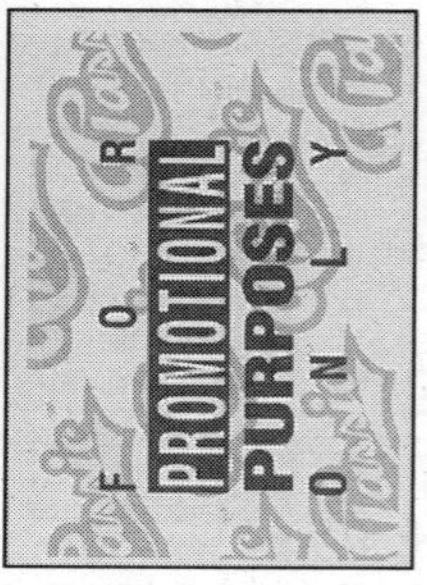

There are 360,000 sets available. Both English and bilingual cards sell at the same price.

Imprint: 1991 Classic Games, Inc., a subsidiary of The Scoreboard, Inc. - all rights reserved. Classic is a registered trademark of The Scoreboard, Inc.

Complete Set (50 cards): 6.00

	Promos	NRMT-MT
☐	Eric Lindros	8.00
☐	Pat Falloon	2.00

	No.	Player	NRMT-MT
☐ ☐	1	Eric Lindros, Oshawa	3.00
☐ ☐	2	Pat Falloon, Spokane	.25
☐ ☐	3	Scott Niedermayer, WHL All-Stars	.50
☐ ☐	4	Scott Lachance, Boston U.	.25
☐ ☐	5	Peter Forsberg, Pha.	2.00
☐ ☐	6	Alek Stojanov, Hamilton	.10
☐ ☐	7	Richard Matvichuk, Saskatoon	.10
☐ ☐	8	Patrick Poulin, St. Hyacinthe	.10
☐ ☐	9	Martin Lapointe, Laval	.25
☐ ☐	10	Tyler Wright, Swift Current	.10
☐ ☐	11	Philippe Boucher, Granby	.10
☐ ☐	12	Pat Peake, Detroit-OHL, Error	.25
☐ ☐	13	Markus Naslund, Pgh.	.25

	No.	Player	NRMT-MT
☐☐	14	Brent Bilodeau, Seattle	.10
☐☐	15	Glen Murray, Sudbury	.10
☐☐	16	Niklas Sundblad, Cgy.	.10
☐☐	17	Martin Rucinsky, CSR.	.25
☐☐	18	Trevor Halverson, North Bay	.10
☐☐	19	Dean McAmmond, Prince Albert	.10
☐☐	20	Ray Whitney, Spokane	.10
☐☐	21	René Corbet, Drummonville	.10
☐☐	22	Eric Lavigne, Hull	.10
☐☐	23	Zigmund Palffy, CSR.	.75
☐☐	24	Steve Staios, Niagara Falls	.10
☐☐	25	Jim Campbell, Northwood	.50
☐☐	26	Jassen Cullimore, Peterborough	.10
☐☐	27	Martin Hamrlik, CSR.	.10
☐☐	28	Jamie Pushor, Lethbridge	.10
☐☐	29	Donevan Hextall, Prince Albert	.10
☐☐	30	Andrew Verner (G), Peterborough	.10
☐☐	31	Jason Dawe, Peterborough	.10
☐☐	32	Jeff Nelson, Prince Albert	.10
☐☐	33	Darcy Werenka, Lethbridge	.10
☐☐	34	Jozef Stumpel, CSR.	.25
☐☐	35	François Groleau, Shawinigan	.10
☐☐	36	Guy Léveque, Cornwall	.10
☐☐	37	Jamie Matthews, Sudbury	.10
☐☐	38	Dody Wood, Seattle	.10
☐☐	39	Yanic Perreault, Trois-Rivières	.25
☐☐	40	Jamie McLennan (G), Lethbridge	.35
☐☐	41	Yanick Dupré, Drummondville	.10
☐☐	42	Sandy McCarthy, Laval	.10
☐☐	43	Chris Osgood (G), Medicine Hat	.75
☐☐	44	Fredrik Lindquist , Djugarden	.10
☐☐	45	Jason Young, Sudbury	.10
☐☐	46	Steve Konowalchuk, Portland	.10
☐☐	47	Michael Nylander, Hfd.	.10
☐☐	48	Shane Peacock, Lethbridge	.10
☐☐	49	Yves Sarault , St.-Jean	.10
☐☐	50	Marcel Cousineau (G), Beauport	.10
		Player	**NRMT-MT**
☐☐		Raghib "Rocket" Ismail	1.00

1991 - 92 CLASSIC GAMES FOUR-SPORT

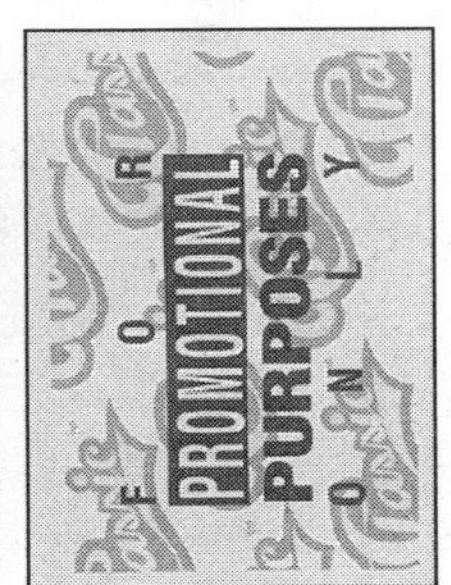

This 230-card four-sport set features only 50 hockey players. Both English and bilingual cards sell at the same price. A 230-card set sells at $18.

Imprint:

		Promo	**NRMT-MT**
☐		Pat Falloon	2.00
	No.	**Player**	**NRMT-MT**
☐☐	1	Future Stars (Eric Lindros)	2.00
☐☐	2	Pat Falloon	.50
☐☐	3	Scott Niedermayer, Kamloops	.35
☐☐	4	Scott Lachance, Boston U.	.25
☐☐	5	Peter Forsberg, Pha.	2.00
☐☐	6	Alek Stojanov, Hamilton	.10
☐☐	7	Richard Matvichuk, Saskatoon	.10
☐☐	8	Patrick Poulin, St.-Hyacinthe	.10
☐☐	9	Martin Lapointe, Laval	.25
☐☐	10	Tyler Wright , WHL All-Stars	.10
☐☐	11	Philippe Boucher, QMJHL All-Stars	.10
☐☐	12	Pat Peake, Detroit-OHL	.25
☐☐	13	Markus Naslund, Pgh.	.25
☐☐	14	Brent Bilodeau, WHL All-Stars	.10
☐☐	15	Glen Murray	.10
☐☐	16	Niklas Sundblad, Cgy.	.10
☐☐	17	Martin Rucinsky, CSR.	.25
☐☐	18	Trevor Halverson, North Bay	.10
☐☐	19	Dean McAmmond, Prince Albert	.10
☐☐	20	Ray Whitney, Spokane	.10
☐☐	21	René Corbet , Drummondville	.10
☐☐	22	Eric Lavigne, QMJHL All-Stars	.10
☐☐	23	Zigmund Palffy, CSR.	.75
☐☐	24	Steve Staios, Niagara Falls	.10
☐☐	25	Jim Campbell, Northwood	.50
☐☐	26	Jassen Cullimore, Peterborough	.10
☐☐	27	Martin Hamrlik, CSR.	.10
☐☐	28	Jamie Pushor, Lethbridge	.10
☐☐	29	Donevan Hextall, Prince Albert	.10
☐☐	30	Andrew Verner (G), Peterborough	.10
☐☐	31	Jason Dawe, Peterborough	.10
☐☐	32	Jeff Nelson, WHL All-Stars	.10
☐☐	33	Darcy Werenka, Lethbridge	.10
☐☐	34	Jozef Stumpel, CSR.	.25
☐☐	35	François Groleau, Shawinigan	.10
☐☐	36	Guy Lévèque, Cornwall	.10
☐☐	37	Jamie Matthews, Sudbury	.10
☐☐	38	Dody Wood, Seattle	.35
☐☐	39	Yanic Perreault, QMJHL All-Stars	.25
☐☐	40	Jamie McLennan (G), Lethbridge	.10
☐☐	41	Yanick Dupré, Drummondville	.10
☐☐	42	Sandy McCarthy, Laval	.10
☐☐	43	Chris Osgood (G), Medicine Hat	.75
☐☐	44	Fredrik Lindquist, Djugarden	.10
☐☐	45	Jason Young, Sudbury	.10
☐☐	46	Steve Konowalchuk, Portland-WHL	.10
☐☐	47	Michael Nylander, Hfd.	.25
☐☐	48	Shane Peacock, Lethbridge	.10
☐☐	49	Yves Sarault, St.-Jean	.10
☐☐	50	Marcel Cousineau (G), Beauport	.10

	Autographs	**NRMT-MT**
☐	Brent Bilodeau	5.00
☐	Philippe Boucher	5.00
☐	Jim Campbell	15.00
☐	René Corbet	8.00
☐	Marcel Cousineau (G)	8.00
☐	Jassen Cullimore	5.00
☐	Jason Dawe	5.00
☐	Yanick Dupré	15.00
☐	Pat Falloon	8.00
☐	François Groleau	5.00
☐	Trevor Halverson	5.00
☐	Donevan Hextall	5.00
☐	Steve Konowalchuk	5.00
☐	Scott Lachance	8.00
☐	Eric Lavigne	5.00
☐	Guy Lévêque	5.00
☐	Fred Lindqvist	5.00
☐	Jamie Matthews	5.00
☐	Dean McAmmond	5.00
☐	Sandy McCarthy	8.00
☐	Jamie McLennan (G)	15.00
☐	Glen Murray	5.00
☐	Jeff Nelson	5.00
☐	Scott Niedermayer	10.00
☐	Michael Nylander	8.00
☐	Chris Osgood (G)	35.00
☐	Shane Peacock	5.00
☐	Pat Peake	8.00
☐	Yanic Perreault	10.00
☐	Patrick Poulin	5.00
☐	Jamie Pushor	5.00
☐	Martin Rucinsky	10.00
☐	Yves Sarault	5.00
☐	Steve Staios	5.00
☐	Alek Stojanov	5.00
☐	Niklas Sundblad	5.00
☐	Andrew Verner (G)	5.00
☐	Darcy Werenka	5.00
☐	Ray Whitney	5.00
☐	Dody Wood	5.00
☐	Tyler Wright	5.00
☐	Jason Young	5.00

1991 - 92 FUTURE TRENDS '72 HOCKEY CANADA

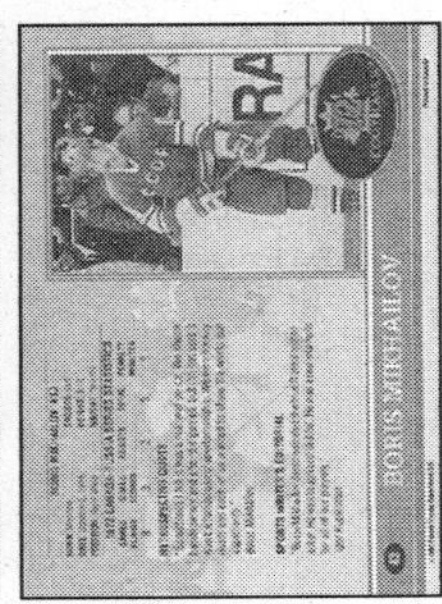

These cards have two versions: an English issue and a French issue. 36 players have a third autographed version signed in gold ink. Cards were produced by 7th Inning Sketch and distributed through Hudson Bay stores in Canada.

Imprint: 1991 Future Trends Experience Ltd. Printed in Canada

Complete Set (101 cards):	**11.00**	**11.00**
Common Player:	**.05**	**.25**
Promo Card Esposito:	**3.00**	
Promo Card Henderson:	**3.00**	
Promo Card Tretiak:	**3.00**	

	No.	**Player**	**Auto.**	**Eng.**	**French**
☐☐	1	In the Beginning	.–	.05	.25
☐☐	2	The Backyard Rink/More Months a Year	.–	.05	.25
☐☐	3	It Didn't Take Long/7-2	.–	.05	.25
☐☐	4	The Patriarch/Anatoli Tarasov	.–	.05	.25
☐☐	5	More Hours a Day	.–	1.00	2.00
☐☐	6	Coming Out Party	.–	.05	.25
☐☐	7	Never in Doubt	.–	.05	.25
☐☐	8	Team Canada	.–	.20	.50
☐☐☐	9	Pat Stapleton	15.00	.05	.25
☐☐	10	Vsevolod Bobrov, Coach	.–	.05	.25
☐☐☐	11	Vladislav Tretiak (G)	100.00	1.00	2.00
☐☐	12	Faceoff	.–	.05	.25
☐☐	13	30 Seconds	.–	.05	.25
☐☐	14	Yevgeny Zimin	.–	.05	.25
☐☐☐	15	Bill White	15.00	.05	.25
☐☐	16	7-3/Game 1 Statistics	.–	.05	.25
☐☐☐	17	Don Awrey	15.00	.05	.25
☐☐☐	18	Mickey Redmond	15.00	.05	.25
☐☐	19	Alexander Gusev	.–	.05	.25
☐☐	20	Alexander Maltsev	.–	.05	.25
☐☐☐	21	Rod Seiling	15.00	.05	.25
☐☐☐	22	Dale Tallon	15.00	.05	.25
☐☐	23	Coming Back	.–	.05	.25
☐☐	24	Unforgettable/Game 2 Statistics	.–	.05	.25
☐☐☐	25	Wayne Cashman	20.00	.20	.50
☐☐☐	26	Frank Mahovlich	35.00	.50	1.00
☐☐☐	27	Peter Mahovlich	15.00	.05	.25
☐☐	28	A. Sidelnikov/V. Solodukhin	.–	.05	.25
☐☐	29	Yuri Shatalov	.–	.05	.25
☐☐	30	Brothers: Phil and Tony Esposito Frank and Peter Mahovlich	.–	.50	1.00
☐☐	31	The Goalies: Ken Dryden, Tony Esposito, V. Tretiak	.–	1.25	2.50
☐☐	32	Alexander Bodunov	.–	.05	.25
☐☐	33	All Even/Game 3 Statistics	.–	.05	.25
☐☐	34	Yuri Blinov	.–	.05	.25
☐☐☐	35	Jocelyn Guevremont	15.00	.05	.25
☐☐☐	36	Vic Hadfield	15.00	.05	.25
☐☐	37	Yuri Lebedev	.–	.05	.25
☐☐	38	V. Starshinov/Y. Poladiev	.–	.05	.25
☐☐	39	Disaster/Game 4 Statistics	.–	.05	.25
☐☐	40	Address to the Nation	.–	.20	.50
☐☐	41	Victor Kuzkin	.–	.05	.25
☐☐	42	Vladimir Lutchenko	.–	.05	.25
☐☐	43	Boris Mikhailov	.–	.05	.25
☐☐	44	Grace Under Pressure	.–	.05	.25
☐☐	45	Afraid to Lose...	.–	.05	.25
☐☐	46	Ready to Win/Game 5 Statistics	.–	.05	.25
☐☐	47	Vladimir Vikulov	.–	.05	.25
☐☐☐	48	Red Berenson	15.00	.05	.25
☐☐☐	49	Richard Martin	20.00	.20	.50
☐☐	50	Alexander Martynyuk	.–	.05	.25
☐☐☐	51	Gilbert Perreault	25.00	.50	1.00
☐☐	52	Vladimir Petrov	.–	.05	.25
☐☐☐	53	Serge Savard	20.00	.35	.75

	No.	Player			
□□	54	Vladimir Shadrin	.–	.05	.25
□□	55	Da Da Ka-na-da/Nyet Nyet Sov-j-et	.–	.05	.25
□□	56	One Step Back/Game 6 Statistics	.–	.05	.25
□□□	57	Bobby Clarke	35.00	.50	1.00
□□	58	Valeri Kharlamov	.–	.75	1.50
□□	59	Alexander Volchkov	.–	.05	.25
□□	60	Standing Guard	.–	.05	.25
□□□	61	Stan Mikita	30.00	.50	1.00
□□	62	One More to Go/Game 7 Statistics	.–	.05	.25
□□	63	The Winner	.–	.05	.25
□□	64	The Fans Go Wild	.–	.05	.25
□□	65	Alexander Ragulin	.–	.05	.25
□□□	66	Jean Ratelle	25.00	.35	.75
□□	67	Gennady Tsygankov	.–	.05	.25
□□	68	Valeri Vasiliev	.–	.05	.25
□□	69	International Dialogue	.–	.05	.25
□□	70	Series Stars: P. Esposito/Yakushev	.–	.60	1.25
□□	71	Series Stars: Henderson/Tretiak	.–	1.50	3.00
□□	72	No Solitudes/The Telegrams	.–	.05	.25
□□	73	2 - 2/3 - 3	.–	.05	.25
□□□	74	Rod Gilbert	25.00	.35	.75
□□	75	Yevgeny Mishakov	.–	.05	.25
□□□	76	Ron Ellis	15.00	.05	.25
□□	77	5 - 4/5 - 5	.–	.05	.25
□□	78	Different Games/Interlude	.–	.05	.25
□□□	79	Bill Goldsworthy	45.00	.05	.25
□□	80	The Huddle.../...1:30 To Go	.–	.05	.25
□□	81	The Moment	.–	.05	.25
□□□	82	Yvan Cournoyer	25.00	.05	.25
□□	83	Yuri Liapkin	.–	.05	.25
□□□	84	Phil Esposito	50.00	.60	1.25
□□□	85	Ken Dryden (G)	110.00	1.00	2.00
□□	86	Peace/Game 8 Statistics	.–	.05	.25
□□□	87	Gary Bergman	15.00	.05	.25
□□□	88	Brian Glennie	15.00	.05	.25
□□□	89	Dennis Hull	15.00	.05	.25
□□	90	Vyacheslav Anisin	.–	.05	.25
□□□	91	Marcel Dionne	30.00	.50	1.00
□□□	92	Guy Lapointe	20.00	.35	.75
□□□	93	Ed Johnston (G)	18.00	.05	.25
□□□	94	Harry Sinden, Coach	20.00	.05	.25
□□□	95	Brad Park	25.00	.35	.75
□□□	96	Tony Esposito (G)	35.00	.60	1.25
□□	97	Alexander Yakushev	.–	.35	.75
□□□	98	Paul Henderson	35.00	1.00	2.00
□□□	99	J. P. Parise	15.00	.05	.25
□□	100	V. Kharlamov 1948-1981	.–	.50	1.00
□□	101	Checklist	.–	.05	.25

1991 - 92 GILLETTE

Imprint: Gillette
Complete Set (48 cards): **25.00**

	No.	Player	NRMT-MT
□		Title Card: Smythe Division	.25
□	1	Luc Robitaille, L.A.	.50
□	2	Esa Tikkanen, Edm.	.25
□	3	Pat Falloon, S.J.	.25
□	4	Theoren Fleury, Cgy.	1.00
□	5	Trevor Linden, Van.	.50
□	6	Rob Blake, L.A.	.50
□	7	Al MacInnis, Cgy.	.50
□	8	Bob Essensa (G), Wpg.	.25
□	9	Bill Ranford (G), Edm.	.50
□	10	Pavel Bure, Van.	2.50
□		Title Card: Norris Division	.25
□	11	Wendel Clark, Tor.	.50
□	12	Sergei Fedorov, Det.	1.50
□	13	Jeremy Roenick, Chi.	1.00
□	14	Brett Hull, Stl.	1.50
□	15	Mike Modano, Min.	1.50
□	16	Chris Chelios, Chi.	1.25
□	17	Dave Ellett, Tor.	.25
□	18	Ed Belfour (G), Chi.	1.00
□	19	Grant Fuhr (G), Tor.	.50
□	20	Martin Lapointe, Det.	.25
□		Title Card: Adams Division	.25
□	21	Kirk Muller, Mtl.	.25
□	22	Joe Sakic, Que.	2.50
□	23	Pat LaFontaine, Buf.	.50
□	24	Pat Verbeek, Hfd.	.25
□	25	Owen Nolan, Que.	.50
□	26	Ray Bourque, Bos.	1.50
□	27	Eric Desjardins, Mtl.	.50
□	28	Patrick Roy (G), Mtl.	4.00
□	29	Andy Moog (G), Bos.	.50
□	30	Valeri Kamensky, Que.	.50
□		Title Card: Patrick Division	.25
□	31	Mark Messier, NYR.	1.50
□	32	Mike Ricci, Pha.	.25
□	33	Mario Lemieux, Pgh.	4.00
□	34	Jaromir Jagr, Pgh.	3.00
□	35	Pierre Turgeon, Buf.	.50
□	36	Kevin Hatcher, Wsh.	.25
□	37	Paul Coffey, Pgh.	.50
□	38	Chris Terreri (G), N.J.	.25
□	39	Mike Richter (G), NYR..	1.00
□	40	Kevin Todd, N.J.	.25
□		Trivia Card	.25
□		Trivia Card	.25
□		Trivia Card	.25
□		Trivia Card	.25

1991 - 92 JYVAS HYVA HOCKEY LIIGA

A set of 12 unnumbered team logos and 72 numbered stickers from the Finnish National League. We have little pricing information on this set. Teemu Selänne is the most expensive single at $15.00. Singles start at 20¢.

Card Size: 1 5/8" x 4 1/4"
Imprint:
Complete Set (84 stickers):
Common Player: **.20**

	No.	Player
□		HIFK Helsinki
□	1	Sakari Lindfors (G)
□	2	Jukka Seppo
□	3	Pekka Tuomisto
□	4	Harri Tuohimaa
□	5	Pertti Lehtonen
□	6	Simo Saarinen
□		HPK Hameenlinna
□	7	Timo Lehkonen (G)
□	8	Teppo Kivela
□	9	Markku Piikkio
□	10	Pekka Peltola
□	11	Hannu Henriksson
□	12	Jari Haapamaki
□		Ilves Tampere
□	13	Jukka Tammi (G)
□	14	Risto Jalo
□	15	Timo Peltomaa
□	16	Raimo Summanen
□	17	Ville Siren
□	18	Risto Siltanen
□		Jokerit Helsinki
□	19	Markus Ketterer (G)
□	20	Pekka Jarvela
□	21	Teemu Selänne
□	22	Keijo Sailynoja
□	23	Mika Stromberg
□	24	Waltteri Immonen
□		JyPHT Jyvaskyla
□	25	AriPekka Siekkinen (G)
□	26	Jari Lindroos
□	27	Ari Haanpaa
□	28	Jiri Dolezal
□	29	Harri Laurila
□	30	Leo Gudas
□		KalPa Kuopio
□	31	Mika Rautio (G)
□	32	Pekka Tirkkonen
□	33	Jarmo Kekalainen
□	34	Juha Jokiharju
□	35	Juha Tuohimaa
□	36	Erik Hamalainen
□		Joensuun Kiekkopojat
□	37	Juha Jaaskelainen (G)
□	38	Rostislav Vlach
□	39	Jouni Mustonen
□	40	Markku Kyllonen
□	41	Antonin Stavjana
□	42	Ossi Piitulainen
□		Rauman Lukko
□	43	Petr Briza (G)
□	44	Mika Nieminen
□	45	Jari Torkki
□	46	Tommi Pullola
□	47	Jarmo Kuusisto
□	48	Pasi Huura
□		Hockey Reipa Lahti
□	49	Jaromir Sindel (G)
□	50	Marko Jantunen
□	51	Erkki Laine
□	52	Erkki Makela
□	53	Niko Marttila
□	54	Erik Kakko
□		Tappara Tampere
□	55	Jari Halme (G)
□	56	Kari Heikkinen
□	57	Jiri Kucera
□	58	Vesa Viitakoski
□	59	Jukka Marttila
□	60	Pekka Laksola
□		Turun Palloseura
□	61	Jouni Rokama (G)
□	62	Esa Keskinen
□	63	Jukka Vilander
□	64	Jari Pulliainen
□	65	Jouko Narvanmaa
□	66	Hannu Virta
□		Assat Pori
□	67	Kari Takko (G)
□	68	Janne Virtanen
□	69	Arto Javanainen
□	70	Oleg Znarok
□	71	Tapio Levo
□	72	Harry Nikander

1991 - 92 KELLOGG'S - SCORE

Two of 24 different were available in specially marked boxes of Kellogg's cereal.

Imprint:
Complete Set (24 cards): **15.00**
Album: **5.00**

	No.	Player	NRMT-MT
□	1	Patrick Roy (G), Mtl.	4.00
□	2	Rick Tocchet, Pha.	.35

	No.	Player	Price
☐	3	Wendel Clark, Tor.	.50
☐	4	Mike Modano, Min.	1.50
☐	5	Jeremy Roenick, Chi.	1.00
☐	6	Pierre Turgeon, Buf.	.50
☐	7	Kevin Hatcher, Wsh.	.35
☐	8	Brian Leetch, NYR.	1.00
☐	9	Mark Recchi, Pgh.	.50
☐	10	Andy Moog (G), Bos.	.50
☐	11	Kevin Dineen, Hfd.	.35
☐	12	Joe Sakic, Que.	2.00
☐	13	John MacLean, N.J.	.35
☐	14	Steve Yzerman, Det.	3.00
☐	15	Pat LaFontaine, NYI.	.50
☐	16	Al MacInnis, Cgy.	.50
☐	17	Petr Klima, Edm.	.35
☐	18	Ed Olczyk, Wpg.	.35
☐	19	Doug Wilson, S.J.	.50
☐	20	Trevor Linden, Van.	.50
☐	21	Brett Hull, Stl.	1.50
☐	22	Rob Blake, L.A.	.50
☐	23	Dave Ellett, Tor.	.35
☐	24	Cornelius Rooster, Kelloggs	.35

1991 - 92 KRAFT

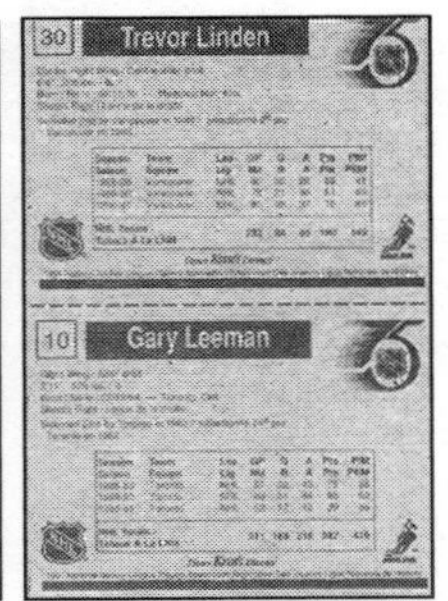

Cards: 1 to 40 and 64: Red backs; Issued on Kraft Dinner packages.
Cards: 41 to 56: Red backs; Issued on Kraft Spirals packages.
Cards: 21 and 57 to 63: Red backs; Issued on Kraft Noodles packages.
Disks: 67 to 88: Yellow backs; Issued in Kraft Peanut Butter.
Subset: Unnumbered: Maroon backs; Issued in the "Special Edition" album.
Factory-cut cards were available and command a 200% price premium over the cards cut from boxes. Three "Original Six" and one "Stanley Cup" unnumbered cards were issued with an album to hold the complete set.

Imprint: KRAFT
Disk Diameter: 2 3/4"
Imprint: KRAFT

Factory Set (92 cards w/album):			**135.00**
Complete Set (88 cards):			**95.00**
Album:			**40.00**

	No.	Player	NRMT-MT
☐	1	Mario Lemieux, Pgh.	5.00
☐	2	Mark Recchi, Pgh.	1.25
☐	3	Jaromir Jagr, Pgh.	4.00
☐	4	Mats Sundin, Que.	2.00
☐	5	Adam Oates, Stl.	1.50
☐	6	M. Richard; J. Plante (G)	3.00
☐	7	Brendan Shanahan, Stl.	2.50
☐	8	Pat Falloon, S.J.	.60
☐	9	Grant Fuhr (G), Tor.	1.00
☐	10	Gary Leeman, Tor.	.60
☐	11	Petr Nedved, Van.	1.00
☐	12	Kirk Muller, Mtl.	.60
☐	13	Theoren Fleury, Cgy.	1.50
☐	14	Dino Ciccarelli, Wsh.	1.00
☐	15	Geoff Courtnall, Van.	.60
☐	16	Mark Messier, NYR.	2.00
☐	17	Ken Hodge, Bos.	.60
☐	18	Chris Chelios, Chi.	1.50
☐	19	Mike Vernon (G), Cgy.	1.00
☐	20	Kevin Hatcher, Wsh.	.60
☐	21	Stéphane Richer, N.J.	.60
☐	22	Mark Tinordi, Min.	.60
☐	23	Pat Verbeek, Hfd.	.60
☐	24	John Cullen, Hfd.	.60
☐	25	Pat LaFontaine, Buf.	1.00
☐	26	Stéphan Lebeau, Mtl.	.60
☐	27	Mike Gartner, NYR.	1.00
☐	28	Bobby Baun, Last Leaf Dynasty	1.00
☐	29	Shayne Corson, Mtl.	1.00
☐	30	Trevor Linden, Van.	1.00
☐	31	Craig Janney, Bos.	.60
☐	32	Al MacInnis, Cgy.	1.00
☐	33	Phil Housley, Wpg.	.60
☐	34	Doug Wilson, S.J.	1.00
☐	35	Tony Granato, L.A.	.60
☐	36	Dale Hawerchuk, Buf.	1.00
☐	37	Bill Durnan, Mtl.; Turk Broda, Tor.	1.25
☐	38	Brian Bellows, Min.	.60
☐	39	Bob Gainey, Mtl.	1.50
☐	40	Darryl Sittler, Tor.	1.00
☐	41	Joe Sakic, Que.	3.00
☐	42	Wendel Clark, Tor.	1.00
☐	43	Brent Sutter, Chi.	.60
☐	44	Bill Ranford (G), Edm.	1.00
☐	45	Rick Tocchet, Pha.	.60
☐	46	Paul Ysebaert, Det.	.60
☐	47	Adam Creighton, NYI.	.60
☐	48	Mike Modano, Min.	2.00
☐	49	Russ Courtnall, Mtl.	.60
☐	50	Syl Apps, Tor.	1.00
☐	51	Sergei Fedorov, Det.	2.00
☐	52	Mike Ricci, Pha.	.60
☐	53	Scott Stevens, N.J.	1.00
☐	54	Bobby Clarke, Pha.	1.50
☐	55	Owen Nolan, Que.	.75
☐	56	Jeremy Roenick, Chi.	1.50
☐	57	Ray Bourque, Bos.	2.00
☐	58	Gerard Gallant, Det.	.60
☐	59	Andy Moog (G), Bos.	1.00
☐	60	Alexander Mogilny, Buf.	1.50
☐	61	Denis Potvin, NYI.	1.50
☐	62	Ed Olczyk, Wpg.	.60
☐	63	Tomas Sandström, L.A.	.60
☐	64	Checklist 1 (1-56)	.60

1991 KRAFT DISKS

	No.	Player	NRMT-MT
☐	65	Wayne Gretzky, L.A./ Maurice Richard, Mtl.	15.00
☐	66	Brett Hull, Stl./ Guy Lafleur, Mtl.	3.00
☐	67	Jari Kurri, L.A./ Bobby Clarke, Pha.	1.50
☐	68	Steve Yzerman, Det./ Jean Béliveau, Mtl.	5.00
☐	69	Steve Larmer, Chi./ Pat Stapleton, Chi.	1.00
☐	70	Luc Robitaille, L.A./ Ted Lindsay, Det.	1.50
☐	71	Larry Murphy, Phi./ Doug Harvey, Mtl.	1.50
☐	72	Denis Potvin, NYI../ Gary Suter, Cgy.	1.50
☐	73	Brian Leetch, NYR../ Harry Howell, NYR.	1.75
☐	74	Paul Coffey, Pit./ Bill Gadsby, Det.	1.75
☐	75	Jon Casey (G), Min./ Terry Sawchuk (G), Det.	2.25
☐	76	Patrick Roy (G), Mtl./ Jacques Plante (G), Mtl.	8.50
☐	77	Denis Savard, Mtl./ Serge Savard, Mtl.	1.50
☐	78	Doug Gilmour, Cgy./ Bob Baun, Tor.	2.00
☐	79	Guy Carbonneau, Mtl./ Yvan Cournoyer, Mtl.	1.50
☐	80	Gilbert Perreault, Buf./ Larry Robinson, L.A.	2.00
☐	81	Red Kelly, Tor./ Craig Simpson, Edm.	1.00
☐	82	Bobby Smith, Min./ Rod Gilbert, NYR.	1.50
☐	83	Syl Apps, Tor./ Peter Stastny, N.J.	1.50
☐	84	Bernie Geoffrion, Mtl./ Vince Damphousse, Edm.	1.75
☐	85	Marcel Dionne, L.A./ Steve Smith, Chi.	1.50
☐	86	Tim Horton, Tor./ Kevin Dineen, Hfd.	2.00
☐	87	Michel Goulet, Chi./ Frank Mahovlich, Tor.	2.00
☐	88	Mike Richter, NYR../ Henri Richard, Mtl.	2.00

ORIGINAL SIX TEAM LOGOS/STANLEY CUP

☐	Montréal Canadiens/Toronto Maple Leafs	1.25
☐	Chicago Blackhawks/Detroit Red Wings	1.25
☐	Boston Bruins/New York Rangers	1.25
☐	Stanley Cup	1.50

1991 - 92 McDONALD'S - UPPER DECK

Imprint: 1991 The Upper Deck Co. All Rights Reserved. Printed in the U.S.A.

	No.	Holograms	NRMT-MT
Complete Set (31 cards):			**25.00**
☐	McH1	Wayne Gretzky, L.A.	4.50
☐	McH2	Chris Chelios, Chi.	1.50
☐	McH3	Ray Bourque, Bos.	1.50
☐	McH4	Brett Hull, Stl.	1.50
☐	McH5	Cam Neely, Bos.	1.00
☐	McH6	Patrick Roy (G), Mtl.	3.50
	No.	**All-Stars**	**NRMT-MT**
☐	Mc 1	Cam Neely, Bos.	.35
☐	Mc 2	Rick Tocchet, Pha.	.25
☐	Mc 3	Kevin Stevens, Pgh.	.25
☐	Mc 4	Mark Recchi, Pgh.	.75
☐	Mc 5	Joe Sakic, Que.	1.50
☐	Mc 6	Pat LaFontaine, Buf.	1.00
☐	Mc 7	Darren Turcotte, NYR.	.25
☐	Mc 8	Patrick Roy (G), Mtl.	2.75
☐	Mc 9	Andy Moog (G), Bos.	.35
☐	Mc10	Ray Bourque, Bos.	1.00
☐	Mc11	Paul Coffey, Pgh.	.35
☐	Mc12	Brian Leetch, NYR.	1.00
☐	Mc13	Brett Hull, Stl.	1.00
☐	Mc14	Luc Robitaille, L.A.	.35
☐	Mc15	Steve Larmer, Chi.	.35
☐	Mc16	Vincent Damphousse, Edm.	.50
☐	Mc17	Wayne Gretzky, L.A.	3.25
☐	Mc18	Theoren Fleury, Cgy.	.75
☐	Mc19	Steve Yzerman, Det.	1.75
☐	Mc20	Mike Vernon (G), Cgy.	.35
☐	Mc21	Bill Ranford (G), Edm.	.35
☐	Mc22	Chris Chelios, Chi.	1.00
☐	Mc23	Al MacInnis, Cgy.	.35
☐	Mc24	Scott Stevens, Stl.	.35
☐	Mc25	Checklist	.50

1991 - 92 O-PEE-CHEE / TOPPS

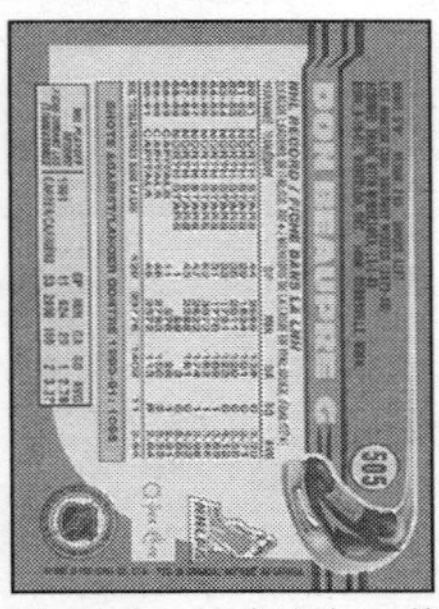

These promo cards were issued as a nine-card promo sheet along with your Bowman promo cards. The regular cards have two versions: the O-Pee-Chee (Canadian, Bilingual) issue and the Topps (American, English) issue. Pricing for both issues is identical.

OPC Imprint: © 1991 O-Pee-Chee Co. Ltd.
Topps Imprint: © 1991 The Topps Company, Inc.

Complete Set (528 cards):			**15.00**
Common Player:			**.10**
		Promo	**NRMT-MT**
☐		Ed Belfour (G), Chi.	2.00
☐		Brett Hull, Stl.	2.00
☐		Pat LaFontaine, NYI.	2.00
☐		Mario Lemieux, Pgh.	5.00
☐		Joe Sakic, Que.	3.00
	No.	**Player**	**Reg.**
☐ ☐	1	Goodbye Guy!!	.50
☐ ☐	2	Gueeey's Last Hoorah	.50
☐ ☐	3	Guy Bids Farewell	.50
☐ ☐	4	Ed Belfour (G), Chi.	.25
☐ ☐	5	Ken Hodge, Bos.	.10
☐ ☐	6	Rob Blake, L.A.	.25
☐ ☐	7	Bobby Holik, Hfd.	.10
☐ ☐	8	Sergei Fedorov, Det., Error (Federov)	.25
☐ ☐	9	Jaromir Jagr, Pgh.	.50
☐ ☐	10	Eric Weinrich, N.J.	.10
☐ ☐	11	Mike Richter (G), NYR..	.25
☐ ☐	12	Mats Sundin, Que.	.25
☐ ☐	13	Mike Ricci, Pha.	.10

	No.	Player	Price
☐☐	14	Eric Desjardins, Mtl.	.10
☐☐	15	Paul Ranheim, Cgy.	.10
☐☐	16	Joe Sakic, Que.	.75
☐☐	17	Curt Giles, Min.	.10
☐☐	18	Mike Foligno, Tor.	.10
☐☐	19	Brad Marsh, Det.	.10
☐☐	20	Ed Belfour (G), Chi.	.35
☐☐	21	Steve Smith, Edm.	.10
☐☐	22	Kirk Muller, N.J.	.10
☐☐	23	Kelly Chase, Stl.	.10
☐☐	**24**	**Jim McKenzie, Hfd., RC**	**.10**
☐☐	25	Mick Vukota, NYI.	.10
☐☐	**26**	**Tony Amonte, NYR.., RC**	**.75**
☐☐	27	Danton Cole, Wpg.	.10
☐☐	**28**	**Jay Mazur, Van., RC**	**.10**
☐☐	29	Pete Peeters (G), Pha.	.10
☐☐	30	Petri Skriko, Bos.	.10
☐☐	31	Steve Duchesne, L.A. (Pha.)	.10
☐☐	32	TC: A. Mogilny/B. Hogue/D. Hawerchuk, Buf.	.25
☐☐	33	Phil Bourque, Pgh.	.10
☐☐	34	Tim Bergland, Wsh.	.10
☐☐	35	Tim Cheveldae (G), Det.	.10
☐☐	**36**	**Bill Armstrong, Pha., RC**	**.10**
☐☐	37	John McIntyre, L.A.	.10
☐☐	38	Dave Andreychuk, Buf.	.25
☐☐	39	Curtis Leschyshyn, Que.	.10
☐☐	40	Jaromir Jagr, Pgh.	1.00
☐☐	41	Craig Janney, Bos.	.10
☐☐	42	Doug Brown, N.J.	.10
☐☐	43	Ken Sabourin, Wsh.	.10
☐☐	44	TC: Brian Bellows, Min.	.10
☐☐	45	Fredrik Olausson, Wpg., Error (Clausson)	.10
☐☐	46	Mike Gartner, NYR.	.25
☐☐	47	Mark Fitzpatrick (G), NYI.	.10
☐☐	48	Joe Murphy, Edm.	.10
☐☐	49	Doug Wilson, Chi.	.25
☐☐	50	Brian MacLellan, Cgy., (Det.)	.10
☐☐	51	Bob Bassen, Stl.	.10
☐☐	52	Robert Kron, Van.	.10
☐☐	53	Roger Johansson, Cgy.	.10
☐☐	54	Guy Carbonneau, Mtl.	.10
☐☐	55	Rob Ramage, Tor. (Min.)	.10
☐☐	56	Bobby Holik, Hfd.	.10
☐☐	57	Alan May, Wsh.	.10
☐☐	58	Rick Meagher, Stl.	.10
☐☐	59	Cliff Ronning, Van.	.10
☐☐	60	TC: B. McCrimmon/S. Yzerman/S. Chiasson, Det.	.35
☐☐	61	Bob Kudelski, L.A.	.10
☐☐	62	Wayne McBean, NYI.	.10
☐☐	63	Craig MacTavish, Edm.	.10
☐☐	64	Owen Nolan, Que.	.25
☐☐	65	Dale Hawerchuk, Buf.	.25
☐☐	66	Ray Bourque, Bos.	.50
☐☐	67	Sean Burke (G), N.J.	.25
☐☐	68	Frantisek Musil, Cgy.	.10
☐☐	69	Joe Mullen, Pgh.	.10
☐☐	70	Drake Berehowsky, Tor.	.10
☐☐	71	Darren Turcotte, NYR.	.10
☐☐	72	Randy Carlyle, Wpg.	.10
☐☐	73	Paul Cyr, Hfd.	.10
☐☐	74	Dave Gagner, Min.	.10
☐☐	75	Steve Larmer, Chi.	.25
☐☐	76	Petr Svoboda, Mtl.	.10
☐☐	77	Keith Acton, Pha.	.10
☐☐	78	Dmitri Khristich, Wsh.	.10
☐☐	79	Brad McCrimmon, Det.	.10
☐☐	80	Pat LaFontaine, NYI.	.25
☐☐	81	Jeff Reese (G), Tor.	.10
☐☐	82	Mario Marois, Stl.	.10
☐☐	83	Rob Brown, Hfd.	.10
☐☐	84	Grant Fuhr (G), Edm.	.25
☐☐	85	Carey Wilson, Cgy.	.10
☐☐	86	Garry Galley, Bos.	.10
☐☐	87	Troy Murray, Chi., (Wpg.)	.10
☐☐	88	Tony Granato, L.A.	.10
☐☐	89	Gord Murphy, Pha.	.10
☐☐	90	Brent Gilchrist, Mtl.	.10
☐☐	91	Mike Richter (G), NYR..	.35
☐☐	92	Eric Weinrich, N.J.	.10
☐☐	93	Marc Bureau, Min.	.10
☐☐	94	Bob Errey, Pgh.	.10
☐☐	95	Dave McLlwain, Wpg.	.10
☐☐	96	TC: J. Sakic/L. DeBlois, Que.	.25
☐☐	97	Clint Malarchuk (G), Buf.	.10
☐☐	98	Shawn Antoski, Van.	.10
☐☐	99	Bob Sweeney, Bos.	.10
☐☐	100	Stephen Leach, Wsh., (Bos.)	.10
☐☐	101	Gary Nylund, NYI.	.10
☐☐	102	Lucien DeBlois, Tor.	.10
☐☐	103	TC: Norm Maciver, Edm.	.10
☐☐	104	Jimmy Carson, Det.	.10
☐☐	105	Rod Langway, Wsh.	.10
☐☐	106	Jeremy Roenick, Chi.	.35
☐☐	107	Mike Vernon (G), Cgy.	.25
☐☐	108	Brian Leetch, NYR.	.35
☐☐	109	Mark Hunter, Hfd.	.10
☐☐	110	Brian Bellows, Min.	.10
☐☐	111	Per-Erik Eklund, Pha.	.10
☐☐	112	Rob Blake, L.A.	.25
☐☐	113	Mike Hough, Que.	.10
☐☐	114	Frank Pietrangelo (G), Pgh.	.10
☐☐	115	Christian Ruuttu, Buf.	.10
☐☐	**116**	**Bryan Marchment, Wpg., RC**	**.10**
☐☐	117	Garry Valk, Van.	.10
☐☐	118	Ken Daneyko, N.J.	.10
☐☐	119	Russ Courtnall, Mtl.	.10
☐☐	120	Ron Wilson, Stl.	.10
☐☐	121	Shayne Stevenson, Bos.	.10
☐☐	**122**	**Bill Berg, NYI.., RC**	**.10**
☐☐	123	TC: Luke Richardson, Tor.	.10
☐☐	124	Glenn Anderson, Edm.	.10
☐☐	125	Kevin Miller, Det.	.10
☐☐	126	Calle Johansson, Wsh.	.10
☐☐	127	Jim Waite (G), Chi.	.10
☐☐	128	Allen Pedersen, Bos., (Min.)	.10
☐☐	129	Brian Mullen, S.J.	.10
☐☐	130	Ron Francis, Pgh.	.35
☐☐	131	Jergus Baca, Hfd.	.10
☐☐	132	Checklist 1 (1 to 132)	.10
☐☐	133	Tony Tanti, Buf.	.10
☐☐	134	Wes Walz, Bos.	.10
☐☐	135	Stéphan Lebeau, Mtl.	.10
☐☐	136	Ken Wregget (G), Pha.	.10
☐☐	137	Scott Arniel, Wpg.	.10
☐☐	138	Dave Taylor, L.A.	.10
☐☐	139	Steven Finn, Que.	.10
☐☐	140	Brendan Shanahan, N.J., (Stl.)	.35
☐☐	141	Petr Nedved, Van.	.10
☐☐	142	Chris Dahlquist, Min.	.10
☐☐	143	Rich Sutter, Stl.	.10
☐☐	144	Joe Reekie, NYI.	.10
☐☐	145	Peter Ing (G), Tor.	.10
☐☐	146	Ken Linseman, Edm.	.10
☐☐	147	Dave Barr, Det.	.10
☐☐	148	Al Iafrate, Wsh.	.10
☐☐	149	Greg Gilbert, Chi.	.10
☐☐	150	Craig Ludwig, Mtl., (Min.)	.10
☐☐	151	Gary Suter, Cgy.	.10
☐☐	152	Jan Erixon, NYR.	.10
☐☐	153	Mario Lemieux, Pgh.	1.00
☐☐	154	Mike Liut (G), Wsh.	.10
☐☐	155	Uwe Krupp, Buf.	.10
☐☐	156	Darin Kimble, Stl.	.10
☐☐	157	Shayne Corson, Mtl.	.25
☐☐	158	Winnipeg Jets	.10
☐☐	159	Stéphane Morin, Que., Error (Jeff Jackson)	.10
☐☐	160	Rick Tocchet, Pha.	.10
☐☐	161	John Tonelli, L.A.	.10
☐☐	162	Adrien Plavsic, Van.	.10
☐☐	163	Jason Miller, N.J.	.10
☐☐	164	TIm Kerr, Pha. (NYR.)	.10
☐☐	165	Brent Sutter, NYI.	.10
☐☐	166	Michel Petit, Tor.	.10
☐☐	167	Adam Graves, Edm.	.10
☐☐	168	Jamie Macoun, Cgy.	.10
☐☐	169	Terry Yake, Hfd.	.10
☐☐	170	TC: R. Bourque/C. Neely/C. Nilan, Bos.	.20
☐☐	171	Alexander Mogilny, Buf.	.35
☐☐	172	Karl Dykhuis, Chi.	.10
☐☐	173	Tomas Sandström, L.A.	.10
☐☐	174	Bernie Nicholls, NYR.	.10
☐☐	175	Viacheslav Fetisov, N.J.	.25
☐☐	176	Andrew Cassels, Mtl.	.10
☐☐	177	Ulf Dahlen, Min.	.10
☐☐	178	Brian Hayward (G), S.J.	.10
☐☐	179	Doug Lidster, Van.	.10
☐☐	180	Dave Lowry, Stl.	.10
☐☐	181	Ron Tugnutt (G), Que.	.10
☐☐	182	Ed Olczyk, Wpg.	.10
☐☐	183	Paul Coffey, Pgh.	.25
☐☐	184	Shawn Burr, Det.	.10
☐☐	185	TC: Hartford Whalers	.10
☐☐	186	Mark Janssens, NYR.	.10
☐☐	187	Mike Craig, Min.	.10
☐☐	188	Gary Leeman, Tor.	.10
☐☐	189	Phil Sykes, Wpg.	.10
☐☐	190	Brett Hull, Stl.	.35
☐☐	191	TC: B. Shanahan/D. Brown/K. Muller P. Stastny/P. Sundstrom, N.J.	.20
☐☐	192	Cam Neely, Bos.	.25
☐☐	193	Petr Klima, Edm.	.10
☐☐	194	Mike Ricci, Pha.	.10
☐☐	195	Kelly Hrudey (G), LA	.10
☐☐	196	Mark Recchi, Pgh.	.25
☐☐	197	Mikael Andersson, Hfd.	.10
☐☐	198	Bob Probert, Det.	.10
☐☐	199	Craig Wolanin, Que.	.10
☐☐	200	Scott Mellanby, Pha. (Edm.)	.10
☐☐	201	HL:Gretzky Scores 2000th Point	1.00
☐☐	202	Laurie Boschman, N.J.	.10
☐☐	203	Gino Odjick, Van.	.10
☐☐	204	Garth Butcher, Stl.	.10
☐☐	205	Randy Wood, NYI.	.10
☐☐	206	John Druce, Wsh.	.10
☐☐	207	Doug Bodger, Buf.	.10
☐☐	208	Doug Gilmour, Cgy.	.35
☐☐	**209**	**John LeClair, Mtl., RC**	**1.50**
☐☐	210	Steve Thomas, Chi,	.10
☐☐	211	Kjell Samuelsson, Pha.	.10
☐☐	212	Daniel Marois, Tor.	.10
☐☐	213	Jiri Hrdina, Pgh.	.10
☐☐	214	Darrin Shannon, Buf.	.10
☐☐	215	TC: B. Leetch/J. Erixon/P. Broten, NYR.	.10
☐☐	216	Robert McGill, S.J.	.10
☐☐	217	Dirk Graham, Chi.	.10
☐☐	218	Thomas Steen, Wpg.	.10
☐☐	219	Mats Sundin, Que.	.50
☐☐	220	Kevin Lowe, Edm.	.10
☐☐	221	Kirk McLean (G), Van.	.25
☐☐	222	Jeff Brown, Stl.	.10
☐☐	223	Joe Nieuwendyk, Cgy.	.25
☐☐	224	LL: Wayne Gretzky, L.A.	1.00
☐☐	225	Marty McSorley, L.A.	.10
☐☐	226	John Cullen, Hfd.	.10
☐☐	227	Brian Propp, Min.	.10
☐☐	228	Yves Racine, Det.	.10
☐☐	229	Dale Hunter, Wsh.	.10
☐☐	**230**	**Dennis Vaske, NYI.., RC**	**.10**
☐☐	231	Sylvain Turgeon, Mtl.	.10
☐☐	232	Ron Sutter, Pha.	.10
☐☐	233	Chris Chelios, Chi.	.35
☐☐	234	Brian Bradley, Tor.	.10
☐☐	235	Scott Young, Pgh.	.10
☐☐	236	Mike Ramsey, Buf.	.10
☐☐	237	Jon Casey (G), Min.	.10
☐☐	238	Nevin Markwart, Bos.	.10
☐☐	239	John MacLean, N.J.	.10
☐☐	240	Brent Ashton, Wpg.	.10
☐☐	241	Tony Hrkac, S.J.	.10
☐☐	242	TC: Steve Bozek, Van.	.10
☐☐	243	Jeff Norton, NYI.	.10
☐☐	244	Martin Gelinas, Edm.	.10
☐☐	245	Mike Ridley, Wsh.	.10
☐☐	246	Pat Jablonski, (G), Stl.	.10
☐☐	247	TC: Mike Vernon, Cgy.	.25
☐☐	248	Paul Ysebaert, Det.	.10
☐☐	249	Sylvain Côté, Hfd.	.10
☐☐	250	Marc Habscheid, Det. (Cgy.)	.10
☐☐	251	Todd Elik, L.A., (Min.)	.10
☐☐	252	Mike McPhee, Mtl.	.10
☐☐	253	James Patrick, NYR.	.10
☐☐	254	Murray Craven, Pha.	.10
☐☐	255	Trent Yawney, Chi.	.10
☐☐	256	Rob Cimetta, Tor.	.10
☐☐	257	LL: Wayne Gretzky	1.00
☐☐	258	AS: Wayne Gretzky, L.A.	1.00
☐☐	259	AS: Brett Hull, Stl.	.25
☐☐	260	Luc Robitaille, L.A.	.25
☐☐	261	AS: Ray Bourque, Bos.	.25
☐☐	262	AS: Al MacInnis, Cgy.	.10
☐☐	263	AS: Ed Belfour (G), Chi.	.25
☐☐	264	AS: Checklist 2 (133 to 264)	.10
☐☐	265	AS: Adam Oates, Stl.	.25
☐☐	266	AS: Cam Neely, Bos.	.25
☐☐	267	AS: Kevin Stevens, Pgh.	.10

	No.	Card	Value
☐☐	268	AS: Chris Chelios, Chi.	.25
☐☐	269	AS: Brian Leetch, NYR.	.25
☐☐	270	AS: Patrick Roy (G), Mtl.	.50
☐☐	271	LL: Ed Belfour (G), Chi.	.25
☐☐	272	Rob Zettler, S.J.	.10
☐☐	273	Donald Audette, Buf.	.10
☐☐	274	Teppo Numminen, Wpg.	.10
☐☐	275	Peter Stastny, N.J.	.25
☐☐	276	David Christian, Bos.	.10
☐☐	277	Larry Murphy, Pgh.	.25
☐☐	278	Johan Garpenlov, Det.	.10
☐☐	279	Tom Fitzgerald, NYI.	.10
☐☐	280	Gerald Diduck, Van.	.10
☐☐	281	Gino Cavallini, Stl.	.10
☐☐	282	Theoren Fleury, Cgy.	.35
☐☐	283	TC: Brian Benning, L.A.	.10
☐☐	284	Jeff Beukeboom, Edm.	.10
☐☐	285	Kevin Dineen, Hfd.	.10
☐☐	286	Jacques Cloutier (G), Que.	.10
☐☐	287	Tom Chorske, Mtl.	.10
☐☐	288	LL: Ed Belfour, Chi.	.25
☐☐	289	Ray Sheppard, NYR.	.10
☐☐	290	Olaf Kolzig (G), Wsh.	.35
☐☐	291	Terry Carkner, Pha.	.10
☐☐	292	Benoît Hogue, Buf.	.10
☐☐	293	Mike Peluso, Chi.	.10
☐☐	294	Bruce Driver, N.J.	.10
☐☐	295	Jari Kurri, Edm. (L.A.)	.25
☐☐	296	Peter Sidorkiewicz (G), Hfd.	.10
☐☐	297	Scott Pearson, Que.	.10
☐☐	298	TC: S. Richer/S. Corson/B. Skrudland, Mtl.	.10
☐☐	299	Vincent Damphousse, Tor.	.25
☐☐	300	John Carter, Bos.	.10
☐☐	301	Geoff Smith, Edm.	.10
☐☐	302	Steve Kasper, Bos. (Pha.)	.10
☐☐	303	Brett Hull, Stl.	.50
☐☐	304	Ray Ferraro, NYI.	.10
☐☐	305	Geoff Courtnall, Van.	.10
☐☐	306	David Shaw, NYR.	.10
☐☐	307	Bob Essensa (G), Wpg.	.10
☐☐	308	Mark Tinordi, Min.	.10
☐☐	309	Keith Primeau, Det.	.25
☐☐	310	Kevin Hatcher, Wsh.	.10
☐☐	311	Chris Nilan, Bos.	.10
☐☐	312	Trevor Kidd (G), Cgy.	.25
☐☐	313	Daniel Berthiaume (G), L.A.	.10
☐☐	314	Adam Creighton, Chi.	.10
☐☐	315	Everett Sanipass, Que.	.10
☐☐	316	Ken Baumgartner, NYI.	.10
☐☐	317	Sheldon Kennedy, Det.	.10
☐☐	318	Dave Capuano, Van.	.10
☐☐	319	Don Sweeney, Bos.	.10
☐☐	320	Gary Roberts, Cgy.	.25
☐☐	321	Wayne Gretzky, L.A.	1.75
☐☐	322	LL: T. Fleury, Cgy./M. McSorley, L.A.	.20
☐☐	323	Ulf Samuelsson, Pgh.	.10
☐☐	324	Mike Krushelnyski, Tor.	.10
☐☐	325	Dean Evason, Hfd.	.10
☐☐	326	Pat Elynuik, Wpg.	.10
☐☐	327	Michal Pivonka, Wsh.	.10
☐☐	328	Paul Cavallini, Stl.	.10
☐☐	329	Philadelphia Flyers	.10
☐☐	330	Denis Savard, Mtl.	.25
☐☐	331	Paul Fenton, Cgy.	.10
☐☐	332	Jon Morris, N.J.	.10
☐☐	333	Daren Puppa (G), Buf.	.10
☐☐	334	Doug Smail, Min.	.10
☐☐	335	Kelly Kisio, S.J.	.10
☐☐	336	Michel Goulet, Chi.	.25
☐☐	337	Mike Sillinger, Det.	.10
☐☐	338	Andy Moog (G), Bos.	.25
☐☐	339	Paul Stanton, Pgh.	.10
☐☐	340	Greg Adams, Van.	.10
☐☐	341	Doug Crossman, Det.	.10
☐☐	342	Kelly Miller, Wsh.	.10
☐☐	343	Patrick Flatley, NYI.	.10
☐☐	344	Zarley Zalapski, Hfd.	.10
☐☐	345	Mark Osborne, Wpg.	.10
☐☐	346	Mark Messier, Edm.	.50
☐☐	347	TC: Adam Oates, Stl.	.25
☐☐	348	Neil Wilkinson, S.J.	.10
☐☐	349	Brian Skrudland, Mtl.	.10
☐☐	350	Lyle Odelein, Mtl.	.10
☐☐	351	Luke Richardson, Tor.	.10
☐☐	352	Zdeno Ciger, N.J.	.10
☐☐	353	John Vanbiesbrouck (G), NYR..	.60
☐☐	354	Lou Franceschetti, Buf.	.10
☐☐	355	Alexei Gusarov, Que.	.10
☐☐	356	Bill Ranford (G), Edm.	.25
☐☐	357	Normand Lacombe, Pha.	.10
☐☐	358	Randy Burridge, Bos. (Wsh.)	.10
☐☐	359	Brian Benning, L.A.	.10
☐☐	360	Dave Hannan, Tor.	.10
☐☐	361	Todd Gill, Tor.	.10
☐☐	362	Peter Bondra, Wsh.	.35
☐☐	363	Mike Hartman, Buf.	.10
☐☐	364	Trevor Linden, Van.	.25
☐☐	365	John Ogrodnick, NYR.	.10
☐☐	366	Steve Konroyd, Chi.	.10
☐☐	367	Mike Modano, Min.	.50
☐☐	368	Glenn Healy (G), NYI.	.10
☐☐	369	Stéphane Richer, Mtl.	.10
☐☐	370	Vincent Riendeau (G), Stl.	.10
☐☐	371	Randy Moller, NYR.	.10
☐☐	372	TC: Tom Barrasso, Pgh.	.25
☐☐	373	Murray Baron, Pha.	.10
☐☐	374	Troy Crowder, N.J.	.10
☐☐	375	Rick Tabaracci (G), Wpg.	.10
☐☐	376	Brent Fedyk, Det.	.10
☐☐	377	Randy Velischek, Que.	.10
☐☐	378	Esa Tikkanen, Edm.	.10
☐☐	379	Richard Pilon, NYI.	.10
☐☐	**380**	**Jeff Lazaro, Bos., RC**	**.10**
☐☐	381	David Ellett, Tor.	.10
☐☐	382	Jeff Hackett (G), S.J.	.25
☐☐	383	Stéphane Matteau, Cgy.	.10
☐☐	384	TC: Dave Tippett, Hfd.	.10
☐☐	385	Wayne Presley, Chi.	.10
☐☐	386	Grant Ledyard, Buf.	.10
☐☐	387	Kip Miller, Que.	.10
☐☐	388	Dean Kennedy, Buf.	.10
☐☐	389	Hubie McDonough, NYI.	.10
☐☐	390	Anatoli Semenov, Edm.	.10
☐☐	391	Daryl Reaugh (G), Hfd.	.10
☐☐	392	Mathieu Schneider, Mtl.	.10
☐☐	393	Dan Quinn, Stl.	.10
☐☐	394	Claude Lemieux, N.J.	.10
☐☐	395	Phil Housley, Wpg.	.10
☐☐	396	Checklist 3 (265 - 396)	.10
☐☐	397	Steven Bozek, Van.	.10
☐☐	398	Bobby Smith, Min.	.10
☐☐	399	Mark Pederson, Pha.	.10
☐☐	400	Kevin Todd, N.J.	.10
☐☐	401	Sergei Fedorov, Det.	.50
☐☐	402	Tom Barrasso (G), Pgh.	.25
☐☐	403	HL: Brett Hull, Stl.	.25
☐☐	404	Bob Carpenter, Bos.	.10
☐☐	405	Luc Robitaille, L.A.	.25
☐☐	406	Mark Hardy, NYR.	.10
☐☐	407	Neil Sheehy, Wsh.	.10
☐☐	408	Mike McNeill, Que.	.10
☐☐	409	Dave Manson, Chi.	.10
☐☐	410	Mike Tomlak, Hfd.	.10
☐☐	411	Robert Reichel, Cgy.	.10
☐☐	412	New York Islanders	.10
☐☐	413	Patrick Roy (G), Mtl.	1.00
☐☐	**414**	**Shaun Van Allen, Edm., RC**	**.10**
☐☐	415	Dale Kushner, Pha.	.10
☐☐	416	Pierre Turgeon, Buf.	.10
☐☐	417	Curtis Joseph (G), Stl.	.60
☐☐	418	Randy Gilhen, Pgh. (LA)	.10
☐☐	419	Jyrki Lumme, Van.	.10
☐☐	420	Neal Broten, Min.	.10
☐☐	421	Kevin Stevens, Pgh.	.10
☐☐	422	Chris Terreri (G), N.J.	.10
☐☐	423	David Reid, Tor.	.10
☐☐	424	Steve Yzerman, Det.	1.00
☐☐	425	LL: Ed Belfour, Chi.	.25
☐☐	426	Jim Johnson, Min.	.10
☐☐	427	Joey Kocur, NYR.	.10
☐☐	428	Joel Otto, Cgy.	.10
☐☐	429	Dino Ciccarelli, Wsh.	.25
☐☐	430	TC: Chicago Blackhawks	.10
☐☐	431	Claude Lapointe, Que.	.10
☐☐	432	Chris Joseph, Edm.	.10
☐☐	433	Gaetan Duchesne, Min.	.10
☐☐	434	Mike Keane, Mtl.	.10
☐☐	435	David Chyzowski, NYI.	.10
☐☐	436	Glen Featherstone, Stl.	.10
☐☐	**437**	**Jim Paek, Pgh., RC**	**.10**
☐☐	438	Doug Evans, Wpg.	.10
☐☐	439	Alexei Kasatonov, N.J., Error (Alexi)	.10
☐☐	440	Ken Hodge, Bos.	.10
☐☐	441	Dave Snuggerud, Stl.	.10
☐☐	442	Brad Shaw, Hfd.	.10
☐☐	443	Gerard Gallant, Det.	.10
☐☐	444	Jiri Latal, Pha.	.10
☐☐	445	Peter Zezel, Tor.	.10
☐☐	446	Troy Gamble (G), Van.	.10
☐☐	447	Craig Coxe, S.J.	.10
☐☐	448	Adam Oates, Stl.	.35
☐☐	449	Todd Krygier, Hfd.	.10
☐☐	**450**	**André Racicot (G), Mtl., RC**	**.10**
☐☐	451	Patrik Sundstrom, N.J.	.10
☐☐	452	Glen Wesley, Bos.	.10
☐☐	453	Jocelyn Lemieux, Chi.	.10
☐☐	454	Rick Zombo, Det.	.10
☐☐	455	Derek King, NYI.	.10
☐☐	456	J.J. Daigneault, Mtl.	.10
☐☐	457	Rick Vaive, Buf.	.10
☐☐	458	Larry Robinson, L.A.	.25
☐☐	459	Rick Wamsley (G), Cgy.	.10
☐☐	460	Craig Simpson, Edm.	.10
☐☐	**461**	**Corey Millen, NYR.., RC**	**.10**
☐☐	462	Sergio Momesso, Van.	.10
☐☐	463	Paul MacDermid, Wpg.	.10
☐☐	464	Wendel Clark, Tor.	.25
☐☐	465	Mikhail Tatarinov, Wsh., (Que.)	.10
☐☐	466	Mark Howe, Pha.	.25
☐☐	467	Jay Miller, L.A.	.10
☐☐	468	Grant Jennings, Pgh.	.10
☐☐	469	Paul Gillis, Chi.	.10
☐☐	470	Ron Hextall (G), Pha.	.25
☐☐	**471**	**A. Godynyuk, Tor., RC, Error (Godynuk)**	**.10**
☐☐	472	Bryan Trottier, Pgh.	.25
☐☐	**473**	**Kevin Haller, Buf., RC**	**.10**
☐☐	474	Troy Mallette, NYR.	.10
☐☐	475	James Wiemer, Bos.	.10
☐☐	476	David Maley, N.J.	.10
☐☐	477	Moe Mantha, Wpg.	.10
☐☐	**478**	**Brad Jones, L.A., RC**	**.10**
☐☐	479	Craig Muni, Edm	.10
☐☐	480	Igor Larionov, Van.	.25
☐☐	481	Scott Stevens, Stl.	.25
☐☐	482	Sergei Makarov, Cgy.	.10
☐☐	483	Mike Lalor, Wsh.	.10
☐☐	484	Tony McKegney, Chi.	.10
☐☐	485	Perry Berezan, Min.	.10
☐☐	486	Derrick Smith, Pha.	.10
☐☐	487	Jim Hrivnak (G), Wsh.	.10
☐☐	488	David Volek, NYI.	.10
☐☐	489	Sylvain Lefebvre, Mtl.	.10
☐☐	490	Rod Brind'Amour, Stl.	.25
☐☐	491	Al MacInnis, Cgy.	.25
☐☐	492	Jamie Leach, Pgh.	.10
☐☐	493	Robert Dirk, Van.	.10
☐☐	494	Gord Roberts, Pgh.	.10
☐☐	495	Mike Hudson, Chi.	.10
☐☐	496	François Breault, L.A.	.10
☐☐	497	Réjean Lemelin (G), Bos.	.10
☐☐	498	Kris King, NYR.	.10
☐☐	499	Pat Verbeek, Hfd.	.10
☐☐	500	Bryan Fogarty, Que.	.10
☐☐	**501**	**Perry Anderson, S.J., RC**	**.10**
☐☐	502	Joe Cirella, NYR.	.10
☐☐	503	Mikko Makela, Buf.	.10
☐☐	504	HL: Coffey Scores 1000th Point	.25
☐☐	505	Donald Beaupré (G), Wsh.	.10
☐☐	506	Brian Glynn, Min.	.10
☐☐	507	Dave Poulin, Bos.	.10
☐☐	508	Steve Chiasson, Det.	.10
☐☐	**509**	**Myles O'Connor, N.J., RC**	**.10**
☐☐	510	Ilkka Sinisalo, L.A.	.10
☐☐	511	Nick Kypreos, Wsh.	.10
☐☐	512	Doug Houda, Hfd.	.10
☐☐	513	Valeri Kamensky, Que.	.25
☐☐	514	Sergei Nemchinov, NYR.	.10
☐☐	515	Dimitri Mironov, Tor.	.10
☐☐	516	AW: Brett Hull, Stl.	.25
☐☐	517	AW: Ray Bourque, Bos.	.25
☐☐	518	AW: Ed Belfour, Chi.	.25
☐☐	519	AW: Ed Belfour, Chi.	.25
☐☐	520	AW: Wayne Gretzky, L.A.	1.00
☐☐	521	AW: Dirk Graham, Chi.	.10
☐☐	522	AW: Wayne Gretzky, L.A.	1.00

	No.	Player	
□ □	523	AW: Mario Lemieux, Pgh.	.50
□ □	524	HL: Gretzky Joins the 700 Club	1.00
□ □	525	San Jose Sharks Roster	.10
□ □	526	Tampa Bay Lightning	.10
□ □	527	Ottawa Senators	.10
□ □	528	Checklist 4 (397 to 528)	.10

TOPPS SCORING LEADERS

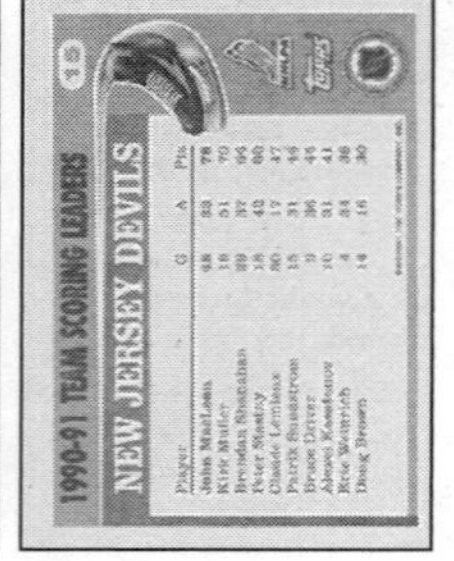

Imprint: © 1991 THE TOPPS COMPANY, INC.
Insert Set (21 cards): **8.00**

	No.	Player	NRMT-MT
□	1	Pat Verbeek, Hfd.	.25
□	2	Dale Hawerchuk, Buf.	.35
□	3	Steve Yzerman, Det.	1.50
□	4	Brian Leetch, NYR.	.50
□	5	Mark Recchi, Pgh.	.35
□	6	Esa Tikkanen, Edm.	.25
□	7	Dave Gagner, Min.	.25
□	8	Joe Sakic, Que.	1.25
□	9	Vincent Damphousse, Tor.	.35
□	10	Wayne Gretzky, L.A.	3.00
□	11	Phil Housley, Wpg.	.25
□	12	Pat LaFontaine, NYI.	.35
□	13	Rick Tocchet, Pha.	.25
□	14	Theoren Fleury, Cgy.	.50
□	15	John MacLean, N.J.	.25
□	16	Kevin Hatcher, Wsh.	.25
□	17	Trevor Linden, Van.	.35
□	18	Russ Courtnall, Mtl.	.25
□	19	Ray Bourque, Bos.	1.00
□	20	Brett Hull, Stl.	1.00
□	21	Steve Larmer, Chi.	.35

O-PEE-CHEE INSERT SET - SAN JOSE / RUSSIA

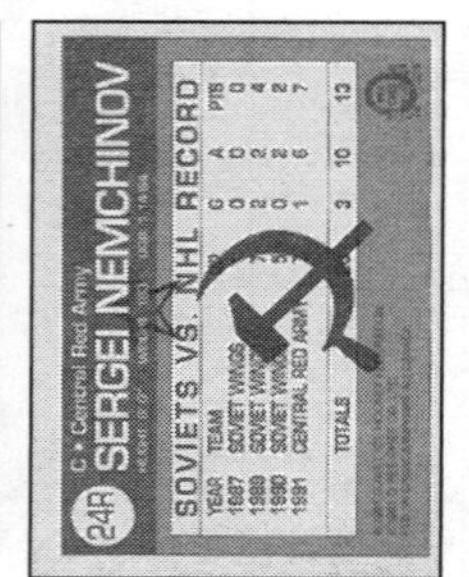

Insert Set (66 cards): **10.00**
Common Player: **.15**

	No.	Player	NRMT-MT
□	1S	Link Gaetz, S.J.	.15
□	2S	Bengt Gustafsson, S.J.	.15
□	3S	Dan Keczmer, S.J.	.15
□	4S	Dean Kolstad, S.J.	.15
□	5S	Peter Lappin, S.J.	.15
□	6S	Jeff Madill, S.J.	.15
□	7S	Michael McHugh, S.J.	.15
□	8S	Jarmo Myllys (G), S.J.	.25
□	9S	Doug Zmolek, S.J.	.15
□	10S	San Jose Sharks Checklist	.15
□	11R	Vadim Brezgunov, CSKA	.15
□	12R	Vyacheslav Butsayev, CSKA	.15
□	13R	Ilya Byakin, CSKA	.15
□	14R	Igor Chibirev, CSKA	.15
□	15R	Viktor Gordijuk, CSKA	.15
□	16R	Yuri Khmylev, CSKA	.25
□	17R	Pavel Kostichkin, CSKA	.15
□	18R	Andrei Kovalenko, CSKA	.75
□	19R	Igor Kravchuk, CSKA	.25
□	20R	Igor Malykhin, CSKA	.15
□	21R	Igor Maslennikov, CSKA	.15
□	22R	Maxim Mikhailovsky, CSKA	.15
□	23R	Dimitri Mironov, CSKA	.25
□	24R	Sergei Nemchinov, CSKA	.25
□	25R	Alexander Prokopjev, CSKA	.15
□	26R	Igor Stelnov, CSKA	.15
□	27R	Sergei Vostrikov, CSKA	.15
□	28R	Sergei Zubov, CSKA	.75
□	29R	Maxin Mikhailovsky (G), CSKA	.15
□	30R	S. Zubov/M. Mikhailovsky, CSKA	.15
□	31R	Alexander Andreivsky, Dynamo	.15
□	32R	Igor Dorofeyev, Dynamo	.15
□	33R	Alexander Galchenyuk, Dynamo	.15
□	34R	Roman Ilyin, Dynamo	.15
□	35R	Alexander Karpovtsev, Dynamo	.25
□	36R	Ravil Khaidarov, Dynamo	.15
□	37R	Igor Korolev, Dynamo	.25
□	38R	Andrei Kovalyov, Dynamo	.15
□	39R	Yuri Leonov, Dynamo	.15
□	40R	Andrei Lomakin, Dynamo	.15
□	41R	Evgeny Popikhin, Dynamo	.15
□	42R	Alexander Semak, Dynamo	.25
□	43R	Mikhail Shtalenkov (G), Dynamo	.50
□	44R	Sergei Sorokin, Dynamo, Error	.15
□	45R	Andrei Trefilov (G), Dynamo	.50
□	46R	Ravil Yakubov, Dynamo	.15
□	47R	Alexander Yudin, Dynamo	.15
□	48R	Alexei Zhamnov, Dynamo	1.00
□	49R	Andrei Basalgin, Khimik	.15
□	50R	Lev Berdichevsky, Khimik	.15
□	51R	Konstantin Kapkaikin (G, Khimik)	.15
□	52R	Konstantin Kurashov,Khimik	.15
□	53R	Andrei Kvartalnov, Khimik	.15
□	54R	Albert Malgin, Khimik	.15
□	55R	Nikolai Maslov, Khimik	.15
□	56R	Anatoli Naida, Khimik	.15
□	57R	Roman Oksiuta, Khimik	.15
□	58R	Sergei Selyanin, Khimik	.15
□	59R	Valeri Shiryev, Khimik	.15
□	60R	Alexander Smirnov, Khimik	.15
□	61R	Leonid Trukhno, Khimik	.15
□	62R	Igor Ulanov, Khimik	.15
□	63R	Andrei Yakovenko, Khimik	.15
□	64R	Oleg Yashin, Khimik	.15
□	65R	Valeri Zelepukin, Khimik	.25
□	66R	Checklist	.15

1991 - 92 O-PEE-CHEE PREMIER

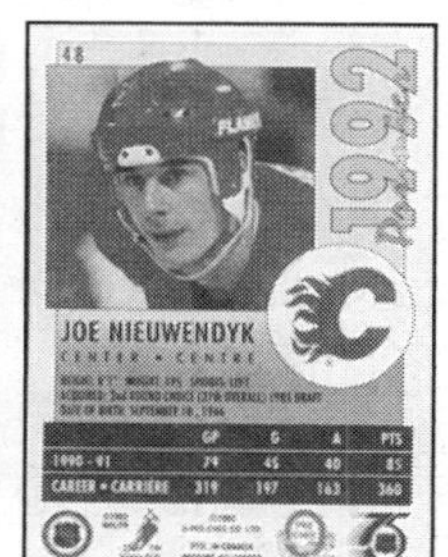

Imprint: © 1992 O-PEE-CHEE CO. LTD.
Complete Set (198 cards): **12.00**
Common Player: **.10**

	No.	Player	NRMT-MT
□	1	Dale Hawerchuk, Buf.	.25
□	2	Ray Sheppard, Det.	.10
□	3	Wayne Gretzky, L.A.	2.00
□	4	John MacLean, N.J.	.10
□	5	Pat Verbeek, Hfd.	.10
□	6	Doug Wilson, S.J.	.25
□	7	Adam Oates, Stl.	.35
□	8	Robert McGill, S.J.	.10
□	9	Mike Vernon (G), Cgy.	.25
□	10	Glenn Anderson, Tor.	.10
□	**11**	**Tony Amonte, NYR.., RC**	**1.00**
□	12	Stephen Leach, Bos.	.10
□	13	Steve Duchesne, Pha.	.10
□	14	Patrick Roy (G), Mtl.	1.50
□	15	Jarmo Myllys (G), S.J.	.10
□	**16**	**Yanic Dupré, Pha., RC**	**.10**
□	17	Chris Chelios, Chi.	.35
□	18	Bill Ranford (G), Edm.	.25
□	19	Ed Belfour (G), Chi.	.35
□	**20**	**Michel Picard, Hfd., RC**	**.10**
□	21	Rob Zettler, S.J.	.10
□	**22**	**Kevin Todd, N.J., RC**	**.10**
□	23	Mike Ricci, Pha.	.10
□	24	Jaromir Jagr, Pgh.	1.00
□	25	Sergei Nemchinov, NYR.	.10
□	26	Kevin Stevens, Pgh.	.10
□	27	Dan Quinn, Pha.	.10
□	28	Adam Graves, NYR.	.10
□	**29**	**Pat Jablonski (G), Stl., RC**	**.10**
□	30	Scott Mellanby, Edm.	.10
□	31	Tomas Forslund, Cgy.	.10
□	**32**	**Doug Weight, NYR.., RC**	**1.00**
□	33	Peter Ing (G), Edm.	.10
□	34	Luc Robitaille, L.A.	.25
□	35	Scott Niedermayer, N.J.	.25
□	36	Dean Evason, S.J.	.10
□	37	John Tonelli, Chi.	.10
□	38	Ron Hextall (G), Pha.	.25
□	39	Troy Mallette, Edm.	.10
□	40	Tony Hrkac, S.J.	.10
□	41	Ken Hodge, Bos.	.10
□	42	Kip Miller, Que.	.10
□	43	Randy Burridge, Wsh.	.10
□	44	Rob Blake, L.A.	.25
□	45	Sergei Makarov, Cgy.	.10
□	46	Luke Richardson, Edm.	.10
□	47	Craig Berube, Tor.	.10
□	48	Joe Nieuwendyk, Cgy.	.25
□	49	Brett Hull, Stl.	.50
□	50	Phil Housley, Wpg.	.10
□	51	Mark Messier, NYR.	.50
□	52	Jeremy Roenick, Chi.	.35
□	53	David Christian, Stl.	.10
□	54	Dave Barr, N.J.	.10
□	55	Sergio Momesso, Van.	.10
□	56	Pat Falloon, S.J.	.10
□	57	Brian Leetch, NYR.	.50
□	58	Russ Courtnall, Mtl.	.10
□	59	Pierre Turgeon, NYI.	.20
□	60	Steve Larmer, Chi.	.20
□	61	Petr Klima, Edm.	.10
□	62	Mikhail Tatarinov, Que.	.10
□	63	Rick Tocchet, Pha.	.10
□	64	Pat LaFontaine, Buf.	.25
□	**65**	**Rob Pearson, Tor., RC**	**.10**
□	66	Glen Featherstone, Bos.	.10
□	67	Pavel Bure, Van.	1.00
□	68	Sergei Fedorov, Det.	.50
□	69	Kelly Kisio, S.J.	.10
□	70	Joe Sakic, Que.	.85
□	71	Denis Savard, Mtl.	.25
□	72	Andrew Cassels, Hfd.	.10
□	73	Steve Yzerman, Det.	1.00
□	74	Todd Elik, Min.	.10
□	75	Troy Murray, Wpg.	.10
□	76	Rob Ramage, Min.	.10
□	77	Trevor Linden, Van.	.25
□	78	Mike Richter (G), NYR..	.35
□	79	Paul Coffey, Pgh.	.25
□	80	Craig Ludwig, Min.	.10
□	81	Al MacInnis, Cgy.	.25
□	82	Tomas Sandström, L.A.	.10
□	83	Tim Kerr, NYR.	.10
□	84	Scott Stevens, N.J.	.25
□	85	Steve Kasper, Pha.	.10
□	86	Kirk Muller, Mtl.	.10
□	**87**	**Pat MacLeod, S.J., RC**	**.10**
□	88	Kevin Hatcher, Wsh.	.10
□	89	Wayne Presley, S.J.	.10
□	90	Darryl Sydor, L.A.	.10
□	91	Tom Chorske, N.J.	.10
□	92	Theoren Fleury, Cgy.	.35
□	93	Craig Janney, Bos.	.10
□	94	Rod Brind'Amour, Pha.	.25
□	95	Ron Sutter, Stl.	.10
□	**96**	**Matt DelGuidice (G), Bos., RC**	**.10**
□	97	Rollie Melanson (G), Mtl.	.10
□	98	Tom Kurvers, NYI.	.10
□	**99**	**Bryan Marchment, Chi., RC**	**.10**
□	100	Grant Fuhr (G), Tor.	.25
□	101	Geoff Courtnall, Van.	.10
□	102	Joel Otto, Cgy.	.10

	No.	Player	Price
☐	103	Tom Barrasso (G), Pgh.	.25
☐	104	Vincent Damphousse, Edm.	.35
☐	**105**	**John LeClair, Mtl., RC**	**1.75**
☐	106	Gary Leeman, Tor.	.10
☐	107	Cam Neely, Bos.	.25
☐	108	Jeff Hackett (G), S.J.	.25
☐	109	Stu Barnes, Wpg.	.10
☐	110	Neil Wilkinson, S.J.	.10
☐	111	Jari Kurri, L.A.	.25
☐	112	Jon Casey (G), Min.	.10
☐	113	Stéphane Richer, N.J.	.10
☐	114	Mario Lemieux, Pgh.	1.75
☐	**115**	**Brad Jones, Pha., RC**	**.10**
☐	116	Wendel Clark, Tor.	.25
☐	**117**	**Nicklas Lidström, Det., RC**	**.60**
☐	**118**	**V. Konstantinov, Det., RC, Err. (/b: Lidström)**	**15.00**
☐	**118**	**Vladimir Konstantinov, Det., RC, Corrected**	**.50**
☐	119	Ray Bourque, Bos.	.50
☐	120	Ron Francis, Pgh.	.35
☐	121	Esa Tikkanen, Edm.	.10
☐	122	Randy Hillier, Buf.	.10
☐	123	Randy Gilhen, L.A.	.10
☐	124	Barry Pederson, Hfd.	.10
☐	125	Charlie Huddy, L.A.	.10
☐	126	Gary Roberts, Cgy.	.25
☐	127	John Cullen, Hfd.	.10
☐	128	Dave Gagner, Min.	.10
☐	129	Bob Kudelski, L.A.	.10
☐	130	Brendan Shanahan, Stl.	.60
☐	131	Dirk Graham, Chi.	.10
☐	132	Checklist 1 (1 to 99)	.10
☐	133	Andy Moog (G), Bos.	.25
☐	134	06: Gary Leeman, Tor.	.10
☐	135	06: Steve Larmer, Chi.	.25
☐	136	Steve Smith, Chi.	.10
☐	137	Dave Manson, Edm.	.10
☐	138	Nelson Emerson, Stl.	.10
☐	139	06: Doug Weight, NYR.	.35
☐	140	Uwe Krupp, NYI.	.10
☐	141	06: Peter Douris, Bos.	.10
☐	142	06: Steve Yzerman, Det.	.50
☐	143	Derian Hatcher, Min.	.20
☐	144	06: Vladimir Ruzicka, Bos.	.10
☐	145	06: Kirk Muller, Mtl.	.10
☐	146	Darrin Shannon, Wpg.	.10
☐	147	06: Mike Gartner, NYR.	.25
☐	148	06: Bob Carpenter, Bos.	.10
☐	**149**	**Josef Beranek, Edm., RC**	**.10**
☐	150	06: Chris Chelios, Chi.	.25
☐	151	06: Bob Rouse, Tor.	.10
☐	152	06: Guy Carbonneau, Mtl.	.10
☐	153	Joe Mullen, Pgh.	.25
☐	154	06: Ken Hodge, Bos.	.10
☐	155	06: Vladimir Konstantinov, Det.	.25
☐	156	Brent Sutter, Chi.	.10
☐	157	06: Eric Desjardins, Mtl.	.25
☐	158	Kirk McLean (G), Van.	.25
☐	159	06: John Tonelli, Chi.	.10
☐	160	06: Rob Cimetta, Tor.	.10
☐	161	Shayne Corson, Mtl.	.25
☐	**162**	**Russ Romaniuk, Wpg., RC**	**.10**
☐	163	06: Nicklas Lidström, Det.	.25
☐	164	Mike Gartner, NYR.	.25
☐	165	Curtis Joseph (G), Stl.	.60
☐	166	Brian Mullen, S.J.	.10
☐	167	Jimmy Carson, Det.	.10
☐	168	06: Petr Svoboda, Mtl.	.10
☐	169	Troy Crowder, Det.	.10
☐	170	06: Patrick Roy (G), Mtl.	1.00
☐	171	Adam Creighton, NYI.	.10
☐	172	06: James Patrick, NYR.	.10
☐	173	06: Sergei Fedorov, Det.	.35
☐	174	06: Jeremy Roenick, Chi.	.25
☐	175	06: Tim Cheveldae (G), Det.	.10
☐	176	Dimitri Khristich, Wsh.	.10
☐	177	06: Wendel Clark, Tor.	.25
☐	178	Andrei Lomakin, Pha.	.10
☐	179	Benoît Hogue, NYI.	.10
☐	180	06: David Ellett, Tor.	.10
☐	181	06: Mathieu Schneider, Mtl.	.10
☐	182	Kay Whitmore (G), Hfd.	.10
☐	183	06: Brian Leetch, NYR.	.25
☐	184	06: Sylvain Turgeon, NYR.	.10
☐	185	06: Brian Bradley, Tor.	.10
☐	186	06: John LeClair, Mtl.	.60
☐	187	Paul Fenton, S.J.	.10
☐	188	06: Alain Côté, Mtl.	.10
☐	189	06: M. Krushelnyski, Tor. Error (Krushelnynski)	.10
☐	190	Brian Bradley, Tor.	.10
☐	191	06: Grant Fuhr (G), Tor.	.25
☐	192	06: Ray Bourque, Bos.	.25
☐	193	Owen Nolan, Que.	.25
☐	194	06: Russ Courtnall, Mtl.	.10
☐	195	Steve Thomas, NYI.	.10
☐	196	Ed Olczyk, Wpg.	.10
☐	197	Chris Terreri (G), N.J.	.10
☐	198	Checklist 2 (100 to 198)	.10

1991 - 92 PANINI STICKERS

One of four different wrappers were available: Wayne Gretzky/Al MacInnis, Mario Lemieux/Steve Yzerman, Ray Bourque/Mark Recchi and Brett Hull/Patrick Roy.

Sticker Size: 1 13/16" x 2 7/8"
Imprint:
Complete Set (344 stickers): **20.00**
Common Player: **.10**
Album: **5.00**

	No.	Logo / Player	NRMT-MT
☐	1	NHL Logo	.10
☐	2	NHLPA Logo	.10
☐	3	NHL 75th Anniversary Logo	.10
☐	4	NHL 75th Anniversary Logo	.10
☐	5	Clarence Campbell Conference Logo	.10
☐	6	Prince of Wales Converence Logo	.10
☐	7	Stanley Cup Championship Logo	.10
☐	8	Steve Larmer, Chi.	.25
☐	9	Ed Belfour (G), Chi.	.35
☐	10	Chris Chelios, Chi.	.35
☐	11	Michel Goulet, Chi.	.25
☐	12	Jeremy Roenick, Chi.	.35
☐	13	Adam Creighton, Chi.	.10
☐	14	Steve Thomas, Chi.	.10
☐	15	Dave Manson, Chi.	.10
☐	16	Dirk Graham, Chi.	.10
☐	17	Troy Murray, Chi.	.10
☐	18	Doug Wilson, Chi.	.10
☐	19	Wayne Presley, Chi.	.10
☐	20	Jocelyn Lemieux, Chi.	.10
☐	21	Keith Brown, Chi.	.10
☐	22	Curtis Joseph (G), Stl.	.60
☐	23	Jeff Brown, Stl.	.10
☐	24	Gino Cavallini, Stl.	.10
☐	25	Brett Hull, Stl.	.50
☐	26	Scott Stevens, Stl.	.25
☐	27	Dan Quinn, Stl.	.10
☐	28	Garth Butcher, Stl.	.10
☐	29	Bob Bassen, Stl.	.10
☐	30	Rod Brind'Amour, Stl.	.25
☐	31	Adam Oates, Stl.	.35
☐	32	Dave Lowry, Stl.	.10
☐	33	Rich Sutter, Stl.	.10
☐	34	Ron Wilson, Stl.	.10
☐	35	Paul Cavallini, Stl.	.10
☐	36	Trevor Linden, Van.	.25
☐	37	Troy Gamble (G), Van.	.10
☐	38	Geoff Courtnall, Van.	.10
☐	39	Greg Adams, Van.	.10
☐	40	Doug Lidster, Van.	.10
☐	41	Dave Capuano, Van.	.10
☐	42	Igor Larionov, Van.	.25
☐	43	Tom Kurvers, Van.	.10
☐	44	Sergio Momesso, Van.	.10
☐	45	Kirk McLean (G), Van.	.25
☐	46	Cliff Ronning, Van.	.10
☐	47	Robert Kron, Van.	.10
☐	48	Steve Bozek, Van.	.10
☐	49	Petr Nedved, Van.	.25
☐	50	Al MacInnis, Cgy.	.25
☐	51	Theoren Fleury, Cgy.	.35
☐	52	Gary Roberts, Cgy.	.25
☐	53	Joe Nieuwendyk, Cgy.	.25
☐	54	Paul Ranheim, Cgy.	.10
☐	55	Mike Vernon (G), Cgy.	.25
☐	56	Carey Wilson, Cgy.	.10
☐	57	Gary Suter, Cgy.	.10
☐	58	Sergei Makarov, Cgy.	.10
☐	59	Doug Gilmour, Cgy.	.35
☐	60	Joel Otto, Cgy.	.10
☐	61	Jamie Macoun, Cgy.	.10
☐	62	Stéphane Matteau, Cgy.	.10
☐	63	Robert Reichel, Cgy.	.25
☐	64	Ed Olczyk, Wpg.	.10
☐	65	Phil Housley, Wpg.	.10
☐	66	Pat Elynuik, Wpg.	.10
☐	67	Fredrik Olausson, Wpg.	.10
☐	68	Thomas Steen, Wpg.	.10
☐	69	Paul MacDermid, Wpg.	.10
☐	70	Brent Ashton, Wpg.	.10
☐	71	Teppo Numminen, Wpg.	.10
☐	72	Danton Cole, Wpg.	.10
☐	73	Dave McLlwain, Wpg.	.10
☐	74	Scott Arniel, Wpg.	.10
☐	75	Bob Essensa (G), Wpg.	.10
☐	76	Randy Carlyle, Wpg.	.10
☐	77	Mark Osborne, Wpg.	.10
☐	78	Wayne Gretzky, L.A.	1.75
☐	79	Tomas Sandström, L.A.	.10
☐	80	Steve Duchesne, L.A.	.10
☐	81	Kelly Hrudey (G), L.A.	.10
☐	82	Larry Robinson, L.A.	.25
☐	83	Tony Granato, L.A.	.10
☐	84	Marty McSorley, L.A.	.10
☐	85	Todd Elik, L.A.	.10
☐	86	Rob Blake, L.A.	.25
☐	87	Bob Kudelski, L.A.	.10
☐	88	Steve Kasper, L.A.	.10
☐	89	Dave Taylor, L.A.	.10
☐	90	John Tonelli, L.A.	.10
☐	91	Luc Robitaille, L.A.	.25
☐	92	Vincent Damphousse, Tor.	.35
☐	93	Brian Bradley, Tor.	.10
☐	94	Dave Ellett, Tor.	.10
☐	95	Daniel Marois, Tor.	.10
☐	96	Rob Ramage, Tor.	.10
☐	97	Mike Krushelnyski, Tor.	.10
☐	98	Michel Petit, Tor.	.10
☐	99	Peter Ing (G), Tor.	.10
☐	100	Lucien DeBlois, Tor.	.10
☐	101	Bob Rouse, Tor.	.10
☐	102	Wendel Clark, Tor.	.25
☐	103	Peter Zezel, Tor.	.10
☐	104	David Reid, Tor.	.10
☐	105	Aaron Broten, Tor.	.10
☐	106	Brian Hayward (G), Min.	.10
☐	107	Neal Broten, Min.	.10
☐	108	Brian Bellows, Min.	.10
☐	109	Mark Tinordi, Min.	.10
☐	110	Ulf Dahlen, Min.	.10
☐	111	Doug Smail, Min.	.10
☐	112	Dave Gagner, Min.	.10
☐	113	Bobby Smith, Min.	.10
☐	114	Brian Glynn, Min.	.10
☐	115	Brian Propp, Min.	.10
☐	116	Mike Modano, Min.	.25
☐	117	Gaetan Duchesne, Min.	.10
☐	118	Jon Casey (G), Min.	.10
☐	119	Basil McRae, Min.	.10
☐	120	Glenn Anderson, Edm.	.10
☐	121	Steve Smith, Edm.	.10
☐	122	Adam Graves, Edm.	.10
☐	123	Esa Tikkanen, Edm.	.10
☐	124	Mark Messier, Edm.	.50
☐	125	Bill Ranford (G), Edm.	.25
☐	126	Petr Klima, Edm.	.10
☐	127	Anatoli Semenov, Edm.	.10
☐	128	Martin Gelinas, Edm.	.10
☐	129	Charlie Huddy, Edm.	.10

☐ 130 Craig Simpson, Edm. .10
☐ 131 Kevin Lowe, Edm. .10
☐ 132 Craig MacTavish, Edm. .10
☐ 133 Craig Muni, Edm. .10
☐ 134 Steve Yzerman, Det. 1.00
☐ 135 Shawn Burr, Det. .10
☐ 136 Tim Cheveldae (G), Det. .10
☐ 137 Rick Zombo, Det. .10
☐ 138 Marc Habscheid, Det. .10
☐ 139 Jimmy Carson, Det. .10
☐ 140 Brent Fedyk, Det. .10
☐ 141 Yves Racine, Det. .10
☐ 142 Gerard Gallant, Det. .10
☐ 143 Steve Chiasson, Det. .10
☐ 144 Johan Garpenlov, Det. .10
☐ 145 Sergei Fedorov, Det. .50
☐ 146 Bob Probert, Det. .10
☐ 147 Rick Green, Det. .10
☐ 148 Chicago Blackhawks .10
☐ 149 Detroit Red Wings .10
☐ 150 Minnesota North Stars .10
☐ 151 St. Louis Blues .10
☐ 152 Toronto Maple Leafs .10
☐ 153 Calgary Flames .10
☐ 154 Edmonton Oilers .10
☐ 155 Los Angeles Kings .10
☐ 156 San Jose Sharks .10
☐ 157 Vancouver Canucks .10
☐ 158 Winnipeg Jets .10
☐ 159 Boston Bruins .10
☐ 160 Buffalo Sabres .10
☐ 161 Hartford Whalers .10
☐ 162 Montréal Canadiens .10
☐ 163 Québec Nordiques .10
☐ 164 New Jersey Devils .10
☐ 165 New York Islanders .10
☐ 166 New York Rangers .10
☐ 167 Philadelphia Flyers .10
☐ 168 Pittsburgh Penguins .10
☐ 169 Washington Capitals .10
☐ 170 Craig Janney, Bos. .10
☐ 171 Ray Bourque, Bos. .50
☐ 172 Réjean Lemelin (G), Bos. .10
☐ 173 Dave Christian, Bos. .10
☐ 174 Randy Burridge, Bos. .10
☐ 175 Garry Galley, Bos. .10
☐ 176 Cam Neely, Bos. .25
☐ 177 Bob Sweeney, Bos. .10
☐ 178 Ken Hodge, Bos. .10
☐ 179 Andy Moog (G), Bos. .25
☐ 180 Don Sweeney, Bos. .10
☐ 181 Bob Carpenter, Bos. .10
☐ 182 Glen Wesley, Bos. .10
☐ 183 Chris Nilan, Bos. .10
☐ 184 Patrick Roy (G), Mtl. 1.25
☐ 185 Petr Svoboda, Mtl. .10
☐ 186 Russ Courtnall, Mtl. .10
☐ 187 Denis Savard, Mtl. .25
☐ 188 Mike McPhee, Mtl. .10
☐ 189 Eric Desjardins, Mtl. .25
☐ 190 Mike Keane, Mtl. .10
☐ 191 Stéphan Lebeau, Mtl. .10
☐ 192 J.J. Daigneault, Mtl. .10
☐ 193 Stéphane Richer, Mtl. .10
☐ 194 Brian Skrudland, Mtl. .10
☐ 195 Mathieu Schneider, Mtl. .10
☐ 196 Shayne Corson, Mtl. .25
☐ 197 Guy Carbonneau, Mtl. .10
☐ 198 Kevin Hatcher, Wsh. .10
☐ 199 Mike Ridley, Wsh. .10
☐ 200 John Druce, Wsh. .10
☐ 201 Don Beaupré (G), Wsh. .10
☐ 202 Kelly Miller, Wsh. .10
☐ 203 Dale Hunter, Wsh. .10
☐ 204 Nick Kypreos, Wsh. .10
☐ 205 Calle Johansson, Wsh. .10
☐ 206 Michal Pivonka, Wsh. .10
☐ 207 Dino Ciccarelli, Wsh. .25
☐ 208 Al Iafrate, Wsh. .10
☐ 209 Rod Langway, Wsh. .10
☐ 210 Mikhail Tatarinov, Wsh. .10
☐ 211 Stephen Leach, Wsh. .10
☐ 212 Sean Burke (G), N.J. .25
☐ 213 John MacLean, N.J. .10
☐ 214 Lee Norwood, N.J. .10
☐ 215 Laurie Boschman, N.J. .10
☐ 216 Alexei Kasatonov, N.J. .10
☐ 217 Patrik Sundstrom, N.J. .10
☐ 218 Ken Daneyko, N.J. .10
☐ 219 Kirk Muller, N.J. .10
☐ 220 Peter Stastny, N.J. .10
☐ 221 Chris Terreri (G), N.J. .10
☐ 222 Brendan Shanahan, N.J. .60
☐ 223 Eric Weinrich, N.J. .10
☐ 224 Claude Lemieux, N.J. .10
☐ 225 Bruce Driver, N.J. .10
☐ 226 Tim Kerr, Pha. .10
☐ 227 Ron Hextall (G), Pha. .25
☐ 228 Per-Erik Eklund, Pha. .10
☐ 229 Rick Tocchet, Pha. .10
☐ 230 Gord Murphy, Pha. .10
☐ 231 Mike Ricci, Pha. .10
☐ 232 Derrick Smith, Pha. .10
☐ 233 Ron Sutter, Pha. .10
☐ 234 Murray Craven, Pha. .10
☐ 235 Terry Carkner, Pha. .10
☐ 236 Ken Wregget (G), Pha. .10
☐ 237 Keith Acton, Pha. .10
☐ 238 Scott Mellanby, Pha. .10
☐ 239 Kjell Samuelsson, Pha. .10
☐ 240 Jeff Hackett (G), NYI. .25
☐ 241 David Volek, NYI. .10
☐ 242 Craig Ludwig, NYI. .10
☐ 243 Pat LaFontaine, NYI. .25
☐ 244 Randy Wood, NYI. .10
☐ 245 Patrick Flatley, NYI. .10
☐ 246 Brent Sutter, NYI. .10
☐ 247 Derek King, NYI. .10
☐ 248 Jeff Norton, NYI. .10
☐ 249 Glenn Healy (G), NYI. .10
☐ 250 Ray Ferraro, NYI. .10
☐ 251 Gary Nylund, NYI. .10
☐ 252 Joe Reekie, NYI. .10
☐ 253 David Chyzowski, NYI. .10
☐ 254 Mike Hough, Que. .10
☐ 255 Mats Sundin, Que. .50
☐ 256 Curtis Leschyshyn, Que. .10
☐ 257 Joe Sakic, Que. .85
☐ 258 Stéphane Fiset (G), Que. .25
☐ 259 Bryan Fogarty, Que. .10
☐ 260 Alexei Gusarov, Que. .10
☐ 261 Steven Finn, Que. .10
☐ 262 Everett Sanipass, Que. .10
☐ 263 Stéphane Morin, Que. .10
☐ 264 Craig Wolanin, Que. .10
☐ 265 Randy Velischek, Que. .10
☐ 266 Owen Nolan, Que. .25
☐ 267 Ron Tugnutt (G), Que. .10
☐ 268 Mario Lemieux, Pgh. 1.25
☐ 269 Kevin Stevens, Pgh. .10
☐ 270 Larry Murphy, Pgh. .25
☐ 271 Tom Barrasso (G), Pgh. .25
☐ 272 Phil Bourque, Pgh. .10
☐ 273 Scott Young, Pgh. .10
☐ 274 Paul Stanton, Pgh. .10
☐ 275 Jaromir Jagr, Pgh. 1.00
☐ 276 Paul Coffey, Pgh. .25
☐ 277 Ulf Samuelsson, Pgh. .10
☐ 278 Joe Mullen, Pgh. .10
☐ 279 Bob Errey, Pgh. .10
☐ 280 Mark Recchi, Pgh. .25
☐ 281 Ron Francis, Pgh. .35
☐ 282 John Vanbiesbrouck (G), NYR.. .60
☐ 283 Jan Erixon, NYR. .10
☐ 284 Brian Leetch, NYR. .35
☐ 285 Darren Turcotte, NYR. .10
☐ 286 Ray Sheppard, NYR. .10
☐ 287 James Patrick, NYR. .10
☐ 288 Bernie Nicholls, NYR. .10
☐ 289 Brian Mullen, NYR. .10
☐ 290 Mike Richter (G), NYR.. .35
☐ 291 Kelly Kisio, NYR. .10
☐ 292 Mike Gartner, NYR. .25
☐ 293 John Ogrodnick, NYR. .10
☐ 294 David Shaw, NYR. .10
☐ 295 Troy Mallette, NYR. .10
☐ 296 Dale Hawerchuk, Buf. .25
☐ 297 Rick Vaive, Buf. .10
☐ 298 Daren Puppa (G), Buf. .10
☐ 299 Mike Ramsey, Buf. .10
☐ 300 Benoît Hogue, Buf. .10
☐ 301 Clint Malarchuk (G), Buf. .10
☐ 302 Mikko Makelä, Buf. .10
☐ 303 Pierre Turgeon, Buf. .25
☐ 304 Alexander Mogilny, Buf. .35
☐ 305 Uwe Krupp, Buf. .10
☐ 306 Christian Ruuttu, Buf. .10
☐ 307 Doug Bodger, Buf. .10
☐ 308 Dave Snuggerud, Buf. .10
☐ 309 Dave Andreychuk, Buf. .25
☐ 310 Peter Sidorkiewicz (G), Hfd. .10
☐ 311 Brad Shaw, Hfd. .10
☐ 312 Dean Evason, Hfd. .10
☐ 313 Pat Verbeek, Hfd. .10
☐ 314 John Cullen, Hfd. .10
☐ 315 Rob Brown, Hfd. .10
☐ 316 Bobby Holik, Hfd. .10
☐ 317 Todd Krygier, Hfd. .10
☐ 318 Adam Burt, Hfd. .10
☐ 319 Mike Tomlak, Hfd. .10
☐ 320 Randy Cunneyworth, Hfd. .10
☐ 321 Paul Cyr, Hfd. .10
☐ 322 Zarley Zalapski, Hfd. .10
☐ 323 Kevin Dineen, Hfd. .10
☐ 324 AS: Luc Robitaille .25
☐ 325 AS: Brett Hull .25
☐ 326 All-Star Game Logo .10
☐ 327 AS: Wayne Gretzky .75
☐ 328 AS: Mike Vernon (G) .25
☐ 329 AS: Chris Chelios .25
☐ 330 AS: Al MacInnis .10
☐ 331 AS: Rick Tocchet .10
☐ 332 AS: Cam Neely .25
☐ 333 AS: Patrick Roy (G) .60
☐ 334 AS: Joe Sakic .35
☐ 335 AS: Ray Bourque .25
☐ 336 AS: Paul Coffey .25
☐ 337 Ed Belfour (G) .25
☐ 338 Mike Ricci .10
☐ 339 Rob Blake .25
☐ 340 Sergei Fedorov .25
☐ 341 Ken Hodge .10
☐ 342 Bobby Holik .10
☐ 343 Robert Reichel .10
☐ 344 Jaromir Jagr .50

1991 - 92 PARKHURST

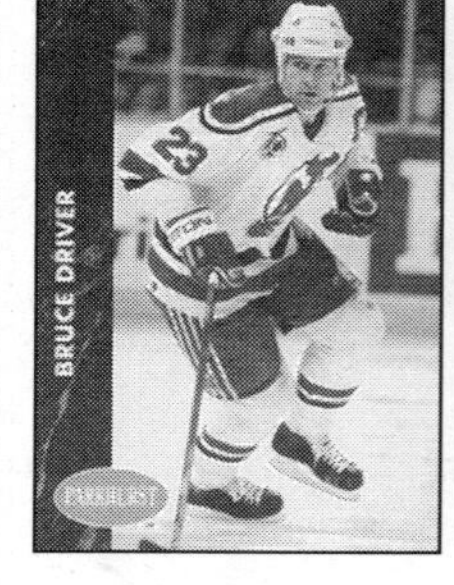

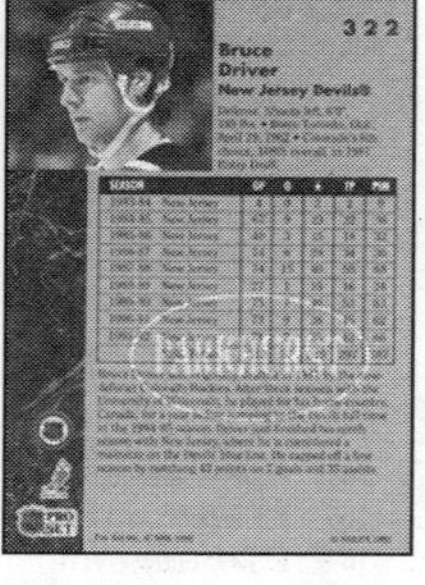

These cards have two versions: an English (1-475) issue and a French issue (1-450). Both English and French cards sell at the same price.

Imprint: Pro Set Inc.

Series 1 Set (225 cards):	**15.00**
Series 2 Set (225 cards):	**15.00**
Final Update (25 cards):	**60.00**
Common Player (1-450):	**.10**
Common Player (451-475):	**1.00**
Promo Card (Doug Gilmour):	**8.00**
Promo Card (Robert Reichel):	**4.00**

	No.	Player	NRMT-MT
☐☐	**1**	**Matt DelGuidice (G), Bos., RC**	**.10**
☐☐	2	Ken Hodge, Bos.	.10
☐☐	3	Vladimir Ruzicka, Bos., Error (Ruzika)	.10
☐☐	4	Craig Janney, Bos.	.10
☐☐	5	Glen Wesley, Bos.	.10
☐☐	6	Stephen Leach, Bos.	.10
☐☐	7	Garry Galley, Bos.	.10
☐☐	8	Andy Moog (G), Bos.	.20
☐☐	9	Ray Bourque, Bos.	.50
☐☐	10	Brad May, Buf.	.10

	No.	Player	Price
□□	11	Donald Audette, Buf.	.10
□□	12	Alexander Mogilny, Buf.	.35
□□	13	Randy Wood, Buf.	.10
□□	14	Daren Puppa (G), Buf.	.10
□□	15	Doug Bodger, Buf.	.10
□□	16	Pat LaFontaine, Buf.	.25
□□	17	Dave Andreychuk, Buf.	.25
□□	18	Dale Hawerchuk, Buf.	.25
□□	19	Mike Ramsey, Buf.	.10
□□	**20**	**Tomas Forslund, Cgy., RC**	**.10**
□□	21	Robert Reichel, Cgy.	.25
□□	22	Theoren Fleury, Cgy.	.35
□□	23	Joe Nieuwendyk, Cgy.	.25
□□	24	Gary Roberts, Cgy.	.25
□□	25	Gary Suter, Cgy.	.10
□□	26	Doug Gilmour, Cgy.	.35
□□	27	Mike Vernon (G), Cgy.	.25
□□	28	Al MacInnis, Cgy.	.25
□□	29	Jeremy Roenick, Chi.	.35
□□	30	Ed Belfour (G), Chi.	.35
□□	31	Steve Smith, Chi.	.10
□□	32	Chris Chelios, Chi.	.35
□□	33	Dirk Graham, Chi.	.10
□□	34	Steve Larmer, Chi.	.25
□□	35	Brent Sutter, Chi.	.10
□□	36	Michel Goulet, Chi.	.25
□□	**37**	**Nicklas Lidström, Det., RC, Error (Niklas)**	**.60**
□□	38	Sergei Fedorov, Det.	.50
□□	39	Tim Cheveldae (G), Det.	.10
□□	40	Kevin Miller, Det.	.10
□□	41	Ray Sheppard, Det.	.10
□□	42	Paul Ysebaert, Det.	.10
□□	43	Jimmy Carson, Det.	.10
□□	44	Steve Yzerman, Det.	1.00
□□	45	Shawn Burr, Det.	.10
□□	**46**	**Vladimir Konstantinov, Det., RC**	**.50**
□□	**47**	**Josef Beranek, Edm., RC**	**.10**
□□	48	Vincent Damphousse, Edm.	.35
□□	49	Dave Manson, Edm.	.10
□□	50	Scott Mellanby, Edm.	.10
□□	51	Kevin Lowe, Edm.	.10
□□	52	Joe Murphy, Edm.	.10
□□	53	Bill Ranford (G), Edm.	.25
□□	54	Craig Simpson, Edm.	.10
□□	55	Esa Tikkanen, Edm.	.10
□□	**56**	**Michel Picard, Hfd., RC**	**.10**
□□	**57**	**Geoff Sanderson, Hfd., RC**	**.75**
□□	58	Kay Whitmore (G), Hfd.	.10
□□	59	John Cullen, Hfd.	.10
□□	60	Rob Brown, Hfd.	.10
□□	61	Zarley Zalapski, Hfd.	.10
□□	62	Brad Shaw, Hfd.	.10
□□	63	Mikael Andersson, Hfd.	.10
□□	64	Patrick Verbeek, Hfd.	.10
□□	**65**	**Peter Ahola, L.A., RC**	**.10**
□□	66	Tony Granato, L.A.	.10
□□	67	Dave Taylor, L.A.	.10
□□	68	Luc Robitaille, L.A.	.25
□□	69	Marty McSorley, L.A.	.10
□□	70	Tomas Sandström, L.A.	.25
□□	71	Kelly Hrudey (G), L.A.	.10
□□	72	Jari Kurri, L.A.	.25
□□	73	Wayne Gretzky, L.A.	2.00
□□	74	Larry Robinson, L.A.	.20
□□	75	Derian Hatcher, Min.	.25
□□	76	Ulf Dahlen, Min.	.25
□□	77	Jon Casey (G), Min.	.10
□□	78	Dave Gagner, Min.	.10
□□	79	Brian Bellows, Min.	.10
□□	80	Neal Broten, Min.	.10
□□	81	Mike Modano, Min.	.50
□□	82	Brian Propp, Min.	.10
□□	83	Bobby Smith, Min.	.10
□□	**84**	**John LeClair, Mtl., RC**	**3.00**
□□	85	Eric Desjardins, Mtl.	.25
□□	86	Shayne Corson, Mtl.	.25
□□	87	Stéphan Lebeau, Mtl.	.10
□□	88	Mathieu Schneider, Mtl.	.10
□□	89	Kirk Muller, Mtl.	.10
□□	90	Patrick Roy (G), Mtl.	1.75
□□	91	Sylvain Turgeon, Mtl.	.10
□□	92	Guy Carbonneau, Mtl.	.10
□□	93	Denis Savard, Mtl.	.25
□□	94	Scott Niedermayer, N.J.	.25
□□	95	Tom Chorske, N.J.	.10
□□	96	Viacheslav Fetisov, N.J.	.25
□□	**97**	**Kevin Todd, N.J., RC**	**.10**
□□	98	Chris Terreri (G), N.J.	.10
□□	99	David Maley, N.J.	.10
□□	100	Stéphane Richer, N.J.	.10
□□	101	Claude Lemieux, N.J.	.10
□□	102	Scott Stevens, N.J.	.25
□□	103	Peter Stastny, N.J.	.25
□□	104	David Volek, NYI.	.10
□□	105	Steve Thomas, NYI.	.10
□□	106	Pierre Turgeon, NYI.	.25
□□	107	Glenn Healy (G), NYI., Error (b/ Healey)	.10
□□	108	Derek King, NYI.	.10
□□	109	Uwe Krupp, NYI.	.10
□□	110	Ray Ferraro, NYI.	.10
□□	111	Patrick Flatley, NYI.	.10
□□	112	Tom Kurvers, NYI.	.10
□□	113	Adam Creighton, NYI.	.10
□□	**114**	**Tony Amonte, NYR.., RC**	**1.50**
□□	115	John Ogrodnick, NYR.	.10
□□	**116**	**Doug Weight, NYR.., RC**	**1.50**
□□	117	Mike Richter (G), NYR..	.35
□□	118	Darren Turcotte, NYR.	.10
□□	119	Brian Leetch, NYR.	.35
□□	120	James Patrick, NYR.	.10
□□	121	Mark Messier, NYR.	.50
□□	122	Mike Gartner, NYR.	.20
□□	123	Mike Ricci, Pha.	.10
□□	124	Rod Brind'Amour, Pha.	.25
□□	125	Steve Duchesne, Pha.	.10
□□	126	Ron Hextall (G), Pha.	.25
□□	**127**	**Brad Jones, Pha., RC**	**.10**
□□	128	Per-Erik Eklund, Pha.	.10
□□	129	Rick Tocchet, Pha.	.10
□□	130	Mark Howe, Pha.	.25
□□	131	Andrei Lomakin, Pha.	.10
□□	132	Jaromir Jagr, Pgh.	1.00
□□	**133**	**Jim Paek, Pgh., RC**	**.10**
□□	134	Mark Recchi, Pgh.	.25
□□	135	Kevin Stevens, Pgh.	.10
□□	136	Phil Bourque, Pgh.	.10
□□	137	Mario Lemieux, Pgh.	1.50
□□	138	Bob Errey, Pgh.	.10
□□	139	Tom Barrasso (G), Pgh.	.25
□□	140	Paul Coffey, Pgh.	.25
□□	141	Joe Mullen, Pgh.	.25
□□	**142**	**Kip Miller, Que., RC**	**.10**
□□	143	Owen Nolan, Que.	.25
□□	144	Mats Sundin, Que.	.50
□□	145	Mikhail Tatarinov, Que.	.10
□□	146	Bryan Fogarty, Que.	.10
□□	147	Stéphane Morin, Que.	.10
□□	148	Joe Sakic, Que.	.85
□□	149	Ron Tugnutt (G), Que.	.10
□□	150	Mike Hough, Que.	.10
□□	**151**	**Nelson Emerson, Stl., RC**	**.10**
□□	152	Curtis Joseph (G), Stl.	.60
□□	153	Brendan Shanahan, Stl.	.60
□□	154	Paul Cavallini, Stl.	.10
□□	155	Adam Oates, Stl.	.35
□□	156	Jeff Brown, Stl.	.10
□□	157	Brett Hull, Stl.	.50
□□	158	Ron Sutter, Stl.	.10
□□	159	Dave Christian, Stl.	.10
□□	160	Pat Falloon, S.J.	.10
□□	**161**	**Pat MacLeod, S.J., RC**	**.10**
□□	162	Jarmo Myllys (G), S.J.	.10
□□	163	Wayne Presley, S.J.	.10
□□	**164**	**Perry Anderson, S.J., RC**	**.10**
□□	165	Kelly Kisio, S.J.	.10
□□	166	Brian Mullen, S.J.	.10
□□	167	Brian Lawton, S.J.	.10
□□	168	Doug Wilson, S.J.	.25
□□	**169**	**Rob Pearson, Tor., RC**	**.10**
□□	170	Wendel Clark, Tor.	.20
□□	171	Brian Bradley, Tor.	.25
□□	172	Dave Ellett, Tor.	.10
□□	173	Gary Leeman, Tor.	.10
□□	174	Peter Zezel, Tor.	.10
□□	175	Grant Fuhr (G), Tor.	.25
□□	176	Bob Rouse, Tor.	.10
□□	177	Glenn Anderson, Tor.	.10
□□	178	Petr Nedved, Van.	.10
□□	179	Trevor Linden, Van.	.25
□□	180	Jyrki Lumme, Van.	.10
□□	181	Kirk McLean (G), Van.	.25
□□	182	Cliff Ronning, Van.	.10
□□	183	Greg Adams, Van.	.10
□□	184	Doug Lidster, Van.	.10
□□	185	Sergio Momesso, Van.	.10
□□	186	Geoff Courtnall, Van.	.10
□□	187	Dave Babych, Van.	.10
□□	188	Peter Bondra, Wsh.	.35
□□	189	Dimitri Khristich, Wsh.	.10
□□	190	Randy Burridge, Wsh.	.10
□□	191	Kevin Hatcher, Wsh.	.10
□□	192	Mike Ridley, Wsh.	.10
□□	193	Dino Ciccarelli, Wsh.	.25
□□	194	Al Iafrate, Wsh.	.10
□□	195	Dale Hunter, Wsh.	.10
□□	196	Mike Liut (G), Wsh.	.10
□□	**198**	**Russ Romaniuk, Wpg., RC**	**.10**
□□	199	Bob Essensa (G), Wpg.	.10
□□	200	Teppo Numminen, Wpg.	.10
□□	201	Darrin Shannon, Wpg.	.10
□□	202	Pat Elynuik, Wpg.	.10
□□	203	Fredrik Olausson, Wpg.	.10
□□	204	Ed Olczyk, Wpg.	.10
□□	205	Phil Housley, Wpg.	.10
□□	206	Troy Murray, Wpg.	.10
□□	207	Wayne Gretzky, L.A.	1.00
□□	208	Bryan Trottier, Pgh.	.25
□□	209	Peter Stastny, N.J.	.25
□□	210	Jari Kurri, L.A.	.25
□□	211	Denis Savard, Mtl.	.25
□□	212	Paul Coffey, Pgh.	.25
□□	213	Mark Messier, NYR.	.25
□□	214	Dave Taylor, L.A.	.10
□□	215	Michel Goulet, Chi.	.25
□□	216	Dale Hawerchuk, Buf.	.25
□□	217	Bobby Smith, Min.	.10
□□	218	Ed Belfour (G), Chi.	.25
□□	219	Brett Hull, Stl.	.25
□□	220	Patrick Roy (G), Mtl.	.85
□□	221	Ray Bourque, Bos.	.25
□□	222	Wayne Gretzky, Stl.	1.00
□□	223	Jari Kurri, L.A.	.25
□□	224	Luc Robitaille, L.A.	.25
□□	225	Paul Coffey, Pgh.	.25
□□	226	Bob Carpenter, Bos.	.10
□□	227	Gord Murphy, Bos.	.10
□□	228	Don Sweeney, Bos.	.10
□□	**229**	**Glen Murray, Bos., RC**	**.10**
□□	**230**	**Ted Donato, Bos., RC**	**.10**
□□	**231**	**Josef Stumpel, Bos., RC**	**.35**
□□	**232**	**Stephen Heinze, Bos., RC**	**.10**
□□	233	Adam Oates, Bos.	.35
□□	**234**	**Joé Juneau, Bos., RC**	**.75**
□□	**235**	**Rookie: Gord Hynes, Bos., RC**	**.10**
□□	236	Tony Tanti, Buf.	.10
□□	237	Petr Svoboda, Buf.	.10
□□	238	Bob Corkum, Buf.	.10
□□	**239**	**Ken Sutton, Buf., RC**	**.10**
□□	**240**	**Tom Draper (G), Buf., RC**	**.10**
□□	241	Grant Ledyard, Buf.	.10
□□	242	Christian Ruuttu, Buf.	.10
□□	243	Brad Miller, Buf.	.10
□□	244	Clint Malarchuk (G), Buf.	.10
□□	245	Trent Yawney, Cgy.	.10
□□	246	Craig Berube, Cgy.	.10
□□	247	Sergei Makarov, Cgy.	.10
□□	248	Alexander Godynyuk, Cgy.	.10
□□	249	Paul Ranheim, Cgy.	.10
□□	250	Jeff Reese (G), Cgy.	.10
□□	**251**	**Chris Lindberg, Cgy., RC**	**.10**
□□	252	Michel Petit, Cgy.	.10
□□	253	Joel Otto, Cgy.	.10
□□	254	Gary Leeman, Cgy.	.10
□□	**255**	**Ray LeBlanc (G), Chi., RC**	**.10**
□□	256	Jocelyn Lemieux, Chi.	.10
□□	**257**	**Igor Kravchuk, Chi., RC**	**.10**
□□	258	Rob Brown, Chi.	.10
□□	259	Stéphane Matteau, Chi.	.10
□□	260	Mike Hudson, Chi.	.10
□□	261	Keith Brown, Chi.	.10
□□	262	Karl Dykhuis, Chi.	.10
□□	**263**	**Dominik Hasek (G), Chi., RC**	**5.00**
□□	264	Brian Noonan, Chi.	.10
□□	265	Yves Racine, Det.	.10
□□	**266**	**Vyacheslav Kozlov, Det., RC**	**1.00**

	No.	Player	NRMT-MT
□ □	267	Martin Lapointe, Det.	.10
□ □	268	Steve Chiasson, Det.	.10
□ □	269	Gerard Gallant, Det.	.10
□ □	270	Brent Fedyk, Det.	.10
□ □	271	Brad McCrimmon, Det.	.10
□ □	272	Bob Probert, Det.	.10
□ □	273	Alan Kerr, Det.	.10
□ □	274	Luke Richardson, Edm.	.10
□ □	275	Kelly Buchberger, Edm.	.10
□ □	276	Craig MacTavish, Edm.	.10
□ □	277	Ron Tugnutt (G), Edm.	.10
□ □	278	Bernie Nicholls, Edm.	.10
□ □	279	Anatoli Semenov, Edm.	.10
□ □	280	Petr Klima, Edm.	.10
□ □	**281**	**Louie DeBrusk, Edm., RC**	**.10**
□ □	**282**	**Norm Maciver, Edm., RC**	**.10**
□ □	283	Martin Gelinas, Edm.	.25
□ □	284	Randy Cunneyworth, Hfd.	.10
□ □	285	Andrew Cassels, Hfd.	.10
□ □	286	Peter Sidorkiewicz (G), Hfd.	.10
□ □	287	Steve Konroyd, Hfd.	.10
□ □	288	Murray Craven, Hfd.	.10
□ □	289	Randy Ladouceur, Hfd.	.10
□ □	290	Bobby Holik, Hfd.	.10
□ □	291	Adam Burt, Hfd.	.10
□ □	**292**	**Corey Millen, L.A., RC**	**.10**
□ □	293	Rob Blake, L.A.	.25
□ □	**294**	**Mike Donnelly, L.A., RC**	**.10**
□ □	**295**	**Kyosti Karjalainen, L.A., RC**	**.10**
□ □	296	John McIntyre, L.A.	.10
□ □	297	Paul Coffey, L.A.	.25
□ □	298	Charlie Huddy, L.A.	.10
□ □	299	Bob Kudelski, L.A.	.10
□ □	300	Todd Elik, Min.	.10
□ □	301	Mike Craig, Min.	.10
□ □	302	Marc Bureau, Min.	.10
□ □	303	Jim Johnson, Min.	.10
□ □	304	Mark Tinordi, Min.	.10
□ □	305	Gaetan Duchesne, Min.	.10
□ □	**306**	**Darcy Wakaluk (G), Min., RC**	**.10**
□ □	307	Sylvain Lefebvre, Mtl.	.10
□ □	308	Russ Courtnall, Mtl.	.10
□ □	309	Patrice Brisebois, Mtl.	.10
□ □	310	Mike McPhee, Mtl.	.10
□ □	311	Mike Keane, Mtl.	.10
□ □	312	J.J. Daigneault, Mtl.	.10
□ □	**313**	**Gilbert Dionne, Mtl., RC**	**.10**
□ □	314	Brian Skrudland, Mtl.	.10
□ □	315	Brent Gilchrist, Mtl.	.10
□ □	316	Laurie Boschman, N.J.	.10
□ □	317	Ken Daneyko, N.J.	.10
□ □	318	Eric Weinrich, N.J.	.10
□ □	319	Alexei Kasatonov, N.J.	.10
□ □	**320**	**Craig Billington (G), N.J., RC**	**.10**
□ □	321	Claude Vilgrain, N.J.	.10
□ □	322	Bruce Driver, N.J.	.10
□ □	**323**	**Alexander Semak, N.J., RC**	**.10**
□ □	**324**	**Valeri Zelepukin, N.J., RC**	**.10**
□ □	325	Rob DiMaio, NYI.	.10
□ □	**326**	**Scott Lachance, NYI.., RC**	**.25**
□ □	**327**	**Marty McInnis, NYI.., RC**	**.10**
□ □	328	Joe Reekie, NYI.	.10
□ □	329	Daniel Marois, NYI.	.10
□ □	330	Wayne McBean, NYI.	.10
□ □	331	Jeff Norton, NYI.	.10
□ □	332	Benoît Hogue, NYI.	.10
□ □	333	Tie Domi, NYR.	.10
□ □	334	Sergei Nemchinov, NYR.	.10
□ □	335	Randy Gilhen, NYR.	.10
□ □	336	Paul Broten, NYR.	.10
□ □	337	Kris King, NYR.	.10
□ □	338	John Vanbiesbrouck (G), NYR..	.60
□ □	339	Adam Graves, NYR.	.10
□ □	340	Joe Cirella, NYR.	.10
□ □	341	Jeff Beukeboom, NYR.	.10
□ □	342	Terry Carkner, Pha.	.10
□ □	**343**	**Mark Freer, Pha., RC**	**.10**
□ □	**344**	**Corey Foster, Pha., RC**	**.10**
□ □	345	Mark Pederson, Pha.	.10
□ □	**346**	**Kimbi Daniels, Pha., RC**	**.10**
□ □	347	Mark Recchi, Pha.	.25
□ □	348	Kevin Dineen, Pha.	.10
□ □	349	Kerry Huffman, Pha.	.10
□ □	350	Garry Galley, Pha.	.10
□ □	351	Dan Quinn, Pha.	.10
□ □	352	Troy Loney, Pgh.	.10
□ □	353	Ron Francis, Pgh.	.35
□ □	354	Rick Tocchet, Pgh.	.10
□ □	**355**	**Shawn McEachern, Pgh., RC**	**.25**
□ □	356	Kjell Samuelsson, Pgh.	.10
□ □	357	Ken Wregget (G), Pgh.	.10
□ □	358	Larry Murphy, Pgh.	.25
□ □	359	Ken Priestlay, Pgh.	.10
□ □	360	Bryan Trottier, Pgh.	.25
□ □	361	Ulf Samuelsson, Pgh.	.10
□ □	**362**	**Valeri Kamensky, Que., RC**	**.75**
□ □	363	Stéphane Fiset (G), Que.	.25
□ □	**364**	**Alexei Gusarov, Que., RC**	**.10**
□ □	365	Gregory Paslawski, Que.	.10
□ □	**366**	**Martin Rucinsky, Que., RC**	**.75**
□ □	367	Curtis Leschyshyn, Que.	.10
□ □	368	Jacques Cloutier (G), Que.	.10
□ □	369	Craig Wolanin, Que.	.10
□ □	**370**	**Rookie: Claude Lapointe, Que., RC**	**.10**
□ □	**371**	**Adam Foote, Que., RC**	**.50**
□ □	372	Rich Sutter, Stl.	.10
□ □	373	Lee Norwood, Stl.	.10
□ □	374	Garth Butcher, Stl.	.10
□ □	**375**	**Philippe Bozon, Stl., RC**	**.10**
□ □	376	Dave Lowry, Stl.	.10
□ □	377	Darin Kimble, Stl.	.10
□ □	378	Craig Janney, Stl.	.10
□ □	379	Bob Bassen, Stl.	.10
□ □	380	Rick Zombo, Stl.	.10
□ □	381	Perry Berezan, S.J.	.10
□ □	382	Neil Wilkinson, S.J.	.10
□ □	**383**	**Mike Sullivan, S.J., RC**	**.10**
□ □	**384**	**David Bruce, S.J., RC**	**.10**
□ □	385	Johan Garpenlov, S.J.	.10
□ □	**386**	**Jeff Odgers, S.J., RC**	**.10**
□ □	**387**	**Jayson More, S.J., RC**	**.10**
□ □	388	Dean Evason, S.J.	.10
□ □	389	Dale Craigwell, S.J.	.10
□ □	**390**	**Darryl Shannon, Tor., RC**	**.10**
□ □	391	Dimitri Mironov, Tor.	.10
□ □	392	Kent Manderville, Tor.	.10
□ □	393	Todd Gill, Tor.	.10
□ □	394	Rick Wamsley (G), Tor.	.10
□ □	**395**	**Joe Sacco, Tor., RC**	**.10**
□ □	396	Doug Gilmour, Tor.	.35
□ □	397	Mike Bullard, Tor.	.10
□ □	398	Félix Potvin (G), Tor.	.50
□ □	**399**	**Guy Larose, Tor., RC**	**.10**
□ □	400	Tom Fergus, Van.	.10
□ □	401	Ryan Walter, Van.	.10
□ □	402	Troy Gamble (G), Van.	.10
□ □	403	Robert Dirk, Van.	.10
□ □	404	Pavel Bure, Van.	1.00
□ □	405	Jim Sandlak, Van.	.10
□ □	406	Igor Larionov, Van.	.25
□ □	407	Gerald Diduck, Van.	.10
□ □	408	Todd Krygier, Wsh.	.10
□ □	409	Tim Bergland, Wsh.	.10
□ □	410	Calle Johansson, Wsh.	.10
□ □	411	Nick Kypreos, Wsh.	.10
□ □	412	Michal Pivonka, Wsh.	.10
□ □	**413**	**Brad Schlegel, Wsh., RC**	**.10**
□ □	414	Kelly Miller, Wsh.	.10
□ □	415	John Druce, Wsh.	.10
□ □	416	Don Beaupré (G), Wsh.	.10
□ □	417	Alan May, Wsh.	.10
□ □	418	Randy Carlyle, Wpg.	.10
□ □	419	Stu Barnes, Wpg.	.10
□ □	420	Mike Eagles, Wpg.	.10
□ □	**421**	**Igor Ulanov, Wpg., RC**	**.10**
□ □	**422**	**Evgeny Davydov, Wpg., RC**	**.10**
□ □	423	Shawn Cronin, Wpg.	.10
□ □	**424**	**Keith Tkachuk, Wpg., RC**	**3.00**
□ □	**425**	**Luciano Borsato, Wpg., RC**	**.10**
□ □	426	Stéphane Beauregard (G), Wpg.	.10
□ □	427	Mike Lalor, Wpg.	.10
□ □	428	Michel Goulet, Chi.	.25
□ □	429	Wayne Gretzky, L.A.	1.00
□ □	430	Mike Gartner, NYR.	.25
□ □	431	Bryan Trottier, NYI.	.25
□ □	432	LL: Brett Hull, Stl.	.30
□ □	433	LL: Wayne Gretzky, L.A.	1.00
□ □	434	LL: Steve Yzerman, Det.	.50
□ □	435	LL: Paul Ysebaert, Det.	.10
□ □	436	LL: Gary Roberts, Cgy.	.25
□ □	437	LL: Dave Andreychuk, Buf.	.25
□ □	438	LL: Brian Leetch, NYR.	.25
□ □	439	LL: Jeremy Roenick, Chi.	.25
□ □	440	LL: Kirk McLean (G), Van.	.25
□ □	441	LL: Tim Cheveldae (G), Det.	.10
□ □	442	LL: Patrick Roy (G), Mtl.	.85
□ □	443	LL: Tony Amonte, NYR.	.50
□ □	444	LL: Kevin Todd, N.J.	.10
□ □	445	LL: Nicklas Lidström, Det.	.25
□ □	446	LL: Pavel Bure, Van.	.60
□ □	447	LL: Gilbert Dionne, Mtl.	.10
□ □	448	LL: Tom Draper (G), Buf.	.10
□ □	449	LL: Dominik Hasek (G), Chi.	1.50
□ □	450	LL: Dominic Roussel (G), Pha.	.10

FINAL UPDATE

	No.	Player	NRMT-MT
□	451	CL: Parkhurst Cover card	1.00
□	452	CL: Trent Klatt, Min.,	1.50
□	453	CL: Bill Guerin, N.J.	4.00
□	454	CL: Ray Whitney, S.J.	3.00
□	455	P. DiPietro/C. Winnes	1.00
□	456	L. Murphy/D. Trucotte	1.00
□	457	M. Goulet/V. Konstantinov/R. Sheppard	1.00
□	458	P. Klima/J. Murphy	1.00
□	459	R. Lemelin/D. Sweeney/M. Lemieux	1.00
□	460	B. Ranford/L. Richardson/ Bre. Sutter	1.00
□	461	I. Kravchuk/B. Trottier/C. Chelios	1.00
□	462	Pavel Bure, Van.	8.00
□	463	Patrick Roy (G), Mtl.	12.00
□	464	Brian Leetch, NYR.	2.50
□	465	Wayne Gretzky, L.A.	15.00
□	466	Guy Carbonneau, Mtl.	1.50
□	467	Mario Lemieux, Pgh.	12.00
□	468	Mark Messier, NYR.	4.00
□	469	Ray Bourque, Bos.	4.00
□	470	Patrick Roy (G), Mtl.	12.00
□	471	Brian Leetch, NYR.	2.50
□	472	Raymond Bourque, Bos.	4.00
□	473	Kevin Stevens, Pgh.	1.00
□	474	Brett Hull, Stl.	4.00
□	475	Mark Messier, NYR.	4.00

COLLECTOR'S CARDS

These cards have two versions: an English issue and a French issue. Both English and French cards have the same value.

Insert Set (10 cards): **18.00**

	No.	Player	NRMT-MT
□ □		Happy Holidays, Santa Claus	1.00
□ □	PHC1	Gordie Howe, Det.	5.00
□ □	PHC2	Alex Delvecchio, Det.	1.50
□ □	PHC3	Ken Hodge, Bos.	.75
□ □	PHC4	Robert Kron, Van.	.75
□ □	PHC5	Sergei Fedorov, Det.	2.50
□ □	PHC6	Brett Hull, Stl.	2.50
□ □	PHC7	Mario Lemieux, Pgh.	7.50
□ □	PHC8	Gartner/Messier/Leetch	2.50
□ □	PHC9	Terry Sawchuk (G), Det.	3.00

1991 - 92 PINNACLE

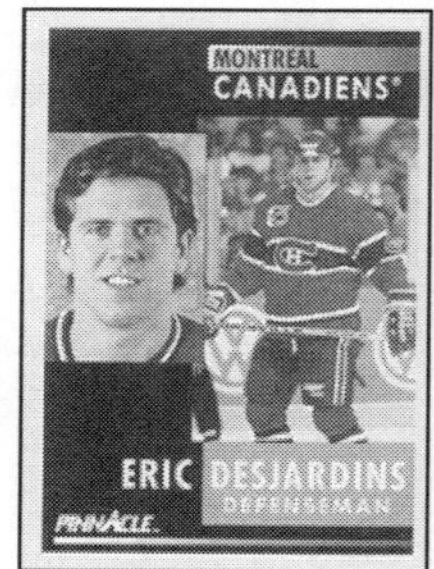

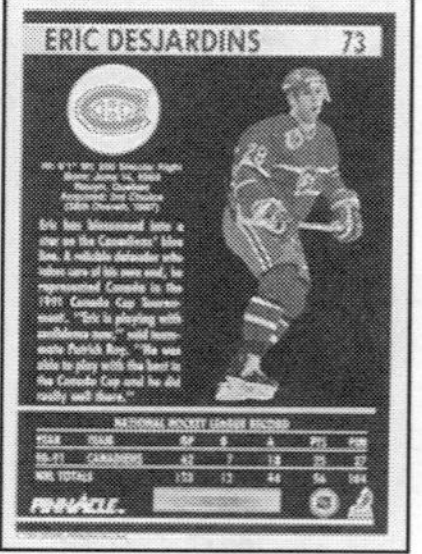

These cards have two versions: an English issue and a French issue.

Imprint: © 1991 SCORE

		English	French
Complete Set (420 cards):		**40.00**	**50.00**
Common Player:		**.10**	**.15**
Promo Panel (#s: 73, 78, 82, 87):			**5.00**
Promo Panel (#s: 12, 17, 23, 28):			**5.00**

	No.	Player	English	French
□ □	1	Mario Lemieux,Pgh.	2.50	3.00
□ □	2	Trevor Linden, Van.	.25	.35
□ □	3	Kirk Muller, Mtl.	.10	.15

	No.	Player		
□□	4	Phil Housley, Wpg.	.10	.15
□□	5	Mike Modano, Min.	.75	1.00
□□	6	Adam Oates, Stl.	.50	.75
□□	7	Tom Kurvers, NYI.	.10	.15
□□	8	Doug Bodger, Buf.	.10	.15
□□	9	Rod Brind'Amour, Pha.	.25	.35
□□	10	Mats Sundin, Que.	.75	1.00
□□	11	Gary Suter, Cgy.	.10	.15
□□	12	Glenn Anderson, Tor.	.10	.15
□□	13	Doug Wilson, S.J.	.25	.35
□□	14	Stéphane Richer, N.J.	.10	.15
□□	15	Ray Bourque, Bos.	.75	1.00
□□	16	Adam Graves, NYR.	.10	.15
□□	17	Luc Robitaille, L.A.	.25	.35
□□	18	Steve Smith, Chi.	.10	.15
□□	19	Uwe Krupp, NYI.	.10	.15
□□	20	Rick Tocchet, Pha.	.10	.15
□□	21	Tim Cheveldae (G), Det.	.10	.15
□□	22	Kay Whitmore (G), Hfd.	.10	.15
□□	23	Kelly Miller, Wsh.	.10	.15
□□	24	Esa Tikkanen, Edm.	.10	.15
□□	25	Pat LaFontaine, Buf.	.25	.35
□□	26	James Patrick, NYR.	.10	.15
□□	27	Daniel Marois, Tor.	.10	.15
□□	28	Denis Savard, Mtl.	.25	.35
□□	29	Steve Larmer, Chi.	.10	.15
□□	30	Pierre Turgeon, NYI.	.25	.35
□□	31	Gary Leeman, Tor.	.10	.15
□□	32	Mike Ricci, Pha.	.10	.15
□□	33	Troy Murray, Wpg.	.10	.15
□□	34	Sergio Momesso, Van.	.10	.15
□□	35	Marty McSorley, L.A.	.10	.15
□□	36	Paul Ysebaert, Det.	.10	.15
□□	37	Gary Roberts, Cgy.	.25	.35
□□	38	Mike Hudson, Chi.	.10	.15
□□	39	Kelly Hrudey (G), L.A.	.10	.15
□□	40	Dale Hunter, Wsh.	.10	.15
□□	41	Brendan Shanahan, Stl.	1.00	1.25
□□	42	Steve Duchesne, Pha.	.10	.15
□□	43	Pat Verbeek, Hfd.	.10	.15
□□	44	Tom Barrasso (G), Pgh.	.25	.35
□□	45	Scott Mellanby, Edm.	.10	.15
□□	46	Stephen Leach, Bos.	.10	.15
□□	47	Darren Turcotte, NYR.	.10	.15
□□	48	Jari Kurri, L.A.	.25	.35
□□	49	Michel Petit, Tor.	.10	.15
□□	50	Mark Messier, NYR.	1.00	1.25
□□	51	Terry Carkner, Pha.	.10	.15
□□	52	Tim Kerr, NYR.	.10	.15
□□	53	Jaromir Jagr, Pgh.	1.50	2.00
□□	54	Joe Nieuwendyk, Cgy.	.25	.35
□□	55	Randy Burridge, Wsh.	.10	.15
□□	56	Robert Reichel, Cgy.	.10	.15
□□	57	Craig Janney, Bos.	.10	.15
□□	58	Chris Chelios, Chi.	.50	.75
□□	59	Bryan Fogarty, Que.	.10	.15
□□	60	Christian Ruuttu, Buf.	.10	.15
□□	61	Steven Bozek, S.J.	.10	.15
□□	62	Dave Manson, Edm.	.10	.15
□□	63	Bruce Driver, N.J.	.10	.15
□□	64	Mikel Ramsey, Buf.	.10	.15
□□	65	Bobby Holik, Hfd.	.10	.15
□□	66	Bob Essensa (G), Wpg.	.10	.15
□□	67	Patrick Flatley, NYI.	.10	.15
□□	68	Wayne Presley, S.J.	.10	.15
□□	69	Mike Bullard, Tor.	.10	.15
□□	70	Claude Lemieux, N.J.	.10	.15
□□	71	Dave Gagner, Min.	.10	.15
□□	72	Jeff Brown, Stl.	.10	.15
□□	73	Eric Desjardins, Mtl.	.25	.35
□□	74	Fredrik Olausson, Wpg.	.10	.15
□□	75	Steve Yzerman, Det.	1.50	2.00
□□	76	Tony Granato, L.A.	.10	.15
□□	77	Adam Burt, Hfd.	.10	.15
□□	78	Cam Neely, Bos.	.25	.35
□□	79	Brent Sutter, Chi.	.10	.15
□□	80	Dale Hawerchuk, Buf.	.25	.35
□□	81	Scott Stevens, N.J.	.10	.15
□□	82	Adam Creighton, NYI.	.10	.15
□□	83	Brian Hayward (G), S.J.	.10	.15
□□	84	Dan Quinn, Pha.	.10	.15
□□	85	Garth Butcher, Stl.	.10	.15
□□	86	Shawn Burr, Det.	.10	.15
□□	87	Peter Bondra, Wsh.	.50	.75
□□	88	Brad Shaw, Hfd.	.10	.15
□□	89	Eric Weinrich, N.J.	.10	.15
□□	90	Brian Bradley, Tor.	.10	.15
□□	91	Vincent Damphousse, Edm.	.50	.75
□□	92	Doug Gilmour, Cgy.	.50	.75
□□	93	Martin Gelinas, Edm.	.10	.15
□□	94	Mike Ridley, Wsh.	.10	.15
□□	95	Ron Sutter, Stl.	.10	.15
□□	96	Mark Osborne, Wpg.	.10	.15
□□	97	Mikhail Tatarinov, Que.	.10	.15
□□	98	Bob McGill, S.J.	.10	.15
□□	99	Bob Carpenter, Bos.	.10	.15
□□	100	Wayne Gretzky, L.A.	3.00	4.00
□□	101	Viacheslav Fetisov, N.J.	.25	.35
□□	102	Shayne Corson, Mtl.	.25	.35
□□	103	Clint Malarchuk (G), Buf.	.10	.15
□□	104	Randy Wood, Buf.	.10	.15
□□	105	Curtis Joseph (G), Stl.	.75	1.00
□□	106	Cliff Ronning, Van.	.10	.15
□□	107	Derek King, NYI.	.10	.15
□□	108	Neil Wilkinson, S.J.	.10	.15
□□	109	Michel Goulet, Chi.	.25	.35
□□	110	Zarley Zalapski, Hfd.	.10	.15
□□	111	Dave Ellett, Tor.	.10	.15
□□	112	Glen Wesley, Bos.	.10	.15
□□	113	Bob Kudelski, L.A.	.10	.15
□□	114	Jamie Macoun, Cgy.	.10	.15
□□	115	John MacLean, N.J.	.10	.15
□□	116	Steve Thomas, NYI.	.10	.15
□□	117	Pat Elynuik, Wpg.	.10	.15
□□	118	Ron Hextall (G), Pha.	.25	.35
□□	119	Jeff Hackett (G), S.J.	.25	.35
□□	120	Jeremy Roenick, Chi.	.35	.50
□□	121	John Vanbiesbrouck (G), NYR..	1.25	1.50
□□	122	Dave Andreychuk, Buf.	.25	.35
□□	123	Ray Ferraro, NYI.	.10	.15
□□	124	Ron Tugnutt (G), Que.	.10	.15
□□	125	John Cullen, Hfd.	.10	.15
□□	126	Andy Moog (G), Bos.	.25	.35
□□	127	Ed Belfour (G), Chi.	.50	.75
□□	128	Dino Ciccarelli, Wsh.	.25	.35
□□	129	Brian Bellows, Min.	.10	.15
□□	130	Guy Carbonneau, Mtl.	.10	.15
□□	131	Kevin Hatcher, Wsh.	.10	.15
□□	132	Mike Vernon (G), Cgy.	.25	.35
□□	133	Kevin Miller, Det.	.10	.15
□□	134	Per-Erik Eklund, Pha.	.10	.15
□□	135	Brian Mullen, S.J.	.50	.15
□□	136	Brian Leetch, NYR.	.60	.75
□□	137	Daren Puppa (G), Buf.	.10	.15
□□	138	Steven Finn, Que.	.10	.15
□□	139	Stéphan Lebeau, Mtl.	.10	.15
□□	140	Gord Murphy, Pha.	.10	.15
□□	141	Rob Brown, Hfd.	.10	.15
□□	142	Ken Daneyko, N.J.	.10	.15
□□	143	Larry Murphy, Pgh.	.25	.35
□□	144	Jon Casey (G), Min.	.10	.15
□□	145	John Ogrodnick, NYR.	.10	.15
□□	146	Benoît Hogue, NYI.	.10	.15
□□	147	Mike McPhee, Mtl.	.10	.15
□□	148	Don Beaupré (G), Wsh.	.10	.15
□□	149	Kjell Samuelsson, Pha.	.10	.15
□□	150	Joe Sakic, Que.	1.25	1.50
□□	151	Mark Recchi, Pgh.	.25	.35
□□	152	Ulf Dahlen, Min.	.10	.15
□□	153	Dean Evason, S.J.	.10	.15
□□	154	Keith Brown, Chi.	.10	.15
□□	155	Ray Sheppard, Det.	.10	.15
□□	156	Owen Nolan, Que.	.25	.35
□□	157	Sergei Fedorov, Det.	.75	1.00
□□	158	Kirk McLean (G), Van.	.25	.35
□□	159	Petr Klima, Edm.	.10	.15
□□	160	Brian Skrudland, Mtl.	.10	.15
□□	161	Neal Broten, Min.	.10	.15
□□	162	Dimitri Khristich, Wsh.	.10	.15
□□	163	Alexander Mogilny, Buf.	.50	.75
□□	164	Mike Richter (G), NYR..	.50	.75
□□	165	Daniel Berthiaume (G), L.A.	.10	.15
□□	166	Teppo Numminen, Wpg.	.10	.15
□□	167	Ron Francis, Pgh.	.50	.75
□□	168	Grant Fuhr (G), Tor.	.25	.35
□□	169	Mike Liut (G), Wsh.	.10	.15
□□	170	Bill Ranford (G), Edm.	.25	.35
□□	171	Garry Galley, Bos.	.10	.15
□□	172	Jeff Norton, NYI.	.10	.15
□□	173	Jimmy Carson, Det.	.10	.15
□□	174	Peter Zezel, Tor.	.10	.15
□□	175	Patrick Roy (G), Mtl.	2.50	3.00
□□	176	Joe Mullen, Pgh.	.10	.15
□□	177	Murray Craven, Hfd.	.10	.15
□□	178	Tomas Sandström, L.A.	.10	.15
□□	179	Joel Otto, Cgy.	.10	.15
□□	180	Steve Konroyd, Chi.	.10	.15
□□	181	Vladimir Ruzicka, Bos.	.10	.15
□□	182	Paul Cavallini, Stl.	.10	.15
□□	183	Bob Probert, Det.	.10	.15
□□	184	Brian Propp, Min.	.10	.15
□□	185	Glenn Healy (G), NYI.	.10	.15
□□	186	Paul Coffey, Pgh.	.25	.35
□□	187	Jan Erixon, NYR.	.10	.15
□□	188	Kevin Lowe, Edm.	.10	.15
□□	189	Doug Lidster, Van.	.10	.15
□□	190	Theoren Fleury, Cgy.	.50	.75
□□	191	Kevin Stevens, Pgh.	.25	.35
□□	192	Petr Nedved, Van.	.25	.35
□□	193	Ed Olczyk, Wpg.	.10	.15
□□	194	Mike Hough, Que.	.10	.15
□□	195	Rod Langway, Wsh.	.10	.15
□□	196	Craig Simpson, Edm.	.10	.15
□□	197	Petr Svoboda, Mtl.	.10	.15
□□	198	David Volek, NYI.	.10	.15
□□	199	Mark Tinordi, Min.	.10	.15
□□	200	Brett Hull, Stl.	.75	1.00
□□	201	Rob Blake, L.A.	.25	.35
□□	202	Mike Gartner, NYR.	.25	.35
□□	203	Ken Hodge, Bos.	.15	.150
□□	204	Murray Baron, Stl.	.10	.15
□□	205	Gerard Gallant, Det.	.10	.15
□□	206	Joe Murphy, Edm.	.10	.15
□□	207	Al Iafrate, Wsh.	.10	.15
□□	208	Larry Robinson, L.A.	.25	.35
□□	209	Mathieu Schneider, Mtl.	.10	.15
□□	210	Bobby Smith, Min.	.10	.15
□□	211	Gerald Diduck, Van.	.10	.15
□□	212	Luke Richardson, Edm.	.10	.15
□□	213	Rob Zettler, S.J.	.10	.15
□□	214	Brad McCrimmon, Det.	.10	.15
□□	215	Craig MacTavish, Edm.	.10	.15
□□	216	Gino Cavallini, Stl.	.10	.15
□□	217	Craig Wolanin, Que.	.10	.15
□□	218	Greg Adams, Van.	.10	.15
□□	219	Mike Craig, Min.	.10	.15
□□	220	Al MacInnis, Cgy.	.25	.35
□□	221	Sylvain Côté, Wsh.	.10	.15
□□	222	Bob Sweeney, Bos.	.10	.15
□□	223	Dave Snuggerud, Buf.	.10	.15
□□	224	Randy Ladouceur, Hfd.	.10	.15
□□	225	Charlie Huddy, L.A.	.10	.15
□□	226	Sylvain Turgeon, Mtl.	.10	.15
□□	227	Phil Bourque, Pgh.	.10	.15
□□	228	Rob Ramage, Min.	.10	.15
□□	229	Jeff Beukeboom, NYR.	.10	.15
□□	**230**	**Alexei Gusarov, Que., RC**	**.10**	**.15**
□□	231	Kelly Kisio, S.J.	.10	.15
□□	232	Calle Johansson, Wsh.	.10	.15
□□	233	Yves Racine, Det.	.10	.15
□□	234	Peter Sidorkiewicz (G), Hfd.	.10	.15
□□	235	Jim Johnson, Min.	.10	.15
□□	236	Brent Gilchrist, Mtl.	.10	.15
□□	237	Jyrki Lumme, Van.	.10	.15
□□	238	Randy Gilhen, L.A.	.10	.15
□□	239	Ken Baumgartner, NYI.	.10	.15
□□	240	Joey Kocur, NYR.	.10	.15
□□	241	Bryan Trottier, Pgh.	.25	.35
□□	242	Todd Krygier, Wsh.	.10	.15
□□	243	Darrin Shannon, Wpg.	.10	.15
□□	244	Dave Christian, Stl.	.10	.15
□□	245	Stéphane Morin, Que.	.10	.15
□□	246	Kevin Dineen, Pha.	.10	.15
□□	247	Chris Terreri (G), N.J.	.10	.15
□□	248	Craig Ludwig, Min.	.10	.15
□□	249	Dave Taylor, L.A.	.10	.15
□□	250	Wendel Clark, Tor.	.25	.35
□□	251	David Shaw, Edm.	.10	.15
□□	252	Paul Ranheim, Cgy.	.10	.15
□□	253	Mark Hunter, Hfd.	.10	.15
□□	254	Russ Courtnall, Mtl.	.10	.15
□□	255	Alexei Kasatonov, N.J.	.10	.15
□□	256	Randy Moller, NYR.	.10	.15
□□	257	Bob Errey, Pgh.	.10	.15
□□	258	Curtis Leschyshyn, Que.	.10	.15

	No.	Player		
☐ ☐	259	Rick Zombo, Stl.	.10	.15
☐ ☐	260	Dana Murzyn, Van.	.10	.15
☐ ☐	261	Dirk Graham, Chi.	.10	.15
☐ ☐	262	Craig Muni, Edm.	.10	.15
☐ ☐	263	Geoff Courtnall, Van.	.10	.15
☐ ☐	264	Todd Elik, Min.	.10	.15
☐ ☐	265	Mike Keane, Mtl.	.10	.15
☐ ☐	266	Peter Stastny, N.J.	.25	.35
☐ ☐	267	Ulf Samuelsson,Pgh.	.10	.15
☐ ☐	268	Rich Sutter, Stl.	.10	.15
☐ ☐	269	Mike Krushelnyski, Tor.	.10	.15
☐ ☐	270	Dave Babych, Van.	.10	.15
☐ ☐	271	Sergei Makarov, Cgy.	.10	.15
☐ ☐	272	David Maley, N.J.	.10	.15
☐ ☐	273	Normand Rochefort, NYR.	.10	.15
☐ ☐	274	Gord Roberts,Pgh.	.10	.15
☐ ☐	275	Thomas Steen, Wpg.	.10	.15
☐ ☐	276	Dave Lowry, Stl.	.10	.15
☐ ☐	277	Michal Pivonka, Wsh.	.10	.15
☐ ☐	278	Todd Gill, Tor.	.10	.15
☐ ☐	279	Paul MacDermid, Wpg.	.10	.15
☐ ☐	280	Brent Ashton, Bos.	.10	.15
☐ ☐	281	Randy Hillier, Buf.	.10	.15
☐ ☐	282	Frantisek Musil, Cgy.	.10	.15
☐ ☐	283	Geoff Smith, Edm.	.10	.10
☐ ☐	284	John Tonelli, Chi.	.10	.15
☐ ☐	285	Joe Reekie, NYI.	.10	.15
☐ ☐	286	Greg Paslawski, Que.	.10	.15
☐ ☐	287	Perry Berezan, S.J.	.10	.15
☐ ☐	288	Randy Carlyle, Wpg.	.10	.15
☐ ☐	289	Chris Nilan, Bos.	.10	.15
☐ ☐	290	Patrik Sundstrom, N.J.	.10	.15
☐ ☐	291	Garry Valk, Van.	.10	.15
☐ ☐	292	Mike Foligno, Tor.	.10	.15
☐ ☐	293	Igor Larionov, Van.	.25	.35
☐ ☐	294	Jim Sandlak, Van.	.10	.15
☐ ☐	295	Tom Chorske, N.J.	.10	.15
☐ ☐	296	Claude Loiselle, Tor.	.10	.15
☐ ☐	297	Mark Howe, Pha.	.25	.35
☐ ☐	298	Steve Chiasson, Det.	.10	.15
☐ ☐	**299**	**Mike Donnelly, L.A., RC**	**.10**	**.15**
☐ ☐	300	Bernie Nicholls, Edm.	.10	.15
☐ ☐	**301**	**Tony Amonte, NYR.., RC**	**2.00**	**2.50**
☐ ☐	302	Brad May, Buf.	.10	.15
☐ ☐	**303**	**Josef Beranek, Edm., RC**	**.10**	**.15**
☐ ☐	**304**	**Rob Pearson, Tor., RC**	**.10**	**.15**
☐ ☐	305	Andrei Lomakin, Pha.	.10	.15
☐ ☐	306	Kip Miller, Que.	.10	.15
☐ ☐	**307**	**Kevin Haller, Buf., RC**	**.10**	**.15**
☐ ☐	**308**	**Kevin Todd, N.J., RC**	**.10**	**.15**
☐ ☐	**309**	**Geoff Sanderson, Hfd., RC**	**1.00**	**1.25**
☐ ☐	**310**	**Doug Weight, NYR.., RC**	**2.00**	**2.50**
☐ ☐	**311**	**Vladimir Konstantinov, Det., RC**	**.85**	**1.00**
☐ ☐	**312**	**Peter Ahola, L.A., RC**	**.10**	**.15**
☐ ☐	**313**	**Claude Lapointe, Que., RC**	**.10**	**.15**
☐ ☐	314	Nelson Emerson, Stl.	.10	.15
☐ ☐	315	Pavel Bure, Van.	1.00	1.50
☐ ☐	316	Jimmy Waite (G), Chi.	.10	.15
☐ ☐	317	Sergei Nemchinov, NYR.	.10	.15
☐ ☐	318	Alexander Godynyuk, Tor.	.10	.15
☐ ☐	319	Stu Barnes, Wpg.	.10	.15
☐ ☐	**320**	**Nicklas Lidström, Det., RC**	**.75**	**1.00**
☐ ☐	321	Darryl Sydor, L.A.	.10	.15
☐ ☐	**322**	**John LeClair, Mtl., RC**	**3.50**	**4.00**
☐ ☐	323	Arturs Irbe (G), S.J.	.10	.15
☐ ☐	**324**	**Russ Romaniuk, Wpg., RC**	**.10**	**.15**
☐ ☐	**325**	**Ken Sutton, Buf., RC**	**.10**	**.15**
☐ ☐	326	Bob Beers, Bos.	.10	.15
☐ ☐	**327**	**Michel Picard, Hfd., RC**	**.10**	**.15**
☐ ☐	328	Derian Hatcher, Min.	.25	.35
☐ ☐	329	Pat Falloon, S.J.	.25	.35
☐ ☐	330	Donald Audette, Buf.	.10	.15
☐ ☐	**331**	**Pat Jablonski, Stl., RC**	**.10**	**.15**
☐ ☐	**332**	**Corey Foster, Pha., RC**	**.10**	**.15**
☐ ☐	**333**	**Tomas Forslund, Cgy., RC**	**.10**	**.15**
☐ ☐	334	Steven Rice, Edm.	.10	.15
☐ ☐	335	Marc Bureau, Min.	.10	.15
☐ ☐	336	Kimbi Daniels, Pha.	.10	.15
☐ ☐	**337**	**Adam Foote, Que., RC**	**.50**	**.75**
☐ ☐	**338**	**Dan Kordic, Pha., RC**	**.10**	**.15**
☐ ☐	339	Link Gaetz, S.J.	.10	.15
☐ ☐	**340**	**Valeri Kamensky, Que., RC**	**1.25**	**1.50**
☐ ☐	**341**	**Tom Draper, Buf., RC**	**.10**	**.15**
☐ ☐	**342**	**Jayson More, S.J., RC**	**.10**	**.15**
☐ ☐	**343**	**Dominic Roussel (G), Pha., RC**	**.10**	**.15**
☐ ☐	**344**	**Jim Paek, Pgh., RC**	**.10**	**.15**
☐ ☐	345	Félix Potvin (G), Tor.	.75	1.00
☐ ☐	**346**	**Dan Lambert, Que., RC**	**.10**	**.15**
☐ ☐	347	Louis DeBrusk, Edm.	.10	.15
☐ ☐	**348**	**Jamie Baker, Que., RC**	**.10**	**.15**
☐ ☐	349	Scott Niedermayer, N.J.	.25	.35
☐ ☐	**350**	**Paul DiPietro, Mtl., RC**	**.10**	**.15**
☐ ☐	**351**	**Chris Winnes, Bos., RC**	**.10**	**.15**
☐ ☐	352	Mark Greig, Hfd.	.10	.15
☐ ☐	**353**	**Luciano Borsato, Wpg., RC**	**.10**	**.15**
☐ ☐	**354**	**Valeri Zelepukin, N.J., RC**	**.10**	**.15**
☐ ☐	355	Martin Lapointe, Det.	.10	.15
☐ ☐	356	Brett Hull, Stl.	.35	.50
☐ ☐	357	Steve Larmer, Chi.	.10	.15
☐ ☐	358	Theoren Fleury, Cgy.	.25	.35
☐ ☐	359	Jeremy Roenick, Chi.	.25	.35
☐ ☐	360	Mark Recchi, Pgh.	.25	.35
☐ ☐	361	Brad Marsh, Det.	.10	.15
☐ ☐	362	Kris King, NYR.	.10	.15
☐ ☐	363	Doug Brown, N.J.	.10	.15
☐ ☐	364	Carey Wilson, Cgy.	.10	.15
☐ ☐	365	Eric Lindros, Cdn.	5.00	6.00
☐ ☐	366	Kevin Dineen, Pha.	.10	.15
☐ ☐	367	John Vanbiesbrouck (G), NYR..	.50	.75
☐ ☐	368	Ray Bourque, Bos.	.35	.50
☐ ☐	369	Doug Wilson, S.J.	.10	.15
☐ ☐	370	Keith Brown, Chi.	.10	.15
☐ ☐	371	Kevin Lowe, Edm.	.10	.15
☐ ☐	372	Kelly Miller, Wsh.	.10	.15
☐ ☐	373	Dave Taylor, L.A.	.10	.15
☐ ☐	374	Guy Carbonneau, Mtl.	.10	.15
☐ ☐	375	Tim Hunter, Cgy.	.10	.15
☐ ☐	376	Brett Hull, Stl.	.35	.50
☐ ☐	377	Paul Coffey, Pgh.	.25	.35
☐ ☐	378	Adam Oates, Stl.	.25	.35
☐ ☐	379	Andy Moog (G), Bos.	.25	.35
☐ ☐	380	Mario Lemieux, Pgh.	1.50	2.00
☐ ☐	381	Joe Sakic/Wayne Gretzky	1.50	2.00
☐ ☐	382	Rob Blake/Larry Robinson	.25	.35
☐ ☐	383	Doug Weight/Steve Yzerman	.50	.75
☐ ☐	384	Mike Richter/Bernie Parent	.25	.35
☐ ☐	385	Luc Robitaille/Marcel Dionne	.25	.35
☐ ☐	386	Ed Olczyk/Bobby Clarke	.25	.35
☐ ☐	387	Patrick Roy/Rogatien Vachon	1.00	1.50
☐ ☐	388	Ed Belfour/Tony Esposito	.25	.35
☐ ☐	389	Mats Sundin/Mats Naslund	.25	.35
☐ ☐	390	Tony Amonte/Mark Messier	.25	.35
☐ ☐	391	John Cullen/Barry Cullen	.10	.15
☐ ☐	392	Gary Suter/Bobby Orr	1.00	1.50
☐ ☐	393	Rick Zombo/Glen Resch	.10	.15
☐ ☐	394	Todd Krygier, Wsh.	.10	.15
☐ ☐	395	John Druce, Wsh.	.10	.15
☐ ☐	396	Bob Carpenter, Bos.	.10	.15
☐ ☐	397	Clint Malarchuk (G) Buf.	.10	.15
☐ ☐	398	Jim Kyte, Cgy.	.10	.15
☐ ☐	399	Al MacInnis, Cgy.	.25	.35
☐ ☐	400	Ed Belfour (G), Chi.	.25	.35
☐ ☐	401	Brad Marsh, Det.	.10	.15
☐ ☐	402	Brian Benning, L.A.	.10	.15
☐ ☐	403	Larry Robinson, L.A.	.25	.35
☐ ☐	404	Craig Ludwig, Min.	.10	.15
☐ ☐	405	Patrick Flatley, NYI.	.10	.15
☐ ☐	406	Gary Nylund, NYI.	.10	.15
☐ ☐	407	Kjell Samuelsson, Pha.	.10	.15
☐ ☐	408	Dan Quinn, Pha.	.10	.15
☐ ☐	409	Garth Butcher, Stl.	.10	.15
☐ ☐	410	Rick Zombo, Stl.	.10	.15
☐ ☐	411	Paul Cavallini, Stl.	.10	.15
☐ ☐	412	Link Gaetz, S.J.	.10	.15
☐ ☐	413	David Hannan, Tor.	.10	.15
☐ ☐	414	Peter Zezel, Tor.	.10	.15
☐ ☐	415	Randy Gregg, Van.	.10	.15
☐ ☐	416	Pat Elynuik, Wpg.	.10	.15
☐ ☐	417	Rod Buskas, Chi.	.10	.15
☐ ☐	418	Mark Howe, Pha.	.25	.35
☐ ☐	419	Don Sweeney, Bos.	.10	.15
☐ ☐	420	Mark Hardy, NYR.	.10	.15

TEAM PINNACLE

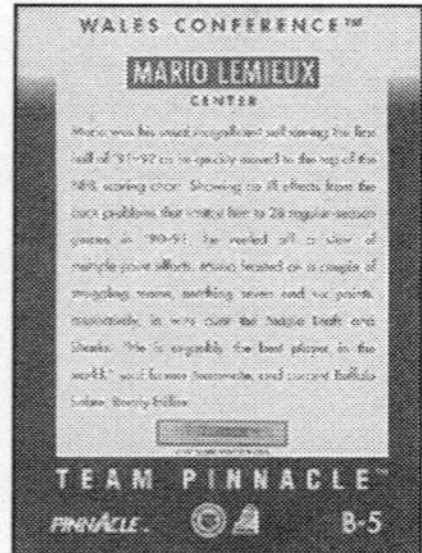

These inserts have two versions: an English issue and a French issue.

Insert Set (12 cards): **500.00** **550.00**

	No.	Player	English	French
☐ ☐	B-1	Patrick Roy (G), Mtl.	115.00	125.00
☐ ☐	B-2	Ray Bourque, Bos.	50.00	60.00
☐ ☐	B-3	Brian Leetch, NYR.	30.00	35.00
☐ ☐	B-4	Kevin Stevens,Pgh.	20.00	20.00
☐ ☐	B-5	Mario Lemieux,Pgh.	115.00	125.00
☐ ☐	B-6	Cam Neely, Bos.	20.00	20.00
☐ ☐	B-7	Bill Ranford (G), Edm.	20.00	20.00
☐ ☐	B-8	Al MacInnis, Cgy.	20.00	20.00
☐ ☐	B-9	Chris Chelios, Chi.	30.00	35.00
☐ ☐	B-10	Luc Robitaille, L.A.	20.00	20.00
☐ ☐	B-11	Wayne Gretzky, L.A.	125.00	135.00
☐ ☐	B-12	Brett Hull, Stl.	50.00	60.00

1991 - 92 PRO CARDS TEAM SETS

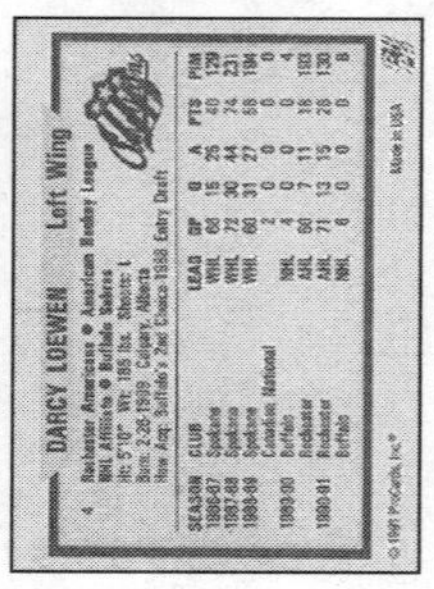

Imprint: 1991 ProCards, Inc. Made in USA

Complete Set (620 cards): **100.00**

Common Player: **.25**

ROCHESTER AMERICANS - AHL

Team Set (24 cards): **6.00**

	No.	Player	NRMT-MT
☐	1	Bill Houlder	.50
☐	2	Brian Curran	.25
☐	3	Dan Frawley	.25
☐	4	Darcy Loewen	.25
☐	5	Jiri Sejba	.25
☐	6	Lindy Ruff	.75
☐	7	Chris Snell	.25
☐	8	Bob Corkum	.35
☐	9	Dave Baseggio	.25
☐	10	Sean O'Donnell	.35
☐	11	Brad Rubachuk	.25
☐	12	Peter Ciavaglia	.35
☐	13	Joel Savage	.25
☐	14	Jason Winch	.25
☐	15	Steve Ludzik	.25
☐	16	Don McSween	.25
☐	17	David DiVita	.25
☐	18	Greg Brown	.35
☐	19	David Littman (G)	.35
☐	20	Tom Draper (G)	.35
☐	21	Jody Gage	.35
☐	22	Terry Martin, Asst. Coach	.25
☐	23	Don Lever, Coach	.35
☐	24	Rochester Americans Checklist	.25

PEORIA RIVERMEN - IHL

Team Set (23 cards): 7.00

	No.	Player	NRMT-MT
☐	25	Jason Marshall	.35
☐	26	Michel Mongeau	.25
☐	27	Derek Frenette	.25
☐	28	Kevin Miehm	.25
☐	29	Guy Hebert (G)	3.00
☐	30	Greg Poss	.25
☐	31	Dave Mackey	.25
☐	32	Dan Fowler	.25
☐	33	Mark Bassen	.25
☐	34	Yves Heroux	.25
☐	35	Harold Snepsts, Coach	.50
☐	36	Bruce Shoebottom	.25
☐	37	Jaan Luik	.25
☐	38	Alain Raymond (G)	.35
☐	39	Kyle Reeves	.25
☐	40	Brian McKee	.25
☐	41	Steve Tuttle	.25
☐	42	Rob Tustian	.25
☐	43	Richard Pion	.25
☐	44	Joe Hawley	.25
☐	45	Brian Pellerin	.25
☐	46	Jason Ruff	.25
☐	47	Peoria Rivermen Checklist	.25

MAINE MARINERS - AHL

Team Set (22 cards): 5.00

	No.	Player	NRMT-MT
☐	48	Wes Walz	.25
☐	49	Steve Bancroft	.25
☐	50	John Blue (G)	.35
☐	51	Rick Allain	.25
☐	52	Mike Walsh	.25
☐	53	Dave Thomlinson	.25
☐	54	Dennis Smith	.25
☐	55	Jack Capuano	.25
☐	56	Mike Rossetti	.25
☐	57	Petr Prajsler	.25
☐	58	Matt Glennon	.25
☐	59	John Byce	.25
☐	60	Howie Rosenblatt	.35
☐	61	Brad Tiley	.25
☐	62	Lou Crawford	.25
☐	63	Matt Hervey	.25
☐	64	Peter Douris	.25
☐	65	Jeff Lazaro	.25
☐	66	Dave Reid	.25
☐	67	E. J. McGuire, Coach	.35
☐	68	Frank Bathe, Asst. Coach	.25
☐	69	Maine Mariners Checklist	.25

FREDERICTON CANADIENS - AHL

Team Set (23 cards): 6.00

	No.	Player	NRMT-MT
☐	70	Paul DiPietro	.35
☐	71	Darcy Simon	.25
☐	72	Patrick Lebeau	.25
☐	73	Gilbert Dionne	.35
☐	74	John Ferguson	.25
☐	75	Norman Desjardins	.25
☐	76	Luc Gauthier	.25
☐	77	J.C. Bergeron (G)	.35
☐	78	André Racicot (G)	.35
☐	79	Steve Veilleux	.25
☐	80	Patrice Brisebois	.75
☐	81	Tom Sagissor	.25
☐	82	Lindsay Vallis	.25
☐	83	Steve Larouche	.50
☐	84	Sean Hill	.25
☐	85	Jesse Belanger	.35
☐	86	Stéphane Richer	.25
☐	87	Marc Labelle	.25
☐	88	Pierre Sévigny	.50
☐	89	Eric Charron	.25
☐	90	Ed Ronan	.25
☐	91	Paulin Bordeleau, Coach	.75
☐	92	Fredericton Canadiens Checklist	.25

SPRINGFIELD INDIANS - AHL

Team Set (25 cards): 5.00

	No.	Player	NRMT-MT
☐	93	Daryl Reaugh (G)	.35
☐	94	Jergus Baca	.25
☐	95	Karl Johnston	.25
☐	96	Shawn Evans	.25
☐	97	Scott Humeniuk	.25
☐	98	Cam Brauer	.25
☐	99	Scott Eichstadt	.25
☐	100	Paul Cyr	.25
☐	101	James Black	.25
☐	102	Chris Govedaris	.25
☐	103	Joe Day	.25
☐	104	Chris Tancill	.25
☐	105	Kerry Russell	.25
☐	106	Denis Chalifoux	.25
☐	107	Blair Atcheynum	.75
☐	108	John Stevens	.25
☐	109	Brian Chapman	.25
☐	110	Chris Bright	.25
☐	111	Jim Burke	.25
☐	112	Scott Daniels	.25
☐	113	Kelly Ens	.25
☐	114	Mike Tomlak	.25
☐	115	Mario Gosselin (G)	.35
☐	116	Jay Leach, Coach	.25
☐	117	Springfield Indians Checklist	.25

ADIRONDACK RED WINGS - AHL

Team Set (25 cards): 9.00

	No.	Player	NRMT-MT
☐	118	Allan Bester (G)	.50
☐	119	Daniel Shank	.25
☐	120	Lonnie Loach	.25
☐	121	Mark Reimer (G)	.35
☐	122	Kirk Tomlinson	.25
☐	123	Stewart Malgunas	.25
☐	124	Serge Anglehart	.25
☐	125	Chris Luongo	.25
☐	126	Keith Primeau	5.00
☐	127	Ken Quinney	.25
☐	128	Dave Flanagan	.25
☐	129	Pete Stauber	.25
☐	130	Mike Sillinger	1.00
☐	131	Micah Aivazoff	.25
☐	132	Gary Shuchuk	.25
☐	133	Bill McDougall	.25
☐	134	Sheldon Kennedy	1.00
☐	135	Derek Mayer	.25
☐	136	Darin Bannister	.25
☐	137	Guy Dupuis	.25
☐	138	Gord Kruppke	.25
☐	139	Jason York	1.00
☐	140	Barry Melrose, Coach	.75
☐	141	Glenn Merkosky, Asst. Coach	.25
☐	142	Adirondack Red Wings Checklist	.25

KALAMAZOO WINGS - IHL

Team Set (21 cards): 5.00

	No.	Player	NRMT-MT
☐	143	Larry Dyck (G)	.35
☐	144	Roy Mitchell	.25
☐	145	Greg Spenrath	.25
☐	146	Steve Herniman	.25
☐	147	Brad Berry	.25
☐	148	Jim Nesich	.25
☐	149	Tim Lenardon	.25
☐	150	Steve Guenette (G)	.35
☐	151	Paul Jerrard	.25
☐	152	Cal McGowan	.25
☐	153	Scott Robinson	.25
☐	154	Mitch Messier	.25
☐	155	Tony Joseph	.25
☐	156	Steve Maltais	.25
☐	157	Steve Gotaas	.25
☐	158	Doug Barrault	.25
☐	159	Dave Moylan	.25
☐	160	Mario Thyer	.25
☐	161	Bob Hoffmeyer, Coach	.25
☐	162	Wade Dawson, Asst. Coach	.25
☐	163	Kalamazoo Wings Checklist	.25

MONCTON HAWKS - AHL

Team Set (26 cards): 6.00

	No.	Player	NRMT-MT
☐	164	Rob Murray	.25
☐	165	Chris Kiene	.25
☐	166	Lee Davidson	.25
☐	167	Rudy Poeschek	.25
☐	168	Kent Paynter	.25
☐	169	John LeBlanc	.25
☐	170	Dallas Eakins	.25
☐	171	Claude Julien	.35
☐	172	Bob Joyce	.25
☐	173	Derek Langille	.25
☐	174	Rob Cowie	.25
☐	175	Warren Rychel	.35
☐	176	Tom Karalis	.25
☐	177	Kris Draper	.25
☐	178	Ken Gernander	.25
☐	179	Tod Hartje	.25
☐	180	Sean Gauthier (G)	.35
☐	181	Tyler Larter	.25
☐	182	Scott Levins	.25
☐	183	Jason Cirone	.25
☐	184	Mark Kumpel	.25
☐	185	Rick Tabaracci (G)	1.00
☐	186	Luciano Borsato	.35
☐	187	Dave Farrish, Head Coach/GM	.25
☐	188	Dave Prior, Goaltender Coach	.25
☐	189	Moncton Hawks Checklist	.25

BINGHAMTON RANGERS - AHL

Team Set (25 cards): 6.00

	No.	Player	NRMT-MT
☐	190	Peter Fiorentino	.25
☐	191	Glen Goodall	.25
☐	192	John Mokosak	.25
☐	193	Sam St. Laurent (G)	.25
☐	194	Daniel Lacroix	.35
☐	195	Guy LaRose	.25
☐	196	Mike Hurlbut	.25
☐	197	Peter Laviolette	.25
☐	198	Rick Bennett	.25
☐	199	Steven King	.35
☐	200	Boris Rousson (G)	.35
☐	201	Jody Hull	.50
☐	202	Shaun Sabol	.25
☐	203	Joe Paterson	.25
☐	204	Rob Zamuner	1.50
☐	205	Don Biggs	.25
☐	206	Chris Cichocki	.25
☐	207	Ross Fitzpatrick	.25
☐	208	Mark LaForest	.25
☐	209	Brian McReynolds	.25
☐	210	Jeff Bloemberg	.25
☐	211	Kord Cernich	.25
☐	212	Ron Smith, Coach	.25
☐	213	Al Hill, Asst. Coach	.35
☐	214	Binghamton Rangers Checklist	.25

CAPE BRETON OILERS - AHL

Team Set (24 cards): 7.00

	No.	Player	NRMT-MT
☐	215	François Leroux	.35
☐	216	Marc Laforge	.25
☐	217	Max Middendorf	.25
☐	218	Shjon Podein	.25
☐	219	Jason Soules	.25
☐	220	Collin Bauer	.25
☐	221	Shaun Van Allen	.50
☐	222	Eldon Reddick (G)	.35
☐	223	Eugeny Belosheikin (G)	.35
☐	224	David Haas	.25
☐	225	Norm Foster (G)	.35
☐	226	Greg Hawgood	.25
☐	227	Steven Rice	1.00
☐	228	Dan Currie	.25
☐	229	Peter Soberlak	.25
☐	230	Martin Rucinksy	2.00
☐	231	Tomas Kapusta	.25
☐	232	Dean Antos	.25
☐	233	Craig Fisher	.25
☐	234	Tomas Srsen	.25
☐	235	Don MacAdam, Coach	.25
☐	236	Norm Ferguson, Asst. Coach	.25
☐	237	Coaching Staff,	.25
☐	238	Cape Breton Oilers Checklist	.25

FORT WAYNE KOMETS - IHL

Team Set (24 cards): 5.00

	No.	Player	NRMT-MT
☐	239	Peter Hankinson	.25
☐	240	Chris McRae	.25

No.	Player	NRMT-MT
241	Craig Martin	.35
242	Carey Lucyk	.25
243	Jean-Marc Richard	.25
244	Grant Richison	.25
245	Mark Turner	.25
246	Todd Flichel	.25
247	Scott Shaunessy	.25
248	Darin Smith	.25
249	Ian Boyce	.25
250	Colin Chin	.25
251	Bob Jones	.25
252	Bob Jay	.25
253	Kelly Hurd	.25
254	Scott Gruhl	.25
255	Kory Kocur	.25
256	Steven Fletcher	.25
257	Bob Lakso	.25
258	Dusty Imoo (G)	.35
259	Mike O'Neill (G)	.35
260	Bruce Boudreau, Asst. Coach	.25
261	Al Sims, Coach	.35
262	Fort Wayne Komets Checklist	.25

HERSHEY BEARS - AHL

Team Set (25 cards): 5.00

No.	Player	NRMT-MT
263	Ray Letourneau (G)	.35
264	Marc D'Amour (G)	.35
265	Dominic Roussel (G)	.75
266	Bill Armstrong	.25
267	Al Conroy	.25
268	Dale Kushner	.25
269	Toni Porkka	.25
270	Mike Stothers	.25
271	Darren Rumble	.35
272	Reid Simpson	.25
273	Claude Boivin	.25
274	Len Barrie	.35
275	Chris Jensen	.25
276	Pat Murray	.25
277	Eric Dandenault	.25
278	Rod Dallman	.25
279	Mark Freer	.25
280	Bill Armstrong	.25
281	Tim Tookey	.25
282	Jamie Cooke	.25
283	David Fenyves	.25
284	Steve Morrow	.25
285	Martin Hostak	.25
286	Mike Eaves, Coach	.25
287	Hershey Bears Checklist	.25

MUSKEGON LUMBERJACKS - IHL

Team Set (23 cards): 5.00

No.	Player	NRMT-MT
288	Dave Michayluk	.25
289	Glenn Mulvenna	.25
290	Jean Blouin	.25
291	Jock Callander	.25
292	Perry Ganchar	.25
293	Paul Laus	.25
294	Mark Major	.25
295	Bruce Racine (G)	.35
296	Daniel Gauthier	.25
297	Mike Needham	.25
298	Jeff Daniels	.25
299	Sandy Smith	.25
300	Gilbert Delorme	.25
301	Rob Dopson (G)	.35
302	Eric Brule	.25
303	Alain Morissette (G)	.35
304	Paul Dyck	.25
305	Jason Smart	.25
306	Gord Dineen	.35
307	Todd Nelson	.25
308	Jamie Heward	.25
309	Phil Russell, Coach	.25
310	Muskegon Lumberjacks Checklist	.25

SAN DIEGO GULLS - IHL

Team Set (24 cards): 6.00

No.	Player	NRMT-MT
311	Soren True	.25
312	Murray Duval	.25
313	Dmitri Kvartalnov	.35
314	Larry Floyd	.25
315	Alan Leggett	.25
316	Alan Hepple	.25
317	Ron Duguay	.75
318	Len Hachborn	.25
319	Steve Martinson	.25
320	Rick Knickle (G)	.35
321	Darcy Norton	.25
322	Keith Gretzky	.75
323	Brian Straub	.25
324	Denny Lambert	.25
325	Jason Prosofsky	.25
326	Bruce Hoffort (G)	.35
327	Sergei Starikov	.35
328	Dave Korol	.25
329	Robbie Nichols	.25
330	Kord Cernich	.25
331	Brent Sapergia	.25
332	Don Waddell, Coach	.25
333	Charlie Simmer, Asst. Coach	.25
334	San Diego Gulls Checklist	.25

ST. JOHN'S MAPLE LEAFS - AHL

Team Set (25 cards): 15.00

No.	Player	NRMT-MT
235	Rob Mendel	.25
336	Curtis Hunt	.25
337	Jeff Serowik	.25
338	Bruce Bell	.25
339	Yanic Perreault	1.00
340	Brad Aitken	.25
341	Keith Osborne	.25
342	Todd Hawkins	.25
343	Andrew McKim	.25
344	Kevin McClelland	.25
345	Mike Stevens	.25
346	Dave Tomlinson	.25
347	Kevin Maguire	.25
348	Mike MacWilliam	.25
349	Greg Walters	.25
350	Guy Lehoux	.25
351	Todd Gillingham	.25
352	Len Esau	.25
353	Greg Johnston	.25
354	Félix Potvin (G)	10.00
355	Damian Rhodes (G)	2.00
356	Joel Quenneville, Asst. Coach	1.50
357	Marc Crawford, Coach	2.00
358	Mike Eastwood	.50
359	St. John's Maple Leafs Checklist	.25

NEW HAVEN NIGHTHAWKS - AHL

Team Set (24 cards): 5.00

No.	Player	NRMT-MT
360	Lou Franceschetti	.25
361	John Anderson	.25
362	Scott Schneider	.25
363	Jerome Bechard	.25
364	Mario Doyon	.25
365	Jeff Jackson	.25
366	John Tanner (G)	.35
367	Al Tuer	.25
368	Paul Willett	.25
369	Darryl Williams	.25
370	George Maneluk (G)	.35
371	Eric Ricard	.25
372	Trevor Stienburg	.25
373	Jerry Tarrant	.25
374	Michael McEwen	.25
375	Brian Dobbin	.25
376	David Latta	.25
377	Jim Sprott	.25
378	Trevor Pochipinksi	.25
379	Stan Drulia	.25
380	Kent Hulst	.25
381	Brad Turner	.25
382	Doug Carpenter, Coach	.35
383	New Haven Nighthawks Checklist	.25

PHOENIX ROADRUNNERS - IHL

Team Set (24 cards): 5.00

No.	Player	NRMT-MT
384	Bob Berg	.25
385	Steve Jaques	.25
386	Chris Norton	.25
387	Vern Smith	.25
388	Kevin MacDonald	.25
389	Ross Wilson	.25
390	Shawn McCosh	.25
391	Mike Vukonich	.25
392	Marc Saumier	.25
393	Mike Ruark	.25
394	Kris Miller	.25
395	Tim Breslin	.25
396	Paul Holden	.25
397	Jeff Rohlicek	.25
398	Kyosti Karjalainen	.25
399	David Goverde (G)	.35
400	John Van Kessel	.25
401	Sean Whyte	.25
402	Brent Thompson	.25
403	Darryl Gilmour (G)	.35
404	Scott Bjugstad	.25
405	Ralph Backstrom, Coach, Error	.25
406	Rick Kozuback, Asst. Coach, Error	.25
407	Phoenix Roadrunners Checklist	.25

UTICA DEVILS - AHL

Team Set (20 cards): 5.00

No.	Player	NRMT-MT
408	Brent Severyn	.25
409	Dean Malkoc	.25
410	Matt Ruchty	.25
411	Jarrod Skalde	.25
412	Brian Sullivan	.25
413	Ben Hankinson, Error	.25
414	Bill Huard	.25
415	Jeff Christian	.25
416	Corey Schwab (G)	1.00
417	Kevin Dean	.25
418	Todd Copeland	.25
419	Mike Bodnarchuk	.25
420	Jason Miller	.25
421	Chad Erickson (G)	.35
422	David Craievich	.25
423	Jim Dowd	.35
424	Jamie Huscroft	.25
425	Myles O'Connor	.35
426	Jon Morris	.25
427	Valeri Zelepukin	.75
428	Utica Devils Checklist	.25

FLINT BULLDOGS - COLONIAL LEAGUE

Team Set (23 cards): 5.00

No.	Player	NRMT-MT
429	Brad Beck	.25
430	Brett MacDonald	.25
431	Jacques Mailhot	.25
432	Francis Ouellette	.25
433	Ron Kinghorn (G)	.35
434	Dennis Miller	.25
435	Darren Miciak	.25
436	Tom Sasso	.25
437	Peter Corbett	.25
438	Brian Horan	.25
439	John Messuri	.25
440	E. J. Sauer	.25
441	Tom Mutch	.25
442	Jason Simon	.25
443	Steve Sullivan	.25
444	Scott Allen	.25
445	Stéphane Brochu	.25
446	Ken Spangler	.25
447	Lee Odelein	.25
448	Antti Autere	.25
449	John Reid	.25
450	Skip Probst, Coach/G.M.	.25
451	Flint Bulldogs Checklist	.25

CAPITAL DISTRICT ISLANDERS - AHL

Team Set (25 cards): 7.00

No.	Player	NRMT-MT
452	Dean Ewen	.25
453	Brent Grieve	.25
454	Jim Culhane	.25
455	Joni Lehto	.25
456	Graeme Townshend	.25
457	Danny Lorenz (G)	.35
458	Phil Huber	.25
459	Kevin Cheveldayoff	.25

	No.	Player	NRMT-MT
☐	460	Dennis Vaske	.25
☐	461	Wayne Doucet	.25
☐	462	Greg Parks	.25
☐	463	Dean Chynoweth	.25
☐	464	Lee Giffin	.25
☐	465	Richard Kromm	.25
☐	466	Derek Laxdal	.25
☐	467	Travis Green	1.50
☐	468	Iain Fraser	.25
☐	469	Rick Hayward	.25
☐	470	Jeff Finley	.25
☐	471	Dave Chyzowski	.35
☐	472	Mark Fitzpatrick (G)	1.50
☐	473	Hubie McDonough	.25
☐	474	Sean LeBrun	.25
☐	475	Chris Pryor	.25
☐	476	Capital District Islanders Checklist	.25

INDIANAPOLIS ICE - IHL

Team Set (28 cards): 18.00

	No.	Player	NRMT-MT
☐	477	Jeff Sirkka	.25
☐	478	Owen Lessard	.25
☐	479	Jim Playfair	.25
☐	480	Dan Vincelette	.25
☐	481	Tracey Egeland	.25
☐	482	Shawn Byram	.25
☐	483	Trevor Dam	.25
☐	484	Martin Desjardins	.25
☐	485	Milan Tichy	.25
☐	486	Cam Russell	.35
☐	487	Mike Speer	.25
☐	488	Sean Williams	.25
☐	489	Paul Gillis	.25
☐	490	Brad Laurer	.25
☐	491	Trent Yawney	.35
☐	492	Craig Woodcroft	.25
☐	493	Justin Lafayette	.25
☐	494	Robb Conn	.25
☐	495	Frantisek Kucera	.35
☐	496	Mike Peluso	.75
☐	497	Roch Belley (G)	.35
☐	498	Ryan McGill	.25
☐	499	Kerry Toporowski	.25
☐	500	Dominik Hasek (G)	12.00
☐	501	Adam Bennett	.25
☐	502	Ray LeBlanc (G)	.35
☐	503	John Marks, Coach	.25
☐	504	Indianapolis Ice Checklist	.25

KANSAS CITY BLADES - IHL

Team Set (23 cards): 5.00

	No.	Player	NRMT-MT
☐	505	Mikhail Kravets	.25
☐	506	Gary Emmons	.25
☐	507	Ed Courtenay	.25
☐	508	Claudio Scremin	.25
☐	509	Jarmo Myllys (G)	.75
☐	510	Mike Colman	.25
☐	511	Kevin Evans	.25
☐	512	Troy Frederick	.25
☐	513	Ron Handy	.25
☐	514	Murray Garbutt	.25
☐	515	Gord Frantti	.25
☐	516	Dale Craigwell	.25
☐	517	Wade Flaherty (G)	.50
☐	518	Dean Kolstad	.25
☐	519	Rick Lessard	.25
☐	520	Craig Coxe	.25
☐	521	Jeff Madill	.25
☐	522	Peter Lappin	.25
☐	523	Duane Joyce	.25
☐	524	Larry DePalma	.25
☐	525	Pat MacLeod	.25
☐	526	Andy Akervik	.25
☐	527	Kansas City Blades Checklist	.25

HALIFAX CITADELS - AHL

Team Set (19 cards): 6.00

	No.	Player	NRMT-MT
☐	528	Mike Dagenais	.25
☐	529	Gerald Bzdel	.25
☐	530	Stéphane Fiset (G)	2.50
☐	531	David Espe	.25
☐	532	Patrick Labrecque (G)	.35
☐	533	Niclas Andersson	.50
☐	534	Jon Klemm	.50
☐	535	Denis Chassé	.35
☐	536	Stéphane Charbonneau	.25
☐	537	Ivan Matulik	.25
☐	538	Serge Roberge	.25
☐	539	Daniel Doré	.25
☐	540	Sergei Kharin	.25
☐	541	Jamie Baker	.75
☐	542	Ken McRae	.25
☐	543	Dave Marcinyshyn	.25
☐	544	Clément Jodoin, Coach	.25
☐	545	Dean Hopkins, Asst. Coach	.25
☐	546	Halifax Citadels Checklist	.25

BALTIMORE SKIPJACKS - AHL

Team Set (27 cards): 8.00

	No.	Player	NRMT-MT
☐	547	Jeff Greenlaw	.25
☐	548	Byron Dafoe (G)	1.00
☐	549	Jim Hrivnak (G)	.50
☐	550	Olaf Kolzig (G)	5.00
☐	551	John Purves	.25
☐	552	Bobby Reynolds	.25
☐	553	Simon Wheeldon	.25
☐	554	Jim Mathieson	.25
☐	555	Trevor Halverson	.25
☐	556	Steve Seftel	.25
☐	557	Ken Lovsin	.25
☐	558	Victor Gervais	.25
☐	559	Steve Martell	.25
☐	560	Chris Clarke	.25
☐	561	Brent Hughes	.25
☐	562	Jiri Vykoukal	.25
☐	563	Tim Taylor	.35
☐	564	Richie Walcott	.25
☐	565	Harry Mews	.25
☐	566	Craig Duncanson	.25
☐	567	Todd Hlushko	.25
☐	568	Mark Ferner	.25
☐	569	Bob Babcock	.25
☐	570	Reggie Savage	.25
☐	571	Rob Laird, Coach	.25
☐	572	Barry Trotz, Asst. Coach	.25
☐	573	Baltimore Skipjacks Checklist	.25

SALT LAKE GOLDEN EAGLES - IHL

Team Set (21 cards): 5.00

	No.	Player	NRMT-MT
☐	574	Kevan Melrose	.25
☐	575	Kevin Grant	.25
☐	576	Kevan Guy	.25
☐	577	Darryl Olsen	.25
☐	578	Kevin Wortman	.25
☐	579	Darren Stolk	.25
☐	580	Bryan Deasley	.25
☐	581	Paul Kruse	.25
☐	582	Darren Banks	.25
☐	583	Corey Lyons	.25
☐	584	Kerry Clark	.35
☐	585	Todd Strueby	.25
☐	586	Rich Chernomaz	.25
☐	587	Tim Harris	.25
☐	588	Shawn Heaphy	.25
☐	589	Todd Harkins	.25
☐	590	Richard Zemlak	.25
☐	591	Warren Sharples (G)	.35
☐	592	Jason Muzzatti (G)	1.00
☐	593	Dennis Holland	.25
☐	594	Salt Lake Golden Eagles Checklist	.25

MILWAUKEE ADMIRALS - IHL

Team Set (26 cards): 5.00

	No.	Player	NRMT-MT
☐	595	Shawn Antoski	.50
☐	596	Peter Bakovic	.25
☐	597	Robin Bawa	.25
☐	598	Cam Brown	.25
☐	599	Neil Eisenhut	.25
☐	600	Jason Herter	.25
☐	601	Ian Kidd	.25
☐	602	Troy Neumeier	.25
☐	603	Carl Valimont	.25
☐	604	Phil Von Stefenelli	.25
☐	605	Andrew McBain	.35
☐	606	Eric Murano	.25
☐	607	Rob Murphy	.25
☐	608	Brian Blad	.25
☐	609	Randy Boyd	.25
☐	610	Don Gibson	.25
☐	611	Paul Guay	.25
☐	612	Jay Mazur	.25
☐	613	Jeff Larmer	.25
☐	614	Ladislav Tresl	.25
☐	615	Dennis Snedden	.25
☐	616	Corrie D'Alessio (G)	.35
☐	617	Bob Mason (G)	.35
☐	618	Jack McIlhargey, Coach	.35
☐	619	Curt Fraser, Asst. Coach, Error	.35
☐	620	Milwaukee Admirals Checklist	.25

1991 - 92 PRO SET

THE 1991 HOCKEY HALL OF FAME INDUCTION DINNER & CEREMONIES

These cards were issued for the 1991 Hockey Hall of Fame Dinner and Ceremonies held in Toronto on September 23rd, 1991.

Imprint: 1991 Pro Set Inc.

Complete Set (14 cards): 90.00

	No.	Player/Team	NRMT-MT
☐		Title Card	8.00
☐	1	Mike Bossy, NYI.	16.00
☐	2	Denis Potvin, NYI.	16.00
☐	3	Bob Pulford, Tor.	12.00
☐	4	Scott Bowman, Wales All-Stars	12.00
☐	5	Neil P. Armstrong, Lineman	8.00
☐	6	Clint Smith, NYR.	12.00
☐	7	1903-04 Ottawa Silver Seven	8.00
☐	8	1905-06 Ottawa Silver Seven	8.00
☐	9	1908-09 Ottawa Senators	8.00
☐	10	1910-11 Ottawa Senators	8.00
☐	11	1919-20 Ottawa Senators	8.00
☐	12	1922-23 Ottawa Senators	8.00
☐	13	1926-27 Ottawa Senators	8.00

HOCKEY HALL OF FAME NHL 75TH ANNIVERSARY TRIBUTE

This set was issued in a polyethylene pack of eight cards for the Hockey Hall of Fame's 75th Anniversary Tribute to the NHL.

Imprint: 1991 Pro Set Inc.

	No.	Team	NRMT-MT
☐		Title Card: Hockey Hall of Fame NHL 75th Anniversary Tribute	1.00
☐	HHF1	Hockey Hall of Fame Collectible Excellence Education Entertainment	1.00

ST. LOUIS BLUES MID WEST COLLECTOR SHOW

Issued for the Mid West Collector Show held at St. Louis during October 1991, these cards are identical to the regular issue except for a blue stripe at the right side of the card. The cards are numbered in gold within the strip.

Imprint: Pro Set NHL & NHLPA 1991

Complete Set (4 cards): 20.00

	No.	Player	NRMT-MT
☐	1 of 4	Adam Oates	8.00
☐	2 of 4	Paul Cavallini	3.00
☐	3 of 4	Rick Meagher	3.00
☐	4 of 4	Brett Hull	12.00

TOUR PROMO CARD

During the 1991-92 season Pro Set sponsored a Hockey Card Collectibles and Memorabilia Show which toured several NHL cities. A limited number of cards were given out at each city the tour visited. The card was not numbered.

Imprint: NHL Pro Set 1991

	No.	Player	NRMT-MT
☐		National Hockey Tour	1.00

PRO SET

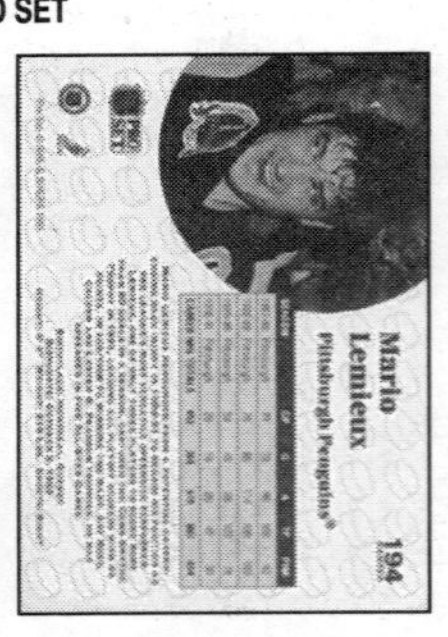

These cards have two versions: an English issue and a French issue. The French issue was released a little later than the English edition and shows the new Minnesota North Stars logos instead of the old ones.

Imprint: Pro Set

Complete Set (615 cards): 15.00

Common Player: .10

	Promo	NRMT-MT
☐	Title Card:	.15
☐	Bob Essensa (G), Win.	.15
☐	Gord Murphy, Phi.	.15
☐	Dave Reid, Tor.	.15
☐	Craig Wolanin, Que.	.15
☐	Randy Wood, NYI	.15

	No.	Player	NRMT-MT
☐ ☐	1	Glen Wesley, Bos.	.10
☐ ☐	2	Craig Janney, Bos.	.10
☐ ☐	3	Ken Hodge, Bos.	.10
☐ ☐	4	Randy Burridge, Bos., (Wsh.)	.10
☐ ☐	5	Cam Neely, Bos.	.20
☐ ☐	6	Bob Sweeney, Bos.	.10
☐ ☐	7	Garry Galley, Bos.	.10
☐ ☐	8	Petri Skriko, Bos.	.10
☐ ☐	9	Ray Bourque, Bos.	.35
☐ ☐	10	Andy Moog (G), Bos.	.20
☐ ☐	11	David Christian, Bos.	.10
☐ ☐	12	Dave Poulin, Bos.	.10
☐ ☐	**13**	**Jeff Lazaro, Bos., RC**	**.10**
☐ ☐	14	Darrin Shannon, Buf.	.10
☐ ☐	15	Pierre Turgeon, Buf., Error (8-28)	.20
☐ ☐	16	Alexander Mogilny, Buf.	.20
☐ ☐	17	Benoît Hogue, Buf., Error (b/ Wpg.)	.10
☐ ☐	18	Dave Snuggerud, Buf.	.10
☐ ☐	19	Doug Bodger, Buf.	.10
☐ ☐	20	Uwe Krupp, Buf.	.10
☐ ☐	21	Daren Puppa (G), Buf.	.10
☐ ☐	22	Christian Ruuttu, Buf.	.10
☐ ☐	23	Dave Andreychuk, Buf.	.20
☐ ☐	24	Dale Hawerchuk, Buf.	.20
☐ ☐	25	Mike Ramsey, Buf.	.10
☐ ☐	26	Rick Vaive, Buf.	.10
☐ ☐	27	Stéphane Matteau, Cgy.	.10
☐ ☐	28	Theoren Fleury, Cgy.	.20
☐ ☐	29	Joe Nieuwendyk, Cgy.	.20
☐ ☐	30	Gary Roberts, Cgy.	.20
☐ ☐	31	Paul Ranheim, Cgy.	.10
☐ ☐	32	Gary Suter, Cgy.	.10
☐ ☐	33	Al MacInnis, Cgy.	.20
☐ ☐	34	Doug Gilmour, Cgy.	.20
☐ ☐	35	Mike Vernon (G), Cgy.	.20
☐ ☐	36	Carey Wilson, Cgy.	.10
☐ ☐	37	Joel Otto, Cgy.	.10
☐ ☐	38	Jamie Macoun, Cgy.	.10
☐ ☐	39	Sergei Makarov, Cgy.	.10
☐ ☐	40	Jeremy Roenick, Chi.	.20
☐ ☐	41	Dave Manson, Chi.	.10
☐ ☐	42	Adam Creighton, Chi.	.10
☐ ☐	43	Ed Belfour (G), Chi.	.25
☐ ☐	44	Wayne Presley, Chi.	.10
☐ ☐	45	Steve Thomas, Chi.	.10
☐ ☐	46	Troy Murray, Chi.	.10
☐ ☐	47	Bob McGill, Chi. (S.J.)	.10
☐ ☐	48	Chris Chelios, Chi.	.20
☐ ☐	49	Steve Larmer, Chi.	.20
☐ ☐	50	Michel Goulet, Chi.	.20
☐ ☐	51	Dirk Graham, Chi.	.10
☐ ☐	52	Doug Wilson, Chi.	.20
☐ ☐	53	Sergei Fedorov, Det.	.35
☐ ☐	54	Yves Racine, Det.	.10
☐ ☐	55	Jimmy Carson, Det.	.10
☐ ☐	56	Johan Garpenlov, Det.	.10
☐ ☐	57	Tim Cheveldae (G), Det.	.10
☐ ☐	58	Shawn Burr, Det.	.10
☐ ☐	59	Paul Ysebaert, Det.	.10
☐ ☐	60	Kevin Miller, Det.	.10
☐ ☐	61	Bob Probert, Det.	.10
☐ ☐	62	Steve Yzerman, Det.	.75
☐ ☐	63	Gerard Gallant, Det.	.10
☐ ☐	64	Rick Zombo, Det.	.10
☐ ☐	65	David Barr, Det.	.10
☐ ☐	66	Martin Gelinas, Edm.	.10
☐ ☐	67	Adam Graves, Edm.	.10
☐ ☐	68	Joe Murphy, Edm.	.10
☐ ☐	69	Craig Simpson, Edm.	.10
☐ ☐	70	Bill Ranford (G), Edm.	.20
☐ ☐	71	Esa Tikkanen, Edm.	.10
☐ ☐	72	Petr Klima, Edm.	.10
☐ ☐	73	Steve Smith, Edm.	.10
☐ ☐	74	Mark Messier, Edm.	.35
☐ ☐	75	Glenn Anderson, Edm.	.10
☐ ☐	76	Kevin Lowe, Edm.	.10
☐ ☐	77	Craig MacTavish, Edm.	.10
☐ ☐	78	Grant Fuhr (G), Edm.	.20
☐ ☐	79	Bobby Holik, Hfd.	.10
☐ ☐	80	Rob Brown, Hfd.	.10
☐ ☐	81	Doug Houda, Hfd.	.10
☐ ☐	82	Sylvain Côté, Hfd.	.10
☐ ☐	83	Todd Krygier, Hfd.	.10
☐ ☐	84	Dean Evason, Hfd.	.10
☐ ☐	85	John Cullen, Hfd.	.10
☐ ☐	86	Pat Verbeek, Hfd.	.10
☐ ☐	87	Brad Shaw, Hfd.	.10
☐ ☐	88	Paul Cyr, Hfd.	.10
☐ ☐	89	Kevin Dineen, Hfd.	.10
☐ ☐	90	Peter Sidorkiewicz (G), Hfd.	.10
☐ ☐	91	Zarley Zalapski, Hfd.	.10
☐ ☐	92	Rob Blake, L.A.	.20
☐ ☐	93	Jari Kurri, L.A.	.20
☐ ☐	94	Todd Elik, L.A. (Min.)	.10
☐ ☐	95	Luc Robitaille, L.A.	.20
☐ ☐	96	Steve Duchesne, L.A. (Pha.)	.10
☐ ☐	97	Tomas Sandström, L.A.	.10
☐ ☐	98	Tony Granato, L.A.	.10
☐ ☐	99	Bob Kudelski, L.A.	.10
☐ ☐	100	Marty McSorley, L.A.	.10
☐ ☐	101	Wayne Gretzky, L.A.	1.50
☐ ☐	102	Kelly Hrudey (G), L.A.	.10
☐ ☐	103	Dave Taylor, L.A.	.10
☐ ☐	104	Larry Robinson, L.A.	.20
☐ ☐	105	Mike Modano, Min.	.35
☐ ☐	106	Ulf Dahlen, Min.	.10
☐ ☐	107	Mark Tinordi, Min.	.10
☐ ☐	108	Dave Gagner, Min.	.10
☐ ☐	109	Brian Bellows, Min.	.10
☐ ☐	110	Gaetan Duchesne, Min.	.10
☐ ☐	111	Jon Casey (G), Min.	.10
☐ ☐	112	Neal Broten, Min.	.10
☐ ☐	113	Brian Propp, Min.	.10
☐ ☐	114	Curt Giles, Min.	.10
☐ ☐	115	Bobby Smith, Min.	.10
☐ ☐	116	Jim Johnson, Min.	.10
☐ ☐	117	Doug Smail, Min.	.10
☐ ☐	118	Eric Desjardins, Mtl.	.20
☐ ☐	119	Mathieu Schneider, Mtl.	.10
☐ ☐	120	Stéphan Lebeau, Mtl.	.10
☐ ☐	121	Mike Keane, Mtl.	.10
☐ ☐	122	Stéphane Richer, Mtl.	.10
☐ ☐	123	Petr Svoboda, Mtl.	.10
☐ ☐	124	J.J. Daigneault, Mtl.	.10
☐ ☐	125	Patrick Roy (G), Mtl.	1.00
☐ ☐	126	Russ Courtnall, Mtl.	.10
☐ ☐	127	Brian Skrudland, Mtl.	.10
☐ ☐	128	Denis Savard, Mtl.	.20
☐ ☐	129	Mike McPhee, Mtl.	.10
☐ ☐	130	Guy Carbonneau, Mtl.	.10
☐ ☐	131	Brendan Shanahan, N.J.	.35
☐ ☐	132	Sean Burke (G), N.J.	.20
☐ ☐	133	Eric Weinrich, N.J.	.10
☐ ☐	134	Kirk Muller, N.J.	.10
☐ ☐	135	Claude Lemieux, N.J.	.10
☐ ☐	136	John MacLean, N.J.	.10
☐ ☐	137	Chris Terreri (G), N.J.	.10
☐ ☐	138	Doug Brown, N.J.	.10
☐ ☐	139	Ken Daneyko, N.J.	.10
☐ ☐	140	Bruce Driver, N.J.	.10
☐ ☐	141	Patrik Sundstrom, N.J.	.10
☐ ☐	142	Viacheslav Fetisov, N.J.	.20
☐ ☐	143	Peter Stastny, N.J.	.10
☐ ☐	144	Wayne McBean, NYI.	.10
☐ ☐	**145**	**Bill Berg, NYI., RC**	**.10**
☐ ☐	146	Derek King, NYI.	.10
☐ ☐	147	David Volk, NYI.	.10
☐ ☐	148	Jeff Norton, NYI.	.10
☐ ☐	149	Pat LaFontaine, NYI.	.20
☐ ☐	150	Gary Nylund, NYI.	.10
☐ ☐	151	Randy Wood, NYI.	.10
☐ ☐	152	Patrick Flatley, NYI.	.10
☐ ☐	153	Glenn Healy (G), NYI.	.10
☐ ☐	154	Brent Sutter, NYI.	.10
☐ ☐	155	Craig Ludwig, NYI. (Min.)	.10
☐ ☐	156	Ray Ferraro, NYI.	.10
☐ ☐	157	Troy Mallette, NYR.	.10
☐ ☐	158	Mark Janssens, NYR.	.10
☐ ☐	159	Brian Leetch, NYR.	.20
☐ ☐	160	Darren Turcotte, NYR.	.10
☐ ☐	161	Mike Richter (G), NYR.	.20
☐ ☐	162	Ray Sheppard, NYR.	.10
☐ ☐	163	Randy Moller, NYR.	.10
☐ ☐	164	James Patrick, NYR.	.10
☐ ☐	165	Brian Mullen, NYR. (S.J.)	.10
☐ ☐	166	Bernie Nicholls, NYR.	.10
☐ ☐	167	Mike Gartner, NYR.	.20
☐ ☐	168	Kelly Kisio, NYR., (Min.)	.10
☐ ☐	169	John Ogrodnick, NYR.	.10
☐ ☐	170	Mike Ricci, Pha.	.10
☐ ☐	171	Gord Murphy, Pha.	.10
☐ ☐	172	Scott Mellanby, Pha. (Edm.)	.10
☐ ☐	173	Terry Carkner, Pha.	.10
☐ ☐	174	Derrick Smith, Pha.	.10
☐ ☐	175	Murray Craven, Pha.	.10
☐ ☐	176	Ron Hextall (G), Pha.	.20
☐ ☐	177	Rick Tocchet, Pha.	.10
☐ ☐	178	Ron Sutter, Pha.	.10
☐ ☐	179	Per-Erik Eklund, Pha.	.10
☐ ☐	180	Tim Kerr, Pha. (NYR)	.10
☐ ☐	181	Kjell Samuelsson, Pha.	.10
☐ ☐	182	Mark Howe, Pha.	.20
☐ ☐	183	Jaromir Jagr, Pgh.	.75
☐ ☐	184	Mark Recchi, Pgh.	.20
☐ ☐	185	Kevin Stevens, Pgh.	.10
☐ ☐	186	Tom Barrasso (G), Pgh.	.20
☐ ☐	187	Bob Errey, Pgh.	.10
☐ ☐	188	Ron Francis, Pgh.	.20
☐ ☐	189	Phil Bourque, Pgh.	.10
☐ ☐	190	Paul Coffey, Pgh.	.20
☐ ☐	191	Joe Mullen, Pgh.	.10
☐ ☐	192	Bryan Trottier, Pgh.	.20
☐ ☐	193	Larry Murphy, Pgh.	.20
☐ ☐	194	Mario Lemieux, Pgh.	1.00
☐ ☐	195	Scott Young, Pgh.	.10
☐ ☐	196	Owen Nolan, Que.	.20
☐ ☐	197	Mats Sundin, Que.	.35
☐ ☐	198	Curtis Leschyshyn, Que.	.10
☐ ☐	199	Joe Sakic, Que.	.65
☐ ☐	200	Bryan Fogarty, Que.	.10
☐ ☐	201	Stéphane Morin, Que.	.10
☐ ☐	202	Ron Tugnutt (G), Que.	.10
☐ ☐	203	Craig Wolanin, Que.	.10
☐ ☐	204	Steven Finn, Que.	.10
☐ ☐	205	Tony Hrkac, Que., (S.J.)	.10
☐ ☐	206	Randy Velischek, Que.	.10
☐ ☐	**207**	**Alexei Gusarov, Que., RC**	**.10**
☐ ☐	208	Scott Pearson, Que.	.10
☐ ☐	209	Dan Quinn, Stl.	.10
☐ ☐	210	Garth Butcher, Stl.	.10
☐ ☐	211	Rod Brind'Amour, Stl.	.20
☐ ☐	212	Jeff Brown, Stl.	.10
☐ ☐	213	Vincent Riendeau (G), Stl.	.10
☐ ☐	214	Paul Cavallini, Stl.	.10
☐ ☐	215	Brett Hull, Stl.	.35
☐ ☐	216	Scott Stevens, Stl.	.10
☐ ☐	217	Rich Sutter, Stl.	.10
☐ ☐	218	Gino Cavallini, Stl.	.10
☐ ☐	219	Adam Oates, Stl.	.20
☐ ☐	220	Ron Wilson, Stl.	.10
☐ ☐	221	Bob Bassen, Stl.	.10
☐ ☐	222	Peter Ing (G), Tor.	.10
☐ ☐	223	Daniel Marois, Tor.	.10
☐ ☐	224	Vincent Damphousse, Tor.	.20
☐ ☐	225	Wendel Clark, Tor.	.20

☐☐ 226 Todd Gill, Tor. .10
☐☐ 227 Peter Zezel, Tor. .10
☐☐ 228 Bob Rouse, Tor. .10
☐☐ 229 David Reid, Tor. .10
☐☐ 230 Dave Ellett, Tor. .10
☐☐ 231 Gary Leeman, Tor. .10
☐☐ 232 Rob Ramage, Tor. (Min.) .10
☐☐ 233 Mike Krushelnyski, Tor. .10
☐☐ 234 Tom Fergus, Tor. .10
☐☐ 235 Petr Nedved, Van. .10
☐☐ 236 Trevor Linden, Van. .20
☐☐ 237 Dave Capuano, Van. .10
☐☐ 238 Troy Gamble (G), Van. .10
☐☐ 239 Robert Kron, Van. .10
☐☐ 240 Jyrki Lumme, Van. .10
☐☐ 241 Cliff Ronning, Van. .10
☐☐ 242 Sergio Momesso, Van. .10
☐☐ 243 Greg Adams, Van. .10
☐☐ 244 Tom Kurvers, Van. (NYI.) .10
☐☐ 245 Geoff Courtnall, Van. .10
☐☐ 246 Igor Larionov, Van. .20
☐☐ 247 Doug Lidster, Van. .10
☐☐ 248 Calle Johansson, Wsh. .10
☐☐ 249 Kevin Hatcher, Wsh. .10
☐☐ 250 Al Iafrate, Wsh. .10
☐☐ 251 John Druce, Wsh. .10
☐☐ 252 Michal Pivonka, Wsh. .10
☐☐ 253 Stephen Leach, Wsh. (Bos.) .10
☐☐ 254 Mike Ridley, Wsh. .10
☐☐ 255 Mike Lalor, Wsh. .10
☐☐ 256 Kelly Miller, Wsh. .10
☐☐ 257 Don Beaupré (G), Wsh. .10
☐☐ 258 Dino Ciccarelli, Wsh. .20
☐☐ 259 Rod Langway, Wsh. .10
☐☐ 260 Dimitri Khristich, Wsh. .10
☐☐ 261 Teppo Numminen, Wpg. .10
☐☐ 262 Pat Elynuik, Wpg. .10
☐☐ 263 Danton Cole, Wpg. .10
☐☐ 264 Fredrik Olausson, Wpg. .10
☐☐ 265 Ed Olczyk, Wpg. .10
☐☐ 266 Bob Essensa (G), Wpg. .10
☐☐ 267 Phil Housley, Wpg. .10
☐☐ 268 Shawn Cronin, Wpg. .10
☐☐ 269 Paul MacDermid, Wpg. .10
☐☐ 270 Mark Osborne, Wpg. .10
☐☐ 271 Thomas Steen, Wpg. .10
☐☐ 272 Brent Ashton, Wpg. .10
☐☐ 273 Randy Carlyle, Wpg. .10
☐☐ 274 AS: Theoren Fleury, Cgy. .20
☐☐ 275 AS: Al MacInnis, Cgy. .20
☐☐ 276 AS: Gary Suter, Cgy. .10
☐☐ 277 AS: Mike Vernon (G), Cgy. .20
☐☐ 278 AS: Chris Chelios, Chi. .20
☐☐ 279 AS: Steve Larmer, Chi. .20
☐☐ 280 AS: Jeremy Roenick, Chi. .20
☐☐ 281 AS: Steve Yzerman, Det. .35
☐☐ 282 AS: Mark Messier, Edm. .20
☐☐ 283 AS: Bill Ranford (G), Edm. .20
☐☐ 284 AS: Steve Smith, Edm. .10
☐☐ 285 AS: Wayne Gretzky, L.A. .75
☐☐ 286 AS: Luc Robitaille, L.A. .20
☐☐ 287 AS: Tomas Sandström, L.A. .10
☐☐ 288 AS: Dave Gagner, Min. .10
☐☐ 289 AS: Bobby Smith, Min. .10
☐☐ 290 AS: Brett Hull, Stl. .20
☐☐ 291 AS: Adam Oates, Stl. .20
☐☐ 292 AS: Scott Stevens, Stl. .10
☐☐ 293 AS: Vincent Damphousse, Tor. .20
☐☐ 294 AS: Trevor Linden, Van. .20
☐☐ 295 AS: Phil Housley, Wpg. .10
☐☐ 296 AS: Ray Bourque, Bos. .20
☐☐ 297 AS: David Christian, Bos. .10
☐☐ 298 AS: Garry Galley, Bos. .10
☐☐ 299 AS: Andy Moog (G), Bos. .20
☐☐ 300 AS: Cam Neely, Bos. .20
☐☐ 301 AS: Uwe Krupp, Buf. .10
☐☐ 302 AS: John Cullen, Hfd. .10
☐☐ 303 AS: Pat Verbeek, Hfd. .10
☐☐ 304 AS: Patrick Roy (G), Mtl. .50
☐☐ 305 AS: Denis Savard, Mtl. .20
☐☐ 306 AS: Brian Skrudland, Mtl. .10
☐☐ 307 AS: John MacLean, N.J. .10
☐☐ 308 AS: Pat LaFontaine, NYI .20
☐☐ 309 AS: Brian Leetch, NYR .20
☐☐ 310 AS: Darren Turcotte, NYR .10
☐☐ 311 AS: Rick Tocchet, Pha. .10
☐☐ 312 AS: Paul Coffey, Pgh. .20
☐☐ 313 AS: Mark Recchi, Pgh. .20
☐☐ 314 AS: Kevin Stevens, Pgh. .10
☐☐ 315 AS: Joe Sakic, Que. .35
☐☐ 316 AS: Kevin Hatcher, Wsh. .10
☐☐ 317 AS: Guy Lafleur, Que. .35
☐☐ 318 Mario Lemieux, Pgh. .50
☐☐ 319 AW: Pittsburgh Penguins .50
☐☐ 320 AW: Brett Hull, Stl. .20
☐☐ 321 AW: Ed Belfour (G), Chi. .20
☐☐ 322 AW: Ray Bourque, Bos. .20
☐☐ 323 AW: Dirk Graham, Chi. .10
☐☐ 324 AW: Wayne Gretzky, L.A. .75
☐☐ 325 AW: Dave Taylor, L.A. .10
☐☐ 326 AW: Brett Hull, Stl. .20
☐☐ 327 Brian Hayward (G), S.J. .10
☐☐ 328 Neil Wilkinson, S.J. .10
☐☐ 329 Craig Coxe, S.J. .10
☐☐ 330 Rob Zettler, S.J. .10
☐☐ 331 Jeff Hackett (G), S.J. .10
☐☐ 332 Phantom Joe Malone .20
☐☐ 333 Georges Vézina, The First Ironman .20
☐☐ 334 The Modern Arena .10
☐☐ 335 Ace Bailey Benefit Game .10
☐☐ 336 Howie Morenz, The Stratford Streak .20
☐☐ 337 M. Richard/ E. Lach/ T. Blake .50
☐☐ 338 J. Primeau/ H. Jackson/ C. Conacher .20
☐☐ 339 Before the Zamboni .10
☐☐ 340 Bill Barilko, The End of the Innocence .20
☐☐ 341 Jacques Plante, The Innovator .20
☐☐ 342 Arena Designs, Separate and Not Equal .10
☐☐ 343 Terry Sawchuk, The True Mr. Zero .20
☐☐ 344 Gordie Howe, Mr. Hockey .25
☐☐ 345 Guy Carbonneau, Mtl. .10
☐☐ 346 Stephen Leach, Bos. .10
☐☐ 347 Peter Douris, Bos. .10
☐☐ 348 David Reid, Bos. .10
☐☐ 349 Bob Carpenter, Bos. .10
☐☐ 350 Stéphane Quintal, Bos. .10
☐☐ 351 Barry Pederson, Bos. .10
☐☐ 352 Brent Ashton, Bos. .10
☐☐ 353 Vladimir Ruzicka, Bos. .10
☐☐ 354 Brad Miller, Buf. .10
☐☐ 355 Rob Ray, Buf. .10
☐☐ 356 Colin Patterson, Buf. .10
☐☐ 357 Gord Donnelly, Buf. .10
☐☐ 358 Pat LaFontaine, Buf. .20
☐☐ 359 Randy Wood, Buf. .10
☐☐ 360 Randy Hillier, Buf. .10
☐☐ 361 Robert Reichel, Cgy. .10
☐☐ 362 Ron Stern, Cgy. .10
☐☐ 363 Ric Nattress Cgy. (Tor.) .10
☐☐ 364 Tim Sweeney, Cgy. .10
☐☐ 365 Marc Habscheid, Cgy. .10
☐☐ 366 Tim Hunter, Cgy. .10
☐☐ 367 Rick Wamsley (G), Cgy. (Tor.) .10
☐☐ 368 Frankisek Musil, Cgy. .10
☐☐ 369 Mike Hudson, Chi. .10
☐☐ 370 Steve Smith, Chi. .10
☐☐ 371 Keith Brown, Chi. .10
☐☐ 372 Greg Gilbert, Chi. .10
☐☐ 373 John Tonelli, Chi. .10
☐☐ 374 Brent Sutter, Chi. .10
☐☐ 375 Brad Lauer, Chi. .10
☐☐ 376 Alan Kerr, Det. .10
☐☐ 377 Brad McCrimmon, Det. .10
☐☐ 378 Brad Marsh, Det. .10
☐☐ 379 Brent Fedyk, Det. .10
☐☐ 380 Ray Sheppard, Det. .10
☐☐ 381 Vincent Damphousse, Edm. .20
☐☐ 382 Craig Muni, Edm. .10
☐☐ 383 Scott Mellanby, Edm. .10
☐☐ 384 Geoff Smith, Edm. .10
☐☐ 385 Kelly Buchberger, Edm. .10
☐☐ 286 Bernie Nicholls, Edm. .10
☐☐ 387 Luke Richardson, Edm. .10
☐☐ 388 Peter Ing (G), Edm. .10
☐☐ 389 Dave Manson, Edm. .10
☐☐ 390 Mark Hunter, Hfd. .10
☐☐ **391 Jim McKenzie, Hfd., RC .10**
☐☐ 392 Randy Cunneyworth, Hfd. .10
☐☐ 393 Murray Craven, Hfd. .10
☐☐ 394 Mikael Andersson, Hfd. .10
☐☐ 395 Andrew Cassels, Hfd. .10
☐☐ 396 Randy Ladouceur, Hfd. .10
☐☐ 397 Marc Bergevin, Hfd. .10
☐☐ 398 Brian Benning, Hfd. .10
☐☐ **399 Mike Donnelly, L.A., RC .10**
☐☐ 400 Charlie Huddy, L.A. .10
☐☐ 401 John McIntyre, L.A. .10
☐☐ 402 Jay Miller, L.A. .10
☐☐ 403 Randy Gilhen, L.A. .10
☐☐ 404 Stewart Gavin, Min. .10
☐☐ 405 Mike Craig, Min. .10
☐☐ 406 Brian Glynn, Min. .10
☐☐ 407 Rob Ramage, Min. .10
☐☐ 408 Chris Dahlquist, Min. .10
☐☐ 409 Basil McRae, Min. .10
☐☐ 410 Todd Elik, Min. .10
☐☐ 411 Craig Ludwig, Min. .10
☐☐ 412 Kirk Muller, Mtl. .10
☐☐ 413 Shayne Corson, Mtl. .20
☐☐ 414 Brent Gilchrist, Mtl. .10
☐☐ **415 Mario Roberge, Mtl., RC .10**
☐☐ 416 Sylvain Turgeon, Mtl. .10
☐☐ 417 Alain Côté, Mtl. .10
☐☐ 418 Donald Dufresne, Mtl. .10
☐☐ 419 Todd Ewen, Mtl. .10
☐☐ 420 Stéphane Richer, N.J. .10
☐☐ 421 David Maley, N.J. .10
☐☐ 422 Randy McKay, N.J. .10
☐☐ 423 Scott Stevens, N.J. .20
☐☐ 424 Jon Morris, N.J. .10
☐☐ 425 Claude Vilgrain, N.J. .10
☐☐ 426 Laurie Boschman, N.J. .10
☐☐ 427 Pat Conacher, N.J. .10
☐☐ 428 Tom Kurvers, NYI. .10
☐☐ 429 Joe Reekie, NYI. .10
☐☐ 430 Rob DiMaio, NYI. .10
☐☐ 431 Tom Fitzgerald, NYI. .10
☐☐ 432 Ken Baumgartner, NYI. .10
☐☐ 433 Pierre Turgeon, NYI. .20
☐☐ 434 Dave McLlwain, NYI. .10
☐☐ 435 Benoît Hogue, NYI. .10
☐☐ 436 Uwe Krupp, NYI. .10
☐☐ 437 Adam Creighton, NYI. .10
☐☐ 438 Steve Thomas, NYI. .10
☐☐ 439 Mark Messier, NYR. .35
☐☐ 440 Tie Domi, NYR. .10
☐☐ 441 Sergei Nemchinov, NYR. .10
☐☐ 442 Mark Hardy, NYR. .10
☐☐ 443 Adam Graves, NYR. .10
☐☐ 444 Jeff Beukeboom, NYR. .10
☐☐ 445 Kris King, NYR. .10
☐☐ 446 Tim Kerr, NYR. .10
☐☐ 447 John Vanbiesbrouck (G), NYR. .50
☐☐ 448 Steve Duchesne, Pha. .10
☐☐ 449 Steve Kasper, Pha. .10
☐☐ 450 Ken Wregget (G), Pha. .10
☐☐ 451 Kevin Dineen, Pha. .10
☐☐ 452 Dave Brown, Pha. .10
☐☐ 453 Rod Brind'Amour, Pha. .20
☐☐ 454 Jiri Latal, Pha. .10
☐☐ 455 Tony Horacek, Pha. .10
☐☐ **456 Brad Jones, Pha., RC .10**
☐☐ 457 Paul Stanton, Pgh. .10
☐☐ 458 Gord Roberts, Pha. .10
☐☐ 459 Ulf Samuelsson, Pha. .10
☐☐ **460 Ken Priestlay, Pha., RC .10**
☐☐ 461 Jiri Hrdina, Pha. .10
☐☐ 462 Mikhail Tatarinov, Que. .10
☐☐ 463 Mike Hough, Que. .10
☐☐ 464 Don Barber, Que. .10
☐☐ **465 Greg Smyth, Que., RC .10**
☐☐ 466 Doug Smail, Que. .10
☐☐ 467 Mike McNeill, Que. .10
☐☐ 468 John Kordic, Que. .10
☐☐ 469 Greg Paslawski, Que. .10
☐☐ 470 Herb Raglan, Que. .10
☐☐ 471 David Christian, Stl. .10
☐☐ 472 Murray Baron, Stl. .10
☐☐ 473 Curtis Joseph (G), Stl. .35
☐☐ 474 Rick Zombo, Stl. .10
☐☐ 475 Brendan Shanahan, Stl. .35
☐☐ 476 Ron Sutter, Stl. .10
☐☐ 477 Mario Marois, Stl. (Wpg.) .10
☐☐ 478 Doug Wilson, S.J. .20
☐☐ 479 Kelly Kisio, S.J. .10
☐☐ 480 Bob McGill, S.J. .10

	No.	Player	
□ □	**481**	**Perry Anderson, S.J., RC**	**.10**
□ □	482	Brian Lawton, S.J.	.10
□ □	483	Neil Wilkinson, S.J.	.10
□ □	484	Ken Hammond, S.J.	.10
□ □	**485**	**David Bruce, S.J., RC**	**.10**
□ □	486	Steven Bozek, S.J.	.10
□ □	487	Perry Berezan, S.J.	.10
□ □	488	Wayne Presley, S.J.	.10
□ □	489	Brian Bradley, Tor.	.10
□ □	**490**	**Darryl Shannon, Tor., RC**	**.10**
□ □	491	Lucien DeBlois, Tor.	.10
□ □	492	Michel Petit, Tor. (Cgy.)	.10
□ □	493	Claude Loiselle, Tor.	.10
□ □	494	Grant Fuhr (G), Tor.	.20
□ □	495	Craig Berube, Tor. (Cgy.)	.10
□ □	496	Mike Bullard, Tor.	.10
□ □	497	Jim Sandlak, Van.	.10
□ □	498	Dana Murzyn, Van.	.10
□ □	499	Garry Valk, Van.	.10
□ □	500	Andrew McBain, Van.	.10
□ □	501	Kirk McLean (G), Van.	.20
□ □	502	Gerald Diduck, Van.	.10
□ □	503	Dave Babych, Van.	.10
□ □	504	Ryan Walter, Van.	.10
□ □	505	Gino Odjick, Van.	.10
□ □	506	Dale Hunter, Wsh.	.10
□ □	507	Tim Bergland, Wsh.	.10
□ □	508	Alan May, Wsh.	.10
□ □	509	Jim Hrivnak (G), Wsh.	.10
□ □	510	Randy Burridge, Wsh.	.10
□ □	511	Peter Bondra, Wsh.	.10
□ □	512	Sylvain Côté, Wsh.	.10
□ □	513	Nick Kypreos, Wsh.	.10
□ □	514	Troy Murray, Wpg.	.10
□ □	515	Darrin Shannon, Wpg.	.10
□ □	516	Bryan Erickson, Wpg.	.10
□ □	517	Petri Skriko, Wpg.	.10
□ □	518	Mike Eagles, Wpg.	.10
□ □	519	Mike Hartman, Wpg.	.10
□ □	**520**	**Bob Beers, Bos., RC**	**.10**
□ □	**521**	**Matt DelGuidice (G), Bos., RC**	**.10**
□ □	**522**	**Chris Winnes, Bos., RC**	**.10**
□ □	523	Brad May, Buf.	.10
□ □	524	Donald Audette, Buf.	.10
□ □	**525**	**Kevin Haller, Buf., RC**	**.10**
□ □	**526**	**Martin Simard, Cgy., RC**	**.10**
□ □	**527**	**Tomas Forslund, Cgy., RC**	**.10**
□ □	**528**	**Mark Osiecki, Cgy., RC**	**.10**
□ □	**529**	**Dominik Hasek (G), Chi.. RC**	**2.00**
□ □	530	Jimmy Waite (G), Chi.	.10
□ □	**531**	**Nicklas Lidström, Det., RC, Err. (Niklas)**	**.35**
□ □	532	Martin Lapointe, Det.	.10
□ □	**533**	**Vladimir Konstantinov, Det., RC**	**.25**
□ □	**534**	**Josef Beranek, Edm., RC**	**.10**
□ □	**535**	**Louie DeBrusk, Edm., RC**	**.10**
□ □	**536**	**Geoff Sanderson, Hfd., RC**	**.50**
□ □	**537**	**Mark Greig, Hfd., RC**	**.10**
□ □	**538**	**Michel Picard, Hfd., RC**	**.10**
□ □	**539**	**Chris Tancill, Hfd. (Det.), RC,**	**.10**
□ □	**540**	**Peter Ahola, L.A., RC**	**.10**
□ □	**541**	**François Breault, L.A., RC**	**.10**
□ □	542	Darryl Sydor, L.A.	.10
□ □	543	Derian Hatcher, Min.	.20
□ □	**544**	**Marc Bureau, Min., RC**	**.10**
□ □	**545**	**John LeClair, Mtl., RC**	**1.50**
□ □	**546**	**Paul DiPietro, Mtl., RC**	**.10**
□ □	547	Scott Niedermayer, N.J., Err. (Neid.)	.20
□ □	**548**	**Kevin Todd, N.J., RC**	**.10**
□ □	**549**	**Doug Weight, NYR., RC**	**.60**
□ □	**550**	**Tony Amonte, NYR., RC**	**.60**
□ □	**551**	**Corey Foster, Pha., RC**	**.10**
□ □	**552**	**Dominic Roussel (G), Pha., RC**	**.10**
□ □	**553**	**Dan Kordic, Pha., RC**	**.10**
□ □	**554**	**Jim Paek, Pgh., RC**	**.10**
□ □	555	Kip Miller, Que.	.10
□ □	**556**	**Claude Lapointe. Que., RC**	**.10**
□ □	557	Nelson Emerson, Stl.	.10
□ □	558	Pat Falloon, S.J.	.10
□ □	**559**	**Pat MacLeod, S.J., RC**	**.10**
□ □	**560**	**Rick Lessard, S.J., RC**	**.10**
□ □	**561**	**Link Gaetz, S.J., RC**	**.10**
□ □	**562**	**Rob Pearson, Tor., RC**	**.10**
□ □	**563**	**Alexander Godynyuk, Tor. (Cgy.), RC**	**.10**
□ □	564	Pavel Bure, Van.	1.00
□ □	**565**	**Russ Romaniuk, Wpg., RC**	**.10**
□ □	566	Stu Barnes, Wpg.	.10
□ □	567	Ray Bourque, Bos.	.20
□ □	568	Mike Ramsey, Buf.	.10
□ □	569	Joe Nieuwendyk, Cgy.	.10
□ □	570	Dirk Graham, Chi.	.10
□ □	571	Steve Yzerman, Det.	.35
□ □	572	Kevin Lowe, Edm.	.10
□ □	573	Randy Ladouceur, Hfd.	.10
□ □	574	Wayne Gretzky, L.A.	.75
□ □	575	Mark Tinordi, Min.	.10
□ □	576	Guy Carbonneau, Mtl.	.10
□ □	577	Bruce Driver, N.J.	.10
□ □	578	Pat Flatley, NYI.	.10
□ □	579	Mark Messier, NYR.	.20
□ □	580	Rick Tocchet, Pha.	.10
□ □	581	Mario Lemieux, Pgh.	.50
□ □	582	Mike Hough, Que.	.10
□ □	583	Garth Butcher, Stl.	.10
□ □	584	Doug Wilson, S.J.	.10
□ □	585	Wendel Clark, Tor.	.20
□ □	586	Trevor Linden, Van.	.20
□ □	587	Rod Langway, Wsh.	.10
□ □	588	Troy Murray, Wpg.	.10
□ □	589	Montréal Canadiens Practice Outdoors	.10
□ □	590	Shape Up or Ship Out	.10
□ □	591	Boston Bruins Cartoon	.10
□ □	592	Opening Night at Maple Leaf Gardens	.10
□ □	593	Rod Gilbert	.20
□ □	594	Phil Esposito	.20
□ □	595	Dale Tallon	.10
□ □	596	Gilbert Perreault	.20
□ □	597	Bernie Federko	.20
□ □	598	History of the HNL All-Star Game	.10
□ □	599	Patrick Roy (G), Mtl.	.50
□ □	600	Ed Belfour (G), Chi.	.20
□ □	601	Don Beaupré (G), Wsh.	.10
□ □	602	Bob Essensa (G), Wpg.	.10
□ □	603	Kirk McLean (G), Van., Error	..20
□ □	604	Mike Gartner, NYR.	.20
□ □	605	Jeremy Roenick, Chi.	.20
□ □	606	Rob Brown, Hfd.	.10
□ □	607	Ulf Dahlen, Min.	.10
□ □	608	Paul Ysebaert, Det.	.10
□ □	609	Brad McCrimmon, Det.	.10
□ □	610	Nicklas Lidström, Det.	.20
□ □	611	Kelly Miller, Wsh.	.10
□ □	612	Jim Kyte, Cgy., Hockey is For Everyone	.10
□ □	613	Patrick Roy (G), Mtl., Study Hard	.50
□ □	614	Alan May, Wsh., Stay in School	.10
□ □	615	Kelly Miller, Wsh., Get Involved	.10

COLLECTOR CARDS INSERT SET

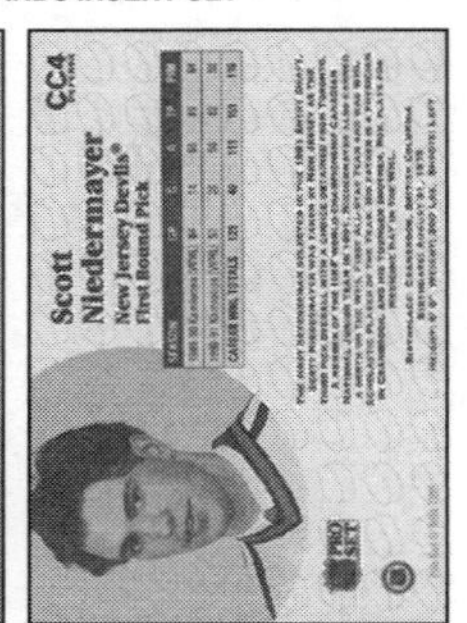

These inserts have two versions: an English (1-9) and a French issue (1-2/5-9).

Insert Set (9 cards): 35.00
French Insert Set (7 cards): 15.00

	No.	Player	English	French
□ □	CC1	1991 Draft Entry	.75	.75
□ □	CC2	The Mask	6.00	6.00
□	CC3	Pat Falloon	7.00	—
□	CC4	Scott Niedermayer	12.00	—
□ □	CC5	Wayne Gretzky, L.A.	5.00	5.00
□ □	CC6	Brett Hull, Stl.	2.00	2.00
□ □	CC7	Adam Oates, Stl.	1.50	1.50
□ □	CC8	Mark Recchi, Pgh.	1.00	1.00
□ □	CC9	John Cullen, Hfd.	.75	.75

AUTOGRAPHED CARD

Patrick Roy's first autograph (#125, serial numbers 1-1000) was inserted into Series One French packs while his second autograph (#599, serial numbered 1001-2000) was inserted into Series Two French packs. The McLean autograph was inserted into English packs.

	No.	Player	NRMT-MT
□	125	Patrick Roy (#/1,000)	250.00
□	501	Kirk McLean	40.00
□	599	Patrick Roy (#/1,000)	250.00

PLAYER OF THE MONTH

Imprint: Pro Set NHL 1991
Complete Set (7 cards): 60.00

	No.	Player	NRMT-MT
□	P1	October: Kirk McLean (G), Van.	10.00
□	P2	November: Kevin Stevens, Pgh.	5.00
□	P3	December: Mario Lemieux, Pgh.	30.00
□	P4	January: Pat LaFontaine, NYI	10.00
□	P5	January: Andy Moog (G), Bos.	10.00
□	P6	February: Luc Robitaille, L,A,	10.00

PRO SET GAZETTE COLLECTIBLES

The Gazette was published by Pro Set as a product information magazine. Sample packs produced specially for the magazine, were inserted into the Gazette with each mailing. These packs could contain two types of cards: (1) Promotional which are regular issue cards from the various Pro Set products and (2) Pro Set Gazette cards.

Imprint: Pro Set Inc. NHL 1992 NHLPA 1992

	No.	Player	NRMT-MT
□	2	Patrick Roy (G), Mtl.	5.00

PRO SET HOLOGRAM

These cards are serial numbered of 10,000.

	Player	NRMT-MT
□	Holographic 75th Anniversary Logo	70.00

1991 - 92 PRO SET PLATINUM

Imprint: Series One: Pro Set NHL & NHLPA 1991
Series Two: PRO SET NHL AND NHLPA 1992
Complete Set (300) 12.00
Common Player: .10

	No.	Player	NRMT-MT
□	1	Cam Neely, Bos.	.20
□	2	Ray Bourque, Bos.	.35
□	3	Craig Janney, Bos.	.10
□	4	Andy Moog (G), Bos.	.20
□	5	Dave Poulin, Bos.	.10
□	6	Ken Hodge, Bos.	.10
□	7	Glen Wesley, Bos.	.10
□	8	Dave Andreychuk, Buf.	.20
□	9	Daren Puppa (G), Buf.	.10
□	10	Pierre Turgeon, Buf.	.20
□	11	Dale Hawerchuk, Buf.	.20
□	12	Doug Bodger, Buf.	.10
□	13	Mike Ramsey, Buf.	.10
□	14	Alexander Mogilny, Buf.	.20
□	15	Sergei Makarov, Cgy.	.10
□	16	Theoren Fleury, Cgy.	.20
□	17	Joel Otto, Cgy.	.10
□	18	Joe Nieuwendyk, Cgy.	.20
□	19	Al MacInnis, Cgy.	.20
□	20	Gary Suter, Cgy.	.10
□	21	Mike Vernon (G), Cgy.	.20
□	22	John Tonelli, Chi.	.10
□	23	Dirk Graham, Chi.	.10
□	24	Jeremy Roenick, Chi.	.20
□	25	Chris Chelios, Chi.	.25
□	26	Ed Belfour (G), Chi.	.25

	No.	Card	Price
☐	27	Steve Smith, Chi.	.10
☐	28	Steve Larmer, Chi.	.20
☐	29	Johan Garpenlov, Det.	.10
☐	30	Sergei Fedorov, Det.	.35
☐	31	Tim Cheveldae (G), Det.	.10
☐	32	Steve Yzerman, Det.	.75
☐	33	Jimmy Carson, Det.	.10
☐	34	Bob Probert, Det.	.10
☐	35	Vincent Damphousse, Edm.	.20
☐	36	Bill Ranford (G), Edm.	.20
☐	37	Petr Klima, Edm.	.10
☐	38	Kevin Lowe, Edm.	.10
☐	39	Esa Tikkanen, Edm.	.10
☐	40	Craig Simpson, Edm.	.10
☐	41	Peter Ing (G), Edm.	.10
☐	42	Rob Brown, Hfd.	.10
☐	43	Bobby Holik, Hfd.	.10
☐	44	Pat Verbeek, Hfd.	.10
☐	45	Brad Shaw, Hfd.	.10
☐	46	Kevin Dineen, Hfd.	.10
☐	47	Zarley Zalapski, Hfd.	.10
☐	48	Jari Kurri, L.A.	.20
☐	49	Tony Granato, L.A.	.10
☐	50	Luc Robitaille, L.A.	.20
☐	51	Rob Blake, L.A.	.20
☐	52	Wayne Gretzky, L.A.	1.50
☐	53	Tomas Sandström, L.A.	.10
☐	54	Kelly Hrudey (G), L.A.	.10
☐	55	Mike Modano, Min.	.20
☐	56	Jon Casey, Min.	.10
☐	57	Todd Elik, Min.	.10
☐	58	Mark Tinordi, Min.	.10
☐	59	Brian Bellows, Min.	.10
☐	60	Dave Gagner, Min.	.10
☐	61	Patrick Roy (G), Mtl.	1.00
☐	62	Russ Courtnall, Mtl.	.10
☐	63	Guy Carbonneau, Mtl.	.10
☐	64	Denis Savard, Mtl.	.20
☐	65	Petr Svoboda, Mtl.	.10
☐	66	Kirk Muller, Mtl.	.10
☐	67	Stéphane Richer, N.J.	.10
☐	68	Chris Terreri (G), N.J.	.10
☐	69	Bruce Driver, N.J.	.10
☐	70	John MacLean, N.J.	.10
☐	71	Patrik Sundstrom, N.J.	.10
☐	72	Scott Stevens, N.J.	.10
☐	73	Glenn Healy (G), NYI.	.10
☐	74	Brent Sutter, NYI.	.10
☐	75	David Volek, NYI.	.10
☐	76	Ray Ferraro, NYI.	.10
☐	77	Patrick Flatley, NYI.	.10
☐	78	Jeff Norton, NYI.	.10
☐	79	Brian Leetch, NYR.	.20
☐	80	Tim Kerr, NYR.	.10
☐	81	Mark Messier, NYR.	.35
☐	82	James Patrick, NYR.	.10
☐	83	Mike Richter (G), NYR.	.20
☐	84	Mike Gartner, NYR.	.20
☐	85	Mike Ricci, Pha.	.10
☐	86	Steve Duchesne, Pha.	.10
☐	87	Ron Hextall (G), Pha.	.20
☐	88	Rick Tocchet, Pha.	.10
☐	89	Per-Erik Eklund, Pha.	.10
☐	90	Rod Brind'Amour, Pha.	.20
☐	91	Mario Lemieux, Pgh.	1.00
☐	92	Jaromir Jagr, Pgh.	.75
☐	93	Kevin Stevens, Pgh.	.10
☐	94	Paul Coffey, Pgh.	.20
☐	95	Ulf Samuelsson, Pgh.	.10
☐	96	Tom Barrasso (G), Pgh.	.20
☐	97	Mark Recchi, Pgh.	.20
☐	98	Ron Tugnutt (G), Que.	.10
☐	99	Mats Sundin, Que.	.35
☐	100	Stéphane Morin, Que.	.10
☐	101	Owen Nolan, Que.	.20
☐	102	Joe Sakic, Que.	.65
☐	103	Bryan Fogarty, Que.	.10
☐	104	Kelly Kisio, S.J.	.10
☐	105	Tony Hrkac, S.J.	.10
☐	106	Brian Mullen, S.J.	.10
☐	107	Doug Wilson, S.J.	.20
☐	108	Rich Sutter, Stl.	.10
☐	109	Brett Hull, Stl.	.35
☐	110	Dave Christian, Stl.	.10
☐	111	Brendan Shanahan, Stl.	.35

	No.	Card	Price
☐	112	Vincent Riendeau (G), Stl.	.10
☐	113	Adam Oates, Stl.	.20
☐	114	Jeff Brown, Stl.	.10
☐	115	Gary Leeman, Tor.	.10
☐	116	Dave Ellett, Tor.	.10
☐	117	Grant Fuhr (G), Tor.	.20
☐	118	Daniel Marois, Tor.	.10
☐	119	Mike Krushelnyski, Tor.	.10
☐	120	Wendel Clark, Tor.	.20
☐	121	Troy Gamble (G), Van.	.10
☐	122	Robert Kron, Van.	.10
☐	123	Geoff Courtnall, Van.	.10
☐	124	Trevor Linden, Van.	.20
☐	125	Greg Adams, Van.	.10
☐	126	Igor Larionov, Van.	.20
☐	127	Kevin Hatcher, Wsh.	.10
☐	128	Mike Ridley, Wsh.	.10
☐	129	John Druce, Wsh.	.10
☐	130	Al Iafrate, Wsh.	.10
☐	131	Dino Ciccarelli, Wsh.	.20
☐	132	Michal Pivonka, Wsh.	.10
☐	133	Fredrik Olausson, Wpg.	.10
☐	134	Ed Olczyk, Wpg.	.10
☐	135	Bob Essensa (G), Wpg.	.10
☐	136	Pat Elynuik, Wpg.	.10
☐	137	Phil Housley, Wpg.	.10
☐	138	Thomas Steen, Wpg.	.10
☐	139	Don Beaupré (G), Wsh.	.10
☐	140	Boston Bruins	.10
☐	141	Chicago Blackhawks	.10
☐	142	Los Angeles Kings (/b: Gretzky)	.35
☐	143	Minnesota North Stars	.10
☐	144	Pittsburgh Penguins	.25
☐	145	Boston Bruins	.10
☐	146	Chicago Black Hawks	.10
☐	147	Detroit Red Wings	.10
☐	148	Montréal Canadiens	.10
☐	149	New York Rangers	.10
☐	150	Toronto Maple Leafs	.10
☐	151	Stephen Leach, Bos.	.10
☐	152	Vladimir Ruzicka, Bos.	.10
☐	153	Don Sweeney, Bos.	.10
☐	154	Bob Carpenter, Bos.	.10
☐	155	Brent Ashton, Bos.	.10
☐	156	Gord Murphy, Bos.	.10
☐	157	Pat LaFontaine, Buf.	.20
☐	158	Randy Hillier, Buf.	.10
☐	159	Clint Malarchuk, Buf.	.10
☐	160	Randy Wood, Buf.	.10
☐	161	Gary Roberts, Cgy.	.20
☐	162	Gary Leeman, Cgy.	.10
☐	163	Robert Reichel, Cgy.	.20
☐	164	Brent Sutter, Chi.	.10
☐	165	Brian Noonan, Chi.	.10
☐	166	Michel Goulet, Chi.	.20
☐	167	Paul Ysebaert, Det.	.10
☐	168	Kevin Miller, Det.	.10
☐	169	Ray Sheppard, Det.	.10
☐	170	Brad McCrimmon, Det.	.10
☐	171	Joe Murphy, Edm.	.10
☐	172	Dave Manson, Edm.	.10
☐	173	Scott Mellanby, Edm.	.10
☐	174	Bernie Nicholls, Edm.	.10
☐	175	John Cullen, Hfd.	.10
☐	176	Marc Bergevin, Hfd.	.10
☐	177	Steve Konroyd, Hfd.	.10
☐	178	Kay Whitmore (G), Hfd.	.10
☐	179	Murray Craven, Hfd.	.10
☐	180	Mikael Andersson, Hfd.	.10
☐	181	Bob Kudelski, L.A.	.10
☐	182	Brian Benning, L.A.	.10
☐	183	Mike Donnelly, L.A.	.10
☐	184	Marty McSorley, L.A.	.10
☐	**185**	**Corey Millen, L.A., RC**	**.10**
☐	186	Ulf Dahlen, Min.	.10
☐	187	Brian Propp, Min.	.10
☐	188	Neal Broten, Min.	.10
☐	189	Mike Craig, Min.	.10
☐	190	Stéphan Lebeau, Mtl.	.10
☐	191	Mike Keane, Mtl.	.10
☐	192	Brent Gilchrist, Mtl.	.10
☐	193	Eric Desjardins, Mtl.	.20
☐	194	Peter Stastny, N.J.	.20
☐	195	Claude Vilgrain, N.J.	.10
☐	196	Claude Lemieux, N.J.	.10

	No.	Card	Price
☐	**197**	**Craig Billington (G), N.J., RC, Error (C. Terreri)**	**.10**
☐	198	Alexei Kasatonov, N.J.	.10
☐	199	Viacheslav Fetisov, N.J.	.20
☐	200	Benoît Hogue, NYI.	.10
☐	201	Derek King, NYI.	.10
☐	202	Uwe Krupp, NYI.	.10
☐	203	Steve Thomas, NYI.	.10
☐	204	John Ogrodnick, NYR.	.10
☐	205	Sergei Nemchinov, NYR.	.10
☐	206	Jeff Beukeboom, NYR.	.10
☐	207	Adam Graves, NYR.	.10
☐	208	Andrei Lomakin, Pha.	.10
☐	209	Dan Quinn, Pha.	.10
☐	210	Ken Wreggett (G), Pha.	.10
☐	211	Garry Galley, Pha.	.10
☐	212	Terry Carkner, Pha.	.10
☐	213	Larry Murphy, Pgh.	.20
☐	214	Ron Francis, Pgh.	.20
☐	215	Bob Errey, Pgh.	.10
☐	216	Bryan Trottier, Pgh.	.20
☐	217	Mike Hough, Que.	.10
☐	218	Mikhail Tatarinov, Que.	.10
☐	219	Jacques Cloutier, Que.	.10
☐	220	Greg Paslawski, Que.	.10
☐	**221**	**Alexei Gusarov, Que., RC**	**.10**
☐	222	Ron Sutter, Stl.	.10
☐	223	Garth Butcher, Stl.	.10
☐	224	Paul Cavallini, Stl.	.10
☐	225	Curtis Joseph (G), Stl.	.35
☐	226	Jeff Hackett (G), S.J.	.10
☐	**227**	**David Bruce, S.J., RC**	**.10**
☐	228	Wayne Presley, S.J.	.10
☐	229	Neil Wilkinson, S.J.	.10
☐	230	Dean Evason, S.J.	.10
☐	231	Brian Bradley, Tor.	.10
☐	232	Peter Zezel, Tor.	.10
☐	233	Mike Bullard, Tor.	.10
☐	234	Doug Gilmour, Tor.	.20
☐	235	Jamie Macoun, Tor.	.10
☐	236	Cliff Ronning, Van.	.10
☐	237	Jyrki Lumme, Van.	.10
☐	238	Tom Fergus, Van.	.10
☐	239	Kirk McLean (G), Van.	.20
☐	240	Sergio Momesso, Van.	.10
☐	241	Randy Burridge, Wsh.	.10
☐	242	Dimitri Khristich, Wsh.	.10
☐	243	Calle Johansson, Wsh.	.10
☐	244	Peter Bondra, Wsh.	.20
☐	245	Dale Hunter, Wsh.	.10
☐	246	Darrin Shannon, Wpg.	.10
☐	247	Troy Murray, Wpg.	.10
☐	248	Teppo Numminen, Wpg.	.10
☐	249	Donald Audette, Buf.	.10
☐	**250**	**Kevin Haller, Buf., RC**	**.10**
☐	**251**	**Alexander Godynyuk, Cgy., RC**	**.10**
☐	**252**	**Dominik Hasek (G), Chi., RC**	**2.00**
☐	**253**	**Nicklas Lidström, Det., RC**	**.35**
☐	**254**	**Vladimir Konstantinov, Det., RC**	**.25**
☐	**255**	**Josef Beranek, Edm., RC**	**.10**
☐	**256**	**Geoff Sanderson, Hfd., RC**	**.50**
☐	**257**	**Peter Ahola, L.A., RC**	**.10**
☐	258	Derian Hatcher, Min.	.20
☐	**259**	**John LeClair, Mtl., RC**	**1.50**
☐	**260**	**Kevin Todd, N.J., RC**	**.10**
☐	**261**	**Valeri Zelepukin, N.J., RC**	**.10**
☐	**262**	**Tony Amonte, NYR., RC**	**.75**
☐	**263**	**Doug Weight, NYR., RC**	**.75**
☐	**264**	**Claude Boivin, Pha., RC**	**.10**
☐	**265**	**Corey Foster, Pha., RC**	**.10**
☐	**266**	**Jim Paek, Pgh., RC**	**.10**
☐	**267**	**Claude Lapointe, Que., RC**	**.10**
☐	**268**	**Adam Foote, Que., RC**	**.20**
☐	269	Nelson Emerson, Stl.	.10
☐	270	Arturs Irbe (G), S.J.	.10
☐	271	Pat Falloon, S.J.	.10
☐	272	Pavel Bure, Van.	.50
☐	273	Stu Barnes, Wpg.	.10
☐	**274**	**Russ Romaniuk, Wpg., RC**	**.10**
☐	**275**	**Luciano Borsato, Wpg., RC**	**.10**
☐	276	Al MacInnis, Cgy.	.20
☐	277	Sergei Fedorov, Det.	.20
☐	278	Ray Bourque, Bos.	.20
☐	279	Mike Richter (G), NYR.	.20
☐	280	Campbell Conference	.10
☐	281	Wales Conference	.10

No.	Player	NRMT-MT
282	Brett Hull, Stl.	.20
283	Alexander Mogilny, Buf.	.20
284	Brian Leetch, NYR.	.20
285	Bob Essensa (G), Wpg.	.10
286	Derek King, NYI.	.10
287	Steve Larmer, Chi.	.20
288	Chris Terreri (G), N.J.	.10
289	Terry O'Reilly, Bos.	.10
290	Burton Cummins, Wpg.	.10
291	Marv Albert, NYR.	.10
292	Larry King, Wsh.	.10
293	Jim Kelly, Buf.	.20
294	David Wheaton, Min.	.10
295	Ralph Macchio, NYI.	.10
296	Rick Hansen, Van.	.10
297	Fred Rogers, Pgh.	.10
298	Gaetan Boucher, Que.	.10
299	Susan Saint James, Hfd.	.10
300	James Belushi, Chi.	.10

PLATINUM COLLECTOR CARDS

Insert Set (20 cards): **20.00**

No.	Player	NRMT-MT
PC1	John Vanbiesbrouck (G), NYR.	1.75
PC2	Pete Peeters (G), Pha.	.50
PC3	Tom Barrasso (G), Pgh.	.75
PC4	Wayne Gretzky, L.A.	6.00
PC5	Brett Hull, Stl.	1.50
PC6	Kelly Hrudey (G), L.A.	.50
PC7	Sergei Fedorov, Det.	1.50
PC8	Rob Blake, L.A.	.75
PC9	Ken Hodge, Bos.	.50
PC10	Eric Weinrich, N.J.	.50
PC11	Mike Gartner, NYR.	.75
PC12	Paul Coffey, Pgh.	.75
PC13	Bobby Smith, Min.	.50
PC14	Wayne Gretzy, L.A.	6.00
PC15	Michel Goulet, Chi.	.75
PC16	Mike Liut (G), Wsh.	.50
PC17	Brian Propp, Min.	.50
PC18	Denis Savard, Mtl.	.75
PC19	Bryan Trottier, Pgh.	1.00
PC20	Mark Messier, NYR.	1.50

1991 - 92 PRO SET THE PUCK

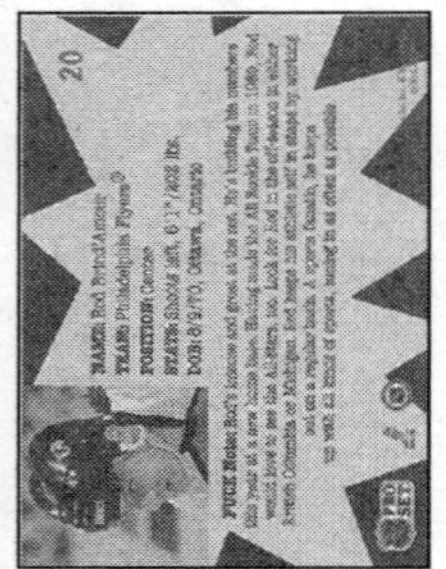

Three of 30 different cards were packaged with a chocolate, peanut and caramel candy bar.

Imprint: Pro Set Inc. NHL 1992 NHLPA 1992

Complete Set (30 cards): **25.00**

Promo	NRMT-MT
Andy Moog (G), Bos.	2.00
Kirk McLean (G), Van.	2.00
Pat Verbeek, Hfd.	1.50

No.	Player	NRMT-MT
1	Ray Bourque, Bos.	1.25
2	Andy Moog (G), Bos.	.25
3	Doug Bodger, Buf.	.10
4	Theoren Fleury, Cgy.	.75
5	Al MacInnis, Cgy.	.25
6	Jeremy Roenick, Chi.	.75
7	Tim Cheveldae (G), Det.	.10
8	Steve Yzerman, Det.	2.50
9	Craig Simpson, Edm.	.10
10	Patrick Verbeek, Hfd.	.10
11	Wayne Gretzky, L.A.	5.00
12	Luc Robitaille, L.A.	.25
13	Brian Bellows, Min.	.10
14	Patrick Roy (G), Mtl.	4.00
15	Guy Carbonneau, Mtl.	.10
16	Peter Stastny, N.J.	.25
17	Adam Creighton, NYI.	.10
18	Glenn Healy (G), NYI.	.10
19	Mark Messier, NYR.	1.25
20	Rod Brind'Amour, Pha.	.25
21	Paul Coffey, Pgh.	.25
22	Tom Barrasso (G), Pgh.	.25
23	Joe Sakic, Que.	2.00
24	Brett Hull, Stl.	1.25
25	Adam Oates, Stl.	.75
26	Kelly Kisio, S.J.	.10
27	Grant Fuhr, Tor.	.25
28	Kirk McLean (G), Van.	.25
29	Kevin Hatcher (G), Wsh.	.10
30	Phil Housley, Wpg.	.10

1991 - 92 RED ACE INTERNATIONAL RUSSIAN NHL STARS

There are 50,000 sets available.

Complete Set (17 cards with folder): **15.00**

Player	NRMT-MT
Pavel Bure	4.00
Evgeny Davydov	.50
Sergei Fedorov	3.00
Viacheslav Fetisov	1.50
Alexei Gusarov	.50
Valeri Kamensky	1.00
Alexei Kasatonov	.50
Ravil Khaidarov	.50
Vladimir Konstantinov	1.00
Igor Kravchuk	.50
Alexander Mogilny	2.00
Igor Larionov	1.50
Andrei Lomakin	.50
Sergei Makarov	1.00
Sergei Nemchinov	.50
Anatoli Semenov	.50
Mikhail Tatarinov	.50

1991 - 92 SCORE

PROMOTIONAL

These cards were handed out at the 12th National Sports Collectors Convention in Anaheim, the National Candy Wholesalers Convention and the Toronto Baseball Fanfest. Fanfest versions do not mention which event cards were given out at.

No.	Player	NSCC	NCWA	Toronto
1	Wayne Gretzky, L.A.	10.00	10.00	12.00
2	Brett Hull, Stl.	4.00	4.00	5.00
3	Ray Bourque, Bos.	4.00	4.00	5.00
4	Al MacInnis, Cgy.	1.00	1.00	1.50
5	Luc Robitaille, L.A.	1.50	1.50	2.00
6	Ed Belfour (G), Chi.	2.00	2.00	3.00
7	Steve Yzerman, Det.	6.00	6.00	8.00
8	Cam Neely, Bos.	1.50	1.50	2.00
9	Paul Coffey, Pgh.	2.00	2.00	3.00
10	Patrick Roy (G), Mtl.	8.00	8.00	10.00

CANADIAN PROMOTIONAL CARDS

The fronts of these cards are identical to the regular cards. The back contains two variations. First, the stats table is printed completely in blue while on the regular cards, the table is blue and red. Second, the Score logo is followed by the letters TM., instead of R on the regular cards.

Imprint: 1991 SCORE, PRINTED IN U.S.A.

Complete Set (6 cards): **35.00** **35.00**

No.	Player	English	Bilingual
1	Brett Hull, Stl.	4.00	4.00
2	Al MacInnis, Cgy.	2.00	2.00
3	Luc Robitaille, L.A.	2.00	2.00
50	Ray Bourque, Bos.	4.00	4.00
75	Patrick Roy (G), Mtl.	15.00	15.00
100	Wayne Gretzky, L.A.	25.00	25.00

SCORE CANADIAN

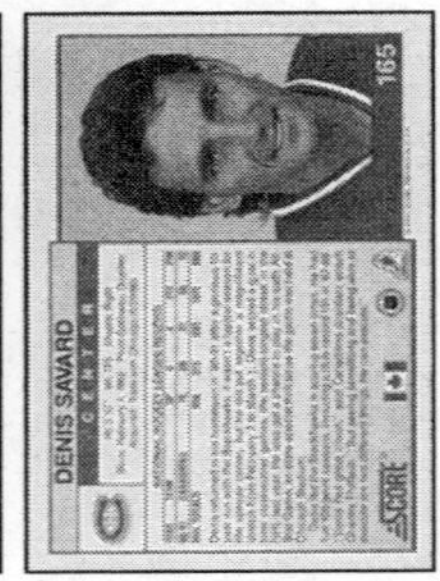

The Canadian issue has two versions: a card with English only text and a card with both French and English test. Series One cards (1-330) have a red border, while Series Two cards (331-660) have a blue border. Pricing for both versions are the same.

Imprint: © 1991 SCORE

Complete Set (660 cards): **14.00** **14.00**

Common Player: **.10** **.10**

No.	Player	NRMT-MT
1	Brett Hull, Stl.	.35
2	Al MacInnis, Cgy.	.10
3	Luc Robitaille, L.A.	.20
4	Pierre Turgeon, Buf.	.20
5	Brian Leetch, NYR.	.20
6	Cam Neely, Bos.	.20
7	John Cullen, Hfd.	.10
8	Trevor Linden, Van.	.20
9	Rick Tocchet, Pha.	.10
10	John Vanbiesbrouck (G), NYR.	.50
11	Steve Smith, Edm.	.10
12	Doug Smail, Min.	.10
13	Craig Ludwig, NYI.	.10
14	Paul Fenton, Cgy.	.10
15	Dirk Graham, Chi.	.10
16	Brad McCrimmon, Det.	.10
17	Dean Evason, Hfd.	.10
18	Fredrik Olausson, Wpg.	.10
19	Guy Carbonneau, Mtl.	.10
20	Kevin Hatcher, Wsh.	.10
21	Paul Ranheim, Cgy.	.10
22	Claude Lemieux, N.J.	.10
23	Vincent Riendeau (G), Stl.	.10
24	Garth Butcher, Stl.	.10
25	Joe Sakic, Que.	.50
26	Rick Vaive, Buf.	.10
27	Rob Blake, L.A.	.20
28	Mike Ricci, Pha.	.10
29	Patrick Flatley, NYI.	.10
30	Bill Ranford (G), Edm.	.20
31	Larry Murphy, Pgh.	.20
32	Bobby Smith, Min.	.10
33	Mike Krushelnyski, Tor.	.10
34	Gerard Gallant, Det.	.10
35	Doug Wilson, Chi.	.20
36	John Ogrodnick, NYR.	.10
37	Mikhail Tatarinov, Wsh.	.10
38	Doug Crossman, Det.	.10
39	Mark Osborne, Wpg.	.10
40	Scott Stevens, Stl.	.20
41	Ron Tugnutt (G), Que.	.10
42	Russ Courtnall, Mtl.	.10
43	Gord Murphy, Pha.	.10
44	Greg Adams, Van.	.10
45	Christian Ruuttu, Buf.	.10
46	Ken Daneyko, N.J.	.10
47	Glenn Anderson, Edm.	.10
48	Ray Ferraro, NYI.	.10
49	Tony Tanti, Buf.	.10
50	Ray Bourque, Bos.	.35
51	Sergei Makarov, Cgy.	.10
52	Jim Johnson, Min.	.10
53	Troy Murray, Chi.	.10
54	Shawn Burr, Det.	.10

	#	Card	Value
□ □	55	Peter Ing (G), Tor.	.10
□ □	56	Dale Hunter, Wsh.	.10
□ □	57	Tony Granato, L.A.	.10
□ □	58	Curtis Leschyshyn, Que.	.10
□ □	59	Brian Mullen, NYR.	.10
□ □	60	Ed Olczyk, Wpg.	.10
□ □	61	Mike Ramsey, Buf.	.10
□ □	62	Dan Quinn, Stl.	.10
□ □	63	Rich Sutter, Stl.	.10
□ □	64	Terry Carkner, Pha.	.10
□ □	65	Shayne Corson, Mtl.	.20
□ □	66	Peter Stastny, N.J.	.20
□ □	67	Craig Muni, Edm.	.10
□ □	68	Glenn Healy (G), NYI.	.10
□ □	69	Phil Bourque, Pgh.	.10
□ □	70	Pat Verbeek, Hfd.	.10
□ □	71	Garry Galley, Bos.	.10
□ □	72	Dave Gagner, Min.	.10
□ □	73	Bob Probert, Det.	.10
□ □	74	Craig Wolanin, Que.	.10
□ □	75	Patrick Roy (G), Mtl.	1.00
□ □	76	Keith Brown, Chi.	.10
□ □	77	Gary Leeman, Tor.	.10
□ □	78	Brent Ashton, Wpg.	.10
□ □	79	Randy Moller, NYR.	.10
□ □	80	Mike Vernon (G), Cgy.	.20
□ □	81	Kelly Miller, Wsh.	.10
□ □	82	Ulf Samuelsson, Pgh.	.10
□ □	83	Todd Elik, L.A.	.10
□ □	84	Uwe Krupp, Buf.	.10
□ □	85	Rod Brind'Amour, Stl.	.20
□ □	86	Dave Capuano, Van.	.10
□ □	87	Geoff Smith, Edm.	.10
□ □	88	David Volek, NYI.	.10
□ □	89	Bruce Driver, N.J.	.10
□ □	90	Andy Moog (G), Bos.	.20
□ □	91	Per-Erik Eklund, Pha.	.10
□ □	92	Joey Kocur, NYR.	.10
□ □	93	Mark Tinordi, Min.	.10
□ □	94	Steve Thomas, Chi.	.10
□ □	95	Petr Svoboda, Mtl.	.10
□ □	96	Joel Otto, Cgy.	.10
□ □	97	Todd Krygier, Hfd.	.10
□ □	98	Jaromir Jagr, Pgh.	1.00
□ □	99	Mike Liut (G), Wsh.	.10
□ □	100	Wayne Gretzky, L.A.	1.50
□ □	101	Teppo Numminen, Wpg.	.10
□ □	102	Randy Burridge, Bos.	.10
□ □	103	Michel Petit, Tor.	.10
□ □	104	Tony McKegney, Chi.	.10
□ □	105	Mathieu Schneider, Mtl.	.10
□ □	106	Daren Puppa (G), Buf	.10
□ □	107	Paul Cavallini, Stl.	.10
□ □	108	Tim Kerr, Pha.	.10
□ □	109	Kevin Lowe, Edm.	.10
□ □	110	Kirk Muller, N.J.	.10
□ □	111	Zarley Zalapski, Hfd.	.10
□ □	112	Mike Hough, Que.	.10
□ □	113	Ken Hodge, Bos.	.10
□ □	114	Grant Fuhr (G), Edm.	.20
□ □	115	Paul Coffey, Pgh.	.20
□ □	116	Wendel Clark, Tor.	.20
□ □	117	Patrik Sundstrom, N.J.	.10
□ □	118	Kevin Dineen, Hfd.	.10
□ □	119	Eric Desjardins, Mtl.	.20
□ □	120	Mike Richter (G), NYR.	.20
□ □	121	Sergio Momesso, Van.	.10
□ □	122	Tony Hrkac, Que.	.10
□ □	123	Joe Reekie, NYI.	.10
□ □	124	Petr Nedved, Van.	.10
□ □	125	Randy Carlyle, Wpg.	.10
□ □	126	Kevin Miller, Det.	.10
□ □	127	Réjean Lemelin (G), Bos.	.10
□ □	128	Dino Ciccarelli, Wsh.	.20
□ □	129	Sylvain Côté, Hfd.	.10
□ □	130	Mats Sundin, Que.	.35
□ □	131	Eric Weinrich, N.J.	.10
□ □	132	Daniel Berthiaume (G), L.A.	.10
□ □	133	Keith Acton, Pha.	.10
□ □	134	Benoît Hogue, Buf.	.10
□ □	135	Mike Gartner, NYR.	.20
□ □	136	Petr Klima, Edm.	.10
□ □	137	Curt Giles, Min.	.10
□ □	138	Scott Pearson, Que.	.10
□ □	139	Luke Richardson, Tor.	.10
□ □	140	Steve Larmer, Chi.	.20
□ □	141	Ken Wregget (G), Pha.	.10
□ □	142	Frantisek Musil, Cgy.	.20
□ □	143	Owen Nolan, Que.	.20
□ □	144	Keith Primeau, Det.	.20
□ □	145	Mark Recchi, Pgh.	.10
□ □	146	Don Sweeney, Bos.	.10
□ □	147	Mike McPhee, Mtl.	.10
□ □	148	Ken Baumgartner, NYI.	.10
□ □	149	Dave Lowry, Stl.	.10
□ □	150	Geoff Courtnall, Van.	.10
□ □	151	Chris Terreri (G), N.J.	.10
□ □	152	Dave Manson, Chi.	.10
□ □	153	Bobby Holik, Hfd.	.10
□ □	154	Bob Kudelski, L.A.	.10
□ □	155	Calle Johansson, Wsh.	.10
□ □	156	Mark Hunter, Hfd.	.10
□ □	157	Randy Gilhen, Pgh.	.10
□ □	158	Yves Racine, Det.	.10
□ □	159	Martin Gelinas, Edm.	.10
□ □	160	Brian Bellows, Min.	.10
□ □	161	David Shaw, NYR.	.10
□ □	162	Bob Carpenter, Bos.	.10
□ □	163	Doug Brown, N.J.	.10
□ □	164	Ulf Dahlen, Min.	.10
□ □	165	Denis Savard, Mtl.	.20
□ □	166	Paul Ysebaert, Det.	.10
□ □	167	Derek King, NYI.	.10
□ □	168	Igor Larionov, Van.	.20
□ □	169	Bob Errey, Pgh.	.10
□ □	170	Joe Nieuwendyk, Cgy.	.20
□ □	171	Normand Rochefort, NYR.	.10
□ □	172	John Tonelli, L.A.	.10
□ □	173	David Reid, Tor.	.10
□ □	174	Tom Kurvers, Van.	.10
□ □	175	Dimitri Khristich, Wsh.	.10
□ □	176	Bob Sweeney, Bos.	.10
□ □	177	Rick Zombo, Det.	.10
□ □	178	Troy Mallette, NYR.	.10
□ □	179	Bob Bassen, Stl.	.10
□ □	180	John Druce, Wsh.	.10
□ □	181	Mike Craig, Min.	.10
□ □	182	John McIntyre, L.A.	.10
□ □	183	Murray Baron, Pha.	.10
□ □	184	Viacheslav Fetisov, N.J.	.20
□ □	185	Don Beaupré (G), Wsh.	.10
□ □	186	Brian Benning, L.A.	.10
□ □	187	Dave Barr, Det.	.10
□ □	188	Petri Skriko, Bos.	.10
□ □	189	Steve Konroyd, Chi.	.10
□ □	190	Steve Yzerman, Det.	.75
□ □	191	Jon Casey (G), Min.	.10
□ □	192	Gary Nylund, NYI.	.10
□ □	193	Michal Pivonka, Wsh.	.10
□ □	194	Alexei Kasatonov, N.J.	.10
□ □	195	Garry Valk, Van.	.10
□ □	196	Darren Turcotte, NYR.	.10
□ □	197	Chris Nilan, Bos.	.10
□ □	198	Thomas Steen, Wpg.	.10
□ □	199	Gary Roberts, Cgy.	.20
□ □	200	Mario Lemieux, Pgh.	1.00
□ □	201	Michel Goulet, Chi.	.20
□ □	202	Craig MacTavish, Edm.	.10
□ □	203	Peter Sidorkiewicz (G), Hfd.	.10
□ □	204	Johan Garpenlov, Det.	.10
□ □	205	Steve Duchesne, L.A.	.10
□ □	206	Dave Snuggerud, Buf.	.10
□ □	207	Kjell Samuelsson, Pha.	.10
□ □	208	Sylvain Turgeon, Mtl.	.10
□ □	209	Al Iafrate, Wsh.	.10
□ □	210	John MacLean, N.J.	.10
□ □	211	Brian Hayward (G), Min.	.10
□ □	212	Cliff Ronning, Van.	.10
□ □	213	Ray Sheppard, NYR.	.10
□ □	214	Dave Taylor, L.A.	.10
□ □	215	Doug Lidster, Van.	.10
□ □	216	Peter Bondra, Wsh.	.20
□ □	217	Marty McSorley, L.A.	.10
□ □	218	Doug Gilmour, Cgy.	.20
□ □	219	Paul MacDermid, Wpg.	.10
□ □	220	Jeremy Roenick, Chi.	.20
□ □	221	Wayne Presley, Chi.	.10
□ □	222	Jeff Norton, NYI.	.10
□ □	223	Brian Propp, Min.	.10
□ □	224	Jimmy Carson, Det.	.10
□ □	225	Tom Barrasso (G), Pgh.	.20
□ □	226	Theoren Fleury, Cgy.	.20
□ □	227	Carey Wilson, Cgy.	.10
□ □	228	Rod Langway, Wsh.	.10
□ □	229	Bryan Trottier, Pgh.	.20
□ □	230	James Patrick, NYR.	.10
□ □	231	Dana Murzyn, Van.	.10
□ □	232	Rick Wamsley (G), Cgy.	.10
□ □	233	Dave McLlwain, Wpg.	.10
□ □	234	Tom Fergus, Tor.	.10
□ □	235	Adam Graves, Edm.	.10
□ □	236	Jacques Cloutier (G), Que.	.10
□ □	237	Gino Odjick, Van.	.10
□ □	238	Andrew Cassels, Mtl.	.10
□ □	239	Ken Linseman, Edm.	.10
□ □	240	Danton Cole, Wpg.	.10
□ □	241	Dave Hannan, Tor.	.10
□ □	242	Stéphane Matteau, Cgy.	.10
□ □	243	Gerald Diduck, Van.	.10
□ □	244	Rick Tabaracci (G), Wpg.	.10
□ □	245	Sylvain Lefebvre, Mtl.	.10
□ □	246	Bob Rouse, Tor.	.10
□ □	247	Charlie Huddy, Edm.	.10
□ □	248	Mike Foligno, Tor.	.10
□ □	249	Ric Nattress, Cgy.	.10
□ □	250	Aaron Broten, Tor.	.10
□ □	251	Mike Keane, Mtl.	.10
□ □	252	Steven Bozek, Van.	.10
□ □	253	Jeff Beukeboom, Edm.	.10
□ □	254	Stéphane Morin, Que.	.10
□ □	255	Brian Bradley, Tor.	.10
□ □	256	Scott Arniel, Wpg.	.10
□ □	257	Robert Kron, Van.	.10
□ □	258	Anatoli Semenov, Edm.	.10
□ □	259	Brent Gilchrist, Mtl.	.10
□ □	260	Jim Sandlak, Van.	.10
□ □	261	HL: Brett Hull, Stl.	.20
□ □	262	HL: Paul Coffey, Pgh.	.20
□ □	263	HL: Mark Messier, Edm.	.20
□ □	264	HL: Dave Taylor, L.A.	.10
□ □	265	HL: Michel Goulet, Chi.	.10
□ □	266	HL: Dale Hawerchuk, Buf.	.20
□ □	267	Pierre & Sylvain Turgeon	.10
□ □	268	Rich, Brian & Ron Sutter	.10
□ □	269	Brian & Joe Mullen	.10
□ □	270	Geoff & Russ Courtnall	.10
□ □	271	Trevor Kidd (G), Cgy.	.20
□ □	272	Patrice Brisebois, Mtl.	.10
□ □	273	Mark Greig, Hfd.	.10
□ □	274	Kip Miller, Que.	.10
□ □	275	Drake Berehowsky, Tor.	.10
□ □	**276**	**Kevin Haller, Buf., RC**	**.10**
□ □	277	David Gagnon (G), Det.	.10
□ □	278	Jason Marshall, Stl.	.10
□ □	279	Don Audette, Buf.	.10
□ □	**280**	**Patrick Lebeau, Mtl., RC**	**.10**
□ □	**281**	**Alexander, Godynyuk, Tor., RC**	**.10**
□ □	**282**	**Jarrod Skalde, N.J., RC**	**.10**
□ □	**283**	**Ken Sutton, Buf., RC**	**.10**
□ □	**284**	**Sergei Kharin, Wpg., RC**	**.10**
□ □	**285**	**André Racicot (G), Mtl., RC**	**.10**
□ □	**286**	**Doug Weight, NYR., RC**	**.75**
□ □	**287**	**Kevin Todd, N.J., RC**	**.10**
□ □	**288**	**Tony Amonte, NYR., RC**	**.75**
□ □	**289**	**Kimbi Daniels, Pha., RC**	**.10**
□ □	**290**	**Jeff Daniels, Pgh., RC**	**.10**
□ □	291	Speed and Grace: Guy Lafleur	.35
□ □	292	Awards and Achievements: Guy Lafleur	.35
□ □	293	A Hall of Famer: Guy Lafleur	.35
□ □	294	LL: Brett Hull, Stl.	.20
□ □	295	LL: Wayne Gretzky, L.A.	.75
□ □	296	LL: Wayne Gretzky, L.A.	.75
□ □	297	LL: T. Fleury, Cgy./M. McSorley, L.A.	.20
□ □	298	LL: Sergei Fedorov, Det.	.20
□ □	299	LL: Al MacInnis, Cgy.	.10
□ □	300	LL: Ed Belfour (G), Chi.	.20
□ □	301	LL: Ed Belfour (G), Chi.	.20
□ □	302	Brett Hull 50 Goals/50 Games	.20
□ □	303	Wayne Gretzky's 700th Career Goal	.75
□ □	304	San Jose Sharks Checklist	.10
□ □	305	Cam Neely, Bos.	.20
□ □	306	Rick Tocchet, Pha.	.10
□ □	307	Scott Stevens, Stl.	.10
□ □	308	Ulf Samuelsson, Pgh.	.10
□ □	309	Jeremy Roenick, Chi.	.20

	No.	Card	Price
□ □	310	Mark Messier, Edm.	.20
□ □	311	John Cullen, Hfd.	.10
□ □	312	Wayne Gretzky, L.A.	.75
□ □	313	Mike Modano, Min.	.20
□ □	314	Patrick Roy (G), Mtl.	.50
□ □	315	Pittsburgh Penguins	.25
□ □	316	Mario Lemieux, Pgh.	.50
□ □	317	Wayne Gretzky, L.A.	.75
□ □	318	Brett Hull, Stl.	.20
□ □	319	Ray Bourque, Bos.	.20
□ □	320	Ed Belfour (G), Chi.	.20
□ □	321	Ed Belfour (G), Chi.	.20
□ □	322	Dirk Graham	.10
□ □	323	Ed Belfour (G), Chi.	.20
□ □	324	Wayne Gretzky, L.A./ Dave Taylor, L.A.	.50
□ □	325	Dave Taylor, L.A.	.10
□ □	326	Jeff Hackett (G), S.J.	.20
□ □	327	Robert McGill, S.J.	.10
□ □	328	Neil Wilkinson, S.J.	.10
□ □	329	Eric Lindros	1.25
□ □	330	Eric Lindros	1.25
□ □	331	TF: Ray Bourque, Bos.	.20
□ □	332	TF: Pierre Turgeon, Buf.	.20
□ □	333	TF: Al MacInnis, Cgy.	.20
□ □	334	TF: Jeremy Roenick, Chi.	.20
□ □	335	TF: Steve Yzerman, Det.	.25
□ □	336	Dale and Mark Hunter	.10
□ □	337	Aaron and Neal Broten	.10
□ □	338	Gino and Paul Cavallini	.10
□ □	339	Kelly and Kevin Miller	.10
□ □	**340**	**Dennis Vaske, NYI., RC**	**.10**
□ □	**341**	**Rob Pearson, Tor., RC**	**.10**
□ □	**342**	**Jason Miller, N.J., RC**	**.10**
□ □	**343**	**John LeClair, Mtl., RC**	**1.50**
□ □	**344**	**Bryan Marchment, Wpg., RC**	**.10**
□ □	**345**	**Gary Shuchuk, Det., RC**	**.10**
□ □	**346**	**Dominik Hasek (G), Chi., RC**	**2.00**
□ □	**347**	**Michel Picard, Hfd., RC**	**.10**
□ □	**348**	**Corey Millen, NYR., RC**	**.10**
□ □	**349**	**Joe Sacco, Tor., RC**	**.10**
□ □	**350**	**Reggie Savage, Wsh., RC**	**.10**
□ □	351	Pat Murray, Pha.	.10
□ □	**352**	**Myles O'Connor, N.J., RC**	**.10**
□ □	353	Shawn Antoski, Van.	.10
□ □	**354**	**Geoff Sanderson, Hfd., RC**	**.25**
□ □	355	Chris Govedaris, Hfd.	.10
□ □	**356**	**Alexei Gusarov, Que., RC**	**.10**
□ □	357	Mike Sillinger, Det.	.10
□ □	**358**	**Bob Wilkie, Det., RC**	**.10**
□ □	**359**	**Pat Jablonski (G), Stl., RC**	**.10**
□ □	360	Spokane Chiefs	.20
□ □	361	TF: Kirk Muller, N.J.	.10
□ □	362	TF: Pat LaFontaine, NYI.	.20
□ □	363	TF: Brian Leetch, NYR.	.20
□ □	364	TF: Rick Tocchet, Pha.	.10
□ □	365	TF: Mario Lemieux, Pgh.	.50
□ □	366	TF: Joe Sakic, Que.	.25
□ □	367	TF: Brett Hull, Stl.	.20
□ □	368	TF: Vincent Damphousse, Tor.	.20
□ □	369	TF: Trevor Linden, Van.	.20
□ □	370	TF: Kevin Hatcher, Wsh.	.10
□ □	371	TF: Pat Elynuik, Wpg.	.10
□ □	372	Patrick Roy (G), Mtl.	.50
□ □	373	Brian Leetch, NYR.	.20
□ □	374	Ray Bourque, Bos.	.20
□ □	375	Luc Robitaille, L.A.	.20
□ □	376	Wayne Gretzky, L.A.	.75
□ □	377	Brett Hull, Stl.	.20
□ □	378	Ed Belfour (G), Chi.	.20
□ □	379	Rob Blake, L.A.	.20
□ □	380	Eric Weinrich, N.J.	.10
□ □	381	Jaromir Jagr	.50
□ □	382	Sergei Fedorov, Det.	.20
□ □	383	Ken Hodge, Bos.	.10
□ □	384	Eric Lindros	1.25
□ □	385	Eric Lindros/ Rob Pearson	1.25
□ □	386	Senators, Lightning	.10
□ □	387	Mick Vukota, NYI.	.10
□ □	388	Lou Franceschetti, Buf.	.10
□ □	389	Mike Hudson, Chi.	.10
□ □	390	Frantisek Kucera, Chi.	.10
□ □	391	Basil McRae, Min.	.10
□ □	392	Donald Dufresne, Mtl.	.10
□ □	393	Tommy Albelin, N.J.	.10
□ □	394	Normand Lacombe, Pha.	.10
□ □	395	Lucien DeBlois, Tor.	.10
□ □	**396**	**Tony Twist, Que., RC**	**.10**
□ □	397	Rob Murphy, Van.	.10
□ □	398	Ken Sabourin, Wsh.	.10
□ □	399	Doug Evans, Wpg.	.10
□ □	400	Walt Poddubny, N.J.	.10
□ □	401	Grant Ledyard, Buf.	.10
□ □	402	Kris King, NYR.	.10
□ □	403	Paul Gillis, Chi.	.10
□ □	404	Chris Dahlquist, Min.	.10
□ □	405	Zdeno Ciger, N.J.	.10
□ □	406	Paul Stanton, Pgh.	.10
□ □	407	Randy Ladouceur, Hfd.	.10
□ □	408	Ron Stern, Cgy.	.10
□ □	409	Dave Tippett, Wsh.	.10
□ □	410	Jeff Reese (G), Tor.	.10
□ □	411	Vladimir Ruzicka, Bos.	.10
□ □	412	Brent Fedyk, Det.	.10
□ □	413	Paul Cyr, Hfd.	.10
□ □	414	Mike Eagles, Wpg.	.10
□ □	415	Chris Joseph, Edm.	.10
□ □	416	Brad Marsh, Cgy.	.10
□ □	417	Rich Pilon, NYI.	.10
□ □	418	Jiri Hrdina, Pgh.	.10
□ □	419	Clint Malarchuk (G), Buf.	.10
□ □	420	Steven Rice, NYR.	.10
□ □	421	Mark Janssens, NYR.	.10
□ □	422	Gord Roberts, Pgh.	.10
□ □	423	Shawn Cronin, Wpg.	.10
□ □	424	Randy Cunneyworth, Hfd.	.10
□ □	425	Frank Pietrangelo (G), Pgh.	.10
□ □	426	David Maley, N.J.	.10
□ □	427	Rod Buskas, L.A.	.10
□ □	428	Dennis Vial, Det.	.10
□ □	429	Kelly Buchberger, Edm.	.10
□ □	430	Wes Walz, Bos.	.10
□ □	431	Dean Kennedy, Buf.	.10
□ □	432	Nick Kypreos, Wsh.	.10
□ □	433	Stewart Gavin, Min.	.10
□ □	**434**	**Norm Maciver, Edm., RC**	**.10**
□ □	435	Mark Pederson, Pha.	.10
□ □	436	Laurie Boschman, N.J.	.10
□ □	437	Stéphane Quintal, Bos.	.10
□ □	438	Darrin Shannon, Buf.	.10
□ □	439	Trent Yawney, Chi.	.10
□ □	440	Gaetan Duchesne, Min.	.10
□ □	441	Joe Cirella, NYR.	.10
□ □	442	Doug Houda, Hfd.	.10
□ □	443	Dave Chyzowski, NYI.	.10
□ □	444	Derrick Smith, Pha.	.10
□ □	445	Jeff Lazaro, Bos.	.10
□ □	446	Brian Glynn, Min.	.10
□ □	447	Jocelyn Lemieux, Chi.	.10
□ □	448	Peter Taglianetti, Pgh.	.10
□ □	449	Adam Burt, Hfd.	.10
□ □	450	Hubie McDonough, NYI.	.10
□ □	451	Kelly Hrudey (G), L.A.	.10
□ □	452	Dave Poulin, Bos.	.10
□ □	453	Mark Hardy, NYR.	.10
□ □	454	Mike Hartman, Buf.	.10
□ □	455	Chris Chelios, Chi.	.25
□ □	456	Alexander Mogilny, Buf.	.25
□ □	457	Bryan Fogarty, Que.	.10
□ □	458	Adam Oates, Stl.	.20
□ □	459	Ron Hextall (G), Pha.	.20
□ □	460	Bernie Nicholls, NYR.	.10
□ □	461	Esa Tikkanen, Edm.	.10
□ □	462	Jyrki Lumme, Van.	.10
□ □	463	Brent Sutter, NYI.	.10
□ □	464	Gary Suter, Cgy.	.10
□ □	465	Sean Burke (G), N.J.	.20
□ □	466	Rob Brown, Hfd.	.10
□ □	467	Mike Modano, Min.	.35
□ □	468	Kevin Stevens, Pgh.	.10
□ □	469	Mike Lalor, Wsh.	.10
□ □	470	Sergei Fedorov, Det.	.35
□ □	471	Bob Essensa (G), Wpg.	.10
□ □	472	Mark Howe, Pha.	.20
□ □	473	Craig Janney, Bos.	.10
□ □	474	Daniel Marois, Tor.	.10
□ □	475	Craig Simpson, Edm.	.10
□ □	476	Marc Bureau, Min.	.10
□ □	477	Randy Velischek, Que.	.10
□ □	478	Gino Cavallini, Stl.	.10
□ □	479	Dale Hawerchuk, Buf.	.20
□ □	480	Pat LaFontaine, NYI.	.20
□ □	481	Kirk McLean (G), Van.	.20
□ □	482	Murray Craven, Pha.	.10
□ □	483	Robert Reichel, Cgy.	.20
□ □	484	Jan Erixon, NYR.	.10
□ □	485	Adam Creighton, Chi.	.10
□ □	486	Mark Fitzpatrick (G), NYI.	.10
□ □	487	Ron Francis, Pgh.	.20
□ □	488	Joe Mullen, Pgh.	.10
□ □	489	Peter Zezel, Tor.	.10
□ □	490	Tomas Sandström, L.A.	.10
□ □	491	Phil Housley, Wpg.	.10
□ □	492	Tim Cheveldae (G), Det.	.10
□ □	493	Glen Wesley, Bos.	.10
□ □	494	Stéphan Lebeau, Mtl.	.10
□ □	495	David Ellett, Tor.	.10
□ □	496	Jeff Brown, Stl.	.10
□ □	497	Dave Andreychuk, Buf.	.20
□ □	498	Steven Finn, Que.	.10
□ □	**499**	**Mike Donnelly, L.A., RC**	**.10**
□ □	500	Neal Broten, Min.	.10
□ □	501	Randy Wood, NYI.	.10
□ □	502	Troy Gamble (G), Van.	.10
□ □	503	Mike Ridley, Wsh.	.10
□ □	504	Jamie Macoun, Cgy.	.10
□ □	505	Mark Messier, Edm.	.35
□ □	506	Moe Mantha, Wpg.	.10
□ □	507	Scott Young, Pgh.	.10
□ □	508	Robert Dirk, Van.	.10
□ □	509	Brad Shaw, Hfd.	.10
□ □	510	Ed Belfour (G), Chi.	.20
□ □	511	Larry Robinson, L.A.	.20
□ □	512	Dale Kushner, Pha.	.10
□ □	513	Steve Chiasson, Det.	.10
□ □	514	Brian Skrudland, Mtl.	.10
□ □	515	Pat Elynuik, Wpg.	.10
□ □	516	Curtis Joseph (G), Stl.	.20
□ □	517	Doug Bodger, Buf.	.10
□ □	518	Greg Brown, Buf.	.10
□ □	519	Joe Murphy, Edm.	.10
□ □	520	J. J. Daigneault, Mtl.	.10
□ □	521	Todd Gill, Tor.	.10
□ □	522	Troy Loney, Pgh.	.10
□ □	523	Tim Watters, L.A.	.10
□ □	524	Jody Hull, NYR.	.10
□ □	525	Colin Patterson, Cgy.	.10
□ □	526	Darin Kimble, Stl.	.10
□ □	527	Perry Berezan, Min.	.10
□ □	528	Lee Norwood, N.J.	.10
□ □	529	Mike Peluso, Chi.	.10
□ □	530	Wayne McBean, NYI.	.10
□ □	531	Grant Jennings, Pgh.	.10
□ □	532	Claude Loiselle, Tor.	.10
□ □	533	Ron Wilson, Stl.	.10
□ □	534	Phil Sykes, Wpg.	.10
□ □	535	Jim Wiemer, Bos.	.10
□ □	536	Herb Raglan, Que.	.10
□ □	537	Tim Hunter, Cgy.	.10
□ □	538	Mike Tomlak, Hfd.	.10
□ □	539	Greg Gilbert, Chi.	.10
□ □	540	Jiri Latal, Pha.	.10
□ □	**541**	**Bill Berg, NYI., RC**	**.10**
□ □	542	Shane Churla, Min.	.10
□ □	543	Jay Miller, L.A.	.10
□ □	544	Pete Peeters (G), Pha.	.10
□ □	545	Alan May, Wsh.	.10
□ □	546	Mario Marois, Stl.	.10
□ □	547	Jim Kyte, Cgy.	.10
□ □	548	Jon Morris, N.J.	.10
□ □	549	Mikko Makelä, Buf.	.10
□ □	550	Nelson Emerson, Stl.	.10
□ □	551	Doug Wilson, S.J.	.10
□ □	552	Brian Mullen, S.J.	.10
□ □	553	Kelly Kisio, S.J.	.10
□ □	554	Brian Hayward (G), S.J.	.10
□ □	555	Tony Hrkac, S.J.	.10
□ □	556	Steve Bozek, S.J.	.10
□ □	557	John Carter, S.J.	.10
□ □	558	Neil Wilkinson, S.J.	.10
□ □	559	Wayne Presley, S.J.	.10
□ □	560	Robert McGill, S.J.	.10
□ □	561	Craig Ludwig, Min.	.10
□ □	562	Mikhail Tatarinov, Que.	.10
□ □	563	Todd Elik, Min.	.10
□ □	564	Randy Burridge, Wsh.	.10

	No.	Player	
☐☐	565	Tim Kerr, NYR.	.10
☐☐	566	Randy Gilhen, L.A.	.10
☐☐	567	John Tonelli, Chi.	.10
☐☐	568	Tom Kurvers, NYI.	.10
☐☐	569	Steve Duchesne, Pha.	.10
☐☐	570	Charlie Huddy, L.A.	.10
☐☐	571	Alan Kerr, Det.	.10
☐☐	572	Shawn Chambers	.10
☐☐	573	Rob Ramage, Min.	.10
☐☐	574	Steve Kasper, Pha.	.10
☐☐	575	Scott Mellanby, Edm.	.10
☐☐	576	Stephen Leach, Bos.	.10
☐☐	577	Scott Niedermayer, N.J.	.20
☐☐	578	Craig Berube, Tor.	.10
☐☐	579	Gregory Paslawski, Que.	.10
☐☐	580	Randy Hillier, NYI.	.10
☐☐	581	Stéphane Richer, N.J.	.10
☐☐	582	Brian MacLellan, Det.	.10
☐☐	583	Marc Habscheid, Cgy.	.10
☐☐	584	Dave Babych, Van.	.10
☐☐	585	Troy Murray, Wpg.	.10
☐☐	586	Ray Sheppard, Det.	.10
☐☐	587	Glen Featherstone, Bos.	.10
☐☐	588	Brendan Shanahan, Stl.	.35
☐☐	589	Dave Christian, Stl.	.10
☐☐	590	Mike Bullard, Tor.	.10
☐☐	591	Ryan Walter, Van.	.10
☐☐	592	Doug Smail, Que.	.10
☐☐	593	Paul Fenton, Hfd.	.10
☐☐	594	Adam Graves, NYR.	.10
☐☐	595	Scott Stevens, N.J.	.20
☐☐	596	Sylvain Côté, Wsh.	.10
☐☐	597	David Barr, N.J.	.10
☐☐	598	Randy Gregg, Van.	.10
☐☐	599	Allen Pedersen, Min.	.10
☐☐	600	Jari Kurri, L.A.	.20
☐☐	601	Troy Mallette, Edm.	.10
☐☐	602	Troy Crowder, Det.	.10
☐☐	603	Brad Jones, Pha.	.10
☐☐	604	Randy McKay, N.J.	.10
☐☐	605	Scott Thornton, Edm.	.10
☐☐	**606**	**Bryan Marchment, Chi., RC**	**.10**
☐☐	607	Andrew Cassels, Hfd.	.10
☐☐	608	Grant Fuhr (G), Tor.	.20
☐☐	609	Vincent Damphousse, Edm.	.20
☐☐	610	Rob Ray, Buf.	.10
☐☐	611	Glenn Anderson, Tor.	.10
☐☐	612	Peter Ing (G), Edm.	.10
☐☐	613	Tom Chorske, N.J.	.10
☐☐	614	Kirk Muller, Mtl.	.10
☐☐	615	Dan Quinn, Pha.	.10
☐☐	616	Murray Baron, Stl.	.10
☐☐	617	Sergei Nemchinov, NYR.	.10
☐☐	618	Rod Brind'Amour, Pha.	.20
☐☐	619	Ron Sutter, Stl.	.10
☐☐	620	Luke Richardson, Edm.	.10
☐☐	**621**	**Nicklas Lidström, Det., RC**	**.25**
☐☐	622	Ken Linseman, Tor.	.10
☐☐	623	Steve Smith, Chi.	.10
☐☐	624	Dave Manson, Edm.	.10
☐☐	625	Kay Whitmore (G), Hfd.	.10
☐☐	626	Jeff Chychrun, L.A.	.10
☐☐	**627**	**Russ Romaniuk, Wpg., RC**	**.10**
☐☐	628	Brad May, Buf.	.10
☐☐	**629**	**Tomas Forslund, Cgy., RC**	**.10**
☐☐	630	Stu Barnes, Wpg.	.10
☐☐	631	Darryl Sydor, L.A.	.10
☐☐	632	Jimmy Waite (G), Chi.	.10
☐☐	633	Peter Douris, Bos.	.10
☐☐	634	Dave Brown, Pha.	.10
☐☐	635	Mark Messier, NYR.	.35
☐☐	636	Neil Sheehy, Cgy.	.10
☐☐	637	Todd Krygier, Wsh.	.10
☐☐	638	Stéphane Beauregard (G), Wpg.	.10
☐☐	639	Barry Pederson, Hfd.	.10
☐☐	640	Pat Falloon, S.J.	.10
☐☐	641	Dean Evason, S.J.	.10
☐☐	642	Jeff Hackett (G), S.J.	.20
☐☐	643	Rob Zettler, S.J.	.10
☐☐	**644**	**David Bruce, S.J., RC**	**.10**
☐☐	**645**	**Pat MacLeod, S.J., RC**	**.10**
☐☐	646	Craig Coxe, S.J.	.10
☐☐	**647**	**Ken Hammond, S.J., RC**	**.10**
☐☐	648	Brian Lawton, S.J.	.10
☐☐	**649**	**Perry Anderson, S.J., RC**	**.10**
☐☐	**650**	**Kevin Evans, S.J., RC**	**.10**
☐☐	**651**	**Mike McHugh, S.J., RC**	**.10**
☐☐	652	Mark Lamb, Edm.	.10
☐☐	**653**	**Darcy Wakaluk (G), Min., RC**	**.10**
☐☐	654	Pat Conacher, N.J.	.10
☐☐	655	Martin Lapointe, Det.	.10
☐☐	656	Derian Hatcher, Min.	.20
☐☐	657	Bryan Erickson, Wpg.	.10
☐☐	**658**	**Ken Priestlay, Pgh., RC**	**.10**
☐☐	**659**	**Vladimir Konstantinov, Det., RC**	**.25**
☐☐	660	Andrei Lomakin, Pha.	.10

SCORE AMERICAN

The American issue of 1991-92 Score features a purple border as compared to the red or blue border in Score Canadian. The U.S. set was released as a single 440 card series.

Imprint: © 1991 SCORE

Complete Set (400 cards): **12.00**

Common Player: **.10**

	No.	Player	NRMT-MT
☐	1	Brett Hull, Stl.	.35
☐	2	Al MacInnis, Cgy.	.20
☐	3	Luc Robitaille, L.A.	.20
☐	4	Pierre Turgeon, Buf.	.20
☐	5	Brian Leetch, NYR.	.20
☐	6	Cam Neely, Bos.	.20
☐	7	John Cullen, Hfd.	.10
☐	8	Trevor Linden, Van.	.20
☐	9	Rick Tocchet, Pha.	.10
☐	10	John Vanbiesbrouck (G), NYR.	.50
☐	11	Steve Smith, Edm.	.10
☐	12	Doug Smail, Min.	.10
☐	13	Craig Ludwig, NYI.	.10
☐	14	Paul Fenton, Cgy.	.10
☐	15	Dirk Graham, Chi.	.10
☐	16	Brad McCrimmon, Det.	.10
☐	17	Dean Evason, Hfd.	.10
☐	18	Fredrik Olausson, Wpg.	.10
☐	19	Guy Carbonneau, Mtl.	.10
☐	20	Kevin Hatcher, Wsh.	.10
☐	21	Paul Ranheim, Cgy.	.10
☐	22	Claude Lemieux, N.J.	.10
☐	23	Vincent Riendeau (G), Stl.	.10
☐	24	Garth Butcher, Stl.	.10
☐	25	Joe Sakic, Que.	.60
☐	26	Rick Vaive, Buf.	.10
☐	27	Rob Blake, L.A.	.20
☐	28	Mike Ricci, Pha.	.10
☐	29	Patrick Flatley, NYI.	.10
☐	30	Bill Ranford (G), Edm.	.20
☐	31	Larry Murphy, Pgh.	.20
☐	32	Bobby Smith, Min.	.10
☐	33	Mike Krushelnyski, Tor.	.10
☐	34	Gerard Gallant, Det.	.10
☐	35	Doug Wilson, Chi.	.20
☐	36	John Ogrodnick, NYR.	.10
☐	37	Mikhail Tatarinov, Wsh.	.10
☐	38	Doug Crossman, Det.	.10
☐	39	Mark Osborne, Wpg.	.10
☐	40	Scott Stevens, Stl.	.10
☐	41	Ron Tugnutt (G), Que.	.10
☐	42	Russ Courtnall, Mtl.	.10
☐	43	Gord Murphy, Pha.	.10
☐	44	Greg Adams, Van.	.10
☐	45	Christian Ruuttu, Stl.	.10
☐	46	Ken Daneyko, N.J.	.10
☐	47	Glenn Anderson, Edm.	.10
☐	48	Ray Ferraro, NYI.	.10
☐	49	Tony Tanti, Buf.	.10
☐	50	Ray Bourque, Bos.	.35
☐	51	Sergei Makarov, Cgy.	.10
☐	52	Jim Johnson, Min.	.10
☐	53	Troy Murray, Chi.	.10
☐	54	Shawn Burr, Det.	.10
☐	55	Peter Ing (G), Tor.	.10
☐	56	Dale Hunter, Wsh.	.10
☐	57	Tony Granato, L.A.	.10
☐	58	Curtis Leschyshyn, Que.	.10
☐	59	Brian Mullen, NYR.	.10
☐	60	Ed Olczyk, Wpg.	.10
☐	61	Mike Ramsey, Buf.	.10
☐	62	Dan Quinn, Stl.	.10
☐	63	Rich Sutter, Stl.	.10
☐	64	Terry Carkner, Pha.	.10
☐	65	Shayne Corson, Mtl.	.20
☐	66	Peter Stastny, N.J.	.20
☐	67	Craig Muni, Edm.	.10
☐	68	Glenn Healy (G), NYI.	.10
☐	69	Phil Bourque, Pgh.	.10
☐	70	Pat Verbeek, Hfd.	.10
☐	71	Garry Galley, Bos.	.10
☐	72	Dave Gagner, Min.	.10
☐	73	Bob Probert, Det.	.10
☐	74	Craig Wolanin, Que.	.10
☐	75	Patrick Roy (G), Mtl.	1.00
☐	76	Keith Brown, Chi.	.10
☐	77	Gary Leeman, Tor.	.10
☐	78	Brent Ashton, Wpg.	.10
☐	79	Randy Moller, NYR.	.10
☐	80	Mike Vernon (G), Cgy.	.20
☐	81	Kelly Miller, Wsh.	.10
☐	82	Ulf Samuelsson, Pgh.	.10
☐	83	Todd Elik, L.A.	.10
☐	84	Uwe Krupp, Buf.	.10
☐	85	Rod Brind'Amour, Stl.	.20
☐	86	Dave Capuano, Van.	.10
☐	87	Geoff Smith, Edm.	.10
☐	88	David Volek, NYI.	.10
☐	89	Bruce Driver, N.J.	.10
☐	90	Andy Moog (G), Bos.	.20
☐	91	Per-Erik Eklund, Pha.	.10
☐	92	Joey Kocur, NYR.	.10
☐	93	Mark Tinordi, Min.	.10
☐	94	Steve Thomas, Chi.	.10
☐	95	Petr Svoboda, Mtl.	.10
☐	96	Joel Otto, Cgy.	.10
☐	97	Todd Krygier, Hfd.	.10
☐	98	Jaromir Jagr, Pgh.	.75
☐	99	Mike Liut (G), Wsh.	.10
☐	100	Wayne Gretzky, L.A.	1.50
☐	101	Teppo Numminen, Wpg.	.10
☐	102	Randy Burridge, Bos.	.10
☐	103	Michel Petit, Tor.	.10
☐	104	Tony McKegney, Chi.	.10
☐	105	Mathieu Schneider, Mtl.	.10
☐	106	Daren Puppa (G), Stl.	.10
☐	107	Paul Cavallini, Stl.	.10
☐	108	Tim Kerr, Pha.	.10
☐	109	Kevin Lowe, Edm.	.10
☐	110	Kirk Muller, N.J.	.10
☐	111	Zarley Zalapski, Hfd.	.10
☐	112	Mike Hough, Que.	.10
☐	113	Ken Hodge, Bos.	.10
☐	114	Grant Fuhr (G), Edm.	.20
☐	115	Paul Coffey, Pgh.	.20
☐	116	Wendel Clark, Tor.	.20
☐	117	Patrik Sundstrom, N.J.	.10
☐	118	Kevin Dineen, Hfd.	.10
☐	119	Eric Desjardins, Mtl.	.20
☐	120	Mike Richter (G), NYR.	.20
☐	121	Sergio Momesso, Van.	.10
☐	122	Tony Hrkac, Que.	.10
☐	123	Joe Reekie, NYI.	.10
☐	124	Petr Nedved, Van.	.10
☐	125	Randy Carlyle, Wpg.	.10
☐	126	Kevin Miller, Det.	.10
☐	127	Réjean Lemelin (G), Bos.	.10
☐	128	Dino Ciccarelli, Wsh.	.20
☐	129	Sylvain Côté, Hfd.	.10
☐	130	Mats Sundin, Que.	.35
☐	131	Eric Weinrich, N.J.	.10
☐	132	Daniel Berthiaume (G), L.A.	.10
☐	133	Keith Acton, Pha.	.10
☐	134	Benoît Hogue, Buf.	.10
☐	135	Mike Gartner, NYR.	.20

☐ 136 Petr Klima, Edm. .10
☐ 137 Curt Giles, Min. .10
☐ 138 Scott Pearson, Que. .10
☐ 139 Luke Richardson, Tor. .10
☐ 140 Steve Larmer, Chi. .20
☐ 141 Ken Wregget (G), Pha. .10
☐ 142 Frantisek Musil, Cgy. .10
☐ 143 Owen Nolan, Que. .20
☐ 144 Keith Primeau, Det. .20
☐ 145 Mark Recchi, Pgh. .20
☐ 146 Don Sweeney, Bos. .10
☐ 147 Mike McPhee, Mtl. .10
☐ 148 Ken Baumgartner, NYI. .10
☐ 149 Dave Lowry, Stl. .10
☐ 150 Geoff Courtnall, Van. .10
☐ 151 Chris Terreri (G), N.J. .10
☐ 152 Dave Manson, Chi. .10
☐ 153 Bobby Holik, Hfd. .10
☐ 154 Bob Kudelski, L.A. .10
☐ 155 Calle Johansson, Wsh. .10
☐ 156 Mark Hunter, Hfd. .10
☐ 157 Randy Gilhen, Pgh. .10
☐ 158 Yves Racine, Det. .10
☐ 159 Martin Gelinas, Edm. .10
☐ 160 Brian Bellows, Min. .10
☐ 161 David Shaw, NYR. .10
☐ 162 Bob Carpenter, Bos. .10
☐ 163 Doug Brown, N.J. .10
☐ 164 Ulf Dahlen, Min. .10
☐ 165 Denis Savard, Mtl. .20
☐ 166 Paul Ysebaert, Det. .10
☐ 167 Derek King, NYI. .10
☐ 168 Igor Larionov, Van. .20
☐ 169 Bob Errey, Pgh. .10
☐ 170 Joe Nieuwendyk, Cgy. .20
☐ 171 Normand Rochefort, NYR. .10
☐ 172 John Tonelli, L.A. .10
☐ 173 David Reid, Tor. .10
☐ 174 Tom Kurvers, Van. .10
☐ 175 Dimitri Khristich, Wsh. .10
☐ 176 Bob Sweeney, Bos. .10
☐ 177 Rick Zombo, Det. .10
☐ 178 Troy Mallette, NYR. .10
☐ 179 Bob Bassen, Stl. .10
☐ 180 John Druce, Wsh. .10
☐ 181 Mike Craig, Min. .10
☐ 182 John McIntyre, L.A. .10
☐ 183 Murray Baron, Pha. .10
☐ 184 Viacheslav Fetisov, N.J. .20
☐ 185 Don Beaupré (G), Wsh. .10
☐ 186 Brian Benning, L.A. .10
☐ 187 David Barr, Det. .10
☐ 188 Petri Skriko, Bos. .10
☐ 189 Steve Konroyd, Chi. .10
☐ 190 Steve Yzerman, Det. .75
☐ 191 Jon Casey (G), Min. .10
☐ 192 Gary Nylund, NYI. .10
☐ 193 Michal Pivonka, Wsh. .10
☐ 194 Alexei Kasatonov, N.J. .10
☐ 195 Garry Valk, Van. .10
☐ 196 Darren Turcotte, NYR. .10
☐ 197 Chris Nilan, Bos. .10
☐ 198 Thomas Steen, Wpg. .10
☐ 199 Gary Roberts, Cgy. .20
☐ 200 Mario Lemieux, Pgh. 1.00
☐ 201 Michel Goulet, Chi. .20
☐ 202 Craig MacTavish, Edm. .10
☐ 203 Peter Sidorkiewicz (G), Hfd. .10
☐ 204 Johan Garpenlov, Det. .10
☐ 205 Steve Duchesne, L.A. .10
☐ 206 Dave Snuggerud, Buf. .10
☐ 207 Kjell Samuelsson, Pha. .10
☐ 208 Sylvain Turgeon, Mtl. .10
☐ 209 Al Iafrate, Wsh. .10
☐ 210 John MacLean, N.J. .10
☐ 211 Brian Hayward (G), Min. .10
☐ 212 Cliff Ronning, Van. .10
☐ 213 Ray Sheppard, NYR. .10
☐ 214 Dave Taylor, L.A. .10
☐ 215 Doug Lidster, Van. .10
☐ 216 Peter Bondra, Wsh. .20
☐ 217 Marty McSorley, L.A. .10
☐ 218 Doug Gilmour, Cgy. .20
☐ 219 Paul MacDermid, Wpg. .10
☐ 220 Jeremy Roenick, Chi. .20
☐ 221 Wayne Presley, Chi. .10
☐ 222 Jeff Norton, NYI. .10
☐ 223 Brian Propp, Min. .10
☐ 224 Jimmy Carson, Det. .10
☐ 225 Tom Barrasso (G), Pgh. .20
☐ 226 Theoren Fleury, Cgy. .20
☐ 227 Carey Wilson, Cgy. .10
☐ 228 Rod Langway, Wsh. .10
☐ 229 Bryan Trottier, Pgh. .20
☐ 230 James Patrick, NYR. .10
☐ 231 Kelly Hrudey (G), L.A. .10
☐ 232 Dave Poulin, Bos. .10
☐ 233 Rob Ramage, Tor. .10
☐ 234 Stéphane Richer, Mtl. .10
☐ 235 Chris Chelios, Chi. .20
☐ 236 Alexander Mogilny, Buf. .20
☐ 237 Bryan Fogarty, Que. .10
☐ 238 Adam Oates, Stl. .20
☐ 239 Ron Hextall (G), Pha. .20
☐ 240 Bernie Nicholls, NYR. .10
☐ 241 Esa Tikkanen, Edm. .10
☐ 242 Jyrki Lumme, Van. .10
☐ 243 Brent Sutter, NYI. .10
☐ 244 Gary Suter, Cgy. .10
☐ 245 Sean Burke (G), N.J. .20
☐ 246 Rob Brown, Hfd. .10
☐ 247 Mike Modano, Min. .35
☐ 248 Kevin Stevens, Pgh. .10
☐ 249 Mike Lalor, Wsh. .10
☐ 250 Sergei Fedorov, Det. .35
☐ 251 Bob Essensa (G), Wpg. .10
☐ 252 Mark Howe, Pha. .20
☐ 253 Craig Janney, Bos. .10
☐ 254 Daniel Marois, Tor. .10
☐ 255 Craig Simpson, Edm. .10
☐ 256 Steve Kasper, L.A. .10
☐ 257 Randy Velischek, Que. .10
☐ 258 Gino Cavallini, Stl. .10
☐ 259 Dale Hawerchuk, Buf. .20
☐ 260 Pat LaFontaine, NYI. .20
☐ 261 Kirk McLean (G), Van. .20
☐ 262 Murray Craven, Pha. .10
☐ 263 Robert Reichel, Cgy. .20
☐ 264 Jan Erixon, NYR. .10
☐ 265 Adam Creighton, Chi. .10
☐ 266 Mark Fitzpatrick (G), NYI. .10
☐ 267 Ron Francis, Pgh. .20
☐ 268 Joe Mullen, Pgh. .10
☐ 269 Peter Zezel, Tor. .10
☐ 270 Tomas Sandström, L.A. .10
☐ 271 Phil Housley, Wpg. .10
☐ 272 Tim Cheveldae (G), Det. .10
☐ 273 Glen Wesley, Bos. .10
☐ 274 Stéphan Lebeau, Mtl. .10
☐ 275 Dave Ellett, Tor. .10
☐ 276 Jeff Brown, Stl. .10
☐ 277 Dave Andreychuk, Buf. .20
☐ 278 Steven Finn, Que. .10
☐ 279 Scott Mellanby, Pha. .10
☐ 280 Neal Broten, Min. .10
☐ 281 Randy Wood, NYI. .10
☐ 282 Troy Gamble (G), Van. .10
☐ 283 Mike Ridley, Wsh. .10
☐ 284 Jamie Macoun, Cgy. .10
☐ 285 Mark Messier, Edm. .35
☐ 286 Brendan Shanahan, N.J. .50
☐ 287 Scott Young, Pgh. .10
☐ 288 Kelly Kisio, NYR. .10
☐ 289 Brad Shaw, Hfd. .10
☐ 290 Ed Belfour (G), Chi. .20
☐ 291 Larry Robinson, L.A. .20
☐ 292 Dave Christian, Bos. .10
☐ 293 Steve Chiasson, Det. .10
☐ 294 Brian Skrudland, Mtl. .10
☐ 295 Pat Elynuik, Wpg. .10
☐ 296 Curtis Joseph (G), Stl. .50
☐ 297 Doug Bodger, Buf. .10
☐ 298 Ron Sutter, Pha. .10
☐ 299 Joe Murphy, Edm. .10
☐ 300 Vincent Damphousse, Tor. .20
☐ 301 Cam Neely, Bos. .20
☐ 302 Rick Tocchet, Pha. .10
☐ 303 Scott Stevens, Stl. .10
☐ 304 Ulf Samuelsson, Pgh. .10
☐ 305 Jeremy Roenick, Chi. .20
☐ 306 Dale and Mark Hunter .10
☐ 307 Aaron and Neal Broten .10
☐ 308 Gino and Paul Cavallini .10
☐ 309 Kelly and Kevin Miller .10
☐ **310 Dennis Vaske, NYI., RC .10**
☐ **311 Rob Pearson, Tor., RC .10**
☐ **312 Jason Miller, N.J., RC .10**
☐ **313 John LeClair, Mtl., RC 1.50**
☐ **314 Bryan Marchment, Wpg., RC .10**
☐ **315 Gary Shuchuk, Det., RC .10**
☐ **316 Dominik Hasek (G), Chi., RC 2.00**
☐ **317 Michel Picard, Hfd., RC .10**
☐ **318 Corey Millen, NYR., RC .10**
☐ **319 Joe Sacco, Tor., RC .10**
☐ **320 Reggie Savage, Wsh., RC .10**
☐ 321 Pat Murray, Pha. .10
☐ **322 Myles O'Connor, N.J., RC .10**
☐ 323 Shawn Antoski, Van. .10
☐ **324 Geoff Sanderson, Hfd., RC .25**
☐ 325 Chris Govedaris, Hfd. .10
☐ **326 Alexei Gusarov, Que., RC .10**
☐ 327 Mike Sillinger, Det. .10
☐ **328 Bob Wilkie, Det., RC .10**
☐ **329 Pat Jablonski (G), Stl., RC .10**
☐ 330 David Emma .10
☐ 331 TF: Kirk Muller, N.J. .10
☐ 332 TF: Pat LaFontaine, NYI. .20
☐ 333 TF: Brian Leetch, NYR. .20
☐ 334 TF: Rick Tocchet, Pha. .10
☐ 335 TF: Mario Lemieux, Pgh. .50
☐ 336 TF: Joe Sakic, Que. .25
☐ 337 TF: Brett Hull, Stl. .20
☐ 338 TF: Vincent Damphousse, Tor. .20
☐ 339 TF: Trevor Linden, Van. .20
☐ 340 TF: Kevin Hatcher, Wsh. .10
☐ 341 TF: Pat Elynuik, Wpg. .10
☐ 342 Patrick Roy (G), Mtl. .50
☐ 343 Brian Leetch, NYR. .20
☐ 344 Ray Bourque, Bos. .25
☐ 345 Luc Robitaille, L.A. .20
☐ 346 Wayne Gretzky, L.A. .75
☐ 347 Brett Hull, Stl. .20
☐ 348 Ed Belfour (G), Chi. .20
☐ 349 Rob Blake, L.A. .20
☐ 350 Eric Weinrich, N.J. .10
☐ 351 Jaromir Jagr, Pgh. .50
☐ 352 Sergei Fedorov, Det. .20
☐ 353 Ken Hodge, Bos. .10
☐ 354 Eric Lindros 1.25
☐ 355 Eric Lindros 1.25
☐ 356 Eric Lindros 1.25
☐ 357 Dana Murzyn, Van. .10
☐ 358 Adam Graves, Edm. .10
☐ 359 Ken Linseman, Edm. .10
☐ 360 Mike Keane, Mtl. .10
☐ 361 Stéphane Morin, Que. .10
☐ 362 Grant Ledyard, Buf. .10
☐ 363 Kris King, NYR. .10
☐ 364 Paul Gillis, Chi. .10
☐ 365 Chris Dahlquist, Min. .10
☐ 366 Paul Stanton, Pgh. .10
☐ 367 Jeff Hackett (G), S.J. .20
☐ 368 Robert McGill, S.J. .10
☐ 369 Neil Wilkinson, S.J. .10
☐ 370 Rob Zettler, S.J. .10
☐ 371 Brett Hull, Stl. .20
☐ 372 Paul Coffey, Pgh. .20
☐ 373 Mark Messier, Edm. .20
☐ 374 Dave Taylor, L.A. .10
☐ 375 Michel Goulet, Chi. .20
☐ 376 Dale Hawerchuk, Buf. .20
☐ 377 Pierre and Sylvain Turgeon .10
☐ 378 Rich, Ron and Brian Sutter .10
☐ 379 Brian and Joe Mullen .10
☐ 380 Geoff and Russ Courtnall .10
☐ 381 Trevor Kidd (G), Cgy. .20
☐ 382 Patrice Brisebois, Mtl. .10
☐ 383 Mark Greig, Hfd. .10
☐ 384 Kip Miller, Que. .10
☐ 385 Drake Berehowsky, Tor. .10
☐ **386 Kevin Haller, Buf., RC .10**
☐ 387 David Gagnon (G), Det. .10
☐ 388 Jason Marshall, Stl. .10
☐ 389 Donald Audette, Buf. .10
☐ **390 Patrick Lebeau, Mtl., RC .10**

	No.	Player	
☐	**391**	**Alexander Godynyuk, Tor., RC**	**.10**
☐	**392**	**Jarrod Skalde, N.J., RC**	**.10**
☐	**393**	**Ken Sutton, Buf., RC**	**.10**
☐	**394**	**Sergei Kharin, Wpg., RC**	**.10**
☐	**395**	**André Racicot (G), Mtl., RC**	**.10**
☐	**396**	**Doug Weight, NYR.., RC**	**.75**
☐	**397**	**Kevin Todd, N.J., RC**	**.10**
☐	**398**	**Tony Amonte, NYR., RC**	**.75**
☐	**399**	**Kimbi Daniels, Pha., RC**	**.10**
☐	**400**	**Jeff Daniels, Pgh., RC**	**.10**
☐	401	Speed and Grace: Guy Lafleur	.35
☐	402	Awards and Achievements: Guy Lafleur	.35
☐	403	A Hall of Famer: Guy Lafleur	.35
☐	404	LL: Brett Hull, Stl.	.20
☐	405	LL: Wayne Gretzky, L.A.	.75
☐	406	LL: Wayne Gretzky, L.A.	.75
☐	407	LL: Theoren Fleury/Marty McSorley	.20
☐	408	LL: Sergei Fedorov, Det	.25
☐	409	LL: Al MacInnis, Cgy.	.20
☐	410	LL: Ed Belfour (G), Chi.	.20
☐	411	LL: Ed Belfour (G), Chi.	.20
☐	412	Brett Hull 50 Goals/50 Games	.20
☐	413	Wayne Gretzky's 700th Career Goal	.75
☐	414	San Jose Sharks Checklist	.10
☐	415	TF: Ray Bourque, Bos.	.20
☐	416	TF: Pierre Turgeon, Buf.	.20
☐	417	TF: Al MacInnis, Cgy.	.20
☐	418	TF: Jeremy Roenick, Chi.	.20
☐	419	TF: Steve Yzerman, Det.	.25
☐	420	TF: Mark Messier, Edm.	.20
☐	421	TF: John Cullen, Hfd.	.10
☐	422	TF: Wayne Gretzky, L.A.	.75
☐	423	TF: Mike Modano, Min.	.20
☐	424	TF: Patrick Roy (G), Mtl.	.50
☐	425	Pittsburgh Penguins	.20
☐	426	AW: Mario Lemieux, Pgh.	.50
☐	427	AW: Wayne Gretzky, L.A.	.75
☐	428	AW: Brett Hull, Stl.	.20
☐	429	AW: Ray Bourque, Bos.	.20
☐	430	AW: Ed Belfour (G), Chi.	.20
☐	431	AW: Ed Belfour (G), Chi.	.20
☐	432	AW: Dirk Graham, Chi.	.10
☐	433	AW: Ed Belfour (G), Chi.	.20
☐	434	AW: Wayne Gretzky, L.A.	.75
☐	435	AW: Dave Taylor, L.A.	.10
☐	436	Randy Ladouceur, Hfd.	.10
☐	437	Dave Tippett, Wsh.	.10
☐	438	Clint Malarchuk (G), Buf.	.10
☐	439	Gord Roberts, Pgh.	.10
☐	440	Frank Pietrangelo (G), Pgh.	.10

BOBBY ORR COLLECTOR CARDS

The Bobby Orr collector cards were randomly inserted into the regular foil packs of all three issues, Canadian, Bilingual and American. A total of 270,000 cards were inserted, 45,000 of each. In addition 15,000 autographed cards were inserted, 2500 of each.

The "Junior Star" and "The Scoring Leader" cards were inserted in all three packs. The Stanley Cup Hero" and the "Hall of Famer" cards were inserted in the Canadian and Bilingual packs.

The "Rookie" and "The Award Winner" cards were inserted in the American packs.

Insert Set (6 cards): **55.00** **1,300.00**

	Player	Insert	Autograph
☐☐	Bobby Orr, Junior Star	12.00	285.00
☐☐	Bobby Orr, Scoring Leader	12.00	285.00
☐☐	Bobby Orr, Cup Hero	12.00	285.00
☐☐	Bobby Orr, Hall of Famer	12.00	285.00
☐☐	Bobby Orr, Rookie	12.00	285.00
☐☐	Bobby Orr, Award Winner	12.00	285.00

ERIC LINDROS FIRE ON ICE

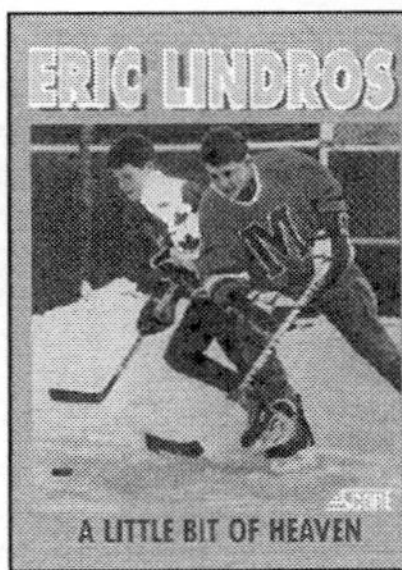

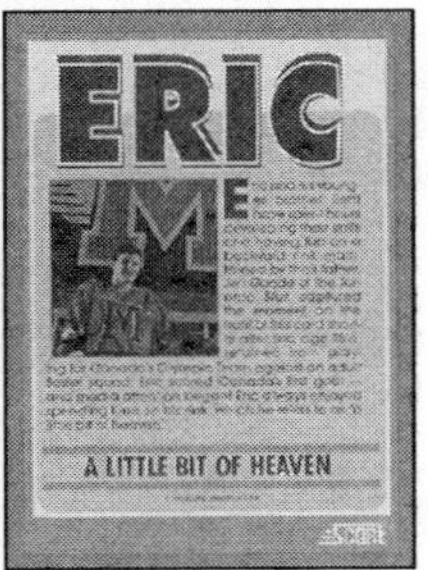

These 3 cards were given out by Score as a premium when purchasing Eric Lindros' book Fire On Ice.

Complete Set (3 cards): **6.00**

	No.	Player	NRMT-MT
☐	1	A Real Corker	3.00
☐	2	A Little Bit of Heaven	3.00
☐	3	Graduation Day	3.00

HOT CARDS

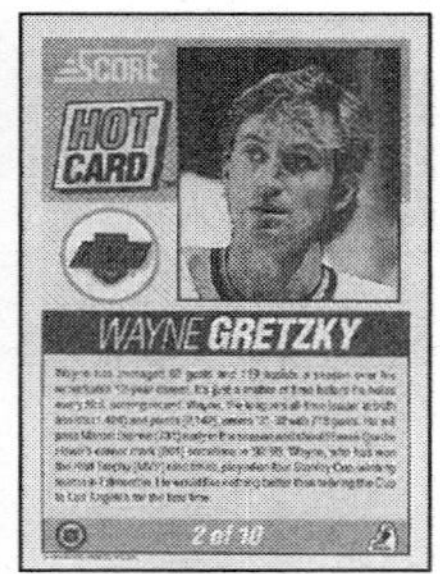

These cards were inserted in Score bubble packs

Insert Set (10 cards): **30.00**

	No.	Player	NRMT-MT
☐	1	Eric Lindros	6.50
☐	2	Wayne Gretzky, L.A.	10.00
☐	3	Brett Hull, Stl.	2.50
☐	4	Sergei Fedorov, Det.	2.50
☐	5	Mario Lemieux, Pgh.	8.00
☐	6	Adam Oates, Stl.	1.50
☐	7	Theoren Fleury, Cgy.	1.50
☐	8	Jaromir Jagr, Pgh.	5.00
☐	9	Ed Belfour (G), Chi.	1.50
☐	10	Jeremy Roenick, Chi.	1.50

ROOKIE AND TRADED

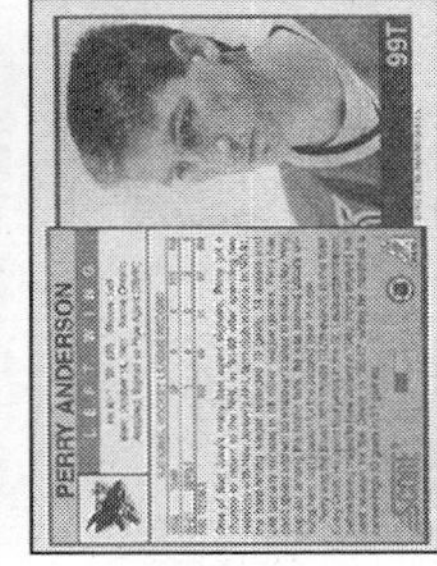

Rookie and Traded cards have a green border and act as an update to the American series. The 110-card set was sold as a set on its own.

Complete Set (110 cards): **5.00**

Common Player: **.10**

	No.	Player	NRMT-MT
☐	1T	Doug Wilson, S.J.	.20
☐	2T	Brian Mullen, S.J.	.10
☐	3T	Kelly Kisio, S.J.	.10
☐	4T	Brian Hayward (G), S.J.	.10
☐	5T	Tony Hrkac, S.J.	.10
☐	6T	Steven Bozek, S.J.	.10
☐	7T	John Carter, S.J.	.10
☐	8T	Neil Wilkinson, S.J.	.10
☐	9T	Wayne Presley, S.J.	.10
☐	10T	Bob McGill, S.J.	.10
☐	11T	Craig Ludwig, Min.	.10
☐	12T	Mikhail Tatarinov, Que.	.10
☐	13T	Todd Elik, Min.	.10
☐	14T	Randy Burridge, Wsh.	.10
☐	15T	Tim Kerr, NYR.	.10
☐	16T	Randy Gilhen, L.A.	.10
☐	17T	John Tonelli, Chi.	.10
☐	18T	Tom Kurvers, NYI.	.10
☐	19T	Steve Duchesne, Pha.	.10
☐	20T	Charlie Huddy, L.A.	.10
☐	21T	Adam Creighton, NYI.	.10
☐	22T	Brent Ashton, Bos.	.10
☐	23T	Rob Ramage, Min.	.10
☐	24T	Steve Kasper, Pha.	.10
☐	25T	Scott Mellanby, Edm.	.10
☐	26T	Steve Leach, Bos.	.10
☐	27T	Scott Niedermayer, N.J.	.20
☐	28T	Craig Berube, Tor.	.10
☐	29T	Greg Paslawski, Que.	.10
☐	30T	Randy Hillier, Buf.	.10
☐	31T	Stéphane Richer, N.J.	.10
☐	32T	Brian MacLellan, Det.	.10
☐	33T	Marc Habscheid, Cgy.	.10
☐	34T	Dave Babych, Van.	.10
☐	35T	Troy Murray, Wpg.	.10
☐	36T	Ray Sheppard, Det.	.10
☐	37T	Glen Featherstone, Bos.	.10
☐	38T	Brendan Shanahan, Stl.	.50
☐	39T	Dave Christian, Stl.	.10
☐	40T	Mike Bullard, Tor.	.10
☐	41T	Ryan Walter, Van.	.10
☐	42T	Randy Wood, Buf.	.10
☐	43T	Vincent Riendeau (G), Det.	.10
☐	44T	Adam Graves, NYR.	.10
☐	45T	Scott Stevens, N.J.	.20
☐	46T	Sylvain Côté, Wsh.	.10
☐	47T	David Barr, N.J.	.10
☐	48T	Randy Gregg, Van.	.10
☐	49T	Pavel Bure, Van.	.50
☐	50T	Jari Kurri, L.A.	.20
☐	51T	Steve Thomas, NYI.	.10
☐	52T	Troy Crowder, Det.	.10
☐	53T	Brad Jones, Pha.	.10
☐	54T	Randy McKay, N.J.	.10
☐	55T	Scott Thornton, Edm.	.10
☐	56T	Bryan Marchment, Chi.	.10
☐	57T	Andrew Cassels, Hfd.	.10
☐	58T	Grant Fuhr (G), Tor,	.20
☐	59T	Vincent Damphousse, Edm.	.20
☐	60T	Rick Zombo, Stl.	.10
☐	61T	Glenn Anderson, Tor.	.10
☐	62T	Peter Ing (G), Edm.	.10
☐	63T	Tom Chorske, N.J.	.10
☐	64T	Kirk Muller, Mtl.	.10
☐	65T	Dan Quinn, Pha.	.10
☐	66T	Murray Baron, Stl.	.10
☐	67T	Sergei Nemchinov, NYR.	.10
☐	68T	Rod Brind'Amour, Pha.	.20
☐	69T	Ron Sutter, Stl.	.10
☐	70T	Luke Richardson, Edm.	.10
☐	71T	Nicklas Lidström, Det., Error	.20
☐	72T	Petri Skriko, Wpg.	.10
☐	73T	Steve Smith, Chi.	.10
☐	74T	Dave Manson, Edm.	.10
☐	75T	Kay Whitmore (G), Hfd.	.10
☐	76T	Valeri Kamensky, Que.	.20
☐	77T	Russ Romaniuk, Wpg.	.10
☐	78T	Brad May, Buf.	.10
☐	79T	Tomas Forslund, Cgy.	.10
☐	80T	Stu Barnes, Wpg.	.10
☐	81T	Darryl Sydor, L.A.	.10
☐	82T	Jimmy Waite (G), Chi.	.10
☐	83T	Vladimir Ruzicka, Bos.	.10
☐	84T	Dave Brown, Pha.	.10
☐	85T	Mark Messier, NYR.	.35
☐	86T	Neil Sheehy, Cgy.	.10
☐	87T	Todd Krygier, Wsh.	.10
☐	88T	Eric Lindros, Cdn.	3.50
☐	89T	Nelson Emerson, Stl.	.10
☐	90T	Pat Falloon, S.J.	.10
☐	91T	Dean Evason, S.J.	.10
☐	92T	Jeff Hackett (G), S.J.	.20
☐	93T	Rob Zettler, S.J.	.10
☐	94T	Perry Berezan, S.J.	.10
☐	95T	Pat MacLeod, S.J.	.10
☐	96T	Craig Coxe, S.J.	.10
☐	97T	Ken Hammond, S.J.	.10
☐	98T	Brian Lawton, S.J.	.10
☐	99T	Perry Anderson, S.J.	.10
☐	100T	Pat LaFontaine, Buf	.20
☐	101T	Pierre Turgeon, NYI.	.20
☐	102T	Dave McLlwain, NYI.	.10
☐	103T	Brent Sutter, Chi.	.10
☐	104T	Uwe Krupp, NYI.	.10
☐	105T	Martin Lapointe, Det.	.10
☐	106T	Derian Hatcher, Min.	.20
☐	107T	Darrin Shannon, Wpg.	.10
☐	108T	Benoît Hogue, NYI.	.10
☐	109T	Vladimir Konstantinov, Det.	.20
☐	110T	Andrei Lomakin, Pha.	.10

YOUNG SUPERSTARS

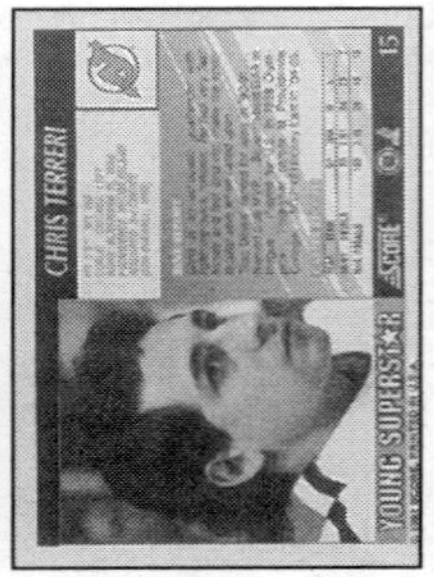

This was sold as a boxed 40-card set.

Imprint: 1991 SCORE, PRINTED IN U.S.A.

Complete Set (40 cards): **6.00**

Common Player: **.10**

	No.	Player	NRMT-MT
☐	1	Sergei Fedorov, Det.	.50
☐	2	Mike Richter (G), NYR.	.35
☐	3	Mats Sundin, Que.	.50
☐	4	Theoren Fleury, Cgy.	.35
☐	5	John Cullen, Hfd.	.10
☐	6	Dimitri Khristich, Wsh.	.10
☐	7	Stéphan Lebeau, Mtl.	.10
☐	8	Rob Blake, L.A.	.25
☐	9	Ken Hodge, Bos.	.10
☐	10	Mike Ricci, Pha.	.10
☐	11	Trevor Linden, Van.	.25
☐	12	Peter Ing (G), Edm.	.10
☐	13	Alexander Mogilny, Buf.	.35
☐	14	Martin Gelinas, Edm.	.10
☐	15	Chris Terreri (G), N.J.	.10
☐	16	Jeff Norton, NYI.	.10
☐	17	Bob Essensa (G), Wpg.	.10
☐	18	Mark Tinordi, Min.	.10
☐	19	Curtis Joseph (G), Stl.	.60
☐	20	Joe Sakic, Que.	.85
☐	21	Jeremy Roenick, Chi.	.35
☐	22	Mark Recchi, Pgh.	.25
☐	23	Eric Desjardins, Mtl.	.25
☐	24	Robert Reichel, Cgy.	.25
☐	25	Tim Cheveldae (G), Det.	.10
☐	26	Eric Weinrich, N.J.	.10
☐	27	Murray Barron, Stl.	.10
☐	28	Darren Turcotte, NYR.	.10
☐	29	Troy Gamble (G), Van.	.10
☐	30	Eric Lindros, Osh.	3.00
☐	31	Benoît Hogue, Buf.	.10
☐	32	Ed Belfour (G), Chi.	.35
☐	33	Ron Tugnutt (G), Que.	.10
☐	34	Pat Elynuik, Wpg.	.10
☐	35	Mike Modano, Min.	.50
☐	36	Bobby Holik, Hfd.	.10
☐	37	Yves Racine, Det.	.10
☐	38	Jaromir Jagr, Pgh.	1.00
☐	39	Stéphane Morin, Que.	.10
☐	40	Kevin Miller, Det.	.10

1991 - 92 SEMIC ELITSERIEN STICKERS

Size: 3" x 2 1/8"

Complete Set (360 stickers) **40.00**

Common Player: **.20**

	No.	Player	NRMT-MT
☐	1	AIK Logo	.20
☐	2	Thomas Ostlund	.20
☐	3	Sam Lindstahl	.20
☐	4	Borje Salming	2.00
☐	5	Petri Liimatainen	.20
☐	6	Mats Thelin	.20
☐	7	Rikard Franzen	.20
☐	8	Petter Sahlsten	.20
☐	9	Daniel Jardemyr	.20
☐	10	Thomas Nilsson	.20
☐	11	Niclas Havelid	.20
☐	12	Mattias Norstrom	.20
☐	13	Peter Gradin	.20
☐	14	Peter Hammarstrom	.20
☐	15	Patrik Ericksson	.20
☐	16	Thomas Bjuhr	.20
☐	17	Thomas Strandberg	.20
☐	18	Tommy Lehmann	.20
☐	19	Mats Lindberg	.20
☐	20	Patric Kjellberg	.20
☐	21	Michael Nylander	1.00
☐	22	Patric Englund	.20
☐	23	Niclas Sundblad	.20
☐	24	Kristian Gahn	.20
☐	25	Erik Andersson	.20
☐	26	Bjorn Ahlstrom	.20
☐	27	Brynas Logo	.20
☐	28	Michael Sundlov	.20
☐	29	Lars Eriksson	.20
☐	30	Lars Karlsson	.20
☐	31	Tommy Sjokin	.20
☐	32	Nikolaj Davydkin	.20
☐	33	Niklas Gallstedt	.20
☐	34	Mikael Lindman	.20
☐	35	Tommy Melkersson	.20
☐	36	Mikael Enander	.20
☐	37	Ruban Molander	.20
☐	38	Stefan Klockare	.20
☐	39	Anders Huss	.20
☐	40	Mikael Lindholm	.20
☐	41	Jan Larsson	.20
☐	42	Anders Gozzi	.20
☐	43	Peter Larsson	.20
☐	44	Thomas Tallberg	.20
☐	45	Peter Gustafsson	.20
☐	46	Joakim Persson	.20
☐	47	Peter Eriksson	.20
☐	48	Ove Molin	.20
☐	49	Jonas Johnson	.20
☐	50	Johan Schillgard	.20
☐	51	Andreas Dackell	.50
☐	52	Tom Bissett	.20
☐	53	Djurgarden Logo	.20
☐	54	Tommy Söderström (G)	1.00
☐	55	Joakim Persson	.20
☐	56	Petter Ronnqvist	.20
☐	57	Thomas Eriksson	.20
☐	58	Kenneth Kennholt	.20
☐	59	Arto Blomsten	.20
☐	60	Orvar Stambert	.20
☐	61	Christian Due-Boje	.20
☐	62	Marcus Ragnarsson	.20
☐	63	Per Nygards	.20
☐	64	Thomas Johansson	.20
☐	65	Mikael Johansson	.20
☐	66	Charles Berglund	.20
☐	67	Jan Viktorsson	.20
☐	68	Ola Josefsson	.20
☐	69	Jens Ohlin	.20
☐	70	Magnus Jansson	.20
☐	71	Peter Nilsson	.20
☐	72	Fredrik Linqvist	.20
☐	73	Mariusz Czerkawski	.50
☐	74	Johan Lindstedt	.20
☐	75	Stefan Ketola	.20
☐	76	Erik Huusko	.20
☐	77	Anders Huusko	.20
☐	78	Farjestad Logo	.20
☐	79	Anders Bergman	.20
☐	80	Jorgen Ryden	.20
☐	81	Patrik Haltia	.20
☐	82	Tommy Samuelsson	.20
☐	83	Per Lundell	.20
☐	84	Leif Carlsson	.20
☐	85	Jesper Duus	.20
☐	86	Mattias Olsson	.20
☐	87	Thomas Rhodin	.20
☐	88	Jacob Karlsson	.20
☐	89	Greger Artursson	.20
☐	90	Thomas Rundqvist	.20
☐	91	Bengt Gustafsson	.35
☐	92	Hakan Loob	1.50
☐	93	Lars Karlsson	.20
☐	94	Magnus Roupe	.20
☐	95	Kjell Dahlin	.20
☐	96	Staffan Lundh	.20
☐	97	Peter Ottosson	.20
☐	98	Niklas Brannstrom	.20
☐	99	Jonas Hoglund	.50
☐	100	Clas Eriksson	.20
☐	101	Andreas Johansson	.20
☐	102	Mathias Johansson	.20
☐	103	HV 71 Logo	.20
☐	104	Peter Aslin	.20
☐	105	Boo Ahl (G)	.20
☐	106	Stefan Magnusson	.20
☐	108	Fredrik Stillman	.20
☐	109	Klas Heed	.20
☐	110	Arto Ruotanen	.20
☐	111	Per Gustafsson	.50
☐	112	Tommy Fritz	.20
☐	113	Mathias Svedberg	.20
☐	114	Kristian Pedersen	.20
☐	115	Peter Eriksson	.20
☐	116	Risto Kurkinen	.20
☐	117	Ove Thornberg	.20
☐	118	Stefan Ornskog	.20
☐	119	Thomas Ljungberg	.20
☐	120	Patrik Ross	.20
☐	121	Eddy Ericsson	.20
☐	122	Dennis Strom	.20
☐	123	Torbjorn Persson	.20
☐	124	Jonas Jonsson	.20
☐	125	Peter Ekelund	.20
☐	126	Stefan Falk	.20
☐	127	Ronny Nilsson	.20
☐	128	Leksand Logo	.20
☐	129	Olow Sundstrom	.20
☐	130	Jonas Leven	.20
☐	131	Tomas Jonsson	.20
☐	132	Ricard Persson	.20
☐	133	Magnus Svensson	.20
☐	134	Mattias Andersson	.20
☐	135	Henric Bjorkman	.20
☐	136	Orjan Lindmark	.20
☐	137	Orjan Nilsson	.20
☐	138	Tomas Ring	.20
☐	139	Roger Johansson	.20
☐	140	Marcus Thuresson	.20
☐	141	Per-Olof Carlsson	.20
☐	142	Jens Nielsen	.20
☐	143	Cenneth Soderlund	.20
☐	144	Markus Akerblom	.20
☐	145	Fredrik Jax	.20
☐	146	Reine Rauhala	.20
☐	147	Niklas Eriksson	.20
☐	148	Martin Wiita	.20
☐	149	Jonas Bergqvist	.20
☐	150	Hannu Jarvenpaa	.20
☐	151	Lulea Logo	.20
☐	152	Robert Skoog	.20
☐	153	Erik Granqvist	.20
☐	154	Timo Jutila	.50
☐	155	Tomas Lilja	.20
☐	156	Lars Modig	.20
☐	157	Per Ljusterang	.20
☐	158	Jari Gronstrand	.20
☐	159	Torbjorn Lindberg	.20
☐	160	Patrik Hoglund	.20
☐	161	Petter Nilsson	.20
☐	162	Daniel Behm	.20
☐	163	Johan Stromvall	.20
☐	164	Pauli Jarvinen	.20
☐	165	Lars Edstrom	.20
☐	166	Lars-Gunnar Pettersson	.20
☐	167	Stefan Nilsson	.20
☐	168	Lars Hurtig	.20
☐	169	Tomas Berglund	.20
☐	170	Robert Nordberg	.20
☐	171	Mikael Renberg	.20
☐	172	Ulf Sandstrom	.20
☐	173	Jens Hellgren	.20
☐	174	Mikael engstrom	.20
☐	175	Malmo Logo	.20
☐	176	Peter Lindmark	.20
☐	177	Roger Nordström (G)	.20
☐	178	Johan Mansson	.20
☐	179	Timo Blomqvist	.20
☐	180	Peter Andersson	.20
☐	181	Mats Lusth	.20
☐	182	Roger Ohman	.20
☐	183	Johan Salle	.20
☐	184	Anders Svensson	.20
☐	185	Johan Norgren	.20
☐	186	Raimo Helminen	.20

	No.	Player	Price
☐	187	Mats Hallin	.20
☐	188	Mats Naslund	2.00
☐	189	Robert Burakovsky	.20
☐	190	Hakan Ahlund	.20
☐	191	Peter Sundstrom	.20
☐	192	Daniel Rydmark	.20
☐	193	Matti Pauna	.20
☐	194	Roger Hansson	.20
☐	195	Patrik Gustavsson	.20
☐	196	Rick Erdall	.20
☐	197	Bo Svanberg	.20
☐	198	Jesper Mattsson	.35
☐	199	Jonas Hakansson	.20
☐	200	MoDo Logo	.20
☐	201	Fredrik Andersson	.20
☐	202	Goran Arnmark	.20
☐	203	Miroslav Horava	.20
☐	204	Hans Lodin	.20
☐	205	Iras Jansson	.20
☐	206	Jorgen Eriksson	.20
☐	208	Anders Berglund	.20
☐	208	Osmo Soutokorva	.20
☐	209	Tomas Nanzen	.20
☐	210	Hans Jonsson	.20
☐	211	Fredrik Bergqvist	.20
☐	212	Erik Holmberg	.20
☐	213	Peter Forsberg	15.00
☐	214	Markus Naslund	1.00
☐	215	Magnus Wernblom	.20
☐	216	Lars Bystrom	.20
☐	217	Kent Lantz	.20
☐	218	Per Wallin	.20
☐	219	Lennart Henriksson	.20
☐	220	Ingemar Strom	.20
☐	221	Ulf Odmark	.20
☐	222	Jens Ohman	.20
☐	223	Tommy Pettersson	.20
☐	224	Andreas Salomonsson	.20
☐	225	Sodertalje Logo	.20
☐	226	Reino Sundberg	.20
☐	227	Stefan Dernestal	.20
☐	228	Mats Kilstrom	.20
☐	229	Stefan Jonsson	.20
☐	230	Jan Bergman	.20
☐	231	Peter Ekroth	.20
☐	232	Stefan Nyman	.20
☐	233	Thomas Carlsson	.20
☐	234	Stefan Claesson	.20
☐	235	Oto Hascak	.20
☐	236	Morgan Samuelsson	.20
☐	237	Tomax Eriksson	.20
☐	238	Thom Eklund	.20
☐	239	Conny Jansson	.20
☐	240	Bjorn Carlsson	.20
☐	241	Scott Moore	.20
☐	242	Reine Landgren	.20
☐	243	Ola Rosander	.20
☐	244	Stefan Olsson	.20
☐	245	Anders Frykbo	.20
☐	246	Ola Andersson	.20
☐	247	Joe Tracy	.20
☐	248	Christer Ljungberg	.20
☐	249	Patrik Nyberg	.20
☐	250	Joakim Skold	.20
☐	251	Västerås logo	.20
☐	252	Mats Ytter (G)	.20
☐	253	Par Hellenberg	.20
☐	254	Tommy Salo (G)	1.00
☐	255	Nicklas Lidström	3.00
☐	256	Robert Nordmark	.20
☐	257	Leif Rohlin	.20
☐	258	Roger Akerstrom	.20
☐	259	Peter Popovic	.35
☐	260	Jan Karlsson	.20
☐	261	Tore Lindgren	.20
☐	262	Peter Jacobsson	.20
☐	263	Pierre Ivarsson	.20
☐	264	Mishat Fahrutdinov	.20
☐	265	Paul Andersson	.20
☐	266	Patrik Juhlin	.35
☐	267	Henrik Nilsson	.20
☐	268	Anders Berglund	.20
☐	269	Claes Lindblom	.20
☐	270	Jorgen Holmberg	.20
☐	271	Stefan Hellkvist	.20
☐	272	Fredrik Nilsson	.20
☐	274	Micael Karlberg	.20
☐	275	Niclas Lundberg	.20
☐	276	Vastra Frolunda Logo	.20
☐	277	Ake Lilljebjorn	.20
☐	278	Hakan Algotsson	.20
☐	279	Hakan Nordin	.20
☐	280	Jonas Heed	.20
☐	281	Joacim Esbjors	.20
☐	282	Stefan Larsson	.20
☐	283	Stefan Axelsson	.20
☐	284	Oscar Ackestrom	.20
☐	285	Jerk Hogstrom	.20
☐	286	Patric Aberg	.20
☐	287	Patrok Carnback	.20
☐	288	Serge Boisvert	.20
☐	289	Mats Lundstrom	.20
☐	290	Miael Andersson	.20
☐	291	Kari Jaako	.20
☐	292	Terho Koskela	.20
☐	293	Lars Dahlstrom	.20
☐	294	Jerry Persson	.20
☐	295	Peter Berndtsson	.20
☐	296	Thomas Sjogren	.20
☐	297	Par Edlund	.20
☐	298	Christian Lechtaler	.20
☐	299	Jonas Esbjors	.20
☐	300	Dennis Fredriksson	.20
☐	301	Mats Hjalmarsson	.20
☐	302	Leif Holmgren, Coach	.20
☐	303	Tommy Sandlin, Coach	.20
☐	304	Lars Falk, Coach	.20
☐	305	Harald Luckner, Coach	.20
☐	306	Lars-Erik Lundstrom, Coach	.20
☐	307	Staffan Tholson, Coach	.20
☐	309	Freddy Lindfors, Coach	.20
☐	309	Timo Lahtinen, Coach	.20
☐	310	Jan-Ake Andersson, Coach	.20
☐	311	Claes-Goran Wallin, Coach	.20
☐	312	Mikael Lundstrom, Coach	.20
☐	313	Leif Boork, Coach	.20
☐	314	Thomas Rundqvist	.20
☐	315	Hakan Loob	1.00
☐	316	Tommy Söderström (G)	.75
☐	317	Niklas Andersson	.20
☐	318	Hakan Loob	1.00
☐	319	Tomas Sandström	1.00
☐	320	Rolf Ridderwall	.20
☐	321	Thomas Eriksson	.20
☐	322	Niklas Lidström	3.00
☐	323	Mats Sundin	8.00
☐	324	Thomas Rundqvist	.20
☐	325	Hakan Loob	1.00
☐	326	Marcus Karlsson	.20
☐	327	Anders Eriksson	.35
☐	328	Mats Lindgren	.35
☐	329	Mikael Hakansson	.20
☐	330	Mathias Johansson	.20
☐	331	Niklas Sundstrom	1.50
☐	332	Jesper Mattsson	.20
☐	333	Anders Soderberg	.20
☐	334	Swedish Ice Hockey	.20
☐	335	1991 World Champions	.20
☐	336	Rolf Ridderwall	.20
☐	337	Peter Lindmark	.20
☐	338	Tommy Söderström (G)	.20
☐	339	Kjell Samuelsson	.20
☐	340	Calle Johansson	.20
☐	341	Nicklas Lidström	3.00
☐	342	Tomas Jonsson	.20
☐	343	Peter Andersson	.20
☐	344	Kenneth Kennholt	.20
☐	345	Fredrik Stillman	.20
☐	346	Thomas Rundqvist	.20
☐	347	Hakan Loob	1.00
☐	348	Bengt Gustafsson	.20
☐	349	Mats Naslund	1.50
☐	350	Mikael Johansson	.20
☐	351	Charles Berglund	.20
☐	352	Jan Viktorsson	.20
☐	353	Johan Garpenlov	.35
☐	354	Anders Carlsson	.20
☐	355	Patrik Ericksson	.20
☐	356	Jonas Bergqvist	.20
☐	357	Mats Sundin	8.00
☐	358	Per-Erik Eklun	.20
☐	359	Conny Evensson	.20
☐	360	Curt Lundmark	.20

1991 - 92 7TH INNING SKETCH AWARD WINNERS

Imprint: 1992 Seventh Inning Sketch "Tomorrows Stars Today". Printed in Canada

Complete Set (30 cards): 12.00

	No.	Player	NRMT-MT
☐	1	Eric Lindros, Oshawa	3.00
☐	2	Dale Craigwell, Oshawa	.15
☐	3	Nathan LaFayette, Cornwall	.15
☐	4	Chris Snell, Ottawa-OHL	.15
☐	5	Cory Stillman, Windsor	.15
☐	6	Mike Torchia (G), Kitchener	.15
☐	7	George Burnett, Niagara Falls	.15
☐	8	Eric Lindros, Oshawa	3.00
☐	9	Sherwood Bassin, S.S.Marie	.15
☐	10	Player of the Year: Eric Lindros, Osh.	3.00
☐	11	Scott Niedermayer, Kamloops	.50
☐	12	Pat Falloon, Spokane	.25
☐	13	Scott Niedermayer, Kamloops	.50
☐	14	Darryl Sydor, Kamloops	.25
☐	15	Donevan Hextall	.15
☐	16	Jamie McLennan, Lethbridge	.50
☐	17	Tom Renney, Kamloops	.25
☐	18	Frank Evans, Spokane	.15
☐	19	Bob Brown, Kamloops	.15
☐	20	Ray Whitney, Spokane	.50
☐	21	Phillippe Boucher, Granby	.15
☐	22	Yanic Perreault, Trois-Rivières	.25
☐	23	Benoît Larose, Laval	.15
☐	24	Patrice Brisebois, Drummondville	.25
☐	25	Phillippe Boucher, Granby	.15
☐	26	Félix Potvin Chicoutimi	1.00
☐	27	Joe Canale, Chicoutimi	.15
☐	28	Christian Larivière, St-Hyacinthe	.15
☐	29	Roland Janellem Drummondville	.15
☐	30	Yanic Perreault, Trois-Rivières	.25

1991 - 92 7TH INNING SKETCH OHL

There are several card number errors in this set. Card 293 is unknown.

Imprint: 1991 7TH Inning Sketch Printed in Canada

Complete Set (383 cards): 20.00

Common Player: .10

	No.	Player	NRMT-MT
☐		The Dream	5.00
☐	1	John Slaney, Cornwall	.25
☐	2	Jason Meloch , Cornwall	.10
☐	3	Mark DeSantis, Cornwall	.10
☐	4	Richard Raymond, Cornwall	.10
☐	5	Dave Lemay, Cornwall	.10

	No.	Player	Price
☐	6	Matt McGuffin, Cornwall	.10
☐	7	Sam Oliveira, Cornwall	.10
☐	8	Jeremy Stevenson, Cornwall	.10
☐	9	Todd Walker, Cornwall	.10
☐	10	Jean-Alain Schneider, Cornwall	.10
☐	11	Guy Lévêque, Cornwall	.25
☐	12	Shayne Gaffar, Cornwall	.10
☐	13	Mike Prokopec, Cornwall	.50
☐	14	Nathan Lafayette, Cornwall	.50
☐	15	Larry Courville, Cornwall	.10
☐	16	Chris Clancy, Cornwall	.10
☐	17	Thomas Nemeth , Cornwall	.10
☐	18	Jeff Reid , Cornwall	.10
☐	19	Ilpo Kauhanen (G), Cornwall	.15
☐	20	Rob Dykeman (G), Cornwall	.15
☐	21	Rival Fullum, Cornwall	.10
☐	22	Ryan VandenBussche, Cornwall	.50
☐	23	Gordon Pell, Cornwall	.10
☐	24	Paul Andrea, Cornwall, Error (Generals)	.10
☐	25	John Lovell, Coach, Cornwall, Error (Generals)	.10
☐	26	Alan Letang, Cornwall	.10
☐	27	Chris Phelps, Detroit	.10
☐	28	John Wynne, Detroit	.10
☐	29	Rob Kinghan, Detroit	.10
☐	30	Glen Craig, Detroit	.10
☐	31	Eric Cairns, Detroit	.50
☐	32	John Pinches, Detroit	.10
☐	33	Todd Harvey, Detroit	.75
☐	34	Craig Fraser, Detroit	.10
☐	35	Pat Peake, Detroit	.50
☐	36	Chris Skoryna, Detroit	.10
☐	37	Bob Wren, Detroit	.25
☐	38	Chris Varga, Detroit	.10
☐	39	David Benn, Detroit	.10
☐	40	Mark Lawrence, Detroit	.25
☐	41	Jeff Kostuch, Detroit	.10
☐	42	J. D. Eaton, Detroit	.10
☐	43	Derek Etches, Detroit	.10
☐	44	Jeff Gardiner, Detroit	.10
☐	45	James Shea (G), Detroit	.15
☐	46	Brad Teichmann (G), Detroit	.15
☐	47	Jim Rutherford, GM-Coach, Detroit	.10
☐	48	Derek Wilkinson, Detroit	.10
☐	49	OHL Action	.10
☐	50	OHL Action	.10
☐	51	Sandy Allan (G), North Bay	.15
☐	52	Ron Bertrand (G), North Bay	.15
☐	53	Brad Brown, North Bay	.25
☐	54	Dennis Bonvie, North Bay	.25
☐	55	Bradley Shepard, North Bay	.10
☐	56	Allan Cox, North Bay	.10
☐	57	Jack Williams, North Bay	.10
☐	58	Chad Penney, North Bay	.25
☐	59	Jason Firth, North Bay	.10
☐	60	Bill Lang, North Bay	.10
☐	61	Ryan Merritt, North Bay	.10
☐	62	Michael Burman, North Bay	.10
☐	63	Billy Wright, North Bay	.10
☐	64	Dave Szabo, North Bay	.10
☐	65	James Sheehan, North Bay	.10
☐	66	John Spoltore, North Bay	.10
☐	67	Paul Rushforth, North Bay	.10
☐	68	Jeff Shevalier, North Bay	.50
☐	69	Robert Thorpe, North Bay	.10
☐	70	Drake Berehowsky, North Bay, Error	.25
☐	71	Patrick Barton, North Bay	.10
☐	72	Bert Templeton, Coach, North Bay	.10
☐	73	Wade Gibson, Ottawa	.10
☐	74	C. Jay Denomme (G), Kitchener	.15
☐	75	Mike Torchia (G), Kitchener	.50
☐	76	Mike Polano, Kitchener	.10
☐	77	Tony McCabe, Kitchener	.10
☐	78	Chris Kraemer, Kitchener	.10
☐	79	Tim Spitzig, Kitchener	.10
☐	80	Trevor Gallant, Kitchener	.10
☐	81	Yvan Corbin, Kitchener	.10
☐	82	Norman Dezainde, Kitchener	.10
☐	83	Marc Robillard, Kitchener	.10
☐	84	Derek Gauthier, Kitchener	.10
☐	85	Gib Tucker, Kitchener	.10
☐	86	Paul McCallion, Kitchener	.25
☐	87	Eric Manlow, Kitchener	.10
☐	88	James Caruso, Kitchener	.10
☐	89	Gary Miller, Kitchener	.10
☐	90	Jason Stevenson, Kitchener	.10
☐	91	Shayne McCosh, Kitchener	.10
☐	92	Jason Gladney, Kitchener	.10
☐	93	Brad Barton, Kitchener	.10
☐	94	Chris LiPuma, Kitchener	.25
☐	95	Justin Cullen, Kitchener	.10
☐	96	Bill Smith, Scout, Kitchener	.10
☐	97	Joe McDonnell, Coach, Kitchener	.10
☐	98	C. Schucask, Kitchener, Error (Card 000)	.10
☐	99	Brent Gretzky, Belleville	.50
☐	100	Gairin Smith, Belleville	.10
☐	101	Blair Scott, Belleville	.10
☐	102	Daniel Godbout, Belleville	.10
☐	103	Dan Preston, Belleville	.10
☐	104	Ian Keiller, Belleville	.10
☐	105	Rick Marshall, Belleville	.10
☐	106	Aaron Morrison, Belleville	.10
☐	107	Dominic Belanger, Belleville	.10
☐	108	Kevin Brown, Belleville	.25
☐	109	Tony Cimellaro, Belleville	.10
☐	110	Larry Mavety, Coach, Belleville	.10
☐	111	Jake Grimes, Belleville	.10
☐	112	Greg Dreveny (G), Belleville	.15
☐	113	Darren McCarty, Belleville	.50
☐	114	Doug Doull, Belleville	.10
☐	115	Scott Boston, Belleville	.10
☐	116	Dale Chokan, Belleville	.10
☐	117	Darren Hurley, Belleville	.10
☐	118	B. Mielko, Belleville, Error (Card 61)	.10
☐	119	R. Gallace, Belleville, Error (Card 65)	.10
☐	120	Shayne Antoski, Belleville	.10
☐	121	Greg Bailey, Belleville	.10
☐	122	Keith Redmond, Belleville	.10
☐	123	Dick Todd, Coach, Peterborough	.10
☐	124	Scott Turner, Peterborough	.10
☐	125	Colin Wilson, Peterborough	.10
☐	126	Mike Tomlinson, Peterborough	.10
☐	127	Dale McTavish, Peterborough	.10
☐	128	Chris Longo, Peterborough	.10
☐	129	Chad Lang (G), Peterborough	.15
☐	130	Brent Tully, Peterborough	.25
☐	131	Shawn Heins, Peterborough	.10
☐	132	Geordie Kinnear, Peterborough	.25
☐	133	Jeff Walker, Peterborough	.10
☐	134	Chris Pronger, Peterborough	1.25
☐	135	Chad Grills, Peterborough	.10
☐	136	Michael Harding, Peterborough	.10
☐	137	Matt St. Germain, Peterborough	.10
☐	138	Don O'Neill, Peterborough	.10
☐	139	Dave Roche, Peterborough	.25
☐	140	Doug Searle, Peterborough	.10
☐	141	Bryan Gendron, Peterborough	.10
☐	142	Kelly Vipond, Peterborough	.10
☐	143	Andrew Verner (G), Peterborough	.25
☐	144	Ryan Black, Peterborough	.10
☐	145	Jason Dawe, Peterborough	.25
☐	146	Jassen Cullimore, Peterborough	.50
☐	148	Jason Arnott, Oshawa	2.50
☐	149	Jan Benda, Oshawa	.10
☐	150	Todd Bradley, Oshawa	.10
☐	151	Markus Brunner, Oshawa	.10
☐	152	Jason Campeau, Oshawa	.10
☐	153	Mark Deazeley, Oshawa	.10
☐	154	Matt Hoffman, Oshawa	.10
☐	155	Scott Hollis, Oshawa	.10
☐	156	Neil Iserhoff, Oshawa	.10
☐	157	Darryl LaFrance, Oshawa	.10
☐	158	B. J. MacPherson, Oshawa	.10
☐	159	Troy Swee, Oshawa	.10
☐	160	Jason Weaver, Oshawa	.10
☐	161	Stéphane Yelle, Oshawa	.50
☐	162	Trevor Burgess, Oshawa	.10
☐	163	Joe Cook, Oshawa	.10
☐	164	Jean-Paul Davis, Oshawa	.10
☐	165	Brian Grieve, Oshawa	.10
☐	166	Rob Leask, Oshawa	.10
☐	167	Wade Simpson, Oshawa	.10
☐	168	Kevin Spero, Oshawa	.10
☐	169	Fred Brathwaite (G), Oshawa	.50
☐	170	Mike Fountain (G), Oshawa	.50
☐	171	Rick Cornacchia, Coach, Oshawa	.10
☐	172	Checklist 1 (1 to 98)	.10
☐	173	Todd Warriner, Windsor	.50
☐	174	Reuben Castella, Windsor	.10
☐	175	Cory Stillman, Windsor	.50
☐	176	Steve Gibson, Windsor	.10
☐	177	Trent Cull, Windsor	.25
☐	178	John Copley, Windsor	.10
☐	179	Craig Binns, Windsor	.10
☐	180	Ryan O'Neill, Windsor	.10
☐	181	Matthew Mullin (G), Windsor	.15
☐	182	Todd Hunter, Windsor	.10
☐	183	Jason Stos, Windsor	.10
☐	184	Robert Frayn, Windsor, Error	.10
☐	185	Leonard MacDonald, Windsor	.10
☐	186	Tom Sullivan, Windsor	.10
☐	187	Steve Smith, Windsor	.10
☐	188	Bill Bowler, Windsor	.10
☐	189	James Allison, Windsor	.50
☐	190	Kevin MacKay, Windsor	.10
☐	191	David Myles, Windsor	.10
☐	192	Wayne Maxner, GM-Coach, Windsor	.10
☐	193	Dave Prpich, Asst. Coach, Windsor	.10
☐	194	Brady Blain, Windsor	.10
☐	195	Eric Stamp, Windsor	.10
☐	196	OHL Action	.10
☐	197	David Babcock, Niagara Falls	.10
☐	198	Brad Love, Niagara Falls	.10
☐	199	Dale Junkin, Niagara Falls	.10
☐	200	Rick Corriveau, Niagara Falls	.10
☐	201	Scott Campbell, Niagara Falls	.10
☐	202	Jason Clarke, Niagara Falls	.10
☐	203	George Burnett, Coach-GM, Niagara Falls	.10
☐	204	Ryan Tocher, Niagara Falls	.10
☐	205	Dennis Maxwell, Niagara Falls	.10
☐	206	Greg Scott (G), Niagara Falls	.15
☐	207	Mark Cardiff, Niagara Falls	.10
☐	208	Neil Fewster, Niagara Falls	.10
☐	209	Jason Coles, Niagara Falls	.10
☐	210	Randy Hall, Asst. Coach, Niagara Falls	.10
☐	211	Todd Simon, Niagara Falls	.25
☐	212	Ethan Moreau, Niagara Falls	.75
☐	213	Todd Wetzel, Niagara Falls	.10
☐	214	Tom Moores, Niagara Falls	.10
☐	215	Geoff Rawson, Niagara Falls	.10
☐	216	Dan Krisko, Niagara Falls	.10
☐	217	Manny Legacé (G), Niagara Falls	.50
☐	218	Kevin Brown, Niagara Falls	.10
☐	219	Steve Staios, Niagara Falls	.50
☐	220	Checklist 2 (99 to 196), Error	.10
☐	221	Checklist 3 (197 to 290), Error	.10
☐	222	Tony Bella, Kingston	.10
☐	223	Shawn Caplice, Kingston	.10
☐	224	Keli Corpse, Kingston	.10
☐	225	Chris Gratton, Kingston	1.75
☐	226	Gord Harris, Kingston	.10
☐	227	Cory Johnson, Kingston	.10
☐	228	Kevin King, Kingston	.10
☐	229	Justin Morrison, Kingston	.10
☐	230	Alastair Still, Kingston	.10
☐	231	Chris Scharf, Kingston	.10
☐	232	Brian Stagg, Kingston	.10
☐	233	Mike Dawson, Kingston	.10
☐	234	Rod Pasma, Kingston	.10
☐	235	Craig Rivet, Kingston	.25
☐	236	Dave Stewart, Kingston	.10
☐	237	John Vary, Kingston	.10
☐	238	Jason Wadel, Kingston	.10
☐	239	Joel Yates, Kingston	.10
☐	240	Marc Lamothe (G), Kingston	.25
☐	241	Pete McGlynn (G), Kingston	.15
☐	242	OHL Action	.10
☐	243	Checklist 4 (291 to 383), Error	.10
☐	244	Joel Sandie, Sudbury	.10
☐	245	Glen Murray, Sudbury	.50
☐	246	Derek Armstrong, Sudbury	.25
☐	247	Michael Peca, Sudbury	2.00
☐	248	Barry Young, Sudbury	.10
☐	249	Bernie Joh, Sudbury	.10
☐	250	Terry Chitaroni, Sudbury	.10
☐	251	Jason Young, Sudbury	.10
☐	252	Rod Hinks, Sudbury	.10
☐	253	Michael Yeo, Sudbury	.10
☐	254	Kyle Blacklock, Sudbury	.10
☐	255	Dan Ryder (G), Sudbury	.15
☐	256	Doug Mason, Asst. Coach, Sudbury	.10
☐	257	Jamie Rivers, Sudbury	.35
☐	258	Brandon Convery, Sudbury	.50
☐	259	Barrie Moore, Sudbury	.50
☐	260	Shawn Rivers, Sudbury	.10
☐	261	Jamie Matthews, Sudbury	.10

☐ 262 Tim Favot, Sudbury .10
☐ 263 Bob MacIsaac, Sudbury .10
☐ 264 Sean Gagnon, Sudbury .10
☐ 265 Ken MacKenzie, Coach-GM, Sudbury .10
☐ 266 George Dourian, Sudbury, Error .10
☐ 267 Brian MacKenzie, Asst. Coach, Sudbury .10
☐ 268 Jason Zohil, Sudbury .10
☐ 269 Rick Tarasuk, Coach, Owen Sound .10
☐ 270 James Storr (G), Owen Sound .75
☐ 271 Sean Basilio (G), Owen Sound .15
☐ 272 Rick Morton, Owen Sound .10
☐ 273 Jason Hughes, Owen Sound .10
☐ 274 Scott Walker, Owen Sound .50
☐ 275 Willie Skilliter, Owen Sound .10
☐ 276 Shawn Krueger, Owen Sound .10
☐ 277 Jason MacDonald, Owen Sound .10
☐ 278 Kirk Maltby, Owen Sound .25
☐ 279 Brock Woods, Owen Sound .10
☐ 280 Troy Hutchinson, Owen Sound .10
☐ 281 Geordie Maynard, Owen Sound .10
☐ 282 Luigi Calce, Owen Sound .10
☐ 283 Steven Parson, Owen Sound .10
☐ 284 Andrew Brunette, Owen Sound .25
☐ 285 Robert MacKenzie, Owen Sound .10
☐ 286 Jason Buetow, Owen Sound .10
☐ 287 Wyatt Buckland, Owen Sound .10
☐ 288 Jim Brown, Owen Sound .10
☐ 289 Gord Dickie, Owen Sound .10
☐ 290 Jeff Smith, Owen Sound .10
☐ 291 Peter Ambroziak, Ottawa .25
☐ 292 Mark O'Donnell, Ottawa .10
☐ 294 Grayden Reid, Owen Sound, Error .10
☐ 295 Sean Spencer (G), Ottawa .15
☐ 296 Gerry Skrypec, Owen Sound .10
☐ 297 Billy Hall, Owen Sound .10
☐ 298 Sean Gawley, Owen Sound .10
☐ 299 Grant Marshall, Owen Sound .50
☐ 300 Michael Johnson, Owen Sound .10
☐ 301 Brett Seguin, Owen Sound .10
☐ 302 Chris Coveny, Owen Sound .10
☐ 303 Ryan Kuwabara, Owen Sound .10
☐ 304 Jeff Ricciardi, Owen Sound .10
☐ 305 Curt Bowen, Owen Sound .25
☐ 306 Zbynek Kukacka, Owen Sound .10
☐ 307 Chris Gignac, Owen Sound .10
☐ 308 Steve Washburn, Owen Sound .50
☐ 309 Brian Kilrea, Coach, Owen Sound .50
☐ 310 Mike Lenarduzzi (G), Owen Sound .15
☐ 311 Matt Stone, Owen Sound .10
☐ 312 Ken Belanger, Owen Sound .50
☐ 313 Chris Simon, Sault Ste. Marie 1.00
☐ 314 Kiley Hill, Sault Ste. Marie .10
☐ 315 Chris Grenville, Sault Ste. Marie .10
☐ 316 Aaron Gavey, Sault Ste. Marie .50
☐ 317 Briane Thompson, Sault Ste. Marie .10
☐ 318 Ted Nolan, Coach, Sault Ste. Marie .50
☐ 319 Perry Pappas, Sault Ste. Marie .10
☐ 320 Kevin Hodson (G), Sault Ste. Marie .75
☐ 321 Colin Miller, Sault Ste. Marie .10
☐ 322 Tom MacDonald, Sault Ste. Marie .10
☐ 323 Shaun Imber, Sault Ste. Marie .10
☐ 324 Jarret Reid, Sault Ste. Marie .10
☐ 325 Tony Iob, Sault Ste. Marie .10
☐ 326 Mark Matier, Sault Ste. Marie .10
☐ 327 Drew Bannister, Sault Ste. Marie .50
☐ 328 Jason Denomme, Sault Ste. Marie .10
☐ 329 David Matsos, Sault Ste. Marie .10
☐ 330 Rick Kowalsky, Sault Ste. Marie .10
☐ 331 Tim Bacik (G), Sault Ste. Marie .10
☐ 332 Ralph Intranuovo, Sault Ste. Marie .25
☐ 333 Jonas Rudberg, Sault Ste. Marie .10
☐ 334 Jeff Toms, Sault Ste. Marie .50
☐ 335 Jason Julian, Sault Ste. Marie .10
☐ 336 Brian Goudie, Sault Ste. Marie .25
☐ 337 Gary Roach, Sault Ste. Marie .10
☐ 338 Brad Baber, Sault Ste. Marie .10
☐ 339 Todd Gleason, Sault Ste. Marie .10
☐ 340 Chris McMurty, Guelph .10
☐ 341 Matt Turek, Guelph .10
☐ 342 Shane Johnson, Guelph .10
☐ 343 Grant Pritchett, Guelph .10
☐ 344 Mike Cote, Guelph .10
☐ 345 Duane Harmer, Guelph .10
☐ 346 Jeff Bes, Guelph .10
☐ 347 Wade Whitten, Guelph .10
☐ 347 Dan Taveski, Guelph .10
☐ 348 Bill Kovacs, Guelph .10
☐ 349 Kayle Short, Guelph .10
☐ 350 Sylvain Cloutier, Guelph .10
☐ 351 Brent Watson, Guelph .10
☐ 352 Brent Pope, Guelph .10
☐ 353 Craig Lutes, Guelph .10
☐ 354 Michael Hartwick, Guelph .10
☐ 355 Kevin Reid, Guelph .10
☐ 356 Toby Burkitt, Guelph .10
☐ 357 Todd Bertuzzi, Guelph 1.00
☐ 358 Angelo Amore (G), Guelph .15
☐ 359 Jeff Pawluk, Guelph .25
☐ 361 Gordon Ross, London .10
☐ 362 Dennis Purdie, London .10
☐ 363 Dave Gilmore, London .10
☐ 364 Brent Brownlee (G), London .10
☐ 365 Aaron Nagy, London .10
☐ 366 Barry Potomski, London .25
☐ 367 Steve Smillie, London .10
☐ 368 Kelly Reed, London .10
☐ 369 Gary Agnew, Coach, London .10
☐ 370 Chris Taylor, London .25
☐ 371 Brett Marietti, London .10
☐ 372 Cory Evans, London .10
☐ 373 Brian Stacey, London .10
☐ 374 Chris Crombie, London .10
☐ 375 Derrick Crane, London .10
☐ 376 Scott McKay, London .10
☐ 377 Gregory Ryan, London .10
☐ 378 Mark Visheau, London .10
☐ 379 Gerry Arcella, London .10
☐ 380 Nick Stajduhar, London .25
☐ 381 Jason Allison, London 3.50
☐ 382 Sean O'Reilly, London .10
☐ 383 Paul Wolanski, London .10

THE TEAMS

Insert Set (16 cards): 6.00

No. Player NRMT-MT

☐ O1 Cornwall Royals .50
☐ O2 Detroit Ambassadors .50
☐ O3 Guelph Storm .50
☐ O4 Kingston Frontenacs .50
☐ O5 London Knights .50
☐ O6 Niagara Falls Thunder .50
☐ O7 North Bay Centennials .50
☐ O8 Oshawa Generals .50
☐ O9 Ottawa 67's .50
☐ O10 Kitchener Rangers .50
☐ O11 Owen Sound Platers .50
☐ O12 Peterborough Petes .50
☐ O13 Sault Ste. Marie Greyhounds .50
☐ O14 Sudbury Wolves .50
☐ O15 Windsor Spitfires .50
☐ O16 Belleville Bulls .50

1991 - 92 7TH INNING SKETCH QMJHL

Card numbers 66 and 256 do not exist.

Imprint: 1991 7th Inning Sketch Printed in Canada

Complete Set (298 cards): 18.00

Common Player: .10

No. Player NRMT-MT

☐ 1 Martin Brodeur (G), St-Hyacinthe 4.50
☐ 2 Normand Paquet, St-Hyacinthe .10
☐ 3 David Desnoyers, St-Hyacinthe .10
☐ 4 Carlo Colombi, St-Hyacinthe .10
☐ 5 Stéphane Ménard (G), St-Hyacinthe .15
☐ 6 Sébastien Bérubé, St-Hyacinthe .10
☐ 7 Marc Desgagne, St-Hyacinthe .10
☐ 8 Mil Sukovic, St-Hyacinthe .10
☐ 9 Patrick Belisle, St-Hyacinthe .10
☐ 10 Patrick Poulin, St-Hyacinthe .50
☐ 11 Martin Trudel, St-Hyacinthe .10
☐ 12 Charles Poulin, St-Hyacinthe .10
☐ 13 Etienne Thibault, St-Hyacinthe .10
☐ 14 Pierre Allard, St-Hyacinthe .10
☐ 15 François Gagnon, St-Hyacinthe .10
☐ 16 Stéphane Huard, St-Hyacinthe .10
☐ 17 Yannik Lemay, St-Hyacinthe .10
☐ 18 Dany Fortin, St-Hyacinthe .10
☐ 19 Carl Ménard, St-Hyacinthe .10
☐ 20 Serge Labelle, St-Hyacinthe .10
☐ 21 Dean Melanson, St-Hyacinthe .25
☐ 22 Yves Meunier, St-Hyacinthe .10
☐ 23 Pierre Petroni, Coach, St-Hyacinthe .10
☐ 24 Mario Pouliot, Asst. Coach, St-Hyacinthe, Error .10
☐ 25 Alain Côté, St-Hyacinthe, Error .10
☐ 26 Hugues Laliberté, St-Hyacinthe .10
☐ 27 Martin Gendron, St-Hyacinthe .25
☐ 28 Stan Melanson, St-Hyacinthe .10
☐ 29 Carl Leblanc, Granby .10
☐ 30 Patrick Grisé, Granby .10
☐ 31 Yves Charron, Granby .10
☐ 32 Hughes Mongeon, Granby .10
☐ 33 Christian Tardif, Granby .10
☐ 34 Patrick Tessier, Granby .10
☐ 35 Christian Campeau, Granby .10
☐ 36 Mario Thérrien, Granby .10
☐ 37 Martin Balleux, Granby .10
☐ 38 Joel Brassard, Granby .10
☐ 39 Sébastien Fortier, Granby .10
☐ 40 Jocelyn Langlois, Granby .10
☐ 41 Guiseppe Argentos, Granby .10
☐ 42 Sylvain Brisson, Granby .10
☐ 43 Philippe Boucher, Granby .50
☐ 44 Martin Brochu (G), Granby .15
☐ 45 Marc Rodgers, Granby .10
☐ 46 Pascal Gagnon, Granby .10
☐ 47 Benoît Thérrien, Granby .10
☐ 48 Robin Bouchard, Granby .10
☐ 49 Michel Savoie, Granby .10
☐ 50 Jean-Sébastien Boiteau .10
☐ 51 Patrick Lamoureux, Granby .10
☐ 52 Stéphane Giard (G), Granby .15
☐ 53 Maxime Jean, Shawinigan .10
☐ 54 Alain Côté, Shawinigan .10
☐ 55 François Groleau, Shawinigan .25
☐ 56 Richard Hamelin, Shawinigan .10
☐ 57 Eric Beauvis, Shawinigan .10
☐ 58 Steve Laplante, Shawinigan .10
☐ 59 Yves Meunier, Shawinigan .10
☐ 60 Steve Dontigny, Shawinigan .10
☐ 61 Simon Roy, Shawinigan .10
☐ 62 Jean-François Laroche, Shawinigan .10
☐ 63 Patrick Traverse, Shawinigan .25
☐ 64 Eric Joyal, Shawinigan .10
☐ 65 Jean-François Gregoire, Shawinigan .10
☐ 67 Jean Imbeau, Shawinigan .10
☐ 68 François Bourdeau, Shawinigan .10
☐ 69 Alain Savage, Jr., Shawinigan .10
☐ 70 Johnny Lorenzo (G), Shawinigan .15
☐ 71 Patrick Lalime (G), Shawinigan .50
☐ 72 Patrick Melfi, Shawinigan .10
☐ 73 Marc Tardif, Shawinigan .10
☐ 74 Marc Savard, Shawinigan .10
☐ 75 Alain Sanscartier, Coach, Shawinigan .10
☐ 76 Pascal Lebrasseur, Shawinigan .10
☐ 77 Checklist 1 (1 to 101) .10
☐ 78 Dany Girard, Chicoutimi .10
☐ 79 Eddy Gervais, Chicoutimi .10
☐ 80 Dave Tremblay, Chicoutimi .10
☐ 81 Dany Larochelle, Chicoutimi .10
☐ 82 Michel St-Jacques, Chicoutimi .10
☐ 83 Rodney Petawabano, Chicoutimi .10
☐ 84 Eric Duchesne, Chicoutimi .10
☐ 85 Patrick Clement, Chicoutimi .10
☐ 86 Steve Gosselin, Chicoutimi .10
☐ 87 Patrick Lacombe, Chicoutimi .10
☐ 88 Patrice Martineau, Chicoutimi .10
☐ 89 Danny Beauregard, Chicoutimi .10
☐ 90 Martin Lamarche, Chicoutimi .10
☐ 91 Sébastien Parent, Chicoutimi .10
☐ 92 Christian Caron, Chicoutimi .10

	No.	Player	Value
☐	93	Sylvain Careau (G), Chicoutimi	.15
☐	94	Martin Beaupré, Chicoutimi	.10
☐	95	Daniel Paradis, Chicoutimi	.10
☐	96	Sylvain Rodrigue (G), Chicoutimi	.10
☐	97	Joe Canale, Coach, Chicoutimi	.10
☐	98	Patrick Lampron, Chicoutimi	.10
☐	99	Carl Blondin, Chicoutimi	.10
☐	100	Carl Wiseman, Chicoutimi	.10
☐	101	Hugo Hamelin, Chicoutimi	.10
☐	102	Claude Poirier, Trois Rivières	.10
☐	103	Charles Paquette, Trois Rivières	.25
☐	104	Carl Fleury, Trois Rivières	.10
☐	105	Paolo Racicot, Trois Rivières	.10
☐	106	Sébastien Moreau, Trois Rivières	.10
☐	107	Pascal Trépanier, Trois Rivières	.10
☐	108	Dominic Maltais, Trois Rivières	.10
☐	109	Steve Arés, Trois Rivières	.10
☐	110	Daniel Thibault, Trois Rivières	.10
☐	111	Eric Messier, Trois Rivières	.10
☐	112	Stéphane Julien, Trois Rivières	.10
☐	113	Dave Paquet, Trois Rivières	.10
☐	114	Nicolas Turmel, Trois Rivières	.10
☐	115	Pascal Rhéaume, Trois Rivières	.25
☐	116	Carl Boudreau, Trois Rivières	.10
☐	117	Dave Boudreault, Trois Rivières	.10
☐	118	Eric Bellerose, Trois Rivières	.10
☐	119	Steve Searles, Trois Rivières	.10
☐	120	Patrick Nadeau, Trois Rivières	.10
☐	121	Stephan Viens, Trois Rivières	.10
☐	122	Jean-François Labbé (G), Trois Rivières	.10
☐	123	Jocelyn Thibault (G), Trois Rivières	3.50
☐	124	Gaston Drapeau, Coach, Trois Rivières	.10
☐	125	Checklist 2 (102 - 198)	.10
☐	126	Martin Lajeaunes, Verdun	.10
☐	127	Etienne Lavoie, Verdun	.10
☐	128	Dominic Rhéaume, Verdun	.10
☐	129	Robert Guillet, Verdun	.10
☐	130	François Rivard, Verdun	.10
☐	131	Phillippe DeRouville (G), Verdun)	.50
☐	132	Andrej Dobrota, Verdun	.10
☐	133	Pierre Gendron, Verdun	.10
☐	134	Dave Chouinard, Verdun	.10
☐	135	Martin Tanguay, Verdun	.10
☐	136	Jacques Blouin, Verdun	.10
☐	137	Martin Larochelle, Verdun	.10
☐	138	Jean-Martin Morin, Verdun	.10
☐	139	Donald Brashear, Verdun	.50
☐	140	Stéphane Paradis, Verdun	.10
☐	141	Jan Simcik, Verdun	.10
☐	142	Yan Arsenault, Verdun	.10
☐	143	Joel Bouchard, Verdun	.50
☐	144	Jean-Sébastien Lefebvre, Verdun	.10
☐	145	David St. Pierre, Verdun	.10
☐	146	Mario Nobili, Verdun	.10
☐	147	Stacy Dallaire, Verdun	.10
☐	148	Carl Lamothe, Verdun	.10
☐	149	André Bouliane (G), Verdun	.15
☐	150	Simon Arial, Verdun	.10
☐	151	Stéphane Madore, St-Jean	.10
☐	152	Hughes Bouchard, St-Jean	.10
☐	153	Steve Decaen, St-Jean	.10
☐	154	Jason Downey, St-Jean	.10
☐	155	Raymond Delarosbil, St-Jean	.10
☐	156	Lino Salvo, St-Jean	.10
☐	157	Réginald Brézeault, St-Jean	.10
☐	158	Nathan Morin, St-Jean	.10
☐	159	Samuel Groleau, St-Jean	.10
☐	160	Patrick Carignan, St-Jean	.10
☐	161	Stéphane St-Amour, St-Jean	.10
☐	162	Marquis Mathieu, St-Jean	.10
☐	163	Yves Sarault, St-Jean	.25
☐	164	Dave Belliveau, St-Jean	.10
☐	165	Trevor Duhaime, St-Jean	.10
☐	166	Eric O'Connor, St-Jean	.10
☐	167	Christian Proulx, St-Jean	.25
☐	168	Martin Lavallée (G), St-Jean	.15
☐	169	Jean François Gagnon (G), St-Jean	.10
☐	170	Eric Lafrance, St-Jean	.10
☐	171	Enrico Scardocchio, St-Jean	.10
☐	172	David Bergeron, St-Jean	.10
☐	173	Guillaume Morin (G), Beauport	.15
☐	174	Charlie Boucher, Beauport	.10
☐	175	Marti Rozon, Beauport	.10
☐	176	Brandon Piccarreto, Beauport	.10
☐	177	Simon Toupin, Beauport	.10
☐	178	Jamie Bird, Beauport	.10
☐	179	Hervé Lapointe, Beauport	.10
☐	180	Ian Mclantyre, Beauport	.10
☐	181	Jean-François Rivard (G), Beauport	.10
☐	182	Alain Chainey, Coach, Beauport	.10
☐	183	Daniel Laflamme, Beauport	.10
☐	184	Patrice Paquin, Beauport	.10
☐	185	Patrick Déraspé, Beauport	.10
☐	186	Martin Roy, Beauport	.10
☐	187	Jeannot Ferland, Beauport	.10
☐	188	Patrick Genest, Beauport	.10
☐	189	Matthew Barnaby, Beauport	1.00
☐	190	Jean-Guy Trudel, Beauport	.10
☐	191	Eric Moreau, Beauport	.10
☐	192	Eric Cool, Beauport	.10
☐	193	Alexandre Legault, Beauport	.10
☐	194	Gregg Pineo, Beauport	.10
☐	195	LHJMQ Action - Québec	.10
☐	196	Radoslav Balaz, Beauport	.10
☐	197	Stefan Simoes, Beauport	.10
☐	198	LHJMQ Action - Québec	.10
☐	199	François Paquette, Hull	.10
☐	200	Paul Macdonald, Hull	.10
☐	201	Shane Doiron, Hull	.10
☐	202	Michal Longauer, Hull	.10
☐	203	Joe Crowley, Hull	.10
☐	204	Joey Deliva, Hull	.10
☐	205	Pierre-François Lalonde, Hull	.10
☐	206	Paul Brousseau, Hull	.10
☐	207	Martin Lepage, Hull	.10
☐	208	Yanick DeGrâce (G), Hull	.15
☐	209	Jim Campbell, Hull	2.50
☐	210	Sébastien Bordeleau, Hull	.50
☐	211	Marc Legault (G), Hull	.10
☐	212	Joel Blain, Hull	.10
☐	213	Claude Jutras, Hull	.10
☐	214	Eric Lavigne, Hull	.25
☐	215	Todd Sparks, Hull	.10
☐	216	Sylvain Lapointe, Hull	.10
☐	217	Eric Lecompte, Hull	.25
☐	218	Thierry Mayer, Hull	.10
☐	219	Harold Hersh, Hull, Error	.10
☐	219	Harold Hersh, Corrected, Hull	.10
☐	220	Frédéric Boivin, Hull	.10
☐	221	Steven Dion, Hull	.10
☐	222	Alain Vigneault, Coach, Hull	.50
☐	223	Checklist 3 (199 - 298)	.10
☐	224	Petr Valenta, Laval	.10
☐	225	LHJMQ Action - Québec	.10
☐	226	Jim Bermingham, Laval	.10
☐	227	Yanick Dubé, Laval	.10
☐	228	Sandy McCarthy, Laval	.50
☐	229	Dany Michaud, Laval	.10
☐	230	Jason Brousseau, Laval	.10
☐	231	Marc Beaucage, Laval	.10
☐	232	Eric Cardinal, Laval	.10
☐	233	Martin Chaput, Laval	.10
☐	234	Jean Roberge, Laval	.10
☐	235	Philip Gathercole, Laval	.10
☐	236	Michael Gaule, Laval	.10
☐	237	Yannick Fréchette, Laval	.10
☐	238	Sylvain Bloiun, Laval	.10
☐	239	David Pekorek, Laval	.10
☐	240	John Kovacs, Laval	.10
☐	241	Eric Raymond (G), Laval	.15
☐	242	Manny Fernandez (G), Laval	.50
☐	243	Yan St. Pierre, Laval	.10
☐	244	Brant Blackned, Laval	.10
☐	245	Eric Veilleux, Laval	.25
☐	246	Pascal Vincent, Laval	.10
☐	247	Benoît Larose, Laval	.10
☐	248	Olivier Guillaume, Laval	.10
☐	249	Alain Gauthier (G), Victoriaville	.15
☐	250	Bruno Ducharme (G), Victoriaville	.15
☐	251	Patrick Charbonneau (G), Victoriaville	.25
☐	252	Daniel Germain, Victoriaville	.10
☐	253	Pascal Chiasson, Victoriaville	.10
☐	254	Marc Thibeault, Victoriaville	.10
☐	255	Martin Woods, Victoriaville	.10
☐	257	Dominique Grandmaison, Victoriaville	.10
☐	258	Carl Poirier, Victoriaville	.10
☐	259	Stéphane Larocque, Victoriaville	.10
☐	260	Mario Dumoulin, Victoriaville	.10
☐	261	Yvan Laterreur, Victoriaville	.10
☐	262	Claude Savoie, Victoriaville	.10
☐	263	Denis Beauchamp, Victoriaville	.10
☐	264	Patrick Bisaillon, Victoriaville	.10
☐	265	Pascal Bernier, Victoriaville	.10
☐	266	Nicolas Lefebvre, Victoriaville	.10
☐	267	LHJMQ Action	.10
☐	268	Joseph Napolitano, Victoriaville	.10
☐	269	Sébastien Tremblay, Victoriaville	.10
☐	270	Alexandre Daigle, Victoriaville	2.00
☐	271	Pierre Pillion, Victoriaville	.10
☐	272	Yves Lambert, Asst. Coach, Victoriaville	.10
☐	273	Pierre Aubry, Coach, Victoriaville	.10
☐	274	Yves Loubier (G), Drummondville	.15
☐	275	Peter Sandke, Drummondville	.10
☐	276	Louis Bernard, Drummondville	.10
☐	277	Alain Nasreddine, Drummondville	.10
☐	278	Sylvain Ducharme, Drummondville	.10
☐	279	Jeremy Caissie, Drummondville	.10
☐	280	Eric Meloche, Drummondville	.10
☐	281	Ian Laperrière, Drummondville	.50
☐	282	Hugo Proulx, Drummondville	.10
☐	283	Dave Whittom, Drummondville	.10
☐	284	Yannick Dupré, Drummondville	.50
☐	285	Eric Plante, Drummondville	.10
☐	286	Stéphane Desjardins, Drummondville	.10
☐	287	René Corbet, Drummondville	.50
☐	288	David Lessard, Drummondville	.10
☐	289	Eric Marcoux, Drummondville	.10
☐	290	Alexandre Duchesne, Drummondville	.10
☐	291	Maxime Petitclerc, Drummondville	.10
☐	292	Pierre Gagnon (G), Drummondville	.15
☐	293	Roger Larche, Drummondville	.10
☐	294	Jeam Hamel, Coach, Drummondville	.10
☐	295	Alexandre Gaumond, Drummondville	.10
☐	296	Paul-Emile Exantus, Drummondville	.10
☐	297	LHJMQ Action	.10
☐	298	LHJMQ Action	.10

THE TEAMS

Insert Set (12 cards): 5.00

	No.	Player	Nrmt-mt
☐	Q1	Les Harfangs de Beauport	.50
☐	Q2	Les Saguenéens de Chicoutimi	.50
☐	Q3	Les Voltigeurs de Drummondville	.50
☐	Q4	Les Olympiques de Hull	.50
☐	Q5	Le Titan de Laval	.50
☐	Q6	Le College François de Verdun	.50
☐	Q7	Le Laser de St-Hyacinthe	.50
☐	Q8	Les Lynx de St-Jean	.50
☐	Q9	Les Cataractes de Shawinigan	.50
☐	Q10	Les Draveurs de Trois-Rivières	.50
☐	Q11	Les Tigres de Victoriaville	.50
☐	Q12	Les Bisons de Granby	.50

1991 - 92 7TH INNING SKETCH - WHL

Card numbers 233 and 234 do not exist.

Imprint: 1991 7th Inning Sketch, Printed in Canada.

Complete Set (360 cards): 15.00

Common Player: .10

	No.	Player	NRMT-MT
☐	1	Valeri Bure, Spokane	1.25
☐	2	Hardy Sauter, Spokane	.10
☐	3	Bryan Maxwell, Coach, Spokane	.10
☐	4	Scott Bailey, Spokane	.50
☐	5	Mike Gray, Spokane	.10
☐	6	Mark Szoke, Spokane	.10
☐	7	Mike Jickling, Spokane	.10
☐	8	Frank Evans, Spokane	.10
☐	9	Steve Junker, Spokane	.25
☐	10	Greg Gatto, Spokane	.10

- ☐ 11 Jared Bednar, Spokane .10
- ☐ 12 Justin Hocking, Spokane .25
- ☐ 13 Paxton Schulte, Spokane .25
- ☐ 14 Brad Toporowski, Spokane .10
- ☐ 15 Shane Maitland, Spokane .10
- ☐ 16 Aaron Boh, Spokane .10
- ☐ 17 Ryan Duthie, Spokane .25
- ☐ 18 Craig Reichert, Spokane .25
- ☐ 19 Danny Faassen, Spokane .10
- ☐ 20 Randy Toye, Spokane .10
- ☐ 21 Geoff Grandberg, Spokane .10
- ☐ 22 Jeremy Warring (G), Spokane .10
- ☐ 23 Tyler Romanchuck, Spokane .10
- ☐ 24 Jamie Linden, Spokane .25
- ☐ 25 90/91 Champs, Spokane .10
- ☐ 26 Corey Jones (G), Portland .10
- ☐ 27 Brandon Smith, Portland .10
- ☐ 28 Mike Williamson, Portland .10
- ☐ 29 Adam Murray, Portland .10
- ☐ 30 Steve Konowalchuk, Portland .50
- ☐ 31 Shawn Stone, Portland .10
- ☐ 32 Adam Deadmarsh, Portland 2.50
- ☐ 33 Rick Mearns, Portland .10
- ☐ 34 Chris Rowland, Portland .10
- ☐ 35 Brandon Coates, Portland .10
- ☐ 36 Dave Cammock, Portland .10
- ☐ 37 Colin Foley, Portland .10
- ☐ 38 Dennis Saharchuk, Portland .10
- ☐ 39 Jiri Beranek, Portland .10
- ☐ 40 Chad Seibel, Portland .10
- ☐ 41 Kelly Harris, Portland .10
- ☐ 42 Layne Roland, Portland .10
- ☐ 43 Cale Hulse, Portland .25
- ☐ 44 Ken Hodge, Coach, Portland .10
- ☐ 45 Peter Cox, Moose Jaw .10
- ☐ 46 Joaquin Cage (G), Portland .50
- ☐ 47 Brent Peterson, Co-Coach, Portland .10
- ☐ 48 Jason McBain, Lethbridge .10
- ☐ 49 John Badduke, Portland .25
- ☐ 50 Rick Hopper, GM, Victoria .10
- ☐ 51 Dave Hamilton (G), Victoria .10
- ☐ 52 Dwayne Newman, Victoria .10
- ☐ 53 Chris Catellier, Victoria .10
- ☐ 54 Fran Defrenza, Victoria .10
- ☐ 55 Randy Chadney, Victoria .10
- ☐ 56 David Hebky, Tri-City .10
- ☐ 57 Craig Fletcher, Victoria .10
- ☐ 58 Kane Chaloner, Victoria .10
- ☐ 59 Ross Harris, Victoria .10
- ☐ 60 Mike Barrie, Victoria .10
- ☐ 61 Steve Lingren, Victoria .10
- ☐ 62 Shea Esselmont, Victoria .10
- ☐ 63 Matt Smith, Victoria .10
- ☐ 64 Gerry St. Cyr, Victoria .10
- ☐ 65 Andrew Laming, Victoria .10
- ☐ 66 Jeff Fancy, Tri-City .10
- ☐ 67 Ryan Pellaers, Victoria .10
- ☐ 68 Scott Fukami, Victoria .10
- ☐ 69 Darcy Mattersdorfer, Victoria .10
- ☐ 70 Chris Hawes, Victoria .10
- ☐ 72 The Goalies 1 .10
- ☐ 73 Checklist 1 (1 to 97) .10
- ☐ 74 Riverside Coliseum, Kamloops .10
- ☐ 75 Tom Renney, Coach, Kamloops .25
- ☐ 76 Corey Hirsch (G), Kamloops 1.00
- ☐ 77 Scott Ferguson, Kamloops .25
- ☐ 78 Steve Yule, Kamloops .10
- ☐ 79 Todd Johnson, Moose Jaw .10
- ☐ 80 Jarrett Bousquet, Kamloops .10
- ☐ 81 Mike Mathers, Kamloops .10
- ☐ 82 Rod Stevens, Kamloops .25
- ☐ 83 Lance Johnson, Kamloops .10
- ☐ 84 Zac Boyer, Kamloops .10
- ☐ 85 Craig Lyons, Kamloops .10
- ☐ 86 Dale Masson (G), Kamloops .10
- ☐ 87 Scott Loucks, Kamloops .10
- ☐ 88 Darcy Tucker, Kamloops .75
- ☐ 89 Shayne Green, Kamloops .10
- ☐ 90 Micheal Sup, Kamloops .10
- ☐ 91 Craig Bonner, Kamloops .10
- ☐ 92 Jeff Watchorn, Kamloops .10
- ☐ 93 Jarrett Dueling, Kamloops .25
- ☐ 94 Ed Patterson, Kamloops .25
- ☐ 95 David Wilkie, Kamloops .50
- ☐ 96 The Goalies III .10
- ☐ 97 A Goal .10
- ☐ 98 Andy MacIntyre, Seattle .25
- ☐ 99 Rhett Trombley, Tacoma .10
- ☐ 100 Lorne Molleken, Coach, Saskatoon .10
- ☐ 101 Trevor Robins (G), Saskatoon .10
- ☐ 102 Jeff Buchanan, Saskatoon .25
- ☐ 103 Mark Raiter, Saskatoon .10
- ☐ 104 Bryce Goebel, Saskatoon .10
- ☐ 105 Paul Buczkowski, Saskatoon .10
- ☐ 106 James Startup, Saskatoon .10
- ☐ 107 Chad Rusnak, Saskatoon .10
- ☐ 108 Sean McFatridge, Saskatoon .10
- ☐ 109 Shane Calder, Saskatoon .10
- ☐ 110 Ryan Fujita, Saskatoon .10
- ☐ 111 Derek Tibbatts, Saskatoon .10
- ☐ 112 Glen Gulutzan, Saskatoon .10
- ☐ 113 Richard Matvichuk, Saskatoon .50
- ☐ 114 Chad Michalchuk, Saskatoon .10
- ☐ 115 Mark Wotton, Saskatoon .25
- ☐ 116 Mark Franks, Saskatoon .10
- ☐ 117 Norm Maracle (G), Saskatoon .25
- ☐ 118 Jason Becker, Saskatoon .10
- ☐ 119 Shawn Yakimishyn, Saskatoon .10
- ☐ 120 Ed Chynoweth, WHL President .10
- ☐ 121 Checklist 2 (98 to 195) .10
- ☐ 122 Craig Chapman, Seattle .10
- ☐ 123 Jeff Jubenville, Seattle .10
- ☐ 124 George Zajankala, Seattle .10
- ☐ 125 Turner Stevenson, Seattle .50
- ☐ 126 Rob Tallas (G), Seattle .25
- ☐ 127 Ryan Brown, Seattle .10
- ☐ 128 Andrew Kemper, Seattle .10
- ☐ 129 Brendan Witt, Seattle .50
- ☐ 130 Troy Hyatt, Seattle .10
- ☐ 131 Mike Kennedy, Seattle .10
- ☐ 132 Jesse Wilson, Seattle .10
- ☐ 133 Kurt Seher, Swift Current .10
- ☐ 134 Dody Wood, Seattle .35
- ☐ 135 Darren McAusland, Seattle .10
- ☐ 136 Jeff Sebastian, Seattle .10
- ☐ 137 Eric Bouchard, Seattle .10
- ☐ 138 Joel Dyck, Swift Current .10
- ☐ 139 Blake Knox, Swift Current .10
- ☐ 140 Peter Anholt, Coach, Seattle .10
- ☐ 141 Chris Wells, Seattle .25
- ☐ 142 Andrew Reimer (G), Seattle .10
- ☐ 143 Along The Boards .10
- ☐ 144 Which Way Is Up .10
- ☐ 145 Checklist 3 (196 to 287) .10
- ☐ 146 Tacoma Dome, Tacoma .10
- ☐ 147 Opening Ceremonies, Tacoma .10
- ☐ 148 Marcel Comeau, Coach, Tacoma .10
- ☐ 149 Donn Clark, Asst. Coach, Tacoma .10
- ☐ 150 John Varga, Tacoma .10
- ☐ 151 Joey Young, Tacoma .10
- ☐ 152 Laurie Billeck, Tacoma .10
- ☐ 153 Jeff Calvert (G), Tacoma .10
- ☐ 154 Tuomas Gronman, Tacoma .25
- ☐ 155 Jason Knox, Tacoma .10
- ☐ 156 Kevin Malgunas, Tacoma .10
- ☐ 157 Dave McMillen, Tacoma .10
- ☐ 158 Darryl Onofrychuk (G), Tacoma .10
- ☐ 159 Mike Piersol, Tacoma .10
- ☐ 160 Lasse Pirjeta, Tacoma .10
- ☐ 161 Drew Schoneck, Tacoma .10
- ☐ 162 Corey Stock, Tacoma .10
- ☐ 163 Ryan Strain, Tacoma .10
- ☐ 164 Michal Sykora, Tacoma .50
- ☐ 165 Scott Thomas, Tacoma .25
- ☐ 166 Toby Weishaar, Tacoma .10
- ☐ 167 Jeff Whittle, Tacoma .10
- ☐ 168 The Rockettes, Tacoma .10
- ☐ 169 Allan Egeland, Tacoma .25
- ☐ 170 Van Burgess, Tacoma .10
- ☐ 171 Trever Fraser, Tacoma .10
- ☐ 172 Jamie Black, Tacoma .10
- ☐ 173 WHL Action .10
- ☐ 174 Andy Schneider, Swift Current .25
- ☐ 175 John McMulkin, Swift Current .10
- ☐ 176 Rick Girard, Swift Current .25
- ☐ 177 Shane Hnidy, Swift Current .10
- ☐ 178 Jason Krywulak, Swift Current .10
- ☐ 179 Jeremy Riehl, Swift Current .10
- ☐ 180 Brent Bilodeau, Seattle .25
- ☐ 181 Mark McCoy, Swift Current .10
- ☐ 182 Matt Young, Swift Current .10
- ☐ 183 Dan Sherstenka, Swift Current .10
- ☐ 184 Jarrod Daniel (G), Swift Current .10
- ☐ 185 Lennie MacAusland, Swift Current .10
- ☐ 186 Keith McCambridge, Swift Current .10
- ☐ 187 Jason Horvath, Swift Current .10
- ☐ 188 Kevin Koopman (G), Swift Current .10
- ☐ 189 Chris Herperger, Swift Current .10
- ☐ 190 Trent McCleary, Swift Current .50
- ☐ 191 Tyler Wright, Swift Current .25
- ☐ 192 Todd Holt, Swift Current .10
- ☐ 193 Ashley Buckberger, Swift Current .25
- ☐ 194 Bram Vanderkracht, Spokane .10
- ☐ 195 Ken Zilka, Swift Current .10
- ☐ 196 Chris Osgood (G), Medicine Hat 3.50
- ☐ 197 Rob Puchniak, Brandon .10
- ☐ 198 Todd Dutiaume, Brandon .10
- ☐ 199 Mike Maneluk, Brandon .10
- ☐ 200 Shawn Dietrich (G), Brandon .10
- ☐ 201 Chris Johnston, Brandon .10
- ☐ 202 Brian Purdy, Brandon .10
- ☐ 203 Mike Chrun, Brandon .10
- ☐ 204 Dan Kopec, Brandon .10
- ☐ 205 Ryan Smith, Brandon .10
- ☐ 206 Marty Murray, Brandon .10
- ☐ 207 Merv Priest, Brandon .10
- ☐ 208 Bobby House, Brandon .25
- ☐ 209 Chris Constant, Brandon .10
- ☐ 210 Dwayne Gylywoychuk, Brandon .10
- ☐ 211 Stu Scantlebury, Brandon .10
- ☐ 212 Mark Kolesar, Brandon .25
- ☐ 213 Craig Geekie, Brandon .10
- ☐ 214 Terran Sandwith, Brandon .10
- ☐ 215 Jeff Hoad, Brandon .10
- ☐ 216 Kelly McCrimmon, Coach, Brandon .10
- ☐ 217 Carlos Bye, Brandon .10
- ☐ 218 Trevor Hanas, Regina .10
- ☐ 219 Jeff Shantz, Regina .50
- ☐ 220 Heath Weenk, Regina .10
- ☐ 221 Nathan Dempsey, Regina .10
- ☐ 222 Louis Dumont, Regina .10
- ☐ 223 Garry Pearce, Regina .10
- ☐ 224 Terry Bendera, Regina .10
- ☐ 225 Hal Christiansen, Regina .10
- ☐ 226 Jason Smith, Regina .50
- ☐ 227 K. Biette, Regina .10
- ☐ 228 Barry Becker (G), Regina .10
- ☐ 229 Derek Eberle, Regina .10
- ☐ 230 Ken Richardson, Regina .10
- ☐ 231 Niklas Barklund, Regina .10
- ☐ 232 Frank Kovacs, Regina .10
- ☐ 235 Lloyd Pelletier, Regina .10
- ☐ 236 Dale Vossen, Asst. Coach, Regina .10
- ☐ 237 A. J. Kelham, Regina .10
- ☐ 238 Mike Risdale (G), Regina .10
- ☐ 239 Brad Bagu, Victoria .10
- ☐ 240 Niko Ovaska, Regina .10
- ☐ 241 Brad Tippett, Coach, Regina .10
- ☐ 242 The Goalies II .10
- ☐ 243 Lee J. Leslie, Prince Albert .10
- ☐ 244 Darren Perkins, Prince Albert .10
- ☐ 245 Jason Kwiatkowski, Prince Albert .10
- ☐ 246 J. Renard, Prince Albert .10
- ☐ 247 Dan Kesa, Prince Albert .25
- ☐ 248 Jason Klassen, Prince Albert .10
- ☐ 249 Nick Polychronopoulus, Prince Albert .10
- ☐ 250 David Neilson, Prince Albert .10
- ☐ 251 Merv Haney, Prince Albert .10
- ☐ 252 Troy Hjertaas, Prince Albert .10
- ☐ 253 Curt Regnier, Prince Albert .10
- ☐ 254 Dean McAmmond, Prince Albert .50
- ☐ 255 Travis Laycock (G), Prince Albert .10
- ☐ 256 Jeff Lank, Prince Albert .10
- ☐ 257 Barkley Swenson, Prince Albert .10
- ☐ 258 Darren Van Impe, Prince Albert .10
- ☐ 259 Ryan Pisiak, Prince Albert .10
- ☐ 260 Jeff Gorman, Prince Albert .10
- ☐ 261 Stan Matwijiw (G), Prince Albert .10
- ☐ 262 Mike Fedorko, Coach, Prince Albert .10
- ☐ 263 Mark Odnokon, Asst. Coach, Prince Albert .10
- ☐ 264 Shane Zulyniak, Prince Albert .10
- ☐ 265 Jeff Nelson, Prince Albert .25
- ☐ 266 Donevan Hextall, Prince Albert .10
- ☐ 267 Kevin Masters, Moose Jaw .10
- ☐ 268 C. Schmidt, Moose Jaw .10

	No.	Player	NRMT-MT
☐	269	Jeff Budai, Moose Jaw	.10
☐	270	Bill Hooson, Moose Jaw	.10
☐	271	Fred Hettle, Kamloops	.10
☐	272	Kent Staniforth, Moose Jaw	.10
☐	273	T. Stevenson, Moose Jaw	.10
☐	274	David Jesiolowski, Moose Jaw	.10
☐	275	Mike Babcock, Coach, Moose Jaw	.10
☐	276	Scott Allison, Moose Jaw	.10
☐	277	Travis Thiessen, Moose Jaw	.25
☐	278	Marc Hussey, Moose Jaw	.10
☐	279	Kevin Smyth, Moose Jaw	.25
☐	280	Jason Fitzsimmons (G), Moose Jaw	.10
☐	281	Jeff Petruic, Moose Jaw	.10
☐	282	Russ West, Moose Jaw	.10
☐	283	Derek Kletzel, Moose Jaw	.10
☐	284	Jarrett Zukiwsky, Kamloops	.10
☐	285	J. Carey, Kamloops	.10
☐	286	Close Checking, Kamloops	.10
☐	287	Checklist 3 (288 to W15)	.10
☐	288	Jason Bowen, Tri-City	.25
☐	289	Dean Tiltgen, Tri-City	.10
☐	290	Terry Degner, Tri-City	.10
☐	291	J. Murphy, Tri-City	.10
☐	292	Brian Sakic, Tri-City	.10
☐	293	Jamie Barnes, Tri-City	.10
☐	294	Darren Hastman, Tri-City	.10
☐	295	Todd Klassen, Tri-City	.10
☐	296	Mirsad Mujcin, Tri-City	.10
☐	297	Trevor Sherban, Tri-City	.10
☐	298	Chadden Cabana, Tri-City	.10
☐	299	Adam Rettschlag, Tri-City	.10
☐	300	Mark Toljanich, Tri-City	.10
☐	301	Kory Mullin, Tri-City	.10
☐	302	Byron Penstock (G), Tri-City	.10
☐	303	Vladimir Vujtek, Tri-City	.25
☐	304	Bill Lindsay, Tri-City	.50
☐	305	Jeff Cej, Tri-City	.10
☐	306	Mike Busniak, Coach, Tri-City	.10
☐	307	Todd Harris, Victoria	.10
☐	308	Cory Dosdall, Tri-City	.10
☐	309	Jason Smith, Tri-City	.10
☐	310	Mark Dawkins (G), Tri-City	.10
☐	311	Dan O'Rourke, Tri-City	.10
☐	312	Darby Walker, Medicine Hat	.10
☐	313	Olaf Kjenstadt, Medicine Hat	.10
☐	314	Sonny Mignacca (G), Medicine Hat	.10
☐	315	Jon Duval, Medicine Hat	.10
☐	316	Lorne Toews, Medicine Hat	.10
☐	317	Dana Rieder, Medicine Hat	.10
☐	318	Clayton Norris, Medicine Hat	.25
☐	319	David Cooper, Medicine Hat	.50
☐	320	Lanny Watkins, Medicine Hat	.10
☐	321	Evan Marble, Medicine Hat	.10
☐	322	Scott Lindsay, Medicine Hat	.10
☐	323	Ryan Petz, Medicine Hat	.10
☐	324	Jeramie Heistad, Medicine Hat	.10
☐	325	Scott Townsend, Medicine Hat	.10
☐	326	Stacy Roest, Medicine Hat	.10
☐	327	Rob Niedermayer, Medicine Hat	1.25
☐	328	Tim Bothwell, Coach, Medicine Hat	.25
☐	329	Kevin Riehl, Medicine Hat	.10
☐	330	Mike Rathje, Medicine Hat	.50
☐	331	Bryan McCabe, Medicine Hat	1.00
☐	332	MHT Tiger, Medicine Hat	.10
☐	333	Dean Intwert (G), Brandon	.10
☐	334	Mike Vandenberghe, Brandon	.10
☐	335	Cam Danyluk, Spokane	.10
☐	336	Darcy Austin (G), Lethbridge	.10
☐	337	Jason Knight, Lethbridge	.10
☐	338	Lee Sorochan, Lethbridge	.10
☐	339	Al Kinisky, Lethbridge	.10
☐	340	Rob Hartnell, Lethbridge	.10
☐	341	Radek Sip, Lethbridge	.10
☐	342	Jamie Pushor, Lethbridge	.50
☐	343	Shane Peacock, Lethbridge	.10
☐	344	Cadrin Smart, Lethbridge	.10
☐	345	Maurice Meagher, Lethbridge	.10
☐	346	Lance Burns, Lethbridge	.10
☐	347	Dominic Pittis, Lethbridge	.25
☐	348	Todd MacIsaac, Lethbridge	.10
☐	349	Brad Zimmer, Lethbridge	.10
☐	350	Jason Sorochan, Lethbridge	.10
☐	351	Darcy Werenka, Lethbridge	.10
☐	352	Kevin St. Jacques, Lethbridge	.10
☐	353	David Trofimenkoff, Lethbridge	.10
☐	354	Terry Hollinger, Lethbridge	.25
☐	355	Travis Munday, Lethbridge	.10
☐	356	Slade Stephenson, Lethbridge	.10
☐	357	Jason Widmer, Lethbridge	.10
☐	358	Brad Zavisha, Portland	.10
☐	359	Bob Loucks, Coach, Lethbridge	.10
☐	360	Brantt Myrhes, Lethbridge	.10
☐		Garfield Henderson, Moose Jaw	.10

THE TEAMS

Insert Set (15 cards): 6.00

	No.	Player	NRMT-MT
☐	W1	Spokane Chiefs	.50
☐	W2	Portland Winterhawks	.10
☐	W3	Victoria Cougars	.10
☐	W4	Kamloops Blazers	.10
☐	W5	Saskatoon Blades	.50
☐	W6	Seattle Thunderbirds	.10
☐	W7	Tacoma Rockets	.10
☐	W8	Swift Current Broncos	.50
☐	W9	Brandon Wheat Kings	.10
☐	W10	Regina Pats	.10
☐	W11	Prince Albert Raiders	.10
☐	W12	Moose Jaw Warriors	.10
☐	W13	Tri-City Americans	.10
☐	W14	Medicine Hat Tigers	.10
☐	W15	Lethbridge Hurricanes	.10

1991 - 92 STAR PICS PROSPECTS

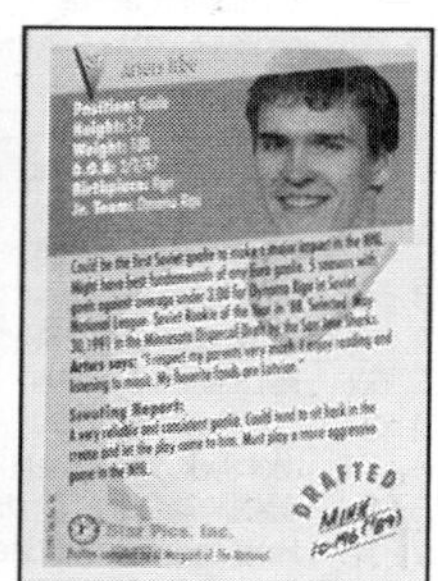

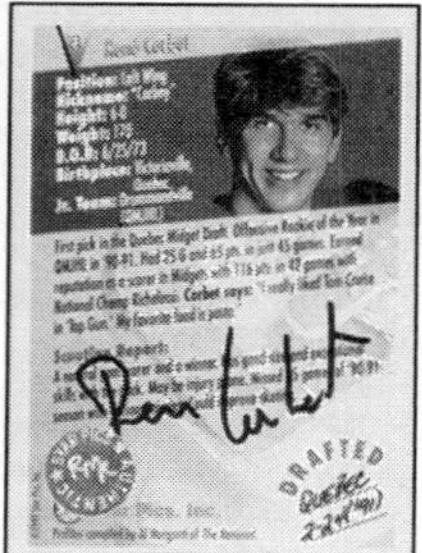

A number of players also signed cards in this series.

Imprint: © 1991 Star Pics, Inc.

Complete Set (72 cards): 7.00

Common Player: .10

	No.	Player	Aut.	Reg.
☐	1	Draft Overview		.10
☐	2	Pat Falloon		.10
☐	3	Jamie Pushor		.10
☐	4	HOF: Jean Béliveau		1.00
☐	5	Martin Lapointe		.10
☐	6	Jamie Matthews		.10
☐	7	HOF: Rod Gilbert		.25
☐	8	Niklas Sunblad		.10
☐	9	Steve Konowalchuk		.10
☐	10	HOF: Alex Delvecchio		.25
☐	11	Donevan Hextall		.10
☐	12	Dody Wood		.10
☐	13	Scott Niedermayer		.50
☐	14	Trevor Halverson		.10
☐	15	Terry Chitaroni		.10
☐	16	Tyler Wright		.10
☐	17	Andrey Lomakin		.10
☐	18	Martin Hamrlik		.10
☐	19	Dmitry Filimonov		.10
☐	20	Flashback: Ed Belfour (G)		.50
☐	21	Andrew Verner (G)		.10
☐	22	Yanic Perreault		.25
☐	23	Michael Nylander		.10
☐	24	Scott Lachance		.10
☐	25	Pavel Bure		1.50
☐	26	Mike Torchia (G)		.10
☐	27	HOF: Frank Mahovlich		.25
☐	28	Philippe Boucher		.10
☐	29	Jiri Slegr		.10
☐	30	Sergei Fedorov		1.00
☐☐	31	René Corbet	5.00	.10
☐	32	Jamie McLennan (G)		.10
☐	33	Shane Peacock		.10
☐	34	Mario Nobili		.10
☐	35	Peter Forsberg		3.00
☐	36	P. Falloon/ T. Wright/ P. Poulin/ P. Boucher/ A. Verner/ S. Lachance		.10
☐	37	Arturs Irbe (G)		.10
☐	38	Alexei Zhitnik		.10
☐	39	Pat Peake		.10
☐	40	Adam Oates		.50
☐	41	Markus Naslund		.10
☐	42	Eric Lavigne		.10
☐	43	Jeff Nelson		.10
☐	44	Yanick Dupré		.10
☐	45	Justin Morrison		.10
☐	46	Alek Stojanov		.10
☐	47	Marcel Cousineau (G)		.10
☐	48	Alexei Kovalev		.50
☐	49	Andrey Trefilov (G)		.10
☐	50	Mats Sundin		1.00
☐	51	Steve Staios		.25
☐	52	HOF: Glenn Hall (G)		.50
☐	53	Brent Bilodeau		.10
☐	54	Darcy Werenka		.10
☐	55	Chris Osgood (G)		.75
☐	56	Nathan LaFayette		.10
☐	57	Richard Matvichuk		.10
☐	58	Dmitri Mironov		.10
☐	59	Jason Dawe		.10
☐	60	Mike Ricci		.10
☐	61	HOF: Gerry Cheevers		.50
☐	62	Jim Campbell		.50
☐	63	François Groleau		.10
☐	64	Glen Murray		.10
☐	65	Jason Young		.10
☐	66	Dean McAmmond		.10
☐	67	Guy Lévêque		.10
☐	68	Patrick Poulin		.10
☐	69	Bobby House		.10
☐	70	Jaromir Jagr		2.00
☐	71	Jassen Cullimore		.10
☐	72	Checklist		.10

1991 - 92 TOPPS STADIUM CLUB

Imprint: © 1991 THE TOPPS COMPANY, INC.

Complete Set (440 cards): 30.00

Common Player: .10

	No.	Player	NRMT-MT
☐	1	Wayne Gretzky, L.A.	3.00
☐	2	Randy Moller, NYR.	.10
☐	3	Ray Ferraro, NYI.	.10
☐	4	Craig Wolanin, Que.	.10
☐	5	Shayne Corson, Mtl.	.10
☐	6	Chris Chelios, Chi.	.50
☐	7	Joe Mullen, Pgh.	.10
☐	8	Ken Wregget (G), Pha.	.10
☐	9	Rob Cimetta, Tor.	.10
☐	10	Mike Liut (G), Wsh.	.10

	No.	Player	Value
☐	11	Martin Gelinas, Edm.	.10
☐	12	Mario Marois, Stl.	.10
☐	13	Rick Vaive, Buf.	.10
☐	14	Brad McCrimmon, Det.	.10
☐	15	Mark Hunter, Hfd.	.10
☐	16	Jim Wiemer, Bos.	.10
☐	17	Sergio Momesso, Van.	.10
☐	18	Claude Lemieux, N.J.	.10
☐	19	Brian Hayward (G), (S.J.)	.10
☐	20	Patrick Flatley, NYI.	.10
☐	21	Mark Osborne, Wpg.	.10
☐	22	Mike Hudson, Chi.	.10
☐	23	Réjean Lemelin (G), Bos.	.10
☐	24	Viacheslav Fetisov, N.J.	.25
☐	25	Bobby Smith, Min.	.10
☐	26	Kris King, NYR.	.10
☐	27	Randy Velischek, Que.	.10
☐	28	Steve Bozek, (S.J.)	.10
☐	29	Mike Foligno, Tor.	.10
☐	30	Scott Arniel, Wpg.	.10
☐	31	Sergei Makarov, Cgy.	.10
☐	32	Rick Zombo, Det.	.10
☐	33	Christian Ruuttu, Buf.	.10
☐	34	Gino Cavallini, Stl.	.10
☐	35	Rick Tocchet, Pha.	.10
☐	36	Jiri Hrdina, Pgh.	.10
☐	37	Peter Bondra, Wsh.	.60
☐	38	Craig Ludwig, (Min.)	.10
☐	39	Mikael Anderson, Hfd.	.10
☐	40	Bob Kudelski, L.A.	.10
☐	41	Guy Carbonneau, Mtl.	.10
☐	42	Geoff Smith, Edm.	.10
☐	43	Russ Courtnall, Mtl.	.10
☐	44	Michal Pivonka, Wsh.	.10
☐	45	Todd Krygier, Hfd.	.10
☐	46	Jeremy Roenick, Chi.	.50
☐	47	Doug Brown, N.J.	.10
☐	48	Paul Cavallini, Stl.	.10
☐	49	Ron Sutter, Pha.	.10
☐	50	Paul Ranheim, Cgy.	.10
☐	51	Mike Gartner, NYR.	.25
☐	52	Greg Adams, Van.	.10
☐	53	Dave Capuano, Van.	.10
☐	54	Mike Krushelnyski, Tor.	.10
☐	55	Ulf Dahlen, Min.	.10
☐	56	Steven Finn, Que.	.10
☐	57	Ed Olczyk, Wpg.	.10
☐	58	Steve Duchesne, Pha.	.10
☐	59	Bob Probert, Det.	.10
☐	60	Joe Nieuwendyk, Cgy.	.25
☐	61	Petr Klima, Edm.	.10
☐	62	Uwe Krupp, Buf.	.10
☐	63	Jay Miller, L.A.	.10
☐	64	Cam Neely, Bos.	.25
☐	65	Phil Housley, Wpg.	.10
☐	66	Michel Goulet, Chi.	.25
☐	67	Brett Hull, Stl.	.75
☐	68	Mike Ridley, Wsh.	.10
☐	69	Esa Tikkanen, Edm.	.10
☐	70	Kjell Samuelsson, Pha.	.10
☐	**71**	**Corey Millen, NYR., RC**	**.10**
☐	72	Doug Lidster, Van.	.10
☐	73	Ron Francis, Pgh.	.50
☐	74	Scott Young, Pgh.	.10
☐	75	Bob Sweeney, Bos.	.10
☐	76	Sean Burke (G), N.J.	.25
☐	77	Pierre Turgeon, Buf.	.25
☐	78	Dave Reid, Tor.	.10
☐	79	Al MacInnis, Cgy.	.25
☐	80	Mike Hough, Que.	.10
☐	81	Steve Yzerman, Det.	1.50
☐	82	Derek King, NYI.	.10
☐	83	Brad Shaw, Hfd.	.10
☐	84	Trevor Linden, Van.	.25
☐	85	Rick Meagher, Stl.	.10
☐	86	Stéphane Richer, Mtl.	.10
☐	87	Brian Bellows, Min.	.10
☐	88	Pete Peeters (G), Pha.	.10
☐	89	Adam Creighton, Chi.	.10
☐	90	Brent Ashton, Pgh.	.10
☐	91	Bryan Trottier, Pgh.	.25
☐	92	Mike Richter (G), NYR.	.50
☐	93	Dave Andreychuk, Buf.	.25
☐	94	Randy Carlyle, Wpg.	.10
☐	95	Dave Christian, (Stl.)	.10
☐	96	Doug Gilmour, Cgy.	.50
☐	97	Tony Granato, L.A.	.10
☐	98	Jeff Norton, NYR.	.10
☐	99	Neal Broten, Min.	.10
☐	100	Jody Hull, NYR.	.10
☐	101	Shawn Burr, Det.	.10
☐	102	Pat Verbeek, Hfd., Error (/b: Sarina)	.10
☐	103	Ken Daneyko, N.J.	.10
☐	104	Peter Zezel, Tor.	.10
☐	105	Kirk McLean (G), Van.	.25
☐	106	Kelly Miller, Wsh.	.10
☐	107	Patrick Roy (G), Mtl.	2.50
☐	108	Adam Oates, Stl.	.50
☐	109	Steve Thomas, Chi.	.10
☐	110	Scott Mellanby, (Edm.)	.10
☐	111	Mark Messier, Edm.	.75
☐	112	Larry Murphy, Pgh.	.25
☐	113	Mark Janssens, NYR.	.10
☐	114	Doug Bodger, Buf.	.10
☐	115	Ron Tugnutt (G), Que.	.10
☐	116	Glenn Anderson, Edm.	.10
☐	117	Dave Gagner, Min.	.10
☐	118	Dino Ciccarelli, Wsh.	.25
☐	119	Randy Burridge, Bos. (Wsh.)	.10
☐	120	Kelly Hrudey (G) L.A.	.10
☐	121	Jimmy Carson, Det.	.10
☐	122	Bruce Driver, N.J.	.10
☐	123	Pat LaFontaine, NYI.	.25
☐	124	Wendel Clark, Tor.	.25
☐	125	Peter Sidorkiewicz (G), Hfd.	.10
☐	126	Gary Roberts, Cgy.	.25
☐	127	Petr Svoboda, Mtl.	.10
☐	128	Vincent Riendeau (G), Stl.	.10
☐	129	Brian Skrudland, Mtl.	.10
☐	130	Tim Kerr, NYR.	.10
☐	131	Doug Wilson, Chi. (S.J.)	.25
☐	132	Pat Elynuik, Wpg.	.10
☐	133	Craig MacTavish, Edm.	.10
☐	134	Troy Mallette, NYR.	.10
☐	135	Mike Ramsey, Buf.	.10
☐	136	Tony Hrkac, Stl. (S.J.)	.10
☐	137	Craig Simpson, Edm.	.10
☐	138	Jon Casey (G), Min.	.10
☐	139	Steve Kasper, (Pha.)	.10
☐	140	Kevin Hatcher, Wsh.	.10
☐	141	Dave Barr, (N.J.)	.10
☐	142	Brad Lauer, NYI.	.10
☐	143	Gary Suter, Cgy.	.10
☐	144	John MacLean, N.J.	.10
☐	145	Dean Evason, Hfd.	.10
☐	146	Vincent Damphousse, Tor.	.50
☐	147	Craig Janney, Bos.	.10
☐	148	Jeff Brown, Stl.	.10
☐	149	Geoff Courtnall, Van.	.10
☐	150	Igor Larionov, Van.	.25
☐	151	Jan Erixon, NYR.	.10
☐	152	Bob Essensa (G), Wpg.	.10
☐	153	Gaetan Duchesne, Min.	.10
☐	154	Jyrki Lumme, Van.	.10
☐	155	Tom Barrasso (G), Pgh.	.25
☐	156	Curtis Leschyshyn, Que.	.10
☐	157	Benoît Hogue, Buf.	.10
☐	158	Gary Leeman, Tor.	.10
☐	159	Luc Robitaille, L.A.	.25
☐	160	Jamie Macoun, Cgy.	.10
☐	161	Bob Carpenter, Bos.	.10
☐	162	Gary Nylund, Hfd.	.10
☐	163	Kevin Dineen, NYI.	.10
☐	164	Dale Hunter, Wsh.	.10
☐	165	Gerard Gallant, Det.	.10
☐	166	Jacques Cloutier (G), Que.	.10
☐	167	Troy Murray, (Wpg.)	.10
☐	168	Phil Bourque, Pgh.	.10
☐	169	Grant Ledyard, Buf.	.10
☐	170	Joel Otto, Cgy.	.10
☐	171	Paul Ysebaert, Det., Error (Mike Sillinger)	.10
☐	172	Luke Richardson, Tor.	.10
☐	173	Ron Hextall (G), Pha.	.25
☐	174	Mario Lemieux, Pgh.	2.50
☐	175	Garry Galley, Bos.	.10
☐	176	Murray Craven, Pha.	.10
☐	177	Walt Poddubny, N.J.	.10
☐	178	Scott Pearson, Que.	.10
☐	179	Kevin Lowe, Edm.	.10
☐	180	Brent Sutter, NYI.	.10
☐	181	Dirk Graham, Chi.	.10
☐	182	Pelle Eklund, Pha.	.10
☐	183	Sylvain Côté, (Wsh.)	.10
☐	184	Rod Brind'Amour, Stl.	.25
☐	185	Fredrik Olausson, Wpg.	.10
☐	186	Kelly Kisio, S.J.	.10
☐	187	Mike Modano, Min.	.75
☐	188	Calle Johansson, Wsh.	.10
☐	189	John Tonelli, (Chi.)	.10
☐	190	Glen Wesley, Bos.	.10
☐	191	Bob Errey, Pgh.	.10
☐	192	Rich Sutter, Stl.	.10
☐	193	Kirk Muller, N.J.	.10
☐	194	Rob Zettler, S.J.	.10
☐	195	Alexander Mogilny, Buf.	.50
☐	196	Adrien Plavsic, Van.	.10
☐	197	Daniel Marois, Tor.	.10
☐	198	Yves Racine, Det.	.10
☐	199	Brendan Shanahan, Stl.	1.00
☐	200	Rob Brown, Hfd.	.10
☐	201	Brian Leetch, NYR.	.50
☐	202	Dave McLlwain, Wpg.	.10
☐	203	Charlie Huddy, L.A.	.10
☐	204	David Volek, NYI.	.10
☐	205	Trent Yawney, Chi.	.10
☐	206	Brian MacLellan, (Det.)	.10
☐	207	Thomas Steen, Wpg.	.10
☐	208	Sylvain Lefebvre, Mtl.	.10
☐	209	Tomas Sandström, L.A.	.10
☐	210	Mike McPhee, Mtl.	.10
☐	211	Andy Moog (G), Bos.	.25
☐	212	Paul Coffey, Pgh.	.25
☐	213	Denis Savard, Mtl.	.10
☐	214	Eric Desjardins, Mtl.	.25
☐	215	Wayne Presley, Chi.	.10
☐	216	Stéphane Morin, Que.	.10
☐	217	Ric Nattress, Cgy.	.10
☐	218	Troy Gamble (G), Van.	.10
☐	219	Terry Carkner, Pha.	.10
☐	220	Dave Hannan, Tor.	.10
☐	221	Randy Wood, NYI.	.10
☐	222	Brian Mullen, (S.J.)	.10
☐	223	Garth Butcher, Stl.	.10
☐	224	Tim Cheveldae (G), Det.	.10
☐	225	Rod Langway, Wsh.	.10
☐	226	Stephen Leach, (Bos.)	.10
☐	227	Perry Berezan, Min.	.10
☐	228	Zarley Zalapski, Hfd.	.10
☐	229	Patrik Sundstrom, N.J.	.10
☐	230	Steve Smith, Edm.	.10
☐	231	Daren Puppa (G), Buf.	.10
☐	232	Dave Taylor, L.A.	.10
☐	233	Ray Bourque, Bos.	.75
☐	234	Kevin Stevens, Pgh.	.10
☐	235	Frank Musil, Cgy.	.10
☐	236	Mike Keane, Mtl.	.10
☐	237	Brian Propp, Min.	.10
☐	238	Brent Fedyk, Det.	.10
☐	239	Rob Ramage, (Min.)	.10
☐	240	Robert Kron, Van.	.10
☐	241	Mike McNeil, Que.	.10
☐	242	Greg Gilbert, Chi.	.10
☐	243	Dan Quinn, Stl.	.10
☐	244	Chris Nilan, Bos.	.10
☐	245	Bernie Nicholls, NYR.	.10
☐	246	Don Beaupré (G), Wsh.	.10
☐	247	Keith Acton, Pha.	.10
☐	248	Gord Murphy, Pha.	.10
☐	249	Bill Ranford (G), Edm.	.25
☐	250	Dave Chyzowski, NYI.	.10
☐	251	Clint Malarchuk (G), Buf.	.10
☐	252	Larry Robinson, L.A.	.25
☐	253	Dave Poulin, Bos.	.10
☐	254	Paul MacDermid, Wpg.	.10
☐	255	Doug Smail, (Que.)	.10
☐	256	Mark Recchi, Pgh.	.25
☐	257	Brian Bradley, Tor.	.10
☐	258	Grant Fuhr (G), Edm.	.25
☐	259	Owen Nolan, Que.	.25
☐	260	Hubie McDonough, NYI.	.10
☐	261	Mikko Makela, Buf.	.10
☐	262	Mathieu Schneider, Mtl.	.10
☐	263	Peter Stastny, N.J.	.25
☐	264	Jim Hrivnak (G), Wsh.	.10
☐	265	Scott Stevens, Stl.	.25

	No.	Player	Price
☐	266	Mike Tomlak, Hfd.	.10
☐	267	Marty McSorley, L.A.	.10
☐	268	Johan Garpenlov, Det.	.10
☐	269	Mike Vernon (G), Cgy.	.25
☐	270	Steve Larmer, Chi.	.10
☐	271	Phil Sykes, Wpg.	.10
☐	**272**	**Jay Mazur, Van., RC**	**.10**
☐	273	John Ogrodnick, NYR.	.10
☐	274	Dave Ellett, Tor.	.10
☐	275	Randy Gilhen, (L.A.)	.10
☐	276	Tom Chorske, Mtl.	.10
☐	277	James Patrick, NYR.	.10
☐	278	Darin Kimble, Stl.	.10
☐	279	Paul Cyr, Hfd.	.10
☐	280	Petr Nedved, Van.	.10
☐	281	Tony McKegney, Chi.	.10
☐	282	Alexei Kasatonov, N.J.	.10
☐	283	Stéphan Lebeau, Mtl.	.10
☐	284	Everett Sanipass, Que.	.10
☐	285	Tony Tanti, Buf.	.10
☐	286	Kevin Miller, Det.	.10
☐	287	Moe Mantha, Wpg.	.10
☐	288	Alan May, Wsh.	.10
☐	289	John Cullen, Hfd.	.10
☐	290	Daniel Berthiaume (G), L.A.	.10
☐	291	Mark Pederson, Pha.	.10
☐	292	Laurie Boschman, N.J.	.10
☐	293	Neil Wilkinson, S.J.	.10
☐	294	Rick Wamsley (G), Cgy.	.10
☐	295	Ken Linseman, Edm.	.10
☐	296	Jamie Leach, Pgh.	.10
☐	297	Chris Terreri (G), N.J.	.10
☐	298	Cliff Ronning, Van.	.10
☐	299	Bobby Holik, Hfd.	.10
☐	300	Mats Sundin, Que.	.75
☐	301	Carey Wilson, Cgy.	.10
☐	302	Teppo Numminen, Wpg.	.10
☐	303	Dave Lowry, Stl.	.10
☐	304	Joe Reekie, NYI.	.10
☐	305	Keith Primeau, Det.	.25
☐	306	David Shaw, NYR.	.10
☐	307	Nick Kypreos, Wsh.	.10
☐	308	Dave Manson, Chi.	.10
☐	309	Mick Vukota, NYI.	.10
☐	310	Todd Elik, (Min.)	.10
☐	311	Michel Petit, Tor.	.10
☐	312	Dale Hawerchuk, Buf.	.25
☐	313	Joe Murphy, Edm.	.10
☐	314	Chris Dahlquist, Min.	.10
☐	315	Petri Skriko, Bos.	.10
☐	316	Sergei Fedorov, Det.	.75
☐	317	Lee Norwood, N.J.	.10
☐	318	Garry Valk, Van.	.10
☐	319	Glen Featherstone, (Bos.)	.10
☐	320	Dave Snuggerud, Buf.	.10
☐	321	Doug Evans, Wpg.	.10
☐	322	Marc Bureau, Min.	.10
☐	323	John Vanbiesbrouck (G), NYR.	1.00
☐	324	John McIntyre, L.A.	.10
☐	325	Wes Walz, Bos.	.10
☐	326	Daryl Reaugh (G), Hfd.	.10
☐	327	Paul Fenton, (Hfd.)	.10
☐	328	Ulf Samuelsson, Pgh.	.10
☐	329	Andrew Cassels, Mtl.	.10
☐	**330**	**Alexei Gusarov, Que., RC**	**.10**
☐	331	John Druce, Wsh.	.10
☐	332	Adam Graves, (NYR.)	.10
☐	333	Ed Belfour (G), Chi.	.50
☐	334	Murray Baron, Pha.	.10
☐	335	John Tucker, NYI.	.10
☐	336	Todd Gill, Tor.	.10
☐	337	Martin Hostak, Pha.	.10
☐	338	Gino Odjick, Van.	.10
☐	339	Eric Weinrich, N.J.	.10
☐	340	Todd Ewen, Mtl.	.10
☐	341	Mike Hartman, Buf.	.10
☐	342	Danton Cole, Wpg.	.10
☐	343	Jaromir Jagr, Pgh.	1.50
☐	344	Mike Craig, Min.	.10
☐	345	Mark Fitzpatrick (G), NYI.	.10
☐	346	Darren Turcotte, NYR.	.10
☐	347	Ron Wilson, Stl.	.10
☐	348	Rob Blake, L.A.	.25
☐	349	Dale Kushner, Pha.	.10
☐	350	Jeff Beukeboom, Edm.	.10
☐	351	Tim Bergland, Wsh.	.10
☐	352	Peter Ing, Tor.	.10
☐	353	Wayne McBean, NYI.	.10
☐	**354**	**Jim McKenzie, Hfd., RC**	**.10**
☐	355	Theoren Fleury, Cgy.	.50
☐	356	Jocelyn Lemieux, Chi.	.10
☐	357	Ken Hodge, Bos.	.10
☐	358	Shawn Anderson, Que.	.10
☐	359	Dmitri Khristich, Wsh.	.10
☐	360	Jon Morris, N.J.	.10
☐	361	Darrin Shannon, Buf.	.10
☐	362	Chris Joseph, Edm.	.10
☐	363	Norman Lacombe, Pha.	.10
☐	364	Frank Pietrangelo (G), Pgh	.10
☐	365	Joey Kocur, NYR.	.10
☐	366	Anatoli Semenov, Edm.	.10
☐	367	Bob Bassen, Stl.	.10
☐	**368**	**Brad Jones, (Pha.), RC**	**.10**
☐	369	Glenn Healy (G) NYI.	.10
☐	370	Don Sweeney, Bos.	.10
☐	371	Brad Dalgarno, NYI.	.10
☐	372	Al Iafrate, Wsh.	.10
☐	**373**	**Patrick Lebeau, Mtl., RC, (Brent Gilchrist)**	**.10**
☐	374	Terry Yake, Hfd.	.10
☐	375	Roger Johansson, Cgy.	.10
☐	376	Paul Broten, NYR.	.10
☐	**377**	**André Racicot (G), Mtl., RC**	**.10**
☐	378	Scott Thornton, Tor.	.10
☐	379	Zdeno Ciger, N.J.	.10
☐	380	Paul Stanton, Pgh.	.10
☐	381	Ray Sheppard, (Det.)	.10
☐	**382**	**Kevin Haller, Buf., RC**	**.10**
☐	383	Vladimir Ruzicka, Bos.	.10
☐	**384**	**Bryan Marchment, (Chi.), RC**	**.10**
☐	**385**	**Bill Berg, NYI., RC**	**.10**
☐	386	Mike Ricci, Pha.	.10
☐	387	Pat Conacher, N.J.	.10
☐	**388**	**Brian Glynn, Min., RC**	**.10**
☐	389	Joe Sakic, Que.	1.25
☐	390	Mikhail Tatarinov, (Que.)	.10
☐	391	Stephane Matteau, Cgy.	.10
☐	392	Mark Tinordi, Min.	.10
☐	393	Robert Reichel, Cgy.	.25
☐	394	Tim Sweeney, Cgy.	.10
☐	395	Rick Tabaracci (G), Wpg.	.10
☐	396	Ken Sabourin, Wsh.	.10
☐	**397**	**Jeff Lazaro, Bos., RC**	**.10**
☐	398	Checklist	.10
☐	399	Checklist	.10
☐	400	Checklist	.10

1991 - 92 STADIUM CLUB CHARTER MEMBERS SET

This multi-sport set was issued in redemption form. Cards either say "Member Only" or "Charter Member" on the face.

Imprint: © 1991 THE TOPPS COMPANY, INC.

Complete Set (22 cards): 15.00

	Player	NRMT-MT
☐	Ed Belfour (Vezina)	.50
☐	Ed Belfour (Top Goalie)	.50
☐	Ray Bourque	.75
☐	Pavel Bure	1.00
☐	Guy Carbonneau	.25
☐	Paul Coffey (1,000)	.50
☐	Paul Coffey	.50
☐	Mike Gartner	.50
☐	Mike Gartner (500)	.50
☐	Michel Goulet	.50
☐	Wayne Gretzky	3.00
☐	Wayne Gretzky (700)	3.00
☐	Wayne Gretzky (2,000)	3.00
☐	Brett Hull	.75
☐	Brett Hull (Hart)	.75
☐	Brett Hull (50 in 50)	.75
☐	Brian Leetch	.50
☐	Mario Lemieux (Art Ross)	2.50
☐	Mario Lemieux (MVP)	2.50
☐	Mario Lemieux (Club MVP)	2.50
☐	Mark Messier (Hart)	.75
☐	Patrick Roy	2.50

1991 - 92 TRI-GLOBE INTERNATIONAL MAGNIFICENT FIVE

SERGEI FEDOROV

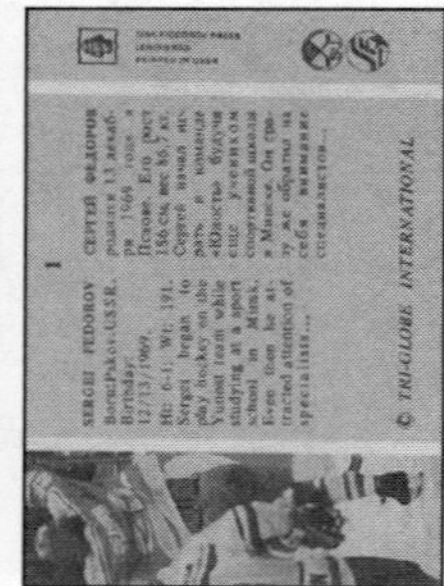

Complete Set (5 cards): 6.00

	No.	Player	NRMT-MT
☐	1	Sergei Fedorov	1.50
☐	2	Sergei Fedorov (Some Men Are Faster)	1.50
☐	3	Sergei Fedorov (Some Men Are Tougher)	1.50
☐	4	Sergei Fedorov (Some Men Are Stronger)	1.50
☐	5	Sergei Fedorov (Some Men Are Better)	1.50

MAGNIFICENT FIVE

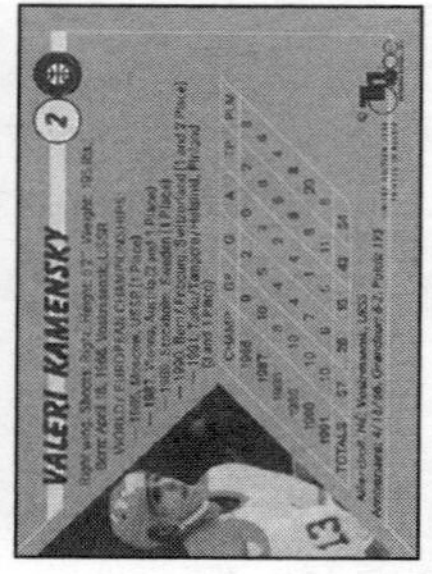

Complete Set (21 cards): 15.00

	No.	Player	NRMT-MT
☐	1	Valeri Kamensky (One Of The Worlds Best)	1.00
☐	2	Valeri Kamensky (A World Champion)	1.00
☐	3	Valeri Kamensky (A World Class Forward)	1.00
☐	4	Valeri Kamensky (Champion Of The USSR)	1.00
☐	5	Valeri Kamensky (There Are Only Few Of Them)	1.00
☐	6	Pavel Bure (One Of The Worlds Best)	2.00
☐	7	Pavel Bure (A World Champion)	2.00
☐	8	Pavel Bure (A World Class Forward)	2.00
☐	9	Pavel Bure (Champion Of The USSR)	2.00
☐	10	Pavel Bure (A European Champion)	2.00
☐	11	Anatoli Semenov (One Of The Worlds Best)	.75
☐	12	Anatoli Semenov (An Olympic Champion)	.75
☐	13	Anatoli Semenov (A World Class Forward)	.75
☐	14	Anatoli Semenov (Champion Of The USSR)	.75
☐	15	Anatoli Semenov (There Are Only Few Of Them)	.75
☐	16	Arturs Irbe (One Of The Worlds Best)	.75
☐	17	Arturs Irbe (A European Champion)	.75
☐	18	Arturs Irbe (A World Class Goaltender)	.75
☐	19	Arturs Irbe (A World Champion)	.75
☐	20	Arturs Irbe (There Are Only Few Of Them)	.75
☐		Sergei Fedorov (Checklist)	1.00

1991 - 92 TRI-GLOBE INTERNATIONAL FROM RUSSIA WITH PUCK

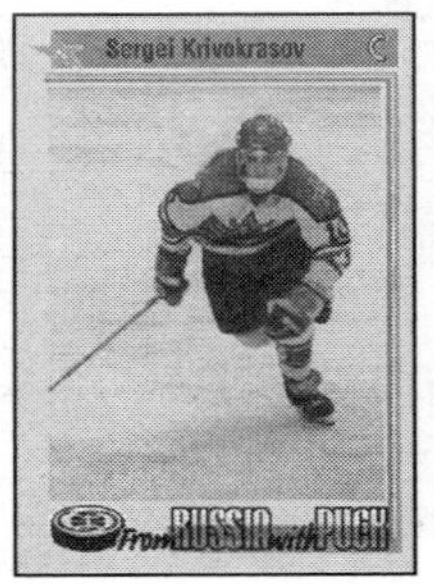

There are 50,000 sets available. Each player has two cards.

Complete Set (24 cards): 10.00

	No.	Player	NRMT-MT
□	1	Igor Larionov	1.00
□	2	Igor Larionov	1.00
□	3	Andrei Lomakin	.20
□	4	Andrei Lomakin	.20
□	5	Pavel Bure	3.00
□	6	Pavel Bure	3.00
□	7	Alexei Zhamnov	1.00
□	8	Alexei Zhamnov	1.00
□	9	Sergei Krivokrasov	.20
□	10	Sergei Krivokrasov	.20
□	11	Valeri Kamensky	1.00
□	12	Valeri Kamensky	1.00
□	13	Vyacheslav Kozlov	.50
□	14	Vyacheslav Kozlov	.50
□	15	Valeri Zelepukin	.20
□	16	Valeri Zelepukin	.20
□	17	Igor Kravchuk	.20
□	18	Igor Kravchuk	.20
□	19	Vladimir Malakhov	.50
□	20	Vladimir Malakhov	.50
□	21	Boris Mironov	.20
□	22	Boris Mironov	.20
□	23	Arturs Irbe (G)	.25
□	24	Arturs Irbe (G)	.25

1991 - 92 ULTIMATE DRAFT CARDS

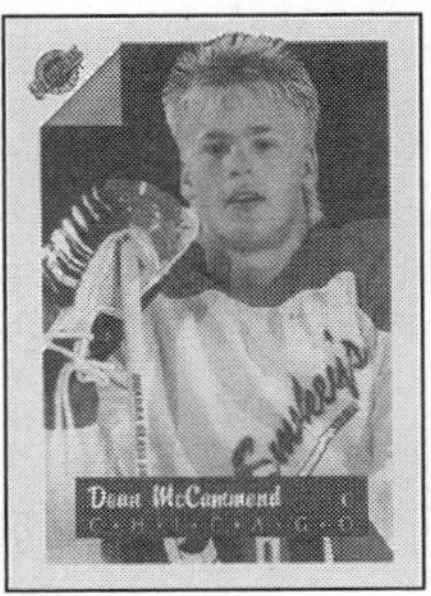

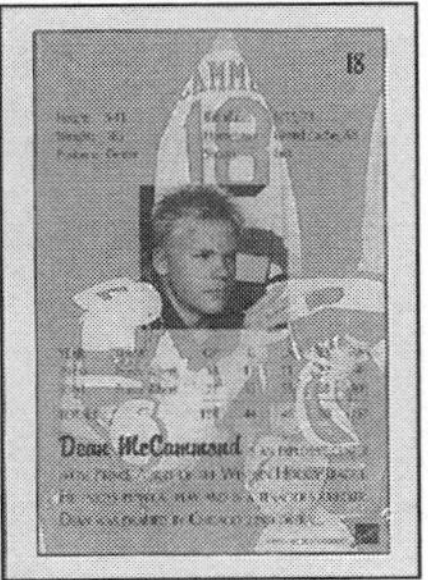

These cards have two versions an English issue and a French issue. 51 players have also signed both English and French cards.

Imprint: 1991 - ALL RIGHTS RESERVED (SMOKEY'S) logo

Complete Set (90 cards): 8.00

Common Player: .10 .10

	Promo	NRMT-MT
□	Pat Falloon	1.00
□	Alex Stojanov	1.00
□	Mike Torchia (G)	1.00

	No.	Player	Aut.	Card
□□	1	Ultimate / Preview	-	.10
□□	2	Pat Falloon	-	.10
□□□□	3	Scott Niedermayer	10.00	.35
□□	4	Scott Lachance	-	.10
□□□□	5	Peter Forsberg	50.00	2.00
□□	6	Alek Stojanov	-	.10
□□	7	Richard Matvichuk	-	.10
□□□□	8	Patrick Poulin	5.00	.10
□□	9	Martin Lapointe	-	.10
□□□□	10	Tyler Wright	5.00	.10
□□	11	Philippe Boucher	-	.10
□□□□	12	Pat Peake	8.00	.10
□□	13	Markus Naslund	-	.10
□□□□	14	Brent Bilodeau	5.00	.10
□□□□	15	Glen Murray	5.00	.10
□□□□	16	Niklas Sundblad	5.00	.10
□□	17	Trevor Halverson	-	.10
□□	18	Dean McAmmond	-	.10
□□□□	19	Jim Campbell	15.00	.10
□□□□	20	René Corbet	8.00	.10
□□□□	21	Eric Lavigne	5.00	.10
□□□□	22	Steve Staios	5.00	.10
□□□□	23	Jassen Cullimore	5.00	.10
□□□□	24	Jamie Pushor	5.00	.10
□□□□	25	Donevan Hextall	5.00	.10
□□□□	26	Andrew Verner (G)	8.00	.10
□□□□	27	Jason Dawe	8.00	.10
□□□□	28	Jeff Nelson	5.00	.10
□□□□	29	Darcy Werenka	5.00	.10
□□□□	30	François Groleau	5.00	.10
□□□□	31	Guy Lévêque	5.00	.10
□□□□	32	Jamie Matthews	5.00	.10
□□□□	33	Dody Wood	5.00	.10
□□□□	34	Yanic Perreault	10.00	.25
□□□□	35	Jamie McLellan (G)	8.00	.10
□□□□	36	Yanick Dupré	15.00	.10
□□	37	Checklist 1: First Round Group Shot	-	.10
□□□□	38	Chris Osgood (G)	25.00	.75
□□□□	39	Fredrik Lindqvist	5.00	.10
□□□□	40	Jason Young	5.00	.10
□□□□	41	Steve Konowalchuk	8.00	.10
□□□□	42	Michael Nylander	5.00	.10
□□□□	43	Shane Peacock	8.00	.10
□□□□	44	Yves Sarault	5.00	.10
□□□□	45	Marcel Cousineau (G)	5.00	.10
□□□□	46	Nathan Lafayette	5.00	.10
□□□□	47	Bobby House	5.00	.10
□□□□	48	Terry Toporowski	5.00	.10
□□□□	49	Terry Chitaroni	5.00	.10
□□□□	50	Mike Torchia (G)	5.00	.10
□□□□	51	Mario Nobil	5.00	.10
□□□□	52	Justin Morrison	5.00	.10
□□□□	53	Grayden Reid	5.00	.10
□□	54	Yanick Perreault	-	.10
□□	55	Checklist 2: Second Round Group Shot	-	.10
□□	56	Niedermayer/Falloon/Lachance	-	.10
□□	57	The Goalies: A. Verner/C. Osgood./ J. McLellan/M. Cousineau./M. Torchia	-	.25
□□	58	Pat Falloon	8.00	.10
□□	59	Scott Niedermayer	-	.25
□□	60	Scott Lachance	-	.10
□□	61	Peter Forsberg	-	1.50
□□	62	Alek Stojanov	5.00	.10
□□	63	Richard Matvichuk	5.00	.10
□□	64	Patrick Poulin	-	.10
□□	65	Martin Lapointe	10.00	.10
□□	66	Tyler Wright	-	.10
□□	67	Philippe Boucher	5.00	.10
□□	68	Pat Peake	-	.10
□□	69	Markus Naslund	-	.10
□□	70	Brent Bilodeau	-	.10
□□	71	Glen Murray	-	.10
□□	72	Niklas Sundblad	-	.10
□□	73	Trevor Halverson	5.00	.10
□□	74	Dean McAmmond	5.00	.10
□□	75	P. Boucher/J. Nelson/S. Niedermayer	-	.10
□□	76	M. Naslund/P. Forsberg/M Nylander	-	1.00
□□	77	Checklist 3: 3rd & 4th Round Group Shot	-	.10
□□	78	Pat Falloon	-	.10
□□	79	Scott Niedermayer	-	.25
□□	80	P. Falloon/R. Niedermayer	-	.10
□□	81	Scott Lachance	8.00	.10
□□	82	Philippe Boucher	-	.10
□□	83	Markus Naslund	8.00	.10
□□	84	Glen Murray	-	.10
□□	85	Niklas Sundblad	-	.10
□□	86	Jason Dawe	-	.10
□□	87	Yanick Perreault	-	.10
□□	88	Y. Dupré/M. Nylander	-	.10
□□	89	Overview	-	.10
□□	90	Face The Future/Ultimate	-	.10

1991 - 92 ULTIMATE ORIGINAL SIX

These cards have two versions: an english and a french card. 59 players have a third autographed version.

Complete Set (100 cards): 7.00 15.00

Common Player: .10 .20

	Promo	NRMT-MT
□	Bernie Geoffrion, Mtl.	4.00
□	Bobby Hull, Chi.	5.00

	No.	Player	Aut.	Eng.	Fr.
□□	1	Montréal Canadiens	-	.10	.20
□□	2	New York Rangers	-	.10	.20
□□	3	Toronto Maple Leafs	-	.10	.20
□□	4	Boston Bruins	-	.10	.20
□□	5	Chicago Blackhawks	-	.10	.20
□□	6	Detroit Red Wings	-	.10	.20
□□□	7	Ralph Backstrom, Mtl.	15.00	.10	.20
□□□	8	Emile Bouchard, Mtl.	15.00	.15	.25
□□□	9	John Ferguson, Mtl.	10.00	.10	.20
□□	10	Bernie Geoffrion, Mtl.	-	.35	.50
□□□	11	Phil Goyette, Mtl.	10.00	.10	.20
□□	12	Doug Harvey, Mtl.	-	.35	.50
□□□	13	Don Marshall, Mtl.	10.00	.10	.20
□□□	14	Henri Richard, Mtl.	25.00	.35	.50
□□□	15	Dollard St. Laurent, Mtl.	15.00	.10	.20
□□	16	Jean-Guy Talbot, Mtl.	-	.10	.20
□□□	17	Gump Worsley (G), Mtl.	35.00	.35	.50
□□□	18	Andy Bathgate, NYR.	15.00	.15	.25
□□□	19	Lou Fontinato, NYR.	15.00	.10	.20
□□□	20	Ed Giacomin (G), NYR.	35.00	.35	.50
□□□	21	Vic Hadfield, NYR.	15.00	.10	.20
□□□	22	Camille Henry, NYR.	30.00	.10	.20
□□□	23	Harry Howell, NYR.	15.00	.15	.25
□□□	24	Orland Kurtenbach, NYR.	10.00	.10	.20
□□□	25	Jim Neilson, NYR.	10.00	.10	.20
□□□	26	Bob Nevin, NYR.	10.00	.10	.20
□□□	27	Dean Prentice, NYR.	10.00	.10	.20
□□□	28	Leo Reise, NYR.	10.00	.10	.20
□□□	29	Red Sullivan, NYR.	10.00-	.10	.20
□□	30	Bob Baun, Tor.	-	.10	.20
□□□	31	Gus Bodnar, Tor.	10.00-	.10	.20
□□	32	Johnny Bower (G), Tor.	-	.35	.50
□□□	33	Bob Davidson, Tor.	30.00	.10	.20
□□□	34	Ron Ellis, Tor.	10.00	.10	.20
□□□	35	Billy Harris, Tor.	10.00	.10	.20
□□□	36	Larry Hillman, Tor.	10.00	.10	.20
□□	37	Tim Horton, Tor.	-	.50	.75
□□	38	Red Kelly, Tor.	-	.25	.35
□□□	39	Dave Keon, Tor.	20.00	.25	.35
□□□	40	Frank Mahovlich, Tor.	35.00	.50	.75
□□□	41	Eddie Shack, Tor.	25.00	.25	.35
□□□	42	Tod Sloan, Tor.	15.00	.10	.20
□□□	43	Sid Smith, Tor.	10.00	.10	.20
□□□	44	Allan Stanley, Tor.	15.00	.15	.25
□□□	45	Gaye Stewart, Tor.	10.00	.10	.20
□□□	46	Harry Watson, Tor.	15.00	.15	.25
□□□	47	Wayne Carleton, Bos.	10.00	.10	.20
□□□	48	Fern Flaman, Bos.	15.00	.15	.25
□□□	49	Ken Hodge, Bos.	10.00	.10	.20
□□□	50	Leo Labine, Bos.	10.00	.10	.20
□□□	51	Harry Lumley (G), Bos.	15.00	.35	.50
□□□	52	John McKenzie, Bos.	10.00	.10	.20
□□□	53	Doug Mohns, Bos.	10.00	.10	.20
□□□	54	Fred Stanfield, Bos.	10.00	.10	.20
□□	55	Jerry Toppazzini, Bos.	-	.10	.20
□□□	56	Ed Westfall, Bos.	15.00	.10	.20
□□	57	Bobby Hull, Chi.	-	.75	1.00
□□	58	Ed Litzenberger, Chi.	-	.10	.20
□□□	59	Gilles Marotte, Chi.	10.00	.10	.20
□□□	60	Ab McDonald, Chi.	10.00	.10	.20

	No.	Player			
□□□	61	Bill Mosienko, Chi.	40.00	.25	.35
□□□	62	Jim Pappin, Chi.	15.00	.10	.20
□□□	63	Pierre Pilote, Chi.	15.00	.25	.35
□□□	64	Elmer Vasko, Chi.	15.00	.10	.20
□□□	65	Johnny Wilson, Chi.	10.00	.10	.20
□□□	66	Sid Abel, Det.	20.00	.15	.25
□□□	67	Gary Bergman, Det.	10.00	.10	.20
□□□	68	Alex Delvecchio, Det.	15.00	.35	.50
□□□	69	Bill Gadsby, Det.	15.00	.15	.25
□□□	70	Ted Lindsay, Det.	35.00	.35	.50
□□□	71	Marcel Pronovost, Det.	15.00	.10	.20
□□□	72	Norm Ullman, Det.	15.00	.25	.35
□□	73	Bernie Geoffrion, Mtl.	-	.35	.50
□□	74	Andy Bathgate, NYR.	-	.15	.25
□□	75	Allan Stanley, Tor.	-	.15	.25
□□	76	Fern Flaman, Bos.	-	.15	.25
□□	77	Bobby Hull, Chi.	-	.75	1.00
□□	78	Norm Ullman, Det.	-	.25	.35
□□□	79	Red Kelly, Tor.	25.00	.25	.35
□□□	80	Johnny Bower (G), Tor.	25.00	.35	.50
□□	81	Henri Richard, Mtl.	-	.35	.50
□□	82	Bobby Hull, Chi.	-	.75	1.00
□□□	83	Bernie Geoffrion, Mtl.	35.00	.35	.50
□□	84	Tim Horton, Tor.	-	.50	.75
□□	85	Bill Friday, Referee	-	.15	.25
□□	86	Bruce Hood, Referee	-	.15	.25
□□	87	Ron Wicks, Referee	-	.15	.25
□□	88	Bobby Hull	-	.50	.75
□□	89	Bobby Hull	-	.50	.75
□□	90	Bobby Hull	-	.50	.75
□□	91	Bobby Hull	-	.50	.75
□□	92	Bobby Hull	-	.50	.75
□□	93	HL: Bob Baun, Tor.	-	.10	.20
□□	94	HL: Ted Lindsay, Det.	-	.35	.50
□□	95	HL: Henri Richard, Mtl.	-	.35	.50
□□	96	HL: Bobby Hull, Chi.	-	.75	1.00
□□	97	HL: Tim Horton, Tor.	-	.50	.75
□□	98	Keith McCreary, Mtl.	-	.10	.20
□□	99	75th Anniversary Checklist 1	-	.10	.20
□□	100	75th Anniversary Checklist 2	-	.10	.20

	Hologram	**NRMT-MT**
□	Bobby Hull, Autographed Hologram	150.00
□	Bobby Hull, Hologram	30.00

1991 - 92 UPPER DECK

These cards have two versions: an English issue and a French issue. Both versions sell at the same price.

Imprint: © 1991 or 1992 Upper Deck Co.

Low Numbers Set (500 cards): 30.00
High Numbers Set (200 cards): 15.00
Common Player: .10

	No.	Player	NRMT-MT
□□	**1**	**Vladimir Malakhov, CIS., RC**	**.25**
□□	**2**	**Alexei Zhamnov, CIS., RC**	**1.00**
□□	**3**	**Dimitri Filimonov, CIS., RC**	**.25**
□□	**4**	**Alexander Semak, CIS., RC**	**.25**
□□	5	Vyacheslav Kozlov, CIS.	.75
□□	6	Sergei Fedorov, CIS.	.50
□□	7	CL: Brett Hull/Eric Lindros	1.00
□□	8	Al MacInnis, Cdn.	.25
□□	9	Eric Lindros, Cdn.	6.00
□□	10	Bill Ranford (G), Cdn.	.25
□□	11	Paul Coffey, Cdn.	.25
□□	12	Dale Hawerchuk, Cdn.	.20
□□	13	Wayne Gretzky, Cdn.	1.50
□□	14	Mark Messier, Cdn.	.35
□□	15	Steve Larmer, Cdn.	.25
□□	16	Zigmund Palffy, Cze.	2.50
□□	17	Josef Beranek, Cze.	.10
□□	18	Jiri Slegr, Cze.	.10
□□	19	Martin Rucinsky, Cze.	.60
□□	20	Jaromir Jagr, Cze.	1.00
□□	**21**	**Teemu Selänne, Fin., RC**	**8.00**
□□	**22**	**Janne Laukkanen, Fin., RC**	**.10**
□□	**23**	**Markus Ketterer (G), Fin., RC**	**.10**
□□	24	Jari Kurri, Fin.	.25
□□	25	Janne Ojanen, Fin.	.10
□□	26	Nicklas Lidström, Swe., Error (Niklas)	.50
□□	27	Tomas Forslund, Swe.	.10
□□	28	Johan Garpenlov, Swe.	.10
□□	29	Niclas Andersson, Swe.	.10
□□	30	Tomas Sandström, Swe.	.10
□□	31	Mats Sundin, Swe.	.25
□□	32	Mike Modano, USA.	.25
□□	33	Brett Hull, USA.	.35
□□	34	Mike Richter (G), USA.	.25
□□	35	Brian Leetch, USA.	.25
□□	36	Jeremy Roenick, USA.	.25
□□	37	Chris Chelios, USA.	.35
□□	38	Wayne Gretzky Art	1.00
□□	39	Ed Belfour (G), Chi.	.25
□□	40	Sergei Fedorov, Det.	.35
□□	41	Ken Hodge, Bos.	.10
□□	42	Jaromir Jagr, Pgh.	.85
□□	43	Rob Blake, L.A.	.25
□□	44	Eric Weinrich, N.J.	.10
□□	45	M. Lemieux/W. Gretzky/B. Hull	1.00
□□	**46**	**Russ Romaniuk, Wpg., RC**	**.10**
□□	47	Mario Lemieux/ President George Bush	1.00
□□	**48**	**Michel Picard, Hfd., RC**	**.10**
□□	**49**	**Dennis Vaske, NYI,. RC**	**.10**
□□	**50**	**Eric Murano, Van., RC**	**.10**
□□	**51**	**Enrico Ciccone, Min., RC**	**.10**
□□	**52**	**Shaun Van Allen, Edm., RC**	**.10**
□□	53	Stu Barnes, Wpg.	.10
□□	54	Pavel Bure, Van.	.75
□□	55	Neil Wilkinson, S.J.	.10
□□	56	Tony Hrkac, S.J.	.10
□□	57	Brian Mullen, S.J.	.10
□□	58	Jeff Hackett (G), S.J.	.25
□□	59	Brian Hayward (G), S.J.	.10
□□	60	Craig Coxe, S.J.	.10
□□	61	Rob Zettler, S.J.	.10
□□	62	Robert McGill, S.J.	.10
□□	63	CL: M. Lapointe/J. Pushor	.10
□□	**64**	**Peter Forsberg, Pha., RC**	**10.00**
□□	**65**	**Patrick Poulin, Hfd., RC**	**.10**
□□	**66**	**Martin Lapointe, Det., RC**	**.25**
□□	**67**	**Tyler Wright, Edm., RC**	**.10**
□□	**68**	**Philippe Boucher, Buf., RC**	**.10**
□□	**69**	**Glen Murray, Bos., RC**	**.10**
□□	**70**	**Martin Rucinsky, Edm., RC**	**.75**
□□	**71**	**Zigmund Palffy, NYI., RC**	**3.50**
□□	**72**	**Jassen Cullimore, Van., RC**	**.10**
□□	**73**	**Jamie Pushor, Det., RC**	**.10**
□□	**74**	**Andrew Verner (G), Edm., RC**	**.10**
□□	**75**	**Jason Dawe, Buf., RC**	**.10**
□□	**76**	**Jamie Mathews, Chi., RC**	**.10**
□□	**77**	**Sandy McCarthy, Cgy., RC**	**.10**
□□	78	CL: Cam Neely, Bos.	.25
□□	79	CL: Dale Hawerchuk, Buf.	.25
□□	80	CL: Theoren Fleury, Cgy.	.25
□□	81	CL: Ed Belfour (G), Chi.	.25
□□	82	CL: Sergei Fedorov, Det.	.25
□□	83	CL: Esa Tikkanen, Edm.	.10
□□	84	CL: John Cullen, Hfd.	.10
□□	85	CL: Tomas Sandström, L.A.	.10
□□	86	CL: Dave Gagner, Min.	.10
□□	87	CL: Russ Courtnall, Mtl.	.10
□□	88	CL: John MacLean, N.J.	.10
□□	89	CL: David Volek, NYI.	.10
□□	90	CL: Darren Turcotte, NYR.	.10
□□	91	CL: Rick Tocchet, Pha.	.10
□□	92	CL: Mark Recchi, Pgh.	.25
□□	93	CL: Mats Sundin, Que.	.25
□□	94	CL: Adam Oates, Stl.	.25
□□	95	CL: Neil Wilkinson, S.J.	.10
□□	96	CL: David Ellett, Tor.	.10
□□	97	CL: Trevor Linden, Van.	.25
□□	98	CL: Kevin Hatcher, Wsh.	.10
□□	99	CL: Ed Olczyk, Wpg.	.10
□□	100	Checklist 1 (1 - 100)	.10
□□	101	Bob Essensa (G), Wpg.	.10
□□	102	Uwe Krupp, Buf.	.10
□□	103	Per-Erik Eklund, Pha.	.10
□□	104	Christian Ruuttu, Buf.	.10
□□	105	Kevin Dineen, Hfd.	.10
□□	106	Phil Housley, Wpg.	.10
□□	**107**	**Pat Jablonski (G), Stl., RC**	**.10**
□□	**108**	**Jarmo Kekalainen, Bos., RC**	**.10**
□□	109	Pat Elynuik, Wpg.	.10
□□	**110**	**Corey Millen, NYR., RC**	**.10**
□□	111	Petr Klima, Edm.	.10
□□	112	Mike Ridley, Wsh.	.10
□□	113	Peter Stastny, N.J.	.25
□□	114	Jyrki Lumme, Van.	.10
□□	115	Chris Terreri (G), N.J.	.10
□□	116	Tom Barrasso (G), Pgh.	.25
□□	117	Bill Ranford (G), Edm.	.25
□□	118	Peter Ing (G), Tor.	.10
□□	119	John Tanner (G), Que.	.10
□□	120	Troy Gamble (G), Van.	.10
□□	121	Stéphane Matteau, Cgy.	.10
□□	122	Rick Tocchet, Pha.	.10
□□	123	Wes Walz, Bos.	.10
□□	124	Dave Andreychuk, Buf.	.25
□□	125	Mike Craig, Min.	.10
□□	126	Dale Hawerchuk, Buf.	.10
□□	127	Dean Evason, Hfd.	.10
□□	128	Craig Janney, Bos.	.10
□□	129	Tim Cheveldae (G), Det.	.10
□□	130	Rick Wamsley (G), Cgy.	.10
□□	131	Peter Bondra, Wsh.	.35
□□	132	Scott Stevens, Stl.	.10
□□	133	Kelly Miller, Wsh.	.10
□□	134	Mats Sundin, Que.	.50
□□	135	Mick Vukota, NYI.	.10
□□	136	Vincent Damphousse, Tor.	.35
□□	137	Patrick Roy (G), Mtl.	1.50
□□	138	Hubie McDonough, NYI.	.10
□□	139	Curtis Joseph (G), Stl.	.60
□□	140	Brent Sutter, NYI.	.10
□□	141	Tomas Sandström, L.A.	.10
□□	142	Kevin Miller, Det.	.10
□□	143	Mike Ricci, Pha.	.10
□□	144	Sergei Fedorov, Det.	.50
□□	145	Luc Robitaille, L.A.	.25
□□	146	Steve Yzerman, Det.	1.00
□□	147	Andy Moog (G), Bos.	.25
□□	148	Rob Blake, L.A.	.25
□□	149	Kirk Muller, N.J.	.10
□□	150	Daniel Berthiaume (G), L.A.	.10
□□	151	John Druce, Wsh.	.10
□□	152	Garry Valk, Van.	.10
□□	153	Brian Leetch, NYR.	.35
□□	154	Kevin Stevens, Pgh.	.10
□□	155	Darren Turcotte, NYR.	.10
□□	156	Mario Lemieux, Pgh.	1.50
□□	157	Dimitri Khristich, Wsh.	.10
□□	**158**	**Brian Glynn, Min., RC**	**.10**
□□	159	Benoît Hogue, Buf.	.10
□□	160	Mike Modano, Min.	.50
□□	161	Jimmy Carson, Det.	.10
□□	162	Steve Thomas, Chi.	.10
□□	163	Mike Vernon (G), Cgy.	.25
□□	164	Ed Belfour (G), Chi.	.35
□□	165	Joel Otto, Cgy.	.10
□□	166	Jeremy Roenick, Chi.	.35
□□	167	Johan Garpenlov, Det.	.10
□□	168	Russ Courtnall, Mtl.	.10
□□	169	John MacLean, N.J.	.10
□□	170	J.J. Daigneault, Mtl.	.10
□□	171	Sylvain Lefebvre, Mtl.	.10
□□	172	Tony Granato, L.A.	.10
□□	173	David Volek, NYI.	.10
□□	174	Trevor Linden, Van.	.25
□□	175	Mike Richter (G), NYR.	.35
□□	176	Pierre Turgeon, Buf.	.25
□□	177	Paul Coffey, Pgh.	.25
□□	178	Jan Erixon, NYR.	.10
□□	179	Rick Vaive, Buf.	.10
□□	180	Dave Gagner, Min.	.10
□□	181	Thomas Steen, Wpg.	.10
□□	182	Esa Tikkanen, Edm.	.10
□□	183	Sean Burke (G), N.J.	.25
□□	184	Paul Cavallini, Stl.	.10
□□	185	Alexei Kasatonov, N.J.	.10
□□	186	Kevin Lowe, Edm.	.10
□□	187	Gino Cavallini, Stl.	.10

	No.	Card	Value
☐ ☐	188	Doug Gilmour, Cgy.	.35
☐ ☐	189	Rod Brind'Amour, Stl.	.25
☐ ☐	190	Gary Roberts, Cgy.	.10
☐ ☐	191	Kirk McLean (G), Van.	.25
☐ ☐	**192**	**Kevin Haller, Buf., RC**	**.10**
☐ ☐	193	Pat Verbeek, Hfd.	.10
☐ ☐	194	Dave Snuggerud, Buf.	.10
☐ ☐	195	Gino Odjick, Van.	.10
☐ ☐	196	David Ellett, Tor.	.10
☐ ☐	197	Don Beaupré (G), Wsh.	.10
☐ ☐	198	Rob Brown, Hfd.	.10
☐ ☐	199	Marty McSorley, L.A.	.10
☐ ☐	200	Checklist 2 (101 - 200)	.10
☐ ☐	201	Joe Mullen, Pgh.	.25
☐ ☐	202	Dave Capuano, Van.	.10
☐ ☐	203	Paul Stanton, Pgh.	.10
☐ ☐	204	Terry Carkner, Pha.	.10
☐ ☐	205	Jon Casey (G), Min.	.10
☐ ☐	206	Ken Wregget (G), Pha.	.10
☐ ☐	207	Gaetan Duchesne, Min.	.10
☐ ☐	208	Cliff Ronning, Van.	.10
☐ ☐	209	Dale Hunter, Wsh.	.10
☐ ☐	210	Danton Cole, Wpg.	.10
☐ ☐	211	Jeff Brown, Stl.	.10
☐ ☐	212	Mike Foligno, Tor.	.10
☐ ☐	213	Michel Mongeau, Stl.	.10
☐ ☐	214	Doug Brown, N.J.	.10
☐ ☐	215	Todd Krygier, Hfd.	.10
☐ ☐	216	Jon Morris, N.J.	.10
☐ ☐	217	David Reid, Tor.	.10
☐ ☐	218	John McIntyre, L.A.	.10
☐ ☐	219	Lafleur's Farewell	.75
☐ ☐	220	Vincent Riendeau (G), Stl.	.10
☐ ☐	221	Tim Hunter, Cgy.	.10
☐ ☐	222	Dave McLlwain, Wpg.	.10
☐ ☐	223	Robert Reichel, Cgy.	.25
☐ ☐	224	Glenn Healy (G), NYI.	.10
☐ ☐	225	Robert Kron, Van.	.10
☐ ☐	226	Patrick Flatley, NYI.	.10
☐ ☐	227	Petr Nedved, Van.	.10
☐ ☐	228	Mark Janssens, NYR.	.10
☐ ☐	229	Michal Pivonka, Wsh.	.10
☐ ☐	230	Ulf Samuelsson, Pgh.	.10
☐ ☐	231	Zarley Zalapski, Hfd.	.10
☐ ☐	232	Neal Broten, Min.	.10
☐ ☐	233	Bobby Holik, Hfd.	.10
☐ ☐	234	Cam Neely, Bos.	.25
☐ ☐	235	John Cullen, Hfd.	.10
☐ ☐	236	Brian Bellows, Min.	.10
☐ ☐	237	Chris Nilan, Bos.	.10
☐ ☐	238	Mikael Andersson, Hfd.	.10
☐ ☐	239	Bob Probert, Det.	.10
☐ ☐	240	Teppo Numminen, Wpg.	.10
☐ ☐	241	Peter Zezel, Tor.	.10
☐ ☐	242	Denis Savard, Mtl.	.25
☐ ☐	243	Al MacInnis, Cgy.	.25
☐ ☐	244	Stéphane Richer, Mtl.	.10
☐ ☐	245	Theoren Fleury, Cgy.	.35
☐ ☐	246	Mark Messier, Edm.	.50
☐ ☐	247	Mike Gartner, NYR.	.25
☐ ☐	248	Daren Puppa (G), Buf.	.10
☐ ☐	249	Louie DeBrusk, NYR.	.10
☐ ☐	250	Glenn Anderson, Edm.	.10
☐ ☐	251	Ken Hodge, Bos.	.10
☐ ☐	252	Adam Oates, Stl.	.35
☐ ☐	253	Pat LaFontaine, NYI.	.25
☐ ☐	254	Adam Creighton, Chi.	.10
☐ ☐	255	Ray Bourque, Bos.	.50
☐ ☐	256	Jaromir Jagr, Pgh.	1.00
☐ ☐	257	Steve Larmer, Chi.	.10
☐ ☐	258	Keith Primeau, Det.	.25
☐ ☐	259	Mikel Liut (G), Wsh.	.10
☐ ☐	260	Brian Propp, Min.	.10
☐ ☐	261	Stéphan Lebeau, Mtl.	.10
☐ ☐	262	Kelly Hrudey (G), L.A.	.10
☐ ☐	263	Joe Nieuwendyk, Cgy.	.25
☐ ☐	264	Grant Fuhr (G), Edm.	.25
☐ ☐	265	Guy Carbonneau, Mtl.	.10
☐ ☐	266	Martin Gelinas, Edm.	.10
☐ ☐	267	Alexander Mogilny, Buf.	.35
☐ ☐	268	Adam Graves, Edm.	.10
☐ ☐	269	Anatoli Semenov, Edm.	.10
☐ ☐	270	Dave Taylor, L.A.	.10
☐ ☐	271	Dirk Graham, Chi.	.10
☐ ☐	272	Gary Leeman, Tor.	.10
☐ ☐	**273**	**Valeri Kamensky, Que., RC**	**1.00**
☐ ☐	274	Marc Bureau, Min.	.10
☐ ☐	275	James Patrick, NYR.	.10
☐ ☐	276	Dino Ciccarelli, Wsh.	.25
☐ ☐	277	Ron Tugnutt (G), Que.	.10
☐ ☐	278	Paul Ysebaert, Det.	.10
☐ ☐	279	Laurie Boschman, N.J.	.10
☐ ☐	280	Dave Manson, Chi.	.10
☐ ☐	281	David Chyzowski, NYI.	.10
☐ ☐	282	Shayne Corson, Mtl.	.25
☐ ☐	283	Steve Chiasson, Det.	.10
☐ ☐	284	Craig MacTavish, Edm.	.10
☐ ☐	285	Petr Svoboda, Mtl.	.10
☐ ☐	286	Craig Simpson, Edm.	.10
☐ ☐	**287**	**Ron Hoover, Bos., RC**	**.10**
☐ ☐	288	Vladimir Ruzicka, Bos.	.10
☐ ☐	289	Randy Wood, NYI.	.10
☐ ☐	290	Doug Lidster, Van.	.10
☐ ☐	291	Kay Whitmore (G), Hfd.	.10
☐ ☐	292	Bruce Driver, N.J.	.10
☐ ☐	293	Bobby Smith, Min.	.10
☐ ☐	294	Claude Lemieux, N.J.	.10
☐ ☐	295	Mark Tinordi, Min.	.10
☐ ☐	296	Mark Osborne, Wpg.	.10
☐ ☐	297	Brad Shaw, Hfd.	.10
☐ ☐	298	Igor Larionov, Van.	.25
☐ ☐	299	Ron Francis, Pgh.	.35
☐ ☐	300	Checklist 3 (201 - 300)	.10
☐ ☐	301	Bob Kudelski, L.A.	.10
☐ ☐	302	Larry Murphy, Pgh.	.25
☐ ☐	303	Brent Ashton, Wpg.	.10
☐ ☐	**304**	**Brad Jones, L.A., RC**	**.10**
☐ ☐	305	Gord Donnelly, Wpg.	.10
☐ ☐	306	Murray Craven, Pha.	.10
☐ ☐	307	Chris Dahlquist, Min.	.10
☐ ☐	**308**	**Jim Paek, Pgh., RC**	**.10**
☐ ☐	309	Ron Sutter, Pha.	.10
☐ ☐	310	Mike Tomlak, Hfd.	.10
☐ ☐	311	Ray Ferraro, NYI.	.10
☐ ☐	312	Dave Hannan, Tor.	.10
☐ ☐	313	Randy McKay, Det.	.10
☐ ☐	314	Rod Langway, Wsh.	.10
☐ ☐	315	Shawn Burr, Det.	.10
☐ ☐	316	Calle Johansson, Wsh.	.10
☐ ☐	317	Rich Sutter, Stl.	.10
☐ ☐	318	Al Iafrate, Wsh.	.10
☐ ☐	319	Bob Bassen, Stl.	.10
☐ ☐	320	Mike Krushelnyski, Tor.	.10
☐ ☐	321	Sergei Makarov, Cgy.	.10
☐ ☐	322	Darrin Shannon, Buf.	.10
☐ ☐	323	Terry Yake, Hfd.	.10
☐ ☐	324	John Vanbiesbrouck (G), NYR.	.60
☐ ☐	325	Peter Sidorkiewicz (G), Hfd.	.10
☐ ☐	326	Troy Mallette, NYR.	.10
☐ ☐	327	Ron Hextall (G), Pha.	.25
☐ ☐	328	Mathieu Schneider, Mtl.	.10
☐ ☐	329	Bryan Trottier, Pgh.	.25
☐ ☐	330	Kris King, NYR.	.10
☐ ☐	331	Daniel Marois, Tor.	.10
☐ ☐	332	Shayne Stevenson, Bos.	.10
☐ ☐	333	Joe Sakic, Que.	.85
☐ ☐	334	Petri Skriko, Bos.	.10
☐ ☐	**335**	**Dominik Hasek (G), Chi., RC**	**5.00**
☐ ☐	336	Scott Pearson, Que.	.10
☐ ☐	337	Bryan Fogarty, Que.	.10
☐ ☐	338	Don Sweeney, Bos.	.10
☐ ☐	339	Rick Tabaracci (G), Wpg.	.10
☐ ☐	340	Steven Finn, Que.	.10
☐ ☐	341	Gary Suter, Cgy.	.10
☐ ☐	342	Troy Crowder, N.J.	.10
☐ ☐	343	Jim Hrivnak (G), Wsh.	.10
☐ ☐	344	Eric Weinrich, N.J.	.10
☐ ☐	**345**	**John LeClair, Mtl., RC**	**3.50**
☐ ☐	346	Mark Recchi, Pgh.	.25
☐ ☐	**347**	**Dan Currie, Edm., RC**	**.10**
☐ ☐	348	Ulf Dahlen, Min.	.10
☐ ☐	349	Rob Ray, Buf.	.10
☐ ☐	350	Steve Smith, Edm.	.10
☐ ☐	351	Shawn Antoski, Van.	.10
☐ ☐	352	Cam Russell, Chi.	.10
☐ ☐	353	Scott Thornton, Tor.	.10
☐ ☐	354	Chris Chelios, Chi.	.35
☐ ☐	355	Sergei Nemchinov, NYR.	.10
☐ ☐	356	Bernie Nicholls, NYR.	.10
☐ ☐	357	Jeff Norton, NYI.	.10
☐ ☐	358	Dan Quinn, Stl.	.10
☐ ☐	359	Michel Petit, Tor.	.10
☐ ☐	360	Eric Desjardins, Mtl.	.25
☐ ☐	361	Kevin Hatcher, Wsh.	.10
☐ ☐	**362**	**Jiri Sejba, Buf., RC**	**.10**
☐ ☐	363	Mark Pederson, Pha.	.10
☐ ☐	**364**	**Jeff Lazaro, Bos., RC**	**.10**
☐ ☐	**365**	**Alexei Gusarov, Que., RC**	**.10**
☐ ☐	366	Jari Kurri, L.A.	.25
☐ ☐	367	Owen Nolan, Que.	.25
☐ ☐	368	Clint Malarchuk (G), Buf.	.10
☐ ☐	369	Patrik Sundstrom, N.J.	.10
☐ ☐	370	Glen Wesley, Bos.	.10
☐ ☐	371	Wayne Presley, Chi.	.10
☐ ☐	372	Craig Muni, Edm.	.10
☐ ☐	373	Brent Fedyk, Det.	.10
☐ ☐	374	Michel Goulet, Chi.	.10
☐ ☐	375	Tim Sweeney, Cgy.	.10
☐ ☐	**376**	**Gary Shuchuk, Det., RC**	**.10**
☐ ☐	**377**	**André Racicot (G), Mtl., RC**	**.10**
☐ ☐	**378**	**Jay Mazur, Van., RC**	**.10**
☐ ☐	379	Andrew Cassels, Mtl.	.10
☐ ☐	380	Brian Noonan, Chi.	.10
☐ ☐	**381**	**Sergei Kharin, Wpg., RC**	**.10**
☐ ☐	382	Derek King, NYI.	.10
☐ ☐	383	Fredrik Olausson, Wpg.	.10
☐ ☐	384	Thomas Fergus, Tor.	.10
☐ ☐	385	Zdeno Ciger, N.J.	.10
☐ ☐	386	Wendel Clark, Tor.	.25
☐ ☐	387	Ed Olczyk, Wpg.	.10
☐ ☐	388	Basil McRae, Min.	.10
☐ ☐	389	Tom Fitzgerald, NYI.	.10
☐ ☐	390	Ray Sheppard, NYR.	.10
☐ ☐	391	Bob Sweeney, Bos.	.10
☐ ☐	392	Gord Murphy, Pha.	.10
☐ ☐	393	John Chabot, Det.	.10
☐ ☐	394	Jeff Beukeboom, Edm.	.10
☐ ☐	395	Rick Zombo, Det.	.10
☐ ☐	396	Kjell Samuelsson, Pha.	.10
☐ ☐	397	Garth Butcher, Stl.	.10
☐ ☐	398	Phil Bourque, Pgh.	.10
☐ ☐	399	Lou Franceschetti, Buf.	.10
☐ ☐	400	Checklist 4 (301 - 400)	.10
☐ ☐	**401**	**Kevin Todd, N.J., RC**	**.10**
☐ ☐	402	Ken Baumgartner, NYI.	.10
☐ ☐	403	Peter Douris, Bos.	.10
☐ ☐	404	Jiri Latal, Pha.	.10
☐ ☐	**405**	**Marc Potvin, Det., RC**	**.10**
☐ ☐	406	Gary Nylund, NYI.	.10
☐ ☐	407	Yvon Corriveau, Hfd.	.10
☐ ☐	408	Sheldon Kennedy, Det.	.10
☐ ☐	409	David Shaw, NYR.	.10
☐ ☐	410	Viacheslav Fetisov, N.J.	.25
☐ ☐	**411**	**Mario Doyon, Que., RC**	**.10**
☐ ☐	412	Jamie Macoun, Cgy.	.10
☐ ☐	413	Curtis Leschyshyn, Que.	.10
☐ ☐	414	Mike Peluso, Chi.	.10
☐ ☐	415	Brian Benning, L.A.	.10
☐ ☐	**416**	**Stu Grimson, Chi., RC**	**.10**
☐ ☐	417	Ken Sabourin, Was.	.10
☐ ☐	418	Luke Richardson, Tor.	.10
☐ ☐	**419**	**Ken Quinney, Que., RC**	**.10**
☐ ☐	**420**	**Mike Donnelly, L.A., RC**	**.10**
☐ ☐	**421**	**Darcy Loewen, Buf., RC**	**.10**
☐ ☐	422	Brian Skrudland, Mtl.	.10
☐ ☐	423	Joel Savage, Buf.	.10
☐ ☐	424	Adrien Plavsic, Van.	.10
☐ ☐	425	Jergus Baca, Hfd.	.10
☐ ☐	426	Greg Adams, Van.	.10
☐ ☐	427	Tom Chorske, Mtl.	.10
☐ ☐	428	Scott Scissons, NYI.	.10
☐ ☐	429	Dale Kushner, Pha.	.10
☐ ☐	**430**	**Todd Richards, Hfd., RC**	**.10**
☐ ☐	431	Kip Miller, Que.	.10
☐ ☐	**432**	**Jason Prosofsky, NYR., RC**	**.10**
☐ ☐	433	Stéphane Morin, Que.	.10
☐ ☐	**434**	**Brian McReynolds, NYR., RC**	**.10**
☐ ☐	435	Ken Daneyko, N.J.	.10
☐ ☐	436	Chris Joseph, Edm.	.10
☐ ☐	437	Wayne Gretzky, L.A.	2.00
☐ ☐	438	Jocelyn Lemieux, Chi.	.10
☐ ☐	439	Garry Galley, Bos.	.10
☐ ☐	440	CL: D. Weight/S. Rice/T. Amonte	.25
☐ ☐	441	Steven Rice, NYR.	.10
☐ ☐	442	Patrice Brisebois, Mtl.	.10

	No.	Card	Price
☐ ☐	443	Jim Waite (G), Chi.	.10
☐ ☐	**444**	**Doug Weight, NYR., RC**	**1.50**
☐ ☐	445	Nelson Emerson, Stl.	.10
☐ ☐	**446**	**Jarrod Skalde, N.J., RC**	**.10**
☐ ☐	447	Jamie Leach, Pgh.	.10
☐ ☐	**448**	**Gilbert Dionne, Mtl., RC**	**.10**
☐ ☐	449	Trevor Kidd (G), Cgy.	.25
☐ ☐	**450**	**Tony Amonte, NYR., RC**	**1.50**
☐ ☐	451	Pat Murray, Pha.	.10
☐ ☐	452	Stéphane Fiset (G), Que.	.25
☐ ☐	**453**	**Patrick Lebeau, Mtl., RC**	**.10**
☐ ☐	**454**	**Chris Taylor, NYI., RC**	**.10**
☐ ☐	**455**	**Chris Tancill, Hfd., RC**	**.10**
☐ ☐	456	Mark Greig, Hfd.	.10
☐ ☐	457	Mike Sillinger, Det.	.10
☐ ☐	**458**	**Ken Sutton, Buf., RC**	**.10**
☐ ☐	**459**	**Len Barrie, Pha., RC**	**.10**
☐ ☐	460	Félix Potvin (G), Tor.	.50
☐ ☐	**461**	**Brian Sakic, Wsh., RC**	**.10**
☐ ☐	**462**	**Vyacheslav Kozlov, Det., RC**	**1.00**
☐ ☐	**463**	**Matt DelGuidice (G), Bos., RC**	**.10**
☐ ☐	464	Brett Hull, Stl.	.50
☐ ☐	**465**	**Norm Foster (G), Bos., RC**	**.10**
☐ ☐	**466**	**Alexander Godynyuk, Tor., RC**	**.10**
☐ ☐	467	Geoff Courtnall, Van.	.10
☐ ☐	468	Frantisek Kucera, Chi	.10
☐ ☐	**469**	**Benoît Brunet, Mtl., RC**	**.10**
☐ ☐	**470**	**Mark Vermette, Que., RC**	**.10**
☐ ☐	471	Tim Watters, L.A.	.10
☐ ☐	472	Paul Ranheim, Cgy.	.10
☐ ☐	473	Martin Hostak, Pha.	.10
☐ ☐	474	Joe Murphy, Edm.	.10
☐ ☐	**475**	**Claude Boivin, Pha., RC**	**.10**
☐ ☐	476	John Ogrodnick, NYR.	.10
☐ ☐	477	Doug Bodger, Buf.	.10
☐ ☐	478	Shawn Cronin, Wpg.	.10
☐ ☐	479	Mark Hunter, Hfd.	.10
☐ ☐	480	Dave Tippett, Wsh.	.10
☐ ☐	481	Rob DiMaio, NYI.	.10
☐ ☐	482	Lyle Odelein, Mtl.	.10
☐ ☐	483	Joe Reekie, NYI.	.10
☐ ☐	484	Randy Velischek, Que.	.10
☐ ☐	**485**	**Myles O'Connor, N.J., RC**	**.10**
☐ ☐	486	Craig Wolanin, Que.	.10
☐ ☐	487	Mike McPhee, Mtl.	.10
☐ ☐	**488**	**Claude Lapointe, Que., RC**	**.10**
☐ ☐	489	Troy Loney, Pgh.	.10
☐ ☐	490	Bob Beers, Bos.	.10
☐ ☐	**491**	**Sylvain Couturier, L.A., RC**	**.10**
☐ ☐	**492**	**Kimbi Daniels, Pha., RC**	**.10**
☐ ☐	**493**	**Darryl Shannon, Tor., RC**	**.10**
☐ ☐	**494**	**Jim McKenzie, Hfd., RC**	**.10**
☐ ☐	**495**	**Don Gibson, Van., RC**	**.10**
☐ ☐	**496**	**Ralph Barahona, Bos., RC**	**.10**
☐ ☐	497	Murray Baron, Pha.	.10
☐ ☐	498	Yves Racine, Det.	.10
☐ ☐	499	Larry Robinson, .LA.	.25
☐ ☐	500	Checklist 5 (401 to 500)	.10
☐ ☐	501	CL: Paul Coffey/Wayne Gretzky	.75
☐ ☐	502	Dirk Graham, Cdn.	.10
☐ ☐	503	Rick Tocchet, Cdn.	.10
☐ ☐	504	Eric Desjardins, Cdn.	.25
☐ ☐	505	Shayne Corson, Cdn.	.25
☐ ☐	506	Theoren Fleury, Cdn.	.25
☐ ☐	507	Luc Robitaille, Cdn.	.25
☐ ☐	508	Tony Granato, USA.	.10
☐ ☐	509	Eric Weinrich, USA.	.10
☐ ☐	510	Gary Suter, USA.	.10
☐ ☐	511	Kevin Hatcher, USA.	.10
☐ ☐	512	Craig Janney, USA.	.10
☐ ☐	513	Darren Turcotte, USA.	.10
☐ ☐	**514**	**Chris Winnes, Bos., RC**	**.10**
☐ ☐	515	Kelly Kisio, S.J.	.10
☐ ☐	**516**	**Joe Day, Hfd., RC**	**.10**
☐ ☐	**517**	**Ed Courtenay, S.J., RC**	**.10**
☐ ☐	518	Andrei Lomakin, Pha.	.10
☐ ☐	519	Kirk Muller, Mtl.	.10
☐ ☐	520	Rick Lessard, S.J.	.10
☐ ☐	521	Scott Thornton, Edm.	.10
☐ ☐	522	Luke Richardson, Edm.	.10
☐ ☐	523	Mike Eagles, Wpg.	.10
☐ ☐	524	Michael McNeill, Que.	.10
☐ ☐	525	Ken Priestlay, Pgh.	.10
☐ ☐	526	Louie DeBrusk, Edm.	.10
☐ ☐	527	Dave McLlwain, NYI.	.10
☐ ☐	528	Gary Leeman, Cgy.	.10
☐ ☐	**529**	**Adam Foote, Que., RC**	**.50**
☐ ☐	530	Kevin Dineen, Pha.	.10
☐ ☐	531	David Reid, Bos.	.10
☐ ☐	532	Arturs Irbe (G), S.J.	.10
☐ ☐	**533**	**Mark Osiecki, Cgy., RC**	**.10**
☐ ☐	534	Steve Thomas, NYI.	.10
☐ ☐	535	Vincent Damphousse, Edm.	.35
☐ ☐	536	Stéphane Richer, N.J.	.10
☐ ☐	**537**	**Jarmo Myllys (G), S.J., RC**	**.10**
☐ ☐	538	Carey Wilson, Cgy.	.10
☐ ☐	539	Scott Stevens, N.J.	.10
☐ ☐	540	Uwe Krupp, NYI.	.10
☐ ☐	541	Dave Christian, Stl.	.10
☐ ☐	542	Scott Mellanby, Edm.	.10
☐ ☐	**543**	**Peter Ahola, L.A., RC**	**.10**
☐ ☐	544	Todd Elik, Min.	.10
☐ ☐	545	Mark Messier, NYR.	.50
☐ ☐	546	Derian Hatcher, Min.	.25
☐ ☐	547	Rod Brind'Amour, Pha.	.25
☐ ☐	548	Dave Manson, Edm.	.10
☐ ☐	549	Darryl Sydor, L.A.	.10
☐ ☐	550	Paul Broten, NYR.	.10
☐ ☐	551	Andrew Cassels, Hfd.	.10
☐ ☐	**552**	**Tom Draper (G), Buf., RC**	**.10**
☐ ☐	553	Grant Fuhr (G), Tor.	.25
☐ ☐	554	Pierre Turgeon, NYI.	.25
☐ ☐	555	Pavel Bure, Van.	.75
☐ ☐	556	Pat LaFontaine, Buf.	.25
☐ ☐	557	Dave Thomlinson, Bos.	.10
☐ ☐	558	Doug Gilmour, Tor.	.50
☐ ☐	**559**	**Craig Billington (G), N.J., RC**	**.10**
☐ ☐	560	Dean Evason, S.J.	.10
☐ ☐	561	Brendan Shanahan, Stl.	.60
☐ ☐	562	Mike Hough, Que.	.10
☐ ☐	563	Dan Quinn, Pha.	.10
☐ ☐	564	Jeff Daniels, Pgh.	.10
☐ ☐	565	Troy Murray, Wpg.	.10
☐ ☐	566	Bernie Nicholls, Edm.	.10
☐ ☐	567	Randy Burridge, Wsh.	.10
☐ ☐	**568**	**Todd Hartje, Wpg., RC**	**.10**
☐ ☐	569	Charlie Huddy, L.A.	.10
☐ ☐	570	Steve Duchesne, Pha.	.10
☐ ☐	571	Sergio Momesso, Van.	.10
☐ ☐	572	Brian Lawton, S.J.	.10
☐ ☐	573	Ray Sheppard, Det.	.10
☐ ☐	574	Adam Graves, NYR.	.10
☐ ☐	575	Rollie Melanson (G), Mtl.	.10
☐ ☐	576	Steve Kasper, Pha.	.10
☐ ☐	577	Jim Sandlak, Van.	.10
☐ ☐	**578**	**Pat MacLeod, S.J., RC**	**.10**
☐ ☐	579	Sylvain Turgeon, Mtl.	.10
☐ ☐	**580**	**James Black, Hfd., RC**	**.10**
☐ ☐	581	Darrin Shannon, Wpg.	.10
☐ ☐	582	Todd Krygier, Wsh.	.10
☐ ☐	**583**	**Dominic Roussel (G), Pha., RC**	**.10**
☐ ☐	584	CL: Nicklas Lidström, Det.	.25
☐ ☐	585	Donald Audette, Buf.	.10
☐ ☐	586	Tomas Forslund, Cgy.	.10
☐ ☐	**587**	**Nicklas Lidström, Det., RC**	**.60**
☐ ☐	**588**	**Geoff Sanderson, Hfd., RC**	**.75**
☐ ☐	**589**	**Valeri Zelepukin, N.J., RC**	**.10**
☐ ☐	**590**	**Igor Ulanov, Wpg., RC**	**.10**
☐ ☐	**591**	**Corey Foster, Pha., RC**	**.10**
☐ ☐	**592**	**Dan Lambert, Que., RC**	**.10**
☐ ☐	593	Pat Falloon, S.J.	.10
☐ ☐	**594**	**Vladimir Konstantinov, Det., RC**	**.75**
☐ ☐	595	Josef Beranek, Edm.	.10
☐ ☐	596	Brad May, Buf.	.10
☐ ☐	**597**	**Jeff Odgers, S.J., RC**	**.10**
☐ ☐	**598**	**Rob Pearson, Tor., RC**	**.10**
☐ ☐	**599**	**Luciano Borsato, Wpg., RC**	**.10**
☐ ☐	600	Checklist 1 (501-600)	.10
☐ ☐	601	Peter Douris, Bos.	.10
☐ ☐	602	Mark Fitzpatrick (G), NYI.	.10
☐ ☐	603	Randy Gilhen, NYR.	.10
☐ ☐	604	Corey Millen, L.A.	.10
☐ ☐	**605**	**Jason Cirone, Wpg., RC**	**.10**
☐ ☐	**606**	**Kyosti Karjalainen, L.A., RC**	**.10**
☐ ☐	607	Garry Galley, Pha.	.10
☐ ☐	**608**	**Brent Thompson, L.A., RC**	**.10**
☐ ☐	**609**	**Alexander Godynyuk, Cgy., RC**	**.10**
☐ ☐	610	CL: M. Richter/M. Messier/B. Leetch	.25
☐ ☐	611	AS: Mario Lemieux, Pgh.	.85
☐ ☐	612	AS: Brian Leetch, NYR.	.25
☐ ☐	613	AS: Kevin Stevens, Pgh.	.10
☐ ☐	614	AS: Patrick Roy (G), Mtl.	.85
☐ ☐	615	AS: Paul Coffey, Pgh.	.25
☐ ☐	616	AS: Joe Sakic, Que.	.50
☐ ☐	617	AS: Jaromir Jagr, Pgh.	.75
☐ ☐	618	AS: Alexander Mogilny, Buf.	.25
☐ ☐	619	AS: Owen Nolan, Que.	.25
☐ ☐	620	AS: Mark Messier, NYR.	.25
☐ ☐	621	AS: Wayne Gretzky, L.A.	1.00
☐ ☐	622	AS: Brett Hull, Stl.	.35
☐ ☐	623	AS: Luc Robitaille, L.A.	.25
☐ ☐	624	AS: Phil Housley, Wpg.	.10
☐ ☐	625	AS: Ed Belfour (G), Chi.	.25
☐ ☐	626	AS: Steve Yzerman, Det.	.50
☐ ☐	627	AS: Adam Oates, Stl.	.25
☐ ☐	628	AS: Trevor Linden, Van.	.25
☐ ☐	629	AS: Jeremy Roenick, Chi.	.25
☐ ☐	630	AS: Theoren Fleury, Cgy.	.25
☐ ☐	631	AS: Sergei Fedorov, Det.	.25
☐ ☐	632	AS: Al MacInnis, Cgy.	.25
☐ ☐	633	AS: Ray Bourque, Bos.	.25
☐ ☐	634	AS: Mike Richter (G), NYR.	.25
☐ ☐	635	Al Secord, Chi.	.10
☐ ☐	636	Marcel Dionne, L.A.	.25
☐ ☐	637	Ken Morrow, NYI.	.10
☐ ☐	638	Guy Lafleur, Mtl.	.75
☐ ☐	639	Ed Mio (G), NYR.	.10
☐ ☐	640	Clark Gillies, NYI.	.10
☐ ☐	641	Bob Nystrom, NYI.	.10
☐ ☐	642	Pete Peeters (G), Wsh.	.10
☐ ☐	643	Ulf Nilsson, NYR.	.10
☐ ☐	644	Stéphan and Patrick Lebeau	.10
☐ ☐	645	The Sutter Brothers	.10
☐ ☐	646	Gino and Paul Cavallini	.10
☐ ☐	647	Valeri and Pavel Bure	1.25
☐ ☐	648	Chris and Peter Ferraro	.10
☐ ☐	649	CL: Team C.I.S.	.25
☐ ☐	**650**	**Darius Kasparaitis, CIS., RC**	**.25**
☐ ☐	**651**	**Alexei Yashin, CIS., RC**	**4.00**
☐ ☐	**652**	**Nikolai Khablbulin (G), CIS., RC**	**2.00**
☐ ☐	**653**	**Denis Metlyuk, CIS., RC**	**.10**
☐ ☐	**654**	**Konstantin Korotkov, CIS., RC**	**.10**
☐ ☐	**655**	**Alexei Kovalev, CIS., RC**	**1.50**
☐ ☐	**656**	**Alexander Kuzminsky, CIS., RC**	**.10**
☐ ☐	**657**	**Alexander Cherbayev, CIS., RC**	**.10**
☐ ☐	**658**	**Sergei Krivokrasov, CIS., RC**	**.25**
☐ ☐	**659**	**Sergei Zholtok, CIS., RC**	**.25**
☐ ☐	**660**	**Alexei Zhitnik, CIS., RC**	**.35**
☐ ☐	**661**	**Sandis Ozolinsh, CIS., RC**	**1.50**
☐ ☐	**662**	**Boris Mironov, CIS., RC**	**.25**
☐ ☐	**663**	**Pauli Jaks (G), Sui., RC**	**.10**
☐ ☐	**664**	**Gaetan Voisard, Sui., RC**	**.10**
☐ ☐	**665**	**Nicola Celio, Sui., RC**	**.10**
☐ ☐	**666**	**Marc Weber, Sui., RC**	**.10**
☐ ☐	**667**	**Bernhard Schumperli, Sui., RC**	**.10**
☐ ☐	**668**	**Laurent Bucher, Sui., RC**	**.10**
☐ ☐	**669**	**Michael Blaha, Sui., RC**	**.10**
☐ ☐	**670**	**Tiziano Gianini, Sui., RC**	**.10**
☐ ☐	**671**	**Marko Kiprusoff, Fin., RC**	**.10**
☐ ☐	**672**	**Janne Gronvall, Fin., RC**	**.10**
☐ ☐	**673**	**Juha Ylönen, Fin., RC**	**.10**
☐ ☐	**674**	**Sami Kapanen, Fin., RC**	**.50**
☐ ☐	**675**	**Marko Tuomainen, Fin., RC**	**.10**
☐ ☐	**676**	**Jarkko Varvio, Fin., RC**	**.10**
☐ ☐	**677**	**Tuomas Grönman, Fin., RC**	**.10**
☐ ☐	**678**	**Andreas Naumann, Ger., RC**	**.10**
☐ ☐	**679**	**Steffan Ziesche, Ger., RC**	**.10**
☐ ☐	**680**	**Jens Schwabe, Ger., RC**	**.10**
☐ ☐	**681**	**Thomas Schubert, Ger., RC**	**.10**
☐ ☐	**682**	**Hans-Jörg Mayer, Ger., RC**	**.10**
☐ ☐	**683**	**Marc Seliger (G), Ger., RC**	**.10**
☐ ☐	684	Trevor Kidd (G), Cdn.	.25
☐ ☐	685	Martin Lapointe, Cdn.	.10
☐ ☐	**686**	**Tyler Wright, Cdn., RC**	**.10**
☐ ☐	**687**	**Kimbi Daniels, Cdn., RC**	**.10**
☐ ☐	688	Karl Dykhuis, Cdn.	.10
☐ ☐	689	Jeff Nelson, Cdn.	.10
☐ ☐	690	Jassen Cullimore, Cdn.	.10
☐ ☐	691	Turner Stevenson, Cdn.	.10
☐ ☐	**692**	**Scott Lachance, USA., RC**	**.35**
☐ ☐	**693**	**Mike Dunham (G), USA., RC**	**.50**
☐ ☐	**694**	**Brent Bilodeau, USA., RC**	**.10**
☐ ☐	**695**	**Ryan Sittler, USA., RC**	**.10**
☐ ☐	**696**	**Peter Ferraro, USA., RC**	**.35**
☐ ☐	**697**	**Pat Peake, USA., RC**	**.35**

	No.	Player	NRMT-MT
□□	**698**	**Keith Tkachuk, USA., RC**	**4.00**
□□	**699**	**Brian Rolston, USA., RC**	**.50**
□□	700	Checklist 2 (601-700)	.10
	No.	**Insert**	**NRMT-MT**
□□	SP1	W. Gretzky/V. Kamensky/B. Hull	4.00

BOX BOTTOMS

Card size: 5-1/2" x 9"

	Player	NRMT-MT
□□	W. Gretzky, L.A.	3.00
□□	Brett Hull, Stl.	1.00
□□	Mark Messier, Edm.	1.25
□□	Mark Messier, NYR.	1.25
□□	Steve Yzerman, Det.	1.50

HOCKEY HEROES

2,500 cards were autographed by Brett Hull.

Insert Set (10 cards): 12.00

	No.	Player	NRMT-MT
□□		"Hockey Heroes": Brett Hull	5.00
□□	1	'83-84 Penticton's 105-Goal Man	1.00
□□	2	1984 Feeling The Draft	1.00
□□	3	'85-86 NCAA's Goal-Scoring Leader	1.00
□□	4	'86-87 AHL's Rookie-of-the-Year	1.00
□□	5	1987 A Full-Time Flame	1.00
□□	6	'88-89 40-Goal Plateau	1.00
□□	7	'89-90 NHL's New 70-Goal Scorer	1.00
□□	8	'90-91 A Season With Hart	1.00
□□	9	CL: Brett Hull,	1.00
	No.	**Autograph**	**NRMT-MT**
□□	9	Autographed card: Brett Hull, #9	200.00

AWARD WINNERS

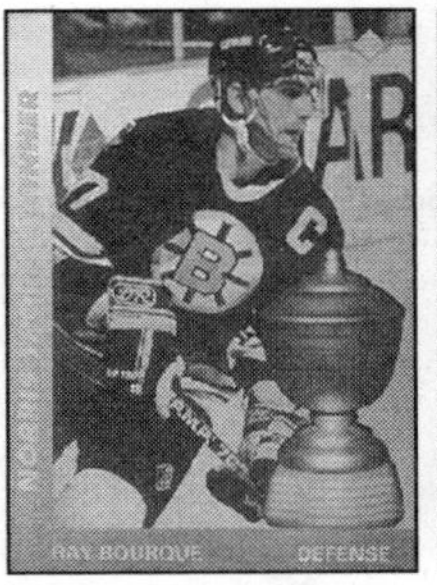

Ray Bourque has a variation without "Best Defenseman" on the card back.

Insert Set (9 cards): 10.00

	No.	Player	English
□	AW1	Wayne Gretzky, L.A.	3.00
□	AW2	Ed Belfour (G), Chi.	1.00
□	AW3	Brett Hull, Stl.	1.50
□	AW4	Ed Belfour (G), Chi.	1.00
□□	AW5	Ray Bourque, Bos.	1.50
□	AW6	Wayne Gretzy, L.A..	3.00
□	AW7	Ed Belfour (G), Chi.	1.00
□	AW8	Dirk Graham, Chi.	.50
□	AW9	Mario Lemieux, Pgh.	2.50

EURO STARS

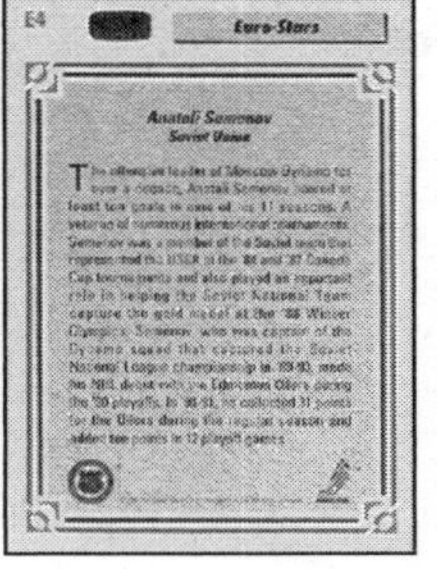

Insert Set (18 cards): 12.00

	No.	Player	French
□□	E1	Jarmo Kekalainen, Bos.	.50
□□	E2	Alexander Mogilny, Buf.	1.50
□□	E3	Bobby Holik, Hfd.	.50
□□	E4	Anatoli Semenov, Edm.	.50
□□	E5	Petr Nedved, Van.	1.00
□□	E6	Jaromir Jagr, Pgh.	4.50
□□	E7	Tomas Sandström, L.A.	.50
□□	E8	Robert Kron, Van.	.50
□□	E9	Sergei Fedorov, Det.	3.00
□□	E10	Esa Tikkanen, Edm.	.50
□□	E11	Christian Ruuttu, Buf.	.50
□□	E12	Peter Bondra, Wsh.	1.75
□□	E13	Mats Sundin, Tor.	1.75
□□	E14	Dominik Hasek (G), Chi.	4.50
□□	E15	Johan Garpenlov, S.J.	.50
□□	E16	Alexander Godynyuk, Tor.	.50
□□	E17	Ulf Samuelsson, Pgh.	.50
□□	E18	Igor Larionov, Van.	1.00

1992 - 93 UPPER DECK COMMEMORATIVE SHEETS

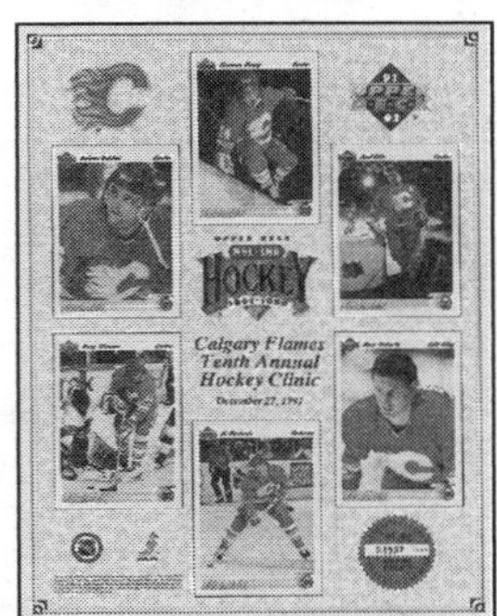

Upper Deck sheets were given out free at home games. Each sheet is limited to different quanitities and features 1991-92 Upper Deck hockey cards. Not all photos on the sheet were actual Upper Deck cards.

Card Size: 8 1/2" x 11"

Complete Set (18 cards): 120.00

	No.	Sheet	NRMT-MT
□	1	L.A. Kings vs. Edm. Oilers, Oct 8/91	10.00
□	2	N.Y. Rangers vs. Cgy. Flames, Nov.4/91	6.00
□	3	Stl. Blues vs. Pha. Flyers, Nov. 5/91	6.00
□	4	N.J. Devils vs. Chi. Blackhawks, Dec 21/91	6.00
□	5	Cgy. Flames 10th Annual Clinic, Dec. 27/91	6.00
□	6	N.Y. Rangers vs. Stl. Blues, Jan. 8/92	6.00
□	7	Flyers Alumni vs. NHL Heroes, Jan. 17/92	6.00
□	8	Campbell Conference All Stars, Jan. 18/92	12.00
□	9	Wales Conference All Stars, Jan. 18/92	12.00
□	10	Det. Red Wings vs. Tor. Maple Leafs, Feb. 7/92	6.00
□	11	Wsh. Capitals vs. N.Y. Rangers, Feb. 7/92	6.00
□	12	Min. North Stars: Dream Team, Feb 15/92	6.00
□	13	Pgh. Penquins vs. Tor. Maple Leafs, Feb. 18/92	8.00
□	14	N.Y. Rangers vs. Pha. Flyers, Feb. 23/92	6.00
□	15	Edm. Oilers vs. Pha. Flyers, Feb. 28/92	6.00
□	16	Min. North Stars vs. Det. Red Wings, Mar. 14/92	6.00
□	17	Cgy. Flames vs. Min. North Stars, Mar. 28/92	6.00
□	18	Det. Red Wings vs. Chi. Blackhaws, Mar. 31/92	6.00
□	19	Pha. Flyers vs. Tor. Maple Leafs, Apr. 5/92	6.00

1991 - 92 UPPER DECK WORLD JUNIOR CHAMPIONSHIPS

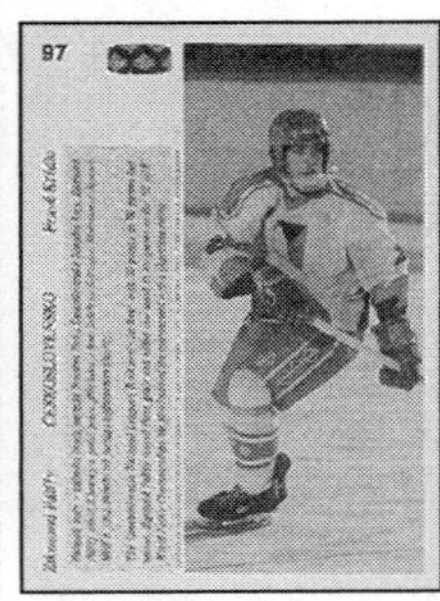

This set was released for the 1992 World Junior Games in the Czech Republic.

Imprint: 1992 The Upper Deck Company Printed in the U.S.A.

Complete Set (100 cards): 65.00

Common Player: .20

Album: 6.00

	No.	Player	NRMT-MT
□	1	Description Card	.20
□	2	Vladislav Buljin	.20
□	3	Ravil Gusmanov	.20
□	4	Denis Vinokurov	.20
□	5	Mikhail Volkov	.20
□	6	Alexei Troschinsky	.20
□	7	Andrei Nikolishin	.60
□	8	Alexander Sverztov	.20
□	9	Artim Kopot	.20
□	10	Ildar Mukhometov	.20
□	11	Darius Kasparaitis	.75
□	12	Alexei Yashin	6.00
□	13	Nikolai Khabibulin (G)	3.00
□	14	Denis Metlyuk	.20
□	15	Konstantin Korotkov	.20
□	16	Alexei Kovalev	2.50
□	17	Alexander Kuzminsky	.20
□	18	Slexander Cherbayev	.20
□	19	Sergei Krivokrasov	.50
□	20	Sergei Zholtok	.50
□	21	Alexei Zhitnik	.60
□	22	Sandis Ozolinsh	3.00
□	23	Boris Mironov	.60
□	24	Pauli Jaks (G)	.20
□	25	Gaetan Voisard	.20
□	26	Nicola Celio	.20
□	27	Marc Weber	.20
□	28	Bernhard Schumperli	.20
□	29	Laurent Bucher	.20
□	30	Michael Blaha	.20
□	31	Tiziano Gianini	.20
□	32	Tero Lehtera	.20
□	33	Mikko Luovi	.20
□	34	Marko Kiprusoff	.20
□	35	Janne Gronvall	.20
□	36	Juha Ylonen	.20
□	37	Sami Kapanen	1.50
□	38	Marko Tuomainen	.20
□	39	Jarkko Varvio	.35
□	40	Tuomas Gronman	.35
□	41	Andreas Naumann	.20
□	42	Steffen Ziesche	.20
□	43	Jens Schwabe	.20
□	44	Thomas Schubert	.20
□	45	Hans-Jorg Mayer	.20
□	46	Marc Seliger (G)	.20
□	47	Ryan Hughes	.20
□	48	Richard Matvichuk	.60
□	49	David St. Pierre	.20
□	50	Paul Kariya	35.00
□	51	Patrick Poulin	.50
□	52	Mike Fountain (G)	.50
□	53	Scott Niedermayer	1.00
□	54	John Slaney	.35
□	55	Brad Bombardir	.20
□	56	Andy Schneider	.20
□	57	Steve Junker	.20
□	58	Trevor Kidd (G)	1.00
□	59	Martin Lapointe	.50

	No.	Player	Price
☐	60	Tyler Wright	.35
☐	61	Kimbi Daniels	.20
☐	62	Karl Dykhuis	.35
☐	63	Jeff Nelson	.20
☐	64	Jassen Cullimore	.35
☐	65	Turner Stevenson	.50
☐	66	Brian Mueller	.20
☐	67	Chris Tucker	.20
☐	68	Marty Schriner	.20
☐	69	Mike Pendergast	.20
☐	70	John Lilley	.20
☐	71	Jim Campbell	2.50
☐	72	Brian Holzinger	1.00
☐	73	Steve Konowalchuk	.50
☐	74	Chris Ferraro	.50
☐	75	Chris Imes	.20
☐	76	Rich Brennan	.20
☐	77	Todd Hall	.20
☐	78	Brian Rafalski	.20
☐	79	Scott Lachance	1.00
☐	80	Mike Dunham (G)	1.00
☐	81	Brent Bilodeau	.20
☐	82	Ryan Sittler	.35
☐	83	Peter Ferraro	.75
☐	84	Pat Peake	.75
☐	85	Keith Tkachuk	8.00
☐	86	Brian Rolston	1.50
☐	87	Milan Hnilicka	.20
☐	88	Roman Hamrlik	3.00
☐	89	Milan Nedoma	.20
☐	90	Patrik Luza	.20
☐	91	Jan Caloun	.50
☐	92	Viktor Ujcik	.20
☐	93	Robert Petrovicky	.35
☐	94	Roman Meluzin	.20
☐	95	Jan Vopat	.50
☐	96	Martin Prochazka	.35
☐	97	Zigmund Palffy	6.00
☐	98	Ivan Droppa	.20
☐	99	Martin Straka	.50
☐	100	Checklist (1-100)	.35
☐		Hologram: Wayne Gretzky, Art Ross	4.00
☐		Hologram: Wayne Gretzky, Lady Byng	4.00

1992 CANADIAN WINTER OLYMPICS

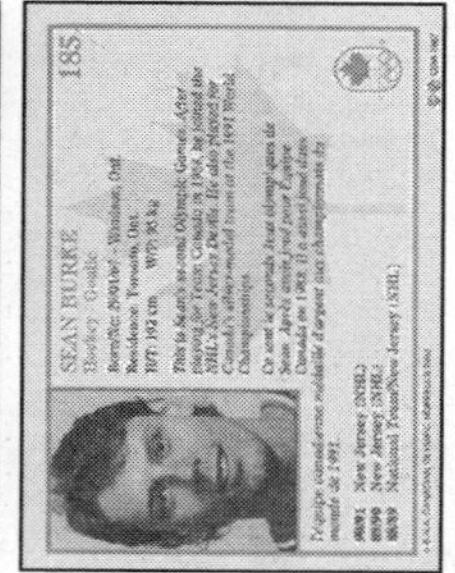

This 200-card multi-sport set features 18 hockey players. A 200-card set sells at $25.00

Imprint: © B.N.A. CANADIAN OLYMPIC HOPEFULS 1992

	No.	Player	NRMT-MT
☐	174	Kevin Dahl	.20
☐	175	Stéphane Roy	.20
☐	179	Curt Giles	.20
☐	180	Dave Archibald	.20
☐	184	Chris Kontos	.20
☐	185	Sean Burke (G)	1.00
☐	189	Adrien Plasvic, Err. (Plausic)	.20
☐	190	Chris Lindberg	.20
☐	191	Todd Brost	.20
☐	192	Joé Juneau	.75
☐	193	Randy Smith	.20
☐	194	Jason Woolley, Err. (Wooley)	.20
☐	195	Dan Ratushny	.20
☐	196	Fabian Joseph	.20
☐	197	Kent Manderville	.20
☐	198	Brad Schlegel	.20
☐	199	Karl Dykhuis	.20
☐	200	Trevor Kidd (G)	1.00

1992 NATIONAL GAME

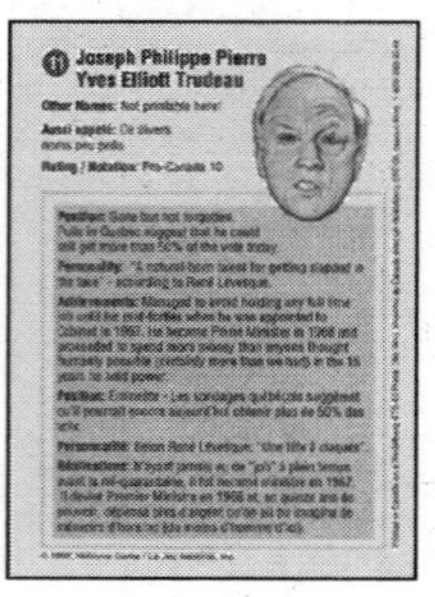

Artwork by Paul Beare. We have no pricing information on this set.

Imprint:

Complete Set (29 cards):

	No.	Player
☐		Title Card
☐	1	Brian "Muldoon" Mulroney
☐	2	Robert "Boubou" Bourassa
☐	3	Joe "Joe Who" Clark
☐	4	Jacques Parizeau
☐	5	Preston "Presto" Manning
☐	6	Jean Chrétien
☐	7	Clyde Kirby Wells
☐	8	"Buffalo" Bob Rae
☐	9	Donald Getty
☐	10	Ovide "Chief" Mecredi
☐	11	Pierre Elliot Trudeau
☐	12	William Vander Zalm
☐	13	Mordecai Richler
☐	14	Keith Spicer
☐	15	Réné Levesque
☐	16	Joseph Smallwood
☐	17	Samuel de Champelain
☐	18	Marquis de Montcalm & Général James Wolfe
☐	19	Sir John A. Macdonald
☐	20	Louis Riel
☐	21	Eric Lindros
☐	22	Don Cherry
☐	23	John Candy
☐	24	Joe Canuck
☐	25	J.P. Canuck
☐	26	Camrose Canuck
☐	27	Team Canuck
☐		Referendum Card (3.5" x 5")

1992 SEMIC STICKERS

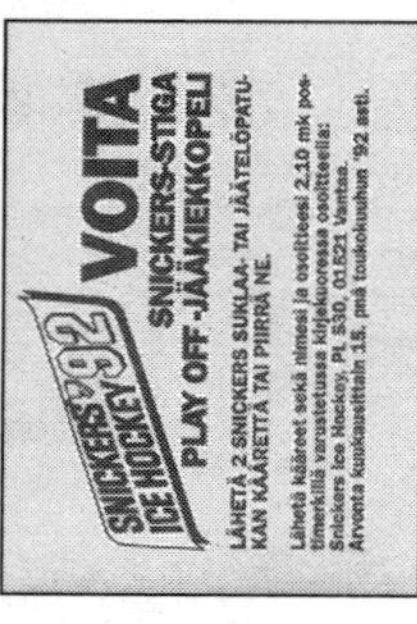

These stickers were issued for the 1992 World Championships.

Complete Set (288 stickers): 50.00

Common Player: .15

	No.	Player	NRMT-MT
☐	1	Finland	.15
☐	2	Pentti Matikainen, Coach, Fin.	.15
☐	3	Markus Ketterer (G), Fin.	.25
☐	4	Sakari Lindfors (G), Fin.	.15
☐	5	Teppo Numminen, Fin.	.25
☐	6	Jyrki Lumme, Fin.	.25
☐	7	Janne Laukkanen, Fin.	.15
☐	8	Ville Siren, Fin.	.15
☐	9	Mikko Haapakoski, Fin.	.15
☐	10	Simo Saarinen, Fin.	.15
☐	11	Teemu Selänne, Fin.	4.00
☐	12	Petri Skriko, Fin.	.25
☐	13	Iiro Järvi, Fin.	.15
☐	14	Esa Tikkanen, Fin.	.15
☐	15	Christian Ruuttu, Fin.	.15
☐	16	Raimo Summanen, Fin.	.15
☐	17	Jari Kurri, Fin.	1.00
☐	18	Time Peltomaa, Fin.	.15
☐	19	Mika Nieminen, Fin.	.15
☐	20	Mikko Mäkelä, Fin.	.15
☐	21	Janne Ojanen, Fin.	.15
☐	22	Jarmo Kekäläinen, Fin.	.15
☐	23	Keijo Säilynoja, Fin.	.15
☐	24	Esa Keskinen, Fin.	.15
☐	25	Norway	.15
☐	26	Bengt Ohlsson, Coach, Nor.	.15
☐	27	Jim Marthinsen, Nor.	.15
☐	28	Steven Allman, Nor.	.15
☐	29	Fetter Salsten, Nor.	.15
☐	30	Åge Ellingsen, Nor.	.15
☐	31	Kim Sogaard, Nor.	.15
☐	32	Jan Roar Fagerli, Nor.	.15
☐	33	Tommy Jakobsen, Nor.	.15
☐	34	Cato Tom Andersen, Nor.	.15
☐	35	Arne Billkvam, Nor.	.15
☐	36	Öystein Olsen, Nor.	.15
☐	37	Geir Hoff, Nor.	.15
☐	38	Erik Kristiansen, Nor.	.15
☐	39	Örjan Lijvdal, Nor.	.15
☐	40	Espen Knutsen, Nor.	.15
☐	41	Ole Eskild Dahlstöm, Nor.	.15
☐	42	Rune Gulliksen, Nor.	.15
☐	43	Marius Rath, Nor.	.15
☐	44	Petter Thoresen, Nor.	.15
☐	45	Tom Johansen, Nor.	.15
☐	46	Stephen Foyn, Nor.	.15
☐	47	Stig Johansen, Nor.	.15
☐	48	Per Christian Knold, Nor.	.15
☐	49	Sweden	.15
☐	50	Conny Evensson, Coach, Swe.	.15
☐	51	Tommy Söderström (G) Swe.	.50
☐	52	Fredrik Andersson Swe.	.15
☐	53	Thomas Eriksson Swe.	.15
☐	54	Peter Andersson Swe.	.15
☐	55	Peter Andersson Swe.	.15
☐	56	Nicklas Lidström Swe.	1.00
☐	57	Calle Johansson Swe.	.25
☐	58	Ulf Samuelsson Swe.	.25
☐	59	Fredrik Olausson Swe.	.15
☐	60	Börje Salming Swe.	.50
☐	61	Håkan Loob Swe.	.25
☐	62	Thomas Rundqvist Swe.	.15
☐	63	Mats Näslund Swe.	.25
☐	64	Mikael Johansson Swe.	.15
☐	65	Bengt-Åke Gustavsson Swe.	.15
☐	66	Peter Ottoson Swe.	.15
☐	67	Markus Näslund Swe.	1.00
☐	68	Daniel Rydmark Swe.	.15
☐	69	Tomas Sandström Swe.	.25
☐	70	Thomas Steen Swe.	.25
☐	71	Per-Erik Eklund Swe.	.25
☐	72	Mats Sundin Swe.	2.50
☐	73	Canada	.15
☐	74	Dave King, Coach, Cdn.	.15
☐	75	Bill Ranford (G), Cdn.	.50
☐	76	Ed Belfour (G), Cdn.	1.50
☐	77	Al MacInnis, Cdn.	.50
☐	78	Scott Stevens, Cdn.	.50
☐	79	Steve Smith, Cdn.	.25
☐	80	Ray Bourque, Cdn.	2.50
☐	81	Paul Coffey, Cdn.	.50
☐	82	Larry Murphy, Cdn.	.25
☐	83	Mark Tinordi, Cdn.	.25
☐	84	Wayne Gretzky, Cdn.	10.00
☐	85	Mark Messier, Cdn.	2.50
☐	86	Mario Lemieux, Cdn.	8.00
☐	87	Steve Yzerman, Cdn.	5.00
☐	88	Eric Lindros, Cdn.	6.50
☐	89	Luc Robitaille, Cdn.	.50
☐	90	Theoren Fleury, Cdn.	1.50
☐	91	Steve Larmer, Cdn.	.25
☐	92	Brent Sutter, Cdn.	.25
☐	93	Shayne Corson, Cdn.	.50
☐	94	Dale Hawerschuk, Cdn.	.50
☐	95	Russ Courtnall, Cdn.	.25
☐	96	Rick Tocchet, Cdn.	.25
☐	97	Soviet Union	.15

☐ 98 Victor Tikhonov, Coach, CIS. .15
☐ 99 Andrei Trefilov (G), CIS. .50
☐ 100 Mikhail Shtalenkov (G), CIS. .50
☐ 101 Alexei Kasatonov, CIS. .25
☐ 102 Mikhail Tatarinov, CIS. .25
☐ 103 Igor Kravchuk, CIS. .25
☐ 104 Vladimir Malakhov, CIS. .25
☐ 105 Alex Gusarov, CIS. .25
☐ 106 Dimitri Filimonov, CIS. .25
☐ 107 Dimitri Mironov, CIS. .25
☐ 108 Viadimir Konstantinov, CIS. 1.50
☐ 109 Sergei Fedorov, CIS. 2.50
☐ 110 Alexei Zhamnov, CIS. 1.00
☐ 111 Vyacheslav Kozlov, CIS. 1.00
☐ 112 Valeri Kamensky, CIS. 1.00
☐ 113 Alexander Semak, CIS. .25
☐ 114 Viatcheslav Butsayev, CIS. .15
☐ 115 Andrei Lomakin, CIS. .25
☐ 116 Pavel Bure, CIS. 3.50
☐ 117 Andrei Kovalenko, CIS. .50
☐ 118 Ravil Khaidarov, CIS. .15
☐ 119 Victor Gordiouk, CIS. .15
☐ 120 Vitali Prokhorov, CIS. .15
☐ 121 Czechoslovakia .15
☐ 122 Ivan Hlinka Coach, CSR. .15
☐ 123 Oldrich Svoboda (G), CSR. .15
☐ 124 Dominik Hasek (G), CSR. 3.50
☐ 125 Leo Gudas, CSR. .15
☐ 126 Frantisek Musil, CSR. .15
☐ 127 Kamil Prachar, CSR. .15
☐ 128 Frantisek Kucera, CSR. .25
☐ 129 Richard Smehlik, CSR. .25
☐ 130 Jergus Baca, CSR. .15
☐ 131 Jiri Slegr, CSR. .15
☐ 132 Petr Hrbek, CSR. .15
☐ 133 Kamil Kastak .15
☐ 134 Richard Zemlicka, CSR. .15
☐ 135 Jaromir Jagr, CSR. 5.00
☐ 136 Martin Rucinsky, CSR. .25
☐ 137 Josef Beranek, CSR. .25
☐ 138 Michael Pivonka, CSR. .25
☐ 139 Robert Kron, CSR. .15
☐ 140 Zigmund Palffy, CSR. 1.50
☐ 141 Tomas Jelinek, CSR. .15
☐ 142 Robert Reichel, CSR. .50
☐ 143 Lubomir Kolnik, CSR. .15
☐ 144 Zdeno Ciger, CSR. .15
☐ 145 USA .15
☐ 146 Tim Taylor, Coach, USA. .15
☐ 147 John Vanbiesbrouck (G), USA. 3.00
☐ 148 Mike Richter (G), USA. 1.50
☐ 149 Phil Housley, USA. .25
☐ 150 Brian Leetch, USA. 1.50
☐ 151 Kevin Hatcher, USA. .25
☐ 152 Gary Suter, USA. .25
☐ 153 Chris Chelios, USA. 2.00
☐ 154 Erich Weinrich, USA. .25
☐ 155 Jim Johnson, USA. .25
☐ 156 Brett Hull, USA. 2.50
☐ 157 Mike Modano, USA. 2.50
☐ 158 Jeremy Roenick, USA. 1.50
☐ 159 Pat LaFontaine, USA. .50
☐ 160 Craig Janney, USA. .25
☐ 161 Ed Olczyk, USA. .25
☐ 162 Tony Granato, USA. .25
☐ 163 Joe Mullen, USA. .25
☐ 164 Dave Christian, USA. .25
☐ 165 Doug Brown, USA. .25
☐ 166 Kevin Miller, USA. .25
☐ 167 Joel Otto, USA. .25
☐ 168 Randy Wood, USA. .25
☐ 169 Germany .15
☐ 170 Ludek Bukac, Coach, Ger. .15
☐ 171 Klaus Merk (G), Ger. .15
☐ 172 Josef Heiss (G), Ger. .15
☐ 173 Harold Kreiss, Ger. .15
☐ 174 Michael Heidt, Ger. .15
☐ 175 Jörg Mayr, Ger. .15
☐ 176 Marco Rentzsch, Ger. .15
☐ 177 Heinrich Schiffel, Ger. .15
☐ 178 Stefan Steinecker, Ger. .15
☐ 179 Torsten Kienass, Ger. .15
☐ 180 Raimund Hilger, Ger. .15
☐ 181 Ernst Köpf, Ger. .15
☐ 182 Peter Draisatl, Ger. .15
☐ 183 Axel Kammerer, Ger. .15
☐ 184 Michael Rumrich, Ger. .15
☐ 185 Jurgen Rumrich, Ger. .15
☐ 186 Georg Holzmann, Ger. .15
☐ 187 Lorenz Funk, Ger. .15
☐ 188 Thomas Schinko, Ger. .15
☐ 189 Andreas Lupzig, Ger. .15
☐ 190 Tobias Abstreiter, Ger. .15
☐ 191 Michael Pohl, Ger. .15
☐ 192 Antony Vogel, Ger. .15
☐ 193 Switzerland .15
☐ 194 Juhani Tamminen, Coach, Sui. .15
☐ 195 Renato Tosio (G), Sui. .15
☐ 196 Reto Pavoni, Sui. .15
☐ 197 Rick Tschumi, Sui. .15
☐ 198 Patrice Brasey, Sui. .15
☐ 199 Didier Massy, Sui. .15
☐ 200 Sandro Bertaggia, Sui. .15
☐ 201 Sven Leuenberger, Sui. .15
☐ 202 Samuel Palmer, Sui. .15
☐ 203 Martin Rauch, Sui. .15
☐ 204 Dino Kessler, Sui. .15
☐ 205 Raymond Walder, Sui. .15
☐ 206 Peter Jaks, Sui. .15
☐ 207 Andy Ton, Sui. .15
☐ 208 Jörg Eberle, Sui. .15
☐ 209 Felix Hollenstein, Sui. .15
☐ 210 Fredy Luthi, Sui. .15
☐ 211 Manuele Celio, Sui. .15
☐ 212 Christian Weber, Sui. .15
☐ 213 Andre Rotheli, Sui. .15
☐ 214 Gil Montandon, Sui. .15
☐ 215 Thomas Vrabec, Sui. .15
☐ 216 Patrick Howald, Sui. .15
☐ 217 France .15
☐ 218 Kjell Larsson, Coach, Fra. .15
☐ 219 Jean-Marc Dijan (G), Fra. .15
☐ 220 Petri Ylönen (G), Fra. .15
☐ 221 Stéphane Botteri, Fra. .15
☐ 222 Michel Leblanc, Fra. .15
☐ 223 Jean-Philippe Lemoine, Fra. .15
☐ 224 Denis Perez, Fra. .15
☐ 225 Bruno Saunier, Fra. .15
☐ 226 Steven Woodburn, Fra. .15
☐ 227 Serge Poudrier, Fra. .15
☐ 228 Michael Babin, Fra. .15
☐ 229 Stéphane Barin, Fra. .15
☐ 230 Philippe Bozon, Fra. .15
☐ 231 Arnaud Briand, Fra. .15
☐ 232 Yves Crettenand, Fra. .15
☐ 233 Patrick Dunn, Fra. .15
☐ 234 Yannick Goicoechea, Fra. .15
☐ 235 Benoît Laporte, Fra. .15
☐ 236 Christian Pouget, Fra. .15
☐ 237 Antoine Richer, Fra. .15
☐ 238 Christophe Ville, Fra. .15
☐ 239 Peter Almasy, Fra. .15
☐ 240 Pierre Pousse, Fra. .15
☐ 241 Italy .15
☐ 242 Gene Ubriaco, Coach, Ita. .15
☐ 243 David Delfino (G), Ita. .15
☐ 244 Mike Zanier (G), Ita. .15
☐ 245 Erwin Kostner, Ita. .15
☐ 246 Roberto Oberrauch, Ita. .15
☐ 247 Jim Camazzola, Ita. .15
☐ 248 Anthony Circelli, Ita. .15
☐ 249 Michael de Angelis, Ita. .15
☐ 250 Giovanni Marchetti, Ita. .15
☐ 251 Alessandro Batiani, Ita. .15
☐ 252 Georg Comploi, Ita. .15
☐ 253 Gaetano Orlando, Ita. .15
☐ 254 Bruno Zarrilo, Ita. .15
☐ 255 Emilio Iovio, Ita. .15
☐ 256 Frank Nigro, Ita. .15
☐ 257 Marco Scapinello, Ita. .15
☐ 258 Giuseppe Foglietta, Ita. .15
☐ 259 Rick Morocco, Ita. .15
☐ 260 Santino Pellegrino, Ita. .15
☐ 261 Lucio Topatigh, Ita. .15
☐ 262 Mario Simioni, Ita. .15
☐ 263 Ivano Cloch, Ita. .15
☐ 264 Martino Soracreppa, Ita. .15
☐ 265 Poland .15
☐ 266 Leszek Lejcyk, Coach, Pol. .15
☐ 267 Andrzej Hanisz (G), Pol. .15
☐ 268 Mariusz Kieca (G), Pol. .15
☐ 269 Henryk Gruth, Pol. .15
☐ 270 Janusz Syposz, Pol. .15
☐ 271 Robert Szopinski, Pol. .15
☐ 272 Marek Cholewa, Pol. .15
☐ 273 Jacek Zamojski, Pol. .15
☐ 274 Rafal Stroka, Pol. .15
☐ 275 Dariusz Garbocz, Pol. .15
☐ 276 Stanislaw Cyrwus, Pol. .15
☐ 277 Janusz Adamiec, Pol. .15
☐ 278 Miloslaw Copija, Pol. .15
☐ 279 Piotr Zdunek, Pol. .15
☐ 280 Krzysztof Bujar, Pol. .15
☐ 281 Ludwik Czapka, Pol. .15
☐ 282 Andrzej Kotonski, Pol. .15
☐ 283 Janusz Hajnos, Pol. .15
☐ 284 Slawomir Wieloch, Pol. .15
☐ 285 Wojciech Matczak, Pol. .15
☐ 286 Jedrzej Kasperczyk, Pol. .15
☐ 287 Wojciech Tkacs, Pol. .15
☐ 288 Mariusz Czerkawski, Pol. .25

1992 SEVEN ELEVEN / COKE CUPS

We have little information on this set. Cups were released at 7-Eleven stores in Western Canada. Other singles exist.

	Player	NRMT-MT
☐	Grant Fuhr (G), Tor.	2.00

1992 - 93 AMERICAN LICORICE SOUR PUNCH CAPS

Imprint: 1993 American Licorice Co.
Complete Set (9 cards): 9.00

	No.	Player	NRMT-MT
☐	1	Theoren Fleury, Cgy.	1.50
☐	2	Guy Lafleur, Mtl.	2.50
☐	3	Chris Chelios, Chi.	1.50
☐	4	Stan Mikita, Chi.	2.00
☐	5	Maurice Richard, Mtl.	3.00
☐	6	Steve Thomas, Chi.	1.00
☐	7	Checklist 1	.50
☐	8	Checklist 2	.50
☐	P	Bobby Hull (Promo)	2.50

1992 - 93 BAYBANK BOBBY ORR

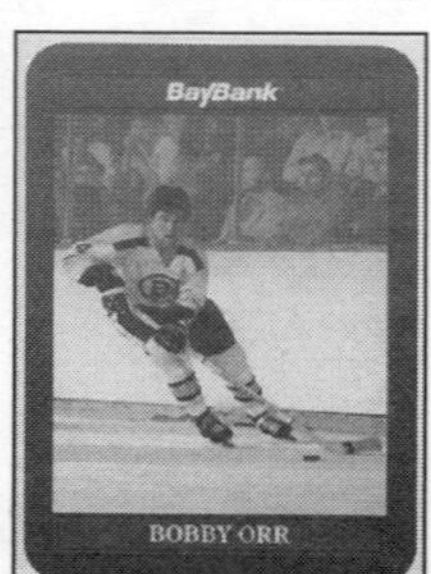

Imprint: ® Baybank

Complete Set (3 cards): 30.00

	No.	Player	NRMT-MT
☐	1	Bobby Orr	10.00
☐	2	Bobby Orr	10.00
☐	3	Bobby Orr	10.00

1992 - 93 BLEACHERS MANON RHÉAUME

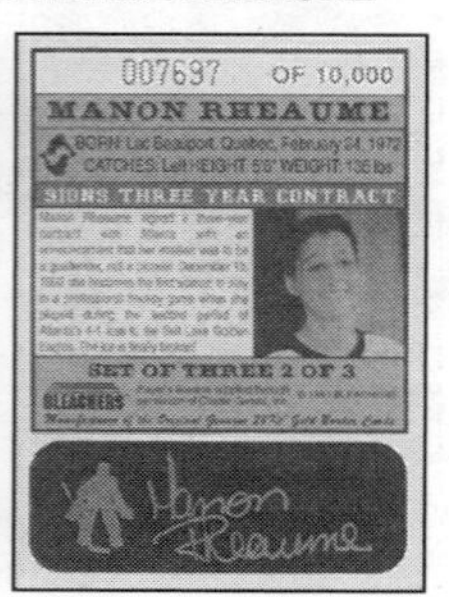

These cards came packaged in a three card lucite holder and are serial numbered of 10,000.

Imprint: © 1993 Bleachers

Complete Set (3 cards): 20.00

	No.	Player	NRMT-MT
☐	1	Trois Rivières	8.00
☐	2	Atlanta Knights	8.00
☐	3	Tampa Bay	8.00

1992 - 93 B.C.J.H.L.

Imprint: None

Complete Set (246 cards): 20.00

Common Player: .15

	No.	Player	NRMT-MT
☐	1	Tom Wittenberg	.15
☐	2	Kendel Kelly	.15
☐	3	Gus Rettschlag	.15
☐	4	Don Barr	.15
☐	5	Dav Kirkpatrick	.15
☐	6	Josh Flett	.15
☐	7	Paul McKenna	.15
☐	8	Brad Wingfield	.15
☐	9	Kerek Gesce	.15
☐	10	Garry Gulash	.15
☐	11	Tim Bell	.15
☐	12	Dean Stork	.15
☐	13	Wes Reusse	.15
☐	14	Jason Peipmann	.15
☐	15	Tyler Johnston	.15
☐	16	Jason Delesoy	.15
☐	17	The Ice Man	.15
☐	18	Don Barr	.15
☐	19	Brad Swain	.15
☐	20	Wes Rudy	.15
☐	21	Michael Sigouin	.15
☐	22	Kevan Rilcof	.15
☐	23	Brian Preston	.15
☐	24	Doug Ast	.15
☐	25	Knut Engqvist	.15
☐	26	Zac George	.15
☐	27	Clint Black	.15
☐	28	Cameron Campbell	.15
☐	29	Dan Davies	.15
☐	30	Bryce Munro	.15
☐	31	Ryan Dayman	.15
☐	32	Kevin Kimura	.15
☐	33	Paul Nicolls	.15
☐	34	Thomas Kraft	.15
☐	35	Erin Thornton	.15
☐	36	Brad Loring	.15
☐	37	Jag Bal	.15
☐	38	Jeff Grabinsky	.15
☐	39	Johan Ahrgren	.15
☐	40	The Lethal Weapon	.15
☐	41	Chilliwach Chiefs	.15
☐	42	Judd Lambert	.15
☐	43	Brian Schiebel	.15
☐	44	Dennis Archibald	.15
☐	45	David Longbroek	.15
☐	46	Silverio Mirao	.15
☐	47	Jason Haakstad	.15
☐	48	Lee Grant	.15
☐	49	Ryan Esselmont	.15
☐	50	Steve Roberts	.15
☐	51	Curtis Fry	.15
☐	52	Daid Dollard	.15
☐	53	Diano Zol	.15
☐	54	Bob Needham	.15
☐	55	Dustin Green	.15
☐	56	Darren Tymchyshyn	.15
☐	57	Peter Arvanitis	.15
☐	58	Don Hearn	.15
☐	59	Title Card	.15
☐	60	Martin Masa	.15
☐	61	Steffon Walby	.15
☐	62	Joel Irwin	.15
☐	63	Brent Bradford	.15
☐	64	Dieter Kochan	.15
☐	65	Brendan Kenny	.15
☐	66	Marty Craigdallie	.15
☐	67	Graeme Harder	.15
☐	68	Pavel Suchanek	.15
☐	69	Shane Johnson	.15
☐	70	Burt Henderson	.15
☐	71	Tyler Willis	.15
☐	72	Mike Olaski	.15
☐	73	Daivd Green	.15
☐	74	Tom Mix	.15
☐	75	Walter (Guy) Prince	.15
☐	76	Joseph Rybar	.15
☐	77	Bill Muckalt	.15
☐	78	Jason Mansoff	.15
☐	79	Duane Puga	.15
☐	80	Aaron Hoffman	.15
☐	81	Dan Blasko	.15
☐	82	Rob Szatmary	.15
☐	83	Mike Minnis	.15
☐	84	Pat Meehan	.15
☐	85	Andre Robichaud	.15
☐	86	The Terminator	.15
☐	87	Derrek Harper	.15
☐	88	Dan Morrissey	.15
☐	89	Joey Kennedy	.15
☐	90	Derrek Harper	.15
☐	91	Lawrence Klyne	.15
☐	92	Ryan Beamin	.15
☐	93	Sjon Wynia	.15
☐	94	Jason Disiewich	.15
☐	95	Jason Sanford	.15
☐	96	Casey Hungle	.15
☐	97	Brent Murcheson	.15
☐	98	Glenn Calder	.15
☐	99	Jade Kersey	.15
☐	100	Shawn York	.15
☐	101	Bob Quinnell	.15
☐	102	Geordie Dunstan	.15
☐	103	Cory Crowther	.15
☐	104	Jason Hodson	.15
☐	105	Chris Jones	.15
☐	106	Cory Green	.15
☐	107	Chris Buie	.15
☐	108	Shaun Peet	.15
☐	109	Jason Wood	.15
☐	110	Dan Murphy	.15
☐	111	Jason Disiewich	.15
☐	112	Cory Dayley	.15
☐	113	Brian Veale	.15
☐	114	Jason Northard	.15
☐	115	Phil Valk	.15
☐	116	Wade Dayley	.15
☐	117	Brendan Morrison	6.00
☐	118	Marcel Sakac	.15
☐	119	Tyler Boucher	.15
☐	120	Ray Guze	.15
☐	121	Brian Barnes	.15
☐	122	Jason Given	.15
☐	123	Michael Dairon	.15
☐	124	Mike Newman	.15
☐	125	Craig Fletcher	.15
☐	126	Ty Davidson	.15
☐	127	Miki Antonik	.15
☐	128	Rob Pennoyer	.15
☐	129	Dave Whitworth	.15
☐	130	Steve Williams	.15
☐	131	Robbie Trampuh	.15
☐	132	Mark Filipenko	.15
☐	133	Clint MacDonald	.15
☐	134	Colin Ryder	.15
☐	135	David Kilduff	.15
☐	136	Mickey McGuire	.15
☐	137	Randy Polacik	.15
☐	138	Jeff Tory	.15
☐	139	Chris Buckman	.15
☐	140	Bill Moddy	.15
☐	141	Rick McLarren	.15
☐	142	The Phantom	.15
☐	143	Jason Zaichkowski	.15
☐	144	Tony Hrycukk	.15
☐	145	Cameron Knox	.15
☐	146	Mike Warriner	.15
☐	147	Robb Gordon	.15
☐	148	Mike Pawluk	.15
☐	149	Tim Harris	.15
☐	150	Mike Bzdel	.15
☐	151	Chad Wilson	.15
☐	152	Andrew Plumb	.15
☐	153	Andy MacIntosh	.15
☐	154	Stefan Brannare	.15
☐	155	Matt Sharrers	.15
☐	156	Brent Berry	.15
☐	157	Ryan Douglas	.15
☐	158	Heath Dennison	.15
☐	159	Chad Vizzutti	.15
☐	160	Adam Lord	.15
☐	161	Brad Klyn	.15
☐	162	Andrew Young	.15
☐	163	Casey Lemanski	.15
☐	164	Mike McKinlay	.15
☐	165	Derek Robinson	.15
☐	166	Kees Roodbol	.15
☐	167	Scott Boucher	.15
☐	168	Shawn Gervais	.15
☐	169	Ryan Schaffer	.15
☐	170	Kevin Robertson	.15
☐	171	Ryan Donovan	.15
☐	172	Bart Tyalor	.15
☐	173	Greg Hunt	.15
☐	174	Darcy George	.15
☐	175	Shane Tidsbury	.15
☐	176	Rob Smillie	.15
☐	177	Chad Vestergaard	.15
☐	178	Al Kinisky	.15
☐	179	Patrick O'Flaherty	.15
☐	180	Loui Mellios	.15
☐	181	Lorin Murdock	.15
☐	182	Jason Genik	.15
☐	183	Rob Herrington	.15
☐	184	Loui Mellios	.15
☐	185	Cal Benazic	.15
☐	186	Richard Kraus	.15
☐	187	Geoff White	.15
☐	188	Kirk Buchanan	.15
☐	189	Peter Zurba	.15
☐	190	John Morabito	.15
☐	191	Corey Kruchkowski	.15
☐	192	Spencer Ward	.15
☐	193	Danny Shermerhorn	.15
☐	194	Mark Davies	.15
☐	195	Jason Rushton	.15
☐	196	Chad Buckle	.15
☐	197	Serge Beauchesne	.15

	No.	Player	Price
☐	198	Todd Kelman	.15
☐	199	Jason Switzer	.15
☐	200	Eon MacFarlane	.15
☐	201	Terry Ryan	2.50
☐	202	Shawn Bourgeois	.15
☐	203	Chad Schraeder	.15
☐	204	Dusty McLellan	.15
☐	205	The Predator	.15
☐	206	Danny Shermerhorn	.15
☐	207	Chris Godard	.15
☐	208	Jason Chipman	.15
☐	209	Christian Twomey	.15
☐	210	Ryan Loxam	.15
☐	211	Greg Buchanan	.15
☐	212	Kees Roodbol	.15
☐	213	Ryan Keller	.15
☐	214	Kevin Paschal	.15
☐	215	David Hebky	.15
☐	216	Vince Devlin	.15
☐	217	Mike Cole	.15
☐	218	Daljit Takhar	.15
☐	219	Scott Hall	.15
☐	220	Derek Lawrence	.15
☐	221	Mark Basanta	.15
☐	222	Jan Kloboucek	.15
☐	223	Randy Barker	.15
☐	224	Kris Gailloux	.15
☐	225	Tyson Scheuer	.15
☐	226	Brent Wormald	.15
☐	227	Vince Devlin	.15
☐	228	Gus Miller	.15
☐	229	Todd McKave	.15
☐	230	Lawrence Oliver	.15
☐	231	Scott Garvin	.15
☐	232	Rob Milliken	.15
☐	233	Roman Kobrc	.15
☐	234	Dan Skene	.15
☐	235	Blair Marsh	.15
☐	236	Maco Balkovec	.15
☐	237	Scott Kirton	.15
☐	238	Blaine Moore	.15
☐	239	Nigel Creightney	.15
☐	240	Bill Zapt	.15
☐	241	Jason Elders	.15
☐	242	BCJHL Officials	.15
☐	243	Black Panther	.15
☐	244	Puck Pirate	.15
☐	245	Mike Pawluk	.15
☐	246	Steffon Walby	.15

1992 - 93 BOWMAN

Gold foil all-stars (199-220 / 222-243 /441) were inserted one per pack. Short printed all-stars are marked with an asterisk (•).

Imprint: 1992 THE TOPPS COMPANY, INC.

Complete Set (442 cards): **300.00**

Common Player: **.25**

	No.	Player	NRMT-MT
☐	1	Wayne Gretzky, L.A.	8.00
☐	2	Mike Krushelnyski, Tor.	.25
☐	3	Ray Bourque, Bos.	2.00
☐	4	Keith Brown, Chi.	.25
☐	5	Bob Sweeney, Bos.	.25
☐	6	Dave Christian, Stl.	.25
☐	7	Frantisek Kucera, Chi.	.25
☐	8	John LeClair, Mtl.	2.00
☐	9	Jamie Macoun, Tor.	.25
☐	10	Bob Carpenter, Bos.	.25
☐	11	Garry Galley, Pha.	.25
☐	12	Bob Kudelski, L.A.	.25
☐	13	Doug Bodger, Buf.	.25
☐	14	Craig Janney, Stl.	.25
☐	15	Glen Wesley, Bos.	.25
☐	16	Daren Puppa (G) Buf.	.35
☐	17	Andy Brickley, Bos.	.25
☐	18	Stephen Konroyd, Hfd.	.25
☐	19	Dave Poulin, Bos.	.25
☐	20	Phil Housley, Wpg.	.25
☐	21	Kevin Todd, N.J.	.25
☐	22	Tomas Sandström, L.A.	.25
☐	23	Pierre Turgeon, NYI.	.50
☐	24	Steve Smith, Chi.	.25
☐	25	Ray Sheppard, Det.	.25
☐	26	Stu Barnes, Wpg.	.25
☐	27	Grant Ledyard, Buf.	.25
☐	28	Benoît Hogue, NYI.	.25
☐	29	Randy Burridge, Wsh.	.25
☐	30	Clint Malarchuk (G), Buf.	.35
☐	31	Steve Duchesne, Pha.	.25
☐	**32**	**Guy Hebert (G), Stl., RC**	**2.00**
☐	33	Steve Kasper, Pha.	.25
☐	34	Alexander Mogilny, Buf.	1.00
☐	35	Marty McSorley, L.A.	.25
☐	36	Doug Weight, NYR.	1.00
☐	37	Dave Taylor, L.A.	.35
☐	38	Guy Carbonneau, Mtl.	.35
☐	39	Brian Benning, Pha.	.25
☐	40	Nelson Emerson, Stl.	.25
☐	41	Craig Wolanin, Que.	.25
☐	42	Kelly Hrudey (G), L.A.	.35
☐	43	Chris Chelios, Chi.	2.00
☐	44	Davie Andreychuk, Buf.	.25
☐	45	Russ Courtnall, Mtl.	.25
☐	46	Stéphane Richer, N.J.	.25
☐	47	Petr Svoboda, Buf.	.25
☐	48	Barry Pederson, Bos.	.25
☐	49	Claude Lemieux, N.J.	.25
☐	50	Tony Granato, L.A.	.50
☐	51	Al MacInnis, Cgy.	.35
☐	52	Luciano Borsato, Wpg.	.25
☐	53	Sergei Makarov, Cgy.	.25
☐	54	Bobby Smith, Min.	.25
☐	55	Gary Suter, Cgy.	.25
☐	56	Tom Draper (G), Buf.	.35
☐	57	Corey Millen, L.A.	.25
☐	58	Joe Mullen, Pgh.	.25
☐	59	Joe Nieuwendyk, Cgy.	.50
☐	60	Brian Hayward (G), S.J.	.35
☐	61	Steve Larmer, Chi.	.25
☐	62	Cam Neely, Bos.	.50
☐	63	Ric Nattress, Tor.	.25
☐	64	Denis Savard, Mtl.	.50
☐	65	Gerald Diduck, Van.	.25
☐	66	Pat Jablonski (G), Stl.	.35
☐	67	Brad McCrimmon, Det.	.25
☐	68	Dirk Graham, Chi.	.25
☐	69	Joel Otto, Cgy.	.25
☐	70	Luc Robitaille, L.A.	.50
☐	71	Dana Murzyn, Van.	.25
☐	72	Jocelyn Lemieux, Chi.	.25
☐	73	Mike Hudson, Chi.	.25
☐	74	Patrick Roy (G), Mtl.	6.50
☐	75	Doug Wilson, S.J.	.25
☐	76	Wayne Presley, Buf.	.25
☐	77	Félix Potvin (G), Tor.	2.00
☐	78	Jeremy Roenick Chi.	1.00
☐	79	Andy Moog (G), Bos.	.50
☐	80	Joey Kocur, NYR.	.25
☐	81	Neal Broten, Min.	.25
☐	82	Shayne Corson, Mtl.	.50
☐	83	Doug Gilmour, Tor.	1.00
☐	84	Rob Zettler, S.J.	.25
☐	85	Bob Probert, Det.	.25
☐	86	Mike Vernon (G), Cgy.	.50
☐	87	Rick Zombo, Stl.	.25
☐	88	Adam Creighton, NYI.	.25
☐	89	Mike McPhee, Mtl.	.25
☐	90	Ed Belfour (G), Chi.	1.50
☐	91	Steve Chiasson, Det.	.25
☐	92	Dominic Roussel (G), Pha.	.35
☐	93	Troy Murray, Wpg.	.25
☐	94	Jari Kurri, L.A.	.50
☐	95	Geoff Smith, Edm.	.25
☐	96	Paul Ranheim, Det.	.25
☐	97	Rick Wamsley (G), Tor.	.35
☐	98	Brian Noonan, Chi.	.25
☐	99	Kevin Lowe, Edm.	.25
☐	100	Josef Beranek, Edm.	.25
☐	101	Michel Petit, Cgy.	.25
☐	102	Craig Billington (G), N.J.	.35
☐	103	Steve Yzerman, Det.	4.00
☐	104	Glenn Anderson, Tor.	.25
☐	105	Perry Berezan, S.J.	.25
☐	106	Bill Ranford (G), Edm.	.50
☐	107	Randy Ladouceur, Hfd.	.25
☐	108	Jimmy Carson, Det.	.25
☐	109	Gary Roberts, Cgy.	.50
☐	110	Checklist #1 (1 -110)	.25
☐	111	Brad Shaw, Ott.	.25
☐	112	Pat Verbeek, Hfd.	.25
☐	113	Mark Messier, NYR.	2.00
☐	114	Grant Fuhr (G), Tor.	.50
☐	115	Sylvain Côté, Wsh.	.25
☐	116	Mike Sullivan, S.J.	.25
☐	117	Steve Thomas, NYI.	.25
☐	118	Craig MacTavish, Edm.	.25
☐	119	Dave Babych Van.	.25
☐	120	Jim Waite. (G), Chi.	.35
☐	121	Kevin Dineen, Pha.	.25
☐	122	Shawn Burr, Det.	.25
☐	123	Ron Francis, Pgh.	1.00
☐	124	Garth Butcher, Stl.	.25
☐	125	Jarmo Myllys (G), Tor.	.35
☐	126	Doug Brown, N.J.	.25
☐	127	James Patrick, NYR.	.25
☐	128	Ray Ferraro, NYI.	.25
☐	129	Terry Carkner, Pha.	.25
☐	130	John MacLean, N.J.	.25
☐	131	Randy Velischek, Que.	.25
☐	132	John Vanbiesbrouck (G), NYR.	2.50
☐	133	Dean Evason, S.J.	.25
☐	134	Patrick Flatley, NYI.	.25
☐	135	Petr Klima, Edm.	.25
☐	136	Geoff Sanderson, Hfd.	.35
☐	137	Joe Reekie, T.B.	.25
☐	138	Kirk Muller, Mtl.	.25
☐	139	Brian Mullen, S.J.	.25
☐	140	Daniel Berthiaume (G), Bos.	.35
☐	141	David Shaw, Min.	.25
☐	142	Pat LaFontaine, Buf.	.50
☐	143	Ulf Dahlen, Mln.	.25
☐	144	Esa Tikkanen, Edm.	.25
☐	145	Viacheslav Fetisov, N.J.	.50
☐	146	Mike Gartner, NYR.	.50
☐	147	Brent Sutter, Chi.	.25
☐	148	Darcy Wakaluk (G), Min.	.25
☐	149	Brian Leetch, NYR.	1.00
☐	150	Craig Simpson, Edm.	.25
☐	151	Mike Modano, Min.	2.00
☐	152	Bryan Trottier, Pgh.	.50
☐	153	Larry Murphy, Pgh.	.50
☐	154	Pavel Bure, Van.	3.00
☐	155	Kay Whitmore (G), Hfd.	.35
☐	156	Darren Turcotte, NYR.	.25
☐	157	Frank Musil, Cgy.	.25
☐	158	Mikael Andersson, T.B.	.25
☐	159	Rick Tocchet, Pgh.	.25
☐	160	Scott Stevens, N.J.	.50
☐	161	Bernie Nicholls, Edm.	.25
☐	162	Peter Sidorkiewicz (G), Ott.	.35
☐	163	Scott Mellanby, Edm.	.25
☐	164	Alexander Semak, N.J.	.25
☐	165	Kjell Samuelsson, Pgh.	.25
☐	166	Kelly Kisio, S.J.	.25
☐	167	Sylvain Turgeon, Ott.	.25
☐	168	Rob Brown, Chi.	.25
☐	169	Gerard Gallant, Det.	.25
☐	170	Jyrki Lumme, Van.	.25
☐	171	Dave Gagner, Min.	.25
☐	172	Tony Tanti, Buf.	.25
☐	173	Zarley Zalapski, Hfd.	.25
☐	174	Joe Murphy, Edm.	.25
☐	175	Ron Sutter, Stl.	.25
☐	176	Dino Ciccarelli, Det.	.50
☐	177	Jim Johnson, Min.	.25
☐	178	Mike Hough, Que.	.25
☐	179	Per-Erik Eklund, Pha.	.25
☐	180	John Druce, Wsh.	.25
☐	181	Paul Coffey, L.A.	.50
☐	182	Ken Wregget (G), Pgh.	.35

	No.	Player	Price
☐	183	Brendan Shanahan, Stl.	2.50
☐	184	Keith Acton, Pha.	.25
☐	185	Steven Finn, Que.	.25
☐	186	Brett Hull, Stl.	2.00
☐	187	Rollie Melanson (G), Mtl.	.35
☐	188	Derek King, NYI.	.25
☐	189	Mario Lemieux, Pgh.	7.00
☐	190	Mathieu Schneider, Mtl.	.25
☐	191	Claude Vilgrain, N.J.	.25
☐	192	Gary Leeman, Cgy.	.25
☐	193	Paul Cavallini, Stl.	.25
☐	194	John Cullen, Hfd.	.25
☐	195	Ron Hextall (G), Que.	.50
☐	196	David Volek, NYI.	.25
☐	197	Gord Roberts, Bos.	.25
☐	198	Dale Craigwell, S.J.	.25
☐	199	AS: Ed Belfour (G), Chi.	3.00
☐	200	AS: Brian Bellows, Min., (*)	7.00
☐	201	AS: Chris Chelios, Chi.	4.00
☐	202	AS: Tim Cheveldae (G), Det., (*)	7.00
☐	203	AS: Vincent Damphousse, Error	3.50
☐	203	AS: Vincent Damphousse, Corrected	3.50
☐	204	AS: Dave Ellett, Tor.	1.25
☐	205	AS: Sergei Fedorov, Det., (*)	30.00
☐	206	AS: Theoren Fleury, Cgy.	3.00
☐	207	AS: Wayne Gretzky, L.A.	20.00
☐	208	AS: Phil Housley, Wpg.	1.25
☐	209	AS: Brett Hull, Stl.	5.00
☐	210	AS: Trevor Linden, Van., (*)	12.00
☐	211	AS: Al MacInnis, Cgy., (*)	7.00
☐	212	AS: Kirk McLean (G), Van., (*)	12.00
☐	213	AS: Adam Oates, Stl.	3.00
☐	214	AS: Gary Roberts, Cgy., (*)	10.00
☐	215	AS: Larry Robinson, L.A.	2.00
☐	216	AS: Luc Robitaille, L.A.	1.50
☐	217	AS: Jeremy Roenick, Chi., (*)	22.00
☐	218	AS: Mark Tinordi, Min.	1.25
☐	219	AS: Doug Wilson, S.J.	1.25
☐	220	AS: Steve Yzerman, Det.	10.00
☐	221	Checklist #2 (111 - 220)	.25
☐	222	Donald Beaupré (G), Wsh., (*)	7.00
☐	223	AS: Ray Bourque, Bos.	5.00
☐	224	AS: Rod Brind'Amour Pha., (*)	12.00
☐	225	AS: Randy Burridge, Wsh., (*)	7.00
☐	226	AS: Paul Coffey, Pgh., (*)	12.00
☐	227	AS: John Cullen, Hfd., (*)	7.00
☐	228	AS: Eric Desjardins, Mtl., (*)	7.00
☐	229	AS: Ray Ferraro, NYI., (*)	7.00
☐	230	AS: Kevin Hatcher, Wsh.	1.25
☐	231	AS: Jaromir Jagr, Pgh.	10.00
☐	232	AS: Brian Leetch, NYR., (*)	12.00
☐	233	AS: Mario Lemieux, Pgh.	15.00
☐	234	AS: Mark Messier, NYR.	5.00
☐	235	AS: Alexander Mogilny, Buf.	3.00
☐	236	AS: Kirk Muller, Mtl.	1.25
☐	237	AS: Owen Nolan, Que.	1.50
☐	238	AS: Mike Richter (G), NYR.	3.00
☐	239	AS: Patrick Roy (G), Mtl.	15.00
☐	240	AS: Joe Sakic, Que., (*)	30.00
☐	241	AS: Kevin Stevens, Pgh.	1.25
☐	242	AS: Scott Stevens, N.J.	1.25
☐	243	AS: Bryan Trottier, Pgh., (*)	10.00
☐	244	Joe Sakic, Que.	3.50
☐	245	Daniel Marois, NYI.	.25
☐	246	Randy Wood, Buf.	.25
☐	247	Jeff Brown, Stl.	.25
☐	248	Peter Bondra, Wsh.	1.50
☐	249	Peter Stastny, N.J.	.50
☐	250	Tom Barrasso (G), Pgh.	.50
☐	251	Al Iafrate, Wsh.	.25
☐	252	James Black, Hfd.	.25
☐	253	Jan Erixon, NYR.	.25
☐	254	Brian Lawton, S.J.	.25
☐	255	Luke Richardson, Edm.	.25
☐	256	Rich Sutter, Stl.	.25
☐	257	Jeff Chychrun, Pgh. Error	.25
☐	258	Adam Oates, Bos.	1.00
☐	259	Tom Kurvers, NYI.	.25
☐	260	Brian Bellows, Min.	.25
☐	261	Trevor Linden, Van.	.50
☐	262	Vincent Riendeau (G), Det.	.35
☐	263	Peter Zezel, Tor.	.25
☐	264	Rich Pilon, NYI.	.25
☐	265	Paul Broten, NYR.	.25
☐	266	Gaetan Duchesne, Min.	.25
☐	267	Doug Lidster, Van.	.25
☐	268	Rod Brind'Amour, Pha.	.50
☐	269	Jon Casey (G), Min.	.35
☐	270	Pat Elynuik, Wpg.	.25
☐	271	Kevin Hatcher, Wsh.	.25
☐	272	Brian Propp, Min.	.25
☐	273	Thomas Fergus, Van.	.25
☐	274	Steve Weeks (G), Ott.	.35
☐	275	Calle Johansson, Wsh.	.25
☐	276	Russ Romaniuk, Wpg.	.25
☐	277	Greg Paslawski, Que.	.25
☐	278	Ed Olczyk, Wpg.	.25
☐	279	Rod Langway, Wsh.	.25
☐	280	Murray Craven, Hfd.	.25
☐	281	Guy Larose, Tor.	.25
☐	282	Paul MacDermid, Wsh.	.25
☐	283	Brian Bradley, T.B.	.25
☐	284	Paul Stanton, Pgh.	.25
☐	285	Kirk McLean (G), Van.	.50
☐	286	Andrei Lomakin, Pha.	.25
☐	287	Randy Carlyle, Wpg.	.25
☐	288	Donald Audette, Buf.	.25
☐	289	Dan Quinn, Pha.	.25
☐	290	Mike Keane, Mtl.	.25
☐	291	Dave Ellett. Tor.	.25
☐	292	Joé Juneau, Bos.	.25
☐	293	Phil Bourque, Pgh.	.25
☐	294	Michal Pivonka, Wsh.	.25
☐	295	Fredrik Olausson, Wpg.	.25
☐	296	Randy McKay, N.J.	.25
☐	297	Don Beaupré (G), Wsh.	.25
☐	298	Stephen Leach, Bos.	.25
☐	299	Teppo Numminen, Wpg.	.25
☐	300	Viacheslav Kozlov, Det.	.35
☐	301	Kevin Haller, Mtl.	.25
☐	302	Jaromir Jagr, Pgh.	4.00
☐	303	Dale Hunter, Wsh.	.25
☐	304	Bob Errey, Pgh.	.25
☐	305	Nicklas Lidström, Det.	.25
☐	306	Bob Essensa (G), Wpg.	.35
☐	307	Sylvain Lefebvre, Mtl.	.25
☐	308	Dale Hawerchuk, Buf.	.50
☐	309	Dave Snuggerud, S.J.	.25
☐	310	Michel Goulet, Chi.	.50
☐	311	Eric Desjardins, Mtl.	.50
☐	312	Thomas Steen, Wpg.	.25
☐	313	Scott Niedermayer, N.J.	.50
☐	314	Mark Recchi, Pha.	.50
☐	315	Gord Murphy, Bos.	.25
☐	316	Sergio Momesso, Van.	.25
☐	317	Todd Elik, Min.	.25
☐	318	Louie DeBrusk, Edm.	.25
☐	319	Mike Lalor, Wpg.	.25
☐	320	Jamie Leach, Pgh.	.25
☐	321	Darryl Sydor, L.A.	.25
☐	322	Brent Gilchrist, Mtl.	.25
☐	323	Alexei Kasatonov, N.J.	.25
☐	324	Rick Tabaracci (G), Wpg.	.35
☐	325	Wendel Clark, Tor.	.50
☐	326	Vladimir Konstantinov, Det.	.35
☐	327	Randy Gilhen, NYR.	.25
☐	328	Owen Nolan, Que.	.50
☐	329	Vincent Damphousse, Edm.	1.00
☐	330	Checklist #3 (221-331)	.25
☐	331	Yves Racine, Det.	.25
☐	332	Jacques Cloutier (G), Que.	.35
☐	333	Greg Adams, Van.	.25
☐	334	Mike Craig, Min.	.25
☐	335	Curtis Leschyshyn, Que.	.25
☐	336	John McIntyre, L.A.	.25
☐	337	Stéphane Quintal, Stl.	.25
☐	338	Kelly Miller, Wsh.	.25
☐	339	Dave Manson. Edm.	.25
☐	340	Stéphane Matteau, Chi.	.25
☐	341	Christian Ruuttu, Wpg.	.25
☐	342	Mike Donnelly, L.A.	.25
☐	343	Eric Weinrich, N.J.	.25
☐	344	Mats Sundin, Que.	2.00
☐	345	Geoff Courtnall, Van.	.25
☐	346	Stéphan Lebeau, Mtl.	.25
☐	347	Jeff Beukeboom, NYR.	.25
☐	348	Jeff Hackett (G), S.J.	.50
☐	349	Uwe Krupp, NYI.	.25
☐	350	Igor Larionov, Van.	.50
☐	351	Ulf Samuelsson, Pgh.	.25
☐	352	Marty McInnis, NYI.	.25
☐	353	Peter Ahola, L.A.	.25
☐	354	Mike Richter (G), NYR.	1.00
☐	355	Theoren Fleury, Cgy.	1.00
☐	356	Dan Lambert, Que.	.25
☐	357	Brent Ashton, Bos.	.25
☐	358	David Bruce, S.J.	.25
☐	359	Chris Dahlquist, Min.	.25
☐	360	Mike Ridley, Wsh.	.25
☐	361	Pat Falloon, S.J.	.60
☐	362	Doug Smail, Que.	.25
☐	363	Adrien Plavsic, Van.	.25
☐	364	Ron Wilson, Stl.	.25
☐	365	Derian Hatcher, Min.	.50
☐	366	Kevin Stevens, Pgh.	.25
☐	367	Rob Blake, L.A.	.50
☐	368	Curtis Joseph (G), Stl.	2.50
☐	369	Tom Fitzgerald, NYI.	.25
☐	370	Dave Lowry, Stl.	.25
☐	371	J. J. Daigneault, Mtl.	.25
☐	372	Jim Hrivnak (G), Wsh.	.35
☐	373	Adam Graves, NYR.	.35
☐	374	Brad May, Buf.	.25
☐	375	Todd Gill, Tor.	.25
☐	376	Paul Ysebaert, Det.	.25
☐	**377**	**David Williams, S.J., RC**	**.25**
☐	378	Bob Bassen, Stl.	.25
☐	379	Brian Glynn, Edm.	.25
☐	380	Kris King, NYR.	.25
☐	381	Rob Pearson, Tor.	.25
☐	382	Marc Bureau, Min.	.25
☐	383	Jim Paek, Pgh.	.25
☐	384	Tomas Forslund, Cgy.	.25
☐	385	Darrin Shannon, Wpg.	.25
☐	386	Chris Terreri (G), N.J.	.35
☐	387	Andrew Cassels, Hfd.	.25
☐	388	Jayson More, S.J.	.25
☐	389	Tony Amonte, NYR.	.50
☐	390	Mark Pederson, Pha.	.25
☐	391	Kevin Miller, Det. (Wsh.)	.25
☐	392	Igor Ulanov, Wpg.	.25
☐	393	Kelly Buchberger, Edm.	.25
☐	394	Mark Fitzpatrick (G), NYI.	.35
☐	395	Mikhail Tatarinov, Que.	.25
☐	396	Petr Nedved, Van.	.25
☐	397	Jeff Odgers, S.J.	.25
☐	398	Stéphane Fiset (G), Que.	.50
☐	399	Mark Tinordi, Min.	.25
☐	400	Johan Garpenlov, S.J.	.25
☐	401	Robert Reichel, Cgy.	.50
☐	402	Don Sweeney, Bos.	.25
☐	403	Rob DiMaio, T.B.	.25
☐	**404**	**Bill Lindsay, Que., RC**	**.25**
☐	405	Stéphane Beauregard (G), Wpg.	.35
☐	406	Mike Ricci, Que.	.25
☐	407	Bobby Holik, Hfd.	.25
☐	408	Igor Kravchuk, Chi.	.25
☐	409	Murray Baron, Stl.	.25
☐	410	Troy Gamble (G), Van.	.35
☐	411	Cliff Ronning, Van.	.25
☐	412	Jeff Reese (G), Cgy.	.35
☐	413	Robert Kron, Van.	.25
☐	414	Benoît Brunet, Mtl.	.25
☐	415	Shawn McEachern, Pgh.	.25
☐	416	Sergei Fedorov, Det.	2.00
☐	417	Joe Sacco, Tor.	.25
☐	418	Bryan Marchment, Chi.	.25
☐	**419**	**John LeBlanc, Wpg., RC**	**.25**
☐	420	Tim Cheveldae (G), Det.	.35
☐	421	Claude Lapointe, Que.	.25
☐	422	Ken Sutton, Buf.	.25
☐	423	Anatoli Semenov, Edm. (T.B.)	.25
☐	424	Michael McNeill, Que.	.25
☐	425	Norm Maciver, Edm.	.25
☐	426	Sergei Nemchinov, NYR.	.25
☐	427	Dimitri Khristich, Wsh.	.25
☐	428	Dominik Hasek (G), Chi.	3.00
☐	429	Bob McGill, T.B.	.25
☐	430	Valeri Zelepukin, N.J.	.25
☐	431	Vladimir Ruzicka, Bos.	.25
☐	432	Valeri Kamensky, Que.	.50
☐	**433**	**Pat MacLeod, S.J., RC**	**.25**
☐	434	Glenn Healy (G), NYI.	.25
☐	435	Patrice Brisebois, Mtl.	.25
☐	436	Jamie Baker, Que.	.25

	No.	Player	NRMT-MT
☐	437	Michel Picard, Hfd.	.25
☐	438	Scott Lachance, NYI.	.25
☐	439	Gilbert Dionne, Mtl.	.25
☐	440	Mario Lemieux, Pgh. (Gold Foil)	15.00
☐	441	Checklist #4 (332-441)	.25
☐	442	Eric Lindros, Pha.	20.00

1992 - 93 CANADIAN OLYMPIC TEAM - ALBERTA LOTTERIES

Complete Set (22 cards): 18.00

	Player	NRMT-MT
☐	Dominic Amodeo	.75
☐	Mark Astley	.75
☐	Adrian Aucoin	.75
☐	Mark Bassen	.75
☐	Eric Bellerose	.75
☐	Mike Brewer	.75
☐	Dany Dubé	.75
☐	Mike Fountain (G)	1.50
☐	Todd Hlushko	.75
☐	Hank Lammens	.75
☐	Derek Laxdal	.75
☐	Derek Mayer	.75
☐	Keith Morris	.75
☐	Jackson Penney	.75
☐	Garth Premak	.75
☐	Tom Renney	.75
☐	Allain Roy	.75
☐	Stéphane Roy	.75
☐	Trevor Sim	.75
☐	Vladislav Tretiak	2.00
☐	Title Card	.75
☐	Mike Myers	2.00

1992 - 93 CANADIAN SPORTSCARD COLLECTOR PREMIUM SHEET

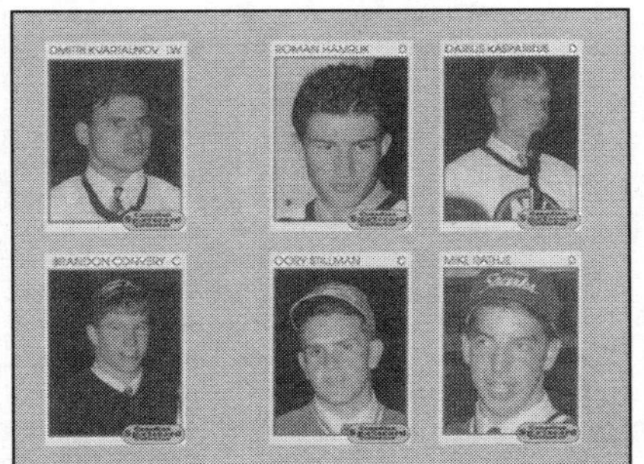

The six cards on this sheet cut out to the standard 2 1/2" x 3 1/2" size. The sheet was an insert in CSC presents 1992-93 Hockey Card Preview.
Size: 8 1/2" x 11"

	No.	Player	NRMT-MT
☐	5	Roman Hamrlik, T.B.	4.00
	6	Darius Kasparaitis, NYI.	
	7	Cory Stillman, Cgy.	
	8	Mike Rathje, S.J.	
	9	Dmitri Kvartalnov, Bos.	
	10	Brandon Convery, Tor.	

1992 - 93 CLARK MARIO LEMIEUX

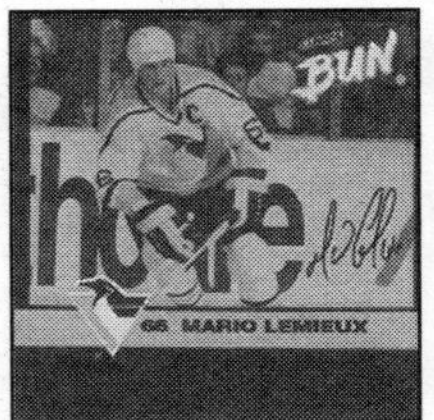

MARIO LEMIEUX 66
Center
6'4" 210 lbs. Shoots: Right
Born: Montreal, Quebec Oct. 5, 1965
Acquired: Pittsburgh's 1st round choice, 1st overall in 1984 Entry Draft.
1991-92: Mario won his third scoring title in the last five years, recording 131 points. One of only eight players in league history to win the Art Ross Trophy at least three times and one of only three players in NHL history to win the Art Ross, Hart, Calder and Conn Smythe Trophies.

One of three different cards were found inside Clark Candy Mario Buns.
Imprint: None
Complete Set (3 cards): 5.00

	Player	NRMT-MT
☐	Mario Lemieux, Pgh.	2.00
☐	Mario Lemieux, Pgh.	2.00
☐	Mario Lemieux, Pgh.	2.00

1992-93 CLASSIC DRAFT PICKS

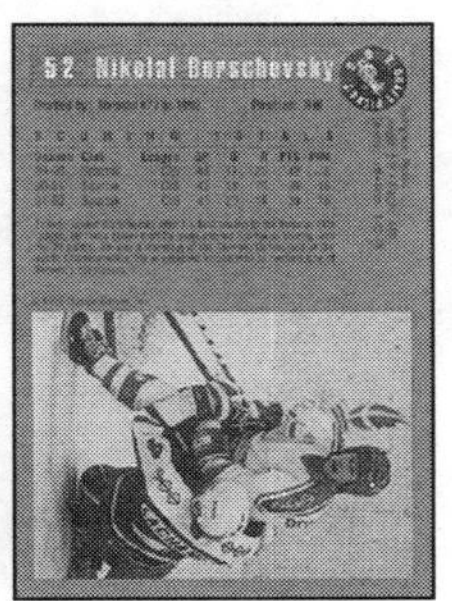

Imprint: 1992 Classic Games, Inc.
Complete Set (120 cards): 10.00
Gold Set (120 cards): 75.00
Common Player: .10 .25
Promo Card Roman Hamrlik: 2.00
Promo Card Mario Lemieux: 6.00
Promo Card RayWhitney: 1.00

	No.	Player	Reg.	Gold
☐☐	1	Roman Hamrlik, Cze.	.25	.50
☐☐	2	Alexei Yashin, CIS.	.50	2.00
☐☐	3	Mike Rathje, Medicine Hat	.10	.25
☐☐	4	Darius Kasparaitis, CIS.	.10	.25
☐☐	5	Cory Stillman, Windsor	.10	.25
☐☐	6	Robert Petrovicky, Cze.	.10	.25
☐☐	7	Andrei Nazarov, CIS.	.10	.25
☐☐	8	CL: Cory Stillman, Windsor	.10	.25
☐☐	9	Jason Bowen, Tri-City	.10	.25
☐☐	10	Jason Smith, Regina	.10	.25
☐☐	11	David Wilkie, Kamloops	.10	.25
☐☐	12	Curtis Bowen, Ottawa	.10	.25
☐☐	13	Grant Marshall, Ottawa	.10	.25
☐☐	14	Valeri Bure, Spokane	.10	.25
☐☐	15	Jeff Shantz, Regina	.10	.25
☐☐	16	Justin Hocking, Spokane	.10	.25
☐☐	17	Michael Peca, Sudbury	.25	.50
☐☐	18	Marc Hussey, Moose Jaw	.10	.25
☐☐	19	Sandy Allan (G), North Bay	.10	.25
☐☐	20	Kirk Maltby, Owen Sound	.10	.25
☐☐	21	Cale Hulse, Portland	.10	.25
☐☐	22	Sylvain Cloutier, Guelph	.10	.25
☐☐	23	Martin Gendron, St. Hyacinthe	.10	.25
☐☐	24	Kevin Smyth, Moose Jaw	.10	.25
☐☐	25	Jason McBain, Portland	.10	.25
☐☐	26	Lee J. Leslie, Prince Albert	.10	.25
☐☐	27	Ralph Intranuovo, S.S. Marie	.10	.25
☐☐	28	Martin Reichel, Freiburg	.10	.25
☐☐	29	Stefan Ustorf, Ger.	.10	.25
☐☐	30	Jarkko Varvio, Fin.	.10	.25
☐☐	31	Jere Lehtinen, Fin.	.25	.50
☐☐	32	Janne Gronvall, Fin.	.10	.25
☐☐	33	Martin Straka, Cze.	.10	.25
☐☐	34	Libor Polasek, Cze.	.10	.25
☐☐	35	Jozef Cierny, Cze.	.10	.25
☐☐	36	Jan Vopat, Cze.	.10	.25
☐☐	37	Ondrej Steiner, Cze.	.10	.25
☐☐	38	Jan Caloun, Cze.	.10	.25
☐☐	39	Petr Hrbek, Cze.	.10	.25
☐☐	40	Richard Smehlik, Cze.	.10	.25
☐☐	41	CL: Sergei Gonchar, CIS	.10	.25
☐☐	42	Sergei Krivokrasov, CIS.	.10	.25
☐☐	43	Sergei Gonchar, CIS.	.10	.25
☐☐	44	Boris Mironov, CIS.	.10	.25
☐☐	45	Denis Metliuk, CIS.	.10	.25
☐☐	46	Sergei Klimovich, CIS.	.10	.25
☐☐	47	Sergei Brylin, CIS.	.10	.25
☐☐	48	Andrei Nikolishin,CIS.	.10	.25
☐☐	49	Alexander Cherbayev, CIS.	.10	.25
☐☐	50	Sergei Zholtok, CIS.	.10	.25
☐☐	51	Vitali Prokhorov , USSR	.10	.25
☐☐	52	Nikolai Borschevsky, CIS.	.10	.25
☐☐	53	Vitali Tomilin, CIS.	.10	.25
☐☐	54	Alexander Alexeyev, Tacoma	.10	.25
☐☐	55	Roman Zolotov, CIS.	.10	.25
☐☐	56	Konstantin Korotkov, CIS.	.10	.25
☐☐	57	Jacques and Daniel Laperrière,	.10	.25
☐☐	58	Martin and Eric Lacroix	.10	.25
☐☐	59	Manon Rhéaume (G)	6.00	30.00
☐☐	60	CL: Hamrlik/Yashin/Rathje	.10	.25
☐☐	61	CL: Viktor Kozlov, CIS.	.10	.25
☐☐	62	Victor Kozlov, CIS.	.10	.25
☐☐	63	CL: Denny Felsner, Michigan	.10	.25
☐☐	64	Denny Felsner, Michigan	.10	.25
☐☐	65	Darrin Madeley (G), Lake Superior	.10	.25
☐☐	66	Flashback: Mario Lemieux, Laval	1.00	8.00
☐☐	67	Sandy Moger, Lake Superior	.10	.25
☐☐	68	Dave Karpa, Ferris State	.10	.25
☐☐	69	Martin Jiranek, Bowling Green	.10	.25
☐☐	70	Dwayne Norris, Michigan State	.10	.25
☐☐	71	Michael Stewart, Michigan State	.10	.25
☐☐	72	Joby Messier, Michigan State	.10	.25
☐☐	73	Mike Bales (G), Pro-AM	.10	.25
☐☐	74	Scott Thomas, Clarkson	.10	.25
☐☐	75	Daniel Laperrière, St. Lawrence	.10	.25
☐☐	76	Mike Lappin, St. Lawrence	.10	.25
☐☐	77	Eric Lacroix, St. Lawrence	.10	.25
☐☐	78	Martin Lacroix, St. Lawrence	.10	.25
☐☐	79	Scott LaGrand (G), Boston College	.10	.25
☐☐	80	Jean-Yves Roy, Maine	.10	.25
☐☐	81	Scott Pellerin, Maine	.10	.25
☐☐	82	Rob Gaudreau, Providence	.10	.25
☐☐	83	Mike Boback, Providence	.10	.25
☐☐	84	Dixon Ward, North Dakota	.10	.25
☐☐	85	Jeff McLean, North Dakota	.10	.25
☐☐	86	Dallas Drake, North Michigan	.10	.25
☐☐	87	Bret Hedican, USA.	.10	.25
☐☐	88	Doug Zmolek, Minnesota	.10	.25
☐☐	89	Trent Klatt, Minnesota	.10	.25
☐☐	90	Larry Olimb, Minnesota	.10	.25
☐☐	91	Duane Derksen (G), Wisonsin	.10	.25
☐☐	92	Doug MacDonald, Wisonsin	.10	.25
☐☐	93	CL: Dmitri Kvartalnov, San Diego	.10	.25
☐☐	94	Jim Cummins, Adirondack	.10	.25
☐☐	95	Lonnie Loach, Adirondack	.10	.25
☐☐	96	Keith Jones, Baltimore	.10	.25
☐☐	97	Jason Woolley, Baltimore	.10	.25
☐☐	98	Rob Zamuner, Bingampton	.25	.50
☐☐	99	Brad Werenka, North Michigan	.10	.25
☐☐	100	Brent Grieve, Captial District	.10	.25
☐☐	101	Sean Hill, Fredericton	.10	.25
☐☐	102	Keith Carney, Rochester	.10	.25
☐☐	103	Peter Ciavagglia, Rochester	.10	.25
☐☐	104	David Littman (G), Rochester	.10	.25
☐☐	105	Bill Guerin, USA.	.25	.50
☐☐	106	Mikhail Kravets, Kansas City	.10	.25
☐☐	107	J. F. Quintin, Kansas City	.10	.25
☐☐	108	Mike Needham, Muskegon	.10	.25
☐☐	109	Jason Ruff, Peoria	.10	.25
☐☐	110	Mike Vukonich, Phoenix	.10	.25
☐☐	111	Shawn McCosh, Phoenix	.10	.25
☐☐	112	Dave Tretowicz, Phoenix	.10	.25
☐☐	113	Todd Harkins, Salt Lake	.10	.25
☐☐	114	Jason Muzzatti (G), Salt Lake	.10	.25
☐☐	115	Paul Kruse, Salt Lake	.10	.25
☐☐	116	Kevin Wortman, Salt Lake	.10	.25
☐☐	117	Sean Burke (G), San Diego	.25	.50
☐☐	118	Keith Gretzky, San Diego	.25	.50
☐☐	119	Ray Whitney, San Diego	.10	.25
☐☐	120	Dmitri Kvartalnov, San Diego	.10	.25

	Autograph	NRMT-MT
☐	Pavel and Varleri Bure (#/6,000)	50.00
☐	Mario Lemieux (#\2,000)	150.00

	No.	Flashback	NRMT-MT
☐	SP1	Mario Lemieux	25.00

LIMITED PRINT

These cards are limited to 1500 copies
Insert Set (10 cards): 12.00

	No.	Player	NRMT-MT
☐	LP1	Roman Hamrlik, Cze.	3.00
☐	LP2	Alexei Yashin, CIS.	5.00
☐	LP3	Mike Rathje, Medicine Hat	1.00
☐	LP4	Darius Kasparaitis, CIS.	1.00
☐	LP5	Cory Stillman, Windsor	1.00
☐	LP6	Dmitri Kvartalnov, San Diego	1.00
☐	LP7	David Wilkie	1.00
☐	LP8	Curtis Bowen	1.00
☐	LP9	Valeri Bure, CIS.	1.00
☐	LP10	Joby Messier	1.00

1992 - 93 CLASSIC FOUR-SPORT

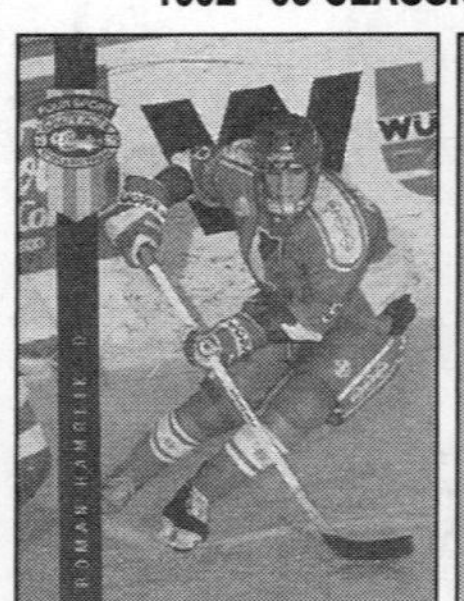

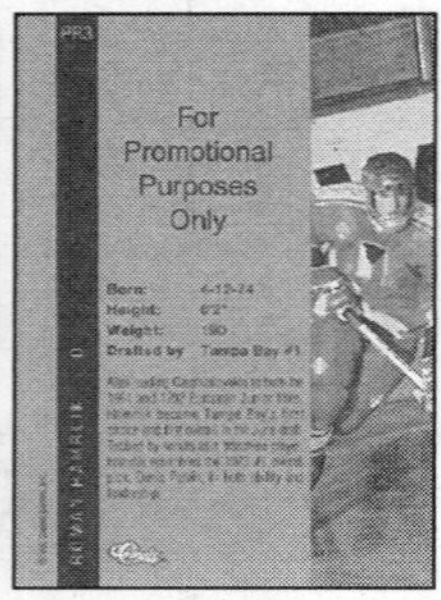

This 225-card four-sport set features only 75 hockey cards. A 225-card set sells for $20.

No.	Promo	NRMT-MT
PR3	Roman Hamrlik, Cze. (Promo)	3.00

No.	Player	NRMT-MT
151	Roman Hamrlik	.25
152	Alexei Yashin	.50
153	Mike Rathje	.10
154	Darius Kasparaitis	.10
155	Cory Stillman	.10
156	Robert Petrovicky	.10
157	Andrei Nazarov	.10
158	Jason Bowen	.10
159	Jason Smith	.10
160	David Wilkie	.10
161	Curtis Bowen	.10
162	Grant Marshall	.10
163	Valeri Bure	.10
164	Jeff Shantz	.10
165	Justin Hocking	.10
166	Michael Peca	.10
167	Marc Hussey	.10
168	Sandy Allen (G)	.10
169	Kirk Maltby	.10
170	Cale Hulse	.10
171	Sylvain Cloutier	.10
172	Martin Gendron	.10
173	Kevin Smyth	.10
174	Jason McBain	.10
175	Lee J. Leslie	.10
176	Ralph Intranuovo	.10
177	Martin Reichel	.10
178	Stefan Ustorf	.10
179	Jarkko Varvio	.10
180	Martin Straka	.10
181	Libor Polasek	.10
182	Jozef Cierny	.10
183	Sergei Krivokrasov	.10
184	Sergei Gonchar	.10
185	Boris Mironov	.10
186	Denis Metliuk	.10
187	Sergei Klimovich	.10
188	Sergei Brylin	.10
189	Andrei Nikolishin	.10
190	Alexander Cherbayev	.10
191	Vitali Tomilin	.10
192	Sandy Moger	.10
193	Darrin Madeley (G)	.10
194	Denny Felsner	.10
195	Dwayne Norris	.10
196	Joby Messier	.10
197	Michael Stewart	.10
198	Scott Thomas	.10
199	Daniel LaPerriere	.10
200	Martin Lacroix	.10
201	Scott Lagrand (G)	.10
202	Scott Pellerin	.10
203	Jean-Yves Roy	.10
204	Rob Gaudreau	.10
205	Jeff McLean	.10
206	Dallas Drake	.10
207	Doug Zmolek	.10
208	Duane Derksen (G)	.10
209	Jim Cummins	.10
210	Lonnie Loach	.10
211	Rob Zamuner	.25
212	Brad Werenka	.10
213	Brent Grieve	.10
214	Sean Hill	.10
215	Peter Ciavaglia	.10
216	Jason Ruff	.10
217	Shawn McCosh	.10
218	Dave Tretowicz	.10
219	Mike Vukonich	.10
220	Kevin Wortman	.10
221	Jason Muzzatti (G)	.10
222	Dmitri Kvartalnov	.10
223	Ray Whitney	.10
224	Manon Rhéaume (G)	5.00
225	Viktor Kozlov	.25

AUTOGRAPHS

Player	NRMT-MT
Roman Hamrlik (#/1,550)	15.00
Mike Rathje (#/2,075)	5.00
Cory Stillman (#/2,125)	5.00
Jason Bowen (#/2,075)	5.00
Jason Smith (#/2,075)	5.00
Justin Hocking (#/2,075)	5.00
Cale Hulse (#/1,850)	5.00
Libor Polasek (#/1,950)	5.00
Boris Mironov (#/2,075)	8.00
Sandy Moger (#/1,075)	5.00
Dwayne Norris (#/1,075)	5.00
Joby Messier (#/1,075)	5.00
Doug Zmolek (#/1,075)	5.00

BONUS CARDS

This 20-card four-sport set features only six hockey cards.

No.	Player	NRMT-MT
BC7	Roman Hamrlik	.50
BC8	Valeri Bure	.25
BC9	Dallas Drake	.25
BC10	Dmitri Kvartalnov	.25
BC11	Manon Rhéaume	10.00
BC12	Viktor Kozlov	.25

LIMITED PRINT

This 25-card four-sport set features only four hockey cards.

No.	Player	NRMT-MT
LP22	Roman Hamrlik	1.00
LP23	Mike Rathje	.75
LP24	Valeri Bure	.75
LP25	Alexei Yashin	2.00

1992 - 93 CLASSIC PRO PROSPECTS

Imprint: © 1993 Classic Games, Inc.

Complete Set (150 cards):	**15.00**
Common Player:	**.10**
Promo Card Steve King (#PR1):	**2.00**
Promo Card Manon Rhéaume (#PR2):	**6.00**

No.	Player	NRMT-MT
1	Manon Rhéaume	3.00
2	Manon Rhéaume	3.00
3	Manon Rhéaume	3.00
4	Manon Rhéaume	3.00
5	Manon Rhéaume	3.00
6	Manon Rhéaume	3.00
7	Manon Rhéaume	3.00
8	Oleg Petrov, Fredericton	.10
9	Shjon Podein, Cape Breton	.10
10	AS: Alexei Kovalev	.25
11	Roman Oksiuta	.10
12	Dave Tomlinson, St. John's	.10
13	Jason Miller	.10
14	Andrew McKim	.10
15	Dallas Drake	.10
16	Rob Gaudreau, Kansas City	.10
17	Darrin Madeley (G), New Haven	.10
18	Scott Pellerin	.10
19	Scott Thomas	.10
20	AS: Chris Tancil	.10
21	Patric Kjellberg	.10
22	Jim Dowd	.10
23	Daniel Gauthier, Cleveland	.10
24	Mark Beaufait	.10
25	AS: Milan Tichy	.10
26	Chris Osgood (G), Adirondack	.75
27	Charles Poulin, Fredericton	.10
28	Patrick Lebeau	.10
29	Chris Govedaris	.10
30	AS: Andrei Trefilov (G)	.10
31	Kevin Stevens	.10
32	Dmitri Kvartalnov	.10
33	Patrick Roy (G)	2.00
34	Mark Recchi	.35
35	Adam Oates	.50
36	Patrik Augusta. St. John's	.10
37	Gerry Fleming, Fredericton	.10
38	Sergei Krivokrasov	.10
39	Mike O'Neill (G)	.10
40	AS: Darrin Madeley (G), New Haven	.10
41	Lindsay Vallis, Fredericton	.10
42	Todd Nelson	.10
43	Keith Jones	.25
44	"The Legend": Howie Rosenblatt	.10
45	AS: Jason Ruff	.10
46	Robert Lang	.10
47	André Faust	.10
48	Steve Bancroff, Indianapolis	.10
49	Iain Fraser	.10
50	AS: Roman Hamrlik	.25
51	Pierre Sévigny	.10
52	Jeff Levy (G), Hershey	.10
53	Len Barrie, Hershey	.10
54	David Goverde (G), Phoenix	.10
55	AS: Vladimir Malakhov, Capital District	.25
56	Scott White, New Haven	.10
57	Dmitri Motkov	.10
58	Jason Herter, Hamilton	.10
59	Drake Berehowsky	.10
60	AS: Steve King	.10
61	Doug Barrault	.10
62	Martin Hamrlik	.10
63	Kevin Miehm	.10
64	Shaun Van Allen	.10
65	AS: Corey Hirsch (G), Binghampton	.10
66	Dwayne Norris	.10
67	Petr Hrbek, Adirondack	.10
68	Philippe Boucher	.10
69	Denis Chervyakov, Providence	.10
70	AS: Sergei Zubov, Binghampton	.25
71	Geoff Sarjeant (G), Peoria	.10
72	Les Kuntar (G)	.10
73	Byron Dafoe (G), Baltimore	.25
74	CL: Kovalev/Zubov/King/Hirsch	.10
75	AS: Alexandr Andrievski	.10
76	CL: Joby Messier/Mitch Messier	.10
77	Brian Sullivan, Utica	.10
78	Steve Larouche, Fredericton	.10
79	Denis Chassé, Halifax	.10
80	AS: Félix Potvin (G)	1.00
81	Josef Beranek	.10
82	Ken Klee, Baltimore	.10
83	Jozef Stumpel, Providence	.25
84	Andrew Verner (G)	.10
85	AS: Keith Osborne	.10
86	Igor Malykhin	.10
87	Gilbert Dionne	.10
88	Viktor Gordijuk	.10
89	Glen Murray	.10
90	AS: Scott Pellerin	.10
91	Tommy Söderström (G), Hershey	.25
92	Terry Chitaroni, St. John's	.10
93	Viktor Kozlov, CIS.	.25
94	Mikhail Shtalenkov (G)	.25
95	Leonid Toropchenko, Springfield	.10
96	Alex Galchenyuk	.10
97	Anatoli Fedotov	.10
98	Igor Chibirev	.10
99	Keith Gretzky, San Diego	.10

	No.	Player	NRMT-MT
☐	100	Manon Rhéaume (G)	3.00
☐	101	Sean Whyte, Phoenix	.10
☐	102	Steve Konowalchuk	.10
☐	103	Richard Borgo, Cape Breton	.10
☐	104	Paul DiPietro	.10
☐	105	AS: Patrik Carnback	.10
☐	106	Mike Fountain (G)	.25
☐	107	Jamie Heward, Cleveland	.10
☐	108	David St. Pierre, Salt Lake	.10
☐	109	Sean O'Donnell, Rochester	.10
☐	110	AS: Greg Andrusak, Cleveland	.10
☐	111	Damian Rhodes (G), St. John's	.10
☐	112	Ted Crowley, St. John's	.10
☐	113	Chris Taylor, Capital District	.10
☐	114	Terran Sandwith	.10
☐	115	AS: Jesse Belanger	.10
☐	116	Justin Duberman	.10
☐	117	Arturs Irbe (G)	.25
☐	118	Chris LiPuma, Atlanta	.10
☐	119	Mike Torchia (G), Kalamazoo	.10
☐	120	AS: Niclas Andersson	.10
☐	121	Rick Knickle (G)	.10
☐	122	RB: Scott Gruh, Fort Wayne	.10
☐	123	HL: Dave Michayluk, Cleveland	.10
☐	124	Guy Levêque	.15
☐	125	AS: Scott Thomas	.10
☐	126	Travis Green	.10
☐	127	Joby Messier	.10
☐	128	Victor Ignatjev, Kansas City	.10
☐	129	Brad Tiley, Binghampton	.10
☐	130	AS: Grigori Panteleyev	.10
☐	131	Vyacheslav Butsayev	.10
☐	132	Danny Lorenz (G)	.10
☐	133	Marty McInnis	.10
☐	134	Ed Ronan	.20
☐	135	AS: Vyacheslav Kozlov	.25
☐	136	Kevin St. Jacques, Indianapolis	.10
☐	137	Pavel Kostichkin, Moncton	.10
☐	138	Mike Hurlbut, Binghampton	.10
☐	139	Tomas Forslund	.10
☐	140	AS: Rob Gaudreau	.10
☐	141	Shawn Heaphy, Salt Lake	.10
☐	142	Radek Hamr	.10
☐	143	Jaroslav Otevrel	.10
☐	144	Keith Redmond	.10
☐	145	AS: Tom Pederson	.10
☐	146	Jaroslav Modry, Utica	.10
☐	147	Darren McCarty	.25
☐	148	Terry Yake	.10
☐	149	Ivan Droppa	.10
☐	150	Shawn Van Allen/Dan/Currie/Steven Rice	.10
		Autographs	**NRMT-MT**
☐		Dmitri Kvartalnov (#/4,000)	5.00
☐		Manon Rhéaume (#/6,500)	75.00

LIMITED PRINT

Insert Set (5 cards): 30.00

	No.	Player	NRMT-MT
☐	LP1	Manon Rhéaume (G)	20.00
☐	LP2	Alexei Kovalev	4.00
☐	LP3	Rob Gaudreau, Kansas City	3.00
☐	LP4	Viktor Kozlov, Russia	3.00
☐	LP5	Dallas Drake, Adirondack	3.00

BONUS CARDS

Insert Set (20 cards): 25.00

	No.	Player	NRMT-MT
☐	BC1	Alexei Kovalev, Binghampton	1.00
☐	BC2	Andrei Trefilov (G), Salt Lake	.50
☐	BC3	Roman Hamrlik, Atlanta	1.00
☐	BC4	Vladimir Malakov, Capital District	.50
☐	BC5	Corey Hirsch (G), Binghampton	.50
☐	BC6	Sergei Zubov, Binghampton	1.00
☐	BC7	Félix Potvin (G)	6.00
☐	BC8	Tommy Söderström (G), Hershey	1.00
☐	BC9	Victor Kozlov, Russia	1.00
☐	BC10	Manon Rhéaume (G)	12.00
☐	BC11	Jesse Belanger	.50
☐	BC12	Rick Knickle (G), San Diego	.50
☐	BC13	Joby Messier, Binghampton	.50
☐	BC14	Viacheslav Butsayev	.50
☐	BC15	Tomas Forslund, Salt Lake	.50
☐	BC16	Jozef Stumpel, Providence	1.00
☐	BC17	Dmitri Kvartlanov	.50
☐	BC18	Adam Oates	3.00
☐	BC19	Dallas Drake	.50
☐	BC20	Mark Recchi, Muskegon	1.00

1992 - 93 DURIVAGE / DIANA - PANINI STICKERS

LES GRANDS HOCKEYEURS QUEBECOIS

This 50-sticker set was randomly inserted in packages of Durivage Bread during the regular season. It is not uncommon to find creases or bread stains on these stickers as they were inserted into the packages while the bread was still hot, and the stickers were often damaged by heat and moisture. There is also an autographed Patrick Roy card limited to 1,000. All of these are individually numbered. A 20-page album was available to hold the 50-sticker collection.

Imprint: IMPRIMÉ EN ITALIE, PANINI PRINTED IN ITALY

Complete Set (50 stickers): 25.00

Album: 3.00

	No.	Player	NRMT-MT
☐	1	Guy Carbonneau, Mtl.	.35
☐	2	Lucien DeBlois, Wpg.	.35
☐	3	Benoît Hogue, NYI.	.35
☐	4	Steve Kasper, Pha.	.35
☐	5	Mike Krushelnyski, Tor.	.35
☐	6	Claude Lapointe, Que.	.35
☐	7	Stéphan Lebeau, Mtl.	.35
☐	8	Mario Lemieux, Pgh.	5.00
☐	9	Stéphane Morin, Que.	.35
☐	10	Denis Savard, Mtl.	1.00
☐	11	Pierre Turgeon, NYI.	1.00
☐	12	Kevin Dineen, Pha.	.35
☐	13	Gord Donnelly, Buf.	.35
☐	14	Claude Lemieux, N.J.	.35
☐	15	Jocelyn Lemieux, Chi.	.35
☐	16	Daniel Marois, NYI.	.35
☐	17	Scott Mellanby, Edm.	.35
☐	18	Stéphane Richer, N.J.	.50
☐	19	Benoît Brunet, Mtl.	.35
☐	20	Vincent Damphousse, Mtl.	1.25
☐	21	Gilbert Dionne, Mtl.	.35
☐	22	Gaetan Duchesne, Min.	.35
☐	23	Bob Errey, Pgh.	.35
☐	24	Michel Goulet, Chi.	1.00
☐	25	Mike Hough, Que.	.35
☐	26	Sergio Momesso, Van.	.35
☐	27	Mario Roberge, Mtl.	.35
☐	28	Luc Robitaille, L.A.	1.00
☐	29	Sylvain Turgeon, Ott.	.35
☐	30	Marc Bergevin, T.B.	.35
☐	31	Ray Bourque, Bos.	2.00
☐	32	Patrice Brisebois, Mtl.	.35
☐	33	Jeff Chychrun, Pgh.	.35
☐	34	Sylvain Côté, Wsh.	.35
☐	35	J. J. Daigneault, Mtl.	.35
☐	36	Eric Desjardins, Mtl.	1.00
☐	37	Gord Dineen, Ott.	.35
☐	38	Steve Duchesne, Que.	.35
☐	39	Donald Dufresne, Mtl.	.35
☐	40	Steven Finn, Que.	.35
☐	41	Garry Galley, Pha.	.35
☐	42	Kevin Lowe, Edm.	.50
☐	43	Michel Petit, Cgy.	.35
☐	44	Normand Rochefort, NYR.	.35
☐	45	Randy Velischek, Que.	.35
☐	46	Jacques Cloutier (G) Que.	.50
☐	47	Stéphane Fiset (G), Que.	1.00
☐	48	Réjean Lemelin (G), Bos.	.50
☐	49	André Racicot (G), Mtl.	.50
☐	50	Patrick Roy (G), Mtl.	5.00
		Autograph	**NRMT-MT**
☐		Patrick Roy (G), Mtl., Autographed	125.00

1992 - 93 FLEER ULTRA

Imprint: © 1992 FLEER CORP.

Series One Set (250 cards): 20.00

Series Two Set (200 cards): 15.00

Common Player: .10

	No.	Player	NRMT-MT
☐	1	Brent Ashton, Bos.	.10
☐	2	Ray Bourque, Bos.	.50
☐	3	Steve Heinze, Bos.	.10
☐	4	Joé Juneau, Bos.	.10
☐	5	Stephen Leach, Bos.	.10
☐	6	Andy Moog (G), Bos.	.25
☐	7	Cam Neely, Bos.	.25
☐	8	Adam Oates, Bos.	.35
☐	9	Dave Poulin, Bos.	.10
☐	10	Vladimir Ruzicka, Bos.	.10
☐	11	Glen Wesley, Bos.	.10
☐	12	Dave Andreychuk, Buf.	.25
☐	**13**	**Keith Carney, Buf., RC**	**.10**
☐	14	Tom Draper (G), Buf.	.10
☐	15	Dale Hawerchuk, Buf.	.25
☐	16	Pat LaFontaine, Buf.	.25
☐	17	Brad May, Buf.	.10
☐	18	Alexander Mogilny, Buf.	.35
☐	19	Mike Ramsey, Buf.	.10
☐	20	Ken Sutton, Buf.	.10
☐	21	Theoren Fleury, Cgy.	.35
☐	22	Gary Leeman, Cgy.	.10
☐	23	Al MacInnis, Cgy.	.25
☐	24	Sergei Makarov, Cgy.	.10
☐	25	Joe Nieuwendyk, Cgy.	.25
☐	26	Joel Otto, Cgy.	.10
☐	27	Paul Ranheim, Cgy.	.10
☐	28	Robert Reichel, Cgy.	.25
☐	29	Gary Roberts, Cgy.	.25
☐	30	Gary Suter, Cgy.	.10
☐	31	Mike Vernon (G)	.25
☐	32	Ed Belfour (G), Chi.	.35
☐	33	Rob Brown, Chi.	.10
☐	34	Chris Chelios, Chi.	.35
☐	35	Michel Goulet, Chi.	.25
☐	36	Dirk Graham, Chi.	.10
☐	37	Mike Hudson, Chi.	.10
☐	38	Igor Kravchuk, Chi.	.10
☐	39	Steve Larmer, Chi.	.10
☐	**40**	**Dean McAmmond, Chi., RC**	**.10**
☐	41	Jeremy Roenick, Chi.	.35
☐	42	Steve Smith, Chi.	.10
☐	43	Brent Sutter, Chi.	.10
☐	44	Shawn Burr, Det.	.10
☐	45	Jimmy Carson, Det.	.10
☐	46	Tim Cheveldae (G), Det.	.10
☐	47	Dino Ciccarelli, Det.	.25
☐	48	Sergei Fedorov, Det.	.50
☐	49	Vladimir Konstantinov, Det.	.25
☐	50	Vyacheslav Kozlov, Det.	.25
☐	51	Nicklas Lidström, Det.	.25
☐	52	Brad McCrimmon, Det.	.10
☐	53	Bob Probert, Det.	.10
☐	54	Paul Ysebaert, Det.	.10
☐	55	Steve Yzerman, Det.	1.25
☐	56	Josef Beranek, Edm.	.10
☐	57	Shayne Corson, Mtl. (Edm.)	.25
☐	58	Brian Glynn, Edm.	.10
☐	59	Petr Klima, Edm.	.10
☐	60	Kevin Lowe, Edm.	.10
☐	61	Norm Maciver, Edm.	.10
☐	62	Dave Manson, Edm.	.10
☐	63	Joe Murphy, Edm.	.10

No.	Player	Price
64	Bernie Nicholls, Edm.	.10
65	Bill Ranford (G), Edm.	.25
66	Craig Simpson, Edm.	.10
67	Esa Tikkanen, Edm.	.10
68	Sean Burke (G), Hfd.	.25
69	Adam Burt, Hfd.	.10
70	Andrew Cassels, Hfd.	.10
71	Murray Craven, Hfd.	.10
72	John Cullen, Hfd.	.10
73	Randy Cunneyworth, Hfd.	.10
74	Tim Kerr, Hfd.	.10
75	Geoff Sanderson, Hfd.	.10
76	Eric Weinrich, Hfd.	.10
77	Zarley Zalapski, Hfd.	.10
78	Peter Ahola, L.A.	.10
79	Rob Blake, L.A.	.25
80	Paul Coffey, L.A.	.25
81	Mike Donnelly, L.A.	.10
82	Tony Granato, L.A.	.10
83	Wayne Gretzky, L.A.	2.50
84	Kelly Hrudey (G), L.A.	.10
85	Jari Kurri, L.A.	.25
86	Corey Millen, L.A.	.10
87	Luc Robitaille, L.A.	.25
88	Tomas Sandström, L.A.	.10
89	Neal Broten, Min.	.10
90	Jon Casey (G), Min.	.10
91	Russ Courtnall, Min.	.10
92	Ulf Dahlen, Min.	.10
93	Todd Elik, Min.	.10
94	Dave Gagner, Min.	.10
95	Jim Johnson, Min.	.10
96	Mike Modano, Min.	.50
97	Bobby Smith, Min.	.10
98	Mark Tinordi, Min.	.10
99	Darcy Wakaluk (G), Min.	.10
100	Brian Bellows, Mtl.	.10
101	Benoît Brunet, Mtl.	.10
102	Guy Carbonneau, Mtl.	.10
103	Vincent Damphousse, Mtl.	.35
104	Eric Desjardins, Mtl.	.25
105	Gilbert Dionne, Mtl.	.10
106	Mike Keane, Mtl.	.10
107	Kirk Muller, Mtl.	.10
108	Patrick Roy (G), Mtl.	2.00
109	Denis Savard, Mtl.	.25
110	Mathieu Schneider, Mtl.	.10
111	Brian Skrudland, Mtl.	.10
112	Tom Chorske, N.J.	.10
113	Zdeno Ciger, N.J.	.10
114	Claude Lemieux, N.J.	.10
115	John MacLean, N.J.	.10
116	Scott Niedermayer, N.J.	.25
117	Stéphane Richer, N.J.	.10
118	Peter Stastny, N.J.	.10
119	Scott Stevens, N.J.	.25
120	Chris Terreri (G), N.J.	.10
121	Kevin Todd, N.J.	.10
122	Valeri Zelepukin, N.J.	.10
123	Ray Ferraro, NYI.	.10
124	Mark Fitzpatrick (G), NYI.	.10
125	Patrick Flatley, NYI.	.10
126	Glenn Healy (G), NYI.	.10
127	Benoît Hogue, NYI.	.10
128	Derek King, NYI.	.10
129	Uwe Krupp, NYI.	.10
130	Scott Lachance, NYI.	.10
131	Steve Thomas, NYI.	.10
132	Pierre Turgeon, NYI.	.25
133	Tony Amonte, NYR.	.25
134	Paul Broten, NYR.	.10
135	Mike Gartner, NYR.	.25
136	Adam Graves, NYR.	.10
137	Alexei Kovalev, NYR.	.10
138	Brian Leetch, NYR.	.35
139	Mark Messier, NYR.	.50
140	Sergei Nemchinov, NYR.	.10
141	James Patrick, NYR.	.10
142	Mike Richter (G), NYR.	.35
143	Darren Turcotte, NYR.	.10
144	John Vanbiesbrouck (G), NYR.	.60
145	Dominic Lavoie, Ott.	.10
146	**Lonnie Loach, Ott., RC**	**.10**
147	Andrew McBain, Ott.	.10
148	**Darren Rumble, Ott., RC**	**.10**
149	Sylvain Turgeon, Ott.	.10
150	Peter Sidorkiewicz (G), Ott.	.10
151	Brian Benning, Pha.	.10
152	Rod Brind'Amour, Pha.	.25
153	**Vyatcheslav Butsayev, Pha., RC**	**.10**
154	Kevin Dineen, Pha.	.10
155	Per-Erik Eklund, Pha.	.10
156	Garry Galley, Pha.	.10
157	Eric Lindros, Pha.	2.00
158	Mark Recchi, Pha.	.25
159	Dominic Roussel (G), Pha.	.10
160	**Tommy Söderström, (G) Pha., RC**	**.25**
161	**Dimitri Yushkevich, Pha., RC**	**.10**
162	Tom Barrasso (G), Pgh.	.25
163	Ron Francis, Pgh.	.35
164	Jaromir Jagr, Pgh.	1.25
165	Mario Lemieux, Pgh.	2.00
166	Joe Mullen, Pgh.	.10
167	Larry Murphy, Pgh.	.25
168	Jim Paek, Pgh.	.10
169	Kjell Samuelsson, Pgh.	.10
170	Ulf Samuelsson, Pgh.	.10
171	Kevin Stevens, Pgh.	.10
172	Rick Tocchet, Pgh.	.10
173	Alexei Gusarov, Que.	.10
174	Ron Hextall (G), Que.	.25
175	Mike Hough, Que.	.10
176	Claude Lapointe, Que.	.10
177	Owen Nolan, Que.	.25
178	Mike Ricci, Que.	.10
179	Joe Sakic, Que.	1.00
180	Mats Sundin, Que.	.50
181	Mikhail Tatarinov, Que.	.10
182	Bob Bassen, Stl.	.10
183	Jeff Brown, Stl.	.10
184	Garth Butcher, Stl.	.10
185	Paul Cavallini, Stl.	.10
186	Brett Hull, Stl.	.50
187	Craig Janney, Stl.	.10
188	Curtis Joseph (G), Stl.	.60
189	Brendan Shanahan, Stl.	.60
190	Ron Sutter, Stl.	.10
191	David Bruce, S.J.	.10
192	Dale Craigwell, S.J.	.10
193	Dean Evason, S.J.	.10
194	Pat Falloon, S.J.	.10
195	Jeff Hackett (G), S.J.	.25
196	Kelly Kisio, S.J.	.10
197	Brian Lawton, S.J.	.10
198	Neil Wilkinson, S.J.	.10
199	Doug Wilson, S.J.	.10
200	Marc Bergevin, T.B.	.10
201	**Roman Hamrlik, T.B., RC**	**.50**
202	Pat Jablonski (G), T.B.	.10
203	Michel Mongeau, T.B.	.10
204	Peter Taglianetti, T.B.	.10
205	Steve Tuttle, T.B.	.10
206	Wendell Young (G), T.B.	.10
207	Glenn Anderson, Tor.	.10
208	Wendel Clark, Tor.	.25
209	David Ellett, Tor.	.10
210	Grant Fuhr (G), Tor.	.25
211	Doug Gilmour, Tor.	.35
212	Jamie Macoun, Tor.	.10
213	Félix Potvin (G), Tor.	.50
214	Bob Rouse, Tor.	.10
215	Joe Sacco, Tor.	.10
216	Peter Zezel, Tor.	.10
217	Greg Adams, Van.	.10
218	Dave Babych, Van.	.10
219	Pavel Bure, Van.	.75
220	Geoff Courtnall, Van.	.10
221	Doug Lidster, Van.	.10
222	Trevor Linden, Van.	.35
223	Jyrki Lumme, Van.	.10
224	Kirk McLean (G), Van.	.25
225	Sergio Momesso, Van.	.10
226	Peter Nedved, Van.	.10
227	Cliff Ronning, Van.	.10
228	Jim Sandlak, Van.	.10
229	Don Beaupré (G), Wsh.	.10
230	Peter Bondra, Wsh.	.35
231	Kevin Hatcher, Wsh.	.10
232	Dale Hunter, Wsh.	.10
233	Al Iafrate, Wsh.	.10
234	Calle Johansson, Wsh.	.10
235	Dimitri Khristich, Wsh.	.10
236	Kelly Miller, Wsh.	.10
237	Michal Pivonka, Wsh.	.10
238	Mike Ridley, Wsh.	.10
239	Luciano Borsato, Wpg.	.10
240	Bob Essensa (G), Wpg.	.10
241	Phil Housley, Wpg.	.10
242	Troy Murray, Wpg.	.10
243	Teppo Numminen, Wpg.	.10
244	Fredrik Olausson, Wpg.	.10
245	Ed Olczyk, Wpg.	.10
246	Darrin Shannon, Wpg.	.10
247	Thomas Steen, Wpg.	.10
248	Checklist 1 (1 - 88)	.10
249	Checklist 2 (89 - 172)	.10
250	Checklist 3 (173 - 250)	.10
251	Ted Donato, Bos.	.10
252	**Dmitri Kvartalnov, Bos., RC**	**.10**
253	Gord Murphy, Bos.	.10
254	**Gregori Panteleyev, Bos., RC**	**.10**
255	Gord Roberts, Bos.	.10
256	David Shaw, Bos.	.10
257	Don Sweeney, Bos.	.10
258	Doug Bodger, Buf.	.10
259	Gord Donnelly, Buf.	.10
260	**Yuri Khmylev, Buf., RC**	**.10**
261	Daren Puppa (G), Buf.	.10
262	**Richard Smehlik, Buf., RC**	**.10**
263	Petr Svoboda, Buf.	.10
264	Rob Sweeney, Buf.	.10
265	Randy Wood, Buf.	.10
266	**Kevin Dahl, Cgy., RC**	**.10**
267	Chris Dahlquist, Cgy.	.10
268	Roger Johansson, Cgy.	.10
269	Chris Lindberg, Cgy.	.10
270	Frank Musil, Cgy.	.10
271	Ron Stern, Cgy.	.10
272	Carey Wilson, Cgy.	.10
273	Dave Christian, Chi.	.10
274	Karl Dykhuis, Chi.	.10
275	Greg Gilbert, Chi.	.10
276	**Sergei Krivokrasov, Chi., RC**	**.10**
277	Frantisek Kucera, Chi.	.10
278	Bryan Marchment, Chi.	.10
279	Stéphane Matteau, Chi.	.10
280	Brian Noonan, Chi.	.10
281	Christian Ruuttu, Chi.	.10
282	Steve Chiasson, Det.	.10
283	Dino Ciccarelli, Det.	.25
284	Gerard Gallant, Det.	.10
285	Mark Howe, Det.	.25
286	Keith Primeau, Det.	.25
287	Yves Racine, Det.	.10
288	Vincent Riendeau (G), Det.	.10
289	Ray Sheppard, Det.	.10
290	Mike Sillinger, Det.	.10
291	Kelly Buchberger, Edm.	.10
292	Shayne Corson, Edm.	.25
293	Brent Gilchrist, Edm.	.10
294	Craig MacTavish, Edm.	.10
295	Scott Mellanby, Edm.	.10
296	Craig Muni, Edm.	.10
297	Luke Richardson, Edm.	.10
298	Ron Tugnutt (G), Edm.	.10
299	Shaun Van Allen, Edm.	.10
300	Steve Konroyd, Hfd.	.10
301	Nick Kypreos, Hfd.	.10
302	**Robert Petrovicky, Hfd., RC**	**.10**
303	Frank Pietrangelo (G), Hfd.	.10
304	Patrick Poulin, Hfd.	.10
305	Pat Verbeek, Hfd.	.10
306	Eric Weinrich, Hfd.	.10
307	**Jim Hiller, L.A., RC**	**.10**
308	Charlie Huddy, L.A.	.10
309	Lonnie Loach, L.A.	.10
310	Marty McSorley, L.A.	.10
311	Robb Stauber (G), L.A.	.10
312	Darryl Sydor, L.A.	.10
313	Dave Taylor, L.A.	.10
314	**Alexei Zhitnik, L.A., RC**	**.10**
315	Shane Churla, Min.	.10
316	Russ Courtnall, Min.	.10
317	Mike Craig, Min.	.10
318	Gaetan Duchesne, Min.	.10

	No.	Player	Price
☐	319	Derian Hatcher, Min.	.25
☐	320	Craig Ludwig, Min.	.10
☐	**321**	**Richard Matvichuk, Min., RC**	**.10**
☐	322	Mike McPhee, Min.	.10
☐	**323**	**Tommy Sjodin, Min., RC**	**.10**
☐	324	Brian Bellows, Mtl.	.10
☐	325	Patrice Brisebois, Mtl.	.10
☐	326	J.J. Daigneault, Mtl.	.10
☐	327	Kevin Haller, Mtl.	.10
☐	**328**	**Sean Hill, Mtl., RC**	**.10**
☐	329	Stéphan Lebeau, Mtl.	.10
☐	330	John LeClair, Mtl.	.50
☐	331	Lyle Odelein, Mtl.	.10
☐	332	André Racicot (G), Mtl.	.10
☐	**333**	**Ed Ronan, Mtl., RC**	**.10**
☐	334	Craig Billington (G), N.J.	.10
☐	335	Ken Daneyko, N.J.	.10
☐	336	Bruce Driver, N.J.	.10
☐	337	Viacheslav Fetisov, N.J.	.25
☐	**338**	**Bill Guerin, N.J., RC**	**.35**
☐	339	Bobby Holik, N.J.	.10
☐	340	Alexei Kasatonov, N.J.	.10
☐	341	Alexander Semak, N.J.	.10
☐	342	Tom Fitzgerald, NYI.	.10
☐	**343**	**Travis Green, NYI., RC**	**.10**
☐	344	Darius Kasparaitis, NYI.	.10
☐	**345**	**Danny Lorenz (G), NYI., RC**	**.10**
☐	346	Vladimir Malakhov, NYI.	.10
☐	347	Marty McInnis, NYI.	.10
☐	348	Brian Mullen, NYI.	.10
☐	349	Jeff Norton, NYI.	.10
☐	350	David Volek, NYI.	.10
☐	351	Jeff Beukeboom, NYR.	.10
☐	352	Phil Bourque, NYR.	.10
☐	353	Paul Broten, NYR.	.10
☐	354	Mark Hardy, NYR.	.10
☐	**355**	**Steven King, NYR., RC**	**.10**
☐	356	Kevin Lowe, NYR.	.10
☐	357	Ed Olczyk, NYR.	.10
☐	358	Doug Weight, NYR.	.35
☐	**359**	**Sergei Zubov, NYR., RC**	**.75**
☐	360	Jamie Baker, Ott.	.10
☐	361	Daniel Berthiaume (G), Ott.	.10
☐	**362**	**Chris Luongo, Ott., RC**	**.10**
☐	363	Norm Maciver, Ott.	.10
☐	364	Brad Marsh, Ott.	.10
☐	365	Mike Peluso, Ott.	.10
☐	366	Brad Shaw, Ott.	.10
☐	367	Peter Sidorkiewicz (G), Ott.	.10
☐	368	Keith Acton, Pha.	.10
☐	369	Stéphane Beauregard (G), Pha.	.10
☐	370	Terry Carkner, Pha.	.10
☐	371	Brent Fedyk, Pha.	.10
☐	372	Andrei Lomakin, Pha.	.10
☐	**373**	**Ryan McGill, Pha., RC**	**.10**
☐	374	Ric Nattress, Pha.	.10
☐	375	Greg Paslawski, Pha.	.10
☐	376	Peter Ahola, Pgh.	.10
☐	377	Jeff Daniels, Pgh.	.10
☐	378	Troy Loney, Pgh.	.10
☐	379	Shawn McEachern, Pgh.	.10
☐	**380**	**Mike Needham, Pgh., RC**	**.10**
☐	381	Paul Stanton, Pgh.	.10
☐	**382**	**Martin Straka, Pgh., RC**	**.10**
☐	383	Ken Wregget (G), Pgh.	.10
☐	384	Steve Duchesne, Que.	.10
☐	385	Ron Hextall (G), Que.	.25
☐	386	Kerry Huffman, Que.	.10
☐	**387**	**Andrei Kovalenko, Que., RC**	**.50**
☐	**388**	**Bill Lindsay, Que., RC**	**.10**
☐	389	Mike Ricci, Que.	.10
☐	390	Martin Rucinsky, Que.	.10
☐	391	Scott Young, Que.	.10
☐	392	Philippe Bozon, Stl.	.10
☐	393	Nelson Emerson, Stl.	.10
☐	**394**	**Guy Hebert (G), Stl., RC**	**1.00**
☐	**395**	**Igor Korolev, Stl., RC**	**.10**
☐	396	Kevin Miller, Stl.	.10
☐	**397**	**Vitali Prokhorov, Stl., RC**	**.10**
☐	398	Rich Sutter, Stl.	.10
☐	399	John Carter, S.J.	.10
☐	400	Johan Garpenlov, S.J.	.10
☐	401	Arturs Irbe (G), S.J.	.10
☐	402	Sandis Ozolinsh, S.J.	.25
☐	**403**	**Tom Pederson, S.J., RC**	**.10**
☐	404	Michel Picard, S.J.	.10
☐	**405**	**Doug Zmolek, S.J., RC**	**.10**
☐	406	Mikael Andersson, T.B.	.10
☐	407	Bob Beers, T.B.	.10
☐	408	Brian Bradley, T.B.	.10
☐	409	Adam Creighton, T.B.	.10
☐	410	Doug Crossman, T.B.	.10
☐	411	Ken Hodge, T.B.	.10
☐	**412**	**Chris Kontos, T.B., RC**	**.10**
☐	413	Rob Ramage, T.B.	.10
☐	414	John Tucker, T.B.	.10
☐	**415**	**Rob Zamuner, T.B., RC**	**.50**
☐	416	Ken Baumgartner, Tor.	.10
☐	417	Drake Berehowsky, Tor.	.10
☐	**418**	**Nikolai Borschevsky, Tor., RC**	**.10**
☐	419	John Cullen, Tor.	.10
☐	420	Mike Foligno, Tor.	.10
☐	421	Mike Krushelnyski, Tor.	.10
☐	422	Dmitri Mironov, Tor.	.10
☐	423	Rob Pearson, Tor.	.10
☐	424	Gerald Diduck, Van.	.10
☐	425	Robert Dirk, Van.	.10
☐	426	Tom Fergus, Van.	.10
☐	427	Gino Odjick, Van.	.10
☐	428	Adrien Plavsic, Van.	.10
☐	429	Anatoli Semenov, Van.	.10
☐	430	Jiri Slegr, Van.	.10
☐	**431**	**Dixon Ward, Van., RC**	**.10**
☐	432	Paul Cavallini, Wsh.	.10
☐	433	Sylvain Côté, Wsh.	.10
☐	434	Pat Elynuik, Wsh.	.10
☐	435	Jim Hrivnak (G), Wsh.	.10
☐	**436**	**Keith Jones, Wsh., RC**	**.25**
☐	**437**	**Steve Konowalchuk, Wsh., RC**	**.10**
☐	438	Todd Krygier, Wsh.	.10
☐	439	Paul MacDermid, Wsh.	.10
☐	**440**	**Sergei Bautin, Wpg., RC**	**.10**
☐	441	Evgeny Davydov, Wpg.	.10
☐	442	John Druce, Wpg.	.10
☐	443	Troy Murray, Wpg.	.10
☐	444	Teemu Selänne, Wpg.	.75
☐	445	Rick Tabaracci (G), Wpg.	.10
☐	446	Keith Tkachuk, Wpg.	.35
☐	447	Alexei Zhamnov, Wpg.,	.25
☐	448	Series 2 Checklist (251 - 314)	.10
☐	449	Series 2 Checklist (315 - 383)	.10
☐	450	Series 2 Checklist (384 - 450)	.10

JEREMY ROENICK HIGHLIGHTS

Cards 1-10 were available in Fleer Ultra Series One packs while cards 11 and 12 were available via mail redemption.

Insert Set (12 cards): 35.00

	No.	Player	NRMT-MT
☐	1	Blast from the Past	3.00
☐	2	Early Days on the Road	3.00
☐	3	Prep School Phenom	3.00
☐	4	Blackhawk Bound	3.00
☐	5	Breakfast with a Champion	3.00
☐	6	The Fast Track	3.00
☐	7	Boy to Man	3.00
☐	8	Great Expectations	3.00
☐	9	Changing of the Guard	3.00
☐	10	Superstar	3.00
☐	11	Mail in Card	4.00
☐	12	Mail in Card	4.00

	Player	NRMT-MT
☐	Jeremy Roenick Autographed Card	140.00

ULTRA ROOKIES

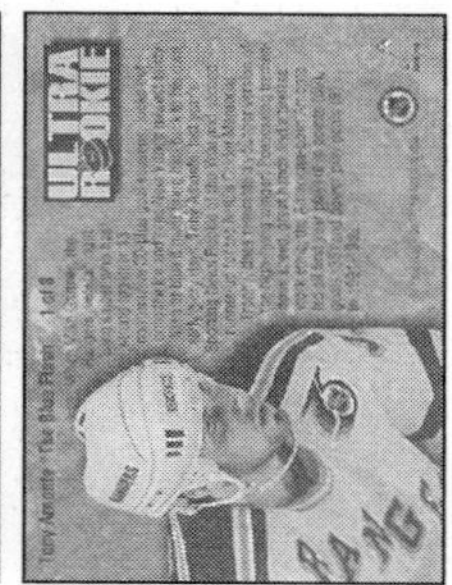

Series One Insert Set (8 cards): 12.00

	No.	Player	NRMT-MT
☐	1	Tony Amonte, NYR.	2.00
☐	2	Donald Audette, Buf.	1.00
☐	3	Pavel Bure, Van.	5.00
☐	4	Gilbert Dionne, Mtl.	1.00
☐	5	Nelson Emerson, Stl.	1.00
☐	6	Pat Falloon, S.J.	1.00
☐	7	Nicklas Lidström, Det.	2.00
☐	8	Kevin Todd, N.J.	1.00

NHL ALL-STAR

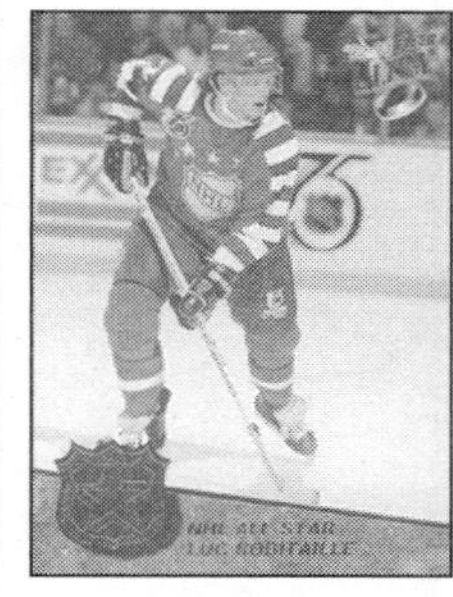

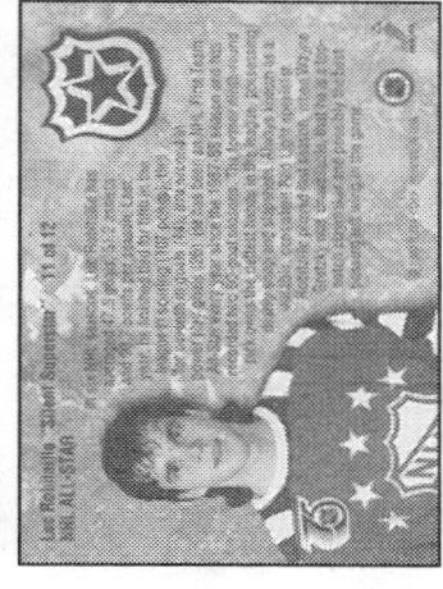

Series One Insert Set (12 cards): 30.00

	No.	Player	NRMT-MT
☐	1	Paul Coffey, L.A., Error	1.00
☐	2	Ray Bourque, Bos.	2.00
☐	3	Patrick Roy (G), Mtl.	6.50
☐	4	Mario Lemieux, Pgh.	6.50
☐	5	Kevin Stevens, Pgh., Error	1.00
☐	6	Jaromir Jagr, Pgh.	4.00
☐	7	Chris Chelios, Chi.	1.50
☐	8	Al McInnis, Cgy.	1.00
☐	9	Ed Belfour, (G), Chi.	1.25
☐	10	Wayne Gretzky, L.A.	8.00
☐	11	Luc Robitaille, L.A.	1.00
☐	12	Brett Hull, Stl.	2.00

AWARD WINNERS

Series One Insert Set (10 cards): 25.00

	No.	Player	NRMT-MT
☐	1	Mark Messier, NYR.	2.00
☐	2	Brian Leetch, NYR.	1.25
☐	3	Guy Carbonneau, Mtl.	.75
☐	4	Patrick Roy, (G), Mtl.	6.50
☐	5	Mario Lemieux, Pgh.	6.50
☐	6	Wayne Gretzky, L.A.	8.00
☐	7	Mark Fitzpatrick, NYI.	.75
☐	8	Ray Bourque, Bos.	2.00
☐	9	Pavel Bure, Van.	3.00
☐	10	Mark Messier, NYR.	2.00

ULTRA IMPORTS

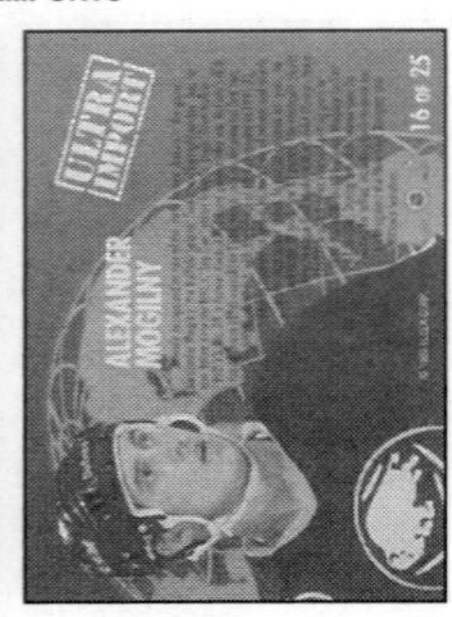

Series Two Insert Set (25 cards):		**45.00**
No.	**Player**	**NRMT-MT**
□ 1	Nikolai Borschevsky, Tor.	1.00
□ 2	Pavel Bure, Van.	5.50
□ 3	Sergei Fedorov, Det.	4.00
□ 4	Roman Hamrlik, T.B.	2.00
□ 5	Arturs Irbe (G), S.J.	1.00
□ 6	Jaromir Jagr, Pgh.	8.00
□ 7	Dimitri Khristich, Wsh.	1.00
□ 8	Petr Klima, Edm.	1.00
□ 9	Andrei Kovalenko, Que.	1.00
□ 10	Alexei Kovalev, NYR.	1.00
□ 11	Jari Kurri, L.A.	2.00
□ 12	Dmitri Kvartalnov, Bos.	1.00
□ 13	Nicklas Lidström, Det.	2.00
□ 14	Vladimir Malakhov, NYI.	1.00
□ 15	Dmitri Mironov, Tor.	1.00
□ 16	Alexander Mogilny, Buf.	3.00
□ 17	Petr Nedved, Van.	1.00
□ 18	Fredrick Olausson, Wpg.	1.00
□ 19	Sandis Ozolinsh, S.J.	2.00
□ 20	Ulf Samuelsson, Pgh.	1.00
□ 21	Teemu Selänne, Wpg.	5.50
□ 22	Richard Smehlik, Buf.	1.00
□ 23	Tommy Söderström (G), Pha.	1.00
□ 24	Peter Stastny, N.J.	1.00
□ 25	Mats Sundin, Que.	4.00

1992 - 93 FUTURE TRENDS CANADA CUP '76

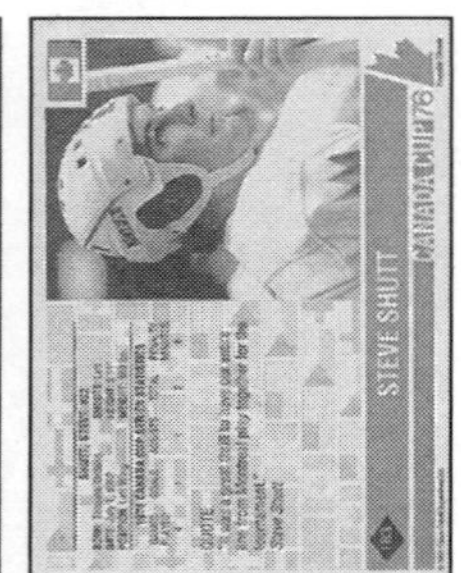

These cards were produced by 7th Inning Sketch. Cards 1-101 are part of the 1991 Future Trends Canada '72 series.

Imprint: 1992 Future Trends Experience Ltd.

Complete Set (100 cards):		**11.00**
Common Player:		**.05**
Promo Sheet Canada Cup '76:		**5.00**
Promo Sheet Team Canada:		**5.00**
Promo Sheet Team U.S.A.:		**5.00**
	Promo	**NRMT-MT**
□	Vladislav Tretiak (G), Promo	5.00
No.	**Player**	**NRMT-MT**
□ 102	Sergeant Pepper, Phil Esposito	.35
□ 103	Soviet Ambassador, Vladislav Tretiak	.75
□ 104	Impossible, Bobby Orr	1.25
□ 105	The Goal	.05
□ 106	IF, Alexander Yakishov	.05
□ 107	The Golden Jet, Bobby Hull	.35
□ 108	Soviet Superstar, Vladislav Tretiak	.75
□ 109	Great Goalies	.60
□ 110	What If Series?	.75
□ 111	A Soviet Suprise	.05
□ 112	World Champs	.05
□ 113	Tournament Underdogs	.05
□ 114	Sweden's Best Ever	.05
□ 115	Team U.S.A. Trains	.05
□ 116	Canada Cup Camp	.05
□ 117	Serge Savard	.25
□ 118	Team Finland	.05
□ 119	Team Sweden	.05
□ 120	Team Czechoslovakia	.05
□ 121	Soviets	.05
□ 122	Team U.S.A.	.05
□ 123	Team Canada	.25
□ 124	The Opening Barrage	.05
□ 125	Richard Martin	.05
□ 126	Bobby Orr	1.25
□ 127	Power Play	.05
□ 128	Ivan Hlinka	.05
□ 129	CSSR 5 - CCCP 3	.05
□ 130	Helmut Balderis	.05
□ 131	Peter Stastny	.15
□ 132	Valeri Vasiliev	.05
□ 133	Out Of Contention	.05
□ 134	Standing Alone	.05
□ 135	"The Miracle on Ice" ...Almost	.05
□ 136	Josef Augusta	.05
□ 137	A Soviet Rout	.05
□ 138	Viktor Zhluktov	.05
□ 139	Hull's A Hit	.05
□ 140	Bob Gainey	.25
□ 141	Anders Hedberg	.05
□ 142	Bobby Hull	.75
□ 143	Ulf Nilsson	.05
□ 144	Sergei Kapustin	.05
□ 145	Borje Salming	.15
□ 146	Well Enough to Win	.05
□ 147	Biggest Upset	.05
□ 148	Matti Hagman	.05
□ 149	Unbeatable	.05
□ 150	Boris Alexandrov	.05
□ 151	A Goaltending Duel	.05
□ 152	Vladimir Dzurilla (G)	.05
□ 153	Phil Esposito	.50
□ 154	Rogatien Vachon (G)	.15
□ 155	Milan Novy	.05
□ 156	Vladimir Martinec	.05
□ 157	Good For Hockey	.05
□ 158	Bill Nyrop	.05
□ 159	Pride	.05
□ 160	Another Summit	.05
□ 161	Alexander Maltsev	.05
□ 162	Gilbert Perreault	.50
□ 163	Vladislav Tretiak (G)	1.00
□ 164	Vladimir Vikulov	.05
□ 165	Canada Cup Final, Game 1	.05
□ 166	Not There Yet	.05
□ 167	Fast & Furious, Game 2	.05
□ 168	4 - 3(Front) 4 - 4 (Back)	.05
□ 169	Bill Barber	.25
□ 170	The Grapevine	.05
□ 171	Guy Lapointe	.25
□ 172	Reggie Leach	.05
□ 173	Sittler's Goal	.75
□ 174	Lanny McDonald	.25
□ 175	Darryl Sittler	.50
□ 176	The Canada Cup	.05
□ 177	Bobby Clarke	.50
□ 178	Last Time For #9	.25
□ 179	Marcel Dionne	.50
□ 180	Peter Mahovlich	.05
□ 181	Denis Potvin	.25
□ 182	Larry Robinson	.25
□ 183	Steve Shutt	.25
□ 184	Tournament MVP: Bobby Orr	1.25
□ 185	M.V.P. Canada: Rogatien Vachon (G)	.15
□ 186	M.V.P. CSSR: Milan Novy	.05
□ 187	M.V.P. Finland: Matti Hagman	.05
□ 188	M.V.P. Sweden: Borje Salming	.15
□ 189	M.V.P. USA: Robbie Ftorek	.05
□ 190	M.V.P. USSR: Alexander Maltsev	.05
□ 191	Canada Final Series Totals	.05
□ 192	Canada Series Totals	.05
□ 193	CSSR Final Series Totals	.05
□ 194	CSSR Series Totals	.05
□ 195	All Star Team: Rogatien Vachon (G)	.15
□ 196	All Star Team: Bobby Orr	1.25
□ 197	All Star Team: Borje Salming	.15
□ 198	All Star Team: Milan Novy	.05
□ 199	All Star Team: Darryl Sittler	.25
□ 200	All STar Team: Alexander Maltsev	.05
□ 201	Checklist	.05

AUTOGRAPHED CARDS

Complete Set (5 cards)		**300.00**
	Player	**NRMT-MT**
□	Bobby Clarke, Pha.	60.00
□	Bobby Hull, Chi.	100.00
□	Bobby Orr, Bos.	145.00
□	Darryl Sittler, Tor.	60.00
□	Rogatien Vachon (G), Mtl.	45.00

1992 - 93 HIGH FIVE PROMOS

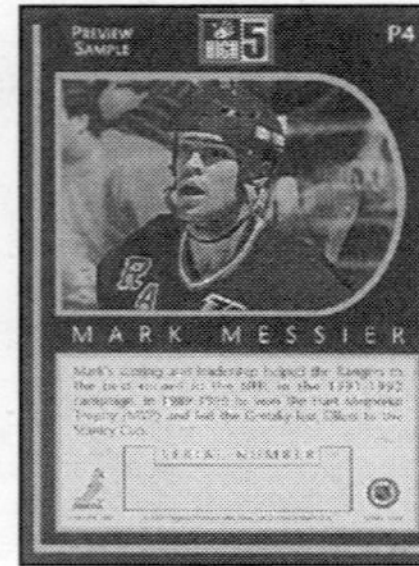

These promos were intended for a never released High Five hockey set. Ed Belfour's and Ray Bourque's cards were double printed. These sample were later repackaged with the Collector's Edge 1995-96 Future Legends product.

Imprint:

Complete Set (6 cards):		**50.00**
No.	**Player**	**NRMT-MT**
□ P1	Ray Bourque, Bos. (**)	5.00
□ P2	Brett Hull, Stl.	8.00
□ P3	Wayne Gretzky, L.A.	30.00
□ P4	Mark Messier, NYR.	8.00
□ P5	Mario Lemieux, Pgh.	25.00
□ P6	Ed Belfour (G), Chi. (**)	5.00

1992 - 93 HIGH LINER CENTENNIAL SERIES

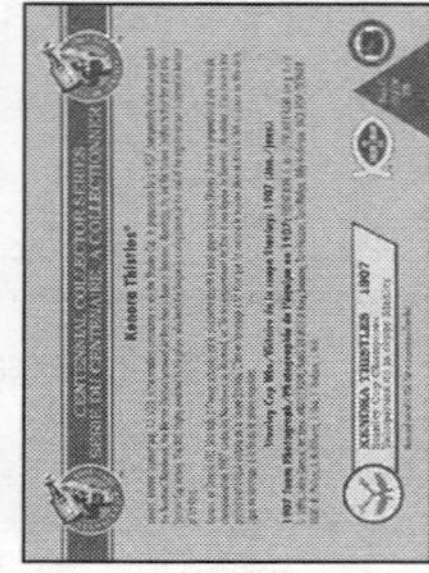

Two of 28 different cards were found in specially marked boxes of High Liner.

Imprint: Made and printed in USA. Fait et imprimé aux États-Unis

Complete Set (28 cards):		**65.00**
No.	**Team**	**NRMT-MT**
□ 1	Montréal AAA, 1893	3.00
□ 2	Winnipeg Victorias, 1896	3.00
□ 3	Montréal Victorias, 1896	3.00
□ 4	Montréal Shamrocks, 1899	3.00
□ 5	Ottawa Silver Seven, 1903	3.00
□ 6	Kenora Thistles, 1907	3.00
□ 7	Montréal Wanderers, 1910	3.00
□ 8	Québec Bulldogs, 1913	3.00
□ 9	Toronto Blueshirts, 1914	3.00
□ 10	Vancouver Millionaires, 1915	3.00
□ 11	Seattle Metropolitans, 1917	3.00
□ 12	Toronto Arenas, 1918	3.00
□ 13	Toronto St. Patricks, 1922	3.00
□ 14	Victoria Cougars, 1925	3.00
□ 15	Ottawa Senators, 1927	3.00
□ 16	Montréal Maroons, 1935	3.00
□ 17	New York Rangers, 1940	3.00
□ 18	Detroit Red Wings, 1955	3.50

	No.	Player	Price
☐	19	Montréal Canadiens, 1956	4.00
☐	20	Chicago Black Hawks, 1961	3.50
☐	21	Toronto Maple Leafs, 1967	3.50
☐	22	Boston Bruins, 1970	3.50
☐	23	Philadelphia Flyers, 1974	3.00
☐	24	New York Islanders, 1980	3.00
☐	25	Edmonton Oilers, 1984	5.00
☐	26	Calgary Flames, 1989	3.00
☐	27	Pittsburgh Penguins, 1991	3.50
☐	28	Checklist	3.00

1992 - 93 HOCKEY HALL OF FAME LEGENDS

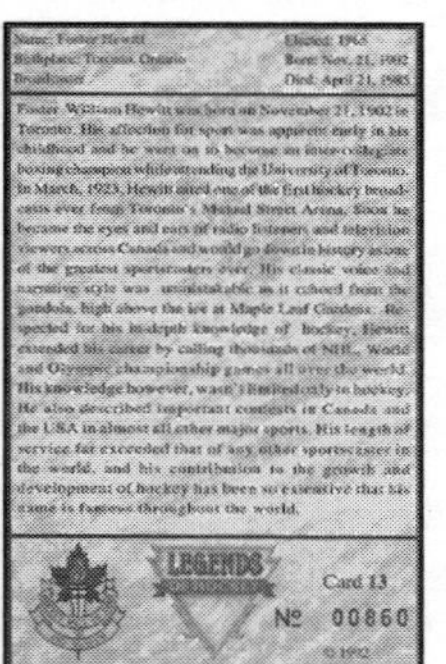

Artwork by Doug West.
Card Size: 3 1/2" x 5 1/2"
Imprint:
Series One Set (18 cards): 135.00

	No.	Player	NRMT-MT
☐	1	Harry Lumley (G), Tor.	10.00
☐	2	Conn Smythe, M.C.	8.00
☐	3	Maurice Richard, Mtl.	14.00
☐	4	Bobby Orr, Bos.	20.00
☐	5	Bernie (Boom Boom) Geoffrion, Mtl.	10.00
☐	6	Hobey Baker	8.00
☐	7	Phil Esposito, Bos.	12.00
☐	8	Francis (King) Clancy, Tor.	8.00
☐	9	Gordie Howe, Det.	15.00
☐	10	Emile Francis (G)	8.00
☐	11	Jacques Plante (G), Mtl.	12.00
☐	12	Sid Abel, Det.	8.00
☐	13	Foster Hewitt, Broadcaster	8.00
☐	14	Charlie Conacher, Tor.	8.00
☐	15	Stan Mikita, Chi.	12.00
☐	16	Bobby Clarke, Pha.	12.00
☐	17	Norm Ullman, Det.	10.00
☐	18	Lord Stanley of Preston	8.00

1992 - 93 HUMPTY DUMPTY

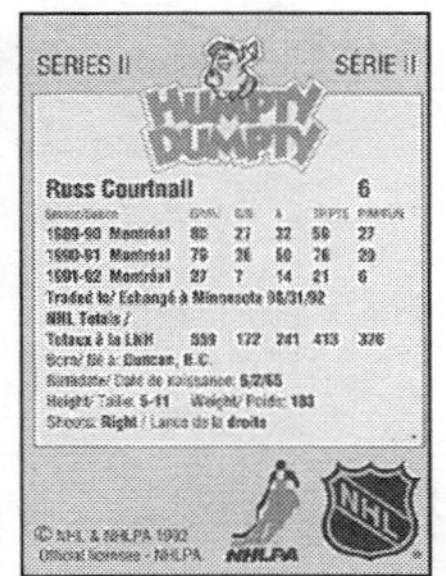

Card Size: 1 1/2" x 2"
Imprint: NHL & NHLPA 1992
Series One Set (26 cards): 18.00
Series Two Set (26 cards): 15.00
Album: 10.00

	Player	NRMT-MT
SERIES ONE		
☐	Ray Bourque, Bos.	1.00
☐	Rod Brind'Amour, Pha.	.50
☐	Chris Chelios, Chi.	.75
☐	Wendel Clark, Tor.	.50
☐	Gilbert Dionne, Mtl.	.35
☐	Pat Falloon, S.J.	.35
☐	Ray Ferraro, NYI.	.35
☐	Theoren Fleury, Cgy.	.75
☐	Grant Fuhr (G), Tor.	.50
☐	Wayne Gretzky, L.A.	4.00
☐	Kevin Hatcher, Wsh.	.35
☐	Valeri Kamensky, Que.	.50
☐	Mike Keane, Mtl.	.35
☐	Brian Leetch, NYR.	.75
☐	Kirk McLean (G), Van.	.50
☐	Alexander Mogilny, Buf.	.75
☐	Troy Murray, Wpg.	.35
☐	Patrick Roy (G), Mtl.	3.00
☐	Joe Sakic, Que.	1.75
☐	Brendan Shanahan, Stl.	1.25
☐	Kevin Stevens, Pgh.	.35
☐	Scott Stevens, N.J.	.35
☐	Mark Tinordi, Min.	.35
☐	Steve Yzerman, Det.	2.00
☐	Zarley Zalapski, Hfd.	.35
☐	Checklist: Series I	.50
SERIES TWO		
☐	Drake Berehowsky, Tor.	.35
☐	Shayne Corson, Mtl.	.50
☐	Russ Courtnall, Mtl.	.35
☐	Dave Ellett, Tor.	.35
☐	Sergei Fedorov, Det.	1.00
☐	Dave Gagner, Min.	.35
☐	Doug Gilmour, Tor.	.75
☐	Phil Housley, Wpg.	.35
☐	Brett Hull, Stl.	1.00
☐	Jaromir Jagr, Pgh.	2.00
☐	Pat LaFontaine, Buf.	.50
☐	Mario Lemieux, Pgh.	3.00
☐	Trevor Linden, Van.	.50
☐	Al MacInnis, Cgy.	.50
☐	Mark Messier, NYR.	1.00
☐	Cam Neely, Bos.	.50
☐	Owen Nolan, Que.	.50
☐	Bill Ranford (G), Edm.	.50
☐	Jeremy Roenick, Chi.	.75
☐	Luc Robitaille, L.A.	.50
☐	Mats Sundin, Que.	1.00
☐	Pat Verbeek, Hfd.	.35
☐	Chris Terreri (G), N.J.	.35
☐	Steve Thomas, NYI.	.35
☐	Neil Wilkinson, S.J.	.35
☐	Checklist: Series II	.50

1992 - 93 JYVAS HYVA HOCKEY LIIGA

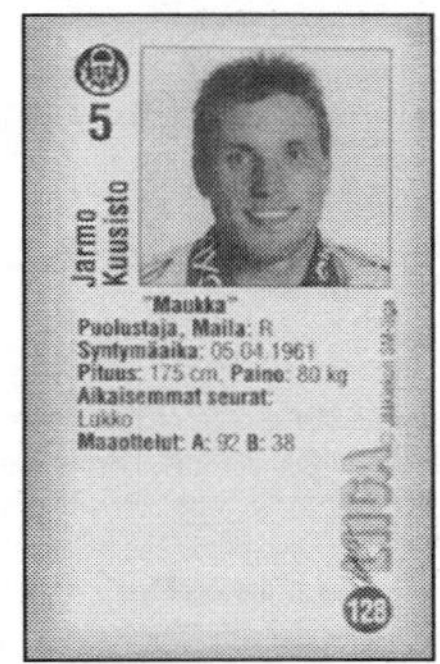

A set of 204 stickers plus a collecting album for the Finnish National League. We have little pricing information on this set. Koivu is the most expensive single at $15.00. Singles start at .20¢

Size: 2" x 3 1/4"
Imprint:
Complete Set (204 cards):
Common Player: .20

	No.	Player
☐	1	Harri Rindell, HIFK
☐	2	Sakari Lindfors (G), HIFK
☐	3	Simo Saarinen, HIFK
☐	4	Pertti Lehtonen, HIFK
☐	5	Kari Laitinen, HIFK
☐	6	Teppo Kivela, HIFK
☐	7	Darren Boyko, HIFK
☐	8	Kai Rautio, HIFK
☐	9	Drahomir Kadlec, HIFK
☐	10	Mika Kortelainen, HIFK
☐	11	Jukka Seppo, HIFK
☐	12	Pekka Tuomisto, HIFK
☐	13	Pasi Sormunen, HIFK
☐	14	Kai Tervonen, HIFK
☐	15	Ville Peltonen, HIFK
☐	16	Valeri Krykov, HIFK
☐	17	Iiro Jarvi, HIFK
☐	18	Hannu Jortikka, HPK.
☐	19	Timo Lehkonen (G), HPK.
☐	20	Timo Nykopp, HPK.
☐	21	Janne Laukkanen, HPK.
☐	22	Marko Palo, HPK.
☐	23	Juha Ylonen, HPK.
☐	24	Jarkko Varvio, HPK.
☐	25	Marko Allen, HPK.
☐	26	Marko Tuulola, HPK.
☐	27	Jarkko Nikander, HPK.
☐	28	Radek Toupal, HPK.
☐	29	Tommi Varjonen, HPK.
☐	30	Niko Marttila, HPK.
☐	31	Jari Haapamaki, HPK.
☐	32	Pasi Kivela, HPK.
☐	33	Tony Virta, HPK.
☐	34	Markku Piikkila, HPK.
☐	35	Anatoli Bogdanov, Ilves
☐	36	Jukka Tammi (G), Ilves
☐	37	Jani Nikko, Ilves
☐	38	Jukka Ollila, Ilves
☐	39	Tommi Kiiski, Ilves
☐	40	Mikko Luovi, Ilves
☐	41	Juha Jarvenpaa, Ilves
☐	42	Juha Lampinen, Ilves
☐	43	Janne Seva, Ilves
☐	44	Timo Peltomaa, Ilves
☐	45	Mika Arvaja, Ilves
☐	46	Esa Tommila, Ilves
☐	47	Kristian Taubert, Ilves
☐	48	Jarkko Glad, Ilves
☐	49	Hannu Mattila, Ilves
☐	50	Pasi Maattanen, Ilves
☐	51	Petri Sullamaa, Ilves
☐	52	Boris Majorov, Jokerit
☐	53	Markus Ketterer (G), Jokerit
☐	54	Waltteri Immonen, Jokerit
☐	55	Mika Stromberg, Jokerit
☐	56	Keijo Sailynoja, Jokerit
☐	57	Otakar Janecky, Jokerit
☐	58	Jiri Sejba, Jokerit
☐	59	Kari Martikainen, Jokerit
☐	60	Erik Hamalainen, Jokerit
☐	61	Timo Norppa, Jokerit
☐	62	Pekka Jarvela, Jokerit
☐	63	Juha Salo, Jokerit
☐	64	Heikki Riihijarvi, Jokerit
☐	65	Ari Salo, Jokerit
☐	66	Hannu Jarvenpaa, Jokerit
☐	67	Jali Wahlsten, Jokerit
☐	68	Juha Jokiharju, Jokerit
☐	69	Hannu Aravirta, Jypht Jyvaskyla
☐	70	Ari-Pekka Siekkinen (G), Jypht Jyvaskyla
☐	71	Jarmo Jokilahti, Jypht Jyvaskyla
☐	72	Harri Laurila, Jypht Jyvaskyla
☐	73	Juha Riihijarvi, Jypht Jyvaskyla
☐	74	Jari Lindroos, Jypht Jyvaskyla
☐	75	Marko Virtanen, Jypht Jyvaskyla
☐	76	Jari Munck, Jypht Jyvaskyla
☐	77	Markku Heikkinen, Jypht Jyvaskyla
☐	78	Lasse Nieminen, Jypht Jyvaskyla
☐	79	Tero Lehikoinen, Jypht Jyvaskyla
☐	80	Ari Haanpaa, Jypht Jyvaskyla
☐	81	Jarmo Rantanen, Jypht Jyvaskyla
☐	82	VeliPekka Hard, Jypht Jyvaskyla
☐	83	Mika Paananen, Jypht Jyvaskyla
☐	84	Joni Lius, Jypht Jyvaskyla
☐	85	Risto Kurkinen, Jypht Jyvaskyla
☐	86	Juha Junno, Kalpa Kuopio
☐	87	Pasi Kuivalainen (G), Kalpa Kuopio
☐	88	Jari Jarvinen, Kalpa Kuopio
☐	89	Vesa Salo, Kalpa Kuopio
☐	90	Vesa Karjalainen, Kalpa Kuopio
☐	91	Darius Rusnak, Kalpa Kuopio
☐	92	Arto Sirvio, Kalpa Kuopio
☐	93	Vesa Ruotsalainen, Kalpa Kuopio
☐	94	Juha Tuohimaa, Kalpa Kuopio

	No.	Player
☐	95	Jari Hamalainen, Kalpa Kuopio
☐	96	Pekka Tirkkonen, Kalpa Kuopio
☐	97	Jari Laukkanen, Kalpa Kuopio
☐	98	Antti Tuomenoksa, Kalpa Kuopio
☐	99	Janne Leppanen, Kalpa Kuopio
☐	100	Marko Jantunen, Kalpa Kuopio
☐	101	Dusan Pasek, Kalpa Kuopio
☐	102	Sami Kapanen, Kalpa Kuopio
☐	103	Martti Merra, Kiekkoespoo
☐	104	Sami Aikaa (G), Kiekkoespoo
☐	105	Teemu Sillanpaa, Kiekkoespoo
☐	106	Sami Nuutinen, Kiekkoespoo
☐	107	Jere Lehtinen, Kiekkoespoo
☐	108	Jan Langbacka, Kiekkoespoo
☐	109	Tero Lehtera, Kiekkoespoo
☐	110	Robert Salo, Kiekkoespoo
☐	111	Jimi Helin, Kiekkoespoo
☐	112	Sami Kokko, Kiekkoespoo
☐	113	Riku Kuusisto, Kiekkoespoo
☐	114	Markku Tiinus, Kiekkoespoo
☐	115	Pasi Heinisto, Kiekkoespoo
☐	116	Petri Pulkkinen, Kiekkoespoo
☐	117	Tom Laaksonen, Kiekkoespoo
☐	118	Jarmo Muukkonen, Kiekkoespoo
☐	119	Petro Koivunen, Kiekkoespoo
☐	120	Matti Keinonen, Rauman Kukko
☐	121	Petr Briza (G), Rauman Kukko
☐	122	Timo Kulonen, Rauman Kukko
☐	123	Allan Measures, Rauman Kukko
☐	124	Harri Suvanto, Rauman Kukko
☐	125	Timo Saarikoski, Rauman Kukko
☐	126	Mika Alatalo, Rauman Kukko
☐	127	Kari-Pekka Friman, Rauman Kukko
☐	128	Jarmo Kuusisto, Rauman Kukko
☐	129	Mika Valila, Rauman Kukko
☐	130	Jari Torkki, Rauman Kukko
☐	131	Pekka Peltola, Rauman Kukko
☐	132	Pasi Huura, Rauman Kukko
☐	133	Matti Forss, Rauman Kukko
☐	134	Kalle Sahlstedt, Rauman Kukko
☐	135	Tommi Pullola, Rauman Kukko
☐	136	Tero Arkiomaa, Rauman Kukko
☐	137	Esko Nokelainen, Reipas Lahti
☐	138	Petri Engman (G), Reipas Lahti
☐	139	Timo Kahelin, Reipas Lahti
☐	140	Pasi Ruponen, Reipas Lahti
☐	141	Petteri Sihvonen, Reipas Lahti
☐	142	Toni Sihvonen, Reipas Lahti
☐	143	Sami Wikstrom, Reipas Lahti
☐	144	Erik Kakko, Reipas Lahti
☐	145	Jari Parviainen, Reipas Lahti
☐	146	Jonni Vauhkonen, Reipas Lahti
☐	147	Jari Kauppila, Reipas Lahti
☐	148	Erkki Makela, Reipas Lahti
☐	149	Jarkko Hamalainen, Reipas Lahti
☐	150	Petri Koski, Reipas Lahti
☐	151	Sami Lekkerimaki, Reipas Lahti
☐	152	Toni Koivunen, Reipas Lahti
☐	153	Jani Uski, Reipas Lahti
☐	154	Pertti Hasanen, Tappara
☐	155	Jaromir Sindel (G), Tappara
☐	156	Tommi Haapsaari, Tappara
☐	157	Jukka Marttila, Tappara
☐	158	Jarmo Kekalainen, Tappara
☐	159	Tommi Pohja, Tappara
☐	160	Pauli Jarvinen, Tappara
☐	161	Timo Jutila, Tappara
☐	162	Janne Gronvall, Tappara
☐	163	Jussi-Pekka Jarvinen, Tappara
☐	164	Kari Heikkinen, Tappara
☐	165	Marko Ek, Tappara
☐	166	VeliPekka Kautonen, Tappara
☐	167	Pekka Laksola, Tappara
☐	168	Pasi Forsberg, Tappara
☐	169	Marko Lapinkoski, Tappara
☐	170	Mikko Peltola, Tappara
☐	171	Vladimir Yursinov, Turun Palloseura
☐	172	Jouni Rokama (G), Turun Palloseura
☐	173	Mikko Haapakoski, Turun Palloseura
☐	174	Kari Harila, Turun Palloseura
☐	175	Kari Kanervo, Turun Palloseura
☐	176	Esa Keskinen, Turun Palloseura
☐	177	Saku Koivu, Turun Palloseura
☐	178	Jouko Narvanmaa, Turun Palloseura
☐	179	Alexander Smirnov, Turun Palloseura
☐	180	Reijo Mikkolainen, Turun Palloseura
☐	181	Mikko Makela, Turun Palloseura
☐	182	Raimo Summanen, Turun Palloseura
☐	183	Hannu Virta, Turun Palloseura
☐	184	Jukka Virtanen, Turun Palloseura
☐	185	German Titov, Turun Palloseura
☐	186	Jukka Vilander, Turun Palloseura
☐	187	Ari Vuori, Turun Palloseura
☐	188	Vasili Tihonov, Assat Pori
☐	189	Kari Takko (G), Assat Pori
☐	190	Sami Saarinen, Assat Pori
☐	191	Marko Sten, Assat Pori
☐	192	Arto Javanainen, Assat Pori
☐	193	Janne Virtanen, Assat Pori
☐	194	Arto Heiskanen, Assat Pori
☐	195	Jouni Vento, Assat Pori
☐	196	Olli Kaski, Assat Pori
☐	197	Vjatseslav Fandul, Assat Pori
☐	198	Jokke Heinanen, Assat Pori
☐	199	Petri Varis, Assat Pori
☐	200	Harry Nikander, Assat Pori
☐	201	Jarno Miikkulainen, Assat Pori
☐	202	Jari Korpisalo, Assat Pori
☐	203	Rauli Raitanen, Assat Pori
☐	204	Jari Levonen, Assat Pori

1992 - 93 KELLOGG'S POSTERS

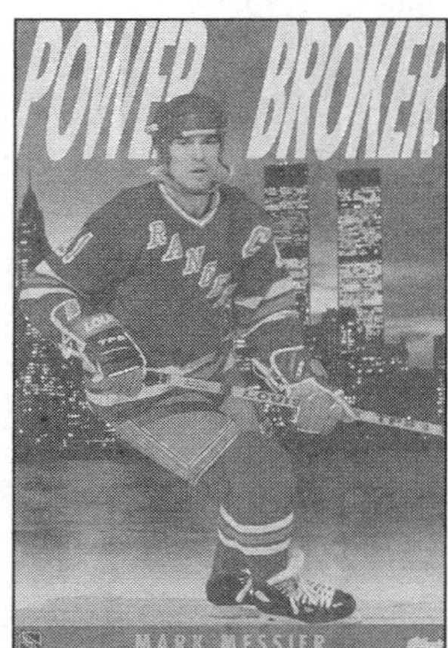

This 5-poster set was inserted in specially marked boxes of Kellogg's Corn Flakes of 525g and 675g sizes. The set has four NHL superstars and features Kellogg's Cornelius Rooster. The posters are bilingual, one side English the other French. There were 700,000 of each poster produced and distributed.

Poster Size: 9 1/4" x 14 1/8"

Imprint: *Registered trademark of /*Marque deposee de KELLOGG'S CANADA INC. 1992

Complete Set (5 posters): 15.00

	Player	NRMT-MT
☐	Mario Lemieux, Man of Steel / L'Homme de Fer	5.00
☐	Mark Messier, Power Broker / LA Super Star	3.00
☐	Luc Robitaille, Robo Shot / Le Coupe De Maitre	2.00
☐	Patrick Roy (G), "Road Block" / Le Baraque	5.00
☐	Cornelius Rooster, "Frequent Flyer" / Vol-Au-Vent	1.00

1992 - 93 KELLOGG'S TROPHIES

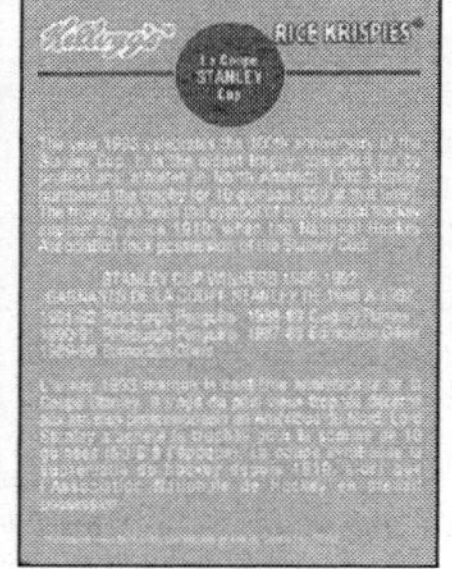

Card Size: 2 1/2" x 3 1/2"

Imprint: *Registered trademark of /*Marque déposée de KELLOGG'S CANADA INC. 1992

Complete Set (11 cards): 5.00

	No.	Trophy	NRMT-MT
☐	1	Stanley Cup	1.00
☐	2	Presidents' Trophy	.50
☐	3	Hart Memorial Trophy	.50
☐	4	Conn Smythe Trophy	.50
☐	5	Vezina Trophy	.50
☐	6	James Norris Memorial Trophy	.50
☐	7	Calder Memorial Trophy	.50
☐	8	Frank J. Selke Trophy	.50
☐	9	Lady Byng Trophy	.50
☐	10	Art Ross Trophy	.50
☐	11	Jack Adams Award	.50

1992 - 93 KRAFT

Complete Set (48 cards): 75.00

Album: 25.00

TEAM PANELS

One of 24 different team photos were found on the back of specially marked Kraft Dinner boxes.

Panel Size: 3 1/2" x 5 1/4"

	Team	NRMT-MT
☐	Boston Bruins, 1924-1993	1.25
☐	Buffalo Sabres, 1970-1993	1.25
☐	Calgary Flames	1.25
☐	Chicago Blackhawks, 1926-1993	1.25
☐	Detroit Red Wings, 1926-1993	1.25
☐	Edmonton Oilers	1.25
☐	Hartford Whalers	1.25
☐	Los Angeles Kings, 1967-1993	1.25
☐	Minnesota North Stars, 1967-1993	1.25
☐	Montréal Canadiens, 1917-1993	1.25
☐	New Jersey Devils	1.25
☐	New York Islander	1.25
☐	New York Rangers, 1926-1993	1.25
☐	Ottawa Senators, 1992-1993	1.25
☐	Philadelphia Flyers	1.25
☐	Pittsburgh Penguins	1.25
☐	Québec Nordiques, 1979-1993	1.25
☐	St. Louis Blues	1.25
☐	San Jose Sharks	1.25
☐	Tampa Bay Lightning	1.25
☐	Toronto Maple Leafs	1.25
☐	Vancouver Canucks, 1970-1993	1.25
☐	Washington Capitals	1.25
☐	Winnipeg Jets	1.25

GOALIE DISKS

One of 12 different disks were found under the lids of specially marked jars of Kraft Peanut Butter.

Disk Diameter: 2 1/2"

	Player	NRMT-MT
☐	Andy Moog (G)/ Mark Fitzpatrick (G)	1.50
☐	Dominik Hasek (G)/ Chris Terreri (G)	3.50

☐	Mike Vernon (G)/ Ed. Belfour (G)	2.00
☐	Tim Cheveldae (G)/ Sean Burke (G)	1.50
☐	Bill Ranford (G)/ Kelly Hrudey (G)	1.50
☐	Jon Casey (G)/ Dominic Roussel (G)	1.50
☐	Patrick Roy (G)/ John Vanbiesbrouk (G)	7.50
☐	Peter Sidorkiewicz (G)/ Grant Fuhr (G)	1.50
☐	Tom Barrasso (G)/ Wendal Young (G)	1.50
☐	Ron Hextall (G)/ Curtis Joseph (G)	3.00
☐	Jeff Hackett (G)/ Kirk McLean (G)	1.50
☐	Don Beaupré (G)/ Bob Essensa (G)	1.50

ALL-STAR PANELS

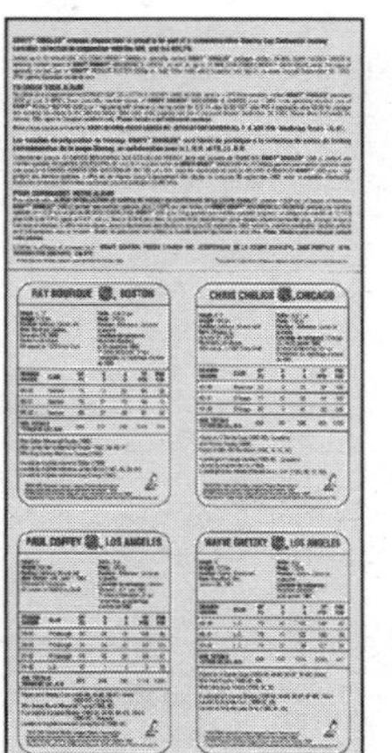

One of 3 different panels was found in specially marked packages of Kraft Singles. Each panel could be cut out into 4 cards each measuring 1 3/4" x 2 1/2". Gretzky is the most expensive cut-out single at $5.00.

Panel Size: 3 1/2" x 7 1/2"

	Player	NRMT-MT
☐	Chris Chelios, Chi/ Wayne Gretzky, L.A. Ray Bourque, Bos./ Paul Coffey, L.A.	8.00
☐	Brett Hull, Stl./ Trevor Linden, Van. Jaromir Jagr, Pgh./ Mario Lemieux, Pgh.	7.00
☐	Jeremy Roenick, Chi./ Steve Yzerman, Det. Mark Messier, NYR./ Patrick Roy (G), Mtl.	6.50

1992 - 93 McDONALD'S TRANSFERS

Imprint: None
Complete Set (26 transfers): 20.00
Common Team: 1.00

☐	Boston Bruins	☐	Buffalo Sabres
☐	Calgary Flames	☐	Chicago Blackhawks
☐	Dallas Stars	☐	Detroit Red Wings
☐	Edmonton Oilers	☐	Hartford Whalers
☐	Los Angeles Kings	☐	Montréal Canadiens
☐	New Jersey Devils	☐	New York Islanders
☐	New York Rangers	☐	Ottawa Senators
☐	Philadelphia Flyers	☐	Pittsburgh Penguins
☐	Québec Nordiques	☐	St. Louis Blues
☐	San Jose Sharks	☐	Tampa Bay Lightning
☐	Toronto Maple Leafs	☐	Vancouver Canucks
☐	Washington Capitals	☐	Winnipeg Jets

1992 - 93 McDONALD'S - UPPER DECK

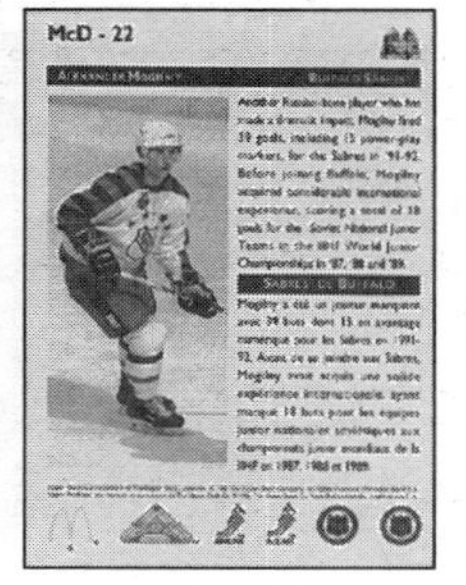

Imprint: 1992 The Upper Deck Co.
Complete Set (34 cards): 25.00

No.	Holograms	NRMT-MT
☐ McH01	Mark Messier, NYR.	3.00
☐ McH02	Brett Hull, Stl.	3.00
☐ McH03	Kevin Stevens, Pgh.	2.00
☐ McH04	Ray Bourque, Bos.	3.00
☐ McH05	Brian Leetch, NYR.	2.50
☐ McH06	Patrick Roy (G), Mtl.	5.00
No.	**All-Stars**	**NRMT-MT**
☐	Checklist	.50
☐ McD01	Ed Belfour (G), Chi.	.75
☐ McD02	Brian Bellows, Mtl.	.35
☐ McD03	Chris Chelios, Chi.	.75
☐ McD04	Vincent Damphousse, Mtl.	.50
☐ McD05	David Ellet, Tor.	.35
☐ McD06	Sergei Fedorov, Det.	1.00
☐ McD07	Theoren Fleury, Cgy.	.75
☐ McD08	Phil Housley, Wpg.	.35
☐ McD09	Trevor Linden, Van.	.50
☐ McD10	Al MacInnis, Cgy.	.50
☐ McD11	Adam Oates, Bos	.75
☐ McD12	Luc Robitaille, L.A.	.50
☐ McD13	Jeremy Roenick, Chi.	.75
☐ McD14	Steve Yzerman, Det.	1.75
☐ McD15	Don Beaupré (G), Wsh.	.35
☐ McD16	Rod Brind'Amour, Pha.	.50
☐ McD17	Paul Coffey, Det.	.50
☐ McD18	John Cullen, Tor.	.35
☐ McD19	Kevin Hatcher, Wsh.	.35
☐ McD20	Jaromir Jagr, Pgh.	1.75
☐ McD21	Mario Lemieux, Pgh.	2.75
☐ McD22	Alexander Mogilny, Buf.	.75
☐ McD23	Kirk Muller, Mtl.	.35
☐ McD24	Owen Nolan, Que.	.50
☐ McD25	Mike Richter (G), NYR.	.75
☐ McD26	Joe Sakic, Que.	1.50
☐ McD27	Scott Stevens, N.J.	.50

1992 - 93 MPS PHOTOGRAPHICS SASKATCHEWAN JUNIOR HOCKEY LEAGUE

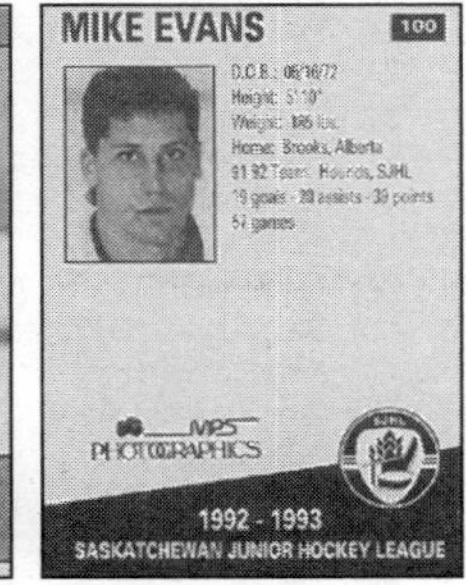

This 168-card set represents the players of the 1992-93 Saskatchewan Junior Hockey League.

Imprint:
Complete Set (168 cards): 30.00
Common Player: .15

	No.	Player	NRMT-MT
☐	1	Troy Edwards, Estevan Bruins	.15
☐	2	Simon Olivier, Estevan Bruins	.15
☐	3	Gerald Tallaire, Estevan Bruins	.15
☐	4	Blair Allison (G), Estevan Bruins	.25
☐	5	Mads True, Estevan Bruins	.15
☐	6	Steve Brent, Estevan Bruins	.15
☐	7	Jay Dobrescu, Estevan Bruins	.15
☐	8	Dave Debusschere, Estevan Bruins	.15
☐	9	Bryan Cossette, Estevan Bruins	.15
☐	10	Brooke Battersby, Estevan Bruins	.15
☐	11	Kyle Niemegeers, Estevan Bruins	.15
☐	12	Darren McLean, Estevan Bruins	.15
☐	13	Carson Cardinal, Estevan Bruins	.15
☐	14	Bill McKay, Estevan Bruins	.15
☐	15	Chris Hatch, Flin Flon Bombers	.15
☐	16	Nolan Weir, Flin Flon Bombers	.15
☐	17	Karl Johnson, Flin Flon Bombers	.15
☐	18	Jason Brown, Flin Flon Bombers	.15
☐	19	Tyler Kuhn, Flin Flon Bombers	.15
☐	20	Daniel Dennis (G), Flin Flon Bombers	.15
☐	21	Wally Spence, Flin Flon Bombers	.15
☐	22	Rob Beck, Flin Flon Bombers	.15
☐	23	Aaron Cain, Flin Flon Bombers	.15
☐	24	Darryl Dickson, Flin Flon Bombers	.15
☐	25	Travis Cheyne, Flin Flon Bombers	.15
☐	26	Mark Leoppky, Flin Flon Bombers	.15
☐	27	Jason Ahenakew, Flin Flon Bombers	.15
☐	28	Kyle Paul, Flin Flon Bombers	.15
☐	29	Dean Normand, Humboldt Broncos	.15
☐	30	Brett Kinaschuk, Humboldt Broncos	.15
☐	31	Darren Schmidt, Humboldt Broncos	.15
☐	32	Chris Schinkel (G), Humboldt Broncos	.25
☐	33	David Foster, Humboldt Broncos	.15
☐	34	Jason Zimmerman, Humboldt Broncos	.15
☐	35	Tom Perry, Humboldt Broncos	.15
☐	36	Kent Kinsachuk, Humboldt Broncos	.15
☐	37	Colin Froese, Humboldt Broncos	.15
☐	38	Shawn Zimmerman, Humboldt Broncos	.15
☐	39	Lary Empey, Humboldt Broncos	.15
☐	40	Curtis Knight, Humboldt Broncos	.15
☐	41	Blake Shipley, Humboldt Broncos	.15
☐	42	Cory Heon, Humboldt Broncos	.15
☐	43	Steve Pashulka, Melfort Mustangs	.15
☐	44	Rob Kinch, Melville Millionaires	.15
☐	45	Dean Gerard, Melfort Mustangs	.15
☐	46	Matt Desmarais, Melfort Mustangs	.15
☐	47	Chad Rusnak, Melfort Mustangs	.15
☐	48	Brad Bagu, Melfort Mustangs	.15
☐	49	Cam Bristow, Melfort Mustangs	.15
☐	50	Derek Simonson, Melfort Mustangs	.15
☐	51	Ken Ruddock, Melfort Mustangs	.15
☐	52	Tyler Deis, Melfort Mustangs	.15
☐	53	Steve Tansowny (G), Melfort Mustangs	.25
☐	54	Bill Stait, Melfort Mustangs	.15
☐	55	Garfield Henderson, Melfort Mustangs	.15
☐	56	Lonny Deobald, Melfort Mustangs	.15
☐	57	Lyle Ehrmantraut, Minot Americans	.15
☐	58	Layne Humenny, Flin Flon Bombers	.15
☐	59	Darren Balcombe, Minot Americans	.15
☐	60	Jeff McCutheon, Minot Americans	.15
☐	61	Trevor Wathen, Minot Americans	.15
☐	62	Derek Wynne, Minot Americans	.15
☐	63	Matt Russo, Minot Americans	.15
☐	64	Bruce Matatall, Minot Americans	.15
☐	65	Derek Crimin, Minot Americans	.15
☐	66	Chad Crumley, Minot Americans	.15
☐	67	Mike Hillock, Minot Americans	.15
☐	68	Art Houghton (G), Minot Americans	.25
☐	69	Lee Materi, Minot Americans	.15
☐	70	Nick Dyhr, Minot Americans	.15
☐	71	Darren Maloney, Melville Millionaires	.15
☐	72	Kurtise Souchotte, Melville Millionaires	.15
☐	73	Noel Kamel, Melville Millionaires	.15
☐	74	Trent Harper, Melville Millionaires	.15
☐	75	Ted Grayling, Melville Millionaires	.15
☐	76	Keith Harris, Melville Millionaires	.15
☐	77	Corri Moffat, Melville Millionaires	.15
☐	78	Travis Vantighem, Melville Millionaires	.15
☐	79	Darren Houghton, Melville Millionaires	.15
☐	80	Wade Welte, Melville Millionaires	.15
☐	81	Dave Doucet, Melville Millionaires	.15
☐	82	Jason Prokopetz, Melville Millionaires	.15
☐	83	Gordon McCann, Melville Millionaires	.15
☐	84	Clint Hooge (G), Melville Millionaires	.25
☐	85	Glen McGillvary, North Battleford North Stars	.15
☐	86	Regan Simpson, North Battleford North Stars	.15
☐	87	Mike Masse, North Battleford North Stars	.15
☐	88	Jeremy Procyshyn, North Battleford North Stars	.15
☐	89	Jim Nellis, North Battleford North Stars	.15

No.	Player	Price
90	Todd Kozak, North Battleford North Stars	.15
91	Brent Hoiness, North Battleford North Stars	.15
92	Josh Welter, Wilkie Youngbloods	.15
	Jason Welter, Wilkie Youngbloods	.15
93	Eldon Barker, Trainer, Weyburn Red Wings	.15
94	Duane Vandale, North Battleford North Stars	.15
95	Brad McEwen, Coach, Melville Millionaires	.15
96	Trent Tibbatts, North Battleford North Stars	.15
97	Jody Reiter, North Battleford North Stars	.15
98	Greg Moore, North Battleford North Stars	.15
99	Jon Rowe, Notre Dame Hounds	.15
100	Mike Evans, Notre Dame Hounds	.15
101	Jason Krug, Notre Dame Hounds	.15
102	Jon Bracco (G), Notre Dame Hounds	.25
103	Ryan Sandholm, Notre Dame Hounds	.15
104	Darryl Sangster, Notre Dame Hounds	.15
105	Brett Colborne, Notre Dame Hounds	.15
106	Dean Moore, Notre Dame Hounds	.15
107	Chris Dechaine, Notre Dame Hounds	.15
108	Steve McKenna, Notre Dame Hounds	.25
109	Tony Bergin, Notre Dame Hounds	.15
110	Tim Murray, Notre Dame Hounds	.15
111	Casey Kesselring, Notre Dame Hounds	.15
112	Todd Barth, Notre Dame Hounds	.15
113	Ryan McConnell, Nipawin Hawks	.15
114	Ian Adamson, Nipawin Hawks	.15
115	Warren Pickford, Nipawin Hawks	.15
116	Todd Murphy, Nipawin Hawks	.15
117	Rob Phillips, Nipawin Hawks	.15
118	Trevor Demmans, Nipawin Hawks	.15
119	Jeff Greenwood, Nipawin Hawks	.15
120	Kevin Messer, Nipawin Hawks	.15
121	Dion Johnson, Nipawin Hawks	.15
122	Rejean Stringer, Nipawin Hawks	.15
123	Scott Mead, Nipawin Hawks	.15
124	Jeff Lawson, Nipawin Hawks	.15
125	Scot Newberry, Nipawin Hawks	.15
126	Bill Reid, Melfort Mustangs	.15
127	Chris Winkler, Saskatoon Titans	.15
128	Kyle Girgan, Saskatoon Titans	.15
129	Trevor Warrener, Saskatoon Titans	.15
130	Richard Boscher (G), Saskatoon Titans	.25
131	Tom Thomson, Saskatoon Titans	.15
132	Mike Wevers, Saskatoon Titans	.15
133	Barton Holt, Saskatoon Titans	.15
134	Kent Rogers, Saskatoon Titans	.15
135	Richard Gibbs, Saskatoon Titans	.15
136	Jared Witt, Saskatoon Titans	.15
137	Jamie Stelmak, Saskatoon Titans	.15
138	Greg Wahl, Saskatoon Titans	.15
139	J. Sotropa, Saskatoon Titans	.15
140	Mark Pivetz, Saskatoon Titans	.15
141	Travis Kirby (G), Weyburn Red Wings	.25
142	Jason Scanzano, Weyburn Red Wings	.15
143	Tyson Balog, Weyburn Red Wings	.15
144	Daryl Krauss, Weyburn Red Wings	.15
145	Mike Harder, Weyburn Red Wings	.15
146	Tyler McMillan, Weyburn Red Wings	.15
147	Darcy Herlick, Weyburn Red Wings	.15
148	Dave Zwyer, Weyburn Red Wings	.15
149	Craig McKechnie, Weyburn Red Wings	.15
150	Cam Cook, Weyburn Red Wings	.15
151	Derek Bruselinck, Weyburn Red Wings	.15
152	Travis Smith, Weyburn Red Wings	.15
153	Daryl Jones, Weyburn Red Wings	.15
154	Mike Savard (G), Weyburn Red Wings	.25
155	Jeremy Matthies, Yorkton Terriers	.15
156	Michel Cook, Yorkton Terriers	.15
157	Leigh Brookbank, Yorkton Terriers	.15
158	Christian Dutil (G), Yorkton Terriers	.25
159	Scott Heshka, Yorkton Terriers	.15
160	Danny Galarneau, Yorkton Terriers	.15
161	Jamie Dunn, Yorkton Terriers	.15
162	Nigel Werenka, Yorkton Terriers	.15
163	Steve Sabo, Yorkton Terriers	.15
164	Tony Toth, Yorkton Terriers	.15
165	Sebastien Moreau, Yorkton Terriers	.15
166	Tim Slukynsky, Yorkton Terriers	.15
167	Sheldon Bylsma, Yorkton Terriers	.15
168	Stacy Prevost, Yorkton Terriers	.15

1992 - 93 O-PEE-CHEE

The 1992-93 season was the 25th Anniversary of continuous hockey card production by O-Pee-Chee.

O-Pee-Chee (396 cards): 18.00
Factory Set Price (396 cards): 25.00
25th Anniversary Factory Set: 85.00
Common Player: .10
9-Card Promo Sheet: 15.00

No.	Player	NRMT-MT
1	Kevin Todd, N.J.	.10
2	Robert Kron, Van.	.10
3	David Volek, NYI.	.10
4	Teppo Numminen, Wpg.	.10
5	Paul Coffey, L.A.	.25
6	Luc Robitaille, L.A.	.25
7	Steven Finn, Que.	.10
8	**Gord Hynes, Bos., RC**	**.10**
9	Dave Ellett, Tor.	.10
10	Alexander Godynyuk, Cgy.	.10
11	Darryl Sydor, L.A.	.10
12	Randy Carlyle, Wpg.	.10
13	Chris Chelios, Chi.	.35
14	Kent Manderville, Tor.	.10
15	Wayne Gretzky, L.A.	1.50
16	Jon Casey (G), Min.	.10
17	Mark Tinordi, Min.	.10
18	Dale Hunter, Wsh.	.10
19	Martin Gelinas, Edm.	.10
20	Todd Elik, Min.	.10
21	Bob Sweeney, Bos.	.10
22	Chris Dahlquist, Min.	.10
23	Joe Mullen, Pgh.	.10
24	Shawn Burr, Det.	.10
25	Pavel Bure, Van.	.50
26	Randy Gilhen, NYR.	.10
27	Brian Bradley, Tor. (T.B.)	.10
28	Don Beaupré (G), Wsh.	.10
29	Kevin Stevens, Pgh.	.10
30	Michal Pivonka, Wsh.	.10
31	Grant Fuhr (G), Tor.	.25
32	Steve Larmer, Chi.	.25
33	Gary Leeman, Cgy.	.10
34	Tony Tanti, Buf.	10
35	Denis Savard, Mtl.	.25
36	Paul Ranheim, Cgy.	.10
37	Andrei Lomakin, Pha.	.10
38	Perry Anderson, S.J.	.10
39	Stu Barnes, Wpg.	.10
40	Don Sweeney, Bos.	.10
41	Jamie Baker, Que.	.10
42	Ray Ferraro, NYI.	.10
43	Bobby Clarke, (1970 Style)	.35
44	Kelly Hrudey (G), L.A.	.10
45	Brian Skrudland, Mtl.	.10
46	Paul Ysebaert, Det.	.10
47	Pierre Turgeon, NYI.	.25
48	Keith Brown, Chi.	.10
49	Rod Brind'Amour, Pha.	.25
50	Wayne McBean, NYI.	.10
51	Doug Lidster, Van.	.10
52	Bernie Nicholls, Edm.	.10
53	Daren Puppa (G), Buf.	.10
54	Joe Sakic, Que.	.60
55	Joe Sakic, (1989 Style)	.60
56	Dave Manson, Edm.	.10
57	Denis Potvin, NYI. (1974 Style)	.35
58	Daniel Marois, Mtl.	.10
59	Martin Brodeur (G), N.J.	.50
60	Brent Sutter, Chi.	.10
61	Steve Yzerman, Det.	.75
62	Neal Broten, Min.	.10
63	Darcy Wakaluk (G), Min.	.10
64	Troy Murray, Wpg.	.10
65	Tony Granato, L.A.	.10
66	Frantisek Musil, Cgy.	.10
67	Claude Lemieux, N.J.	.10
68	Brian Benning, Pha.	.10
69	Stéphane Matteau, Chi.	.10
70	Tomas Forslund, Cgy.	.10
71	Dimitri Mironov, Tor.	.10
72	Gary Roberts, Cgy.	.25
73	Félix Potvin (G), Tor.	.35
74	Glenn Murray, Bos.	.10
75	Stéphane Fiset (G), Que.	.25
76	Stéphane Richer, N.J.	.10
77	Jeff Reese (G), Cgy.	.10
78	Marc Bureau, Min.	.10
79	Derek King, NYI.	.10
80	Dave Gagner, Min.	.10
81	Ed Belfour (G), Chi.	.25
82	Joel Otto, Cgy.	.10
83	Anatoli Semenov, Edm. (T.B.)	.10
84	Ron Hextall (G), Que.	.25
85	Adam Creighton, NYI.	.10
86	Kris King, NYR.	.10
87	Brett Hull, Stl.	.35
88	Zdeno Ciger, N.J.	.10
89	Petr Nedved, Van.	.10
90	Sergei Makarov, Cgy.	.10
91	Tomas Sandström, L.A.	.10
92	Steve Heinze, Bos.	.10
93	Robert Reichel, Cgy.	.10
94	Cliff Ronning, Van.	.10
95	Eric Weinrich, N.J.	.10
96	Wendel Clark, Tor.	.25
97	Rick Zombo, Stl.	.10
98	Ric Nattress, Tor.	.10
99	Theoren Fleury, Cgy.	.25
100	Joe Murphy, Edm.	.10
101	Gord Murphy, Bos.	.10
102	Jaromir Jagr, Pgh.	.75
103	Mike Craig, Min.	.10
104	John Cullen, Hfd.	.10
105	John Druce, Wsh.	.10
106	Peter Bondra, Wsh.	.35
107	Bryan Trottier, (1976 Style)	.35
108	Steve Smith, Chi.	.10
109	Petr Svoboda, Buf.	.10
110	Mats Sundin, Que.	.35
111	Patrick Roy (G), (1986 Style)	2.50
112	Stephen Leach, Bos.	.10
113	Jacques Cloutier (G), Que.	.10
114	Doug Weight, NYR.	.25
115	Frank Pietrangelo (G), Hfd.	.10
116	**Guy Hebert (G), Stl., RC**	**.75**
117	Donald Audette, Buf.	.10
118	Craig MacTavish, Edm.	.10
119	Grant Fuhr (G), (1982 Style)	.25
120	Trevor Linden, Van.	.25
121	Fredrick Olausson, Wpg.	.10
122	Geoff Sanderson, Hfd.	.10
123	Derian Hatcher, Min.	.25
124	Brett Hull, (1988 Style)	.35
125	Kelly Buchberger, Edm.	.10
126	Ray Bourque, Bos.	.35
127	Murray Craven, Hfd.	.10
128	Tim Cheveldae (G), Det.	.10
129	Ulf Dahlen, Min.	.10
130	Bryan Trottier, Pgh.	.25
131	Bob Carpenter, Bos. (Wsh.)	.10
132	Benoît Hogue, NYI.	.10
133	Claude Vilgrain, N.J.	.10
134	Glenn Anderson, Tor.	.10
135	Marty McInnis, NYI.	.10
136	Rob Pearson, Tor.	.10
137	Bill Ranford (G), Edm.	.25
138	Mario Lemieux, Pgh.	1.25
139	Bob Bassen, Stl.	.10
140	Scott Mellanby, Edm.	.10
141	Dave Andreychuk, Buf.	.25
142	Kelly Miller, Wsh.	.10
143	Gaetan Duchesne, Min.	.10
144	Mike Sullivan, S.J.	.10
145	Kevin Hatcher, Wsh.	.10

☐ 146 Doug Bodger, Buf. .10
☐ 147 Craig Berube, Cgy. .10
☐ 148 Rick Tocchet, Pgh. .10
☐ 149 Luciano Borsato, Wpg. .10
☐ 150 Glen Wesley, Bos. .10
☐ 151 Mike Donnelly, L.A. .10
☐ 152 Jimmy Carson, Det. .10
☐ 153 Jocelyn Lemieux, Chi. .10
☐ 154 Ray Sheppard, Det. .10
☐ 155 Tony Amonte, NYR. .25
☐ 156 Adrien Plavsic, Van. .10
☐ 157 Mark Pederson, Pha. .10
☐ 158 Adam Graves, NYR. .10
☐ 159 Igor Larionov, Van. .25
☐ 160 Steve Chiasson, Det. .10
☐ 161 Igor Kravchuk, Chi. .10
☐ 162 Viacheslav Fetisov, N.J. .25
☐ 163 Gerard Gallant, Det. .10
☐ 164 Patrick Roy (G), Mtl. 1.25
☐ 165 Ken Sutton, Buf. .10
☐ 166 Mathieu Schneider, Mtl. .10
☐ 167 Larry Robinson, (1973 Style) .35
☐ 168 Jim Sandlak, Van. .10
☐ 169 Joey Kocur, NYR. .10
☐ 170 Rob Brown, Chi. .10
☐ 171 Luke Richardson, Edm. .10
☐ 172 Adam Oates, (1987 Style) .25
☐ 173 Uwe Krupp, NYI. .10
☐ 174 Cam Neely, Bos. .25
☐ 175 Peter Sidorkiewicz (G), Ott. .10
☐ 176 Geoff Courtnall, Van. .10
☐ 177 Doug Gilmour, Tor. .25
☐ 178 Josef Beranek, Edm. .10
☐ 179 Michel Picard, Hfd. .10
☐ 180 Terry Carkner, Pha. .10
☐ 181 Nelson Emerson, Stl. .10
☐ 182 Perry Berezan, S.J. .10
☐ 183 Checklist C .10
☐ 184 Andy Moog (G), Bos. .25
☐ 185 Michel Petit, Cgy. .10
☐ 186 Mark Greig, Hfd. .10
☐ 187 Paul Coffey, (1981 Style) .25
☐ 188 Ron Francis, Pgh. .25
☐ 189 Joé Juneau, Bos. .10
☐ 190 Jeff Odgers, S.J. .10
☐ 191 Darry Sittler, (1975 Style) .35
☐ 192 Vincent Damphousse, Edm. .25
☐ 193 Greg Paslawski, Que. .10
☐ 194 Tony Esposito (G), (1969 Style) .35
☐ 195 Sergei Fedorov, Det. .35
☐ 196 Doug Smail, Que. .10
☐ 197 Pat Verbeek, Hfd. .10
☐ 198 Dominic Roussel (G), Pha. .10
☐ 199 Mike McPhee, Mtl. .10
☐ 200 Kevin Dineen, Pha. .10
☐ 201 Pat Elyniuk, Wpg. .10
☐ 202 Tom Kurvers, NYI. .10
☐ 203 Chris Joseph, Edm. .10
☐ 204 Mark Fitzpatrick (G), NYI. .10
☐ 205 Jari Kurri, L.A. .25
☐ 206 Guy Carbonneau, Mtl. .10
☐ 207 Jan Erixon, NYR. .10
☐ 208 Mark Messier, NYR. .35
☐ 209 Larry Murphy, Pgh. .25
☐ 210 Dirk Graham, Chi. .10
☐ 211 Ron Tugnutt (G), Edm. .10
☐ 212 Dale Hawerchuk, Buf. .25
☐ 213 Dave Babych, Van. .10
☐ 214 Mikael Andersson, Hfd. .10
☐ 215 James Patrick, NYR. .10
☐ 216 Peter Stastny, N.J. .10
☐ 217 Bernie Parent (G), (1968 Style) .35
☐ 218 Jeff Hackett (G), S.J. .10
☐ 219 Dave Lowry, Stl. .10
☐ 220 Wayne Gretzky, (1979 Style) 3.00
☐ 221 Brent Gilchrist, Mtl. .10
☐ 222 Andrew Cassels, Hfd. .10
☐ 223 Calle Johansson, Wsh. .10
☐ 224 Joe Reekie, NYI. (TB) .10
☐ 225 Craig Simpson, Edm. .10
☐ 226 Bob Essensa (G), Wpg. .10
☐ 227 Pat Falloon, S.J. .10
☐ 228 Vladimir Ruzicka, Bos. .10
☐ 229 Igor Ulanov, Wpg. .10
☐ 230 Kjell Samuelsson, Pgh. .10
☐ 231 Shayne Corson, Mtl. .25
☐ 232 Kelly Kisio, S.J. .10
☐ 233 Gord Roberts, (Bos.) .10
☐ 234 Brian Noonan, Chi. .10
☐ 235 Vyacheslav Kozlov, Det. .20
☐ 236 Checklist B .10
☐ 237 Jeff Beukeboom, NYR. .10
☐ 238 Steve Konroyd, Hfd. .10
☐ 239 Patrice Brisebois, Mtl. .10
☐ 240 MVP: Mario Lemieux, Pgh. .65
☐ 241 Dana Murzyn, Van. .10
☐ 242 Per-Erik Eklund, Pha. .10
☐ 243 Rob Blake, L.A. .25
☐ 244 Brendan Shanahan, Stl. .35
☐ 245 HL: Michael Gartner, NYR. .25
☐ 246 David Bruce, S.J. .10
☐ 247 Mike Vernon (G), Cgy. .25
☐ 248 Zarley Zalapski, Hfd. .10
☐ 249 Dino Ciccarelli, Wsh. (Det.) .25
☐ **250 David Williams, S.J., RC .10**
☐ 251 Scott Stevens, (1983 Style) .25
☐ 252 Bob Probert, Det. .10
☐ 253 Mikhail Tatarinov, Que. .10
☐ 254 Bobby Holik, Hfd. .10
☐ 255 Tony Amonte, (1991 Style) .25
☐ 256 Brad May, Buf. .10
☐ 257 Philippe Bozon, Stl. .10
☐ 258 Mark Messier, (1980 Style) .35
☐ 259 Mike Richter (G), NYR. .25
☐ 260 Brian Mullen, S.J. .10
☐ 261 Marty McSorley, L.A. .10
☐ 262 Glenn Healy (G), NYI. .10
☐ 263 Rus Romaniuk, Wpg. .10
☐ 264 Dan Quinn, Pha. .10
☐ 265 Jyrki Lumme, Van. .10
☐ 266 Valeri Kamensky, Que. .25
☐ 267 Vladimir Konstantinov, Det. .10
☐ 268 Peter Ahola, L.A. .10
☐ **269 Guy Larose, Tor., RC .10**
☐ 270 Ulf Samuelsson, Pgh. .10
☐ 271 Dale Craigwell, S.J. .10
☐ 272 Adam Oates, Bos. .25
☐ 273 Pat MacLeod, S.J. .10
☐ 274 Mike Keane, Mtl. .10
☐ 275 John Vanbiesbrouck (G), NYR. .35
☐ 276 Brian Lawton, S.J. .10
☐ 277 Sylvain Côté, Wsh. .10
☐ 278 Gary Suter, Cgy. .10
☐ 279 Alexander Mogilny, Buf. .25
☐ 280 Garth Butcher, Stl. .10
☐ 281 Doug Wilson, S.J. .10
☐ 282 Chris Terreri (G), N.J. .10
☐ 283 Phil Esposito, (1977 Style) .35
☐ 284 Russ Courtnall, Mtl. .10
☐ 285 Pat LaFontaine, Buf. .25
☐ 286 Dimitri Khristich, Wsh. .10
☐ **287 John LeBlanc, Wpg., RC .10**
☐ 288 Randy Velischek, Que. .10
☐ 289 Dave Christian, Stl. .10
☐ 290 Kevin Haller, Mtl. .10
☐ 291 Kevin Miller, Det. (Wsh.) .10
☐ 292 Mario Lemieux, (1985 Style) 2.50
☐ 293 Stéphan Lebeau, Mtl. .10
☐ 294 Marcel Dionne, (1971 Style) .35
☐ 295 Barry Pederson, Bos. .10
☐ 296 Steve Duchesne, Pha. (Que.) .10
☐ 297 Yves Racine, Det. .10
☐ 298 Phil Housley, Wpg. .10
☐ 299 Randy Ladouceur, Hfd. .10
☐ 300 Mike Gartner, NYR. .25
☐ 301 Dominik Hasek (G), Chi. .50
☐ 302 Kevin Lowe, Edm. .10
☐ 303 Sylvain Lefebvre, Mtl. .10
☐ 304 J. J. Daigneault, Mtl. .10
☐ 305 Mike Ridley, Wsh. .10
☐ 306 Curtis Leschyshyn, Que. .10
☐ 307 Gilbert Dionne, Mtl., .10
☐ **308 Bill Guerin, N.J., RC .25**
☐ 309 Gerald Diduck, Van. .10
☐ 310 Rick Wamsley (G), Tor. .10
☐ 311 Pat Jablonski (G), Stl. (Ott.) .10
☐ **312 Jayson More, S.J., RC .10**
☐ 313 Mike Modano, Min. .35
☐ 314 Checklist A .10
☐ 315 Sylvain Turgeon, Hfd. (Ott.) .10
☐ 316 Sergei Nemchinov, NYR. .10
☐ 317 Garry Galley, Pha. .10
☐ 318 HL: Paul Coffey, Pgh. .25
☐ 319 Esa Tikkanen, Edm. .10
☐ 320 Claude Lapointe, Que. .10
☐ 321 Steve Yzerman, (1984 Style) .75
☐ 322 Mark Lamb, Edm. (Ott.) .10
☐ 323 Bob Errey, Pgh. .10
☐ 324 Pavel Bure, (1992 Premier Style) .50
☐ 325 Craig Janney, Stl. .10
☐ 326 Bob Kudelski, L.A. .10
☐ 327 Kirk Muller, Mtl. .10
☐ 328 Jim Paek, Pgh. .10
☐ 329 Mike Ricci, Pha. (Que.) .10
☐ 330 Al MacInnis, Cgy. .25
☐ 331 Mike Hudson, Chi. .10
☐ 332 Darrin Shannon, Wpg. .10
☐ 333 Doug Brown, N.J. .10
☐ 334 Corey Mullen, L.A. .10
☐ 335 Mike Krushelnyski, Tor. .10
☐ 336 Scott Stevens, N.J. .25
☐ 337 Peter Zezel, Tor. .10
☐ 338 Geoff Smith, Edm. .10
☐ 339 Curtis Joseph (G), Stl. .35
☐ 340 Tom Barrasso (G), Pgh. .25
☐ 341 Al Iafrate, Wsh. .10
☐ 342 Patrick Flatley, NYI. .10
☐ 343 Gerry Cheevers (G), (1972 Style) .35
☐ 344 Norm Maciver, Edm. .10
☐ 345 Jeremy Roenick, Chi. .25
☐ 346 Keith Tkachuk, Wpg., Error .35
☐ 347 Rod Langway, Wsh. .10
☐ 348 HL: Ray Bourque, Bos. .25
☐ 349 Kirk McLean (G), Van. .25
☐ 350 Brian Propp, Min. .10
☐ 351 John Ogrodnick, NYR. .10
☐ 352 Benoît Brunet, Mtl. .10
☐ 353 Alexei Kasatonov, N.J. .10
☐ 354 Joe Nieuwendyk, Cgy. .25
☐ 355 Joe Sacco, Tor. .10
☐ 356 Tom Fergus, Van. .10
☐ 357 Dan Lambert, Que. .10
☐ 358 Michel Goulet, Chi. .10
☐ 359 Shawn McEachern, Pgh. .10
☐ 360 Eric Desjardins, Mtl. .25
☐ 361 Paul Stanton, Pgh. .10
☐ 362 Ron Sutter, Stl. .10
☐ 363 Derrick Smith, Min. .10
☐ 364 Paul Broten, NYR. .10
☐ 365 Greg Adams, Van. .10
☐ 366 Rob Zettler, S.J. .10
☐ 367 Dave Poulin, Bos. .10
☐ 368 Keith Acton, Pha. .10
☐ 369 Nicklas Lidström, Det. .25
☐ 370 Randy Burridge, Wsh. .10
☐ 371 Jamie Macoun, Tor. .10
☐ 372 Craig Billington (G), N.J. .10
☐ 373 Mark Recchi, Pha. .25
☐ 374 Kris Draper, Wpg. .10
☐ 375 Ed Olczyk, Wpg. .10
☐ 376 Tom Draper (G), Buf. .10
☐ 377 Sergio Momesso, Van. .10
☐ 378 Brian Leetch, NYR. .25
☐ 379 Paul Cavallini, Stl. .10
☐ 380 Paul Fenton, S.J. .10
☐ 381 Dean Evason, S.J. .10
☐ 382 Owen Nolan, Que. .25
☐ 383 Jeremy Roenick, (1990 Style) .25
☐ 384 Brian Bellows, Min. .10
☐ 385 Thomas Steen, Wpg. .10
☐ 386 John LeClair, Mtl. .35
☐ 387 Darren Turcotte, NYR. .10
☐ 388 James Black, Hfd. .10
☐ 389 Alexei Gusarov, Que. .10
☐ 390 Scott Lachance, NYI. .10
☐ 391 Mike Bossy, (1978 Style) .35
☐ 392 Mike Hough, Que. .10
☐ 393 Grant Ledyard .10
☐ 394 Tom Fitzgerald .10
☐ 395 Steve Thomas .10
☐ 396 Bobby Smith, Min. .10

25TH ANNIVERSARY

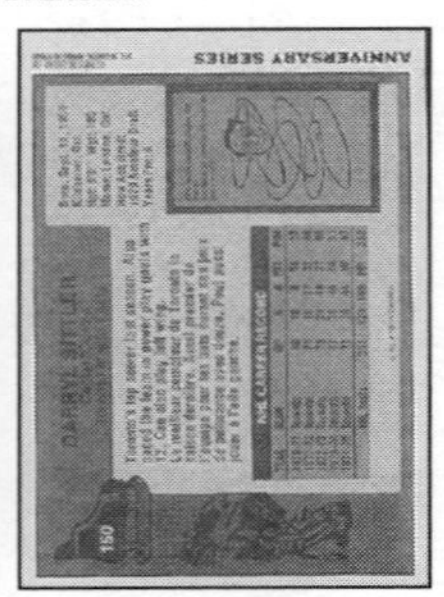

This one-per-pack inserts set features reproductions of twenty five years of O-Pee-Chee cards.

Insert Set (26 cards): 10.00

	No.	Player	NRMT-MT
☐	1	Bernie Parent (G), Pha.	.50
☐	2	Tony Esposito (G), Chi.	.50
☐	3	Bobby Clarke, Pha.	.50
☐	4	Marcel Dionne, Det.	.35
☐	5	Gerry Cheevers (G), Cincinatti	.35
☐	6	Larry Robinson, Mtl.	.35
☐	7	Denis Potvin, NYI.	.35
☐	8	Darryl Sittler, Tor.	.35
☐	9	Bryan Trottier, NYI.	.35
☐	10	Phil Esposito, NYR.	.50
☐	11	Mike Bossy, NYI.	.50
☐	12	Wayne Gretzky, Edm.	3.00
☐	13	Mark Messier, Edm.	.75
☐	14	Paul Coffey, Edm.	.25
☐	15	Grant Fuhr (G), Edm.	.25
☐	16	Scott Stevens, Wsh.	.25
☐	17	Steve Yzerman, Det.	1.50
☐	18	Mario Lemieux, Pgh.	2.50
☐	19	Patrick Roy (G), Mtl.	2.50
☐	20	Adam Oates, Det.	.25
☐	21	Brett Hull, Stl.	.75
☐	22	Joe Sakic, Que.	1.25
☐	23	Jeremy Roenick, Chi.	.25
☐	24	Tony Amonte, NYR.	.25
☐	25	Pavel Bure, Van.	1.00
☐		Checklist: 25th Anniversary Series	.25

BOX BOTTOMS

One of four different large size cards were found on the bottom of O-Pee-Chee boxes.

Card Size: 5" x 6 3/4"

Complete Set (4 cards): 8.00

	Player	NRMT-MT
☐	AW: Pavel Bure, Van.	2.50
☐	AW: Brian Leetch, NYR.	1.00
☐	AW: Mark Messier, NYR.	1.50
☐	AW: Patrick Roy (G), Mtl.	5.00

1992 - 93 O-PEE-CHEE PREMIER

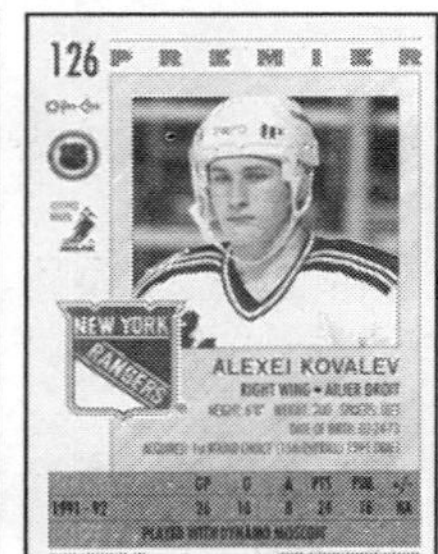

Imprint: © 1993 O-PEE-CHEE CO. LTD

Complete Set (132 cards): 10.00

Common Player: .10

	No.	Player	NRMT-MT
☐	1	Dave Christian, Chi.	.10
☐	2	Christian Ruuttu, Chi.	.10
☐	3	Vincent Damphousse, Mtl.	.25
☐	4	Chris Lindberg, Cgy.	.10
☐	**5**	**Bill Lindsay, Que., RC**	**.10**
☐	**6**	**Dmitri Kvartalnov, Bos., RC**	**.10**
☐	**7**	**Darcy Loewen, Ott., RC**	**.10**
☐	**8**	**Ed Courtenay, S.J., RC**	**.10**
☐	9	Sergei Krivokrasov, Chi.	.10
☐	10	Shawn Antoski, Van.	.10
☐	11	André Racicot (G), Mtl.	.10
☐	12	Marty McInnis, NYI.	.10
☐	13	Alexei Zhamnov, Wpg.	.25
☐	**14**	**Keith Jones, Wsh., RC**	**.10**
☐	**15**	**Steve Konowalchuk, Wsh., RC**	**.10**
☐	16	Darryl Sydor, L.A.	.10
☐	17	Janne Ojanen, N.J.	.10
☐	**18**	**Doug Zmolek, S.J., RC**	**.10**
☐	**19**	**Mikael Nylander, Hfd., RC**	**.10**
☐	20	Russ Courtnall, Min.	.10
☐	**21**	**Martin Straka, Pgh., RC**	**.10**
☐	**22**	**Kevin Dahl, Cgy., RC**	**.10**
☐	23	Kent Manderville, Tor.	.10
☐	24	Steve Heinze, Bos.	.10
☐	25	Philippe Bozon, Stl.	.10
☐	26	Brent Fedyk, Pha.	.10
☐	27	Kris Draper, Wpg.	.10
☐	28	Brad Schlegel, Wsh.	.10
☐	**29**	**Patrik Kjellberg, Mtl., RC**	**.10**
☐	30	Ted Donato, Bos.	.10
☐	**31**	**Vyacheslav Butsayev, Pha., RC**	**.10**
☐	32	Tyler Wright, Edm.	.10
☐	**33**	**Tom Pederson, S.J., RC**	**.10**
☐	**34**	**Jim Hiller, L.A., RC**	**.10**
☐	**35**	**Chris Luongo, Ott., RC**	**.10**
☐	**36**	**Robert Petrovicky, Hfd, RC**	**.10**
☐	**37**	**Jean-François Quintin, S.J., RC**	**.10**
☐	38	Chris Dahlquist, Cgy.	.10
☐	**39**	**Daniel Laperrière, Stl., RC**	**.10**
☐	**40**	**Guy Hebert (G), Stl., RC**	**.50**
☐	**41**	**Ed Ronan, Mtl., RC**	**.10**
☐	42	Shawn Cronin, Pha.	.10
☐	43	Keith Tkachuk, Wpg.	.35
☐	44	Dino Ciccarelli, Det.	.25
☐	45	Doug Evans, Pha.	.10
☐	**46**	**Roman Hamrlik, T.B., RC**	**.35**
☐	**47**	**Robert Lang, L.A., RC**	**.10**
☐	48	Kerry Huffman, Que.	.10
☐	49	Pat Conacher, L.A.	.10
☐	50	Dominik Hasek (G), Buf.	.50
☐	51	Dominic Roussel (G), Pha.	.10
☐	52	Glen Murray, Bos.	.10
☐	**53**	**Igar Korolev, Stl., RC**	**.10**
☐	54	Jiri Slegr, Van.	.10
☐	55	Mikael Andersson, T.B.	.10
☐	**56**	**Bob Babcock, Wsh., RC**	**.10**
☐	57	Ron Hextall (G), Que.	.25
☐	58	Jeff Daniels, Pgh.	.10
☐	59	Doug Crossman, T.B.	.10
☐	**60**	**Viktor Gordijuk, Buf., RC**	**.10**
☐	61	Adam Creighton, T.B.	.10
☐	62	Rob DiMaio, T.B.	.10
☐	63	Eric Weinrich, Hfd.	.10
☐	**64**	**Vitali Prokhorov, Stl., RC**	**.10**
☐	**65**	**Dimitri Yushkevich, Pha., RC**	**.10**
☐	66	Evgeny Davydov, Wpg.	.10
☐	**67**	**Dixon Ward, Van., RC**	**.10**
☐	68	Teemu Selänne, Wpg.	.50
☐	**69**	**Rob Zamuner, T.B., RC**	**.35**
☐	70	Joe Reekie, T.B.	.10
☐	71	Vyacheslav Kozlov, Det.	.10
☐	72	Philippe Boucher, Buf.	.10
☐	73	Phil Bourque, NYR.	.10
☐	74	Yvon Corriveau, S.J.	.10
☐	75	Brian Bellows. Mtl.	.10
☐	76	Wendell Young (G), T.B.	.10
☐	77	Bobby Holik, N.J.	.10
☐	78	Bob Carpenter, Wsh.	.10
☐	79	Scott Lachance, NYI.	.10
☐	80	John Druce, Wpg.	.10
☐	**81**	**Keith Carney, Buf., RC**	**.10**
☐	82	Neil Brady, Ott.	.10
☐	**83**	**Richard Matvichuk, Min., RC**	**.10**
☐	**84**	**Sergei Bautin, Wpg., RC**	**.10**
☐	85	Patrick Poulin, Hfd.	.10
☐	86	Gord Roberts, Bos.	.10
☐	87	Kay Whitmore (G), Van.	.10
☐	88	Stéphane Beauregard (G), Pha.	.10
☐	89	Vladimir Malakhov, NYI.	.10
☐	**90**	**Richard Smehilk, Buf., RC**	**.10**
☐	91	Mike Ricci, Que.	.10
☐	92	Sean Burke (G), Hfd.	.25
☐	**93**	**Andrei Kovalenko, Que., RC**	**.10**
☐	94	Shawn McEachern, Pgh.	.10
☐	95	Pat Jablonski (G), T.B.	.10
☐	**96**	**Oleg Petrov, Mtl., RC**	**.10**
☐	**97**	**Glenn Mulvenna, Pha., RC**	**.10**
☐	**98**	**Jason Woolley, Wsh., RC**	**.10**
☐	99	Mark Greig, Hfd., RC	.10
☐	**100**	**Nikolai Borschevsky, Tor., RC**	**.10**
☐	101	Joé Juneau, Bos.	.10
☐	102	Eric Lindros, Pha.	1.00
☐	103	Darius Kasparaitis, NYI.	.10
☐	104	Sandis Ozolinsh, S.J.	.25
☐	**105**	**Stan Drulla, T.B., RC**	**.10**
☐	**106**	**Mike Needham, Pgh., RC**	**.10**
☐	107	Norm Maciver, Ott.	.10
☐	108	Sylvain Lefebvre, Tor.	.10
☐	**109**	**Tommy Sjodin, Min., RC**	**.10**
☐	110	Bob Sweeney, Buf.	.10
☐	111	Brian Mullen, NYI.	.10
☐	112	Peter Sidorkiewicz (G), Ott.	.10
☐	113	Scott Niedermayer, N.J.	.25
☐	114	Félix Potvin (G), Tor.	.35
☐	115	Robb Stauber (G), L.A.	.10
☐	116	Sylvain Turgeon, Ott.	.10
☐	117	Mark Janssens, Hfd.	.10
☐	**118**	**Darren Banks, Bos., RC**	**.10**
☐	119	Pat Elynuik, Wsh.	.10
☐	**120**	**Bill Guerin, N.J., RC**	**.35**
☐	121	Reggie Savage, Wsh.	.10
☐	122	Enrico Ciccone, Min.	.10
☐	**123**	**Chris Kontos, T.B., RC**	**.10**
☐	124	Martin Rucinsky, Que.	.10
☐	125	Alexei Zhitnik, L.A.	.10
☐	126	Alexei Kovalev, NYR.	.10
☐	127	Tim Kerr, Hfd.	.10
☐	**128**	**Guy Larose, Tor., RC**	**.10**
☐	129	Brent Gilchrist, Edm.	.10
☐	130	Steve Duchesne, Que.	.10
☐	131	Drake Berehowsky, Tor.	.10
☐	132	Checklist	.10

STAR PERFORMERS

Insert Set (22 cards): 8.00

Common Player: .10

	No.	Player	NRMT-MT
☐	1	Ray Ferraro, NYI.	.10
☐	2	Dale Hunter, Wsh.	.10
☐	3	Murray Craven, Hfd.	.10
☐	4	Paul Coffey, L.A.	.25
☐	5	Jeremy Roenick, Chi.	.50
☐	6	Denis Savard, Mtl.	.25
☐	7	Jon Casey (G), Min.	.10
☐	8	Doug Gilmour, Tor.	.50
☐	9	Rod Brind'Amour Pha.	.25
☐	10	Pavel Bure, Van.	1.00
☐	11	Joe Sakic, Que.	1.25
☐	12	Pat Falloon, S.J.	.10
☐	13	Adam Oates, Bos.	.50
☐	14	Gary Roberts, Cgy.	.25
☐	15	Mark Messier, NYR.	.75
☐	16	Phil Housley, Wpg.	.10
☐	17	Pat LaFontaine, Buf.	.25
☐	18	Stéphane Richer, N.J.	.10
☐	19	Bill Ranford (G), Edm.	.25
☐	20	Sergei Fedorov, Det.	.75
☐	21	Brett Hull, Stl.	.75
☐	22	Mario Lemieux, Pgh.	2.50

TOP ROOKIES

Insert Set (4 cards): 7.00

	No.	Player	NRMT-MT
□	1	Eric Lindros, Pha.	5.00
□	2	Roman Hamrlik, T.B.	1.00
□	3	Dominic Roussel (G), Pha.	.50
□	4	Félix Potvin (G), Tor.	2.00

1992 - 93 PANINI STICKERS

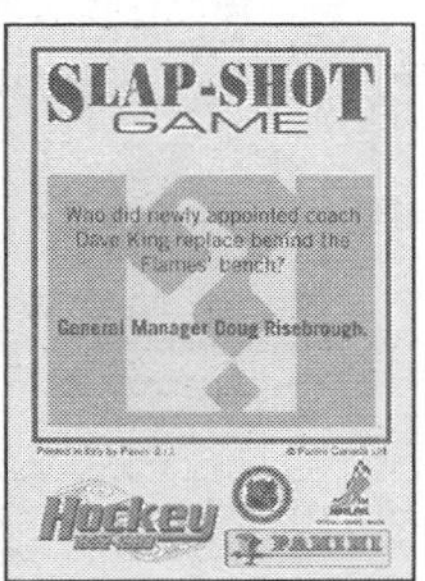

These stickers have two versions: an English issue and a French issue.

Sticker Size: 2 1/2" x 3 1/2"

Imprint: Panini S.r.l. Panini Canada Ltd.

			English	French
Complete Set (330 stickers):			20.00	25.00
Common Player:			.10	.15
Album:			3.00	4.00

	No.	Player	English	French
□ □	1	Stanley Cup	.25	.35
□ □	2	Chicago Blackhawks Logo	.10	.15
□ □	3	Ed Belfour (G), Chi.	.25	.35
□ □	4	Jeremy Roenick, Chi.	.25	.35
□ □	5	Steve Larmer, Chi.	.20	.25
□ □	6	Michel Goulet, Chi.	.20	.25
□ □	7	Dirk Graham, Chi.	.10	.15
□ □	8	Jocelyn Lemieux, Chi.	.10	.15
□ □	9	Brian Noonan, Chi.	.10	.15
□ □	10	Rob Brown, Chi.	.10	.15
□ □	11	Chris Chelios, Chi.	.35	.50
□ □	12	Steve Smith, Chi.	.10	.15
□ □	13	Keith Brown, Chi.	.10	.15
□ □	14	St. Louis Blues Logo	.10	.15
□ □	15	Curtis Joseph (G), Stl.	.35	.60
□ □	16	Brett Hull, Stl.	.35	.50
□ □	17	Brendan Shanahan, Stl.	.35	.60
□ □	18	Ron Wilson, Stl.	.10	.15
□ □	19	Rich Sutter, Stl.	.10	.15
□ □	20	Ron Sutter, Stl.	.10	.15
□ □	21	Dave Lowry, Stl.	.10	.15
□ □	22	Craig Janney, Stl.	.10	.15
□ □	23	Paul Cavallini, Stl.	.10	.15
□ □	24	Garth Butcher, Stl.	.10	.15
□ □	25	Jeff Brown, Stl.	.10	.15
□ □	26	Vancouver Canucks Logo	.10	.15
□ □	27	Kirk McLean (G), Van.	.20	.25
□ □	28	Trevor Linden, Van.	.20	.25
□ □	29	Geoff Courtnall, Van.	.10	.15
□ □	30	Cliff Ronning, Van.	.10	.15
□ □	31	Petr Nedved, Van.	.20	.25
□ □	32	Igor Larionov, Van.	.20	.25
□ □	33	Robert Kron, Van.	.10	.15
□ □	34	Jim Sandlak, Van.	.10	.15
□ □	35	Dave Babych, Van.	.10	.15
□ □	36	Jyrki Lumme, Van.	.10	.15
□ □	37	Doug Lidster, Van.	.10	.15
□ □	38	Calgary Flames Logo	.10	.15
□ □	39	Mike Vernon (G), Cgy.	.20	.25
□ □	40	Joe Nieuwendyk, Cgy.	.20	.25
□ □	41	Gary Leeman, Cgy.	.10	.15
□ □	42	Robert Reichel, Cgy.	.10	.15
□ □	43	Joel Otto, Cgy.	.10	.15
□ □	44	Paul Ranheim, Cgy.	.10	.15
□ □	45	Gary Roberts, Cgy.	.20	.25
□ □	46	Theoren Fleury, Cgy.	.25	.35
□ □	47	Sergei Makarov, Cgy.	.10	.15
□ □	48	Gary Suter, Cgy.	.10	.15
□ □	49	Al MacInnis, Cgy.	.20	.25
□ □	50	Winnipeg Jets Logo	.10	.15
□ □	51	Bob Essensa (G), Wpg.	.10	.15
□ □	52	Teppo Numminen, Wpg.	.10	.15
□ □	53	Thomas Steen, Wpg.	.10	.15
□ □	54	Pat Elynuik, Wpg.	.10	.15
□ □	55	Ed Olczyk, Wpg.	.10	.15
□ □	56	Danton Cole, Wpg.	.10	.15
□ □	57	Troy Murray, Wpg.	.10	.15
□ □	58	Darrin Shannon, Wpg.	.10	.15
□ □	59	Russ Romaniuk, Wpg.	.10	.15
□ □	60	Fredrik Olausson, Wpg.	.10	.15
□ □	61	Phil Housley, Wpg.	.10	.15
□ □	62	Los Angeles Kings Logo	.10	.15
□ □	63	Kelly Hrudey (G), L.A.	.10	.15
□ □	64	Wayne Gretzky, L.A.	1.50	2.00
□ □	65	Luc Robitaille, L.A.	.20	.25
□ □	66	Jari Kurri, L.A.	.20	.25
□ □	67	Tomas Sandström, L.A.	.10	.15
□ □	68	Tony Granato, L.A.	.10	.15
□ □	69	Bob Kudelski, L.A.	.10	.15
□ □	70	Corey Millen, L.A.	.10	.15
□ □	71	Rob Blake, L.A.	.20	.25
□ □	72	Paul Coffey, L.A.	.20	.25
□ □	73	Marty McSorley, L.A.	.10	.15
□ □	74	Toronto Maple Leafs Logo	.10	.15
□ □	75	Grant Fuhr (G), Tor.	.20	.25
□ □	76	Glenn Anderson, Tor.	.10	.15
□ □	77	Doug Gilmour, Tor.	.25	.35
□ □	78	Mike Krushelnyski, Tor.	.10	.15
□ □	79	Wendel Clark, Tor.	.20	.25
□ □	80	Rob Pearson, Tor.	.10	.15
□ □	81	Peter Zezel, Tor.	.10	.15
□ □	82	Todd Gill, Tor.	.10	.15
□ □	83	Dave Ellett, Tor.	.10	.15
□ □	84	Mike Foligno, Tor.	.10	.15
□ □	85	Ken Baumgartner, Tor.	.10	.15
□ □	86	Minnesota North Stars Logo	.10	.15
□ □	87	Jon Casey (G), Min.	.10	.15
□ □	88	Brian Bellows, Min.	.10	.15
□ □	89	Neal Broten, Min.	.10	.15
□ □	90	Dave Gagner, Min.	.10	.15
□ □	91	Mike Modano, Min.	.35	.50
□ □	92	Ulf Dahlen, Min.	.10	.15
□ □	93	Brian Propp, Min.	.10	.15
□ □	94	Jim Johnson, Min.	.10	.15
□ □	95	Mike Craig, Min.	.10	.15
□ □	96	Bobby Smith, Min.	.10	.15
□ □	97	Mark Tinordi, Min.	.10	.15
□ □	98	Edmonton Oilers Logo	.10	.15
□ □	99	Bill Ranford (G), Edm.	.20	.25
□ □	100	Joe Murphy, Edm.	.10	.15
□ □	101	Craig MacTavish, Edm.	.10	.15
□ □	102	Craig Simpson, Edm.	.10	.15
□ □	103	Esa Tikkanen, Edm.	.10	.15
□ □	104	Vincent Damphousse, Edm.	.25	.35
□ □	105	Petr Klima, Edm.	.10	.15
□ □	106	Martin Gelinas, Edm.	.10	.15
□ □	107	Kevin Lowe, Edm.	.10	.15
□ □	108	Dave Manson, Edm.	.10	.15
□ □	109	Bernie Nicholls, Edm.	.10	.15
□ □	110	Detroit Red Wings Logo	.10	.15
□ □	111	Tim Cheveldae (G), Det.	.10	.15
□ □	112	Steve Yzerman, Det.	.75	1.00
□ □	113	Sergei Fedorov, Det.	.35	.50
□ □	114	Jimmy Carson, Det.	.10	.15
□ □	115	Kevin Miller, Det.	.10	.15
□ □	116	Gerard Gallant, Det.	.10	.15
□ □	117	Keith Primeau, Det.	.20	.25
□ □	118	Paul Ysebaert, Det.	.10	.15
□ □	119	Yves Racine, Det.	.10	.15
□ □	120	Steve Chiasson, Det.	.10	.15
□ □	121	Ray Sheppard, Det.	.10	.15
□ □	122	San Jose Sharks Logo	.10	.15
□ □	123	Jeff Hackett (G), S.J.	.20	.25
□ □	124	Kelly Kisio, S.J.	.10	.15
□ □	125	Brian Mullen, S.J.	.10	.15
□ □	126	David Bruce, S.J.	.10	.15
□ □	127	Rob Zettler, S.J.	.10	.15
□ □	128	Neil Wilkinson, S.J.	.10	.15
□ □	129	Doug Wilson, S.J.	.10	.15
□ □	130	Jeff Odgers, S.J.	.10	.15
□ □	131	Dean Evason, S.J.	.10	.15
□ □	132	Brian Lawton, S.J.	.10	.15
□ □	133	Dale Craigwell, S.J.	.10	.15
□ □	134	Boston Bruins Logo	.10	.15
□ □	135	Andy Moog (G), Bos.	.20	.25
□ □	136	Adam Oates, Bos.	.25	.35
□ □	137	Dave Poulin, Bos.	.10	.15
□ □	138	Vladimir Ruzicka, Bos.	.10	.15
□ □	139	Jeff Lazaro, Bos.	.10	.15
□ □	140	Bob Carpenter, Bos.	.10	.15
□ □	141	Peter Douris, Bos.	.10	.15
□ □	142	Glen Murray, Bos.	.10	.15
□ □	143	Cam Neely, Bos.	.20	.25
□ □	144	Ray Bourque, Bos.	.35	.50
□ □	145	Glen Wesley, Bos.	.10	.15
□ □	146	Montréal Canadiens Logo	.10	.15
□ □	147	Patrick Roy (G), Mtl.	1.25	1.50
□ □	148	Kirk Muller, Mtl.	.10	.15
□ □	149	Guy Carbonneau, Mtl.	.10	.15
□ □	150	Shayne Corson, Mtl.	.20	.25
□ □	151	Stéphan Lebeau, Mtl.	.10	.15
□ □	152	Denis Savard, Mtl.	.20	.25
□ □	153	Brent Gilchrist, Mtl.	.10	.15
□ □	154	Russ Courtnall, Mtl.	.10	.15
□ □	155	Patrice Brisebois, Mtl.	.10	.15
□ □	156	Eric Desjardins, Mtl.	.20	.25
□ □	157	Mathieu Schneider, Mtl.	.10	.15
□ □	158	Washington Capitals Logo	.10	.15
□ □	159	Don Beaupré (G), Wsh.	.10	.15
□ □	160	Dino Ciccarelli, Wsh.	.20	.25
□ □	161	Michal Pivonka, Wsh.	.10	.15
□ □	162	Mike Ridley, Wsh.	.10	.15
□ □	163	Randy Burridge, Wsh.	.10	.15
□ □	164	Peter Bondra, Wsh.	.25	.35
□ □	165	Dale Hunter, Wsh.	.10	.15
□ □	166	Kelly Miller, Wsh.	.10	.15
□ □	167	Kevin Hatcher, Wsh.	.10	.15
□ □	168	Al Iafrate, Wsh.	.10	.15
□ □	169	Rod Langway, Wsh.	.10	.15
□ □	170	New Jersey Devils Logo	.10	.15
□ □	171	Chris Terreri (G), N.J.	.10	.15
□ □	172	Claude Lemieux, N.J.	.10	.15
□ □	173	Stéphane Richer, N.J.	.10	.15
□ □	174	Peter Stastny, N.J.	.10	.15
□ □	175	Zdeno Ciger, N.J.	.10	.15
□ □	176	Alexander Semak, N.J.	.10	.15
□ □	177	Valeri Zelepukin, N.J.	.10	.15
□ □	178	Bruce Driver, N.J.	.10	.15
□ □	179	Scott Niedermayer, N.J.	.20	.25
□ □	180	Alexei Kasatonov, N.J.	.10	.15
□ □	181	Scott Stevens, N.J.	.20	.25
□ □	182	Philadelphia Flyers Logo	.10	.15
□ □	183	Dominic Roussel (G), Pha.	.10	.15
□ □	184	Mike Ricci, Pha.	.10	.15
□ □	185	Mark Recchi, Pha.	.20	.25
□ □	186	Kevin Dineen, Pha.	.10	.15
□ □	187	Rod Brind'Amour, Pha.	.20	.25
□ □	188	Mark Pederson, Pha.	.10	.15
□ □	189	Per-Erik Eklund, Pha.	.10	.15
□ □	190	Terry Carkner, Pha.	.10	.15
□ □	191	Mark Howe, Pha.	.20	.25
□ □	192	Steve Duchesne, Pha.	.10	.15
□ □	193	Andrei Lomakin, Pha.	.10	.15
□ □	194	New York Islanders Logo	.10	.15
□ □	195	Mark Fitzpatrick (G), NYI.	.10	.15
□ □	196	Pierre Turgeon, NYI.	.20	.25
□ □	197	Benoît Hogue, NYI.	.10	.15
□ □	198	Ray Ferraro, NYI.	.10	.15
□ □	199	Derek King, NYI.	.10	.15
□ □	200	David Volek, NYI.	.10	.15
□ □	201	Patrick Flatley, NYI.	.10	.15
□ □	202	Uwe Krupp, NYI.	.10	.15
□ □	203	Steve Thomas, NYI.	.10	.15
□ □	204	Adam Creighton, NYI.	.10	.15
□ □	205	Jeff Norton, NYI.	.10	.15
□ □	206	Québec Nordiques Logo	.10	.15
□ □	207	Stéphane Fiset (G), Que.	.20	.25
□ □	208	Mikhail Tatarinov, Que.	.10	.15

No.	Player		
209	Joe Sakic, Que.	.60	.85
210	Owen Nolan, Que.	.20	.25
211	Mike Hough, Que.	.10	.15
212	Mats Sundin, Que.	.35	.50
213	Claude Lapointe, Que.	.10	.15
214	Stéphane Morin, Que.	.10	.15
215	Alexei Gusarov, Que.	.10	.15
216	Steven Finn, Que.	.10	.15
217	Curtis Leschyshyn	.10	.15
218	Pittsburgh Penguins Logo	.10	.15
219	Tom Barrasso (G), Pgh.	.20	.25
220	Mario Lemieux, Pgh.	1.25	1.50
221	Kevin Stevens, Pgh.	.10	.15
222	Shawn McEachern, Pgh.	.10	.15
223	Joe Mullen, Pgh.	.10	.15
224	Ron Francis, Pgh.	.25	.35
225	Phil Bourque, Pgh.	.10	.15
226	Rick Tocchet, Pgh.	.10	.15
227	Bryan Trottier, Pgh.	.20	.25
228	Larry Murphy, Pgh.	.20	.25
229	Ulf Samuelsson, Pgh.	.10	.15
230	New York Rangers Logo	.10	.15
231	Mike Richter (G), NYR.	.25	.35
232	John Vanbiesbrouck (G), NYR.	.35	.60
233	Mark Messier, NYR.	.35	.50
234	Sergei Nemchinov, NYR.	.10	.15
235	Darren Turcotte, NYR.	.10	.15
236	Doug Weight, NYR.	.25	.35
237	Mike Gartner, NYR.	.20	.25
238	Adam Graves, NYR.	.10	.15
239	Brian Leetch, NYR.	.25	.35
240	James Patrick, NYR.	.10	.15
241	Jan Erixon, NYR.	.10	.15
242	Buffalo Sabres Logo	.10	.15
243	Tom Draper (G), Buf.	.10	.15
244	Grant Ledyard, Buf.	.10	.15
245	Doug Bodger, Buf.	.10	.15
246	Pat LaFontaine, Buf.	.20	.25
247	Dale Hawerchuk, Buf.	.20	.25
248	Alexander Mogilny, Buf.	.25	.35
249	Dave Andreychuk, Buf.	.20	.25
250	Christian Ruuttu, Buf.	.10	.15
251	Randy Wood, Buf.	.10	.15
252	Brad May, Buf.	.10	.15
253	Mike Ramsey, Buf.	.10	.15
254	Hartford Whalers Logo	.10	.15
255	Kay Whitmore (G), Hfd.	.10	.15
256	Pat Verbeek, Hfd.	.10	.15
257	John Cullen, Hfd.	.10	.15
258	Mikael Andersson, Hfd.	.10	.15
259	Yvon Corriveau, Hfd.	.10	.15
260	Randy Cunneyworth, Hfd.	.10	.15
261	Bobby Holik, Hfd.	.10	.15
262	Murray Craven, Hfd.	.10	.15
263	Zarley Zalapski, Hfd.	.10	.15
264	Adam Burt, Hfd.	.10	.15
265	Brad Shaw, Hfd.	.10	.15
266	Tampa Bay Lightning Logo	.10	.15
267	Tampa Bay Lighning Jersey	.10	.15
268	Ottawa Senators Logo	.10	.15
269	Ottawa Senators Jersey	.10	.15
270	Tony Amonte, NYR.	.20	.25
271	Pavel Bure, Van.	.50	.75
272	Gilbert Dionne, Mtl.	.10	.15
273	Pat Falloon, S.J.	.10	.15
274	Nicklas Lidström, Det.	.20	.25
275	Kevin Todd, N.J.	.10	.15
276	Prince of Wales Conference Logo	.10	.15
277	AS: Patrick Roy (G), Mtl.	.75	1.00
278	AS: Paul Coffey, L.A.	.20	.25
279	AS: Ray Bourque, Bos.	.35	.50
280	AS: Mario Lemieux, Pgh.	.75	1.00
281	AS: Kevin Stevens, Pgh.	.10	.15
282	AS: Jaromir Jagr, Pgh.	.60	.75
283	Clarence Campbell Conference Logo	.10	.15
284	AS: Ed Belfour (G), Chi.	.25	.35
285	AS: Al MacInnis, Cgy.	.20	.25
286	AS: Chris Chelios, Chi.	.25	.35
287	AS: Wayne Gretzky, L.A.	1.00	1.50
288	AS: Luc Robitaille, L.A.	.20	.25
289	AS: Brett Hull, Stl.	.35	.50
290	Pavel Bure, Van.	.50	.75
291	Sergei Fedorov, Det.	.35	.50
292	Dominik Hasek (G), Chi.	.50	.75
293	Bobby Holik, Hfd.	.10	.15
294	Jaromir Jagr, Pgh.	.60	.75
295	Valeri Kamensky, Que.	.20	.25
296	Alexander Semak, N.J.	.10	.15
297	Igor Kravchuk, Chi.	.10	.15
298	Nicklas Lidström, Det.	.20	.25
299	Alexander Mogilny, Buf.	.25	.35
300	Petr Nedved, Van.	.20	.25
301	Robert Reichel, Cgy.	.10	.15
302	Mats Sundin, Que.	.25	.35
303	Calder Trophy	.10	.15
304	Hart Trophy	.10	.15
305	Lady Byng Trophy	.10	.15
306	Norris Trophy	.10	.15
307	Frank J. Selke Trophy	.10	.15
308	Vezina Trophy	.10	.15
A	Igor Kravchuk, Chi	.25	.35
B	Nelson Emerson, Stl.	.25	.35
C	Pavel Bure, Van.	1.00	1.50
D	Tomas Forslund, Cgy.	.25	.35
E	Luciano Borsato, Wpg.	.25	.35
F	Darryl Sydor, L.A.	.25	.35
G	Félix Potvin (G), Tor.	.50	.75
H	Derian Hatcher, Min.	.35	.50
I	Josef Beranek, Edm.	.25	.35
J	Nicklas Lidström, Det.	.35	.50
K	Pat Falloon, S.J.	.25	.35
L	Joé Juneau, Bos.	.25	.35
M	Gilbert Dionne, Mtl.	.25	.35
N	Dimitri Khristich, Wsh.	.25	.35
O	Kevin Todd, N.J.	.25	.35
P	Eric Lindros, Pha.	3.00	4.00
Q	Scott Lachance, NYI.	.25	.35
R	Valeri Kamensky, Que.	.35	.50
S	Jaromir Jagr, Pgh.	1.50	2.00
T	Tony Amonte, NYR.	.35	.50
U	Donald Audette, Buf.	.25	.35
V	Geoff Sanderson, Hfd.	.25	.35

1992 - 93 PANINI ACTION FREAKS

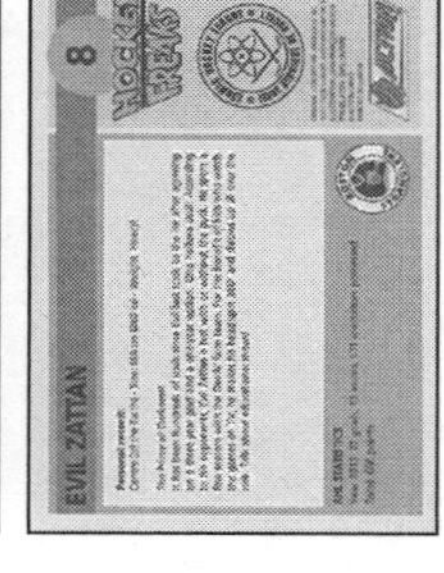

Imprint: None

Complete Set (110 stickers):	**10.00**
French Set (110 stickers):	**10.00**
Common Sticker:	**.10**

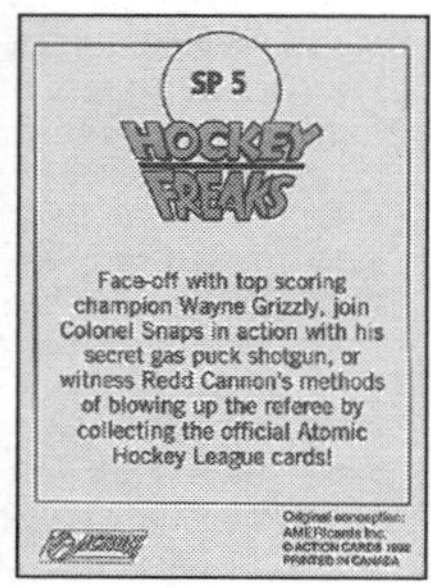

1992 - 93 PARKHURST

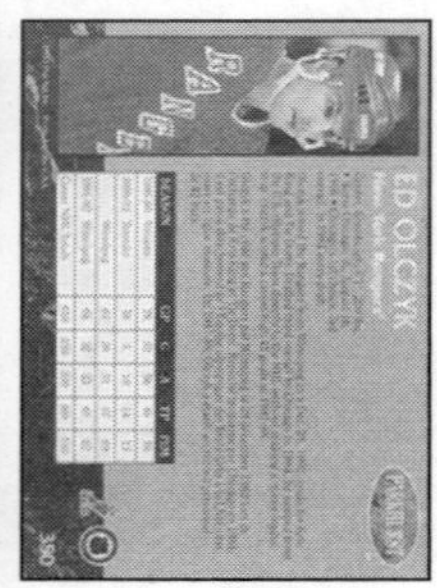

These cards have two versions: the regular card and an Emerald Ice parallel .

Imprint: © 1993 Pro Set Inc.

Series 1 Set (240 cards):	**18.00**	**125.00**
Series 2 Set (240 cards):	**12.00**	**80.00**
Final Update set (30 cards):	**12.00**	**30.00**
Common Player (1-480):	**.10**	**.35**
Common Player (481-510):	**.25**	**.50**

No.	Player	Regular	Emerald
1	Ray Bourque, Bos.	.50	2.50
2	Joé Juneau, Bos.	.10	.35
3	Andy Moog (G), Bos.	.25	.50
4	Adam Oates, Bos.	.10	.35
5	Vladimir Ruzicka, Bos.	.10	.35
6	Glen Wesley, Bos.	.10	.35
7	**Dmitri Kvartalnov, Bos., RC**	**.10**	**.35**
8	Ted Donato, Bos.	.10	.35
9	Glen Murray, Bos.	.10	.35
10	Dave Andreychuk, Buf.	.25	.50
11	Dale Hawerchuk, Buf.	.25	.50
12	Pat LaFontaine, Buf.	.25	.50
13	Alexander Mogilny, Buf.	.35	1.00
14	**Richard Smehlik, Buf., RC**	**.10**	**.35**
15	**Keith Carney, Buf., RC**	**.10**	**.35**
16	Philippe Boucher, Buf.	.10	.35
17	**Viktor Gordijuk, Buf., RC**	**.10**	**.35**
18	Donald Audette, Buf.	.10	.35
19	Theoren Fleury, Cgy.	.35	1.00
20	Al MacInnis, Cgy.	.25	.50
21	Joe Nieuwendyk, Cgy.	.25	.50
22	Gary Roberts, Cgy.	.25	.50
23	Gary Suter, Cgy.	.10	.35
24	Mike Vernon (G), Cgy.	.25	.50
25	Sergei Makarov, Cgy.	.10	.35
26	Robert Reichel, Cgy.	.10	.35
27	Chris Lindberg, Cgy.	.10	.35
28	Ed Belfour (G), Chi.	.35	1.00
29	Chris Chelios, Chi.	.35	1.50
30	Steve Larmer, Chi.	.25	.50
31	Jeremy Roenick, Chi.	.35	1.00
32	Steve Smith, Chi.	.10	.35
33	Brent Sutter, Chi.	.10	.35
34	Christian Ruuttu, Chi.	.10	.35
35	Igor Kravchuk, Chi.	.10	.35
36	Sergei Krivokrasov, Chi.	.10	.35
37	Tim Cheveldae (G), Det.	.10	.35
38	Mike Sillinger, Det.	.10	.35
39	Sergei Fedorov, Det.	.50	2.50
40	Vyacheslav Kozlov, Det.	.10	.35
41	Bob Probert, Det.	.10	.35
42	Nicklas Lidström, Det.	.25	.50
43	Paul Ysebaert, Det.	.25	.35
44	Steve Yzerman, Det.	1.00	5.00
45	Dino Ciccarelli, Det.	.25	.50
46	Esa Tikkanen, Edm.	.10	.35
47	Dave Manson, Edm.	.10	.35
48	Craig MacTavish, Edm.	.10	.35
49	Bernie Nicholls, Edm.	.10	.35
50	Bill Ranford (G), Edm.	.25	.50
51	Craig Simpson, Edm.	.10	.35
52	Scott Mellanby, Edm.	.10	.35
53	Shayne Corson, Edm.	.25	.50
54	Petr Klima, Edm.	.10	.35
55	Murray Craven, Hfd.	.10	.35
56	Eric Weinrich, Hfd.	.10	.35
57	Sean Burke (G), Hfd.	.25	.50
58	Pat Verbeek, Hfd.	.10	.35

	No.	Player		
☐☐	59	Zarley Zalapski, Hfd.	.10	.35
☐☐	60	Patrick Poulin, Hfd.	.10	.35
☐☐	61	Robert Petrovicky, Hfd.	.10	.35
☐☐	62	Geoff Sanderson, Hfd.	.10	.35
☐☐	63	Paul Coffey, L.A.	.25	.50
☐☐	**64**	**Robert Lang, L.A., RC**	**.10**	**.35**
☐☐	65	Wayne Gretzky, L.A.	2.00	10.00
☐☐	66	Kelly Hrudey (G), L.A.	.10	.35
☐☐	67	Jari Kurri, L.A.	.25	.50
☐☐	68	Luc Robitaille, L.A.	.25	.50
☐☐	69	Darryl Sydor, L.A.	.10	.35
☐☐	**70**	**Jim Hiller, L.A., RC**	**.10**	**.35**
☐☐	71	Alexei Zhitnik, L.A.	.10	.35
☐☐	72	Derian Hatcher, Min.	.25	.50
☐☐	73	Jon Casey (G), Min.	.10	.35
☐☐	**74**	**Richard Matvichuk, Min., RC**	**.10**	**.35**
☐☐	75	Mike Modano, Min.	.50	2.50
☐☐	76	Mark Tinordi, Min.	.10	.35
☐☐	77	Todd Elik, Min.	.10	.35
☐☐	78	Russ Courtnall, Min.	.10	.35
☐☐	**79**	**Tommy Sjodin, Min., RC**	**.10**	**.35**
☐☐	80	Eric Desjardins, Mtl.	.10	.35
☐☐	81	Gilbert Dionne, Mtl.	.10	.35
☐☐	82	Stéphan Lebeau, Mtl.	.10	.35
☐☐	83	Kirk Muller, Mtl.	.10	.35
☐☐	84	Patrick Roy (G), Mtl.	1.50	8.00
☐☐	85	Denis Savard, Mtl.	.25	.50
☐☐	86	Vincent Damphousse, Mtl.	.35	1.00
☐☐	87	Brian Bellows, Mtl.	.10	.35
☐☐	**88**	**Ed Ronan, Mtl., RC**	**.10**	**.35**
☐☐	89	Claude Lemieux, N.J.	.10	.35
☐☐	90	John MacLean, N.J.	.10	.35
☐☐	91	Stéphane Richer, N.J.	.10	.35
☐☐	92	Scott Stevens, N.J.	.10	.35
☐☐	93	Chris Terreri (G), N.J.	.10	.35
☐☐	94	Kevin Todd, N.J.	.10	.35
☐☐	95	Scott Niedermayer, N.J.	.25	.50
☐☐	96	Bobby Holik, N.J.	.10	.35
☐☐	**97**	**Bill Guerin, N.J., RC**	**.35**	**.50**
☐☐	98	Ray Ferraro, NYI.	.10	.35
☐☐	99	Mark Fitzpatrick (G), NYI.	.10	.35
☐☐	100	Derek King, NYI.	.10	.35
☐☐	101	Uwe Krupp, NYI.	.10	.35
☐☐	102	Darius Kasparaitis, NYI.	.10	.35
☐☐	103	Pierre Turgeon, NYI.	.25	.50
☐☐	104	Benoît Hogue, NYI.	.10	.35
☐☐	105	Scott Lachance, NYI.	.10	.35
☐☐	106	Marty McInnis, NYI.	.10	.35
☐☐	107	Tony Amonte, NYR.	.25	.50
☐☐	108	Mike Gartner, NYR.	.25	.50
☐☐	109	Alexei Kovalev, NYR.	.10	.35
☐☐	110	Brian Leetch, NYR.	.35	1.00
☐☐	111	Mark Messier, NYR.	.50	2.50
☐☐	112	Mike Richter (G), NYR.	.35	1.00
☐☐	113	James Patrick, NYR.	.10	.35
☐☐	114	Sergei Nemchinov, NYR.	.10	.35
☐☐	115	Doug Weight, NYR.	.35	1.00
☐☐	116	Mark Lamb, Ott.	.10	.35
☐☐	117	Norm Maciver, Ott.	.10	.35
☐☐	118	Mike Peluso, Ott.	.10	.35
☐☐	119	Jody Hull, Ott.	.10	.35
☐☐	120	Peter Sidorkiewicz (G), Ott.	.10	.35
☐☐	121	Sylvain Turgeon, Ott.	.10	.35
☐☐	122	Laurie Boschman, Ott.	.10	.35
☐☐	123	Brad Marsh, Ott.	.10	.35
☐☐	124	Neil Brady, Ott.	.10	.35
☐☐	125	Brian Benning, Pha.	.10	.35
☐☐	126	Rod Brind'Amour, Pha.	.10	.35
☐☐	127	Kevin Dineen, Pha.	.10	.35
☐☐	128	Eric Lindros, Pha.	2.00	8.00
☐☐	129	Dominic Roussel (G), Pha.	.10	.35
☐☐	130	Mark Recchi, Pha.	.25	.50
☐☐	131	Brent Fedyk, Pha.	.10	.35
☐☐	132	Greg Paslawski, Pha.	.10	.35
☐☐	**133**	**Dimitri Yushkevich, Pha., RC**	**.10**	**.35**
☐☐	134	Tom Barrasso (G), Pgh.	.25	.50
☐☐	135	Jaromir Jagr, Pgh.	1.00	1.50
☐☐	136	Mario Lemieux, Pgh.	1.50	8.00
☐☐	137	Larry Murphy, Pgh.	.25	.50
☐☐	138	Kevin Stevens, Pgh.	.10	.35
☐☐	139	Rick Tocchet, Pgh.	.10	.35
☐☐	**140**	**Martin Straka, Pgh., RC**	**.10**	**.35**
☐☐	141	Ron Francis, Pgh.	.35	1.00
☐☐	142	Shawn McEachern, Pgh.	.10	.35
☐☐	143	Steve Duchesne, Que.	.10	.35
☐☐	144	Ron Hextall (G), Que.	.25	.50
☐☐	145	Owen Nolan, Que.	.25	.50
☐☐	146	Mike Ricci, Que.	.10	.35
☐☐	147	Joe Sakic, Que.	.85	4.00
☐☐	148	Mats Sundin, Que.	.50	2.50
☐☐	149	Martin Rucinsky, Que.	.10	.35
☐☐	**150**	**Andrei Kovalenko, Que., RC**	**.35**	**.50**
☐☐	**151**	**Dave Karpa, Que., RC**	**.10**	**.35**
☐☐	152	Nelson Emerson, Stl.	.10	.35
☐☐	153	Brett Hull, Stl.	.50	2.50
☐☐	154	Craig Janney, Stl.	.10	.35
☐☐	155	Curtis Joseph (G), Stl.	.60	3.00
☐☐	156	Brendan Shanahan, Stl.	.60	3.00
☐☐	**157**	**Vitali Prokhorov, Stl., RC**	**.10**	**.35**
☐☐	**158**	**Igor Korolev, Stl., RC**	**.10**	**.35**
☐☐	159	Philippe Bozon, Stl.	.10	.35
☐☐	**160**	**Ray Whitney, S.J., RC**	**.10**	**.35**
☐☐	161	Pat Falloon, S.J.	.10	.35
☐☐	162	Jeff Hackett (G), S.J.	.25	.50
☐☐	163	Brian Lawton, S.J.	.10	.35
☐☐	164	Sandis Ozolinsh, S.J.	.25	.50
☐☐	165	Neil Wilkinson, S.J.	.10	.35
☐☐	166	Kelly Kisio, S.J.	.10	.35
☐☐	167	Doug Wilson, S.J.	.10	.35
☐☐	168	Dale Craigwell, S.J.	.10	.35
☐☐	169	Mikael Andersson, T.B.	.10	.35
☐☐	170	Wendell Young (G), T.B.	.10	.35
☐☐	**171**	**Rob Zamuner, T.B., RC**	**.35**	**.50**
☐☐	172	Adam Creighton, T.B.	.10	.35
☐☐	**173**	**Roman Hamrlik, T.B., RC**	**.35**	**.50**
☐☐	174	Brian Bradley, T.B.	.10	.35
☐☐	175	Rob Ramage, T.B.	.10	.35
☐☐	**176**	**Chris Kontos, T.B., RC**	**.10**	**.35**
☐☐	**177**	**Stan Drulia, T.B., RC**	**.10**	**.35**
☐☐	178	Glenn Anderson, Tor.	.10	.35
☐☐	179	Wendel Clark, Tor.	.25	.50
☐☐	180	John Cullen, Tor.	.10	.35
☐☐	181	Dave Ellett, Tor.	.10	.35
☐☐	182	Grant Fuhr (G), Tor.	.25	.50
☐☐	183	Doug Gilmour, Tor.	.35	1.00
☐☐	184	Kent Manderville, Tor.	.10	.35
☐☐	185	Joe Sacco, Tor.	.10	.35
☐☐	**186**	**Nikolai Borschevsky, Tor., RC**	**.10**	**.35**
☐☐	187	Félix Potvin (G), Tor.	.50	2.50
☐☐	188	Pavel Bure, Van.	.75	3.50
☐☐	189	Geoff Courtnall, Van.	.10	.35
☐☐	190	Trevor Linden, Van.	.25	.50
☐☐	191	Jyrki Lumme, Van.	.10	.35
☐☐	192	Kirk McLean (G), Van.	.25	.50
☐☐	193	Cliff Ronning, Van.	.10	.35
☐☐	**194**	**Dixon Ward, Van., RC**	**.10**	**.35**
☐☐	195	Greg Adams, Van.	.10	.35
☐☐	196	Jiri Slegr, Van.	.10	.35
☐☐	197	Don Beaupré (G), Wsh.	.10	.35
☐☐	198	Kevin Hatcher, Wsh.	.10	.35
☐☐	199	Brad Schlegel, Wsh.	.10	.35
☐☐	200	Mike Ridley, Wsh.	.10	.35
☐☐	201	Calle Johansson, Wsh.	.10	.35
☐☐	**202**	**Steve Konowalchuk, Wsh., RC**	**.10**	**.35**
☐☐	203	Al Iafrate, Wsh.	.10	.35
☐☐	204	Peter Bondra, Wsh.	.35	1.50
☐☐	205	Pat Elynuik, Wsh.	.10	.35
☐☐	206	Keith Tkachuk, Wpg.	.35	1.50
☐☐	207	Bob Essensa (G), Wpg.	.10	.35
☐☐	208	Phil Housley, Wpg.	.10	.35
☐☐	209	Teemu Selänne, Wpg.	.75	3.50
☐☐	210	Alexei Zhamnov, Wpg.	.25	.50
☐☐	211	Evgeny Davydov, Wpg.	.10	.35
☐☐	212	Fredrik Olausson, Wpg.	.10	.35
☐☐	213	Ed Olczyk, Wpg.	.10	.35
☐☐	214	Thomas Steen, Wpg.	.10	.35
☐☐	215	Darius Kasparaitis, NYI.	.10	.35
☐☐	216	Nikolai Borschevsky, Tor.	.10	.35
☐☐	217	Teemu Selänne, Wpg.	.50	1.75
☐☐	218	Alexander Mogilny, Buf.	.25	.50
☐☐	219	Sergei Fedorov, Det.	.35	1.25
☐☐	220	Jaromir Jagr, Pgh.	.75	2.50
☐☐	221	Mats Sundin, Que.	.35	1.25
☐☐	222	Dmitri Kvartalnov, Bos.	.10	.35
☐☐	223	Andrei Kovalenko, Que.	.10	.35
☐☐	224	Tommy Sjodin, Min.	.10	.35
☐☐	225	Alexei Kovalev, NYR.	.10	.35
☐☐	226	Evgeny Davydov, Wpg.	.10	.35
☐☐	227	Robert Lang, L.A.	.10	.35
☐☐	228	Valeri Zelepukin, N.J.	.10	.35
☐☐	229	Doug Weight, NYR.	.25	.50
☐☐	230	Valeri Kamensky, Que.	.25	.50
☐☐	231	Donald Audette, Buf.	.10	.35
☐☐	232	Nelson Emerson, Stl.	.10	.35
☐☐	233	Pat Falloon, S.J.	.10	.35
☐☐	234	Pavel Bure, Van.	.50	1.75
☐☐	235	Tony Amonte. NYR.	.25	.50
☐☐	236	Sergei Nemchinov, NYR.	.10	.35
☐☐	237	Gilbert Dionne, Mtl.	.10	.35
☐☐	238	Kevin Todd, N.J.	.10	.35
☐☐	239	Nicklas Lidström, Det.	.25	.50
☐☐	240	Brad May, Buf.	.10	.35
☐☐	241	Stephen Leach, Bos.	.10	.35
☐☐	242	Dave Poulin, Bos.	.10	.35
☐☐	**243**	**Grigori Panteleyev, Bos., RC**	**.10**	**.35**
☐☐	244	Don Sweeney, Bos.	.10	.35
☐☐	**245**	**John Blue (G), Bos., RC**	**.10**	**.35**
☐☐	**246**	**C.J. Young, Bos., RC**	**.10**	**.35**
☐☐	247	Steve Heinze, Bos.	.10	.50
☐☐	248	Cam Neely, Bos.	.25	.50
☐☐	249	Dave Reid, Bos.	.10	.35
☐☐	250	Grant Fuhr (G), Buf.	.25	.50
☐☐	251	Bob Sweeney, Buf.	.10	.35
☐☐	252	Rob Ray, Buf.	.10	.35
☐☐	253	Doug Bodger, Buf.	.10	.35
☐☐	254	Ken Sutton, Buf.	.10	.35
☐☐	**255**	**Yuri Khmylev, Buf., RC**	**.10**	**.35**
☐☐	256	Mike Ramsey, Buf.	.10	.35
☐☐	257	Brad May, Buf.	.10	.35
☐☐	258	Brent Ashton, Cgy.	.10	.35
☐☐	259	Joel Otto, Cgy.	.10	.35
☐☐	260	Paul Ranheim, Cgy.	.10	.35
☐☐	**261**	**Kevin Dahl, Cgy., RC**	**.10**	**.35**
☐☐	262	Trent Yawney, Cgy.	.10	.35
☐☐	263	Roger Johansson, Cgy.	.10	.35
☐☐	264	Jeff Reese (G), Cgy.	.10	.35
☐☐	265	Ron Stern, Cgy.	.10	.35
☐☐	266	Brian Skrudland, Cgy.	.10	.35
☐☐	267	Bryan Marchment, Chi.	.10	.35
☐☐	268	Stéphane Matteau, Chi.	.10	.35
☐☐	269	Frantisek Kucera, Chi.	.10	.35
☐☐	270	Jimmy Waite (G), Chi.	.10	.35
☐☐	271	Dirk Graham, Chi.	.10	.35
☐☐	272	Michel Goulet, Chi.	.10	.35
☐☐	273	Joe Murphy, Chi.	.10	.35
☐☐	274	Keith Brown, Chi.	.10	.35
☐☐	275	Jocelyn Lemieux, Chi.	.10	.35
☐☐	276	Paul Coffey, Det.	.25	.50
☐☐	277	Keith Primeau, Det.	.25	.50
☐☐	278	Vincent Riendeau (G), Det.	.10	.35
☐☐	279	Mark Howe, Det.	.25	.50
☐☐	280	Ray Sheppard, Det.	.10	.35
☐☐	**281**	**Jim Hiller, Det., RC**	**.10**	**.35**
☐☐	282	Steve Chiasson, Det.	.10	.35
☐☐	283	Vladimir Konstantinov, Det.	.25	.50
☐☐	284	Brian Benning, Edm.	.10	.35
☐☐	285	Kevin Todd, Edm.	.10	.35
☐☐	286	Zdeno Ciger, Edm.	.10	.35
☐☐	287	Brian Glynn, Edm.	.10	.35
☐☐	288	Shaun Van Allen, Edm.	.10	.35
☐☐	**289**	**Brad Werenka, Edm., RC**	**.10**	**.35**
☐☐	290	Ron Tugnutt (G), Edm.	.10	.35
☐☐	291	Igor Kravchuk, Edm.	.10	.35
☐☐	292	Todd Elik, Edm.	.10	.35
☐☐	293	Terry Yake, Hfd.	.10	.35
☐☐	**294**	**Michael Nylander, Hfd., RC**	**.10**	**.35**
☐☐	295	Yvon Corriveau, Hfd.	.10	.35
☐☐	296	Frank Pietrangelo (G), Hfd.	.10	.35
☐☐	297	Nick Kypreos, Hfd.	.10	.35
☐☐	298	Andrew Cassels, Hfd.	.10	.35
☐☐	299	Steve Konroyd, Hfd.	.10	.35
☐☐	300	Allen Pedersen, Hfd.	.10	.35
☐☐	301	Tony Granato, L.A.	.10	.35
☐☐	302	Rob Blake, L.A.	.25	.50
☐☐	303	Robb Stauber (G), L.A.	.10	.35
☐☐	304	Martin McSorley, L.A.	.10	.35
☐☐	**305**	**Lonnie Loach, L.A., RC**	**.10**	**.35**
☐☐	306	Corey Millen, L.A.	.10	.35
☐☐	307	Dave Taylor, L.A.	.10	.35
☐☐	308	Jimmy Carson, L.A.	.10	.35
☐☐	**309**	**Warren Rychel, L.A., RC**	**.10**	**.35**
☐☐	310	Ulf Dahlen, Min.	.10	.35
☐☐	311	Dave Gagner, Min.	.10	.35
☐☐	**312**	**Brad Berry, Min., RC**	**.10**	**.35**
☐☐	313	Neal Broten, Min.	.10	.35

No.	Player		
314	Mike Craig, Min.	.10	.35
315	Darcy Wakaluk (G), Min.	.10	.35
316	Shane Churla, Min.	.10	.35
317	**Trent Klatt, Min., RC**	**.10**	**.35**
318	Mike Keane, Mtl.	.10	.35
319	Mathieu Schneider, Mtl.	.10	.35
320	Patrice Brisebois, Mtl.	.10	.35
321	André Racicot (G), Mtl.	.10	.35
322	**Mario Roberge, Mtl., RC**	**.10**	**.35**
323	Gary Leeman, Mtl.	.10	.35
324	J. J. Daigneault, Mtl.	.10	.35
325	Lyle Odelein, Mtl.	.10	.35
326	John LeClair, Mtl.	.50	2.50
327	Valeri Zelepukin, N.J.	.10	.35
328	Bernie Nicholls, N.J.	.10	.35
329	Alexander Semak, N.J.	.10	.35
330	Craig Billington (G), N.J.	.10	.35
331	Randy McKay, N.J.	.10	.35
332	Ken Daneyko, N.J.	.10	.35
333	Bruce Driver, N.J.	.10	.35
334	Viacheslav Fetisov, N.J.	.25	.50
335	Dennis Vaske, NYI.	.10	.35
336	Brad Dalgarno, NYI.	.10	.35
337	Jeff Norton, NYI.	.10	.35
338	Steve Thomas, NYI.	.10	.35
339	Vladimir Malakhov, NYI.	.10	.35
340	David Volek, NYI.	.10	.35
341	Glenn Healy (G), NYI.	.10	.35
342	Patrick Flatley, NYI.	.10	.35
343	**Travis Green, NYI. ,RC**	**.10**	**.35**
344	**Corey Hirsch (G), NYR., RC**	**.25**	**.35**
345	Darren Turcotte, NYR.	.10	.35
346	Adam Graves, NYR.	.10	.35
347	**Steven King, NYR., RC**	**.10**	**.35**
348	Kevin Lowe, NYR.	.10	.35
349	John Vanbiesbrouck (G), NYR.	.60	3.00
350	Ed Olczyk, NYR.	.10	.35
351	**Sergei Zubov, NYR., RC**	**.35**	**.50**
352	Brad Shaw, Ott.	.10	.35
353	Jamie Baker, Ott.	.10	.35
354	**Mark Freer, Ott., RC**	**.10**	**.35**
355	**Darcy Loewen, Ott., RC**	**.10**	**.35**
356	**Darren Rumble, Ott., RC**	**.10**	**.35**
357	Bob Kudelski, Ott.	.10	.35
358	Ken Hammond, Ott.	.10	.35
359	Daniel Berthiaume (G), Ott.	.10	.35
360	Josef Beranek, Pha.	.10	.35
361	Greg Hawgood, Pha.	.10	.35
362	Terry Carkner, Pha.	.10	.35
363	**Vyacheslav Butsayev, Pha., RC**	**.10**	**.35**
364	Garry Galley, Pha.	.10	.35
365	**André Faust, Pha., RC**	**.10**	**.35**
366	**Ryan McGill, Pha., RC**	**.10**	**.35**
367	**Tommy Söderström (G), Pha., RC**	**.25**	**.35**
368	Joe Mullen, Pgh.	.10	.35
369	Ulf Samuelsson, Pgh.	.10	.35
370	**Mike Needham, Pgh., RC**	**.10**	**.35**
371	Ken Wregget (G), Pgh.	.10	.35
372	Dave Tippett, Pgh.	.10	.35
373	Kjell Samuelsson, Pgh.	.10	.35
374	Bob Errey, Pgh.	.10	.35
375	Jim Paek, Pgh.	.10	.35
376	**Bill Lindsay, Que., RC**	**.10**	**.35**
377	Valeri Kamensky, Que.	.25	.50
378	Stéphane Fiset (G), Que.	.25	.50
379	Steven Finn, Que.	.10	.35
380	Mike Hough, Que.	.10	.35
381	Scott Pearson, Que.	.10	.35
382	Kerry Huffman, Que.	.10	.35
383	Scott Young, Que.	.10	.35
384	Stéphane Quintal, Stl.	.10	.35
385	**Bret Hedican, Stl., RC**	**.10**	**.35**
386	**Guy Hebert (G), Stl., RC**	**.35**	**.50**
387	**Vitali Karamnov, Stl., RC**	**.10**	**.35**
388	Doug Crossman, Stl.	.10	.35
389	Ron Sutter, Stl.	.10	.35
390	Garth Butcher, Stl.	.10	.35
391	Basil McRae, Stl.	.10	.35
392	Dean Evason, S.J.	.10	.35
393	**Doug Zmolek, S.J., RC**	**.10**	**.35**
394	Jayson More, S.J.	.10	.35
395	Mike Sullivan, S.J.	.10	.35
396	Arturs Irbe (G), S.J.	.10	.35
397	Johan Garpenlov, S.J.	.10	.35
398	Jeff Odgers, S.J.	.10	.35
399	**Jaroslav Otevrel, S.J., RC**	**.10**	**.35**
400	Marc Bureau, T.B.	.10	.35
401	Bob Beers, T.B.	.10	.35
402	Rob DiMaio, T.B.	.10	.35
403	Steve Kasper, T.B.	.10	.35
404	Pat Jablonski (G), T.B.	.10	.35
405	John Tucker, T.B.	.10	.35
406	Shawn Chambers, T.B.	.10	.35
407	Mike Hartman, T.B.	.10	.35
408	Danton Cole, T.B.	.10	.35
409	Dave Andreychuk, Tor.	.25	.50
410	Peter Zezel, Tor.	.10	.35
411	Mike Krushelnyski, Tor.	.10	.35
412	Daren Puppa (G), Tor.	.10	.35
413	Ken Baumgartner, Tor.	.10	.35
414	Rob Pearson, Tor.	.10	.35
415	Mike Foligno, Tor.	.10	.35
416	Sylvain Lefebvre, Tor.	.10	.35
417	Dimitri Mironov, Tor.,	.10	.35
418	Petr Nedved, Van.	.10	.35
419	Gerald Diduck, Van.	.10	.35
420	Anatoli Semenov, Van.	.10	.35
421	Sergio Momesso, Van.	.10	.35
422	Gino Odjick, Van.	.10	.35
423	Kay Whitmore (G), Van.	.10	.35
424	Dave Babych, Van.	.10	.35
425	Robert Dirk, Van.	.10	.35
426	Reggie Savage, Wsh.	.10	.35
427	**Keith Jones, Wsh., RC**	**.25**	**.35**
428	Dimitri Khristich, Wsh.	.10	.35
429	**Jason Woolley, Wsh., RC**	**.10**	**.35**
430	Jim Hrivnak (G), Wsh.	.10	.35
431	Sylvain Côté, Wsh.	.10	.35
432	Michal Pivonka, Wsh.	.10	.35
434	Tie Domi, Wpg.	.10	.35
435	**Sergei Bautin, Wpg., RC**	**.10**	**.35**
436	Darrin Shannon, Wpg.	.10	.35
437	John Druce, Wpg.	.10	.35
438	Teppo Numminen, Wpg.	.10	.35
439	Luciano Borsato, Wpg.	.10	.35
440	Igor Ulanov, Wpg.	.10	.35
441	**Mike O'Neil (G), Wpg., RC**	**.10**	**.35**
442	Kris King, Wpg.	.10	.35
443	Roman Hamrlik, T.B.	.25	.50
444	Steve Smith, Chi.	.10	.35
445	Jari Kurri, L.A.	.25	.50
446	Ulf Samuelsson, Pgh.	.10	.35
447	Sergei Nemchinov, NYR.	.10	.35
448	**Tommy Söderström, (G), Pha., RC**	**.10**	**.35**
449	Petr Nedved, Van.	.10	.35
450	Peter Sidorkiewicz (G), Ott.	.10	.35
451	Nicklas Lidström, Det.	.25	.50
452	Philippe Bozon, Stl.	.10	.35
453	Uwe Krupp, NYI.	.10	.35
454	Steve Thomas, NYI.	.10	.35
455	Owen Nolan, Que.	.25	.50
456	AS: Steve Yzerman, Det.	.75	2.50
457	AS: Chris Chelios, Chi.	.25	.75
458	AS: Paul Coffey, Det.	.25	.50
459	AS: Brett Hull, Stl.	.35	1.25
460	AS: Pavel Bure, Van	.50	1.75
461	AS: Ed Belfour (G), Chi.	.25	.50
462	AS: Mario Lemieux, Pgh.	1.00	4.00
463	AS: Patrick Roy (G), Mtl.	1.00	4.00
464	AS: Ray Bourque, Bos.	.35	1.25
465	AS: Jaromir Jagr, Pgh.	.75	2.50
466	AS: Kevin Stevens, Pgh.	.10	.35
467	AS: Brian Leetch, NYR.	.25	.50
468	Bobby Clarke	.35	1.50
469	Bill Barber	.25	.50
470	Bernie Parent (G)	.35	1.50
471	Reggie Leach	.10	.35
472	Rick MacLeish	.10	.35
473	Dave Schultz	.10	.35
474	Joe Watson	.10	.35
475	Bobby Taylor (G)	.10	.35
476	Orest Kindrachuk	.10	.35
477	Bob Kelly	.10	.35
478	Bill Clement	.10	.35
479	Ed Van Impe	.10	.35
480	Fred Shero, Coach	.25	.50
481	**Bryan Smolinski, Bos., RC**	**.75**	**1.50**
482	Sergei Zholtok, Bos.	.25	.50
483	**Matthew Barnaby, Buf., RC**	**.25**	**.50**
484	**Gary Shuchuk, L.A., RC**	**.25**	**.50**
485	Guy Carbonneau, Mtl.	.25	.50
486	**Oleg Petrov, Mtl., RC**	**.25**	**.50**
487	**Sean Hill, Mtl., RC**	**.25**	**.50**
488	**Jesse Belanger, Mtl., RC**	**.25**	**.50**
489	Paul DiPietro, Mtl.	.25	.50
490	Richard Pilon, NYI.	.25	.50
491	**Greg Parks, NYI., RC**	**.25**	**.50**
492	**Jeff Daniels, Pgh., RC**	**.25**	**.50**
493	**Denny Felsner, Stl., RC**	**.25**	**.50**
494	**Mike Eastwood, Tor., RC**	**.25**	**.50**
495	Murray Craven, Van.	.25	.50
496	Vincent Damphousse, Mtl.	.25	.50
497	Grant Fuhr (G), Buf.	.35	.75
498	Mario Lemieux, Pgh.	4.00	12.00
499	Ray Ferraro, NYI.	.25	.50
500	Teemu Selänne, Wpg.	1.75	5.00
501	Luc Robitaille, L.A.	.50	1.00
502	Doug Gilmour, Tor.	.75	2.00
503	Curtis Joseph (G), Stl.	1.50	4.50
504	Kirk Muller, Mtl.	.25	.50
505	Glenn Healy (G), NYI.	.25	.50
506	Pavel Bure, Van.	1.75	5.00
507	Félix Potvin (G), Tor.	1.25	3.50
508	Guy Carbonneau, Mtl.	.25	.50
509	Wayne Gretzky, L.A.	5.00	15.00
510	Patrick Roy (G), Mtl.	4.00	12.00

PARKHURST REPRINT CARDS

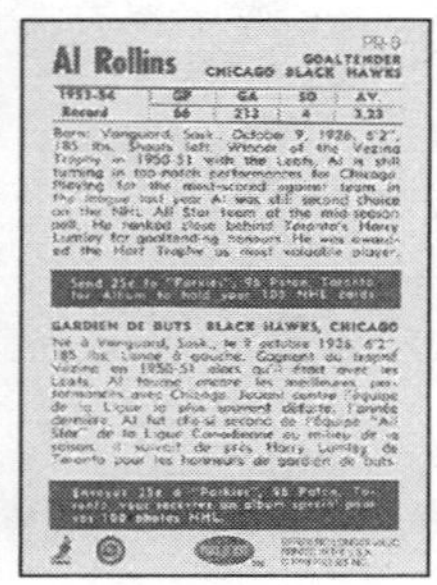

Series 1 Regular Pack (1-8/CL1): 85.00
Series 1 Jumbo Pack (9-16/CL2): 65.00
Series 2 Regular Pack (17-24/CL3): 85.00
Series 2 Jumbo Pack (25-32/CL4): 65.00
Common Player (1-32): 6.00

No.	Player	NRMT-MT
	Checklist #1 ('55-56)	15.00
PR-1	Jacques Plante (G), Mtl. ('55-56)	20.00
PR-2	Terry Sawchuk (G), Det. ('51-52)	20.00
PR-3	Johnny Bower (G), Tor. ('59-60)	10.00
PR-4	Gump Worsley (G), NYR. ('53-54)	15.00
PR-5	Harry Lumley (G), Tor. ('53-54)	10.00
PR-6	Turk Broda (G), Tor. ('51-52)	10.00
PR-7	Jim Henry (G), Bos. ('52-53)	10.00
PR-8	Al Rollins (G), Chi. ('54-55)	10.00
	Checklist #2 ('53-54)	15.00
PR-9	Bill Gadsby, Chi. ('53-54)	6.00
PR-10	Red Kelly, Det. ('54-55)	6.00
PR-11	Allan Stanley, NYR. ('52-53)	6.00
PR-12	Bobby Baun, Tor. ('59-60)	6.00
PR-13	Carl Brewer, Tor. ('62-63)	6.00
PR-14	Doug Harvey, Mtl. ('54-55)	12.00
PR-15	Harry Howell, NYR. ('53-54)	6.00
PR-16	Tim Horton, Tor., ('55-56)	20.00
	Checklist #3 ('58-59)	15.00
PR-17	George Armstrong, Tor.	6.00
PR-18	Ralph Backstrom, Mtl. ('58-59)	6.00
PR-19	Alex Delvecchio, Det.	6.00
PR-20	Bill Mosienko, Chi. ('53-54)	6.00
PR-21	Dave Keon, Tor.	6.00
PR-22	Andy Bathgate, NYR. ('53-54)	6.00
PR-23	Milton Schmidt, Bos. ('52-53)	6.00
PR-24	Dick Duff, Tor. ('58-59)	6.00
	Checklist #4 ('54-55)	15.00
PR-25	Norm Ullman, Det. ('62-63)	6.00
PR-26	Dickie Moore, Mtl. ('55-56)	6.00
PR-27	Jerry Toppazzini, Bos.	6.00
PR-28	Henri Richard, Mtl.	10.00
PR-29	Frank Mahovlich, Tor.	10.00
PR-30	Jean Béliveau, Mtl.	20.00
PR-31	Ted Lindsay, Det.	10.00
PR-32	Bernie Geoffrion, Mtl.	10.00

DON CHERRY REPRINT CARD

The Don Cherry card is a reprint of the 1954-55 Parkhurst card no. 56 of Warren Godfrey. The reprint has Don Cherry's portrait superimposed on Godfrey's and the card number changed to 101. The cards are found only in Canadian distributed Series Two regular and jumbo foils. They were inserted approximately one per case and are thus scarce. There are also 300 autographed Don Cherry Reprint cards.

	No.	Player	NRMT-MT
□	101	Don Cherry	55.00
□	101	Don Cherry, Autographed	225.00

CHERRY PICKS

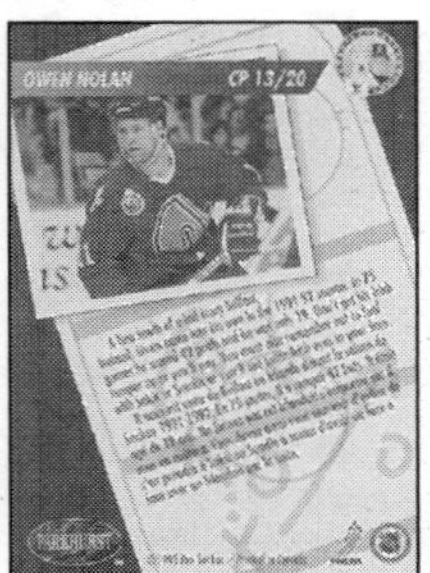

This 21-card set was randomly inserted in the Series Two regular and jumbo foil packs. The Don Cherry Thumbs Up autographed card was inserted only in jumbo Series Two foil packs.

Series Two Insert Set (CP1-CP20): **80.00**

	No.	Player	NRMT-MT
□		Don Cherry Checklist	25.00
□		Don Cherry Redemption	12.00
□		Don Cherry Autograph	225.00
□	CP1	Doug Gilmour, Tor.	5.00
□	CP2	Jeremy Roenick, Chi.	5.00
□	CP3	Brent Sutter, Chi.	4.00
□	CP4	Mark Messier, NYR.	8.00
□	CP5	Kirk Muller, Mtl.	4.00
□	CP6	Eric Lindros, Pha.	25.00
□	CP7	Dale Hunter, Wsh.	4.00
□	CP8	Gary Roberts, Cgy.	4.00
□	CP9	Bob Probert, Det.	4.00
□	CP10	Brendan Shanahan, Stl.	10.00
□	CP11	Wendel Clark, Tor.	4.00
□	CP12	Rick Tocchet, Pgh.	4.00
□	CP13	Owen Nolan, Que.	4.00
□	CP14	Cam Neely, Bos.	4.00
□	CP15	Dave Manson, Edm.	4.00
□	CP16	Chris Chelios, Chi.	6.00
□	CP17	Marty McSorely, L.A.	4.00
□	CP18	Scott Stevens, N.J.	4.00
□	CP19	John Blue (G), Bos.	4.00
□	CP20	Ron Hextall (G), Que.	4.00

DON CHERRY'S PICK OFF THE YEAR

One chase card was randomly inserted into the Final Update sets.

	Player	NRMT-MT
□	Cherry's Pick of the Year: Douglas Gilmour	12.00

COMMEMORATIVE SHEETS

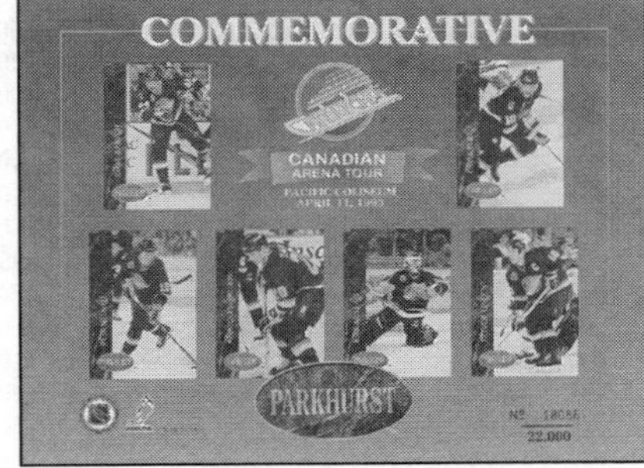

Five different commemorative sheets were issued during the 1992-93 season, first as promos and then as regular issue in regular and jumbo foil cases.

Sheet Size: 8 1/2" x 11"

	No.	Player	NRMT-MT
□		Goalies Promo Sheet	15.00
□		Defense Promo Sheet	15.00
□		Forwards # 1 Promo Sheet	15.00
□		Forwards # 2 Promo Sheet	15.00
□		The Stanley Cup Update Promo Sheet	15.00
□	1	Goalies (#/7,000)	10.00
□	2	Defense (#/3,000)	15.00
□	3	Forwards #1 (#/7,000)	10.00
□	4	Forwards #2 (#/3,000)	15.00
□	5	The Stanley Cup Update Sheet (#/7,000)	10.00
□		Toronto Maple Leafs vs. Montréal Canadiens April 4, 1993 Maple Leaf Gardens	15.00
□	1	Calgary Flames, April 1, 1993, (#/22,000)	5.00
□	2	Edmonton Oilers, April 3, 1993, (#/22,000)	5.00
□	3	Québec Nordiques, April 6, 1993, (#/22,000)	5.00
□	4	Vancouver Canucks, April 11, 1993, (#/22,000)	5.00
□	5	Montréal Canadiens, April 12, 1993, (#/22,000)	8.00
□	6	Toronto Maple Leafs, April 13, 1993, (#/22,000)	5.00
□	7	Ottawa Senators, April 14, 1993, (#/22,000)	5.00
□	8	Winnipeg Jets, April 15, 1993, (#22,000)	5.00
□		Promo Don Cherry Sheet	50.00
□		Regular Don Cherry Sheet	50.00

1992 - 93 PINNACLE

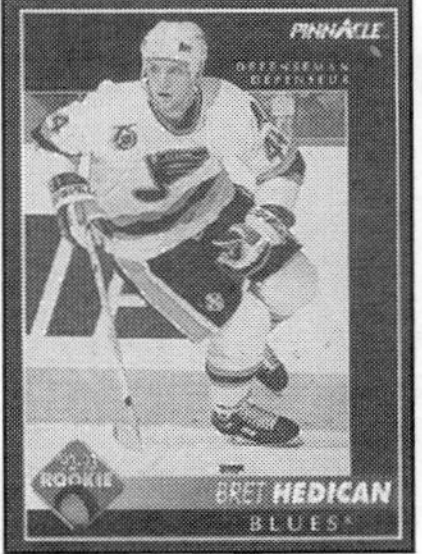

These cards have two versions: an American (English only) and a Canadian (bilingual) issue. Player photos for both series are different.

Complete Set (420 cards): **35.00**
Common Player: **.10**
Promo Sheet (#'s: 111, 165, 288, 387): **4.00**
Promo Sheet (#'s: 66, 80, 110, 280): **5.00**
Promo Sheet (#'s: 77, 175, 279, 406): **5.00**
Promo Sheet (#'s: 6, 22, 36, 61, 88, 91): **8.00**

	No.	Player	NRMT-MT
□ □	1	Mark Messier, NYR.	.50
□ □	2	Ray Bourque, Bos.	.50
□ □	3	Gary Roberts, Cgy.	.25
□ □	4	Bill Ranford (G), Edm.	.25
□ □	5	Gilbert Dionne, Mtl.	.10
□ □	6	Owen Nolan, Que.	.25
□ □	7	Pat LaFontaine, Buf.	.25
□ □	8	Nicklas Lidström, Det.	.25
□ □	9	Pat Falloon, S.J.	.10
□ □	10	Jeremy Roenick, Chi.	.35
□ □	11	Kevin Hatcher, Wsh.	.10
□ □	12	Cliff Ronning, Van.	.10
□ □	13	Jeff Brown, Stl.	.10
□ □	14	Kevin Dineen, Pha.	.10
□ □	15	Brian Leetch, NYR.	.35
□ □	16	Eric Desjardins, Mtl.	.10
□ □	17	Derek King, NYI.	.10
□ □	18	Mark Tinordi, Min.	.10
□ □	19	Kelly Hrudey (G), L.A.	.10
□ □	20	Sergei Fedorov, Det.	.50
□ □	21	Mike Ramsey, Buf.	.10
□ □	22	Michel Goulet, Chi.	.10
□ □	23	Joe Murphy, Edm.	.10
□ □	24	Mark Fitzpatrick (G), NYI.	.10
□ □	25	Cam Neely, Bos.	.25
□ □	26	Rod Brind'Amour, Pha.	.25
□ □	27	Neil Wilkinson, S.J.	.10
□ □	28	Greg Adams, Van.	.10
□ □	29	Thomas Steen, Wpg.	.10
□ □	30	Calle Johansson, Wsh.	.10
□ □	31	Joe Nieuwendyk, Cgy.	.25
□ □	32	Rob Blake, L.A.	.25
□ □	33	Darren Turcotte, NYR.	.10
□ □	34	Derian Hatcher, Min.	.25
□ □	35	Mikhail Tatarinov, Que.	.10
□ □	36	Nelson Emerson, Stl.	.10
□ □	37	Tim Cheveldae, (G), Det.	.10
□ □	38	Donald Audette, Buf.	.10
□ □	39	Brent Sutter, Chi.	.10
□ □	40	Adam Oates, Bos.	.35
□ □	41	Luke Richardson, Edm.	.10
□ □	42	Jon Casey, (G), Min.	.10
□ □	43	Guy Carbonneau, Mtl.	.10
□ □	44	Patrick Flatley, NYI.	.10
□ □	45	Brian Benning, Pha.	.10
□ □	46	Curtis Leschyshyn, Que.	.10
□ □	47	Trevor Linden, Van.	.25
□ □	48	Don Beaupré (G), Wsh.	.10
□ □	49	Troy Murray, Wpg.	.10
□ □	50	Paul Coffey, L.A.	.25
□ □	51	Frantisek Musil, Cgy.	.10
□ □	52	Doug Wilson, S.J.	.10
□ □	53	Pat Elynuik, Wsh.	.10
□ □	54	Curtis Joseph (G), Stl.	.75
□ □	55	Tony Amonte, NYR.	.25
□ □	56	Bob Probert, Det.	.10
□ □	57	Steve Smith, Chi.	.10
□ □	58	Dave Andreychuk, Buf.	.25
□ □	59	Vladimir Ruzicka, Bos.	.10
□ □	60	Jari Kurri, L.A.	.25
□ □	61	Denis Savard, Bos.	.25
□ □	62	Benoît Hogue, NYI.	.10
□ □	63	Terry Carkner, Pha.	.10
□ □	64	Valeri Kamensky, Que.	.25
□ □	65	Jyrki Lumme, Van.	.10
□ □	66	Al Iafrate, Wsh.	.10
□ □	67	Paul Ranheim, Cgy.	.10
□ □	68	Ulf Dahlen, Min.	.10
□ □	69	Tony Granato, L.A.	.10
□ □	70	Phil Housley, Wpg.	.10
□ □	71	Brian Lawton, S.J.	.10
□ □	72	Garth Butcher, Stl.	.10
□ □	73	Stephen Leach, Bos.	.10
□ □	74	Steve Larmer, Chi.	.10
□ □	75	Mike Richter (G), NYR.	.35
□ □	76	Vladimir Konstantinov, Det.	.25
□ □	77	Alexander Mogilny, Buf.	.35
□ □	78	Craig MacTavish, Edm.	.10
□ □	79	Mathieu Schneider, Mtl.	.10
□ □	80	Mark Recchi, Pha.	.25
□ □	81	Gerald Diduck, Van.	.10
□ □	82	Peter Bondra, Wsh.	.35
□ □	83	Al MacInnis, Cgy.	.10
□ □	84	Bob Kudelski, L.A.	.25
□ □	85	Dave Gagner, Min.	.10
□ □	86	Uwe Krupp, NYI.	.10
□ □	87	Randy Carlyle, Wpg.	.10
□ □	88	Eric Lindros, Pha.	2.00
□ □	89	Rob Zettler, S.J.	.10
□ □	90	Mats Sundin, Que.	.50
□ □	91	Andy Moog (G), Bos.	.25
□ □	92	Keith Brown, Chi.	.10
□ □	93	Paul Ysabaert, Det.	.10
□ □	94	Mike Gartner, NYR.	.25
□ □	95	Kelly Buchberger, Edm.	.10
□ □	96	Dominic Roussel (G), Pha.	.10
□ □	97	Doug Bodger, Buf.	.10
□ □	98	Mike Donnelly, L.A.	.10
□ □	99	Mike Craig, Min.	.10
□ □	100	Brett Hull, Stl.	.50
□ □	101	Robert Reichel, Cgy.	.10
□ □	102	Jeff Norton, NYI.	.10
□ □	103	Garry Galley, Pha.	.10
□ □	104	Dale Hunter, Wsh.	.10
□ □	105	Jeff Hackett (G), S.J.	.25
□ □	106	Darrin Shannon, Wpg.	.10
□ □	107	Craig Wolanin, Que.	.10
□ □	108	Adam Graves, NYR.	.10
□ □	109	Chris Chelios, Chi.	.35
□ □	110	Pavel Bure, Van.	.85
□ □	111	Kirk Muller, Mtl.	.10
□ □	112	Jeff Beukeboom, NYR.	.10
□ □	113	Mike Hough, Que.	.10
□ □	114	Brendan Shanahan, Stl.	.75
□ □	115	Randy Burridge, Wsh.	.10
□ □	116	Dave Poulin, Bos.	.10
□ □	117	Petr Svoboda, Buf.	.10
□ □	118	Ed Belfour (G), Chi.	.35
□ □	119	Ray Sheppard, Det.	.10
□ □	120	Bernie Nicholls, Edm.	.10
□ □	121	Glenn Healy (G), NYI.	.10
□ □	122	Johan Garpenlov, S.J.	.10
□ □	123	Mike Lalor, Wpg.	.10

	No.	Player	Price
□□	124	Brad McCrimmon, Det.	.10
□□	125	Theoren Fleury, Cgy.	.35
□□	126	Randy Gilhen, NYR.	.10
□□	127	Petr Nedved, Van.	.10
□□	128	Steve Thomas, NYI.	.10
□□	129	Rick Zombo, Stl.	.10
□□	130	Patrick Roy (G), Mtl.	2.00
□□	131	Rod Langway, Wsh.	.10
□□	132	Gord Murphy, Bos.	.10
□□	133	Randy Wood, Buf.	.10
□□	134	Mike Hudson, Chi.	.10
□□	135	Gerard Gallant, Det.	.10
□□	136	Brian Glynn, Edm.	.10
□□	137	Jim Johnson, Min.	.10
□□	138	Corey Millen, L.A.	.10
□□	139	Daniel Marois, NYI.	.10
□□	140	James Patrick, NYR.	.10
□□	141	Claude Lapointe, Que.	.10
□□	142	Bobby Smith, Min.	.10
□□	143	Charlie Huddy, L.A.	.10
□□	144	Murray Baron, Stl.	.10
□□	145	Ed Olczyk, Wpg.	.10
□□	146	Dimitri Khristich, Wsh.	.10
□□	147	Doug Lidster, Van.	.10
□□	148	Perry Berezan, S.J.	.10
□□	149	Per-Erik Eklund, Pha.	.10
□□	150	Joe Sakic, Que.	1.00
□□	151	Michal Pivonka, Wsh.	.10
□□	152	Joey Kocur, NYR.	.10
□□	153	Patrice Brisebois, Mtl.	.10
□□	154	Ray Ferraro, NYI.	.10
□□	155	Mike Modano, Min.	.50
□□	156	Marty McSorley, L.A.	.10
□□	157	Norm Maciver, Ott.	.10
□□	158	Sergei Nemchinov, NYR.	.10
□□	159	David Bruce, S.J.	.10
□□	160	Kelly Miller, Wsh.	.10
□□	161	Alexei Gusarov, Que.	.10
□□	162	Andrei Lomakin, Pha.	.10
□□	163	Sergio Momesso, Van.	.10
□□	164	Mike Keane, Mtl.	.10
□□	165	Pierre Turgeon, NYI.	.20
□□	166	Martin Gelinas, Edm.	.10
□□	167	Chris Dahlquist, Cgy.	.10
□□	168	Kris King, NYR.	.10
□□	169	Dean Evason, S.J.	.10
□□	170	Mike Ridley, Wsh.	.10
□□	171	Shawn Burr, Det.	.10
□□	172	Dana Murzyn, Van.	.10
□□	173	Dirk Graham, Chi.	.10
□□	174	Trent Yawney, Cgy.	.10
□□	175	Luc Robitaille, L.A.	.25
□□	176	Randy Moller, Buf.	.10
□□	177	Vincent Riendeau (G), Det.	.10
□□	178	Brian Propp, Min.	.10
□□	179	Don Sweeney, Bos.	.10
□□	180	Stéphane Matteau, Chi.	.10
□□	181	Garry Valk, Van.	.10
□□	182	Sylvain Côté, Wsh.	.10
□□	183	Dave Snuggerud, S.J.	.10
□□	184	Gary Leeman, Cgy.	.10
□□	185	John Druce, Wpg.	.10
□□	186	John Vanbiesbrouck (G), NYR.	.75
□□	187	Geoff Courtnall, Van.	.10
□□	188	David Volek, NYI.	.10
□□	189	Doug Weight, NYR.	.35
□□	190	Bob Essensa (G), Wpg.	.10
□□	191	Jan Erixon, NYR.	.10
□□	192	Geoff Smith, Edm.	.10
□□	193	Dave Christian, Chi.	.10
□□	194	Brian Noonan, Chi.	.10
□□	195	Gary Suter, Cgy.	.10
□□	196	Craig Janney, Stl.	.10
□□	197	Brad May, Buf.	.10
□□	198	Gaetan Duchesne, Min.	.10
□□	199	Adam Creighton, TB	.10
□□	200	Wayne Gretzky, L.A.	2.50
□□	201	Dave Babych, Van.	.10
□□	202	Fredrik Olausson, Wpg.	.10
□□	203	Bob Bassen, Stl.	.10
□□	204	Todd Krygier, Wsh.	.10
□□	205	Grant Ledyard. Buf.	.10
□□	206	Michel Petit, Cgy.	.10
□□	207	Todd Elik, Min.	.10
□□	208	Josef Beranek, Edm.	.10
□□	209	Neal Broten, Min.	.10
□□	210	Jim Sandlak, Van.	.10
□□	211	Kevin Haller, Mtl.	.10
□□	212	Paul Broten, NYR.	.10
□□	213	Mark Pederson, Pha.	.10
□□	214	John McIntyre, L.A.	.10
□□	215	Teppo Numminen, Wpg.	.10
□□	216	Ken Sutton, Buf.	.10
□□	217	Ron Stern, Cgy.	.10
□□	218	Luciano Borsato, Wpg.	.10
□□	219	Claude Loiselle, NYI.	.10
□□	220	Mark Hardy, NYR.	.10
□□	221	Joé Juneau, Bos.	.10
□□	222	Keith Tkachuk, Wpg.	.50
□□	223	Scott Lachance, NYI.	.10
□□	224	Glen Murray, Bos.	.10
□□	225	Igor Kravchuk, Chi.	.10
□□	226	Evgeny Davydov, Wpg.	.10
□□	**227**	**Ray Whitney, S.J., RC**	**.10**
□□	**228**	**Bret Hedican, Stl., RC**	**.10**
□□	**229**	**Keith Carney, Buf., RC**	**.10**
□□	230	Vyacheslav Kozlov, Det.	.10
□□	231	Drake Berehowsky, Tor.	.10
□□	232	Cam Neely, Bos.	.25
□□	233	Doug Gilmour, Tor.	.25
□□	234	Randy Wood, Buf.	.10
□□	235	Luke Richardson, Edm.	.10
□□	236	Eric Lindros, Pha.	1.50
□□	237	Dale Hunter, Wsh.	.10
□□	238	Pat Falloon, S.J.	.10
□□	239	Dean Kennedy, Wpg.	.10
□□	240	Uwe Krupp, NYI.	.10
□□	241	Scott Niedermayer/Steve Yzerman	.50
□□	242	Gary Roberts/Lanny McDonald	.25
□□	243	Peter Ahola/Jari Kurri	.25
□□	244	Scott Lachance/Mark Howe	.25
□□	245	Rob Pearson/Mike Bossy	.25
□□	246	Kirk McLean/Bernie Parent	.25
□□	247	Dmitri Mironov/Viacheslav Fetisov	.25
□□	248	Brendan Shanahan/Darryl Sittler	.25
□□	249	Petr Nedved/Wayne Gretzky	1.00
□□	250	Todd Ewen/Clark Gilles	.15
□□	251	Luc Robitaille, L.A.	.25
□□	252	Mark Tinordi, Min.	.10
□□	253	Kris King, NYR.	.10
□□	254	Pat LaFontaine, Buf.	.25
□□	255	Ryan Walter, Van.	.10
□□	256	Jeremy Roenick, Chi.	.25
□□	257	Brett Hull, Stl.	.25
□□	258	Steve Yzerman, Det.	.50
□□	259	Claude Lemieux, N.J.	.10
□□	260	Mike Modano, Min.	.25
□□	261	Vincent Damphousse, Mtl.	.25
□□	262	Tony Granato, L.A.	.10
□□	263	Andy Moog Mask	3.00
□□	264	Curtis Joseph Mask	4.00
□□	265	Ed Belfour Mask	3.50
□□	266	Brian Hayward Mask	3.50
□□	267	Grant Fuhr Mask	3.00
□□	268	Don Beaupré Mask	2.00
□□	269	Tim Cheveldae Mask	2.00
□□	270	Mike Richter Mask	3.50
□□	271	Zarley Zalapski. Hfd.	.10
□□	272	Kevin Todd, N.J.	.10
□□	273	David Ellett, Tor.	.10
□□	274	Chris Terreri, (G), N.J.	.10
□□	275	Jaromir Jagr, Pgh.	1.25
□□	276	Wendel Clark, Tor.	.25
□□	277	Bobby Holik, N.J.	.10
□□	278	Bruce Driver, N.J.	.10
□□	279	Doug Gilmour, Tor.	.35
□□	280	Scott Stevens, N.J.	.10
□□	281	Murray Craven, Hfd.	.10
□□	282	Rick Tocchet, Pgh.	.10
□□	283	Peter Zezel, Tor.	.10
□□	284	Claude Lemieux, N.J.	.10
□□	285	John Cullen, Hfd.	.10
□□	286	Valeri Zelepukin, N.J.	.10
□□	287	Rob Pearson, Tor.	.10
□□	288	Kevin Stevens, Pgh.	.10
□□	289	Alexei Kasatonov, N.J.	.10
□□	290	Todd Gill, Tor.	.10
□□	291	Randy Ladouceur, Hfd.	.10
□□	292	Larry Murphy, Pgh.	.25
□□	293	Tom Chorske, N.J.	.10
□□	294	Jamie Macoun, Tor.	.10
□□	295	Sean Burke (G), Hfd.	.25
□□	296	Ulf Samuelsson, Pgh.	.10
□□	297	Eric Weinrich, Hfd.	.10
□□	298	Tom Barrasso (G), Pgh.	.10
□□	299	Viacheslav Fetisov, N.J.	.25
□□	300	Mario Lemieux, Pgh.	2.00
□□	301	Grant Fuhr (G), Tor.	.25
□□	302	Zdeno Ciger, N.J.	.10
□□	303	Ron Francis, Pgh.	.35
□□	304	Scott Niedermayer, N.J.	.25
□□	305	Mark Osborne, Tor.	.10
□□	306	Kjell Samuelsson, Pgh.	.10
□□	307	Geoff Sanderson, Hfd.	.10
□□	308	Paul Stanton, Pgh.	.10
□□	309	Frank Pietrangelo (G), Hfd.	.10
□□	310	Bob Errey, Pgh.	.10
□□	311	Dino Ciccarelli, Det.	.25
□□	312	Gord Roberts, Bos.	.25
□□	313	Kevin Miller, Wsh.	.10
□□	314	Mike Ricci, Que.	.10
□□	315	Bob Carpenter, Wsh.	.10
□□	316	Dale Hawerchuk, Buf.	.25
□□	317	Christian Ruuttu, Chi.	.10
□□	318	Mike Vernon (G), Cgy.	.25
□□	319	Paul Cavallini, Stl.	.10
□□	320	Steve Duchesne, Que.	.10
□□	321	Craig Simpson, Edm.	.10
□□	322	Mark Howe, Det.	.25
□□	323	Shayne Corson, Edm.	.25
□□	324	Tom Kurvers, NYI.	.10
□□	325	Brian Bellows, Mtl.	.10
□□	326	Glen Wesley, Bos.	.10
□□	327	Daren Puppa (G), Buf.	.10
□□	328	Joel Otto, Cgy.	.10
□□	329	Jimmy Carson, Det.	.10
□□	330	Kirk McLean (G), Van.	.25
□□	331	Rob Brown, Chi.	.10
□□	332	Yves Racine, Det.	.10
□□	333	Brian Mullen, NYI.	.10
□□	334	Dave Manson, Edm.	.10
□□	335	Sergei Makarov, Cgy.	.10
□□	336	Esa Tikkanen, Edm.	.10
□□	337	Russ Courtnall, Min.	.10
□□	338	Kevin Lowe, Edm.	.10
□□	339	Steve Chaisson, Det.	.10
□□	340	Ron Hextall (G), Que.	.25
□□	341	Stéphan Lebeau, Mtl.	.10
□□	342	Mike McPhee, Min.	.10
□□	343	David Shaw, Bos.	.10
□□	344	Petr Klima, Edm.	.10
□□	345	Tomas Sandström, L.A.	.10
□□	346	Scott Mellanby, Edm.	.10
□□	347	Brian Skrudland, Mtl.	.10
□□	348	Pat Verbeek, Hfd.	.10
□□	349	Vincent Damphousse, Mtl.	.35
□□	350	Steve Yzerman, Det.	1.25
□□	351	John MacLean, N.J.	.10
□□	352	Steve Konroyd, Hfd.	.10
□□	353	Phil Bourque, NYR.	.10
□□	354	Ken Daneyko, N.J.	.10
□□	355	Glenn Anderson, Tor.	.10
□□	356	Ken Wregget (G), Pgh.	.10
□□	357	Brent Gilchrist, Edm.	.10
□□	358	Bob Rouse, Tor.	.10
□□	359	Peter Stastny, N.J.	.10
□□	360	Joe Mullen, Pgh.	.10
□□	361	Stéphane Richer, N.J.	.10
□□	362	Kelly Kisio, S.J.	.10
□□	363	Keith Acton, Pha.	.10
□□	364	Félix Potvin (G), Tor.	.50
□□	365	Martin Lapointe, Det.	.20
□□	366	Ron Tugnutt (G), Edm.	.10
□□	367	Dave Taylor, L.A.	.10
□□	368	Tim Kerr, Hfd.	.10
□□	369	Carey Wilson, Cgy.	.10
□□	370	Greg Paslawski, Pha.	.10
□□	371	Peter Sidorkiewick (G), Ott.	.10
□□	372	Brad Shaw, Ott.	.10
□□	373	Sylvain Turgeon, Ott.	.10
□□	374	Mark Lamb, Ott.	.10
□□	375	Laurie Boschman, Ott.	.10
□□	376	Mark Osiecki, Ott.	.10
□□	377	Doug Smail, Ott.	.10
□□	378	Brad Marsh, Ott.	.10

	No.	Player	Price
☐ ☐	379	Mike Peluso, Ott.	.10
☐ ☐	380	Steve Weeks (G), Ott.	.10
☐ ☐	381	Wendell Young (G), T.B.	.10
☐ ☐	382	Joe Reekie, T.B.	.10
☐ ☐	383	Peter Taglianetti, T.B.	.10
☐ ☐	384	Mikael Andersson, T.B.	.10
☐ ☐	385	Marc Bergevin, T.B.	.10
☐ ☐	386	Anatoli Semenov, T.B.	.10
☐ ☐	387	Brian Bradley, T.B.	.10
☐ ☐	388	Michel Mongeau, T.B.	.10
☐ ☐	389	Rob Ramage, T.B.	.10
☐ ☐	390	Ken Hodge, T.B.	.10
☐ ☐	**391**	**Richard Matvichuk, Min., RC**	**.10**
☐ ☐	392	Alexei Zhitnik, L.A.	.10
☐ ☐	**393**	**Richard Smehlik, Buf., RC**	**.10**
☐ ☐	**394**	**Dimitri Yushkevich, Pha., RC**	**.10**
☐ ☐	**395**	**Andrei Kovalenko, Que., RC**	**.25**
☐ ☐	**396**	**Vladimir Vujtek, Edm., RC**	**.10**
☐ ☐	**397**	**Nikolai Borschevsky, Tor., RC**	**.10**
☐ ☐	**398**	**Vitali Karamnov, Stl., RC**	**.10**
☐ ☐	**399**	**Jim Hiller, L.A., RC**	**.10**
☐ ☐	**400**	**Michael Nylander, Min., RC**	**.10**
☐ ☐	**401**	**Tommy Sjodin, Min., RC**	**.10**
☐ ☐	**402**	**Robert Petrovicky, Hfd., RC**	**.10**
☐ ☐	403	Alexei Kovalev, NYR.	.10
☐ ☐	**404**	**Vatali Prokhorov, Stl., RC**	**.10**
☐ ☐	**405**	**Dmitri Kvartalnov, Bos., RC**	**.10**
☐ ☐	406	Teemu Selänne, Wpg.	.75
☐ ☐	407	Darius Kasparaitis, NYI.	.10
☐ ☐	**408**	**Roman Hamrlik, T.B., RC**	**.25**
☐ ☐	409	Vladimir Malakhov, NYI.	.10
☐ ☐	410	Sergei Krivokrasov, Chi.	.10
☐ ☐	**411**	**Robert Lang, L.A., RC**	**.10**
☐ ☐	412	Josef Stumpel, Bos.	.10
☐ ☐	**413**	**Denny Felsner, Stl., RC**	**.10**
☐ ☐	**414**	**Rob Zamuner, T.B., RC**	**.35**
☐ ☐	**415**	**Jason Woolley, Wsh., RC**	**.10**
☐ ☐	416	Alexei Zhamnov, Wpg.	.25
☐ ☐	**417**	**Igor Korolev, Stl., RC**	**.10**
☐ ☐	418	Patrick Poulin, Hfd.	.10
☐ ☐	419	Dmitri Mironov, Tor.	.10
☐ ☐	420	Shawn McEachern, Pgh.	.10

TEAM PINNACLE

These cards have two versions: an American issue and a Canadian issue.

Insert Set (6 cards): **65.00**

	No.	Player	NRMT-MT
☐ ☐	1	Ed Belfour/Mike Richter	10.00
☐ ☐	2	Chris Chelios/Ray Bourque	8.00
☐ ☐	3	Paul Coffey/Brian Leetch	6.00
☐ ☐	4	Pavel Bure/Kevin Stevens	10.00
☐ ☐	5	Wayne Gretzky/Eric Lindros	30.00
☐ ☐	6	Brett Hull/Jaromir Jagr	15.00

TEAM 2000

These cards have two versions: an American issue and a Canadian issue.

Insert Set (30 cards): **30.00**

	No.	Player	NRMT-MT
☐ ☐	1	Eric Lindros, Pha.	6.50
☐ ☐	2	Mike Modano, Min.	2.50
☐ ☐	3	Nicklas Lidström, Det.	.50
☐ ☐	4	Tony Amonte, NYR.	.50
☐ ☐	5	Félix Potvin (G), Tor.	2.50
☐ ☐	6	Scott Lachance, NYI.	.25
☐ ☐	7	Mats Sundin, Que.	2.50
☐ ☐	8	Pavel Bure, Van.	3.50
☐ ☐	9	Eric Desjardins, Mtl.	.25
☐ ☐	10	Owen Nolan, Que.	.50
☐ ☐	11	Dominic Roussel (G), Pha.	.25
☐ ☐	12	Scott Niedermayer, N.J.	.50
☐ ☐	13	Vyacheslav Kozlov, Det.	.25
☐ ☐	14	Patrick Poulin, Hfd.	.25
☐ ☐	15	Jaromir Jagr, Pgh.	5.00
☐ ☐	16	Rob Blake, L.A.	.50
☐ ☐	17	Pierre Turgeon, NYI.	.50
☐ ☐	18	Rod Brind'Amour, Pha.	.50
☐ ☐	19	Joé Juneau, Bos.	.25
☐ ☐	20	Tim Cheveldae (G), Det.	.25
☐ ☐	21	Joe Sakic, Que.	4.00
☐ ☐	22	Kevin Todd, N.J.	.25
☐ ☐	23	Rob Pearson, Tor.	.25
☐ ☐	24	Trevor Linden, Van.	.50
☐ ☐	25	Dimitri Khristich, Wsh.	.25
☐ ☐	26	Pat Falloon, S.J.	.25
☐ ☐	27	Jeremy Roenick, Chi.	1.25
☐ ☐	28	Alexander Mogilny, Buf.	1.25
☐ ☐	29	Gilbert Dionne, Mtl.	.25
☐ ☐	30	Sergei Fedorov, Det.	2.50

1992 - 93 PINNACLE ERIC LINDROS

Imprint: © 1992 SCORE, PRINTED IN U.S.A.

Complete Set (30 cards): **30.00**

	No.	Player	NRMT-MT
☐	1	St. Michael's Buzzers	1.50
☐	2	Detroit Compuware	1.50
☐	3	Oshawa Generals	1.50
☐	4	Oshawa Generals	1.50
☐	5	Oshawa Generals	1.50
☐	6	Oshawa Generals	1.50
☐	7	Memorial Cup	1.50
☐	8	World Junior Championships	1.50
☐	9	World Junior Championships	1.50
☐	10	World Junior Championships	1.50
☐	11	Canada Cup	1.50
☐	12	Canada Cup	1.50
☐	13	Canadian National Team	1.50
☐	14	Canadian National Team	1.50
☐	15	Canadian National Team	1.50
☐	16	Canadian National Team	1.50
☐	17	First-Round Draft Pick	1.50
☐	18	Trade to Philadelphia	1.50
☐	19	Happy Flyer	1.50
☐	20	Preseason Action	1.50
☐	21	Preseason Action	1.50
☐	22	Regular Season Debut	1.50
☐	23	First NHL Goal	1.50
☐	24	Game-Winning Goal Home Debut	1.50
☐	25	First NHL Hat Trick	1.50
☐	26	Playing Golf	1.50
☐	27	Backyard Fun	1.50
☐	28	Fan Favorite	1.50
☐	29	Welcome to Philly	1.50
☐	30	Philly Hero	1.50

1992 - 93 PRO SET

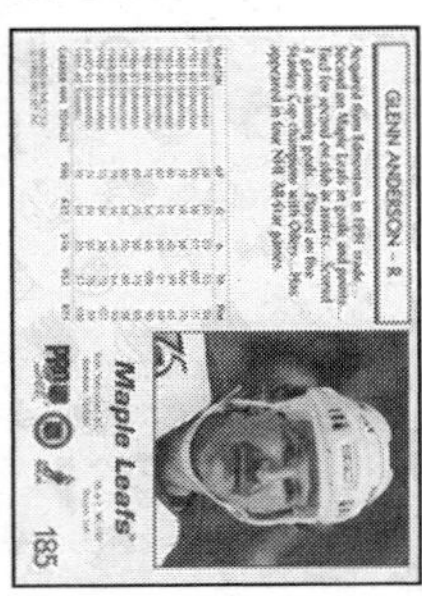

An intended second series was never issued.

Imprint: © 1992 PRO SET INC.

Complete Set (270 cards): **14.00**

Common Player: **.10**

	No.	Player	NRMT-MT
☐	1	Mario Lemieux, Pgh.	.65
☐	2	Patrick Roy (G), Mtl.	.65
☐	3	Adam Oates, Bos.	.25
☐	4	Ray Bourque, Bos.	.35
☐	5	Vladimir Ruzicka, Bos.	.10
☐	6	Stephen Leach, Bos.	.10
☐	7	Andy Moog (G), Bos.	.25
☐	8	Cam Neely, Bos.	.25
☐	9	Dave Poulin, Bos.	.10
☐	10	Glen Wesley, Bos.	.10
☐	11	Gord Murphy, Bos.	.10
☐	12	Dale Hawerchuk, Buf.	.25
☐	13	Pat LaFontaine, Buf.	.25
☐	14	Tom Draper (G), Buf.	.10
☐	15	Dave Andreychuk, Buf.	.25
☐	16	Petr Svoboda, Buf.	.10
☐	17	Doug Bodger, Buf.	.10
☐	18	Donald Audette, Buf.	.10
☐	19	Alexander Mogilny, Buf.	.35
☐	20	Randy Wood, Buf.	.10
☐	21	Gary Roberts, Cgy.	.25
☐	22	Al MacInnis, Cgy.	.25
☐	23	Theoren Fleury, Cgy.	.35
☐	24	Sergei Makarov, Cgy.	.10
☐	25	Mike Vernon (G), Cgy.	.25
☐	26	Joe Nieuwendyk, Cgy.	.25
☐	27	Gary Suter, Cgy.	.10
☐	28	Joel Otto, Cgy.	.10
☐	29	Paul Ranheim, Cgy.	.10
☐	30	Jeremy Roenick, Chi.	.35
☐	31	Steve Larmer, Chi.	.25
☐	32	Michel Goulet, Chi.	.10
☐	33	Ed Belfour (G), Chi.	.25
☐	34	Chris Chelios, Chi.	.35
☐	35	Igor Kravchuk, Chi.	.10
☐	36	Brent Sutter, Chi.	.10
☐	37	Steve Smith, Chi.	.10
☐	38	Dirk Graham, Chi.	.10
☐	39	Steve Yzerman, Det.	.75
☐	40	Sergei Fedorov, Det.	.35
☐	41	Paul Ysebaert, Det.	.10
☐	42	Nicklas Lidström, Det.	.25
☐	43	Tim Cheveldae (G), Det.	.10
☐	44	Vladimir Konstantinov, Det.	.25
☐	45	Shawn Burr, Det.	.10
☐	46	Bob Probert, Det.	.10
☐	47	Ray Sheppard, Det.	.10
☐	48	Kelly Buchberger, Edm.	.10
☐	49	Joe Murphy, Edm.	.10
☐	50	Norm Maciver, Edm.	.10
☐	51	Bill Ranford (G), Edm.	.25
☐	52	Bernie Nicholls, Edm.	.10
☐	53	Esa Tikkanen, Edm.	.10
☐	54	Scott Mellanby, Edm.	.10
☐	55	Dave Manson, Edm.	.10
☐	56	Craig Simpson, Edm.	.10
☐	57	John Cullen, Hfd.	.10
☐	58	Pat Verbeek, Hfd.	.10
☐	59	Zarley Zalapski, Hfd.	.10
☐	60	Murray Craven, Hfd.	.10
☐	61	Bobby Holik, Hfd. (N.J.)	.10
☐	62	Steve Konroyd, Hfd.	.10
☐	63	Geoff Sanderson, Hfd.	.10

	No.	Player	Price
☐	64	Frank Pietrangelo (G), Hfd.	.10
☐	65	Mikael Andersson, Hfd. (T.B.)	.10
☐	66	Wayne Gretzky, L.A.	1.50
☐	67	Rob Blake, L.A.	.25
☐	68	Jari Kurri, L.A.	.25
☐	69	Marty McSorley, L.A.	.10
☐	70	Kelly Hrudey (G), L.A.	.10
☐	71	Paul Coffey, L.A.	.25
☐	72	Luc Robitaille, L.A.	.25
☐	73	Peter Ahola, L.A.	.10
☐	74	Tony Granato, L.A.	.10
☐	75	Derian Hatcher, Min.	.25
☐	76	Mike Modano, Min.	.35
☐	77	Dave Gagner, Min.	.10
☐	78	Mark Tinordi, Min.	.10
☐	79	Craig Ludwig, Min.	.10
☐	80	Ulf Dahlen, Min.	.10
☐	81	Bobby Smith, Min.	.10
☐	82	Jon Casey (G), Min.	.10
☐	83	Jim Johnson, Min.	.10
☐	84	Denis Savard, Mtl.	.10
☐	85	Patrick Roy (G), Mtl.	1.25
☐	86	Eric Desjardins, Mtl.	.25
☐	87	Kirk Muller, Mtl.	.10
☐	88	Guy Carbonneau, Mtl.	.10
☐	89	Shayne Corson, Mtl. (Edm.)	.25
☐	90	Brent Gilchrist, Mtl. (Edm.)	.10
☐	91	Mathieu Schneider, Mtl.	.10
☐	92	Gilbert Dionne, Mtl.	.10
☐	93	Stéphane Richer, N.J.	.10
☐	94	Kevin Todd, N.J.	.10
☐	95	Scott Stevens, N.J.	.10
☐	96	Viacheslav Fetisov, N.J.	.25
☐	97	Chris Terreri (G), N.J.	.10
☐	98	Claude Lemieux, N.J.	.10
☐	99	Bruce Driver, N.J.	.10
☐	100	Peter Stastny, N.J.	.10
☐	101	Alexei Kasatonov, N.J.	.10
☐	102	Patrick Flatley, NYI.	.10
☐	103	Adam Creighton, NYI. (T.B.)	.10
☐	104	Pierre Turgeon, NYI.	.25
☐	105	Ray Ferraro, NYI.	.10
☐	106	Steve Thomas, NYI.	.10
☐	107	Mark Fitzpatrick (G), NYI.	.10
☐	108	Benoît Hogue, NYI.	.10
☐	109	Uwe Krupp, NYI.	.10
☐	110	Derek King, NYI.	.10
☐	111	Mark Messier, NYR.	.35
☐	112	Brian Leetch, NYR.	.25
☐	113	Mike Gartner, NYR.	.25
☐	114	Darren Turcotte, NYR.	.10
☐	115	Adam Graves, NYR.	.10
☐	116	Mike Richter (G), NYR.	.25
☐	117	Sergei Nemchinov, NYR.	.10
☐	118	Tony Amonte, NYR.	.10
☐	119	James Patrick, NYR.	.10
☐	120	Andrew McBain, Ott.	.10
☐	121	Rob Murphy, Ott.	.10
☐	122	Mike Peluso, Ott.	.10
☐	123	Sylvain Turgeon, Ott.	.10
☐	124	Brad Shaw, Ott.	.10
☐	125	Peter Sidorkiewicz (G), Ott.	.10
☐	126	Brad Marsh, Ott.	.10
☐	127	Mark Freer, Ott.	.10
☐	128	Marc Fortier, Ott.	.10
☐	129	Ron Hextall (G), Pha. (Que.)	.25
☐	130	Claude Boivin, Pha.	.10
☐	131	Mark Recchi, Pha.	.25
☐	132	Rod Brind'Amour, Pha.	.25
☐	133	Mike Ricci, Pha. (Que.)	.10
☐	134	Kevin Dineen, Pha.	.10
☐	135	Brian Benning, Pha.	.10
☐	136	Kerry Huffman, Pha. (Que.)	.10
☐	137	Steve Duchesne, Pha. (Que.)	.10
☐	138	Rick Tocchet, Pgh.	.10
☐	139	Mario Lemieux, Pgh.	1.25
☐	140	Kevin Stevens, Pgh.	.10
☐	141	Jaromir Jagr, Pgh.	.75
☐	142	Joe Mullen, Pgh.	.10
☐	143	Ulf Samuelsson, Pgh.	.10
☐	144	Ron Francis, Pgh.	.25
☐	145	Tom Barrasso (G), Pgh.	.25
☐	146	Larry Murphy, Pgh.	.10
☐	147	Alexei Gusarov, Que.	.10
☐	148	Valeri Kamensky, Que.	.25
☐	149	Mats Sundin, Que.	.35
☐	150	Joe Sakic, Que.	.60
☐	151	Claude Lapointe, Que.	.10
☐	152	Stéphane Fiset (G), Que.	.25
☐	153	Owen Nolan, Que.	.25
☐	154	Mike Hough, Que.	.10
☐	155	Greg Paslawski, Que.	.10
☐	156	Brett Hull, Stl.	.35
☐	157	Craig Janney, Stl.	.10
☐	158	Jeff Brown, Stl.	.10
☐	159	Paul Cavallini, Stl.	.10
☐	160	Garth Butcher, Stl.	.10
☐	161	Nelson Emerson, Stl.	.10
☐	162	Ron Sutter, Stl.	.10
☐	163	Brendan Shanahan, Stl.	.35
☐	164	Curtis Joseph (G), Stl.	.35
☐	165	Doug Wilson, S.J.	.10
☐	166	Pat Falloon, S.J.	.10
☐	167	Kelly Kisio, S.J.	.10
☐	168	Neil Wilkinson, S.J.	.10
☐	169	Jay More, S.J.	.10
☐	170	David Bruce, S.J.	.10
☐	171	Jeff Hackett (G), S.J.	.10
☐	**172**	**David Williams, S.J., RC**	**.10**
☐	173	Brian Lawton, S.J.	.10
☐	174	Brian Bradley, T.B.	.10
☐	**175**	**Jock Callander, T.B., RC**	**.10**
☐	176	Basil McRae, T.B.	.10
☐	177	Rob Ramage, T.B.	.10
☐	178	Pat Jablonski (G), T.B.	.10
☐	179	Joe Reekie, T.B.	.10
☐	180	Doug Crossman, T.B.	.10
☐	181	Jim Benning, T.B.	.10
☐	182	Ken Hodge., T.B.	.10
☐	183	Grant Fuhr (G), Tor.	.25
☐	184	Doug Gilmour, Tor.	.25
☐	185	Glenn Anderson, Tor.	.10
☐	186	David Ellett, Tor.	.10
☐	187	Peter Zezel, Tor.	.10
☐	188	Jamie Macoun, Tor.	.10
☐	189	Wendel Clark, Tor.	.25
☐	**190**	**Bob Halkidis, Tor., RC**	**.10**
☐	191	Rob Pearson, Tor.	.10
☐	192	Pavel Bure, Van.	.50
☐	193	Kirk McLean (G), Van.	.25
☐	194	Sergio Momesso, Van.	.10
☐	195	Cliff Ronning, Van.	.10
☐	196	Jyrki Lumme, Van.	.10
☐	197	Trevor Linden, Van.	.25
☐	198	Geoff Courtnall, Van.	.10
☐	199	Doug Lidster, Van.	.10
☐	200	Dave Babych, Van.	.10
☐	201	Michal Pivonka, Wsh.	.10
☐	202	Dale Hunter, Wsh.	.10
☐	203	Calle Johansson, Wsh.	.10
☐	204	Kevin Hatcher, Wsh.	.10
☐	205	Al Iafrate, Wsh.	.10
☐	206	Don Beaupré (G), Wsh.	.10
☐	207	Randy Burridge, Wsh.	.10
☐	208	Dimitri Khristich, Wsh.	.10
☐	209	Peter Bondra, Wsh.	.25
☐	210	Teppo Numminen, Wpg.	.10
☐	211	Bob Essensa (G), Wpg.	.10
☐	212	Phil Housley, Wpg.	.10
☐	213	Ed Olczyk, Wpg.	.10
☐	214	Pat Elynuik, Wpg., (Wsh.)	.10
☐	215	Troy Murray, Wpg.	.10
☐	216	Igor Ulanov, Wpg.	.10
☐	217	Thomas Steen, Wpg.	.10
☐	218	Darrin Shannon, Wpg.	.10
☐	219	Joé Juneau, Bos.	.10
☐	220	Steve Heinze, Bos.	.10
☐	221	Ted Donato, Bos.	.10
☐	222	Glen Murray, Bos.	.10
☐	**223**	**Keith Carney, Buf., RC**	**.10**
☐	**224**	**Dean McAmmond, Chi., RC**	**.10**
☐	225	Vyacheslav Kozlov, Det.	.25
☐	226	Martin Lapointe, Det.	.10
☐	227	Patrick Poulin, Hfd.	.10
☐	228	Darryl Sydor, L.A.	.10
☐	**229**	**Trent Klatt, Min., RC**	**.10**
☐	**230**	**Bill Guerin, N.J., RC**	**.35**
☐	231	Jerrod Skalde, N.J.	.10
☐	232	Scott Niedermayer, N.J.	.25
☐	233	Marty McInnis, NYI.	.10
☐	234	Scott Lachance, NYI.	.10
☐	235	Dominic Roussel (G), Pha.	.10
☐	236	Eric Lindros, Pha.	1.50
☐	237	Shawn McEachern, Pgh.	.10
☐	238	Martin Rucinsky, Que.	.10
☐	**239**	**Bill Lindsay, Que., RC**	**.10**
☐	**240**	**Bret Hedican, Stl., RC**	**.10**
☐	**241**	**Ray Whitney, S.J., RC**	**.10**
☐	242	Félix Potvin (G), Tor.	.35
☐	243	Keith Tkachuk, Wpg.	.35
☐	244	Evgeny Davydov, Wpg.	.10
☐	245	Brett Hull, Stl.	.25
☐	246	Wayne Gretzky, L.A.	.75
☐	247	Steve Yzerman, Det.	.35
☐	248	Paul Ysebaert, Det.	.10
☐	249	Dave Andreychuk, Buf.	.10
☐	250	Kirk McLean, Van.	.25
☐	251	Tim Cheveldae, Det.	.10
☐	252	Jeremy Roenick, Chi.	.25
☐	253	NHL Pro Set Youth Clinic	.10
☐	254	NHL Pro Set Hockey Clinic	.10
☐	255	NHL All-Time Team	.10
☐	256	Mike Gartner, NYR.	.25
☐	257	Brian Propp, Min.	.10
☐	258	Dave Taylor, L.A.	.10
☐	259	Bobby Smith, Min.	.10
☐	260	Denis Savard, Mtl.	.25
☐	261	Ray Bourque, Bos.	.25
☐	262	Joe Mullen, Pgh.	.10
☐	263	John Tonelli, Que.	.10
☐	264	Brad Marsh, Det.	.10
☐	265	Randy Carlyle, Wpg.	.10
☐	266	Mike Hough, Que.	.10
☐	267	Bob Essensa (G), Wpg.	.10
☐	268	Mike Lalor, Wpg.	.10
☐	269	Terry Carkner, Pha.	.10
☐	270	Todd Krygier, Wsh.	.10

AWARD WINNERS

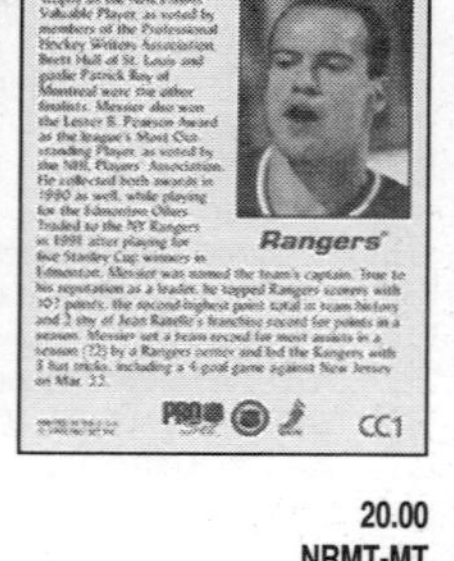

Insert Set (5 cards): 20.00

	No.	Player	NRMT-MT
☐	CC1	Mark Messier, NYR.	3.50
☐	CC2	Partick Roy (G), Mtl.	12.00
☐	CC3	Pavel Bure, Van.	5.00
☐	CC4	Brian Leetch, NYR.	3.00
☐	CC5	Guy Carbonneau, Mtl.	2.00

ROOKIE GOAL LEADERS

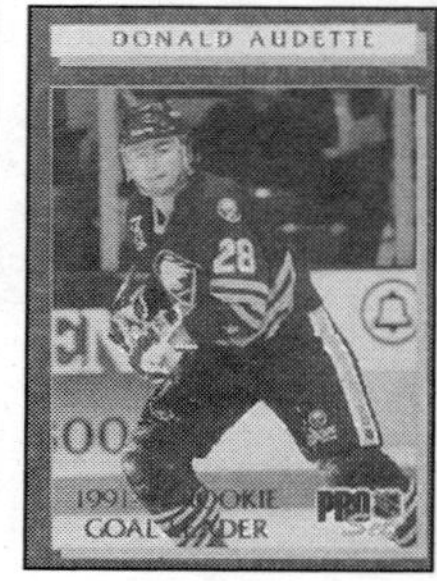

Insert Set (12 cards): 20.00

	No.	Player	NRMT-MT
☐	1	Tony Amonte, NYR.	3.00
☐	2	Pavel Bure, Van.	5.00
☐	3	Donald Audette, Buf.	1.50
☐	4	Pat Falloon, S.J.	1.50
☐	5	Nelson Emerson, Stl.	1.50
☐	6	Gilbert Dionne, Mtl.	1.50

	No.	Player	NRMT-MT
☐	7	Kevin Todd, N.J.	1.50
☐	8	Luciano Borsato, Wpg.	1.50
☐	9	Rob Pearson, Tor.	1.50
☐	10	Valeri Zelepukin, N.J.	1.50
☐	11	Geoff Sanderson, Hfd.	1.50
☐	12	Claude Lapointe, Que.	1.50

TEAM LEADERS

Insert Set (15 cards): 25.00

	No.	Player	NRMT-MT
☐	1	Gary Roberts, Cgy.	1.00
☐	2	Jeremy Roenick, Chi.	1.50
☐	3	Steve Yzerman, Det.	5.00
☐	4	Nicklas Lidström, Det.	1.00
☐	5	Vincent Damphousse, Edm.	1.00
☐	6	Wayne Gretzky, L.A.	10.00
☐	7	Mike Modano, Min.	2.50
☐	8	Brett Hull, Stl.	2.50
☐	9	Nelson Emerson, Stl.	.75
☐	10	Pat Falloon, S.J.	.75
☐	11	Doug Gilmour, Tor.	1.50
☐	12	Trevor Linden, Van.	1.00
☐	13	Pavel Bure, Van.	3.50
☐	14	Phil Housley, Wpg.	.75
☐	15	Luciano Borsato, Wpg.	.75

PARKHURST PREVIEWS

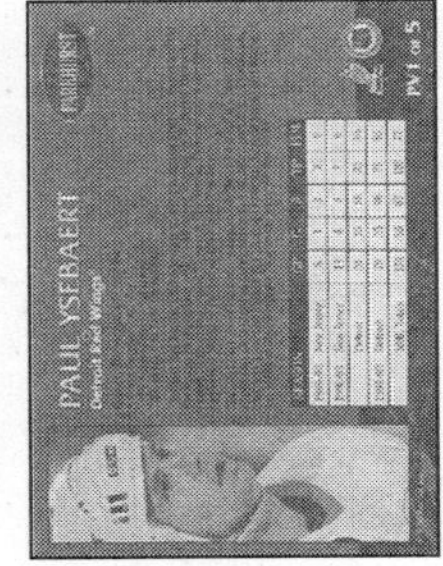

This 5-card set was randomly inserted in the Pro Set foil packs, a marketing strategy to promote their 1992-93 Parkhurst cards.

Insert Set (5 cards): 5.00

	No.	Player	NRMT-MT
☐	PV1	Paul Ysebaert, Det.	1.00
☐	PV2	Sean Burke (G), Hfd.	1.50
☐	PV3	Gilbert Dionne, Mtl.	1.00
☐	PV4	Ken Hammond, Ott.	1.00
☐	PV5	Grant Fuhr (G), Tor.	2.00

1992 - 93 RED ACE INTERNATIONAL RUSSIAN STARS

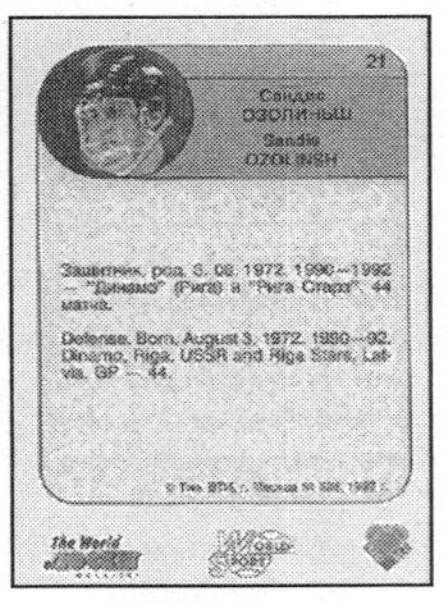

This set was co-sponsered by the World of Hockey magazine and World Sport. Cards have a light blue border.

Complete Set (36 cards with folder): 5.00

	No.	Player	NRMT-MT
☐	1	Darius Kasparaitis, Dynamo	.20
☐	2	Alexei Zhamnov, USSR	1.00
☐	3	Dmitri Khristich, USSR	.20
☐	4	Andrei Trefilov (G), Rus.	.20
☐	5	Vitali Prokhorov, USSR	.20
☐	6	Dmitri Filimonov, Dynamo	.20
☐	7	Valeri Zelepukin, USSR	.20
☐	8	Alexei Kovalev, Dynamo	.50
☐	9	Dmitri Kvartalnov	.20
☐	10	Igor Korolev, Dynamo	.20
☐	11	Nikolai Borschevsky, Spartak	.20
☐	12	Igor Boldin, Spartak	.20
☐	13	Arturs Irbe (G), Dynamo Riga	.50
☐	14	Vyacheslav Butsayev, CSKA	.20
☐	15	Boris Mironov, CSKA	.20
☐	16	Sergei Bautin, Rus.	.20
☐	17	Alexander Kharlamov, CSKA	.20
☐	18	Vyacheslav Kozlov, USSR	.50
☐	19	Mikhail Shtalenkov (G), Rus.	.50
☐	20	Roman Oksyuta, Rus.	.20
☐	21	Sandis Ozolnish, Dynamo Riga	1.00
☐	22	Dmitri Mironov, Krylja	.20
☐	23	Sergei Brylin, CSKA	.20
☐	24	Vladimir Grachev	.20
☐	25	Dmitri Starostenko	.20
☐	26	Andrei Nazarov	.20
☐	27	Alexei Yashin, Dynamo	2.00
☐	28	Vladimir Malakhov, USSR	.50
☐	29	Ravil Yakubov	.20
☐	30	Sergei Klimovich, Dynamo	.20
☐	31	Artur Oktjabrev	.20
☐	32	Lev Berdichevsky, Khimik	.20
☐	33	Yan Kaminski	.20
☐	34	Andrei Kovalenko, Rus.	.50
☐	35	Dmitri Yushkevich, Dynamo	.20
☐		Title card/Checklist, (No#)	.20

1992 - 93 RED ACE INTERNATIONAL RUSSIAN NHL STARS

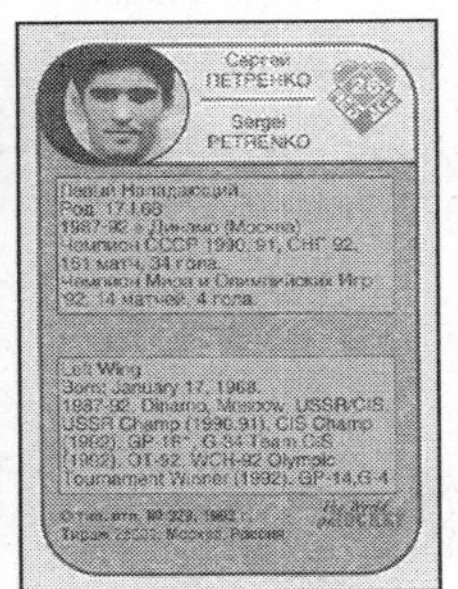

There are 25,000 sets available. Cards have a white and violet border.

Imprint:

Complete Set (37 cards): 5.00

	No.	Player	NRMT-MT
☐	1	Alexander Barkov	.20
☐	2	Sergei Bautin	.20
☐	3	Igor Boldin	.20
☐	4	Nikolai Borshevsky	.20
☐	5	Sergei Brylin	.20
☐	6	Vyacheslav Butsayev	.20
☐	7	Alexander Cherbayev	.20
☐	8	Evgeny Garanin	.20
☐	9	Sergei Gonchar	.50
☐	10	Alexander Karpovtsev	.20
☐	11	Darius Kasparaitis	.20
☐	12	Alexander Kharlamov	.20
☐	13	Yuri Khmylev	.20
☐	14	Sergei Klimovich	.20
☐	15	Igor Korolev	.20
☐	16	Andrei Kovalenko	.20
☐	17	Alexei Kovalev	.50
☐	18	Dmitri Kvartalnov	.20
☐	19	Vladimir Malakhov	.50
☐	20	Maxim Mikhailovsky (G)	.50
☐	21	Boris Mironov	.20
☐	22	Dmitri Mironov	.20
☐	23	Andrei Nazarov	.20
☐	24	Roman Oksiuta	.20
☐	25	Arthur Oktjabrev	.20
☐	26	Sergei Petrenko	.20
☐	27	Oleg Petrov	.20
☐	28	Andrei Potaichuk	.20
☐	29	Vitali Prokhorov	.20
☐	30	Alexander Semak	.20
☐	31	Dmitri Starostenko	.20
☐	32	Ravil Yakubov	.20
☐	33	Alexei Yashin	2.00
☐	34	Dmitri Yushkevich	.20
☐	35	Alexei Zhamnov	1.00
☐	36	Alexei Zhitnik	.50
☐	37	Checklist	.20

1992 - 93 RICE KRISPIES ALL-STAR TEAM POSTERS

Poster Size:14" x 9 1/4"

Imprint: *Registered trademark of /*Marque déposée de KELLOGG'S CANADA INC. 1992

Complete Set (3 posters): 5.00

	Player	NRMT-MT
☐	Campbell Conference All-Stars	2.00
☐	Wales Conference All-Stars	2.00
☐	All-Stars Snap, Crackle, Pop	2.00

1992 - 93 SCORE

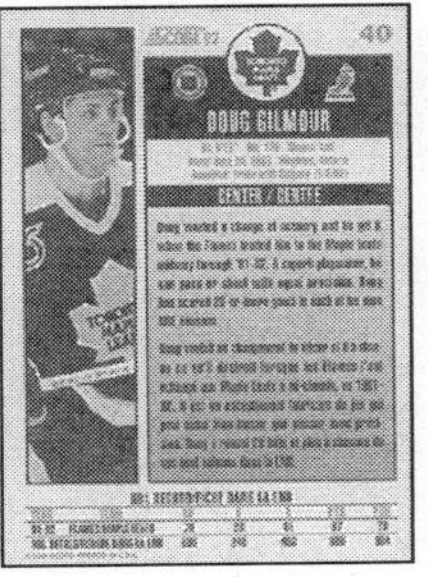

The Canadian set has a blue border, while the U.S. set has a white border.

Imprint: © 1992 SCORE

Complete Cdn. Set (550 cards):	**18.00**
Common Player:	**.10**
Promo Sheet (#'s: 8, 16, 23, 25):	**3.00**
Promo Sheet (#'s: 2, 6, 16, 25):	**3.00**

No.	Player	NRMT-MT
1	Wayne Gretzky, L.A.	1.50
2	Chris Chelios, Chi.	.25
3	Joe Mullen, Pgh.	.10
4	Russ Courtnall, Mtl.	.10
5	Mike Richter (G), NYR.	.25
6	Pat LaFontaine, Buf.	.25
7	Mark Tinordi, Min.	.10
8	Claude Lemieux, N.J.	.10
9	Jimmy Carson, Det.	.10
10	Cam Neely, Bos.	.25
11	Al Iafrate, Wsh.	.10
12	Steve Thomas, NYI.	.10
13	Fredrik Olausson, Wpg.	.10
14	Pavel Bure, Van.	.50
15	Doug Wilson, S.J.	.10
16	Esa Tikkanen, Edm.	.10
17	Gary Suter, Cgy.	.10
18	Murray Craven, Hfd.	.10
19	Garry Galley, Pha.	.10
20	Grant Fuhr (G), Tor.	.25
21	Craig Wolanin, Que.	.10
22	Paul Cavallini, Stl.	.10
23	Eric Desjardins, Mtl.	.25
24	Joey Kocur, NYR.	.10
25	Kevin Stevens, Pgh.	.10
26	Marty McSorley, L.A.	.10
27	Dirk Graham, Chi.	.10
28	Mike Ramsey, Buf.	.10
29	Gord Murphy, Bos.	.10
30	John MacLean, N.J.	.10
31	Vladimir Konstantinov, Det.	.25
32	Neal Broten, Min.	.10
33	Dimitri Khristich, Wsh.	.10
34	Gerald Diduck, Van.	.10
35	Ken Baumgartner, Tor.	.10
36	Darrin Shannon, Wpg.	.10
37	Steven Bozek, S.J.	.10
38	Michel Petit, Cgy.	.10
39	Kevin Lowe, Edm.	.10
40	Doug Gilmour, Tor.	.25
41	Peter Sidorkiewicz (G), Hfd.	.10
42	Gino Cavallini, Que.	.10
43	Dan Quinn, Pha.	.10
44	Steven Finn, Que.	.10
45	Larry Murphy, Pgh.	.25
46	Brent Gilchrist, Mtl.	.10
47	Darren Puppa (G), Buf.	.10
48	Steve Smith, Chi.	.10
49	Dave Taylor, L.A.	.10
50	Mike Gartner, NYR.	.25
51	Derian Hatcher, Min.	.25
52	Bob Probert, Det.	.10
53	Ken Daneyko, N.J.	.10
54	Stephen Leach, Bos.	.10
55	Kelly Miller, Wsh.	.10
56	Jeff Norton, NYI.	.10
57	Kelly Kisio, S.J.	.10
58	Igor Larionov, Van.	.25
59	Paul MacDermid, Wsh.	.10
60	Mike Vernon (G), Cgy.	.25
61	Randy Ladouceur, Hfd.	.10
62	Luke Richardson, Edm.	.10
63	Daniel Marois, NYI.	.10
64	Mike Hough, Que.	.10
65	Garth Butcher, Stl.	.10
66	Terry Carkner, Pha.	.10
67	Mike Donnelly, L.A.	.10
68	Keith Brown, Chi.	.10
69	Mathieu Schneider, Mtl.	.10
70	Tom Barrasso (G), Pgh.	.25
71	Adam Graves, NYR.	.10
72	Brian Propp, Min.	.10
73	Randy Wood, Buf.	.10
74	Yves Racine, Det.	.10
75	Scott Stevens, N.J.	.25
76	Chris Nilan, Mtl.	.10
77	Uwe Krupp, NYI.	.10
78	Sylvain Côté, Wsh.	.10
79	Sergio Momesso, Van.	.10
80	Thomas Steen, Wpg.	.10
81	Craig Muni, Edm.	.10
82	Jeff Hackett. (G), S.J.	.25
83	Frantisek Musil, Cgy.	.10
84	Mike Ricci, Pha.	.10
85	Brad Shaw, Hfd.	.10
86	Ron Sutter, Stl.	.10
87	Curtis Leschyshyn, Que.	.10
88	Jamie Macoun, Tor.	.10
89	Brian Noonan, Chi.	.10
90	Ulf Samuelsson, Pgh.	.10
91	Mike McPhee, Mtl.	.10
92	Charlie Huddy, L.A.	.10
93	Tim Kerr, NYR.	.10
94	Craig Ludwig, Min.	.10
95	Paul Ysebaert, Det.	.10
96	Brad May, Buf.	.10
97	Viacheslav Fetisov, N.J.	.25
98	Todd Krygier, Wsh.	.10
99	Patrick Flatley, NYI.	.10
100	Ray Bourque, Bos.	.35
101	Petr Nedved, Van.	.10
102	Teppo Numminen, Wpg.	.10
103	Dean Evason, S.J.	.10
104	Ron Hextall (G), Pha.	.25
105	Josef Beranek, Edm.	.10
106	Robert Reichel, Cgy.	.10
107	Mikhail Tatarinov, Que.	.10
108	Geoff Sanderson, Hfd.	.10
109	Dave Lowry, Stl.	.10
110	Wendel Clark, Tor.	.25
111	Corey Millen, L.A.	.10
112	Brent Sutter, Chi.	.10
113	Jaromir Jagr, Pgh.	.75
114	Petr Svoboda, Buf.	.10
115	Sergei Nemchinov, NYR.	.10
116	Tony Tanti, Buf.	.10
117	Stewart Gavin, Min	.10
118	Doug Brown, N.J.	.10
119	Gerard Gallant, Det.	.10
120	Andy Moog (G), Bos.	.25
121	John Druce, Wsh.	.10
122	Dave McLlwain, Tor.	.10
123	Bob Essensa (G), Wpg.	.10
124	Doug Lidster, Van.	.10
125	Pat Falloon, S.J.	.10
126	Kelly Buchberger, Edm.	.10
127	Carey Wilson, Cgy.	.10
128	Bobby Holik, Hfd.	.10
129	Andrei Lomakin, Pha.	.10
130	Bob Rouse, Tor.	.10
131	Adam Foote, Que.	.25
132	Bob Bassen, Stl.	.10
133	Brian Benning, Pha.	.10
134	Greg Gilbert, Chi.	.10
135	Paul Stanton, Pgh.	.10
136	Brian Skrudland, Mtl.	.10
137	Jeff Beukeboom, NYR.	.10
138	Clint Malarchuk (G), Buf.	.10
139	Mike Modano, Min.	.35
140	Stéphane Richer, N.J.	.10
141	Brad McCrimmon, Det.	.10
142	Bob Carpenter, Bos.	.10
143	Rod Langway, Wsh.	.10
144	Adam Creighton, NYI.	.10
145	Ed Olczyk, Wpg.	.10
146	Greg Adams, Van.	.10
147	Jayson More, S.J.	.10
148	Scott Mellanby, Edm.	.10
149	Paul Ranheim, Cgy.	.10
150	John Cullen, Hfd.	.10
151	Steve Duchesne, Pha.	.10
152	Dave Ellett, Tor.	.10
153	Mats Sundin, Que.	.35
154	Rick Zombo, Stl.	.10
155	Kelly Hrudey (G), L.A.	.10
156	Mike Hudson, Chi.	.10
157	Bryan Trottier, Pgh.	.25
158	Shayne Corson, Mtl.	.25
159	Kevin Haller, Mtl.	.10
160	John Vanbiesbrouck (G), NYR.	.50
161	Jim Johnson, Min.	.10
162	Kevin Todd, N.J.	.10
163	Ray Sheppard, Det.	.10
164	Brent Ashton, Bos.	.10
165	Peter Bondra, Wsh.	.35
166	Dave Volek, NYI.	.10
167	Randy Carlyle, Wpg.	.10
168	Dana Murzyn, Van.	.10
169	Perry Berezan, S.J.	.10
170	Vincent Damphousse, Edm.	.25
171	Gary Leeman, Cgy.	.10
172	Steve Konroyd, Hfd.	.10
173	Per-Erik Eklund, Pha.	.10
174	Peter Zezel, Tor.	.10
175	Greg Paslawski, Que	.10
176	Murray Baron, Stl.	.10
177	Rob Blake, L.A.	.25
178	Ed Belfour (G), Chi.	.25
179	Mike Keane, Mtl.	.10
180	Mark Recchi, Pha.	.25
181	Kris King, NYR.	.10
182	Dave Snuggerud, S.J.	.10
183	David Shaw, Min.	.10
184	Tom Chorske, N.J.	.10
185	Steve Chiasson, Det.	.10
186	Don Sweeney, Bos.	.10
187	Mike Ridley, Wsh.	.10
188	Glenn Healy (G), NYI.	.10
189	Troy Murray, Wpg.	.10
190	Tom Fergus, Van.	.10
191	Rob Zettler, S.J.	.10
192	Geoff Smith, Edm.	.10
193	Joe Nieuwendyk, Cgy.	.25
194	Mark Hunter, Hfd.	.10
195	Kjell Samuelsson, Pgh.	.10
196	Todd Gill, Tor.	.10
197	Doug Smail, Que.	.10
198	Dave Christian, Stl.	.10
199	Tomas Sandström, L.A.	.10
200	Jeremy Roenick, Chi.	.25
201	Gord Roberts, Pgh.	.10
202	Denis Savard, Mtl.	.25
203	James Patrick, NYR.	.10
204	Dave Andreychuk, Buf.	.10
205	Bobby Smith, Min.	.10
206	Valeri Zelepukin, N.J.	.10
207	Shawn Burr, Det.	.10
208	Vladimir Ruzicka, Bos.	.10
209	Calle Johansson, Wsh.	.10
210	Mark Fitzpatrick (G), NYI.	.10
211	Dean Kennedy, Wpg.	.10
212	Dave Babych, Van.	.10
213	Wayne Presley, Buf.	.10
214	Dave Manson, Edm.	.10
215	Mikael Andersson, Hfd.	.10
216	Trent Yawney, Cgy.	.10
217	Mark Howe, Pha.	.10
218	Mike Bullard, Tor.	.10
219	Claude Lapointe, Que.	.10
220	Jeff Brown, Stl.	.10
221	Bob Kudelski, L.A.	.10
222	Michel Goulet, Chi.	.10
223	Phil Bourque, Pgh.	.10
224	Darren Turcotte, NYR.	.10
225	Kirk Muller, Mtl.	.10
226	Doug Bodger, Buf.	.10
227	Dave Gagner, Min.	.10
228	Craig Billington (G), N.J.	.10
229	Kevin Miller, Det.	.10
230	Glen Wesley, Bos.	.10
231	Dale Hunter, Wsh.	.10
232	Tom Kurvers, NYI.	.10
233	Pat Elynuik, Wpg.	.10
234	Geoff Courtnall, Van.	.10
235	Neil Wilkinson, S.J.	.10
236	Bill Ranford (G), Edm.	.25
237	Ron Stern, Cgy.	.10
238	Zarley Zalapski, Hfd.	.10
239	Kerry Huffman, Pha.	.10
240	Joe Sakic, Que.	.60
241	Glenn Anderson, Tor.	.10
242	Stéphane Quintal, Stl.	.10
243	Tony Granato, L.A.	.10
244	Rob Brown, Chi.	.10
245	Rick Tocchet, Pgh.	.10
246	Stéphan Lebeau, Mtl.	.10
247	Mark Hardy, NYR.	.10
248	Alexander Mogilny, Buf.	.50
249	Jon Casey (G), Min.	.10
250	Adam Oates, Bos.	.25
251	Bruce Driver, N.J.	.10
252	Sergei Fedorov, Det.	.35
253	Michal Pivonka, Wsh.	.10
254	Cliff Ronning, Van.	.10

□□ 255 Derek King, NYI. .10
□□ 256 Luciano Borsato, Wpg. .10
□□ 257 Paul Fenton, S.J. .10
□□ 258 Craig Berube, Cgy. .10
□□ 259 Brian Bradley, Tor. .10
□□ 260 Craig Simpson, Edm. .10
□□ 261 Adam Burt, Hfd. .10
□□ 262 Curtis Joseph (G), Stl., Error .35
□□ 263 Mark Pederson, Pha. .10
□□ 264 Alexei Gusarov, Que. .10
□□ 265 Paul Coffey, L.A. .25
□□ 266 Steve Larmer, Chi. .10
□□ 267 Ron Francis, Pgh. .25
□□ 268 Randy Gilhen, NYR. .10
□□ 269 Guy Carbonneau, Mtl. .10
□□ 270 Chris Terreri (G), N.J. .10
□□ 271 Mike Craig, Min. .10
□□ 272 Dale Hawerchuk, Buf. .25
□□ 273 Kevin Hatcher, Wsh. .10
□□ 274 Ken Hodge, Bos. .10
□□ 275 Tim Cheveldae (G), Det. .10
□□ 276 Benoît Hogue, NYI. .10
□□ 277 Mark Osborne, Tor. .10
□□ 278 Brian Mullen, S.J. .10
□□ 279 Robert Dirk, Van. .10
□□ 280 Theoren Fleury, Cgy. .25
□□ 281 Martin Gelinas, Edm. .10
□□ 282 Pat Verbeek, Hfd. .10
□□ 283 Mike Krushelnyski, Tor. .10
□□ 284 Kevin Dineen, Pha. .10
□□ 285 Craig Janney, Stl. .10
□□ 286 Owen Nolan, Que. .25
□□ 287 Bob Errey, Pgh. .10
□□ 288 Bryan Marchment, Chi. .10
□□ 289 Randy Moller, Buf. .10
□□ 290 Luc Robitaille, L.A. .25
□□ 291 Peter Stastny, N.J. .10
□□ 292 Ken Sutton, Buf. .10
□□ 293 Brad Marsh, Det. .10
□□ 294 Chris Dahlquist, Min. .10
□□ 295 Patrick Roy (G), Mtl. 1.25
□□ 296 Andy Brickley, Bos. .10
□□ 297 Randy Burridge, Wsh. .10
□□ 298 Ray Ferraro, NYI. .10
□□ 299 Phil Housley, Wpg. .10
□□ 300 Mark Messier, NYR. .35
□□ 301 David Bruce, S.J. .10
□□ 302 Al MacInnis, Cgy. .25
□□ 303 Craig MacTavish, Edm. .10
□□ 304 Kay Whitmore (G), Hfd. .10
□□ 305 Trevor Linden, Van. .25
□□ 306 Steve Kasper, Pha. .10
□□ 307 Todd Elik, Min. .10
□□ 308 Eric Weinrich, N.J. .10
□□ 309 Jocelyn Lemieux, Chi. .10
□□ 310 Peter Ahola, L.A. .10
□□ 311 J.J. Daigneault, Mtl. .10
□□ 312 Colin Patterson, Buf. .10
□□ 313 Darcy Wakaluk (G), Min. .10
□□ 314 Doug Weight, NYR. .25
□□ 315 David Barr, N.J. .10
□□ 316 Keith Primeau, Det. .25
□□ 317 Bob Sweeney, Bos. .10
□□ 318 Jyrki Lumme, Van. .10
□□ 319 Stu Barnes, Wpg. .10
□□ 320 Don Beaupré (G), Wsh. .10
□□ 321 Joe Murphy, Edm. .10
□□ 322 Gary Roberts, Cgy. .25
□□ 323 Andrew Cassels, Hfd. .10
□□ 324 Rod Brind'Amour, Pha. .25
□□ 325 Pierre Turgeon, NYI. .25
□□ 326 Claude Vilgrain, N.J. .10
□□ 327 Rich Sutter, Stl. .10
□□ 328 Claude Loiselle, NYI. .10
□□ 329 John Ogrodnick, NYR. .10
□□ 330 Ulf Dahlen, Min. .10
□□ 331 Gilbert Dionne, Mtl. .10
□□ 332 Joel Otto, Cgy. .10
□□ 333 Rob Pearson, Tor. .10
□□ 334 Christian Ruuttu, Buf. .10
□□ 335 Brian Bellows, Min. .10
□□ 336 Anatoli Semenov, Edm. .10
□□ 337 Brent Fedyk, Det. .10
□□ 338 Gaetan Duchesne, Min. .10
□□ 339 Randy McKay, N.J. .10
□□ 340 Bernie Nicholls, Edm. .10
□□ 341 Keith Acton, Pha. .10
□□ 342 John Tonelli, Que. .10
□□ 343 Brian Lawton, S.J. .10
□□ 344 Ric Nattress, Tor. .10
□□ 345 Mike Eagles, Wpg. .10
□□ 346 Frantisek Kucera, Chi. .10
□□ 347 John McIntyre, L.A. .10
□□ 348 Troy Loney, Pgh. .10
□□ 349 Norm Maciver, Edm. .10
□□ 350 Brett Hull, Stl. .35
□□ 351 Rob Ramage, Min. .10
□□ 352 Claude Boivin, Pha. .10
□□ 353 Paul Broten, NYR. .10
□□ 354 Stéphane Fiset (G), Que. .25
□□ 355 Garry Valk, Van. .10
□□ 356 Basil McRae, Min. .10
□□ 357 Alan May, Wsh. .10
□□ 358 Grant Ledyard, Buf. .10
□□ 359 Dave Poulin, Bos. .10
□□ 360 Valeri Kamensky, Que. .25
□□ 361 Brian Glynn, Edm. .10
□□ 362 Jan Erixon, NYR. .10
□□ 363 Mike Lalor, Wpg. .10
□□ 364 Jeff Chychrun, Pgh. .10
□□ 365 Ron Wilson, Stl. .10
□□ 366 Shawn Cronin, Wpg. .10
□□ 367 Sylvain Turgeon, Mtl. .10
□□ 368 Mike Liut (G), Wsh. .10
□□ 369 Joe Cirella, NYR. .10
□□ 370 David Maley, Edm. .10
□□ 371 Lucien DeBlois, Wpg. .10
□□ 372 Per Djoos, NYR. .10
□□ 373 Dominik Hasek (G), Chi. .50
□□ 374 Laurie Boschman, N.J. .10
□□ 375 Brian Leetch, NYR. .25
□□ 376 Nelson Emerson, Stl. .10
□□ 377 Normand Rochefort, NYR. .10
□□ 378 Jacques Cloutier (G), Que. .10
□□ 379 Jim Sandlak, Van. .10
□□ 380 David Reid, Bos. .10
□□ 381 Gary Nylund, NYI. .10
□□ 382 Sergei Makarov, Cgy. .10
□□ 383 Petr Klima, Edm. .10
□□ 384 Peter Douris, Bos. .10
□□ 385 Kirk McLean (G), Van. .25
□□ 386 Robert McGill, Det. .10
□□ 387 Ron Tugnutt (G), Edm. .10
□□ 388 Patrice Brisebois, Mtl. .10
□□ 389 Tony Amonte, NYR. .25
□□ 390 Mario Lemieux, Pgh. 1.25
□□ 391 Nicklas Lidström, Det. .25
□□ 392 Brendan Shanahan, Stl. .35
□□ 393 Donald Audette, Buf. .10
□□ 394 Alexei Kasatonov, N.J. .10
□□ 395 Dino Ciccarelli, Wsh. .25
□□ 396 Vincent Riendeau (G), Det. .10
□□ 397 Joe Reekie, NYI. .10
□□ 398 Jari Kurri, L.A. .25
□□ 399 Ken Wregget (G), Pgh. .10
□□ 400 Steve Yzerman, Det. .75
□□ 401 Scott Niedermayer, N.J. .25
□□ 402 Stéphane Beauregard (G), Wpg. .10
□□ 403 Tim Hunter, Cgy. .10
□□ 404 Marc Bergevin, Hfd. .10
□□ 405 Sylvain Lefebvre, Mtl. .10
□□ 406 Johan Garpenlov, S.J. .10
□□ 407 Tony Hrkac, Chi. .10
□□ 408 Tie Domi, NYR. .10
□□ 409 Martin Lapointe, Det. .10
□□ 410 Darryl Sydor, L.A. .10
□□ 411 LL: Brett Hull, Stl. .25
□□ 412 LL: Wayne Gretzky, L.A. 1.00
□□ 413 LL: Mario Lemieux, Pgh. .75
□□ 414 LL: Paul Ysebaert, Det. .10
□□ 415 LL: Tony Amonte, NYR. .25
□□ 416 LL: Brian Leetch, NYR. .25
□□ 417 LL: McLean/Cheveldae .10
□□ 418 LL: Patrick Roy (G), Mtl. .75
□□ 419 Ray Bourque, Bos. .25
□□ 420 Pat LaFontaine, Buf. .25
□□ 421 Al MacInnis, Cgy. .25
□□ 422 Jeremy Roenick, Chi. .25
□□ 423 Steve Yzerman, Det. .35
□□ 424 Bill Ranford (G), Edm. .25
□□ 425 John Cullen, Hfd. .10
□□ 426 Wayne Gretzky, L.A. 1.00
□□ 427 Mike Modano, Min. .25
□□ 428 Patrick Roy (G), Mtl. .75
□□ 429 Scott Stevens, N.J. .25
□□ 430 Pierre Turgeon, NYI. .25
□□ 431 Mark Messier, NYR. .25
□□ 432 Eric Lindros, Pha. .75
□□ 433 Mario Lemieux, Pgh. .75
□□ 434 Joe Sakic, Que. .50
□□ 435 Brett Hull, Stl. .25
□□ 436 Pat Falloon, S.J. .10
□□ 437 Grant Fuhr (G), Tor. .25
□□ 438 Trevor Linden, Van. .25
□□ 439 Kevin Hatcher, Wsh. .10
□□ 440 Phil Housley, Wpg. .10
□□ 441 HL: Paul Coffey, Pgh. .25
□□ 442 HL: Brett Hull, Stl. .25
□□ 443 HL: Mike Gartner, NYR. .25
□□ 444 HL: Michel Goulet, Chi. .25
□□ 445 HL: Mike Gartner, NYR. .25
□□ 446 HL: Bobby Smith, Min. .10
□□ 447 HL: Ray Bourque, Bos .25
□□ 448 HL: Mario Lemieux, Pgh. .75
□□ 449 Scott Lachance, NYI. .10
□□ 450 Keith Tkachuk, Wpg. .35
□□ 451 Alexander Semak, N.J. .10
□□ 452 John Tanner (G), Que. .10
□□ 453 Joé Juneau, Bos. .10
□□ 454 Igor Kravchuk, Chi. .10
□□ 455 Brent Thompson, L.A. .10
□□ 456 Evgeny Davydov, Wpg. .10
□□ 457 Arturs Irbe (G), S.J. .10
□□ 458 Kent Manderville, Tor. .10
□□ 459 Shawn McEachern, Pgh. .10
□□ **460 Guy Hebert (G), Stl., RC .35**
□□ **461 Keith Carney, Buf., RC .10**
□□ 462 Karl Dykhuis, Chi. .10
□□ **463 Bill Lindsay, Que., RC .10**
□□ 464 Dominic Roussel (G), Pha. .10
□□ 465 Marty McInnis, NYI. .10
□□ 466 Dale Craigwell, S.J. .10
□□ 467 Igor Ulanov, Wpg. .10
□□ 468 Dimitri Mironov, Tor. .10
□□ **469 Dean McAmmond, Chi., RC .10**
□□ **470 Bill Guerin, N.J., RC .35**
□□ 471 Bret Hedican, Stl. .10
□□ 472 Félix Potvin (G), Tor. .35
□□ 473 Vyacheslav Kozlov, Det. .20
□□ 474 Martin Rucinsky, Que. .10
□□ **475 Ray Whitney, S.J., RC .10**
□□ 476 Stephen Heinze, Bos. .10
□□ 477 Brad Schlegel, Wsh. .10
□□ 478 Patrick Poulin, Hfd. .10
□□ 479 Ted Donato, Bos. .10
□□ 480 Martin Brodeur (G), N.J. .50
□□ **481 Denny Felsner, Stl., RC .10**
□□ **482 Trent Klatt, Min., RC .10**
□□ 483 Gord Hynes, Bos. .10
□□ 484 Glen Murray, Bos. .10
□□ 485 Chris Lindberg, Cgy. .10
□□ 486 Ray LeBlanc (G), Chi. .10
□□ **487 Yanic Perreault, Tor., RC .25**
□□ **488 Jean-François Quintin, S.J., RC .10**
□□ 489 Patrick Roy (G), Mtl. .75
□□ 490 Ray Bourque, Bos. .25
□□ 491 Brian Leetch, NYR. .25
□□ 492 Kevin Stevens, Pgh. .10
□□ 493 Mark Messier, NYR. .25
□□ 494 Jaromir Jagr, Pgh. .50
□□ 495 Bill Ranford (G), Edm. .25
□□ 496 Al MacInnis, Cgy. .25
□□ 497 Chris Chelios, Chi. .25
□□ 498 Luc Robitaille, L.A. .25
□□ 499 Jeremy Roenick, Chi. .25
□□ 500 Brett Hull, Stl. .25
□□ 501 Félix Potvin (G), Tor. .25
□□ 502 Nicklas Lidström, Det. .25
□□ 503 Vladimir Konstantinov, Det. .10
□□ 504 Pavel Bure, Van. .35
□□ 505 Nelson Emerson, Stl. .10
□□ 506 Tony Amonte, NYR. .25
□□ 507 Tampa Bay Lightning Checklist .10
□□ 508 Shawn Chambers .10
□□ 509 Basil McRae, T.B. .10

	No.	Player	NRMT-MT
□ □	510	Joe Reekie, T.B.	.10
□ □	511	Wendell Young (G), T.B.	.10
□ □	512	Ottawa Senators Checklist	.10
□ □	513	Laurie Boschman, Ott.	.10
□ □	514	Mark Lamb, Ott.	.10
□ □	515	Peter Sidorkiewicz (G), Ott.	.10
□ □	516	Sylvain Turgeon, Ott.	.10
□ □	517	Kevin and Bill Dineen, Pha.	.10
□ □	518	1992 Stanley Cup Champs, Pgh.	.10
□ □	519	AW: Mario Lemieux, Pgh.	.75
□ □	520	AW: Ray Bourque, Bos.	.25
□ □	521	AW: Mark Messier, NYR.	.25
□ □	522	AW: Brian Leetch, NYR.	.25
□ □	523	AW: Pavel Bure, Van.	.35
□ □	524	AW: Guy Carbonneau, Mtl.	.10
□ □	525	AW: Wayne Gretzky, L.A.	1.00
□ □	526	AW: Mark Fitzpatrick, NYI.	.10
□ □	527	AW: Patrick Roy (G), Mtl.	.75
□ □	528	Kamloops Blazers	.10
□ □	529	Rick Tabaracci (G), Wpg.	.20
□ □	530	Tom Draper (G), Buf.	.10
□ □	531	Adrien Plavsic, Van.	.10
□ □	532	Joe Sacco, Tor.	.10
□ □	533	Mike Sullivan, S.J.	.10
□ □	534	Zdeno Ciger, N.J.	.10
□ □	535	Frank Pietrangelo (G), Hfd.	.10
□ □	536	Mike Peluso, Chi.	.10
□ □	537	Jim Paek, Pgh.	.10
□ □	538	Dave Hannan, Buf.	.10
□ □	**539**	**David Williams, S.J., RC**	**.10**
□ □	540	Gino Odjick, Van.	.10
□ □	541	Yvon Corriveau, Hfd.	.10
□ □	542	Grant Jennings, Pgh.	.10
□ □	543	Stéphane Matteau, Chi.	.10
□ □	544	Patrick Conacher, N.J.	.10
□ □	545	Steven Rice, Edm.	.10
□ □	546	Marc Habscheid, Cgy.	.10
□ □	547	Steve Weeks (G), L.A.	.10
□	548	Maurice Richard, Mtl.	1.00
□	548	Jay Wells, NYR.	.10
□	549	Maurice Richard, Mtl.	1.00
□	549	Mick Vukota, NYI.	.10
□ □	550	Eric Lindros, Pha.	1.50

CANADIAN OLYMPIC HEROES

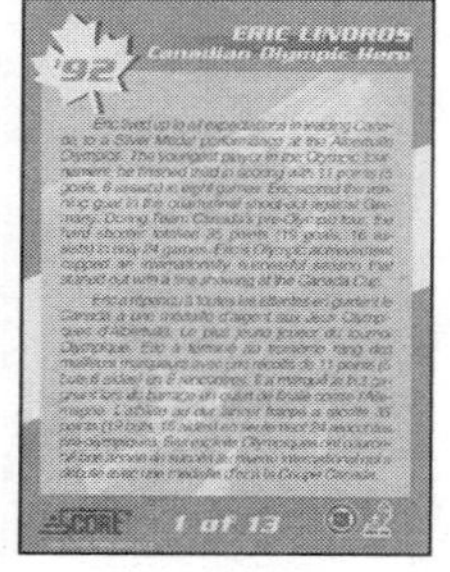

Canadian Insert Set (13 cards): **80.00**

	No.	Player	NRMT-MT
□	1	Eric Lindros	35.00
□	2	Joé Juneau	6.00
□	3	Dave Archibald	4.00
□	4	Randy Smith	4.00
□	5	Gord Hynes	4.00
□	6	Chris Lindberg	4.00
□	7	Jason Woolley	4.00
□	8	Fabian Joseph	4.00
□	9	Brad Schlegel	4.00
□	10	Kent Manderville	4.00
□	11	Adrien Plavsic	4.00
□	12	Trevor Kidd (G)	8.00
□	13	Sean Burke (G)	8.00

MAURICE RICHARD

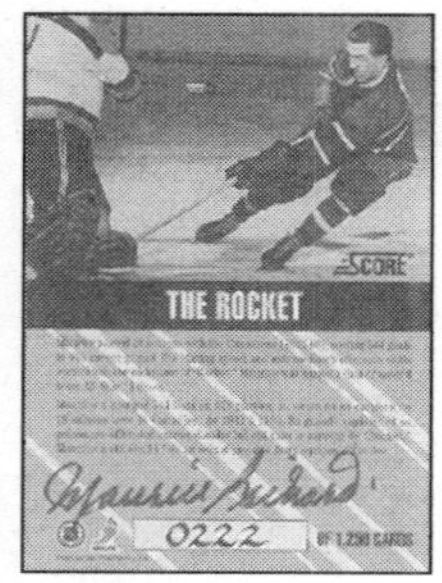

	Player	Reg.	Auto.
□ □	Maurice Richard	20.00	250.00
□ □	Maurice Richard	20.00	250.00

SHARP SHOOTERS

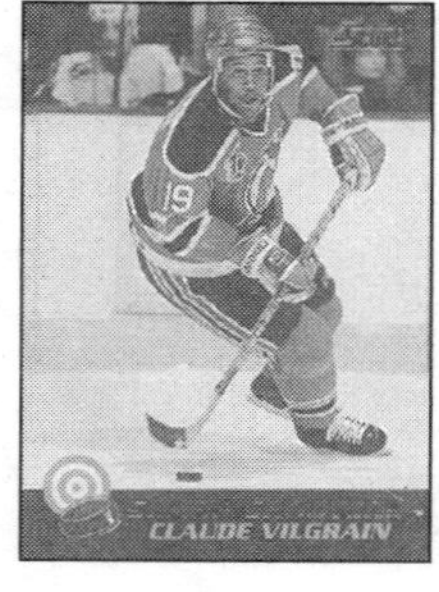

These cards have two versions: an American and a Canadian issue.

Insert Set (30 cards): **8.00**

	No.	Player	NRMT-MT
□ □	1	Gary Roberts, Cgy.	.50
□ □	2	Sergei Makarov, Cgy.	.50
□ □	3	Ray Ferraro, NYI.	.20
□ □	4	Dale Hunter, Wsh.	.20
□ □	5	Sergei Nemchinov, NYR.	.20
□ □	6	Mike Ridley, Wsh.	.20
□ □	7	Gilbert Dionne, Mtl.	.20
□ □	8	Pat LaFontaine, Buf.	.50
□ □	9	Jimmy Carson, Det.	.20
□ □	10	Jeremy Roenick. Chi.	1.50
□ □	11	Kelly Buchberger, Edm.	.20
□ □	12	Owen Nolan, Que.	.50
□ □	13	Igor Larionov, Van.	.50
□ □	14	Claude Vilgrain, N.J.	.20
□ □	15	Derek King, NYI.	.20
□ □	16	Greg Paslawski, Que.	.20
□ □	17	Bob Probert, Det.	.20
□ □	18	Mark Recchi, Pha.	.50
□ □	19	Donald Audette, Buf.	.20
□ □	20	Ray Sheppard, Det.	.20
□ □	21	Benoît Hogue, NYI.	.20
□ □	22	Rob Brown, Chi.	.20
□ □	23	Pat Elynuik, Wpg.	.20
□ □	24	Petr Klima, Edm.	.20
□ □	25	Pierre Turgeon, NYI.	.50
□ □	26	Corey Millen, L.A.	.20
□ □	27	Dimitri Khristich, Wsh.	.20
□ □	28	Anatoli Semenov, Edm.	.20
□ □	29	Kirk Muller, Mtl.	.20
□ □	30	Craig Simpson, Edm.	.20

USA GREATS

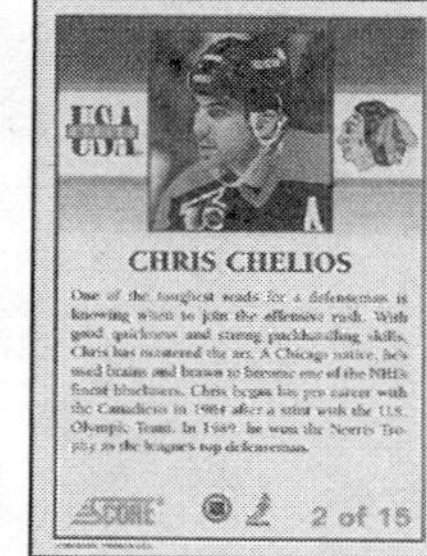

American Insert Set (15 cards): **40.00**

	No.	Player	NRMT-MT
□	1	Pat LaFontaine, Buf.	2.00
□	2	Chris Chelios, Chi.	3.50
□	3	Jeremy Roenick, Chi.	3.50
□	4	Tony Granato, L.A.	2.00
□	5	Mike Modano, Min.	6.00
□	6	Mike Richter (G), NYR.	3.50
□	7	John Vanbiesbrouck (G), NYR.	8.00
□	8	Brian Leetch, NYR.	3.50
□	9	Joe Mullen, Pgh.	2.00
□	10	Kevin Stevens, Pgh.	2.00
□	11	Craig Janney, Stl.	2.00
□	12	Brian Mullen, S.J.	2.00
□	13	Kevin Hatcher, Wsh.	2.00
□	14	Kelly Miller, Wsh.	2.00
□	15	Ed Olczyk, Wpg.	2.00

ERIC LINDROS PRESS CONFERENCE CARD

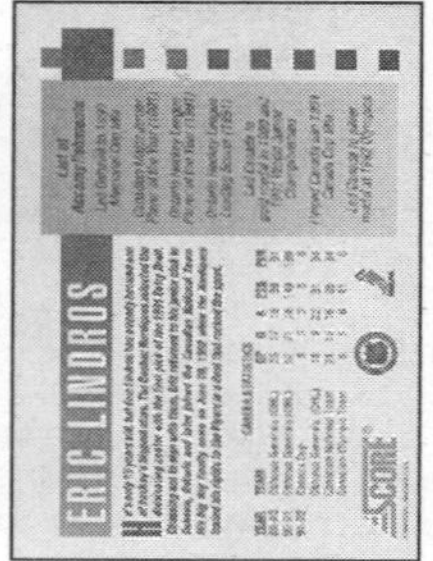

	Player	NRMT-MT
□	Eric Lindros	40.00

1992 - 93 SCORE YOUNG SUPERSTARS

Imprint:

Complete Set (40 cards): **6.00**

	No.	Player	NRMT-MT
□	1	Eric Lindros, Pha.	2.00
□	2	Tony Amonte, NYR.	.25
□	3	Mats Sundin, Que.	.75
□	4	Jaromir Jagr, Pgh.	1.50
□	5	Sergei Fedorov, Det.	.75
□	6	Gilbert Dionne, Mtl.	.10
□	7	Mark Recchi, Pha.	.25
□	8	Alexander Mogilny, Buf.	.50
□	9	Mike Richter (G), NYR.	.50
□	10	Jeremy Roenick, Chi.	.50
□	11	Nicklas Lidström, Det.	.25
□	12	Scott Lachance, NYI.	.10
□	13	Nelson Emerson, S.J.	.10
□	15	Pat Falloon, S.J.	.10
□	15	Dimitri Khristich, Wsh.	.10
□	16	Trevor Linden, Van.	.25
□	17	Curtis Joseph (G), Stl.	.85
□	18	Rob Pearson, Tor.	.10
□	19	Kevin Todd, N.J.	.10
□	20	Joe Sakic, Que.	1.25
□	21	Tim Cheveldae (G), Det.	.10
□	22	Joé Juneau, Wsh.	.10
□	23	Vladimir Konstantinov, Det.	.10
□	24	Valeri Kamensky, Que.	.25
□	25	Ed Belfour (G), Chi.	.50
□	26	Rod Brind'Amour, Pha.	.25
□	27	Pierre Turgeon, NYI.	.25
□	28	Eric Desjardins, Mtl.	.25
□	29	Keith Tkachuk, Wpg.	.75

	No.	Player	Price
☐	30	Pavel Bure, Van.	1.00
☐	31	Patrick Poulin, Hfd.	.10
☐	32	Vyacheslav Kozlov, Det.	.10
☐	33	Scott Niedermayer, N.J.	.25
☐	34	Jyrki Lumme, Van.	.10
☐	35	Paul Ysebaert, Det.	.10
☐	36	Dominic Roussel (G), Pha.	.10
☐	37	Owen Nolan, Que.	.25
☐	38	Rob Blake, L.A.	.25
☐	39	Félix Potvin (G), Tor.	.75
☐	40	Mike Modano, Dal.	.75

1992 - 93 SEASON'S ACTION PLAYER PATCHES

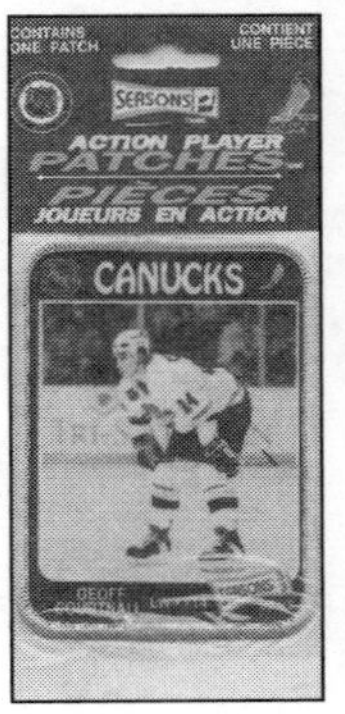

The patches were made of soft cloth and intended to patch clothing. The set is considered complete without the prototype patch (#22, Grant Mulvey).

Patch Size: 3 1/8" x 4 3/8"
Imprint: (on packaging) SEASONS TM/MC
Complete Set (70 patches): 200.00
Common Player: 2.00

	No.	Player	NRMT-MT
☐	1	Jeremy Roenick, Chi.	3.00
☐	2	Steve Larmer, Chi.	2.00
☐	3	Ed Belfour (G), Chi.	3.00
☐	4	Chris Chelios, Chi.	3.00
☐	5	Sergei Fedorov, Det.	4.00
☐	6	Steve Yzerman, Det.	8.00
☐	7	Tim Cheveldae (G), Det.	2.00
☐	8	Bob Probert, Det.	2.00
☐	9	Wayne Gretzky, L.A.	15.00
☐	10	Luc Robitaille, L.A.	2.00
☐	11	Tony Granato, L.A.	2.00
☐	12	Kelly Hrudey (G), L.A.	2.00
☐	13	Brett Hull, Stl.	4.00
☐	14	Curtis Joseph (G), Stl.	5.00
☐	15	Brendan Shanahan, Stl.	5.00
☐	16	Nelson Emerson, Bos.	2.00
☐	17	Ray Bourque, Bos.	4.00
☐	18	Joé Juneau, Bos.	2.00
☐	19	Andy Moog (G), Bos.	3.00
☐	20	Adam Oates, Bos.	3.00
☐	21	Patrick Roy (G), Mtl.	12.00
☐	22	Prototype: Grant Mulvey	20.00
☐	23	Denis Savard, Mtl.	2.00
☐	24	Gilbert Dionne, Mtl.	2.00
☐	25	Kirk Muller, Mtl.	2.00
☐	26	Mark Messier, NYR.	4.00
☐	27	Tony Amonte, NYR.	2.00
☐	28	Brian Leetch, NYR.	3.00
☐	29	Mike Richter (G), NYR.	3.00
☐	30	Trevor Linden, Van.	2.00
☐	31	Pavel Bure, Van.	6.00
☐	32	Cliff Ronning, Van.	2.00
☐	33	Geoff Courtnall, Van.	2.00
☐	34	Mario Lemieux, Pgh.	12.00
☐	35	Jaromir Jagr, Pgh.	8.00
☐	36	Tom Barrasso (G), Pgh.	3.00
☐	37	Rick Tocchet, Pha.	2.00
☐	38	Eric Lindros, Pha.	10.00
☐	39	Rod Brind'Amour, Pha.	2.00
☐	40	Dominic Roussel (G) Pha.	2.00
☐	41	Mark Recchi, Pha.	2.00
☐	42	Pat LaFontaine, Buf.	2.00
☐	43	Donald Audette, Buf.	2.00
☐	44	Pat Verbeek, Hfd.	2.00
☐	45	John Cullen, Hfd.	2.00
☐	46	Owen Nolan, Que.	2.00
☐	47	Joe Sakic, Que.	7.00
☐	48	Kevin Hatcher Wsh.	2.00
☐	49	Don Beaupré (G), Wsh.	2.00
☐	50	Scott Stevens, N.J.	2.00
☐	51	Chris Terreri (G), N.J.	2.00
☐	52	Scott Lachance, N.J.	2.00
☐	53	Pierre Turgeon, NYI.	2.00
☐	54	Grant Fuhr (G), Tor.	3.00
☐	55	Doug Gilmour, Tor.	3.00
☐	56	Dave Manson, Edm.	2.00
☐	57	Bill Ranford (G), Edm.	2.00
☐	58	Troy Murray, Chi.	2.00
☐	59	Phil Housley, Wpg.	2.00
☐	60	Al MacInnis, Cgy.	2.00
☐	61	Mike Vernon (G), Cgy.	3.00
☐	62	Pat Falloon, S.J.	2.00
☐	63	Doug Wilson, S.J.	2.00
☐	64	Jon Casey (G), Min.	2.00
☐	65	Mike Modano, Min.	4.00
☐	66	Kevin Stevens, Pgh.	2.00
☐	67	Al Iafrate, Wsh.	2.00
☐	68	Dale Hawerchuk, Wpg.	2.00
☐	69	Igor Kravchuk, Chi.	2.00
☐	70	Wendel Clark, Tor.	3.00
☐	71	Kirk McLean (G), Van.	3.00

1992 - 93 SEMIC ELITSERIEN STICKERS

Size: 3" x 2 1/8"
Imprint:
Complete Set (356 stickers): 40.00
Common Player: .20

	No.	Player	NRMT-MT
☐	1	AIK Photo LH	.20
☐	2	AIK Photo RH	.20
☐	3	Brynas Photo LH	.20
☐	4	Brynas Photo RH	.20
☐	5	Djurgardens Photo LH	.20
☐	6	Djurgardens Photo RH	.20
☐	7	Farjestad Photo LH	.20
☐	8	Farjestad Photo RH	.20
☐	9	HV 71 Photo LH	.20
☐	10	HV 71 Photo RH	.20
☐	11	Leksands Photo LH	.20
☐	12	Leksands Photo RH	.20
☐	13	Lulea Photo LH	.20
☐	14	Lulea Photo RH	.20
☐	15	Malmo Photo LH	.20
☐	16	Malmo Photo RH	.20
☐	17	MoDo Photo LH	.20
☐	18	MoDo Photo RH	.20
☐	19	Rogle Photo LH	.20
☐	20	Rogle Photo RH	.20
☐	21	Västerås Photo LH	.20
☐	22	Västerås Photo RH	.20
☐	23	Vastra Frolunda Photo LH	.20
☐	24	Vastra Frolunda Photo RH	.20
☐	25	AIK Logo	.20
☐	26	Rolf Ridderwall	.20
☐	27	Sam Lindstahl	.20
☐	28	Ronnie Karlsson	.20
☐	29	Mats Thelin	.20
☐	30	Mattias Norstrom	.20
☐	31	Dick Tarnstrom	.20
☐	32	Petri Liimatainen	.20
☐	33	Rikard Franzen	.20
☐	34	Daniel Jardemyr	.20
☐	35	Niclas Havelid	.20
☐	36	Borje Salming	2.00
☐	37	Thomas Bjuhr	.20
☐	38	Peter Hammarstrom	.20
☐	39	Thomas Strandberg	.20
☐	40	Mats Lindberg	.20
☐	41	Anders Bjork	.20
☐	42	Anders Johnson	.20
☐	43	Patrik Erickson	.20
☐	44	Torbjorn Ohrlund	.20
☐	45	Bjorn Ahlstrom	.20
☐	46	Niclas Sundblad	.20
☐	47	Patric Englund	.20
☐	48	Kristian Gahn	.20
☐	49	Morgan Samuelsson	.20
☐	50	Brynas Logo	.20
☐	51	Michael Sundlov	.20
☐	52	Lars Karlsson	.20
☐	53	Bedrick Scerban	.20
☐	54	Mikael Lindman	.20
☐	55	Tommy Melkersson	.20
☐	56	Stefan Klockare	.20
☐	57	Mikael Enander	.20
☐	58	Roger Karlsson	.20
☐	59	Niklas Gallstedt	.20
☐	60	Christer Olsson	.20
☐	61	Anders Carlsson	.20
☐	62	Thomas Tallberg	.20
☐	63	Tom Bissett	.20
☐	64	Andreas Dackell	.50
☐	65	Mikael Wahlberg	.20
☐	66	Jan Larsson	.20
☐	67	Anders Gozzi	.20
☐	68	Ove Molin	.20
☐	69	Anders Huss	.20
☐	70	Peter Gustafsson	.20
☐	71	Jonas Johnson	.20
☐	72	Peter Larsson	.20
☐	73	Mikael Lindholm	.20
☐	74	Djurgarden Logo	.20
☐	75	Thomas Ostlund	.20
☐	76	Petter Ronnquist	.20
☐	77	Christian Due-Boje	.20
☐	78	Arto Blomsten	.20
☐	79	Kenneth Kennholt	.20
☐	80	Marcus Ragnarsson	.20
☐	81	Thomas Johansson	.20
☐	82	Joakim Lundberg	.20
☐	83	Thomas Eriksson	.20
☐	84	Bjorn Nord	.20
☐	85	Mikael Magnusson	.20
☐	86	Charles Berglund	.20
☐	87	Erik Huusko	.20
☐	88	Anders Huusko	.20
☐	89	Tony Skopac	.20
☐	90	Jens Ohling	.20
☐	91	Peter Nilsson	.20
☐	94	Mikael Hakansson	.20
☐	95	Ola Josefsson	.20
☐	96	Jerry Friman	.20
☐	97	Fredrik Lindquist	.20
☐	98	Mathias Hallback	.20
☐	99	Jan Viktorsson	.20
☐	100	Farjestad Logo	.20
☐	101	Anders Bergman	.20
☐	102	Jonas Eriksson	.20
☐	103	Patrik Haltia	.20
☐	104	Tommy Samuelsson	.20
☐	105	Jesper Duus	.20
☐	106	Leif Carlsson	.20
☐	107	Per Lundell	.20
☐	108	Jacob Karlsson	.20
☐	109	Thomas Rhodin	.20
☐	110	Mattias Olsson	.20
☐	111	Hakan Loob	1.50
☐	112	Thomas Rundqvist	.20
☐	113	Andreas Johansson	.20
☐	114	Staffan Lundh	.20
☐	115	Jonas Hoglund	.50
☐	116	Bengt-Ake Gustafsson	.20
☐	117	Mattias Johansson	.20
☐	118	Clas Eriksson	.20
☐	119	Peter Ottosson	.20
☐	120	Niklas Brannstrom	.20
☐	121	Lars Karlsson	.20
☐	122	Peter Hagstrom	.20
☐	123	Kjell Dahlin	.20
☐	124	HV 71 Logo	.20
☐	125	Peter Aslin	.20
☐	126	Boo Ahl	.20
☐	127	Antonin Stavjana	.20
☐	128	Klas Heed	.20
☐	129	Tommy Fritz	.20
☐	130	Kristian Pedersen	.20
☐	131	Per Gustafsson	.20
☐	132	Mathias Svedberg	.20
☐	133	Niclas Rahm	.20
☐	134	Martin Canielsson	.20
☐	135	Fredrik Stillman	.20
☐	136	Lars Ivarsson	.20

	No.	Player	Price
☐	137	Ove Thornberg	.20
☐	138	Peter Ekelund	.20
☐	139	Eddy Eriksson	.20
☐	140	Stefan Ornskog	.20
☐	141	Patrik Ross	.20
☐	142	Torbjorn Persson	.20
☐	143	Kamil Kastak	.20
☐	144	Dennis Strom	.20
☐	145	Peter Eriksson	.20
☐	146	Magnus Axelsson	.20
☐	147	Stefan Falk	.20
☐	148	Thomas Ljungberg	.20
☐	149	Leksand Logo	.20
☐	150	Ake Lilljeborn	.20
☐	151	Jonas Leven	.20
☐	152	Johan Hedberg	.20
☐	153	Tomas Jonsson	.20
☐	154	Henric Bjorkman	.20
☐	155	Mattias Andersson	.20
☐	156	Rickard Persson	.20
☐	157	Orjan Nilsson	.20
☐	158	Magnus Svensson	.20
☐	159	Orjan Lindmark	.20
☐	160	Jan Huokko	.20
☐	161	Reine Rauhala	.20
☐	162	Emil Skoglund	.20
☐	163	Jens Nielsen	.20
☐	164	Marcus Thuresson	.20
☐	165	Niklas Eriksson	.20
☐	166	Tomas Srsen	.20
☐	167	Jonas Bergqvist	.20
☐	168	Per-Olof Carlsson	.20
☐	169	Markus Akerblom	.20
☐	170	Greg Parks	.20
☐	171	Mattias Loof	.20
☐	172	Cenneth Soderlund	.20
☐	173	Jarmo Makitalo	.20
☐	174	Lulea Logo	.20
☐	175	Robert Skoog	.20
☐	176	Erik Grankvist	.20
☐	177	Lars Modig	.20
☐	178	Patrik Hoglund	.20
☐	179	Niklas Bjornoft	.20
☐	180	Torbjorn Lindberg	.20
☐	181	Ville Siren	.20
☐	182	Petter Nilsson	.20
☐	183	Joakim Gunler	.20
☐	184	Tomas Lilja	.20
☐	185	Stefan Jonsson	.20
☐	186	Stefan Nilsson	.20
☐	187	Johan Stromvall	.20
☐	188	Robert Nordberg	.20
☐	189	Tomas Berglund	.20
☐	190	Mikael Renberg	5.00
☐	191	Lars-Gunnar Pettersson	.20
☐	192	Lars Edstrom	.20
☐	193	Kyosti Karjalainen	.20
☐	194	Lars Hurtig	.20
☐	195	Fredrik Oberg	.20
☐	196	Mikael Engstrom	.20
☐	197	Mika Nieminen	.20
☐	198	Malmo Logo	.20
☐	199	Peter Lindmark	.20
☐	200	Roger Nordström (G)	.20
☐	201	Johan Mansson	.20
☐	202	Anders Svensson	.20
☐	203	Timo Blomqvist	.20
☐	204	Johan Norgren	.20
☐	205	Mats Lusth	.20
☐	206	Peter Hasselblad	.20
☐	207	Robert Svehla	1.50
☐	208	Johan Salle	.20
☐	209	Roger Ohman	.20
☐	210	Raimo Helminen	.20
☐	211	Roger Hansson	.20
☐	212	Per Rosenqvist	.20
☐	213	Bo Svanberg	.20
☐	214	Daniel Rydmark	.20
☐	215	Patrik Sylvegard	.20
☐	216	Jonas Hakansson	.20
☐	217	Jesper Mattsson	.20
☐	218	Hakan Ahlund	.20
☐	219	peter Sundstrom	.20
☐	220	Mats Naslund	2.00
☐	221	Robert Burakovsky	.20
☐	222	MoDo Logo	.20
☐	223	Fredrik Andersson	.20
☐	224	Anders Nasstrom	.20
☐	225	Anders Berglund	.20
☐	226	Miroslav Horava	.20
☐	227	Hans Lodin	.20
☐	228	Lars Jansson	.20
☐	229	Jorgen Eriksson	.20
☐	230	Anders Eriksson	.20
☐	231	Hans Jonsson	.20
☐	232	Tomas Nazen	.20
☐	233	Mattias Timander	.20
☐	234	Fredrik Bergqvist	.20
☐	235	Magnus Wernblom	.20
☐	236	Martin Hostak	.20
☐	237	Mikael Pettersson	.20
☐	238	Lennart Hermansson	.20
☐	239	Tommy Lehmann	.20
☐	240	Markus Naslund	1.00
☐	241	Ulf Odmark	.20
☐	242	Peter Forsberg	10.00
☐	243	Andreas Salomonsson	.20
☐	244	Niklas Sundstrom	1.50
☐	245	Lars Bystrom	.20
☐	246	Erik Holmberg	.20
☐	247	Henrik Gradin	.20
☐	248	Rogle Logo	.20
☐	249	Kenneth Johansson	.20
☐	250	Billy Nilsson	.20
☐	251	Orjan Jacobsson	.20
☐	252	Daniel Johansson	.20
☐	253	Kenny Jonsson	1.00
☐	254	Kari Eloranta	.35
☐	255	Kari Suoraniemi	.20
☐	256	Hakan Persson	.20
☐	257	Rikar Gronborg	.20
☐	258	Stefan Nilsson	.20
☐	259	Per Ljusterang	.20
☐	260	Igor Stelnov	.20
☐	261	Peter Lundmark	.20
☐	262	Heinz Ehlers	.20
☐	263	Michael Hjalm	.20
☐	264	Jan Ericson	.20
☐	265	Pelle Svensson	.20
☐	266	Mats Loov	.20
☐	267	Stefan Elvenes	.20
☐	268	Roger Elvenes	.20
☐	269	Peter Wennberg	.20
☐	270	Per Wallin	.20
☐	271	Torgny Lowgren	.20
☐	272	Jorgen Jonsson	.20
☐	273	Vasteras Logo	.20
☐	274	Mats Ytter(G)	.20
☐	275	Tommy Salo (G)	1.00
☐	276	Erik Bergstrom	.20
☐	277	Pierre Iversson	.20
☐	278	Peter Popovic	.35
☐	279	Sergei Fokin	.20
☐	280	Edvin Frylen	.20
☐	281	Leif Rohlin	.35
☐	282	Peter Karlsson	.20
☐	283	Peter Jacobsson	.20
☐	294	Roger Akerstrom	.20
☐	285	Robert Nordmark	.20
☐	286	Patrik Juhlin	.35
☐	287	Mishat Fahrutdinov	.20
☐	288	Henrik Nilsson	.20
☐	289	Mikael Pettersson	.20
☐	290	Fredrik Nilsson	.20
☐	291	Stefan Hellkvist	.20
☐	292	Henrik Pettersson	.20
☐	293	Micael Karlberg	.20
☐	294	Anders Berglund	.20
☐	295	Claes Lindblom	.20
☐	296	Johan Brummer	.20
☐	297	Patrik Ulin	.20
☐	298	Paul Andersson	.20
☐	299	Vastra Frolunda Logo	.20
☐	300	Hakan Algotsson	.20
☐	301	Miael Sandberg	.20
☐	302	Patric Aberg	.20
☐	303	Joacim Esbjors	.20
☐	304	Oscar Ackestrom	.20
☐	305	Jonas Heed	.20
☐	306	Stefan Axelsson	.20
☐	308	Ronnie Sundin	.20
☐	308	Stefan Larsson	.20
☐	309	Jonathan Hagrenius	.20
☐	310	Serge Boisvert	.20
☐	311	Jerry Persson	.20
☐	312	Trond Magnussen	.20
☐	313	Terho Koskela	.20
☐	314	Peter Derndtsson	.20
☐	315	Mikael Persson	.20
☐	316	Mats Hjalmarsson	.20
☐	317	Henrik Lundin	.20
☐	318	Jonas Esbjors	.20
☐	319	Daniel Alfredsson	5.00
☐	320	Stefan Ketola	.20
☐	321	Lars Dahlstrom	.20
☐	322	Par Edlund	.20
☐	323	Thomas Sjogren	.20
☐	324	Leif Holmgren, Coach	.20
☐	325	Tommy Sandlin, Coach	.20
☐	326	Lars Falk, Coach	.20
☐	327	Harald Luckner, Coach	.20
☐	328	Lars-Erik Lundstrom, Coach	.20
☐	329	Wayne Fleming, Coach	.20
☐	330	Freddy Lindfors, Coach	.20
☐	331	Timo Cahtinen, Coach	.20
☐	332	Kent Forsberg, Coach	.20
☐	333	Christer Abrahamsson, Coach	.20
☐	334	Mikael Lundstrom, Coach	.20
☐	335	Leif Boork, Coach	.20
☐	336	Tommy Sjodin	.35
☐	337	Hakan Loob	1.00
☐	338	Michael Nylander	.75
☐	339	Michael Nylander	.75
☐	340	Hakan Loob	1.00
☐	341	Calle Johansson	.20
☐	342	Tommy Sandlin	.20
☐	343	Tommy Söderström (G)	.75
☐	344	Tommy Sjodin	.35
☐	345	Peter Andersson	.20
☐	346	Hakan Loob	1.00
☐	347	Peter Forsberg	8.00
☐	348	Mats Sundin	6.00
☐	349	Jonas Forsberg	.20
☐	350	Stefan Bjork	.20
☐	351	Edvin Frylen	.20
☐	352	Mikael Tjallden	.20
☐	353	Johan Davidsson	.35
☐	354	Markus Eriksson	.20
☐	355	Fredrik Lindh	.20
☐	356	Peter Nylander	.50

1992 - 93 TOPPS

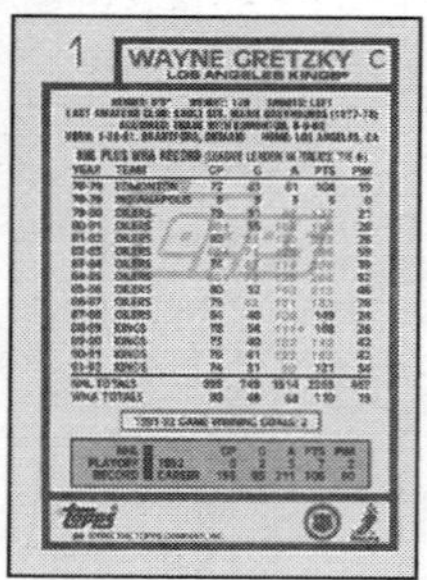

These cards have two versions: the regular issue and a one per pack Topps Gold parallel. Short prints in the Topps Gold series are priced accordingly.

Imprint: © 1992 THE TOPPS COMPANY, INC.

Complete Set (529 cards):			20.00	350.00
Common Player:			.10	.35
	No.	**Player**	**TOPPS**	**GOLD**
☐ ☐	1	Wayne Gretzky, L.A.	1.50	50.00
☐ ☐	2	Brett Hull, Stl.	.50	15.00
☐ ☐	3	Félix Potvin (G), Tor.	.50	15.00
☐ ☐	4	Mark Tinordi, Min.	.10	.35
☐ ☐	5	Highlight: Paul Coffey, L.A.	.25	1.00
☐ ☐	6	Tony Amonte, NYR.	.20	1.00
☐ ☐	7	Pat Falloon, S.J.	.10	.35
☐ ☐	8	Pavel Bure, Van.	.25	4.00
☐ ☐	9	Nicklas Lidström, Det.	.25	1.00

	No.	Player		
□□	10	Dominic Roussel (G) Pha.	.10	.35
□□	11	Nelson Emerson, Stl.	.10	.35
□□	12	Donald Audette, Buf.	.10	.35
□□	13	Gilbert Dionne, Mtl.	.10	.35
□□	14	Vladimir Konstantinov, Det.	.25	1.00
□□	15	Kevin Todd, N.J.	.10	.35
□□	16	Stephen Leach, Bos.	.10	.35
□□	17	Ed Olczyk, Wpg.	.10	.35
□□	18	Jim Hrivnak (G), Wsh.	.10	.35
□□	19	Gilbert Dionne, Mtl.	.10	.35
□□	20	Mike Vernon (G), Cgy.	.25	1.00
□□	21	Dave Christian, Stl.	.10	.35
□□	22	Ed Belfour (G), Chi.	.25	2.00
□□	23	Andrew Cassels, Hfd.	.10	.35
□□	24	Jaromir Jagr, Pgh.	.75	25.00
□□	25	Arturs Irbe (G), S.J.	.10	.35
□□	26	Petr Klima, Ed	.10	.35
□□	27	Randy Gilhen, NYR.	.10	.35
□□	28	Ulf Dahlen, Min.	.10	.35
□□	29	Kelly Hrudey (G), LA	.10	.35
□□	30	Dave Ellett, Tor.	.10	.35
□□	31	Tom Fitzgerald, NYI.	.10	.35
□□	32	Cam Neely, Bos.	.25	1.00
□□	33	Greg Paslawski, Que.	.10	.35
□□	34	Brad May, Buf.	.10	.35
□□	35	Vyacheslav Kozlov, Det.	.10	5.00
□□	36	Mark Hunter, Wsh.	.10	.35
□□	37	Steve Chiasson, Det.	.10	.35
□□	38	Joe Murphy, Edm.	.10	.35
□□	39	Darryl Sydor, L.A.	.10	.35
□□	40	Ron Hextall (G), Que.	.10	.35
□□	41	Jim Sandlak, Van.	.10	.35
□□	42	Dave Lowry, Stl.	.10	.35
□□	43	Claude Lemieux, N.J.	.10	.35
□□	44	Gerald Diduck, Van.	.10	.35
□□	45	Mike McPhee, Mtl.	.10	.35
□□	46	Rod Langway, Wsh.	.10	.35
□□	47	Guy Larose, Tor.	.10	.35
□□	48	Craig Billington (G), N.J.	.10	.35
□□	49	Daniel Marois, NYI.	.10	.35
□□	**50**	**Todd Nelson, Pigh, RC**	**.10**	**.35**
□□	51	Jari Kurri, L.A.	.25	1.00
□□	52	Keith Brown, Chi.	.10	.35
□□	53	Valeri Kamensky, Que.	.25	3.00
□□	54	Jim Johnson, Min.	.10	.35
□□	55	Vincent Damphousse, Edm.	.25	2.00
□□	56	Pat Elynuik, Wpg.	.10	.35
□□	57	Jeff Beukeboom, NYR.	.10	.35
□□	58	Paul Ysebaert, Det.	.10	.35
□□	59	Ken Sutton, Buf.	.10	.35
□□	60	Dale Craigwell, S.J.	.10	.35
□□	61	Marc Bergevin, T.B.	.10	.35
□□	62	Stéphane Beauregard (G), Wpg.	.10	.35
□□	63	Bob Probert, Det.	.10	.35
□□	64	Jergus Baca, Hfd.	.10	.35
□□	65	Brian Propp, Min.	.10	.35
□□	66	Jacques Cloutier (G), Que.	.10	.35
□□	**67**	**Jim Thomson, Ott., RC**	**.10**	**.35**
□□	68	Anatoli Semenov, T.B.	.10	.35
□□	69	Stéphan Lebeau, Mtl.	.10	.35
□□	70	Rick Tocchet, Pgh.	.10	.35
□□	71	James Patrick, NYR.	.10	.35
□□	72	Rob Brown, Chi.	.10	.35
□□	73	Peter Ahola, L.A.	.10	.35
□□	74	Bob Corkum, Buf.	.10	.35
□□	75	Brent Sutter, Chi.	.10	.35
□□	76	Neil Wilkinson, S.J.	.10	.35
□□	77	Mark Osborne, Tor.	.10	.35
□□	78	Ronald Wilson, Stl.	.10	.35
□□	79	Todd Richards, Hfd.	.10	.35
□□	80	Robert Kron, Van.	.10	.35
□□	81	Cliff Ronning, Van.	.10	.35
□□	82	Zarley Zalapski, Hfd.	.10	.35
□□	83	Randy Burridge, Wsh.	.10	.35
□□	84	Jarrod Skalde, N.J.	.10	.35
□□	85	Gary Leeman, Cgy.	.10	.35
□□	86	Mike Ricci, Que.	.10	.35
□□	87	Dennis Vaske, NYI.	.10	.35
□□	**88**	**John LeBlanc, Wpg., RC**	**.10**	**.35**
□□	89	Brad Shaw, Hfd. (Ott.)	.10	.35
□□	90	Rod Brind'Amour, Pha. (*HOR)	.25	6.00
□□	91	Colin Patterson, Buf.	.10	.35
□□	92	Gerard Gallant, Det.	.10	.35
□□	93	Per Djoos, NYR.	.10	.35
□□	94	Claude Lapointe, Que.	.10	.35
□□	95	Bob Errey, Pgh.	.10	.35
□□	96	Norm Maciver, Edm.	.10	.35
□□	97	Todd Elik, Min.	.10	.35
□□	98	Chris Chelios, Chi.	.25	3.00
□□	99	Keith Primeau, Det.	.20	1.00
□□	100	Jimmy Waite (G), Chi.	.10	.35
□□	101	Luc Robitaille, L.A.	.25	1.00
□□	102	Keith Tkachuk, Wpg.	.35	10.00
□□	103	Benoît Hogue, NYI.	.10	.35
□□	104	Brian Mullen, S.J.	.10	.35
□□	105	Joe Nieuwendyk, Cgy.	.10	.35
□□	106	Randy McKay, N.J.	.10	.35
□□	107	Michal Pivonka, Wsh.	.10	.35
□□	108	Darcy Wakaluk (G), Min.	.10	.35
□□	109	Andy Brickley, Bos.	.10	.35
□□	110	Patrick Roy (G), Mtl.	.65	15.00
□□	111	Bob Sweeney, Bos.	.10	.35
□□	**112**	**Guy Hebert (G), Stl., RC**	**.25**	**3.00**
□□	113	Joe Mullen, Pgh.	.10	.35
□□	114	Gord Murphy, Bos.	.10	.35
□□	115	Evgeny Davydov, Wpg.	.10	.35
□□	116	Gary Roberts, Cgy.	.25	1.00
□□	117	Per-Erik Eklund, Pha.	.10	.35
□□	118	Tom Kurvers, NYI.	.10	.35
□□	119	John Tonelli, Que.	.10	.35
□□	120	Fredrik Olausson, Wpg.	.10	.35
□□	121	Mike Donnelly, L.A.	.10	.35
□□	122	Doug Gilmour, Tor.	.25	2.00
□□	123	Wayne Gretzky, L.A.	.75	25.00
□□	124	Curtis Leschyshyn, Que.	.10	.35
□□	125	Guy Carbonneau, Mtl.	.10	.35
□□	126	Bill Ranford (G), Edm.	.25	1.00
□□	127	Ulf Samuelsson, Pgh.	.10	.35
□□	128	Joey Kocur, NYR.	.10	.35
□□	129	Kevin Miller, Det. (Wsh.)	.10	.35
□□	130	Kirk McLean (G), Van.	.25	1.00
□□	131	Kevin Dineen, Pha.	.10	.35
□□	132	John Cullen, Hfd.	.10	.35
□□	133	Al Iafrate, Wsh.	.10	.35
□□	134	Craig Janney, Stl.	.10	.35
□□	135	Patrick Flatley, NYI.	.10	.35
□□	136	Dominik Hasek (G), Chi.	.50	18.00
□□	137	Benoît Brunet, Mtl.	.10	.35
□□	138	Dave Babych, Van.	.10	.35
□□	139	Doug Brown, N.J.	.10	.35
□□	140	Mike Lalor, Wpg.	.10	.35
□□	141	Thomas Steen, Wpg.	.10	.35
□□	142	Frantisek Musil, Cgy.	.10	.35
□□	143	Dan Quinn, Pha.	.10	.35
□□	144	Dmitri Mironov, Tor.	.10	.35
□□	145	Bob Kudelski, L.A.	.10	.35
□□	146	Mike Bullard, Tor.	.10	.35
□□	147	Randy Carlyle, Wpg.	.10	.35
□□	148	Kent Manderville, Tor.	.10	.35
□□	149	Kevin Hatcher, Wsh.	.10	.35
□□	150	Steve Kasper, Pha.	.10	.35
□□	151	Mikael Andersson, T.B.	.10	.35
□□	152	Alexei Kasatonov, N.J.	.10	.35
□□	153	Jan Erixon, NYR.	.10	.35
□□	154	Craig Ludwig, Min.	.10	.35
□□	155	Dave Poulin, Bos.	.10	.35
□□	156	Scott Stevens, N.J.	.25	1.00
□□	157	Robert Reichel, Cgy.	.10	.35
□□	158	Uwe Krupp, NYI.	.10	.35
□□	159	Brian Noonan, Chi.	.10	.35
□□	160	Stéphane Richer, N.J.	.10	.35
□□	161	Brent Thompson, L.A.	.10	.35
□□	162	Glenn Anderson, Tor.	.10	.35
□□	163	Joe Cirella, NYR.	.10	.35
□□	164	Dave Andreychuk, Buf. (*HOR)	.25	6.00
□□	165	Vladimir Konstantinov, Det.	.25	1.00
□□	166	Michael McNeill, Que.	.10	.35
□□	167	Darrin Shannon, Wpg.	.10	.35
□□	168	Rob Pearson, Tor.	.10	.35
□□	169	John Vanbiesbrouck (G), NYR.	.50	10.00
□□	170	Randy Wood, Buf.	.10	.35
□□	171	Marty McSorley, L.A.	.10	.35
□□	172	Mike Hudson, Chi.	.10	.35
□□	173	Paul Fenton, S.J.	.10	.35
□□	174	Jeff Brown, Stl.	.10	.35
□□	175	Mark Greig, Hfd.	.10	.35
□□	176	Gord Roberts, Bos.	.10	.35
□□	177	Josef Beranek, Edm.	.10	.35
□□	178	Shawn Burr, Det.	.10	.35
□□	179	Marc Bureau, Min.	.10	.35
□□	180	Mikhail Tatarinov, Que.	.10	.35
□□	181	Rob Cimetta, Tor.	.10	.35
□□	182	Paul Coffey, L.A.	.25	1.00
□□	183	Bob Essensa (G), Wpg.	.10	.35
□□	184	Joe Reekie, T.B.	.10	.35
□□	185	Jeff Hackett (G), S.J.	.25	1.00
□□	186	Tomas Forslund, Cgy.	.10	.35
□□	187	Claude Vilgrain, N.J.	.10	.35
□□	188	John Druce, Wsh.	.10	.35
□□	189	Patrice Brisebois, Mtl.	.10	.35
□□	190	Peter Douris, Bos.	.10	.35
□□	191	Brent Ashton, Bos.	.10	.35
□□	192	Eric Desjardins, Mtl.	.25	1.00
□□	193	Nick Kypreos, Wsh. (Hfd.)	.10	.35
□□	194	Dana Murzyn, Van.	.10	.35
□□	195	Don Beaupré (G), Wsh. (*HOR)	.10	5.00
□□	196	Jeff Chychrun, Pgh.	.10	.35
□□	197	Dave Barr, N.J.	.10	.35
□□	198	Brian Glynn, Edm.	.10	.35
□□	199	Keith Acton, Pha.	.10	.35
□□	200	Igor Kravchuk, Chi.	.10	.35
□□	201	Shayne Corson, Mtl.	.10	.35
□□	202	Curt Giles, Stl.	.10	.35
□□	203	Darren Turcotte, NYR.	.10	.35
□□	204	David Volek, NYI.	.10	.35
□□	**205**	**Ray Whitney, S.J., RC**	**.10**	**.35**
□□	206	Donald Audette, Buf.	.10	.35
□□	207	Steve Yzerman, Det.	.75	20.00
□□	208	Craig Berube, Cgy. (XCX: Fleury)	.10	.35
□□	209	Robert McGill, T.B.	.10	.35
□□	210	Stu Barnes, Wpg.	.10	.35
□□	211	Rob Blake, L.A.	.10	.35
□□	212	Mario Lemieux, Pgh.	1.25	30.00
□□	213	Dominic Roussel (G), Pha.	.10	.35
□□	214	Sergio Momesso, Van.	.10	.35
□□	215	Brad Marsh, Ott.	.10	.35
□□	216	Mark Fitzpatrick (G), NYI.	.10	.35
□□	217	Ken Baumgartner, Tor.	.10	.35
□□	218	Greg Gilbert, Chi.	.10	.35
□□	219	Ric Nattress, Tor.	.10	.35
□□	220	Theoren Fleury, Cgy.	.25	2.00
□□	221	Ray Bourque, Bos.	.35	5.00
□□	222	Steve Thomas, NYI.	.10	.35
□□	223	Scott Niedermayer, N.J.	.25	1.00
□□	224	Jeff Lazaro, Ott.	.10	.35
□□	225	Kirk McLean (G), Van. (*HOR)	.25	6.00
□□	225	Tim Cheveldae (G), Det.	.10	.35
□□	226	Marc Fortier, Que.	.10	.35
□□	227	Rob Zettler, S.J.	.10	.35
□□	228	Kevin Todd, N.J.	.10	.35
□□	229	Tony Amonte, NYR.	.25	1.00
□□	230	Mark Lamb, Ott.	.10	.35
□□	231	Chris Dahlquist, Min.	.10	.35
□□	232	James Black, Hfd.	.10	.35
□□	233	Paul Cavallini, Stl.	.10	.35
□□	234	Gino Cavallini, Que.	.10	.35
□□	235	Tony Tanti, Buf.	.10	.35
□□	236	Mike Ridley, Wsh.	.10	.35
□□	237	Curtis Joseph (G), Stl.	.50	8.00
□□	238	Mike Craig, Min.	.10	.35
□□	239	Luciano Borsato, Wpg.	.10	.35
□□	240	Brian Bellows, Min.	.10	.35
□□	241	Barry Pederson, Bos.	.10	.35
□□	242	Tony Granato, L.A.	.10	.35
□□	243	Jim Paek, Pgh.	.10	.35
□□	244	Tim Bergland, T.B.	.10	.35
□□	245	Jayson More, S.J.	.10	.35
□□	246	Laurie Boschman, Ott.	.10	.35
□□	247	Doug Bodger, Buf.	.10	.35
□□	248	Murray Craven, Hfd.	.10	.35
□□	249	Kris Draper, Wpg.	.10	.35
□□	250	Brian Benning, Pha.	.10	.35
□□	251	Jarmo Myllys (G), Tor.	.10	.35
□□	252	Sergei Fedorov, Det.	.35	5.00
□□	253	Mathieu Schneider, Mtl.	.10	.35
□□	254	Dave Gagner, Min.	.10	.35
□□	255	Michel Goulet, Chi.	.25	1.00
□□	256	Alexander Godynyuk, Cgy.	.10	.35
□□	257	Ray Sheppard, Det.	.10	.35
□□	258	AS: Mark Messier, NYR.	.25	2.50
□□	259	AS: Kevin Stevens, Pgh.	.10	.35
□□	260	AS: Brett Hull, Stl.	.25	2.50
□□	261	AS: Brian Leetch, NYR.	.25	1.00
□□	262	AS: Ray Bourque, Bos.	.25	2.50
□□	263	AS: Patrick Roy (G), Mtl.	.65	15.00

□ □	264	HL: Mike Gartner, NYR.	.25	.75
□ □	265	AS: Mario Lemieux, Pgh.	.65	15.00
□ □	266	AS: Luc Robitaille, L.A.	.25	.75
□ □	267	AS: Mark Recchi, Pha.	.25	.75
□ □	268	AS: Phil Housley, Wpg.	.10	.35
□ □	269	AS: Scott Stevens, N.J.	.10	.35
□ □	270	AS: Kirk McLean (G), Van.	.25	.75
□ □	271	Steve Duchesne, Que.	.10	.35
□ □	272	Jiri Hrdina, Pgh. (*HOR)	.10	5.00
□ □	273	John MacLean, N.J.	.10	.35
□ □	274	Mark Messier, NYR.	.35	10.00
□ □	275	Geoff Smith, Edm.	.10	.35
□ □	276	Russ Courtnall, Mtl.	.10	.35
□ □	277	Yves Racine, Det.	.10	.35
□ □	278	Tom Draper (G), Buf.	.10	.35
□ □	279	Charlie Huddy, L.A.	.10	.35
□ □	280	Trevor Kidd (G), Cgy.	.25	1.00
□ □	281	Garth Butcher, Stl.	.10	.35
□ □	282	Mike Sullivan, S.J.	.10	.35
□ □	283	Adam Burt, Hfd.	.10	.35
□ □	284	Troy Murray, Wpg.	.10	.35
□ □	285	Stéphane Fiset (G), Que.	.10	.35
□ □	286	Perry Anderson, S.J.	.10	.35
□ □	287	Sergei Nemchinov, NYR.	.10	.35
□ □	288	Rick Zombo, Stl.	.10	.35
□ □	289	Pierre Turgeon, NYI.	.25	1.00
□ □	290	Kevin Lowe, Edm.	.10	.35
□ □	291	Brian Bradley, T.B.	.10	.35
□ □	292	Martin Gelinas, Edm.	.10	.35
□ □	293	Brian Leetch, NYR.	.25	2.00
□ □	294	Peter Bondra, Wsh.	.25	3.00
□ □	295	Brendan Shanahan, Stl.	.35	8.00
□ □	296	Dale Hawerchuk, Buf.	.25	1.00
□ □	297	Mike Hough, Que.	.10	.35
□ □	298	Rollie Melanson (G), Mtl.	.10	.35
□ □	299	Brad Jones, Pha.	.10	2.00
□ □	300	Jocelyn Lemieux, Chi.	.10	.35
□ □	301	Brad McCrimmon, Det.	.10	.35
□ □	302	Marty McInnis, NYI.	.10	.35
□ □	303	Chris Terreri (G), N.J.	.10	.35
□ □	304	Dean Evason, S.J.	.10	.35
□ □	305	Glenn Healy (G), NYI.	.10	.35
□ □	306	Ken Hodge, Bos.	.10	.35
□ □	307	Mike Liut (G), Wsh. (*HOR)	.10	5.00
□ □	308	Gary Suter, Cgy.	.10	.35
□ □	309	Neal Broten, Min.	.10	.35
□ □	310	Tim Cheveldae (G), Det.	.10	.35
□ □	311	Tom Fergus, Van.	.10	.35
□ □	312	Petr Svoboda, Buf.	.10	.35
□ □	313	Tom Chorske, N.J.	.10	.35
□ □	314	Paul Ysebaert, Det.	.10	.35
□ □	315	Steve Smith, Chi.	.10	.35
□ □	316	Stéphane Morin, Que.	.10	.35
□ □	317	Pat MacLeod, S.J.	.10	.35
□ □	318	Dino Ciccarelli, Det.	.25	1.00
□ □	319	Peter Zezel, Tor.	.10	.35
□ □	320	Chris Lindberg, Cgy.	.10	.35
□ □	321	Grant Ledyard, Buf.	.10	.35
□ □	322	Ron Francis, Pgh.	.25	2.00
□ □	323	Adrien Plavsic, Van.	.10	.35
□ □	324	Ray Ferraro, NYI. (*HOR)	.10	5.00
□ □	325	Wendel Clark, Tor.	.25	1.00
□ □	326	Corey Millen, L.A.	.10	.35
□ □	327	Mark Pederson, Pha.	.10	.35
□ □	328	Patrick Poulin, Hfd.	.10	.35
□ □	329	Adam Graves, NYR.	.10	.35
□ □	330	Bobby Holik, Hfd.	.10	.35
□ □	331	Kelly Kisio, S.J.	.10	.35
□ □	332	Peter Sidorkiewicz (G), Ott.	.10	.35
□ □	333	Vladimir Ruzicka, Bos.	.10	.35
□ □	334	J. J. Daigneault, Mtl.	.10	.35
□ □	335	Troy Mallette, N.J.	.10	.35
□ □	336	Craig MacTavish, Edm.	.10	.35
□ □	337	Michel Petit, Cgy. (*HOR)	.10	5.00
□ □	338	Claude Loiselle, NYI.	.10	.35
□ □	339	Teppo Numminen, Wpg.	.10	.35
□ □	340	Brett Hull, Stl.	.35	5.00
□ □	341	Sylvain Lefebvre, Mtl.	.10	.35
□ □	342	Perry Berezan, S.J.	.10	.35
□ □	343	Kevin Stevens, Pgh.	.10	.35
□ □	344	Randy Ladouceur, Hfd.	.10	.35
□ □	345	Pat LaFontaine, Buf.	.25	1.00
□ □	346	Glen Wesley, Bos.	.10	.35
□ □	347	HL: Michel Goulet, Chi.	.10	.35
□ □	348	Jamie Macoun, Tor.	.10	.35
□ □	349	Owen Nolan, Que.	.25	1.00
□ □	350	Grant Fuhr (G), Tor. (*HOR)	.25	6.00
□ □	351	Tim Kerr, Hfd.	.10	.35
□ □	352	Kjell Samuelsson, Pgh.	.10	.35
□ □	353	Pavel Bure, Van.	.50	15.00
□ □	354	Murray Baron, Stl.	.10	.35
□ □	355	Paul Broten, NYR.	.10	.35
□ □	356	Craig Simpson, Edm.	.10	.35
□ □	357	Ken Daneyko N.J.	.10	.35
□ □	358	Greg Hawgood, Edm.	.10	.35
□ □	359	Johan Garpenlov, S.J.	.10	.35
□ □	360	Garry Galley, Pha.	.10	.35
□ □	361	Paul DiPietro, Mtl.	.10	.35
□ □	362	Jamie Leach, Pgh.	.10	.35
□ □	363	Clint Malarchuk (G), Buf.	.10	.35
□ □	364	Dan Lambert, Que.	.10	.35
□ □	365	Joé Juneau, Bos.	.10	.35
□ □	366	Scott Lachance, NYI. (*HOR)	.10	5.00
□ □	367	Mike Richter (G), NYR.	.35	2.00
□ □	368	Sheldon Kennedy, Det.	.10	.35
□ □	369	John McIntyre, L.A.	.10	.35
□ □	370	Glen Murray, Bos.	.10	.35
□ □	371	Ron Sutter, Stl.	.10	.35
□ □	**372**	**Dave Williams, S.J., RC**	**.10**	**.35**
□ □	**373**	**Bill Lindsay, Que., RC**	**.10**	**.35**
□ □	374	Todd Gill, Tor.	.10	.35
□ □	375	Sylvain Turgeon, Ott.	.10	.35
□ □	376	Dirk Graham, Chi.	.10	.35
□ □	377	Brad Schlegel, Wsh.	.10	.35
□ □	378	Bob Carpenter, Wsh.	.10	.35
□ □	379	Jon Casey (G), Min.	.10	.35
□ □	380	Andrei Lomakin, Pha.	.10	.35
□ □	381	Kay Whitmore (G), Hfd.	.10	.35
□ □	382	Alexander Mogilny, Buf.	.25	6.00
□ □	383	Garry Valk, Van.	.10	.35
□ □	384	Bruce Driver, N.J.	.10	.35
□ □	385	Jeff Reese (G), Cgy.	.10	.35
□ □	386	Brent Gilchrist, Mtl.	.10	.35
□ □	387	Kerry Huffman, Que.	.10	.35
□ □	388	Bobby Smith, Min.	.10	.35
□ □	389	Dave Manson, Edm.	.10	.35
□ □	390	Russ Romaniuk, Wpg.	.10	.35
□ □	391	Paul MacDermid, Wsh.	.10	.35
□ □	392	Louie DeBrusk, Edm.	.10	.35
□ □	393	Dave McLlwain, Tor.	.10	.35
□ □	394	Andy Moog (G), Bos.	.25	1.00
□ □	395	Tie Domi, NYR.	.10	.35
□ □	396	Pat Jablonski (G), Stl. (T.B.)	.10	.35
□ □	397	Troy Loney, Pgh.	.10	.35
□ □	398	Jimmy Carson, Det.	.10	.35
□ □	399	Eric Weinrich, N.J.	.10	.35
□ □	400	Jeremy Roenick, Chi.	.25	2.00
□ □	401	Brent Fedyk, Det.	.10	.35
□ □	402	Geoff Sanderson, Hfd.	.10	.35
□ □	403	Doug Lidster, Van.	.10	.35
□ □	404	Mike Gartner, NYR.	.25	1.00
□ □	405	Derian Hatcher, Min.	.25	1.00
□ □	406	Gaetan Duchesne, Min.	.10	.35
□ □	407	Randy Moller, Buf.	.10	.35
□ □	408	Brian Skrudland, Mtl.	.10	.35
□ □	409	Luke Richardson, Edm.	.10	.35
□ □	410	Mark Recchi, Pha.	.25	1.00
□ □	411	Steve Konroyd, Hfd.	.10	.35
□ □	412	Troy Gamble (G), Van.	.10	.35
□ □	413	Greg Johnston, Tor. (*HOR)	.10	5.00
□ □	414	Denis Savard, Mtl.	.10	.35
□ □	415	Mats Sundin, Que.	.35	5.00
□ □	416	Bryan Trottier, Pgh.	.25	1.00
□ □	417	Don Sweeney, Bos.	.10	.35
□ □	418	Pat Falloon, S.J.	.10	.35
□ □	419	Alexander Semak, N.J.	.10	.35
□ □	420	David Shaw, Min. (*HOR)	.10	5.00
□ □	421	Tomas Sandström, L.A.	.10	.35
□ □	422	Petr Nedved, Van.	.10	.35
□ □	423	Peter Ing (G), Edm.	.10	.35
□ □	424	Wayne Presley, Buf.	.10	.35
□ □	425	Rick Wamsley (G), Tor.	.10	.35
□ □	**426**	**Rob Zamuner, T.B., RC**	**.35**	**.50**
□ □	427	Claude Boivin, Pha.	.10	.35
□ □	428	Sylvain Côté, Wsh.	.10	.35
□ □	429	HL: Kevin Stevens, Pgh.	.10	.35
□ □	430	Randy Velischek, Que.	.10	.35
□ □	431	Derek King, NYI.	.10	.35
□ □	432	Terry Yake, Hfd.	.10	.35
□ □	433	Phillipe Bozon, Stl.	.10	.35
□ □	434	Richard Sutter, Stl.	.10	.35
□ □	435	Brian Lawton, S.J.	.10	.35
□ □	436	Brian Hayward (G), S.J.	.10	.35
□ □	437	Robert Dirk, Van.	.10	.35
□ □	438	Bernie Nicholls, Edm.	.10	.35
□ □	439	Michel Picard, Hfd.	.10	.35
□ □	440	Nicklas Lidström, Det.	.25	1.00
□ □	441	Mike Modano, Min.	.35	5.00
□ □	442	Phil Bourque, Pgh.	.10	.35
□ □	443	Wayne McBean, NYI.	.10	.35
□ □	444	Scott Mellanby, Edm.	.10	.35
□ □	445	Kevin Haller, Mtl.	.10	.35
□ □	446	Dave Taylor, L.A.	.10	.35
□ □	447	Larry Murphy, Pgh.	.25	1.00
□ □	448	David Bruce, S.J.	.10	.35
□ □	449	Steven Finn, Que.	.10	.35
□ □	450	Mike Krushelnyski, Tor.	.10	.35
□ □	451	Adam Creighton, NYI.	.10	.35
□ □	452	Al MacInnis, Cgy.	.25	1.00
□ □	453	Rick Tabaracci, Wpg.	.10	.35
□ □	454	Bob Bassen, Stl.	.10	.35
□ □	455	Kelly Buchberger, Edm.	.10	.35
□ □	456	Phil Housley, Wpg.	.10	.35
□ □	457	Daren Puppa (G), Buf.	.10	.35
□ □	458	Viacheslav Fetisov, N.J.	.25	1.00
□ □	459	Doug Smail, Que.	.10	.35
□ □	460	Paul Stanton, Pgh.	.10	.35
□ □	461	Steve Weeks (G), Wsh.	.10	.35
□ □	462	Valeri Zelepukin, N.J.	.10	.35
□ □	463	Stéphane Matteau, Chi.	.10	.35
□ □	464	Dale Hunter, Wsh.	.10	.35
□ □	465	Terry Carkner, Pha.	.10	.35
□ □	466	Vincent Riendeau (G), Det.	.10	.35
□ □	467	Sergei Makarov, Cgy.	.10	.35
□ □	468	Igor Ulanov, Wpg.	.10	.35
□ □	469	Peter Stastny, N.J.	.10	.35
□ □	470	Dimitri Khristich, Wsh.	.10	.35
□ □	471	Joel Otto, Cgy.	.10	.35
□ □	472	Geoff Courtnall, Van.	.10	.35
□ □	473	Mike Ramsey, Buf.	.10	.35
□ □	474	Yvon Corriveau, Hfd.	.10	.35
□ □	475	Adam Oates, Bos.	.25	2.00
□ □	476	Esa Tikkanen, Edm.	.10	.35
□ □	477	Doug Weight, NYR.	.25	2.00
□ □	478	Mike Keane, Mtl.	.10	.35
□ □	479	Kelly Miller, Wsh.	.10	.35
□ □	480	Nelson Emerson, Stl.	.10	.35
□ □	481	Shawn McEachern, Pgh.	.10	.35
□ □	482	Doug Wilson, S.J.	.10	.35
□ □	483	Jeff Odgers, S.J.	.10	.35
□ □	484	Stéphane Quintal, Stl.	.10	.35
□ □	485	Christian Ruuttu, Wpg.	.10	.35
□ □	486	Paul Ranheim, Cgy.	.10	.35
□ □	487	Craig Wolanin, Que.	.10	.35
□ □	488	Robert DiMaio, T.B.	.10	.35
□ □	489	Shawn Cronin. Wpg.	.10	.35
□ □	490	Kirk Muller, Mtl.	.10	.35
□ □	491	Patrick Roy (G), Mtl.	.65	15.00
□ □	492	Richard Pilon, NYI.	.10	.35
□ □	493	Pat Verbeek, Hfd.	.10	.35
□ □	494	Ken Wregget (G), Pgh.	.10	.35
□ □	495	Joe Sakic, Que.	.75	15.00
□ □	496	Zdeno Ciger, N.J.	.10	.35
□ □	497	Steve Larmer, Chi. (*)	.25	8.00
□ □	498	Calle Johansson, Wsh.	.10	.35
□ □	499	Trevor Linden, Van.	.25	1.00
□ □	500	John LeClair, Mtl.	.35	8.00
□ □	501	Bryan Marchment, Chi.	.10	.35
□ □	502	Todd Krygier, Wsh.	.10	.35
□ □	503	Tom Barrasso (G), Pgh.	.10	.35
□ □	504	Mario Lemieux, Pgh.	.65	15.00
□ □	505	Daniel Berthiaume (G), Wpg.	.10	.35
□ □	506	Jamie Baker, Que.	.10	.35
□ □	507	Greg Adams, Van.	.10	.35
□ □	508	Patrick Roy (G), Mtl. (*HOR)	1.25	30.00
□ □	509	Kris King, NYR.	.10	.35
□ □	510	Jyrki Lumme, Van.	.10	.35
□ □	511	Darin Kimble, T.B.	.10	.35
□ □	512	Igor Larionov, Van.	.10	.35
□ □	513	Martin Brodeur (G), N.J.	.50	20.00
□ □	**514**	**Denny Felsner, Stl., RC**	**.10**	**.35**
□ □	515	Yanic Dupré, Pha.	.10	.35
□ □	**516**	**Bill Guerin, N.J., RC**	**.35**	**.50**
□ □	**517**	**Brett Hedican, Stl., RC**	**.10**	**.35**
□ □	518	Mike Hartman, Wpg. (T.B.)	.10	.35

	No.	Player		
☐☐	519	Stephen Heinze, Bos.	.10	.35
☐☐	520	Frantisek Kucera, Chi.	.10	.35
☐☐	521	David Reid, Bos.	.10	.35
☐☐	522	Frank Pietrangelo (G), Hfd.	.10	.35
☐☐	523	Martin Rucinsky, Que.	.10	.35
☐☐	524	Tony Hrkac, Chi.	.10	.35
☐	525	Checklist 1 (1 - 132)	.10	
☐	525	Allan Conroy, Pha.		.75
☐	526	Checklist 2 (133 - 264)	.10	
☐	526	Jeff Norton, NYI.		.75
☐	527	Checklist 3 (265 - 396	.10	
☐	527	Rob Robinson, T.B.		.75
☐	528	Checklist 4 (397 - 528)	.10	
☐	528	Adam Foote, Que.		1.00
☐☐	529	Eric Lindros, Pha.	1.50	40.00

1992 - 93 TOPPS STADIUM CLUB

Imprint: © 1992 THE TOPPS COMPANY, INC.

Complete Set (501 cards): 25.00

Common Player: .10

	No.	Player	NRMT-MT
☐	1	Brett Hull, Stl.	.50
☐	2	Theoren Fleury, Cgy.	.35
☐	3	Joe Sakic, Que.	1.00
☐	4	Mike Modano, Min.	.50
☐	5	Dmitri Mironov, Tor.	.10
☐	6	Yves Racine, Det.	.10
☐	7	Igor Kravchuk, Chi.	.10
☐	8	Philippe Bozon, Stl.	.10
☐	9	Stéphane Richer, N.J.	.10
☐	10	Dave Lowry, Stl.	.10
☐	11	Dean Evason, S.J.	.10
☐	12	Mark Fitzpatrick (G), NYI.	.10
☐	13	Dave Poulin, Bos.	.10
☐	14	Phil Housley, Wpg.	.10
☐	15	Adrien Plavsic, Van.	.10
☐	16	Claude Boivin, Pha.	.10
☐	**17**	**Bill Guerin, N.J., RC**	**.10**
☐	18	Wayne Gretzky, L.A.	2.50
☐	19	Steve Yzerman, Det.	1.25
☐	20	Joe Mullen, Pgh.	.10
☐	21	Brad McCrimmon, Det.	.10
☐	22	Dan Quinn, Pha.	.10
☐	23	Rob Blake, L.A.	.25
☐	24	Wayne Presley, Buf.	.10
☐	25	Zarley Zalapski, Hfd.	.10
☐	26	Bryan Trottier, Pgh.	.25
☐	27	Peter Sidorkiewicz (G), Ott.	.10
☐	28	John MacLean, N.J.	.10
☐	29	Brad Schlegel, Wsh.	.10
☐	30	Marc Bureau, Min.	.10
☐	31	Troy Murray, Wpg.	.10
☐	32	Tony Amonte, NYR.	.25
☐	33	Rob Dimaio, T.B.	.10
☐	34	Joe Murphy, Edm.	.10
☐	35	Jim Waite (G), Chi.	.10
☐	36	Ron Sutter, Stl.	.10
☐	37	Joe Nieuwendyk, Cgy.	.25
☐	38	Kevin Haller, Mtl.	.10
☐	39	Andrew Cassels, Hfd.	.10
☐	40	Dale Hunter, Wsh.	.10
☐	41	Craig Janney, Stl.	.10
☐	42	Sergio Momesso, Van.	.10
☐	43	Nicklas Lidström, Det.	.10
☐	44	Luc Robitaille, L.A.	.25
☐	45	Adam Creighton, NYI.	.10
☐	46	Norm Maciver, Edm.	.10
☐	47	Mikhail Tatarinov, Que.	.10
☐	48	Gary Roberts, Cgy.	.25
☐	49	Gord Hynes, Bos.	.10
☐	50	Claude Lemieux, N.J.	.10
☐	51	Brad May, Buf.	.10
☐	52	Paul Stanton, Pgh.	.10
☐	53	Rick Wamsley (G) Tor.	.10
☐	54	Steve Larmer, Chi.	.25
☐	55	Darrin Shannon, Wpg.	.10
☐	56	Pat Falloon, S.J.	.10
☐	57	Chris Dahlquist, Min.	.10
☐	58	John Vanbiesbrouck (G), NYR.	.75
☐	59	Sylvain Turgeon, Ott.	.10
☐	60	Jayson More, S.J.	.10
☐	61	Randy Burridge, Wsh.	.10
☐	62	Vyacheslav Kozlov, Det.	.10
☐	63	Daniel Marois, NYI.	.10
☐	64	Curt Giles, Stl.	.10
☐	65	Brad Shaw, Ott.	.10
☐	66	Bill Ranford (G), Edm.	.25
☐	67	Frantisek Musil, Cgy.	.10
☐	68	Steve Leach, Bos.	.10
☐	69	Michel Goulet, Chi.	.25
☐	70	Mathieu Schneider, Mtl.	.10
☐	71	Steve Kasper, Pha.	.10
☐	72	Darryl Sydor, L.A.	.10
☐	73	Brian Leetch, NYR.	.35
☐	74	Chris Terreri (G), N.J.	.10
☐	75	Jim Johnson, Min.	.10
☐	76	Rick Tocchet, Pgh.	.10
☐	77	Teppo Numminen, Wpg.	.10
☐	78	Owen Nolan, Que.	.25
☐	79	Grant Ledyard, Buf.	.10
☐	80	Trevor Linden, Van.	.25
☐	81	Luciano Borsato, Wpg.	.10
☐	82	Derek King, NYI.	.10
☐	83	Rob Cimetta, Tor.	.10
☐	84	Geoff Smith, Edm.	.10
☐	85	Ray Sheppard, Det.	.10
☐	86	Dimitri Khristich, Wsh.	.10
☐	87	Chris Chelios, Chi.	.35
☐	88	Alexander Godynyuk, Cgy.	.10
☐	89	Perry Anderson, S.J.	.10
☐	90	Neal Broten, Min.	.10
☐	91	Brian Benning, Pha.	.10
☐	92	Brent Thompson, L.A.	.10
☐	93	Claude Lapointe, Que.	.10
☐	94	Mario Lemieux, Pgh.	2.00
☐	95	Pat LaFontaine, Buf.	.25
☐	96	Frank Pietrangelo (G), Hfd.	.10
☐	97	Gerald Diduck, Van.	.10
☐	98	Paul DiPietro, Mtl.	.10
☐	99	Valeri Zelepukin, N.J.	.10
☐	100	Rick Zombo, Stl.	.10
☐	101	Daniel Berthiaume (G), Wpg.	.10
☐	102	Tom Fitzgerald, NYI.	.10
☐	103	Ken Baumgartner, Tor.	.10
☐	104	Esa Tikkanen, Edm.	.10
☐	105	Steve Chiasson, Det.	.10
☐	106	Bobby Holik, Hfd.	.10
☐	107	Dominik Hasek (G), Chi.	.85
☐	108	Jeff Hackett (G), S.J.	.25
☐	109	Paul Broten, NYR.	.10
☐	110	Kevin Stevens, Pgh.	.10
☐	111	Geoff Sanderson, Hfd.	.10
☐	112	Donald Audette, Buf.	.10
☐	113	Jarmo Myllys (G), Tor.	.10
☐	114	Brian Skrudland, Mtl.	.10
☐	115	Andrei Lomakin, Pha.	.10
☐	116	Keith Tkachuk, Wpg.	.35
☐	117	John McIntyre, L.A.	.10
☐	118	Jacques Cloutier (G), Que.	.10
☐	119	Michel Picard, Hfd.	.10
☐	120	Dave Babych, Van.	.10
☐	121	Dave Gagner, Min.	.10
☐	122	Bob Carpenter, Wsh.	.10
☐	123	Ray Ferraro, NYI.	.10
☐	124	Glenn Anderson, Tor.	.10
☐	125	Craig MacTavish, Edm.	.10
☐	126	Shawn Burr, Det.	.10
☐	127	Tim Bergland, T.B.	.10
☐	128	Al MacInnis, Cgy	.25
☐	129	Jeff Beukeboom, NYR.	.10
☐	130	Ken Wregget (G), Pgh.	.10
☐	131	Arturs Irbe (G), S.J.	.10
☐	132	Dave Andreychuk, Buf.	.25
☐	133	Patrick Roy (G), Mtl.	2.00
☐	134	Benoît Brunet, Mtl.	.10
☐	135	Rick Tabaracci (G), Wpg.	.10
☐	136	Jamie Baker, Que.	.10
☐	137	Yanic Dupré, Pha.	.10
☐	138	Jari Kurri, L.A.	.25
☐	139	Adam Burt, Hfd.	.10
☐	140	Peter Stastny, N.J.	.10
☐	141	Brad Jones, Pha.	.10
☐	142	Jeff Odgers, S.J.	.10
☐	143	Anatoli Semenov, Edm. (T.B.)	.10
☐	144	Paul Ranheim, Cgy.	.10
☐	145	Sylvain Côté, Wsh.	.10
☐	146	Brent Ashton, Bos.	.10
☐	147	Doug Bodger, Buf.	.10
☐	148	Bryan Marchment, Chi.	.10
☐	149	Bob Kudelski, L.A.	.10
☐	150	Adam Graves, NYR.	.10
☐	151	Scott Stevens, N.J.	.10
☐	152	Russ Courtnall, Mtl.	.10
☐	153	Darcy Wakaluk (G), Min.	.10
☐	154	Per-Erik Eklund, Pha.	.10
☐	155	Robert Kron, Van.	.10
☐	156	Randy Ladouceur, Hfd.	.10
☐	157	Ed Olczyk, Wpg.	.10
☐	158	Jiri Hrdina, Pgh.	.10
☐	159	John Tonelli, Que.	.10
☐	160	John Cullen, Hfd.	.10
☐	161	Jan Erixon, Hfd.	.10
☐	162	David Shaw, Min.	.10
☐	163	Brian Bradley, T.B.	.10
☐	164	Russ Romaniuk, Wpg.	.10
☐	165	Eric Weinrich, N.J.	.10
☐	166	Steve Heinze, Bos.	.10
☐	167	Jeremy Roenick, Chi.	.35
☐	168	Mark Pederson, Pha.	.10
☐	169	Paul Coffey, L.A.	.25
☐	170	Bob Errey, Pgh.	.10
☐	171	Brian Lawton, S.J.	.10
☐	172	Vincent Riendeau (G), Det.	.10
☐	173	Marc Fortier, Que.	.10
☐	174	Marc Bergevin, T.B.	.10
☐	175	Jim Sandlak, Van.	.10
☐	176	Bob Bassen, Stl.	.10
☐	177	Uwe Krupp, NYI.	.10
☐	178	Paul MacDermid, Wsh.	.10
☐	179	Bob Corkum, Buf.	.10
☐	180	Robert Reichel, Cgy.	.10
☐	181	John LeClair, Mtl.	.35
☐	182	Mike Hudson, Chi.	.10
☐	183	Mark Recchi, Pha.	.25
☐	184	Rollie Melanson (G), Mtl.	.10
☐	185	Gord Roberts, Bos.	.10
☐	186	Clint Malarchuk (G), Buf.	.10
☐	187	Kris King, NYR.	.10
☐	188	Adam Oates, Bos.	.35
☐	189	Jarrod Skalde, N.J.	.10
☐	190	Mike Lalor, Wpg.	.10
☐	191	Vincent Damphousse, Edm.	.35
☐	192	Peter Ahola, L.A.	.10
☐	193	Kirk McLean (G), Van.	.25
☐	194	Murray Baron, Stl.	.10
☐	195	Michel Petit, Cgy.	.10
☐	196	Stéphane Fiset (G), Que.	.25
☐	197	Pat Verbeek, Hfd.	.10
☐	198	Jon Casey (G), Min.	.10
☐	199	Tim Cheveldae (G), Det.	.10
☐	200	Mike Ridley, Wsh.	.10
☐	201	Scott Lachance, NYI.	.10
☐	202	Rod Brind'Amour, Pha.	.25
☐	**203**	**Bret Hedican, Stl., RC, Error (Brett)**	**.10**
☐	204	Wendel Clark, Tor.	.25
☐	205	Shawn McEachern, Pgh.	.10
☐	206	Randy Wood, Buf.	.10
☐	207	Ulf Dahlen, Min.	.10
☐	208	Andy Brickley, Bos.	.10
☐	209	Scott Niedermayer, N.J.	.25
☐	210	Bob Essensa (G), Wpg.	.10
☐	211	Patrick Poulin, Hfd.	.10
☐	212	Johan Garpenlov, S.J.	.10
☐	213	Marty McInnis, NYI.	.10
☐	214	Josef Beranek, Edm.	.10
☐	215	Rod Langway, Wsh.	.10
☐	216	Dave Christian, Stl.	.10
☐	217	Sergei Makarov, Cgy.	.10
☐	218	Gerard Gallant, Det.	.10

	No.	Player	Price
☐	219	Neil Wilkinson, S.J.	.10
☐	220	Tomas Sandström, L.A.	.10
☐	221	Shayne Corson, Mtl.	.25
☐	222	John Ogrodnick, NYR.	.10
☐	223	Keith Acton, Pha.	.10
☐	224	Paul Fenton, S.J.	.10
☐	225	Rob Zettler, S.J.	.10
☐	226	Todd Elik, Min.	.10
☐	227	Petr Svoboda, Buf.	.10
☐	228	Zdeno Ciger, N.J.	.10
☐	229	Kevin Miller, Wsh.	.10
☐	230	Rich Pilon, NYI.	.10
☐	231	Pat Jablonski (G), T.B.	.10
☐	232	Greg Adams, Van.	.10
☐	233	Martin Brodeur (G), N.J.	.85
☐	234	Dave Taylor, L.A.	.10
☐	235	Kelly Buchberger, Edm.	.10
☐	236	Steve Konroyd, Hfd.	.10
☐	237	Guy Larose, Tor.	.10
☐	238	Patrice Brisebois, Mtl.	.10
☐	239	Checklist 1-125	.10
☐	240	Checklist 126-250	.10
☐	241	MC: Mark Messier, NYR.	.35
☐	242	MC: Mike Richter (G), NYR.	.25
☐	243	MC: Ed Belfour (G), Chi.	.25
☐	244	MC: Sergei Fedorov, Det.	.35
☐	245	MC: Adam Oates, Bos.	.25
☐	246	MC: Pavel Bure, Van.	.50
☐	247	MC: Luc Robitaille, L.A.	.25
☐	248	MC: Brian Leetch, NYR.	.25
☐	249	MC: Ray Bourque, Bos.	.35
☐	250	MC: Tony Amonte, NYR.	.25
☐	251	MC: Mario Lemieux, Pgh.	1.00
☐	252	MC: Patrick Roy (G), Mtl.	1.00
☐	253	MC: Nicklas Lidström, Det.	.25
☐	254	MC: Steve Yzerman, Det.	.50
☐	255	MC: Jeremy Roenick, Chi.	.25
☐	256	MC: Wayne Gretzky, L.A.	1.75
☐	257	MC: Kevin Stevens, Pgh.	.10
☐	258	MC: Brett Hull, Stl.	.35
☐	259	MC: Pat Falloon, S.J.	.10
☐	260	MC: Guy Carbonneau, Mtl.	.10
☐	261	Todd Gill, Tor.	.10
☐	262	Mike Sullivan, S.J.	.10
☐	263	Jeff Brown, Stl.	.10
☐	264	Joe Reekie, T.B.	.10
☐	265	Geoff Courtnall, Van.	.10
☐	266	Mike Richter (G), NYR.	.35
☐	267	Ray Bourque, Bos.	.50
☐	268	Mike Craig, Min.	.10
☐	269	Scott King (G), Det.	.10
☐	270	Don Beaupré (G), Wsh.	.10
☐	271	Ted Donato, Bos.	.10
☐	272	Gary Leeman, Cgy.	.10
☐	273	Steve Weeks (G), Wsh.	.10
☐	274	Keith Brown, Chi.	.10
☐	275	Greg Paslawski, Que.	.10
☐	276	Pierre Turgeon, NYI.	.25
☐	277	Jimmy Carson, Det.	.10
☐	278	Tom Fergus, Van.	.10
☐	279	Glen Wesley, Bos.	.10
☐	280	Tomas Forslund, Cgy.	.10
☐	281	Tony Granato, L.A.	.10
☐	282	Phil Bourque, Pgh.	.10
☐	283	Dave Ellett, Tor.	.10
☐	284	David Bruce, S.J.	.10
☐	285	Stu Barnes, Wpg.	.10
☐	286	Peter Bondra, Wsh.	.35
☐	287	Garth Butcher, Stl.	.10
☐	288	Ron Hextall (G), Que.	.25
☐	289	Guy Carbonneau, Mtl.	.10
☐	290	Louie DeBrusk, Edm.	.10
☐	291	Dave Barr, N.J.	.10
☐	292	Ken Sutton, Buf.	.10
☐	293	Brian Bellows, Min.	.10
☐	294	Mike McNeill, Que.	.10
☐	295	Rob Brown, Chi.	.10
☐	296	Corey Millen, L.A.	.10
☐	297	Joé Juneau, Bos.	.10
☐	298	Jeff Chychrun, Pgh., Error (Chychurn)	.10
☐	299	Igor Larionov, Van.	.25
☐	300	Sergei Fedorov, Det.	.50
☐	301	Kevin Hatcher, Wsh.	.10
☐	302	Al Iafrate, Wsh.	.10
☐	303	James Black, Hfd.	.10
☐	304	Stéphane Beauregard (G), Wpg.	.10
☐	305	Joel Otto, Cgy.	.10
☐	306	Nelson Emerson, Stl.	.10
☐	307	Gaetan Duchesne, Min.	.10
☐	308	J.J. Daigneault, Mtl.	.10
☐	309	Jamie Macoun, Tor.	.10
☐	310	Laurie Boschman, Ott.	.10
☐	311	Mike Gartner, NYR.	.25
☐	312	Tony Tanti, Buf.	.10
☐	313	Steve Duchesne, Que.	.10
☐	314	Martin Gelinas, Edm.	.10
☐	315	Dominic Roussel (G) Pha.	.10
☐	316	Cam Neely, Bos.	.25
☐	317	Craig Wolanin, Que.	.10
☐	318	Randy Gilhen, NYR.	.10
☐	319	David Volek, NYI.	.10
☐	320	Alexander Mogilny, Buf.	.35
☐	321	Jyrki Lumme, Van.	.10
☐	322	Jeff Reese (G), Cgy.	.10
☐	323	Greg Gilbert, Chi.	.10
☐	324	Jeff Norton, NYI.	.10
☐	325	Jim Hrivnak (G), Wsh.	.10
☐	326	Eric Desjardins, Mtl.	.25
☐	327	Curtis Joseph (G), Stl.	.60
☐	328	Ric Nattress, Tor.	.10
☐	329	Jamie Leach, Pgh.	.10
☐	330	Christian Ruutu, Wpg.	.10
☐	331	Doug Brown, N.J.	.10
☐	332	Randy Carlyle, Wpg.	.10
☐	333	Ed Belfour (G), Chi.	.35
☐	334	Doug Smail, Que.	.10
☐	335	Hubie McDonough, NYI.	.10
☐	336	Pat MacLeod, S.J.	.10
☐	337	Don Sweeney, Bos.	.10
☐	338	Félix Potvin (G), Tor.	.50
☐	339	Kent Manderville, Tor.	.10
☐	340	Sergei Nemchinov, NYR.	.10
☐	341	Calle Johansson, Wsh.	.10
☐	342	Dirk Graham, Chi.	.10
☐	343	Craig Billington (G), N.J.	.10
☐	344	Valeri Kamensky, Que.	.25
☐	345	Mike Vernon (G), Cgy.	.25
☐	346	Fredrik Olausson, Wpg.	.10
☐	347	Peter Ing (G), Edm.	.10
☐	348	Mikael Andersson, T.B.	.10
☐	349	Mike Keane, Mtl.	.10
☐	350	Stéphane Quintal, Stl.	.10
☐	351	Tom Chorske, N.J.	.10
☐	352	Ron Francis, Pgh.	.35
☐	353	Dana Murzyn, Van.	.10
☐	354	Craig Ludwig, Min.	.10
☐	355	Bob Probert, Det.	.10
☐	356	Glenn Healy (G), NYI.	.10
☐	357	Troy Loney, Pgh.	.10
☐	358	Vladimir Ruzicka, Bos.	.10
☐	359	Doug Gilmour, Tor.	.35
☐	360	Darren Turcotte, NYR.	.10
☐	361	Kelly Miller, Wsh.	.10
☐	362	Dennis Vaske, NYI.	.10
☐	363	Stéphane Matteau, Chi.	.10
☐	364	Brian Hayward (G), S.J.	.10
☐	365	Kevin Dineen, Pha.	.10
☐	366	Igor Ulanov, Wpg.	.10
☐	367	Sylvain Lefebvre, Mtl.	.10
☐	368	Petr Klima, Edm.	.10
☐	369	Steve Thomas, NYI.	.10
☐	370	Daren Puppa (G), Buf.	.10
☐	371	Brendan Shanahan, Stl.	.75
☐	372	Charlie Huddy, L.A.	.10
☐	373	Cliff Ronning, Van.	.10
☐	374	Brian Propp, Min.	.10
☐	375	Larry Murphy, Pgh.	.25
☐	376	Bruce Driver, N.J.	.10
☐	377	Rob Pearson, Tor.	.10
☐	378	Paul Ysebaert, Det.	.10
☐	379	Mark Osborne, Tor.	.10
☐	380	Doug Weight, NYR.	.35
☐	381	Kerry Huffman, Pha.	.10
☐	382	Michal Pivonka, Wsh.	.10
☐	383	Steve Smith, Chi.	.10
☐	384	Steven Finn, Que.	.10
☐	385	Kevin Lowe, Edm.	.10
☐	386	Mike Ramsey, Buf.	.10
☐	387	Kirk Muller, Mtl.	.10
☐	**388**	**John LeBlanc, Wpg., RC**	**.10**
☐	389	Rich Sutter, Stl.	.10
☐	390	Brent Fedyk, Det.	.10
☐	391	Kelly Hrudey (G), L.A.	.10
☐	392	Viacheslav Fetisov, N.J.	.25
☐	393	Glen Murray, Bos., Error (Glenn)	.10
☐	394	James Patrick, NYR.	.10
☐	395	Tom Draper (G), Buf.	.10
☐	396	Mark Hunter, Wsh.	.10
☐	397	Wayne McBean, NYI.	.10
☐	398	Joe Sacco, Tor.	.10
☐	399	Dino Ciccarelli, Det.	.25
☐	400	Brian Noonan, Chi.	.10
☐	**401**	**Guy Hebert (G), Stl., RC**	**.50**
☐	402	Peter Douris, Bos.	.10
☐	403	Gilbert Dionne, Mtl.	.10
☐	404	Doug Lidster, Van.	.10
☐	405	John Druce, Wpg.	.10
☐	406	Alexei Kasatonov, N.J.	.10
☐	407	Chris Lindberg, Cgy.	.10
☐	408	Mike Ricci, Que.	.10
☐	409	Tom Kurvers, NYI.	.10
☐	410	Pat Elynuik, Wpg.	.10
☐	411	Mike Donnelly, L.A.	.10
☐	412	Grant Fuhr (G), Tor.	.25
☐	413	Curtis Leschyshyn, Que.	.10
☐	414	Derian Hatcher, Min.	.25
☐	415	Michel Mongeau, T.B.	.10
☐	416	Tom Barrasso (G), Pgh.	.25
☐	417	Joey Kocur, NYR.	.10
☐	418	Vladimir Konstantinv, Det.	.10
☐	419	Dale Hawerchuk, Buf.	.25
☐	420	Brian Mullen, S.J.	.10
☐	421	Mark Greig, Hfd.	.10
☐	422	Claude Vilgrain, N.J.	.10
☐	423	Gary Suter, Cgy.	.10
☐	424	Garry Galley, Pha.	.10
☐	425	Benoît Hogue, NYI.	.10
☐	**426**	**Jeff Finley, NYI., RC**	**.10**
☐	427	Bobby Smith, Min.	.10
☐	428	Brent Sutter, Chi.	.10
☐	429	Ron Wilson, Stl.	.10
☐	430	Andy Moog (G), Bos.	.25
☐	431	Stéphane Lebeau, Mtl.	.10
☐	432	Troy Mallette, N.J.	.10
☐	433	Peter Zezel, Tor.	.10
☐	434	Mike Hough, Que.	.10
☐	435	Mark Tinordi, Min.	.10
☐	436	Dave Manson, Edm.	.10
☐	437	Jim Paek, Pgh.	.10
☐	438	Frantisek Kucera, Chi.	.10
☐	**439**	**Rob Zamuner, T.B., RC**	**.35**
☐	440	Ulf Samuelsson, Pgh.	.10
☐	441	Perry Berezan, S.J.	.10
☐	442	Murray Craven, Hfd.	.10
☐	443	Mark Messier, NYR.	.50
☐	444	Alexander Semak, N.J.	.10
☐	445	Gord Murphy, Bos.	.10
☐	446	Jocelyn Lemieux, Chi.	.10
☐	447	Paul Cavallini, Stl.	.10
☐	448	Bernie Nicholls, Edm.	.10
☐	449	Brent Gilchrist, Mtl.	.10
☐	450	Randy McKay, N.J.	.10
☐	451	Alexei Gusarov, Que.	.10
☐	452	Mike McPhee, Mtl.	.10
☐	453	Kimbi Daniels, Pha.	.10
☐	454	Kelly Kisio, S.J.	.10
☐	455	Bob Sweeney, Bos.	.10
☐	456	Luke Richardson, Edm.	.10
☐	457	Petr Nedved, Van.	.10
☐	458	Craig Berube, Cgy.	.10
☐	459	Kay Whitmore (G), Hfd.	.10
☐	460	Randy Velischek, Que.	.10
☐	461	David Williams, Edm.	.10
☐	462	Scott Mellanby, Pha.	.10
☐	463	Terry Carkner, Pha.	.10
☐	464	Dale Craigwell, S.J.	.10
☐	465	Kevin Todd, N.J.	.10
☐	466	Kjell Samuelsson, Pgh.	.10
☐	467	Denis Savard, Mtl.	.25
☐	468	Adam Foote, Que.	.25
☐	469	Stéphane Morin, Que.	.10
☐	470	Doug Wilson, S.J.	.10
☐	471	Shawn Cronin, Wpg.	.10
☐	472	Brian Glynn, Edm.	.10
☐	473	Craig Simpson, Edm.	.10

	No.	Player	Price
☐	474	Todd Krygier, Wsh.	.10
☐	475	Brad Miller, Ott.	.10
☐	476	Yvon Corriveau, Hfd.	.10
☐	477	Patrick Flatley, NYI.	.10
☐	478	Mats Sundin, Que.	.50
☐	479	Joe Cirella, NYR.	.10
☐	480	Gino Cavallini, Que.	.10
☐	481	Marty McSorley, L.A.	.10
☐	482	Brad Marsh, Ott.	.10
☐	483	Bob McGill, T.B.	.10
☐	484	Randy Moller, Buf.	.10
☐	485	Keith Primeau, Det.	.25
☐	486	Darin Kimble, T.B.	.10
☐	487	Mike Krushelnyski, Tor.	.10
☐	488	Ron Sutter/Rich Sutter, Stl.	.10
☐	489	Pavel Bure, Van.	.85
☐	490	Ray Whitney, S.J.	.10
☐	491	Dave McLlwain, Tor.	.10
☐	**492**	**Per Djoos, NYR., RC**	**.10**
☐	493	Garry Valk, Van.	.10
☐	494	Mike Bullard, Tor.	.10
☐	495	Greg Hawgood, Edm.	.10
☐	496	Terry Yake, Hfd.	.10
☐	497	Mike Hartman, T.B.	.10
☐	498	Jaromir Jagr, Pgh.	1.25
☐	499	Checklist	.10
☐	500	Checklist	.10
☐	501	Eric Lindros, Pha.	2.50

1992 - 93 TOPPS STADIUM CLUB MEMBERS ONLY

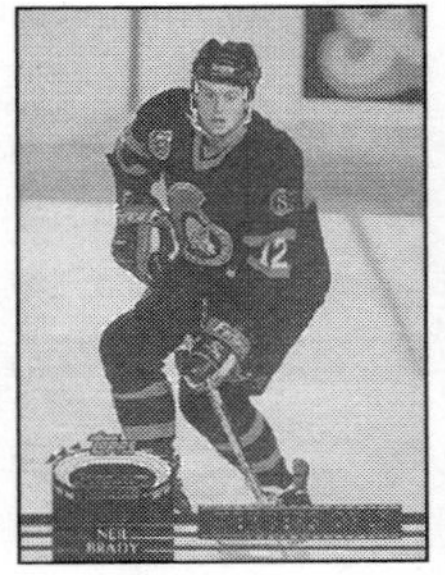

Imprint: **© 1992 THE TOPPS COMPANY, INC.

Complete Set (5 cards): 3.50

	No.	Player	NRMT-MT
☐	1	Neil Nets 1st: Neil Brady, Ott.	.25
☐	2	Lightning Has Struck: Chris Kontos, T.B.	.25
☐	3	Kurri Joins 500 Club: Jari Kurri, L.A.	.50
☐	4	Lindros Makes Debut: Eric Lindros, Pha.	3.00
☐	5	Reggie Makes History: Reggie Savage, Wsh.	.25

1992 - 93 UPPER DECK

Card 88 (Eric Lindros) was only inserted into Low Series packs.

Imprint: 1992 The Upper Deck Company

Low Numbers Set (440 cards): 20.00

High Numbers Set (200 cards): 40.00

Common Player: .10

	No.	Player	NRMT-MT
☐	1	CL: Andy Moog (G), Bos.	.25
☐	2	CL: Donald Audette, Buf.	.10
☐	3	CL: Tomas Forslund, Cgy.	.10
☐	4	CL: Steve Larmer, Chi.	.10
☐	5	CL: Tim Cheveldae (G), Det.	.10
☐	6	CL: Vincent Damphousse, Edm.	.25
☐	7	CL: Pat Verbeek, Hfd.	.10
☐	8	CL: Luc Robitaille, L.A.	.25
☐	9	CL: Mike Modano, Min.	.25
☐	10	CL: Denis Savard, Mtl.	.25
☐	11	CL: Kevin Todd, N.J.	.10
☐	12	CL: Ray Ferraro, NYI	.10
☐	13	CL: Tony Amonte, NYR	.25
☐	14	CL: Peter Sidorkiewicz (G), Ott.	.10
☐	15	CL: Rod Brind'Amour, Pha.	.25
☐	16	CL: Jaromir Jagr, Pgh.	.75
☐	17	CL: Owen Nolan, Que.	.25
☐	18	CL: Nelson Emerson, Stl.	.10
☐	19	CL: Pat Falloon, S.J.	.10
☐	20	CL: Anatoli Semenov, T.B.	.10
☐	21	CL: Doug Gilmour, Tor.	.25
☐	22	CL: Kirk McLean (G), Van.	.25
☐	23	CL: Don Beaupré (G), Wsh.	.10
☐	24	CL: Phil Housley, Wpg.	.10
☐	25	Wayne Gretzky, L.A.	2.00
☐	26	Mario Lemieux, Pgh.	1.50
☐	27	Valeri Kamensky, Que.	.25
☐	28	Jaromir Jagr, Pgh.	1.00
☐	29	Brett Hull, Stl.	.50
☐	30	Neil Wilkinson, S.J.	.10
☐	31	Dominic Roussel (G), Pha.	.10
☐	32	Kent Manderville, Tor.	.10
☐	33	1500th Assist: Wayne Gretzky, L.A.	1.00
☐	34	Presidents' Trophy: New York Rangers	.10
☐	35	Kevin, Kelly and Kip Miller	.10
☐	36	Joe and Brian Sakic	.50
☐	37	Keith, Brent and Wayne Gretzky	1.25
☐	38	Trevor and Jamie Linden	.25
☐	39	Russ and Geoff Courtnall	.10
☐	40	Dale Craigwell, S.J.	.10
☐	41	Peter Ahola, L.A.	.10
☐	42	Robert Reichel, Cgy.	.10
☐	43	Chris Terreri (G), N.J.	.10
☐	44	John Vanbiesbrouck (G), NYR.	.60
☐	45	Alexander Semak, N.J.	.10
☐	46	Mike Sullivan, S.J.	.10
☐	47	Bob Sweeney, Bos.	.10
☐	48	Corey Millen, L.A.	.10
☐	49	Murray Craven, Hfd.	.10
☐	50	Dennis Vaske, NYI.	.10
☐	**51**	**David Williams, S.J., RC**	**.10**
☐	52	Tom Fitzgerald, NYI.	.10
☐	53	Corey Foster, Pha.	.10
☐	54	Al Iafrate, Wsh.	.10
☐	55	John LeClair, Mtl.	.50
☐	56	Stéphane Richer, N.J.	.10
☐	57	Claude Boivin, Pha.	.10
☐	58	Rick Tabaracci (G), Wpg.	.10
☐	59	Johan Garpenlov, S.J.	.10
☐	60	Checklist (1-110)	.10
☐	61	Stephen Leach, Bos.	.10
☐	**62**	**Trent Klatt, Min., RC**	**.10**
☐	63	Darryl Sydor, LA	.10
☐	64	Brian Glynn, Edm.	.10
☐	65	Mike Craig, Min.	.10
☐	66	Gary Leeman, Cgy.	.10
☐	67	Jimmy Waite (G), Chi.	.10
☐	68	Jason Marshall, Stl.	.10
☐	69	Robert Kron, Van.	.10
☐	**70**	**Yanic Perreault, Tor., RC**	**.25**
☐	71	Daniel Marois, NYI.	.10
☐	72	Mark Osborne, Tor.	.10
☐	73	Mark Tinordi, Min.	.10
☐	74	Brad May, Buf.	.10
☐	75	Kimbi Daniels, Pha.	.10
☐	76	Kay Whitmore (G), Hfd.	.10
☐	77	Luciano Borsato, Wpg.	.10
☐	78	Kris King, NYR.	.10
☐	79	Félix Potvin (G), Tor.	.50
☐	80	Benoît Brunet, Mtl.	.10
☐	81	Shawn Antoski, Van.	.10
☐	82	Randy Gilhen, NYR.	.10
☐	83	Dmitri Mironov, Tor	.10
☐	84	Dave Manson, Edm.	.10
☐	85	Sergio Momesso, Van.	.10
☐	86	Cam Neely, Bos.	.25
☐	87	Mike Krushelnyski, Tor.	.10
☐	88	Eric Lindros, Pha. (*)	4.00
☐	89	Wendel Clark, Tor.	.25
☐	90	Enrico Ciccone, Min.	.10
☐	91	Jarrod Skalde, N.J.	.10
☐	92	Dominik Hasek (G), Chi.	.75
☐	93	Dave McLlwain, Tor.	.10
☐	94	Russ Courtnall, Mtl.	.10
☐	95	Tim Sweeney, Cgy.	.10
☐	96	Alexei Kasatonov, N.J.	.10
☐	97	Chris Lindberg, Cgy.	.10
☐	98	Steven Rice, Edm.	.10
☐	99	Tie Domi, NYR.	.10
☐	100	Paul Stanton, Pgh.	.10
☐	101	Brad Schlegel, Wsh.	.10
☐	102	David Bruce, S.J.	.10
☐	103	Mikael Andersson, T.B.	.10
☐	104	Shawn Chambers, T.B.	.10
☐	105	Rob Ramage, T.B.	.10
☐	106	Joe Reekie, T.B.	.10
☐	107	Sylvain Turgeon, Ott.	.10
☐	108	Rob Murphy, Ott.	.10
☐	109	Brad Shaw, Ott.	.10
☐	**110**	**Darren Rumble, Ott., RC**	**.10**
☐	**111**	**Kyosti Karjalainen, L.A., RC**	**.10**
☐	112	Mike Vernon (G), Cgy.	.25
☐	113	Michel Goulet, Chi.	.25
☐	114	Garry Valk, Van.	.10
☐	115	Peter Bondra, Wsh.	.35
☐	116	Paul Coffey, L.A.	.25
☐	117	Brian Noonan, Chi.	.10
☐	118	John McIntyre, L.A.	.10
☐	119	Scott Mellanby, Edm.	.10
☐	120	Jim Sandlak, Van.	.10
☐	121	Mats Sundin, Que.	.50
☐	122	Brendan Shanahan, Stl.	.60
☐	123	Kelly Buchberger, Edm.	.10
☐	124	Doug Smail, Que.	.10
☐	125	Craig Janney, Stl.	.10
☐	126	Mike Gartner, NYR.	.25
☐	127	Alexei Gusarov, Que.	.10
☐	128	Joe Nieuwendyk, Cgy.	.25
☐	129	Troy Murray, Wpg.	.10
☐	130	Jamie Baker, Que.	.10
☐	131	Dale Hunter, Wsh.	.10
☐	132	Darrin Shannon, Wpg.	.10
☐	133	Adam Oates, Bos.	.35
☐	134	Trevor Kidd (G), Cgy.	.25
☐	135	Steve Larmer, Chi.	.10
☐	136	Fredrik Olausson, Wpg.	.10
☐	137	Jyrki Lumme, Van.	.10
☐	138	Tony Amonte, NYR.	.25
☐	139	Calle Johansson, Wsh.	.10
☐	140	Rob Blake, L.A.	.25
☐	141	Phil Bourque, Pgh.	.10
☐	142	Yves Racine, Det.	.10
☐	143	Rich Sutter, Stl.	.10
☐	144	Joe Mullen, Pgh.	.10
☐	145	Mike Richter (G), NYR.	.35
☐	146	Pat MacLeod, S.J.	.10
☐	147	Claude Lapointe. Que.	.10
☐	148	Paul Broten, NYR.	.10
☐	149	Patrick Roy (G), Mtl.	1.50
☐	150	Doug Wilson, S.J.	.10
☐	151	Jim Hrivnak (G), Wsh.	.10
☐	152	Joe Murphy, Edm.	.10
☐	153	Randy Burridge, Wsh.	.10
☐	154	Thomas Steen, Wpg.	.10
☐	155	Steve Yzerman, Det.	1.00
☐	156	Pavel Bure, Van.	.75
☐	157	Sergei Fedorov, Det.	.50
☐	158	Trevor Linden, Van.	.25
☐	159	Chris Chelios, Chi.	.35
☐	160	Cliff Ronning, Van.	.10
☐	161	Jeff Beukeboom, NYR.	.10
☐	162	Denis Savard, Mtl.	.10
☐	163	Claude Lemieux, N.J.	.10
☐	164	Mike Keane, Mtl.	.10
☐	165	Pat LaFontaine, Buf.	.25
☐	166	Nelson Emerson, Stl.	.10
☐	167	Alexander Mogilny, Buf.	.35
☐	168	Jamie Leach, Pgh.	.10
☐	169	Darren Turcotte, NYR.	.10
☐	170	Checklist (111 - 220)	.10
☐	171	Steve Thomas, NYI.	.10
☐	172	Brian Bellows, Min.	.10
☐	173	Mike Ridley, Wsh.	.10
☐	174	Dave Gagner, Min.	.10
☐	175	Pierre Turgeon, NYI.	.25

☐ 176 Paul Ysabaert, Det. .10
☐ 177 Brian Propp, Min. .10
☐ 178 Nicklas Lidstrom, Det. .25
☐ 179 Kelly Miller, Wsh. .10
☐ 180 Kirk Muller, Mtl. .10
☐ 181 Bob Bassen, Stl. .10
☐ 182 Tony Tanti, Buf. .10
☐ 183 Mikhail Tatarinov, Que. .10
☐ 184 Ron Sutter, Stl. .10
☐ 185 Tony Granato, L.A. .10
☐ 186 Curtis Joseph (G), Stl. .60
☐ 187 Uwe Krupp, NYI. .10
☐ 188 Esa Tikkanen, Edm. .10
☐ 189 Ulf Samuelsson, Pgh. .10
☐ 190 Jon Casey (G), Min. .10
☐ 191 Derek King, NYI. .10
☐ 192 Greg Adams, Van. .10
☐ 193 Ray Ferraro, NYI. .10
☐ 194 Dave Christian, Stl. .10
☐ 195 Eric Weinrich, N.J. .10
☐ 196 Josef Beranek, Edm. .10
☐ 197 Tim Cheveldae (G), Det. .10
☐ 198 Kevin Hatcher, Wsh. .10
☐ 199 Brent Sutter, Chi. .10
☐ 200 Bruce Driver, N.J. .10
☐ 201 Tom Draper (G), Buf. .10
☐ 202 Ted Donato, Bos. .10
☐ 203 Ed Belfour (G), Chi. .35
☐ 204 Pat Verbeek, Hfd. .10
☐ 205 John Druce, Wsh. .10
☐ 206 Neal Broten, Min. .10
☐ 207 Doug Bodger, Buf. .10
☐ 208 Troy Loney, Pgh. .10
☐ 209 Mark Pederson, Pha. .10
☐ 210 Todd Elik, Min. .10
☐ 211 Ed Olczyk, Wpg. .10
☐ 212 Paul Cavallini, Stl. .10
☐ 213 Stéphan Lebeau, Mtl. .10
☐ 214 Dave Ellett, Tor. .10
☐ 215 Doug Gilmour, Tor. .35
☐ 216 Luc Robitaille, L.A. .25
☐ 217 Bob Essensa (G), Wpg. .10
☐ 218 Jari Kurri, L.A. .25
☐ 219 Dimitri Khristich, Wsh. .10
☐ 220 Joel Otto, Cgy. .10
☐ 221 Checklist (222-236) .10
☐ **222 Jonas Hoglund, Swe., RC .50**
☐ **223 Rolf Wanhainen (G), Swe., RC .10**
☐ **224 Stefan Klockare, Swe., RC .10**
☐ **225 Johan Norgren, Swe., RC .10**
☐ **226 Roger Kyro, Swe., RC .10**
☐ **227 Niklas Sundblad, Swe., RC .10**
☐ **228 Calle Carlsson, Swe., RC .10**
☐ **229 Jakob Karlsson, Swe., RC .10**
☐ **230 Fredrik Jax, Swe., RC .10**
☐ **231 Bjorn Nord, Swe., RC .10**
☐ **232 Kristian Gahn, Swe., RC .10**
☐ **233 Mikael Renberg, Swe., RC 1.50**
☐ **234 Markus Naslund, Swe., RC .75**
☐ 235 Peter Forsberg, Swe. 2.00
☐ **236 Michael Nylander, Swe., RC .50**
☐ 237 Stanley Cup Centennial 1893-1993 .10
☐ 238 Rick Tocchet, Pgh. .10
☐ 239 Igor Kravchuk, Chi. .10
☐ 240 Geoff Courtnall, Van. .10
☐ 241 Larry Murphy, Pgh. .25
☐ 242 Mark Messier, NYR. .50
☐ 243 Tom Barrasso (G), Pgh. .25
☐ 244 Glen Wesley, Bos. .10
☐ 245 Randy Wood, Buf. .10
☐ 246 Gerard Gallant, Det. .10
☐ 247 Kip Miller, Min. .10
☐ 248 Bob Probert, Det. .10
☐ 249 Gary Suter, Cgy. .10
☐ 250 Ulf Dahlen, Min. .10
☐ 251 Dan Lambert, Que. .10
☐ 252 Bobby Holik, Hfd. .10
☐ 253 Jimmy Carson, Det. .10
☐ 254 Ken Hodge, Bos. .10
☐ 255 Joe Sakic, Que. .85
☐ 256 Kevin Dineen, Pha. .10
☐ 257 Al MacInnis, Cgy. .25
☐ 258 Vladimir Ruzicka, Bos. .10
☐ 259 Ken Daneyko, N.J. .10
☐ 260 Guy Carbonneau, Mtl. .10

☐ 261 Michal Pivonka, Wsh. .10
☐ 262 Bill Ranford (G), Edm. .25
☐ 263 Petr Nedved, Van. .10
☐ 264 Rod Brind'Amour, Pha. .25
☐ 265 Ray Bourque, Bos. .50
☐ 266 Joe Sacco, Tor. .10
☐ 267 Vladimir Konstantinov, Det. .25
☐ 268 Eric Desjardins, Mtl. .25
☐ 269 Dave Andreychuk, Buf. .25
☐ 270 Kelly Hrudey (G), L.A. .10
☐ 271 Grant Fuhr (G),Tor. .25
☐ 272 Dirk Graham, Chi. .10
☐ 273 Frank Pietrangelo (G), Hfd. .10
☐ 274 Jeremy Roenick, Chi. .35
☐ 275 Kevin Stevens, Pgh. .10
☐ 276 Phil Housley, Wpg. .10
☐ 277 Patrice Brisebois. Mtl. .10
☐ 278 Viacheslav Fetisov, N.J. .25
☐ 279 Doug Weight, NYR. .35
☐ 280 Checklist (221-330) .10
☐ 281 Dean Evason, S.J. .10
☐ 282 Martin Gelinas, Edm. .10
☐ 283 Philippe Bozon, Stl. .10
☐ 284 Brian Leetch, NYR. .35
☐ 285 Theoren Fleury, Cgy. .35
☐ 286 Pat Falloon, S.J. .10
☐ 287 Derian Hatcher, Min. .25
☐ 288 Andrew Cassels, Hfd. .10
☐ 289 Gary Roberts, Cgy. .25
☐ 290 Bernie Nicholls, Edm. .10
☐ 291 Ron Francis, Pgh. .35
☐ 292 Tom Kurvers, NYI. .10
☐ 293 Geoff Sanderson, Hfd. .10
☐ 294 Vyacheslav Kozlov, Det. .10
☐ 295 Valeri Zelepukin, N.J. .10
☐ 296 Ray Sheppard, Det. .10
☐ 297 Scott Stevens, N.J. .10
☐ 298 Sergei Nemchinov, NYR. .10
☐ 299 Kirk McLean (G), Van. .25
☐ 300 Igor Ulanov, Wpg. .10
☐ 301 Brian Benning, Pha. .10
☐ 302 Dale Hawerchuk, Buf. .25
☐ 303 Kevin Todd, N.J. .10
☐ 304 John Cullen, Hfd. .10
☐ 305 Mike Modano, Min. .50
☐ 306 Donald Audette, Buf. .10
☐ 307 Vincent Damphousse, Edm. .35
☐ 308 Jeff Hackett (G), S.J. .25
☐ 309 Craig Simpson, Edm. .10
☐ 310 Don Beaupré (G), Wsh. .10
☐ 311 Adam Creighton, NYI. .10
☐ 312 Pat Elynuik, Wpg. .10
☐ 313 David Volek, NYI. .10
☐ 314 Sergei Makarov, Cgy. .10
☐ 315 Craig Billington (G), N.J. .10
☐ 316 Zarley Zalapski, Hfd. .10
☐ 317 Brian Mullen, S.J. .10
☐ 318 Rob Pearson, Tor. .10
☐ 319 Garry Galley, Pha. .10
☐ 320 James Patrick, NYR. .10
☐ 321 Owen Nolan, Que. .25
☐ 322 Marty McSorley, L.A. .10
☐ 323 James Black, Hfd. .10
☐ 324 Jacques Cloutier (G), Que. .10
☐ 325 Benoît Hogue, NYI. .10
☐ 326 Teppo Numminen, Wpg. .10
☐ 327 Mark Recchi, Pha. .25
☐ 328 Paul Ranheim, Cgy. .10
☐ 329 Andy Moog (G), Bos. .25
☐ 330 Shayne Corson, Mtl. .25
☐ 331 J.J. Daigneault, Mtl. .10
☐ 332 Mark Fitzpatrick (G), NYI. .10
☐ 333 Russian Stars Checklist (342-350) .10
☐ 334 Alexei Yashin, Dynamo .50
☐ 335 Darius Kasparaitis, Dynamo .10
☐ **336 Alexander Yudin, Dynamo, RC .10**
☐ **337 Sergei Bautin, Dynamo, RC .10**
☐ **338 Igor Korolov, Dynamo, RC .25**
☐ **339 Sergei Klimovich, Dynamo, RC .10**
☐ **340 Andrei Nikolishin, Dynamo, RC .10**
☐ **341 Vitali Karamnov, Dynamo, RC .10**
☐ **342 Alexander Andriyevski, Dynamo, RC .10**
☐ **343 Sergei Sorokin, Dynamo, RC .10**
☐ **344 Yan Kaminsky, Dynamo, RC .10**
☐ **345 Andrei Trefilov (G), Dynamo, RC .25**

☐ **346 Sergei Petrenko, Dynamo, RC .10**
☐ **347 Ravil Khaidarov, Dynamo, RC .10**
☐ **348 Dmitri Frolov, Dynamo, RC .10**
☐ **349 Ravil Yakubov, Dynamo, RC .10**
☐ **350 Dmitri Yushkevich, Dynamo, RC .10**
☐ **351 Alexander Karpovtsev, Dynamo, RC .10**
☐ **352 Igor Dorofeyev, Dynamo, RC .10**
☐ **353 Alexander Galchenyuk, Dynamo, RC .10**
☐ 354 Joé Juneau, Bos. .10
☐ 355 Pat Falloon, S.J. .10
☐ 356 Gilbert Dionne, Mtl. .10
☐ 357 Vladimir Konstantinov, Det. .10
☐ 358 Rick Tabaracci (G), Wpg. .10
☐ 359 Tony Amonte, NYR. .25
☐ 360 Scott Lachance, NYI. .10
☐ 361 Tom Draper (G), Buf. .10
☐ 362 Pavel Bure, Van. .50
☐ 363 Nicklas Lidström, Det. .25
☐ 364 Keith Tkachuk, Wpg. .35
☐ 365 Kevin Todd, N.J. .10
☐ 366 Dominik Hasek (G), Chi. .50
☐ 367 Igor Kravchuk, Chi. .10
☐ 368 Shawn McEachern, Pgh. .10
☐ 369 Checklist .50
☐ **370 Dieter Hegen, Ger., RC .10**
☐ **371 Stefan Ustorf, Ger., RC .10**
☐ **372 Ernst Kopf, Ger., RC .10**
☐ **373 Raimond Hilger, Ger., RC .10**
☐ 374 Mats Sundin, Swe. .25
☐ 375 Peter Forsberg, Swe. 2.00
☐ **376 Arto Blomsten, Swe., RC .10**
☐ 377 Tommy Söderström (G), Swe. .10
☐ 378 Michael Nylander, Swe. .25
☐ **379 David Jensen, USA., RC .10**
☐ 380 Chris Winnes, USA. .10
☐ **381 Ray LeBlanc (G), USA., RC .10**
☐ 382 Joe Sacco, USA. .10
☐ 383 Dennis Vaske, USA. .10
☐ 384 Jorg Eberle, Sui. .10
☐ 385 Trevor Kidd (G), Cdn. .25
☐ 386 Pat Falloon, Cdn. .10
☐ 387 Rob Brown, Chi. .10
☐ 388 Adam Graves, NYR. .10
☐ 389 Peter Zezel, Tor. .10
☐ 390 Checklist (331-440) .10
☐ 391 Don Sweeney, Bos. .10
☐ 392 Sean Hill, USA. .10
☐ 393 Ted Donato, USA. .10
☐ 394 Marty McInnis, USA. .10
☐ 395 C.J. Young, USA. .10
☐ 396 Ted Drury, USA. .10
☐ 397 Scott Young, USA. .10
☐ 398 CL: S. Lachance/ K. Tkachuk .25
☐ 399 Joé Juneau, Bos. .10
☐ 400 Stephen Heinze, Bos. .10
☐ 401 Glen Murray, Bos. .10
☐ **402 Keith Carney, Buf., RC .10**
☐ **403 Dean McAmmond, Chi., RC .10**
☐ 404 Karl Dykhuis, Chi. .10
☐ 405 Martin Lapointe, Det. .10
☐ 406 Scott Niedermayer, N.J. .25
☐ **407 Ray Whitney, S.J., RC .10**
☐ 408 Martin Brodeur (G), N.J. .75
☐ 409 Scott Lachance, NYI. .10
☐ 410 Marty McInnis, NYI. .10
☐ **411 Bill Guerin, N.J., RC .50**
☐ 412 Shawn McEachern, Pgh. .10
☐ **413 Denny Felsner, Stl., RC .10**
☐ **414 Bret Hedican, Stl., RC .10**
☐ 415 Drake Berehowsky, Tor. .10
☐ 416 Patrick Poulin, Hfd. .10
☐ **417 Vladimir Vujtek, Mtl., RC .10**
☐ **418 Steve Konowalchuk, Wsh., RC .10**
☐ 419 Keith Tkachuk, Wpg. .50
☐ 420 Evgeny Davydov, Wpg. .10
☐ 421 Yanick Dupré, Pha. .10
☐ **422 Jason Woolley, Wsh., RC .10**
☐ 423 Brett Hull/Wayne Gretzky 1.00
☐ 424 Tomas Sandström, L.A. .10
☐ 425 Craig MacTavish, Edm. .10
☐ 426 Stu Barnes, Wpg. .10
☐ 427 Gilbert Dionne, Mtl. .10
☐ 428 Andrei Lomakin, Pha. .10
☐ 429 Tomas Forslund, Cgy. .10
☐ 430 André Racicot (G), Mtl. .10

	No.	Player	Value
☐	431	AW: Pavel Bure, Van.	.50
☐	432	AW: Mark Messier, NYR.	.35
☐	433	AW: Mario Lemieux, Pgh.	.85
☐	434	AW: Brian Leetch, NYR.	.25
☐	435	AW: Wayne Gretzky, L.A.	1.00
☐	436	AW: Mario Lemieux, Pgh.	.85
☐	437	AW: Mark Messier, NYR.	.35
☐	438	AW: Patrick Roy (G), Mtl.	.85
☐	439	AW: Guy Carbonneau, Mtl.	.10
☐	440	AW: Patrick Roy (G), Mtl.	.85
☐	441	Russ Courtnall, Min.	.10
☐	442	Jeff Reese (G), Cgy.	.10
☐	443	Brent Fedyk, Pha.	.10
☐	444	Kerry Huffman, Que.	.10
☐	445	Mark Freer, Ott.	.10
☐	446	Christian Ruuttu, Chi.	.10
☐	447	Nick Kypreos, Hfd.	.10
☐	**448**	**Mike Hurlbut, NYR., RC**	**.10**
☐	449	Bob Sweeney, Buf.	.10
☐	450	Checklist (441 - 540)	.10
☐	451	Perry Berezan, S.J.	.10
☐	452	Phil Bourque, NYR.	.10
☐	453	Messier/Amonte/Graves, NYR.	.35
☐	454	Lemieux/Stevens/Tocchet, Pgh.	.75
☐	455	Oates/Juneau/Kvartalnov, Bos.	.25
☐	456	LaFontaine/Andreychuk/ Mogilny, Buf.	.25
☐	457	Zdeno Ciger, N.J.	.10
☐	458	Pat Jablonski (G) T.B.	.10
☐	459	Brent Gilchrist, Edm.	.10
☐	460	Yvon Corriveau, S.J.	.10
☐	461	Dino Ciccarelli. Det.	.25
☐	462	David Emma, N.J.	.10
☐	**463**	**Corey Hirsch (G), NYR., RC**	**.25**
☐	464	Jamie Baker, Ott.	.10
☐	465	John Cullen, Tor.	.10
☐	**466**	**Lonnie Loach, L.A., RC**	**.10**
☐	467	Louie DeBrusk, Edm.	.10
☐	468	Brian Mullen, NYI.	.10
☐	469	Gaetan Duchesne, Min.	.10
☐	470	Eric Lindros, Pha.	3.00
☐	471	Brian Bellows, Mtl.	.10
☐	**472**	**Bill Lindsay, Que., RC**	**.10**
☐	473	Dave Archibald, Ott.	.10
☐	474	Reggie Savage, Wsh.	.10
☐	**475**	**Tommy Söderström (G), Pha., RC**	**.35**
☐	476	Vincent Damphousse, Mtl.	.10
☐	477	Mike Ricci, Que.	.10
☐	478	Bob Carpenter, Wsh.	.10
☐	479	Kevin Haller, Mtl.	.10
☐	480	Peter Sidorkiewicz (G), Ott.	.10
☐	**481**	**Peter Andersson, NYR., RC**	**.10**
☐	482	Kevin Miller, Stl.	.10
☐	**483**	**Jean-François Quintin, S.J., RC**	**.10**
☐	484	Philippe Boucher, Buf.	.10
☐	485	Jozef Stumpel, Bos.	.25
☐	**486**	**Vitali Prokhorov, Stl., RC**	**.10**
☐	**487**	**Stan Drulia, T.B., RC**	**.10**
☐	488	Jayson More, S.J.	.10
☐	**489**	**Mike Needham, Pgh., RC**	**.10**
☐	**490**	**Glenn Mulvenna, Pha., RC**	**.10**
☐	**491**	**Ed Ronan, Mtl., RC**	**.10**
☐	**492**	**Grigori Panteleyev, Bos., RC**	**.10**
☐	**493**	**Kevin Dahl, Cgy., RC**	**.10**
☐	**494**	**Ryan McGill, Pha., RC**	**.10**
☐	495	Robb Stauber (G), L.A.	.10
☐	496	Vladimir Vujtek, Edm.	.10
☐	**497**	**Tomas Jelinek, Ott., RC**	**.10**
☐	**498**	**Patrik Kjellberg, Mtl., RC**	**.10**
☐	499	Sergei Bautin, Wpg.	.10
☐	500	Bobby Holik, N.J.	.10
☐	**501**	**Guy Hebert (G), Stl., RC**	**1.00**
☐	**502**	**Chris Kontos, T.B., RC**	**.10**
☐	**503**	**Vyacheslav Butsayev, Pha., RC**	**.10**
☐	**504**	**Yuri Khmylev, Buf., RC**	**.10**
☐	**505**	**Richard Matvichuk, Min., RC**	**.10**
☐	506	Dominik Hasek (G), Buf.	.75
☐	507	Ed Courtenay, S.J.	.10
☐	508	Jeff Daniels, Pgh.	.10
☐	**509**	**Doug Zmolek, S.J., RC**	**.10**
☐	**510**	**Vitali Karamnov, Stl., RC**	**.10**
☐	511	Norm Maciver, Ott.	.10
☐	512	Terry Yake, Hfd.	.10
☐	513	Steve Duchesne, Que.	.10
☐	514	Andrei Trefilov (G), Cgy.	.10
☐	515	Jiri Slegr, Van.	.10
☐	**516**	**Sergei Zubov, NYR., RC**	**.50**
☐	**517**	**Dave Karpa, Que., RC**	**.10**
☐	518	Sean Burke (G), Hfd.	.25
☐	519	Adrien Plavsic, Van.	.10
☐	520	Michael Nylander, Hfd.	.10
☐	521	John MacLean, N.J.	.10
☐	**522**	**Jason Ruff, Stl., RC**	**.10**
☐	**523**	**Sean Hill, Mtl., RC**	**.10**
☐	524	Mike Sillinger, Det.	.10
☐	**525**	**Daniel Laperrière, Stl., RC**	**.10**
☐	526	Peter Ahola, Pgh.	.10
☐	527	Guy Larose, Tor.	.10
☐	**528**	**Tommy Sjodin, Min., RC**	**.10**
☐	529	Rob DiMaio, T.B.	.10
☐	530	Mark Howe, Det.	.10
☐	531	Greg Paslawski, Pha.	.10
☐	532	Ron Hextall (G), Que.	.25
☐	**533**	**Keith Jones, Wsh., RC**	**.35**
☐	**534**	**Chris Luongo, Ott., RC**	**.10**
☐	535	Anatoli Semenov, Van.	.10
☐	536	Stéphane Beauregard (G), Pha.	.10
☐	537	Pat Elynuik, Wsh.	.10
☐	538	Mike McPhee, Min.	.10
☐	539	Jody Hull, Ott.	.10
☐	540	Stéphane Matteau, Chi.	.10
☐	541	Shayne Corson, Edm.	.25
☐	**542**	**Mikhail Kravets, S.J., RC**	**.10**
☐	**543**	**Kevin Miehm, Stl., RC**	**.10**
☐	544	Brian Bradley, T.B.	.10
☐	545	Mathieu Schneider, Mtl.	.10
☐	546	Steve Chiasson, Det.	.10
☐	**547**	**Warren Rychel, L.A., RC**	**.10**
☐	548	John Tucker, T.B.	.10
☐	549	Todd Ewen, Mtl.	.10
☐	550	Checklist (541-640)	.10
☐	551	Petr Klima, Edm.	.10
☐	**552**	**Robert Lang, L.A., RC**	**.10**
☐	553	Eric Weinrich, Hfd.	.10
☐	554	CL: D. Kasparaitis/V. Malakhov	.10
☐	**555**	**Roman Hamrlik, T.B., RC**	**.50**
☐	556	Martin Rucinsky, Que.	.10
☐	557	Patrick Poulin, Hfd.	.10
☐	558	Tyler Wright, Edm.	.10
☐	**559**	**Martin Straka, Pgh., RC**	**.10**
☐	**560**	**Jim Hiller, L.A., RC**	**.10**
☐	**561**	**Dmitri Kvartalnov, Bos., RC**	**.10**
☐	562	Scott Niedermayer, N.J.	.25
☐	563	Darius Kasparaitis, NYI.	.10
☐	**564**	**Richard Smehlik, Buf., RC**	**.10**
☐	565	Shawn McEachern, Pgh.	.10
☐	566	Alexei Zhitnik, L.A.	.10
☐	**567**	**Andrei Kovalenko, Que., RC**	**.60**
☐	568	Sandis Ozolinsh, S.J.	.25
☐	**569**	**Robert Petrovicky, Hfd., RC**	**.10**
☐	**570**	**Dimitri Yushkevich, Pha., RC**	**.10**
☐	571	Scott Lachance, NYI.	.10
☐	**572**	**Nikolai Borschevsky, Tor., RC**	**.10**
☐	573	Alexei Kovalev, NYR.	.25
☐	574	Teemu Selänne, Wpg.	.75
☐	**575**	**Steven King, NYR., RC**	**.10**
☐	**576**	**Guy Lévêque, L.A., RC**	**.10**
☐	577	Vladimir Malakhov, NYI.	.10
☐	578	Alexei Zhamnov, Wpg.	.10
☐	**579**	**Viktor Gordijuk, Buf., RC**	**.10**
☐	**580**	**Dixon Ward, Van., RC**	**.25**
☐	**581**	**Igor Korolev, Stl., RC**	**.10**
☐	582	Sergei Krivokrasov, Chi.	.10
☐	**583**	**Rob Zamuner, T.B., RC**	**.35**
☐	584	CL: Aucoi/Lapointe/Wright	.10
☐	**585**	**Manny Legacé (G), Cdn., RC**	**.25**
☐	**586**	**Paul Kariya, Cdn., RC**	**25.00**
☐	**587**	**Alexandre Daigle, Cdn., RC**	**2.00**
☐	**588**	**Nathan Lafayette, Cdn., RC**	**.25**
☐	**589**	**Mike Rathje, Cdn., RC**	**.25**
☐	**590**	**Chris Gratton, Cdn., RC**	**2.00**
☐	**591**	**Chris Pronger, Cdn., RC**	**2.00**
☐	**592**	**Brent Tully, Cdn., RC**	**.10**
☐	**593**	**Rob Niedermayer, Cdn., RC**	**1.50**
☐	**594**	**Darcy Werenka, Cdn., RC**	**.10**
☐	595	Peter Forsberg, Swe.	1.50
☐	**596**	**Kenny Jonsson, Swe., RC**	**.35**
☐	**597**	**Niklas Sundstrom,S we., RC**	**.75**
☐	**598**	**Reine Rauhala, Swe., RC**	**.10**
☐	**599**	**Daniel Johansson, Swe., RC**	**.10**
☐	**600**	**David Vyborny, Cze., RC**	**.10**
☐	**601**	**Jan Vopat, Cze., RC**	**.10**
☐	**602**	**Pavol Demitra, Cze., RC**	**.10**
☐	**603**	**Michal Cerny, Cze., RC**	**.10**
☐	**604**	**Ondrej Steiner, Cze., RC**	**.10**
☐	**605**	**Jim Campbell, USA., RC**	**1.50**
☐	**606**	**Todd Marchant, USA., RC**	**.10**
☐	**607**	**Mike Pomichter, USA., RC**	**.10**
☐	**608**	**John Emmons, USA., RC**	**.10**
☐	**609**	**Adam Deadmarsh, USA., RC**	**2.00**
☐	**610**	**Nikolai Semin, Rus. RC**	**.10**
☐	**611**	**Igor Alexandrov, Rus. RC**	**.10**
☐	**612**	**Vadim Sharifjanov, Rus. RC**	**.25**
☐	**613**	**Viktor Kozlov, Rus. RC**	**.50**
☐	**614**	**Nikolai Tsulygin, Rus. RC**	**.10**
☐	**615**	**Jere Lehtinen, Fin., RC**	**1.00**
☐	**616**	**Ville Peltonen, Fin., RC**	**.10**
☐	**617**	**Saku Koivu, Fin., RC**	**10.00**
☐	**618**	**Kimmo Rintanen, Fin., RC**	**.10**
☐	**619**	**Jonni Vauhkonen, Fin., RC**	**.10**
☐	620	Brett Hull, Stl.	.35
☐	621	Wayne Gretzky, L.A.	1.00
☐	622	Jaromir Jagr, Pgh.	.75
☐	623	Darius Kasparaitis, NYI.	.10
☐	624	Bernie Nicholls, Edm.	.10
☐	625	Gibert Dionne, Mtl.	.10
☐	626	Ray Bourque, Bos.	.35
☐	627	Mike Ricci, Que.	.10
☐	628	Phil Housley, Wpg.	.10
☐	629	Chris Chelios, Chi.	.25
☐	630	Kevin Stevens, Pgh.	.10
☐	631	Roman Hamrlik, T.B.	.25
☐	632	Sergei Fedorov, Det.	.35
☐	633	Alexei Kovalev, NYR.	.10
☐	634	Shawn McEachern, Pgh.	.10
☐	635	Tony Amonte, NYR.	.25
☐	636	Brian Bellows, Mtl.	.10
☐	637	Adam Oates, Bos.	.25
☐	638	Denis Savard, Mtl.	.10
☐	639	Doug Gilmour, Tor.	.25
☐	640	Brian Leetch, NYR.	.25

	No.	Player	NRMT-MT
☐	SP2	Pavel Bure, Top Vote-Getter	4.00
☐	SP3	1993 World Junior Champions	3.00
☐	SP3	1993 World Junior Champions 3.9" x 5.4"	5.00

HOCKEY HEROES- WAYNE GRETZKY

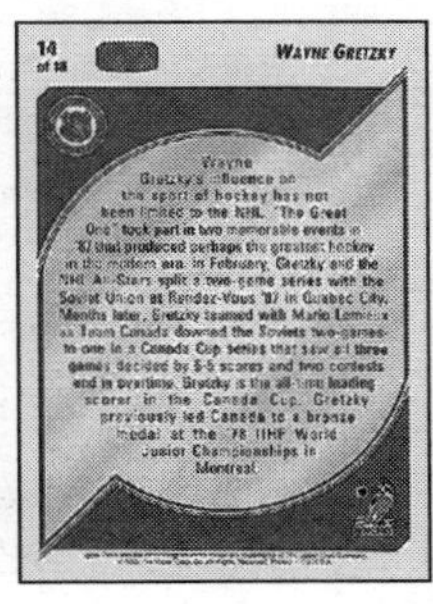

Insert Set (10 cards): 50.00

	No.	Player	NRMT-MT
☐		Title Card: Hockey Heroes Wayne Gretzky	10.00
☐	10	The Untouchable Greyhound	5.50
☐	11	17 Year Old Pro	5.50
☐	12	Hart Trophy In NHL Debut	5.50
☐	13	Four Cups in Five Seasons (w/Messier)	6.00
☐	14	Wrapped In The Maple Leaf	5.50
☐	15	The Trade that Rocked Sports	5.50
☐	16	Athlete of the Decade	5.50
☐	17	New Goals	5.50
☐	18	Checklist	5.50

HOCKEY HEROES - GORDIE HOWE

	No.	Player	NRMT-MT
		Insert Set (10 cards):	18.00
□		Title Card: Hockey Heroes Gordie Howe	3.00
□	19	The Early Years	2.50
□	20	Dynasty in Detroit	2.50
□	21	The First Production Line	2.50
□	22	'50s Scoring Champion	2.50
□	23	Six-Time Hart Trophy Winner	2.50
□	24	Hall of Fame	2.50
□	25	The Comeback	2.50
□	26	Mr Hockey and The Great One	4.00
□	27	Hockey Heroes Checklist	2.50

EURO ROOKIES

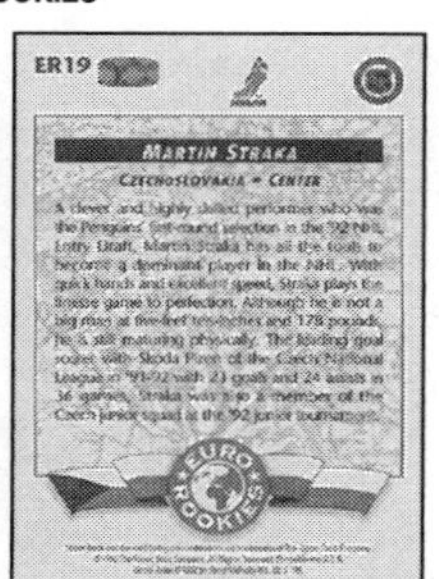

	No.	Player	NRMT-MT
		Insert Set (20 cards):	18.00
□	ER1	Richard Smehlik, Buf.	.75
□	ER2	Michael Nylander, Hfd.	.75
□	ER3	Igor Korolev, Stl.	.75
□	ER4	Robert Lang, L.A.	.75
□	ER5	Sergei Krivokrasov, Chi.	.75
□	ER6	Teemu Selänne, Wpg.	5.00
□	ER7	Darius Kasparaitis, NYI.	.75
□	ER8	Alexei Zhamnov, Wpg.	1.50
□	ER9	Jiri Slegr, Van.	.75
□	ER10	Alexei Kovalev, NYR.	.75
□	ER11	Roman Hamrlik, T.B.	1.50
□	ER12	Dimitri Yushkevich, Pha.	.75
□	ER13	Alexei Zhitnik, L.A.	.75
□	ER14	Andrei Kovalenko, Que.	.75
□	ER15	Vladimir Malakhov, NYI.	.75
□	ER16	Sandis Ozolinsh, S.J.	1.50
□	ER17	Evgeny Davydov, Wpg.	.75
□	ER18	Viktor Gordijuk, Buf.	.75
□	ER19	Martin Straka, Pgh.	.75
□	ER20	Robert Petrovicky, Hfd.	.75

CALDER CANDIDATES

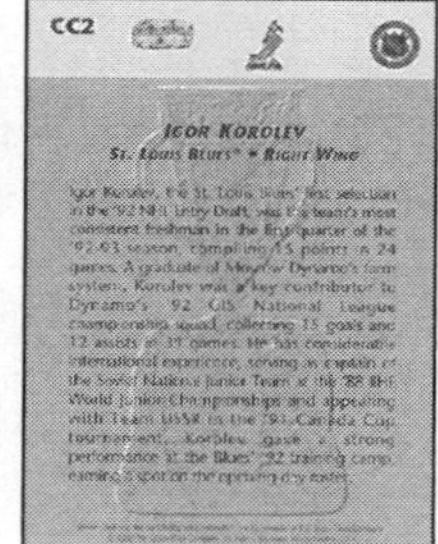

	No.	Player	NRMT-MT
		Insert Set (20 cards):	45.00
□	CC1	Dixon Ward, Van.	1.50
□	CC2	Igor Korolev, Stl.	1.50
□	CC3	Félix Potvin (G), Tor.	5.00
□	CC4	Rob Zamuner, T.B.	2.50
□	CC5	Scott Niedermayer, N.J.	2.50
□	CC6	Eric Lindros, Pha.	12.00
□	CC7	Alexei Zhitnik, L.A.	1.50
□	CC8	Roman Hamrlik, T.B.	2.50
□	CC9	Joé Juneau, Bos.	1.50
□	CC10	Teemu Selänne, Wpg.	7.00
□	CC11	Alexei Kovalev, NYR.	1.50
□	CC12	Vladimir Malakhov, NYI.	1.50
□	CC13	Darius Kasparaitis, NYI.	1.50
□	CC14	Shawn McEachern, Pgh.	1.50
□	CC15	Keith Tkachuk, Wpg.	4.00
□	CC16	Scott Lachance, NYI.	1.50
□	CC17	Andrei Kovalenko, Que.	1.50
□	CC18	Patrick Poulin, Hfd.	1.50
□	CC19	Evgeny Davydov, Wpg.	1.50
□	CC20	Dimitri Yushkevich, Pha.	1.50

EURO STARS

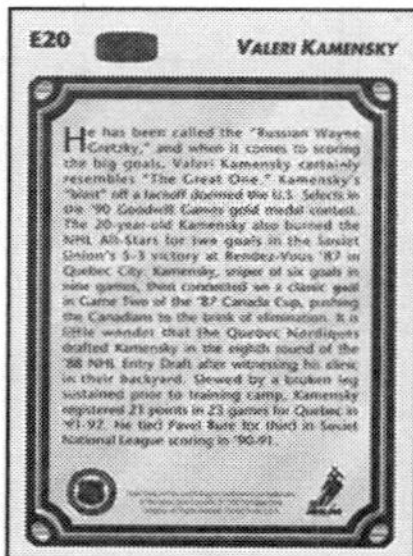

	No.	Player	NRMT-MT
		Insert Set (20 cards):	25.00
□	E1	Sergei Fedorov, Det.	2.50
□	E2	Pavel Bure, Van.	3.50
□	E3	Dominik Hasek (G), Chi.	3.50
□	E4	Vladimir Ruzicka, Bos.	.75
□	E5	Peter Ahola, L.A.	.75
□	E6	Kyosti Karjalainen, L.A.	.75
□	E7	Igor Kravchuk, Chi.	.75
□	E8	Evgeny Davydov, Wpg.	.75
□	E9	Nicklas Lidström, Det.	1.25
□	E10	Vladimir Konstantinov, Det.	.75
□	E11	Josef Beranek, Edm.	.75
□	E12	Valeri Zelepukin, N.J.	.75
□	E13	Sergei Nemchinov, NYR.	.75
□	E14	Jaromir Jagr, Pgh.	5.00
□	E15	Igor Ulanov, Wpg.	.75
□	E16	Sergei Makarov, Cgy.	.75
□	E17	Andrei Lomakin, Pha.	.75
□	E18	Mats Sundin, Que.	2.50
□	E19	Jarmo Myllys, S.J.	.75
□	E20	Valeri Kamensky, Que.	1.25

ALL ROOKIE TEAM

	No.	Player	NRMT-MT
		Insert Set (7 cards):	30.00
□	AR1	Tony Amonte	4.00
□	AR2	Gilbert Dionne	3.00
□	AR3	Kevin Todd	3.00
□	AR4	Nicklas Lidstrom	4.00
□	AR5	Vladimir Konstantinov	3.00
□	AR6	Dominik Hasek (G)	15.00
□	AR7	Checklist	10.00

ALL WORLD TEAM

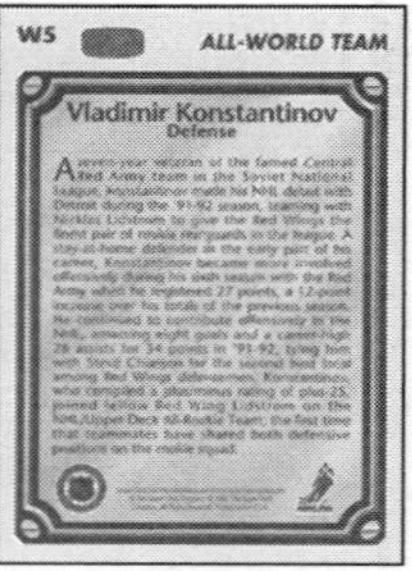

	No.	Player	NRMT-MT
		Insert Set (6 cards):	20.00
□	W1	Wayne Gretzky, L.A.	8.00
□	W2	Brett Hull, Stl.	2.00
□	W3	Jaromir Jagr, Pgh.	4.00
□	W4	Nicklas Lidström, Det.	1.50
□	W5	Vladimir Konstantinov, Det.	1.50
□	W6	Patrick Roy (G), Mtl.	6.50

AMERI / CAN ROOKIE TEAM HOLOGRAMS

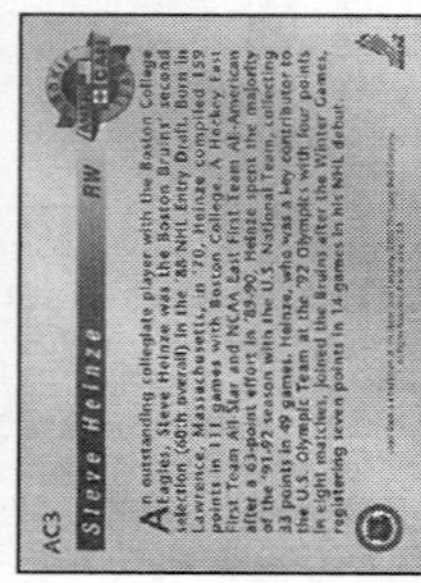

	No.	Player	NRMT-MT
		Insert Set (6 cards):	10.00
□	AC1	Joé Juneau, Bos.	1.00
□	AC2	Keith Tkachuk, Wpg.	6.00
□	AC3	Steve Heinze, Bos.	1.00
□	AC4	Scott Lachance, NYI.	1.00
□	AC5	Scott Niedermayer, N.J.	2.00
□	AC6	Dominic Roussel (G), Pha.	1.00

EURO - ROOKIE TEAM

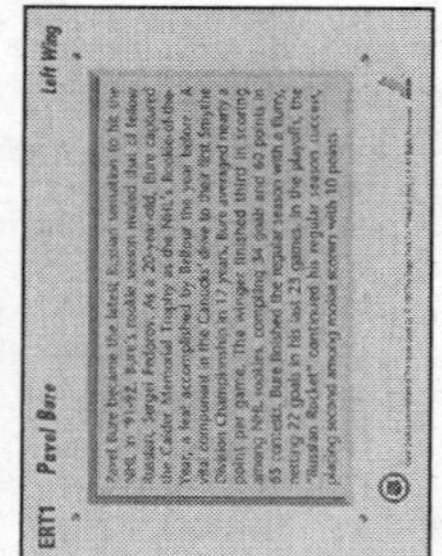

	No.	Player	NRMT-MT
		Insert Set (6 cards):	15.00
□	ERT1	Pavel Bure, Van.	6.00
□	ERT2	Nicklas Lidstrom, Det.	1.50
□	ERT3	Dominik Hasek (G), Chi.	6.00
□	ERT4	Peter Ahola, L.A.	1.00
□	ERT5	Alexander Semak, N.J.	1.00
□	ERT6	Tomas Forslund, Cgy.	1.00

WORLD JUNIOR GRADS

	No.	Player	NRMT-MT
Insert Set (20 cards):			**100.00**
☐	WG1	Scott Niedermayer, N.J.	3.00
☐	WG2	Vyacheslav Kozlov, Det.	2.00
☐	WG3	Chris Chelios, Chi.	5.00
☐	WG4	Jari Kurri, L.A.	3.00
☐	WG5	Pavel Bure, Van.	8.00
☐	WG6	Jaromir Jagr, Pgh.	12.00
☐	WG7	Steve Yzerman, Det.	12.00
☐	WG8	Joe Sakic, Que.	10.00
☐	WG9	Alexei Kovalev, NYR.	2.00
☐	WG10	Wayne Gretzky, L.A.	25.00
☐	WG11	Mario Lemieux, Pgh.	20.00
☐	WG12	Eric Lindros, Pha.	15.00
☐	WG13	Pat Falloon, S.J.	2.00
☐	WG14	Trevor Linden, Van.	3.00
☐	WG15	Brian Leetch, NYR.	4.00
☐	WG16	Sergei Fedorov, Det.	6.00
☐	WG17	Mats Sundin, Que.	6.00
☐	WG18	Alexander Mogilny, Buf.	4.00
☐	WG19	Jeremy Roenick, Chi.	4.00
☐	WG20	Luc Robitaille, L.A.	4.00

GORDIE HOWE SELECTS

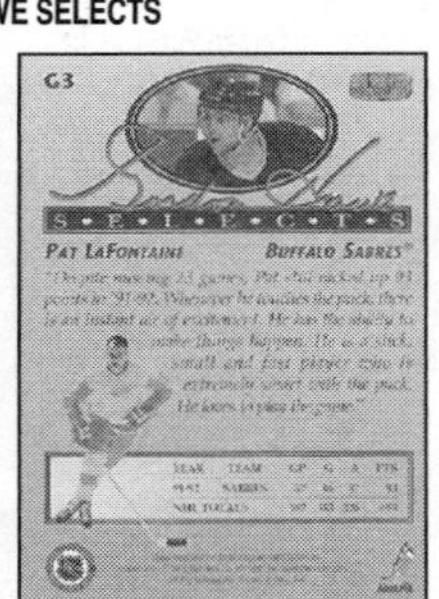

	No.	Player	NRMT-MT
Insert Set (20 cards):			**55.00**
☐	G1	Brian Bellows, Mtl.	1.50
☐	G2	Luc Robitaille, L.A.	1.50
☐	G3	Pat LaFontaine, Buf.	1.50
☐	G4	Kevin Stevens, Pgh.	1.50
☐	G5	Wayne Gretzky, L.A.	12.00
☐	G6	Steve Larmer, Chi.	1.50
☐	G7	Brett Hull, Stl.	3.00
☐	G8	Jeremy Roenick, Chi.	2.00
☐	G9	Mario Lemieux, Pgh.	10.00
☐	G10	Steve Yzerman, Det.	6.00
☐	G11	Joé Juneau, Bos.	1.50
☐	G12	Vladimir Malakhov, NYI.	1.50
☐	G13	Alexei Kovalev, NYR.	1.50
☐	G14	Eric Lindros, Pha.	8.00
☐	G15	Teemu Selänne, Wpg.	4.00
☐	G16	Dave Poulin, Bos.	1.50
☐	G17	Shawn McEachern, Pgh.	1.50
☐	G18	Keith Tkachuk, Wpg.	2.50
☐	G19	Andrei Kovalenko, Que.	1.50
☐	G20	Ted Donato, Bos.	1.50

1992 - 93 UPPER DECK ALL-STAR LOCKER SET

This 60-card set was produced after the 1992-93 NHL All-Star game in Montréal.

Imprint:

	No.	Player	NRMT-MT
Complete Set (60 cards):			**20.00**
Locker Box:			**2.00**
☐	1	Peter Bondra, Wsh.	.50
☐	2	Steve Duchesne, Que.	.15
☐	3	Jaromir Jagr, Pgh.	1.75
☐	4	Pat LaFontaine, Buf.	.35
☐	5	Brian Leetch, NYR.	.50
☐	6	Mario Lemieux, Pgh.	2.50
☐	7	Mark Messier, NYR.	.75
☐	8	Alexander Mogilny, Buf.	.50
☐	9	Kirk Muller, Mtl.	.15
☐	10	Adam Oates, Bos.	.50
☐	11	Mark Recchi, Pha.	.35
☐	12	Patrick Roy (G), Mtl.	2.50
☐	13	Joe Sakic, Que.	1.25
☐	14	Kevin Stevens, Pgh.	.15
☐	15	Scott Stevens, N.J.	.15
☐	16	Rick Tocchet, Pgh.	.15
☐	17	Pierre Turgeon, N.J.	.35
☐	18	Zarley Zalapski, Hfd.	.15
☐	19	Ed Belfour (G), Chi.	.50
☐	20	Brian Bradley, T.B.	.15
☐	21	Pavel Bure, Van.	1.00
☐	22	Chris Chelios, Chi.	.50
☐	23	Paul Coffey, Det.	.50
☐	24	Doug Gilmour, Tor.	.50
☐	25	Wayne Gretzky, L.A.	3.00
☐	26	Phil Housley, Wpg.	.15
☐	27	Brett Hull, Stl.	.75
☐	28	Kelly Kisio, S.J.	.15
☐	29	Jari Kurri, L.A.	.35
☐	30	Dave Manson, Edm.	.15
☐	31	Mike Modano, Min.	.75
☐	32	Gary Roberts, Cgy.	.15
☐	33	Luc Robitaille, L.A.	.35
☐	34	Jeremy Roenick, Chi.	.35
☐	35	Teemu Selänne, Wpg.	1.00
☐	36	Steve Yzerman, Det.	1.50
☐	37	Hardest Shot: Al Iafrate, Wsh.	.15
☐	38	Fastest Skater: Mike Gartner, NYR.	.35
☐	39	Shooting Accuracy: Ray Bourque, Bos.	.75
☐	40	Jon Casey (G), Min.	.15
☐	41	Bob Gainey, Mtl.	.35
☐	42	Gordie Howe, Det.	2.00
☐	43	Bobby Hull, Chi.	.75
☐	44	Frank Mahovlich, Mtl.	.50
☐	45	Lanny McDonald, Cgy.	.35
☐	46	Stan Mikita, Chi.	.50
☐	47	Henri Richard, Mtl.	.50
☐	48	Larry Robinson, Mtl.	.35
☐	49	Glen Sather, NYR.	.35
☐	50	Bryan Trottier, NYI.	.35
☐	51	Tony Amonte, NYR.	.35
☐	52	Pat Falloon, S.J.	.15
☐	53	Joé Juneau, Bos.	.15
☐	54	Alexei Kovalev, NYR.	.15
☐	55	Dmitri Kvartalnov, Bos.	.15
☐	56	Eric Lindros, Pha.	2.00
☐	57	Vladimir Malakhov, NYI.	.15
☐	58	Félix Potvin (G), Tor.	.75
☐	59	Mats Sundin, Que.	.75
☐	60	Alexei Zhamnov, Wpg.	.35
		Autograph	**NRMT-MT**
☐		Gordie Howe Autograph	300.00

1992 - 93 ZELLER'S MASTERS OF HOCKEY

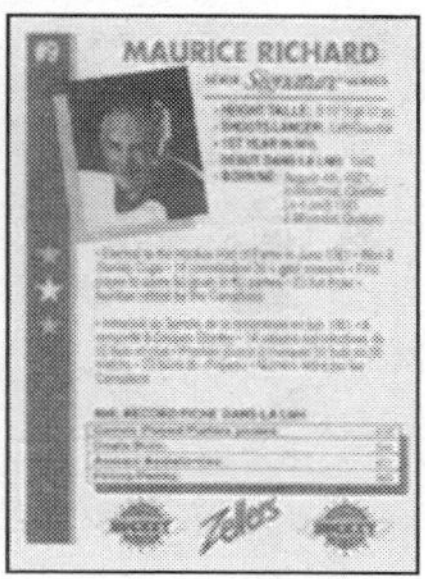

There are 10,000 copies of each card and 1,000 copies of each autographed card.

Imprint: ZELLERS

	Player	Auto.	Reg.
Complete Set (7 cards):			**17.00**
Certificate of Authenticity:			**1.00**
☐ ☐	Johnny Bower (G), Tor.	80.00	3.50
☐ ☐	Rod Gilbert, NYR.	60.00	2.50
☐ ☐	Ted Lindsay, Det.	60.00	2.50
☐ ☐	Frank Mahovlich, Tor.	100.00	4.00
☐ ☐	Stan Mikita, Chi.	80.00	3.50
☐ ☐	Maurice Richard, Mtl.	150.00	6.00

1993 KOULULAINEN

A 9 card sheet issued by the magazine Koululainen. We have no pricing information on this set.

Card Size: 2 5/8" x 3 4/16"

Imprint:

	Player		Player
☐	Jari Kurri	☐	Mario Lemieux
☐	Jyrki Lumme	☐	Teppo Numminen
☐	Janne Ojanen	☐	Christian Ruuttu
☐	Teemu Selänne	☐	Esa Tikkanen
☐	Title card		

1993 SEMIC STICKERS

These stickers were issued for the 1993 World Championships.

Imprint:

	No.	Player	NRMT-MT
Complete Set (288 stickers):			**50.00**
Common Player:			**.20**
Album:			**6.00**
☐	1	Peter Åslin, Swe.	.20
☐	2	Håkan Algotsson, Swe.	.20
☐	3	Kenneth Kennholt, Swe.	.20
☐	4	Arto Blomsten, Swe.	.20
☐	5	Tomas Jonsson, Swe.	.25
☐	6	Fredrik Stillman, Swe.	.20
☐	7	Stefan Larsson, Swe.	.20
☐	8	Peter Popovic, Swe.	.20
☐	9	Håkan Loob, Swe.	.25
☐	10	Thomas Rundqvist, Swe.	.20
☐	11	Patrick Juhlin, Swe.	.20
☐	12	Mikael Renberg	1.50
☐	13	Peter Forsberg	5.00
☐	14	Markus Näslund, Swe.	.50
☐	15	Bengt-Åke Gustafsson, Swe.	.20
☐	16	Jan Larsson, Swe.	.20
☐	17	Fredrik Nilsson, Swe.	.20

	No.	Player	Price
☐	18	Roger Hansson, Swe.	.20
☐	19	Tommy Söderström (G), Swe.	.50
☐	20	Anders Eldebrink, Swe.	.20
☐	21	Ulf Samuelsson, Swe.	.25
☐	22	Kjell Samuelsson, Swe.	.25
☐	23	Nicklas Lidström, Swe.	1.00
☐	24	Tommy Sjödin, Swe.	.20
☐	25	Calle Johansson, Swe.	.20
☐	26	Fredrik Olaussen, Swe.	.20
☐	27	Peter Andersson, Swe.	.20
☐	28	Tommy Albelin, Swe.	.20
☐	29	Roger Johansson, Swe.	.20
☐	30	Per Djoos, Swe.	.20
☐	31	Mikael Johansson, Swe.	.20
☐	32	Tomas Sandström, Swe.	.25
☐	33	Mats Sundin	2.50
☐	34	Ulf Dahlen, Swe.	.25
☐	35	Jan Erixon, Swe.	.25
☐	36	Thomas Steen, Swe.	.25
☐	37	Mikael Andersson, Swe.	.20
☐	38	Johan Garpenlöv, Swe.	.20
☐	39	Per-Erik Eklund, Swe.	.25
☐	40	Michael Nylander, Swe.	.25
☐	41	Thomas Forslund, Swe.	.20
☐	42	Patric Kjelberg, Swe.	.20
☐	43	Patrick Carnbäck, Swe.	.20
☐	44	Niclas Andersson, Swe.	.20
☐	45	Markus Ketterer (G), Fin.	.20
☐	46	Sakari Lindfors (G), Fin.	.20
☐	47	Jarmo Myllys (G), Fin.	.25
☐	48	Peter Ahola, Fin.	.20
☐	49	Mikko Haapakoski, Fin.	.20
☐	50	Kari Harila, Fin.	.20
☐	51	Pasi Huura, Fin.	.20
☐	52	Waltteri Immonen, Fin.	.20
☐	53	Timo Jutila, Fin.	.20
☐	54	Janne Laukkanen, Fin.	.20
☐	55	Harri Laurila, Fin.	.20
☐	56	Jyrki Lumme, Fin.	.25
☐	57	Teppo Numminen, Fin.	.25
☐	58	Sami Nuutinen, Fin.	.20
☐	59	Ville Siren, Fin.	.20
☐	60	Pasi Sormunen, Fin.	.20
☐	61	Mika Strömberg, Fin.	.20
☐	62	Mika Alatalo, Fin.	.20
☐	63	Raimo Helminen, Fin.	.20
☐	64	Pauli Järvinen, Fin.	.20
☐	65	Jarmo Kekäläinen, Fin.	.20
☐	66	Jari Korpisalo, Fin.	.20
☐	67	Jari Kurri, Fin.	1.00
☐	68	Mikko Mäkelä, Fin.	.20
☐	69	Mika Nieminen, Fin.	.20
☐	70	Timo Norppa, Fin.	.20
☐	71	Janne Ojanen, Fin.	.20
☐	72	Timo Norppa, Fin.	.20
☐	73	Rauli Raitanen, Fin.	.20
☐	74	Juha Riihijärvi, Fin.	.20
☐	75	Christian Ruuttu, Fin.	.20
☐	76	Timo Saarikoski, Fin.	.20
☐	77	Teemu Selänne, Fin.	3.50
☐	78	Jukka Seppo, Fin.	.20
☐	79	Petri Skriko, Fin.	.25
☐	80	Esa Tikkanen, Fin.	.25
☐	81	Pekka Tuomisto, Fin.	.20
☐	82	Petri Varis, Fin.	.20
☐	83	Jarkko Varvio, Fin.	.25
☐	84	Vesa Viitakoski, Fin.	.20
☐	85	Marko Virtanen, Fin.	.20
☐	86	Jali Wahlsten, Fin.	.20
☐	87	Sami Wahlsten, Fin.	.20
☐	88	Pentti Matikainen, Fin.	.20
☐	89	Petr Briza (G), Cze.	.20
☐	90	Roman Turek (G), Cze.	.50
☐	91	Milos Holan, Cze.	.20
☐	92	Drahomir Kadlec, Cze.	.20
☐	93	Bedrich Scerban, Cze.	.20
☐	94	Frantisek Prochazka, Cze.	.20
☐	95	Richard Zemlicka, Cze.	.20
☐	96	Roman Horak, Cze.	.20
☐	97	Lubos Rob, Cze.	.20
☐	98	Jiri Kucera, Cze.	.20
☐	99	Tomas Kapusta, Cze.	.20
☐	100	Roman Rysanek, Cze.	.20
☐	101	Roman Hamrlik	1.50
☐	102	Robert Svehla	1.50
☐	103	Tomas Jelinek, Cze.	.20
☐	104	Petr Klima, Cze.	.20
☐	105	Josef Beranek, Cze.	.25
☐	106	Robert Petrovecky, Cze.	.25
☐	107	Kamil Kastak, Cze.	.20
☐	108	David Volek, Cze.	.20
☐	109	Renato Tosio, Sui.	.20
☐	110	Patrick Schöpf, Sui.	.20
☐	111	Samuel Palmer, Sui.	.20
☐	112	Andreas Beautler, Sui.	.20
☐	113	Patrice Brasey, Sui.	.20
☐	114	Rick Tschumi, Sui.	.20
☐	115	Sven Leuenberger, Sui.	.20
☐	116	Sandro Bertaggia, Sui.	.20
☐	117	Patrick Howard, Sui.	.20
☐	118	Andy Ton, Sui.	.20
☐	119	Keith Fair, Sui.	.20
☐	120	Mario Brodman, Sui.	.20
☐	121	Fredy Luthi, Sui.	.20
☐	122	Jörg Eberle, Sui.	.20
☐	123	Roman Wäger, Sui.	.20
☐	124	Manuel Celio, Sui.	.20
☐	125	Christian Weber, Sui.	.20
☐	126	Roger Thöny, Sui.	.20
☐	127	Felix Hollenstein, Sui.	.20
☐	128	Gil Montandon, Sui.	.20
☐	129	Nikolai Khalibulin (G), Rus.	1.00
☐	130	Alexei Cherviakov, Rus.	.20
☐	131	Ilja Byakin, Rus.	.20
☐	132	Dmitri Filimonov, Rus.	.20
☐	133	Alexander Karpovstev, Rus.	.25
☐	134	Sergei Sorokin, Rus.	.20
☐	135	Andrei Sapozhnikov, Rus.	.20
☐	136	Alexei Yashin, Rus.	2.00
☐	137	Alexander Cherbayev, Rus.	.20
☐	138	Konstantin Astrakhantsev, Rus.	.20
☐	139	Sergei Petrenko, Rus.	.20
☐	140	Viktor Kozlov, Rus.	1.50
☐	141	Roman Oksiuta, Rus.	.25
☐	142	Vladimir Malakhov, Rus.	.25
☐	143	Andrei Lomakin, Rus.	.20
☐	144	Dmitri Yushkevich, Rus.	.20
☐	145	Igor Korolev, Rus.	.25
☐	146	Darius Kasparaitis, Rus.	.25
☐	147	Vyacheslav Bykov, Rus.	.25
☐	148	Andrei Khomutov, Rus.	.25
☐	149	Helmut de Raaf (G), Ger.	.20
☐	150	Klaus Merk (G), Ger.	.20
☐	151	Michael Heidt, Ger.	.20
☐	152	Michael Schmidt, Ger.	.20
☐	153	Uli Hiemer, Ger.	.20
☐	154	Andreas Niederberg, Ger.	.20
☐	155	Rick Amann, Ger.	.20
☐	156	Andreas Brockmann, Ger.	.20
☐	157	Gerd Truntschka, Ger.	.20
☐	158	Dieter Hegen, Ger.	.20
☐	159	Stefan Usdorf, Ger.	.20
☐	160	Georg Holzmann, Ger.	.20
☐	161	Ernst Köpf, Ger.	.20
☐	162	Bernd Truntschka, Ger.	.20
☐	163	Raimund Hilger, Ger.	.20
☐	164	Wolfgang Kummer, Ger.	.20
☐	165	Georg Franz, Ger.	.20
☐	166	Thomas Brandl, Ger.	.20
☐	167	Michael Rumrich, Ger.	.20
☐	168	Uwe Krupp, Ger.	.25
☐	169	Tom Barraso (G), USA.	.75
☐	170	Mike Richter (G), USA.	1.50
☐	171	Brian Leetch, USA.	1.50
☐	172	Chris Chelios, USA.	2.00
☐	173	Al Iafrate, USA.	.25
☐	174	Phil Housley, USA.	.25
☐	175	Kevin Hatcher, USA.	.25
☐	176	Gary Suter, USA.	.25
☐	177	Mathieu Schneider, USA.	.25
☐	178	Joe Mullen, USA.	.25
☐	179	Kevin Stevens, USA.	.25
☐	180	Jeremy Roenick, USA.	1.50
☐	181	Tony Granato, USA.	.25
☐	182	Mike Modano, USA.	2.50
☐	183	Pat LaFontaine, USA.	.50
☐	184	Ed Olczyk, USA.	.25
☐	185	Brett Hull, USA.	2.00
☐	186	Craig Janney, USA.	1.00
☐	187	Jimmy Carson, USA.	.25
☐	188	Tony Amonte, USA.	.50
☐	189	Patrick Roy (G), Cdn.	8.00
☐	190	Kirk McLean (G), Cdn.	.50
☐	191	Larry Murphy, Cdn.	.25
☐	192	Ray Bourque, Cdn.	2.50
☐	193	Al MacInnis, Cdn.	.75
☐	194	Steve Duchesne, Cdn.	.25
☐	195	Eric Desjardins, Cdn.	.25
☐	196	Scott Stevens, Cdn.	.25
☐	197	Paul Coffey, Cdn.	1.00
☐	198	Mario Lemieux, Cdn.	8.00
☐	199	Wayne Gretzky, Cdn.	10.00
☐	200	Rick Tocchet, Cdn.	.25
☐	201	Eric Lindros, Cdn.	6.00
☐	202	Mark Messier, Cdn.	2.50
☐	203	Steve Yzerman, Cdn.	5.00
☐	204	Luc Robitaille, Cdn.	.50
☐	205	Mark Recchi, Cdn.	1.00
☐	206	Joe Sakic, Cdn.	4.00
☐	207	Owen Nolan, Cdn.	.50
☐	208	Gary Roberts, Cdn.	.50
☐	209	David Delfino, Ita.	.20
☐	210	Mike Rosati, Ita.	.20
☐	211	Robert Oberrauch, Ita.	.20
☐	212	Jim Camazzola, Ita.	.20
☐	213	Bill Stewart, Ita.	.20
☐	214	Mike de Angelis, Ita.	.20
☐	215	Anthony Circelli, Ita.	.20
☐	216	Georg Comploy, Ita.	.20
☐	217	Frank di Muzio, Ita.	.20
☐	218	Gates Orlando, Ita.	.20
☐	219	John Vecchiarelli, Ita.	.20
☐	220	Joe Foglietta, Ita.	.20
☐	221	Lucio Topatigh, Ita.	.20
☐	222	Carmine Vani, Ita.	.20
☐	223	Lino de Toni, Ita.	.20
☐	224	Mario Chitarroni, Ita.	.20
☐	225	Bruno Zarillo, Ita.	.20
☐	226	Maurizio Mansi, Ita.	.20
☐	227	Stefan Figliuzzi, Ita.	.20
☐	228	Santino Pellegrina, Ita.	.20
☐	229	Jim Marthinsen, Nor.	.20
☐	230	Rob Schistad, Nor.	.20
☐	231	Petter Salsten, Nor.	.20
☐	232	Cato Tom Andersen, Nor.	.20
☐	233	Tommy Jakobsen, Nor.	.20
☐	234	Svein E. Nöstebö, Nor.	.20
☐	235	Jon Magne Karlstad, Nor.	.20
☐	236	Klm Sögaard, Nor.	.20
☐	237	Geir Hoff, Nor.	.20
☐	238	Erik Kristiansen, Nor.	.20
☐	239	Petter Thoresen, Nor.	.20
☐	240	Ole Eskil Dahlström, Nor.	.20
☐	241	Espen Knutsen, Nor.	.20
☐	242	Öystein Olsen, Nor.	.20
☐	243	Roy Johansen, Nor.	.20
☐	244	Trond Magnussen, Nor.	.20
☐	245	Arne Billkvam, Nor.	.20
☐	246	Marius Rath, Nor.	.20
☐	247	Tom Erik Olsen, Nor.	.20
☐	248	Morten Finstad, Nor.	.20
☐	249	Petri Ylönen (G), Fra.	.20
☐	250	Michel Vallière, Fra.	.20
☐	251	Stéphane Boteri, Fra.	.20
☐	252	Serge Poudrier, Fra.	.20
☐	253	Eric Durand, Fra.	.20
☐	254	Jean-Philippe Lemoine, Fra.	.20
☐	255	Denis Perez, Fra.	.20
☐	256	Sébastian Marquet, Fra.	.20
☐	257	Michael Babin, Fra.	.20
☐	258	Stéphane Barin, Fra.	.20
☐	259	Arnaud Briand, Fra.	.20
☐	260	Yves Crettenand, Fra.	.20
☐	261	Laurent Deschaume, Fra.	.20
☐	262	Roger Dubé, Fra.	.20
☐	263	Patrick Dunn, Fra.	.20
☐	264	Franck Pajonkowski, Fra.	.20
☐	265	Pierre Pousse, Fra.	.20
☐	266	Antoine Richer, Fra.	.20
☐	267	Christophe Ville, Fra.	.20
☐	268	Mario Schaden, Fra.	.20
☐	269	Brian Stankiewicz, Aut.	.20
☐	270	Claus Dalpiaz, Aut.	.20
☐	271	Michael Shea, Aut.	.20
☐	272	Robin Doyle, Aut.	.20

	No.	Player	Price
☐	273	Martin Ulrich, Aut.	.20
☐	274	Martin Krainz, Aut.	.20
☐	275	Erich Solderer, Aut.	.20
☐	276	Michael Guntner, Aut.	.20
☐	277	Friedrich Ganster, Aut.	.20
☐	278	Wayne Groulx, Aut.	.20
☐	279	Dieter Kalt, Aut.	.20
☐	280	Werner Kerth, Aut.	.20
☐	281	Arno Maier, Aut.	.20
☐	282	Richard Nasheim, Aut.	.20
☐	283	Christian Perthaler, Aut.	.20
☐	284	Andreas Puschning, Aut.	.20
☐	285	Gerhard Punschnik, Aut.	.20
☐	286	Walter Putnik, Aut.	.20
☐	287	Reinhard Lampert, Aut.	.20
☐	288	Mario Schaden, Aut.	.20

1993 TITREX GUY LAFLEUR

This card was issued as a premium with Titrex Power Bar.

Imprint:

	Player	NRMT-MT
☐	Guy Lafleur	4.00

1993 UPPER DECK WORLD CUP SOCCER HONOURARY CAPTAINS

This 4-card insert set features one hockey player. There is a regular card and a gold parallel.

Imprint: © 1993 The Upper Deck Company

	No.	Player	Gold	Reg.
☐☐	H4	Wayne Gretzky	40.00	20.00

1993 - 94 ACTION PACKED PROMOS

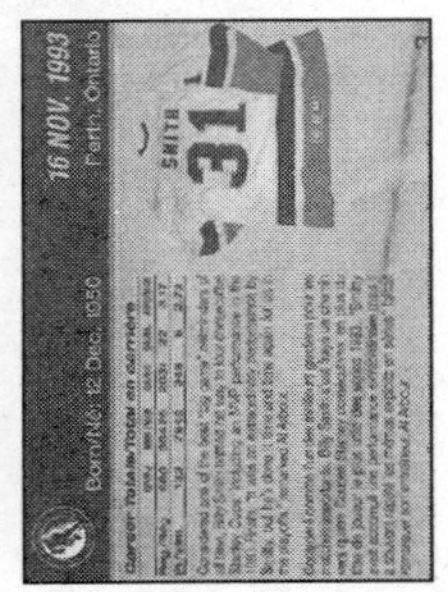

Imprint: Action Packed, Inc. Copyright 1993 Pat. #315,364. Printed in U.S.A.

Action Packed Hull Set (2 cards): 10.00
Action Packed HOF Set (10 cards): 40.00

	No.	Player	NRMT-MT
☐	BH1	Bobby Hull, Chi.	5.00
☐	BH2	Bobby Hull (Gold), Chi.	5.00
☐	1	Edgar Laprade	6.00
☐	2	Guy Lapointe	6.00
☐	3	Billy Smith, NYI.	10.00
☐	4	Steve Shutt, Mtl.	8.00
☐	5	John D'Amico	4.00
☐	6	Al Shaver	4.00
☐	7	Seymour Knox	4.00
☐	8	Frank Griffiths	4.00
☐	9	Fred Page	4.00
☐	10	Al Strachan	4.00

1993 - 94 CANADIAN OLYMPIC TEAM - ALBERTA LOTTERIES

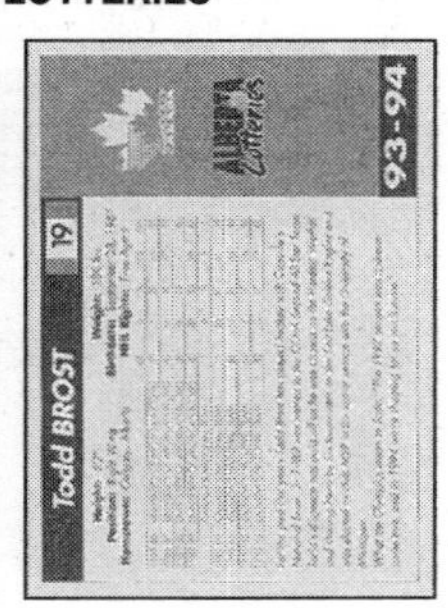

Imprint:

Complete Set (23 cards): 25.00

	Player	NRMT-MT
☐	Adrian Aucion	.75
☐	Todd Brost	.75
☐	Dany Dubé	.75
☐	David Harlock	.75
☐	Corey Hirsch (G)	1.25
☐	Todd Hlushko	.75
☐	Fabian Joseph	.75
☐	Paul Kariya	10.00
☐	Chris Kontos	.75
☐	Manny Legacé (G)	1.25
☐	Brett Lindros	1.25
☐	Ken Lovsin	.75
☐	Jason Marshall	.75
☐	Derek Mayer	.75
☐	Dwayne Norris	.75
☐	Tom Renney	2.00
☐	Russ Romaniuk	.75
☐	Brian Savage	2.50
☐	Trevor Sim	.75
☐	Chris Therien	.75
☐	Todd Warriner	1.25
☐	Craig Woodcroft	.75
☐	Sponsor Card	.75

1993 - 94 CLASSIC HOCKEY DRAFT

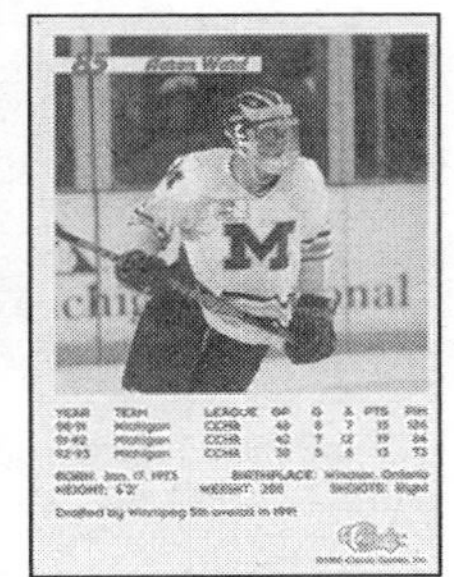

Imprint: © 1993 Classic Games, Inc.

Complete Set (150 cards): 15.00
Common Player: .10
Preview Card (Pavel Bure, PR3): 5.00
Promo Postcard (Kariya, Rhéame, Mogilny; 5 1/4" x 7 3/4"): 5.00

	No.	Player	NRMT-MT
☐	1	Alexandre Daigle, Victoriaville	.35
☐	2	Chris Pronger, Peterborough	.35
☐	3	Chris Gratton, Kingston	.35
☐	4	Paul Kariya, Cdn.	2.00
☐	5	Rob Niedermayer, Medicine Hat	.25
☐	6	Viktor Kozlov, Rus.	.10
☐	7	Jason Arnott , Oshawa	.50
☐	8	Niklas Sundstrom, Binghampton	.10
☐	9	Todd Harvey, Detroit-OHL	.25
☐	10	Jocelyn Thibault (G), Sherbrooke	.75
☐	11	CL: (Draft Picks 1-5, 7, 10)	.35
☐	12	Pat Peake, Detroit-OHL	.10
☐	13	Jason Allison, London	.75
☐	14	Todd Bertuzzi	.25
☐	15	Maxim Bets, USSR	.10
☐	16	Curtis Bowen, Ottawa-OHL	.10
☐	17	Kevin Brown, Detroit-OHL	.10
☐	18	Valeri Bure, Spokane	.25
☐	19	Jason Dawe, Peterborough	.10
☐	20	Adam Deadmarsh, Portland-WHL	.25
☐	21	Aaron Gavey, S.S. Marie	.10
☐	22	Nathan Lafayette, Newmarket	.10
☐	23	Eric Lecompte, Hull	.10
☐	24	Manny Legacé (G), Nigara Falls	.10
☐	25	Michael Peca	.50
☐	26	Denis Pederson, Prince Albert	.10
☐	27	Jeff Shantz, Regina	.10
☐	28	Nick Stadjuhar, London	.10
☐	29	Cory Stillman, Peterborough	.10
☐	30	Michal Sykora, Tacoma	.10
☐	31	Brent Tully	.10
☐	32	Mike Wilson, Sudbury	.10
☐	33	Kevin Brown/Pat Peake/Bob Wren	.10
☐	34	CL: Alexandre Daigle/Alexei Yashin	.25
☐	35	Antti Aalto, Fin.	.10
☐	36	Radim Bicanek, Cze.	.10
☐	37	Vladimir Chebaturkin, Rus.	.10
☐	38	Alexander Cherbayev , Rus.	.10
☐	39	Markus Ketterer (G) , Fin.	.10
☐	40	Saku Koivu, Fin.	1.00
☐	41	Vladimir Krechin, Rus.	.10
☐	42	Alexei Kudashov, USSR	.10
☐	43	Janne Laukkanen, Fin.	.10
☐	44	Janne Niinimaa, Fin.	.50
☐	45	Juha Riihijarvi, Fin.	.10
☐	46	Nikolai Tsulygin, Rus.	.10
☐	47	Vesa Viitakoski, Fin.	.10
☐	48	David Vyborny, Rus.	.10
☐	49	Nikolai Zavarukhin, Rus.	.10
☐	50	Alexandre Daigle, Victoriaville	.25
☐	51	Alexandre Daigle, Victoriaville	.25
☐	52	Alexandre Daigle, Victoriaville	.25
☐	53	Alexandre Daigle, Victoriaville	.25
☐	54	Alexandre Daigle, Victoriaville	.25
☐	55	Jim Montgomery, Maine	.10
☐	56	Mike Dunham (G), Maine	.25
☐	57	Matt Martin, Maine	.10
☐	58	Garth Snow (G), Maine	.25
☐	59	Shawn Walch, Maine, Coach	.10
☐	60	Mike Bavis/Mark Bavis, Boston U.	.10
☐	61	Scott Chartier, W. Michigan	.10
☐	62	Craig Darby, Providence	.10
☐	63	Ted Drury, Harvard	.10
☐	64	Steve Dubinsky, Clarkson	.10
☐	65	Joe Frederick, N. Michigan	.10
☐	66	Cammi Granato, Providence (XCY: T. Granato)	1.50
☐	67	Brett Hauer, Minn.-Duluth	.10
☐	68	Jon Hillebrandt (G), Chicago-CCHA	.10
☐	69	Ryan Hughes, Cornell	.10
☐	70	Dean Hullet, Lake Superior	.10
☐	71	Kevin O'Sullivan, Boston U.	.10
☐	72	Dan Plante, Wisconsin	.10
☐	73	Derek Plante, Minn.-Duluth	.25
☐	74	Travis Richards, Minnesota	.10
☐	75	Barry Richter, Wisconsin	.10
☐	76	David Roberts, Michigan	.10
☐	77	Chris Rogles (G), Clarkson	.10
☐	78	Jon Rohloff, Minn.-Duluth	.10
☐	79	Brian Rolston, Lake Superior	.10
☐	80	David Sacco	.10
☐	81	Brian Savage, Miami	.10
☐	82	Mike Smith, Lake Superior	.10
☐	83	Chris Tamer, Michigan	.10
☐	84	Chris Therien, Providence	.10
☐	85	Aaron Ward, Michigan	.25
☐	86	Russian Celebration	.10
☐	87	Viacheslav Butsayev, Rus.	.10
☐	88	Yan Kaminsky, Rus.	.10
☐	89	Alexander Karpovtsev, Rus.	.10
☐	90	Valeri Karpov, Rus.	.10
☐	91	Sergei Petrenko, Rus.	.10
☐	92	Andrei Sapozhniko, Rus.	.10
☐	93	Sergei Sorokin, Rus.	.10
☐	94	German Titov, Rus.	.10
☐	95	Andrei Trefilov (G), Rus.	.10
☐	96	Alexei Yashin, Rus.	.50
☐	97	Dimitri Yushkevich, Rus.	.10
☐	98	Radek Bonk , Las Vegas	.25
☐	99	Jason Bonsignore, Newmarket	.10
☐	100	Brad Brown, North Bay	.10
☐	101	Chris Drury, PRO-AM	.10

	No.	Player	NRMT-MT
☐	102	Jeff Freisen, Regina	.50
☐	103	Sean Haggerty,	.10
☐	104	Jeff Kealty, PRO-AM	.10
☐	105	Alexander Kharlamov, Rus.	.10
☐	106	Stanislav Neckar, Cze.	.10
☐	107	Tom O'Connor, PRO-AM	.10
☐	108	Jeff O'Neill, Guelph	.10
☐	109	Deron Quint, PRO-AM	.10
☐	110	Vadim Sharifianov, Rus.	.10
☐	111	Oleg Tverdovsky, Rus.	.25
☐	112	Manon Rhéaume, Atlanta	2.00
☐	113	Paul Kariya, Cdn.	1.50
☐	114	Alexandre Daigle, Victorianville	.25
☐	115	Jeff O'Neill, Guelph	.25
☐	116	Mike Bossy, NYI.	.50
☐	117	Pavel Bure, USSR	.75
☐	118	Chris Chelios, Wisconsin	.35
☐	119	Doug Gilmour, Cornwall	.35
☐	120	Roman Hamrlik, Atlanta	.25
☐	121	Jari Kurri, Fin.	.25
☐	122	Alexander Mogilny, USSR	.50
☐	123	Félix Potvin (G), St. John's	.60
☐	124	Teemu Selänne, Fin.	.75
☐	125	Tommy Soderström (G), Hershey	.10
☐	126	Mike Bales (G), Providence	.10
☐	127	Jozef Cierny, Rochester	.10
☐	128	Ivan Droppa, Indianapolis	.10
☐	129	Anders Eriksson, Adirondack	.25
☐	130	Anatoli Fedotov, Moncton	.10
☐	131	Martin Gendron, Baltimore	.10
☐	132	Daniel Guérard, New Haven	.10
☐	133	Corey Hirsch (G), Binghampton	.10
☐	134	Milos Holan, Hershey	.10
☐	135	Kenny Jonsson, St. John's	.10
☐	136	Steven King, Binghampton	.10
☐	137	Alexei Kovalev, Binghampton	.10
☐	138	Sergei Krivokrasov, IHL All-Star	.10
☐	139	Mats Lindgren, Moncton	.10
☐	140	Grant Marshall,	.10
☐	141	Jesper Mattsson, Las Vegas	.10
☐	142	Sandy McCarthy, Salt Lake	.10
☐	143	Dean Melanson, Rochester	.10
☐	144	Robert Petrovicky	.10
☐	145	Mike Rathje, Kansas City	.10
☐	146	Manon Rhéaume (G), Atlanta	3.00
☐	147	Claude Savoie, New Haven	.10
☐	148	Mikhail Shtalenkov (G), Milwaukee	.10
☐	149	Manon Rhéaume (G), Atlanta	3.00
☐	150	Manon Rhéaume (Up Close) (G)	3.00
	No.	**Acetate Insert**	**NRMT-MT**
☐	MR1	Manon Rhéaume (G), Atlanta	25.00
		Autographs	**NRMT-MT**
☐		Mike Bossy (#/975)	35.00
☐		Pavel Bure (#/900)	75.00
☐		Chris Chelios (#/1,800)	35.00
☐		Doug Gilmour (#/1,850)	25.00
☐		Alexander Mogilny (#/950)	30.00
☐		Jim Montgomery (#/1,800)	5.00
☐		Rob Niedermayer (#/2,500)	20.00
☐		Jeff O'Neill (#/2,225)	20.00
☐		Pat Peake (#/790)	10.00
☐		Mark Recchi (#/1,725)	25.00
☐		Manon Rhéaume (G) (#/1,500)	125.00
☐		Geoff Sanderson (#/875)	15.00

CLASS OF 1994

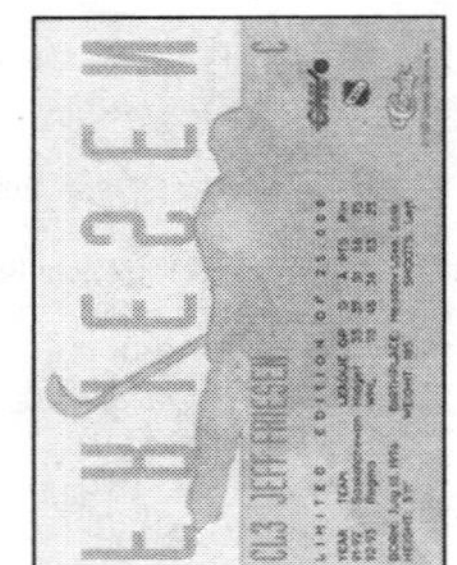

Insert Set (7 cards): 15.00

	No.	Player	NRMT-MT
☐	CL1	Jeff O'Neill, Guelph	4.00
☐	CL2	Jason Bonsignore	2.00
☐	CL3	Jeff Friesen, Regina	4.00
☐	CL4	Radek Bonk, Las Vegas	2.00
☐	CL5	Deron Quint	2.00
☐	CL6	Vadim Sharifjanov	2.00
☐	CL7	Tom O'Connor, PRO-AM	2.00

CRASH NUMBERED

Insert Set (10 cards): 100.00

	No.	Player	NRMT-MT
☐	N1	Alexandre Daigle, Victoriaville	5.00
☐	N2	Paul Kariya, Cdn.	30.00
☐	N3	Jeff O'Neill, Guelph	5.00
☐	N4	Jason Bonsignore, Newmarket	4.00
☐	N5	Teemu Selänne, Fin.	15.00
☐	N6	Pavel Bure, USSR	15.00
☐	N7	Alexandre Mogilny, USSR	6.00
☐	N8	Manon Rhéaume (G), Atlanta	30.00
☐	N9	Félix Potvin (G), St. John's	10.00
☐	N10	Radek Bonk, Las Vegas	4.00

TEAM CANADA

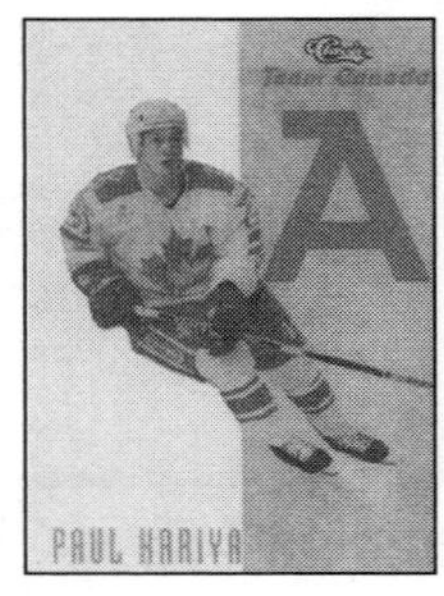

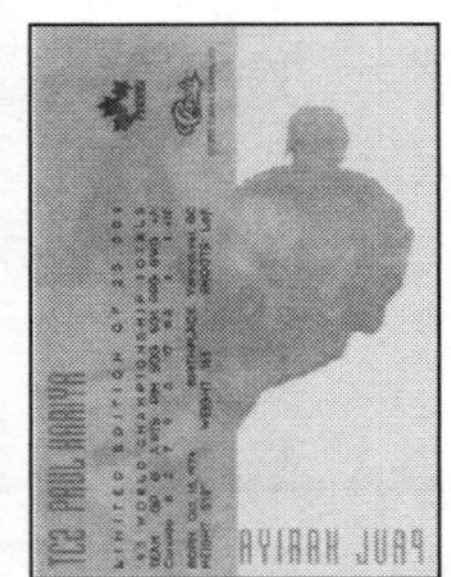

Insert Set (7 cards): 18.00

	No.	Player	NRMT-MT
☐	TC1	Greg Johnson, Cdn.	2.00
☐	TC2	Paul Kariya, Cdn.	10.00
☐	TC3	Brian Savage, Cdn.	2.00
☐	TC4	Bill Ranford (G), Cdn.	4.00
☐	TC5	Mark Recchi, Cdn.	4.00
☐	TC6	Geoff Sanderson, Cdn.	2.00
☐	TC7	Adam Graves, Cdn.	2.00

TOP TEN

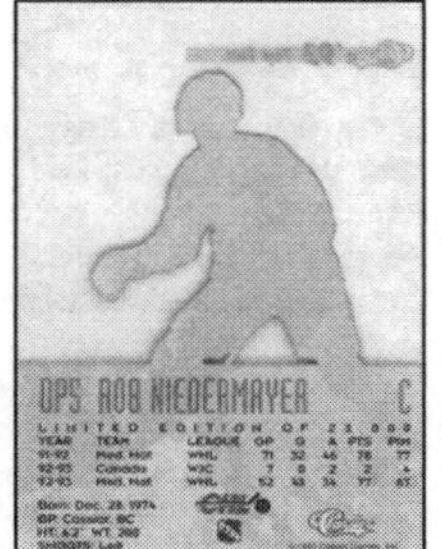

Insert Set (10 cards): 20.00

	No.	Player	NRMT-MT
☐	DP1	Alexandre Daigle, Victoriaville	2.00
☐	DP2	Chris Pronger, Peterborough	2.00
☐	DP3	Chris Gratton, Kingston	2.00
☐	DP4	Paul Kariya, Cdn.	10.00
☐	DP5	Rob Niedermayer, CHL All-Stars	2.00
☐	DP6	Viktor Kozlov, Russia	1.00
☐	DP7	Jason Arnott, Oshawa	2.00
☐	DP8	Niklas Sundstrom, Binghampton	1.00
☐	DP9	Todd Harvey, Detroit	1.00
☐	DP10	Jocelyn Thibault (G), CHL All-Stars	3.00

1993 - 94 CLASSIC FOUR-SPORT

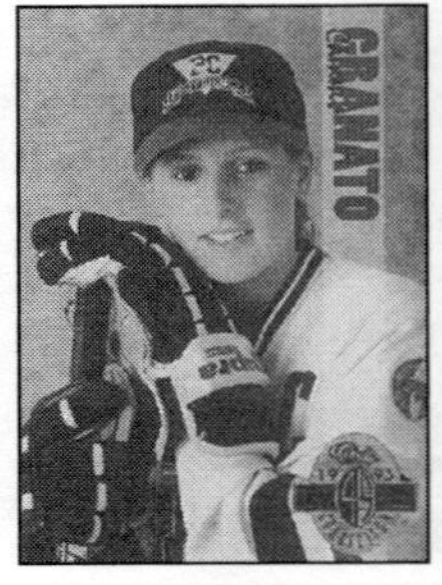

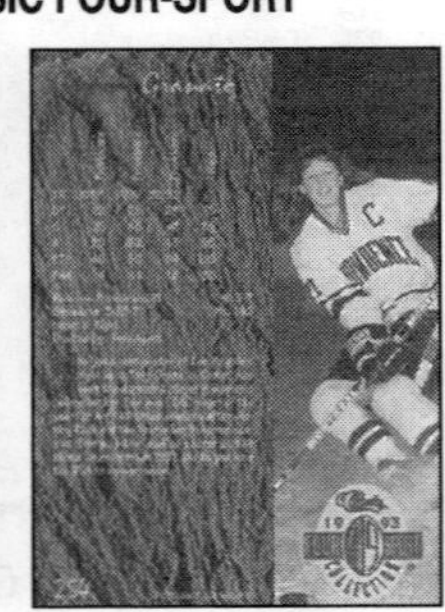

This 325-card four-sport set features 75 hockey players. Each card has two versions: the regular card and a gold parallel. A 325-card set sells at $15.

Imprint: © 1993 Classic Games, Inc.

	No.	Player	NRMT-MT
☐	185	Alexandre Daigle, Victoriaville	.35
☐	186	Chris Pronger	.35
☐	187	Chris Gratton	.35
☐	188	Paul Kariya	2.00
☐	189	Rob Niedermayer	.25
☐	190	Viktor Kozlov	.10
☐	191	Jason Arnott	.50
☐	192	Niklas Sundstrom, Binghampton	.10
☐	193	Todd Havery, Detroit-OHL	.25
☐	194	Jocelyn Thibault (G)	.75
☐	195	Kenny Jonsson, St. John's	.10
☐	196	Denis Pederson	.10
☐	197	Adam Deadmarsh	.25
☐	198	Mats Lindgren, Moncton	.10
☐	199	Nick Stajduhar	.10
☐	200	Jason Allison	.75
☐	201	Jesper Mattsson, Las Vegas	.10
☐	202	Saku Koivu	1.25
☐	203	Anders Eriksson	.25
☐	204	Todd Bertuzzi, Guelph	.25
☐	205	Eric Lecompte	.10
☐	206	Nikolai Tsulygin	.10
☐	207	Janne Niinimaa	.50
☐	208	Maxim Bets	.10
☐	209	Rory Fitzpatrick	.10
☐	210	Eric Manlow	.10
☐	211	David Roche, Peterborough	.10
☐	212	Vladimir Chebaturkin	.10
☐	213	Bill McCauley	.10
☐	214	Chad Lang	.10
☐	215	Cosmo Dupaul	.10
☐	216	Bob Wren, Detroit-OHL	.10
☐	217	Chris Simon	.25
☐	218	Ryan Brown, Swift Current	.10
☐	219	Mikhail Shtalenkov (G)	.10
☐	220	Vladimir Krechin, Rus.	.10
☐	221	Jason Saal (G), Detroit-OHL	.10
☐	222	Dion Darling, Spokane	.10
☐	223	Chris Kelleher, PRO-AM	.10
☐	224	Antti Aalto	.10
☐	225	Alain Nasreddine, Drummondville	.10
☐	226	Paul Vincent, PRO-AM	.10
☐	227	Manny Legacé (G)	.10
☐	228	Igor Chibirev	.10
☐	229	Tom Noble (G), PRO-AM	.10
☐	230	Mike Bales (G)	.10
☐	231	Jozef Cierny	.10
☐	232	Ivan Droppa	.10
☐	233	Anatoli Fedotov	.10
☐	234	Martin Gendron	.10
☐	235	Daniel Guerard	.10
☐	236	Corey Hirsch (G)	.10
☐	237	Steven King	.10
☐	238	Sergei Krivokrasov	.10
☐	239	Darrin Madeley (G), New Haven	.10
☐	240	Grant Marshall	.10
☐	241	Sandy McCarthy	.10
☐	242	Bill McDougall, Cape Breton	.10
☐	243	Dean Melanson	.10

☐	244	Roman Oksiuta, Cape Breton	.10
☐	245	Robert Petrovicky	.10
☐	246	Mike Rathje	.10
☐	247	Eldon Reddick (G), Fort Wayne	.10
☐	248	Andrei Trefilov (G)	.10
☐	249	Jiri Slegr	.10
☐	250	Leonid Toropchenko, Springfield	.10
☐	251	Dody Wood	.10
☐	252	Kevin Paden	.10
☐	253	Manon Rhéaume (G)	3.00
☐	254	Cammi Granato	1.50
☐	255	Patrick Charboneaum, Victoriaville	.10
☐	256	Curtis Bowen	.10
☐	257	Kevin Brown	.10
☐	258	Valeri Bure	.25
☐	259	Janne Laukkanen, Fin.	.10

AUTOGRAPHS

This 30-card four-sport insert set features five hockey players.

	Player	NRMT-MT
☐	Adam Deadmarsh (#/4250)	15.00
☐	Chris Gratton (#/3900)	25.00
☐	Rob Niedermayer (#/4500)	15.00
☐	Denis Pederson (#/2050)	5.00
☐	Manon Rhéaume (#/1250)	150.00

ACETATE

This 12-card four-sport insert set features only two hockey players. A 12-card set sells at $50.

	No.	Player	NRMT-MT
☐	11	Alexandre Daigle	3.00
☐	12	Chris Pronger	3.00

DRAFT STARS

This 20-card four-sport insert set (DS41-DS60) features three hockey players. A 20-card set sells at $20.

	No.	Player	NRMT-MT
☐	DS58	Alexandre Daigle	.75
☐	DS59	Chris Pronger	.75
☐	DS60	Chris Gratton	.75

LIMITED PRINT

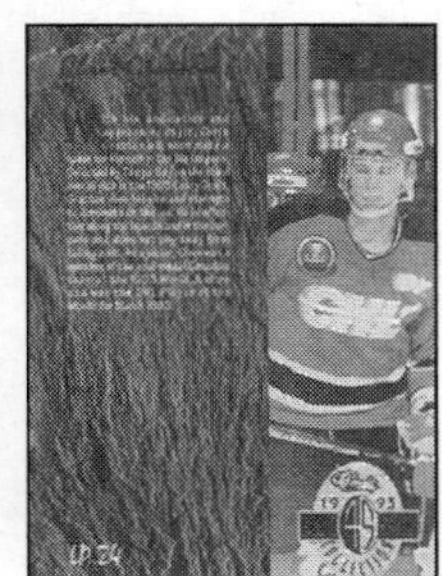

This 25-card four-sport insert set features four hockey players. A 25-card set sells at $35.

	No.	Player	NRMT-MT
☐	LP22	Alexandre Daigle	1.50
☐	LP23	Chris Pronger	1.50
☐	LP24	Chris Gratton	1.50
☐	LP25	Paul Kariya	8.00

POWER PICKS

This 20-card four-sport insert set features three hockey players. A 20-card set sells at $20.

	No.	Player	NRMT-MT
☐	PP18	Alexandre Daigle	1.00
☐	PP19	Chris Pronger	1.00
☐	PP20	Chris Gratton	1.00

TRI CARDS

This five-card four-sport insert set features only one hockey trio.

	No.	Player	NRMT-MT
☐	TC4	A. Daigle/C. Pronger/C. Gratton	4.00

1993 - 94 CLASSIC IMAGES FOUR SPORT

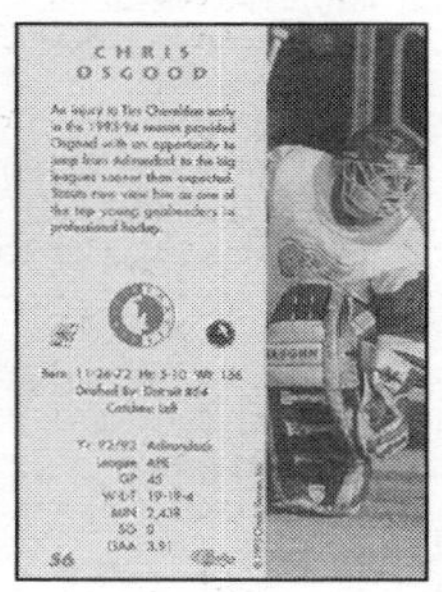

This 150-card four sport set features only 29 hockey players. A 150-card set sells at $15.

Imprint:

	No.	Player	NRMT-MT
☐	4	Alexandre Daigle	.35
☐	8	Chris Pronger, Peterborough	.35
☐	16	Jim Montgomery, Maine	.20
☐	17	Todd Marchant, USA.	.20
☐	20	Mike Dunham (G), USA.	.35
☐	21	Garth Snow (G), USA.	.35
☐	24	Barry Richter, Wisconsin	.20
☐	28	Matt Martin, USA.	.20
☐	30	Rob Niedermayer, CHL All-Stars	.35
☐	32	Jesse Belanger, Fredericton	.20
☐	35	Peter Ferraro USA.	.20
☐	38	Ted Drury, USA.	.20
☐	43	Derek Plante	.35
☐	46	Jim Campbell, USA.	.35
☐	56	Chris Osgood (G), Adirondack	1.00
☐	62	Jason Arnott, Oshawa	.50
☐	74	Jocelyn Thibault (G), Sherbrooke	1.00
☐	86	Chris Gratton, Kingston	.35
☐	92	Mike Rathje, Kansas City	.20
☐	101	Martin Brodeur (G)	1.50
☐	106	Paul Kariya, Cdn.	2.00
☐	111	Manon Rhéaume (G)	3.00
☐	121	Félix Potvin (G)	1.00
☐	125	Alexei Yashin	.50
☐	130	Alexei Yashin, Rus.	.50
☐	135	Chris Pronger	.35
☐	138	Chris Gratton, Kingston	.35
☐	142	Jason Arnott	.50
☐	147	Manon Rhéaume (G)	3.00

CHROME

This 20-card four sport insert set features only four hockey players.

	No.	Player	NRMT-MT
☐	CC13	Alexei Yashin	6.00
☐	CC14	Alexandre Daigle	4.00
☐	CC15	Manon Rhéaume (G)	15.00
☐	CC16	Radek Bonk	3.00

SUDDEN IMPACT

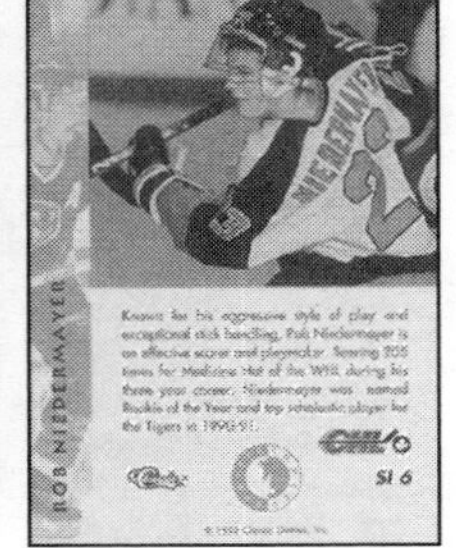

This 20-card four sport insert set features only three hockey players. A 20-card set sells at $15.

	No.	Player	NRMT-MT
☐	SI6	Rob Niedermayer	.75
☐	SI7	Jocelyn Thibault (G)	1.00
☐	SI8	Derek Plante	.25

1993 - 94 CLASSIC PRO PROSPECTS

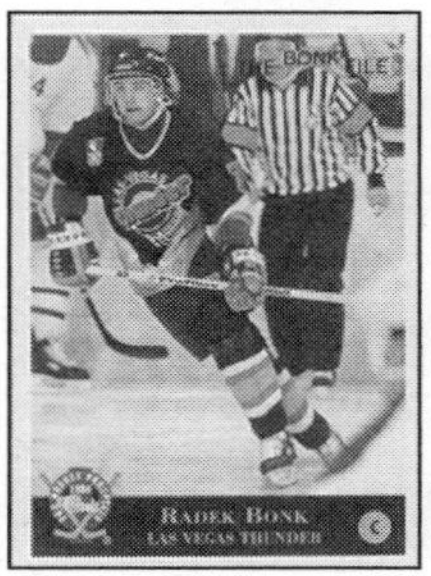

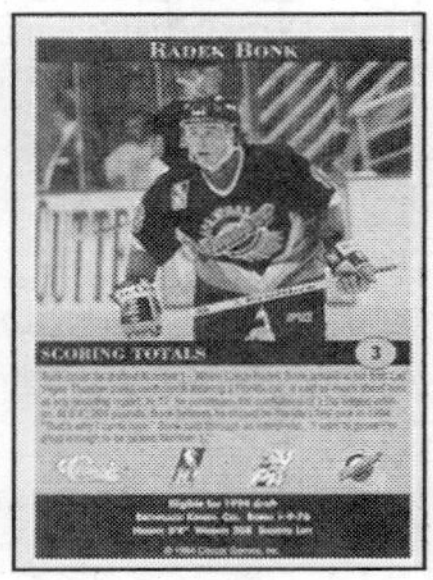

Imprint: © 1994 Classic Games, Inc.

Complete Set (250 cards): 15.00

Common Player: .10

	No.	Player	NRMT-MT
☐	1	Radek Bonk, Las Vegas	.25
☐	2	Radek Bonk, Las Vegas	.25
☐	3	Radek Bonk, Las Vegas	.25
☐	4	Vlastimil Kroupa	.10
☐	5	Mattias Norstrom	.10
☐	6	Jaroslav Nedved, Cincinnati	.10
☐	7	Steve Dubinsky	.10
☐	8	Christian Proulx	.10
☐	9	Michal Grosek	.10
☐	10	Pat Neaton	.10
☐	11	Jason Arnott	.50
☐	12	Martin Brodeur (G)	1.00
☐	13	Alexandre Daigle	.25
☐	14	Ted Drury	.10
☐	15	Iain Fraser	.10
☐	16	Chris Gratton	.35
☐	17	Greg Johnson	.10
☐	18	Paul Kariya	2.00
☐	19	Alexander Karpovtsev	.10
☐	20	Chris LiPuma	.10
☐	21	Kirk Maltby	.10
☐	22	Sandy McCarthy	.10
☐	23	Darren McCarty	.25
☐	24	Jaroslav Modry	.10
☐	25	Jim Montgomery	.10
☐	26	Markus Naslund	.10
☐	27	Rob Niedermayer	.25
☐	28	Chris Osgood (G)	.75
☐	29	Pat Peake	.10
☐	30	Derek Plante	.25
☐	31	Chris Pronger	.35
☐	32	Mike Rathje	.10
☐	33	Mikael Renberg, Swe.	.25
☐	34	Damian Rhodes (G)	.25
☐	35	Garth Snow (G)	.25
☐	36	Cam Stewart	.10
☐	37	Jim Storm, USA.	.10
☐	38	Michal Sykora	.10
☐	39	Jocelyn Thibault (G)	.75
☐	40	Alexei Yashin	.50
☐	41	Checklist 1 (1 - 84)	.10
☐	42	Vesa Viitakoski	.10
☐	43	Jake Grimes	.10
☐	44	Jim Dowd	.10
☐	45	Craig Ferguson	.10
☐	46	Mike Boback	.10
☐	47	François Groleau	.10
☐	48	Juha Riihijarvi, Cape Breton	.10
☐	49	Mikhail Shtalenkov (G)	.10
☐	50	Zigmund Palffy	.50
☐	51	Félix Potvin (G), Tor.	.75
☐	52	Alexei Kovalev, NYR.	.10
☐	53	Larry Robinson, Mtl.	.50
☐	54	John LeClair, Mtl.	.75
☐	55	Dominic Roussel (G)	.10
☐	56	Geoff Sanderson, Hfd.	.25
☐	57	Greg Pankewicz, P.E.I.	.10
☐	58	Brent Bilodeau	.10
☐	59	Brandon Convery	.10
☐	60	Fred Knipscheer	.10
☐	61	Igor Chibirev	.10
☐	62	Anatoli Fedotov	.10
☐	63	Bob Kellogg, Indianapolis	.10
☐	64	Mike Maurice	.10

	No.	Player	NRMT-MT
☐	65	Chad Penney	.10
☐	66	Mike Bavis, Rochester	.10
☐	67	Eric Veilleux, Cornwall	.10
☐	68	Parris Duffus (G), Peoria	.10
☐	69	Daniel Lacroix, Binghampton	.10
☐	70	Milos Holan, Hershey	.10
☐	71	Mike Muller, Moncton	.10
☐	72	Michah Aivazoff, Adirondack	.10
☐	73	Krzysztop Oliwa, Albany	.10
☐	74	Ryan Hughes, Cornwall	.10
☐	75	Christian Soucy (G), Indianapolis	.10
☐	76	Keith Redmond, Phoenix	.10
☐	77	Mark DeSantis	.10
☐	78	Craig Martin	.10
☐	79	Mike Kennedy, Kalamazoo	.10
☐	80	Pauli Jaks (G)	.10
☐	81	Colin Chin, Fort Wayne	.10
☐	82	Jody Gage	.10
☐	83	Don Biggs, Cincinnati	.10
☐	84	Tim Tookey, Hershey	.10
☐	85	Clint Malarchuk (G)	.10
☐	86	Jozef Cierny	.10
☐	87	Radek Hamr	.10
☐	88	Jason Dawe	.10
☐	89	Chris Longo	.10
☐	90	Brian Rolston	.10
☐	91	Mike McKee	.10
☐	92	Vitali Prokhorov	.10
☐	93	Chris Snell	.10
☐	94	Martin Brochu (G)	.10
☐	95	Dan Plante	.10
☐	96	Darcy Werenka	.10
☐	97	Steffon Walby, St. John's	.10
☐	98	David Emma	.10
☐	99	Dan Stiver, St. John's	.10
☐	100	Radek Bonk	.25
☐	101	Mark Visheau	.10
☐	102	Dean Melanson	.10
☐	103	Vladimir Tsyplakov, Fort Wayne	.10
☐	104	Mikhail Volkov, Rochester	.10
☐	105	Aaron Miller, Cornwall	.10
☐	106	Alexei Kudashov	.10
☐	107	Shawn Rivers	.10
☐	108	Ladislav Karabin	.10
☐	109	Matt Mallgrave	.10
☐	110	Craig Darby	.10
☐	111	Marcel Cousineau (G)	.10
☐	112	Jamie McLennan (G)	.25
☐	113	Yanic Perreault	.25
☐	114	Zac Boyer, Indianapolis	.10
☐	115	Sergei Zubov	.25
☐	116	Dan Kesa	.10
☐	117	Jim Hiller	.10
☐	118	Dmitri Starostenko	.10
☐	119	Chris Tamer	.10
☐	120	Aaron Ward	.25
☐	121	Claude Savoie	.10
☐	122	Jamie Black	.10
☐	123	Jean-François Jomphe	.10
☐	124	Paxton Schulte	.10
☐	125	Jarkko Varvio	.10
☐	126	Jaroslav Otevrel	.10
☐	127	Dane Jackson, Hamilton	.10
☐	128	Brent Grieve	.10
☐	129	CL: Rhéaume Family	1.50
☐	130	René Corbet	.10
☐	131	Joe Frederick	.10
☐	132	Martin Tanguay, Atlanta	.10
☐	133	Fredrik Jax	.10
☐	134	Jamie Linden, Cincinnati	.10
☐	135	Jason Smith	.10
☐	136	Rick Kowalsky	.10
☐	137	Dino Grossi, Indianapolis	.10
☐	138	Aris Brimanis, Hershey	.10
☐	130	Jeff McLean	.10
☐	140	Tyler Wright	.10
☐	141	Roman Gorev, Providence	.10
☐	142	Dean Hulett	.10
☐	143	Niklas Sundblad	.10
☐	144	Jeff Bes	.10
☐	145	Pascal Rhéaume, Albany	.10
☐	146	Donald Brashear	.10
☐	147	Hugo Belanger, Indianapolis	.10
☐	148	Blair Scott	.10
☐	149	Steve Staios, Peoria	.10
☐	150	Matt Martin	.10
☐	151	Richard Matvichuk	.10
☐	152	Paul Brousseau	.10
☐	153	Evgeny Namestnikov	.10
☐	154	Michael Peca	.50
☐	155	Jeff Nelson	.10
☐	156	Greg Andrusak, Cleveland	.10
☐	157	Norm Batherson, P.E.I.	.10
☐	158	Martin Bakula, Cape Breton	.10
☐	159	Ed Patterson	.10
☐	160	Steve Larouche	.10
☐	161	Libor Polasek, Hamilton	.10
☐	162	Jon Hillebrandt (G)	.10
☐	163	Guy Lévesque	.10
☐	164	Eric Lacroix	.10
☐	165	Scott Walker	.10
☐	166	Robert Burakovsky	.10
☐	167	Markus Ketterer (G)	.10
☐	168	Mike Speer	.10
☐	169	Martin Jiranek	.10
☐	170	Andy Schneider, P.E.I.	.10
☐	171	Terry Hollinger	.10
☐	172	Mark Lawrence	.10
☐	173	Martin Lapointe	.10
☐	174	Vaclav Prospal	.50
☐	175	Mike Fountain (G)	.25
☐	176	Alexander Kerch	.10
☐	177	Oleg Petrov	.10
☐	178	Derek Armstrong	.10
☐	179	Matthew Barnaby	.10
☐	180	Andrei Nazarov	.10
☐	181	Andrei Trefilov (G)	.10
☐	182	Jean-Yves Roy	.10
☐	183	Boris Rousson (G)	.10
☐	184	Daniel Laperrière, Peoria	.10
☐	185	Yan Kaminsky	.10
☐	186	Ralph Intranuovo	.10
☐	187	Sandy Moger	.10
☐	188	Grant Marshall	.10
☐	189	Denny Felsner	.10
☐	190	Cory Stillman	.10
☐	191	Eric Lavigne	.10
☐	192	Jarrod Skalde	.10
☐	193	Steve Junker	.10
☐	194	Alexander Cherbayev	.10
☐	195	Nathan Lafayette	.10
☐	196	Ed Ward, Cornwall	.10
☐	197	Harijs Vitolinsh	.10
☐	198	Jarmo Kekäläinen	.10
☐	199	Neil Eisenhut, Hamilton	.10
☐	200	Radek Bonk	.25
☐	201	Jason Bonsignore	.10
☐	202	Jeff Friesen	.25
☐	203	Ed Jovanovski	.50
☐	204	Brett Lindros, Cdn.	.25
☐	205	Jeff O'Neill	.25
☐	206	Deron Quint	.10
☐	207	Vadim Sharifjanov	.10
☐	208	Oleg Tverdovsky	.25
☐	209	CL: Jeff Friesen/Jeff O'Neill	.25
☐	210	David Cooper, Rochester	.10
☐	211	Doug MacDonald	.10
☐	212	Leonid Toropchenko	.10
☐	213	Chris Rogles (G)	.10
☐	214	Vyacheslav Kozlov, Adirondack	.10
☐	215	Denis Metlyuk, Hersey	.10
☐	216	Scott McKay	.10
☐	217	Brian Loney	.10
☐	218	Kevin Hodson (G)	.25
☐	219	Bobby House	.10
☐	220	Sergei Krivokrasov, Indianapolis	.10
☐	221	Brett Harkins, Adirondack	.10
☐	222	Cale Hulse	.10
☐	223	Marc Tardif, Atlanta	.10
☐	224	Jon Rohloff	.10
☐	225	Kevin Smyth	.10
☐	226	Jason Young	.10
☐	227	Sergei Zholtok	.10
☐	228	Todd Simon	.10
☐	229	Jerome Bechard	.10
☐	230	Matt Robbins, Charlotte	.10
☐	231	Joe Cook, Columbus	.10
☐	232	John Brill, Dayton	.10
☐	233	Dan Goldie, Erie	.10
☐	234	Dan Gravelle, Greensboro	.10
☐	235	Shawn Wheeler, Hampton	.10
☐	236	Brad Harrison, Huntington	.10
☐	237	Joe Dragon, Huntsville	.10
☐	238	Jason Jennings, Johnstown	.10
☐	239	Manon Rhéaume (G)	3.00
☐	240	Jamie Steer, Louisville	.10
☐	241	Scott Rogers, Nashville	.10
☐	242	Lyle Wildgoose, Raleigh	.10
☐	243	Darren Colbourne, Richmond	.10
☐	244	Mike Smith, Roanoke	.10
☐	245	Chris Bright, South Carolina	.10
☐	246	Chris Belanger, Toledo	.10
☐	247	Darren Schwartz	.10
☐	248	Cammi Granato	1.50
☐	249	Erin Whitten (G)	1.00
☐	250	Manon Rhéaume (G)	3.00

		Autographs	**NRMT-MT**
☐		Radek Bonk (#/2,400)	15.00
☐		Jason Bonsignore (#/2,450)	5.00
☐		Jeff Friesen (#/2,450)	20.00
☐		Joé Juneau (#/1,370)	15.00
☐		Alexei Kovalev (#/1,900)	10.00
☐		Chris Pronger (#/1,400)	15.00
☐		Manon Rhéaume (G) (#/1,900)	100.00
☐		Erin Whitten (G) (#/1,800)	30.00
☐		Alexei Yashin (#/1,400)	30.00

ICE AMBASSADORS

Insert Set (20 cards):

	No.	Player	NRMT-MT
☐	IA1	Adrian Aucoin, Cdn.	.50
☐	IA2	Corey Hirsch (G), Cdn.	.75
☐	IA3	Paul Kariya, Cdn.	5.00
☐	IA4	David Harlock, Cdn.	.50
☐	IA5	Manny Legacé (G), Cdn.	.75
☐	IA6	Chris Therien, Cdn.	.50
☐	IA7	Todd Warriner, Cdn.	.50
☐	IA8	Todd Marchant, USA.	.75
☐	IA9	Matt Martin, USA.	.50
☐	IA10	Peter Ferraro, USA.	.50
☐	IA11	Brian Rolston, USA.	.75
☐	IA12	Jim Campbell, USA.	.75
☐	IA13	Mike Dunham (G), USA.	.50
☐	IA14	Craig Johnson, USA.	.50
☐	IA15	Saku Koivu, Fin.	2.75
☐	IA16	Jere Lehtinen, Fin.	.75
☐	IA17	Viktor Kozlov, CIS.	.50
☐	IA18	Andrei Nikolishin, CIS.	.50
☐	IA19	Sergei Gonchar, CIS.	.50
☐	IA20	Valeri Karpov, CIS.	.50

INTERNATIONAL HEROES

Insert Set (25 cards): 50.00

	No.	Player	NRMT-MT
☐	LP1	Jim Campbell, USA.	2.50
☐	LP2	Ted Drury, USA.	1.50
☐	LP3	Mike Dunham (G), USA.	1.50
☐	LP4	Chris Ferraro, USA.	1.50
☐	LP5	Peter Ferraro, USA.	1.50
☐	LP6	Darby Hendrickson, USA.	1.50
☐	LP7	Craig Johnson, USA.	1.50
☐	LP8	Todd Marchant, USA.	2.50
☐	LP9	Matt Martin, USA.	1.50
☐	LP10	Brian Rolston, USA.	2.50
☐	LP11	Adrian Aucoin, Cdn.	1.50
☐	LP12	Martin Gendron, Cdn.	1.50
☐	LP13	David Harlock, Cdn.	1.50
☐	LP14	Corey Hirsch (G), Cdn.	2.50
☐	LP15	Paul Kariya, Cdn.	12.00
☐	LP16	Manny Legacé (G), Cdn.	1.50
☐	LP17	Brett Lindros, Cdn.	2.50

	No.	Player	NRMT-MT
☐	LP18	Brian Savage, Cdn.	2.50
☐	LP19	Chris Terrien, Cdn.	1.50
☐	LP20	Todd Warriner, Cdn.	1.50
☐	LP21	Radek Bonk	2.50
☐	LP22	Pavel Bure	7.00
☐	LP23	Teemu Selänne	7.00
☐	LP24	Mark Recchi	2.50
☐	LP25	Alexei Yashin	4.00

1993 - 94 DONRUSS

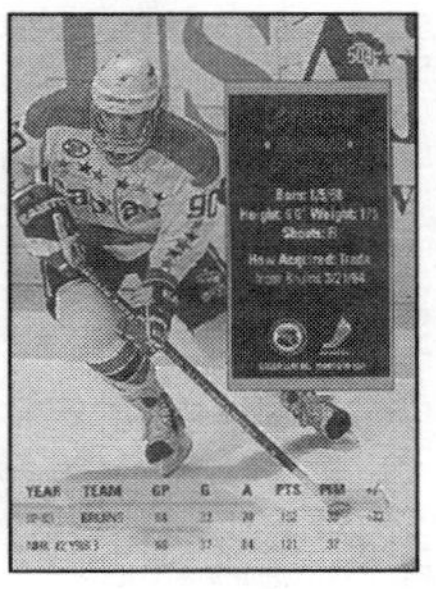

Imprint: 1993 LEAF INC.

Series One Set (400 cards):			**32.00**
Update Set (110 cards):			**8.00**
Common Player:			**.15**
	No.	**Player**	**NRMT-MT**
☐	1	Steven King, Ana.	.15
☐	2	Joe Sacco, Ana.	.15
☐	3	Anatoli Semenov, Ana.	.15
☐	4	Terry Yake, Ana.	.15
☐	5	Alexei Kasatonov, Ana.	.15
☐	**6**	**Patrik Carnback, Ana., RC**	**.15**
☐	7	Sean Hill, Ana.	.15
☐	8	Bill Houlder, Ana.	.15
☐	9	Todd Ewen, Ana.	.15
☐	10	Bob Corkum, Ana.	.15
☐	11	Tim Sweeney, Ana.	.15
☐	12	Ron Tugnutt (G), Ana.	.15
☐	13	Guy Hebert (G), Ana.	.25
☐	14	Shaun Van Allen, Ana.	.15
☐	15	Stu Grimson, Ana.	.15
☐	16	Jon Casey (G), Bos.	.15
☐	17	Daniel Marois, Bos.	.15
☐	18	Adam Oates, Bos.	.35
☐	19	Glen Wesley, Bos.	.15
☐	**20**	**Cam Stewart, Bos., RC**	**.15**
☐	21	Don Sweeney, Bos.	.15
☐	22	Glen Murray, Bos.	.15
☐	23	Jozef Stumpel, Bos.	.15
☐	24	Ray Bourque, Bos.	.50
☐	25	Ted Donato, Bos.	.15
☐	26	Joé Juneau, Bos.	.15
☐	27	Dmitri Kvartalnov, Bos.	.15
☐	28	Steve Leach, Bos.	.15
☐	29	Cam Neely, Bos.	.25
☐	30	Bryan Smolinski, Bos.	.15
☐	31	Craig Simpson, Buf.	.15
☐	32	Donald Audette, Buf.	.15
☐	33	Doug Bodger, Buf.	.15
☐	34	Grant Fuhr (G), Buf.	.25
☐	35	Dale Hawerchuk, Buf.	.25
☐	36	Yuri Khmylev, Buf.	.15
☐	37	Pat LaFontaine, Buf.	.25
☐	38	Brad May, Buf.	.15
☐	39	Alexander Mogilny, Buf.	.35
☐	40	Richard Smehlik, Buf.	.15
☐	41	Petr Svoboda, Buf.	.15
☐	42	Matthew Barnaby, Buf.	.15
☐	**43**	**Sergei Petrenko, Buf., RC**	**.15**
☐	44	Mark Astley, Buf.	.15
☐	**45**	**Derek Plante, Buf., RC**	**.25**
☐	46	Theoren Fleury, Cgy.	.35
☐	47	Al MacInnis, Cgy.	.25
☐	48	Joe Nieuwendyk, Cgy.	.25
☐	49	Joel Otto, Cgy.	.15
☐	50	Paul Ranheim, Cgy.	.15
☐	51	Robert Reichel, Cgy.	.15
☐	52	Gary Roberts, Cgy.	.25
☐	53	Gary Suter, Cgy.	.15
☐	54	Mike Vernon (G), Cgy.	.25
☐	55	Kelly Kisio, Cgy.	.15
☐	**56**	**German Titov, Cgy., RC**	**.15**
☐	57	Wes Walz, Cgy.	.15
☐	**58**	**Ted Drury, Cgy., RC**	**.15**
☐	59	Sandy McCarthy, Cgy.	.15
☐	**60**	**Vesa Viitakoski, Cgy., RC**	**.15**
☐	61	Jeff Hackett (G), Chi.	.25
☐	62	Neil Wilkinson, Chi.	.15
☐	63	Dirk Graham, Chi.	.15
☐	64	Ed Belfour (G), Chi.	.35
☐	65	Chris Chelios, Chi.	.35
☐	66	Joe Murphy, Chi.	.15
☐	67	Jeremy Roenick, Chi.	.35
☐	68	Steve Smith, Chi.	.15
☐	69	Brent Sutter, Chi.	.15
☐	**70**	**Steve Dubinsky, Chi., RC**	**.15**
☐	71	Michel Goulet, Chi.	.25
☐	72	Christian Ruuttu, Chi.	.15
☐	73	Bryan Marchment, Chi.	.15
☐	74	Sergei Krivokrasov, Chi.	.15
☐	**75**	**Jeff Shantz, Chi., RC**	**.15**
☐	76	Mike Modano, Dal.	.50
☐	77	Derian Hatcher, Dal.	.25
☐	78	Ulf Dahlen, Dal.	.15
☐	79	Mark Tinordi, Dal.	.15
☐	80	Russ Courtnall, Dal.	.15
☐	81	Mike Craig, Dal.	.15
☐	82	Trent Klatt, Dal.	.15
☐	83	Dave Gagner, Dal.	.15
☐	**84**	**Chris Tancill, Dal., RC**	**.15**
☐	85	James Black, Dal.	.15
☐	86	Dean Evason, Dal.	.15
☐	87	Andy Moog (G), Dal.	.25
☐	88	Paul Cavallini, Dal.	.15
☐	89	Grant Ledyard, Dal.	.15
☐	90	Jarkko Varvio, Dal.	.15
☐	91	Vyacheslav Kozlov, Det.	.15
☐	92	Mike Sillinger, Det.	.15
☐	**93**	**Aaron Ward, Det., RC**	**.25**
☐	94	Greg Johnson, Det.	.15
☐	95	Steve Yzerman, Det.	1.50
☐	96	Tim Cheveldae (G), Det.	.15
☐	97	Steve Chiasson, Det.	.15
☐	98	Dino Ciccarelli, Det.	.25
☐	99	Paul Coffey, Det.	.25
☐	**100**	**Dallas Drake, Det., RC**	**.15**
☐	101	Sergei Fedorov, Det.	.50
☐	102	Nicklas Lidstrom, Det.	.25
☐	**103**	**Darren McCarty, Det., RC**	**.25**
☐	104	Bob Probert, Det.	.15
☐	105	Ray Sheppard, Det.	.15
☐	106	Scott Pearson, Edm.	.15
☐	107	Steven Rice, Edm.	.15
☐	108	Louie DeBrusk, Edm.	.15
☐	109	Dave Manson, Edm.	.15
☐	110	Dean McAmmond, Edm.	.15
☐	**111**	**Roman Oksiuta, Edm., RC**	**.15**
☐	112	Geoff Smith, Edm.	.15
☐	113	Zdeno Ciger, Edm.	.15
☐	114	Shayne Corson, Edm.	.25
☐	115	Luke Richardson, Edm.	.15
☐	116	Igor Kravchuk, Edm.	.15
☐	117	Bill Ranford (G), Edm.	.25
☐	118	Doug Weight, Edm.	.35
☐	**119**	**Fred Brathwaite (G), Edm., RC**	**.15**
☐	**120**	**Jason Arnott, Edm., RC**	**1.50**
☐	121	Tom Fitzgerald, Fla.	.15
☐	122	Mike Hough, Fla.	.15
☐	**123**	**Jesse Belanger, Fla., RC**	**.15**
☐	124	Brian Skrudland, Fla.	.15
☐	125	Dave Lowry, Fla.	.15
☐	126	Scott Mellanby, Fla.	.15
☐	127	Eugeny Davydov, Fla.	.15
☐	128	Andrei Lomakin, Fla.	.15
☐	129	Brian Benning, Fla.	.15
☐	**130**	**Scott Levins, Fla., RC**	**.15**
☐	131	Gord Murphy, Fla.	.15
☐	132	John Vanbiesbrouck (G), Fla.	.75
☐	133	Mark Fitzpatrick (G), Fla.	.15
☐	134	Rob Niedermayer, Fla.	.25
☐	135	Alexander Godynyuk, Fla.	.15
☐	136	Eric Weinrich, Hfd.	.15
☐	137	Mark Greig, Hfd.	.15
☐	138	Jim Sandlak, Hfd.	.15
☐	139	Adam Burt, Hfd.	.15
☐	140	Nick Kypreos, Hfd.	.15
☐	141	Sean Burke (G), Hfd.	.25
☐	142	Andrew Cassels, Hfd.	.15
☐	143	Robert Kron, Hfd.	.15
☐	144	Mikael Nylander, Hfd.	.15
☐	145	Robert Petrovicky, Hfd.	.15
☐	146	Patrick Poulin, Hfd.	.15
☐	147	Geoff Sanderson, Hfd.	.15
☐	148	Pat Verbeek, Hfd.	.15
☐	149	Zarley Zalapski, Hfd.	.15
☐	150	Chris Pronger, Hfd.	.35
☐	151	Jari Kurri, L.A.	.25
☐	152	Wayne Gretzky, L.A.	2.50
☐	153	Patrick Conacher, L.A.	.15
☐	154	Shawn McEachern, L.A.	.15
☐	155	Mike Donnelly, L.A.	.15
☐	156	Warren Rychel, L.A.	.15
☐	157	Gary Shuchuk, L.A.	.15
☐	158	Rob Blake, L.A.	.25
☐	159	Jimmy Carson, L.A.	.15
☐	160	Tony Granato, L.A.	.15
☐	161	Kelly Hrudey (G), L.A.	.15
☐	162	Luc Robitaille, L.A.	.25
☐	163	Tomas Sandström, L.A.	.15
☐	164	Darryl Sydor, L.A.	.15
☐	165	Alexei Zhitnik, L.A.	.15
☐	166	Benoît Brunet, Mtl.	.15
☐	167	Lyle Odelein, Mtl.	.15
☐	168	Kevin Haller, Mtl.	.15
☐	169	Pierre Sévigny, Mtl.	.15
☐	170	Brian Bellows, Mtl.	.15
☐	171	Patrice Brisebois, Mtl.	.15
☐	172	Vincent Damphousse, Mtl.	.35
☐	173	Eric Desjardins, Mtl.	.25
☐	174	Gilbert Dionne, Mtl.	.15
☐	175	Stéphan Lebeau, Mtl.	.15
☐	176	John LeClair, Mtl.	.75
☐	177	Kirk Muller, Mtl.	.15
☐	178	Patrick Roy (G), Mtl.	2.00
☐	179	Mattieu Schneider, Mtl.	.15
☐	180	Peter Popovic, Mtl.	.15
☐	181	Corey Millen, N.J.	.15
☐	**182**	**Jason Smith, N.J., RC**	**.15**
☐	183	Bobby Holik, N.J.	.15
☐	184	John MacLean, N.J.	.15
☐	185	Bruce Driver, N.J.	.15
☐	186	Bill Guerin, N.J.	.25
☐	187	Claude Lemieux, N.J.	.15
☐	188	Bernie Nicholls, N.J.	.15
☐	189	Scott Niedermayer, N.J.	.25
☐	190	Stéphane Richer, N.J.	.15
☐	191	Alexander Semak, N.J.	.15
☐	192	Scott Stevens, N.J.	.25
☐	193	Valeri Zelepukin, N.J.	.15
☐	194	Chris Terreri (G), N.J.	.15
☐	195	Martin Brodeur (G), N.J.	1.00
☐	196	Ron Hextall (G), NYI.	.25
☐	197	Brad Dalgarno, NYI.	.15
☐	198	Ray Ferraro, NYI.	.15
☐	199	Patrick Flatley, NYI.	.15
☐	200	Travis Green, NYI.	.15
☐	201	Benoit Hogue, NYI.	.15
☐	**202**	**Steve Junker, NYI., RC**	**.15**
☐	203	Darius Kasparaitis, NYI.	.15
☐	204	Derek King, NYI.	.15
☐	205	Uwe Krupp, NYI.	.15
☐	206	Scott Lachance, NYI.	.15
☐	207	Vladimir Malakhov, NYI.	.15
☐	208	Steve Thomas, NYI.	.15
☐	209	Pierre Turgeon, NYI.	.25
☐	210	Scott Scissons, NYI.	.15
☐	211	Glenn Healy (G), NYR.	.15
☐	**212**	**Alexander Karpovtsev, NYR., RC**	**.15**
☐	213	James Patrick, NYR.	.15
☐	214	Sergei Nemchinov, NYR.	.15
☐	215	Esa Tikkanen, NYR.	.15
☐	216	Corey Hirsch (G), NYR.	.25
☐	217	Tony Amonte, NYR.	.25
☐	218	Mike Gartner, NYR.	.25
☐	219	Adam Graves, NYR.	.15
☐	220	Alexei Kovalev, NYR.	.15
☐	221	Brian Leetch, NYR.	.35
☐	222	Mark Messier, NYR.	.50
☐	223	Mike Richter (G), NYR.	.35

	No.	Player	Price
☐	224	Darren Turcotte, NYR.	.15
☐	225	Sergei Zubov, NYR.	.25
☐	226	Craig Billington (G), Ott.	.15
☐	227	Troy Mallette, Ott.	.15
☐	228	Vladimir Ruzicka, Ott.	.15
☐	**229**	**Darrin Madeley (G), Ott., RC**	**.15**
☐	230	Mark Lamb, Ott.	.15
☐	231	Dave Archibald, Ott.	.15
☐	232	Bob Kudelski, Ott.	.15
☐	233	Norm Maciver, Ott.	.15
☐	234	Brad Shaw, Ott.	.15
☐	235	Sylvain Turgeon, Ott.	.15
☐	236	Brian Glynn, Ott.	.15
☐	237	Alexandre Daigle, Ott.	.35
☐	238	Alexei Yashin, Ott.	.75
☐	239	Dimitri Filimonov, Ott.	.15
☐	240	Pavol Demitra, Ott.	.15
☐	**241**	**Jason Bowen, Pha., RC**	**.15**
☐	242	Eric Lindros, Pha.	2.00
☐	243	Dominic Roussel (G), Pha.	.15
☐	**244**	**Milos Holan, Pha., RC**	**.15**
☐	245	Greg Hawgood, Pha.	.15
☐	246	Yves Racine, Pha.	.15
☐	247	Josef Beranek, Pha.	.15
☐	248	Rod Brind'Amour, Pha.	.25
☐	249	Kevin Dineen, Pha.	.15
☐	250	Per-Erik Eklund, Pha.	.15
☐	251	Garry Galley, Pha.	.15
☐	252	Mark Recchi, Pha.	.25
☐	253	Tommy Söderström (G), Pha.	.15
☐	254	Dimitri Yushkevich, Pha.	.15
☐	255	Mikael Renberg, Pha.	.25
☐	256	Marty McSorley, Pgh.	.15
☐	257	Joe Mullen, Pgh.	.25
☐	258	Doug Brown, Pgh.	.15
☐	259	Kjell Samuelsson, Pgh.	.15
☐	260	Tom Barrasso (G), Pgh.	.25
☐	261	Ron Francis, Pgh.	.35
☐	262	Mario Lemieux, Pgh.	2.00
☐	263	Larry Murphy, Pgh.	.25
☐	264	Ulf Samuelsson, Pgh.	.15
☐	265	Kevin Stevens, Pgh.	.15
☐	266	Martin Straka, Pgh.	.15
☐	267	Rick Tocchet, Pgh.	.15
☐	268	Bryan Trottier, Pgh.	.25
☐	269	Markus Naslund, Pgh.	.15
☐	270	Jaromir Jagr, Pgh.	1.50
☐	271	Martin Gelinas, Que.	.15
☐	272	Adam Foote, Que.	.25
☐	273	Curtis Leschyshyn, Que.	.15
☐	274	Stéphane Fiset (G), Que.	.25
☐	**275**	**Jocelyn Thibault (G), Que., RC**	**2.00**
☐	276	Steve Duchesne, Que.	.15
☐	277	Valeri Kamensky, Que.	.25
☐	278	Andrei Kovalenko, Que.	.15
☐	279	Owen Nolan, Que.	.25
☐	280	Mike Ricci, Que.	.15
☐	281	Martin Rucinsky, Que.	.15
☐	282	Joe Sakic, Que.	1.25
☐	283	Mats Sundin, Que.	.50
☐	284	Scott Young, Que.	.15
☐	285	Claude Lapointe, Que.	.15
☐	286	Brett Hull, Stl.	.50
☐	**287**	**Vitali Karamnov, Stl., RC**	**.15**
☐	288	Ron Sutter, Stl.	.15
☐	289	Garth Butcher, Stl.	.15
☐	**290**	**Vitali Prokhorov, Stl., RC**	**.15**
☐	291	Bret Hedican, Stl.	.15
☐	292	Tony Hrkac, Stl.	.15
☐	293	Jeff Brown, Stl.	.15
☐	294	Phil Housley, Stl.	.15
☐	295	Craig Janney, Stl.	.15
☐	296	Curtis Joseph (G), Stl.	.75
☐	**297**	**Igor Korolev, Stl., RC**	**.15**
☐	298	Kevin Miller, Stl.	.15
☐	299	Brendan Shanahan, Stl.	.75
☐	**300**	**Jim Montgomery, Stl., RC**	**.15**
☐	301	Gaetan Duchesne, S.J.	.15
☐	302	Jimmy Waite (G), S.J.	.15
☐	303	Jeff Norton, S.J.	.15
☐	304	Sergei Makarov, S.J.	.15
☐	305	Igor Larionov, S.J.	.25
☐	306	Mike Lalor, S.J.	.15
☐	307	Michal Sykora, S.J.	.15
☐	308	Pat Falloon, S.J.	.15
☐	309	Johan Garpenlov, S.J.	.15
☐	310	Rob Gaudreau, S.J.	.15
☐	311	Arthurs Irbe (G), S.J.	.15
☐	312	Sandis Ozolinsh, S.J.	.25
☐	313	Doug Zmolek, S.J.	.15
☐	314	Mike Rathje, S.J.	.15
☐	315	Vlastimil Kroupa, S.J.	.15
☐	316	Daren Puppa (G), T.B.	.15
☐	317	Petr Klima, T.B.	.15
☐	318	Brent Gretzky, T.B.	.15
☐	319	Denis Savard, T.B.	.25
☐	320	Gerard Gallant, T.B.	.15
☐	321	Joe Reekie, T.B.	.15
☐	322	Mikael Andersson, T.B.	.15
☐	323	Bill McDougall, T.B.	.15
☐	324	Brian Bradley, T.B.	.15
☐	325	Shawn Chambers, T.B.	.15
☐	326	Adam Creighton, T.B.	.15
☐	327	Roman Hamrlik, T.B.	.25
☐	328	John Tucker, T.B.	.15
☐	329	Rob Zamuner, T.B.	.15
☐	330	Chris Gratton, T.B.	.35
☐	331	Sylvain Lefebvre, Tor.	.15
☐	332	Nikolai Borschevsky, Tor.	.15
☐	333	Bob Rouse, Tor.	.15
☐	334	John Cullen, Tor.	.15
☐	335	Todd Gill, Tor.	.15
☐	336	Drake Berehowsky, Tor.	.15
☐	337	Wendel Clark, Tor.	.25
☐	338	Peter Zezel, Tor.	.15
☐	339	Rob Pearson, Tor.	.15
☐	340	Glenn Anderson, Tor.	.15
☐	341	Doug Gilmour, Tor.	.35
☐	342	Dave Andreychuk, Tor.	.15
☐	343	Félix Potvin (G), Tor.	.50
☐	344	Dave Ellett, Tor.	.15
☐	345	Alexei Kudashov, Tor.	.15
☐	346	Gino Odjick, Van.	.15
☐	347	Jyrki Lumme, Van.	.15
☐	348	Dana Murzyn, Van.	.15
☐	349	Sergio Momesso, Van.	.15
☐	350	Greg Adams, Van.	.15
☐	351	Pavel Bure, Van.	1.00
☐	352	Geoff Courtnall, Van.	.15
☐	353	Murray Craven, Van.	.15
☐	354	Trevor Linden, Van.	.25
☐	355	Kirk McLean (G), Van.	.25
☐	356	Petr Nedved, Van.	.15
☐	357	Cliff Ronning, Van.	.15
☐	358	Jiri Slegr, Van.	.15
☐	359	Kay Whitmore (G), Van.	.15
☐	360	Gerald Diduck, Van.	.15
☐	361	Pat Peake, Wsh.	.15
☐	362	Dave Poulin, Wsh.	.15
☐	363	Rick Tabaracci (G), Wsh.	.15
☐	364	Jason Woolley, Wsh.	.15
☐	365	Kelly Miller, Wsh.	.15
☐	366	Peter Bondra, Wsh.	.35
☐	367	Sylvain Côté, Wsh.	.15
☐	368	Pat Elynuik, Wsh.	.15
☐	369	Kevin Hatcher, Wsh.	.15
☐	370	Dale Hunter, Wsh.	.15
☐	371	Al Iafrate, Wsh.	.15
☐	372	Calle Johansson, Wsh.	.15
☐	373	Dimitri Khristich, Wsh.	.15
☐	374	Michal Pivonka, Wsh.	.15
☐	375	Mike Ridley, Wsh.	.15
☐	376	Paul Ysebaert, Wpg.	.15
☐	377	Stu Barnes, Wpg.	.15
☐	**378**	**Sergei Bautin, Wpg., RC**	**.15**
☐	379	Kris King, Wpg.	.15
☐	380	Alexei Zhamnov, Wpg.	.25
☐	381	Tie Domi, Wpg.	.15
☐	382	Bob Essensa (G), Wpg.	.15
☐	383	Nelson Emerson, Wpg.	.15
☐	**384**	**Boris Mironov, Wpg., RC**	**.15**
☐	385	Teppo Numminen, Wpg.	.15
☐	386	Fredrik Olausson, Wpg.	.15
☐	387	Teemu Selänne, Wpg.	1.00
☐	388	Darrin Shannon, Wpg.	.15
☐	389	Thomas Steen, Wpg.	.15
☐	390	Keith Tkachuk, Wpg.	.50
☐	391	Opening Night: Florida Panthers	1.00
☐	392	Opening Night: Mighty Ducks of Anaheim	1.00
☐	393	Alexandre Daigle/Chris Pronger/Chris Gratton	.25
☐	394	HL: Joé Juneau/Teemu Selänne	.50
☐	395	Record Breaking Kings: Luc Robitaille; Wayne Gretzky	1.25
☐	396	Subset Checklist	.15
☐	397	Checklist: Atlantic Division (1 - 100)	.15
☐	398	Checklist: North East Division (101 - 200)	.15
☐	399	Checklist: Central Division (201-300)	.15
☐	400	Checklist: Pacific Division (301-400)	.15
☐	401	Garry Valk, Ana.	.15
☐	402	Al Iafrate, Bos	.15
☐	403	David Reid, Bos.	.15
☐	404	Jason Dawe, Buf.	.15
☐	405	Craig Muni, Buf.	.15
☐	**406**	**Dan Keczmer, Cgy., RC**	**.15**
☐	407	Mikael Nylander, Cgy.	.15
☐	408	James Patrick, Cgy.	.15
☐	**409**	**Andrei Trefilov (G), Cgy., RC**	**.15**
☐	410	Zarley Zalapski, Cgy.	.15
☐	411	Tony Amonte, Chi.	.15
☐	**412**	**Keith Carney, Chi., RC**	**.15**
☐	413	Randy Cunneyworth, Chi.	.15
☐	414	Ivan Droppa, Chi.	.15
☐	415	Gary Suter, Chi.	.15
☐	416	Eric Weinrich, Chi.	.15
☐	417	Paul Ysebaert, Chi.	.15
☐	418	Richard Matvichuk, Dal.	.15
☐	419	Alan May, Dal.	.15
☐	420	Darcy Wakaluk (G), Dal.	.15
☐	**421**	**Micah Aivazoff, Det., RC**	**.15**
☐	422	Terry Carkner, Det.	.15
☐	423	Kris Draper, Det.	.15
☐	**424**	**Chris Osgood (G), Det., RC**	**2.50**
☐	425	Keith Primeau, Det.	.25
☐	426	Bob Beers, Edm.	.15
☐	**427**	**Ilya Byakin, Edm., RC**	**.15**
☐	**428**	**Kirk Maltby, Edm., RC**	**.15**
☐	**429**	**Boris Mironov, Edm., RC**	**.15**
☐	430	Fredrik Olausson, Edm.	.15
☐	**431**	**Peter White, Edm., RC**	**.15**
☐	432	Stu Barnes, Fla.	.15
☐	433	Mike Foligno, Fla.	.15
☐	434	Bob Kudelski, Fla.	.15
☐	435	Geoff Smith, Fla.	.15
☐	**436**	**Igor Chibirev, Hfd., RC**	**.15**
☐	**437**	**Ted Drury, Hfd., RC**	**.15**
☐	438	Alexander Godynyuk, Hfd.	.15
☐	439	Frantisek Kucera, Hfd.	.15
☐	440	Jocelyn Lemieux, Hfd.	.15
☐	441	Brian Propp, Hfd.	.15
☐	442	Paul Ranheim, Hfd.	.15
☐	443	Jeff Reese (G), Hfd.	.15
☐	**444**	**Kevin Smyth, Hfd., RC**	**.15**
☐	**445**	**Jim Storm, Hfd., RC**	**.15**
☐	**446**	**Phil Crowe, L.A., RC**	**.15**
☐	447	Marty McSorley, L.A.	.15
☐	**448**	**Keith Redmond, L.A., RC**	**.15**
☐	449	Dixon Ward, L.A.	.15
☐	450	Guy Carbonneau, Mtl.	.15
☐	451	Mike Keane, Mtl.	.15
☐	**452**	**Oleg Petrov, Mtl., RC**	**.15**
☐	453	Ron Tugnutt (G), Mtl.	.15
☐	454	Randy McKay, N.J.	.15
☐	**455**	**Jaroslav Modry, N.J., RC**	**.15**
☐	456	Yan Kaminsky, NYI.	.15
☐	457	Marty McInnis, NYI.	.15
☐	**458**	**Jamie McLennan (G), NYI., RC**	**.50**
☐	459	Zigmund Palffy, NYI.	.50
☐	460	Glenn Anderson, NYR.	.15
☐	461	Steve Larmer, NYR.	.15
☐	462	Craig MacTavish, NYR.	.15
☐	463	Stéphane Matteau, NYR.	.15
☐	464	Brian Noonan, NYR.	.15
☐	**465**	**Mattias Norstrom, NYR., RC**	**.15**
☐	**466**	**Scott Levins, Ott., RC**	**.15**
☐	**467**	**Derek Mayer, Ott., RC**	**.15**
☐	**468**	**Andy Schneider, Ott., RC**	**.15**
☐	**469**	**Todd Hlushko, Pha., RC**	**.15**
☐	**470**	**Stewart Malgunas, Pha., RC**	**.15**
☐	**471**	**Justin Duberman, Pgh., RC**	**.15**
☐	**472**	**Ladislav Karabin, Pgh., RC**	**.15**
☐	473	Shawn McEachern, Pgh.	.15
☐	474	Ed Patterson, Pgh.	.15
☐	475	Tomas Sandström, Pgh.	.15
☐	476	Bob Bassen, Que.	.15
☐	477	Garth Butcher, Que.	.15
☐	**478**	**Iain Fraser, Que., RC**	**.15**

	No.	Player	NRMT-MT
☐	**479**	**Mike McKee, Que., RC**	**.15**
☐	**480**	**Dwayne Norris, Que., RC**	**.15**
☐	**481**	**Garth Snow (G), Que., RC**	**.25**
☐	482	Ron Sutter, Que.	.15
☐	483	Kelly Chase, Stl.	.15
☐	484	Steve Duchesne, Stl.	.15
☐	485	Daniel Laperrière, Stl.	.15
☐	486	Petr Nedved, Stl.	.15
☐	487	Peter Stastny, Stl.	.15
☐	488	Ulf Dahlen, S.J.	.15
☐	489	Todd Elik, S.J.	.15
☐	**490**	**Andrei Nazarov, S.J., RC**	**.15**
☐	**491**	**Danton Cole, T.B., RC**	**.15**
☐	**492**	**Chris Joseph, T.B., RC**	**.15**
☐	**493**	**Chris LiPuma, T.B., RC**	**.15**
☐	494	Mike Gartner, Tor.	.25
☐	495	Mark Greig, Tor.	.15
☐	**496**	**David Harlock, Tor., RC**	**.15**
☐	**497**	**Matt Martin, Tor., RC**	**.15**
☐	498	Shawn Antoski, Van.	.15
☐	499	Jeff Brown, Van.	.15
☐	500	Jimmy Carson, Van.	.15
☐	501	Martin Gelinas, Van.	.15
☐	**502**	**John Namestnikov, Van., RC**	**.15**
☐	503	Randy Burridge, Wsh.	.15
☐	504	Joé Juneau, Wsh.	.15
☐	**505**	**Kevin Kaminski, Wsh., RC**	**.15**
☐	506	Arto Blomsten, Wpg.	.15
☐	507	Tim Cheveldae (G), Wpg.	.15
☐	508	Dallas Drake, Wpg.	.15
☐	509	Dave Manson, Wpg.	.15
☐	510	Checklist (401 - 510)	.15

	No.	Premier Edition	NRMT-MT
☐	WC	Luc Robitaille, L.A.	8.00
☐	EC	Mario Lemieux, Pgh.	35.00

ELITE SERIES

These cards are serial numbered out of 10,000.

Insert Set (15 cards): **300.00**

	No.	Player	NRMT-MT
☐	1	Mario Lemieux, Pgh.	50.00
☐	2	Alexandre Daigle, Ott.	10.00
☐	3	Teemu Selänne, Wpg.	25.00
☐	4	Eric Lindros, Pha.	40.00
☐	5	Brett Hull, Stl.	15.00
☐	6	Jeremy Roenick, Chi.	10.00
☐	7	Doug Gilmour, Tor.	10.00
☐	8	Alexander Mogilny, Buf.	10.00
☐	9	Patrick Roy (G), Mtl.	50.00
☐	10	Wayne Gretzky, L.A.	60.00
☐	U1	Mikael Renberg, Pha.	10.00
☐	U2	Sergei Fedorov, Det.	15.00
☐	U3	Félix Potvin (G), Tor.	20.00
☐	U4	Cam Neely, Bos.	10.00
☐	U5	Alexei Yashin, Ott.	10.00

ICE KINGS

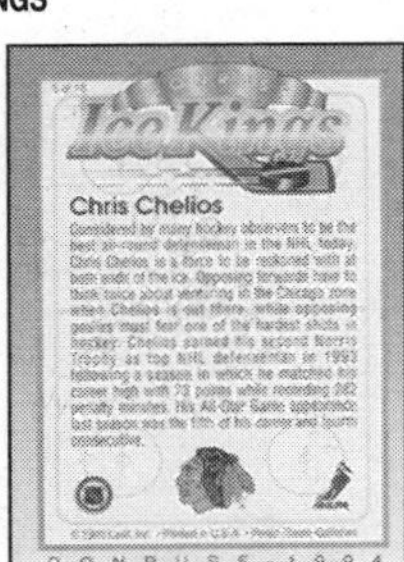

Artwork by Dick Perez.

Insert Set (10 cards): **35.00**

	No.	Player	NRMT-MT
☐	1	Patrick Roy (G), Mtl.	6.50
☐	2	Pat LaFontaine, Buf.	1.50
☐	3	Jaromir Jagr, Pgh.	4.00
☐	4	Wayne Gretzky, L.A.	8.00
☐	5	Chris Chelios, Chi.	1.50
☐	6	Félix Potvin (G), Tor.	2.75
☐	7	Mario Lemieux, Pgh.	6.50
☐	8	Pavel Bure, Van.	3.00
☐	9	Eric Lindros, Pha.	5.00
☐	10	Teemu Selänne, Wpg.	3.00

RATED ROOKIES

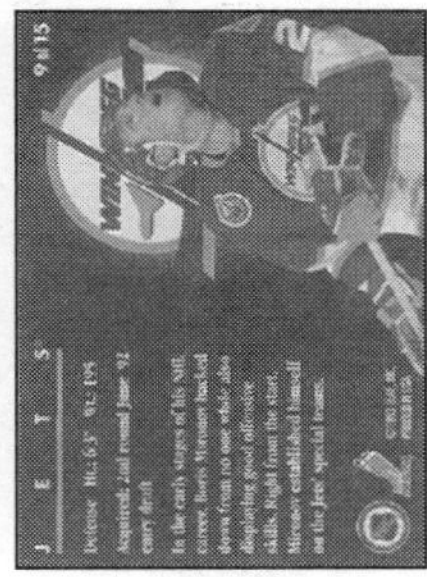

Insert Set (15 cards): **25.00**

	No.	Player	NRMT-MT
☐	1	Alexandre Daigle, Ott.	2.00
☐	2	Chris Gratton, T.B.	2.00
☐	3	Chris Pronger, Hfd.	2.00
☐	4	Rob Niedermayer, Fla.	1.50
☐	5	Mikael Renberg, Pha.	1.50
☐	6	Jarkko Varvio, Dal.	.75
☐	7	Alexei Yashin, Ott.	3.00
☐	8	Markus Naslund, Pgh.	.75
☐	9	Boris Mironov, Wpg.	.75
☐	10	Martin Brodeur (G), N.J.	6.00
☐	11	Jocelyn Thibault (G), Que.	4.00
☐	12	Jason Arnott, Edm.	3.00
☐	13	Jim Montgomery, Stl.	.75
☐	14	Ted Drury, Cgy.	.75
☐	15	Roman Oksiuta, Edm.	.75

SPECIAL PRINT

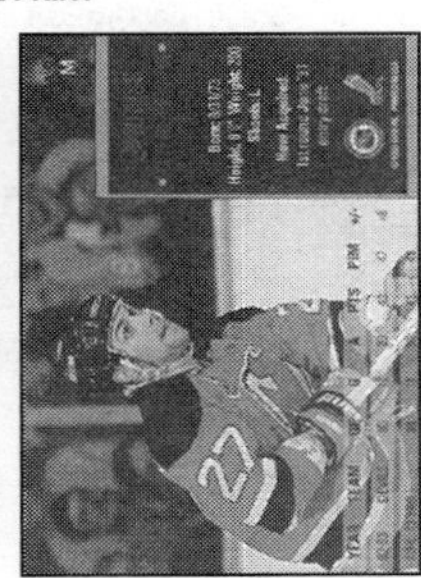

These cards parallel the regular issue cards.

Insert Set (26 cards): **160.00**

	No.	Player	NRMT-MT
☐	A	Ron Tugnutt (G), Ana.	1.50
☐	B	Adam Oates, Bos.	3.50
☐	C	Alexander Mogilny, Buf.	3.50
☐	D	Theoren Fleury, Cgy.	3.50
☐	E	Jeremy Roenick, Chi.	3.50
☐	F	Mike Modano, Dal.	6.00
☐	G	Steve Yzerman, Det.	12.00
☐	H	Jason Arnott, Edm.	6.00
☐	I	Rob Niedermayer, Fla.	2.00
☐	J	Chris Pronger, Hfd.	3.50
☐	K	Wayne Gretzky, L.A.	25.00
☐	L	Patrick Roy (G), Mtl.	18.00
☐	M	Scott Niedermayer, N.J.	2.00
☐	N	Pierre Turgeon, NYI.	2.00
☐	O	Mark Messier, NYR.	6.00
☐	P	Alexandre Daigle, Ott.	3.50
☐	Q	Eric Lindros, Pha.	15.00
☐	R	Mario Lemieux, Pgh.	18.00
☐	S	Mats Sundin, Que.	6.00
☐	T	Pat Falloon, S.J.	1.50
☐	U	Brett Hull, Stl.	6.00
☐	V	Chris Gratton, T.B.	3.50
☐	W	Félix Potvin (G), Tor.	8.00
☐	X	Pavel Bure, Van.	10.00
☐	Y	Al Iafrate, Wsh.	1.50
☐	Z	Teemu Selänne, Wpg.	10.00

1994 WORLD JUNIOR CHAMPIONSHIPS

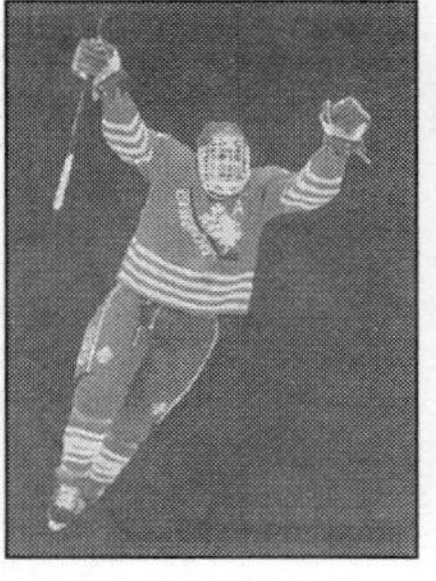

Insert Set (45 cards): **25.00**

	No.	Player	NRMT-MT
☐	CAN1	Jason Allison, Cdn.	3.00
☐	CAN2	Chris Armstrong, Cdn.	.50
☐	CAN3	Drew Bannister, Cdn.	.50
☐	CAN4	Jason Botterill, Cdn.	.75
☐	CAN5	Joel Bouchard, Cdn.	.50
☐	CAN6	Curtis Bowen, Cdn.	.50
☐	CAN7	Anson Carter, Cdn.	1.00
☐	CAN8	Brandon Convery, Cdn.	.50
☐	CAN9	Yannick Dubé, Cdn.	.50
☐	CAN10	Manny Fernandez (G), Cdn.	.75
☐	CAN11	Jeff Friesen, Cdn.	2.50
☐	CAN12	Aaron Gavey, Cdn.	.50
☐	CAN13	Martin Gendron, Cdn.	.50
☐	CAN14	Rick Girard, Cdn.	.50
☐	CAN15	Todd Harvey, Cdn.	.75
☐	CAN16	Bryan McCabe, Cdn.	1.00
☐	CAN17	Marty Murray, Cdn.	.50
☐	CAN18	Mike Peca, Cdn.	2.00
☐	CAN19	Nick Stajduhar, Cdn.	.50
☐	CAN20	Jamie Storr (G), Cdn.	1.00
☐	CAN21	Brent Tully, Cdn.	.50
☐	CAN22	Brendan Witt, Cdn.	.75
☐	USA1	Kevyn Adams, USA.	.50
☐	USA2	Jason Bonsignore, USA.	.50
☐	USA3	Andy Brink, USA.	.50
☐	USA4	Joe Coleman, USA.	.50
☐	USA5	Adam Deadmarsh, USA.	2.00
☐	USA6	Aaron Ellis (G), USA.	.50
☐	USA7	John Emmons, USA.	.50
☐	USA8	Ashlin Halfnight, USA.	.50
☐	USA9	Kevin Hilton, USA.	.50
☐	USA10	Jason Karmanos, USA.	.50
☐	USA11	Toby Kvalevog (G), USA.	.50
☐	USA12	Bob Lachance, USA.	.50
☐	USA13	Jamie Langenbrunner, USA.	1.75
☐	USA14	Jason McBain, USA.	.50
☐	USA15	Chris O'Sullivan, USA.	.50
☐	USA16	Jay Pandolfo, USA.	.50
☐	USA17	Richard Park, USA.	.50
☐	USA18	Deron Quint, USA.	.50
☐	USA19	Ryan Sittler, USA.	.50
☐	USA20	Blake Sloan, USA.	.50
☐	USA21	John Varga, USA.	.50
☐	USA22	David Wilkie, USA.	.50
☐		Checklist	2.00

1993 - 94 DURIVAGE / DIANA - SCORE

Imprint: Imprimé en États-Unis Printed in USA

Complete Set (51 cards): **25.00**

	No.	Player	NRMT-MT
☐	1	Alexandre Daigle, Ott.	1.25
☐	2	Pierre Sévigny, Mtl.	.35

	No.	Player	Price
☐	3	Jocelyn Thibault (G), Que.	2.50
☐	4	Philippe Boucher, Buf.	.35
☐	5	Martin Brodeur (G), N.J.	4.00
☐	6	Martin Lapointe, Det.	.35
☐	7	Patrice Brisebois, Mtl.	.35
☐	8	Benoît Brunet, Mtl.	.35
☐	9	Guy Carbonneau, Mtl.	.35
☐	10	J. J. Daigneault, Mtl.	.35
☐	11	Vincent Damphousse, Mtl.	1.00
☐	12	Eric Desjardins, Mtl.	.35
☐	13	Gilbert Dionne, Mtl.	.35
☐	14	Stéphan Lebeau, Mtl.	.35
☐	15	André Racicot (G), Mtl.	.50
☐	16	Mario Roberge, Mtl.	.35
☐	17	Patrick Roy (G), Mtl.	4.50
☐	18	Jacques Cloutier (G), Que.	.50
☐	19	Alain Côté, Que.	.35
☐	20	Steve Finn, Que.	.35
☐	21	Stéphane Fiset (G), Que.	.75
☐	22	Martin Gélinas, Que.	.35
☐	23	Reginald Savage, Que.	.35
☐	24	Claude Lapointe, Que.	.35
☐	25	Denis Savard, T.B.	.50
☐	26	Ray Bourque, Bos.	2.00
☐	27	Joé Juneau, Bos.	.35
☐	28	Ron Stern, Cgy.	.35
☐	29	Benoît Hogue, NYI.	.35
☐	30	Pierre Turgeon, NYI.	.75
☐	31	Mike Krushelnyski, Tor.	.35
☐	32	Félix Potvin (G), Tor.	3.00
☐	33	Sergio Momesso, Van.	.35
☐	34	Yves Racine, Pha.	.35
☐	35	Sylvain Côté, Wsh.	.35
☐	36	Sylvain Turgeon, Ott.	.35
☐	37	Kevin Dineen, Pha.	.35
☐	38	Garry Galley, Pha.	.35
☐	39	Dominic Roussel (G), Pha.	.50
☐	40	Gaetan Duchesne, Dal.	.35
☐	41	Luc Robitaille, L.A.	.75
☐	42	Michel Goulet, Chi.	.50
☐	43	Jocelyn Lemieux, Chi.	.35
☐	44	Stéphane Matteau, Chi.	.35
☐	45	Mike Hough, Fla.	.35
☐	46	Scott Mellanby, Fla.	.35
☐	47	Claude Lemieux, N.J.	.50
☐	48	Stéphane Richer, N.J.	.50
☐	49	Jimmy Waite (G), S.J.	.50
☐	50	Patrick Poulin, Hfd.	.35
☐		Checklist 1 (1 - 50)	.35
		Autographs	**NRMT-MT**
☐		Patrick Roy (G), Mtl.	115.00
☐		Jocelyn Thibault (G), Que.	50.00

1993 - 94 E.A. SPORTS - SEGA

Imprint: None

Complete Set (225 cards): 65.00

Common Player: .25

	No.	Player	NRMT-MT
☐	1	Alexei Kasatonov, N.J. (Ana.)	.25
☐	2	Randy Ladouceur, Hfd. (Ana.)	.25
☐	3	Terry Yake, Hfd. (Ana.)	.25
☐	4	Troy Loney, Pgh. (Ana.)	.25
☐	5	Anatoli Semenov, Edm. (Ana.)	.25
☐	6	Guy Hebert (G), Stl. (Ana.)	.75
☐	7	Ray Bourque, Bos.	2.50
☐	8	Don Sweeney, Bos.	.25
☐	8	Adam Oates, Bos.	1.50
☐	19	Joé Juneau, Bos.	.25
☐	11	Cam Neely, Bos.	.75
☐	12	Andy Moog (G), Bos.	.75
☐	13	Doug Bodger, Buf.	.25
☐	14	Petr Svoboda, Buf.	.25
☐	15	Pat LaFontaine, Buf.	.75
☐	16	Dale Hawerchuk, Buf.	.75
☐	17	Alexander Mogilny, Buf.	1.50
☐	18	Grant Fuhr (G), Buf.	.75
☐	19	Gary Suter, Cgy.	.25
☐	20	Al MacInnis, Cgy.	.75
☐	21	Joe Nieuwendyk, Cgy.	.75
☐	22	Gary Roberts, Cgy.	.75
☐	23	Theoren Fleury, Cgy.	1.50
☐	24	Mike Vernon (G), Cgy.	.75
☐	25	Chris Chelios, Chi.	2.00
☐	26	Steve Smith, Chi.	.25
☐	27	Jeremy Roenick, Chi.	1.50
☐	28	Michel Goulet, Chi.	.75
☐	29	Steve Larmer, Chi.	.50
☐	30	Ed Belfour (G), Chi.	1.50
☐	31	Mark Tinordi, Dal.	.25
☐	32	Tommy Sjodin, Dal.	.25
☐	33	Mike Modano, Dal.	2.50
☐	34	Dave Gagner, Dal.	.25
☐	35	Russ Courtnall, Dal.	.25
☐	36	Jon Casey (G), Dal.	.50
☐	37	Paul Coffey, Det.	.75
☐	38	Steve Chiasson, Det.	.25
☐	39	Steve Yzerman, Det.	5.00
☐	40	Sergei Fedorov, Det.	2.50
☐	41	Dino Ciccarelli, Det.	.75
☐	42	Tim Cheveldae (G), Det.	.50
☐	43	Dave Manson, Edm.	.25
☐	44	Igor Kravchuk, Edm.	.25
☐	45	Doug Weight, Edm.	1.50
☐	46	Shayne Corson, Edm.	.75
☐	47	Petr Klima, Edm.	.25
☐	48	Bill Ranford (G), Edm.	.75
☐	49	Joe Cirella, NYR. (Fla.)	.25
☐	50	Gord Murphy, Pha. (Fla.)	.25
☐	51	Brian Skrudland, Cgy. (Fla.)	.25
☐	52	Andrei Lomakin, Pha. (Fla.)	.25
☐	53	Scott Mellanby, Edm. (Fla.)	.25
☐	54	John Vanbiesbrouck (G), NYR. (Fla.)	3.00
☐	55	Zarley Zalapski, Hfd.	.25
☐	56	Eric Weinrich, Hfd.	.25
☐	57	Andrew Cassels, Hfd.	.25
☐	58	Geoff Sanderson, Hfd.	.50
☐	59	Pat Verbeek, Hfd.	.50
☐	60	Sean Burke (G), Hfd.	.75
☐	61	Rob Blake, L.A.	.75
☐	62	Marty McSorley, L.A.	.25
☐	63	Wayne Gretzky, L.A.	10.00
☐	64	Luc Robitaille, L.A.	.75
☐	65	Tomas Sandström, L.A.	.25
☐	66	Kelly Hrudey (G), L.A.	.50
☐	67	Eric Desjardins, Mtl.	.75
☐	68	Mathieu Schneider, Mtl.	.25
☐	69	Kirk Muller, Mtl.	.50
☐	70	Vincent Damphousse, Mtl.	1.50
☐	71	Brian Bellows, Mtl.	.25
☐	72	Patrick Roy (G), Mtl.	7.50
☐	73	Scott Stevens, N.J.	.75
☐	74	Viacheslav Fetisov, N.J.	.75
☐	75	Alexander Semak, N.J.	.25
☐	76	Stéphane Richer, N.J.	.50
☐	77	Claude Lemieux, N.J.	.50
☐	78	Chris Terreri (G), N.J.	.50
☐	79	Vladimir Malakhov, NYI.	.25
☐	80	Darius Kasparaitis, NYI.	.25
☐	81	Pierre Turgeon, NYI.	.75
☐	82	Steve Thomas, NYI.	.25
☐	83	Benoit Hogue, NYI.	.25
☐	84	Glenn Healy (G), NYI.	.50
☐	85	Brian Leetch, NYR.	1.50
☐	86	James Patrick, NYR.	.25
☐	87	Mark Messier, NYR.	2.50
☐	88	The Wong	.25
☐	89	Mike Gartner, NYR.	.75
☐	90	Mike Richter (G), NYR.	1.50
☐	91	Norm Maciver, Ott.	.25
☐	92	Brad Shaw, Ott.	.25
☐	93	Jamie Baker, Ott.	.25
☐	94	Sylvain Turgeon, Ott.	.25
☐	95	Bob Kudelski, Ott.	.25
☐	96	Peter Sidorkiewicz (G), Ott.	.50
☐	97	Garry Galley, Pha.	.25
☐	98	Dimitri Yushkevitch, Pha.	.25
☐	99	Eric Lindros, Pha.	6.50
☐	100	Rod Brind'Amour, Pha.	.75
☐	101	Mark Recchi, Pha.	.75
☐	102	Tommy Soderström (G), Pha.	.50
☐	103	Larry Murphy, Pgh.	.50
☐	104	Ulf Samuelsson, Pgh.	.25
☐	105	Mario Lemieux, Pgh.	7.50
☐	106	Kevin Stevens, Pgh.	.50
☐	107	Jaromir Jagr, Pgh.	5.00
☐	108	Tom Barrasso (G), Pgh.	.75
☐	109	Steve Duchesne, Que.	.50
☐	110	Curtis Leschyshyn, Que.	.25
☐	111	Mats Sundin, Que.	2.50
☐	112	Joe Sakic, Que.	4.50
☐	113	Owen Nolan, Que.	.75
☐	114	Ron Hextall (G), Que.	.75
☐	115	Doug Wilson, S.J.	.50
☐	116	Neil Wilkinson, S.J.	.25
☐	117	Kelly Kisio, S.J.	.25
☐	118	Johan Garpenlov, S.J.	.25
☐	119	Pat Falloon, S.J.	.25
☐	120	Arturs Irbe (G), S.J.	.50
☐	121	Jeff Brown, Stl.	.25
☐	122	Garth Butcher, Stl., Error (/b: R. Bourque)	.50
☐	123	Craig Janney, Stl.	.25
☐	124	Brendan Shanahan, Stl.	3.00
☐	125	Brett Hull, Stl.	2.50
☐	126	Curtis Joseph (G), Stl.	3.00
☐	127	Bob Beers, T.B.	.25
☐	128	Roman Hamrlik, T.B.	.75
☐	129	Brian Bradley, T.B.	.25
☐	130	Mikael Andersson, T.B.	.25
☐	131	Chris Kontos, T.B.	.25
☐	132	Wendell Young (G), T.B.	.50
☐	133	Todd Gill, Tor.	.25
☐	134	Dave Ellett, Tor.	.25
☐	135	Doug Gilmour, Tor., Error (/b: Bure)	1.50
☐	136	Dave Andreychuk, Tor.	.50
☐	137	Nikolai Borschevsky, Tor.	.25
☐	138	Félix Potvin (G), Tor.	2.50
☐	139	Jyrki Lumme, Van.	.25
☐	140	Doug Lidster, Van.	.25
☐	141	Cliff Ronning, Van.	.25
☐	142	Geoff Courtnall, Van.	.25
☐	143	Pavel Bure, Van.	3.50
☐	144	Kirk McLean (G), Van.	.75
☐	145	Phil Housley, Wpg.	.25
☐	146	Teppo Numminen, Wpg.	.25
☐	147	Alexei Zhamnov, Wpg.	.75
☐	148	Thomas Steen, Wpg.	.25
☐	149	Teemu Selänne, Wpg.	3.50
☐	150	Bob Essensa (G), Wpg.	.25
☐	151	Kevin Hatcher, Wsh.	.25
☐	152	Al Iafrate, Wsh.	.25
☐	153	Mike Ridley, Wsh.	.25
☐	154	Dimitri Khristich, Wsh.	.25
☐	155	Peter Bondra, Wsh.	2.00
☐	156	Don Beaupré (G), Wsh.	.50
☐	157	All Star Standings Statistics East	.25
☐	158	All Star Standings Statistics West	.25
☐	159	Mighty Ducks of Anaheim	.25
☐	160	Boston Bruins	.25
☐	161	Buffalo Sabres	.25
☐	162	Calgary Flames	.25
☐	163	Chicago Blackhawks	.25
☐	164	Detroit Red Wings	.25
☐	165	Edmonton Oilers	.25
☐	166	Florida Panthers	.25
☐	167	Hartford Whalers	.25
☐	168	Los Angeles Kings	.25
☐	169	Dallas Stars	.25
☐	170	Montréal Canadiens	.25
☐	171	New Jersey Devils	.25
☐	172	New York Islanders	.25
☐	173	New York Rangers	.25
☐	174	Ottawa Senators	.25
☐	175	Philadelphia Flyers	.25
☐	176	Pittsburgh Penguins	.25
☐	177	Québec Nordiques	.25
☐	178	San Jose Sharks	.25
☐	179	St. Louis Blues	.25
☐	180	Tampa Bay Lightning	.25
☐	181	Toronto Maple Leafs	.25

	No.	Player	Price
☐	182	Vancouver Canucks	.25
☐	183	Washington Capitals	.25
☐	184	Winnipeg Jets	.25
☐	185	Checking: Ray Bourque, Bos.	1.50
☐	186	Defense: Chris Chelios, Chi.	1.00
☐	187	Goaltending: Ed Belfour, Chi.	.75
☐	188	Passing: Adam Oates, Bos.	.50
☐	189	Shot Accuracy: Mario Lemieux, Pgh.	4.00
☐	190	Shot Power: Al Iafrate, Wsh.	.25
☐	191	Skating: Alexander Mogilny, Buf.	.75
☐	192	Stickhandling: Wayne Gretzky, L.A.	6.00
☐	193	4 Way Play	.25
☐	194	Auto Line Changes (Derian Hatcher)	.25
☐	195	Bench Checks (Dimitri Kvartalnov)	.25
☐	196	Board Checks (Randy Wood)	.25
☐	197	Clear Zone (Gord Murphy)	.25
☐	198	Crowd Records	.25
☐	199	Expansion Teams	.25
☐	200	Goalie Control: Jimmy Waite, S.J.	.50
☐	201	Hot/Cold Streaks (Terry Yake)	.25
☐	202	Local Organ Music (Mark Fitzpatick)	.25
☐	203	More Stats (Brad Shaw)	.25
☐	204	NHL Logos	.25
☐	205	One Timers (Jyrki Lumme)	.25
☐	206	Penalty Shots (Peter Sidorkiewicz)	.25
☐	207	Player Cards (Gord Murphy)	.25
☐	208	Player Profiles (Viacheslav Fetisov)	.25
☐	209	Player Records (Stéphan Lebeau)	.25
☐	210	Reverse Angle	.25
☐	211	Shootout Game (Dominik Hasek)	1.00
☐	212	User Records (Cam Neely)	.50
☐	213	The Brook: Delayed Slap Shot	.25
☐	214	The Costa: Skate Away From Goal	.25
☐	215	The Hogan: Slide Into Goal	.25
☐	216	The Lange: Use Goalie To Take Out Shooter	.25
☐	217	The Lesser: Screen To Take Out Goalie	.25
☐	218	The Matulac: Fake Outside Shoot Inside	.25
☐	219	The Scott: Fake Inside Shoot Outside	.25
☐	220	The Probin: One Timer In The Slot	.25
☐	221	The Rogers: One Timer Across The Crease	.25
☐	222	The Rubinelli: Fake Outside Fake Inside Shoot	.25
☐	223	The Shin: Wrap Around Goal Shoot Wide	.25
☐	224	The White: Deflection At The Goal Mouth	.25
☐	225	The Wike: One Timer From Behind The Goal	.25

1993 - 94 FAX-PAX WORLD OF SPORT

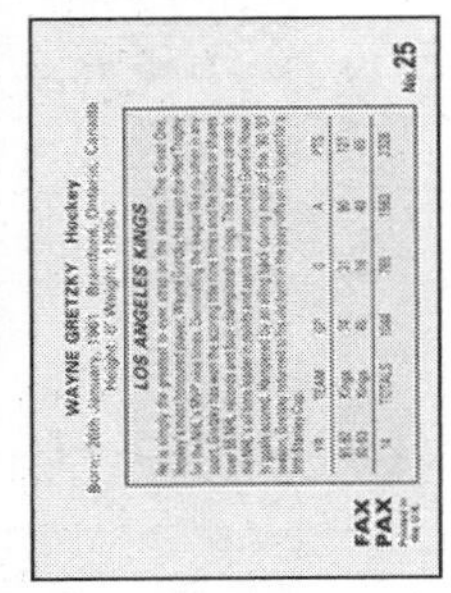

This 40-card multi-sport set was printed in the U.K. and features three hockey players. A 40-card set sells for $15.

Imprint: Fax Pax

	No.	Player	NRMT-MT
☐	25	Wayne Gretzky, L.A.	3.00
☐	26	Brett Hull, Stl.	.75
☐	27	Eric Lindros, Pha.	2.00

1993 - 94 FLEER ULTRA

Imprint:

Series One Set (250 cards): **25.00**

Series Two Set (250 cards): **25.00**

Common Player: **.15**

8-card Promo Sheet: **10.00**

	No.	Player	NRMT-MT
☐	1	Ray Bourque, Bos.	.50
☐	2	Andy Moog, (G), Bos. (Dal.)	.25
☐	3	Brian Benning, Edm.	.15
☐	4	Brian Bellows, Mtl.	.15
☐	5	Claude Lemieux, N.J.	.15
☐	6	Jamie Baker, Ott.	.15
☐	7	Steve Duchesne, Que.	.15
☐	8	Ed Courtenay, S.J.	.15
☐	9	Glenn Anderson, Tor.	.15
☐	10	Sergei Bautin, Wpg.	.15
☐	11	Al Iafrate, Wsh.	.15
☐	**12**	**Gary Shuchuk, L.A., RC**	**.15**
☐	**13**	**Matthew Barnaby, Buf., RC**	**.15**
☐	14	Tim Cheveldae (G), Det.	.15
☐	15	Sean Burke (G), Hfd.	.25
☐	16	Ray Ferraro, NYI.	.15
☐	17	Josef Beranek, Pha.	.15
☐	18	Bob Beers, T.B.	.15
☐	19	Greg Adams, Van.	.15
☐	20	John Cullen, Tor.	.15
☐	21	Kirk Muller, Mtl.	.15
☐	22	Ed Belfour (G), Chi.	.35
☐	23	Kevin Dahl, Cgy.	.15
☐	24	Rob Blake, L.A.	.25
☐	25	Mike Gartner, NYR.	.25
☐	26	Tom Barrasso (G), Pgh.	.25
☐	27	Garth Butcher, Stl.	.15
☐	28	Don Beaupré (G), Wsh.	.15
☐	29	Kirk McLean (G), Van.	.25
☐	30	Félix Potvin (G), Tor.	.50
☐	31	Doug Bodger, Buf.	.15
☐	32	Dino Ciccarelli, Det.	.25
☐	33	Andrew Cassels, Hfd.	.15
☐	34	Patrick Flatley, NYI.	.15
☐	**35**	**Jason Bowen, Pha., RC**	**.15**
☐	36	Brian Bradley, T.B.	.15
☐	37	Pavel Bure, Van.	1.00
☐	38	Dave Ellett, Tor.	.15
☐	39	Patrick Roy (G), Mtl.	2.00
☐	40	Chris Chelios, Chi.	.35
☐	41	Theoren Fleury, Cgy.	.35
☐	42	Jimmy Carson, L.A.	.15
☐	43	Adam Graves, NYR.	.15
☐	44	Ron Francis, Pgh.	.35
☐	45	Nelson Emerson, Stl.	.15
☐	46	Peter Bondra, Wsh.	.35
☐	47	Sergio Momesso, Van.	.15
☐	48	Teemu Selänne, Wpg.	1.00
☐	49	Joé Juneau, Bos.	.25
☐	50	Russ Courtnall, Dal.	.15
☐	51	Shayne Corson, Edm.	.25
☐	52	Patrice Brisebois, Mtl.	.15
☐	53	John MacLean, N.J.	.15
☐	54	Daniel Berthiaume, (G), Ott.	.15
☐	55	Stéphane Fiset, (G), Que.	.25
☐	56	Pat Falloon, S.J.	.15
☐	57	Dave Andreychuk, Tor.	.25
☐	58	Evgeny Davydov, Wpg.	.15
☐	59	Dimitri Khristich, Wsh.	.15
☐	60	Daryl Sydor, L.A.	.15
☐	61	Dirk Graham, Chi.	.15
☐	62	Chris Lindberg, Cgy.	.15
☐	63	Tony Granato, L.A.	.15
☐	64	Corey Hirsch (G), NYR.	.25
☐	65	Jaromir Jagr, Pgh.	1.50
☐	66	Bret Hedican, Stl.	.15
☐	67	Pat Elynuik, Wsh.	.15
☐	68	Petr Nedved, Van.	.15
☐	69	Thomas Steen, Wpg.	.15
☐	**70**	**Philippe Boucher, Buf., RC**	**.15**
☐	71	Paul Coffey, Det.	.25
☐	**72**	**Mike Lenarduzzi (G), Hfd., RC**	**.15**
☐	**73**	**Iain Fraser, Que., RC**	**.15**
☐	74	Rod Brind'Amour, Pha.	.25
☐	75	Shawn Chambers, T.B.	.15
☐	76	Geoff Courtnall, Van.	.15
☐	77	Todd Gill, Tor.	.15
☐	78	Mathieu Schneider, Mtl.	.15
☐	79	Vincent Damphousse, Mtl.	.25
☐	80	Igor Kravchuk, Edm.	.15
☐	81	Ulf Dahlen, Dal.	.15
☐	82	Dmitri Kvartalnov, Bos.	.15
☐	83	Johan Garpenlov, S.J.	.15
☐	84	Valeri Kamensky, Que.	.25
☐	85	Bob Kudelski, Ott.	.15
☐	86	Bernie Nicholls, N.J.	.15
☐	87	Alexei Zhitnik, L.A.	.15
☐	88	Kelly Miller, Wsh.	.15
☐	89	Bob Essensa (G), Wpg.	.15
☐	90	Drake Berehowsky, Tor.	.15
☐	91	Jon Casey (G), Dal. (Bos.)	.15
☐	92	Dave Gagner, Dal.	.15
☐	93	Dave Manson, Edm.	.15
☐	94	Eric Desjardins, Mtl.	.25
☐	95	Scott Niedermayer, N.J.	.25
☐	96	Chris Luongo, NYI.	.15
☐	**97**	**Dave Karpa, Que., RC**	**.15**
☐	**98**	**Rob Gaudreau, S.J., RC**	**.15**
☐	99	Nikolai Borschevsky, Tor.	.15
☐	100	Phil Housley, Wpg.	.15
☐	101	Michal Pivonka, Wsh.	.15
☐	102	Dixon Ward, Van.	.15
☐	103	Grant Fuhr (G), Buf.	.25
☐	**104**	**Dallas Drake, Det., RC**	**.15**
☐	105	Michael Nylander, Hfd.	.15
☐	106	Glenn Healy (G), NYI. (NYR.)	.15
☐	107	Kevin Dineen, Pha.	.15
☐	108	Roman Hamrlik, T.B.	.25
☐	109	Trevor Linden, Van.	.25
☐	110	Doug Gilmour, Tor.	.35
☐	111	Keith Tkachuk, Wpg.	.50
☐	112	Sergei Krivokrasov, Chi.	.15
☐	113	Al MacInnis, Cgy.	.25
☐	114	Wayne Gretzky, L.A.	2.50
☐	115	Alexei Kovalev, NYR.	.15
☐	116	Mario Lemieux, Pgh.	2.00
☐	117	Brett Hull, Stl.	.50
☐	118	Kevin Hatcher, Wsh.	.15
☐	119	Cliff Ronning, Van.	.15
☐	**120**	**Viktor Gordiouk, Buf., RC**	**.15**
☐	121	Sergei Fedorov, Det.	.50
☐	122	Patrick Poulin, Hfd.	.15
☐	123	Benoît Hogue, NYI.	.15
☐	124	Garry Galley, Pha.	.15
☐	125	Pat Jablonski (G), T.B.	.15
☐	126	Jyrki Lumme, Van.	.15
☐	127	Dimitri Mironov, Tor.	.15
☐	128	Alexei Zhamnov, Wpg.	.25
☐	129	Steve Larmer, Chi.	.15
☐	130	Joe Nieuwendyk, Cgy.	.25
☐	131	Kelly Hrudey (G), L.A.	.15
☐	132	Brian Leetch, NYR.	.35
☐	133	Shawn McEachern, Pgh.	.15
☐	134	Craig Janney, Stl.	.15
☐	135	Dale Hunter, Wsh.	.15
☐	136	Jiri Slegr, Van.	.15
☐	137	Mats Sundin, Que.	.50
☐	138	Cam Neely, Bos.	.25
☐	139	Derian Hatcher, Dal.	.25
☐	**140**	**Shjon Podein, Edm., RC**	**.15**
☐	141	Gilbert Dionne, Mtl.	.15
☐	**142**	**Scott Pellerin, N.J., RC**	**.15**
☐	143	Norm MacIver, Ott.	.15
☐	144	Andrei Kovalenko, Que.	.15
☐	145	Artus Irbe (G), S.J.	.15
☐	146	Wendel Clark, Tor.	.25
☐	147	Fredrik Oalusson, Wpg.	.15

	No.	Player	Price
☐	148	Mike Ridley, Wsh.	.15
☐	149	Dale Hawerchuk, Buf.	.25
☐	150	Vladimir Konstantinov, Det.	.15
☐	151	Geoff Sanderson, Hfd.	.15
☐	152	Stéphane Richer, N.J.	.15
☐	153	Darren Rumble, Ott.	.15
☐	154	Owen Nolan, Que.	.25
☐	155	Kelly Kisio, S.J.	.15
☐	156	Adam Oates, Bos.	.35
☐	157	Trent Klatt, Dal.	.15
☐	158	Bill Ranford (G), Edm.	.25
☐	159	Paul DiPietro, Mtl.	.15
☐	160	Darius Kasparaitis, NYI.	.15
☐	161	Eric Lindros, Pha.	2.00
☐	162	Chris Kontos, T.B.	.15
☐	163	Joe Murphy, Chi.	.15
☐	164	Robert Reichel, Cgy.	.15
☐	165	Jari Kurri, L.A.	.25
☐	166	Alexander Semak, N.J.	.15
☐	167	Brad Shaw, Ott.	.15
☐	168	Mike Ricci, Que.	.15
☐	169	Sandis Ozolinsh, S.J.	.25
☐	**170**	**Joby Messier, NYR., RC**	**.15**
☐	171	Joe Mullen, Pgh.	.25
☐	172	Curtis Joseph (G), Stl.	.75
☐	173	Yuri Khmylev, Buf.	.15
☐	174	Vyacheslav Kozlov, Det.	.15
☐	175	Pat Verbeek, Hfd.	.15
☐	176	Derek King, NYI.	.15
☐	177	Ryan McGill, Pha.	.15
☐	**178**	**Chris LiPuma, T.B., RC**	**.15**
☐	179	Gregori Pantaleyev, Bos.	.15
☐	180	Richard Matvichuk, Dal.	.15
☐	181	Steven Rice, Edm.	.15
☐	182	Sean Hill, Mtl. (Ana.)	.15
☐	183	Mark Messier, NYR.	.50
☐	184	Larry Murphy, Pgh.	.25
☐	185	Igor Korolev, Stl.	.15
☐	186	Jeremy Roenick, Chi.	.35
☐	187	Gary Roberts, Cgy.	.25
☐	188	Robert Lang, L.A.	.15
☐	189	Scott Stevens, N.J.	.25
☐	190	Sylvain Turgeon, Ott.	.15
☐	191	Martin Rucinsky, Que.	.15
☐	192	Jean-François Quintin, S.J.	.15
☐	193	David Poulin, Bos.	.15
☐	194	Mike Modano, Dal.	.50
☐	195	Doug Weight, Edm.	.35
☐	196	Mike Keane, Mtl.	.15
☐	197	Pierre Turgeon, NYI.	.25
☐	198	Dimitri Yushkevich, Pha.	.15
☐	199	Rob Zamuner, T.B.	.25
☐	200	Richard Smehlik, Buf.	.15
☐	201	Steve Yzerman, Det.	1.50
☐	202	Tony Amonte, NYR.	.25
☐	203	Sergei Nemchinov, NYR.	.15
☐	204	Ulf Samuelsson, Pgh.	.15
☐	**205**	**Kevin Miehm, Stl., RC**	**.15**
☐	206	Brent Sutter, Chi.	.15
☐	207	Mike Vernon (G), Cgy.	.25
☐	208	Luc Robitaille, L.A.	.25
☐	209	Chris Terreri (G), N.J.	.15
☐	210	Philippe Bozon, Stl.	.15
☐	211	John Tucker, T.B.	.15
☐	212	Jozef Stumpel, Bos.	.15
☐	213	Mark Tinordi, Dal.	.15
☐	214	Bruce Driver, N.J.	.15
☐	215	John LeClair, Mtl.	.75
☐	216	Steve Thomas, NYI.	.15
☐	217	Tommy Soderström (G), Pha.	.15
☐	218	Kevin Miller, Stl.	.15
☐	219	Pat LaFontaine, Buf.	.25
☐	220	Nicklas Lidstrom, Det.	.25
☐	221	Terry Yake, Hfd. (Ana.)	.15
☐	222	Valeri Zelepukin, N.J.	.15
☐	223	Jeff Brown, Stl.	.15
☐	**224**	**Chris Simon, Que., RC**	**.25**
☐	225	Rick Tocchet, Pgh.	.15
☐	226	Gary Suter, Cgy.	.15
☐	227	Marty McSorley, L.A.	.15
☐	228	Mike Richter (G), NYR.	.35
☐	229	Kevin Stevens, Pgh.	.15
☐	230	Doug Wilson, S.J.	.15
☐	231	Steve Smith, Chi.	.15
☐	**232**	**Bryan Smolinski, Bos., RC**	**.15**
☐	233	Tommy Sjodin, Dal.	.15
☐	234	Zarley Zalapski, Hfd.	.15
☐	235	Vladimir Malakhov, NYI.	.15
☐	236	Mark Recchi, Pha.	.25
☐	**237**	**David Littman, T.B., RC**	**.15**
☐	238	Alexander Mogilny, Buf.	.35
☐	239	Keith Primeau, Det.	.25
☐	**240**	**Tyler Wright, Edm., RC**	**.15**
☐	241	Stéphan Lebeau, Mtl.	.15
☐	242	Joe Sakic, Que.	1.25
☐	243	Sergei Zubov, NYR.	.25
☐	244	Martin Straka, Pgh.	.15
☐	245	Brendan Shanahan, Stl.	.75
☐	246	Tomas Sandström, L.A.	.15
☐	**247**	**Milan Tichy, Chi. (Fla.), RC**	**.15**
☐	**248**	**C.J. Young, Bos., RC**	**.15**
☐	249	Checklist 1	.15
☐	250	Checklist 2	.15
☐	**251**	**Patrik Carnback, Ana., RC**	**.15**
☐	252	Todd Ewen, Ana.	.15
☐	253	Stu Grimson, Ana.	.15
☐	254	Guy Hebert (G), Ana.	.25
☐	255	Sean Hill, Ana.	.15
☐	256	Bill Houlder, Ana.	.15
☐	257	Alexei Kasatonov, Ana.	.15
☐	258	Steven King, Ana.	.15
☐	259	Troy Loney, Ana.	.15
☐	260	Joe Sacco, Ana.	.15
☐	261	Anatoli Semenov, Ana.	.15
☐	262	Tim Sweeney, Ana.	.15
☐	263	Ron Tugnutt (G), Ana.	.15
☐	264	Shaun Van Allen, Ana.	.15
☐	265	Terry Yake, Ana.	.15
☐	266	Jon Casey (G), Bos.	.15
☐	267	Ted Donato, Bos.	.15
☐	268	Steven Leach, Bos.	.15
☐	269	David Reid, Bos.	.15
☐	**270**	**Cam Stewart, Bos., RC**	**.15**
☐	271	Don Sweeney, Bos.	.15
☐	272	Glen Wesley, Bos.	.15
☐	273	Donald Audette, Buf.	.15
☐	274	Dominik Hasek (G), Buf.	1.00
☐	**275**	**Sergei Petrenko, Buf., RC**	**.15**
☐	**276**	**Derek Plante, Buf., RC**	**.25**
☐	277	Craig Simpson, Buf.	.15
☐	278	Bob Sweeney, Buf.	.15
☐	279	Randy Wood, Buf.	.15
☐	**280**	**Ted Drury, Cgy., RC**	**.15**
☐	281	Trevor Kidd (G), Cgy.	.25
☐	282	Kelly Kisio, Cgy.	.15
☐	283	Frantisek Musil, Cgy.	.15
☐	**284**	**Jason Muzzatti (G), Cgy., RC**	**.15**
☐	285	Joel Otto, Cgy.	.15
☐	286	Paul Ranheim, Cgy.	.15
☐	287	Wes Walz, Cgy.	.15
☐	**288**	**Ivan Droppa, Chi., RC**	**.15**
☐	289	Michel Goulet, Chi.	.25
☐	290	Stéphane Matteau, Chi.	.15
☐	291	Brian Noonan, Chi.	.15
☐	292	Patrick Poulin, Chi.	.15
☐	293	Rich Sutter, Chi.	.15
☐	294	Kevin Todd, Chi.	.15
☐	295	Eric Weinrich, Chi.	.15
☐	296	Neal Broten, Dal.	.15
☐	297	Mike Craig, Dal.	.15
☐	298	Dean Evason, Dal.	.15
☐	299	Grant Ledyard, Dal.	.15
☐	300	Mike McPhee, Dal.	.15
☐	301	Andy Moog (G), Dal.	.25
☐	**302**	**Jarkko Varvio, Dal., RC**	**.15**
☐	**303**	**Micah Aivazoff, Det., RC**	**.15**
☐	304	Terry Carkner, Det.	.15
☐	305	Steve Chiasson, Det.	.15
☐	306	Greg Johnson, Det.	.15
☐	**307**	**Darren McCarty, Det., RC**	**.25**
☐	**308**	**Chris Osgood (G), Det., RC**	**2.50**
☐	309	Bob Probert, Det.	.15
☐	310	Ray Sheppard, Det.	.15
☐	311	Mike Sillinger, Det.	.15
☐	**312**	**Jason Arnott, Edm., RC**	**1.50**
☐	**313**	**Fred Brathwaite (G), Edm., RC**	**.15**
☐	314	Kelly Buchberger, Edm.	.15
☐	315	Zdeno Ciger, Edm.	.15
☐	316	Craig MacTavish, Edm.	.15
☐	317	Deam McAmmond, Edm.	.15
☐	318	Luke Richardson, Edm.	.15
☐	319	Vladimir Vujtek, Edm.	.15
☐	320	Jesse Belanger, Fla.	.15
☐	321	Brian Benning, Fla.	.15
☐	322	Keith Brown, Fla.	.15
☐	323	Evgeny Davydov, Fla.	.15
☐	324	Tom Fitzgerald, Fla.	.15
☐	325	Alexander Godynyuk, Fla.	.15
☐	**326**	**Scott Levins, Fla., RC**	**.15**
☐	327	Andrei Lomakin, Fla.	.15
☐	328	Scott Mellanby, Fla.	.15
☐	329	Gord Murphy, Fla.	.15
☐	330	Rob Niedermayer, Fla.	.25
☐	**331**	**Brent Severyn, Fla., RC**	**.15**
☐	332	Brian Skrudland, Fla.	.15
☐	333	John Vanbiesbrouck (G), Fla.	.75
☐	334	Mark Greig, Hfd.	.15
☐	335	Bryan Marchment, Hfd.	.15
☐	336	James Patrick, Hfd.	.15
☐	337	Robert Petrovicky, Hfd.	.15
☐	338	Frank Pietrangelo (G), Hfd.	.15
☐	339	Chris Pronger, Hfd.	.35
☐	340	Brian Propp, Hfd.	.15
☐	341	Darren Turcotte, Hfd.	.15
☐	342	Patrick Conacher, L.A.	.15
☐	343	Mark Hardy, L.A.	.15
☐	344	Charlie Huddy, L.A.	.15
☐	345	Shawn McEachern, L.A.	.15
☐	346	Warren Rychel, L.A.	.15
☐	347	Robb Stauber (G), L.A.	.15
☐	348	Dave Taylor, L.A.	.15
☐	349	Benoît Brunet, Mtl.	.15
☐	350	Guy Carbonneau, Mtl.	.15
☐	351	J. J. Daigneault, Mtl.	.15
☐	352	Kevin Haller, Mtl.	.15
☐	353	Gary Leeman, Mtl.	.15
☐	354	Lyle Odelein, Mtl.	.15
☐	355	André Racicot (G), Mtl.	.15
☐	356	Ron Wilson, Mtl.	.15
☐	357	Martin Brodeur (G), N.J.	1.00
☐	358	Ken Daneyko, N.J.	.15
☐	359	Bill Guerin, N.J.	.25
☐	360	Bobby Holik, N.J.	.15
☐	361	Corey Millen, N.J.	.15
☐	**362**	**Jaroslav Modry, N.J., RC**	**.15**
☐	**363**	**Jason Smith, N.J., RC**	**.15**
☐	**364**	**Brad Dalgarno, NYI., RC**	**.15**
☐	**365**	**Travis Green, NYI., RC**	**.15**
☐	366	Ron Hextall (G), NYI.	.25
☐	**367**	**Steve Junker, NYI., RC**	**.15**
☐	368	Tom Kurvers, NYI.	.15
☐	369	Scott Lachance, NYI.	.15
☐	370	Marty McInnis, NYI.	.15
☐	371	Glenn Healy (G), NYR.	.15
☐	**372**	**Alexander Karpovtsev, NYR., RC**	**.15**
☐	373	Steve Larmer, NYR.	.15
☐	374	Doug Lidster, NYR.	.15
☐	375	Kevin Lowe, NYR.	.15
☐	**376**	**Mattias Norstrom, NYR., RC**	**.15**
☐	377	Esa Tikkanen, NYR.	.15
☐	378	Craig Billington (G), Ott.	.15
☐	**379**	**Robert Burakovsky, Ott., RC**	**.15**
☐	380	Alexandre Daigle, Ott.	.35
☐	381	Dmitri Filimonov, Ott.	.15
☐	**382**	**Darrin Madeley, Ott., RC**	**.15**
☐	383	Vladimir Ruzicka, Ott.	.15
☐	384	Alexei Yashin, Ott.	.75
☐	385	Viacheslav Butsayev, Pha.	.15
☐	386	Per-Erik Eklund, Pha.	.15
☐	387	Brent Fedyk, Pha.	.15
☐	388	Greg Hawgood, Pha.	.15
☐	**389**	**Milos Holan, Pha., RC**	**.15**
☐	**390**	**Stewart Malgunas, Pha., RC**	**.15**
☐	391	Mikael Renberg, Pha.	.25
☐	392	Dominic Roussel (G), Pha.	.15
☐	393	Doug Brown, Pgh.	.15
☐	394	Marty McSorley, Pgh.	.15
☐	395	Markus Naslund, Pgh.	.15
☐	396	Mike Ramsey, Pgh.	.15
☐	397	Peter Taglianetti, Pgh.	.15
☐	398	Bryan Trottier, Pgh.	.25
☐	399	Ken Wregget (G), Pgh.	.25
☐	**400**	**Iain Fraser, RC, Que.**	**.15**
☐	401	Martin Gelinas, Que.	.15
☐	402	Kerry Huffman, Que.	.15

	No.	Player	Price
☐	403	Claude Lapointe, Que.	.15
☐	404	Curtis Leschyshyn, Que.	.15
☐	**405**	**Chris Lindberg, Que., RC**	**.15**
☐	**406**	**Jocelyn Thibault (G), Que., RC**	**2.00**
☐	407	Murray Baron, Stl.	.15
☐	408	Bob Bassen, Stl.	.15
☐	409	Phil Housley, Stl.	.15
☐	410	Jim Hrivnak, Stl.	.15
☐	411	Tony Hrkac, Stl.	.15
☐	**412**	**Vitali Karamnov, Stl., RC**	**.15**
☐	**413**	**Jim Montgomery, Stl., RC**	**.15**
☐	**414**	**Vlastimil Kroupa, S.J., RC**	**.15**
☐	415	Igor Larionov, S.J.	.25
☐	416	Sergei Makarov, S.J.	.15
☐	417	Jeff Norton, S.J.	.15
☐	**418**	**Mike Rathje, S.J., RC**	**.15**
☐	419	Jim Waite (G), S.J.	.15
☐	420	Ray Whitney, S.J.	.15
☐	421	Mikael Andersson, T.B.	.15
☐	422	Donald Dufresne, T.B.	.15
☐	423	Chris Gratton, T.B.	.35
☐	**424**	**Brent Gretzky, T.B., RC**	**.15**
☐	425	Petr Klima, T.B.	.15
☐	**426**	**Bill McDougall, T.B., RC**	**.15**
☐	427	Daren Puppa (G), T.B.	.15
☐	428	Denis Savard, T.B.	.25
☐	429	Ken Baumgartner, Tor.	.15
☐	430	Sylvain Lefebvre, Tor.	.15
☐	431	Jamie Macoun, Tor.	.15
☐	**432**	**Matt Martin, Tor., RC**	**.15**
☐	433	Mark Osborne, Tor.	.15
☐	434	Rob Pearson, Tor.	.15
☐	**435**	**Damian Rhodes (G), Tor., RC**	**.50**
☐	436	Peter Zezel, Tor.	.15
☐	437	Shawn Antoski, Van.	.15
☐	438	José Charbonneau, Van.	.15
☐	439	Murray Craven, Van.	.15
☐	440	Gerald Diduck, Van.	.15
☐	441	Dana Murzyn, Van.	.15
☐	442	Gino Odjick, Van.	.15
☐	443	Kay Whitmore (G), Van.	.15
☐	444	Randy Burridge, Wsh.	.15
☐	445	Sylvain Côté, Wsh.	.15
☐	446	Keith Jones, Wsh.	.15
☐	447	Olaf Kolzig (G), Wsh.	.35
☐	448	Todd Krygier, Wsh.	.15
☐	449	Pat Peake, Wsh.	.15
☐	450	Dave Poulin, Wsh.	.15
☐	451	Stéphane Beauregard (G), Wpg.	.15
☐	452	Luciano Borsata, Wpg.	.15
☐	453	Nelson Emerson, Wpg.	.15
☐	**454**	**Boris Mironov, Wpg., RC**	**.15**
☐	455	Teppo Numminen, Wpg.	.15
☐	456	Stéphane Quintal, Wpg.	.15
☐	457	Paul Ysebaert, Wpg.	.15
☐	**458**	**Adrian Aucoin, Cdn., RC**	**.15**
☐	**459**	**Todd Brost, Cdn., RC**	**.15**
☐	**460**	**Martin Gendron, Cdn., RC**	**.15**
☐	**461**	**David Harlock, Cdn., RC**	**.15**
☐	462	Corey Hirsch (G), Cdn.	.15
☐	**463**	**Todd Hlushko, Cdn., RC**	**.15**
☐	**464**	**Fabian Joseph, Cdn., RC**	**.15**
☐	465	Paul Kariya, Cdn.	8.00
☐	**466**	**Brett Lindros, Cdn., RC**	**.15**
☐	**467**	**Ken Lovsin, Cdn., RC**	**.15**
☐	468	Jason Marshall, Cdn.	.15
☐	**469**	**Derek Mayer, Cdn., RC**	**.15**
☐	**470**	**Dwayne Norris, Cdn., RC**	**.15**
☐	471	Russ Romaniuk, Cdn.	.15
☐	**472**	**Brian Savage, Cdn., RC**	**.50**
☐	**473**	**Trevor Sim, Cdn., RC**	**.15**
☐	**474**	**Chris Therien, Cdn., RC**	**.15**
☐	**475**	**Brad Turner, Cdn., RC**	**.15**
☐	**476**	**Todd Warriner, Cdn., RC**	**.25**
☐	**477**	**Craig Woodcroft, Cdn., RC**	**.15**
☐	**478**	**Mark Beaufait, USA., RC**	**.15**
☐	479	Jim Campbell, USA.	.25
☐	**480**	**Ted Crowley, USA., RC**	**.15**
☐	481	Mike Dunham (G), USA.	.15
☐	**482**	**Chris Ferraro, USA., RC**	**.15**
☐	483	Peter Ferraro, USA.	.15
☐	**484**	**Brett Hauer, USA., RC**	**.15**
☐	**485**	**Darby Hendrickson, USA., RC**	**.15**
☐	**486**	**Chris Imes, USA., RC**	**.15**
☐	487	Craig Johnson, USA.	.15
☐	**488**	**Peter Laviolette, USA., RC**	**.15**
☐	489	Jeff Lazaro, USA.	.15
☐	**490**	**John Lilley, USA., RC**	**.15**
☐	491	Todd Marchant, USA.	.15
☐	**492**	**Ian Moran, USA., RC**	**.15**
☐	**493**	**Travis Richards, USA., RC**	**.15**
☐	**494**	**Barry Richter, USA., RC**	**.15**
☐	**495**	**David Roberts, USA., RC**	**.15**
☐	496	Brian Rolston, USA.	.15
☐	497	David Sacco, USA.	.15
☐	498	Checklist	.15
☐	499	Checklist	.15
☐	500	Checklist	.15

ADAM OATES CAREER HIGHLIGHTS

Cards 11 and 12 were available by mail.

Complete Set (12 cards): 8.00

Autographed Adam Oates card: 110.00

	No.	Player	NRMT-MT
☐	1	A Challenge Met	.50
☐	2	Sowing His Oates, Boston Bruins	.50
☐	3	Wanted Man, Detroit Red Wings	.50
☐	4	Making The Grade, Detroit Red Wings	.50
☐	5	Motor City Motion	.50
☐	6	Hello and Goodbye, St. Louis Blues 1989-1992	.50
☐	7	Blues' Brother, St. Louis Blues 1989-1992	.50
☐	8	Hit the Ignition, St. Louis Blues 1989-1992	.50
☐	9	The Break-up	.50
☐	10	The Spotlight Shines	.50
☐	11	North American Dream	2.50
☐	12	Giving till it Hurts	2.50

ALL-ROOKIE SERIES

Insert Set (10 cards): 45.00

	No.	Player	NRMT-MT
☐	1	Philippe Boucher, Buf.	5.00
☐	2	Viktor Gordiouk, Buf.	5.00
☐	3	Corey Hirsch (G), NYR.	8.00
☐	4	Chris LiPuma, T.B.	5.00
☐	5	David Littman, T.B.	5.00
☐	6	Joby Messier, NYR.	5.00
☐	7	Chris Simon, Que.	5.00
☐	8	Bryan Smolinski, Bos.	5.00
☐	9	Jozef Stumpel, Bos.	8.00
☐	10	Milan Tichy, Chi.	5.00

NHL ALL-STARS

Insert Set (18 cards): 40.00

	No.	Player	NRMT-MT
☐	1	Patrick Roy (G), Mtl.	8.00
☐	2	Ray Bourque, Bos.	2.50
☐	3	Pierre Turgeon, NYI.	1.00
☐	4	Pat LaFontaine, Buf.	1.00
☐	5	Alexander Mogilny, Buf.	1.50
☐	6	Kevin Stevens, Pgh.	1.00
☐	7	Adam Oates, Bos.	1.50
☐	8	Al Iafrate, Wsh.	1.00
☐	9	Kirk Muller, Mtl.	1.00
☐	10	Ed Belfour (G), Chi.	1.50
☐	11	Teemu Selänne, Wpg.	3.50
☐	12	Steve Yzerman, Det.	5.00
☐	13	Luc Robitaille, L.A.	1.00
☐	14	Chris Chelios, Chi.	2.00
☐	15	Wayne Gretzky, L.A.	10.00
☐	16	Doug Gilmour, Tor.	1.50
☐	17	Pavel Bure, Van.	3.50
☐	18	Phil Housley, Wpg.	1.00

AWARD WINNERS

Insert Set (6 cards): 15.00

	No.	Player	NRMT-MT
☐	1	Ed Belfour, Chi.	1.50
☐	2	Chris Chelios, Chi.	2.00
☐	3	Doug Gilmour, Tor.	2.00
☐	4	Mario Lemieux, Pgh.	8.00
☐	5	Dave Poulin, Bos.	1.00
☐	6	Teemu Selänne, Wpg.	3.50

PREMIER PIVOTS

Insert Set (10 cards): 25.00

	No.	Player	NRMT-MT
☐	1	Doug Gilmour, Tor.	1.25
☐	2	Wayne Gretzky, L.A.	8.00
☐	3	Pat LaFontaine, Buf.	.75
☐	4	Mario Lemieux, Pgh.	6.00
☐	5	Eric Lindros, Pha.	5.00
☐	6	Mark Messier, NYR.	2.00
☐	7	Adam Oates, Bos.	1.25
☐	8	Jeremy Roenick, Chi.	.75
☐	9	Pierre Turgeon, NYI.	.75
☐	10	Steve Yzerman, Det.	4.00

ULTRA PROSPECTS

Insert Set (10 cards): 10.00

	No.	Player	NRMT-MT
☐	1	Iain Fraser, NYI.	1.50
☐	2	Rob Gaudreau, S.J.	1.50

	No.	Player	NRMT-MT
☐	3	Dave Karpa, Que.	1.50
☐	4	Trent Klatt, Min.	1.50
☐	5	Mike Lenarduzzi (G), Hfd.	1.50
☐	6	Kevin Miehm, Stl.	1.50
☐	7	Michael Nylander, Hfd.	1.50
☐	8	J.F. Quintin, S.J.	1.50
☐	9	Gary Shuchuk, L.A.	1.50
☐	10	Tyler Wright, Edm.	1.50

RED LIGHT SPECIALS

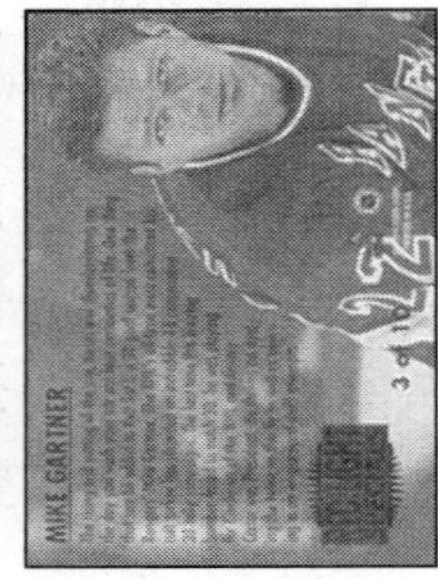

Insert Set (10 cards): 25.00

	No.	Player	NRMT-MT
☐	1	Dave Andreychuk, Tor.	1.00
☐	2	Pavel Bure, Van.	3.50
☐	3	Mike Gartner, NYR.	1.00
☐	4	Brett Hull, Stl.	2.50
☐	5	Jaromir Jagr, Pgh.	5.00
☐	6	Mario Lemieux, Pgh.	8.00
☐	7	Alexander Mogilny, Buf.	1.50
☐	8	Mark Recchi, Pha.	1.00
☐	9	Luc Robitaille, L.A.	1.00
☐	10	Teemu Selänne, Wpg.	3.50

SCORING KINGS

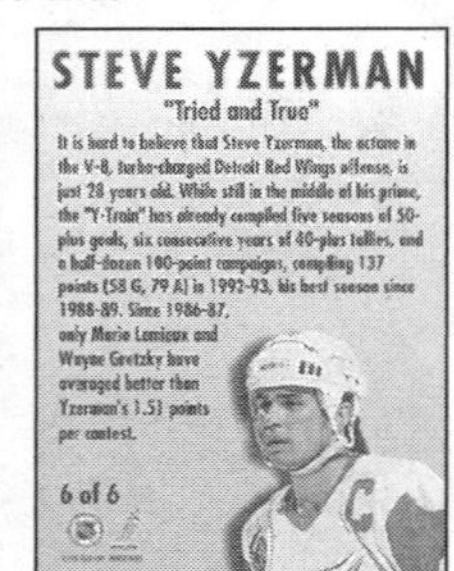

Insert Set (6 cards): 25.00

	No.	Player	NRMT-MT
☐	1	Pat LaFontaine, Buf.	1.00
☐	2	Wayne Gretzky, L.A.	10.00
☐	3	Brett Hull, Stl.	2.50
☐	4	Mario Lemieux, Pgh.	8.00
☐	5	Pierre Turgeon, NYI.	1.00
☐	6	Steve Yzerman, Det.	5.00

SPEED MERCHANTS

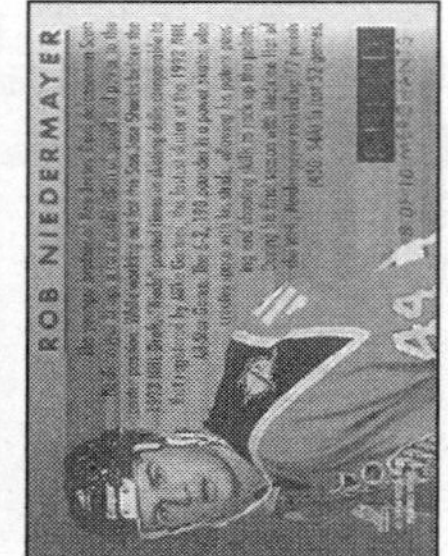

Insert Set (10 cards): 90.00

	No.	Player	NRMT-MT
☐	1	Pavel Bure, Van.	20.00
☐	2	Russ Courtnall, Dal.	6.00
☐	3	Sergei Fedorov, Det.	15.00
☐	4	Mike Gartner, NYR.	8.00
☐	5	Al Iafrate, Wsh.	6.00
☐	6	Pat LaFontaine, Buf.	8.00
☐	7	Alexander Mogilny, Buf.	9.00
☐	8	Rob Niedermayer, Fla.	8.00
☐	9	Geoff Sanderson, Hfd.	6.00
☐	10	Teemu Selänne, Wpg.	20.00

WAVE OF THE FUTURE

Insert Set (20 cards): 30.00

	No.	Player	NRMT-MT
☐	1	Jason Arnott, Edm.	3.00
☐	2	Martin Brodeur (G), N.J.	6.00
☐	3	Alexandre Daigle, Ott.	2.00
☐	4	Ted Drury, Cgy.	.75
☐	5	Chris Gratton, T.B.	2.00
☐	6	Milos Holan, Pha.	.75
☐	7	Greg Johnson, Det.	.75
☐	8	Boris Mironov, Wpg.	.75
☐	9	Jaroslav Modry, N.J.	.75
☐	10	Markus Naslund, Cgy.	.75
☐	11	Rob Niedermayer, Fla.	1.50
☐	12	Chris Osgood (G), Det.	5.00
☐	13	Derek Plante, Buf.	.75
☐	14	Chris Pronger, Hfd.	2.00
☐	15	Mike Rathje, S.J.	.75
☐	16	Mikael Renberg, Pha.	1.50
☐	17	Jason Smith, Cgy.	.75
☐	18	Jocelyn Thibault (G), Que.	4.00
☐	19	Jarkko Varvio, Dal.	.75
☐	20	Alexei Yashin, Ott.	3.00

1993 - 94 HIGH LINER GREATEST GOALIES

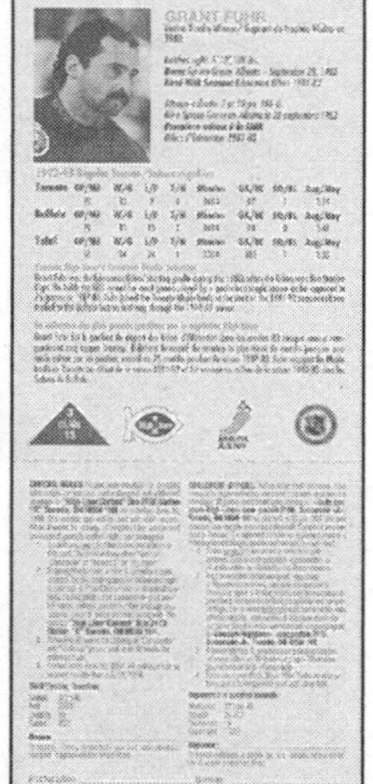

One of 15 cards was found in specially marked boxes of High Liner. A factory-cut set and album was also available through the mail.

Imprint:

Complete Set (15 cards): 18.00

Album: 5.00

	No.	Player	NRMT-MT
☐	1	Patrick Roy (G), Mtl.	3.50
☐	2	Ed Belfour (G), Chi.	1.25
☐	3	Grant Fuhr (G), Buf.	1.00
☐	4	Ron Hextall (G), Que.	.75
☐	5	John Vanbiesbrouck (G), NYR.	1.75
☐	6	Tom Barrasso (G), Pgh.	.75
☐	7	Bernie Parent (G), Pha.	1.75
☐	8	Tony Esposito (G), Chi.	1.75
☐	9	Johnny Bower (G), Tor.	1.50
☐	10	Jacques Plante (G), Mtl.	2.50
☐	11	Terry Sawchuk (G), Det.	2.50
☐	12	Bill Durnan (G), Mtl.	1.50
☐	13	Félix Potvin (G), Tor.	1.50
☐	14	The Evolution of the Goalie Mask	1.25
☐	15	The Vezina Trophy	.75

1993 - 94 HOCKEY HALL OF FAME LEGENDS

Artwork by Doug West.

Card Size: 3 1/2" x 5 1/2"

Imprint:

Series Two Set (18 cards): 135.00

Common Player: 8.00

	No.	Player	NRMT-MT
☐	19	Ted Lindsay	11.00
☐	20	Duke Keats	8.00
☐	21	Jack Adams	8.00
☐	22	Bill Mosienko	10.00
☐	23	Johnny Bower (G)	11.00
☐	24	Tim Horton	12.00
☐	25	Punch Imlach	8.00
☐	26	Georges Vézina (G)	10.00
☐	27	Earl Seibert	8.00
☐	28	Bryan Hextall	8.00
☐	29	Babe Pratt	8.00
☐	30	Gump Worsley (G)	11.00
☐	31	Ed Giacomin (G)	12.00
☐	32	Ace Bailey	8.00
☐	33	Harry Sinden	8.00
☐	34	Lanny McDonald	12.00
☐	35	Tommy Ivan	8.00
☐	36	Frank Calder	8.00

1993 - 94 HOCKEY WIT

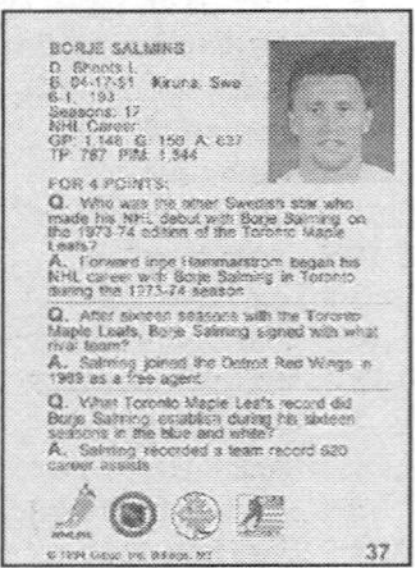

Card Size: 2 1/2" x 3 7/16"

Imprint:

Complete Set (108 cards): 16.00

Common Player: .10

	No.	Player	NRMT-MT
☐	1	Mike Richter (G), NYR.	.25
☐	2	Tony Amonte, NYR.	.25
☐	3	Patrick Roy (G), Mtl.	3.00
☐	4	Craig Janney, Stl.	.10
☐	5	Adam Oates, Bos.	.50
☐	6	Geoff Sanderson, Hfd.	.10
☐	7	Pavel Bure, Van.	1.50
☐	8	Steve Duchesne, Stl.	.10
☐	9	Gordie Howe, Det.	3.00
☐	10	Brad Park, NYR.	.10
☐	11	Brian Bellows, Min.	.10
☐	12	Chris Chelios, Chi.	.75
☐	13	Bill Barber, Pha.	.25
☐	14	Gump Worsley (G), NYR.	.75
☐	15	Stanley Cup	.50
☐	16	Maurice Richard, Mtl.	2.75
☐	17	Kevin Hatcher, Wsh.	.10
☐	18	Ed Belfour (G), Chi.	.50
☐	19	Kirk Muller, Mtl.	.10
☐	20	Kevin Stevens, Pgh.	.10
☐	21	Dave Taylor, L.A.	.10
☐	22	Dale Hawerchuk, Buf.	.25
☐	23	Jean Béliveau, Mtl.	2.00
☐	24	Rogatien Vachon (G), L.A.	.25
☐	25	Tom Barrasso (G), Pgh.	.25
☐	26	Rod Langway, Wsh.	.10

	No.	Player	Price
☐	27	Pierre Turgeon, NYI.	.25
☐	28	Derek King, NYI.	.10
☐	29	Brendan Shanahan, Stl.	1.25
☐	30	Darren Turcotte, NYR.	.10
☐	31	Chris Terreri (G), N.J.	.10
☐	32	Tony Granato, L.A.	.10
☐	33	Michel Goulet, Que.	.10
☐	34	Félix Potvin (G), Tor.	1.00
☐	35	Curtis Joseph (G), Stl.	1.25
☐	36	Cam Neely, Bos.	.50
☐	37	Borje Salming, Tor.	.50
☐	38	Denis Savard, Mtl.	.25
☐	39	Stan Mikita, Chi.	1.50
☐	40	Grant Fuhr (G), Buf.	.25
☐	41	Gary Suter, Cgy.	.10
☐	42	Serge Savard, Mtl.	.25
☐	43	Steve Larmer, NYR.	.10
☐	44	Bryan Trottier, Pgh.	.50
☐	45	Mike Vernon (G), Cgy.	.25
☐	46	Paul Coffey, Det.	.25
☐	47	Bernie Federko, Stl.	.10
☐	48	Larry Murphy, Pgh.	.25
☐	49	Scotty Bowman, Det.	.50
☐	50	Glenn Anderson, NYR.	.10
☐	51	Mats Sundin, Que.	1.00
☐	52	Henri Richard, Mtl.	.50
☐	53	Ron Francis, Pgh.	.50
☐	54	Scott Niedermayer, N.J.	.25
☐	55	Teemu Selänne, Wpg.	1.50
☐	56	Frank Mahovlich, Tor.	.75
☐	57	Owen Nolan, Que.	.25
☐	58	Rick Tocchet, Pgh.	.10
☐	59	Rod Brind'Amour, Pha.	.25
☐	60	Mike Modano, Dal.	1.00
☐	61	Doug Gilmour, Tor.	.50
☐	62	Jimmy Carson, Van.	.10
☐	63	Mike Keane, Mtl.	.10
☐	64	Bernie Nicholls, N.J.	.10
☐	65	Scott Stevens, N.J.	.10
☐	66	Mario Lemieux, Pgh.	3.00
☐	67	Keith Primeau, Det.	.25
☐	68	Bobby Carpenter, N.J.	.10
☐	69	Sergei Fedorov, Det.	1.00
☐	70	Peter Stastny, Stl.	.15
☐	71	Brian Leetch, NYR.	.50
☐	72	Vincent Damphousse, Mtl.	.25
☐	73	Darryl Sittler, Tor.	.50
☐	74	Al Iafrate, Bos.	.10
☐	75	Alexander Mogilny, Buf.	.50
☐	76	Bill Ranford (G), Edm.	.25
☐	77	Ray Bourque, Bos.	1.00
☐	78	Joey Mullen, Pgh.	.10
☐	79	Mike Ricci, Que.	.10
☐	80	Bobby Clarke, Pha.	.50
☐	81	Gerry Cheevers (G), Bos.	.25
☐	82	Joe Nieuwendyk, Cgy.	.25
☐	83	Terry Sawchuk (G), Det.	2.00
☐	84	Ray Ferraro, Hfd.	.10
☐	85	Lanny McDonald, Cgy.	.25
☐	86	Adam Graves, NYR.	.10
☐	87	Tomas Sandström, L.A.	.10
☐	88	Eric Lindros, Pha.	2.50
☐	89	Jari Kurri, L.A.	.25
☐	90	Al MacInnis, Cgy.	.25
☐	91	Alexandre Daigle, Ott.	.25
☐	92	Larry Robinson, Mtl.	.25
☐	93	Kelly Hrudey (G), L.A.	.10
☐	94	Theoren Fleury, L.A.	.25
☐	95	Billy Smith (G), NYI.	.25
☐	96	Luc Robitaille, L.A.	.25
☐	97	Brett Hull, Stl.	1.00
☐	98	Pat Falloon, S.J.	.10
☐	99	Wayne Gretzky, L.A.	4.00
☐	100	Joe Sakic, Que.	1.75
☐	101	Phil Housley, Stl.	.10
☐	102	Mark Messier, NYR.	1.00
☐	103	Jeremy Roenick, Chi.	.75
☐	104	Mark Recchi, Pha.	.25
☐	105	Pat LaFontaine, Buf.	.25
☐	106	Trevor Linden, Van.	.25
☐	107	Jaromir Jagr, Pgh.	2.00
☐	108	Steve Yzerman, Det.	2.00

1993 - 94 JYVAS HYVA HOCKEY LIIGA

Tero Lehterä 197 — Vladimir Jursinov 313 — Erik Hämäläinen 106

A set of 348 stickers plus a collecting album for the Finnish National League. There are three player stickers to each panel. Team panels are made up of 12 stickers. Stickers numbered 30, 60, 90, 120, 150, 180, 210, 240, 270, 300 and 330 were never issued. We have little pricing information on this set. The Saku Koivu panel is the most expensive single at $10.00. Singles start at 20¢.

Size: 2" x 3 3/8"

Imprint:

	No.	Player
☐	1	HIFK Helsinki
☐	2	HIFK Helsinki
☐	3	HIFK Helsinki
☐	4	HIFK Helsinki
☐	5	HIFK Helsinki
☐	6	HIFK Helsinki
☐	7	HIFK Helsinki
☐	8	HIFK Helsinki
☐	9	HIFK Helsinki
☐	10	HIFK Helsinki
☐	11	HIFK Helsinki
☐	12	HIFK Helsinki
☐	13	Harri Rindell
☐	14	Sakari Lindfors (G)
☐	15	Simo Saarinen
☐	16	Pertti Lehtonen
☐	17	Jari Laukkanen
☐	18	Valeri Krykov
☐	19	Iiro Jarvi
☐	20	Jari Munck
☐	21	Pasi Sormunen
☐	22	Pekka Peltola
☐	23	Teppo Kivela
☐	24	Pekka Tuomisto
☐	25	Kai Tervonen
☐	26	Dan Lambert
☐	27	Marco Poulsen
☐	28	Ville Peltonen
☐	29	Kim Ahlroos
☐	31	HPK Hameenlinna
☐	32	HPK Hameenlinna
☐	33	HPK Hameenlinna
☐	34	HPK Hameenlinna
☐	35	HPK Hameenlinna
☐	36	HPK Hameenlinna
☐	37	HPK Hameenlinna
☐	38	HPK Hameenlinna
☐	39	HPK Hameenlinna
☐	40	HPK Hameenlinna
☐	41	HPK Hameenlinna
☐	42	HPK Hameenlinna
☐	43	Pentti Matikainen
☐	44	Kari Rosenberg (G)
☐	45	Mikko Myllykoski
☐	46	Janne Laukkanen
☐	47	Jarkko Nikander
☐	48	Tomas Kapusta
☐	49	Mika Lartama
☐	50	Niko Marttila
☐	51	Jari Haapamaki
☐	52	Tommi Varjonen
☐	53	Toni Virta
☐	54	Marko Palo
☐	55	Marko Allen
☐	56	Miikka Ruohonen
☐	57	Jani Hassinen
☐	58	Pasi Kivila
☐	59	Markku Piikkila
☐	61	Ilves Tampere
☐	62	Ilves Tampere
☐	63	Ilves Tampere
☐	64	Ilves Tampere
☐	65	Ilves Tampere
☐	66	Ilves Tampere
☐	67	Ilves Tampere
☐	68	Ilves Tampere
☐	69	Ilves Tampere
☐	70	Ilves Tampere
☐	71	Ilves Tampere
☐	72	Ilves Tampere
☐	73	Jukka Jalonen
☐	74	Jukka Tammi (G)
☐	75	Jani Nikko
☐	76	Hannu Henriksson
☐	77	Juha Jarvenpaa
☐	78	Hannu Mattila
☐	79	Timo Peltomaa
☐	80	Jukka Ollila
☐	81	JuhaMatti Marijarvi
☐	82	Mikko Luovi
☐	83	Jarno Peltonen
☐	84	Pasi Maattanen
☐	85	Juha Lampinen
☐	86	Allan Measures
☐	87	Janne Seva
☐	88	Risto Jalo
☐	89	Esa Tommila
☐	91	Jokerit Helsinki
☐	92	Jokerit Helsinki
☐	93	Jokerit Helsinki
☐	94	Jokerit Helsinki
☐	95	Jokerit Helsinki
☐	96	Jokerit Helsinki
☐	97	Jokerit Helsinki
☐	98	Jokerit Helsinki
☐	99	Jokerit Helsinki
☐	100	Jokerit Helsinki
☐	101	Jokerit Helsinki
☐	102	Jokerit Helsinki
☐	103	Alpo Suhonen
☐	104	Ari Sulander (G)
☐	105	Kari Martikainen
☐	106	Erik Hamalainen
☐	107	Juha Jokiharju
☐	108	Otakar Janecky
☐	109	Petri Varis
☐	110	Waltteri Immonen
☐	111	Mika Stromberg
☐	112	Keijo Sailynoja
☐	113	Timo Saarikoski
☐	114	Juha Ylonen
☐	115	Ari Salo
☐	116	Heikki Riihijarvi
☐	117	Timo Norppa
☐	118	Jali Wahlsten
☐	119	Rami Koivisto
☐	121	JyP HT Jyvaskyla
☐	122	JyP HT Jyvaskyla
☐	123	JyP HT Jyvaskyla
☐	124	JyP HT Jyvaskyla
☐	125	JyP HT Jyvaskyla
☐	126	JyP HT Jyvaskyla
☐	127	JyP HT Jyvaskyla
☐	128	JyP HT Jyvaskyla
☐	129	JyP HT Jyvaskyla
☐	130	JyP HT Jyvaskyla
☐	131	JyP HT Jyvaskyla
☐	132	JyP HT Jyvaskyla
☐	133	Kari Savolainen
☐	134	AriPekka Siekkinen (G)
☐	135	Harri Laurila
☐	136	Markku Heikkinen
☐	137	Jari Lindroos
☐	138	Lasse Nieminen
☐	139	Risto Kurkinen
☐	140	Jarmo Jokilahti
☐	141	VeliPekka Hard
☐	142	Joni Lius
☐	143	Jyrki Jokinen
☐	144	Mika Arvaja
☐	145	Vesa Ponto
☐	146	Jarmo Rantanen
☐	147	Mika Paananen
☐	148	Marko Virtanen
☐	149	Marko Ek
☐	151	Kalpa Kuopio

☐ 152 Kalpa Kuopio
☐ 153 Kalpa Kuopio
☐ 154 Kalpa Kuopio
☐ 155 Kalpa Kuopio
☐ 156 Kalpa Kuopio
☐ 157 Kalpa Kuopio
☐ 158 Kalpa Kuopio
☐ 159 Kalpa Kuopio
☐ 160 Kalpa Kuopio
☐ 161 Kalpa Kuopio
☐ 162 Kalpa Kuopio
☐ 163 Hannu Kapanen
☐ 164 Pasi Kuivalainen (G)
☐ 165 Kimmo Timonen
☐ 166 Vesa Salo
☐ 167 Jani Rautio
☐ 168 Pekka Tirkkonen
☐ 169 Dimitri Zinine
☐ 170 Antti Tuomenoksa
☐ 171 Jari Jarvinen
☐ 172 Tuomas Kalliomaki
☐ 173 Tommi Miettinen
☐ 174 Sami Kapanen
☐ 175 Vesa Ruotsalainen
☐ 176 Mikko Tavi
☐ 177 Sami Mettovaara
☐ 178 VeliPekka Pekkarinen
☐ 179 Arto Sirvio
☐ 181 Kiekko-Espoo
☐ 182 Kiekko-Espoo
☐ 183 Kiekko-Espoo
☐ 184 Kiekko-Espoo
☐ 185 Kiekko-Espoo
☐ 186 Kiekko-Espoo
☐ 187 Kiekko-Espoo
☐ 188 Kiekko-Espoo
☐ 189 Kiekko-Espoo
☐ 190 Kiekko-Espoo
☐ 191 Kiekko-Espoo
☐ 192 Kiekko-Espoo
☐ 193 Martti Merra
☐ 194 Timo Maki (G)
☐ 195 Sami Nuutinen
☐ 196 Teemu Sillanpaa
☐ 197 Tero Lehtera
☐ 198 Jan Langbacka
☐ 199 Jukka Tiilikainen
☐ 200 Petri Pulkkinen
☐ 201 Robert Salo
☐ 202 Petro Koivunen
☐ 203 Juha Ikonen
☐ 204 Mikko Lempiainen
☐ 205 Marko Halonen
☐ 206 Jimi Helin
☐ 207 Timo Hirvonen
☐ 208 Mikko Halonen
☐ 209 Kimmo MakiKokkila
☐ 211 Rauman Lukko
☐ 212 Rauman Lukko
☐ 213 Rauman Lukko
☐ 214 Rauman Lukko
☐ 215 Rauman Lukko
☐ 216 Rauman Lukko
☐ 217 Rauman Lukko
☐ 218 Rauman Lukko
☐ 219 Rauman Lukko
☐ 220 Rauman Lukko
☐ 221 Rauman Lukko
☐ 222 Rauman Lukko
☐ 223 Vaclav Sykora
☐ 224 Jarmo Myllys (G)
☐ 225 KariPekka Friman
☐ 226 Timo Kulonen
☐ 227 Pasi Saarela
☐ 228 Kalle Sahlstedt
☐ 229 Kimmo Rintanen
☐ 230 Jarmo Kuusisto
☐ 231 Tuomas Gronman
☐ 232 Tero Arkiomaa
☐ 233 Petr Korinek
☐ 234 Mika Alatalo
☐ 235 Marko Tuulola
☐ 236 Pasi Huura
☐ 237 Tommi Pullola
☐ 238 Mika Valila
☐ 239 Jari Torkki
☐ 241 Reipas Lahti
☐ 242 Reipas Lahti
☐ 243 Reipas Lahti
☐ 244 Reipas Lahti
☐ 245 Reipas Lahti
☐ 246 Reipas Lahti
☐ 247 Reipas Lahti
☐ 248 Reipas Lahti
☐ 249 Reipas Lahti
☐ 250 Reipas Lahti
☐ 251 Reipas Lahti
☐ 252 Reipas Lahti
☐ 253 Kari Makinen
☐ 254 Oldrich Svoboda (G)
☐ 255 Timo Kahelin
☐ 256 Pasi Ruponen
☐ 257 Tommy Kiviaho
☐ 258 Jari Multanen
☐ 259 Erkki Makela
☐ 260 Jari Parviainen
☐ 261 Petri Koski
☐ 262 Jonni Vauhkonen
☐ 263 Toni Koivunen
☐ 264 Sami Wikstrom
☐ 265 Jarkko Hamalainen
☐ 266 Sami Helenius
☐ 267 Sami Lekkerimaki
☐ 268 Jari Kauppila
☐ 269 Jani Uski
☐ 271 Tappara Tampere
☐ 272 Tappara Tampere
☐ 273 Tappara Tampere
☐ 274 Tappara Tampere
☐ 275 Tappara Tampere
☐ 276 Tappara Tampere
☐ 277 Tappara Tampere
☐ 278 Tappara Tampere
☐ 279 Tappara Tampere
☐ 280 Tappara Tampere
☐ 281 Tappara Tampere
☐ 282 Tappara Tampere
☐ 283 Boris Majorov
☐ 284 Timo Hankela (G)
☐ 285 Timo Jutila
☐ 286 Samuli Rautio
☐ 287 Ari Haanpaa
☐ 288 Mikko Peltola
☐ 289 Pauli Jarvinen
☐ 290 Pekka Laksola
☐ 291 Janne Gronvall
☐ 292 Kari Heikkinen
☐ 293 Tommi Pohja
☐ 294 Petri Aaltonen
☐ 295 Petri Kalteva
☐ 296 Tommi Haapsaari
☐ 297 Teemu Numminen
☐ 298 Pasi Forsberg
☐ 299 VeliPekka Kautonen
☐ 301 TPS Turku
☐ 302 TPS Turku
☐ 303 TPS Turku
☐ 304 TPS Turku
☐ 305 TPS Turku
☐ 306 TPS Turku
☐ 307 TPS Turku
☐ 308 TPS Turku
☐ 309 TPS Turku
☐ 310 TPS Turku
☐ 311 TPS Turku
☐ 312 TPS Turku
☐ 313 Vladimir Yursinov
☐ 314 Jouni Rokama (G)
☐ 315 Hannu Virta
☐ 316 Erik Kakko
☐ 317 Jukka Vilander
☐ 318 Esa Keskinen
☐ 319 Ari Vuori
☐ 320 Jouko Narvanmaa
☐ 321 Marko Kiprusoff
☐ 322 Jere Lehtinen
☐ 323 Saku Koivu
☐ 324 Marko Jantunen
☐ 325 Kari Harila
☐ 326 Aleksander Smirnov
☐ 327 Toni Sihvonen
☐ 328 Harri Sillgren
☐ 329 Kai Nurminen
☐ 331 Assat Pori
☐ 332 Assat Pori
☐ 333 Assat Pori
☐ 334 Assat Pori
☐ 335 Assat Pori
☐ 336 Assat Pori
☐ 337 Assat Pori
☐ 338 Assat Pori
☐ 339 Assat Pori
☐ 340 Assat Pori
☐ 341 Assat Pori
☐ 342 Assat Pori
☐ 343 VeliPekka Ketola
☐ 344 Kari Takko (G)
☐ 345 Olli Kaski
☐ 346 Karri Kivi
☐ 347 Arto Heiskanen
☐ 348 Janne Virtanen
☐ 349 Mikael Kotkaniemi
☐ 350 Stanislav Meciar
☐ 351 Jarmo Miikkulainen
☐ 352 Jokke Heinanen
☐ 353 Vjatseslav Fandul
☐ 354 Ari Saarinen
☐ 355 Jouni Vento
☐ 356 Arto Javanainen
☐ 357 Jari Korpisalo
☐ 358 Rauli Raitanen
☐ 359 Jari Levonen

1993 - 94 KENNER STARTING LINEUP

Each figurine came with two cards. Canadian cards have bilingual text.

Figurine Size: 3 1/2" to 5 1/2"

Canadian Set (11 figurines): 300.00

American Set (12 figurines): 550.00

	Player	U.S.	Cdn.
☐☐	Ed Belfour (G), Chi.	110.00	75.00
☐☐	Ray Bourque, Bos.	25.00	18.00
☐	Grant Fuhr (G), Buf.	200.00	–
☐☐	Brett Hull, Stl.	16.00	15.00
☐☐	Jarmir Jagr, Pgh.	40.00	30.00
☐☐	Pat LaFontaine, Buf.	100.00	50.00
☐☐	Mario Lemieux, Pgh.	30.00	25.00
☐☐	Eric Lindros, Pha.	50.00	35.00
☐☐	Mark Messier, NYR.	40.00	25.00
☐☐	Jeremy Roenick, Chi.	25.00	20.00
☐☐	Patrick Roy (G), Mtl.	110.00	90.00
☐☐	Steve Yzerman, Det.	35.00	28.00

1993 - 94 KRAFT

Imprint:

Complete Set (69 cards): 100.00

Album: 35.00

GOLD EDITION

This set was orginally issued as a six card panel. Panels were inserted in specially marked 12-box cases of Kraft Dinner.

Card Size: 3 1/2" x 5 1/4"

	Player	NRMT-MT
☐	Jason Arnott, Edm.	3.50
☐	Chris Chelios, Chi.	3.00
☐	Mario Lemieux, Pgh.	4.50
☐	Rob Niedermayer, Fla.	2.00
☐	Chris Pronger, Hfd.	2.00
☐	Patrick Roy (G), Mtl.	4.50

PANEL CARDS

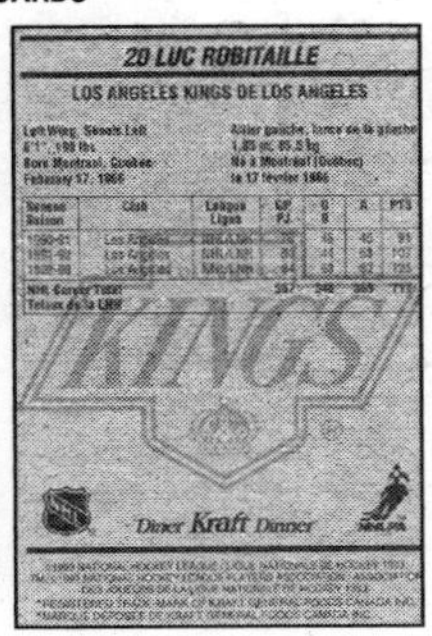

One of 26 different cards was issued on the backs of specially marked boxes of Kraft Dinner.

Card Size: 3 1/2" x 5 1/4"

	Player	NRMT-MT
☐	Ed Belfour (G), Chi.	2.00
☐	Brian Bradley, T.B.	1.00
☐	Pavel Bure, Van.	3.00
☐	Paul Coffey, Det.	1.50
☐	Russ Courtnall, Dal.	1.00
☐	Alexandre Daigle, Ott.	1.50
☐	Pat Falloon, S.J.	1.00
☐	Theoren Fleury, Cgy.	2.00
☐	Doug Gilmour, Tor.	2.00
☐	Adam Graves, NYR.	1.00
☐	Stu Grimson, Ana.	1.00
☐	Al Iafrate, Wsh.	1.00
☐	Jaromir Jagr, Pgh.	3.75
☐	Joé Juneau, Bos.	1.00
☐	Eric Lindros, Pha.	4.50
☐	Alexander Mogilny, Buf.	2.00
☐	Kirk Muller, Mtl.	1.00
☐	Bill Ranford (G), Edm.	1.50
☐	Mike Ricci, Que.	1.00
☐	Luc Robitaille, L.A.	1.50
☐	Geoff Sanderson, Hfd.	1.00
☐	Teemu Selänne, Wpg.	3.00
☐	Brendan Shanahan, Stl.	2.75
☐	Pierre Turgeon, NYI.	1.50
☐	John Vanbiesbrouck (G), Fla.	2.75
☐	Valeri Zelepukin, N.J.	1.00

DISKS

Two of 23 different captains and coaches disks were found under the lids of specially marked jars of Kraft Peanut Butter.

Disk Diameter: 2 1/2"

	Player	NRMT-MT
☐	Ray Bourque, Bos. / Patrick Flatley, NYI.	3.00
☐	Guy Carbonneau, Mtl. / Jeremy Roenick, Chi.	2.50
☐	Kevin Dineen, Pha. / Kevin Hatcher, Wsh.	2.00
☐	Wayne Gretzky, L.A. / Wendel Clark, Tor.	8.00
☐	Brett Hull, Stl. / Brad Shaw, Ott.	3.00
☐	Dean Kennedy, Wpg. / Denis Savard, T.B.	2.50
☐	Pat LaFontaine, Buf. / Pat Verbeek, Hfd.	2.50
☐	Mike Lalor, S.J. / Mark Tinordi, Dal.	2.00
☐	Mario Lemieux, Pgh. / Mark Messier, NYR.	6.00
☐	Trevor Linden, Van. / Troy Loney, Ana.	2.50
☐	Craig MacTavish, Edm. / Brian Skrudland, Fla.	2.00
☐	Joe Nieuwendyk, Cgy. / Joe Sakic, Mtl.	3.50
☐	Scott Stevens, N.J. / Steve Yzerman, Det.	4.00
☐	Al Arbour, Coach, NYI.	2.00
☐	Bob Berry, Coach, Stl.	1.50
☐	Scott Bowman, Coach, Det.	2.50
☐	Pat Burns, Coach, Tor.	2.00
☐	Jacques Demers, Coach, Mtl.	1.50
☐	Eddie Johnston, Coach, Pgh.	1.50
☐	Dave King, Coach, Cgy.	2.00
☐	Barry Melrose, Coach, L.A.	1.50
☐	John Muckler, Coach, Buf.	1.50
☐	Pierre Pagé, Coach, Que.	1.50

POP-OUT PANELS

One of 8 different panels were found under tops of specially marked boxes of JELL-O pudding (4x142g).

Panel Size: 3 11/16" x 5 3/16"

	Player	NRMT-MT
☐	Stéphane Fiset / Joe Sakic	3.50
☐	Eric Lindros / Dominic Roussel	5.00
☐	Félix Potvin / Doug Gilmour	3.00
☐	Kirk Muller / Patrick Roy	5.50
☐	Tom Barrasso / Mario Lemieux	5.50
☐	Wayne Gretzky / Kelly Hrudey	7.00
☐	Kirk McLean / Pavél Bure	3.00
☐	Joe Nieuwendyk / Mike Vernon	2.00

1993 - 94 LEAF

Imprint: 1993 Leaf, Inc.
Series One Set (220 cards): 20.00
Series Two Set (220 cards): 20.00
Common Player: .15

	No.	Player	NRMT-MT
☐	1	Mario Lemieux, Pgh.	2.00
☐	2	Curtis Joseph (G), Stl.	.75
☐	3	Stephen Leach, Bos.	.15
☐	4	Vincent Damphousse, Mtl.	.35
☐	5	Murray Craven, Van.	.15
☐	6	Pat Elynuik, Wsh.	.15
☐	7	Bill Guerin, N.J.	.25
☐	8	Zarley Zalapski, Hfd.	.15
☐	**9**	**Rob Gaudreau, S.J., RC**	**.15**
☐	10	Pavel Bure, Van.	1.00
☐	11	Brad Shaw, Ott.	.15
☐	12	Pat LaFontaine, Buf.	.25
☐	13	Teemu Selänne, Wpg.	1.00
☐	14	Trent Klatt, Dal.	.15
☐	15	Kevin Todd, Edm.	.15
☐	16	Larry Murphy, Pgh.	.25
☐	17	Tony Amonte, NYR.	.25
☐	18	Dino Ciccarelli, Det.	.25
☐	19	Doug Bodger, Buf.	.15
☐	20	Luc Robitaille, L.A.	.25
☐	21	John Tucker, T.B.	.15
☐	22	Todd Gill, Tor.	.15
☐	23	Mike Ricci, Que.	.15
☐	24	Evgeny Davydov, Wpg.	.15
☐	25	Pierre Turgeon, NYI.	.25
☐	26	Rod Brind'Amour, Pha.	.25
☐	27	Jeremy Roenick, Chi.	.25
☐	28	Joel Otto, Cgy.	.15
☐	29	Jeff Brown, Stl.	.15
☐	30	Brendan Shanahan, Stl.	.75
☐	31	Jiri Slegr, Van.	.15
☐	32	Vladimir Malakhov, NYI.	.15
☐	33	Patrick Roy (G), Mtl.	2.00
☐	34	Kevin Hatcher, Wsh.	.15
☐	35	Alexander Semak, N.J.	.15
☐	36	Gary Roberts, Cal.	.25
☐	37	Tommy Söderström (G), Pha.	.15
☐	38	Bob Essensa (G), Wpg.	.15
☐	39	Kelly Hurdey (G), L.A.	.15
☐	40	Shawn Chambers, T.B.	.15
☐	41	Glenn Anderson, Tor.	.15
☐	42	Owen Nolan, Que.	.25
☐	43	Patrick Flatley, NYI.	.15
☐	44	Ray Sheppard, Det.	.15
☐	45	Darren Turcotte, NYR.	.15
☐	46	Shayne Corson, Edm.	.25
☐	47	Brad May, Buf.	.15
☐	48	Bob Kudelski, Ott.	.15
☐	49	Pat Falloon, S.J.	.15
☐	50	Andrew Cassels, Hfd.	.15
☐	51	Chris Chelios, Chi.	.35
☐	52	Sylvain Côté, Wsh.	.15
☐	53	Mathieu Schneider, Mtl.	.15
☐	54	Ted Donato, Bos.	.15
☐	55	Kirk McLean (G), Van.	.25
☐	56	Bruce Driver, N.J.	.15
☐	57	Uwe Krupp, NYI.	.15
☐	58	Brent Fedyk, Pha.	.15
☐	59	Robert Reichel, Cgy.	.15
☐	60	Scott Stevens, N.J.	.25
☐	61	Phil Housley, Wpg.	.15
☐	62	Ed Belfour (G), Chi.	.35
☐	63	Dave Andreychuk, Tor.	.15
☐	64	Claude Lapointe, Que.	.15
☐	65	Russ Courtnall, Min.	.15
☐	66	Grant Fuhr (G), Buf.	.25
☐	67	Paul Coffey, Det.	.25
☐	68	Bill Ranford (G), Edm.	.25
☐	69	Kevin Stevens, Pgh.	.15
☐	70	Brian Leetch, NYR.	.35
☐	71	Dale Hawerchuk, Buf.	.25
☐	72	Geoff Courtnall, Van.	.15
☐	73	Sandis Ozolinsh, S.J.	.25
☐	74	Sylvain Turgeon, Ott.	.15
☐	75	Nelson Emerson, Stl.	.15
☐	76	Brian Bellows, Mtl.	.15
☐	77	Geoff Sanderson, Hfd.	.15
☐	78	Petr Nedved, Van.	.15
☐	79	Peter Bondra, Wsh.	.35
☐	80	Scott Niedermayer, N.J.	.25
☐	81	Steve Thomas, NYI.	.15
☐	82	Dimitri Yushkevitch, Pha.	.15
☐	83	Mike Vernon (G), Cgy.	.25
☐	84	Alexei Zhamnov, Wpg.	.25
☐	85	Adam Creighton, T.B.	.15
☐	86	Dave Ellett, Tor.	.15
☐	87	Joe Sakic, Que.	1.25
☐	88	Mike Craig, Min.	.15
☐	89	Nicklas Lidstrom, Det.	.25
☐	90	Ed Olczyk, NYR.	.15
☐	91	Alexander Mogilny, Buf.	.35
☐	92	Ulf Samuelsson, Pgh.	.15
☐	93	Doug Gilmour, Tor.	.35
☐	94	Mikael Nylander, Hfd.	.15
☐	95	Steve Smith, Chi.	.15
☐	96	Igor Korolev, Stl.	.15
☐	97	Dixon Ward, Van.	.15
☐	98	John LeClair, Mtl.	.75
☐	99	Cam Neely, Bos.	.25
☐	100	Stanley Cup Champions / P. Roy (G)	2.00
☐	101	Darius Kasparaitis, NYI.	.15
☐	102	Mike Ridley, Wsh.	.15
☐	103	Josef Beranek, Edm.	.15
☐	104	Valeri Zelepukin, N.J.	.15
☐	105	Keith Tkachuk, Wpg.	.50
☐	106	Tomas Sandström, L.A.	.15
☐	107	Peter Zezel, Tor.	.15
☐	108	Scott Young, Que.	.15
☐	109	Rick Tocchet, Pgh.	.15
☐	110	CL: Teemu Selänne, Wpg.	.50
☐	111	Steve Chiasson, Det.	.15
☐	112	Doug Zmolek, S.J.	.15
☐	113	Patrick Poulin, Hfd.	.15
☐	114	Stéphane Matteau, Chi.	.15
☐	115	Yves Racine, Det.	.15
☐	116	Steve Heinze, Bos.	.15
☐	117	Gilbert Dionne, Mtl.	.15
☐	118	Dale Hunter, Wsh.	.15
☐	119	Derek King, NYI.	.15
☐	120	Garry Galley, Pha.	.15
☐	121	Ray Ferraro, NYI.	.15
☐	122	Andrei Kovalenko, Que.	.15
☐	123	Alexei Zhitnik, L.A.	.15
☐	124	Fredrik Olausson, Wpg.	.15
☐	125	Claude Lemieux, N.J.	.15
☐	126	Joe Nieuwendyk, Cgy.	.25
☐	127	Travis Green, NYI.	.15
☐	128	Dave Gagner, Min.	.15
☐	129	Sergei Fedorov, Det.	.50
☐	130	Adam Graves, NYR.	.15
☐	131	Petr Svoboda, Buf.	.15
☐	132	Sean Burke (G), Hfd.	.25
☐	133	Johan Garpenlov, S.J.	.15

	No.	Player	Price
☐	134	Jamie Baker, Ott.	.15
☐	135	Teppo Numminen, Wpg.	.15
☐	136	Mats Sundin, Que.	.50
☐	137	Nikolai Borschevsky, Tor.	.15
☐	138	Stéphane Richer, N.J.	.15
☐	139	Scott Lachance, NYI.	.15
☐	140	Gary Suter, Cgy.	.15
☐	141	Al Iafrate, Wsh.	.15
☐	142	Brent Sutter, Chi.	.15
☐	143	Dmitri Kvartalnov, Bos.	.15
☐	144	Pat Verbeek, Hfd.	.15
☐	145	Ed Courtenay, S.J.	.15
☐	146	Mark Tinordi, Min.	.15
☐	147	Alexei Kovalev, NYR.	.15
☐	**148**	**Dallas Drake, Det., RC**	**.15**
☐	149	Jimmy Carson, L.A.	.15
☐	150	Florida Panthers Logo	.75
☐	151	Roman Hamrlik, T.B.	.25
☐	152	Martin Rucinsky, Que.	.15
☐	153	Calle Johansson, Wsh.	.15
☐	154	Theoren Fleury, Cgy.	.35
☐	155	Benoît Hogue, NYI.	.15
☐	156	Kevin Dineen, Pha.	.15
☐	157	Jody Hull, Ott.	.15
☐	158	Mark Messier, NYR.	.50
☐	159	Dave Manson, Edm.	.15
☐	160	Chris Kontos, T.B.	.15
☐	161	Ron Francis, Pgh.	.35
☐	162	Steve Yzerman, Det.	1.50
☐	163	Igor Kravchuk, Edm.	.15
☐	164	Sergei Zubov, NYR.	.25
☐	165	Thomas Steen, Wpg.	.15
☐	166	Wendel Clark, Tor.	.25
☐	**167**	**Scott Pellerin, N.J., RC**	**.15**
☐	168	Dimitri Khristich, Wsh.	.15
☐	169	Bernie Nicholls, N.J.	.15
☐	170	Paul Ranheim, Cgy.	.15
☐	171	Robert Kron, Hfd.	.15
☐	172	Rob Blake, L.A.	.25
☐	173	Rob Zamuner, T.B.	.25
☐	174	Rob Pearson, Tor.	.15
☐	175	CL: Ed Belfour, Chi.	.25
☐	176	Steve Duchesne, Que.	.15
☐	177	Pelle Eklund, Pha.	.15
☐	178	Michal Pivonka, Wsh.	.15
☐	179	Joe Murphy, Chi.	.15
☐	180	Al MacInnis, Cgy.	.25
☐	181	Craig Janney, Stl.	.15
☐	182	Kirk Muller, Mtl.	.15
☐	183	Cliff Ronning, Van.	.15
☐	184	Doug Weight, Edm.	.35
☐	185	Mike Richter (G), NYR.	.35
☐	186	Bob Probert, Det.	.15
☐	187	Robert Petrovicky, Hfd.	.15
☐	188	Richard Smehlik, Buf.	.15
☐	189	Norm Maciver, Ott.	.15
☐	190	Stéphan Lebeau, Mtl.	.15
☐	191	Patrice Brisebois, Mtl.	.15
☐	192	Kevin Miller, Stl.	.15
☐	193	Trevor Linden, Van.	.25
☐	194	Darrin Shannon, Wpg.	.15
☐	195	Tim Cheveldae (G), Det.	.15
☐	196	Tom Barrasso (G), Pgh.	.25
☐	197	Zdeno Ciger, Edm.	.15
☐	198	Ulf Dahlen, Min.	.15
☐	199	Arturs Irbe (G), S.J.	.15
☐	200	Anaheim Mighty Ducks Logo	.75
☐	201	Tony Granato, L.A.	.15
☐	202	Mike Modano, Min.	.50
☐	203	Eric Desjardins, Mtl.	.25
☐	204	Bryan Smolinski, Bos.	.15
☐	205	Mark Recchi, Pha.	.25
☐	206	Darryl Sydor, L.A.	.15
☐	207	Valeri Kamensky, Que.	.25
☐	208	Kelly Kisio, S.J.	.15
☐	209	Brian Bradley, T.B.	.15
☐	210	CL: Mario Lemieux, Pgh.	1.00
☐	211	Yuri Khmylev, Buf.	.15
☐	212	Derian Hatcher, Min.	.25
☐	213	Mike Gartner, NYR.	.25
☐	214	Mike Needham, Pgh.	.15
☐	215	Ray Bourque, Bos.	.50
☐	216	Tie Domi, Wpg.	.15
☐	217	Shawn McEachern, Pgh.	.15
☐	218	Joé Juneau, Bos.	.15
☐	219	Greg Adams, Van.	.15
☐	220	Martin Straka, Pgh.	.15
☐	221	Tom Fitzgerald, Fla.	.15
☐	222	Gary Shuchuk, L.A.	.15
☐	223	Kevin Haller, Mtl.	.15
☐	224	Bryan Marchment, Chi.	.15
☐	225	Louie DeBrusk, Edm.	.15
☐	226	Randy Wood, Buf.	.15
☐	227	Bobby Holik, N.J.	.15
☐	228	Troy Mallette, Ott.	.15
☐	229	Adam Foote, Que.	.25
☐	230	Bob Rouse, Tor.	.15
☐	231	Jyrki Lumme, Van.	.15
☐	232	James Patrick, NYR.	.15
☐	233	Eric Lindros, Pha.	2.00
☐	234	Joe Reekie, T.B.	.15
☐	235	Adam Oates, Bos.	.35
☐	236	Frank Musil, Cgy.	.15
☐	237	Vladimir Konstantinov, Det.	.15
☐	238	Dave Lowry, Fla.	.15
☐	239	Garth Butcher, Stl.	.15
☐	240	Jari Kurri, L.A.	.25
☐	241	Rick Tabaracci (G), Wsh.	.15
☐	242	Sergei Bautin, Wpg.	.15
☐	243	Scott Scissons, NYI.	.15
☐	244	Dominic Roussel (G), Pha.	.15
☐	245	John Cullen, Tor.	.15
☐	246	Sheldon Kennedy, Det.	.15
☐	247	Mike Hough, Fla.	.15
☐	248	Paul DiPietro, Mtl.	.15
☐	249	David Shaw, Bos.	.15
☐	250	Sergio Momesso, Van.	.15
☐	251	Jeff Daniels, Pgh.	.15
☐	252	Sergei Nemchinov, NYR.	.15
☐	253	Kris King, Wpg.	.15
☐	254	Kelly Miller, Wsh.	.15
☐	255	Brett Hull, Stl.	.50
☐	256	Dominik Hasek (G), Buf.	1.00
☐	257	Chris Pronger, Hfd.	.35
☐	**258**	**Derek Plante, Buf., RC**	**.25**
☐	259	Mark Howe, Det.	.15
☐	**260**	**Oleg Petrov, Mtl., RC**	**.15**
☐	261	Ronnie Stern, Cgy.	.15
☐	262	Scott Mellanby, Fla.	.15
☐	263	Warren Rychel, L.A.	.15
☐	264	John MacLean, N.J.	.15
☐	**265**	**Radek Hamr, Ott., RC**	**.15**
☐	266	Greg Hawgood, Pha.	.15
☐	267	Sylvain Lefebvre, Tor.	.15
☐	268	Glen Wesley, Bos.	.15
☐	269	Joe Cirella, Fla.	.15
☐	270	Dirk Graham, Chi.	.15
☐	271	Eric Weinrich, Hfd.	.15
☐	272	Donald Audette, Buf.	.15
☐	273	Jason Woolley, Wsh.	.15
☐	274	Kjell Samuelsson, Pha.	.15
☐	275	Ron Sutter, Stl.	.15
☐	276	Keith Primeau, Det.	.25
☐	277	Ron Tugnutt (G), Ana.	.15
☐	**278**	**Jesse Belanger, Fla., RC**	**.15**
☐	279	Mike Keane, Mtl.	.15
☐	280	Adam Burt, Hfd.	.15
☐	281	Don Sweeney, Bos.	.15
☐	282	Mike Donnelly, L.A.	.15
☐	283	Lyle Odelein, Mtl.	.15
☐	284	Gord Murphy, Fla.	.15
☐	285	Mikael Andersson, T.B.	.15
☐	286	Bret Hedican, Stl.	.15
☐	287	Bill Berg, Tor.	.15
☐	288	Esa Tikkanen, NYR.	.15
☐	289	Markus Naslund, Pgh.	.15
☐	290	CL: Chris Chelios, Chi.	.25
☐	291	Kerry Huffman, Que.	.15
☐	292	Dana Murzyn, Van.	.15
☐	293	Rob Niedermayer, Fla.	.25
☐	294	André Racicot (G), Mtl.	.15
☐	295	Ken Sutton, Buf.	.15
☐	296	Shawn Burr, Det.	.15
☐	297	Scott Pearson, Edm.	.15
☐	**298**	**Joby Messier, NYR., RC**	**.15**
☐	**299**	**Darrin Madeley (G), Ott., RC**	**.15**
☐	300	Joe Mullen, Pgh.	.25
☐	301	Stéphane Fiset (G), Que.	.25
☐	302	Geoff Smith, Edm.	.15
☐	303	Vyacheslav Kozlov, Det.	.15
☐	304	Wayne Gretzky, L.A.	2.50
☐	305	Curtis Leschyshyn, Que.	.15
☐	306	Mike Sillinger, Det.	.15
☐	307	Vyacheslav Butsayev, Pha.	.15
☐	308	Mark Lamb, Ott.	.15
☐	**309**	**German Titov, Cgy., RC**	**.15**
☐	310	Gerard Gallant, T.B.	.15
☐	311	Alexandre Daigle, Ott.	.35
☐	312	Jim Hrivnak (G), Stl.	.15
☐	313	Corey Hirsch (G), NYR.	.15
☐	314	Craig Berube, Wsh.	.15
☐	315	Bill Houlder, Ana.	.15
☐	316	Ron Wilson, Mtl.	.15
☐	317	Glen Murray, Bos.	.15
☐	318	Bryan Trottier, Pgh.	.25
☐	319	Jeff Hackett (G), Chi.	.15
☐	320	Brad Dalgarno, NYI.	.15
☐	321	Petr Klima, T.B.	.15
☐	322	Jon Casey (G), Bos.	.15
☐	323	Mikael Renberg, Pha.	.25
☐	324	Jimmy Waite (G), S.J.	.15
☐	325	Brian Skrudland, Fla.	.15
☐	326	Vitali Prokhorov, Stl.	.15
☐	327	Glenn Healy (G), NYR.	.15
☐	328	Brian Benning, Fla.	.15
☐	329	Tony Hrkac, Stl.	.15
☐	330	Stu Grimson, Ana.	.15
☐	331	Chris Gratton, T.B.	.35
☐	332	Dave Poulin, Wsh.	.15
☐	333	Jarrod Skalde, Ana.	.15
☐	334	Christian Ruuttu, Chi.	.15
☐	335	Mark Fitzpatrick (G), Fla.	.15
☐	336	Martin Lapointe, Det.	.15
☐	**337**	**Cam Stewart, Bos., RC**	**.15**
☐	338	Anatoli Semenov, Ana.	.15
☐	339	Gaetan Duchesne, S.J.	.15
☐	340	CL: Pierre Turgeon, NYI.	.25
☐	341	Ron Hextall (G), NYI.	.25
☐	342	Mikhail Tatarinov, Bos.	.15
☐	343	Danny Lorenz (G), NYI.	.15
☐	344	Craig Simpson, Buf.	.15
☐	345	Martin Brodeur (G), N.J.	1.00
☐	346	Jaromir Jagr, Pgh.	1.50
☐	347	Tyler Wright, Edm.	.15
☐	348	Greg Gilbert, NYR.	.15
☐	349	Dave Tippett, Pha.	.15
☐	350	Stu Barnes, Wpg.	.15
☐	351	Daniel Lacroix, NYR.	.15
☐	352	Marty McSorley, Pgh.	.15
☐	353	Sean Hill, Ana.	.15
☐	354	Craig Billington (G), Ott.	.15
☐	355	Donald Dufresne, T.B.	.15
☐	356	Guy Hebert (G), Ana.	.25
☐	357	Neil Wilkinson, Chi.	.15
☐	358	Sandy McCarthy, Cgy.	.15
☐	**359**	**Aaron Ward, Det., RC**	**.25**
☐	**360**	**Scott Thomas, Buf., RC**	**.15**
☐	361	Corey Millen, N.J.	.15
☐	362	Matthew Barnaby, Buf.	.15
☐	363	Benoît Brunet, Mtl.	.15
☐	364	Boris Mironov, Wpg.	.15
☐	365	Doug Lidster, NYR.	.15
☐	366	Pavol Demitra, Ott.	.15
☐	**367**	**Damian Rhodes (G), Tor., RC**	**.50**
☐	368	Shawn Antoski, Van.	.15
☐	369	Andy Moog (G), Dal.	.25
☐	370	Greg Johnson, Det.	.15
☐	371	John Vanbiesbrouck (G), Fla.	.75
☐	372	Denis Savard, T.B.	.25
☐	373	Michel Goulet, Chi.	.25
☐	374	Dave Taylor, L.A.	.15
☐	375	Enrico Ciccone, Wsh.	.15
☐	376	Sergei Zholtok, Bos.	.15
☐	377	Bob Errey, S.J.	.15
☐	378	Doug Brown, Pgh.	.15
☐	**379**	**Bill McDougall, T.B., RC**	**.15**
☐	380	Pat Conacher, L.A.	.15
☐	381	Alexei Kasatonov, Ana.	.15
☐	**382**	**Jason Arnott, Edm., RC**	**1.50**
☐	383	Jarkko Varvio, Dal.	.15
☐	384	Sergei Makarov, S.J.	.15
☐	385	Trevor Kidd (G), Cgy.	.25
☐	386	Alexei Yashin, Ott.	.75
☐	387	Gerald Diduck, Van.	.15
☐	388	Paul Ysebaert, Wpg.	.15

	No.	Player	Price
☐	**389**	**Jason Smith, N.J., RC**	**.15**
☐	390	Jeff Norton, S.J.	.15
☐	391	Igor Larionov, S.J.	.25
☐	392	Pierre Sévigny, Mtl.	.15
☐	393	Wes Walz, Cgy.	.15
☐	394	Grant Ledyard, Dal.	.15
☐	395	Brad McCrimmon, Hfd.	.15
☐	396	Martin Gelinas, Que.	.15
☐	397	Paul Cavallini, Dal.	.15
☐	398	Brian Noonan, Chi.	.15
☐	399	Mike Lalor, S.J.	.15
☐	400	Dimitri Filimonov, Ott.	.15
☐	401	Andrei Lomakin, Fla.	.15
☐	**402**	**Steve Junker, NYI., RC**	**.15**
☐	403	Daren Puppa (G), T.B.	.15
☐	404	Jozef Stumpel, Bos.	.15
☐	405	Jeff Shantz, Chi.	.15
☐	406	Terry Yake, Ana.	.15
☐	407	Mike Peluso, N.J.	.15
☐	408	Vitali Karamnov, Stl.	.15
☐	409	Félix Potvin (G), Tor.	.50
☐	410	Steven King, Ana.	.15
☐	**411**	**Roman Oksiuta, Edm., RC**	**.15**
☐	412	Mark Greig, Hfd.	.15
☐	413	Wayne McBean, NYI.	.15
☐	414	Nick Kypreos, Hfd.	.15
☐	415	Dominic Lavoie, L.A.	.15
☐	**416**	**Chris Simon, Que., RC**	**.25**
☐	**417**	**Peter Popovic, Mtl., RC**	**.15**
☐	418	Gino Odjick, Van.	.15
☐	419	Mike Rathje, S.J.	.15
☐	420	Keith Acton, Wsh.	.15
☐	421	Bob Carpenter, N.J.	.15
☐	422	Steven Finn, Que.	.15
☐	**423**	**Ian Herbers, Edm., RC**	**.15**
☐	**424**	**Ted Drury, Cgy., RC**	**.15**
☐	**425**	**Sergei Petrenko, Buf., RC**	**.15**
☐	**426**	**Mattias Norstrom, NYR., RC**	**.15**
☐	427	Todd Ewen, Ana.	.15
☐	**428**	**Jocelyn Thibault (G), Que., RC**	**2.00**
☐	429	Robert Burakovsky, Ott.	.15
☐	430	Chris Terreri (G), N.J.	.15
☐	**431**	**Michal Sykora, S.J., RC**	**.15**
☐	432	Craig Ludwig, Dal.	.15
☐	**433**	**Vesa Viitakoski, Cgy., RC**	**.15**
☐	434	Sergei Krivokrasov, Chi.	.15
☐	**435**	**Darren McCarty, Det., RC**	**.25**
☐	436	Dean McAmmond, Edm.	.15
☐	437	J. J. Daigneault, Mtl.	.15
☐	438	Vladimir Ruzicka, Ott.	.15
☐	439	Vlastimil Kroupa, S.J.	.15
☐	440	CL: Doug Gilmour, Tor.	.25

FRESHMAN PHENOMS

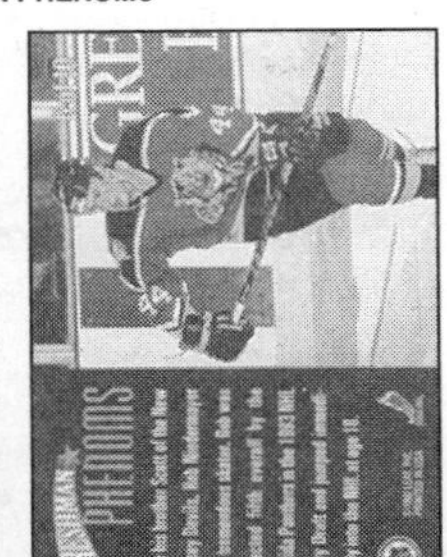

Insert Set (10 cards): **15.00**

	No.	Player	NRMT-MT
☐	1	Alexandre Daigle, Ott.	2.00
☐	2	Chris Pronger, Hfd.	2.00
☐	3	Chris Gratton, T.B.	2.00
☐	4	Markus Naslund, Pgh.	.75
☐	5	Mikael Renberg, Pha.	1.50
☐	6	Rob Niedermayer, Fla.	1.50
☐	7	Jason Arnott, Edm.	3.00
☐	8	Jarkko Varvio, Dal.	.75
☐	9	Alexei Yashin, Ott.	3.00
☐	10	Jocelyn Thibault (G), Que.	4.00

GOLD LEAF ALL-STARS

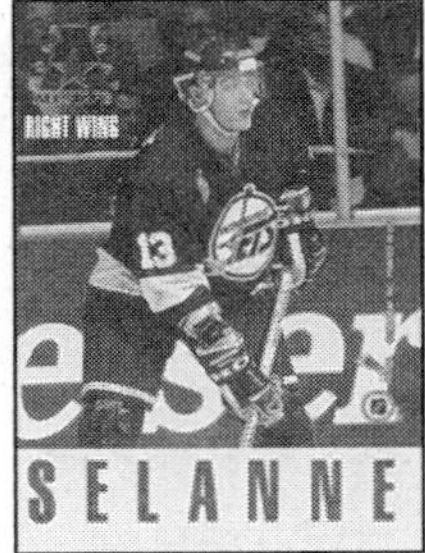

Insert Set (10 cards): **55.00**

	No.	Player	NRMT-MT
☐	1	M. Lemieux, Pgh./P. LaFontaine, Buf.	12.00
☐	2	C. Chelios, Chi./L. Murphy, Pgh.	3.00
☐	3	B. Hull, Stl./T. Selänne, Wpg.	5.00
☐	4	K. Stevens, Pgh./D. Andreychuk, Tor.	2.00
☐	5	P. Roy (G), Mtl./T. Barrasso (G), Pgh.	12.00
☐	6	W. Gretzky, L.A./D. Gilmour, Tor.	15.00
☐	7	R. Bourque, Bos./P. Coffey, Det.	3.50
☐	8	A. Mogilny, Buf./P. Bure, Van.	5.00
☐	9	L. Robitaille, L.A./B. Shanahan, Stl.	4.00
☐	10	E. Belfour (G), Chi./F. Potvin (G), Tor.	4.00

GOLD LEAF ROOKIES

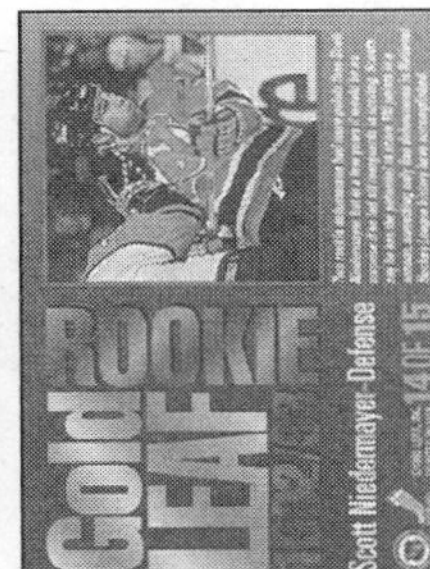

Series One Insert Set (15 cards): **18.00**

	No.	Player	NRMT-MT
☐	1	Teemu Selänne, Wpg.	3.00
☐	2	Joé Juneau, Bos.	.75
☐	3	Eric Lindros, Pha.	5.00
☐	4	Félix Potvin (G), Tor.	2.50
☐	5	Alexei Zhamnov, Wpg.	1.00
☐	6	Andrei Kovalenko, Que.	.75
☐	7	Shawn McEachern, Pgh.	.75
☐	8	Alexei Zhitnik, L.A.	.75
☐	9	Vladimir Malakhov, NYI.	.75
☐	10	Patrick Poulin, Hfd.	.75
☐	11	Keith Tkachuk, Wpg.	2.00
☐	12	Tommy Soderström (G), Pha.	1.00
☐	13	Darius Kasparaitis, NYI.	.75
☐	14	Scott Niedermayer, N.J.	1.00
☐	15	Darryl Sydor, L.A.	.75

HAT TRICK ARTISTS

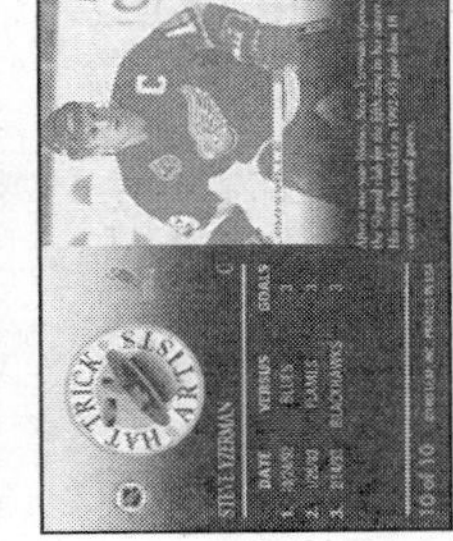

Insert Set (10 cards): **20.00**

	No.	Player	NRMT-MT
☐	1	Title Card, Mario Lemieux	4.00
☐	2	Alexander Mogilny, Buf.	1.50
☐	3	Teemu Selänne, Wpg.	3.00
☐	4	Mario Lemieux, Pgh.	6.50
☐	5	Pierre Turgeon, NYI.	.75
☐	6	Kevin Dineen, Pha.	.75
☐	7	Eric Lindros, Pha.	5.00
☐	8	Adam Oates, Bos.	1.50
☐	9	Kevin Stevens, Pgh.	.75
☐	10	Steve Yzerman, Det.	4.00

MARIO LEMIEUX COLLECTION

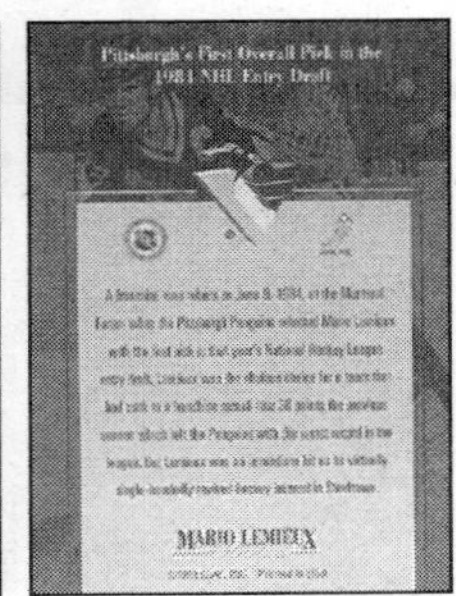

Insert Set (10 cards): **25.00**

	No.	Player	NRMT-MT
☐	1	Title Card	3.00
☐	2	1st Pick in 1984 NHL Draft	3.00
☐	3	1984 QMJHL Player of the Year	3.00
☐	4	1984/85 Calder Trophy Winner	3.00
☐	5	1987/88 Hart & Art Ross Trophy Winner	3.00
☐	6	Two Time Conn Smythe Trophy Winner	3.00
☐	7	Six-Time NHL All Star	3.00
☐	8	Penguins Capture First Stanley Cup	3.00
☐	9	1992-93: Mario Lemieux Best Season Ever	3.00
☐	10	Mario's Magnificent Career	3.00
		Autograph	**NRMT-MT**
☐		Mario Lemieux, Autograph	300.00

PAINTED WARRIORS

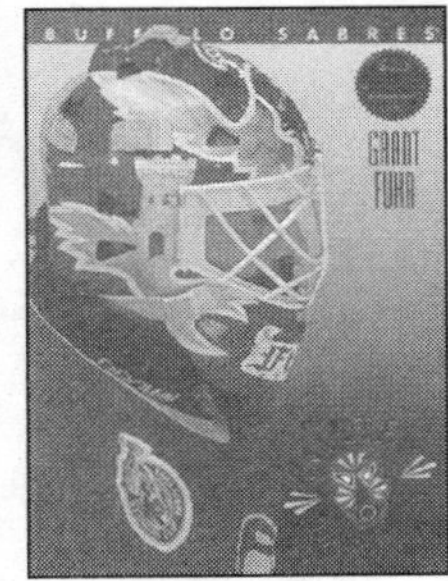

Insert Set (10 cards): **20.00**

	No.	Player	NRMT-MT
☐	1	Félix Potvin (G), Tor.	2.50
☐	2	Curtis Joseph (G), Stl.	3.00
☐	3	Kirk McLean (G), Van.	1.50
☐	4	Patrick Roy (G), Mtl.	8.00
☐	5	Grant Fuhr (G), Buf.	1.50
☐	6	Ed Belfour (G), Chi.	1.50
☐	7	Mike Vernon (G), Cgy.	1.50
☐	8	John Vanbiesbrouk (G), Fla.	3.00
☐	9	Tom Barrasso (G), Pgh.	1.50
☐	10	Bill Ranford (G), Edm.	1.50

STUDIO SIGNATURE

Insert Set (10 cards): **35.00**

	No.	Player	NRMT-MT
☐	1	Doug Gilmour, Tor.	1.50
☐	2	Pat Falloon, S.J.	1.00

	No.	Player	NRMT-MT
☐	3	Pat LaFontaine, Buf.	1.00
☐	4	Wayne Gretzky, L.A.	10.00
☐	5	Steve Yzerman, Det.	5.00
☐	6	Patrick Roy (G), Mtl.	8.00
☐	7	Jeremy Roenick, Chi.	1.50
☐	8	Brett Hull, Stl.	2.50
☐	9	Alexandre Daigle, Ott.	1.50
☐	10	Eric Lindros, Pha.	6.50

1993 - 94 McDONALD'S - UPPER DECK

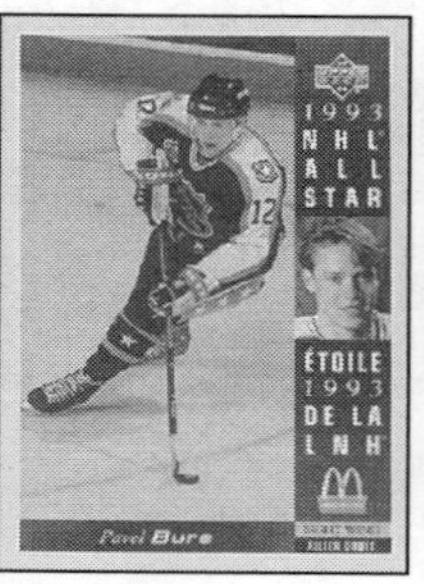

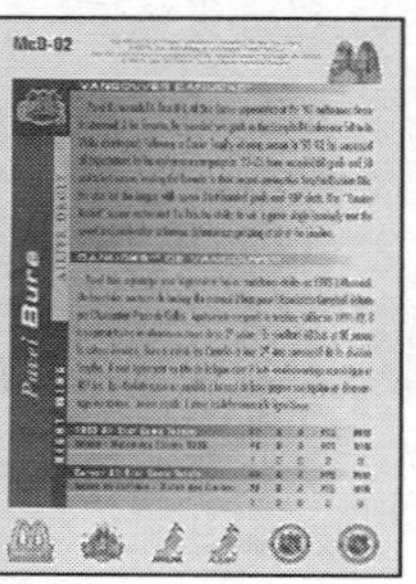

Imprint: © 1993 The Upper Deck Company
Complete Set (34 cards): 25.00

	No.	Holograms	NRMT-MT
☐	McH-01	Mario Lemieux, Pgh.	5.00
☐	McH-02	Teemu Selänne, Wpg.	3.50
☐	McH-03	Luc Robitaille, L.A.	2.50
☐	McH-04	Ray Bourque, Bos.	3.00
☐	McH-05	Chris Chelios, Chi.	2.50
☐	McH-06	Ed Belfour (G), Chi.	2.50

	No.	All-Stars	NRMT-MT
☐		Checklist	3.00
☐	McD-01	Brian Bradley, T.B.	.20
☐	McD-02	Pavel Bure, Van.	1.00
☐	McD-03	Jon Casey (G), Min.	.20
☐	McD-04	Paul Coffey, Det.	.35
☐	McD-05	Doug Gilmour, Tor.	.60
☐	McD-06	Phil Housley, Wpg.	.20
☐	McD-07	Brett Hull, Stl.	.85
☐	McD-08	Jari Kurri, L.A.	.35
☐	McD-09	Dave Manson, Edm.	.20
☐	McD-10	Mike Modano, Min.	.85
☐	McD-11	Gary Roberts, Cgy.	.35
☐	McD-12	Jeremy Roenick, Chi.	.60
☐	McD-13	Steve Yzerman, Det.	1.50
☐	McD-14	Steve Duchesne, Que.	.20
☐	McD-15	Mike Gartner, NYR.	.35
☐	McD-16	Al Iaftrate, Wsh.	.20
☐	McD-17	Jaromir Jagr, Pgh.	1.50
☐	McD-18	Pat LaFontaine, Buf.	.35
☐	McD-19	Alexander Mogilny, Buf.	.60
☐	McD-20	Kirk Muller, Mtl.	.20
☐	McD-21	Adam Oates, Bos.	.60
☐	McD-22	Mark Recchi, Pha.	.35
☐	McD-23	Patrick Roy (G), Mtl.	2.00
☐	McD-24	Joe Sakic, Que.	1.25
☐	McD-25	Kevin Stevens, Pgh.	.20
☐	McD-26	Scott Stevens, N.J.	.35
☐	McD-27	Pierre Turgeon, NYI.	.35
☐	McD-23	Patrick Roy, 5" x 7" MVP Card	9.00

1993 - 94 PANINI STICKERS

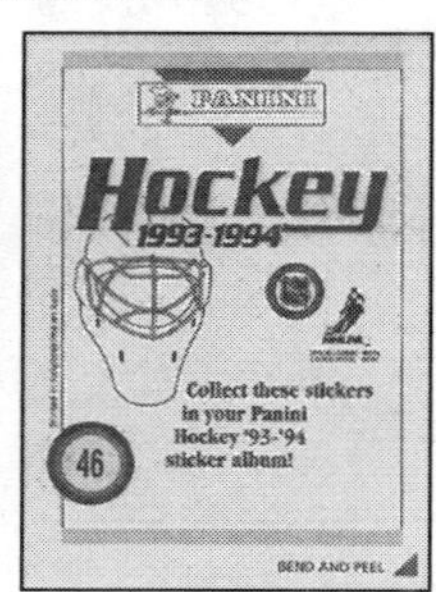

Sticker Size: 2 1/2" x 3 1/2"
Imprint: Printed in Italy. Imprimé en Italie
Complete Set (300 stickers): 15.00
Common Player: .10
English Album: 2.00
French Album: 2.00

	No.	Players	NRMT-MT
☐	1	Boston Bruin Team Logo	.10
☐	2	Adam Oates, Bos.	.35
☐	3	Cam Neely, Bos.	.25
☐	4	David Poulin, Bos.	.10
☐	5	Stephen Leach, Bos.	.10
☐	6	Glen Wesley, Bos.	.10
☐	7	Dmitri Kvartalnov, Bos.	.10
☐	8	Ted Donato, Bos.	.10
☐	9	Andy Moog (G), Bos.	.25
☐	10	Ray Bourque, Bos.	.75
☐	11	Don Sweeney, Bos.	.10
☐	12	Montréal Canadiens Team Logo	.10
☐	13	Vincent Damphousse, Mtl.	.35
☐	14	Kirk Muller, Mtl.	.10
☐	15	Brian Bellows, Mtl.	.10
☐	16	Stéphan Lebeau, Mtl.	.10
☐	17	Denis Savard, Mtl.	.25
☐	18	Gilbert Dionne, Mtl.	.10
☐	19	Guy Carbonneau, Mtl.	.10
☐	20	Benoît Brunet, Mtl.	.10
☐	21	Eric Desjardins, Mtl.	.25
☐	22	Mathieu Schneider, Mtl.	.10
☐	23	Washington Capitals Team Logo	.10
☐	24	Peter Bondra, Wsh.	.50
☐	25	Mike Ridley, Wsh.	.10
☐	26	Dale Hunter, Wsh.	.10
☐	27	Michal Pivonka, Wsh.	.10
☐	28	Dimitri Khristich, Wsh.	.10
☐	29	Pat Elynuik, Wsh.	.10
☐	30	Kelly Miller, Wsh.	.10
☐	31	Calle Johansson, Wsh.	.10
☐	32	Al Iafrate, Wsh.	.10
☐	33	Don Beaupré (G), Wsh.	.10
☐	34	New Jersey Devils Team Logo	.10
☐	35	Claude Lemieux, N.J.	.10
☐	36	Alexander Semak, N.J.	.10
☐	37	Stéphane Richer, N.J.	.10
☐	38	Valeri Zelepukin, N.J.	.10
☐	39	Bernie Nicholls, N.J.	.10
☐	40	John MacLean, N.J.	.10
☐	41	Peter Stastny, N.J.	.10
☐	42	Scott Niedermayer, N.J.	.25
☐	43	Scott Stevens, N.J.	.25
☐	44	Bruce Driver, N.J.	.10
☐	45	Philadelphia Flyers Team Logo	.10
☐	46	Mark Recchi, Pha.	.25
☐	47	Rod Brind'Amour, Pha.	.25
☐	48	Brent Fedyk, Pha.	.10
☐	49	Kevin Dineen, Pha.	.10
☐	50	Keith Acton, Pha.	.10
☐	51	Per-Erik Eklund, Pha.	.10
☐	52	Andrei Lomakin, Pha.	.10
☐	53	Garry Galley, Pha.	.10
☐	54	Terry Carkner, Pha.	.10
☐	55	Tommy Söderström (G), Pha.	.10
☐	56	New York Islanders Team Logo	.10
☐	57	Steve Thomas, NYI.	.10
☐	58	Derek King, NYI.	.10
☐	59	Benoit Hogue, NYI.	.10
☐	60	Patrick Flatley, NYI.	.10
☐	61	Brian Mullen, NYI.	.10
☐	62	Marty McInnis, NYI.	.10
☐	63	Scott Lachance, NYI.	.10
☐	64	Jeff Norton, NYI.	.10
☐	65	Glenn Healy (G), NYI.	.10
☐	66	Mark Fitzpatrick (G), NYI.	.10
☐	67	Québec Nordiques Team Logo	.10
☐	68	Mats Sundin, Que.	.75
☐	69	Mike Ricci, Que.	.10
☐	70	Owen Nolan, Que.	.25
☐	71	Andrei Kovalenko, Que.	.10
☐	72	Valeri Kamensky, Que.	.25
☐	73	Scott Young, Que.	.10
☐	74	Martin Rucinsky, Que.	.10
☐	75	Steven Finn, Que.	.10
☐	76	Steve Duchesne, Que.	.10
☐	77	Ron Hextall (G), Que.	.25
☐	78	Pittsburgh Penguins Team Logo	.10
☐	79	Kevin Stevens, Pgh.	.10
☐	80	Rick Tocchet, Pgh.	.10
☐	81	Ron Francis, Pgh.	.35
☐	82	Jaromir Jagr, Pgh.	2.00
☐	83	Joe Mullen, Pgh.	.10
☐	84	Shawn McEachern, Pgh.	.10
☐	85	Dave Tippett, Pgh.	.10
☐	86	Larry Murphy, Pgh.	.25
☐	87	Ulf Samuelsson, Pgh.	.10
☐	88	Tom Barrasso (G), Pgh.	.25
☐	89	New York Rangers Team Logo	.10
☐	90	Tony Amonte, NYR.	.25
☐	91	Mike Gartner, NYR.	.25
☐	92	Adam Graves, NYR.	.10
☐	93	Sergei Nemchinov, NYR.	.10
☐	94	Darren Turcotte, NYR.	.10
☐	95	Esa Tikkanen, NYR.	.10
☐	96	Brian Leetch, NYR.	.35
☐	97	Kevin Lowe, NYR.	.10
☐	98	John Vanbiesbrouck (G), NYR.	1.00
☐	99	Mike Richter (G), NYR.	.35
☐	100	Buffalo Sabres Team Logo	.10
☐	101	Pat LaFontaine, Buf.	.25
☐	102	Dale Hawerchuk, Buf.	.25
☐	103	Donald Audette, Buf.	.10
☐	104	Bob Sweeney, Buf.	.10
☐	105	Randy Wood, Buf.	.10
☐	106	Yuri Khmylev, Buf.	.10
☐	107	Wayne Presley, Buf.	.10
☐	108	Grant Fuhr (G), Buf.	.25
☐	109	Doug Bodger, Buf.	.10
☐	110	Richard Smehlik, Buf.	.10
☐	111	Ottawa Senators Team Logo	.10
☐	112	Norm Maciver, Ott.	.10
☐	113	Jamie Baker, Ott.	.10
☐	114	Bob Kudelski, Ott.	.10
☐	115	Jody Hull, Ott.	.10
☐	116	Mike Peluso, Ott.	.10
☐	117	Mark Lamb, Ott.	.10
☐	118	Mark Freer, Ott.	.10
☐	119	Neil Brady, Ott.	.10
☐	120	Brad Shaw, Ott.	.10
☐	121	Peter Sidorkiewicz (G), Ott.	.10
☐	122	Hartford Whalers Team Logo	.10
☐	123	Andrew Cassels, Hfd.	.10
☐	124	Pat Verbeek, Hfd.	.10
☐	125	Terry Yake, Hfd.	.10
☐	126	Patrick Poulin, Hfd.	.10
☐	127	Mark Janssens, Hfd.	.10
☐	128	Mikael Nylander, Hfd.	.10
☐	129	Zarley Zalapski, Hfd.	.10
☐	130	Eric Weinrich, Hfd.	.10
☐	131	Sean Burke (G), Hfd.	.25
☐	132	Frank Pietrangelo (G), Hfd.	.10
☐	133	LL: Phil Housley, Wpg.	.10
☐	134	LL: Paul Coffey, Det.	.25
☐	135	LL: Larry Murphy, Pgh.	.25
☐	136	LL: Mario Lemieux, Pgh.	2.50
☐	137	LL: Pat LaFontaine, Buf.	.25
☐	138	LL: Adam Oates, Bos.	.25
☐	139	LL: Félix Potvin (G), Tor.	.35
☐	140	LL: Ed Belfour (G), Chi.	.25
☐	141	LL: Tom Barasso (G), Pgh.	.25
☐	142	LL: Teemu Selänne, Wpg.	.75
☐	143	LL: Joé Juneau, Bos.	.10
☐	144	LL: Eric Lindros, Pha.	2.50
☐	145	Chicago Blackhawks Team Logo	.10
☐	146	Steve Larmer, Chi.	.10

	No.	Player	Price
☐	147	Dirk Graham, Chi.	.10
☐	148	Michel Goulet, Chi.	.25
☐	149	Brian Noonan, Chi.	.10
☐	150	Stéphane Matteau, Chi.	.10
☐	151	Brent Sutter, Chi.	.10
☐	152	Jocelyn Lemieux, Chi.	.10
☐	153	Chris Chelios, Chi.	.50
☐	154	Steve Smith, Chi.	.10
☐	155	Ed Belfour (G), Chi.	.35
☐	156	St. Louis Blues Team Logo	.10
☐	157	Craig Janney, Stl.	.10
☐	158	Brendan Shanahan, Stl.	1.00
☐	159	Nelson Emerson, Stl.	.10
☐	160	Rich Sutter, Stl.	.10
☐	161	Ron Sutter, Stl.	.10
☐	162	Ron Wilson, Stl.	.10
☐	163	Bob Bassen, Stl.	.10
☐	164	Garth Butcher, Stl.	.10
☐	165	Jeff Brown, Stl.	.10
☐	166	Curtis Joseph (G), Stl.	1.00
☐	167	Vancouver Canucks Team Logo	.10
☐	168	Cliff Ronning, Van.	.10
☐	169	Murray Craven, Van.	.10
☐	170	Geoff Courtnall, Van.	.10
☐	171	Petr Nedved, Van.	.10
☐	172	Trevor Linden, Van.	.25
☐	173	Greg Adams, Van.	.10
☐	174	Anatoli Semenov, Van.	.10
☐	175	Jyrki Lumme, Van.	.10
☐	176	Doug Lidster, Van.	.10
☐	177	Kirk McLean (G), Van.	.25
☐	178	Calgary Flames Team Logo	.10
☐	179	Theoren Fleury, Cgy.	.35
☐	180	Robert Reichel, Cgy.	.10
☐	181	Gary Roberts, Cgy.	.25
☐	182	Joe Nieuwendyk, Cgy.	.25
☐	183	Sergei Makarov, Cgy.	.10
☐	184	Paul Ranheim, Cgy.	.10
☐	185	Joel Otto, Cgy.	.10
☐	186	Gary Suter, Cgy.	.10
☐	187	Jeff Reese (G), Cgy.	.10
☐	188	Mike Vernon (G), Cgy.	.25
☐	189	Winnipeg Jets Team Logo	.10
☐	190	Alexei Zhamnov, Wpg.	.25
☐	191	Thomas Steen, Wpg.	.10
☐	192	Darrin Shannon, Wpg.	.10
☐	193	Keith Tkachuk, Wpg.	.75
☐	194	Evgeny Davydov, Wpg.	.10
☐	195	Luciano Borsato, Wpg.	.10
☐	196	Phil Housley, Wpg.	.10
☐	197	Teppo Numminen, Wpg.	.10
☐	198	Fredrik Olausson, Wpg.	.10
☐	199	Bob Essensa (G), Wpg.	.10
☐	200	Los Angeles Kings Team Logo	.10
☐	201	Luc Robitaille, L.A.	.25
☐	202	Jari Kurri, L.A.	.25
☐	203	Tony Granato, L.A.	.10
☐	204	Jimmy Carson, L.A.	.10
☐	205	Tomas Sandström, L.A.	.10
☐	206	David Taylor, L.A.	.10
☐	207	Corey Millen, L.A.	.10
☐	208	Marty McSorley, L.A.	.10
☐	209	Rob Blake, L.A.	.25
☐	210	Kelly Hrudey (G), L.A.	.10
☐	211	Tampa Bay Lightning Team Logo	.10
☐	212	John Tucker, T.B.	.10
☐	213	Chris Kontos, T.B.	.10
☐	214	Rob Zamuner, T.B.	.25
☐	215	Adam Creighton, T.B.	.10
☐	216	Mikael Andersson, T.B.	.10
☐	217	Bob Beers, T.B.	.10
☐	218	Rob DiMaio, T.B.	.10
☐	219	Shawn Chambers, T.B.	.10
☐	220	J.C. Bergeron (G), T.B.	.10
☐	221	Wendell Young (G), T.B.	.10
☐	222	Toronto Maple Leafs Team Logo	.10
☐	223	Dave Andreychuk, Tor.	.10
☐	224	Nikolai Borschevsky, Tor.	.10
☐	225	Glenn Anderson, Tor.	.10
☐	226	John Cullen, Tor.	.10
☐	227	Wendel Clark, Tor.	.25
☐	228	Mike Foligno, Tor.	.10
☐	229	Mike Krushelnyski, Tor.	.10
☐	230	Jamie Macoun, Tor.	.10
☐	231	Dave Ellett, Tor.	.10
☐	232	Félix Potvin (G), Tor.	.75
☐	233	Edmonton Oilers Team Logo	.10
☐	234	Petr Klima, Edm.	.10
☐	235	Doug Weight, Edm.	.35
☐	236	Shayne Corson, Edm.	.25
☐	237	Craig Simpson, Edm.	.10
☐	238	Todd Elik, Edm.	.10
☐	239	Zdeno Ciger, Edm.	.10
☐	240	Craig MacTavish, Edm.	.10
☐	241	Kelly Buchberger, Edm.	.10
☐	242	Dave Manson, Edm.	.10
☐	243	Scott Mellanby, Edm.	.10
☐	244	Detroit Red Wings Team Logo	.10
☐	245	Dino Ciccarelli, Det.	.25
☐	246	Sergei Fedorov, Det.	.75
☐	247	Ray Sheppard, Det.	.10
☐	248	Paul Ysebaert, Det.	.10
☐	249	Bob Probert, Det.	.10
☐	250	Keith Primeau, Det.	.25
☐	251	Steve Chiasson, Det.	.10
☐	252	Paul Coffey, Det.	.25
☐	253	Nicklas Lidstrom, Det.	.25
☐	254	Tim Cheveldae (G), Det.	.10
☐	255	San Jose Sharks Team Logo	.10
☐	256	Kelly Kisio, S.J.	.10
☐	257	Johan Garpenlov, S.J.	.10
☐	258	Robert Gaudreau, S.J.	.10
☐	259	Dean Evason, S.J.	.10
☐	260	Jeff Odgers, S.J.	.10
☐	261	Ed Courtenay, S.J.	.10
☐	262	Mike Sullivan, S.J.	.10
☐	263	Doug Zmolek, S.J.	.10
☐	264	Doug Wilson, S.J.	.10
☐	265	Brian Hayward (G), S.J.	.10
☐	266	Dallas Stars Team Logo	.10
☐	267	Brian Propp, Dal.	.10
☐	268	Russ Courtnall, Dal.	.10
☐	269	Dave Gagner, Dal.	.10
☐	270	Ulf Dahlen, Dal.	.10
☐	271	Mike Craig, Dal.	.10
☐	272	Neal Broten, Dal.	.10
☐	273	Gaetan Duchesne, Dal.	.10
☐	274	Derian Hatcher, Dal.	.20
☐	275	Mark Tinordi, Dal.	.10
☐	276	Jon Casey (G), Dal.	.10
☐	A	Joé Juneau, Bos.	.25
☐	B	Patrick Roy (G), Mtl.	3.00
☐	C	Kevin Hatcher, Wsh.	.25
☐	D	Chris Terreri (G), N.J.	.25
☐	E	Eric Lindros, Pha.	3.00
☐	F	Pierre Turgeon, NYI.	.35
☐	G	Joe Sakic, Que.	2.00
☐	H	Mario Lemieux, Pgh.	3.00
☐	I	Mark Messier, NYR.	1.00
☐	J	Alexander Mogilny, Buf.	.50
☐	K	Sylvain Turgeon, Ott.	.25
☐	L	Geoff Sanderson, Hfd.	.25
☐	M	Jeremy Roenick, Chi.	.50
☐	N	Brett Hull, Stl.	1.00
☐	O	Pavel Bure, Van.	1.50
☐	P	Al MacInnis, Cgy.	.35
☐	Q	Teemu Selänne, Wpg.	1.50
☐	R	Wayne Gretzky, L.A.	4.00
☐	S	Doug Gilmour, Tor.	.50
☐	T	Brian Bradley, T.B.	.25
☐	U	Bill Ranford (G), Edm.	.35
☐	V	Steve Yzerman, Det.	2.50
☐	W	Pat Falloon, S.J.	.25
☐	X	Mike Modano, Dal.	1.00

1993 - 94 PARKHURST

These cards have two versions: the regular card and an Emerald Ice parallel. Cards 404 and 478 are repeated while cards 398 and 498 were never issued.

Imprint: © 1993 The Upper Deck Company

	Reg.	E.I.
Series One Set (270 cards):	**20.00**	**160.00**
Series Two (270 cards):	**20.00**	**160.00**
Common Player:	**.10**	**.35**

	No.	Player	Reg.	E.I.
☐☐	1	Steven King, Ana.	.10	.35
☐☐	2	Sean Hill, Ana.	.10	.35
☐☐	3	Anatoli Semenov, Ana.	.10	.35
☐☐	4	Garry Valk, Ana.	.10	.35
☐☐	5	Todd Ewen, Ana.	.10	.35
☐☐	6	Bob Corkum, Ana.	.10	.35
☐☐	7	Tim Sweeney, Ana.	.10	.35
☐☐	**8**	**Patrik Carnback, Ana., RC**	**.10**	**.35**
☐☐	9	Troy Loney, Ana.	.10	.35
☐☐	10	Cam Neely, Bos.	.25	.50
☐☐	11	Adam Oates, Bos.	.35	1.00
☐☐	12	Jon Casey (G), Bos.	.10	.35
☐☐	13	Don Sweeney, Bos.	.10	.35
☐☐	14	Ray Bourque, Bos.	.50	2.50
☐☐	15	Jozef Stumpel, Bos.	.10	.35
☐☐	16	Glen Murray, Bos.	.10	.35
☐☐	17	Glen Wesley, Bos.	.10	.35
☐☐	**18**	**Fred Knipscheer, Bos., RC**	**.10**	**.35**
☐☐	19	Craig Simpson, Buf.	.10	.35
☐☐	20	Richard Smehlik, Buf.	.10	.35
☐☐	21	Alexander Mogilny, Buf.	.35	1.00
☐☐	22	Grant Fuhr (G), Buf.	.25	.50
☐☐	23	Dale Hawerchuk, Buf.	.25	.50
☐☐	24	Philippe Boucher, Buf.	.10	.35
☐☐	**25**	**Scott Thomas, Buf., RC**	**.10**	**.35**
☐☐	26	Donald Audette, Buf.	.10	.35
☐☐	27	Brad May, Buf.	.10	.35
☐☐	28	Theoren Fleury, Cgy.	.35	1.00
☐☐	29	Andrei Trefilov (G), Cgy.	.10	.35
☐☐	**30**	**Sandy McCarthy, Cgy., RC**	**.10**	**.35**
☐☐	31	Joe Nieuwendyk, Cgy.	.25	.50
☐☐	32	Paul Ranheim, Cgy.	.10	.35
☐☐	33	Kelly Kisio, Cgy.	.10	.35
☐☐	34	Joel Otto, Cgy.	.10	.35
☐☐	35	Ted Drury, Cgy.	.10	.35
☐☐	36	Al MacInnis, Cgy.	.25	.50
☐☐	37	Kevin Todd, Chi.	.10	.35
☐☐	38	Joe Murphy, Chi.	.10	.35
☐☐	39	Christian Ruuttu, Chi.	.10	.35
☐☐	**40**	**Steve Dubinsky, Chi., RC**	**.10**	**.35**
☐☐	41	Stéphane Matteau, Chi.	.10	.35
☐☐	**42**	**Ivan Droppa, Chi., RC**	**.10**	**.35**
☐☐	43	Jocelyn Lemieux, Chi.	.10	.35
☐☐	44	Ed Belfour (G), Chi.	.35	1.00
☐☐	45	Chris Chelios, Chi.	.35	1.50
☐☐	46	Derian Hatcher, Dal.	.25	.50
☐☐	47	Andy Moog (G), Dal.	.25	.50
☐☐	48	Trent Klatt, Dal.	.10	.35
☐☐	49	Mike Modano, Dal.	.50	2.50
☐☐	50	Paul Cavallini, Dal.	.10	.35
☐☐	51	Mike McPhee, Dal.	.10	.35
☐☐	52	Brent Gilchrist, Dal.	.10	.35
☐☐	53	Russ Courtnall, Dal.	.10	.35
☐☐	54	Neal Broten, Dal.	.10	.35
☐☐	55	Steve Chiasson, Det.	.10	.35
☐☐	56	Paul Coffey, Det.	.25	.50
☐☐	57	Vyacheslav Kozlov, Det.	.10	.35
☐☐	58	Sergei Fedorov, Det.	.50	2.50
☐☐	59	Tim Cheveldae (G), Det.	.10	.35
☐☐	60	Dino Ciccarelli, Det.	.25	.50

□□	**61**	**Dallas Drake, Det., RC**	**.10**	**.35**
□□	62	Nicklas Lidstrom, Det.	.25	.50
□□	63	Martin Lapointe, Det.	.10	.35
□□	64	Dean McAmmond, Edm.	.10	.35
□□	65	Igor Kravchuk, Edm.	.10	.35
□□	**66**	**Shjon Podein, Edm., RC**	**.10**	**.35**
□□	67	Bill Ranford (G), Edm.	.25	.50
□□	68	Brad Werenka, Edm.	.10	.35
□□	69	Doug Weight, Edm.	.35	1.00
□□	**70**	**Ian Herbers, Edm., RC**	**.10**	**.35**
□□	71	Todd Elik, Edm.	.10	.35
□□	72	Steve Rice, Edm.	.10	.35
□□	73	John Vanbiesbrouck (G), Fla.	.60	3.00
□□	74	Alexander Godynyuk, Fla.	.10	.35
□□	75	Brian Skrudland, Fla.	.10	.35
□□	76	Jody Hull, Fla.	.10	.35
□□	**77**	**Brent Severyn, Fla., RC**	**.10**	**.35**
□□	78	Evgeny Davydov, Fla.	.10	.35
□□	79	Dave Lowry, Fla.	.10	.35
□□	**80**	**Scott Levins, Fla., RC**	**.10**	**.35**
□□	81	Scott Mellanby, Fla.	.10	.35
□□	82	Dan Keczmer, Hfd.	.10	.35
□□	83	Michael Nylander, Hfd.	.10	.35
□□	84	Jim Sandlak, Hfd.	.10	.35
□□	85	Brian Propp, Hfd.	.10	.35
□□	86	Geoff Sanderson, Hfd.	.10	.35
□□	**87**	**Mike Lenarduzzi (G), Hfd., RC**	**.10**	**.35**
□□	88	Zarley Zalapski, Hfd.	.10	.35
□□	89	Robert Petrovicky, Hfd.	.10	.35
□□	90	Robert Kron, Hfd.	.10	.35
□□	91	Luc Robitaille, L.A.	.25	.50
□□	92	Alexei Zhitnik, L.A.	.10	.35
□□	93	Tony Granato, L.A.	.10	.35
□□	94	Rob Blake, L.A.	.25	.50
□□	95	Gary Shuchuk, L.A.	.10	.35
□□	96	Darryl Sydor, L.A.	.10	.35
□□	97	Kelly Hrudey (G), L.A.	.10	.35
□□	98	Warren Rychel, L.A.	.10	.35
□□	99	Wayne Gretzky, L.A.	2.00	10.00
□□	100	Patrick Roy (G), Mtl.	1.50	8.00
□□	101	Gilbert Dionne, Mtl.	.10	.35
□□	102	Eric Desjardins, Mtl.	.25	.50
□□	**103**	**Peter Popovic, Mtl., RC**	**.10**	**.35**
□□	104	Vincent Damphousse, Mtl.	.35	1.00
□□	105	Patrice Brisebois, Mtl.	.10	.35
□□	106	Pierre Sévigny, Mtl.	.10	.35
□□	107	John LeClair, Mtl.	.60	3.00
□□	108	Paul DiPietro, Mtl.	.10	.35
□□	109	Alexander Semak, N.J.	.10	.35
□□	110	Claude Lemieux, N.J.	.10	.35
□□	111	Scott Niedermayer, N.J.	.25	.50
□□	112	Chris Terreri (G), N.J.	.10	.35
□□	113	Stéphane Richer, N.J.	.10	.35
□□	114	Scott Stevens, N.J.	.25	.50
□□	115	John MacLean, N.J.	.10	.35
□□	**116**	**Scott Pellerin, N.J., RC**	**.10**	**.35**
□□	117	Bernie Nicholls, N.J.	.10	.35
□□	118	Ron Hextall (G), NYI.	.25	.50
□□	119	Derek King, NYI.	.10	.35
□□	120	Scott Lachance, NYI.	.10	.35
□□	121	Scott Scissons, NYI.	.10	.35
□□	122	Darius Kasparaitis, NYI.	.10	.35
□□	123	Ray Ferraro, NYI.	.10	.35
□□	124	Steve Thomas, NYI.	.10	.35
□□	125	Vladimir Malakhov, NYI.	.10	.35
□□	126	Travis Green, NYI.	.10	.35
□□	127	Mark Messier, NYR.	.50	2.50
□□	128	Sergei Nemchinov, NYR.	.10	.35
□□	129	Mike Richter (G), NYR.	.35	1.00
□□	130	Alexei Kovalev, NYR.	.10	.35
□□	131	Brian Leetch, NYR.	.35	1.00
□□	132	Tony Amonte, NYR.	.25	.50
□□	133	Sergei Zubov, NYR.	.25	.50
□□	134	Adam Graves, NYR.	.10	.35
□□	135	Esa Tikkanen, NYR.	.10	.35
□□	136	Sylvain Turgeon, Ott.	.10	.35
□□	137	Norm Maciver, Ott.	.10	.35
□□	138	Craig Billington (G), Ott.	.10	.35
□□	139	Dmitri Filimonov, Ott.	.10	.35
□□	140	Pavol Demitra, Ott.	.10	.35
□□	141	Brian Glynn, Ott.	.10	.35
□□	**142**	**Darrin Madeley (G), Ott., RC**	**.10**	**.35**
□□	**143**	**Rader Hamr, Ott., RC**	**.10**	**.35**
□□	**144**	**Robert Burakovsky, Ott., RC**	**.10**	**.35**
□□	145	Dimitri Yushkevich, Pha.	.10	.35
□□	146	Claude Boivin, Pha.	.10	.35
□□	147	Per-Erik Eklund, Pha.	.10	.35
□□	148	Brent Fedyk, Pha.	.10	.35
□□	149	Mark Recchi, Pha.	.25	.50
□□	150	Tommy Söderström (G), Pha.	.10	.35
□□	151	Vyacheslav Butsayev, Pha.	.10	.35
□□	152	Rod Brind'Amour, Pha.	.25	.50
□□	153	Josef Beranek, Pha.	.10	.35
□□	154	Jaromir Jagr, Pgh.	1.25	6.00
□□	155	Ulf Samuelsson, Pgh.	.10	.35
□□	156	Martin Straka, Pgh.	.10	.35
□□	157	Tom Barrasso (G), Pgh.	.25	.50
□□	158	Kevin Stevens, Pgh.	.10	.35
□□	159	Joe Mullen, Pgh.	.25	.50
□□	160	Ron Francis, Pgh.	.35	1.00
□□	161	Marty McSorley, Pgh.	.10	.35
□□	162	Larry Murphy, Pgh.	.25	.50
□□	163	Owen Nolan, Que.	.25	.50
□□	164	Stéphane Fiset (G), Que.	.25	.50
□□	165	Dave Karpa, Que.	.10	.35
□□	166	Martin Gelinas, Que.	.10	.35
□□	167	Andrei Kovalenko, Que.	.10	.35
□□	168	Steve Duchesne, Que.	.10	.35
□□	169	Joe Sakic, Que.	1.00	4.00
□□	170	Martin Rucinsky, Que.	.10	.35
□□	**171**	**Chris Simon, Que., RC**	**.25**	**.50**
□□	172	Brendan Shanahan, Stl.	.60	3.00
□□	173	Jeff Brown, Stl.	.10	.35
□□	174	Phil Housley, Stl.	.10	.35
□□	175	Curtis Joseph (G), Stl.	.60	3.00
□□	**176**	**Jim Montgomery, Stl., RC**	**.10**	**.35**
□□	177	Bret Hedican, Stl.	.10	.35
□□	178	Kevin Miller, Stl.	.10	.35
□□	179	Philippe Bozon, Stl.	.10	.35
□□	180	Brett Hull, Stl.	.50	2.50
□□	181	Jimmy Waite (G), S.J.	.10	.35
□□	182	Ray Whitney, S.J.	.10	.35
□□	183	Pat Falloon, S.J.	.10	.35
□□	184	Tom Pederson, S.J.	.10	.35
□□	185	Igor Larionov, S.J.	.25	.50
□□	**186**	**Dody Wood, S.J., RC**	**.10**	**.35**
□□	187	Sandis Ozolinsh, S.J.	.25	.50
□□	188	Sergei Makarov, S.J.	.10	.35
□□	**189**	**Rob Gaudreau, S.J., RC**	**.10**	**.35**
□□	190	Roman Hamrlik, T.B.	.25	.50
□□	191	Stan Drulia, T.B.	.10	.35
□□	192	Pat Jablonski (G), T.B.	.10	.35
□□	193	Denis Savard, T.B.	.25	.50
□□	194	Rob Zamuner, T.B.	.25	.50
□□	195	Petr Klima, T.B.	.10	.35
□□	196	Rob DiMaio, T.B.	.10	.35
□□	197	Chris Kontos, T.B.	.10	.35
□□	198	Mikael Andersson, T.B.	.10	.35
□□	199	Drake Berehowsky, Tor.	.10	.35
□□	200	Dave Andreychuk, Tor.	.10	.35
□□	201	Glenn Anderson, Tor.	.10	.35
□□	202	Félix Potvin (G), Tor.	.50	2.50
□□	203	Nikolai Borschevsky, Tor.	.10	.35
□□	204	Kent Manderville, Tor.	.10	.35
□□	205	Dave Ellett, Tor.	.10	.35
□□	206	Peter Zezel, Tor.	.10	.35
□□	207	Ken Baumgartner, Tor.	.10	.35
□□	208	Murray Craven, Van.	.10	.35
□□	209	Dixon Ward, Van.	.10	.35
□□	210	Cliff Ronning, Van.	.10	.35
□□	211	Pavel Bure, Van.	.75	3.50
□□	212	Sergio Momesso, Van.	.10	.35
□□	213	Kirk McLean (G), Van.	.25	.50
□□	214	Jiri Slegr, Van.	.10	.35
□□	215	Trevor Linden, Van.	.25	.50
□□	216	Geoff Courtnall, Van.	.10	.35
□□	217	Al Iafrate, Wsh.	.10	.35
□□	218	Mike Ridley, Wsh.	.10	.35
□□	219	Enrico Ciccone, Wsh.	.10	.35
□□	220	Dimitri Khristich, Wsh.	.10	.35
□□	221	Kevin Hatcher Wsh.	.10	.35
□□	222	Peter Bondra, Wsh.	.35	1.50
□□	223	Steve Konowalchuk, Wsh.	.10	.35
□□	224	Pat Elynuik, Wsh.	.10	.35
□□	225	Don Beaupré (G), Wsh.	.10	.35
□□	226	Stu Barnes, Wpg.	.10	.35
□□	227	Fredrik Olausson, Wpg.	.10	.35
□□	228	Keith Tkachuk, Wpg.	.50	2.50
□□	229	Mike Eagles, Wpg.	.10	.35
□□	230	Tie Domi, Wpg.	.10	.35
□□	231	Teppo Numminen, Wpg.	.10	.35
□□	232	Arto Blomsten, Wpg.	.10	.35
□□	233	Teemu Selänne, Wpg.	.75	3.50
□□	234	Bob Essensa (G), Wpg.	.10	.35
□□	235	Teemu Selänne, Wpg.	.50	2.00
□□	236	Eric Lindros, Pha.	1.00	5.00
□□	237	Félix Potvin (G), Tor.	.50	1.50
□□	238	Alexei Kovalev, NYR.	.10	.35
□□	239	Vladimir Malakhov, NYI.	.10	.35
□□	240	Scott Niedermayer, N.J.	.10	.35
□□	241	Joé Juneau, Bos.	.10	.35
□□	242	Shawn McEachern, L.A.	.10	.35
□□	243	Alexei Zhamnov, Wpg.	.10	.35
□□	244	Alexandre Daigle, Ott.	.35	.50
□□	245	Markus Naslund, Pgh.	.10	.35
□□	246	Rob Niedermayer, Fla.	.25	.50
□□	**247**	**Jocelyn Thibault (G), Que., RC**	**1.50**	**4.00**
□□	**248**	**Brent Gretzky, T.B., RC**	**.10**	**.35**
□□	249	Chris Pronger, Hfd.	.35	.50
□□	250	Chris Gratton, T.B.	.35	.50
□□	251	Mikael Renberg, Pha.	.25	.50
□□	**252**	**Jarkko Varvio, Dal., RC**	**.10**	**.35**
□□	**253**	**Micah Aivazoff, Det., RC**	**.10**	**.35**
□□	254	Alexei Yashin, Ott.	.75	2.50
□□	**255**	**German Titov (G), Cgy., RC**	**.10**	**.35**
□□	**256**	**Mattias Norstrom, NYR., RC**	**.10**	**.35**
□□	**257**	**Michal Sykora, S.J., RC**	**.10**	**.35**
□□	**258**	**Roman Oksiuta, Edm., RC**	**.10**	**.35**
□□	259	Bryan Smolinski, Bos.	.10	.35
□□	**260**	**Alexei Kudashov, Tor., RC**	**.10**	**.35**
□□	**261**	**Jason Arnott, Edm., RC**	**1.50**	**4.00**
□□	**262**	**Aaron Ward, Det., RC**	**.25**	**.50**
□□	**263**	**Vesa Viitakoski, Cgy., RC**	**.10**	**.35**
□□	**264**	**Boris Mironov, Wpg., RC**	**.10**	**.35**
□□	**265**	**Darren McCarty, Det., RC**	**.25**	**.50**
□□	**266**	**Vlastimil Kroupa, S.J., RC**	**.10**	**.35**
□□	**267**	**Denny Felsner, Stl., RC**	**.10**	**.35**
□□	**268**	**Milos Holan, Pha., RC**	**.10**	**.35**
□□	**269**	**Alexander Karpovtsev, NYR., RC**	**.10**	**.35**
□□	270	Greg Johnson, Det.	.10	.35
□□	271	Terry Yake, Ana.	.10	.35
□□	272	Bill Houlder, Ana.	.10	.35
□□	273	Joe Sacco, Ana.	.10	.35
□□	274	Myles O'Connor, Ana.	.10	.35
□□	**275**	**Mark Ferner, Ana., RC**	**.10**	**.35**
□□	276	Alexei Kasatonov, Ana.	.10	.35
□□	277	Stu Grimson, Ana.	.10	.35
□□	278	Shaun Van Allen, Ana.	.10	.35
□□	279	Guy Hebert (G), Ana.	.25	.50
□□	280	Joé Juneau, Bos.	.10	.35
□□	281	Sergei Zholtok, Bos.	.10	.35
□□	282	Daniel Marois, Bos.	.10	.35
□□	283	Ted Donato, Bos.	.10	.35
□□	**284**	**Cam Stewart, Bos., RC**	**.10**	**.35**
□□	285	Stephen Leach, Bos.	.10	.35
□□	286	Darren Banks, Bos.	.10	.35
□□	287	Dmitri Kvartalnov, Bos.	.10	.35
□□	288	Paul Stanton, Bos.	.10	.35
□□	289	Pat LaFontaine, Buf.	.25	.50
□□	290	Bob Sweeney, Buf.	.10	.35
□□	291	Craig Muni, Buf.	.10	.35
□□	292	Sergei Petrenko, Buf.	.10	.35
□□	**293**	**Derek Plante, Buf., RC**	**.25**	**.50**
□□	294	Wayne Presley, Buf.	.10	.35
□□	**295**	**Mark Astley, Buf., RC**	**.10**	**.35**
□□	296	Matthew Barnaby, Buf.	.10	.35
□□	297	Randy Wood, Buf.	.10	.35
□□	298	Kevin Dahl, Cgy.	.10	.35
□□	299	Gary Suter, Cgy.	.10	.35
□□	300	Robert Reichel, Cgy.	.10	.35
□□	301	Mike Vernon (G), Cgy.	.25	.50
□□	302	Gary Roberts, Cgy.	.25	.50
□□	303	Ron Stern, Cgy.	.10	.35
□□	304	Michel Petit, Cgy.	.10	.35
□□	305	Wes Walz, Cgy.	.10	.35
□□	306	Brad Miller, Cgy.	.10	.35
□□	307	Patrick Poulin, Chi.	.10	.35
□□	308	Brent Sutter, Chi.	.10	.35
□□	309	Jeremy Roenick, Chi.	.35	1.00
□□	310	Steve Smith, Chi.	.10	.35
□□	311	Eric Weinrich, Chi.	.10	.35
□□	312	Jeff Hackett (G), Chi.	.10	.35
□□	313	Michel Goulet, Chi.	.25	.50
□□	**314**	**Jeff Shantz, Chi., RC**	**.10**	**.35**
□□	315	Neil Wilkinson, Chi.	.10	.35

	No.	Player		
☐ ☐	316	Shane Churla, Dal.	.10	.35
☐ ☐	317	Dave Gagner, Dal.	.10	.35
☐ ☐	318	Chris Tancill, Dal.	.10	.35
☐ ☐	319	Dean Evason, Dal.	.10	.35
☐ ☐	320	Mark Tinordi, Dal.	.10	.35
☐ ☐	321	Grant Ledyard, Dal.	.10	.35
☐ ☐	322	Ulf Dahlen, Dal.	.10	.35
☐ ☐	323	Mike Craig, Dal.	.10	.35
☐ ☐	324	Paul Broten, Dal.	.10	.35
☐ ☐	325	Vladimir Konstantinov, Det.	.10	.35
☐ ☐	326	Steve Yzerman, Det.	1.25	6.00
☐ ☐	327	Keith Primeau, Det.	.25	.50
☐ ☐	328	Shawn Burr, Det.	.10	.35
☐ ☐	**329**	**Chris Osgood (G), Det., RC**	**2.00**	**6.00**
☐ ☐	330	Ray Sheppard, Det.	.10	.35
☐ ☐	331	Mike Sillinger, Det.	.10	.35
☐ ☐	332	Terry Carkner, Det.	.10	.35
☐ ☐	333	Bob Probert, Det.	.10	.35
☐ ☐	334	Adam Bennett, Edm.	.10	.35
☐ ☐	335	Dave Manson, Edm.	.10	.35
☐ ☐	336	Zdeno Ciger, Edm.	.10	.35
☐ ☐	337	Louie DeBrusk, Edm.	.10	.35
☐ ☐	338	Shayne Corson, Edm.	.10	.35
☐ ☐	339	Vladimir Vujtek, Edm.	.10	.35
☐ ☐	340	Tyler Wright, Edm.	.10	.35
☐ ☐	**341**	**Ilya Byakin, Edm., RC**	**.10**	**.35**
☐ ☐	342	Craig MacTavish, Edm.	.10	.35
☐ ☐	343	Brian Benning, Fla.	.10	.35
☐ ☐	344	Mark Fitzpatrick (G), Fla.	.10	.35
☐ ☐	345	Gord Murphy, Fla.	.10	.35
☐ ☐	346	Jesse Belanger, Fla.	.10	.35
☐ ☐	347	Joe Cirella, Fla.	.10	.35
☐ ☐	348	Tom Fitzgerald, Fla.	.10	.35
☐ ☐	349	Anrei Lomakin, Fla.	.10	.35
☐ ☐	350	Bill Lindsay, Fla.	.10	.35
☐ ☐	351	Len Barrie, Fla.	.10	.35
☐ ☐	352	Frank Pietrangelo (G), Hfd.	.10	.35
☐ ☐	353	Pat Verbeek, Hfd.	.10	.35
☐ ☐	354	Jim Storm, Hfd.	.10	.35
☐ ☐	355	Mark Janssens, Hfd.	.10	.35
☐ ☐	356	Darren Turcotte, Hfd.	.10	.35
☐ ☐	357	Jim McKenzie, Hfd.	.10	.35
☐ ☐	358	Brad McCrimmon, Hfd.	.10	.35
☐ ☐	359	Andrew Cassels, Hfd.	.10	.35
☐ ☐	360	James Patrick, Hfd.	.10	.35
☐ ☐	**361**	**Bob Jay, L.A., RC**	**.10**	**.35**
☐ ☐	362	Tomas Sandström, L.A.	.10	.35
☐ ☐	363	Pat Conacher, L.A.	.10	.35
☐ ☐	364	Shawn McEachern, L.A.	.10	.35
☐ ☐	365	Jari Kurri, L.A.	.25	.50
☐ ☐	366	Dominic Lavoie, L.A.	.10	.35
☐ ☐	367	Dave Taylor, L.A.	.10	.35
☐ ☐	368	Jimmy Carson, L.A.	.10	.35
☐ ☐	369	Mike Donnelley, L.A.	.10	.35
☐ ☐	370	Lyle Odelein, Mtl.	.10	.35
☐ ☐	371	Brian Bellows, Mtl.	.10	.35
☐ ☐	372	Guy Carbonneau, Mtl.	.10	.35
☐ ☐	373	Mathieu Schneider, Mtl.	.10	.35
☐ ☐	374	Stéphan Lebeau, Mtl.	.10	.35
☐ ☐	375	Benoît Brunet, Mtl.	.10	.35
☐ ☐	376	Kevin Haller, Mtl.	.10	.35
☐ ☐	377	J. J. Daigneault, Mtl.	.10	.35
☐ ☐	378	Kirk Muller, Mtl.	.10	.35
☐ ☐	**379**	**Jason Smith, N.J., RC**	**.10**	**.35**
☐ ☐	380	Martin Brodeur (G), N.J.	.75	3.50
☐ ☐	381	Corey Millen, N.J.	.10	.35
☐ ☐	382	Bill Guerin, N.J.	.25	.50
☐ ☐	383	Valeri Zelepukin, N.J.	.10	.35
☐ ☐	384	Tom Chorske, N.J.	.10	.35
☐ ☐	385	Bobby Holik, N.J.	.10	.35
☐ ☐	**386**	**Jaroslav Modry, N.J., RC**	**.10**	**.35**
☐ ☐	387	Ken Daneyko, N.J.	.10	.35
☐ ☐	388	Uwe Krupp, NYI.	.10	.35
☐ ☐	389	Pierre Turgeon, NYI.	.25	.50
☐ ☐	390	Marty McInnis, NYI.	.10	.35
☐ ☐	391	Patrick Flatley, NYI.	.10	.35
☐ ☐	392	Tom Kurvers, NYI.	.10	.35
☐ ☐	393	Brad Dalgarno, NYI.	.10	.35
☐ ☐	**394**	**Steve Junker, NYI., RC**	**.10**	**.35**
☐ ☐	395	David Volek, NYI.	.10	.35
☐ ☐	396	Benoît Hogue, NYI.	.10	.35
☐ ☐	397	Zigmund Palffy, NYI.	.50	2.50
☐ ☐	**399**	**Joby Messier, NYR., RC**	**.10**	**.35**
☐ ☐	400	Mike Gartner, NYR.	.25	.50
☐ ☐	401	Joey Kocur, NYR.	.10	.35
☐ ☐	402	Ed Olczyk, NYR.	.10	.35
☐ ☐	403	Doug Lidster, NYR.	.10	.35
☐ ☐	404	Greg Gilbert, NYR.	.10	.35
☐ ☐	404	Steve Larmer, NYR.	.20	.50
☐ ☐	405	Glenn Healy (G), NYR.	.10	.35
☐ ☐	406	Dennis Vial, Ott.	.10	.35
☐ ☐	407	Darcy Loewen, Ott.	.10	.35
☐ ☐	408	Bob Kudelski, Ott.	.10	.35
☐ ☐	**409**	**Hank Lammens, Ott., RC**	**.10**	**.35**
☐ ☐	410	Jarmo Kekäläinen, Ott.	.10	.35
☐ ☐	411	Darren Rumble, Ott.	.10	.35
☐ ☐	412	François Leroux, Ott.	.10	.35
☐ ☐	413	Troy Mallette, Ott.	.10	.35
☐ ☐	**414**	**Bill Huard, Ott., RC**	**.10**	**.35**
☐ ☐	415	Ryan McGill, Pha.	.10	.35
☐ ☐	416	Eric Lindros, Pha.	1.50	7.50
☐ ☐	417	Dominic Roussel (G), Pha.	.10	.35
☐ ☐	**418**	**Jason Bowen, Pha., RC**	**.10**	**.35**
☐ ☐	419	André Faust, Pha.	.10	.35
☐ ☐	**420**	**Stewart Malgunas, Pha., RC**	**.10**	**.35**
☐ ☐	421	Kevin Dineen, Pha.	.10	.35
☐ ☐	422	Yves Racine, Pha.	.10	.35
☐ ☐	423	Garry Galley, Pha.	.10	.35
☐ ☐	424	Doug Brown, Pgh.	.10	.35
☐ ☐	425	Mario Lemieux, Pgh.	1.50	8.00
☐ ☐	426	Ladislav Karabin, Pgh.	.10	.35
☐ ☐	427	Grant Jennings, Pgh.	.10	.35
☐ ☐	428	Rick Tocchet, Pgh.	.10	.35
☐ ☐	429	Jeff Daniels, Pgh.	.10	.35
☐ ☐	430	Peter Taglianetti, Pgh.	.10	.35
☐ ☐	431	Bryan Trottier, Pgh.	.25	.50
☐ ☐	432	Kjell Samuelsson, Pgh.	.10	.35
☐ ☐	**433**	**René Corbet, Que., RC**	**.10**	**.35**
☐ ☐	**434**	**Iain Fraser, Que., RC**	**.10**	**.35**
☐ ☐	435	Mats Sundin, Que.	.50	2.50
☐ ☐	436	Curtis Leschyshyn, Que.	.10	.35
☐ ☐	437	Claude Lapointe, Que.	.10	.35
☐ ☐	438	Valeri Kamensky, Que.	.25	.50
☐ ☐	439	Mike Ricci, Que.	.10	.35
☐ ☐	440	Chris Lindberg, Que.	.10	.35
☐ ☐	441	Alexei Gusarov, Que.	.10	.35
☐ ☐	442	Tom Tilley, Stl.	.10	.35
☐ ☐	443	Craig Janney, Stl.	.10	.35
☐ ☐	444	Vitali Karamnov, Stl.	.10	.35
☐ ☐	445	Bob Bassen, Stl.	.10	.35
☐ ☐	446	Igor Korolev, Stl.	.10	.35
☐ ☐	**447**	**Kevin Miehm, Stl., RC**	**.10**	**.35**
☐ ☐	448	Tony Hrkac, Stl.	.10	.35
☐ ☐	449	Garth Butcher, Stl.	.10	.35
☐ ☐	**450**	**Vitali Prokhorov, Stl., RC**	**.10**	**.35**
☐ ☐	451	Arturs Irbe (G), S.J.	.10	.35
☐ ☐	452	Jayson More, S.J.	.10	.35
☐ ☐	453	Bob Errey, S.J.	.10	.35
☐ ☐	454	Mike Sullivan, S.J.	.10	.35
☐ ☐	455	Jeff Norton, S.J.	.10	.35
☐ ☐	456	Gaetan Duchesne, S.J.	.10	.35
☐ ☐	457	Doug Zmolek, S.J.	.10	.35
☐ ☐	**458**	**Mike Rathje, S.J., RC**	**.10**	**.35**
☐ ☐	459	Jamie Baker, S.J.	.10	.35
☐ ☐	460	Joe Reekie, T.B.	.10	.35
☐ ☐	461	Marc Bureau, T.B.	.10	.35
☐ ☐	462	John Tucker, T.B.	.10	.35
☐ ☐	**463**	**Bill McDougall, T.B., RC**	**.10**	**.35**
☐ ☐	464	Danton Cole, T.B.	.10	.35
☐ ☐	465	Brian Bradley, T.B.	.10	.35
☐ ☐	466	Jason Lafrenière, T.B.	.10	.35
☐ ☐	467	Donald Dufresne, T.B.	.10	.35
☐ ☐	468	Daren Puppa (G), T.B.	.10	.35
☐ ☐	469	Doug Gilmour, Tor.	.35	1.00
☐ ☐	**470**	**Damian Rhodes (G), Tor., RC**	**.50**	**1.50**
☐ ☐	**471**	**Matt Martin, Tor., RC**	**.10**	**.35**
☐ ☐	472	Bill Berg, Tor.	.10	.35
☐ ☐	473	John Cullen, Tor.	.10	.35
☐ ☐	474	Rob Pearson, Tor.	.10	.35
☐ ☐	475	Wendel Clark, Tor.	.25	.50
☐ ☐	476	Mark Osborne, Tor.	.10	.35
☐ ☐	477	Dmitri Mironov, Tor.	.10	.35
☐ ☐	478	Kay Whitmore (G), Van.	.10	.35
☐ ☐	478	Kris King, Wpg.	.10	.35
☐ ☐	479	Shawn Antoski, Van.	.10	.35
☐ ☐	480	Greg Adams, Van.	.10	.35
☐ ☐	481	Dave Babych, Van.	.10	.35
☐ ☐	482	John McIntyre, Van.	.10	.35
☐ ☐	483	Jyrki Lumme, Van.	.10	.35
☐ ☐	484	José Charbonneau, Van.	.10	.35
☐ ☐	485	Gino Odjick, Van.	.10	.35
☐ ☐	486	Dana Murzyn, Van.	.10	.35
☐ ☐	487	Michal Pivonka, Wsh.	.10	.35
☐ ☐	488	David Poulin, Wsh.	.10	.35
☐ ☐	489	Sylvain Côté, Wsh.	.10	.35
☐ ☐	490	Pat Peake, Wsh.	.10	.35
☐ ☐	491	Kelly Miller, Wsh.	.10	.35
☐ ☐	492	Randy Burridge, Wsh.	.10	.35
☐ ☐	**493**	**Kevin Kaminski, Wsh., RC**	**.10**	**.35**
☐ ☐	494	John Slaney, Wsh.	.10	.35
☐ ☐	495	Keith Jones, Wsh.	.10	.35
☐ ☐	496	Harijs Vitolinsh, Wpg.	.10	.35
☐ ☐	497	Nelson Emerson, Wpg.	.10	.35
☐ ☐	499	Darrin Shannon, Wpg.	.10	.35
☐ ☐	500	Stéphane Quintal, Wpg.	.10	.35
☐ ☐	501	Luciano Borsato, Wpg.	.10	.35
☐ ☐	502	Thomas Steen, Wpg.	.10	.35
☐ ☐	503	Alexei Zhamnov, Wpg.	.25	.50
☐ ☐	504	Paul Ysebaert, Wpg.	.10	.35
☐ ☐	**505**	**Jeff Friesen, Cdn. RC**	**1.00**	**3.00**
☐ ☐	506	Niklas Sundstrom, Swe.	.10	.35
☐ ☐	**507**	**Nick Stajduhar, Cdn. RC**	**.10**	**.35**
☐ ☐	**508**	**Jamie Storr (G), Cdn. RC**	**.50**	**1.50**
☐ ☐	509	Valeri Bure, Rus.	.25	.50
☐ ☐	**510**	**Jason Bonsignore, USA. RC**	**.10**	**.35**
☐ ☐	511	Mats Lindgren, Swe.	.10	.35
☐ ☐	**512**	**Yanick Dubé, Cdn. RC**	**.10**	**.35**
☐ ☐	**513**	**Todd Harvey, Cdn. RC**	**.25**	**.50**
☐ ☐	**514**	**Ladislav Prokupek, Cze., RC**	**.10**	**.35**
☐ ☐	**515**	**Tomas Vlasak, Cze., RC**	**.10**	**.35**
☐ ☐	**516**	**Josef Marha, Cze., RC**	**.10**	**.35**
☐ ☐	**517**	**Tomas Blazek, Cze., RC**	**.10**	**.35**
☐ ☐	**518**	**Zdenek Nedved, Cze., RC**	**.10**	**.35**
☐ ☐	**519**	**Jaroslav Miklenda, Cze., RC**	**.10**	**.35**
☐ ☐	**520**	**Janne Niinimaa, Fin., RC**	**2.50**	**6.00**
☐ ☐	521	Saku Koivu, Fin.	2.25	6.00
☐ ☐	**522**	**Tommi Miettinen, Fin., RC**	**.10**	**.35**
☐ ☐	**523**	**Tuomas Gronman, Fin., RC**	**.10**	**.35**
☐ ☐	**524**	**Jani Nikko, Fin., RC**	**.10**	**.35**
☐ ☐	**525**	**Jonni Vauhkonen, Fin., RC**	**.10**	**.35**
☐ ☐	**526**	**Nikolai Tsulygin, Fin., RC**	**.10**	**.35**
☐ ☐	**527**	**Vadim Sharifjanov, Rus., RC**	**.25**	**.50**
☐ ☐	**528**	**Valeri Bure, Rus., RC**	**.50**	**1.50**
☐ ☐	**529**	**Alexander Kharlamov, Rus., RC**	**.10**	**.35**
☐ ☐	**530**	**Nikolai Zavarukhin, Rus., RC**	**.10**	**.35**
☐ ☐	**531**	**Oleg Tverdovsky, Rus., RC**	**.50**	**1.50**
☐ ☐	**532**	**Sergei Kondrashkin, Rus., RC**	**.10**	**.35**
☐ ☐	**533**	**Evgeni Ryabchikov (G), Rus., RC**	**.10**	**.35**
☐ ☐	**534**	**Mats Lindgren, Swe., RC**	**.25**	**.50**
☐ ☐	535	Kenny Jonsson, Swe.	.10	.35
☐ ☐	**536**	**Edvin Frylen, Swe., RC**	**.10**	**.35**
☐ ☐	**537**	**Mathias Johansson, Swe., RC**	**.10**	**.35**
☐ ☐	**538**	**Johan Davidsson, Swe., RC**	**.10**	**.35**
☐ ☐	**539**	**Mikael Hakansson, Swe., RC**	**.10**	**.35**
☐ ☐	**540**	**Anders Eriksson, Swe., RC**	**.50**	**1.50**

	No.	**Inserts**	**Silver**	**Gold**
☐ ☐	99	Wayne Gretzky Upper Deck	25.00	12.00

CALDER CANDIDATES

Series Two Insert Set (20 cards): **55.00** **85.00**

	No.	**Player**	**Silver**	**Gold**
☐ ☐	C1	Alexandre Daigle, Ott.	4.00	6.00
☐ ☐	C2	Chris Pronger, Hfd.	4.00	6.00
☐ ☐	C3	Chris Gratton, T.B.	4.00	6.00
☐ ☐	C4	Rob Niedermayer, Fla.	3.00	4.00
☐ ☐	C5	Markus Naslund, Pgh.	1.50	2.00
☐ ☐	C6	Jason Arnott, Edm.	6.00	10.00
☐ ☐	C7	Pierre Sévigny, Mtl.	1.50	2.00
☐ ☐	C8	Jarkko Varvio, Dal.	1.50	2.00
☐ ☐	C9	Dean McAmmond, Edm.	1.50	2.00
☐ ☐	C10	Alexei Yashin, Ott.	6.00	10.00

	No.	Player	Silver	Gold
□ □	C11	Phillippe Boucher, Buf.	1.50	2.00
□ □	C12	Mikael Renberg, Pha.	3.00	4.00
□ □	C13	Chris Simon, Que.	1.50	2.00
□ □	C14	Brent Gretzky, T.B.	1.50	2.00
□ □	C15	Jesse Belanger, Fla.	1.50	2.00
□ □	C16	Jocelyn Thibault (G), Que.	8.00	12.00
□ □	C17	Chris Osgood (G), Det.	10.00	15.00
□ □	C18	Derek Plante, Buf.	1.50	2.00
□ □	C19	Iain Fraser, Que.	1.50	2.00
□ □	C20	Vesa Viitakoski, Cgy.	1.50	2.00
		Trade Cards	**Silver**	**Gold**
□		Silver Trade Card	1.00	
□		Gold Trade Card	1.00	

CHERRY'S PLAYOFF HEROES

Insert Set (20 cards): **300.00**

	No.	Player	NRMT-MT
□	D1	Wayne Gretzky, L.A.	60.00
□	D2	Mario Lemieux, Pgh.	45.00
□	D3	Al MacInnis, Cgy.	5.00
□	D4	Mark Messier, NYR.	15.00
□	D5	Dino Ciccarelli, Det.	5.00
□	D6	Dale Hunter, Wsh.	5.00
□	D7	Grant Fuhr (G), Buf.	5.00
□	D8	Paul Coffey, Det.	5.00
□	D9	Doug Gilmour, Tor.	5.00
□	D10	Patrick Roy (G), Mtl.	45.00
□	D11	Alexandre Daigle, Ott.	10.00
□	D12	Chris Gratton, T.B.	10.00
□	D13	Chris Pronger, Hfd.	10.00
□	D14	Félix Potvin (G), Tor.	20.00
□	D15	Eric Lindros, Pha.	40.00
□	D16	Maurice Richard, Mtl.	20.00
□	D17	Gordie Howe, Det.	25.00
□	D18	Henri Richard, Mtl.	10.00
□	D19	Reggie Leach, Pha.	6.00
□	D20	Don Cherry Checklist	20.00

EAST / WEST STARS

Series Two Set (20 cards): **175.00**

	No.	Player	NRMT-MT
□	E1	Eric Lindros, Pha.	20.00
□	E2	Mario Lemieux, Pgh.	25.00
□	E3	Alexandre Daigle, Ott.	4.00
□	E4	Patrick Roy (G), Mtl.	25.00
□	E5	Rob Niedermayer, Fla.	3.00
□	E6	Chris Gratton, T.B.	4.00
□	E7	Alexei Yashin, Ott.	5.00
□	E8	Pat LaFontaine, Buf.	3.00
□	E9	Joe Sakic, Que.	12.00
□	E10	Pierre Turgeon, NYI.	3.00
□	W1	Wayne Gretzky, L.A.	30.00
□	W2	Pavel Bure, Van.	10.00
□	W3	Teemu Selänne, Wpg.	10.00
□	W4	Doug Gilmour, Tor.	4.00
□	W5	Steve Yzerman, Det.	15.00
□	W6	Jeremy Roenick, Chi.	4.00
□	W7	Brett Hull, Stl.	8.00
□	W8	Jason Arnott, Edm.	5.00
□	W9	Félix Potvin (G), Tor.	9.00
□	W10	Sergei Fedorov, Det.	8.00

FIRST OVERALL

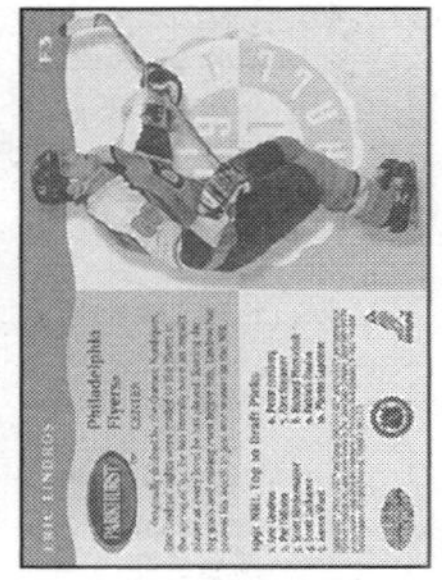

Series One Insert Set (10 cards): **70.00**

	No.	Player	NRMT-MT
□	F1	Alexandre Daigle, Ott.	4.00
□	F2	Roman Hamrlik, T.B.	3.00
□	F3	Eric Lindros, Pha.	20.00
□	F4	Owen Nolan, Que.	3.00
□	F5	Mats Sundin, Que.	8.00
□	F6	Mike Modano, Dal.	8.00
□	F7	Pierre Turgeon, NYI.	3.00
□	F8	Joe Murphy, Chi.	3.00
□	F9	Wendel Clark, Tor.	3.00
□	F10	Mario Lemieux, Pgh.	20.00

CANADA / USA GOLD

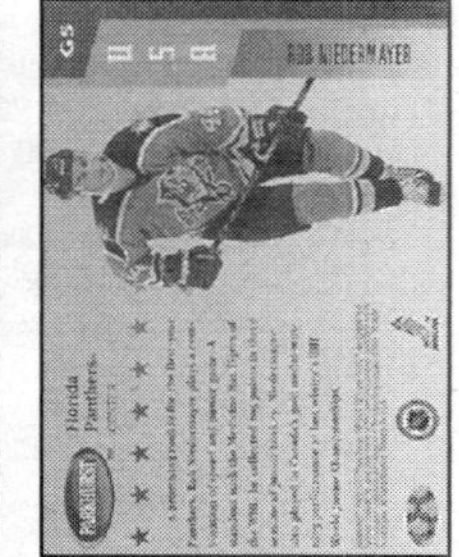

Insert Set (10 cards): **100.00**

	No.	Player	NRMT-MT
□	G1	Wayne Gretzky, L.A.	25.00
□	G2	Mario Lemieux, Pgh.	20.00
□	G3	Eric Lindros, Pha.	15.00
□	G4	Brett Hull, Stl.	6.00
□	G5	Rob Niedermayer, Fla.	3.00
□	G6	Alexandre Daigle, Ott.	3.00
□	G7	Pavel Bure, Van.	9.00
□	G8	Teemu Selänne, Wpg.	9.00
□	G9	Patrick Roy (G), Mtl.	20.00
□	G10	Doug Gilmour, Tor.	4.00

PARKIE REPRINTS

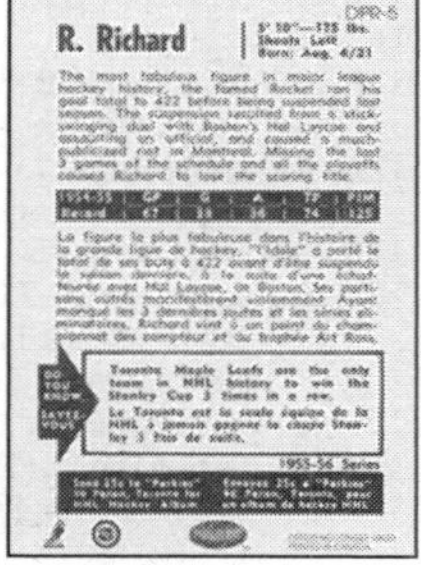

Series 1 Regular Pack Set (33-41/CL5): **80.00**
Series 1 Jumbo Pack Set (42-50/CL6): **90.00**
Series 2 Regular Pack Set (51-59/CL7): **85.00**
Series 2 Jumbo Pack Set (60-68/CL8): **85.00**
Series 1 Case Inserts (DPR1-DPR6): **35.00**
Series 2 Case Insers (DPR7-DPR12) **30.00**

	No.	Player	NRMT-MT
□		Checklist No. 5 ('61-62)	15.00
□	PR33	Gordie Howe	20.00
□	PR34	Tim Horton ('52-53)	15.00
□	PR35	Bill Barilko ('51-52)	15.00
□	PR36	Elmer Lach/Maurice Richard ('53-54)	10.00
□	PR37	Terry Sawchuk ('61-62)	18.00
□	PR38	George Armstrong ('59-60)	6.00
□	PR39	Billy Harris ('63-64)	6.00
□	PR40	Doug Harvey ('57-58)	6.00
□	PR41	Gump Worsley (G) ('63-64)	10.00
□		Checklist No. 6 ('57-58)	15.00
□	PR42	Gordie Howe ('51-52)	20.00
□	PR43	Jacques Plante ('60-61)	18.00
□	PR44	Frank Mahovlich ('62-63)	6.00
□	PR45	Fern Flaman	6.00
□	PR46	Bernie Geoffrion	6.00
□	PR47	Toe Blake ('63-64)	6.00
□	PR48	Maurice Richard	20.00
□	PR49	Ted Lindsay	6.00
□	PR50	Camille Henry ('54-55)	6.00
□		Checklist No. 7 ('63-64)	15.00
□	PR51	Gordie Howe ('61-62)	20.00
□	PR52	Jean Guy Talbot ('59-60)	6.00
□	PR53	Terry Sawchuk (G) ('54-55)	18.00
□	PR54	Warren Godfrey ('53-54)	6.00
□	PR55	Tom Johnson ('55-56)	6.00
□	PR56	Bert Olmstead ('60-61)	6.00
□	PR57	Cal Gardner ('53-54)	6.00
□	PR58	Red Kelly ('63-64)	6.00
□	PR59	Phil Goyette ('59-60)	6.00
□		Checklist No. 8 ('63-64)	15.00
□	PR60	Gordie Howe	20.00
□	PR61	Lou Fontinato	6.00
□	PR62	Bill Dineen	6.00
□	PR63	Maurice Richard	20.00
□	PR64	Vic Stasiuk	6.00
□	PR65	Marcel Pronovost	6.00
□	PR66	Ed Litzenberger	6.00
□	PR67	Dave Keon	6.00
□	PR68	Dollard St. Laurent ('55-56)	6.00
□	DPR-1	Gordie Howe ('63-64)	20.00
□	DPR-2	Milt Schmidt ('54-55)	6.00
□	DPR-3	Tim Horton ('62-63)	12.00
□	DPR-4	Al Rollins ('51-52)	6.00
□	DPR-5	Maurice Richard ('55-56)	18.00
□	DPR-6	Harry Howell ('54-55)	6.00
□	DPR-7	Gordie Howe	20.00
□	DPR-8	Johnny Bower (G)	12.00
□	DPR-9	Dean Prentice ('54-55)	6.00
□	DPR-10	Leo Labine ('53-54)	6.00
□	DPR-11	Harry Watson	6.00
□	DPR-12	Dickie Moore	6.00

1993 - 94 PARKHURST 1956 - 57 MISSING LINK

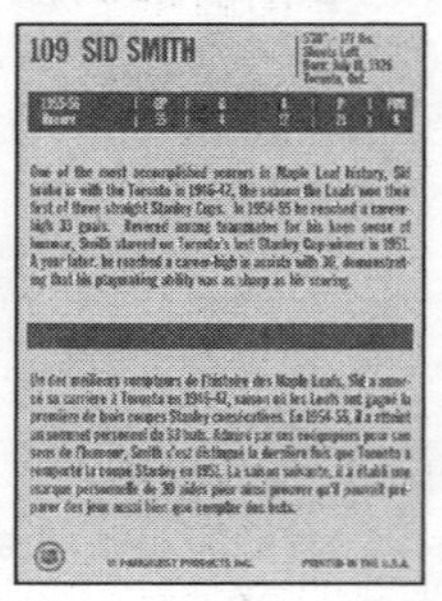

Complete Set (180 cards): **35.00**
Common Player: **.20**
Album: **18.00**
Promo Doug Harvey (#136): **1.00**

	No.	Player	NRMT-MT
□	1	Jerry Toppazzini, Bos.	.20
□	2	Fern Flaman, Bos.	.20
□	3	Fleming MacKell, Bos.	.20
□	4	Léo Labine, Bos.	.20
□	5	John Peirson, Bos.	.20
□	6	Don McKenney, Bos.	.20
□	7	Bob Armstrong, Bos.	.20
□	8	Réal Cheverfils, Bos.	.20
□	9	Vic Stasiuk, Bos.	.20
□	10	Cal Gardner, Bos.	.20
□	11	Léo Boivin, Bos.	.20
□	12	Jack Caffery, Bos.	.20
□	13	Bob Beckett, Bos.	.20
□	14	Jack Bionda, Bos.	.20

☐ 15 Claude Pronovost, Bos. .20
☐ 16 Lerry Regan, Bos. .20
☐ 17 Terry Sawchuk (G), Bos. 3.00
☐ 18 Doug Mohns, Bos. .20
☐ 19 Marcel Bonin, Bos. .20
☐ 20 Allan Stanley, Bos. .50
☐ 21 Milt Schmidt, Coach, Bos. .20
☐ 22 Al Dewsbury, Chi. .20
☐ 23 Glen Skov, Chi. .20
☐ 24 Ed Litzenberger, Chi. .20
☐ 25 Nick Mickoski, Chi. .20
☐ 26 Wally Hergesheimer, Chi. .20
☐ 27 Jack McIntyre, Chi. .20
☐ 28 Al Rollins (G), Chi. .20
☐ 29 Hank Ciesla, Chi. .20
☐ 30 Gus Mortson, Chi. .20
☐ 31 Elmer Vasko, Chi. .20
☐ 32 Pierre Pilote, Chi. .20
☐ 33 Ron Ingram, Chi. .20
☐ 34 Frank Martin, Chi. .20
☐ 35 Forbes Kennedy, Chi. .20
☐ 36 Harry Watson, Chi. .75
☐ 37 Eddie Kachur, Chi. .20
☐ 38 Hec Lalonde, Chi. .20
☐ 39 Eric Nesterenko, Chi. .20
☐ 40 Ben Woit, Chi. .20
☐ 41 Ken Mosdell, Chi. .20
☐ 42 Tommy Ivan, Coach, Chi. .20
☐ 43 Gordie Howe, Det. 4.00
☐ 44 Ted Lindsay, Det. 1.00
☐ 45 Norm Ullman, Det. 1.00
☐ 46 Glenn Hall (G), Det. 2.25
☐ 47 Billy Dea, Det. .20
☐ 48 Bill McNeill, Det. .20
☐ 49 Earl Reibel, Det. .20
☐ 50 Bill Dineen, Det. .20
☐ 51 Warren Godfrey, Det. .20
☐ 52 Red Kelly, Det. 1.00
☐ 53 Marty Pavelich, Det. .20
☐ 54 Lorne Ferguson, Det. .20
☐ 55 Larry Hillman, Det. .20
☐ 56 John Bucyk, Det. 1.25
☐ 57 Metro Prystai, Det. .20
☐ 58 Marcel Pronovost, Det. .20
☐ 59 Alex Delvecchio, Det. 1.25
☐ 60 Murray Costello, Det. .20
☐ 61 Al Arbour, Det. .20
☐ 62 Bucky Hollingworth, Det. .20
☐ 63 Jim Skinner, Coach, Det. .20
☐ 64 Jean Béliveau, Mtl. 2.50
☐ 65 Maurice Richard, Mtl. 3.50
☐ 66 Henri Richard, Mtl. 1.50
☐ 67 Doug Harvey, Mtl. 1.25
☐ 68 Bernie Geoffrion, Mtl. 1.25
☐ 69 Dollard St. Laurent, Mtl. .20
☐ 70 Dickie Moore, Mtl. 1.00
☐ 71 Bert Olmstead, Mtl. .20
☐ 72 Jacques Plante (G), Mtl. 3.00
☐ 73 Claude Provost, Mtl. .20
☐ 74 Phil Goyette, Mtl. .20
☐ 75 André Pronovost, Mtl. .20
☐ 76 Don Marshall, Mtl. .20
☐ 77 Ralph Backstrom, Mtl. .20
☐ 78 Floyd Curry, Mtl. .20
☐ 79 Tom Johnson, Mtl. .20
☐ 80 Jean-Guy Talbot, Mtl. .20
☐ 81 Bob Turner, Mtl. .20
☐ 82 Connie Broden, Mtl. .20
☐ 83 Jackie Leclair, Mtl. .20
☐ 84 Toe Blake, Mtl. .20
☐ 85 Frank Selke, Coach, Mtl. .20
☐ 86 George Sullivan, NYR. .20
☐ 87 Larry Cahan, NYR. .20
☐ 88 Jean-Guy Gendron, NYR. .20
☐ 89 Bill Gadsby, NYR. .50
☐ 90 Andy Bathgate, NYR. .75
☐ 91 Dean Prentice, NYR. .20
☐ 92 Gump Worsley (G), NYR. 2.00
☐ 93 Lou Fontinato, NYR. .20
☐ 94 Gerry Foley, NYR. .20
☐ 95 Larry Popein, NYR. .20
☐ 96 Harry Howell, NYR. .50
☐ 97 Andy Hebenton, NYR. .20
☐ 98 Danny Lewicki, NYR. .20
☐ 99 Dave Creighton, NYR. .20
☐ 100 Camille Henry, NYR. .20
☐ 101 Jack Evans, NYR. .20
☐ 102 Ron Murphy, NYR. .20
☐ 103 Johnny Bower (G), NYR. 1.75
☐ 104 Parker MacDonald, NYR. .20
☐ 105 Bronco Horvath, NYR. .20
☐ 106 Bruce Cline, NYR. .20
☐ 107 Ivan Irwin, NYR. .20
☐ 108 Phil Watson, Coach, NYR. .20
☐ 109 Sid Smith, Tor. .20
☐ 110 Ron Stewart, Tor. .20
☐ 111 Rudy Migay, Tor. .20
☐ 112 Tod Sloan, Tor. .20
☐ 113 Bob Pulford, Tor. .75
☐ 114 Marc Réaume, Tor. .20
☐ 115 Jim Morrison, Tor. .20
☐ 116 Ted Kennedy, Tor. 1.25
☐ 117 Gerry James, Tor. .20
☐ 118 Brian Cullen, Tor. .20
☐ 119 Jim Thompson, Tor. .20
☐ 120 Barry Cullen, Tor. .20
☐ 121 Al MacNeil, Tor. .20
☐ 122 Gary Aldcorn, Tor. .20
☐ 123 Bob Baun, Tor. .20
☐ 124 Hugh Bolton, Tor. .20
☐ 125 George Armstrong, Tor. 1.00
☐ 126 Dick Duff, Tor. .20
☐ 127 Tim Horton, Tor. 2.50
☐ 128 Ed Chadwick (G), Tor. .20
☐ 129 Billy Harris, Tor. .20
☐ 130 Mike Nykoluk, Tor. .20
☐ 131 Noel Price, Tor. .20
☐ 132 Ken Girard, Tor. .20
☐ 133 Howie Meeker, Tor. .20
☐ 134 Hap Day, Coach, Tor. .20
☐ 135 AS: Jacques Plante (G), Mtl. 1.75
☐ 136 AS: Doug Harvey, Mtl. .75
☐ 137 AS: Bill Gadsby, NYR. .20
☐ 138 AS: Jean Béliveau, Mtl. 1.50
☐ 139 AS: Maurice Richard, Mtl. 2.00
☐ 140 AS: Ted Lindsay, Det. .60
☐ 141 AS: Glenn Hall (G), Det. 1.25
☐ 142 AS: Red Kelly, Det. .60
☐ 143 AS: Tom Johnson, Mtl. .20
☐ 144 AS: Tod Sloan, Tor. .20
☐ 145 AS: Gordie Howe, Det. 2.25
☐ 146 AS: Bert Olmstead, Mtl. .20
☐ 147 AW: Earl Reibel, Det. .20
☐ 148 AW: Doug Harvey, Mtl. .75
☐ 149 AW: Jean Béliveau, Mtl. 1.50
☐ 150 AW: Jean Béliveau, Mtl. 1.50
☐ 151 AW: Jacques Plante (G), Mtl. .20
☐ 152 AW: Glenn Hall (G), Det. .20
☐ 153 Terry Sawchuk (G) (Action) 1.00
☐ 154 Action Shot .20
☐ 155 Action Shot .20
☐ 156 Jean Béliveau (Action) 1.00
☐ 157 Jean Béliveau (Action) 1.00
☐ 158 Action Shot .20
☐ 159 Action Shot (Action) .20
☐ 160 Gordie Howe (Action) 1.50
☐ 161 Jacques Plante (G) (Action) 1.00
☐ 162 Gordie Howe (Action) 1.50
☐ 163 Jacques Plante (G) (Action) 1.00
☐ 164 Action Shot .20
☐ 165 Action Shot .20
☐ 166 Action Shot .20
☐ 167 Terry Sawchuk (G) (Action) 1.00
☐ 168 Terry Sawchuk (G) (Action) 1.00
☐ 169 LL: Vic Stasiuk, Bos. .20
☐ 170 LL: Red Sullivan, Chi. .20
☐ 171 LL: Gordie Howe, Det. 2.25
☐ 172 LL: Jean Béliveau, Mtl. 1.50
☐ 173 LL: Andy Bathgate, NYR. .35
☐ 174 LL: Tod Sloan, Tor. .20
☐ 175 Stanley Cup Playoffs .20
☐ 176 Stanley Cup Playoffs .20
☐ 177 Stanley Cup Playoffs .20
☐ 178 Stanley Cup Playoffs .20
☐ 179 Checklist 1 .20
☐ 180 Checklist 2 .20

AUTOGRAPHS

Autographed cards were limited to 956 copies.

Insert Set (6 cards): 800.00

	No.	Player	NRMT-MT
☐	1	Gordie Howe, Det.	250.00
☐	2	Maurice Richard, Mtl.	225.00
☐	3	Bernie Geoffrion, Mtl.	130.00
☐	4	Gump Worsley (G), NYR.	125.00
☐	5	Jean Béliveau, Mtl.	175.00
☐	6	Frank Mahovlich, Tor.	130.00

FUTURE STARS

Insert Set (6 cards): 75.00

	No.	Player	NRMT-MT
☐	FS1	Carl Brewer	10.00
☐	FS2	Dave Keon	12.00
☐	FS3	Stan Mikita	22.00
☐	FS4	Eddie Shack	15.00
☐	FS5	Frank Mahovlich	25.00
☐	FS6	Charlie Hodge (G)	12.00

POP-UPS

Cards 1-6 were inserted into Canadian packs while cards 7-12 were inserted into American packs.

Insert Set (12 cards): 400.00

	No.	Player	NRMT-MT
☐	P1	Howie Morenz, Mtl.	70.00
☐	P2	George Hainsworth (G), Mtl.	35.00
☐	P3	Georges Vézina (G), Mtl.	65.00
☐	P4	King Clancy, Tor.	45.00
☐	P5	Syl Apps, Tor.	35.00
☐	P6	Turk Broda (G), Tor.	45.00
☐	P7	Eddie Shore, Bos.	65.00
☐	P8	Bill Cook, NYR.	35.00
☐	P9	Woody Dumart, Bos.	25.00
☐	P10	Lester Patrick, NYR.	45.00
☐	P11	Doug Bentley, Chi.	25.00
☐	P12	Earl Seibert, NYR.	25.00

1993 - 94 PINNACLE

These cards have two versions: an American (English text) issue and a Canadian (Bilingual) issue. Card 512 (Wayne Gretzky) was a late addition in Series Two.

Imprint: Series One: © 1993 SCORE
Series Two: 1994 PINNACLE BRANDS, INC. PRINTED IN U.S.A.

Series One Set (236 cards): 20.00
Series Two Set (276 cards): 25.00
Common Player: .15
Promo Panel (Cards 1-6): 6.00

	No.	Player	NRMT-MT
☐ ☐	1	Eric Lindros, Pha.	2.00
☐ ☐	2	Mats Sundin, Que.	.50
☐ ☐	3	Tom Barrasso (G), Pgh.	.25
☐ ☐	4	Teemu Selänne, Pgh.	1.00
☐ ☐	5	Joé Juneau, Bos.	.15
☐ ☐	6	Tony Amonte, NYR.	.25
☐ ☐	7	Bob Probert, Det.	.15
☐ ☐	8	Chris Kontos, T.B.	.15
☐ ☐	9	Geoff Sanderson, Hfd.	.15
☐ ☐	10	Alexander Mogilny, Buf.	.35
☐ ☐	11	Kevin Lowe, NYR.	.15
☐ ☐	12	Nikolai Borschevsky, Tor.	.15
☐ ☐	13	Dale Hunter, Wsh.	.15
☐ ☐	14	Gary Suter, Cgy.	.15
☐ ☐	15	Curtis Joseph (G), Stl.	.75
☐ ☐	16	Mark Tinordi, Dal.	.15
☐ ☐	17	Doug Weight, Edm.	.35
☐ ☐	18	Benoît Hogue, NYI.	.15

	No.	Player	Price
☐ ☐	19	Tommy Söderström (G), Pha.	.15
☐ ☐	20	Pat Falloon, S.J.	.15
☐ ☐	21	Jyrki Lumme, Van.	.15
☐ ☐	22	Brian Bellows, Mtl.	.15
☐ ☐	23	Alexei Zhitnik, L.A.	.15
☐ ☐	24	Dirk Graham, Chi.	.15
☐ ☐	25	Scott Stevens, N.J.	.25
☐ ☐	26	Adam Foote, Que.	.25
☐ ☐	27	Mike Gartner, NYR.	.25
☐ ☐	**28**	**Dallas Drake, Det., RC**	**.15**
☐ ☐	29	Ulf Samuelsson, Pgh.	.15
☐ ☐	30	Cam Neely, Bos.	.25
☐ ☐	31	Sean Burke (G), Hfd.	.25
☐ ☐	32	Petr Svoboda, Buf.	.15
☐ ☐	33	Keith Tkachuk, Pgh.	.50
☐ ☐	34	Roman Hamrlik, T.B.	.25
☐ ☐	35	Robert Reichel, Cgy.	.15
☐ ☐	36	Igor Kravchuk, Edm.	.15
☐ ☐	37	Mathieu Schneider, Mtl.	.15
☐ ☐	38	Bob Kudelski, Ott.	.15
☐ ☐	39	Jeff Brown, Stl.	.15
☐ ☐	40	Mke Modano, Dal.	.50
☐ ☐	**41**	**Rob Gaudreau, S.J., RC**	**.15**
☐ ☐	42	Dave Andreychuk, Tor.	.15
☐ ☐	43	Trevor Linden, Van.	.25
☐ ☐	44	Dimitri Khristich, Wsh.	.15
☐ ☐	45	Joe Murphy, Chi.	.15
☐ ☐	46	Rob Blake, L.A.	.25
☐ ☐	47	Alexander Semak, N.J.	.15
☐ ☐	48	Ray Ferraro, NYI.	.15
☐ ☐	49	Curtis Leschyshyn, Que.	.15
☐ ☐	50	Mark Recchi, Pha.	.25
☐ ☐	51	Sergei Nemchinov, NYR.	.15
☐ ☐	52	Larry Murphy, Pgh.	.25
☐ ☐	53	Stephen Heinze, Bos.	.15
☐ ☐	54	Sergei Fedorov, Det.	.50
☐ ☐	55	Gary Roberts, Cgy.	.15
☐ ☐	56	Alexei Zhamnov, Pgh.	.15
☐ ☐	57	Derian Hatcher, Dal.	.25
☐ ☐	58	Kelly Buchberger, Edm.	.15
☐ ☐	59	Eric Desjardins, Mtl.	.25
☐ ☐	60	Brian Bradley, T.B.	.15
☐ ☐	61	Patrick Poulin, Hfd.	.15
☐ ☐	62	Scott Lachance, NYI.	.15
☐ ☐	63	Johan Garpenlov, S.J.	.15
☐ ☐	64	Sylvain Turgeon, Ott.	.15
☐ ☐	65	Grant Fuhr (G), Buf.	.25
☐ ☐	66	Garth Butcher, Stl.	.15
☐ ☐	67	Michal Pivonka, Wsh.	.15
☐ ☐	68	Todd Gill, Tor.	.15
☐ ☐	69	Cliff Ronning, Van.	.15
☐ ☐	70	Steve Smith, Chi.	.15
☐ ☐	71	Bobby Holik, N.J.	.15
☐ ☐	72	Garry Galley, Pha.	.15
☐ ☐	73	Stephen Leach, Bos.	.15
☐ ☐	74	Ron Francis, Pgh.	.25
☐ ☐	75	Jari Kurri, L.A.	.25
☐ ☐	76	Alexei Kovalev, NYR.	.15
☐ ☐	77	Dave Gagner, Dal.	.15
☐ ☐	78	Steve Duchesne, Que.	.15
☐ ☐	79	Theoren Fleury, Cgy.	.35
☐ ☐	80	Paul Coffey, Det.	.25
☐ ☐	81	Bill Ranford (G), Edm.	.25
☐ ☐	82	Doug Bodger, Buf.	.15
☐ ☐	83	Nick Kypreos, Hfd.	.15
☐ ☐	84	Darius Kasparaitis, NYI.	.15
☐ ☐	85	Vincent Damphousse, Mtl.	.35
☐ ☐	86	Arturs Irbe (G), S.J.	.15
☐ ☐	87	Shawn Chambers, T.B.	.15
☐ ☐	88	Murray Craven, Van.	.15
☐ ☐	89	Rob Pearson, Tor.	.15
☐ ☐	90	Kevin Hatcher, Wsh.	.15
☐ ☐	91	Brent Sutter, Chi.	.15
☐ ☐	92	Teppo Numminen, Pgh.	.15
☐ ☐	93	Shawn Burr, Det.	.15
☐ ☐	94	Valeri Zelepukin, N.J.	.15
☐ ☐	95	Ron Sutter, Stl.	.15
☐ ☐	96	Craig MacTavish, Edm.	.15
☐ ☐	97	Dominic Roussel (G), Pha.	.15
☐ ☐	98	Nicklas Lidström, Det.	.25
☐ ☐	99	Adam Graves, NYR.	.15
☐ ☐	100	Doug Gilmour, Tor.	.35
☐ ☐	101	Frantisek Musil, Cgy.	.15
☐ ☐	102	Ted Donato, Bos.	.15
☐ ☐	103	Andrew Cassels, Hfd.	.15
☐ ☐	104	Vladimir Malakhov, NYI.	.15
☐ ☐	105	Shawn McEachern, Pgh.	.15
☐ ☐	106	Petr Nedved, Van.	.15
☐ ☐	107	Calle Johansson, Wsh.	.15
☐ ☐	108	Rich Sutter, Stl.	.15
☐ ☐	109	Evgeny Davydov, Pgh.	.15
☐ ☐	110	Mike Ricci, Que.	.15
☐ ☐	111	Scott Niedermayer, N.J.	.25
☐ ☐	112	John LeClair, Mtl.	.75
☐ ☐	113	Darryl Sydor, L.A.	.15
☐ ☐	114	Paul DiPietro, Mtl.	.15
☐ ☐	115	Stéphane Fiset (G), Que.	.25
☐ ☐	116	Christian Ruuttu, Chi.	.15
☐ ☐	117	Doug Zmolek, S.J.	.15
☐ ☐	118	Bob Sweeney, Buf.	.15
☐ ☐	119	Brent Fedyk, Pha.	.15
☐ ☐	120	Norm Maciver, Ott.	.15
☐ ☐	121	Rob Zamuner, T.B.	.25
☐ ☐	122	Joe Mullen, Pgh.	.25
☐ ☐	123	Trent Yawney, Cgy.	.15
☐ ☐	124	David Shaw, Bos.	.15
☐ ☐	125	Mark Messier, NYR.	.50
☐ ☐	126	Kevin Miller, Stl.	.15
☐ ☐	127	Dino Ciccarelli, Det.	.25
☐ ☐	128	Derek King, NYI.	.15
☐ ☐	129	Scott Young, Que.	.15
☐ ☐	130	Craig Janney, Stl.	.15
☐ ☐	131	Jamie Macoun, Tor.	.15
☐ ☐	132	Geoff Courtnall, Van.	.15
☐ ☐	133	Bob Essensa (G), Pgh.	.15
☐ ☐	134	Ken Daneyko, N.J.	.15
☐ ☐	135	Mike Ridley, Wsh.	.15
☐ ☐	136	Stéphan Lebeau, Mtl.	.15
☐ ☐	137	Tony Granato, L.A.	.15
☐ ☐	138	Kay Whitmore (G), Van.	.15
☐ ☐	139	Luke Richardson, Edm.	.15
☐ ☐	140	Jeremy Roenick, Chi.	.35
☐ ☐	141	Brad May, Buf.	.15
☐ ☐	142	Sandis Ozolinsh, S.J.	.25
☐ ☐	143	Stéphane Richer, N.J.	.15
☐ ☐	144	John Tucker, T.B.	.15
☐ ☐	145	Luc Robitaille, L.A.	.25
☐ ☐	146	Dimitri Yushkievich, Pha.	.15
☐ ☐	147	Sean Hill, Ana.	.15
☐ ☐	148	John Vanbiesbrouck (G), Fla.	.75
☐ ☐	149	Kevin Stevens, Pgh.	.15
☐ ☐	150	Patrick Roy (G), Mtl.	2.00
☐ ☐	151	Owen Nolan, Que.	.25
☐ ☐	152	Richard Smehlik, Buf.	.15
☐ ☐	153	Ray Sheppard, Det.	.15
☐ ☐	154	Ed Olczyk, NYR.	.15
☐ ☐	155	Al MacInnis, Cgy.	.25
☐ ☐	156	Sergei Zubov, NYR.	.25
☐ ☐	157	Wendel Clark, Tor.	.25
☐ ☐	158	Kirk McLean (G), Van.	.25
☐ ☐	159	Thomas Steen, Pgh.	.15
☐ ☐	160	Pierre Turgeon, NYI.	.25
☐ ☐	161	Dmitri Kvartalnov, Bos.	.15
☐ ☐	162	Brian Noonan, Chi.	.15
☐ ☐	163	Mike McPhee, Dal.	.15
☐ ☐	164	Peter Bondra, Wsh.	.35
☐ ☐	165	Bernie Nicholls, N.J.	.15
☐ ☐	166	Michael Nylander, Hfd.	.15
☐ ☐	167	Guy Hebert (G), Ana.	.25
☐ ☐	168	Scott Mellanby, Fla.	.15
☐ ☐	169	Bob Bassen, Stl.	.15
☐ ☐	170	Rod Brind'Amour, Pha.	.25
☐ ☐	171	Andrei Kovalenko, Que.	.15
☐ ☐	172	Mike Donnelley, L.A.	.15
☐ ☐	173	Steve Thomas, NYI.	.15
☐ ☐	174	Rick Tocchet, Pgh.	.15
☐ ☐	175	Steve Yzerman, Det.	1.50
☐ ☐	176	Dixon Ward, Van.	.15
☐ ☐	177	Randy Wood, Buf.	.15
☐ ☐	178	Dean Kennedy, Pgh.	.15
☐ ☐	179	Joel Otto, Cgy.	.15
☐ ☐	180	Kirk Muller, Mtl.	.15
☐ ☐	181	Chris Chelios, Chi.	.35
☐ ☐	182	Richard Matvichuk, Dal.	.15
☐ ☐	183	John MacLean, N.J.	.15
☐ ☐	184	Joe Kocur, NYR.	.15
☐ ☐	185	Adam Oates, Bos.	.35
☐ ☐	186	Bob Beers, T.B.	.15
☐ ☐	187	Ron Tugnutt (G), Ana.	.15
☐ ☐	188	Brian Skrudland, Fla.	.15
☐ ☐	189	Al Iafrate, Wsh.	.15
☐ ☐	190	Félix Potvin (G), Tor.	.50
☐ ☐	191	David Reid, Bos.	.15
☐ ☐	192	Jim Johnson, Dal.	.15
☐ ☐	193	Kevin Haller, Mtl.	.15
☐ ☐	194	Steve Chiasson, Det.	.15
☐ ☐	195	Jaromir Jagr, Pgh.	1.50
☐ ☐	196	Martin Rucinsky, Que.	.15
☐ ☐	197	Sergei Bautin, Pgh.	.15
☐ ☐	198	Joe Nieuwendyk, Cgy.	.25
☐ ☐	199	Gilbert Dionne, Mtl.	.15
☐ ☐	200	Brett Hull, Stl.	.50
☐ ☐	201	Yuri Khmylev, Buf.	.15
☐ ☐	202	Todd Elik, Edm.	.15
☐ ☐	203	Patrick Flatley, NYI.	.15
☐ ☐	204	Martin Straka, Pgh.	.15
☐ ☐	205	Brendan Shanahan, Stl.	.75
☐ ☐	**206**	**Mark Beaufait, S.J., RC**	**.15**
☐ ☐	**207**	**Mike Lenarduzzi (G), Hfd., RC**	**.15**
☐ ☐	208	Chris LiPuma, T.B.	.15
☐ ☐	209	André Faust, Pha.	.15
☐ ☐	**210**	**Ben Hankinson, N.J., RC**	**.15**
☐ ☐	**211**	**Darrin Madeley (G), Ott., RC**	**.15**
☐ ☐	**212**	**Oleg Petrov, Mtl., RC**	**.15**
☐ ☐	213	Philippe Boucher, Buf.	.15
☐ ☐	214	Tyler Wright, Edm.	.15
☐ ☐	**215**	**Jason Bowen, Pha., RC**	**.15**
☐ ☐	216	Matthew Barnaby, Buf.	.15
☐ ☐	217	Bryan Smolinski, Bos.	.15
☐ ☐	218	Dan Keczmer, Hfd.	.15
☐ ☐	**219**	**Chris Simon, Que., RC**	**.25**
☐ ☐	220	Corey Hirsch (G), NYR.	.15
☐ ☐	221	AW: Mario Lemieux, Pgh.	1.00
☐ ☐	222	AW: Teemu Selänne, Pgh.	.50
☐ ☐	223	AW: Chris Chelios, Chi.	.25
☐ ☐	224	AW: Ed Belfour (G), Chi.	.25
☐ ☐	225	AW: Pierre Turgeon, NY	.25
☐ ☐	226	AW: Doug Gilmour, Tor.	.25
☐ ☐	227	AW: Ed Belfour (G), Chi.	.25
☐ ☐	228	AW: Patrick Roy (G), Mtl.	1.00
☐ ☐	229	AW: Dave Poulin, Bos.	.15
☐ ☐	230	AW: Mario Lemieux, Pgh.	1.00
☐ ☐	231	Mike Vernon (G), Cgy.	.25
☐ ☐	232	Vincent Damphousse, Mtl.	.25
☐ ☐	233	Chris Chelios, Chi.	.25
☐ ☐	234	Cliff Ronning, Van.	.15
☐ ☐	235	Mark Howe, Det.	.15
☐ ☐	236	Alexandre Daigle, Ott.	.35
☐ ☐	237	Wayne Gretzky, L.A.	1.50
☐ ☐	238	Mark Messier, NYR.	.25
☐ ☐	239	Dino Ciccarelli, Det.	.25
☐ ☐	240	Joe Mullen, Pgh.	.15
☐ ☐	241	Mike Gartner, NYR.	.25
☐ ☐	242	Mike Richter (G), NYR.	.50
☐ ☐	243	Pat Verbeek, Hfd.	.15
☐ ☐	244	Valeri Kamensky, Que.	.25
☐ ☐	245	Nelson Emerson, Wpg.	.15
☐ ☐	246	James Patrick, Hfd.	.15
☐ ☐	247	Greg Adams, Van.	.15
☐ ☐	248	Ulf Dahlen, Dal.	.15
☐ ☐	249	Shayne Corson, Edm.	.25
☐ ☐	250	Ray Bourque, Bos.	.50
☐ ☐	251	Claude Lemieux, N.J.	.15
☐ ☐	252	Kelly Hrudey (G), L.A.	.15
☐ ☐	253	Patrice Brisebois, Mtl.	.15
☐ ☐	254	Mark Howe, Det.	.15
☐ ☐	255	Ed Belfour (G), Chi.	.35
☐ ☐	256	Per-Erik Eklund, Pha.	.15
☐ ☐	257	Zarley Zalapski, Hfd.	.15
☐ ☐	258	Sylvain Côté, Wsh.	.15
☐ ☐	259	Uwe Krupp, NYI.	.15
☐ ☐	260	Dale Hawerchuk, Buf.	.25
☐ ☐	261	Alexei Gusarov, Que.	.15
☐ ☐	262	Dave Ellett, Tor.	.15
☐ ☐	263	Tomas Sandström, L.A.	.15
☐ ☐	264	Vladimir Konstantinov, Det.	.15
☐ ☐	265	Paul Ranheim, Cgy.	.15
☐ ☐	266	Darrin Shannon, Pgh.	.15
☐ ☐	267	Chris Terreri (G), N.J.	.15
☐ ☐	268	Russ Courtnall, Dal.	.15
☐ ☐	269	Don Sweeney, Bos.	.15
☐ ☐	270	Kevin Todd, Chi.	.15
☐ ☐	271	Brad Shaw, Ott.	.15
☐ ☐	272	Adam Creighton, T.B.	.15
☐ ☐	273	Dana Murzyn, Van.	.15

□ □ 274 Donald Audette, Buf. .15
□ □ 275 Brian Leetch, NYR. .35
□ □ 276 Kevin Dineen, Pha. .15
□ □ 277 Bruce Driver, N.J. .15
□ □ 278 Jim Paek, Pgh. .15
□ □ 279 Esa Tikkanen, NYR. .15
□ □ 280 Guy Carbonneau, Mtl. .15
□ □ 281 Eric Weinrich, Chi. .15
□ □ 282 Tim Cheveldae (G), Det. .15
□ □ 283 Bryan Marchment, Hfd. .15
□ □ 284 Kelly Miller, Wsh. .15
□ □ 285 Jimmy Carson, L.A. .15
□ □ 286 Terry Carkner, Det. .15
□ □ 287 Mike Sullivan, S.J. .15
□ □ 288 Joe Reekie, T.B. .15
□ □ 289 Robert Rouse, Tor. .15
□ □ 290 Joe Sakic, Que. 1.25
□ □ 291 Gerald Diduck, Van. .15
□ □ 292 Don Beaupré (G), Wsh. .15
□ □ 293 Kjell Samuelsson, Pgh. .15
□ □ 294 Claude Lapointe, Que. .15
□ □ 295 Tie Domi, Pgh. .15
□ □ 296 Charlie Huddy, L.A. .15
□ □ 297 Peter Zezel, Tor. .15
□ □ 298 Craig Muni, Buf. .15
□ □ 299 Richard Tabaracci (G), Wsh. .15
□ □ 300 Pat LaFontaine, Buf. .25
□ □ 301 Lyle Odelein, Mtl. .15
□ □ 302 Jocelyn Lemieux, Chi. .15
□ □ 303 Craig Ludwig, Dal. .15
□ □ 304 Marc Bergevin, T.B. .15
□ □ 305 Bill Guerin, N.J. .25
□ □ 306 Rick Zombo, Stl. .15
□ □ 307 Steven Finn, Que. .15
□ □ 308 Gino Odjick, Van. .15
□ □ 309 Jeff Beukeboom, NYR. .15
□ □ 310 Mario Lemieux, Pgh. 2.00
□ □ 311 J.J. Daigneault, Mtl. .15
□ □ 312 Vincent Riendeau (G), Det. .15
□ □ 313 Adam Burt, Hfd. .15
□ □ 314 Mike Craig, Dal. .15
□ □ 315 Bret Hedican, Stl. .15
□ □ 316 Kris King, Pgh. .15
□ □ 317 Sylvain Lefebvre, Tor. .15
□ □ 318 Troy Murray, Chi. .15
□ □ 319 Gord Roberts, Bos. .15
□ □ 320 Pavel Bure, Van. 1.00
□ □ 321 Marc Bureau, T.B. .15
□ □ 322 Randy McKay, N.J. .15
□ □ 323 Mark Lamb, Ott. .15
□ □ 324 Brian Mullen, NYI. .15
□ □ 325 Ken Wregget (G), Pgh. .25
□ □ 326 Stéphane Quintal, Wpg. .15
□ □ 327 Robert Dirk, Van. .15
□ □ 328 Mike Krushelnyski, Tor. .15
□ □ 329 Mikael Andersson, T.B. .15
□ □ 330 Paul Stanton, Bos. .15
□ □ 331 Phil Bourque, NYR. .15
□ □ 332 André Racicot (G), Mtl. .15
□ □ 333 Brad Dalgarno, NYI. .15
□ □ 334 Neal Broten, Dal. .15
□ □ 335 John Blue (G), Bos. .15
□ □ 336 Ken Sutton, Buf. .15
□ □ 337 Greg Paslawski, Cgy. .15
□ □ 338 Rob Stauber (G), L.A. .15
□ □ 339 Mike Keane, Mtl. .15
□ □ 340 Terry Yake, Ana. .15
□ □ 341 Brian Benning, Fla. .15
□ □ 342 Brian Propp, Hfd. .15
□ □ 343 Frank Pietrangelo (G), Hfd. .15
□ □ 344 Stéphane Matteau, Chi. .15
□ □ 345 Steven King, Ana. .15
□ □ 346 Joe Cirella, Fla. .15
□ □ 347 Andy Moog (G), Dal. .25
□ □ 348 Paul Ysebaert, Pgh. .15
□ □ 349 Petr Klima, T.B. .15
□ □ 350 Corey Millen, N.J. .15
□ □ 351 Phil Housley, Stl. .15
□ □ 352 Craig Billington (G), Ott. .15
□ □ 353 Jeff Norton, S.J. .15
□ □ 354 Neil Wilkinson, Chi. .15
□ □ 355 Doug Lidster, NYR. .15
□ □ 356 Steve Larmer, NYR. .15
□ □ 357 Jon Casey (G), Bos. .15
□ □ 358 Brad McCrimmon, Hfd. .15
□ □ 359 Alexei Kasatonov, Ana. .15
□ □ 360 Andrei Lomakin, Fla. .15
□ □ 361 Daren Puppa (G), T.B. .15
□ □ 362 Sergei Makarov, S.J. .15
□ □ 363 Dave Manson, Edm. .15
□ □ 364 Jim Sandlak, Hfd. .15
□ □ 365 Glenn Healy (G), NYR. .15
□ □ 366 Martin Gelinas, Que. .15
□ □ 367 Igor Larionov, S.J. .25
□ □ 368 Anatoli Semenov, Ana. .15
□ □ 369 Mark Fitzpatrick (G), Fla. .15
□ □ 370 Paul Cavallini, Dal. .15
□ □ 371 Jimmy Waite (G), S.J. .15
□ □ 372 Yves Racine, Pha. .15
□ □ 373 Jeff Hackett (G), Chi. .25
□ □ 374 Marty McSorley, Pgh. .15
□ □ 375 Scott Pearson, Edm. .15
□ □ 376 Ron Hextall (G), NYI. .25
□ □ 377 Gaetan Duchesne, S.J. .15
□ □ 378 Jamie Baker, S.J. .15
□ □ 379 Troy Loney, Ana. .15
□ □ 380 Gord Murphy, Fla. .15
□ □ 381 Peter Sidorkiewicz (G), N.J. .15
□ □ 382 Pat Elynuik T.B. .15
□ □ 383 Glen Wesley, Bos. .15
□ □ 384 Dean Evason, Dal. .15
□ □ 385 Mike Peluso, N.J. .15
□ □ 386 Darren Turcotte, Hfd. .15
□ □ 387 Dave Poulin, Wsh. .15
□ □ 388 John Cullen, Tor. .15
□ □ 389 Randy Ladouceur, Ana. .15
□ □ 390 Tom Fitzgerald, Fla. .15
□ □ 391 Denis Savard, T.B. .25
□ □ 392 Fredrick Olausson, Edm. .15
□ □ 393 Sergio Momesso, Van. .15
□ □ 394 Mike Ramsey, Pgh. .15
□ □ 395 Kelly Kisio, Cgy. .15
□ □ 396 Craig Simpson, Buf. .15
□ □ 397 Viacheslav Fetisov, N.J. .25
□ □ 398 Glenn Anderson, Tor. .15
□ □ 399 Michel Goulet, Chi. .25
□ □ 400 Wayne Gretzky, L.A. 2.50
□ □ 401 Stu Grimson, Ana. .15
□ □ 402 Mike Hough, Fla. .15
□ □ 403 Dominik Hasek (G), Buf. 1.00
□ □ 404 Gerard Gallant, T.B. .15
□ □ 405 Greg Gilbert, NYR. .15
□ □ 406 Vladimir Ruzicka, Ott. .15
□ □ 407 Jim Hrivnak (G), Stl. .15
□ □ 408 Dave Lowry, Fla. .15
□ □ 409 Todd Ewen, Ana. .15
□ □ 410 Bob Errey, S.J. .15
□ □ 411 Bryan Trottier, Pgh. .25
□ □ 412 Dave Taylor, L.A. .15
□ □ 413 Grant Ledyard, Dal. .15
□ □ 414 Chris Dahlquist, Cgy. .15
□ □ 415 Brent Gilchrist, Dal. .15
□ □ 416 Geoff Smith, Edm. .15
□ □ 417 Jiri Slegr, Van. .15
□ □ 418 Randy Burridge, Wsh. .15
□ □ 419 Sergei Krivokrasov, Chi. .15
□ □ 420 Keith Primeau, Det. .25
□ □ 421 Robert Kron, Hfd. .15
□ □ 422 Keith Brown, Fla. .15
□ □ 423 David Volek, NYI. .15
□ □ 424 Josef Beranek, Pha. .20
□ □ 425 Wayne Presley, Buf. .15
□ □ 426 Stu Barnes, Pgh. .15
□ □ **427 Milos Holan, Pha., RC .15**
□ □ 428 Jeff Shantz, Chi. .15
□ □ **429 Brent Gretzky, T.B., RC .15**
□ □ 430 Jarkko Varvio, Dal. .15
□ □ **431 Chris Osgood (G), Det., RC 2.50**
□ □ **432 Aaron Ward, Det., RC .25**
□ □ **433 Jason Smith, N.J., RC .15**
□ □ **434 Cam Stewart, Bos., RC .15**
□ □ **435 Derek Plante, Buf., RC .25**
□ □ 436 Pat Peake, Wsh. .15
□ □ 437 Alexander Karpovtsev, NYR. .15
□ □ **438 Jim Montgomery, Stl., RC .15**
□ □ 439 Rob Niedermayer, Fla. .25
□ □ **440 Jocelyn Thibault (G), Que., RC 2.00**
□ □ **441 Jason Arnott, Edm., RC 1.50**
□ □ **442 Mike Rathje, S.J., RC .15**
□ □ 443 Chris Gratton, T.B. .35
□ □ **444 Vesa Viitakoski, Cgy., RC .15**
□ □ **445 Alexei Kudashov, Tor., RC .15**
□ □ 446 Pavol Demitra, Ott. .15
□ □ 447 Ted Drury, Cgy. .15
□ □ **448 René Corbet, Que., RC .15**
□ □ 449 Markus Naslund, Pgh. .15
□ □ 450 Dmitri Filimonov, Ott. .15
□ □ **451 Roman Oksiuta, Edm., RC .15**
□ □ **452 Michal Sykora, S.J., RC .15**
□ □ 453 Greg Johnson, Det. .15
□ □ 454 Mikael Renberg, Pha. .25
□ □ 455 Alexei Yashin, Ott. .75
□ □ 456 Chris Pronger, Hfd. .35
□ □ **457 Manny Fernandez (G), Cdn., RC .25**
□ □ **458 Jamie Storr (G), Cdn., RC .50**
□ □ **459 Chris Armstrong, Cdn., RC .15**
□ □ **460 Drew Bannister, Cdn., RC .15**
□ □ **461 Joel Bouchard, Cdn., RC .15**
□ □ **462 Bryan McCabe, Cdn., RC .50**
□ □ **463 Nick Stajduhar, Cdn., RC .15**
□ □ **464 Brent Tully, Cdn., RC .15**
□ □ **465 Brendan Witt, Cdn., RC .25**
□ □ **466 Jason Allison, Cdn., RC 2.00**
□ □ **467 Jason Botterill, Cdn., RC .25**
□ □ **468 Curtis Bowen, Cdn., RC .15**
□ □ **469 Anson Carter, Cdn., RC .50**
□ □ **470 Brandon Convery, Cdn., RC .15**
□ □ **471 Yanick Dubé, Cdn., RC .15**
□ □ **472 Jeff Friesen, Cdn., RC 1.25**
□ □ **473 Aaron Gavey, Cdn., RC .15**
□ □ **474 Martin Gendron, RC .15**
□ □ **475 Rick Girard, Cdn., RC .15**
□ □ **476 Todd Harvey, Cdn., RC .25**
□ □ **477 Marty Murray, Cdn., RC .25**
□ □ **478 Michael Peca, Cdn., RC 1.00**
□ □ **479 Aaron Ellis (G), USA., RC .15**
□ □ **480 Toby Kvalevog (G), USA., RC .15**
□ □ **481 Joe Coleman, USA., RC .15**
□ □ **482 Ashlin Halfnight, USA., RC .15**
□ □ **483 Jason McBain, USA., RC .15**
□ □ **484 Chris O'Sullivan, USA., RC .15**
□ □ **485 Deron Quint, USA., RC .15**
□ □ **486 Blake Sloan, USA., RC .15**
□ □ **487 David Wilkie, USA., RC .15**
□ □ **488 Kevyn Adams, USA., RC .15**
□ □ **489 Jason Bonsignore, USA., RC .15**
□ □ **490 Andy Brink, USA., RC .15**
□ □ 491 Adam Deadmarsh, USA. .35
□ □ **492 John Emmons, USA., RC .15**
□ □ **493 Kevin Hilton, USA., RC .15**
□ □ **494 Jason Karmanos, USA., RC .15**
□ □ **495 Bob Lachance, USA., RC .15**
□ □ **496 Jamie Langenbrunner, USA., RC .85**
□ □ **497 Jay Pandolfo, USA., RC .15**
□ □ **498 Richard Park, USA., RC .15**
□ □ 499 Ryan Sittler, USA. .15
□ □ **500 John Varga, USA., RC .15**
□ □ **501 Valeri Bure, Rus., RC .50**
□ □ **502 Maxim Bets, Rus., RC .15**
□ □ **503 Vadim Sharifjanov, Rus., RC .25**
□ □ **504 Alexander Kharlamov, Rus., RC .15**
□ □ **505 Pavel Desyatkov, Rus., RC .15**
□ □ **506 Oleg Tverdovsky, Rus., RC .75**
□ □ **507 Nikolai Tsulygin, Rus., RC .15**
□ □ **508 Evgeni Ryabchikov (G), Rus., RC .15**
□ □ **509 Sergei Brylin, Rus., RC .25**
□ □ **510 Maxim Sushinski, Rus., RC .15**
□ □ **511 Sergei Kondrashkin, Rus., RC .15**
□ □ 512 Wayne Gretzky (802) 12.00

No. Inserts NRMT-MT

□ 236 Alexandre Daigle Autograph 50.00
□ Eric Lindros Autograph 235.00
□ □ Eric Lindros/Brett Lindros 20.00

TEAM CAPTAINS

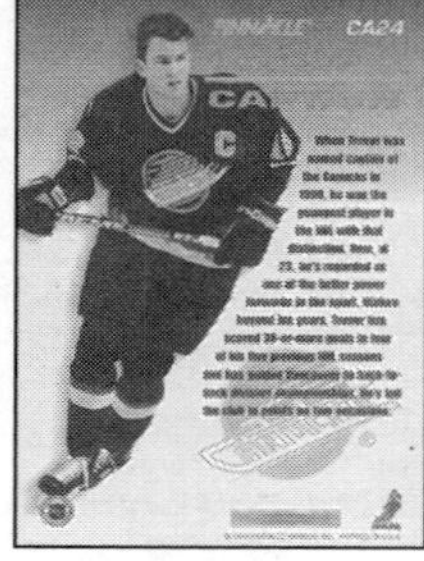

These cards have two versions: an American issue and a Canadian issue. Photos in each set are different.

Insert Set (27 cards): 180.00

	No.	Player	NRMT-MT
☐ ☐	CA1	Troy Loney, Ana.	4.00
☐ ☐	CA2	Ray Bourque, Bos.	10.00
☐ ☐	CA3	Pat LaFontaine, Buf.	6.00
☐ ☐	CA4	Joe Nieuwendyk, Cgy.	4.00
☐ ☐	CA5	Dirk Graham, Chi.	4.00
☐ ☐	CA6	Mark Tinordi, Dal.	4.00
☐ ☐	CA7	Steve Yzerman, Det.	20.00
☐ ☐	CA8	Craig MacTavish, Edm.	4.00
☐ ☐	CA9	Brian Skrudland, Fla.	4.00
☐ ☐	CA10	Pat Verbeek, Hfd.	4.00
☐ ☐	CA11	Wayne Gretzky, L.A.	40.00
☐ ☐	CA12	Guy Carbonneau, Mtl.	4.00
☐ ☐	CA13	Scott Stevens, N.J.	4.00
☐ ☐	CA14	Pat Flatley, NYI.	4.00
☐ ☐	CA15	Mark Messier, NYR.	10.00
☐ ☐	CA16	Mark Lamb, Ott.	4.00
☐ ☐	CA17	Kevin Dineen, Pha.	4.00
☐ ☐	CA18	Mario Lemieux, Pgh.	30.00
☐ ☐	CA19	Joe Sakic, Que.	18.00
☐ ☐	CA20	Brett Hull, Stl.	10.00
☐ ☐	CA21	Bob Errey, S.J.	4.00
☐ ☐	CA22	Bergevin/Savard/Tucker, T.B.	4.00
☐ ☐	CA23	Wendel Clark, Tor.	6.00
☐ ☐	CA24	Trevor Linden, Van.	6.00
☐ ☐	CA25	Kevin Hatcher, Wsh.	4.00
☐ ☐	CA26	Keith Tkachuk, Pgh.	10.00
☐ ☐	CA27	Checklist	15.00

EXPANSION

Insert Set (6 cards): 15.00

	No.	Player	NRMT-MT
☐	1	John Vanbiesbrouck/Guy Hebert	8.00
☐	2	Gord Murphy/Randy Ladouceur	2.00
☐	3	Joe Cirella/Sean Hill	2.00
☐	4	Dave Lowry/Troy Loney	2.00
☐	5	Brian Skrudland/Terry Yake	2.00
☐	6	Scott Mellanby/Steven King	2.00

MASKS

Insert Set (10 cards): 165.00

	No.	Player	NRMT-MT
☐	1	Grant Fuhr (G), Buf.	20.00
☐	2	Mike Vernon (G), Van.	20.00
☐	3	Rob Stauber (G), L.A.	15.00
☐	4	Dominic Roussel (G), Pha.	15.00
☐	5	Pat Jablonski (G), T.B.	15.00
☐	6	Stéphane Fiset (G), Que.	20.00
☐	7	Wendell Young (G), T.B.	15.00
☐	8	Ron Hextall (G), NYI.	20.00
☐	9	John Vanbiesbrouck (G), Fla.	35.00
☐	10	Peter Sidorkiewicz (G), N.J.	15.00

NIFTY FIFTY

Insert Set (15 cards): 175.00

	No.	Player	NRMT-MT
☐	1	Checklist	30.00
☐	2	Alexander Mogilny, Buf.	8.00
☐	3	Teemu Selänne, Pgh.	18.00
☐	4	Mario Lemieux, Pgh.	40.00
☐	5	Luc Robitaille, L.A.	6.00
☐	6	Pavel Bure, Van.	18.00
☐	7	Pierre Turgeon, NYI.	6.00
☐	8	Steve Yzerman, Det.	25.00
☐	9	Kevin Stevens, Pgh.	6.00
☐	10	Brett Hull, Stl.	12.00
☐	11	Dave Andreychuk, Tor.	6.00
☐	12	Pat LaFontaine, Buf.	6.00
☐	13	Mark Recchi, Pha.	6.00
☐	14	Brendan Shanahan, Stl.	15.00
☐	15	Jeremy Roenick, Chi.	6.00

SUPER ROOKIES

These cards have two versions: an American issue and a Canadain issue. Photos in each series are different.

Insert Set (9 cards): 15.00

	No.	Player	NRMT-MT
☐ ☐	SR1	Alexandre Daigle, Ott	2.00
☐ ☐	SR2	Chris Pronger, Hfd.	2.00
☐ ☐	SR3	Chris Gratton, T.B.	2.00
☐ ☐	SR4	Rob Niedermayer, Fla.	1.50
☐ ☐	SR5	Alexei Yashin, Ott.	3.00
☐ ☐	SR6	Mikael Renberg, Pha.	1.50
☐ ☐	SR7	Jason Arnott, Edm.	3.00
☐ ☐	SR8	Markus Naslund, Cgy.	.75
☐ ☐	SR9	Pat Peake, Wsh.	.75

TEAM PINNACLE

These cards have two verions: an American issue and a Canadian issue.

Insert Set (12 cards): 350.00

	No.	Player	NRMT-MT
☐ ☐	1	P. Roy/E. Belfour	60.00
☐ ☐	2	B. Leetch/C. Chelios	20.00
☐ ☐	3	A. MacInnis/S. Stevens	15.00
☐ ☐	4	L. Robitaille/K. Stevens	15.00
☐ ☐	5	W. Gretzky/M. Lemieux	125.00
☐ ☐	6	B. Hull/J. Jagr	50.00
☐ ☐	7	T. Barrasso/K. McLean,	15.00
☐ ☐	8	P. Coffey/R. Bourque	20.00
☐ ☐	9	A. Iafrate/P. Housley	15.00
☐ ☐	10	V. Damphousse/P. Bure	30.00
☐ ☐	11	E. Lindros/J. Roenick	50.00
☐ ☐	12	T. Selänne/A. Mogilny	35.00

TEAM 2001

These cards have two versions: an American issue and a Canadian issue.

Insert Set (30 cards): 50.00

	No.	Player	NRMT-MT
☐ ☐	1	Eric Lindros, Pha.	10.00
☐ ☐	2	Alexander Mogilny, Buf.	2.00
☐ ☐	3	Pavel Bure, Van.	5.00
☐ ☐	4	Joé Juneau, Bos.	1.00
☐ ☐	5	Félix Potvin (G), Tor.	4.00
☐ ☐	6	Niklas Lidstrom, Det.	1.50
☐ ☐	7	Alexei Kovalev, NYR.	1.00
☐ ☐	8	Pat Poulin, Hfd.	1.00
☐ ☐	9	Shawan McEachern, Pgh.	1.00
☐ ☐	10	Teemu Selänne, Pgh.	5.00
☐ ☐	11	Rod Brind'Amour, Pha.	1.50
☐ ☐	12	Jaromir Jagr, Pgh.	8.00
☐ ☐	13	Pierre Turgeon, NYI.	1.50
☐ ☐	14	Scott Niedermayer, N.J.	1.50
☐ ☐	15	Mats Sundin, Que.	3.00
☐ ☐	16	Trevor Linden, Van.	1.50
☐ ☐	17	Mike Modano, Dal.	3.00
☐ ☐	18	Roman Hamrlik, T.B.	1.50
☐ ☐	19	Tony Amonte, NYR.	1.50
☐ ☐	20	Jeremy Roenick, Chi.	2.00
☐ ☐	21	Scott Lachance, NYI.	1.00
☐ ☐	22	Mike Ricci, Que.	1.00
☐ ☐	23	Dmitri Khristich, Wsh.	1.00
☐ ☐	24	Sergei Fedorov, Det.	3.00
☐ ☐	25	Joe Sakic, Que.	6.00
☐ ☐	26	Pat Falloon, S.J.	1.00
☐ ☐	27	Mathieu Schneider, Mtl.	1.00
☐ ☐	28	Owen Nolan, Que.	1.50
☐ ☐	29	Brendan Shanahan, Stl.	4.00
☐ ☐	30	Mark Recchi, Pha.	1.50

1993 - 94 POWER PLAY

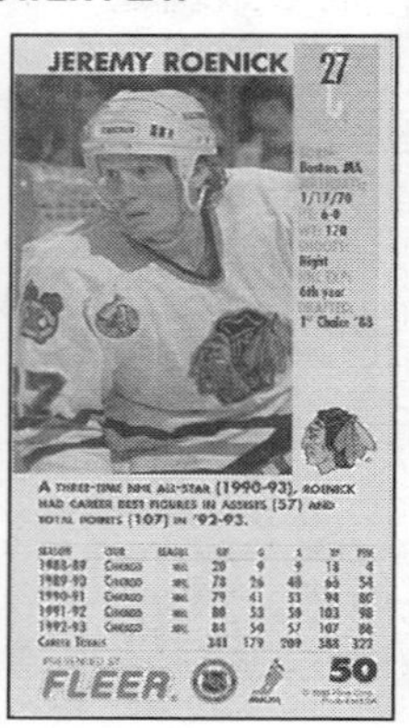

Chris Ponger was featured on the Series 2 packaging.

Card Size: 2 1/2" x 4 3/4"

Imprint: © 1993 Fleer Corp.

Series One Set (280 cards): 35.00

Series Two Set (240 cards): 35.00

Common Player .15

	No.	Player	NRMT-MT
☐	1	Stu Grimson, Ana.	.15
☐	2	Guy Hebert (G), Ana.	.25
☐	3	Sean Hill, Ana.	.15
☐	4	Bill Houlder, Ana.	.15
☐	5	Alexei Kasatonov, Ana.	.15
☐	6	Steven King, Ana.	.15
☐	7	Lonnie Loach, Ana.	.15
☐	8	Troy Loney, Ana.	.15
☐	9	Joe Sacco, Ana.	.15
☐	10	Anatoli Semenov, Ana.	.15
☐	11	Jarrod Skalde, Ana.	.15
☐	12	Tim Sweeney, Ana.	.15
☐	13	Ron Tugnutt (G), Ana.	.15
☐	14	Terry Yake, Ana.	.15
☐	15	Shaun Van Allen, Ana.	.15
☐	16	Ray Bourque, Bos.	.75
☐	17	Jon Casey (G), Bos.	.15
☐	18	Ted Donato, Bos.	.15
☐	19	Joé Juneau, Bos.	.15
☐	20	Dmitri Kvartalnov, Bos.	.15
☐	21	Stephen Leach, Bos.	.15
☐	22	Cam Neely, Bos.	.25
☐	23	Adam Oates, Bos.	.35
☐	24	Don Sweeney, Bos.	.15
☐	25	Glen Wesley, Bos.	.15
☐	26	Doug Bodger, Buf.	.15
☐	27	Grant Fuhr (G), Buf.	.25
☐	28	Viktor Gordijuk, Buf.	.15
☐	29	Dale Hawerchuk, Buf.	.25
☐	30	Yuri Khmylev, Buf.	.15
☐	31	Pat LaFontaine, Buf.	.25
☐	32	Alexander Mogilny, Buf.	.35
☐	33	Richard Smehlik, Buf.	.15
☐	34	Bob Sweeney, Buf.	.15
☐	35	Randy Wood, Buf.	.15
☐	36	Theoren Fleury, Cgy.	.35
☐	37	Kelly Kisio, Cgy.	.15
☐	38	Al MacInnis, Cgy.	.25
☐	39	Joe Nieuwendyk, Cgy.	.25
☐	40	Joel Otto, Cgy.	.15

	No.	Player	Price
☐	41	Robert Reichel, Cgy.	.15
☐	42	Gary Roberts, Cgy.	.25
☐	43	Ron Stern, Cgy.	.15
☐	44	Gary Suter, Cgy.	.15
☐	45	Mike Vernon (G), Cgy.	.25
☐	46	Ed Belfour (G), Chi.	.35
☐	47	Chris Chelios, Chi.	.50
☐	48	Karl Dykhuis, Chi.	.15
☐	49	Michel Goulet, Chi.	.25
☐	50	Dirk Graham, Chi.	.15
☐	51	Sergei Krivokrasov, Chi.	.15
☐	52	Steve Larmer, Chi.	.15
☐	53	Joe Murphy, Chi.	.15
☐	54	Jeremy Roenick, Chi.	.35
☐	55	Steve Smith, Chi.	.15
☐	56	Brent Sutter, Chi.	.15
☐	57	Neal Broten, Dal.	.15
☐	58	Russ Courtnall, Dal.	.15
☐	59	Ulf Dahlen, Dal.	.15
☐	60	Dave Gagner, Dal.	.15
☐	61	Derian Hatcher, Dal.	.25
☐	62	Trent Klatt, Dal.	.15
☐	63	Mike Modano, Dal.	.75
☐	64	Andy Moog (G), Dal.	.25
☐	65	Tommy Sjodin, Dal.	.15
☐	66	Mark Tinordi, Dal.	.15
☐	67	Tim Cheveldae (G), Det.	.15
☐	68	Steve Chiasson, Det.	.15
☐	69	Dino Ciccarelli, Det.	.25
☐	70	Paul Coffey, Det.	.25
☐	**71**	**Dallas Drake, Det., RC**	**.15**
☐	72	Sergei Fedorov, Det.	.75
☐	73	Vladimir Konstantinov, Det.	.15
☐	74	Nicklas Lidström, Det.	.25
☐	75	Keith Primeau, Det.	.25
☐	76	Ray Sheppard, Det.	.15
☐	77	Steve Yzerman, Det.	2.00
☐	78	Zdeno Ciger, Edm.	.15
☐	79	Shayne Corson, Edm.	.15
☐	80	Todd Elik, Edm.	.15
☐	81	Igor Kravchuk, Edm.	.15
☐	82	Craig MacTavish, Edm.	.15
☐	83	Dave Manson, Edm.	.15
☐	**84**	**Shjon Podein, Edm., RC**	**.15**
☐	85	Bill Ranford (G), Edm.	.25
☐	86	Steven Rice, Edm.	.15
☐	87	Doug Weight, Edm.	.35
☐	**88**	**Doug Barrault, Fla., RC**	**.15**
☐	89	Jesse Belanger, Fla.	.15
☐	90	Brian Benning, Fla.	.15
☐	91	Joe Cirella, Fla.	.15
☐	92	Mark Fitzpatrick (G), Fla.	.15
☐	93	Randy Gilhen, Fla.	.15
☐	94	Mike Hough, Fla.	.15
☐	95	Bill Lindsay, Fla.	.15
☐	96	Andrei Lomakin, Fla.	.15
☐	97	Dave Lowry, Fla.	.15
☐	98	Scott Mellanby, Fla.	.15
☐	99	Gord Murphy, Fla.	.15
☐	100	Brian Skrudland, Fla.	.15
☐	**101**	**Milan Tichy, Fla., RC**	**.15**
☐	102	John Vanbiesbrouck (G), Fla.	1.00
☐	103	Sean Burke (G), Hfd.	.25
☐	104	Andrew Cassels, Hfd.	.15
☐	105	Nick Kypreos, Hfd.	.15
☐	106	Mikael Nylander, Hfd.	.15
☐	107	Robert Petrovicky, Hfd.	.15
☐	108	Patrick Poulin, Hfd.	.15
☐	109	Geoff Sanderson, Hfd.	.15
☐	110	Pat Verbeek, Hfd.	.15
☐	111	Eric Weinrich, Hfd.	.15
☐	112	Zarley Zalapski, Hfd.	.15
☐	113	Rob Blake, L.A.	.25
☐	114	Jimmy Carson, L.A.	.15
☐	115	Tony Granato, L.A.	.15
☐	116	Wayne Gretzky, L.A.	3.50
☐	117	Kelly Hrudey (G), L.A.	.15
☐	118	Jari Kurri, L.A.	.25
☐	119	Shawn McEachern, L.A.	.15
☐	120	Luc Robitaille, L.A.	.25
☐	121	Tomas Sandström, L.A.	.15
☐	122	Darryl Sydor, L.A.	.15
☐	123	Alexei Zhitnik, L.A.	.15
☐	124	Brian Bellows, Mtl.	.15
☐	125	Patrice Brisebois, Mtl.	.15
☐	126	Guy Carbonneau, Mtl.	.15
☐	127	Vincent Damphousse, Mtl.	.35
☐	128	Eric Desjardins, Mtl.	.25
☐	129	Mike Keane, Mtl.	.15
☐	130	Stéphan Lebeau, Mtl.	.15
☐	131	Kirk Muller, Mtl.	.15
☐	132	Lyle Odelein, Mtl.	.15
☐	133	Patrick Roy (G), Mtl.	3.00
☐	134	Mathieu Schneider, Mtl.	.15
☐	135	Bruce Driver, N.J.	.15
☐	136	Viacheslav Fetisov, N.J.	.25
☐	137	Claude Lemieux, N.J.	.15
☐	138	John MacLean, N.J.	.15
☐	139	Bernie Nicholls, N.J.	.15
☐	140	Scott Niedermayer, N.J.	.25
☐	141	Stephane Richer, N.J.	.15
☐	142	Alexander Semak, N.J.	.15
☐	143	Scott Stevens, N.J.	.25
☐	144	Chris Terreri (G), N.J.	.15
☐	145	Valeri Zelepukin, N.J.	.15
☐	146	Patrick Flatley, NYI.	.15
☐	147	Ron Hextall (G), NYI.	.25
☐	148	Benoît Hogue, NYI.	.15
☐	149	Darius Kasparaitis, NYI.	.15
☐	150	Derek King, NYI.	.15
☐	151	Uwe Krupp, NYI.	.15
☐	152	Scott Lachance, NYI.	.15
☐	153	Vladimir Malakhov, NYI.	.15
☐	154	Steve Thomas, NYI.	.15
☐	155	Pierre Turgeon, NYI.	.25
☐	156	Tony Amonte, NYR.	.25
☐	157	Mike Gartner, NYR.	.25
☐	158	Adam Graves, NYR.	.15
☐	159	Alexei Kovalev, NYR.	.15
☐	160	Brian Leetch, NYR.	.35
☐	**161**	**Joby Messier, NYR., RC**	**.15**
☐	162	Sergei Nemchinov, NYR.	.15
☐	163	James Patrick, NYR.	.15
☐	164	Mike Richter (G), NYR.	.35
☐	166	Darren Turcotte, NYR.	.15
☐	167	Sergei Zubov, NYR.	.25
☐	168	Dave Archibald, Ott.	.15
☐	169	Craig Billington (G), Ott.	.15
☐	170	Bob Kudelski, Ott.	.15
☐	171	Mark Lamb, Ott.	.15
☐	172	Norm Maciver, Ott.	.15
☐	173	Darren Rumble, Ott.	.15
☐	174	Vladimir Ruzicka, Ott.	.15
☐	175	Brad Shaw, Ott.	.15
☐	176	Sylvain Turgeonv, Ott.	.15
☐	177	Josef Beranek, Pha.	.15
☐	178	Rod Brind'Amour, Pha.	.25
☐	179	Kevin Dineen, Pha.	.15
☐	180	Per-Erik Eklund, Pha.	.15
☐	181	Brent Fedyk, Pha.	.15
☐	182	Garry Galley, Pha.	.15
☐	183	Eric Lindros, Pha.	3.00
☐	184	Mark Recchi, Pha.	.25
☐	185	Tommy Söderström (G), Pha.	.15
☐	186	Dimitri Yushkevich, Pha.	.15
☐	187	Tom Barrasso (G), Pgh.	.25
☐	188	Ron Francis, Pgh.	.35
☐	189	Jaromir Jagr, Pgh.	2.00
☐	190	Mario Lemieux, Pgh.	3.00
☐	191	Marty McSorley, Pgh.	.15
☐	192	Joe Mullen, Pgh.	.25
☐	193	Larry Murphy, Pgh.	.25
☐	194	Ulf Samuelsson, Pgh.	.15
☐	195	Kevin Stevens, Pgh.	.15
☐	196	Rick Tocchet, Pgh.	.15
☐	197	Steve Duchesne, Que.	.15
☐	198	Stéphane Fiset (G), Que.	.25
☐	199	Valeri Kamensky, Que.	.25
☐	200	Andrei Kovalenko, Que.	.15
☐	201	Owen Nolan, Que.	.25
☐	202	Mike Ricci, Que.	.15
☐	203	Martin Rucinsky, Que.	.15
☐	204	Joe Sakic, Que.	1.50
☐	205	Mats Sundin, Que.	.75
☐	206	Scott Young, Que.	.15
☐	207	Jeff Brown, Stl.	.15
☐	208	Garth Butcher, Stl.	.15
☐	209	Nelson Emerson, Stl.	.15
☐	210	Bret Hedican, Stl.	.15
☐	211	Brett Hull, Stl.	.75
☐	212	Craig Janney, Stl.	.15
☐	213	Curtis Joseph (G), Stl.	1.00
☐	214	Igor Korolev, Stl.	.15
☐	215	Kevin Miller, Stl.	.15
☐	216	Brendan Shanahan, Stl.	1.00
☐	217	Ed Courtnay, S.J.	.15
☐	218	Pat Falloon, S.J.	.15
☐	219	Johan Garpenlov, S.J.	.15
☐	**220**	**Rob Gaudreau, S.J., RC**	**.15**
☐	221	Arturs Irbe (G), S.J.	.15
☐	222	Sergei Makarov, S.J.	.15
☐	223	Jeff Norton, S.J.	.15
☐	224	Jeff Odgers, S.J.	.15
☐	225	Sandis Ozolinsh, S.J.	.25
☐	226	Tom Pederson, S.J.	.15
☐	227	Bob Beers, T.B.	.15
☐	228	Brian Bradley, T.B.	.15
☐	229	Shawn Chambers, T.B.	.15
☐	230	Gerard Gallant, T.B.	.15
☐	231	Roman Hamrlik, T.B.	.25
☐	232	Petr Klim, T.B.	.15
☐	233	Chris Kontos, T.B.	.15
☐	234	Daren Puppa (G), T.B.	.15
☐	235	John Tucker, T.B.	.15
☐	236	Rob Zamuner, T.B.	.15
☐	237	Glenn Anderson, Tor.	.15
☐	238	Dave Andreychuk, Tor.	.15
☐	239	Drake Berehowsky, Tor.	.15
☐	240	Nikolai Borschevsky, Tor.	.15
☐	241	Wendel Clark, Tor.	.25
☐	242	John Cullen, Tor.	.15
☐	243	Dave Ellett, Tor.	.15
☐	244	Doug Gilmour, Tor.	.35
☐	245	Dimitri Mironov, Tor.	.15
☐	246	Félix Potvin (G), Tor.	.75
☐	247	Greg Adams, Van.	.15
☐	248	Pavel Bure, Van.	1.25
☐	249	Geoff Courtnall, Van.	.15
☐	250	Gerald Diduck, Van.	.15
☐	251	Trevor Linden, Van.	.25
☐	252	Jyrki Lumme, Van.	.15
☐	253	Kirk McLean (G), Van.	.25
☐	254	Petr Nedved, Van.	.15
☐	255	Cliff Ronning, Van.	.15
☐	256	Jiri Slegr, Van.	.15
☐	257	Dixon Ward, Van.	.15
☐	258	Peter Bondra, Wsh.	.50
☐	259	Sylvain Côté, Wsh.	.15
☐	260	Pat Elynuik, Wsh.	.15
☐	261	Kevin Hatcher, Wsh.	.15
☐	262	Dale Hunter, Wsh.	.15
☐	263	Al Iafrate, Wsh.	.15
☐	264	Dimitri Khristich, Wsh.	.15
☐	265	Michal Pivonka, Wsh.	.15
☐	266	Mike Ridley, Wsh.	.15
☐	267	Rick Tabaracci (G), Wsh.	.15
☐	268	Sergei Bautin, Wpg.	.15
☐	269	Evgeny Davydov, Wpg.	.15
☐	270	Bob Essensa (G), Wpg.	.15
☐	271	Phil Housley, Wpg.	.15
☐	272	Teppo Numminen, Wpg.	.15
☐	273	Fredrik Olausson, Wpg.	.15
☐	274	Teemu Selänne, Wpg.	1.25
☐	275	Thomas Steen, Wpg.	.15
☐	276	Keith Tkachuk, Wpg.	.75
☐	277	Paul Ysebaert, Wpg.	.15
☐	278	Alexei Zhamnov, Wpg.	.15
☐	279	Checklist 1 (1 - 164)	.15
☐	280	Checklist 2 (165 - 280, Insert Sets)	.15
☐	**281**	**Patrick Carnback, Ana., RC**	**.15**
☐	282	Bob Corkum, Ana.	.15
☐	283	Bobby Dollas, Ana.	.15
☐	284	Peter Douris, Ana.	.15
☐	285	Todd Ewen, Ana.	.15
☐	286	Garry Valk, Ana.	.15
☐	287	John Blue (G), Bos.	.25
☐	288	Glen Featherstone, Bos.	.15
☐	289	Stephen Heinze, Bos.	.15
☐	290	David Reid, Bos.	.15
☐	291	Bryan Smolinski, Bos.	.15
☐	**292**	**Cam Stewart, Bos., RC**	**.15**
☐	293	Jozef Stumpel, Bos.	.15
☐	294	Sergei Zholtok, Bos.	.15
☐	295	Donald Audette, Buf.	.15
☐	296	Philippe Boucher, Buf.	.15

	No.	Player	Price
☐	297	Dominik Hasek (G), Buf.	1.25
☐	298	Brad May, Buf.	.15
☐	299	Craig Muni, Buf.	.15
☐	**300**	**Derek Plante, Buf., RC**	**.25**
☐	301	Craig Simpson, Buf.	.15
☐	**302**	**Scott Thomas, Buf., RC**	**.15**
☐	303	Ted Drury, Cgy.	.15
☐	**304**	**Dan Keczmer, Cgy., RC**	**.15**
☐	305	Trevor Kidd (G), Cgy.	.25
☐	306	Sandy McCarthy, Cgy.	.15
☐	307	Frantisek Musil, Cgy.	.15
☐	308	Michel Petit, Cgy.	.15
☐	309	Paul Ranheim, Cgy.	.15
☐	**310**	**German Titov, Cgy., RC**	**.15**
☐	311	Andrei Trefilov (G), Cgy.	.15
☐	312	Jeff Hackett (G), Chi.	.25
☐	313	Stéphane Matteau, Chi.	.15
☐	314	Brian Noonan, Chi.	.15
☐	315	Patrick Poulin, Chi.	.15
☐	**316**	**Jeff Shantz, Chi., RC**	**.15**
☐	317	Rich Sutter, Chi.	.15
☐	318	Kevin Todd, Chi.	.15
☐	319	Eric Weinrich, Chi.	.15
☐	320	Dave Barr, Dal.	.15
☐	321	Paul Cavallini, Dal.	.15
☐	322	Mike Craig, Dal.	.15
☐	323	Dean Evason, Dal.	.15
☐	324	Brent Gilchrist, Dal.	.15
☐	325	Grant Ledyard, Dal.	.15
☐	326	Mike McPhee, Dal.	.15
☐	327	Darcy Wakaluk (G), Dal.	.15
☐	328	Terry Carkner, Det.	.15
☐	329	Mark Howe, Det.	.15
☐	330	Greg Johnson, Det.	.15
☐	331	Vyacheslav Kozlov, Det.	.15
☐	332	Martin Lapointe, Det.	.15
☐	**333**	**Darren McCarty, Det., RC**	**.25**
☐	**334**	**Chris Osgood (G), Det., RC**	**3.25**
☐	335	Bob Probert, Det.	.15
☐	336	Mike Sillinger, Det.	.15
☐	**337**	**Jason Arnott, Edm., RC**	**2.00**
☐	338	Bob Beers, Edm.	.15
☐	**339**	**Fred Brathwaite (G), Edm., RC**	**.15**
☐	340	Kelly Buchberger, Edm.	.15
☐	**341**	**Ilya Byakin, Edm., RC**	**.15**
☐	342	Fredrik Olausson, Edm.	.15
☐	343	Vladimir Vujtek, Edm.	.15
☐	**344**	**Peter White, Edm., RC**	**.15**
☐	345	Stu Barnes, Fla.	.15
☐	346	Mike Foligno, Fla.	.15
☐	347	Greg Hawgood, Fla.	.15
☐	348	Bob Kudelski, Fla.	.15
☐	349	Rob Niedermayer, Fla.	.25
☐	**350**	**Igor Chibirev, Hfd., RC**	**.15**
☐	351	Robert Kron, Hfd.	.15
☐	352	Bryan Marchment, Hfd.	.15
☐	353	James Patrick, Hfd.	.15
☐	354	Chris Pronger, Hfd.	.35
☐	355	Jeff Reese (G), Hfd.	.15
☐	356	Jim Storm, Hfd.	.15
☐	357	Darren Turcotte, Hfd.	.15
☐	358	Pat Conacher, L.A.	.15
☐	359	Mike Donnelly, L.A.	.15
☐	360	John Druce, L.A.	.15
☐	361	Charlie Huddy, L.A.	.15
☐	352	Warren Rychel, L.A.	.15
☐	363	Robb Stauber (G), L.A.	.15
☐	364	Dave Taylor, L.A.	.15
☐	365	Dixon Ward, L.A.	.15
☐	366	Benoît Brunet, Mtl.	.15
☐	367	J.J. Daigneault, Mtl.	.15
☐	368	Gilbert Dionne, Mtl.	.15
☐	369	Paul DiPietro, Mtl.	.15
☐	370	Kevin Haller, Mtl.	.15
☐	371	Oleg Petrov, Mtl.	.15
☐	**372**	**Peter Popovic, Mtl., RC**	**.15**
☐	373	Ron Wilson, Mtl.	.15
☐	374	Martin Brodeur (G), N.J.	1.25
☐	375	Tom Chorske, N.J.	.15
☐	**376**	**Jim Dowd, N.J., RC**	**.15**
☐	377	David Emma, N.J.	.15
☐	378	Bobby Holik, N.J.	.15
☐	379	Corey Millen, N.J.	.15
☐	**380**	**Jaroslav Modry, N.J., RC**	**.15**
☐	**381**	**Jason Smith, N.J., RC**	**.15**
☐	382	Ray Ferraro, NYI.	.15
☐	383	Travis Green, NYI.	.15
☐	384	Tom Kurvers, NYI.	.15
☐	385	Marty McInnis, NYI.	.15
☐	**386**	**Jamie McLennan (G), NYI., RC**	**.75**
☐	387	Dennis Vaske, NYI.	.15
☐	388	David Volek, NYI.	.15
☐	389	Jeff Beukeboom, NYR.	.15
☐	390	Glenn Healy (G), NYR.	.15
☐	391	Alexander Karpovtsev, NYR.	.15
☐	392	Steve Larmer, NYR.	.15
☐	393	Kevin Lowe, NYR.	.15
☐	394	Ed Olczyk, NYR.	.15
☐	395	Esa Tikkanen, NYR.	.15
☐	396	Alexandre Daigle, Ott.	.35
☐	397	Evgeny Davydov, Ott.	.15
☐	398	Dimitri Filimonov, Ott.	.15
☐	399	Brian Glynn, Ott.	.15
☐	**400**	**Darrin Madeley (G), Ott., RC**	**.15**
☐	401	Troy Mallette, Ott.	.15
☐	402	Dave McLlwain, Ott.	.15
☐	403	Alexei Yashin, Ott.	.75
☐	**404**	**Jason Bowen, Pha., RC**	**.15**
☐	405	Jeff Finley, Pha.	.15
☐	406	Yves Racine, Pha.	.15
☐	407	Rob Ramage, Pha.	.15
☐	408	Mikael Renberg, Pha.	.25
☐	409	Dominic Roussel (G), Pha.	.15
☐	410	Dave Tippett, Pha.	.15
☐	411	Doug Brown, Pgh.	.15
☐	412	Markus Naslund, Pgh.	.15
☐	**413**	**Pat Neaton, Pgh., RC**	**.15**
☐	414	Kjell Samuelsson, Pgh.	.15
☐	415	Martin Straka, Pgh.	.15
☐	416	Bryan Trottier, Pgh.	.25
☐	417	Ken Wregget (G), Pgh.	.25
☐	418	Adam Foote, Que.	.25
☐	**419**	**Iain Fraser, Que., RC**	**.15**
☐	420	Alexei Gusarov, Que.	.15
☐	421	Dave Karpa, Que.	.15
☐	422	Claude Lapointe, Que.	.15
☐	423	Curtis Leschyshyn, Que.	.15
☐	424	Mike McKee, Que.	.15
☐	**425**	**Garth Snow (G), Que., RC**	**.25**
☐	**426**	**Jocelyn Thibault (G), Que., RC**	**2.50**
☐	427	Phil Housley, Stl.	.15
☐	428	Jim Hrivnak (G), Stl.	.15
☐	429	Vitali Karamnov, Stl.	.15
☐	430	Basil McRae, Stl.	.15
☐	**431**	**Jim Montgomery, Stl., RC**	**.15**
☐	432	Vitali Prokhorov, Stl.	.15
☐	433	Gaetan Duchesne, S.J.	.15
☐	434	Todd Elik, S.J.	.15
☐	435	Bob Errey, S.J.	.15
☐	436	Igor Larionov, S.J.	.25
☐	437	Mike Rathje, S.J.	.15
☐	438	Jimmy Waite (G), S.J.	.15
☐	439	Ray Whitney, S.J.	.15
☐	440	Mikael Andersson, T.B.	.15
☐	441	Danton Cole, T.B.	.15
☐	442	Pat Elynuik, T.B.	.15
☐	443	Chris Gratton, T.B.	.35
☐	444	Pat Jablonski (G), T.B.	.15
☐	445	Chris Joseph, T.B.	.15
☐	**446**	**Chris LiPuma, T.B., RC**	**.15**
☐	447	Denis Savard, T.B.	.25
☐	448	Ken Baumgartner, Tor.	.15
☐	449	Todd Gill, Tor.	.15
☐	450	Sylvain Lefebvre, Tor.	.15
☐	451	Jamie Macoun, Tor.	.15
☐	452	Mark Osborne, Tor.	.15
☐	453	Rob Pearson, Tor.	.15
☐	**454**	**Damian Rhodes (G), Tor., RC**	**.75**
☐	455	Peter Zezel, Tor.	.15
☐	456	Dave Babych, Van.	.15
☐	**457**	**José Charbonneau, Van., RC**	**.15**
☐	458	Murray Craven, Van.	.15
☐	**459**	**Neil Eisenhut, Van., RC**	**.15**
☐	**460**	**Dan Kesa, Van., RC**	**.15**
☐	461	Gino Odjick, Van.	.15
☐	462	Kay Whitmore (G), Van.	.15
☐	463	Don Beaupré (G), Wsh.	.15
☐	464	Randy Burridge, Wsh.	.15
☐	465	Calle Johansson, Wsh.	.15
☐	466	Keith Jones, Wsh.	.15
☐	467	Todd Krygier, Wsh.	.15
☐	468	Kelly Miller, Wsh.	.15
☐	469	Pat Peake, Wsh.	.15
☐	470	Dave Poulin, Wsh.	.15
☐	471	Luciano Borsato, Wpg.	.15
☐	472	Nelson Emerson, Wpg.	.15
☐	473	Randy Gilhen, Wpg.	.15
☐	474	Boris Mironov, Wpg.	.15
☐	475	Stéphane Quintal, Wpg.	.15
☐	476	Thomas Steen, Wpg.	.15
☐	477	Igor Ulanov, Wpg.	.15
☐	**478**	**Adrian Aucoin, Cdn., RC**	**.15**
☐	**479**	**Todd Brost, Cdn., RC**	**.15**
☐	**480**	**Martin Gendron, Cdn., RC**	**.15**
☐	481	David Harlock, Cdn.	.15
☐	482	Corey Hirsch (G), Cdn.	.15
☐	**483**	**Todd Hlushko, Cdn., RC**	**.15**
☐	**484**	**Fabian Joseph, Cdn., RC**	**.15**
☐	485	Paul Kariya, Cdn.	9.00
☐	**486**	**Brett Lindros, Cdn., RC**	**.15**
☐	**487**	**Ken Lovsin, Cdn., RC**	**.15**
☐	488	Jason Marshall, Cdn.	.15
☐	**489**	**Derek Mayer, Cdn., RC**	**.15**
☐	490	Petr Nedved, Cdn.	.15
☐	**491**	**Dwayne Norris, Cdn., RC**	**.15**
☐	492	Russ Romaniuk, Cdn.	.15
☐	493	Brian Savage, Cdn.	.75
☐	**494**	**Trevor Sim, Cdn., RC**	**.15**
☐	**495**	**Chris Therien, Cdn., RC**	**.15**
☐	**496**	**Todd Warriner, Cdn., RC**	**.25**
☐	**497**	**Craig Woodcroft, Cdn., RC**	**.15**
☐	**498**	**Mark Beaufait, USA., RC**	**.15**
☐	499	Jim Campbell, USA.	.25
☐	**500**	**Ted Crowley, USA., RC**	**.15**
☐	501	Mike Dunham (G), USA.	.15
☐	**502**	**Chris Ferraro, USA., RC**	**.15**
☐	503	Peter Ferraro, USA.	.15
☐	**504**	**Brett Hauer, USA., RC**	**.15**
☐	**505**	**Darby Hendrickson, USA., RC**	**.15**
☐	**506**	**Chris Imes, USA., RC**	**.15**
☐	**507**	**Craig Johnson, USA., RC**	**.15**
☐	**508**	**Peter Laviolette, USA., RC**	**.15**
☐	509	Jeff Lazaro, USA.	.15
☐	**510**	**John Lilley, USA., RC**	**.15**
☐	511	Todd Marchant, USA.	.15
☐	**512**	**Ian Moran, USA., RC**	**.15**
☐	**513**	**Travis Richards, USA, RC.**	**.15**
☐	**514**	**Barry Richter, USA., RC**	**.15**
☐	**515**	**David Roberts, USA., RC**	**.15**
☐	516	Brian Rolston, USA.	.15
☐	**517**	**David Sacco, USA., RC**	**.15**
☐	518	Checklist (281 - 373)	.15
☐	519	Checklist (374 - 462)	.15
☐	520	Checklist (463 - 520, Insert Sets)	.15

GAMEBREAKERS

Card Size: 2 1/2" x 4 3/4"
Series Two Insert Set (10 cards): 30.00

	No.	Player	NRMT-MT
☐	1	Sergei Fedorov, Det.	2.00
☐	2	Doug Gilmour, Tor.	1.00
☐	3	Wayne Gretzky, L.A.	8.00
☐	4	Curtis Joseph (G), Stl.	2.50
☐	5	Mario Lemieux, Pgh.	6.50
☐	6	Eric Lindros, Pha.	5.00
☐	7	Félix Potvin (G), Tor.	2.00
☐	8	Jeremy Roenick, Det.	1.00
☐	9	Patrick Roy (G), Mtl.	6.50
☐	10	Steve Yzerman, Det.	4.00

GLOBAL GREATS

Card Size: 2 1/2" x 4 3/4"
Series Two Insert Set (10 cards): 20.00

	No.	Player	NRMT-MT
☐	1	Pavel Bure, Van.	3.50
☐	2	Sergei Fedorov, Det.	2.50
☐	3	Jaromir Jagr, Pgh.	5.00
☐	4	Jarri Kurri, L.A.	1.00
☐	5	Alexander Mogilny, Buf.	1.50
☐	6	Mikael Renberg, Pha.	1.00
☐	7	Teemu Selänne, Wpg.	3.50
☐	8	Mats Sundin, Que.	2.50
☐	9	Esa Tikkanen, NYR.	.50
☐	10	Alexei Yashin, Ott.	2.50

NETMINDERS

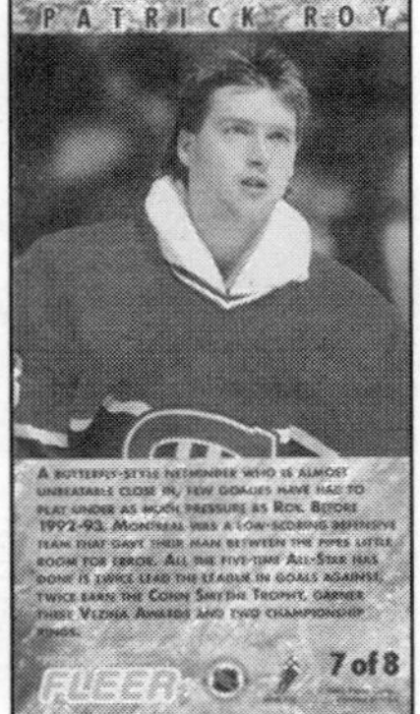

Card Size: 2 1/2" x 4 3/4"
Series One Insert Set (8 cards): 50.00

	No.	Player	NRMT-MT
☐	1	Tom Barrasso (G), Pgh.	4.00
☐	2	Ed Belfour (G), Chi.	5.00
☐	3	Grant Fuhr (G), Buf.	4.00
☐	4	Curtis Joseph (G), Stl.	10.00
☐	5	Félix Potvin (G), Tor.	8.00
☐	6	Bill Ranford (G), Edm.	4.00
☐	7	Patrick Roy (G), Mtl.	25.00
☐	8	Tommy Söderström (G), Pha.	3.00

POINT LEADERS

Card Size: 2 1/2" x 4 3/4"
Series One Insert Set (20 cards): 25.00

	No.	Player	NRMT-MT
☐	1	Pavel Bure, Van.	2.00
☐	2	Doug Gilmour, Tor.	.75
☐	3	Wayne Gretzky, L.A.	6.00
☐	4	Brett Hull, Stl.	1.50
☐	5	Jaromir Jagr, Pgh.	3.00
☐	6	Joé Juneau, Bos.	.50
☐	7	Pat LaFontaine, Buf.	.50
☐	8	Mario Lemieux, Pgh.	5.00
☐	9	Mark Messier, NYR.	1.50
☐	10	Alexander Mogilny, Buf.	.75
☐	11	Adam Oates, Bos.	.75
☐	12	Mark Recchi, Pha.	.50
☐	13	Luc Robitaille, L.A.	.50
☐	14	Jeremy Roenick, Chi.	.75
☐	15	Joe Sakic, Que.	2.50
☐	16	Teemu Selänne. Wpg.	2.00
☐	17	Kevin Stevens, Pgh.	.50
☐	18	Mats Sundin, Que.	1.50
☐	19	Pierre Turgeon, NYI.	.50
☐	20	Steve Yzerman, Det.	2.00

RISING STARS

Card Size: 2 1/2" x 4 3/4"
Series Two Insert Set (10 cards): 30.00

	No.	Player	NRMT-MT
☐	1	Arturs Irbe (G), S.J.	2.00
☐	2	Vyacheslav Kozlov, Det.	2.00
☐	3	Félix Potvin (G), Tor.	10.00
☐	4	Keith Primeau, Det.	4.00
☐	5	Robert Reichel, Cgy.	2.00
☐	6	Geoff Sanderson, Hfd.	2.00
☐	7	Martin Straka, Pgh.	2.00
☐	8	Keith Tkachuk, Wpg.	8.00
☐	9	Alexei Zhamnov, Wpg.	4.00
☐	10	Sergei Zubov, NYR.	4.00

ROOKIE STANDOUTS

Card Size: 2 1/2" x 4 3/4"
Series Two Insert Set (16 cards): 25.00

	No.	Player	NRMT-MT
☐	1	Jason Arnott, Edm.	3.00
☐	2	Jesse Belanger, Fla.	.75
☐	3	Alexandre Daigle, Ott.	2.00
☐	4	Iain Fraser, Que.	.75
☐	5	Chris Gratton, T.B.	2.00
☐	6	Boris Mironov, Wpg.	.75
☐	7	Jaroslav Modry, N.J.	.75
☐	8	Rob Niedermayer, Fla.	1.50
☐	9	Chris Osgood (G), Det.	5.00
☐	10	Pat Peake, Wsh.	.75
☐	11	Derek Plante, Buf.	.75
☐	12	Chris Pronger, Hfd.	2.00
☐	13	Mikael Renberg, Pha.	1.50
☐	14	Bryan Smolinski, Bos.	.75
☐	15	Jocelyn Thibault (G), Que.	4.00
☐	16	Alexei Yashin, Ott.	3.00

SECOND YEAR STARS

Card Size: 2 1/2" x 4 3/4"
Series One Insert Set (12 cards): 12.00

	No.	Player	NRMT-MT
☐	1	Rob Gaudreau, S.J.	.50
☐	2	Joé Juneau, Bos.	.50
☐	3	Darius Kasparaitis. NYI.	.50
☐	4	Dmitri Kvartalnov, Bos.	.50
☐	5	Eric Lindros, Pha.	5.00
☐	6	Vladimir Malakhov, NYI.	.50
☐	7	Shawn McEachern, Pgh.	.50
☐	8	Félix Potvin (G), Tor.	2.50
☐	9	Patrick Poulin, Hfd.	.50
☐	10	Teemu Selänne, Wpg.	3.00
☐	11	Tommy Söderström (G), Pha.	.50
☐	12	Alexei Zhamnov, Wpg.	1.00

SLAPSHOT ARTISTS

Card Size: 2 1/2" x 4 3/4"
Series Two Insert Set (10 cards): 25.00

	No.	Player	NRMT-MT
☐	1	Dave Andreychuk, Tor.	1.00
☐	2	Ray Bourque, Bos.	4.00
☐	3	Sergei Fedorov, Det.	4.00
☐	4	Brett Hull, Stl.	4.00
☐	5	Al Iafrate, Wsh.	1.00
☐	6	Brian Leetch, NYR.	2.50
☐	7	Al MacInnis, Cgy.	1.00
☐	8	Mike Modano, Dal.	4.00
☐	9	Teemu Selänne, Wpg.	6.00
☐	10	Brendan Shanahan, Stl.	5.00

1993 - 94 PREMIER (O-PEE-CHEE / TOPPS)

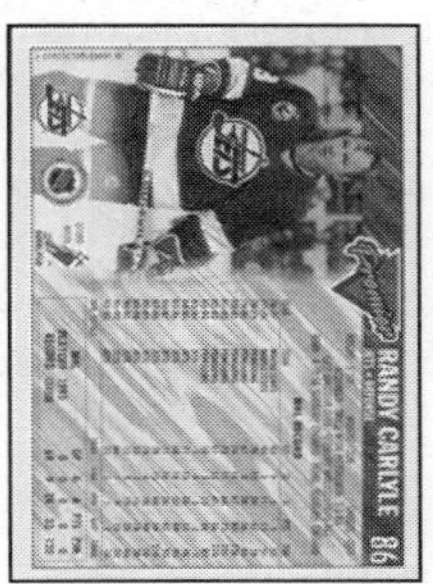

There are four versions to this series: an O-Pee-Chee card, a Topps card, an O-Pee-Chee Gold parallel and a Topps Gold parallel. O-Pee-Chee and Topps cards have the same value.

Complete Set (528 cards): 24.00 150.00 200.00
9-card Promo Sheet: 8.00
Common Player: .10 .25 .35

	No.	Player	OPC/Topps Premier	Topps Gold	OPC Gold
☐☐☐☐	1	Patrick Roy (G), Mtl.	1.50	8.00	10.00
☐☐☐☐	2	Alexei Zhitnik, L.A.	.10	.25	.35
☐☐☐☐	3	Uwe Krupp, NYI.	.10	.25	.35
☐☐☐☐	4	Todd Gill, Tor.	.10	.25	.35
☐☐☐☐	5	Paul Stanton, Pgh.	.10	.25	.35
☐☐☐☐	6	Sergio Momesso, Van.	.10	.25	.35
☐☐☐☐	7	Dale Hawerchuck, Buf.	.25	.50	.60
☐☐☐☐	8	Kevin Miller, Stl.	.10	.25	.35
☐☐☐☐	9	Nicklas Lidstrom, Det.	.25	.50	.60
☐☐☐☐	10	Joe Sakic, Que.	.85	4.00	6.00
☐☐☐☐	11	Thomas Steen, Wpg.	.10	.25	.35
☐☐☐☐	12	Peter Bondra, Wsh.	.35	1.00	1.50
☐☐☐☐	13	Brian Noonan, Chi.	.10	.25	.35
☐☐☐☐	14	Glen Featherstone, Bos.	.10	.25	.35
☐☐☐☐	15	Mike Vernon (G), Cgy.	.25	.50	.60
☐☐☐☐	16	Janne Ojanen, N.J.	.10	.25	.35
☐☐☐☐	17	Neil Brady, Ott.	.10	.25	.35
☐☐☐☐	18	Dimitri Yushkievich, Pha.	.10	.25	.35
☐☐☐☐	19	Rob Zamuner, T.B.	.25	.50	.60
☐☐☐☐	20	Zarley Zalapski, Hfd.	.10	.25	.35
☐☐☐☐	21	Mike Sullivan, S.J.	.10	.25	.35
☐☐☐☐	22	Jamie Baker, Ott.	.10	.25	.35
☐☐☐☐	23	Craig MacTavish, Edm.	.10	.25	.35
☐☐☐☐	24	Mark Tinordi, Dal.	.10	.25	.35
☐☐☐☐	25	Brian Leetch, NYR.	.35	.75	1.00
☐☐☐☐	26	Brian Skrudland, Fla.	.10	.25	.35
☐☐☐☐	27	Keith Tkachuk, Wpg.	.50	1.50	2.00
☐☐☐☐	28	Patrick Flatley, NYI.	.10	.25	.35
☐☐☐☐	29	Doug Bodger, Buf.	.10	.25	.35
☐☐☐☐	30	Félix Potvin (G), Tor.	.50	1.50	2.00
☐☐☐☐	31	Shawn Antoski, Van.	.10	.25	.35
☐☐☐☐	32	Eric Desjardins, Mtl.	.25	.50	.60
☐☐☐☐	33	Mike Donnelley, L.A.	.10	.25	.35
☐☐☐☐	34	Kjell Samuelsson, Pgh.	.10	.25	.35
☐☐☐☐	35	Nelson Emerson, Stl.	.10	.25	.35
☐☐☐☐	36	Phil Housley, Wpg.	.10	.25	.35
☐☐☐☐	37	LL: M. Lemieux, Pgh.	.75	4.50	6.00
☐☐☐☐	38	Shayne Corson, Edm.	.25	.50	.60
☐☐☐☐	39	Steve Smith, Chi.	.10	.25	.35
☐☐☐☐	40	Bob Kudelski, Ott.	.10	.25	.35
☐☐☐☐	41	Joe Cirella, Fla.	.10	.25	.35
☐☐☐☐	42	Sergei Nemchinov, NYR.	.10	.25	.35
☐☐☐☐	43	Kerry Huffman, Que.	.10	.25	.35
☐☐☐☐	44	Bob Beers, T.B.	.10	.25	.35
☐☐☐☐	45	Al Iafrate, Wsh.	.10	.25	.35
☐☐☐☐	46	Mike Modano, Dal.	.50	1.50	2.00
☐☐☐☐	47	Pat Verbeek, Hfd.	.10	.35	.50
☐☐☐☐	48	Joel Otto, Cgy.	.10	.25	.35
☐☐☐☐	49	Dino Ciccarelli, Det.	.25	.50	.60
☐☐☐☐	50	Adam Oates, Bos.	.35	.75	1.00
☐☐☐☐	51	Pat Elynuik, Wsh.	.10	.25	.35
☐☐☐☐	52	Bobby Holik, N.J.	.10	.25	.35
☐☐☐☐	53	Johan Garpenlov, S.J.	.10	.25	.35
☐☐☐☐	54	Jeff Beukeboom, NYR.	.10	.25	.35
☐☐☐☐	55	Tommy Söderström (G), Pha.	.10	.35	.50
☐☐☐☐	56	Rob Blake, L.A.	.25	.50	.60
☐☐☐☐	57	Marty McInnis, NYI.	.10	.25	.35
☐☐☐☐	58	Dixon Ward, Van.	.10	.25	.35
☐☐☐☐	59	Patrice Brisebois, Mtl.	.10	.25	.35
☐☐☐☐	60	Ed Belfour (G), Chi.	.35	.75	1.00

	No.	Player			
□□□□	61	Donald Audette, Buf.	.10	.25	.35
□□□□	62	Mike Ricci, Que.	.10	.35	.50
□□□□	63	Frederik Olausson, Wpg.	.10	.25	.35
□□□□	64	Norm Maciver, Ott.	.10	.25	.35
□□□□	65	Andrew Cassels, Hfd.	.10	.25	.35
□□□□	66	Tim Cheveldae (G), Det.	.10	.35	.50
□□□□	67	Dave Reid, Bos.	.10	.25	.35
□□□□	68	Philippe Bozon, Stl.	.10	.25	.35
□□□□	69	Drake Berehowsky, Tor.	.10	.25	.35
□□□□	70	Tony Amonte, NYR.	.25	.50	.60
□□□□	71	Dave Manson, Edm.	.10	.25	.35
□□□□	72	Rick Tocchet, Pgh.	.10	.35	.50
□□□□	73	Steve Kasper, T.B.	.10	.25	.35
□□□□	74	LL: Adam Oates, Bos.	.25	.50	.60
□□□□	75	Ulf Dahlen, Dal.	.10	.25	.35
□□□□	76	Chris Lindberg, Cgy.	.10	.25	.35
□□□□	77	Doug Wilson, S.J.	.10	.35	.50
□□□□	78	Mike Ridley, Wsh.	.10	.25	.35
□□□□	79	Vyacheslav Butsayev, Pha.	.10	.25	.35
□□□□	80	Scott Stevens, N.J.	.25	.50	.60
□□□□	81	Cliff Ronning, Van.	.10	.25	.35
□□□□	82	Andrei Lomakin, Fla.	.10	.25	.35
□□□□	83	Shawn Burr, Det.	.10	.25	.35
□□□□	84	Benoît Brunet, Mtl.	.10	.25	.35
□□□□	85	Valeri Kamensky, Que.	.25	.50	.60
□□□□	86	Randy Carlyle, Wpg.	.10	.25	.35
□□□□	87	Chris Joseph, Edm.	.10	.25	.35
□□□□	88	Dirk Graham, Chi.	.10	.25	.35
□□□□	89	Ken Sutton, Buf.	.10	.25	.35
□□□□	90	AS: Luc Robitaille, L.A.	.25	.50	.60
□□□□	91	AS: Mario Lemieux, Pgh.	.75	4.50	6.00
□□□□	92	AS: Teemu Selänne, Wpg.	.35	1.75	2.50
□□□□	93	AS: Ray Bourque, Bos.	.25	.75	1.00
□□□□	94	AS: Chris Chelios, Chi.	.25	.50	.60
□□□□	95	AS: Ed Belfour (G), Chi.	.25	.50	.60
□□□□	96	Keith Jones, Wsh.	.10	.25	.35
□□□□	97	Sylvain Turgeon, Ott.	.10	.25	.35
□□□□	98	Jim Johnson, Dal.	.10	.25	.35
□□□□	99	Mikael Nylander, Hfd.	.10	.25	.35
□□□□	100	Theoren Fleury, Cgy.	.35	.75	1.00
□□□□	101	Shawn Chambers, T.B.	.10	.25	.35
□□□□	102	Alexander Semak, N.J.	.10	.25	.35
□□□□	103	Ron Sutter, Stl.	.10	.25	.35
□□□□	104	Glenn Anderson, Tor.	.10	.25	.35
□□□□	105	Jaromir Jagr, Pgh.	1.00	6.00	8.00
□□□□	106	Adam Graves, NYR.	.10	.35	.50
□□□□	107	Nikolai Borschevsky, Tor.	.10	.25	.35
□□□□	108	Vladimir Konstantinov, Det.	.10	.35	.50
□□□□	109	Robb Stauber (G), L.A.	.10	.35	.50
□□□□	110	Arturs Irbe (G), S.J.	.10	.25	.35
□□□□	111	LL: Félix Potvin (G), Tor.	.35	1.00	1.50
□□□□	112	Darius Kasparaitis, NYI.	.10	.25	.35
□□□□	113	Kirk McLean (G), Van.	.25	.50	.60
□□□□	114	Glen Wesley, Bos.	.10	.25	.35
□□□□	115	Rod Brind'Amour, Pha.	.25	.50	.60
□□□□	116	Mike Eagles, Wpg.	.10	.25	.35
□□□□	117	Brian Bradley, T.B.	.10	.25	.35
□□□□	118	Dave Christian, Chi.	.10	.25	.35
□□□□	119	Randy Wood, Buf.	.10	.25	.35
□□□□	120	Craig Janney, Stl.	.10	.25	.35
□□□□	121	Eric Lindros, Pha.	.75	4.50	6.00
□□□□	122	Tommy Söderström (G), Pha.	.10	.35	.50
□□□□	123	Shawn McEachern, Pgh.	.10	.25	.35
□□□□	124	Andrew Kovalenko. Que.	.10	.25	.35
□□□□	125	Joé Juneau, Bos.	.10	.25	.35
□□□□	126	Félix Potvin (G), Tor.	.35	1.25	1.75
□□□□	127	Dixon Ward, Van.	.10	.25	.35
□□□□	128	Alexei Zhamnov, Wpg.	.25	.50	.60
□□□□	129	Vladimir Malakhov, NYI.	.10	.25	.35
□□□□	130	Teemu Selänne, Wpg.	.35	1.75	2.50
□□□□	131	Neal Broten, Dal.	.10	.35	.50
□□□□	132	Ulf Samuelsson, Pgh.	.10	.25	.35
□□□□	133	Mark Janssens, Hfd.	.10	.25	.35
□□□□	134	Claude Lemieux, Edm.	.10	.35	.50
□□□□	135	Mike Richter (G), NYR.	.35	.75	1.00
□□□□	136	Doug Weight, NYR.	.35	.75	1.00
□□□□	137	Rob Pearson, Tor.	.10	.25	.35
□□□□	138	Sylvain Côté, Wsh.	.10	.25	.35
□□□□	139	Mike Keane, Mtl.	.10	.25	.35
□□□□	140	Benoît Hogue, NYI.	.10	.25	.35
□□□□	141	Michel Petit, Cgy.	.10	.25	.35
□□□□	142	Mark Freer, Ott.	.10	.25	.35
□□□□	143	Doug Zmolek, S.J.	.10	.25	.35
□□□□	144	Tony Granato, L.A.	.10	.25	.35
□□□□	145	Paul Coffey, Det.	.25	.50	.60
□□□□	146	Ted Donato, Bos.	.10	.25	.35
□□□□	147	Brent Sutter, Chi.	.10	.25	.35
□□□□	148	LL: Selänne, Wpg./Mogilny, Buf.	.35	1.25	1.75
□□□□	149	James Patrick, NYR.	.10	.25	.35
□□□□	150	Mikael Andersson, T.B.	.10	.25	.35
□□□□	151	Steve Duchesne, Que.	.10	.25	.35
□□□□	152	Terry Carkner, Pha.	.10	.25	.35
□□□□	153	Russ Courtnall, Dal.	.10	.25	.35
□□□□	154	Brian Mullen, NYI.	.10	.25	.35
□□□□	155	Martin Straka, Pgh.	.10	.25	.35
□□□□	156	Geoff Sanderson, Hfd.	.10	.35	.50
□□□□	157	Mark Howe, Det.	.10	.35	.50
□□□□	158	Stéphane Richer, N.J.	.10	.35	.50
□□□□	159	Doug Crossman, Stl.	.10	.25	.35
□□□□	160	John Vanbiesbrouck (G), Fla.	.60	3.00	4.25
□□□□	161	Bob Essensa (G), Wpg.	.10	.25	.35
□□□□	162	Wayne Presley, Buf.	.10	.25	.35
□□□□	163	Mathieu Schneider, Mtl.	.10	.25	.35
□□□□	164	Jiri Slegr, Van.	.10	.25	.35
□□□□	165	Stéphane Fiset (G), Que.	.25	.50	.60
□□□□	166	Wendell Young (G), T.B.	.10	.35	.50
□□□□	167	Kevin Dineen, Pha.	.10	.25	.35
□□□□	168	Sandis Ozolinsh, S.J.	.25	.50	.60
□□□□	169	Mike Krushelnyski, Tor.	.10	.25	.35
□□□□	170	AS: Kevin Stevens, Pgh.	.10	.35	.50
□□□□	171	AS: Pat LaFontaine, Buf.	.25	.50	.60
□□□□	172	AS: Alexander Mogilny, Buf.	.25	.50	.60
□□□□	173	AS: Larry Murphy, Pgh.	.25	.50	.60
□□□□	174	AS: Al Iafrate, Wsh.	.10	.25	.35
□□□□	175	AS: Tom Barrasso (G), Pgh.	.25	.50	.60
□□□□	176	Derek King, NYI.	.10	.25	.35
□□□□	177	Bob Probert. Det.	.10	.25	.35
□□□□	178	Gary Suter, Cgy.	.10	.25	.35
□□□□	179	David Shaw, Bos.	.10	.25	.35
□□□□	180	Luc Robitaille, L.A.	.25	.50	.60
□□□□	181	John LeClair, Mtl.	.60	2.00	3.00
□□□□	182	Troy Murray, Chi.	.10	.25	.35
□□□□	183	Dave Gagner, Dal.	.10	.25	.35
□□□□	184	Darcy Loewen, Ott.	.10	.25	.35
□□□□	185	LL: Mario Lemieux, Pgh.	.75	4.50	6.00
□□□□	186	Pat Jablonski (G), T.B.	.10	.35	.50

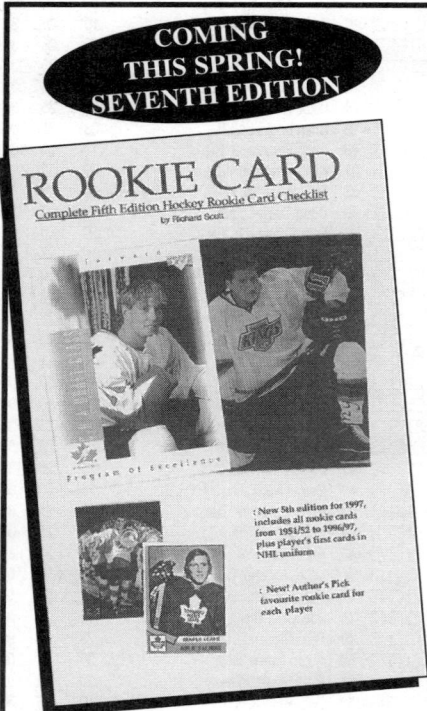

	No.	Player			
□□□□	187	Alexei Kovalev, NYR.	.10	.25	.35
□□□□	188	Todd Krygier, Wsh.	.10	.25	.35
□□□□	189	Larry Murphy, Pgh.	.25	.50	.60
□□□□	190	Pierre Turgeon, NYI.	.25	.50	.60
□□□□	191	Craig Ludwig, Dal.	.10	.25	.35
□□□□	192	Brad May, Buf.	.10	.25	.35
□□□□	193	John MacLean, N.J.	.10	.25	.35
□□□□	194	Ron Wilson, Stl.	.10	.25	.35
□□□□	195	Eric Weinrich, Hfd.	.10	.25	.35
□□□□	196	Steve Chiasson, Det.	.10	.25	.35
□□□□	197	Dmitri Kvartalnov, Bos.	.10	.25	.35
□□□□	198	Andrei Kovalenko, Que.	.10	.25	.35
□□□□	199	Rob Gaudreau, S.J.	.10	.25	.35
□□□□	200	Evgeny Davydov, Wpg.	.10	.25	.35
□□□□	201	Adrien Plavsic, Van.	.10	.25	.35
□□□□	202	Brian Bellows, Mtl.	.10	.25	.35
□□□□	203	Doug Evans, Pha.	.10	.25	.35
□□□□	204	LL: Tom Barrasso (G), Pgh.	.25	.50	.60
□□□□	205	Joe Nieuwendyk, Cgy.	.25	.50	.60
□□□□	206	Jari Kurri, L.A.	.25	.50	.60
□□□□	207	Robert Rouse, Tor.	.10	.25	.35
□□□□	208	Yvon Corriveau, Hfd.	.10	.25	.35
□□□□	209	John Blue (G), Bos.	.10	.35	.50
□□□□	210	Dimitri Khristich, Wsh.	.10	.25	.35
□□□□	211	Brent Fedyk, Pha.	.10	.25	.35
□□□□	212	Jody Hull, Ott.	.10	.25	.35
□□□□	213	Chris Terreri (G), N.J.	.10	.25	.35
□□□□	214	Mike McPhee, Dal.	.10	.25	.35
□□□□	215	Chris Kontos, T.B.	.10	.25	.35
□□□□	216	Greg Gilbert, Chi.	.10	.25	.35
□□□□	217	Sergei Zubov, NYR.	.25	.50	.60
□□□□	218	Grant Fuhr (G), Buf.	.25	.50	.60
□□□□	219	Charlie Huddy, L.A.	.10	.25	.35
□□□□	220	Mario Lemieux, Pgh.	1.50	8.00	10.00
□□□□	221	Sheldon Kennedy, Det.	.10	.25	.35
□□□□	222	LL: Curtis Joseph (G), Stl.	.25	1.00	1.50
□□□□	223	Brad Dalgarno, NYI.	.10	.25	.35
□□□□	224	Bret Hedican, Stl.	.10	.25	.35
□□□□	225	Trevor Linden, Van.	.25	.50	.60
□□□□	226	Darryl Sydor, L.A.	.10	.25	.35
□□□□	227	Jayson More, S.J.	.10	.25	.35
□□□□	228	Dave Poulin, Bos.	.10	.25	.35
□□□□	229	Frantisek Musil, Cgy.	.10	.25	.35
□□□□	230	Mark Recchi, Pha.	.25	.50	.60
□□□□	231	Craig Simpson, Edm.	.10	.25	.35
□□□□	232	Gino Cavallini, Que.	.10	.25	.35
□□□□	233	Vincent Damphousse, Mtl.	.35	.75	1.00
□□□□	234	Luciano Borsato, Wpg.	.10	.25	.35
□□□□	235	Dave Andreychuk, Tor.	.10	.35	.50
□□□□	236	Ken Daneyko, N.J.	.10	.25	.35
□□□□	237	Chris Chelios, Chi.	.35	1.00	1.50
□□□□	238	Andrew McBain, Ott.	.10	.25	.35
□□□□	239	Rick Tabaracci (G), Wsh.	.10	.35	.50
□□□□	240	Steve Larmer, Chi.	.10	.35	.50
□□□□	241	Sean Burke (G), Hfd.	.25	.50	.60
□□□□	242	Rob DiMaio, T.B.	.10	.25	.35
□□□□	243	Jim Paek, Pgh.	.10	.25	.35
□□□□	244	Dave Lowry, Fla.	.10	.25	.35
□□□□	245	Alexander Mogilny, Buf.	.25	.50	.60
□□□□	246	Darren Turcotte, NYR.	.10	.25	.35
□□□□	247	Brendan Shanahan, Stl.	.35	1.75	2.50
□□□□	248	Peter Taglianetti, Pgh.	.10	.25	.35
□□□□	249	Scott Mellanby, Fla.	.10	.25	.35
□□□□	250	Guy Carbonneau, Mtl.	.10	.35	.50
□□□□	251	Claude Lapointe, Que.	.10	.25	.35
□□□□	252	Pat Conacher, L.A.	.10	.25	.35
□□□□	253	Roger Johansson, Cgy.	.10	.25	.35
□□□□	254	Cam Neely, Bos.	.25	.50	.60
□□□□	255	Garry Galley, Pha.	.10	.25	.35
□□□□	256	Keith Primeau, Det.	.25	.50	.60
□□□□	257	Scott Lachance, NYI.	.10	.25	.35
□□□□	258	Bill Ranford (G), Edm.	.25	.50	.60
□□□□	259	Pat Falloon, S.J.	.10	.25	.35
□□□□	260	Pavel Bure, Van.	.75	3.50	5.00
□□□□	261	Darrin Shannon, Wpg.	.10	.25	.35
□□□□	262	Mike Foligno, Tor.	.10	.25	.35
□□	263	Checklist 1-132	.15	.–	–
□□	263	Martin Lapointe, Det.	.–	.50	.60
□□	264	Checklist 133-264	.15	.–	.–
□□	264	Kevin Miehm, Stl.	.–	.50	.60
□□□□	265	Peter Douris, S.J.	.10	.25	.35
□□□□	266	Warren Rychel, L.A.	.10	.25	.35
□□□□	267	Owen Nolan, Que.	.25	.50	.60
□□□□	268	Mark Osborne, Tor.	.10	.25	.35
□□□□	269	Teppo Numminen, Wpg.	.10	.25	.35
□□□□	270	Rob Niedermayer, Fla.	.25	.50	.60
□□□□	271	Mark Lamb, Ott.	.10	.25	.35
□□□□	272	Curtis Joseph (G), Stl.	.60	2.00	3.00
□□□□	273	Joe Murphy, Chi.	.10	.25	.35
□□□□	274	Bernie Nicholls, N.J.	.10	.25	.35
□□□□	275	Gord Roberts, Bos.	.10	.25	.35
□□□□	276	Al MacInnis, Cgy.	.25	.50	.60
□□□□	277	Ken Wregget (G), Pgh.	.25	.50	.60
□□□□	278	Calle Johansson, Wsh.	.10	.25	.35
□□□□	279	Tom Kurvers, NYI.	.10	.25	.35
□□□□	280	Steve Yzerman, Det.	1.50	3.00	4.25
□□□□	281	Roman Hamrlik, T.B.	.25	.50	.60
□□□□	282	Esa Tikkanen, NYR.	.10	.25	.35
□□□□	**283**	**Darrin Madeley (G), Ott, RC**	**.10**	**.35**	**.50**
□□□□	284	Robert Dirk, Van.	.10	.25	.35
□□□□	**285**	**Derek Plante, Buf., RC**	**.25**	**.50**	**.60**
□□□□	286	Ron Tugnutt (G), Ana.	.10	.35	.50
□□□□	287	Frank Pietrangelo (G), Hfd.	.10	.35	.50
□□□□	288	Paul DiPietro, Mtl.	.10	.25	.35
□□□□	289	Alexander Godynyuk, Fla.	.10	.25	.35
□□□□	**290**	**Kirk Maltby, Edm., RC**	**.10**	**.25**	**.35**
□□□□	291	Olaf Kolzig (G), Wsh.	.35	1.00	1.50
□□□□	292	Vitali Karamnov, Stl.	.10	.25	.35
□□□□	293	Alexei Gusarov, Que.	.10	.25	.35
□□□□	294	Bryan Erickson, Wpg.	.10	.25	.35
□□□□	295	Jocelyn Lemieux, Chi.	.10	.25	.35
□□□□	296	Bryan Trottier, Pgh.	.25	.50	.60
□□□□	297	Dave Ellett, Tor.	.10	.25	.35
□□□□	298	Tim Watters, L.A.	.10	.25	.35
□□□□	299	José Juneau, Bos.	.10	.25	.35
□□□□	300	Steve Thomas, NYI.	.10	.25	.35
□□□□	301	Mark Greig, Hfd.	.10	.25	.35
□□□□	302	Jeff Reese (G), Cgy.	.10	.35	.50
□□□□	303	Steven King, Ana.	.10	.25	.35
□□□□	304	Don Beaupré (G), Wsh.	.10	.35	.50
□□□□	305	Denis Savard, T.B.	.25	.50	.60
□□□□	306	Greg Smyth, Fla.	.10	.25	.35
□□□□	**307**	**Jaroslav Modry, N.J., RC**	**.10**	**.25**	**.35**
□□□□	308	Petr Svoboda, Buf.	.10	.25	.35
□□□□	309	Mike Craig, Dal.	.10	.25	.35
□□□□	310	Eric Lindros, Pha.	1.50	8.00	10.00
□□□□	311	Dana Murzyn, Van.	.10	.25	.35
□□□□	312	Sean Hill, Ana.	.10	.25	.35
□□□□	313	André Racicot (G), Mtl.	.10	.35	.50
□□□□	314	John Vanbiesbrouck (G), Fla.	.60	2.00	3.00
□□□□	315	Doug Lidster, NYR.	.10	.25	.35
□□□□	316	Garth Butcher, Stl.	.10	.25	.35
□□□□	317	Alexei Yashin, Ott.	.60	2.00	3.00
□□□□	318	Sergei Fedorov, Det.	.50	1.50	2.00
□□□□	319	Louie DeBrusk, Edm.	.10	.25	.35
□□□□	320	Dominik Hasek (G), Buf.	.75	3.50	5.00
□□□□	321	Michal Pivonka, Wsh.	.10	.25	.35
□□□□	322	Bobby Holik, N.J.	.10	.25	.35
□□□□	323	Roman Hamrlik, T.B.	.25	.50	.60
□□□□	324	Petr Svoboda, Buf.	.10	.25	.35
□□□□	325	Jaromir Jagr, Pgh.	1.00	6.00	8.00
□□□□	326	Steven Finn, Que.	.10	.25	.35
□□□□	327	Stéphane Richer, Fla.	.10	.25	.35
□□□□	328	Claude Loiselle, NYI.	.10	.25	.35
□□□□	329	Joé Sacco, Ana.	.10	.25	.35
□□□□	330	Wayne Gretzky, L.A.	2.00	10.00	15.00
□□□□	331	Sylvain Lefebvre, Tor.	.10	.25	.35
□□□□	332	Sergei Bautin, Wpg.	.10	.25	.35
□□□□	333	Craig Simpson, Buf.	.10	.25	.35
□□□□	334	Don Sweeney, Bos.	.10	.25	.35
□□□□	335	Dominic Roussel (G), Pha.	.10	.35	.50
□□□□	**336**	**Scott Thomas, Buf., RC**	**.10**	**.25**	**.35**
□□□□	337	Geoff Courtnall, Van.	.10	.25	.35
□□□□	338	Tom Fitzgerald, Fla.	.10	.25	.35
□□□□	339	Kevin Haller, Mtl.	.10	.25	.35
□□□□	340	Troy Loney, Ana.	.10	.25	.35
□□□□	341	Ron Stern, Cgy.	.10	.25	.35
□□□□	**342**	**Mark Astley, Buf., RC**	**.10**	**.25**	**.35**
□□□□	343	Jeff Daniels, Pgh.	.10	.25	.35
□□□□	344	Marc Bureau, T.B.	.10	.25	.35
□□□□	**345**	**Micah Aivazoff, Det., RC**	**.10**	**.25**	**.35**
□□□□	346	Matthew Barnaby, Buf.	.10	.35	.50
□□□□	347	C.J. Young, Fla.	.10	.25	.35
□□□□	348	Dale Craigwell, S.J.	.10	.25	.35
□□□□	349	Ray Ferraro, NYI.	.10	.25	.35
□□□□	350	Ray Bourque, Bos.	.50	1.50	2.00
□□□□	351	Stu Barnes, Wpg.	.10	.25	.35
□□□□	**352**	**Allan Conroy, Pha., RC**	**.10**	**.25**	**.35**
□□□□	353	Shawn McEachern, L.A.	.10	.25	.35
□□□□	354	Garry Valk, Ana.	.10	.25	.35
□□□□	355	Christian Ruuttu, Chi.	.10	.25	.35
□□□□	356	Darren Rumble, Ott.	.10	.25	.35
□□□□	357	Stu Grimson, Ana.	.10	.25	.35
□□□□	358	Alexander Karpovtsev, NYR.	.10	.25	.35
□□□□	359	Wendel Clark, Tor.	.25	.50	.60
□□□□	360	Michal Pivonka, Wsh.	.10	.25	.35
□□□□	**361**	**Peter Popovic, Mtl., RC**	**.10**	**.25**	**.35**
□□□□	362	Kevin Dahl, Cgy.	.10	.25	.35
□□□□	363	Jeff Brown, Stl.	.10	.25	.35
□□□□	364	Daren Puppa (G), T.B.	.10	.35	.50
□□□□	**365**	**Dallas Drake, Det., RC**	**.10**	**.25**	**.35**
□□□□	366	Dean McAmmond, Edm.	.10	.25	.35
□□□□	367	Martin Rucinsky, Que.	.10	.25	.35
□□□□	368	Shane Churla, Dal.	.10	.25	.35
□□□□	369	Todd Ewen, Ana.	.10	.25	.35
□□□□	370	Kevin Stevens, Pgh.	.10	.35	.50
□□□□	371	David Volek, NYI.	.10	.25	.35
□□□□	372	J.J. Daigneault, Mtl.	.10	.25	.35
□□□□	373	Marc Bergevin, T.B.	.10	.25	.35
□□□□	374	Craig Billington (G), Ott.	.10	.35	.50
□□□□	375	Mike Gartner, NYR.	.25	.50	.60
□□□□	376	Jimmy Carson, L.A.	.10	.25	.35
□□□□	377	Bruce Driver, N.J.	.10	.25	.35
□□□□	378	Steve Heinze, Bos.	.10	.25	.35
□□□□	379	Patrick Carnback, Ana.	.10	.25	.35
□□□□	380	Wayne Gretzky, L.A.	1.00	6.00	8.00
□□□□	381	Jeff Brown, Stl.	.10	.25	.35
□□□□	382	Gary Roberts, Cgy.	.25	.50	.60
□□□□	383	Ray Bourque, Bos.	.25	.75	1.00
□□□□	384	Mike Gartner, NYR.	.25	.50	.60
□□□□	385	Félix Potvin (G), Tor.	.35	1.00	2.00
□□□□	386	Michel Goulet, Chi.	.25	.50	.60
□□□□	387	Dave Tippett, Pha.	.10	.25	.35
□□□□	388	Jim Waite (G), S.J.	.10	.35	.50
□□□□	389	Yuri Khmylev, Buf.	.10	.25	.35
□□□□	390	Doug Gilmour, Tor.	.25	.50	.60
□□□□	391	Brad McCrimmon, Hfd.	.10	.25	.35
□□□□	**392**	**Brent Severyn, Fla., RC**	**.10**	**.25**	**.35**
□□□□	**393**	**Jocelyn Thibault (G), Que., RC**	**1.50**	**6.00**	**8.00**
□□□□	394	Boris Mironov, Wpg.	.10	.25	.35
□□□□	395	Marty McSorley, Pgh.	.10	.25	.35
□□□□	396	Shaun Van Allen, Ana.	.10	.25	.35
□□□□	397	Gary Leeman, Mtl.	.10	.25	.35
□□□□	398	Ed Olczyk, NYR.	.10	.25	.35
□□□□	399	Darcy Wakaluk (G), Dal.	.10	.35	.50
□□□□	400	Murray Craven, Van.	.10	.25	.35
□□□□	401	Martin Brodeur (G), N.J.	.75	3.50	5.00
□□□□	402	Paul Laus, Fla.	.10	.25	.35
□□□□	403	Bill Houlder, Ana.	.10	.25	.35
□□□□	404	Robert Reichel, Cgy.	.10	.25	.35
□□□□	405	Alexandre Daigle, Ott.	.35	.75	1.00
□□□□	406	Brent Thompson, L.A.	.10	.25	.35
□□□□	407	Keith Acton, NYI.	.10	.25	.35
□□□□	408	Dave Karpa, Que.	.10	.25	.35
□□□□	409	Igor Korolev, Stl.	.10	.25	.35
□□□□	410	Chris Gratton. T.B.	.35	.75	1.00
□□□□	411	Vincent Riendeau (G), Det.	.10	.35	.50
□□□□	**412**	**Darren McCarty, Det., RC**	**.25**	**.50**	**.60**
□□□□	413	Bob Carpenter, N.J.	.10	.25	.35
□□□□	414	Joe Cirella, Fla.	.10	.25	.35
□□□□	415	Stéphane Matteau, Chi.	.10	.25	.35
□□□□	416	Jozef Stumpel, Bos.	.10	.25	.35
□□□□	417	Richard Pilon, NYI.	.10	.25	.35
□□□□	**418**	**Mattias Norstrom, NYR., RC**	**.10**	**.25**	**.35**
□□□□	419	Dmitri Mironov, Tor.	.10	.25	.35
□□□□	420	Alexei Zhamnov, Wpg.	.25	.50	.60
□□□□	421	Bill Guerin, N.J.	.25	.50	.60
□□□□	422	Greg Hawgood, Pha.	.10	.25	.35
□□□□	423	Randy Cunneyworth, Hfd.	.10	.25	.35
□□□□	424	Ron Francis, Pgh.	.35	.75	1.00
□□□□	425	Brett Hull, Stl.	.50	1.50	2.00
□□□□	426	Tim Sweeney, Ana.	.10	.25	.35
□□□□	427	Mike Rathje, S.J.	.10	.25	.35
□□□□	428	Dave Babych, Van.	.10	.25	.35
□□□□	**429**	**Chris Tancill, Dal., RC**	**.10**	**.25**	**.35**
□□□□	430	Mark Messier, NYR.	.50	1.50	2.00
□□□□	431	Bob Sweeney, Buf.	.10	.25	.35
□□□□	432	Terry Yake, Ana.	.10	.25	.35
□□□□	433	Joe Reekie, T.B.	.10	.25	.35
□□□□	434	Tomas Sandström, L.A.	.10	.25	.35
□□□□	435	Kevin Hatcher, Wsh.	.10	.25	.35
□□□□	436	Bill Lindsay, Fla.	.10	.25	.35
□□□□	437	Jon Casey (G), Bos.	.10	.35	.50
□□□□	438	Dennis Vaske, NYI.	.10	.25	.35
□□□□	439	Allen Pedersen, Hfd.	.10	.25	.35

	No.	Player			
□□□□	440	Pavel Bure, Van.	.75	3.50	5.00
□□□□	441	Sergei Fedorov, Det.	.50	1.50	2.00
□□□□	442	Arturs Irbe (G), S.J.	.10	.35	.50
□□□□	443	Darius Kasparaitis, NYI.	.10	.25	.35
□□□□	444	Evgeny Davydov, Fla.	.10	.25	.35
□□□□	445	Vladimir Malakhov, NYI.	.10	.25	.35
□□□□	446	Tom Barrasso (G), Pgh.	.25	.50	.60
□□□□	447	Jeff Norton, S.J.	.10	.25	.35
□□□□	448	David Emma, N.J.	.10	.25	.35
□□□□	449	Per-Erik Eklund, Pha.	.10	.25	.35
□□□□	450	Jeremy Roenick. Chi.	.35	.75	1.00
□□□□	451	Jesse Belanger, Fla.	.10	.25	.35
□□□□	452	Vitali Prokhorov, Stl.	.10	.25	.35
□□□□	453	Arto Blomsten, Wpg.	.10	.25	.35
□□□□	454	Peter Zezel, Tor.	.10	.25	.35
□□□□	455	Kelly Kisio, Cgy.	.10	.25	.35
□□□□	456	Zdeno Ciger, Edm.	.10	.25	.35
□□□□	457	Greg Johnson, Det.	.10	.25	.35
□□□□	458	Dave Archibald, Ott.	.10	.25	.35
□□□□	459	Vladimir Vujtek, Edm.	.10	.25	.35
□□□□	460	Mats Sundin, Que.	.50	1.50	2.00
□□□□	461	Dan Keczmer, Hfd.	.10	.25	.35
□□□□	462	Stéphan Lebeau, Mtl.	.10	.25	.35
□□□□	463	Dominik Hasek (G), Buf.	.75	3.50	5.00
□□□□	464	Kevin Lowe, NYR.	.10	.25	.35
□□□□	465	Gord Murphy, Fla.	.10	.25	.35
□□□□	466	Bryan Smolinski, Bos.	.10	.25	.35
□□□□	467	Josef Beranek, Pha.	.10	.25	.35
□□□□	468	Ron Hextall (G), NYI.	.25	.50	.60
□□□□	469	Randy Ladouceur, Ana.	.10	.25	.35
□□□□	470	Scott Niedermayer, N.J.	.25	.50	.60
□□□□	471	Kelly Hrudey (G), L.A.	.10	.35	.50
□□□□	472	Mike Needham, Pgh.	.10	.25	.35
□□□□	473	John Tucker, T.B.	.10	.25	.35
□□□□	474	Kelly Miller, Wsh.	.10	.25	.35
□□□□	475	Jyrki Lumme, Van.	.10	.25	.35
□□□□	476	Andy Moog (G), Dal.	.25	.50	.60
□□□□	477	Glen Murray, Bos.	.10	.25	.35
□□□□	**478**	**Mark Ferner, Ana., RC**	**.10**	**.25**	**.35**
□□□□	479	John Cullen, Tor.	.10	.25	.35
□□□□	480	Gilbert Dionne, Mtl.	.10	.25	.35
□□□□	481	Paul Ranheim, Cgy.	.10	.25	.35
□□□□	482	Mike Hough, Fla.	.10	.25	.35
□□□□	483	Teemu Selänne, Wpg.	.75	3.50	5.00
□□□□	**484**	**Aaron Ward, Det., RC**	**.25**	**.50**	**.60**
□□□□	485	Chris Pronger, Hfd.	.35	.75	1.00
□□□□	486	Glenn Healy (G), NYR.	.10	.35	.50
□□□□	487	Curtis Leschyshyn, Que.	.10	.25	.35
□□□□	**488**	**Jim Montgomery, Stl., RC**	**.10**	**.25**	**.35**
□□□□	489	Travis Green, NYI.	.10	.25	.35
□□□□	490	Pat LaFontaine, Buf.	.25	.50	.60
□□□□	**491**	**Bobby Dollas, Ana., RC**	**.10**	**.25**	**.35**
□□□□	492	Alexei Kasatonov, Bos.	.10	.25	.35
□□□□	493	Corey Millen, N.J.	.10	.25	.35
□□□□	494	Vyacheslav Kozlov, Det.	.10	.25	.35
□□□□	495	Igor Kravchuk, Edm.	.10	.25	.35
□□□□	496	Dimitri Filimonov, Ott.	.10	.25	.35
□□□□	497	Jeff Odgers, S.J.	.10	.25	.35
□□□□	498	Joe Mullen, Pgh.	.25	.50	.60
□□□□	499	Gary Shuchuk, L.A.	.10	.25	.35
□□□□	500	Jeremy Roenick, Chi.	.25	.50	.60
□□□□	501	Tom Barrasso (G), Pgh.	.25	.50	.60
□□□□	502	Keith Tkachuk, Wpg.	.25	.75	1.00
□□□□	503	Phil Housley, Stl.	.10	.25	.35
□□□□	504	Tony Granato, L.A.	.10	.25	.35
□□□□	505	Brian Leetch, NYR.	.25	.50	.60
□□□□	506	Anatoli Semenov, Ana.	.10	.25	.35
□□□□	507	Stephen Leach, Bos.	.10	.25	.35
□□□□	508	Brian Skrudland, Fla.	.10	.25	.35
□□□□	509	Kirk Muller, Mtl.	.10	.35	.50
□□□□	510	Gary Roberts, Cgy.	.25	.50	.60
□□□□	511	Gerard Gallant, T.B.	.10	.25	.35
□□□□	512	Joey Kocur, NYR.	.10	.25	.35
□□□□	513	Tie Domi, Wpg.	.10	.25	.35
□□□□	514	Kay Whitmore (G), Van.	.10	.35	.50
□□□□	515	Vladimir Malakhov, NYI.	.10	.25	.35
□□□□	**516**	**Stewart Malgunas, Pha., RC**	**.10**	**.25**	**.35**
□□□□	517	Jamie Macoun, Tor.	.10	.25	.35
□□□□	518	Alan May, Wsh.	.10	.25	.35
□□□□	519	Guy Hebert (G), Stl.	.25	.50	.60
□□□□	520	Derian Hatcher, Dal.	.25	.50	.60
□□□□	521	Richard Smehlik, Buf.	.10	.25	.35
□□□□	**522**	**Joby Messier, NYR., RC**	**.10**	**.25**	**.35**
□□□□	523	Trent Klatt, Dal.	.10	.25	.35
□□□□	524	Tom Chorske, N.J.	.10	.25	.35
□□□□	**525**	**Iain Fraser, Que., RC**	**.10**	**.25**	**.35**
□□□□	526	Daniel Laperrière, Stl.	.10	.25	.35
□□	527	Checklist (265-396)	.15	.–	.–
□□	527	Myles O'Connor	.–	.50	.60
□□	528	Checklist (397-528)	.15	.–	.–
□□	528	Jamie Leach	.–	.50	.60

OPC BLACK GOLD

Insert Set (24 cards): 125.00

	No.	Player	NRMT-MT
□	1	Wayne Gretzky, L.A.	20.00
□	2	Vincent Damphousse, Mtl.	3.00
□	3	Adam Oates, Bos.	3.00
□	4	Phil Housley, Wpg.	1.50
□	5	Mike Vernon (G), Cgy.	1.50
□	6	Mats Sundin, Que.	5.00
□	7	Pavel Bure, Van.	7.00
□	8	Patrick Roy (G), Mtl.	16.00
□	9	Tom Barrasso (G), Pgh.	1.50
□	10	Alexander Mogilny, Buf.	3.00
□	11	Doug Gilmour, Tor.	3.00
□	12	Eric Lindros, Pha.	12.00
□	13	Theoren Fleury, Cgy.	3.00
□	14	Pat LaFontaine, Buf.	1.50
□	15	Joe Sakic, Que.	8.00
□	16	Ed Belfour (G), Chi.	3.00
□	17	Félix Potvin (G), Tor.	5.00
□	18	Mario Lemieux, Pgh.	16.00
□	19	Jaromir Jagr, Pgh.	10.00
□	20	Teemu Selänne, Wpg.	7.00
□	21	Ray Bourque, Bos.	5.00
□	22	Brett Hull, Stl.	5.00
□	23	Steve Yzerman, Det.	10.00
□	24	Kirk Muller, Mtl.	1.50

FINEST

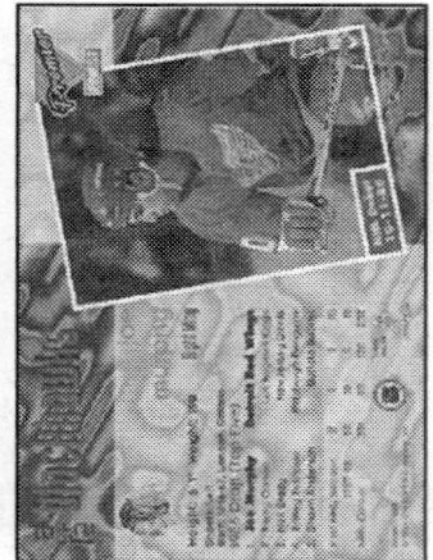

Insert Set (12 cards): 40.00

	No.	Player	NRMT-MT
□	1	Alexandre Daigle, Ott.	3.00
□	2	Roman Hamrlik, T.B.	1.50
□	3	Eric Lindros, Pha.	12.00
□	4	Owen Nolan, Que.	1.50
□	5	Mats Sundin, Que.	5.00
□	6	Mike Modano, Dal.	5.00
□	7	Pierre Turgeon, NYI.	1.50
□	8	Joe Murphy, Det.	1.50
□	9	Wendel Clark, Tor.	1.50
□	10	Mario Lemieux, Pgh.	15.00
□	11	Dale Hawerchuk, Buf.	1.50
□	12	Rob Ramage, Pha.	1.50
□		Redemption Card (Single)	1.00
□		Redemption Card (Set)	2.50

TEAM CANADA

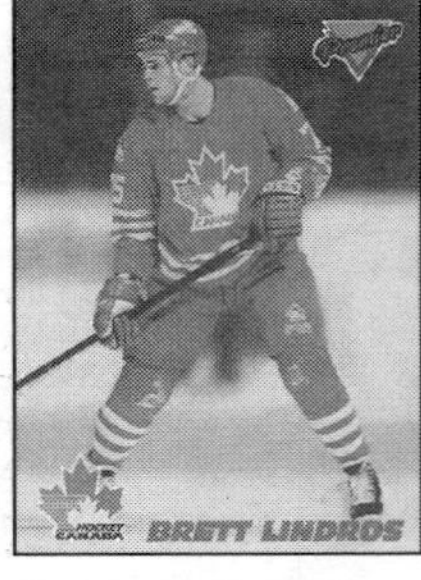

O-Pee-Chee Insert Set (19 cards): 50.00

	No.	Player	NRMT-MT
□	1	Brett Lindros	3.00
□	2	Manny Legacé (G)	2.00
□	3	Adrian Aucoin	1.50
□	4	Ken Lovsin	1.50
□	5	Craig Woodcroft	1.50
□	6	Derek Mayer	1.50
□	7	Fabian Joseph	1.50
□	8	Todd Brost	1.50
□	9	Chris Therien	1.50
□	10	Brad Turner	1.50
□	11	Trevor Sim	1.50
□	12	Todd Hlushko	1.50
□	13	Dwayne Norris	1.50
□	14	Chris Kontos	1.50
□	15	Petr Nedved	5.00
□	16	Brian Savage	3.00
□	17	Paul Kariya	25.00
□	18	Corey Hirsch (G)	3.00
□	19	Todd Warriner	1.50

TOPPS BLACK GOLD

Topps Insert Set (24 cards): 60.00

	No.	Player	NRMT-MT
□	1	Teemu Selänne, Wpg.	4.00
□	2	Steve Duchesne, Que.	1.00
□	3	Félix Potvin (G), Tor.	3.00
□	4	Shawn McEachern, Pgh.	1.00
□	5	Adam Oates, Bos.	1.50
□	6	Paul Coffey, Det.	1.00
□	7	Wayne Gretzky, L.A.	12.00
□	8	Alexei Zhamnov, Wpg.	1.00
□	9	Mario Lemieux, Pgh.	9.00
□	10	Gary Suter, Cgy.	1.00
□	11	Tom Barrasso (G), Pgh.	1.00
□	12	Joé Juneau, Bos.	1.00
□	13	Eric Lindros, Pha.	7.50
□	14	Ed Belfour (G), Chi.	1.50
□	15	Ray Bourque, Bos.	3.00
□	16	Steve Yzerman, Det.	6.00
□	17	Andrei Kovalenko, Que.	1.00
□	18	Curtis Joseph (G), Stl.	3.50
□	19	Phil Housley, Stl.	1.00
□	20	Pierre Turgeon, NYI.	1.00
□	21	Brett Hull, Stl.	3.00
□	22	Patrick Roy (G), Mtl.	9.00
□	23	Larry Murphy, Pgh.	1.00
□	24	Pat LaFontaine, Buf.	1.00
		Description	**NRMT-MT**
□		Winner A (1-12)	1.00
□		Winner B (13-24)	1.00
□		Winner A and B (1-24)	2.50

TEAM U.S.A.

Insert Set (23 cards): 20.00

	No.	Player	NRMT-MT
☐	1	Mike Dunham (G)	1.50
☐	2	Peter Laviolette	1.00
☐	4	Darby Hendrickson	1.00
☐	5	Brian Rolston	1.00
☐	6	Mark Beaufait	1.00
☐	7	Travis Richards	1.00
☐	8	John Lilley	1.00
☐	9	Chris Ferraro	1.00
☐	10	Jon Hillebrandt (G)	1.00
☐	11	Chris Imes	1.00
☐	12	Ted Crowley	1.00
☐	13	David Sacco	1.00
☐	14	Todd Marchant	1.00
☐	15	Peter Ferraro	1.00
☐	16	David Roberts	1.00
☐	17	Jim Cambell	2.00
☐	18	Barry Richter	1.00
☐	19	Craig Johnson	1.00
☐	20	Brett Hauer	1.00
☐	21	Jeff Lazaro	1.00
☐	22	Jim Storm	1.00
☐	23	Matt Martin	1.00

1993 - 94 SCORE

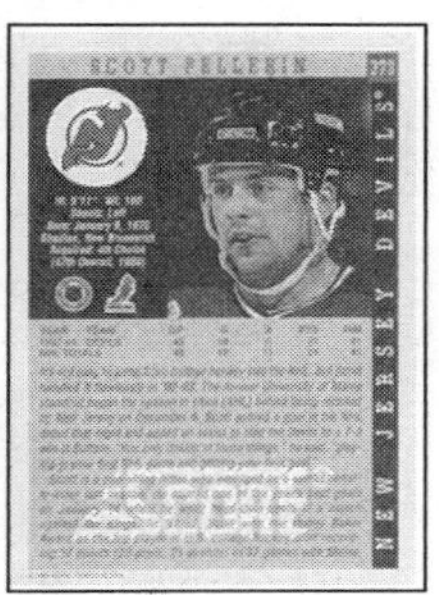

These cards have two versions: an American (English) card and a Canadian (bilingual) card. Series two cards (497-662) have a third American Gold Rush parallel and fourth Canadian Gold Rush parallel version. Pricing for Canadian and American versions is the same. Six promo cards exist.

Series One Set (496 cards): 17.00
Series Two Set (166 cards): 8.00
Score Gold Rush Set (166 cards): 55.00
Common Player: .10

	No.	Player	NRMT-MT
☐☐☐	1	Eric Lindros, Pha.	1.50
☐☐☐	2	Mike Gartner, NYR.	.25
☐☐☐	3	Steve Larmer, Chi.	.10
☐☐☐	4	Brian Bellows, Mtl.	.10
☐☐☐	5	Félix Potvin (G), Tor.	.50
☐☐☐	6	Pierre Turgeon, NYI.	.25
☐☐	7	Joe Mullen, Pgh.	.25
☐☐	8	Craig MacTavish, Edm.	.10
☐☐	9	Mats Sundin, Que.	.50
☐☐	10	Pat Verbeek, Hfd.	.10
☐☐	11	Andy Moog (G), Bos.	.25
☐☐	12	Dirk Graham, Chi.	.10
☐☐	13	Gary Suter, Cgy.	.10
☐☐	14	Brent Fedyk, Pha.	.10
☐☐	15	Brad Shaw, Ott.	.10
☐☐	16	Benoît Hogue, NYI.	.10
☐☐	17	Cliff Ronning, Van.	.10
☐☐	18	Mathieu Schneider, Mtl.	.10
☐☐	19	Bernie Nicholls, N.J.	.10
☐☐	20	Vladimir Konstantinov, Det.	.10
☐☐	21	Doug Bodger, Buf.	.10
☐☐	22	Peter Stastny, N.J.	.10
☐☐	23	Larry Murphy, Pgh.	.25
☐☐	24	Darren Turcotte, NYR.	.10
☐☐	25	Doug Crossman, Stl.	.10
☐☐	26	Bob Essensa, Wpg.	.10
☐☐	27	Kelly Kisio, S.J.	.10
☐☐	28	Nelson Emerson, Stl.	.10
☐☐	29	Ray Bourque, Bos.	.50
☐☐	30	Kelly Miller, Wsh.	.10
☐☐	31	Peter Zezel, Tor.	.10
☐☐	32	Owen Nolan, Que.	.25
☐☐	33	Sergei Makarov, Cgy.	.10
☐☐	34	Stéphane Richer, N.J.	.10
☐☐	35	Adam Graves, NYR.	.10
☐☐	36	Rob Ramage, Mtl.	.10
☐☐	37	Ed Olczyk, NYR.	.10
☐☐	38	Jeff Hackett (G), S.J.	.10
☐☐	39	Ron Sutter, Stl.	.10
☐☐	40	Dale Hunter, Wsh.	.10
☐☐	41	Nikolai Borschevsky, Tor.	.10
☐☐	42	Curtis Leschyshyn, Que.	.10
☐☐	43	Mike Vernon, Cgy.	.25
☐☐	44	Brent Sutter, NYI.	.10
☐☐	45	Rod Brind'Amour, Pha.	.25
☐☐	46	Sylvain Turgeon, Ott.	.10
☐☐	47	Kirk McLean (G), Van.	.25
☐☐	48	Derek King, NYI.	.10
☐☐	49	Murray Craven, Van.	.10
☐☐	50	Jaromir Jagr, Pgh.	1.00
☐☐	51	Guy Carbonneau, Mtl.	.10
☐☐	52	Tony Granato, L.A.	.10
☐☐	53	Mark Tinordi, Dal.	.10
☐☐	54	Brad McCrimmon, Det.	.10
☐☐	55	Randy Wood, Buf.	.10
☐☐	56	Scott Young, Que.	.10
☐☐	57	Jamie Baker, Ott.	.10
☐☐	58	Don Beaupré (G), Wsh.	.10
☐☐	59	Bob Probert, Det.	.10
☐☐	60	Ray Ferraro, NYI.	.10
☐☐	61	Alexei Kasatonov, N.J.	.10
☐☐	62	Corey Millen, L.A.	.10
☐☐	63	Scott Mellanby, Edm.	.10
☐☐	64	Brian Benning, Edm.	.10
☐☐	65	Doug Lidster, Van.	.10
☐☐	66	Doug Gilmour, Tor.	.35
☐☐	67	Shawn McEachern, Pgh.	.10
☐☐	68	Tim Cheveldae (G), Det.	.10
☐☐	69	Jeff Norton, NYI.	.10
☐☐	70	Ed Belfour (G), Chi.	.35
☐☐	71	Thomas Steen, Wpg.	.10
☐☐	72	Stéphan Lebeau, Mtl.	.10
☐☐	73	James Patrick, NYR.	.10
☐☐	74	Joel Otto, Cgy.	.10
☐☐	75	Grant Fuhr (G), Buf.	.25
☐☐	76	Calle Johansson, Wsh.	.10
☐☐	77	Donald Audette, Buf.	.10
☐☐	78	Geoff Courtnall, Van.	.10
☐☐	79	Fredrik Olausson, Wpg.	.10
☐☐	80	Dimitri Khristich, Wsh.	.10
☐☐	81	John MacLean (G), N.J.	.10
☐☐	82	Dominic Roussel (G), Pha.	.10
☐☐	83	Ray Sheppard, Det.	.10
☐☐	84	Christian Ruuttu, Chi.	.10
☐☐	85	Mike McPhee, Dal.	.10
☐☐	86	Adam Creighton, NYI.	.10
☐☐	87	Uwe Krupp, NYI.	.10
☐☐	88	Steve Leach, Bos.	.10
☐☐	89	Kevin Miller, Stl.	.10
☐☐	90	Charlie Huddy, L.A.	.10
☐☐	91	Mark Howe, Det.	.10
☐☐	92	Sylvain Côté, Wsh.	.10
☐☐	93	Anatoli Semenov, Van.	.10
☐☐	94	Jeff Beukeboom, NYR.	.10
☐☐	95	Gord Murphy, Bos.	.10
☐☐	96	Rob Pearson, Tor.	.10
☐☐	97	Esa Tikkanen, NYR.	.10
☐☐	98	Dave Gagner, Dal.	.10
☐☐	99	Mike Richter (G), NYR.	.35
☐☐	100	Jari Kurri, L.A.	.25
☐☐	101	Chris Chelios, Chi.	.35
☐☐	102	Peter Sidorkiewicz (G), Ott.	.10
☐☐	103	Scott Lachance, NYI.	.10
☐☐	104	Zarley Zalapski, Hfd.	.10
☐☐	105	Denis Savard, Mtl.	.25
☐☐	106	Paul Coffey, Det.	.25
☐☐	107	Ulf Dahlen, S.J.	.10
☐☐	108	Shayne Corson, Edm.	.25
☐☐	109	Jimmy Carson, L.A.	.10
☐☐	110	Petr Svoboda, Buf.	.10
☐☐	111	Scott Stevens, N.J.	.25
☐☐	112	Kevin Lowe, NYR.	.10
☐☐	113	Chris Kontos, T.B.	.10
☐☐	114	Evgeny Davydov, Wpg.	.10
☐☐	115	Doug Wilson, S.J.	.10
☐☐	116	Curtis Joseph (G), Stl.	.60
☐☐	117	Trevor Linden, Van.	.25
☐☐	118	Michal Pivonka, Wsh.	.10
☐☐	119	Dave Ellet, Tor.	.10
☐☐	120	Mike Ricci, Que.	.10
☐☐	121	Al MacInnis, Cgy.	.25
☐☐	122	Kevin Dineen, Pha.	.10
☐☐	123	Norm Maciver, Ott.	.10
☐☐	124	Darius Kasparaitis, NYI.	.10
☐☐	125	Adam Oates, Bos.	.35
☐☐	126	Sean Burke (G), Hfd.	.25
☐☐	127	Dave Manson, Edm.	.10
☐☐	128	Eric Desjardins, Mtl.	.10
☐☐	129	Tomas Sandström, L.A.	.10
☐☐	130	Russ Courtnall, Dal.	.10
☐☐	131	Roman Hamrlik, T.B.	.25
☐☐	132	Teppo Numminen, Wpg.	.10
☐☐	133	Pat Falloon, S.J.	.10
☐☐	134	Jyrki Lumme, Van.	.10
☐☐	135	Joe Sakic, Que.	.85
☐☐	136	Kevin Hatcher, Wsh.	.10
☐☐	137	Wendel Clark, Tor.	.25
☐☐	138	Neil Wilkinson, S.J.	.10
☐☐	139	Craig Simpson, Edm.	.10
☐☐	140	Kelly Hrudey (G). L.A.	.10
☐☐	141	Steve Thomas, NYI.	.10
☐☐	142	Mike Modano, Dal.	.50
☐☐	143	Garry Galley, Pha.	.10
☐☐	144	Jim Johnson, Dal.	.10
☐☐	145	Rod Langway, Wsh.	.10
☐☐	146	Bob Sweeney, Buf.	.10
☐☐	147	Gary Leeman, Mtl.	.10
☐☐	148	Alexei Zhitnik, L.A.	.10
☐☐	149	Adam Foote, Que.	.25
☐☐	150	Mark Recchi, Pha.	.25
☐☐	151	Ron Francis, Pgh.	.35
☐☐	152	Ron Hextall (G), Que.	.25
☐☐	153	Michel Goulet, Chi.	.25
☐☐	154	Vladimir Ruzicka, Bos.	.10
☐☐	155	Bill Ranford (G), Edm.	.25
☐☐	156	Mike Craig, Dal.	.10
☐☐	157	Vladimir Malakhov, NYI.	.10
☐☐	158	Nicklas Lidstrom, Det.	.25
☐☐	159	Dale Hawerchuk, Buf.	.25
☐☐	160	Claude Lemieux, N.J.	.10
☐☐	161	Ulf Samuelsson, Pgh.	.10
☐☐	162	John Vanbiesbrouck (G), NYR.	.60
☐☐	163	Patrice Brisebois, Mtl.	.10
☐☐	164	Andrew Cassels, Hfd.	.10
☐☐	165	Paul Ranheim, Cgy.	.10
☐☐	166	Neal Broten, Dal.	.10
☐☐	167	Joe Reekie, T.B.	.10
☐☐	168	Derian Hatcher, Dal.	.25
☐☐	169	Don Sweeney, Bos.	.10
☐☐	170	Mike Keane, Mtl.	.10
☐☐	171	Mark Fitzpatrick (G), NYI.	.10
☐☐	172	Paul Cavallini, Wsh.	.10
☐☐	173	Garth Butcher, Stl.	.10
☐☐	174	Andrei Kovalenko, Que.	.10
☐☐	175	Shawn Burr, Det.	.10
☐☐	176	Mike Donnelly, L.A.	.10
☐☐	177	Glenn Healy (G), NYI.	.10
☐☐	178	Gilbert Dionne, Mtl.	.10
☐☐	179	Mike Ramsey, Pgh.	.10
☐☐	180	Glenn Anderson, Tor.	.10
☐☐	181	Pelle Eklund, Pha.	.10
☐☐	182	Kerry Huffman, Que.	.10
☐☐	183	Johan Garpenlov, S.J.	.10
☐☐	184	Kjell Samuelsson, Pgh.	.10
☐☐	185	Todd Elik, Dal.	.10
☐☐	186	Craig Janney, Stl.	.10
☐☐	187	Dmitri Kvartalnov, Bos.	.10
☐☐	188	Al Iafrate, Wsh.	.10
☐☐	189	John Cullen, Tor.	.10
☐☐	190	Steve Duchesne, Que.	.10
☐☐	191	Theoren Fleury, Cgy.	.35
☐☐	192	Steve Smith, Chi.	.10
☐☐	193	Jon Casey (G), Dal.	.10
☐☐	194	Jeff Brown, Stl.	.10
☐☐	195	Keith Tkachuk, Wpg.	.50
☐☐	196	Greg Adams, Van.	.10
☐☐	197	Mike Ridley, Wsh.	.10
☐☐	198	Bobby Holik, N.J.	.10
☐☐	199	Joe Nieuwendyk, Cgy.	.25
☐☐	200	Mark Messier, NYR.	.50
☐☐	201	Jim Hrivnak (G), Wpg.	.10
☐☐	202	Patrick Poulin, Hfd.	.10
☐☐	203	Alexei Kovalev, NYR.	.10

	No.	Player	Price
☐☐	204	Robert Reichel, Cgy.	.10
☐☐	205	David Shaw, Bos.	.10
☐☐	206	Brent Gilchrist, Det.	.10
☐☐	207	Craig Billington (G), N.J.	.10
☐☐	208	Bob Errey, Buf.	.10
☐☐	209	Dmitri Mirinov, Tor.	.10
☐☐	210	Dixon Ward, Van.	.10
☐☐	211	Rick Zombo, Stl.	.10
☐☐	212	Marty McSorley, L.A.	.10
☐☐	213	Geoff Sanderson, Hfd.	.10
☐☐	214	Dino Ciccarelli, Det.	.25
☐☐	215	Tony Amonte, NYR.	.25
☐☐	216	Dimitri Yushkevich, Pha.	.10
☐☐	217	Scott Niedermayer, N.J.	.25
☐☐	218	Sergei Nemchinov, NYR.	.10
☐☐	219	Steve Konroyd, Det.	.10
☐☐	220	Patrick Flatley, NYI.	.10
☐☐	221	Steve Chiasson, Det.	.10
☐☐	222	Alexander Mogilny, Buf.	.35
☐☐	223	Pat Elynuik, Wsh.	.10
☐☐	224	Jamie Macoun, Tor.	.10
☐☐	225	Tom Barrasso (G), Pgh.	.25
☐☐	226	Gaetan Duchesne, Det.	.10
☐☐	227	Eric Weinrich, Hfd.	.10
☐☐	228	Dave Poulin, Bos.	.10
☐☐	229	Viacheslav Fetisov, N.J.	.25
☐☐	230	Brian Bradley, T.B.	.10
☐☐	231	Petr Nedved, Van.	.10
☐☐	232	Phil Housley, Wpg.	.10
☐☐	233	Terry Carkner, Pha.	.10
☐☐	234	Kirk Muller, Mtl.	.10
☐☐	235	Brian Leetch, NYR.	.35
☐☐	236	Rob Blake, L.A.	.25
☐☐	237	Chris Terreri (G), N.J.	.10
☐☐	238	Brendan Shanahan, Stl.	.60
☐☐	239	Paul Ysebaert, Det.	.10
☐☐	240	Jeremy Roenick, Chi.	.35
☐☐	241	Gary Roberts, Cgy.	.25
☐☐	242	Petr Klima, Edm.	.10
☐☐	243	Glen Wesley, Bos.	.10
☐☐	244	Vincent Damphousse, Mtl.	.35
☐☐	245	Luc Robitaille, L.A.	.25
☐☐	**246**	**Dallas Drake, Det., RC**	**.10**
☐☐	**247**	**Rob Gaudreau, S.J., RC**	**.10**
☐☐	248	Tommy Sjodin, Det.	.10
☐☐	249	Richard Smehlik, S.J.	.10
☐☐	250	Sergei Fedorov, Det.	.50
☐☐	251	Stephen Heinze, Bos.	.10
☐☐	252	Luke Richardson, Edm.	.10
☐☐	253	Doug Weight, Edm.	.35
☐☐	254	Martin Rucinsky, Que.	.10
☐☐	255	Sergio Memesso, Van.	.10
☐☐	256	Alexei Zhamnov, Wpg.	.25
☐☐	257	Bob Kudelski, Ott.	.10
☐☐	258	Brian Skrudland, Cgy.	.10
☐☐	259	Terry Yake, Hfd.	.10
☐☐	260	Alexei Gusarov, Que.	.10
☐☐	261	Sandis Ozolinsh, S.J.	.25
☐☐	262	Ted Donato, Bos.	.10
☐☐	263	Bruce Driver, N.J.	.10
☐☐	264	Yves Racine, Det.	.10
☐☐	265	Mike Peluso, Ott.	.10
☐☐	266	Craig Muni, Edm.	.10
☐☐	267	Bob Carpenter, Wsh.	.10
☐☐	268	Kevin Haller, Mtl.	.10
☐☐	269	Brad May, Buf.	.10
☐☐	270	Joe Kocur, NYR.	.10
☐☐	271	Igor Korolev, Stl.	.10
☐☐	272	Troy Murray, Chi.	.10
☐☐	273	Daren Puppa (G), Tor.	.10
☐☐	274	Gord Roberts, Bos.	.10
☐☐	275	Michel Petit, Cgy.	.10
☐☐	276	Vincent Riendeau (G), Det.	.10
☐☐	277	Robert Petrovicky, Hfd.	.10
☐☐	278	Valeri Zelepukin, N.J.	.10
☐☐	279	Bob Bassen, Stl.	.10
☐☐	280	Darrin Shannon, Wpg.	.10
☐☐	281	Dominik Hasek (G), Buf.	.75
☐☐	282	Craig Ludwig, Cgy.	.10
☐☐	283	Lyle Odelein, Mtl.	.10
☐☐	284	Alexander Semak, N.J.	.10
☐☐	285	Richard Matvichuk, Det.	.10
☐☐	286	Ken Daneyko, N.J.	.10
☐☐	287	Jan Erixon, NYR.	.10
☐☐	288	Robert Dirk, Van.	.10
☐☐	289	Laurie Boschman, Ott.	.10
☐☐	290	Greg Paslawski, Cgy.	.10
☐☐	291	Rob Zamuner, T.B.	.25
☐☐	292	Todd Gill, Tor.	.10
☐☐	293	Neil Brady, Ott.	.10
☐☐	294	Murray Baron, Stl.	.10
☐☐	295	Peter Taglianetti, Pgh.	.10
☐☐	296	Wayne Presley, Buf.	.10
☐☐	297	Paul Broten, NYR.	.10
☐☐	298	Dana Murzyn, Van.	.10
☐☐	299	J.J. Daigneault, Mtl.	.10
☐☐	300	Wayne Gretzky, L.A.	2.00
☐☐	301	Keith Acton, Pha.	.10
☐☐	302	Yuri Khmylev, Buf.	.10
☐☐	303	Frantisek Musil, Cgy.	.10
☐☐	304	Bob Rouse, Tor.	.10
☐☐	305	Greg Gilbert, Chi.	.10
☐☐	306	Geoff Smith, Edm.	.10
☐☐	307	Adam Burt, Hfd.	.10
☐☐	308	Phil Bourque, NYR.	.10
☐☐	309	Igor Kravchuk, Edm.	.10
☐☐	310	Steve Yzerman, Det.	1.00
☐☐	311	Darryl Sydor, L.A.	.10
☐☐	312	Tie Domi, Wpg.	.10
☐☐	313	Sergei Zubov, NYR.	.25
☐☐	314	Chris Dahlquist, Cgy.	.10
☐☐	315	Patrick Roy (G), Mtl.	1.50
☐☐	316	Mark Osborne, Tor.	.10
☐☐	317	Kelly Buchberger, Edm.	.10
☐☐	318	John LeClair, Mtl.	.60
☐☐	319	Randy McKay, N.J.	.10
☐☐	320	Jody Hull, Ott.	.10
☐☐	321	Paul Stanton, Pgh.	.10
☐☐	322	Steven Finn, Que.	.10
☐☐	323	Rich Sutter, Stl.	.10
☐☐	324	Ray Whitney, S.J.	.10
☐☐	325	Kevin Stevens, Pgh.	.10
☐☐	326	Valeri Kamensky, Que.	.25
☐☐	327	Doug Zmolek, S.J.	.10
☐☐	328	Mikhail Tatarinov, Que.	.10
☐☐	329	Ken Wregget (G), Pgh.	.10
☐☐	330	Joé Juneau, Bos.	.10
☐☐	331	Teemu Selänne, Wpg.	.75
☐☐	332	Trent Yawney, Cgy.	.10
☐☐	333	Pavel Bure, Van.	.75
☐☐	334	Jim Paek, Pgh.	.10
☐☐	335	Brett Hull, Stl.	.50
☐☐	336	Tommy Söderström (G), Pha.	.10
☐☐	337	Grigori Panteleyev, Bos.	.10
☐☐	338	Kevin Todd, Edm.	.10
☐☐	339	Mark Janssens, Hfd.	.10
☐☐	340	Rick Tocchet, Pgh.	.10
☐☐	341	Wendell Young (G), T.B.	.10
☐☐	342	Cam Neely, Bos.	.25
☐☐	343	Dave Andreychuk, Tor.	.10
☐☐	344	Peter Bondra, Wsh.	.35
☐☐	345	Pat LaFontaine, Buf.	.25
☐☐	346	Robb Stauber (G), L.A.	.10
☐☐	347	Brian Mullen, NYI.	.10
☐☐	348	Joe Murphy, Chi.	.10
☐☐	349	Pat Jablonski (G), T.B.	.10
☐☐	350	Mario Lemieux, Pgh.	1.50
☐☐	351	Sergei Bautin, Wpg.	.10
☐☐	352	Claude Lapointe, Que.	.10
☐☐	353	Dean Evason, Stl.	.10
☐☐	354	John Tucker, T.B.	.10
☐☐	355	Drake Berehowsky, Tor.	.10
☐☐	356	Gerald Diduck, Van.	.10
☐☐	357	Todd Krygier, Wsh.	.10
☐☐	358	Adrien Plavsic, Van.	.10
☐☐	359	Sylvain Lefebvre, Tor.	.10
☐☐	360	Kay Whitmore (G), Van.	.10
☐☐	361	Sheldon Kennedy, Det.	.10
☐☐	362	Kris King, Wpg.	.10
☐☐	363	Marc Bergevin, T.B.	.10
☐☐	364	Keith Primeau, Det.	.25
☐☐	365	Jimmy Waite, Chi.	.10
☐☐	366	Dean Kennedy, Wpg.	.10
☐☐	367	Mike Krushelnyski, Tor.	.10
☐☐	368	Ron Tugnutt (G), Edm.	.10
☐☐	369	Bob Beers, T.B.	.10
☐☐	370	Randy Burridge, Wsh.	.10
☐☐	371	Dave Reid, Bos.	.10
☐☐	372	Frantisek Kucera, Chi.	.10
☐☐	373	Scott Pellerin, N.J.	.10
☐☐	374	Brad Dalgarno, NYI.	.10
☐☐	375	Martin Straka, Pgh.	.10
☐☐	376	Scott Pearson, Que.	.10
☐☐	377	Arturs Irbe (G), S.J.	.10
☐☐	378	Jiri Slegr, Van.	.10
☐☐	379	Stéphane Fiset (G), Que.	.25
☐☐	380	Stu Barnes, Wpg.	.10
☐☐	381	Ric Nattress, Pha.	.10
☐☐	382	Steven King, NYR.	.10
☐☐	383	Michael Nylander, Hfd.	.10
☐☐	384	Keith Brown, Chi.	.10
☐☐	385	Gino Odjick, Van.	.10
☐☐	386	Bryan Marchment, Chi.	.10
☐☐	387	Mike Foligno, Tor.	.10
☐☐	388	Zdeno Ciger, Edm.	.10
☐☐	389	Dave Taylor, L.A.	.10
☐☐	390	Mike Sullivan, S.J.	.10
☐☐	391	Shawn Chambers, T.B.	.10
☐☐	392	Brad Marsh, Ott.	.10
☐☐	393	Mike Hough, Que.	.10
☐☐	394	Jeff Reese, Cgy.	.10
☐☐	395	Bill Guerin, N.J.	.25
☐☐	396	Greg Hawgood, Pha.	.10
☐☐	397	Jim Sandlak, Van.	.10
☐☐	398	Stéphane Matteau, Chi.	.10
☐☐	399	John Blue (G), Bos.	.10
☐☐	400	Tony Twist, Que.	.10
☐☐	401	Luciano Borsato, Wpg.	.10
☐☐	402	Gerard Gallant, Det.	.10
☐☐	403	Rick Tabaracci (G), Wsh.	.10
☐☐	404	Nick Kypreos, Hfd.	.10
☐☐	405	Marty McInnis, NYI.	.10
☐☐	406	Craig Wolanin, Que.	.10
☐☐	407	Mark Lamb, Ott.	.10
☐☐	408	Martin Gelinas, Edm.	.10
☐☐	409	Ronnie Stern, Cgy.	.10
☐☐	410	Ken Sutton, Buf.	.10
☐☐	411	Brian Noonan, Chi.	.10
☐☐	412	Stéphane Quintal, Stl.	.10
☐☐	413	Rob Zettler, S.J.	.10
☐☐	414	Gino Cavallini, Que.	.10
☐☐	415	Mark Hardy, L.A.	.10
☐☐	416	Jay Wells, NYR.	.10
☐☐	417	Keith Jones, Wsh.	.10
☐☐	418	Dave McLlwain, Tor.	.10
☐☐	419	Frank Pietrangelo (G), Hfd.	.10
☐☐	420	Jocelyn Lemieux, Chi.	.10
☐☐	421	Vyacheslav Kozlov, Det.	.10
☐☐	422	Randy Moller, Buf.	.10
☐☐	423	Kevin Dahl, Cgy.	.10
☐☐	**424**	**Shjon Podein, Edm., RC**	**.10**
☐☐	425	Shane Churla, Dal.	.10
☐☐	426	Guy Hebert (G), Stl.	.25
☐☐	427	Mikael Andersson, T.B.	.10
☐☐	428	Robert Kron, Hfd.	.10
☐☐	429	Mike Eagles, Wpg.	.10
☐☐	430	Alan May, Wsh.	.10
☐☐	431	Ron Wilson, Stl.	.10
☐☐	432	Darcy Wakaluk (G), Dal.	.10
☐☐	433	Rob Ray, Buf.	.10
☐☐	434	Brent Ashton, Cgy.	.10
☐☐	435	Jason Woolley, Wsh.	.10
☐☐	436	Basil McRae, Stl.	.10
☐☐	437	André Racicot (G), Mtl.	.10
☐☐	438	Brad Werenka, Edm.	.10
☐☐	439	Josef Beranek, Pha.	.10
☐☐	440	Dave Christian, Chi.	.10
☐☐	441	Theoren Fleury, Cgy.	.35
☐☐	442	Mark Recchi, Pha.	.25
☐☐	443	Cliff Ronning, Van.	.10
☐☐	444	Tony Granato, L.A.	.10
☐☐	445	John Vanbiesbrouck (G), NYR.	.25
☐☐	446	HL: Jarri Kurri, L.A.	.25
☐☐	447	HL: Mike Gartner, NYR.	.25
☐☐	448	HL: Steve Yzerman, Det.	.50
☐☐	449	HL: Glenn Anderson, Tor.	.10
☐☐	450	HL: A. Iafrate/ S. Côté/ K. Hatcher	.10
☐☐	451	HL: Luc Robitaille, L.A.	.25
☐☐	452	Pittsburgh Penguins	.10
☐☐	453	Corey Hirsch (G), NYR.	.10
☐☐	**454**	**Jesse Belanger, Mtl., RC**	**.10**
☐☐	455	Philippe Boucher, Buf.	.10
☐☐	**456**	**Robert Lang, L.A., RC**	**.10**
☐☐	**457**	**Doug Barrault, Dal., RC**	**.10**
☐☐	458	Steve Konowalchuk, Wsh.	.10

	No.	Player	Price
□□	**459**	**Oleg Petrov, Mtl., RC**	**.10**
□□	460	Niclas Andersson, Que.	.10
□□	461	Milan Tichy, Chi.	.10
□□	**462**	**Darrin Madeley (G), Ott., RC**	**.10**
□□	463	Tyler Wright, Edm.	.10
□□	464	Sergei Krivokrasov, Chi.	.10
□□	**465**	**Vladimir Vujtek, Edm., RC**	**.10**
□□	**466**	**Rick Knickle (G), L.A., RC**	**.10**
□□	**467**	**Gord Kruppke, Det., RC**	**.10**
□□	468	David Emma, N.J.	.10
□□	**469**	**Scott Thomas, Buf., RC**	**.10**
□□	**470**	**Shawn Rivers, T.B., RC**	**.10**
□□	**471**	**Jason Bowen, Pha., RC**	**.10**
□□	**472**	**Bryan Smolinski, Bos., RC**	**.10**
□□	**473**	**Chris Simon, Que., RC**	**.25**
□□	**474**	**Peter Ciavaglia, Buf., RC**	**.10**
□□	475	Sergei Zholtok, Bos.	.10
□□	**476**	**Radek Hamr, Ott., RC**	**.10**
□□	477	LL: Teemu Selänne/Alexander Mogilny	.20
□□	478	LL: Adam Oates, Bos.	.20
□□	479	LL: Mario Lemieux, Pgh.	.60
□□	480	LL: Mario Lemieux, Pgh.	.60
□□	481	LL: Dave Andreychuk, Tor.	.10
□□	482	LL: Phil Housley, Wpg.	.10
□□	483	LL: Tom Barrasso (G), Pgh.	.10
□□	484	LL: Félix Potvin (G), Tor.	.25
□□	485	LL: Ed Belfour (G), Chi.	.25
□□	486	Sault Ste. Marie Greyhounds	.10
□□	487	Stanley Cup Champions, Montreal	.35
□□	488	Mighty Ducks of Anaheim	.50
□□	489	Guy Hebert (G), Ana.	.25
□□	490	Sean Hill, Ana.	.10
□□	491	Florida Panthers	.50
□□	492	John Vanbiesbrouck (G), Fla.	.60
□□	493	Tom Fitzgerald (G), Fla.	.10
□□	494	Paul DePietro, Mtl.	.10
□□	495	David Volek, NYI.	.10
□□	496	Alexandre Daigle Redemption Card	.75
□□	496	Alexandre Daigle, Ott.	1.00

	No.	Player	Reg.	Gold
□□□□	497	Shawn McEachern, L.A.	.10	.35
□□□□	498	Rich Sutter, Chi.	.10	.35
□□□□	499	Evgeny Davydov, Ott.	.10	.35
□□□□	500	Sean Hill, Ana.	.10	.35
□□□□	501	John Vanbiesbrouck (G), Fla.	.60	3.00
□□□□	502	Guy Hebert (G), Ana.	.25	.50
□□□□	503	Scott Mellanby, Fla.	.10	.35
□□□□	504	Ron Tugnutt (G), Ana.	.10	.35
□□□□	505	Brian Skrudland, Fla.	.10	.35
□□□□	506	Nelson Emerson, Wpg.	.10	.35
□□□□	507	Kevin Todd, Chi.	.10	.35
□□□□	508	Terry Carkner, Det.	.10	.35
□□□□	509	Stéphane Quintal, Wpg.	.10	.35
□□□□	510	Paul Stanton, Bos.	.10	.35
□□□□	511	Terry Yake, Ana.	.10	.35
□□□□	512	Brain Benning, Fla.	.10	.35
□□□□	513	Brian Propp, Hfd.	.10	.35
□□□□	514	Steven King, Ana.	.10	.35
□□□□	515	Joe Cirella, Fla.	.10	.35
□□□□	516	Andy Moog (G), Dal.	.25	.50
□□□□	517	Paul Ysebaert, Wpg.	.10	.35
□□□□	518	Petr Klima, T.B.	.10	.35
□□□□	519	Corey Millen, N.J.	.10	.35
□□□□	520	Phil Housley, Stl.	.10	.35
□□□□	521	Craig Billington (G), Ott.	.10	.35
□□□□	522	Jeff Norton, S.J.	.10	.35
□□□□	523	Neil Wilkinson, Chi.	.10	.35
□□□□	524	Doug Lidster, NYR.	.10	.35
□□□□	525	Steve Larmer, NYR.	.10	.35
□□□□	526	Jon Casey (G), Bos.	.10	.35
□□□□	527	Brad McCrimmon, Hfd.	.10	.35
□□□□	528	Alexei Kasatonov, Ana.	.10	.35
□□□□	529	Andrei Lomakin, Fla.	.10	.35
□□□□	530	Daren Puppa (G), T.B.	.10	.35
□□□□	531	Sergei Makarov, S.J.	.10	.35
□□□□	532	Jim Sandlak, Hfd.	.10	.35
□□□□	533	Glenn Healy (G), NYR.	.10	.35
□□□□	534	Martin Gelinas, Van.	.10	.35
□□□□	535	Igor Larionov, S.J.	.10	.50
□□□□	536	Anatoli Semenov, Ana.	.10	.35
□□□□	537	Mark Fitzpatrick (G), Fla.	.10	.35
□□□□	538	Paul Cavallini, Dal.	.10	.35
□□□□	539	Jimmy Waite (G), S.J.	.10	.35
□□□□	540	Yves Racine, Pha.	.10	.35
□□□□	541	Jeff Hackett (G), Chi.	.10	.35
□□□□	542	Marty McSorley, Pgh.	.10	.35
□□□□	543	Scott Pearson, Edm.	.10	.35
□□□□	544	Ron Hextall (G), NYI.	.25	.50
□□□□	545	Gaetan Duchesne, S.J.	.10	.35
□□□□	546	Jamie Baker, S.J.	.10	.35
□□□□	547	Troy Loney, Ana.	.10	.35
□□□□	548	Gord Murphy, Fla.	.10	.35
□□□□	549	Bob Kudelski, Fla.	.10	.35
□□□□	550	Dean Evason, Dal.	.10	.35
□□□□	551	Mike Peluso, N.J.	.10	.35
□□□□	552	Dave Poulin, Wsh.	.10	.35
□□□□	553	Randy Ladouceur, Ana.	.10	.35
□□□□	554	Tom Fitzgerald, Fla.	.10	.35
□□□□	555	Denis Savard, T.B.	.25	.50
□□□□	556	Kelly Kisio, Cgy.	.10	.35
□□□□	557	Craig Simpson, Buf.	.10	.35
□□□□	558	Stu Grimson, Ana.	.10	.35
□□□□	559	Mike Hough, Fla.	.10	.35
□□□□	560	Gerard Gallant, T.B.	.10	.35
□□□□	561	Greg Gilbert, NYR.	.10	.35
□□□□	562	Vladimir Ruzicka, Ott.	.10	.35
□□□□	563	Jim Hrivnak (G), Stl.	.10	.35
□□□□	564	Dave Lowry, Fla.	.10	.35
□□□□	565	Todd Ewen, Ana.	.10	.35
□□□□	566	Bob Errey, S.J.	.10	.35
□□□□	567	Bryan Trottier, Pgh.	.25	.50
□□□□	568	Grant Ledyard, Dal.	.10	.35
□□□□	569	Keith Brown, Fla.	.10	.35
□□□□	570	Darren Turcotte, Har.	.10	.35
□□□□	571	Patrick Poulin, Chi.	.10	.35
□□□□	572	Jimmy Carson, Van.	.10	.35
□□□□	573	Eric Weinrich, Chi.	.10	.35
□□□□	574	James Patrick, Hfd.	.10	.35
□□□□	575	Bob Beers, Edm.	.10	.35
□□□□	576	Chris Joseph, T.B.	.10	.35
□□□□	577	Bryan Marchment, Hfd.	.10	.35
□□□□	578	Bob Carpenter, N.J.	.10	.35
□□□□	579	Craig Muni, Buf.	.10	.35
□□□□	580	Pat Elynuik, T.B.	.10	.35
□□□□	581	Todd Elik, S.J.	.10	.35
□□□□	582	Doug Brown, Pgh.	.10	.35
□□□□	583	Dave McLlwain, Ott.	.10	.35
□□□□	584	Dave Tippett, Pha.	.10	.35
□□□□	585	Jesse Belanger, Fla.	.10	.35
□□□□	586	Chris Pronger, Hfd.	.35	.75
□□□□	587	Alexandre Daigle, Ott.	.35	.75
□□□□	**588**	**Cam Stewart, Bos., RC**	**.10**	**.35**
□□□□	**589**	**Derek Plante, Buf., RC**	**.25**	**.50**
□□□□	590	Pat Peake, Wsh.	.10	.35
□□□□	**591**	**A. Karpovtsev, NYR., RC**	**.10**	**.35**
□□□□	592	Rob Niedermayer, Fla.	.25	.50
□□□□	**593**	**J. Thibault (G), Que., RC**	**1.50**	**4.00**
□□□□	**594**	**Jason Arnott, Edm., RC**	**1.00**	**3.00**
□□□□	595	Mike Rathje, S.J.	.10	.35
□□□□	596	Chris Gratton, T.B.	.35	.75
□□□□	597	Markus Naslund, Pgh.	.10	.35
□□□□	598	Dmitri Filimonov, Ott.	.10	.35
□□□□	599	Andrei Trefilov (G), Cgy.	.10	.35
□□□□	600	Michal Sykora, S.J.	.10	.35
□□□□	601	Greg Johnson, Det.	.10	.35
□□□□	602	Mikael Renberg, Pha.	.25	.50
□□□□	603	Alexei Yashin, Ott.	.60	2.00
□□□□	**604**	**Damian Rhodes (G), Tor., RC**	**.50**	**1.50**
□□□□	**605**	**Jeff Shantz, Chi., RC**	**.10**	**.35**
□□□□	**606**	**Brent Gretzky, T.B., RC**	**.10**	**.35**
□□□□	**607**	**Boris Mironov, Wpg., RC**	**.10**	**.35**
□□□□	**608**	**Ted Drury, Cgy., RC**	**.10**	**.35**
□□□□	**609**	**Chris Osgood (G), Det., RC**	**2.00**	**5.00**
□□□□	**610**	**Jim Storm, Hfd., RC**	**.10**	**.35**
□□□□	**611**	**Dave Karpa, Que., RC**	**.10**	**.35**
□□□□	**612**	**Stewart Malgunas, Pha., RC**	**.10**	**.35**
□□□□	**613**	**Jason Smith, N.J., RC**	**.10**	**.35**
□□□□	**614**	**German Titov, Cgy., RC**	**.10**	**.35**
□□□□	**615**	**Patrik Carnback, Ana., RC**	**.10**	**.35**
□□□□	**616**	**Jaroslav Modry, N.J., RC**	**.10**	**.35**
□□□□	**617**	**Scott Levins, Ott., RC**	**.10**	**.35**
□□□□	**618**	**F. Brathwaite (G), Edm., RC**	**.10**	**.35**
□□□□	**619**	**Ilya Byakin, Edm., RC**	**.10**	**.35**
□□□□	**620**	**Jarkko Varvio, Dal., RC**	**.10**	**.35**
□□□□	**621**	**Jim Montgomery, Stl., RC**	**.10**	**.35**
□□□□	**622**	**Vesa Viitakoski, Cgy., RC**	**.10**	**.35**
□□□□	**623**	**Alexei Kudashov, Tor., RC**	**.10**	**.35**
□□□□	624	Pavol Demitra, Ott.	.10	.35
□□□□	**625**	**Iain Fraser, Que., RC**	**.10**	**.35**
□□□□	**626**	**Peter Popovic, Mtl., RC**	**.10**	**.35**
□□□□	**627**	**Kirk Maltby, Edm., RC**	**.10**	**.35**
□□□□	**628**	**Garth Snow (G), Que., RC**	**.25**	**.50**
□□□□	**629**	**Peter White, Edm., RC**	**.10**	**.35**
□□□□	**630**	**Mike McKee, Que., RC**	**.10**	**.35**
□□□□	**631**	**Darren McCarty, Det., RC**	**.25**	**.50**
□□□□	**632**	**Pat Neaton, Pgh., RC**	**.10**	**.35**
□□□□	633	Sandy McCarthy, Cgy.	.10	.35
□□□□	634	Pierre Sévigny, Mtl.	.10	.35
□□□□	**635**	**Matt Martin, Tor., RC**	**.10**	**.35**
□□□□	636	John Slaney, Wsh.	.10	.35
□□□□	637	Bob Corkum, Ana.	.10	.35
□□□□	638	Mike Stapleton, Pgh.	.10	.35
□□□□	639	Bill Houlder, Ana.	.10	.35
□□□□	640	Ron Sutter, Que.	.10	.35
□□□□	641	Garry Valk, Ana.	.10	.35
□□□□	642	Greg Hawgood, Fla.	.10	.35
□□□□	643	Bob Bassen, Que.	.10	.35
□□□□	644	Stu Barnes, Fla.	.10	.35
□□□□	645	Fredrik Olausson, Edm.	.10	.35
□□□□	646	Geoff Smith, Fla.	.10	.35
□□□□	647	Mike Foligno, Fla.	.10	.35
□□□□	648	Martin Brodeur (G), N.J.	.75	3.50
□□□□	649	Ryan McGill, Pha.	.10	.35
□□□□	650	Jeff Reese (G), Hfd.	.10	.35
□□□□	651	Mike Sillinger, Det.	.10	.35
□□□□	652	Brent Severyn, Fla.	.10	.35
□□□□	653	Rob Ramage, Pha.	.10	.35
□□□□	654	Dixon Ward, L.A.	.10	.35
□□□□	655	Danton Cole, T.B.	.10	.35
□□□□	656	Vyacheslav Butsayev, S.J.	.10	.35
□□□□	657	Garth Butcher, Que.	.10	.35
□□□□	658	Paul Broten, Dal.	.10	.35
□□□□	659	Steve Duchesne, Stl.	.10	.35
□□□□	660	Trevor Kidd (G), Cgy.	.25	.50
□□□□	661	Travis Green, NYI.	.10	.35
□□□□	662	Wayne Gretzky, L.A. (802)	3.00	18.00

	1994 All-Star	**NRMT-MT**
□	Eric Lindros	40.00

DREAM TEAM

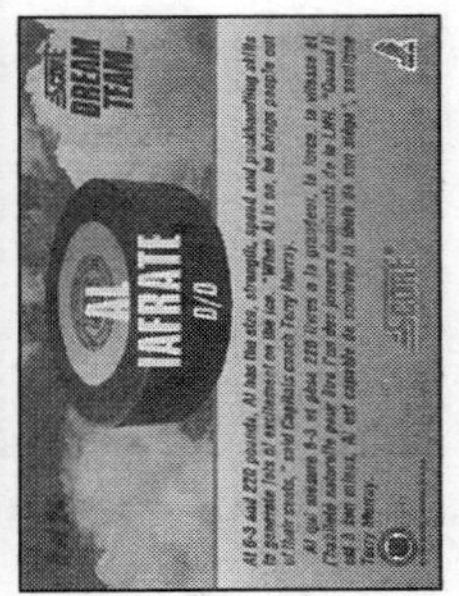

Series One Canadian Insert Set (24 cards): 185.00

	No.	Player	NRMT-MT
□	1	Tom Barrasso (G), Pgh.	3.00
□	2	Patrick Roy (G), Mtl.	25.00
□	3	Chris Chelios, Chi.	6.00
□	4	Al MacInnis, Cgy.	3.00
□	5	Scott Stevens, N.J.	3.00
□	6	Brian Leetch, NYR.	6.00
□	7	Ray Bourque, Bos.	8.00
□	8	Paul Coffey, Det.	3.00
□	9	Al Iafrate, Wsh.	3.00
□	10	Mario Lemieux, Pgh.	25.00
□	11	Wayne Gretzky, L.A.	30.00
□	12	Eric Lindros, Pha.	20.00
□	13	Pat LaFontaine, Buf.	3.00
□	14	Joe Sakic, Que.	12.00

	No.	Player	NRMT-MT
☐	15	Pierre Turgeon, NYI.	3.00
☐	16	Steve Yzerman, Det.	15.00
☐	17	Adam Oates, Bos.	4.00
☐	18	Brett Hull, Stl.	8.00
☐	19	Pavel Bure, Van.	10.00
☐	20	Alexander Mogilny, Buf.	4.00
☐	21	Teemu Selänne, Wpg.	10.00
☐	22	Steve Larmer, Chi.	3.00
☐	23	Kevin Stevens, Pgh.	3.00
☐	24	Luc Robitaille, L.A.	3.00

DYNAMIC DUOS

Series Two Canadian Insert Set (9 cards): 100.00
Series Two American Insert Set (9 cards): 150.00

	No.	Canadian Inserts	NRMT-MT
☐	DD1	D. Gilmour/D. Andreychuk	6.00
☐	DD2	T. Selänne/A. Zhamnov	15.00
☐	DD3	A. Daigle/A. Yashin	6.00
☐	DD4	G. Roberts/J. Nieuwendyk	5.00
☐	DD5	J. Sakic/M. Sundin	25.00
☐	DD6	B. Bellows/K. Muller	5.00
☐	DD7	S. Corson/J. Arnott	6.00
☐	DD8	M. Lemieux/K. Stevens	45.00
☐	DD9	P. Turgeon/D. King	5.00

	No.	American Inserts	NRMT-MT
☐	DD1	M. Recchi/E. Lindros	40.00
☐	DD2	P. LaFontaine/A. Mogilny	6.00
☐	DD3	A. Oates/J. Juneau	6.00
☐	DD4	B. Hull/C. Janney	12.00
☐	DD5	M. Messier/A. Graves	12.00
☐	DD6	J. Roenick/J. Murphy	6.00
☐	DD7	J. Kurri/W. Gretzky	65.00
☐	DD8	S. Makarov/I. Larionov	5.00
☐	DD9	S. Yzerman/S. Fedorov	30.00

THE FRANCHISE

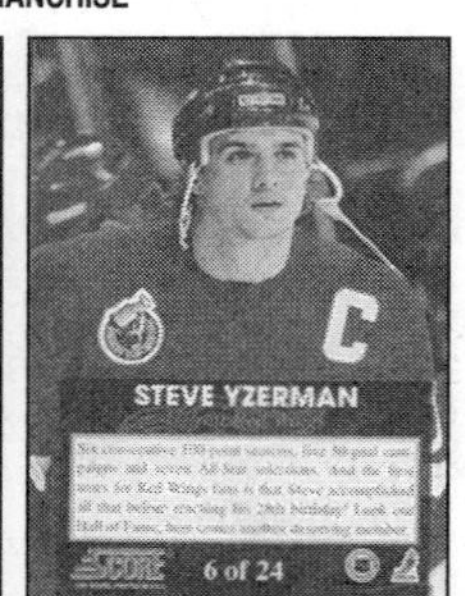

Series One American Insert Set (24 cards): 185.00

	No.	Player	NRMT-MT
☐	1	Ray Bourque, Bos.	8.00
☐	2	Pat LaFontaine, Buf.	4.00
☐	3	Al MacInnis, Cgy.	3.00
☐	4	Jeremy Roenick, Chi.	4.00
☐	5	Mike Modano, Dal.	8.00
☐	6	Steve Yzerman, Det.	15.00
☐	7	Bill Ranford (G), Edm.	3.00
☐	8	Sean Burke (G), Hfd.	3.00
☐	9	Wayne Gretzky, L.A.	30.00
☐	10	Patrick Roy (G), Mtl.	25.00
☐	11	Scott Stevens, N.J.	3.00
☐	12	Pierre Turgeon, NYI.	3.00
☐	13	Brian Leetch, NYR.	4.00
☐	14	Peter Sidorkiewicz (G), Ott.	3.00
☐	15	Eric Lindros, Pha.	20.00
☐	16	Mario Lemieux, Pgh.	25.00
☐	17	Joe Sakic, Que.	12.00
☐	18	Brett Hull, Stl.	8.00
☐	19	Pat Falloon, S.J.	3.00
☐	20	Brian Bradley, T.B.	3.00
☐	21	Doug Gilmour, Tor.	4.00
☐	22	Pavel Bure, Van.	10.00
☐	23	Kevin Hatcher, Wsh.	3.00
☐	24	Teemu Selänne, Wpg.	10.00

44TH ALL-STAR GAME - PINNACLE

These cards have two versions: an American issue and a Canadian issue. Photo variations for the Canadian [CDN] and American [U.S.] series are explained in brackets.

Insert Set (45 cards): 10.00
Redemption Set (46-50): 10.00
Common Player: .20

	No.	Player	NRMT-MT
☐	1	Craig Billington (G) [CDN-Net to his right]	.20
☐	1	Craig Billington (G) [U.S.]	.20
☐	2	Zarley Zalapski [CDN-McDonald's ad.]	.20
☐	2	Zarley Zalapski [U.S.-Molson Canadian ad.]	.20
☐	3	Kevin Lowe [CDN-Coca-Cola ad.]	.20
☐	3	Kevin Lowe [U.S.-XZX: K. Kisio]	.20
☐	4	Scott Stevens [CDN-Blue line visible]	.20
☐	4	Scott Stevens [U.S.-UPS ad.]	.20
☐	5	Pierre Turgeon [CDN-XZX: Z. Zalapski]	.20
☐	5	Pierre Turgeon [U.S.-XZX: Wales bench]	.20
☐	6	Mark Recchi [CDN-Goal crease visible]	.35
☐	6	Mark Recchi [U.S.-Coca-Cola ad.]	.35
☐	7	Kirk Muller [CDN-McDonald's ad.]	.20
☐	7	Kirk Muller [U.S.-XZX: Oates, Recchi & Duchesne]	.20
☐	8	Mike Gartner [CDN-XZX: Wayne Gretzky]	.20
☐	8	Mike Gartner [U.S.-XZX: Bourque, Lowe]	.20
☐	9	Adam Oates [CDN-Kellogg's ad.]	.35
☐	9	Adam Oates [U.S.-Referee visible]	.35
☐	10	Brad Marsh [CDN-Coca-Cola ad.]	.20
☐	10	Brad Marsh [U.S.-Molson Export ad.]	.20
☐	11	Pat LaFontaine [CDN-XZX: Wayne Gretzky]	.20
☐	11	Pat LaFontaine [U.S.-Gillette Sensor ad.]	.20
☐	12	Peter Bondra [CDN-Molson Export ad.]	.35
☐	12	Peter Bondra [U.S.-Molson Canadian ad.]	.35
☐	13	Joe Sakic [CDN-XZX: Campbell bench]	.85
☐	13	Joe Sakic [U.S.]	.85
☐	14	Rick Tocchet [CDN-XZX: P. Housley]	.20
☐	14	Rick Tocchet [U.S.]	.20
☐	15	Kevin Stevens [CDN-XZX: Campbell bench]	.20
☐	15	Kevin Stevens [U.S.-XZX: K. Kisio]	.20
☐	16	Steve Duchesne [CDN-XZX: Wales bench]	.20
☐	16	Steve Duchesne [U.S.-Molson Canadian ad.]	.20
☐	17	Peter Sidorkiewicz (G) [CDN-Net mid-left]	.20
☐	17	Peter Sidorkiewicz (G) [U.S.]	.20
☐	18	Patrick Roy (G) [CDN-Hugging post]	1.50
☐	18	Patrick Roy (G) [U.S.]	1.50
☐	19	Al Iafrate [CDN-XZX: L. Robitaille]	.20
☐	19	Al Iafrate [U.S.-Molson Canadian ad.]	.20
☐	20	Jaromir Jagr [CDN-Sony ad.]	1.00
☐	20	Jaromir Jagr [U.S.-68 mirror image]	1.00
☐	21	Ray Bourque [CDN-McDonald's ad.]	.50
☐	21	Ray Bourque [U.S.-XZX: D. Gilmour]	.50
☐	22	Alexander Mogilny [CDN-XZX: M. Vernon]	.35
☐	22	Alexander Mogilny [U.S.-XZX: S. Chiasson]	.35
☐	23	Steve Chiasson [CDN-XZX: Wales bench]	.20
☐	23	Steve Chiasson [U.S.-McDonald's ad.]	.20
☐	24	Garth Butcher [CDN-Front view]	.20
☐	24	Garth Butcher [U.S.-Esso ad.]	.20
☐	25	Phil Housley [CDN-XZX: M. Gartner]	.20
☐	25	Phil Housley [U.S.-XZX: A. Mogilny]	.20
☐	26	Chris Chelios [CDN-XZX: J. Jagr]	.35
☐	26	Chris Chelios [U.S.-Coca-Cola ad.]	.35
☐	27	Randy Carlyle [CDN-Photo from ankles up]	.20
☐	27	Randy Carlyle [U.S.-Photo from skates up]	.20
☐	28	Mike Modano [CDN-McDonald's ad.]	.50
☐	28	Mike Modano [U.S.]	.50
☐	29	Gary Roberts [CDN-Molson Export ad.]	.20
☐	29	Gary Roberts [U.S.-McDonald's ad.]	.20
☐	30	Kelly Kisio [CDN-Coca-Cola ad.]	.20
☐	30	Kelly Kisio [U.S.-XZX: Wayne Gretzky]	.20
☐	31	Pavel Bure [CDN-Glidden ad.]	.75
☐	31	Pavel Bure [U.S.-XZX: A. Iafrate]	.75
☐	32	Teemu Selänne [CDN-Someone's stick blade]	.75
☐	32	Teemu Selänne [U.S.]	.75
☐	33	Brian Bradley [CDN-McDonald's ad.]	.20
☐	33	Brian Bradley [U.S.-XZX: Robitaille, Selänne, Roenick]	.20
☐	34	Brett Hull [CDN-UPS ad.]	.50
☐	34	Brett Hull [U.S]	.50
☐	35	Jari Kurri [CDN-UPS ad.]	.20
☐	35	Jari Kurri [U.S.]	.20
☐	36	Steve Yzerman [CDN-Esso ad.]	1.00
☐	36	Steve Yzerman [U.S.-XZX: M.Gartner]	1.00
☐	37	Luc Robitaille [CDN-XZX: P. Sidorkiewicz]	.20
☐	37	Luc Robitaille [U.S.-Esso ad.]	.20
☐	38	Dave Manson [CDN-Kellogg's ad.]	.20
☐	38	Dave Manson [U.S.]	.20
☐	39	Jeremy Roenick [CDN-Gillette ad.]	.20
☐	39	Jeremy Roenick [U.S.-Open ice]	.20
☐	40	Mike Vernon (G) [CDN-Molson Export ad.]	.20
☐	40	Mike Vernon (G) [U.S.]	.20
☐	41	Jon Casey (G) [CDN-Coca-Cola ad.]	.20
☐	41	Jon Casey (G) [U.S.-Esso ad.]	.20
☐	42	Ed Belfour (G) [CDN-Photo from pads up]	.35
☐	42	Ed Belfour (G) [U.S.-Canadian stick]	.35
☐	43	Paul Coffey [CDN-Photo from skates up]	.20
☐	43	Paul Coffey [U.S.-Photo from ankles up]	.20
☐	44	Doug Gilmour [CDN-Opponent's skates]	.35
☐	44	Doug Gilmour [U.S.-Esso ad.]	.35
☐	45	Wayne Gretzky [CDN-XZX: J. Sakic]	2.00
☐	45	Wayne Gretzky [U.S.]	2.00
☐☐	46	Mike Gartner, NYR. [Esso ad.]	2.00
☐☐	47	Al Iafrate, Wsh. [Coca-Cola ad.]	1.50
☐☐	48	Ray Bourque, Bos.	4.00
☐☐	49	Jon Casey (G), Bos.	1.50
☐☐	50	Teemu Selänne/ Brian Bradley [XCY: J.Roenick]	2.00

INTERNATIONAL STARS

These cards have two versions: an American issue and a Canadian issue.

Insert Set (22 cards): 40.00

	No.	Player	NRMT-MT
☐☐	1	Pavel Bure, Van.	7.00
☐☐	2	Teemu Selänne, Wpg.	7.00
☐☐	3	Sergei Fedorov, Det.	5.00
☐☐	4	Peter Bondra, Wsh.	4.00
☐☐	5	Tommy Söderström (G), NYI.	.75
☐☐	6	Robert Reichel, Cgy.	.75
☐☐	7	Jari Kurri, L.A.	1.50
☐☐	8	Alexander Mogilny, Buf.	2.00
☐☐	9	Jaromir Jagr, Pgh.	10.00
☐☐	10	Mats Sundin, Que.	5.00
☐☐	11	Uwe Krupp, NYI.	.75
☐☐	12	Nikolai Borschevsky, Tor.	.75
☐☐	13	Ulf Dahlen, Min.	.75
☐☐	14	Alexander Semak, N.J.	.75
☐☐	15	Michal Pivonka, Wsh.	.75
☐☐	16	Sergei Nemchinov, NYR.	.75
☐☐	17	Darius Kasparaitis, NYI.	.75
☐☐	18	Sandis Ozolinsh, S.J.	1.50
☐☐	19	Alexei Kovalev, NYR.	.75
☐☐	20	Dimitri Khristich, Wsh.	.75
☐☐	21	Tomas Sandström, L.A.	.75
☐☐	22	Petr Nedved, Van.	.75

1993 - 94 SEASON'S ACTION PATCHES

Patch Size: 3 1/8" x 4 3/8"
Imprint: (on packaging) SEASONS TM/MC
Complete Set (20 patches): 70.00

	No.	Player	NRMT-MT
☐	1	Ed Belfour (G), Chi.	2.00
☐	2	Pavel Bure, Van.	3.50
☐	3	Paul Coffey, Det.	2.00
☐	4	Doug Gilmour, Tor.	2.00
☐	5	Wayne Gretzky, L.A.	10.00
☐	6	Brett Hull, Stl.	2.50
☐	7	Jaromir Jagr, Pgh.	5.00
☐	8	Joé Juneau, Bos.	1.50
☐	9	Mario Lemieux, Pgh.	8.00
☐	10	Eric Lindros, Pha.	6.50

	No.	Player	Price
☐	11	Shawn McEachern, Pgh.	1.50
☐	12	Alexander Mogilny, Buf.	2.00
☐	13	Adam Oates, Bos.	2.00
☐	14	Félix Potvin (G), Tor.	3.00
☐	15	Jeremy Roenick, Chi.	2.00
☐	16	Patrick Roy (G), Mtl.	8.00
☐	17	Joe Sakic, Que.	4.50
☐	18	Teemu Selänne, Wpg.	3.50
☐	19	Kevin Stevens, Pgh.	1.50
☐	20	Steve Yzerman, Det.	5.00

1993 - 94 SISU (FINNISH SM-LIIGA)

Imprint: © 1993 Leaf
Complete Set (396 cards): 40.00
Common Player: .20

	No.	Player	NRMT-MT
☐	1	Jokerit Helsinki Logo	.20
☐	2	Alpo Suhonen, Coach, Jokerit	.20
☐	3	Ari Sulander (G), Jokerit	.50
☐	4	Marko Rantanen, Jokerit	.20
☐	5	Ari Salo, Jokerit	.20
☐	6	Kalle Koskinen, Jokerit	.20
☐	7	Sebastian Sulku, Jokerit	.20
☐	8	Waltteri Immonen, Jokerit	.20
☐	9	Mika Strömberg, Jokerit	.20
☐	10	Heikki Riihijärvi, Jokerit	.20
☐	11	Kari Martikainen, Jokerit	.20
☐	12	Erik Hämäläinen, Jokerit	.20
☐	13	Juha Jokiharju, Jokerit	.20
☐	14	Timo Norppa, Jokerit	.20
☐	15	Rami Koivisto, Jokerit	.20
☐	16	Antti Törmänen, Jokerit	.35
☐	17	Keijo Säilynoja, Jokerit	.20
☐	18	Jere Keskinen, Jokerit	.20
☐	19	Jali Wahlsten, Jokerit	.20
☐	20	Mikko Konttila, Jokerit	.20
☐	21	Juha Ylönen, Jokerit	.20
☐	22	Jussi Veinonen, Jokerit	.20
☐	23	Petri Varis, Jokerit	.20
☐	24	Juha Lind, Jokerit	.20
☐	25	Timo Saarikoski, Jokerit	.20
☐	26	Otakar Janecky, Jokerit	.20
☐	27	TPS Turku Logo	.20
☐	28	Vladimir Yursinov, Coach, TPS	.20
☐	29	Juoni Rokama (G), TPS	.25
☐	30	Kimmo Lecklin, TPS	.20
☐	31	Jouko Narvanmaa, TPS	.20
☐	32	Petteri Nummelin, TPS	.20
☐	33	Erik Kakko, TPS	.20
☐	34	Tom Koivisto, TPS	.20
☐	35	Marko Kiprusoff, TPS	.25
☐	36	Kari Harila, TPS	.20
☐	37	Hannu Virta, TPS	.20
☐	38	Aki Berg, TPS	2.00
☐	39	Alexander Smirnov, TPS	.20
☐	40	Esa Keskinen, TPS	.20
☐	41	Saku Koivu, TPS	10.00
☐	42	Jukka Vilander, TPS	.20
☐	43	Antti Aalto, TPS	.20
☐	44	Mika Karapuu, TPS	.20
☐	45	Toni Sihvonen, TPS	.20
☐	46	Pavel Torgajev, TPS	.20
☐	47	Jere Lehtinen, TPS	4.00
☐	48	Kai Nurminen, TPS	.20
☐	49	Harri Sillgren, TPS	.20
☐	50	Niko Mikkola, TPS	.20
☐	51	Ari Vuori, TPS	.20
☐	52	Lasse Pirjetä, TPS	.20
☐	53	Reijo Mikkolainen, TPS	.20
☐	54	Marko Jantunen, TPS	.20
☐	55	Mikko Virolainen, TPS	.20
☐	56	Tappara Tampere Logo	.20
☐	57	Boris Majorov, Coach, Tappara	.20
☐	58	Jaromir Sindel (G), Tappara	.25
☐	59	Timo Hankela (G), Tappara	.25
☐	60	Teemu Kivinen, Tappara	.20
☐	61	Petri Kalteva, Tappara	.20
☐	62	Jari Harjumäki, Tappara	.20
☐	63	Timo Jutila, Tappara	.25
☐	64	Janne Grönvall, Tappara	.20
☐	65	Jari Grönstand, Tappara	.20
☐	66	Pekka Laksola, Tappara	.20
☐	67	Tommi Haapsaari, Tappara	.20
☐	68	Veli-Pekka Kautonen, Tappara	.20
☐	69	Mikko Peltola, Tappara	.20
☐	70	Kari Heikkinen, Tappara	.20
☐	71	Teemu Numminen, Tappara	.20
☐	72	Jiri Kucera, Tappara	.20
☐	73	Pauli Järvinen, Tappara	.20
☐	74	Pasi Forsberg, Tappara	.20
☐	75	Tero Toivola, Tappara	.20
☐	76	Ari Haanpää, Tappara	.20
☐	77	Tommi Pohja, Tappara	.20
☐	78	Samuli Rautio, Tappara	.20
☐	79	Markus Oijennus, Tappara	.20
☐	80	Petri Aaltonen, Tappara	.20
☐	81	HIFK, Helsinki Logo	.20
☐	82	Harri Rindell, Coach, HIFK	.20
☐	83	Sakari Lindfors (G), HIFK	.25
☐	84	Mikael Granlund (G), HIFK	.25
☐	85	Kimmo Hyttinen, HIFK	.20
☐	86	Jere Karalahti, HIFK	.20
☐	87	Dan Lambert, HIFK	.25
☐	88	Simo Saarinen, HIFK	.20
☐	89	Pasi Sormunen, HIFK	.20
☐	90	Tommi Hämäläinen, HIFK	.20
☐	91	Pertti Lehtonen, HIFK	.20
☐	92	Jari Munck, HIFK	.20
☐	93	Kai Tervonen, HIFK	.20
☐	94	Kim Ahlroos, HIFK	.20
☐	95	Teppo Kivelä, HIFK	.20
☐	96	Darren Boyko, HIFK	.25
☐	97	Pekka Peltola, HIFK	.20
☐	98	Marco Poulsen, HIFK	.20
☐	99	Valeri Krykov, HIFK	.20
☐	100	Jari Laukkanen, HIFK	.20
☐	101	Ville Peltonen, HIFK	.20
☐	102	Pekka Tuomisto, HIFK	.20
☐	103	Miro Haapaniemi, HIFK	.20
☐	104	Mika Kortelainen, HIFK	.20
☐	105	Marko Ojanen, HIFK	.20
☐	106	Iiro Järvi, HIFK	.20
☐	107	Ilves Tampere Logo	.20
☐	108	Jukka Jalonen, Coach, Ilves	.20
☐	109	Jukka Tammi (G), Ilves	.25
☐	110	Mika Manninen (G), Ilves	.25
☐	111	Jani Nikko, Ilves	.20
☐	112	Jukka Ollila, Ilves	.20
☐	113	Juha Lampinen, Ilves	.20
☐	114	Hannu Henriksson, Ilves	.20
☐	115	Sami Lehtonen, Ilves	.20
☐	116	Mikko Niemi, Ilves	.20
☐	117	Juha-Matti Märijärvi, Ilves	.20
☐	118	Jarkko Glad, Ilves	.20
☐	119	Allan Measures, Ilves	.20
☐	120	Mikko Luovi, Ilves	.20
☐	121	Risto Jalo, Ilves	.20
☐	122	Juha Järvenpää, Ilves	.20
☐	123	Jarno Peltonen, Ilves	.20
☐	124	Matti Kaipainen, Ilves	.20
☐	125	Timo Peltomaa, Ilves	.20
☐	126	Esa Tommila, Ilves	.20
☐	127	Hannu Mattila, Ilves	.20
☐	128	Jari Neuvonen, Ilves	.20
☐	129	Pasi Määttänen, Ilves	.20
☐	130	Juha Hautamaa, Ilves	.20
☐	131	Janne Seva, Ilves	.20
☐	132	Sami Ahlberg, Ilves	.20
☐	133	Jari Virtanen, Ilves	.20
☐	134	JyP HT Jyväskylä Logo	.20
☐	135	Kari Savolainen, Coach, JyP HT	.20
☐	136	Ari-Pekka Siekkinen (G), JyP HT	.25
☐	137	Marko Leinonen (G), JyP HT	.25
☐	138	Jan Latvala, JyP HT	.20
☐	139	Markku Heikkinen, JyP HT	.20
☐	140	Jarmo Jokilahti, JyP HT	.20
☐	141	Veli-Pekka Härd, JyP HT	.20
☐	142	Kalle Koskinen, JyP HT	.20
☐	143	Vesa Ponto, JyP HT	.20
☐	144	Petri Kujala, JyP HT	.20
☐	145	Jarmo Rantanen, JyP HT	.20
☐	146	Harri Laurila, JyP HT	.20
☐	147	Lasse Nieminen, JyP HT	.20
☐	148	Mika Paananen, JyP HT	.20
☐	149	Mika Arvaja, JyP HT	.20
☐	150	Marko Virtanen, JyP HT	.20
☐	151	Marko Ek, JyP HT	.20
☐	152	Joni Lius, JyP HT	.20
☐	153	Teemu Kohvakka, JyP HT	.20
☐	154	Jari Lindroos, JyP HT	.20
☐	155	Marko Kupari, JyP HT	.20
☐	156	Markku Ikonen, JyP HT	.20
☐	157	Jyrki Jokinen, JyP HT	.20
☐	158	Risto Kurkinen, JyP HT	.20
☐	159	KalPa Logo	.20
☐	160	Hannu Kapanen, Coach, KalPa	.20
☐	161	Pasi Kuivalainen (G), KalPa	.25
☐	162	Kimmo Kapanen, KalPa	.20
☐	163	Kimmo Timonen, KalPa	.20
☐	164	Jari Järvinen, KalPa	.20
☐	165	Mikko Tavi, KalPa	.20
☐	166	Jermu Pisto, KalPa	.20
☐	167	Antti Tuomenoksa, KalPa	.20
☐	168	Vesa Ruotsalainen, KalPa	.50
☐	169	Vesa Salo, KalPa	.20
☐	170	Veli-Pekka Pekkarinen, KalPa	.20
☐	171	Tuomas Kalliomäki, KalPa	.20
☐	172	Dimitri Zinine, KalPa	.20
☐	173	Jani Rautio, KalPa	.20
☐	174	Janne Kekäläinen, KalPa	.20
☐	175	Arto Sirviö, KalPa	.20
☐	176	Sami Mettovaara, KalPa	.20
☐	177	Sami Simonen, KalPa	.20
☐	178	Pekka Tirkkonen, KalPa	.20
☐	179	Sami Kapanen, KalPa	.20
☐	180	Jussi Tarvainen, KalPa	.20
☐	181	Lukko Logo	.20
☐	182	Vaclav Sykora, Coach, Kukko	.50
☐	183	Jarmo Myllys (G), Kukko	.50
☐	184	Kimmo Vesa (G), Kukko	.25
☐	185	Mika Yli-Mäenpää, Kukko	.20
☐	186	Jarmo Kuusisto, Kukko	.20
☐	187	Marko Tuulola, Kukko	.20
☐	188	Tuomas Grönman, Kukko	.25
☐	189	Timo Kulonen, Kukko	.20
☐	190	Kari-Pekka Friman, Kukko	.20
☐	191	Pasi Huura, Kukko	.20
☐	192	Harri Suvanto, Kukko	.20
☐	193	Kamil Kastak, Kukko	.20
☐	194	Jari Torkki, Kukko	.20
☐	195	Kalle Sahlstedt, Kukko	.20
☐	196	Tommi Pullola, Kukko	.20
☐	197	Mika Välilä, Kukko	.20
☐	198	Tero Arkiomaa, Kukko	.20
☐	199	Pasi Saarela, Kukko	.20
☐	200	Matti Forss, Kukko	.20
☐	201	Jussi Kiuru, Kukko	.20
☐	202	Mika Alatalo, Kukko	.20
☐	203	Kimmo Rintanen, Kukko	.20
☐	204	Petri Lätti, Kukko	.20
☐	205	Petr Korinek, Kukko	.20
☐	206	Assat Pori Logo	.20
☐	207	Veli-Pekka Ketola, Coach, Assat Pori	.35
☐	208	Kari Takko (G), Assat Pori	.35
☐	209	Timo Järvinen (G), Assat Pori	.25
☐	210	Marko Sten, Assat Pori	.20
☐	211	Pasi Peltonen, Assat Pori	.20
☐	212	Olli Kaski, Assat Pori	.20
☐	213	Jarno Miikkulainen, Assat Pori	.20
☐	214	Juoni Vento, Assat Pori	.20
☐	215	Karri Kivi, Assat Pori	.20
☐	216	Stanislav Meciar, Assat Pori	.20
☐	217	Nemo Nokkosmäki, Assat Pori	.20
☐	218	Arto Javanainen, Assat Pori	.20
☐	219	Janne Virtanen, Assat Pori	.20
☐	220	Vjatseslav Fandul, Assat Pori	.20
☐	221	Jari Levonen, Assat Pori	.20
☐	222	Jarno Levonen, Assat Pori	.20

	No.	Player	Price
☐	223	Jari Korpisalo, Assat Pori	.20
☐	224	Jokke Heinänen, Assat Pori	.20
☐	225	Harri Lönnberg, Assat Pori	.20
☐	226	Ari Saarinen, Assat Pori	.20
☐	227	Kari Syväsalmi, Assat Pori	.20
☐	228	Jarno Mäkelä, Assat Pori	.20
☐	229	Rauli Raitanen, Assat Pori	.20
☐	230	Arto Heiskanen, Assat Pori	.20
☐	231	Mikael Kotkaniemi, Assat Pori	.20
☐	232	HPK Hämeenlinna Logo	.25
☐	233	Pentti Matikainen, Coach, HPK	.20
☐	234	Kari Rosenberg (G), HPK	.25
☐	235	Petri Vilen (G), HPK	.25
☐	236	Marko Allen, HPK	.20
☐	237	Mikko Myllykoski, HPK	.20
☐	238	Kim Vähänen, HPK	.20
☐	239	Janne Laukkanen, HPK	.20
☐	240	Jari Haapamäki, HPK	.20
☐	241	Niko Marttila, HPK	.20
☐	242	Esa Sateri, HPK	.20
☐	243	Toni Virta, HPK	.20
☐	244	Marko Palo, HPK	.20
☐	245	Markku Piikkilä, HPK	.20
☐	246	Jani Hassinen, HPK	.20
☐	247	Jarkko Nikander, HPK	.20
☐	248	Pasi Kivilä, HPK	.20
☐	249	Mika Lartama, HPK	.20
☐	250	Tomas Kapusta, HPK	.20
☐	251	Tommi Varjonen, HPK	.20
☐	252	Teemu Tamminen, HPK	.20
☐	253	Jukka Seppo, HPK	.20
☐	254	Kiekko-Espoo Logo	.20
☐	255	Martti Merra, Coach, Kiekko-Espoo	.20
☐	256	Scott Brower (G), Kiekko-Espoo	.25
☐	257	Timo Mäki (G), Kiekko-Espoo	.25
☐	258	Petri Pulkkinen, Kiekko-Espoo	.20
☐	259	Robert Salo, Kiekko-Espoo	.20
☐	260	Sami Nuutinen, Kiekko-Espoo	.20
☐	261	Teemu Sillanpää, Kiekko-Espoo	.20
☐	262	Marko Halonen, Kiekko-Espoo	.20
☐	263	Jimi Helin, Kiekko-Espoo	.20
☐	264	Kari Haakana, Kiekko-Espoo	.20
☐	265	Jukka Tiilikainen, Kiekko-Espoo	.20
☐	266	Jan Långbacka, Kiekko-Espoo	.20
☐	267	Jarmo Muukkonen, Kiekko-Espoo	.20
☐	268	Timo Hirvonen, Kiekko-Espoo	.20
☐	269	Pasi Heinistö, Kiekko-Espoo	.20
☐	270	Kimmo Maki-Kokkila, Kiekko-Espoo	.20
☐	271	Mikko Lempiäinen, Kiekko-Espoo	.20
☐	272	Tero Lehterä, Kiekko-Espoo	.40
☐	273	Hannu Järvenpää, Kiekko-Espoo	.75
☐	274	Riku Kuusisto, Kiekko-Espoo	.20
☐	275	Mikko Halonen, Kiekko-Espoo	.20
☐	276	Markku Takala, Kiekko-Espoo	.20
☐	277	Petro Koivunen, Kiekko-Espoo	.20
☐	278	Reipas Lahti Logo	.20
☐	279	Kari Mäkinen, Coach, Reipas Lahti	.20
☐	280	Oldrich Svoboda (G), Reipas Lahti	.25
☐	281	Pekka Ilmivalta (G), Reipas Lahti	.25
☐	282	Matti Vuorio, Reipas Lahti	.20
☐	283	Jari Parviainen, Reipas Lahti	.20
☐	284	Timo Kahelin, Reipas Lahti	.20
☐	285	Ville Skinnari, Reipas Lahti	.20
☐	286	Petri Koski, Reipas Lahti	.20
☐	287	Jarkko Hämäläinen, Reipas Lahti	.20
☐	288	Pasi Ruponen, Reipas Lahti	.20
☐	289	Oldrich Valek, Reipas Lahti	.20
☐	290	Juha Nurminen, Reipas Lahti	.20
☐	291	Erkki Laine, Reipas Lahti	.20
☐	292	Sami Lekkerimaki, Reipas Lahti	.20
☐	293	Tommy Kiviaho, Reipas Lahti	.20
☐	294	Jyrki Poikolainen, Reipas Lahti	.20
☐	295	Sami Wikström, Reipas Lahti	.20
☐	296	Jonni Vauhkonen, Reipas Lahti	.20
☐	297	Erkki Mäkelä, Reipas Lahti	.20
☐	298	Jani Uski, Reipas Lahti	.20
☐	299	Jari Multanen, Reipas Lahti	.20
☐	300	Toni Koivunen, Reipas Lahti	.20
☐	301	Runkosarjan 1. Kierros	.20
☐	302	Runkosarjan 2. Kierros	.20
☐	303	Runkosarjan 3. Kierros	.20
☐	304	Runkosarjan 4. Kierros	.20
☐	305	Runkosarjan 5. Kierros	.20
☐	306	Runkosarjan 6. Kierros	.20
☐	307	Runkosarjan 7. Kierros	.20
☐	308	Runkosarjan 8. Kierros	.20
☐	309	Runkosarjan 9. Kierros	.20
☐	310	Runkosarjan 10. Kierros	.20
☐	311	Runkosarjan 11. Kierros	.20
☐	312	Runkosarjan 12. Kierros	.20
☐	313	Runkosarjan 13. Kierros	.20
☐	314	Runkosarjan 14. Kierros	.20
☐	315	Runkosarjan 15. Kierros	.20
☐	316	Runkosarjan 16. Kierros	.20
☐	317	Runkosarjan 17. Kierros	.20
☐	318	Runkosarjan 18. Kierros	.20
☐	319	Runkosarjan 19. Kierros	.20
☐	320	Runkosarjan 20. Kierros	.20
☐	321	Runkosarjan 21. Kierros	.20
☐	322	Runkosarjan 22. Kierros	.20
☐	323	Runkosarjan 23. Kierros	.20
☐	324	Runkosarjan 24. Kierros	.20
☐	325	Runkosarjan 25. Kierros	.20
☐	326	Runkosarjan 26. Kierros	.20
☐	327	Runkosarjan 27. Kierros	.20
☐	328	Runkosarjan 28. Kierros	.20
☐	329	Runkosarjan 29. Kierros	.20
☐	330	Runkosarjan 30. Kierros	.20
☐	331	Runkosarjan 31. Kierros	.20
☐	332	Runkosarjan 32. Kierros	.20
☐	333	Runkosarjan 33. Kierros	.20
☐	334	Runkosarjan 34. Kierros	.20
☐	335	Runkosarjan 35. Kierros	.20
☐	336	Runkosarjan 36. Kierros	.20
☐	337	Runkosarjan 37. Kierros	.20
☐	338	Runkosarjan 38. Kierros	.20
☐	339	Runkosarjan 39. Kierros	.20
☐	340	Runkosarjan 40. Kierros	.20
☐	341	Runkosarjan 41. Kierros	.20
☐	342	Runkosarjan 42. Kierros	.20
☐	343	Runkosarjan 43. Kierros	.20
☐	344	Runkosarjan 44. Kierros	.20
☐	345	Paikallisottelut 1.	.20
☐	346	Paikallisottelut 2.	.20
☐	347	Paikallisottelut 3.	.20
☐	348	Paikallisottelut 4.	.20
☐	349	Puoliväleria HPK - Lukko	.20
☐	350	Puoliväleria Jokerit - éssät	.20
☐	351	Puoliväleria Jokerit - éssät	.20
☐	352	Puoliväleria TPS - Ilves	.20
☐	353	Väleriä HPK - JyP HT	.20
☐	354	Väleriä TPS - éssät	.20
☐	355	Pronssiottelu	.20
☐	356	Finaali	.20
☐	357	Finaali	.20
☐	358	Finaali	.20
☐	359	Finaali	.20
☐	360	Most Points - Esa Keskinen	.20
☐	361	Most goals - Tomas Kapusta	.20
☐	362	+/- Leader - Erik Hamalainen	.20
☐	363	Penalty minutes - Brian Tutt	.20
☐	364	Otakar Janecky	.20
☐	365	Ville Peltonen	.20
☐	366	AS: Petr Briza (G)	.20
☐	367	AS: Janne Laukkanen	.35
☐	368	AS: Timo Jutila	.35
☐	369	AS: Juha Riihijarvi	.25
☐	370	AS: Esa Keskinen	.25
☐	371	AS: Jarkko Varvio	.75
☐	372	Esa Keskinen	.20
☐	373	Vladimir Yursinov	.20
☐	374	Erik Hämäläinen	.20
☐	375	Timo Lehkonen (G)	.20
☐	376	German Titov	.50
☐	377	Raimo Summanen	.20
☐	378	Mikko Haapakoski	.20
☐	379	Marko Palo	.20
☐	380	Seppo Mäkelä, Referee	.20
☐	381	TPS Turku Team Card	.20
☐	382	HPK Hämeenlinna	.20
☐	383	JyP HT Jyväskylä	.20
☐	384	Juha Riihijärvi	.20
☐	385	Jukka Virtanen	.20
☐	386	Kari Jalonen	.20
☐	387	Matti Forss	.20
☐	388	Arto Javanainen	.20
☐	389	Saku Koivu	5.00
☐	390	Janne Niinimaa	4.00
☐	391	Ville Peltonen	.50
☐	392	Jonni Vauhkonen	.20
☐	393	Petri Varis	.20
☐	394	Antti Aalto	.25
☐	395	Jere Karalaht	.20
☐	396	Kimmo Timonen	.25

1993 - 94 SLAPSHOT TEAM SETS

These team sets were released between November, 1993 and February, 1994. 3,000 sets were issued for each team (except the Greyhounds with 3,400). Numbered uncut sheets were also available or every team except for the Wolves.

Imprint:

PROMOTIONAL CARD

	Player	NRMT-MT
☐	Trevor Gallant	1.00

DETROIT JR. RED WINGS

Complete Set (25 cards): 15.00

	No.	Player		No.	Player
☐	1	Todd Harvey	☐	2	Jason Saal (G)
☐	3	Aaron Ellis (G)	☐	4	Chris Mailloux (G)
☐	5	Robin Lacour	☐	6	Mike Rucinski
☐	7	Eric Cairns	☐	8	Matt Ball
☐	9	Dale Junkin	☐	10	Bill McCauley
☐	11	Jeremy Meehan	☐	12	Mike Harding
☐	13	Brad Cook	☐	14	Jeff Mitchell
☐	15	Jamie Allison	☐	16	Dan Pawlaczyk
☐	17	Kevin Brown	☐	18	Duane Harmer
☐	19	Gerry Skrypec	☐	20	Shayne McCosh
☐	21	Sean Haggerty	☐	22	Nic Beaudoin
☐	23	Paul Maurice, Coach	☐	24	Pete DeBoer, A. Coach
☐	25	Bob Wren			

LES VOLTIGEURS DE DRUMMONDVILLE

Complete Set (28 cards): 10.00

	No.	Player		No.	Player
☐	1	Checklist	☐	2	Stéphane Routhier (G)
☐	3	Yannick Gagnon (G)	☐	4	Sébastien Bety
☐	5	Martin Latulippe	☐	6	Nicolas Savage
☐	7	Sylvain Ducharme	☐	8	Yan St. Pierre
☐	9	Emmanuel Labranche	☐	10	Ian Laperrière
☐	11	Louis Bernard	☐	12	Stéphane St Amour
☐	13	Vincent Tremblay	☐	14	Denis Gauthier
☐	15	Eric Plante	☐	16	Christian Marcoux
☐	17	Patrice Charbonneau	☐	18	Raymond Delarosbil
☐	19	Patrick Livernoche	☐	20	Luc Decelles
☐	21	François Sasseville	☐	22	Steve Tardif
☐	23	Mathieu Sunderland	☐	24	Alexandre Duchesne
☐	25	Jean Hamel, Head Trainer	☐	26	Mario Carrier, A.Trainer
☐	27	André Lepage, Trainer	☐	28	Slapshot Calender

GUELPH STORM

Complete Set (30 cards): 12.00

	No.	Player		No.	Player
☐	1	Title Card	☐	2	Jeff O'Neill
☐	3	Mark McArthur (G)	☐	4	Kayle Short
☐	5	Ryan Risidore	☐	6	Mike Rusk
☐	7	Regan Stocco	☐	8	Duane Harmer
☐	9	Sylvain Cloutier	☐	10	Eric Landry
☐	11	Jamie Wright	☐	12	Todd Norman
☐	13	Mike Pittman	☐	14	Ken Belanger
☐	15	Viktor Reuta	☐	16	Mike Prokopec
☐	17	Jeff Williams	☐	18	Chris Skoryna
☐	19	Stéphane Lefebvre	☐	20	Jeff Cowan
☐	21	Murray Hogg	☐	22	Andy Adams (G)
☐	23	Todd Bertuzzi	☐	24	Grant Pritchett
☐	25	Rumun Ndur	☐	26	Jeff O'Neill
☐	27	Paul Brydges, A Coach	☐	28	John Lovell, Coach

☐ 29	Team Picture	☐ 30	Domino's Pizza

KINGSTON FRONTENACS

Complete Set (24 cards): 10.00

No.	Player	No.	Player
☐ 1	Greg Lovell (G)	☐ 2	Marc Lamothe (G)
☐ 3	T. J. Moss (G)	☐ 4	Marc Moro
☐ 5	Trevor Doyle	☐ 6	Jeff Dacosta
☐ 7	Gord Walsh	☐ 8	Brian Scott
☐ 9	Jason Disher	☐ 10	Alexander Zhurik
☐ 11	Ken Boone	☐ 12	Cail Maclean
☐ 13	Bill Marandiuk	☐ 14	Martin Sychra
☐ 15	Duncan Fader	☐ 16	David Ling
☐ 17	Chad Kilger	☐ 18	Greg Kraemer
☐ 19	Trent Cull	☐ 20	Steve Parson
☐ 21	Craig Rivet	☐ 22	Keli Corpse
☐ 23	Brett Lindros	☐ 24	D. Allison/ M. Allison

KITCHENER RANGERS

Complete Set (30 cards): 10.00

No.	Player	No.	Player
☐ 1	Checklist	☐ 2	David Belitski (G)
☐ 3	Darryl Whyte (G)	☐ 4	Greg McLean
☐ 5	Jason Hughes	☐ 6	Gord Dickie
☐ 7	Travis Riggin	☐ 8	Norm Dezainde
☐ 9	Tim Spitzig	☐ 10	Trevor Gallant
☐ 11	Chris Pittman	☐ 12	Ryan Pawluk
☐ 13	Jason Morgan	☐ 14	James Boyd
☐ 15	Todd Warriner	☐ 16	Mark Donahue
☐ 17	Peter Brearley	☐ 18	Andrew Taylor
☐ 19	Jason Gladney	☐ 20	Wes Swinson
☐ 21	Matt O'Dette	☐ 22	Darren Schmidt
☐ 23	Jason Johnson	☐ 24	Eric Manlow
☐ 25	Jeff Lillie (G)	☐ 26	Sergei Olympiev
☐ 27	Joe McDonnell, Coach	☐ 28	Rick Chambers, Trainer
☐ 29	Taylor/ Riggin/ Belitski	☐ 30	Domino's Pizza

NIAGARA FALLS THUNDER

Complete Set (28 cards): 10.00

No.	Player	No.	Player
☐ 1	Checklist	☐ 2	Jimmy Hibbert (G)
☐ 3	Darryl Foster (G)	☐ 4	Gerry Skrypec
☐ 5	Greg de Vries	☐ 6	Tim Thompson
☐ 7	Joel Yates	☐ 8	Yianni Loannou
☐ 9	Steve Nimigon	☐ 10	Jeff Johnstone
☐ 11	Brandon Convery	☐ 12	Dale Junkin
☐ 13	Ethan Moreau	☐ 14	Derek Grant
☐ 15	Neil Fewster	☐ 16	Jason Reesor
☐ 17	Tom Moores	☐ 18	Matthew Mayo
☐ 19	Bogdon Savenko	☐ 20	Corey Bricknell
☐ 21	Derek Sylvester	☐ 22	Anatoli Filatov
☐ 23	Jason Bonsignore	☐ 24	Mike Perna
☐ 25	Manny Legacé (G)	☐ 26	Randy Hall, Coach/GM
☐ 27	Chris Johnstone, A.G.M.	☐ 28	Bonsignore/Moreau/Convery

NORTH BAY CENTENNIALS

Complete Set (25 cards): 10.00

No.	Player	No.	Player
☐ 1	Brad Brown	☐ 2	Sandy Allan (G)
☐ 3	Rob Lave	☐ 4	Steve McLaren
☐ 5	Andy Delmore	☐ 6	Corey Neilson
☐ 7	Jason Campeau	☐ 8	Jim Ensom
☐ 9	Bill Lang	☐ 10	Ryan Gillis
☐ 11	Michael Burman	☐ 12	Stefan Rivard
☐ 13	B. J. MacPherson	☐ 14	Lee Jinman
☐ 15	Scott Cherrey	☐ 16	Damien Bloye
☐ 17	Denis Gaudet	☐ 18	Bob Thornton
☐ 19	John Guirestante	☐ 20	Jeff Shevalier
☐ 21	Scott Roche (G)	☐ 22	Vitali Yachmenev
☐ 23	Bert Templeton, Coach	☐ 24	Rob Kirsch, Asst. Coach
☐ 25	B. Brown/ V.Yachmenev		

OSHAWA GENERALS

Complete Set (26 cards): 10.00

No.	Player	No.	Player
☐ 1	Checklist	☐ 2	Joel Gagnon (G)
☐ 3	Ken Shepard (G)	☐ 4	Jan Snopek
☐ 5	David Froh	☐ 6	Brandon Gray
☐ 7	Damon Hardy	☐ 8	Sean Brown
☐ 9	Jeff Andrews	☐ 10	Stéphane Yelle
☐ 11	Stéphane Soullière	☐ 12	Andrew Power
☐ 13	Todd Bradley	☐ 14	Darryl Lafrance
☐ 15	Darryl Moxam	☐ 16	Robert Dubois
☐ 17	Kevin Vaughan	☐ 18	Rob McQuat
☐ 19	B. J. Johnston	☐ 20	Paul Doherty
☐ 21	Eric Boulton	☐ 22	Marc Savard
☐ 23	Chris Hall	☐ 24	Jason McQuat
☐ 25	Ryan Lindsay	☐ 26	Cornacchia/Daniels/Drumm

PETERBOROUGH PETES

Complete Set (30 cards): 10.00

No.	Player	No.	Player
☐ 1	1992-93 OHL Champions	☐ 2	Jonathan Murphy
☐ 3	Dave Roche	☐ 4	Rob Giffin
☐ 5	Mike Harding	☐ 6	Tim Hill
☐ 7	Darryl Moxam	☐ 8	Pat Paone
☐ 9	Brent Tully	☐ 10	Zac Bierk (G)
☐ 11	Chad Grills	☐ 12	Matt St. Germain
☐ 13	Henrik Eppers	☐ 14	Rick Emmett
☐ 15	Chad Lang (G)	☐ 16	Cameron Mann
☐ 17	Steve Hogg	☐ 18	Mike Williams
☐ 19	Ryan Nauss	☐ 20	Jamie Langenbrunner
☐ 21	Ryan Douglas (G)	☐ 22	Matt Johnson
☐ 23	Kelvin Solari	☐ 24	Dan Delmonte
☐ 25	Quade Loghtbody	☐ 26	Adrain Murray
☐ 27	Jason Dawe	☐ 28	Mike Harding
☐ 29	Chris Pronger	☐ 30	Cardball Heroes

SAULT STE. MARIE GREYHOUNDS

Complete Set (30 cards): 10.00

No.	Player	No.	Player
☐ 1	Andrea Carpano (G)	☐ 2	Ryan Douglas (G)
☐ 3	Dan Cloutier (G)	☐ 4	Oliver Pastinsky
☐ 5	Scott King	☐ 6	Drew Bannister
☐ 7	Sean Gagnon	☐ 8	Andre Payette
☐ 9	Peter Mackeller	☐ 10	Richard Uniacke
☐ 11	Steve Zoryk	☐ 12	Brad Baber
☐ 13	Gary Roach	☐ 14	Jeff Gies
☐ 15	Tom MacDonald	☐ 16	Rhett Trombley
☐ 17	Jon VanVolsen	☐ 18	Andrew Clark
☐ 19	Briane Thompson	☐ 20	Aaron Gavey
☐ 21	Wade Gibson	☐ 22	Chad Grills
☐ 23	Jeff Toms	☐ 24	Steve Sullivan
☐ 25	Jeremy Stevenson	☐ 26	Corey Moylan
☐ 27	Steve Spina	☐ 28	Dave Mayville, GM
☐ 29	Ted Nolan, Coach	☐ 30	D.Flynn/ M.Zuke

SUDBURY WOLVES

Complete Set (24 cards): 10.00

No.	Player	No.	Player
☐ 1	Shawn Silver (G)	☐ 2	Jeff Melnechuk (G)
☐ 3	Jay McKee	☐ 4	Chris McMurtry
☐ 5	Rory Fitzpatrick	☐ 6	Mike Wilson
☐ 7	Shawn Frappier	☐ 8	Jamie Rivers
☐ 9	Zdenek Nedved	☐ 10	Ryan Shanahan
☐ 11	Sean Venedam	☐ 12	Andrew Dale
☐ 13	Mark Giannetti	☐ 14	Rick Bodkin
☐ 15	Barrie Moore	☐ 16	Jamie Matthews
☐ 17	Gary Coupal	☐ 18	Ilya Lysenko
☐ 19	Simon Sherry	☐ 20	Steve Potvin
☐ 21	Joel Poirier	☐ 22	Mike Yeo
☐ 23	Bob MacIssac	☐ 24	Legend: Paul DiPietro

WINDSOR SPITFIRES

Complete Set (26 cards): 10.00

No.	Player	No.	Player
☐ 1	Ed Jovanovski	☐ 2	Shawn Silver (G)
☐ 3	Travis Scott (G)	☐ 4	Mike Martin
☐ 5	Daryl Lavoie	☐ 6	Craig Lutes
☐ 7	David Pluck	☐ 8	Bill Bowler
☐ 9	David Green	☐ 10	Adam Young
☐ 11	Mike Loach	☐ 12	Brady Blain
☐ 13	Shayne McCosh	☐ 14	Rob Shearer
☐ 15	Joel Poirier	☐ 16	Cory Evans
☐ 17	Vladimir Kretchine	☐ 18	Dave Roche
☐ 19	Ryan Stewart	☐ 20	Dave Geris
☐ 21	Dan West	☐ 22	Luke Clowes
☐ 23	John Cooper	☐ 24	Akil Adams
☐ 25	Pizza Hut	☐ 26	Steve Bell, AM800

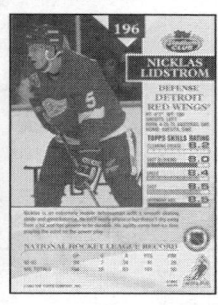

1993 - 94 TOPPS STADIUM CLUB

This series features up to five versions: a Topps card (1-500), an O-Pee-Chee (1-250, "PTD in U.S.A."), a Topps First Day Issue (1-500), an O-Pee-Chee First Day Issue (1-250, "PTD. in U.S.A") and a Members Only parallel (1-500). O-Pee-Chee regular cards may carry a 10-50% premium over Topps regular cards and O-Pee-Chee First Day Issues carry a 10-25% premium over Topps First Day Issues.

Imprint: © 1993 THE TOPPS COMPANY, INC.

Series One (250 cards):	16.00	1,400.00	–
Series Two (250 cards):	16.00	1,400.00	–
Members Only Set (500 cards):			3,500.00
Common Player:	.10	3.50	6.00

No.	Player	Topps	F.D.	M.O.
☐☐☐☐☐ 1	Guy Carbonneau, Mtl., Error	.10	3.50	8.00
☐☐☐☐☐ 2	Joe Cirella, Fla.	.10	3.50	6.00
☐☐☐☐☐ 3	Laurie Boschman, Ott.	.10	3.50	6.00
☐☐☐☐☐ 4	Arturs Irbe, (G), S.J.	.10	3.50	8.00
☐☐☐☐☐ 5	Adam Creighton, T.B.	.10	3.50	6.00
☐☐☐☐☐ 6	Mike McPhee, Dal.	.10	3.50	6.00
☐☐☐☐☐ 7	Jeff Beukeboom, NYR.	.10	3.50	6.00
☐☐☐☐☐ 8	Kevin Todd, Edm.	.10	3.50	6.00
☐☐☐☐☐ 9	Yvon Corriveau, Hfd.	.10	3.50	6.00
☐☐☐☐☐ 10	Eric Lindros, Pha.	1.50	125.00	185.00
☐☐☐☐☐ 11	Martin Rucinsky, Que.	.10	3.50	6.00
☐☐☐☐☐ 12	Michel Goulet, Chi.	.25	6.00	10.00
☐☐☐☐☐ 13	Scott Pellerin, N.J.	.10	3.50	6.00
☐☐☐☐☐ 14	Mike Eagles, Wpg.	.10	3.50	6.00
☐☐☐☐☐ 15	Steve Heinze, Bos.	.10	3.50	6.00
☐☐☐☐☐ 16	Gerald Gallant, Det.	.10	3.50	6.00
☐☐☐☐☐ 17	Kelly Miller, Wsh.	.10	3.50	6.00
☐☐☐☐☐ 18	Petr Nedved, Van.	.10	3.50	8.00
☐☐☐☐☐ 19	Joe Mullen, Pgh.	.25	6.00	10.00
☐☐☐☐☐ 20	Pat LaFontaine, Buf.	.25	6.00	12.00
☐☐☐☐☐ 21	Garth Butcher, Stl.	.10	3.50	6.00
☐☐☐☐☐ 22	Jeff Reese (G), Cgy.	.10	3.50	6.00
☐☐☐☐☐ 23	Dave Andreychuk, Tor.	.10	3.50	8.00
☐☐☐☐☐ 24	Patrick Flatley, NYI.	.10	3.50	6.00
☐☐☐☐☐ 25	Tomas Sandström, L.A.	.10	3.50	6.00
☐☐☐☐☐ 26	André Racicot (G), Mtl.	.10	3.50	6.00
☐☐☐☐☐ 27	Patrice Brisebois, Mtl.	.10	3.50	6.00
☐☐☐☐☐ 28	Neal Broten, Dal.	.10	3.50	8.00
☐☐☐☐☐ 29	Mark Freer, Ott.	.10	3.50	6.00
☐☐☐☐☐ 30	Kelly Kisio, S.J.	.10	3.50	6.00
☐☐☐☐☐ 31	Scott Mellanby, Fla.	.10	3.50	8.00
☐☐☐☐☐ 32	Joe Sakic, Que.	1.00	80.00	120.00
☐☐☐☐☐ 33	Kerry Huffman, Que.	.10	3.50	6.00
☐☐☐☐☐ 34	Evgeny Davydov, Wpg.	.10	3.50	6.00
☐☐☐☐☐ 35	Mark Messier, NYR.	.50	35.00	50.00
☐☐☐☐☐ 36	Pat Verbeek, Hfd.	.10	3.50	8.00
☐☐☐☐☐ 37	Greg Gilbert, NYR.	.10	3.50	6.00
☐☐☐☐☐ 38	John Tucker, T.B.	.10	3.50	6.00
☐☐☐☐☐ 39	Claude Lemieux, N.J.	.10	3.50	8.00
☐☐☐☐☐ 40	Shayne Corson, Edm.	.25	6.00	10.00
☐☐☐☐☐ 41	Gord Roberts, Bos.	.25	6.00	10.00
☐☐☐☐☐ 42	Jiri Slegr, Van.	.10	3.50	6.00
☐☐☐☐☐ 43	Kevin Dineen, Pha.	.10	3.50	6.00
☐☐☐☐☐ 44	Johan Garpenlov, S.J.	.10	3.50	6.00
☐☐☐☐☐ 45	Sergei Fedorov, Det.	.50	35.00	50.00
☐☐☐☐☐ 46	Rich Sutter, Stl.	.10	3.50	6.00
☐☐☐☐☐ 47	Dave Hannan, Buf.	.10	3.50	6.00
☐☐☐☐☐ 48	Sylvain Lefebvre, Tor.	.10	3.50	6.00
☐☐☐☐☐ 49	Pat Elynuik, Wsh.	.10	3.50	6.00
☐☐☐☐☐ 50	Ray Ferraro, NYI.	.10	3.50	6.00
☐☐☐☐☐ 51	Brent Ashton, Cgy.	.10	3.50	6.00
☐☐☐☐☐ 52	Paul Stanton, Pgh.	.10	3.50	6.00
☐☐☐☐☐ 53	Kevin Haller, Mtl.	.10	3.50	6.00
☐☐☐☐☐ 54	Kelly Hrudey (G), L.A.	.10	3.50	8.00
☐☐☐☐☐ 55	Russ Courtnall, Dal.	.10	3.50	6.00
☐☐☐☐☐ 56	Alexei Zhamnov, Wpg.	.25	6.00	10.00

	No.	Player			
□□□□□	57	Andrei Lomakin, Fla.	.10	3.50	6.00
□□□□□	58	Keith Brown, Chi.	.10	3.50	6.00
□□□□□	59	Glenn Murray, Bos.	.10	3.50	8.00
□□□□□	60	Kay Whitmore (G), Van.	.10	3.50	6.00
□□□□□	61	Stéphane Richer, N.J.	.10	3.50	8.00
□□□□□	62	Todd Gill, Tor.	.10	3.50	6.00
□□□□□	63	Bob Sweeney, Buf.	.10	3.50	6.00
□□□□□	64	Mike Richter (G), NYR.	.35	12.00	20.00
□□□□□	65	Brett Hull, Stl.	.50	35.00	45.00
□□□□□	66	Sylvain Côté, Wsh.	.10	3.50	6.00
□□□□□	67	Kirk Muller, Mtl.	.10	3.50	8.00
□□□□□	68	Ronnie Stern, Cgy.	.10	3.50	6.00
□□□□□	69	Josef Beranek, Pha.	.10	3.50	6.00
□□□□□	70	Steve Yzerman, Det.	1.25	100.00	150.00
□□□□□	71	Don Beaupré (G), Wsh.	.10	3.50	6.00
□□□□□	72	Ed Courtenay, S.J.	.10	3.50	6.00
□□□□□	73	Zdeno Ciger, Edm.	.10	3.50	6.00
□□□□□	74	Andrew Cassels, Hfd.	.10	3.50	6.00
□□□□□	75	Roman Hamrlik, T.B.	.25	6.00	10.00
□□□□□	76	Benoît Hogue, NYI.	.10	3.50	6.00
□□□□□	77	Andrei Kovalenko, Que.	.10	3.50	6.00
□□□□□	78	Rod Brind'Amour, Pha.	.25	6.00	10.00
□□□□□	79	Tom Barrasso (G), Pgh.	.25	6.00	10.00
□□□□□	80	Al Iafrate, Wsh.	.10	3.50	6.00
□□□□□	81	Bret Hedican, Stl.	.10	3.50	6.00
□□□□□	82	Peter Bondra, Wsh.	.35	20.00	30.00
□□□□□	83	Ted Donato, Bos.	.10	3.50	6.00
□□□□□	84	Chris Lindberg, Cgy.	.10	3.50	6.00
□□□□□	85	John Vanbiesbrouck (G), Fla.	.60	45.00	60.00
□□□□□	86	Ron Sutter, Stl.	.10	3.50	6.00
□□□□□	87	Luc Robitaille, L.A.	.25	6.00	10.00
□□□□□	88	Brian Leetch, NYR.	.35	12.00	20.00
□□□□□	89	Randy Wood, Buf.	.10	3.50	6.00
□□□□□	90	Dirk Graham, Chi.	.10	3.50	6.00
□□□□□	91	Alexander Mogilny, Buf.	.35	12.00	20.00
□□□□□	92	Mike Keane, Mtl.	.10	3.50	6.00
□□□□□	93	Adam Oates, Bos.	.35	12.00	20.00
□□□□□	94	Viacheslav Butsayev, Pha.	.10	3.50	6.00
□□□□□	95	John LeClair, Mtl.	.60	45.00	60.00
□□□□□	96	Joe Nieuwendyk, Cgy.	.25	6.00	10.00
□□□□□	97	Mikael Andersson, T.B.	.10	3.50	6.00
□□□□□	98	Jaromir Jagr, Pgh.	1.25	100.00	150.00
□□□□□	99	Ed Belfour (G), Chi.	.35	12.00	20.00
□□□□□	100	Dave Reid, Bos.	.10	3.50	6.00
□□□□□	101	Darius Kasparaitis, NYI.	.10	3.50	6.00
□□□□□	102	Zarley Zalapski, Hfd.	.10	3.50	6.00
□□□□□	103	Christian Ruuttu, Chi.	.10	3.50	6.00
□□□□□	104	Phil Housley, Wpg.	.10	3.50	6.00
□□□□□	105	Al MacInnis, Cgy.	.25	6.00	10.00
□□□□□	106	Tommy Sjodin, Dal.	.10	3.50	6.00
□□□□□	107	Richard Smehlik, Buf.	.10	3.50	6.00
□□□□□	108	Jyrki Lumme, Van.	.10	3.50	6.00
□□□□□	109	Dominic Roussel (G), Pha.	.10	3.50	6.00
□□□□□	110	Mike Gartner, NYR.	.25	6.00	10.00
□□□□□	111	Bernie Nicholls, N.J.	.10	3.50	6.00
□□□□□	112	Mark Howe, Det.	.10	3.50	6.00
□□□□□	113	Rich Pilon, NYI.	.10	3.50	6.00
□□□□□	114	Jeff Odgers, S.J.	.10	3.50	6.00
□□□□□	115	Gilbert Dionne, Mtl.	.10	3.50	6.00
□□□□□	116	Peter Zezel, Tor.	.10	3.50	6.00
□□□□□	117	Don Sweeney, Bos.	.10	3.50	6.00
□□□□□	118	Jimmy Carson, L.A.	.10	3.50	6.00
□□□□□	119	Igor Korolev, Stl.	.10	3.50	6.00
□□□□□	120	Bob Kudelski, Ott.	.10	3.50	6.00
□□□□□	121	Dave Lowry, Fla.	.10	3.50	6.00
□□□□□	122	Steve Kasper, T.B.	.10	3.50	6.00
□□□□□	123	Mike Ridley, Wsh.	.10	3.50	6.00
□□□□□	124	Dave Tippett, Pgh	.10	3.50	6.00
□□□□□	125	Cliff Ronning, Van.	.10	3.50	6.00
□□□□□	126	Bruce Driver, N.J.	.10	3.50	6.00
□□□□□	127	Stéphane Matteau, Chi.	.10	3.50	6.00
□□□□□	128	Joel Otto, Cgy.	.10	3.50	6.00
□□□□□	129	Alexei Kovalev, NYR.	.10	3.50	6.00
□□□□□	130	Mike Modano, Dal.	.50	35.00	50.00
□□□□□	131	Bill Ranford (G) Edm.	.25	6.00	10.00
□□□□□	132	Petr Svoboda, Buf.	.10	3.50	6.00
□□□□□	133	Roger Johansson, Cgy.	.10	3.50	6.00
□□□□□	134	Marc Bureau, T.B.	.10	3.50	6.00
□□□□□	135	Keith Tkachuk, Wpg.	.50	35.00	50.00
□□□□□	136	Mark Recchi, Pha.	.25	6.00	12.00
□□□□□	137	Bob Probert, Det.	.10	3.50	8.00
□□□□□	138	Uwe Krupp, NYI.	.10	3.50	6.00
□□□□□	139	Mike Sullivan, S.J.	.10	3.50	6.00
□□□□□	140	Doug Gilmour, Tor.	.35	12.00	20.00
□□□□□	141	AW: Teemu Selänne, Wpg.	.35	25.00	35.00
□□□□□	142	AW: Dave Poulin, Bos.	.10	3.50	6.00
□□□□□	143	AW: Mario Lemieux, Pgh.	.75	60.00	85.00
□□□□□	144	AW: Ed Belfour (G), Chi.	.25	10.00	18.00
□□□□□	145	AW: Pierre Turgeon, NYI.	.25	6.00	10.00
□□□□□	146	AW: Mario Lemieux, Pgh.	.75	60.00	85.00
□□□□□	147	AW: Chris Chelios, Chi.	.25	10.00	18.00
□□□□□	148	AW: Mario Lemieux, Pgh.	.75	60.00	85.00
□□□□□	149	AW: Doug Gilmour, Tor.	.25	10.00	18.00
□□□□□	150	AW: Ed Belfour (G), Chi.	.25	10.00	18.00
□□□□□	151	Paul Ranheim, Cgy.	.10	3.50	6.00
□□□□□	152	Gino Cavallini, Que.	.10	3.50	6.00
□□□□□	153	Kevin Hatcher, Wsh.	.10	3.50	8.00
□□□□□	154	Marc Bergevin, T.B.	.10	3.50	6.00
□□□□□	155	Marty McSorley, L.A.	.10	3.50	6.00
□□□□□	156	Brian Bellows, Mtl.	.10	3.50	6.00
□□□□□	157	Patrick Poulin, Hfd.	.10	3.50	6.00
□□□□□	158	Kevin Stevens, Pgh.	.10	3.50	8.00
□□□□□	159	Bobby Holik, N.J.	.10	3.50	6.00
□□□□□	160	Ray Bourque, Bos.	.50	35.00	50.00
□□□□□	161	Bryan Marchment, Chi.	.10	3.50	6.00
□□□□□	162	Curtis Joseph (G), Stl.	.60	45.00	60.00
□□□□□	163	Kirk McLean (G), Van.	.25	6.00	10.00
□□□□□	164	Teppo Numminen, Wpg.	.10	3.50	6.00
□□□□□	165	Kevin Lowe, NYR.	.10	3.50	6.00
□□□□□	166	Tim Cheveldae (G), Det.	.10	3.50	6.00
□□□□□	167	Brad Dalgarno, NYI.	.10	3.50	6.00
□□□□□	168	Glenn Anderson, Tor.	.10	3.50	6.00
□□□□□	169	Frantisek Musil, Cgy.	.10	3.50	6.00
□□□□□	170	Eric Desjardins, Mtl.	.25	6.00	10.00
□□□□□	171	Doug Zmolek, S.J.	.10	3.50	6.00
□□□□□	172	Mark Lamb, Ott.	.10	3.50	6.00
□□□□□	173	Craig Ludwig, Dal.	.10	3.50	6.00
□□□□□	174	Rob Gaudreau, S.J.	.10	3.50	6.00
□□□□□	175	Bob Carpenter, Wsh.	.10	3.50	6.00
□□□□□	176	Mike Ricci, Que.	.10	3.50	8.00
□□□□□	177	Brian Skrudland, Fla.	.10	3.50	8.00
□□□□□	178	Dominik Hasek (G), Buf.	.75	60.00	80.00
□□□□□	179	Pat Conacher, L.A.	.10	3.50	6.00
□□□□□	180	Mark Janssens, Hfd.	.10	3.50	6.00
□□□□□	181	Brent Fedyk, Pha.	.10	3.50	6.00
□□□□□	182	Rob DiMaio, T.B.	.10	3.50	6.00
□□□□□	183	Dave Manson, Edm.	.10	3.50	6.00
□□□□□	184	Janne Ojanen, N.J.	.10	3.50	6.00
□□□□□	185	Ryan Walter, Van.	.10	3.50	6.00
□□□□□	186	Michael Nylander, Hfd.	.10	3.50	6.00
□□□□□	187	Steve Leach, Bos.	.10	3.50	6.00
□□□□□	188	Jeff Brown, Stl.	.10	3.50	6.00
□□□□□	189	Shawn McEachern, Pgh.	.10	3.50	8.00
□□□□□	190	Jeremy Roenick, Chi.	.35	12.00	20.00
□□□□□	191	Darrin Shannon, Wpg.	.10	3.50	6.00
□□□□□	192	Wendel Clark, Tor.	.25	6.00	12.00
□□□□□	193	Kevin Miller, Stl.	.10	3.50	6.00
□□□□□	194	Paul DiPietro, Mtl.	.10	3.50	6.00
□□□□□	195	Steve Thomas, NYI	.10	3.50	6.00
□□□□□	196	Nicklas Lidstrom, Det.	.25	6.00	10.00
□□□□□	197	Ed Olczyk, NYR.	.10	3.50	6.00
□□□□□	198	Robert Reichel, Cgy.	.10	3.50	8.00
□□□□□	199	Neil Brady, Ott.	.10	3.50	6.00
□□□□□	200	Wayne Gretzky, L.A.	2.00	160.00	300.00
□□□□□	201	Adrien Plavsic, Van.	.10	3.50	6.00
□□□□□	202	Joé Juneau, Bos.	.10	3.50	8.00
□□□□□	203	Brad May, Buf.	.10	3.50	6.00
□□□□□	204	Igor Kravchuk, Edm.	.10	3.50	6.00
□□□□□	205	Keith Acton, Pha.	.10	3.50	6.00
□□□□□	206	Ken Daneyko, N.J.	.10	3.50	6.00
□□□□□	207	Sean Burke (G), Hfd.	.25	6.00	10.00
□□□□□	208	Jayson More, S.J.	.10	3.50	6.00
□□□□□	209	John Cullen, Tor.	.10	3.50	6.00
□□□□□	210	Teemu Selänne, Wpg.	.75	60.00	80.00
□□□□□	211	Brent Sutter, Chi.	.10	3.50	6.00
□□□□□	212	Brian Bradley, T.B.	.10	3.50	6.00
□□□□□	213	Donald Audette, Buf.	.10	3.50	6.00
□□□□□	214	Philippe Bozon, Stl.	.10	3.50	6.00
□□□□□	215	Derek King, NYI.	.10	3.50	6.00
□□□□□	216	Cam Neely, Bos.	.25	6.00	10.00
□□□□□	217	Keith Primeau, Det.	.25	6.00	10.00
□□□□□	218	Steve Smith, Chi.	.10	3.50	6.00
□□□□□	219	Ken Sutton, Buf.	.10	3.50	6.00
□□□□□	220	Dale Hawerchuk, Buf.	.25	6.00	10.00
□□□□□	221	Alexei Zhitnik, L.A.	.10	3.50	6.00
□□□□□	222	Glen Wesley, Bos.	.10	3.50	6.00
□□□□□	223	Nelson Emerson, Stl.	.10	3.50	6.00
□□□□□	224	Pat Falloon, S.J.	.10	3.50	6.00
□□□□□	225	Darryl Sydor, L.A.	.10	3.50	6.00
□□□□□	226	Tony Amonte, NYR.	.25	6.00	10.00
□□□□□	227	Brian Mullen, NYI.	.10	3.50	6.00
□□□□□	228	Gary Suter, Cgy.	.10	3.50	6.00
□□□□□	229	David Shaw, Bos.	.10	3.50	6.00
□□□□□	230	Troy Murray, Chi.	.10	3.50	6.00
□□□□□	231	Patrick Roy (G), Mtl.	1.50	125.00	200.00
□□□□□	232	Michel Petit, Cgy.	.10	3.50	6.00
□□□□□	233	Wayne Presley, Buf.	.10	3.50	6.00
□□□□□	234	Keith Jones, Wsh.	.10	3.50	6.00
□□□□□	235	Gary Roberts, Cgy.	.25	6.00	10.00
□□□□□	236	Steve Larmer, Chi.	.10	3.50	8.00
□□□□□	237	Valeri Kamensky, Que.	.25	6.00	10.00
□□□□□	238	Ulf Dahlen, T.B.	.10	3.50	6.00
□□□□□	239	Danton Cole, Mtl.	.10	3.50	6.00
□□□□□	240	Vincent Damphousse, Mtl.	.35	12.00	20.00
□□□□□	241	Yuri Khmylev, Buf.	.10	3.50	6.00
□□□□□	242	Stéphane Quintal, Stl.	.10	3.50	6.00
□□□□□	243	Peter Taglianetti, Pgh.	.10	3.50	6.00
□□□□□	244	Gary Leeman, Mtl.	.10	3.50	6.00
□□□□□	245	Sergei Nemchinov, NYR.	.10	3.50	6.00
□□□□□	246	Rob Blake, L.A.	.25	6.00	10.00
□□□□□	247	Steve Chiasson, Det.	.10	3.50	6.00
□□□□□	248	Vladimir Malakhov, NYI.	.10	3.50	6.00
□□□□□	249	Checklist 1-125	.10	3.50	6.00
□□□□□	250	Checklist 126-250	.10	3.50	6.00
□□□	251	Kjell Samuelsson, Pgh.	.10	3.50	6.00
□□□	252	Terry Carkner, Det.	.10	3.50	6.00
□□□	253	Bill Lindsay, Fla.	.10	3.50	6.00
□□□	254	Bob Essensa (G), Wpg.	.10	3.50	6.00
□□□	255	Jocelyn Lemieux, Chi.	.10	3.50	6.00
□□□	256	Joe Sacco, Ana.	.10	3.50	6.00
□□□	257	Marty McInnis, NYI.	.10	3.50	6.00
□□□	258	Warren Rychel, L.A.	.10	3.50	6.00
□□□	259	David Maley, S.J.	.10	3.50	6.00
□□□	260	Grant Fuhr (G), Buf.	.25	6.00	12.00
□□□	261	Scott Young, Que.	.10	3.50	6.00
□□□	262	Ed Ronan, Que.	.10	3.50	6.00
□□□	**263**	**Micah Aivazoff, Det., RC**	**.10**	**3.50**	**6.00**
□□□	264	Murray Craven, Van.	.10	3.50	6.00
□□□	265	Viacheslav Fetisov, N.J.	.25	6.00	10.00
□□□	266	Chris Dahlquist, Cgy.	.10	3.50	6.00
□□□	267	Norm MacIver, Ott.	.10	3.50	6.00
□□□	268	Alexander Godynyuk, Fla.	.10	3.50	6.00
□□□	269	Mikael Renberg, Pha.	.25	6.00	10.00
□□□	270	Adam Graves, NYR.	.10	3.50	8.00
□□□	271	Randy Ladouceur, Ana.	.10	3.50	6.00
□□□	272	Frank Pietrangelo (G), Ana.	.10	3.50	6.00
□□□	273	Basil McRae, Stl.	.10	3.50	6.00
□□□	274	Bryan Smolinski, Bos.	.10	3.50	6.00
□□□	275	Daren Puppa (G), T.B.	.10	3.50	8.00
□□□	276	Darcy Wakaluk (G), Dal.	.10	3.50	6.00
□□□	277	Dimitri Khristich, Wsh.	.10	3.50	8.00
□□□	278	Vladimir Vujtek, Edm.	.10	3.50	6.00
□□□	279	Tom Kurvers, NYI.	.10	3.50	6.00
□□□	280	Félix Potvin (G), Tor.	.50	35.00	50.00
□□□	281	Keith Brown, Fla.	.10	3.50	6.00
□□□	282	Thomas Steen, Wpg.	.10	3.50	6.00
□□□	283	Larry Murphy, Pgh.	.25	6.00	10.00
□□□	284	Bob Corkum, Ana.	.10	3.50	6.00
□□□	285	Tony Granato, L.A.	.10	3.50	6.00
□□□	**286**	**Cam Russell, Chi., RC**	**.10**	**3.50**	**6.00**
□□□	287	John MacLean, N.J.	.10	3.50	6.00
□□□	288	Shawn Antoski, Van.	.10	3.50	6.00
□□□	289	Per-Erik Eklund, Pha.	.10	3.50	6.00
□□□	290	Chris Pronger, Hfd.	.35	10.00	15.00
□□□	**291**	**Alexander Karpovtsev, NYR., RC**	**.10**	**3.50**	**6.00**
□□□	**292**	**Paul Laus, Fla., RC**	**.10**	**3.50**	**6.00**
□□□	**293**	**Jaroslav Otevrel, S.J., RC**	**.10**	**3.50**	**6.00**
□□□	294	Dino Ciccarelli, Det.	.25	6.00	10.00
□□□	295	Guy Hebert (G), Ana.	.25	6.00	10.00
□□□	296	Dave Karpa, Que.	.10	3.50	6.00
□□□	297	Denis Savard, T.B.	.25	6.00	10.00
□□□	298	Jim Johnson, Dal.	.10	3.50	6.00
□□□	**299**	**Kirk Maltby, Edm., RC**	**.10**	**3.50**	**6.00**
□□□	300	Alexandre Daigle, Ott.	.35	10.00	15.00
□□□	301	Dave Poulin, Wsh.	.10	3.50	6.00
□□□	302	James Patrick, Hfd.	.10	3.50	6.00
□□□	303	Jon Casey (G), Bos.	.10	3.50	8.00
□□□	304	Yves Racine, Pha.	.10	3.50	6.00
□□□	305	Craig Simpson, Buf.	.10	3.50	6.00
□□□	306	Mike Krushelnyski, Tor.	.10	3.50	6.00
□□□	307	Mark Fitzpatrick (G), Fla.	.10	3.50	6.00
□□□	308	Charlie Huddy, L.A.	.10	3.50	6.00
□□□	309	Todd Ewen, Ana.	.10	3.50	6.00
□□□	310	Mario Lemieux, Pgh.	1.75	135.00	200.00
□□□	311	Dan Keczmer, Hfd.	.10	3.50	6.00

	No.	Player			
□□□	312	Sergei Zubov, NYR.	.25	6.00	10.00
□□□	313	Shawn Burr, Det.	.10	3.50	6.00
□□□	314	Valeri Zelepukin, N.J.	.10	3.50	6.00
□□□	315	Stéphane Fiset (G), Que.	.25	6.00	10.00
□□□	316	C.J. Young, Fla.	.10	3.50	6.00
□□□	317	Luciano Borsato, Wpg.	.10	3.50	6.00
□□□	318	Darcy Loewen, Ott.	.10	3.50	6.00
□□□	319	Mike Vernon (G), Cgy.	.25	6.00	12.00
□□□	320	Chris Gratton, T.B.	.35	10.00	15.00
□□□	321	Matthew Barnaby, Buf.	.10	3.50	6.00
□□□	322	Mike Rathje, S.J.	.10	3.50	6.00
□□□	323	Sergio Momesso, Van.	.10	3.50	6.00
□□□	324	David Volek, NYR.	.10	3.50	6.00
□□□	325	Ron Tugnutt (G), Ana.	.10	3.50	8.00
□□□	326	Jeff Hackett (G), Chi.	.25	6.00	10.00
□□□	327	Robb Stauber (G), L.A.	.10	3.50	6.00
□□□	328	Chris Terreri (G), N.J.	.10	3.50	8.00
□□□	329	Rick Tocchet, Pgh.	.10	3.50	8.00
□□□	330	John Vanbiesbrouck (G), Fla.	.60	45.00	60.00
□□□	331	Drake Berehowsky, Tor.	.10	3.50	6.00
□□□	332	Alexei Kasatonov, Ana.	.10	3.50	6.00
□□□	333	Vladimir Konstantinv, Det.	.10	3.50	8.00
□□□	334	John Blue (G), Bos.	.10	3.50	6.00
□□□	335	Craig Janney, Stl.	.10	3.50	6.00
□□□	336	Curtis Leschyshyn, Que.	.10	3.50	6.00
□□□	337	Todd Krygier, Wsh.	.10	3.50	6.00
□□□	338	Boris Mironov, Wpg.	.10	3.50	6.00
□□□	**339**	**Joby Messier, NYR., RC**	**.10**	**3.50**	**6.00**
□□□	340	Tommy Söderström (G), Pha.	.10	3.50	6.00
□□□	341	Randy Cunneyworth, Hfd.	.10	3.50	6.00
□□□	**342**	**Mark Ferner, Ana., RC**	**.10**	**3.50**	**6.00**
□□□	343	Stéphan Lebeau, Mtl.	.10	3.50	6.00
□□□	344	Jody Hull, Fla.	.10	3.50	6.00
□□□	**345**	**Jason Arnott, Edm., RC**	**1.50**	**35.00**	**45.00**
□□□	346	Gerard Gallant, T.B.	.10	3.50	6.00
□□□	347	Stéphane Richer, Fla.	.10	3.50	6.00
□□□	**348**	**Jeff Shantz, Chi., RC**	**.10**	**3.50**	**6.00**
□□□	349	Brian Skrudland, Fla.	.10	3.50	8.00
□□□	**350**	**Chris Osgood (G), Det., RC**	**2.50**	**65.00**	**80.00**
□□□	351	Gary Shuchuk, L.A.	.10	3.50	6.00
□□□	352	Martin Brodeur (G), N.J.	.75	60.00	80.00
□□□	353	Bob Rouse, Tor.	.10	3.50	6.00
□□□	354	Doug Bodger, Buf.	.10	3.50	6.00
□□□	355	Mike Craig, Dal.	.10	3.50	6.00
□□□	356	Ulf Samuelsson, Pgh.	.10	3.50	6.00
□□□	357	Trevor Linden, Van.	.25	6.00	10.00
□□□	358	Dennis Vaske, NYI.	.10	3.50	6.00
□□□	359	Alexei Yashin, Ott.	.75	30.00	45.00
□□□	360	Paul Ysebaert, Wpg.	.10	3.50	6.00
□□□	361	Shaun Van Allen, Ana.	.10	3.50	6.00
□□□	362	Sandis Ozolinsh, S.J.	.25	6.00	10.00
□□□	363	Todd Elik, S.J.	.10	3.50	6.00
□□□	**364**	**German Titov, Cgy., RC**	**.10**	**3.50**	**6.00**
□□□	365	Alexander Semak, N.J.	.10	3.50	6.00
□□□	366	Allen Pedersen, Hfd.	.10	3.50	6.00
□□□	367	Greg Johnson, Det.	.10	3.50	6.00
□□□	368	Anatoli Semenov, Ana.	.10	3.50	6.00
□□□	369	Scott Mellanby, Fla.	.10	3.50	6.00
□□□	370	Mats Sundin, Que.	.50	35.00	50.00
□□□	**371**	**Mattias Norstrom, NYR., RC**	**.10**	**3.50**	**6.00**
□□□	372	Glen Featherstone, Bos.	.10	3.50	6.00
□□□	**373**	**Sergei Petrenko, Buf., RC**	**.10**	**3.50**	**6.00**
□□□	374	Mike Donnelly, L.A.	.10	3.50	6.00
□□□	375	Nikolai Borschevsky, Tor.	.10	3.50	6.00
□□□	376	Rob Zamuner, T.B.	.25	6.00	10.00
□□□	377	Steven King, Ana.	.10	3.50	6.00
□□□	378	Rick Tabaracci (G), Wsh.	.10	3.50	6.00
□□□	379	Dave Lowry, Fla.	.10	3.50	6.00
□□□	380	Pierre Turgeon, NYI.	.25	6.00	12.00
□□□	381	Garry Galley, Pha.	.10	3.50	6.00
□□□	382	Doug Weight, Edm.	.35	12.00	20.00
□□□	383	Scott Stevens, N.J.	.10	3.50	8.00
□□□	384	Mark Tinordi, Dal.	.10	3.50	6.00
□□□	385	Ron Francis, Pgh.	.35	12.00	20.00
□□□	386	Mark Greig, Hfd.	.10	3.50	6.00
□□□	387	Sean Hill, Ana.	.10	3.50	6.00
□□□	388	Vyacheslav Kozlov, Det.	.10	3.50	8.00
□□□	389	Brendan Shanahan, Stl.	.60	45.00	60.00
□□□	390	Theoren Fleury, Cgy.	.35	12.00	20.00
□□□	391	Mathieu Schneider, Mtl.	.10	3.50	6.00
□□□	392	Tom Fitzgerald, Fla.	.10	3.50	6.00
□□□	393	Markus Naslund, Pgh.	.10	3.50	6.00
□□□	394	Travis Green, NYI.	.10	3.50	6.00
□□□	395	Troy Loney, Ana.	.10	3.50	6.00
□□□	396	Gord Donnelly, Buf.	.10	3.50	6.00
□□□	397	Owen Nolan, Que.	.25	6.00	10.00
□□□	398	Steve Larmer, NYR.	.10	3.50	8.00
□□□	399	Dave Archibald, Ott.	.10	3.50	6.00
□□□	400	Jari Kurri, L.A.	.25	6.00	12.00
□□□	401	Jim Paek, Pgh.	.10	3.50	6.00
□□□	402	Andrei Lomakin, Fla.	.10	3.50	6.00
□□□	403	Scott Niedermayer, N.J.	.25	6.00	10.00
□□□	404	Bob Errey, S.J.	.10	3.50	6.00
□□□	405	Michal Pivonka, Wsh.	.10	3.50	6.00
□□□	406	Doug Lidster, NYR.	.10	3.50	6.00
□□□	407	Garry Valk, Ana.	.10	3.50	6.00
□□□	408	Geoff Sanderson, Hfd.	.10	3.50	8.00
□□□	**409**	**Stewart Malgunas, Pha., RC**	**.10**	**3.50**	**6.00**
□□□	410	Craig MacTavish, Edm.	.10	3.50	6.00
□□□	**411**	**Jaroslav Modry, N.J., RC**	**.10**	**3.50**	**6.00**
□□□	412	Shawn Chambers, T.B.	.10	3.50	6.00
□□□	413	Geoff Courtnall, Van.	.10	3.50	6.00
□□□	414	Mark Hardy, L.A.	.10	3.50	6.00
□□□	415	Martin Straka, Pgh.	.10	3.50	6.00
□□□	416	Randy Burridge, Wsh.	.10	3.50	6.00
□□□	417	Kent Manderville, Tor.	.10	3.50	6.00
□□□	418	Darren Rumble, Ott.	.10	3.50	6.00
□□□	419	Bill Houlder, Ana.	.10	3.50	6.00
□□□	420	Chris Chelios, Chi.	.35	20.00	30.00
□□□	421	Jim Hrivnak (G), Stl.	.10	3.50	6.00
□□□	422	Benoît Brunet, Mtl.	.10	3.50	6.00
□□□	**423**	**Aaron Ward, Det., RC**	**.25**	**5.00**	**8.00**
□□□	424	Alexei Gusarov, Que.	.10	3.50	6.00
□□□	425	Mats Sundin, Que.	.35	15.00	25.00
□□□	426	Kjell Samuelsson, Pgh.	.10	3.50	6.00
□□□	427	Mikael Andersson, T.B.	.10	3.50	6.00
□□□	428	Ulf Dahlen, Dal.	.10	3.50	6.00
□□□	429	Nicklas Lidstrom, Det.	.25	6.00	10.00
□□□	430	Tommy Söderström (G), Pha.	.10	3.50	6.00
□□□	**431**	**Darrin Madeley (G), Ott., RC**	**.10**	**3.50**	**6.00**
□□□	432	Kevin Dahl, Cgy.	.10	3.50	6.00
□□□	433	Ron Hextall (G), NYI.	.25	6.00	10.00
□□□	**434**	**Patrik Carnback, Ana., RC**	**.10**	**3.50**	**6.00**
□□□	435	Randy Moller, Buf.	.10	3.50	6.00
□□□	436	Dave Gagner, Dal.	.10	3.50	6.00
□□□	437	Corey Millen, N.J.	.10	3.50	6.00
□□□	438	Olaf Kolzig (G), Wsh.	.35	12.00	20.00
□□□	439	Gord Murphy, Fla.	.10	3.50	6.00
□□□	**440**	**Cam Stewart, Bos., RC**	**.10**	**3.50**	**6.00**
□□□	**441**	**Darren McCarty, Det., RC**	**.25**	**5.00**	**8.00**
□□□	442	Frantisek Kucera, Chi.	.10	3.50	6.00
□□□	**443**	**Ted Drury, Cgy., RC**	**.10**	**3.50**	**6.00**
□□□	444	Troy Mallette, Ott.	.10	3.50	6.00
□□□	**445**	**Robin Bawa, Ana., RC**	**.10**	**3.50**	**6.00**
□□□	446	Steve Rice, Edm.	.10	3.50	6.00
□□□	447	Pat Elynuik, T.B.	.10	3.50	6.00
□□□	**448**	**Jim Cummins, Pha., RC**	**.10**	**3.50**	**6.00**
□□□	449	Rob Niedermayer, Fla.	.25	6.00	10.00
□□□	450	Paul Coffey, Det.	.25	6.00	12.00
□□□	451	Calle Johansson, Wsh.	.10	3.50	6.00
□□□	452	Mike Needham, Pgh.	.10	3.50	6.00
□□□	453	Glenn Healy (G), NYR.	.10	3.50	8.00
□□□	454	Dixon Ward, Van.	.10	3.50	6.00
□□□	455	Al Iafrate, Wsh.	.10	3.50	6.00
□□□	456	Jon Casey (G), Bos.	.10	3.50	6.00
□□□	457	Kevin Stevens, Pgh.	.10	3.50	8.00
□□□	458	Tony Amonte, NYR.	.25	6.00	10.00
□□□	459	Chris Chelios, Chi.	.25	6.00	10.00
□□□	460	Pat LaFontaine, Buf.	.25	6.00	10.00
□□□	461	Jamie Baker, S.J.	.10	3.50	6.00
□□□	462	André Faust, Pha.	.10	3.50	6.00
□□□	463	Bobby Dollas, Ana.	.10	3.50	6.00
□□□	464	Steven Finn, Que.	.10	3.50	6.00
□□□	465	Scott Lachance, NYI.	.10	3.50	6.00
□□□	466	Mike Hough, Fla.	.10	3.50	6.00
□□□	467	Bill Guerin, N.J.	.25	6.00	10.00
□□□	468	Dimitri Filimonov, Ott.	.10	3.50	6.00
□□□	469	Dave Ellett, Tor.	.10	3.50	6.00
□□□	470	Andy Moog (G), Dal.	.25	6.00	12.00
□□□	**471**	**Scott Thomas, Buf., RC**	**.10**	**3.50**	**6.00**
□□□	472	Trent Yawney, Cgy.	.10	3.50	6.00
□□□	473	Tim Sweeney, Ana.	.10	3.50	6.00
□□□	**474**	**Shjon Podein, Edm., RC**	**.10**	**3.50**	**6.00**
□□□	475	J.J. Daigneault, Mtl.	.10	3.50	6.00
□□□	476	Darren Turcotte, Hfd.	.10	3.50	6.00
□□□	477	Esa Tikkanen, NYR.	.10	3.50	6.00
□□□	478	Vitali Karamnov, Stl.	.10	3.50	6.00
□□□	**479**	**Jocelyn Thibault (G), Que., RC**	**2.00**	**45.00**	**60.00**
□□□	480	Pavel Bure, Van.	.75	60.00	80.00
□□□	481	Steve Konowalchuk, Wsh.	.10	3.50	6.00
□□□	482	Sylvain Turgeon, Ott.	.10	3.50	6.00
□□□	483	Jeff Daniels, Pgh.	.10	3.50	6.00
□□□	**484**	**Dallas Drake, Det., RC**	**.10**	**3.50**	**6.00**
□□□	**485**	**Iain Fraser, Que., RC**	**.10**	**3.50**	**6.00**
□□□	486	Joe Reekie, T.B.	.10	3.50	6.00
□□□	487	Evgeny Davydov, Fla.	.10	3.50	6.00
□□□	488	Jozef Stumpel, Bos.	.10	3.50	8.00
□□□	489	Brent Thompson, L.A.	.10	3.50	6.00
□□□	490	Terry Yake, Ana.	.10	3.50	6.00
□□□	**491**	**Derek Plante, Buf., RC**	**.25**	**5.00**	**8.00**
□□□	492	Dimitri Yushkevich, Pha.	.10	3.50	6.00
□□□	493	Wayne McBean, NYI.	.10	3.50	6.00
□□□	494	Derian Hatcher, Dal.	.25	5.00	10.00
□□□	495	Jeff Norton, S.J.	.10	3.50	6.00
□□□	496	Adam Foote, Que.	.25	6.00	10.00
□□□	497	Mike Peluso, N.J.	.10	3.50	6.00
□□□	498	Rob Pearson, Tor.	.10	3.50	6.00
□□□	499	Checklist	.10	3.50	6.00
□□□	500	Checklist	.10	3.50	6.00

NHL ALL-STARS

These cards have three versions: a Topps version, an O-Pee-Chee version and a Members Only version.

	Series One Insert Set (23 cards):	110.00	140.00	300.00
	Player	Topps	OPC	M.O.
□□□	Patrick Roy/Ed Belfour	20.00	25.00	65.00
□□□	Ray Bourque/Paul Coffey	4.00	6.00	18.00
□□□	Al Iafrate/Chris Chelios	3.00	4.00	12.00
□□□	Jaromir Jagr/Brett Hull	12.00	14.00	40.00
□□□	Pat LaFontaine/Steve Yzerman	8.00	10.00	30.00
□□□	Pavel Bure/Kevin Stevens	6.00	8.00	25.00
□□□	Craig Billington/Jon Casey	1.50	2.00	6.00
□□□	Steve Duchesne/Steve Chiasson	1.50	2.00	6.00
□□□	Scott Stevens/Phil Housley	1.50	2.00	6.00
□□□	Peter Bondra/Kelly Kisio	3.00	4.00	12.00
□□□	Adam Oates/Brian Bradley	2.00	3.00	8.00
□□□	Alexander Mogilny/Jari Kurri	3.00	4.00	12.00
□□□	Peter Sidoriewicz/Mike Vernon	1.50	2.00	6.00
□□□	Zarley Zalapski/Dave Manson	1.50	2.00	6.00
□□□	Brad Marsh/Randy Carlyle	1.50	2.00	6.00
□□□	Kirk Muller/Gary Roberts	2.00	3.00	8.00
□□□	Doug Gilmour/Joe Sakic	8.00	10.00	30.00
□□□	Mark Recchi/Luc Robitaille	2.00	3.00	8.00
□□□	Kevin Lowe/Garth Butcher	1.50	2.00	6.00
□□□	Rick Tocchet/Jeremy Roenick	2.00	3.00	8.00
□□□	Pierre Turgeon/Mike Modano	4.00	6.00	18.00
□□□	Teemu Selänne/Mike Gartner	6.00	8.00	25.00
□□□	Wayne Gretzky/Mario Lemieux	30.00	40.00	120.00

FINEST

These cards have two versions: the insert and a Members Only version.

	Series Two Insert Set (12 cards):		50.00	250.00
	No.	Player	Insert	M.O.
□□	1	Wayne Gretzky, L.A.	15.00	90.00
□□	2	Jeff Brown, Stl.	1.00	6.00
□□	3	Brett Hull, Stl.	4.00	30.00

	No.	Player		
☐☐	4	Paul Coffey, Det.	2.00	15.00
☐☐	5	Félix Potvin (G), Tor.	5.00	35.00
☐☐	6	Mike Gartner, NYR.	1.50	10.00
☐☐	7	Luc Robitaille, L.A.	1.50	10.00
☐☐	8	Marty McSorley, Pgh.	1.00	6.00
☐☐	9	Gary Roberts, Cgy.	1.50	10.00
☐☐	10	Mario Lemieux, Pgh.	12.00	70.00
☐☐	11	Patrick Roy (G), Mtl.	12.00	70.00
☐☐	12	Ray Bourque, Bos.	4.00	30.00

MASTER PHOTOS

These cards have two versions: a 5" x 7" box insert and a standard size insert card.

Insert Set (24 cards): 35.00 45.00

	No.	Player	5"x7"	Insert
☐☐	1	Pat LaFontaine, Buf.	.75	1.00
☐☐	2	Doug Gilmour, Tor.	1.50	1.50
☐☐	3	Ray Bourque, Bos.	2.00	2.50
☐☐	4	Teemu Selänne, Wpg.	3.00	3.50
☐☐	5	Eric Lindros, Pha.	5.00	8.00
☐☐	6	Ray Ferraro, NYI.	.50	.75
☐☐	7	Patrick Roy (G), Mtl.	6.50	8.00
☐☐	8	Wayne Gretzky, L.A.	8.00	10.00
☐☐	9	Brett Hull, Stl.	2.00	2.50
☐☐	10	John Vanbiesbrouck (G), Fla.	2.50	3.00
☐☐	11	Adam Oates, Bos.	1.00	1.50
☐☐	12	Tom Barrasso (G), Pgh.	.50	.75
☐☐	1	Esa Tikkanen, Edm.	.50	.75
☐☐	2	Jari Kurri, L.A.	.75	1.00
☐☐	3	Grant Fuhr (G), Buf.	.75	1.00
☐☐	4	Scott Lachance, NYI.	.50	.75
☐☐	5	Theoren Fleury, Cgy.	1.00	1.50
☐☐	6	Adam Graves, NYR.	.50	.75
☐☐	7	Rick Tabaracci (G), Wsh.	.50	.75
☐☐	8	Pierre Turgeon, NYI.	.75	1.50
☐☐	9	Steven Finn, Que.	.50	.75
☐☐	10	Craig Janney, Stl.	.50	.75
☐☐	11	Mathieu Schneider, Mtl.	.50	.75
☐☐	12	Félix Potvin (G), Tor.	2.50	3.00

TEAM U.S.A.

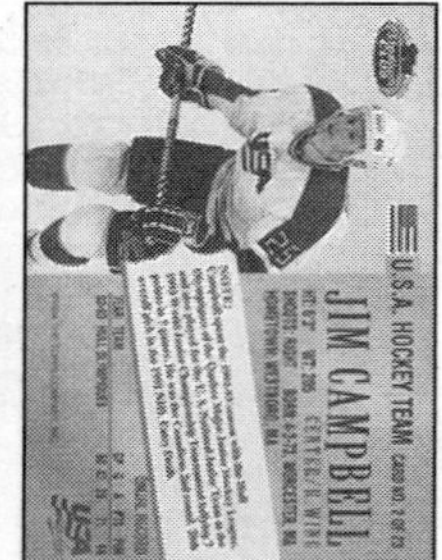

These cards have two versions: The insert and a Members Only version.

Series Two Insert Set (23 cards): 20.00 120.00

	No.	Player	Insert	M.O.
☐☐	1	Mark Beaufait	1.00	6.00
☐☐	2	Jim Campbell	2.00	10.00
☐☐	3	Ted Crowley	1.00	6.00
☐☐	4	Mike Dunham (G)	1.25	6.00
☐☐	5	Chris Ferraro	1.00	6.00
☐☐	6	Peter Ferraro	1.00	6.00
☐☐	7	Brett Hauer	1.00	6.00
☐☐	8	Darby Hendrickson	1.00	6.00
☐☐	9	Jon Hillebrandt	1.00	6.00
☐☐	10	Chris Imes	1.00	6.00
☐☐	11	Craig Johnson	1.00	6.00
☐☐	12	Peter Laviolette	1.00	6.00
☐☐	13	Jeff Lazaro	1.00	6.00
☐☐	14	John Lilley	1.00	6.00
☐☐	15	Todd Marchant	1.25	8.00
☐☐	16	Matt Martin	1.00	6.00
☐☐	17	Ian Moran	1.00	6.00
☐☐	18	Travis Richards	1.00	6.00
☐☐	19	Barry Richter	1.00	6.00
☐☐	20	David Roberts	1.00	6.00
☐☐	21	Brian Rolston	1.00	6.00
☐☐	22	David Sacco	1.00	6.00
☐☐	23	Jim Storm	1.00	6.00

1993 - 94 TOPPS STADIUM CLUB MEMBERS ONLY

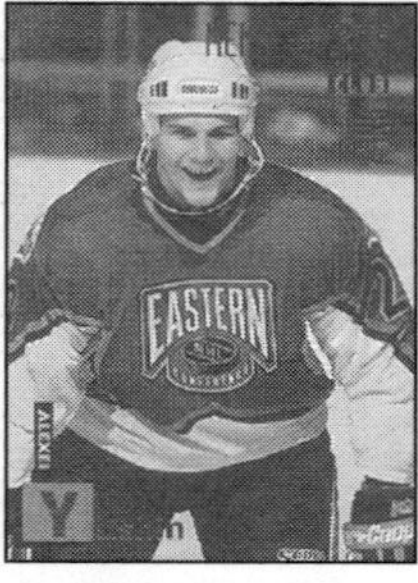

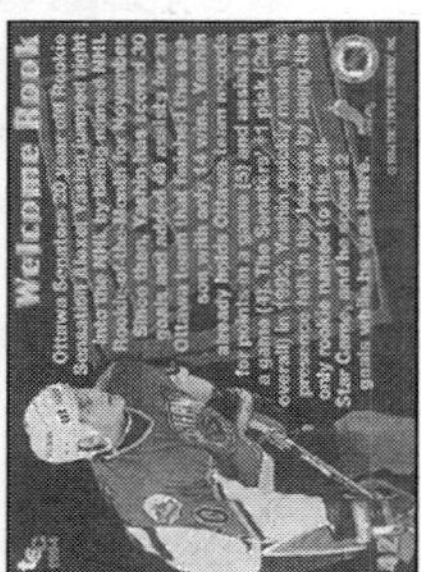

Complete Set (50 cards): 25.00

	No.	Player	NRMT-MT
☐	1	Félix Potvin (G), Tor.	1.00
☐	2	Chris Chelios, Chi.	.50
☐	3	Paul Coffey, Det.	.35
☐	4	Pavel Bure, Van.	1.25
☐	5	Wayne Gretzky, L.A.	4.00
☐	6	Brett Hull, Stl.	.75
☐	7	Al MacInnis, Cgy.	.35
☐	8	Rob Blake, L.A.	.35
☐	9	Alexei Kasatonov, Ana.	.20
☐	10	Teemu Selänne, Wpg.	1.25
☐	11	Sandis Ozolinsh, S.J.	.35
☐	12	Shayne Corson, Edm.	.35
☐	13	Dave Andreychuk, Tor.	.20
☐	14	Dave Taylor, L.A.	.20
☐	15	Sergei Fedorov, Det.	.75
☐	16	Brendan Shanahan, Stl.	1.00
☐	17	Arturs Irbe (G), S.J.	.20
☐	18	Joe Nieuwendyk, Cgy.	.35
☐	19	Russ Courtnall, Dal.	.20
☐	20	Jeremy Roenick, Chi.	.50
☐	21	Doug Gilmour, Tor.	.50
☐	22	Curtis Joseph (G), Stl.	.50
☐	23	Patrick Roy (G), Mtl.	3.00
☐	24	Brian Leetch, NYR.	.50
☐	25	Ray Bourque, Bos.	.75
☐	26	Alexander Mogilny, Buf.	.50
☐	27	Mark Messier, NYR.	.75
☐	28	Eric Lindros, Pha.	3.00
☐	29	Garry Galley, Pha.	.20
☐	30	Scott Stevens, N.J.	.35
☐	31	Al Iafrate, Bos.	.20
☐	32	Larry Murphy, Pgh.	.35
☐	33	Joe Mullen, NYR.	.35
☐	34	Mark Recchi, Pha.	.35
☐	35	Adam Graves, NYR.	.20
☐	36	Geoff Sanderson, Hfd.	.20
☐	37	Adam Oates, Bos.	.50
☐	38	Pierre Turgeon, NYI.	.35
☐	39	Joe Sakic, Que.	1.50
☐	40	John Vanbiesbrouck (G), Fla.	1.00
☐	41	Brian Bradley, T.B.	.20
☐	42	Alexei Yashin, Ott.	.75
☐	43	Bob Kudelski, Fla.	.20
☐	44	Jaromir Jagr, Pgh.	2.00
☐	45	Mike Richter (G), NYR.	.50
☐	46	Martin Brodeur (G), N.J.	1.25
☐	47	Mikael Renberg, Pha.	.35
☐	48	Derek Plante, Buf.	.35
☐	49	Jason Arnott, Edm.	.75
☐	50	Alexandre Daigle, Ott.	.50

1993 - 94 UPPER DECK

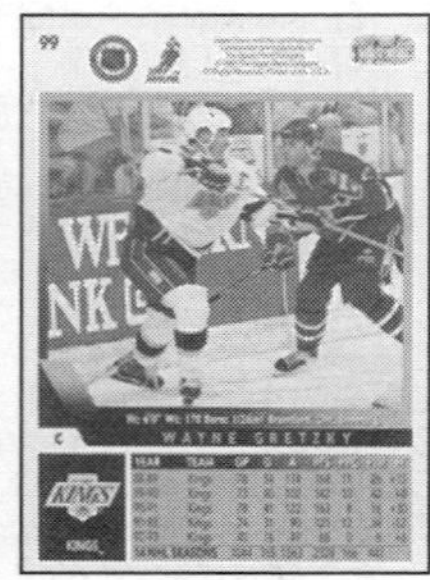

Wayne Gretzky was featured on the packaging.

Imprint: © 1993 The Upper Deck Company

Series One Set (310 cards): 20.00

Series Two Set (265 cards): 20.00

Common Player: .10

	No.	Player	NRMT-MT
☐	1	Guy Hebert (G), Ana.	.25
☐	2	Bob Bassen, Stl.	.10
☐	3	Theoren Fleury, Cgy.	.35
☐	4	Ray Whitney, S.J.	.10
☐	5	Donald Audette, Buf.	.10
☐	6	Martin Rucinsky, Que.	.10
☐	7	Lyle Odelein, Mtl.	.10
☐	8	John Vanbiesbrouck (G), Fla.	.50
☐	9	Tim Cheveldae (G), Det.	.10
☐	10	Jock Callander, T.B.	.10
☐	11	Nick Kypreos, Hfd.	.10
☐	12	Jarrold Skalde, Ana.	.10
☐	13	Gary Shuchuk, L.A.	.10
☐	14	Kris King, Wpg.	.10
☐	15	Josef Beranek, Pha.	.10
☐	16	Sean Hill, Ana.	.10
☐	17	Bob Kudelski, Ott.	.10
☐	18	Jiri Slegr, Van.	.10
☐	19	Dmitri Kvartalnov, Bos.	.10
☐	20	Drake Berehowsky, Tor.	.10
☐	21	Jean-François Quintin, S.J.	.10
☐	22	Randy Wood, Buf.	.10
☐	23	Jim McKenzie, Hfd.	.10
☐	24	Steven King, Ana.	.10
☐	25	Scott Niedermayer, N.J.	.25
☐	26	Alexander Andrijevski, Chi.	.10
☐	27	Alexei Kovalev, NYR.	.10
☐	28	Steve Konowalchuk, Wsh.	.10
☐	29	Vladimir Malakhov, NYI.	.10
☐	30	Eric Lindros, Pha.	1.50
☐	31	Mathieu Schneider, Mtl.	.10
☐	32	Russ Courtnall, Dal.	.10
☐	33	Ron Sutter, Stl.	.10
☐	**34**	**Radek Hamr, Ott., RC**	**.10**
☐	35	Pavel Bure, Van.	.75
☐	36	Joe Sacco, Ana.	.10
☐	37	Robert Petrovicky, Hfd.	.10
☐	**38**	**Anatoli Fedotov, Ana., RC**	**.10**
☐	39	Pat Falloon, S.J.	.10
☐	40	Martin Straka, Pgh.	.10
☐	41	Brad Werenka, Edm.	.10
☐	42	Mike Richter (G), NYR.	.35
☐	43	Mike McPhee, Dal.	.10
☐	44	Sylvain Turgeon, Ott.	.10
☐	45	Tom Barrasso (G), Pgh.	.25
☐	46	Anatoli Semenov, Ana.	.10
☐	47	Joe Murphy, Chi.	.10
☐	48	Rob Pearson, Tor.	.10
☐	49	Patrick Roy (G), Mtl.	1.50
☐	**50**	**Dallas Drake, Det., RC**	**.10**
☐	51	Mark Messier, NYR.	.50
☐	**52**	**Scott Pellerin, N.J., RC**	**.10**
☐	53	Teppo Numminen, Wpg.	.10
☐	54	Chris Kontos, T.B.	.10
☐	55	Richard Matvichuk, Dal.	.10
☐	56	Dale Craigwell, S.J.	.10
☐	57	Mke Eastwood, Tor.	.10
☐	58	Bernie Nicholls, N.J.	.10
☐	59	Travis Green, NYI.	.10
☐	**60**	**Shjon Podein, Edm., RC**	**.10**
☐	**61**	**Darrin Madeley (G), Ott., RC**	**.10**
☐	62	Dixon Ward, Van.	.10

	No.	Card	Value
☐	63	André Faust, Pha.	.10
☐	64	Tony Amonte, NYR.	.25
☐	65	Joe Cirella, Fla.	.10
☐	66	Michel Petit, Cgy.	.10
☐	67	Dave Lowry, Fla.	.10
☐	68	Shawn Chambers, T.B.	.10
☐	69	Joe Sakic, Que.	.85
☐	70	Michael Nylander, Hfd.	.10
☐	71	Peter Andersson, NYR.	.10
☐	72	Sandis Ozolinsh, S.J.	.25
☐	**73**	**Joby Messier, NYR., RC**	**.10**
☐	74	John Blue (G), Bos.	.10
☐	75	Pat Elynuik, Wsh.	.10
☐	**76**	**Keith Osborne, T.B., RC**	**.10**
☐	77	Greg Adams, Van.	.10
☐	78	Chris Gratton, T.B.	.35
☐	79	Louie DeBrusk, Edm.	.10
☐	**80**	**Todd Harkins, Cgy., RC**	**.10**
☐	81	Neil Brady, Ott.	.10
☐	82	Philippe Boucher, Buf.	.10
☐	83	Darryl Sydor, L.A.	.10
☐	**84**	**Oleg Petrov, Mtl., RC**	**.10**
☐	85	Andrei Kovalenko, Que.	.10
☐	86	Dave Andreychuk, Tor.	.10
☐	87	Jeff Daniels, Pgh.	.10
☐	88	Kevin Todd, Edm.	.10
☐	89	Mark Tinordi, Dal.	.10
☐	90	Garry Galley, Pha.	.10
☐	91	Shawn Burr, Det.	.10
☐	92	Tom Pederson, S.J.	.10
☐	93	Warren Rychel, L.A.	.10
☐	94	Stu Barnes, Wpg.	.10
☐	95	Peter Bondra, Wsh.	.35
☐	96	Brian Skrudland, Fla.	.10
☐	97	Doug MacDonald, Buf.	.10
☐	98	Rob Niedermayer, Fla.	.25
☐	99	Wayne Gretzky, L.A.	2.00
☐	100	Peter Taglianetti, Pgh.	.10
☐	101	Don Sweeney, Bos.	.10
☐	102	Andrei Lomakin, Fla.	.10
☐	103	Checklist 1 (1 - 103)	.10
☐	104	Sergio Momesso, Van.	.10
☐	105	Dave Archibald, Ott.	.10
☐	106	Karl Dykhuis, Chi.	.10
☐	107	Scott Mellanby, Fla.	.10
☐	108	Paul DiPietro, Mtl.	.10
☐	109	Neal Broten, Dal.	.10
☐	110	Chris Terreri (G), N.J.	.10
☐	111	Craig MacTavish, Edm.	.10
☐	112	Jody Hull, Ott.	.10
☐	113	Philippe Bozon, Stl.	.10
☐	114	Geoff Courtnall, Van.	.10
☐	115	Ed Olczyk, NYR.	.10
☐	116	Ray Bourque, Bos.	.50
☐	117	Gilbert Dionne, Mtl.	.10
☐	118	Valeri Kamensky, Que.	.25
☐	119	Scott Stevens, N.J.	.25
☐	120	Per-Erik Eklund, Pha.	.10
☐	121	Brian Bradley, T.B.	.10
☐	122	Steve Thomas, NYI.	.10
☐	123	Don Beaupré (G), Wsh.	.10
☐	124	Joel Otto, Cgy.	.10
☐	125	Arturs Irbe (G), S.J.	.10
☐	126	Kevin Stevens, Pgh.	.10
☐	127	Dimitri Yushkevich, Pha.	.10
☐	128	Adam Graves, NYR.	.10
☐	129	Chris Chelios, Chi.	.35
☐	130	Jeff Brown, Stl.	.10
☐	131	Paul Ranheim, Cgy.	.10
☐	132	Shayne Corson, Edm.	.25
☐	133	Curtis Leschyshyn, Que.	.10
☐	134	John MacLean, N.J.	.10
☐	135	Dimitri Khristich, Wsh.	.10
☐	136	Dino Ciccarelli, Det.	.25
☐	137	Pat LaFontaine, Buf.	.25
☐	138	Pat Poulin, Hfd.	.10
☐	139	Jaromir Jagr, Pgh.	1.25
☐	140	Kevin Hatcher, Wsh.	.10
☐	141	Christian Ruuttu, Chi.	.10
☐	142	Ulf Samuelsson, Pgh.	.10
☐	143	Ted Donato, Bos.	.10
☐	144	Bob Essensa (G), Wpg.	.10
☐	145	Dave Gagner, Dal.	.10
☐	146	Tony Granato, L.A.	.10
☐	147	Ed Belfour (G), Chi.	.35
☐	148	Kirk Muller, Mtl.	.10
☐	**149**	**Rob Gaudreau, S.J., RC**	**.10**
☐	150	Nicklas Lidstrom, Det.	.25
☐	151	Gary Roberts, Cgy.	.25
☐	152	Trent Klatt, Dal.	.10
☐	153	Ray Ferraro, NYI.	.10
☐	154	Michal Pivonka, Wsh.	.10
☐	155	Mike Foligno, Tor.	.10
☐	156	Kirk McLean (G), Van.	.25
☐	157	Curtis Joseph (G), Stl.	.60
☐	158	Roman Hamrlik, T.B.	.10
☐	159	Félix Potvin (G), Tor.	.50
☐	160	Brett Hull, Stl.	.50
☐	161	Alexei Zhitnik, L.A.	.10
☐	162	Alexei Zhamnov, Wpg.	.25
☐	163	Grant Fuhr (G), Buf.	.25
☐	164	Nikolai Borschevsky, Tor.	.10
☐	165	Tomas Jelinek, Ott.	.10
☐	166	Thomas Steen, Wpg.	.10
☐	167	John LeClair, Mtl.	.60
☐	168	Vladimir Vujtek, Edm.	.10
☐	169	Richard Smehlik, Buf.	.10
☐	170	Alexandre Daigle, Ott.	.35
☐	171	Sergei Fedorov, Det.	.50
☐	172	Steve Larmer, Chi.	.10
☐	173	Darius Kasparaitis, NYI.	.10
☐	174	Igor Kravchuk, Edm.	.10
☐	175	Owen Nolan, Que.	.25
☐	176	Rob DiMaio, T.B.	.10
☐	177	Mike Vernon (G), Cgy.	.35
☐	178	Alexander Semak, N.J.	.10
☐	179	Rick Tocchet, Pgh.	.10
☐	180	Bill Ranford (G), Edm.	.20
☐	181	Sergei Zubov, NYR.	.20
☐	182	Tommy Söderström (G), Pha.	.10
☐	183	Al Iafrate, Wsh.	.10
☐	184	Eric Desjardins, Mtl.	.25
☐	185	Bret Hedican, Stl.	.10
☐	186	Joe Mullen, Pgh.	.25
☐	187	Doug Bodger, Buf.	.10
☐	188	Tomas Sandström, L.A.	.10
☐	189	Glen Murray, Bos.	.10
☐	190	Chris Pronger, Hfd.	.35
☐	191	Mike Craig, Dal.	.10
☐	192	Jim Paek, Pgh.	.10
☐	193	Doug Zmolek, S.J.	.10
☐	194	Yves Racine, Det.	.10
☐	195	Keith Tkachuk, Wpg.	.50
☐	196	Chris Lindberg, Cgy.	.10
☐	197	Kelly Buchberger, Edm.	.10
☐	198	Mark Janssens, Hfd.	.10
☐	199	Peter Zezel, Tor.	.10
☐	200	Bob Probert, Det.	.10
☐	201	Brad May, Buf.	.10
☐	202	Rob Zamuner, T.B.	.25
☐	203	Stéphane Fiset (G), Que.	.25
☐	204	Derian Hatcher, Dal.	.25
☐	205	Mike Gartner, NYR.	.25
☐	206	Checklist 2 (104 - 206)	.10
☐	207	Todd Krygier, Wsh.	.10
☐	208	Glen Wesley, Bos.	.10
☐	209	Fredrik Olausson, Wpg.	.10
☐	210	Patrick Flatley, NYI.	.10
☐	211	Cliff Ronning, Van.	.10
☐	212	Kevin Dineen, Pha.	.10
☐	213	Zarley Zalapski, Hfd.	.10
☐	214	Stéphane Matteau, Chi.	.10
☐	215	Dave Ellett, Tor.	.10
☐	216	Kelly Hrudey (G), L.A.	.10
☐	217	Steve Duchesne, Que.	.10
☐	218	Bobby Holik, N.J.	.10
☐	219	Brad Dalgarno, NYI.	.10
☐	220	Checklist No. 3	.10
☐	221	Pat LaFontaine, Buf.	.25
☐	222	Mark Recchi, Pha.	.25
☐	223	Joe Sakic, Que.	.50
☐	224	Pierre Turgeon, NYI.	.10
☐	225	Craig Janney, Stl.	.10
☐	226	Adam Oates, Bos.	.25
☐	227	Steve Yzerman, Det.	.50
☐	228	Mats Sundin, Que.	.25
☐	229	Theoren Fleury, Cgy.	.25
☐	230	Kevin Stevens, Pgh.	.10
☐	231	Luc Robitaille, L.A.	.25
☐	232	Brett Hull, Stl.	.25
☐	233	Rick Tocchet, Pgh.	.10
☐	234	Alexander Mogilny, Buf.	.25
☐	235	Jeremy Roenick, Chi.	.25
☐	236	CL: G. Lévêque, L.A./T. Stevenson, Mtl.	.10
☐	**237**	**Adam Bennett, Chi., RC**	**.10**
☐	**238**	**Dody Wood, S.J., RC**	**.10**
☐	**239**	**Niclas Andersson, Que., RC**	**.10**
☐	**240**	**Jason Bowen, Pha., RC**	**.10**
☐	**241**	**Steve Junker, NYI., RC**	**.10**
☐	242	Bryan Smolinski, Bos.	.10
☐	**243**	**Chris Simon, Que., RC**	**.25**
☐	244	Sergei Zholtok, Bos.	.10
☐	**245**	**Dan Ratushny, Van., RC**	**.10**
☐	246	Guy Lévêque, L.A.	.10
☐	**247**	**Scott Thomas, Buf., RC**	**.10**
☐	248	Turner Stevenson, Mtl.	.10
☐	249	Dan Keczmer, Hfd.	.10
☐	250	CL: Alexandre Daigle, Ott.	.10
☐	**251**	**Adrian Aucoin, Cdn., RC**	**.10**
☐	**252**	**Jason Smith, Cdn., RC**	**.10**
☐	**253**	**Ralph Intranuovo, Cdn., RC**	**.10**
☐	254	Jason Dawe, Cdn.	.10
☐	**255**	**Jeff Bes, Cdn., RC**	**.10**
☐	256	Tyler Wright, Cdn.	.10
☐	257	Martin Lapointe, Cdn.	.10
☐	**258**	**Jeff Shantz, Cdn., RC**	**.10**
☐	**259**	**Martin Gendron, Cdn., RC**	**.10**
☐	**260**	**Philippe DeRouville (G), Cdn., RC**	**.10**
☐	**261**	**Frantisek Kaberle,Cze., RC**	**.10**
☐	**262**	**Radim Bicanek, Cze., RC**	**.10**
☐	**263**	**Tomas Klimt, Cze., RC**	**.10**
☐	**264**	**Tomas Nemcicky, Cze., RC**	**.10**
☐	**265**	**Richard Kapus, Cze., RC**	**.10**
☐	**266**	**Patrik Krisak, Cze., RC**	**.10**
☐	**267**	**Roman Kadera, Cze., RC**	**.10**
☐	268	Kimmo Timonen, Fin.	.10
☐	**269**	**Jukka Ollila, Fin., RC**	**.10**
☐	270	Tuomas Gronman, Fin.	.10
☐	**271**	**Mikko Luovi, Fin., RC**	**.10**
☐	**272**	**Sergei Gonchar, Rus., RC**	**.25**
☐	**273**	**Maxim Golanov, Rus., RC**	**.10**
☐	**274**	**Oleg Belov, Rus., RC**	**.10**
☐	**275**	**Sergei Klimovich, Rus., RC**	**.10**
☐	**276**	**Sergei Brylin, Rus., RC, Error (Unkown player)**	**.10**
☐	277	Alexei Yashin, Rus.	.35
☐	**278**	**Vitali Tomilin, Rus., RC**	**.10**
☐	**279**	**Alexander Cherbayev, Rus., RC**	**.10**
☐	280	Eric Lindros, Pha.	.75
☐	281	Teemu Selänne, Wpg.	.35
☐	282	Joé Juneau, Bos.	.10
☐	283	Vladimir Malakhov, NYI.	.10
☐	284	Scott Niedermayer, N.J.	.10
☐	285	Félix Potvin (G), Tor.	.35
☐	286	TL: Adam Oates, Bos.	.20
☐	287	TL: Pat LaFontaine, Buf.	.25
☐	288	TL: Theoren Fleury, Cgy.	.25
☐	289	TL: Jeremy Roenick, Chi.	.25
☐	290	TL: Steve Yzerman, Det.	.50
☐	291	TL: Petr Klima/Doug Weight, Edm.	.25
☐	292	TL: Geoff Sanderson, Hfd.	.10
☐	293	TL: Luc Robitaille, L.A.	.25
☐	294	TL: Mike Modano, Dal.	.25
☐	295	TL: Vincent Damphousse, Mtl.	.25
☐	296	TL: Claude Lemieux, N.J.	.10
☐	297	TL: Pierre Turgeon, NYI.	.25
☐	298	TL: Mark Messier, NYR.	.25
☐	299	TL: Norm Maciver, Ott.	.10
☐	300	TL: Mark Recchi, Pha.	.25
☐	301	TL: Mario Lemieux, Pgh.	1.00
☐	302	TL: Mats Sundin, Que.	.25
☐	303	TL: Craig Janney, Stl.	.10
☐	304	TL: Kelly Kisio, S.J.	.10
☐	305	TL: Brian Bradley, T.B.	.10
☐	306	TL: Doug Gilmour, Tor.	.25
☐	307	TL: Pavel Bure, Van.	.35
☐	308	TL: Peter Bondra, Wsh.	.25
☐	309	TL: Teemu Selänne, Wpg.	.35
☐	310	Checklist 3 (207 - 310)	.10
☐	311	Terry Yake, Ana.	.10
☐	312	Bob Sweeney, Buf.	.10
☐	313	Robert Reichel, Cgy.	.10
☐	314	Jeremy Roenick, Chi.	.35
☐	315	Paul Coffey, Det.	.25
☐	316	Geoff Sanderson, Hfd.	.10
☐	317	Rob Blake, L.A.	.25

	No.	Player	Price
☐	318	Patrice Brisebois, Mtl.	.10
☐	**319**	**Jaroslav Modry, N.J., RC**	**.10**
☐	320	Scott Lachance, NYI.	.10
☐	321	Glenn Healy (G), NYR.	.10
☐	322	Martin Gelinas, Que.	.10
☐	323	Craig Janney, Stl.	.10
☐	**324**	**Bill McDougall, T.B., RC**	**.10**
☐	325	Shawn Antoski, Van.	.10
☐	326	Olaf Kolzig (G), Wsh.	.35
☐	327	Adam Oates, Bos.	.25
☐	328	Dirk Graham, Chi.	.10
☐	329	Brent Gilchrist, Dal.	.10
☐	330	Zdeno Ciger, Edm.	.10
☐	331	Pat Verbeek, Hfd.	.10
☐	332	Jari Kurri, L.A.	.25
☐	333	Kevin Haller, Mtl.	.10
☐	334	Martin Brodeur (G), N.J.	.75
☐	335	Norm Maciver, Ott.	.10
☐	336	Dominic Roussel (G), Pha.	.10
☐	**337**	**Iain Fraser, Que., RC**	**.10**
☐	338	Vitali Karamnov, Stl.	.10
☐	**339**	**René Corbet, Que., RC**	**.10**
☐	340	Wendel Clark, Tor.	.25
☐	341	Mike Ridley, Wsh.	.10
☐	342	Nelson Emerson, Wpg.	.10
☐	343	Joé Juneau, Bos.	.10
☐	**344**	**Vesa Viitakoski, Cgy., RC**	**.10**
☐	345	Steve Chiasson, Det.	.10
☐	346	Andrew Cassels, Hfd.	.10
☐	347	Pierre Turgeon, NYI.	.25
☐	348	Brian Leetch, NYR.	.35
☐	349	Alexei Yashin, Ott.	.60
☐	350	Mark Recchi, Pha.	.25
☐	351	Ron Francis, Pgh.	.35
☐	352	Mike Ricci, Que.	.10
☐	353	Igor Korolev, Stl.	.10
☐	**354**	**Brent Gretzky, T.B., RC**	**.10**
☐	355	Dave Poulin, Wsh.	.10
☐	356	Cam Neely, Bos.	.25
☐	357	Gary Suter, Cgy.	.10
☐	358	Dave Manson, Edm.	.10
☐	359	Robert Kron, Hfd.	.10
☐	360	Ulf Dahlen, Dal.	.10
☐	361	Rod Brind'Amour, Pha.	.25
☐	362	Alexei Gusarov, Que.	.10
☐	363	Vitali Prokhorov, Stl.	.10
☐	**364**	**Damian Rhodes (G), Tor., RC**	**.50**
☐	365	Paul Ysebaert, Wpg.	.10
☐	366	Vladimir Konstantinov, Det.	.10
☐	367	Steve Rice, Edm.	.10
☐	368	Brian Propp, Hfd.	.10
☐	369	Valeri Zelepukin, N.J.	.10
☐	370	David Volek, NYI.	.10
☐	371	Sergei Nemchinov, NYR.	.10
☐	372	Pavol Demitra, Ott.	.10
☐	373	Brent Fedyk, Pha.	.10
☐	374	Larry Murphy, Pgh.	.25
☐	375	Dave Karpa, Que.	.10
☐	376	Dave Babych, Van.	.10
☐	377	Keith Jones, Wsh.	.10
☐	378	Neil Wilkinson, Chi.	.10
☐	379	Jozef Stumpel, Bos.	.10
☐	380	Vincent Damphousse, Mtl.	.35
☐	381	Tom Kurvers, NYI.	.10
☐	382	Doug Gilmour, Tor.	.35
☐	383	Trevor Linden, Van.	.25
☐	384	Kelly Miller, Wsh.	.10
☐	385	Tim Sweeney, Ana.	.10
☐	386	Mikhail Tatarinov, Bos.	.10
☐	387	Dominik Hasek (G), Buf.	.75
☐	388	Steve Yzerman, Det.	1.25
☐	389	Scott Pearson, Edm.	.10
☐	390	Brian Bellows, Mtl.	.10
☐	391	Claude Lemieux, N.J.	.10
☐	392	Marty McInnis, NYI.	.10
☐	393	Jim Sandlak, Hfd.	.10
☐	**394**	**Jocelyn Thibault (G), Que., RC**	**2.00**
☐	395	John Cullen, Tor.	.10
☐	396	Joe Nieuwendyk, Cgy.	.25
☐	397	Mike Modano, Dal.	.50
☐	398	Ray Sheppard, Det.	.10
☐	399	Trevor Kidd (G), Cgy.	.25
☐	400	Checklist 1 (311 - 400)	.10
☐	401	Frank Pietrangelo (G), Hfd.	.10
☐	402	Stéphan Lebeau, Mtl.	.10
☐	403	Stéphane Richer, N.J.	.10
☐	404	Greg Gilbert, NYR.	.10
☐	405	Dmitri Filimonov, Ott.	.10
☐	406	Vjateslav Butsayev, Pha.	.10
☐	407	Mario Lemieux, Pgh.	1.50
☐	408	Kevin Miller, Stl.	.10
☐	409	John Tucker, T.B.	.10
☐	410	Murray Craven, Van.	.10
☐	411	Dale Hawerchuk, Buf.	.25
☐	412	Al MacInnis, Cgy.	.25
☐	413	Keith Primeau, Det.	.25
☐	414	Luc Robitaille, L.A.	.25
☐	415	Benoît Brunet, Mtl.	.10
☐	416	Tom Chorske, N.J.	.10
☐	417	Derek King, NYI.	.10
☐	418	Troy Mallette, Ott.	.10
☐	419	Mats Sundin, Que.	.50
☐	420	Kent Manderville, Tor.	.10
☐	421	Kip Miller, S.J.	.10
☐	422	Jarkko Varvio, Dal.	.10
☐	**423**	**Jason Arnott, Edm., RC**	**1.50**
☐	424	Craig Billington (G), Ott.	.10
☐	**425**	**Stewart Malgunas, Pha., RC**	**.10**
☐	426	Ron Tugnutt (G), Ana.	.10
☐	**427**	**Alexei Kudashov, Tor., RC**	**.10**
☐	**428**	**Harijs Vitolinsh, Wpg., RC**	**.10**
☐	429	Bill Houlder, Ana.	.10
☐	430	Craig Simpson, Buf.	.10
☐	431	Wes Walz, Cgy.	.10
☐	**432**	**Micah Aivazoff, Det., RC**	**.10**
☐	**433**	**Scott Levins, Fla., RC**	**.10**
☐	434	Ron Hextall (G), NYI.	.25
☐	**435**	**Fred Brathwaite (G), Edm., RC**	**.10**
☐	**436**	**Chad Penney, Ott., RC**	**.10**
☐	**437**	**Vlastimil Kroupa, S.J., RC**	**.10**
☐	438	Troy Loney, Ana.	.10
☐	439	Matthew Barnaby, Buf.	.10
☐	440	Kevin Todd, Chi.	.10
☐	441	Paul Cavallini, Dal.	.10
☐	442	Doug Weight, Edm.	.35
☐	443	Evgeny Davydov, Fla.	.10
☐	444	Dominic Lavoie, L.A.	.10
☐	**445**	**Peter Popovic, Mtl., RC**	**.10**
☐	446	Sergei Makarov, S.J.	.10
☐	**447**	**Matt Martin, Tor., RC**	**.10**
☐	448	Teemu Selänne, Wpg.	.75
☐	449	Todd Ewen, Ana.	.10
☐	**450**	**Sergei Petrenko, Buf., RC**	**.10**
☐	**451**	**Jeff Shantz, Chi., RC**	**.10**
☐	**452**	**Greg Johnson, Det., RC**	**.10**
☐	**453**	**Brent Severyn, Fla., RC**	**.10**
☐	454	Shawn McEachern, L.A.	.10
☐	455	Pierre Sévigny, Mtl.	.10
☐	456	Benoît Hogue, NYI.	.10
☐	457	Esa Tikkanen, NYR.	.10
☐	458	Brian Glynn, Ott.	.10
☐	459	Doug Brown, Pgh.	.10
☐	**460**	**Mike Rathje, S.J., RC**	**.10**
☐	**461**	**Rudy Poeschek, T.B., RC**	**.10**
☐	462	Jason Woolley, Wsh.	.10
☐	**463**	**Patrik Carnback, Ana., RC**	**.10**
☐	**464**	**Cam Stewart, Bos., RC**	**.10**
☐	465	Petr Svoboda, Buf.	.10
☐	**466**	**Ted Drury, Cgy., RC**	**.10**
☐	**467**	**Ladislav Karabin, Pgh., RC**	**.10**
☐	468	Paul Broten, Dal.	.10
☐	469	Alexander Godynyuk, Fla.	.10
☐	**470**	**Bob Jay, L.A., RC**	**.10**
☐	471	Steve Larmer, NYR.	.10
☐	**472**	**Jim Montgomery, Stl., RC**	**.10**
☐	473	Daren Puppa (G), Tor.	.10
☐	474	Alexei Kasatonov, Ana.	.10
☐	**475**	**Derek Plante, Buf., RC**	**.25**
☐	**476**	**German Titov, Cgy., RC**	**.10**
☐	477	Steve Dubinsky, Chi.	.10
☐	478	Andy Moog (G), Dal.	.25
☐	**479**	**Aaron Ward, Det., RC**	**.25**
☐	480	Dean McAmmond, Edm.	.10
☐	481	Randy Gilhen, Fla.	.10
☐	**482**	**Jason Muzzatti (G), Cgy., RC**	**.10**
☐	483	Corey Millen, N.J.	.10
☐	484	Alexander Karpovtsev, NYR.	.10
☐	**485**	**Bill Huard, Ott., RC**	**.10**
☐	486	Mikael Renberg, Pha.	.25
☐	487	Marty McSorley, Pgh.	.10
☐	488	Alexander Mogilny, Buf.	.35
☐	**489**	**Michal Sykora, S.J., RC**	**.10**
☐	490	Checklist 2 (401 - 490)	.10
☐	491	Tom Tilley, Stl.	.10
☐	**492**	**Boris Mironov, Wpg., RC**	**.10**
☐	493	Sandy McCarthy, Cgy.	.10
☐	**494**	**Mark Astley, Buf., RC**	**.10**
☐	495	Vyacheslav Kozlov, Det.	.10
☐	496	Brian Benning, Fla.	.10
☐	497	Eric Weinrich, Chi.	.10
☐	**498**	**Robert Burakovsky, Ott., RC**	**.10**
☐	499	Patrick Lebeau, Fla.	.10
☐	500	Markus Naslund, Pgh.	.10
☐	501	Jimmy Waite (G), S.J.	.10
☐	502	Denis Savard, T.B.	.25
☐	503	José Charbonneau, Van.	.10
☐	504	Randy Burridge, Wsh.	.10
☐	505	Arto Blomsten, Wpg.	.10
☐	506	Shaun Van Allen, Ana.	.10
☐	507	Jon Casey (G), Bos.	.10
☐	**508**	**Darren McCarty, Det., RC**	**.25**
☐	**509**	**Roman Oksiuta, Edm., RC**	**.10**
☐	510	Jody Hull, Fla.	.10
☐	511	Scott Scissons NYI.	.10
☐	512	Jeff Norton, S.J.	.10
☐	513	Dmitri Mironov, Tor.	.10
☐	514	Sergei Bautin, Wpg.	.10
☐	515	Garry Valk, Ana.	.10
☐	516	Keith Carney, Chi.	.10
☐	517	James Black, Dal.	.10
☐	518	Pat Peake, Wsh.	.10
☐	**519**	**Chris Osgood (G), Det., RC**	**2.50**
☐	520	Kirk Maltby, Edm.	.10
☐	521	Gord Murphy, Fla.	.10
☐	**522**	**Mattias Norstrom, NYR., RC**	**.10**
☐	**523**	**Milos Holan, Pha., RC**	**.10**
☐	524	Dave McLlwain, Ott.	.10
☐	525	Phil Housley, Stl.	.10
☐	526	Petr Klima, T.B.	.10
☐	527	John McIntyre, Van.	.10
☐	528	Enrico Ciccone, Wsh.	.10
☐	529	Stéphane Quintal, Wpg.	.10
☐	530	CL: Brent Tully, Cdn.	.10
☐	**531**	**Anson Carter, Cdn., RC**	**.50**
☐	**532**	**Jeff Friesen, Cdn., RC**	**1.25**
☐	**533**	**Yanick Dubé, Cdn., RC**	**.10**
☐	**534**	**Jason Botterill, Cdn., RC**	**.25**
☐	**535**	**Todd Harvey, Cdn., RC**	**.25**
☐	**536**	**Manny Fernandez (G), Cdn., RC**	**.25**
☐	**537**	**Jason Allison, Cdn., RC**	**2.00**
☐	**538**	**Jamie Storr (G), Cdn., RC**	**.50**
☐	**539**	**Rick Girard, Cdn., RC**	**.10**
☐	**540**	**Martin Gendron, Cdn., RC**	**.10**
☐	**541**	**Joel Bouchard, Cdn., RC**	**.10**
☐	**542**	**Michael Peca, Cdn., RC**	**1.00**
☐	**543**	**Nick Stajduhar, Cdn., RC**	**.10**
☐	**544**	**Brendan Witt, Cdn., RC**	**.25**
☐	**545**	**Aaron Gavey, Cdn., RC**	**.10**
☐	**546**	**Chris Armstrong, Cdn., RC**	**.10**
☐	**547**	**Curtis Bowen, Cdn., RC**	**.10**
☐	**548**	**Brandon Convery, Cdn., RC**	**.10**
☐	**549**	**Bryan McCabe, Cdn., RC**	**.50**
☐	**550**	**Marty Murray, Cdn., RC**	**.10**
☐	551	Ryan Sittler, USA.	.10
☐	**552**	**Jason McBain, USA., RC**	**.10**
☐	**553**	**Richard Park, USA., RC**	**.10**
☐	**554**	**Aaron Ellis (G), USA., RC**	**.10**
☐	**555**	**Toby Kvalevog (G), USA., RC**	**.10**
☐	**556**	**Jay Pandolfo, USA., RC**	**.10**
☐	**557**	**John Emmons, USA., RC**	**.10**
☐	**558**	**David Wilkie, USA., RC**	**.10**
☐	**559**	**John Varga, USA., RC**	**.10**
☐	**560**	**Jason Bonsignore, USA., RC**	**.10**
☐	**561**	**Deron Quint, USA., RC**	**.10**
☐	562	Adam Deadmarsh, USA.	.35
☐	**563**	**Joe Coleman, USA., RC**	**.10**
☐	**564**	**Bob Lachance, USA., RC**	**.10**
☐	**565**	**Chris O'Sullivan, USA., RC**	**.10**
☐	**566**	**Jamie Langenbrunner, USA., RC**	**.85**
☐	**567**	**Kevin Hilton, USA., RC**	**.10**
☐	**568**	**Kevin Adams, USA., RC**	**.10**
☐	569	Saku Koivu, Fin.	2.00
☐	**570**	**Mats Lindgren, Swe., RC**	**.25**
☐	**571**	**Valeri Bure, Rus. RC**	**.50**
☐	**572**	**Edvin Frylen, Swe., RC**	**.10**

	No.	Player	NRMT-MT
☐	**573**	**Jaroslav Miklenda, Cze., RC**	**.10**
☐	**574**	**Vadim Sharifjanov, Rus., RC**	**.25**
☐	575	Checklist 3 (491 - 575)	.10
	No.	**Collector Card**	**NRMT-MT**
☐	SP4	Teemu Selänne Hologram	2.50

AWARD WINNERS

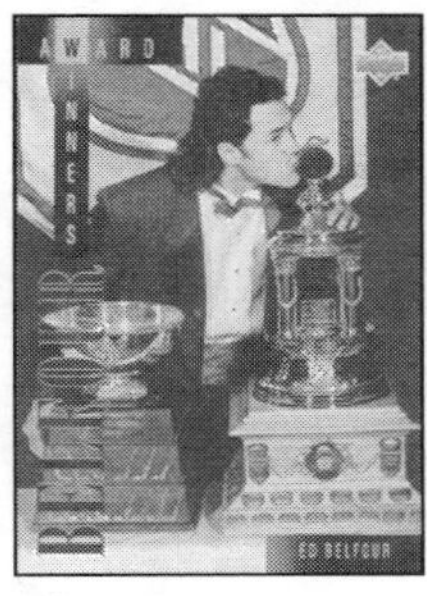

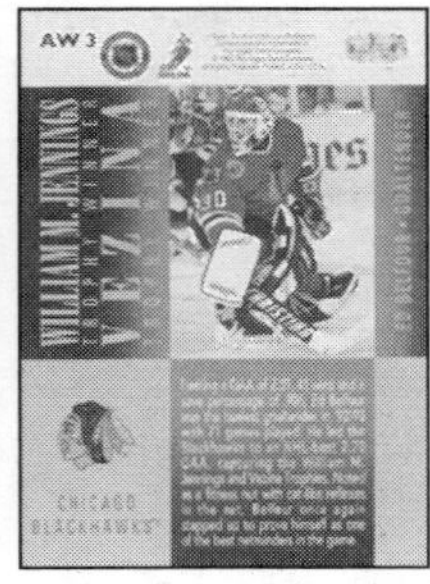

Insert Set (8 cards): **40.00**

	No.	Player	NRMT-MT
☐	AW1	Mario Lemieux, Pgh.	15.00
☐	AW2	Teemu Selänne, Wpg.	7.00
☐	AW3	Ed Belfour (G), Chi.	2.00
☐	AW4	Patrick Roy (G), Mtl.	15.00
☐	AW5	Chris Chelios, Chi.	3.00
☐	AW6	Doug Gilmour, Tor.	2.00
☐	AW7	Pierre Turgeon, NYI.	1.50
☐	AW8	Dave Poulin, Bos.	1.00

FUTURE HEROES

Insert Set (10 cards): **140.00**

	No.	Player	NRMT-MT
☐		Title Card	12.00
☐	28	Félix Potvin (G), Tor.	15.00
☐	29	Pat Falloon, S.J.	5.00
☐	30	Pavel Bure, Van.	18.00
☐	31	Eric Lindros, Pha.	35.00
☐	32	Teemu Selänne, Wpg.	18.00
☐	33	Jaromir Jagr, Pgh.	25.00
☐	34	Alexander Mogilny, Buf.	10.00
☐	35	Joé Juneau, Bos.	5.00
☐	36	Checklist	20.00

GRETZKY'S GREAT ONES

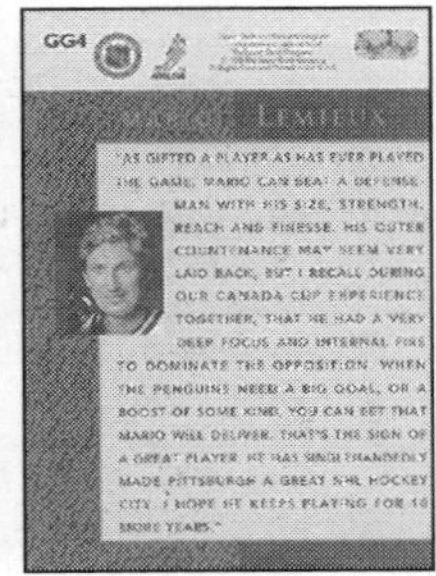

Insert Set (10 cards): **10.00**

	No.	Player	NRMT-MT
☐	GG1	Denis Savard, Mtl.	.50
☐	GG2	Chris Chelios, Chi.	1.25
☐	GG3	Brett Hull, Stl.	1.50
☐	GG4	Mario Lemieux, Pgh.	5.00
☐	GG5	Mark Messier, NYR.	1.50
☐	GG6	Paul Coffey, Pgh.	.50
☐	GG7	Theoren Fleury, Cgy.	.75
☐	GG8	Luc Robitaille, L.A.	.50
☐	GG9	Marty McSorley, L.A.	.50
☐	GG10	Grant Fuhr (G), Edm.	.75

HAT TRICKS

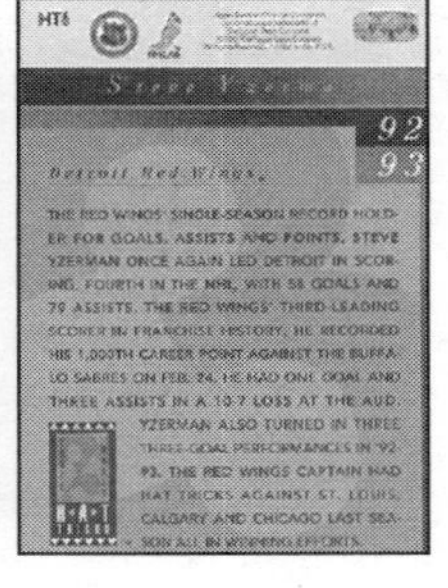

Insert Set (20 cards): **10.00**

	No.	Player	NRMT-MT
☐	HT1	Adam Graves, NYR.	.50
☐	HT2	Geoff Sanderson, Hfd.	.50
☐	HT3	Gary Roberts, Cgy.	.50
☐	HT4	Robert Reichel, Cgy.	.50
☐	HT5	Adam Oates, Bos.	.75
☐	HT6	Steve Yzerman, Det.	3.00
☐	HT7	Alexei Kovalev, NYR.	.50
☐	HT8	Vincent Damphousse, Mtl.	.50
☐	HT9	Rob Gaudreau, S.J.	.50
☐	HT10	Pat LaFontaine, Buf.	.50
☐	HT11	Pierre Turgeon, NYI.	.50
☐	HT12	Rick Tocchet, Pgh.	.50
☐	HT13	Michael Nylander, Hfd.	.50
☐	HT14	Steve Larmer, Det.	.50
☐	HT15	Alexander Mogilny, Buf.	.75
☐	HT16	Owen Nolan, Que.	.50
☐	HT17	Luc Robitaille, L.A.	.50
☐	HT18	Jeremy Roenick, Chi.	.75
☐	HT19	Kevin Stevens, Pgh.	.50
☐	HT20	Mats Sundin, Que.	1.50

NEXT IN LINE

Insert Set (6 cards): **15.00**

	No.	Player	NRMT-MT
☐	NL1	Wayne Gretzky/Michael Nylander	6.00
☐	NL2	Brett Hull/ Patrick Poulin	1.50
☐	NL3	Steve Yzerman/Joe Sakic	3.00
☐	NL4	Ray Bourque/Brian Leetch	1.50
☐	NL5	Doug Gilmour/Keith Tkachuk	1.00
☐	NL6	Patrick Roy/Félix Potvin	6.00

NHL'S BEST

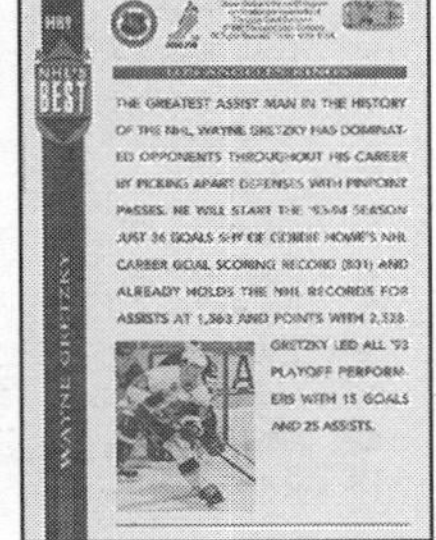

Insert Set (10 cards): **150.00**

	No.	Player	NRMT-MT
☐	HB1	Alexander Mogilny, Buf.	8.00
☐	HB2	Rob Gaudreau, S.J.	5.00
☐	HB3	Brett Hull, Stl.	12.00
☐	HB4	Dallas Drake, Det.	5.00
☐	HB5	Pavel Bure, Van.	18.00
☐	HB6	Alexei Kovalev, NYR.	5.00
☐	HB7	Mario Lemieux, Pgh.	40.00
☐	HB8	Eric Lindros, Pha.	35.00
☐	HB9	Wayne Gretzky, L.A.	50.00
☐	HB10	Joé Juneau, Bos.	5.00

PROGRAM OF EXCELLENCE

Insert Set (15 cards): **300.00**

	No.	Player	NRMT-MT
☐	E1	Adam Smith, Cdn.	10.00
☐	E2	Jason Podollan, Cdn.	10.00
☐	E3	Jason Wiemer, Cdn.	10.00
☐	E4	Jeff O'Neill, Cdn.	20.00
☐	E5	Daniel Goneau, Cdn.	10.00
☐	E6	Christian Laflamme, Cdn.	10.00
☐	E7	Daymond Langkow, Cdn.	12.00
☐	E8	Jeff Friesen, Cdn.	20.00
☐	E9	Wayne Primeau, Cdn.	10.00
☐	E10	Paul Kariya, Cdn.	70.00
☐	E11	Rob Niedermayer, Fla.	12.00
☐	E12	Eric Lindros, Pha.	60.00
☐	E13	Mario Lemieux, Pgh.	70.00
☐	E14	Steve Yzerman, Det.	45.00
☐	E15	Alexandre Daigle, Ott.	15.00

SILVER SKATES

Silver Trade and Gold Trade could be redeemed until July 31, 1994, for either a silver or gold Retail Silver Skate set.

Hobby Insert Set (10 cards): **50.00**
Retail Insert Set (10 cards): **60.00**
Gold Trade Card (Gretzky): **100.00**
Silver Trade Card (Gretzky): **50.00**

	No.	Hobby Singles	Silver
☐	H1	Mario Lemieux, Pgh.	15.00
☐	H2	Pavel Bure, Van.	7.00
☐	H3	Eric Lindros, Pha.	12.00
☐	H4	Rob Niedermayer. Fla.	2.00
☐	H5	Chris Pronger, Edm.	3.00
☐	H6	Adam Oates, Bos.	3.00
☐	H7	Pierre Turgeon, NYI.	2.00
☐	H8	Alexei Yashin, Ott.	4.00
☐	H9	Joe Sakic, Que.	9.00
☐	H10	Alexander Mogilny, Buf.	3.00

	No.	Retail Singles	Gold	Silver
☐ ☐	R1	Wayne Gretzky, L.A.	30.00	20.00
☐ ☐	R2	Teemu Selänne, Wpg.	10.00	7.00
☐ ☐	R3	Alexandre Daigle, Ott.	4.50	3.00
☐ ☐	R4	Chris Gratton, T.B.	4.50	3.00
☐ ☐	R5	Brett Hull, Stl.	7.50	5.00
☐ ☐	R6	Steve Yzerman, Det.	15.00	10.00
☐ ☐	R7	Doug Gilmour, Tor.	6.00	4.00
☐ ☐	R8	Jaromir Jagr, Pgh.	15.00	10.00
☐ ☐	R9	Jason Arnott, Edm.	4.50	3.00
☐ ☐	R10	Jeremy Roenick, Chi.	4.50	3.00

SPECIAL PRINT

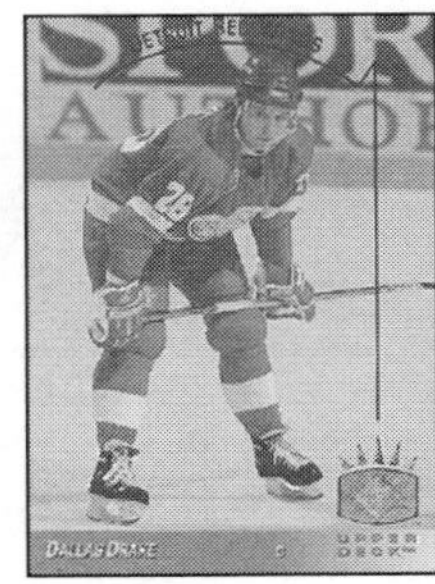

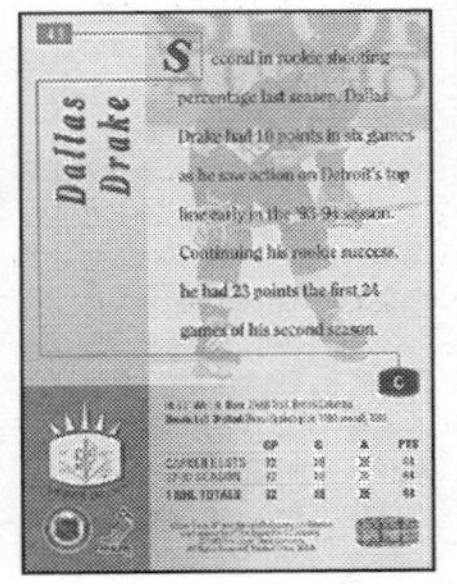

Insert Set (180 cards): **100.00**
Common Player: **.35**

	No.	Player	NRMT-MT
☐	1	Sean Hill, Ana.	.35
☐	2	Troy Loney, Ana.	.35
☐	3	Joe Sacco, Ana.	.35
☐	4	Anatoli Semenov, Ana.	.35
☐	5	Ron Tugnutt (G), Ana.	.50
☐	6	Terry Yake, Ana.	.35
☐	7	Ray Bourque, Bos.	2.00
☐	8	Jon Casey (G), Bos.	.35
☐	9	Joé Juneau, Bos.	.35
☐	10	Cam Neely, Bos.	.75
☐	11	Adam Oates, Bos.	1.00

No.	Player	Price
12	Bryan Smolinski, Bos.	.35
13	Matthew Barnaby, Buf.	.35
14	Philippe Boucher, Buf.	.35
15	Grant Fuhr (G), Buf.	.75
16	Dale Hawerchuk, Buf.	.75
17	Pat LaFontaine, Buf.	.75
18	Alexander Mogilny, Buf.	1.00
19	Craig Simpson, Buf.	.35
20	Ted Drury, Cgy.	.35
21	Theoren Fleury, Cgy.	1.00
22	Al MacInnis, Cgy.	.75
23	Joe Nieuwendyk, Cgy.	.75
24	Joel Otto, Cgy.	.35
25	Gary Roberts, Cgy.	.75
26	Vesa Viitakoski, Cgy.	.35
27	Ed Belfour (G), Chi.	1.00
28	Chris Chelios, Chi.	1.50
29	Joe Murphy, Chi.	.35
30	Patrick Poulin, Chi.	.35
31	Jeremy Roenick, Chi.	1.00
32	Jeff Shantz, Chi.	.35
33	Kevin Todd, Chi.	.35
34	Neal Broten, Dal.	.50
35	Paul Cavallini, Dal.	.35
36	Russ Courtnall, Dal.	.35
37	Derian Hatcher, Dal.	.50
38	Mike Modano, Dal.	2.00
39	Andy Moog (G), Dal.	.75
40	Jarkko Varvio, Dal.	.35
41	Dino Ciccarelli, Det.	.75
42	Paul Coffey, Det.	.75
43	Dallas Drake, Det.	.35
44	Sergei Fedorov, Det.	2.00
45	Keith Primeau, Det.	.75
46	Bob Probert, Det.	.35
47	Steve Yzerman, Det.	5.00
48	Jason Arnott, Edm.	2.50
49	Shayne Corson, Edm.	.75
50	Dave Manson, Edm.	.35
51	Dean McAmmond, Edm.	.35
52	Bill Ranford (G), Edm.	.75
53	Doug Weight, Edm.	1.00
54	Brad Werenka, Edm.	.35
55	Evgeny Davydov, Fla.	.35
56	Scott Levins, Fla.	.35
57	Scott Mellanby, Fla.	.35
58	Rob Niedermayer, Fla.	.75
59	Brian Skrudland, Fla.	.35
60	John Vanbiesbrouck (G), Fla.	3.00
61	Robert Kron, Hfd.	.35
62	Michael Nylander, Hfd.	.35
63	Robert Petrovicky, Hfd.	.35
64	Chris Pronger, Hfd.	1.00
65	Geoff Sanderson, Hfd.	.50
66	Darren Turcotte, Hfd.	.35
67	Pat Verbeek, Hfd.	.50
68	Rob Blake, L.A.	.75
69	Tony Granato, L.A.	.35
70	Wayne Gretzky, L.A.	12.00
71	Kelly Hrudey (G), L.A.	.50
72	Shawn McEachern, L.A.	.35
73	Luc Robitaille, L.A.	.75
74	Darryl Sydor, L.A.	.35
75	Alexei Zhitnik, L.A.	.35
76	Brian Bellows, Mtl.	.35
77	Vincent Damphousse, Mtl.	1.00
78	Stéphan Lebeau, Mtl.	.35
79	John LeClair, Mtl.	2.50
80	Kirk Muller, Mtl.	.35
81	Patrick Roy (G), Mtl.	8.00
82	Pierre Sévigny, Mtl.	.35
83	Claude Lemieux, N.J.	.50
84	Corey Millen, N.J.	.35
85	Bernie Nicholls, N.J.	.35
86	Scott Niedermayer, N.J.	.75
87	Stéphane Richer, N.J.	.50
88	Alexander Semak, N.J.	.35
89	Scott Stevens, N.J.	.75
90	Ray Ferraro, NYI.	.35
91	Darius Kasparaitis, NYI.	.35
92	Scott Lachance, NYI.	.35
93	Vladimir Malakhov, NYI.	.35
94	Marty McInnis, NYI.	.35
95	Steve Thomas, NYI.	.35
96	Pierre Turgeon, NYI.	.75
97	Tony Amonte, NYR.	.75
98	Mike Gartner, NYR.	.75
99	Adam Graves, NYR.	.50
100	Alexander Karpovtsev, NYR.	.35
101	Alexei Kovalev, NYR.	.50
102	Brian Leetch, NYR.	1.00
103	Mark Messier, NYR.	2.00
104	Esa Tikkanen, NYR.	.35
105	Craig Billington (G), Ott.	.50
106	Robert Burakovsky, Ott.	.35
107	Alexandre Daigle, Ott.	1.00
108	Pavel Demitra, Ott.	.35
109	Alexei Kovalev, Ott.	.35
110	Bob Kudelski, Ott.	.35
111	Norm Maciver, Ott.	.35
112	Alexei Yashin, Ott.	2.50
113	Josef Beranek, Pha.	.35
114	Rod Brind'Amour, Pha.	.75
115	Milos Holan, Pha.	.35
116	Eric Lindros, Pha.	7.00
117	Mark Recchi, Pha.	.75
118	Mikael Renberg, Pha.	.75
119	Dimitri Yushkevich, Pha.	.35
120	Tom Barrasso (G), Pgh.	.75
121	Jaromir Jagr, Pgh.	5.00
122	Mario Lemieux, Pgh.	8.00
123	Markus Naslund, Pgh.	.35
124	Kevin Stevens, Pgh.	.50
125	Martin Straka, Pgh.	.35
126	Rick Tocchet, Pgh.	.50
127	Martin Gelinas, Que.	.50
128	Owen Nolan, Que.	.75
129	Mike Ricci, Que.	.35
130	Joe Sakic, Que.	4.00
131	Chris Simon, Que.	.75
132	Mats Sundin, Que.	2.00
133	Jocelyn Thibault (G), Que.	3.00
134	Philippe Bozon, Stl.	.35
135	Jeff Brown, Stl.	.35
136	Phil Housley, Stl.	.35
137	Brett Hull, Stl.	2.00
138	Craig Janney, Stl.	.35
139	Curtis Joseph (G), Stl.	3.00
140	Brendan Shanahan, Stl.	3.00
141	Pat Falloon, S.J.	.35
142	Johan Garpenlov, S.J.	.35
143	Rob Gaudreau, S.J.	.35
144	Vlastimal Kroupa, S.J.	.35
145	Sergei Makarov, S.J.	.35
146	Sandis Ozolinsh, S.J.	.75
147	Mike Rathje, S.J.	.35
148	Brian Bradley, T.B.	.35
149	Chris Gratton, T.B.	1.00
150	Brent Gretzky, T.B.	.35
151	Roman Hamrlik, T.B.	.75
152	Petr Klima, T.B.	.35
153	Denis Savard, T.B.	.75
154	Rob Zamuner, T.B.	.75
155	Dave Andreychuk, Tor.	.50
156	Nickolai Borschevsky, Tor.	.35
157	Dave Ellett, Tor.	.35
158	Doug Gilmour, Tor.	1.00
159	Alexei Kudashov, Tor.	.35
160	Félix Potvin (G), Tor.	2.00
161	Greg Adams, Van.	.35
162	Pavel Bure, Van.	3.50
163	Geoff Courtnall, Van.	.35
164	Trevor Linden, Van.	.75
165	Kirk McLean (G), Van.	.75
166	Jiri Slegr, Van.	.35
167	Dixon Ward, Van.	.35
168	Peter Bondra, Wsh.	1.50
169	Kevin Hatcher, Wsh.	.50
170	Al Iafrate, Wsh.	.35
171	Dimitri Khristich, Wsh.	.35
172	Pat Peake, Wsh.	.35
173	Mike Ridley, Wsh.	.35
174	Arto Blomsten, Wpg.	.35
175	Nelson Emerson, Wpg.	.35
176	Boris Mironov, Wpg.	.35
177	Teemu Selänne, Wpg.	3.50
178	Keith Tkachuk, Wpg.	2.00
179	Paul Ysebaert, Wpg.	.35
180	Alexei Zhamnov, Wpg.	.75

1993 - 94 UPPER DECK BE A PLAYER

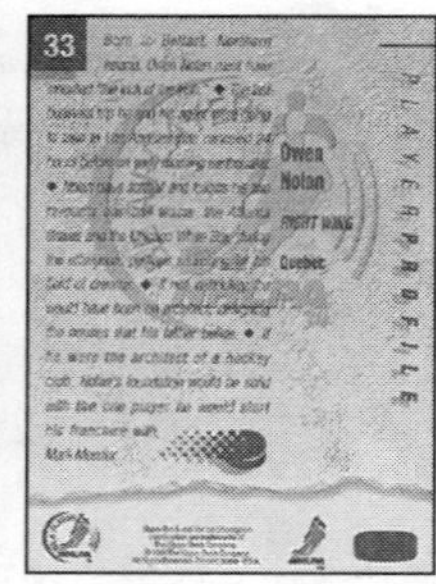

Cards 1-18 feature the photography of Walter Iooss.

Complete Set (45 cards): 30.00

No.	Players	NRMT-MT
1	Tony Amonte	.50
2	Chris Chelios	1.00
3	Alexandre Daigle	.75
4	Dave Ellett	.25
5	Sergei Fedorov	1.50
6	Chris Gratton	.75
7	Wayne Gretzky	5.00
8	Brett Hull	1.50
9	Brian Leetch	1.00
10	Rob Niedermayer	.50
11	Félix Potvin (G)	2.00
12	Luc Robitaille	.50
13	Jeremy Roenick	.75
14	Joe Sakic	3.00
15	Teemu Selänne	2.50
16	Brendan Shanahan	2.00
17	Alexei Yashin	1.00
18	Steve Yzerman	3.50
19	Jason Arnott	2.00
20	Pavel Bure	2.50
21	Theoren Fleury	.75
22	Mike Gartner	.50
23	Kevin Haller	.25
24	Derian Hatcher	.50
25	Mark and Gordie Howe	3.00
26	Al Iafrate	.25
27	Joé Juneau	.25
28	Pat LaFontaine	.50
29	Eric Lindros	4.00
30	Dave Manson	.25
31	Mike Modano	1.50
32	Scott Niedermayer	.50
33	Owen Nolan	.50
34	Joel Otto	.25
35	Chris Pronger	.75
36	Scott Stevens	.50
37	Pierre Turgeon	.50
38	Pat Verbeek	.25
39	Doug Weight	.75
40	Terry Yake	.25
41	Doug Gilmour	.75
42	Doug Gilmour	.75
43	Doug Gilmour	.75
44	Doug Gilmour	.75
45	Doug Gilmour	.75

1993 - 94 UPPER DECK - ROOTS BE A PLAYER

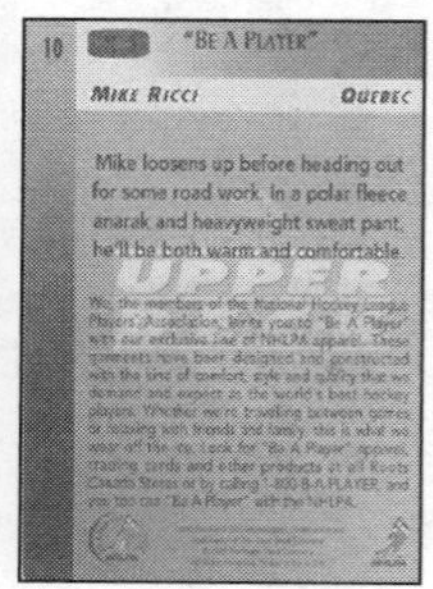

These cards were issued with the NHLPA's Roots/Be A Player line of clothing.

Series One Set (10 cards):			**10.00**
Series Two Set (10 cards):			**10.00**
Series Three Set (10 cards):			**10.00**
	No.	**Player**	**NRMT-MT**
☐	1	Trevor Linden	1.00
☐	2	Guy Carbonneau	.50
☐	3	Félix Potvin (G)	2.25
☐	4	Steve Yzerman	3.50
☐	5	Doug Gilmour	1.50
☐	6	Wendel Clark	1.00
☐	7	Kirk McLean (G)	1.00
☐	8	Larry Murphy	1.00
☐	9	Patrick Roy (G)	5.00
☐	10	Mike Ricci	.50
☐	11	Doug Gilmour	1.50
☐	12	Sergei Fedorov	2.00
☐	13	Shayne Corson	1.00
☐	14	Alexei Yashin	2.00
☐	15	Pavel Bure	2.50
☐	16	Joe Sakic	3.00
☐	17	Teemu Selänne	2.50
☐	18	Dave Andreychuk	.50
☐	19	Al MacInnis	1.00
☐	20	Rob Blake	1.00
☐	21	Doug Gilmour	1.50
☐	22	Steve Larmer	.50
☐	23	Eric Lindros	4.00
☐	24	Mike Modano	2.00
☐	25	Vincent Damphousse	1.50
☐	26	Mike Gartner	1.00
☐	27	John Vanbiesbrouck (G)	2.25
☐	28	Theoren Fleury	1.50
☐	29	Ken Baumgartner	.50
☐	30	Jeremy Roenick	1.50

1993 - 94 ZELLERS MASTERS OF HOCKEY

This 8-card set is unnumbered and listed here alphabetically. There are 10,000 copies of each card and 2,100 copies of each autographed card.

Imprint: ZELLERS

Complete Set (8 cards):			**20.00**
	Player	**Auto.**	**Reg.**
☐☐	Andy Bathgate	50.00	2.00
☐☐	John Bucyk	55.00	2.50
☐☐	Yvan Cournoyer	85.00	3.00
☐☐	Marcel Dionne	90.00	3.25
☐☐	Bobby Hull	125.00	6.50
☐☐	Brad Park	60.00	2.50
☐☐	Jean Ratelle	60.00	2.50
☐☐	Gump Worsley (G)	100.00	4.00

1994 COCA COLA THE GREAT ONE

These milk caps were available at Mac's Milk stores in Canada.

Cap Diameter: 1 3/4"

Imprint: © 1994 WPF

Complete Set (18 caps):			**20.00**
	No.	**Player**	**NRMT-MT**
☐	1	Wayne Gretzky, L.A.	2.00
☐	2	Wayne Gretzky, L.A. (HL1851)	2.00
☐	3	Wayne Gretzky, L.A.	2.00
☐	4	Wayne Gretzky, L.A.	2.00
☐	5	Wayne Gretzky, Edm.	2.00
☐	6	Wayne Gretzky, Edm.	2.00
☐	7	Wayne Gretzky, Edm.	2.00
☐	8	Wayne Gretzky, Edm.	2.00
☐	9	Wayne Gretzky, Edm.	2.00
☐	10	Wayne Gretzky, L.A.	2.00
☐	11	Wayne Gretzky, Edm.	2.00
☐	12	Wayne Gretzky, A.S. (L.A.)	2.00
☐	13	Wayne Gretzky, A.S. (Edm.)	2.00
☐	14	Wayne Gretzky, Edm.	2.00
☐	15	Wayne Gretzky, L.A.	2.00
☐	16	Wayne Gretzky, Edm.	2.00
☐	17	Wayne Gretzky, L.A.	2.00
☐	18	Wayne Gretzky, L.A.	2.00

1994 KOULULAINEN

A 9 card sheet issued by the magazine Koululainen. We have no pricing information on this set.

Card Size: 2 5/8" x 3 3/8"

Imprint:

	Player		**Player**
☐	Ray Bourque, Bos.	☐	Sergei Fedorov, Det.
☐	Doug Gilmour, Tor.	☐	Wayne Gretzky, L.A.
☐	Mario Lemieux, Pgh.	☐	Eric Lindros, Pha.
☐	Mark Messier, NYR.	☐	Alexander Mogilny, Buf.
☐	Patrick Roy (G), Mtl.		

1994 SEMIC

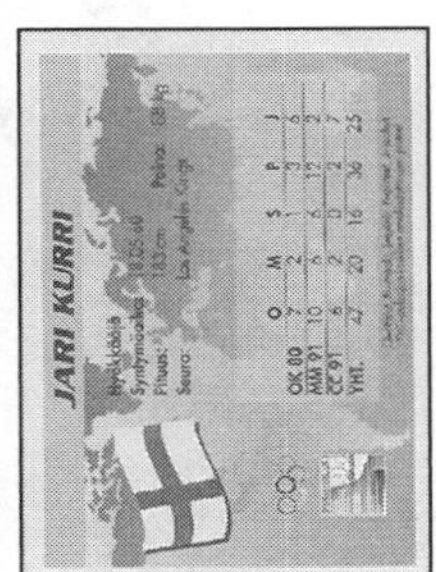

Imprint: None

Complete Set (360 cards):			**50.00**
Common Player:			**.10**
Album:			**10.00**
	No.	**Player**	**NRMT-MT**
☐	1	Jarmo Mylls (G), Fin.	.25
☐	2	Pasi Kuivalainen (G), Fin.	.10
☐	3	Jukka Tammi (G), Fin.	.10
☐	4	Markus Ketterer (G), Fin.	.20
☐	5	Timo Jutila, Fin.	.25
☐	6	Mikko Jaapakoski, Fin.	.10
☐	7	Marko Tuulola, Fin.	.10
☐	8	Jyrki Lumme, Fin.	.20
☐	9	Kari Harila, Fin.	.10
☐	10	Teppo Numminen, Fin.	.20
☐	11	Pasi Sormunen, Fin.	.10
☐	12	Petteri Nummelin, Fin.	.10
☐	13	Harri Laurila, Fin.	.10
☐	14	Mika Strömberg, Fin.	.10
☐	15	Ville Siren, Fin.	.10
☐	16	Pekka Laksola, Fin.	.10
☐	17	Janne Laukkanen, Fin.	.10
☐	18	Marko Kiprusoff, Fin.	.10
☐	19	Waltteri Immonen, Fin.	.10
☐	20	Teemu Selänne, Fin.	2.00
☐	21	Mlka Alatalo, Fin.	.10
☐	22	Vesa Viitakoski, Fin.	.10
☐	23	Tero Arkiomaa, Fin.	.10
☐	24	Jari Kurri, Fin.	.75
☐	25	Pekka Tirkkonen, Fin.	.10
☐	26	Jarmo Kekäläinen, Fin.	.10
☐	27	Saku Koivu, Fin.	2.00
☐	28	Antti Törmänen, Fin.	.10
☐	29	Mikko Mäkelä, Fin.	.20
☐	30	Jere Lehtinen, Fin.	.75
☐	31	Raimo Helminen, Fin.	.10
☐	32	Marko Jantunen, Fin.	.10
☐	33	Ville Peltonen, Fin.	.10
☐	34	Esa Tikkanen, Fin.	.25
☐	35	Janne Ojanen, Fin.	.10
☐	36	Mika Nieminen, Fin.	.10
☐	37	Marko Palo, Fin.	.10
☐	38	Rauli Raitanen, Fin.	.10
☐	39	Sami Kapanen, Fin.	.35
☐	40	Juha Riihijärvi, Fin.	.10
☐	41	Esa Keskinen, Fin.	.10
☐	42	Jari Korpisalo, Fin.	.10
☐	43	Christian Ruutu, Fin.	.20
☐	44	Jarkko Varvio, Fin.	.10
☐	45	Sami Wahlsten, Fin.	.10
☐	46	Petri Varis, Fin.	.10
☐	47	Timo Saarikoski, Fin.	.10
☐	48	Timo Norppa, Fin.	.10
☐	49	Marko Virtanen, Fin.	.10
☐	50	Pauli Järvinen, Fin.	.10
☐	51	Håkan Algotsson (G), Swe.	.10
☐	52	Tommy Söderström (G), Swe.	.25
☐	53	Rolf Riddervall, Swe.	.10
☐	54	Tomas Jonsson, Swe.	.10
☐	55	Christer Due-Boje, Swe.	.10
☐	56	Peter Popovic, Swe.	.10
☐	57	Fredrik Stillman, Swe.	.10
☐	58	Magnus Svensson, Swe.	.10
☐	59	Fredrik Nilsson, Swe.	.10
☐	60	Tommy Albelin, Swe.	.10
☐	61	Joacim Esbjörs, Swe.	.10
☐	62	Roger Johansson, Swe.	.10
☐	63	Stefan Nilsson, Swe.	.10
☐	64	Håkan Loob, Swe.	.50
☐	65	Peter Ottosson, Swe.	.10
☐	66	Daniel Rydmark, Swe.	.10
☐	67	Mikael Renberg, Swe.	.50
☐	68	Patrik Juhlin, Swe.	.20
☐	69	Thomas Rundqvist, Swe.	.10
☐	70	Andreas Johansson, Swe.	.10
☐	71	Stefan Örnskog, Swe.	.10
☐	72	Niklas Eriksson, Swe.	.10
☐	73	Jonas Bergqvist, Swe.	.10
☐	74	Mats Sundin, Swe.	1.50
☐	75	Peter Forsberg, Swe.	3.00
☐	76	Stefan Elvenes, Swe.	.10
☐	77	Tomas Forslund, Swe.	.10
☐	78	Patric Kjelberg, Swe.	.10
☐	79	Bill Ranford (G), Cdn.	.50
☐	80	Corey Hirsh (G), Cdn.	.25
☐	81	Larry Murphy, Cdn.	.50
☐	82	Mark Tinordi, Cdn.	.25
☐	83	Scott Stevens, Cdn.	.25
☐	84	Al MacInnis, Cdn.	.50
☐	85	Steve Smith, Cdn.	.25
☐	86	Paul Coffey, Cdn.	.50
☐	87	Eric Desjardins, Cdn.	.50
☐	88	Eric Lindros, Cdn.	4.00
☐	89	Dale Hawerchuk, Cdn.	.50
☐	90	Steve Larmer, Cdn.	.25
☐	91	Brent Sutter, Cdn.	.25
☐	92	Luc Robitaille, Cdn.	.50
☐	93	Shayne Corson, Cdn.	.25
☐	94	Mark Messier, Cdn.	1.50
☐	95	Rick Tocchet, Cdn.	.25
☐	96	Theoren Fleury, Cdn.	1.00
☐	97	Dirk Graham, Cdn.	.25
☐	98	Russ Courtnall, Cdn.	.25
☐	99	Wayne Gretzky, Cdn.	6.00
☐	100	Brendan Shanahan, Cdn.	1.75
☐	101	Mark Recchi, Cdn.	.50
☐	102	David Harlock, Cdn.	.20
☐	103	Craig Woodcroft, Cdn.	.20
☐	104	Paul Kariya, Cdn.	4.00
☐	105	Jason Marshall, Cdn.	.20
☐	106	Brett Lindros, Cdn.	.25
☐	107	Mike Richter (G), USA.	1.00
☐	108	Mike Dunham (G), USA.	.50
☐	109	Craig Wolanin, USA.	.25
☐	110	Jim Johnson, USA.	.25
☐	111	Chris Chelios, USA.	1.25
☐	112	Eric Weinrich, USA.	.25
☐	113	Brian Leetch, USA.	1.00
☐	114	Kevin Hatcher, USA.	.25
☐	115	Ed Olczyk, USA.	.25
☐	116	Kevin Miller, USA.	.25

	No.	Player	Price
☐	117	Doug Brown, USA.	.25
☐	118	Joe Mullen, USA.	.25
☐	119	Craig Janney, USA.	.25
☐	120	Pat LaFontaine, USA.	.50
☐	121	Gary Suter, USA.	.25
☐	122	Jeremy Roenick, USA.	1.00
☐	123	Brett Hull, USA.	1.50
☐	124	Joel Otto, USA.	.25
☐	125	Mike Modano, USA.	1.50
☐	126	Tony Granato, USA.	.25
☐	127	Dave Christian, USA.	.20
☐	128	Brian Mullen, USA.	.20
☐	129	Chris Ferraro, USA.	.20
☐	130	John Lilley, USA.	.20
☐	131	Jeff Lazaro, USA.	.20
☐	132	Peter Ferraro, USA.	.25
☐	133	Brian Rolston, USA.	.25
☐	134	Dave Roberts, USA.	.20
☐	135	Nikolai Khabibulin (G), Rus.	1.00
☐	136	Andrei Trefilov (G), Rus.	.25
☐	137	Vladimir Malakhov, Rus.	.25
☐	138	Alexander Karpovstev, Rus.	.20
☐	139	Alexander Smirnov, Rus.	.10
☐	140	Sergei Zubov, Rus.	.50
☐	141	Sergei Seljanin, Rus.	.10
☐	142	Sergei Shendelev, Rus.	.10
☐	143	Alexei Kasatonov, Rus.	.10
☐	144	Sergei Sorokin, Rus.	.10
☐	145	Vjatseslav Bykov, Rus.	.10
☐	146	Sergei Fedorov, Rus.	1.50
☐	147	Alexei Yashin, Rus.	1.25
☐	148	Vjatseslav Butsajev, Rus.	.10
☐	149	Konstantin Astrahantsev, Rus.	.10
☐	150	Alexei Zhamnov, Rus.	.50
☐	151	Dimitri Frolov, Rus.	.10
☐	152	Vyacheslav Kozlov, Rus.	.25
☐	153	Sergei Pushkov, Rus.	.10
☐	154	Andrei Khomutov, Rus.	.25
☐	155	Sergei Makarov, Rus.	.25
☐	156	Igor Larionov, Rus.	.50
☐	157	Valeri Kamensky, Rus.	.50
☐	158	Alexander Semak, Rus.	.20
☐	159	Alexei Gusarov, Rus.	.20
☐	160	Andrei Lomakin, Rus.	.10
☐	161	Igor Korolev, Rus.	.25
☐	162	Ravil Khaidarov, Rus.	.10
☐	163	Dominik Hasek (G), Cze.	2.00
☐	164	Oldrich Svoboda (G), Cze.	.20
☐	165	Peter Briza (G), Cze.	.20
☐	166	Leov Gudas, Cze.	.10
☐	167	Kamil Prachar, Cze.	.10
☐	168	Richard Smehlik, Cze.	.20
☐	169	Frantisek Kucera, Cze.	.10
☐	170	Drahomir Kadlec, Cze.	.10
☐	171	Jan Vopat, Cze.	.20
☐	172	Frantisek Prohazka, Cze.	.10
☐	173	Antonin Stavjana, Cze.	.10
☐	174	Bedrich Scerban, Cze.	.10
☐	175	Kamil Kastak, Cze.	.10
☐	176	Josef Beranek, Cze.	.20
☐	177	Martin Rucinsky, Cze.	.25
☐	178	Michal Pivonka, Cze.	.25
☐	179	Tomas Jelinek, Cze.	.10
☐	180	Richard Zemlicka, Cze.	.10
☐	181	Robert Kron, Cze.	.20
☐	182	Jiri Slegr, Cze.	.20
☐	183	Jaromir Jagr, Cze.	3.00
☐	184	Robert Reichel, Cze.	.50
☐	185	David Vyborny, Cze.	.10
☐	186	Robert Lang, Cze.	.10
☐	187	Petr Rosol, Cze.	.10
☐	188	Otakar Janeckv, Cze.	.10
☐	189	Martin Hostak, Cze.	.10
☐	190	Jiri Kucera, Cze.	.10
☐	191	Eduard Hartman (G), Slo.	.10
☐	192	Lubomir Sekeras, Slo.	.10
☐	193	Marian Smerciak, Slo.	.10
☐	194	Jan Varholik, Slo.	.10
☐	195	Lubomir Rybovic, Slo.	.10
☐	196	Miroslav Marcinko, Slo.	.10
☐	197	Stanislav Medrik, Slo.	.10
☐	198	Zdeno Ciger, Slo.	.20
☐	199	Jergus Baca, Slo.	.10
☐	200	Peter Stastny, Slo.	.50
☐	201	Peter Veselovsky, Slo.	.10
☐	202	Anton Stastny, Slo.	.20
☐	203	Lubomir Kolnik, Slo.	.10
☐	204	Roman Kontsek, Slo.	.10
☐	205	Rene Pucher, Slo.	.10
☐	206	Slavomir Ilavsky, Slo.	.10
☐	207	Zigmund Palffy, Slo.	1.25
☐	208	Vlastimil Plavucha, Slo.	.10
☐	209	Dusan Pohorelec, Slo.	.10
☐	210	Robert Petrovicky, Slo.	.10
☐	211	Michel Valliere (G), Fra.	.10
☐	212	Petri Ylönen, Fra.	.10
☐	213	Jean-Philippe Lemoin, Fra.	.10
☐	214	Christophe Moyon, Fra.	.10
☐	215	Denis Perez, Fra.	.10
☐	216	Bruno Saunier, Fra.	.10
☐	217	Stéphane Botteri, Fra.	.10
☐	218	Michel Breistroff, Fra.	.10
☐	219	Gerald Guennelon, Fra.	.10
☐	220	Serge Poudrier, Fra.	.10
☐	221	Bemjamin Agnel, Fra.	.10
☐	222	Stéphane Arcangeloni, Fra.	.10
☐	223	Pierrick Maia, Fra.	.10
☐	224	Antoine Richer, Fra.	.10
☐	225	Christophe Ville, Fra.	.10
☐	226	Michael Babin, Fra.	.10
☐	227	Lionel Orsolini, Fra.	.10
☐	228	Stéphane Barin, Fra.	.10
☐	229	Amauld Briand, Fra.	.10
☐	230	Franck Pajonkowski, Fra.	.10
☐	231	Claus Dalpiaz (G), Aut.	.10
☐	232	Brian Stankiewicz, Aut.	.10
☐	233	Robin Doyle, Aut.	.10
☐	234	Michael Guntner, Aut.	.10
☐	235	Martin Krainz, Aut.	.10
☐	236	Michael Shea, Aut.	.10
☐	237	Martin Ulrich, Aut.	.10
☐	238	Erich Solderer, Aut.	.10
☐	239	Wayne Groulx, Aut.	.10
☐	240	Andreas Puschnig, Aut.	.10
☐	241	Dieter Kalt, Aut.	.10
☐	242	Gerhard Puschnik, Aut.	.10
☐	243	Werner Kerth, Aut.	.10
☐	244	Richard Nasheim, Aut.	.10
☐	245	Arno Maier, Aut.	.10
☐	246	Mario Schaden, Aut.	.10
☐	247	Reinhart Lampert, Aut.	.10
☐	248	Karl Heinzle, Aut.	.10
☐	249	Wolfgang Kromp, Aut.	.10
☐	250	Marty Dallman , Aut.	.10
☐	251	Jim Marthinsen (G), Nor.	.10
☐	252	Robert Schistad, Nor.	.10
☐	253	Cato Tom Andersen, Nor.	.10
☐	254	Anders Myrvold, Nor.	.10
☐	255	Svein Enok Norstebb, Nor.	.10
☐	256	Tommy Jakobsen, Nor.	.10
☐	257	Pål Kristiansen, Nor.	.10
☐	258	Petter Salsten, Nor.	.10
☐	259	Ole Eskild Dahlström, Nor.	.10
☐	260	Morten Finstad, Nor.	.10
☐	261	Espen Knutsen, Nor.	.10
☐	262	Erik Kristiansen, Nor.	.10
☐	263	Geir Hoff, Nor.	.10
☐	264	Roy Johansen, Nor.	.10
☐	265	Trend Magnussen, Nor.	.10
☐	266	Marius Rath, Nor.	.10
☐	267	Vegar Barlie, Nor.	.10
☐	268	Arne Billkvam, Nor.	.10
☐	269	Tom Johanssen, Nor.	.10
☐	270	Petter Thoresen, Nor.	.10
☐	271	Klaus Merk (G), Ger.	.10
☐	272	Josef Heiss, Ger.	.10
☐	273	Rick Amann, Ger.	.10
☐	274	Torsten Kienass, Ger.	.10
☐	275	Mirco Ludemann, Ger.	.10
☐	276	Jason Meyer, Ger.	.10
☐	277	Uli Hiemer, Ger.	.10
☐	278	Karsten Mende, Ger.	.10
☐	279	Andreas Niederberger, Ger.	.10
☐	280	Thomas Brandl, Ger.	.10
☐	281	Benoit Doucet, Ger.	.10
☐	282	Robert Hock, Ger.	.10
☐	283	Georg Franz, Ger.	.10
☐	284	Ernst Kopf, Ger.	.10
☐	285	Reemt Pyka, Ger.	.10
☐	286	Jurgen Rumrich, Ger.	.10
☐	287	Dieter Hegen, Ger.	.10
☐	288	Raimund Hilger, Ger.	.10
☐	289	Thomas Schinko, Ger.	.10
☐	290	Leo Stefan, Ger.	.10
☐	291	David Delfino (G), Ita.	.10
☐	292	Elmar Parth, Ita.	.10
☐	293	Luigi Da Corte, Ita.	.10
☐	294	Phil Gaetano, Ita.	.10
☐	295	Ralph Di Fiore, Ita.	.10
☐	296	Giorgio Comploi, Ita.	.10
☐	297	Alexander Thaler, Ita.	.10
☐	298	Giovanni Marchetti, Ita.	.10
☐	299	Gates Orlando, Ita.	.10
☐	300	Frank Di Muzio, Ita.	.10
☐	301	Joe Foglietta, Ita.	.10
☐	302	Stefan Figliuzzi, Ita.	.10
☐	303	John Vecchiarelli, Ita.	.10
☐	304	Maurizio Mansi, Ita.	.10
☐	305	Santino Pellegrino, Ita.	.10
☐	306	Line De Toni, Ita.	.10
☐	307	Mario Chitarroni, Ita.	.10
☐	308	Bruno Zarillo, Ita.	.10
☐	309	Armando Chelodi, Ita.	.10
☐	310	Carmine Vani, Ita.	.10
☐	311	Martin McKay (G), G.B.	.10
☐	312	Scott O'Connor, G.B.	.10
☐	:313	John McCrone, G.B.	.10
☐	314	Stephen Cooper, G.B.	.10
☐	315	Mike O'Connor, G.B.	.10
☐	316	Chris Kelland, G.B.	.10
☐	317	Graham Waghorn, G.B.	.10
☐	318	Nickey Chinn, G.B.	.10
☐	319	Damien Smith, G.B.	.10
☐	320	Tim Cranston, G.B.	.10
☐	321	Scott Morrison, G.B.	.10
☐	322	Anthony Johnson, G.B.	.10
☐	323	Tony Hand, G.B.	.10
☐	324	Kevin Conway, G.B.	.10
☐	325	Rick Fera, G.B.	.10
☐	326	Doug McEwen, G.B.	.10
☐	327	Scott Neil, G.B.	.10
☐	328	John Iredale, G.B.	.10
☐	329	Iain Robertson, G.B.	.10
☐	330	Ian Cooper, G.B.	.10
☐	331	Bill Ranford (G), Cdn.	.35
☐	332	Jarmo Myllys (G), Fin.	.20
☐	333	Dominik Hasek (G), Cze.	2.00
☐	334	Tommy Söderström (G), Swe.	.20
☐	335	Teppo Numminen, Fin.	.20
☐	336	Mikhail Tatarinov, Rus.	.10
☐	337	Paul Coffey, Cdn.	1.00
☐	338	Chris Chelios, USA.	1.00
☐	339	Brian Leetch, USA.	1.00
☐	340	Al MacInnis, Cdn.	.25
☐	341	Vladimir Malakhov, Rus.	.20
☐	342	Kevin Hatcher, USA.	.20
☐	343	Jiri Slegr, Cze.	.20
☐	344	Wayne Gretzky, Cdn.	6.00
☐	345	Teemu Selänne, Fin.	2.00
☐	346	Jari Kurri, Fin.	.50
☐	347	Brett Hull, USA.	1.50
☐	348	Sergei Fedorov, Rus.	1.50
☐	349	Esa Tikkanen, Fin.	.25
☐	350	Mark Messier, Cdn.	1.50
☐	351	Jaromir Jagr, Cze.	3.00
☐	352	Jeremy Roenick, USA.	.75
☐	353	Luc Robitaille, Cdn.	.35
☐	354	Tomas Sandström, Swe.	.25
☐	355	Peter Forsberg, Fin.	3.00
☐	356	Alexei Zhamnov, Rus.	.35
☐	357	Theoren Fleury, Cdn.	.75
☐	358	Rick Tocchet, Cdn.	.20
☐	359	Pat LaFontaine, USA.	.35
☐	360	Eric Lindros, Cdn.	4.00

1994 SPORTSFLICS PROMOS

This four-card set features only two hockey palyers. These cards were given out at the 1994 National Sports Collectors Convention in Houston.

Imprint:

	Player	NRMT-MT
☐	Mike Modano, Dal.	5.00
☐	Derian Hatcher, Dal.	2.00

1994 TOPPS FINEST BRONZE

Each card is "bonded to a bed of solid bronze".

Imprint:

Complete Set (6 cards): 125.00

	No.	Player	NRMT-MT
☐	1	Jaromir Jagr, Pgh.	35.00
☐	2	Eric Lindros, Pha.	45.00
☐	3	Patrick Roy (G), Mtl.	50.00
☐	4	Pavel Bure, Van.	25.00
☐	5	Teemu Selänne, Wpg.	25.00
☐	6	Doug Gilmour, Tor.	20.00

1994 UPPER DECK WORLD CUP SOCCER HONOURARY SITE CAPTAINS

This 10-card insert set features two hockey players.

Imprint: © 1994 The Upper Deck Company

	No.	Player	NRMT-MT
☐	C5	Gordie Howe	15.00
☐	C6	Wayne Gretzky	25.00

1994 -95 ACTION PACKED PROMOS

Action Packed had plans of releasing a series of player pins (Badges of Honour), player coasters, oversized photos and an 84-card Big Picture set. Promos were released for most if not all of these sets. Big Picture cards are standard-sized issues with a 5 3/4" x 6 1/2" paper photo folded inside. The cards open up at bottom to unfold the oversize action shot. Two different styles of Jeremy Roenick's Big Picture card are known to exist: one card that opens up at the bottom (like a notepad) and one card that opens up from the side (like a booklet). A 4" x 5" checklist card was also available that listed the 84 intended players for this never released product. We have no pricing information on these promos and little information on excatly which cards were released in each series.

Imprint:

	Player
☐ ☐	Jeremy Roenick - Big Picture
☐	John Vanbiesbrouck (G) - Big Picture
☐	Steve Yzerman - Big Picture
☐	Jaromir Jagr - Big Picture
☐	Mario Lemieux - Coaster

1994 - 95 APS CZECH LEAGUE

Imprint:

Complete Set (300 cards): 85.00

Common Player: .20

	No.	Player	NRMT-MT
☐	1	Pavel Cagas	.20
☐	2	Ladislav Blazek	.20
☐	3	Ales Flasar	.20
☐	4	Petr Tejkl	.20
☐	5	Jaromir Latal	.20
☐	6	Ales Tomasek	.20
☐	7	Jiri Kuntos	.20
☐	8	Jan Vavrecka	.20
☐	9	Martin Smetak	.20
☐	10	Patrik Rimmel	.20
☐	11	Michal Slavik	.20
☐	12	Milan Navratil	.20
☐	13	Petr Fabian	.20
☐	14	Zdenek Eichenmann	.20
☐	15	Miroslav Chalanek	.20
☐	16	Pavel Nohel	.20
☐	17	Radim Radevic	.20
☐	18	Tomas Martinec	.20
☐	19	Alex Zima	.20
☐	20	Ivo Hrstka	.20
☐	21	Richard Brancik	.20
☐	22	Martin Janecek	.20
☐	23	Robert Holy	.20
☐	24	Radovan Biegl	.20
☐	25	Dusan Salficky	.20
☐	26	Jiri Malinsky	.20
☐	27	Jan Filip	.20
☐	28	Jaroslav Spelda	.20
☐	29	Petr Jancarik	.20
☐	30	Robert Kostka	.20
☐	31	Kamil Ioupal	.20
☐	32	Tomas Pacal	.20
☐	33	Ales Pisa	.20
☐	34	Milan Hejduk	.20
☐	35	Josef Zajic	.20
☐	36	Stanislav Prochazka	.20
☐	37	Jiri Sejba	.20
☐	38	Marek Zadina	.20
☐	39	Milan Filipi	.20
☐	40	David Pospisil	.20
☐	41	Tomas Blazek	.20
☐	42	Patrik Weber	.20
☐	43	Richard Kral	.20
☐	44	Martin Sekera	.20
☐	45	Ladislav Lubina	.20
☐	46	Jiri Provznik	.20
☐	47	Martin Chlad	.20
☐	48	Tomas Vokoun (G)	1.00
☐	49	Pavel Trnka	.20
☐	50	Petr Kuda	.20
☐	51	Frantisek Kaberle	.20
☐	52	Libor Prochazka	.20
☐	53	Jan Dlouhy	.20
☐	54	Otakar Cerny	.20
☐	55	Martin Ancicka	.20
☐	56	Marke Zidlicky	.20
☐	57	Martin Prochazka	.50
☐	58	Pavel Patera	.20
☐	59	Otakar Vejvoda	.20
☐	60	Jan Blaha	.20
☐	61	David Cernak	.20
☐	62	Petr Ton	.20
☐	63	Miroslav Mach	.20
☐	64	Patrik Elias	.20
☐	65	Martin Stepanek	.20
☐	66	Tomas Mikolasek	.20
☐	67	Milan Ruchar	.20
☐	68	Jaromir Jagr	50.00
☐	69	Milos Kajer	.20
☐	70	Jaromir Sindel	.20
☐	71	Ivo Capek	.20
☐	72	Jan Bohacek	.20
☐	73	Zdenek Touzimsky	.20
☐	74	Jan Krulis	.20
☐	75	Frantisek Musil	.50
☐	76	Jaroslav Nedved	.20
☐	77	Frantisek Ptacek	.20
☐	78	Pavel Taborsky	.20
☐	79	Frantisek Kucera	.50
☐	80	Pavel Srek	.20
☐	81	Martin Simek	.20
☐	82	Zbynek Kukacka	.20
☐	83	Jiri Zelenka	.20
☐	84	Jan Hlavac	.50
☐	85	Patrik Martinec	.20
☐	86	David Bruk	.20
☐	87	Pavel Geffert	.20
☐	88	Michal Sup	.20
☐	89	Jaromir Kverka	.20
☐	90	Miroslav Hlinka	.20
☐	91	Milan Kastner	.20
☐	92	Andrej Potajcuk	.20
☐	93	Roman Turek (G)	3.00
☐	94	Ladislav Gula	.20
☐	95	Robert Slavik	.20

	No.	Player	Price
☐	96	Jiri Hala	.20
☐	97	Jaroslav Modry	.50
☐	98	Petr Sedy	.20
☐	99	Petr Hodek	.20
☐	100	Petr Mainer	.20
☐	101	Michael Kubicek	.20
☐	102	Milan Nedoma	.20
☐	103	Rudolf Suchanek	.20
☐	104	Libor Zabransky	.20
☐	105	Jaroslav Brabec	.20
☐	106	Lubos Rob	.20
☐	107	Zdenek Sperger	.20
☐	108	Ondrej Vosta	.20
☐	109	Filip Turek	.20
☐	110	Radek Belohlav	.20
☐	111	Frantisek Sevcik	.20
☐	112	Roman Bozek	.20
☐	113	Roman Horak	.20
☐	114	Pavel Pycha	.20
☐	115	Arpad Gyori	.20
☐	116	Tomas Vasicek	.20
☐	117	Michal Hlinka	.20
☐	118	Daniel Kysela	.20
☐	119	Rudolf Wolf	.20
☐	120	Antonin Planovsky	.20
☐	121	Tomas Kramny	.20
☐	122	Vitezslav Skuta	.20
☐	123	Pavel Marecek	.20
☐	124	Miroslav Javin	.20
☐	125	Kamil Pribyia	.20
☐	126	Michal Cerny	.20
☐	127	Juris Opulskis	.20
☐	128	Richard Smehlik	.20
☐	129	Ales Badal	.20
☐	130	Robert Simicek	.20
☐	131	Vladimir Vujtek	.20
☐	132	Tomas Chlubna	.20
☐	133	Michal Piskor	.20
☐	134	Petr Folta	.20
☐	135	Roman Kadera	.20
☐	136	Lumir Kotala	.20
☐	137	Jan Peterek	.20
☐	138	Roman Rysanek	.20
☐	139	Rudolf Pejchar	.20
☐	140	Jiri Kucera	.20
☐	141	Stanislav Benes	.20
☐	142	Karel Smid	.20
☐	143	Martin Kovarik	.20
☐	144	Kiri Jonak	.20
☐	145	Alexander Savickij	.20
☐	146	Vaclav Ruprecht	.20
☐	147	Ivan Vlcek	.20
☐	149	Jaroslav Spacek	.20
☐	150	Peter Veselovsky	.20
☐	150	Milan Cerny	.20
☐	151	Milan Volak	.20
☐	152	Dusan Huml	.20
☐	153	Tomas Kucharcik	.20
☐	154	Martin Zivny	.20
☐	155	Martin Straka	2.00
☐	156	Michal Straka	.20
☐	157	Jiri Beranek	.20
☐	158	Ondrej Steiner	.20
☐	159	Josef Rybar	.20
☐	160	Jaroslav Kreuzmann	.20
☐	161	David Trachta	.20
☐	162	Marek Novotny	.20
☐	163	Pavel Falta	.20
☐	164	Antonin Necas	.20
☐	165	Roman Cech	.20
☐	166	Pavel Zmrhal	.20
☐	167	Petr Buzek	.20
☐	168	Jaroslav Benak	.20
☐	169	Michael Vyhlidal	.20
☐	170	Petr Kuchyna	.20
☐	171	Josef Marha	.50
☐	172	Leos Pipa	.20
☐	173	Jiri Poukar	.20
☐	174	Libor Dolana	.20
☐	175	Viktor Ujcik	.20
☐	176	Ladislav Prokupek	.20
☐	177	Jiri Cihlar	.20
☐	178	Patrik Fink	.20
☐	179	Oldrich Valek	.20
☐	180	Zdenek Cely	.20
☐	181	Jaroslav Kames	.20
☐	182	Pavel Malac	.20
☐	183	Martin Maskarinec	.20
☐	184	Pavel Rajnoha	.20
☐	185	Pavel Kowalczyk	.20
☐	186	Miloslav Guren	.20
☐	187	Radim Tesarik	.20
☐	188	Jan Krajicek	.20
☐	189	Patrik Hucko	.20
☐	190	Roman Kankovsky	.20
☐	191	Jaroslav Hub	.20
☐	192	Petr Kankovsky	.20
☐	193	Pavel Janku	.20
☐	194	Miroslav Okal	.20
☐	195	Zdenek Okal	.20
☐	196	Roman Mejzlik	.20
☐	197	Juraj Jurik	.20
☐	198	Roman Meluzin	.20
☐	199	Josef Straub	.20
☐	200	Martin Kotasek	.20
☐	201	Zdenek Sedlak	.20
☐	202	Petr Cajanek	.20
☐	203	Zdenek Orct	.20
☐	204	Petr Franek	.20
☐	205	Petr Svoboda	.20
☐	206	Angel Nikolov	.20
☐	207	Petr Molnar	.20
☐	208	Kamil Prachar	.20
☐	209	Jiri Slegr	.50
☐	210	Radek Mrazek	.20
☐	211	Jan Vopat	.20
☐	212	Ondrej Zetek	.20
☐	213	Martin Stelcich	.20
☐	214	Zdenek Skorepa	.20
☐	215	Stanislav Rosa	.20
☐	216	Radek Sip	.20
☐	217	Martin Rousek	.20
☐	218	Tomas Vlasak	.20
☐	219	Radim Piroutek	.20
☐	220	Robert Kysela	.20
☐	221	Martin Rucinsky	2.00
☐	222	Robert Lang	.50
☐	223	Ivo Prorok	.20
☐	224	Jan Alinc	.20
☐	225	Vladimir Machulda	.20
☐	226	Kamil Kolacek	.20
☐	227	David Balazs	.20
☐	228	Roman Cechmanek	.20
☐	229	Ivo Pesat	.20
☐	230	Antonin Stavjana	.20
☐	231	Pavel Augusta	.20
☐	232	Daniel Vria	.20
☐	233	Alexej Jaskin	.20
☐	234	Radek Mesicek	.20
☐	235	Marek Tichy	.20
☐	236	Stanislav Pavelec	.20
☐	237	Jan Srdinko	.20
☐	238	Zbynek Marak	.20
☐	239	Andrej Galkin	.20
☐	240	Miroslav Stavjana	.20
☐	241	Libor Forch	.20
☐	242	Roman Stantien	.20
☐	243	Josef Beranek	.50
☐	244	Lubos Jenacek	.20
☐	245	Michal Tomek	.20
☐	246	Rostislav Vlach	.20
☐	247	Miroslav Barus	.20
☐	248	Josef Podlaha	.20
☐	249	Pavel Rohlik	.20
☐	250	Martin Altrichter	.20
☐	251	Radek Toth	.20
☐	252	Vladimir Hudacek	.20
☐	253	Miloslav Horava	.20
☐	254	Meptr Macek	.20
☐	255	Pavel Blaha	.20
☐	256	Radomir Brazda	.20
☐	257	Jiri Hes	.20
☐	258	Romas Arnost	.20
☐	259	Miroslav Hosek	.20
☐	260	Jan Penk	.20
☐	261	Tomas Jelinek	.20
☐	262	Jiri Hlinka	.20
☐	263	Lubos Pazler	.20
☐	264	Roman Blazek	.20
☐	265	Vladimir Ruzicka	.20
☐	266	Tomas Kupka	.20
☐	267	Lubos Dpoita	.20
☐	268	Ladislav Slizek	.20
☐	269	Milan Antos	.20
☐	270	Vadim Kulabuchov	.20
☐	271	Anatoli Naida	.20
☐	272	Tomas Hyka	.20
☐	273	Vaclav Eiselt	.20
☐	274	Tomas Placatka	.20
☐	275	Jan Nemecek	.20
☐	276	Josef Augusta	.20
☐	277	Lubomir Fischer	.20
☐	278	Jaromir Piecechtel	.20
☐	279	Marek Sykora	.20
☐	280	Petr Hemsky	.20
☐	281	Jan Neliba	.20
☐	282	Zdenek Muller	.20
☐	283	Frantisek Vyborny	.20
☐	284	Stanislav Berger	.20
☐	285	Karel Prazak	.20
☐	286	Vladimir Caldr	.20
☐	287	Alois Hadamczik	.20
☐	288	Bretislav Bochensky	.20
☐	289	Karel Trachta	.20
☐	290	Jindrich Setikovsky	.20
☐	291	Jaroslav Holik	.20
☐	292	Jan Hrbaty	.20
☐	293	Vladimir Vujtek, Sr.	.20
☐	294	Zdenek Cech	.20
☐	295	Frantisek Vorlicek	.20
☐	296	Ondrej Weissmann	.20
☐	297	Horst Valasek	.20
☐	298	Zdislav Tabara	.20
☐	299	Pavel Richter	.20
☐	300	Bretislav Kopriva	.20

1994 - 95 ASSETS

This 100-card four-sport set features only 14 hockey players. Half the cards (excluding the checklists) have a Silver Signatures parallel, a one minute Sprint phone card and a $2 Sprint phone card. A 100-card regular set sells at $25 while a 48-card Silver Signatures set sells for $135. A 48-card one-minute set sells at $150 while a 48-card $2 set sells at $275.

Bonk, Jovanovski and Rhéaume (Canadian national team uniform) were available in series one while Fichaud, O'Neill, Sykora and Rhéaume (Las Vegas Thunder uniform) were available in series two. There are reportedly 20,605 first series one minute phone cards, 2,587 first series $2 phone cards and 3,117 second series $2 phone cards.

Rhéaume's series one card has a $25 phone card version (808 copies) and a $1,000 phone card version (4 copies) while her series two card has a $5 phone card version (2,562 copies) and a $2,000 phone card version (4 copies). All phone cards are unnumbered. Prices below are for unused phone cards.

	No.	Player	1-min	$2	Silver	Reg.
☐☐☐☐	8	Ed Jovanovski, Windsor	5.00	10.00	3.00	.50
☐☐☐☐	20	Radek Bonk, Las Vegas	2.50	5.00	1.25	.25
☐☐☐☐	21	Manon Rhéaume (G), Cdn.	8.00	15.00	12.00	2.00
☐	33	Ed Jovanovski, Windsor	.–	.–	.–	.50
☐	45	Radek Bonk, Las Vegas	.–	.–	.–	.25
☐	46	Manon Rhéaume (G), Cdn.	.–	.–	.–	2.00
☐☐☐☐	57	Jeff O'Neill, Guelph	3.00	6.00	1.75	.35
☐☐☐☐	60	Petr Sykora, Detroit	2.50	5.00	1.25	.25
☐☐☐☐	62	Eric Fichaud (G), Chicoutimi	4.00	8.00	2.50	.50
☐☐☐☐	72	Manon Rhéaume (G), Las Vegas	8.00	15.00	12.00	2.00
☐	82	Jeff O'Neill, Guelph	.–	.–	.–	.35
☐	85	Petr Sykora, Detroit	.–	.–	.–	.25
☐	87	Eric Fichaud (G), Chicoutimi	.–	.–	.–	.50
☐	97	Manon Rhéaume (G), Las Vegas	.–	.–	.–	2.00

Den.	Player	NRMT-MT
☐ $25	Manon Rhéaume (G), Cdn.	60.00
☐ $1000	Manon Rhéaume (G), Cdn.	1600.00
☐ $5	Manon Rhéaume (G), Las Vegas	10.00
☐ $2000	Manon Rhéaume (G), Las Vegas	3000.00

DIE-CUTS

This 25-card four-sport insert set features three hockey players. A 25-card set sells at $200.

No.	Player	NRMT-MT
☐ DC9	Ed Jovanovski, Windsor	7.50
☐ DC10	Manon Rhéaume (G), Cdn.	20.00
☐ DC24	Eric Fichaud (G), Chicoutimi	6.50

1994 - 95 BE A PLAYER MAGAZINE CARDS

These cards were inserted in the NHLPA's Be A Player magazine.

Imprint:

No.	Player	NRMT-MT
☐	Teemu Selänne (no #)	2.50
☐	Félix Potvin (G) (no #)	1.50
☐ 3	Paul Kariya	4.00
☐ 4	Joe Sakic	3.00

1994 - 95 CANADA GAMES POGs

Cap Diameter: 1 5/8"
Imprint: 1994 CGCL TM/MC & 1994 WPF
Complete Set (376 POGs): 100.00
Common Player: .15

No.	Team	NRMT-MT
☐ 1	Los Angeles Kings' Kini	1.00
☐ 2	New York Rangers' Kini	1.00
☐ 3	Pittsburgh Penguins' Kini	1.00
☐ 4	Dallas Stars' Kini	1.00
☐ 5	Ottawa Senators' Kini	1.00
☐ 6	Winnipeg Jets' Kini	1.00
☐ 7	Vancouver Canucks' Kini	1.00
☐ 8	Washington Capitals' Kini	1.00
☐ 9	Anaheim Mighty Ducks' Kini	1.00
☐ 10	Boston Bruins' Kini	1.00
☐ 11	Buffalo Sabres' Kini	1.00
☐ 12	Calgary Flames' Kini	1.00
☐ 13	Chicago Blackhawks' Kini	1.00
☐ 14	Detroit Red Wings' Kini	1.00
☐ 15	Edmonton Oilers' Kini	1.00
☐ 16	Florida Panthers' Kini	1.00
☐ 17	Hartford Whalers' Kini	1.00
☐ 18	Montréal Canadiens' Kini	1.00
☐ 19	New Jersey Devils' Kini	1.00
☐ 20	New York Islanders' Kini	1.00
☐ 21	Philadelphia Flyers' Kini	1.00
☐ 22	Québec Nordiques' Kini	1.00
☐ 23	San Jose Sharks' Kini	1.00
☐ 24	St. Louis Blues' Kini	1.00
☐ 25	Tampa Bay Lightning's Kini	1.00
☐ 26	Toronto Maple Leafs' Kini	1.00
☐ 27	Cliff Ronning, Van.	.15
☐ 28	Bob Corkum, Ana.	.15
☐ 29	Joe Sacco, Ana.	.15
☐ 30	Peter Douris, Ana.	.15
☐ 31	Shaun Van Allen, Ana.	.15
☐ 32	Stéphan Lebeau, Ana.	.15
☐ 33	Stu Grimson, Ana.	.15
☐ 34	Tim Sweeney, Ana.	.15
☐ 35	Adam Oates, Bos.	.75
☐ 36	Al Iafrate, Bos.	.15
☐ 37	Alexei Kasatonov, Bos.	.15
☐ 38	Bryan Smolinski, Bos.	.15
☐ 39	Cam Neely, Bos.	.35
☐ 40	Don Sweeney, Bos.	.15
☐ 41	Glen Murray, Bos.	.15
☐ 42	Ray Bourque, Bos.	1.25
☐ 43	Ted Donato, Bos.	.15
☐ 44	Alexander Mogilny, Buf.	.75
☐ 45	Doug Gilmour, Tor.	.75
☐ 46	Dale Hawerchuk, Buf.	.35
☐ 47	Derek Plante, Buf.	.15
☐ 48	Donald Audette, Buf.	.15
☐ 49	Doug Bodger, Buf.	.15
☐ 50	Pat LaFontaine, Buf.	.35
☐ 51	Randy Wood, Buf.	.15
☐ 52	Richard Smehlik, Buf.	.15
☐ 53	Yuri Khmylev, Buf.	.15
☐ 54	Theoren Fleury, Cgy.	.75
☐ 55	Kelly Kisio, Cgy.	.15
☐ 56	Joe Nieuwendyk, Cgy.	.35
☐ 57	Michael Nylander, Cgy.	.15
☐ 58	Joel Otto, Cgy.	.15
☐ 59	James Patrick, Cgy.	.15
☐ 60	Robert Reichel, Cgy.	.35
☐ 61	Gary Roberts, Cgy	.35
☐ 62	Wes Walz, Cgy.	.15
☐ 63	Ulf Dahlen, S.J.	.15
☐ 64	Zarley Zalapski, Cgy.	.15
☐ 65	Tony Amonte, Chi.	.35
☐ 66	Dirk Graham, Chi	.15
☐ 67	Joe Murphy, Chi.	.15
☐ 68	Bernie Nicholls, Chi.	.15
☐ 69	Patrick Poulin, Chi.	.15
☐ 70	Jeremy Roenick, Chi.	.75
☐ 71	Christian Ruuttu, Chi.	.15
☐ 72	Brent Sutter, Chi.	.15
☐ 73	Chris Chelios, Chi.	1.00
☐ 74	Steve Smith, Chi.	.15
☐ 75	Gary Suter, Chi.	.15
☐ 76	Neal Broten, Dal.	.15
☐ 77	Russ Courtnall, Dal.	.15
☐ 78	Dean Evason, Dal.	.15
☐ 79	Dave Gagner, Dal.	.15
☐ 80	Mike McPhee, Dal.	.15
☐ 81	Mike Modano, Dal.	1.25
☐ 82	Paul Cavallini, Dal.	.15
☐ 83	Derian Hatcher, Dal.	.35
☐ 84	Grant Ledyard, Dal.	.15
☐ 85	Mark Tinordi, Dal.	.15
☐ 86	Dino Ciccarelli, Det.	.35
☐ 87	Sergei Fedorov, Det.	1.25
☐ 88	Vyacheslav Kozlov, Det.	.15
☐ 89	Darren McCarty, Det.	.15
☐ 90	Keith Primeau, Det.	.35
☐ 91	Ray Sheppard, Det.	.15
☐ 92	Steve Yzerman, Det.	2.50
☐ 93	Paul Coffey, Det.	.75
☐ 94	Vladimir Konstantinov, Det.	.15
☐ 95	Nicklas Lidstrom, Det.	.35
☐ 96	Greg Adams, Van.	.15
☐ 97	Jason Arnott, Edm.	.35
☐ 98	Kelly Buchberger, Edm.	.15
☐ 99	Shayne Corson, Edm.	.35
☐ 100	Scott Pearson, Edm.	.15
☐ 101	Doug Weight, Edm.	.75
☐ 102	Boris Mironov, Edm.	.15
☐ 103	Fredrik Olausson, Edm.	.15
☐ 104	Stu Barnes, Fla.	.15
☐ 105	Bob Kudelski, Fla.	.15
☐ 106	Andrei Lomakin, Fla.	.15
☐ 107	Dave Lowry, Fla.	.15
☐ 108	Scott Mellanby, Fla.	.15
☐ 109	Rob Niedermayer, Fla.	.35
☐ 110	Brian Skrudland, Fla.	.15
☐ 111	Brian Benning, Fla.	.15
☐ 112	Gord Murphy, Fla.	.15
☐ 113	Andrew Cassels, Hfd.	.15
☐ 114	Robert Kron, Hfd.	.15
☐ 115	Jocelyn Lemieux, Hfd.	.15
☐ 116	Paul Ranheim, Hfd.	.15
☐ 117	Geoff Sanderson, Hfd.	.15
☐ 118	Jim Sandlak, Hfd.	.15
☐ 119	Darren Turcotte, Hfd.	.15
☐ 120	Pat Verbeek, Hfd.	.15
☐ 121	Chris Pronger, Hfd	.35
☐ 122	Pat Conacher, L.A.	.15
☐ 123	Mike Donnelly, L.A.	.15
☐ 124	John Druce, L.A.	.15
☐ 125	Tony Granato, L.A.	.15
☐ 126	Wayne Gretzky, L.A.	5.00
☐ 127	Jari Kurri, L.A.	.35
☐ 128	Warren Rychel, L.A.	.15
☐ 129	Rob Blake, L.A.	.35
☐ 130	Marty McSorley, L.A.	.15
☐ 131	Alexei Zhitnik, L.A.	.15
☐ 132	Brian Bellows, Mtl.	.15
☐ 133	Vincent Damphousse, Mtl.	.35
☐ 134	Gilbert Dionne, Mtl.	.15
☐ 135	Mike Keane, Mtl.	.15
☐ 136	John LeClair, Mtl.	1.25
☐ 137	Kirk Muller, Mtl.	.15
☐ 138	Oleg Petrov, Mtl.	.15
☐ 139	Eric Desjardins, Mtl.	.35
☐ 140	Lyle Odelein, Mtl.	.15
☐ 141	Peter Popovic, Mtl.	.15
☐ 142	Mathieu Schneider, Mtl.	.15
☐ 143	Trent Klatt, Dal.	.15
☐ 144	Bobby Holik, N.J.	.15
☐ 145	Claude Lemieux, N.J.	.15
☐ 146	John MacLean, N.J.	.15
☐ 147	Corey Millen, N.J.	.15
☐ 148	Stéphane Richer, N.J.	.15
☐ 149	Valeri Zelepukin, N.J.	.15
☐ 150	Bruce Driver, N.J.	.15
☐ 151	Gino Odlick, Van.	.15
☐ 152	Scott Stevens, N.J.	.15
☐ 153	Brad Dalgarno, NYI.	.15
☐ 154	Ray Ferraro, NYI.	.15
☐ 155	Patrick Flatley, NYI.	.15
☐ 156	Travis Green, NYI.	.15
☐ 157	Derek King, NYI.	.15
☐ 158	Marty McInnis, NYI.	.15
☐ 159	Steve Thomas, NYI.	.15
☐ 160	Pierre Turgeon, NYI.	.35
☐ 161	Darius Kasparaitis, NYI.	.15
☐ 162	Vladimir Malakhov, NYI.	.15
☐ 163	Alexei Kovalev, NYR.	.15
☐ 164	Steve Larmer, NYR.	.15
☐ 165	Stéphane Matteau, NYR.	.15
☐ 166	Mark Messier, NYR.	1.25
☐ 167	Sergei Nemchinov, NYR.	.15
☐ 168	Brian Noonan, NYR.	.15
☐ 169	Petr Nedved, NYR.	.15
☐ 170	Brian Leetch, NYR.	.75
☐ 171	Kevin Lowe, NYR.	.15
☐ 172	Sergei Zubov, NYR.	.35
☐ 173	Sylvain Turgeon, Ott.	.15
☐ 174	Alexei Yashin, Ott.	1.00
☐ 175	Norm Maciver, Ott.	.15
☐ 176	Brad Shaw, Ott.	.15
☐ 177	Brent Fedyk, Pha.	.15
☐ 178	Mark Lamb, Pha.	.15
☐ 179	Don McSweeney, Ana.	.15
☐ 180	Mark Recchi, Pha.	.35
☐ 181	Mikael Renberg, Pha.	.15
☐ 182	Garry Galley, Pha.	.15
☐ 183	Ron Francis, Pgh.	.75
☐ 184	Jaromir Jagr, Pgh.	2.50
☐ 185	Mario Lemieux, Pgh.	4.00
☐ 186	Shawn McEachern, Pgh.	.15
☐ 187	Joe Mullen, Pgh.	.15
☐ 188	Tomas Sandström, Pgh.	.15
☐ 189	Kevin Stevens, Pgh.	.15
☐ 190	Martin Straka, Pgh.	.15
☐ 191	Larry Murphy, Pgh.	.35
☐ 192	Kjell Samuelsson, Pgh.	.15
☐ 193	Ulf Samuelsson, Pgh.	.15
☐ 194	Wendel Clark, Que.	.35
☐ 195	Valeri Kamensky, Que.	.35
☐ 196	Andrei Kovalev, Que.	.15

	No.	Player	NRMT-MT
☐	197	Owen Nolan, Que.	.35
☐	198	Mike Ricci, Que.	.15
☐	199	Joe Sakic, Que.	2.00
☐	200	Scott Young, Que.	.15
☐	201	Uwe Krupp, Que.	.15
☐	202	Curtis Leschyshyn, Que.	.15
☐	203	Brett Hull, Stl.	1.25
☐	204	Craig Janney, Stl.	.15
☐	205	Kevin Miller, Stl.	.15
☐	206	Vitali Prokhorov, Stl.	.15
☐	207	Brendan Shanahan, Stl.	1.50
☐	208	Peter Stastny, Stl.	.15
☐	209	Esa Tikkanen, Stl.	.15
☐	210	Steve Duchesne, Stl.	.15
☐	211	Gaetan Duchesne, S.J.	.15
☐	212	Todd Elik, S.J.	.15
☐	213	POG Man	.15
☐	214	Pat Falloon, S.J.	.15
☐	215	Johan Garpenlov, S.J.	.15
☐	216	Igor Larionov, S.J.	.35
☐	217	Sergei Makarov, S.J.	.15
☐	218	Jeff Norton, S.J.	.15
☐	219	Sandis Ozolinsh, S.J.	.35
☐	220	Mikael Andersson, T.B.	.15
☐	221	Brian Bradley, T.B.	.15
☐	222	Danton Cole, T.B.	.15
☐	223	Chris Gratton, T.B.	.35
☐	224	Petr Klima, T.B.	.15
☐	225	Denis Savard, T.B.	.35
☐	226	John Tucker, T.B.	.15
☐	227	Shawn Chambers, T.B.	.15
☐	228	Chris Joseph, T.B.	.15
☐	229	Dave Andreychuk, Tor.	.15
☐	230	Nikolai Borschevsky, Tor.	.15
☐	231	Mike Craig, Tor.	.15
☐	232	Mike Eastwood, Tor.	.15
☐	233	Mike Gartner, Tor.	.35
☐	234	Doug Gilmour, Tor.	.75
☐	235	Kent Manderville, Tor.	.15
☐	236	Mike Ridley, Tor.	.15
☐	237	Mats Sundin, Tor.	1.25
☐	238	Dave Ellett, Tor.	.15
☐	239	Todd Gill, Tor.	.15
☐	240	Jamie Macoun, Tor.	.15
☐	241	Dmitri Mironov, Tor.	.15
☐	242	Peter Bondra, Wsh.	1.00
☐	243	Randy Burridge, Wsh.	.15
☐	244	Dale Hunter, Wsh.	.15
☐	245	Joé Juneau, Wsh.	.15
☐	246	Dmitri Khristich, Wsh.	.15
☐	247	Kelly Miller, Wsh.	.15
☐	248	Michal Pivonka, Wsh.	.15
☐	249	Sylvain Côté, Wsh.	.15
☐	250	Tie Domi, Wpg.	.15
☐	251	Dallas Drake, Wpg.	.15
☐	252	Nelson Emerson, Wpg.	.15
☐	253	Teemu Selänne, Wpg.	1.75
☐	254	Darrin Shannon, Wpg.	.15
☐	255	Thomas Steen, Wpg.	.15
☐	256	Keith Tkachuk, Wpg.	1.00
☐	257	Dave Manson, Wpg.	.15
☐	258	Stéphane Quintal, Wpg.	.15
☐	259	AS: Adam Graves, NYR.	.15
☐	260	AS: Brian Leetch, NYR.	.50
☐	261	AS: John Vanbiesbrouck (G), Fla.	.75
☐	262	AS: Scott Stevens. N.J.	.15
☐	263	AS: Ray Bourque, Bos.	.60
☐	264	AS: Al MacInnis, Cgy.	.35
☐	265	AS: Brendan Shanahan, Stl.	.75
☐	266	AS: Pavel Bure, Van.	1.00
☐	267	AS: Sergei Fedorov, Det.	.60
☐	268	AS: Wayne Gretzky, L.A.	3.00
☐	269	Guy Hebert (G), Ana.	.35
☐	270	Kirk McLean (G), Van.	.35
☐	271	John Blue (G), Bos.	.25
☐	272	Vincent Riendeau (G), Bos.	.25
☐	273	Grant Fuhr (G), Buf.	.15
☐	274	Dominik Hasek (G), Buf.	1.75
☐	275	Trevor Kidd (G), Cgy.	.35
☐	276	Ed Belfour (G), Chi.	.50
☐	277	Andy Moog (G), Dal.	.35
☐	278	Mike Vernon (G), Det.	.35
☐	279	Bill Ranford (G), Edm.	.35
☐	280	John Vanbiesbrouck (G), Fla.	1.50
☐	281	Sean Burke (G), Hfd.	.35
☐	282	Kelly Hrudey (G), L.A.	.35
☐	283	Patrick Roy (G), Mtl.	4.00
☐	284	Martin Brodeur (G), N.J.	1.75
☐	285	Chris Terreri (G), N.J.	.25
☐	286	Jamie McLennan (G), NYI.	.35
☐	287	Glenn Healy (G), NYR.	.25
☐	288	Mike Richter (G), NYR.	.75
☐	289	Craig Billington (G), Ott.	.25
☐	290	Dominic Roussel (G), Pha.	.25
☐	291	Tom Barrasso (G), Pgh.	.25
☐	292	Stéphane Fiset (G), Que.	.35
☐	293	Curtis Joseph (G), Stl.	1.50
☐	294	Arturs Irbe (G), S.J.	.25
☐	295	Daren Puppa (G), T.B.	.25
☐	296	Félix Potvin (G), Tor.	1.50
☐	297	Tim Cheveldae (G), Wpg.	.25
☐	298	Don Beaupré (G), Wsh.	.25
☐	299	Rick Tabaracci (G), Wsh.	.25
☐	300	Anaheim Mighty Ducks Logo	.15
☐	301	Boston Bruins Logo	.15
☐	302	Buffalo Sabres Logo	.15
☐	303	Calgary Flames Logo	.15
☐	304	Chicago Blackhawks Logo	.15
☐	305	Dallas Stars Logo	.15
☐	306	Detroit Red Wings Logo	.15
☐	307	Edmonton Oilers Logo	.15
☐	308	Florida Panthers Logo	.15
☐	309	Hartford Whalers Logo	.15
☐	310	Los Angeles Kings Logo	.15
☐	311	Montréal Canadiens Logo	.15
☐	312	New Jersey Devils Logo	.15
☐	313	Jeff Brown, Van.	.15
☐	314	New York Rangers Logo	.15
☐	315	Ottawa Senators Logo	.15
☐	316	Philadelphia Flyers Logo	.15
☐	317	Pittsburgh Penguins Logo	.15
☐	318	Québec Nordiques Logo	.15
☐	319	St. Louis Blues Logo	.15
☐	320	San Jose Sharks Logo	.15
☐	321	Tampa Bay Lightning Logo	.15
☐	322	Toronto Maple Leafs Logo	.15
☐	323	Vancouver Canucks Logo	.15
☐	324	Washington Capitals Logo	.15
☐	325	Winnipeg Jets Logo	.15
☐	326	AW: Martin Brodeur (G), N.J.	1.75
☐	327	AW: Ray Bourque, Bos.	.75
☐	328	AW: Cam Neely, Bos.	.35
☐	329	Geoff Courtnall, Van.	.15
☐	330	The World POG Federation	.15
☐	331	AW: Wayne Gretzky, L.A.	3.00
☐	332	AW: Dominik Hasek (G), Buf.	1.00
☐	333	AW: Dominik Hasek (G), Buf.	1.00
☐	334	AW: Brian Leetch, NYR.	.50
☐	335	Martin Gelinas, Van.	.15
☐	336	AW: Cam Neely, Bos.	.35
☐	337	LL: Mike Richter, NYR.	.50
☐	338	Luke Richardson, Edm.	.15
☐	339	Jyrki Lumme, Van.	.15
☐	340	Nathan LaFayette, Van.	.15
☐	341	Pavel Bure, Van.	1.75
☐	342	Sergio Momesso, Van.	.15
☐	343	Randy Burridge, Wsh.	.15
☐	344	LL: Tie Domi, Wpg.	.15
☐	345	LL: Scott Stevens, N.J.	.15
☐	346	Teppo Numminen, Wpg.	.15
☐	347	Anatoli Semenov, Ana.	.15
☐	348	Stephen Heinze, Bos.	.15
☐	349	Tom Chorske, N.J.	.15
☐	350	Bill Guerin, N.J.	.15
☐	351	Scott Niedermayer, N.J.	.35
☐	352	Adam Graves, NYR.	.15
☐	353	Alexandre Daigle, Ott.	.35
☐	354	Troy Mallette, Ott.	.15
☐	355	Dave McLean, Ott.	.15
☐	356	Josef Beranek, Pha.	.15
☐	357	Kevin Dineen, Pha.	.15
☐	358	Eric Lindros, Pha.	3.00
☐	359	Bob Rouse, Det.	.15
☐	360	AW: Sergei Fedorov, Det.	.75
☐	361	Bob Errey, S.J.	.15
☐	362	Brad May, Buf.	.15
☐	363	Kevin Hatcher, Wsh.	.15
☐	364	New York Islanders Logo	.15
☐	365	Randy Ladouceur, Ana.	.15
☐	366	Bobby Dollas, Ana.	.15
☐	367	Igor Kravchuk, Edm.	.15
☐	368	Jesse Belanger, Fla.	.15
☐	369	POG Logo	.15
☐	370	Garry Valk, Ana.	.15
☐	371	POG Logo	.15
☐	372	Ron Hextall (G), Pha.	.35
☐	373	Rod Brind'Amour, Pha.	.35
☐	374	Benoît Hogue, NYI.	.15
☐	375	Alexei Zhamnov, Wpg.	.35
☐	376	LL: Pavel Bure, Van.	1.00

	Checklist (2 1/8" x 3 1/2")	**NRMT-MT**
☐	Checklist 1 (1-47)	.25
☐	Checklist 2 (48-94)	.25
☐	Checklist 3 (95-141)	.25
☐	Checklist 4 (142-188)	.25
☐	Checklist 5 (189-235)	.25
☐	Checklist 6 (236-282)	.25
☐	Checklist 7 (283-329)	.25
☐	Checklist 8 (330-376)	.25

1994 - 95 CLASSIC

There are two versions: the regular card and gold parallel.

Imprint: 1994 Classic Games, Inc.

Complete Set (120 cards):		12.00	60.00
Common Player:		.10	.25

	Promo	**NRMT-MT**
☐	Jason Arnott	5.00

	No.	**Player**	**Reg.**	**Gold**
☐☐	1	Ed Jovanovski, CHL All-Stars	.50	1.50
☐☐	2	Oleg Tverdovsky, Rus.	.20	.35
☐☐	3	Radek Bonk, Las Vegas	.20	.35
☐☐	4	Jason Bonsignore, Niagara Falls	.10	.25
☐☐	5	Jeff O'Neill, Guelph	.20	.35
☐☐	6	Ryan Smyth, CHL All-Stars	1.00	3.00
☐☐	7	Jamie Storr (G), Owen Sound	.20	.35
☐☐	8	Jason Wiemer, Portland-WHL	.10	.25
☐☐	9	Nolan Baumgartner, Kamloops	.10	.25
☐☐	10	Jeff Friesen, Regina	.20	.35
☐☐	11	Wade Belak, Saskatoon	.10	.25
☐☐	12	Ethan Moreau, Niagara Falls	.20	.35
☐☐	13	Alexander Kharlamov, CSKA	.10	.25
☐☐	14	Eric Fichaud (G), Chicautimi	.50	1.50
☐☐	15	Wayne Primeau, Owen Sound	.20	.35
☐☐	16	Brad Brown, North Bay	.10	.25
☐☐	17	Chris Dingman, Brandon	.10	.25
☐☐	18	Evgeni Ryabchikov (G), Rus.	.10	.25
☐☐	19	Yan Golubovsky, CSKA	.10	.25
☐☐	20	Chris Wells, Seattle	.10	.25
☐☐	21	Vadim Sharifjanov, Rus.	.10	.25
☐☐	22	Dan Cloutier (G), S.S. Marie	.50	1.50
☐☐	23	CL: Portland Pirates	.10	.25
☐☐	24	Jamie Langenbrunner, Peterborough	.20	.35
☐☐	25	Kenny Jonsson, Swe.	.20	.35
☐☐	26	Curtis Bowen, Ottawa-OHL	.10	.25
☐☐	27	Sergei Gonchar, Portland-AHL	.20	.35
☐☐	28	Stefan Bergqvist, Swe.	.10	.25
☐☐	29	Vaclav Prospal, Hershey	.50	1.50
☐☐	30	Valeri Bure, Rus.	.20	.35
☐☐	31	Richard Shulmistra (G), CCHA All-Stars	.10	.25
☐☐	32	Chris Armstrong, CHL All-Stars	.10	.25
☐☐	33	Brian Farrell, Harvard	.10	.25
☐☐	34	Brian Savage	.20	.35
☐☐	35	Blaine Lacher (G), Lake Superior	.10	.25
☐☐	36	Kevin Brown, Detroit-OHL	.10	.25
☐☐	37	Joe Dziedzic, Minnesota	.10	.25
☐☐	38	Peter Ferraro, Maine	.10	.25
☐☐	39	Chris Ferraro, Maine	.10	.25
☐☐	40	Todd Harvey, Detroit-OHL	.20	.35
☐☐	41	Eric Lecompte, Hull	.10	.25

	No.	Player		
□ □	42	Dean Grillo, North Dakota	.10	.25
□ □	43	Valeri Karpov, Rus.	.10	.25
□ □	44	Andrew Shier, Wisconsin	.10	.25
□ □	45	Vesa Viitakoski, Saint John	.10	.25
□ □	46	Xavier Majic, R.P.I.	.10	.25
□ □	47	Kevin Smyth, Springfield	.10	.25
□ □	48	Jeff Nelson, Portland-AHL	.10	.25
□ □	49	Cory Stillman, Saint John	.10	.25
□ □	50	Clayton Beddoes, Lake Superior	.10	.25
□ □	51	Craig Conroy, Clarkson	.10	.25
□ □	52	Dean Fedorchuk, Alaska	.10	.25
□ □	53	John Gruden, Ferris State	.10	.25
□ □	54	Chris McAlpine, Minnesota	.10	.25
□ □	55	Sean McCann, Harvard	.10	.25
□ □	56	Derek Maguire, Harvard	.10	.25
□ □	57	David Oliver, Michigan	.20	.35
□ □	58	Mike Pomichter, Boston U.	.10	.25
□ □	59	Jamie Ram (G), Michigan	.10	.25
□ □	60	Shawn Reid, WCHA All-Stars	.10	.25
□ □	61	Dwayne Roloson (G), Lowell	.10	.25
□ □	62	Steve Shields (G), Michigan	.20	.35
□ □	63	Brian Wiseman, Michigan	.10	.25
□ □	64	Drew Bannister, CHL All-Stars	.10	.25
□ □	65	Matt Johnson, Peterborough	.10	.25
□ □	66	Scott Malone, New Hampshire	.10	.25
□ □	67	Sergei Berezin, Rus.	.35	.75
□ □	68	Chad Penney, P.E.I.	.10	.25
□ □	69	Ian Laperrière, Drummondville	.10	.25
□ □	70	Andrei Nikolishin, Rus.	.10	.25
□ □	71	Kelly Fairchild, Wisconsin	.10	.25
□ □	72	Jere Lehtinen, Fin.	.20	.35
□ □	73	Ravil Gusmanov, CIS.	.10	.25
□ □	74	CL: Atlanta Knights	.10	.25
□ □	75	Neil Little (G), R.P.I.	.10	.25
□ □	76	Brian Rolston, Albany	.20	.35
□ □	77	David Vyborny, Cze.	.10	.25
□ □	78	Nikolai Tsulygin, Rus.	.10	.25
□ □	79	Niklas Sundstrom, Swe.	.20	.35
□ □	80	Patrik Juhlin, Swe.	.10	.25
□ □	81	Dan Plante, Salt Lake	.10	.25
□ □	82	Brandon Convery, Belleville	.10	.25
□ □	83	Nick Stajduhar, London	.10	.25
□ □	84	Garth Snow (G), Cornwall	.20	.35
□ □	85	Corey Hirsch (G), Binghampton	.20	.35
□ □	86	Craig Darby, Fredericton	.10	.25
□ □	87	Andrei Nazarov, Kansas City	.10	.25
□ □	88	Todd Marchant, Cape Breton	.20	.35
□ □	89	Jeff Nielson, Minnesota	.10	.25
□ □	90	Brendan Witt, Seattle	.20	.35
□ □	91	Denis Metlyuk, Hershey	.10	.25
□ □	92	Maxim Bets, San Diego	.10	.25
□ □	93	Sean Pronger, Bowling Green	.25	.35
□ □	94	Chris Tamer, Cleveland	.10	.25
□ □	95	Saku Koivu, Fin.	1.00	3.00
□ □	96	Mattias Norstrom, Binghampton	.10	.25
□ □	97	Ville Peltonen, Fin.	.10	.25
□ □	98	René Corbet, Cornwall	.10	.25
□ □	99	Brent Gretzky, Atlanta	.10	.25
□ □	100	Chris Marinucci, Minn.-Duluth	.10	.25
□ □	101	Ian Moran, Clevland	.10	.25
□ □	102	Janne Laukkanen, Fin.	.10	.25
□ □	103	Todd Bertuzzi, Guelph	.20	.35
□ □	104	Darby Hendrickson, St. John's	.10	.25
□ □	105	Janne Niinimaa, Fin.	.35	.75
□ □	106	David Roberts, Peoria	.10	.25
□ □	107	Pat Neaton, Cleveland	.10	.25
□ □	108	Todd Warriner, Cornwall	.20	.35
□ □	109	Mats Lindgren, Swe.	.10	.25
□ □	110	Jason Allison, London	.50	1.50
□ □	111	Radim Bicanek, Belleville	.10	.25
□ □	112	Denis Pederson, Prince Albert	.10	.25
□ □	113	Viktor Kozlov, Rus.	.20	.35
□ □	114	Mike Murray, Lowell	.10	.25
□ □	115	Aaron Gavey, S.S. Marie	.10	.25
□ □	116	Michael Peca, Ottawa-OHL	.35	.75
□ □	117	Jason Zent, Wisconsin	.10	.25
□ □	118	Jason MacDonald, Owen Sound	.10	.25
□ □	119	Aaron Israel (G), Harvard	.10	.25
□ □	120	Manon Rhéaume (G), Cdn.	3.00	8.00

WOMEN OF HOCKEY

Insert Set (40 cards): 15.00

	No.	Player	NRMT-MT
□	W1	Manon Rhéaume (G)	5.00
□	W2	France St. Louis	.75
□	W3	Cheryl Pounder	.35
□	W4	Thérèse Brisson	.35
□	W5	Cassie Campbell	1.50
□	W6	Angela James	.75
□	W7	Danielle Goyette	.35
□	W8	Jane Robinson	.35
□	W9	Stacy Wilson	.35
□	W10	Margot Page	.35
□	W11	Laura Leslie	.35
□	W12	Judy Diduck	.35
□	W13	Hayley Wickenheiser	1.50
□	W14	Nathalie Picard	.35
□	W15	Leslie Reddon (G)	.35
□	W16	Marianne Grnak	.35
□	W17	Andria Hunter	.35
□	W18	Nancy Drolet	.35
□	W19	Geraldine Heaney	.75
□	W20	Karen Nystrom	.35
□	W21	CL: Rhéaume/Grnak/Heaney	2.00
□	W22	Kelly Dyer	.35
□	W23	Vicki Movsessian	.35
□	W24	Lisa Brown	.35
□	W25	Shawna Davidson	.35
□	W26	Colleen Coyne	.35
□	W27	Karyne Bye	.35
□	W28	Suzanne Merz	.35
□	W29	Gretzhen Ulion	.35
□	W30	Sandra Whyte	.35
□	W31	Cindy Curley	.35
□	W32	Michele DiFronze	.35
□	W33	Stephanie Boyd	.35
□	W34	Shelley Looney	.35
□	W35	Jeanine Sobek	.35
□	W36	Beth Beagan	.35
□	W37	Cammi Granato	2.00
□	W38	Christina Bailey	.35
□	W39	Kelly O'Leary	.35
□	W40	Erin Whitten (G)	1.50

AUTOGRAPHS

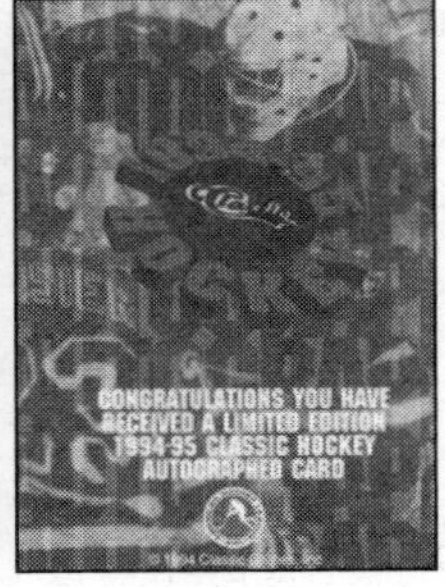

	Player	NRMT-MT
□	Mark Bavis (#/1,955)	5.00
□	Radek Bonk(#/4,940)	15.00
□	Jason Bonsignore(#/4,300)	5.00
□	Scott Chartier (#/1,930)	5.00
□	Craig Darby (#/1,915)	5.00
□	Dallas Drake (#/960)	5.00
□	Ted Drury (#/1,920)	5.00
□	Mike Dunham (G) (#/1,955)	10.00
□	Eric Fenton (#/1,845)	5.00
□	Peter Ferraro (#/4,875)	5.00
□	Chris Ferraro (#/4,770)	5.00
□	Jeff Friesen (#/6,145)	20.00
□	Doug Gilmour (#/1,950)	35.00
□	Chris Gratton (#/2,000)	15.00
□	Brett Harkins (#/1,885)	5.00
□	Brett Hauer (#/1,930)	5.00
□	Jon Hillebrandt (#/1,570)	5.00
□	Ryan Hughes (#/1,940)	5.00
□	Dean Hullet (#/1,955)	5.00
□	Fred Knipsheer (#/1,945)	5.00
□	John Lilley (#/2,460)	5.00
□	Stanislav Neckar (#/4,645)	5.00
□	Cam Neely (#/1,850)	25.00
□	Rob Niedermayer (#/950)	25.00
□	Jeff O'Neill (#/5,380)	15.00
□	Derek Plante (#/1,970)	5.00
□	Manon Rhéaume (#/2,400)	90.00
□	Travis Richards (#/1,950)	5.00
□	Barry Richter (#/1,935)	5.00
□	David Roberts (#/1,970)	5.00
□	Chris Rogles (#/1,920)	5.00
□	Jon Rohloff (#/2,010)	5.00
□	Brian Rolston (#/2,400)	10.00
□	David Sacco (#/1,975)	5.00
□	Brian Savage (#/4,930)	10.00
□	Cam Stewart (#/970)	5.00
□	Jim Storm (#1,950)	5.00
□	Chris Tamer (#/1,900)	5.00
□	Aaron Ward (#1,965)	5.00

CLASSIC DRAFT PROSPECTS

Insert Set (10 cards): 55.00

	No.	Player	NRMT-MT
□	DP1	Bubba Berenzweig	4.00
□	DP2	Aki Berg, Fin.	6.00
□	DP3	Chad Kilger	6.00
□	DP4	Daymond Langkow	6.00
□	DP5	Alyn McCauley	15.00
□	DP6	Igor Melyakov, Rus.	4.00
□	DP7	Erik Rasmussen	8.00
□	DP8	Marty Reasoner	8.00
□	DP9	Scott Roche	4.00
□	DP10	Petr Sykora, Cleveland	6.00

ALL-AMERICANS

Insert Set (10 cards): 20.00

	No.	Player	NRMT-MT
□	AA1	Craig Conroy	2.00
□	AA2	John Gruden	2.00
□	AA3	Chris Marinucci	2.00
□	AA4	Chris McAlpine	2.00
□	AA5	Sean McCann	2.00
□	AA6	David Oliver	3.00
□	AA7	Mike Pomichter	2.00
□	AA8	Jamie Ram (G)	3.00
□	AA9	Shawn Reid	2.00
□	AA10	Dwayne Roloson (G)	3.00

ALL-ROOKIE TEAM

Insert Set (6 cards): 30.00

	No.	Player	NRMT-MT
☐	AR1	Martin Brodeur (G), Utica	15.00
☐	AR2	Jason Arnott	5.00
☐	AR3	Alexei Yashin	8.00
☐	AR4	Oleg Petrov	3.00
☐	AR5	Chris Pronger	5.00
☐	AR6	Alexander Karpovtsev	3.00

CHL ALL-STARS

These cards are limited to 2,000 copies.

Insert Set (10 cards): 50.00

	No.	Player	NRMT-MT
☐	C1	Jason Allison	10.00
☐	C2	Yannick Dubé	4.00
☐	C3	Eric Fichaud (G)	8.00
☐	C4	Jeff Friesen	6.00
☐	C5	Aaron Gavey	5.00
☐	C6	Ed Jovanovski	8.00
☐	C7	Jeff O'Neill	6.00
☐	C8	Ryan Smyth	15.00
☐	C9	Jamie Storr (G)	6.00
☐	C10	Brendan Witt	5.00

CHL PREVIEW

Insert Set (6 cards): 20.00

	No.	Player	NRMT-MT
☐	CP1	Wayne Primeau, Owen Sound	4.00
☐	CP2	Eric Fichaud (G), Chicoutimi	6.00
☐	CP3	Wade Redden, Brandon	5.00
☐	CP4	Jason Doig, St-Jean	4.00
☐	CP5	Vitali Yachmenev, North Bay	4.00
☐	CP6	Nolan Baumgartner, Kamloops	4.00

ENFORCERS

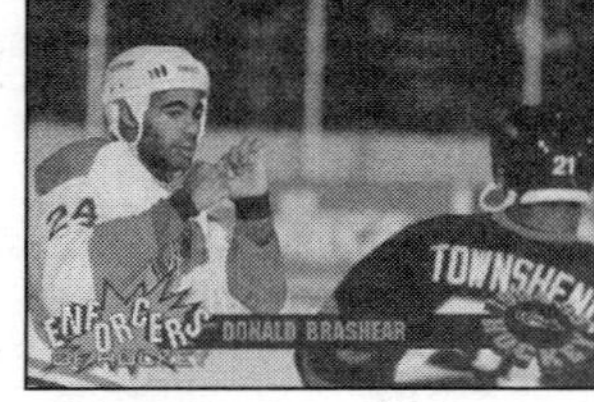

Insert Set (10 cards): 15.00

Promo Card (Richard Zemlak, #PR1): 2.00

	No.	Player	NRMT-MT
☐	E1	Donald Brashear, Fredericton	3.00
☐	E2	Daniel Lacroix, Binghampton	2.00
☐	E3	Dale Henry, Milwaukee	2.00
☐	E4	John Badduke, Hamilton	2.00
☐	E5	Corey Schwab (G), Albany	3.00
☐	E6	Craig Martin, Adirondack	2.00
☐	E7	Kerry Clark, Portland-AHL	2.00
☐	E8	Kevin Kaminski, Portland-AHL	2.00
☐	E9	Jim Kyte, Las Vegas	2.00
☐	E10	Mark DeSantis, San Diego	2.00

DRAFT PICKS

Insert Set (5 cards): 35.00

	No.	Player	NRMT-MT
☐	CP11	Ed Jovanovski	8.00
☐	CP12	Oleg Tverdovsky	4.00
☐	CP13	Radek Bonk	4.00
☐	CP14	Jason Allison	10.00
☐	CP15	Manon Rhéaume	20.00

R.O.Y. SWEEPSTAKES

Insert Set (20 cards): 35.00

	No.	Player	NRMT-MT
☐	R1	Jason Allison, Portland-AHL	8.00
☐	R2	Radek Bonk	2.00
☐	R3	Jason Bonsignore	2.00
☐	R4	Valeri Bure	2.00
☐	R5	Jeff Friesen	3.00
☐	R6	Aaron Gavey	2.00
☐	R7	Todd Harvey	2.00
☐	R8	Kenny Jonnson, Swe.	2.00
☐	R9	Ed Jovanovski	6.00
☐	R10	Patrik Juhlin	2.00
☐	R11	Valeri Karpov	2.00
☐	R12	Viktor Kozlov	2.00
☐	R13	Blaine Lacher (G)	2.00
☐	R14	Andrei Nikolishin	2.00
☐	R15	Jeff O'Neill	2.00
☐	R16	David Oliver	2.00
☐	R17	Garth Snow (G)	2.00
☐	R18	Jamie Storr (G), Owen Sound	4.00
☐	R19	Oleg Tverdovsky	2.00
☐	R20	Field Card	2.00

CLASSIC DRAFT TRI-CARDS

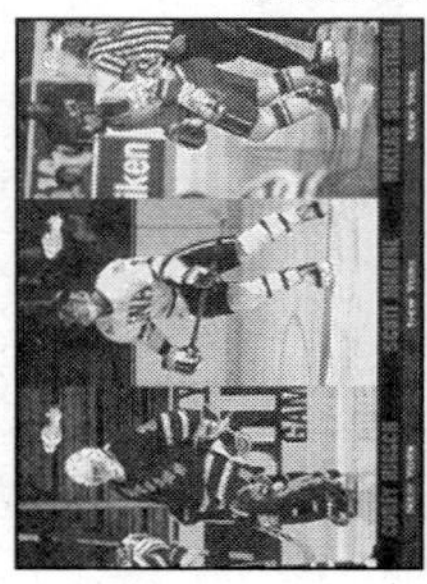

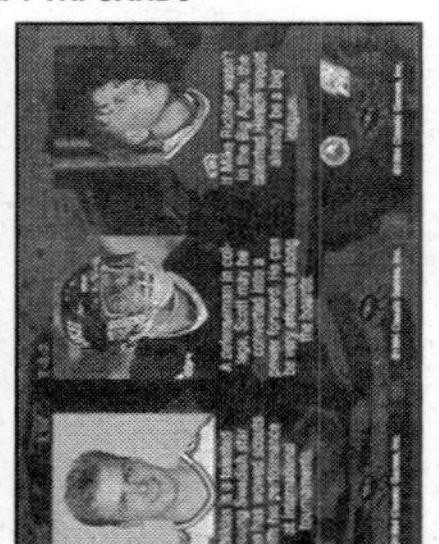

Insert Set (26 cards): 65.00

	No.	Player	NRMT-MT
☐	T1-3	V. Karpov / N. Tsulygin / O.Tverdovsky	3.00
☐	T4-6	F. Knipscheeer / B. Lacher (G) / E. Ryabchikov (G)	2.00
☐	T7-10	D. Cooper / W. Primeau / S. Shields (G)	2.00
☐	T10-12	C. Dingman / C. Stillman / V. Vitakoski	2.00
☐	T13-15	E. Lecompte / E. Moreau / M. Pomichter	3.00
☐	T16-18	T. Harvey / J. Langenbrunner / J. Lehtinen	3.00
☐	T19-21	C. Bowen / Y. Golubovsky / K. Hodson (G)	3.00
☐	T22-24	J. Bonsignore / M. Lindgren / D. Oliver	2.00
☐	T25-27	C. Armstrong / E. Jovanovski / J. Podollan	4.00
☐	T28-30	A. Nikolishin / J. O'Neill / K. Smyth	3.00
☐	T31-33	K. Brown / M. Johnson / J. Storr (G)	3.00
☐	T34-36	V. Bure / S. Koivu / B. Savage	8.00
☐	T37-39	D. Pederson / B. Rolston / V. Sharifijanov	3.00
☐	T40-42	T. Bertuzzi / C. Marinucci / D. Plante	2.00
☐	T43-45	C. Hirsch (G) / N. Sundstrom / S. Malone	3.00
☐	T46-48	R. Bicanek / R. Bonk / C. Penney	2.00
☐	T49-51	P. Juhlin / D. Metlyuk / J. Niinimaa	3.00
☐	T52-54	G. Andrusak / P. Neaton / C. Wells	2.00
☐	T55-57	R. Corbet / A. Deadmarsh / G. Snow (G)	3.00
☐	T58-60	D. Roberts / I. Laperrière / P. Tardif	2.00
☐	T61-63	J. Friesen / V. Kozlov / V. Peltonen	3.00
☐	T64-66	A. Gavey / B. Gretzky / J. Weimer	2.00
☐	T67-69	B. Convery / E. Fichaud (G) / K. Jonsson	3.00
☐	T70-72	M. Fountain / R. Girard / M. Peca	4.00
☐	T73-75	J. Allison / A. Kharlamov / B. Witt	5.00
☐	T76-78	M. Alatalo / R. Gusmanov / D. Quint	2.00

CLASSIC DRAFT DAY

Complete Set (10 cards): 35.00

	Player	NRMT-MT
☐	Ana.: Radek Bonk, Las Vegas	3.00
☐	Fla.: Radek Bonk, Las Vegas	3.00
☐	Ott.: Radek Bonk, Las Vegas	3.00
☐	Edm.: Jason Bonsignore, Niagara Falls	3.00
☐	Ana.: Ed Jovanovski, Windsor	6.00
☐	Fla.: Ed Jovanovski, Windsor	6.00
☐	Ott.: Ed Jovanovski, Windsor	6.00
☐	Ana.: Jeff O'Neill, Guelph	4.00
☐	Fla.: Jeff O'Neill, Guelph	4.00
☐	Ott.: Jeff O'Neill, Guelph	4.00

1994 - 95 CLASSIC FOUR-SPORT

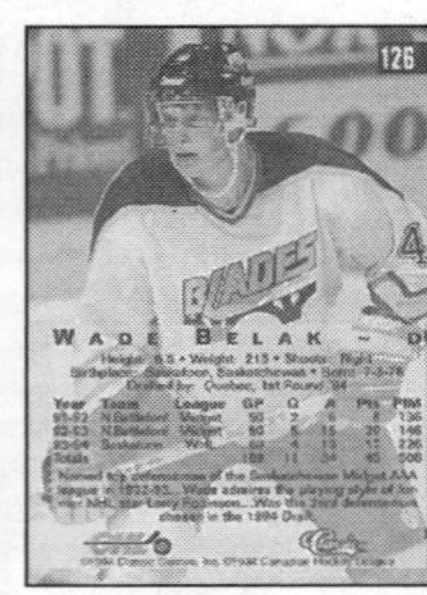

This 200-card four-sport set features 46 hockey players. Each card has two verions: the regular card and a gold parallel. A 200-card regular set sells at $15 and a 200-card gold set sells at $40.

Imprint:

	No.	Player	Reg.	Gold
☐☐	115	Ed Jovanovski, Windsor	.50	1.50
☐☐	116	Oleg Tverdovsky, Rus.	.25	.75
☐☐	117	Radek Bonk, Las Vegas	.35	1.00
☐☐	118	Jason Bonsignore, Niagara Falls	.10	.25
☐☐	119	Jeff O'Neill, Guelph	.35	1.00
☐☐	120	Ryan Smyth, Moose Jaw	1.00	3.00
☐☐	121	Jamie Storr (G), Owen Sound	.25	.75
☐☐	122	Jason Wiemer, Portland-WHL	.10	.25
☐☐	123	Evgeni Ryabchikov (G), Rus.	.10	.25
☐☐	124	Nolan Baumgartner	.10	.25
☐☐	125	Jeff Friesen	.25	.75
☐☐	126	Wade Belak, Saskatoon	.10	.25
☐☐	127	Maxim Bets, San Diego	.10	.25
☐☐	128	Ethan Moreau, Niagara Falls	.20	.50
☐☐	129	Alexander Kharlamov, Rus.	.10	.25
☐☐	130	Eric Fichaud (G), Chicoutimi	.25	.75
☐☐	131	Wayne Primeau, Owen Sound	.20	.50
☐☐	132	Brad Brown	.10	.25
☐☐	133	Chris Dingman, Brandon	.10	.25
☐☐	134	Craig Darby, Fredericton	.10	.25
☐☐	135	Darby Hendrickson, St. John's	.10	.25
☐☐	136	Yan Golubovsky, CSKA	.10	.25
☐☐	137	Chris Wells, Seattle	.10	.25
☐☐	138	Vadim Sharifjanov, Rus.	.10	.25
☐☐	139	Dan Cloutier (G), S.S. Marie	.50	1.50
☐☐	140	Todd Marchant, Cape Breton	.20	.50
☐☐	141	David Roberts, Peoria	.10	.25
☐☐	142	Brian Rolston, Albany	.20	.50
☐☐	143	Garth Snow (G), Cornwall	.25	.75
☐☐	144	Cory Stillman, Saint John	.20	.50
☐☐	145	Chad Penney, P.E.I.	.10	.25
☐☐	146	Jeff Nelson, Portland-AHL	.10	.25
☐☐	147	Michael Stewart, Binghampton	.10	.25
☐☐	148	Mike Dunham (G), Albany	.20	.50
☐☐	149	Joe Frederick, Adirondack	.10	.25
☐☐	150	Mark DeSantis, San Diego	.10	.25
☐☐	151	David Cooper	.10	.25
☐☐	152	Andrei Buschan, Kansas City	.10	.25
☐☐	153	Mike Greenlay	.10	.25
☐☐	154	Geoff Sarjeant (G), Peoria	.10	.25
☐☐	155	Pauli Jaks (G), Phoenix	.10	.25
☐☐	156	Greg Andrusak, Cleveland	.10	.25
☐☐	157	Denis Metlyuk, Hershey	.10	.25
☐☐	158	Mike Fountain (G), Hamilton	.20	.50
☐☐	159	Brent Gretzky, Atlanta	.20	.50
☐☐	160	Jason Allison, Portland-AHL	.50	1.50

HIGH VOLTAGE

This 20-card four-sport insert set features five hockey players.

	No.	Player	NRMT-MT
☐	HV4	Ed Jovanovski	15.00
☐	HV8	Oleg Tverdovsky	5.00
☐	HV12	Radek Bonk	5.00
☐	HV16	Jason Bonsignore	5.00
☐	HV19	Jeff O'Neill	6.00

CLASSIC PICKS

This 10-card four-sport insert set (16-25) features only one hockey player.

	No.	Player	NRMT-MT
☐	25	Ethan Moreau	4.00

BONUS CARDS

This 20-card four-sport insert set (jumbo packs) features four hockey players. A 20-card set sells at $25.

	No.	Player	NRMT-MT
☐	BC17	Ed Jovanovski	1.50
☐	BC18	Radek Bonk	.50
☐	BC19	Jeff O'Neill	.75
☐	BC20	Ethan Moreau	.50

TRI-CARDS

This five-card four-sport insert set features only one hockey trio. A five-card set sells at $30.

	No.	Player	NRMT-MT
☐	TC4	Radek Bonk/Chris Wells/Jeff O'Neill	6.00

SPRINT PHONE CARDS

This eight-card four-sport insert set features two hockey players. Each card has five denominations: A one dollar, a two dollar, a three dollar, a four dollar and a five dollar card. Prices below are for unused phone cards.

	Player	$1	$2	$3	$4	$5
☐☐☐☐☐	Ed Jovanovski	5.00	10.00	15.00	20.00	30.00
☐☐☐☐☐	Jeff O'Neill	3.00	6.00	9.00	12.00	18.00

FOUR-IN-ONE INSERT

	Players	NRMT-MT
☐	Ed Jovanovski (w/Glenn Robinson, Dan Wilkinson and Paul Wilson)	25.00

1994 - 95 CLASSIC IMAGES

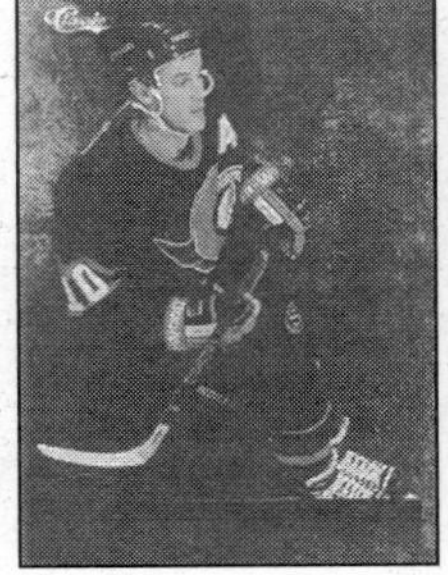

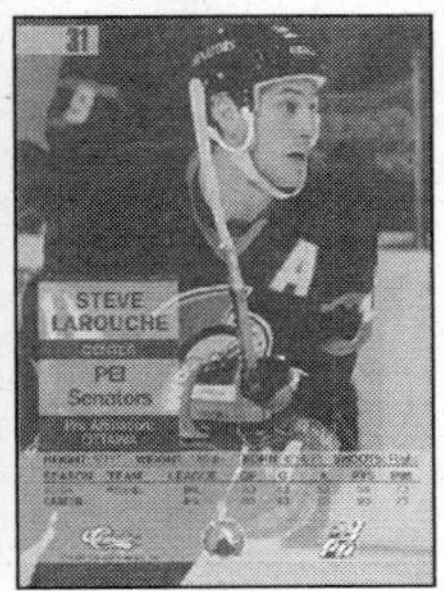

These cards have two versions: the regular card and a gold parallel. Twenty-two players also have a third autographed version (no card number, serial numbered). Each player signed between 970 (Radek Bonk) and 1,500 autographs. NHL logos are covered in this set.

Imprint:

Complete Set (100 cards): 25.00 65.00

	No.	Player	Aut.	Reg.	Gold
☐☐	1	Bryan Berard, Detroit-OHL	.–	2.00	5.00
☐☐☐	2	Jeff Friesen, Regina	30.00	.50	1.25
☐☐	3	Tommy Salo (G), Denver	.–	.35	1.00
☐☐	4	Jim Carey (G), Portland-AHL	.–	.35	1.00
☐☐	5	Wade Redden, Brandon	.–	.50	1.25
☐☐☐	6	Jocelyn Thibault (G), Sherbrooke	50.00	.75	1.75
☐☐	7	Ian Laperriere, Peoria	.–	.20	.50
☐☐	8	Todd Marchant, Cape Breton	.–	.35	1.00
☐☐☐	9	Blaine Lacher (G), Providence	6.00	.20	.50
☐☐	10	Pavel Bure, Van.	.–	2.00	5.00
☐☐	11	Alexei Vasilevski, Prince George	.–	.20	.50
☐☐	12	Jason Doig, Laval	.–	.35	.75
☐☐	13	Eric Fichaud (G), Chicoutimi	.–	.50	1.25
☐☐	14	Eric Dazé, Beauport	.–	1.00	2.50
☐☐	15	Ed Jovanovski, Windsor	.–	1.00	2.50
☐☐	16	Alexander Selivanov, Chicago	.–	.35	.75
☐☐	17	Brent Gretzky, Atlanta	.–	.35	.75
☐☐	18	Terry Ryan, Tri-City	.–	.35	1.00
☐☐	19	Chris Wells, Seattle	.–	.20	.50
☐☐	20	Wade Belak, Saskatoon	.–	.20	.50
☐☐	21	Kevin Dineen, Houston	.–	.20	.50
☐☐	22	Craig Fisher, Indianpolis	.–	.20	.50
☐☐	23	Jan Caloun, Kansas City	.–	.20	.50
☐☐	24	Manny Fernandez (G), Kalamazoo	.–	.35	.75
☐☐☐	25	Radek Bonk, Las Vegas	25.00	.35	1.00
☐☐	26	Dave Christian, Minnesota	.–	.20	.50
☐☐	27	Patrice Tardif, Peoria	.–	.20	.50
☐☐	28	Kevin Brown, Phoenix	.–	.20	.50
☐☐	29	Hubie McDonough, San Diego	.–	.20	.50
☐☐☐	30	Yan Golubovsky, Adirondack	6.00	.20	.50
☐☐	31	Steve Larouche, P.E.I.	.–	.20	.50
☐☐	32	Chris Therien, Hershey	.–	.20	.50
☐☐	33	Craig Darby, Fredericton	.–	.20	.50
☐☐	34	Dwayne Norris, Cornwall	.–	.20	.50
☐☐	35	Roman Oksiuta, Cape Breton	.–	.20	.50
☐☐☐	36	Steve Washburn, Ottawa	6.00	.20	.50
☐☐	37	Todd Bertuzzi, Guelph	.–	.35	1.00
☐☐	38	Cory Stillman, Saint John	.–	.20	.50
☐☐	39	Steve Kelly, Prince Albert	.–	.35	.75
☐☐	40	Nathan Lafayette, Syracuse	.–	.20	.50
☐☐☐	41	Dwayne Roloson (G), Saint John	10.00	.35	.75
☐☐	42	Nikolai Khabibulin (G), Springfield	.–	.75	1.75
☐☐	43	Radim Bicanek, Belleville	.–	.20	.50
☐☐	44	Jeff O'Neill, Guelph	.–	.50	1.25
☐☐☐	45	Jason Bonsignore, Sudbury	10.00	.35	.75
☐☐☐	46	Shean Donovan, Ottawa	10.00	.35	.75
☐☐	47	Wayne Primeau, Owen Sound	.–	.35	.75
☐☐☐	48	Jamie Langenbrunner, Peterborough	20.00	.35	1.00
☐☐	49	Dan Cloutier (G), S.S.Marie	.–	1.00	2.50
☐☐	50	Ethan Moreau, Sudbury	.–	.35	1.00
☐☐	51	Brad Bombardir, Albany	.–	.20	.50
☐☐	52	Jason Muzzatti (G), Saint John	.–	.35	.75
☐☐	53	Jassen Cullimore, Syracuse	.–	.35	.75
☐☐☐	54	Jason Zent, P.E.I.	6.00	.20	.50
☐☐	55	Sergei Gonchar, Portland-AHL	.–	.35	.75
☐☐	56	Steve Rucchin, San Diego	.–	.35	1.00
☐☐	57	Rob Cowie, Phoenix	.–	.20	.50
☐☐	58	Miroslav Satan, Detroit-IHL	.–	.35	1.00
☐☐☐	59	Kenny Jonsson, St. John's	15.00	.35	1.00
☐☐☐	60	Adam Deadmarsh, Portland-WHL	20.00	.35	1.00
☐☐	61	Mike Dunham (G), Albany	.–	.35	1.00
☐☐	62	Corey Hirsch (G), Binghampton	.–	.35	1.00
☐☐	63	Janne Laukkanen, Cornwall	.–	.20	.50
☐☐☐	64	Craig Conroy, Fredericton	6.00	.20	.50
☐☐	65	Ryan Sittler, Hershey	.–	.20	.50
☐☐	66	Jeff Nelson, Portland-AHL	.–	.20	.50
☐☐	67	Michel Picard, P.E.I.	.–	.20	.50
☐☐	68	Mark Astley, Rochester	.–	.20	.50
☐☐	69	Lonny Bohonos, Syracuse	.–	.20	.50
☐☐	70	Evgeny Ryabchikov (G), Providence	.–	.20	.50
☐☐	71	Chris Osgood (G), Adirondack	.–	1.00	2.50
☐☐	72	Manon Rhéaume (G), Las Vegas	.–	4.00	10.00
☐☐	73	Mike Kennedy, Kalamazoo	.–	.35	.75
☐☐☐	74	Deron Quint, Seattle	10.00	.35	.75
☐☐	75	Jamie Storr (G), Windsor	.–	.50	1.25
☐☐☐	76	Aris Brimanis, Hershey	6.00	.20	.50
☐☐	77	Valeri Bure, Fredericton	.–	.35	1.00
☐☐	78	René Corbet, Cornwall	.–	.35	.75
☐☐☐	79	David Oliver, Cape Breton	15.00	.35	1.00
☐☐☐	80	Chris McAlpine, Albany	6.00	.20	.50
☐☐☐	81	Petr Sykora, Detroit-IHL	30.00	.50	1.25
☐☐	82	Brad Church, Prince Albert	.–	.20	.50
☐☐	83	Daymond Langkow, Tri-City	.–	.35	1.00
☐☐	84	Chad Kilger, Kingston	.–	.35	.75
☐☐	85	Shane Doan, Kamloops	.–	.35	.75
☐☐	86	Jeff Ware, Oshawa	.–	.35	.75
☐☐	87	Christian Laflamme, Beauport	.–	.20	.50
☐☐	88	Cory Cross, Atlanta	.–	.20	.50
☐☐	89	Al Secord, Chicago	.–	.20	.50
☐☐	90	Jason Woolley, Detroit-IHL	.–	.20	.50
☐☐	91	Bryan McCabe, Spokane	.–	.20	.50
☐☐	92	Travis Richards, Kalamazoo	.–	.20	.50
☐☐	93	Andrei Nazarov, Kansas City	.–	.20	.50
☐☐☐	94	Mike Pomichter, Indianapolis	6.00	.20	.50
☐☐☐	95	Chris Marinucci, Denver	6.00	.20	.50
☐☐	96	Jean-Yves Roy, Binghampton	.–	.20	.50
☐☐	97	Brian Rolston, Albany	.–	.35	.75
☐☐☐	98	Aaron Ward, Adirondack	10.00	.35	1.00
☐☐	99	CL: Jim Carey (G), Portland-AHL	.–	.20	.50
☐☐	100	CL: Pavel Bure, Van.	.–	1.00	2.50

CLEAR EXCITEMENT

These cards are serial numbered out of 350.

Insert Set (20 cards): 350.00

Promo Card (Jim Carey, #CE4): 10.00

	No.	Player	NRMT-MT
☐	CE1	Bryan Berard, Detroit-OHL	40.00
☐	CE2	Jeff Friesen, Regina	15.00
☐	CE3	Tommy Salo (G), Denver	10.00
☐	CE4	Jim Carey (G), Portland-AHL	15.00
☐	CE5	Wade Redden, Brandon	15.00
☐	CE6	Jocelyn Thibault, Sherbrooke	25.00
☐	CE7	Ian Laperrière, Peoria	8.00
☐	CE8	Todd Marchant, Cape Breton	10.00
☐	CE9	Blaine Lacher (G), Providence	8.00
☐	CE10	Pavel Bure, Van.	50.00
☐	CE11	Petr Sykora, Detroit-IHL	15.00
☐	CE12	Manny Fernandez (G), Kalamazoo	10.00
☐	CE13	Radek Bonk, Las Vegas	12.00
☐	CE14	Patrice Tardif, Peoria	8.00
☐	CE15	Jeff Nelson, Portland-AHL	8.00
☐	CE16	Jeff O'Neill, Guelph	15.00
☐	CE17	Ed Jovanovski, Windsor	25.00
☐	CE18	Jason Doig, Laval	10.00
☐	CE19	Chris Marinucci, Denver	8.00
☐	CE20	Manon Rhéaume (G), Las Vegas	120.00

PLATINUM PLAYERS

Insert Set (10 cards): 40.00

Promo Card (Claude Lemieux, #PL5): 1.00

	No.	Player	NRMT-MT
☐	PL1	Pavel Bure, Van.	20.00
☐	PL2	Tony Granato, L.A.	3.00
☐	PL3	Kevin Dineen, Pha.	3.00
☐	PL4	Ron Hextall (G), Pha.	5.00
☐	PL5	Claude Lemieux, N.J.	3.00
☐	PL6	Mark Recchi	5.00
☐	PL7	Benoît Hogue	3.00
☐	PL8	Tim Cheveldae (G), Wpg.	3.00
☐	PL9	Darcy Wakaluk (G)	3.00
☐	PL10	Todd Gill, Tor.	3.00

PREMIER DRAFT CHOICES

The Bryan Berard winner card could be redeemed for a Manon Rhéaume autographed phone card.

Insert Set (10 cards): 45.00

	No.	Player	NRMT-MT
☐	PD1	Bryan Berard, Detroit-OHL	20.00
☐	PD2	Wade Redden, Brandon	6.00
☐	PD3	Steve Kelly, London	3.00
☐	PD4	Petr Sykora, Detroit-IHL	6.00
☐	PD5	Brad Church, Prince Albert	3.00
☐	PD6	Daymond Langkow, Tri-City	4.00
☐	PD7	Chad Kilger, Kingston	3.00
☐	PD8	Terry Ryan, Tri-City	6.00
☐	PD9	Jason Doig, Laval	3.00
☐	PD10	Field Card (Brandon players)	3.00
		Autograph	**NRMT-MT**
☐		Manon Rhéaume	65.00

PLATINUM PROSPECTS

Insert Set (10 cards): 40.00

	No.	Player	NRMT-MT
☐	PR1	Jeff Nelson, Portland-AHL	3.00
☐	PR2	Jim Carey (G), Portland-AHL	5.00
☐	PR3	Ian Laperrière, Peoria	3.00
☐	PR4	Chris Osgood (G), Adirondack	15.00
☐	PR5	Todd Marchant, Cape Breton	4.00
☐	PR6	Radek Bonk, Las Vegas	4.00
☐	PR7	Chris Marinucci, Denver	3.00
☐	PR8	Tommy Salo (G), Denver	4.00
☐	PR9	Manny Fernandez (G), Kalamazoo	4.00
☐	PR10	Jan Caloun, Kansas City	3.00

1994 - 95 CLASSIC IMAGES FOUR SPORT

This 120 card set features only 25 hockey players. A 120-card regular set sells at $35.

Imprint:

	No.	Player	NRMT-MT
☐	94	Ed Jovanovski, Windsor	.75
☐	95	Oleg Tverdovsky, Rus.	.35
☐	96	Radek Bonk, Las Vegas	.35
☐	97	Jason Bonsignore, Sudbury	.25
☐	98	Jeff O'Neill, Guelph	.50
☐	99	Ryan Smyth, Moose Jaw	1.00
☐	100	Jamie Storr (G)	.50
☐	101	Jason Wiemer, Portland-WHL	.25
☐	102	Nolan Baumgartner, Kamloops	.35
☐	103	Jeff Friesen, Regina	.50
☐	104	Wade Belak, Saskatoon	.25
☐	105	Ethan Moreau, Sudbury	.35
☐	106	Alexander Kharlamov, Rus.	.35
☐	107	Eric Fichaud (G), Chicoutimi	.50
☐	108	Wayne Primeau, Owen Sound	.25
☐	109	Brad Brown, North Bay	.25
☐	110	Chris Dingman, Brandon	.25
☐	111	Chris Wells, Seattle	.25
☐	112	Vadim Sharifjanov, Rus.	.25
☐	113	Dan Cloutier (G), S.S. Marie	.75
☐	114	Jason Allison, Portland-AHL	.75
☐	115	Todd Marchant, Cape Breton	.35
☐	116	Brent Gretzky, Atlanta	.35
☐	117	Petr Sykora, Detroit-IHL	.50
☐	118	Manon Rhéaume (G), Las Vegan	4.00

CLASSIC PERFORMANCES

This 20-card insert set features only two hockey players.

	No.	Player	NRMT-MT
☐	CP19	Ed Jovanovski	8.00
☐	CP20	Eric Fichaud (G)	6.00

CLEAR EXCITEMENT

This 5-card hobby pack insert set features only one hockey player.

	No.	Player	NRMT-MT
☐	E5	Manon Rhéaume (G)	100.00

1994 - 95 DEL EISHOCKEY

Imprint:

Complete Set (440 cards): 60.00

Common Player: .20

	No.	Player	NRMT-MT
☐	1	International Hockey	.20
☐	2	DEL 1994-95	.20
☐	3	Season 1994-95	.20
☐	4	TC: Augsburger Panther	.20
☐	5	Gunnar Leiborg	.20
☐	6	Gary Prior	.20
☐	7	Scott Campbell	.20
☐	8	Dieter Medicus	.20
☐	9	Duanne Moeser	.20
☐	10	Daniel Naud	.20
☐	11	Andy Romer	.20
☐	12	Thomas Groger	.20
☐	13	Sven Zywitza	.20
☐	14	Fritz Meyer	.20
☐	15	Christian Curth	.20
☐	16	Toni Krinner	.20
☐	17	Patrik Pysz	.20
☐	18	Heinrich Romer	.20
☐	19	Ales Polcar	.20
☐	20	Philip Kukuk	.20
☐	21	Dietrich Adam	.20
☐	22	Tim Schnobrich	.20
☐	23	Tim Ferguson	.20
☐	24	Robert Heidt	.20
☐	25	Alfred Burkhard	.20
☐	26	Charly Fliegauf	.20
☐	27	Robert Paclik	.20
☐	28	Stefan Mayer	.20
☐	29	Reinhard Haider	.20
☐	30	Dennis Schrapp	.20
☐	31	TC: Eisbaren Berlin	.20
☐	32	Walter Jaroslav	.20
☐	33	Klaus Schroder	.20
☐	34	Andre Dietsch	.20
☐	35	Juri Stumpf	.20
☐	36	Torsten Deutscher	.20
☐	37	Frank Kannewurf	.20
☐	38	Thomas Graul	.20
☐	39	Sven Felski	.20
☐	40	Moritz Schmidt	.20
☐	41	Marco Swibenko	.20
☐	42	Holger Mix	.20
☐	43	Jiri Dopita	.20
☐	44	Dirk Perschau	.20
☐	45	Guido Hiller	.20
☐	46	Daniel Held	.20
☐	47	Richard Zemlicka	.20
☐	48	Jan Schertz	.20
☐	49	Mike Iosch	.20
☐	50	Patrick Solf	.20
☐	51	Rupert Meister	.20
☐	52	TC: BSC Preussen	.20
☐	53	Billy Flynn	.20
☐	54	Tony Tanti	.20
☐	55	Jochen Molling	.20
☐	56	Andreas Schubert	.20
☐	57	Stefan Steinecker	.20
☐	58	Josef Lebner	.20
☐	59	Tom O'Regan	.20
☐	60	Gaetan Malo	.20
☐	61	Michael Komma	.20
☐	62	Marco Schinko	.20
☐	63	Marco Rentzsch	.20
☐	64	Georg Holzmann	.20
☐	65	Mark Kosturik	.20
☐	66	Jurgen Rumrich	.20
☐	67	John Chabot	.50
☐	68	Harald Windler	.20
☐	69	Mark Teevens	.20
☐	70	Klaus Merk	.20
☐	71	Stephen Sinner	.20
☐	72	Mark Gronau	.20
☐	73	Bruce Hardy	.20
☐	74	Fabian Brannstrom	.20
☐	75	Daniel Poudrier	.20
☐	76	TC: Dusseldorfer EG	.20
☐	77	Hans Zach	.20
☐	78	Helmut DeRaaf	.20
☐	79	Markus Kehle	.20
☐	80	Christian Schmitz	.20
☐	81	Lorenz Funk	.20
☐	82	Chris Valentine	.50
☐	83	Rafael Jedamzik	.20
☐	84	Torsten Keinass	.20
☐	85	Christopher Kreutzer	.20
☐	86	Benoît Doucet	.20
☐	87	Bernd Kuhnhauser	.20
☐	88	Andreas Niederberger	.20
☐	89	Rick Amann	.20
☐	90	Thorsten Van Leyen	.20
☐	91	Bruce Eakin	.20
☐	92	Pierre Rioux	.20
☐	93	Andreas Brockmann	.20
☐	94	Uli Heimer	.20
☐	95	Bernd Truntschka	.20
☐	96	Wolfgang Kummer	.20
☐	97	Carsten Gossman	.20
☐	98	Ernst Kopf	.20
☐	99	Robert Sterflinger	.20
☐	100	Kevin LaVallée	.20
☐	101	Rainer Zerwesz	.20
☐	102	TC: Frankfurt Lions	.20
☐	103	Pjotr Vorobiev	.20
☐	104	Peter Obresa	.20
☐	105	Vladimir Quapp	.20
☐	106	Florian Storf	.20
☐	107	Alexander Wedl	.20
☐	108	Olaf Scholz	.20
☐	109	Ilya Vorobjev	.20
☐	110	Ladislav Stompf	.20
☐	111	Udo Dohler	.20
☐	112	Alexander Wunsch	.20
☐	113	Jiri Lala	.20
☐	114	Andrej Jaufmann	.20
☐	115	Thomas Muhlbauer	.20
☐	116	Markus Kempf	.20
☐	117	Igor Schultz	.20
☐	118	Martin Schultz	.20
☐	119	Michael Raubal	.20
☐	120	Rudi Gorgenlander	.20
☐	121	Jurgen Schaal	.20
☐	122	Patrick Vozar	.20
☐	123	Rochus Schneider	.20
☐	124	Toni Raubal	.20
☐	125	Stefan Koniger	.20
☐	126	TC: EC Hannover	.20
☐	127	Hartmut Nickel	.20
☐	128	Joachim Lempio	.20
☐	129	Torsten Hanusch	.20
☐	130	Thomas Jungwirth	.20
☐	131	David Reierson	.20
☐	132	Friedhelm Bogelsack	.20
☐	133	Thomas Werner	.20
☐	134	Dirk Rohrbach	.20
☐	135	Harald Kuhnke	.20
☐	136	Florian Funk	.20
☐	137	Mark Maroste	.20
☐	138	Anton Maidl	.20
☐	139	Rene Reuter	.20
☐	140	Rene Ledock	.20
☐	141	Marco Hebst	.20
☐	142	Milos Vanik	.20
☐	143	Gunther Preuss	.20
☐	144	Troy Tumbach	.20
☐	145	Marc Wittbrock	.20
☐	146	Roger Mede	.20
☐	147	Craig Topolinsky	.20
☐	148	Josef Schlickenriede	.20
☐	149	Marcus Bleicher	.20
☐	150	TC: EC Kassel	.20
☐	151	Ross Yates	.20
☐	152	Josef Kontny	.20
☐	153	Milan Mokros	.20
☐	154	Alexander Engel	.20
☐	155	Greg Johnston	.20
☐	156	Jedrzej Kasperczyk	.20
☐	157	Dave Morrison	.20
☐	158	Jaro Mucha	.20
☐	159	Mike Millar	.20
☐	160	Ireneusz Pacula	.20
☐	161	Vitalij Grossmann	.20
☐	162	Murray McIntosh	.20
☐	163	Manfred Ahne	.20
☐	164	Peter Kwasigroch	.20
☐	165	Georg Guttler	.20
☐	166	Falk Ozellis	.20
☐	167	Mario Naster	.20
☐	168	Sergej Wikulow	.20
☐	169	Gerhard Hegen	.20
☐	170	Brian Hannon	.20
☐	171	Tino Boos	.20
☐	172	TC: Kaufbeurer Adler	.20
☐	173	Peter Kathan	.20
☐	174	Kenneth Karpuk	.20
☐	175	Michael Olbrich	.20
☐	176	Drahomir Kadlec	.20
☐	177	Christian Seeberger	.20
☐	178	Elmar Boiger	.20
☐	179	Otto Hascak	.20
☐	180	Thorsten Rau	.20
☐	181	Tomas Martinec	.20
☐	182	Norbert Zabel	.20
☐	183	Daniel Kunce	.20
☐	184	Hans-Jorg Mayer	.20
☐	185	Manfred Jorde	.20
☐	186	Roland Timoschuk	.20
☐	187	Jim Hoffmann	.20
☐	188	Andreas Volland	.20
☐	189	Rolf Hammer	.20

- ☐ 190 Manuel Hess .20
- ☐ 191 Timo Gschwill .20
- ☐ 192 Marc Pethke .20
- ☐ 193 Axel Kammerer .20
- ☐ 194 Jurgen Simon .20
- ☐ 195 Patrick Lange .20
- ☐ 196 Ronny Martin .20
- ☐ 197 TC: Kolner EC .20
- ☐ 198 Vladimir Vassiliev .20
- ☐ 199 Bernd Haake .20
- ☐ 200 Joseph Heiss .20
- ☐ 201 Jorg Mayr .20
- ☐ 202 Thomas Brandl .20
- ☐ 203 Stephan Mann .20
- ☐ 204 Tony Reddo .20
- ☐ 205 Mirco Ludemann .20
- ☐ 206 Leo Stefan .20
- ☐ 207 Andreas Pokorny .20
- ☐ 208 Peter Draisaitl .20
- ☐ 209 Ralf Dobrzynski .20
- ☐ 210 Andreas Lupzig .20
- ☐ 211 Karsten Mende .20
- ☐ 212 Frank Hohenadl .20
- ☐ 213 Marco Heinrichs .20
- ☐ 214 Michael Rumrich .20
- ☐ 215 Martin Ondrejka .20
- ☐ 216 Herbert Hohenberger .20
- ☐ 217 Thorsten Sendt .20
- ☐ 218 Thorsten Koslowski .20
- ☐ 219 Olaf Grundmann .20
- ☐ 220 Franz Demmel .20
- ☐ 221 Sergei Berezin 5.00
- ☐ 222 TC: Krefelder EV .20
- ☐ 223 Michael Zettel .20
- ☐ 224 Frank Brunsing .20
- ☐ 225 Karel Lang .20
- ☐ 226 Markus Krawinkel .20
- ☐ 227 Earl Spry .20
- ☐ 228 Andre Grein .20
- ☐ 229 Greg Evtushevski .20
- ☐ 230 Herberts Vasiljevs .20
- ☐ 231 Ken Petrash .20
- ☐ 232 Greg Thomson .20
- ☐ 233 Reemt Pyka .20
- ☐ 234 Brad Bergen .20
- ☐ 235 Chris Lindberg .20
- ☐ 236 Markus Kranwinkel .20
- ☐ 237 Martin Gebel .20
- ☐ 238 François Sills .20
- ☐ 239 Klaus Micheller .20
- ☐ 240 Peter Ihnacak .50
- ☐ 241 Marek Strebnicki .20
- ☐ 242 Johnny Walker .20
- ☐ 243 Gunter Oswald .20
- ☐ 244 James Hanlon .20
- ☐ 245 Rene Bielke .20
- ☐ 246 TC: EV Landshut .20
- ☐ 247 Bernhard Johnston .20
- ☐ 248 Mark Stuckey .20
- ☐ 249 Michael Bresagk .20
- ☐ 250 Bernd Wagner .20
- ☐ 251 Eduard Uvria .20
- ☐ 252 Mike Smazal .20
- ☐ 253 Jacek Plachta .20
- ☐ 254 Georg Franz .20
- ☐ 255 Stephan Retzer .20
- ☐ 256 Henri Macoux .20
- ☐ 257 Andreas Loth .20
- ☐ 258 Mike Bullard 1.00
- ☐ 259 Markus Berwanger .20
- ☐ 260 Petr Briza (G) 2.00
- ☐ 261 Wally Schreiber .20
- ☐ 262 Peter Gulda .20
- ☐ 263 Ralf Hantschke .20
- ☐ 264 Steve McNeill .20
- ☐ 265 Christian Kunast .20
- ☐ 266 Jorg Hendrick .20
- ☐ 267 Helmut Steiger .20
- ☐ 268 Udo Kiessling .20
- ☐ 269 Mike Lay .20
- ☐ 270 TC: Adler Mannheim .20
- ☐ 271 Lance Nethery .20
- ☐ 272 Marcus Kuhl .20
- ☐ 273 Joachim Appel .20
- ☐ 274 Harold Kries .20
- ☐ 275 Mike Heidt .20
- ☐ 276 Mario Gehrig .20
- ☐ 277 Pavel Gross .20
- ☐ 278 Steffen Michel .20
- ☐ 279 Daniel Korber .20
- ☐ 280 Robert Cimetta .20
- ☐ 281 Dale Krentz .20
- ☐ 282 Jochen Hecht .50
- ☐ 283 Till Feser .20
- ☐ 284 Lars Bruggemann .20
- ☐ 285 Toni Plattner .20
- ☐ 286 Alexander Schuster .20
- ☐ 287 Dieter Willmann .20
- ☐ 288 Markus Flemming .20
- ☐ 289 Rick Goldmann .20
- ☐ 290 Damian Adamus .20
- ☐ 291 Frederik Ledlin .20
- ☐ 292 David Musial .20
- ☐ 293 Michael Gabler .20
- ☐ 294 Sven Valenti .20
- ☐ 295 TC: Maddogs Munchen .20
- ☐ 296 Robert Murdoch .20
- ☐ 297 Alexander Genze .20
- ☐ 298 Greg Muller .20
- ☐ 299 Mike Schmidt .20
- ☐ 300 Zdenek Travnicek .20
- ☐ 301 Christian Lukes .20
- ☐ 302 Gordon Sherven .20
- ☐ 303 Anthony Vogel .20
- ☐ 304 Michael Hreuss .20
- ☐ 305 Dale Derkatch .20
- ☐ 306 Sergei Schendelew .20
- ☐ 307 Christian Brittig .20
- ☐ 308 Harald Waibel .20
- ☐ 309 Rainer Lutz .20
- ☐ 310 Ewald Steiger .20
- ☐ 311 Didi Hegen .20
- ☐ 312 Ralf Reisinger .20
- ☐ 313 Henrik Holscher .20
- ☐ 314 Karl Friesen .20
- ☐ 315 Christian Frutel .20
- ☐ 316 Tobias Abstreiter .20
- ☐ 317 Christopher Sandner .20
- ☐ 318 Harald Birk .20
- ☐ 319 Chris Strausse .20
- ☐ 320 TC: EHC 80 Nurnberg .20
- ☐ 321 Josef Golonka .20
- ☐ 322 Christian Gerum .20
- ☐ 323 Paul Geddes .20
- ☐ 324 Ian Young .20
- ☐ 325 Stefan Steinbock .20
- ☐ 326 Doug Irwin .20
- ☐ 327 Christian Flugge .20
- ☐ 328 Klaus Birk .20
- ☐ 329 Jurgen Lechl .20
- ☐ 330 Thomas Popiesch .20
- ☐ 331 Miroslav Maly .20
- ☐ 332 Stephan Eder .20
- ☐ 333 Arno Brux .20
- ☐ 334 Jiri Dolezal .20
- ☐ 335 Reiner Vorderbruggen .20
- ☐ 336 Thomas Sterflinger .20
- ☐ 337 Bernhard Engelbrecht .20
- ☐ 338 Michael Weinfurther .20
- ☐ 339 Sepp Wassermann .20
- ☐ 340 Stephan Bauer .20
- ☐ 341 Otto Sykora .20
- ☐ 342 TC: Ratingen Die Lowen .20
- ☐ 343 Bill Lochead .20
- ☐ 344 Pavel Mann .20
- ☐ 345 Christian Kohmann .20
- ☐ 346 Sven Prusa .20
- ☐ 347 Otto Keresztes .20
- ☐ 348 Frank Kovacs .20
- ☐ 349 Jiri Smicek .20
- ☐ 350 Richard Brodnicke .20
- ☐ 351 Andrej Fuchs .20
- ☐ 352 Oliver Kasper .20
- ☐ 353 Michael Kratz .20
- ☐ 354 Klaus Striemitzer .20
- ☐ 355 Oliver Schwartz .20
- ☐ 356 Boris Fuchs .20
- ☐ 357 Christian Althoff .20
- ☐ 358 Waldemar Novosjolov .20
- ☐ 359 Thomas Imdahl .20
- ☐ 360 Helmut Elters .20
- ☐ 361 Andrej Hanisz .20
- ☐ 362 Peter Lutter .20
- ☐ 363 Martem Janov .20
- ☐ 364 Mark Bassen .20
- ☐ 365 Udo Schmid .20
- ☐ 366 Mark Bassen .20
- ☐ 367 TC: Rosenheim Star Bulls .20
- ☐ 368 Ernst Hofner .20
- ☐ 369 Ludek Bukac .20
- ☐ 370 Markus Wieland .20
- ☐ 371 Andreas Schneider .20
- ☐ 372 Raphael Kruger .20
- ☐ 373 Michael Tattner .20
- ☐ 374 Rick Boehm .20
- ☐ 375 Robert Hock .20
- ☐ 376 Joachim Reil .20
- ☐ 377 Radek Toupal .20
- ☐ 378 Martin Reichel .20
- ☐ 379 Ron Fischer .20
- ☐ 380 Raimund Hilger .20
- ☐ 381 Petr Hrbek .20
- ☐ 382 Oliver Hausler .20
- ☐ 383 Christian Gegenfurth .20
- ☐ 384 Marc Seliger .20
- ☐ 385 Venci Sebek .20
- ☐ 386 Florian Keller .20
- ☐ 387 Heinrich Schiffl .20
- ☐ 388 Michael Pohl .20
- ☐ 389 TC: Fuchse Sachsen .20
- ☐ 390 Jiri Kochta .20
- ☐ 391 Boris Capla .20
- ☐ 392 Matthias Kliemann .20
- ☐ 393 Josef Rednicek .20
- ☐ 394 Branjo Heisig .20
- ☐ 395 Jens Schwabe .20
- ☐ 396 Frank Peschke .20
- ☐ 397 Thomas Schubert .20
- ☐ 398 Torsten Eisebitt .20
- ☐ 399 Marcel Lichnovsky .20
- ☐ 400 Jari Gronstrand .20
- ☐ 401 Thomas Knobloch .20
- ☐ 402 Falk Herzig .20
- ☐ 403 Thomas Wagner .20
- ☐ 404 Jan Tabor .20
- ☐ 405 Sebastian Klenner .20
- ☐ 406 Peter Hofmann .20
- ☐ 407 Terry Cambell .20
- ☐ 408 Antonio Fonso .20
- ☐ 409 Thomas Bresagk .20
- ☐ 410 Peter Franke .20
- ☐ 411 Andreas Ott .20
- ☐ 412 Michael Flemming .20
- ☐ 413 Janusz Janikowski .20
- ☐ 414 TC: Schwenningen .20
- ☐ 415 Miroslav Berek .20
- ☐ 416 Bob Burns .20
- ☐ 417 Thomas Gaus .20
- ☐ 418 Richard Trojan .20
- ☐ 419 Ilmar Toman .20
- ☐ 420 Alan Young .20
- ☐ 421 Michael Pastika .20
- ☐ 422 Thomas Schadler .20
- ☐ 423 Andrei Kovalev .20
- ☐ 424 Alexander Horn .20
- ☐ 425 Petr Kopta .20
- ☐ 426 Robert Brezina .20
- ☐ 427 Wayne Hynes .20
- ☐ 428 Frantisek Frosch .20
- ☐ 429 Carsten Solbach .20
- ☐ 430 George Fritz .20
- ☐ 431 Mike Bader .20
- ☐ 432 Thomas Deiter .20
- ☐ 433 Daniel Nowak .20
- ☐ 434 Peter Heinold .20
- ☐ 435 Matthias Hoppe .20
- ☐ 436 Grant Martin .20
- ☐ 437 Roger Bruns .20
- ☐ 438 Andreas Renz .20
- ☐ 439 Karsten Schulz .20
- ☐ 440 Alfie Turcotte .20

1994 - 95 DONRUSS

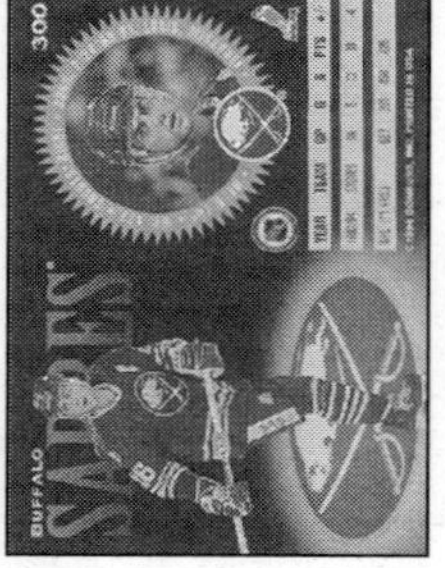

Imprint: © 1994 DONRUSS, INC.
Complete Set (330 cards): 20.00
Common Player: .10

No.	Player	NRMT-MT
1	Steve Yzerman, Det.	1.25
2	Paul Ysebaert, Chi.	.10
3	Doug Weight, Edm.	.35
4	Trevor Kidd (G), Cgy.	.25
5	Mario Lemieux, Pgh.	2.00
6	Andrei Kovalenko, Que.	.10
7	Arturs Irbe (G), S.J.	.10
8	Doug Gilmour, Tor.	.35
9	Mark Messier, NYR.	.50
10	Milos Holan, Pha.	.10
11	Kevin Miller, Stl.	.10
12	Félix Potvin (G), Tor.	.50
13	Josef Beranek, Pha.	.10
14	Mikael Andersson, T.B.	.10
15	Stéphane Matteau, NYR.	.10
16	Todd Simon, Buf.	.10
17	Darcy Wakaluk (G), Min.	.10
18	Kelly Buchberger, Edm.	.10
19	Pavel Bure, Van.	.75
20	Dave Lowry, Fla.	.10
21	Bryan Smolinski, Bos.	.10
22	Kirk McLean (G), Van.	.25
23	Pierre Turgeon, NYI.	.25
24	Martin Brodeur (G), N.J.	.75
25	Jason Arnott, Edm.	.35
26	Steve Dubinsky, Chi.	.10
27	Larry Murphy, Pgh.	.25
28	Craig Janney, Stl.	.10
29	Patrick Carnback, Ana.	.10
30	Derek King, NYI.	.10
31	Peter Bondra, Wsh.	.35
32	Jason Bowen, Pha.	.10
33	Maxim Bets, Ana.	.10
34	Matt Martin, Tor.	.10
35	Jeff Hackett (G), Chi.	.25
36	Kevin Dineen, Pha.	.10
37	Trent Klatt, Min.	.10
38	Joe Murphy, Chi.	.10
39	Sandy McCarthy, Cgy.	.10
40	Brian Bradley, T.B.	.10
41	Scott Lachance, NYI.	.10
42	Scott Mellanby, Fla.	.10
43	Adam Graves, NYR.	.10
44	Dale Hawerchuk, Buf.	.25
45	Owen Nolan, Que.	.25
46	Keith Primeau, Det.	.25
47	Jim Dowd, N.J.	.10
48	Dan Plante, NYI.	.10
49	Rick Tabaracci (G), Wsh.	.10
50	Geoff Courtnall, Van.	.10
51	Markus Naslund, Pgh.	.10
52	Kelly Miller, Wsh.	.10
53	Mark Maltby, Edm.	.10
54	Paul Coffey, Det.	.25
55	Gord Murphy, Fla.	.10
56	Joe Nieuwendyk, Cgy.	.25
57	Ulf Dahlen, S.J.	.10
58	Dmitri Mironov, Tor.	.10
59	Kevin Smyth, Hfd.	.10
60	Tie Domi, Wpg.	.10
61	Oleg Petrov, Mtl.	.10
62	Bill Guerin, N.J.	.25
63	Alexei Yashin, Ott.	.35
64	Joe Sacco, Ana.	.10
65	Aris Brimanis, Pha.	.10
66	Randy Burridge, Wsh.	.10
67	Neal Broten, Min.	.10
68	Ray Bourque, Bos.	.50
69	Ron Tugnutt (G), Mtl.	.10
70	Darryl Sydor, L.A.	.10
71	Jocelyn Thibault (G), Que.	.35
72	Shawn Chambers, T.B.	.10
73	Alexei Zhamnov, Wpg.	.25
74	Michael Nylander, Cgy.	.10
75	Travis Green, NYI.	.10
76	Brad May, Buf.	.10
77	Geoff Sanderson, Hfd.	.10
78	Derek Plante, Buf.	.10
79	Stéphane Richer, N.J.	.10
80	Rod Brind'Amour, Pha.	.25
81	Guy Hebert (G), Ana.	.25
82	Claude Lemieux, N.J.	.10
83	Pat Falloon, S.J.	.10
84	Alexei Kudashov, Tor.	.10
85	Andrei Lomakin, Fla.	.10
86	Dino Ciccarelli, Det.	.25
87	John Tucker, T.B.	.10
88	Jamie McLennan (G), NYI.	.25
89	Peter Taglianetti, Pgh.	.10
90	Bobby Holik, N.J.	.10
91	Sergei Krivokrasov, Chi.	.10
92	Alexander Mogilny, Buf.	.35
93	Jari Kurri, L.A.	.25
94	Domink Hasek (G), Buf.	.75
95	Shawn McEachern, Pgh.	.10
96	Ron Corkum, Ana.	.10
97	Dimitri Filimonov, Ott.	.10
98	John LeClair, Mtl.	.50
99	Theoren Fleury, Cgy.	.35
100	Daren Puppa (G), T.B.	.10
101	Greg Adams, Van.	.10
102	Joel Otto, Cgy.	.10
103	Sergei Makarov, S.J.	.10
104	Mike Ricci, Que.	.10
105	Sylvain Turgeon, Ott.	.10
106	Igor Larionov, S.J.	.25
107	Tony Amonte, Chi.	.25
108	Andy Moog (G), Min.	.25
109	Jeff Brown, Van.	.10
110	Checklist 1 (1-83)	.10
111	Mike Gartner, Tor.	.25
112	Craig Simpson, Buf.	.10
113	Rob Niedermayer, Fla.	.25
114	Robert Kron, Hfd.	.10
115	**Jason York, Det., RC**	**.10**
116	Valeri Kamensky, Que.	.25
117	Ray Whitney, S.J.	.10
118	Chris Chelios, Chi.	.35
119	Scott Levins, Ott.	.10
120	Sandis Ozolinsh, S.J.	.25
121	Mark Recchi, Pha.	.25
122	Ron Francis, Pgh.	.25
123	Dean McAmmond, Edm.	.10
124	Terry Yake, Ana.	.10
125	Sergei Nemchinov, NYR.	.10
126	Vitali Prokhorov, Buf.	.10
127	Wayne Gretzky, L.A.	2.50
128	Roman Hamrlik, T.B.	.25
129	Jarkko Varvio, Min.	.10
130	Brian Skrudland, Fla.	.10
131	Murray Craven, Van.	.10
132	Jeff Norton, S.J.	.10
133	Pavol Demitra, Ott.	.10
134	Mike Keane, Mtl.	.10
135	Paul Cavallini, Min.	.10
136	Richard Smehlik, Buf.	.10
137	Eric Lindros, Pha.	2.00
138	**Mariusz Czerkawski, Bos., RC**	**.10**
139	Darrin Shannon, Wpg.	.10
140	Brian Noonan, NYR.	.10
141	Joe Sakic, Que.	1.00
142	Steve Thomas, NYI.	.10
143	Gary Roberts, Cgy.	.25
144	Patrick Poulin, Chi.	.10
145	Tony Granato, L.A.	.10
146	**Donald Brashear, Mtl., RC**	**.10**
147	Ron Hextall (G), NYI.	.25
148	Corey Millen, N.J.	.10
149	Dale Hunter, Wsh.	.10
150	Greg Johnson, Det.	.10
151	John MacLean, N.J.	.10
152	Brian Leetch, NYR.	.35
153	Sylvain Côté, Wsh.	.10
154	Thomas Steen, Wpg.	.10
155	Ted Donato, Bos.	.10
156	Nathan Lafayette, Van.	.10
157	Kelly Chase, Stl.	.10
158	Sean Burke (G), Hfd.	.25
159	Jaromir Jagr, Pgh.	1.25
160	Checklist 2 (84-166)	.10
161	Scott Niedermayer, N.J.	.25
162	Ray Ferraro, NYI.	.10
163	Todd Elik, S.J.	.10
164	Dave Gagner, Min.	.10
165	Mike Richter (G), NYR.	.35
166	Garry Galley, Pha.	.10
167	Russ Courtnall, Min.	.10
168	Marty McSorley, L.A.	.10
169	Robert Reichel, Cgy.	.10
170	Mike Rathje, S.J.	.10
171	Bill Ranford (G), Edm.	.25
172	Danton Cole, T.B.	.10
173	Sergei Federov, Det.	.50
174	Brendan Shanahan, Stl.	.60
175	**Byron Dafoe (G), Wsh., RC**	**.25**
176	John Vanbiesbrouck (G), Fla.	.60
177	Eric Desjardins, Mtl.	.10
178	Andrew Cassels, Hfd.	.10
179	**John Gruden, Bos., RC**	**.10**
180	Vyacheslav Kozlov, Det.	.10
181	Trevor Linden, Van.	.25
182	Kris Draper, Det.	.10
183	Steve Smith, Chi.	.10
184	André Faust, Pha.	.10
185	James Patrick, Cgy.	.10
186	Ted Drury, Hfd.	.10
187	**Dan Laperrière, Stl., RC**	**.10**
188	Benoît Hogue, NYI.	.10
189	Chris Gratton, T.B.	.25
190	Jyrki Lumme, Van.	.10
191	Peter Stastny, Stl.	.10
192	Keith Tkachuk, Wpg.	.35
193	Mike Modano, Dal.	.50
194	Nicklas Lidstrom, Dal.	.25
195	Pierre Sévigny, Mtl.	.10
196	Scott Pearson, Edm.	.10
197	Jaroslav Modry, N.J.	.10
198	Gary Valk, Ana.	.10
199	Kevin Hatcher, Wsh.	.10
200	Denis Tsygurov, Buf.	.10
201	**Paul Laus, Fla., RC**	**.10**
202	Alexander Godynyuk, Hfd.	.10
203	Brian Bellows, Mtl.	.10
204	Michal Sykora, S.J.	.10
205	Al Iafrate, Bos.	.10
206	Mark Tinordi, Dal.	.10
207	Kelly Hrudey (G), L.A.	.10
208	Tom Barrasso (G), Pgh.	.25
209	Craig Billington (G), Ott.	.10
210	Teemu Selänne, Wpg.	.75
211	Alexandre Daigle, Ott.	.25
212	Grant Fuhr (G), Buf.	.25
213	Doug Brown, Pgh.	.10
214	Tim Sweeney, Ana.	.10
215	Chris Pronger, Hfd.	.25
216	Alexei Gusarov, Que.	.10
217	Gary Suter, Chi.	.10
218	Boris Mironov, Edm.	.10
219	Sergei Zubov, NYR.	.25
220	Checklist 3 (167-249)	.10
221	Shayne Corson, Edm.	.25
222	Jeremy Roenick, Chi.	.35
223	John Druce, L.A.	.10
224	Martin Straka, Pgh.	.10
225	Stéphane Fiset (G), Que.	.25
226	Vincent Damphousse, Mtl.	.35
227	Bob Kudelski, Fla.	.10
228	German Titov, Cgy.	.10
229	Kevin Stevens, Pgh.	.10
230	Dave Ellett, Tor.	.10
231	Steve Larmer, NYR.	.10
232	Glen Wesley, Bos.	.10
233	Mathieu Schneider, Mtl.	.10

No.	Player	
234	Stéphan Lebeau, Ana.	.10
235	Mark Fitzpatrick (G), Fla.	.10
236	Mikael Renberg, Pha.	.25
237	Darren McCarty, Det.	.10
238	Todd Nelson, Wsh.	.10
239	Igor Korolev, Stl.	.10
240	Warren Rychel, L.A.	.10
241	Gino Odjick, Van.	.10
242	Dave Manson, Wpg.	.10
243	Calle Johansson, Wsh.	.10
244	Andrei Trefilov (G), Cgy.	.10
245	Jason Dawe, Buf.	.10
246	Glen Murray, Bos.	.10
247	Jeff Shantz, Chi.	.10
248	Zarley Zalapski, Cgy.	.10
249	Petr Klima, T.B.	.10
250	Patrice Brisebois, Mtl.	.10
251	Chris Osgood (G), Det.	.35
252	Darius Kasparaitis, NYI.	.10
253	Chris Joseph, T.B.	.10
254	Glenn Anderson, NYR.	.10
255	Kirk Muller, Mtl.	.10
256	**Jason Smith, N.J., RC**	**.10**
257	Bob Bassen, Que.	.10
258	Joé Juneau, Wsh.	.10
259	Igor Kravchuk, Edm.	.10
260	John Lilley, Ana.	.10
261	Philippe Bozon, Stl.	.10
262	Scott Stevens, N.J.	.10
263	Dominic Roussel (G), Pha.	.10
264	Dimitri Khristich, Wsh.	.10
265	**Ed Patterson, Pgh., RC**	**.10**
266	Michael Peca, Van.	.25
267	Teppo Numminen, Wpg.	.10
268	Alexei Kovalev, NYR.	.10
269	Cam Neely, Bos.	.25
270	Iain Fraser, Que.	.10
271	Tomas Sandström, Pgh.	.10
272	Lyle Odelein, Mtl.	.10
273	Norm Maciver, Ott.	.10
274	Zdeno Ciger, Edm.	.10
275	Ed Belfour (G), Chi.	.35
276	Brian Savage, Mtl.	.10
277	Vlastimil Kroupa, S.J.	.10
278	Cliff Ronning, Van.	.10
279	Alexei Zhitnik, L.A.	.10
280	Jim Storm, Hfd.	.10
281	Don Sweeney, Bos.	.10
282	Mike Donnelly, L.A.	.10
283	Glenn Healy (G), NYR.	.10
284	Denis Savard, T.B.	.25
285	Chris Terreri (G), N.J.	.10
286	Darren Turcotte, Hfd.	.10
287	Curtis Joseph (G), Stl.	.60
288	Ken Baumgartner, Tor.	.10
289	Matthew Barnaby, Buf.	.10
290	Brent Sutter, Chi.	.10
291	Valeri Zelepukin, N.J.	.10
292	Michal Pivonka, Wsh.	.10
293	Ray Sheppard, Det.	.10
294	Jiri Slegr, Van.	.10
295	**Vesa Viitakoski, Cgy., RC**	**.10**
296	Ulf Samuelsson, Pgh.	.10
297	Nelson Emerson, Wpg.	.10
298	John Slaney, Wsh.	.10
299	Pat Verbeek, Hfd.	.10
300	Pat LaFontaine, Buf.	.25
301	Johan Garpenlov, S.J.	.10
302	Eric Weinrich, Chi.	.10
303	Richard Matvichuk, Dal.	.10
304	Steve Duchesne, Stl.	.10
305	Donald Audette, Buf.	.10
306	Stu Barnes, Fla.	.10
307	Vladimir Malakhov, NYI.	.10
308	Dimitri Yushkevich, Pha.	.10
309	David Sacco, Tor.	.10
310	Scott Young, Que.	.10
311	Marty McInnis, NYI.	.10
312	Grant Ledyard, Dal.	.10
313	Peter Popovic, Mtl.	.10
314	**Mikhail Shtalenkov, Ana., RC**	**.10**
315	Dave McLlwain, Ott.	.10
316	Cam Stewart, Bos.	.10
317	Derian Hatcher, Dal.	.25
318	Pat Peake, Wsh.	.10
319	Wes Walz, Cgy.	.10
320	**Fred Braithwaite (G), Edm., RC**	**.10**
321	Jesse Belanger, Fla.	.10
322	Jozef Stumpel, Bos.	.25
323	Dave Andreychuk, Tor.	.10
324	Yuri Khmylev, Buf.	.10
325	Tim Cheveldae (G), Wpg.	.10
326	Anatoli Semenov, Ana.	.10
327	Alexander Karpovtsev, NYR.	.10
328	Patrick Roy (G), Mtl.	2.00
329	Troy Mallette, Ott.	.10
330	Checklist 4 (250-330)	.10

DOMINATORS

Insert Set (8 cards): 100.00

No.	Player	NRMT-MT
1	Mark Messier/Mario Lemieux/Eric Lindros	20.00
2	Brian Leetch/Ray Bourque/Scott Stevens	8.00
3	Patrick Roy/Dominik Hasek/John Vanbiesbrouck	20.00
4	Jaromir Jagr/Mikael Renberg/Cam Neely	12.00
5	Wayne Gretzky/Jeremy Roenick/Sergei Fedorov	25.00
6	Al McInnis/Paul Coffey/Chris Chelios	6.00
7	Félix Potvin/Ed Belfour/Arturs Irbe	10.00
8	Pavel Bure/Brett Hull/Teemu Selänne	12.00

ELITE SERIES

These inserts are serial numbered out of 10,000.

Insert Set (10 cards): 275.00

No.	Player	NRMT-MT
1	Jason Arnott, Edm.	12.00
2	Martin Brodeur (G), N.J.	25.00
3	Pavel Bure, Van.	25.00
4	Sergei Fedorov, Det.	15.00
5	Wayne Gretzky, L.A.	65.00
6	Mario Lemieux, Pgh.	50.00
7	Eric Lindros, Pha.	45.00
8	Félix Potvin (G), Tor.	15.00
9	Jeremy Roenick, Chi	12.00
10	Patrick Roy (G), Mtl.	50.00

ICE MASTERS – by Dick Perez

Insert Set (10 cards): 35.00

No.	Player	NRMT-MT
1	Ed Belfour (G), Chi.	1.50
2	Sergei Fedorov, Det.	2.50
3	Doug Gilmour, Tor.	1.50
4	Wayne Gretzky, L.A.	10.00
5	Mario Lemieux, Pgh.	8.00
6	Eric Lindros, Pha.	6.50
7	Mark Messier, NYR.	2.50
8	Mike Modano, Dal.	2.50
9	Luc Robitaille, Pgh.	1.50
10	John Vanbiesbrouck (G), Fla.	3.00

MASKED MARVELS

Insert Set (10 cards): 50.00

No.	Player	NRMT-MT
1	Ed Belfour (G), Chi.	3.50
2	Martin Brodeur (G), N.J.	7.00
3	Dominik Hasek (G), Buf.	7.00
4	Arturs Irbe (G), S.J.	3.00
5	Curtis Joseph (G), Stl.	6.00
6	Kirk McLean (G), Van.	3.00
7	Félix Potvin (G), Tor.	4.50
8	Mike Richter (G), NYR.	3.50
9	Patrick Roy (G), Mtl.	15.00
10	John Vanbiesbrouck (G), Fla.	6.00

1994 - 95 FLAIR

Imprint: © 1994 FLEER CORP.

Complete Set (225 cards): 45.00

Common Player: .20

No.	Player	NRMT-MT
1	Bob Corkum, Ana.	.20
2	Bobby Dallas, Ana.	.20
3	Guy Hebert (G), Ana.	.50
4	Paul Kariya, Ana.	4.50
5	Anatoli Semenov, Ana.	.20
6	Tim Sweeney, Ana.	.20
7	Garry Valk, Ana.	.20
8	Ray Bourque, Bos.	1.50
9	**Mariusz Czerkawski, Bos., RC**	**.20**
10	Al Iafrate, Bos.	.20
11	Cam Neely, Bos.	.50
12	Adam Oates, Bos.	.75
13	Vincent Riendeau (G), Bos.	.20
14	Don Sweeney, Bos.	.20
15	Donald Audette, Buf.	.20
16	Doug Bodger, Buf.	.20
17	Dominik Hasek (G), Buf.	2.00
18	Dale Hawerchuk, Buf.	.50
19	Pat LaFontaine, Buf.	.50
20	Alexander Mogilny, Buf.	.75
21	Craig Muni, Buf.	.20
22	Richard Smehlik, Buf.	.20
23	Denis Tsygurov, Buf.	.20
24	Theoren Fleury, Cgy.	.75
25	Trevor Kidd (G), Cgy.	.50
26	James Patrick, Cgy.	.20
27	Robert Reichel, Cgy.	.50
28	Gary Roberts, Cgy.	.50
29	German Titov, Cgy.	.20
30	Zarley Zalapski, Cgy.	.20
31	Ed Belfour (G), Chi.	.75
32	Chris Chelios, Chi.	1.00
33	Dirk Graham, Chi.	.20
34	Joe Murphy, Chi.	.20
35	Bernie Nicholls, Chi.	.20
36	Jeremy Roenick, Chi.	.75
37	Steve Smith, Chi.	.20
38	Gary Suter, Chi.	.20
39	Neal Broten, Dal.	.20
40	Russ Courtnall, Dal.	.20
41	Todd Harvey, Dal.	.20
42	Grant Ledyard, Dal.	.20
43	Mike Modano, Dal.	1.50
44	Andy Moog (G), Dal.	.50
45	Mark Tinordi, Dal.	.20
46	Dino Ciccarelli, Det.	.50
47	Paul Coffey, Det.	.50
48	Sergei Fedorov, Det.	1.50
49	Vladimir Konstantinov, Det.	.20
50	Vyacheslav Kozlov, Det.	.20
51	Keith Primeau, Det.	.50
52	Ray Sheppard, Det.	.20
53	Mike Vernon (G), Det.	.75
54	**Jason York, Det., RC**	**.20**
55	Steve Yzerman, Det.	3.00

No.	Player	NRMT-MT
56	Jason Arnott, Edm.	.50
57	Shayne Corson, Edm.	.20
58	Igor Kravchuk, Edm.	.20
59	Dean McAmmond, Edm.	.20
60	**David Oliver, Edm., RC**	**.20**
61	Bill Ranford (G), Edm.	.50
62	Doug Weight, Edm.	.75
63	Jesse Belanger, Fla.	.20
64	Bob Kudelski, Fla.	.20
65	Scott Mellanby, Fla.	.20
66	Gord Murphy, Fla.	.20
67	Rob Niedermayer, Fla.	.50
68	Brian Skrudland, Fla.	.20
69	John Vanbiesbrouck (G), Fla.	1.75
70	Sean Burke (G), Hfd.	.50
71	Andrew Cassels, Hfd.	.20
72	Alexander Godynyuk, Hfd.	.20
73	Chris Pronger, Hfd.	.50
74	Geoff Sanderson, Hfd.	.20
75	Darren Turcotte, Hfd.	.20
76	Pat Verbeek, Hfd.	.20
77	Rob Blake, L.A.	.50
78	Mike Donnelly, L.A.	.20
79	Wayne Gretzky, L.A.	6.00
80	Kelly Hrudey (G), L.A.	.20
81	Jari Kurri, L.A.	.50
82	Marty McSorley, L.A.	.20
83	Rick Tocchet, L.A.	.20
84	Brian Bellows, Mtl.	.20
85	Patrice Brisebois, Mtl.	.20
86	Valeri Bure, Mtl.	.20
87	Vincent Damphousse, Mtl.	.75
88	Eric Desjardins, Mtl.	.20
89	Kirk Muller, Mtl.	.20
90	Oleg Petrov, Mtl.	.20
91	Patrick Roy (G), Mtl.	4.50
92	Martin Brodeur (G), N.J.	2.00
93	David Emma, N.J.	.20
94	Bill Guerin, N.J.	.50
95	John MacLean, N.J.	.20
96	Scott Niedermayer, N.J.	.50
97	Stéphane Richer, N.J.	.20
98	Brian Rolston, N.J.	.20
99	Alexander Semak, N.J.	.20
100	Scott Stevens, N.J.	.20
101	Valeri Zelepukin, N.J.	.20
102	Patrick Flatley, NYI.	.20
103	Derek King, NYI.	.20
104	Brett Lindros, NYI.	.20
105	Vladimir Malakhov, NYI.	.20
106	Marty McInnis, NYI.	.20
107	Jamie McLennan (G), NYI.	.50
108	Steve Thomas, NYI.	.20
109	Pierre Turgeon, NYI.	.50
110	Jeff Beukeboom, NYR.	.20
111	Adam Graves, NYR.	.20
112	Alexei Kovalev, NYR.	.20
113	Steve Larmer, NYR.	.20
114	Brian Leetch, NYR.	.75
115	Mark Messier, NYR.	1.50
116	Sergei Nemchinov, NYR.	.20
117	Mike Richter (G), NYR.	.75
118	Sergei Zubov, NYR.	.50
119	Craig Billington (G), Ott.	.20
120	Alexandre Daigle, Ott.	.50
121	Sean Hill, Ott.	.20
122	Norm Maciver, Ott.	.20
123	Dave McLlwain, Ott.	.20
124	Alexei Yashin, Ott.	1.00
125	Vladislav Boulin, Pha.	.20
126	Rod Brind'Amour, Pha.	.50
127	Ron Hextall (G), Pha.	.50
128	Patrik Juhlin, Pha.	.20
129	Eric Lindros, Pha.	4.00
130	Mark Recchi, Pha.	.50
131	Mikael Renberg, Pha.	.50
132	Chris Therien, Pha.	.20
133	Tom Barrasso (G), Pgh.	.20
134	Ron Francis, Pgh.	.75
135	Mario Lemieux, Pgh.	4.50
136	Shawn McEachern, Pgh.	.20
137	Larry Murphy, Pgh.	.50
138	Luc Robitaille, Pgh.	.50
139	Ulf Samuelsson, Pgh.	.20
140	Kevin Stevens, Pgh.	.20
141	Martin Straka, Pgh.	.20
142	Wendel Clark, Que.	.50
143	René Corbet, Que.	.20
144	Adam Deadmarsh, Que.	.50
145	Stéphane Fiset (G), Que.	.50
146	Peter Forsberg, Que.	3.50
147	Valeri Kamensky, Que.	.50
148	Janne Laukkanen, Que.	.20
149	Sylvain Lefebvre, Que.	.20
150	Mike Ricci, Que.	.20
151	Joe Sakic, Que.	2.50
152	Steve Duchesne, Stl.	.20
153	Brett Hull, Stl.	1.50
154	Craig Janney, Stl.	.20
155	Craig Johnson, Stl.	.20
156	Curtis Joseph (G), Stl.	1.50
157	Al MacInnis, Stl.	.50
158	Brendan Shanahan, Stl.	1.75
159	Peter Stastny, Stl.	.20
160	Esa Tikkanen, Stl.	.20
161	Ulf Dahlen, S.J.	.20
162	Todd Elik, S.J.	.20
163	Pat Falloon, S.J.	.20
164	Jeff Friesen, S.J.	.50
165	Johan Garpenlov, S.J.	.20
166	Arturs Irbe (G), S.J.	.20
167	Sergei Makarov, S.J.	.20
168	Jeff Norton, S.J.	.20
169	Sandis Ozolinsh, S.J.	.50
170	Brian Bradley, T.B.	.20
171	Shawn Chambers, T.B.	.20
172	**Aaron Gavey, T.B., RC**	**.20**
173	Chris Gratton, T.B.	.50
174	Petr Klima, T.B.	.20
175	Daren Puppa (G), T.B.	.20
176	Jason Wiemer, T.B.	.20
177	Dave Andreychuk, Tor.	.20
178	Dave Ellett, Tor.	.20
179	**Éric Fichaud (G), Tor., RC**	**1.25**
180	Mike Gartner, Tor.	.50
181	Doug Gilmour, Tor.	.75
182	Kenny Jonsson, Tor.	.20
183	Dmitri Mironov, Tor.	.20
184	Félix Potvin (G), Tor.	1.50
185	Mike Ridley, Tor.	.20
186	Mats Sundin, Tor.	1.50
187	Greg Adams, Van.	.20
188	Jeff Brown, Van.	.20
189	Pavel Bure, Van.	2.00
190	Nathan Lafayette, Van.	.20
191	Trevor Linden, Van.	.50
192	Jyrki Lumme, Van.	.20
193	Kirk McLean (G), Van.	.50
194	Cliff Ronning, Van.	.20
195	Jason Allison, Wsh.	.75
196	Peter Bondra, Wsh.	1.00
197	Randy Burridge, Wsh.	.20
198	Sylvain Côté, Wsh.	.20
199	Dale Hunter, Wsh.	.20
200	Joé Juneau, Wsh.	.20
201	Dimitri Khristich, Wsh.	.20
202	Todd Nelson, Wsh.	.20
203	Pat Peake, Wsh.	.20
204	Rick Tabaracci (G), Wsh.	.20
205	Tim Cheveldae (G), Wpg.	.20
206	Dallas Drake, Wpg.	.20
207	Dave Manson, Wpg.	.20
208	Teppo Numminen, Wpg.	.20
209	Teemu Selänne, Wpg.	2.00
210	Darrin Shannon, Wpg.	.20
211	Keith Tkachuk, Wpg.	1.00
212	Alexei Zhamnov, Wpg.	.50
213	Sergei Fedorov The Bank	.60
214	Sergei Fedorov Over There	.60
215	Sergei Fedorov Wonderblades-BFM	.60
216	Sergei Fedorov The Red	.60
217	Sergei Fedorov Midnight Run	.60
218	Sergei Fedorov In The Shadows	.60
219	Sergei Fedorov Flight Leader	.60
220	Sergei Fedorov Flying Machine	.60
221	Sergei Fedorov Candle Burning	.60
222	Sergei Fedorov Gotta Have Hart	.60
223	Checklist #1 (1-88)	.20
224	Checklist #2 (89-176)	.20
225	Checklist #3 (177-225)	.20

CENTRE SPOTLIGHT

Insert Set (10 cards): 30.00

No.	Player	NRMT-MT
1	Jason Arnott, Edm.	1.50
2	Sergei Fedorov, Det.	2.50
3	Doug Gilmour, Tor.	1.50
4	Wayne Gretzky, L.A.	10.00
5	Pat LaFontaine, Buf.	1.50
6	Mario Lemieux, Pgh.	8.00
7	Eric Lindros, Pha.	6.50
8	Mark Messier, NYR.	2.50
9	Mike Modano, Dal.	2.50
10	Jeremy Roenick, Chi.	1.50

HOT NUMBERS

Insert Set (10 cards): 120.00

No.	Player	NRMT-MT
1	Pavel Bure, Van.	10.00
2	Wayne Gretzky, L.A.	30.00
3	Dominik Hasek (G), Buf.	10.00
4	Brett Hull, Stl.	7.00
5	Mario Lemieux, Pgh.	25.00
6	Adam Oates, Bos.	5.00
7	Luc Robitaille, Pgh.	5.00
8	Patrick Roy (G), Mtl.	25.00
9	Brendan Shanahan, Stl.	9.00
10	Steve Yzerman, Det.	15.00

SCORING POWER

Insert Set (10 cards): 25.00

No.	Player	NRMT-MT
1	Pavel Bure, Van.	4.00
2	Alexandre Daigle, Ott.	1.50
3	Sergei Fedorov, Det.	3.00
4	Alexei Kovalev, NYR.	1.50
5	Brian Leetch, NYR.	2.50
6	Eric Lindros, Pha.	8.00
7	Mike Modano, Dal.	3.00
8	Alexander Mogilny, Buf.	2.00
9	Jeremy Roenick, Chi.	2.00
10	Alexei Yashin, Ott.	2.50

1994 - 95 FLEER

Imprint: © 1995 FLEER CORP.

Complete Set (250 cards): 25.00

Common Player: .10

No.	Player	NRMT-MT
1	Patrik Carnback, Ana.	.10
2	Bob Corkum, Ana.	.10
3	Paul Kariya, Ana.	2.00
4	**Valeri Karpov, Ana., RC**	**.10**
5	Tom Kurvers, Ana.	.10
6	**John Lilley, Ana., RC**	**.10**
7	**Mikhail Shtalenkov (G), Ana., RC**	**.10**
8	Oleg Tverdovsky, Ana.	.20
9	Ray Bourque, Bos.	.50
10	**Mariusz Czerkawski, Bos., RC**	**.10**
11	**John Gruden, Bos., RC**	**.10**
12	Al Iafrate, Bos.	.10
13	**Blaine Lacher (G), Bos., RC**	**.10**
14	Mats Naslund, Bos.	.10
15	Cam Neely, Bos.	.25
16	Adam Oates, Bos.	.35
17	Bryan Smolinski, Bos.	.10
18	Don Sweeney, Bos.	.10
19	Donald Audette, Buf.	.10
20	Dominik Hasek (G), Buf.	.75
21	Dale Hawerchuk, Buf.	.25

	No.	Player	Price
☐	22	Yuri Khmylev, Buf.	.10
☐	23	Pat LaFontaine, Buf.	.25
☐	24	Brad May, Buf.	.10
☐	25	Alexander Mogilny, Buf.	.35
☐	26	Derek Plante, Buf.	.10
☐	27	Richard Smehlik, Buf.	.10
☐	28	Steve Chiasson, Cgy.	.10
☐	29	Theoren Fleury, Cgy.	.35
☐	30	Phil Housley, Cgy.	.10
☐	31	Tevor Kidd (G), Cgy.	.25
☐	32	Joe Nieuwendyk, Cgy.	.25
☐	33	James Patrick, Cgy.	.10
☐	34	Robert Reichel, Cgy.	.10
☐	35	Gary Roberts, Cgy.	.25
☐	36	German Titov, Cgy.	.10
☐	37	Tony Amonte, Chi.	.10
☐	38	Ed Belfour (G), Chi.	.35
☐	39	Chris Chelios, Chi.	.35
☐	40	Dirk Graham, Chi.	.10
☐	41	Sergei Krivokrasov, Chi.	.10
☐	42	Joe Murphy, Chi.	.10
☐	43	Bernie Nicholls, Chi.	.10
☐	44	Patrick Poulin, Chi.	.10
☐	45	Jeremy Roenick, Chi.	.35
☐	46	Steve Smith, Chi.	.10
☐	47	Gary Suter, Chi.	.10
☐	48	Russ Courtnall, Dal.	.10
☐	49	Dave Gagner, Dal.	.10
☐	50	Brent Gilchrist, Dal.	.10
☐	51	Todd Harvey, Dal.	.10
☐	52	Derian Hatcher, Dal.	.25
☐	53	Kevin Hatcher, Dal.	.10
☐	**54**	**Mike Kennedy, Dal., RC**	**.10**
☐	55	Mike Modano, Dal.	.50
☐	56	Andy Moog (G), Dal.	.25
☐	57	Dino Ciccarelli, Det.	.25
☐	58	Paul Coffey, Det.	.25
☐	59	Sergei Fedorov, Det.	.50
☐	60	Vladimir Konstantinov, Det.	.10
☐	61	Vyacheslav Kozlov, Det.	.10
☐	62	Nicklas Lidstrom, Det.	.25
☐	63	Chris Osgood (G), Det.	.35
☐	64	Keith Primeau, Det.	.25
☐	65	Ray Sheppard, Det.	.10
☐	66	Mike Vernon (G), Det.	.25
☐	67	Steve Yzerman, Det.	1.25
☐	68	Jason Arnott, Edm.	.25
☐	69	Shayne Corson, Edm.	.25
☐	70	Igor Kravchuk, Edm.	.10
☐	71	Todd Marchant, Edm.	.10
☐	72	Roman Oksiuta, Edm.	.10
☐	73	Fredrik Olausson, Edm.	.10
☐	**74**	**David Oliver, Edm., RC**	**.10**
☐	75	Bill Ranford (G), Edm.	.25
☐	76	Stu Barnes, Fla.	.10
☐	77	Jesse Belanger, Fla.	.10
☐	78	Keith Brown, Fla.	.10
☐	79	Bob Kudelski, Fla.	.10
☐	80	Scott Mellanby, Fla.	.10
☐	81	Gord Murphy, Fla.	.10
☐	82	Rob Niedermayer, Fla.	.25
☐	83	John Vanbiesbrouck (G), Fla.	.60
☐	84	Sean Burke (G), Hfd.	.25
☐	85	Jimmy Carson, Hfd.	.10
☐	86	Andrew Cassels, Hfd.	.10
☐	**87**	**Andrei Nikolishin, Hfd., RC**	**.10**
☐	88	Chris Pronger, Hfd.	.25
☐	89	Geoff Sanderson, Hfd.	.10
☐	90	Darren Turcotte, Hfd.	.10
☐	91	Pat Verbeek, Hfd. (NYR.)	.10
☐	92	Glen Wesley, Hfd.	.10
☐	93	Rob Blake, L.A.	.25
☐	94	Wayne Gretzky, L.A.	2.50
☐	95	Kelly Hrudey (G), L.A.	.10
☐	96	Jari Kurri, L.A.	.25
☐	**97**	**Eric Lacroix, L.A., RC**	**.10**
☐	98	Marty McSorley, L.A.	.10
☐	99	Jamie Storr (G), L.A.	.25
☐	100	Rick Tocchet, L.A.	.10
☐	101	Brian Bellows, Mtl.	.10
☐	102	Patrice Brisebois, Mtl.	.10
☐	103	Vincent Damphousse, Mtl.	.35
☐	104	Kirk Muller, Mtl.	.10
☐	105	Lyle Odelein, Mtl.	.10
☐	106	Mark Recchi, Mtl.	.25
☐	107	Patrick Roy (G), Mtl.	2.00
☐	108	Brian Savage, Mtl.	.10
☐	109	Mathieu Schneider, Mtl.	.10
☐	110	Turner Stevenson, Mtl.	.10
☐	111	Martin Brodeur (G), N.J.	.75
☐	112	Bill Guerin, N.J.	.25
☐	113	Claude Lemieux, N.J.	.10
☐	114	John MacLean, N.J.	.10
☐	115	Scott Niedermayer, N.J.	.25
☐	116	Stéphane Richer, N.J.	.10
☐	117	Brian Rolston, N.J.	.10
☐	118	Alexander Semak, N.J.	.10
☐	119	Scott Stevens, N.J.	.10
☐	120	Ray Ferraro, NYI.	.10
☐	121	Patrick Flatley, NYI.	.10
☐	122	Darius Kasparaitis, NYI.	.10
☐	123	Derek King, NYI.	.10
☐	124	Scott Lachance, NYI.	.10
☐	125	Brett Lindros, NYI.	.10
☐	126	Vladimir Malakhov, NYI.	.10
☐	127	Jamie McLennan (G), NYI.	.25
☐	128	Zigmund Palffy, NYI.	.35
☐	129	Steve Thomas, NYI.	.10
☐	130	Pierre Turgeon, NYI.	.25
☐	131	Jeff Beukeboom, NYR.	.10
☐	132	Adam Graves, NYR.	.10
☐	133	Alexei Kovalev, NYR.	.10
☐	134	Steve Larmer, NYR.	.10
☐	135	Brian Leetch, NYR.	.35
☐	136	Mark Messier, NYR.	.50
☐	137	Petr Nedved, NYR.	.10
☐	138	Sergei Nemchinov, NYR.	.10
☐	139	Mike Richter (G), NYR.	.25
☐	140	Sergei Zubov, NYR.	.25
☐	141	Don Beaupré (G), Ott.	.10
☐	**142**	**Radek Bonk, Ott., RC**	**.25**
☐	143	Alexandre Daigle, Ott.	.25
☐	144	Pavol Demitra, Ott.	.10
☐	145	Pat Elynuik, Ott.	.10
☐	146	Rob Gaudreau, Ott.	.10
☐	147	Sean Hill, Ott.	.10
☐	148	Sylvain Turgeon, Ott.	.10
☐	149	Alexei Yashin, Ott.	.35
☐	150	Rod Brind'Amour, Pha.	.25
☐	151	Eric Desjardins, Pha.	.25
☐	152	Gilbert Dionne, Pha.	.10
☐	153	Garry Galley, Pha.	.10
☐	154	Ron Hextall (G), Pha.	.25
☐	155	Patrik Juhlin, Pha.	.10
☐	156	John LeClair, Pha.	.50
☐	157	Eric Lindros, Pha.	2.00
☐	158	Mikael Renberg, Pha.	.25
☐	159	Chris Therien, Pha.	.10
☐	160	Dimitri Yushkevich, Pha.	.10
☐	**161**	**Len Barrie, Pgh., RC**	**.10**
☐	162	Ron Francis, Pgh.	.35
☐	163	Jaromir Jagr, Pgh.	1.25
☐	164	Shawn McEachern, Pgh.	.10
☐	165	Joe Mullen, Pgh.	.10
☐	166	Larry Murphy, Pgh.	.25
☐	167	Luc Robitaille, Pgh.	.25
☐	168	Ulf Samuelsson, Pgh.	.10
☐	169	Tomas Sandström, Pgh.	.10
☐	170	Kevin Stevens, Pgh.	.10
☐	171	Martin Straka, Pgh.	.10
☐	172	Ken Wregget (G), Pgh.	.10
☐	173	Wendel Clark, Que.	.25
☐	174	Adam Deadmarsh, Que.	.25
☐	175	Stéphane Fiset (G), Que.	.25
☐	176	Peter Forsberg, Que.	1.50
☐	177	Valeri Kamensky, Que.	.25
☐	178	Andrei Kovalenko, Que.	.10
☐	179	Uwe Krupp, Que.	.10
☐	180	Sylvain Lefebvre, Que.	.10
☐	181	Owen Nolan, Que.	.25
☐	182	MIke Ricci, Que.	.10
☐	183	Joe Sakic, Que.	1.00
☐	**184**	**Denis Chassé, Stl., RC**	**.10**
☐	185	Adam Creighton, Stl.	.10
☐	186	Steve Duchesne, Stl.	.10
☐	187	Brett Hull, Stl.	.50
☐	188	Curtis Joseph (G), Stl.	.60
☐	189	Ian Laperrière, Stl.	.10
☐	190	Al MacInnis, Stl.	.25
☐	191	Brendan Shanahan, Stl.	.60
☐	**192**	**Patrice Tardif, Stl., RC**	**.10**
☐	193	Esa Tikkanen, Stl.	.10
☐	194	Ulf Dahlen, S.J.	.10
☐	195	Pat Falloon, S.J.	.10
☐	196	Jeff Friesen, S.J.	.25
☐	197	Arturs Irbe (G), S.J.	.10
☐	198	Sergei Makarov, S.J.	.10
☐	**199**	**Andrei Nazarov, S.J., RC**	**.10**
☐	200	Sandis Ozolinsh, S.J.	.25
☐	201	Michal Sykora, S.J.	.10
☐	202	Ray Whitney, S.J.	.10
☐	203	Brian Bradley, T.B.	.10
☐	204	Shawn Chambers, T.B.	.10
☐	**205**	**Eric Charron, T.B., RC**	**.10**
☐	206	Chris Gratton, T.B.	.25
☐	207	Roman Hamrlik, T.B.	.25
☐	208	Petr Klima, T.B.	.10
☐	209	Daren Puppa (G), T.B.	.10
☐	**210**	**Alexander Selivanov, T.B., RC**	**.10**
☐	**211**	**Jason Wiemer, T.B., RC**	**.10**
☐	212	Dave Andreychuk, Tor.	.10
☐	213	Dave Ellett, Tor.	.10
☐	214	Mike Gartner, Tor.	.25
☐	215	Doug Gilmour, Tor.	.35
☐	216	Kenny Jonsson, Tor.	.10
☐	217	Dmitri Mironov, Tor.	.10
☐	218	Félix Potvin (G), Tor.	.50
☐	219	Mike Ridley, Tor.	.10
☐	220	Mats Sundin, Tor.	.50
☐	221	Josef Beranek, Van.	.10
☐	222	Jeff Brown, Van.	.10
☐	223	Pavel Bure, Van.	.75
☐	224	Geoff Courtnall, Van.	.10
☐	225	Trevor Linden, Van.	.25
☐	226	Jurki Lumme, Van.	.10
☐	227	Kirk McLean (G), Van.	.25
☐	228	Gino Odjick, Van.	.10
☐	229	Michael Peca, Van.	.25
☐	230	Cliff Ronning, Van.	.10
☐	231	Jason Allison, Wsh.	.35
☐	232	Peter Bondra, Wsh.	.35
☐	**233**	**Jim Carey (G), Wsh., RC**	**.25**
☐	234	Sylvain Côté, Wsh.	.10
☐	235	Dale Hunter, Wsh.	.10
☐	236	Joé Juneau, Wsh.	.10
☐	237	Dimitri Khristich, Wsh.	.10
☐	238	Pat Peake, Wsh.	.10
☐	239	Mark Tinordi, Wsh.	.10
☐	240	Nelson Emerson, Wpg.	.10
☐	**241**	**Michal Grosek,Wpg., RC**	**.10**
☐	242	Nikolai Khabibulin (G), Wpg.	.35
☐	243	Dave Manson, Wpg.	.10
☐	244	Stéphane Quintal, Wpg.	.10
☐	245	Teemu Selänne, Wpg.	.75
☐	246	Keith Tkachuk, Wpg.	.35
☐	247	Alexei Zhamnov, Wpg.	.25
☐	248	Checklist #1 (1-110)	.10
☐	249	Checklist #2 (111-211)	.10
☐	250	Checklist #3 (212-250)	.10

FRANCHISE FUTURES

Insert Set (10 cards): 10.00

	No.	Player	NRMT-MT
☐	1	Jason Arnott, Edm.	1.00
☐	2	Rob Blake, L.A.	1.00
☐	3	Adam Graves, NYR.	.50
☐	4	Arturs Irbe (G), S.J.	.50
☐	5	Joé Juneau, Wsh.	.50
☐	6	Sandis Ozolinsh, S.J.	1.00
☐	7	Mikael Renberg, Pha.	1.00
☐	8	Keith Tkachuk, Wpg.	4.00

	No.	Player	NRMT-MT
☐	9	Alexei Yashin, Ott.	4.00
☐	10	Sergei Zubov, NYR.	1.00

HEADLINERS

Insert Set (10 cards): 12.00

	No.	Player	NRMT-MT
☐	1	Pavel Bure, Van.	1.75
☐	2	Sergei Fedorov, Det.	1.25
☐	3	Doug Gilmour, Tor.	.75
☐	4	Wayne Gretzky, L.A.	5.00
☐	5	Brian Leetch, NYR.	.75
☐	6	Eric Lindros, Pha.	3.00
☐	7	Mark Messier, NYR.	1.25
☐	8	Cam Neely, Bos.	.50
☐	9	Mark Recchi, Mtl.	.50
☐	10	Brendan Shanahan, Stl.	1.50

NETMINDERS

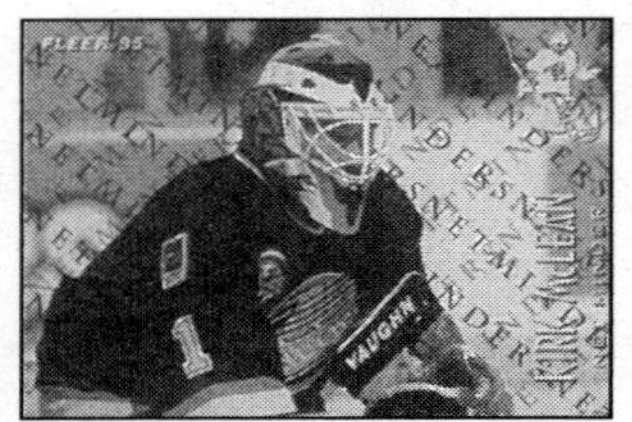

Insert Set (10 cards): 10.00

	No.	Player	NRMT-MT
☐	1	Ed Belfour (G), Chi.	.75
☐	2	Martin Brodeur (G), N.J.	1.75
☐	3	Dominik Hasek (G), Buf.	1.75
☐	4	Arturs Irbe (G), S.J.	.50
☐	5	Curtis Joseph (G), Stl.	1.50
☐	6	Kirk McLean (G), Van.	.50
☐	7	Félix Potvin (G), Tor.	1.25
☐	8	Mike Richter (G), NYR.	.75
☐	9	Patrick Roy (G), Mtl.	4.00
☐	10	John Vanbiesbrouck (G), Fla.	1.50

ROOKIE SENSATIONS

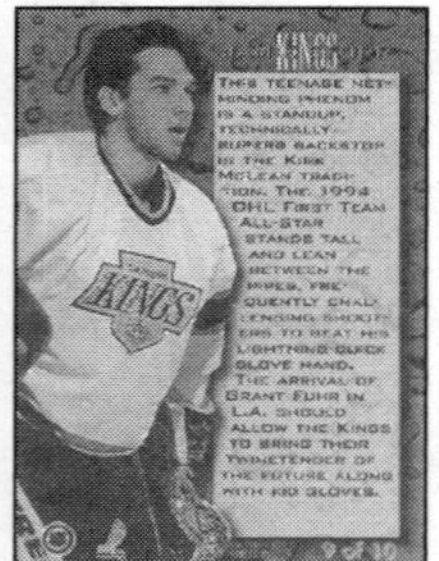

Insert Set (10 cards): 75.00

	No.	Player	NRMT-MT
☐	1	Radek Bonk, Ott.	3.00
☐	2	Peter Forsberg, Que.	25.00
☐	3	Jeff Friesen, S.J.	6.00
☐	4	Todd Harvey, Dal.	3.00
☐	5	Paul Kariya, Ana.	30.00
☐	6	Blaine Lacher (G), Bos.	3.00
☐	7	Brett Lindros, NYI.	3.00
☐	8	Michael Peca, Van.	6.00
☐	9	Jamie Storr (G), L.A.	6.00
☐	10	Oleg Tverdovsky, Ana.	3.00

SLAPSHOT ARTISTS

Insert Set (10 cards): 30.00

	No.	Player	NRMT-MT
☐	1	Wendel Clark, Que.	2.00
☐	2	Brett Hull, Stl.	6.00
☐	3	Al Iafrate, Bos.	1.00
☐	4	Jaromir Jagr, Pgh.	12.00
☐	5	Al MacInnis, Stl.	2.00
☐	6	Mike Modano, Dal.	6.00
☐	7	Stéphane Richer, N.J.	1.00
☐	8	Jeremy Roenick, Chi.	3.50
☐	9	Geoff Sanderson, Hfd.	1.00
☐	10	Steve Thomas, NYI.	1.00

1994 - 95 FLEER ULTRA

Sergei Fedorov was featured on series one packaging while Wendel Clark was featured on series two packaging.

Imprint: © 1994 FLEER CORP. or © 1995 FLEER CORP.

Series One Set (250 cards): 25.00

Series Two Set (150 cards): 20.00

Common Player: .15

	No.	Player	NRMT-MT
☐	1	Bob Corkum, Ana.	.15
☐	2	Todd Ewen, Ana.	.15
☐	3	Guy Hebert (G), Ana.	.25
☐	4	Bill Houlder, Ana.	.15
☐	5	Stéphan Lebeau, Ana.	.15
☐	6	Joe Sacco, Ana.	.15
☐	7	Anatoli Semenov, Ana.	.15
☐	8	Tim Sweeney, Ana.	.15
☐	9	Terry Yake, Ana.	.15
☐	10	Ray Bourque, Bos.	.50
☐	**11**	**Mariusz Czerkawski, Bos., RC**	**.15**
☐	12	Ted Donato, Bos.	.15
☐	13	Cam Neely, Bos.	.25
☐	14	Adam Oates, Bos.	.35
☐	15	Vincent Riendeau (G), Bos.	.15
☐	16	Bryan Smolinski, Bos.	.15
☐	17	Don Sweeney, Bos.	.15
☐	18	Glen Wesley, Bos.	.15
☐	19	Donald Audette, Buf.	.15
☐	20	Doug Bodger, Buf.	.15
☐	21	Jason Dawe, Buf.	.15
☐	22	Dominik Hasek (G), Buf.	.75
☐	23	Dale Hawerchuk, Buf.	.25
☐	24	Pat LaFontaine, Buf.	.25
☐	25	Brad May, Buf.	.15
☐	26	Alexander Mogilny, Buf.	.35
☐	27	Derek Plante, Buf.	.15
☐	28	Richard Smehlik, Buf.	.15
☐	29	Theoren Fleury, Cgy.	.35
☐	30	Trevor Kidd (G), Cgy.	.25
☐	31	Frank Musil, Cgy.	.15
☐	32	Mikael Nylander, Cgy.	.15
☐	33	James Patrick, Cgy.	.15
☐	34	Robert Reichel, Cgy.	.15
☐	35	Gary Roberts, Cgy.	.25
☐	36	German Titov, Cgy.	.15
☐	37	Wes Walz, Cgy.	.15
☐	38	Zarley Zalapski, Cgy.	.15
☐	39	Ed Belfour (G), Chi.	.35
☐	40	Chris Chelios, Chi.	.35
☐	41	Dirk Graham, Chi.	.15
☐	42	Bernie Nicholls, N.J. (Chi.)	.15
☐	43	Patrick Poulin, Chi.	.15
☐	44	Jeremy Roenick, Chi.	.35
☐	45	Steve Smith, Chi.	.15
☐	46	Gary Suter, Chi.	.15
☐	47	Brent Sutter, Chi.	.15
☐	48	Neal Broten, Dal.	.15
☐	49	Paul Cavallini, Dal.	.15
☐	50	Dean Evason, Dal.	.15
☐	51	Dave Gagner, Dal.	.15
☐	52	Derian Hatcher, Dal.	.35
☐	53	Trent Klatt, Dal.	.15
☐	54	Grant Ledyard, Dal.	.15
☐	55	Mike Modano, Dal.	.50
☐	56	Andy Moog (G), Dal.	.25
☐	57	Mark Tinordi, Dal.	.15
☐	58	Dino Ciccarelli, Det.	.25
☐	59	Paul Coffey, Det.	.25
☐	60	Sergei Fedorov, Det.	.50
☐	61	Vladimir Konstantinov, Det.	.15
☐	62	Nicklas Lidstrom, Det.	.25
☐	63	Darren McCarty, Det.	.15
☐	64	Chris Osgood (G), Det.	.35
☐	65	Keith Primeau, Det.	.25
☐	66	Ray Sheppard, Det.	.15
☐	67	Steve Yzerman, Det.	1.25
☐	68	Jason Arnott, Edm.	.25
☐	69	Bob Beers, Edm.	.15
☐	70	Ilya Byakin, Edm.	.15
☐	71	Zdeno Ciger, Edm.	.15
☐	72	Igor Kravchuk, Edm.	.15
☐	73	Boris Mironov, Edm.	.15
☐	74	Fredrik Olausson, Edm.	.15
☐	75	Scott Pearson, Edm.	.15
☐	76	Bill Ranford (G), Edm.	.25
☐	77	Doug Weight, Edm.	.35
☐	78	Stu Barnes, Fla.	.15
☐	79	Jesse Belanger, Fla.	.15
☐	80	Bob Kudelski, Fla.	.15
☐	81	Andrei Lomakin, Fla.	.15
☐	82	Dave Lowry, Fla.	.15
☐	83	Gord Murphy, Fla.	.15
☐	84	Rob Niedermayer, Fla.	.25
☐	85	Brian Skrudland, Fla.	.15
☐	86	John Vanbiesbrouck (G), Fla.	.60
☐	87	Sean Burke (G), Hfd.	.25
☐	88	Ted Drury, Hfd.	.15
☐	89	Alexander Godynyuk, Hfd.	.15
☐	90	Robert Kron, Hfd.	.15
☐	91	Chris Pronger, Hfd.	.25
☐	92	Brian Propp, Hfd.	.15
☐	93	Geoff Sanderson, Hfd.	.15
☐	94	Darren Turcotte, Hfd.	.15
☐	95	Pat Verbeek, Hfd.	.10
☐	96	Rob Blake, L.A.	.25
☐	97	Mike Donnelly, L.A.	.15
☐	98	John Druce, L.A.	.15
☐	99	Kelly Hrudey (G), L.A.	.15
☐	100	Jari Kurri, L.A.	.25
☐	101	Robert Lang, L.A.	.15
☐	102	Marty McSorley, L.A.	.15
☐	103	Luc Robitaille, L.A.	.25
☐	104	Alexei Zhitnik, L.A.	.15
☐	105	Brian Bellows, Mtl.	.15
☐	106	Patrice Brisebois, Mtl.	.15
☐	107	Vincent Damphousse, Mtl.	.25
☐	108	Eric Desjardins, Mtl.	.25
☐	109	Gilbert Dionne, Mtl.	.15
☐	110	Mike Keane, Mtl.	.15
☐	111	John LeClair, Mtl.	.50
☐	112	Lyle Odelein, Mtl.	.15
☐	113	Patrick Roy (G), Mtl.	2.00
☐	114	Mathieu Schneider, Mtl.	.15
☐	115	Martin Brodeur (G), N.J.	.75
☐	116	Jim Dowd, N.J.	.15
☐	117	Bill Guerin, N.J.	.25

	No.	Card	Value
☐	118	Claude Lemieux, N.J.	.15
☐	119	John MacLean, N.J.	.15
☐	120	Corey Millen, N.J.	.15
☐	121	Scott Niedermayer, N.J.	.25
☐	122	Stéphane Richer, N.J.	.15
☐	123	Scott Stevens, N.J.	.15
☐	124	Valeri Zelepukin, N.J.	.15
☐	125	Patrick Flatley, NYI.	.15
☐	126	Travis Green, NYI.	.15
☐	127	Ron Hextall (G), NYI.	.25
☐	128	Benoît Hogue, NYI.	.15
☐	129	Darius Kasparaitis, NYI.	.15
☐	130	Vladimir Malakhov, NYI.	.15
☐	131	Marty McInnis, NYI.	.15
☐	132	Steve Thomas, NYI.	.15
☐	133	Pierre Turgeon, NYI.	.25
☐	134	Dennis Vaske, NYI.	.15
☐	135	Glenn Anderson, NYR.	.15
☐	136	Jeff Beukeboom, NYR.	.15
☐	137	Adam Graves, NYR.	.15
☐	138	Steve Larmer, NYR.	.15
☐	139	Brian Leetch, NYR.	.35
☐	140	Mark Messier, NYR.	.50
☐	141	Petr Nedved, Stl. (NYR.)	.15
☐	142	Sergei Nemchinov, NYR.	.15
☐	143	Mike Richter (G), NYR.	.35
☐	144	Sergei Zubov, NYR.	.25
☐	145	Craig Billington (G), Ott.	.15
☐	146	Alexandre Daigle, Ott.	.25
☐	147	Evgeny Davydov, Ott.	.15
☐	148	Scott Levins, Ott.	.15
☐	149	Norm Maciver, Ott.	.15
☐	150	Troy Mallette, Ott.	.15
☐	151	Brad Shaw, Ott.	.15
☐	152	Alexei Yashin, Ott.	.35
☐	153	Josef Beranek, Pha.	.15
☐	154	Jason Bowen, Pha.	.15
☐	155	Rod Brind'Amour, Pha.	.25
☐	156	Kevin Dineen, Pha.	.15
☐	157	Garry Galley, Pha.	.15
☐	158	Mark Recchi, Pha.	.25
☐	159	Mikael Renberg, Pha.	.25
☐	160	Tommy Söderström (G), Pha.	.15
☐	161	Dimitri Yushkevich, Pha.	.15
☐	162	Tom Barrasso (G), Pgh.	.25
☐	163	Ron Francis, Pgh.	.35
☐	164	Jaromir Jagr, Pgh.	1.25
☐	165	Mario Lemieux, Pgh.	2.00
☐	166	Shawn McEachern, Pgh.	.15
☐	167	Joe Mullen, Pgh.	.15
☐	168	Larry Murphy, Pgh.	.25
☐	169	Ulf Samuelsson, Pgh.	.15
☐	170	Kevin Stevens, Pgh.	.15
☐	171	Martin Straka, Pgh.	.15
☐	172	Wendel Clark, Tor. (Que.)	.25
☐	173	Stéphane Fiset (G), Que.	.25
☐	174	Iain Fraser, Que.	.15
☐	175	Andrei Kovalenko, Que.	.15
☐	176	Sylvain Lefebvre, Tor. (Que.)	.15
☐	177	Owen Nolan, Que.	.25
☐	178	Mike Ricci, Que.	.15
☐	179	Martin Rucinsky, Que.	.15
☐	180	Joe Sakic, Que.	1.00
☐	181	Scott Young, Que.	.15
☐	182	Steve Duchesne, Stl.	.15
☐	183	Brett Hull, Stl.	.50
☐	184	Curtis Joseph (G), Stl.	.60
☐	185	Al MacInnis, Cgy. (Stl.)	.15
☐	186	Kevin Miller, Stl.	.15
☐	187	Jim Montgomery, Stl.	.15
☐	188	Vitali Prokhorov, Stl.	.15
☐	189	Brendan Shanahan, Stl.	.60
☐	190	Peter Stastny, Stl.	.15
☐	191	Esa Tikkanen, NYR. (Stl.)	.15
☐	192	Ulf Dahlen, S.J.	.15
☐	193	Todd Elik, S.J.	.15
☐	194	Johan Garpenlov, S.J.	.15
☐	195	Arturs Irbe (G), S.J.	.15
☐	196	Vlastimil Kroupa, S.J.	.15
☐	197	Igor Larionov, S.J.	.25
☐	198	Sergei Makarov, S.J.	.15
☐	199	Jeff Norton, S.J.	.15
☐	200	Sandis Ozolinsh, S.J.	.25
☐	201	Mike Rathje, S.J.	.15
☐	202	Brian Bradley, T.B.	.15
☐	203	Shawn Chambers, T.B.	.15
☐	204	Danton Cole, T.B.	.15
☐	205	Chris Gratton, T.B.	.25
☐	206	Roman Hamrlik, T.B.	.25
☐	207	Chris Joseph, T.B.	.15
☐	208	Petr Klima, T.B.	.15
☐	209	Daren Puppa (G), T.B.	.15
☐	210	John Tucker, T.B.	.15
☐	211	Dave Andreychuk, Tor.	.15
☐	212	Ken Baumgartner, Tor.	.15
☐	213	Dave Ellett, Tor.	.15
☐	214	Mike Gartner, Tor.	.25
☐	215	Todd Gill, Tor.	.15
☐	216	Doug Gilmour, Tor.	.35
☐	217	Jamie Macoun, Tor.	.15
☐	218	Dmitri Mironov, Tor.	.15
☐	219	Félix Potvin (G), Tor.	.50
☐	220	Mats Sundin, Que. (Tor.)	.50
☐	221	Jeff Brown, Van.	.15
☐	222	Pavel Bure, Van.	.75
☐	223	Murray Craven, Van.	.15
☐	224	Bret Hedican, Van.	.15
☐	225	Nathan Lafayette, Van.	.15
☐	226	Trevor Linden, Van.	.25
☐	227	Jyrki Lumme, Van.	.15
☐	228	Kirk McLean (G), Van.	.25
☐	229	Gino Odjick, Van.	.15
☐	230	Cliff Ronning, Van.	.15
☐	231	Peter Bondra, Wsh.	.35
☐	232	Sylvain Côté, Wsh.	.15
☐	233	Kevin Hatcher, Wsh.	.15
☐	234	Dale Hunter, Wsh.	.15
☐	235	Calle Johansson, Wsh.	.15
☐	236	Dimitri Khristich, Wsh.	.15
☐	237	Pat Peake, Wsh.	.15
☐	238	Michal Pivonka, Wsh.	.15
☐	239	Rick Tabaracci (G), Wsh.	.15
☐	240	Tim Cheveldae (G), Wpg.	.15
☐	241	Dallas Drake, Wpg.	.15
☐	242	Nelson Emerson, Wpg.	.15
☐	243	Dave Manson, Wpg.	.15
☐	244	Teppo Numminen, Wpg.	.15
☐	245	Stéphane Quintal, Wpg.	.15
☐	246	Teemu Selänne, Wpg.	.75
☐	247	Keith Tkachuk, Wpg.	.35
☐	248	Checklist	.15
☐	249	Checklist	.15
☐	250	Checklist	.15
☐	251	John Lilley, Ana.	.15
☐	**252**	**Mikhail Shtalenkov (G), Ana., RC**	**.15**
☐	253	Garry Valk, Ana.	.15
☐	**254**	**John Gruden, Bos., RC**	**.15**
☐	255	Brent Hughes, Bos.	.15
☐	256	Al Iafrate, Bos.	.15
☐	257	Alexei Kasatonov, Bos.	.15
☐	258	Mikko Makela, Bos.	.15
☐	259	Marc Potvin, Bos.	.15
☐	**260**	**Jon Rohloff, Bos., RC**	**.15**
☐	261	Jozef Stumpel, Bos.	.15
☐	262	Grant Fuhr (G), Buf.	.25
☐	263	Viktor Gordiouk, Buf.	.15
☐	264	Yuri Khmylev, Buf.	.15
☐	265	Craig Muni, Buf.	.15
☐	266	Craig Simpson, Buf.	.15
☐	**267**	**Denis Tsygurov, Buf., RC**	**.15**
☐	268	Steve Chiasson, Cgy.	.15
☐	269	Phil Housley, Cgy.	.15
☐	270	Joel Otto, Cgy.	.15
☐	271	Andrei Trefilov (G), Cgy.	.15
☐	272	Vesa Viitakoski, Cgy.	.15
☐	273	Tony Amonte, Chi.	.25
☐	274	Brent Grieve, Chi.	.15
☐	275	Bernie Nicholls, Chi.	.15
☐	276	Christian Soucy, Chi.	.15
☐	277	Paul Ysebaert, Chi.	.15
☐	278	Shane Churla, Dal.	.15
☐	279	Russ Courtnall, Dal.	.15
☐	280	Craig Ludwig, Dal.	.15
☐	281	Jarkko Varvio, Dal.	.15
☐	282	Darcy Wakaluk (G), Dal.	.15
☐	283	Greg Johnson, Det.	.15
☐	284	Vyaheslav Kozlov, Det.	.15
☐	285	Martin Lapointe, Det.	.15
☐	**286**	**Tim Taylor, Det., RC**	**.15**
☐	287	Mike Vernon (G), Det.	.25
☐	**288**	**Jason York, Det., RC**	**.15**
☐	**289**	**Fred Brathwaite (G), Edm., RC**	**.15**
☐	290	Kelly Buchberger, Edm.	.15
☐	291	Shayne Corson, Edm.	.25
☐	292	Dean McAmmond, Edm.	.15
☐	293	Vladimir Vujtek, Edm.	.15
☐	294	Doug Barrault, Fla.	.15
☐	295	Keith Brown, Fla.	.15
☐	296	Mark Fitzpatrick (G), Fla.	.15
☐	297	Mike Hough, Fla.	.15
☐	298	Scott Mellanby, Fla.	.15
☐	299	Jimmy Carson, Hfd.	.15
☐	300	Andrew Cassels, Hfd.	.15
☐	301	Andrei Nikolishin, Hfd.	.15
☐	302	Steven Rice, Hfd.	.15
☐	303	Glen Wesley, Hfd.	.15
☐	304	Rob Brown, L.A.	.15
☐	305	Tony Granato, L.A.	.15
☐	306	Wayne Gretzky, L.A.	2.50
☐	307	Dan Quinn, L.A.	.15
☐	308	Darryl Sydor, L.A.	.15
☐	309	Rick Tocchet, L.A.	.15
☐	**310**	**Donald Brashear, Mtl., RC**	**.15**
☐	311	Valeri Bure, Mtl.	.15
☐	312	Jim Montgomery, Mtl.	.15
☐	313	Kirk Muller, Mtl.	.15
☐	314	Oleg Petrov, Mtl.	.15
☐	315	Peter Popovic, Mtl.	.15
☐	316	Yves Racine, Mtl.	.15
☐	317	Turner Stevenson, Mtl.	.15
☐	318	Ken Daneyko, N.J.	.15
☐	319	David Emma, N.J.	.15
☐	320	Brian Rolston, N.J.	.15
☐	321	Alexander Semak, N.J.	.15
☐	322	Jason Smith, N.J.	.15
☐	323	Chris Terreri (G), N.J.	.15
☐	324	Ray Ferraro, NYI.	.15
☐	325	Derek King, NYI.	.15
☐	326	Scott Lachance, NYI.	.15
☐	327	Brett Lindros, NYI.	.15
☐	328	Jamie McLennan (G), NYI.	.25
☐	320	Zigmund Palffy, NYI.	.35
☐	330	Corey Hirsch (G), NYR.	.15
☐	331	Alexei Kovalev, NYR.	.15
☐	332	Stéphane Matteau, NYR.	.15
☐	333	Petr Nedved, NYR.	.15
☐	334	Mattias Norstrom, NYR.	.15
☐	335	Mark Osbourne, NYR.	.15
☐	336	Randy Cunneyworth, Ott.	.15
☐	337	Pavol Demitra, Ott.	.15
☐	338	Pat Elynuik, Ott.	.15
☐	339	Sean Hill, Ott.	.15
☐	340	Darrin Madeley (G), Ott.	.15
☐	341	Sylvain Turgeon, Ott.	.15
☐	342	Vladislav Boulin, Pha.	.15
☐	343	Ron Hextall (G), Pha.	.25
☐	344	Patrik Juhlin, Pha.	.15
☐	345	Eric Lindros, Pha.	2.00
☐	346	Shjon Podein, Pha.	.15
☐	347	Chris Therien, Pha.	.15
☐	348	John Cullen, Pgh.	.15
☐	349	Markus Naslund, Pgh.	.15
☐	350	Luc Robitaille, Pgh.	.25
☐	351	Kjell Samuelsson, Pgh.	.15
☐	352	Tomas Sandström, Pgh.	.15
☐	353	Ken Wregget (G), Pgh.	.15
☐	354	Wendel Clark, Que.	.25
☐	355	Adam Deadmarsh, Que.	.25
☐	356	Peter Forsberg, Que.	2.00
☐	357	Valeri Kamensky, Que.	.25
☐	358	Uwe Krupp, Que.	.15
☐	359	Janne Laukkanen, Que.	.15
☐	360	Sylvain Lefebvre, Que.	.15
☐	361	Jocelyn Thibault (G), Que.	.35
☐	362	Bill Houlder, Stl.	.15
☐	363	Craig Janney, Stl.	.15
☐	364	Pat Falloon, S.J.	.25
☐	365	Jeff Friesen, S.J.	.15
☐	366	Viktor Kozlov, S.J.	.35
☐	367	Andrei Nazarov, S.J.	.15
☐	368	Jeff Odgers, S.J.	.15
☐	369	Michal Sykora, S.J.	.15
☐	370	Mikael Andersson, T.B.	.15
☐	371	Eric Charron, T.B.	.15
☐	372	Chris Lipuma, T.B.	.15

	No.	Player	NRMT-MT
☐	373	Denis Savard, T.B.	.25
☐	374	Jason Wiemer, T.B.	.15
☐	375	Nikolai Borschevsky, Tor.	.15
☐	**376**	**Eric Fichaud (G), Tor., RC**	**.50**
☐	377	Kenny Jonsson, Tor.	.15
☐	378	Mike Ridley, Tor.	.15
☐	379	Mats Sundin, Tor.	.50
☐	380	Greg Adams, Van.	.15
☐	381	Shawn Antoski, Van.	.15
☐	382	Geoff Courtnall, Van.	.15
☐	383	Martin Gelinas, Van.	.15
☐	384	Sergio Momesso, Van.	.15
☐	385	Jiri Slegr, Van.	.15
☐	386	Jason Allison, Wsh.	.35
☐	387	Don Beaupré (G), Wsh.	.15
☐	388	Joé Juneau, Wsh.	.15
☐	389	Steve Konowalchuk, Wsh.	.15
☐	390	Kelly Miller, Wsh.	.15
☐	391	Dave Poulin, Wsh.	.15
☐	392	Tie Domi, Wpg.	.15
☐	393	Michal Grosek, Wpg.	.15
☐	394	Russ Romaniuk, Wpg.	.15
☐	395	Darrin Shannon, Wpg.	.15
☐	396	Thomas Steen, Wpg.	.15
☐	397	Igor Ulanov, Wpg.	.15
☐	398	Alexei Zhamnov, Wpg.	.25
☐	399	Checklist #1 (251-353)	.15
☐	400	Checklist #2 (354-400)	.15

ALL-ROOKIE SERIES

Insert Set (10 cards): **95.00**

	No.	Player	NRMT-MT
☐	1	Jason Arnott, Edm.	8.00
☐	2	Martin Brodeur (G), N.J.	40.00
☐	3	Alexandre Daigle, Ott.	8.00
☐	4	Chris Gratton, T.B.	8.00
☐	5	Boris Mironov, Edm.	5.00
☐	6	Derek Plante, Buf.	5.00
☐	7	Chris Pronger, Hfd.	8.00
☐	8	Mikael Renberg, Pha.	8.00
☐	9	Bryan Smolinshi, Bos.	5.00
☐	10	Alexei Yashin, Ott.	15.00

GLOBAL GREATS

Series Two Insert Set (10 cards): **115.00**

	No.	Player	NRMT-MT
☐	1	Sergei Fedorov, Det.	15.00
☐	2	Dominik Hasek (G), Buf.	20.00
☐	3	Arturs Irbe (G), S.J.	5.00
☐	4	Jaromir Jagr, Pgh.	30.00
☐	5	Jari Kurri, L.A.	8.00
☐	6	Alexander Mogilny, Buf.	10.00
☐	7	Petr Nedved, NYR.	5.00
☐	8	Mikael Renberg, Pha.	8.00
☐	9	Teemu Selänne, Wpg.	20.00
☐	10	Alexei Yashin, Ott.	12.00

NHL ALL-STARS

Series One Insert Set (12 cards): **10.00**

	No.	Player	NRMT-MT
☐	1	Ray Bourque, Bos.	.75
☐	2	Brian Leetch, NYR.	.50
☐	3	Eric Lindros, Pha.	2.00
☐	4	Mark Messier, NYR.	1.75
☐	5	Alexander Mogilny, Buf.	.50
☐	6	Patrick Roy (G), Mtl.	2.50
☐	7	Pavel Bure, Van.	1.00
☐	8	Chris Chelios, Chi.	.50
☐	9	Paul Coffey, Det.	.50
☐	10	Wayne Gretzky, L.A.	3.00
☐	11	Brett Hull, Stl.	.75
☐	12	Félix Potvin (G), Tor.	.75

NHL AWARD WINNERS

Series One Insert Set (8 cards): **12.00**

	No.	Player	NRMT-MT
☐	1	Ray Bourque, Bos.	1.50
☐	2	Martin Brodeur (G), N.J.	2.00
☐	3	Sergei Fedorov, Det.	1.50
☐	4	Adam Graves, NYR.	.50
☐	5	Wayne Gretzky, L.A.	6.00
☐	6	Dominik Hasek (G), Buf.	2.00
☐	7	Brian Leetch, NYR.	1.00
☐	8	Cam Neely, Bos.	.50

SERGEI FEDOROV HIGHLIGHTS

Series One Insert Set (12 cards): **15.00**
Autographed Sergei Fedorov card: **175.00**

	No.	Player	NRMT-MT
☐	1	Sergei Fedorov	1.50
☐	2	Sergei Fedorov	1.50
☐	3	Sergei Fedorov	1.50
☐	4	Sergei Fedorov	1.50
☐	5	Sergei Fedorov	1.50
☐	6	Sergei Fedorov	1.50
☐	7	Sergei Fedorov	1.50
☐	8	Sergei Fedorov	1.50
☐	9	Sergei Fedorov	1.50
☐	10	Sergei Fedorov	1.50
☐	11	Sergei Fedorov Mail-In	2.50
☐	12	Sergei Fedorov Mail-In	2.50

PREMIER PAD MEN

Series One Insert Set (6 cards): **55.00**

	No.	Player	NRMT-MT
☐	1	Dominik Hasek (G), Buf.	12.00
☐	2	Arturs Irbe (G), S.J.	4.00
☐	3	Curtis Joseph (G), Stl.	10.00
☐	4	Félix Potvin (G), Tor.	7.50
☐	5	Mike Richter (G), NYR.	5.00
☐	6	Patrick Roy (G), Mtl.	25.00

PREMIER PIVOTS

Series Two Insert Set (10 cards): **18.00**

	No.	Player	NRMT-MT
☐	1	Jason Arnott, Edm.	.50
☐	2	Sergei Fedorov, Det.	1.50
☐	3	Doug Gilmour, Tor.	1.00
☐	4	Wayne Gretzky, L.A.	6.00
☐	5	Pat LaFontaine, Buf.	.50
☐	6	Eric Lindros, Pha.	4.00
☐	7	Mark Messier, NYR.	1.50
☐	8	Mike Modano, Dal.	1.50
☐	9	Adam Oates, Bos.	1.00
☐	10	Steve Yzerman, Det.	3.00

ULTRA PROSPECT

Series Two Insert Set (10 cards): **50.00**

	No.	Player	NRMT-MT
☐	1	Peter Forsberg, Que.	15.00
☐	2	Todd Harvey, Dal.	2.50
☐	3	Paul Kariya, Ana.	20.00
☐	4	Viktor Kozlov, S.J.	2.50
☐	5	Bret Lindros, NYI.	2.50
☐	6	Michael Peca, Van.	5.00
☐	7	Brian Rolston, N.J.	2.50
☐	8	Jamie Storr (G), L.A.	5.00
☐	9	Oleg Tverdovsky, Ana.	2.50
☐	10	Jason Wiemer, T.B.	2.50

RED LIGHT SPECIALS

Series Two Insert Set (10 cards): **18.00**

	No.	Player	NRMT-MT
☐	1	Dave Andreychuk, Tor.	1.00
☐	2	Pavel Bure, Van.	4.00
☐	3	Mike Gartner, Tor.	1.00
☐	4	Adam Graves, NYR.	1.00
☐	5	Brett Hull, Stl.	3.00
☐	6	Cam Neely, Bos.	1.00
☐	7	Gary Roberts, Cgy.	1.00
☐	8	Teemu Selänne, Wpg.	4.00
☐	9	Brendan Shanahan, Stl.	3.50
☐	10	Kevin Stevens, Pgh.	1.00

SCORING KINGS

Series One Insert Set (7 cards): **25.00**

	No.	Player	NRMT-MT
☐	1	Pavel Bure, Van.	3.00
☐	2	Sergei Fedorov, Det.	2.00
☐	3	Doug Gilmour, Tor.	1.25
☐	4	Wayne Gretzky, L.A.	8.00
☐	5	Mario Lemieux, Pgh.	6.50
☐	6	Eric Lindros, Pha.	5.00
☐	7	Steve Yzerman, Det.	4.00

SPEED MERCHANTS

Series Two Insert Set (10 cards): **10.00**

	No.	Player	NRMT-MT
☐	1	Pavel Bure, Van.	3.00
☐	2	Russ Courtnall, Dal.	.50
☐	3	Sergei Fedorov, Det.	2.00
☐	4	Al lafrate, Bos.	.50
☐	5	Pat Lafontaine, Buf.	.50
☐	6	Brian Leetch, NYR.	1.00
☐	7	Mike Modano, Dal.	2.00
☐	8	Alexander Mogilny,Buf.	1.00
☐	9	Jeremy Roenick, Chi.	1.00
☐	10	Geoff Sanderson, Hfd.	.50

ULTRA POWER

Series One Insert Set (10 cards): **40.00**

	No.	Player	NRMT-MT
☐	1	Dave Andreychuk, Tor.	2.50
☐	2	Jason Arnott, Edm.	2.50
☐	3	Chris Gratton, T.B.	2.50
☐	4	Adam Graves, NYR.	2.50
☐	5	Eric Lindros, Pha.	15.00
☐	6	Cam Neely, Bos.	2.50
☐	7	Mikael Renberg, Pha.	2.50
☐	8	Jeremy Roenick, Chi.	3.50
☐	9	Brendan Shanahan, Stl.	7.50
☐	10	Keith Tkachuk, Wpg.	5.00

1994 - 95 HOCKEY HALL OF FAME LEGENDS

Artwork by Doug West.
Card Size: 3 1/2" x 5 1/2"
Imprint:
Series Three Set (18 cards): **135.00**
Common Player: **8.00**

	No.	Player	NRMT-MT
☐	37	Red Storey	11.00
☐	38	Harry Oliver	8.00
☐	39	Tony Esposito	12.00
☐	40	Milt Schmidt	10.00
☐	41	Ivan Johnson	8.00
☐	42	Brad Park	11.00
☐	43	Frank Mahovlich	13.00
☐	44	Syd Howe	8.00

☐	45	Woody Dumart	10.00
☐	46	Jean Béliveau	14.00
☐	47	Jack Walker	8.00
☐	48	Frank Patrick	8.00
☐	49	Hap Holmes	8.00
☐	50	Elmer Lach	10.00
☐	51	Cecil Dye	8.00
☐	52	Sir Montagu Allan	8.00
☐	53	Red Kelly	10.00
☐	54	Marcel Dionne	11.00

1994 - 95 INCOMNET PHONE CARDS

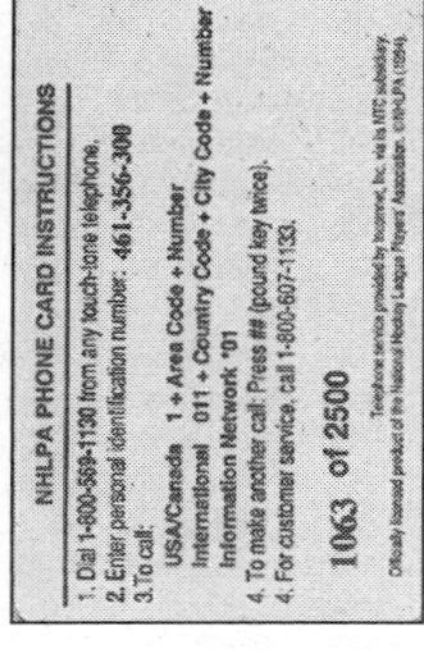

These $20 (U.S.) phone cards were issued by Incomnet. The NHLPA - licensed cards feature photos from the 1994 Four on Four Challenge. Prices are for unused telecards.

Imprint:

	Player	NRMT-MT
☐	Doug Gilmour, Post/Ontario	20.00
☐	Brett Hull, Radio Shack/U.S.A.	25.00
☐	Paul Kariya, Microplay/West	35.00
☐	Eric Lindros, Post/Ontario	35.00
☐	Luc Robitaille, Kraft/Québec	20.00
☐	Jeremy Roenick, Radio Shack/U.S.A.	20.00
☐	Patrick Roy (G), Kraft/Québec	40.00
☐	John Vanbiesbrouck (G), Radio Shack/U.S.A.	28.00
☐	Team Ontario	20.00

1994 - 95 KENNER STARTING LINEUP

The card was a 93-94 Score card with a "Starting Lineup" logo on the front.

Imprint: 1994 NHLPA

Canadian Set (13 figurines): 250.00

American Set (20 figurines): 400.00

	Player	U.S.	Cdn.
☐	Tom Barrasso (G), Buf.	40.00	–
☐	Ray Bourque, Bos.	30.00	–
☐ ☐	Pavel Bure, Van.	20.00	18.00
☐ ☐	Sergei Fedorov, Det.	22.00	20.00
☐	Grant Fuhr (G), Buf.	–	85.00
☐ ☐	Doug Gilmour, Tor.	18.00	15.00
☐	Brett Hull, Stl.	15.00	–
☐	Arturs Irbe (G), S.J.	40.00	–
☐	Jaromir Jagr, Pgh.	22.00	–
☐	Pat LaFontaine, Buf.	18.00	–
☐ ☐	Brian Leetch, NYR.	18.00	15.00
☐ ☐	Mario Lemieux, Pgh.	30.00	22.00
☐ ☐	Eric Lindros, Pha.	35.00	25.00
☐	Mark Messier, NYR.	60.00	–
☐ ☐	Alexander Mogilny, Buf.	20.00	18.00
☐ ☐	Adam Oates, Bos.	20.00	18.00
☐ ☐	Mike Richter (G), NYR.	40.00	35.00
☐ ☐	Luc Robitaille, L.A.	25.00	18.00
☐	Jeremy Roenick, Chi.	20.00	–
☐ ☐	Teemu Selänne, Wpg.	25.00	22.00
☐ ☐	Steve Yzerman, Det.	25.00	20.00

1994 - 95 KRAFT

Imprint:

Complete Set (108 cards): 100.00

Album: 40.00

MASKED DEFENDERS

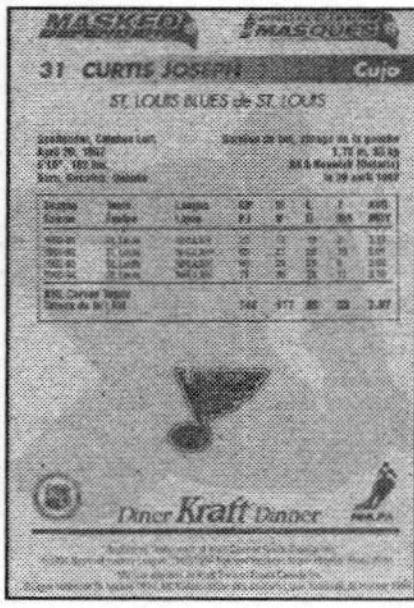

One of 26 different cards was found on the back of specially marked Kraft Dinner.

Card Size: 3" x 5"

	Player	NRMT-MT
☐	Tom Barrasso (G), Pgh.	1.50
☐	Don Beaupré (G), Wsh.	1.50
☐	Ed Belfour (G), Chi.	2.00
☐	Craig Billington (G), Ott.	1.50
☐	Martin Brodeur (G), N.J.	3.50
☐	Sean Burke (G), Hfd.	1.50
☐	Tim Cheveldae (G), Wpg.	1.50
☐	Stéphane Fiset (G), Que.	1.50
☐	Dominik Hasek (G), Buf.	3.50
☐	Guy Hebert (G), Ana.	1.50
☐	Ron Hextall (G), Pha.	1.50
☐	Kelly Hrudey (G), L.A.	1.50
☐	Arturs Irbe (G), S.J.	1.50
☐	Curtis Joseph (G), Edm.	3.00
☐	Trevor Kidd (G), Cgy.	1.50
☐	Kirk McLean (G), Van.	1.50
☐	Jamie McLennan (G), NYI.	1.50
☐	Andy Moog (G), Dal.	1.50
☐	Félix Potvin (G), Tor.	2.50
☐	Darren Puppa (G), T.B.	1.50
☐	Bill Ranford (G), Edm.	1.50
☐	Mike Richter (G), NYR.	2.00
☐	Vincent Riendeau (G), Bos.	1.50
☐	Patrick Roy (G), Mtl.	6.00
☐	John Vanbiesbrouck (G), Fla.	3.00
☐	Mike Vernon (G), Det.	1.50

AWARD WINNERS & ALL-STARS

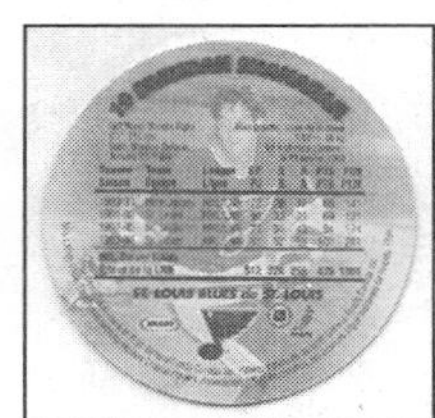

Two of 16 different disks were found under caps of specially marked Kraft Peanut Butter.

Disk Diameter: 2 3/4"

	Player	NRMT-MT
☐	Ray Bourque, Bos.	2.50
☐	Martin Brodeur (G), Buf.	3.00
☐	Sergei Fedorov, Det.	2.50
☐	Adam Graves, NYR.	1.50
☐	Wayne Gretzky, L.A.	8.00
☐	Dominik Hasek (G), Buf.	3.00
☐	Brian Leetch, NYR.	2.00
☐	Jacques Lemaire, N.J.	2.00
☐	Cam Neely, Bos.	1.50
☐	New York Rangers	2.50
☐	Ray Bourque, Bos.	1.50
☐	Pavel Bure, Van.	3.00
☐	Sergei Fedorov, Det.	2.50
☐	Domink Hasek (G), Buf.	3.00
☐	Brendan Shanahan, Stl.	2.75
☐	Scott Stevens, N.J.	1.50

SHARP SHOOTERS

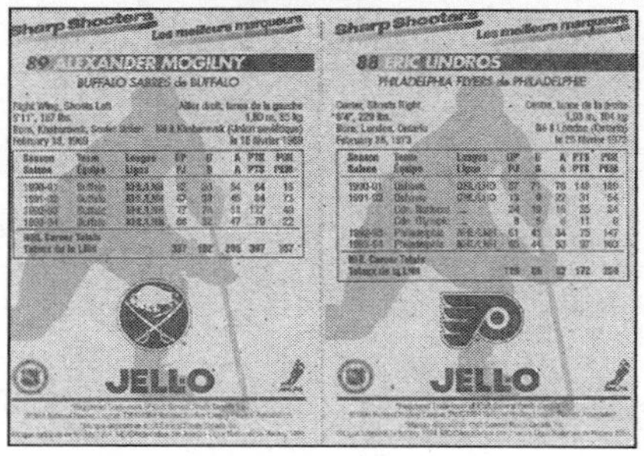

Two of 16 different cards was found under the tops of specially marked JELL-O pudding.

	Player	NRMT-MT
☐	Jason Arnott, Edm.	1.00
☐	Vincent Damphousse, Mtl.	1.00
☐	Doug Gilmour, Tor.	1.00
☐	Craig Janney, Stl.	1.00
☐	Joé Juneau, Wsh.	1.00
☐	Trevor Linden, Van.	1.00
☐	Eric Lindros, Pha.	3.50
☐	Mark Messier, NYR.	2.00
☐	Mike Modano, Dal.	2.00
☐	Alexander Mogilny, Buf.	1.00
☐	Adam Oates, Bos.	1.00
☐	Robert Reichel, Cgy.	1.00
☐	Jeremy Roenick, Chi.	1.00
☐	Joe Sakic, Que.	2.50
☐	Keith Tkachuk, Wpg.	1.50
☐	Alexei Yashin, Ott.	1.50

HOCKEY HEROES

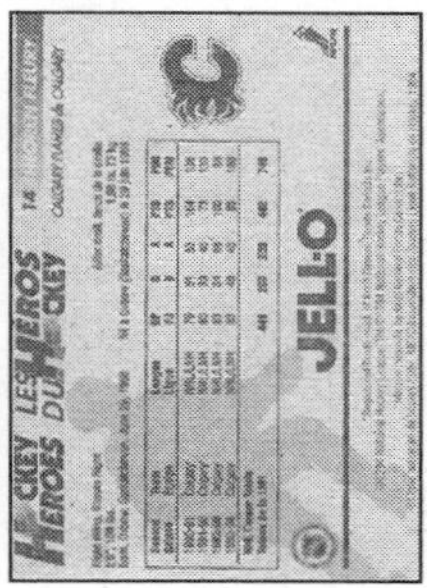

One of 14 different cards were found on the backs of specially marked boxes of JELL-O instant pudding.

Card Size: 3" x 4 1/4"

	Player	NRMT-MT
☐	Dave Andreychuk, Tor.	1.00
☐	Chris Chelios, Chi.	1.00
☐	Wendel Clark, Tor.	1.00
☐	Theoren Fleury, Cgy.	1.00
☐	Wayne Gretzky, L.A.	6.00
☐	Al Iafrate, Bos.	1.00
☐	Brett Hull, Stl.	2.00
☐	Jaromir Jagr, Pgh.	3.00
☐	Pat LaFontaine, Buf.	1.00
☐	Kirk Muller, Mtl.	1.00
☐	Mark Recchi, Mtl.	1.00
☐	Gary Roberts, Cgy.	1.00
☐	Mats Sundin, Tor.	2.00
☐	Steve Yzerman, Det.	3.00

1994 - 95 KRAFT JUMBO MASKS

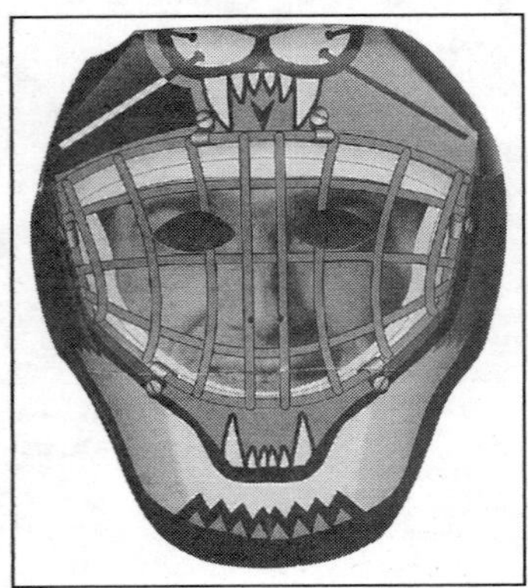

	Player	NRMT-MT
☐	Ed Belfour (G), Chi.	1.50
☐	Guy Hebert (G), Ana.	1.00
☐	Curtis Joseph (G), Stl.	2.50
☐	Andy Moog (G), Dal.	1.00
☐	Félix Potvin (G), Tor.	2.00
☐	Vincent Riendeau (G), Bos.	1.00
☐	Patrick Roy (G), Mtl.	6.00
☐	John Vanbiesbrouck (G), Fla.	2.50

1994 - 1995 LEAF

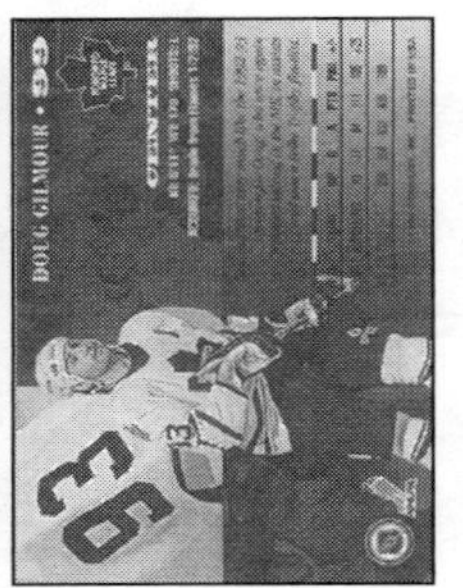

Imprint: © 1994 DONRUSS, INC.

Series One Set (330 cards):	**22.00**
Series Two Set (220 cards):	**18.00**
Common Player:	**.10**
Doug Gilmour Swiss card 8" x 10" (#/2,500):	**30.00**

	No.	Player	NRMT-MT
☐	1	Mario Lemieux, Pgh.	2.00
☐	2	Tony Amonte, Chi.	.25
☐	3	Steve Duchesne, Stl.	.10
☐	4	Glen Murray, Bos.	.10
☐	5	John LeClair, Mtl.	.50
☐	6	Glen Wesley, Bos.	.10
☐	7	Chris Chelios, Chi.	.35
☐	8	Alexei Zhitnik, L.A.	.10
☐	9	Mike Modano, Dal.	.50
☐	10	Pavel Bure, Van.	.75
☐	11	Mark Messier, NYR.	.50
☐	12	Rob Blake, L.A.	.25
☐	13	Tony Twist, Que.	.10
☐	14	Glenn Anderson, NYR.	.10
☐	**15**	**Keith Redmond, L.A., RC**	**.10**
☐	16	Brett Hull, Stl.	.50
☐	17	Valeri Zelepukin, N.J.	.10
☐	18	Mike Richter (G), NYR.	.25
☐	19	Alexei Yashin, Ott.	.35
☐	20	Luc Robitaille, L.A.	.25
☐	21	Tim Sweeney, Ana.	.10
☐	22	Ted Drury, Hfd.	.10
☐	23	Guy Carbonneau, Mtl.	.10
☐	24	Stéphane Richer, N.J.	.10
☐	25	Ulf Dahlen, S.J.	.10
☐	**26**	**Fred Braithwaite (G), Edm., RC**	**.10**
☐	27	Darius Kasparaitis, NYI.	.10
☐	28	Kris Draper, Det.	.10
☐	29	Alexander Godynyuk, Hfd.	.10
☐	30	Brent Sutter, Chi.	.10
☐	31	Josef Beranek, Pha.	.10
☐	32	Stéphane Matteau, NYR.	.10
☐	33	Derek Plante, Buf.	.10
☐	34	Vesa Viitakoski, Cgy.	.10
☐	35	Dave Ellett, Tor.	.10
☐	36	Martin Straka, Pgh.	.10
☐	37	Dimitri Yushkevich, Pha.	.10
☐	38	John Tucker, T.B.	.10
☐	39	Rob Gaudreau, S.J.	.10
☐	40	Doug Weight, Edm.	.35
☐	41	Patrick Roy (G), Mtl.	2.00
☐	42	Brian Bradley, T.B.	.10
☐	43	Bob Beers, Edm.	.10
☐	44	Dino Ciccarelli, Det.	.25
☐	45	Dean Evason, Dal.	.10
☐	46	Ron Tugnutt (G), Mtl.	.10
☐	47	Andy Moog (G), Dal.	.25
☐	48	Jason Dawe, Buf.	.10
☐	49	Ted Donato, Bos.	.10
☐	50	Ron Hextall (G), NYI.	.25
☐	51	Derek Armstrong, NYI.	.10
☐	52	Craig Janney, Stl.	.10
☐	53	Geoff Courtnall, Van.	.10
☐	54	Mikael Renberg, Pha.	.25
☐	55	Theoren Fleury, Cgy.	.35
☐	56	Martin Brodeur (G), N.J.	.75
☐	**57**	**Mattias Norstrom, NYR., RC**	**.10**
☐	58	David Sacco, Tor.	.10
☐	59	Jeff Reese (G), Hfd.	.10
☐	60	Bill Ranford (G), Edm.	.25
☐	61	Dan Quinn, Ott.	.10
☐	62	Joé Juneau, Wsh.	.10
☐	63	Jeremy Roenick, Chi.	.35
☐	64	Donald Audette, Buf.	.10
☐	65	Zdeno Ciger, Edm.	.10
☐	66	Cliff Ronning, Van.	.10
☐	67	Steve Thomas, NYI.	.10
☐	68	Norm Maciver, Ott.	.10
☐	69	Vincent Damphousse, Mtl.	.35
☐	70	John Vanbiesbrouck (G), Fla.	.60
☐	71	Andrei Kovalenko, Que.	.10
☐	72	Dave Andreychuk, Tor.	.10
☐	73	Stu Barnes, Fla.	.10
☐	74	Jamie McLennan (G), NYI.	.25
☐	75	Rudy Poeschek, T.B.	.10
☐	76	Ken Wregget (G), Pgh.	.10
☐	77	Ray Bourque, Bos.	.50
☐	78	Grant Fuhr (G), Buf.	.25
☐	79	Paul Cavallini, Dal.	.10
☐	80	Nelson Emerson, Wpg.	.10
☐	81	Tim Cheveldae (G), Wpg.	.10
☐	**82**	**Mariusz Czerkawski, Bos., RC**	**.10**
☐	83	Pat Peake, Wsh.	.10
☐	84	Craig Billington (G), Ott.	.10
☐	85	Sean Burke (G), Hfd.	.25
☐	86	Chris Gratton, T.B.	.25
☐	87	Andrei Trefilov (G), Cgy.	.10
☐	88	Terry Yake, Ana.	.10
☐	89	Mark Recchi, Pha.	.25
☐	90	Igor Korolev, Stl.	.10
☐	91	Mark Tinordi, Dal.	.10
☐	92	Alexei Kovalev, NYR.	.10
☐	93	Bob Essensa (G), Det.	.10
☐	94	Keith Tkachuk, Wpg.	.35
☐	95	Pat Falloon, S.J.	.10
☐	96	John Slaney, Wsh.	.10
☐	97	Alexei Zhamnov, Wpg.	.25
☐	98	Jeff Norton, S.J.	.10
☐	99	Doug Gilmour, Tor.	.35
☐	100	Rick Tocchet, Pgh.	.10
☐	101	Robert Kron, Hfd.	.10
☐	102	Patrik Carnback, Ana.	.10
☐	103	Tom Barrasso (G), Pgh.	.25
☐	104	Jari Kurri, L.A.	.25
☐	105	Iain Fraser, Que.	.10
☐	106	Mike Donnelly, L.A.	.10
☐	107	Ray Sheppard, Det.	.10
☐	108	Scott Young, Que.	.10
☐	109	Kirk McLean (G), Van.	.25
☐	110	Checklist #1 (1-83)	.10
☐	111	Sergei Zubov, NYR.	.25
☐	112	Ivan Droppa, Chi.	.10
☐	113	Brendan Shanahan, Stl.	.60
☐	114	Michal Pivonka, Wsh.	.10
☐	115	Pavol Demitra, Ott.	.10
☐	116	Doug Brown, Pgh.	.10
☐	117	Valeri Kamensky, Que.	.25
☐	118	Alexander Karpovtsev, NYR.	.10
☐	119	Alexandre Daigle, Ott.	.25
☐	120	Dominik Hasek (G), Buf.	.75
☐	121	Murray Craven, Van.	.10
☐	122	Michal Sykora, S.J.	.10
☐	123	Aris Brimanis, Pha.	.10
☐	124	Benoît Hogue, NYI.	.10
☐	125	Arto Blomsten, Wpg.	.10
☐	126	Russ Courtnall, Dal.	.10
☐	127	Bryan Marchment, Hfd.	.10
☐	128	Jeff Hackett (G), Chi.	.25
☐	129	Kevin Miller, Stl.	.10
☐	130	Bryan Smolinski, Bos.	.10
☐	131	John Druce, L.A.	.10
☐	132	Roman Hamrlik, T.B.	.25
☐	133	Jason Arnott, Edm.	.25
☐	134	Chris Terreri (G), N.J.	.10
☐	135	Mike Gartner, Tor.	.25
☐	136	Daryl Sydor, L.A.	.10
☐	137	Lyle Odelein, Mtl.	.10
☐	138	Martin Gelinas, Van.	.10
☐	139	Mike Rathje, S.J.	.10
☐	140	Sylvain Côté, Wsh.	.10
☐	141	Nicklas Lidstrom, Det.	.25
☐	142	Guy Hebert (G), Ana.	.25
☐	143	Jozef Stumpel, Bos.	.25
☐	144	Owen Nolan, Que.	.25
☐	145	Jesse Belanger, Fla.	.10
☐	146	Bill Guerin, N.J.	.25
☐	147	Mike Stapleton, Edm.	.10
☐	148	Steve Yzerman, Det.	1.25
☐	149	Michael Nylander, Cgy.	.10
☐	150	Rod Brind'Amour, Pha.	.25
☐	151	Jaromir Jagr, Pgh.	1.25
☐	152	Darcy Wakaluk (G), Dal.	.10
☐	153	Sergei Nemchinov, NYR.	.10
☐	154	Wes Walz, Cgy.	.10
☐	155	Sergei Fedorov, Det.	.50
☐	156	Daniel Laperrière, Stl.	.10
☐	157	Marty McInnis, NYI.	.10
☐	158	Chris Joseph, T.B.	.10
☐	159	Matt Martin, Tor.	.10
☐	160	Checklist #2 (84-166)	.10
☐	**161**	**Denis Tsygurov, Buf., RC**	**.10**
☐	162	Stéphan Lebeau, Ana.	.10
☐	163	Kirk Muller, NYI.	.10
☐	164	Shayne Corson, Edm.	.25
☐	165	Joe Sakic, Que.	1.00
☐	166	Denis Savard, Chi.	.25
☐	167	Kevin Dineen, Pha.	.10
☐	168	Paul Coffey, Det.	.25
☐	169	Sandis Ozolinsh, S.J.	.25
☐	170	Stewart Malgunas, Pha.	.10
☐	171	Peter Klima, T.B.	.10
☐	172	Pat Verbeek, Hfd.	.10
☐	173	Yan Kaminsky, NYI.	.10
☐	174	Marty McSorley, L.A.	.10
☐	175	Arturs Irbe (G), S.J.	.10
☐	176	Peter Popovic, Mtl.	.10
☐	177	Brian Skrudland, Fla.	.10
☐	178	John Lilley, Ana.	.10
☐	179	Boris Mironov, Edm.	.10
☐	180	Garth Snow (G), Que.	.10
☐	181	Alexei Kudashov, Tor.	.10
☐	182	Scott Mellanby, Fla.	.10
☐	183	Dale Hunter, Wsh.	.10
☐	184	Tommy Söderström (G), Pha.	.10
☐	185	Claude Lemieux, N.J.	.10
☐	186	Félix Potvin (G), Tor.	.50
☐	187	Corey Millen, N.J.	.10
☐	188	Derek King, NYI.	.10
☐	189	Kelly Hrudey (G), L.A.	.10
☐	190	Dimitri Khristich, Wsh.	.10
☐	191	Sylvain Turgeon, Ott.	.10
☐	192	John Gruden, Bos.	.10
☐	193	Michael Peca, Van.	.25
☐	194	Vladimir Malakhov, NYI.	.10
☐	195	Mathieu Schneider, Mtl.	.10
☐	196	Jeff Shantz, Chi.	.10
☐	197	Darren McCarty, Det.	.10
☐	198	Craig Simpson, Buf.	.10
☐	199	Jarkko Varvio, Dal.	.10
☐	200	Gino Odjick, Van.	.10

	No.	Card	Value
☐	201	Martin Lapointe, Det.	.10
☐	202	Paul Ysebaert, Chi.	.10
☐	203	Mike McPhee, Dal.	.10
☐	204	John MacLean, N.J.	.10
☐	205	Ulf Samuelsson, Pgh.	.10
☐	206	Garry Valk, Ana.	.10
☐	207	Tomas Sandström, Pgh.	.10
☐	208	Curtis Joseph (G), Stl.	.60
☐	**209**	**Mikhail Shtalenkov (G), Ana., RC**	**.10**
☐	210	Darren Turcotte, NYR	.10
☐	211	Markus Naslund, Pgh.	.10
☐	212	Al Iafrate, Wsh.	.10
☐	213	Jim Storm, Hfd.	.10
☐	214	Dan Plante, NYI.	.10
☐	215	Brad May, Buf.	.10
☐	216	Nathan Lafayette, Van.	.10
☐	217	Brian Noonan, NYR.	.10
☐	218	Brent Hughes, Wpg.	.10
☐	219	Geoff Sanderson, Hfd.	.10
☐	220	Checklist #3 (167-248)	.10
☐	221	Eric Weinrich, Chi.	.10
☐	222	Greg Adams, Van.	.10
☐	223	Dominic Roussel (G), Pha.	.10
☐	224	Daren Puppa (G), T.B.	.10
☐	225	Rob Niedermayer, Fla.	.25
☐	226	Todd Elik, S.J.	.10
☐	227	Donald Brashear, Mtl.	.10
☐	228	Joe Nieuwendyk, Cgy.	.25
☐	229	Tony Granato, L.A.	.10
☐	230	Kirk Maltby, Edm.	.10
☐	231	Jocelyn Thibault (G), Que.	.35
☐	232	Shawn McEachern, Pgh.	.10
☐	233	Teppo Numminen, Wpg.	.10
☐	234	Johan Garpenlov, S.J.	.10
☐	235	Ron Francis, Pgh.	.35
☐	236	Vyacheslav Kozlov, Det.	.10
☐	237	Scott Niedermayer, N.J.	.25
☐	238	Sergei Krivokrasov, Chi.	.10
☐	239	Dave Manson, Wpg.	.10
☐	240	Mike Ricci, Que.	.10
☐	241	Chad Penney, Ott.	.10
☐	242	Calle Johansson, Wsh.	.10
☐	243	Robert Reichel, Cgy.	.25
☐	244	Igor Kravchuk, Edm.	.10
☐	245	Jason Smith, N.J.	.10
☐	246	Neal Broten, Dal.	.10
☐	247	Jeff Brown, Van.	.10
☐	248	Jason Bowen, Pha.	.10
☐	249	Larry Murphy, Pgh.	.25
☐	250	Gord Murphy, Fla.	.10
☐	251	Darrin Shannon, Wpg.	.10
☐	252	Bobby Holik, N.J.	.10
☐	253	Zigmund Palffy, NYI.	.35
☐	254	Dimitri Mironov, Tor.	.10
☐	255	Adam Graves, NYR.	.10
☐	256	Alexander Mogilny, Buf.	.35
☐	257	Steve Smith, Chi.	.10
☐	258	Jim Montgomery, Stl.	.10
☐	259	Danton Cole, T.B.	.10
☐	260	Dave McLlwain, Ott.	.10
☐	261	German Titov, Cgy.	.10
☐	262	Tom Chorske, N.J.	.10
☐	263	Grant Ledyard, Dal.	.10
☐	264	Garry Galley, Pha.	.10
☐	265	Vlastimil Kroupa, S.J.	.10
☐	266	Keith Primeau, Det.	.25
☐	267	Cam Neely, Bos.	.25
☐	268	Chris Pronger, Hfd.	.25
☐	269	Richard Matvichuk, Dal.	.10
☐	270	Steve Larmer, NYR.	.10
☐	271	James Patrick, Cgy.	.10
☐	272	Joel Otto, Cgy.	.10
☐	273	Todd Nelson, Wsh.	.10
☐	274	Joe Sacco, Ana.	.10
☐	275	Jason York, Det.	.10
☐	276	Andrew Cassels, Hfd.	.10
☐	277	Peter Bondra, Wsh.	.35
☐	278	Pat LaFontaine, Buf.	.25
☐	279	Nikolai Borschevsky, Tor.	.10
☐	280	Dave Mackey, Stl.	.10
☐	281	Cameron Stewart, Bos.	.10
☐	282	Sergei Makarov, S.J.	.10
☐	**283**	**Byron Dafoe (G), Wsh., RC**	**.25**
☐	284	Joe Murphy, Chi.	.10
☐	285	Matthew Barnaby, Buf.	.10
☐	286	Derian Hatcher, Dal.	.25
☐	287	Jyrki Lumme, Van.	.10
☐	288	Travis Green, NYI.	.10
☐	289	Milos Holan, Pha.	.10
☐	290	Ed Patterson, Pgh.	.10
☐	291	Randy Burridge, Wsh.	.10
☐	292	Brian Savage, Mtl.	.10
☐	293	Stéphane Quintal, Wpg.	.10
☐	294	Zarley Zalapski, Cgy.	.10
☐	295	Vitali Prokhorov, Stl.	.10
☐	296	Ed Belfour (G), Chi.	.35
☐	297	Yuri Khmylev, Buf.	.10
☐	298	Dean McAmmond, Edm.	.10
☐	299	Bob Corkum, Ana.	.10
☐	300	Darrin Madeley (G), Ott.	.10
☐	301	Brian Bellows, Mtl.	.10
☐	302	Andrei Lomakin, Fla.	.10
☐	303	Anatoli Semenov, Ana.	.10
☐	304	Claude Lapointe, Que.	.10
☐	305	Adam Oates, Bos.	.35
☐	306	Richard Smehlik, Buf.	.10
☐	307	Jim Dowd, N.J.	.10
☐	308	Mark Fitzpatrick (G), Fla.	.10
☐	309	Pierre Sévigny, Mtl.	.10
☐	310	Glenn Healy (G), NYR.	.10
☐	311	Igor Larionov, S.J.	.25
☐	312	Aaron Ward, Det.	.10
☐	313	Dale Hawerchuk, Buf.	.25
☐	314	Bob Kudelski, Fla.	.10
☐	315	Chris Osgood (G), Det.	.35
☐	316	Trent Klatt, Dal.	.10
☐	317	Gary Suter, Chi.	.10
☐	318	Tie Domi, Wpg.	.10
☐	319	Dave Gagner, Dal.	.10
☐	320	Kevin Smyth, Hfd.	.10
☐	321	Philippe Bozon, Stl.	.10
☐	322	Trevor Kidd (G), Cgy.	.25
☐	323	Warren Rychel, L.A.	.10
☐	324	Steven Rice, Edm.	.10
☐	325	Patrice Brisebois, Mtl.	.10
☐	326	Gary Roberts, Cgy.	.25
☐	327	Fredrik Olausson, Edm.	.10
☐	328	Andrei Nazarov, S.J.	.10
☐	329	Stéphane Fiset (G), Que.	.25
☐	330	Checklist #4 (249-330)	.10
☐	331	Fred Knipscheer, Bos.	.10
☐	332	Shawn Chambers, T.B.	.10
☐	333	Kelly Buchberger, Edm.	.10
☐	334	Ray Ferraro, NYI	.10
☐	335	Dirk Graham, Chi.	.10
☐	336	Ken Daneyko, N.J.	.10
☐	337	Mark Lamb, Pha.	.10
☐	338	Shaun Van Allen, Ana.	.10
☐	339	Chris Simon, Que.	.10
☐	340	Brent Gilchrist, Dal.	.10
☐	341	Greg Gilbert, NYR.	.10
☐	342	Brent Severyn, Fla.	.10
☐	343	Craig Berube, Wsh.	.10
☐	344	Randy Moller, Fla.	.10
☐	345	Wayne Gretzky, L.A.	2.50
☐	346	Shawn Anderson, Pha.	.10
☐	347	Mikael Andersson, T.B.	.10
☐	348	Jim Montgomery, Mtl.	.10
☐	349	Scott Pearson, Edm.	.10
☐	350	Kevin Todd, L.A.	.10
☐	351	Ron Sutter, NYI.	.10
☐	352	Paul Kruse, Cgy.	.10
☐	353	Doug Lidster, Stl.	.10
☐	354	Oleg Petrov, Mtl.	.10
☐	355	Greg Johnson, Det.	.10
☐	356	Kevin Stevens, Pgh.	.10
☐	357	Doug Bodger, Buf.	.10
☐	358	Troy Mallette, Ott.	.10
☐	359	Keith Carney, Chi.	.10
☐	360	Petr Nedved, NYR.	.10
☐	361	Mark Janssens, Hfd.	.10
☐	362	Teemu Selänne, Wpg.	.75
☐	363	Scott Stevens, N.J.	.10
☐	364	Shane Churla, Dal.	.10
☐	365	John McIntyre, Van.	.10
☐	366	Geoff Smith, Fla.	.10
☐	367	Pierre Turgeon, NYI.	.25
☐	368	Shawn Burr, Det.	.10
☐	369	Kevin Hatcher, Wsh.	.10
☐	370	Paul Ranheim, Hfd.	.10
☐	371	Kevin Haller, Pha.	.10
☐	372	Scott Lachance, NYI.	.10
☐	373	Craig Muni, Buf.	.10
☐	374	Mike Ridley, Tor.	.10
☐	375	Joby Messier, NYR.	.10
☐	376	Thomas Steen, Wpg.	.10
☐	377	Bruce Driver, N.J.	.10
☐	378	Mike Eastwood, Tor.	.10
☐	379	Brian Benning, Fla.	.10
☐	380	Dallas Drake, Wpg.	.10
☐	381	Patrick Flatley, NYI.	.10
☐	382	Cam Russell, Chi.	.10
☐	383	Bobby Dollas, Ana.	.10
☐	384	Marc Bergevin, T.B.	.10
☐	385	Joe Mullen, Pgh.	.10
☐	386	Chris Dahlquist, Ott.	.10
☐	387	Robert Petrovicky, Hfd.	.10
☐	388	Yves Racine, Mtl.	.10
☐	389	Adam Bennett, Edm.	.10
☐	390	Patrick Poulin, Chi.	.10
☐	391	Vladimir Konstantinov, Det.	.10
☐	392	Frantisek Kucera, Hfd.	.10
☐	393	Petr Svoboda, Buf.	.10
☐	394	Mike Sillinger, Det.	.10
☐	395	Kris King, Wpg.	.10
☐	396	Kelly Chase, Stl.	.10
☐	397	Peter Douris, Ana.	.10
☐	398	Bob Errey, S.J.	.10
☐	399	Ron Stern, Cgy.	.10
☐	400	Randy McKay, N.J.	.10
☐	401	Benoît Brunet, Mtl.	.10
☐	402	Gerald Diduck, Van.	.10
☐	403	Brian Leetch, NYR.	.35
☐	404	Stephen Heinze, Bos.	.10
☐	405	Jimmy Waite (G), S.J.	.10
☐	406	Nick Kypreos, NYR.	.10
☐	407	J.J. Daigneault, Mtl.	.10
☐	408	Alexei Gusarov, Que.	.10
☐	409	Paul Broten, Dal.	.10
☐	410	Drake Berehowsky, Tor.	.10
☐	411	Sandy McCarthy, Cgy.	.10
☐	412	John Cullen, Pgh.	.10
☐	413	Dan Quinn, L.A.	.10
☐	414	Dave Lowry, Fla.	.10
☐	415	Eric Lindros, Pha.	1.75
☐	416	Igor Ulanov, Wpg.	.10
☐	417	Bob Sweeney, Buf.	.10
☐	418	Jamie Macoun, Tor.	.10
☐	419	Brian Mullen, NYI.	.10
☐	420	Stephen Leach, Bos.	.10
☐	421	Jamie Baker, S.J.	.10
☐	422	Uwe Krupp, Que.	.10
☐	423	Steve Konowalchuk, Wsh.	.10
☐	424	Craig Ludwig, Dal.	.10
☐	425	Bret Hedican, Van.	.10
☐	426	Steve Dubinsky, Chi.	.10
☐	427	Rob Zamuner, T.B.	.25
☐	428	Dave Brown, Pha.	.10
☐	429	Robert Lang, L.A.	.10
☐	430	Dave Babych, Van.	.10
☐	431	Scott Thornton, Edm.	.10
☐	432	Dave Archibald, Ott.	.10
☐	433	Eric Desjardins, Mtl.	.25
☐	434	Jim Cummins, T.B.	.10
☐	435	Troy Loney, NYI.	.10
☐	436	Bob Carpenter, N.J.	.10
☐	437	Joe Reekie, Wsh.	.10
☐	438	Mike Krushelnyski, Det.	.10
☐	439	Jeff Odgers, S.J.	.10
☐	440	Checklist (331-404)	.10
☐	441	Brian Rolston, N.J.	.10
☐	442	Adam Deadmarsh, Que.	.25
☐	**443**	**Eric Fichaud (G), Tor., RC**	**.50**
☐	444	Michel Petit, L.A.	.10
☐	445	Brett Lindros, NYI	.10
☐	446	Pat Jablonski (G), Tor.	.10
☐	447	Janne Laukkanen, Que.	.10
☐	448	Ray Whitney, S.J.	.10
☐	449	Tom Kurvers, Ana.	.10
☐	450	Phil Housley, Cgy.	.10
☐	451	Viktor Kozlov, S.J.	.10
☐	452	Aaron Gavey, T.B.	.10
☐	453	Doug Zmolek, Dal.	.10
☐	454	Tony Twist, Stl.	.10
☐	455	Paul Kariya, Ana.	2.25

	No.	Player	NRMT-MT
☐	456	Vladislav Boulin, Pha.	.10
☐	457	Kevin Brown, L.A.	.10
☐	458	David Wilkie, Mtl.	.10
☐	459	Jamie Pushor, Det.	.10
☐	460	Glen Wesley, Hfd.	.10
☐	461	Al MacInnis, Stl.	.25
☐	462	Bernie Nicholls, Chi.	.10
☐	463	Luc Robitaille, Pgh.	.25
☐	464	Mike Vernon (G), Det.	.25
☐	465	Alex Cherbayev, S.J.	.10
☐	466	Garth Butcher, Tor.	.10
☐	467	Todd Harvey, Dal.	.10
☐	468	Viktor Gordijuk, Buf.	.10
☐	469	Pat Neaton, Pgh.	.10
☐	470	Jason Muzzatti (G), Cgy.	.10
☐	471	Valeri Bure, Mtl.	.10
☐	472	Kenny Jonsson, Tor.	.10
☐	473	Alexei Kasatonov, Bos.	.10
☐	474	Rick Tocchet, L.A.	.10
☐	475	Peter Forsberg, Que.	2.00
☐	476	Sean Hill, Ott.	.10
☐	477	Steven Rice, Hfd.	.10
☐	478	Dave Roberts, Stl.	.10
☐	**479**	**Justin Hocking, L.A., RC**	**.10**
☐	480	Chris Therien, Pha.	.10
☐	481	Cale Hulse, N.J.	.10
☐	482	Jeff Friesen, S.J.	.10
☐	**483**	**Brandon Convery, Tor., RC**	**.10**
☐	484	Ian Laperrière, Stl.	.10
☐	485	Brent Grieve, Chi.	.10
☐	**486**	**Valeri Karpov, Ana., RC**	**.10**
☐	487	Steve Chiasson, Cgy.	.10
☐	**488**	**Jassen Cullimore, Van., RC**	**.10**
☐	**489**	**Jason Wiemer, T.B., RC**	**.10**
☐	490	Checklist (405-478)	.10
☐	**491**	**Len Barrie, Pgh., RC**	**.10**
☐	492	Turner Stevenson, Mtl.	.10
☐	493	Kelly Kisio, Cgy.	.10
☐	494	Dwayne Norris, Que.	.10
☐	495	Ron Hextall (G), Pha.	.25
☐	496	Jaroslav Modry, N.J.	.10
☐	497	Todd Gill, Tor.	.10
☐	498	Ken Sutton, Buf.	.10
☐	499	Sergio Momesso, Van.	.10
☐	500	Dean Kennedy, Wpg.	.10
☐	501	David Reid, Bos.	.10
☐	502	Jocelyn Lemieux, Hfd.	.10
☐	503	Mark Osborne, NYR.	.10
☐	504	Mike Hough, Fla.	.10
☐	505	Todd Marchant, Edm.	.10
☐	506	Keith Jones, Wsh.	.10
☐	507	Sylvain Lefebvre, Que.	.10
☐	508	Sergei Zholtok, Bos.	.25
☐	**509**	**Jay More, S.J., RC**	**.10**
☐	510	Mike Craig, Tor.	.10
☐	511	Jason Allison, Wsh.	.35
☐	512	Jim Paek, Ott.	.10
☐	513	Chris Tamer, Pgh.	.10
☐	514	Craig MacTavish, Pha.	.10
☐	515	Mikko Mäkelä, Bos.	.10
☐	516	Tom Fitzgerald, Fla.	.10
☐	517	Brent Fedyk, Pha.	.10
☐	518	Don Sweeney, Bos.	.10
☐	519	Kelly Miller, Wsh.	.10
☐	520	Jiri Slegr, Van.	.10
☐	521	Wayne Presley, Buf.	.10
☐	522	Mark Greig, Cgy.	.10
☐	523	Doug Houda, Buf.	.10
☐	524	Kay Whitmore (G), Van.	.10
☐	525	Craig Ferguson, Mtl.	.10
☐	526	Kent Manderville, Tor.	.10
☐	527	Trevor Linden, Van.	.25
☐	528	Jeff Beukeboom, NYR.	.10
☐	529	Adam Foote, Que.	.25
☐	530	Mats Sundin, Tor.	.50
☐	531	Shjon Podein, Pha.	.10
☐	532	Louie DeBrusk, Edm.	.10
☐	533	Peter Zezel, Dal.	.10
☐	534	Greg Hawgood, Pgh.	.10
☐	535	Pat Elynuik, Ott.	.10
☐	536	Mike Ramsey, Det.	.10
☐	537	Bob Beers, NYI.	.10
☐	538	David Williams, Ana.	.10
☐	539	Philippe Boucher, Buf.	.10
☐	540	Rob Brown, L.A.	.10
☐	541	Marc Potvin, Bos.	.10
☐	542	Wendel Clark, Que.	.25
☐	543	Alexander Semak, N.J.	.10
☐	544	Randy Wood, Buf.	.10
☐	545	Frantisek Musil, Cgy.	.10
☐	546	Mike Peluso, N.J.	.10
☐	547	Gaetan Duchesne, S.J.	.10
☐	548	Curtis Leschyshyn, Que.	.10
☐	549	Rob DiMaio, Pha.	.10
☐	550	Checklist (479-550)	.10

CREASE PATROL

Insert Set (10 cards): 10.00

	No.	Player	NRMT-MT
☐	1	Patrick Roy (G), Mtl.	4.00
☐	2	Ed Belfour (G), Chi.	.75
☐	3	Curtis Joseph (G), Stl.	1.50
☐	4	Félix Potvin (G), Tor.	1.25
☐	5	John Vanbiesbrouck (G), Fla.	1.50
☐	6	Dominik Hasek (G), Buf.	2.00
☐	7	Kirk McLean (G), Van.	.50
☐	8	Mike Richter (G), NYR.	.75
☐	9	Martin Brodeur (G), N.J.	2.00
☐	10	Bill Ranford (G), Edm.	.50

FIRE ON ICE

Insert Set (12 cards): 35.00

	No.	Player	NRMT-MT
☐	1	Sergei Fedorov, Det.	2.50
☐	2	Jeremy Roenick, Chi.	1.50
☐	3	Pavel Bure, Van.	3.50
☐	4	Wayne Gretzky, L.A.	10.00
☐	5	Doug Gilmour, Tor.	1.50
☐	6	Eric Lindros, Pha.	6.50
☐	7	Joé Juneau, Bos.	1.00
☐	8	Paul Coffey, Det.	1.00
☐	9	Mario Lemieux, Pgh.	8.00
☐	10	Alexander Mogilny, Buf.	1.50
☐	11	Mike Gartner, Tor.	1.00
☐	12	Teemu Selänne, Wpg.	3.50

GOLD LEAF ROOKIES

Insert Set (15 cards): 50.00

	No.	Player	NRMT-MT
☐	1	Martin Brodeur (G), N.J.	12.00
☐	2	Jason Arnott, Edm.	3.00
☐	3	Alexei Yashin, Ott.	7.00
☐	4	Chris Gratton, T.B.	3.00
☐	5	Alexandre Daigle, Ott.	3.00
☐	6	Mikael Renberg, Pha.	3.00
☐	7	Rob Niedermayer, Fla.	3.00
☐	8	Boris Mironov, Wpg.	2.00
☐	9	Chris Pronger, Hfd.	3.00
☐	10	Chris Osgood (G), Det.	7.00
☐	11	Derek Plante, Buf.	2.00
☐	12	Pat Peake, Wsh.	2.00
☐	13	Jason Allison, Wsh.	5.00
☐	14	Bryan Smolinski, Bos.	2.00
☐	15	Jocelyn Thibault (G), Que.	5.00

GOLD LEAF STARS

Insert Set (15 cards): 500.00

	No.	Player	NRMT-MT
☐	1	S. Fedorov, Det./W. Gretzky, L.A.	100.00
☐	2	D. Gilmour, Tor./J. Roenick, Chi.	20.00
☐	3	P. Roy (G), Mtl./M. Richter (G), NYR.	65.00
☐	4	B. Hull, Stl./P. Bure, Van.	35.00
☐	5	M. Messier, NYR./A. Yashin, Ott.	25.00
☐	6	R. Bourque, Bos./B. Leetch, NYR.	25.00
☐	7	C. Joseph (G), Stl./E. Belfour (G), Chi.	30.00
☐	8	M. Brodeur (G), N.J./D. Hasek (G), Buf.	35.00
☐	9	C. Neely, Bos./M. Renberg, Pha.	20.00
☐	10	M. Modano, Dal./J. Arnott, Edm.	25.00
☐	11	E. Lindros, Pha./M. Lemieux, Pgh.	80.00
☐	12	S. Stevens N.J./R. Blake, L.A.	20.00
☐	13	F. Potvin (G), Tor./J. Vanbiesbrouck (G), Fla.	30.00
☐	14	A. Oates, Bos./P. LaFontaine, Buf.	20.00
☐	15	J. Jagr, Pgh./M. Recchi, Mtl.	45.00

LIMITED

Insert Set (28 cards): 140.00

	No.	Player	NRMT-MT
☐	1	Guy Hebert (G), Ana.	2.00
☐	2	Adam Oates, Bos.	3.00
☐	3	Dominik Hasek (G), Buf.	6.00
☐	4	Robert Reichel, Cgy.	2.00
☐	5	Jeremy Roenick, Chi.	3.00
☐	6	Mike Modano, Dal.	4.50
☐	7	Sergei Fedorov, Det.	4.50
☐	8	Jason Arnott, Edm.	2.00
☐	9	John Vanbiesbrouck (G), Fla.	5.00
☐	10	Chris Pronger, Hfd.	2.00
☐	11	Wayne Gretzky, L.A.	18.00
☐	12	Patrick Roy (G), Mtl.	15.00
☐	13	Martin Brodeur (G), N.J.	6.00
☐	14	Pierre Turgeon, NYI.	2.00
☐	15	Mark Messier, NYR.	4.50
☐	16	Alexei Yashin, Ott.	3.50
☐	17	Eric Lindros, Pha.	12.00
☐	18	Mario Lemieux, Pgh.	158.00
☐	19	Joe Sakic, Que.	8.00
☐	20	Brendan Shanahan, Stl.	5.00
☐	21	Arturs Irbe (G), S.J.	1.50
☐	22	Chris Gratton, T.B.	2.00
☐	23	Doug Gilmour, Tor.	3.00
☐	24	Pavel Bure, Van.	6.00
☐	25	Joé Juneau, Wsh.	1.50
☐	26	Teemu Selänne, Wpg.	6.00
☐	27	Paul Kariya, Ana.	12.00
☐	28	Peter Forsberg, Que.	10.00

PHENOMS

Insert Set (10 cards): 35.00

No.	Player	MINT
1	Jamie Storr (G), L.A.	4.00
2	Brett Lindros, NYI.	2.00
3	Peter Forsberg, Que.	10.00
4	Jason Weimer, T.B.	2.00
5	Paul Kariya, Ana.	12.00
6	Oleg Tverdovsky, Ana.	2.00
7	Eric Fichaud (G), Tor.	4.00
8	Viktor Kozlov, S.J.	2.00
9	Jeff Friesen, S.J.	4.00
10	Valeri Karpov, Ana.	2.00

1994 - 95 LEAF ELIT SET

Series One Set (160 cards): 30.00
Series Two Set (160 cards): 50.00
Common Player: .20

No.	Player	NRMT-MT
1	Thomas Tallberg	.20
2	Hakan Algotsson (G)	.20
3	Mikael Magnusson	.20
4	Per Lundell	.20
5	Kenneth Kennholt	.20
6	Jan Huokko	.20
7	Petter Nilsson	.20
8	Johan Norgren	.20
9	Anders Berglund	.20
10	Kari Eloranta	.20
11	Sam Lindstahi	.20
12	Johan Rosen	.20
13	Jonas Johnsson	.20
14	Erik Huusko	.20
15	Thomas Rhodin	.20
16	Patric Kjellberg	.20
17	Fredrik Andersson	.20
18	Stefan Nilsson	.20
19	Petri Liimatainen	.20
20	Lars Jansson	.20
21	Per Wallin	.20
22	Mika Nieminen	.20
23	Lars Ivarsson	.20
24	Ronnie Sundin	.20
25	Bedrich Scerban	.20
26	Anders Huusko	.20
27	Erik Grenkvist	.20
28	Stefan Ornskog	.20
29	Marcus Thuresson	.20
30	John Stromvall	.20
31	Peter Hasselblad	.20
32	Anders Eriksson	.50
33	Roger Elvenes	.20
34	Stefan Larsson	.20
35	Alexei Salomatin	.20
36	Niclas Havelid	.20
37	Mikael Lindman	.20
38	Jens Ohling	.20
39	Hakan Loob	1.00
40	Johan Hedberg (G)	.20
41	Niklas Eriksson	.20
42	Robert Norberg	.20
43	Robert Svehla	.75
44	Hans Honsson	.20
45	Thomas Srsen	.20
46	Thomas Sjogren	.20
47	Mishat Fahrutdinov	.20
48	Thomas Standberg	.20
49	Andreas Dackell	.50
50	Peter Nilsson	.20
51	Andreas Johnsson	.20
52	Stefan Falk	.20
53	Marcus Akerblom	.20
54	Peter Aslin (G)	.20
55	Ricard Persson	.20
56	Tomas Nanzen	.20
57	Per-Johan Svensson	.20
58	Terhom Koskela	.20
59	Henrik Nelsson	.20
60	Mats Lindberg	.20
61	Anders Huss	.20
62	Magnus Hansson	.20
63	Mats Lindgren	.50
64	Thomas Ljungberg	.20
65	Tomas Forslund	.20
66	Thomas Ostlund	.20
67	Raimo Helminen	.20
68	Magnus Wenblom	.20
69	Jorgen Jonsson	.20
70	Peter Berndtsson	.20
71	Stefan Hellkvist	.20
72	Tommy Lehmann	.20
73	Stefan Klockare	.20
74	Ola Josefsson	.20
75	Peter Lindmark (G)	.20
76	Ove Thornberg	.20
77	Jarno Kakitalo	.20
78	Tomas Berglund	.20
79	Bo Svanberg	.20
80	Lennart Hermansson	.20
81	Stefan Elvenes	.20
82	Daniel Alfredsson	5.00
83	Claes Lindblom	.20
84	Bjorn Ahlstrom	.20
85	Ove Molin	.20
86	Fredrik Lindquist	.20
87	Clas Ericksson	.20
88	Pter Hammarstrom	.20
89	Magnus Swardh	.20
90	Lars Hurtig	.20
91	Daniel Rydmark	.20
92	Lars Bystrom	.20
93	Mats Loov	.20
94	Lars Dahlstrom	.20
95	Johan Brummer	.20
96	Patric Englund	.20
97	Christer Olsson	.20
98	Patrik Erickson	.20
99	Peter Ottsosson	.20
100	Tomas Jonsson	.20
101	Lars Modig	.20
102	Ake Lilljebjorn (G)	.20
103	Patrik Sylvegard	.20
104	Danel Johansson	.20
105	Edvin Frylen	.20
106	Par Edlund	.20
107	Paul Andersson	.20
108	Rikard Franzen	.20
109	Christian Due-Boje	.20
110	Tommy Samuelsson	.20
111	Mathias Svedberg	.20
112	Hans Lodin	.20
113	Jonas Eriksson	.20
114	Mikael Engstrom	.20
115	Hakan Ahlund	.20
116	Kari Suoraniemi	.20
117	Peter Jacobsson	.20
118	Kristian Gahn	.20
119	Tommy Melkersson	.20
120	Oscar Ackestrom	.20
121	Thomas Johansson	.20
122	Jesper Duus	.20
123	Hans Abrahamsson	.20
124	Orjan Lindmark	.20
125	Torbjorn Lindberg	.20
126	Michael Sundlov	.20
127	Peter Sundstrom	.20
128	Pierre Johnsson	.20
129	Thomas Carlsson	.20
130	Stefan Axelsson	.20
131	Robert Norkmark	.20
132	Torbjorn Persson	.20
133	Bjorn Nord	.20
134	Mats Ytter	.20
135	AIK	.20
136	Brynas	.20
137	Djurgardens	.20
138	Vastra Frolunda	.20
139	Farjestads	.20
140	HV 71	.20
141	Leksands	.20
142	Lulea	.20
143	Malmo	.20
144	MoDo Hockey	.20
145	Rögle BK	.20
146	Västerås	.20
147	A.I.K.	.20
148	Brynas	.20
149	Djurgardens	.20
150	Vastra Frolunda	.20
151	Farjestads	.20
152	HV 71 Logo	.20
153	Leksands	.20
154	Lulea	.20
155	Malmo	.20
156	MoDo	.20
157	Rögle	.20
158	Västerås	.20
159	Checklist	.20
160	Checklist	.20
161	Kenneth Johansson, Rögle	.20
162	Stefan Jonsson	.20
163	Mikael Wahlberg, Brynas	.20
164	Per Djoos, Vastra Frolunda	.20
165	Andreas Schultz, HV71	.20
166	Sacha Molin, A.I.K.	.20
167	Marcus Ramén, MoDo	.20
168	Jergus Baca, Leksands	.20
169	Erik Bergström, Västerås	.20
170	Jonas Forsberg, Djurgardens	.20
171	Olli Kaski, Farjestads	.20
172	Morgan Samuelsson	.20
173	Anders Burström, Lulea	.20
174	Staninslav Meciar, Rögle	.20
175	Leif Rohlin, Västerås	.35
176	Lars Edström, Vastra Frolunda	.20
177	Esa Keskinen, HV71	.20
178	Daniel Casselstahl, Brynas	.20
179	Mattias Timander, MoDo	.35
180	Peter Nordström, Leksands	.20
181	Patric Aberg, A.I.K.	.20
182	Mikael Enander	.20
183	Charles Berglund	.20
184	Jonas Andersson-Junkka, Vastra Frolunda	.20
185	Sergei Fokin	.20
186	Boo Ahl (G), HV71	.20
187	Jiri Kucera, Lulea	.20
188	Roger Nordström (G)	.20
189	Peter Forsberg, MoDo	12.00
190	Arto Ruotanen	.20
191	Mikael Wiklander, Västerås	.20
192	Joakim Persson, A.I.K.	.20
193	Peter Larsson, Brynas	.20
194	Per Eklund, Djurgardens	.20
195	Joacim Esbjörs, Vastra Frolunda	.20
196	Magnus Arvedsson	.20
197	Marko Palo	.20
198	Mikael Homberg	.20
199	Mikael Renberg, Lulea	5.00
200	Tero Lehterä, Malmo	.20
201	Fredrik Lindh, MoDo	.20
202	Johan Finnström, Rögle	.20
203	Peter Popovic	.50
204	Tony Barthelson	.20
205	Stefan Pöllä, Brynas	.20
206	Jonas Esbjörs	.20
207	Roger Hansson	.20
208	Mikael Håkanson, MoDo	.20
209	Daniel Tjarnqvist	.20
210	Anders Carlsson, Västerås	.20
211	Dick Tarnstrom	.20
212	Johan Tornberg	.20
213	Joakim Lundberg, Djurgardens	.20
214	Marko Jantunen	.20
215	Patrik Haltia	.20
216	Fredrik Stillman	.20
217	Andy Schneider, Lulea	.20
218	Tomas Holmstrom	.50
219	Jens Hemström, Malmo	.20
220	Anders Soderberg	.20
221	Peter Lundmark, Rögle	.20

No.	Player	Price
222	Patrik Juhlin, Västerås	.35
223	Anders Gozzi	.20
224	Marcus Ragnarsson	.50
225	Mattias Olsson	.20
226	Andreas Karlsson	.20
227	Thomas Lilja	.20
228	Stefan Ohman	.20
229	Jarmo Kekalainen	.20
230	Tony Skopac, A.I.K.	.20
231	Lars Karlsson, Brynas	.20
232	Mats Sundin	8.00
233	Peter Ström, Vastra Frolunda	.20
234	Mattias Johansson	.20
235	Johan Lindbom	.20
236	Mats Lusth, Leksands	.20
237	Marcus Magnertoft, Malmo	.20
238	Martin Hostak	.20
239	Mikael Pettersson, Västerås	.20
240	Johan Akerman	.20
241	Mathias Hällback, Djurgardens	.20
242	Johan Davidsson, HV71	.35
234	Per-Erik Eklund, Leksands	.50
244	Johan Sälle, Malmo	.20
245	Per Svartvadet, MoDo	.20
246	Ville Siren, Västerås	.20
247	Mattias Lööf, Rögle	.20
248	Per-Johan Axelsson, Vastra Frolunda	.20
249	Peter Gerhardsson, A.I.K.	.20
250	Jonas Bergqvist	.20
251	Per-Johan Johansson	.20
252	Mattias Bosson, Malmo	.20
253	Andreas Olsson, MoDo	.20
254	Patrik Zetterberg, Västerås	.20
255	Michael Johansson	.20
256	Stefan Gustavson	.20
257	Jerry Persson	.20
258	Stefan Nilsson, Farjestads	.20
259	Roger Johansson, Lulea	.35
260	Jarmo Myllys (G), Lulea	.50
261	Kyosti Karjalainen	.20
262	Thomas Eriksson, Västerås	.20
263	Michael Hjälm, Rögle	.20
264	Espen Knutsen, Djurgardens	1.00
265	Andreas Salomonsson	.20
266	Patrik Hoglund	.20
267	Peter Andersson, Malmo	.20
268	Brett Hauer, A.I.K.	.20
269	Stefan Ketola	.20
270	Patrik Carnbäck, Vastra Frolunda	.35
271	Petter Rönnqvist, MoDo	.20
272	Roger Ohman, Malmo	.20
273	Fredrik Modin, Brynas	.75
274	Alexander Beliavski, Vastra Frolunda	.20
275	Niklas Brännström, Farjestads	.20
276	Per Gustafsson, HV71	.50
277	Nicklas Nordquist	.20
278	Roger Akerström, Lulea	.20
279	Jiri Vykoukal, MoDo	.20
280	Jesper Mattsson, Malmo	.35
281	Henrik Nordfeldt, Västerås	.20
282	Joakim Musakka, Djurgardens	.20
283	Anders Johnson, A.I.K.	.20
284	Niklas Sundstrom, MoDo	3.00
285	Nicklas Lidstrom	5.00
286	Tomas Sandström, Malmo	3.00
287	Jens Nielsen	.20
288	Mattias Ohlund, Lulea	4.00
289	Markus Eriksson, Leksands	.20
290	Mikael Sandberg	.20
291	Sergei Pushkov	.20
292	Jonas Hoglund	.35
293	Peter Ekelund, HV71	.20
294	Fredrik Bergqvist	.20
295	Torgny Bendelin, Coach, A.I.K.	.20
296	Tommy Sandlin, Coach, Brynas	.20
297	Tommy Boustedt, Coach, Djurgardens	.20
298	Conny Evensson, Coach, Farjestads	.20
299	Sune Bergman, Coach, HV71	.20
300	Wayne Fleming, Coach, Leksands	.35
301	Lars Bergstrom, Coach, Lulea	.20
302	Hannu Jortikka, Coach, Malmo	.20
303	Leif Boork, Coach, MoDo	.20
304	Christer Abranhamsson, Coach, Rögle	.20
305	Randy Edmonds, Coach, Västerås	.20
306	Ulf Labraaten, Coach, Vastra Frolunda	.20
307	AIK Team Photo	.20
308	Brynas Team Photo	.20
309	Djurgardesn Team Photo	.20
310	Farjestads Team Photo	.20
311	HV 71 Team Photo	.20
312	Leksands Team Photo	.20
313	LuleaTeam Photo	.20
314	Malmo Team Photo	.20
315	MoDo Team Photo	.20
316	Rogle Team Photo	.20
317	Vasteras Team Photo	.20
318	Vastra Frolunda Team Photo	.20
319	Checklist	.20
320	Checklist	.20

CLEAN SWEEPERS

Series One Insert Set (10 cards): 45.00

No.	Player	NRMT-MT
1	Peter Lindmark (G)	5.00
2	Michael Sundlov (G)	5.00
3	Thomas Ostlund (G)	5.00
4	Jonas Eriksson (G)	5.00
5	Peter Aslin (G)	5.00
6	Ake Lilljebjorn (G)	5.00
7	Johan Hedberg (G)	5.00
8	Henrik Arvsell (G)	5.00
9	Frederik Andersson (G)	5.00
10	Hakan Algotsson (G)	5.00

GOLD CARDS

Series One Insert Set (24 cards): 90.00

No.	Player	NRMT-MT
1	Title Card	3.00
2	Andreas Dackell	4.00
3	Charles Berglund	3.00
4	Christian Due-Boje	3.00
5	Daniel Rydmark	3.00
6	Fredrik Stillman	3.00
7	Hakan Algotsson	3.00
8	Hakan Loob	8.00
9	Jonas Bergqvist	3.00
10	Jorgen Jonsson	3.00
11	Kenny Jonsson	4.00
12	Leif Rohlin	3.00
13	Magnus Svensson	3.00
14	Mats Naslund	8.00
15	Michael Sundlov	3.00
16	Niklas Eriksson	3.00
17	Patric Kjellberg	3.00
18	Patrick Juhlin	4.00
19	Peter Forsberg	30.00
20	Roger Hansson	3.00
21	Roger Johansson	3.00
22	Stafan Ornskog	3.00
23	Tomas Jonsson	4.00
24	Tommy Salo (G)	6.00

PLAYMAKERS

Series One Insert Set (6 cards): 18.00

No.	Player	NRMT-MT
1	Title Card	3.00
2	Stefan Nilsson	3.00
3	Mika Nieminen	3.00
4	Raimo Helminen	3.00
5	Peter Larsson	3.00
6	Hakan Loob	6.00

TOP GUNS

Series One Insert Set (10 cards): 40.00

No.	Player	NRMT-MT
1	Thomas Srsen	4.00
2	Hakan Loob	8.00
3	Lars Hurtig	4.00
4	Stefan Elvenes	4.00
5	Jorgen Jonsson	4.00
6	Robert Svehla	6.00
7	Daniel Rydmark	4.00
8	Ove Thornberg	4.00
9	Patric Kjellberg	4.00
10	Mats Loov	4.00

FOREIGN AFFAIRS

Series One Insert Set (10 cards): 30.00

No.	Player	NRMT-MT
1	Espen Knutsen	5.00
2	Esa Keskinen	3.00
3	Marko Jantunen	3.00
4	Jarmo Myllys (G)	4.00
5	Jiri Kucera	3.00
6	Jiri Vykoukal	3.00
7	Jarmo Kekalainen	3.00
8	Olli Kaski	3.00
9	Jergus Baca	3.00
10	Tero Lehtera	3.00

GUEST SPECIALS

Series Two Insert Set (8 cards): 80.00

No.	Player	NRMT-MT
1	Mats Sundin	20.00
2	Tomas Sandström	6.00
3	Peter Forsberg	40.00
4	Nicklas Lidstrom	10.00
5	Mikael Renberg	8.00
6	Roger Johansson	5.00
7	Peter Popovic	5.00
8	Patrick Juhlin	5.00

NHL DRAFT

Series Two Insert Set (10 cards): 35.00

No.	Player	NRMT-MT
1	Mattias Ohlund	10.00
2	Johan Davidsson	4.00
3	Fredrik Modin	4.00
4	Johan Finnstrom	3.00
5	Edvin Frylen	3.00
6	Daniel Alfredsson	15.00
7	Patrik Haltia	3.00
8	Peter Strom	3.00
9	Thomas Holmstrom	5.00
10	Dick Tarnstrom	3.00

ROOKIE ROCKETS

Series Two Insert Set (10 cards): 30.00

No.	Player	NRMT-MT
1	Fredrik Modin	5.00
2	Jonas Andersson-Junkka	3.00
3	Thomas Holmstrom	5.00
4	Mattias Ohlund	10.00
5	Per Eklund	3.00
6	Daniel Tjarnqvist	3.00
7	Joakim Persson	3.00
8	Patrik Haltia	3.00
9	Andreas Karlsson	3.00
10	Stefan Nilsson	3.00

STUDIO SIGNATURES

Series Two Insert Set (12 cards): 30.00

No.	Player	NRMT-MT
1	Rikard Franzen	3.00
2	Anders Huuss	3.00
3	Jens Ohling	3.00

	No.	Player	NRMT-MT
☐	4	Tommy Samuelsson	3.00
☐	5	Fredrik Stillman	3.00
☐	6	Jonas Bergqvist	3.00
☐	7	Johan Stromvall	3.00
☐	8	Roger Nordstrom	3.00
☐	9	Lars Bystrom	3.00
☐	10	Roger Elvenes	3.00
☐	11	Leif Rohlin	3.00
☐	12	Tero Koskela	3.00

1994 - 95 LEAF LIMITED

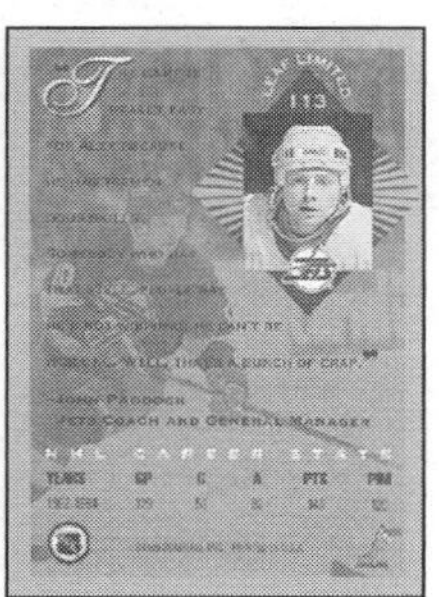

Imprint: © 1995 DONRUSS, INC.
Complete Set (120 cards): 70.00
Common Player: .35

	No.	Player	NRMT-MT
☐	1	Mario Lemieux, Pgh.	8.00
☐	2	Brett Hull, Stl.	2.50
☐	3	Ed Belfour (G), Chi.	1.50
☐	4	Brian Rolston, N.J.	.35
☐	5	Garry Galley, Pha.	.35
☐	6	Steve Thomas, NYI.	.35
☐	7	Kevin Brown, L.A.	.35
☐	8	Doug Gilmour, Tor.	1.50
☐	9	Bill Ranford (G), Edm.	.75
☐	10	Wayne Gretzky, L.A.	10.00
☐	11	Rob Niedermayer, Fla.	.75
☐	12	Larry Murphy, Pgh.	.75
☐	13	Glen Wesley, Hfd.	.35
☐	14	Pat Falloon, S.J.	.35
☐	15	Jocelyn Thibault (G), Que.	1.50
☐	16	Félix Potvin (G), Tor.	2.50
☐	17	Mike Richter (G), NYR.	1.50
☐	18	Jeff Brown, Van.	.35
☐	19	Jesse Belanger, Fla.	.35
☐	20	Benoît Hogue, NYI.	.35
☐	21	Viktor Kozlov, S.J.	.35
☐	22	Chris Pronger, Hfd.	.75
☐	23	Kirk McLean (G), Van.	.75
☐	24	Oleg Tverdovsky, Ana.	.35
☐	25	Derian Hatcher, Dal.	.75
☐	26	Ray Sheppard, Det.	.35
☐	27	Pat Verbeek, Hfd.	.35
☐	28	Patrick Roy (G), Mtl.	6.50
☐	**29**	**Mariusz Czerkawski, Bos., RC**	**.35**
☐	30	Ron Francis, Pgh.	1.50
☐	31	Wendel Clark, Que.	.75
☐	32	Rob Blake, L.A.	.75
☐	33	Brian Leetch, NYR.	1.50
☐	34	Dave Andreychuk, Tor.	.35
☐	35	Russ Courtnall, Dal.	.35
☐	36	Alexander Mogilny, Buf.	1.50
☐	37	Kirk Muller, Mtl.	.35
☐	38	Joé Juneau, Wsh.	.35
☐	39	Robert Reichel, Cgy.	.35
☐	40	Scott Niedermayer, N.J.	.75
☐	41	Owen Nolan, Que.	.75
☐	42	Mats Sundin, Tor.	2.50
☐	43	Sandis Ozolinsh, S.J.	.75
☐	44	Derek Plante, Buf.	.35
☐	**45**	**Eric Fichaud (G), Tor., RC**	**2.50**
☐	46	Kevin Stevens, Pgh.	.35
☐	47	Igor Larionov, S.J.	.75
☐	48	Mikael Renberg, Pha.	.75
☐	49	Cam Neely, Bos.	.75
☐	50	Brett Lindros, NYI.	.35
☐	**51**	**Valeri Karpov, Ana., RC**	**.35**
☐	52	Pierre Turgeon, NYI.	.75
☐	53	Doug Weight, Edm.	1.50
☐	54	Geoff Sanderson, Hfd.	.35
☐	55	Vyacheslav Kozlov, Det.	.35
☐	56	Chris Gratton, T.B.	.75
☐	57	Bryan Smolinski, Bos.	.35
☐	58	Eric Lindros, Pha.	6.50
☐	59	Alexei Kovalev, NYR.	.35
☐	60	Mike Modano, Dal.	2.50
☐	61	Jeremy Roenick, Chi.	1.50
☐	62	Martin Straka, Pgh.	.35
☐	63	Pat LaFontaine, Buf.	.75
☐	64	Vlastimil Kroupa, S.J.	.35
☐	65	Sergei Zubov, NYR.	.75
☐	66	Jason Arnott, Edm.	.75
☐	67	Petr Nedved, NYR.	.35
☐	68	Teemu Selänne, Wpg.	3.50
☐	69	Geoff Courtnall, Van.	.35
☐	70	Martin Brodeur (G), N.J.	3.50
☐	71	Mark Recchi, Pha.	.75
☐	72	John Vanbiesbrouck (G), Fla.	3.00
☐	73	Adam Graves, NYR.	.35
☐	74	Arturs Irbe (G), S.J.	.35
☐	75	Paul Coffey, Det.	.75
☐	76	Ulf Dahlen, S.J.	.35
☐	77	Phil Housley, Cgy.	.35
☐	78	Rod Brind'Amour, Pha.	.75
☐	79	Al McInnis, Stl.	.35
☐	80	Alexei Yashin, Ott.	2.00
☐	81	Sergei Fedorov, Det.	2.50
☐	82	Joe Nieuwendyk, Cgy.	.75
☐	83	Chris Chelios, Chi.	2.00
☐	84	Ray Bourque, Bos.	2.50
☐	85	Scott Stevens, N.J.	.35
☐	86	Jaromir Jagr, Pgh.	5.00
☐	87	Alexandre Daigle, Ott.	.75
☐	88	Luc Robitaille, Pgh.	.75
☐	89	Mark Messier, NYR.	2.50
☐	90	Vincent Damphousse, Mtl.	1.50
☐	91	Craig Janney, Stl.	.35
☐	92	John MacLean, N.J.	.35
☐	93	Steve Duchesne, Stl.	.35
☐	94	Dale Hawerchuk, Buf.	.75
☐	95	Curtis Joseph (G), Stl.	3.00
☐	96	Chris Osgood (G), Det.	1.50
☐	97	Brendan Shanahan, Stl.	3.00
☐	98	Jason Allison, Wsh.	1.50
☐	99	Theoren Fleury, Cgy.	1.50
☐	100	Pavel Bure, Van.	3.50
☐	101	Mathieu Schneider, Mtl.	.35
☐	102	Dominik Hasek (G), Buf.	3.50
☐	103	Scott Mellanby, Fla.	.35
☐	104	Adam Oates, Bos.	1.50
☐	105	Jari Kurri, L.A.	.75
☐	106	Joe Sakic, Que.	4.00
☐	107	Paul Kariya, Ana.	6.50
☐	108	Keith Tkachuk, Wpg.	2.00
☐	109	Daren Puppa (G), T.B.	.35
☐	110	Keith Primeau, Det.	.75
☐	111	Alexei Zhitnik, L.A.	.35
☐	112	Trevor Linden, Van.	.75
☐	113	Alexei Zhamnov, Wpg.	.75
☐	114	Gary Roberts, Cgy.	.75
☐	115	Kenny Jonsson, Tor.	.35
☐	116	Peter Forsberg, Que.	5.00
☐	117	Rick Tocchet, L.A.	.35
☐	118	Aaron Gavey, T.B.	.35
☐	**119**	**Jason Wiemer, T.B., RC**	**.35**
☐	120	Steve Yzerman, Det.	5.00

GOLD CARDS

Insert Set (10 cards): 525.00

	No.	Player	NRMT-MT
☐	1	Mario Lemieux, Pgh.	100.00
☐	2	Brett Hull, Stl.	30.00
☐	3	Doug Gilmour, Tor.	18.00
☐	4	Eric Lindros, Pha.	80.00
☐	5	Paul Kariya, Ana.	80.00
☐	6	Jaromir Jagr, Pgh.	60.00
☐	7	Wayne Gretzky, L.A.	125.00
☐	8	Jeremy Roenick, Chi.	18.00
☐	9	Sergei Fedorov, Det.	30.00
☐	10	Pavel Bure, Van.	45.00

WORLD JUNIORS

Team Canada Insert Set (10 cards): 155.00
Team U.S.A. Insert Set (10 cards): 110.00

	No.	Player	NRMT-MT
☐	1	Nolan Baumgartner, Cdn.	12.00
☐	2	Eric Dazé, Cdn.	20.00
☐	3	Jeff Friesen, Cdn.	18.00
☐	4	Todd Harvey, Cdn.	12.00
☐	5	Ed Jovanovski, Cdn.	20.00
☐	6	Jeff O'Neill, Cdn.	18.00
☐	7	Wade Redden, Cdn.	15.00
☐	8	Jamie Rivers, Cdn.	12.00
☐	9	Ryan Smyth, Cdn.	30.00
☐	10	Jamie Storr (G), Cdn.	18.00
☐	1	Bryan Berard, USA.	25.00
☐	2	Doug Bonner, USA.	10.00
☐	3	Jason Bonsignore, USA.	12.00
☐	4	Adam Deadmarsh, USA.	20.00
☐	5	Rory Fitzpatrick, USA.	10.00
☐	6	Sean Haggerty, USA.	10.00
☐	7	Jamie Langenbrunner, USA.	15.00
☐	8	Jeff Mitchell, USA.	10.00
☐	9	Richard Park, USA.	10.00
☐	10	Deron Quint, USA.	10.00

1994 - 95 MCDONALD'S - UPPER DECK

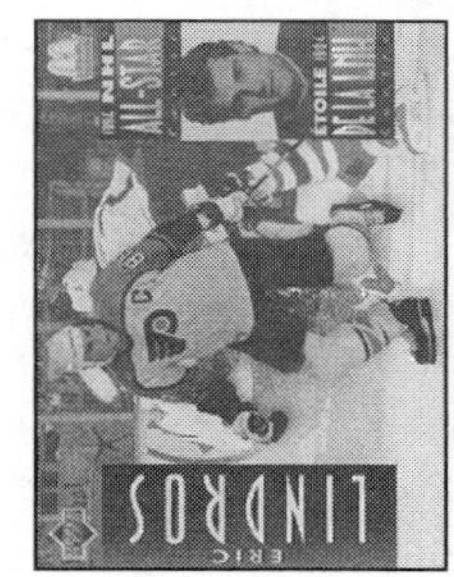
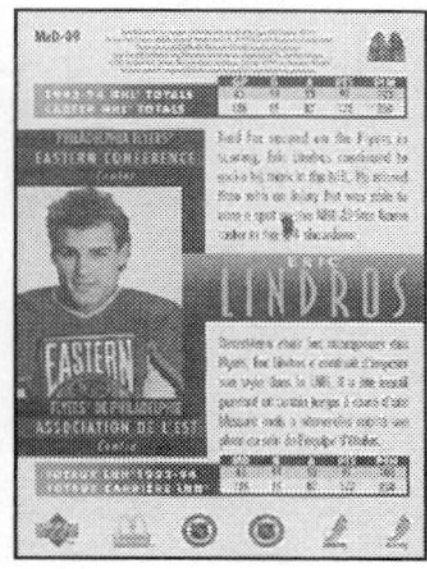

Imprint: © 1995 The Upper Deck Compnay
Complete Set (40 cards): 20.00

	No.	Player	NRMT-MT
☐	McD-01	Joe Sakic, Que.	1.25
☐	McD-02	Adam Graves, NYR.	.25
☐	McD-03	Alexei Yashin, Ott.	.60
☐	McD-04	Patrick Roy (G), Mtl.	2.50
☐	McD-05	Ray Bourque, Bos	.75
☐	McD-06	Brian Leetch, NYR.	.50
☐	McD-07	Scott Stevens, N.J.	.25
☐	McD-08	Alexander Mogilny, Buf.	.50
☐	McD-09	Eric Lindros, Pha.	2.00
☐	McD-10	Jaromir Jagr, Pgh.	1.50
☐	McD-11	Sandis Ozolinsh, S.J.	.25
☐	McD-12	Sergei Fedorov, Det.	.75
☐	McD-13	Brett Hull, Stl.	.75
☐	McD-14	Félix Potvin (G), Tor.	.75
☐	McD-15	Al MacInnis, Stl.	.25
☐	McD-16	Chris Chelios, Chi.	.60
☐	McD-17	Rob Blake, L.A.	.25
☐	McD-18	Dave Andreychuk, Tor.	.25
☐	McD-19	Paul Coffey, Det.	.25
☐	McD-20	Jeremy Roenick, Chi.	.50
☐	McD-21	Joe Nieuwendyk, Cgy.	.25
☐	McD-22	Cam Neely, Bos.	.25
☐	McD-23	Pavel Bure, Van.	1.00
☐	McD-24	Wendel Clark, Que.	.25
☐	McD-25	Teemu Selänne, Wpg.	1.00
☐	McD-26	Pierre Turgeon, NYI.	.25
☐	McD-27	Alexei Zhamnov, Wpg.	.25
☐	McD-28	Doug Gilmour, Tor.	.50
☐	McD-29	Vincent Damphousse, Mtl.	.50
☐	McD-30	Brendan Shanahan, Stl.	.85
☐	McD-31	Peter Forsberg, Que.	1.50
☐	McD-32	Paul Kariya, Ana.	2.00
☐	McD-33	Viktor Kozlov, S.J.	.25
☐	McD-34	Brett Lindros, NYI.	.25
☐	McD-35	Martin Brodeur, N.J.	1.00
☐	McD-36	Alexandre Daigle, Ott.	.25
☐	McD-37	Jason Arnott, Edm.	.25
☐	McD-38	Alexei Kovalev, NYR.	.25
☐	McD-39	Mikael Renberg, Pha.	.25
☐		Checklist/Mike Richter	.35

1994 - 95 PANINI STICKERS

Imprint: Panini S. r. l. - Modena

Complete Set (276 stickers):	**25.00**
Common Player:	**.10**
Album:	**2.00**

	No.	Player	NRMT-MT
☐	A	Bryan Smolinski, Bos.	.20
☐	1	Adam Oates, Bos.	.50
☐	2	Ted Donato, Bos.	.10
☐	3	Cam Neely, Bos.	.25
☐	4	Brent Hughes, Bos.	.10
☐	5	Boston Bruins	.20
☐	6	Glen Wesley, Bos.	.10
☐	7	Al Iafrate, Bos.	.10
☐	8	Ray Bourque, Bos.	1.00
☐	9	Jon Casey (G), Bos.	.10
☐	B	Oleg Petrov, Mtl.	.20
☐	10	Guy Carbonneau, Mtl.	.10
☐	11	Pierre Sévigny, Mtl.	.10
☐	12	Kirk Muller, Mtl.	.10
☐	13	Montréal Canadiens	.20
☐	14	Vincent Damphousse, Mtl.	.50
☐	15	Gilbert Dionne, Mtl.	.10
☐	16	Mathieu Schneider, Mtl.	.10
☐	17	Eric Desjardins, Mtl.	.25
☐	18	Patrick Roy (G), Mtl.	3.00
☐	C	Pat Peake, Wsh.	.20
☐	19	Joé Juneau, Wsh.	.10
☐	20	Dimitri Khristich, Wsh.	.10
☐	21	Dale Hunter, Wsh.	.10
☐	22	Washington Capitals	.20
☐	23	Mike Ridley, Wsh.	.10
☐	24	Peter Bondra, Wsh.	.75
☐	25	Sylvain Côté, Wsh.	.10
☐	26	Kevin Hatcher, Wsh.	.10
☐	27	Don Beaupré (G), Wsh.	.10
☐	D	Jaroslav Modry, N.J.	.20
☐	28	Bernie Nicholls, N.J.	.10
☐	29	Alexander Semak, N.J.	.10
☐	30	John MacLean, N.J.	.10
☐	31	New Jersey Devils	.20
☐	32	Stéphane Richer, N.J.	.10
☐	33	Valeri Zelepukin, N.J.	.10
☐	34	Scott Stevens, N.J.	.10
☐	35	Martin Brodeur (G), N.J.	1.50
☐	36	Chris Terreri (G), N.J.	.10
☐	E	Mikael Renberg, Pha.	.20
☐	37	Rod Brind'Amour, Pha.	.25
☐	38	Eric Lindros, Pha.	2.50
☐	39	Mark Recchi, Pha.	.25
☐	40	Philadelphia Flyers	.20
☐	41	Kevin Dineen, Pha.	.10
☐	42	Brent Fedyk, Pha.	.10
☐	43	Garry Galley, Pha.	.10
☐	44	Ryan McGill, Pha.	.10
☐	45	Dominic Roussel (G), Pha.	.10
☐	F	Yan Kaminsky, NYI.	.20
☐	46	Ray Ferraro, NYI.	.10
☐	47	Benoît Hogue, NYI.	.10
☐	48	Pierre Turgeon, NYI.	.25
☐	49	New York Islanders	.20
☐	50	Patrick Flatley, NYI.	.10
☐	51	Steve Thomas, NYI.	.10
☐	52	Darius Kasparaitis, NYI.	.10
☐	53	Vladimir Malakhhov, NYI.	.10
☐	54	Ron Hextall (G), NYI.	.25
☐	G	Iain Fraser, Que.	.20
☐	55	Mats Sundin, Que.	1.00
☐	56	Joe Sakic, Que.	1.75
☐	57	Québec Nordiques	.20
☐	58	Claude Lapointe, Que.	.10
☐	59	Scott Young, Que.	.10
☐	60	Valeri Kamensky, Que.	.25
☐	61	Steven Finn, Que.	.10
☐	62	Jocelyn Thibault (G), Que.	.50
☐	63	Stéphane Fiset (G), Que.	.25
☐	H	Rob Niedrmayer, Fla.	.35
☐	64	Brian Skrudland, Fla.	.10
☐	65	Bob Kudelski, Fla.	.10
☐	66	Jody Hull, Fla.	.10
☐	67	Scott Mellanby, Fla.	.10
☐	68	Florida Panthers	.20
☐	69	Dave Lowry, Fla.	.10
☐	70	Mike Hough, Fla.	.10
☐	71	Gord Murphy, Fla.	.10
☐	72	John Vanbiesbrouck (G), Fla.	1.25
☐	I	Markus Naslund, Pgh.	.20
☐	73	Ron Francis, Pgh.	.50
☐	74	Mario Lemieux, Pgh.	3.00
☐	75	Pittsburgh Penguins	.20
☐	76	Jaromir Jagr, Pgh.	2.00
☐	77	Rick Tocchet, Pgh.	.10
☐	78	Kevin Stevens, Pgh.	.10
☐	79	Ulf Samuelsson, Pgh.	.10
☐	80	Larry Murphy, Pgh.	.25
☐	81	Tom Barrasso (G), Pgh.	.25
☐	J	Alex Karpovtsev, NYR.	.20
☐	82	Mark Messier, NYR.	1.00
☐	83	Alexei Kovalev, NYR.	.10
☐	84	New York Rangers	.20
☐	85	Sergei Nemchinov, NYR.	.10
☐	86	Steve Larmer, NYR.	.10
☐	87	Adam Graves, NYR.	.10
☐	88	Brian Leetch, NYR.	.50
☐	89	Sergei Zubov, NYR.	.25
☐	90	Mike Richter (G), NYR.	.25
☐	K	Derek Plante, Buf.	.20
☐	91	Dale Hawerchuk, Buf.	.25
☐	92	Pat LaFontaine, Buf.	.25
☐	93	Donald Audette, Buf.	.10
☐	94	Alexander Mogilny, Buf.	.50
☐	95	Buffalo Sabres	.20
☐	96	Yuri Khmylev, Buf.	.10
☐	97	Brad May, Buf.	.10
☐	98	Richard Smehlik, Buf.	.10
☐	99	Dominik Hasek (G), Buf.	1.50
☐	L	Alexei Yashin, Ott.	.75
☐	100	Dave McLlwain, Ott.	.10
☐	101	Alexandre Daigle, Ott.	.25
☐	102	David Archibald, Ott.	.10
☐	103	Ottawa Senators	.20
☐	104	Troy Murray, Ott.	.10
☐	105	Sylvain Turgeon, Ott.	.10
☐	106	Gord Dineen, Ott.	.10
☐	107	Darren Rumble, Ott.	.10
☐	108	Craig Billington (G), Ott.	.10
☐	M	Chris Pronger, Hfd.	.35
☐	109	Geoff Sanderson, Hfd.	.10
☐	110	Andrew Cassels, Hfd.	.10
☐	111	Hartford Whalers	.20
☐	112	Pat Verbeek, Hfd.	.10
☐	113	Jim Sandlak, Hfd.	.10
☐	114	Jocelyn Lemieux, Hfd.	.10
☐	115	Brian Propp, Hfd.	.10
☐	116	Frantisek Kucera, Hfd.	.10
☐	117	Sean Burke (G), Hfd.	.25
☐	AA	Wayne Gretzky, L.A.	5.00
☐	BB	Sergei Fedorov, Det.	1.25
☐	CC	Adam Oates, Bos.	.75
☐	DD	Mark Recchi, Pha.	.35
☐	EE	Brendan Shanahan, Stl.	1.50
☐	FF	Doug Gilmour, Tor.	.75
☐	GG	Pavel Bure, Van.	1.75
☐	HH	Jeremy Roenick, Chi.	.75
☐	II	Jaromir Jagr, Pgh.	2.50
☐	JJ	Dave Andreychuck, Tor.	.20
☐	N	Patrick Carnback, Ana.	.20
☐	118	Anatoli Semenov, Ana.	.10
☐	119	Stéphan Lebeau, Ana.	.10
☐	120	Anaheim Mighty Ducks	.20
☐	121	Terri Yake, Ana.	.10
☐	122	Joe Sacco, Ana.	.10
☐	123	Todd Ewen, Ana.	.10
☐	124	Troy Loney, Ana.	.10
☐	125	Sean Hill, Ana.	.10
☐	126	Guy Hebert (G), Ana.	.25
☐	O	Jeff Shantz, Chi.	.20
☐	127	Jeremy Roenick, Chi.	.25
☐	128	Tony Amonte, Chi.	.25
☐	129	Joe Murphy, Chi.	.10
☐	130	Chicago Blackhawks	.20
☐	131	Michel Goulet, Chi.	.25
☐	132	Paul Ysebaert, Chi.	.10
☐	133	Gary Suter, Chi.	.10
☐	134	Chris Chelios, Chi.	.75
☐	135	Ed Belfour (G), Chi.	.50
☐	P	Vitali Karamnov, Stl.	.20
☐	136	Craig Janney, Stl.	.10
☐	137	Petr Nedved, Stl.	.10
☐	138	St. Louis Blues	.20
☐	139	Kevin Miller, Stl.	.10
☐	140	Brett Hull, Stl.	1.00
☐	141	Brendan Shanahan, Stl.	1.25
☐	142	Phil Housley, Stl.	.10
☐	143	Steve Duchesne, Stl.	.10
☐	144	Curtis Joseph (G), Stl.	1.25
☐	Q	Nathan Lafayette, Van.	.20
☐	145	Cliff Ronning, Van.	.10
☐	146	Pavel Bure, Van.	1.50
☐	147	Trevor Linden, Van.	.25
☐	148	Vancouver Canucks	.20
☐	149	Geoff Courtnall, Van.	.10
☐	150	Gino Odjick, Van.	.10
☐	151	Jyrki Lumme, Van.	.10
☐	152	Jeff Brown, Van.	.10
☐	153	Kirk McLean (G), Van.	.25
☐	R	Trevor Kidd, Cgy.	.35
☐	154	Robert Reichel, Cgy.	.25
☐	155	Joel Otto, Cgy.	.10
☐	156	Joe Nieuwendyk, Cgy.	.25
☐	157	Calgary Flames	.20
☐	158	German Titov, Cgy.	.10
☐	159	Theoren Fleury, Cgy.	.50
☐	160	Gary Roberts, Cgy.	.25
☐	161	Al MacInnis, Cgy.	.25
☐	162	Mike Vernon (G), Cgy.	.25
☐	S	Dave Tomlinson, Wpg.	.20
☐	163	Alexei Zhamnov, Wpg.	.25
☐	164	Nelson Emerson, Wpg.	.10
☐	165	Winnipeg Jets	.20
☐	166	Teemu Selänne, Wpg.	1.50
☐	167	Tie Domi, Wpg.	.10
☐	168	Keith Tkachuk, Wpg.	.75
☐	169	Teppo Numminen, Wpg.	.10
☐	170	Stéphane Quintal, Wpg.	.10
☐	171	Tim Cheveldae (G), Wpg.	.10
☐	T	Robert Lang, L.A.	.20
☐	172	Wayne Gretzky, L.A.	4.00
☐	173	Jari Kurri, L.A.	.25
☐	174	Luc Robitaille, L.A.	.25
☐	175	Los Angeles Kings	.20
☐	176	Tony Granato, L.A.	.10
☐	177	Rob Blake, L.A.	.25
☐	178	Marty McSorley, L.A.	.10
☐	179	Alexei Zhitnik, L.A.	.10
☐	180	Kelly Hrudey (G), L.A.	.10
☐	U	Chris Gratton, T.B.	.35
☐	181	Denis Savard, T.B.	.25
☐	182	Brian Bradley, T.B.	.10
☐	183	Tampa Bay Lightning	.20
☐	184	Danton Cote, T.B.	.10
☐	185	Petr Klima, T.B.	.10
☐	186	Mikael Andersson, T.B.	.10
☐	187	Shawn Chambers, T.B.	.10
☐	188	Roman Hamrlik, T.B.	.25
☐	189	Daren Puppa (G), T.B.	.10
☐	V	Alexei Kudashov,Tor.	.20
☐	190	Doug Gilmour, Tor.	.50
☐	191	Mike Gartner, Tor.	.25
☐	192	Nikolai Borschevsky, Tor.	.10
☐	193	Toronto Maple Leafs	.20
☐	194	Dave Andreychuk, Tor.	.10
☐	195	Wendel Clark, Tor.	.25
☐	196	Sylvain Lefebvre, Tor.	.10
☐	197	Dave Ellett, Tor.	.10
☐	198	Félix Potvin (G), Tor.	1.00
☐	W	Jason Arnott, Edm.	.35
☐	199	Doug Weight, Edm.	.50
☐	200	Zdeno Ciger, Edm.	.10

	No.	Player	Price
☐	201	Kelly Buchberger, Edm.	.10
☐	202	Shayne Corson, Edm.	.25
☐	203	Edmonton Oilers	.20
☐	204	Scott Pearson, Edm.	.10
☐	205	Igor Kravchuk, Edm.	.10
☐	206	Luke Richardson, Edm.	.10
☐	207	Bill Ranford (G), Edm.	.25
☐	X	Chris Osgood, Det.	.75
☐	208	Vyacheslav Kozlov, Det.	.10
☐	209	Steve Yzerman, Det.	2.00
☐	210	Sergei Fedorov, Det.	1.00
☐	211	Ray Sheppard, Det.	.10
☐	212	Detroit Red Wings	.20
☐	213	Bob Probert, Det.	.10
☐	214	Keith Primeau, Det.	.25
☐	215	Paul Coffey, Det.	.25
☐	216	Nicklas Lidstrom, Det.	.25
☐	Y	Mike Rathje, S.J.	.20
☐	217	Igor Larionov, S.J.	.25
☐	218	Todd Elik, S.J.	.10
☐	219	Pat Falloon, S.J.	.10
☐	220	San Jose Sharks	.20
☐	221	Ulf Dahlen, S.J.	.10
☐	222	Sergei Makarov, S.J.	.10
☐	223	Sandis Ozolinsh, S.J.	.25
☐	224	Jeff Norton, S.J.	.10
☐	225	Arturs Irbe (G), S.J.	.10
☐	Z	Jarkko Varvio, Dal.	.20
☐	226	Mike Modano, Dal.	1.00
☐	227	Dave Gagner, Dal.	.10
☐	228	Mike Craig, Dal.	.10
☐	229	Dallas Stars	.20
☐	230	Russ Courtnall, Dal.	.10
☐	231	Derian Hatcher, Dal.	.25
☐	232	Mark Tinordi, Dal.	.10
☐	233	Craig Ludwig, Dal.	.10
☐	234	Darcy Wakaluk (G), Dal.	.10
☐	235a	Pavel Bure, Van.	1.00
	235b	Brett Hull, Stl.	
☐	236a	Sergei Fedorov, Det.	.75
	236b	Dave Andreychuk, Tor.	
☐	237a	Brendan Shanahan, Stl.	.75
	237b	Ray Sheppard, Det.	
☐	238a	Adam Graves, NYR.	.50
	238b	Cam Neely, Bos.	
☐	239a	50+ Goal Club	.75
	239b	Mike Modano, Dal.	

1994 - 95 PARKHURST

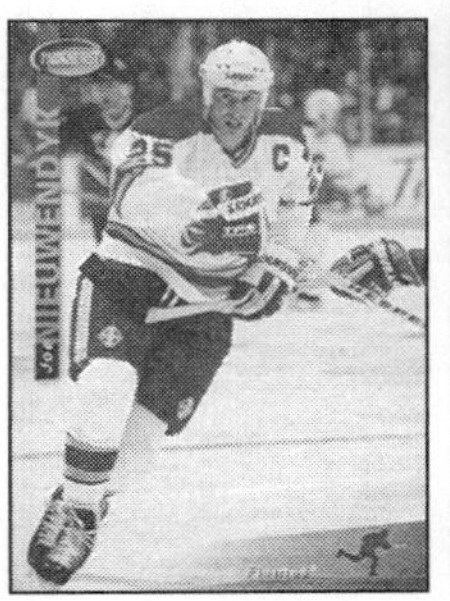

These cards have two versions: the regular cards and a Parkie Gold parallel. An intended second series was never released.

Imprint: © 1994 The Upper Deck Company

Complete Set (315 cards): 20.00 850.00

Common Player: .10 2.00

	No.	Player	Reg.	Gold
☐☐	1	Anatoli Semenov, Ana.	.10	2.00
☐☐	2	Stéphan Lebeau, Ana.	.10	2.00
☐☐	3	Stu Grimson, Ana.	.10	2.00
☐☐	**4**	**Mikhail Shtalenkov (G), Ana., RC**	**.10**	**2.00**
☐☐	5	Troy Loney, Ana.	.10	2.00
☐☐	6	Sean Hill, Ana.	.10	2.00
☐☐	7	Patrik Carnback, Ana.	.10	2.00
☐☐	8	John Lilley, Ana.	.10	2.00
☐☐	9	Tim Sweeney, Ana.	.10	2.00
☐☐	10	Maxim Bets, Ana.	.10	2.00
☐☐	11	Cam Neely, Bos.	.25	5.00
☐☐	12	Bryan Smolinski, Bos.	.10	2.00
☐☐	13	Ray Bourque, Bos.	.50	12.00
☐☐	14	Vincent Riendeau (G), Bos.	.10	2.00
☐☐	15	Al Iafrate, Bos.	.10	2.00
☐☐	**16**	**Andrew McKim, Bos., RC**	**.10**	**2.00**
☐☐	17	Glen Wesley, Bos.	.10	2.00
☐☐	18	Daniel Marois, Bos.	.10	2.00
☐☐	19	Jozef Stumpel, Bos.	.25	5.00
☐☐	**20**	**Mariusz Czerkawski, Bos., RC**	**.10**	**2.00**
☐☐	21	Alexander Mogilny, Buf.	.35	7.00
☐☐	22	Yuri Khmylev, Buf.	.10	2.00
☐☐	23	Donald Audette, Buf.	.10	2.00
☐☐	24	Dominik Hasek, Buf.	.75	20.00
☐☐	25	Randy Wood, Buf.	.10	2.00
☐☐	26	Brad May, Buf.	.10	2.00
☐☐	27	Wayne Presley, Buf.	.10	2.00
☐☐	28	Richard Smehlik, Buf.	.10	2.00
☐☐	29	Dale Hawerchuk, Buf.	.25	5.00
☐☐	30	Rob Ray, Buf.	.10	2.00
☐☐	31	Zarley Zalapski, Cgy.	.10	2.00
☐☐	32	Michael Nylander, Cgy.	.10	2.00
☐☐	33	Joe Nieuwendyk, Cgy.	.10	2.00
☐☐	34	Robert Reichel, Cgy.	.10	2.00
☐☐	35	Al MacInnis, Cgy.	.25	5.00
☐☐	36	Andrei Trefilov (G), Cgy.	.25	5.00
☐☐	37	Guy Larose, Cgy.	.25	5.00
☐☐	38	Wes Walz, Cgy.	.10	2.00
☐☐	39	Michel Petit, Cgy.	.10	2.00
☐☐	40	James Patrick, Cgy.	.10	2.00
☐☐	41	Ed Belfour (G), Chi.	.35	7.00
☐☐	42	Christian Ruuttu, Chi.	.10	2.00
☐☐	43	Eric Weinrich, Chi.	.10	2.00
☐☐	44	Joe Murphy, Chi.	.10	2.00
☐☐	45	Chris Chelios, Chi.	.35	9.00
☐☐	46	Jeff Shantz, Chi.	.10	2.00
☐☐	47	Gary Suter, Chi.	.10	2.00
☐☐	48	Paul Ysebaert, Chi.	.10	2.00
☐☐	49	Ivan Droppa, Chi.	.10	2.00
☐☐	50	Sergei Krivokrasov, Chi.	.10	2.00
☐☐	51	Andy Moog (G), Dal.	.25	5.00
☐☐	52	Russ Courtnall, Dal.	.10	2.00
☐☐	53	Neal Broten, Dal.	.10	2.00
☐☐	54	Mike Craig, Dal.	.10	2.00
☐☐	55	Brent Gilchrist, Dal.	.10	2.00
☐☐	56	Per-Erik Eklund, Dal.	.10	2.00
☐☐	57	Richard Matvichuk, Dal.	.10	2.00
☐☐	58	Dave Gagner, Dal.	.10	2.00
☐☐	59	Mark Tinordi, Dal.	.10	2.00
☐☐	60	Paul Broten, Dal.	.10	2.00
☐☐	61	Nicklas Lidstrom, Det.	.25	5.00
☐☐	62	Shawn Burr, Det.	.10	2.00
☐☐	63	Paul Coffey, Det.	.25	5.00
☐☐	64	Bob Essensa (G), Det.	.10	2.00
☐☐	65	Dino Ciccarelli, Det.	.25	5.00
☐☐	66	Vyacheslav Kozlov, Det.	.10	2.00
☐☐	67	Keith Primeau, Det.	.25	5.00
☐☐	68	Steve Chiasson, Det.	.10	2.00
☐☐	69	Terry Carkner, Det.	.10	2.00
☐☐	70	Martin Lapointe, Det.	.10	2.00
☐☐	71	Bob Probert, Det.	.10	2.00
☐☐	72	Bill Ranford (G), Edm.	.25	5.00
☐☐	73	Scott Thornton, Edm.	.10	2.00
☐☐	74	Doug Weight, Edm.	.35	7.00
☐☐	75	Shayne Corson, Edm.	.25	5.00
☐☐	76	Zdeno Ciger, Edm.	.10	2.00
☐☐	77	Adam Bennett, Edm.	.10	2.00
☐☐	78	Scott Pearson, Edm.	.10	2.00
☐☐	**79**	**Brent Grieve, Edm., RC**	**.10**	**2.00**
☐☐	**80**	**Gord Mark, Edm., RC**	**.10**	**2.00**
☐☐	81	Shjon Podein, Edm.	.10	2.00
☐☐	82	Geoff Smith, Edm.	.10	2.00
☐☐	83	Bob Kudelski, Fla.	.10	2.00
☐☐	84	Andrei Lomakin, Fla.	.10	2.00
☐☐	85	Scott Mellanby, Fla.	.10	2.00
☐☐	86	Jesse Belanger, Fla.	.10	2.00
☐☐	87	Mark Fitzpatrick (G), Fla.	.10	2.00
☐☐	88	Peter Andersson, Fla.	.10	2.00
☐☐	89	Jody Hull, Fla.	.10	2.00
☐☐	90	Brent Severyn, Fla.	.10	2.00
☐☐	91	Jim Sandlak, Hfd.	.10	2.00
☐☐	92	Pat Verbeek, Hfd.	.10	2.00
☐☐	**93**	**Ted Crowley, Hfd., RC**	**.10**	**2.00**
☐☐	94	Robert Petrovicky, Hfd.	.10	2.00
☐☐	95	Geoff Sanderson, Hfd.	.10	2.00
☐☐	96	Ted Drury, Hfd.	.10	2.00
☐☐	97	Andrew Cassels, Hfd.	.10	2.00
☐☐	98	Igor Chibirev, Hfd.	.10	2.00
☐☐	99	Kevin Smyth, Hfd.	.10	2.00
☐☐	100	Alexander Godynyuk, Hfd.	.10	2.00
☐☐	101	Alexei Zhitnik, L.A.	.10	2.00
☐☐	102	Dixon Ward, L.A.	.10	2.00
☐☐	103	Wayne Gretzky, L.A.	2.00	85.00
☐☐	104	Jari Kurri, L.A.	.25	5.00
☐☐	105	Rob Blake, L.A.	.25	5.00
☐☐	106	Marty McSorley, L.A.	.10	2.00
☐☐	107	Pat Conacher, L.A.	.10	2.00
☐☐	108	Kevin Todd, L.A.	.10	2.00
☐☐	109	Robb Stauber (G), L.A.	.10	2.00
☐☐	**110**	**Keith Redmond, L.A., RC**	**.10**	**2.00**
☐☐	111	John LeClair, Mtl.	.50	12.00
☐☐	112	Brian Bellows, Mtl.	.10	2.00
☐☐	113	Patrick Roy (G), Mtl.	1.50	65.00
☐☐	**114**	**Les Kuntar (G), Mtl., RC**	**.10**	**2.00**
☐☐	115	Vincent Damphousse, Mtl.	.35	7.00
☐☐	116	Patrice Brisebois, Mtl.	.10	2.00
☐☐	117	Pierre Sévigny, Mtl.	.10	2.00
☐☐	118	Eric Desjardins, Mtl.	.25	5.00
☐☐	119	Oleg Petrov, Mtl.	.10	2.00
☐☐	120	Kevin Haller, Mtl.	.10	2.00
☐☐	121	Christian Proulx, Mtl.	.10	2.00
☐☐	122	Corey Millen, N.J.	.10	2.00
☐☐	123	Jaroslav Modry, N.J.	.10	2.00
☐☐	124	Valeri Zelepukin, N.J.	.10	2.00
☐☐	125	John MacLean, N.J.	.10	2.00
☐☐	126	Martin Brodeur (G), N.J.	.75	20.00
☐☐	127	Bill Guerin, N.J.	.25	5.00
☐☐	128	Bobby Holik, N.J.	.10	2.00
☐☐	129	Claude Lemieux, N.J.	.10	2.00
☐☐	130	Jason Smith, N.J.	.10	2.00
☐☐	131	Ken Daneyko, N.J.	.10	2.00
☐☐	132	Derek King, NYI.	.10	2.00
☐☐	133	Darius Kasparaitis, NYI.	.10	2.00
☐☐	134	Ray Ferraro, NYI.	.10	2.00
☐☐	135	Pierre Turgeon, NYI.	.25	5.00
☐☐	136	Ron Hextall (G), NYI.	.25	5.00
☐☐	137	Travis Green, NYI.	.10	2.00
☐☐	**138**	**Joe Day, NYI., RC**	**.10**	**2.00**
☐☐	139	David Volek, NYI.	.10	2.00
☐☐	140	Scott Lachance, NYI.	.10	2.00
☐☐	141	Dennis Vaske, NYI.	.10	2.00
☐☐	142	Alexei Kovalev, NYR.	.10	2.00
☐☐	143	Brian Noonan, NYR.	.10	2.00
☐☐	144	Sergei Zubov, NYR.	.25	5.00
☐☐	145	Craig MacTavish, NYR.	.10	2.00
☐☐	146	Steve Larmer, NYR.	.10	2.00
☐☐	147	Adam Graves, NYR.	.10	2.00
☐☐	148	Jeff Beukeboom, NYR.	.10	2.00
☐☐	149	Corey Hirsch (G), NYR.	.10	2.00
☐☐	150	Stéphane Matteau, NYR.	.10	2.00
☐☐	151	Brian Leetch, NYR.	.35	7.00
☐☐	152	Mattias Norstrom, NYR.	.10	2.00
☐☐	153	Sylvain Turgeon, Ott.	.10	2.00
☐☐	154	Norm Maciver, Ott.	.10	2.00
☐☐	155	Scott Levins, Ott.	.10	2.00
☐☐	156	Derek Mayer, Ott.	.10	2.00
☐☐	157	Dave McLlwain, Ott.	.10	2.00
☐☐	158	Craig Billington (G), Ott.	.10	2.00
☐☐	159	Claude Boivin, Ott.	.10	2.00
☐☐	160	Troy Mallette, Ott.	.10	2.00
☐☐	161	Evgeny Davydov, Ott.	.10	2.00
☐☐	162	Dimitri Filimonov, Ott.	.10	2.00
☐☐	163	Dimitri Yushkevich, Pha.	.10	2.00
☐☐	164	Rob Zettler, Pha.	.10	2.00
☐☐	165	Mark Recchi, Pha.	.25	5.00
☐☐	166	Josef Beranek, Pha.	.10	2.00
☐☐	167	Rod Brind'Amour, Pha.	.25	5.00
☐☐	168	Yves Racine, Pha.	.10	2.00
☐☐	169	Dominic Roussel, Pha.	.10	2.00
☐☐	170	Brent Fedyk, Pha.	.10	2.00
☐☐	**171**	**Bob Wilkie, Pha., RC**	**.10**	**2.00**
☐☐	172	Kevin Dineen, Pha.	.10	2.00
☐☐	173	Shawn McEachern, Pgh.	.10	2.00
☐☐	174	Jaromir Jagr, Pgh.	1.00	40.00
☐☐	175	Tomas Sandström, Pgh.	.10	2.00
☐☐	176	Ron Francis, Pgh.	.35	7.00
☐☐	177	Kevin Stevens, Pgh.	.10	2.00
☐☐	178	Jim McKenzie, Pgh.	.10	2.00
☐☐	179	Larry Murphy, Pgh.	.25	5.00
☐☐	180	Joe Mullen, Pgh.	.10	2.00
☐☐	181	Greg Hawgood, Pgh.	.10	2.00
☐☐	182	Tom Barrasso (G), Pgh.	.25	5.00
☐☐	183	Ulf Samuelsson, Pgh.	.10	2.00

	No.	Player		
☐☐	184	Bob Bassen, Que.	.10	2.00
☐☐	185	Mats Sundin, Que.	.50	12.00
☐☐	186	Mike Ricci, Que.	.10	2.00
☐☐	187	Iain Fraser, Que.	.10	2.00
☐☐	188	Garth Butcher, Que.	.10	2.00
☐☐	189	Jocelyn Thibault, Que.	.35	7.00
☐☐	190	Valeri Kamensky, Que.	.25	5.00
☐☐	191	Martin Rucinsky, Que.	.10	2.00
☐☐	192	Dwayne Norris, Que.	.10	2.00
☐☐	193	René Corbet, Que.	.10	2.00
☐☐	194	Reggie Savage, Que.	.10	2.00
☐☐	195	Alexei Kasatonov, Stl.	.10	2.00
☐☐	196	Brendan Shanahan, Stl.	.60	15.00
☐☐	197	Phil Housley, Stl.	.10	2.00
☐☐	198	Jim Montgomery, Stl.	.10	2.00
☐☐	199	Curtis Joseph (G), Stl.	.60	15.00
☐☐	200	Craig Janney, Stl.	.10	2.00
☐☐	201	David Roberts, Stl.	.10	2.00
☐☐	**202**	**Dave Mackey, Stl., RC**	**.10**	**2.00**
☐☐	203	Peter Stastny, Stl.	.10	2.00
☐☐	204	Terry Hollinger, Stl.	.10	2.00
☐☐	205	Steve Duchesne, Stl.	.10	2.00
☐☐	206	Vitali Prokhorov, Stl.	.10	2.00
☐☐	207	Rob Gaudreau, S.J.	.10	2.00
☐☐	208	Sandis Ozolinsh, S.J.	.25	5.00
☐☐	209	Johan Garpenlov, S.J.	.10	2.00
☐☐	210	Todd Elik, S.J.	.10	2.00
☐☐	211	Sergei Makarov, S.J.	.10	2.00
☐☐	212	Jean-François Quintin, S.J.	.10	2.00
☐☐	213	Vyacheslav Butsayev, S.J.	.10	2.00
☐☐	214	Jimmy Waite (G), S.J.	.10	2.00
☐☐	215	Ulf Dahlen, S.J.	.10	2.00
☐☐	216	Andrei Nazarov, S.J.	.10	2.00
☐☐	217	Denis Savard, T.B.	.10	2.00
☐☐	218	Brent Gretzky, T.B.	.10	2.00
☐☐	219	Petr Klima, T.B.	.10	2.00
☐☐	220	Chris Gratton, T.B.	.25	5.00
☐☐	221	Brian Bradley, T.B.	.10	2.00
☐☐	222	Adam Creighton, T.B.	.10	2.00
☐☐	223	Shawn Chambers, T.B.	.10	2.00
☐☐	224	Rob Zamuner, T.B.	.25	5.00
☐☐	225	Daren Puppa, T.B.	.10	2.00
☐☐	226	Mikael Andersson, T.B.	.10	2.00
☐☐	227	Dave Ellett, Tor.	.10	2.00
☐☐	228	Mike Gartner, Tor.	.25	5.00
☐☐	229	Félix Potvin (G), Tor.	.50	12.00
☐☐	230	Yanic Perreault, Tor.	.10	2.00
☐☐	231	Nikolai Borschevsky, Tor.	.10	2.00
☐☐	232	Dmitri Mironov, Tor.	.10	2.00
☐☐	233	Todd Gill, Tor.	.10	2.00
☐☐	234	Eric Lacroix, Tor.	.10	2.00
☐☐	235	Kent Manderville, Tor.	.10	2.00
☐☐	236	Chris Goverdans, Tor.	.10	2.00
☐☐	**237**	**Frank Bialowas, Tor., RC**	**.10**	**2.00**
☐☐	238	Kirk McLean (G), Van.	.25	5.00
☐☐	239	Jimmy Carson, Van.	.10	2.00
☐☐	240	Geoff Courtnall, Van.	.10	2.00
☐☐	241	Trevor Linden, Van.	.25	5.00
☐☐	242	Murray Craven, Van.	.10	2.00
☐☐	243	Bret Hedican, Van.	.10	2.00
☐☐	244	Jeff Brown, Van.	.10	2.00
☐☐	245	Michael Peca, Van.	.25	5.00
☐☐	246	John Namestnikov, Van.	.10	2.00
☐☐	247	Nathan Lafayette, Van.	.10	2.00
☐☐	248	Shawn Antoski, Van.	.10	2.00
☐☐	249	Sergio Momesso, Van.	.10	2.00
☐☐	250	Mike Ridley, Wsh.	.10	2.00
☐☐	251	Peter Bondra, Wsh.	.35	9.00
☐☐	252	Dimitri Khristich, Wsh.	.10	2.00
☐☐	253	Dave Poulin, Wsh.	.10	2.00
☐☐	254	Dale Hunter, Wsh.	.10	2.00
☐☐	255	Rick Tabaracci (G), Wsh.	.10	2.00
☐☐	256	Kelly Miller, Wsh.	.10	2.00
☐☐	257	John Slaney, Wsh.	.10	2.00
☐☐	258	Todd Krygier, Wsh.	.10	2.00
☐☐	259	Kevin Hatcher, Wsh.	.10	2.00
☐☐	260	Alexei Zhamnov, Wpg.	.25	5.00
☐☐	261	Dallas Drake, Wpg.	.10	2.00
☐☐	262	Dave Manson, Wpg.	.10	2.00
☐☐	263	Thomas Steen, Wpg.	.10	2.00
☐☐	264	Keith Tkachuk, Wpg.	.35	9.00
☐☐	265	Russ Romaniuk, Wpg.	.10	2.00
☐☐	266	Michal Grosek, Wpg.	.10	2.00
☐☐	267	Nelson Emerson, Wpg.	.10	2.00
☐☐	268	Michael O'Neill (G), Wpg.	.10	2.00
☐☐	269	Kris King, Wpg.	.10	2.00
☐☐	270	Teppo Numminen, Wpg.	.10	2.00
☐☐	271	Jason Arnott, Edm.	.25	5.00
☐☐	272	Mikael Renberg, Pha.	.25	5.00
☐☐	273	Alexei Yashin, Ott.	.35	9.00
☐☐	274	Chris Pronger, Hfd.	.25	5.00
☐☐	275	Jocelyn Thibault (G), Que.	.35	7.00
☐☐	276	Bryan Smolinski, Fla.	.10	2.00
☐☐	277	Derek Plante, Buf.	.10	2.00
☐☐	278	Martin Brodeur (G), N.J.	.35	12.00
☐☐	279	Jim Dowd, N.J.	.10	2.00
☐☐	280	Iain Fraser, Que.	.10	2.00
☐☐	281	Pat Peake, Wsh.	.10	2.00
☐☐	282	Chris Gratton, T.B.	.25	5.00
☐☐	283	Chris Osgood (G), Det.	.35	9.00
☐☐	284	Jesse Belanger, Fla.	.10	2.00
☐☐	285	Alexandre Daigle, Ott.	.25	5.00
☐☐	286	Robert Lang, L.A.	.10	2.00
☐☐	287	Markus Naslund, Pgh.	.10	2.00
☐☐	288	Trevor Kidd (G), Cgy.	.25	5.00
☐☐	289	Jeff Shantz, Chi.	.10	2.00
☐☐	290	Jaroslav Modry, N.J.	.10	2.00
☐☐	291	Oleg Petrov, Mtl.	.10	2.00
☐☐	292	Scott Levins, Ott.	.10	2.00
☐☐	293	Jozef Stumpel, Bos.	.10	2.00
☐☐	294	Rob Niedermayer, Fla.	.25	5.00
☐☐	295	Brent Gretzky, T.B.	.10	2.00
☐☐	296	Mario Lemieux, Pgh.	1.25	65.00
☐☐	297	Pavel Bure, Van.	.75	20.00
☐☐	298	Brendan Shanahan, Stl.	.60	15.00
☐☐	299	Steve Yzerman, Det.	1.00	70.00
☐☐	300	Teemu Selänne, Wpg.	.75	20.00
☐☐	301	Eric Lindros, Pha.	1.00	65.00
☐☐	302	Jeremy Roenick, Chi.	.25	5.00
☐☐	303	Dave Andreychuk, Tor.	.10	2.00
☐☐	304	Ray Bourque, Bos.	.25	8.00
☐☐	305	Sergei Fedorov, Det.	.50	12.00
☐☐	306	Wayne Gretzky, L.A.	1.50	65.00
☐☐	307	Adam Graves, NYR.	.10	2.00
☐☐	308	Mike Modano, Dal.	.50	12.00
☐☐	309	Brett Hull, Stl.	.50	12.00
☐☐	310	Pat LaFontaine, Buf.	.25	5.00
☐☐	311	Adam Oates, Bos.	.35	7.00
☐☐	312	Patrick Roy (G), Mtl.	1.00	40.00
☐☐	313	Doug Gilmour, Tor.	.35	7.00
☐☐	314	Jaromir Jagr, Pgh.	.75	30.00
☐☐	315	Mark Recchi, Pha.	.25	5.00

"YOU CRASH THE GAME"

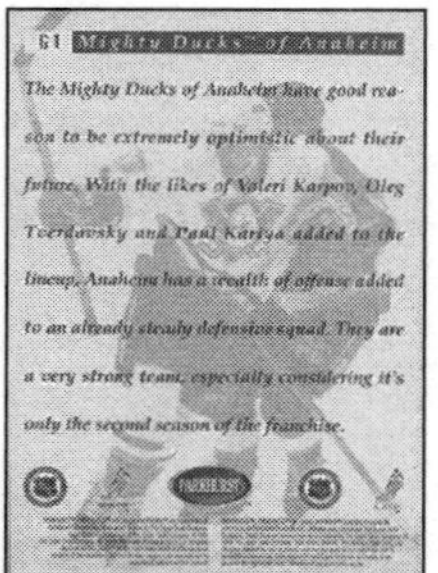

These cards have four versions: a Canadian insert (prefix C, red), a Hobby insert (prefix H, green), a Retail insert (prefix R, blue) and a redeemed card (prefix G, gold). Canadian, Hobby and Retail inserts all have identical pricing. Since the 1994-95 hockey season was shortened by an NHL-lockout, any insert could be redeemed for a complete gold set.

Insert Set (28 cards): 110.00 20.00

	No.	Player	Insert	Gold
☐☐☐☐	1	Stéphan Lebeau, Ana.	.50	.10
☐☐☐☐	2	Ray Bourque, Bos.	4.00	1.00
☐☐☐☐	3	Pat LaFontaine, Buf.	1.00	.25
☐☐☐☐	4	Joe Nieuwendyk, Cgy.	1.00	.25
☐☐☐☐	5	Jeremy Roenick, Chi.	2.00	.50
☐☐☐☐	6	Mike Modano, Dal.	4.00	1.00
☐☐☐☐	7	Sergei Fedorov, Det.	4.00	1.00
☐☐☐☐	8	Jason Arnott, Edm.	1.00	.25
☐☐☐☐	9	John Vanbiesbrouck (G), Fla.	4.50	1.25
☐☐☐☐	10	Geoff Sanderson, Hfd.	.50	.10
☐☐☐☐	11	Wayne Gretzky, L.A.	15.00	4.00
☐☐☐☐	12	Patrick Roy (G), Mtl.	12.00	3.00
☐☐☐☐	13	Scott Stevens, N.J.	.50	.10
☐☐☐☐	14	Pierre Turgeon, NYI.	1.00	.25
☐☐☐☐	15	Adam Graves, NYR.	.50	.10
☐☐☐☐	16	Alexei Yashin, Ott.	3.00	.75
☐☐☐☐	17	Eric Lindros, Pha.	10.00	2.50
☐☐☐☐	18	Mario Lemieux, Pgh.	12.00	3.00
☐☐☐☐	19	Joe Sakic, Que.	6.00	1.75
☐☐☐☐	20	Brett Hull, Stl.	4.00	1.00
☐☐☐☐	21	Sandis Ozolinsh, S.J.	1.00	.25
☐☐☐☐	22	Chris Gratton, T.B.	1.00	.25
☐☐☐☐	23	Doug Gilmour, Tor.	2.00	.50
☐☐☐☐	24	Pavel Bure, Van.	5.00	1.50
☐☐☐☐	25	Joé Juneau, Wsh.	.50	.10
☐☐☐☐	26	Teemu Selänne, Wpg.	5.00	1.50
☐☐☐☐	27	Mark Messier	4.00	1.00
☐☐☐☐	28	Wayne Gretzky	15.00	4.00

VINTAGE

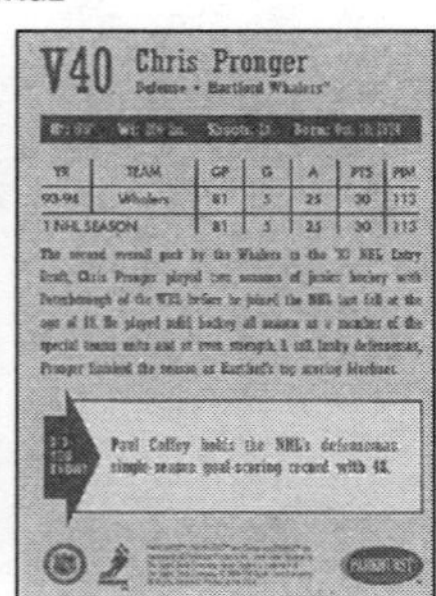

Insert Set (90 cards): 35.00
Common Player: .25

	No.	Player	NRMT-MT
☐	V1	Dominik Hasek (G), Buf.	2.00
☐	V2	Mike Modano, Dal.	1.50
☐	V3	Shayne Corson, Edm.	.50
☐	V4	Kirk Muller, Mtl.	.25
☐	V5	Mike Richter (G), NYR.	1.00
☐	V6	Mario Lemieux, Pgh.	5.00
☐	V7	Sandis Ozolinsh, S.J.	.50
☐	V8	Dave Ellett, Tor.	.25
☐	V9	Dave Manson, Edm.	.25
☐	V10	Terry Yake, Hfd.	.25
☐	V11	Craig Simpson, Buf.	.25
☐	V12	Paul Cavallini, Dal.	.25
☐	V13	John Vanbiesbrouck (G), Fla.	1.75
☐	V14	Gilbert Dionne, Mtl.	.25
☐	V15	Brian Leetch, NYR.	1.00
☐	V16	Martin Straka, Pgh.	.25
☐	V17	Curtis Joseph (G), Stl.	1.75
☐	V18	Pavel Bure, Van.	2.00
☐	V19	Garry Valk, Ana.	.25
☐	V20	Theoren Fleury, Cgy.	1.00
☐	V21	Brent Gilchrist, Dal.	.25
☐	V22	Rob Niedermayer, Fla.	.50
☐	V23	Vincent Damphousse, Mtl.	1.00
☐	V24	Alexei Kovalev, NYR.	.25
☐	V25	Rick Tocchet, Pgh.	.25
☐	V26	Steve Duchesne, Stl.	.25
☐	V27	Jiri Slegr, Van.	.25
☐	V28	Patrick Carnback, Ana.	.25
☐	V29	Gary Roberts, Cgy.	.50
☐	V30	Derian Hatcher, Dal.	.50
☐	V31	Jesse Belanger, Fla.	.25
☐	V32	Mathieu Schneider, Mtl.	.25
☐	V33	Mark Messier, NYR.	1.50
☐	V34	Joe Sakic, Que.	2.50
☐	V35	Brett Hull, Stl.	1.50
☐	V36	Martin Gelinas, Van.	.25
☐	V37	Maxim Bets, Ana.	.25
☐	V38	Joel Otto, Cgy.	.25
☐	V39	Sergei Fedorov, Det.	1.50
☐	V40	Chris Pronger, Hfd.	.50
☐	V41	Scott Stevens, N.J.	.25
☐	V42	Alexandre Daigle, Ott.	.50
☐	V43	Owen Nolan, Que.	.50
☐	V44	Petr Nedved, Stl.	.25
☐	V45	Jeff Brown, Van.	.25
☐	V46	Adam Oates, Bos.	1.00
☐	V47	Robert Reichel, Cgy.	.50
☐	V48	Vyacheslav Kozlov, Det.	.25
☐	V49	Geoff Sanderson, Hfd.	.25
☐	V50	Stéphane Richer, N.J.	.25
☐	V51	Sylvain Turgeon, Ott.	.25

☐	V52	Mike Ricci, Que.	.25
☐	V53	Roman Hamrlik, T.B.	.50
☐	V54	Kevin Hatcher, Wsh.	.25
☐	V55	Mariusz Czerkawski, Bos.	.25
☐	V56	Tony Amonte, Chi.	.50
☐	V57	Steve Yzerman, Det.	3.00
☐	V58	Andrew Cassels, Hfd.	.25
☐	V59	Claude Lemieux, N.J.	.25
☐	V60	Derek Mayer, Ott.	.25
☐	V61	Jocelyn Thibault (G), Que.	1.00
☐	V62	Brent Gretzky, T.B.	.25
☐	V63	Pat Peake, Wsh.	.25
☐	V64	Cam Neely, Bos.	.50
☐	V65	Jeremy Roenick, Chi.	.50
☐	V66	Keith Primeau, Det.	.50
☐	V67	Luc Robitaille, L.A.	.50
☐	V68	Steve Thomas, NYI.	.25
☐	V69	Eric Lindros, Pha.	4.00
☐	V70	Pat Falloon, S.J.	.25
☐	V71	Brian Bradley, T.B.	.25
☐	V72	Kelly Miller, Wsh.	.25
☐	V73	Pat LaFontaine, Buf.	.50
☐	V74	Gary Suter, Cgy.	.25
☐	V75	Bill Ranford (G), Edm.	.50
☐	V76	Tony Granato, L.A.	.25
☐	V77	Vladimir Malakhov, NYI.	.25
☐	V78	Mikael Renberg, Pha.	.50
☐	V79	Arturs Irbe (G), S.J.	.25
☐	V80	Doug Gilmour, Tor.	1.00
☐	V81	Teemu Selänne, Wpg.	2.00
☐	V82	Derek Plante, Buf.	.25
☐	V83	Eric Weinrich, Hfd.	.25
☐	V84	Jason Arnott, Edm.	.50
☐	V85	Rob Blake, L.A.	.50
☐	V86	Ray Ferraso, NYI.	.25
☐	V87	Gary Galley, Pha.	.25
☐	V88	Igor Larionov, S.J.	.50
☐	V89	Dave Andreychuk, Tor.	.25
☐	V90	Dallas Drake, Det.	.25

1994 - 95 PARKHURST "64-65" TALL BOYS

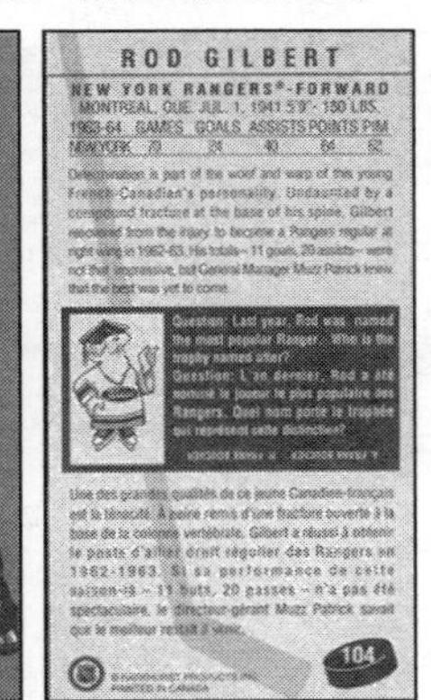

Imprint: © PARKHURST PRODUCTS
Card Size: 2 1/2" x 4 11/16"
Complete Set (180 cards): 18.00
Common Player: .15
Album: 18.00

	No.	Player	NRMT-MT
☐	1	John Bucyk, Bos.	.75
☐	2	Murray Oliver, Bos.	.15
☐	3	Ted Green, Bos.	.15
☐	4	Tom Williams, Bos.	.15
☐	5	Dean Prentice, Bos.	.15
☐	6	Ed Westfall, Bos.	.15
☐	7	Orland Kurtenbach, Bos.	.15
☐	8	Reg Fleming, Bos.	.15
☐	9	Léo Boivin, Bos.	.35
☐	10	Bob McCord, Bos.	.15
☐	11	Bob Leiter, Bos.	.15
☐	12	Tom Johnson, Bos.	.35
☐	13	Bob Woytowich, Bos.	.15
☐	14	Ab MacDonald, Bos.	.15
☐	15	Ed Johnston (G), Bos.	.35
☐	16	Forbes Kennedy, Bos.	.15
☐	17	Murray Balfour, Bos.	.15
☐	18	Wayne Cashman, Bos.	.50
☐	19	Don Awrey, Bos.	.15
☐	20	Gary Dornhoefer, Bos.	.15
☐	21	Ron Schock, Bos.	.15
☐	22	Milt Schmidt, Coach, Bos.	.35
☐	23	Ken Wharram, Chi.	.15
☐	24	Chico Maki, Chi.	.15
☐	25	Bobby Hull, Chi.	2.75
☐	26	Stan Mikita, Chi.	1.00
☐	27	Doug Mohns, Chi.	.15
☐	28	Denis DeJordy (G), Chi.	.35
☐	29	Phil Esposito, Chi.	1.50
☐	30	Elmer Vasko, Chi.	.15
☐	31	Pierre Pilote, Chi.	.35
☐	32	Glenn Hall (G), Chi.	1.75
☐	33	Eric Nesterenko, Chi.	.15
☐	34	Doug Robinson, Chi.	.15
☐	35	Matt Ravlich, Chi.	.15
☐	36	John McKenzie, Chi.	.15
☐	37	Fred Stanfield, Chi.	.15
☐	38	Doug Jarrett, Chi.	.15
☐	39	Dennis Hull, Chi.	.50
☐	40	Al MacNeil, Chi.	.15
☐	41	Wayne Hillman, Chi.	.15
☐	42	Bill Hay, Chi.	.15
☐	43	Billy Reay, Coach, Chi.	.15
☐	44	Parker MacDonald, Det.	.15
☐	45	Floyd Smith, Det.	.15
☐	46	Gordie Howe, Det.	2.75
☐	47	Bruce MacGregor, Det.	.15
☐	48	Ron Murphy, Det.	.15
☐	49	Doug Barkley, Det.	.15
☐	50	Paul Henderson, Det.	.75
☐	51	Pit Martin, Det.	.15
☐	52	Al Langlois, Det.	.15
☐	53	Roger Crozier (G), Det.	1.00
☐	54	Bill Gadsby, Det.	.35
☐	55	Marcel Pronovost, Det.	.35
☐	56	Alex Delvecchio, Det.	.75
☐	57	Gary Bergman, Det.	.15
☐	58	Norm Ullman, Det.	.75
☐	59	Larry Jeffrey, Det.	.15
☐	60	Lowell MacDonald, Det.	.15
☐	61	Pete Goegan, Det.	.15
☐	62	Andre Pronovost, Det.	.15
☐	63	Warren Godfrey, Det.	.15
☐	64	Ted Lindsay, Det.	.75
☐	65	Sid Abel, Coach, Det.	.35
☐	66	John Ferguson, Mtl.	.50
☐	67	Henri Richard, Mtl.	1.25
☐	68	Dave Balon, Mtl.	.15
☐	69	Noel Picard, Mtl.	.15
☐	70	Claude Provost, Mtl.	.15
☐	71	Claude Larose, Mtl.	.15
☐	72	Jacques Laperrière, Mtl.	.75
☐	73	Ralph Backstrom, Mtl.	.15
☐	74	J.C. Tremblay, Mtl.	.15
☐	75	Yvan Cournoyer, Mtl.	1.25
☐	76	Jean-Guy Talbot, Mtl.	.15
☐	77	Gilles Tremblay, Mtl.	.15
☐	78	Ted Harris, Mtl.	.15
☐	79	Jim Roberts, Mtl.	.15
☐	80	Red Berenson, Mtl.	.15
☐	81	Gump Worsley (G), Mtl.	1.50
☐	82	Charlie Hodge (G), Mtl.	.35
☐	83	Terry Harper, Mtl.	.15
☐	84	Bobby Rousseau, Mtl.	.15
☐	85	Jean Béliveau, Mtl.	2.00
☐	86	Bill Hicke, Mtl.	.15
☐	87	Toe Blake, Coach, Mtl.	.35
☐	88	Don Marshall, NYR.	.15
☐	89	Jean Ratelle, NYR.	1.00
☐	90	Vic Hadfield, NYR.	.15
☐	91	Earl Ingarfield, NYR.	.15
☐	92	Harry Howell, NYR.	.35
☐	93	Rod Seiling, NYR.	.15
☐	94	Dave Richardson, NYR.	.15
☐	95	Val Fonteyne, NYR.	.15
☐	96	Lou Angotti, NYR.	.15
☐	97	Arnie Brown, NYR.	.15
☐	98	Don Johns, NYR.	.15
☐	99	Jim Mikol, NYR.	.15
☐	100	Jacques Plante (G), NYR.	2.25
☐	101	Marcel Paille (G), NYR.	.35
☐	102	Jim Neilson, NYR.	.15
☐	103	Bob Nevin, NYR.	.15
☐	104	Rod Gilbert, NYR.	1.00
☐	105	Phil Goyette, NYR.	.15
☐	106	Dick Duff, NYR.	.15
☐	107	Camille Henry, NYR.	.15
☐	108	Red Sullivan, Coach, NYR.	.15
☐	109	Kent Douglas, Tor.	.15
☐	110	Bob Pulford, Tor.	.60
☐	111	Dave Keon, Tor.	1.00
☐	112	Don McKenney, Tor.	.15
☐	113	Pete Stemkowski, Tor.	.15
☐	114	Carl Brewer, Tor.	.15
☐	115	Allan Stanley, Tor.	.15
☐	116	Dickie Moore, Tor.	.15
☐	117	Eddie Shack, Tor.	.15
☐	118	Larry Hillman, Tor.	.15
☐	119	Terry Sawchuk (G), Tor.	2.25
☐	120	Bob Baun, Tor.	.15
☐	121	Brit Selby, Tor.	.15
☐	122	George Armstrong, Tor.	.75
☐	123	Jim Pappin, Tor.	.15
☐	124	Andy Bathgate, Tor.	.35
☐	125	Ron Ellis, Tor.	.15
☐	126	Billy Harris, Tor.	.15
☐	127	Red Kelly, Tor.	.75
☐	128	Ron Stewart, Tor.	.15
☐	129	Johnny Bower (G), Tor.	1.50
☐	130	Frank Mahovlich, Tor.	1.50
☐	131	Tim Horton, Tor.	2.00
☐	132	King Clancy, Ass. G.M., Tor.	.35
☐	133	AS: Glenn Hall (G), Chi.	1.00
☐	134	AS: Pierre Pilote, Chi.	.25
☐	135	AS: Tim Horton, Tor.	1.00
☐	136	AS: Bobby Hull, Chi.	1.50
☐	137	AS: Ken Wharram, Chi.	.15
☐	138	AS: Stan Mikita, Chi.	.50
☐	139	AS: Charlie Hodge (G), Mtl.	.25
☐	140	AS: Jacques Laperrière, Mtl.	.35
☐	141	AS: Elmer Vasko, Chi.	.15
☐	142	AS: Jean Béliveau, Mtl.	1.00
☐	143	AS: Frank Mahovlich, Tor.	.75
☐	144	AS: Gordie Howe, Det.	1.50
☐	145	AW: Pierre Pilote, Chi.	.25
☐	146	AW: Jean Béliveau, Mtl.	1.00
☐	147	AW: Stan Mikita, Chi.	.50
☐	148	AW: Charlie Hodge (G), Mtl.	.25
☐	149	AW: Jacques Laperrière, Mtl.	.35
☐	150	AW: Ken Wharram, Chi.	.15
☐	151	1964 All-Star Game	.50
☐	152	Jean Ratelle Invades Crease	.50
☐	153	Center Ice Action	.50
☐	154	Old Teammates Duel	.50
☐	155	All Eyes On The Puck	.50
☐	156	Detroit Defense Stands Tall	.50
☐	157	Roger Crozier Makes The Stretch	.50
☐	158	Roger Crozier Plays Center Field	.50
☐	159	Hawks Eye Jean Béliveau	1.00
☐	160	Montreal's Speedy Rookie	.60
☐	161	Jacques Laperrière Wins Race	.35
☐	162	Ron Ellis Robbed By Habs	.25
☐	163	Terry Sawchuk Eyes Bouncing Disc	1.25
☐	164	Eddie Shack Entertains	.50
☐	165	"Mr Goalie" In Action	1.00
☐	166	Glenn Hall Holds His Ground	1.00
☐	167	Ed Johnston Freezes Action	.25
☐	168	Ron Ellis Robbed By Ed Johnston	.25
☐	169	LL: Murray Oliver, Bos.	.15
☐	170	LL: Stan Mikita, Chi.	.50
☐	171	LL: Gordie Howe, Det.	1.50
☐	172	LL: Jean Béliveau, Mtl.	1.00
☐	173	LL: Phil Goyette, NYR.	.15
☐	174	LL: Andy Bathgate, Tor.	.25
☐	175	Stanley Cup Semi-Finals	.75
☐	176	Stanley Cup Semi-Finals	.75
☐	177	Stanley Cup Finals	1.50
☐	178	Stanley Cup	.50
☐	179	Checklist 1	.15
☐	180	Checklist 2	.15

AUTOGRAPHS

These cards are serial numbered out of 964.
Card Size: 2 1/2" x 4 11/16"
Insert Set (6 cards): 500.00

	No.	Player	NRMT-MT
☐	A1	Rod Gilbert, Mtl.	70.00

	No.	Player	NRMT-MT
☐	A2	Yvan Cournoyer, Mtl.	85.00
☐	A3	Bobby Hull, Chi.	160.00
☐	A4	Phil Esposito, Chi.	140.00
☐	A5	Gordie Howe, Det.	175.00
☐	A6	Dave Keon, Tor.	100.00

FUTURE STARS

Card Size: 2 1/2" x 4 11/16"
Insert Set (6 cards): 75.00

	No.	Player	NRMT-MT
☐	FS1	Jacques Lemaire	16.00
☐	FS2	Gerry Cheevers (G)	22.00
☐	FS3	Ken Hodge	14.00
☐	FS4	Bernie Parent (G)	22.00
☐	FS5	Rogatien Vachon (G)	16.00
☐	FS6	Derek Sanderson	20.00

ALL-TIME GREATS

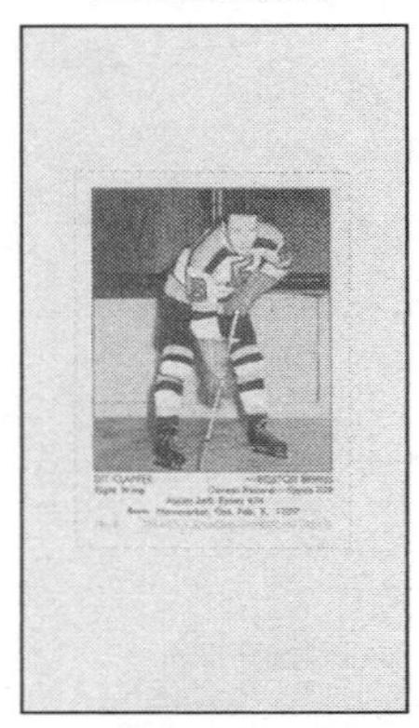

Cards 1-6 were issued in Canadian packs while cards 7-12 were issued in American packs. These cards are limited to 1,000 copies.
Card Size: 2 1/2" x 4 11/16"
Insert Set (12 cards): 275.00

	No.	Player	NRMT-MT
☐	1	Ace Bailey	40.00
☐	2	Alex Levinsky	20.00
☐	3	Babe Pratt	25.00
☐	4	Elmer Lach	30.00
☐	5	Maurice Richard	60.00
☐	6	Bill Durnan (G)	40.00
☐	7	Frank Brimsek	40.00
☐	8	Dit Clapper	30.00
☐	9	Tiny Thompson (G)	40.00
☐	10	Bun Cook	25.00
☐	11	Ching Johnson	30.00
☐	12	Lionel Conacher	40.00

REDEMPTION

Each six card set was available through a wrapper redemption.
Card Size: 2 1/2" x 4 11/16"
All-Stars Set (6 cards): 18.00
Award Winners Set (6 cards): 30.00
League Leaders Set (6 cards): 15.00

	No.	Player	NRMT-MT
☐	AS1	Roger Crozier (G)	3.50
☐	AS2	Pierre Pilote	1.50
☐	AS3	Jacques Laperrière	2.50
☐	AS4	Norm Ullman	2.50
☐	AS5	Bobby Hull	10.00
☐	AS6	Claude Provost	1.00
☐	TW1	Pierre Pilote	1.50
☐	TW2	Bobby Hull	10.00
☐	TW3	Stan Mikita	3.50
☐	TW4	Terry Sawchuk/Johnny Bower	6.00
☐	TW5	Roger Crozier	3.50
☐	TW6	Bobby Hull	10.00
☐	SL1	John Bucyk	2.50
☐	SL2	Stan Mikita	3.50
☐	SL3	Norm Ullman	2.50
☐	SL4	Claude Provost	1.00
☐	SL5	Rod Gilbert	3.50
☐	SL6	Frank Mahovlich	5.00

1994 - 95 PARKHURST SE

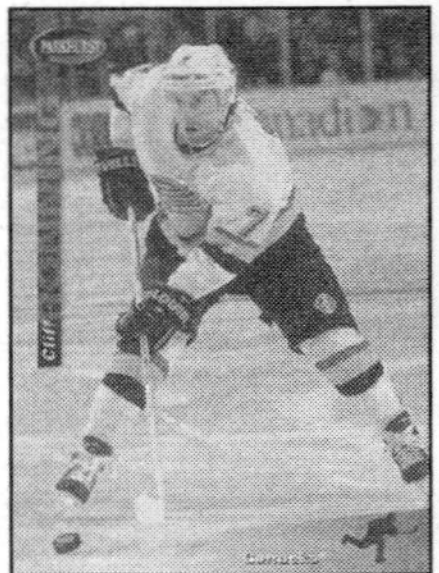

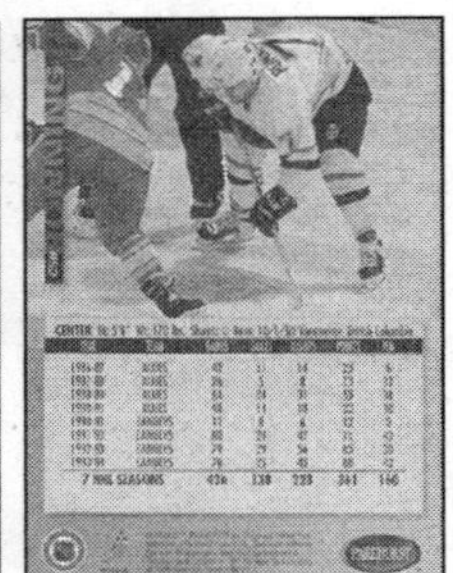

These cards have two versions: the regular card and a "Parkie" gold parallel.
Imprint: © 1994 The Upper Deck Company
Complete Set (270 cards): 20.00 200.00
Common Player: .10 .25

	No.	Player	Regular	Gold
☐ ☐	SE1	Guy Hebert (G), Ana.	.25	.50
☐ ☐	SE2	Bob Corkum, Ana.	.10	.25
☐ ☐	SE3	Randy Ladouceur, Ana.	.10	.25
☐ ☐	SE4	Tom Kurvers, Ana.	.10	.25
☐ ☐	SE5	Joe Sacco, Ana.	.10	.25
☐ ☐	SE6	Valeri Karpov, Ana.	.10	.25
☐ ☐	SE7	Garry Valk, Ana.	.10	.25
☐ ☐	SE8	Paul Kariya, Ana.	2.00	10.00
☐ ☐	SE9	Alexei Kasatonov, Ana.	.10	.25
☐ ☐	SE10	Sergei Zholtok, Ana.	.25	.50
☐ ☐	SE11	Glenn Murray, Bos.	.10	.25
☐ ☐	SE12	Dave Reid, Bos.	.10	.25
☐ ☐	SE13	Adam Oates, Bos.	.35	1.00
☐ ☐	SE14	Ted Donato, Bos.	.10	.25
☐ ☐	SE15	Don Sweeney, Bos.	.10	.25
☐ ☐	SE16	Philippe Boucher, Buf.	.10	.25
☐ ☐	SE17	Bob Sweeney, Buf.	.10	.25
☐ ☐	SE18	Pat LaFontaine, Buf.	.25	.50
☐ ☐	SE19	Derek Plante, Buf.	.10	.25
☐ ☐	SE20	Jason Dawe, Buf.	.10	.25
☐ ☐	SE21	Petr Svoboda, Buf.	.10	.25
☐ ☐	SE22	Craig Simpson, Buf.	.10	.25
☐ ☐	SE23	Viktor Gordiouk, Cgy.	.10	.25
☐ ☐	SE24	Trevor Kidd (G), Cgy.	.25	.50
☐ ☐	SE25	Todd Hlushko, Cgy.	.10	.25
☐ ☐	SE26	German Titov, Cgy.	.10	.25
☐ ☐	SE27	Gary Roberts, Cgy.	.25	.50
☐ ☐	SE28	Theoren Fleury, Cgy.	.35	1.00
☐ ☐	SE29	Cory Stillman, Cgy.	.10	.25
☐ ☐	SE30	Phil Housley, Cgy.	.10	.25
☐ ☐	SE31	Joel Otto, Cgy.	.10	.25
☐ ☐	SE32	Patrick Poulin, Cgy.	.10	.25
☐ ☐	SE33	Christian Soucy, Cgy.	.10	.25
☐ ☐	SE34	Karl Dykhuis, Chi.	.10	.25
☐ ☐	SE35	Jeremy Roenick, Chi.	.35	1.00
☐ ☐	SE36	Tony Amonte, Chi.	.25	.50
☐ ☐	SE37	Sergei Krivokrasov, Chi.	.10	.25
☐ ☐	SE38	Bernie Nicholls, Chi.	.10	.25
☐ ☐	SE39	Todd Harvey, Dal.	.10	.25
☐ ☐	SE40	Jarkko Varvio, Dal.	.10	.25
☐ ☐	SE41	Shane Churla, Dal.	.10	.25
☐ ☐	SE42	Paul Cavallini, Dal.	.10	.25
☐ ☐	SE43	Trent Klatt, Dal.	.10	.25
☐ ☐	SE44	Darcy Wakaluk (G), Dal.	.10	.25
☐ ☐	SE45	Derian Hatcher, Dal.	.25	.50
☐ ☐	SE46	Dean Evason, Dal.	.10	.25
☐ ☐	SE47	Mike Modano, Dal.	.50	2.50
☐ ☐	SE48	Greg Johnson, Det.	.10	.25
☐ ☐	SE49	Ray Sheppard, Det.	.10	.25
☐ ☐	SE50	Sergei Fedorov, Det.	.50	2.50
☐ ☐	SE51	Bob Rouse, Det.	.10	.25
☐ ☐	SE52	Mike Vernon (G), Det.	.25	.50
☐ ☐	SE53	Vladimir Konstantinov, Det.	.10	.25
☐ ☐	SE54	Chris Osgood (G), Det.	.35	1.50
☐ ☐	SE55	Steve Yzerman, Det.	1.00	5.00
☐ ☐	**SE56**	**Jason York, Det., RC**	**.10**	**.25**
☐ ☐	SE57	Boris Mironov, Edm.	.10	.25
☐ ☐	SE58	Igor Kravchuk, Edm.	.10	.25
☐ ☐	SE59	Jason Arnott, Edm.	.25	.50
☐ ☐	**SE60**	**David Oliver, Edm., RC**	**.10**	**.25**
☐ ☐	SE61	Todd Marchant, Edm.	.10	.25
☐ ☐	SE62	Dean McAmmond, Edm.	.10	.25
☐ ☐	SE63	Brian Skrudland, Fla.	.10	.25
☐ ☐	SE64	Tom Fitzgerald (G), Fla.	.10	.25
☐ ☐	SE65	Brian Benning, Fla.	.10	.25
☐ ☐	SE66	Stu Barnes, Fla.	.10	.25
☐ ☐	SE67	John Vanbiesbrouck (G), Fla.	.60	3.00
☐ ☐	SE68	Rob Niedermayer, Fla.	.25	1.50
☐ ☐	SE69	Jimmy Carson, Fla.	.10	.25
☐ ☐	SE70	Mark Janssens, Hfd.	.10	.25
☐ ☐	SE71	Sean Burke (G), Hfd.	.25	.50
☐ ☐	SE72	Andre Nikolishin, Hfd.	.10	.25
☐ ☐	SE73	Chris Pronger, Hfd.	.25	.50
☐ ☐	SE74	Jeff Reese, Hfd.	.10	.25
☐ ☐	SE75	Darren Turcotte, Hfd.	.10	.25
☐ ☐	SE76	Robert Kron, Hfd.	.10	.25
☐ ☐	SE77	Kevin Brown, Hfd.	.10	.25
☐ ☐	SE78	Robert Lang, L.A.	.10	.25
☐ ☐	SE79	Rick Tocchet, L.A.	.10	.25
☐ ☐	SE80	Jamie Storr (G), L.A.	.25	.50
☐ ☐	SE81	Kelly Hrudey (G), L.A.	.10	.25
☐ ☐	SE82	Darryl Sydor, L.A.	.10	.25
☐ ☐	SE83	Tony Granato, L.A.	.10	.25
☐ ☐	SE84	Warren Rychel, L.A.	.10	.25
☐ ☐	SE85	Gary Shuchuk, L.A.	.10	.25
☐ ☐	SE86	Peter Popovic, Mtl.	.10	.25
☐ ☐	SE87	Valeri Bure, Mtl.	.10	.25
☐ ☐	SE88	Kirk Muller, Mtl.	.10	.25
☐ ☐	SE89	Lyle Odelein, Mtl.	.10	.25
☐ ☐	SE90	Brian Savage, Mtl.	.10	.25
☐ ☐	SE91	Gilbert Dionne, Mtl.	.10	.25
☐ ☐	SE92	Mathieu Schneider, Mtl.	.10	.25
☐ ☐	SE93	Jim Montgomery, Mtl.	.10	.25
☐ ☐	SE94	Chris Terreri, N.J.	.10	.25
☐ ☐	SE95	Scott Niedermayer, N.J.	.25	.50
☐ ☐	SE96	Bob Carpenter, N.J.	.10	.25
☐ ☐	SE97	Scott Stevens, N.J.	.10	.25
☐ ☐	SE98	Jim Dowd, N.J.	.10	.25
☐ ☐	SE99	Brian Rolston, N.J.	.10	.25
☐ ☐	SE100	Stéphane Richer, N.J.	.10	.25
☐ ☐	SE101	Mick Vukota, NYI.	.10	.25
☐ ☐	SE102	Steve Thomas, NYI.	.10	.25
☐ ☐	SE103	Patrick Flatley, NYI.	.10	.25
☐ ☐	SE104	Marty McInnis, NYI.	.10	.25
☐ ☐	SE105	Rich Pilon, NYI.	.10	.25
☐ ☐	SE106	Benoît Hogue, NYI.	.10	.25
☐ ☐	SE107	Zigmund Palffy, NYI.	.35	1.50
☐ ☐	SE108	Vladimir Malakhov, NYI.	.10	.25
☐ ☐	SE109	Brett Lindros, NYI.	.10	.25
☐ ☐	SE110	Mike Richter (G), NYR.	.35	1.00
☐ ☐	SE111	Greg Gilbert, NYR.	.10	.25
☐ ☐	SE112	Kevin Lowe, NYR.	.10	.25
☐ ☐	SE113	Mark Messier, NYR	.50	2.50
☐ ☐	SE114	Alexander Karpovtsev, NYR.	.10	.25
☐ ☐	SE115	Sergei Nemchinov, NYR.	.10	.25
☐ ☐	SE116	Petr Nedved, NYR.	.10	.25
☐ ☐	SE117	Glenn Healy (G), NYR.	.10	.25
☐ ☐	SE118	Dave Archibald, Ott.	.10	.25
☐ ☐	SE119	Alexandre Daigle, Ott.	.25	.50
☐ ☐	SE120	Darrin Madeley, Ott.	.10	.25
☐ ☐	SE121	Pavol Demitra, Ott.	.10	.25
☐ ☐	SE122	Brad Shaw, Ott.	.10	.25
☐ ☐	SE123	Alexei Yashin, Ott.	.35	1.50
☐ ☐	SE124	Sean Hill, Ott.	.10	.25
☐ ☐	**SE125**	**Vladislav Boulin, Pha., RC**	**.10**	**.25**
☐ ☐	SE126	Kevin Haller, Pha.	.10	.25
☐ ☐	SE127	Chris Therien, Pha.	.10	.25
☐ ☐	SE128	Garry Galley, Pha.	.10	.25
☐ ☐	SE129	Mikael Renberg, Pha.	.25	.50
☐ ☐	SE130	Ron Hextall (G), Pha.	.25	.50
☐ ☐	SE131	Eric Lindros, Pha.	1.75	10.00
☐ ☐	SE132	Craig MacTavish, Pha.	.10	.25

	No.	Player		
☐ ☐	SE133	Patrik Juhlin, Pha.	.10	.25
☐ ☐	SE134	Martin Straka, Pgh.	.10	.25
☐ ☐	SE135	Doug Brown, Pgh.	.10	.25
☐ ☐	SE136	Markus Naslund, Pgh.	.10	.25
☐ ☐	SE137	Luc Robitaille, Pgh.	.25	.50
☐ ☐	SE138	Kjell Samuelsson, Pgh.	.10	.25
☐ ☐	SE139	Ken Wregget (G), Pgh.	.10	.25
☐ ☐	SE140	John Cullen, Pgh.	.10	.25
☐ ☐	SE141	Peter Taglianetti, Pgh.	.10	.25
☐ ☐	SE142	Janne Laukkenen, Pgh.	.10	.25
☐ ☐	SE143	Owen Nolan, Que.	.25	.50
☐ ☐	SE144	Adam Deadmarsh, Que.	.25	.50
☐ ☐	SE145	Dave Karpa, Que.	.10	.25
☐ ☐	SE146	Wendel Clark, Que.	.25	.50
☐ ☐	SE147	Joe Sakic, Que.	.85	4.50
☐ ☐	SE148	Alexei Gusarov, Que.	.10	.25
☐ ☐	SE149	Peter Forsberg, Que.	1.75	8.00
☐ ☐	SE150	Kevin Miller, Stl.	.10	.25
☐ ☐	SE151	Denny Felsner, Stl.	.10	.25
☐ ☐	SE152	Al MacInnis, Stl.	.10	.25
☐ ☐	SE153	Philippe Bozon, Stl.	.10	.25
☐ ☐	SE154	Brett Hull, Stl.	.50	2.50
☐ ☐	SE155	Guy Carbonneau, Stl.	.10	.25
☐ ☐	SE156	Igor Korolev, Stl.	.10	.25
☐ ☐	SE157	Esa Tikkanen, Stl.	.10	.25
☐ ☐	SE158	Jon Casey (G), Stl.	.10	.25
☐ ☐	SE159	Viktor Kozlov, S.J.	.10	.25
☐ ☐	SE160	Mike Rathje, S.J.	.10	.25
☐ ☐	SE161	Bob Errey, S.J.	.10	.25
☐ ☐	SE162	Arturs Irbe (G), S.J.	.10	.25
☐ ☐	SE163	Ray Whitney, S.J.	.10	.25
☐ ☐	SE164	Igor Larionov, S.J.	.25	.50
☐ ☐	SE165	Pat Falloon, S.J.	.10	.25
☐ ☐	SE166	Jeff Friesen, S.J.	.10	.25
☐ ☐	SE167	Vlastimil Kroupa, S.J.	.10	.25
☐ ☐	SE168	Chris Joseph, T.B.	.10	.25
☐ ☐	SE169	Danton Cole, T.B.	.10	.25
☐ ☐	SE170	John Tucker, T.B.	.10	.25
☐ ☐	SE171	Roman Hamrlik, T.B.	.25	.50
☐ ☐	SE172	Jason Wiemer, T.B.	.10	.25
☐ ☐	SE173	Kenny Jonsson, Tor.	.10	.25
☐ ☐	**SE174**	**Eric Fichaud (G), Tor., RC**	**.50**	**1.00**
☐ ☐	SE175	Mats Sundin, Tor.	.50	2.50
☐ ☐	SE176	Doug Gilmour, Tor.	.35	1.00
☐ ☐	SE177	Drake Berehowsky, Tor.	.10	.25
☐ ☐	SE178	Mike Ridley, Tor.	.10	.25
☐ ☐	SE179	Jamie Macoun, Tor.	.10	.25
☐ ☐	SE180	Alexei Kudashov, Tor.	.10	.25
☐ ☐	SE181	Bill Berg, Tor.	.10	.25
☐ ☐	SE182	Dave Andreychuk, Tor.	.10	.25
☐ ☐	SE183	Mike Eastwood, Tor.	.10	.25
☐ ☐	ES184	Martin Gelinas, Van.	.10	.25
☐ ☐	SE185	Greg Adams, Van.	.10	.25
☐ ☐	SE186	Gino Odjick, Van.	.10	.25
☐ ☐	SE187	Pavel Bure, Van.	.75	3.50
☐ ☐	SE188	Cliff Ronning, Van.	.10	.25
☐ ☐	SE189	Jiri Slegr, Van.	.10	.25
☐ ☐	SE190	Jyrki Lumme, Van.	.10	.25
☐ ☐	SE191	Jassen Cullimore, Wsh.	.10	.25
☐ ☐	SE192	Steve Konowalchuk, Wsh.	.10	.25
☐ ☐	SE193	Sylvain Côté, Wsh.	.10	.25
☐ ☐	SE194	Jason Allison, Wsh.	.35	1.50
☐ ☐	SE195	Sergei Gonchar, Wsh.	.10	.25
☐ ☐	SE196	Pat Peake, Wsh.	.10	.25
☐ ☐	SE197	Calle Johansson, Wsh.	.10	.25
☐ ☐	SE198	Joé Juneau, Wsh.	.10	.25
☐ ☐	SE199	Jeff Nelson, Wsh.	.10	.25
☐ ☐	SE200	Luciano Borsato, Wpg.	.10	.25
☐ ☐	SE201	Teemu Selänne, Wpg.	.75	3.50
☐ ☐	SE202	Tie Domi, Wpg.	.10	.25
☐ ☐	SE203	Tim Cheveldae (G), Wpg.	.10	.25
☐ ☐	SE204	Darrin Shannon, Wpg.	.10	.25
☐ ☐	SE205	Ravil Gusmanov, Wpg.	.10	.25
☐ ☐	SE206	Todd Harvey, Cdn.	.20	.35
☐ ☐	**SE207**	**Ed Jovanovski, Cdn., RC**	**1.50**	**3.00**
☐ ☐	SE208	Jason Allison, Cdn.	.35	1.50
☐ ☐	SE209	Bryan McCabe, Cdn.	.10	.25
☐ ☐	**SE210**	**Dan Cloutier (G), Cdn., RC**	**1.50**	**3.00**
☐ ☐	**SE211**	**Ladislav Kohn, Cze., RC**	**.10**	**.25**
☐ ☐	**SE212**	**Marek Malik, Cze., RC**	**.10**	**.25**
☐ ☐	**SE213**	**Jan Hlavac, Cze., RC**	**.10**	**.25**
☐ ☐	**SE214**	**Petr Cajanek, Cze., RC**	**.10**	**.25**
☐ ☐	**SE215**	**Jussi Markkannen, Cze., RC**	**.10**	**.25**
☐ ☐	**SE216**	**Jere Karalahti, Cze., RC**	**.10**	**.25**
☐ ☐	SE217	Janne Niinimaa, Fin.	.25	.50
☐ ☐	SE218	Kimmo Timonen, Fin.	.10	.25
☐ ☐	**SE219**	**Mikko Helisten, Fin., RC**	**.10**	**.25**
☐ ☐	**SE220**	**Niko Halttunen, Fin., RC**	**.10**	**.25**
☐ ☐	SE221	T. Miettinen, Fin.	.10	.25
☐ ☐	**SE222**	**Velli-Pekka Nutikka, Fin., RC**	**.10**	**.25**
☐ ☐	**SE223**	**Timo Salonen, Fin., RC**	**.10**	**.25**
☐ ☐	**SE224**	**Tommi Sova, Fin., RC**	**.10**	**.25**
☐ ☐	**SE225**	**Jussi Tarvainen, Fin., RC**	**.10**	**.25**
☐ ☐	**SE226**	**Tommi Rajamaki, Fin., RC**	**.10**	**.25**
☐ ☐	**SE227**	**Antti Aalto, Fin., RC**	**.10**	**.25**
☐ ☐	**SE228**	**Alexandre Koroliouk, Rus., RC**	**.10**	**.25**
☐ ☐	**SE229**	**Vitali Yachmenenv, Rus., RC**	**.50**	**1.00**
☐ ☐	**SE230**	**Nikolai Zavarukhim, Rus., RC**	**.10**	**.25**
☐ ☐	**SE231**	**Vadim Epantchinsev, Rus., RC**	**.10**	**.25**
☐ ☐	**SE232**	**Dmitri Klevakin, Rus., RC**	**.10**	**.25**
☐ ☐	SE233	Anders Eriksson, Swe.	.10	.25
☐ ☐	**SE234**	**Anders Soderberg, Swe., RC**	**.10**	**.25**
☐ ☐	**SE235**	**Per Svartvadet, Swe., RC**	**.10**	**.25**
☐ ☐	SE236	Johan Davidsson, Swe.	.10	.25
☐ ☐	SE237	Niklas Sundstrom, Swe.	.10	.25
☐ ☐	**SE238**	**Jonas Andersson-Junkka, Swe., RC**	**.10**	**.25**
☐ ☐	**SE239**	**Dick Tarnstrom, Swe., RC**	**.10**	**.25**
☐ ☐	**SE240**	**Per-Johan Axelsson, Swe., RC**	**.10**	**.25**
☐ ☐	**SE241**	**Fredrik Johansson, Swe., RC**	**.10**	**.25**
☐ ☐	**SE242**	**Peter Strom, Swe., RC**	**.10**	**.25**
☐ ☐	**SE243**	**Mattias Ohlund, Swe., RC**	**2.00**	**4.00**
☐ ☐	SE244	Jesper Mattsson, Swe.	.10	.25
☐ ☐	**SE245**	**Jonas Forsberg (G), Swe., RC**	**.10**	**.25**
☐ ☐	SE246	Adam Deadmarsh, USA.	.25	.50
☐ ☐	SE247	Deron Quint, USA.	.10	.25
☐ ☐	SE248	Jamie Langenbrunner, USA.	.10	.25
☐ ☐	SE249	Richard Park, USA.	.10	.25
☐ ☐	**SE250**	**Bryan Berard, USA., RC**	**2.50**	**5.00**
☐ ☐	**SE251**	**David Belitski (G), Cdn., RC**	**.25**	**.50**
☐ ☐	**SE252**	**Mike McBain, Cdn., RC**	**.20**	**.35**
☐ ☐	**SE253**	**Hugh Hamilton, Cdn., RC**	**.20**	**.35**
☐ ☐	**SE254**	**Jason Doig, Cdn., RC**	**.25**	**.50**
☐ ☐	**SE255**	**Xavier Delisle, Cdn., RC**	**.20**	**.35**
☐ ☐	**SE256**	**Wade Redden, Cdn., RC**	**.60**	**1.25**
☐ ☐	**SE257**	**Jeffrey Ware, Cdn., RC**	**.25**	**.50**
☐ ☐	**SE258**	**Christian Dubé, Cdn., RC**	**.75**	**1.50**
☐ ☐	**SE259**	**Louis-Phillip Sévigny, Cdn., RC**	**.20**	**.35**
☐ ☐	**SE260**	**Jarome Iginla, Cdn., RC**	**2.50**	**5.00**
☐ ☐	**SE261**	**Daniel Brière, Cdn., RC**	**1.50**	**3.00**
☐ ☐	**SE262**	**Justin Kurtz, Cdn., RC**	**.20**	**.35**
☐ ☐	**SE263**	**Marc Savard, Cdn., RC**	**.50**	**1.00**
☐ ☐	**SE264**	**Alyn McCauley, Cdn., RC**	**2.50**	**5.00**
☐ ☐	**SE265**	**Brad Mehalko, Cdn., RC**	**.20**	**.35**
☐ ☐	**SE266**	**Jeffrey Ambrosio, Cdn., RC**	**.20**	**.35**
☐ ☐	**SE267**	**Todd Norman, Cdn., RC**	**.25**	**.50**
☐ ☐	**SE268**	**Brian Scott, Cdn., RC**	**.20**	**.35**
☐ ☐	**SE269**	**Brad Larsen, Cdn., RC**	**.25**	**.50**
☐ ☐	**SE270**	**J. S. Giguère (G), Cdn., RC**	**.75**	**1.50**

EURO-STARS

Insert Set (20 cards): 30.00

	No.	Player	NRMT-MT
☐	ES-1	Peter Forsberg, Que.	6.00
☐	ES-2	Mats Sundin, Tor.	2.50
☐	ES-3	Mikael Renberg, Pha.	1.00
☐	ES-4	Nicklas Lidström, Det.	1.00
☐	ES-5	Mariusz Czerkawski, Bos.	.50
☐	ES-6	Ulf Dahlen, S.J.	.50
☐	ES-7	Kjell Samuelsson, Hfd.	.50
☐	ES-8	Jyrki Lumme, Van.	.50
☐	ES-9	Jari Kurri, L.A.	1.00
☐	ES-10	Teppo Nummunen, Wpg.	.50
☐	ES-11	Esa Tikkanen, Stl.	.50
☐	ES-12	Christian Ruuttu, Chi.	.50
☐	ES-13	Teemu Selänne, Wpg.	3.50
☐	ES-14	Alexander Mogilny, Buf.	1.50
☐	ES-15	Pavel Bure, Van.	3.50
☐	ES-16	Sergei Fedorov, Det.	2.50
☐	ES-17	Arturs Irbe (G), S.J.	.50
☐	ES-18	Alexei Kovalev, NYR.	.50
☐	ES-19	Dominik Hasek (G), Buf.	3.50
☐	ES-20	Jaromir Jagr, Pgh.	5.00

VINTAGE PARKHURST

Insert Set (45 cards): 40.00

	No.	Player	NRMT-MT
☐	seV1	Paul Kariya, Ana.	6.50
☐	seV2	Dino Ciccarelli, Det.	.75
☐	seV3	Patrick Roy (G), Mtl.	8.00
☐	seV4	Markus Naslund, Pgh.	.35
☐	seV5	Trevor Linden, Van.	.75
☐	seV6	Valeri Karpov, Ana.	.35
☐	seV7	Pat Verbeek, NYR	.35
☐	seV8	Martin Brodeur (G), N.J.	3.50
☐	seV9	Kevin Stevens, Bos.	.35
☐	seV10	Kirk McLean (G), Van.	.75
☐	seV11	Stéphan Lebeau, Mtl.	.35
☐	seV12	Scott Niedermayer, N.J.	.75
☐	seV13	Peter Bondra, Wsh.	2.00
☐	seV14	Ed Belfour (G), Chi.	1.50
☐	seV15	Paul Coffey, Det.	.75
☐	seV16	Chris Gratton, T.B.	.75
☐	seV17	Joé Juneau, Wsh.	.35
☐	seV18	Ray Bourque, Bos.	2.50
☐	seV19	Sergei Krivokrasov, Chi.	.35
☐	seV20	Wayne Gretzky, L.A.	10.00
☐	seV21	Alexei Yashin, Ott.	2.00
☐	seV22	Al Iafrate, Bos.	.35
☐	seV23	Doug Weight, Edm.	1.50
☐	seV24	Jari Kurri, L.A.	.75
☐	seV25	Rod Brind'Amour, Pha.	.75
☐	seV26	Bryan Smolinski, Pgh.	.35
☐	seV27	Darius Kasparaitis, NYI.	.35
☐	seV28	Mark Recchi, Mtl.	.75
☐	seV29	Mike Gartner, Tor.	.75
☐	seV30	Russ Courtnall, Van.	.35
☐	seV31	Pierre Turgeon, Mtl.	.75
☐	seV32	Félix Potvin (G), Tor.	2.50
☐	seV33	Nelson Emerson, Wpg.	.35
☐	seV34	Alexander Mogilny, Buf.	1.50
☐	seV35	Bob Kudelski, Fla.	.35
☐	seV36	Brett Lindros, NYI.	.35
☐	seV37	Mats Sundin, Tor.	2.50
☐	seV38	Keith Tkachuk, Wpg.	2.00
☐	seV39	Derek Plante, Buf.	.35
☐	seV40	Oleg Petrov, Mtl.	.35
☐	seV41	Adam Graves, NYR.	.75
☐	seV42	Jaromir Jagr, Pgh.	5.00
☐	seV43	Viktor Kozlov, S.J.	.35
☐	seV44	Nathan Lafayette, Van.	.35
☐	seV45	Alexei Zhamnov, Wpg.	.75

1994 - 95 PINNACLE

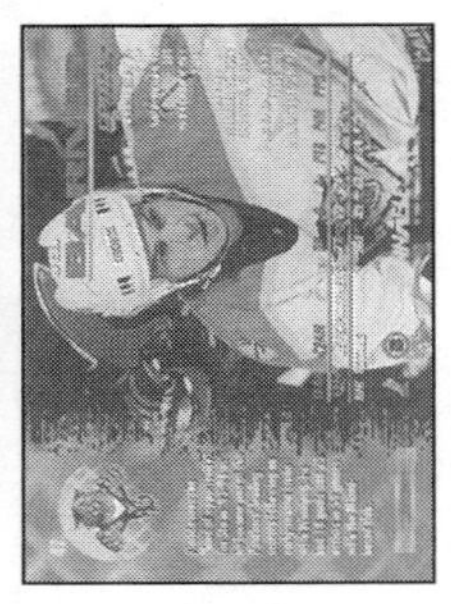

These cards have three versions: the regular card, a Rink Collection parallel and an Artist's Proof parallel. Rink Collection parallels for cards 246-266 and 521-540 were available via redemption. Trade cards for each of these cards were inserted into packs. Expired trade cards sell at $1.00.

Imprint: © 1994 PINNACLE BRANDS, INC.

Series One Set (270 cards):	**15.00**	**550.00**	**3,000.00**
Series Two Set (270 cards):	**15.00**	**550.00**	**3,000.00**
Common Player:	**.10**	**1.00**	**5.00**

	No.	Player	Reg.	Rink	A/P
□□□	1	Eric Lindros, Pha.	2.00	50.00	275.00
□□□	2	Alexandre Daigle, Ott.	.25	3.00	10.00
□□□	3	Mike Modano, Dal.	.50	10.00	30.00
□□□	4	Vincent Damphousse, Mtl.	.35	5.00	15.00
□□□	5	Dave Andreychuk, Tor.	.10	1.00	5.00
□□□	6	Curtis Joseph (G), Stl.	.60	12.00	40.00
□□□	7	Joé Juneau, Wsh.	.10	1.00	5.00
□□□	8	Trevor Linden, Van.	.25	3.00	10.00
□□□	9	Rob Blake, L.A.	.25	3.00	10.00
□□□	10	Mike Richter (G), NYR.	.35	5.00	15.00
□□□	11	Chris Pronger, Hfd.	.25	3.00	10.00
□□□	12	Robert Reichel, Cgy.	.10	1.00	5.00
□□□	13	Bryan Smolinski, Bos.	.10	1.00	5.00
□□□	14	Ray Sheppard, Det.	.10	1.00	5.00
□□□	15	Guy Hebert (G), Ana.	.25	3.00	10.00
□□□	16	Tony Amonte, Chi.	.25	3.00	10.00
□□□	17	Richard Smehlik, Buf.	.10	1.00	5.00
□□□	18	Doug Weight, Edm.	.35	5.00	15.00
□□□	19	Chris Gratton, T.B.	.25	3.00	10.00
□□□	20	Tom Barrasso (G), Pgh.	.25	3.00	10.00
□□□	21	Brian Skrudland, Fla.	.10	1.00	5.00
□□□	22	Sandis Ozolinsh, S.J.	.25	3.00	10.00
□□□	23	Bill Guerin, N.J.	.25	3.00	10.00
□□□	24	Curtis Leschyshyn, Que.	.10	1.00	5.00
□□□	25	Teemu Selänne, Wpg.	.75	18.00	60.00
□□□	26	Darius Kasparaitis, NYI.	.10	1.00	5.00
□□□	27	Garry Galley, Pha.	.10	1.00	5.00
□□□	28	Alexei Yashin, Ott.	.35	8.00	20.00
□□□	29	Mark Tinordi, Dal.	.10	1.00	5.00
□□□	30	Patrick Roy (G), Mtl.	2.00	50.00	275.00
□□□	31	Mike Gartner, Tor.	.25	3.00	10.00
□□□	32	Brendan Shanahan, Stl.	.60	12.00	40.00
□□□	33	Sylvain Côté, Wsh.	.10	1.00	5.00
□□□	34	Jeff Brown, Van.	.10	1.00	5.00
□□□	35	Jari Kurri, L.A.	.25	3.00	10.00
□□□	36	Sergei Zubov, NYR.	.25	3.00	10.00
□□□	37	Pat Verbeek, Hfd.	.10	1.00	5.00
□□□	38	Theoren Fleury, Cgy.	.35	5.00	15.00
□□□	39	Al Iafrate, Bos.	.10	1.00	5.00
□□□	40	Keith Primeau, Det.	.25	3.00	10.00
□□□	41	Bobby Dollas, Ana.	.10	1.00	5.00
□□□	42	Ed Belfour (G), Chi.	.35	5.00	15.0
□□□	43	Dale Hawerchuk, Buf.	.25	3.00	10.00
□□□	44	Shayne Corson, Edm.	.25	3.00	10.00
□□□	45	Danton Cole, T.B.	.10	1.00	5.00
□□□	46	Ulf Samuelsson, Pgh.	.10	1.00	5.00
□□□	47	Stu Barnes, Fla.	.10	1.00	5.00
□□□	48	Ulf Dahlen, S.J.	.10	1.00	5.00
□□□	49	Valeri Zelepukin, N.J.	.10	1.00	5.00
□□□	50	Joe Sakic, Que.	1.00	25.00	100.00
□□□	51	Dave Manson, Wpg.	.10	1.00	5.00
□□□	52	Steve Thomas, NYI.	.10	1.00	5.00
□□□	53	Mark Recchi, Pha.	.25	3.00	10.00
□□□	54	Dave McLlwain, Ott.	.10	1.00	5.00
□□□	55	Derian Hatcher, Dal.	.25	3.00	10.00
□□□	56	Mathieu Schneider, Mtl.	.10	1.00	5.00
□□□	57	Bill Berg, Tor.	.10	1.00	5.00
□□□	58	Petr Nedved, Stl.	.10	1.00	5.00
□□□	59	Dimitri Khristich, Wsh.	.10	1.00	5.00
□□□	60	Kirk McLean (G), Van.	.25	3.00	10.00
□□□	61	Marty McSorley, L.A.	.10	1.00	5.00
□□□	62	Adam Graves, NYR.	.10	1.00	5.00
□□□	63	Geoff Sanderson, Hfd.	.10	1.00	5.00
□□□	64	Frantisek Musil, Cgy.	.10	1.00	5.00
□□□	65	Cam Neely, Bos.	.25	3.00	10.00
□□□	66	Nicklas Lidstrom, Det.	.25	3.00	10.00
□□□	67	Stéphan Lebeau, Ana.	.10	1.00	5.00
□□□	68	Joe Murphy, Chi.	.10	1.00	5.00
□□□	69	Yuri Khmylev, Buf.	.10	1.00	5.00
□□□	70	Zdeno Ciger, Edm.	.10	1.00	5.00
□□□	71	Daren Puppa (G), T.B.	.10	1.00	5.00
□□□	72	Ron Francis, Pgh.	.35	5.00	15.00
□□□	73	Scott Mellanby, Fla.	.10	1.00	5.00
□□□	74	Igor Larionov, S.J.	.25	3.00	10.00
□□□	75	Scott Niedermayer, N.J.	.25	3.00	10.00
□□□	76	Owen Nolan, Que.	.25	3.00	10.00
□□□	77	Teppo Numminen, Wpg.	.10	1.00	5.00
□□□	78	Pierre Turgeon, NYI.	.25	3.00	10.00
□□□	79	Mikael Renberg, Pha.	.25	3.00	10.00
□□□	80	Norm Maciver, Ott.	.10	1.00	5.00
□□□	81	Paul Cavallini, Dal.	.10	1.00	5.00
□□□	82	Kirk Muller, Mtl.	.10	1.00	5.00
□□□	83	Félix Potvin (G), Tor.	.50	10.00	30.00
□□□	84	Craig Janney, Stl.	.10	1.00	5.00
□□□	85	Dale Hunter, Wsh.	.10	1.00	5.00
□□□	86	Jyrki Lumme, Van.	.10	1.00	5.00
□□□	87	Alexei Zhitnik, L.A.	.10	1.00	5.00
□□□	88	Steve Larmer, NYR.	.10	1.00	5.00
□□□	89	Jocelyn Lemieux, Hfd.	.10	1.00	5.00
□□□	90	Joe Nieuwendyk, Cgy.	.25	3.00	10.00
□□□	91	Don Sweeney, Bos.	.10	1.00	5.00
□□□	92	Vyacheslav Kozlov, Det.	.10	1.00	5.00
□□□	93	Tim Sweeney, Ana.	.10	1.00	5.00
□□□	94	Chris Chelios, Chi.	.35	8.00	20.00
□□□	95	Derek Plante, Buf.	.10	1.00	5.00
□□□	96	Igor Kravchuk, Edm.	.10	1.00	5.00
□□□	97	Shawn Chambers, T.B.	.10	1.00	5.00
□□□	98	Jaromir Jagr, Pgh.	1.25	35.00	150
□□□	99	Jeff Norton, S.J.	.10	1.00	5.00
□□□	100	John Vanbiesbrouck (G), Fla.	.60	12.00	40.00
□□□	101	John MacLean, N.J.	.10	1.00	5.00
□□□	102	Stéphane Fiset (G), Que.	.25	3.00	10.00
□□□	103	Keith Tkachuk, Wpg.	.35	8.00	20.00
□□□	104	Vladimir Malakhov, NYI.	.10	1.00	5.00
□□□	105	Mike McPhee, Dal.	.10	1.00	5.00
□□□	106	Eric Desjardins, Mtl.	.25	3.00	10.00
□□□	107	Alexei Kovalev, NYR.	.10	1.00	5.00
□□□	108	Steve Duchesne, Stl.	.10	1.00	5.00
□□□	109	Peter Zezel, Tor.	.10	1.00	5.00
□□□	110	Randy Burridge, Wsh.	.10	1.00	5.00
□□□	111	Jason Bowen, Pha.	.10	1.00	5.00
□□□	112	Phil Bourque, Ott.	.10	1.00	5.00
□□□	113	Cliff Ronning, Van.	.10	1.00	5.00
□□□	114	Sean Burke (G), Hfd.	.25	3.00	10.00
□□□	115	Gary Roberts, Cgy.	.25	3.00	10.00
□□□	116	Vladimir Konstantinov, Det.	.10	1.00	5.00
□□□	117	Brent Sutter, Chi.	.10	1.00	5.00
□□□	118	Tony Granato, L.A.	.10	1.00	5.00
□□□	119	Garry Valk, Ana.	.10	1.00	5.00
□□□	120	Adam Oates, Bos.	.35	5.00	15.00
□□□	121	Arturs Irbe (G), S.J.	.10	1.00	5.00
□□□	122	Jesse Belanger, Fla.	.10	1.00	5.00
□□□	123	Roman Hamrlik, T.B.	.25	3.00	10.00
□□□	124	Jason Arnott, Edm.	.25	3.00	10.00
□□□	125	Alexander Mogilny, Buf.	.35	5.00	15.00
□□□	126	Bruce Driver, N.J.	.10	1.00	5.00
□□□	127	Shawn McEachern, Pgh.	.10	1.00	5.00
□□□	128	Andrei Kovalenko, Que.	.10	1.00	5.00
□□□	129	Benoît Hogue, NYI.	.10	1.00	5.00
□□□	130	Tim Cheveldae (G), Wpg.	.10	1.00	5.00
□□□	131	Brian Noonan, NYR.	.10	1.00	5.00
□□□	132	Lyle Odelein, Mtl.	.10	1.00	5.00
□□□	133	Russ Courtnall, Dal.	.10	1.00	5.00
□□□	134	Peter Stastny, Stl.	.10	1.00	5.00
□□□	135	Doug Gilmour, Tor.	.35	5.00	15.00
□□□	136	Pat Peake, Wsh.	.10	1.00	5.00
□□□	137	Gary Suter, Chi.	.10	1.00	5.00
□□□	138	Paul Ranheim, Hfd.	.10	1.00	5.00
□□□	139	Troy Murray, Ott.	.10	1.00	5.00
□□□	140	Pavel Bure, Van.	.75	18.00	60.00
□□□	141	Gord Murphy, Fla.	.10	1.00	5.00
□□□	142	Michael Nylander, Cgy.	.10	1.00	5.00
□□□	143	Craig Muni, Buf.	.10	1.00	5.00
□□□	144	Bob Corkum, Ana.	.10	1.00	5.00
□□□	145	Martin Brodeur (G), N.J.	.75	18.00	60.00
□□□	146	Ted Donato, Bos.	.10	1.00	5.00
□□□	147	Alexei Zhamnov, Wpg.	.25	3.00	10.00
□□□	148	Josef Beranek, Pha.	.10	1.00	5.00
□□□	149	Joe Mullen, Pgh.	.10	1.00	5.00
□□□	150	Sergei Fedorov, Det.	.50	10.00	30.00
□□□	151	Mike Keane, Mtl.	.10	1.00	5.00
□□□	152	Sergei Makarov, S.J.	.10	1.00	5.00
□□□	153	Marty McInnis, NYI.	.10	1.00	5.00
□□□	154	Steven Rice, Edm.	.10	1.00	5.00
□□□	155	Brian Leetch, NYR.	.35	5.00	15.00
□□□	156	Chris Joseph, T.B.	.10	1.00	5.00
□□□	157	Darcy Wakaluk (G), Dal.	.10	1.00	5.00
□□□	158	Kelly Miller, Wsh.	.10	1.00	5.00
□□□	159	Jim Montgomery, Stl.	.10	1.00	5.00
□□□	160	Nikolai Borschevsky, Tor.	.10	1.00	5.00
□□□	161	Darren Turcotte, Hfd.	.10	1.00	5.00
□□□	162	Brad Shaw, Ott.	.10	1.00	5.00
□□□	163	Mark Lamb, Pha.	.10	1.00	5.00
□□□	164	Alexei Gusarov, Que.	.10	1.00	5.00
□□□	165	Jeremy Roenick, Chi.	.25	3.00	10.00
□□□	166	Stéphane Richer, N.J.	.10	1.00	5.00
□□□	167	German Titov, Cgy.	.10	1.00	5.00
□□□	168	Rob Niedermayer, Fla.	.25	3.00	10.00
□□□	169	Glen Murray, Bos.	.10	1.00	5.00
□□□	170	Mario Lemieux, Pgh.	2.00	50.00	275.00
□□□	171	Thomas Steen, Wpg.	.10	1.00	5.00
□□□	172	Ron Tugnutt (G), Mtl.	.10	1.00	5.00
□□□	173	Pat Falloon, S.J.	.10	1.00	5.00
□□□	174	Esa Tikkanen, NYR. (Stl.)	.75	18.00	60.00
□□□	175	Dominik Hasek (G), Buf.	1.00	25.00	75.00
□□□	176	Patrick Flatley, NYI.	.10	1.00	5.00
□□□	177	Gino Odjick, Van.	.10	1.00	5.00
□□□	178	Charlie Huddy, L.A.	.10	1.00	5.00
□□□	179	Dave Poulin, Wsh.	.10	1.00	5.00
□□□	180	Darren McCarty, Det.	.10	1.00	5.00
□□□	181	Todd Gill, Tor.	.10	1.00	5.00
□□□	182	Tom Chorske, N.J.	.10	1.00	5.00
□□□	183	Marc Bergevin, T.B.	.10	1.00	5.00
□□□	184	Dave Lowry, Fla.	.10	1.00	5.00
□□□	185	Brent Gilchrist, Dal.	.10	1.00	5.00
□□□	186	Eric Weinrich, Chi.	.10	1.00	5.00
□□□	187	Ted Drury, Hfd.	.10	1.00	5.00
□□□	188	Boris Mironov, Edm.	.10	1.00	5.00
□□□	189	Patrick Carnback, Ana.	.10	1.00	5.00
□□□	190	Ray Bourque, Bos.	.50	10.00	30.00
□□□	191	Patrice Brisebois, Mtl.	.10	1.00	5.00
□□□	192	Bob Errey, S.J.	.10	1.00	5.00
□□□	193	Scott Lachance, NYI.	.10	1.00	5.00
□□□	194	Brad May, Buf.	.10	1.00	5.00
□□□	195	Jeff Beukeboom, NYR.	.10	1.00	5.00
□□□	196	James Patrick, Cgy.	.10	1.00	5.00
□□□	197	Doug Brown, Pgh.	.10	1.00	5.00
□□□	198	Dana Murzyn, Van.	.10	1.00	5.00
□□□	199	Chris Osgood (G), Det.	.35	8.00	20.00
□□□	200	Wayne Gretzky, L.A.	2.50	60.00	450.00
□□□	201	Bob Carpenter, N.J.	.10	1.00	5.00
□□□	202	Evgeny Davydov, Ott.	.10	1.00	5.00
□□□	203	Oleg Petrov, Mtl.	.10	1.00	5.00
□□□	204	Grant Ledyard, Dal.	.10	1.00	5.00
□□□	205	Jocelyn Thibault (G), Que.	.35	5.00	15.0
□□□	206	Bill Houlder, Ana.	.10	1.00	5.00
□□□	207	Tom Fitzgerald, Fla.	.10	1.00	5.00
□□□	208	Dominic Roussel (G), Pha.	.10	1.00	5.00
□□□	209	Dave Ellett, Tor.	.10	1.00	5.00
□□□	210	Frantisek Kucera, Hfd.	.10	1.00	5.00
□□□	211	Steve Smith, Chi.	.10	1.00	5.00
□□□	212	Vincent Riendeau (G), Bos.	.10	1.00	5.00
□□□	213	Scott Pearson, Edm.	.10	1.00	5.00
□□□	214	John Slaney, Wsh.	.10	1.00	5.00
□□□	215	Larry Murphy, Pgh.	.25	3.00	10.00
□□□	216	Travis Green, NYI.	.10	1.00	5.00
□□□	217	Joel Otto, Cgy.	.10	1.00	5.00
□□□	218	Randy Wood, Buf.	.10	1.00	5.00
□□□	219	Gaetan Duchesne, S.J.	.10	1.00	5.00
□□□	220	Sergei Nemchinov, NYR.	.10	1.00	5.00
□□□	221	Terry Carkner, Det.	.10	1.00	5.00
□□□	222	Randy McKay, N.J.	.10	1.00	5.00
□□□	223	Mike Donnelly, L.A.	.10	1.00	5.00
□□□	224	J.J. Daigneault, Mtl.	.10	1.00	5.00
□□□	225	Dallas Drake, Wpg.	.10	1.00	5.00
□□□	226	John Tucker, T.B.	.10	1.00	5.00
□□□	227	Dimitri Yushkevich, Pha.	.10	1.00	5.00
□□□	228	Mike Stapleton, Edm.	.10	1.00	5.00
□□□	229	Dimitri Mironov, Tor.	.10	1.00	5.00

□□□	230 Ken Wregget (G), Pgh.	.10	1.00	5.00
□□□	231 Claude Lapointe, Que.	.10	1.00	5.00
□□□	232 Joe Sacco, Ana.	.10	1.00	5.00
□□□	233 Craig Ludwig, Dal.	.10	1.00	5.00
□□□	234 David Reid, Bos.	.10	1.00	5.00
□□□	235 Rich Sutter, Chi.	.10	1.00	5.00
□□□	236 Mark Fitzpatrick (G), Fla.	.10	1.00	5.00
□□□	237 Jim Storm, Hfd.	.10	1.00	5.00
□□□	238 Brad Dalgarno, NYI.	.10	1.00	5.00
□□□	239 Dixon Ward, L.A.	.10	1.00	5.00
□□□	240 Greg Adams, Van.	.10	1.00	5.00
□□□	241 Dino Ciccarelli, Det.	.10	1.00	5.00
□□□	242 Vlastimil Kroupa, S.J.	.10	1.00	5.00
□□□	243 Joe Kocur, NYR.	.10	1.00	5.00
□□□	244 Donald Audette, Buf.	.10	1.00	5.00
□□□	245 Trent Yawney, Cgy.	.10	1.00	5.00
□□□	**246 Mariusz Czerkawski, Bos., RC**	**.10**	**1.00**	**5.00**
□□□	247 Jason Allison, Wsh.	.35	5.00	15.00
□□□	248 Brian Savage, Mtl.	.10	1.00	5.00
□□□	249 Fred Knipscheer, Bos.	.10	1.00	5.00
□□□	250 Jamie McLennen (G), NYI.	.25	3.00	10.00
□□□	251 Aaron Gavey, T.B.	.10	1.00	5.00
□□□	252 Jeff Friesen, S.J.	.25	3.00	10.00
□□□	253 Adam Deadmarsh, Que.	.25	3.00	10.00
□□□	254 Jamie Storr (G), L.A.	.25	3.00	10.00
□□□	255 Brian Rolston, N.J.	.10	1.00	5.00
□□□	256 Zigmund Palffy, NYI.	.35	8.00	20.00
□□□	257 Brett Lindros, NYI.	.10	1.00	5.00
□□□	258 Denis Tsygurov, Buf.	.10	1.00	5.00
□□□	259 Chris Tamer, Pgh.	.10	1.00	5.00
□□□	260 Michael Peca, Van.	.25	3.00	10.00
□□□	261 Oleg Tverdovsky, Ana.	.10	1.00	5.00
□□□	262 Todd Harvey, Dal.	.10	1.00	5.00
□□□	263 Yan Kaminsky, NYI.	.10	1.00	5.00
□□□	264 Kenny Jonsson, Tor.	.10	1.00	5.00
□□□	265 Paul Kariya, Ana.	2.00	40.00	200.00
□□□	266 Peter Forsberg, Que.	1.75	35.00	150.00
□□□	267 Atlantic Division Checklist	.10	1.00	5.00
□□□	268 Northeast Division Checklist	.10	1.00	5.00
□□□	269 Central Division Checklist	.10	1.00	5.00
□□□	270 Pacific Division Checklist	.10	1.00	5.00
□□□	271 Steve Yzerman, Det.	1.25	5.00	150.00
□□□	272 John LeClair, Mtl.	.50	10.00	30.00
□□□	273 Rod Brind'Amour, Pha.	.25	3.00	10.00
□□□	274 Ron Hextall (G), Pha.	.25	3.00	10.00
□□□	275 Todd Elik, S.J.	.10	1.00	5.00
□□□	276 Geoff Courtnall, Van.	.10	1.00	5.00
□□□	277 Ulf Samuelsson, Pgh.	.10	1.00	5.00
□□□	278 Brian Bradley, T.B.	.10	1.00	5.00
□□□	279 Darrin Shannon, Wpg.	.10	1.00	5.00
□□□	280 Mike Ricci, Que.	.10	1.00	5.00
□□□	281 Peter Bondra, Wsh.	.35	8.00	20.00
□□□	282 Terry Yake, Ana. (Tor.)	.10	1.00	5.00
□□□	283 Patrick Poulin, Chi.	.10	1.00	5.00
□□□	284 Bob Kudelski, Fla.	.10	1.00	5.00
□□□	285 Bill Ranford (G), Edm.	.25	3.00	10.00
□□□	286 Alexander Godynyuk, Hfd.	.10	1.00	5.00
□□□	287 Claude Lemieux, N.J.	.10	1.00	5.00
□□□	288 Sylvain Turgeon, Ott.	.10	1.00	5.00
□□□	289 Kevin Miller, Stl.	.10	1.00	5.00
□□□	290 Brian Bellows, Mtl.	.10	1.00	5.00
□□□	291 Murray Craven, Van.	.10	1.00	5.00
□□□	292 Kelly Hrudey (G), L.A.	.10	1.00	5.00
□□□	293 Neal Broten, Dal.	.10	1.00	5.00
□□□	294 Craig Simpson, Buf.	.10	1.00	5.00
□□□	295 Mark Howe, Det.	.10	1.00	5.00
□□□	296 Johan Garpenlov, S.J.	.10	1.00	5.00
□□□	297 Jamie Macoun, Tor.	.10	1.00	5.00
□□□	298 Stephen Leach, Bos.	.10	1.00	5.00
□□□	299 Kevin Stevens, Pgh.	.10	1.00	5.00
□□□	300 Mark Messier, NYR.	.50	10.00	30.00
□□□	301 Paul Ysebaert, Chi.	.10	1.00	5.00
□□□	302 Derek King, NYI.	.10	1.00	5.00
□□□	303 Fredrik Olausson, Edm.	.10	1.00	5.00
□□□	304 John Druce, L.A.	.10	1.00	5.00
□□□	305 Calle Johansson, Wsh.	.10	1.00	5.00
□□□	306 Kelly Kisio, Cgy.	.10	1.00	5.00
□□□	307 Sergio Momesso, Van.	.10	1.00	5.00
□□□	308 Joe Cirella, Fla.	.10	1.00	5.00
□□□	309 Tommy Söderström (G), NYI.	.10	1.00	5.00
□□□	310 Scott Stevens, N.J.	.10	1.00	5.00
□□□	311 Petr Klima, T.B.	.10	1.00	5.00
□□□	312 Steven Finn, Que.	.10	1.00	5.00
□□□	313 Tomas Sandström, Pgh.	.10	1.00	5.00
□□□	314 Ray Ferraro, NYI.	.10	1.00	5.00
□□□	315 Andy Moog (G), Dal.	.25	3.00	10.00
□□□	316 Ray Whitney, S.J.	.10	1.00	5.00
□□□	317 Dirk Graham, Chi.	.10	1.00	5.00
□□□	318 Shawn Burr, Det.	.10	1.00	5.00
□□□	319 Andrew Cassels, Hfd.	.10	1.00	5.00
□□□	320 Craig Billington (G), Ott.	.10	1.00	5.00
□□□	321 Wayne Presley, Buf.	.10	1.00	5.00
□□□	322 Anatoli Semenov, Ana.	.10	1.00	5.00
□□□	323 Michal Pivonka, Wsh.	.10	1.00	5.00
□□□	324 Martin Gelinas, Van.	.10	1.00	5.00
□□□	325 Nelson Emerson, Wpg.	.10	1.00	5.00
□□□	326 Brent Fedyk, Pha.	.10	1.00	5.00
□□□	327 Bob Bassen, Que.	.10	1.00	5.00
□□□	328 Darryl Sydor, L.A.	.10	1.00	5.00
□□□	329 Stéphane Matteau, NYR.	.10	1.00	5.00
□□□	330 Ken Daneyko, N.J.	.10	1.00	5.00
□□□	331 Mikhail Shtalenkov (G), Ana.	.10	1.00	5.00
□□□	332 Kelly Buchberger, Edm.	.10	1.00	5.00
□□□	333 Mike Hough, Fla.	.10	1.00	5.00
□□□	334 Dave Gagner, Dal.	.10	1.00	5.00
□□□	335 Chris Terreri (G), N.J.	.10	1.00	5.00
□□□	336 Robert Kron, Hfd.	.10	1.00	5.00
□□□	337 Andrei Lomakin, Fla.	.10	1.00	5.00
□□□	338 Kevin Lowe, NYR.	.10	1.00	5.00
□□□	339 Steve Konroyd, Ott.	.10	1.00	5.00
□□□	340 Denis Savard, T.B.	.25	3.00	10.00
□□□	341 Stephen Heinze, Bos.	.10	1.00	5.00
□□□	342 Zarley Zalapski, Cgy.	.10	1.00	5.00
□□□	343 Valeri Kamensky, Que.	.25	3.00	10.00
□□□	344 Tie Domi, Wpg.	.10	1.00	5.00
□□□	345 Kevin Hatcher, Wsh.	.10	1.00	5.00
□□□	346 Dean Evason, Dal.	.10	1.00	5.00
□□□	347 Bobby Holik, N.J.	.10	1.00	5.00
□□□	348 Steve Konowalchuk, Wsh.	.10	1.00	5.00
□□□	349 Rob Gaudreau, S.J.	.10	1.00	5.00
□□□	350 Pat LaFontaine, Buf.	.25	3.00	10.00
□□□	351 Joe Reekie, Wsh.	.10	1.00	5.00
□□□	352 Martin Straka, Pgh.	.10	1.00	5.00
□□□	353 Dave Babych, Van.	.10	1.00	5.00
□□□	354 Geoff Smith, Fla.	.10	1.00	5.00
□□□	355 Don Beaupré (G), Wsh.	.10	1.00	5.00
□□□	356 Adam Burt, Hfd.	.10	1.00	5.00
□□□	357 Doug Bodger, Buf.	.10	1.00	5.00
□□□	358 Dean McAmmond, Edm.	.10	1.00	5.00
□□□	359 Gerald Diduck, Van.	.10	1.00	5.00
□□□	360 Rob DiMaio, Pha.	.10	1.00	5.00
□□□	361 Scott Young, Que.	.10	1.00	5.00
□□□	362 Alexander Semak, N.J.	.10	1.00	5.00
□□□	363 Mike Rathje, Pgh.	.10	1.00	5.00
□□□	364 Alexander Karpovtsev, NYR.	.10	1.00	5.00
□□□	365 Trevor Kidd (G), Cgy.	.25	3.00	10.00
□□□	366 Jason Dawe, Buf.	.10	1.00	5.00
□□□	367 Vitali Prokhorov, Stl.	.10	1.00	5.00
□□□	368 Keith Brown, Fla.	.10	1.00	5.00
□□□	369 Bret Hedican, Van.	.10	1.00	5.00
□□□	370 Markus Naslund, Pgh.	.10	1.00	5.00
□□□	371 Rick Tocchet, L.A.	.10	1.00	5.00
□□□	372 Guy Carbonneau, Stl.	.10	1.00	5.00
□□□	373 Kevin Haller, Pha.	.10	1.00	5.00
□□□	374 Bob Rouse, Det.	.10	1.00	5.00
□□□	375 Rob Pearson, Wsh.	.10	1.00	5.00
□□□	376 Steve Chiasson, Cgy.	.10	1.00	5.00
□□□	377 Mike Vernon (G), Det.	.25	3.00	10.00
□□□	378 Keith Jones, Wsh.	.10	1.00	5.00
□□□	379 Sylvain Lefebvre, Que.	.10	1.00	5.00
□□□	380 Tom Kurvers, Ana.	.10	1.00	5.00
□□□	381 Pat Elynuik, Ott.	.10	1.00	5.00
□□□	382 Uwe Krupp, Que.	.10	1.00	5.00
□□□	383 Ron Sutter, NYI.	.10	1.00	5.00
□□□	384 Mike Ridley, Tor.	.10	1.00	5.00
□□□	385 Wendel Clark, Que.	.25	3.00	10.00
□□□	386 Mats Sundin, Tor.	.50	10.00	30.00
□□□	387 Al MacInnis, Stl.	.25	3.00	10.00
□□□	388 Glen Wesley, Hfd.	.10	1.00	5.00
□□□	389 Jim Paek, Ott.	.10	1.00	5.00
□□□	390 Rudy Poeschek, T.B.	.10	1.00	5.00
□□□	391 Yves Racine, Mtl.	.10	1.00	5.00
□□□	392 Craig MacTavish, Pha.	.10	1.00	5.00
□□□	393 Jon Casey (G), Stl.	.10	1.00	5.00
□□□	394 Garth Butcher, Tor.	.10	1.00	5.00
□□□	395 Sean Hill, Ott.	.10	1.00	5.00
□□□	396 Troy Loney, NYI.	.10	1.00	5.00
□□□	397 John Cullen, Pgh.	.10	1.00	5.00
□□□	398 Alexei Kasatonov, Bos.	.10	1.00	5.00
□□□	399 Mike Craig, Tor.	.10	1.00	5.00
□□□	400 Luc Robitaille, Pgh.	.25	3.00	10.00
□□□	401 Randy Moller, Fla.	.10	1.00	5.00
□□□	402 Chris Dahlquist, Ott.	.10	1.00	5.00
□□□	403 Pat Conacher, L.A.	.10	1.00	5.00
□□□	404 Bob Probert, Chi.	.10	1.00	5.00
□□□	405 Robert Dirk, Ana.	.10	1.00	5.00
□□□	406 Randy Cunneyworth, Ott.	.10	1.00	5.00
□□□	407 Bryan Marchment, Edm.	.10	1.00	5.00
□□□	408 Nick Kypreos, NYR.	.10	1.00	5.00
□□□	409 Doug Lidster, Stl.	.10	1.00	5.00
□□□	410 Phil Housley, Cgy.	.10	1.00	5.00
□□□	411 Bob Sweeney, Buf.	.10	1.00	5.00
□□□	412 Mike Ramsey, Det.	.10	1.00	5.00
□□□	413 Robert Lang, L.A.	.10	1.00	5.00
□□□	414 Brian Benning, Fla.	.10	1.00	5.00
□□□	415 Greg Gilbert, NYR.	.10	1.00	5.00
□□□	416 Martin Rucinsky, Que.	.10	1.00	5.00
□□□	417 Jason Smith, N.J.	.10	1.00	5.00
□□□	418 Jozef Stumpel, Bos.	.10	1.00	5.00
□□□	419 Bob Beers, NYI.	.10	1.00	5.00
□□□	420 Ed Olczyk, NYR.	.10	1.00	5.00
□□□	421 Grant Fuhr (G), Buf.	.25	3.00	10.00
□□□	422 Gilbert Dionne, Mtl.	.10	1.00	5.00
□□□	423 Mike Peluso, N.J.	.10	1.00	5.00
□□□	424 Petr Svoboda, Buf.	.10	1.00	5.00
□□□	425 Corey Millen. N.J.	.10	1.00	5.00
□□□	426 Kevin Dineen, Pha.	.10	1.00	5.00
□□□	427 Brad McCrimmon, Hfd.	.10	1.00	5.00
□□□	428 Bob Essensa (G), Det.	.10	1.00	5.00
□□□	429 Paul Coffey, Det.	.25	3.00	10.00
□□□	430 Glenn Healy (G), NYR.	.10	1.00	5.00
□□□	431 Luke Richardson, Edm.	.10	1.00	5.00
□□□	432 Adam Foote, Que.	.25	3.00	10.00
□□□	433 Paul Broten, Dal.	.10	1.00	5.00
□□□	434 Christian Ruutu, Chi.	.10	1.00	5.00
□□□	435 David Shaw, Bos.	.10	1.00	5.00
□□□	436 Jimmy Carson, Hfd.	.10	1.00	5.00
□□□	437 Ken Sutton, Buf.	.10	1.00	5.00
□□□	438 Kay Whitmore (G), Van.	.10	1.00	5.00
□□□	439 Jim Dowd, N.J.	.10	1.00	5.00
□□□	440 Jim Johnson, Wsh.	.10	1.00	5.00
□□□	441 Kirk Maltby, Edm.	.10	1.00	5.00
□□□	442 Trent Klatt, Dal.	.10	1.00	5.00
□□□	443 Paul DiPietro, Mtl.	.10	1.00	5.00
□□□	444 Rick Tabaracci (G), Wsh.	.10	1.00	5.00
□□□	445 Craig Wolanin, Que.	.10	1.00	5.00
□□□	446 Dave Hannan, Buf.	.10	1.00	5.00
□□□	447 Rick Zombo, Stl.	.10	1.00	5.00
□□□	448 Tom Pederson, S.J.	.10	1.00	5.00
□□□	449 Martin Lapointe, Det.	.10	1.00	5.00
□□□	450 Brett Hull, Stl.	.50	10.00	30.00
□□□	451 Mikael Andersson, T.B.	.10	1.00	5.00
□□□	452 Benoît Brunet, Mtl.	.10	1.00	5.00
□□□	453 Nathan Lafayette, Van.	.10	1.00	5.00
□□□	454 Kent Manderville, Tor.	.10	1.00	5.00
□□□	455 Todd Krygier, Wsh.	.10	1.00	5.00
□□□	456 Dennis Vaske, NYI.	.10	1.00	5.00
□□□	457 Peter Popovic, Mtl.	.10	1.00	5.00
□□□	458 Jeff Shantz, Chi.	.10	1.00	5.00
□□□	459 Darrin Madeley (G), Ott.	.10	1.00	5.00
□□□	460 René Corbet, Que.	.10	1.00	5.00
□□□	461 Alexandre Daigle, Ott.	.25	3.00	10.00
□□□	462 Martin Brodeur (G), N.J.	.75	18.00	60.00
□□□	463 Jason Arnott, Edm.	.25	3.00	10.00
□□□	464 Mikael Renberg, Pha.	.25	3.00	10.00
□□□	465 Alexei Yashin, Ott.	.35	5.00	15.00
□□□	466 Chris Pronger, Hfd.	.25	3.00	10.00
□□□	467 Mariusz Czerkawski, Bos.	.10	1.00	5.00
□□□	468 Chris Gratton, T.B.	.25	3.00	10.00
□□□	469 Rob Niedermayer, Fla.	.25	3.00	10.00
□□□	470 Bryan Smolinski, Bos.	.10	1.00	5.00
□□□	471 Chris Osgood (G), Det.	.35	8.00	20.00
□□□	472 Derek Plante, Buf.	.10	1.00	5.00
□□□	473 Brian Rolston, N.J.	.10	1.00	5.00
□□□	474 Jason Allison, Wsh.	.35	5.00	15.00
□□□	475 Jamie Storr (G), L.A.	.25	3.00	10.00
□□□	476 Kenny Jonsson, Tor.	.10	1.00	5.00
□□□	477 Viktor Kozlov, S.J.	.10	1.00	5.00
□□□	478 Brett Lindros, NYI.	.10	1.00	5.00
□□□	479 Peter Forsberg, Que.	1.75	35.00	150
□□□	480 Paul Kariya, Ana.	2.00	40.00	200
□□□	481 Viktor Kozlov, S.J.	.10	1.00	5.00
□□□	**482 Michal Grosek, Wpg., RC**	**.10**	**1.00**	**5.00**
□□□	**483 Maxim Bets, Ana., RC**	**.10**	**1.00**	**5.00**
□□□	484 Jason Wiemer, T.B.	.10	1.00	5.00

	No.	Player			
□□□	485	Janne Laukkanen, Que.	.10	1.00	5.00
□□□	**486**	**Valeri Karpov, Ana., RC**	**.10**	**1.00**	**5.00**
□□□	487	Andrei Nikolishin, Hfd.	.10	1.00	5.00
□□□	488	Dan Plante, NYI.	.10	1.00	5.00
□□□	489	Mattias Norstrom, NYR.	.10	1.00	5.00
□□□	**490**	**David Oliver, Edm., RC**	**.10**	**1.00**	**5.00**
□□□	491	Todd Simon, Buf.	.10	1.00	5.00
□□□	492	Valeri Bure, Mtl.	.10	1.00	5.00
□□□	**493**	**Eric Fichaud (G), Tor., RC**	**.50**	**5.00**	**15.00**
□□□	494	Cory Stillman, Cgy.	.10	1.00	5.00
□□□	495	Chris Therien, Pha.	.10	1.00	5.00
□□□	**496**	**Matt Johnson, L.A., RC**	**.10**	**1.00**	**5.00**
□□□	497	Joby Messier, NYR.	.10	1.00	5.00
□□□	498	Viacheslav Butsayev, S.J.	.10	1.00	5.00
□□□	499	Bernie Nicholls, Chi.	.10	1.00	5.00
□□□	500	Mark Osborne, NYR.	.10	1.00	5.00
□□□	501	Stéphane Quintal, Wpg.	.10	1.00	5.00
□□□	502	Jamie Baker, S.J.	.10	1.00	5.00
□□□	503	Todd Ewen, Ana.	.10	1.00	5.00
□□□	504	Dan Quinn, L.A.	.10	1.00	5.00
□□□	505	Peter Taglianetti, Pgh.	.10	1.00	5.00
□□□	506	Chris Simon, Que.	.10	1.00	5.00
□□□	507	Jay Wells, NYR.	.10	1.00	5.00
□□□	508	Tommy Albelin, N.J.	.10	1.00	5.00
□□□	509	Warren Rychel, L.A.	.10	1.00	5.00
□□□	510	Brent Hughes, Bos.	.10	1.00	5.00
□□□	511	Greg Johnson, Det.	.10	1.00	5.00
□□□	512	Stu Grimson, Ana.	.10	1.00	5.00
□□□	513	Iain Fraser, Que.	.10	1.00	5.00
□□□	514	Rob Ray, Buf.	.10	1.00	5.00
□□□	515	Craig Berube, Wsh.	.10	1.00	5.00
□□□	516	Shane Churla, Dal.	.10	1.00	5.00
□□□	517	Atlantic Division Checklist	.10	1.00	5.00
□□□	518	Central Division Checklist	.10	1.00	5.00
□□□	519	Northeast Division Checklist	.10	1.00	5.00
□□□	520	Pacific Division Checklist	.10	1.00	5.00
□□□	521	Jamie Storr (G), Cdn.	.25	3.00	10.00
□□□	**522**	**Dan Cloutier (G), Cdn., RC**	**1.50**	**15.00**	**60.00**
□□□	523	Bryan McCabe, Cdn.	.10	1.00	5.00
□□□	**524**	**Ed Jovanovski, Cdn., RC**	**1.50**	**20.00**	**75.00**
□□□	**525**	**Nolan Baumgartner, Cdn., RC**	**.10**	**1.00**	**5.00**
□□□	526	Jamie Rivers, Cdn.	.10	1.00	5.00
□□□	**527**	**Wade Redden, Cdn., RC**	**.60**	**5.00**	**20.00**
□□□	**528**	**Lee Sorochan, Cdn., RC**	**.10**	**1.00**	**5.00**
□□□	**529**	**Eric Dazé, Cdn., RC**	**1.50**	**15.00**	**60.00**
□□□	530	Jason Allison, Cdn.	.35	5.00	15.00
□□□	531	Alexandre Daigle, Cdn.	.25	3.00	10.00
□□□	532	Jeff Friesen, Cdn.	.25	3.00	10.00
□□□	533	Todd Harvey, Cdn.	.10	1.00	5.00
□□□	**534**	**Jeff O'Neill, Cdn., RC**	**.75**	**8.00**	**30.00**
□□□	**535**	**Ryan Smyth, Cdn., RC**	**3.00**	**30.00**	**100.00**
□□□	536	Marty Murray, Cdn.	.10	1.00	5.00
□□□	537	Darcy Tucker, Cdn.	.10	1.00	5.00
□□□	**538**	**Denis Pederson, Cdn., RC**	**.10**	**1.00**	**5.00**
□□□	**539**	**Shean Donovan, Cdn., RC**	**.10**	**1.00**	**5.00**
□□□	**540**	**Larry Courville, Cdn., RC**	**.10**	**1.00**	**5.00**

No.	MVP Inserts	NRMT-MT
□ MVPC	Pavel Bure, Van.	40.00
□ MVPU	Dominik Hasek (G), Buf.	40.00

BOOMERS

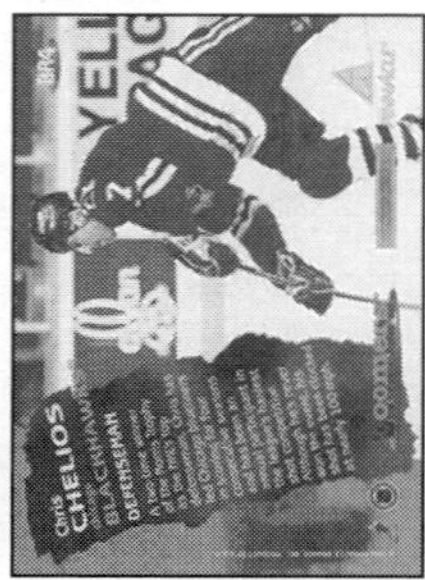

Series One U.S. Insert Set (18 cards): 80.00

No.	Player	NRMT-MT
□ BR1	Al Iafrate, Bos.	2.00
□ BR2	Vladamir Malakhov, NYI.	2.00
□ BR3	Al MacInnis, Stl.	3.00
□ BR4	Chris Chelios, Chi.	5.00
□ BR5	Mike Modano, Dal.	6.00
□ BR6	Brendan Shanahan, Stl.	7.50
□ BR7	Ray Bourque, Bos.	6.00
□ BR8	Geoff Sanderson, Hfd.	2.00
□ BR9	Brett Hull, Stl.	6.00
□ BR10	Rob Blake, L.A.	3.00
□ BR11	Steve Thomas, NYI.	2.00
□ BR12	Cam Neely, Bos.	3.00
□ BR13	Pavel Bure, Van.	9.00
□ BR14	Stéphane Richer, N.J.	2.00
□ BR15	Teemu Selänne, Wpg.	9.00
□ BR16	Eric Lindros, Pha.	18.00
□ BR17	Alexander Mogilny, Buf.	4.00
□ BR18	Rick Tocchet, L.A.	2.00

GAMERS

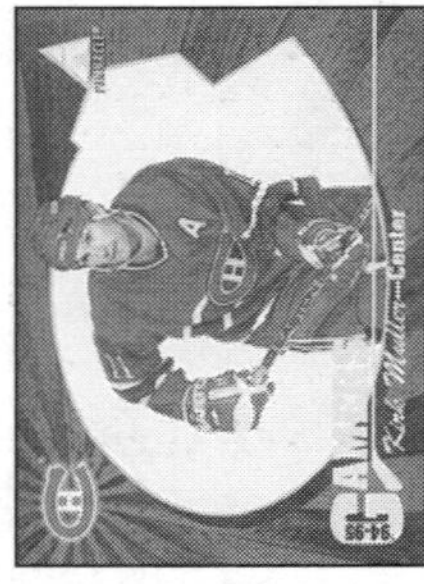

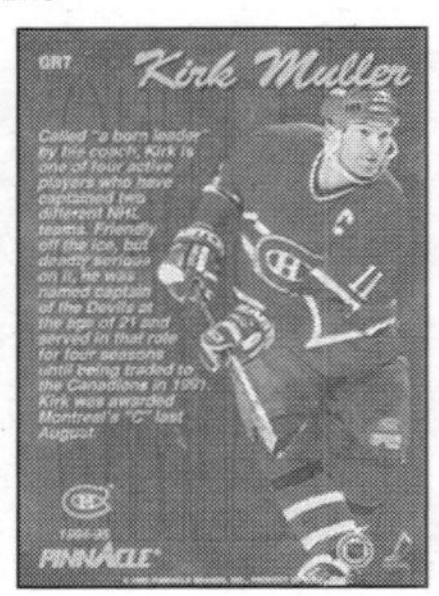

Series Two Insert Set (18 cards): 145.00

No.	Player	NRMT-MT
□ GR1	Teemu Selänne, Wpg.	15.00
□ GR2	Pat LaFontaine, Buf.	4.00
□ GR3	Sergei Fedorov, Det.	10.00
□ GR4	Pavel Bure, Van.	15.00
□ GR5	Jaromir Jagr, Pgh.	20.00
□ GR6	Alexander Mogilny, Buf.	6.00
□ GR7	Kirk Muller, Mtl.	4.00
□ GR8	Mike Modano, Dal.	10.00
□ GR9	Mark Messier, NYR.	10.00
□ GR10	Brendan Shanahan, Stl.	12.00
□ GR11	Doug Gilmour, Tor.	6.00
□ GR12	Rick Tocchet, L.A.	4.00
□ GR13	Wendel Clark, Que.	4.00
□ GR14	Jeremy Roenick, Chi.	6.00
□ GR15	Adam Graves, NYR.	4.00
□ GR16	Eric Lindros, Pha.	25.00
□ GR17	Cam Neely, Bos.	4.00
□ GR18	Keith Tkachuk, Wpg.	8.00

GOALTENDING GREATS

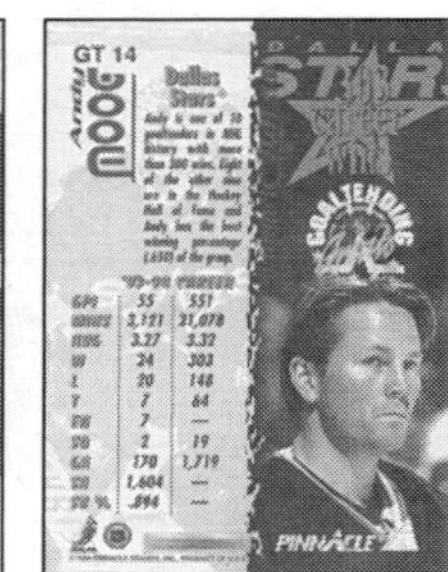

Series One Jumbo Pack Insert Set (18 cards): 165.00

No.	Player	NRMT-MT
□ GT1	Dominik Hasek (G), Buf.	18.00
□ GT2	Mike Richter (G), NYR.	8.00
□ GT3	John Vanbiesbrouck (G), Fla.	15.00
□ GT4	Ed Belfour (G), Chi.	8.00
□ GT5	Patrick Roy (G), Mtl.	40.00
□ GT6	Bill Ranford (G), Edm.	5.00
□ GT7	Martin Brodeur (G), N.J.	18.00
□ GT8	Félix Potvin (G), Tor.	12.00
□ GT9	Arturs Irbe (G), S.J.	5.00
□ GT10	Mike Vernon (G), Det.	5.00
□ GT11	Kirk McLean (G), Van.	5.00
□ GT12	Sean Burke (G), Hfd.	5.00
□ GT13	Curtis Joseph (G), Stl.	15.00
□ GT14	Andy Moog (G), Dal.	5.00
□ GT15	Daren Puppa (G), T.B.	5.00
□ GT16	Chris Osgood (G), Det.	10.00
□ GT17	Tom Barrasso (G), Pgh.	5.00
□ GT18	Jocelyn Thibault (G), Que.	8.00

MASKS

Series One Canadian Insert Set (10 cards): 425.00

No.	Player	NRMT-MT
□ MA1	Patrick Roy (G), Mtl.	135.00
□ MA2	John Vanbiesbrouck (G), Fla.	50.00
□ MA3	Kelly Hrudey (G), L.A.	35.00
□ MA4	Guy Hebert (G), Ana.	40.00
□ MA5	Rick Tabaracci (G), Wpg.	35.00
□ MA6	Ron Hextall (G), NYI.	40.00
□ MA7	Trevor Kidd (G), Cgy.	40.00
□ MA8	Andy Moog (G), Dal.	40.00
□ MA9	Jimmy Waite (G), Chi.	35.00
□ MA10	Curtis Joseph (G), Stl.	50.00

NORTHERN LIGHTS

Series One Insert Set (18 cards): 150.00

No.	Player	NRMT-MT
□ NL1	Patrick Roy (G), Mtl.	35.00
□ NL2	Kirk Muller, Mtl.	3.00
□ NL3	Vincent Damphousse, Mtl.	6.00
□ NL4	Joe Sakic, Que.	20.00
□ NL5	Wendel Clark, Que.	4.00
□ NL6	Alexandre Daigle, Ott.	4.00
□ NL7	Alexei Yashin, Ott.	8.00
□ NL8	Doug Gilmour, Tor.	6.00
□ NL9	Félix Potvin (G), Tor.	12.00
□ NL10	Mats Sundin, Que.	12.00
□ NL11	Teemu Selänne, Wpg.	15.00
□ NL12	Keith Tkachuk, Wpg.	10.00
□ NL13	Bill Ranford (G), Edm.	4.00
□ NL14	Jason Arnott, Edm.	4.00
□ NL15	Theoren Fleury, Cgy.	6.00
□ NL16	Gary Roberts, Cgy.	4.00
□ NL17	Pavel Bure, Van.	15.00
□ NL18	Trevor Linden, Van.	4.00

ROOKIE TEAM PINNACLE

These inserts can be found with dufex printing on either side.

Series Two Insert Set (12 cards): 235.00

No.	Player	NRMT-MT
□□ RTP1	Corey Hirsch (G)/Jamie Storr (G)	15.00
□□ RTP2	Mattias Norstrom/Oleg Tverdovsky	10.00
□□ RTP3	Denis Tsygurov/ Janne Laukkanen	10.00
□□ RTP4	Chris Tamer/Kenny Jonsson	10.00
□□ RTP5	Zigmund Palffy/Viktor Kozlov	25.00
□□ RTP6	René Corbet/ Maxim Bets	10.00
□□ RTP7	Jason Allison/Jeff Friesen	20.00
□□ RTP8	Brian Rolston/Michael Peca	15.00
□□ RTP9	Peter Forsberg/Paul Kariya	125.00
□□ RTP10	Brian Savage/Todd Harvey	10.00
□□ RTP11	Brett Lindros/Valeri Karpov	10.00
□□ RTP12	Maruisz Czerkawski/Sergei Krivokravsov	10.00

TEAM PINNACLE

These inserts can be found with dufex printing on either side.

Series One U.S. Insert Set (12 cards): 475.00

	No.	Player	NRMT-MT
☐☐	TP1	Félix Potvin (G)/Patrick Roy (G)	85.00
☐☐	TP2	Curtis Joseph (G)/Mike Richter (G)	25.00
☐☐	TP3	Chris Chelios/Ray Bourque	20.00
☐☐	TP4	Brian Leetch/Rob Blake	15.00
☐☐	TP5	Scott Stevens/Paul Coffey	15.00
☐☐	TP6	Brendan Shanahan/Adam Graves	25.00
☐☐	TP7	Luc Robitaille/Kevin Stevens	15.00
☐☐	TP8	Sergei Fedorov/Eric Lindros	70.00
☐☐	TP9	Wayne Gretzky/Mark Messier	125.00
☐☐	TP10	Doug Gilmour/Mario Lemieux	70.00
☐☐	TP11	Brett Hull/Jaromir Jagr	50.00
☐☐	TP12	Pavel Bure/Cam Neely	35.00

WORLD EDITION

Series Two Hobby Insert Set (18 cards): 65.00

	No.	Player	NRMT-MT
☐	WE1	Teemu Selänne, Wpg.	7.00
☐	WE2	Doug Gilmour, Tor.	3.00
☐	WE3	Jeremy Roenick, Chi.	3.00
☐	WE4	Ulf Dahlen, S.J.	1.00
☐	WE5	Sergei Fedorov, Det.	5.00
☐	WE6	Dominik Hasek (G), Buf.	7.00
☐	WE7	Jari Kurri, L.A.	2.00
☐	WE8	Mario Lemieux, Pgh.	15.00
☐	WE9	Mike Modano, Dal.	5.00
☐	WE10	Mikael Renberg, Pha.	2.00
☐	WE11	Sandis Ozolinsh, S.J.	2.00
☐	WE12	Alexei Kovalev, NYR.	1.00
☐	WE13	Robert Reichel, Cgy.	2.00
☐	WE14	Eric Lindros, Pha.	12.00
☐	WE15	Brian Leetch, NYR.	3.00
☐	WE16	Nicklas Lidstrom, Det.	2.00
☐	WE17	Alexei Yashin, Ott.	4.00
☐	WE18	Petr Nedved, NYR.	1.00

1994 - 95 POST BE A PLAYER

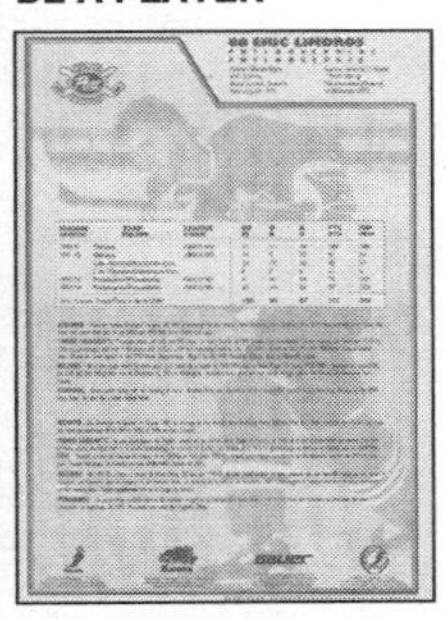

This series was licensed by the NHLPA and issued on the backs of specially marked boxes of Post Honey Comb and Post Sugar Crisp cereal. A complete 25-card factory set was available by mail. The title card was only available in the redeemed sets.

Card Size: 8 3/4" x 12 1/4"

Imprint:

Complete Set (25 cards): 60.00

	Player	NRMT-MT
☐	Title Card	2.00
☐	Tony Amonte	3.00
☐	Jason Arnott	3.00
☐	Ray Bourque	4.00
☐	Martin Brodeur (G)	5.00
☐	Pavel Bure	5.00
☐	Chris Chelios	3.50
☐	Geoff Courtnall	2.50
☐	Russ Courtnall	2.50
☐	Steve Duchesne	2.50
☐	Sergei Fedorov	4.00
☐	Theoren Fleury	3.00
☐	Doug Gilmour	3.00
☐	Wayne Gretzky	12.00
☐	Jari Kurri	3.00
☐	Eric Lindros	8.00
☐	Marty McSorley	2.50
☐	Alexander Mogilny	3.00
☐	Kirk Muller	2.50
☐	Rob Niedermayer	3.00
☐	Félix Potvin (G)	4.00
☐	Luc Robitaille	3.00
☐	Joe Sakic	6.00
☐	Teemu Selänne	5.00
☐	Alexei Yashin	3.50

1994 - 95 PREMIER (O-PEE-CHEE / TOPPS)

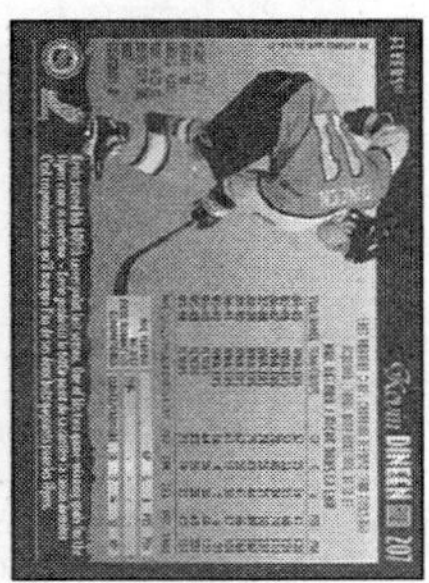

These cards have foour versions: an O-Pee-Chee regular card, an O-Pee-Chee Special FX parallel, a Topps regular card and a Topps Special FX parallel. The OPC and Topps regular cards have the same value.

Series One Imprint: © 1994 THE TOPPS COMPANY, INC.

Series Two Imprint: © 1995 THE TOPPS COMPANY, INC.

Complete Set (550 cards): 30.00 400 600

Common Player: .10 .35 .50

	No.	Player	OPC/ Topps	Topps FX	OPC FX
☐☐☐☐	1	Mark Messier, NYR.	.50	5.00	7.50
☐☐☐☐	2	Darren Turcotte, Hfd.	.10	.35	.50
☐☐☐☐	**3**	**Mikhail Shtalenkov (G), Ana., RC**	**.10**	**.35**	**.50**
☐☐☐☐	4	Rob Gaudreau, S.J.	.10	.35	.50
☐☐☐☐	5	Tony Amonte, Chi.	.25	1.00	1.50
☐☐☐☐	6	Stéphane Quintal, Wpg.	.10	.35	.50
☐☐☐☐	7	Iain Fraser, Que.	.10	.35	.50
☐☐☐☐	8	Doug Weight, Edm.	.35	2.00	3.00
☐☐☐☐	9	German Titov, Cgy.	.10	.35	.50
☐☐☐☐	10	Larry Murphy, Pgh.	.25	1.00	1.50
☐☐☐☐	11	Danton Cole, T.B.	.10	.35	.50
☐☐☐☐	12	Pat Peake, Wsh.	.10	.35	.50
☐☐☐☐	13	Chris Terreri (G), N.J.	.10	.35	.50
☐☐☐☐	14	Yuri Khmylev, Buf.	.10	.35	.50
☐☐☐☐	15	Paul Coffey, Det.	.25	1.00	1.50
☐☐☐☐	16	Brian Savage, Mtl.	.10	.35	.50
☐☐☐☐	17	Rod Brind'Amour, Pha.	.25	1.00	1.50
☐☐☐☐	18	Nathan Lafayette, Van.,	.10	.35	.50
☐☐☐☐	19	Gord Murphy, Fla.	.10	.35	.50
☐☐☐☐	20	Al Iafrate, Bos.	.10	.35	.50
☐☐☐☐	21	Kevin Miller, Stl.	.10	.35	.50
☐☐☐☐	22	Peter Zezel, Tor.	.10	.35	.50
☐☐☐☐	23	Sylvain Turgeon, Ott.	.10	.35	.50
☐☐☐☐	24	Mark Tinordi, Dal.	.10	.35	.50
☐☐☐☐	25	Jari Kurri, L.A.	.25	1.00	1.50
☐☐☐☐	26	Benoît Hogue, NYI.	.10	.35	.50
☐☐☐☐	27	Jeff Reese (G), Hfd.	.10	.35	.50
☐☐☐☐	28	Brian Noonan, NYR.	.10	.35	.50
☐☐☐☐	**29**	**Denis Tsygurov, Buf., RC**	**.10**	**.35**	**.50**
☐☐☐☐	30	James Patrick, Cgy.	.10	.35	.50
☐☐☐☐	31	Robert Corkum, Ana.	.10	.35	.50
☐☐☐☐	32	Valeri Kamensky, Que.	.25	1.00	1.50
☐☐☐☐	33	Ray Whitney, S.J.	.10	.35	.50
☐☐☐☐	34	Joe Murphy, Chi.	.10	.35	.50
☐☐☐☐	35	AS: Dominik Hasek (G), Buf.	.35	3.75	5.00
☐☐☐☐	36	AS: Ray Bourque, Bos.	.25	2.50	3.50
☐☐☐☐	37	AS: Brian Leetch, NYR.	.25	2.00	3.00
☐☐☐☐	38	AS: Dave Andreychuk, Tor.	.10	.35	.50
☐☐☐☐	39	AS: Pavel Bure, Van.	.35	3.75	5.00
☐☐☐☐	40	AS: Sergei Fedorov, Det.	.25	2.50	3.50
☐☐☐☐	41	Bob Beers, Edm.	.10	.35	.50
☐☐☐☐	**42**	**Byron Dafoe, Wsh., RC**	**.25**	**1.00**	**1.50**
☐☐☐☐	43	Lyle Odelein, Mtl.	.10	.35	.50
☐☐☐☐	44	Markus Naslund, Pgh.	.10	.35	.50
☐☐☐☐	45	Dean Chynoweth, NYI.	.10	.35	.50
☐☐☐☐	46	Trent Klatt, Dal.	.10	.35	.50
☐☐☐☐	47	Murray Craven, Van.	.10	.35	.50
☐☐☐☐	48	David Mackey, Stl.	.10	.35	.50
☐☐☐☐	49	Norm Maciver, Ott.	.10	.35	.50
☐☐☐☐	50	Alexander Mogilny, Buf.	.35	2.00	3.00
☐☐☐☐	51	David Reid, Bos.	.10	.35	.50
☐☐☐☐	52	Nicklas Lidstrom, Det.	.25	1.00	1.50
☐☐☐☐	53	Tom Fitzgerald, Fla.	.10	.35	.50
☐☐☐☐	54	Roman Hamrlik, T.B.	.25	1.00	1.50
☐☐☐☐	55	Wendel Clark, Tor.	.25	1.00	1.50
☐☐☐☐	56	Dominic Roussel (G), Pha.	.10	.35	.50
☐☐☐☐	57	Alexei Zhitnik, L.A.	.10	.35	.50
☐☐☐☐	58	Valeri Zelepukin, N.J.	.10	.35	.50
☐☐☐☐	59	Calle Johansson, Wsh.	.10	.35	.50
☐☐☐☐	60	Craig Janney, Stl.	.10	.35	.50
☐☐☐☐	61	Randy Wood, Buf.	.10	.35	.50
☐☐☐☐	62	Curtis Leschyshyn, Que.	.10	.35	.50
☐☐☐☐	63	Stéphan Lebeau, Ana.	.10	.35	.50
☐☐☐☐	64	Dallas Drake, Wpg.	.10	.35	.50
☐☐☐☐	65	Vincent Damphousse, Mtl.	.35	2.00	3.00
☐☐☐☐	66	Scott Lachance, NYI.	.10	.35	.50
☐☐☐☐	67	Dirk Graham, Chi.	.10	.35	.50
☐☐☐☐	68	Kevin Smyth, Hfd.	.10	.35	.50
☐☐☐☐	69	Denis Savard, T.B.	.10	.35	.50
☐☐☐☐	70	Mike Richter (G), NYR.	.35	2.00	3.00
☐☐☐☐	71	Ron Stern, Cgy.	.10	.35	.50
☐☐☐☐	72	Kirk Maltby, Edm.	.10	.35	.50
☐☐☐☐	73	Kjell Samuelsson, Pgh.	.10	.35	.50
☐☐☐☐	74	Neal Broten, Dal.	.10	.35	.50
☐☐☐☐	75	Trevor Linden, Van.	.25	1.00	1.50
☐☐☐☐	76	Todd Elik, S.J.	.10	.35	.50
☐☐☐☐	77	Andrew McBain, Ott.	.10	.35	.50
☐☐☐☐	78	Alexei Kudashov, Tor.	.10	.35	.50
☐☐☐☐	79	Ken Daneyko, N.J.	.10	.35	.50
☐☐☐☐	80	Dominik Hasek/Grant Fuhr	.50	5.00	7.50
☐☐☐☐	81	Andy Moog/Darcy Wakaluk	.25	1.00	1.50
☐☐☐☐	82	John Vanbiesbrouck/Mark Fitzpatrick	.35	3.75	5.00
☐☐☐☐	83	Martin Brodeur/Chris Terreri	.50	5.00	7.50
☐☐☐☐	84	Tom Barrasso/Ken Wregget	.25	1.00	1.50
☐☐☐☐	85	Kirk McLean/Kay Whitmore	.25	1.00	1.50
☐☐☐☐	86	Darryl Sydor, L.A.	.10	.35	.50
☐☐☐☐	87	Chris Osgood (G), Det.	.35	3.50	5.00
☐☐☐☐	88	Ted Donato, Bos.	.10	.35	.50
☐☐☐☐	89	Dave Lowry, Fla.	.10	.35	.50
☐☐☐☐	90	Mark Recchi, Pha.	.25	1.00	1.50
☐☐☐☐	91	Jim Montgomery, Stl.	.10	.35	.50
☐☐☐☐	92	Bill Houlder, Ana.	.10	.35	.50
☐☐☐☐	93	Richard Smehlik, Buf.	.10	.35	.50
☐☐☐☐	94	Benoît Brunet, Mtl.	.10	.35	.50
☐☐☐☐	95	Teemu Selänne, Wpg.	.75	7.50	12.00
☐☐☐☐	96	Paul Ranheim, Hfd.	.10	.35	.50
☐☐☐☐	97	Andrei Kovalenko, Que.	.10	.35	.50
☐☐☐☐	98	Grant Ledyard, Dal.	.10	.35	.50
☐☐☐☐	99	Brent Grieve, Edm.	.10	.35	.50
☐☐☐☐	100	Joé Juneau, Wsh.	.10	.35	.50
☐☐☐☐	101	Martin Gelinas, Van.	.10	.35	.50
☐☐☐☐	102	Jamie Macoun, Tor.	.10	.35	.50
☐☐☐☐	103	Craig MacTavish, NYR.	.10	.35	.50
☐☐☐☐	104	Micah Aivazoff, Det.	.10	.35	.50
☐☐☐☐	105	Stéphane Richer, N.J.	.10	.35	.50
☐☐☐☐	106	Eric Weinrich, Chi.	.10	.35	.50
☐☐☐☐	107	Pat Elynuik, T.B.	.10	.35	.50
☐☐☐☐	108	Tomas Sandström, Pgh.	.10	.35	.50
☐☐☐☐	109	Darrin Madeley (G), Ott.	.10	.35	.50
☐☐☐☐	110	Al MacInnis, Cgy.	.25	1.00	1.50
☐☐☐☐	111	Cam Stewart, Bos.	.10	.35	.50
☐☐☐☐	112	Dixon Ward, L.A.	.10	.35	.50
☐☐☐☐	113	Vlastimil Kroupa, S.J.	.10	.35	.50
☐☐☐☐	114	Rob DiMaio, Pha.	.10	.35	.50
☐☐☐☐	115	Pierre Turgeon, NYI.	.25	1.00	1.50
☐☐☐☐	116	Mike Hough, Fla.	.10	.35	.50
☐☐☐☐	117	John LeClair, Mtl.	.50	5.00	7.50
☐☐☐☐	118	Dave Hannan, Buf.	.10	.35	.50
☐☐☐☐	119	Todd Ewen, Ana.	.10	.35	.50
☐☐☐☐	120	New York Rangers	.25	1.00	1.50
☐☐☐☐	121	Dave Manson, Wpg.	.10	.35	.50
☐☐☐☐	122	Jocelyn Lemieux, Hfd.	.10	.35	.50
☐☐☐☐	123	Jocelyn Thibault (G), Que.	.35	2.00	3.00
☐☐☐☐	124	Scott Pearson, Edm.	.10	.35	.50
☐☐☐☐	125	AS: Patrick Roy (G), Mtl.	.75	10.00	15.00
☐☐☐☐	126	AS: Scott Stevens, N.J.	.10	.35	.50
☐☐☐☐	127	AS: Al MacInnis, Cgy.	.25	1.00	1.50
☐☐☐☐	128	AS: Adam Graves, NYR.	.10	.35	.50
☐☐☐☐	129	AS: Cam Neely, Bos.	.25	.50	1.00
☐☐☐☐	130	AS: Wayne Gretzky, L.A.	1.00	15.00	20.00
☐☐☐☐	131	Tom Chorske, N.J.	.10	.35	.50
☐☐☐☐	132	John Tucker, T.B.	.10	.35	.50
☐☐☐☐	133	Steve Smith, Chi.	.10	.35	.50
☐☐☐☐	134	Kay Whitmore (G), Van.	.10	.35	.50
☐☐☐☐	135	Adam Oates, Bos.	.35	2.00	3.00
☐☐☐☐	136	Bill Berg, Tor.	.10	.35	.50
☐☐☐☐	137	Wes Walz, Cgy.	.10	.35	.50

□□□□ 138 Jeff Beukeboom, NYR. .10 .35 .50
□□□□ 139 Ron Francis, Pgh. .35 2.00 3.00
□□□□ 140 Alexandre Daigle, Ott. .25 .50 1.00
□□□□ 141 Josef Beranek, Pha. .10 .35 .50
□□□□ 142 Tom Pederson, S.J. .10 .35 .50
□□□□ 143 Jamie McLennan (G), NYI. .25 .50 1.00
□□□□ 144 Scott Mellanby, Fla. .10 .35 .50
□□□□ 145 Vyacheslav Kozlov, Det. .10 .35 .50
□□□□ 146 Marty McSorley, L.A. .10 .35 .50
□□□□ 147 Tim Sweeney, Ana. .10 .35 .50
□□□□ 148 Luciano Borsato, Wpg. .10 .35 .50
□□□□ 149 Jason Dawe, Buf. .10 .35 .50
□□□□ 150 Wayne Gretzky, L.A. 1.00 15.00 20.00
□□□□ 151 Pavel Bure, Van. .35 3.75 5.00
□□□□ 152 Dominik Hasek (G), Buf. .35 3.75 5.00
□□□□ 153 Scott Stevens, N.J. .10 .35 .50
□□□□ 154 Wayne Gretzky, L.A. 1.00 15.00 20.00
□□□□ 155 Mike Richter (G), NYR. .25 1.00 1.50
□□□□ 156 Dominik Hasek (G), Buf. .35 3.75 5.00
□□□□ 157 Ted Drury, Hfd. .10 .35 .50
□□□□ 158 Peter Popovic, Mtl. .10 .35 .50
□□□□ 159 Alexei Kasatonov, Stl. .10 .35 .50
□□□□ 160 Mats Sundin, Que. .50 5.00 7.50
□□□□ 161 Brad Shaw, Ott. .10 .35 .50
□□□□ 162 Bret Hedican, Van. .10 .35 .50
□□□□ 163 Mike McPhee, Dal. .10 .35 .50
□□□□ 164 Martin Straka, Pgh. .10 .35 .50
□□□□ 165 Dmitri Mironov, Tor. .10 .35 .50
□□□□ 166 Andrei Trefilov (G), Cgy. .10 .35 .50
□□□□ 167 Joe Reekie, Wsh. .10 .35 .50
□□□□ 168 Gary Suter, Chi. .10 .35 .50
□□□□ 169 Greg Gilbert, NYR. .10 .35 .50
□□□□ 170 Igor Larionov, S.J. .25 1.00 1.50
□□□□ 171 Mike Sillinger, Det. .10 .35 .50
□□□□ 172 Igor Kravchuk, Edm. .10 .35 .50
□□□□ 173 Glen Murray, Bos. .10 .35 .50
□□□□ 174 Shawn Chambers, T.B. .10 .35 .50
□□□□ 175 John MacLean, N.J. .10 .35 .50
□□□□ 176 Yves Racine, Pha. .10 .35 .50
□□□□ 177 Andrei Lomakin, Fla. .10 .35 .50
□□□□ 178 Patrick Flatley, NYI. .10 .35 .50
□□□□ 179 Igor Ulanov, Wpg. .10 .35 .50
□□□□ 180 Pat LaFontaine, Buf. .25 1.00 1.50
□□□□ 181 Mathieu Schneider, Mtl. .10 .35 .50
□□□□ 182 Peter Stastny, Stl. .10 .35 .50
□□□□ 183 Tony Granato, L.A. .10 .35 .50
□□□□ 184 Peter Douris, Ana. .10 .35 .50
□□□□ 185 Alexei Kovalev, NYR. .10 .35 .50
□□□□ 186 Geoff Courtnall, Van. .10 .35 .50
□□□□ 187 Richard Matvichuk, Dal. .10 .35 .50
□□□□ 188 Troy Murray, Ott. .10 .35 .50
□□□□ 189 Todd Gill, Tor. .10 .35 .50
□□□□ 190 Martin Brodeur (G), N.J. .35 3.75 5.00
□□□□ 191 Mikael Renberg, Pha. .25 1.00 1.50
□□□□ 192 Alexei Yashin, Ott. .25 1.50 2.00
□□□□ 193 Jason Arnott, Edm. .25 1.00 1.50
□□□□ 194 Derek Plante, Buf. .10 .35 .50
□□□□ 195 Alexandre Daigle, Ott. .25 1.00 1.50
□□□□ 196 Bryan Smolinski, Bos. .10 .35 .50
□□□□ 197 Jesse Belanger, Fla. .10 .35 .50
□□□□ 198 Chris Pronger, Hfd. .25 1.00 1.50
□□□□ 199 Chris Osgood (G), Det. .35 3.50 5.00
□□□□ 200 Jeremy Roenick, Chi. .25 1.00 1.50
□□□□ 201 Johan Garpenlov, S.J. .10 .35 .50
□□□□ 202 Dave Karpa, Que. .10 .35 .50
□□□□ 203 Darren McCarty, Det. .10 .35 .50
□□□□ 204 Claude Lemieux, N.J. .10 .35 .50
□□□□ 205 Geoff Sanderson, Hfd. .10 .35 .50
□□□□ 206 Tom Barrasso (G), Pgh. .25 1.00 1.50
□□□□ 207 Kevin Dineen, Pha. .10 .35 .50
□□□□ 208 Sylvain Côté, Wsh. .10 .35 .50
□□□□ 209 Brent Gretzky, T.B. .10 .35 .50
□□□□ 210 Shayne Corson, Edm. .25 1.00 1.50
□□□□ 211 Darius Kasparaitis, NYI. .10 .35 .50
□□□□ 212 Peter Andersson, Fla. .10 .35 .50
□□□□ 213 Robert Reichel, Cgy. .25 1.00 1.50
□□□□ 214 Jozef Stumpel, Bos. .25 1.00 1.50
□□□□ 215 Brendan Shanahan, Stl. .60 6.00 9.00
□□□□ 216 Craig Muni, Buf. .10 .35 .50
□□□□ 217 Alexei Zhamnov, Wpg. .25 1.00 1.50
□□□□ 218 Robert Lang, L.A. .10 .35 .50
□□□□ 219 Brian Bellows, Mtl. .10 .35 .50
□□□□ 220 Steven King, Ana. .10 .35 .50
□□□□ 221 Sergei Zubov, NYR. .25 1.00 1.50
□□□□ 222 Kelly Miller, Wsh. .10 .35 .50
□□□□ 223 Ilya Byakin, Edm. .10 .35 .50
□□□□ 224 Chris Tamer, Pgh. .10 .35 .50
□□□□ 225 Doug Gilmour, Tor. .35 2.00 3.00
□□□□ 226 Shawn Antoski, Van. .10 .35 .50
□□□□ 227 Andrew Cassels, Hfd. .10 .35 .50
□□□□ 228 Craig Wolanin, Que. .10 .35 .50
□□□□ 229 Jon Casey (G), Bos. .10 .35 .50
□□□□ 230 Mike Modano, Dal. .50 5.00 7.50
□□□□ 231 Bill Guerin, N.J. .25 1.00 1.50
□□□□ 232 Gaetan Duchesne, S.J. .10 .35 .50
□□□□ 233 Steve Dubinsky, Chi. .10 .35 .50
□□□□ 234 Jason Bowen, Pha. .10 .35 .50
□□□□ 235 Steve Yzerman, Det. 1.00 10.00 15.00
□□□□ 236 Dave Poulin, Wsh. .10 .35 .50
□□□□ 237 Mikael Nylander, Cgy. .10 .35 .50
□□□□ 238 Félix Potvin (G), Tor. .25 2.50 3.50
□□□□ 239 Sandis Ozolinsh, S.J. .25 1.00 1.50
□□□□ 240 Scott Niedermayer, N.J. .25 1.00 1.50
□□□□ 241 Eric Lindros, Pha. .75 10.00 15.00
□□□□ 242 Keith Tkachuk, Wpg. .25 2.00 3.00
□□□□ 243 Teemu Selänne, Wpg. .25 2.75 3.75
□□□□ 244 Marty McInnis, NYI. .10 .35 .50
□□□□ 245 Bob Kudelski, Fla. .10 .35 .50
□□□□ 246 Paul Cavallini, T.B. .10 .35 .50
□□□□ 247 Brian Bradley, T.B. .10 .35 .50
□□□□ 248 Robb Stauber, L.A. .10 .35 .50
□□□□ 249 Jay Wells, NYR. .10 .35 .50
□□□□ 250 Mario Lemieux, Pgh. 1.50 25.00 35.00
□□□□ 251 Tommy Albelin, N.J. .10 .35 .50
□□□□ 252 Paul DiPietro, Mtl. .10 .35 .50
□□□□ 253 Mike Gartner, Tor. .25 1.00 1.50
□□□□ 254 Darrin Shannon, Wpg. .10 .35 .50
□□□□ 255 Alexander Karpovtsev, NYR. .10 .35 .50
□□□□ 256 Dave Babych, Van. .10 .35 .50
□□□□ 257 Greg Johnson, Det. .10 .35 .50
□□□□ 258 Frantisek Musil, Cgy. .10 .35 .50
□□□□ 259 Michal Pivonka, Wsh. .10 .35 .50
□□□□ 260 Arturs Irbe (G), S.J. .10 .35 .50
□□□□ 261 Paul Broten, Dal. .10 .35 .50
□□□□ 262 Don Sweeney, Bos. .10 .35 .50
□□□□ 263 Doug Brown, Pgh. .10 .35 .50
□□□□ 264 Bobby Dollas, Ana. .10 .35 .50
□□□□ 265 Brian Skrudland, Fla. .10 .35 .50
□□□□ **266 Dan Plante, NYI., RC .10 .35 .50**
□□□□ **267 Chad Penney, Ott., RC .10 .35 .50**
□□□□ 268 Stephen Leach, Bos. .10 .35 .50
□□□□ 269 Damian Rhodes (G), Tor. .10 .35 .50
□□□□ 270 Glenn Anderson, NYR. .10 .35 .50
□□□□ 271 Randy McKay, N.J. .10 .35 .50
□□□□ 272 Jeff Brown, Van. .10 .35 .50
□□□□ 273 Steve Konowalchuk, Wsh. .10 .35 .50
□□ 274 Checklist (1 - 136) .15 .– .–
□□ 274 Rudy Poeschek, T.B. .– .50 .75
□□ 275 Checklist (137 - 275) .15 .– .–
□□ 275 Michael Peca, Van. .– 1.00 1.50
□□□□ 276 Sergei Fedorov, Det. .25 2.75 3.75
□□□□ 277 Adam Oates, Bos. .25 1.00 1.50
□□□□ 278 Mark Messier, NYR. .25 2.75 3.75
□□□□ 279 Doug Gilmour, Tor. .25 1.00 1.50
□□□□ 280 Wayne Gretzky, L.A. 1.00 15.00 20.00
□□□□ 281 Rick Tocchet, L.A. .10 .35 .50
□□□□ 282 Guy Carbonneau, Stl. .10 .35 .50
□□□□ 283 Peter Bondra, Wsh. .35 3.50 5.00
□□□□ **284 Valeri Karpov, Ana., RC .10 .35 .50**
□□□□ 285 Ed Belfour (G), Chi. .35 2.00 3.00
□□□□ 286 Petr Nedved, NYR. .10 .35 .50
□□□□ 287 Mikael Andersson, T.B. .10 .35 .50
□□□□ 288 Boris Mironov, Edm. .10 .35 .50
□□□□ 289 Donald Audette, Buf. .10 .35 .50
□□□□ 290 Kevin Stevens, Pgh. .10 .35 .50
□□□□ 291 Cliff Ronning, Van. .10 .35 .50
□□□□ 292 Bruce Driver, N.J. .10 .35 .50
□□□□ **293 Mariusz Czerkawski, Bos., RC .10 .35 .50**
□□□□ 294 Mikael Renberg, Pha. .10 .35 .50
□□□□ 295 Theoren Fleury, Cgy. .35 2.00 3.00
□□□□ 296 Robert Kron, Hfd. .10 .35 .50
□□□□ 297 Wendel Clark, Que. .25 1.00 1.50
□□□□ 298 Dave Gagner, Dal. .10 .35 .50
□□□□ 299 Ulf Dahlen, S.J. .10 .35 .50
□□□□ 300 Keith Tkachuk, Wpg. .35 3.50 5.00
□□□□ 301 Mike Ridley, Tor. .10 .35 .50
□□□□ 302 Mike Vernon (G), Det. .25 1.00 1.50
□□□□ 303 Troy Mallette, Ott. .10 .35 .50
□□□□ 304 Derek King, NYI. .10 .35 .50
□□□□ 305 Kirk Muller, Mtl. .10 .35 .50
□□□□ 306 Rob Niedermayer, Fla. .25 1.00 1.50
□□□□ 307 Ian Laperrière, Stl. .10 .35 .50
□□□□ 308 Mike Donnelly, L.A. .10 .35 .50
□□□□ 309 Joe Sacco, Ana. .10 .35 .50
□□□□ 310 Patrick Roy (G), Mtl. .75 10.00 15.00
□□□□ 311 Tom Barrasso (G), Pgh. .25 1.00 1.50
□□□□ 312 Dominik Hasek (G), Buf. .35 3.75 5.00
□□□□ 313 Félix Potvin (G), Tor. .25 2.50 3.50
□□□□ 314 Mike Richter (G), NYR. .25 1.00 1.50
□□□□ 315 Bobby Holik, N.J. .10 .35 .50
□□□□ 316 Patrick Poulin, Chi. .10 .35 .50
□□□□ 317 Stéphane Matteau, NYR. .10 .35 .50
□□□□ 318 Petr Klima, T.B. .10 .35 .50
□□□□ 319 Fredrik Olausson, Edm. .10 .35 .50
□□□□ 320 Dale Hawerchuk, Buf. .10 .35 .50
□□□□ 321 Jim Dowd, N.J. .10 .35 .50
□□□□ 322 Chris Therien, Phi. .10 .35 .50
□□□□ **323 Ravil Gusmanov, Wpg., RC .10 .35 .50**
□□□□ 324 Vincent Riendeau (G), Bos. .10 .35 .50
□□□□ 325 Pavel Bure, Van. .75 7.50 12.00
□□□□ 326 Jimmy Carson, Hfd. .10 .35 .50
□□□□ 327 Steve Chiasson, Cgy. .10 .35 .50
□□□□ 328 Ken Wregget (G), Pgh. .10 .35 .50
□□□□ 329 Kenny Jonsson, Tor. .10 .35 .50
□□□□ 330 Keith Primeau, Det. .25 1.00 1.50
□□□□ 331 Bob Errey, S.J. .10 .35 .50
□□□□ 332 Derian Hatcher, Dal. .25 1.00 1.50
□□□□ 333 Stéphane Fiset (G), Que. .25 1.00 1.50
□□□□ 334 Brent Severyn, Fla. .10 .35 .50
□□□□ 335 Ray Ferraro, NYI. .10 .35 .50
□□□□ 336 Pavol Demitra, Ott. .10 .35 .50
□□□□ 337 Valeri Bure, Mtl. .10 .35 .50
□□□□ 338 Guy Hebert (G), Ana. .10 .35 .50
□□□□ **339 Matt Johnson, L.A., RC .10 .35 .50**
□□□□ 340 Curtis Joseph (G), Stl. .60 6.00 9.00
□□□□ 341 Rob Pearson, Wsh. .10 .35 .50
□□□□ 342 Jeff Shantz, Chi. .10 .35 .50
□□□□ 343 Eric Charron, T.B. .10 .35 .50
□□□□ 344 Jason Smith, N.J. .10 .35 .50
□□□□ 345 Mats Sundin/Wendel Clark .25 1.00 1.50
□□□□ 346 Luc Robitaille/Rick Tocchet .25 1.00 1.50
□□□□ 347 Phil Housley/Al MacInnis .25 1.00 1.50
□□□□ 348 Mike Vernon (G)/Steve Chiasson .25 1.00 1.50
□□□□ 349 Craig Simpson, Buf. .10 .35 .50
□□□□ 350 Adam Graves, NYR. .10 .35 .50
□□□□ 351 Kevin Haller, Pha. .10 .35 .50
□□□□ 352 Nelson Emerson, Wpg. .10 .35 .50
□□□□ 353 Phil Housley, Cgy. .10 .35 .50
□□□□ 354 Shawn McEachern, Pgh. .10 .35 .50
□□□□ 355 Félix Potvin (G), Tor. .50 5.00 7.50
□□□□ 356 Sergio Momesso, Van. .10 .35 .50
□□□□ 357 Glen Wesley, Hfd. .10 .35 .50
□□□□ 358 David Shaw, Bos. .10 .35 .50
□□□□ 359 Terry Carkner, Det. .10 .35 .50
□□□□ 360 John Vanbiesbrouck (G), Fla. .60 6.00 9.00
□□□□ 361 Dean Evason, Dal. .10 .35 .50
□□□□ 362 Michal Sykora, S.J. .10 .35 .50
□□□□ 363 Troy Loney, NYI. .10 .35 .50
□□□□ 364 Sylvlain Lefebvre, Que. .10 .35 .50
□□□□ 365 Alexei Yashin, Ott. .35 3.50 5.00
□□□□ 366 Gilbert Dionne, Mtl. .10 .35 .50
□□□□ 367 Rick Tabaracci (G), Wsh. .10 .35 .50
□□□□ 368 Paul Ysebaert, Chi. .10 .35 .50
□□□□ **369 Craig Johnson, Stl., RC .10 .35 .50**
□□□□ 370 Scott Stevens, N.J. .10 .35 .50
□□□□ 371 Philippe Boucher, Buf. .10 .35 .50
□□□□ 372 Garry Valk, Ana. .10 .35 .50
□□□□ 373 Jason Muzzatti (G), Cgy. .10 .35 .50
□□□□ 374 Chris Joseph, T.B. .10 .35 .50
□□□□ 375 Wayne Gretzky, L.A. 2.00 30.00 45.00
□□□□ 376 Teppo Numminen, Wpg. .10 .35 .50
□□□□ 377 Oleg Petrov, Mtl. .10 .35 .50
□□□□ **378 Patrik Juhlin, Pha., RC .10 .35 .50**
□□□□ 379 Zarley Zalapski, Cgy. .10 .35 .50
□□□□ 380 Martin Brodeur (G), N.J. .35 3.75 5.00
□□□□ 381 Chris Pronger, Hfd. .25 1.00 1.50
□□□□ 382 Sergei Zubov, NYR. .25 1.00 1.50
□□□□ 383 Mikael Renberg, Pha. .25 1.00 1.50
□□□□ 384 Brett Lindros, NYI. .10 .35 .50
□□□□ 385 Peter Forsberg, Que. .75 8.50 11.00
□□□□ **386 Brandon Convery, Tor., RC .10 .35 .50**
□□□□ 387 Stephen Heinze, Bos. .10 .35 .50
□□□□ 388 Glenn Healy (G), NYR. .10 .35 .50
□□□□ 389 Brian Benning, Fla. .10 .35 .50
□□□□ 390 Pat Verbeek, Hfd. .10 .35 .50

	No.	Player			
□□□□	391	Ulf Samuelsson, Pgh.	.10	.35	.50
□□□□	392	Turner Stevenson, Mtl.	.10	.35	.50
□□□□	393	Bob Rouse, Det.	.10	.35	.50
□□□□	394	Steve Konroyd, Ott.	.10	.35	.50
□□□□	395	Russ Courtnall, Dal.	.10	.35	.50
□□□□	396	Sergei Makarov, S.J.	.10	.35	.50
□□□□	397	Kirk McLean (G), Van.	.25	1.00	1.50
□□□□	398	Steven Finn, Que.	.10	.35	.50
□□□□	399	Yan Kaminsky, NYI.	.10	.35	.50
□□□□	400	Eric Lindros, Pha.	1.50	20.00	30.00
□□□□	401	Steve Duschesne, Stl.	.10	.35	.50
□□□□	402	John Slaney, Wsh.	.10	.35	.50
□□□□	403	Bernie Nicholls, Chi.	.10	.35	.50
□□□□	404	Kelly Buchberger, Edm.	.10	.35	.50
□□□□	405	Paul Kariya, Ana.	1.50	18.00	25.00
□□□□	406	Michel Petit, L.A.	.10	.35	.50
□□□□	**407**	**Cale Hulse, N.J., RC**	**.10**	**.35**	**.50**
□□□□	408	Sheldon Kennedy, Wpg.	.10	.35	.50
□□□□	409	Brad May, Buf.	.10	.35	.50
□□□□	410	Daren Puppa (G), T.B.	.10	.35	.50
□□□□	**411**	**Janne Laukkanen, Que.**	**.10**	**.35**	**.50**
□□□□	412	Mats Sundin, Tor.	.50	5.00	7.50
□□□□	413	Trevor Kidd (G), Cgy.	.25	1.00	1.50
□□□□	414	Greg Adams, Van.	.10	.35	.50
□□□□	415	Pavel Bure, Van.	.35	3.75	5.00
□□□□	416	Teemu Selänne, Wpg.	.25	2.75	3.75
□□□□	417	Brett Hull, Stl.	.25	2.50	3.50
□□□□	418	Steve Larmer, NYR.	.10	.35	.50
□□□□	419	Cam Neely, Bos.	.25	1.00	1.50
□□□□	420	Ray Bourque, Bos.	.35	4.00	6.00
□□□□	421	Andrei Nikolishin, Hfd.	.10	.35	.50
□□□□	422	Jim Paek, Ott.	.10	.35	.50
□□□□	423	John Cullen, Pgh.	.10	.35	.50
□□□□	424	Darcy Wakaluk (G), Dal.	.10	.35	.50
□□□□	425	Peter Forsberg, Que.	1.50	18.00	25.00
□□□□	426	Yves Racine, Mtl.	.10	.35	.50
□□□□	427	Jody Hull, Fla.	.10	.35	.50
□□□□	428	Ron Sutter, NYI.	.10	.35	.50
□□□□	429	Ray Sheppard, Det.	.10	.35	.50
□□□□	430	Sandis Ozolinsh, S.J.	.25	1.00	1.50
□□□□	431	Brent Grieve, Chi.	.10	.35	.50
□□□□	432	Shaun Van Allen, Ana.	.10	.35	.50
□□□□	433	Criag Berube, Wsh.	.10	.35	.50
□□□□	**434**	**Vladislav Boulin, Pha., RC**	**.10**	**.35**	**.50**
□□□□	435	Bill Ranford (G), Edm.	.25	1.00	1.50
□□□□	436	Denny Felsner, Stl.	.10	.35	.50
□□□□	437	Jamie Storr, (G), L.A.	.25	1.00	1.50
□□□□	**438**	**Brian Rolston, N.J., RC**	**.10**	**.35**	**.50**
□□□□	439	Chris Gratton, T.B.	.25	1.00	1.50
□□□□	440	Dominik Hasek (G), Buf.	.75	7.50	11.00
□□□□	441	Garth Butcher, Tor.	.10	.35	.50
□□□□	442	Jyrki Lumme, Van.	.10	.35	.50
□□□□	443	Sergei Nemchinov, NYR.	.10	.35	.50
□□□□	444	Tie Domi, Wpg.	.10	.35	.50
□□□□	445	Gary Roberts, Cgy.	.25	1.00	1.50
□□□□	446	Dave McLlwain, Ott.	.10	.35	.50
□□□□	**447**	**John Gruden, Bos., RC**	**.10**	**.35**	**.50**
□□□□	448	Vladimir Konstantinov, Det.	.10	.35	.50
□□□□	449	Adam Deadmarsh, Que.	.25	1.00	1.50
□□□□	450	Brian Leetch, NYR.	.35	2.00	3.00
□□□□	451	Scott Stevens, N.J.	.10	.35	.50
□□□□	452	Mark Tinordi, Dal.	.10	.35	.50
□□□□	453	Al Iafrate, Bos.	.10	.35	.50
□□□□	454	Ray Bourque, Bos.	.25	2.50	3.50
□□□□	455	Patrick Roy (G), Mtl.	1.50	25.00	35.00
□□□□	456	Viktor Gordiouk, Buf.	.10	.35	.50
□□□□	457	Owen Nolan, Que.	.10	.35	.50
□□□□	458	Stu Barnes, Fla.	.10	.35	.50
□□□□	459	Zigmund Palffy, NYI.	.35	2.00	3.00
□□□□	460	Jaromir Jagr, Pgh.	1.00	18.00	25.00
□□□□	461	Andrei Nazarov, S.J.	.10	.35	.50
□□□□	462	Kelly Hrudey (G), L.A.	.10	.35	.50
□□□□	**463**	**Jason Wiemer, T.B., RC**	**.10**	**.35**	**.50**
□□□□	464	Oleg Tverdovsky, Ana.	.10	.35	.50
□□□□	465	Brett Hull, Stl.	.50	5.00	7.50
□□□□	466	Luke Richardson, Edm.	.10	.35	.50
□□□□	467	Jason Allison, Wsh.	.35	2.00	3.00
□□□□	468	Dimitri Yushkevich, Pha.	.10	.35	.50
□□□□	469	Todd Simon, Buf.	.10	.35	.50
□□□□	470	Martin Brodeur (G), N.J.	.75	7.50	11.00
□□□□	471	Thomas Steen, Wpg.	.10	.35	.50
□□□□	472	Vesa Viitakoski, Cgy.	.10	.35	.50
□□□□	473	Todd Harvey, Dal.	.10	.35	.50
□□□□	474	Kent Manderville, Tor.	.10	.35	.50
□□□□	475	Chris Chelios, Chi.	.35	3.50	5.00
□□□□	476	Joby Messier, NYR.	.10	.35	.50
□□□□	477	Jassen Cullimore, Van.	.10	.35	.50
□□□□	**478**	**Jamie Pushor, Det., RC**	**.10**	**.35**	**.50**
□□□□	479	Bryan Smolinski, Bos.	.10	.35	.50
□□□□	480	Joe Sakic, Que.	.85	8.50	12.00
□□□□	**481**	**David Wilkie, Mtl., RC**	**.10**	**.35**	**.50**
□□□□	482	Craig Billington (G), Ott.	.10	.35	.50
□□□□	483	Pat Neaton, Pgh.	.10	.35	.50
□□□□	484	Chris Pronger, Hfd.	.25	1.00	1.50
□□□□	485	Brian Leetch, NYR.	.25	1.00	1.50
□□□□	486	Chris Chelios, Chi.	.25	1.00	1.50
□□□□	487	Jeff Brown, Van.	.10	.35	.50
□□□□	488	Al MacInnis, Stl.	.25	1.00	1.50
□□□□	489	Paul Coffey, Det.	.25	1.00	1.50
□□□□	490	Ray Bourque, Bos.	.25	1.00	1.50
□□□□	491	Phil Housley, Cgy.	.10	.35	.50
□□□□	492	Larry Murphy, Pgh.	.25	1.00	1.50
□□□□	493	Sergei Zubov, NYR.	.25	1.00	1.50
□□□□	494	Scott Stevens, N.J.	.10	.35	.50
□□□□	495	Steve Thomas, NYI.	.10	.35	.50
□□□□	496	Jimmy Waite (G), S.J.	.10	.35	.50
□□□□	497	Mike Keane, Mtl.	.10	.35	.50
□□□□	498	Rob Blake, L.A.	.25	1.00	1.50
□□□□	499	John Lilley, Ana.	.10	.35	.50
□□□□	500	Brian Leetch, NYR.	.35	2.00	3.00
□□□□	501	Derek Plante, Buf.	.10	.35	.50
□□□□	502	Tim Cheveldae (G), Wpg.	.10	.35	.50
□□□□	503	Vladimir Vujtek, Edm.	.10	.35	.50
□□□□	504	Esa Tikkanen, Stl.	.10	.35	.50
□□□□	505	Cam Neely, Bos.	.25	1.00	1.50
□□□□	506	Dale Hunter, Wsh.	.10	.35	.50
□□□□	507	Marc Bergevin, T.B.	.10	.35	.50
□□□□	508	Joel Otto, Cgy.	.10	.35	.50
□□□□	509	Brent Fedyk, Pha.	.10	.35	.50
□□□□	510	Dave Andreychuk, Tor.	.10	.35	.50
□□□□	511	Andy Moog (G), Dal.	.25	1.00	1.50
□□□□	512	Jaroslav Modry, N.J.	.10	.35	.50
□□□□	513	Sergei Krivokrasov, Chi.	.10	.35	.50
□□□□	514	Brett Lindros, NYI.	.10	.35	.50
□□□□	**515**	**Cory Stillman, Cgy., RC**	**.10**	**.35**	**.50**
□□□□	**516**	**Jon Rohloff, Bos., RC**	**.10**	**.35**	**.50**
□□□□	517	Joe Mullen, Pgh.	.10	.35	.50
□□□□	518	Evgeny Davydov, Ott.	.10	.35	.50
□□□□	519	Scott Young, Que.	.10	.35	.50
□□□□	520	Sergei Fedorov, Det.	.50	5.00	7.50
□□□□	521	Pat Falloon, S.J.	.10	.35	.50
□□□□	522	Bill Lindsay, Fla.	.10	.35	.50
□□□□	523	Ron Tugnutt (G), Mtl.	.10	.35	.50
□□□□	524	Anatoli Semenov, Ana.	.10	.35	.50
□□□□	525	Geoff Courtnall, Van.	.10	.35	.50
□□□□	526	Luc Robitaille, Pgh.	.25	1.00	1.50
□□□□	527	Geoff Sanderson, Hfd.	.10	.35	.50
□□□□	528	Esa Tikkanen, Stl.	.10	.35	.50
□□□□	529	Brendan Shanahan, Stl.	.35	2.00	3.00
□□□□	530	Jason Arnott, Edm.	.25	1.00	1.50
□□□□	**531**	**Michal Grosek, Wpg., RC**	**.10**	**.35**	**.50**
□□□□	532	Steve Larmer, NYR.	.10	.35	.50
□□□□	**533**	**Eric Fichaud (G), Tor., RC**	**.50**	**2.50**	**3.50**
□□□□	534	Dimitri Khristich, Wsh.	.10	.35	.50
□□□□	535	Garry Galley, Pha.	.10	.35	.50
□□□□	**536**	**Aaron Gavey, T.B., RC**	**.10**	**.35**	**.50**
□□□□	537	Joe Nieuwendyk, Cgy.	.25	1.00	1.50
□□□□	538	Mike Craig, Tor.	.10	.35	.50
□□□□	539	Scott Niedermayer, N.J.	.25	1.00	1.50
□□□□	540	Luc Robitaille, Pgh.	.25	1.00	1.50
□□□□	541	Dino Ciccarelli, Det.	.25	1.00	1.50
□□□□	542	Sean Burke (G), Hfd.	.25	1.00	1.50
□□□□	543	Jiri Slegr, Van.	.10	.35	.50
□□□□	544	Jesse Belanger, Fla.	.10	.35	.50
□□□□	545	Sean Hill, Ott.	.10	.35	.50
□□□□	546	Vladimir Malakhov, NYI.	.10	.35	.50
□□□□	547	Jeff Friesen, S.J.	.25	1.00	1.50
□□□□	548	Mike Ricci, Que.	.10	.35	.50
□□	549	Checklist (276-413)	.15	.–	.–
□□	549	John Druce, L.A.	.–	.50	.75
□□	550	Checklist (414-550)	.15	.–	.–
□□	550	Matt Martin, Tor.	.–	.50	.75

O-PEE-CHEE FINEST

O-Pee-Chee Insert Set (23 cards): **1010.00**

	No.	Player	NRMT-MT
□	1	Patrik Carnback, Ana.	2.00
□	2	Bryan Smolinski, Bos.	2.00
□	3	Derek Plante, Buf.	2.00
□	4	Alexander Karpovtsev, Que.	2.00
□	5	Trevor Kidd (G), Cgy.	4.00
□	6	Iain Fraser, Que.	2.00
□	7	Alexandre Daigle, Ott.	4.00
□	8	Chris Osgood (G), Det.	15.00
□	9	Rob Niedermayer, Fla.	4.00
□	10	Jason Arnott, Edm.	6.00
□	11	Chris Pronger, Hfd.	4.00
□	12	Jesse Belanger, Fla.	2.00
□	13	Oleg Petrov, Mtl.	2.00
□	14	Martin Brodeur (G), N.J.	25.00
□	15	Alexei Yashin, Ott.	15.00
□	16	Mikael Renberg, Pha.	4.00
□	17	Boris Mironov, Wpg.	2.00
□	18	Damian Rhodes (G), Tor.	4.00
□	19	Darren McCarty, Det.	2.00
□	20	Chris Gratton, T.B.	4.00
□	21	Jamie McLennan, NYI.	4.00
□	22	Nathan Lafayette, Van.	2.00
□	23	Jeff Shantz, Chi.	2.00

THE GO TO GUY

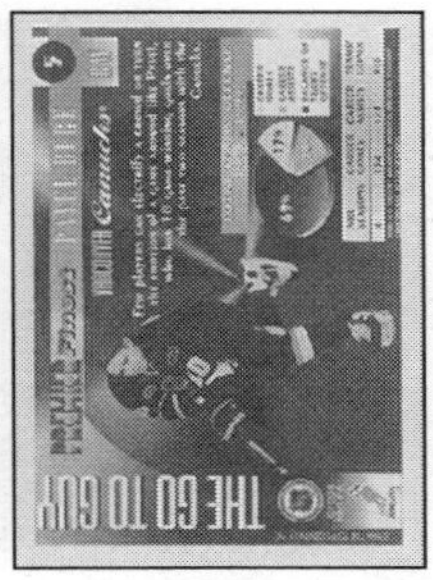

Insert Set (15 cards): **75.00**

	No.	Player	NRMT-MT
□	1	Wayne Gretzky, L.A.	20.00
□	2	Joe Sakic, Que.	8.00
□	3	Brett Hull, Stl.	5.00
□	4	Mike Modano, Dal.	5.00
□	5	Pavel Bure, Van.	7.00
□	6	Pat LaFontaine, Buf.	1.50
□	7	Theoren Fleury, Cgy.	3.00
□	8	Jeremy Roenick, Chi.	3.00
□	9	Sergei Fedorov, Det.	5.00
□	10	Eric Lindros, Pha.	12.00
□	11	Kirk Muller, Mtl.	1.50
□	12	Steve Yzerman, Det.	10.00
□	13	Alexander Mogilny, Buf.	3.00
□	14	Doug Gilmour, Tor.	3.00
□	15	Mark Messier, NYR.	5.00

TOPPS FINEST

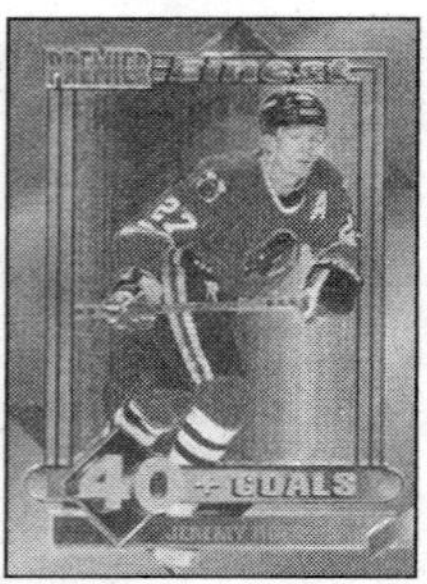

Topps Insert Set (23 cards): 95.00

	No.	Player	NRMT-MT
☐	1	Pavel Bure, Van.	10.00
☐	2	Brett Hull, Stl.	7.50
☐	3	Sergei Fedorov, Det.	7.50
☐	4	Dave Andreychuk, Tor.	1.50
☐	5	Brendan Shanahan, Stl.	9.00
☐	6	Ray Sheppard, Det.	1.50
☐	7	Adam Graves, NYR.	1.50
☐	8	Cam Neely, Bos.	3.00
☐	9	Mike Modano, Dal.	7.50
☐	10	Wendel Clark, Tor.	3.00
☐	11	Jeremy Roenick, Chi.	4.50
☐	12	Eric Lindros, Pha.	20.00
☐	13	Luc Robitaille, L.A.	3.00
☐	14	Steve Thomas, NYI.	1.50
☐	15	Geoff Sanderson, Hfd.	1.50
☐	16	Gary Roberts, Cgy.	3.00
☐	17	Kevin Stevens, Pgh.	1.50
☐	18	Keith Tkachuk, Wpg.	6.00
☐	19	Theoren Fleury, Cgy.	4.50
☐	20	Robert Reichel, Cgy.	3.00
☐	21	Mark Recchi, Pha.	3.00
☐	22	Vincent Damphousse, Mtl.	4.50
☐	23	Bob Kudelski, Fla.	1.50

1994 - 95 SCORE

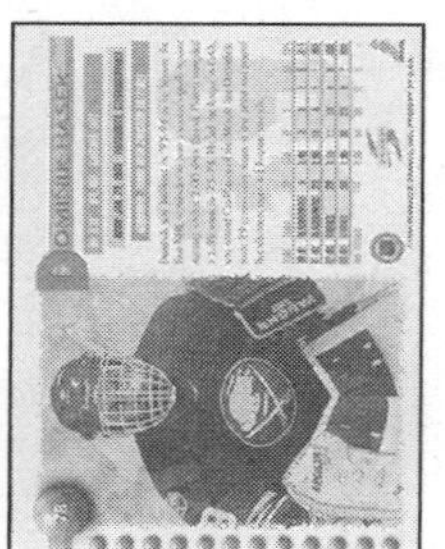

These cards have two or three versions: a regular card (1-275), a Gold Line card and a Platinum (1-200, 219-262). There are two versions of the Gold Line parallel: the gold band crosses either to the right or to the left. This variation appears only in cards 219-262. Gold Line team sets could be redeemed for Platinum Team sets. Only NHL team cards were redeemed in Platinum. Common Platinum Team sets sell for $15.00-20.00. The Kings' Platinum set sells for $90.00 and the Flyers' Platinum set sells for $70.00. Gold Line cards were returned with a perforation of the Pinnacle logo.

Imprint: © 1994 PINNACLE BRANDS, INC.

Complete Set (275 cards): 95.00

Common Player: 2.00 .35 .10

	No.	Player	Promo	Plat.	G. L.	Reg.
☐☐☐☐	1	Eric Lindros, Pha.	1.00	55.00	10.00	1.00
☐☐☐☐	2	Pat LaFontaine, Buf.	.25	3.00	.50	.25
☐☐☐☐	3	Wendel Clark, Tor.	.25	3.00	.50	.25
☐☐☐☐	4	Cam Neely, Bos.	.25	3.00	.50	.60
☐☐☐☐	5	Larry Murphy, Pgh.	.25	3.00	.50	.60
☐☐☐☐	6	Patrick Poulin, Chi.	.10	2.00	.35	.10
☐☐☐☐	7	Bob Beers, Edm.	.10	2.00	.35	.10
☐☐☐	8	James Patrick, Cgy.		2.00	.35	.10
☐☐☐	9	Gino Odjick, Van.		2.00	.35	.10
☐☐☐	10	Arturs Irbe (G), S.J.		2.00	.35	.10
☐☐☐	11	Darius Kasparaitis, NYI.		2.00	.35	.10
☐☐☐	12	Peter Bondra, Wsh.		7.50	1.50	.25
☐☐☐	13	Garth Butcher, Que.		2.00	.35	.10
☐☐☐	14	Sergei Nemchinov, NYR.		2.00	.35	.10
☐☐☐	15	Doug Brown, Pgh.		2.00	.35	.10
☐☐☐	16	Anatoli Semenov, NYR.		2.00	.35	.10
☐☐☐	17	Mike McPhee, Dal.		2.00	.35	.10
☐☐☐	18	Joel Otto, Cgy.		2.00	.35	.10
☐☐☐	19	Dino Ciccarelli, Det.		3.00	.50	.25
☐☐☐	20	Marty McSorley, L.A.		2.00	.35	.10
☐☐☐	21	Ron Tugnutt (G), Ana.		2.00	.35	.10
☐☐☐	22	Scott Niedermayer, N.J.		3.00	.50	.25
☐☐☐	23	John Tucker, Buf.		2.00	.35	.10
☐☐☐	24	Norm Maciver, Ott.		2.00	.35	.10
☐☐☐	25	Kevin Miller, Stl.		2.00	.35	.10
☐☐☐	26	Garry Galley, Pha.		2.00	.35	.10
☐☐☐	27	Ted Donato, Bos.		2.00	.35	.10
☐☐☐	28	Bob Kudelski, Ott.		2.00	.35	.10
☐☐☐	29	Craig Muni, Buf.		2.00	.35	.10
☐☐☐	30	Nikolai Borschevsky, Tor.		2.00	.35	.10
☐☐☐	31	Tom Barrasso (G), Pgh.		3.00	.50	.25
☐☐☐	32	Brent Sutter, Chi.		2.00	.35	.10
☐☐☐	33	Igor Kravchuk, Chi.		2.00	.35	.10
☐☐☐	34	Andrew Cassels, Hfd.		2.00	.35	.10
☐☐☐	35	Jyrki Lumme, Van.		2.00	.35	.10
☐☐☐	36	Sandis Ozolinsh, S.J.		3.00	.50	.25
☐☐☐	37	Steve Thomas, NYI.		2.00	.35	.10
☐☐☐	38	Dave Poulin, Wsh.		2.00	.35	.10
☐☐☐	39	Andrei Kovalenko, Que.		2.00	.35	.10
☐☐☐	40	Steve Larmer, NYR.		2.00	.35	.10
☐☐☐	41	Nelson Emerson, Wpg.		2.00	.35	.10
☐☐☐	42	Guy Hebert (G), Ana.		3.00	.50	.25
☐☐☐	43	Russ Courtnall, Dal.		2.00	.35	.10
☐☐☐	44	Gary Suter, Cgy.		2.00	.35	.10
☐☐☐	45	Steve Chiasson, Det.		2.00	.35	.10
☐☐☐	46	Guy Carbonneau, Mtl.		2.00	.35	.10
☐☐☐	47	Rob Blake, L.A.		3.00	.50	.25
☐☐☐	48	Roman Hamrlik, T.B.		3.00	.50	.25
☐☐☐	49	Valeri Zepelukin, N.J.		2.00	.35	.10
☐☐☐	50	Mark Recchi, Pha.		3.00	.50	.25
☐☐☐	51	Darrin Madeley (G), Ott.		2.00	.35	.10
☐☐☐	52	Steve Duchesne, Stl.		2.00	.35	.10
☐☐☐	53	Brian Skrudland, Cgy.		2.00	.35	.10
☐☐☐	54	Craig Simpson, Edm.		2.00	.35	.10
☐☐☐	55	Todd Gill, Tor.		2.00	.35	.10
☐☐☐	56	Dirk Graham, Chi.		2.00	.35	.10
☐☐☐	57	Joe Mullen, Pgh.		2.00	.35	.10
☐☐☐	58	Doug Weight, Edm.		5.00	1.00	.25
☐☐☐	59	Mikael Nylander, Cgy.		2.00	.35	.10
☐☐☐	60	Kirk McLean (G), Van.		3.00	.50	.25
☐☐☐	61	Igor Larionov, S.J.		3.00	.50	.25
☐☐☐	62	Vladimir Malakhov, NYI.		2.00	.35	.10
☐☐☐	63	Kelly Miller, Wsh.		2.00	.35	.10
☐☐☐	64	Curtis Leschyshyn, Que.		2.00	.35	.10
☐☐☐	65	Thomas Steen, Wpg.		2.00	.35	.10
☐☐☐	66	Jeff Beukeboom, NYR.		2.00	.35	.10
☐☐☐	67	Troy Loney, Ana.		2.00	.35	.10
☐☐☐	68	Mark Tinordi, Dal.		2.00	.35	.10
☐☐☐	69	Theoren Fleury, Cgy.		5.00	1.00	.25
☐☐☐	70	Vyacheslav Kozlov, Det.		2.00	.35	.10
☐☐☐	71	Tony Granato, L.A.		2.00	.35	.10
☐☐☐	72	Daren Puppa (G), T.B.		2.00	.35	.10
☐☐☐	73	Brian Bellows, Mtl.		2.00	.35	.10
☐☐☐	74	Bernie Nicholls, N.J.		2.00	.35	.10
☐☐☐	75	Rick Zombo, Stl.		2.00	.35	.10
☐☐☐	76	Brad Shaw, Ott.		2.00	.35	.10
☐☐☐	77	Josef Beranek, Pha.		2.00	.35	.10
☐☐☐	78	Dominik Hasek (G), Buf.		20.00	4.00	.50
☐☐☐	79	Stephen Leach, Bos.		2.00	.35	.10
☐☐☐	80	David Reid, Bos.		2.00	.35	.10
☐☐☐	81	Dave Lowry, Fla.		2.00	.35	.10
☐☐☐	82	Martin Straka, Pgh.		2.00	.35	.10
☐☐☐	83	Dave Ellett, Tor.		2.00	.35	.10
☐☐☐	84	Sean Burke (G), Hfd.		2.00	.35	.10
☐☐☐	85	Craig MacTavish, NYR.		2.00	.35	.10
☐☐☐	86	Cliff Ronning, Van.		2.00	.35	.10
☐☐☐	87	Bob Errey, S.J.		2.00	.35	.10
☐☐☐	88	Marty McInnis, NYI.		2.00	.35	.10
☐☐☐	89	Mats Sundin, Que.		15.00	3.00	.35
☐☐☐	90	Randy Burridge, Wsh.		2.00	.35	.10
☐☐☐	91	Teppo Numminen, Wpg.		2.00	.35	.10
☐☐☐	92	Tony Amonte, NYR.		3.00	.50	.25
☐☐☐	93	Terry Yake, Ana.		2.00	.35	.10
☐☐☐	94	Paul Cavallini, Dal.		2.00	.35	.10
☐☐☐	95	German Titov, Cgy.		2.00	.35	.10
☐☐☐	96	Vladimir Konstantinov, Det.		2.00	.35	.10
☐☐☐	97	Darryl Sydor, L.A.		2.00	.35	.10
☐☐☐	98	Chris Joseph, T.B.		2.00	.35	.10
☐☐☐	99	Corey Millen, L.A.		2.00	.35	.10
☐☐☐	100	Brett Hull, Stl.		15.00	3.00	.35
☐☐☐	101	Don Sweeney, Bos.		2.00	.35	.10
☐☐☐	102	Scott Mellanby, Fla.		2.00	.35	.10
☐☐☐	103	Mathieu Schneider, Mtl.		2.00	.35	.10
☐☐☐	104	Brad May, Buf.		2.00	.35	.10
☐☐☐	105	Dominic Roussel (G), Bos.		2.00	.35	.10
☐☐☐	106	Jamie Macoun, Tor.		2.00	.35	.10
☐☐☐	107	Bryan Marchment, Hfd.		2.00	.35	.10
☐☐☐	108	Shawn McEachern, Pgh.		2.00	.35	.10
☐☐☐	109	Murray Craven, Van.		2.00	.35	.10
☐☐☐	110	Eric Desjardins, Mtl.		3.00	.50	.25
☐☐☐	111	Jon Casey (G), Bos.		2.00	.35	.10
☐☐☐	112	Mike Gartner, Tor.		3.00	.50	.25
☐☐☐	113	Neal Broten, Dal.		2.00	.35	.10
☐☐☐	114	Jari Kurri, L.A.		3.00	.50	.25
☐☐☐	115	Bruce Driver, N.J.		2.00	.35	.10
☐☐☐	116	Patrick Flatley, NYI.		2.00	.35	.10
☐☐☐	117	Gord Murphy, Fla.		2.00	.35	.10
☐☐☐	118	Dimitri Khristich, Wsh.		2.00	.35	.10
☐☐☐	119	Nicklas Lidstrom, Det.		3.00	.50	.25
☐☐☐	120	Al MacInnis, Cgy.		3.00	.50	.25
☐☐☐	121	Steve Smith, Chi.		2.00	.35	.10
☐☐☐	122	Zdeno Ciger, Edm.		2.00	.35	.10
☐☐☐	123	Tie Domi, Wpg.		2.00	.35	.10
☐☐☐	124	Joé Juneau, Wsh.		2.00	.35	.10
☐☐☐	125	Todd Elik, S.J.		2.00	.35	.10
☐☐☐	126	Stéphane Fiset (G), Que.		3.00	.50	.25
☐☐☐	127	Craig Janney, Stl.		2.00	.35	.10
☐☐☐	128	Stéphan Lebeau, Ana.		2.00	.35	.10
☐☐☐	129	Richard Smehlik, Buf.		2.00	.35	.10
☐☐☐	130	Mike Richter (G), NYR.		5.00	1.00	.25
☐☐☐	131	Danton Cole, T.B.		2.00	.35	.10
☐☐☐	132	Rod Brind'Amour, Pha.		3.00	.50	.25
☐☐☐	133	Dave Archibald, Ott.		2.00	.35	.10
☐☐☐	134	Dana Murzyn, Van.		2.00	.35	.10
☐☐☐	135	Jaromir Jagr, Pgh.		30.00	6.00	.75
☐☐☐	136	Esa Tikkanen, NYR.		2.00	.35	.10
☐☐☐	137	Rob Pearson, Tor.		2.00	.35	.10
☐☐☐	138	Stu Barnes, Wpg.		2.00	.35	.10
☐☐☐	139	Frantisek Musil, Cgy.		2.00	.35	.10
☐☐☐	140	Ron Hextall (G), NYI.		3.00	.50	.25
☐☐☐	141	Adam Oates, Bos.		5.00	1.00	.25
☐☐☐	142	Ken Daneyko, N.J.		2.00	.35	.10
☐☐☐	143	Dale Hunter, Wsh.		2.00	.35	.10
☐☐☐	144	Geoff Sanderson, Hfd.		2.00	.35	.10
☐☐☐	145	Kelly Hrudey (G), L.A.		2.00	.35	.10
☐☐☐	146	Kirk Muller, Mtl.		2.00	.35	.10
☐☐☐	147	Fredrik Olausson, Wpg.		2.00	.35	.10
☐☐☐	148	Derian Hatcher, Dal.		5.00	1.00	.25
☐☐☐	149	Ed Belfour (G), Chi.		5.00	1.00	.25
☐☐☐	150	Steve Yzerman, Det.		30.00	6.00	.75
☐☐☐	151	Adam Foote, Que.		3.00	.50	.25
☐☐☐	152	Pat Falloon, S.J.		2.00	.35	.10
☐☐☐	153	Shawn Chambers, T.B.		2.00	.35	.10
☐☐☐	154	Alexei Zhamnov, Wpg.		3.00	.50	.25
☐☐☐	155	Brendan Shanahan, Stl.		18.00	3.50	.50
☐☐☐	156	Ulf Samuelsson, Pgh.		2.00	.35	.10
☐☐☐	157	Donald Audette, Buf.		2.00	.35	.10
☐☐☐	158	Bob Corkum, Ana.		2.00	.35	.10
☐☐☐	159	Joe Nieuwendyk, Cgy.		2.00	.35	.10
☐☐☐	160	Félix Potvin (G), Tor.		15.00	3.00	.35
☐☐☐	161	Geoff Courtnall, Van.		2.00	.35	.10
☐☐☐	162	Yves Racine, Pha.		2.00	.35	.10
☐☐☐	163	Tom Fitzgerald, Fla.		2.00	.35	.10
☐☐☐	164	Adam Graves, NYR.		2.00	.35	.10
☐☐☐	165	Vincent Damphousse, Mtl.		5.00	1.00	.25
☐☐☐	166	Pierre Turgeon, NYI.		3.00	.50	.25
☐☐☐	167	Craig Billington (G), Ott.		2.00	.35	.10
☐☐☐	168	Al Iafrate, Bos.		2.00	.35	.10
☐☐☐	169	Darren Turcotte, Hfd.		2.00	.35	.10
☐☐☐	170	Joe Murphy, Chi.		2.00	.35	.10
☐☐☐	171	Alexei Zhitnik, NYI.		2.00	.35	.10
☐☐☐	172	John MacLean, N.J.		2.00	.35	.10
☐☐☐	173	Andy Moog (G), Dal.		3.00	.50	.25
☐☐☐	174	Shayne Corson, Edm.		3.00	.50	.25
☐☐☐	175	Ray Sheppard, Det.		2.00	.35	.10
☐☐☐	176	Johan Garpenlov, S.J.		2.00	.35	.10
☐☐☐	177	Ron Sutter, Stl.		2.00	.35	.10
☐☐☐	178	Teemu Selänne, Wpg.		20.00	4.00	.50
☐☐☐	179	Brian Bradley, T.B.		2.00	.35	.10
☐☐☐	180	Ray Bourque, Bos.		15.00	3.00	.35
☐☐☐	181	Curtis Joseph (G), Stl.		18.00	3.50	.50
☐☐☐	182	Kevin Stevens, Pgh.		2.00	.35	.10
☐☐☐	183	Alexei Kasatonov, Ana.		2.00	.35	.10
☐☐☐	184	Brian Leetch, NYR.		7.50	1.50	.25

	No.	Player			
☐☐☐	185	Doug Gilmour, Tor.	7.50	1.50	.25
☐☐☐	186	Gary Roberts, Cgy.	3.00	.50	.25
☐☐☐	187	Mike Keane, Mtl.	2.00	.35	.10
☐☐☐	188	Mike Modano, Dal.	15.00	3.00	.35
☐☐☐	189	Chris Chelios, Chi.	7.50	1.50	.25
☐☐☐	190	Pavel Bure, Van.	20.00	4.00	.50
☐☐☐	191	Bob Essensa (G), Det.	2.00	.35	.10
☐☐☐	192	Dale Hawerchuk, Buf.	3.00	.50	.20
☐☐☐	193	Scott Stevens, N.J.	2.00	.35	.10
☐☐☐	194	Claude Lapointe, Que.	2.00	.35	.10
☐☐☐	195	Scott Lachance, NYI.	2.00	.35	.10
☐☐☐	196	Gaetan Duchesne, Dal.	2.00	.35	.10
☐☐☐	197	Kevin Dineen, Pha.	2.00	.35	.10
☐☐☐	198	Doug Bodger, NYR.	2.00	.35	.10
☐☐☐	199	Mike Ridley, Wsh.	2.00	.35	.10
☐☐☐	200	Alexander Mogilny, Buf.	1.50	1.00	.25

	No.	Player	Gold	Regular
☐☐	201	Jamie Storr (G), Cdn.	.50	.25
☐☐	202	Jason Botterill, Cdn.	.35	.10
☐☐	203	Jeff Friesen, Cdn.	.50	.25
☐☐	204	Todd Harvey, Cdn.	.35	.10
☐☐	205	Brendan Witt, Cdn.	.35	.10
☐☐	206	Jason Allison, Cdn.	1.00	.25
☐☐	207	Aaron Gavey, Cdn.	.35	.10
☐☐	208	Deron Quint, USA.	.35	.10
☐☐	209	Jason Bonsignore, USA.	.35	.10
☐☐	210	Richard Park, USA.	.35	.10
☐☐	211	Kevyn Adams, USA.	.35	.10
☐☐	212	Vadim Sharifjanov, Rus.	.35	.10
☐☐	213	Alexander Kharlamov, Rus.	.35	.10
☐☐	214	Oleg Tverdovsky, Rus.	.35	.10
☐☐	215	Valeri Bure, Rus.	.35	.10

	No.	Player	Plat.	G.L.	Reg.
☐☐☐☐	**216**	**Dane Jackson, Van., RC**	**2.00**	**.35**	**.10**
☐☐☐☐	**217**	**Jozef Cierny, Edm., RC**	**2.00**	**.35**	**.10**
☐☐☐☐	218	Yevgeny Namestnikov, Van.	2.00	.35	.10
☐☐☐☐	219	Daniel Laperrière, Stl.	2.00	.35	.10
☐☐☐☐	220	Fred Knipscheer, Bos.	2.00	.35	.10
☐☐☐☐	221	Yan Kaminsky, NYI.	2.00	.35	.10
☐☐☐☐	222	David Roberts, Stl.	2.00	.35	.10
☐☐☐☐	223	Derek Mayer, Ott.	2.00	.35	.10
☐☐☐☐	224	Jamie McLennan (G), NYI.	3.00	.50	.25
☐☐☐☐	225	Kevin Smyth, Hfd.	2.00	.35	.10
☐☐☐☐	226	Todd Marchant, Edm.	2.00	.35	.10
☐☐☐☐	**227**	**Mariusz Czerkawski, Bos., RC**	**2.00**	**.35**	**.10**
☐☐☐☐	228	John Lilley, Ana.	2.00	.35	.10
☐☐☐☐	229	Aaron Ward, Det.	2.00	.35	.10
☐☐☐☐	230	Brian Savage, Mtl.	2.00	.35	.10
☐☐☐☐	231	Jason Allison, Wsh.	.25	1.00	5.00
☐☐☐☐	232	Maxim Bets, Ana.	2.00	.35	.10
☐☐☐☐	233	Ted Crowley, Hfd.	2.00	.35	.10
☐☐☐☐	234	Todd Simon, Buf.	2.00	.35	.10
☐☐☐☐	235	Zigmund Palffy, NYI.	7.50	1.50	.25
☐☐☐☐	236	René Corbet, Que.	2.00	.35	.10
☐☐☐☐	237	Michael Peca, Van.	3.00	.50	.25
☐☐☐☐	238	Dwayne Norris, Que.	2.00	.35	.10
☐☐☐☐	239	Andrei Nazarov, Stl.	2.00	.35	.10
☐☐☐☐	240	David Sacco, Tor.	2.00	.35	.10
☐☐☐☐	241	Wayne Gretzky, L.A.	75.00	15.00	1.50
☐☐☐☐	242	Mike Gartner, NYR.	2.00	.35	.25
☐☐☐☐	243	Dino Ciccarelli, Det.	2.00	.35	.25
☐☐☐☐	244	Ron Francis, Pgh.	5.00	1.00	.25
☐☐☐☐	245	Bernie Nicholls, N.J.	2.00	.35	.10
☐☐☐☐	246	Dino Ciccarelli, Det.	3.00	.50	.25
☐☐☐☐	247	Brian Propp, Dal.	2.00	.35	.10
☐☐☐☐	248	Alexandre Daigle, Ott.	3.00	.50	.25
☐☐☐☐	249	Mikael Renberg, Pha.	3.00	.50	.25
☐☐☐☐	250	Jocelyn Thibault (G), Que.	5.00	1.00	.25
☐☐☐☐	251	Derek Plante, Buf.	2.00	.35	.10
☐☐☐☐	252	Chris Pronger, Hfd.	3.00	.50	.25
☐☐☐☐	253	Alexei Yashin, Ott.	7.50	1.50	.25
☐☐☐☐	254	Jason Arnott, Edm.	3.00	.50	.25
☐☐☐☐	255	Boris Mironov, Wpg.	2.00	.35	.10
☐☐☐☐	256	Chris Osgood (G), Det.	7.50	1.50	.25
☐☐☐☐	257	Jesse Belanger, Fla.	2.00	.35	.10
☐☐☐☐	258	Darren McCarty, Det.	2.00	.35	.10
☐☐☐☐	259	Trevor Kidd (G), Cgy.	3.00	.50	.25
☐☐☐☐	260	Oleg Petrov, Mtl.	2.00	.35	.10
☐☐☐☐	261	Mike Rathje, S.J.	2.00	.35	.10
☐☐☐☐	262	John Slaney, Wsh.	2.00	.35	.10

	No.	Player	Gold	Regular
☐☐	263	CL: Mighty Ducks / Bruins	.35	.10
☐☐	264	CL: Sabres / Flames	.35	.10
☐☐	265	CL: Blackhawks / Stars	.35	.10
☐☐	266	CL: Red Wings / Oilers	.35	.10
☐☐	267	CL: Panthers / Whalers	.35	.10
☐☐	268	CL: Kings / Canadiens	.35	.10
☐☐	269	CL: Devils / Islanders	.35	.10
☐☐	270	CL: Rangers / Senators	.35	.10
☐☐	271	CL: Flyers / Penguins	.35	.10
☐☐	272	CL: Nordiques / Blues	.35	.10
☐☐	273	CL: Sharks / Lightning	.35	.10
☐☐	274	CL: Maple Leafs / Canucks	.35	.10
☐☐	275	CL: Capitals / Jets	.35	.10

CHECK IT

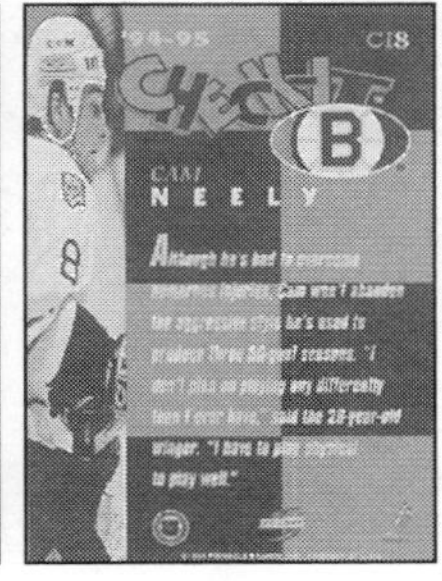

Insert Set (18 cards): 500.00

	No.	Player	NRMT-MT
☐	CI1	Eric Lindros, Pha.	225.00
☐	CI2	Scott Stevens, N.J.	15.00
☐	CI3	Darius Kasparaitis, NYI.	15.00
☐	CI4	Kevin Stevens, Pgh.	15.00
☐	CI5	Brendan Shanahan, Stl.	65.00
☐	CI6	Jeremy Roenick. Chi.	30.00
☐	CI7	Ulf Samuelsson, Pgh.	15.00
☐	CI8	Cam Neely, Bos.	20.00
☐	CI9	Adam Graves, NYR.	15.00
☐	CI10	Kirk Muller, Mtl.	15.00
☐	CI11	Rick Tocchet, Pgh.	15.00
☐	CI12	Gary Roberts, Cgy.	20.00
☐	CI13	Wendel Clark, Tor.	20.00
☐	CI14	Keith Tkachuk, Wpg.	40.00
☐	CI15	Theoren Fleury, Cgy.	30.00
☐	CI16	Claude Lemieux, N.J.	15.00
☐	CI17	Chris Chelios, Chi.	40.00
☐	CI18	Pat Verbeek, Hfd.	15.00

DREAM TEAM

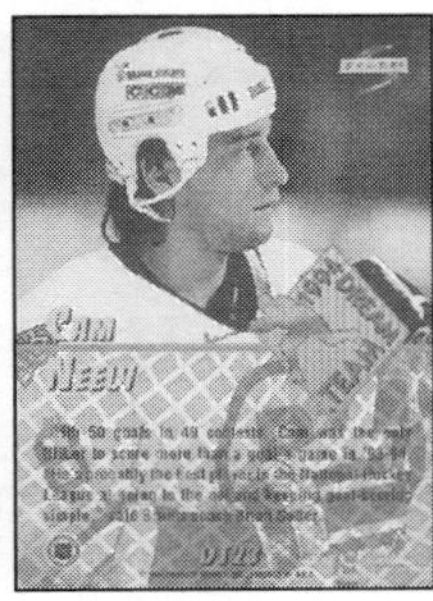

Insert Set (24 cards): 200.00

	No.	Player	NRMT-MT
☐	DT1	Patrick Roy (G), Mtl.	28.00
☐	DT2	Félix Potvin (G), Tor.	9.00
☐	DT3	Ray Bourque, Bos.	9.00
☐	DT4	Brian Leetch, NYR.	5.00
☐	DT5	Scott Stevens, N.J.	3.00
☐	DT6	Paul Coffey, Det.	4.00
☐	DT7	Al MacInnis, Cgy.	4.00
☐	DT8	Chris Chelios, Chi.	7.00
☐	DT9	Adam Graves, NYR.	3.00
☐	DT10	Luc Robitaille, L.A.	4.00
☐	DT11	Dave Andreychuk, Tor.	3.00
☐	DT12	Sergei Fedorov, Det.	9.00
☐	DT13	Doug Gilmour, Tor.	5.00
☐	DT14	Wayne Gretzky, L.A.	35.00
☐	DT15	Mario Lemieux, Pgh.	28.00
☐	DT16	Mark Messier, NYR.	9.00
☐	DT17	Mike Modano, Dal.	9.00
☐	DT18	Jeremy Roenick, Chi.	5.00
☐	DT19	Eric Lindros, Pha.	25.00
☐	DT20	Steve Yzerman, Det.	18.00
☐	DT21	Alexandre Daigle, Ott.	4.00
☐	DT22	Brett Hull, Stl.	9.00
☐	DT23	Cam Neely, Bos.	4.00
☐	DT24	Pavel Bure, Van.	12.00

THE FRANCHISE

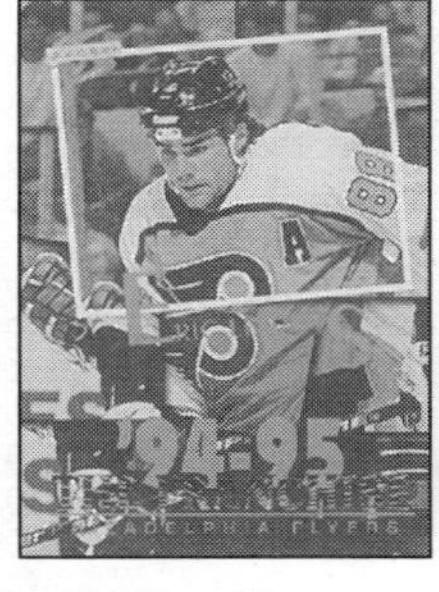
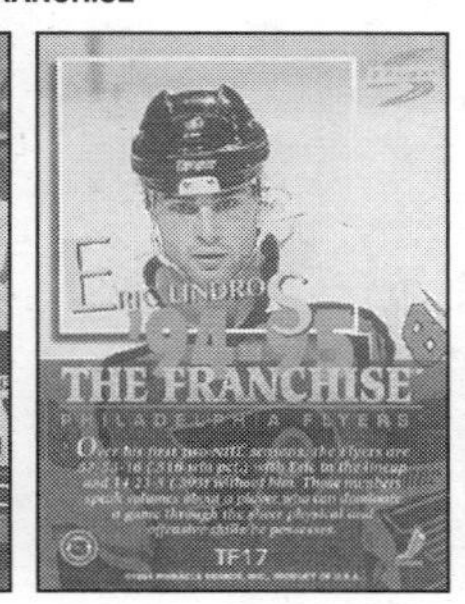

Insert Set (26 cards): 600.00

	No.	Player	NRMT-MT
☐	TF1	Guy Hebert (G), Ana.	10.00
☐	TF2	Cam Neely, Bos.	10.00
☐	TF3	Pat LaFontaine, Buf.	10.00
☐	TF4	Theoren Fleury, Cgy.	15.00
☐	TF5	Jeremy Roenick, Chi.	15.00
☐	TF6	Mike Modano, Dal.	25.00
☐	TF7	Sergei Fedorov, Det.	25.00
☐	TF8	Jason Arnott, Edm.	10.00
☐	TF9	John Vanbiesbrouck (G), Fla.	30.00
☐	TF10	Geoff Sanderson, Hfd.	5.00
☐	TF11	Wayne Gretzky, L.A.	100.00
☐	TF12	Patrick Roy (G), Mtl.	80.00
☐	TF13	Scott Stevens, N.J.	5.00
☐	TF14	Pierre Turgeon, NYI.	10.00
☐	TF15	Mark Messier, NYR.	25.00
☐	TF16	Alexandre Daigle, Ott.	10.00
☐	TF17	Eric Lindros, Pha.	65.00
☐	TF18	Mario Lemieux, Pgh.	80.00
☐	TF19	Joe Sakic, Que.	40.00
☐	TF20	Brett Hull, Stl.	25.00
☐	TF21	Arturs Irbe (G), S.J.	5.00
☐	TF22	Darren Puppa (G), T.B.	5.00
☐	TF23	Doug Gilmour, Tor.	15.00
☐	TF24	Pavel Bure, Van.	35.00
☐	TF25	Joé Juneau, Wsh.	5.00
☐	TF26	Teemu Selänne, Wpg.	35.00

NINETY PLUS CLUB

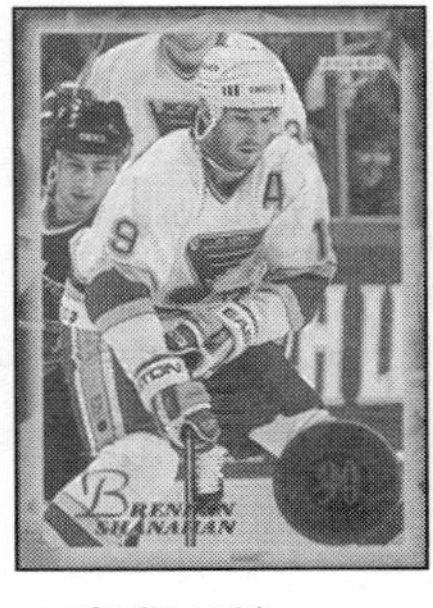

Insert Set (21 cards): 155.00

	No.	Player	NRMT-MT
☐	NP1	Wayne Gretzky, L.A.	35.00
☐	NP2	Sergei Fedorov, Det.	8.00
☐	NP3	Adam Oates, Bos.	4.00
☐	NP4	Doug Gilmour, Tor.	4.00
☐	NP5	Pavel Bure, Van.	12.00
☐	NP6	Jeremy Roenick, Chi.	4.00
☐	NP7	Mark Recchi, Pha.	2.50
☐	NP8	Brendan Shanahan, Stl.	10.00
☐	NP9	Jaromir Jagr, Pgh.	18.00
☐	NP10	Dave Andreychuk, Tor.	1.50
☐	NP11	Brett Hull, Stl.	8.00
☐	NP12	Eric Lindros, Pha.	25.00
☐	NP13	Rod Brind'Amour, Pha.	2.50
☐	NP14	Pierre Turgeon, NYI.	2.50
☐	NP15	Ray Sheppard, Det.	1.50
☐	NP16	Mike Modano, Dal.	8.00
☐	NP17	Robert Reichel, Cgy.	2.50
☐	NP18	Ron Francis, Pgh.	4.00
☐	NP19	Joe Sakic, Que.	15.00

	No.	Player	NRMT-MT
□	NP20	Vincent Damphousse, Mtl.	4.00
□	NP21	Ray Bourque, Bos.	9.00

1994 CANADIAN TEAM

Insert Set (24 cards): 120.00

	No.	Player	NRMT-MT
□	CT1	Paul Kariya, Cdn.	25.00
□	CT2	Petr Nedved, Cdn.	8.00
□	CT3	Todd Warriner, Cdn.	5.00
□	CT4	Corey Hirsch (G), Cdn.	8.00
□	CT5	Greg Johnson, Cdn.	5.00
□	CT6	Chris Kontos, Cdn.	5.00
□	CT7	Dwayne Norris, Cdn.	5.00
□	CT8	Brian Savage, Cdn.	5.00
□	CT9	Todd Hlushko, Cdn.	5.00
□	CT10	Fabian Joseph, Cdn.	5.00
□	CT11	Greg Parks, Cdn.	5.00
□	CT12	Jean-Yves Roy, Cdn.	5.00
□	CT13	Mark Astley, Cdn.	5.00
□	CT14	Adrien Aucoin, Cdn.	5.00
□	CT15	David Harlock, Cdn.	5.00
□	CT16	Ken Lovsin, Cdn.	5.00
□	CT17	Derek Mayer, Cdn.	5.00
□	CT18	Brad Schlegel, Cdn.	5.00
□	CT19	Chris Therien, Cdn.	5.00
□	CT20	Manny Legacé (G), Cdn.	5.00
□	CT21	Brad Werenka, Cdn.	5.00
□	CT22	Wally Schreiber, Cdn.	5.00
□	CT23	Allain Roy, Cdn.	5.00
□	CT24	Brett Lindros, Cdn.	8.00

TOP ROOKIE

Redemption Set (10 cards): 80.00
Expired Pro Debut cards: .50

	No.	Player	NRMT-MT
□	TR1	Paul Kariya, Ana.	35.00
□	TR2	Peter Forsberg, Que.	30.00
□	TR3	Brett Lindros, NYI.	3.00
□	TR4	Oleg Tverdovsky, Ana.	3.00
□	TR5	Jamie Storr (G), L.A.	6.00
□	TR6	Kenny Jonsson, Tor.	3.00
□	TR7	Brian Rolston, N.J.	3.00
□	TR8	Jeff Friesen, S.J.	6.00
□	TR9	Todd Harvey, Dal.	3.00
□	TR10	Viktor Kozlov, S.J.	3.00

1994 - 95 SELECT

Imprint: © 1995 PINNACLE BRANDS, INC.

			Select	Gold
Complete Set (200 cards):			**20.00**	**350.00**
Common Player:			**.10**	**.50**
	No.	**Player**	**Select**	**Gold**
□ □	1	Mark Messier, NYR.	.50	8.00
□ □	2	Rick Tocchet, L.A.	.10	.50
□ □	3	Alexandre Daigle, Ott.	.25	1.50
□ □	4	Owen Nolan, Que.	.25	1.50
□ □	5	Bill Ranford (G), Edm.	.25	1.50
□ □	6	Dave Gagner, Dal.	.10	.50
□ □	7	John Vanbiesbrouck (G), Fla.	.60	10.00
□ □	8	Sergei Makarov, S.J.	.10	.50
□ □	9	Derek King, NYI.	.10	.50
□ □	10	Sergei Fedorov, Det.	.50	8.00
□ □	11	Trevor Linden, Van.	.25	1.50
□ □	12	Don Beaupré (G), Ott.	.10	.50
□ □	13	Dave Manson, Wpg.	.10	.50
□ □	14	Sergei Zubov, NYR.	.25	1.50
□ □	15	Keith Primeau, Det.	.25	1.50
□ □	16	Joe Mullen, Pgh.	.10	.50
□ □	17	Bernie Nicholls, Chi.	.10	.50
□ □	18	Ray Bourque, Bos.	.50	8.00
□ □	19	Mike Ridley, Tor.	.10	.50
□ □	20	Wendel Clark, Que.	.25	1.50
□ □	21	Mats Sundin, Tor.	.50	8.00
□ □	22	Alexander Mogilny, Buf.	.35	3.50
□ □	23	Mathieu Schneider, Mtl.	.10	.50
□ □	24	Brian Leetch, NYR.	.35	3.50
□ □	25	Rob Niedermayer, Fla.	.25	1.50
□ □	26	Donald Audette, Buf.	.10	.50
□ □	27	Doug Weight, Edm.	.35	3.50
□ □	28	Al MacInnis, Stl.	.10	.50
□ □	29	Jeremy Roenick, Chi.	.35	3.50
□ □	30	Mark Recchi, Pha.	.25	1.50
□ □	31	Chris Chelios, Chi.	.35	5.00
□ □	32	Luc Robitaille, Pgh.	.25	1.50
□ □	33	Dale Hunter, Wsh.	.10	.50
□ □	34	Kelly Hrudey (G), L.A.	.10	.50
□ □	35	Steve Yzerman, Det.	1.25	25.00
□ □	36	Martin Straka, Pgh.	.10	.50
□ □	37	Arturs Irbe (G), S.J.	.10	.50
□ □	38	Mike Modano, Dal.	.50	8.00
□ □	39	Cam Neely, Bos.	.25	1.50
□ □	40	Igor Larionov, S.J.	.25	1.50
□ □	41	Ray Ferraro, NYI.	.10	.50
□ □	42	Dale Hawerchuk, Buf.	.25	1.50
□ □	43	Brian Bradley, T.B.	.10	.50
□ □	44	Joe Murphy, Chi.	.10	.50
□ □	45	Daren Puppa (G), T.B.	.10	.50
□ □	46	Pierre Turgeon, NYI.	.25	1.50
□ □	47	Shayne Corson, Edm.	.25	1.50
□ □	48	Adam Graves, NYR.	.10	.50
□ □	49	Craig Billington (G), Ott.	.10	.50
□ □	50	Derian Hatcher, Dal.	.25	1.50
□ □	51	Alexei Zhamnov, Wpg.	.25	1.50
□ □	52	Dominik Hasek (G), Buf.	.75	15.00
□ □	53	Ed Belfour (G), Chi.	.35	3.50
□ □	54	Mike Vernon (G), Det.	.25	1.50
□ □	55	Bob Kudelski, Fla.	.10	.50
□ □	56	Ray Sheppard, Det.	.10	.50
□ □	57	Pat LaFontaine, Buf.	.25	1.50
□ □	58	Adam Oates, Bos.	.35	3.50
□ □	59	Vincent Damphousse, Mtl.	.35	3.50
□ □	60	Jaromir Jagr, Pgh.	1.00	20.00
□ □	61	Mikael Renberg, Pha.	.25	1.50
□ □	62	Joe Sakic, Que.	.85	18.00
□ □	63	Sandis Ozolinsh, S.J.	.25	1.50
□ □	64	Kirk McLean (G), Van.	.25	1.50
□ □	65	Stéphan Lebeau, Ana.	.10	.50
□ □	66	Alexei Kovalev, NYR.	.10	.50
□ □	67	Ron Hextall (G), Pha.	.25	1.50
□ □	68	Geoff Sanderson, Hfd.	.10	.50
□ □	69	Doug Gilmour, Tor.	.35	3.50
□ □	70	Russ Courtnall, Dal.	.10	.50
□ □	71	Jari Kurri, L.A.	.25	1.50
□ □	72	Paul Coffey, Det.	.25	1.50
□ □	73	Claude Lemieux, N.J.	.10	.50
□ □	74	Teemu Selänne, Wpg.	.75	15.00
□ □	75	Keith Tkachuk, Wpg.	.35	5.00
□ □	76	Pat Verbeek, Hfd.	.10	.50
□ □	77	Chris Gratton, T.B.	.25	1.50
□ □	78	Martin Brodeur (G), N.J.	.75	15.00
□ □	79	Guy Hebert (G), Ana.	.25	1.50
□ □	80	Al Iafrate, Bos.	.10	.50
□ □	81	Glen Wesley, Hfd.	.10	.50
□ □	82	Scott Stevens, N.J.	.10	.50
□ □	83	Wayne Gretzky, L.A.	2.50	50.00
□ □	84	Ron Francis, Pgh.	.35	3.50
□ □	85	Scott Mellanby, Fla.	.10	.50
□ □	86	Joé Juneau, Wsh.	.10	.50
□ □	87	Jason Arnott, Edm.	.25	1.50
□ □	88	Tom Barrasso (G), Pgh.	.25	1.50
□ □	89	Peter Bondra, Wsh.	.35	5.00
□ □	90	Félix Potvin (G), Tor.	.50	8.00
□ □	91	Brian Bellows, Mtl.	.10	.50
□ □	92	Pavel Bure, Van.	.75	15.00
□ □	93	Grant Fuhr (G), Buf.	.25	1.50
□ □	94	Andy Moog (G), Dal.	.25	1.50
□ □	95	Mike Gartner, Tor.	.25	1.50
□ □	96	Patrick Roy, Mtl.	2.00	40.00
□ □	97	Brett Hull, Stl.	.50	8.00
□ □	98	Rob Blake, L.A.	.25	1.50
□ □	99	Dave Andreychuk, Tor.	.10	.50
□ □	100	Eric Lindros, Pha.	1.75	35.00
□ □	101	Scott Niedermayer, N.J.	.25	1.50
□ □	102	Tim Cheveldae (G), Wpg.	.10	.50
□ □	103	Vyacheslav Kozlov, Det.	.10	.50
□ □	104	Dimitri Khristich, Wsh.	.10	.50
□ □	105	Steve Thomas, NYI.	.10	.50
□ □	106	Kevin Stevens, Pgh.	.10	.50
□ □	107	Kirk Muller, Mtl.	.10	.50
□ □	108	Stéphane Richer, N.J.	.10	.50
□ □	109	Theoren Fleury, Cgy.	.35	3.50
□ □	110	Jeff Brown, Van.	.10	.50
□ □	111	Chris Pronger, Hfd.	.25	1.50
□ □	112	Steve Larmer, NYR.	.10	.50
□ □	113	Eric Desjardins, Mtl.	.25	1.50
□ □	114	Mike Ricci, Que.	.10	.50
□ □	115	Tony Amonte, Chi.	.25	1.50
□ □	116	Pat Falloon, S.J.	.10	.50
□ □	117	Garry Galley, Pha.	.10	.50
□ □	118	Dino Ciccarelli, Det.	.25	1.50
□ □	119	Rod Brind'Amour, Pha.	.25	1.50
□ □	120	Petr Nedved, NYR.	.10	.50
□ □	121	Curtis Joseph (G), Stl.	.60	10.00
□ □	122	Cliff Ronning, Van.	.10	.50
□ □	123	Ulf Dahlen, S.J.	.10	.50
□ □	124	Marty McSorley, L.A.	.10	.50
□ □	125	Nelson Emerson, Wpg.	.10	.50
□ □	126	Brian Skrudland, Fla.	.10	.50
□ □	127	Sean Burke (G), Hfd.	.25	1.50
□ □	128	Sylvain Côté, Wsh.	.10	.50
□ □	129	Brendan Shanahan, Stl.	.60	10.00
□ □	130	Benoît Hogue, NYI.	.10	.50
□ □	131	Joe Nieuwendyk, Cgy.	.25	1.50
□ □	132	Bryan Smolinski, Bos.	.10	.50
□ □	133	Mike Richter (G), NYR.	.35	3.50
□ □	134	Nicklas Lidstrom, Det.	.25	1.50
□ □	135	Alexei Yashin, Ott.	.35	5.00
□ □	136	John MacLean, N.J.	.10	.50
□ □	137	Geoff Courtnall, Van.	.10	.50
□ □	138	Robert Reichel, Cgy.	.25	1.50
□ □	139	Craig Janney, Stl.	.10	.50
□ □	140	Zarley Zalapski, Cgy.	.10	.50
□ □	141	Andrew Cassels, Hfd.	.10	.50
□ □	142	Kevin Dineen, Pha.	.10	.50
□ □	143	Larry Murphy, Pgh.	.25	1.50
□ □	144	Valeri Kamensky, Que.	.25	1.50
□ □	145	Steve Duchesne, Stl.	.10	.50
□ □	146	Phil Housley, Cgy.	.10	.50
□ □	147	Gary Roberts, Cgy.	.25	1.50
□ □	148	Kevin Hatcher, Dal.	.10	.50
□ □	**149**	**Bryan Berard, USA., RC**	**2.00**	**16.00**
□ □	**150**	**Marty Reasoner, USA., RC**	**.35**	**1.00**
□ □	**151**	**Andrew Berenzweig, USA., RC**	**.20**	**.50**
□ □	**152**	**Erik Rasmussen, USA., RC**	**.65**	**4.00**
□ □	**153**	**Luke Curtin, USA., RC**	**.20**	**.50**
□ □	**154**	**Dan Lacouture, USA., RC**	**.20**	**.50**
□ □	**155**	**Brian Boucher (G), USA., RC**	**1.50**	**12.00**
□ □	**156**	**Wyatt Smith, USA., RC**	**.20**	**.50**
□ □	**157**	**Maxim Kusnetsov, Rus., RC**	**.20**	**.50**
□ □	**158**	**Alexei Morozov, Rus., RC**	**6.00**	**30.00**
□ □	**159**	**Dmitri Nabokov, Rus., RC**	**.75**	**5.00**
□ □	**160**	**Wade Redden, Cdn., RC**	**.65**	**4.00**
□ □	**161**	**Jason Doig, Cdn., RC**	**.35**	**1.00**
□ □	**162**	**Alyn McCauley, Cdn., RC**	**3.50**	**25.00**
□ □	**163**	**Jeff Ware, Cdn., RC**	**.35**	**1.00**
□ □	**164**	**Brad Larsen, Cdn., RC**	**.35**	**1.00**
□ □	**165**	**Jarome Iginla, Cdn., RC**	**2.50**	**20.00**
□ □	**166**	**Christian Dubé, Cdn., RC**	**1.25**	**10.00**
□ □	**167**	**Mike McBain, Cdn., RC**	**.35**	**1.00**
□ □	**168**	**Todd Norman, Cdn., RC**	**.35**	**1.00**
□ □	169	Oleg Tverdovsky, Ana.	.10	.50
□ □	170	Jamie Storr (G), L.A.	.25	1.50
□ □	171	Jason Wiemer, T.B.	.10	.50
□ □	172	Kenny Jonsson, Tor.	.10	.50
□ □	173	Paul Kariya, Ana.	2.00	35.00
□ □	174	Viktor Kozlov, S.J.	.10	1.50
□ □	175	Peter Forsberg, Que.	1.75	30.00
□ □	176	Jeff Friesen, S.J.	.25	1.50
□ □	177	Brian Rolston, N.J.	.10	.50
□ □	178	Brett Lindros, NYI.	.10	.50
□ □	179	Adam Deadmarsh, Que.	.25	1.50
□ □	180	Aaron Gavey, T.B.	.10	.50
□ □	181	Janne Laukkanen, Que.	.10	.50
□ □	182	Todd Harvey, Dal.	.10	.50
□ □	**183**	**Valeri Karpov, Ana., RC**	**.10**	**.50**
□ □	184	Andrei Nikolishin, Hfd.	.10	.50
□ □	185	Pavol Demitra, Ott.	.10	.50
□ □	**186**	**Radek Bonk, Ott., RC**	**.25**	**1.00**
□ □	187	Valeri Bure, Mtl.	.10	.50
□ □	**188**	**Eric Fichaud (G), Tor., RC**	**.50**	**4.00**

	No.	Player		
☐☐	189	Jamie McLennan (G), NYI.	.25	1.50
☐☐	**190**	**Mariusz Czerkawski, Bos., RC**	**.10**	**.50**
☐☐	**191**	**John Lilley, Ana., RC**	**.10**	**.50**
☐☐	192	Brian Savage, Mtl.	.10	.50
☐☐	193	Jason Allison, Wsh.	.35	3.50
☐☐	194	Mattias Norstrom, NYR.	.10	.50
☐☐	195	Todd Simon, Buf.	.10	.50
☐☐	196	Zigmund Palffy, NYI.	.35	5.00
☐☐	197	René Corbet, Que.	.10	.50
☐☐	198	Michael Peca, Van.	.25	1.50
☐☐	199	Checklist #1 (1-100)	.10	.50
☐☐	200	Checklist #2 (101-200)	.10	.50

FIRST LINE

Complete Set (12 cards): 175.00

	No.	Player	NRMT-MT
☐	FL1	Patrick Roy (G), Mtl.	40.00
☐	FL2	Ray Bourque, Bos.	12.00
☐	FL3	Brian Leetch, NYR.	8.00
☐	FL4	Brendan Shanahan, Stl.	15.00
☐	FL5	Eric Lindros, Pha.	35.00
☐	FL6	Pavel Bure, Van.	18.00
☐	FL7	Mike Richter (G), NYR.	8.00
☐	FL8	Scott Stevens, N.J.	5.00
☐	FL9	Chris Chelios, Chi.	10.00
☐	FL10	Luc Robitaille, Pgh.	5.00
☐	FL11	Wayne Gretzky, L.A.	50.00
☐	FL12	Brett Hull, Stl.	12.00

YOUTH EXPLOSION

Complete Set (12 cards): 80.00

	No.	Player	NRMT-MT
☐	YE1	Jamie Storr (G), L.A.	6.00
☐	YE2	Oleg Tverdovsky, Ana.	4.00
☐	YE3	Janne Laukkanen, Que.	4.00
☐	YE4	Kenny Jonsson, Tor.	4.00
☐	YE5	Paul Kariya, Ana.	25.00
☐	YE6	Viktor Kozlov, S.J.	4.00
☐	YE7	Peter Forsberg, Que.	20.00
☐	YE8	Jason Allison, Wsh.	8.00
☐	YE9	Jeff Friesen, S.J.	6.00
☐	YE10	Brian Rolston, N.J.	4.00
☐	YE11	Mariusz Czerkawski, Buf.	4.00
☐	YE12	Brett Lindros, NYI.	4.00

1994 - 95 SIGNATURE ROOKIES

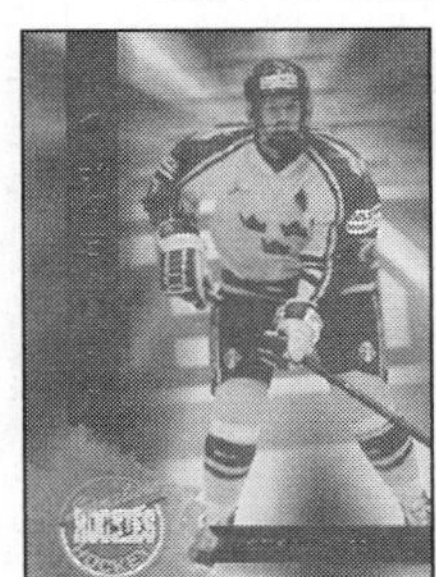

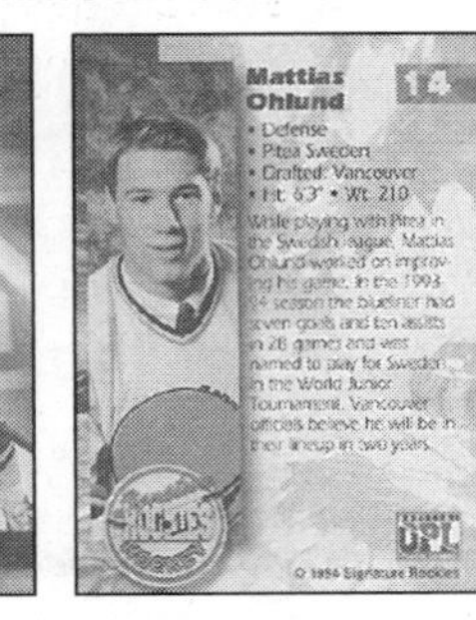

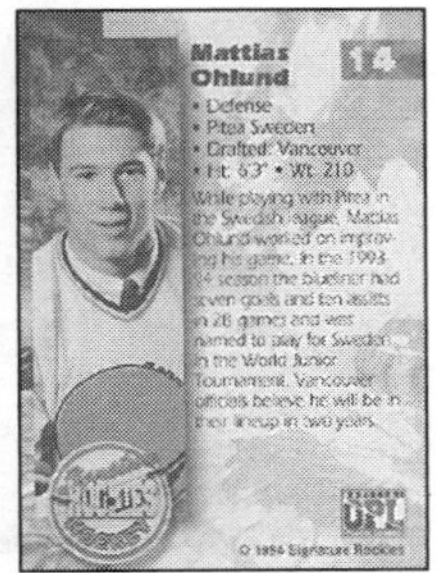

Each player card has two versions: the regular card and a one per pack autograph parallel. Regular cards are limited to 45,000 copies while autographed cards are limited to 7,750 copies.

Imprint: © 1994 Signature Rookies

Complete Set (70 cards): 15.00 300.00

Common Player: .20 4.00

	No.	Player	Reg.	Aut.
☐☐	1	Vaclav Varada, Cze.	.50	15.00
☐☐	2	Roman Vopat, Cze.	.35	5.00
☐☐	3	Yannick Dubé, Cdn.	.20	4.00
☐☐	4	Colin Cloutier, Brandon	.20	4.00
☐☐	5	Scott Cherrey, North Bay	.20	4.00
☐☐	6	Johan Finnstrom, Swe.	.20	4.00
☐☐	7	Fredrik Modin, Swe.	.50	15.00
☐☐	8	Stéphane Roy, Vald'or	.20	4.00
☐☐	9	Evgeni Ryabchikov (G), Rus.	.20	4.00
☐☐	10	José Théodore (G), St. Hyacinthe	2.00	30.00
☐☐	11	Jason Holland, Kamloops	.35	5.00
☐☐	12	Richard Park, Belleville	.35	5.00
☐☐	13	Jason Podollan, Fla.	.35	5.00
☐☐	14	Mattias Ohlund, Swe.	1.50	25.00
☐☐	15	Chris Wells, Pgh.	.20	4.00
☐☐	16	Hugh Hamilton, Spokane	.20	4.00
☐☐	17	Edvin Frylen, Swe.	.20	4.00
☐☐	18	Wade Belak, Que.	.35	5.00
☐☐	19	Sébastien Bety, Drummondville	.20	4.00
☐☐	20	Chris Dingman, Brandon	.20	4.00
☐☐	21	Peter Nylander, Swe.	.35	5.00
☐☐	22	Daymond Langkow, Tri-City	.50	15.00
☐☐	23	Kelly Fairchild, St. John's	.20	4.00
☐☐	24	Norm Dezainde, Kitchener	.20	4.00
☐☐	25	Nolan Baumgartner, Kamloops	.20	4.00
☐☐	26	Deron Quint, USA.	.20	4.00
☐☐	27	Sheldon Souray, N.J.	.20	4.00
☐☐	28	Stefan Ustorf, Ger.	.35	5.00
☐☐	29	Juha Vuovirta, Fin.	.20	4.00
☐☐	30	Mark Seliger (G), Rosenheim	.20	4.00
☐☐	31	Ryan Smyth, Edm.	2.00	30.00
☐☐	32	Dimitri Tabarin, CIS.	.20	4.00
☐☐	33	Nikolai Tsulygin, Rus.	.20	4.00
☐☐	34	Paul Vincent, Tor.	.20	4.00
☐☐	35	Rhett Warrener, Fla.	.35	8.00
☐☐	36	Jamie Rivers, Stl.	.35	5.00
☐☐	37	Rumun Ndur, Buf.	.20	4.00
☐☐	38	Phil Huber	.20	4.00
☐☐	39	Radek Dvorak, Cze.	.50	15.00
☐☐	40	Mike Barrie, Seattle	.20	4.00
☐☐	41	Chris Hynnes	.20	4.00
☐☐	42	Mike Dubinsky, Van.	.20	4.00
☐☐	43	Steve Cheredaryk, Wpg.	.20	4.00
☐☐	44	Jim Carey (G), Wsh.	.35	8.00
☐☐	45	Dorian Anneck, Edm.	.20	4.00
☐☐	46	Jorgen Jonsson, Swe.	.20	4.00
☐☐	47	Alyn McCauley, Ottawa-OHL	1.50	25.00
☐☐	48	Corey Nielson, Edm.	.20	4.00
☐☐	49	Daniel Tjarnqvist, Swe.	.20	4.00
☐☐	50	Vadim Epantchisev, Rus.	.20	4.00
☐☐	51	Sean Haggerty, Detroit-OHL	.35	8.00
☐☐	52	Milan Hejduk	.20	4.00
☐☐	53	Adam Magarrell, Pha.	.20	4.00
☐☐	54	Dave Scatchard, Van.	.35	5.00
☐☐	55	Sébastien Vallée, Pha.	.20	4.00
☐☐	56	Milos Guren, Cze.	.20	4.00
☐☐	57	Johan Davidsson, Ana.	.20	4.00
☐☐	58	Byron Briske, Ana.	.20	4.00
☐☐	59	Sylvain Blouin, NYR.	.20	4.00
☐☐	60	Bryan Berard, Detroit-OHL, Error (Brian)	2.00	30.00
☐☐	61	Tim Findlay, Windsor	.20	4.00
☐☐	62	Doug Bonner, Seattle	.20	4.00
☐☐	63	Curtis Brown, Buf.	.35	5.00
☐☐	64	Brad Symes, Wpg.	.20	4.00
☐☐	65	Andrew Taylor, Kitchener	.20	4.00
☐☐	66	Brad Bombardir, Albany	.20	4.00
☐☐	67	Joe Dziedzic, Pgh.	.35	5.00
☐☐	68	Valentin Morozov, CSKA	.20	4.00
☐☐	69	Mark McArthur, Que.	.20	4.00
☐	70	Checklist, Error (wrong numbering)	.20	–

COOL FIVE

These cards have two versions: the regular insert (1 of 7,000) and an autographed version (serial numbered).

Insert Set (5 cards): 25.00 150.00

	No.	Player	Reg.	Aut.
☐☐	CF1	Radek Bonk, Las Vegas	3.50	20.00
☐☐	CF2	Brad Park, Bos.	4.00	25.00
☐☐	CF3	Brian Leetch, NYR.	5.00	35.00
☐☐	CF4	Maurice Richard, Mtl.	12.00	60.00
☐☐	CF5	Henri Richard, Mtl.	6.00	40.00

FUTURE FLASH

These cards have two versions: the regular insert (1 of 7,000) and an autographed version (serial numbered).

Insert Set (10 cards): 20.00 75.00

	No.	Player	Reg.	Aut.
☐☐	FF1	Jeff Ambrosio	2.50	6.00
☐☐	FF2	Brad Brown, North Bay	2.50	6.00
☐☐	FF3	Patrik Juhlin	2.50	6.00
☐☐	FF4	Sergei Gorbachev, Dynamo	2.50	6.00
☐☐	FF5	Vasili Kamenev	2.50	6.00
☐☐	FF6	Oleg Orekhovski	2.50	6.00
☐☐	FF7	Maxim Kuznetsov	2.50	6.00
☐☐	FF8	Sergei Luchinkin, Rus.	2.50	6.00
☐☐	FF9	Scotte Roche	2.50	6.00
☐☐	FF10	Alexei Morozov	6.00	25.00

REDEMPTION SET

Insert Set (5 cards): 8.00

	No.	Player	NRMT-MT
☐	1	Sergei Luchinkin	1.50
☐	2	Stefan Ustorf	1.50
☐	3	Brad Brown	1.50
☐	4	Yannick Dubé	1.50
☐	5	Vitali Yachmenev	3.00

1994 - 95 SIGNATURE ROOKIES AUTO-PHONEX

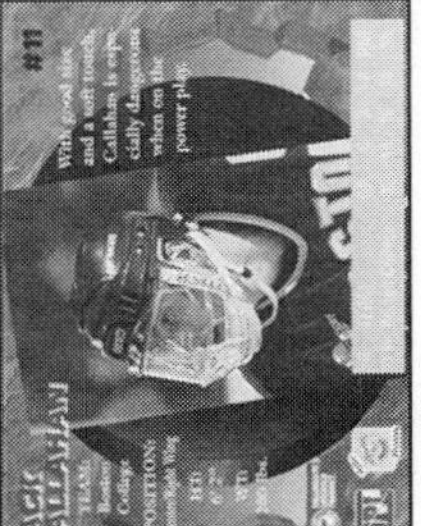

These cards have two versions: the regular card and a one per pack autographed $3 Sprint phone card. Shane Doan (#14) did not sign. Autographs are serial numbered out of 3,000. Autograph prices below are for unused phone cards. Used autographed cards sell at 50-60% of the unused value.

Imprint:

Complete Set (40 cards): 20.00 .–

Autographed Set (39 cards): .– 300.00

	No.	Player	Reg.	Aut.
☐☐	1	Mika Alatalo	.20	5.00
☐☐	2	Chad Allan	.35	8.00
☐☐	3	Jonas Andersson-Junkka	.20	5.00
☐☐	4	Serge Aubin	.20	5.00
☐☐	5	David Belitski (G)	.35	10.00
☐☐	6	Aki Berg	.35	10.00
☐☐	7	Zac Bierk (G)	.50	15.00
☐☐	8	Lou Boddy	.20	5.00
☐☐	9	Kevin Bolibruck	.35	8.00
☐☐	10	Brian Boucher (G)	.50	20.00
☐☐	11	Jack Callahan	.20	5.00
☐☐	12	Jake Deadmarsh	.20	5.00
☐☐	13	Andy Delmore	.20	5.00
☐☐	14	Shane Doan	.35	10.00
☐☐	15	Dan Cleary	1.50	30.00
☐☐	16	Ian Gordon	.20	5.00
☐☐	17	Jochen Hecht, Ger.	.20	5.00
☐☐	18	Martin Hohenberger	.20	5.00
☐☐	19	Tomas Holmstrom	.50	15.00
☐☐	20	Cory Keenan	.20	5.00
☐☐	21	Shane Kenny, Owen Sound	.20	5.00
☐☐	22	Pavel Kriz	.20	5.00
☐☐	23	Justin Kurtz	.20	5.00
☐☐	24	Jan Labraaten	.20	5.00
☐☐	25	Brad Larsen	.35	10.00

	No.	Player		
□□	26	Donald MacLean	.35	8.00
□□	27	Tavis MacMillan	.20	5.00
□□	28	Mike Martin	.20	5.00
□□	29	Bryan Berard	2.00	35.00
□□	30	Dimitri Nabokov	.50	15.00
□□	31	Todd Norman	.35	8.00
□□	32	Cory Peterson	.20	5.00
□□	33	Johan Ramstedt	.20	5.00
□□	34	Wade Redden	.50	15.00
□□	35	Kevin Riehl	.20	5.00
□□	36	David Roberts	.20	5.00
□□	37	Terry Ryan	.35	10.00
□□	38	Brian Scott	.20	5.00
□□	39	Alexander Selivanov	.50	12.00
□□	40	Peter Wallin	.20	5.00

PHONE CARDS

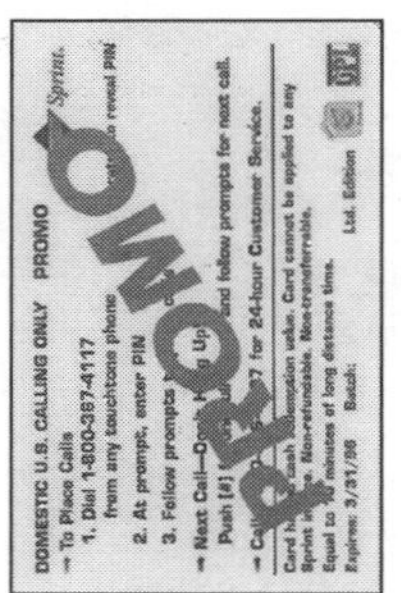

We have little information on these Sprint phone card inserts. Other singles may exist. Prices are for unused phone cards.

Promo Card (Wade Redden, $1,000): 2.00 -
Promo Card (Ryan Smith $6): 4.00 -

	Den.	Player	NRMT-MT
□	$6	Terry Ryan	10.00
□	$6	Wade Redden	10.00

BEYOND 2000

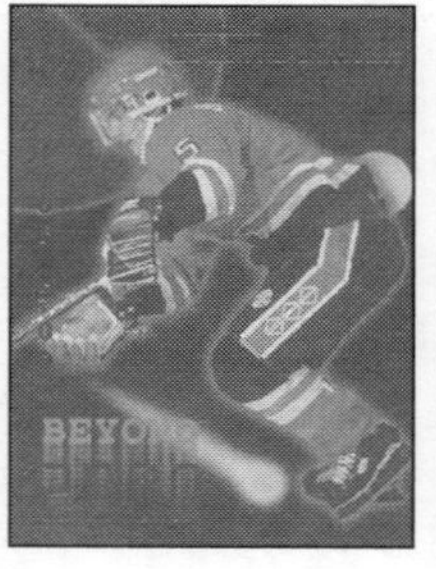
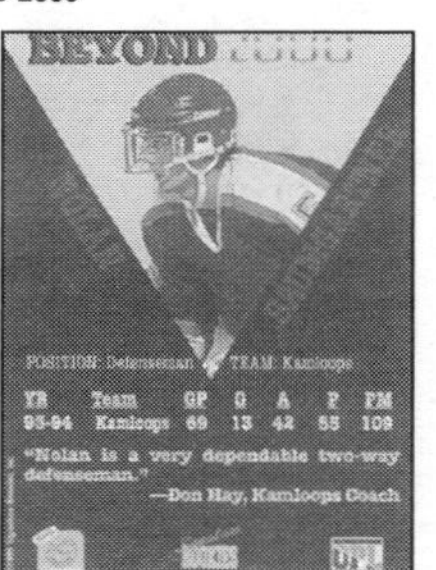

These cards have two versions: the regular card and an autographed card.

Insert Set (5 cards): 25.00 100.00

	No.	Player	Insert	Aut.
□□	B1	Jamie Rivers	2.00	10.00
□□	B2	Terry Ryan	2.50	12.00
□□	B3	Ryan Smyth	10.00	45.00
□□	B4	Nolan Baumgartner	2.00	10.00
□□	B5	José Théodore (G)	10.00	45.00

JAROMIR JAGR

These cards have two versions: the regular card and an autographed card.

Insert Set (5 cards): 25.00 350.00
Promo Card (Jaromir Jagr): 5.00 .–

	No.	Player	Insert	Aut.
□□	JJ1	Jaromir Jagr	6.00	75.00
□□	JJ2	Jaromir Jagr	6.00	75.00
□□	JJ3	Jaromir Jagr	6.00	75.00
□□	JJ4	Jaromir Jagr	6.00	75.00
□□	JJ5	Jaromir Jagr	6.00	75.00

PRODIGIES

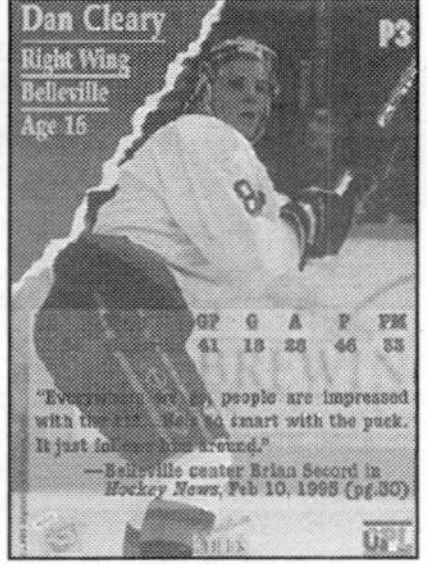

These cards have two versions: the regular card and an autographed card.

Insert Set (5 cards): 20.00 90.00
Promo Card (Wade Redden, P5): 2.00 .–

	No.	Player	Insert	Aut.
□□	P1	Bryan Berard	10.00	45.00
□□	P2	Daymond Langkow	4.00	20.00
□□	P3	Daniel Cleary	8.00	35.00
□□	P4	Aki Berg	3.00	15.00
□□	P5	Wade Redden	5.00	20.00

1994 - 95 SIGNATURE ROOKIES GOLD STANDARD

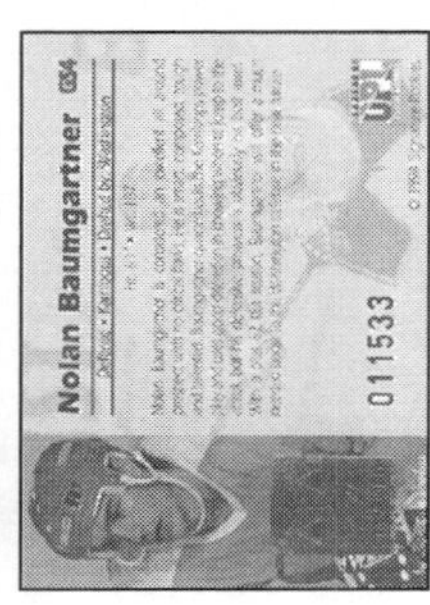

Imprint:

	No.	Player	NRMT-MT
□	76	Nolan Baumgartner	.20
□	77	Wade Belak	.20
□	78	Radek Bonk	.50
□	79	Brad Brown	.50
□	80	Dan Cloutier (G)	1.00
□	81	Johan Davidsson	1.50
□	82	Yannick Dubé	.20
□	83	Eric Fichaud (G)	1.50
□	84	Johan Finnstrom	.20
□	85	Edvin Frylin	.20
□	86	Patrik Juhlin	.20
□	87	Valeri Karpov	.20
□	88	Nikolai Khabibulin (G)	1.00
□	89	Mattias Ohlund	2.00
□	90	Jason Podollan	.20
□	91	Vadim Sharifjanov	.25
□	92	Ryan Smyth	3.00
□	93	Dimitri Tabarin	.20
□	94	Nikolai Tsulygin	.20
□	95	Stefan Ustorf	.20
□	96	Paul Vincent	.20
□	97	Roman Vopat	.20
□	98	Rhett Warrener	.20
□	99	Vitali Yachmenev	.50
□	100	Vadim Epenchintrev	.20
□	GS2	Nolan Baumgartner	.50
□	GS3	Radek Bonk, Las Vegas	.50
□	GS9	Valeri Karpov	.50
□	GS18	Ryan Smyth	5.00
□	HOF7	Tony Esposito (G)	3.00
□	L1	Brian Leetch	3.00

1994 - 95 SIGNATURE ROOKIES MIRACLE ON ICE

We have little information on this set. Cards have two versions: the regular card and an autographed parallel. It is unsure whether players signed one or both of their cards. Action cards (45-50) were not signed. The most expensive autographs are Mike Eruzione at $30 and Neal Broten at $20. Common autographs start at $5.

Imprint:

Complete Set (50 cards): 20.00

	No.	Player	NRMT-MT
□	1	Bill Baker	.20
□	2	Bill Baker	.20
□	3	Neal Broten	1.00
□	4	Neal Broten	1.00
□	5	Dave Christian	.35
□	6	Dave Christian	.35
□	7	Steve Christoff	.35
□	8	Steve Christoff	.35
□	9	Jim Craig (G)	.75
□	10	Jim Craig (G)	.75
□	11	Mike Eruzione	1.50
□	12	Mike Eruzione	1.50
□	13	John Harrington	.20
□	14	John Harrington	.20
□	15	Steve Janasak	.20
□	16	Steve Janasak	.20
□	17	Mark Johnson	.50
□	18	Mark Johnson	.50
□	19	Rob McClanahan	.20
□	20	Rob McClanahan	.20
□	21	Ken Morrow	.50
□	22	Ken Morrow	.50
□	23	Jack O'Callahan	.35
□	24	Jack O'Callahan	.35
□	25	Mark Pavelich	.35
□	26	Mark Pavelich	.35
□	27	Mike Ramsey	.50
□	28	Mike Ramsey	.50
□	29	Buzz Schneider	.20
□	30	Buzz Schneider	.20
□	31	Dave Silk	.20
□	32	Dave Silk	.20
□	33	Bob Suter	.20
□	34	Bob Suter	.20
□	35	Eric Strobel	.20
□	36	Eric Strobel	.20
□	37	Phil Verchota	.20
□	38	Phil Verchota	.20
□	39	Marc Wells	.20
□	40	Marc Wells	.20
□	41	Herb Brooks	.35
□	42	Herb Brooks	.35
□	43	Craig Patrick	.50
□	44	Craig Patrick	.50
□	45	U.S.A. Action	.25
□	46	U.S.A. Action	.25
□	47	Mike Eruzione (Action)	.25
□	48	U.S.A. Celebration	.25
□	49	U.S.A. Action (Neal Broten)	.25
□	50	Checklist	.20

1994 - 95 SIGNATURE ROOKIES TETRAD

This 120-card multi-sport set has only 16 hockey cards. Each card has a regular version and autographed version.

Imprint: © 1994 Signature Rookies

	No.	Player	Reg.	Auto.
□ □	CIV	Sven Butenschon	.20	4.00
□ □	CV	Dan Cloutier (G)	.75	12.00
□ □	CVI	Pat Jablonski (G)	.20	4.00
□ □	CVII	Valeri Karpov, Rus.	.20	4.00
□ □	CVIII	Nikolai Khabibulin (G), CSKA	.75	12.00
□ □	CIX	Sergei Klimentiev, Buf. (Medicine Hat)	.20	4.00
□ □	CX	Krzysztof Oliwa, N.J. (Raleigh)	.20	4.00
□ □	CXI	Dimitri Rjabykin, Cgy. (CSKA)	.20	4.00
□ □	CXII	Ryan Risidore, Hfd. (Guelph)	.20	4.00
□ □	CXIII	Shawn Rivers, Atlanta	.20	4.00
□ □	CXIV	Vadim Shariljanov, Rus.	.25	5.00
□ □	CXV	Mika Stromberg, Fin.	.20	4.00
□ □	CXVI	Tim Taylor	.20	4.00
□ □	CXVII	Vitali Yachmenev, North Bay	.50	8.00
□ □	CXVIII	Wendell Young (G), t.B.	.25	5.00
□ □	CXXII	Bobby Hull	3.00	35.00

1994 - 95 SISU

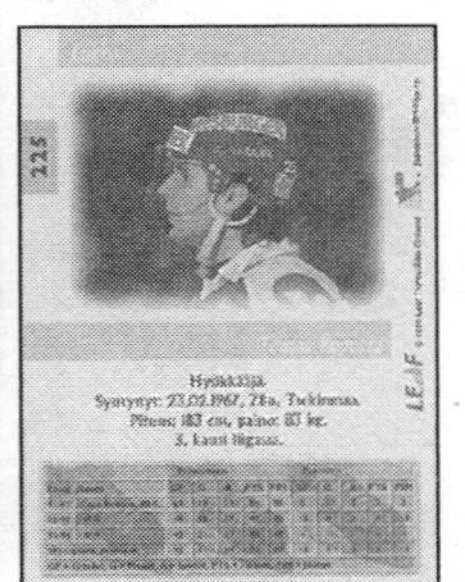

Imprint:

Series One Set (200 cards):	**35.00**
Series Two Set (200 cards):	**50.00**
Common Player:	**.20**

	No.	Player	NRMT-MT
□	1	Pasi Kuivalainen	.20
□	2	Jere Karalahti	.20
□	3	Markku Heikkinen	.20
□	4	Marko Allen	.20
□	5	Jarmo Kuusisto	.20
□	6	Marko Tuulola	.20
□	7	Marko Kiprusoff	.50
□	8	Vesa Ponto	.20
□	9	Tero Lehtera	.20
□	10	Darren Boyko	.25
□	11	Kari Heikkinen	.20
□	12	Niko Marttila	.20
□	13	Jari Torkki	.20
□	14	Jiri Kucera	.20
□	15	Jari Levonen	.20
□	16	Juha Ikonen	.20
□	17	Joni Lius	.20
□	18	Pekka Tuomisto	.20
□	19	Petri Kokko	.20
□	20	Jere Lehtinen	2.00
□	21	Janne Kekalainen	.20
□	22	Ari Haanpaa	.20
□	23	Hannu Jarvenpaa	.20
□	24	Waltteri Immonen	.20
□	25	Jari Lindroos	.20
□	26	Jan Langbacka	.20
□	27	Kari Takko (G)	.35
□	28	Pasi Maattanen	.20
□	29	Jan Latvala	.20
□	30	Arto Heiskanen	.20
□	31	Iiro Jarvi	.20
□	32	Igor Boldin	.20
□	33	Sami Simonen	.20
□	34	Kari Rosenberg (G)	.35
□	35	Sakari Lindfors (G)	.35
□	36	Veli-Pekka Hard	.20
□	37	Jari Halme	.20
□	38	Jukka Tammi (G)	.35
□	39	Kalle Koskinen	.20
□	40	Pekka Tirkkonen	.20
□	41	Ari Sulander (G)	.35
□	42	Jani Hassinen	.20
□	43	Timo Peltomaa	.20
□	44	Sami Mettovaara	.20
□	45	Mika Yli-Maenpaa	.20
□	46	Toni Virta	.20
□	47	Kimmo Lecklin	.20
□	48	Rauli Raitanen	.20
□	49	Juha Lind	.20
□	50	Ari-Pekka Siekkinen (G)	.35
□	51	Kim Ahlroos	.20
□	52	Jarkko Nikander	.20
□	53	Jouni Vento	.20
□	54	Juha Lampinen	.20
□	55	Kalle Sahlstedt	.20
□	56	Teemu Sillanpaa	.20
□	57	Lasse Nieminen	.20
□	58	Janne Niinimaa	3.00
□	59	Timo Jutila	.50
□	60	Tommi Haapsaari	.20
□	61	Allan Measures	.20
□	62	Petteri Nummelin	.20
□	63	Antti Tormanen	.35
□	64	Pekka Laksola	.20
□	65	Esa Sateri	.20
□	66	Petro Koivunen	.20
□	67	Janne Virtanen	.20
□	68	Pekka Peltola	.20
□	69	Matti Kaipainen	.20
□	70	Sami Pekki	.20
□	71	Jussi Tarvainen	.20
□	72	Jari Virtanen	.20
□	73	Kimmo Salminen	.20
□	74	Tommi Varjonen	.20
□	75	Pauli Jarvinen	.20
□	76	Hannu Mattila	.20
□	77	Aleksander Smirnov	.30
□	78	Arto Kulmala	.20
□	79	Roland Karlsson	.20
□	80	Jarno Miikkulainen	.20
□	81	Jarmo Muukkonen	.20
□	82	Mika Paananen	.20
□	83	Pasi Kivila	.20
□	84	Jari Laukkanen	.20
□	85	Tero Arkiomaa	.20
□	86	Tommi Miettinen	.20
□	87	Juha Järvenpää	.20
□	88	Niko Mikkola	.20
□	89	Antti Tuomenoksa	.20
□	90	Ilkka Sinisalo	.35
□	91	Otakar Janecky	.20
□	92	Arto Sirvio	.20
□	93	Robert Salo	.20
□	94	Ari Saarinen	.20
□	95	Kari Martikainen	.20
□	96	Miro Haapaniemi	.20
□	97	Fredrik Norrena (G)	.20
□	98	Erik Hamalainen	.20
□	99	Simo Saarinen	.20
□	100	Harri Suvanto	.20
□	101	Kai Nurminen	.20
□	102	Rami Koivisto	.20
□	103	Pasi Peltonen	.20
□	104	Kari-Pekka Friman	.20
□	105	Mika Kortelainen	.20
□	106	Timo Hirvonen	.20
□	107	Jari Haapamaki	.20
□	108	Mika Manninen	.20
□	109	Ari Vuori	.20
□	110	Markku Ikonen	.20
□	111	Mikko Konttila	.20
□	112	Harri Sillgren	.20
□	113	Mikko Tavi	.20
□	114	Markus Oijennus	.20
□	115	Kimmo Hyttinen	.20
□	116	Jokke Heinanen	.20
□	117	Sami Ahlberg	.20
□	118	Mika Rautio	.20
□	119	Ari Salo	.20
□	120	Juha Hautamaa	.20
□	121	Kari Haakana	.20
□	122	Sami Nuutinen	.20
□	123	Lasse Pirjeta	.20
□	124	Keijo Sailynoja	.20
□	125	Mikael Kotkaniemi	.20
□	126	Samuli Rautio	.20
□	127	Veli-Pekka Pekkarinen	.20
□	128	Hannu Henriksson	.20
□	129	Antti Aalto	.35
□	130	Jyrki Jokinen	.20
□	131	Marko Ek	.20
□	132	Marko Ojanen	.50
□	133	Mika Arvaja	.20
□	134	Karri Kivi	.20
□	135	Timo Saarikoski	.20
□	136	Toni Sihvonen	.20
□	137	Mika Laaksonen	.20
□	138	HIFK, Helsinki	.20
□	139	HPK, Hameenlinna	.20
□	140	Ilves, Tampere	.20
□	141	Jokerit, Helsinki	.20
□	142	JyP HT, Jyvaskyla	.20
□	143	KalPa, Kuopio	.20
□	144	Kiekko-Espoo	.20
□	145	Lukko, Rauma	.20
□	146	Tappara, Tampere	.20
□	147	TPS, Turku	.20
□	148	TuTo, Turku	.20
□	149	Assat, Pori	.20
□	150	Checklist 1, Juha Lind (G)	.20
□	151	Checklist 2, Kari Takko (G)	.35
□	152	Checklist 3, V. Yursinov	.20
□	153	Checklist 4, P. Nummelin	.20
□	154	Marko Jantunen	.25
□	155	Jere Lehtinen	1.50
□	156	Esa Keskinen	.25
□	157	Jere Lehtinen	1.50
□	158	Timo Peltomaa	.25
□	159	Janne Grönvall	.25
□	160	AS: Jarmo Myllys (G)	.50
□	161	AS: Marko Kiprusoff	.50
□	162	AS: Timo Jutila	.50
□	163	AS: Sami Kapaner	.50
□	164	AS: Esa Keskinen	.50
□	165	AS: Mika Alatalo	.25
□	166	Ville Peltonen	.25
□	167	Igor Boldin	.25
□	168	Sami Lehtonen	.25
□	169	Juha Jokiharju	.25
□	170	Harri Laurila	.25
□	171	Pekka Tirkkonen	.25
□	172	Mikko Halonen	.25
□	173	Tero Arkiomaa	.25
□	174	Jonni Vauhkonen	.25
□	175	Janne Grönvall	.25
□	176	Marko Jantunen	.25
□	177	Jouni Vento	.20
□	178	HIFK/ottelut	.20
□	179	HPK/ottelut	.20
□	180	Ilves/ottelut	.20
□	181	Jokerit/ottelut	.20
□	182	JyP HT/ottelut	.20
□	183	KalPa/ottelut	.20
□	184	Kiekko-Espoo/ottelut	.20
□	185	Lukko/ottelut	.20
□	186	Reipas/ottelut	.20
□	187	Tappara/ottelut	.20
□	188	TPS/ottelut	.20
□	189	Assat/ottelut	.20
□	190	SM-kulta/Jokerit	.20
□	191	SM-hopea/TPS	.20
□	192	SM-pronssi/Lukko	.20
□	193	EM-kulta/TPS	.20
□	194	Puolivalierat	.20

	No.	Player	Price
☐	195	Valierat	.20
☐	196	Pronssiottelu	.20
☐	197	1. finaali	.20
☐	198	2. finaali	.20
☐	199	3. finaali	.20
☐	200	4. finaali	.20
☐	201	Jouni Rokama	.20
☐	202	Sami Leinonen	.20
☐	203	Jani Nikko	.20
☐	204	Arto Vuoti	.20
☐	205	Petr Pavlas	.20
☐	206	Reijo Mikkolainen	.20
☐	207	Jari Kurri	3.00
☐	208	Janne Ojanen	.35
☐	209	Sami Kapanen	.20
☐	210	Teppo Kivelä	.20
☐	211	Saku Koivu	6.00
☐	212	Pekka Virta	.20
☐	213	Risto Jalo	.20
☐	214	Serjei Prjakhin	.20
☐	215	Aleksander Barkov	.20
☐	216	Ville Peltonen	.50
☐	217	Jari Korpisalo	.20
☐	218	Jari Liikkanen	.20
☐	219	Timo Lehkonen	.20
☐	220	Juha Ylönen	.20
☐	221	Harri Lönnberg	.20
☐	222	Teemu Vuorinen	.20
☐	223	Pertti Lehtonen	.20
☐	224	Tommi Pullola	.20
☐	225	Tomas Kapusta	.20
☐	226	Joonas Jääskeläinen	.20
☐	227	Jukka Tiilikainen	.20
☐	228	Jarno Kultanen	.20
☐	229	Kimmo Kapanen	.20
☐	230	Jari Kauppila	.20
☐	231	Jarkko Glad	.20
☐	232	Nemo Nokkosmäki	.20
☐	233	Petri Matikainen	.20
☐	234	Christian Ruuttu	.50
☐	235	Matti Järventie	.20
☐	236	Sami Salo	.20
☐	237	Timo Kulonen	.20
☐	238	Pasi Sormunen	.20
☐	239	Timo Nurmberg	.20
☐	240	Jari Hirsimäki	.20
☐	241	Tommi Hämäläinen	.20
☐	242	Vesa Salo	.20
☐	243	Juha Nurminen	.20
☐	244	Petr Korinek	.20
☐	245	Kimmo Vesa	.20
☐	246	Jukka Seppo	.20
☐	247	Jarno Mäkelä	.20
☐	248	Petri Varis	.20
☐	249	Marko Virtanen	.20
☐	250	Risto Siltanen	.35
☐	251	Juha Järvenpää	.20
☐	252	Raimo Summanen	.20
☐	253	Markus Hätinen	.20
☐	254	Kimmo Nurro	.20
☐	255	Timo Salonen	.20
☐	256	Jari Munck	.20
☐	257	Kimmo Rintanen	.20
☐	258	Jarno Levonen	.20
☐	259	Jarno Peltonen	.20
☐	260	Valeri Krykov	.20
☐	261	Kai Rautio	.20
☐	262	Timo Blomqvist	.20
☐	263	Teemu Selänne	6.00
☐	264	Juha Virtanen	.20
☐	265	Veli-Pekka Kautonen	.20
☐	266	Mikko Koivunoro	.20
☐	267	Mikko Luovi	.20
☐	268	Jaroslav Otevrel	.20
☐	269	Erik Kakko	.20
☐	270	Peter Ahola	.20
☐	271	Miikka Kemppi	.20
☐	272	Toni Mäkiaho	.20
☐	273	Pekka Poikolainen	.20
☐	274	Timo Norppa	.20
☐	275	Sebastian Sulku	.20
☐	276	Esa Tikkanen	1.50
☐	277	Pasi Saarela	.20
☐	278	Ilpo Kauhanen	.20
☐	279	Mika Alatalo	.20
☐	280	Jukka Suomalainen	.20
☐	281	Tony Arima	.20
☐	282	Mika Puhakka	.20
☐	283	Jussi Kiuru	.20
☐	284	Jarkko Isotalo	.20
☐	285	Esa Tommila	.20
☐	286	Jouni Loponen	.20
☐	287	Jermu Pisto	.20
☐	288	Pasi Heinistö	.20
☐	289	Toni Porkka	.20
☐	290	Juha Vuorivirta	.20
☐	291	Vesa Karjalainen	.20
☐	292	Tom Koivisto	.20
☐	293	Markku Hurme	.20
☐	294	Mika Kannisto	.20
☐	295	Marko Rantanen	.20
☐	296	Petri Kalteva	.20
☐	297	Pasi Huura	.20
☐	298	Miikka Ruokonen	.20
☐	299	Tuomo Räty	.20
☐	300	Vadim Shaidullin	.20
☐	301	Juha Riihijärvi	.35
☐	302	Brad Turner	.20
☐	303	Marko Toivola	.20
☐	304	Kimmo Timonen	.20
☐	305	Kai Nurminen	.20
☐	306	Vesa Lehtonen	.20
☐	307	Mika Niittymäki	.20
☐	308	Sami Wahlsten	.20
☐	309	Pavel Torgajev	.20
☐	310	Pasi Kemppainen	.20
☐	311	Markku Kallio	.20
☐	312	Timo Mäki	.20
☐	313	Mika Strömberg	.20
☐	314	Tuomas Grönman	.35
☐	315	Tommi Rajamäki	.20
☐	316	Juri Kuznetsov	.20
☐	317	Mikko Myllykoski	.20
☐	318	Brian Tutt	.25
☐	319	Teemu Numminen	.20
☐	320	Juha Jokiharju	.20
☐	321	Mika Lehtinen	.20
☐	322	Jari Pulliainen	.20
☐	323	Kimmo Mäki-Kokkila	.20
☐	324	Mikko Peltola	.20
☐	325	Risto Kurkinen	.20
☐	326	Harri Laurila	.20
☐	327	Vjatcheslav Fandul	.20
☐	328	Niklas Hede	.20
☐	329	Boris Rousson	.20
☐	330	Jukka Ollila	.20
☐	331	Jouni Tuominen	.20
☐	332	Marko Härkönen	.20
☐	333	Petri Engman	.20
☐	334	Mikko Halonen	.20
☐	335	Aki Berg	2.00
☐	336	Kristian Fagerström	.20
☐	337	Jiri Veber	.20
☐	338	Tommy Kiviaho	.20
☐	339	Konstantin Astrahantsev	.20
☐	340	Jukka Mäkitalo	.20
☐	341	Timo Nykopp	.20
☐	342	Sami Lehtonen	.20
☐	343	Joni Lehto	.20
☐	344	Jouko Myrrä	.20
☐	345	Mikko Mäkelä	.50
☐	346	Marco Poulsen	.20
☐	347	Janne Seva	.20
☐	348	Shawn McEachern	1.50
☐	349	Jarkko Varvio	.50
☐	350	Mikko Konttila	.20
☐	351	Veli-Pekka Ahonen	.20
☐	352	Michael Nylander	1.50
☐	353	Kristian Taubert	.20
☐	354	Ismo Kuoppala	.20
☐	355	Kimmo Hyttinen	.20
☐	356	Petri Lätti	.20
☐	357	Ted Donato	1.50
☐	358	Jari Harjumäki	.20
☐	359	Teppo Numminen	.20
☐	360	Jyrki Lumme	1.50
☐	361	German Titov	1.00
☐	362	Kari Eloranta	.20
☐	363	Raimo Helminen	.20
☐	364	Marko Jantunen	.20
☐	365	Olli Kaski	.20
☐	366	Jarmo Kekäläinen	.20
☐	367	Esa Keskinen	.20
☐	368	Jarmo Mäkitalo	.20
☐	369	Mika Nieminen	.20
☐	370	Marko Palo	.20
☐	371	Ville Siren	.20
☐	372	Kari Suoraniemi	.20
☐	373	Otakar Janecky	.20
☐	374	Jari Lindroos	.20
☐	375	Teppo Kivelä	.20
☐	376	Petri Varis	.20
☐	377	Pekka Laksola	.20
☐	378	Jari Korpisalo	.20
☐	379	Iiro Järvi	.20
☐	380	Timo Saarikoski	.20
☐	381	Rauli Raitanen	.20
☐	382	Juha Riihijärvi	.20
☐	383	Juha Jokiharju	.20
☐	384	Vesa Salo	.20
☐	385	Kari Nieminen	.20
☐	386	Marko Jantunen	.20
☐	387	Jere Lehtinen	1.50
☐	388	Ari Sulander (G)	.35
☐	389	Hannu Kapanen	.20
☐	390	Hannu Savolainen	.20
☐	391	Heikki Vesala	.20
☐	392	Hannu Aravirta	.20
☐	393	Kari Savolainen	.20
☐	394	Anatoli Bogdanov	.20
☐	395	Harri Rindell	.20
☐	396	Vaclav Sykora	.20
☐	397	Boris Majorov	.20
☐	398	Vladimir Yursinov	.20
☐	399	Seppo Suoraniemi	.20
☐	400	Veli-Pekka Ketola	.50

SISU SPECIALS

Insert Set (10 cards): 30.00

	No.	Player	NRMT-MT
☐	1	Mika Alatalo	1.50
☐	2	Jari Korpisalo	1.50
☐	3	Petteri Nummelin	1.50
☐	4	Janne Ojanen	1.50
☐	5	Sami Kapanen	2.00
☐	6	Kari Takko (G)	2.50
☐	7	Esa Keskinen	2.00
☐	8	Ari Sulander (G)	2.50
☐	9	Jarmo Myllys (G)	3.00
☐	10	Saku Koivu	20.00

NOLLAKORTIT

Insert Set (10 cards): 40.00

	No.	Player	NRMT-MT
☐	1	Mika Manninen (G)	4.00
☐	2	Kari Takko (G)	6.00
☐	3	Ari Sulander (G)	6.00
☐	4	Jouni Rokama (G)	4.00
☐	5	Kari Rosenberg (G)	5.00
☐	6	Ari-Pekka Siekkinen (G)	4.00
☐	7	Allain Roy (G)	4.00
☐	8	Pasi Kuivalainen (G)	4.00
☐	9	Sakari Lindfors (G)	4.00
☐	10	Mika Rautio (G)	4.00

FIRE ON ICE

Insert Set (20 cards): 40.00

	No.	Player	NRMT-MT
☐	1	Saku Koivu	15.00
☐	2	Esa Keskinen	3.00

	No.	Player	NRMT-MT
☐	3	Igor Boldin	2.00
☐	4	Juha Nurminen	2.00
☐	5	Marko Jantunen	2.00
☐	6	Janne Ojanen	2.50
☐	7	Sami Kapanen	3.00
☐	8	Kai Nurminen	3.00
☐	9	Jari Korpisalo	2.00
☐	10	Tero Lehtera	2.00
☐	11	Timo Jutila	4.00
☐	12	Vjatseslav Fandul	2.00
☐	13	Otakar Janecky	2.00
☐	14	Tero Arkiomaa	2.00
☐	15	Jari Torkki	2.00
☐	16	Risto Kurkinen	2.00
☐	17	Petr Korinek	2.00
☐	18	Petro Koivunen	2.00
☐	19	Tomas Kapusta	2.00
☐	20	Pauli Jarvinen	2.00

JUNIOR

Insert Set (10 cards): 25.00

	No.	Player	NRMT-MT
☐	1	Saku Koivu	15.00
☐	2	Jokke Heinanen	1.50
☐	3	Tommi Miettinen	1.50
☐	4	Jere Karalahti	1.50
☐	5	Kalle Koskinen	1.50
☐	6	Kari Rosenberg (G)	2.50
☐	7	Mika Manninen (G)	2.00
☐	8	Jussi Tarvainen	1.50
☐	9	Mika Stromberg	2.00
☐	10	Kalle Sahlstedt	1.50

SUPER CHASE

	Player	NRMT-MT
☐	The Canada Bowl	20.00
☐	Saku Koivu Autograph	80.00

SPECIAL GUEST STARS

Insert Set (12 cards): 45.00

	No.	Player	NRMT-MT
☐	1	Ted Donato	3.00
☐	2	Jari Kurri	6.00
☐	3	Jyrki Lumme	3.00
☐	4	Shawn McEachern	3.00
☐	5	Mikko Mäkelä	2.00
☐	6	Teppo Numminen	2.00
☐	7	Michael Nylander	3.00
☐	8	Christian Ruuttu	2.00
☐	9	Teemu Selänne	15.00
☐	10	Esa Tikkanen	3.00
☐	11	German Titov	2.00
☐	12	Jarkko Varvio	2.00

MAGIC NUMBERS

Insert Set (10 cards): 10.00

	No.	Player	NRMT-MT
☐	1	Pasi Kuivalainen	1.00
☐	2	Petteri Nummelin	1.00
☐	3	Jarmo Kuusisto	1.00
☐	4	Janne Ojanen	1.50
☐	5	Sami Kapanen	1.50
☐	6	Pekka Virta	1.00
☐	7	Antti Törmänen	1.50
☐	8	Jari Korpisalo	1.00
☐	9	Kimmo Salminen	1.00
☐	10	Jukka Tammi (G)	1.50

HOROSCOPES

Insert Set (20 cards): 15.00

	No.	Player	NRMT-MT
☐	1	Juha Lind	1.00
☐	2	Jukka Seppo	1.50
☐	3	Antti Tuomenoksa	1.00
☐	4	Tuomas Grönman	1.50
☐	5	Peter Ahola	1.00
☐	6	Ville Peltonen	2.00
☐	7	Timo Saarikoski	1.00
☐	8	Timo Peltomaa	1.00
☐	9	Jari Levonen	1.00
☐	10	Teppo Kivelä	1.00
☐	11	Valeri Krykov	1.00
☐	12	Juha Riihijärvi	2.00
☐	13	Kai Nurminen	1.50
☐	14	Mikko Luovi	1.00
☐	15	Raimo Summanen	1.00
☐	16	Tommy Kiviaho	1.00
☐	17	Hannu Järvenpää	1.00
☐	18	Marko Virtanen	1.00
☐	19	Sami Lehtonen	1.00
☐	20	Mika Alatalo	1.00

NHL DRAFT

Insert Set (8 cards): 20.00

	No.	Player	NRMT-MT
☐	1	Title Card	3.00
☐	2	Marko Kiprusoff	4.00
☐	3	Jussi Tarvainen	3.00
☐	4	Arto Kuki	3.00
☐	5	Tommi Rajamäki	3.00
☐	6	Tero Lehterä	3.00
☐	7	Tommi Miettinen	3.00
☐	8	Antti Törmänen	4.00

1994 - 95 SLAPSHOT TEAM SETS

PROMO CARDS

	Player	NRMT-MT
☐	David Belitski (G)	2.00
☐	Todd Norman	2.00
☐	Steve Rice	2.00
☐	Zdenek Nedved/Jason Bonsignore Jamie Rivers/Rory Fitzpatrick	2.00

BRANTFORD SMOKE

Complete Set (25 cards): 9.00

	No.	Player		No.	Player
☐	1	Checklist	☐	2	Bob Decomimière
☐	3	Todd Francis	☐	4	Petr Liptrolt
☐	5	Lorne Knauft	☐	6	Paul Polillo
☐	7	Rob Arabski	☐	8	Derek Gauthier
☐	9	Joe Simon	☐	10	Brad Barton
☐	11	Terry Chitaroni	☐	12	Paul Mitton
☐	13	Wayne MacPhee	☐	14	Brian Blad
☐	15	John Laan	☐	16	Shane MacEachern
☐	17	Wayne Muir	☐	18	Ted Miskolczi
☐	19	Marc Delorme	☐	20	Mike Speer
☐	21	Bob Baird/Ken Crabb	☐	22	Ken Gratton, Coach
☐	23	Team/Sponsor Card	☐	24	Craig Newton
☐	25	Joe Lowes			

DETROIT JR. RED WINGS

Complete Set (25 cards): 15.00

	No.	Player		No.	Player
☐	1	Checklist	☐	2	Darryl Foster
☐	3	Quade Lightbody	☐	4	Ryan MacDonald
☐	5	Mike Rucinski	☐	6	Murray Sheehan
☐	7	Matt Ball	☐	8	Gerry Lanigan
☐	9	Mike Morrone	☐	10	Tom Buckley
☐	11	Eric Manlow	☐	12	Bill McCauley
☐	13	Andrew Taylor	☐	14	Scott Blair
☐	15	Jeff Mitchell	☐	16	Jason Saal (G)
☐	17	Jamie Allison	☐	18	Bryan Berard
☐	19	Dan Pawlaczyk	☐	20	Milan Kostolny
☐	21	Duane Harmer	☐	22	Shayne McCosh
☐	23	Sean Haggerty	☐	24	Nic Beaudoin
☐	25	Paul Maurice, Coach			

GUELPH STORM

Complete Set (30 cards): 12.00

	No.	Player		No.	Player
☐	1	Checklist	☐	2	Mark McArthur
☐	3	Andy Adams	☐	4	Bryan McKinney
☐	5	Ryan Risidore	☐	6	Joel Cort
☐	7	Chris Hajt	☐	8	Regan Stocco
☐	9	Dwayne Hay	☐	10	Andrew Clark
☐	11	Neil Fewster	☐	12	Jamie Wright
☐	13	Jason Jackman	☐	14	Pat Barton
☐	15	Tom Johnson	☐	16	Brian Wesenberg
☐	17	Mike Pittman	☐	18	Jeff Williams
☐	19	Todd Norman	☐	20	Mike Rusk
☐	21	David Lylyk	☐	22	Todd Bertuzzi
☐	23	Jeff Cowan	☐	24	Rumun Ndur
☐	25	Jeff O'Neill	☐	26	Andrew Long
☐	27	Craig Hartsburg, Coach	☐	28	Paul Brydges, A. Coach
☐	29	Burger King Sponsor	☐	30	Domino's Pizza

KITCHENER RANGERS

Complete Set (30 cards): 10.00
Update Set (5 cards): 3.00

	No.	Player		No.	Player
☐	1	Checklist	☐	2	David Belitski (G)
☐	3	Darryl Whyte	☐	4	Daniel Godbout
☐	5	Greg McLean	☐	6	Jason Hughes
☐	7	Jason Byrnes	☐	8	Paul Traynor
☐	9	Travis Riggin	☐	10	Tim Spitzig
☐	11	Trevor Gallant	☐	12	Chris Pittman
☐	13	Rick Emmett	☐	14	Jason Morgan
☐	15	Luch Nasato	☐	16	Ryan Pepperall
☐	17	Keith Welsh	☐	18	Bill McGuigen
☐	19	Chris Brassard	☐	20	Andrew Taylor
☐	21	Rob Deciantis	☐	22	Wes Swinson
☐	23	Lucas Miller	☐	24	Sergei Olympiev
☐	25	Rob Maric	☐	26	Eric Manlow
☐	27	Geoff Ward, Coach	☐	28	Bob Ertel, G.M.
☐	29	R. Chambers/D. Nicholls	☐	30	Domino's Pizza
	No.	**Player**		**No.**	**Player**
☐	31	Brian Scott	☐	32	Robin LaCour
☐	33	Jim Ensom	☐	34	Dylan Seca
☐	35	Garrett Burnett			

NORTH BAY CENTENNIALS

Complete Set (25 cards): 10.00

	No.	Player		No.	Player
☐	1	Joel Gagnon	☐	2	Scott Roche
☐	3	Derek Lahnalampi	☐	4	Brad Brown
☐	5	Steve McLaren	☐	6	Cam White
☐	7	Corey Neilson	☐	8	Jason Campeau
☐	9	Steve Carpenter	☐	10	Trevor Gallant
☐	11	Alex Matvichuk	☐	12	Ryan Gillis
☐	13	Kris Cantu	☐	14	Stefan Rivard
☐	15	Brian Whitley	☐	16	Dustin Virag
☐	17	Lee Jinman	☐	18	Scott Cherrey
☐	19	Damian Bloye	☐	20	Justin Robinson
☐	21	Kody Grigg	☐	22	John Guirestante
☐	23	Gary Roach	☐	24	Vitali Yachmenev
☐	25	Shane Parker/ Tom Hedica			

SARNIA STING

Complete Set (30 cards): 10.00

No.	Player	No.	Player
1	Checklist	2	Ken Carroll
3	Scott Hay	4	Kam White
5	Joe Doyle	6	Tom Brown
7	Jeremy Miculinic	8	Darren Mortier
9	Aaron Brand	10	Chris George
11	Stephane Soulliere	12	Paul McInnes
13	Trevor Letowski	14	Dustin McArthur
15	Rob Massa	16	Brendan Yarema
17	Dan DelMonte	18	B.J. Johnston
19	Wes Mason	20	Rob Guinn
21	Jeff Brown	22	Dennis Maxwell
23	Damon Hardy	24	Alan Letang
25	Matt Hogan	26	Sasha Cucuz
27	Rich Brown, Coach	28	Gord Hamilton, Trainer
29	D. Ciccarelli/S. Burr	30	Mascot Buzz

SUDBURY WOLVES

Complete Set (25 cards): 10.00

No.	Player	No.	Player
1	Checklist	2	Dave MacDonald
3	Rory Fitzpatrick	4	Mike Wilson
5	Neal Martin	6	Shwan Frappier
7	Jamie Rivers	8	Zdenek Nedved
9	Ryan Shanahan	10	Sean Venedam
11	Andrew Dale	12	Rick Bodkin
13	Luc Gagne	14	Barrie Moore
15	Richard Rochefort	16	Krystof Secemski
17	Jason Bonsignore	18	Liam MacEachern
19	Simon Sherry	20	Ethan Moreau
21	Matt Mulin (G)	22	Aaron Starnyski
23	Ron Newhook	24	G. Merkosky/T. Lalonde
25	Dan Lebold/Jason Allen		

WINDSOR SPITFIRES

Complete Set (28 cards): 12.00

No.	Player	No.	Player
1	Checklist	2	Jamie Storr (G)
3	Travis Scott	4	Paul Beazley
5	Mike Martin	6	Chris Van Dyk
7	Denis Smith	8	Glenn Crawford
9	David Pluck	10	Bill Bowler
11	David Green	12	Adam Young
13	Wes Ward	14	Ed Jovanovski
15	Kevin Paden	16	Rob Shearer
17	Joel Poirier	18	Cory Evans
19	Vladimir Kretchine	20	David Roche
21	Rick Emmett	22	David Geris
23	Caleb Ward	24	Luke Clowes
25	John Cooper	26	Tim Findlay
27	Pizza Hut Sponsor	28	AM 800 Sponsor

1994 - 95 SLAPSHOT MEMORIAL CUP

Complete Set (110 cards): 35.00
Common Player: .25

No.	Player	NRMT-MT
01	Rod Branch (G), Kamloops	.35
02	Jeff Oldenborger, Kamloops	.25
03	Jason Holland, Kamloops	.25
04	Nolan Baumgartner, Kamloops	.50
05	Keith McCambridge, Kamloops	.25
06	Ivan Vologjaninov, Kamloops	.25
07	Aaron Keller, Kamloops	.25
08	Greg Hart, Kamloops	.25
09	Jarome Iginla, Kamloops	4.00
10	Ryan Huska, Kamloops	.25
11	Jeff Ainsworth, Kamloops	.25
12	Darcy Tucker, Kamloops	.75
13	Hnat Domenichelli, Kamloops	2.00
14	Tyson Nash, Kamloops	.25
15	Shane Doan, Kamloops	.50
16	Jeff Antonovich, Kamloops	.25
17	Donnie Kinney, Kamloops	.25
18	Ashley Buckberger, Kamloops	.25
19	Brad Lukowich, Kamloops	.25
20	Bob Westerby, Kamloops	.25
21	Jason Strudwick, Kamloops	.25
22	Bob Maudie, Kamloops	.25
23	Randy Petruk (G), Kamloops	.35
24	Shawn McNeil, Kamloops	.25
25	Don Hay, Head Coach, Kamloops	.25
26	Byron Penstock (G), Brandon	.35
27	Brian Elder (G), Brandon	.35
28	Jeff Staples, Brandon	.25
29	Scott Laluk, Brandon	.25
30	Kevin Pozzo, Brandon	.25
31	Wade Redden, Brandon	2.50
32	Jusin Kurtz, Brandon	.25
33	Sven Butenschon, Brandon	.25
34	Bryan McCabe, Brandon	1.50
35	Kelly Smart, Brandon	.25
36	Bobby Brown, Brandon	.25
37	Mike Dubinsky, Brandon	.25
38	Mike Leclerc, Brandon	.25
39	Dean Kletzel, Brandon	.25
40	Darren Ritchie, Brandon	.25
41	Mark Dutiaume, Brandon	.25
42	Ryan Robson, Brandon	.25
43	Chris Dingman, Brandon	.50
44	Darren Van Oene, Brandon	.25
45	Colin Cloutier, Brandon	.25
46	Darryl Stoclham, Brandon	.25
47	Peter Schaefer, Brandon	2.00
48	Marty Murray, Brandon	1.00
49	Alex Vasilevski, Brandon	.35
50	Bob Lowes, Head Coach, Brandon	.25
51	Michael Coveny, Hull	.25
52	Jan Nemecek, Hull	.25
53	Chris Hall, Hull	.25
54	Jason Groleau, Hull	.25
55	Alex Rodrigue, Hull	.25
56	Jamie Bird, Hull	.25
57	Jarold Hersh, Hull	.25
58	Carl Prud'homme, Hull	.25
59	Sean Farmer, Hull	.25
60	Carl Beaudoin, Hull	.25
61	Gordie Dwyer, Hull	.25
62	Richard Safarik, Hull	.25
63	Carl Charland, Hull	.25
64	Jean-Guy Trudel, Hull	.25
65	François Cloutier, Hull	.25
66	Roddie MacKenzie, Hull	.25
67	Colin White, Hull	.25
68	Marin Menard, Hull	.25
69	Sébastien Bordeleau, Hull	1.00
70	Jonathan Delisle, Hull	.25
71	Peter Worrell, Hull	.75
72	Louis-Philippe Charbonneau, Hull	.25
73	José Théodore (G), Hull	4.00
74	Neil Savary (G), Hull	.25
75	Michael McKay, Hull	.25
76	Darryl Foster (G), Detroit-OHL	.35
77	Quade Lightbody, Detroit-OHL	.25
78	Ryan MacDonald, Detroit-OHL	.25
79	Mike Rucinski, Detroit-OHL	.25
80	Murray Sheehan, Detroit-OHL	.25
81	Matt Ball, Detroit-OHL	.25
82	Gerry Lanigan, Detroit-OHL	.25
83	Mike Morrone, Detroit-OHL	.25
84	Tom Buckley, Detroit-OHL	.25
85	Eric Manlow, Detroit-OHL	.25
86	Bill McCauley, Detroit-OHL	.25
87	Andrew Taylor, Detroit-OHL	.25
88	Scott Blair, Detroit-OHL	.25
89	Jeff Mitchell, Detroit-OHL	.25
90	Jason Saal (G), Detroit-OHL	.35
91	Jamie Allison, Detroit-OHL	.25
92	Bryan Berard, Detroit-OHL	4.00
93	Dan Pawlaczyk, Detroit-OHL	.25
94	Milan Kostolny, Detroit-OHL	.25
95	Duane Harmer, Detroit-OHL	.25
96	Shayne McCosh, Detroit-OHL	.25
97	Sean Haggerty, Detroit-OHL	.50
98	Nic Beaudoin, Detroit-OHL	.25
99	Paul Maurice, Coach/GM, Detroit-OHL	.25
100	Pete DeBoe, Asst. Coach, Detroit-OHL	.25
101	CL: Kamloops	.25
102	CL: Brandon	.25
103	CL: Hull	.25
104	CL: Detroit	.25
105	Kamloops Blazers	.25
106	Detroit Jr. Red Wings	.25
107	Hull Olympiques	.25
	WHL Card	.25
	OHL Card	.25
	QMJHL Card	.25

1994 - 95 SP

Imprint: © 1995 The Upper Deck Company

		SP	Die-Cut
Complete Set (195 cards):		50.00	100.00
Common Player:		.20	.35
No.	**Player**	**SP**	**Die-Cut**
1	Paul Kariya, Ana.	3.00	5.00
2	Oleg Tverdovsky, Ana.	.20	.35
3	Stephan Lebeau, Ana.	.20	.35
4	Bob Corkum, Ana.	.20	.35
5	Guy Hebert (G), Ana.	.35	.75
6	Ray Bourque, Bos.	1.00	2.00
7	**Blaine Lacher (G), Bos., RC**	**.20**	**.35**
8	Adam Oates, Bos.	.50	1.00
9	Cam Neely, Bos.	.35	.75
10	Mariusz Czerkawski, Bos.	.20	.35
11	Bryan Smolinski, Bos.	.20	.35
12	Pat LaFontaine, Buf.	.35	.75
13	Alexander Mogilny, Buf.	.50	1.00
14	Dominik Hasek (G), Buf.	1.50	3.00
15	Dale Hawerchuk, Buf.	.35	.75
16	Alexei Zhitnik, Buf.	.20	.35
17	Theoren Fleury, Cgy.	.50	1.00
18	German Titov, Cgy.	.20	.35
19	Phil Housley, Cgy.	.20	.35
20	Joe Nieuwendyk, Cgy.	.35	.75
21	Trevor Kidd (G), Cgy.	.35	.75
22	Jeremy Roenick, Chi.	.50	1.00
23	Chris Chelios, Chi.	.75	1.50
24	Ed Belfour (G), Chi.	.50	1.00
25	Bernie Nicholls, Chi.	.20	.35
26	Tony Amonte, Chi.	.35	.75
27	Joe Murphy, Chi.	.20	.35
28	Mike Modano, Dal.	1.00	2.00
29	Trent Klatt, Dal.	.20	.35
30	Dave Gagner, Dal.	.20	.35
31	Kevin Hatcher, Dal.	.20	.35
32	Andy Moog (G), Dal.	.35	.75
33	Sergei Fedorov, Det.	1.00	2.00
34	Steve Yzerman, Det.	2.00	4.00
35	Vyacheslav Kozlov, Det.	.20	.35
36	Paul Coffey, Det.	.35	.75
37	Keith Primeau, Det.	.35	.75
38	Ray Sheppard, Det.	.20	.35
39	Doug Weight, Edm.	.50	1.00
40	Jason Arnott, Edm.	.35	.75
41	Bill Ranford (G), Edm.	.35	.75
42	Shayne Corson, Edm.	.35	.75
43	Stu Barnes, Fla.	.20	.35
44	John Vanbiesbrouck (G), Fla.	1.25	2.50
45	Johan Garpenlov, Fla.	.20	.35
46	Bob Kudelski, Fla.	.20	.35
47	Scott Mellanby, Fla.	.20	.35

	No.	Player		
□□	48	Chris Pronger, Hfd.	.35	.75
□□	49	Darren Turcotte, Hfd.	.20	.35
□□	50	Andrew Cassels, Hfd.	.20	.35
□□	51	Sean Burke (G), Hfd.	.35	.75
□□	52	Geoff Sanderson, Hfd.	.20	.35
□□	53	Rob Blake, L.A.	.35	.75
□□	54	Wayne Gretzky, L.A.	4.00	8.00
□□	55	Rick Tocchet, L.A.	.20	.35
□□	56	Tony Granato, L.A.	.20	.35
□□	57	Jari Kurri, L.A.	.35	.75
□□	58	Vincent Damphousse, Mtl.	.50	1.00
□□	59	Patrick Roy (G), Mtl.	3.00	6.00
□□	60	Vladimir Malakhov, Mtl.	.20	.35
□□	61	Pierre Turgeon, Mtl.	.35	.75
□□	62	Mark Recchi, Mtl.	.35	.75
□□	63	Martin Brodeur (G), N.J.	1.50	3.00
□□	64	Stéphane Richer, N.J.	.20	.35
□□	65	John MacLean, N.J.	.20	.35
□□	66	Scott Stevens, N.J.	.20	.35
□□	67	Scott Niedermayer, N.J.	.35	.75
□□	68	Kirk Muller, NYI.	.20	.35
□□	69	Ray Ferraro, NYI.	.20	.35
□□	70	Brett Lindros, NYI.	.20	.35
□□	71	Steve Thomas, NYI.	.20	.35
□□	72	Pat Verbeek, NYR.	.20	.35
□□	73	Mark Messier, NYR.	1.00	2.00
□□	74	Brian Leetch, NYR.	.50	1.00
□□	75	Mike Richter (G), NYR.	.50	1.00
□□	76	Alexei Kovalev, NYR.	.20	.35
□□	77	Adam Graves, NYR.	.20	.35
□□	78	Sergei Zubov, NYR.	.35	.75
□□	79	Alexei Yashin, Ott.	.75	1.50
□□	**80**	**Radek Bonk, Ott., RC**	**.50**	**1.00**
□□	81	Alexandre Daigle, Ott.	.35	.75
□□	82	Don Beaupré (G), Ott.	.20	.35
□□	83	Mikael Renberg, Pha.	.35	.75
□□	84	Eric Lindros, Pha.	2.50	5.00
□□	85	John LeClair, Pha.	1.00	2.00
□□	86	Rod Brind'Amour, Pha.	.35	.75
□□	87	Ron Hextall (G), Pha.	.35	.75
□□	88	Ken Wregget (G), Pgh.	.20	.35
□□	89	Jaromir Jagr, Pgh.	2.00	4.00
□□	90	Tomas Sandström, Pgh.	.20	.35
□□	91	John Cullen, Pgh.	.20	.35
□□	92	Ron Francis, Pgh.	.50	1.00
□□	93	Luc Robitaille, Pgh.	.35	.75
□□	94	Joe Sakic, Que.	1.75	3.50
□□	95	Owen Nolan, Que.	.35	.75
□□	96	Peter Forsberg, Que.	2.50	4.00
□□	97	Wendel Clark, Que.	.35	.75
□□	98	Mike Ricci, Que.	.20	.35
□□	99	Stéphane Fiset (G), Que.	.35	.75
□□	100	Brett Hull, Stl.	1.00	2.00
□□	101	Brendan Shanahan, Stl.	1.25	2.50
□□	102	Curtis Joseph (G), Stl.	1.25	2.50
□□	103	Esa Tikkanen, Stl.	.20	.35
□□	104	Al MacInnis, Stl.	.35	.75
□□	105	Arturs Irbe (G), S.J.	.20	.35
□□	106	Ray Whitney, S.J.	.20	.35
□□	107	Sergei Makarov, S.J.	.20	.35
□□	108	Sandis Ozolinsh, S.J.	.35	.75
□□	109	Craig Janney, S.J.	.20	.35
□□	110	Petr Klima, T.B.	.20	.35
□□	111	Chris Gratton, T.B.	.35	.75
□□	112	Roman Hamrlik, T.B.	.35	.75
□□	**113**	**Alexander Selivanov, T.B., RC**	**.20**	**.35**
□□	114	Brian Bradley, T.B.	.20	.35
□□	115	Doug Gilmour, Tor.	.50	1.00
□□	116	Mats Sundin, Tor.	1.00	2.00
□□	117	Félix Potvin (G), Tor.	1.00	2.00
□□	118	Mike Ridley, Tor.	.20	.35
□□	119	Dave Andreychuk, Tor.	.20	.35
□□	120	Dmitri Mironov, Tor.	.20	.35
□□	121	Pavel Bure, Van.	1.50	3.00
□□	122	Trevor Linden, Van.	.35	.75
□□	123	Jeff Brown, Van.	.20	.35
□□	124	Kirk McLean (G), Van.	.35	.75
□□	125	Geoff Courtnall, Van.	.20	.35
□□	126	Joé Juneau, Wsh.	.20	.35
□□	127	Dale Hunter, Wsh.	.20	.35
□□	**128**	**Jim Carey (G), Wsh., RC**	**.75**	**1.00**
□□	129	Peter Bondra, Wsh.	.75	1.50
□□	130	Dimitri Khristich, Wsh.	.20	.35
□□	131	Teemu Selänne, Wpg.	1.50	3.00
□□	132	Keith Tkachuk, Wpg.	.75	1.50
□□	133	Alexei Zhamnov, Wpg.	.35	.75
□□	134	Dave Manson, Wpg.	.20	.35
□□	135	Nelson Emerson, Wpg.	.20	.35
□□	136	Alexandre Daigle, Cdn.	.35	.75
□□	137	Jamie Storr (G), Cdn.	.35	.75
□□	138	Todd Harvey, Cdn.	.20	.35
□□	**139**	**Wade Redden, Cdn., RC**	**.75**	**1.00**
□□	**140**	**Ed Jovanovski, Cdn., RC**	**2.00**	**2.50**
□□	**141**	**Jamie Rivers, , Cdn., RC**	**.20**	**.35**
□□	**142**	**Ryan Smyth, Cdn., RC**	**4.00**	**5.00**
□□	**143**	**Jason Botterill, Cdn., RC**	**.20**	**.35**
□□	**144**	**Denis Pederson, Cdn., RC**	**.20**	**.35**
□□	145	Jeff Friesen, Cdn.	.35	.75
□□	**146**	**Dan Cloutier (G), Cdn., RC**	**2.00**	**2.50**
□□	**147**	**Lee Sorochan, Cdn., RC**	**.20**	**.35**
□□	148	Marty Murray, Cdn.	.20	.35
□□	**149**	**Shean Donovan, Cdn., RC**	**.20**	**.35**
□□	**150**	**Larry Courville, Cdn., RC**	**.20**	**.35**
□□	151	Jason Allison, Cdn.	.50	1.00
□□	**152**	**Jeff O'Neill, Cdn., RC**	**1.00**	**1.50**
□□	**153**	**Bryan McCabe, Cdn., RC**	**.50**	**.75**
□□	**154**	**Miloslav Guren, Cze. , RC**	**.20**	**.35**
□□	**155**	**Petr Buzek, Cze. , RC**	**.20**	**.35**
□□	156	Tomas Blazek, Cze.	.20	.35
□□	157	Josef Marha, Cze.	.20	.35
□□	**158**	**Jan Hlavac, Cze. , RC**	**.20**	**.35**
□□	**159**	**Veli-Pekka Nutikka, Fin., RC**	**.20**	**.35**
□□	160	Kimmo Timonen, Fin.	.20	.35
□□	161	Antti Aalto, Fin.	.20	.35
□□	162	Janne Niinimaa, Fin.	.35	.75
□□	163	Nikolai Zavarukhin, Rus.	.20	.35
□□	**164**	**Vadim Epantchinsev, Rus., RC**	**.20**	**.35**
□□	**165**	**Alexandre Koroliouk, Rus., RC**	**.20**	**.35**
□□	**166**	**Dmitri Klevakin, Rus., RC**	**.20**	**.35**
□□	**167**	**Vitali Yachmenev, Rus., RC**	**.50**	**.75**
□□	168	Niklas Sundstrom, Swe.	.20	.35
□□	**169**	**Anders Soderberg, Swe., RC**	**.20**	**.35**
□□	170	Anders Eriksson, Swe.	.20	.35
□□	171	Jesper Mattsson, Swe.	.20	.35
□□	**172**	**Mattias Ohlund, Swe., RC**	**3.00**	**3.75**
□□	173	Jason Bonsignore, USA.	.20	.35
□□	**174**	**Bryan Berard, USA., RC**	**4.00**	**5.00**
□□	175	Richard Park, USA.	.20	.35
□□	**176**	**Mike McBain, Cdn., RC**	**.35**	**.50**
□□	**177**	**Jason Doig, Cdn., RC**	**.50**	**.75**
□□	**178**	**Xavier Delisle, Cdn., RC**	**.35**	**.50**
□□	**179**	**Christian Dubé, Cdn., RC**	**1.50**	**1.75**
□□	**180**	**Louis-Philippe Sévigny, Cdn., RC**	**.35**	**.50**
□□	**181**	**Jarome Iginla, Cdn., RC**	**4.00**	**5.00**
□□	**182**	**Marc Savard, Cdn., RC**	**.75**	**1.00**
□□	**183**	**Alyn McCauley, Cdn., RC**	**4.00**	**5.00**
□□	**184**	**Brad Mehalko, Cdn., RC**	**.35**	**.50**
□□	**185**	**Todd Norman, Cdn., RC**	**.35**	**.50**
□□	**186**	**Brian Scott, Cdn., RC**	**.35**	**.50**
□□	**187**	**Brad Larsen, Cdn., RC**	**.35**	**.50**
□□	**188**	**Jeffrey Ware, Cdn., RC**	**.35**	**.50**
□□	**189**	**Sergei Samsonov, Rus., RC**	**20.00**	**25.00**
□□	**190**	**Andrei Petrunin, Rus., RC**	**.35**	**.50**
□□	**191**	**Sean Haggerty, USA., RC**	**.50**	**.75**
□□	**192**	**Rory Fitzpatrick, USA., RC**	**.35**	**.50**
□□	**193**	**Deron Quint, USA., RC**	**.35**	**.50**
□□	194	Jamie Langenbrunner, USA.	.35	.75
□□	**195**	**Jeff Mitchell, USA., RC**	**.35**	**.50**

	Player	Die-Cut
□	Wayne Gretzky 2,500 points	115.00

SP PREMIER

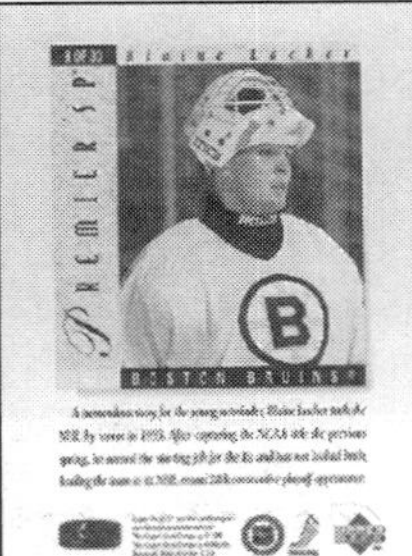

These cards have two versions: the regular insert and a die-cut parallel.

Insert Set (30 cards): **150.00** **350.00**

	No.	Player	Premier	Die-Cut
□□	1	Paul Kariya, Ana.	15.00	75.00
□□	2	Peter Forsberg, Que.	12.00	60.00
□□	3	Viktor Kozlov, S.J.	3.00	10.00
□□	4	Todd Marchant, Edm.	3.00	10.00
□□	5	Oleg Tverdovsky, Ana.	3.00	10.00
□□	6	Todd Harvey, Dal.	3.00	10.00
□□	7	Kenny Jonsson, Tor.	3.00	10.00
□□	8	Blaine Lacher (G), Bos.	3.00	10.00
□□	9	Radek Bonk, Ott.	4.00	12.00
□□	10	Brett Lindros, NYI.	3.00	10.00
□□	11	Valeri Bure, Mtl.	3.00	10.00
□□	12	Brial Rolston, N.J.	3.00	10.00
□□	13	David Oliver, Edm.	3.00	10.00
□□	14	Ian Laperrière, Stl.	3.00	10.00
□□	15	Adam Deadmarsh, Que.	4.00	15.00
□□	16	Pavel Bure, Van.	8.00	40.00
□□	17	Wayne Gretzky, L.A.	25.00	125.00
□□	18	Jeremy Roenick, Chi.	4.00	15.00
□□	19	Dominik Hasek (G), Buf.	8.00	40.00
□□	20	Ray Bourque, Bos.	4.00	15.00
□□	21	Doug Gilmour, Tor.	5.00	20.00
□□	22	Teemu Selänne, Wpg.	8.00	40.00
□□	23	Cam Neely, Bos.	4.00	15.00
□□	24	Sergei Fedorov, Det.	6.00	30.00
□□	25	Bernie Nicholls, Chi.	3.00	10.00
□□	26	Jaromir Jagr, Pgh.	12.00	60.00
□□	27	Joe Sakic, Que.	10.00	50.00
□□	28	Mark Messier, NYR.	6.00	30.00
□□	29	Brett Hull, Stl.	6.00	30.00
□□	30	Eric Lindros, Pha.	15.00	75.00

1994 - 95 TOPPS FINEST

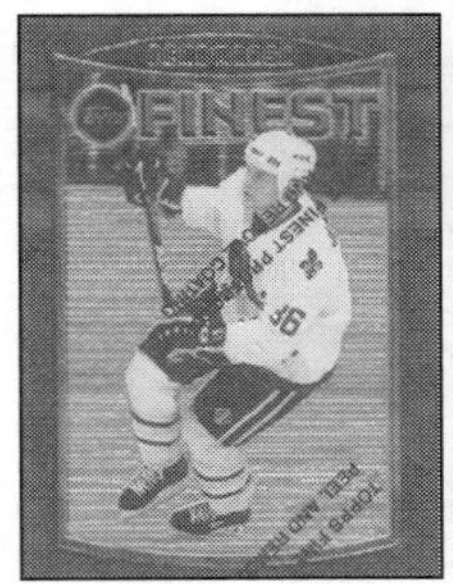

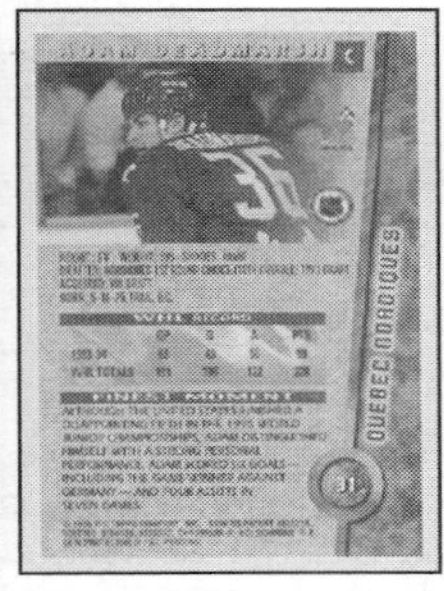

These cards have up to five versions: the regular card (1-165), a Refractor parallel (1-165), a Stanley Cup Champions card (1-165), a Conference Winners card (Red Wings and Devils only) and a Division Winners card (Red Wings, Flames, Flyers and Nordiques only). Stanley Cup Champions, Conference Winners and Division Winners all have identical pricing. Box Top versions for each card also exist.

Imprint: © 1995 THE TOPPS COMPANY, INC

			Reg.	Ref.	S.C.
Complete Set (165 cards):			**80.00**	**2,100.00**	**150.00**
Common Player:			**.35**	**6.00**	**.75**
	No.	**Player**	**Reg.**	**Ref.**	**S.C.**
□□□□	1	Peter Forsberg, Que.	5.00	150.00	18.00
□□□	2	Oleg Tverdovsky, Ana.	.35	6.00	.75
□□□	**3**	**Radek Bonk, Ott., RC**	**1.00**	**10.00**	**2.00**
□□□□	4	Brian Rolston, N.J.	.35	6.00	.75
□□□	5	Kenny Jonsson, Tor., Error (b/A. Yashin)	.35	6.00	.75
□□□□	6	Patrik Juhlin, Pha.	.35	6.00	.75
□□□	7	Paul Kariya, Ana.	6.00	175.00	20.00
□□□□	8	Janne Laukkanen, Que.	.35	6.00	.75
□□□	9	Brett Lindros, NYI.	.35	6.00	.75
□□□	10	Andrei Nikolishin, Hfd.	.35	6.00	.75
□□□	11	Jeff Friesen, S.J.	.50	10.00	1.50
□□□	12	Jamie Storr (G), L.A.	.50	10.00	1.50
□□□□	13	Chris Therien, Pha.	.35	6.00	.75
□□□	14	Alexander Cherbayev, S.J.	.35	6.00	.75
□□□	15	Kevin Brown, L.A.	.35	6.00	.75
□□□	16	Mark Messier, NYR.	2.50	50.00	7.00
□□□	17	Kevin Hatcher, Dal.	.35	6.00	.75
□□□	18	Scott Stevens, N.J.	.35	6.00	.75
□□□	19	Keith Tkachuk, Wpg.	2.00	40.00	5.00
□□□	20	Guy Hebert (G), Ana.	.50	10.00	1.50
□□□	21	Jason Arnott, Edm.	.75	10.00	1.50
□□□	22	Cam Neely, Bos.	.50	10.00	1.50
□□□	23	Adam Graves, NYR.	.35	6.00	.75
□□□	24	Pavel Bure, Van.	2.50	50.00	7.00

	No.	Player			
□□□	25	Mark Tinordi, Wsh.	.35	6.00	.75
□□□	26	Félix Potvin (G), Tor.	3.00	70.00	8.00
□□□	27	Nikolai Khabibulin (G), Wpg.	1.50	20.00	4.00
□□□□	28	Theoren Fleury, Cgy.	1.50	20.00	4.00
□□□	29	Curtis Joseph (G), Stl.	3.00	60.00	8.00
□□□	30	Patrick Roy (G), Mtl.	8.00	250.00	20.00
□□□□	31	Adam Deadmarsh, Que.	.75	10.00	3.00
□□□	32	Pat Falloon, S.J.	.35	6.00	.75
□□□	33	Jaromir Jagr, Pgh.	5.00	150.00	18.00
□□□	34	Chris Chelios, Chi.	2.00	40.00	5.00
□□□	35	Ray Bourque, Bos.	2.50	50.00	7.00
□□□□□	36	Mike Vernon (G), Det.	.75	10.00	3.00
□□□	37	Steve Thomas, NYI.	.35	6.00	.75
□□□□	38	Eric Lindros, Pha.	6.50	250.00	20.00
□□□	39	Dave Andreychuk, Tor.	.35	6.00	.75
□□□	40	John Vanbiesbrouck (G), Fla.	3.00	60.00	8.00
□□□	41	Wayne Gretzky, L.A.	10.00	350.00	30.00
□□□	42	Brett Hull, Stl.	2.50	50.00	7.00
□□□	43	Dominik Hasek (G), Buf.	3.50	75.00	9.00
□□□	44	Kirk Muller, Mtl.	.35	6.00	.75
□□□	45	Rob Blake, L.A.	.75	10.00	1.50
□□□	46	Viktor Kozlov, S.J.	.35	6.00	.75
□□□	47	Todd Harvey, Dal.	.35	6.00	.75
□□□	48	Valeri Bure, Mtl.	.35	6.00	.75
□□□	49	Brian Leetch, NYR.	1.50	20.00	4.00
□□□□□	50	Ray Sheppard, Det.	.35	6.00	.75
□□□	51	Ed Belfour (G), Chi.	1.50	20.00	4.00
□□□	52	Rick Tocchet, L.A.	.35	6.00	.75
□□□	53	Daren Puppa (G), T.B.	.35	6.00	.75
□□□	54	Russ Courtnall, Dal.	.35	6.00	.75
□□□	55	Jason Allison, Wsh.	1.50	20.00	4.00
□□□	56	A. Yashin, Ott., Err (b/K. Jonsson)	2.00	40.00	5.00
□□□	57	Sandis Ozolinsh, S.J.	.75	10.00	1.50
□□□	58	Chris Gratton, T.B.	.75	10.00	1.50
□□□	59	Michael Peca, Van.	.75	10.00	1.50
□□□	60	Glen Wesley, Hfd.	.35	6.00	.75
□□□	61	Kirk McLean (G), Van.	.50	10.00	1.50
□□□	62	Chris Pronger, Hfd.	.75	10.00	1.50
□□□	63	Steve Larmer, NYR.	.35	6.00	.75
□□□	64	Michal Grosek, Wpg.	.35	6.00	.75
□□□□□	65	Sergei Fedorov, Det.	2.50	50.00	7.00
□□□	66	Stu Barnes, Fla.	.35	6.00	.75
□□□	67	Adam Oates, Bos.	.50	10.00	1.50
□□□□□	68	Paul Coffey, Det., Error (b/A. Mogilny)	.75	10.00	1.50
□□□□	69	Joe Sakic, Que.	4.00	80.00	10.00
□□□	70	Pat LaFontaine,Buf.	.50	10.00	1.50
□□□□	71	Martin Brodeur (G), N.J.	3.50	75.00	9.00
□□□	72	Bob Corkum, Ana.	.35	6.00	.75
□□□	73	Jeremy Roenick, Chi.	1.50	20.00	4.00
□□□	74	Shayne Corson, Edm.	.75	10.00	.75
□□□□	75	German Titov, Cgy.	.35	6.00	1.50
□□□	76	Teemu Selänne, Wpg.	3.50	75.00	9.00
□□□	**77**	**Eric Fichaud (G), Tor., RC**	**2.00**	**15.00**	**3.00**
□□□	78	Pierre Turgeon, NYI.	.75	10.00	1.50
□□□	**79**	**Alexander Selivanov, T.B., RC**	**.35**	**6.00**	**.75**
□□□	80	Kevin Stevens, Pgh.	.35	6.00	.75
□□□	81	Jari Kurri, L.A.	.75	10.00	1.50
□□□□	82	Gary Roberts, Cgy.	.75	10.00	1.50
□□□	83	Geoff Courtnall, Van.	.35	6.00	.75
□□□□□	84	Steve Yzerman, Det.	5.00	100.00	15.00
□□□□	85	Rod Brind'Amour, Pha.	.75	10.00	.75
□□□	86	Mike Richter (G), NYR.	1.50	30.00	5.00
□□□	87	Bernie Nicholls, Chi.	.35	6.00	.75
□□□	88	Alexander Daigle, Ott.	.75	10.00	1.50
□□□	89	Luc Robitaille, Pgh.	.75	10.00	1.50
□□□□	90	John MacLean, N.J.	.35	6.00	.75
□□□□	91	Phil Housley, Cgy.	.35	6.00	.75
□□□	92	Brendan Shanahan, Stl.	3.00	60.00	8.00
□□□	93	Joé Juneau, Wsh.	.35	6.00	.75
□□□□	94	Stéphane Richer, N.J.	.35	6.00	.75
□□□	**95**	**Blaine Lacher (G), Bos., RC**	**.35**	**6.00**	**.75**
□□□	96	Mike Gartner, Tor.	.75	10.00	1.50
□□□□	97	René Corbet, Que.	.35	6.00	.75
□□□	98	Vincent Damphousse, Mtl.	1.50	30.00	4.00
□□□	99	Alexander Mogilny, Buf., Error (b/K. Jonsson)	1.50	30.00	4.00
□□□	100	Doug Gilmour, Tor.	1.50	30.00	4.00
□□□□	101	Petr Nedved, NYR.	.35	6.00	.75
□□□	102	Alexei Zhamnov, Wpg.	.75	10.00	1.50
□□□	103	Wendel Clark, Que.	.75	10.00	1.50
□□□	104	Arturs Irbe, S.J.	.35	6.00	.75
□□□	105	Brian Bellows, Mtl.	.35	6.00	.75
□□□	106	Mike Modano, Dal.	2.50	50.00	7.00
□□□	107	Ravil Gusmanov, Wpg.	.35	6.00	.75
□□□	108	Geoff Sanderson, Hfd.	.35	6.00	.75
□□□	109	Mark Recchi, Mtl.	.75	10.00	1.50
□□□	110	Mats Sundin, Tor.	2.50	50.00	7.00
□□□	111	Pavol Demitra, Ott.	.35	6.00	.75
□□□	112	Richard Park, USA.	.50	6.00	1.00
□□□	**113**	**Doug Bonner (G), USA., RC**	**.50**	**6.00**	**1.00**
□□□	**114**	**Bryan Berard, USA., RC**	**8.00**	**80.00**	**15.00**
□□□	**115**	**Rory Fitzpatrick, USA., RC**	**.50**	**6.00**	**1.00**
□□□	116	Deron Quint, USA.	.50	6.00	1.00
□□□	117	Jason Bonsignore, USA.	.50	6.00	1.00
□□□	118	Adam Deadmarsh, USA.	.75	10.00	1.50
□□□	**119**	**Sean Haggerty, USA., RC**	**.75**	**8.00**	**1.50**
□□□	120	Jamie Langenbrunner, USA.	.75	10.00	1.50
□□□	**121**	**Jeff Mitchell, USA., RC**	**.50**	**6.00**	**1.00**
□□□	122	Antti Aalto, Fin.	.50	6.00	1.00
□□□	**123**	**Tommi Rajamaki, Fin., RC**	**.50**	**6.00**	**1.00**
□□□	**124**	**Jusi Markkanen (G), Fin., RC**	**.50**	**6.00**	**1.00**
□□□	**125**	**Mikka Kiprusoff (G), Fin., RC Error (b: J. Markkanen)**	**.50**	**6.00**	**1.00**
□□□	**126**	**Jere Karalahti, Fin., RC**	**.50**	**6.00**	**1.00**
□□□	**127**	**Petri Kokko, Fin., RC**	**.50**	**6.00**	**1.00**
□□□	128	Janne Niinimaa, Fin.	.75	10.00	1.50
□□□	**129**	**Kimmo Timonen, Fin., RC**	**.50**	**6.00**	**1.00**
□□□	**130**	**Martti Jarventie, Fin., RC**	**.50**	**6.00**	**1.00**
□□□	**131**	**Mikko Helisten, Fin., RC**	**.50**	**6.00**	**1.00**
□□□	**132**	**Niko Halttunen, Fin., RC**	**.50**	**6.00**	**1.00**
□□□	**133**	**Tommi Miettinen, Fin., RC**	**.50**	**6.00**	**1.00**
□□□	**134**	**Miska Kangasniemi, Fin., RC**	**.50**	**6.00**	**1.00**
□□□	**135**	**Veli-Pekka Nutikka, Fin., RC**	**.50**	**6.00**	**1.00**
□□□	**136**	**Jani Hassinen, Fin., RC**	**.50**	**6.00**	**1.00**
□□□	**137**	**Timo Salonen, Fin., RC**	**.50**	**6.00**	**1.00**
□□□	**138**	**Tommi Sova, Fin., RC**	**.50**	**6.00**	**1.00**
□□□	**139**	**Toni Makiaho, Fin., RC**	**.50**	**6.00**	**1.00**
□□□	**140**	**Tommi Hamalainen, Fin., RC**	**.50**	**6.00**	**1.00**
□□□	**141**	**Juha Vuorivirta, Fin., RC**	**.50**	**6.00**	**1.00**
□□□	**142**	**Jussi Tarvainen, Fin., RC**	**.50**	**6.00**	**1.00**
□□□	**143**	**Miikka Elomo, Fin., RC**	**.75**	**8.00**	**1.50**
□□□	**144**	**Jason Botterill, Cdn., RC**	**.50**	**6.00**	**1.00**
□□□	**145**	**Dan Cloutier (G), Cdn., RC**	**4.00**	**40.00**	**8.00**
□□□	146	Jamie Storr (G), Cdn.	.75	10.00	1.50
□□□	**147**	**Chad Allan, Cdn., RC**	**.50**	**6.00**	**1.00**
□□□	**148**	**Nolan Baumgartner, Cdn., RC**	**.75**	**8.00**	**1.50**
□□□	**149**	**Ed Jovanovski, Cdn., RC**	**3.50**	**35.00**	**7.00**
□□□	150	Bryan McCabe, Cdn.	.50	6.00	1.00
□□□	**151**	**Wade Redden, Cdn., RC**	**1.25**	**12.00**	**2.50**
□□□	**152**	**Jamie Rivers, Cdn., RC**	**.50**	**6.00**	**1.00**
□□□	**153**	**Lee Sorochan, Cdn., RC**	**.50**	**6.00**	**1.00**
□□□	154	Jason Allison, Cdn.	.50	6.00	1.00
□□□	155	Alexandre Daigle, Cdn.	.75	10.00	1.50
□□□	**156**	**Larry Courville, Cdn., RC**	**.50**	**6.00**	**1.00**
□□□	**157**	**Eric Dazé, Cdn., RC**	**3.50**	**35.00**	**10.00**
□□□	**158**	**Shean Donovan, Cdn., RC**	**.50**	**6.00**	**1.00**
□□□	159	Jeff Friesen, Cdn.	.75	10.00	1.50
□□□	160	Todd Harvey, Cdn.	.50	6.00	1.00
□□□	161	Marty Murray, Cdn.	.50	6.00	1.00
□□□	**162**	**Jeff O'Neill, Cdn., RC**	**1.50**	**15.00**	**3.00**
□□□	**163**	**Denis Pederson, Cdn., RC**	**.75**	**8.00**	**1.50**
□□□	**164**	**Darcy Tucker, Cdn., RC**	**.75**	**8.00**	**1.50**
□□□	**165**	**Ryan Smyth, Cdn., RC**	**10.00**	**90.00**	**20.00**

BOWMAN'S BEST

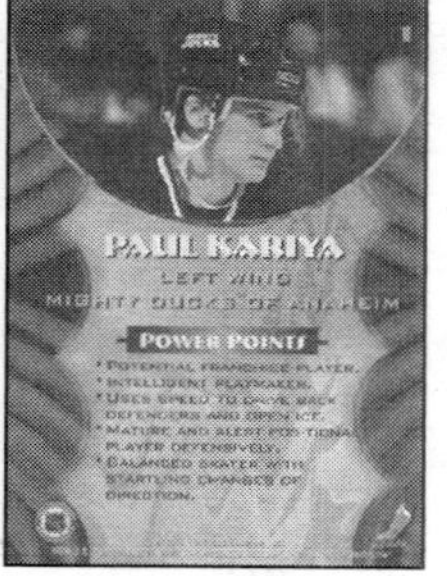

These cards have two versions: the regular insert and a Refractor parallel. Rookies have a red background while veterans have a blue background.

Insert Set (25 cards): 200.00 1,300.00

	No.	Player	Insert	Ref.
□□	1	Paul Kariya, Ana.	18.00	90.00
□□	2	Oleg Tverdovsky, Ana.	3.00	15.00
□□	3	Blaine Lacher (G), Bos.	3.00	15.00
□□	4	Todd Harvey, Dal.	3.00	15.00
□□	5	Roman Oksiuta, Van.	3.00	15.00
□□	6	David Oliver, Edm.	3.00	15.00
□□	7	Jamie Storr (G), L.A.	5.00	18.00
□□	8	Brian Savage, Mtl.	3.00	15.00
□□	9	Brian Rolston, N.J.	3.00	15.00
□□	10	Brett Lindros, NYI.	3.00	15.00
□□	11	Radek Bonk, Ott.	5.00	18.00
□□	12	Peter Forsberg, Que.	15.00	75.00
□□	13	Adam Deadmarsh, Que.	5.00	18.00
□□	14	Jeff Friesen, S.J.	5.00	20.00
□□	15	Denis Chassé, Stl.	3.00	15.00
□□	16	Jason Wiemer, T.B.	3.00	15.00
□□	17	Alexander Selivanov, T.B.	3.00	15.00
□□	18	Kenny Jonsson, Tor.	3.00	15.00
□□	19	Todd Marchant, Edm.	3.00	15.00
□□	20	Mariusz Czerkawski, Bos.	3.00	15.00
□□	1	Ray Bourque, Bos.	8.00	40.00
□□	2	Mark Messier, NYR.	8.00	40.00
□□	3	Cam Neely, Bos.	5.00	20.00
□□	4	Theoren Fleury, Cgy.	6.00	25.00
□□	5	Jeremy Roenick, Chi.	6.00	25.00
□□	6	Mike Modano, Dal.	8.00	40.00
□□	7	Sergei Fedorov, Det.	8.00	40.00
□□	8	John Vanbiesbrouck (G), Fla.	9.00	45.00
□□	9	Pierre Turgeon, Mtl.	5.00	20.00
□□	10	Kirk Muller, NYI.	3.00	15.00
□□	11	Pavel Bure, Van.	10.00	50.00
□□	12	Brian Leetch, NYR.	6.00	25.00
□□	13	Mike Richter (G), NYR.	6.00	25.00
□□	14	Teemu Selänne, Wpg.	10.00	50.00
□□	15	Brett Hull, Stl.	8.00	40.00
□□	16	Eric Lindros, Pha.	18.00	90.00
□□	17	Keith Tkachuk, Wpg.	7.00	30.00
□□	18	Joe Sakic, Que.	12.00	75.00
□□	19	Doug Gilmour, Tor.	6.00	25.00
□□	20	Jaromir Jagr, Pgh.	15.00	90.00
□□	1	Paul Kariya, Ana./Theoren Fleury, Cgy.	10.00	60.00
□□	2	Doug Gilmour, Tor./Peter Forsberg, Que.	8.00	45.00
□□	3	Joe Sakic, Que./Radek Bonk, Ott.	7.00	40.00
□□	4	Brian Leetch, NYR./Oleg Tverdovsky, Ana.	6.00	25.00
□□	5	Cam Neely, Bos./Jason Wiemer, T.B.	4.00	15.00

DIVISION'S FINEST

These cards feature ClearChrome technology.

Insert Set (20 cards): 140.00

	No.	Player	NRMT-MT
□	1	Patrick Roy (G), Mtl.	25.00
□	2	Ray Bourque, Bos.	7.50
□	3	Adam Oates, Bos.	5.00
□	4	Luc Robitaille, Pgh.	3.50
□	5	Mark Recchi, Mtl.	3.50
□	6	Mike Richter (G), NYR.	5.00
□	7	Scott Stevens, N.J.	3.00
□	8	Eric Lindros, Pha.	20.00
□	9	Adam Graves, NYR.	3.00
□	10	Stéphane Richer, N.J.	3.00
□	11	Ed Belfour (G), Chi.	5.00
□	12	Al MacInnis, Stl.	3.50
□	13	Sergei Fedorov, Det.	7.50
□	14	Brendan Shanahan, Stl.	9.00
□	15	Brett Hull, Stl.	7.50
□	16	Arturs Irbe (G), S.J.	3.00
□	17	Sandis Ozolinsh, S.J.	3.50
□	18	Wayne Gretzky, L.A.	30.00
□	19	Gary Roberts, Cgy.	3.50
□	20	Pavel Bure, Van.	10.00

RING LEADERS

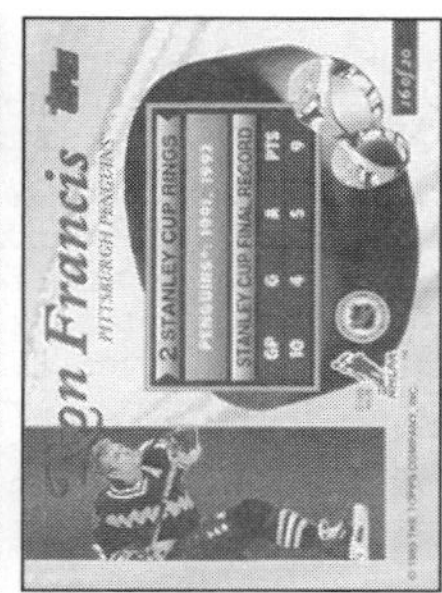

Insert Set (20 cards): 225.00

	No.	Player	NRMT-MT
□	1	Mark Messier, NYR.	18.00
□	2	Kevin Lowe, NYR.	4.00
□	3	Jari Kurri, L.A.	6.00
□	4	Grant Fuhr (G), L.A.	6.00
□	5	Wayne Gretzky, L.A.	75.00
□	6	Paul Coffey, Det.	6.00
□	7	Craig Simpson, Buf.	4.00
□	8	Craig MacTavish, NYR.	4.00
□	9	Jeff Beukeboom, NYR.	4.00
□	10	Joe Mullen, Pgh.	4.00
□	11	Marty McSorley, L.A.	4.00
□	12	Steve Smith, Chi.	4.00
□	13	Kevin Stevens, Pgh.	4.00
□	14	Patrick Roy (G), Mtl.	60.00
□	15	Jaromir Jagr, Pgh.	35.00
□	16	Ron Francis, Pgh.	10.00
□	17	Bill Ranford (G), Edm.	6.00
□	18	Larry Murphy, Pgh.	6.00
□	19	Tom Barrasso (G), Pgh.	6.00
□	20	Adam Graves, NYR.	4.00

1994 - 95 TOPPS STADIUM CLUB

These card have up to six versions: the regular card (1-270), a First Day Issue (1-270), a Stanley Cup Champions card (1-270), a Conference Winners card (Red Wings and Devils only); a Division Winners card (Red Wings, Flames, Flyers and Nordiques only) and a Members Only card (1-270). Stanley Cup. Conference and Division Winners all have the same value. An intended second series for 1994-95 Topps Stadium Club was never released. Instead, Topps released Topps Finest.

Imprint: © 1994 THE TOPPS COMPANY, INC.

			Reg.	F.D.	S.C.	M.O.
Complete Set (275 cards):			30.00	1,200.	15.00	500.00
Common Player:			.15	4.00	.50	1.50
	No.	**Player**	**Reg.**	**F.D.**	**S.C.**	**M.O.**
□□□□	1	Mark Messier, NYR.	.50	25.00	6.00	15.00
□□□□	2	Brad May, Buf.	.15	4.00	.50	1.50
□□□□□	3	Mike Ricci, Que.	.15	4.00	.50	1.50
□□□□□	4	Scott Stevens, N.J.	.15	4.00	.50	1.50
□□□□	5	Keith Tkachuk, Wpg.	.35	20.00	4.00	10.00
□□□□	6	Guy Hebert (G), Ana.	.25	8.00	1.00	3.00
□□□□	7	Jason Arnott, Edm.	.25	8.00	1.00	3.00
□□□□	8	Cam Neely, Bos.	.25	8.00	1.00	3.00
□□□□	9	Adam Graves, NYR.	.15	4.00	.50	1.50
□□□□	10	Pavel Bure, Van.	.75	40.00	8.00	25.00
□□□□	11	Jeff Odgers, S.J.	.15	4.00	.50	1.50
□□□□	12	Dimitri Khristich, Wsh.	.15	4.00	.50	1.50
□□□□	13	Patrick Poulin, Chi.	.15	4.00	.50	1.50
□□□□	14	Mike Donnelly, L.A.	.15	4.00	.50	1.50
□□□□	15	Félix Potvin (G), Tor.	.50	25.00	6.00	15.00
□□□□□□	16	Keith Primeau, Det.	.25	8.00	1.00	3.00
□□□□	17	Fred Knipscheer, Bos.	.15	4.00	.50	1.50
□□□□	18	Mike Keane, Mtl.	.15	4.00	.50	1.50
□□□□	19	Vitali Prokhorov, Stl.	.15	4.00	.50	1.50
□□□□	20	Ray Ferraro, NYI.	.15	4.00	.50	1.50
□□□□	21	Shane Churla, Dal.	.15	4.00	.50	1.50
□□□□	22	Rob Niedermayer, Fla.	.25	8.00	1.00	3.00
□□□□	23	Adam Creighton, T.B.	.15	4.00	.50	1.50
□□□□□	24	Tommy Söderström (G), Pha.	.15	4.00	.50	1.50
□□□□□	25	Theoren Fleury, Cgy.	.35	15.00	2.00	6.00
□□□□	26	Jim Storm, Hfd.	.15	4.00	.50	1.50
□□□□	27	Bret Hedican, Van.	.15	4.00	.50	1.50
□□□□	28	Sean Hill, Ana.	.15	4.00	.50	1.50
□□□□	29	Bill Ranford (G), Edm.	.25	8.00	1.00	3.00
□□□□	30	Derek Plante, Buf.	.15	4.00	.50	1.50
□□□□	31	Dave McLlwain, Ott.	.15	4.00	.50	1.50
□□□□□	32	Iain Fraser, Que.	.15	4.00	.50	1.50
□□□□	33	Patrick Roy (G), Mtl.	2.00	135.00	20.00	75.00
□□□□	34	Martin Straka, Pgh.	.15	4.00	.50	1.50
□□□□□	35	Bruce Driver, N.J.	.15	4.00	.50	1.50
□□□□	36	Brian Skrudland, Fla.	.15	4.00	.50	1.50
□□□□	37	Bob Errey, S.J.	.15	4.00	.50	1.50
□□□□	38	Randy Cunneyworth, Chi.	.15	4.00	.50	1.50
□□□□	39	John Slaney, Wsh.	.15	4.00	.50	1.50
□□□□□□	40	Ray Sheppard, Det.	.15	4.00	.50	1.50
□□□□	41	Sergei Nemchinov, NYR.	.15	4.00	.50	1.50
□□□□	42	Dave Ellett, Tor.	.15	4.00	.50	1.50
□□□□	43	Vincent Riendeau (G), Bos.	.15	4.00	.50	1.50
□□□□□	44	Trent Yawney, Cgy.	.15	4.00	.50	1.50
□□□□	45	Dave Gagner, Dal.	.15	4.00	.50	1.50
□□□□	46	Igor Korolev, Stl.	.15	4.00	.50	1.50
□□□□	47	Gary Shuchuk, L.A.	.15	4.00	.50	1.50
□□□□	48	Rob Zamuner, T.B.	.25	8.00	1.00	3.00
□□□□	49	Frantisek Kucera, Hfd.	.15	4.00	.50	1.50
□□□□	50	Joe Mullen, Pgh.	.15	4.00	.50	1.50
□□□□	51	Ron Hextall (G), NYI.	.25	8.00	1.00	3.00
□□□□	52	J.J. Daigneault, Mtl.	.15	4.00	.50	1.50
□□□□	53	Patrik Carnback, Ana.	.15	4.00	.50	1.50
□□□□	54	Steven Rice, Edm.	.15	4.00	.50	1.50
□□□□	55	Brian Leetch, NYR.	.50	20.00	4.00	10.00
□□□□□	56	Al MacInnis, Cgy.	.25	8.00	1.00	3.00
□□□□	57	Luc Robitaille, L.A.	.25	8.00	1.00	3.00
□□□□	58	Dave Andreychuk, Tor.	.15	4.00	.50	1.50
□□□□	59	Jeremy Roenick, Chi.	.35	15.00	2.00	6.00
□□□□	60	Mario Lemieux, Pgh.	2.00	135.00	20.00	75.00
□□□□	61	Dave Manson, Wpg.	.15	4.00	.50	1.50
□□□□	62	Pat Falloon, S.J.	.15	4.00	.50	1.50
□□□□	63	Jesse Belanger, Fla.	.15	4.00	.50	1.50
□□□□	64	Philippe Boucher, Buf.	.15	4.00	.50	1.50
□□□□	65	Sergio Momesso, Van.	.15	4.00	.50	1.50
□□□□	66	Evgeny Davydov, Ott.	.15	4.00	.50	1.50
□□□□□	67	Alexei Gusarov, Que.	.15	4.00	.50	1.50
□□□□	68	Jaromir Jagr, Pgh.	1.25	80.00	15.00	20.00
□□□□	69	Randy Ladouceur, Ana.	.15	4.00	.50	1.50
□□□□	70	Chris Chelios, Chi.	.35	20.00	4.00	10.00
□□□□	71	John Druce, L.A.	.15	4.00	.50	1.50
□□□□□□	72	Kris Draper, Det.	.15	4.00	.50	1.50
□□□□	73	Joey Kocur, NYR.	.15	4.00	.50	1.50
□□□□	74	Rick Tabaracci (G), Wsh.	.15	4.00	.50	1.50
□□□□	75	Mikael Andersson, T.B.	.15	4.00	.50	1.50
□□□□	76	Mark Osborne, Tor.	.15	4.00	.50	1.50
□□□□	77	Ray Bourque, Bos.	.50	25.00	6.00	15.00
□□□□□	78	Dimitri Yushkevich, Pha.	.15	4.00	.50	1.50
□□□□□	79	Mike Vernon (G), Cgy.	.25	8.00	1.00	3.00
□□□□	80	Steve Thomas, NYI.	.15	4.00	.50	1.50
□□□□	81	Steve Duchesne, Stl.	.15	4.00	.50	1.50
□□□□	82	Dean Evason, Dal.	.15	4.00	.50	1.50
□□□□	83	Jason Smith, N.J.	.15	4.00	.50	1.50
□□□□	84	Bryan Marchment, Hfd.	.15	4.00	.50	1.50
□□□□	85	Boris Mironov, Edm.	.15	4.00	.50	1.50
□□□□	86	Jeff Norton, S.J.	.15	4.00	.50	1.50
□□□□	87	Donald Audette, Buf.	.15	4.00	.50	1.50
□□□□□	88	Eric Lindros, Pha.	1.75	125.00	20.00	70.00
□□□□	89	Garry Valk, Ana.	.15	4.00	.50	1.50
□□□□□	90	Mats Sundin, Que.	.50	25.00	6.00	15.00
□□□□	91	Gerald Diduck, Van.	.15	4.00	.50	1.50
□□□□	92	Jeff Shantz, Chi.	.15	4.00	.50	1.50
□□□□	93	Scott Niedermayer, N.J.	.25	8.00	1.00	3.00
□□□□	94	Troy Mallette, Ott.	.15	4.00	.50	1.50
□□□□	95	John Vanbiesbrouck (G), Fla.	.60	30.00	7.00	20.00
□□□□	96	Ron Francis, Pgh.	.35	15.00	2.00	6.00
□□□□□□	97	Vyacheslav Kozlov, Det.	.15	4.00	.50	1.50
□□□□	98	Ken Baumgartner, Tor.	.15	4.00	.50	1.50
□□□□	99	Wayne Gretzky, L.A.	2.50	200.00	25.00	100.00
□□□□	100	Brett Hull, Stl.	.50	25.00	6.00	15.00
□□□□	101	Marc Bergevin, T.B.	.15	4.00	.50	1.50
□□□□□	102	Owen Nolan, Que.	.25	8.00	1.00	3.00
□□□□	103	Bryan Smolinski, Bos.	.15	4.00	.50	1.50
□□□□	104	Lyle Odelein, Mtl.	.15	4.00	.50	1.50
□□□□	105	Mike Ridley, Wsh.	.15	4.00	.50	1.50
□□□□□	106	Trevor Kidd (G), Cgy.	.25	8.00	1.00	3.00
□□□□	107	Derian Hatcher, Dal.	.25	8.00	1.00	3.00
□□□□	108	Derek King, NYI.	.15	4.00	.50	1.50
□□□□□	109	Rob Zettler, Pha.	.15	4.00	.50	1.50
□□□□	110	Alexander Daigle, Ott.	.25	8.00	1.00	3.00
□□□□	111	Chris Pronger, Hfd.	.25	8.00	1.00	3.00
□□□□	112	Chris Gratton, T.B.	.25	8.00	1.00	3.00
□□□□	113	John Slaney, Wsh.	.15	4.00	.50	1.50
□□□□□	114	Jocelyn Thibault (G), Que.	.75	35.00	7.50	20.00
□□□□	115	Jason Arnott, Edm.	.25	8.00	1.00	3.00
□□□□	116	Alexei Yashin, Ott.	.35	20.00	4.00	10.00
□□□□	117	Rob Niedermayer, Fla.	.25	8.00	1.00	3.00
□□□□	118	Jason Allison, Wsh.	.35	15.00	2.00	6.00
□□□□□	119	Martin Brodeur (G), N.J.	.75	40.00	8.00	25.00
□□□□	120	Pat Verbeek, Hfd.	.15	4.00	.50	1.50
□□□□	121	Kelly Buchberger, Edm.	.15	4.00	.50	1.50
□□□□	122	Doug Lidster, NYR.	.15	4.00	.50	1.50
□□□□	123	Sergei Makarov, S.J.	.15	4.00	.50	1.50
□□□□	124	Kris King, Wpg.	.15	4.00	.50	1.50
□□□□	125	Dominik Hasek (G), Buf.	.75	40.00	8.00	25.00
□□□□□	126	Martin Rucinsky, Que.	.15	4.00	.50	1.50
□□□□	127	Kerry Huffman, Ott.	.15	4.00	.50	1.50
□□□□	128	Gord Murphy, Fla.	.15	4.00	.50	1.50
□□□□□	129	Bobby Holik, N.J.	.15	4.00	.50	1.50
□□□□	130	Kirk Muller, Mtl.	.15	4.00	.50	1.50
□□□□	131	Christian Ruutu, Chi.	.15	4.00	.50	1.50
□□□□	132	Jyrki Lumme, Van.	.15	4.00	.50	1.50
□□□□	133	Ken Wregget (G), Pgh.	.15	4.00	.50	1.50
□□□□	134	Dale Hunter, Wsh.	.15	4.00	.50	1.50
□□□□	135	Rob Blake, L.A.	.25	8.00	1.00	3.00
□□□□	136	Petr Klima, T.B.	.15	4.00	.50	1.50
□□□□	137	Steve Heinze, Bos.	.15	4.00	.50	1.50
□□□□□□	138	Chris Osgood (G), Det.	.35	15.00	2.00	6.00
□□□□	139	John Lilley, Ana.	.15	4.00	.50	1.50
□□□□	140	Dave Andreychuk, Tor.	.15	4.00	.50	1.50
□□□□□	141	Zarley Zalapski, Cgy.	.15	4.00	.50	1.50
□□□□	142	Curtis Joseph (G), Stl.	.60	30.00	7.00	20.00
□□□□	143	Brent Gilchrist, Dal.	.15	4.00	.50	1.50
□□□□	144	Vladimir Malakhov, NYI.	.15	4.00	.50	1.50
□□□□□	145	Mikael Renberg, Pha.	.25	8.00	1.00	3.00
□□□□	146	Robert Kron, Hfd.	.15	4.00	.50	1.50
□□□□	147	Dean McAmmond, Edm.	.15	4.00	.50	1.50
□□□□	148	Doug Bodger, Buf.	.15	4.00	.50	1.50
□□□□	149	Ray Whitney, S.J.	.15	4.00	.50	1.50
□□□□	150	Brian Leetch, NYR.	.35	15.00	2.00	6.00
□□□□□□	151	Martin Lapointe, Det.	.15	4.00	.50	1.50
□□□□	152	Teppo Numminen, Wpg.	.15	4.00	.50	1.50
□□□□□	153	Scott Young, Que.	.15	4.00	.50	1.50
□□□□	154	Nick Kypreos, NYR.	.15	4.00	.50	1.50
□□□□	155	Ed Belfour (G), Chi.	.50	20.00	4.00	10.00
□□□□	156	Greg Adams, Van.	.15	4.00	.50	1.50
□□□□	157	Brian Benning, Fla.	.15	4.00	.50	1.50
□□□□□	158	Bob Carpenter, N.J.	.15	4.00	.50	1.50
□□□□□	159	Vladimir Konstantinov, Det.	.15	4.00	.50	1.50
□□□□	160	Rick Tocchet, Pgh.	.15	4.00	.50	1.50
□□□□	161	Joe Sacco, Ana.	.15	4.00	.50	1.50
□□□□	162	Daren Puppa (G), T.B.	.15	4.00	.50	1.50
□□□□	163	Randy Burridge, Wsh.	.15	4.00	.50	1.50
□□□□	164	Darryl Sydor, L.A.	.15	4.00	.50	1.50
□□□□	165	Jay More, S.J.	.15	4.00	.50	1.50
□□□□□	166	Joe Nieuwendyk, Cgy.	.25	8.00	1.00	3.00
□□□□	167	Mike Eastwood, Tor.	.15	4.00	.50	1.50
□□□□	168	Murray Baron, Stl.	.15	4.00	.50	1.50
□□□□□	169	Brent Fedyk, Pha.	.15	4.00	.50	1.50
□□□□	170	Russ Courtnall, Dal.	.15	4.00	.50	1.50
□□□□	171	Sean Burke (G), Hfd.	.25	8.00	1.00	3.00
□□□□	172	Uwe Krupp, NYI.	.15	4.00	.50	1.50
□□□□	173	Kevin Lowe, NYR.	.15	4.00	.50	1.50
□□□□	174	Guy Carbonneau, Mtl.	.15	4.00	.50	1.50
□□□□	175	Alexei Yashin, Ott.	.35	20.00	4.00	10.00
□□□□	176	Thomas Steen, Wpg.	.15	4.00	.50	1.50
□□□□	177	Sandis Ozolinsh, S.J.	.25	8.00	1.00	3.00
□□□□	178	Patrick Roy (G), Mtl.	1.00	50.00	10.00	30.00
□□□□	179	Dominik Hasek (G), Buf.	.75	40.00	8.00	25.00
□□□□	180	Ed Belfour (G), Chi.	.35	15.00	2.00	6.00
□□□□	181	Mike Richter (G), NYR.	.35	15.00	2.00	6.00
□□□□	182	Ron Hextall (G), NYI.	.25	8.00	1.00	3.00
□□□□	183	Daren Puppa (G), T.B.	.15	4.00	.50	1.50
□□□□	184	Jon Casey (G), Bos.	.15	4.00	.50	1.50
□□□□	185	Félix Potvin (G), Tor.	.50	25.00	6.00	15.00
□□□□□	186	Martin Brodeur (G), N.J.	.75	40.00	8.00	25.00
□□□□	187	Darcy Wakaluk (G), Dal.	.15	4.00	.50	1.50
□□□□	188	Kirk McLean (G), Van.	.25	8.00	1.00	3.00

No.	Player				
189	Mike Vernon (G), Cgy.	.25	8.00	1.00	3.00
190	Arturs Irbe (G), S.J.	.15	4.00	.50	1.50
191	Dino Ciccarelli, Det.	.25	8.00	1.00	3.00
192	Steven Finn, Que.	.15	4.00	.50	1.50
193	Pierre Sévigny, Mtl.	.15	4.00	.50	1.50
194	Jim Dowd, N.J.	.15	4.00	.50	1.50
195	Chris Gratton, T.B.	.25	8.00	1.00	3.00
196	Wayne Presley, Buf.	.15	4.00	.50	1.50
197	Joel Otto, Cgy.	.15	4.00	.50	1.50
198	Fredrik Olausson, Edm.	.15	4.00	.50	1.50
199	Jody Hull, Fla.	.15	4.00	.50	1.50
200	Cliff Ronning, Van.	.15	4.00	.50	1.50
201	Darren Turcotte, Hfd.	.15	4.00	.50	1.50
202	Al Iafrate, Bos.	.15	4.00	.50	1.50
203	Eric Lindros, Pha.	1.00	70.00	12.00	40.00
204	Sandis Ozolinsh, S.J.	.25	8.00	1.00	3.00
205	Petr Nedved, Stl.	.15	4.00	.50	1.50
206	Mark Lamb, Pha.	.15	4.00	.50	1.50
207	Shaun Van Allen, Ana.	.15	4.00	.50	1.50
208	Kelly Hrudey (G), L.A.	.15	4.00	.50	1.50
209	Nikolai Borschevsky, Tor.	.15	4.00	.50	1.50
210	Glen Wesley, Bos.	.15	4.00	.50	1.50
211	Shawn McEachern, Pgh.	.15	4.00	.50	1.50
212	Mark Janssens, Hfd.	.15	4.00	.50	1.50
213	Brian Mullen, NYI.	.15	4.00	.50	1.50
214	Craig Ludwig, Dal.	.15	4.00	.50	1.50
215	Mike Rathje, S.J.	.15	4.00	.50	1.50
216	Stéphane Matteau, NYR.	.15	4.00	.50	1.50
217	Tim Cheveldae (G), Wpg.	.15	4.00	.50	1.50
218	Brent Sutter, Chi.	.15	4.00	.50	1.50
219	Gord Dineen, Ott.	.15	4.00	.50	1.50
220	Kevin Hatcher, Wsh.	.15	4.00	.50	1.50
221	Todd Simon, Buf.	.15	4.00	.50	1.50
222	Bill Lindsay, Fla.	.15	4.00	.50	1.50
223	Kirk McLean (G), Van.	.25	8.00	1.00	3.00
224	Chris Joseph, T.B.	.15	4.00	.50	1.50
225	Valeri Zelepukin, N.J.	.15	4.00	.50	1.50
226	Terry Yake, Ana.	.15	4.00	.50	1.50
227	Benoît Brunet, Mtl.	.15	4.00	.50	1.50
228	Nicklas Lidström, Det.	.25	8.00	1.00	3.00
229	Zdeno Ciger, Edm.	.15	4.00	.50	1.50
230	Gary Roberts, Cgy.	.25	8.00	1.00	3.00
231	Andy Moog (G), Dal.	.25	8.00	1.00	3.00
232	Ed Patterson, Pgh.	.15	4.00	.50	1.50
233	Philippe Bozon, Stl.	.15	4.00	.50	1.50
234	Brent Hughes, Bos.	.15	4.00	.50	1.50
235	Chris Pronger, Hfd.	.25	8.00	1.00	3.00
236	Travis Green, NYI.	.15	4.00	.50	1.50
237	Pat Conacher, L.A.	.15	4.00	.50	1.50
238	Bob Rouse, Tor.	.15	4.00	.50	1.50
239	Yves Racine, Pha.	.15	4.00	.50	1.50
240	Nelson Emerson, Wpg.	.15	4.00	.50	1.50
241	Oleg Petrov, Mtl.	.15	4.00	.50	1.50
242	Steve Larmer, NYR.	.15	4.00	.50	1.50
243	Daniel Laperrière, Stl.	.15	4.00	.50	1.50
244	John McIntyre, Van.	.15	4.00	.50	1.50
245	Alexander Semak, N.J.	.15	4.00	.50	1.50
246	Stéphane Fiset (G), Que.	.25	8.00	1.00	3.00
247	Peter Bondra, Wsh.	.35	20.00	4.00	10.00
248	Dale Hawerchuk, Buf.	.25	8.00	1.00	3.00
249	Jamie Baker, S.J.	.15	4.00	.50	1.50
250	Sergei Fedorov, Det.	.50	25.00	6.00	15.00
251	Derek Mayer, Ott.	.15	4.00	.50	1.50
252	Ivan Droppa, Chi.	.15	4.00	.50	1.50
253	Kent Manderville, Tor.	.15	4.00	.50	1.50
254	Sergei Zholtok, Bos.	.25	8.00	1.00	3.00
255	Murray Craven, Van.	.15	4.00	.50	1.50
256	Todd Krygier, Wsh.	.15	4.00	.50	1.50
257	Brent Grieve, Edm.	.15	4.00	.50	1.50
258	Esa Tikkanen, NYR.	.15	4.00	.50	1.50
259	Brad Dalgarno, NYI.	.15	4.00	.50	1.50
260	Russ Romaniuk, Wpg.	.15	4.00	.50	1.50
261	Stu Barnes, Fla.	.15	4.00	.50	1.50
262	Dan Keczmer, Cgy.	.15	4.00	.50	1.50
263	Eric Desjardins, Mtl.	.25	8.00	1.00	3.00
264	AW: Martin Brodeur (G), N.J.	.75	40.00	8.00	25.00
265	AW: Adam Graves, NYR.	.15	4.00	.50	1.50
266	AW: Cam Neely, Bos.	.25	8.00	1.00	3.00
267	AW: Ray Bourque, Bos.	.35	15.00	4.00	8.00
268	AW: Sergei Fedorov, Det.	.35	15.00	4.00	8.00
269	AW: Dominik Hasek (G), Buf.	.50	25.00	5.00	15.00
270	AW: Wayne Gretzky, L.A.	1.75	135.00	18.00	70.00

DYNASTY AND DESTINY

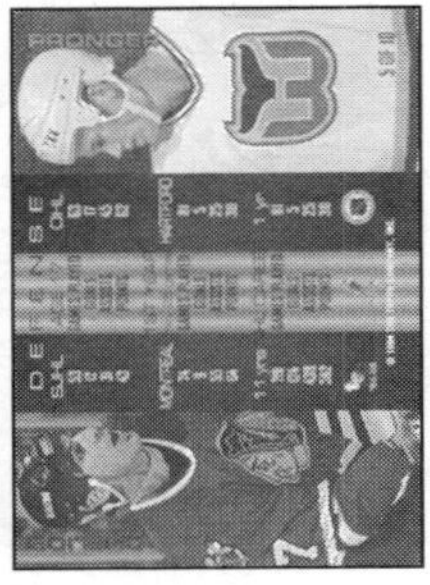

These cards have two versions: the insert and a Members Only card.

Insert Set (5 cards): 30.00 35.00

No.	Player	Insert	M.O.
1	Tom Barrasso (G), Pgh./Arturs Irbe (G), S.J.	3.00	5.00
2	Mark Messier, NYR./Eric Lindros, Pha.	15.00	25.00
3	Pavel Bure, Van./Brett Hull, Stl.	8.50	10.00
4	Luc Robitaille, L.A./Mikael Renberg, Pha.	3.00	5.00
5	Chris Chelios, Chi./Chris Pronger, Hfd.	4.00	6.00

FINEST

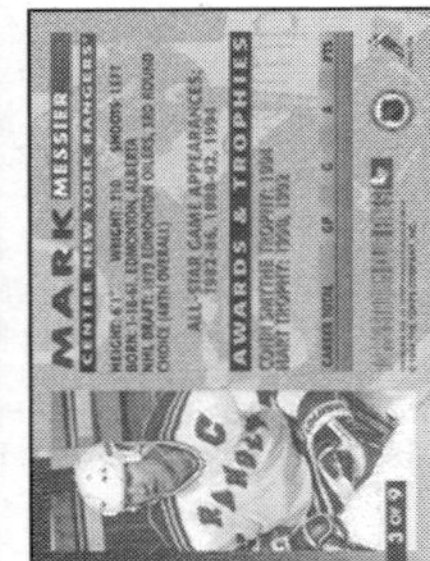

These cards have two versions: the insert and a Members Only card.

Insert Set (9 cards): 75.00 125.00

No.	Player	Insert	M.O.
1	Mario Lemieux, Pgh.	15.00	30.00
2	Brett Hull, Stl.	5.00	10.00
3	Mark Messier, NYR.	5.00	10.00
4	Wayne Gretzky, L.A.	25.00	50.00
5	Pavel Bure, Van.	7.00	15.00
6	Sergei Fedorov, Det.	5.00	10.00
7	Brian Leetch, NYR.	3.00	6.00
8	Ray Bourque, Bos.	5.00	10.00
9	Patrick Roy (G), Mtl.	15.00	30.00

SUPER TEAMS

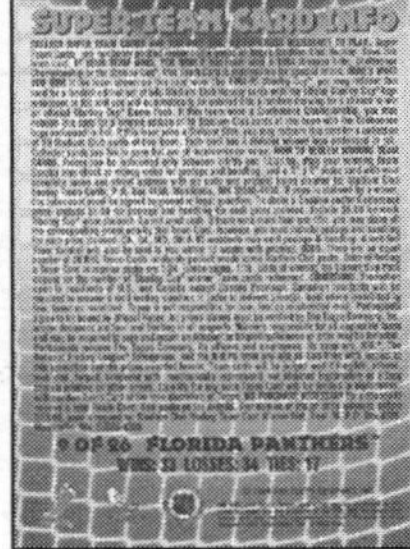

These cards have up to five versions: the Insert (1-26), a Stanley Cup Champions redeemed card (#13 only), a Conference Winners redeemed card (#s 7 and 13 only), a Division Winners redeemed card (#s 4, 7, 17 and 19 only), a Members Only card (1-26) and a Test Proof (1-26). A winner card was redeemed for a gold-stamped Topps Stadium Club/Topps Finest team set or in the case of the Devils, a complete 435-card gold-stamped Stanley Cup Champions set. "Redeemed" Super Team cards sell at 33% of the insert's value. A redeemed Devils Conference Winners set sells at $18; a redeemed Red Wings Conference Winners or Division Winners set sells at $20; a redeemed Flyers Division Winners set sells at $25; a redeemed Nordiques Division Winners set sells at $25; and a redeemed Flames set sells at $15.

Insert Set (26 cards): 110.00 50.00

No.	Player	Insert	M.O.
1	Ana.: Backs (B.Corkum, G.Valk, etc.)	3.00	1.50
2	Bos.: Adam Oates and Cam Neely	5.00	2.50
3	Buf.: Aerial (D.Hasek (G), K.Sutton, R.Ray, R.Smehlik, Der.Plante)	3.00	1.50
4	Cgy.: A. Trefilov and T. Fleury	6.00	3.00
5	Chi.: E. Belfour (G), J. Roenick (Group: Brent Sutter, etc.)	3.00	1.50
6	Dal.: Paul Broten (& Mike Modano, Trent Klatt's back)	3.00	1.50
7	Det.: Bench (C.Osgood, R.Sheppard, S. Fedorov, G.Johnson, etc.)	15.00	7.50
8	Edm.: Backs (B. Beers, B. Ranford (G))	3.00	1.50
9	Fla.: Rob Niedermayer, Mike Foligno (bench: A. Lomakin, etc.)	3.00	1.50
10	Hfd.: J. Storm, S. Burke (G), T. Crowley	3.00	1.50
11	L.A.: Blueline (T. Granato, R. Blake, A. Zhitnik, L.A-51, M.Donnelly)	3.00	1.50
12	Mtl.: Lyle Odelein and Patrick Roy (G)	10.00	5.00
13	N.J.: K. Daneyko, M. Brodeur (G), S. Stevens	15.00	7.50
14	NYI.: Darius Kasparaitis, Yan Kaminsky (& M. McInnis)	3.00	1.50
15	NYR.: Parade (Backs: S. Larmer, B.Leetch, M. Richter (G), M. Messier w/ Cup, A. Graves)	10.00	5.00
16	Ott.: Aerial (Senators warm-up stretches)	3.00	1.50
17	Pha.: Mark Recchi (& Eric Lindros' back, etc.)	12.00	6.00
18	Pgh.: R. Francis (talking to J. Mullen)	3.00	1.50
19	Que.: O. Nolan (& J. Sakic's back, etc.)	7.00	3.50
20	Stl.: C. Joseph, B. Shanahan	6.00	3.00
21	S.J.: T. Pederson and S. Makarov	3.00	1.50
22	T.B.: D. Savard (& P.Klima, S. Chambers)	3.00	1.50
23	Tor.: Gilmour and D. Andreychuk	5.00	2.50
24	Van.: Pavel Bure (bench: N.Lafayette, G.Adams, B.Glynn, etc.)	7.00	3.50
25	Wsh.: Aerial (D. Poulin, K.Hatcher, B. Dafoe (G), C. Johansson)	3.00	1.50
26	Wpg.: Backs (A. Zhamnov, T. Selänne, etc.)	6.00	3.00

1994 - 95 TOPPS STADIUM CLUB – MEMBERS ONLY SET –

Imprint: © 1995 THE TOPPS COMPANY, INC.

Complete Set (50 cards): 20.00

No.	Player	NRMT-MT
1	Patrick Roy (G), Mtl.	3.00
2	Ray Bourque, Bos.	1.00
3	Brian Leetch, NYR.	.50
4	Cam Neely, Bos.	.35
5	Jaromir Jagr, Pgh.	2.00
6	Alexander Mogilny, Buf.	.50
7	John Vanbiesbrouck (G), Fla.	1.25
8	Geoff Sanderson, Hfd.	.20
9	Mark Recchi, Mtl.	.35
10	Scott Stevens, N.J.	.20
11	Roman Hamrlik, T.B.	.35
12	Dominik Hasek (G), Buf.	1.50
13	Joe Sakic, Que.	1.75
14	Alexei Yashin, Ott.	.75
15	Eric Lindros, Pha.	2.50
16	Adam Oates, Bos.	.50
17	Ulf Samuelsson, Pgh.	.20
18	Wendel Clark, Que.	.35
19	Mark Messier, NYR.	1.00
20	Pierre Turgeon, NYI.	.35
21	Mark Tinordi, Min.	.20
22	Ron Francis, Pgh.	.50

No.	Player	Price
23	Jeff Brown, Stl.	.20
24	Tom Kurvers, NYI.	.20
25	Mike Modano, Dal.	1.00
26	Mats Sundin, Tor.	1.00
27	Jeremy Roenick, Chi.	.50
28	Kevin Hatcher, Pgh.	.20
29	Curtis Joseph (G), Stl.	1.25
30	Paul Coffey, Det.	.35
31	Jason Arnott, Edm.	.35
32	Wayne Gretzky, L.A.	4.00
33	Theoren Fleury, Cgy.	.50
34	Al MacInnis, Stl.	.35
35	Ed Belfour (G), Chi.	.50
36	Sergei Fedorov, Det.	1.00
37	Brett Hull, Stl.	1.00
38	Chris Chelios, Chi.	.75
39	Keith Tkachuk, Wpg.	.75
40	Félix Potvin (G), Tor.	1.00
41	Pavel Bure, Van.	1.50
42	Ulf Dahlen, S.J.	.20
43	Teemu Selänne, Wpg.	1.50
44	Doug Gilmour, Tor.	.50
45	Phil Housley, Cgy.	.20
46	Paul Kariya, Ana.	4.00
47	Peter Forsberg, Que.	4.00
48	Jim Carey (G), Wsh.	.35
49	Todd Marchant, Edm.	.20
50	Blaine Lacher (G), Bos.	.20

1994 - 95 UPPER DECK

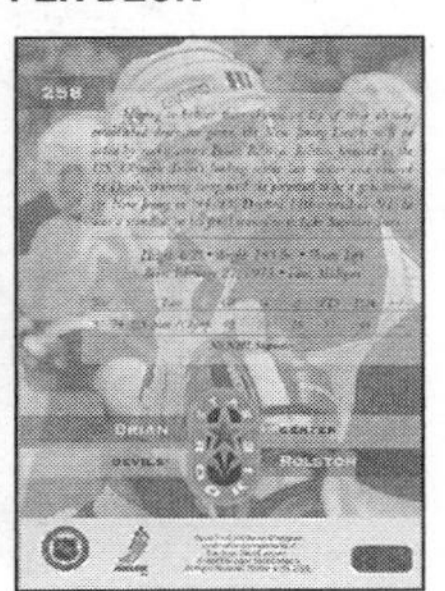

These cards have two versions: the regular card and an Electric Ice parallel.

Series One Imprint: © 1994 THE UPPER DECK COMPANY
Series Two Imprint: © 1995 THE UPPER DECK COMPANY

Series One Set (270 cards):	**30.00**	**1,200.00**
Series Two Set (300 cards):	**35.00**	**1,300.00**
Common Player:	**.10**	**2.50**
Series One Box Bottom (Gretzky):		**3.00**
Series Two Box Bottom (Renberg):		**1.00**
5" x 7" Wayne Gretzky Promo (#1):		**10.00**

No.	Player	Regular	Electric
1	Wayne Gretzky, L.A.	2.50	100.00
2	German Titov, Cgy.	.10	2.50
3	Guy Hebert (G), Ana.	.25	4.00
4	Tony Amonte, Chi.	.25	4.00
5	Dino Ciccarelli, Det.	.25	4.00
6	Geoff Sanderson, Hfd.	.10	2.50
7	Alexei Zhamnov, Wpg.	.25	4.00
8	John MacLean, N.J.	.10	2.50
9	Brent Fedyk, Pha.	.10	2.50
10	Adam Graves, NYR.	.10	2.50
11	Adam Oates, Bos.	.35	6.00
12	Ron Francis, Pgh.	.35	6.00
13	Bobby Dollas, Ana.	.10	2.50
14	Ray Ferraro, NYI.	.10	2.50
15	Paul Broten, Dal.	.10	2.50
16	Ulf Dahlen, S.J.	.10	2.50
17	Pat LaFontaine, Buf.	.25	4.00
18	Craig Janney, Stl.	.10	2.50
19	Garry Galley, Pha.	.10	2.50
20	Gary Roberts, Cgy.	.10	2.50
21	Bill Ranford (G), Edm.	.25	4.00
22	Mario Lemieux, Pgh.	2.00	80.00
23	Glen Murray, Bos.	.10	2.50
24	Paul Coffey, Det.	.25	4.00
25	Corey Millen, N.J.	.10	2.50
26	Chris Chelios, Chi.	.35	8.00
27	Ron Stern, Cgy.	.10	2.50
28	Zdeno Ciger, Edm.	.10	2.50
29	Tony Granato, L.A.	.10	2.50
30	Donald Audette, Buf.	.10	2.50
31	Russ Courtnall, Dal.	.10	2.50
32	Mike Gartner, Tor.	.25	4.00
33	Marty McSorley, L.A.	.10	2.50
34	Jeff Brown, Van.	.10	2.50
35	Mark Janssens, Hfd.	.10	2.50
36	Patrick Poulin, Chi.	.10	2.50
37	Sergei Fedorov, Det.	.50	12.00
38	Tim Sweeney, Ana.	.10	2.50
39	John Slaney, Wsh.	.10	2.50
40	Steve Larmer, NYR.	.10	2.50
41	Dave Karpa, Que.	.10	2.50
42	Esa Tikkanen, Stl.	.10	2.50
43	Joel Otto, Cgy.	.10	2.50
44	Doug Weight, Edm.	.35	6.00
45	Murray Craven, Van.	.10	2.50
46	John Vanbiesbrouck (G), Fla.	.60	15.00
47	Nelson Emerson, Wpg.	.10	2.50
48	Dean Evason, Dal.	.10	2.50
49	Evgeny Davydov, Ott.	.10	2.50
50	Craig Simpson, Buf.	.10	2.50
51	Mats Sundin, Tor.	.50	12.00
52	Chris Pronger, Hfd.	.25	4.00
53	Stéphan Lebeau, Ana.	.10	2.50
54	Martin Gelinas, Van.	.10	2.50
55	Bob Rouse, Det.	.10	2.50
56	Christian Ruutu, Chi.	.10	2.50
57	Gilbert Dionne, Mtl.	.10	2.50
58	Mike Modano, Dal.	.50	12.00
59	Derek King, NYI.	.10	2.50
60	Peter Stastny, Stl.	.10	2.50
61	Ted Donato, Bos.	.10	2.50
62	Mark Messier, NYR.	.50	12.00
63	Dave Manson, Wpg.	.10	2.50
64	Johan Garpenlov, S.J.	.10	2.50
65	Sergio Momesso, Van.	.10	2.50
66	Kirk Muller, Mtl.	.10	2.50
67	David Ellett, Tor.	.10	2.50
68	Dale Hunter, Wsh.	.10	2.50
69	Brent Gretzky, T.B.	.10	2.50
70	Tom Barrasso (G), Pgh.	.25	4.00
71	Philippe Boucher, Buf.	.10	2.50
72	Jesse Belanger, Fla.	.10	2.50
73	Scott Stevens, N.J.	.10	2.50
74	Gary Suter, Chi.	.10	2.50
75	Tim Cheveldae (G), Wpg.	.10	2.50
76	Dimitri Khristich, Wsh.	.10	2.50
77	Pierre Turgeon, NYI.	.25	4.00
78	Mike Richter (G), NYR.	.35	6.00
79	Michael Nylander, Cgy.	.10	2.50
80	Sergei Krivokrasov, Chi.	.10	2.50
81	Andy Moog (G), Dal.	.25	4.00
82	Al Iafrate, Bos.	.10	2.50
83	Bernie Nicholls, Chi.	.10	2.50
84	Darren Turcotte, Hfd.	.10	2.50
85	Igor Larionov, S.J.	.25	4.00
86	Petr Klima, T.B.	.10	2.50
87	Alexandre Daigle, Ott.	.25	4.00
88	Joé Juneau, Wsh.	.10	2.50
89	Glen Wesley, Hfd.	.10	2.50
90	Teemu Selänne, Wpg.	.75	20.00
91	Curtis Joseph (G), Stl.	.60	15.00
92	Scott Mellanby, Fla.	.10	2.50
93	Jaromir Jagr, Pgh.	1.25	40.00
94	Mark Recchi, Pha.	.25	4.00
95	Jiri Slegr, Van.	.10	2.50
96	Martin Brodeur (G), N.J.	.75	20.00
97	Scott Pearson, Edm.	.10	2.50
98	Eric Lindros, Pha.	2.00	80.00
99	Larry Murphy, Pgh.	.25	4.00
100	Sergei Zubov, NYR.	.25	4.00
101	Mathieu Schneider, Mtl.	.10	2.50
102	Dale Hawerchuk, Buf.	.25	4.00
103	Owen Nolan, Que.	.25	4.00
104	Darryl Sydor, L.A.	.10	2.50
105	Anatoli Semenov, Ana.	.10	2.50
106	Marty McInnis, NYI.	.10	2.50
107	Derek Mayer, Ott.	.10	2.50
108	Steve Duchesne, Stl.	.10	2.50
109	Geoff Smith, Fla.	.10	2.50
110	Zarley Zalapski, Cgy.	.10	2.50
111	Rod Brind'Amour, Pha.	.25	4.00
112	Nicklas Lidstrom, Det.	.25	4.00
113	Teppo Numminen, Wpg.	.10	2.50
114	Denny Felsner, Stl.	.10	2.50
115	Wendel Clark, Que.	.25	4.00
116	Arturs Irbe (G), S.J.	.10	2.50
117	Josef Beranek, Pha.	.10	2.50
118	Brian Bradley, T.B.	.10	2.50
119	Eric Weinrich, Chi.	.10	2.50
120	Kevin Todd, L.A.	.10	2.50
121	Patrick Roy (G), Mtl.	2.00	80.00
122	Guy Carbonneau, Stl.	.10	2.50
123	Tom Kurvers, Ana.	.10	2.50
124	Sergei Makarov, S.J.	.10	2.50
125	Pat Peake, Wsh.	.10	2.50
126	Danton Cole, T.B.	.10	2.50
127	Derian Hatcher, Dal.	.25	4.00
128	Kjell Samuelsson, Pgh.	.10	2.50
129	Alexei Yashin, Ott.	.35	8.00
130	Chris Osgood (G), Det.	.35	8.00
131	Kent Manderville, Tor.	.10	2.50
132	Jim Montgomery, Mtl.	.10	2.50
133	Kirk McLean (G), Van.	.25	4.00
134	Kelly Buchberger, Edm.	.10	2.50
135	Peter Bondra, Wsh.	.35	8.00
136	Stéphane Matteau, NYR.	.10	2.50
137	Oleg Petrov, Mtl.	.10	2.50
138	Doug Gilmour, Tor.	.35	6.00
139	Vladimir Malakhov, NYI.	.10	2.50
140	Peter Zezel, Dal.	.10	2.50
141	Mike Vernon (G), Det.	.25	4.00
142	Derek Plante, Buf.	.10	2.50
143	Valeri Zelepukin, N.J.	.10	2.50
144	Kevin Haller, Pha.	.10	2.50
145	Keith Tkachuk, Wpg.	.35	8.00
146	Claude Boivin, Ott.	.10	2.50
147	Jocelyn Thibault (G), Que.	.35	8.00
148	Jyrki Lumme, Van.	.10	2.50
149	Ray Whitney, S.J.	.10	2.50
150	Al MacInnis, Stl.	.25	4.00
151	Kelly Miller, Wsh.	.10	2.50
152	Ray Sheppard, Det.	.10	2.50
153	Aaron Ward, Det.	.10	2.50
154	Damian Rhodes (G), Tor.	.10	2.50
155	Jozef Stumpel, Bos.	.25	4.00
156	Sergei Nemchinov, NYR.	.10	2.50
157	Richard Matvichuk, Dal.	.10	2.50
158	Sean Burke (G), Hfd.	.25	4.00
159	Todd Marchant, Edm.	.10	2.50
160	Ryan McGill, Pha.	.10	2.50
161	Sean Hill, Ott.	.10	2.50
162	Iain Fraser, Que.	.10	2.50
163	Shawn McEachern, Pgh.	.10	2.50
164	Petr Nedved, NYR.	.10	2.50
165	John Lilley, Ana.	.10	2.50
166	Joe Sacco, Ana.	.10	2.50
167	Jason Dawe, Buf.	.10	2.50
168	Mike Rathje, S.J.	.10	2.50
169	Phil Housley, Cgy.	.10	2.50
170	Ron Hextall (G), Pha.	.25	4.00
171	Yves Racine, Mtl.	.10	2.50
172	Boris Mironov, Edm.	.10	2.50
173	Vitali Prokhorov, Stl.	.10	2.50
174	Roman Hamrlik, T.B.	.25	4.00
175	Robert Lang, L.A.	.10	2.50
176	Jody Hull, Fla.	.10	2.50
177	Mike Ridley, Tor.	.10	2.50
178	Dimitri Filimonov, Ott.	.10	2.50
179	René Corbet, Que.	.10	2.50
180	Rob Pearson, Wsh.	.10	2.50
181	Richard Smehlik, Buf.	.10	2.50
182	Rob Gaudreau, S.J.	.10	2.50
183	Bill Houlder, Stl.	.10	2.50
184	Igor Korolev, Stl.	.10	2.50
185	Chris Joseph, T.B.	.10	2.50
186	Shane Churla, Dal.	.10	2.50
187	Rick Tabaracci (G), Wsh.	.10	2.50
188	Alexander Godynyuk, Hfd.	.10	2.50
189	Vladimir Konstantinov, Det.	.10	2.50
190	Markus Naslund, Pgh.	.10	2.50
191	Tom Chorske, N.J.	.10	2.50
192	Thomas Steen, Wpg.	.10	2.50
193	Patrice Brisebois, Mtl.	.10	2.50
194	Luc Robitaille, Pgh.	.20	4.00
195	Michal Sykora, S.J.	.10	2.50
196	Troy Mallette, Ott.	.10	2.50
197	Steve Chiasson, Cgy.	.10	2.50

	No.	Player		
☐☐	198	Jimmy Carson, Hfd.	.10	2.50
☐☐	199	Mike Donnelly, L.A.	.10	2.50
☐☐	200	Mike Sillinger, Det.	.10	2.50
☐☐	201	Martin Rucinsky, Que.	.10	2.50
☐☐	202	Adam Bennett, Edm.	.10	2.50
☐☐	**203**	**Matt Johnson, L.A., RC**	**.10**	**2.50**
☐☐	204	Daren Puppa (G), T.B.	.10	2.50
☐☐	205	Ted Drury, Hfd.	.10	2.50
☐☐	206	Jon Casey (G), Stl.	.10	2.50
☐☐	207	Alexei Kovalev, NYR.	.10	2.50
☐☐	208	Alexei Kasatonov, Bos.	.10	2.50
☐☐	209	Ulf Samuelsson, Pgh.	.10	2.50
☐☐	210	Justin Hocking, L.A.	.10	2.50
☐☐	211	Greg Adams, Van.	.10	2.50
☐☐	212	Greg Johnson, Det.	.10	2.50
☐☐	213	Mike Craig, Tor.	.10	2.50
☐☐	214	Steve Konowalchuk, Wsh.	.10	2.50
☐☐	215	Luke Richardson, Edm.	.10	2.50
☐☐	216	Pavol Demitra, Ott.	.10	2.50
☐☐	217	Brian Benning, Fla.	.10	2.50
☐☐	218	Corey Hirsch (G), NYR.	.10	2.50
☐☐	219	Alexander Semak, N.J.	.10	2.50
☐☐	220	Travis Green, NYI.	.10	2.50
☐☐	221	Turner Stevenson, Mtl.	.10	2.50
☐☐	222	Dmitri Mironov, Tor.	.10	2.50
☐☐	223	Christian Soucy, Chi.	.10	2.50
☐☐	224	Rick Tocchet, L.A.	.10	2.50
☐☐	225	Craig MacTavish, Pha.	.10	2.50
☐☐	226	Wayne Gretzky, L.A. (802)	2.50	100.00
☐☐	227	Pavel Bure, Van.	.35	10.00
☐☐	228	Wayne Gretzky, L.A.	2.00	80.00
☐☐	229	Brett Hull, Stl.	.25	7.50
☐☐	230	Mike Gartner, Tor.	.25	4.00
☐☐	231	Brian Leetch, NYR.	.25	4.00
☐☐	232	Al MacInnis, Stl.	.25	4.00
☐☐	233	Dominik Hasek, Buf.	.35	10.00
☐☐	234	Mark Messier, NYR.	.25	7.50
☐☐	235	Paul Kariya, Ana.	2.25	65.00
☐☐	236	Jamie Storr (G), L.A.	.25	4.00
☐☐	237	Jeff Friesen, S.J.	.25	4.00
☐☐	238	Kenny Jonsson, Tor.	.10	2.50
☐☐	**239**	**Mariusz Czerkawski, Bos., RC**	**.10**	**2.50**
☐☐	240	Brett Lindros, NYI.	.10	2.50
☐☐	241	Andrei Nikolishin, Hfd.	.10	2.50
☐☐	242	Jason Allison, Wsh.	.35	6.00
☐☐	243	Oleg Tverdovsky, Ana.	.10	2.50
☐☐	244	Brian Savage, Mtl.	.10	2.50
☐☐	245	Peter Forsberg, Que.	2.00	50.00
☐☐	246	Patrik Juhlin, Pha.	.10	2.50
☐☐	247	Jassen Cullimore, Van.	.10	2.50
☐☐	248	Chris Therien, Pha.	.10	2.50
☐☐	249	Kevin Brown, L.A.	.10	2.50
☐☐	250	Jeff Nelson, Wsh.	.10	2.50
☐☐	251	Janne Laukkanen, Que.	.10	2.50
☐☐	252	Jamie McLennan (G), NYI.	.25	4.00
☐☐	253	Craig Johnson, Stl.	.10	2.50
☐☐	**254**	**Ravil Gusmanov, Wpg., RC**	**.10**	**2.50**
☐☐	255	Valeri Bure, Mtl.	.10	2.50
☐☐	256	Valeri Karpov, Ana.	.10	2.50
☐☐	257	Michael Peca, Van.	.25	4.00
☐☐	258	Brian Rolston, N.J.	.10	2.50
☐☐	259	Brandon Convery, Tor.	.10	2.50
☐☐	**260**	**Mark Lawrence, Dal., RC**	**.10**	**2.50**
☐☐	261	Adam Deadmarsh, Que.	.10	2.50
☐☐	262	Jason Wiemer, T.B.	.10	2.50
☐☐	263	Alexander Cherbayev, S.J.	.10	2.50
☐☐	264	Sergei Gonchar, Wsh.	.10	2.50
☐☐	265	Viktor Kozlov, S.J.	.10	2.50
☐☐	266	Vladislav Boulin, Pha.	.10	2.50
☐☐	267	Todd Harvey, Dal.	.10	2.50
☐☐	268	Cory Stillman, Cgy.	.10	2.50
☐☐	**269**	**David Oliver, Edm., RC**	**.10**	**2.50**
☐☐	270	Andrei Nazarov, S.J.	.10	2.50
☐☐	271	Mikael Renberg, Pha.	.25	4.00
☐☐	272	Andrei Kovalenko, Que.	.10	2.50
☐☐	273	Neal Broten, Dal.	.10	2.50
☐☐	274	Ed Olczyk, NYR.	.10	2.50
☐☐	275	Steve Thomas, NYI.	.10	2.50
☐☐	276	Joe Nieuwendyk, Cgy.	.25	4.00
☐☐	277	Rob Gaudreau, Ott.	.10	2.50
☐☐	278	Pat Verbeek, Hfd.	.10	2.50
☐☐	279	Eric Desjardins, Pha.	.25	4.00
☐☐	280	Vincent Damphousse, Mtl.	.25	4.00
☐☐	281	John Cullen, Pgh.	.10	2.50
☐☐	282	Garry Valk, Ana.	.10	2.50
☐☐	283	Daniel Lacroix, Bos.	.10	2.50
☐☐	284	Mike Ricci, Que.	.10	2.50
☐☐	285	Dominik Hasek (G), Buf.	.75	20.00
☐☐	286	Geoff Courtnall, Van.	.10	2.50
☐☐	287	Rob Niedermayer, Fla.	.25	4.00
☐☐	288	Alexander Karpovtsev, NYR.	.10	2.50
☐☐	289	Martin Straka, Pgh.	.10	2.50
☐☐	290	Ed Belfour (G), Chi.	.35	6.00
☐☐	291	Dave Lowry, Fla.	.10	2.50
☐☐	292	Brendan Shanahan, Stl.	.60	15.00
☐☐	293	Jari Kurri, L.A.	.25	4.00
☐☐	294	Steven Rice, Hfd.	.10	2.50
☐☐	295	Scott Levins, Ott.	.10	2.50
☐☐	296	Ray Bourque, Bos.	.50	12.00
☐☐	297	Mikael Andersson, T.B.	.10	2.50
☐☐	298	Darius Kasparaitis, NYI.	.10	2.50
☐☐	299	Chris Simon, Que.	.10	2.50
☐☐	300	Steve Yzerman, Det.	1.25	40.00
☐☐	301	Don McSween, Ana.	.10	2.50
☐☐	302	Brian Noonan, NYR.	.10	2.50
☐☐	303	Claude Lemieux, N.J.	.10	2.50
☐☐	**304**	**Radek Bonk, Ott., RC**	**.25**	**4.00**
☐☐	305	Jason Arnott, Edm.	.25	4.00
☐☐	**306**	**Ian Laperrière, Stl., RC**	**.10**	**2.50**
☐☐	307	Pat Falloon, S.J.	.10	2.50
☐☐	308	Kris King, Wpg.	.10	2.50
☐☐	309	Brian Bellows, Mtl.	.10	2.50
☐☐	310	Uwe Krupp, Que.	.10	2.50
☐☐	311	Paul Cavallini, Dal.	.10	2.50
☐☐	312	Shaun Van Allen, Ana.	.10	2.50
☐☐	313	Dave Andreychuk, Tor.	.10	2.50
☐☐	314	Bobby Holik, N.J.	.10	2.50
☐☐	315	Theoren Fleury, Cgy.	.35	6.00
☐☐	316	Mark Osborne, NYR.	.10	2.50
☐☐	317	Andrew Cassels, Hfd.	.10	2.50
☐☐	318	Chris Tamer, Pgh.	.10	2.50
☐☐	319	Trevor Linden, Van.	.25	4.00
☐☐	320	Tom Fitzgerald, Fla.	.10	2.50
☐☐	321	Ron Tugnutt (G), Mtl.	.10	2.50
☐☐	322	Jeremy Roenick, Chi.	.35	6.00
☐☐	323	Todd Marchant, Edm.	.10	2.50
☐☐	324	Scott Niedermayer, N.J.	.25	4.00
☐☐	**325**	**Tim Taylor, Det., RC**	**.10**	**2.50**
☐☐	326	Mike Kennedy, Dal.	.10	2.50
☐☐	327	Stephen Heinze, Bos.	.10	2.50
☐☐	328	David Sacco, Ana.	.10	2.50
☐☐	329	Sergei Brylin, N.J.	.10	2.50
☐☐	330	John LeClair, Pha.	.50	12.00
☐☐	331	Brian Skrudland, Fla.	.10	2.50
☐☐	332	Kevin Hatcher, Dal.	.10	2.50
☐☐	333	Brett Hull, Stl.	.50	12.00
☐☐	334	Alexander Mogilny, Buf.	.35	6.00
☐☐	335	Sylvain Lefebvre, Que.	.10	2.50
☐☐	336	Sylvain Turgeon, Ott.	.10	2.50
☐☐	337	Keith Primeau, Det.	.25	4.00
☐☐	**338**	**Eric Fichaud (G), Tor., RC**	**.50**	**8.00**
☐☐	339	Jeff Beukeboom, NYR.	.10	2.50
☐☐	340	Cory Cross, T.B.	.10	2.50
☐☐	341	J.J. Daigneault, Mtl.	.10	2.50
☐☐	342	Stephen Leach, Bos.	.10	2.50
☐☐	343	Zigmund Palffy, NYI.	.35	8.00
☐☐	344	Igor Korolev, Wpg.	.10	2.50
☐☐	345	Chris Gratton, T.B.	.25	4.00
☐☐	346	Joe Mullen, Pgh.	.10	2.50
☐☐	347	Brent Gilchrist, Dal.	.10	2.50
☐☐	348	Adam Creighton, Stl.	.10	2.50
☐☐	349	Dimitri Yushkevich, Pha.	.10	2.50
☐☐	350	Wes Walz, Cgy.	.10	2.50
☐☐	351	Shayne Corson, Edm.	.25	4.00
☐☐	352	Eric Lacroix, L.A.	.10	2.50
☐☐	353	Maxim Bets, Ana.	.10	2.50
☐☐	354	Sylvain Côté, Wsh.	.10	2.50
☐☐	355	Valeri Kamensky, Que.	.25	4.00
☐☐	356	Shjon Podein, Pha.	.10	2.50
☐☐	357	Robert Reichel, Cgy.	.25	4.00
☐☐	358	Cliff Ronning, Van.	.10	2.50
☐☐	359	Bill Guerin, N.J.	.25	4.00
☐☐	360	Dallas Drake, Wpg.	.10	2.50
☐☐	361	Robert Petrovicky, Hfd.	.10	2.50
☐☐	362	Ken Wregget (G), Pgh.	.10	2.50
☐☐	363	Todd Elik, S.J.	.10	2.50
☐☐	364	Cam Neely, Bos.	.20	4.00
☐☐	365	Darren McCarty, Det.	.25	2.50
☐☐	366	Shean Donovan, S.J.	.10	2.50
☐☐	367	Félix Potvin (G), Tor.	.50	12.00
☐☐	368	Yuri Khmylev, Buf.	.10	2.50
☐☐	369	Mark Tinordi, Wsh.	.10	2.50
☐☐	370	Craig Billington (G), Ott.	.10	2.50
☐☐	371	Patrick Flatley, NYI.	.10	2.50
☐☐	372	Jocelyn Lemieux, Hfd.	.10	2.50
☐☐	373	Vyacheslav Kozlov, Det.	.10	2.50
☐☐	374	Trent Klatt, Dal.	.10	2.50
☐☐	**375**	**Geoff Sarjeant, Stl., RC**	**.10**	**2.50**
☐☐	376	Bob Kudelski, Fla.	.10	2.50
☐☐	**377**	**Stanislav Neckar, Ott., RC**	**.25**	**4.00**
☐☐	**378**	**Jon Rohloff, Bos., RC**	**.10**	**2.50**
☐☐	379	Jeff Shantz, Chi.	.10	2.50
☐☐	380	Dale Craigwell, S.J.	.10	2.50
☐☐	381	Adrien Plavsic, Van.	.10	2.50
☐☐	382	Dave Gagner, Dal.	.10	2.50
☐☐	383	Dave Archibald, Ott.	.10	2.50
☐☐	384	Gilbert Dionne, Pha.	.10	2.50
☐☐	385	Troy Loney, NYI.	.10	2.50
☐☐	386	Deam McAmmond, Edm.	.10	2.50
☐☐	387	Pauli Jaks (G), L.A.	.10	4.00
☐☐	388	Stéphane Richer, N.J.	.10	2.50
☐☐	389	Don Beaupré (G), Ott.	.10	2.50
☐☐	390	Kevin Stevens, Pgh.	.10	2.50
☐☐	391	Brad May, Buf.	.10	2.50
☐☐	392	Neil Wilkinson, Wpg.	.10	2.50
☐☐	393	Kevin Lowe, NYR.	.10	2.50
☐☐	394	Fredrik Olausson, Edm.	.10	2.50
☐☐	395	Trevor Kidd (G), Cgy.	.25	4.00
☐☐	396	Brent Grieve, Chi.	.10	2.50
☐☐	397	Dominic Roussel (G), Pha.	.10	2.50
☐☐	398	Bret Hedican, Van.	.10	2.50
☐☐	399	Bryan Smolinski, Bos.	.10	2.50
☐☐	400	Doug Lidster, Stl.	.10	2.50
☐☐	401	Bob Errey, S.J.	.10	2.50
☐☐	402	Pierre Sévigny, Mtl.	.10	2.50
☐☐	403	Rob Brown, L.A.	.10	2.50
☐☐	404	Joe Sakic, Que.	1.00	25.00
☐☐	405	Nikolai Borschevsky, Tor.	.10	2.50
☐☐	406	Martin Lapointe, Det.	.10	2.50
☐☐	**407**	**Jean Yves Roy, NYR., RC**	**.10**	**4.00**
☐☐	408	Robert Kron, Hfd.	.10	2.50
☐☐	409	Tie Domi, Wpg.	.10	2.50
☐☐	410	Jim Dowd, N.J.	.10	2.50
☐☐	411	Keith Jones, Wsh.	.10	2.50
☐☐	412	Scott Lachance, NYI.	.10	2.50
☐☐	413	Bob Corkum, Ana.	.10	2.50
☐☐	**414**	**Denis Chassé, Stl., RC**	**.10**	**2.50**
☐☐	415	Denis Savard, T.B.	.25	4.00
☐☐	416	Joe Murphy, Chi.	.10	2.50
☐☐	417	Viatcheslav Butsayev, S.J.	.10	2.50
☐☐	**418**	**Mattias Norstrom, NYR., RC**	**.10**	**2.50**
☐☐	419	Sergei Zholtok, Bos.	.25	4.00
☐☐	420	Nikolai Khabibulin (G), Wpg.	.35	6.00
☐☐	421	Pat Elynuik, Ott.	.10	2.50
☐☐	422	Doug Brown, Det.	.10	2.50
☐☐	423	Dave McLlwain, Ott.	.10	2.50
☐☐	424	James Patrick, Cgy.	.10	2.50
☐☐	**425**	**Alexander Selivanov, T.B., RC**	**.10**	**2.50**
☐☐	426	Scott Thornton, Edm.	.10	2.50
☐☐	427	Todd Ewen, Ana.	.10	2.50
☐☐	428	Peter Popovic, Mtl.	.10	2.50
☐☐	429	Jarkko Varvio, Dal.	.10	2.50
☐☐	430	Paul Ranheim, Hfd.	.10	2.50
☐☐	431	Kevin Dineen, Pha.	.10	2.50
☐☐	432	Kelly Hrudey (G), L.A.	.10	2.50
☐☐	**433**	**Michal Grosek, Wpg., RC**	**.10**	**2.50**
☐☐	434	Viacheslav Fetisov, N.J.	.25	4.00
☐☐	435	Ivan Droppa, Chi.	.10	2.50
☐☐	436	Benoît Hogue, NYI.	.10	2.50
☐☐	437	Sheldon Kennedy, Cgy.	.10	2.50
☐☐	438	Gord Murphy, Fla.	.10	2.50
☐☐	439	Jamie Baker, S.J.	.10	2.50
☐☐	440	Todd Gill, Tor.	.10	2.50
☐☐	441	Mark Recchi, Mtl.	.25	4.00
☐☐	**442**	**Ted Crowley, Hfd., RC**	**.10**	**2.50**
☐☐	**443**	**Ryan Smyth, Edm., RC**	**3.00**	**35.00**
☐☐	444	Brian Leetch, NYR.	.35	6.00
☐☐	445	Bob Sweeney, Buf.	.10	2.50
☐☐	446	Don Sweeney, Bos.	.10	2.50
☐☐	**447**	**Byron Dafoe (G), Wsh., RC**	**.25**	**4.00**
☐☐	448	Nathan Lafayette, Van.	.10	2.50
☐☐	449	Keith Carney, Chi.	.10	2.50
☐☐	450	Stéphane Fiset (G). Que.	.25	4.00
☐☐	451	Kevin Miller, Stl.	.10	2.50
☐☐	**452**	**Craig Darby, Mtl., RC**	**.10**	**2.50**

	No.	Player		
☐☐	453	Vlastimil Kroupa, S.J.	.10	2.50
☐☐	454	Rob Zettler, Pha.	.10	2.50
☐☐	455	Glenn Healy (G), NYR.	.10	2.50
☐☐	456	Todd Simon, Buf.	.10	2.50
☐☐	457	Mark Fitzpatrick (G), Fla.	.10	2.50
☐☐	458	Drake Berehowsky, Tor.	.10	2.50
☐☐	459	Darcy Wakaluk (G), Hfd.	.10	2.50
☐☐	460	Enrico Ciccone, T.B.	.10	2.50
☐☐	461	Tomas Sandström, Pgh.	.10	2.50
☐☐	**462**	**Mikhail Shtalenkov (G), Ana., RC**	**.10**	**2.50**
☐☐	463	Igor Kravchuk, Edm.	.10	2.50
☐☐	464	Jamie Allison, Cgy.	.10	2.50
☐☐	465	Gino Odjick, Van.	.10	2.50
☐☐	466	Norm Maciver, Ott.	.10	2.50
☐☐	467	Terry Carkner, Det.	.10	2.50
☐☐	468	Rob Zamuner, T.B.	.25	4.00
☐☐	469	Pavel Bure, Van.	.75	20.00
☐☐	**470**	**Patrice Tardiff, Stl., RC**	**.10**	**2.50**
☐☐	471	Andrei Lomakin, Fla.	.10	2.50
☐☐	472	Kirk Maltby, Edm.	.10	2.50
☐☐	473	Jaroslav Modry, N.J.	.10	2.50
☐☐	474	Tommy Söderström (G), NYI.	.10	2.50
☐☐	475	Patrik Carnback, Ana.	.10	2.50
☐☐	476	Jeff Reese (G), Hfd.	.10	2.50
☐☐	477	Todd Krygier, Ana.	.10	2.50
☐☐	478	John McIntyre, Van.	.10	2.50
☐☐	479	Joey Kocur, NYR.	.10	2.50
☐☐	**480**	**Steve Rucchin, Ana., RC**	**.25**	**4.00**
☐☐	481	Bob Bassen, Que.	.10	2.50
☐☐	**482**	**Marek Malik, Hfd., RC**	**.10**	**2.50**
☐☐	483	Darryl Shannon, Wpg.	.10	2.50
☐☐	484	Shawn Burr, Det.	.10	2.50
☐☐	485	Louie DeBrusk, Edm.	.10	2.50
☐☐	486	Olaf Kolzig (G), Wsh.	.35	6.00
☐☐	487	Cam Stewart, Bos.	.10	2.50
☐☐	488	Rob Blake, L.A.	.25	4.00
☐☐	489	Eric Charron, T.B.	.10	2.50
☐☐	490	Sandis Ozolinsh, S.J.	.25	4.00
☐☐	491	Paul Ysebaert, Chi.	.10	2.50
☐☐	492	Kris Draper, Det.	.10	2.50
☐☐	493	Stu Barnes, Fla.	.10	2.50
☐☐	494	Doug Bodger, Buf.	.10	2.50
☐☐	**495**	**Blaine Lacher (G), Bos., RC**	**.10**	**2.50**
☐☐	**496**	**Ed Jovanovski, Cdn., RC**	**1.75**	**25.00**
☐☐	**497**	**Eric Dazé, Cdn., RC**	**1.75**	**25.00**
☐☐	**498**	**Dan Cloutier (G), Cdn., RC**	**1.75**	**25.00**
☐☐	**499**	**Chad Allan, Cdn., RC**	**.10**	**2.50**
☐☐	500	Todd Harvey, Cdn.	.10	2.50
☐☐	**501**	**Jamie Rivers, Cdn., RC**	**.10**	**2.50**
☐☐	502	Bryan McCabe, Cdn.	.10	2.50
☐☐	**503**	**Darcy Tucker, Cdn., RC**	**.10**	**2.50**
☐☐	**504**	**Wade Redden, Cdn., RC**	**.75**	**12.00**
☐☐	**505**	**Nolan Baumgartner, Cdn., RC**	**.10**	**2.50**
☐☐	506	Marek Malik, Cze.	.10	2.50
☐☐	**507**	**Petr Cajanek, Cze., RC**	**.10**	**2.50**
☐☐	**508**	**Jan Hlavac, Cze., RC**	**.10**	**2.50**
☐☐	**509**	**Ladislav Kohn, Cze., RC**	**.10**	**2.50**
☐☐	**510**	**Kimmo Timonen, Fin., RC**	**.10**	**2.50**
☐☐	**511**	**Antti Aalto, Fin., RC**	**.10**	**2.50**
☐☐	**512**	**Tommi Rajamaki, Fin., RC**	**.10**	**2.50**
☐☐	**513**	**Vitali Yachmenev, Rus., RC**	**.50**	**12.00**
☐☐	**514**	**Vadim Epantchinsev, Rus., RC**	**.10**	**2.50**
☐☐	**515**	**Dmitri Klevakin, Rus., RC**	**.10**	**2.50**
☐☐	**516**	**Nikolai Zavarukhin, Rus., RC**	**.10**	**2.50**
☐☐	**517**	**Alexandre Koroliouk, Rus., RC**	**.10**	**2.50**
☐☐	518	Anders Eriksson, Swe.	.10	2.50
☐☐	519	Jesper Mattsson, Swe.	.10	2.50
☐☐	**520**	**Mattias Ohlund, Swe., RC**	**2.50**	**30.00**
☐☐	**521**	**Anders Soderberg, Swe., RC**	**.10**	**2.50**
☐☐	**522**	**Bryan Berard, USA., RC**	**2.75**	**30.00**
☐☐	523	Jason Bonsignore, USA.	.10	2.50
☐☐	524	Deron Quint, USA.	.10	2.50
☐☐	525	Richard Park, USA.	.10	2.50
☐☐	526	Jeff Friesen, S.J.	.10	2.50
☐☐	527	Paul Kariya, Ana.	1.25	40.00
☐☐	528	Peter Forsberg, Que.	1.00	30.00
☐☐	529	Zigmund Palffy, NYI.	.25	4.00
☐☐	530	Kenny Jonsson, Tor.	.10	2.50
☐☐	531	Jamie Storr (G), L.A.	.25	4.00
☐☐	532	Alexander Selivanov, T.B.	.10	2.50
☐☐	533	Michael Peca, Van.	.25	4.00
☐☐	534	Mariusz Czerkawski, Bos.	.10	2.50
☐☐	535	Jason Allison, Wsh.	.10	2.50
☐☐	536	Todd Harvey, Dal.	.10	2.50
☐☐	537	Brett Lindros, NYI.	.10	2.50
☐☐	538	Radek Bonk, Ott.	.10	2.50
☐☐	539	Blaine Lacher (G), Bos.	.10	2.50
☐☐	540	Oleg Tverdovsky, Ana.	.10	2.50
☐☐	541	Wayne Gretzky, L.A.	1.50	50.00
☐☐	542	Radek Bonk, Ott.	.10	2.50
☐☐	543	Mariusz Czerkawski, Bos.	.10	2.50
☐☐	544	Jaromir Jagr, Pgh.	.75	25.00
☐☐	545	Dominik Hasek (G), Buf.	.50	15.00
☐☐	546	Todd Harvey, Dal.	.10	2.50
☐☐	547	Michael Peca, Van.	.25	4.00
☐☐	548	Mats Sundin, Tor.	.25	4.00
☐☐	549	Doug Weight, Edm.	.25	4.00
☐☐	550	Steve Yzerman, Det.	.50	15.00
☐☐	551	Brett Lindros, NYI.	.10	2.50
☐☐	552	Alexander Mogilny, Buf.	.25	4.00
☐☐	553	Patrik Juhlin, Pha.	.10	2.50
☐☐	554	Alexei Yashin, Ott.	.25	4.00
☐☐	555	Peter Forsberg, Que.	.75	25.00
☐☐	556	Michael Nylander, Cgy.	.10	2.50
☐☐	557	Teemu Selänne, Wpg.	.35	10.00
☐☐	558	Marek Malik, Hfd.	.10	2.50
☐☐	559	Jari Kurri, L.A.	.20	4.00
☐☐	560	Kenny Jonsson, Tor.	.10	2.50
☐☐	561	Mikael Renberg, Pha.	.20	4.00
☐☐	562	Adam Deadmarsh, Que.	.10	2.50
☐☐	563	Mark Messier, NYR.	.25	6.00
☐☐	564	Rob Blake, L.A.	.25	4.00
☐☐	565	Janne Laukkanen, Que.	.10	2.50
☐☐	566	Theoren Fleury, Cgy.	.20	4.00
☐☐	567	Alexei Kovalev, NYR.	.10	2.50
☐☐	568	Jamie Storr (G), L.A.	.20	4.00
☐☐	569	Brett Hull, Stl.	.25	6.00
☐☐	570	Valeri Karpov, Ana.	.10	2.50

ICE GALLERY

Insert Set (15 cards): **65.00**

	No.	Player	NRMT-MT
☐	IG1	Steve Yzerman, Det.	10.00
☐	IG2	Jason Arnott, Edm.	2.50
☐	IG3	Jeremy Roenick, Chi.	3.00
☐	IG4	Brendan Shanahan, Stl.	6.00
☐	IG5	Scott Stevens, N.J.	1.50
☐	IG6	Scott Niedermayer, N.J.	2.50
☐	IG7	Adam Graves, NYR.	1.50
☐	IG8	Mike Modano, Dal.	5.00
☐	IG9	Kirk Muller, Mtl.	1.50
☐	IG10	Alexandre Daigle, Ott.	2.50
☐	IG11	Martin Brodeur (G), N.J.	7.00
☐	IG12	Gary Valk, Ana.	1.50
☐	IG13	Teemu Selänne, Wpg.	7.00
☐	IG14	Pat LaFontaine, Buf.	2.50
☐	IG15	Wayne Gretzky, L.A.	20.00

SP INSERTS

Complete Set (180 cards): **100.00** **375.00**
Common Player: **.35** **1.00**

	No.	Player	SP	Die-Cut
☐☐	SP1	Maxim Bets, Ana.	.35	1.00
☐☐	SP2	Stéphan Lebeau, Ana.	.35	1.00
☐☐	SP3	Gary Valk, Ana.	.35	1.00
☐☐	SP4	Ray Bourque, Bos.	2.00	8.00
☐☐	SP5	Mariusz Czerkawski, Bos.	.35	1.00
☐☐	SP6	Cam Neely, Bos.	.75	2.00
☐☐	SP7	Adam Oates, Bos.	1.25	4.00
☐☐	SP8	Dominik Hasek (G), Buf.	3.00	12.00
☐☐	SP9	Dale Hawerchuk, Buf.	.75	2.00
☐☐	SP10	Alexander Mogilny, Buf.	1.25	4.00
☐☐	SP11	Theoren Fleury, Cgy.	1.25	4.00
☐☐	SP12	Trevor Kidd (G), Cgy.	.75	2.00
☐☐	SP13	Joe Nieuwendyk, Cgy.	.75	2.00
☐☐	SP14	Gary Roberts, Cgy.	.75	2.00
☐☐	SP15	Ed Belfour (G), Chi.	1.25	4.00
☐☐	SP16	Chris Chelios, Chi.	1.75	6.00
☐☐	SP17	Jeremy Roenick, Chi.	1.25	4.00
☐☐	SP18	Neal Broten, Dal.	.35	1.00
☐☐	SP19	Russ Courtnall, Dal.	.35	1.00
☐☐	SP20	Derian Hatcher, Dal.	.75	2.00
☐☐	SP21	Mike Modano, Dal.	2.00	8.00
☐☐	SP22	Paul Coffey, Det.	.75	2.00
☐☐	SP23	Vyachaslav Kozlov, Det.	.35	1.00
☐☐	SP24	Keith Primeau, Det.	.75	2.00
☐☐	SP25	Steve Yzerman, Det.	4.00	20.00
☐☐	SP26	Jason Arnott, Edm.	.75	2.00
☐☐	SP27	Bill Ranford (G), Edm.	.75	2.00
☐☐	SP28	Doug Weight, Edm.	1.25	4.00
☐☐	SP29	Bob Kudelski, Fla.	.35	1.00
☐☐	SP30	Rob Niedermayer, Fla.	.75	2.00
☐☐	SP31	John Vanbiesbrouck (G), Fla.	2.50	12.00
☐☐	SP32	Andrew Cassels, Hfd.	.35	1.00
☐☐	SP33	Chris Pronger, Hfd.	.75	2.00
☐☐	SP34	Geoff Sanderson, Hfd.	.35	1.00
☐☐	SP35	Rob Blake, Hfd.	.75	2.00
☐☐	SP36	Wayne Gretzky, L.A.	8.00	40.00
☐☐	SP38	Alexei Zhitnik, L.A.	.35	1.00
☐☐	SP39	Vincent Damphousse, Mtl.	.75	2.00
☐☐	SP40	Kirk Muller, Mtl.	.35	1.00
☐☐	SP41	Oleg Petrov, Mtl.	.35	1.00
☐☐	SP42	Patrick Roy (G), Mtl.	6.50	30.00
☐☐	SP43	Martin Brodeur (G), N.J.	3.00	15.00
☐☐	SP44	Stéphane Richer, N.J.	.35	1.00
☐☐	SP45	Scott Stevens, N.J.	.35	1.00
☐☐	SP46	Darius Kasparaitis, NYI.	.35	1.00
☐☐	SP47	Vladamir Malakhov, NYI.	.35	1.00
☐☐	SP48	Pierre Turgeon, NYI.	.75	2.00
☐☐	SP49	Alexei Kovalev, NYR.	.35	1.00
☐☐	SP50	Brian Leetch, NYR.	1.25	4.00
☐☐	SP51	Mark Messier, NYR.	2.00	8.00
☐☐	SP52	Mike Richter (G), NYR.	1.25	4.00
☐☐	SP53	Craig Billington (G), Ott.	.35	1.00
☐☐	SP54	Alexandre Daigle, Ott.	.75	2.00
☐☐	SP55	Alexei Yashin, Ott.	1.75	6.00
☐☐	SP56	Josef Beranek, Pha.	.35	1.00
☐☐	SP57	Rod Brind'Amour, Pha.	.75	2.00
☐☐	SP58	Mark Recchi, Pha.	.75	2.00
☐☐	SP59	Mikael Renberg, Pha.	.75	2.00
☐☐	SP60	Jaromir Jagr, Pgh.	4.00	20.00
☐☐	SP61	Mario Lemieux, Pgh.	6.50	30.00
☐☐	SP62	Kevin Stevens, Pgh.	.35	1.00
☐☐	SP63	Owen Nolan, Que.	.75	2.00
☐☐	SP64	Mike Ricci, Que.	.35	1.00
☐☐	SP65	Joe Sakic, Que.	3.50	18.00
☐☐	SP66	Brett Hull, Stl.	2.00	8.00
☐☐	SP67	Craig Janney, Stl.	.35	1.00
☐☐	SP68	Curtis Joseph (G), Stl.	2.50	12.00
☐☐	SP69	Brendan Shanahan, Stl.	2.50	12.00
☐☐	SP70	Ulf Dahlen, S.J.	.35	1.00
☐☐	SP71	Arturs Irbe (G), S.J.	.35	1.00
☐☐	SP72	Sergei Makarov, S.J.	.35	1.00
☐☐	SP73	Sandis Ozolinsh, S.J.	.75	2.00
☐☐	SP74	Brian Bradley, T.B.	.35	1.00
☐☐	SP75	Chris Gratton, T.B.	.75	2.00
☐☐	SP76	Denis Savard, T.B.	.75	2.00
☐☐	SP77	Dave Andreychuk, Tor.	.35	1.00
☐☐	SP78	Mike Gartner, Tor.	.75	2.00
☐☐	SP79	Dimitri Mironov, Tor.	.35	1.00
☐☐	SP80	Félix Potvin (G), Tor.	2.00	8.00
☐☐	SP81	Jeff Brown, Van.	.35	1.00
☐☐	SP82	Geoff Courtnall, Van.	.35	1.00
☐☐	SP83	Trevor Linden, Van.	.75	2.00
☐☐	SP84	Kirk McLean (G), Van.	.75	2.00
☐☐	SP85	Peter Bondra, Wsh.	1.75	6.00

No.	Player		
☐☐ SP86	Kevin Hatcher, Wsh.	.35	1.00
☐☐ SP87	Dimitri Khristich, Wsh.	.35	1.00
☐☐ SP88	Teemu Selänne, Wpg.	3.00	12.00
☐☐ SP89	Keith Tkachuk, Wpg.	1.75	6.00
☐☐ SP90	Alexei Zhamnov, Wpg.	.75	2.00
☐☐ SP91	Paul Kariya, Ana.	5.00	25.00
☐☐ SP92	Valeri Karpov, Ana.	.35	1.00
☐☐ SP93	Oleg Tverdovsky, Ana.	.35	2.00
☐☐ SP94	Al Iafrate, Bos.	.35	1.00
☐☐ SP95	Blaine Lacher (G), Bos.	.35	1.00
☐☐ SP96	Bryan Smolinski, Bos.	.35	1.00
☐☐ SP97	Donald Audette, Buf.	.35	1.00
☐☐ SP98	Yuri Khmylev, Buf.	.35	1.00
☐☐ SP99	Pat LaFontaine, Buf.	.75	2.00
☐☐ SP100	Derek Plante, Buf.	.35	1.00
☐☐ SP101	Steve Chiasson, Cgy.	.35	1.00
☐☐ SP102	Phil Housley, Cgy.	.35	1.00
☐☐ SP103	Michael Nylander, Cgy.	.35	1.00
☐☐ SP104	Robert Reichel, Cgy.	.35	1.00
☐☐ SP105	Tony Amonte, Chi.	.50	2.00
☐☐ SP106	Bernie Nicholls, Chi.	.75	2.00
☐☐ SP107	Gary Suter, Chi.	.75	1.00
☐☐ SP108	Paul Cavallini, Dal.	.35	1.00
☐☐ SP109	Todd Harvey, Dal.	.35	1.00
☐☐ SP110	Kevin Hatcher, Dal.	.35	1.00
☐☐ SP111	Andy Moog (G), Dal.	.75	2.00
☐☐ SP112	Dino Ciccarelli, Det.	.75	2.00
☐☐ SP113	Sergei Fedorov, Det.	2.00	8.00
☐☐ SP114	Nicklas Lidstrom, Det.	.75	2.00
☐☐ SP115	Mike Vernon (G), Det.	.75	2.00
☐☐ SP116	Shayne Corson, Edm.	.75	2.00
☐☐ SP117	David Oliver, Edm.	.35	1.00
☐☐ SP118	Ryan Smith, Edm.	4.00	12.00
☐☐ SP119	Jesse Belanger, Fla.	.35	1.00
☐☐ SP120	Mark Fitzpatrick (G), Fla.	.35	1.00
☐☐ SP121	Scott Mellanby, Fla.	.35	1.00
☐☐ SP122	Andrei Nikolishin, Hfd.	.35	1.00
☐☐ SP123	Darren Turcotte, Hfd.	.35	1.00
☐☐ SP124	Pat Verbeek, Hfd.	.35	1.00
☐☐ SP125	Glen Wesley, Hfd.	.35	1.00
☐☐ SP126	Tony Granato, L.A.	.35	1.00
☐☐ SP127	Marty McSorley, L.A.	.35	1.00
☐☐ SP128	Jamie Storr (G), L.A.	.75	2.00
☐☐ SP129	Rick Tocchet, L.A.	.35	1.00
☐☐ SP130	Brian Bellows, Mtl.	.35	1.00
☐☐ SP131	Valeri Bure, Mtl.	.35	1.00
☐☐ SP132	Turner Stevenson, Mtl.	.35	1.00
☐☐ SP133	John MacLean, N.J.	.35	1.00
☐☐ SP134	Scott Niedermayer, N.J.	.75	2.00
☐☐ SP135	Brian Rolston, N.J.	.35	1.00
☐☐ SP136	Brett Lindros, NYI.	.35	1.00
☐☐ SP137	Jamie McLennan (G), NYI.	.75	2.00
☐☐ SP138	Zigmund Palffy, NYI.	1.75	6.00
☐☐ SP139	Steve Thomas, NYI.	.35	1.00
☐☐ SP140	Adam Graves, NYR.	.35	1.00
☐☐ SP141	Petr Nedved, NYR.	.35	1.00
☐☐ SP142	Sergei Zubov, NYR.	.75	2.00
☐☐ SP143	Don Beaupré (G), Ott.	.35	1.00
☐☐ SP144	Radek Bonk, Ott.	.35	1.00
☐☐ SP145	Pavol Demitra, Ott.	.35	1.00
☐☐ SP146	Sylvain Turgeon, Ott.	.35	1.00
☐☐ SP147	Ron Hextall (G), Pha.	.75	2.00
☐☐ SP148	Patrik Juhlin, Pha.	.35	1.00
☐☐ SP149	Eric Lindros, Pha.	5.00	25.00
☐☐ SP150	Ron Francis, Pgh.	1.25	4.00
☐☐ SP151	Markus Naslund, Pgh.	.35	1.00
☐☐ SP152	Luc Robitaille, Pgh.	.75	2.00
☐☐ SP153	Martin Stratka, Pgh.	.35	1.00
☐☐ SP154	Wendel Clark, Que.	.75	2.00
☐☐ SP155	Adam Deadmarsh, Que.	.75	2.00
☐☐ SP156	Peter Forsberg, Que.	4.00	20.00
☐☐ SP157	Janne Laukkanen, Que.	.35	1.00
☐☐ SP158	Steve Duchesne, Stl.	.35	1.00
☐☐ SP159	Al MacInnis, Stl.	.75	2.00
☐☐ SP160	Esa Tikkanen, Stl.	.35	1.00
☐☐ SP161	Jeff Friesen, S.J.	.75	2.00
☐☐ SP162	Viktor Kozlov, S.J.	.35	1.00
☐☐ SP163	Ray Whitney, S.J.	.35	1.00
☐☐ SP164	Roman Hamrlik, T.B.	.75	2.00
☐☐ SP165	Alexander Selivanov, T.B.	.35	1.00
☐☐ SP166	Jason Wiemer, T.B.	.35	1.00
☐☐ SP167	Doug Gilmour, Tor.	1.25	4.00
☐☐ SP168	Kenny Jonsson, Tor.	.35	1.00
☐☐ SP169	Mike Ridley, Tor.	.35	1.00
☐☐ SP170	Mats Sundin, Tor.	2.00	8.00
☐☐ SP171	Pavel Bure, Van.	3.00	12.00
☐☐ SP172	Martin Gelinas, Van.	.35	1.00
☐☐ SP173	Michael Peca, Van.	.75	2.00
☐☐ SP174	Jason Allison, Wsh.	1.25	4.00
☐☐ SP175	Joé Juneau, Wsh.	.35	1.00
☐☐ SP176	Pat Peake, Wsh.	.35	1.00
☐☐ SP177	Mark Tinordi, Wsh.	.35	1.00
☐☐ SP178	Tim Cheveldae (G), Wpg.	.35	1.00
☐☐ SP179	Nelson Emerson, Wpg.	.35	1.00
☐☐ SP180	Dave Manson, Wpg.	.35	1.00

AWARD PREDICTORS

Only C1-C15 and H1-H15 have Silver and Gold redeemed versions. All other Predictor cards have only Gold redeemed versions.

Calder Set (C1-C15):	**40.00**	**20.00**
Pearson Set (C16-C25):	**60.00**	**30.00**
Norris Set (C26-C35):	**25.00**	**12.50**
Hart Set (H1-H15):	**100.00**	**50.00**
Art Ross Set (H16-H25):	**70.00**	**35.00**
Vezina Set (H26-H35):	**50.00**	**25.00**
Goals Set (R1-R10):	**40.00**	**20.00**
Assists Set (R11-R20):	**40.00**	**20.00**
Points Set (R21-R30):	**50.00**	**25.00**
Playoff Goals Set (R31-R40):	**40.00**	**20.00**
Playoff Assists Set (R41-R50):	**40.00**	**20.00**
Playoff Points Set (R51-R60):	**50.00**	**25.00**

No.	Calder	Insert	Silver	Gold
☐☐☐ C1	Peter Forsberg, Que.	10.00	5.00	5.00
☐☐☐ C2	Paul Kariya, Ana.	12.00	6.00	6.00
☐☐☐ C3	Viktor Kozlov, S.J.	2.00	1.00	1.00
☐☐☐ C4	Jason Allison, Wsh.	2.00	1.00	1.00
☐☐☐ C5	Maruisz Czerkawski, Buf.	2.00	1.00	1.00
☐☐☐ C6	Valeri Karpov, Mtl.	2.00	1.00	1.00
☐☐☐ C7	Brett Lindros, NYI.	2.00	1.00	1.00
☐☐☐ C8	Valeri Bure, Mtl.	2.00	1.00	1.00
☐☐☐ C9	Andre Nikolishin, Hfd.	2.00	1.00	1.00
☐☐☐ C10	Michael Peca, Van.	3.00	1.50	1.50
☐☐☐ C11	Kenny Jonsson, Tor.	2.00	1.00	1.00
☐☐☐ C12	Alexander Cherbayev, S.J.	2.00	1.00	1.00
☐☐☐ C13	Brian Rolston, N.J.	2.00	1.00	1.00
☐☐☐ C14	Oleg Tverdovsky, Ana.	2.00	1.00	1.00
☐☐☐ C15	Calder Long Shot	1.00	.50	.50

No.	Pearson / Norris	Insert	Gold
☐☐ C16	Wayne Gretzky, L.A.	20.00	10.00
☐☐ C17	Brett Hull, Stl.	5.00	2.50
☐☐ C18	Doug Gilmour, Tor.	4.00	2.00
☐☐ C19	Jeremy Roenick, Chi.	4.00	2.00
☐☐ C20	John Vanbiesbrouck (G), Fla.	6.00	3.00
☐☐ C21	Sergei Fedorov, Det.	5.00	2.50
☐☐ C22	Mark Messier, NYR.	5.00	2.50
☐☐ C23	Eric Lindros, Pha.	12.00	6.00
☐☐ C24	Jaromir Jagr, Pgh.	10.00	5.00
☐☐ C25	Pearson Long Shot	1.00	.50
☐☐ C26	Ray Bourque, Bos.	5.00	2.50
☐☐ C27	Sandis Ozolinsh, S.J.	3.00	1.50
☐☐ C28	Brian Leetch, NYR.	4.00	2.00
☐☐ C29	Chris Chelios, Chi.	4.00	2.00
☐☐ C30	Scott Stevens, N.J.	2.00	1.00
☐☐ C31	Paul Coffey, Det.	3.00	1.50
☐☐ C32	Rob Blake, L.A.	3.00	1.50
☐☐ C33	Al MacInnis, Stl.	3.00	1.50
☐☐ C34	Scott Niedermayer, N.J.	3.00	1.50
☐☐ C35	Norris Long Shot	1.00	.50

No.	Hart	Insert	Silver	Gold
☐☐☐ H1	Wayne Gretzky, L.A.	20.00	10.00	10.00
☐☐☐ H2	Pavel Bure, Van.	7.00	3.50	3.50
☐☐☐ H3	Doug Gilmour, Tor.	4.00	2.00	2.00
☐☐☐ H4	Mark Messier, NYR.	5.00	2.50	2.50
☐☐☐ H5	Patrick Roy (G), Mtl.	15.00	7.50	7.50
☐☐☐ H6	Sergei Fedorov, Det.	5.00	2.50	2.50
☐☐☐ H7	Chris Chelios, Chi.	4.00	2.00	2.00
☐☐☐ H8	Eric Lindros, Pha.	12.00	6.00	6.00
☐☐☐ H9	Alexander Mogilny, Buf.	4.00	2.00	2.00
☐☐☐ H10	Peter Forsberg, Que.	10.00	5.00	5.00
☐☐☐ H11	Brian Leetch, NYR.	4.00	2.00	2.00
☐☐☐ H12	Martin Brodeur (G), N.J.	7.00	3.50	3.50
☐☐☐ H13	Jeremy Roenick, Chi.	4.00	2.00	2.00
☐☐☐ H14	Paul Kariya, Ana.	12.00	6.00	6.00
☐☐☐ H15	Hart Long Shot	1.00	.50	.50

No.	Art Ross / Vezina	Insert	Gold
☐☐ H16	Wayne Gretzky, L.A.	20.00	10.00
☐☐ H17	Joe Sakic, Que.	8.00	4.00
☐☐ H18	Sergei Fedorov, Det.	5.00	2.50
☐☐ H19	Pavel Bure, Van.	7.00	3.50
☐☐ H20	Adam Oates, Bos.	4.00	2.00
☐☐ H21	Doug Gilmour, Tor.	4.00	2.00
☐☐ H22	Steve Yzerman, Det.	10.00	5.00
☐☐ H23	Eric Lindros, Pha.	12.00	6.00
☐☐ H24	Jaromir Jagr, Pgh.	10.00	5.00
☐☐ H25	Art Ross Long Shot	1.00	.50
☐☐ H26	Patrick Roy (G), Mtl.	15.00	7.50
☐☐ H27	Ed Belfour (G), Chi.	4.00	2.00
☐☐ H28	Félix Potvin (G), Tor.	5.00	2.50
☐☐ H29	Martin Brodeur (G), N.J.	7.00	3.50
☐☐ H30	Mike Richter (G), NYR.	4.00	2.00
☐☐ H31	Dominik Hasek (G), Buf.	7.00	3.50
☐☐ H32	John Vanbiesbrouck (G), Fla.	6.00	3.00
☐☐ H33	Curtis Joseph (G), Stl.	6.00	3.00
☐☐ H34	Kirk McLean (G), Van.	3.00	1.50
☐☐ H35	Vezina Long Shot	1.00	.50

No.	Scoring	Insert	Gold
☐☐ R1	Pavel Bure, Van.	7.00	3.50
☐☐ R2	Brett Hull, Stl.	5.00	2.50
☐☐ R3	Teemu Selänne, Wpg.	7.00	3.50
☐☐ R4	Sergei Fedorov, Det.	5.00	2.50
☐☐ R5	Adam Graves, NYR.	2.00	1.00
☐☐ R6	Dave Andreychuk, Tor.	2.00	1.00
☐☐ R7	Brendan Shanahan, Stl.	6.00	3.00
☐☐ R8	Jeremy Roenick, Chi.	4.00	2.00
☐☐ R9	Eric Lindros, Pha.	12.00	6.00
☐☐ R10	Goals Long Shot	1.00	.50
☐☐ R11	Doug Gilmour, Tor.	4.00	2.00
☐☐ R12	Adam Oates, Bos.	4.00	2.00
☐☐ R13	Brian Leetch, NYR.	4.00	2.00
☐☐ R14	Ray Bourque, Bos.	5.00	2.50
☐☐ R15	Joé Juneau, Wsh.	2.00	1.00
☐☐ R16	Craig Janney, S.J.	2.00	1.00
☐☐ R17	Pat LaFontaine, Buf.	3.00	1.50
☐☐ R18	Jaromir Jagr, Pgh.	10.00	5.00
☐☐ R19	Wayne Gretzky, L.A.	20.00	10.00
☐☐ R20	Assist Long Shot	1.00	.50
☐☐ R21	Wayne Gretzky, L.A.	20.00	10.00
☐☐ R22	Pat LaFontaine, Buf.	3.00	1.50
☐☐ R23	Sergei Fedorov, Det.	5.00	2.50
☐☐ R24	Steve Yzerman, Det.	10.00	5.00
☐☐ R25	Pavel Bure, Van.	7.00	3.50
☐☐ R26	Adam Oates, Bos.	4.00	2.00
☐☐ R27	Doug Gilmour, Tor.	4.00	2.00
☐☐ R28	Eric Lindros, Pha.	12.00	6.00
☐☐ R29	Jaromir Jagr, Pgh.	10.00	5.00
☐☐ R30	Points Long Shot	1.00	.50
☐☐ R31	Pavel Bure, Van.	7.00	3.50
☐☐ R32	Brett Hull, Stl.	5.00	2.50
☐☐ R33	Cam Neely, Bos.	3.00	1.50
☐☐ R34	Mark Messier, NYR.	5.00	2.50
☐☐ R35	Dave Andreychuk, Tor.	2.00	1.00
☐☐ R36	Sergei Fedorov, Det.	5.00	2.50
☐☐ R37	Mike Modano, Dal.	5.00	2.50
☐☐ R38	Adam Graves, NYR.	2.00	1.00
☐☐ R39	Jaromir Jagr, Pgh.	10.00	5.00
☐☐ R40	Playoff Goals Long Shot	1.00	.50
☐☐ R41	Theoren Fleury, Cgy.	4.00	2.00
☐☐ R42	Wayne Gretzky, L.A.	20.00	10.00
☐☐ R43	Steve Yzerman, Det.	10.00	5.00
☐☐ R44	Adam Oates, Bos.	4.00	2.00
☐☐ R45	Brian Leetch, NYR.	4.00	2.00
☐☐ R46	Al MacInnis, Stl.	3.00	1.50
☐☐ R47	Pat LaFontaine, Buf.	3.00	1.50
☐☐ R48	Scott Stevens, N.J.	2.00	1.00
☐☐ R49	Doug Gilmour, Tor.	4.00	2.00
☐☐ R50	Playoff Assist Long Shot	1.00	.50
☐☐ R51	Brian Leetch, NYR.	4.00	2.00
☐☐ R52	Sergei Fedorov, Det.	5.00	2.50
☐☐ R53	Pavel Bure, Van.	7.00	3.50
☐☐ R54	Mark Messier, NYR.	5.00	2.50

	No.	Player		
☐☐	R55	Pat LaFontaine, Buf.	3.00	1.50
☐☐	R56	Doug Gilmour, Tor.	4.00	2.00
☐☐	R57	Brett Hull, Stl.	5.00	2.50
☐☐	R58	Theoren Fleury, Cgy.	4.00	2.00
☐☐	R59	Wayne Gretzky, L.A.	20.00	10.00
☐☐	R60	Playoff Point Long Shot	1.00	.50

1994 - 95 UPPER DECK BE A PLAYER

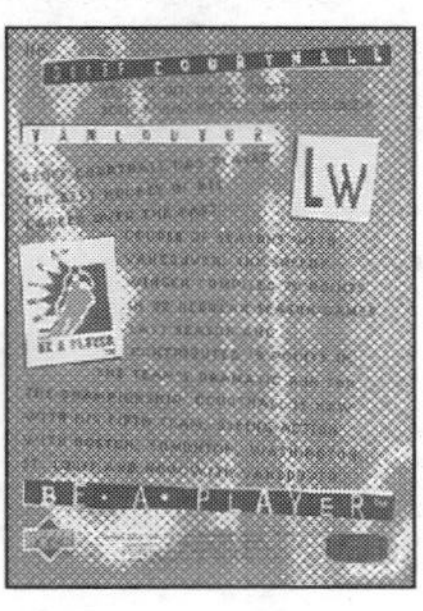

Imprint: © 1995 THE UPPER DECK COMPANY

Complete Set (180 cards): **50.00**

Common Player: **.15**

	No.	Player	NRMT-MT
☐	R1	Doug Gilmour	.50
☐	R2	Joel Otto	.15
☐	R3	Kirk Muller	.15
☐	R4	Marty McInnis	.15
☐	R5	Dave Gagner	.15
☐	R6	Geoff Courtnall	.15
☐	R7	Dale Hawerchuk	.35
☐	R8	Mike Modano	1.00
☐	R9	Roman Hamrlik	.35
☐	R10	Marty McSorley	.15
☐	R11	Teemu Selänne	1.50
☐	R12	Jeremy Roenick	.50
☐	R13	Glenn Healy (G)	.15
☐	R14	Darren Turcotte	.15
☐	R15	Derian Hatcher	.35
☐	R16	Enrico Ciccone	.15
☐	R17	Tony Amonte	.35
☐	R18	Mark Recchi	.35
☐	R19	Eric Weinrich	.15
☐	R20	John Vanbiesbrouck (G)	1.25
☐	R21	Nick Kypreos	.15
☐	R22	Gilbert Dionne	.15
☐	R23	Theoren Fleury	.50
☐	R24	Todd Gill	.15
☐	R25	Jari Kurri	.35
☐	R26	Brad May	.15
☐	R27	Russ Courtnall	.15
☐	R28	Bill Ranford (G)	.35
☐	R29	Steve Yzerman	2.00
☐	R30	Alexandre Daigle	.35
☐	R31	Mike Hudson	.15
☐	R32	Ray Bourque	1.00
☐	R33	Dave Andreychuk	.15
☐	R34	Jason Arnott	.35
☐	R35	Pavel Bure	1.50
☐	R36	Keith Tkachuk	.75
☐	R37	Scott Niedermayer	.35
☐	R38	Johan Garpenlov	.15
☐	R39	Dino Ciccarelli	.35
☐	R40	Rob Blake	.35
☐	R41	Dave Manson	.15
☐	R42	Adam Foote	.35
☐	R43	Chris Pronger	.35
☐	R44	Scott Lachance	.15
☐	R45	Adam Oates	.50
☐	R46	Brian Leetch	.50
☐	R47	Guy Hebert (G)	.35
☐	R48	Brett Hull	1.00
☐	R49	Mike Ricci	.15
☐	R50	Dave Ellett	.15
☐	R51	Owen Nolan	.35
☐	R52	Craig Janney	.15
☐	R53	Trevor Linden	.35
☐	R54	Ray Sheppard	.15
☐	R55	Rob Niedermayer	.35
☐	R56	Kevin Haller	.15
☐	R57	Jeff Norton	.15
☐	R58	Martin Brodeur (G)	1.50
☐	R59	Robb Stauber (G)	.15
☐	R60	Sylvain Turgeon	.15
☐	R61	Pat Verbeek	.15
☐	R62	Steve Smith	.15
☐	R63	Jaromir Jagr	2.00
☐	R64	Steve Duchesne	.15
☐	R65	Tie Domi	.15
☐	R66	Sylvain Lefebvre	.15
☐	R67	Guy Carbonneau	.15
☐	R68	Alexander Mogilny	.50
☐	R69	Mario Lemieux	3.00
☐	R70	Neil Wilkinson	.15
☐	R71	Curtis Joseph (G)	1.25
☐	R72	Wendel Clark	.35
☐	R73	Kirk McLean (G)	.35
☐	R74	Mikael Renberg	.35
☐	R75	Shawn McEachern	.15
☐	R76	Mats Sundin	1.00
☐	R77	Craig Simpson	.15
☐	R78	Phil Housley	.15
☐	R79	Pat LaFontaine	.35
☐	R80	Pierre Turgeon	.35
☐	R81	Félix Potvin (G)	1.00
☐	R82	Kevin Stevens	.15
☐	R83	Steve Chiasson	.15
☐	R84	Robert Petrovicky	.15
☐	R85	Joé Juneau	.15
☐	R86	Brendan Shanahan	1.25
☐	R87	Joe Sacco	.15
☐	R88	David Reid	.15
☐	R89	Louie DeBrusk	.15
☐	R90	Darryl Sydor	.15
☐	R91	Paul Coffey	.35
☐	R92	Alexei Yashin	.75
☐	R93	Jason Arnott	.35
☐	R94	Gary Sute	.15
☐	R95	Luc Robitaille	.35
☐	R96	Joe Sakic	1.75
☐	R97	Chris Chelios	.75
☐	R98	Tony Granato	.15
☐	R99	Wayne Gretzky	4.00
☐	R100	Joé Juneau	.15
☐	R101	Curtis Joseph (G)	1.25
☐	R102	Vincent Damphousse	.50
☐	R103	Paul Kariya	2.50
☐	R104	Brendan Shanahan	1.25
☐	R105	Eric Desjardins	.35
☐	R106	Eric Lindros	2.50
☐	R107	Kirk McLean (G)	.35
☐	R108	Mike Ricci	.15
☐	R109	Chris Chelios	.50
☐	R110	Chris Gratton	.35
☐	R111	Doug Gilmour	.50
☐	R112	Vincent Damphousse	.50
☐	R113	Mark Osborne	.15
☐	R114	Mike Modano	1.00
☐	R115	Steve Yzerman	2.00
☐	R116	Garry Valk	.15
☐	R117	Adam Graves	.15
☐	R118	Doug Weight	.50
☐	R119	Rob Niedermayer	.35
☐	R120	Craig Simpson	.15
☐	R121	Patrick Roy (G)	3.00
☐	R122	Ron Stern	.15
☐	R123	Jiri Slegr	.15
☐	R124	Darren Turcotte	.15
☐	R125	Vladimir Malakhov	.15
☐	R126	Paul Kariya	1.25
☐	R127	Mike Gartner	.35
☐	R128	Scott Niedermayer	.35
☐	R129	Dino Ciccarelli	.35
☐	R130	Martin Brodeur (G)	.75
☐	R131	Kevin Hatcher	.15
☐	R132	Pat LaFontaine	.35
☐	R133	Joel Otto	.15
☐	R134	Jason Arnott	.35
☐	R135	John Vanbiesbrouck (G)	.50
☐	R136	Derian Hatcher	.35
☐	R137	Brendan Shanahan	.50
☐	R138	Félix Potvin (G)	.50
☐	R139	Trevor Linden	.35
☐	R140	Ken Baumgartner	.15
☐	R141	Denis Leary	.15
☐	R142	Wendel Clark	.35
☐	R143	Cam Neely	.35
☐	R144	Jeremy Roenick	.50
☐	R145	Sergei Fedorov	1.00
☐	R146	Scott Stevens	.15
☐	R147	Wayne Gretzky	4.00
☐	R148	Darius Kasparaitis	.15
☐	R149	Brian Leetch	.50
☐	R150	Marty McSorley	.15
☐	R151	Paul Kariya	2.50
☐	R152	Peter Forsberg	2.00
☐	R153	Brett Lindros	.15
☐	R154	Kenny Jonsson	.15
☐	R155	Jason Allison	.50
☐	R156	Aaron Gavey	.15
☐	R157	Jamie Storr (G)	.35
☐	R158	Viktor Kozlov	.15
☐	R159	Valeri Bure	.15
☐	R160	Oleg Tverdovsky	.35
☐	R161	Brent Gretzky	.15
☐	R162	Todd Harvey	.15
☐	R163	Todd Warriner	.15
☐	R164	Jeff Friesen	.35
☐	R165	Adam Deadmarsh	.15
☐	R166	Ken Baumgartner	.15
☐	R167	Terry Carkner	.15
☐	R168	Tie Domi	.15
☐	R169	Steve Larmer	.15
☐	R170	Larry Murphy	.35
☐	R171	Steve Thomas	.15
☐	R172	Alexei Yashin	.75
☐	R173	Félix Potvin (G)	1.00
☐	R174	Curtis Joseph (G)	1.25
☐	R175	Rob Zamuner	.35
☐	R176	Wayne Gretzky	4.00
☐	R177	Pavel Bure	1.50
☐	R178	Eric Lindros	2.50
☐	R179	Patrick Roy (G)	3.00
☐	R180	Doug Gilmour	.50

SIGNATURE SERIES

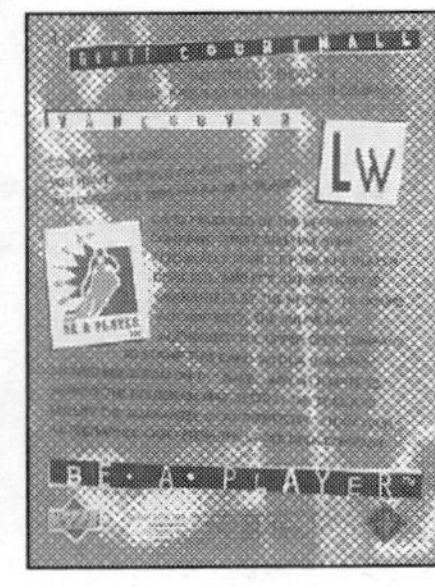

These autographs were inserted one per pack. Most signed approximately 2,400 cards. Short prints are marked with an asterisk. The Jiri Slegr autograph (#119) was only available through the mail.

Insert Set (178 cards): **2,800.00**

Common Player: **5.00**

	No.	Player	NRMT-MT
☐	1	Doug Gilmour (#/1250)	55.00
☐	2	Adam Foote	8.00
☐	3	Martin Brodeur (G)	60.00
☐	4	Alexander Semak	5.00
☐	5	Dale Hawerchuk	15.00
☐	6	Derek King	5.00
☐	7	Mark Recchi	15.00
☐	8	Fredrik Olausson	5.00
☐	9	Dave McLlwain	5.00
☐	10	Marc Bergevin	5.00
☐	11	Teemu Selänne (#/600)	250.00
☐	12	Jeremy Roenick (#/600)	150.00
☐	13	Eric Lacroix	5.00
☐	14	Marty McInnis	5.00
☐	15	Kris King	5.00
☐	16	Bill Ranford (G)	12.00
☐	17	Gary Roberts	8.00
☐	18	Mark Osborne	5.00
☐	19	Dmitri Mironov	5.00
☐	20	John Vanbiesbrouck (G) (#/600)	200.00
☐	21	Alexei Zhamnov	10.00
☐	22	Brad May	5.00
☐	23	Doug Lidster	5.00
☐	24	Mikael Renberg	12.00

	No.	Player	NRMT-MT
☐	25	Kris Draper	8.00
☐	26	Darryl Sydor	5.00
☐	27	Claude Lemieux	8.00
☐	28	Doug Brown	5.00
☐	29	Louie DeBrusk	5.00
☐	30	Andy Moog (G)	15.00
☐	31	Donald Audette	5.00
☐	32	Ray Bourque (#/600)	200.00
☐	33	Brian Rolston	5.00
☐	34	Ted Drury	5.00
☐	35	Darren Turcotte	5.00
☐	36	Gary Shuchuk	5.00
☐	37	Mike Ricci	8.00
☐	38	Kirk Maltby	5.00
☐	39	Doug Bodger	5.00
☐	40	Kirk Muller	8.00
☐	41	Sylvain Lefebvre	5.00
☐	42	Brent Grieve	5.00
☐	43	Bill Holder	5.00
☐	44	Neil Wilkinson	5.00
☐	45	Donald Dufresne	5.00
☐	46	Brian Leetch (#/600)	150.00
☐	47	Bryan Smolinski	5.00
☐	48	Kevin Hatcher	8.00
☐	49	Steven Rice	5.00
☐	50	Bill Guerin	12.00
☐	51	Grant Jennings	5.00
☐	52	Dave Andreychuk	12.00
☐	53	Sean Burke (G)	12.00
☐	54	Nick Kypreos	5.00
☐	55	Drake Berehowsky	5.00
☐	56	Kevin Haller	5.00
☐	57	Bill Berg	5.00
☐	58	Chris Simon	8.00
☐	59	Owen Nolan	12.00
☐	60	Don Sweeney	5.00
☐	61	Johan Garpenlov	5.00
☐	62	Garry Galley	5.00
☐	63	Pat LaFontaine	25.00
☐	64	Craig Berube	5.00
☐	65	Dave Ellett	5.00
☐	66	Robert Kron	5.00
☐	67	Alexander Godynyuk	5.00
☐	68	Markus Naslund	5.00
☐	69	Joel Otto	5.00
☐	70	Igor Ulanov	5.00
☐	71	Pat Verbeek	5.00
☐	72	Craig MacTavish	5.00
☐	73	Gary Leeman	5.00
☐	74	Kevin Todd	5.00
☐	75	Mike Sullivan	5.00
☐	76	Rob Pearson	5.00
☐	77	Dave Gagner	5.00
☐	78	Dirk Graham	5.00
☐	79	Joe Sacco	5.00
☐	80	Jassen Cullimore	5.00
☐	81	Glen Featherstone	5.00
☐	82	Scott Lachance	8.00
☐	83	Kerry Huffman	5.00
☐	84	Troy Loney	5.00
☐	85	Rob Gaudreau	5.00
☐	86	Brendan Shanahan (#/600)	250.00
☐	87	Joe Murphy	5.00
☐	88	Scott Niedermayer	8.00
☐	89	Dan Quinn	5.00
☐	90	Jeff Norton	5.00
☐	91	Jim Dowd	5.00
☐	92	Ray Ferraro	8.00
☐	93	Shawn Burr	5.00
☐	94	Denis Savard	8.00
☐	95	Dave Manson	5.00
☐	96	Joe Nieuwendyk	15.00
☐	97	Tony Amonte	12.00
☐	98	James Patrick	5.00
☐	99	Guy Hebert (G)	18.00
☐	100	Peter Zezel	5.00
☐	101	Shawn McEachern	5.00
☐	102	Dave Lowry	5.00
☐	103	David Reid	5.00
☐	104	Todd Gill	5.00
☐	105	John Cullen	8.00
☐	106	Guy Carbonneau	8.00
☐	107	Jeff Beukeboom	5.00
☐	108	Wayne Gretzky (#/300)	1,300.00
☐	109	Curtis Joseph (G)	30.00
☐	110	Jason Arnott	15.00
☐	111	Eric Desjardins	8.00
☐	112	Gary Suter	5.00
☐	113	Luc Robitaille	15.00
☐	114	Tony Granato	5.00
☐	115	Steve Yzerman (#/600)	400.00
☐	116	Chris Gratton	15.00
☐	117	Doug Weight	20.00
☐	118	Gary Valk	5.00
☐	119	Jiri Slegr	40.00
☐	120	Vincent Damphousse	20.00
☐	121	Vladimir Malakhov	5.00
☐	122	Craig Simpson	5.00
☐	123	Theoren Fleury	25.00
☐	124	Dave Poulin	5.00
☐	125	Derian Hatcher	10.00
☐	126	Jimmy Waite (G)	5.00
☐	127	Norm Maciver	5.00
☐	128	Glenn Healy (G)	8.00
☐	129	Jocelyn Lemieux	5.00
☐	130	Steve Chiasson	5.00
☐	131	Keith Jones	5.00
☐	132	Enrice Ciccone	5.00
☐	133	Martin Lapointe	5.00
☐	134	John MacLean	5.00
☐	135	Geoff Courtnall	5.00
☐	136	David Shaw	5.00
☐	137	Steve Duchesne	5.00
☐	138	Dean Evason	5.00
☐	139	Eric Weinrich	5.00
☐	140	Kelly Hrudey (G)	8.00
☐	141	Ted Donato	5.00
☐	142	Darius Kasparaitis	5.00
☐	143	Tie Domi	5.00
☐	144	Terry Carkner	5.00
☐	145	Steve Thomas	5.00
☐	146	Steve Larmer	10.00
☐	147	Rob Zamuner	8.00
☐	148	Larry Murphy	8.00
☐	149	Ken Baumgartner	5.00
☐	150	Alexei Yashin (#/600)	160.00
☐	151	Paul Kariya (#/600)	400.00
☐	152	Todd Harvey	5.00
☐	153	Viktor Kozlov (Signed V K)	15.00
☐	153	Viktor Kozlov (Signed Viktor Kozlov)	225.00
☐	154	Brent Gretzky	5.00
☐	155	Petr Klima	5.00
☐	156	Kent Manderville	5.00
☐	157	Mike Eagles	5.00
☐	158	Valeri Kamensky	12.00
☐	159	Thomas Steen	5.00
☐	160	Michal Pivonka	5.00
☐	161	Steven Heinze	5.00
☐	162	Nicklas Lidström	12.00
☐	163	Uwe Krupp	5.00
☐	164	Pat Elyniuk	5.00
☐	165	Michael Peca	12.00
☐	166	Sylvain Côté	5.00
☐	167	Trevor Kidd (G)	20.00
☐	168	Patrick Poulin	5.00
☐	169	Shane Churla	5.00
☐	170	Scott Mellanby	5.00
☐	171	Mike Sillinger	5.00
☐	172	Shayne Corson	12.00
☐	173	Micah Alvazoff	5.00
☐	174	Robert Lang	5.00
☐	175	Rod Brind'Amour	15.00
☐	176	Troy Murray	5.00
☐	177	Mike Krushelnyski	5.00
☐	178	Sergio Momesso	5.00

99 ALL-STARS

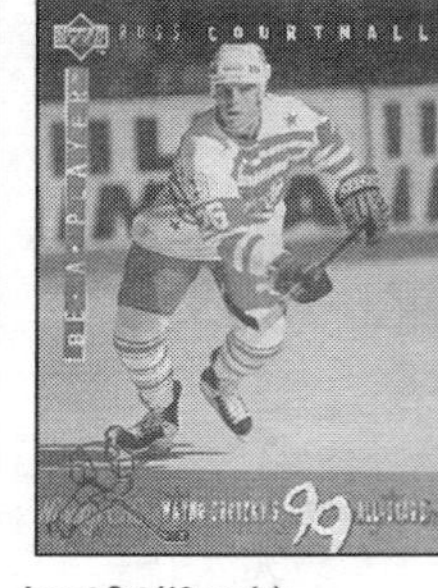

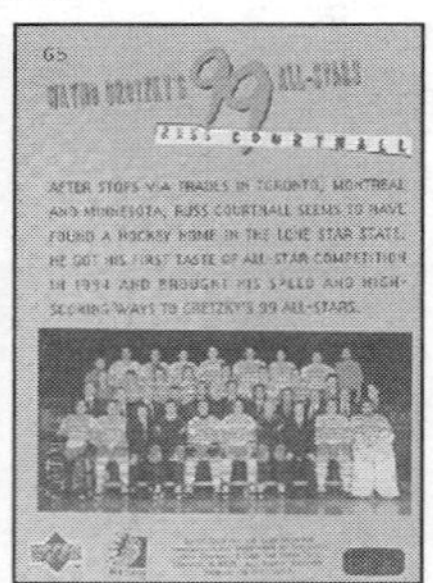

Insert Set (19 cards): **215.00**

	No.	Player	NRMT-MT
☐	G1	Wayne Gretzky	80.00
☐	G2	Paul Coffey	10.00
☐	G3	Rob Blake	8.00
☐	G4	Pat Conacher	5.00
☐	G5	Russ Courtnall	5.00
☐	G6	Sergei Fedorov	20.00
☐	G7	Grant Fuhr (G)	8.00
☐	G8	Todd Gill	5.00
☐	G9	Tony Granato	5.00
☐	G10	Brett Hull	20.00
☐	G11	Charlie Huddy	5.00
☐	G12	Steve Larmer	5.00
☐	G13	Kelly Hrudey (G)	5.00
☐	G14	Al MacInnis	8.00
☐	G15	Marty McSorley	5.00
☐	G16	Jari Kurri	8.00
☐	G17	Kirk Muller	5.00
☐	G18	Rick Tocchet	5.00
☐	G19	Steve Yzerman	35.00

UP CLOSE AND PERSONAL

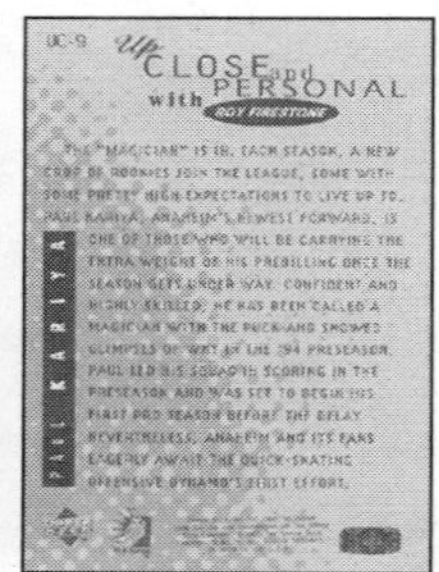

Insert Set (10 cards): **100.00**

	No.	Player	NRMT-MT
☐	UC1	Wayne Gretzky	25.00
☐	UC2	Eric Lindros	18.00
☐	UC3	Pavel Bure	8.00
☐	UC4	Teemu Selänne	8.00
☐	UC5	Steve Yzerman	12.00
☐	UC6	Jeremy Roenick	4.00
☐	UC7	Sergei Fedorov	6.00
☐	UC8	Patrick Roy (G)	20.00
☐	UC9	Paul Kariya	18.00
☐	UC10	Doug Gilmour	4.00

1994 - 95 UPPER DECK CANADIAN WORLD JUNIOR ALUMNI

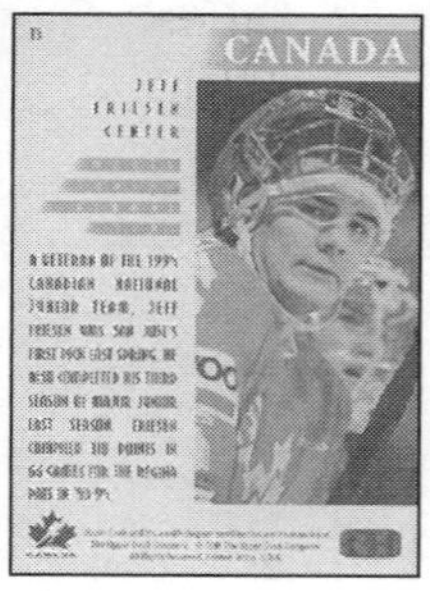

Imprint:

Complete Set (15 cards): **6.00**

	No.	Player	NRMT-MT
☐	1	Title card	.15
☐	2	1993 Manny Legacé (G)	.25
☐	3	1992 Jeff Nelson	.25
☐	4	1993 Alexandre Daigle	.75
☐	5	1993 Paul Kariya	3.00
☐	6	1992 Turner Stevenson	.25
☐	7	1994 Michael Peca	.75
☐	8	1993 Tyler Wright	.25
☐	9	1994 Brent Tully	.25
☐	10	1992 Trevor Kidd (G)	.75
☐	11	1993 Martin Lapointe	.25
☐	12	1992 Scott Niedermayer	.75
☐	13	1994 Jeff Friesen	.75
☐	14	1994 Todd Harvey	.25
☐	15	1994 Jamie Storr (G)	.75

1994 - 95 ZELLERS MASTERS OF HOCKEY

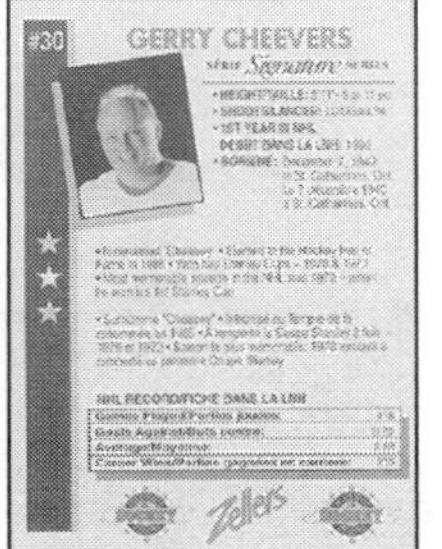

There are 10,850 copies of each card and 1,100 copies of each autographed card.

Imprint: ZELLERS

	No.	Player	Reg.	Auto.
Complete Set (8 cards):			**18.00**	**450.00**
☐☐	1	Jean Béliveau	4.50	115.00
☐☐	2	Gerry Cheevers (G)	3.50	85.00
☐☐	3	Red Kelly	2.50	50.00
☐☐	4	Dave Keon	3.00	65.00
☐☐	5	Lanny McDonald	2.50	55.00
☐☐	6	Pierre Pilote	2.00	40.00
☐☐	7	Henri Richard	3.50	85.00
☐☐	8	Norm Ullman	2.50	50.00

1995 FINNISH ALL-STAR

A set of 8 card covers.

Card Size: 3" x 4 1/2"

Imprint:

	No.	Player	NRMT-MT
Complete Set (8 cards):			**25.00**
☐	1	Jarmo Myllys (G)	2.00
☐	2	Jari Kurri	4.00
☐	3	Saku Koivu	10.00
☐	4	Teemu Selänne	10.00
☐	5	Esa Tikkanen	2.00
☐	6	Christian Ruuttu	1.00
☐	7	Mika Nieminen	1.00
☐	8	Timo Jutila	2.00

1995 GLOBE

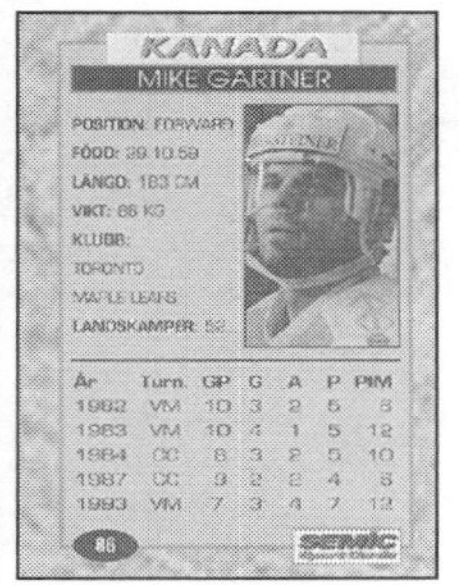

Imprint: Semic Sports Cards

	No.	Player	NRMT-MT
Complete Set (270 cards):			**40.00**
Common Player:			**.10**
Album:			**6.00**
☐	1	Tommy Söderström (G), Swe.	.20
☐	2	Roger Nordström (G), Swe.	.20
☐	3	Tommy Salo (G), Swe.	.20
☐	4	Hakan Algotsson, Swe.	.10
☐	5	Thomas Ostlund, Swe.	.10
☐	6	Johan Hedberg (G), Swe.	.10
☐	7	Ulf Samuelsson, Swe.	.20
☐	8	Calle Johansson, Swe.	.10
☐	9	Nicklas Lidström, Swe.	.20
☐	10	Tommy Albein, Swe.	.10
☐	11	Peter Andersson, Swe.	.10
☐	12	Magnus Svensson, Swe.	.10
☐	13	Mats Sundin, Swe.	.75
☐	14	Tomas Jonsson, Swe.	.10
☐	15	Kenny Jönsson, Swe.	.10
☐	16	Tommy Sjödin, Swe.	.10
☐	17	Fredrik Stillman, Swe.	.10
☐	18	Marcus Ragnarsson, Swe.	.10
☐	19	Peter Popovic, Swe.	.10
☐	20	Arto Blomsten, Swe.	.10
☐	21	Peter Forsberg, Swe.	2.00
☐	22	Roger Johansson, Swe.	.10
☐	23	Leif Rohlin, Swe.	.10
☐	24	Björn Nord, Swe.	.10
☐	25	Stefan Larsson, Swe.	.10
☐	26	Fredrik Olausson, Swe.	.10
☐	27	Kjell Samuelsson, Swe.	.10
☐	28	Tomas Sandström, Swe.	.10
☐	29	Mikael Renberg, Swe.	.50
☐	30	Mikael Johansson, Swe.	.10
☐	31	Patrik Juhlin, Swe.	.10
☐	32	Roger Hansson, Swe.	.10
☐	33	Daniel Rydmark, Swe.	.10
☐	34	Jonas Bergqvist, Swe.	.10
☐	35	Michael Nylander, Swe.	.20
☐	36	Johan Garpenlov, Swe.	.10
☐	37	Charles Berglund, Swe.	.10
☐	38	Jörgen Jönsson, Swe.	.10
☐	39	Stefan Ömskog, Swe.	.10
☐	40	Thomas Steen, Swe.	.10
☐	41	Patrik Carnbäck, Swe.	.10
☐	42	Mikael Andersson, Swe.	.10
☐	43	Markus Näslund, Swe.	.20
☐	44	Andreas Dackell, Swe.	.20
☐	45	Erik Huusko, Swe.	.10
☐	46	Tomas Forslund, Swe.	.10
☐	47	Daniel Alfredsson, Swe.	1.00
☐	48	Ulf Dahlen, Swe.	.20
☐	49	Anders Huusko, Swe.	.10
☐	50	Tomas Holmström, Swe.	.20
☐	51	Niklas Andersson, Swe.	.20
☐	52	Hakan Loob, Swe.	.25
☐	53	Per-Erik Eklund, Swe.	.20
☐	54	Patrik Erickson, Swe.	.10
☐	55	Jonas Forsberg (G), Swe.	.10
☐	56	Daniel Johansson, Swe.	.10
☐	57	Mattias Öhlund, Swe.	.75
☐	58	Anders Eriksson, Swe.	.20
☐	59	Fredrik Modin, Swe.	.20
☐	60	Niklas Sundstrom, Swe.	.20
☐	61	Jesper Mattsson, Swe.	.10
☐	62	Johan Davidsson, Swe.	.10
☐	63	Mats Lindgren, Swe.	.10
☐	64	Leif (Honken) Holmqvist, Swe.	.20
☐	65	Pelle Lindberg, Swe.	.50
☐	66	Lennart (Lill-Strimma) Svedberg, Swe.	.20
☐	67	Börje Salming, Swe.	.50
☐	68	Sven Tumba Johansson, Swe.	.20
☐	69	Ulf Sterner, Swe.	.20
☐	70	Anders Hedberg, Swe.	.25
☐	71	Kent Nilsson, Swe.	.25
☐	72	Mats Näslund, Swe.	.25
☐	73	Patrick Roy (G), Cdn.	3.00
☐	74	Ed Belfour (G), Cdn.	.75
☐	75	Bill Ranford (G), Cdn.	.25
☐	76	Paul Coffey, Cdn.	.25
☐	77	Ray Bourque, Cdn.	1.00
☐	78	Steve Smith, Cdn.	.20
☐	79	Al MacInnis, Cdn.	.25
☐	80	Mark Tinordi, Cdn.	.20
☐	81	Scott Stevens, Cdn.	.20
☐	82	Rob Blake, Cdn.	.25
☐	83	Theoren Fleury, Cdn.	.50
☐	84	Mark Messier, Cdn.	1.00
☐	85	Mike Gartner, Cdn.	.25
☐	86	Brendan Shanahan, Cdn.	1.25
☐	87	Mario Lemieux, Cdn.	3.00
☐	88	Eric Lindros, Cdn.	2.50
☐	89	Steve Yzerman, Cdn.	2.00
☐	90	Adam Oates, Cdn.	.50
☐	91	Paul Kariya, Cdn.	2.50
☐	92	Rick Tocchet, Cdn.	.20
☐	93	Doug Gilmour, Cdn.	.50
☐	94	Luc Robitaille, Cdn.	.25
☐	95	Jason Arnott, Cdn.	.50
☐	96	Adam Graves, Cdn.	.20
☐	97	Petr Nedved, Cdn.	.20
☐	98	Mark Recchi, Cdn.	.50
☐	99	Wayne Gretzky, Cdn.	4.00
☐	100	Mike Richter (G), USA.	.35
☐	101	John Vanbiesbrouck (G), USA.	1.25
☐	102	Tom Barrasso (G), USA.	.25
☐	103	Brian Leetch, USA.	.50
☐	104	Gary Suter, USA.	.20
☐	105	Kevin Hatcher, USA.	.20
☐	106	Phil Housley, USA.	.20
☐	107	Chris Chelios, USA.	.75
☐	108	Eric Weinrich, USA.	.20
☐	109	Derian Hatcher, USA.	.25
☐	110	Craig Wolanin, USA.	.20
☐	111	Mike Modano, USA.	1.00
☐	112	Joe Mullen, USA.	.20
☐	113	Joel Otto, USA.	.20
☐	114	Doug Brown, USA.	.20
☐	115	Brett Hull, USA.	1.00
☐	116	Pat LaFontaine, USA.	.25
☐	117	Jeremy Roenick, USA.	.50
☐	118	Craig Janney, USA.	.20
☐	119	Kevin Miller, USA.	.20
☐	120	Tony Granato, USA.	.20
☐	121	Tony Amonte, USA.	.25
☐	122	Kevin Stevens, USA.	.20
☐	123	Darren Turcotte, USA.	.20
☐	124	Scott Young, USA.	.20
☐	125	Doug Weight, USA.	.50
☐	126	Phil Bourque, USA.	.20
☐	127	Markus Ketterer (G), Fin.	.20
☐	128	Jarmo Myllys (G), Fin.	.20
☐	129	Jyrki Lumme, Fin.	.20
☐	130	Timo Jutila, Fin.	.25
☐	131	Marko Kiprusoff, Fin.	.10
☐	132	Hannu Virta, Fin.	.10
☐	133	Teppo Numminen, Fin.	.20
☐	134	Janne Laukkanen, Fin.	.10
☐	135	Mika Nieminen, Fin.	.10
☐	136	Janne Ojanen, Fin.	.10
☐	137	Jari Kurri, Fin.	.50
☐	138	Esa Tikkanen, Fin.	.20
☐	139	Saku Koivu, Fin.	1.50
☐	140	Teemu Selänne, Fin.	1.50
☐	141	Raimo Helminen, Fin.	.10
☐	142	Mikko Mäkelä, Fin.	.10
☐	143	Christian Ruuttu, Fin.	.10
☐	144	Esa Keskinen, Fin.	.10
☐	145	Dominik Hasek (G), Cze.	1.50
☐	146	Petr Briza (G), Cze.	.25
☐	147	Richard Smehlik, Cze.	.20
☐	148	Leo Gudas, Cze.	.10

	No.	Player	Price
☐	149	Roman Hamrlik, Cze.	.25
☐	150	Antonin Stavjana, Cze.	.10
☐	151	Jiri Slegr, Cze.	.20
☐	152	Jiri Vykoukal, Cze.	.10
☐	153	Tomas Jelinek, Cze.	.10
☐	154	Richard Zemlicka, Cze.	.10
☐	155	Robert Lang, Cze.	.10
☐	156	Michal Pivonka, Cze.	.20
☐	157	Jaromir Jagr, Cze.	2.00
☐	158	Josef Beranek, Cze.	.20
☐	159	Robert Reichel, Cze.	.35
☐	160	Petr Hrbek, Cze.	.10
☐	161	Jiri Kucera, Cze.	.10
☐	162	Kamil Kastak, Cze.	.10
☐	163	Andrei Trefilov (G), Rus.	.20
☐	164	Mikhail Shtalenkov, (G), Rus.	.20
☐	165	Sergei Zubov, Rus.	.35
☐	166	Vladimir Malakhov, Rus.	.20
☐	167	Igor Kravchuk, Rus.	.20
☐	168	Alexei Gusarov, Rus.	.20
☐	169	Alexei Zhitnik, Rus.	.20
☐	170	Alexander Smirnov, Rus.	.10
☐	171	Dimitri Yushkevich, Rus.	.20
☐	172	Alexei Yashin, Rus.	.75
☐	173	Alexei Zhamonov, Rus.	.25
☐	174	Pavel Bure, Rus.	1.50
☐	175	Sergei Fedorov, Rus.	1.00
☐	176	Andrei Kovalenko, Rus.	.20
☐	177	Alexei Kovalev, Rus.	.20
☐	178	Andrei Khomutov, Rus.	.10
☐	179	Valeri Kamensky, Rus.	.25
☐	180	Vyacheslav Bykov, Rus.	.25
☐	181	Claus Dalpiaz (G), Aut.	.10
☐	182	Michael Puschacher, Aut.	.10
☐	183	Ken Strong, Aut.	.10
☐	184	Martin Ulrich, Aut.	.10
☐	185	Andreas Puschnig, Aut.	.10
☐	186	Herbert Hohenberger, Aut.	.10
☐	187	Marty Dallmann, Aut.	.10
☐	188	James Burton, Aut.	.10
☐	189	Michael Shea, Aut.	.10
☐	190	Jim Marthinsen (G), Nor.	.10
☐	191	Örjan Lövdal, Nor.	.10
☐	192	Cato Tom Andersen, Nor.	.10
☐	193	Geir Hoff, Nor.	.10
☐	194	Tommy Jakobsen, Nor.	.10
☐	195	Marius Rath, Nor.	.10
☐	196	Trond Magnussen, Nor.	.10
☐	197	Svein Enok Nörstebö, Nor.	.10
☐	198	Espen Knutsen, Nor.	.25
☐	199	Petri Ylönen (G), Fra.	.10
☐	200	Michel Valliere, Fra.	.10
☐	201	Franck Pajonkowski, Fra.	.10
☐	202	Plerrick Maia, Fra.	.10
☐	203	Christophe Ville, Fra.	.10
☐	204	Serge Poudrier, Fra.	.10
☐	205	Philippe Bozon, Fra.	.10
☐	206	Gerald Guennelon, Fra.	.10
☐	207	Antoine Richer, Fra.	.10
☐	208	Reto Pavoni (G), Sui.	.10
☐	209	Renato Tosio, Sui.	.10
☐	210	Jörg Eberle, Sui.	.10
☐	211	Fredy Luthi, Sui.	.10
☐	212	Christian Weber, Sui.	.10
☐	213	Sandro Bertaggia, Sui.	.10
☐	214	Patrick Howald, Sui.	.10
☐	215	Gil Montandon, Sui.	.10
☐	216	Rick Tschumi, Sui.	.10
☐	217	Klaus Merk (G), Ger.	.10
☐	218	Josef Heiss, Ger.	.10
☐	219	Rich Amann, Ger.	.10
☐	220	Michael Rumrich, Ger.	.10
☐	221	Thomas Brandl, Ger.	.10
☐	222	Andreas Niederberger, Ger.	.10
☐	223	Leo Stefan, Ger.	.10
☐	224	Stefan Ustorf, Ger.	.20
☐	225	Dieter Hegen, Ger.	.10
☐	226	Michael Rosati (G), Ita.	.10
☐	227	Bruno Campese, Ita.	.10
☐	228	Roberto Oberrauch, Ita.	.10
☐	229	Anthony Circelli, Ita.	.10
☐	230	Bill Stewart, Ita.	.10
☐	231	Bruno Zarrillo, Ita.	.10
☐	232	Gaetano Orlando, Ita.	.10
☐	233	Stefan Figliuzzi, Ita.	.10
☐	234	Jimmy Camazzola, Ita.	.10
☐	235	Vladislav Tretiak (G), USSR	1.00
☐	236	Viacheslav Fetisov, USSR	.25
☐	237	Alexei Kasatonov, USSR	.20
☐	238	Sergei Makarov, USSR	.20
☐	239	Igor Larionov, USSR	.25
☐	240	Vladimir Krutov, USSR	.20
☐	241	Valeri Kharlamov, USSR	.50
☐	242	Vladimir Petrov, USSR	.25
☐	243	Boris Mikhailov, USSR	.25
☐	244	OS-GULD 94	.20
☐	245	OS-GULD 94	.20
☐	246	OS-GULD 94	.20
☐	247	VM-GULD 94	.25
☐	248	VM-GULD 94	.25
☐	249	VM-GULD 94	.25
☐	250	Manon Rhéaume	3.00
☐	251	Tomas Brolin/Espen Knutsen	.25
☐	252	Mats Sundin/Roger Andersson	.50
☐	253	Peter Forsberg	1.50
☐	254	Peter Forsberg	1.50
☐	255	Peter Forsberg	1.50
☐	256	Mats Sundin	.75
☐	257	Mats Sundin	.75
☐	258	Mats Sundin	.75
☐	259	Mikael Renberg	.35
☐	260	Mikael Renberg	.35
☐	261	Mikael Renberg	.35
☐	262	Eric Lindros	1.75
☐	263	Eric Lindros	1.75
☐	264	Eric Lindros	1.75
☐	265	Wayne Gretzky	3.00
☐	266	Wayne Gretzky	3.00
☐	267	Wayne Gretzky	3.00
☐	268	CL: Mikael Renberg	.25
☐	269	CL: Mats Sundin	.50
☐	270	CL: Peter Forsberg	1.00

1995 HARTWALL KARJALA

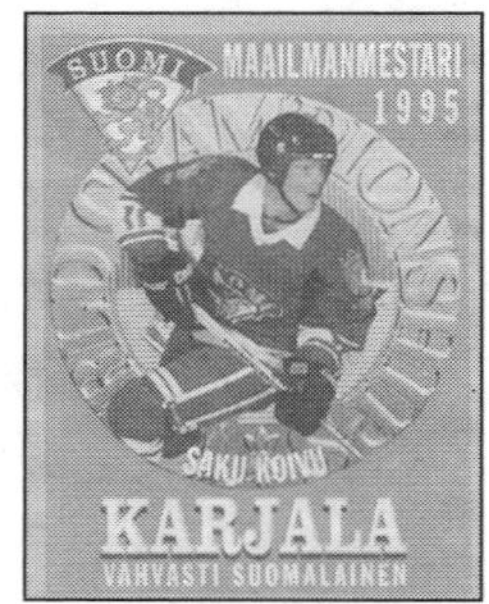

A set of 24 beer labels issued by Hartwall Brewery of the 1995 World Championship Finnish team.

Label Size: 2 1/4" x 3"

Imprint:

Complete Set (24 labels): **45.00**

	Player	NRMT-MT
☐	Raimo Helminen	1.50
☐	Erik Hamalainen	1.50
☐	Timo Jutila	3.00
☐	Sami Kapanen	3.00
☐	Esa Keskinen	1.50
☐	Marko Kiprusoff	1.50
☐	Saku Koivu	15.00
☐	Tero Lehtera	1.50
☐	Jere Lehtinen	5.00
☐	Jarmo Myllys (G)	3.00
☐	Mika Nieminen	1.50
☐	Janne Niinimaa	5.00
☐	Petteri Nummelin	1.50
☐	Janne Ojanen	1.50
☐	Marko Palo	1.50
☐	Ville Peltonen	1.50
☐	Mika Stromberg	1.50
☐	Ari Sulander	1.50
☐	Raimo Summanen	1.50
☐	Jukka Tammi	1.50
☐	Antti Tormanen	1.50
☐	Hannu Virta	1.50
☐	Juha Ylonen	1.50
☐	Curt Lindstrom	1.50

1995 KOULULAINEN

Two 2-card panels issued by the magazine Koululainen. We have no pricing information on this set.

Card Size: 1 7/8" x 4 1/8"

Imprint:

	Player
☐	Wayne Gretzky/Saku Koivu
☐	Jari Kurri/Esa Tikkanen

1995 LEAF LATKALIIGA

A set of 12 candy boxes issued by Leaf for the the Finnish National League. We have no pricing information on this set.

Card Size: 1 7/8" x 2 3/16"

Imprint:

	No.	Player
☐	1	Jere Lehtinen
☐	2	Antti Törmänen
☐	3	Jari Korpisalo
☐	4	Ari-Pekka Siekkinen
☐	5	Ville Peltonen
☐	6	Mika Rautio
☐	7	Juha Riihijarvi
☐	8	Jukka Seppo
☐	9	Pasi Kuivalainen
☐	10	Kari Rosenberg
☐	11	Mika Manninen
☐	12	Janne Ojanen

1995 PANINI WORLD CHAMPIONSHIP STICKERS

These stickers were a European release.

Sticker Size:

Imprint:

Complete Set (300 stickers): **50.00**

Common Player: **.20**

Album (Saku Koivu, et al):

	No.	Player	NRMT-MT
☐	1	Bill Ranford (G), Cdn.	1.00
☐	2	Stéphane Fiset (G), Cdn.	1.00
☐	3	Steve Duchesne, Cdn.	.50
☐	4	Brad Schlegel, Cdn.	.20
☐	5	Luke Richardson, Cdn.	.50
☐	6	Darryl Sydor, Cdn.	.50
☐	7	Yves Racine, Cdn.	.20
☐	8	Rob Blake, Cdn.	1.00
☐	9	Marc Bergevin, Cdn.	.20
☐	10	Paul Coffey, Cdn.	1.00
☐	11	Jason Arnott, Cdn.	1.00
☐	12	Geoff Sanderson, Cdn.	.50
☐	13	Shayne Corson, Cdn.	1.00
☐	14	Mike Ricci, Cdn.	.50
☐	15	Kelly Buchberger, Cdn.	.50
☐	16	Brendan Shanahan, Cdn.	3.00
☐	17	Pat Verbeek, Cdn.	.50
☐	18	Nelson Emerson, Cdn.	.50

☐ 19 Rod Brind'Amour, Cdn. 1.00
☐ 20 Joe Sakic, Cdn. 4.00
☐ 21 Luc Robitaille, Cdn. 1.00
☐ 22 Steve Thomas, Cdn. .50
☐ 23 Paul Kariya, Cdn. 6.50
☐ 24 Theoren Fleury, Cdn. 1.50
☐ 25 Dave Gagner, Cdn. .50
☐ 26 Valeri Ivannikov (G), Rus. .20
☐ 27 Mikhail Shtalenkov (G), Rus. .50
☐ 28 Nikolai Tsulygin, Rus. .20
☐ 29 Dmitri Krasotkin, Rus. .20
☐ 30 Morat Davydov, Rus. .20
☐ 31 Andrei Sklopintsev, Rus. .20
☐ 32 Oleg Davydov, Rus. .20
☐ 33 Evgeny Gribko, Rus. .20
☐ 34 Andrei Yakhanov, Rus. .20
☐ 35 Igor Nikulin, Rus. .20
☐ 36 Valeri Kamensky, Rus. 1.00
☐ 37 Boris Timorfeyev, Rus. .20
☐ 38 Dmitri Denisov, Rus. .20
☐ 39 Rall Muftiyev, Rus. .20
☐ 40 Andrei Tarasyenko, Rus. .20
☐ 41 Oleg Belov, Rus. .20
☐ 42 Andrei Kovalenko, Rus. .50
☐ 43 Igor Varitski, Rus. .20
☐ 44 Ravil Yakubov, Rus. .20
☐ 45 Vyacheslav Kozlov, Rus. .20
☐ 46 Alexander Vinogradov, Rus. .20
☐ 47 Yuri Tsyplakov, Rus. .20
☐ 48 Stanislav Romanov, Rus. .20
☐ 49 Vyacheslav Bykov, Rus. .50
☐ 50 Andrei Khomutov, Rus. .50
☐ 51 Joseph Heiss (G), Ger. .20
☐ 52 Kalus Merk (G), Ger. .20
☐ 53 Mirko Lüdemann, Ger. .20
☐ 54 Ulrich Hiemer, Ger. .20
☐ 55 Torsten Kienass, Ger. .20
☐ 56 Jayson Meyer, Ger. .20
☐ 57 Josef Lehner, Ger. .20
☐ 58 Ron Fischer, Ger. .20
☐ 59 Michael Bresagk, Ger. .20
☐ 60 Andreas Niederberger, Ger. .20
☐ 61 Peter Guida, Ger. .20
☐ 62 Jan Benda, Ger. .50
☐ 63 Thomas Brandl, Ger. .20
☐ 64 Andreas Lupzig, Ger. .20
☐ 65 Michael Rumrich, Ger. .20
☐ 66 Benoit Doucet, Ger. .20
☐ 67 Raimond Hilger, Ger. .20
☐ 68 Georg Franz, Ger. .20
☐ 69 Jörg Handrick, Ger. .20
☐ 70 Dieter Hegen, Ger. .20
☐ 71 Ernst Köpf, Ger. .20
☐ 72 Günter Oswald, Ger. .20
☐ 73 Georg Holzmann, Ger. .20
☐ 74 Jürgen Rumrich, Ger. .20
☐ 75 Leo Stfean, Ger. .20
☐ 76 Bruno Campese (G), Ita. .20
☐ 77 Michael Rosati (G), Ita. .20
☐ 78 Giovanni Marchetti, Ita. .20
☐ 79 Georg Comloi, Ita. .20
☐ 80 Luigi de Corte, Ita. .20
☐ 81 Robert Oberrauch, Ita. .20
☐ 82 Anthony Circelli, Ita. .20
☐ 83 Alex Thaler, Ita. .20
☐ 84 Carlo Lorenzi, Ita. .20
☐ 85 Michael de Angelis, Ita. .20
☐ 86 Emilio Iovio, Ita. .20
☐ 87 Gaetano Orlando, Ita. .20
☐ 88 Lucio Topatigh, Ita. .20
☐ 89 Stefano Figliuzzi, Ita. .20
☐ 90 Bruno Zarrillo, Ita. .20
☐ 91 Mark Montanari, Ita. .20
☐ 92 Armando Chelodi, Ita. .20
☐ 93 Mirko Moroder, Ita. .20
☐ 94 Alex Gschliesser, Ita. .20
☐ 95 Maurizio Mansi, Ita. .20
☐ 96 Petri Ylönen (G), Fra. .20
☐ 97 Michel Valliere (G), Fra. .20
☐ 98 Serge Djelloul, Fra. .20
☐ 99 Christophe Moyon, Fra. .20
☐ 100 Gerald Guennelon, Fra. .20
☐ 101 Philippe Lemoine, Fra. .20
☐ 102 Denis Perez, Fra. .20
☐ 103 Serge Poudrier, Fra. .20
☐ 104 Steven Woodburn, Fra. .20
☐ 105 Michael Babin, Fra. .20
☐ 106 Benjamin Angnel, Fra. .20
☐ 107 Stéphane Arcangeloni, Fra. .20
☐ 108 Laurent Deschaume, Fra. .20
☐ 109 Pierre Pousse, Fra. .20
☐ 110 Patrick Dunn, Fra. .20
☐ 111 Pierrick Maia, Fra. .20
☐ 112 Philippe Bozon, Fra. .20
☐ 113 Christian Pouget, Fra. .20
☐ 114 Antoine Richer, Fra. .20
☐ 115 Richard Aimonetto, Fra. .20
☐ 116 Reto Pavoni (G), Sui. .20
☐ 117 Renato Tosio (G), Sui. .20
☐ 118 Marco Bayer, Sui. .20
☐ 119 Sandro Bertaggia, Sui. .20
☐ 120 Frédy Bobillier, Sui. .20
☐ 121 Dino Kessler, Sui. .20
☐ 122 Sven Leuenberger, Sui. .20
☐ 123 Martin Steinegger, Sui. .20
☐ 124 Andreas Zehnder, Sui. .20
☐ 125 Misko Antisin, Sui. .20
☐ 126 Gian-Marco Crameri, Sui. .20
☐ 127 Jörg Eberle, Sui. .20
☐ 128 Patrick Fischer, Sui. .20
☐ 129 Patrick Howald, Sui. .20
☐ 130 Marcel Jenni, Sui. .20
☐ 131 Gil Montandon, Sui. .20
☐ 132 Pascal Schaller, Sui. .20
☐ 133 Andy Ton, Sui. .20
☐ 134 Roberto Triulzi, Sui. .20
☐ 135 Theo Wittman, Sui. .20
☐ 136 Roger Nordström (G), Swe. .20
☐ 137 Thomas Östlund (G), Swe. .20
☐ 138 Magnus Svensson, Swe. .20
☐ 139 Tommy Sjödin, Swe. .20
☐ 140 Fredrik Stillman, Swe. .20
☐ 141 Tomas Jonsson, Swe. .50
☐ 142 Stefan Larsson, Swe. .20
☐ 143 Leif Rohlin, Swe. .20
☐ 144 Marcus Ragnarsson, Swe. .50
☐ 145 Christer Olsson, Swe. .20
☐ 146 Morgan Samuelsson, Swe. .20
☐ 147 Andreas Dackell, Swe. .50
☐ 148 Jonas Johnsson, Swe. .20
☐ 149 Charles Berglund, Swe. .20
☐ 150 Erik Huusko, Swe. .20
☐ 151 Daniel Rydmark, Swe. .20
☐ 152 Patrik Carnbäck, Swe. .20
☐ 153 Mats Lindgren, Swe. .50
☐ 154 Jonas Bergkvist, Swe. .20
☐ 155 Stefan Örnskog, Swe. .20
☐ 156 Per-Erik Eklund, Swe. .50
☐ 157 Tomas Forslund, Swe. .20
☐ 158 Roger Hansson, Swe. .20
☐ 159 Håkan Åhlund, Swe. .20
☐ 160 Daniel Alfredsson, Swe. 2.00
☐ 161 Jarmo Myllys (G), Fin. .50
☐ 162 Jukka Tammi (G), Fin. .20
☐ 163 Mika Strömberg, Fin. .20
☐ 164 Erik Hämäläinen, Fin. .20
☐ 165 Karri Kivi, Fin. .20
☐ 166 Timo Jutila, Fin. .50
☐ 167 Petteri Nummelin, Fin. .20
☐ 168 Hannu Virta, Fin. .20
☐ 169 Marko Kiprusov, Fin. .20
☐ 170 Waltteri Immonen, Fin. .20
☐ 171 Janne Ojanen, Fin. .20
☐ 172 Esa Keskinen, Fin. .20
☐ 173 Marko Jantunen, Fin. .20
☐ 174 Saku Koivu, Fin. 3.50
☐ 175 Marko Palo, Fin. .20
☐ 176 Tero Lehterä, Fin. .20
☐ 177 Mika Alatalo, Fin. .20
☐ 178 Ville Peltonen, Fin. .20
☐ 179 Raimo Helminen, Fin. .20
☐ 180 Petri Varis, Fin. .20
☐ 181 Jokke Heinänen, Fin. .20
☐ 182 Timo Saarikoski, Fin. .20
☐ 183 Sami Kapanen, Fin. .20
☐ 184 Tero Arkiomaa, Fin. .20
☐ 185 Mika Nieminen, Fin. .20
☐ 186 Petr Briza (G), Cze. .50
☐ 187 Roman Turek (G), Cze. .50
☐ 188 Milos Holan, Cze. .20
☐ 189 Drahomir Kadlec, Cze. .20
☐ 190 Frantisek Kaberle, Cze. .20
☐ 191 Bedrich Scerban, Cze. .20
☐ 192 Roman Hamrlik, Cze. 1.00
☐ 193 Jan Vopat, Cze. .50
☐ 194 Antonin Stavjana, Cze. .20
☐ 195 Jiri Vykoukal, Cze. .20
☐ 196 Jiri Veber, Cze. .20
☐ 197 Frantisek Musil, Cze. .20
☐ 198 Richard Zemlicka, Cze. .20
☐ 199 Kamil Kastak, Cze. .20
☐ 200 Jiri Kucera, Cze. .20
☐ 201 Roman Horak, Cze. .20
☐ 202 Martin Rucinsky, Cze. .50
☐ 203 Josef Beranek, Cze. .50
☐ 204 Bobby Holik, Cze. .50
☐ 205 Otakar Janecky, Cze. .20
☐ 206 Jiri Dolezal, Cze. .20
☐ 207 Martin Straka, Cze. .50
☐ 208 Martin Hostak, Cze. .20
☐ 209 Radek Toupal, Cze. .20
☐ 210 Tomas Kapusta, Cze. .20
☐ 211 Guy Hebert (G), USA. 1.00
☐ 212 Mike Richter (G), USA. 1.50
☐ 213 Shawn Chambers, USA. .20
☐ 214 Sean Hill, USA. .50
☐ 215 Don McSween, USA. .20
☐ 216 Pat Neaton, USA. .20
☐ 217 Barry Richter, USA. .20
☐ 218 Craig Wolanin, USA. .20
☐ 219 Gary Suter, USA. .50
☐ 220 Bob Beers, USA. .20
☐ 221 Brett Hauer, USA. .20
☐ 222 Peter Ciavaglia, USA. .20
☐ 223 Phil Bourque, USA. .20
☐ 224 Shjon Podein, USA. .20
☐ 225 John Lilley, USA. .20
☐ 226 Tim Sweeney, USA. .20
☐ 227 Scott Young, USA. .50
☐ 228 Craig Janney, USA. .20
☐ 229 Joe Sacco, USA. .20
☐ 230 Jeff Lazaro, USA. .20
☐ 231 Doug Weight, USA. 1.50
☐ 232 Thomas Bisset, USA. .20
☐ 233 Jim Campbell, USA. .50
☐ 234 Mark Beaufait, USA. .20
☐ 235 Peter Ferraro, USA. .20
☐ 236 Jim Marthinsen (G), Nor. .20
☐ 237 Robert Schinstad (G), Nor. .20
☐ 238 Jan Roar Fagerli, Nor. .20
☐ 239 Petter Salsten, Nor. .20
☐ 240 Carl Oscar Bøe Andersen, Nor. .20
☐ 241 Svein Enok Nørstebø, Nor. .20
☐ 242 Thommie Eriksen, Nor. .20
☐ 243 Tom Erik Olsen, Nor. .20
☐ 244 Geir Hoff, Nor. .20
☐ 245 Bjørn Anders Dahl, Nor. .20
☐ 246 Trond Magnussen, Nor. .20
☐ 247 Ørjan Løvdal, Nor. .20
☐ 248 Espen Knutsen, Nor. .20
☐ 249 Rune Gulliksen, Nor. .20
☐ 250 Erik Paulsen, Nor. .20
☐ 251 Sjur Robert Nilsen, Nor. .20
☐ 252 Petter Thoresen, Nor. .20
☐ 253 Rune Fjeldstad, Nor. .20
☐ 254 Erik Tveten, Nor. .20
☐ 255 Henrik Aaby, Nor. .20
☐ 256 Michael Puschacher (G), Aut. .20
☐ 257 Claus Dalpiaz (G), Aut. .20
☐ 258 Michael Günter, Aut. .20
☐ 259 Martin Ulrich, Aut. .20
☐ 260 Peter Kasper, Aut. .20
☐ 261 Engelbert Linder, Aut. .20
☐ 262 Herbert Hohenberger, Aut. .20
☐ 263 Gerhard Unterluggauer, Aut. .20
☐ 264 Martin Krainz, Aut. .20
☐ 265 Helmut Karel, Aut. .20
☐ 266 Werner Kerth, Aut. .20
☐ 267 Dieter Kalt, Aut. .20
☐ 268 Patrick Pilloni, Aut. .20
☐ 269 Mario Schaden, Aut. .20
☐ 270 Wolfgang Kromp, Aut. .20
☐ 271 Günter Lanzinger, Aut. .20
☐ 272 Manfred Mühr, Aut. .20
☐ 273 Gerald Ressmann, Aut. .20

	No.	Player	Price
☐	274	Siegfried Habert, Aut.	.20
☐	275	Christoph Brandner, Aut.	.20
☐	276	Wayne Gretzky, Cdn.	10.00
☐	277	Mario Lemieux, Cdn.	8.00
☐	278	Eric Lindros, Cdn.	6.50
☐	279	Mark Messier, Cdn.	2.50
☐	280	Steve Yzerman, Cdn.	5.00
☐	281	Pavel Bure, Rus.	3.50
☐	282	Sergei Fedorov, Rus.	2.50
☐	283	Igor Larionov, Rus.	1.00
☐	284	Sergei Makarov, Rus.	.50
☐	285	Alexander Mogilny, Rus.	1.50
☐	286	Ulf Dahlen, Swe.	.50
☐	287	Peter Forsberg, Swe.	5.00
☐	288	Mikael Renberg, Swe.	1.00
☐	289	Ulf Samuelsson, Swe.	.50
☐	290	Tomas Sandström, Swe.	.50
☐	291	Thomas Steen, Swe.	.50
☐	292	Mats Sundin, Swe.	2.50
☐	293	Jari Kurri, Fin.	1.00
☐	294	Teemu Selänne, Fin.	3.50
☐	295	Esa Tikkanen, Fin.	.50
☐	296	Dominik Hasek (G), Cze.	3.50
☐	297	Jaromir Jagr, Cze.	5.00
☐	298	Robert Reichel, Cze.	1.00
☐	299	Brett Hull, USA.	2.50
☐	300	Brian Leetch, USA.	1.50

1995 PARKHURST PHONE CARDS

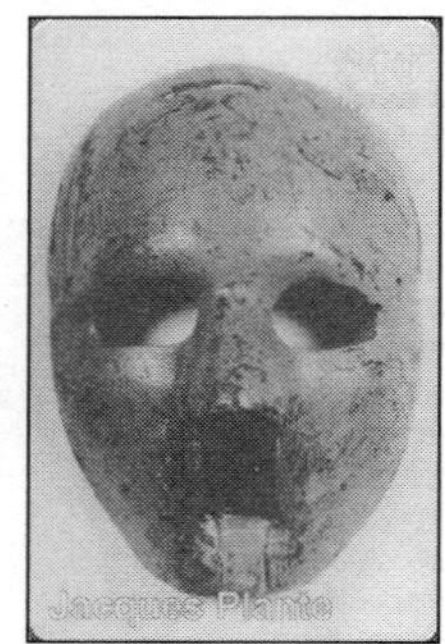

These telecards premiered at the National Sportscard Collectors Convention in St. Louis. These Incomnet telecards are licensed by the NHLPA. We have no pricing information on these cards.

Imprint:

	Player
☐	Ed Belfour (G)
☐	Curtis Joseph (G)
☐	Kirk McLean (G)
☐	Andy Moog (G)
☐	Félix Potvin (G)
☐	John Vanbiesbrouck (G)
☐	Jacques Plante Mask
☐	B. Hull/ B. Shanahan/ C. Joseph (G)

1995 PARKHURST PHONE CARDS

We have no pricing information on these cards.

Imprint: Canada Telecom Network Inc.

	Player
☐	Doug Gilmour
☐	Brett Hull
☐	Jaromir Jagr
☐	Trevor Linden
☐	Eric Lindros
☐	Mark Messier
☐	Félix Potvin (G)
☐	Patrick Roy (G)

1995 SEMIC

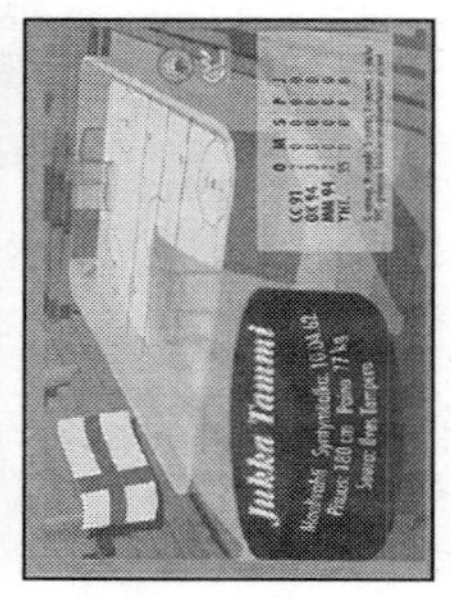

Imprint: Semic Sport Cards

Complete Set (240 cards): 40.00

Common Player: .15

	No.	Player	NRMT-MT
☐	1	Pasi Kuivalainen, Fin.	.15
☐	2	Marko Kiprusoff, Fin.	.15
☐	3	Tuomas Grönman, Fin.	.20
☐	4	Erik Hämäläinen, Fin.	.15
☐	5	Timo Jutila, Fin.	.25
☐	6	Pasi Sormunen, Fin.	.15
☐	7	Waltteri Immonen, Fin.	.15
☐	8	Janne Ojanen, Fin.	.15
☐	9	Esa Keskinen, Fin.	.15
☐	10	Kimmo Timonen, Fin.	.15
☐	11	Saku Koivu, Fin.	1.50
☐	12	Janne Laukkanen, Fin.	.15
☐	13	Marko Pale, Fin.	.15
☐	14	Raimo Helminen, Fin.	.15
☐	15	Mika Alatalo, Fin.	.15
☐	16	Ville Peltonen, Fin.	.15
☐	17	Jari Kurri, Fin.	.50
☐	18	Jari Korpisalo, Fin.	.15
☐	19	Kimmo Rintanen, Fin.	.15
☐	20	Jere Lehtinen, Fin.	.50
☐	21	Kalle Sahlstedt, Fin.	.15
☐	22	Christian Ruuttu, Fin.	.20
☐	23	Hannu Virta, Fin.	.15
☐	24	Sami Kapanen, Fin.	.20
☐	25	Marko Tuulola, Fin.	.15
☐	26	Mika Strömberg, Fin.	.15
☐	27	Tero Lehterä, Fin.	.15
☐	28	Petri Varis, Fin.	.15
☐	29	Mikko Peltola, Fin.	.15
☐	30	Jukka Tammi (G), Fin.	.15
☐	31	Tero Arkiomaa, Fin.	.15
☐	32	Olli Kaski, Fin.	.15
☐	33	Pekka Laksola, Fin.	.15
☐	34	Mika Välilä, Fin.	.15
☐	35	Jarmo Myllys (G), Fin.	.20
☐	36	Harri Laurila, Fin.	.15
☐	37	Teppo Numminen, Fin.	.15
☐	38	Jyrki Lumme, Fin.	.20
☐	39	Petteti Nummelin, Fin.	.15
☐	40	Mika Nieminen, Fin.	.15
☐	41	Teemu Selänne, Fin.	1.50
☐	42	Mikko Mäkelä, Fin.	.15
☐	43	Esa Tikkanen, Fin.	.15
☐	44	Jarkko Varvio, Fin.	.15
☐	45	Vesa Viitakoski, Fin.	.15
☐	46	Juha Riihijärvi, Fin.	.15
☐	47	Markus Ketterer (G), Fin.	.15
☐	48	Mikko Haapakoski, Fin.	.15
☐	49	Antti Törmänen, Fin.	.15
☐	50	Time Peltomaa, Fin.	.15
☐	51	Rauli Raitanen, Fin.	.15
☐	52	Roger Nordström (G), Swe.	.15
☐	53	Tommy Salo (G), Swe.	.20
☐	54	Tommy Söderström (G), Swe.	.20
☐	55	Magnus Svensson, Swe.	.15
☐	56	Fredrik Stillman, Swe.	.15
☐	57	Nicklas Lidstrom, Swe.	.15
☐	58	Roger Johansson, Swe.	.15
☐	59	Kenny Jonsson, Swe.	.20
☐	60	Peter Andersson, Swe.	.15
☐	61	Tommy Sjödin, Swe.	.15
☐	62	Mats Sundin, Swe.	1.00
☐	63	Jonas Bergqvisd, Swe.	.15
☐	64	Peter Forsberg, Swe.	2.00
☐	65	Roger Hansson, Swe.	.15
☐	66	Jargen Jansson, Swe.	.15
☐	67	Charles Berglund, Swe.	.15
☐	68	Mikael Johansson, Swe.	.15
☐	69	Tomas Forslund, Swe.	.15
☐	70	Anders Dackell, Swe.	.20
☐	71	Stefan Öjrnskog, Swe.	.15
☐	72	Mikael Andersson, Swe.	.20
☐	73	Jan Larsson, Swe.	.15
☐	74	Patrik Carnbäck, Swe.	.20
☐	75	Håkan Loob, Swe.	.25
☐	76	Patrik Juhlin, Swe.	.20
☐	77	Bill Ranford (G), Cdn.	.50
☐	78	Ed Belfour (G), Cdn.	.75
☐	79	Rob Blake, Cdn.	.20
☐	80	Yves Racine, Cdn.	.20
☐	81	Steve Smith, Cdn.	.20
☐	82	Paul Coffey, Cdn.	.50
☐	83	Larry Murphy, Cdn.	.50
☐	84	Mark Tinordi, Cdn.	.20
☐	85	Al MacInnis, Cdn.	.20
☐	86	Paul Kariya, Cdn.	4.50
☐	87	Joe Sakic, Cdn.	1.75
☐	88	Brendan Shanahan, Cdn.	3.00
☐	89	Luc Robitaille, Cdn.	.50
☐	90	Rod Brind'Amour, Cdn.	.50
☐	91	Shayne Corson, Cdn.	.50
☐	92	Mike Ricci, Cdn.	.20
☐	93	Mario Lemieux, Cdn.	3.00
☐	94	Eric Lindros, Cdn.	2.50
☐	95	Russ Courtnall, Cdn.	.20
☐	96	Theoren Fleury, Cdn.	.50
☐	97	Mark Messier, Cdn.	1.00
☐	98	Rick Tocchet, Cdn.	.20
☐	99	Wayne Gretzky, Cdn.	4.00
☐	100	Steve Larmer, Cdn.	.20
☐	101	Brett Lindros, Cdn.	.20
☐	102	John Vanbiesbrouck (G), USA.	1.25
☐	103	Craig Wolanin, USA.	.20
☐	104	Chris Chelios, USA.	.75
☐	105	Brian Leetch, USA.	.50
☐	106	Kevin Hatcher, USA.	.20
☐	107	Craig Janney, USA.	.20
☐	108	Tim Sweeney, USA.	.20
☐	109	Shawn Chambers, USA.	.20
☐	110	Scott Young, USA.	.20
☐	111	John Lilley, USA.	.20
☐	112	Joe Sacco, USA.	.20
☐	113	Brett Hull, USA.	1.00
☐	114	Pat LaFontaine, USA.	.50
☐	115	Joel Otto, USA.	.20
☐	116	Mike Modano, USA.	1.00
☐	117	Tony Granato, USA.	.20
☐	118	Jeremy Roenick, USA.	.50
☐	119	Jeff Lazaro, USA.	.20
☐	120	Brian Mullen, USA.	.20
☐	121	Mikhail Shtalenkov (G), Rus.	.25
☐	122	Valeri Ivannikov, Rus.	.15
☐	123	Andrei Nikolishin, Rus.	.15
☐	124	Ilja Byakin, Rus.	.15
☐	125	Aleksander Smirnov, Rus.	.15
☐	126	Dimitri Yushkevich, Rus.	.20
☐	127	Sergei Shendelev, Rus.	.15
☐	128	Alexei Zhitnik, Rus.	.20
☐	129	Igor Ulanov, Rus.	.15
☐	130	Dmitri Frolov, Rus.	.15
☐	131	Valeri Kamensky, Rus.	.50
☐	132	Igor Feduiov, Rus.	.15
☐	133	Andrei Kovalenko, Rus.	.15
☐	134	Valeri Bure, Rus.	.25
☐	135	Sergei Berezin, Rus.	.50
☐	136	Alexei Yashin, Rus.	.75
☐	137	Vyacheslav Kozlov, Rus.	.20
☐	138	Vyacheslav Bykov, Rus.	.25
☐	139	Andrei Khomutov, Rus.	.20
☐	140	Petr Briza (G), Cze.	.20
☐	141	Dominik Hasek (G), Cze.	1.50
☐	142	Roman Turek (G), Cze.	.50
☐	143	Jan Vopat, Cze.	.20
☐	144	Drahomir Kadlec, Cze.	.15
☐	145	Petr Pavlas, Cze.	.15
☐	146	Frantisek Kucera, Cze.	.15
☐	147	Jiri Veber, Cze.	.15
☐	148	David Vyborny, Cze.	.15
☐	149	Radek Toupalv, Cze.	.15

	No.	Player	Price
☐	150	Jiri Kucera, Cze.	.15
☐	151	Richard Zemlicka, Cze.	.15
☐	152	Martin Rucinsky, Cze.	.25
☐	153	Jiri Dolezal, Cze.	.15
☐	154	Josef Beranek, Cze.	.25
☐	155	Martin Prochazka, Cze.	.15
☐	156	Tomas Srsen, Cze.	.15
☐	157	Vavid Bruk, Cze.	.15
☐	158	Jaromir Jagr, Cze.	2.00
☐	159	Jan Caloun, Cze.	.15
☐	160	Martin Straka, Cze.	.25
☐	161	Roman Horak, Cze.	.15
☐	162	Frantisek Musil, Cze.	.20
☐	163	Peter Hrbek, Cze.	.15
☐	164	Jan Alino, Cze.	.15
☐	165	Joseph Heiss (G), Ger.	.15
☐	166	Peter Gulda, Ger.	.15
☐	167	Jayson Meyer, Ger.	.15
☐	168	Ernst Köpf, Ger.	.15
☐	169	Raimund Hilger, Ger.	.15
☐	170	Richard Böhm, Ger.	.15
☐	171	Michael Rosati (G), Ita.	.15
☐	172	Michael de Angelis, Ita.	.15
☐	173	Anthony Circelli, Ita.	.15
☐	174	Gaetano Orlando, Ita.	.15
☐	175	Lucio Topatigh, Ita.	.15
☐	176	Martin Pavlu, Ita.	.15
☐	177	Jim Marthinsen (G), Nor.	.15
☐	178	Petter Salsten, Nor.	.15
☐	179	Tommy Jacobsen, Nor.	.15
☐	180	Morten Finsted, Nor.	.15
☐	181	Tom Andersen, Nor.	.15
☐	182	Magnus Rath, Nor.	.15
☐	183	Michael Puschacher (G), Aut.	.15
☐	184	James Burton, Aut.	.15
☐	185	Michael Shea, Aut.	.15
☐	186	Dieter Kalt, Aut.	.15
☐	187	Manfred Muhr, Aut.	.15
☐	188	Andreas Pusnik, Aut.	.15
☐	189	Renato Tosio (G), Sui.	.15
☐	190	Doug Honneger, Sui.	.15
☐	191	Felix Hollenstein, Sui.	.15
☐	192	Jörg Eberle, Sui.	.15
☐	193	Gil Montandon, Sui.	.15
☐	194	Roberto Triulzi, Sui.	.15
☐	195	Petri Yönen (G), Fra.	.15
☐	196	Bruno Maynort, Fra.	.15
☐	197	Michel Leblanc, Fra.	.15
☐	198	Benoit Laporte, Fra.	.15
☐	199	Christophe Ville, Fra.	.15
☐	200	Antoine Richer, Fra.	.15
☐	201	AS: Bill Ranford (G), Cdn.	.15
☐	202	AS: Timo Jutila, Fin.	.25
☐	203	AS: Magnus Svensson, Swe.	.20
☐	204	AS: Jari Kurri, Fin.	.50
☐	205	AS: Saku Koivu, Fin.	1.50
☐	206	AS: Paul Kariya, Cdn.	2.50
☐	207	Jarmo Myllys (G), Fin.	.20
☐	208	Bill Ranford (G), Cdn.	.50
☐	209	Roger Nordström (G), Swe.	.15
☐	210	Guy Hebert (G), USA.	.50
☐	211	Mikail Shtalenkov (G), Rus.	.25
☐	212	Tommy Söderström (G), Swe.	.25
☐	213	Petr Briza (G), Cze.	.25
☐	214	Dominik Hasek (G), Cze.	1.50
☐	215	Tom Barrasso (G),	.25
☐	216	Jukka Tammi (G), Fin.	.20
☐	217	John Vanbiesbrouck (G), USA.	1.25
☐	218	Mike Richter (G), USA.	.50
☐	219	Saku Koivu, Fin.	1.00
☐	220	Saku Koivu, Fin.	1.00
☐	221	Saku Koivu, Fin.	1.00
☐	222	Saku Koivu, Fin.	1.00
☐	223	Saku Koivu, Fin.	1.00
☐	224	Saku Koivu, Fin.	3.00
☐	225	Tuomas Grönman, Fin.	.20
☐	226	Jani Nikko, Fin.	.15
☐	227	Janne Niinimaa, Fin.	.75
☐	228	Jukka Tiilikainen, Fin.	.15
☐	229	Kimmo Rintanen, Fin.	.15
☐	230	Ville Peltonen, Fin.	.15
☐	231	Sami Kapanen, Fin.	.20
☐	232	Jere Lehtinen, Fin.	.75
☐	233	Kimmo Timonen, Fin.	.15
☐	234	Jonni Vauhkonen, Fin.	.15
☐	235	Juha Lind, Fin.	.15
☐	236	Tommi Miettinen, Fin.	.15
☐	237	Jere Karalahti, Fin.	.15
☐	238	Antti Aalto, Fin.	.20
☐	239	Teemu Kohvakka, Fin.	.15
☐	240	Niko Mikkola, Fin.	.15

1995 SUOMEN BECKETT ALL-STARS

A set of 8 ad cards.
Card Size: 2 7/8" x 4 1/2"
Imprint:
Complete Set (8 cards): 25.00

	No.	Player	NRMT-MT
☐	1	Saku Koivu	12.00
☐	2	Jere Lehtinen	5.00
☐	3	Ville Peltonen	3.00
☐	4	Erik Hamalainen	2.00
☐	5	Sami Kapanen	2.00
☐	6	Marko Kiprusoff	2.00
☐	7	Mika Stromberg	2.00
☐	8	Marko Palo	2.00

1995 TOPPS FINEST BRONZE

These oversized cards were sold by Topps as a complete set.
Imprint:
Series Two Set (7 cards): 150.00

	No.	Player	NRMT-MT
☐	8	Brett Hull, Stl.	20.00
☐	9	Paul Kariya, Ana.	60.00
☐	10	Cam Neely, Bos.	18.00
☐	11	Mats Sundin, Tor.	20.00
☐	12	Martin Brodeur (G), N.J.	35.00
☐	13	Jeremy Roenick, Chi.	18.00
☐	14	Brian Leetch, NYR.	18.00

1995 - 96 APS

We have little pricing information on this set. Our checklist is supposedly incomplete. Jaromir Jagr is the most expensive single at $15-20. Singles start at 25¢.
Imprint:

	No.	Player
☐	1	Horst Valasek, Dadak Vsetin
☐	2	Zdislav Tabara, Dadak Vsetin
☐	3	Roman Cechmanek, Dadak Vsetin
☐	4	Ivo Pesat, Dadak Vsetin
☐	5	Alexei Jaskin, Dadak Vsetin
☐	6	Stanislav Pavelec, Dadak Vsetin
☐	7	Jan Srdinko, Dadak Vsetin
☐	8	Antonin Stavjana, Dadak Vsetin
☐	9	Pavel Taborsky, Dadak Vsetin
☐	10	Jiri Veber, Dadak Vsetin
☐	11	Daniel Vrla, Dadak Vsetin
☐	12	Miroslav Barus, Dadak Vsetin
☐	13	Ivan Padelek, Dadak Vsetin
☐	14	Libor Forch, Dadak Vsetin
☐	15	Andrej Galkin, Dadak Vsetin
☐	16	Lubos Jenacek, Dadak Vsetin
☐	17	Tomas Srsen, Dadak Vsetin
☐	18	Rostislav Vlach, Dadak Vsetin
☐	19	Zbynek Marak, Dadak Vsetin
☐	20	Jiri Dopita, Dadak Vsetin
☐	21	Ales Polcar, Dadak Vsetin
☐	22	Roman Stantien, Dadak Vsetin
☐	23	Michal Tomek, Dadak Vsetin
☐	24	Jiri Zadrazil, Dadak Vsetin
☐	25	Pavel Augusta, Dadak Vsetin
☐	26	Tomas Jakes, Dadak Vsetin
☐	27	Vladimir Vujtek, Sr., ZPS Zlin
☐	28	Zdenek Cech, ZPS Zlin
☐	29	Jaroslav Kames, ZPS Zlin
☐	30	Pavel Malac, ZPS Zlin
☐	31	Jan Vavrecka, ZPS Zlin
☐	32	Miroslav Javin, ZPS Zlin
☐	33	Stanislav Medrik, ZPS Zlin
☐	34	Pavel Kowalczyk, ZPS Zlin
☐	35	Miroslav Guren, ZPS Zlin
☐	36	Radim Tesarik, ZPS Zlin
☐	37	Jan Krajicek, ZPS Zlin
☐	38	Jiri Marusak, ZPS Zlin
☐	39	Josef Straub, ZPS Zlin
☐	40	Pavel Janku, ZPS Zlin
☐	41	Roman Meluzin, ZPS Zlin
☐	42	Miroslav Okal, ZPS Zlin
☐	43	Zdenek Okal, ZPS Zlin
☐	44	David Bruk, ZPS Zlin
☐	45	Jaroslav Hub, ZPS Zlin
☐	46	Petr Cajanek, ZPS Zlin
☐	47	Tomas Nemcicky, ZPS Zlin
☐	48	Martin Kotasek, ZPS Zlin
☐	49	Zdenek Sedlak, ZPS Zlin
☐	50	Petr Leska, ZPS Zlin
☐	51	Vladimir Caldr, Ceske Budejovice
☐	52	Jaroslav Liska, Ceske Budejovice
☐	53	Oldrich Svoboda, Ceske Budejovice
☐	54	Robert Slavik, Ceske Budejovice
☐	55	Rudolf Suchanek, Ceske Budejovice
☐	56	Milan Nedoma, Ceske Budejovice
☐	57	Lukas Zib, Ceske Budejovice
☐	58	Karel Soudek, Ceske Budejovice
☐	59	Petr Sedy, Ceske Budejovice
☐	60	Libor Zabransky, Ceske Budejovice
☐	61	Kamil Toupal, Ceske Budejovice
☐	62	Michal Kubicek, Ceske Budejovice
☐	63	Martin Masak, Ceske Budejovice
☐	64	Radek Belohlav, Ceske Budejovice
☐	65	Radek Toupal, Ceske Budejovice
☐	66	Pavel Pycha, Ceske Budejovice
☐	67	Lubos Rob, Ceske Budejovice
☐	68	Filip Turek, Ceske Budejovice
☐	69	Ondrej Vosta, Ceske Budejovice
☐	70	Roman Bozek, Ceske Budejovice
☐	71	Jaroslav Brabec, Ceske Budejovice
☐	72	Petr Sailer, Ceske Budejovice
☐	73	Martin Strba, Ceske Budejovice
☐	74	Zdenek Sperger, Ceske Budejovice
☐	75	Jan Neliba, Kladno
☐	76	Zdenek Miller, Kladno
☐	77	Martin Chlad, Kladno
☐	78	Jiri Kucera, Kladno
☐	79	Jan Dlouhy, Kladno
☐	80	Tomas Kaberle, Kladno
☐	81	Petr Kasik, Kladno
☐	82	Jan Krulis, Kladno
☐	83	Petr Kuda, Kladno
☐	84	Libor Prochazka, Kladno
☐	85	Martin Stepanek, Kladno
☐	86	Marek Zidlicky, Kladno
☐	87	Jiri Beranek, Kladno
☐	88	Jiri Burger, Kladno
☐	89	David Cermak, Kladno
☐	90	Milos Kajer, Kladno
☐	91	Miroslav Mach, Kladno
☐	92	Tomas Mikolasek, Kladno
☐	93	Pavel Patera, Kladno
☐	94	Martin Prochazka, Kladno
☐	95	Petr Ton, Kladno
☐	96	Otakar Vejvoda, Kladno
☐	97	Josef Zajic, Kladno
☐	98	Josef Augusta, Kladno
☐	99	Lubomir Fischer, Olomouc
☐	100	Jaromir Precechtel, Olomouc
☐	101	Pavel Cagas, Olomouc
☐	102	Ladislav Blazek, Olomouc
☐	103	Jaromir Latal, Olomouc
☐	104	Jiri Latal, Olomouc
☐	105	Petr Tejkl, Olomouc
☐	106	Jiri Kuntos, Olomouc
☐	107	Patrik Rimmel, Olomouc
☐	108	Robert Machalek, Olomouc

☐ 109 Jiri Polak, Olomouc
☐ 110 Martin Bakula, Olomouc
☐ 111 Michal Slavik, Olomouc
☐ 112 Pavel Nohel, Olomouc
☐ 113 Igor Cikl, Olomouc
☐ 114 Zdenek Eichenmann, Olomouc
☐ 115 Milan Navratil, Olomouc
☐ 116 Ales Zima, Olomouc
☐ 117 Tomas Matinec, Olomouc
☐ 118 Richard Brancik, Olomouc
☐ 119 Ondrej Kratena, Olomouc
☐ 120 Michal Bros, Olomouc
☐ 121 Juraj Jurik, Olomouc
☐ 122 Jan Tomajko, Olomouc
☐ 123 Richard Farda, Olomouc
☐ 124 Bretislav Kopriva, Slavia Fraha
☐ 125 Martin Altrichter, Slavia Fraha
☐ 126 Radek Toth, Slavia Fraha
☐ 127 Miroslav Horava, Slavia Fraha
☐ 128 Martin Maskarinec, Slavia Fraha
☐ 129 Jakub Ficenec, Slavia Fraha
☐ 130 Jiri Hes, Slavia Fraha
☐ 131 Andrej Jakovenko, Slavia Fraha
☐ 132 Petr Macek, Slavia Fraha
☐ 133 Jan Penk, Slavia Fraha
☐ 134 Robert Kostka, Slavia Fraha
☐ 135 Vladimir Ruzicka, Slavia Fraha
☐ 136 Viktor Ujcik, Slavia Fraha
☐ 137 Ivo Prorok, Slavia Fraha
☐ 138 Tomas Jelinek, Slavia Fraha
☐ 139 Michal Sup, Slavia Fraha
☐ 140 Milan Antos, Slavia Fraha
☐ 141 Roman Blazek, Slavia Fraha
☐ 142 Jiri Hlinka, Slavia Fraha
☐ 143 Tomas Kupka, Slavia Fraha
☐ 144 Vaclav Eiselt, Slavia Fraha
☐ 145 Jaroslav Bednar, Slavia Fraha
☐ 146 Ladislav Svoboda, Slavia Fraha
☐ 147 Ladislav Kudrna, Slavia Fraha
☐ 148 Josef Beranek, Chemopetrol Litvinov
☐ 149 Vladimir Kyhos, Chemopetrol Litvinov
☐ 150 Zdenek Orct, Chemopetrol Litvinov
☐ 151 Petr Franek, Chemopetrol Litvinov
☐ 152 Kamil Prachar, Chemopetrol Litvinov
☐ 153 Angel Nikolov, Chemopetrol Litvinov
☐ 154 Onderj Zetek, Chemopetrol Litvinov
☐ 155 Tomas Arnost, Chemopetrol Litvinov
☐ 156 Normunds Sejejs, Chemopetrol Litvinov
☐ 157 Petr Kratky, Chemopetrol Litvinov
☐ 158 Sergej Butko, Chemopetrol Litvinov
☐ 159 Petr Molnar, Chemopetrol Litvinov
☐ 160 Radek Mrazek, Chemopetrol Litvinov
☐ 161 Radim Piroutek, Chemopetrol Litvinov
☐ 162 David Balasz, Chemopetrol Litvinov
☐ 163 Jindrich Kotrla, Chemopetrol Litvinov
☐ 164 Jaroslav Buchal, Chemopetrol Litvinov
☐ 165 Josef Straka, Chemopetrol Litvinov
☐ 166 Michail Fadejev, Chemopetrol Litvinov
☐ 167 Radek Sip, Chemopetrol Litvinov
☐ 168 Martin Rousek, Chemopetrol Litvinov
☐ 169 Tomas Vlasak, Chemopetrol Litvinov
☐ 170 Robert Kysela, Chemopetrol Litvinov
☐ 171 Jan Alinc, Chemopetrol Litvinov
☐ 172 Vladimir Machulda, Chemopetrol Litvinov
☐ 173 Vladimir Jerabek, Chemopetrol Litvinov
☐ 174 Frantisek Vorlicek, Dukhla Jihlava
☐ 175 Jan Hrbaty, Dukhla Jihlava
☐ 176 Marek Novotny, Dukhla Jihlava
☐ 177 Lukas Sablik, Dukhla Jihlava
☐ 178 Roman Kankovsky, Dukhla Jihlava
☐ 179 Michael Vyhlidal, Dukhla Jihlava
☐ 180 Jan Bohacek, Dukhla Jihlava
☐ 181 Roman Cech, Dukhla Jihlava
☐ 182 Zdenek Touzimsky, Dukhla Jihlava
☐ 183 Marek Posmyk, Dukhla Jihlava
☐ 184 Pavel Rajnoha, Dukhla Jihlava
☐ 185 Martin Tupa, Dukhla Jihlava
☐ 186 Libor Dolana, Dukhla Jihlava
☐ 187 Petr Vlk, Dukhla Jihlava
☐ 188 Petr Kankovsky, Dukhla Jihlava
☐ 189 Jiri Cihlar, Dukhla Jihlava
☐ 190 Jiri Poukar, Dukhla Jihlava
☐ 191 Jaromir Kverka, Dukhla Jihlava
☐ 192 Leos Pipa, Dukhla Jihlava
☐ 193 Ladislav Prokupek, Dukhla Jihlava
☐ 194 Patrik Fink, Dukhla Jihlava
☐ 195 Marek Melenovsky, Dukhla Jihlava
☐ 196 Jiri Holik, Dukhla Jihlava
☐ 197 Miroslav Bruna, Dukhla Jihlava
☐ 198 Jaroslav Walter, Dukhla Jihlava
☐ 199 Otto Zelezny, BNO
☐ 200 Libor Barta, BNO
☐ 201 Pavel Nestak, BNO
☐ 202 Leo Gudas, BNO
☐ 203 Karel Beran, BNO
☐ 204 Richard Adam, BNO
☐ 205 Pavel Zubicek, BNO
☐ 206 Alexander Elsner, BNO
☐ 207 Robert Kantor, BNO
☐ 208 Ladislav Tresl, BNO
☐ 209 Frantisek Sevcik, BNO
☐ 210 Michal Konecny, BNO
☐ 211 Richard Sebestu, BNO
☐ 212 Roman Mejzlik, BNO
☐ 213 Zdenek Cely, BNO
☐ 214 Jiri Vitek, BNO
☐ 215 Radek Haman, BNO
☐ 216 Tomas Krasny, BNO
☐ 217 Jiri Suhrada, BNO
☐ 218 Jaroslav Smolik, BNO
☐ 219 Alois Hadamczik, TRI
☐ 220 Karel Suchanek, TRI
☐ 221 Michal Hlinka, TRI
☐ 222 Josef Lucak, TRI
☐ 223 Karel Pavlik, TRI
☐ 224 Stanislav Meciar, TRI
☐ 225 Petr Mainer, TRI
☐ 226 Petr Pavlas, TRI
☐ 227 Lubomir Sekeras, TRI
☐ 228 Roman Sindel, TRI
☐ 229 Vaclav Slaby, TRI
☐ 230 Miroslav Cihal, TRI
☐ 231 Martin Palinek, TRI
☐ 232 Petr Zajonc, TRI
☐ 233 Michal Piskor, TRI
☐ 234 Roman Kadera, TRI
☐ 235 Marek Zadina, TRI
☐ 236 Richard Kral, TRI
☐ 237 Miroslav Skovira, TRI
☐ 238 Vladimir Machalek, TRI
☐ 239 Libor Zatopek, TRI
☐ 240 Dusan Adamcik, TRI
☐ 241 Jiri Novotny, TRI
☐ 242 Karel Trachta, Interconex Plzen
☐ 243 Jindrich Setikovsky, Interconex Plzen
☐ 244 Rudolf Pejchar, Interconex Plzen
☐ 245 Michal Marik, Interconex Plzen
☐ 246 Karel Smid, Interconex Plzen
☐ 247 Martin Kovarik, Interconex Plzen
☐ 248 Jiri Hanzlik, Interconex Plzen
☐ 249 Jaroslav Spacek, Interconex Plzen
☐ 250 Stanislav Benes, Interconex Plzen
☐ 251 Robert Jindrich, Interconex Plzen
☐ 252 Vaclav Ruprecht, Interconex Plzen
☐ 253 Tomas Kucharcik, Interconex Plzen
☐ 254 Michal Straka, Interconex Plzen
☐ 255 Ondrej Steiner, Interconex Plzen
☐ 256 Tomas Klimt, Interconex Plzen
☐ 257 Martin Zivny, Interconex Plzen
☐ 258 Milan Volak, Interconex Plzen
☐ 259 Pavel Metlicka, Interconex Plzen
☐ 260 Josef Rybar, Interconex Plzen
☐ 261 Jaroslav Kreuzman, Interconex Plzen
☐ 262 David Trachta, Interconex Plzen
☐ 263 Anatolij Najda, Interconex Plzen
☐ 264 Tomas Ruprecht, Interconex Plzen
☐ 265 Dalibor Sanda, Interconex Plzen
☐ 266 Jaroslav Brabec, Interconex Plzen
☐ 267 Frantisek Vyborny, Sparta Praha
☐ 268 Stanislav Berger, Sparta Praha
☐ 269 Ivo Capek, Sparta Praha
☐ 270 David Volek, Sparta Praha
☐ 271 Jiri Vykoukal, Sparta Praha
☐ 272 Vaclav Burda, Sparta Praha
☐ 273 Petr Kuchyna, Sparta Praha
☐ 274 Pavel Srek, Sparta Praha
☐ 275 Frantisek Ptacek, Sparta Praha
☐ 276 Radek Hamr, Sparta Praha
☐ 277 Jiri Krocak, Sparta Praha
☐ 278 Jaroslav Nedved, Sparta Praha
☐ 279 Jiri Zelenka, Sparta Praha
☐ 280 David Vyborny, Sparta Praha
☐ 281 Petr Hrbek, Sparta Praha
☐ 282 Roman Horak, Sparta Praha
☐ 283 Kamil Kastak, Sparta Praha
☐ 284 Patrik Martinec, Sparta Praha
☐ 285 Zbynek Kukacka, Sparta Praha
☐ 286 Miroslav Hlinka, Sparta Praha
☐ 287 Jaroslav Hlinka, Sparta Praha
☐ 288 Jan Hlavac, Sparta Praha
☐ 289 Andrej Potajcuk, Sparta Praha
☐ 290 Richard Zemlicka, Sparta Praha
☐ 291 Vladimir Stransky, Vitkovice
☐ 292 Ladislav Svozil, Vitkovice
☐ 293 Martin Prusek, Vitkovice
☐ 294 Vladimir Hudacek, Vitkovice
☐ 295 Pavel Marecek, Vitkovice
☐ 296 Rudolf Wolf, Vitkovice
☐ 297 Tomas Kramny, Vitkovice
☐ 298 Pavel Kubina, Vitkovice
☐ 299 Rene Sevecek, Vitkovice
☐ 300 Filip Kuba, Vitkovice
☐ 301 Ales Tomasek, Vitkovice
☐ 302 Roman Rysanek, Vitkovice
☐ 303 Vladimir Vujtek, Vitkovice
☐ 304 Petr Folta, Vitkovice
☐ 305 Jan Peterek, Vitkovice
☐ 306 Roman Simicek, Vitkovice
☐ 307 Pavel Zdrahal, Vitkovice
☐ 308 Pavel Sebesta, Vitkovice
☐ 309 David Moravec, Vitkovice
☐ 310 Tomas Chlubna, Vitkovice
☐ 311 Ludek Krayzel, Vitkovice
☐ 312 Waldemar Klisiak, Vitkovice
☐ 313 Petr Fabian, Vitkovice
☐ 314 Josef Palacek, Pardubice
☐ 315 Florian Strida, Pardubice
☐ 316 Radovan Biegl, Pardubice
☐ 317 Dusan Salficky, Pardubice
☐ 318 Petr Jancarik, Pardubice
☐ 319 Tomas Pacal, Pardubice
☐ 320 Radomir Brazda, Pardubice
☐ 321 Radek Mesicek, Pardubice
☐ 322 Jiri Antonin, Pardubice
☐ 323 Alexander Terechov, Pardubice
☐ 324 Milan Beranek, Pardubice
☐ 325 Ladislav Lubina, Pardubice
☐ 326 David Pospisil, Pardubice
☐ 327 Milan Kastner, Pardubice
☐ 328 Stanislav Prochazka, Pardubice
☐ 329 Patrik Weber, Pardubice
☐ 330 Milan Hejduk, Pardubice
☐ 331 Tomas Blazek, Pardubice
☐ 332 Jiri Jantovsky, Pardubice
☐ 333 Jaroslav Kudrna, Pardubice
☐ 334 Tomas Pisa, Pardubice
☐ 335 Ales Pisa, Pardubice
☐ 336 Ivan Vasilev
☐ 337 Milan Hnilicka
☐ 338 Ales Flasar
☐ 339 Martin Smetak
☐ 340 Libor Polasek
☐ 341 Vitezslav Skuta
☐ 342 Ladislav Benysek
☐ 343 Jaroslav Smolik
☐ 344 Igor Cikl
☐ 345 Jan Czerlinski
☐ 346 Marek Vorel
☐ 347 Martin Ancicka
☐ 348 Pavel Skrbek
☐ 349 Petr Kadlec
☐ 350 Tomas Kucharcik
☐ 351 Ludek Bukac, Cze.
☐ 352 Zdenek Uher, Cze.
☐ 353 Roman Cechmanek
☐ 354 Roman Turek
☐ 355 Petr Briza
☐ 356 Jaroslav Kames
☐ 357 Antonin Stavjana
☐ 358 Berdrich Scerban
☐ 359 Petr Kuchyna
☐ 360 Jiri Vykoukal
☐ 361 Frantisek Kaberle
☐ 362 Jan Vopat
☐ 363 Libor Prochazka

	No.	Player
☐	364	Jiri Kucera
☐	365	Tomas Jelinek
☐	366	Richard Zemlicka
☐	367	Martin Hostak
☐	368	Tomas Srsen
☐	369	Jiri Dopita
☐	370	Martin Prochazka
☐	371	Pavel Patera
☐	372	Otakar Vejvoda
☐	373	Roman Horak
☐	374	Radek Belohlav
☐	375	Pavel Geffert
☐	376	Jan Alinc
☐	377	Roman Kadera
☐	378	Viktor Ujcik
☐	379	Roman Meluzin
☐	380	Pavel Janku
☐	381	Tomas Kucharcik
☐	382	Zbynek Marak
☐	383	Ales Zima
☐	384	Jaromir Jagr
☐	385	Pavel Patera
☐	386	Martin Prochazka
☐	387	Pavel Janku
☐	388	Roman Cechmanek
☐	389	Antonin Stavjana
☐	390	Rostislav Vlach
☐	391	Lubos Jenacek
☐	392	Dominik Hasek
☐	393	Jiri Holik
☐	394	Frantisek Pospisil
☐	395	Ivan Hlinka
☐	396	Vladimir Martinec
☐	397	Jaroslav Pouzar
☐	398	Karel Gut
☐	399	Jan Benda

1995 - 96 BICYCLE SPORTS HOCKEY ACES

Imprint: 1995•1996 Bicycle Sports Collection

Complete Deck (55 cards): 8.00

	No.	Player	NRMT-MT
☐	2♣	Scott Stevens, N.J.	.10
☐	3♣	Bill Ranford (G), Edm.	.25
☐	4♣	Brian Bradley, T.B.	.10
☐	5♣	Ed Belfour (G), Chi.	.35
☐	6♣	Brian Leetch, NYR.	.35
☐	7♣	Ron Francis, Pgh.	.35
☐	8♣	Teemu Selänne, Wpg.	.75
☐	9♣	Martin Brodeur (G), N.J.	.75
☐	10♣	Joe Nieuwendyk, Dal.	.25
☐	J♣	Mark Messier, NYR.	.50
☐	Q♣	Mikael Renberg, Pha.	.10
☐	K♣	Joe Sakic, Que.	.85
☐	A♣	Paul Coffey, Det.	.25
☐	2♦	Al MacInnis, Stl.	.25
☐	3♦	Mike Modano, Dal.	.50
☐	4♦	Alexandre Daigle, Ott.	.25
☐	5♦	Jeremy Roenick, Chi.	.35
☐	6♦	Jason Arnott, Edm.	.25
☐	7♦	Peter Bondra, Wsh.	.35
☐	8♦	Ray Bourque, Bos.	.50
☐	9♦	Pavel Bure, Van.	.75
☐	10♦	Mats Sundin, Tor.	.50
☐	J♦	Brett Hull, Stl.	.50
☐	Q♦	Jaromir Jagr, Pgh.	1.00
☐	K♦	Dominik Hasek (G), Buf.	.75
☐	A♦	Wayne Gretzky, L.A.	2.00
☐	2♥	Craig Janney, S.J.	.10
☐	3♥	Doug Gilmour, Tor.	.35
☐	4♥	Claude Lemieux, N.J.	.10
☐	5♥	Trevor Linden, Van.	.25
☐	6♥	Geoff Sanderson, Hfd.	.10
☐	7♥	Paul Kariya, Ana.	1.25
☐	8♥	Pierre Turgeon, Mtl.	.25
☐	9♥	Peter Forsberg, Que.	1.00
☐	10♥	Adam Oates, Bos.	.35
☐	J♥	Sergei Fedorov, Det.	.50
☐	Q♥	Mario Lemieux, Pgh.	1.50
☐	K♥	Alexei Zhamnov, Wpg.	.25
☐	A♥	Eric Lindros, Pha.	1.25
☐	2♠	Kirk Muller, NYI.	.10
☐	3♠	Steve Yzerman, Det.	1.00
☐	4♠	Félix Potvin (G), Tor.	.65
☐	5♠	Pat LaFontaine, Buf.	.25
☐	6♠	Jim Carey (G), Wsh.	.10
☐	7♠	John Vanbiesbrouck (G), Fla.	.60
☐	8♠	Alexei Yashin, Ott.	.35
☐	9♠	Chris Chelios, Chi.	.35
☐	10♠	Cam Neely, Bos.	.25
☐	J♠	Keith Tkachuk, Wpg.	.35
☐	Q♠	John LeClair, Pha.	.50
☐	K♠	Theoren Fleury, Cgy.	.35
☐	A♠	Patrick Roy (G), Mtl.	1.50
☐		Checklist	.10
☐		Eastern Conference	.10
☐		Western Conference	.10

1995 - 96 BOWMAN

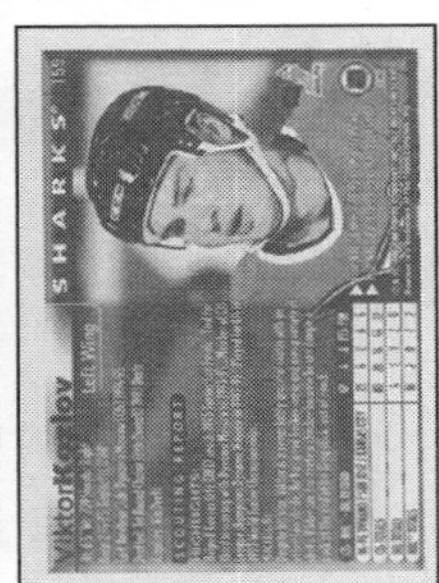

These cards have two versions: the regular card and a foil parallel.

Imprint: © 1996 THE TOPPS COMPANY, INC.

Complete Set (165 cards): 30.00 150.00

Common Player: .10 .50

	No.	Player	Reg.	Foil
☐ ☐	1	Wayne Gretzky, Stl.	2.50	15.00
☐ ☐	2	Ray Bourque, Bos.	.50	3.00
☐ ☐	3	Craig Janney, S.J.	.10	.50
☐ ☐	4	Andrew Cassels, Hfd.	.10	.50
☐ ☐	5	Alexander Mogilny, Van.	.35	1.50
☐ ☐	6	Pierre Turgeon, Mtl.	.25	1.00
☐ ☐	7	Dave Andreychuk, Tor.	.10	.50
☐ ☐	8	Mark Messier, NYR.	.50	3.00
☐ ☐	9	Igor Korolev, Wpg.	.10	.50
☐ ☐	10	Tomas Sandström, Pgh.	.10	.50
☐ ☐	11	Shayne Corson, Stl.	.25	1.00
☐ ☐	12	Chris Chelios, Chi.	.35	2.00
☐ ☐	13	Claude Lemieux, N.J.	.10	.50
☐ ☐	14	Stéphane Richer, Mtl.	.10	.50
☐ ☐	15	Patrick Roy (G), Col.	2.00	12.00
☐ ☐	16	Al MacInnis, Stl.	.25	1.00
☐ ☐	17	Cam Neely, Bos.	.25	1.00
☐ ☐	18	Doug Gilmour, Tor.	.35	1.50
☐ ☐	19	Steve Thomas, N.J.	.10	.50
☐ ☐	20	Jeremy Roenick, Chi.	.35	1.50
☐ ☐	21	Steve Yzerman, Det.	1.25	7.50
☐ ☐	22	Petr Klima, T.B.	.10	.50
☐ ☐	23	Luc Robitaille, NYR.	.25	1.00
☐ ☐	24	Bill Ranford (G), Edm.	.25	1.00
☐ ☐	25	Grant Fuhr (G), Stl.	.25	1.00
☐ ☐	26	Sean Burke (G), Hfd.	.25	1.00
☐ ☐	27	John MacLean, N.J.	.10	.50
☐ ☐	28	Brendan Shanahan, Hfd.	.60	3.50
☐ ☐	29	Pat LaFontaine, Buf.	.25	1.00
☐ ☐	30	John Vanbiesbrouck (G), Fla.	.60	3.50
☐ ☐	31	Ron Francis, Pgh.	.35	1.50
☐ ☐	32	Brian Leetch, NYR.	.35	1.50
☐ ☐	33	Dave Gagner, Tor.	.10	.50
☐ ☐	34	Larry Murphy, Tor.	.25	1.00
☐ ☐	35	Mike Modano, Dal.	.50	3.00
☐ ☐	36	Rick Tocchet, L.A.	.10	.50
☐ ☐	37	Scott Mellanby, Fla.	.10	.50
☐ ☐	38	Ron Hextall (G), Fla.	.25	1.00
☐ ☐	39	Joé Juneau, Wsh.	.10	.50
☐ ☐	40	Mario Lemieux, Pgh.	2.00	12.00
☐ ☐	41	Paul Coffey, Det.	.25	1.00
☐ ☐	42	Joe Sakic, Col.	1.00	6.00
☐ ☐	43	Brett Hull, Stl.	.50	3.00
☐ ☐	44	Adam Oates, Bos.	.35	1.50
☐ ☐	45	Wendel Clark, Tor.	.25	1.00
☐ ☐	46	Trevor Linden, Van.	.25	1.00
☐ ☐	47	Tom Barrasso (G), Pgh.	.25	1.00
☐ ☐	48	Kevin Hatcher, Wsh.	.10	.50
☐ ☐	49	Mats Sundin, Tor.	.50	3.00
☐ ☐	50	Scott Stevens, N.J.	.10	.50
☐ ☐	51	Mark Recchi, Mtl.	.25	1.00
☐ ☐	52	Theoren Fleury, Cgy.	.35	1.50
☐ ☐	53	Ed Belfour (G), Chi.	.35	1.50
☐ ☐	54	Adam Graves, NYR.	.10	.50
☐ ☐	55	Peter Bondra, Wsh.	.35	2.00
☐ ☐	56	Dominik Hasek (G), Buf.	.75	4.50
☐ ☐	57	Jaromir Jagr, Pgh.	1.25	7.50
☐ ☐	58	Owen Nolan, S.J.	.25	1.00
☐ ☐	59	Kevin Stevens, Bos.	.10	.50
☐ ☐	60	Alexei Zhamnov, Wpg.	.25	1.00
☐ ☐	61	Dmitri Khristich, L.A.	.10	.50
☐ ☐	62	Chris Pronger, Stl.	.25	1.00
☐ ☐	63	John LeClair, Pha.	.50	3.00
☐ ☐	64	Scott Niedermayer, N.J.	.25	1.00
☐ ☐	65	Pavel Bure, Van.	.75	4.50
☐ ☐	66	Chris Osgood (G), Det.	.35	2.00
☐ ☐	67	Geoff Sanderson, Hfd.	.10	.50
☐ ☐	68	Doug Weight, Edm.	.35	1.50
☐ ☐	69	Keith Tkachuk, Wpg.	.35	2.00
☐ ☐	70	Martin Brodeur (G), N.J.	.75	4.50
☐ ☐	71	Eric Lindros, Pha.	1.50	9.00
☐ ☐	72	Martin Straka, Ott.	.10	.50
☐ ☐	73	Alexander Selivanov, T.B.	.10	.50
☐ ☐	74	Jim Carey (G), Wsh.	.10	.50
☐ ☐	75	Teemu Selänne, Wpg.	.75	4.50
☐ ☐	76	Rob Niedermayer, Fla.	.10	.50
☐ ☐	77	Vyacheslav Kozlov, Det.	.10	.50
☐ ☐	78	Todd Harvey, Dal.	.10	.50
☐ ☐	79	Félix Potvin (G), Tor.	.50	3.00
☐ ☐	80	Sergei Fedorov, Det.	.50	3.00
☐ ☐	81	Mathieu Schneider, NYI.	.10	.50
☐ ☐	82	Roman Hamrlik, T.B.	.25	1.00
☐ ☐	83	Mikael Renberg, Pha.	.10	.50
☐ ☐	84	Jeff Friesen, S.J.	.25	1.00
☐ ☐	85	Peter Forsberg, Col.	1.25	7.50
☐ ☐	86	Kenny Jonsson, NYI.	.10	.50
☐ ☐	87	Brian Savage, Mtl.	.10	.50
☐ ☐	88	Oleg Tverdovsky, Ana.	.10	.50
☐ ☐	89	Nikolai Khabibulin (G), Wpg.	.35	1.50
☐ ☐	90	Paul Kariya, Ana.	1.50	9.00
☐ ☐	91	Zdenek Nedved, Tor.	.10	.50
☐ ☐	**92**	**Darren Langdon, NYR., RC**	**.10**	**.50**
☐ ☐	**93**	**Lonny Bohonos, Van., RC**	**.10**	**.50**
☐ ☐	**94**	**Mike Wilson, Buf., RC**	**.10**	**.50**
☐ ☐	**95**	**Landon Wilson, Col., RC**	**.10**	**.50**
☐ ☐	96	Bryan McCabe, NYI.	.10	.50
☐ ☐	97	Byron Dafoe (G), L.A.	.10	.50
☐ ☐	**98**	**Denny Lambert, Ana., RC**	**.10**	**.50**
☐ ☐	**99**	**Craig Mills, Wpg., RC**	**.10**	**.50**
☐ ☐	100	Ed Jovanovski, Fla.	.25	1.00
☐ ☐	101	Jason Bonsignore, Edm.	.10	.50
☐ ☐	**102**	**Clayton Beddoes, Bos., RC**	**.10**	**.50**
☐ ☐	103	Jamie Pushor, Det.	.10	.50
☐ ☐	104	Drew Bannister, T.B.	.10	.50
☐ ☐	**105**	**Ed Ward, Cgy., RC**	**.10**	**.50**
☐ ☐	106	Todd Warriner, Tor.	.10	.50
☐ ☐	107	Deron Quint, Wpg.	.10	.50
☐ ☐	**108**	**Rhett Warrener, Fla., RC**	**.25**	**.75**
☐ ☐	109	Marko Kiprusoff, Mtl.	.10	.50
☐ ☐	**110**	**Daniel Alfredsson, Ott., RC**	**.85**	**3.00**
☐ ☐	**111**	**Marcus Ragnarsson, S.J., RC**	**.10**	**.50**
☐ ☐	112	Miroslav Satan, Edm.	.10	.50
☐ ☐	113	Niklas Sundstrom, NYR.	.10	.50
☐ ☐	**114**	**Mathieu Dandenault, Det., RC**	**.10**	**.50**
☐ ☐	115	Vitali Yachmenev, L.A.	.10	.50
☐ ☐	**116**	**Petr Sykora, N.J., RC**	**.25**	**.75**
☐ ☐	**117**	**Antti Törmänen, Ott. RC**	**.10**	**.50**
☐ ☐	118	Jeff O'Neill, Hfd.	.10	.50
☐ ☐	**119**	**David Nemirovsky, Fla., RC**	**.10**	**.50**

	No.	Player		
☐ ☐	120	Jason Doig, Wpg.	.10	.50
☐ ☐	121	Aaron Gavey, T.B.	.10	.50
☐ ☐	122	Ladislav Kohn, Cgy.	.10	.50
☐ ☐	123	Richard Park, Pgh.	.10	.50
☐ ☐	**124**	**Stéphane Yelle, Col., RC**	**.25**	**.75**
☐ ☐	125	Eric Dazé, Chi.	.25	1.00
☐ ☐	126	Niklas Andersson, NYI.	.10	.50
☐ ☐	127	Brendan Witt, Wsh.	.10	.50
☐ ☐	128	Jamie Storr (G), L.A.	.25	1.00
☐ ☐	129	Darby Hendrickson, Tor.	.10	.50
☐ ☐	**130**	**Radek Dvorak, Fla., RC**	**.25**	**.75**
☐ ☐	131	Cory Stillman, Cgy.	.10	.50
☐ ☐	132	Jamie Rivers, Stl.	.10	.50
☐ ☐	133	Ville Peltonen, S.J.	.10	.50
☐ ☐	134	Peter Ferraro, NYR.	.10	.50
☐ ☐	**135**	**Trent McCleary, Ott., RC**	**.10**	**.50**
☐ ☐	**136**	**Chris Wells, Pgh, RC**	**.10**	**.50**
☐ ☐	**137**	**Chad Kilger, Ana., RC**	**.10**	**.50**
☐ ☐	138	Denis Pederson, N.J.	.10	.50
☐ ☐	**139**	**Roman Vopat, Stl., RC**	**.10**	**.50**
☐ ☐	140	Shean Donovan, S.J.	.10	.50
☐ ☐	141	Alek Stojanov, Van.	.10	.50
☐ ☐	**142**	**Mark Kolesar, Tor., RC**	**.10**	**.50**
☐ ☐	**143**	**Scott Walker, Van., RC**	**.10**	**.50**
☐ ☐	**144**	**Dave Roche, Pgh., RC**	**.10**	**.50**
☐ ☐	145	Corey Hirsch (G), Van.	.10	.50
☐ ☐	**146**	**Aki Berg, L.A., RC**	**.25**	**.75**
☐ ☐	147	Stefan Ustorf, Wsh.	.10	.50
☐ ☐	148	Saku Koivu, Mtl.	.75	4.50
☐ ☐	**149**	**Shane Doan, Wpg., RC**	**.10**	**.50**
☐ ☐	150	Jere Lehtinen, Dal.	.25	1.00
☐ ☐	**151**	**Kyle McLaren, Bos, RC**	**.10**	**.50**
☐ ☐	152	Marty Murray, Cgy.	.10	.50
☐ ☐	**153**	**Sean Pronger, Ana., RC**	**.25**	**.75**
☐ ☐	**154**	**Joaquin Gage (G), Edm., RC**	**.10**	**.50**
☐ ☐	155	Eric Fichaud (G), NYI.	.10	.50
☐ ☐	**156**	**Todd Bertuzzi, NYI., RC**	**.50**	**1.50**
☐ ☐	**157**	**Wayne Primeau, Buf., RC**	**.10**	**.50**
☐ ☐	**158**	**Scott Bailey (G), Bos., RC**	**.10**	**.50**
☐ ☐	159	Viktor Kozlov, S.J.	.10	.50
☐ ☐	160	Valeri Bure, Mtl.	.10	.50
☐ ☐	161	Dody Wood, S.J.	.10	.50
☐ ☐	162	Grant Marshall, Dal.	.10	.50
☐ ☐	**163**	**Ken Klee, Wsh., RC**	**.10**	**.50**
☐ ☐	**164**	**Corey Schwab (G), N.J., RC**	**.10**	**.50**
☐ ☐	**165**	**Brian Holzinger, Buf., RC**	**.25**	**.75**

BOWMAN'S BEST

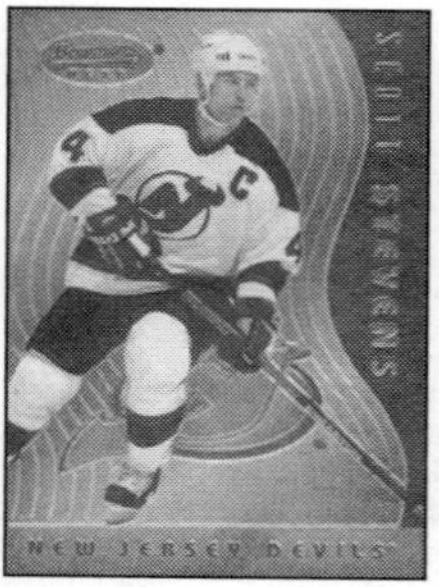

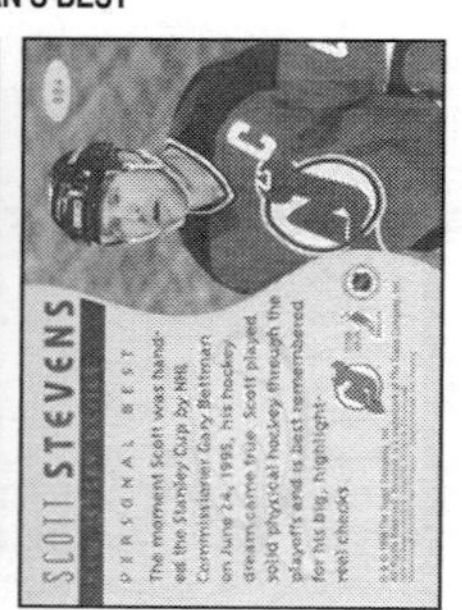

This series has two versions: a regular insert and a refractor version.

Insert Set (30 cards): 200.00 700.00

	No.	Player	Reg.	Ref.
☐ ☐	BB 1	Peter Forsberg, Col.	15.00	50.00
☐ ☐	BB 2	Teemu Selänne, Wpg.	10.00	35.00
☐ ☐	BB 3	Eric Lindros, Pha.	20.00	65.00
☐ ☐	BB 4	Scott Stevens, N.J.	2.00	6.00
☐ ☐	BB 5	Wayne Gretzky, Stl.	30.00	100.00
☐ ☐	BB 6	Mark Messier, NYR.	7.50	25.00
☐ ☐	BB 7	Jaromir Jagr, Pgh.	15.00	50.00
☐ ☐	BB 8	Martin Brodeur (G), N.J.	10.00	35.00
☐ ☐	BB 9	Alexander Mogilny, Van.	4.50	15.00
☐ ☐	BB10	Mario Lemieux, Pgh.	25.00	80.00
☐ ☐	BB11	Joe Sakic, Col.	12.00	40.00
☐ ☐	BB12	Sergei Fedorov, Det.	7.50	25.00
☐ ☐	BB13	Pavel Bure, Van.	10.00	35.00
☐ ☐	BB14	Brian Leetch, NYR.	4.50	15.00
☐ ☐	BB15	Paul Kariya, Ana.	20.00	65.00
☐ ☐	BB16	Daniel Alfredsson, Ott.	6.00	20.00
☐ ☐	BB17	Saku Koivu, Mtl.	10.00	35.00
☐ ☐	BB18	Eric Dazé, Chi.	3.00	10.00
☐ ☐	BB19	Ed Jovanovski, Fla.	3.00	10.00
☐ ☐	BB20	Vitali Yachmenev, L.A.	2.00	6.00
☐ ☐	BB21	Niklas Sundstrom, NYR.	2.00	6.00
☐ ☐	BB22	Radek Dvorak, Fla.	2.00	6.00
☐ ☐	BB23	Byron Dafoe (G), L.A.	2.00	6.00
☐ ☐	BB24	Shane Doan, Wpg.	2.00	6.00
☐ ☐	BB25	Chad Kilger, Ana.	2.00	6.00
☐ ☐	BB26	Jeff O'Neill, Hfd.	3.00	10.00
☐ ☐	BB27	Cory Stillman, Cgy.	2.00	6.00
☐ ☐	BB28	Valeri Bure, Mtl.	2.00	6.00
☐ ☐	BB29	Marcus Ragnarsson, S.J.	2.00	6.00
☐ ☐	BB30	Todd Bertuzzi, NYI.	3.00	10.00

CHL PROSPECTS (ALL-STARS)

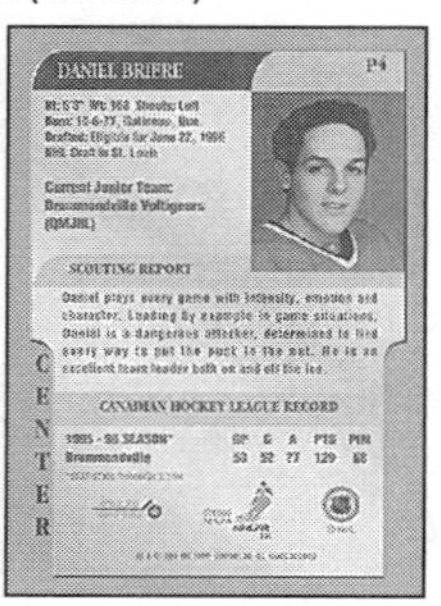

Insert Set (40 cards): 30.00

	No.	Player	NRMT-MT
☐	P1	Johnathan Aitken	.35
☐	P2	Chris Allen	.35
☐	P3	Matt Bradley	1.00
☐	P4	Daniel Brière	3.50
☐	P5	Jeff Brown	.35
☐	P6	Jan Bulis	1.00
☐	P7	Daniel Corso	1.00
☐	P8	Luke Curtin	.35
☐	P9	Mathieu Descôteaux	.50
☐	P10	Boyd Devereaux	1.75
☐	P11	Jason Doyle	.35
☐	P12	Etienne Drapeau	.35
☐	P13	Jean-Pierre Dumont	3.50
☐	P14	Mathieu Garon (G)	1.50
☐	P15	Josh Green	.35
☐	P16	Chris Hajt	.35
☐	P17	Matt Higgins	.35
☐	P18	Craig Hillier (G)	1.25
☐	P19	Josh Holden	1.50
☐	P20	Dan Focht	.35
☐	P21	Henry Kuster	.35
☐	P22	François Larivée	.35
☐	P23	Mario Larocque	.50
☐	P24	Wes Mason	.35
☐	P25	François Methot	.35
☐	P26	Geoff Peters	.35
☐	P27	Randy Petruk	.35
☐	P28	Chris Phillips	3.00
☐	P29	Boris Protsenko	.35
☐	P30	Remi Royer	.35
☐	P31	Cory Sarich	1.50
☐	P32	Jaroslav Svejkovsky	3.00
☐	P33	Curtis Tipler	.35
☐	P34	Darren Van Oene	.35
☐	P35	Jesse Wallin	.35
☐	P36	Kurt Walsh	.35
☐	P37	Lance Ward	.35
☐	P38	Steve Wasylko	.35
☐	P39	Trevor Wasyluk	.35
☐	P40	Jon Zukiwsky	.35

1995 - 96 CANADA GAMES POGs

Kinis come in blue, gold and purple but do not show a player photo.

Cap Diameter: 1 5/8"
Imprint:
Complete Set (296 POGs): 100.00
Common Player: .20

	No.	Player	NRMT-MT
☐	1	Pearson/Eric Lindros	4.00
☐	2	Art Ross/Jaromir Jagr	3.00
☐	3	Masterton/Pat LaFontaine	2.00
☐	4	Calder/Peter Forsberg	3.00
☐	5	Campbell/Detroit Red Wings	2.00
☐	6	Smythe/Claude Lemieux	2.00
☐	7	Selke/Ron Francis	2.00
☐	8	Hart/Eric Lindros	4.00
☐	9	Adams/Marc Crawford	2.00
☐	10	Norris/Paul Coffey	2.00
☐	11	Clancy/Joe Nieuwendyk	2.00
☐	12	Byng/Ron Francis	2.00
☐	13	Wales/New Jersey Devils	2.00
☐	14	Stanley Cup/New Jersey Devils	2.00
☐	15	Vezina/Dominik Hasek (G)	2.50
☐	16	Jennings/Ed Belfour (G)	2.00
☐	17	Paul Kariya, Ana.	3.50
☐	18	Peter Douris, Ana.	.20
☐	19	Valeri Karpov, Ana.	.20
☐	20	Todd Krygier, Ana.	.20
☐	21	Joe Sacco, Ana.	.20
☐	22	Mike Sillinger, Ana.	.20
☐	23	Shaun Van Allen, Ana.	.20
☐	24	Oleg Tverdovsky, Ana.	.20
☐	25	Bobby Dollas, Ana.	.20
☐	26	Steve Rucchin, Ana.	.20
☐	27	Guy Hebert (G), Ana.	.50
☐	28	Shawn McEachern, Bos.	.20
☐	29	Adam Oates, Bos.	.75
☐	30	Ted Donato, Bos.	.20
☐	31	Cam Neely, Bos.	.50
☐	32	Joe Mullen, Bos.	.20
☐	33	Kevin Stevens, Bos.	.20
☐	34	Mariusz Czerkawski, Bos.	.20
☐	35	Don Sweeney, Bos.	.20
☐	36	Ray Bourque, Bos.	1.25
☐	37	Alexei Kasatonov, Bos.	.20
☐	38	Blaine Lacher (G), Bos.	.35
☐	39	Brian Holzinger, Buf.	.20
☐	40	Derek Plante, Buf.	.20
☐	41	Michael Peca, Buf.	.50
☐	42	Pat LaFontaine, Buf.	.50
☐	43	Jason Dawe, Buf.	.20
☐	44	Brad May, Buf.	.20
☐	45	Yuri Khmylev, Buf.	.20
☐	46	Garry Galley, Buf.	.20
☐	47	Alexei Zhitnik, Buf.	.20
☐	48	Dominik Hasek (G), Buf.	1.75
☐	49	Joe Nieuwendyk, Cgy.	.50
☐	50	German Titov, Cgy.	.20
☐	51	Cory Stillman, Cgy.	.20
☐	52	Theoren Fleury, Cgy.	.75
☐	53	Paul Kruse, Cgy.	.20
☐	54	Michael Nylander, Cgy.	.20
☐	55	Gary Roberts, Cgy.	.50
☐	56	Phil Housley, Cgy.	.20
☐	57	Steve Chiasson, Cgy.	.20
☐	58	Zarley Zalapski, Cgy.	.20
☐	59	Ron Stern, Cgy.	.20
☐	60	Trevor Kidd (G), Cgy.	.50
☐	61	Jeremy Roenick, Chi.	.75
☐	62	Denis Savard, Chi.	.50
☐	63	Tony Amonte, Chi.	.50
☐	64	Bernie Nicholls, Chi.	.20
☐	65	Sergei Krivokrasov, Chi.	.20
☐	66	Joe Murphy, Chi.	.20
☐	67	Patrick Poulin, Chi.	.20
☐	68	Bob Probert, Chi.	.20
☐	69	Gary Suter, Chi.	.20
☐	70	Chris Chelios, Chi.	1.00
☐	71	Ed Belfour (G), Chi.	.75
☐	72	Joe Sakic, Col.	2.00
☐	73	Mike Ricci, Col.	.20
☐	74	Valeri Kamensky, Col.	.50
☐	75	Andrei Kovalenko, Col.	.20
☐	76	Owen Nolan, Col.	.50
☐	77	Peter Forsberg, Col.	2.50
☐	78	Scott Young, Col.	.20
☐	79	Uwe Krupp, Col.	.20
☐	80	Curtis Leschyshyn, Col.	.20

	No.	Player	Price
☐	81	Adam Deadmarsh, Col.	.20
☐	82	Stéphane Fiset (G), Col.	.50
☐	83	Bob Bassen, Dal.	.20
☐	84	Corey Millen, Dal.	.20
☐	85	Mike Modano, Dal.	1.25
☐	86	Dave Gagner, Dal.	.20
☐	87	Mike Donnelly, Dal.	.20
☐	88	Trent Klatt, Dal.	.20
☐	89	Kevin Hatcher, Dal.	.20
☐	90	Grant Ledyard, Dal.	.20
☐	91	Grag Adams, Dal.	.20
☐	92	Andy Moog (G), Dal.	.50
☐	93	Keith Primeau, Det.	.50
☐	94	Kris Draper, Det.	.20
☐	95	Sergei Fedorov, Det.	1.25
☐	96	Steve Yzerman, Det.	2.50
☐	97	Vyacheslav Kozlov, Det.	.20
☐	98	Ray Sheppard, Det.	.20
☐	99	Dino Ciccarelli, Det.	.50
☐	100	Viacheslav Fetisov, Det.	.50
☐	101	Nicklas Lidstrom, Det.	.20
☐	102	Paul Coffey, Det.	.50
☐	103	Darren McCarty, Det.	.20
☐	104	Mike Vernon (G), Det.	.50
☐	105	Doug Weight, Edm.	.75
☐	106	Jason Arnott, Edm.	.50
☐	107	Todd Marchant, Edm.	.20
☐	108	David Oliver, Edm.	.20
☐	109	Igor Kravchuk, Edm.	.20
☐	110	Jiri Slegr, Edm.	.20
☐	111	Kelly Buchberger, Edm.	.20
☐	112	Scott Thornton, Edm.	.20
☐	113	Bill Ranford (G), Edm.	.50
☐	114	Jesse Belanger, Fla.	.20
☐	115	Stu Barnes, Fla.	.20
☐	116	Scott Mellanby, Fla.	.20
☐	117	Bill Lindsay, Fla.	.20
☐	118	Dave Lowry, Fla.	.20
☐	119	Gaetan Duchesne, Fla.	.20
☐	120	Johan Garpenlov, Fla.	.20
☐	121	Paul Laus, Fla.	.20
☐	122	Gord Murphy, Fla.	.20
☐	123	John Vanbiesbrouck (G), Fla.	1.50
☐	124	Andrew Cassels, Hfd.	.20
☐	125	Geoff Sanderson, Hfd.	.20
☐	126	Brendan Shanahan, Hfd.	1.50
☐	127	Paul Ranheim, Hfd.	.20
☐	128	Steven Rice, Hfd.	.20
☐	129	Frantisek Kucera, Hfd.	.20
☐	130	Glen Wesley, Hfd.	.20
☐	131	Sean Burke (G), Hfd.	.50
☐	132	Wayne Gretzky, L.A.	5.00
☐	133	Dimitri Khristich, L.A.	.20
☐	134	Jari Kurri, L.A.	.50
☐	135	John Druce, L.A.	.20
☐	136	Pat Conacher, L.A.	.20
☐	137	Rick Tocchet, L.A.	.20
☐	138	Rob Blake, L.A.	.50
☐	139	Tony Granato, L.A.	.20
☐	140	Marty McSorley, L.A.	.20
☐	141	Darryl Sydor, L.A.	.20
☐	142	Eric Lacroix, L.A.	.20
☐	143	Kelly Hrudey (G), L.A.	.20
☐	144	Brian Savage, Mtl.	.20
☐	145	Pierre Turgeon, Mtl.	.50
☐	146	Benoît Brunet, Mtl.	.20
☐	147	Valeri Bure, Mtl.	.20
☐	148	Vincent Damphousse, Mtl.	.75
☐	149	Mike Keane, Mtl.	.20
☐	150	Mark Recchi, Mtl.	.50
☐	151	Vladimir Malakhov, Mtl.	.20
☐	152	Patrice Brisebrois, Mtl.	.20
☐	153	J.J. Daigneault, Mtl.	.20
☐	154	Yves Racine, Mtl.	.20
☐	155	Patrick Roy (G), Mtl.	4.00
☐	156	Bob Carpenter, N.J.	.20
☐	157	Neal Broten, N.J.	.20
☐	158	Steve Thomas, N.J.	.20
☐	159	Bobby Holik, N.J.	.20
☐	160	John MacLean, N.J.	.20
☐	161	Mike Peluso, N.J.	.20
☐	162	Randy McKay, N.J.	.20
☐	163	Stéphane Richer, N.J.	.20
☐	164	Scott Niedermayer, N.J.	.50
☐	165	Scott Stevens, N.J.	.20
☐	166	Bill Guerin, N.J.	.50
☐	167	Martin Brodeur (G), N.J.	1.75
☐	168	Kirk Muller, NYI.	.20
☐	169	Zigmund Palffy, NYI.	1.00
☐	170	Travis Green, NYI.	.20
☐	171	Brett Lindros, NYI.	.20
☐	172	Derek King, NYI.	.20
☐	173	Pat Flatley, NYI.	.20
☐	174	Wendel Clark, NYI.	.50
☐	175	Bryan McCabe, NYI.	.20
☐	176	Mathieu Schneider, NYI.	.20
☐	177	Eric Fichaud (G), NYI.	.20
☐	178	Ray Ferraro, NYR.	.20
☐	179	Adam Graves, NYR.	.20
☐	180	Mark Messier, NYR.	1.25
☐	181	Sergei Nemchinov, NYR.	.20
☐	182	Pat Verbeek, NYR.	.20
☐	183	Luc Robitaille, NYR.	.50
☐	184	Alexei Kovalev, NYR.	.20
☐	185	Jeff Beukeboom, NYR.	.20
☐	186	Brian Leetch, NYR.	.75
☐	187	Ulf Samuelsson, NYR.	.20
☐	188	Alexander Karpovtsev, NYR.	.20
☐	189	Mike Richter (G), NYR.	.75
☐	190	Alexandre Daigle, Ott.	.20
☐	191	Alexei Yashin, Ott.	1.00
☐	192	Dan Quinn, Ott.	.20
☐	193	Martin Straka, Ott.	.20
☐	194	Radek Bonk, Ott.	.20
☐	195	Pavol Demitra, Ott.	.20
☐	196	Steve Duchesne, Ott.	.20
☐	197	Chris Dahlquist, Ott.	.20
☐	198	Sean Hill, Ott.	.20
☐	199	Stanislav Neckar, Ott.	.20
☐	200	Don Beaupré (G), Ott.	.20
☐	201	Eric Lindros, Pha.	3.50
☐	202	Rod Brind'Amour, Pha.	.50
☐	203	Shjon Podein, Pha.	.20
☐	204	Brent Fedyk, Pha.	.20
☐	205	Joel Otto, Pha.	.20
☐	206	John LeClair, Pha.	1.25
☐	207	Kevin Dineen, Pha.	.20
☐	208	Petr Svoboda, Pha.	.20
☐	209	Eric Desjardins, Pha.	.20
☐	210	Ron Hextall (G), Pha.	.50
☐	211	Mario Lemieux, Pgh.	4.00
☐	212	Petr Nedved, Pgh.	.20
☐	213	Bryan Smolinski, Pgh.	.20
☐	214	Tomas Sandström, Pgh.	.20
☐	215	Ron Francis, Pgh.	.75
☐	216	Jaromir Jagr, Pgh.	2.50
☐	217	Sergei Zubov, Pgh.	.50
☐	218	Drake Berehowsky, Pgh.	.20
☐	219	Dmitri Mironov, Pgh.	.20
☐	220	Ken Wregget (G), Pgh.	.20
☐	221	Tom Barrasso (G), Pgh.	.50
☐	222	Igor Larionov, S.J.	.50
☐	223	Jeff Friesen, S.J.	.50
☐	224	Kevin Miller, S.J.	.20
☐	225	Ray Whitney, S.J.	.20
☐	226	Craig Janney, S.J.	.20
☐	227	Pat Falloon, S.J.	.20
☐	228	Ulf Dahlen, S.J.	.20
☐	229	Viktor Kozlov, S.J.	.20
☐	230	Michal Sykora, S.J.	.20
☐	231	Sandis Ozolinsh, S.J.	.50
☐	232	Jamie Baker, S.J.	.20
☐	233	Arturs Irbe (G), S.J.	.20
☐	234	Adam Creighton, Stl.	.20
☐	235	Ian Laperrière, Stl.	.20
☐	236	Brett Hull, Stl.	1.25
☐	237	Brian Noonan, Stl.	.20
☐	238	Dale Hawerchuk, Stl.	.50
☐	239	Esa Tikkanen, Stl.	.20
☐	240	Geoff Courtnall, Stl.	.20
☐	241	Shayne Corson, Stl.	.50
☐	242	Al MacInnis, Stl.	.20
☐	243	Chris Pronger, Stl.	.50
☐	244	Jeff Norton, Stl.	.20
☐	245	Grant Fuhr (G), Stl.	.50
☐	246	Brian Bradley, T.B.	.20
☐	247	Chris Gratton, T.B.	.50
☐	248	John Cullen, T.B.	.20
☐	249	John Tucker, T.B.	.20
☐	250	Paul Ysebaert, T.B.	.20
☐	251	Petr Klima, T.B.	.20
☐	252	Alexander Selivanov, T.B.	.20
☐	253	Brian Bellows, T.B.	.20
☐	254	Enrico Ciccone, T.B.	.20
☐	255	Roman Hamrlik, T.B.	.50
☐	256	Daren Puppa (G), T.B.	.20
☐	257	Doug Gilmour, Tor.	1.25
☐	258	Benoît Hogue, Tor.	.20
☐	259	Mats Sundin, Tor.	1.00
☐	260	Dave Andreychuk, Tor.	.20
☐	261	Mike Gartner, Tor.	.50
☐	262	Randy Wood, Tor.	.20
☐	263	Tie Domi, Tor.	.20
☐	264	Dave Ellett, Tor.	.20
☐	265	Todd Gill, Tor.	.20
☐	266	Larry Murphy, Tor.	.50
☐	267	Kenny Jonsson, Tor.	.20
☐	268	Félix Potvin (G), Tor.	1.25
☐	269	Cliff Ronning, Van.	.20
☐	270	Mike Ridley, Van.	.20
☐	271	Trevor Linden, Van.	.50
☐	272	Alexander Mogilny, Van.	.75
☐	273	Martin Gelinas, Van.	.20
☐	274	Pavel Bure, Van.	1.75
☐	275	Russ Courtnall, Van.	.20
☐	276	Jeff Brown, Van.	.20
☐	277	Jyrki Lumme, Van.	.20
☐	278	Kirk McLean (G), Van.	.50
☐	279	Steve Konowalchuk, Wsh.	.20
☐	280	Kelly Miller, Wsh.	.20
☐	281	Peter Bondra, Wsh.	1.00
☐	282	Keith Jones, Wsh.	.20
☐	283	Joé Juneau, Wsh.	.20
☐	284	Mark Tinordi, Wsh.	.20
☐	285	Calle Johansson, Wsh.	.20
☐	286	Sergei Gonchar, Wsh.	.50
☐	287	Jim Carey (G), Wsh.	.20
☐	288	Dallas Drake, Wpg.	.20
☐	289	Alexei Zhamnov, Wpg.	.50
☐	290	Mike Eastwood, Wpg.	.20
☐	291	Igor Korolev, Wpg.	.20
☐	292	Teemu Selänne, Wpg.	1.75
☐	293	Keith Tkachuk, Wpg.	1.00
☐	294	Teppo Numminen, Wpg.	.20
☐	295	Dave Manson, Wpg.	.20
☐	296	Tim Cheveldae (G), Wpg.	.35

INSERTS

Insert Set (35 caps): 75.00

	No.	Player	NRMT-MT
☐	001	Wayne Gretzky, L.A.	10.00
☐	002	Mario Lemieux, Pgh.	8.00
☐	003	Cam Neely, Bos	1.00
☐	004	Ray Bourque, Bos.	2.50
☐	005	Patrick Roy (G), Col.	8.00
☐	006	Mark Messier, NYR.	2.50
☐	007	Brett Hull, Stl.	2.50
☐	008	Grant Fuhr (G), Stl.	1.00
☐	009	Eric Lindros, Pha.	6.50
☐	010	John LeClair, Pha.	2.50
☐	011	Jaromir Jagr, Pgh.	5.00
☐	012	Chris Chelios, Chi.	2.00
☐	013	Paul Coffey, Det.	1.00
☐	014	Dominik Hasek (G), Buf.	3.50
☐	015	Alexei Zhamnov, Wpg.	1.00
☐	016	Keith Tkachuk, Wpg.	2.00
☐	017	Theoren Fleury, Cgy.	1.50
☐	018	Ray Bourque, Bos.	2.50
☐	019	Larry Murphy, Tor.	1.50
☐	020	Ed Belfour (G), Chi.	1.50
☐	021	Pavel Bure, Van.	3.50
☐	022	Doug Gilmour, Tor.	1.50
☐	023	Brett Hull, Stl.	2.50
☐	024	Mark Messier, NYR.	2.50
☐	025	Cam Neely, Bos.	1.00
☐	026	Jeremy Roenick, Chi.	1.50
☐	027	Patrick Roy (G), Col.	8.00
☐	028	Jim Carey (G), Wsh.	.75
☐	029	Peter Forsberg, Col.	5.00
☐	030	Jeff Friesen, S.J.	1.00
☐	031	Kenny Jonsson, Tor.	.75
☐	032	Paul Kariya, Ana.	6.50
☐	033	Ian Laperrière, Stl.	.75
☐	034	David Oliver, Edm.	.75
☐	035	Kyle McLaren, Bos.	.75

POWER PAC CHECKLISTS

Card Size: 2 1/8" x 3 1/2"

	Checklist	NRMT-MT
□	Checklist (1-16)	.10
□	Checklist (17-64)	.10
□	Checklist (65-112)	.10
□	Checklist (113-160)	.10
□	Checklist (161-208)	.10
□	Checklist (209-256)	.10
□	Checklist (257-296)	.10
□	Checklist (001-035)	.10

1995 - 96 CLASSIC

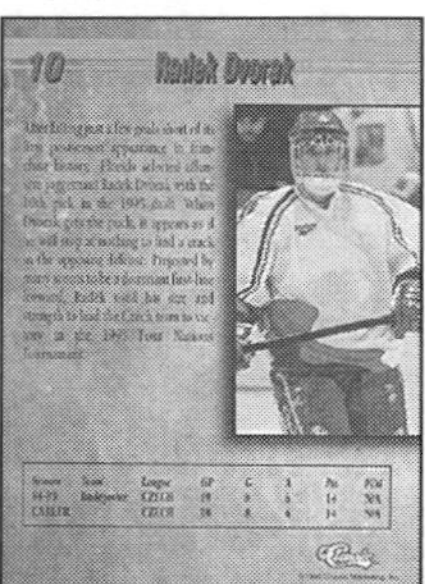

There are five versions to Classic: the regular card, a silver foil-board parallel (Canadian packs), a gold foil-board parallel (American packs), a Printer's Proof parallel (Canadian Packs, "1 of 749") and a Printer's Proof Gold foil-board parallel (American packs, "1 of 249"). Prices for silver and gold parallels are the same.

			Reg.	Gold	Prf.	Prf.G
Complete Set (100 cards):			10.00	50.00	350.00	600.00
Wade Redden Box Bottom:						1.00
Common Player:			.10	.20	3.00	5.00

	No.	Player	Reg.	Gold	Prf.	Prf.G
□□□□□	1	Bryan Berard	.75	2.00	15.00	25.00
□□□□□	2	Wade Redden	.20	.35	4.00	6.00
□□□□□	3	Aki Berg	.20	.35	4.00	6.00
□□□□□	4	Chad Kilger	.10	.20	3.00	5.00
□□□□□	5	Daymond Langkow	.20	.35	4.00	6.00
□□□□□	6	Steve Kelly	.10	.20	3.00	5.00
□□□□□	7	Shane Doan	.10	.20	3.00	5.00
□□□□□	8	Terry Ryan	.20	.35	4.00	6.00
□□□□□	9	Mike Martin	.10	.20	3.00	5.00
□□□□□	10	Radek Dvorak	.20	.35	4.00	6.00
□□□□□	11	Jarome Iginla	.75	2.00	15.00	25.00
□□□□□	12	Teemu Riihijarvi	.10	.20	3.00	5.00
□□□□□	13	J.S. Giguère (G)	.50	1.50	10.00	18.00
□□□□□	14	Peter Schaefer	.35	1.00	7.00	12.00
□□□□□	15	Jeff Ware	.10	.20	3.00	5.00
□□□□□	16	Martin Biron (G)	.20	.35	4.00	6.00
□□□□□	17	Brad Church	.10	.20	3.00	5.00
□□□□□	18	Petr Sykora	.25	.50	5.00	8.00
□□□□□	19	Denis Gauthier	.10	.20	3.00	5.00
□□□□□	20	Sean Brown	.10	.20	3.00	5.00
□□□□□	21	Brad Isbister	.10	.20	3.00	5.00
□□□□□	22	Miikka Elomo	.20	.35	4.00	6.00
□□□□□	23	Mathieu Sunderland	.10	.20	3.00	5.00
□□□□□	24	Marc Moro	.10	.20	3.00	5.00
□□□□□	25	Jan Hlavac	.10	.20	3.00	5.00
□□□□□	26	Brian Wesenberg	.10	.20	3.00	5.00
□□□□□	27	Mike McBain	.10	.20	3.00	5.00
□□□□□	28	Georges Laraque	.10	.20	3.00	5.00
□□□□□	29	Marc Chouinard	.10	.20	3.00	5.00
□□□□□	30	Donald MacLean	.10	.20	3.00	5.00
□□□□□	31	Jason Doig	.10	.20	3.00	5.00
□□□□□	32	Aaron MacDonald	.10	.20	3.00	5.00
□□□□□	33	Patrick Côté	.10	.20	3.00	5.00
□□□□□	34	Christian Dubé	.35	1.00	7.00	12.00
□□□□□	35	Chris McAllister	.10	.20	3.00	5.00
□□□□□	36	Denis Smith	.10	.20	3.00	5.00
□□□□□	37	Mark Dutiaume	.10	.20	3.00	5.00
□□□□□	38	Dwayne Hay	.10	.20	3.00	5.00
□□□□□	39	Nathan Perrott	.10	.20	3.00	5.00
□□□□□	40	Christian Laflamme	.10	.20	3.00	5.00
□□□□□	41	Paxton Schafer (G)	.10	.20	3.00	5.00
□□□□□	42	Shane Kenny	.10	.20	3.00	5.00
□□□□□	43	Nic Beaudoin	.10	.20	3.00	5.00
□□□□□	44	Philippe Audet	.10	.20	3.00	5.00
□□□□□	45	Brad Larsen	.20	.35	4.00	6.00
□□□□□	46	Ryan Pepperall	.10	.20	3.00	5.00
□□□□□	47	Mike Leclerc	.10	.20	3.00	5.00
□□□□□	48	Shane Willis	.20	.35	4.00	6.00
□□□□□	49	Darryl Laplante	.10	.20	3.00	5.00
□□□□□	50	Larry Courville	.10	.20	3.00	5.00
□□□□□	51	Mike O'Grady	.10	.20	3.00	5.00
□□□□□	52	Petr Buzek	.10	.20	3.00	5.00
□□□□□	53	Alyn McCauley	.75	2.00	15.00	25.00
□□□□□	54	Scott Roche (G)	.10	.20	3.00	5.00
□□□□□	55	John Tripp	.10	.20	3.00	5.00
□□□□□	56	Johnathan Aitken	.10	.20	3.00	5.00
□□□□□	57	Blake Bellefeuille	.10	.20	3.00	5.00
□□□□□	58	Daniel Brière	.75	2.00	15.00	25.00
□□□□□	59	Josh DeWolf	.10	.20	3.00	5.00
□□□□□	60	Josh Green	.10	.20	3.00	5.00
□□□□□	61	Chris Hajt	.10	.20	3.00	5.00
□□□□□	62	Josh Holden	.35	1.00	7.00	12.00
□□□□□	63	Henry Kuster	.10	.20	3.00	5.00
□□□□□	64	Dan Lacouture	.10	.20	3.00	5.00
□□□□□	65	Oleg Orekhovsky	.10	.20	3.00	5.00
□□□□□	66	Andrei Petrunin	.10	.20	3.00	5.00
□□□□□	67	Tom Poti	.20	.35	4.00	6.00
□□□□□	68	Peter Ratchuk	.10	.20	3.00	5.00
□□□□□	69	Andrei Zyuzin	.50	1.50	10.00	18.00
□□□□□	70	George Breen	.10	..20	3.00	5.00
□□□□□	71	Greg Bullock	.10	.20	3.00	5.00
□□□□□	72	Kent Fearns	.10	.20	3.00	5.00
□□□□□	73	Eric Flinton	.10	.20	3.00	5.00
□□□□□	74	Brian Holzinger	.25	.50	5.00	8.00
□□□□□	75	Chris Kenady	.10	.20	3.00	5.00
□□□□□	76	Kaj Linna	.10	.20	3.00	5.00
□□□□□	77	Brian Mueller	.10	.20	3.00	5.00
□□□□□	78	Brent Peterson	.10	.20	3.00	5.00
□□□□□	79	Chad Quenneville	.10	.20	3.00	5.00
□□□□□	80	Randy Stevens	.10	.20	3.00	5.00
□□□□□	81	Adam Wiesel	.10	.20	3.00	5.00
□□□□□	82	R. Boyko/J. Cowan/ Y. Ioannou/J. Miculinic	.10	.20	3.00	5.00
□□□□□	83	B. Secord/D. Cleary/ R. Bicanek/S. Brown	.35	1.00	7.00	12.00
□□□□□	84	B. Berard/S. Haggerty/ J. Mitchell/ J. Saal	.35	1.00	7.00	12.00
□□□□□	85	T.Norman/ T. Bertuzzi/ C. Hajt/ B. Wesenberg	.10	.20	3.00	5.00
□□□□□	86	R.Pepperal/R.DeCiantis/ D. Belitski (G)/ B. Devereaux	.25	.50	5.00	8.00
□□□□□	87	C. Kilger/ D. Ling/ T. Moss (G)/ G. Walsh	.10	.20	3.00	5.00
□□□□□	88	S.Bergkvist/D.Gilmore/ A. Colagiacomo/ J. Doyle	.25	.50	5.00	8.00
□□□□□	89	J. Johnstone/ S. Potvin/ G. Peters/ D. Foster	.10	.20	3.00	5.00
□□□□□	90	L.Jinman/V.Yachmenev/ S. Roche/ B. Brown	.20	.35	4.00	6.00
□□□□□	91	M. Savard/ D. LaFrance/ J. Tripp/ J. Ware	.20	.35	4.00	6.00
□□□□□	92	S.Washburn/S.Donovan/ A. McCauley/ N. Boynton	.35	1.00	7.00	12.00
□□□□□	93	J. Kostuch/ W. Primeau/ M. Osborne/ S. Kenny	.10	.20	3.00	5.00
□□□□□	94	C. Lang/ K. Bolibruck/ D. Duerden/ J. Langenbrunner	.10	.20	3.00	5.00
□□□□□	95	S. Lowe/ A. Payette/ D. Cloutier/ J. Thornton	1.00	2.00	15.00	25.00
□□□□□	96	J. Brown/ A. Brand/ R. Guinn/ D. Maxwell	.10	.20	3.00	5.00
□□□□□	97	E. Moreau/ Z. Nedved/ J. Rivers/ J. Bonsignore	.10	.20	3.00	5.00
□□□□□	98	M. Martin/ E. Jovanovski/ G. Crawford/ D. Smith	.25	.50	5.00	8.00
□□□□□	99	CL: Bryan Berard	.35	1.00	7.00	12.00
□□□□□	100	CL: Wade Redden	.25	.50	5.00	8.00

AUTOGRAPHS

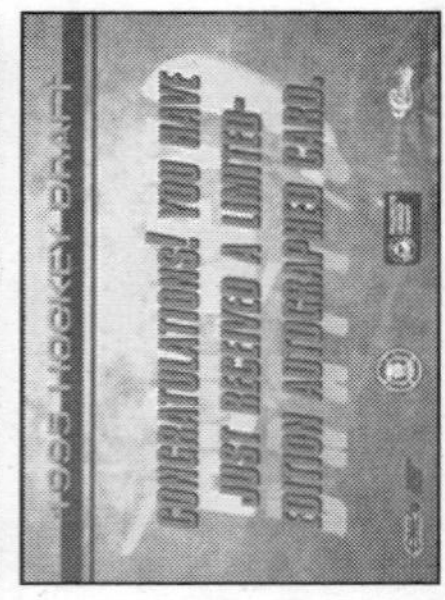

Each player signed a different amount of cards. Petr Sykora signed the least number of autographs (fewer than 1000).

	Player	NRMT-MT
□	George Breen	5.00
□	Greg Bullock	5.00
□	Petr Buzek	5.00
□	Henry Custer	5.00
□	Radek Dvorak	25.00
□	Kent Fearns	5.00
□	Eric Flinton	5.00
□	Josh Green	5.00
□	Josh Holden	15.00
□	Brian Holzinger	15.00
□	Ed Jovanovski	40.00
□	Chris Kenady	5.00
□	Josef Marha	8.00
□	Brian Mueller	5.00
□	Angel Nikolov	5.00
□	Oleg Orekhovsky	5.00
□	Brent Peterson	5.00
□	Andrei Petrunin	5.00
□	Chad Quenneville	5.00
□	Manon Rhéaume	50.00
□	Miroslav Satan	20.00
□	Randy Stevens	5.00
□	Petr Sykora	50.00
□	Adam Wiesel	5.00
□	Andrei Zyuzin	25.00

CHL ALL-STARS

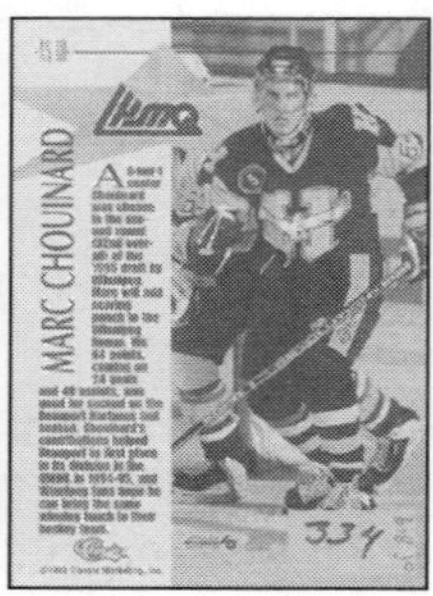

These cards are limited to 849 copies.

Insert Set (18 cards): 100.00

	No.	Player	NRMT-MT
□	AS1	Nolan Baumgartner	4.00
□	AS2	Wade Redden	8.00
□	AS3	Henry Kuster	4.00
□	AS4	Daymond Langkow	6.00
□	AS5	Shane Doan	4.00
□	AS6	Steve Kelly	4.00
□	AS7	Tyler Moss (G)	6.00
□	AS8	Bryan Berard	15.00
□	AS9	Ed Jovanovski	10.00
□	AS10	Chad Kilger	4.00
□	AS11	Daniel Cleary	15.00
□	AS12	Ethan Moreau	6.00
□	AS13	J.S. Giguère (G)	10.00
□	AS14	Daniel Gauthier	4.00
□	AS15	Jason Doig	4.00
□	AS16	Etienne Drapeau	4.00
□	AS17	Daniel Brière	15.00
□	AS18	Marc Chouinard	4.00

ICE BREAKERS

There are two versions to this set: the regular insert card (American packs only) and a die-cut insert (Canadian and American packs, "1 of 1649").

	No.	Player	Reg.	Die-Cut
		Insert Set (20 cards):	**100.00**	**400.00**
□ □	BK1	Bryan Berard	15.00	60.00
□ □	BK2	Wade Redden	8.00	30.00
□ □	BK3	Aki Berg	6.00	20.00
□ □	BK4	Chad Kilger	4.00	12.00
□ □	BK5	Daymond Langkow	6.00	20.00
□ □	BK6	Steve Kelly	4.00	12.00
□ □	BK7	Shane Doan	4.00	12.00
□ □	BK8	Terry Ryan	5.00	15.00
□ □	BK9	Radek Dvorak	6.00	20.00
□ □	BK10	Jarome Iginla	10.00	40.00
□ □	BK11	Teemu Riihijarvi	4.00	12.00
□ □	BK12	J.S. Giguère (G)	10.00	40.00
□ □	BK13	Martin Biron (G)	5.00	15.00
□ □	BK14	Jeff Ware	4.00	12.00
□ □	BK15	Brad Church	4.00	12.00
□ □	BK16	Petr Sykora	6.00	20.00
□ □	BK17	Jason Bonsignore	4.00	12.00
□ □	BK18	Brian Holzinger	6.00	20.00
□ □	BK19	Ed Jovanovski	10.00	40.00
□ □	BK20	Nolan Baumgartner	4.00	12.00

5-SPORT PRINTER'S PROOF PREVIEW

The "Printer's Proof" stamp is in red.

	No.	Player	NRMT-MT
□	SP4	Bryan Berard	4.00

1995 - 96 CLASSIC ASSETS

We have little information on this 50-card multi-sport set. Other hockey singles may exist.

Imprint:

	No.	Player	NRMT-MT
□	8	Radek Dvorak	.25
□	17	Ed Jovanovski	.50
□	45	Petr Sykora	.25

1995 - 96 CLASSIC CLEAR ASSETS

We have little information on this 50-card multi-sport set. Other hockey singles may exist.

Imprint:

	No.	Player	NRMT-MT
□	56	Bryan Berard	.50
□	57	Petr Sykora	.25
□	58	Ed Jovanovksi	.35
□	59	Radek Dvorak	.25

$2 PHONE CARDS

	No.	Player	NRMT-MT
□	5	Wade Redden	3.00
□	11	Manon Rhéaume (G)	6.00
□	22	Petr Sykora	3.00

$5 PHONE CARDS

	No.	Player	NRMT-MT
□	16	Petr Sykora	6.00

1995 - 96 CLASSIC FIVE-SPORT

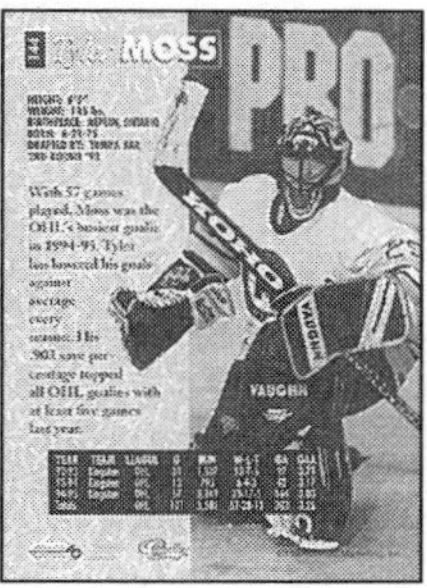

This 200-card five-sport set features only 39 hockey cards. There are four versions to this set: the regular card, a Die-Cut parallel, a Printer's Proof parallel ("1 of 795") and an "Autograph Collection" parallel. A 200-card regular set sells at $15.

Imprint:

	No.	Player	Reg.	D.C.	Prf.	A.C.
□ □ □ □	123	Bryan Berard, Detroit-OHL	.75	6.00	15.00	3.00
□ □ □ □	124	Wade Redden, Brendon	.20	1.00	3.00	.50
□ □ □ □	125	Aki Berg, Fin.	.20	1.00	3.00	.50
□ □ □ □	126	N. Baumgartner, Kamloops	.20	1.00	3.00	.50
□ □ □ □	127	J. Bonsignore, Sudbury	.10	.50	1.50	.25
□ □ □ □	128	Steve Kelly, Edm.	.10	.50	1.50	.25
□ □ □ □	129	George Breen, Providence	.10	.50	1.50	.25
□ □ □ □	130	Terry Ryan, Mtl.	.20	1.00	3.00	.50
□ □ □ □	131	Greg Bullock, Lowell	.10	.50	1.50	.25
□ □ □ □	132	Jarome Iginla, Kamloops	.75	6.00	15.00	3.00
□ □ □ □	133	Petr Buzek, Cze.	.10	.50	1.50	.25
□ □ □ □	134	Brad Church, Prince Albert	.10	.50	1.50	.25
□ □ □ □	135	Jay McKee, Buf.	.10	.50	1.50	.25
□ □ □ □	136	Jan Hlavak, Cze.	.10	.50	1.50	.25
□ □ □ □	137	Petr Sykora, Detroit-IHL	.20	1.00	3.00	.50
□ □ □ □	138	Ed Jovanovski, Windsor	.50	4.00	10.00	2.00
□ □ □ □	139	Chris Kenady, Denver U.	.10	.50	1.50	.25
□ □ □ □	140	Marc Moro, Kingston	.10	.50	1.50	.25
□ □ □ □	141	Kaj Linna, Boston U.	.10	.50	1.50	.25
□ □ □ □	142	A. MacDonald, Swift Current	.10	.50	1.50	.25
□ □ □ □	143	Chad Kilger, Kingston	.10	.50	1.50	.25
□ □ □ □	144	Tyler Moss (G), Kingston	.25	1.50	4.00	.75
□ □ □ □	145	C. Laflamme, Beauport	.10	.50	1.50	.25
□ □ □ □	146	Brian Mueller, Clarkson	.10	.50	1.50	.25
□ □ □ □	147	D. Langkow, Tri-City	.20	1.00	3.00	.50
□ □ □ □	148	Brent Peterson, Michigan	.10	.50	1.50	.25
□ □ □ □	149	C. Quenneville, Providence	.10	.50	1.50	.25
□ □ □ □	150	Chris Van Dyk, Windsor	.10	.50	1.50	.25
□ □ □ □	151	Kent Fearns, Colorado	.10	.50	1.50	.25
□ □ □ □	152	Adam Wiesel, Clarkson	.10	.50	1.50	.25
□ □ □ □	153	Marc Chouinard,Beauport	.10	.50	1.50	.25
□ □ □ □	154	Jason Doig, Laval	.10	.50	1.50	.25
□ □ □ □	155	Denis Smith, Windsor	.10	.50	1.50	.25
□ □ □ □	156	Radek Dvorak, Cze.	.25	1.50	4.00	.75
□ □ □ □	157	D. MacLaren, Beauport	.10	.50	1.50	.25
□ □ □ □	158	S. Kenny, Owen Sound	.10	.50	1.50	.25
□ □ □ □	159	B. Holzinger, Bowling Green	.20	1.00	3.00	.50
□ □ □ □	160	Eric Flinton, U.N.H.	.10	.50	1.50	.25
□ □ □ □	189	George Breen, Providence	.10	.50	1.50	.25

AUTOGRAPHS

Other hockey autographs exist.

	Player	NRMT-MT
□	Nolan Baumgartner	8.00
□	Greg Bullock	5.00
□	Jason Doig	8.00
□	Kent Fearns	5.00
□	Steve Kelly	5.00
□	Aaron MacDonald	5.00
□	Marc Moro	5.00
□	Chad Quenneville	5.00

CLASSIC STANDOUTS

This ten-card insert set features only one hockey card.

	No.	Player	NRMT-MT
□	CS5	Bryan Berard, Detroit-OHL	6.00

FAST TRACK

This 20-card insert set features only two hockey cards.

	No.	Player	NRMT-MT
□	FT5	Bryan Berard	6.00
□	FT14	Petr Sykora	3.00

SPRINT PREPAID FONCARD

Prices are for unused phone cards.

	Player	NRMT-MT
□	($3) Brian Holzinger	8.00
□	($4) Wade Redden	12.00

RED AND BLUE SIGNINGS

This 100-card five-sport set features only nine hockey cards. There are two versions to this set: a blue card and a red card. We have no pricing information on this set.

	No.	Player
□ □	70	Bryan Berard
□ □	71	Wade Redden
□ □	72	Aki Berg
□ □	73	Nolan Baumgartner
□ □	74	Jason Bonsignore
□ □	75	Ed Jovanovski
□ □	76	Radek Dvorak
□ □	77	Brian Holzinger
□ □	78	Brad Church

STRIVE FOR 5 INTERACTIVE GAME CARD

This 65-card five-sport set features only 13 hockey cards.

	No.	Player	NRMT-MT
□	2	Jan Hlavac	2.00
□	3	Brad Church	2.00
□	4	Steve Kelly, Prince Albert	2.00
□	5	Radek Dvorak	3.00
□	6	Jason Bonsignore	2.00
□	7	Petr Sykora	2.50
□	8	Daymond Langkow, Tri-City	2.50
□	9	Chad Kilger	2.00
□	10	Nolan Baumgartner	2.50
□	J	Brian Holzinger	2.50
□	Q	Aki Berg	3.00
□	K	Ed Jovanovski	4.00
□	A	Wade Redden	2.50

1995 - 96 CLASSIC VISIONS

Other hockey singles may exist in this 150-card multi-sport set.

Imprint:

	No.	Player	NRMT-MT
□	82	Bryan Berard	.50
□	91	Petr Sykora	.25
□	92	Ed Jovanovski	.35
□	94	Manon Rhéaume (G)	3.50

1995 - 96 CLASSIC VISIONS SIGNINGS

This 100-card multi-sport set features only 19 hockey cards.

Imprint:

	No.	Player	NRMT-MT
□	61	Boyd Devereaux	.25
□	62	Alexandre Volchkov	.50
□	63	Trevor Wasyluk	.25
□	64	Luke Curtin	.25
□	65	Richard Jackman	.25
□	66	Jonathan Zukiwsky	.25
□	67	Geoff Peters	.25
□	68	Daniel Brière	1.00
□	69	Chris Allen	.25
□	70	Jason Sweitzer	.25
□	71	Steve Nimigon	.25
□	72	Jay McKee	.25
□	73	Henry Kuster	.25
□	74	Johnathan Aitken	.25
□	75	Ed Jovanovski	.35
□	76	Petr Sykora	.25
□	77	Bryan Berard	.50
□	78	Manon Rhéaume (G)	3.50
□	79	Radek Dvorak	.50

CLASSIC CERTIFIED AUTOGRAPHS

Each player signed a different number of autographs. We have no pricing information on this set. Gold parallel autographs possibly exist for the following list.

	Player
□	Boyd Devereaux
□	Alexandre Volchkov
□	Trevor Wasyluk
□	Luke Curtin
□	Richard Jackman

☐ Jonathan Zukiwsky
☐ Geoff Peters
☐ Daniel Brière
☐ Chris Allen
☐ Jason Sweitzer
☐ Steve Nimigon
☐ Jay McKee
☐ Henry Kuster
☐ Johnathan Aitken
☐ Ed Jovanovski
☐ Petr Sykora
☐ Bryan Berard
☐ Manon Rhéaume (G)
☐ Radek Dvorak

ARTISTRY

This 10-card set features only one hockey card.

	No.	Player	NRMT-MT
☐	6	Petr Sykora	15.00

1995 - 96 COOL TRADE

This 20-card set was available as a wrapper redemption offer. Four cards were produced by each company. Cool Trade parallel cards were available via a redemption card. Pinnacle's trade card was inserted into Pinnacle Summit packs; Upper Deck's trade card was inserted into Upper Deck Series Two packs; Fleer/SkyBox's trade card was inserted into Fleer Ultra Extra packs; Donruss' trade card was inserted into Donruss Elite packs; and Topps' trade card was inserted into Bowman packs.

Imprint: © 1995 DONRUSS, INC.

Pack Redemption Set (20 cards): 15.00

PINNACLE SUMMIT / SUMMIT ICE

	No.	Player	Par.	Reg.
☐☐	1	Cam Neely, Bos.	2.00	.50
☐☐	6	Ray Bourque, Bos.	6.00	1.25
☐☐	11	Chris Chelios, Chi.	2.50	.75
☐☐	16	Patrick Roy (G), Col.	12.00	4.00

UPPER DECK / UPPER DECK DIE-CUT

	No.	Player	Par.	Reg.
☐☐	2	Wayne Gretzky, L.A.	20.00	5.00
☐☐	7	Sergei Fedorov, Det.	6.00	1.25
☐☐	12	Peter Forsberg, Col.	7.00	2.50
☐☐	17	Doug Gilmour, Tor.	2.50	.75

SKY BOX EMOTION / EMOTION FOIL

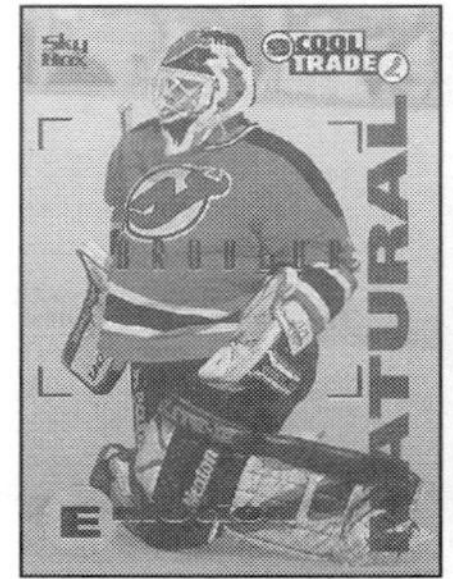

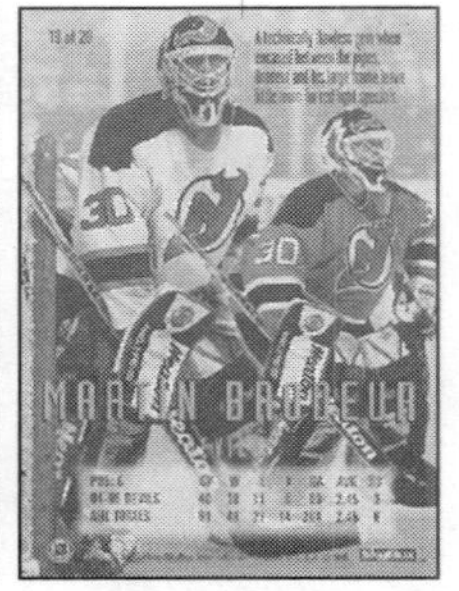

	No.	Player	Par.	Reg.
☐☐	3	Jeremy Roenick Passion, Chi.	15.00	.75
☐☐	8	Paul Kariya Vision, Ana.	50.00	3.00
☐☐	13	Saku Koivu Courage, Mtl.	25.00	1.75
☐☐	18	Martin Brodeur Natural (G), N.J.	30.00	1.75

DONRUSS ELITE / DONRUSS ELITE DIE-CUT

	No.	Player	Par.	Reg.
☐☐	4	Mario Lemieux, Pgh.	9.00	4.00
☐☐	9	Eric Lindros, Pha.	7.00	3.00
☐☐	14	Ed Belfour (G), Chi.	3.00	.75
☐☐	19	Alexander Mogilny, Van.	3.00	.75

TOPPS FINEST / FINEST REFRACTOR

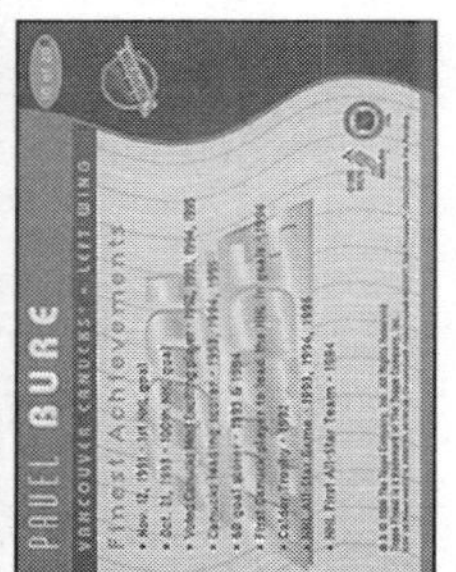

	No.	Player	Par.	Reg.
☐☐	5	Mark Messier, NYR.	6.00	1.25
☐☐	10	Pavel Bure, Van.	12.00	1.75
☐☐	15	Brett Hull, Stl.	6.00	1.25
☐☐	20	Jaromir Jagr, Pgh.	18.00	2.50

1995 - 96 DEL EISHOCKEY

Imprint:

Complete Set (451 cards): 60.00

Common Player: .20

	No.	Player	NRMT-MT
☐	1	Gary Prior	.20
☐	2	Rupert Meister	.20
☐	3	Dennis Schrapp	.20
☐	4	Scott Campbell	.20
☐	5	Fritz Meyer	.20
☐	6	Rob Mendel	.20
☐	7	Ken Collins	.20
☐	8	Stefan Mayer	.20
☐	9	Torsten Fendt	.20
☐	10	Andrei Skopintsev	.20
☐	11	Bob Wilkie	.20
☐	12	Duanne Moeser	.20
☐	13	M Nagler	.20
☐	14	Sven Zywitza	.20
☐	15	Marc Habscheid	.20
☐	16	Daniel Held	.20
☐	17	Heinrich Romer	.20
☐	18	R Laycock	.20
☐	19	R Francz	.20
☐	20	Tim Ferguson	.20
☐	21	Robert Heidt	.20
☐	22	E. Dylla	.20
☐	23	Harald Birk	.20
☐	24	Rochus Schneider	.20
☐	25	Billy Flynn	.20
☐	26	Andre Dietsch	.20
☐	27	Udo Dohler	.20
☐	28	Juri Stumpf	.20
☐	29	Torsten Deutscher	.20
☐	30	Frank Kannewurf	.20
☐	31	Thomas Graul	.20
☐	32	Dirk Perschau	.20
☐	33	Patrick Solf	.20
☐	34	Daniel Poudrier	.20
☐	35	B Kaminski	.20
☐	36	C Hadraschek	.20
☐	37	Sven Felski	.20
☐	38	Marco Swibenko	.20
☐	39	Holger Mix	.20
☐	40	Mark Maroste	.20
☐	41	Troy Tumbach	.20
☐	42	Jan Schertz	.20
☐	43	Mike Losch	.20
☐	44	A Naumann	.20
☐	45	M Garthe	.20
☐	46	I Dorochin	.20
☐	47	T Mitew	.20
☐	48	C Lundmark	.20
☐	49	Chris Panek	.20
☐	50	Klaus Merk	.20
☐	51	Mark Gronau	.20
☐	52	Stefan Steinecker	.20
☐	53	Josef Lehner	.20
☐	54	Tom O'Regan	.20
☐	55	Fredrik Stillmann	.20
☐	56	Marco Rentzsch	.20
☐	57	Stephan Sinner	.20
☐	58	Andreas Schubert	1.00
☐	59	Tony Tanti	.20
☐	60	Gaetan Malo	.20
☐	61	Michael Komma	.20
☐	62	Thomas Schinko	.20
☐	63	Georg Holzmann	.20
☐	64	Mark Kosturik	.20
☐	65	Christian Brittig	.20
☐	66	Jurgen Rumrich	.20
☐	67	John Chabot	.50
☐	68	Andreas Dimbat	.20
☐	69	Ulrich Liebsch	.20
☐	70	Mark Teevens	.20
☐	71	Fabian Brannstom	.20
☐	72	D Meyer	.20
☐	73	L Hoffman	.20
☐	74	Hardy Nilsson, Coach	.20
☐	75	Marcus Karlsson	.20
☐	76	Helmut DeRaaf	.20
☐	77	Kai Fischer	.20
☐	78	Carsten Gossmann	.20
☐	79	Torsten Keinass	.20
☐	80	Christopher Kreutzer	.20
☐	81	Brad Bergen	.20
☐	82	Andreas Niederberger	.20
☐	83	Rick Amann	.20
☐	84	Uli Hiemer	.20
☐	85	Sergei Sorokin	.20
☐	86	Robert Sterflinger	.20
☐	87	Lorenz Funk	.20
☐	88	Chris Valentine	.50
☐	89	Gord Sherven	.20
☐	90	Boris Lingemann	.20
☐	91	Benoit Doucet	.20
☐	92	Bernd Kuhnhauser	.20
☐	93	Bruce Eakin	.20
☐	94	Dieter Hegen	.20
☐	95	Andreas Brockmann	.20
☐	96	Bernd Truntschka	.20
☐	97	Wolfgang Kummer	.20
☐	98	Mikko Makela	.20
☐	99	Nikolaus Mondt	.20
☐	100	Piotr Vorobjew	.20
☐	101	Peter Obresa	.20
☐	102	Thierry Mayer	.20
☐	103	Marc Seliger	.20
☐	104	Florian Storf	.20

☐ 105 Ladislav Stompf .20
☐ 106 Greg Thompson .20
☐ 107 Sergei Schendelev .20
☐ 108 M Duris .20
☐ 109 R Gorgenlander .20
☐ 110 A Raubal .20
☐ 111 Stephan Ziesche .20
☐ 112 Petr Kopta .20
☐ 113 Thomas Popiesch .20
☐ 114 Francois Sills .20
☐ 115 Jiri Lala .20
☐ 116 Robert Reichel .20
☐ 117 Markus Kempf .20
☐ 118 Igor Schultz .20
☐ 119 Martin Schultz .20
☐ 120 Brian Hannon .20
☐ 121 Jurgen Schaal .20
☐ 122 Patrick Vozar .20
☐ 123 Ron Kennedy .20
☐ 124 Friedhelm Bogelsack .20
☐ 125 Marco Herbst .20
☐ 126 Josef Schlickenriede .20
☐ 127 Torsten Hanusch .20
☐ 128 Thomas Jungwirth .20
☐ 129 David Reierson .20
☐ 130 Christian Curth .20
☐ 131 Anton Maidl .20
☐ 132 Marc Wittbrock .20
☐ 133 Brad Schlegel .20
☐ 134 Thomas Werner .20
☐ 135 Dirk Rohrbach .20
☐ 136 Bruce Hardy .20
☐ 137 Harald Kuhnke .20
☐ 138 Florian Funk .20
☐ 139 Rene Reuter .20
☐ 140 Milos Vanik .20
☐ 141 Gunther Preuss .20
☐ 142 Kevin LaVallée .20
☐ 143 Marcus Bleicher .20
☐ 144 Anton Krinner .20
☐ 145 Harald Waibel .20
☐ 146 Hans Zach .20
☐ 147 Josef Kontny .20
☐ 148 Gerhard Hegen .20
☐ 149 Milan Mokros .20
☐ 150 Venci Sebek .20
☐ 151 Alexander Engel .20
☐ 152 Alexander Wedl .20
☐ 153 Jaro Mucha .20
☐ 154 Murray McIntosh .20
☐ 155 Georg Guttler .20
☐ 156 Greg Johnston .20
☐ 157 Jederzej Kaspercyk .20
☐ 158 Dave Morrison .20
☐ 159 Mike Millar .20
☐ 160 Ireneusz Pacula .20
☐ 161 Vitalij Grossmann .20
☐ 162 I Varitsky .20
☐ 163 Peter Kwasigroch .20
☐ 164 Branjo Heisig .20
☐ 165 Greg Evtushevski .20
☐ 166 Falk Ozellis .20
☐ 167 Tino Boos .20
☐ 168 J Tolvanen .20
☐ 169 Dieter Medicus .20
☐ 170 Michael Olbrich .20
☐ 171 Marc Pethke .20
☐ 172 Drahomir Kadlec .20
☐ 173 Christian Seeberger .20
☐ 174 G Kunce .20
☐ 175 Daniel Kunce .20
☐ 176 Timo Gschwill .20
☐ 177 M Ettner .20
☐ 178 Jurgen Simon .20
☐ 179 A Herbst .20
☐ 180 Elmar Boiger .20
☐ 181 Otto Hascak .20
☐ 182 Tim Schnobrich .20
☐ 183 Anthony Vogel .20
☐ 184 Tomas Martinec .20
☐ 185 Hans-Jorg Mayer .20
☐ 186 Roland Timoschuk .20
☐ 187 Jim Hoffmann .20
☐ 188 Andreas Volland .20
☐ 189 Rolf Hammer .20
☐ 190 Manuel Hess .20
☐ 191 Dale Derkatch .20
☐ 192 S Schwele .20
☐ 193 Bob Murdoch .20
☐ 194 Bernd Haake .20
☐ 195 Joseph Heiss .20
☐ 196 Olaf Grundmann .20
☐ 197 Alexander Genze .20
☐ 198 A von Trzcinski .20
☐ 199 Jorg Mayr .20
☐ 200 Mirco Ludemann .20
☐ 201 Andreas Pokorny .20
☐ 202 Jaysen Meyer .20
☐ 203 Karsten Mende .20
☐ 204 Herbert Hohenberger .20
☐ 205 Thomas Brandt .20
☐ 206 Stefan Mann .20
☐ 207 Luciano Borsato .20
☐ 208 Leo Stefan .20
☐ 209 Peter Draisaitl .20
☐ 210 Andreas Lupzig .20
☐ 211 Ralf Reisinger .20
☐ 212 Rainer Zerwesz .20
☐ 213 Michael Rumrich .20
☐ 214 Martin Ondrejka .20
☐ 215 Tobias Abstreiter .20
☐ 216 Franz Demmel .20
☐ 217 Sergei Berezin 4.00
☐ 218 Miroslav Berek, Coach .20
☐ 219 Karel Lang .20
☐ 220 Rene Bieike .20
☐ 221 Markus Krawinkel .20
☐ 222 Kenneth Karpuk .20
☐ 223 Klaus Micheller .20
☐ 224 Earl Spry .20
☐ 225 Andreas Ott .20
☐ 226 Petri Limatainen .20
☐ 227 Andre Grein .20
☐ 228 Ken Petrash .20
☐ 229 James Hanlon .20
☐ 230 Reemt Pyka .20
☐ 231 Thomas Imdahl .20
☐ 232 Chris Lindberg .20
☐ 233 J Luknovsky .20
☐ 234 Peter Ihnacak .20
☐ 235 Marek Strebnicki .20
☐ 236 Johnny Walker .20
☐ 237 Arno Brux .20
☐ 238 R Busch .20
☐ 239 Mark Bassen .20
☐ 240 Martin Gebel .20
☐ 241 Bernhard Johnston .20
☐ 242 Petr Briza (G) 1.00
☐ 243 Christian Kunast .20
☐ 244 Michael Bresagk .20
☐ 245 Eduard Uvria .20
☐ 246 Michael Heidt .20
☐ 247 Peter Gulda .20
☐ 248 Udo Kiessling .20
☐ 249 Dieter Bloem .20
☐ 250 Tony Vogel .20
☐ 251 Jacek Plachta .20
☐ 252 Georg Franz .20
☐ 253 Stephan Retzer .20
☐ 254 Henri Macoux .20
☐ 255 Andreas Loth .20
☐ 256 Mike Bullard 1.00
☐ 257 José Charbonneau .50
☐ 258 Wally Schreiber .20
☐ 259 Jorg Handrick .20
☐ 260 Holger Steiger .20
☐ 261 Marco Sturm 2.00
☐ 262 Lance Nethery .20
☐ 263 Markus Kuhl .20
☐ 264 Joachim Appel .20
☐ 265 Markus Flemming .20
☐ 266 Harold Kreis .20
☐ 267 Paul Stanton .20
☐ 268 Christian Lukes .20
☐ 269 Steffen Michel .20
☐ 270 Stéphane J.G. Richer .50
☐ 271 Jorg Hanft .20
☐ 272 Erich Goldmann .20
☐ 273 Mario Gehrig .20
☐ 274 Pavel Gross .20
☐ 275 Daniel Korber .20
☐ 276 Rob Cimetta .50
☐ 277 Jochen Hecht .20
☐ 278 Till Feser .20
☐ 279 Alexander Serikow .20
☐ 280 Patrik Pysz .20
☐ 281 Darian Adamus .20
☐ 282 David Musial .20
☐ 283 Michael Hreus .20
☐ 284 Chris Strausse .20
☐ 285 Sven Valenti .20
☐ 286 Sebastien Thivierge .20
☐ 287 Jan Eysselt, Coach .20
☐ 288 R Neubauer .20
☐ 289 Roman Turek (G) 2.00
☐ 290 Stefan Lahn .20
☐ 291 Christian Gerum .20
☐ 292 Heiko Smazal .20
☐ 293 Miroslav Maly .20
☐ 294 Thomas Sterflinger .20
☐ 295 M Weinfurter .20
☐ 296 Stephan Bauer .20
☐ 297 Lars Bruggemenn .20
☐ 298 Markus Kehle .20
☐ 299 Paul Geddes .20
☐ 300 Ian Young .20
☐ 301 Stefan Steinbock .20
☐ 302 Jurgen Lechl .20
☐ 303 M Goerlitz .20
☐ 304 Jiri Dolazal .20
☐ 305 Henrik Holscher .20
☐ 306 Sepp Wassermann .20
☐ 307 Otto Sykora .20
☐ 308 Bill Lochead .20
☐ 309 Patrick Lange .20
☐ 310 Ian Wood .20
☐ 311 H Thorn .20
☐ 312 Doug Irwin .20
☐ 313 Christian Schmitz .20
☐ 314 Alexander Wunsch .20
☐ 315 Cory Holden .20
☐ 316 J Bartman .20
☐ 317 Peter Lutter .20
☐ 318 Pavel Mann .20
☐ 319 Greg Muller .20
☐ 320 Christian Kohmann .20
☐ 321 Paul Beraldo .20
☐ 322 Thomas Groger .20
☐ 323 Andrej Fuchs .20
☐ 324 Klaus Birk .20
☐ 325 D Rich .20
☐ 326 Boris Fuchs .20
☐ 327 Thomas Muhlbauer .20
☐ 328 Axel Kammerer .20
☐ 329 Jeff Lazaro .50
☐ 330 Olaf Scholz .20
☐ 331 Bobby Reynolds .20
☐ 332 Jaroslav Sevcik .20
☐ 333 P.M. Arnholt .20
☐ 334 G Stranka .20
☐ 335 Vincent Riendeau .20
☐ 336 Michael Schmidt .20
☐ 337 T Gobel .20
☐ 338 Vladimir Fedosov .20
☐ 339 R Jadamzik .20
☐ 340 Frank Hohendahl .20
☐ 341 A Raubal .20
☐ 342 C Schonmoser .20
☐ 343 A Ludwig .20
☐ 344 K Ostler .20
☐ 345 Markus Berwanger .20
☐ 346 M Holzer .20
☐ 347 J Feller .20
☐ 348 H Domke .20
☐ 349 A Maurer .20
☐ 350 A Gebauer .20
☐ 351 Guntar Oswald .20
☐ 352 H Buchwieser .20
☐ 353 B Stewart .20
☐ 354 Christopher Sandner .20
☐ 355 J Haglsperger .20
☐ 356 Robert Hock .20
☐ 357 Marl Jooris .20
☐ 358 Ernst Hofner .20
☐ 359 Gary Clark, Coach .20

No.	Player	Price
360	Karl Friesen	.20
361	Klaus Dalpiaz	.20
362	Markus Wieland	.20
363	Chris Clarke	.20
364	Markus Pottinger	.20
365	Raphael Kruger	.20
366	Ron Fischer	.20
367	Christian Gegenfurte	.20
368	Heinrich Schiffl	.20
369	Andreas Schneider	.20
370	V Mittelfellner	.20
371	Richard Bohm	.20
372	Dale Krentz	.20
373	T Schraven	.20
374	Florian Keller	.20
375	Doug Gerraugh	.20
376	Martin Reichel	.20
377	M Draxler	.20
378	Raimund Hilger	.20
379	Michael Pohl	.20
380	M Kropf	.20
381	Joel Savage	.20
382	J Eckmaier	.20
383	R.R. Burns	.20
384	Gunnar Leidborg	.20
385	Carsten Solbach	.20
386	Matthias Hoppe	.20
387	Gord Hynes	.20
388	Thomas Gaus	.20
389	Zdenek Travnicek	.20
390	Richard Trojan	.20
391	Frantisek Frosch	.20
392	Daniel Nowak	.20
393	Andreas Renz	.20
394	Alan Young	.20
395	Robert Brezina	.20
396	Wayne Hynes	.20
397	George Fritz	.20
398	Mike Bader	.20
399	Grant Martin	.20
400	Karsten Schulz	.20
401	Mike Lay	.20
402	Jackson Penney	.20
403	Rich Chernomaz	.20
404	Mark MacKay	.20
405	Sana Hassan	.20
406	Jiri Kochta	.20
407	Thomas Bresagk	.20
408	Peter Franke	.20
409	Jochen Molling	.20
410	Frantisek Prochazka	.20
411	Josef Reznicek	.20
412	Thomas Schubert	.20
413	Ronny Martin	.20
414	Marcel Lichnovsky	.20
415	Matthias Kliemann	.20
416	Ronny Reddo	.20
417	Frank Peschke	.20
418	Torsten Eisebitt	.20
419	Janusz Janikowski	.20
420	Thomas Knobloch	.20
421	Falk Herzig	.20
422	Thomas Wagner	.20
423	Jan Tabor	.20
424	J Pohling	.20
425	Pavel Vit	.20
426	Vadim Kulabuchov	.20
427	D. Cup Meister 1995	.20
428	Kingston/Kuhnhauser/Genze	.20
429	Heiss/Lupzig	.20
430	Brandl/Mann	.20
431	Doucet/Nowak	.20
432	Meyer/Pyka	.20
433	Hegen/Kunce	.20
434	Rumrich/Ludemann	.20
435	Benda/Kosturik	.20
436	Kienass/Brockmann/Hanft	.20
437	Draisaitl/Simon/Schneider	.20
438	Andreas Niederberger	.20
439	Martin Reichel	.20
440	Klaus Merk	.20
441	Glenn Anderson	2.00
442	Pavel Bure	30.00
443	Vincent Damphousse	12.00
444	Uwe Krupp	2.00
445	Robert Reichel	6.00
446	Jeremy Roenick	12.00
447	Brendan Shanahan	25.00
448	Jozef Stumpel	6.00
449	Doug Weight	12.00
450	Scott Young	2.00
no#	Hologram Card	15.00

1995 - 96 DONRUSS

Imprint:

Series One Set (205 cards): **20.00**

Series Two Set (205 cards): **15.00**

Common Player: **.10**

No.	Player	NRMT-MT
1	Eric Lindros, Pha.	1.50
2	Steve Larmer, Chi.	.10
3	Oleg Tverdovsky, Wpg.	.10
4	Vladimir Malakhov, Mtl.	.10
5	Ian Laperrière, Stl.	.10
6	Chris Marinucci, N.J.	.10
7	Nelson Emerson, Hfd.	.10
8	David Oliver, Edm.	.10
9	Félix Potvin (G), Tor.	.50
10	Manny Fernandez (G), Dal.	.10
11	Jason Wiemer, T.B.	.10
12	Dale Hunter, Wsh.	.10
13	Wayne Gretzky, L.A	2.50
14	Todd Gill, Tor.	.10
15	Radim Bicanek, Ott.	.10
16	Kirk McLean (G), Van.	.25
17	Esa Tikkanen, NYR.	.10
18	Yuri Khmylev, Buf.	.10
19	Peter Bondra, Wsh.	.35
20	Brian Savage, Mtl.	.10
21	Mariusz Czerkawski, Bos.	.10
22	Rob Blake, L.A.	.25
23	Chris Osgood (G), Det.	.35
24	Bernie Nicholls, Chi.	.10
25	Doug Weight, Edm.	.35
26	Shaun Van Allen, Ana.	.10
27	Jeremy Roenick, Chi.	.35
28	Sean Burke (G), Hfd.	.25
29	Pat Verbeek, NYR.	.10
30	Dino Ciccarelli, Det.	.25
31	Trevor Kidd (G), Cgy.	.25
32	Steve Thomas, N.J.	.10
33	Dominik Hasek (G), Buf.	.75
34	Sandis Ozolinsh, S.J.	.25
35	Bill Guerin, N.J.	.25
36	Scott Young, Col.	.10
37	Scott Mellanby, Fla.	.10
38	Joe Mullen, Pgh.	.10
39	**Steve Larouche, Ott., RC**	**.10**
40	Joe Nieuwendyk, Cgy.	.25
41	Rick Tocchet, L.A.	.10
42	Keith Primeau, Det.	.25
43	Darren Turcotte, Hfd.	.10
44	Jason Arnott, Edm.	.25
45	Brantt Myhres, T.B.	.10
46	Murray Craven, Chi.	.10
47	Martin Gendron, Wsh.	.10
48	Mark Recchi, Mtl.	.25
49	Uwe Krupp, Que.	.10
50	Alexei Zhitnik, Buf.	.10
51	Rob Niedermayer, Fla.	.10
52	Sergei Brylin, N.J.	.10
53	Mats Naslund, Bos.	.10
54	Glenn Healy (G), NYR.	.10
55	Mathieu Schneider, NYI.	.10
56	Marko Tuomainen, Edm.	.10
57	Paul Kariya, Ana.	1.50
58	Dave Gagner, Dal.	.10
59	Mike Richter (G), NYR.	.35
60	Patrik Juhlin, Pha.	.10
61	Pierre Turgeon, Mtl.	.25
62	Mike Modano, Dal.	.50
63	Chris Pronger, Stl.	.25
64	Chris Joseph, Pgh.	.10
65	Peter Forsberg, Que.	1.25
66	Roman Oksiuta, Van.	.10
67	Jamie Storr (G), L.A.	.25
68	Brett Hull, Stl.	.50
69	Steve Chiasson, Cgy.	.10
70	Benoît Hogue, Tor.	.10
71	Guy Hebert (G), Ana.	.25
72	Chris Therien, Pha.	.10
73	Darryl Sydor, L.A.	.10
74	Phil Housley, Cgy.	.10
75	Jason Allison, Wsh.	.35
76	Richard Smehlik, Buf.	.10
77	Shean Donovan, S.J.	.10
78	Keith Tkachuk, Wpg.	.35
79	Cliff Ronning, Van.	.10
80	Mikael Renberg, Pha.	.10
81	Steve Rice, Hfd.	.10
82	Adam Graves, NYR.	.10
83	Nicklas Lidström, Det.	.25
84	Daren Puppa (G), T.B.	.10
85	Todd Warriner, Tor.	.10
86	Jon Rohloff, Bos.	.10
87	Patrice Tardif, Stl.	.10
88	John MacLean, N.J.	.10
89	Ulf Samuelsson, Pgh.	.10
90	Alexander Selivanov, T.B.	.10
91	Chris Chelios, Chi.	.35
92	Ulf Dahlen, S.J.	.10
93	Brad May, Buf.	.10
94	Ron Francis, Pgh.	.35
95	Kevin Hatcher, Dal.	.10
96	Steve Yzerman, Det.	1.25
97	Jocelyn Thibault (G), Mtl.	.35
98	Dave Andreychuk, Tor.	.10
99	Gary Suter, Chi.	.10
100	Teemu Selänne, Wpg.	.75
101	Don Sweeney, Bos.	.10
102	Valeri Bure, Mtl.	.10
103	Todd Harvey, Dal.	.10
104	Luc Robitaille, NYR.	.25
105	Scott Niedermayer, N.J.	.25
106	John Vanbiesbrouck (G), Fla.	.60
107	Alexei Yashin, Ott.	.35
108	Ed Belfour (G), Chi.	.35
109	Jyrki Lumme, Van.	.10
110	Petr Klima, T.B.	.10
111	Tony Granato, L.A.	.10
112	Bob Corkum, Ana.	.10
113	**Chris McAlpine, N.J., RC**	**.10**
114	John LeClair, Pha.	.50
115	Kenny Jonsson, Tor.	.10
116	Garry Galley, Pha.	.10
117	Jeff Norton, Stl.	.10
118	Tomas Sandström, Pgh.	.10
119	Paul Coffey, Det.	.25
120	Mike Ricci, Que.	.10
121	Tony Amonte, Chi.	.25
122	Chris Gratton, T.B.	.25
123	Blaine Lacher (G), Bos.	.10
124	Andrei Nikolishin, Hfd.	.10
125	Michal Grosek, Buf.	.10
126	Shawn Chambers, N.J.	.10
127	Ray Bourque, Bos.	.50
128	Jeff Nelson, Wsh.	.10
129	Kirk Muller, NYI.	.10
130	Sergei Zubov, NYR.	.25
131	Stanislav Neckar, Ott.	.10
132	Stu Barnes, Fla.	.10
133	Jari Kurri, L.A.	.25
134	Vyacheslav Kozlov, Det.	.10
135	Curtis Joseph (G), Stl.	.60
136	Joé Juneau, Wsh.	.10
137	Craig Janney, S.J.	.10
138	Bryan Smolinski, Bos.	.10
139	Brian Bradley, T.B.	.10

	No.	Player	Price
☐	140	Steve Rucchin, Ana.	.10
☐	141	Donald Audette, Buf.	.10
☐	142	Jaromir Jagr, Pgh.	1.25
☐	**143**	**Mike Torchia (G), Dal., RC**	**.10**
☐	144	Ray Ferraro, NYI.	.10
☐	145	Adam Deadmarsh, Que.	.10
☐	146	Joe Murphy, Chi.	.10
☐	147	Ron Hextall (G), Pha.	.25
☐	148	Andrew Cassels, Hfd.	.10
☐	149	Martin Brodeur (G), N.J.	.75
☐	150	Marek Malik, Hfd.	.10
☐	151	Eric Desjardins, Pha.	.10
☐	152	Cory Stillman, Cgy.	.10
☐	153	Owen Nolan, S.J.	.20
☐	154	Randy Wood, Tor.	.10
☐	155	Alexei Zhamnov, Wpg.	.25
☐	156	John Cullen, T.B.	.10
☐	157	Zdenek Nedved, Tor.	.10
☐	158	Greg Adams, Van.	.10
☐	159	Kelly Miller, Wsh.	.10
☐	160	Alexandre Daigle, Ott.	.25
☐	161	Gord Murphy, Fla.	.10
☐	162	Jeff Friesen, S.J.	.25
☐	163	Scott Stevens, N.J.	.10
☐	164	Denis Chassé, Stl.	.10
☐	165	Cam Neely, Bos.	.25
☐	**166**	**Magnus Svensson, Fla., RC**	**.10**
☐	167	Joe Sakic, Que.	1.00
☐	168	Kevin Brown, L.A.	.10
☐	169	Craig Conroy, Mtl.	.10
☐	170	Pavel Bure, Van.	.75
☐	171	Viktor Kozlov, S.J.	.10
☐	172	Pat LaFontaine, Buf.	.25
☐	173	Sergei Gonchar, Wsh.	.10
☐	174	Brett Lindros, NYI.	.10
☐	175	Jassen Cullimore, Van.	.10
☐	176	Mats Sundin, Tor.	.50
☐	177	Zarley Zalapski, Cgy.	.10
☐	178	Stéphane Richer, N.J.	.10
☐	179	Steve Smith, Chi.	.10
☐	180	Brendan Shanahan, Stl.	.75
☐	181	Brian Leetch, NYR.	.35
☐	182	Ken Wregget (G), Pgh.	.10
☐	183	Jeff Brown, Van.	.10
☐	184	Darby Hendrickson, NYI.	.10
☐	185	Nikolai Khabibulin (G), Wpg.	.35
☐	186	Glen Wesley, Hfd.	.10
☐	187	Andrei Nazarov, S.J.	.10
☐	188	Rod Brind'Amour, Pha.	.25
☐	189	Jim Carey (G), Wsh.	.10
☐	190	Derek Plante, Buf.	.10
☐	191	Valeri Karpov, Ana.	.10
☐	192	Mike Kennedy, Dal.	.10
☐	193	Wendel Clark, Tor.	.25
☐	194	Radek Bonk, Ott.	.10
☐	195	Jozef Stumpel, Bos.	.25
☐	**196**	**Tommy Salo (G), NYI., RC**	**.10**
☐	197	Michal Pivonka, Wsh.	.10
☐	198	Ray Sheppard, Det.	.10
☐	199	Russ Courtnall, Van.	.10
☐	200	Todd Marchant, Edm.	.10
☐	201	Geoff Sanderson, Hfd.	.10
☐	202	Vincent Damphousse, Mtl.	.25
☐	203	Sergei Krivokrasov, Chi.	.10
☐	204	Jesse Belanger, Fla.	.10
☐	205	Al MacInnis, Stl.	.10
☐	206	Philippe DeRouville (G), Pgh.	.10
☐	207	Mike Eastwood, Wpg.	.10
☐	208	Travis Green, NYI.	.10
☐	209	Jeff Shantz, Chi.	.10
☐	**210**	**Shane Doan, Wpg., RC**	**.10**
☐	211	Mike Sullivan, S.J.	.10
☐	212	Kevin Dineen, Hfd.	.10
☐	213	Pat Falloon, Pha.	.10
☐	214	Rick Tabaracci (G), Cgy.	.10
☐	215	Kelly Hrudey (G), L.A.	.10
☐	216	Alexei Kovalev, NYR.	.10
☐	217	Matt Johnson, L.A.	.10
☐	218	Turner Stevenson, Mtl.	.10
☐	219	Mike Sillinger, Ana.	.10
☐	220	Bobby Holik, N.J.	.10
☐	221	Kevin Stevens, Bos.	.10
☐	222	Dave Lowry, Fla.	.10
☐	223	Martin Gelinas, Van.	.10
☐	**224**	**Darren Langdon, NYR., RC**	**.10**
☐	225	Tie Domi, Tor.	.10
☐	226	Doug Bodger, S.J.	.10
☐	227	Patrick Flatley, NYI.	.10
☐	**228**	**Anders Myrvold, Col., RC**	**.10**
☐	229	German Titov, Cgy.	.10
☐	230	Pat Peake, Wsh	.10
☐	231	Robert Kron, Hfd.	.10
☐	232	Mike Donnelly, L.A.	.10
☐	233	Denis Savard, Chi.	.25
☐	**234**	**Mathieu Dandenault, Det., RC**	**.10**
☐	**235**	**Joe Dziedzic, Pgh., RC**	**.10**
☐	236	Valeri Kamensky, Que.	.25
☐	**237**	**Joaquin Gage (G), Edm., RC**	**.10**
☐	238	Geoff Courtnall, Stl.	.10
☐	239	Arturs Irbe (G), S.J.	.10
☐	240	Dan Quinn, Pha.	.10
☐	241	J.C. Bergeron (G), T.B.	.10
☐	242	Brian Noonan, Stl.	.10
☐	243	Ulf Samuelsson, NYR.	.10
☐	244	Jeff O'Neill, Hfd.	.10
☐	**245**	**Sandy Moger, Bos., RC**	**.10**
☐	246	Don Beaupré (G), Ott.	.10
☐	247	Bob Probert, Chi.	.10
☐	248	Mattias Norstrom, NYR.	.10
☐	249	Jason Bonsignore, Edm.	.10
☐	250	Mike Ridley, Van.	.10
☐	251	Joe Mullen, Bos.	.10
☐	252	Petr Nedved, Pgh.	.10
☐	253	Jason Doig, Wpg.	.10
☐	254	Olaf Kolzig (G), Wsh.	.35
☐	255	Mark Tinordi, Wsh.	.10
☐	256	Roman Hamrlik, T.B.	.25
☐	257	Denis Pederson, N.J.	.10
☐	258	Paul Ysebaert, T.B.	.10
☐	259	Neal Broten, N.J.	.10
☐	260	Jason Woolley, Fla.	.10
☐	261	Teppo Numminen, Wpg.	.10
☐	262	Scott Thornton, Edm.	.10
☐	263	Ted Donato, Bos.	.10
☐	**264**	**Marcus Ragnarsson, S.J., RC**	**.10**
☐	265	Dimitri Khristich, L.A.	.10
☐	266	Michael Peca, Van.	.25
☐	267	Dominic Roussel (G), Pha.	.10
☐	268	Owen Nolan, S.J.	.25
☐	269	Patrick Poulin, T.B.	.10
☐	270	Mario Lemieux, Pgh.	2.00
☐	271	Mark Messier, NYR.	.50
☐	272	Viacheslav Fetisov, Det.	.25
☐	273	Andrei Trefilov (G), Buf.	.10
☐	274	Damian Rhodes (G), Ott.	.10
☐	275	Alexander Mogilny, Van.	.35
☐	276	Ray Sheppard, S.J.	.10
☐	**277**	**Radek Dvorak, Fla., RC**	**.25**
☐	278	Steve Duchesne, Ott.	.10
☐	279	Jason Smith, N.J.	.10
☐	**280**	**Wade Flaherty (G), S.J., RC**	**.10**
☐	281	Lyle Odelein, Mtl.	.10
☐	282	Keith Jones, Wsh.	.10
☐	283	Saku Koivu, Mtl.	.75
☐	284	Marty Murray, Cgy.	.10
☐	285	Sergei Fedorov, Det.	.50
☐	286	Brian Rolston, N.J.	.10
☐	**287**	**Dave Roche, Pgh., RC**	**.10**
☐	288	Sylvain Lefebvre, Col.	.10
☐	289	Theoren Fleury, Cgy.	.35
☐	290	Andy Moog (G), Dal.	.25
☐	291	Tom Barrasso (G), Pgh.	.25
☐	**292**	**Craig Mills, Wpg., RC**	**.10**
☐	293	Mike Gartner, Tor.	.25
☐	294	Stefan Ustorf, Wsh.	.10
☐	295	Darren Turcotte, Wpg.	.10
☐	296	Steve Konowalchuk, Wsh.	.10
☐	297	Ray Ferraro, NYR.	.10
☐	**298**	**Brian Holzinger, Buf., RC**	**.25**
☐	**299**	**Daniel Alfredsson, Ott., RC**	**.75**
☐	300	Derek King, NYI.	.10
☐	301	Mark Fitzpatrick (G), Fla.	.10
☐	302	Joe Sacco, Ana.	.10
☐	**303**	**Scott Walker, Van, RC**	**.10**
☐	**304**	**Ricard Persson, N.J., RC**	**.10**
☐	305	Mike Rathje, S.J.	.10
☐	306	Petr Svoboda, N.J.	.10
☐	**307**	**Roman Vopat, Stl., RC**	**.10**
☐	308	Ray Whitney, S.J.	.10
☐	309	Calle Johansson, Wsh.	.10
☐	310	Grant Fuhr (G), Stl.	.25
☐	311	John Tucker, T.B.	.10
☐	312	Anatoli Semenov, Ana.	.10
☐	313	Darren McCarty, Det.	.10
☐	314	Stéphane Quintal, Mtl.	.10
☐	315	Jason Dawe, Buf.	.10
☐	316	Zigmund Palffy, NYI.	.35
☐	317	Dave Manson, Wpg.	.10
☐	318	Vitali Yachmenev, L.A.	.10
☐	319	Chris Pronger, Stl.	.25
☐	320	Valeri Zelepukin, N.J.	.10
☐	321	Ryan Smyth, Edm.	.25
☐	322	Johan Garpenlov, Fla.	.10
☐	323	Bill Ranford (G), Edm.	.25
☐	**324**	**Daymond Langkow, T.B., RC**	**.25**
☐	**325**	**Aki Berg, L.A., RC**	**.25**
☐	326	Derian Hatcher, Dal.	.25
☐	327	Bryan Smolinski, Pgh.	.10
☐	328	Michel Picard, Ott.	.10
☐	329	Alek Stojanov, Pgh.	.10
☐	330	Trent Klatt, Dal.	.10
☐	331	Richard Park, Pgh.	.10
☐	332	Jere Lehtinen, Dal.	.25
☐	333	Bryan McCabe, NYI.	.10
☐	**334**	**Kyle McLaren, Bos., RC**	**.10**
☐	335	Todd Krygier, Ana.	.10
☐	336	Adam Creighton, T.B.	.10
☐	337	Jamie Pushor, Det.	.10
☐	338	Patrick Roy (G), Col.	2.00
☐	339	Milos Holan, Ana.	.10
☐	340	Dave Ellett, Tor.	.10
☐	341	Brian Bellows, T.B.	.10
☐	342	Jamie Rivers, Stl.	.10
☐	343	Claude Lemieux, Col.	.10
☐	**344**	**Leif Rohlin, Van., RC**	**.10**
☐	345	Eric Dazé, Chi.	.25
☐	**346**	**Todd Bertuzzi, NYI., RC**	**.10**
☐	**347**	**Antti Törmänen, Ott., RC**	**.10**
☐	348	Luc Robitaille, NYR.	.25
☐	349	Tim Taylor, Det.	.10
☐	**350**	**S. Yelle, Col., RC, Error (Doug Friedman)**	**.25**
☐	351	Marko Kiprusoff, Mtl.	.10
☐	352	Igor Korolev, Wpg.	.10
☐	353	Scott Lachance, NYI.	.10
☐	354	Marty McSorley, L.A.	.10
☐	355	Joel Otto, Pha.	.10
☐	356	Josef Beranek, Pha.	.10
☐	357	Sergei Zubov, Pgh.	.25
☐	**358**	**Rhett Warrener, Fla., RC**	**.25**
☐	359	Jimmy Carson, Hfd.	.10
☐	360	Zdeno Ciger, Edm.	.10
☐	361	Brendan Witt, Wsh.	.10
☐	362	Byron Dafoe (G), L.A.	.10
☐	363	Steve Thomas, N.J.	.10
☐	364	Deron Quint, Wpg.	.10
☐	365	Nelson Emerson, Hfd.	.10
☐	366	Larry Murphy, Tor.	.25
☐	367	Benoît Brunet, Mtl.	.10
☐	368	Kjell Samuelsson, Pha.	.10
☐	369	Aaron Gavey, T.B.	.10
☐	**370**	**Robert Svehla, Fla., RC**	**.25**
☐	371	René Corbet, Col.	.10
☐	372	Gary Roberts, Cgy.	.25
☐	373	Shawn McEachern, Bos.	.10
☐	374	Andrei Kovalenko, Mtl.	.10
☐	375	Yanic Perreault, L.A.	.10
☐	376	Shayne Corson, Stl.	.25
☐	377	Brendan Shanahan, Hfd.	.60
☐	378	Sergei Nemchinov, NYR.	.10
☐	**379**	**Chad Kilger, Ana., RC**	**.10**
☐	380	Sergio Momesso, Tor.	.10
☐	381	Craig Billington (G), Bos.	.10
☐	382	Niklas Sundstrom, NYR.	.10
☐	383	Matthew Barnaby, Buf.	.10
☐	384	Dale Hawerchuk, Stl.	.25
☐	385	Trevor Linden, Van.	.25
☐	386	Adam Oates, Bos.	.35
☐	387	Dimitri Yushkevich, Tor.	.10
☐	388	Todd Elik, Bos.	.10
☐	389	Wendel Clark, Tor.	.25
☐	390	Stéphane Fiset (G), Col.	.25
	No.	**Checklists**	**NRMT-MT**
☐	1	Checklist 1	.10
☐	2	Checklist 2	.10
☐	3	Checklist 3	.10

	No.	Player	NRMT-MT
☐	4	Checklist 4	.10
☐	5	Checklist 5	.10
☐	6	Checklist 6	.10
☐	7	Checklist 7	.10
☐	8	Checklist 8	.10

BETWEEN THE PIPES

These die-cut inserts were found in Series One and Series Two packs.

Insert Set (10 cards): 85.00

	No.	Player	NRMT-MT
☐	1	Blaine Lacher (G), Bos.	4.00
☐	2	Dominik Hasek (G), Buf.	18.00
☐	3	Mike Vernon (G), Det.	4.00
☐	4	Trevor Kidd (G), Cgy.	4.00
☐	5	Martin Brodeur (G), N.J.	18.00
☐	6	Jim Carey (G), Wsh.	4.00
☐	7	Patrick Roy (G), Col.	30.00
☐	8	Sean Burke (G), Hfd.	4.00
☐	9	Félix Potvin (G), Tor.	10.00
☐	10	Ed Belfour (G), Chi.	6.00

CANADA WORLD JUNIOR TEAM

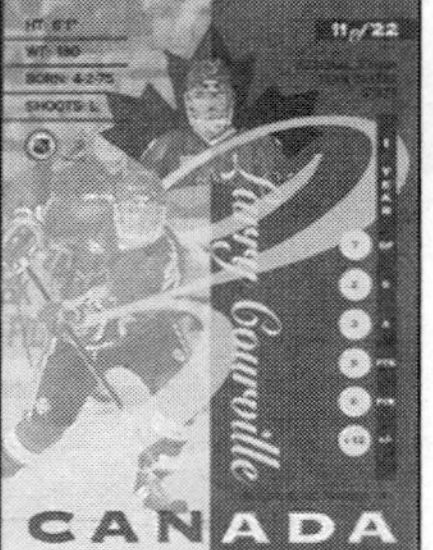

These inserts were found in Series One and Series Two packs.

Insert Set (22 cards): 15.00

	No.	Player	NRMT-MT
☐	1	Jamie Storr (G)	1.00
☐	2	Dan Cloutier (G)	1.00
☐	3	Nolan Baumgartner	.50
☐	4	Chad Allan	.50
☐	5	Wade Redden	.75
☐	6	Ed Jovanovski	1.00
☐	7	Jamie Rivers	.50
☐	8	Bryan McCabe	.50
☐	9	Lee Sorochan	.50
☐	10	Marty Murray	.50
☐	11	Larry Courville	.50
☐	12	Jason Allison	1.50
☐	13	Darcy Tucker	.50
☐	14	Jeff O'Neill	1.00
☐	15	Eric Dazé	1.00
☐	16	Alexandre Daigle	.75
☐	17	Todd Harvey	.50
☐	18	Jason Botterill	.50
☐	19	Shean Donovan	.50
☐	20	Denis Pederson	.50
☐	21	Jeff Friesen	.75
☐	22	Ryan Smyth	4.00

DOMINATORS

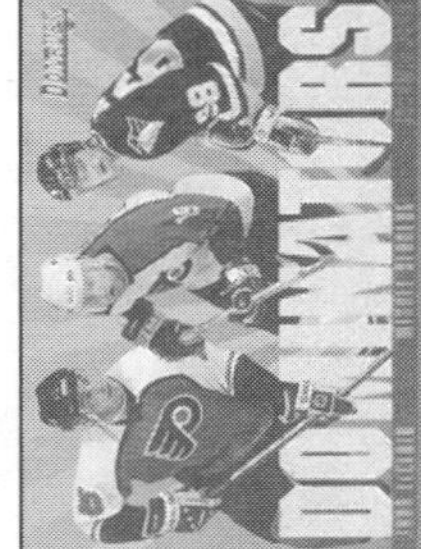

These inserts are serial numbered out of 5000.

Series Two Insert Set (8 cards): 175.00

	No.	Player	NRMT-MT
☐	1	P.Forsberg/E.Lindros/M.Lemieux	50.00
☐	2	J.LeClairM.Renberg/J.Jagr	15.00
☐	3	S.Zubov/R.Bourque/B.Leetch	10.00
☐	4	J.Carey/M.Brodeur/D.Hasek	25.00
☐	5	D.Gilmour/W.Gretzky/S.Fedorov	50.00
☐	6	B.Hull/P.Kariya/P.Bure	30.00
☐	7	P.Coffey/C.Chelios/A.MacInnis	10.00
☐	8	F.Potvin/E.Belfour.T.Kidd	10.00

ELITE

These inserts were found in Series One and Series Two packs. They are serial numbered out of 10,000.

Insert Set (10 cards): 200.00

	No.	Player	NRMT-MT
☐	1	Alexei Zhamnov, Wpg.	6.00
☐	2	Joe Sakic, Que.	20.00
☐	3	Mikael Renberg, Pha.	6.00
☐	4	Sergei Fedorov, Det.	12.00
☐	5	Paul Coffey, Det.	6.00
☐	6	Paul Kariya, Ana.	35.00
☐	7	Wayne Gretzky, L.A.	50.00
☐	8	Eric Lindros, Pha.	35.00
☐	9	Mario Lemieux, Pgh.	40.00
☐	10	Jaromir Jagr, Pgh.	25.00

IGNITERS

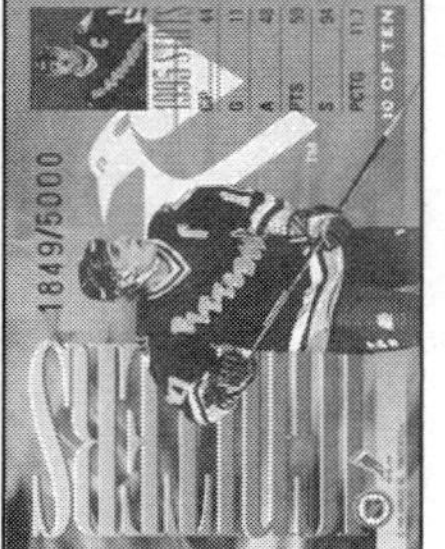

These inserts are serial numbered out of 5000.

Series One Insert Set (10 cards): 120.00

	No.	Player	NRMT-MT
☐	1	Adam Oates, Bos.	12.00
☐	2	Paul Coffey, Det.	8.00
☐	3	Doug Gilmour, Tor.	12.00
☐	4	Pierre Turgeon, Mtl.	8.00
☐	5	Mark Messier, NYR.	20.00
☐	6	Alexei Zhamnov, Wpg.	8.00
☐	7	Jeremy Roenick, Chi.	12.00
☐	8	Steve Yzerman, Det.	40.00
☐	9	Joe Nieuwendyk, Cgy.	8.00
☐	10	Ron Francis, Pgh.	12.00

MARKSMEN

Series One Insert Set (8 cards): 145.00

	No.	Player	NRMT-MT
☐	1	Peter Bondra, Wsh.	15.00
☐	2	Owen Nolan, Que.	7.00
☐	3	Eric Lindros, Pha.	50.00
☐	4	Ray Sheppard, Det.	7.00
☐	5	Jaromir Jagr, Pgh.	35.00
☐	6	Theoren Fleury, Cgy.	10.00
☐	7	Brett Hull, Stl.	18.00
☐	8	Brendan Shanahan, Stl.	25.00

ROOKIE TEAM

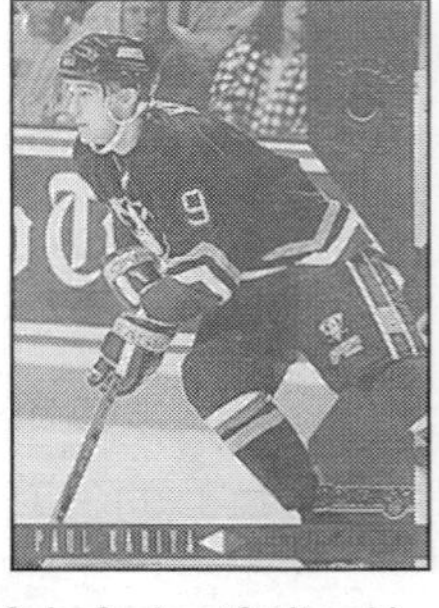

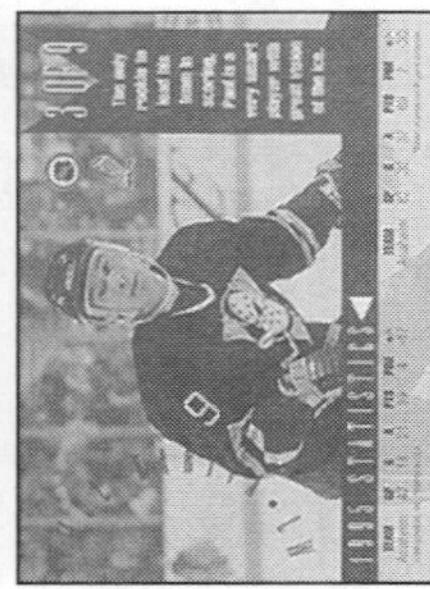

Series One Insert Set (9 cards): 25.00

	No.	Player	NRMT-MT
☐	1	Jim Carey (G), Wsh.	1.50
☐	2	Peter Forsberg, Que.	8.00
☐	3	Paul Kariya, Ana.	10.00
☐	4	David Oliver, Edm.	1.50
☐	5	Blaine Lacher (G), Bos.	1.50
☐	6	Oleg Tverdovsky, Ana.	1.50
☐	7	Jeff Friesen, S.J.	2.50
☐	8	Todd Marchant, Edm.	1.50
☐	9	Todd Harvey, Dal.	1.50

PRO POINTERS

Series Two Insert Set (10 cards): 10.00

	No.	Player	NRMT-MT
☐	1	Jeremy Roenick, USA.	.50
☐	2	Pat LaFontaine, USA.	.25
☐	3	Jason Bonsignore, USA.	.25
☐	4	Chris Chelios, USA.	.50
☐	5	Brian Leetch, USA.	.50
☐	6	Brett Hull, USA.	.75
☐	7	Keith Tkachuk, USA.	.50
☐	8	Mike Modano, USA.	.75
☐	9	Brian Rolston, USA.	.25
☐	10	Darren Turcotte, USA.	.25
☐	11	Jeff Friesen, Cdn.	.25
☐	12	Theoren Fleury, Cdn.	.50
☐	13	Eric Lindros, Cdn.	2.00
☐	14	Mario Lemieux, Cdn.	2.50
☐	15	Jamie Storr (G), Cdn.	.25
☐	16	Trevor Kidd (G), Cdn.	.25
☐	17	Chris Pronger, Cdn.	.25
☐	18	Brendan Witt, Cdn.	.25
☐	19	Paul Kariya, Cdn.	2.00
☐	20	Todd Harvey, Cdn.	.25

RATED ROOKIES

Series Two Insert Set (16 cards): 110.00

	No.	Player	NRMT-MT
☐	1	Saku Koivu, Mtl.	35.00

	No.	Player	
☐	2	Todd Bertuzzi, NYI.	8.00
☐	3	Niklas Sundstrom, NYR.	5.00
☐	4	Jeff O'Neill, Hfd.	8.00
☐	5	Zdenek Nedved, Tor.	5.00
☐	6	Eric Dazé, Chi.	8.00
☐	7	Chad Kilger, Ana.	5.00
☐	8	Shane Doan, Wpg.	5.00
☐	9	Vitali Yachmenev, L.A.	5.00
☐	10	Radek Dvorak, Fla.	5.00
☐	11	Marty Murray, Cgy.	5.00
☐	12	Cory Stillman, Cgy.	5.00
☐	13	Magnus Ragnarsson, S.J.	5.00
☐	14	Daniel Alfredsson, Ott.	20.00
☐	15	Antti Törmänen, Ott.	5.00
☐	16	Petr Sykora, N.J.	5.00

1995 - 96 DONRUSS ELITE

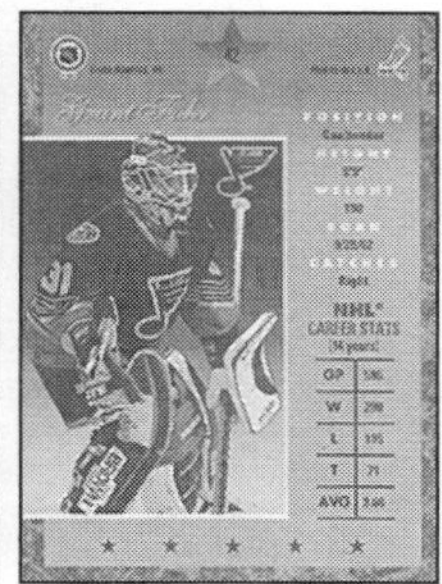

There are three versions to Donruss Elite: a regular card, a Die-Cut Stars parallel and an uncut Die-Cut Stars parallel. There are reportedly 500 copies of each Die-Cut parallel while there is an undetermined number of uncut Die-Cut parallels that were "mistakenly" inserted into the packs.

Imprint: © 1996 DONRUSS, INC.

		Complete Set (110 cards):		**120.00**	**30.00**
		Common Player:	**3.00**	**5.00**	**.20**
	No.	**Player**	**U.D.C.**	**D.C.**	**Reg.**
☐☐☐	1	Jocelyn Thibault (G), Mtl.	10.00	20.00	.75
☐☐☐	2	Nicklas Lidström, Det.	5.00	10.00	.50
☐☐☐	3	Brendan Shanahan, Hfd.	17.50	35.00	1.25
☐☐☐	4	Kenny Jonsson, NYI.	3.00	5.00	.20
☐☐☐	5	Doug Weight, Edm.	10.00	20.00	.75
☐☐☐	6	Oleg Tverdovsky, Wpg.	3.00	5.00	.20
☐☐☐	7	Brett Hull, Stl.	15.00	30.00	1.00
☐☐☐	8	Larry Murphy, Tor.	5.00	10.00	.50
☐☐☐	9	Ray Bourque, Bos.	15.00	30.00	1.00
☐☐☐	10	Adam Graves, NYR.	3.00	5.00	.20
☐☐☐	11	Gary Suter, Chi.	3.00	5.00	.20
☐☐☐	12	Bill Ranford (G), Edm.	5.00	10.00	.50
☐☐☐	13	Zigmund Palffy, NYI.	12.00	25.00	.85
☐☐☐	14	Cam Neely, Bos.	5.00	10.00	.50
☐☐☐	15	Al MacInnis, Stl.	3.00	5.00	.20
☐☐☐	16	Joe Sakic, Col.	25.00	50.00	1.75
☐☐☐	17	Kevin Hatcher, Pgh.	3.00	5.00	.20
☐☐☐	18	Alexander Mogilny, Van.	10.00	20.00	.75
☐☐☐	**19**	**Radek Dvorak, Fla., RC**	**4.00**	**8.00**	**.50**
☐☐☐	20	Ed Belfour (G), Chi.	10.00	20.00	.75
☐☐☐	21	Jeff O'Neill, Hfd.	3.00	5.00	.20
☐☐☐	22	Valeri Kamensky, Que.	5.00	10.00	.50
☐☐☐	23	John MacLean, N.J.	3.00	5.00	.20
☐☐☐	24	Zdeno Ciger, Edm.	3.00	5.00	.20
☐☐☐	**25**	**Daniel Alfredsson, Ott., RC**	**15.00**	**30.00**	**1.50**
☐☐☐	26	Owen Nolan, S.J.	5.00	10.00	.50
☐☐☐	27	Wendel Clark, Tor.	5.00	10.00	.50
☐☐☐	28	Brian Savage, Mtl.	3.00	5.00	.20
☐☐☐	29	Alexei Zhamnov, Wpg.	5.00	10.00	.50
☐☐☐	30	Dominik Hasek (G), Buf.	20.00	40.00	1.50
☐☐☐	31	Paul Kariya, Ana.	40.00	80.00	2.50
☐☐☐	32	Mike Modano, Dal.	15.00	30.00	1.00
☐☐☐	33	Craig Janney, S.J.	3.00	5.00	.20
☐☐☐	34	Todd Harvey, Dal.	3.00	5.00	.20
☐☐☐	35	Jaromir Jagr, Pgh.	30.00	60.00	2.00
☐☐☐	36	Roman Hamrlik, T.B.	5.00	10.00	.50
☐☐☐	37	Sergei Zubov, Dal.	5.00	10.00	.50
☐☐☐	**38**	**Marcus Ragnarsson, S.J., RC**	**3.00**	**5.00**	**.20**
☐☐☐	39	Peter Forsberg, Col.	30.00	60.00	2.00
☐☐☐	40	Ron Francis, Pgh.	10.00	20.00	.75
☐☐☐	41	German Titov, Cgy.	3.00	5.00	.20
☐☐☐	42	Grant Fuhr (G), Stl.	5.00	10.00	.50
☐☐☐	43	Martin Brodeur, N.J.	20.00	40.00	1.50
☐☐☐	44	Claude Lemieux, N.J.	3.00	5.00	.25
☐☐☐	45	Trevor Linden, Van.	5.00	10.00	.50
☐☐☐	46	Mark Messier, NYR.	15.00	30.00	1.00
☐☐☐	47	Jeremy Roenick, Chi.	10.00	20.00	.75
☐☐☐	48	Peter Bondra, Wsh.	12.00	25.00	.85
☐☐☐	49	Donald Audette, Buf.	3.00	5.00	.20
☐☐☐	50	Joe Nieuwendyk, Cgy.	5.00	10.00	.50
☐☐☐	51	CL: Mario Lemieux, Pgh.	25.00	50.00	1.50
☐☐☐	52	Vitali Yachmenev, L.A.	3.00	5.00	.25
☐☐☐	53	Sergei Fedorov, Det.	15.00	30.00	1.00
☐☐☐	54	Kirk Muller, Tor.	3.00	5.00	.20
☐☐☐	**55**	**Chad Kilger, Wpg., RC**	**3.00**	**5.00**	**.20**
☐☐☐	56	John LeClair, Pha.	15.00	30.00	1.00
☐☐☐	**57**	**Todd Bertuzzi, NYI., RC**	**5.00**	**10.00**	**1.00**
☐☐☐	58	Wayne Gretzky, Stl.	60.00	125.00	4.00
☐☐☐	59	Curtis Joseph (G), Edm.	17.50	35.00	1.25
☐☐☐	60	Niklas Sundstrom, NYR.	3.00	5.00	.20
☐☐☐	61	Chris Chelios, Chi.	12.00	25.00	.85
☐☐☐	62	Radek Bonk, Ott.	3.00	5.00	.20
☐☐☐	63	Eric Dazé, Chi.	5.00	10.00	.50
☐☐☐	64	Patrick Roy (G), Col.	50.00	100.00	3.00
☐☐☐	65	Rob Niedermayer, Fla.	5.00	10.00	.50
☐☐☐	66	Mario Lemieux, Pgh.	50.00	100.00	3.00
☐☐☐	67	Saku Koivu, Mtl.	20.00	40.00	1.50
☐☐☐	68	Ed Jovanovski, Fla.	5.00	10.00	.50
☐☐☐	69	Jim Carey (G), Wsh.	3.00	5.00	.20
☐☐☐	70	Scott Stevens, N.J.	3.00	5.00	.20
☐☐☐	71	Steve Thomas, N.J.	3.00	5.00	.20
☐☐☐	72	Mats Sundin, Tor.	15.00	30.00	1.00
☐☐☐	73	Teemu Selänne, Ana.	20.00	40.00	1.50
☐☐☐	74	Tomas Sandström, Pgh.	3.00	5.00	.20
☐☐☐	75	Pat LaFontaine, Buf.	5.00	10.00	.50
☐☐☐	76	Pat Verbeek, NYR.	3.00	5.00	.20
☐☐☐	77	Pavel Bure, Van.	20.00	40.00	1.50
☐☐☐	78	Jeff Brown, Hfd.	3.00	5.00	.20
☐☐☐	79	Alexei Yashin, Ott.	12.00	25.00	.85
☐☐☐	80	Adam Oates, Bos.	10.00	20.00	.75
☐☐☐	81	Keith Tkachuk, Wpg.	12.00	25.00	.85
☐☐☐	82	Brian Bradley, T.B.	3.00	5.00	.20
☐☐☐	83	John Vanbiesbrouck, Fla.	17.50	35.00	1.25
☐☐☐	84	Alexander Selivanov, T.B.	3.00	5.00	.20
☐☐☐	85	Paul Coffey, Det.	5.00	10.00	.50
☐☐☐	86	Scott Mellanby, Fla.	3.00	5.00	.20
☐☐☐	87	Vyachyeslav Kozlov, Det.	3.00	5.00	.20
☐☐☐	88	Eric Lindros, Pha.	40.00	80.00	2.50
☐☐☐	89	Deron Quint, Wpg.	3.00	5.00	.20
☐☐☐	90	Pierre Turgeon, Mtl.	5.00	10.00	.50
☐☐☐	91	Rod Brind'Amour, Pha.	5.00	10.00	.50
☐☐☐	92	Doug Gilmour, Tor.	10.00	20.00	.75
☐☐☐	93	Sandis Ozolinsh, Col.	5.00	10.00	.50
☐☐☐	94	Mikael Renberg, Pha.	3.00	5.00	.20
☐☐☐	95	Kevin Stevens, L.A.	3.00	5.00	.20
☐☐☐	96	Vincent Damphousse, Mtl.	10.00	20.00	.75
☐☐☐	97	Félix Potvin (G), Tor.	15.00	30.00	1.00
☐☐☐	98	Brian Leetch, NYR.	10.00	20.00	.75
☐☐☐	99	Steve Yzerman, Det.	30.00	60.00	2.00
☐☐☐	100	Dale Hawerchuk, Pha.	5.00	10.00	.50
☐☐☐	101	Jason Arnott, Edm.	5.00	10.00	.50
☐☐☐	102	Ray Sheppard, Fla.	3.00	5.00	.20
☐☐☐	103	Mark Recchi, Mtl.	5.00	10.00	.50
☐☐☐	104	Joé Juneau, Wsh.	3.00	5.00	.20
☐☐☐	105	Luc Robitaille, NYR.	5.00	10.00	.50
☐☐☐	106	Theoren Fleury, Cgy.	10.00	20.00	.75
☐☐☐	107	Sean Burke (G), Hfd.	5.00	10.00	.50
☐☐☐	108	Ron Hextall (G), Pha.	5.00	10.000	.50
☐☐☐	**109**	**Shane Doan, Wpg., RC**	**3.00**	**5.00**	**.20**
☐☐☐	110	CL: Eric Lindros	20.00	40.00	1.25

	Autographed Lemieux/Lindros	**NRMT-MT**
☐	M. Lemieux & E. Lindros	500.00

CUTTING EDGE

These inserts are serial numbered out of 5,000.

		Insert Set (15 cards):	**200.00**
	No.	**Player**	**NRMT-MT**
☐	1	Eric Lindros, Pha.	25.00
☐	2	Mario Lemieux, Pgh.	30.00
☐	3	Wayne Gretzky, Stl.	40.00
☐	4	Peter Forsberg, Col.	20.00
☐	5	Paul Kariya, Ana.	25.00
☐	6	Jaromir Jagr, Pgh.	20.00
☐	7	Alexander Mogilny, Van.	6.00
☐	8	Mark Messier, NYR.	10.00
☐	9	Sergei Fedorov, Det.	10.00
☐	10	Pierre Turgeon, Mtl.	5.00
☐	11	Mats Sundin, Tor.	10.00
☐	12	Brett Hull, Stl.	10.00
☐	13	Paul Coffey, Det.	5.00
☐	14	Jeremy Roenick, Chi.	6.00
☐	15	Teemu Selänne, Ana.	15.00

MARIO LEMIEUX SERIES

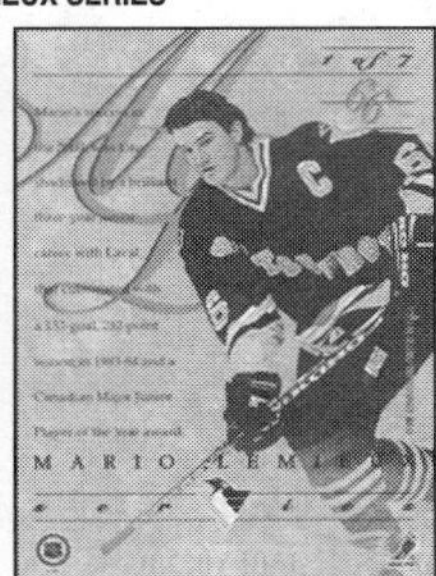

These inserts are serial numbered out of 1,066.

		Insert Set (7 cards):	**500.00**
	No.	**Player**	**NRMT-MT**
☐	1	Mario Lemieux, Pgh.	40.00
☐	2	Mario Lemieux, Pgh.	40.00
☐	3	Mario Lemieux, Pgh.	40.00
☐	4	Mario Lemieux, Pgh.	40.00
☐	5	Mario Lemieux, Pgh.	40.00
☐	6	Mario Lemieux, Pgh.	40.00
☐	7	Mario Lemieux Autograph	350.00

ERIC LINDROS SERIES

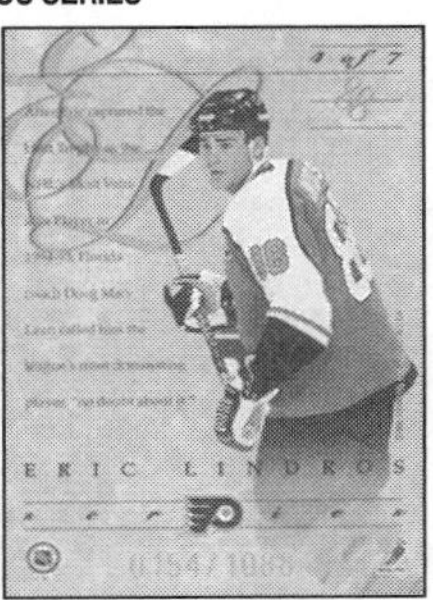

These inserts are serial numbered out of 1,088.

		Insert Set (7 cards):	**450.00**
	No.	**Player**	**NRMT-MT**
☐	1	Eric Lindros, Pha.	35.00
☐	2	Eric Lindros, Pha.	35.00
☐	3	Eric Lindros, Pha.	35.00
☐	4	Eric Lindros, Pha.	35.00
☐	5	Eric Lindros, Pha.	35.00

	No.	Player	NRMT-MT
☐	6	Eric Lindros, Pha.	35.00
☐	7	Eric Lindros Autograph	300.00

PAINTED WARRIORS

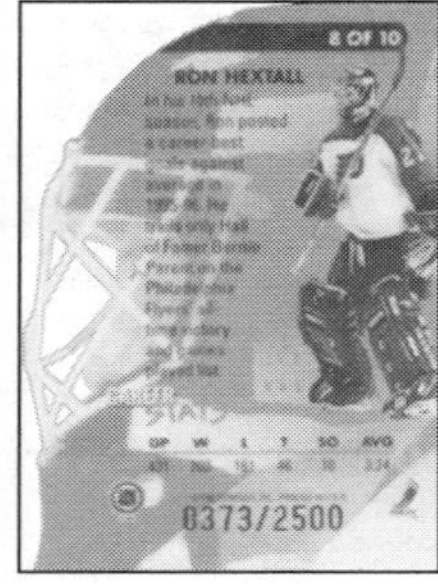

These inserts are serial numbered out of 2,500. Promo cards are numbered "XXXX of 2,500".

	No.	Player	Promo	Reg.
Insert Set (10 cards):			**25.00**	**150.00**
☐☐	1	Patrick Roy (G), Col.	10.00	60.00
☐☐	2	Félix Potvin (G), Tor.	3.00	18.00
☐☐	3	Martin Brodeur (G), N.J.	4.50	25.00
☐☐	4	Ed Belfour (G), Chi.	2.00	12.00
☐☐	5	Guy Hebert (G), Ana.	1.50	8.00
☐☐	6	John Vanbiesbrouck (G), Fla.	3.75	20.00
☐☐	7	Jocelyn Thibault (G), Mtl.	2.00	12.00
☐☐	8	Ron Hextall (G), Pha.	1.50	8.00
☐☐	9	Grant Fuhr (G), Stl.	1.50	8.00
☐☐	10	Jim Carey (G), Wsh.	1.50	8.00

ROOKIES

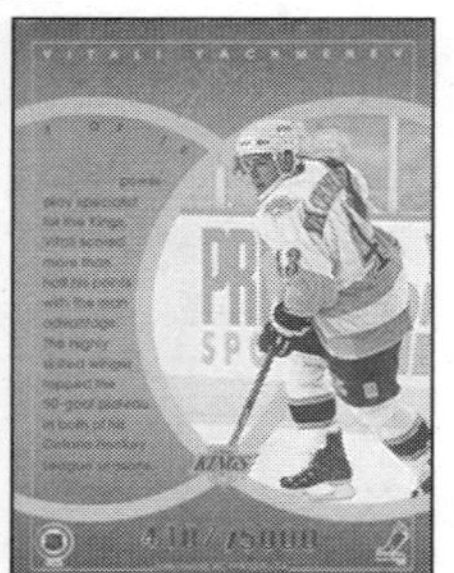

These inserts are serial numbered out of 5000.

	No.	Player	NRMT-MT
Insert Set (15 cards):			**100.00**
☐	1	Eric Dazé, Chi.	8.00
☐	2	Vitali Yachmenev, L.A.	5.00
☐	3	Daniel Alfredsson, Ott.	15.00
☐	4	Todd Bertuzzi, NYI.	8.00
☐	5	Byron Dafoe (G), L.A.	5.00
☐	6	Eric Fichaud (G), NYI.	8.00
☐	7	Marcus Ragnarsson, S.J.	5.00
☐	8	Saku Koivu, Mtl.	20.00
☐	9	Chad Kilger, Ana.	5.00
☐	10	Radek Dvorak, Fla.	5.00
☐	11	Ed Jovanovski, Fla.	8.00
☐	12	Jeff O'Neill, Hfd.	8.00
☐	13	Shane Doan, Wpg.	5.00
☐	14	Niklas Sundstrom, NYR.	5.00
☐	15	Kyle McLaren, Bos.	5.00

WORLD JUNIORS

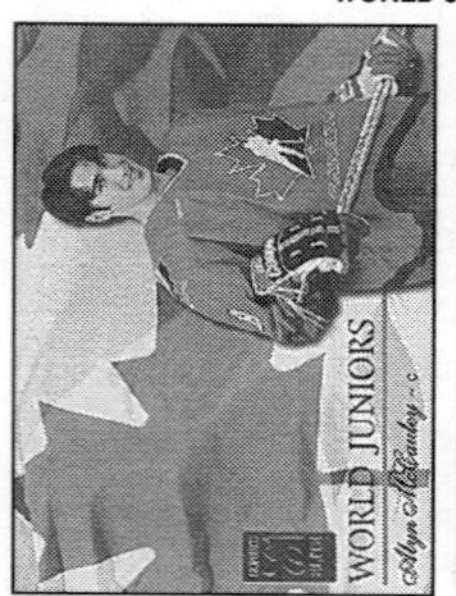

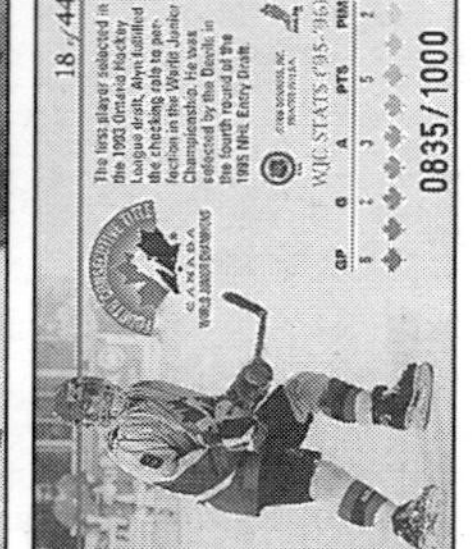

These inserts are serial numbered out of 1,000.

	No.	Player	NRMT-MT
Insert Set (44 cards):			**475.00**
☐	1	Marc Denis (G), Cdn.	30.00
☐	2	José Théodore (G), Cdn.	30.00
☐	3	Chad Allan, Cdn.	8.00
☐	4	Nolan Baumgartner, Cdn.	8.00
☐	5	Denis Gauthier, Cdn.	8.00
☐	6	Jason Holland, Cdn.	8.00
☐	7	Chris Phillips, Cdn.	25.00
☐	8	Wade Redden, Cdn.	12.00
☐	9	Rhett Warrener, Cdn.	8.00
☐	10	Jason Botterill, Cdn.	8.00
☐	11	Curtis Brown, Cdn.	8.00
☐	12	Hnat Domenichelli, Cdn.	15.00
☐	13	Christian Dubé, Cdn.	12.00
☐	14	Robb Gordon, Cdn.	8.00
☐	15	Jarome Iginla, Cdn.	35.00
☐	16	Daymond Langkow, Cdn.	15.00
☐	17	Brad Larsen, Cdn.	8.00
☐	18	Alyn McCauley, Cdn.	25.00
☐	19	Craig Mills, Cdn.	8.00
☐	20	Jason Podollan, Cdn.	8.00
☐	21	Mike Watt, Cdn.	8.00
☐	22	Jamie Wright, Cdn.	8.00
☐	23	Brian Boucher (G), USA.	20.00
☐	24	Marc Magliarditi (G), USA.	10.00
☐	25	Bryan Berard, USA.	30.00
☐	26	Chris Bogas, USA.	8.00
☐	27	Ben Clymer, USA.	8.00
☐	28	Jeff Kealty, USA.	8.00
☐	29	Mike McBain, USA.	8.00
☐	30	Jeremiah McCarthy, USA.	8.00
☐	31	Tom Poti, USA.	8.00
☐	32	Reg Berg, USA.	8.00
☐	33	Matt Cullen, USA.	8.00
☐	34	Chris Drury, USA.	10.00
☐	35	Jeff Farkas, USA.	10.00
☐	36	Casey Hankinson, USA.	8.00
☐	37	Matt Herr, USA.	8.00
☐	38	Mark Parrish, USA.	18.00
☐	39	Erik Rasmussen, USA.	15.00
☐	40	Marty Reasoner, USA.	12.00
☐	41	Wyatt Smith, USA.	8.00
☐	42	Brian Swanson, USA.	8.00
☐	43	Mike Sylvia, USA.	8.00
☐	44	Mike York, USA.	8.00

1995 - 96 EDGE ICE

PROMOS

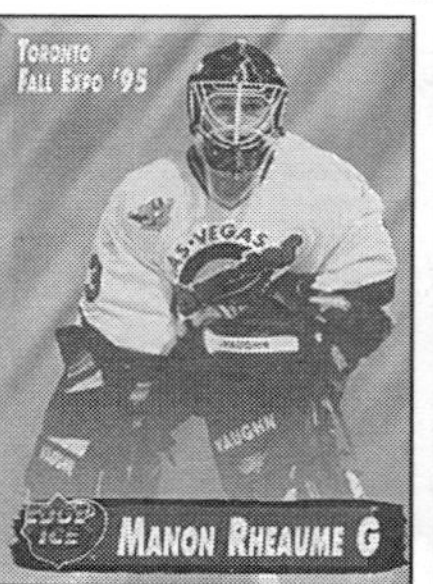

The seven-card promo pack acted as a sample to Edge Ice Hockey. The three Manon Rhéaume cards had a design of their own and were handed out at the Toronto Fall Expo in November 1995.

	No.	Player	NRMT-MT
☐		Title card	1.00
☐	PR-1	Todd Marchant, Cape Breton	1.00
☐	PR-2	Tommy Salo (G), Utah	1.50
☐	PR-3	Mike Dunham (G), Albany	1.50
☐	PR-4	Viktor Kozlov, Kansas City	1.50
☐	PR-5	Dwayne Roloson (G), Saint John	1.50
☐	PR-6	Tony Hrkac, Milwaukee	1.00
☐	1	Manon Rhéaume (G), Las Vegas	5.00
☐	2	Manon Rhéaume (G), Las Vegas	5.00
☐	3	Manon Rhéaume (G), Las Vegas	5.00

EDGE ICE

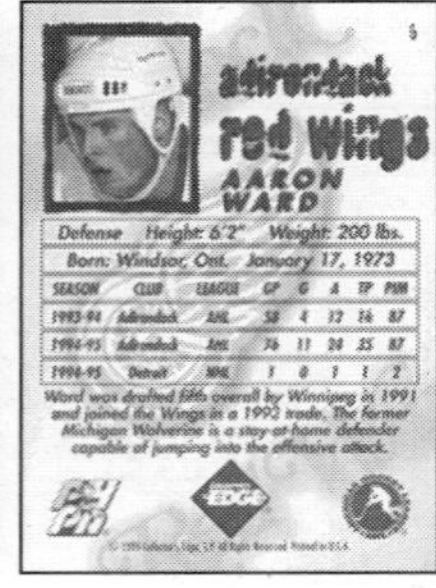

These cards have two versions: a regular card and a holoprism parallel. Holoprism paralllel cards were seeded in specially marked team boxes. There are no holofoil parallels for the checklists.

Imprint:

	No.	Player	Reg.	Par.
Complete Set (200 cards):			**35.00**	**—**
Holoprism Set (196 cards):			**—**	**200.00**
Common Player:			**.15**	**.75**
☐☐	1	Curtis Bowen, Adirondack	.15	.75
☐☐	2	Anders Eriksson, Adirondack	.25	1.25
☐☐	3	Kevin Hodson (G), Adirondack	1.25	6.00
☐☐	4	Martin Lapointe, Adirondack	.25	1.25
☐☐	5	Aaron Ward, Adirondack	.15	.75
☐☐	6	Mike Dunham (G), Albany	.25	1.25
☐☐	7	Chris McAlpine, Albany	.15	.75
☐☐	8	Brian Rolston, Albany	.15	.75
☐☐	9	Corey Schwab (G), Albany	.25	1.25
☐☐	10	Steve Sullivan, Albany	.25	1.25
☐☐	11	Petr Sykora, Albany	.25	1.25
☐☐	12	Darren Van Impe, Albany	.15	.75
☐☐	13	Mike Maneluk, Baltimore	.15	.75
☐☐	14	David Sacco, Baltimore	.15	.75
☐☐	15	Jarrod Skalde, Baltimore	.15	.75
☐☐	16	Nikolai Tsulygin, Baltimore	.15	.75
☐☐	17	Peter Ferraro, Binghampton	.15	.75
☐☐	18	Chris Ferraro, Binghampton	.15	.75
☐☐	19	Corey Hirsch (G), Binghampton	.25	1.25
☐☐	20	Mattias Norstrom, Binghampton	.15	.75
☐☐	21	Jamie Ram (G), Binghampton	.25	1.25
☐☐	22	Chris Armstrong, Carolina	.15	.75
☐☐	23	Alexei Kudashov, Carolina	.15	.75
☐☐	24	Todd MacDonald, Carolina	.15	.75
☐☐	25	Steve Washburn, Carolina	.15	.75
☐☐	26	Kevin Weekes (G), Carolina	.25	1.25
☐☐	27	René Corbet, Cornwall	.15	.75
☐☐	28	Janne Laukkanen, Cornwall	.15	.75
☐☐	29	Aaron Miller, Cornwall	.15	.75
☐☐	30	Landon Wilson, Cornwall	.25	1.25
☐☐	31	Fred Brathwaite (G), Cape Breton	.15	.75
☐☐	32	Ryan Haggerty, Cape Breton	.15	.75
☐☐	33	Ralph Intranuovo, Cape Breton	.15	.75
☐☐	34	Todd Marchant, Cape Breton	.15	.75
☐☐	35	David Oliver, Cape Breton	.25	1.25
☐☐	36	Marko Tuomainen, Cape Breton	.15	.75
☐☐	37	Peter White, Cape Breton	.15	.75
☐☐	38	Sébastien Bordeleau, Fredericton	.25	1.25
☐☐	39	Martin Brochu (G), Fredericton	.25	1.25
☐☐	40	Valeri Bure, Fredericton	.25	1.25
☐☐	41	Craig Conroy, Fredericton	.25	1.25
☐☐	42	Darcy Tucker, Fredericton	.25	1.25
☐☐	43	David Wilkie, Fredericton	.25	1.25
☐☐	44	Paul Healey, Hershey	.15	.75
☐☐	45	Chris Herperger, Hershey	.15	.75
☐☐	46	Jim Montgomery, Hershey	.15	.75
☐☐	47	Chris Therien, Hershey	.15	.75
☐☐	48	Pavol Demitra, P.E.I.	.15	.75
☐☐	49	Michel Picard, P.E.I.	.15	.75
☐☐	50	Jason Zent, P.E.I.	.15	.75
☐☐	51	Patrick Boileau, Portland	.15	.75
☐☐	52	Jim Carey (G), Portland	.25	1.25
☐☐	53	Sergei Gonchar, Portland	.25	1.25
☐☐	54	Jeff Nelson, Portland	.15	.75
☐☐	55	Stefan Ustorf, Portland	.15	.75
☐☐	56	Alexander Kharlamov, Portland	.15	.75
☐☐	57	Ron Tugnutt (G), Portland	.25	1.25
☐☐	58	Scott Bailey (G), Providence	.25	1.25
☐☐	59	Clayton Beddoes, Providence	.15	.75
☐☐	60	André Roy, Providence	.15	.75
☐☐	61	Evgeny Ryabchikov (G), Providence	.15	.75

No.	Player		
62	Mark Astley, Rochester	.15	.75
63	Jody Gage, Rochester	.15	.75
64	Sergei Klimentiev, Rochester	.15	.75
65	Barrie Moore, Rochester	.15	.75
66	Mike Wilson, Rochester	.25	1.25
67	Shayne Wright, Rochester	.15	.75
68	Michal Grosek, Springfield	.15	.75
69	Tavis Hansen, Springfield	.15	.75
70	Nikolai Khabibulin (G), Springfield	1.25	6.00
71	Scott Langkow (G), Sprinfield	.25	1.25
72	Jason McBain, Springfield	.15	.75
73	Dwayne Roloson (G), Saint John	.25	1.25
74	Cory Stillman, Saint John	.25	1.25
75	Jamie Allison, Saint John	.15	.75
76	Jesper Mattson, Saint John	.15	.75
77	David Ling, Saint John	.15	.75
78	Brandon Convery, St. John's	.15	.75
79	Darby Hendrickson, St. John's	.25	1.25
80	Janne Gronvall, St. John's	.15	.75
81	Jason Saal (G), St. John's	.25	1.25
82	Brent Gretzky, St. John's	.25	1.25
83	Kent Manderville, St. John's	.15	.75
84	Shayne Toporowski, St. John's	.15	.75
85	Paul Vincent, St. John's	.15	.75
86	Mark Kolesar, St. John's	.15	.75
87	Lonny Bohonos, Syracuse	.15	.75
88	Larry Courville, Syracuse	.15	.75
89	Jassen Cullimore, Syracuse	.15	.75
90	Scott Walker, Syracuse	.25	1.25
91	Mike Buzak, Worcester	.15	.75
92	Craig Darby, Worcester	.15	.75
93	Eric Fichaud (G), Worcester	.75	3.50
94	Andreas Johansson, Worcester	.15	.75
95	Jamie Rivers, Worcester	.15	.75
96	Jason Strudwick, Worcester	.15	.75
97	Patrice Tardif, Worcester	.15	.75
98	Alex Vasilevski, Worcester	.15	.75
99	Drew Bannister, Atlanta	.15	.75
100	Stan Drulia, Atlanta	.15	.75
101	Aaron Gavey, Atlanta	.15	.75
102	Reggie Sanders, Atlanta	.15	.75
103	Derek Wilkinson, Atlanta	.15	.75
104	Rob Brown, Chicago	.25	1.25
105	Dan Currie, Chicago	.15	.75
106	Kevin MacDonald, Chicago	.15	.75
107	Steve Maltais, Chicago	.15	.75
108	Shawn Rivers, Chicago	.15	.75
109	Wendell Young (G), Chicago	.25	1.25
110	Don Biggs, Cincinnati	.15	.75
111	Dale DeGray, Cincinnati	.15	.75
112	Paul Lawless, Cincinnati	.15	.75
113	Danny Lorenz, Cincinnati	.15	.75
114	Dave Tomlinson, Cincinnati	.15	.75
115	Jock Callander, Cleveland	.15	.75
116	Phillipe DeRouville (G), Cleveland	.25	1.25
117	Ryan Savoia, Cleveland	.15	.75
118	Mike Stevens, Cleveland	.15	.75
119	Chris Tamer, Cleveland	.25	1.25
120	Peter Bondra, Detroit	1.50	7.50
121	Peter Ciavaglia, Detroit	.15	.75
122	Rick Knickle (G), Detroit	.25	1.25
123	Jamie Loach, Detroit	.15	.75
124	Michal Pivonka, Detroit	.25	1.25
125	Andy Bezeau, Fort Wayne	.15	.75
126	Bob Essensa (G), Fort Wayne	.25	1.25
127	Andrew McBain, Fort Wayne	.15	.75
128	Kevin Miehm, Fort Wayne	.15	.75
129	Scott Arniel, Houston	.15	.75
130	Kevin Dineen, Houston	.15	.75
131	Rob Dopson, Houston	.15	.75
132	Mark Freer, Houston	.15	.75
133	Troy Gamble (G), Houston	.25	1.25
134	Ethan Moreau, Indianapolis	.25	1.25
135	Sergei Klimovich, Indianapolis	.15	.75
136	Eric Lecompte, Indianapolis	.15	.75
137	Eric Manlow, Indianaplois	.15	.75
138	Kip Miller, Indianapolis	.15	.75
139	Manny Fernandez (G), Michigan	.25	.1.25
140	Mike Kennedy, Michigan	.25	1.25
141	Jamie Langenbrunner, Michigan	.50	2.50
142	Derrick Smith, Michigan	.15	.75
143	Jordan Willis, Michigan	.15	.75
144	Jan Caloun, Kansas City	.15	.75
145	Viktor Kozlov, Kansas City	.25	1.25
146	Andrei Nazarov, Kansas City	.15	.75
147	Geoff Sarjeant (G), Kansas City	.25	1.25
148	Patrik Augusta, Los Angeles	.15	.75
149	Viktor Gordiouk, Los Angeles	.15	.75
150	Dave Littman (G), Los Angeles	.25	1.25
151	Todd Gillingham, Los Angeles	.15	.75
152	Greg Hawgood, Las Vegas	.15	.75
153	Patrice Lefebvre, Las Vegas	.15	.75
154	Eldon Reddick (G), Las Vegas	.25	1.25
155	Manon Rhéaume (G), Las Vegas	5.00	20.00
156	Jeff Sharples, Las Vegas	.15	.75
157	Todd Simon, Las Vegas	.15	.75
158	Radek Bonk, Las Vegas	.25	1.25
159	Gino Cavallini, Milwaukee	.15	.75
160	Tom Draper (G), Milwaukee	.25	1.25
161	Tony Hrkac, Milwaukee	.15	.75
162	Fabian Joseph, Milwaukee	.15	.75
163	Mark LaForest (G), Milwaukee	.25	1.25
164	Dave Christian, Minnesota	.15	.75
165	Bryan Fogarty, Minnesota	.15	.75
166	Chris Goverdaris, Minnesota	.15	.75
167	Mike Hurlbut, Minnesota	.15	.75
168	Chris Imes, Minnesota	.15	.75
169	Stéphane Morin, Minnesota	.15	.75
170	Allan Bester (G), Orlando	.25	1.25
171	Kerry Clark, Orlando	.25	1.25
172	Neil Eisenhut, Orlando	.15	.75
173	Craig Fisher, Orlando	.15	.75
174	Patrick Neaton, Orlando	.15	.75
175	Todd Richards, Orlando	.15	.75
176	Jon Casey (G), Peoria	.25	1.25
177	Doug Evans, Peoria	.15	.75
178	Michel Mongeau, Peoria	.15	.75
179	Greg Paslawski, Peoria	.15	.75
180	Darren Veitch, Peoria	.15	.75
181	Frederick Beauben, Phoenix	.15	.75
182	Kevin Brown, Phoenix	.15	.75
183	Rob Cowie, Phoenix	.15	.75
184	Yanic Perreault, Phoenix	.25	1.25
185	Chris Snell, Phoenix	.15	.75
186	Jan Vopat, Phoenix	.15	.75
187	Robin Bawa, San Francisco	.15	.75
188	Stéphane Beauregard (G), San Francisco	.15	.75
189	Dale Craigwell, San Francisco	.15	.75
190	John Purves, San Francisco	.15	.75
191	Jeff Madill, San Francisco	.15	.75
192	Gord Dineen, Utah	.15	.75
193	Chris Marinucci, Utah	.15	.75
194	Mark McArthur, Utah	.15	.75
195	Zigmund Palffy, Utah	1.50	7.50
196	Tommy Salo (G), Utah	.25	1.25
197	Checklist	.10	-
198	Checklist	.10	-
199	Checklist	.10	-
200	Checklist	.10	-

CRUCIBLES

Insert Set (24 cards): 85.00

No.	Player	NRMT-MT
C1	David Roberts, Peoria	1.50
C2	Ian Laperrière, Peoria	1.50
C3	Kevin Dineen, Houston	2.00
C4	Kenny Jonsson, St. John's	4.00
C5	Jim Carey (G), Portland	2.00
C6	Todd Marchant, Cape Breton	2.00
C7	David Oliver, Cape Breton	1.50
C8	Yanic Perreault, Phoenix	4.00
C9	Chris Therien, Hershey	1.50
C10	Viktor Kozlov, Kansas City	4.00
C11	Valeri Bure, Fredericton	2.00
C12	Nikolai Khabibulin (G), Springfield	8.00
C13	Steven Rice, Cape Breton	2.00
C14	Mike Kennedy, Kalamazoo	2.00
C15	Peter Bondra, Detroit	12.00
C16	Sergei Zubov, Binghampton	6.00
C17	Vyacheslav Kozlov, Adirondack	4.00
C18	Chris Osgood (G), Adirondack	12.00
C19	Darren McCarty, Adirondack	3.00
C20	Jason Dawe, Rochester	3.00
C21	Trevor Kidd (G), Saint John	6.00
C22	Tommy Salo (G), Utah	3.00
C23	Michal Pivonka, Detroit	3.00
C24	Zigmund Palffy, Utah	12.00

QUANTUM MOTION

These inserts are serial numbered out of 2,000.

Insert Set (12 cards): 40.00

No.	Player	NRMT-MT
1	Manny Fernandez (G), Kalamazoo	5.00
2	Eldon Reddick (G), Las Vegas	3.00
3	Yanic Perreault, Phoenix	6.00
4	Rob Brown, Phoenix	3.00
5	Hubie McDonough	2.00
6	Stan Drulia, Atlanta	2.00
7	Michel Picard, P.E.I.	2.00
8	Jim Carey (G), Portland	5.00
9	Martin Lapointe, Adirondack	3.00
10	Valeri Bure, Fredericton	5.00
11	Martin Brochu (G), Fredericton	3.00
12	Corey Schwab (G), Albany	6.00

LIVIN' LARGE

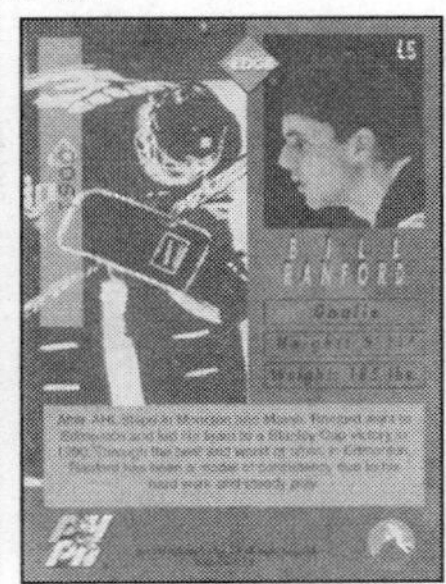

Insert Set (11 cards): 75.00

No.	Player	NRMT-MT
L1	Adam Graves	5.00
L2	Marty McSorley	5.00
L3	Adam Oates	7.50
L4	Keith Primeau	5.00
L5	Bill Ranford (G)	5.00
L6	Curtis Joseph (G)	15.00
L7	Félix Potvin (G)	12.00
L8	Mike Vernon (G)	5.00
L9	Theoren Fleury	7.50
L10	Kevin Stevens	5.00
L11	Martin Brodeur (G)	18.00

THE WALL

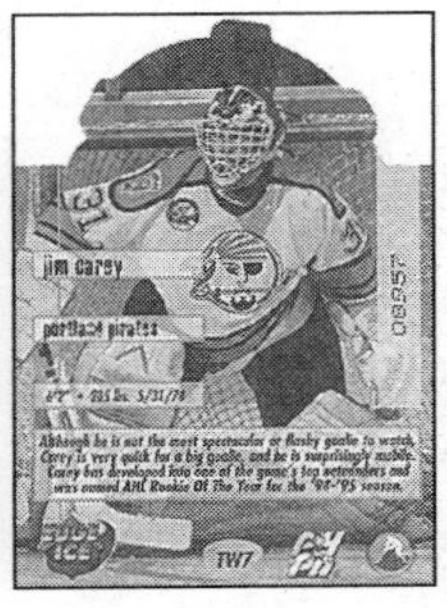

Insert Set (13 cards): 15.00

No.	Player	NRMT-MT
TW1	Ray Leblanc (G), Chicago	1.00
TW2	Manny Fernandez (G), Kalamazoo	1.50
TW3	Rick Knickle (G), Detroit	1.00
TW4	Troy Gamble (G), Houston	1.00
TW5	Eldon Reddick (G), Las Vegas	1.00
TW6	Wendell Young (G), Chicago	1.00
TW7	Jim Carey (G), Portland	1.50
TW8	Dwayne Roloson (G), Saint John	1.00

No.	Player	NRMT-MT
TW9	Les Kuntar (G), Fredericton	1.00
TW10	Mike Dunham (G), Albany	1.50
TW11	Eric Fichaud (G), St. John's	3.00
TW12	Kevin Hodson (G), Adirondack	2.00
	Checklist (No #)	1.50

1995 - 96 FANFEST PHIL ESPOSITO

These cards were handed out at the 1996 All-Star Fanfest in Boston.

Imprint:

Complete Set (5 cards): 20.00

No.	Player	NRMT-MT
	Phil Esposito (Donruss)	5.00
	Phil Esposito (Fleer)	5.00
3	Phil Esposito (Pinnacle)	5.00
	Phil Esposito (Topps)	5.00
	Phil Esposito (UpperDeck)	5.00

1995 - 96 FLEER METAL

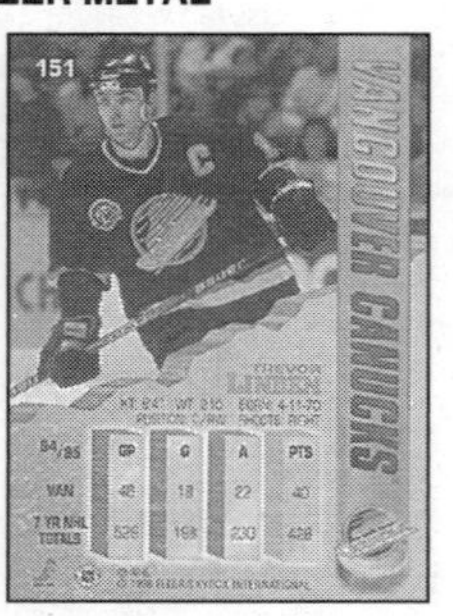

Imprint: © 1996 FLEER/SKYBOX INTERNATIONAL

Complete Set (200 cards): 35.00

Common Player: .20

Four-Card Promo Panel (Potvin/Roenick/Fleury/Park): 3.00

No.	Player	NRMT-MT
1	Guy Hebert (G), Ana.	.50
2	Paul Kariya, Ana.	2.50
3	Todd Krygier, Ana.	.20
4	Steve Rucchin, Ana.	.20
5	Oleg Tverdovsky, Ana.	.20
6	Ray Bourque, Bos.	1.00
7	Blaine Lacher (G), Bos.	.20
8	Shawn McEachern, Bos.	.20
9	Cam Neely, Bos.	.50
10	Adam Oates, Bos.	.75
11	Kevin Stevens, Bos.	.20
12	Donald Audette, Buf.	.20
13	Randy Burridge, Buf.	.20
14	Jason Dawe, Buf.	.20
15	Dominik Hasek (G), Buf.	1.50
16	Pat LaFontaine, Buf.	.50
17	Alexei Zhitnik, Buf.	.20
18	Theoren Fleury, Cgy.	.75
19	Phil Housley, Cgy.	.20
20	Trevor Kidd (G), Cgy.	.50
21	Joe Nieuwendyk, Cgy.	.50
22	Michael Nylander, Cgy.	.20
23	Ed Belfour (G), Chi.	.75
24	Chris Chelios, Chi.	.75
25	Joe Murphy, Chi.	.20
26	Bernie Nicholls, Chi.	.20
27	Patrick Poulin, Chi.	.20
28	Jeremy Roenick, Chi.	.75
29	Gary Suter, Chi.	.20
30	Adam Deadmarsh, Col.	.50
31	Stéphane Fiset (G), Col.	.50
32	Peter Forsberg, Col.	2.00
33	Valeri Kamensky, Col.	.50
34	Claude Lemieux, Col.	.20
35	Sandis Ozolinsh, Col	.50
36	Joe Sakic, Col.	1.75
37	Greg Adams, Dal.	.20
38	Dave Gagner, Dal.	.20
39	Todd Harvey, Dal.	.20
40	Derian Hatcher, Dal.	.50
41	Kevin Hatcher, Dal.	.20
42	Mike Modano, Dal.	1.00
43	Andy Moog (G), Dal.	.50
44	Paul Coffey, Det.	.50
45	Sergei Fedorov, Det.	1.00
46	Vladimir Konstantinov, Det.	.20
47	Vyacheslav Kozlov, Det.	.20
48	Nicklas Lidström, Det.	.50
49	Chris Osgood (G), Det.	.85
50	Keith Primeau, Det.	.50
51	Steve Yzerman, Det.	2.00
52	Jason Arnott, Edm.	.50
53	Zdeno Ciger, Edm.	.20
54	Todd Marchant, Edm.	.20
55	David Oliver, Edm.	.20
56	Bill Ranford (G), Edm.	.50
57	Doug Weight, Edm.	.75
58	Stu Barnes, Fla.	.20
59	Jody Hull, Fla.	.20
60	Scott Mellanby, Fla.	.20
61	Rob Niedermayer, Fla.	.20
62	John Vanbiesbrouck (G), Fla.	1.25
63	Sean Burke (G), Hfd.	.25
64	Andrew Cassels, Hfd.	.20
65	Nelson Emerson, Hfd.	.20
66	Geoff Sanderson, Hfd.	.20
67	Brendan Shanahan, Hfd.	1.25
68	Glen Wesley, Hfd.	.20
69	Rob Blake, L.A.	.50
70	Tony Granato, L.A.	.20
71	Wayne Gretzky, L.A.	4.00
72	Dimitri Khristich, L.A.	.20
73	Yanic Perreault, L.A.	.20
74	Rick Tocchet, L.A.	.20
75	Benoît Brunet, Mtl.	.20
76	Vincent Damphousse, Mtl.	.75
77	Mark Recchi, Mtl.	.50
78	Patrick Roy(G), Mtl.	3.00
79	Brian Savage, Mtl.	.20
80	Pierre Turgeon, Mtl.	.50
81	Martin Brodeur (G), N.J.	1.50
82	Neal Broten, N.J.	.20
83	John MacLean, N.J.	.20
84	Scott Niedermayer, N.J.	.50
85	Scott Stevens, N.J.	.20
86	Stéphane Richer, N.J.	.20
87	Esa Tikkanen, N.J.	.20
88	Steve Thomas, N.J.	.20
89	Wendel Clark, NYI.	.50
90	Travis Green, NYI.	.20
91	Kirk Muller, NYI.	.20
92	Zigmund Palffy, NYI.	.85
93	Mathieu Schneider, NYI.	.20
94	Ray Ferraro, NYR.	.20
95	Alexei Kovalev, NYR.	.20
96	Brian Leetch, NYR.	.75
97	Mark Messier, NYR.	1.00
98	Mike Richter (G), NYR.	.50
99	Luc Robitaille, NYR.	.50
100	Ulf Samuelsson, NYR.	.20
101	Pat Verbeek, NYR.	.20
102	Radek Bonk, Ott.	.20
103	Don Beaupré (G), Ott.	.20
104	Alexandre Daigle, Ott.	.50
105	Steve Duchesne, Ott.	.20
106	Dan Quinn, Ott.	.20
107	Martin Straka, Ott.	.20
108	Rod Brind'Amour, Pha.	.50
109	Eric Desjardins, Pha.	.20
110	Ron Hextall (G), Pha.	.50
111	John LeClair, Pha.	1.00
112	Eric Lindros, Pha.	2.50
113	Mikael Renberg, Pha.	.20
114	Chris Therien, Pha.	.20
115	Tom Barrasso (G), Pgh.	.20
116	Ron Francis, Pgh.	.75
117	Jaromir Jagr, Pgh.	2.00
118	Mario Lemieux, Pgh.	3.00
119	Tomas Sandström, Pgh.	.20
120	Bryan Smolinski, Pgh.	.20
121	Sergei Zubov, Pgh.	.50
122	Shayne Corson, Stl.	.50
123	Grant Fuhr (G), Stl.	.50
124	Dale Hawerchuk, Stl.	.50
125	Brett Hull, Stl.	1.00
126	Al MacInnis, Stl.	.20
127	Chris Pronger, Stl.	.50
128	Ulf Dahlen, S.J.	.20
129	Jeff Friesen, S.J.	.50
130	Arturs Irbe (G), S.J.	.20
131	Craig Janney, S.J.	.20
132	Anderi Nazarov, S.J.	.20
133	Owen Nolan, S.J.	.20
134	Ray Sheppard, S.J.	.20
135	Brian Bradley, T.B.	.20
136	Chris Gratton, T.B.	.50
137	Roman Hamrlik, T.B.	.20
138	Petr Klima, T.B.	.20
139	Daren Puppa (G), T.B.	.20
140	Alexander Selivanov, T.B.	.20
141	Dave Andreychuk, Tor.	.20
142	Mike Gartner, Tor.	.50
143	Doug Gilmour, Tor.	.75
144	Kenny Jonsson, Tor.	.20
145	Larry Murphy, Tor.	.50
146	Félix Potvin (G), Tor.	1.00
147	Mats Sundin, Tor.	1.00
148	Jeff Brown, Van.	.20
149	Pavel Bure, Van.	1.50
150	Russ Courtnall, Van.	.20
151	Trevor Linden, Van.	.50
152	Kirk McLean (G), Van.	.50
153	Alexander Mogilny, Van.	.75
154	Roman Oksiuta, Van.	.20
155	Mike Ridley, Van.	.20
156	Peter Bondra, Wsh.	.85
157	Jim Carey (G)	.20
158	Sylvain Côté, Wsh.	.20
159	Sergei Gonchar, Wsh.	.20
160	Keith Jones, Wsh.	.20
161	Joé Juneau, Wsh.	.20
162	Nikolai Khabibulin (G), Wpg.	.75
163	Igor Korolev, Wpg.	.20
164	Teppo Numminen, Wpg.	.20
165	Teemu Selänne, Wpg.	1.50
166	Keith Tkachuk, Wpg.	.85
167	Darren Turcotte, Wpg.	.20
168	Alexei Zhamnov, Wpg.	.20
169	**Daniel Alfredsson, Ott., RC**	**1.00**
170	**Aki Berg, L.A., RC**	**.20**
171	**Todd Bertuzzi, NYI., RC**	**.75**
172	Jason Bonsignore, Edm.	.20
173	Byron Dafoe (G), L.A.	.20
174	Eric Dazé, Chi.	.50
175	**Shane Doan, Wpg, RC**	**.20**
176	**Radek Dvorak, Fla., RC**	**.50**
177	**Brian Holzinger, Buf., RC**	**.20**
178	Ed Jovanovski, Fla.	.50
179	**Chad Kilger, Ana., RC**	**.20**
180	Saku Koivu, Mtl.	1.50
181	**Darren Langdon, NYR., RC**	**.20**
182	**Daymond Lankow, T.B., RC**	**.20**
183	Jere Lehtinen, Dal.	.50
184	**Kyle McLaren, Bos., RC**	**.20**
185	Marty Murray, Cgy.	.20
186	Jeff O'Neill, Hfd.	.20
187	Richard Park, Pgh.	.20
188	Deron Quint, Wpg.	.20
189	**Marcus Ragnarsson, S.J., RC**	**.20**
190	**Miroslav Satan, Edm., RC**	**.20**
191	**Tommy Salo (G), NYI., RC**	**.20**
192	Jamie Storr (G), L.A.	.20
193	Niklas Sundstrom, NYR.	.20
194	**Robert Svehla, Fla., RC**	**.50**
195	Denis Pederson, N.J.	.20
196	**Antii Törmänen, Ott., RC**	**.20**
197	Brendan Witt, Wsh.	.20
198	Vitali Yachmenev, L.A.	.20
199	Checklist 1	.20
200	Checklist 2	.20

HEAVY METAL

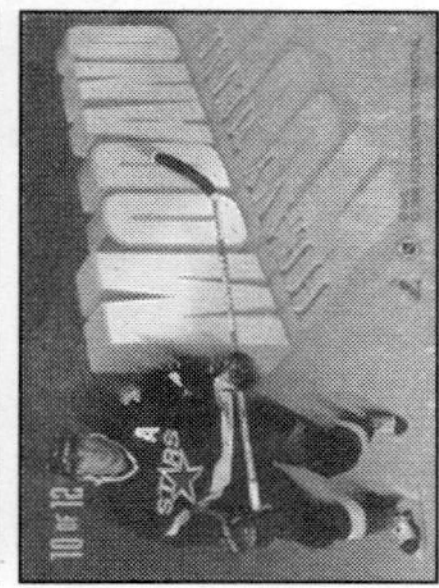

Insert Set (12 cards): 175.00

	No.	Player	NRMT-MT
☐	1	Pavel Bure, Van.	15.00
☐	2	Sergei Fedorov, Det.	10.00
☐	3	Theoren Fleury, Cgy.	6.00
☐	4	Wayne Gretzky, L.A.	40.00
☐	5	Brett Hull, Stl.	10.00
☐	6	Jaromir Jagr, Pgh.	20.00
☐	7	Paul Kariya, Ana.	25.00
☐	8	Brian Leetch, NYR.	6.00
☐	9	Mario Lemieux, Pgh.	30.00
☐	10	Mike Modano, Dal.	10.00
☐	11	Adam Oates, Bos.	6.00
☐	12	Joe Sakic, Col.	18.00

INTERNATIONAL STEEL

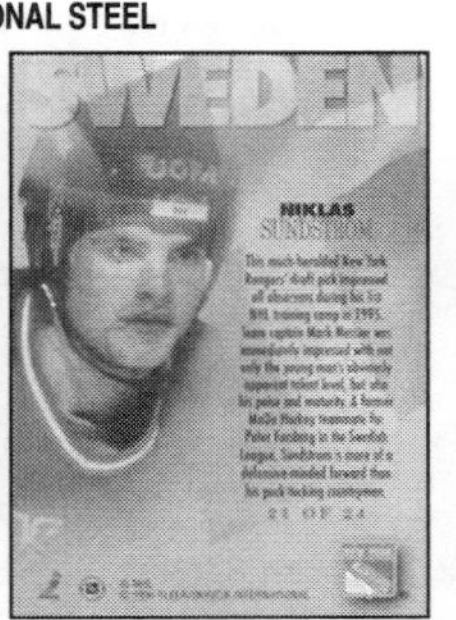

Insert Set (24 cards): 50.00

	No.	Player	NRMT-MT
☐	1	Pavel Bure, Van.	3.50
☐	2	Chris Chelios, Chi.	2.00
☐	3	Sergei Fedorov, Det.	2.50
☐	4	Peter Forsberg, Col.	5.00
☐	5	Wayne Gretzky, L.A.	10.00
☐	6	Roman Hamrlik, T.B.	.75
☐	7	Dominik Hasek (G), Buf.	3.50
☐	8	Brett Hull, Stl.	2.50
☐	9	Jaromir Jagr, Pgh.	5.00
☐	10	Saku Koivu, Mtl.	3.50
☐	11	Pat LaFontaine, Buf.	.75
☐	12	Brian Leetch, NYR.	1.50
☐	13	Jere Lehtinen, Dal.	.75
☐	14	Mario Lemieux, Pgh.	8.00
☐	15	Alexander Mogilny, Van.	1.50
☐	16	Mikael Renberg, Pha.	.75
☐	17	Jeremy Roenick, Chi.	1.50
☐	18	Joe Sakic, Col.	4.00
☐	19	Teemu Selänne, Wpg.	3.50
☐	20	Mats Sundin, Tor.	2.50
☐	21	Niklas Sundstrom, NYR.	.75
☐	22	Vitali Yachmenev, L.A.	.75
☐	23	Alexei Zhamnov, Wpg.	.75
☐	24	Sergei Zubov, Pgh.	.75

IRON WARRIORS

Insert Set (15 cards): 70.00

	No.	Player	NRMT-MT
☐	1	Jason Arnott, Edm.	3.00
☐	2	Ed Belfour (G), Chi.	4.50
☐	3	Theoren Fleury, Cgy.	4.50
☐	4	Ron Francis, Pgh.	4.50
☐	5	John LeClair, Pha.	7.50
☐	6	Claude Lemieux, N.J.	2.00
☐	7	Eric Lindros, Pha.	20.00
☐	8	Mark Messier, NYR.	7.50
☐	9	Cam Neely, Bos.	3.00
☐	10	Keith Primeau, Det.	3.00
☐	11	Kevin Stevens, Bos.	2.00
☐	12	Scott Stevens, N.J.	2.00
☐	13	Brendan Shanahan, Hfd.	9.00
☐	14	Keith Tkachuk, Wpg.	6.00
☐	15	Rick Tocchet, L.A.	2.00

METAL WINNERS

Insert Set (9 cards): 110.00

	No.	Player	NRMT-MT
☐	1	Peter Forsberg, Col.	35.00
☐	2	Saku Koivu, Mtl.	25.00
☐	3	Alexei Kovalev, NYR.	5.00
☐	4	Eric Lindros, Pha.	40.00
☐	5	Alexander Mogilny, Van.	10.00
☐	6	Tommy Salo (G), NYI.	5.00
☐	7	Brian Savage, Mtl.	5.00
☐	8	Sergei Zubov,Pgh.	8.00
☐	9	Alexei Zhamnov, Wpg.	5.00

1995 - 96 FLEER ULTRA

Series One cards (1-200) have two versions: the regular issue and a Gold Medallion parallel. The series two set was called "Ultra Extra".

Series One Imprint: © 1995 FLEER CORP.

Series Two Imprint: © 1996 FLEER/SKYBOX INTERNATIONAL

	G.M.	Reg.
Series One Set (200 cards):	**175.00**	**30.00**
Series Two Set (200 cards):	**—**	**30.00**
Common Player:	**.35**	**.15**

	No.	Player	G.M.	Reg.
☐☐	1	Guy Hebert (G), Ana.	.75	.25
☐☐	2	Milos Holan, Ana.	.35	.15
☐☐	3	Paul Kariya, Ana.	12.00	1.50
☐☐	4	Denny Lambert, Ana., RC	.35	.15
☐☐	5	Stéphan Lebeau, Ana.	.35	.15
☐☐	6	Oleg Tverdovsky, Ana.	.35	.15
☐☐	7	Shaun Van Allen, Ana.	.35	.15
☐☐	8	Ray Bourque, Bos.	3.00	.50
☐☐	9	Mariusz Czerkawski, Bos.	.35	.15
☐☐	10	Blaine Lacher (G), Bos.	.35	.15
☐☐	11	Sandy Moger, Bos, RC	.35	.15
☐☐	12	Cam Neely, Bos.	.75	.25
☐☐	13	Adam Oates, Bos.	1.50	.35
☐☐	14	Bryan Smolinski, Bos.	.35	.15
☐☐	15	Donald Audette, Buf.	.35	.15
☐☐	16	Jason Dawe, Buf.	.35	.15
☐☐	17	Garry Galley, Buf.	.35	.15
☐☐	18	Dominik Hasek (G), Buf.	4.50	.75
☐☐	19	Brian Holzinger, Buf, RC	.50	.25
☐☐	20	Pat LaFontaine, Buf.	.75	.25
☐☐	21	Alexander Mogilny, Buf.	1.50	.35
☐☐	22	Alexei Zhitnik, Buf.	.35	.15
☐☐	23	Steve Chiasson, Cgy.	.35	.15
☐☐	24	Theoren Fleury, Cgy.	1.50	.35
☐☐	25	Phil Housley, Cgy.	.35	.15
☐☐	26	Trevor Kidd (G), Cgy.	.75	.25
☐☐	27	Joel Otto, Cgy.	.35	.15
☐☐	28	Gary Roberts, Cgy.	.75	.25
☐☐	29	Zarley Zalapski, Cgy.	.35	.15
☐☐	30	Ed Belfour (G), Chi.	1.50	.35
☐☐	31	Chris Chelios, Chi.	2.00	.35
☐☐	32	Eric Dazé, Chi.	.75	.25
☐☐	33	Sergei Krivokrasov, Chi.	.35	.15
☐☐	34	Bernie Nicholls, Chi.	.35	.15
☐☐	35	Jeremy Roenick, Chi.	1.50	.35
☐☐	36	Gary Suter, Chi.	.35	.15
☐☐	37	Todd Harvey, Dal.	.35	.15
☐☐	38	Derian Hatcher, Dal.	.75	.25
☐☐	39	Mike Kennedy, Dal.	.35	.15
☐☐	40	Grant Ledyard, Dal.	.35	.15
☐☐	41	Mike Modano, Dal.	3.00	.50
☐☐	42	Andy Moog (G), Dal.	.75	.25
☐☐	**43**	**Mike Torchia (G), Dal., RC**	**.35**	**.15**
☐☐	44	Paul Coffey, Det.	.75	.25
☐☐	45	Sergei Fedorov, Det.	3.00	.50
☐☐	46	Vladimir Konstantinov, Det.	.35	.15
☐☐	47	Vyacheslav Kozlov, Det.	.35	.15
☐☐	48	Keith Primeau, Det.	.75	.25
☐☐	49	Ray Sheppard, Det.	.35	.15
☐☐	50	Mike Vernon (G), Det.	.75	.25
☐☐	51	Steve Yzerman, Det.	10.00	1.25
☐☐	52	Jason Arnott, Edm.	.75	.25
☐☐	53	Shayne Corson, Edm.	.75	.25
☐☐	54	Igor Kravchuk, Edm.	.35	.15
☐☐	55	Todd Marchant, Edm.	.35	.15
☐☐	56	David Oliver, Edm.	.35	.15
☐☐	57	Bill Ranford (G), Edm.	.75	.25
☐☐	58	Doug Weight, Edm.	1.50	.35
☐☐	59	Stu Barnes, Fla.	.35	.15
☐☐	60	Jesse Belanger, Fla.	.35	.15
☐☐	61	Gord Murphy, Fla.	.35	.15
☐☐	62	Rob Niedermayer, Fla.	.35	.15
☐☐	63	Brian Skrudland, Fla.	.35	.15
☐☐	64	John Vanbiesbrouck (G), Fla.	3.50	.60
☐☐	65	Sean Burke (G), Hfd.	.75	.25
☐☐	66	Andrew Cassels, Hfd.	.35	.15
☐☐	67	Frantisek Kucera, Hfd.	.35	.15
☐☐	68	Andrei Nikolishin, Hfd.	.35	.15
☐☐	69	Chris Pronger, Hfd.	.75	.25
☐☐	70	Geoff Sanderson, Hfd.	.35	.15
☐☐	71	Kevin Smyth, Hfd.	.35	.15
☐☐	72	Darren Turcotte, Hfd.	.35	.15
☐☐	73	Rob Blake, L.A.	.75	.25
☐☐	74	Wayne Gretzky, L.A.	20.00	2.50
☐☐	75	Kelly Hrudey (G), L.A.	.35	.15
☐☐	76	Marty McSorley, L.A.	.35	.15
☐☐	77	Jamie Storr (G), L.A.	.75	.25
☐☐	78	Darryl Sydor, L.A.	.35	.15
☐☐	79	Rick Tocchet, L.A.	.35	.15
☐☐	80	Vincent Damphousse, Mtl.	1.50	.35
☐☐	81	Vladimir Malakhov, Mtl.	.35	.15
☐☐	82	Mark Recchi, Mtl.	.75	.25
☐☐	83	Patrick Roy (G), Mtl.	15.00	2.00
☐☐	84	Brian Savage, Mtl.	.35	.15

□ □	85	Pierre Turgeon, Mtl.	.75	.25
□ □	86	Martin Brodeur (G), N.J.	4.50	.75
□ □	87	Neal Broten, N.J.	.35	.15
□ □	88	Sergei Brylin, N.J.	.35	.15
□ □	89	John MacLean, N.J.	.35	.15
□ □	90	Scott Niedermayer, N.J.	.75	.25
□ □	91	Scott Stevens, N.J.	.35	.15
□ □	92	Stéphane Richer, N.J.	.35	.15
□ □	93	Ray Ferraro, NYI.	.35	.15
□ □	94	Scott Lachance, NYI.	.35	.15
□ □	95	Brett Lindros, NYI.	.35	.15
□ □	96	Kirk Muller, NYI.	.35	.15
□ □	**97**	**Tommy Salo (G), NYI., RC**	**.35**	**.15**
□ □	98	Mathieu Schneider, NYI.	.35	.15
□ □	99	Tommy Söderström (G), NYI.	.35	.15
□ □	100	Zigmund Palffy, NYI.	2.00	.35
□ □	101	Glenn Healy (G), NYR.	.35	.15
□ □	**102**	**Darren Langdon, NYR., RC**	**.35**	**.15**
□ □	103	Steve Larmer, NYR.	.35	.15
□ □	104	Brian Leetch, NYR.	1.50	.35
□ □	105	Mark Messier, NYR.	3.00	.50
□ □	106	Mattias Norstrom, NYR.	.35	.15
□ □	107	Pat Verbeek, NYR.	.35	.15
□ □	108	Sergei Zubov, NYR.	.75	.25
□ □	109	Don Beaupré (G), Ott.	.35	.15
□ □	110	Radek Bonk, Ott.	.35	.15
□ □	111	Alexandre Daigle, Ott.	.75	.25
□ □	**112**	**Steve Larouche, Ott., RC**	**.35**	**.15**
□ □	113	Stanislav Neckar, Ott.	.35	.15
□ □	114	Alexei Yashin, Ott.	2.00	.35
□ □	115	Rod Brind'Amour, Pha.	.75	.25
□ □	116	Eric Desjardins, Pha.	.35	.15
□ □	117	Ron Hextall (G), Pha.	.75	.25
□ □	118	John LeClair, Pha.	3.00	.50
□ □	119	Eric Lindros, Pha.	12.00	1.50
□ □	120	Mikael Renberg, Pha.	.35	.15
□ □	121	Chris Therien, Pha.	.35	.15
□ □	122	Ron Francis, Pgh.	1.50	.35
□ □	123	Jaromir Jagr, Pgh.	10.00	1.25
□ □	124	Joe Mullen, Pgh.	.35	.15
□ □	125	Larry Murphy, Pgh.	.75	.25
□ □	126	Ulf Samuelsson, Pgh.	.35	.15
□ □	127	Kevin Stevens, Pgh.	.35	.15
□ □	128	Ken Wregget (G), Pgh.	.35	.15
□ □	129	Wendel Clark, Que.	.75	.25
□ □	130	Adam Deadmarsh, Que.	.35	.15
□ □	131	Stéphane Fiset (G), Que.	.75	.25
□ □	132	Peter Forsberg, Que.	10.00	1.25
□ □	133	Curtis Leschyshyn, Que.	.35	.15
□ □	134	Owen Nolan, Que.	.75	.25
□ □	135	Mike Ricci, Que.	.35	.15
□ □	136	Joe Sakic, Que.	8.00	1.00
□ □	137	Denis Chassé, Stl.	.35	.15
□ □	138	Steve Duchesne, Stl.	.35	.15
□ □	139	Brett Hull, Stl.	3.00	.50
□ □	140	Curtis Joseph (G), Stl.	3.50	.60
□ □	141	Ian Laperrière, Stl.	.35	.15
□ □	142	Brendan Shanahan, Stl.	4.50	.60
□ □	143	Esa Tikkanen, Stl.	.35	.15
□ □	144	Ulf Dahlen, S.J.	.35	.15
□ □	145	Jeff Friesen, S.J.	.75	.25
□ □	146	Arturs Irbe (G), S.J.	.35	.15
□ □	147	Craig Janney, S.J.	.35	.15
□ □	148	Sergei Makarov, S.J.	.35	.15
□ □	149	Sandis Ozolinsh, S.J.	.75	.25
□ □	150	Ray Whitney, S.J.	.35	.15
□ □	151	Chris Gratton, T.B.	.75	.25
□ □	152	Roman Hamrlik, T.B.	.75	.25
□ □	153	Petr Klima, T.B.	.35	.15
□ □	**154**	**Brantt Myhres, T.B., RC**	**.35**	**.15**
□ □	155	Daren Puppa (G), T.B.	.35	.15
□ □	156	Jason Wiemer, T.B.	.35	.15
□ □	157	Paul Ysebaert, T.B.	.35	.15
□ □	158	Dave Andreychuk, Tor.	.35	.15
□ □	159	Tie Domi, Tor.	.35	.15
□ □	160	Doug Gilmour, Tor.	1.50	.35
□ □	161	Kenny Jonsson, Tor.	.35	.15
□ □	162	Félix Potvin (G), Tor.	3.00	.50
□ □	163	Mike Ridley, Tor.	.35	.15
□ □	164	Mats Sundin, Tor.	3.00	.50
□ □	165	Jeff Brown, Van.	.35	.15
□ □	166	Pavel Bure, Van.	4.50	.75
□ □	167	Geoff Courtnall, Van.	.35	.15
□ □	168	Russ Courtnall, Van.	.35	.15
□ □	169	Trevor Linden, Van.	.75	.25
□ □	170	Kirk McLean (G), Van.	.75	.25
□ □	171	Roman Oksiuta, Van.	.35	.15
□ □	172	Peter Bondra, Wsh.	2.00	.35
□ □	173	Jim Carey (G), Wsh.	.35	.15
□ □	174	Martin Gendron, Wsh.	.35	.15
□ □	175	Dale Hunter, Wsh.	.35	.15
□ □	176	Calle Johansson, Wsh.	.35	.15
□ □	177	Michal Pivonka, Wsh.	.35	.15
□ □	178	Mark Tinordi, Wsh.	.35	.15
□ □	179	Nelson Emerson, Wpg.	.35	.15
□ □	180	Nikolai Khabibulin (G), Wpg.	1.50	.35
□ □	181	Dave Manson, Wpg.	.35	.15
□ □	182	Teppo Numminen, Wpg.	.35	.15
□ □	183	Teemu Selänne, Wpg.	4.50	.75
□ □	184	Keith Tkachuk, Wpg.	2.00	.35
□ □	185	Alexei Zhamnov, Wpg.	.35	.15
□ □	186	Martin Brodeur (G), N.J.	4.50	.75
□ □	187	Neal Broten, N.J.	.35	.15
□ □	188	Bob Carpenter, N.J.	.35	.15
□ □	189	Ken Daneyko, N.J.	.35	.15
□ □	190	Bruce Driver, N.J.	.35	.15
□ □	191	Bill Guerin, N.J.	.75	.25
□ □	192	Claude Lemieux, N.J.	.35	.15
□ □	193	John MacLean, N.J.	.35	.15
□ □	194	Scott Niedermayer, N.J.	.75	.25
□ □	195	Stéphane Richer, N.J.	.35	.15
□ □	196	Scott Stevens, N.J.	.35	.15
□ □	197	Scott Stevens, N.J. (w/Cup)	.75	.25
□ □	198	Checklist	.35	.15
□ □	199	Checklist	.35	.15
□ □	200	Checklist	.35	.15

	No.	Player	NRMT-MT
□	201	Todd Krygier, Ana.	.15
□	202	Steve Rucchin, Ana.	.15
□	203	Mike Sillinger, Ana.	.15
□	204	Ted Donato, Bos.	.15
□	205	Shawn McEachern, Bos.	.15
□	206	Joe Mullen, Bos.	.15
□	207	Kevin Stevens, Bos.	.15
□	208	Don Sweeney, Bos.	.15
□	209	Mark Astley, Buf.	.15
□	210	Randy Burridge, Buf.	.15
□	211	Jason Dawe, Buf.	.15
□	212	Michael Peca, Buf.	.25
□	213	Michael Nylander, Cgy.	.15
□	214	Cory Stillman, Cgy.	.15
□	**215**	**Pavel Torgajev, Cgy., RC**	**.15**
□	216	Tony Amonte, Chi.	.25
□	217	Joe Murphy, Chi.	.15
□	218	Bob Probert, Chi.	.15
□	219	Denis Savard, Chi.	.25
□	220	Stéphane Fiset (G), Col.	.25
□	221	Valeri Kamensky, Col.	.25
□	222	Sylvain Lefebvre, Col.	.15
□	223	Claude Lemieux, Col.	.15
□	224	Sandis Ozolinsh, Col.	.25
□	225	Patrick Roy (G), Col.	2.00
□	226	Scott Young, Col.	.15
□	227	Greg Adams, Dal.	.15
□	228	Guy Carbonneau, Dal.	.15
□	229	Dave Gagner, Dal.	.15
□	230	Kevin Hatcher, Dal.	.15
□	231	Darcy Wakaluk (G), Dal.	.15
□	232	Dino Ciccarelli, Det.	.25
□	233	Greg Johnson, Det.	.15
□	234	Igor Larionov, Det.	.25
□	235	Darren McCarty, Det.	.15
□	236	Chris Osgood (G), Det.	.35
□	237	Zdeno Ciger, Edm.	.15
□	238	Bryan Marchment, Edm.	.15
□	239	Boris Mironov, Edm.	.15
□	240	Peter White, Edm.	.15
□	241	Jody Hull, Fla.	.15
□	242	Scott Mellanby, Fla.	.15
□	243	Gord Murphy, Fla.	.15
□	244	Jason Woolley, Fla.	.15
□	245	Gerald Diduck, Hfd.	.15
□	246	Nelson Emerson, Hfd.	.15
□	247	Brendan Shanahan, Hfd.	.60
□	248	Glen Wesley, Hfd.	.15
□	249	Tony Granato, L.A.	.15
□	250	Dimitri Khristich, L.A.	.15
□	251	Jari Kurri, L.A.	.25
□	252	Eric Lacroix, L.A.	.15
□	253	Yanic Perreault, L.A.	.15
□	254	Patrice Brisebois, Mtl.	.15
□	255	Benoît Brunet, Mtl.	.15
□	256	Valeri Bure, Mtl.	.15
□	257	Stéphane Quintal, Mtl.	.15
□	258	Jocelyn Thibault (G), Mtl.	.35
□	259	Shawn Chambers, N.J.	.15
□	260	Jim Dowd, N.J.	.15
□	261	Bill Guerin, N.J.	.25
□	262	Bobby Holik, N.J.	.15
□	263	Steve Thomas, N.J.	.15
□	264	Esa Tikkanen, N.J.	.15
□	265	Wendel Clark, NYI.	.25
□	266	Travis Green, NYI.	.15
□	267	Brett Lindros, NYI.	.15
□	268	Kirk Muller, NYI.	.15
□	269	Zigmund Palffy, NYI.	.35
□	270	Mathieu Schneider, NYI.	.15
□	271	Alexander Semak, NYI.	.15
□	272	Dennis Vaske, NYI.	.15
□	273	Ray Ferraro, NYR.	.15
□	274	Adam Graves, NYR.	.15
□	275	Alexei Kovalev, NYR.	.15
□	276	Mike Richter (G), NYR.	.35
□	277	Luc Robitaille, NYR.	.25
□	278	Ulf Samuelsson, NYR.	.15
□	279	Steve Duchesne, Ott.	.15
□	280	Trent McCleary, Ott.	.15
□	281	Dan Quinn, Ott.	.15
□	282	Martin Straka, Ott.	.15
□	283	Karl Dykhuis, Pha.	.15
□	284	Pat Falloon, Pha.	.15
□	285	Joel Otto, Pha.	.15
□	286	Kjell Samuelsson, Pha.	.15
□	287	Garth Snow (G), Pha.	.15
□	288	Mario Lemieux, Pgh.	2.00
□	289	Norm Maciver, Pgh.	.15
□	290	Dmitri Mironov, Pgh.	.15
□	291	Markus Naslund, Pgh.	.15
□	292	Petr Nedved, Pgh.	.15
□	293	Tomas Sandström, Pgh.	.15
□	294	Bryan Smolinski, Pgh.	.15
□	295	Sergei Zubov, Pgh.	.25
□	296	Shayne Corson, Stl.	.25
□	297	Geoff Courtnall, Stl.	.15
□	298	Grant Fuhr (G), Stl.	.25
□	299	Dale Hawerchuk, Stl.	.25
□	300	Al MacInnis, Stl.	.15
□	301	Brian Noonan, Stl.	.15
□	302	Chris Pronger, Stl.	.25
□	303	Andrei Nazarov, S.J.	.15
□	304	Owen Nolan, S.J.	.25
□	305	Ray Sheppard, S.J.	.15
□	306	Chris Terreri (G), S.J.	.15
□	307	Brian Bellows, T.B.	.15
□	308	Brian Bradley, T.B.	.15
□	309	John Cullen, T.B.	.15
□	310	Alexander Selivanov, T.B.	.15
□	311	Mike Gartner, Tor.	.25
□	312	Benoît Hogue, Tor.	.15
□	313	Sergei Momesso, Tor.	.15
□	314	Larry Murphy, Tor.	.25
□	315	Dave Babych, Van.	.15
□	316	Bret Hedican, Van.	.15
□	317	Alexander Mogilny, Van.	.35
□	318	Mike Ridley, Van.	.15
□	319	Peter Bonrda, Wsh.	.35
□	320	Jim Carey (G), Wsh.	.15
□	321	Sylvain Côté, Wsh.	.15
□	322	Sergei Gonchar, Wsh.	.15
□	323	Joe Juneau, Wsh.	.15
□	324	Steve Konowalchuk, Wsh.	.15
□	325	Pat Peake, Wsh.	.15
□	326	Dallas Drake, Wpg.	.15
□	327	Igor Korolev, Wpg.	.15
□	328	Darren Turcotte, Wpg.	.15
□	**329**	**Daniel Alfredsson, Ott., RC**	**1.00**
□	**330**	**Aki Berg, L.A., RC**	**.25**
□	**331**	**Todd Bertuzzi, NYI., RC**	**.50**
□	332	Jason Bonsignore, Edm.	.15
□	333	Curtis Bowen, Det.	.15
□	334	Byron Dafoe (G), L.A.	.15
□	335	Eric Dazé, Chi.	.25
□	**336**	**Shane Doan, Wpg., RC**	**.15**
□	337	Jason Doig, Wpg.	.15
□	**338**	**Radek Dvorak, Fla., RC**	**.25**

	No.	Player	
☐	**339**	**Joe Dziedzic, Pgh., RC**	**.15**
☐	340	Darby Hendrickson, NYI.	.15
☐	341	Brian Holzinger, Buf.	.25
☐	342	Ed Jovanovski, Fla.	.25
☐	**343**	**Chad Kilger, Ana., RC**	**.15**
☐	344	Saku Koivu, Mtl.	.75
☐	**345**	**Darren Langdon, NYR., RC**	**.15**
☐	346	Jamie Langebrunner, Dal.	.15
☐	347	Jere Lehtinen, Dal.	.25
☐	348	Bryan McCabe, NYI.	.15
☐	**349**	**Kyle McLaren, Bos., RC**	**.15**
☐	350	Marty Murray, Cgy.	.15
☐	351	Jeff O'Neill, Hfd.	.15
☐	352	Deron Quint, Wpg.	.15
☐	**353**	**Marcus Ragnarsson, S.J., RC**	**.15**
☐	**354**	**Tommy Salo (G), NYI., RC**	**.15**
☐	355	Miroslav Satan, Edm.	.15
☐	356	Jamie Storr (G), L.A.	.25
☐	357	Niklas Sundstrom, NYR.	.15
☐	**358**	**Robert Svehla, Fla., RC**	**.25**
☐	359	Denis Pederson, N.J.	.15
☐	**360**	**Antti Törmänen, Ott., RC**	**.15**
☐	361	Brendan Witt, Wsh.	.15
☐	362	Vitali Yachmenev, L.A.	.15
☐	**363**	**Stéphane Yelle, Col., RC**	**.15**
☐	364	Tom Barrasso (G), Pgh.	.25
☐	365	Ed Belfour (G), Chi.	.35
☐	366	Martin Brodeur (G), N.J.	.75
☐	367	Sean Burke (G), Hfd.	.25
☐	368	Jim Carey (G), Wsh.	.15
☐	369	Stéphane Fiset (G), Col.	.25
☐	370	Dominik Hasek (G), Buf.	.75
☐	371	Ron Hextall (G), Pha.	.25
☐	372	Nikolai Khabibulin (G), Pho.	.35
☐	373	Kirk McLean (G), Van.	.25
☐	374	Chris Osgood (G), Det.	.35
☐	375	Félix Potvin (G), Tor.	.50
☐	376	Daren Puppa (G), T.B.	.15
☐	377	Patrick Roy (G), Col.	2.00
☐	378	John Vanbiesbrouck (G), Fla.	.60
☐	379	Pavel Bure, Van.	.75
☐	380	Chris Chelios, Chi.	.35
☐	381	Sergei Fedorov, Det.	.50
☐	382	Theoren Fleury, Cgy.	.35
☐	383	Peter Forsberg, Col.	1.25
☐	384	Ron Francis, Pgh.	.35
☐	385	Wayne Gretzky, Stl.	4.00
☐	386	Brett Hull, Stl.	.50
☐	387	Jaromir Jagr, Pgh.	1.25
☐	388	Paul Kariya, Ana.	1.50
☐	389	Pat LaFontaine, Buf.	.25
☐	390	Brian Leetch, NYR.	.35
☐	391	Mario Lemieux, Pgh.	2.00
☐	392	Eric Lindros, Pha.	1.50
☐	393	Mark Messier, NYR.	.50
☐	394	Mike Modano, Dal.	.50
☐	395	Adam Oates, Bos.	.35
☐	396	Jeremy Roenick, Chi.	.35
☐	397	Joe Sakic, Col.	1.00
☐	398	Alexei Zhamnov, Wpg.	.25
☐	399	Checklist	.15
☐	400	Checklist	.15

ALL-ROOKIES

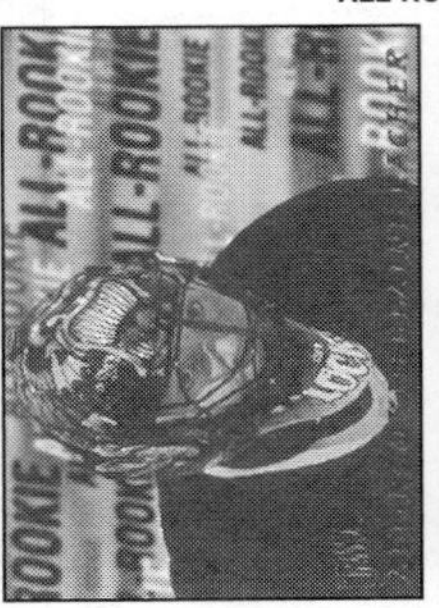

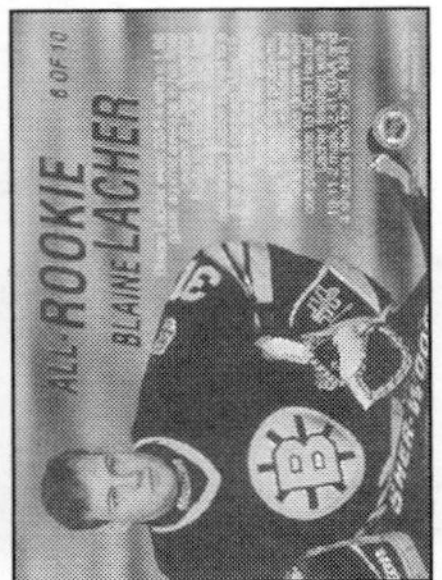

There are two versions to this set: regular inserts and Gold Medallion.

Insert Set (10 cards): **45.00** **80.00**

	No.	Player	Reg.	Gold
☐ ☐	1	Jim Carey (G), Wsh.	3.00	5.00
☐ ☐	2	Mariusz Czerkawski, Bos.	3.00	5.00
☐ ☐	3	Peter Forsberg, Que.	12.00	25.00
☐ ☐	4	Jeff Friesen, S.J.	4.00	7.00
☐ ☐	5	Paul Kariya, Ana.	15.00	30.00
☐ ☐	6	Blaine Lacher (G), Bos.	3.00	5.00
☐ ☐	7	Ian Laperrière, Stl.	3.00	5.00
☐ ☐	8	Todd Marchant, Edm.	3.00	5.00
☐ ☐	9	Roman Oksiuta, Van.	3.00	5.00
☐ ☐	10	David Oliver, Edm.	3.00	5.00

PREMIER PAD MEN

There are two versions to this set: regular inserts and Gold Medallion.

Insert Set (12 cards): **175.00** **350.00**

	No.	Player	Reg.	Gold
☐ ☐	1	Ed Belfour (G), Chi.	10.00	20.00
☐ ☐	2	Sean Burke (G), Hfd.	10.00	20.00
☐ ☐	3	Martin Brodeur (G), N.J.	20.00	40.00
☐ ☐	4	Jim Carey (G), Wsh.	8.00	15.00
☐ ☐	5	Dominik Hasek (G), Buf.	20.00	40.00
☐ ☐	6	Curtis Joseph (G), Stl.	18.00	35.00
☐ ☐	7	Blaine Lacher (G), Bos.	8.00	15.00
☐ ☐	8	Andy Moog (G), Dal.	10.00	20.00
☐ ☐	9	Félix Potvin (G), Tor.	15.00	30.00
☐ ☐	10	Patrick Roy (G), Mtl.	50.00	100.00
☐ ☐	11	John Vanbiesbrouck (G), Fla.	18.00	35.00
☐ ☐	12	Mike Vernon (G), Det.	10.00	20.00

PREMIER PIVOTS

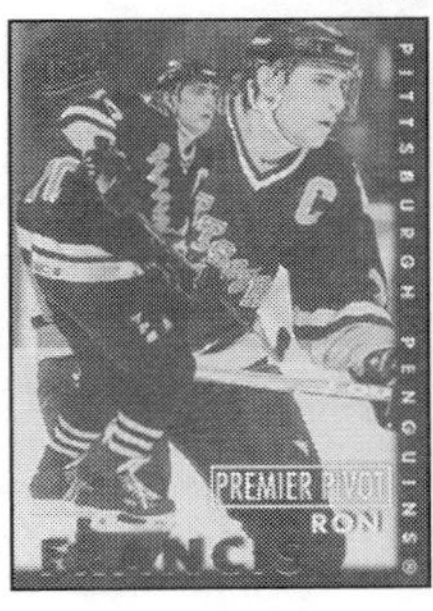

There are two versions to this set: regular inserts and Gold Medallion.

Insert Set (10 cards): **30.00** **60.00**

	No.	Player	Reg.	Gold
☐ ☐	1	Sergei Fedorov, Det.	2.50	5.00
☐ ☐	2	Ron Francis, Pgh.	1.50	3.00
☐ ☐	3	Wayne Gretzky, L.A.	10.00	20.00
☐ ☐	4	Eric Lindros, Pha.	6.50	13.00
☐ ☐	5	Mark Messier, NYR.	2.50	5.00
☐ ☐	6	Adam Oates, Bos.	1.50	3.00
☐ ☐	7	Jeremy Roenick, Chi.	1.50	3.00
☐ ☐	8	Joe Sakic, Que.	4.00	8.00
☐ ☐	9	Mats Sundin, Tor.	2.50	5.00
☐ ☐	10	Alexei Zhamnov, Wpg.	1.00	2.00

RED LIGHT SPECIALS

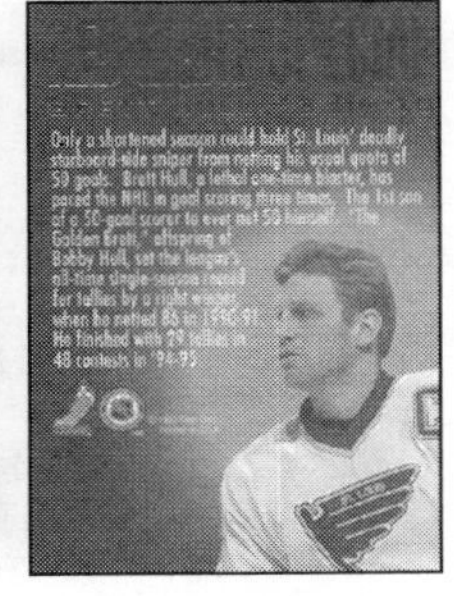

There are two versions to this set: regular inserts and Gold Medallion.

Insert Set (10 cards): **12.50** **25.00**

	No.	Player	Reg.	Gold
☐ ☐	1	Peter Bondra, Wsh.	1.25	2.50
☐ ☐	2	Theoren Fleury, Cgy.	1.00	2.00
☐ ☐	3	Brett Hull, Stl.	1.50	3.00
☐ ☐	4	Jaromir Jagr, Pgh.	3.00	6.00
☐ ☐	5	John LeClair, Pha.	1.50	3.00
☐ ☐	6	Eric Lindros, Pha.	4.00	8.00
☐ ☐	7	Cam Neely, Bos.	.75	1.50
☐ ☐	8	Owen Nolan, Que.	.75	1.50
☐ ☐	9	Ray Sheppard, Det.	.75	1.50
☐ ☐	10	Alexei Zhamnov, Wpg.	.75	1.50

RISING STARS

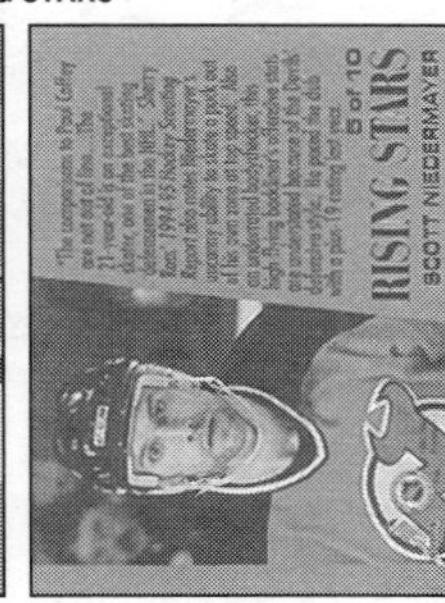

There are two versions to this set: regular inserts and Gold Medallion.

Insert Set (10 cards): **7.50** **15.00**

	No.	Player	Reg.	Gold
☐ ☐	1	Jason Arnott, Edm.	.75	1.50
☐ ☐	2	Alexandre Daigle, Ott.	.75	1.50
☐ ☐	3	Roman Hamrlik, T.B.	.75	1.50
☐ ☐	4	Trevor Kidd (G), Cgy.	.75	1.50
☐ ☐	5	Scott Niedermayer, N.J.	.75	1.50
☐ ☐	6	Keith Primeau, Det.	.75	1.50
☐ ☐	7	Mikael Renberg, Pha.	.50	1.00
☐ ☐	8	Jocelyn Thibault (G), Que.	1.50	3.00
☐ ☐	9	Alexei Yashin, Ott.	2.00	4.00
☐ ☐	10	Alexei Zhitnik, L.A.	.50	1.00

HIGH SPEED

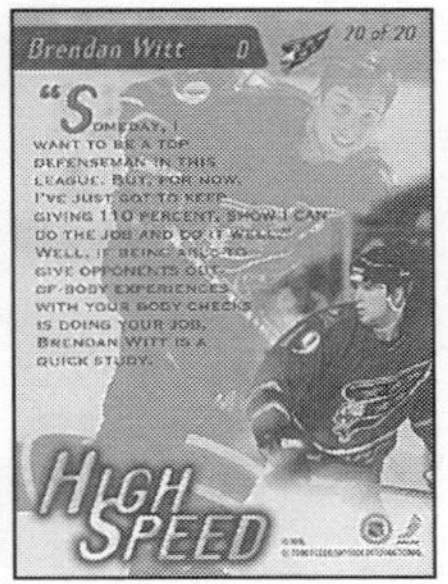

Series Two Insert Set (20 cards): **30.00**

	No.	Player	NRMT-MT
☐	1	Daniel Alfredsson, Ott.	2.50
☐	2	Jason Arnott, Edm.	1.00
☐	3	Todd Bertuzzi, NYI.	1.00
☐	4	Radek Bonk, Ott.	.50
☐	5	Martin Brodeur (G), N.J.	4.00
☐	6	Alexandre Daigle, Ott.	1.00
☐	7	Shane Doan, Wpg.	.50
☐	8	Peter Forsberg, Col.	6.00
☐	9	Roman Hamrlik, T.B.	1.00
☐	10	Todd Harvey, Dal.	.50
☐	11	Paul Kariya, Ana.	8.00
☐	12	Travis Green, NYI.	.50
☐	13	Chris Osgood, Det.	2.50
☐	14	Zigmund Palffy, NYI.	2.50
☐	15	Marcus Ragnarsson, S.J.	.50
☐	16	Mikael Renberg, Pha.	1.00
☐	17	Brian Savage, Mtl.	1.00
☐	18	Robert Svehla, Fla.	1.00
☐	19	Jocelyn Thibault, Mtl.	1.75
☐	20	Brendan Witt, Wsh.	.50

CREASE CRASHERS

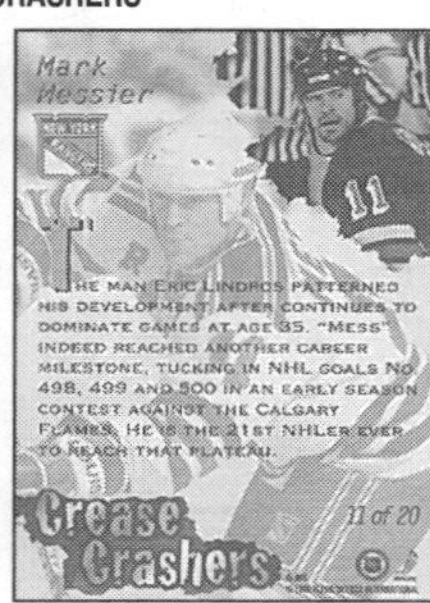

	No.	Player	NRMT-MT
Series Two Insert Set (20 cards):			**240.00**
☐	1	Jason Arnott, Edm.	8.00
☐	2	Rod Brind'Amour, Pha.	8.00
☐	3	Theoren Fleury, Cgy.	15.00
☐	4	Todd Harvey, Dal.	5.00
☐	5	John LeClair, Pha.	25.00
☐	6	Claude Lemieux, Col.	5.00
☐	7	Trevor Linden, Van.	8.00
☐	8	Eric Lindros, Pha.	65.00
☐	9	Darren McCarty, Det.	5.00
☐	10	Scott Mellanby, Fla.	5.00
☐	11	Mark Messier, NYR.	25.00
☐	12	Cam Neely, Bos.	8.00
☐	13	Owen Nolan, Que.	8.00
☐	14	Keith Primeau, Det.	8.00
☐	15	Jeremy Roenick, Chi.	15.00
☐	16	Tomas Sandström, Pgh.	5.00
☐	17	Brendan Shanahan, Hfd.	30.00
☐	18	Kevin Stevens, Bos.	5.00
☐	19	Rick Tocchet, L.A.	5.00
☐	20	Keith Tkachuk, Wpg.	20.00

EXTRA ATTACKERS

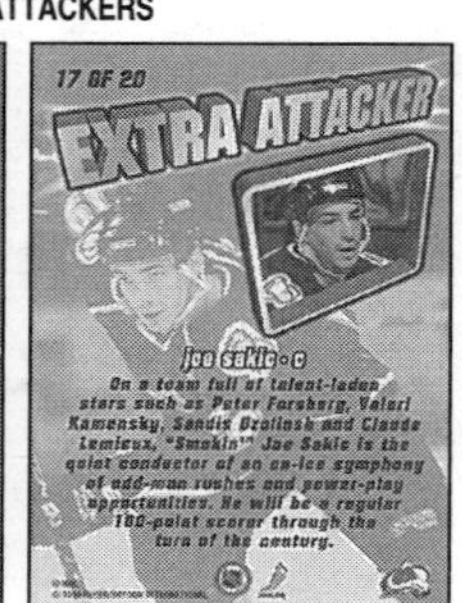

	No.	Player	NRMT-MT
Series Two Insert Set (20 cards):			**225.00**
☐	1	Peter Bondra, Wsh.	8.00
☐	2	Eric Dazé, Chi.	4.00
☐	3	Radek Dvorak, Fla.	3.00
☐	4	Sergei Fedorov, Det.	10.00
☐	5	Peter Forsberg, Col.	20.00
☐	6	Ron Francis, Pgh.	6.00
☐	7	Wayne Gretzky, L.A.	40.00
☐	8	Brett Hull, Stl.	10.00
☐	9	Jaromir Jagr, Pgh.	20.00
☐	10	Ed Jovanovski, Fla.	4.00
☐	11	Paul Kariya, Ana.	25.00
☐	12	Saku Koivu, Mtl.	15.00
☐	13	Mario Lemieux, Pgh.	30.00
☐	14	Mike Modano, Dal.	10.00
☐	15	Alexander Mogilny, Van.	6.00
☐	16	Adam Oates, Bos.	6.00
☐	17	Joe Sakic, Col.	18.00
☐	18	Niklas Sundstrom, NYR.	3.00
☐	19	Mats Sundin, Tor.	10.00
☐	20	Steve Yzerman, Det.	20.00

ULTRA VIEW

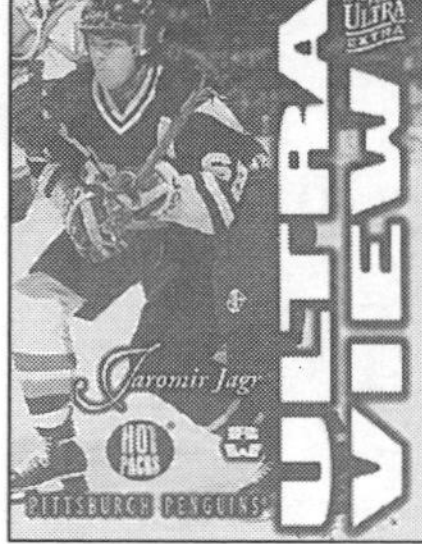

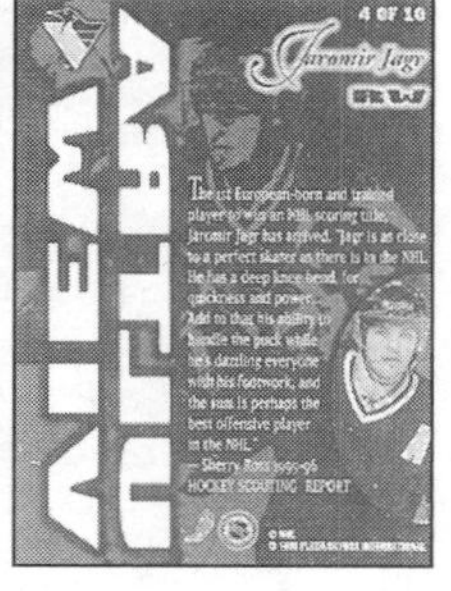

This set has two versions: the regular insert and Hot Packs inserts. "Hot Packs" versions came all in one pack.

	No.	Player	Reg.	H.P.
Series Two Insert Set (10 cards):			**150.00**	**75.00**
Hot Packs Set (10 cards):				**85.00**
☐☐	1	Sergei Fedorov, Det.	10.00	5.00
☐☐	2	Wayne Gretzky, L.A.	40.00	20.00
☐☐	3	Dominik Hasek, Buf.	15.00	7.50
☐☐	4	Jaromir Jagr, Pgh.	20.00	10.00
☐☐	5	Brian Leetch, NYR.	6.00	3.00
☐☐	6	Mario Lemieux, Pgh.	30.00	15.00
☐☐	7	Eric Lindros, Pha.	25.00	12.50
☐☐	8	Jeremy Roenick, Chi.	6.00	3.00
☐☐	9	Joe Sakic, Col.	18.00	9.00
☐☐	10	Alexei Zhamnov, Wpg.	4.00	2.00

1995 - 96 FUTURE LEGENDS

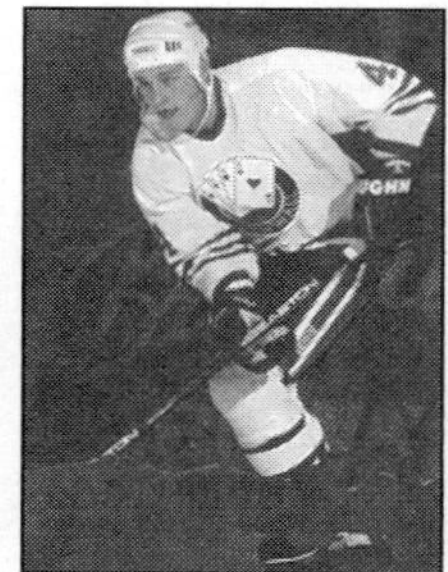
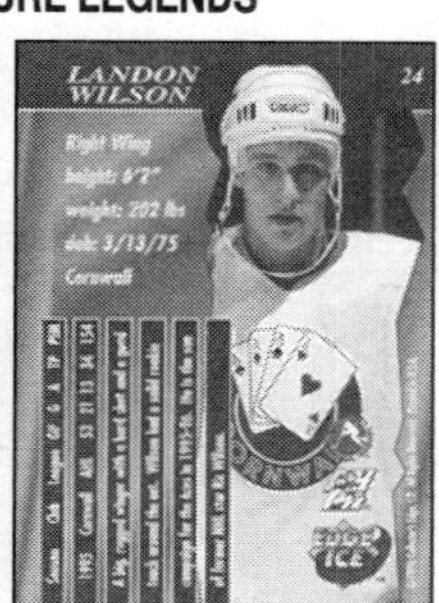

Imprint:

	No.	Player	NRMT-MT
Complete Set (50 cards):			**35.00**
☐	1	Brad Bombardir, Albany	.50
☐	2	Niklas Andersson, Phoenix	.50
☐	3	Mike Dunham (G), Albany	1.50
☐	4	Anders Eriksson, Adirondack	.50
☐	5	Kelly Fairchild, St. John's	.50
☐	6	Chris Ferraro, Binghampton	.50
☐	7	Peter Ferraro, Binghampton	.50
☐	8	Eric Fichaud (G), Worcester	2.00
☐	9	Manny Legacé (G), Springfield	1.00
☐	10	David Ling, Saint John	.50
☐	11	Jim Montgomery, Hershey	.50
☐	12	Chris Murray, Fredericton	.50
☐	13	Rob Brown, Chicago-IHL	.50
☐	14	Rem Murray, Cape Breton	1.00
☐	15	Rob Murray, Springfield	.50
☐	16	Jan Caloun, Kansas City	.50
☐	17	Frédéric Chabot (G), Cincinatti	1.00
☐	18	Craig Fischer, Orlando	.50
☐	19	Dwayne Roloson (G), Saint John	1.00
☐	20	Brad Smyth, Carolina	1.00
☐	21	Steve Sullivan, Albany	1.00
☐	22	Petr Sykora, Albany	1.50
☐	23	Darcy Tucker, Fredericton	.50
☐	24	Landon Wilson, Cornwall	.50
☐	25	Greg Hawgood, Las Vegas	.50
☐	26	Stéphane Beauregard (G), San Francisco	.50
☐	27	Aki Berg, Phoenix	1.00
☐	28	Matt Johnson, Phoenix	.50
☐	29	Curtis Joseph (G), Las Vegas	2.50
☐	30	Dan Lambert, Los Angeles	.50
☐	31	Eric Lecompte, Indianapolis	.50
☐	32	Brett Lievers, Utah	.50
☐	33	Mark McArthur, Utah	.50
☐	34	Ethan Moreau, Indianapolis	.50
☐	35	Marty Murray, Saint John	.50
☐	36	Wayne Primeau, Rochester	.50
☐	37	John Purves, San Francisco	.50
☐	38	Manon Rhéaume (G)	8.00
☐	39	Barry Richter, Binghampton	.50
☐	40	Jamie Rivers, Worcester	.50
☐	41	Tommy Salo (G), Utah	1.50
☐	42	Jamie Storr (G), Phoenix	2.00
☐	43	Tom Tilley, Milwaukee	.50
☐	44	Derek Wilkinson, Atlanta	.50
☐	45	Mike Wilson, Rochester	.50
☐	46	Sandis Ozolinsh, San Francisco	2.00
☐	47	Andrew Brunette, Portland-AHL	1.00
☐	48	James Black, Indianapolis	.50
☐	49	Terry Yake, Milwaukee	.50
☐	50	Mike Prokopec, Indianapolis	.50

HOT PICKS AUTOGRAPHED INSERTS

Two autographed cards came cellophane wrapped in each foil box.

	No.	Player	NRMT-MT
☐	1	Chris Philips	25.00
☐	2	Boyd Devereaux	18.00
☐	3	Richard Jackman	12.00
☐	4	Markus Nilsson	12.00

PLATINUM CLUB

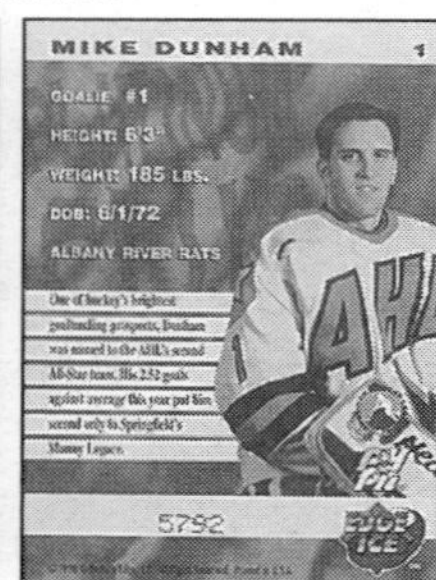

	No.	Player	NRMT-MT
Insert Set (8 cards):			**50.00**
☐	1	Mike Dunham (G), AHL All-Stars	6.00
☐	2	Eric Fichaud (G)	12.00
☐	3	Manny Legacé (G)	5.00
☐	4	Steve Sullivan	6.00
☐	5	Darcy Tucker	5.00
☐	6	Jamie Langenbrunner	10.00
☐	7	Ethan Moreau	6.00
☐	8	Jamie Storr (G)	12.00

SIGNED, SEALED & DELIVERED AUTOGRAPHS

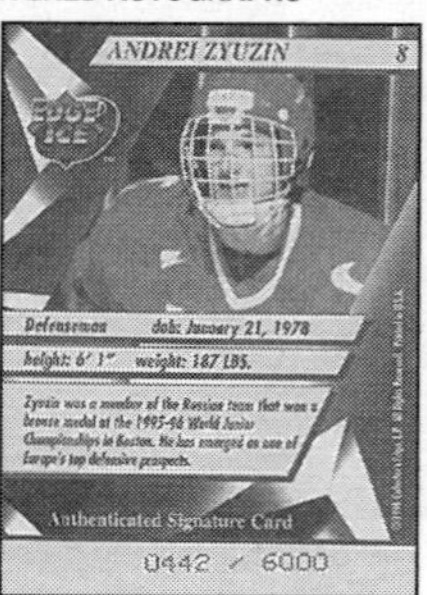

Card number 7 has not been confirmed to exist.

	No.	Player	NRMT-MT
☐	1	Alexandre Volchkov	25.00
☐	2	Chris Allen	10.00
☐	3	Brian Bonin	10.00
☐	4	Josh Green	15.00
☐	5	Chris Hajt	10.00
☐	6	Josh Holden	25.00
☐	8	Andrei Zyuzin, Rus.	20.00

HIGH FIVE AUTOGRAPHED INSERT

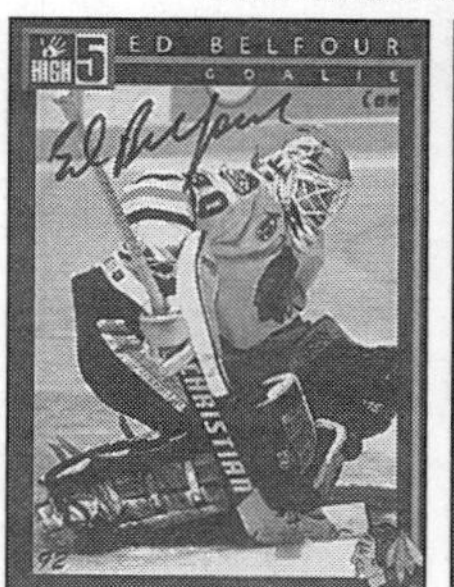

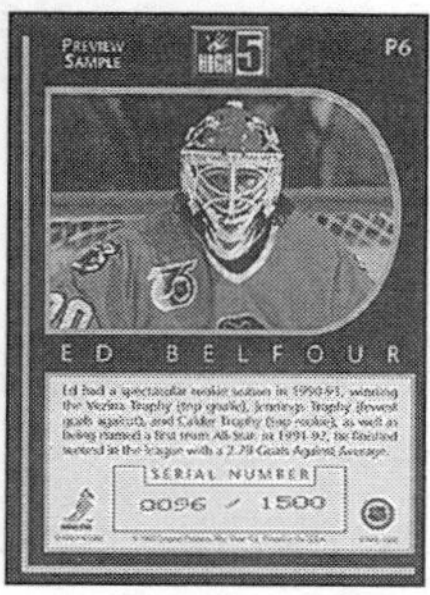

1992-93 High Five Promos were also inserted into Future Legends packs. Only the Belfour card was autographed.

	No.	Player	NRMT-MT
☐	P6	Ed Belfour Autograph (#/1500)	50.00

1995 - 96 HOCKEY HALL OF FAME LEGENDS

Imprint:

Complete Set (18 cards): 120.00

	No.	Player	NRMT-MT
☐	55	Bill Barber	8.00
☐	56	Harry Howell	10.00
☐	57	Dick Irvin	8.00
☐	58	Dave Keon	11.00
☐	59	Clint Smith	10.00
☐	60	Lester Patrick	8.00
☐	61	Rod Gilbert	10.00
☐	62	Hooley Smith	8.00
☐	63	Eddie Shore	8.00
☐	64	Fred Maxwell	8.00
☐	65	Ted Kennedy	10.00
☐	66	Allan Stanley	10.00
☐	67	Darryl Sittler	12.00
☐	68	Red Horner	10.00
☐	69	Howie Morenz	10.00
☐	70	Bill Gadsby	10.00
☐	71	Aurèle Joliat	8.00
☐	72	Joe Malone	8.00

1995 - 96 HOYLE EASTERN CONFERENCE

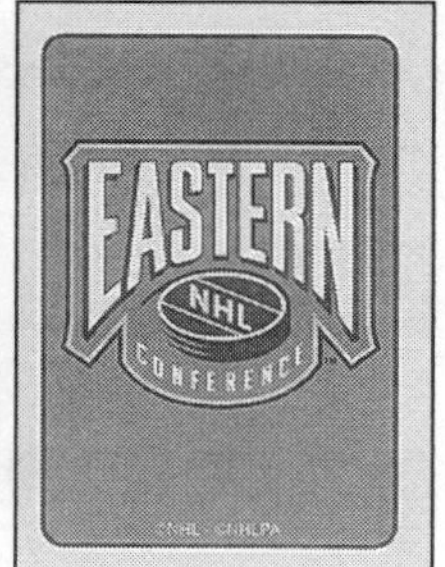

Imprint:

Complete Deck (54 cards): 8.00

	No.	Player	NRMT-MT
☐	JOKER	Alexei Yashin, Ott.	.35
☐	JOKER	Sergei Zubov, NYR.	.25
☐	A♣	Joe Sakic, Que.	.85
☐	2♣	Mikael Renberg, Pha.	.15
☐	3♣	Stéphane Richer, N.J.	.15
☐	4♣	Mike Richter (G), NYR.	.35
☐	5♣	Luc Robitaille, Pgh.	.25
☐	6♣	Geoff Sanderson, Hfd.	.15
☐	7♣	Brian Smolinski, Bos.	.15
☐	8♣	Kevin Stevens, Pgh.	.15
☐	9♣	Scott Stevens, N.J.	.15
☐	10♣	Steve Thomas, N.J.	.15
☐	J♣	Darren Turcotte, Hfd.	.15
☐	Q♣	John Vanbiesbrouck (G), Fla.	.60
☐	K♣	New Jersey Devils	.15
☐	A♦	Mark Messier, NYR.	.50
☐	2♦	Brian Leetch, NYR.	.35
☐	3♦	Alexander Mogilny, Buf.	.35
☐	4♦	Kirk Muller, NYI.	.15
☐	5♦	Cam Neely, Bos.	.25
☐	6♦	Rob Niedermayer, Fla.	.15
☐	7♦	Scott Niedermayer, N.J.	.25
☐	8♦	Owen Nolan, Que.	.25
☐	9♦	Adam Oates, Bos.	.35
☐	10♦	Michal Pivonka, Wsh.	.15
☐	J♦	Derek Plante, Buf.	.15
☐	Q♦	Chris Pronger, Hfd.	.25
☐	K♦	Mark Recchi, Mtl.	.25
☐	A♥	Eric Lindros, Pha.	1.25
☐	2♥	Peter Bondra, Wsh.	.35
☐	3♥	Radek Bonk, Ott.	.15
☐	4♥	Ray Bourque, Bos.	.50
☐	5♥	Brian Bradley, T.B.	.15
☐	6♥	Rod Brind'Amour, Pha.	.25
☐	7♥	Martin Brodeur (G), N.J.	.75
☐	8♥	Wendel Clark, Tor.	.25
☐	9♥	Alexandre Daigle, Ott.	.25
☐	10♥	Vincent Damphousse, Mtl.	.35
☐	J♥	Ray Ferraro, NYR.	.15
☐	Q♥	Stéphane Fiset (G), Que.	.25
☐	K♥	Peter Forsberg, Que.	1.00
☐	A♠	Patrick Roy (G), Mtl.	1.50
☐	2♠	Chris Gratton, T.B.	.25
☐	3♠	Adam Graves, NYR.	.15
☐	4♠	Dominik Hasek (G), Buf.	.75
☐	5♠	Ron Hextall (G), Pha.	.25
☐	6♠	Jaromir Jagr, Pgh.	1.00
☐	7♠	Joé Juneau, Wsh.	.15
☐	8♠	Dmitri Khristich, Wsh.	.15
☐	9♠	Petr Klima, T.B.	.15
☐	10♠	Bob Kudelski, Fla.	.15
☐	J♠	Scott Lachance, NYI.	.15
☐	Q♠	Pat LaFontaine, Buf.	.25
☐	K♠	John LeClair, Pha.	.35

1995 - 96 HOYLE WESTERN CONFERENCE

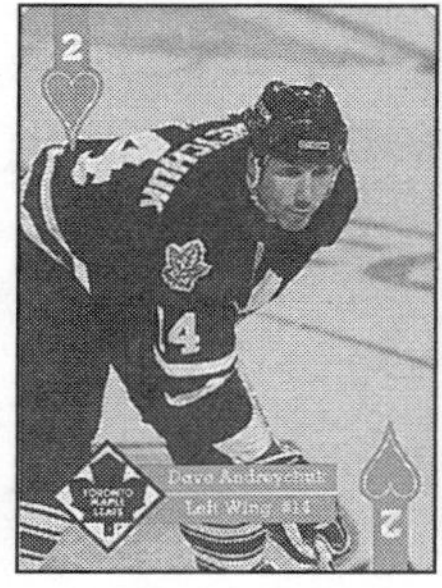

Imprint:

Complete Deck (54 cards): 8.00

	No.	Player	NRMT-MT
☐	JOKER	Alexei Zhamnov, Wpg.	.15
☐	JOKER	Steve Yzerman, Det.	1.00
☐	A♣	Wayne Gretzky, L.A.	2.00
☐	2♣	Joe Sacco, Ana.	.15
☐	3♣	Denis Savard, Chi.	.25
☐	4♣	Teemu Selänne, Wpg.	.75
☐	5♣	Brendan Shanahan, Stl.	.60
☐	6♣	Ray Sheppard, Fla.	.15
☐	7♣	Mats Sundin, Tor.	.50
☐	8♣	Esa Tikkanen, Stl.	.15
☐	9♣	German Titov, Cgy.	.15
☐	10♣	Keith Tkachuk, Wpg.	.35
☐	J♣	Rick Tocchet, L.A.	.15
☐	Q♣	Doug Weight, Edm.	.35
☐	K♣	Detroit Red Wings	.35
☐	A♦	Pavel Bure, Van.	.75
☐	2♦	Jari Kurri, L.A.	.25
☐	3♦	Igor Larionov, S.J.	.25
☐	4♦	Nicklas Lidström, Det.	.25
☐	5♦	Trevor Linden, Van.	.25
☐	6♦	Marty McSorley, L.A.	.15
☐	7♦	Mike Modano, Dal.	.50
☐	8♦	Bernie Nicholls, Chi.	.15
☐	9♦	Joe Nieuwendyk, Cgy.	.25
☐	10♦	David Oliver, Edm.	.15
☐	J♦	Félix Potvin (G), Tor.	.50
☐	Q♦	Bill Ranford (G), Edm.	.25
☐	K♦	Gary Roberts, Cgy.	.25
☐	A♥	Jeremy Roenick, Chi.	.35
☐	2♥	Dave Andreychuk, Tor.	.15
☐	3♥	Jason Arnott, Edm.	.25
☐	4♥	Ed Belfour (G), Chi.	.35
☐	5♥	Rob Blake, L.A.	.25
☐	6♥	Jeff Brown, Stl.	.15
☐	7♥	Patrik Carnback, Ana.	.15
☐	8♥	Chris Chelios, Chi.	.35
☐	9♥	Tim Cheveldae (G), Wpg.	.15
☐	10♥	Paul Coffey, Det.	.35
☐	J♥	Shayne Corson, Stl.	.25
☐	Q♥	Geoff Courtnall, Van.	.15
☐	K♥	Russ Courtnall, Van.	.15
☐	A♠	Sergei Fedorov, Det.	.50
☐	2♠	Ulf Dahlen, S.J.	.15
☐	3♠	Pat Falloon, S.J.	.15
☐	4♠	Theoren Fleury, Cgy.	.35
☐	5♠	Doug Gilmour, Tor.	.35
☐	6♠	Todd Harvey, Dal.	.15
☐	7♠	Kevin Hatcher, Dal.	.15
☐	8♠	Guy Hebert (G), Ana.	.25
☐	9♠	Phil Housley, Cgy.	.15
☐	10♠	Brett Hull, Stl.	.50
☐	J♠	Arturs Irbe (G), S.J.	.15
☐	Q♠	Curtis Joseph (G), Stl.	.35
☐	K♠	Paul Kariya, Ana.	1.25

1995 - 96 KELLOGG'S - DONRUSS

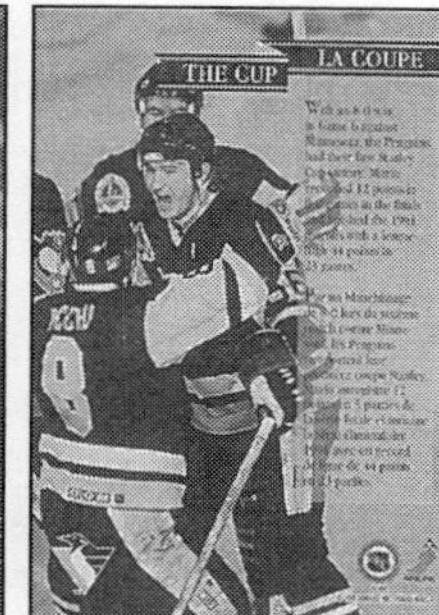

One of six different cards were found in specially marked boxes of Kellogg's cereal.

Imprint:

Complete Set (6 cards): 12.00

	Player	NRMT-MT
☐	Mario Lemieux - 500 Goals	4.00
☐	Mario Lemieux - Return	4.00
☐	Mario Lemieux - The Fiver	4.00
☐	Mario Lemieux - Stanley Cup	4.00
☐	Brett Hull - 50 in 50	2.00
☐	Brett Hull - Hart Trophy	2.00

1995 - 96 KELLOGG'S POP UPS - FINLAND

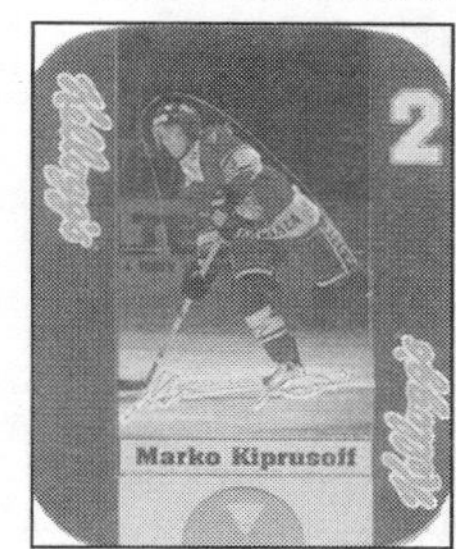

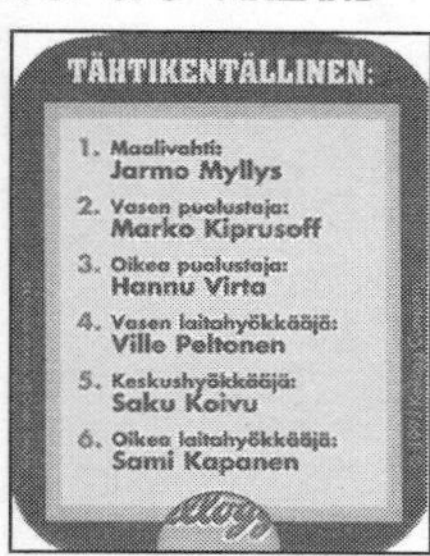

We have no pricing information on this set.

Imprint:

	No.	Player
☐	1	Jarmo Myllys (G)
☐	2	Marko Kiprusoff
☐	3	Hannu Virta
☐	4	Ville Peltonen
☐	5	Saku Koivu
☐	6	Sami Kapanen

1995 - 96 KENNER STARTING LINEUP

Figurines in both the American and Canadian series are the same.

Imprint:

		U.S.	Cdn.
Canadian Set (13 figurines):		—	200.00
U.S. Set (19 figurines):		250.00	—

	Player	U.S.	Cdn.
□	Tom Barrasso (G), Pgh.	-	25.00
□□	Rob Blake, L.A.	12.00	12.00
□□	Martin Brodeur (G), N.J.	30.00	30.00
□	Pavel Bure, Van.	15.00	-
□□	Chris Chelios, Chi.	15.00	15.00
□	Bob Corkum, Ana.	12.00	-
□	Sergei Fedorov, Det.	15.00	-
□□	Theoren Fleury, Cgy.	15.00	15.00
□□	Adam Graves, NYR.	12.00	12.00
□□	Dominik Hasek (G), Buf.	35.00	35.00
□	Brett Hull, Stl.	15.00	-
□	Arturs Irbe (G), S.J.	-	20.00
□□	Mike Modano, Dal.	15.00	15.00
□	Kirk Muller, NYI.	12.00	-
□□	Cam Neely, Bos.	12.00	12.00
□	Sandis Ozolinsh, S.J.	12.00	-
□□	Félix Potvin (G), Tor.	25.00	25.00
□	Luc Robitaille, Pgh.	12.00	-
□□	Brendan Shanahan, Stl.	18.00	18.00
□□	Scott Stevens, N.J.	12.00	12.00
□	Pierre Turgeon, Mtl.	12.00	-

1995 - 96 KENNER STARTING LINEUP LEGENDS

This nine-figurine set features only two hockey players.

Imprint:

	Player	NRMT-MT
□	Gordie Howe, Det.	20.00
□	Bobby Hull, Chi.	20.00

1995 - 96 KENNER STARTING LINEUP CANADIAN LEGENDS

Imprint:

Complete Set (6 figurines): 125.00

	Player	NRMT-MT
□	Jean Béliveau, Mtl.	20.00
□	Phil Esposito, Bos.	18.00
□	Tony Esposito (G), Chi.	30.00
□	Gordie Howe, Det.	25.00
□	Bobby Hull, Chi.	20.00
□	Henri Richard, Mtl.	25.00

1995 - 96 KRAFT FOODS

Imprint:

Master Set (79 cards): 125.00

Album: 25.00

SHOOTING STARS

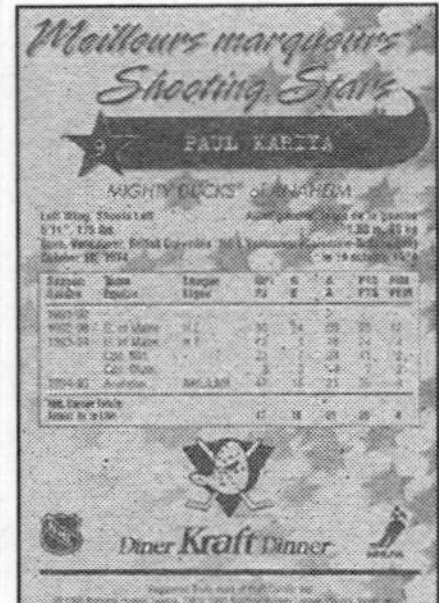

One of 20 different cards could be found on the backs of specially marked 225g boxes of Kraft Dinner and one of six different cards were found on the back of specially marked 225g boxes of Kraft Dinner specialty flavours.

	Player	NRMT-MT
□	Paul Kariya, Ana.	4.00
□	Theoren Fleury, Cgy.	1.00
□	Bernie Nicholls, Chi.	1.00
□	Joe Sakic, Col.	2.75
□	Dave Gagner, Dal.	1.00
□	Paul Coffey, Det.	1.00
□	Andrew Cassels, Hfd.	1.00
□	Wayne Gretzky, L.A.	6.00
□	Mark Recchi, Mtl.	1.50
□	Stéphane Richer, N.J.	1.00
□	Mark Messier, NYR.	2.00
□	Alexandre Daigle, Ott.	1.00
□	Eric Lindros, Pha.	4.00
□	Jaromir Jagr, Pgh.	3.00
□	Ulf Dahlen, S.J.	1.00
□	Brian Bradley, T.B.	1.00
□	Mats Sundin, Tor.	2.00
□	Pavel Bure, Van.	2.50
□	Peter Bondra, Wsh.	1.50
□	Alexei Zhamnov, Wpg.	1.00
CHEESE & TOMATO, SPIRALS, WHITE CHEDDAR		
□	Adam Oates, Bos.	1.00
□	Doug Weight, Edm.	1.00
□	Jesse Belanger, Fla.	1.00
□	Ray Ferraro, NYR.	1.00
□	Brett Hull, Stl.	2.00
□	Alexander Mogilny, Van.	1.00

ALL-STARS

One of 13 different disks were found under the lids of specially marked jars of Kraft Peanut Butter.

	Player	NRMT-MT
□	Dominik Hasek (G), Buf.	2.75
□	Paul Coffey, Det.	2.00
□	Chris Chelios, Chi.	2.00
□	Eric Lindros, Pha.	4.00
□	John LeClair, Pha.	2.50
□	Jaromir Jagr, Pgh.	3.00
□	Ed Belfour (G), Chi.	1.75
□	Ray Bourque, Bos.	2.50
□	Larry Murphy, Tor.	1.50
□	Alexei Zhamnov, Wpg.	1.50
□	Keith Tkachuk, Wpg.	2.00
□	Theoren Fleury, Cgy.	1.75
□	N.J. Devils/Claude Lemieux	10.00

JELL-O INSTANT PUDDING: THEHOTTEST TICKET

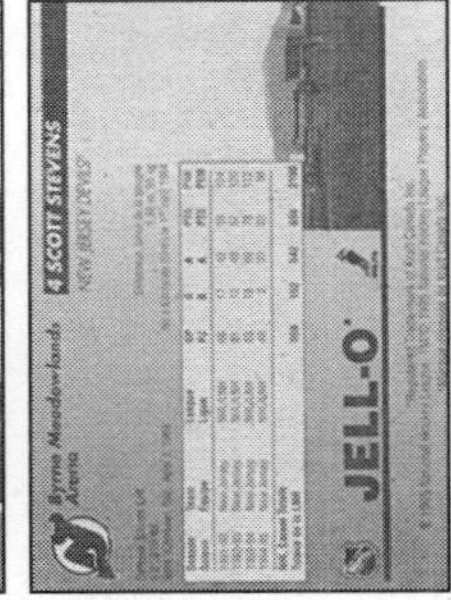

(Cards are on the back of specially marked boxes).

Cards Size: 2 3/4" x 4 1/4"

	Player	NRMT-MT
□	Cam Neely, Bos.	1.75
□	Phil Housley, Cgy.	1.50
□	Peter Forsberg, Col. vs. Buf.	3.00
□	Sergei Fedorov, Det.	2.00
□	Jason Arnott, Edm vs. NYI.	1.75
□	Pierre Turgeon, Mtl. vs. NYR.	1.75
□	Scott Stevens, N.J. vs Fla.	1.50
□	Wendel Clark, NYI.	1.75
□	Alexandre Daigle, Ott	1.75
□	Mario Lemieux, Pgh	4.00
□	Doug Gilmour, Tor	1.75
□	Trevor Linden, Van	1.75
□	Joé Juneau, Wsh	1.50
□	Teemu Selänne, Wpg. vs. Ana.	2.50

CREASE KEEPERS

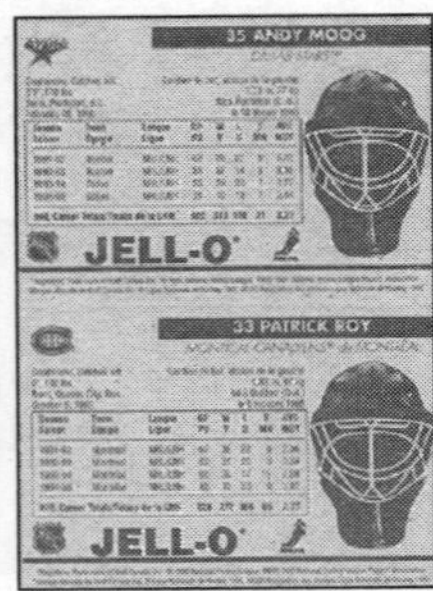

Two of 18 different cards were found under the lid of specially marked packages of JELL-O Pudding. JELL-O flavours and pairings were: Butterscotch (Burke & Hextall or Vanbiesbrouck & Richter); Chocolate (Belfour & Puppa or Kidd & Fuhr); Chocolate Fudge (Belfour & Puppa or Hasek & Fiset); Chocolate Marshmellow (Kidd & Fuhr); Banana (Vernon & McLean); Vanilla (Vernon &McLean); Raspberry (Potvin & Carey); and Strawberry (Moog & Roy).

	Player	NRMT-MT
□	Blaine Lacher (G), Bos.	1.00
□	Martin Brodeur (G), N.J.	3.00
□	Dominik Hasek (G), Buf.	3.00
□	Stéphane Fiset (G), Col.	1.50
□	Trevor Kidd (G), Cgy.	1.50
□	Grant Fuhr (G), Stl.	1.50
□	Ed Belfour (G), Chi.	2.00
□	Daren Puppa (G), T.B.	1.00
□	Andy Moog (G), Bos.	1.50
□	Patrick Roy (G), Mtl.	4.00
□	Mike Vernon (G), Det.	1.50
□	Kirk McLean (G), Van.	1.50
□	John Vanbiesbrouck (G), Fla.	2.75
□	Mike Richter (G), NYR.	2.00
□	Sean Burke (G), Hfd.	1.50
□	Ron Hextall (G), Pha.	1.50
□	Félix Potvin (G), Tor.	2.50
□	Jim Carey (G), Wsh.	1.00

MINI CREASE KEEPERS

Two of 8 different cards were found under the lids of specially marked packages of JELL-O Pudding.

	Player	NRMT-MT
□	Tom Barrasso (G), Pgh.	1.00
□	Kelly Hrudey (G), L.A.	1.00
□	Don Beaupré (G), Ott.	1.00
□	Tommy Söderström (G), NYI.	1.00
□	Guy Hebert (G), Ana.	1.50
□	Tim Cheveldae (G), Wpg.	1.00
□	Arturs Irbe (G), S.J.	1.00
□	Bill Ranford (G), Edm.	1.50

1995 - 96 LEAF

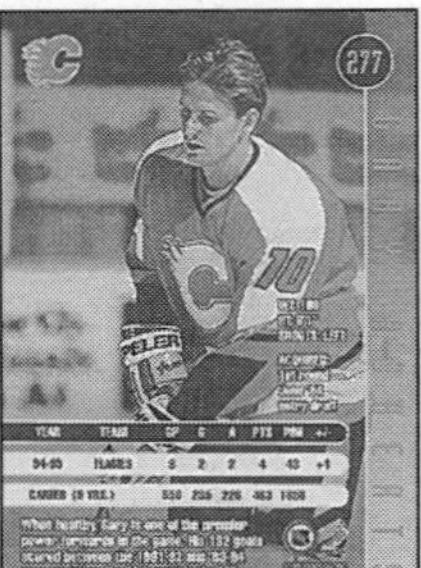

Imprint: © 1995 DONRUSS, INC.

Complete Set (330 cards): 30.00

Common Player: .15

	No.	Player	NRMT-MT
□	1	Mario Lemieux, Pgh.	2.00
□	2	Todd Harvey, Dal.	.15
□	3	Blaine Lacher (G), Bos.	.15
□	4	Alexei Zhitnik, L.A.	.15
□	5	Cory Stillman, Cgy.	.15
□	6	Murray Craven, Chi.	.15
□	7	Mike Kennedy, Dal.	.15
□	8	Mike Vernon (G), Det.	.25

	No.	Card	Price
☐	9	David Oliver, Edm.	.15
☐	**10**	**Magnus Svensson, Fla., RC**	**.15**
☐	11	Andrei Nikolishin, Hfd.	.15
☐	12	Jamie Storr (G), L.A.	.25
☐	13	David Roberts, Stl.	.15
☐	**14**	**Chris McAlpine, N.J., RC**	**.15**
☐	15	Brett Lindros, NYI.	.15
☐	16	Pat Verbeek, NYR.	.15
☐	17	Tony Amonte, Chi.	.25
☐	18	Chris Therien, Pha.	.15
☐	19	Ken Wregget (G), Pgh.	.15
☐	20	Peter Forsberg, Que. (Col.)	1.25
☐	21	Jeff Friesen, S.J.	.25
☐	22	Patrice Tardif, Stl.	.15
☐	23	Jason Wiemer, T.B.	.15
☐	24	Kenny Jonsson, Tor.	.15
☐	25	Jassen Cullimore, Van.	.15
☐	26	Sergei Gonchar, Wsh.	.15
☐	27	Nikolai Khabibulin (G), Wpg.	.35
☐	28	Oleg Tverdovsky, Ana.	.15
☐	29	Rick Tocchet, L.A.	.15
☐	30	Garry Galley, Buf.	.15
☐	31	German Titov, Cgy.	.15
☐	32	Sergei Krivokrasov, Chi.	.15
☐	33	Sylvain Turgeon, Ott.	.15
☐	34	Sergei Fedorov, Det.	.50
☐	35	Ralph Intranuovo, Edm.	.15
☐	36	Stu Barnes, Fla.	.15
☐	37	Mike Gartner, Tor.	.25
☐	38	Kevin Brown, L.A.	.15
☐	39	Valeri Bure, Mtl.	.15
☐	40	Sergei Brylin, N.J.,	.15
☐	41	Kirk Muller, NYI.	.15
☐	42	Mike Richter (G), NYR.	.35
☐	43	Stanislav Neckar, Ott.	.15
☐	44	Patrick Juhlin, Pha.	.15
☐	45	Ron Francis, Pgh.	.35
☐	46	Janne Laukkanen, Ott.	.15
☐	47	Shean Donovan, S.J.	.15
☐	48	Igor Korolev, Stl.	.15
☐	49	Alexander Selivanov, T.B.	.15
☐	50	Frantisek Kucera, Hfd.	.15
☐	51	Russ Courtnall, Van.	.15
☐	52	Don Beaupré, Ott.	.15
☐	53	Michal Grosek, Wpg.	.15
☐	54	Steve Rucchin, Ana.	.15
☐	55	Mariusz Czerkawski, Bos.	.15
☐	56	Dominik Hasek (G), Buf.	.75
☐	57	Trent Klatt, Dal.	.15
☐	58	Sergio Momesso, Van. (Tor.)	.15
☐	**59**	**Mark Lawrence, Dal., RC**	**.15**
☐	60	Steve Yzerman, Det.	1.25
☐	61	Todd Marchant, Edm.	.15
☐	62	Jesse Belanger, Fla.	.15
☐	63	Sean Burke (G), Hfd.	.25
☐	64	Matt Johnson, L.A.	.15
☐	65	Mark Recchi, Mtl.	.25
☐	66	Martin Brodeur (G), N.J.	.75
☐	67	Mathieu Schneider, NYI.	.15
☐	68	Mark Messier, NYR.	.50
☐	69	Radim Bicanek, Ott.	.15
☐	70	Eric Desjardins, Pha.	.15
☐	71	Jaromir Jagr, Pgh.	1.25
☐	72	Adam Deadmarsh, Que. (Col.)	.15
☐	73	Viktor Kozlov, S.J.	.15
☐	74	Jeff Norton, Stl.	.15
☐	**75**	**Brantt Myhres, T.B., RC**	**.15**
☐	76	Darby Hendrickson, NYI.	.15
☐	77	Roman Oksiuta, Van.	.15
☐	78	Jim Carey (G), Wsh., Error	.15
☐	79	Keith Tkachuk, Wpg.	.35
☐	80	Valeri Karpov, Ana.	.15
☐	81	Adam Oates, Bos.	.35
☐	82	Eric Lindros, Pha.	1.50
☐	83	Trevor Kidd (G), Cgy.	.25
☐	84	Bernie Nicholls, Chi.	.15
☐	**85**	**Craig Conroy, Mtl., RC**	**.15**
☐	86	Bill Ranford (G), Edm.	.25
☐	87	Scott Mellanby, Fla.	.15
☐	88	Geoff Sanderson, Hfd.	.15
☐	89	Wayne Gretzky, L.A.	2.50
☐	90	Pierre Turgeon, Mtl.	.25
☐	91	Stéphane Richer, N.J.	.15
☐	**92**	**Chris Marinucci, NYI., RC**	**.15**
☐	93	Brian Leetch, NYR.	.35
☐	**94**	**Steve Larouche, Ott., RC**	**.15**
☐	95	John LeClair, Pha.	.50
☐	96	Dmitri Mironov, Tor. (Pgh)	.15
☐	97	Jocelyn Thibault (G), Que. (Col.)	.35
☐	98	Craig Janney, S.J.	.15
☐	99	Ian Laperrière, Stl.	.15
☐	100	Dino Ciccarelli, Det.	.25
☐	101	Todd Warriner, Tor.	.15
☐	102	Kirk McLean (G), Van.	.25
☐	103	Jason Allison, Wsh.	.35
☐	104	Alexei Zhamnov, Wpg.	.25
☐	105	Keith Jones, Wsh.	.15
☐	106	Ray Bourque, Bos.	.50
☐	107	John Druce, L.A.	.15
☐	108	Scott Walker, Van.	.15
☐	109	Joe Murphy, Chi.	.15
☐	110	Checklist	.15
☐	111	Philippe DeRouville (G), Pgh.	.15
☐	112	Greg Adams, Dal.	.15
☐	113	Cam Neely, Bos.	.25
☐	114	Michael Peca, Van. (Buf.)	.25
☐	115	Theoren Fleury, Cgy.	.35
☐	116	Jeremy Roenick, Chi.	.35
☐	117	Kevin Hatcher, Dal.	.15
☐	118	Ray Sheppard, Det.	.15
☐	119	Jason Arnott, Edm.	.25
☐	120	Mark Fitzpatrick (G), Fla.	.15
☐	121	Brendan Shanahan, Stl. (Hfd)	.60
☐	122	Jari Kurri, L.A.	.25
☐	123	Shayne Corson, Edm. (Stl.)	.25
☐	124	Scott Stevens, N.J.	.15
☐	125	Steve Thomas, NYI.	.15
☐	126	Sergei Zubov, NYR. (Pgh.)	.25
☐	127	Denis Savard, Chi.	.25
☐	128	Mikael Renberg, Pha.	.15
☐	129	Luc Robitaille, Pgh. (NYR.)	.25
☐	130	Andrei Kovalenko, Que. (Col.)	.15
☐	131	Andrei Nazarov, S.J.	.15
☐	132	Denis Chassé, Stl.	.15
☐	133	Chris Gratton, T.B.	.25
☐	134	Benoît Hogue, Dal.	.15
☐	135	Pavel Bure, Van.	.75
☐	136	Peter Bondra, Wsh.	.35
☐	137	Teemu Selänne, Wpg.	.75
☐	**138**	**Darren Van Impe, Ana., RC**	**.15**
☐	139	Dmitri Khristich, Wsh. (L.A.)	.15
☐	140	Pat LaFontaine, Buf.	.25
☐	141	Phil Housley, Cgy.	.15
☐	142	Chris Chelios, Chi.	.35
☐	143	Steve Duchesne, Stl. (Ott.)	.15
☐	144	Paul Coffey, Det.	.25
☐	145	Doug Weight, Edm.	.35
☐	146	Gord Murphy, Fla.	.15
☐	147	Andrew Cassels, Hfd.	.15
☐	148	Rob Blake, L.A.	.25
☐	149	Vladimir Malakhov, Mtl.	.15
☐	150	Scott Niedermayer, N.J.	.25
☐	151	Patrick Flatley, NYI.	.15
☐	152	Adam Graves, NYR.	.15
☐	153	Alexei Yashin, Ott.	.35
☐	154	Rod Brind'Amour, Pha.	.25
☐	155	Joe Mullen, Pgh.	.15
☐	156	Mike Ricci, Que. (Col.)	.15
☐	157	Ulf Dahlen, S.J.	.15
☐	158	Dave Manson, Wpg.	.15
☐	159	Brian Bradley, T.B.	.15
☐	160	Félix Potvin (G), Tor.	.50
☐	161	Trevor Linden, Van.	.25
☐	162	Michal Pivonka, Wsh.	.15
☐	163	Nelson Emerson, Wpg.	.15
☐	164	Joe Sacco, Ana.	.15
☐	165	Todd Elik, Stl. (Bos.)	.15
☐	166	Derek Plante, Buf.	.15
☐	167	Mike Sullivan, S.J.	.15
☐	168	Randy Wood, Tor.	.15
☐	169	Manny Fernandez (G), Dal.	.15
☐	170	Keith Primeau, Det.	.25
☐	171	Marko Tuomainen, Edm.	.15
☐	172	John Vanbiesbrouck (G), Fla.	.60
☐	173	Darren Turcotte, Wpg.	.15
☐	174	Tony Granato, L.A.	.15
☐	175	Brian Savage, Mtl.	.15
☐	176	John MacLean, N.J.	.15
☐	**177**	**Tommy Salo (G), NYI., RC**	**.15**
☐	178	Steve Larmer, NYR.	.15
☐	179	Alexandre Daigle, Ott.	.25
☐	180	Petr Svoboda, Pha.	.15
☐	181	John Cullen, T.B.	.15
☐	182	Joe Sakic, Que. (Col.)	1.00
☐	183	Sandis Ozolinsh, S.J.	.25
☐	184	Dale Hawerchuk, Buf. (Stl.)	.25
☐	185	Paul Ysebaert, T.B.	.15
☐	186	Larry Murphy, Tor.	.25
☐	187	Alexander Mogilny, Buf. (Van.)	.35
☐	188	Joé Juneau, Wsh.	.15
☐	**189**	**Craig Martin, Wpg., RC**	**.15**
☐	190	Jason Marshall, Ana.	.15
☐	191	Don Sweeney, Bos.	.15
☐	192	Ron Hextall (G), Pha.	.25
☐	193	Steve Chiasson, Cgy.	.15
☐	194	Steve Smith, Chi.	.15
☐	195	Lyle Odelein, Mtl.	.15
☐	196	Ryan Smyth, Edm.	.25
☐	197	Rob Niedermayer, Fla.	.15
☐	198	Steven Rice, Hfd.	.15
☐	199	Darryl Sydor, L.A.	.15
☐	200	Patrick Roy (G), Mtl.	2.00
☐	201	Bill Guerin, N.J.	.25
☐	202	Scott Lachance, NYI.	.15
☐	203	Alexei Kovalev, NYR.	.15
☐	204	Ronnie Stern, Cgy.	.15
☐	205	Kevin Dineen, Hfd.	.15
☐	206	Ulf Samuelsson, Pgh. (NYR.)	.15
☐	207	Wendel Clark, Tor.	.25
☐	208	Ray Whitney, S.J.	.15
☐	209	Brett Hull, Stl.	.50
☐	210	Vyacheslav Kozlov, Det.	.15
☐	211	Doug Gilmour, Tor.	.35
☐	212	Mike Ridley, Tor. (Van.)	.15
☐	**213**	**Mike Torchia (G), Dal. (Wsh.), RC**	**.15**
☐	**214**	**Tavis Hansen, Wpg., RC**	**.15**
☐	215	Dale Hunter, Wsh.	.15
☐	216	Kevin Stevens, Pgh. (Bos.)	.15
☐	217	Mike Donnelly, L.A.	.15
☐	218	Sylvain Côté, Wsh.	.15
☐	219	Gary Suter, Chi.	.15
☐	220	Checklist	.15
☐	221	Richard Park, Pgh.	.15
☐	222	Dave Gagner, Dal.	.15
☐	223	Jozef Stumpel, Bos.	.25
☐	224	Brad May, Buf.	.15
☐	225	Zarley Zalapski, Cgy.	.15
☐	226	Eric Dazé, Chi.	.25
☐	227	Mike Modano, Dal.	.50
☐	228	Nicklas Lidström, Det.	.25
☐	229	Jason Bonsignore, Edm.	.15
☐	**230**	**Robert Svehla, Fla., RC**	**.25**
☐	231	Glen Wesley, Bos.	.15
☐	232	Josef Beranek, Edm.	.15
☐	233	Geoff Courtnall, Van. (Stl.)	.15
☐	234	Shawn Chambers, N.J.	.15
☐	235	Darius Kasparaitis, NYI.	.15
☐	236	Sergei Nemchinov, NYR.	.15
☐	237	Patrick Poulin, Chi.	.15
☐	238	Anatoli Semenov, Ana.	.15
☐	239	Bryan Smolinski, Bos. (Pgh.)	.15
☐	240	Owen Nolan, Que. (Col.)	.25
☐	241	Pat Falloon, S.J.	.15
☐	242	Chris Pronger, Hfd. (Stl.)	.25
☐	243	Daren Puppa (G), T.B.	.15
☐	244	Mats Sundin, Tor.	.50
☐	245	Jeff Brown, Van.	.15
☐	246	Jeff Nelson, Wsh.	.15
☐	247	Teppo Numminen, Wpg.	.15
☐	248	Shaun Van Allen, Ana.	.15
☐	249	Yanic Perreault, L.A.	.15
☐	**250**	**Brian Holzinger, Buf., RC**	**.25**
☐	251	Paul Kruse, Cgy.	.15
☐	252	Jeff Shantz, Chi.	.15
☐	253	Martin Straka, Ott.	.15
☐	254	Chris Osgood (G), Det.	.35
☐	**255**	**Joaquin Gage (G), Edm., RC**	**.15**
☐	256	Dave Lowry, Fla.	.15
☐	257	Robert Kron, Hfd.	.15
☐	258	Dan Quinn, L.A. (Ott.)	.15
☐	259	David Wilkie, Mtl.	.15
☐	260	Valeri Zelepukin, N.J.	.15
☐	261	Derek King, NYI.	.15
☐	**262**	**Darren Langdon, NYR., RC**	**.15**
☐	263	Radek Bonk, Ott.	.15

	No.	Player	NRMT-MT
☐	264	Karl Dykhuis, Pha.	.15
☐	265	Tomas Sandström, Pgh.	.15
☐	266	Uwe Krupp, Que. (Col.)	.15
☐	267	Arturs Irbe (G), S.J.	.15
☐	268	Dallas Drake, Wpg.	.15
☐	269	John Tucker, T.B.	.15
☐	270	Dave Andreychuk, Tor.	.15
☐	271	Guy Hebert (G), Ana.	.25
☐	272	Sandy Moger, Bos.	.15
☐	273	Craig Johnson, Stl.	.15
☐	274	Donald Audette, Buf.	.15
☐	275	Cory Cross, T.B.	.15
☐	276	Richard Smehlik, Buf.	.15
☐	277	Gary Roberts, Cgy.	.25
☐	278	Todd Gill, Tor.	.15
☐	279	Derian Hatcher, Dal.	.25
☐	280	Viacheslav Fetisov, Det.	.25
☐	281	Curtis Joseph (G), Stl. (Edm.)	.60
☐	282	Johan Garpenlov, Fla.	.15
☐	283	Vladimir Konstantinov, Det.	.15
☐	284	Ray Ferraro, NYI. (NYR.)	.15
☐	285	Turner Stevenson, Mtl.	.15
☐	286	Neal Broten, N.J.	.15
☐	**287**	**Jason Widmer, NYI., RC**	**.15**
☐	288	Mattias Norstrom, NYR.	.15
☐	289	Michel Picard, Ott.	.15
☐	290	Brent Fedyk, Pha.	.15
☐	291	Dmitri Yushkevich, Pha. (Tor.)	.15
☐	292	Sylvain Lefebvre, Que. (Col.)	.15
☐	293	Sergei Makarov, S.J.	.15
☐	294	Brian Rolston, N.J.	.15
☐	295	Roman Hamrlik, T.B.	.15
☐	**296**	**Mark Wotton, Van., RC**	**.15**
☐	297	Alek Stojanov, Van.	.15
☐	298	Calle Johansson, Wsh.	.15
☐	299	Mike Eastwood, Wpg.	.15
☐	300	Bob Corkum, Ana.	.15
☐	301	Petr Nedved, NYR. (Pgh.)	.15
☐	302	Vincent Damphousse, Mtl.	.35
☐	**303**	**Brett Harkins, Bos. (Fla.), RC**	**.15**
☐	304	Paul Kariya, Ana.	1.50
☐	305	Joe Nieuwendyk, Dal.	.25
☐	**306**	**Dennis Bonvie, Edm., RC**	**.15**
☐	307	Jason Woolley, Fla.	.15
☐	308	Jimmy Carson, Hfd.	.15
☐	309	Marty McSorley, L.A.	.15
☐	**310**	**Craig Rivet, Mtl., RC**	**.15**
☐	311	Claude Lemieux, N.J.	.15
☐	312	Al MacInnis, Stl.	.15
☐	313	Gino Diduck, Chi. (Hfd.)	.15
☐	314	Randy McKay, N.J.	.15
☐	315	Bob Errey, Det.	.15
☐	**316**	**Rusty Fitzgerald, Pgh., RC**	**.15**
☐	317	Scott Young, Que.	.15
☐	318	Igor Larionov, Det.	.25
☐	319	Esa Tikkanen, Stl.	.15
☐	320	Darren McCarty, Det.	.15
☐	321	Petr Klima, T.B.	.15
☐	322	Jon Rohloff, Bos.	.15
☐	323	Steve Konowalchuk, Wsh.	.15
☐	324	Milos Holan, Ana.	.15
☐	325	Checklist	.15
☐	326	Ted Donato, Bos.	.15
☐	327	Grant Marshall, Dal.	.15
☐	328	Jyrki Lumme, Van.	.15
☐	329	Ed Belfour (G), Chi.	.35
☐	330	Checklist	.15

FIRE ON ICE

These cards are serial numbered out of 10,000.

Insert Set (12 cards): 185.00

	No.	Player	NRMT-MT
☐	1	Pavel Bure, Van.	18.00
☐	2	Eric Lindros, Pha.	30.00
☐	3	Alexei Zhamnov, Wpg.	6.00
☐	4	Paul Coffey, Det.	6.00
☐	5	Theoren Fleury, Cgy.	8.00
☐	6	Peter Forsberg, Que.	25.00
☐	7	Sergei Fedorov, Det.	12.00
☐	8	Mats Sundin, Tor.	12.00
☐	9	Brett Hull, Stl.	12.00
☐	10	Wayne Gretzky, L.A.	50.00
☐	11	Paul Kariya, Ana.	30.00
☐	12	Mikael Renberg, Pha.	6.00

FREEZE FRAME

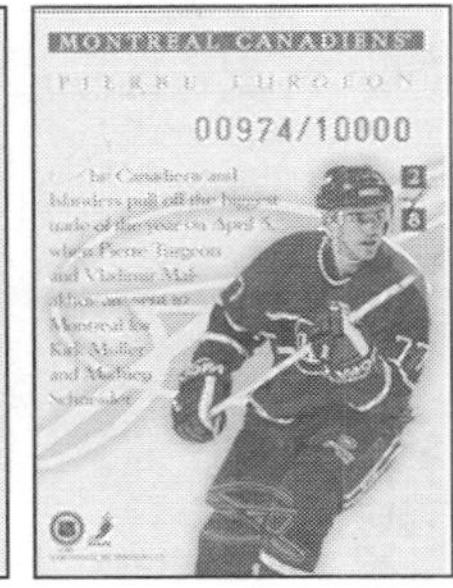

Insert Set (8 cards): 140.00

	No.	Player	NRMT-MT
☐	1	Jim Carey (G), Wsh.	8.00
☐	2	Pierre Turgeon, Mtl. (XCX: Vladimir Malaklov)	10.00
☐	3	Mikael Renberg, Pha.	8.00
☐	4	Jaromir Jagr, Pgh.	35.00
☐	5	Alexei Zhamnov, Wpg.	10.00
☐	6	New Jersey Devils	15.00
☐	7	Mario Lemieux, Pgh.	60.00
☐	8	Alexander Mogilny (XCX: Pavel Bure)	18.00

GOLD LEAF STARS

These retail pack inserts are serial numbered out of 5,000.

Insert Set (6 cards): 125.00

	No.	Player	NRMT-MT
☐	1	Dominik Hasek/Jim Carey	30.00
☐	2	Paul Coffey/Chris Chelios	10.00
☐	3	Ray Bourque/Brian Leetch	15.00
☐	4	Eric Lindros/Alexei Zhamnov	50.00
☐	5	Jaromir Jagr/Theoren Fleury	30.00
☐	6	Brett Hull/Mikael Renberg	15.00

LEMIEUX'S BEST

Insert Set (10 cards): 60.00

	No.	Player	NRMT-MT
☐	1	Mario Lemieux	7.00
☐	2	Mario Lemieux (XCY: Wayne Gretzky)	8.00
☐	3	Mario Lemieux	7.00
☐	4	Mario Lemieux	7.00
☐	5	Mario Lemieux	7.00
☐	6	Mario Lemieux	7.00
☐	7	Mario Lemieux (w/Chris Chelios)	7.00
☐	8	Mario Lemieux (w/Cup)	7.00
☐	9	Mario Lemieux	7.00
☐	10	Mario Lemieux	7.00

ROAD TO THE CUP

These hobby pack inserts are serial numbered out of 5000.

Insert Set (10 cards): 165.00

	No.	Player	NRMT-MT
☐	1	Ray Whitney, S.J.	5.00
☐	2	Martin Brodeur (G), N.J.	30.00
☐	3	Jaromir Jagr, Pgh.	45.00
☐	4	Eric Lindros, Pha.	65.00
☐	5	Paul Coffey, Det.	8.00
☐	6	Chris Chelios, Chi. (XCX: Pavel Bure)	15.00
☐	7	Neal Broten, N.J.	5.00
☐	8	Vyacheslav Kozlov, Det.	5.00
☐	9	Scott Niedermayer, N.J.	8.00
☐	10	Claude Lemieux, N.J.	5.00

STUDIO ROOKIES

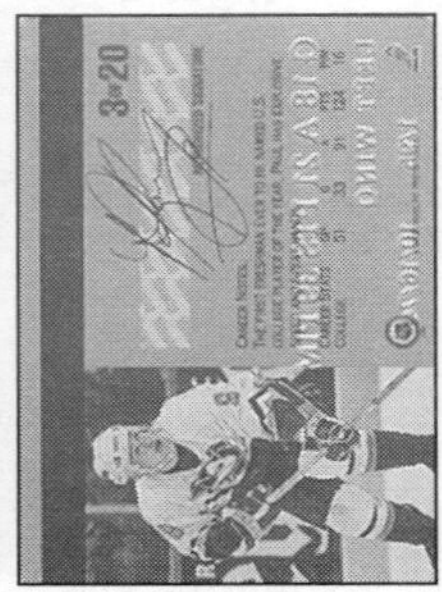

Insert Set (20 cards): 50.00

	No.	Player	NRMT-MT
☐	1	Jim Carey (G), Wsh.	2.00
☐	2	Peter Forsberg, Que.	7.50
☐	3	Paul Kariya, Ana.	10.00
☐	4	David Oliver, Edm.	2.00
☐	5	Blaine Lacher (G), Bos.	2.00
☐	6	Oleg Tverdovsky, Ana.	2.00
☐	7	Jeff Friesen, S.J.	3.00
☐	8	Todd Marchant, Edm.	2.00
☐	9	Todd Harvey, Dal.	2.00
☐	10	Ian Laperrière, Stl.	2.00
☐	11	Eric Dazé, Chi.	3.00
☐	12	Jason Bonsignore, Edm.	2.00
☐	13	Jamie Storr (G), L.A.	3.00
☐	14	Brian Holzinger, Buf.	2.00
☐	15	Brian Savage, Mtl.	2.00
☐	16	Roman Oksiuta, Van.	2.00
☐	17	Mariusz Czerkawski, Bos.	2.00
☐	18	Sergei Krivokrasov, Chi.	2.00
☐	19	Jason Wiemer, T.B.	2.00
☐	20	Radek Bonk, Ott.	2.00

1995 - 96 LEAF ELIT SET

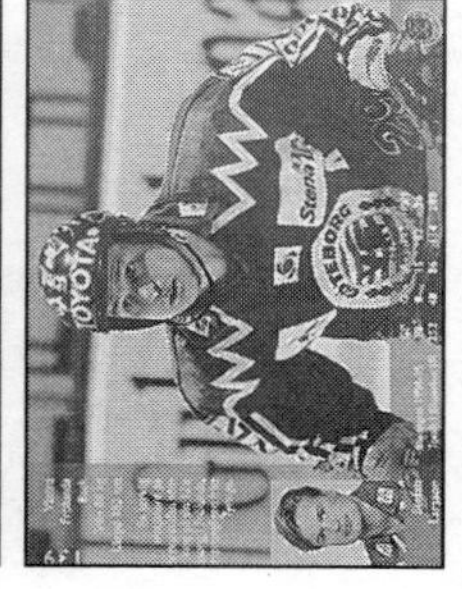

Imprint:
Series One Set (150 cards): 30.00
Series Two Set (160 cards): 30.00
Common Player: .20

	No.	Player	NRMT-MT
☐	1	Hakan Loob	.50
☐	2	AIK logo/checklist	.20
☐	3	AIK stats	.20
☐	4	Joakim Persson (G)	.25
☐	5	Niclas Havelid	.20
☐	6	Tony Barthelsson	.20
☐	7	Patric Aberg	.20
☐	8	Johan Akerman	.20
☐	9	Dick Tarnstrom	.20
☐	10	Stefan Gustavson	.20
☐	11	Anders Gozzi	.20
☐	12	Morgan Samuelsson	.20
☐	13	BRYNAS logo/checklist	.20
☐	14	BRYNAS stats	.20
☐	15	Michael Sundlov (G)	.25
☐	16	Stefan Klockare	.20
☐	17	Bedrich Scerban	.20
☐	18	Andreas Dackell	.50
☐	19	Fredrik Modin	.50
☐	20	Ove Molin	.20
☐	21	Mikael Wahlberg	.20
☐	22	Thomas Tallberg	.20
☐	23	Peter Larsson	.20
☐	24	Stefan Ketola	.20
☐	25	DJURGARDENS Logo/CL	.20
☐	26	DJURGARDENS stats	.20
☐	27	Jonas Forsberg (G)	.25
☐	28	Christian Due-Boje	.20
☐	29	Mikael Magnusson	.20
☐	30	Thomas Johansson	.20
☐	31	Joakim Musakka	.20
☐	32	Erik Huusko	.20
☐	33	Jens Ohling	.20
☐	34	Per Eklund	.20
☐	35	Espen Knutsen	.50
☐	36	Patrik Erickson	.20
☐	37	FARJESTADS logo/CL	.20
☐	38	FARJESTADS stats	.20
☐	39	Patrik Haltia (G)	.25
☐	40	Sergei Fokin	.20
☐	41	Thomas Rhodin	.20
☐	42	Stefan Nilsson	.20
☐	43	Magnus Arvedsson	.20
☐	44	Mattias Johansson	.20
☐	45	Clas Eriksson	.20
☐	46	Peter Ottosson	.20
☐	47	HV71 logo/checklist	.20
☐	48	HV71 stats	.20
☐	49	Boo Ahl (G)	.25
☐	50	Kenneth Kennholt	.20
☐	51	Hans Abrahamsson	.20
☐	52	Peter Hammarstrom	.20
☐	53	Johan Davidsson	.25
☐	54	Stefan Falk	.20
☐	55	Johan Lindbom	.20
☐	56	Esa Keskinen	.25
☐	57	Stefan Ornskog	.20
☐	58	Peter Ekelund	.20
☐	59	LEKSAND logo/checklist	.20
☐	60	LEKSAND stats	.20
☐	61	Johan Hedberg (G)	.25
☐	62	Tomas Jonsson	.20
☐	63	Hans Lodin	.20
☐	64	Orjan Lindmark	.20
☐	65	Jan Huokko	.20
☐	66	Markus Eriksson	.20
☐	67	Andreas Karlsson	.20
☐	68	Mikael Holmberg	.20
☐	69	Jonas Bergqvist	.20
☐	70	Nicklas Eriksson	.20
☐	71	Per-Erik Eklund	.20
☐	72	LULEA logo/checklist	.20
☐	73	LULEA stats	.20
☐	74	Jarmo Myllys (G)	.50
☐	75	Mattias Ohlund	2.00
☐	76	Lars Modig	.20
☐	77	Torbjorn Lindberg	.20
☐	78	Roger Akerstrom	.20
☐	79	Stefan Jonsson	.20
☐	80	Johan Rosen	.20
☐	81	Tomas Berglund	.20
☐	82	Robert Nordberg	.20
☐	83	Jiri Kucera	.20
☐	84	Thomas Holmstrom	.50
☐	85	MALMO logo/checklist	.20
☐	86	MALMO stats	.20
☐	87	Peter Andersson	.20
☐	88	Roger Ohman	.20
☐	89	Marcus Magnertoft	.20
☐	90	Patrik Sylvegard	.20
☐	91	Hakan Ahlund	.20
☐	92	Jesper Matsson	.25
☐	93	Roger Hansson	.20
☐	94	Mattias Bosson	.20
☐	95	Bo Svanberg	.20
☐	96	Raimo Helminen	.20
☐	97	MoDo logo/checklist	.20
☐	98	MoDo stats	.20
☐	99	Petter Ronnqvist (G)	.25
☐	100	Lars Jansson	.25
☐	101	Mattias Timmander	.25
☐	102	Hans Jonsson	.20
☐	103	Anders Soderberg	.20
☐	104	Martin Hostak	.20
☐	105	Kyosti Karjalainen	.20
☐	106	Mikael Hakansson	.20
☐	107	Per Svartvadet	.20
☐	108	Andreas Salomonsson	.20
☐	109	Lars Bystrom	.20
☐	110	Magnus Wernblom	.20
☐	111	ROGLE logo/checklist	.20
☐	112	ROGLE stats	.20
☐	113	Magnus Sward (G)	.25
☐	114	Arto Ruotanen	.20
☐	115	Johan Finnstrom	.20
☐	116	Daniel Tjarnqvist	.20
☐	117	Pierre Johnsson	.20
☐	118	Per Wallin	.20
☐	119	Michael Johansson	.20
☐	120	Per-Johan Svensson	.20
☐	121	Roger Elvenes	.20
☐	122	Mats Loov	.20
☐	123	Michael Hjalm	.20
☐	124	VASTERAS logo/CL	.20
☐	125	VASTERAS stats	.20
☐	126	Mats Ytter (G)	.25
☐	127	Erik Bergstrom	.20
☐	128	Lars Ivarsson	.20
☐	129	Mishat Fahrutdinov	.20
☐	130	Claes Lindblom	.20
☐	131	Paul Andersson	.20
☐	132	Henrik Nordfeldt	.20
☐	133	Alexei Salomatin	.20
☐	134	Mikael Pettersson	.20
☐	135	FROLUNDA logo/CL	.20
☐	136	FROLUNDA stats	.20
☐	137	Hakan Algotsson (G)	.25
☐	138	Jonas Andersson-Junkka	.20
☐	139	Stefan Larsson	.20
☐	140	Par Djoos	.20
☐	141	Ronnie Sundin	.20
☐	142	Par Edlund	.20
☐	143	Peter Berndtsson	.20
☐	144	Joacim Esbjors	.20
☐	145	Alexander Beljavski	.20
☐	146	Jonas Esbjors	.20
☐	147	Marku Jantunen	.20
☐	148	Peter Strom	.20
☐	149	Checklist 1-75	.20
☐	150	Checklist 76-150	.20
☐	151	AIK	.20
☐	152	Tommy Lehmann Captains	.20
☐	153	Mikael Nilsson	.20
☐	154	Juha Jokiharju	.20
☐	155	Stefan Andersson	.20
☐	156	Thomas Strandberg	.20
☐	157	Mats Lindberg	.20
☐	158	Peter Gerhardsson	.20
☐	159	Tommy Lehmann	.20
☐	160	Tommy Hedlund	.20
☐	161	Peter Wallin	.20
☐	162	Bjorn Ahlstrom	.20
☐	163	Erik Hamalainen	.20
☐	164	Patric Englund	.20
☐	165	Rikard Franzen	.20
☐	166	Brynas IF	.20
☐	167	Brynas, Captains	.20
☐	168	Lars Karlsson	.20
☐	169	Jonas Lofstrom	.20
☐	170	Stefan Polla	.20
☐	171	Mikael Lind	.20
☐	172	Brian Rafalski	.20
☐	173	Roger Kyro	.20
☐	174	Per-Johan Johansson	.20
☐	175	Greg Parks	.20
☐	176	Per Lofstrom	.20
☐	177	Jonas Johnson	.20
☐	178	Mikael Lindman	.20
☐	179	Mikael Wiklander	.20
☐	180	Tommy Melkersson	.20
☐	181	Djugardens IF	.20
☐	182	Djugardens, Captains	.20
☐	183	Thomas Ostlund	.20
☐	184	Patrik Hofbauer	.20
☐	185	Magnus Jansson	.20
☐	186	Niklas Falk	.20
☐	187	Ola Josefsson	.20
☐	188	Joakim Lundberg	.20
☐	189	Fredrik Lindquist	.20
☐	190	Patrik Kjellberg	.20
☐	191	Jan Viktorsson	.20
☐	192	Bjorn Nord	.20
☐	193	Tommy Jacobsen	.20
☐	194	Anders Huusko	.20
☐	195	Kristofer Ottosson	.20
☐	196	Vastra Frolunda HC	.20
☐	197	Frolunda, Captains	.20
☐	198	Mikael Sanberg	.20
☐	199	Jerry Persson	.20
☐	200	Peter Hogardh	.20
☐	201	Stefan Axelsson	.20
☐	202	Lars Edstrom	.20
☐	203	Lars-Goran Wiklander	.20
☐	204	Per-Johan Axelsson	.20
☐	205	Henrik Nilsson	.20
☐	206	Petteri Nummelin	.20
☐	207	Christian Ruuttu	.20
☐	208	Oscar Ackerstrom	.20
☐	209	Farjestad BK	.20
☐	210	Farjestad, Captains	.20
☐	211	Markus Ketterer (G)	.25
☐	212	Bjorn Eriksson	.20
☐	213	Jonas Hoglund	.25
☐	214	Peter Nordstrom	.20
☐	215	Jorgen Jonsson	.20
☐	216	Greger Artursson	.20
☐	217	Jesper Duus	.20
☐	218	Roger Johansson	.20
☐	219	Leif Carlsson	.20
☐	220	Per Lundell	.20
☐	221	Vitali Prokhorov	.20
☐	222	HV71	.20
☐	223	HV 71, Captains	.20
☐	224	Kennth Johansson	.20
☐	225	Thomas Gustavsson	.20
☐	226	Marcus Thuresson	.20
☐	227	Vesa Salo	.20
☐	228	Kai Nurminen	.25
☐	229	Johan Brummer	.20
☐	230	Daniel Johansson	.20
☐	231	Per Gustafsson	.50
☐	232	Niklas Rahm	.20
☐	233	Leksands IF	.20

	No.	Player	Price
☐	234	Leksands, Captains	.20
☐	235	Per-Ragnar Bergkvist	.20
☐	236	Anders Carlsson	.20
☐	237	Micael Karlberg	.20
☐	238	Torgny Lowgren	.20
☐	239	Stefan Hellkvist	.20
☐	240	Markus Akerblom	.20
☐	241	Joakim Lindgren	.20
☐	242	Tomas Forslund	.20
☐	243	Torbjorn Johansson	.20
☐	244	Nicklas Nordquist	.20
☐	245	Lulea HF	.20
☐	246	Lulea, Captains	.20
☐	247	Erik Grankvist	.20
☐	248	Mikael Lindholm	.20
☐	249	Johan Stromvall	.20
☐	250	Anders Burstrom	.20
☐	251	Lars Hurtig	.20
☐	252	Stefan Nilsson	.20
☐	253	Jan Mertzig	.20
☐	254	Petter Nilsson	.20
☐	255	Malmo IF	.20
☐	256	Malmo IF, Captains	.20
☐	257	Peter Lindmark	.20
☐	258	Roger Nordstrom	.20
☐	259	Andres Lilja	.20
☐	260	Brian McReynolds	.20
☐	261	Ilja Byakin	.20
☐	262	Robert Burakovsky	.25
☐	263	Mikael Burakovsky	.20
☐	264	Stafn Elvenes	.20
☐	265	Johan Salle	.20
☐	266	Kim Johnsson	.20
☐	267	Peter Hasselblad	.20
☐	268	Marko Palo	.20
☐	269	MoDo Hockey	.20
☐	270	MoDo, Captains	.20
☐	271	Fredrik Andersson	.20
☐	272	Frantisek Kaberle	.20
☐	273	Samuel Pahlsson	.20
☐	274	Jan Larsson	.20
☐	275	Per-Anton Lundstrom	.20
☐	276	Tomas Nansen	.20
☐	277	Marcus Karlsson	.20
☐	278	Jan-Axel Alavaara	.20
☐	279	Kristian Gahn	.20
☐	280	Rogle BK	.20
☐	281	Rogle, Captains	.20
☐	282	Patrick Backlund	.20
☐	283	Peter Lundmark	.20
☐	284	Anders Berglund	.20
☐	285	Harijs Vitolins	.20
☐	286	Jens Nielsen	.20
☐	287	Greg Brown	.20
☐	288	Bjorn Linden	.20
☐	289	Vasteras IK	.20
☐	290	Vasteras, Captains	.20
☐	291	Jacob Karlsson	.20
☐	292	Patrik Zetterberg	.20
☐	293	Mattias Loof	.20
☐	294	Johan Tornberg	.20
☐	295	Andrei Korolev	.20
☐	296	Mattias Olsson	.20
☐	297	Roger Rosen	.20
☐	298	Andrei Lulin	.20
☐	299	Edvin Frylen	.25
☐	300	Mats Lusth	.20
☐	301	Fredrik Oberg	.20
☐	302	AS: Jarmo Myllys (G)	.50
☐	303	AS: Tomas Jonsson	.50
☐	304	AS: Peter Andersson	.25
☐	305	AS: Hakan Loob	.50
☐	306	AS: Esa Keskinen	.25
☐	307	AS: Christian Ruuttu	.25
☐	308	Checklist 151-230	.20
☐	309	Checklist 231-310	.20
☐	310	Checklist Inserts	.20

GOLDIES

Series One Insert Set (10 cards): 40.00

	No.	Player	NRMT-MT
☐	1	Morgan Samuelsson	5.00
☐	2	Ove Molin	5.00
☐	3	Fredrik Lindqvist	5.00
☐	4	Peter Strom	5.00
☐	5	Mattias Johansson	5.00
☐	6	Stefan Ornskog	5.00
☐	7	Niklas Eriksson	5.00
☐	8	Johan Rosen	5.00
☐	9	Roger Ohman	5.00
☐	10	Anders Soderberg	5.00

LEAF MEGA

Series One Insert Set (15 cards): 100.00

	No.	Player	NRMT-MT
☐	1	Michael Sundlov (G)	8.00
☐	2	Jonas Bergqvist	6.00
☐	3	Marko Jantunen	6.00
☐	4	Thomas Ostlund	6.00
☐	5	Tomas Jonsson	6.00
☐	6	Esa Keskinen	7.00
☐	7	Roger Nordstrom	6.00
☐	8	Mattias Ohlund	15.00
☐	9	Hakan Loob	10.00
☐	10	Raimo Helminen	6.00
☐	11	Per-Erik Eklund	8.00
☐	12	Jarmo Myllys (G)	8.00
☐	13	Rikard Franzen	6.00
☐	14	Christer Olsson	6.00
☐	15	Per Gustafsson	7.00

SPIDERMEN

Series Insert Set (14 cards): 90.00

	No.	Player	NRMT-MT
☐	1	Joakim Persson (G)	6.00
☐	2	Michael Sundlov (G)	6.00
☐	3	Thomas Ostlund (G)	6.00
☐	4	Hakan Algotsson (G)	6.00
☐	5	Patrik Haltia (G)	6.00
☐	6	Boo Ahl (G)	6.00
☐	7	Johan Hedberg (G)	6.00
☐	8	Jarmo Myllys (G)	10.00
☐	9	Jonas Forsberg (G)	6.00
☐	10	Petter Ronnqvist (G)	6.00
☐	11	Magnus Swardh (G)	6.00
☐	12	Mats Ytter (G)	6.00
☐	13	Mikael Sandberg (G)	6.00
☐	14	Roger Nordstrom (G)	6.00

CHAMPS

This series is serial numbered out of 3,000.

Series Two Insert Set (15 cards): 60.00

	No.	Player	NRMT-MT
☐	1	Tomas Jonsson	5.00
☐	2	Patrik Kjellberg	5.00
☐	3	Hakan Loob	8.00
☐	4	Peter Lindmark	5.00
☐	5	Anders Carlsson	5.00
☐	6	Raimo Helminen	5.00
☐	7	Esa Keskinen	6.00
☐	8	Jan Larsson	5.00
☐	9	Roger Johansson	5.00
☐	10	Andreas Dackell	6.00
☐	11	Stefan Ornskog	5.00
☐	12	Michael Sundlov	5.00
☐	13	Per-Erik Eklund	6.00
☐	14	Kenneth Kennholt	5.00
☐	15	Jan Viktorsson	5.00

FACE TO FACE

Series Two Insert Set (15 cards): 40.00

	No.	Player	NRMT-MT
☐	1	Morgan Samuelsson/Thomas Strandberg	3.00
☐	2	Bedrich Scerban/Greg Parks	3.00
☐	3	Erik Huusko/Anders Huusko	3.00
☐	4	Stefan Larsson/Marko Jantunen	3.00
☐	5	Hakan Loob/Roger Johansson	5.00
☐	6	Kenneth Kennholt/Per Gustafsson	4.00
☐	7	Stefan Hellkvist/Tomas Forslund	3.00
☐	8	Thomas Holmstrom/Roger Akerstrom	3.00
☐	9	Stefan Elvenes/Robert Burakovsky	3.00
☐	10	Martin Hostak/Mattias Timander	4.00
☐	11	Mats Loov/Michael Hjalm	3.00
☐	12	Alexei Salomatin/Fredrik Oberg	3.00
☐	13	Patrik Erickson/Espen Knutsen	4.00
☐	14	Peter Andersson/Peter Hasselblad	3.00
☐	15	Tomas Jonsson/Markus Akerblom	3.00

ROOKIES

Series Two Insert Set (9 cards): 30.00

	No.	Player	NRMT-MT
☐	1	Peter Wallin	4.00
☐	2	Jan-Axel Alavaara	4.00
☐	3	Niklas Falk	4.00
☐	4	Lars-Goran Wiklander	4.00
☐	5	Torbjorn Johansson	4.00
☐	6	Jan Mertzig	4.00
☐	7	Mikael Burakovsky	4.00
☐	8	Marcus Karlsson	4.00
☐	9	Roger Rosen	4.00

SUPER CHASE

	No.	Player	NRMT-MT
☐		Per-Erik Eklund	30.00
☐	HV71	Swedish Champions (#/2000)	25.00

1995 - 96 LEAF LIMITED

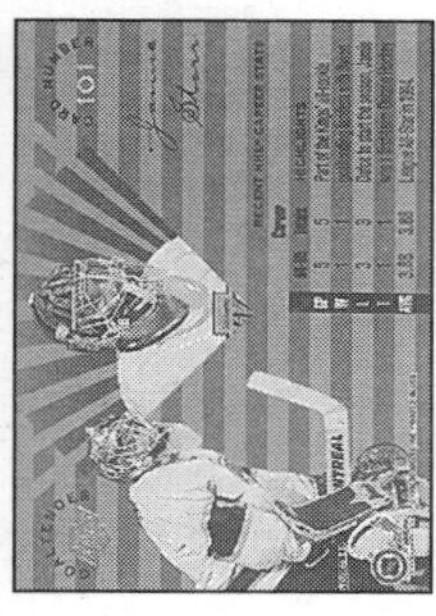

Imprint: © 1996 DONUSS, INC.
Complete Set (120 cards): 75.00
Common Player: .35

	No.	Player	NRMT-MT
☐	1	Mario Lemieux, Pgh.	8.00
☐	2	Peter Forsberg, Col.	5.00
☐	3	Geoff Courtnall, Stl.	.35
☐	4	Vincent Damphousse, Mtl.	1.50
☐	5	Jason Allison, Wsh.	1.50
☐	6	Theoren Fleury, Cgy.	1.50
☐	**7**	**Shane Doan, Wpg., RC**	**.50**
☐	8	Chris Gratton, T.B.	.75
☐	9	Paul Kariya, Ana.	6.50
☐	**10**	**Radek Dvorak, Fla., RC**	**.50**
☐	11	Adam Graves, NYR.	.35
☐	12	Donald Audette, Buf.	.35
☐	13	Craig Janney, S.J.	.35
☐	14	Sean Burke (G), Hfd.	.75
☐	15	Ed Belfour (G), Chi.	1.50
☐	16	Ray Bourque, Bos.	2.50
☐	17	Pavel Bure, Van.	3.50
☐	18	Martin Brodeur (G), N.J.	3.50
☐	**19**	**Todd Bertuzzi, NYI., RC**	**.75**
☐	**20**	**Aki Berg, L.A., RC**	**.35**
☐	21	Dave Andreychuk, Tor.	.35
☐	22	Jason Arnott, Edm.	.75
☐	23	Ron Francis, Pgh.	1.50
☐	24	Paul Coffey, Det.	.75
☐	**25**	**Daniel Alfredsson, Ott., RC**	**3.00**
☐	26	Todd Harvey, Dal.	.35
☐	27	Claude Lemieux, N.J.	.35
☐	28	Brett Hull, Stl.	2.50
☐	29	Félix Potvin (G), Tor.	2.50
☐	30	Peter Bondra, Wsh.	2.00
☐	31	Trevor Kidd (G), Cgy.	.75
☐	32	Igor Korolev, Wpg.	.35
☐	33	Roman Hamrlik, T.B.	.75
☐	**34**	**Chad Kilger, Ana., RC**	**.50**
☐	35	Rob Niedermayer, Fla.	.75
☐	36	Richard Park, Pgh.	.35
☐	**37**	**Mathieu Dandenault, Det., RC**	**.50**
☐	38	Alexandre Daigle, Ott.	.75
☐	39	Jere Lehtinen, Dal.	.75
☐	40	Chris Chelios, Chi.	2.00
☐	41	Blaine Lacher (G), Bos.	.35
☐	42	Trevor Linden, Van.	.75
☐	43	Scott Niedermayer, N.J.	.75
☐	44	Teemu Selänne, Wpg.	3.50
☐	**45**	**Daymond Langkow, T.B., RC**	**.50**
☐	46	Oleg Tverdovsky, Wpg.	.35
☐	47	John Vanbiesbrouck (G), Fla.	3.00
☐	48	Alexei Kovalev, NYR.	.35
☐	49	Sergei Fedorov, Det.	2.50
☐	50	Alexei Yashin, Ott.	2.00
☐	51	Mike Modano, Dal.	2.50
☐	52	Sandis Ozolinsh, Col.	.75
☐	53	Ian Laperrière, Stl.	.35
☐	54	Mark Recchi, Mtl.	.75
☐	55	Jim Carey (G), Wsh.	.75
☐	56	Joe Nieuwendyk, Dal.	.75
☐	57	Keith Tkachuk, Wpg.	2.00
☐	58	Daren Puppa (G), T.B.	.35
☐	59	Jason Bonsignore, Edm.	.35
☐	60	Tomas Sandström, Pgh.	.35
☐	61	Chris Osgood (G), Det.	2.00
☐	62	Jeff Friesen, S.J.	.75
☐	63	Jeff O'Neill, Hfd.	.75
☐	64	Joe Sakic, Col.	4.00
☐	65	Eric Dazé, Chi.	.75
☐	66	Patrick Roy (G), Col.	8.00
☐	67	Kirk McLean (G), Van.	.75
☐	68	Stéphane Richer, N.J.	.35
☐	69	Rod Brind'Amour, Pha.	.75
☐	70	Wendel Clark, Tor.	.75
☐	71	Rob Blake, L.A.	.75
☐	72	Doug Gilmour, Tor.	1.50
☐	73	Jaromir Jagr, Pgh.	5.00
☐	74	Sergei Zubov, Pgh.	.75
☐	75	Mark Messier, NYR.	2.50
☐	76	Dominik Hasek (G), Buf.	3.50
☐	77	Viktor Kozlov, S.J.	.35
☐	**78**	**Marcus Ragnarsson, S.J., RC**	**.50**
☐	79	Jocelyn Thibault (G), Mtl.	1.50
☐	80	Jeremy Roenick, Chi.	1.50
☐	81	Cam Neely, Bos.	.75
☐	82	Brian Savage, Mtl.	.35
☐	83	Alexander Mogilny, Van.	1.50
☐	84	Steve Thomas, N.J.	.35
☐	85	John LeClair, Pha.	2.50
☐	86	Brett Lindros, NYI.	.35
☐	87	Wayne Gretzky, L.A.	10.00
☐	88	Kenny Jonsson, NYI.	.35
☐	89	David Oliver, Edm.	.35
☐	90	Brian Leetch, NYR.	1.50
☐	91	Luc Robitaille, NYR.	.75
☐	92	Keith Primeau, Det.	.75
☐	93	Owen Nolan, S.J.	.75
☐	94	Brendan Shanahan, Hfd.	3.00
☐	95	Al MacInnis, Stl.	.35
☐	96	Kevin Stevens, Bos.	.35
☐	97	Larry Murphy, Tor.	.75
☐	98	Joé Juneau, Wsh.	.35
☐	99	Eric Lindros, Pha.	6.50
☐	100	Travis Green, NYI.	.35
☐	101	Jamie Storr (G), L.A.	.75
☐	102	Pierre Turgeon, Mtl.	.75
☐	103	Bill Ranford (G), Edm.	.75
☐	104	Niklas Sundstrom, NYR.	.35
☐	105	Steve Yzerman, Det.	5.00
☐	106	Ray Sheppard, S.J.	.35
☐	107	Chris Pronger, Stl.	.75
☐	108	Adam Oates, Bos.	1.50
☐	109	Mike Gartner, Tor.	.75
☐	110	Doug Weight, Edm.	1.50
☐	111	Jason Dawe, Buf.	.35
☐	112	Rick Tocchet, L.A.	.35
☐	113	Pat LaFontaine, Buf.	.75
☐	114	Scott Mellanby, Fla.	.35
☐	115	Vitali Yachmenev, L.A.	.35
☐	116	Alexei Zhamnov, Wpg.	.75
☐	117	Brendan Witt, Wsh.	.35
☐	118	Saku Koivu, Mtl.	3.50
☐	119	Mikael Renberg, Pha.	.35
☐	120	Mats Sundin, Tor.	2.50
☐		CL: M.Lemieux/E.Lindros	1.00

STARS OF THE GAME

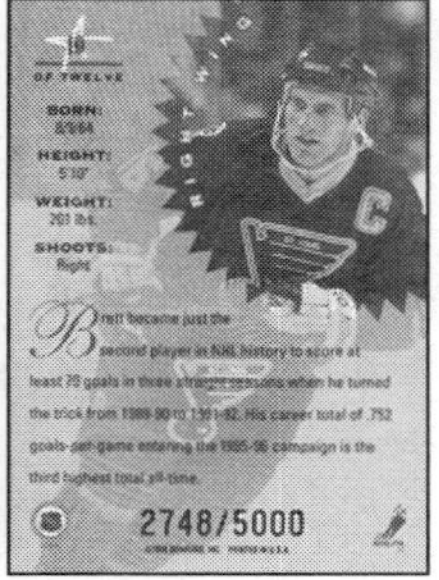

This series is serial numbered out of 5,000. Promo versions supposedly exist.

Insert Set (12 cards): 145.00

	No.	Player	NRMT-MT
☐	1	Mario Lemieux, Pgh.	25.00
☐	2	Eric Lindros, Pha.	20.00
☐	3	Wayne Gretzky, L.A.	30.00
☐	4	Peter Forsberg, Col.	15.00
☐	5	Paul Kariya, Ana.	20.00
☐	6	Alexander Mogilny, Van.	5.00
☐	7	Teemu Selänne, Wpg.	10.00
☐	8	Jaromir Jagr, Pgh.	15.00
☐	9	Mats Sundin, Tor.	7.50
☐	10	Brett Hull, Stl.	7.50
☐	11	Sergei Fedorov, Det.	7.50
☐	12	Jeremy Roenick, Chi.	5.00

ROOKIE PHENOMS

This series is serial numbered out of 5,000.

Insert Set (10 cards): 85.00

	No.	Player	NRMT-MT
☐	1	Marcus Ragnarsson, S.J.	5.00
☐	2	Daniel Alfredsson, Ott.	20.00
☐	3	Chad Kilger, Ana.	5.00
☐	4	Niklas Sundstrom, NYR.	5.00
☐	5	Vitali Yachmenev, L.A.	5.00
☐	6	Eric Dazé, Chi.	10.00
☐	7	Radek Dvorak, Fla.	5.00
☐	8	Jeff O'Neill, Hfd.	10.00
☐	9	Saku Koivu, Mtl.	25.00
☐	10	Todd Bertuzzi, NYI.	10.00

STICK SIDE

This series is serial numbered out of 2,500.

Insert Set (8 cards): 220.00

	No.	Player	NRMT-MT
☐	1	Jim Carey (G), Wsh.	15.00
☐	2	Martin Brodeur (G), N.J.	35.00
☐	3	Félix Potvin (G), Tor.	25.00
☐	4	Patrick Roy (G), Col.	80.00
☐	5	Dominik Hasek (G), Buf.	35.00
☐	6	John Vanbiesbrouck (G), Fla.	30.00
☐	7	Ron Hextall (G), Pha.	15.00
☐	8	Ed Belfour (G), Chi.	18.00

1995 - 96 MCDONALD'S - PINNACLE

Imprint:
Complete Set (41 cards): 22.00

	No.	Player	NRMT-MT
☐		Checklist/Joe Sakic, Col.	.75

No.	Player	Price
□ McD-01	Jaromir Jagr, Pgh.	2.00
□ McD-02	Eric Lindros, Pha.	2.50
□ McD-03	Alexei Zhamnov, Wpg.	.35
□ McD-04	Paul Coffey, Det.	.35
□ McD-05	Mark Messier, NYR.	1.00
□ McD-06	Brett Hull, Stl.	1.00
□ McD-07	Peter Forsberg, Col.	2.00
□ McD-08	Pavel Bure, Van.	1.50
□ McD-09	Doug Gilmour, Tor.	.50
□ McD-10	Owen Nolan, S.J.	.35
□ McD-11	Paul Kariya, Ana.	2.50
□ McD-12	Joe Nieuwendyk, Cgy.	.35
□ McD-13	Pierre Turgeon, Mtl.	.35
□ McD-14	Jason Arnott, Edm.	.35
□ McD-15	Mario Lemieux, Pgh.	3.00
□ McD-16	Jeremy Roenick, Chi.	.50
□ McD-17	Sergei Fedorov, Det.	1.00
□ McD-18	Mats Sundin, Tor.	1.00
□ McD-19	Teemu Selänne, Wpg.	1.50
□ McD-20	John LeClair, Pha.	1.00
□ McD-21	Alexander Mogilny, Van.	.50
□ McD-22	Mikael Renberg, Pha.	.35
□ McD-23	Chris Chelios, Chi.	.75
□ McD-24	Mark Recchi, Mtl.	.35
□ McD-25	Patrick Roy (G), Mtl.	3.00
□ McD-26	Félix Potvin (G), Tor.	1.00
□ McD-27	Martin Brodeur (G), N.J.	1.50
□ McD-28	Dominik Hasek (G), Buf.	1.50
□ McD-29	Ed Belfour (G), Chi.	.50
□ McD-30	Kirk McLean (G), Van.	.35
□ McD-31	Jeff Friesen, S.J.	.35
□ McD-32	Todd Harvey, Dal.	.25
□ McD-33	Brett Lindros, NYI.	.25
□ McD-34	Valeri Bure, Mtl.	.25
□ McD-35	Oleg Tverdovsky, Wpg.	.25
□ McD-36	Kenny Jonsson, NYI.	.25
□ McD-37	Mariusz Czerkawski, Bos.	.25
□ McD-38	Alexandre Daigle, Ott.	.35
□ McD-39	Saku Koivu, Mtl.	1.50
□ McD-40	Jim Carey (G), Wsh.	.25

1995 - 96 MCDONALD'S NHL MUPPET MANIA

The following "Free" teams came on the game card: Chicago, Calgary, Los Angeles, Colorado, Florida, Islanders, Washington, Hartford and Ottawa. We have no pricing information on this set.

Imprint:

	No.	Team		No.	Team
□	501	Dallas Stars	□	502	Detroit Red Wings
□	503	St. Louis Blues	□	504	Tor. Maple Leafs
□	505	Winnipeg Jets	□	506	Edmonton Oilers
□	507	Vancouver Canucks	□	508	San Jose Sharks
□	509	Ana. Mighty Ducks	□	510	Tampa Bay Lightning
□	511	New York Rangers	□	512	New Jersey Devils
□	513	Pha. Flyers	□	514	Pgh. Penguins
□	515	Montréal Canadiens	□	516	Boston Bruins
□	517	Buffalo Sabres			

1995 - 96 PANINI STICKERS

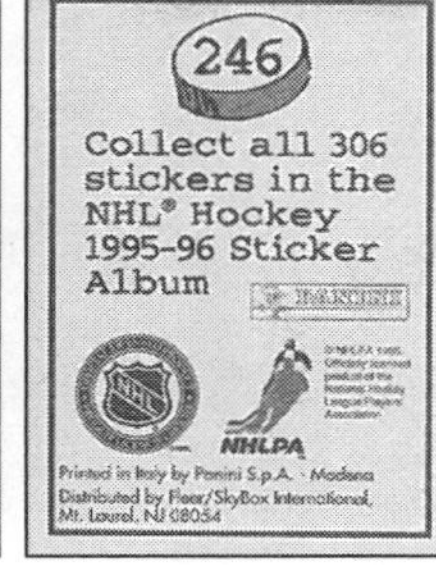

Sticker Size: 2 1/8" x 3"

Imprint:

Complete Set (306 stickers): 20.00

Album: 3.00

	No.	Player	NRMT-MT
□	1	Claude Lemieux LH	.15
□	2	Claude Lemieux RH	.15
□	3	Adam Oates, Bos.	.35
□	4	Ted Donato, Bos.	.15
□	5	Mariusz Czerkawski, Bos.	.15
□	6	Sandy Moger, Bos.	.15
□	7	Kevin Stevens, Bos.	.15
□	8	Cam Neely, Bos.	.25
□	9	Ray Bourque, Bos.	.75
□	10	Boston Bruins Logo	.15
□	11	Don Sweeney, Bos.	.15
□	12	Al Iafrate, Bos.	.15
□	13	Blaine Lacher (G), Bos.	.15
□	14	Brian Holzinger, Buf.	.15
□	15	Pat LaFontaine, Buf.	.25
□	16	Derek Plante, Buf.	.15
□	17	Yuri Khmylev, Buf.	.15
□	18	Jason Dawe, Buf.	.15
□	19	Donald Audette, Buf.	.15
□	20	Alexei Zhitnik, Buf.	.15
□	21	Buffalo Sabres Logo	.15
□	22	Richard Smehlik, Buf.	.15
□	23	Garry Galley, Buf.	.15
□	24	Dominik Hasek (G), Buf.	1.00
□	25	Andrew Cassels, Hfd.	.15
□	26	Jimmy Carson, Hfd.	.15
□	27	Darren Turcotte, Hfd.	.15
□	28	Geoff Sanderson, Hfd.	.15
□	29	Andrei Nikolishin, Hfd.	.15
□	30	Kevyn Smyth, Hfd.	.15
□	31	Brendan Shanahan, Hfd.	.85
□	32	Hartford Whalers Logo	.15
□	33	Steven Rice, Hfd.	.15
□	34	Frantisek Kucera, Hfd.	.15
□	35	Sean Burke (G), Hfd.	.25
□	36	Brian Savage, Mtl.	.15
□	37	Pierre Turgeon, Mtl.	.25
□	38	Vincent Damphousse, Mtl.	.35
□	39	Benoît Brunet, Mtl.	.15
□	40	Mike Keane, Mtl.	.15
□	41	Mark Recchi, Mtl.	.25
□	42	Vladimir Malakhov, Mtl.	.15
□	43	Montréal Canadiens Logo	.15
□	44	Patrice Brisebrois, Mtl.	.15
□	45	Stéphane Quintal, Mtl.	.15
□	46	Patrick Roy (G), Mtl.	2.50
□	47	Alexandre Daigle, Ott.	.25
□	48	Alexei Yashin, Ott.	.35
□	49	Dan Quinn, Ott.	.15
□	50	Radek Bonk, Ott.	.15
□	51	Scott Levins, Ott.	.15
□	52	Sylvain Turgeon, Ott.	.15
□	53	Pavol Demitra, Ott.	.15
□	54	Ottawa Senators Logo	.15
□	55	Steve Larouche, Ott.	.15
□	56	Sean Hill, Ott.	.15
□	57	Don Beaupré (G), Ott.	.15
□	58	Ron Francis, Pgh.	.35
□	59	Mario Lemieux, Pgh.	2.50
□	60	Bryan Smolinski, Pgh.	.15
□	61	Luc Robitaille, Pgh.	.25
□	62	Tomas Sandström, Pgh.	.15
□	63	Jaromir Jagr, Pgh.	1.50
□	64	Joe Mullen, Pgh.	.15
□	65	Pittsburgh Penguins Logo	.15
□	66	Ulf Samuelsson, Pgh.	.15
□	67	Dmitri Mironov, Pgh.	.15
□	68	Ken Wregget (G), Pgh.	.15
□	69	Stu Barnes, Fla.	.15
□	70	Jesse Belanger, Fla.	.15
□	71	Rob Niedermayer, Fla.	.25
□	72	Brian Skrudland, Fla.	.15
□	73	Dave Lowry, Fla.	.15
□	74	Jody Hull, Fla.	.15
□	75	Scott Mellanby, Fla.	.15
□	76	Florida Panthers Logo	.15
□	77	Gord Murphy, Fla.	.15
□	78	Magnus Svensson, Fla.	.15
□	79	John Vanbiesbrouck (G), Fla.	.85
□	80	Neal Broten, N.J.	.15
□	81	Bill Guerin, N.J.	.25
□	82	Claude Lemieux, N.J.	.15
□	83	John MacLean, N.J.	.15
□	84	Randy McKay, N.J.	.15
□	85	Stéphane Richer, N.J.	.15
□	86	Shawn Chambers, N.J.	.15
□	87	New Jersey Devils Logo	.15
□	88	Scott Niedermayer, N.J.	.25
□	89	Scott Stevens, N.J.	.15
□	90	Martin Brodeur (G), N.J.	1.00
□	91	Kirk Muller, NYI.	.15
□	92	Derek King, NYI.	.15
□	93	Patrick Flatley, NYI.	.15
□	94	Brett Lindros, NYI.	.15
□	95	Steve Thomas, NYI.	.15
□	96	Darius Kasparaitis, NYI.	.15
□	97	Scott Lachance, NYI.	.15
□	98	New York Islanders Logo	.15
□	99	Mathieu Schneider, NYI.	.15
□	100	Dennis Vaske, NYI.	.15
□	101	Tommy Salo (G), NYI.	.15
□	102	Mark Messier, NYR.	.75
□	103	Ray Ferraro, NYR.	.15
□	104	Petr Nedved, NYR.	.15
□	105	Adam Graves, NYR.	.15
□	106	Alexei Kovalev, NYR.	.15
□	107	Steve Larmer, NYR.	.15
□	108	Pat Verbeek, NYR.	.15
□	109	New York Rangers Logo	.15
□	110	Brian Leetch, NYR.	.35
□	111	Sergei Zubov, NYR.	.25
□	112	Mike Richter (G), NYR.	.35
□	113	Eric Lindros, Pha.	2.00
□	114	Rod Brind'Amour, Pha.	.25
□	115	Joel Otto, Pha.	.15
□	116	John LeClair, Pha.	.75
□	117	Mikael Renberg, Pha.	.15
□	118	Chris Therien, Pha.	.15
□	119	Eric Desjardins, Pha.	.15
□	120	Philadelphia Flyers Logo	.15
□	121	Dmitri Yushkevich, Pha.	.15
□	122	Karl Dykhuis, Pha.	.15
□	123	Ron Hextall (G), Pha.	.25
□	124	Brian Bradley, T.B.	.15
□	125	John Tucker, T.B.	.15
□	126	Chris Gratton, T.B.	.25
□	127	Alexander Semak, T.B.	.15
□	128	Brian Bellows, T.B.	.15
□	129	Paul Ysebaert, T.B.	.15
□	130	Petr Klima, T.B.	.15
□	131	Tampa Bay Lightning Logo	.15
□	132	Alexander Selivanov, T.B.	.15
□	133	Roman Hamrlik, T.B.	.25
□	134	Daren Puppa (G), T.B.	.15
□	135	Dale Hunter, Wsh.	.15
□	136	Michal Pivonka, Wsh.	.15
□	137	Steve Konowalchuk, Wsh.	.15
□	138	Joé Juneau, Wsh.	.15
□	139	Peter Bondra, Wsh.	.50
□	140	Keith Jones, Wsh.	.15
□	141	Sergei Gonchar, Wsh.	.15
□	142	Washington Capitals Logo	.15
□	143	Calle Johansson, Wsh.	.15
□	144	Mark Tinordi, Wsh.	.15
□	145	Jim Carey (G), Wsh.	.15
□	146	AW: Eric Lindros, Pha.	1.00
□	147	AW: Paul Coffey, Det.	.25
□	148	AW: Peter Forsberg, Col.	.75
□	149	AW: Dominik Hasek, Buf.	.50
□	150	AW: Jaromir Jagr, Pgh.	.75
□	151	LL: Peter Bondra, Wsh.	.25
□	152	LL: Ron Francis, Pgh.	.25
□	153	LL: Cam Neely, Bos.	.25
□	154	LL: Dominik Hasek (G), Buf.	.50
□	155	LL: Ian Laperrière, Stl.	.15
□	156	Bernie Nicholls, Chi.	.15
□	157	Jeremy Roenick, Chi.	.35
□	158	Patrick Poulin, Chi.	.15
□	159	Eric Dazé, Chi.	.25
□	160	Tony Amonte, Chi.	.25
□	161	Sergei Krivokrasov, Chi.	.15
□	162	Joe Murphy, Chi.	.15
□	163	Chicago Blackhawks Logo	.15
□	164	Chris Chelios, Chi.	.50
□	165	Gary Suter, Chi.	.15
□	166	Ed Belfour (G), Chi.	.35
□	167	Dave Gagner, Dal.	.15

	No.	Player	Price
☐	168	Mike Modano, Dal.	.75
☐	169	Todd Harvey, Dal.	.15
☐	170	Mike Donnelly, Dal.	.15
☐	171	Mike Kennedy, Dal.	.15
☐	172	Trent Klatt, Dal.	.15
☐	173	Derian Hatcher, Dal.	.25
☐	174	Dallas Stars Logo	.15
☐	175	Kevin Hatcher, Dal.	.15
☐	176	Grant Ledyard, Dal.	.15
☐	177	Andy Moog (G), Dal.	.25
☐	178	Sergei Fedorov, Det.	.75
☐	179	Steve Yzerman, Det.	1.50
☐	180	Vyacheslav Kozlov, Det.	.15
☐	181	Keith Primeau, Det.	.25
☐	182	Dino Ciccarelli, Det.	.25
☐	183	Ray Sheppard, Det.	.15
☐	184	Paul Coffey, Det.	.25
☐	185	Detroit Red Wings Logo	.15
☐	186	Nicklas Lidström, Det.	.15
☐	187	Chris Osgood (G), Det.	.50
☐	188	Mike Vernon (G), Det.	.25
☐	189	Dale Hawerchuk, Stl.	.25
☐	190	Ian Laperrière, Stl.	.15
☐	191	David Roberts, Stl.	.15
☐	192	Esa Tikkanen, Stl.	.15
☐	193	Geoff Courtnall, Stl.	.15
☐	194	Brett Hull, Stl.	.75
☐	195	Steve Duchesne, Stl.	.15
☐	196	St. Louis Blues Logo	.15
☐	197	Al MacInnis, Stl.	.15
☐	198	Chris Pronger, Stl.	.25
☐	199	Jon Casey (G), Stl.	.15
☐	200	Doug Gilmour, Tor.	.35
☐	201	Mats Sundin, Tor.	.75
☐	202	Benoît Hogue, Tor.	.15
☐	203	Dave Andreychuk, Tor.	.15
☐	204	Mike Gartner, Tor.	.25
☐	205	Dave Ellett, Tor.	.15
☐	206	Todd Gill, Tor.	.15
☐	207	Toronto Maple Leafs Logo	.15
☐	208	Kenny Jonsson, Tor.	.15
☐	209	Larry Murphy, Tor.	.25
☐	210	Félix Potvin (G), Tor.	.75
☐	211	Dallas Drake, Wpg.	.15
☐	212	Alexei Zhamnov, Wpg.	.15
☐	213	Mike Eastwood, Wpg.	.15
☐	214	Keith Tkachuk, Wpg.	.50
☐	215	Igor Korolev, Wpg.	.15
☐	216	Nelson Emerson, Wpg.	.15
☐	217	Teemu Selänne, Wpg.	1.00
☐	218	Winnipeg Jets Logo	.15
☐	219	Dave McLlwain, Wpg.	.15
☐	220	Teppo Numminen, Wpg.	.15
☐	221	Nikolai Khabibulin (G), Wpg.	.35
☐	222	Steve Rucchin, Ana.	.15
☐	223	Shaun Van Allen, Ana.	.15
☐	224	Patrik Carnback, Ana.	.15
☐	225	Peter Douris, Ana.	.15
☐	226	Todd Krygier, Ana.	.15
☐	227	Paul Kariya, Ana.	2.00
☐	228	Bobby Dollas, Ana.	.15
☐	229	Anaheim Mighty Ducks Logo	.15
☐	230	Milan Holan, Ana.	.15
☐	231	Oleg Tverdovsky, Ana.	.15
☐	232	Guy Hebert (G), Ana.	.25
☐	233	Joe Nieuwendyk, Cgy.	.25
☐	234	German Titov, Cgy.	.15
☐	235	Paul Kruse, Cgy.	.15
☐	236	Gary Roberts, Cgy.	.25
☐	237	Theoren Fleury, Cgy.	.35
☐	238	Ronnie Stern, Cgy.	.15
☐	239	Steve Chiasson, Cgy.	.15
☐	240	Calgary Flames Logo	.15
☐	241	Phil Housley, Cgy.	.15
☐	242	Zarley Zalapski, Cgy.	.15
☐	243	Trevor Kidd (G), Cgy.	.25
☐	244	Peter Forsberg, Col.	1.50
☐	245	Mike Ricci, Col.	.15
☐	246	Joe Sakic, Col.	1.25
☐	247	Wendel Clark, Col.	.25
☐	248	Valeri Kamensky, Col.	.25
☐	249	Owen Nolan, Col.	.25
☐	250	Scott Young, Col.	.15
☐	251	Colorado Avalanche Logo	.15
☐	252	Uwe Krupp, Col.	.15

	No.	Player	Price
☐	253	Curtis Leschyshyn, Col.	.15
☐	254	Jocelyn Thibault (G), Col.	.35
☐	255	Jason Arnott, Edm.	.25
☐	256	Jason Bonsignore, Edm.	.15
☐	257	Todd Marchant, Edm.	.15
☐	258	Scott Thornton, Edm.	.15
☐	259	Doug Weight, Edm.	.35
☐	260	Shayne Corson, Edm.	.25
☐	261	Kelly Buchberger, Edm.	.15
☐	262	Edmonton Oilers Logo	.15
☐	263	David Oliver, Edm.	.15
☐	264	Igor Kravchuk, Edm.	.15
☐	265	Curtis Joseph (G), Edm.	.85
☐	266	Wayne Gretzky, L.A.	3.00
☐	267	Tony Granato, L.A.	.15
☐	268	Dmitri Khristich, L.A.	.15
☐	269	John Druce, L.A.	.15
☐	270	Jari Kurri, L.A.	.25
☐	271	Rick Tocchet, L.A.	.15
☐	272	Rob Blake, L.A.	.25
☐	273	Los Angeles Kings Logo	.15
☐	274	Marty McSorley, L.A.	.15
☐	275	Daryl Sydor, L.A.	.15
☐	276	Kelly Hrudey (G), L.A.	.15
☐	277	Craig Janney, S.J.	.15
☐	278	Jeff Friesen, S.J.	.25
☐	279	Viktor Kozlov, S.J.	.15
☐	280	Ray Whitney, S.J.	.15
☐	281	Ulf Dahlen, S.J.	.15
☐	282	Sergei Makarov, S.J.	.15
☐	283	Sandis Ozolinsh, S.J.	.25
☐	284	San Jose Sharks Logo	.15
☐	285	Mike Rathje, S.J.	.15
☐	286	Michal Sykora, S.J.	.15
☐	287	Arturs Irbe (G), S.J.	.15
☐	288	Trevor Linden, Van.	.25
☐	289	Mike Ridley, Van.	.15
☐	290	Cliff Ronning, Van.	.15
☐	291	Josef Beranek, Van.	.15
☐	292	Roman Oksiuta, Van.	.15
☐	293	Pavel Bure, Van.	1.00
☐	294	Alexander Mogilny, Van.	.50
☐	295	Vancouver Canucks Logo	.15
☐	296	Russ Courtnall, Van.	.15
☐	297	Jeff Brown, Van.	.15
☐	298	Kirk McLean (G), Van.	.25
☐	299	FOIL: Peter Forsberg, Col.	1.50
☐	300	FOIL: Paul Kariya, Ana.	2.00
☐	301	FOIL: Chris Therien, Pha.	.25
☐	302	FOIL: Blaine Lacher (G), Bos.	.25
☐	303	FOIL: Jim Carey (G), Wsh.	.25
☐	304	FOIL: Jeff Friesen, S.J.	.35
☐	305	FOIL: Ian Laperrière, Stl.	.25
☐	306	FOIL: Kenny Jonsson, Tor.	.25

1995 - 96 PARKHURST

These cards have two versions: the regular card and an Emerald parallel. Seven cards also have a promo version. The promo card and Emerald Ice card have the same value.

Imprint: PARKHURST PRODUCTS INC.

	Reg.	Emerald
Series One Set (270 cards):	**25.00**	**400.00**
Series Two Set (270 cards):	**30.00**	**400.00**
Common Player:	**.10**	**.75**
Box Insert (Saku Koivu):	**5.00**	

	No.	Player	Reg.	Emerald
☐ ☐	1	Patrick Carnback, Ana.	.10	.75
☐ ☐	2	Milos Holan, Ana.	.10	.75
☐ ☐	3	Paul Kariya, Ana.	1.25	25.00
☐ ☐	4	Guy Hebert (G), Ana.	.25	2.00
☐ ☐	5	Gary Valk, Ana.	.10	.75
☐ ☐	6	Mikail Shtalenkov (G), Ana.	.10	.75
☐ ☐	7	Randy Ladouceur, Ana.	.10	.75
☐ ☐	8	Shaun Van Allen, Ana.	.10	.75
☐ ☐	9	Oleg Tverdovsky, Ana.	.10	.75
☐ ☐	10	Kevin Stevens, Bos.	.10	.75
☐ ☐	11	Ray Bourque, Bos.	.50	8.00
☐ ☐	12	Cam Neely, Bos.	.25	2.00
☐ ☐	13	Josef Stumpel, Bos.	.25	2.00
☐ ☐	14	Blaine Lacher, Bos.	.10	.75
☐ ☐	15	Alexei Kasatonov, Bos.	.10	.75
☐ ☐	16	Adam Oates, Bos.	.35	4.00
☐ ☐	17	Ted Donato, Bos.	.10	.75
☐ ☐	18	Mariusz Czerkawsky, Bos.	.10	.75
☐ ☐	19	Alexei Zhitnik, Buf.	.10	.75
☐ ☐	20	Pat LaFontaine, Buf.	.25	2.00
☐ ☐	21	Garry Galley, Buf.	.10	.75
☐ ☐	22	Scott Pearson, Buf.	.10	.75
☐ ☐	23	Yuri Khmylev, Buf.	.10	.75
☐ ☐	24	Jason Dawe, Buf.	.10	.75
☐ ☐	25	Robb Stauber (G), Buf.	.10	.75
☐ ☐	**26**	**Wayne Primeau, Buf., RC**	**.10**	**.75**
☐ ☐	**27**	**Brian Holzinger, Buf., RC**	**.25**	**1.50**
☐ ☐	28	German Titov, Cgy.	.10	.75
☐ ☐	29	Theoren Fleury, Cgy.	.35	4.00
☐ ☐	30	Phil Housley, Cgy.	.10	.75
☐ ☐	31	Zarley Zalapski, Cgy.	.10	.75
☐ ☐	32	Rick Tabaracci (G), Cgy.	.10	.75
☐ ☐	33	Joe Nieuwendyk, Cgy.	.10	.75
☐ ☐	34	Michael Nylander, Cgy.	.10	.75
☐ ☐	35	Trevor Kidd (G), Cgy.	.25	2.00
☐ ☐	36	Dean Evason, Cgy.	.10	.75
☐ ☐	37	Bernie Nicholls, Chi.	.10	.75
☐ ☐	38	Chris Chelios, Chi.	.35	6.00
☐ ☐	39	Gary Suter, Chi.	.10	.75
☐ ☐	40	Denis Savard, Chi.	.25	2.00
☐ ☐	41	Ed Belfour (G), Chi.	.35	4.00
☐ ☐	42	Patrick Poulin, Chi.	.10	.75
☐ ☐	43	Steve Smith, Chi.	.10	.75
☐ ☐	44	Jeff Hackett (G), Chi.	.25	4.00
☐ ☐	45	Eric Dazé, Chi.	.25	2.00
☐ ☐	46	Joe Sakic, Col.	.85	15.00
☐ ☐	47	John Slaney, Col.	.10	.75
☐ ☐	48	Valeri Kamensky, Col.	.25	2.00
☐ ☐	49	Owen Nolan, Col.	.25	2.00
☐ ☐	50	Uwe Krupp, Col.	.10	.75
☐ ☐	51	Andrei Kovalenko, Col.	.10	.75
☐ ☐	52	Janne Laukkanen, Col.	.10	.75
☐ ☐	53	Jocelyn Thibault (G), Col.	.35	4.00
☐ ☐	54	Adam Deadmarsh, Col.	.25	2.00
☐ ☐	55	Mike Modano, Dal.	.50	8.00
☐ ☐	56	Kevin Hatcher, Dal.	.10	.75
☐ ☐	57	Mike Donnelly, Dal.	.10	.75
☐ ☐	58	Derian Hatcher, Dal.	.25	2.00
☐ ☐	59	Andy Moog (G), Dal.	.25	2.00
☐ ☐	60	Jamie Langenbrunner, Dal.	.25	2.00
☐ ☐	61	Shane Churla, Dal.	.10	.75
☐ ☐	62	Todd Harvey, Dal.	.10	.75
☐ ☐	63	Manny Fernandez (G), Dal.	.10	.75
☐ ☐	64	Nicklas Lidström, Det.	.25	2.00
☐ ☐	65	Vyacheslav Kozlov, Det.	.10	.75
☐ ☐	66	Paul Coffey, Det.	.25	2.00
☐ ☐	67	Chris Osgood (G), Det.	.35	6.00
☐ ☐	68	Viacheslav Fetisov, Det.	.25	2.00
☐ ☐	69	Vladimir Konstantinov, Det.	.10	.75
☐ ☐	70	Steve Yzerman, Det.	1.00	20.00
☐ ☐	71	Aaron Ward, Det.	.10	.75
☐ ☐	72	Keith Primeau, Det.	.25	2.00
☐ ☐	73	Jason Arnott, Edm.	.25	2.00
☐ ☐	74	Igor Kravchuk, Edm.	.10	.75
☐ ☐	75	Boris Mironov, Edm.	.10	.75
☐ ☐	76	David Oliver, Edm.	.10	.75
☐ ☐	77	Kelly Buchberger, Edm.	.10	.75
☐ ☐	78	Bill Ranford (G), Edm.	.25	2.00
☐ ☐	79	Zdeno Ciger, Edm.	.10	.75
☐ ☐	80	Jason Bonsignore, Edm.	.10	.75
☐ ☐	81	Louie DeBrusk, Edm.	.10	.75
☐ ☐	82	Rob Niedermayer, Fla.	.10	.75
☐ ☐	83	Magnus Svensson, Fla.	.10	.75
☐ ☐	**84**	**Robert Svehla, Fla., RC**	**.25**	**1.50**
☐ ☐ ☐	85	John Vanbiesbrouck, Fla.	.60	10.00
☐ ☐	86	Stu Barnes, Fla.	.10	.75
☐ ☐	87	Jesse Belanger, Fla.	.10	.75
☐ ☐	88	Mark Fitzpatrick (G), Fla.	.10	.75

☐☐	89	Jason Woolley, Fla.	.10	.75
☐☐	90	Johan Garpenlov, Fla.	.10	.75
☐☐	91	Geoff Sanderson, Hfd.	.10	.75
☐☐	92	Robert Kron, Hfd.	.10	.75
☐☐	93	Darren Turcotte, Hfd.	.10	.75
☐☐	94	Andrei Nikolishin, Hfd.	.10	.75
☐☐	95	Steven Rice, Hfd.	.10	.75
☐☐	96	Sean Burke (G), Hfd.	.25	2.00
☐☐	97	Brendan Shanahan, Hfd.	.60	10.00
☐☐	98	Glen Wesley, Hfd.	.10	.75
☐☐	99	Marek Malik, Hfd.	.10	.75
☐☐	100	Wayne Gretzky, L.A.	2.00	40.00
☐☐	101	Robert Lang, L.A.	.10	.75
☐☐☐	102	Jari Kurri, L.A.	.25	2.00
☐☐	103	Kelly Hrudey, L.A.	.10	.75
☐☐	104	Jamie Storr (G), L.A.	.25	2.00
☐☐	105	Marty McSorley, L.A.	.10	.75
☐☐	106	Rob Blake, L.A.	.25	2.00
☐☐	107	Eric Lacroix, L.A.	.10	.75
☐☐	108	Dimitri Khristich, L.A.	.10	.75
☐☐	109	Pierre Turgeon, Mtl.	.25	2.00
☐☐	110	Vincent Damphousse, Mtl.	.35	2.00
☐☐	111	Peter Popovic, Mtl.	.10	.75
☐☐	112	Brian Savage, Mtl.	.10	.75
☐☐☐	113	Patrick Roy (G), Mtl.	1.50	30.00
☐☐	114	Valeri Bure, Mtl.	.10	.75
☐☐	115	Vladimir Malakhov, Mtl.	.10	.75
☐☐	116	Benoît Brunet, Mtl.	.10	.75
☐☐	117	Stéphane Quintal, Mtl.	.10	.75
☐☐	118	Stéphane Richer, N.J.	.10	.75
☐☐	119	Sergei Brylin, N.J.	.10	.75
☐☐	120	Neal Broten, N.J.	.10	.75
☐☐	121	Scott Stevens, N.J.	.10	.75
☐☐	122	Martin Brodeur, N.J.	.75	12.00
☐☐	123	John MacLean, N.J.	.10	.75
☐☐	124	Bill Guerin, N.J.	.25	2.00
☐☐	125	Bobby Holik, N.J.	.10	.75
☐☐	126	Tommy Albelin, N.J.	.10	.75
☐☐	127	Tommy Söderström, NYI.	.10	.75
☐☐	128	Tommy Salo, NYI.	.10	.75
☐☐	129	Kirk Muller, NYI.	.10	.75
☐☐	130	Mathieu Schneider, NYI.	.10	.75
☐☐	131	Zigmund Palffy, NYI.	.35	6.00
☐☐	132	Derek King, NYI.	.10	.75
☐☐	133	Brett Lindros, NYI.	.10	.75
☐☐	134	Marty McInnis, NYI.	.10	.75
☐☐	135	Alexander Semak, NYI.	.10	.75
☐☐	136	Mark Messier, NYR.	.50	8.00
☐☐	137	Adam Graves, NYR.	.10	.75
☐☐	138	Mike Richter (G), NYR.	.35	4.00
☐☐	139	Alexei Kovalev, NYR.	.10	.75
☐☐	140	Luc Robitaille, NYR.	.25	2.00
☐☐	141	Sergei Nemchinov, NYR.	.10	.75
☐☐	142	Alexander Karpovtsev, NYR.	.10	.75
☐☐	143	Mattias Norstrom, NYR.	.10	.75
☐☐	144	Brian Leetch, NYR.	.35	4.00
☐☐	145	Martin Straka, Ott.	.10	.75
☐☐	146	Sylvain Turgeon, Ott.	.10	.75
☐☐	147	Radek Bonk, Ott.	.10	.75
☐☐	148	Stanislav Neckar, Ott.	.10	.75
☐☐	149	Pavol Demitra, Ott.	.10	.75
☐☐	150	Alexandre Daigle, Ott.	.25	2.00
☐☐	151	Alexei Yashin, Ott.	.35	6.00
☐☐	152	Don Beaupré (G), Ott.	.10	.75
☐☐	153	Steve Duchesne, Ott.	.10	.75
☐☐	154	Eric Lindros, Pha.	1.25	25.00
☐☐	155	Kjell Samuelsson, Pha.	.10	.75
☐☐	156	Chris Therien, Pha.	.10	.75
☐☐	157	John LeClair, Pha.	.50	8.00
☐☐	158	Rod Brind'Amour, Pha.	.25	2.00
☐☐	159	Ron Hextall (G), Pha.	.25	2.00
☐☐	160	Patrik Juhlin, Pha.	.10	.75
☐☐☐	161	Mikael Renberg, Pha.	.10	.75
☐☐	162	Joel Otto, Pha.	.10	.75
☐☐	163	Markus Naslund, Pgh.	.10	.75
☐☐	164	Ron Francis, Pgh.	.35	6.00
☐☐	165	Jaromir Jagr, Pgh.	1.00	20.00
☐☐	166	Tomas Sandström, Pgh.	.10	.75
☐☐	167	Ken Wregget (G), Pgh.	.10	.75
☐☐	168	Bryan Smolinski, Pgh.	.10	.75
☐☐	169	Richard Park, Pgh.	.10	.75
☐☐	170	Mario Lemieux, Pgh.	1.50	30.00
☐☐	171	Norm Maciver, Pgh.	.10	.75
☐☐	172	Brett Hull, Stl.	.50	8.00
☐☐	173	Esa Tikkanen, Stl.	.10	.75
☐☐	174	Shayne Corson, Stl.	.25	2.00
☐☐	175	Chris Pronger, Stl.	.25	2.00
☐☐	176	Ian Laperrière, Stl.	.10	.75
☐☐	177	Jon Casey (G), Stl.	.10	.75
☐☐	178	Al MacInnis, Stl.	.10	.75
☐☐	179	David Roberts, Stl.	.10	.75
☐☐	180	Dale Hawerchuk, Stl.	.25	2.00
☐☐	181	Michal Sykora, S.J.	.10	.75
☐☐	182	Jeff Friesen, S.J.	.25	2.00
☐☐	183	Ray Whitney, S.J.	.10	.75
☐☐	184	Igor Larionov, S.J.	.25	2.00
☐☐	185	Sandis Ozolinsh, S.J.	.25	2.00
☐☐	186	Andrei Nazarov, S.J.	.10	.75
☐☐	187	Viktor Kozlov, S.J.	.10	.75
☐☐	188	Arturs Irbe (G), S.J.	.10	.75
☐☐	**189**	**Wade Flaherty, S.J., RC**	**.10**	**.75**
☐☐	190	Brian Bradley, T.B.	.10	.75
☐☐	191	Paul Ysebaert, T.B.	.10	.75
☐☐	192	John Tucker, T.B.	.10	.75
☐☐	193	Jason Wiemer, T.B.	.10	.75
☐☐	194	Alexander Selivanov, T.B.	.10	.75
☐☐	195	Daren Puppa (G), T.B.	.10	.75
☐☐	196	Mikael Andersson, T.B.	.10	.75
☐☐	197	Petr Klima, T.B.	.10	.75
☐☐	198	Roman Hamrlik, T.B.	.25	2.00
☐☐	199	Doug Gilmour, Tor.	.35	4.00
☐☐	200	Damian Rhodes (G), Tor.	.10	.75
☐☐	201	Mats Sundin, Tor.	.50	8.00
☐☐	202	Todd Gill, Tor.	.10	.75
☐☐	203	Kenny Jonsson, Tor.	.10	.75
☐☐	204	Félix Potvin (G), Tor.	.50	8.00
☐☐	205	Tie Domi, Tor.	.10	.75
☐☐	206	Mike Gartner, Tor.	.25	2.00
☐☐	207	Larry Murphy, Tor.	.25	2.00
☐☐	208	Josef Beranek, Van.	.10	.75
☐☐	209	Trevor Linden, Van.	.25	2.00
☐☐	210	Russ Courtnall, Van.	.10	.75
☐☐	211	Roman Oksiuta, Van.	.10	.75
☐☐	212	Alexander Mogilny, Van.	.35	4.00
☐☐	213	Kirk McLean (G), Van.	.25	2.00
☐☐	214	Mike Ridley, Van.	.10	.75
☐☐	215	Jyrki Lumme, Van.	.10	.75
☐☐	216	Bret Hedican, Van.	.10	.75
☐☐	217	Keith Jones, Wsh.	.10	.75
☐☐	218	Calle Johansson, Wsh.	.10	.75
☐☐	219	Kelly Miller, Wsh.	.10	.75
☐☐	220	Olaf Kolzig (G), Wsh.	.35	4.00
☐☐	221	Joé Juneau, Wsh.	.10	.75
☐☐	222	Sylvain Côté, Wsh.	.10	.75
☐☐	223	Dale Hunter, Wsh.	.10	.75
☐☐	224	Mark Tinordi, Wsh.	.10	.75
☐☐	225	Sergei Gonchar, Wsh.	.10	.75
☐☐	226	Alexei Zhamnov, Wpg.	.25	2.00
☐☐	227	Igor Korolev, Wpg.	.10	.75
☐☐	228	Teppo Numminen, Wpg.	.10	.75
☐☐	**229**	**Craig Martin, Wpg., Wpg., RC**	**.10**	**.75**
☐☐	230	Nikolai Khabibulin (G), Wpg.	.35	4.00
☐☐	231	Michal Grosek, Wpg.	.10	.75
☐☐☐	232	Teemu Selänne, Wpg.	.75	12.00
☐☐	233	Dave Manson, Wpg.	.10	.75
☐☐	234	Tim Cheveldae (G), Wpg.	.10	.75
☐☐	235	Esa Tikkanen, Stl.	.10	.75
☐☐	236	Dominik Hasek (G), Buf.	.35	6.00
☐☐	237	Peter Forsberg, Col.	.50	10.00
☐☐	238	Sergei Fedorov, Det.	.25	4.00
☐☐	239	Jari Kurri, L.A.	.25	2.00
☐☐	240	Tommy Söderström (G), L.A.	.10	.75
☐☐	241	Alexei Zhamnov, Wpg.	.25	2.00
☐☐	242	Alexei Yashin, Ott.	.25	2.00
☐☐	243	Mikael Renberg, Pha.	.10	.75
☐☐☐	244	Jaromir Jagr, Pgh.	.50	10.00
☐☐	245	Ulf Dahlen, S.J.	.10	.75
☐☐	246	Alexander Mogilny, Van.	.25	2.00
☐☐	247	Mats Sundin, Tor.	.25	2.00
☐☐	248	Pavel Bure, Van.	.35	6.00
☐☐	249	Viacheslav Fetisov, Det.	.25	2.00
☐☐	250	Teemu Selänne, Wpg.	.35	6.00
☐☐	251	Arturs Irbe (G), S.J.	.10	.75
☐☐	252	Nicklas Lidström, Det.	.25	2.00
☐☐	**253**	**Aki Berg, L.A., RC**	**.10**	**.75**
☐☐☐	**254**	**Zdenek Nedved, Tor., RC**	**.10**	**.75**
☐☐	**255**	**Chad Kilger, Ana., RC**	**.10**	**.75**
☐☐	256	Bryan McCabe, NYI.	.10	.75
☐☐	**257**	**Daniel Alfredsson, Ott., RC**	**.75**	**6.00**
☐☐	258	Brendan Witt, Wsh.	.10	.75
☐☐	259	Jeff O'Neill, Hfd.	.10	.75
☐☐	**260**	**Radek Dvorak, Fla., RC**	**.25**	**1.50**
☐☐	261	Niklas Sundstrom, NYR.	.10	.75
☐☐	**262**	**Kyle McLaren, Bos., RC**	**.10**	**.75**
☐☐	263	Saku Koivu, Mtl.	.75	8.00
☐☐	**264**	**Todd Bertuzzi, NYI., RC**	**.50**	**3.00**
☐☐	265	Jere Lehtinen, Dal.	.25	2.00
☐☐	266	Vitali Yachmenev, L.A.	.10	.75
☐☐	267	Shane Doan, Wpg.	.10	.75
☐☐	268	Marko Kiprusoff, Mtl.	.10	.75
☐☐	269	Deron Quint, Wpg.	.10	.75
☐☐	**270**	**Daymond Langkow, T.B., RC**	**.25**	**1.50**
☐☐	**271**	**Alex Hicks, Ana., RC**	**.10**	**.75**
☐☐	272	Steve Rucchin, Ana.	.10	.75
☐☐	273	David Karpa, Ana.	.10	.75
☐☐	274	Mike Sillinger, Ana.	.10	.75
☐☐	275	Teemu Selänne, Ana.	.75	12.00
☐☐	276	Todd Krygier, Ana.	.10	.75
☐☐	277	Valeri Karpov, Ana.	.10	.75
☐☐	278	Peter Douris, Ana.	.10	.75
☐☐	279	Anaheim Checklist	.10	.75
☐☐	280	Shawn McEachern, Bos.	.10	.75
☐☐	281	Dave Reid, Bos.	.10	.75
☐☐	282	Bill Ranford (G), Bos.	.25	2.00
☐☐	283	Don Sweeney, Bos.	.10	.75
☐☐	284	Stephen Leach, Bos.	.10	.75
☐☐	285	Craig Billington (G), Bos.	.10	.75
☐☐	**286**	**Clayton Beddoes, Bos., RC**	**.10**	**.75**
☐☐	287	Rick Tocchet, Bos.	.10	.75
☐☐	288	Boston Checklist	.10	.75
☐☐	289	Brad May, Buf.	.10	.75
☐☐	290	Michael Peca, Bos.	.25	2.00
☐☐	291	Dominik Hasek, Bos.	.75	12.00
☐☐	292	Donald Audette, Bos.	.10	.75
☐☐	293	Randy Burridge, Bos.	.10	.75
☐☐	294	Derek Plante, Bos.	.10	.75
☐☐	**295**	**Martin Biron (G), Bos., RC**	**.50**	**3.00**
☐☐	296	Andrei Trefilov, Bos.	.10	.75
☐☐	297	Buffalo Checklist	.10	.75
☐☐	298	Steve Chiasson, Cgy.	.10	.75
☐☐	299	Cory Stillman, Cgy.	.10	.75
☐☐	300	Mike Sullivan, Cgy.	.10	.75
☐☐	301	Gary Roberts, Cgy.	.25	2.00
☐☐	**302**	**Pavel Torgajev, Cgy., RC**	**.10**	**.75**
☐☐	303	James Patrick, Cgy.	.10	.75
☐☐	304	Corey Millen, Cgy.	.10	.75
☐☐	**305**	**Ed Ward, Cgy., RC**	**.10**	**.75**
☐☐	306	Calgary Checklist	.10	.75
☐☐	307	Jeremy Roenick, Chi.	.35	4.00
☐☐	**308**	**Mike Prokopec, Chi., RC**	**.10**	**.75**
☐☐	309	Joe Murphy, Chi.	.10	.75
☐☐	310	Eric Weinrich, Chi.	.10	.75
☐☐	311	Tony Amonte, Chi.	.25	2.00
☐☐	312	Bob Probert, Chi.	.10	.75
☐☐	313	Murray Craven, Chi.	.10	.75
☐☐	314	Sergei Krivokrasov, Chi.	.10	.75
☐☐	315	Chicago Checklist	.10	.75
☐☐	316	Peter Forsberg, Col.	1.00	20.00
☐☐	317	Stéphane Fiset (G), Col.	.25	2.00
☐☐	318	Mike Ricci, Col.	.10	.75
☐☐	319	Claude Lemieux, Col.	.10	.75
☐☐	320	Sandis Ozolinsh, Col.	.25	2.00
☐☐	321	Sylvain Lefebvre, Col.	.10	.75
☐☐	322	Scott Young, Col.	.10	.75
☐☐	323	Patrick Roy (G), Col.	1.50	35.00
☐☐	324	Colorado Checklist	.10	.75
☐☐	325	Brent Fedyk, Dal.	.10	.75
☐☐	326	Brent Gilchrist, Dal.	.10	.75
☐☐	327	Greg Adams, Dal.	.10	.75
☐☐	328	Richard Matvichuk, Dal.	.10	.75
☐☐	329	Joe Nieuwendyk, Dal.	.25	2.00
☐☐	330	Benoît Hogue, Dal.	.10	.75
☐☐	331	Darcy Wakaluk (G), Dal.	.10	.75
☐☐	332	Guy Carbonneau, Dal.	.10	.75
☐☐	333	Dallas Checklist	.10	.75
☐☐	334	Mike Vernon (G), Det.	.25	2.00
☐☐	**335**	**Mathieu Dandenault, Det., RC**	**.10**	**.75**
☐☐	336	Igor Larionov, Det.	.25	2.00
☐☐	337	Sergei Fedorov, Det.	.50	8.00
☐☐	338	Greg Johnson, Det.	.10	.75
☐☐	339	Dino Ciccarelli, Det.	.25	2.00
☐☐	340	Martin Lapointe, Det.	.10	.75
☐☐	341	Darren McCarty, Det.	.10	.75
☐☐	342	Detroit Checklist	.10	.75
☐☐	**343**	**Joaquin Gage (G), Edm., RC**	**.10**	**.75**

	No.	Player		
☐☐	344	Jiri Slegr, Edm.	.10	.75
☐☐	345	Mariusz Czerkawski, Edm.	.10	.75
☐☐	346	Doug Weight, Edm.	.35	4.00
☐☐	347	Todd Marchant, Edm.	.10	.75
☐☐	**348**	**Miroslav Satan, Edm., RC**	**.10**	**.75**
☐☐	349	Jeff Norton, Edm.	.10	.75
☐☐	350	Curtis Joseph (G), Edm.	.60	10.00
☐☐	351	Edmonton Checklist	.10	.75
☐☐	352	Tom Fitzgerald, Fla.	.10	.75
☐☐	353	Jody Hull, Fla.	.10	.75
☐☐	354	Terry Carkner, Fla.	.10	.75
☐☐	355	Scott Mellanby, Fla.	.10	.75
☐☐	356	Bill Lindsay, Fla.	.10	.75
☐☐	357	Gord Murphy, Fla.	.10	.75
☐☐	358	Brian Skrudland, Fla.	.10	.75
☐☐	359	David Nemirovsky, Fla.	.10	.75
☐☐	360	Florida Checklist	.10	.75
☐☐	361	Paul Ranheim, Hfd.	.10	.75
☐☐	362	Jason Muzzatti (G), Hfd.	.10	.75
☐☐	363	Glen Featherstone, Hfd.	.10	.75
☐☐	364	Andrew Cassels, Hfd.	.10	.75
☐☐	365	Jeff Brown, Hfd.	.10	.75
☐☐	366	Kevin Dineen, Hfd.	.10	.75
☐☐	367	Nelson Emerson, Hfd.	.10	.75
☐☐	368	Gerald Diduck, Hfd.	.10	.75
☐☐	369	Hartford Checklist	.10	.75
☐☐	370	Kevin Stevens, L.A.	.10	.75
☐☐	371	Darryl Sydor, L.A.	.10	.75
☐☐	372	Yanic Perreault, L.A.	.10	.75
☐☐	373	Arto Blomsten, L.A.	.10	.75
☐☐	374	Kevin Todd, L.A.	.10	.75
☐☐	375	Byron Dafoe (G), L.A.	.10	.75
☐☐	376	Tony Granato, L.A.	.10	.75
☐☐	**377**	**Vladimir Tsyplakov, L.A., RC**	**.10**	**.75**
☐☐	378	Los Angeles Checklist	.10	.75
☐☐	379	Martin Rucinsky, Mtl.	.10	.75
☐☐	380	Patric Brisebrois, Mtl.	.10	.75
☐☐	381	Lyle Odelein, Mtl.	.10	.75
☐☐	382	Andrei Kovalenko, Mtl.	.10	.75
☐☐	383	Mark Recchi, Mtl.	.25	2.00
☐☐	384	Jocelyn Thibault (G), Mtl.	.35	4.00
☐☐	385	Turner Stevenson, Mtl.	.10	.75
☐☐	386	Pat Jablonski, Mtl.	.10	.75
☐☐	387	Montreal Checklist	.10	.75
☐☐	388	Scott Niedermayer, N.J.	.25	2.00
☐☐	**389**	**Corey Schwab (G), N.J., RC**	**.10**	**.75**
☐☐	390	Steve Thomas, N.J.	.10	.75
☐☐	391	Valeri Zelepukin, N.J.	.10	.75
☐☐	392	Shawn Chambers, N.J.	.10	.75
☐☐	393	Jocelyn Lemieux, N.J.	.10	.75
☐☐	394	Brian Rolston, N.J.	.10	.75
☐☐	395	Denis Pederson, N.J.	.10	.75
☐☐	396	New Jersey Checklist	.10	.75
☐☐	397	Martin Straka, NYI.	.10	.75
☐☐	398	Niklas Andersson, NYI.	.10	.75
☐☐	399	Wendel Clark, NYI.	.25	2.00
☐☐	400	Travis Green, NYI.	.10	.75
☐☐	401	Chris Marinucci, NYI.	.10	.75
☐☐	402	Darius Kasparaitis, NYI.	.10	.75
☐☐	403	Patrick Flatley, NYI.	.10	.75
☐☐	404	Jamie McLennan (G), NYI.	.25	2.00
☐☐	405	Islanders Checklist	.10	.75
☐☐	406	Glenn Healy (G), NYR.	.10	.75
☐☐	407	Pat Verbeek, NYR.	.10	.75
☐☐	408	Ian Laperrière, NYR.	.10	.75
☐☐	409	Ray Ferraro, NYR.	.10	.75
☐☐	410	Jeff Beukeboom, NYR.	.10	.75
☐☐	411	Ulf Samuelsson, NYR.	.10	.75
☐☐	412	Doug Lidster, NYR.	.10	.75
☐☐	413	Bruce Driver, NYR.	.10	.75
☐☐	414	Rangers Checklist	.10	.75
☐☐	**415**	**Antti Törmänen, Ott., RC**	**.10**	**.75**
☐☐	416	Sean Hill, Ott.	.10	.75
☐☐	417	Damian Rhodes (G), Ott.	.10	.75
☐☐	418	Jaroslav Modry, Ott.	.10	.75
☐☐	**419**	**Mike Bales (G), Ott., RC**	**.10**	**.75**
☐☐	**420**	**Trent McCleary, Ott., RC**	**.10**	**.75**
☐☐	421	Randy Cunneyworth, Ott.	.10	.75
☐☐	422	Ted Drury, Ott.	.10	.75
☐☐	423	Ottawa Checklist	.10	.75
☐☐	424	Pat Falloon, Pha.	.10	.75
☐☐	425	Garth Snow (G), Pha.	.10	.75
☐☐	426	Shjon Podein, Pha.	.10	.75
☐☐	427	Petr Svoboda, Pha.	.10	.75
☐☐	428	Eric Desjardins, Pha.	.10	.75
☐☐	429	Anatoli Semenov, Pha.	.10	.75
☐☐	430	Kevin Haller, Pha.	.10	.75
☐☐	431	Rob DiMaio, Pha.	.10	.75
☐☐	432	Philadelphia Checklist	.10	.75
☐☐	433	Chris Joseph, Pgh.	.10	.75
☐☐	434	Sergei Zubov, Pgh.	.25	2.00
☐☐	435	Tom Barrasso (G), Pgh.	.25	2.00
☐☐	436	Chris Tamer, Pgh.	.10	.75
☐☐	437	Dmitri Mironov, Pgh.	.10	.75
☐☐	438	Petr Nedved, Pgh.	.10	.75
☐☐	439	Neil Wilkinson, Pgh.	.10	.75
☐☐	440	Glen Murray, Pgh.	.10	.75
☐☐	441	Pittsburgh Checklist	.10	.75
☐☐	442	J.J. Daigneault, Stl.	.10	.75
☐☐	443	Grant Fuhr (G), Stl.	.25	2.00
☐☐	444	Adam Creighton, Stl.	.10	.75
☐☐	445	Brian Noonan, Stl.	.10	.75
☐☐	446	Stéphane Matteau, Stl.	.10	.75
☐☐	447	Roman Vopat, Stl.	.10	.75
☐☐	448	Geoff Courtnall, Stl.	.10	.75
☐☐	449	Wayne Gretzky, Stl.	3.50	50.00
☐☐	450	St. Louis Checklist	.10	.75
☐☐	451	Chris Terreri (G), S.J.	.10	.75
☐☐	452	Ulf Dahlen, S.J.	.10	.75
☐☐	453	Owen Nolan, S.J.	.25	2.00
☐☐	454	Doug Bodger, S.J.	.10	.75
☐☐	455	Craig Janney, S.J.	.10	.75
☐☐	456	Ville Peltonen, S.J.	.10	.75
☐☐	457	Ray Sheppard, S.J.	.10	.75
☐☐	458	Shean Donovan, S.J.	.10	.75
☐☐	459	San Jose Checklist	.10	.75
☐☐	460	Jeff Reese (G), T.B.	.10	.75
☐☐	461	Shawn Burr, T.B.	.10	.75
☐☐	462	Chris Gratton, T.B.	.25	2.00
☐☐	463	John Cullen, T.B.	.10	.75
☐☐	464	Bill Houlder, T.B.	.10	.75
☐☐	465	J.C. Bergeron (G), T.B.	.10	.75
☐☐	466	Brian Bellows, T.B.	.10	.75
☐☐	467	Drew Bannister, T.B.	.10	.75
☐☐	468	Tampa Bay Checklist	.10	.75
☐☐	469	Dmitri Yushkevich, Tor.	.10	.75
☐☐	470	Dave Andreychuk, Tor.	.10	.75
☐☐	471	Dave Gagner, Tor.	.10	.75
☐☐	472	Todd Warriner, Tor.	.10	.75
☐☐	473	Sergio Momesso, Tor.	.10	.75
☐☐	474	Kirk Muller, Tor.	.10	.75
☐☐	475	Dave Ellett, Tor.	.10	.75
☐☐	476	Ken Baumgartner, Tor.	.10	.75
☐☐	477	Toronto Checklist	.10	.75
☐☐	478	Esa Tikkanen, Van.	.10	.75
☐☐	479	Cliff Ronning, Van.	.10	.75
☐☐	480	Martin Gelinas, Van.	.10	.75
☐☐	**481**	**Brian Loney, Van., RC**	**.10**	**.75**
☐☐	482	Pavel Bure, Van.	.75	12.00
☐☐	483	Corey Hirsch (G), Van.	.10	.75
☐☐	484	Scott Walker, Van.	.10	.75
☐☐	485	Jim Dowd, Van.	.10	.75
☐☐	486	Vancouver Checklist	.10	.75
☐☐	487	Michal Pivonka, Wsh.	.10	.75
☐☐	488	Pat Peake, Wsh.	.10	.75
☐☐	489	Martin Gendron, Wsh.	.10	.75
☐☐	490	Peter Bondra, Wsh.	.35	6.00
☐☐	491	Nolan Baumgartner, Wsh.	.10	.75
☐☐	492	Jim Carey (G), Wsh.	.10	.75
☐☐	493	Steve Konowalchuk, Wsh.	.10	.75
☐☐	494	Jason Allison, Wsh.	.35	4.00
☐☐	495	Washington Checklist	.10	.75
☐☐	496	Oleg Tverdovsky, Wpg.	.10	.75
☐☐	**497**	**Craig Mills, Wpg., RC**	**.10**	**.75**
☐☐	498	Darren Turcotte, Wpg.	.10	.75
☐☐	499	Norm Maciver, Wpg.	.10	.75
☐☐	500	Chad Kilger, Wpg.	.10	.75
☐☐	501	Keith Tkachuk, Wpg.	.35	6.00
☐☐	502	Kris King, Wpg.	.10	.75
☐☐	503	Dallas Drake, Wpg.	.10	.75
☐☐	504	Winnipeg Checklist	.10	.75
☐☐	505	Saku Koivu, Mtl.	.35	6.00
☐☐	506	Vitali Yachmenev, L.A.	.10	.75
☐☐	507	Daniel Alfredsson, Ott.	.35	3.50
☐☐	508	Radek Dvorak, Fla.	.10	.75
☐☐	509	Miroslav Satan, Edm.	.10	.75
☐☐	510	Aki Berg, L.A	.10	.75
☐☐	511	Valeri Bure, Mtl.	.10	.75
☐☐	512	Petr Sykora, N.J.	.10	.75
☐☐	**513**	**Andrei Vasilyev, NYI., RC**	**.10**	**.75**
☐☐	514	Niklas Sundstrom, NYR.	.10	.75
☐☐	515	Viktor Kozlov, S.J.	.10	.75
☐☐	516	Sami Kapanen, Hfd.	.10	.75
☐☐	517	Anders Myrvold, Col.	.10	.75
☐☐	518	Jere Lehtinen, Dal.	.25	2.00
☐☐	519	Marcus Ragnarsson, S.J.	.10	.75
☐☐	520	Stefan Ustorf, Wsh.	.10	.75
☐☐	521	Ville Peltonen, S.J.	.10	.75
☐☐	**522**	**Antti Törmönen, Ott., RC**	**.10**	**.75**
☐☐	**523**	**Petr Sykora, N.J., RC**	**.35**	**3.00**
☐☐	**524**	**Scott Bailey (G), Bos., RC**	**.10**	**.75**
☐☐	**525**	**Kevin Hodson (G), Det., RC**	**.50**	**3.00**
☐☐	**526**	**Landon Wilson, Col., RC**	**.10**	**.75**
☐☐	527	Aaron Gavey, T.B.	.10	.75
☐☐	**528**	**Darren Langdon, NYR., RC**	**.10**	**.75**
☐☐	529	Jason Doig, Wpg.	.10	.75
☐☐	530	Marty Murray, Cgy.	.10	.75
☐☐	**531**	**Marcus Ragnarsson, S.J., RC**	**.10**	**.75**
☐☐	532	Peter Ferraro, NYR.	.10	.75
☐☐	533	Grant Marshall, Dal.	.10	.75
☐☐	**534**	**Mike Wilson, Buf., RC**	**.10**	**.75**
☐☐	**535**	**Rory Fitzpatrick, Mtl., RC**	**.10**	**.75**
☐☐	536	Ed Jovanovski, Fla.	.25	2.00
☐☐	537	Eric Fichaud (G), NYI.	.25	2.00
☐☐	538	Stefan Ustorf, Wsh.	.10	.75
☐☐	**539**	**Stéphane Yelle, Col., RC**	**.25**	**1.50**
☐☐	540	Eric Dazé, Chi.	.25	2.00

TROPHY WINNERS

Series One Insert Set (6 cards):		**40.00**
No.	**Player**	**NRMT-MT**
☐ 1	Eric Lindros, Pha.	15.00
☐ 2	Jaromir Jagr, Pgh.	12.00
☐ 3	Peter Forsberg, Col.	12.00
☐ 4	Paul Coffey, Det.	4.00
☐ 5	Dominik Hasek, Buf.	8.00
☐ 6	Ron Francis Pgh.	4.00

CROWN COLLECTION

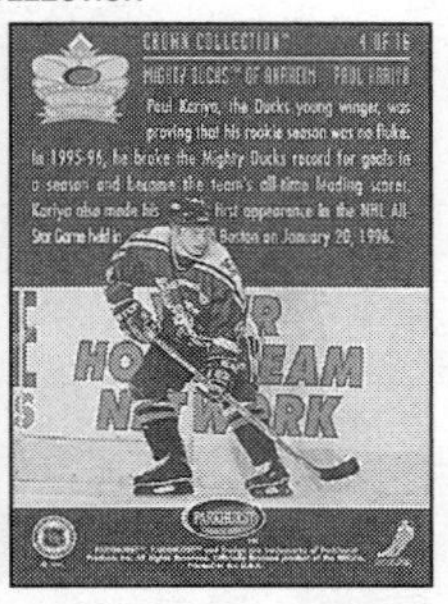

These cards have two versions: the regular insert and a gold parallel. Black border cards were inserted in Series One packs and purple border cards were inserted in Series Two packs.

Black Insert Set (16 cards):			**120.00**	**350.00**
Purple Insert Set (16 cards):			**120.00**	**350.00**
	No.	**Black**	**GCC**	**CC**
☐☐	1	Eric Lindros, Pha.	45.00	15.00
☐☐	2	Félix Potvin, Tor.	18.00	6.00
☐☐	3	Mario Lemieux, Pgh.	60.00	20.00
☐☐	4	Paul Kariya, Ana.	45.00	15.00
☐☐	5	Pavel Bure, Van.	25.00	8.00
☐☐	6	Wayne Gretzky, L.A.	75.00	25.00
☐☐	7	Mikael Renberg, Pha.	6.00	2.00
☐☐	8	Paul Coffey, Det.	9.00	3.00
☐☐	9	Teemu Selänne, Wpg.	25.00	8.00
☐☐	10	Brett Hull, Stl.	18.00	6.00
☐☐	11	Martin Brodeur (G), N.J.	25.00	8.00

	No.	Player	GCC	CC
☐☐	12	Doug Gilmour, Tor.	12.00	4.00
☐☐	13	Peter Forsberg, Col.	35.00	12.00
☐☐	14	Sergei Fedorov, Det.	18.00	6.00
☐☐	15	Saku Koivu, Mtl.	25.00	8.00
☐☐	16	Jim Carey (G), Wsh.	6.00	2.00
	No.	**Purple**	**GCC**	**CC**
☐☐	1	Jaromir Jagr, Pgh.	35.00	12.00
☐☐	2	Patrick Roy (G), Col.	60.00	20.00
☐☐	3	Alexander Mogilny, Van.	12.00	4.00
☐☐	4	Paul Kariya, Ana.	45.00	15.00
☐☐	5	Dominik Hasek (G), Buf.	25.00	8.00
☐☐	6	Peter Forsberg, Col.	35.00	12.00
☐☐	7	Mark Messier, NYR.	18.00	6.00
☐☐	8	Mats Sundin, Tor.	18.00	6.00
☐☐	9	Ray Bourque, Bos.	18.00	6.00
☐☐	10	Wayne Gretzky, Stl.	75.00	25.00
☐☐	11	Eric Lindros, Pha.	45.00	15.00
☐☐	12	John Vanbiesbrouck (G), Fla.	20.00	7.00
☐☐	13	Chris Chelios, Chi.	15.00	5.00
☐☐	14	Brian Leetch, NYR.	12.00	4.00
☐☐	15	Daniel Alfredsson, Ott.	15.00	5.00
☐☐	16	Eric Dazé, Chi.	9.00	3.00

GOAL PATROL

These series one goalie inserts are embossed.

Series One Insert Set (12 cards): 60.00

	No.	Player	NRMT-MT
☐	1	Martin Brodeur (G), N.J.	8.00
☐	2	Félix Potvin (G), Tor.	6.00
☐	3	Patrick Roy (G), Mtl.	20.00
☐	4	Dominik Hasek (G), Buf.	8.00
☐	5	Jim Carey (G), Wsh.	2.00
☐	6	Ed Belfour (G), Chi.	4.00
☐	7	John Vanbiesbrouck (G), Fla.	7.00
☐	8	Trevor Kidd (G), Cgy.	3.00
☐	9	Bill Ranford (G), Edm.	3.00
☐	10	Arturs Irbe (G), S.J.	2.00
☐	11	Kirk McLean (G), NYR.	3.00
☐	12	Mike Richter (G), NYR.	4.00

INTERNATIONAL ALL-STAR

Series One Insert Set (6 cards): 75.00

	No.	Player	NRMT-MT
☐	1	Dominik Hasek/Arturs Irbe	12.00
☐	2	Nicklas Lidström/Sandis Ozolinsh	5.00
☐	3	Sergei Zubov/Alexei Zhitnik	5.00
☐	4	Sergei Fedorov/Peter Forsberg	30.00
☐	5	Jaromir Jagr/Teemu Selänne	30.00
☐	6	Mats Sundin/Mikael Renberg	8.00

AUTOGRAPHED CARDS

These autographed cards were inserted in both Series One and Series Two packs.

	Player	NRMT-MT
☐	Mikael Renberg	35.00
☐	Teemu Selänne	100.00
☐	Martin Brodeur	100.00
☐	Saku Koivu	100.00
☐	Saku Koivu [5"x7"]	100.00

PARKHURST EAST / WEST ALL-STARS

Series Two Insert Set (6 cards): 125.00

	No.	Player	NRMT-MT
☐	1	Mario Lemieux/Wayne Gretzky	75.00
☐	2	Jaromir Jagr/Brett Hull	25.00
☐	3	Brendan Shanahan/Pavel Bure	18.00
☐	4	Scott Stevens/Chris Chelios	5.00
☐	5	Ray Bourque/Paul Coffey	8.00
☐	6	Martin Brodeur/Ed Belfour	15.00

PARKIE PICKS

These cards are limited to 1,000 copies.

Series Two Insert Set (54 cards): 500.00

	No.	Player	NRMT-MT
☐	PP1	Eric Lindros, Pha.	25.00
☐	PP2	Mario Lemieux, Pgh.	30.00
☐	PP3	Sergei Fedorov, Det.	10.00
☐	PP4	Peter Forsberg, Col.	20.00
☐	PP5	John Vanbiesbrouck (G), Fla.	12.00
☐	PP6	Mark Messier, NYR.	10.00
☐	PP7	Jaromir Jagr, Pgh.	20.00
☐	PP8	Joe Sakic, Col.	18.00
☐	PP9	Grant Fuhr (G), Stl.	4.00
☐	PP10	Eric Lindros, Pha.	25.00
☐	PP11	Mario Lemieux, Pgh.	30.00
☐	PP12	Mark Messier, NYR.	10.00
☐	PP13	Peter Forsberg, Col.	15.00
☐	PP14	Jaromir Jagr, Pgh.	20.00
☐	PP15	Paul Kariya, Ana.	25.00
☐	PP16	Joe Sakic, Col.	18.00
☐	PP17	Teemu Selänne, Ana.	15.00
☐	PP18	Alexander Mogilny, Van.	6.00
☐	PP19	Paul Coffey, Det.	4.00
☐	PP20	Chris Chelios, Chi.	8.00
☐	PP21	Brian Leetch, NYR.	6.00
☐	PP22	Ray Bourque, Bos.	10.00
☐	PP23	Larry Murphy, Tor.	4.00
☐	PP24	Nicklas Lidström, Det.	4.00
☐	PP25	Roman Hamrlik, T.B.	4.00
☐	PP26	Gary Suter, Cgy.	2.00
☐	PP27	Sergei Zubov, Pgh.	4.00
☐	PP28	Dominik Hasek (G), Buf.	15.00
☐	PP29	John Vanbiesbrouck (G), Fla.	12.00
☐	PP30	Chris Osgood (G), Det.	8.00
☐	PP31	Mike Richter (G), NYR.	6.00
☐	PP32	Martin Brodeur (G), N.J.	15.00
☐	PP33	Ron Hextall (G), Pha.	4.00
☐	PP34	Grant Fuhr (G), Stl.	4.00
☐	PP35	Patrick Roy (G), Col.	30.00
☐	PP36	Jim Carey (G), Wsh.	2.00
☐	PP37	Vitali Yachmenev, L.A.	2.00
☐	PP38	Daniel Alfredsson, Ott.	10.00
☐	PP39	Saku Koivu, Mtl.	15.00
☐	PP40	Eric Dazé, Chi.	4.00
☐	PP41	Marcus Ragnarsson, S.J.	2.00
☐	PP42	Ed Jovanovski, Fla.	4.00
☐	PP43	Petr Sykora, N.J.	2.00
☐	PP44	Todd Bertuzzi, NYI.	4.00
☐	PP45	Radek Dvorak, Fla.	2.00
☐	PP46	Paul Kariya, Ana.	25.00
☐	PP47	Ron Francis, Pgh.	6.00
☐	PP48	Alexander Mogilny, Van.	6.00
☐	PP49	Pat LaFontaine, Buf.	4.00
☐	PP50	Pierre Turgeon, Mtl.	4.00
☐	PP51	Teemu Selänne, Ana.	15.00
☐	PP52	Sergei Fedorov, Det.	10.00
☐	PP53	Adam Oates, Bos.	6.00
☐	PP54	Brett Hull, Stl.	10.00

1995 - 97 PARKHURST 24 KT. GOLD

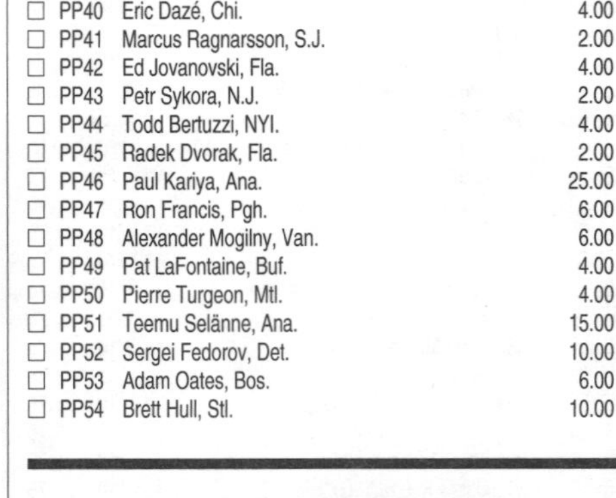

The first nine cards were produced for 1995-96 while the Lemieux card was produced for 1996-97. Each card was serial numbered out of 1,000. The three prototypes for 1996-97 that are known to exist are Ray Bourque, Martin Brodeur and Sergei Fedorov. It is estimated that only a handful of these prototypes exist.

Imprint:

	Player	NRMT-MT
☐	Ed Belfour (G), Chi	70.00
☐	Peter Forsberg, Col.	90.00
☐	Jaromir Jagr, Pgh.	90.00
☐	Paul Kariya, Ana.	100.00
☐	Brian Leetch, NYR.	80.00
☐	Eric Lindros, Pha.	140.00
☐	Jacques Plante (G), Mtl.	75.00
☐	Patrick Roy (G). Mtl.	100.00
☐	Teemu Selänne, Wpg.	90.00
☐	Mario Lemieux, Pgh.	150.00

1995 - 96 PARKHURST "1966 - 67"

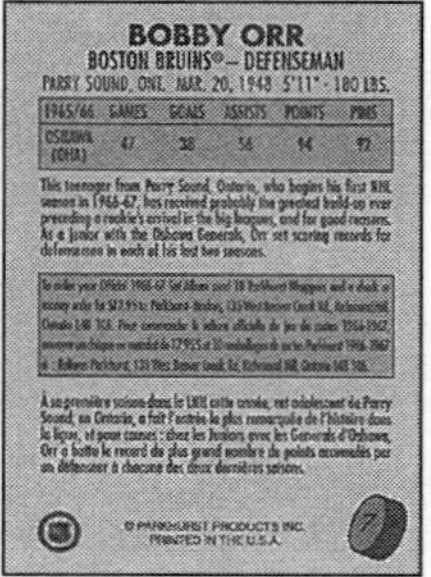

Numbers 1-120 have two versions: the regular card and a one per pack coin parallel. There are also five promo cards. These promo cards are valued at about 2 times the regular issue.

Complete Set (150 cards):				**25.00**
Coin Set (120 coins):			**125.00**	
Album:				**18.00**
Bruins Shield:			**10.00**	
Blackhawks Shield:			**10.00**	
Red Wings Shield:			**10.00**	
Canadiens Shield:			**10.00**	
Rangers Shield:			**10.00**	
Maple Leafs Shield:			**10.00**	
Common Player:			**.50**	**.15**
	No.	**Player**	**Coin**	**Card**
☐☐	1	Pit Martin, Bos.	.50	.15
☐☐	2	Ron Stewart, Bos.	.50	.15

	No.	Player		
☐☐	3	Joe Watson, Bos.	.50	.15
☐☐	4	Ed Westfall, Bos.	.50	.15
☐☐	5	John Bucyk, Bos.	1.50	.75
☐☐	6	Ted Green, Bos.	.50	.15
☐☐	7	Bobby Orr, Bos.	12.00	5.00
☐☐	8	Bob Woytowich, Bos.	.50	.15
☐☐	9	Murray Oliver, Bos.	.50	.15
☐☐	10	John McKenzie, Bos.	.50	.15
☐☐	11	Tom Williams, Bos.	.50	.15
☐☐	12	Don Awrey, Bos.	.50	.15
☐☐	13	Ron Schock, Bos.	.50	.15
☐☐	14	Bernie Parent (G), Bos.	3.00	1.50
☐☐	15	Ron Murphy, Bos.	.50	.15
☐☐☐	16	Gerry Cheevers (G), Bos.	3.00	1.50
☐☐	17	Gilles Marotte, Bos.	.50	.15
☐☐	18	Ed Johnston, Bos.	.75	.35
☐☐	19	Derek Sanderson, Bos.	2.50	1.25
☐☐	20	Wayne Connelly, Bos.	.50	.15
☐☐	21	Bobby Hull, Chi.	7.00	3.00
☐☐	22	Matt Pavelich, Chi.	.50	.15
☐☐	23	Ken Hodge, Chi.	.50	.15
☐☐	24	Stan Mikita, Chi.	3.00	1.50
☐☐	25	Fred Stanfield, Chi.	.50	.15
☐☐	26	Eric Nesterenko, Chi.	.50	.15
☐☐	27	Doug Jarrett, Chi.	.50	.15
☐☐	28	Lou Angotti, Chi.	.50	.15
☐☐	29	Ken Wharram, Chi.	.50	.15
☐☐	30	Bill Hay, Chi.	.50	.15
☐☐	31	Glenn Hall (G), Chi.	4.00	2.00
☐☐	32	Chico Maki, Chi.	.50	.15
☐☐	33	Phil Esposito, Chi.	3.50	1.75
☐☐	34	Pierre Pilote, Chi.	1.00	.35
☐☐	35	Doug Mohns, Chi.	.50	.15
☐☐	36	Ed Van Impe, Chi.	.50	.15
☐☐	37	Dennis Hull, Chi.	.50	.15
☐☐	38	Pat Stapleton, Chi.	.50	.15
☐☐	39	Dennis DeJordy (G), Chi.	.75	.35
☐☐	40	Paul Henderson, Det.	15.00	.35
☐☐	41	Gary Bergman, Det.	.50	.15
☐☐☐	42	Gordie Howe, Det.	10.00	4.00
☐☐	43	Bob McCord, Det.	.50	.15
☐☐	44	Andy Bathgate, Det.	1.25	60
☐☐	45	Norm Ullman, Det.	1.50	.75
☐☐	46	Peter Mahovlich, Det.	.50	.15
☐☐	47	Ted Hampson, Det.	.50	.15
☐☐	48	Léo Boivin, Det.	1.00	.35
☐☐	49	Bruce MacGregor, Det.	.50	.15
☐☐	50	Ab McDonald, Det.	.50	.15
☐☐	51	Dean Prentice, Det.	.50	.15
☐☐	52	Floyd Smith, Det.	.50	.15
☐☐	53	Alex Delvecchio, Det.	1.50	.75
☐☐	54	Pete Goegan, Det.	.50	.15
☐☐	55	Parker McDonald, Det.	.50	.15
☐☐	56	Roger Crozier (G), Det.	.75	.35
☐☐	57	Val Fonteyne, Det.	.50	.15
☐☐	58	Henri Richard, Mtl.	2.50	1.25
☐☐	59	John Ferguson, Mtl.	.50	.15
☐☐	60	Yvan Cournoyer, Mtl.	2.00	1.00
☐☐	61	Claude Provost, Mtl.	.50	.15
☐☐	62	Dave Balon, Mtl.	.50	.15
☐☐	63	Ted Harris, Mtl.	.50	.15
☐☐	64	Ralph Backstrom, Mtl.	.50	.15
☐☐	65	Jacques Laperrière, Mtl.	1.00	.35
☐☐	66	Terry Harper, Mtl.	.50	.15
☐☐	67	J.C. Tremblay, Mtl.	.50	.15
☐☐	68	Jean Guy Talbot, Mtl.	.50	.15
☐☐	69	Claude Larose, Mtl.	.50	.15
☐☐	70	Charlie Hodge (G), Mtl.	.75	.35
☐☐	71	Gilles Tremblay, Mtl.	.50	.15
☐☐	72	Jim Roberts, Mtl.	.50	.15
☐☐	73	Jean Béliveau, Mtl.	5.50	2.25
☐☐	74	Serge Savard, Mtl.	1.50	.75
☐☐	75	Rogatien Vachon (G), Mtl.	2.50	1.25
☐☐	76	Gump Worlsey (G), Mtl.	3.50	1.75
☐☐	77	Bobby Rousseau, Mtl.	.50	.15
☐☐	78	Dick Duff, Mtl.	.50	.15
☐☐	79	Rod Gilbert, NYR.	2.00	1.00
☐☐	80	Harry Howell, NYR.	1.00	.35
☐☐	81	Jim Neilson, NYR.	.50	.15
☐☐	82	Don Marshall, NYR.	.50	.15
☐☐	83	Reg Fleming, NYR.	.50	.15
☐☐	84	Wayne Hillman, NYR.	.50	.15
☐☐	85	Bob Nevin, NYR.	.50	.15
☐☐	86	Arnie Brown, NYR.	.50	.15
☐☐	87	Earl Ingarfield, NYR.	.50	.15
☐☐	88	Jean Ratelle, NYR.	2.00	1.00
☐☐	89	Bernie Geoffrion, NYR.	2.00	1.00
☐☐	90	Orland Kurtenbach, NYR.	.50	.15
☐☐	91	Bill Hicke, NYR.	.50	.15
☐☐	92	Red Berenson, NYR.	.50	.15
☐☐	93	Ed Giacomin (G), NYR.	3.00	1.50
☐☐	94	Al MacNeil, NYR.	.50	.15
☐☐	95	Rod Seiling, NYR.	.50	.15
☐☐	96	Doug Robinson, NYR.	.50	.15
☐☐	97	Cesare Maniago (G), NYR.	.75	.35
☐☐	98	Vic Hadfield, NYR.	.50	.15
☐☐	99	Phil Goyette, NYR.	.50	.15
☐☐	100	Dave Keon, Tor.	2.00	1.00
☐☐	101	Mike Walton, Tor.	.50	.15
☐☐	102	Frank Mahovlich, Tor.	3.50	1.75
☐☐	103	Tim Horton, Tor.	4.00	2.00
☐☐	104	Larry Hillman, Tor.	.50	.15
☐☐	105	Kent Douglas, Tor.	.50	.15
☐☐	106	Ron Ellis, Tor.	.50	.15
☐☐	107	Jim Pappin, Tor.	.50	.15
☐☐	108	Marcel Pronovost, Tor.	1.00	.35
☐☐	109	Red Kelly, Tor.	1.25	.60
☐☐	110	Allan Stanley, Tor.	1.00	.35
☐☐	111	Brit Selby, Tor.	.50	.15
☐☐	112	Pete Stemkowski, Tor.	.50	.15
☐☐	113	Eddie Shack, Tor.	3.00	1.50
☐☐	114	Bob Pulford, Tor.	1.25	.60
☐☐	115	Larry Jeffrey, Tor.	.50	.15
☐☐	116	George Armstrong, Tor.	1.50	.75
☐☐	117	Bob Baun, Tor.	.50	.15
☐☐	118	Bruce Gamble (G), Tor.	.75	.35
☐☐	119	Johnny Bower (G), Tor.	3.00	1.50
☐☐	120	Terry Sawchuk (G), Tor.	5.50	2.25

	No.	Player	Card
☐	121	AS: Glenn Hall/Gump Worsley	1.00
☐	122	AS: Jacques Laperrière/Allan Stanley	.25
☐	123	AS: Pierre Pilote/Pat Stapleton	.25
☐	124	AS: Bobby Hull/Frank Mahovlich	1.50
☐☐	125	AS: Stan Mikita/Jean Béliveau	1.00
☐	126	AS: Gordie Howe/Bobby Rousseau	2.00
☐	127	AW: Alex Delvecchio, Det.	.35
☐☐	128	AW: Jacques Laperrière, Mtl.	.25
☐	129	AW: Bobby Hull, Chi.	1.50
☐	130	AW: Bobby Hull, Chi.	1.50
☐	131	AW: Gump Worsley/Charlie Hodge, Mtl.	.75
☐	132	AW: Brit Selby, Tor.	.25
ACTION CARDS			
☐	133	All-Stars Eye Richard: Vic Hadfield [AS-12] Rod Gilbert [AS], Henri Richard [MTL]	.60
☐	134	Boston Young Stars: Gerry Cheevers [BOS-G] Bobby Orr [4], Jim Pappin [TOR-18]	2.50
☐	135	Gump Stumps Golden Jet: Jim Roberts [MTL-26] Bobby Hull [CHI-9], Lorne Worsley [MTL]	1.50
☐	136	Ellis Beats Crozier: Norm Ullman [DET-7] Roger Crozier [DET-G, Gary Bergman [DET-2], [unknown DET player], Ron Ellis (TOR-8]	.35
☐	137	Habs Protect Rogie: Claude Provost [MTL-14] Roggie Vachon [MTL-G], J.C. Tremblay [MTL-3], Ted Harris [MTL-10]	.60
☐	138	Phil Fills The Crease: Rod Gilbert [NYR-7] Wayne Hillman [NYR-2], Vic Hadfield [NYR-11, Orland Kurtenbach [25], Phil Esposito [BOS-7]	.75
☐	139	All Hands on Deck: Dave Keon (TOR] Pat Stapleton [12], Denis DeJordy [CHI-30], George Armstrong [10], Ed Van Impe [CHI-2]	.50
☐	140	TL: Murray Oliver, Bos.	.25
☐	141	TL: Bobby Hull, Chi.	1.50
☐	142	TL: Gordie Howe, Det.	2.00
☐	143	TL: Bobby Rousseau, Mtl.	.25
☐☐	144	TL: Bob Nevin, NYR.	.25
☐	145	TL: Frank Mahovlich/Bob Pulford, Tor.	.75
PLAYOFF ACTION CARDS			
☐	146	Semi Finals - MTL 4-0, Dave Keon [TOR-14] Claude Provost [MTL-14], F. Mahovlich [TOR-27], G. Armstrong [TOR-10]	.75
☐	147	Semi Finals - DET 4-2, Pierre Pilote [CHI-3] Gordie Howe [DET-9], Glenn Hall [CHI-1], Dean Prentice [DET-20]	2.00
☐	148	Finals - MTL 4-2, Bobby Rousseau [MTL-15] Gordie Howe [DET-9], A. Delvecchio [DET-10], Terry Harper [MTL-19], Dean Prentice [DET-20]	2.00
☐	149	Checklist	.15
☐	150	Checklist	.15

MR. HOCKEY INSERTS

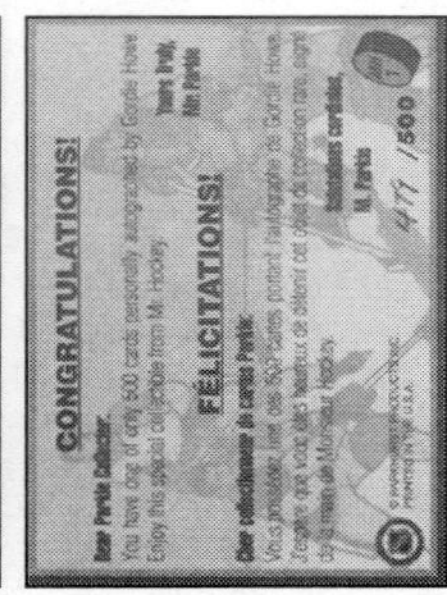

There are four versions to this set: the regular insert, an autographed card, a coin parallel and a 5"x7" promo.

Insert Set (5 cards):			40.00	60.00	50.00	500.00
	No.	Player	Coin	Card	5x7	Auto.
☐☐☐☐	MH1	Gordie Howe	10.00	15.00	12.00	110.00
☐☐☐☐	MH2	Gordie Howe	10.00	15.00	12.00	110.00
☐☐☐☐	MH3	G. Howe/A. Lindsay	10.00	15.00	12.00	110.00
☐☐☐☐	MH4	Gordie Howe [AS]	10.00	15.00	12.00	110.00
☐☐☐☐	MH5	Gordie Howe	10.00	15.00	12.00	110.00

SUPER ROOKIE INSERTS

There are four versions to this set: the regular insert, an autographed card, a coin parallel and a 5"x7" promo.

Insert Set (5 cards):			50.00	75.00	60.00	700.00
	No.	Player	Coin	Card	5x7	Auto.
☐☐☐☐	SR1	Bobby Orr	12.00	20.00	15.00	165.00
☐☐☐☐	SR2	Bobby Orr	12.00	20.00	15.00	165.00
☐☐☐☐	SR3	Bobby Orr	12.00	20.00	15.00	165.00
☐☐☐☐	SR4	Bobby Orr	12.00	20.00	15.00	165.00
☐☐☐☐	SR5	Bobby Orr	12.00	20.00	15.00	165.00

REDEMPTION

Each series of of six cards was available through a redemption offer.

All-Stars Set (6 cards):			**18.00**
Award Winners Set (6 cards):			**25.00**
League Leaders Set (6 cards):			**12.00**
	No.	**Player**	**NRMT-MT**
☐	AS1	Ed Giacomin (G)	5.00
☐	AS2	Pierre Pilote	1.50
☐	AS3	Harry Howell	1.50
☐	AS4	Bobby Hull	8.00
☐	AS5	Stan Mikita	3.50
☐	AS6	Ken Wharram	1.50
☐	TW1	Stan Mikita	3.50
☐	TW2	Stan Mikita	3.50
☐	TW3	Stan Mikita	3.50
☐	TW4	Harry Howell	1.50
☐	TW5	Bobby Orr	15.00
☐	TW6	D. DeJordy (G)/ G. Hall (G)	3.00
☐	SL1	Johnny Bucyk	2.50
☐	SL2	Stan Mikita	3.50
☐	SL3	Norm Ullman	2.50
☐	SL4	Bobby Rousseau	1.50
☐	SL5	Phil Goyette	1.50
☐	SL6	Dave Keon	2.50

1995 - 96 PINNACLE

These cards have three versions: a regular card, a Rink Collection parallel (dufex technology) and an Artist's Proof parallel (dufex with Artist's Proof stamp). Cards 100-125 have horizontal pictures. An intended second series was never released. Seven cards have a clipped promo version. Promo and regular cards have the same value.

Imprint: © 1995 PINNACLE BRANDS, INC.

No.	Player	Reg.	RC	AP
Complete Set (225 cards):		18.00	425.00	2,600.00
Common Player:		.15	1.50	5.00
1	Pavel Bure, Van.	.75	15.00	60.00
2	Paul Kariya, Ana.	1.50	30.00	150.00
3	Adam Oates, Bos.	.35	6.00	20.00
4	Garry Galley, Buf.	.15	1.50	5.00
5	Mark Messier, NYR.	.50	10.00	35.00
6	Theoren Fleury, Cgy.	.35	6.00	20.00
7	Alexandre Daigle, Ott.	.25	3.00	10.00
8	Joe Murphy, Chi.	.15	1.50	5.00
9	Eric Lindros, Pha.	1.50	30.00	150.00
10	Kevin Hatcher, Wsh.	.15	1.50	5.00
11	Jaromir Jagr, Pgh.	1.25	25.00	125.00
12	Owen Nolan, Que.	.25	3.00	10.00
13	Ulf Dahlen, S.J.	.15	1.50	5.00
14	Paul Coffey, Det.	.25	3.00	10.00
15	Brett Hull, Stl.	.50	10.00	35.00
16	Jason Arnott, Edm.	.25	3.00	10.00
17	Paul Ysebaert, T.B.	.15	1.50	5.00
18	Jesse Belanger, Fla.	.15	1.50	5.00
19	Mats Sundin, Tor.	.50	10.00	35.00
20	Darren Turcotte, Wpg.	.15	1.50	5.00
21	Dale Hunter, Wsh.	.15	1.50	5.00
22	Jari Kurri, L.A.	.25	3.00	10.00
23	Alexei Zhamnov, Wpg.	.25	3.00	10.00
24	Mark Recchi, Mtl.	.25	3.00	10.00
25	Dallas Drake, Det.	.15	1.50	5.00
26	John MacLean, N.J.	.15	1.50	5.00
27	Keith Jones, Wsh.	.15	1.50	5.00
28	Matt Schneider, NYI.	.15	1.50	5.00
29	Jeff Brown, Van.	.15	1.50	5.00
30	Patrick Flatley, NYI.	.15	1.50	5.00
31	Dave Andreychuk, Tor.	.15	1.50	5.00
32	Bill Guerin, N.J.	.25	3.00	10.00
33	Chris Gratton, T.B.	.25	3.00	10.00
34	Pierre Turgeon, Mtl.	.25	3.00	10.00
35	Stéphane Richer, N.J.	.15	1.50	5.00
36	Marty McSorley, L.A.	.15	1.50	5.00
37	Craig Janney, Stl.	.15	1.50	5.00
38	Geoff Sanderson, Hfd.	.15	1.50	5.00
39	Ron Francis, Pgh.	.35	6.00	20.00
40	Stu Barnes, Fla.	.15	1.50	5.00
41	Mikael Renberg, Pha.	.15	1.50	5.00
42	David Oliver, Edm.	.15	1.50	5.00
43	Radek Bonk, Ott.	.15	1.50	5.00
44	Sergei Fedorov, Det.	.50	10.00	35.00
45	Adam Graves, NYR.	.15	1.50	5.00
46	Uwe Krupp, Que.	.15	1.50	5.00
47	Mike Richter, NYR.	.25	3.00	10.00
48	Todd Harvey, Dal.	.15	1.50	5.00
49	Stanislav Neckar, Ott.	.15	1.50	5.00
50	Chris Chelios, Chi.	.35	8.00	28.00
51	John LeClair, Pha.	.50	10.00	35.00
52	German Titov, Cgy.	.15	1.50	5.00
53	Garth Butcher, Stl.	.15	1.50	5.00
54	Pat LaFontaine, Buf.	.25	3.00	10.00
55	Jeff Friesen, S.J.	.25	3.00	10.00
56	Ray Bourque, Bos.	.50	10.00	35.00
57	Esa Tikkanen, Stl.	.15	1.50	5.00
58	Steve Rucchin, Ana.	.15	1.50	5.00
59	Roman Hamrlik, T.B.	.25	3.00	10.00
60	Oleg Tverdovsky, Ana.	.15	1.50	5.00
61	Doug Gilmour, Tor.	.35	6.00	20.00
62	Jocelyn Lemieux, Hfd.	.15	1.50	5.00
63	Roman Oksiuta, Ana.	.15	1.50	5.00
64	Alexei Zhitnik, Buf.	.15	1.50	5.00
65	Sylvain Côté, Wsh.	.15	1.50	5.00
66	Paul Kruse, Cgy.	.15	1.50	5.00
67	Teppo Numminen, Wpg.	.15	1.50	5.00
68	Gary Suter, Chi.	.15	1.50	5.00
69	Darrin Shannon, Wpg.	.15	1.50	5.00
70	Derian Hatcher, Dal.	.25	3.00	10.00
71	Sergei Gonchar, Wsh.	.15	1.50	5.00
72	Adam Deadmarsh, Col.	.15	1.50	5.00
73	Jyrki Lumme, Van.	.15	1.50	5.00
74	Dino Ciccarelli, Det.	.25	3.00	10.00
75	Mike Gartner, Tor.	.25	3.00	10.00
76	Todd Marchant, Edm.	.15	1.50	5.00
77	Jason Wiemer, T.B.	.15	1.50	5.00
78	Scott Mellanby, Fla.	.15	1.50	5.00
79	Al MacInnis, Stl.	.15	1.50	5.00
80	Glen Wesley, Hfd.	.15	1.50	5.00
81	Igor Larionov, S.J.	.25	3.00	10.00
82	Eric Lacroix, L.A.	.15	1.50	5.00
83	Mike Keane, Col.	.15	1.50	5.00
84	Vincent Damphousse, Mtl.	.35	6.00	20.00
85	Robert Kron, Hfd.	.15	1.50	5.00
86	Scott Stevens, N.J.	.15	1.50	5.00
87	Don Beaupré (G), Ott.	.15	1.50	5.00
88	Zigmund Palffy, NYI.	.35	8.00	28.00
89	Kevin Lowe, NYR.	.15	1.50	5.00
90	Tommy Söderström (G), NYI.	.15	1.50	5.00
91	Glen Healy (G), NYR.	.15	1.50	5.00
92	Randy McKay, N.J.	.15	1.50	5.00
93	Sean Hill, Ott.	.15	1.50	5.00
94	Brian Savage, Mtl.	.15	1.50	5.00
95	Ron Hextall (G), Pha.	.25	3.00	10.00
96	Darryl Sydor, Dal.	.15	1.50	5.00
97	Tom Barrasso (G), Pgh.	.25	3.00	10.00
98	Andrei Nikolishin, Hfd.	.15	1.50	5.00
99	Viktor Kozlov, S.J.	.15	1.50	5.00
100	Rob Niedermayer, Fla.	.25	3.00	10.00
101	Wayne Gretzky, L.A.	2.50	50.00	250.00
102	Shaun Van Allen, Ana.	.15	1.50	5.00
103	Dave Manson, Wpg.	.15	1.50	5.00
104	Donald Audette, Buf.	.15	1.50	5.00
105	Daren Puppa (G), T.B.	.15	1.50	5.00
106	Jeremy Roenick, Chi.	.35	6.00	20.00
107	Ken Wregget (G), Pgh.	.15	1.50	5.00
108	Mike Modano, Dal.	.50	10.00	35.00
109	Rod Brind'Amour, Pha.	.25	3.00	10.00
110	Eric Desjardins, Pha.	.15	1.50	5.00
111	Pat Verbeek, Hfd.	.15	1.50	5.00
112	Jeff Beukeboom, NYR.	.15	1.50	5.00
113	John Druce, L.A.	.15	1.50	5.00
114	Andy Moog (G), Dal.	.25	3.00	10.00
115	Turner Stevenson, Mtl.	.15	1.50	5.00
116	Alexander Selivanov, T.B.	.15	1.50	5.00
117	Neal Broten N.J.	.15	1.50	5.00
118	Nikolai Khabibulin (G), Pho.	.35	6.00	20.00
119	Claude Lemieux, N.J.	.15	1.50	5.00
120	Sergei Brylin, N.J.	.15	1.50	5.00
121	Bob Corkum, Ana.	.15	1.50	5.00
122	Kelly Hrudey (G), L.A.	.15	1.50	5.00
123	Jason Dawe, Buf.	.15	1.50	5.00
124	Sean Burke (G), Hfd.	.25	3.00	10.00
125	Dave Gagner, Dal.	.15	1.50	5.00
126	Kirk Maltby, Edm.	.15	1.50	5.00
127	Ian Laperriere, Stl.	.15	1.50	5.00
128	Vyacheslav Kozlov, Det.	.15	1.50	5.00
129	Vladimir Konstantinov, Det.	.15	1.50	5.00
130	Kenny Jonsson, Tor.	.15	1.50	5.00
131	Sylvain Lefebvre, Que.	.15	1.50	5.00
132	Kirk McLean (G), Van.	.25	3.00	10.00
133	Brian Leetch, NYR.	.35	6.00	20.00
134	Olaf Kolzig (G), Wsh.	.35	6.00	20.00
135	Patrick Poulin, T.B.	.15	1.50	5.00
136	Tim Cheveldae (G), Wpg.	.15	1.50	5.00
137	Gary Roberts, Cal.	.25	3.00	10.00
138	Jim Carey (G), Wsh.	.15	1.50	5.00
139	Dominik Hasek (G), Buf.	.75	15.00	60.00
140	Josef Beranek, Van.	.15	1.50	5.00
141	Don Sweeney, Bos.	.15	1.50	5.00
142	Félix Potvin (G), Tor.	.50	10.00	35.00
143	Guy Hebert (G), Ana.	.25	3.00	10.00
144	Guy Carbonneau, Dal.	.15	1.50	5.00
145	Mikhail Shtalenkov (G), Ana.	.15	1.50	5.00
146	Kevin Miller, S.J.	.15	1.50	5.00
147	Blaine Lacher (G), Bos.	.15	1.50	5.00
148	Craig MacTavish, Stl.	.15	1.50	5.00
149	Derek Plante, Buf.	.15	1.50	5.00
150	Kevin Dineen, Pha.	.15	1.50	5.00
151	Trevor Kidd (G), Cgy.	.25	3.00	10.00
152	Sergei Nemchinov, NYR.	.15	1.50	5.00
153	Ed Belfour (G), Chi.	.35	6.00	20.00
154	Sergei Krivokrasov, Chi.	.15	1.50	5.00
155	Mike Rathje, S.J.	.15	1.50	5.00
156	Mike Donnelly, L.A.	.15	1.50	5.00
157	David Roberts, Stl.	.15	1.50	5.00
158	Jocelyn Thibault (G), Que.	.35	6.00	20.00
159	Tie Domi, Tor.	.15	1.50	5.00
160	Chris Osgood (G), Det.	.60	12.00	28.00
161	Martin Gelinas, Van.	.15	1.50	5.00
162	Scott Thornton, Edm.	.15	1.50	5.00
163	Bob Rouse, Det.	.15	1.50	5.00
164	Randy Wood, NYI.	.15	1.50	5.00
165	Chris Therien, Pha.	.15	1.50	5.00
166	Steven Rice, Hfd.	.15	1.50	5.00
167	Scott Lachance, NYI.	.15	1.50	5.00
168	Petr Svoboda, Pha.	.15	1.50	5.00
169	Patrick Roy (G), Mtl.	2.00	40.00	200.00
170	Norm Maciver, Ott.	.15	1.50	5.00
171	Todd Gill, Tor.	.15	1.50	5.00
172	Brian Rolston, N.J.	.15	1.50	5.00
173	**Wade Flaherty (G), S.J., RC**	**.15**	**1.50**	**5.00**
174	Valeri Bure, Mtl.	.15	1.50	5.00
175	Mark Fitzpatrick (G), Fla.	.15	1.50	5.00
176	Darren McCarty, Det.	.15	1.50	5.00
177	Ken Danyeko, N.J.	.15	1.50	5.00
178	Yves Racine, Mtl.	.15	1.50	5.00
179	Murray Craven, Van.	.15	1.50	5.00
180	Nicklas Lidström, Det.	.25	3.00	10.00
181	Gord Murphy, Fla.	.15	1.50	5.00
182	Eric Weinrich, Chi.	.15	1.50	5.00
183	Todd Krygier, Wsh.	.15	1.50	5.00
184	Cliff Ronning, Van.	.15	1.50	5.00
185	Mariusz Czerkawski, Bos.	.15	1.50	5.00
186	Benoît Hogue, NYI.	.15	1.50	5.00
187	Richard Smehlik, Buf.	.15	1.50	5.00
188	Jeff Norton, Stl.	.15	1.50	5.00
189	Steve Chiasson, Cgy.	.15	1.50	5.00
190	Andrei Nazarov, S.J.	.15	1.50	5.00
191	Steve Smith, Chi.	.15	1.50	5.00
192	Mario Lemieux, Pgh.	2.00	40.00	200.00
193	Trent Klatt, Dal.	.15	1.50	5.00
194	Valeri Zelepukin, N.J.	.15	1.50	5.00
195	Adam Foote, Que.	.25	3.00	10.00
196	Lyle Odelein, Mtl.	.15	1.50	5.00
197	Keith Primeau, Det.	.25	3.00	10.00
198	Rob Blake, L.A.	.25	3.00	10.00
199	Dave Lowry, Fla.	.15	1.50	5.00
200	Adam Burt, Hfd.	.15	1.50	5.00
201	Martin Gendron, Wsh.	.15	1.50	5.00
202	Tommy Salo (G), NYI.	.15	1.50	5.00
203	Eric Dazé, Chi.	.25	3.00	10.00
204	Ryan Smyth, Edm.	.25	3.00	10.00
205	Brian Holzinger, Buf.	.15	1.50	5.00
206	**Chris Marinucci, NYI., RC**	**.15**	**1.50**	**5.00**
207	Jason Bonsignore, Edm.	.15	1.50	5.00
208	Craig Johnson, Stl.	.15	1.50	5.00
209	**Steve Larouche, Ott., RC**	**.15**	**1.50**	**5.00**
210	**Chris McAlpine, N.J., RC**	**.15**	**1.50**	**5.00**
211	Shean Donovan, S.J.	.15	1.50	5.00
212	Corry Stillman, Cgy.	.15	1.50	5.00
213	Craig Darby, Mtl.	.15	1.50	5.00
214	Phil DeRouville (G), Pgh.	.15	1.50	5.00
215	Kevin Brown, L.A.	.15	1.50	5.00
216	Manny Fernandez (G), Dal.	.15	1.50	5.00
217	Radim Bicanek, Ott.	.15	1.50	5.00
218	Craig Conroy, Mtl.	.15	1.50	5.00
219	Todd Warriner, Tor.	.15	1.50	5.00
220	Richard Park, Pgh.	.15	1.50	5.00
221	Checklist	.15	1.50	5.00
222	Checklist	.15	1.50	5.00
223	Checklist	.15	1.50	5.00
224	Checklist	.15	1.50	5.00
225	Checklist	.15	1.50	5.00

CLEAR SHOTS

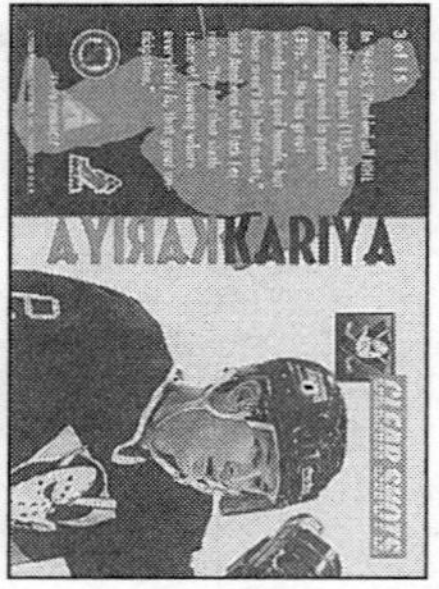

No.	Player	NRMT-MT
Insert Set (15 cards):		225.00
1	Martin Brodeur (G), N.J.	10.00
2	Brett Hull, Stl.	8.00
3	Paul Kariya, Ana.	20.00
4	Eric Lindros, Pha.	20.00
5	Cam Neely, Bos.	5.00
6	Doug Gilmour, Tor.	5.00
7	Sergei Fedorov, Det.	8.00
8	Peter Forsberg, Que.	15.00

	No.	Player	NRMT-MT
☐	9	Wayne Gretzky, L.A.	30.00
☐	10	Patrick Roy (G), Mtl.	25.00
☐	11	Jaromir Jagr, Pgh.	15.00
☐	12	Pavel Bure, Van.	10.00
☐	13	Mario Lemieux, Pgh.	25.00
☐	14	Pierre Turgeon Mtl.	5.00
☐	15	Dominik Hasek (G), Buf.	10.00

FIRST STRIKE

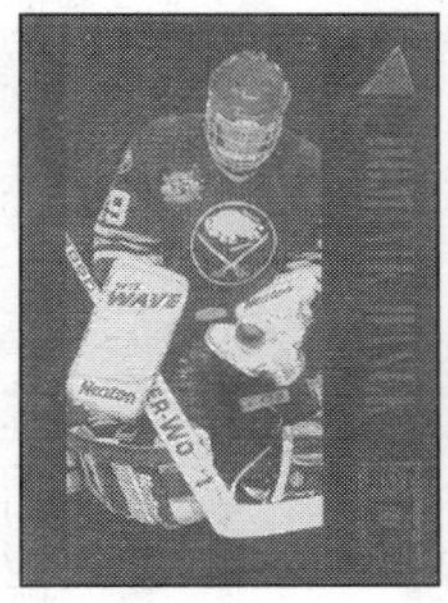

Inset Set (15 cards): 85.00

	No.	Player	NRMT-MT
☐	1	Mark Messier, NYR.	5.00
☐	2	Wayne Gretzky, L.A.	20.00
☐	3	Doug Gilmour, Tor.	3.00
☐	4	Patrick Roy (G), Mtl.	15.00
☐	5	Cam Neely, Bos.	2.00
☐	6	Brian Leetch, NYR.	3.00
☐	7	Ed Belfour (G), Chi.	3.00
☐	8	Wendel Clark, Tor.	2.00
☐	9	Chris Chelios, Chi.	4.00
☐	10	Claude Lemieux, N.J.	2.00
☐	11	Peter Forsberg, Que.	10.00
☐	12	Brett Hull, Stl.	5.00
☐	13	Mario Lemieux, Pgh.	15.00
☐	14	Dominik Hasek (G), Buf.	7.00
☐	15	Theoren Fleury, Cgy.	3.00

FULL CONTACT

Insert Set (12 cards): 50.00

	No.	Player	NRMT-MT
☐	1	Cam Neely, Bos. (vs. Dimitri Yushkevich)	3.00
☐	2	Scott Stevens, N.J. (vs. Fred Knipscheer)	2.00
☐	3	Owen Nolan, Que.	3.00
☐	4	Jeremy Roenick, Chi.	6.00
☐	5	Brendan Shanahan, Stl. (vs. Tony Granato)	12.00
☐	6	Chris Chelios, Chi. (vs. Steve Thomas)	8.00
☐	7	Brett Lindros, NYI. (vs. Paul Laus)	2.00
☐	8	Adam Graves, NYR.	2.00
☐	9	Wendel Clark, NYI. (vs. Valeri Karpov)	3.00
☐	10	Mark Tinordi, Wsh. (vs. John LeClair)	3.00
☐	11	Keith Tkachuk, Wpg. (vs. Chris Chelios)	8.00
☐	12	Mark Messier, NYR. (vs. Brian Savage)	10.00

MASKS

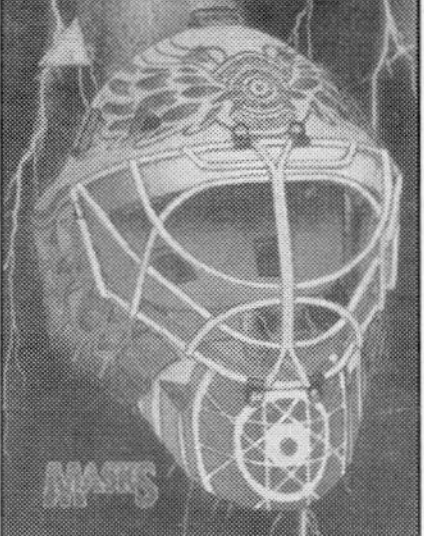

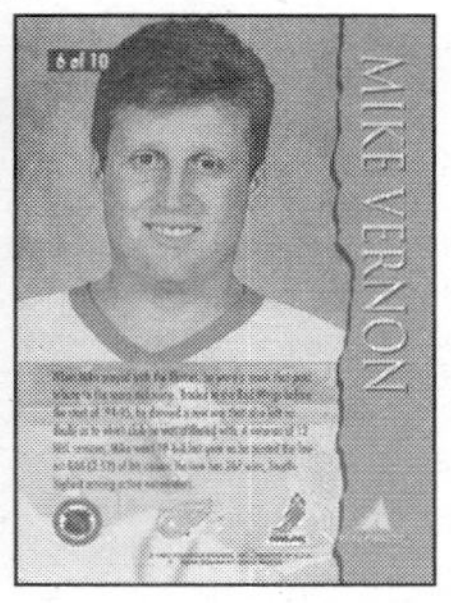

Insert Set (10 cards): 300.00

	No.	Player	NRMT-MT
☐	1	Blaine Lacher (G), Bos.	25.00
☐	2	Martin Brodeur (G), N.J.	80.00
☐	3	Jim Carey (G), Wsh.	25.00
☐	4	Félix Potvin (G), Tor.	50.00
☐	5	Andy Moog (G), Dal.	30.00
☐	6	Mike Vernon (G), Det.	30.00
☐	7	Mark Fitzpatrick, (G), Fla.	25.00
☐	8	Ron Hextall (G), Pha.	30.00
☐	9	Sean Burke (G), Hfd.	30.00
☐	10	Jocelyn Thibault (G), Mtl.	35.00

ROARING 20s

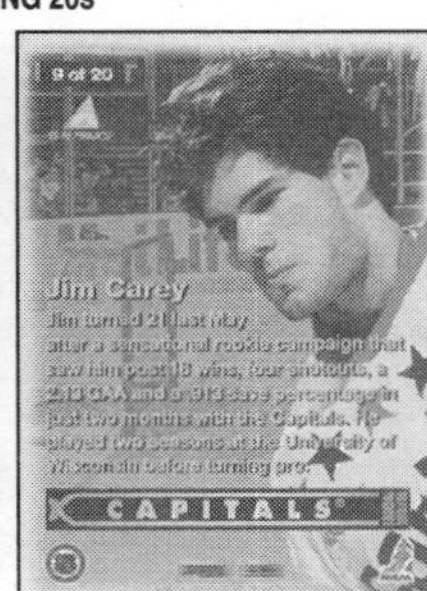

Insert Set (20 cards): 100.00

	No.	Player	NRMT-MT
☐	1	Eric Lindros, Pha.	12.00
☐	2	Paul Kariya, Ana.	12.00
☐	3	Martin Brodeur (G), N.J.	7.00
☐	4	Jeremy Roenick, Chi.	3.00
☐	5	Mike Modano, Dal.	5.00
☐	6	Sergei Fedorov, Det.	5.00
☐	7	Mats Sundin, Tor.	5.00
☐	8	Pavel Bure, Van.	7.00
☐	9	Jim Carey (G), Wsh.	2.00
☐	10	Félix Potvin (G), Tor.	5.00
☐	11	Alexei Zhamnov, Wpg.	2.00
☐	12	Mikael Renberg, Pha.	2.00
☐	13	Jaromir Jagr, Pgh.	10.00
☐	14	Peter Bondra, Wsh.	4.00
☐	15	Peter Forsberg, Que.	10.00
☐	16	John LeClair, Pha.	5.00
☐	17	Joe Sakic, Que.	8.00
☐	18	Brendan Shanahan, Stl.	6.00
☐	19	Teemu Selänne, Wpg.	7.00
☐	20	Pierre Turgeon, Mtl.	2.00

GLOBAL GOLD

These cards are identical to the regular series except for a different numbering system and a Global Gold stamp on the front.

Insert Set (25 cards): 25.00

	No.	Player	NRMT-MT
☐	1	Pavel Bure, Van.	3.50
☐	2	Jaromir Jagr, Pgh.	5.00
☐	3	Mats Sundin, Tor.	2.50
☐	4	Jari Kurri, L.A.	1.00
☐	5	Mikael Renberg, Pha.	.50
☐	6	Radek Bonk, Ott.	.50
☐	7	Sergei Fedorov, Det.	2.50
☐	8	Uwe Krupp, Que.	.50
☐	9	German Titov, Cgy.	.50
☐	10	Esa Tikkanen, Stl.	.50
☐	11	Oleg Tverdovsky, Ana.	.50
☐	12	Teppo Numminen, Wpg.	.50
☐	13	Jyrki Lumme, Van.	2.00
☐	14	Zigmund Palffy, NYI.	.50
☐	15	Tommy Söderström (G), NYI.	.50
☐	16	Viktor Kozlov, S.J.	.50
☐	17	Alexander Selivanov, T.B.	.50
☐	18	Sergei Brylin, N.J.	.50
☐	19	Dominik Hasek (G). Buf.	3.50
☐	20	Sergei Nemchinov, NYR.	.50
☐	21	Petr Svoboda, Pha.	.50
☐	22	Valeri Bure, Mtl.	.50
☐	23	Nicklas Lidström, Det.	1.00
☐	24	Mariusz Czerkawski, Bos.	.50
☐	25	Valeri Zelepukin, N.J.	.50

1995 - 96 PINNACLE FANtasy

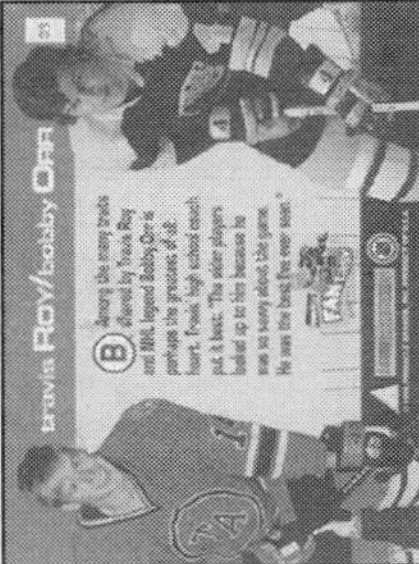

Two-card packs were first handed out at the January 18-21 All-Star Game Fanfest weekend in Boston, Massachusetts.

Imprint:

Complete Set (31 cards): 45.00

	No.	Player	NRMT-MT
☐	1	Cam Neely, Bos.	.75
☐	2	Ray Bourque, Bos.	2.50
☐	3	Alexandre Daigle, Ott.	.75
☐	4	Mariusz Czerkawski, Bos.	.50
☐	5	Adam Oates, Bos.	1.50
☐	6	Brendan Shanahan, Stl.	3.00
☐	7	Arturs Irbe (G), S.J.	.50
☐	8	Mario Lemieux, Pgh.	8.00
☐	9	Theoren Fleury, Cgy.	1.50
☐	10	Patrick Roy (G), Mtl.	8.00
☐	11	Roman Hamrlik, T.B.	.75
☐	12	Pavel Bure, Van.	3.50
☐	13	Wayne Gretzky, L.A.	10.00
☐	14	Mike Modano, Dal.	2.50
☐	15	Teemu Selänne, Wpg.	3.50
☐	16	John Vanbiesbrouck (G), Fla.	3.00
☐	17	Dominik Hasek (G), Buf.	3.50
☐	18	Mark Messier, NYR.	2.50
☐	19	Martin Brodeur (G), N.J.	3.50
☐	20	Jim Carey (G), Wsh.	.50
☐	21	Wendel Clark, Tor.	.75
☐	22	Jason Arnott, Edm.	.75
☐	23	Jeremy Roenick, Chi.	1.50
☐	24	Brett Hull, Stl.	2.50
☐	25	Peter Forsberg, Que.	5.00
☐	26	Paul Kariya, Ana.	6.50
☐	27	Eric Lindros, Pha.	6.50
☐	28	Kevin Stevens, Pgh.	.50
☐	29	Félix Potvin (G), Tor.	2.50
☐	30	Sergei Fedorov, Det.	2.50
☐	31	Bobby Orr/Travis Roy	15.00

1995 - 96 PINNACLE SUMMIT

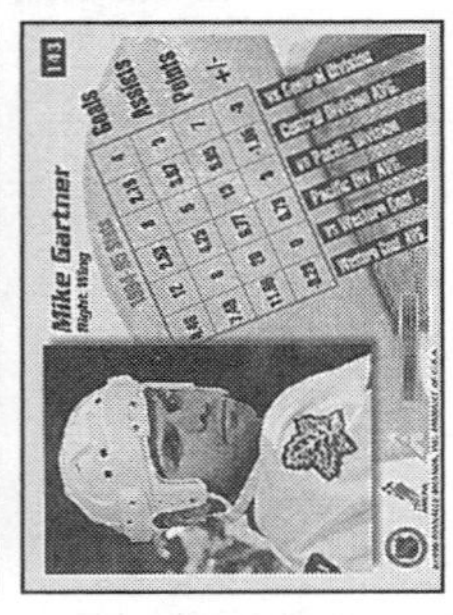

These cards have three versions: a regular card, the Summit Ice parallel and an Artist's Proof parallel. Seven regular cards also have a hole-punched promo version. Promo cards have the same value as the regular card.

Imprint: © 1996 PINNACLE BRANDS, INC.

	Reg.	Ice	AP
Complete Set (200 cards):	**20.00**	**60.00**	**2,600.00**
Common Player:	**.15**	**1.50**	**5.00**

No.	Player	Reg.	Ice	AP
1	Mark Messier, NYR.	.50	8.00	35.00
2	Paul Kariya, Ana.	1.50	25.00	150.00
3	Alexei Zhamnov, Wpg.	.25	3.00	10.00
4	Adam Oates, Bos.	.35	5.00	20.00
5	Dale Hunter, Wsh.	.15	1.50	5.00
6	Valeri Kamensky, Col.	.25	3.00	10.00
7	Pavel Bure, Van.	.75	10.00	60.00
8	Theoren Fleury, Cgy.	.35	5.00	20.00
9	Mats Sundin, Tor.	.50	8.00	35.00
10	Joe Murphy, Chi.	.15	1.50	5.00
11	Brian Bellows, T.B.	.15	1.50	5.00
12	Owen Nolan, S.J.	.25	3.00	10.00
13	Brett Hull, Stl.	.50	8.00	35.00
14	Mike Modano, Dal.	.50	8.00	35.00
15	Ulf Dahlen, S.J.	.15	1.50	5.00
16	Paul Coffey, Det.	.25	3.00	10.00
17	Jaromir Jagr, Pgh.	1.25	18.00	100.00
18	Jason Arnott, Edm.	.25	3.00	10.00
19	Eric Lindros, Pha.	1.50	25.00	150.00
20	Jesse Belanger, Fla.	.15	1.50	5.00
21	Alexandre Daigle, Ott.	.25	3.00	10.00
22	Darren Turcotte, S.J.	.15	1.50	5.00
23	Brian Leetch, NYR.	.35	5.00	20.00
24	Wayne Gretzky, L.A.	2.50	40.00	250.00
25	Mathieu Schneider, NYI.	.15	1.50	5.00
26	Mark Recchi, Mtl.	.25	3.00	10.00
27	Martin Brodeur (G), N.J.	.75	10.00	60.00
28	Igor Korolev, Wpg.	.15	1.50	5.00
29	Jocelyn Thibault (G), Mtl.	.35	5.00	20.00
30	Chris Pronger, Hfd.	.25	3.00	10.00
31	Sergei Fedorov, Det.	.50	8.00	35.00
32	Jari Kurri, L.A.	.25	3.00	10.00
33	Ray Bourque, Bos.	.50	8.00	35.00
34	Pat LaFontaine, Buf.	.25	3.00	10.00
35	Don Beaupré (G), Ott.	.15	1.50	5.00
36	Dave Andreychuk, Tor.	.15	1.50	5.00
37	Oleg Tverdovsky, Wpg.	.15	1.50	5.00
38	Geoff Sanderson, Hfd.	.15	1.50	5.00
39	Chris Chelios, Chi.	.35	6.00	28.00
40	Phil Housley, Cgy.	.15	1.50	5.00
41	Kevin Hatcher, Dal.	.15	1.50	5.00
42	Ron Francis, Pgh.	.35	5.00	20.00
43	Pierre Turgeon, Mtl.	.25	3.00	10.00
44	Mikael Renberg, Pha.	.15	1.50	5.00
45	Chris Gratton, T.B.	.25	3.00	10.00
46	Tommy Söderström (G), NYI.	.15	1.50	5.00
47	Stu Barnes, Fla.	.15	1.50	5.00
48	Alexander Mogilny, Van.	.35	5.00	20.00
49	Craig Janney, Wpg.	.15	1.50	5.00
50	Scott Niedermayer, N.J.	.25	3.00	10.00
51	Jim Carey (G), Wsh.	.15	1.50	5.00
52	Stéphane Richer, N.J.	.15	1.50	5.00
53	Dave Gagner, Dal.	.15	1.50	5.00
54	Teemu Selänne, Wpg.	.75	10.00	60.00
55	Kelly Hrudey (G), L.A.	.15	1.50	5.00
56	Roman Hamrlik, T.B.	.25	3.00	10.00
57	Scott Mellanby, Fla.	.15	1.50	5.00
58	Guy Hebert (G), Ana.	.25	3.00	10.00
59	Gary Suter, Chi.	.15	1.50	5.00
60	Travis Green, NYI.	.15	1.50	5.00
61	Joe Sakic, Col.	1.00	15.00	75.00
62	Doug Gilmour, Tor.	.35	5.00	20.00
63	Peter Bondra, Wsh.	.35	6.00	28.00
64	Vincent Damphousse, Mtl.	.35	5.00	20.00
65	Dino Ciccarelli, T.B.	.25	3.00	10.00
66	Adam Graves, NYR.	.15	1.50	5.00
67	Kevin Stevens, Pgh.	.15	1.50	5.00
68	Jeff Friesen, S.J.	.25	3.00	10.00
69	Kirk McLean (G), Van.	.25	3.00	10.00
70	Brad May, Buf.	.15	1.50	5.00
71	Bill Ranford (G), Edm.	.25	3.00	10.00
72	Derian Hatcher, Dal.	.25	3.00	10.00
73	Glen Wesley, Hfd.	.15	1.50	5.00
74	Sergei Zubov, Pgh.	.25	3.00	10.00
75	John LeClair, Pha.	.50	8.00	35.00
76	Igor Larionov, Det.	.25	3.00	10.00
77	Ray Sheppard, Fla.	.15	1.50	5.00
78	Ulf Samuelsson, Pgh.	.15	1.50	5.00
79	Rod Brind'Amour, Pha.	.25	3.00	10.00
80	Félix Potvin (G), Tor.	.50	8.00	35.00
81	Cam Neely, Bos.	.25	3.00	10.00
82	Jeremy Roenick, Chi.	.35	5.00	20.00
83	Vyacheslav Kozlov, Det.	.15	1.50	5.00
84	Arturs Irbe (G), S.J.	.15	1.50	5.00
85	Daren Puppa (G), T.B.	.15	1.50	5.00
86	Rob Blake, L.A.	.25	3.00	10.00
87	Steve Heinze, Bos.	.15	1.50	5.00
88	Tom Barrasso, Pgh.	.25	3.00	10.00
89	Luc Robitaille, Pgh.	.25	3.00	10.00
90	Al MacInnis, Cgy.	.15	1.50	5.00
91	Petr Nedved, Pgh.	.15	1.50	5.00
92	Joe Mullen, Bos.	.15	1.50	5.00
93	Mark Tinordi, Dal.	.15	1.50	5.00
94	Tomas Sandström, Pgh.	.15	1.50	5.00
95	Dale Hawerchuk, Stl.	.25	3.00	10.00
96	Andy Moog (G), Dal.	.25	3.00	10.00
97	Alexei Kovalev, NYR.	.15	1.50	5.00
98	David Oliver, Edm.	.15	1.50	5.00
99	Patrick Poulin, T.B.	.15	1.50	5.00
100	Tony Granato, L.A.	.15	1.50	5.00
101	Alexei Yashin, Ott.	.35	6.00	28.00
102	Trevor Linden, Van.	.25	3.00	10.00
103	Rick Tocchet, Bos.	.15	1.50	5.00
104	Brett Lindros, NYI.	.15	1.50	5.00
105	Rob Niedermayer, Fla.	.15	1.50	5.00
106	John MacLean, N.J.	.15	1.50	5.00
107	Pat Verbeek, Hfd.	.15	1.50	5.00
108	Ray Ferraro, L.A.	.15	1.50	5.00
109	Mike Ricci, Col.	.15	1.50	5.00
110	Doug Weight, Edm.	.35	5.00	20.00
111	Bill Guerin, N.J.	.25	3.00	10.00
112	Ken Wregget (G), Pgh.	.15	1.50	5.00
113	Teppo Numminen, Wpg.	.15	1.50	5.00
114	Mike Vernon (G), Det.	.25	3.00	10.00
115	Mike Richter (G), NYR.	.35	5.00	20.00
116	Dan Quinn, Ott.	.15	1.50	5.00
117	Peter Forsberg, Col.	1.25	18.00	100.00
119	Geoff Courtnall, Stl.	.15	1.50	5.00
118	Mario Lemieux, Pgh.	2.00	30.00	200.00
120	Ed Belfour (G), Chi.	.35	5.00	20.00
121	Kirk Muller, Tor.	.15	1.50	5.00
122	Chris Osgood (G), Det.	.35	6.00	28.00
123	Radek Bonk, Ott.	.15	1.50	5.00
124	Brendan Shanahan, Hfd.	.60	9.00	50.00
125	Sean Burke (G), Hfd.	.25	3.00	10.00
126	Larry Murphy, Tor.	.25	3.00	10.00
127	Blaine Lacher (G), Bos.	.15	1.50	5.00
128	Russ Courtnall, Van.	.15	1.50	5.00
129	Claude Lemieux, Col.	.15	1.50	5.00
130	John Vanbiesbrouck (G), Fla.	.60	9.00	50.00
131	Wendel Clark, NYI.	.25	3.00	10.00
132	Nelson Emerson, Hfd.	.15	1.50	5.00
133	Ron Hextall (G), Pha.	.25	3.00	10.00
134	Scott Stevens, N.J.	.15	1.50	5.00
135	Bernie Nicholls, Chi.	.15	1.50	5.00
136	Brian Skrudland, Fla.	.15	1.50	5.00
137	Sandis Ozolinsh, Col.	.25	3.00	10.00
138	Trevor Kidd (G), Cgy.	.25	3.00	10.00
139	Joé Juneau, Wsh.	.15	1.50	5.00
140	Keith Primeau, Det.	.25	3.00	10.00
141	Petr Klima, T.B.	.15	1.50	5.00
142	Viktor Kozlov, S.J.	.15	1.50	5.00
143	Mike Gartner, Pha.	.25	3.00	10.00
144	Zigmund Palffy, NYI.	.35	6.00	28.00
145	Steve Duchesne, Ott.	.15	1.50	5.00
146	Brian Bradley, T.B.	.15	1.50	5.00
147	Michal Pivonka, Wsh.	.15	1.50	5.00
148	Todd Harvey, Dal.	.15	1.50	5.00
149	Patrick Roy (G), Mtl.	2.00	30.00	200.00
150	Gary Roberts, Cgy.	.25	3.00	10.00
151	Shayne Corson, Edm.	.25	3.00	10.00
152	Keith Tkachuk, Wpg.	.35	6.00	28.00
153	Dimitri Khristich, L.A.	.15	1.50	5.00
154	Steve Yzerman, Det.	1.25	18.00	100.00
155	Shawn McEachern, Bos.	.15	1.50	5.00
156	Bryan Smolinski, MYI.	.15	1.50	5.00
157	Vladimir Malakhov, Mtl.	.15	1.50	5.00
158	Andrew Cassels, Hfd.	.15	1.50	5.00
159	Dominik Hasek (G), Buf.	.75	10.00	60.00
160	Stéphane Fiset (G), Col.	.25	3.00	10.00
161	Steve Thomas, N.J.	.15	1.50	5.00
162	Joe Nieuwendyk, Dal.	.25	3.00	10.00
163	Sergio Momesso, Tor.	.15	1.50	5.00
164	Jyrki Lumme, Van.	.15	1.50	5.00
165	Tony Amonte, Chi.	.25	3.00	10.00
166	Yanic Perreault, L.A.	.15	1.50	5.00
167	Brian Savage, Mtl.	.15	1.50	5.00
168	**Brian Holzinger, Buf., RC**	**.15**	**2.00**	**8.00**
169	**Radek Dvorak, Fla., RC**	**.25**	**3.00**	**10.00**
170	Jamie Langenbrunner, Dal.	.25	3.00	10.00
171	Ed Jovanovski, Fla.	.25	3.00	10.00
172	Bryan McCabe, NYI.	.15	1.50	5.00
173	Jere Lehtinen, Dal.	.25	3.00	10.00
174	**Antti Tormanen, Ott., RC**	**.15**	**1.50**	**5.00**
175	**Aki Berg, L.A., RC**	**.15**	**1.50**	**5.00**
176	Ryan Smyth, Edm.	.25	3.00	10.00
177	Shean Donovan, S.J.	.15	1.50	5.00
178	Darby Hendrickson, NYI.	.15	1.50	5.00
179	**Chad Kilger, Ana., RC**	**.15**	**1.50**	**5.00**
180	Vitali Yachmenev, L.A.	.15	1.50	5.00
181	Deron Quint, Wpg.	.15	1.50	5.00
182	**Daniel Alfredsson, Ott., RC**	**.85**	**10.00**	**30.00**
183	Jeff O'Neill, Hfd.	.25	3.00	10.00
184	Corey Hirsch (G), Van.	.15	1.50	5.00
185	**Sandy Moger, Bos., RC**	**.15**	**1.50**	**5.00**
186	Saku Koivu, Mtl.	.75	10.00	60.00
187	Niklas Sundstrom, NYR.	.15	1.50	5.00
188	**Shane Doan, Wpg., RC**	**.15**	**1.50**	**5.00**
189	Brendan Witt, Wsh.	.15	1.50	5.00
190	Eric Dazé, Chi.	.25	3.00	10.00
191	Marty Murray, Cgy.	.15	1.50	5.00
192	Byron Dafoe (G), L.A.	.15	1.50	5.00
193	**Todd Bertuzzi, NYI., RC**	**.50**	**3.00**	**10.00**
194	**Kyle McLaren, Bos., RC**	**.15**	**1.50**	**5.00**
195	**Marcus Ragnarsson, S.J., RC**	**.15**	**1.50**	**5.00**
196	**Robert Svehla, Fla., RC**	**.25**	**2.00**	**8.00**
197	Valeri Bure, Mtl.	.15	1.50	5.00
198	HL: Paul Coffey, Det.	.25	3.00	10.00
199	Checklist	.15	1.50	5.00
200	Checklist	.15	1.50	5.00

MAD HATTER

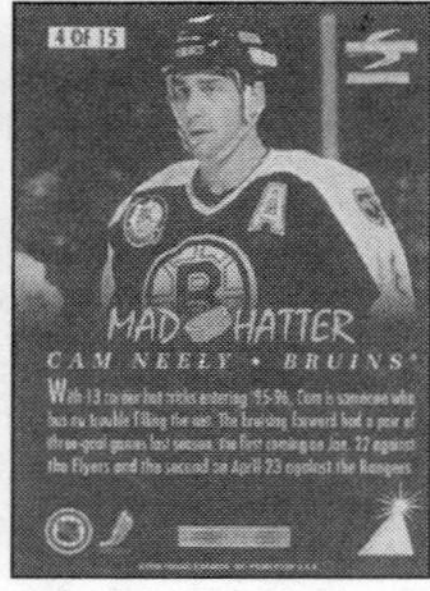

	NRMT-MT
Insert Set (15 cards):	**70.00**
Wendel Clark Promo:	**1.00**

No.	Player	NRMT-MT
1	Eric Lindros/Owen Nolan/Bernie Nicholls	15.00
2	Brett Hull, Stl.	6.00
3	John LeClair, Pha.	6.00
4	Cam Neely, Bos.	3.00
5	Alexei Zhamnov, Wpg.	3.00
6	Jason Arnott, Edm.	3.00
7	Pavel Bure, Van.	8.50
8	Wendel Clark, NYI.	3.00
9	Sergei Fedorov, Det.	6.00
10	Jaromir Jagr, Pgh.	12.00

	No.	Player	NRMT-MT
☐	11	Peter Bondra, Wsh.	4.50
☐	12	Alexei Yashin, Ott.	4.50
☐	13	Joe Nieuwendyk, Dal.	3.00
☐	14	Luc Robitaille, Pgh.	3.00
☐	15	Todd Harvey, Dal.	2.00

IN THE CREASE

Insert Set (15 cards): **350.00**

	No.	Player	NRMT-MT
☐	1	Martin Brodeur (G), N.J.	40.00
☐	2	Dominik Hasek (G), Buf.	40.00
☐	3	Patrick Roy (G), Col.	90.00
☐	4	Ed Belfour (G), Chi.	20.00
☐	5	Félix Potvin (G), Tor.	30.00
☐	6	Jim Carey (G), Wsh.	12.00
☐	7	Jocelyn Thibault (G), Mtl.	20.00
☐	8	Stéphane Fiset (G), Col.	15.00
☐	9	Chris Osgood (G), Det.	25.00
☐	10	Ron Hextall (G), Pha.	15.00
☐	11	Mike Richter (G), NYR.	20.00
☐	12	Andy Moog (G), Dal.	15.00
☐	13	Sean Burke (G), Hfd.	15.00
☐	14	Kirk McLean (G), Van.	15.00
☐	15	John Vanbiesbrouck (G), Fla.	35.00

SUMMIT GM

Insert Set (21 cards): **325.00**

	No.	Player	NRMT-MT
☐	1	Patrick Roy (G), Col.	40.00
☐	2	Martin Brodeur (G), N.J.	17.50
☐	3	Chris Chelios (G), Chi.	10.00
☐	4	Brian Leetch, NYR.	7.50
☐	5	Eric Lindros, Pha.	35.00
☐	6	Keith Tkachuk, Pho.	10.00
☐	7	Pavel Bure, Van.	17.50
☐	8	Scott Stevens, N.J.	3.00
☐	9	Paul Coffey, Det.	5.00
☐	10	Mario Lemieux, Pgh.	40.00
☐	11	Jaromir Jagr, Pgh.	25.00
☐	12	Cam Neely, Bos.	5.00
☐	13	Ray Bourque, Bos.	12.50
☐	14	Al MacInnis, Stl.	3.00
☐	15	Sergei Fedorov, Det.	12.50
☐	16	Mark Messier, NYR.	12.50
☐	17	Brett Hull, Stl.	12.50
☐	18	Wayne Gretzky, L.A.	50.00
☐	19	Paul Kariya, Ana.	35.00
☐	20	Brendan Shanahan, Hfd.	15.00
☐	21	Mike McPhee, General Manager	3.00

1995 - 96 PINNACLE ZENITH

Seven regular cards also have a hole-punched promo version. Neely (#61) also has a second promo without the hole punch.

Imprint: © 1996 PINNACLE BRANDS, INC.

Complete Set (152 cards): **70.00**
Common Player: **.35**

	No.	Player	NRMT-MT
☐	1	Brett Hull, Stl.	2.00
☐	2	Paul Coffey, Det.	.75
☐	3	Jaromir Jagr, Pgh.	4.00
☐	4	Joe Murphy, Stl.	.35
☐	5	Jim Carey (G), Wsh.	.35
☐	6	Eric Lindros, Pha.	5.00
☐	7	Ulf Dahlen, S.J.	.35
☐	8	Mark Recchi, Mtl.	.75
☐	9	Pavel Bure, Van.	3.00
☐	10	Adam Oates, Bos.	1.25
☐	11	Theoren Fleury, Cgy.	1.25
☐	12	Martin Brodeur (G), N.J.	3.00
☐	13	Wayne Gretzky, L.A.	8.00
☐	14	Geoff Sanderson, Hfd.	.35
☐	15	Chris Gratton, T.B.	.75
☐	16	Owen Nolan, S.J.	.75
☐	17	Paul Kariya, Ana.	5.00
☐	18	Mark Messier, NYR.	2.00
☐	19	Mats Sundin, Tor.	2.00
☐ ☐	20	Brian Savage, Mtl.	.35
☐	21	Mathieu Schneider, Tor.	.35
☐	22	Alexandre Daigle, Ott.	.50
☐	23	Jason Arnott, Edm.	.75
☐	24	Mike Modano, Dal.	2.00
☐ ☐	25	Scott Mellanby, Fla.	.35
☐	26	Alexei Zhamnov, Wpg.	.75
☐	27	Scott Niedermayer, N.J.	.75
☐	28	Chris Pronger, Stl.	.75
☐	29	Ray Bourque, Bos.	2.00
☐	30	Sergei Fedorov, Det.	2.00
☐	31	Alexander Mogilny, Van.	1.25
☐ ☐	32	Brian Leetch, NYR.	1.25
☐	33	Adam Graves, NYR.	.35
☐	34	Jocelyn Thibault (G), Mtl.	1.25
☐ ☐	35	Ron Francis, Pgh.	1.25
☐	36	John Vanbiesbrouck (G), Fla.	2.50
☐	37	Chris Chelios, Chi.	1.50
☐	38	Pierre Turgeon, Mtl.	.75
☐	39	Stéphane Richer, N.J.	.35
☐	40	Al MacInnis, Stl.	.35
☐	41	Dave Andreychuk, Tor.	.35
☐	42	Mikael Renberg, Pha.	.35
☐	43	Nelson Emerson, Hfd.	.35
☐	44	Kevin Hatcher, Dal.	.35
☐	45	Kirk Muller, Tor.	.35
☐	46	Bernie Nicholls, S.J.	.35
☐	47	Bill Ranford (G), Edm.	.75
☐	48	Luc Robitaille, Pgh.	.75
☐	49	Peter Bondra, Wsh.	1.50
☐	50	Jari Kurri, L.A.	.75
☐	51	Dino Ciccarelli, Det.	.75
☐	52	Kevin Stevens, Bos.	.35
☐	53	Mike Richter (G), NYR.	1.25
☐	54	Doug Gilmour, Tor.	1.25
☐	55	Kelly Hrudey (G), L.A.	.35
☐	56	Dave Gagner, Dal.	.35
☐	57	Kirk McLean (G), Van.	.50
☐	58	Geoff Courtnall, Stl.	.35
☐	59	John LeClair, Pha.	2.00
☐	60	Mike Vernon (G), Det.	.75
☐ ☐ ☐	61	Cam Neely, Bos.	.75
☐	62	Mike Gartner, Tor.	.75
☐ ☐	63	Igor Korolev, Wpg.	.35
☐	64	Joe Sakic, Col.	3.50
☐	65	Jeff Friesen, S.J.	.75
☐	66	Sergei Zubov, Pgh.	.75
☐	67	Trevor Kidd (G), Cgy.	.75
☐	68	Rod Brind'Amour, Pha.	.75
☐	69	John MacLean, N.J.	.35
☐	70	Peter Forsberg, Col.	4.00
☐	71	Oleg Tverdovsky, Ana.	.35
☐	72	Jeremy Roenick, Chi.	1.25
☐	73	Gary Suter, Chi.	.35
☐ ☐	74	Keith Tkachuk, Wpg.	1.50
☐	75	Todd Harvey, Dal.	.35
☐	76	Félix Potvin (G), Tor.	2.00
☐	77	Vincent Damphousse, Mtl.	1.25
☐	78	Blaine Lacher (G), Bos.	.35
☐	79	Tomas Sandström, L.A.	.35
☐	80	Chris Osgood (G), Det.	1.50
☐	81	Arturs Irbe (G), S.J.	.35
☐	82	Pat Verbeek, NYR.	.35
☐	83	Keith Primeau, Det.	.75
☐	84	Brett Lindros, NYI.	.35
☐	85	Pat LaFontaine, Buf.	.75
☐	86	Brendan Shanahan, Hfd.	2.50
☐	87	Trevor Linden, Van.	.75
☐	88	Rob Blake, L.A.	.75
☐	89	Scott Stevens, N.J.	.35
☐	90	Tom Barrasso (G), Pgh.	.75
☐	91	Mike Ricci, Col.	.35
☐	92	Ray Sheppard, Fla.	.35
☐	93	Steve Yzerman, Det.	4.00
☐	94	Wendel Clark, NYI.	.75
☐	95	Ed Belfour (G), Chi.	1.25
☐	96	Joé Juneau, Wsh.	.35
☐	97	Ron Hextall (G), Pha.	.75
☐	98	Shayne Corson, Stl.	.75
☐	99	Guy Hebert (G), Ana.	.75
☐	100	Sean Burke (G), Hfd.	.75
☐	101	Sandis Ozolinsh, Col.	.75
☐	102	Teemu Selänne, Wpg.	3.00
☐	103	Petr Nedved, Pgh.	.35
☐	104	Phil Housley, N.J.	.35
☐	105	Andy Moog (G), Dal.	.75
☐	106	Larry Murphy, Tor.	.75
☐	107	Grant Fuhr (G), Stl.	.75
☐	108	Mario Lemieux, Pgh.	6.50
☐	109	Dominik Hasek (G), Buf.	3.00
☐	110	Rob Niedermayer, Fla.	.35
☐	111	Steve Duchesne, Ott.	.35
☐	112	Joe Nieuwendyk, Dal.	.75
☐	113	Yanic Perreault, L.A.	.35
☐	114	Steve Thomas, N.J.	.35
☐	115	Russ Courtnall, Van.	.35
☐	116	Claude Lemieux, Col.	.35
☐	117	Patrick Roy (G), Col.	6.50
☐	118	Rick Tocchet, Bos.	.35
☐	119	Stéphane Fiset (G), Col.	.75
☐	120	Daren Puppa (G), T.B.	.35
☐	121	Ed Jovanovski, Fla.	.75
☐	122	Eric Dazé, Chi.	.75
☐	123	Cory Stillman, Cgy.	.35
☐	124	Brendan Witt, Wsh.	.35
☐	125	Valeri Bure, Mtl.	.35
☐	**126**	**Brian Holzinger, Buf., RC**	**.75**
☐	**127**	**Kyle McLaren, Van., RC**	**.35**
☐	128	Niklas Sundstrom, NYR.	.35
☐	129	Jamie Langenbrunner, Dal.	.75
☐	130	Jeff O'Neill, Hfd.	.35
☐	131	Vitali Yachmenev, L.A.	.35
☐	**132**	**Shane Doan, Wpg., RC**	**.35**
☐	133	Byron Dafoe (G), L.A.	.35
☐	134	Corey Hirsch (G), Van.	.35
☐	**135**	**Antti Törmänen, Ott., RC**	**.35**
☐	136	Jason Bonsignore, Edm.	.35
☐	137	Ryan Smyth, Edm.	.75
☐	138	Bryan McCabe, NYI.	.35
☐	**139**	**Chad Kilger, Ana., RC**	**.35**
☐	**140**	**Todd Bertuzzi, NYI., RC**	**1.50**
☐	141	Marcus Ragnarsson, S.J.	.35
☐	142	Marty Murray, Cgy.	.35
☐	**143**	**Daymond Langkow, T.B., RC**	**.35**
☐	144	Saku Koivu, Mtl.	3.00
☐	145	Jere Lehtinen, Dal.	.75
☐	**146**	**Aki Berg, L.A., RC**	**.75**
☐	**147**	**Radek Dvorak, Fla., RC**	**.75**
☐	**148**	**Robert Svehla, Fla., RC**	**.75**
☐	**149**	**Daniel Alfredsson, Ott., RC**	**3.00**
☐	**150**	**Miroslav Satan, Edm., RC**	**.35**
☐		Checklist [1-150] (no #)	.10
☐		Checklist [inserts] (no #)	.10

GIFTED GRINDERS

	No.	Player	NRMT-MT
Insert Set (18 cards):			**40.00**
□	1	Keith Tkachuk, Wpg. (vs. Luke Richardson)	5.00
□	2	Kevin Stevens, Bos. (vs. Steve Duchesne)	2.00
□	3	Wendel Clark, Tor.	3.00
□	4	Claude Lemieux, Col.	2.00
□	5	Rick Tocchet, Bos.	2.00
□	6	Trevor Linden, Van. (vs. Daryl Sydor)	3.00
□	7	John LeClair, Pha. (vs. Chris Pronger)	6.00
□	8	Mikael Renberg, Pha. (vs. Garry Gailey)	2.00
□	9	Owen Nolan, S.J. (vs. Doug Lidster)	3.00
□	10	Todd Harvey, Dal.	2.00
□	11	Dave Gagner, Dal.	2.00
□	12	Dale Hunter, Wsh.	2.00
□	13	Dave Andreychuk, N.J. (vs. Brian Bradley)	2.00
□	14	Mark Recchi, Mtl. (vs. Curtis Lescyshyn)	3.00
□	15	Jason Arnott, Edm.	3.00
□	16	Dino Ciccarelli, Det.	3.00
□	17	Adam Graves, NYR.	2.00
□	18	Steve Thomas, N.J.	2.00

ROOKIE ROLL CALL

	No.	Player	NRMT-MT
Insert Set (18 cards):			**200.00**
□	1	Saku Koivu, Mtl.	40.00
□	2	Radek Dvorak, Fla.	10.00
□	3	Brendan Witt, Wsh.	10.00
□	4	Antti Törmänen, Ott.	10.00
□	5	Brian Holzinger, Buf.	10.00
□	6	Aki Berg, L.A.	10.00
□	7	Ed Jovanovski, Fla.	15.00
□	8	Marcus Ragnarsson, S.J.	10.00
□	9	Todd Bertuzzi, NYI.	15.00
□	10	Daniel Alfredsson, Ott.	30.00
□	11	Vitali Yachmenev, L.A.	10.00
□	12	Chad Kilger, Ana.	10.00
□	13	Eric Dazé, Chi.	15.00
□	14	Niklas Sundstrom, NYR.	10.00
□	15	Shane Doan, Wpg.	10.00
□	16	Cory Stillman, Cgy.	10.00
□	17	Kyle McLaren, Bos.	10.00
□	18	Jeff O'Neill, Hfd.	15.00

Z-TEAM

	No.	Player	NRMT-MT
Insert Set (18 cards):			**1,500.00**
Promo Card (Martin Brodeur):			**5.00**
□	1	Patrick Roy (G), Col.	200.00
□	2	Martin Brodeur (G), N.J.	350.00
□	3	Mario Lemieux, Pgh.	200.00
□	4	Wayne Gretzky, L.A.	250.00
□	5	Mark Messier, NYR.	50.00
□	6	Jeremy Roenick, Chi.	35.00
□	7	Eric Lindros, Pha.	150.00
□	8	Peter Forsberg, Col.	125.00
□	9	Sergei Fedorov, Det.	50.00
□	10	Mike Modano, Dal.	50.00
□	11	Jaromir Jagr, Pgh.	125.00
□	12	Pavel Bure, Van.	75.00
□	13	Joe Sakic, Col.	100.00
□	14	Paul Kariya, Ana.	150.00
□	15	Brett Hull, Stl.	50.00
□	16	Brendan Shanahan, Hfd.	60.00
□	17	Félix Potvin (G), Tor.	50.00
□	18	Jim Carey (G), Wsh.	20.00

1995 - 96 PLAYOFF ONE-ON-ONE HOCKEY CHALLENGE

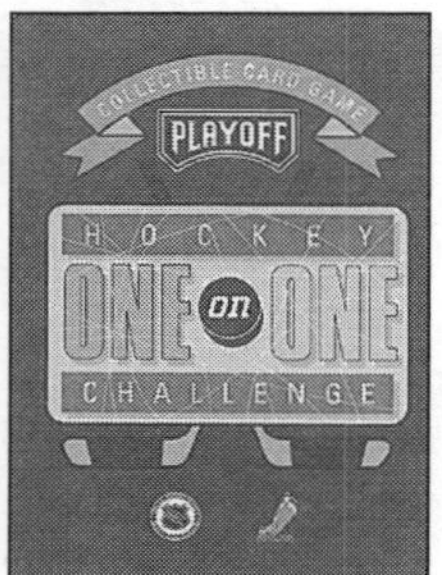

This series was later repackaged with the 1996 - 97 release.

Imprint: © 1995 PLAYOFF CORPORATION

	No.	Player	NRMT-MT
Master Set (330 cards + 26 dice):			**950.00**
Commons Set (110 cards):			**12.00**
Uncommons Set (110 cards):			**20.00**
UNCOMMON - GREEN BAR			
□	1	Guy Hebert (G), Ana.	.25
□	2	Paul Kariya, Ana.	1.25
□	3	Mike Sillinger, Ana.	.10
□	4	Oleg Tverdovsky, Ana.	.10
□	5	Ray Bourque, Bos.	.50
□	6	Alexei Kasatonov, Bos.	.10
□	7	Blaine Lacher (G), Bos.	.10
□	8	Cam Neely, Bos.	.25
□	9	Adam Oates, Bos.	.35
□	10	Kevin Stevens, Bos.	.10
□	11	Donald Audette, Buf.	.10
□	12	Dominik Hasek (G), Buf.	.75
□	13	Pat LaFontaine, Buf.	.25
□	14	Alexei Zhitnik, Buf.	.10
□	15	Steve Chiasson, Cgy.	.10
□	16	Theoren Fleury, Cgy.	.35
□	17	Phil Housley, Cgy.	.10
□	18	Joe Nieuwendyk, Cgy.	.25
□	19	Gary Roberts, Cgy.	.25
□	20	German Titov, Cgy.	.10
□	21	Ed Belfour (G), Chi.	.35
□	22	Chris Chelios, Chi.	.35
□	23	Bernie Nicholls, Chi.	.10
□	24	Jeremy Roenick, Chi.	.35
□	25	Peter Forsberg, Col.	1.00
□	26	Sylvain Lefebvre, Col.	.10
□	27	Owen Nolan, Col.	.25
□	28	Joe Sakic, Col.	.85
□	29	Jocelyn Thibault (G), Col.	.35
□	30	Dave Gagner, Dal.	.10
□	31	Mike Modano, Dal.	.50
□	32	Andy Moog (G), Dal.	.25
□	33	Paul Coffey, Det.	.25
□	34	Sergei Fedorov, Det.	.50
□	35	Keith Primeau, Det.	.25
□	36	Ray Sheppard, Det.	.10
□	37	Jason Arnott, Edm.	.25
□	38	David Oliver, Edm.	.10
□	39	Pat Stapleton, Edm.	.10
□	40	Jesse Belanger, Edm.	.10
□	41	Paul Laus, Fla.	.10
□	42	Rob Niedermayer, Fla.	.10
□	43	Brian Skrudland, Fla.	.10
□	44	John Vanbiesbrouck (G), Fla.	.60
□	45	Sean Burke (G), Hfd.	.25
□	46	Andrew Cassels, Hfd.	.10
□	47	Brendan Shanahan, Hfd.	.60
□	48	Rob Blake, L.A.	.25
□	49	Tony Granato, L.A.	.10
□	50	Wayne Gretzky, L.A.	2.00
□	51	Marty McSorley, L.A.	.10
□	52	Jamie Storr (G), L.A.	.25
□	53	Vincent Damphousse, Mtl.	.35
□	54	Mark Recchi, Mtl.	.25
□	55	Patrick Roy (G), Mtl.	1.50
□	56	Pierre Turgeon, Mtl.	.25
□	57	Martin Brodeur (G), N.J.	.75
□	58	Bill Guerin, N.J.	.25
□	59	Scott Niedermayer, N.J.	.25
□	60	Stéphane Richer, N.J.	.10
□	61	Scott Stevens, N.J.	.10
□	62	Patrick Flatley, NYI.	.10
□	63	Brett Lindros, NYI.	.10
□	64	Mathieu Schneider, NYI.	.10
□	65	Kirk Muller, NYI.	.10
□	66	Adam Graves, NYR.	.10
□	67	Alexei Kovalev, NYR.	.10
□	68	Brian Leetch, NYR.	.35
□	69	Mike Richter (G), NYR.	.35
□	70	Pat Verbeek, NYR.	.10
□	71	Luc Robitaille, NYR.	.10
□	72	Radek Bonk, Ott.	.10
□	73	Alexandre Daigle, Ott.	.25
□	74	Alexei Yashin, Ott.	.35
□	75	Eric Desjardins, Pha.	.10
□	76	Eric Lindros, Pha.	1.25
□	77	Ron Francis, Pgh.	.35
□	78	Jaromir Jagr, Pgh.	1.00
□	79	Mario Lemieux, Pgh.	1.50
□	80	Ken Wregget (G), Pgh.	.10
□	81	François Leroux, Pgh.	.10
□	82	Pat Falloon, S.J.	.10
□	83	Jeff Friesen, S.J.	.25
□	84	Arturs Irbe (G), S.J.	.10
□	85	Igor Larionov, S.J.	.25
□	86	Shayne Corson, Stl.	.25
□	87	Geoff Courtnall, Stl.	.10
□	88	Steve Duchesne, Stl.	.10
□	89	Brett Hull, Stl.	.50
□	90	Al MacInnis, Stl.	.10
□	91	Brian Bellows, T.B.	.10
□	92	Chris Gratton, T.B.	.25
□	93	Dave Andreychuk, Tor.	.10
□	94	Tie Domi, Tor.	.10
□	95	Mike Gartner, Tor.	.25
□	96	Doug Gilmour, Tor.	.35
□	97	Larry Murphy, Tor.	.25
□	98	Félix Potvin (G), Tor.	.50
□	99	Mats Sundin, Tor.	.50
□	100	Pavel Bure, Van.	.75
□	101	Kirk McLean (G), Van.	.25
□	102	Alexander Mogilny, Van.	.10
□	103	Christian Ruuttu, Van.	.10
□	104	Jim Carey (G), Wsh.	.10
□	105	Joé Juneau, Wsh.	.10
□	106	Jason Allison, Wsh.	.35

- ☐ 107 Teppo Numminen, Wsh. .10
- ☐ 108 Teemu Selänne, Wpg. .75
- ☐ 109 Keith Tkachuk, Wpg. .35
- ☐ 110 Alexei Zhamnov, Wpg. .25

COMMON - VIOLET BAR

- ☐ 111 Patrik Carnback, Ana. .20
- ☐ 112 Bobby Dollas, Ana. .20
- ☐ 113 Guy Hebert (G), Ana. .35
- ☐ 114 Paul Kariya, Ana. 2.50
- ☐ 115 Shaun Van Allen, Ana. .20
- ☐ 116 Ray Bourque, Bos. 1.00
- ☐ 117 Mariusz Czerkawski, Bos. .20
- ☐ 118 Todd Elik, Bos. .20
- ☐ 119 Blaine Lacher (G), Bos. .20
- ☐ 120 Cam Neely, Bos. .35
- ☐ 121 Adam Oates, Bos. .50
- ☐ 122 David Reid, Bos. .20
- ☐ 123 Kevin Stevens, Bos. .20
- ☐ 124 Garry Galley, Buf. .20
- ☐ 125 Dominik Hasek (G), Buf. 1.50
- ☐ 126 Brian Holzinger, Buf. .20
- ☐ 127 Pat LaFontaine, Buf. .35
- ☐ 128 Michael Peca, Buf. .35
- ☐ 129 Phil Housley, Cgy. .20
- ☐ 130 Paul Kruse, Cgy. .20
- ☐ 131 Ron Stern, Cgy. .20
- ☐ 132 Zarley Zalapski, Cgy. .20
- ☐ 133 Patrick Poulin, Chi. .20
- ☐ 134 Bob Probert, Chi. .20
- ☐ 135 Jeremy Roenick, Chi. .50
- ☐ 136 Adam Deadmarsh, Col. .20
- ☐ 137 Peter Forsberg, Col. 2.00
- ☐ 138 Andrei Kovalenko, Col. .20
- ☐ 139 Joe Sakic, Col. 1.75
- ☐ 140 Derian Hatcher, Dal. .35
- ☐ 141 Grant Ledyard, Dal. .20
- ☐ 142 Mike Modano, Dal. 1.00
- ☐ 143 Paul Coffey, Det. .35
- ☐ 144 Sergei Fedorov, Det. 1.00
- ☐ 145 Vladimir Konstantinov, Det. .20
- ☐ 146 Nicklas Lidström, Det. .35
- ☐ 147 Steve Yzerman, Det. 2.00
- ☐ 148 Igor Kravchuk, Edm. .20
- ☐ 149 Kirk Maltby, Edm. .20
- ☐ 150 Boris Mironov, Edm. .20
- ☐ 151 Bill Ranford (G), Edm. .35
- ☐ 152 Stu Barnes, Fla. .20
- ☐ 153 Jesse Belanger, Fla. .20
- ☐ 154 Scott Mellanby, Fla. .20
- ☐ 155 Adam Burt, Hfd. .20
- ☐ 156 Steven Rice, Hfd. .20
- ☐ 157 Brendan Shanahan, Hfd. 1.25
- ☐ 158 Glen Wesley, Hfd. .20
- ☐ 159 Wayne Gretzky, L.A. 4.00
- ☐ 160 Darryl Sydor, L.A. .20
- ☐ 161 Rick Tocchet, L.A. .20
- ☐ 162 Benoît Brunet, Mtl. .20
- ☐ 163 J.J. Daigneault, Mtl. .20
- ☐ 164 Saku Koivu, Mtl. 1.50
- ☐ 165 Lyle Odelein, Mtl. .20
- ☐ 166 Patrick Roy (G), Mtl. 3.00
- ☐ 167 Scott Stevens, N.J. .20
- ☐ 168 Valeri Zelepukin, N.J. .20
- ☐ 169 Steve Thomas, N.J. .20
- ☐ 170 Dennis Vaske, NYI. .20
- ☐ 171 Brett Lindros, NYI. .20
- ☐ 172 Zigmund Palffy, NYI. .75
- ☐ 173 Ray Ferraro, NYI. .20
- ☐ 174 Brian Leetch, NYR. .75
- ☐ 175 Mark Messier, NYR. 1.00
- ☐ 176 Ulf Samuelsson, NYR. .20
- ☐ 177 Don Beaupré (G), Ott. .20
- ☐ 178 Alexandre Daigle, Ott. .35
- ☐ 179 Steve Larouche, Ott. .20
- ☐ 180 Scott Levins, Ott. .20
- ☐ 181 Ron Hextall, Pha. .35
- ☐ 182 Eric Lindros, Pha. 2.50
- ☐ 183 Mikael Renberg, Pha. .20
- ☐ 184 Kjell Samuelsson, Pha. .20
- ☐ 185 Jaromir Jagr, Pgh. 2.00
- ☐ 186 Mario Lemieux, Pgh. 3.00
- ☐ 187 Sergei Zubov, Pgh. .35
- ☐ 188 Bryan Smolinski, Pgh. .20
- ☐ 189 Dmitri Mironov, Pgh. .20
- ☐ 190 Ulf Dahlen, S.J. .20
- ☐ 191 Arturs Irbe (G), S.J. .20
- ☐ 192 Craig Janney, S.J. .20
- ☐ 193 Sandis Ozolinsh, S.J. .35
- ☐ 194 Jon Casey (G), Stl. .20
- ☐ 195 Brett Hull, Stl. 1.00
- ☐ 196 Esa Tikkanen, Stl. .20
- ☐ 197 Brian Bradley, T.B. .20
- ☐ 198 Daren Puppa (G), T.B. .20
- ☐ 199 Alexander Selivanov, T.B. .20
- ☐ 200 Rob Zamuner, T.B. .20
- ☐ 201 Ken Baumgartner, Tor. .20
- ☐ 202 Doug Gilmour, Tor. .60
- ☐ 203 Kenny Jonsson, Tor. .20
- ☐ 204 Félix Potvin (G), Tor. 1.00
- ☐ 205 Randy Wood, Tor. .20
- ☐ 206 Jeff Brown, Van. .20
- ☐ 207 Pavel Bure, Van. 1.50
- ☐ 208 Trevor Linden, Van. .35
- ☐ 209 Alexander Mogilny, Van. .50
- ☐ 210 Roman Oksiuta, Van. .20
- ☐ 211 Cliff Ronning, Van. .20
- ☐ 212 Peter Bondra, Wsh. .75
- ☐ 213 Jim Carey (G), Wsh. .20
- ☐ 214 Pat Peake, Wsh. .20
- ☐ 215 Mark Tinordi, Wsh. .20
- ☐ 216 Mike Eastwood, Wpg. .20
- ☐ 217 Nelson Emerson, Wpg. .20
- ☐ 218 Dave Manson, Wpg. .20
- ☐ 219 Teemu Selänne, Wpg. 1.50
- ☐ 220 Keith Tkachuk, Wpg. .75

RARE / SILVER

- ☐ 221 Bob Corkum, Ana. .50
- ☐ 222 Peter Douris, Ana. .50
- ☐ 225 Mike Sillinger, Ana. .50
- ☐ 227 Fred Knipscheer, Bos. .50
- ☐ 229 Adam Oates. Bos. 2.00
- ☐ 230 Jason Dawe, Buf. .50
- ☐ 231 Yuri Khmylev, Buf. .50
- ☐ 233 Trevor Kidd (G), Chi. 1.00
- ☐ 234 Eric Dazé, Chi. 1.00
- ☐ 235 Tony Amonte, Chi. 1.00
- ☐ 237 Denis Savard, Chi. 1.00
- ☐ 238 Gary Suter, Chi. .50
- ☐ 240 Curtis Leschyshyn, Col. .50
- ☐ 243 Valeri Kamensky, Col. 1.00
- ☐ 244 Claude Lemieux, Col. .50
- ☐ 245 Bob Bassen, Dal. .50
- ☐ 246 Shane Churla, Dal. .50
- ☐ 247 Todd Harvey, Dal. .50
- ☐ 249 Richard Matvichuk, Dal. .50
- ☐ 251 Dino Ciccarelli, Det. 1.00
- ☐ 254 Vyacheslav Kozlov, Det. .50
- ☐ 255 Mike Vernon (G), Det. 1.00
- ☐ 256 Jason Bonsignore, Edm. .50
- ☐ 257 Dean McAmmond, Edm. .50
- ☐ 258 Bill Ranford (G), Edm. 1.00
- ☐ 260 Bob Kudelski, Fla. .50
- ☐ 261 Dave Lowry, Fla. .50
- ☐ 262 Gord Murphy, Fla. .50
- ☐ 264 Fratisek Kucera, Hfd. .50
- ☐ 265 Paul Ranheim, Hfd. .50
- ☐ 267 Darren Turcotte, Hfd. .50
- ☐ 268 Pat Conacher, L.A. .50
- ☐ 270 Kelly Hrudey, L.A. .50
- ☐ 271 Jari Kurri, L.A. 1.00
- ☐ 272 Patrice Brisebrois, Mtl. .50
- ☐ 273 Vladimir Malakhov, Mtl. .50
- ☐ 276 Neal Broten, N.J. .50
- ☐ 277 Sergei Brylin, N.J. .50
- ☐ 278 John MacLean, N.J. .50
- ☐ 279 Wendel Clark, NYI. 1.00
- ☐ 280 Travis Green, NYI. .50
- ☐ 282 Tommy Salo (G), NYI. .50
- ☐ 285 Sergei Nemchinov, NYI. .50
- ☐ 287 Sean Hill, Ott. .50
- ☐ 289 Martin Straka, Ott. .50
- ☐ 290 Sylvain Turgeon, Ott. .50
- ☐ 292 Kevin Haller, Pha. .50
- ☐ 293 John LeClair, Pha. 5.00
- ☐ 295 Joel Otto, Pha. .50
- ☐ 296 Chris Therien, Pha .50
- ☐ 299 Glenn Murray, Pgh. .50
- ☐ 300 Petr Nedved, Pgh. .50
- ☐ 301 Jamie Baker, S.J. .50
- ☐ 303 Jayson More, S.J. .50
- ☐ 304 Ray Whitney, S.J. .50
- ☐ 306 Dale Hawerchuk, Stl. 1.00
- ☐ 308 Ian Laperrière, Stl. .50
- ☐ 309 Chris Pronger, Stl. 1.00
- ☐ 310 Roman Hamrlik, T.B. 1.00
- ☐ 312 John Tucker, T.B. .50
- ☐ 314 Ken Baumgartner, Tor. .50
- ☐ 317 Bret Hedican, Van. .50
- ☐ 319 Mike Ridley, Van. .50
- ☐ 320 Peter Bondra, Wsh. 3.00
- ☐ 321 Sylvain Côté, Wsh. .50
- ☐ 322 Dale Hunter, Wsh. .50
- ☐ 324 Kelly Miller, Wsh. .50
- ☐ 325 Tim Cheveldae (G), Wpg. .50
- ☐ 326 Dallas Drake, Wpg. .50
- ☐ 327 Igor Korolev, Wpg. .50
- ☐ 328 Teppo Numminen, Wpg. .50

ULTRA-RARE / GOLD

These cards were inserted in Playoff Booster packs.

	No.	Player	NRMT-MT
☐	223	Paul Kariya, Ana.	65.00
☐	226	Ray Bourque, Bos.	25.00
☐	228	Cam Neely, Bos.	10.00
☐	229	Adam Oates, Bos.	15.00
☐	236	Jeremy Roenick, Chi.	15.00
☐	241	Owen Nolan, Col.	10.00
☐	250	Mike Modano, Dal.	25.00
☐	259	Doug Weight, Edm.	15.00
☐	269	Wayne Gretzky, L.A.	125.00
☐	274	Patrick Roy (G), Mtl.	80.00
☐	283	Brian Leetch, NYR.	15.00
☐	284	Mark Messier, NYR.	25.00
☐	294	Eric Lindros, Pha.	65.00
☐	298	Mario Lemieux, Pgh.	80.00
☐	302	Arturs Irbe (G), S.J.	5.00
☐	307	Brett Hull, Stl.	25.00
☐	313	Paul Ysebaert, T.B.	5.00
☐	315	Doug Gilmour, Tor.	15.00
☐	316	Pavel Bure, Van.	35.00
☐	329	Teemu Selänne, Wpg.	35.00

ULTRA - RARE / GOLD

These cards were inserted in Playoff Starter packs.

	No.	Player	NRMT-MT
☐	224	Todd Krygier, Ana.	5.00
☐	232	Bob Sweeney, Bos.	5.00
☐	239	Peter Forsberg, Col.	50.00
☐	242	Joe Sakic, Col.	40.00
☐	248	Kevin Hatcher, Dal.	5.00
☐	252	Paul Coffey, Det.	10.00
☐	253	Sergei Fedorov, Det.	25.00
☐	263	Rob Niedermayer, Fla.	10.00
☐	266	Geoff Sanderson, Hfd.	5.00
☐	275	Martin Brodeur (G), N.J.	35.00
☐	281	Scott Lachance, NYI.	5.00
☐	286	Luc Robitaille, NYR.	10.00
☐	288	Jim Paek, Ott.	5.00
☐	291	Rod Brind'Amour, Pha.	10.00
☐	297	Jaromir Jagr, Pgh.	50.00
☐	305	Geoff Courtnall, Stl.	5.00
☐	311	Petr Klima, T.B.	5.00
☐	318	Alexander Mogilny, Van.	15.00
☐	323	Keith Jones, Wsh.	5.00
☐	330	Alexei Zhamnov, Wpg.	10.00

ONE-ON-ONE DICE

	Team	NRMT-MT
☐	Anaheim Mighty Ducks	2.25
☐	Boston Bruins	3.00
☐	Buffalo Sabres	2.25
☐	Calgary Flames	3.00
☐	Chicago Blackhawks	3.00
☐	Colorado Avalanche	2.25
☐	Dallas Stars	2.25
☐	Detroit Red Wings	3.00
☐	Edmonton Oilers	3.00
☐	Florida Panthers	2.25
☐	Hartford Whalers	2.25
☐	Los Angeles Kings	2.25
☐	Montréal Canadiens	3.00
☐	New Jersey Devils	2.25
☐	New York Islanders	2.25
☐	New York Rangers	3.00
☐	Ottawa Senators	3.00

	Team	NRMT-MT
□	Philadelphia Flyers	2.25
□	Pittsburgh Penguins	2.25
□	St. Louis Blues	2.25
□	San Jose Sharks	2.25
□	Tampa Bay Lightning	2.25
□	Toronto Maple Leafs	3.00
□	Vancouver Canucks	3.00
□	Washington Capitals	2.25
□	Winnipeg Jets	3.00

1995 - 96 PRO MAGNETS

PROMOS

	No.	Player	NRMT-MT
□	MAG1	Wayne Gretzky, L.A.	10.00
□	MAG2	Ed Belfour (G), Chi.	2.00
□	MAG3	Mike Modano, Dal.	2.50
□	01	Adam Oates, Bos.	2.00
□	02	Pavel Bure, Van.	4.00
□	03	Guy Hebert (G), Ana.	2.00
□	04	Mark Messier, NYR.	3.00
□	05	Sergei Fedorov, Det.	3.00
□	06	Arturs Irbe (G), S.J.	1.00
□		NHL Logo	1.00

PRO MAGNETS

There is believed to be 50-100 copies of each Test Proof. Only 100 of the 130 players in the magnet set have test proof cards. This series was issued by Chris Martin Enterprises.

Card Size: 2 7/16" x 3 11/16"

Imprint:

Complete Set (130 magnets): 125.00

Test Proofs Set (100 cards): 500.00

	No.	Player	Test Proof	Magnet
□□	1	Ed Belfour (G), Chi.	10.00	2.50
□□	2	Chris Chelios, Chi.	15.00	3.00
□□	3	Joe Murphy, Chi.	3.00	1.00
□□	4	Jeremy Roenick, Chi.	10.00	2.50
□□	5	Bernie Nicholls, Chi.	3.00	1.00
□□	6	Brett Hull, Stl.	30.00	4.00
□□	7	Esa Tikkanen, Stl.	3.00	1.00
□□	8	Chris Pronger, Stl.	6.00	2.00
□□	9	Al MacInnis, Stl.	3.00	1.00
□□	10	Geoff Courtnall, Stl.	3.00	1.00
□□	11	Ray Bourque, Bos.	30.00	4.00
□□	12	Blaine Lacher (G), Bos.	3.00	1.00
□□	13	Cam Neely, Bos.	6.00	2.00
□□	14	Adam Oates, Bos.	10.00	2.50
□□	15	Kevin Stevens, Bos.	3.00	1.00
□□	16	Vincent Damphousse, Mtl.	10.00	2.50
□□	17	Mark Recchi, Mtl.	6.00	2.00
□□	18	Pierre Turgeon, Mtl.	6.00	2.00
□□	19	Patrick Roy (G), Mtl.	125.00	12.00
□□	20	Valeri Bure, Mtl.	3.00	1.00
□□	21	Pavel Bure, Van.	45.00	5.00
□□	22	Alexander Mogilny, Van.	10.00	2.50
□□	23	Trevor Linden, Van.	6.00	2.00
□□	24	Kirk McLean (G), Van.	6.00	2.00
□□	25	Cliff Ronning, Van.	3.00	1.00
□	26	Jim Carey (G), Wsh.	.–	1.00
□	27	Brendan Witt, Wsh.	.–	1.00
□	28	Joé Juneau, Wsh.	.–	1.00
□	29	Jason Allison, Wsh.	.–	2.50
□	30	Dale Hunter, Wsh.	.–	1.00
□□	31	Martin Brodeur (G), N.J.	45.00	5.00
□□	32	John MacLean, N.J.	3.00	1.00
□□	33	Scott Niedermayer, N.J.	6.00	2.00
□□	34	Stéphane Richer, N.J.	3.00	1.00
□□	35	Scott Stevens, N.J.	3.00	1.00
□□	36	Patrik Carnback, Ana.	3.00	1.00
□□	37	Oleg Tverdovsky, Ana.	3.00	1.00
□□	38	Guy Hebert (G), Ana.	6.00	2.00
□□	39	Paul Kariya, Ana.	100.00	10.00
□□	40	Garry Valk, Ana.	3.00	1.00
□□	41	Theoren Fleury, Cgy.	10.00	2.50
□□	42	German Titov, Cgy.	3.00	1.00
□□	43	Joe Nieuwendyk, Cgy.	6.00	2.00
□□	44	Gary Roberts, Cgy.	6.00	2.00
□□	45	Trevor Kidd (G), Cgy.	6.00	2.00
□□	46	Rod Brind'Amour, Pha.	6.00	2.00
□□	47	Eric Lindros, Pha.	100.00	10.00
□□	48	John LeClair, Pha.	30.00	4.00
□□	49	Ron Hextall (G), Pha.	6.00	2.00
□□	50	Mikael Renberg, Pha.	3.00	1.00
□	51	Patrick Flatley, NYI.	.–	1.00
□	52	Kirk Muller, NYI.	.–	1.00
□	53	Mathieu Schneider, NYI.	.–	1.00
□	54	Wendel Clark, NYI.	.–	2.00
□	55	Brett Lindros, NYI.	.–	1.00
□	56	Tim Cheveldae (G), Wpg.	.–	2.00
□	57	Dallas Drake, Wpg.	.–	1.00
□	58	Teemu Selänne, Wpg.	.–	5.00
□	59	Keith Tkachuk, Wpg.	.–	3.00
□	60	Alexei Zhamnov, Wpg.	.–	2.00
□□	61	Rob Blake, L.A.	6.00	2.00
□□	62	Wayne Gretzky, L.A.	175.00	15.00
□□	63	Jari Kurri, L.A.	6.00	2.00
□□	64	Jamie Storr (G), L.A.	6.00	2.00
□□	65	Rick Tocchet, L.A.	3.00	1.00
□□	66	Brian Bradley, T.B.	3.00	1.00
□□	67	Roman Hamrlik, T.B.	6.00	2.00
□□	68	Rob Zamuner, T.B.	6.00	2.00
□□	69	Paul Ysebaert, T.B.	3.00	1.00
□□	70	Chris Gratton, T.B.	6.00	2.00
□□	71	Dave Andreychuk, Tor.	3.00	1.00
□□	72	Kenny Jonsson, Tor.	3.00	1.00
□□	73	Doug Gilmour, Tor.	10.00	2.50
□□	74	Félix Potvin (G), Tor.	30.00	4.00
□□	75	Mats Sundin, Tor.	30.00	4.00
□	76	Claude Lemieux, Col.	.–	1.00
□	77	Peter Forsberg, Col.	.–	8.00
□	78	Mike Ricci, Col.	.–	1.00
□	79	Joe Sakic, Col.	.–	6.00
□	80	Stéphane Fiset (G), Col.	.–	2.00
□□	81	Jason Arnott, Edm.	6.00	2.00
□□	82	Jason Bonsignore, Edm.	3.00	1.00
□□	83	Doug Weight, Edm.	10.00	2.50
□□	84	Bill Ranford (G), Edm.	6.00	2.00
□□	85	Todd Marchant, Edm.	3.00	1.00
□□	86	Rob Niedermayer, Fla.	3.00	1.00
□□	87	Jody Hull, Fla.	3.00	1.00
□□	88	Bob Kudelski, Fla.	3.00	1.00
□□	89	Scott Mellanby, Fla.	3.00	1.00
□□	90	John Vanbiesbrouck (G), Fla.	35.00	4.50
□□	91	Bryan Smolinski, Pgh.	3.00	1.00
□□	92	Mario Lemieux, Pgh.	125.00	12.00
□□	93	Jaromir Jagr, Pgh.	80.00	8.00
□□	94	Sergei Zubov, Pgh.	6.00	2.00
□□	95	Ron Francis, Pgh.	10.00	2.50
□□	96	Adam Graves, NYR.	3.00	1.00
□□	97	Brian Leetch, NYR.	10.00	2.50
□□	98	Mark Messier, NYR.	30.00	4.00
□□	99	Mike Richter (G), NYR.	10.00	2.50
□□	100	Luc Robitaille, NYR.	6.00	2.00
□	101	Paul Coffey, Det.	.–	2.00
□	102	Sergei Fedorov, Det.	.–	4.00
□	103	Nicklas Lidström, Det.	.–	2.00
□	104	Ray Sheppard, Det.	.–	1.00
□	105	Steve Yzerman, Det.	.–	8.00
□□	106	Dominik Hasek (G), Buf.	45.00	5.00
□□	107	Alexei Zhitnik, Buf.	3.00	1.00
□□	108	Yuri Khmylev, Buf.	3.00	1.00
□□	109	Pat LaFontaine, Buf.	3.00	2.00
□□	110	Donald Audette, Buf.	3.00	1.00
□□	111	Radek Bonk, Ott.	3.00	1.00
□□	112	Alexandre Daigle, Ott.	6.00	2.00
□□	113	Steve Larouche, Ott.	3.00	1.00
□□	114	Martin Straka, Ott.	3.00	1.00
□□	115	Randy Cunneyworth, Ott.	3.00	1.00
□□	116	Pat Falloon, S.J.	3.00	1.00
□□	117	Arturs Irbe (G), S.J.	3.00	1.00
□□	118	Ulf Dahlen, S.J.	3.00	1.00
□□	119	Craig Janney, S.J.	3.00	1.00
□□	120	Jeff Friesen, S.J.	6.00	1.00
□	121	Shane Churla, Dal.	.–	1.00
□	122	Derian Hatcher, Dal.	.–	2.00
□	123	Todd Harvey, Dal.	.–	1.00
□	124	Mike Modano, Dal.	.–	2.00
□	125	Andy Moog (G), Dal.	.–	2.00
□□	126	Sean Burke (G), Hfd.	6.00	2.00
□□	127	Andrew Cassels, Hfd.	3.00	1.00
□□	128	Darren Turcotte, Hfd.	3.00	1.00
□□	129	Geoff Sanderson, Hfd.	3.00	1.00
□□	130	Brendan Shanahan, Hfd.	35.00	4.50

IRON CURTAIN

	No.	Player
□	IC01	Ed Belfour (G), Chi.
□	IC02	Martin Brodeur (G), N.J.
□	IC03	Arturs Irbe (G), S.J.
□	IC04	Mike Richter (G), NYR.
□	IC05	Mike Vernon (G), Det.
□	IC06	Ron Hextall (G), Pha.

1995 - 96 PRO STAMPS

These sticker/stamps feature the same photos as the Pro Magnets series.

Imprint:

Complete Set (12 panels): 30.00

	Panel		Panel
□	Panel 1	□	Panel 2
□	Panel 3	□	Panel 4
□	Panel 5	□	Panel 6
□	Panel 7	□	Panel 8
□	Panel 9	□	Panel 10
□	Panel 11	□	Panel 12

1995 - 96 RADIO CITY POSTCARDS

We have no pricing information on this set.

Postcard Size: 4 1/4" x 6"

	Player		Player
□	Timo Jutila	□	Jarmo Myllys
□	Petteri Nummelin	□	Christian Ruuttu

1995 - 96 SCORE

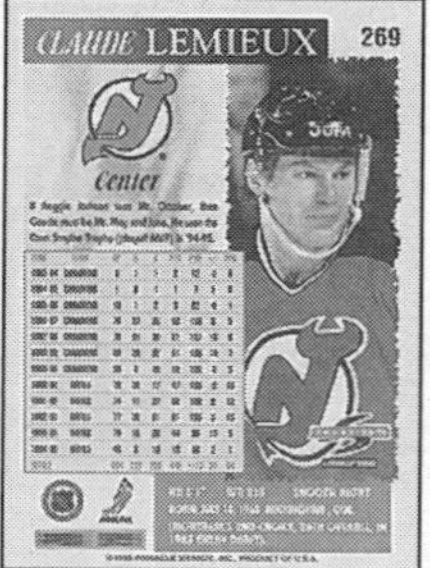

These cards have three versions: a regular card, a Black Ice parallel and a Black Ice Artist's Proof parallel. Seven regular cards also have a promo version. Promo cards and regular cards have the same value.

Imprint: © 1995 PINNACLE BRANDS, INC.

Complete Set (330 cards):	15.00	215.00	1,700.00
Common Player:	.10	.35	3.00

	No.	Player	Reg.	Bl	AP
□□□	1	Jaromir Jagr, Pgh.	1.00	5.00	60.00
□□□	2	Adam Graves, NYR.	.10	.35	3.00
□□□□	3	Chris Chelios, Chi.	.35	1.50	15.00
□□□	4	Félix Potvin (G), Tor.	.50	2.50	30.00
□□□	5	Joe Sakic, Col.	.85	4.50	50.00
□□□	6	Chris Pronger, Stl.	.25	.75	6.00
□□□	7	Teemu Selänne, Ana.	.75	3.75	45.00
□□□□	8	Jason Arnott, Edm.	.25	.75	6.00
□□□□	9	John LeClair, Pha.	.50	2.50	30.00
□□□□	10	Mark Recchi, Mtl.	.25	.75	6.00
□□□	11	Rob Blake, L.A.	.25	.75	6.00
□□□	12	Kevin Hatcher, Pgh.	.10	.35	3.00
□□□	13	Shawn Burr, Det.	.10	.35	3.00
□□□	14	Brett Lindros, NYI.	.10	.35	3.00
□□□	15	Craig Janney, Wpg.	.10	.35	3.00
□□□	16	Oleg Tverdovsky, Ana.	.10	.35	3.00
□□□	17	Blaine Lacher (G), Bos.	.10	.35	3.00
□□□	18	Alexandre Daigle, Ott.	.25	.75	6.00
□□□□	19	Trevor Kidd (G), Cgy.	.25	.75	6.00
□□□	20	Brendan Shanahan, Stl.	.35	1.00	35.00
□□□	21	Alexander Mogilny, Buf.	.35	1.00	10.00
□□□	22	Stu Barnes, Fla.	.10	.35	3.00
□□□	23	Jeff Brown, Van.	.10	.35	3.00
□□□	24	Paul Coffey, Det.	.25	.75	6.00
□□□□	25	Martin Brodeur (G), N.J.	.75	3.75	45.00
□□□	26	Darryl Sydor, Dal.	.10	.35	3.00
□□□	27	Steve Smith, Chi.	.10	.35	3.00
□□□	28	Ted Donato, Bos.	.10	.35	3.00
□□□	29	Bernie Nicholls, Chi.	.10	.35	3.00
□□□	30	Kenny Jonsson, Tor.	.10	.35	3.00
□□□	31	Peter Forsberg, Col.	1.00	5.00	60.00
□□□	32	Sean Burke (G), Hfd.	.25	.75	6.00
□□□□	33	Keith Tkachuk, Wpg.	.35	1.50	15.00
□□□	34	Todd Marchant, Edm.	.10	.35	3.00
□□□	35	Mikael Renberg, Pha.	.10	.35	3.00
□□□	36	Vincent Damphousse, Mtl.	.30	1.00	10.00
□□□	37	Rick Tocchet, Bos.	.10	.35	3.00
□□□	38	Todd Harvey, Dal.	.10	.35	3.00
□□□	39	Chris Gratton, T.B.	.25	.75	6.00
□□□	40	Darius Kasparaitis, NYI.	.10	.35	3.00
□□□	41	Sergei Nemchinov, NYR.	.10	.35	3.00
□□□	42	Bob Corkum, Ana.	.10	.35	3.00
□□□	43	Brian Smolinski, Pgh.	.10	.35	3.00
□□□	44	Kevin Stevens, Bos.	.10	.35	3.00
□□□	45	Phil Housley, N.J.	.10	.35	3.00
□□□	46	Al MacInnis, Stl.	.25	.75	6.00
□□□	47	Alexei Zhitnik, Buf.	.10	.35	3.00
□□□	48	Rob Niedermayer, Fla.	.10	.35	3.00
□□□	49	Kirk McLean (G), Van.	.25	.75	6.00
□□□	50	Mark Messier, NYR.	.50	2.50	30.00
□□□	51	Nicklas Lidström, Det.	.25	.75	6.00
□□□	52	Scott Niedermayer, N.J.	.25	.75	6.00
□□□	53	Peter Bondra, Wsh.	.35	1.50	15.00
□□□	54	Luc Robitaille, Pgh.	.25	.75	6.00
□□□	55	Jeremy Roenick, Chi.	.35	1.00	10.00
□□□	56	Mats Sundin, Tor.	.50	2.50	30.00
□□□	57	Wendel Clark, Tor.	.25	.75	6.00
□□□	58	Todd Elik, Stl.	.10	.35	3.00
□□□	59	Dave Manson, Wpg.	.10	.35	3.00
□□□	60	David Oliver, Edm.	.10	.35	3.00
□□□	61	Yuri Khmylev, Stl.	.10	.35	3.00
□□□	62	Sergei Krivokrasov, Chi.	.10	.35	3.00
□□□	63	Randy Wood, NYI.	.10	.35	3.00
□□□	64	Andy Moog (G), Dal.	.25	.75	6.00
□□□	65	Petr Klima, T.B.	.10	.35	3.00
□□□	66	Ray Ferraro, NYI.	.10	.35	3.00
□□□	67	Sandis Ozolinsh, S.J.	.25	.75	6.00
□□□	68	Joe Sacco, Ana.	.10	.35	3.00
□□□	69	Zarley Zalapski, Cgy.	.10	.35	3.00
□□□	70	Ron Tugnutt (G), Mtl.	.10	.35	3.00
□□□	71	German Titov, Cgy.	.10	.35	3.00
□□□	72	Ian Laperrière, Stl.	.10	.35	3.00
□□□	73	Doug Gilmour, Tor.	.35	1.00	10.00
□□□	74	Brian Skrudland, Fla.	.10	.35	3.00
□□□	75	Cliff Ronning, Van.	.10	.35	3.00
□□□	76	Brian Savage, Mtl.	.10	.35	3.00
□□□	77	John MacLean, N.J.	.10	.35	3.00
□□□	78	Jim Carey (G), Wsh.	.10	.35	3.00
□□□	79	Alexei Kovalev, NYR.	.10	.35	3.00
□□□	80	Brian Rolston, N.J.	.10	.35	3.00
□□□	81	Shawn McEachern, Bos.	.10	.35	3.00
□□□	82	Gary Suter, Chi.	.10	.35	3.00
□□□	83	Owen Nolan, Que.	.25	.75	6.00
□□□	84	Ray Whitney, S.J.	.10	.35	3.00
□□□	85	Alexei Zhamnov, Wpg.	.25	.75	6.00
□□□	86	Shawn Chambers, N.J.	.10	.35	3.00
□□□	87	Ed Belfour (G), Chi.	.35	1.00	10.00
□□□	88	Patrice Tardif, Stl.	.10	.35	3.00
□□□	89	Greg Adams, Van.	.10	.35	3.00
□□□	90	Pierre Turgeon, Mtl.	.25	.75	6.00
□□□	91	Jeff Friesen, S.J.	.25	.75	6.00
□□□	92	Marty McSorley, L.A.	.10	.35	3.00
□□□	93	Dave Gagner, Dal.	.10	.35	3.00
□□□	94	Guy Hebert (G), Ana.	.25	.75	6.00
□□□	95	Keith Jones, Wsh.	.10	.35	3.00
□□□	96	Kirk Muller, Tor.	.10	.35	3.00
□□□	97	Gary Roberts, Cgy.	.25	.75	6.00
□□□	98	Chris Therien, Pha.	.10	.35	3.00
□□□	99	Steve Duchesne, Stl.	.10	.35	3.00
□□□	100	Sergei Fedorov, Det.	.50	2.50	30.00
□□□	101	Donald Audette, Buf.	.10	.35	3.00
□□□	102	Jyrki Lumme, Van.	.10	.35	3.00
□□□	103	Darrin Shannon, Wpg.	.10	.35	3.00
□□□	104	Gord Murphy, Fla.	.10	.35	3.00
□□□	105	John Cullen, T.B.	.10	.35	3.00
□□□	106	Bill Guerin, N.J.	.25	.75	6.00
□□□	107	Dale Hunter, Wsh.	.10	.35	3.00
□□□	108	Uwe Krupp, Col.	.10	.35	3.00
□□□	109	Dave Andreychuk, N.J.	.10	.35	3.00
□□□	110	Joe Murphy, Chi.	.10	.35	3.00
□□□	111	Geoff Sanderson, Hfd.	.10	.35	3.00
□□□	112	Garry Galley, Buf.	.10	.35	3.00
□□□	113	Ron Sutter, NYI.	.10	.35	3.00
□□□	114	Viktor Kozlov, S.J.	.10	.35	3.00
□□□	115	Jari Kurri, L.A.	.25	.75	6.00
□□□	116	Paul Ysebaert, T.B.	.10	.35	3.00
□□□	117	Vladimir Malakhov, Mtl.	.10	.35	3.00
□□□	118	Josef Beranek, Pha.	.10	.35	3.00
□□□	119	Adam Oates, Bos.	.35	1.00	10.00
□□□	120	Mike Modano, Dal.	.50	2.50	30.00
□□□	121	Theoren Fleury, Cgy.	.35	1.00	10.00
□□□	122	Pat Verbeek, Dal.	.10	.35	3.00
□□□	123	Esa Tikkanen, Stl.	.10	.35	3.00
□□□	124	Brian Leetch, NYR.	.35	1.00	10.00
□□□	125	Paul Kariya, Ana.	1.25	6.00	75.00
□□□	126	Ken Wregget (G), Pgh.	.10	.35	3.00
□□□	127	Ray Sheppard, Det.	.10	.35	3.00
□□□	128	Jason Allison, Wsh.	.35	1.00	10.00
□□□	129	Dave Ellett, Tor.	.10	.35	3.00
□□□	130	Stéphane Richer, N.J.	.10	.35	3.00
□□□	131	Jocelyn Thibault (G), Que.	.35	1.00	10.00
□□□	132	Martin Straka, Pgh.	.10	.35	3.00
□□□	133	Tony Amonte, Chi.	.25	.75	6.00
□□□	134	Scott Mellanby, Fla.	.10	.35	3.00
□□□	135	Pavel Bure, Van.	.75	3.75	45.00
□□□	136	Andrew Cassels, Hfd.	.10	.35	3.00
□□□	137	Ulf Dahlen, S.J.	.10	.35	3.00
□□□	138	Valeri Bure, Mtl.	.10	.35	3.00
□□□	139	Teppo Numminen, Wpg.	.10	.35	3.00
□□□	140	Mike Richter (G), NYR.	.35	1.00	10.00
□□□	141	Rob Gaudreau, S.J.	.10	.35	3.00
□□□	142	Nikolai Khabibulin (G), Wpg.	.35	1.00	10.00
□□□	143	Mariusz Czerkawski, Bos.	.10	.35	3.00
□□□	144	Mark Tinordi, Wsh.	.10	.35	3.00
□□□	145	Patrick Roy (G), Mtl.	1.50	7.50	100.00
□□□	146	Steve Chiasson, Cgy.	.10	.35	3.00
□□□	147	Mike Donnelly, L.A.	.10	.35	3.00
□□□	148	Patrice Brisebois, Mtl.	.10	.35	3.00
□□□	149	Jason Wiemer, T.B.	.10	.35	3.00
□□□	150	Eric Lindros, Pha.	1.25	6.00	75.00
□□□	151	Dimitri Khristich, Wsh.	.10	.35	3.00
□□□	152	Tom Barrasso (G), Pgh.	.25	.75	6.00
□□□	153	Curtis Leschyshyn, Que.	.10	.35	3.00
□□□	154	Robert Kron, Hfd.	.10	.35	3.00
□□□	155	Jesse Belanger, Fla.	.10	.35	3.00
□□□	156	Brian Noonan, Stl.	.10	.35	3.00
□□□	157	Michael Peca, Van.	.25	.75	6.00
□□□	158	Patrick Poulin, Hfd.	.10	.35	3.00
□□□	159	Sergei Makarov. S.J.	.10	.35	3.00
□□□	160	Scott Stevens, N.J.	.10	.35	3.00
□□□	161	Sergio Momesso, Van.	.10	.35	3.00
□□□	162	Todd Gill, Tor.	.10	.35	3.00
□□□	163	Don Sweeney, Bos.	.10	.35	3.00
□□□	164	Randy Burridge, Wsh.	.10	.35	3.00
□□□	165	Vyacheslav Kozlov, Det.	.10	.35	3.00
□□□	166	Shaun Van Allen, Ana.	.10	.35	3.00
□□□	167	Steven Rice, Hfd.	.10	.35	3.00
□□□	168	Adam Deadmarsh, Que.	.25	.75	6.00
□□□	169	Andrei Nikolishin, Hfd.	.10	.35	3.00
□□□	170	Valeri Karpov, Ana.	.10	.35	3.00
□□□	171	Doug Bodger, Buf.	.10	.35	3.00
□□□	172	Cory Millen, N.J.	.10	.35	3.00
□□□	173	Mark Fitzpatrick (G), Fla.	.10	.35	3.00
□□□	174	Bob Errey, S.J.	.10	.35	3.00
□□□	175	Dan Quinn, Ott.	.10	.35	3.00
□□□	176	Vladimir Konstantinov, Det.	.10	.35	3.00
□□□	177	Scott Lachance, NYI.	.10	.35	3.00
□□□	178	Jeff Norton, Stl.	.10	.35	3.00
□□□	179	Valeri Zelepukin, N.J.	.10	.35	3.00
□□□	180	Dmitri Mironov, Tor.	.10	.35	3.00
□□□	181	Pat Peake, Wsh.	.10	.35	3.00
□□□	182	Dominic Roussel (G), Pha.	.10	.35	3.00
□□□	183	Sylvain Côté, Wsh.	.10	.35	3.00
□□□	184	Pat Falloon, S.J.	.10	.35	3.00
□□□	185	Roman Hamrlik, T.B.	.25	.75	6.00
□□□	186	Joel Otto, Cgy.	.10	.35	3.00
□□□	187	Ron Francis, Pgh.	.35	1.00	10.00
□□□	188	Sergei Zubov, Pgh.	.25	.75	6.00
□□□	189	Arturs Irbe (G), S.J.	.10	.35	3.00
□□□	190	Radek Bonk, Ott.	.10	.35	3.00
□□□	191	John Tucker, T.B.	.10	.35	3.00
□□□	192	Sylvain Lefebvre, Que.	.10	.35	3.00
□□□	193	Doug Brown, Det.	.10	.35	3.00
□□□	194	Glen Wesley, Hfd.	.10	.35	3.00
□□□	195	Ron Hextall (G), Pha.	.25	.75	6.00
□□□	196	Patrick Flatley, NYI.	.10	.35	3.00
□□□	197	Darcy Wakaluk (G), Dal.	.10	.35	3.00
□□□	198	Kelly Hrudey (G), L.A.	.10	.35	3.00
□□□	199	Ray Bourque, Bos.	.50	2.50	30.00
□□□	200	Dominik Hasek (G), Buf.	.75	3.75	45.00
□□□	201	Pat LaFontaine, Buf.	.25	.75	5.00
□□□	202	Chris Osgood (G), Det.	.35	1.50	20.00
□□□	203	Ulf Samuelsson, Pgh.	.10	.35	3.00
□□□	204	Mike Gartner, Tor.	.25	.75	6.00
□□□	205	Stéphane Fiset (G), Que.	.25	.75	6.00
□□□	206	Mathieu Schneider, NYI.	.10	.35	3.00
□□□	207	Eric Desjardins, Pha.	.10	.35	3.00
□□□	208	Trevor Linden, Van.	.25	.75	6.00
□□□	209	Cam Neely, Bos.	.25	.75	6.00
□□□	210	Daren Puppa (G), T.B.	.10	.35	3.00
□□□	211	Steve Larmer, NYR.	.10	.35	3.00
□□□	212	Tim Cheveldae (G), Det.	.10	.35	3.00
□□□	213	Derek Plante, Buf.	.10	.35	3.00
□□□	214	Murray Craven, Chi.	.10	.35	3.00
□□□	215	Tommy Söderström (G), NYI.	.10	.35	3.00
□□□	216	Bob Bassen, Que.	.10	.35	3.00
□□□	217	Marty McInnis, NYI.	.10	.35	3.00
□□□	218	Dave Lowry, Fla.	.10	.35	3.00
□□□	219	Mike Vernon (G), Det.	.25	.75	6.00
□□□	220	Petr Nedved, Pgh.	.10	.35	3.00
□□□	221	Yves Racine, Mtl.	.10	.35	3.00
□□□	222	Dale Hawerchuk, Stl.	.25	.75	6.00
□□□	223	Wayne Presley, Buf.	.10	.35	3.00
□□□	224	Darren Turcotte, Wpg.	.10	.35	3.00
□□□	225	Derian Hatcher, Dal.	.25	.75	6.00
□□□	226	Steve Thomas, N.J.	.10	.35	3.00
□□□	227	Stéphane Matteau, NYR.	.10	.35	3.00
□□□	228	Grant Fuhr (G), Stl.	.25	.75	6.00
□□□	229	Joe Nieuwendyk, Cgy.	.25	.75	6.00
□□□	230	Alexei Yashin, Ott.	.35	1.50	20.00
□□□	231	Brian Bellows, T.B.	.10	.35	3.00
□□□	232	Brian Bradley, T.B.	.10	.35	3.00
□□□	233	Tony Granato, L.A.	.10	.35	3.00
□□□	234	Mike Ricci, Que.	.10	.35	3.00
□□□	235	Brett Hull, Stl.	.50	2.50	30.00
□□□	236	Mike Ridley, Van.	.10	.35	3.00
□□□	237	Al Iafrate, Wsh.	.10	.35	3.00
□□□	238	Derek King, NYI.	.10	.35	3.00
□□□	239	Bill Ranford (G), Edm.	.25	.75	6.00
□□□	240	Steve Yzerman, Det.	1.00	5.00	60.00
□□□	241	John Vanbiesbrouck (G), Fla.	.60	3.00	35.00
□□□	242	Russ Courtnall, Van.	.10	.35	3.00
□□□	243	Chris Terreri (G), N.J.	.10	.35	3.00
□□□	244	Rod Brind'Amour, Pha.	.25	.75	6.00
□□□	245	Shayne Corson, Stl.	.25	.75	6.00
□□□	246	Don Beaupré (G), Ott.	.10	.35	3.00
□□□	247	Dino Ciccarelli, Det.	.25	.75	6.00
□□□	248	Kevin Lowe, Edm.	.10	.35	3.00
□□□	249	Craig MacTavish, Edm.	.10	.35	3.00
□□□	250	Wayne Gretzky, L.A.	2.00	10.00	120.00
□□□	251	Curtis Joseph (G), Stl.	.60	3.00	35.00
□□□	252	Joe Mullen, Pgh.	.10	.35	3.00
□□□	253	Andrei Kovalenko, Que.	.10	.35	3.00
□□□	254	Igor Larionov, S.J.	.25	.75	6.00

☐☐☐	255	Geoff Courtnall, Van.	.10	.35	3.00
☐☐☐	256	Joé Juneau, Wsh.	.10	.35	3.00
☐☐☐	257	Bruce Driver, N.J.	.10	.35	3.00
☐☐☐	258	Michal Pivonka, Wsh.	.10	.35	3.00
☐☐☐	259	Nelson Emerson, Hfd.	.10	.35	3.00
☐☐☐	260	Larry Murphy, Tor.	.25	.75	6.00
☐☐☐	261	Brent Gilchrist, Dal.	.10	.35	3.00
☐☐☐	262	Benoît Hogue, NYI.	.10	.35	3.00
☐☐☐	263	Doug Weight, Edm.	.35	1.00	10.00
☐☐☐	264	Keith Primeau, Det.	.25	.75	6.00
☐☐☐	265	Neal Broten, N.J.	.10	.35	3.00
☐☐☐	266	Mike Keane, Mtl.	.10	.35	3.00
☐☐☐	267	Norm Maciver, Ott.	.10	.35	3.00
☐☐☐	267	Zigmund Palffy, NYI.	.35	1.50	20.00
☐☐☐	268	Valeri Kamensky, Que.	.25	.75	6.00
☐☐☐	269	Claude Lemieux, N.J.	.10	.35	3.00
☐☐☐	270	Bryan Marchment, Edm.	.10	.35	3.00
☐☐☐	271	Kelly Miller, Wsh.	.10	.35	3.00
☐☐☐	272	Brent Sutter, Chi.	.10	.35	3.00
☐☐☐	273	Glenn Healy (G), NYR.	.10	.35	3.00
☐☐☐	274	Sergei Brylin, N.J.	.10	.35	3.00
☐☐☐	275	Tie Domi, Tor.	.10	.35	3.00
☐☐☐	277	Kevin Dineen, Pha.	.10	.35	3.00
☐☐☐	278	Scott Young, Que.	.10	.35	3.00
☐☐☐	279	Tomas Sandström, Det.	.10	.35	3.00
☐☐☐	280	Guy Carbonneau, Dal.	.10	.35	3.00
☐☐☐	281	Denis Savard, Chi.	.25	.75	6.00
☐☐☐	282	Ed Olczyk, Wpg.	.10	.35	3.00
☐☐☐	283	Adam Creighton, Stl.	.10	.35	3.00
☐☐☐	284	Tom Chorske, Ott.	.10	.35	3.00
☐☐☐	285	Roman Oksiuta, Ana.	.10	.35	3.00
☐☐☐	286	David Roberts, Stl.	.10	.35	3.00
☐☐☐	287	Petr Svoboda, Pha.	.10	.35	3.00
☐☐☐	288	Brad May, Buf.	.10	.35	3.00
☐☐☐	289	Michael Nylander, Hfd.	.10	.35	3.00
☐☐☐	290	Jon Casey (G), Stl., Error (/b: Cu Joseph)	.10	.35	3.00
☐☐☐	291	Philippe DeRouville (G), Pgh.	.10	.35	3.00
☐☐☐	292	Craig Johnson, Stl.	.10	.35	3.00
☐☐☐	**293**	**Chris McAlpine, N.J., RC**	**.10**	**.35**	**3.00**
☐☐☐	294	Ralph Intranuovo, Edm.	.10	.35	3.00
☐☐☐	295	Richard Park, Pgh.	.10	.35	3.00
☐☐☐	296	Todd Warriner, Tor.	.10	.35	3.00
☐☐☐	**297**	**Craig Conroy, Mtl., RC**	**.10**	**.35**	**3.00**
☐☐☐	298	Marek Malik, Hfd.	.10	.35	3.00
☐☐☐	299	Manny Fernandez (G), Dal.	.10	.35	3.00
☐☐☐	300	Cory Stillman, Cgy.	.10	.35	3.00
☐☐☐	301	Kevin Brown, L.A.	.10	.35	3.00
☐☐☐	**302**	**Steve Larouche, Ott., RC**	**.10**	**.35**	**3.00**
☐☐☐	303	Chris Taylor, NYI.	.10	.35	3.00
☐☐☐	304	Ryan Smyth, Edm.	.25	.75	6.00
☐☐☐	305	Craig Darby, NYI.	.10	.35	3.00
☐☐☐	306	Radim Bicanek, Ott.	.10	.35	3.00
☐☐☐	307	Shean Donovan, S.J.	.10	.35	3.00
☐☐☐	308	Jason Bonsignore, Edm.	.10	.35	3.00
☐☐☐	**309**	**Chris Marinucci, NYI., RC**	**.10**	**.35**	**3.00**
☐☐☐	**310**	**Brian Holzinger, Buf., RC**	**.10**	**.35**	**3.00**
☐☐☐	**311**	**Mike Torchia (G), Dal., RC**	**.10**	**.35**	**3.00**
☐☐☐	**312**	**Eric Dazé, Chi., RC**	**.25**	**.75**	**6.00**
☐☐☐☐	**313**	**Jamie Linden, Fla., RC**	**.10**	**.35**	**3.00**
☐☐☐	**314**	**Tommy Salo (G), NYI., RC**	**.10**	**.35**	**3.00**
☐☐☐	315	Martin Gendron, Wsh.	.10	.35	3.00
☐☐☐	316	Félix Potvin (G), Tor.	.25	1.00	15.00
☐☐☐	317	Jim Carey (G), Wsh.	.10	.35	3.00
☐☐☐	318	Ed Belfour (G), Chi.	.25	.75	8.00
☐☐☐	319	Mike Vernon (G), Det.	.25	.75	6.00
☐☐☐	320	Sean Burke (G), Hfd.	.25	.75	6.00
☐☐☐	321	Mike Richter (G), NYR.	.25	.75	8.00
☐☐☐	322	John Vanbiesbrouck (G), Fla.	.25	1.25	20.00
☐☐☐	323	Martin Brodeur (G), N.J.	.35	2.00	30.00
☐☐☐	324	Patrick Roy (G), Mtl.	.75	4.00	60.00
☐☐☐	325	Dominik Hasek (G), Buf.	.35	2.00	30.00
☐☐☐	326	Checklist	.10	.35	3.00
☐☐☐	327	Checklist	.10	.35	3.00
☐☐☐	328	Checklist	.10	.35	3.00
☐☐☐	329	Checklist	.10	.35	3.00
☐☐☐	330	Checklist	.10	.35	3.00

BORDER BATTLE

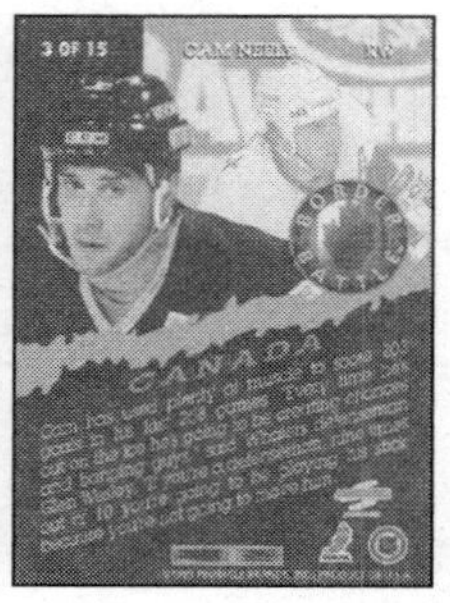

Insert Set (15 cards): 30.00
Promo Card (Cam Neely): 1.00

	No.	Player	NRMT-MT
☐	1	Pierre Turgeon, Mtl.	1.00
☐	2	Wayne Gretzky, L.A.	10.00
☐	3	Cam Neely, Bos.	1.00
☐	4	Joe Sakic, Que.	4.00
☐	5	Doug Gilmour, Tor.	1.50
☐	6	Brett Hull, Stl.	2.50
☐	7	Pat LaFontaine, Buf.	1.00
☐	8	Joe Mullen, Pgh.	1.00
☐	9	Mike Modano, Dal.	2.50
☐	10	Jeremy Roenick, Chi.	1.50
☐	11	Pavel Bure, Van.	3.50
☐	12	Alexei Zhamnov, Wpg.	1.00
☐	13	Sergei Fedorov, Det.	2.50
☐	14	Jaromir Jagr, Pgh.	5.00
☐	15	Mats Sundin, Tor.	2.50

CHECK IT

Insert Set (12 cards): 135.00

	No.	Player	NRMT-MT
☐	1	Eric Lindros, Pha.	50.00
☐	2	Owen Nolan, S.J.	8.00
☐	3	Brett Lindros, NYI.	3.00
☐	4	Chris Gratton, T.B.	8.00
☐	5	Chris Pronger, Hfd.	8.00
☐	6	Adam Deadmarsh, Que.	3.00
☐	7	Peter Forsberg, Que.	40.00
☐	8	Derian Hatcher, Dal.	8.00
☐	9	Rob Blake, L.A.	8.00
☐	10	Jeff Friesen, S.J.	8.00
☐	11	Keith Tkachuk, Wpg.	15.00
☐	12	Mike Ricci, Que.	3.00

DREAM TEAM

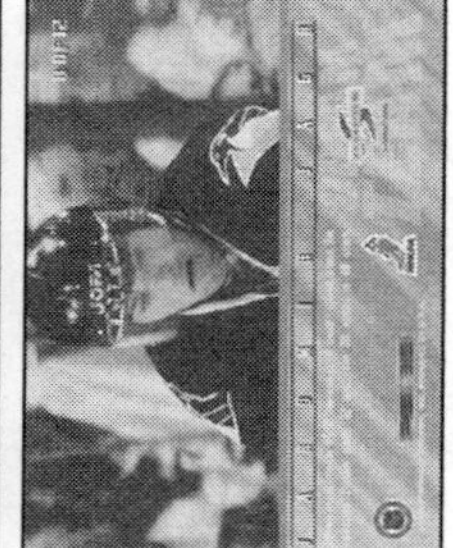

Insert Set (12 cards): 140.00

	No.	Player	NRMT-MT
☐	1	Wayne Gretzky, L.A.	30.00
☐	2	Sergei Fedorov, Det.	7.00
☐	3	Eric Lindros, Pha.	20.00
☐	4	Mark Messier, NYR.	7.00
☐	5	Peter Forsberg, Que.	15.00
☐	6	Doug Gilmour, Tor.	5.00
☐	7	Paul Kariya, Ana.	20.00
☐	8	Jaromir Jagr, Pgh.	15.00
☐	9	Brett Hull, Stl.	7.00
☐	10	Pavel Bure, Van.	10.00
☐	11	Patrick Roy (G), Mtl.	25.00
☐	12	Jim Carey (G), Wsh.	4.00

LAMPLIGHTERS

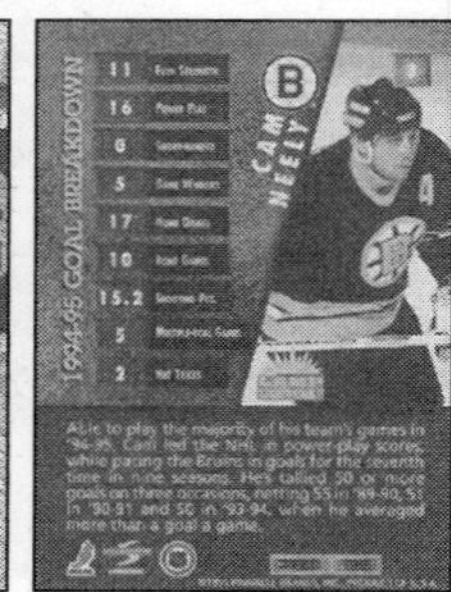

Insert Set (15 cards): 150.00

	No.	Player	NRMT-MT
☐	1	Wayne Gretzky, L.A.	40.00
☐	2	Pavel Bure, Van.	15.00
☐	3	Cam Neely, Bos.	4.00
☐	4	Owen Nolan, S.J.	4.00
☐	5	Sergei Fedorov, Det.	10.00
☐	6	Pierre Turgeon, Mtl.	4.00
☐	7	Peter Bondra, Wsh.	8.00
☐	8	Mikael Renberg, Pha.	2.00
☐	9	Luc Robitaille, Pgh.	4.00
☐	10	Alexei Zhamnov, Chi.	4.00
☐	11	Brett Hull, Stl.	10.00
☐	12	Jaromir Jagr, Pgh.	20.00
☐	13	Theoren Fleury, Cgy.	6.00
☐	14	Teemu Selänne, Wpg.	15.00
☐	15	Eric Lindros, Pha.	25.00

GOLDEN BLADES

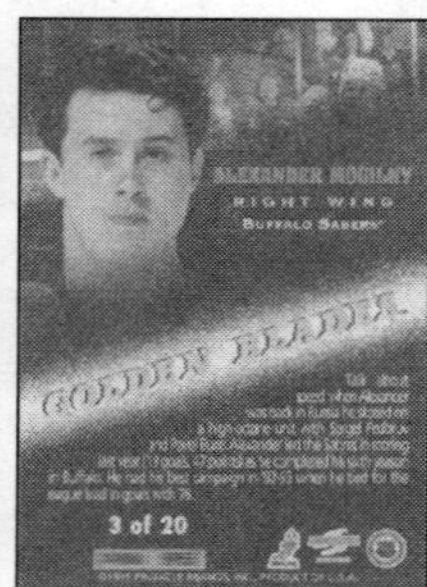

Inset Set (20 cards): 250.00

	No.	Player	NRMT-MT
☐	1	Joe Sakic, Que.	25.00
☐	2	Teemu Selänne, Wpg.	20.00
☐	3	Alexander Mogilny, Buf.	8.00
☐	4	Peter Bondra, Wsh.	12.00
☐	5	Paul Coffey, Det.	6.00
☐	6	Mike Modano, Dal.	15.00
☐	7	Alexei Yashin, Ott.	12.00
☐	8	Pat LaFontaine, Buf.	6.00
☐	9	Paul Kariya, Ana.	40.00
☐	10	Peter Forsberg, Que.	30.00
☐	11	Jeff Friesen, S.J.	6.00
☐	12	Steve Yzerman, Det.	30.00
☐	13	Theoren Fleury, Cgy.	8.00
☐	14	Stéphane Richer, N.J.	4.00
☐	15	Mark Messier, NYR.	15.00
☐	16	Mats Sundin, Tor.	15.00
☐	17	Brendan Shanahan, Stl.	18.00
☐	18	Mark Recchi, Mtl.	6.00
☐	19	Jeremy Roenick, Chi.	10.00
☐	20	Jason Arnott, Edm.	6.00

1995 - 96 SELECT CERTIFIED EDITION

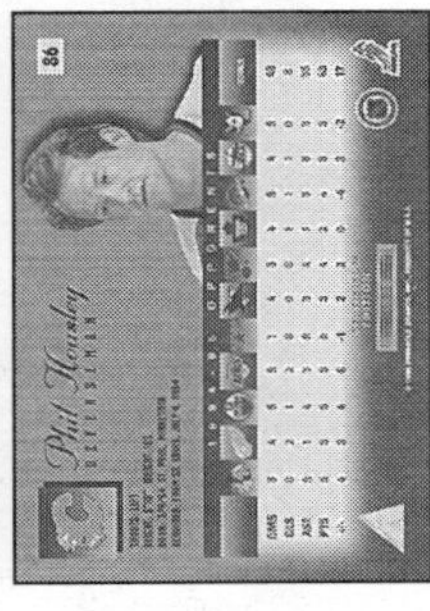

These cards have two versions: a regular card and a Mirror Gold parallel. Seven cards also have a promo version. Regular cards and promos have the same value.

Imprint: © 1996 PINNACLE BRANDS, INC.

Complete Set (144 cards): 70.00 1,300.00
Common Player: .35 5.00

	No.	Player	Reg.	MG
□ □	1	Mario Lemieux, Pgh.	8.00	100.00
□ □	2	Chris Chelios, Chi.	2.00	25.00
□ □	3	Scott Mellanby, Fla.	.35	5.00
□ □	4	Brett Hull, Stl.	2.50	30.00
□ □	5	Theoren Fleury, Cgy.	1.50	18.00
□ □	6	Alexei Zhamnov, Wpg.	.75	10.00
□ □	7	Mats Sundin, Tor.	2.50	30.00
□ □	8	Mathieu Schneider, NYI.	.35	5.00
□ □	9	Jason Arnott, Edm.	.75	10.00
□ □	10	Mark Recchi, Mtl.	.75	10.00
□ □	11	Adam Oates, Bos.	1.50	18.00
□ □ □	12	Jim Carey (G), Wsh.	.35	5.00
□ □ □	13	Paul Kariya, Ana.	6.50	80.00
□ □	14	Mark Messier, NYR.	2.50	30.00
□ □	15	Eric Lindros, Pha.	6.50	80.00
□ □	16	Pavel Bure, Van.	3.50	40.00
□ □ □	17	Mike Modano, Dal.	2.50	30.00
□ □	18	Pat LaFontaine, Buf.	.75	10.00
□ □ □	19	Owen Nolan, S.J.	.75	10.00
□ □	20	Roman Hamrlik, T.B.	.75	10.00
□ □	21	Paul Coffey, Det.	.75	10.00
□ □	22	Alexandre Daigle, Ott.	.75	10.00
□ □	23	Wayne Gretzky, L.A.	10.00	120.00
□ □	24	Martin Brodeur (G), N.J.	3.50	40.00
□ □	25	Ulf Dahlen, S.J.	.35	5.00
□ □	26	Geoff Sanderson, Hfd.	.35	5.00
□ □	27	Brian Leetch, N.J.	1.50	18.00
□ □	28	Dave Andreychuk, Tor.	.35	5.00
□ □	29	Sergei Fedorov, Det.	2.50	30.00
□ □	30	Jocelyn Thibault (G), Mtl.	1.50	18.00
□ □	31	Mikael Renberg, Pha.	.35	5.00
□ □	32	Joe Nieuwendyk, Dal.	.75	10.00
□ □	33	Craig Janney, S.J.	.35	5.00
□ □	34	Ray Bourque, Bos.	2.50	30.00
□ □	35	Jari Kurri, L.A.	.75	10.00
□ □	36	Alexei Yashin, Ott.	2.00	25.00
□ □	37	Keith Tkachuk, Wpg.	2.00	25.00
□ □	38	Jaromir Jagr, Pgh.	5.00	60.00
□ □	39	Stéphane Richer, N.J.	.35	5.00
□ □	40	Trevor Kidd (G), Cgy.	.75	10.00
□ □	41	Kevin Hatcher, Dal.	.35	5.00
□ □	42	Mike Vernon (G), Det.	.75	10.00
□ □ □	43	Alexander Mogilny, Van.	1.50	18.00
□ □	44	John LeClair, Pha.	2.50	30.00
□ □	45	Joe Sakic, Col.	4.00	50.00
□ □	46	Kevin Stevens, Bos.	.35	5.00
□ □	47	Adam Graves, NYR.	.35	5.00
□ □	48	Doug Gilmour, Tor.	1.50	18.00
□ □	49	Pierre Turgeon, Stl.	.75	10.00
□ □	50	Joe Murphy, Chi.	.35	5.00
□ □	51	Peter Bondra, Wsh.	2.00	25.00
□ □	52	Ron Francis, Pgh.	1.50	18.00
□ □	53	Luc Robitaille, NYR.	.75	10.00
□ □	54	Mike Gartner, Tor.	.75	10.00
□ □	55	Bill Ranford (G), Edm.	.75	10.00
□ □	56	Jeff Friesen, S.J.	.75	10.00
□ □	57	Cam Neely, Bos.	.75	10.00
□ □	58	Daren Puppa (G), T.B.	.35	5.00
□ □	59	Rod Brind'Amour, Pha.	.75	10.00
□ □	60	Jeremy Roenick, Chi.	1.50	18.00
□ □	61	Brett Lindros, NYI.	.35	5.00
□ □	62	Todd Harvey, Dal.	.35	5.00
□ □	63	Kirk McLean (G), Van.	.75	10.00
□ □	64	Brendan Shanahan, Hfd.	3.00	30.00
□ □	65	Kelly Hrudey (G), L.A.	.35	5.00
□ □	66	Scott Stevens, N.J.	.35	5.00
□ □	67	Sergei Zubov, Pgh.	.75	10.00
□ □ □	68	Peter Forsberg, Col.	5.00	60.00
□ □ □	69	Félix Potvin (G), Tor.	2.50	30.00
□ □	70	Scott Niedermayer, N.J.	.75	10.00
□ □	71	Keith Primeau, Det.	.75	10.00
□ □	72	Al MacInnis, Stl.	.35	5.00
□ □	73	Mike Richter (G), NYR.	1.50	18.00
□ □	74	Rob Blake, L.A.	.75	10.00
□ □	75	Vincent Damphousse, Mtl.	1.50	18.00
□ □	76	Teemu Selänne, Wpg.	3.50	40.00
□ □	77	Andy Moog (G), Dal.	.75	10.00
□ □	78	Ron Hextall (G), Pha.	.75	10.00
□ □	79	Oleg Tverdovsky, Wpg.	.35	5.00
□ □	80	Joé Juneau, Wsh.	.35	5.00
□ □	81	Patrick Roy (G), Col.	8.00	100.00
□ □	82	Wendel Clark, Tor.	.75	10.00
□ □	83	Brian Bradley, T.B.	.35	5.00
□ □	84	Curtis Joseph (G), Edm.	3.00	35.00
□ □	85	John Vanbiesbrouck (G), Fla.	3.00	35.00
□ □	86	Phil Housley, Wpg.	.35	5.00
□ □	87	Trevor Linden, Van.	.75	10.00
□ □	88	Alexei Kovalev, NYR.	.35	5.00
□ □	89	Dominik Hasek (G), Buf.	3.50	40.00
□ □	90	Larry Murphy, Tor.	.75	10.00
□ □	91	Arturs Irbe (G), S.J.	.35	5.00
□ □	92	John MacLean, N.J.	.35	5.00
□ □	93	Ed Belfour (G), Chi.	1.50	18.00
□ □	94	Steve Yzerman, Det.	5.00	60.00
□ □	95	Tom Barrasso (G), Pgh.	.75	10.00
□ □	96	Rob Niedermayer, Fla.	.35	5.00
□ □	97	Dale Hawerchuk, Stl.	.75	10.00
□ □	98	Rick Tocchet, Bos.	.35	5.00
□ □	99	Claude Lemieux, Col.	.35	5.00
□ □	100	Sean Burke (G), Hfd.	.75	10.00
□ □	101	Shayne Corson, Stl.	.75	10.00
□ □	102	Dino Ciccarelli, Det.	.75	10.00
□ □	103	Kirk Muller, Tor.	.35	5.00
□ □	104	Don Beaupré, Ott.	.35	5.00
□ □	105	Valeri Kamensky, Col.	.75	10.00
□ □	106	Markus Naslund, Van.	.35	5.00
□ □	107	Tomas Sandström, Det.	.35	5.00
□ □	108	Pat Verbeek, NYR.	.35	5.00
□ □	109	Doug Weight, Edm.	1.50	18.00
□ □	**110**	**Brian Holzinger, Buf., RC**	**.75**	**8.00**
□ □	**111**	**Antti Törmänen, Ott., RC**	**.35**	**5.00**
□ □	**112**	**Tommy Salo (G), NYI., RC**	**.35**	**5.00**
□ □	113	Jason Bonsignore, Edm.	.35	5.00
□ □	**114**	**Shane Doan, Wpg., RC**	**.35**	**5.00**
□ □	**115**	**Robert Svehla, Fla., RC**	**.35**	**5.00**
□ □	116	Chad Kilger, Ana.	.35	5.00
□ □	117	Saku Koivu, Mtl.	3.50	40.00
□ □	118	Jeff O'Neill, Hfd.	.75	10.00
□ □	119	Brendan Witt, Wsh.	.35	5.00
□ □	120	Byron Dafoe (G), L.A.	.35	5.00
□ □	121	Ryan Smyth, Edm.	.75	10.00
□ □	**122**	**Daniel Alfredsson, Ott., RC**	**3.50**	**25.00**
□ □	123	Todd Bertuzzi, NYI.	1.50	10.00
□ □	**124**	**Daymond Langkow, T.B., RC**	**.35**	**5.00**
□ □	**125**	**Miroslav Satan, Edm., RC**	**.35**	**5.00**
□ □	126	Bryan McCabe, NYI.	.35	5.00
□ □	**127**	**Aki Berg, L.A., RC**	**.35**	**5.00**
□ □	128	Cory Stillman, Cgy.	.35	5.00
□ □	129	Deron Quint, Wpg.	.35	5.00
□ □	130	Vitali Yachmenev, L.A.	.35	5.00
□ □	131	Valeri Bure, Mtl.	.35	5.00
□ □	132	Eric Dazé, Chi.	.75	10.00
□ □	**133**	**Radek Dvorak, Fla., RC**	**.75**	**8.00**
□ □	**134**	**Landon Wilson, Col., RC**	**.35**	**5.00**
□ □	135	Niklas Sundstrom, NYR.	.35	5.00
□ □	136	Jamie Storr (G), L.A.	.75	10.00
□ □	137	Ed Jovanovski, Fla.	.75	10.00
□ □	**138**	**Marcus Ragnarsson, S.J., RC**	**.35**	**5.00**
□ □	**139**	**Kyle McLaren, Bos., RC**	**.35**	**5.00**
□ □	140	Sandy Moger, Bos.	.35	5.00
□ □	141	Marty Murray, Cgy.	.35	5.00
□ □	142	Darby Hendrickson, NYI.	.35	5.00
□ □	143	Corey Hirsch (G), Van.	.35	5.00
□ □	**144**	**Petr Sykora, N.J., RC**	**.35**	**5.00**

	No.	Player	NRMT-MT
□	1	Checklist	.10
□	2	Checklist	.10
□	3	Checklist	.10
□	4	Checklist	.10
□	5	Checklist	.10
□	6	Checklist	.10
□	7	Checklist	.10

CERTIFIED FUTURE

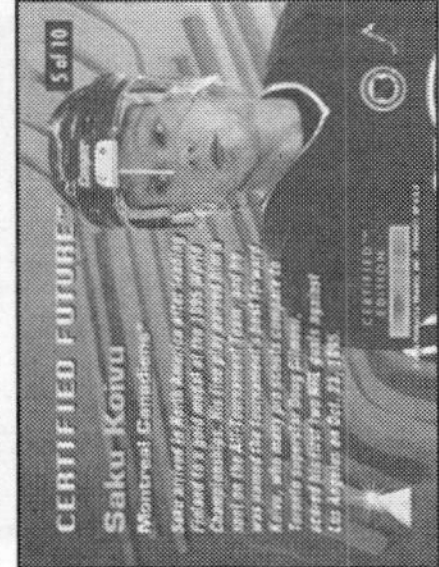

Insert Set (10 cards): 125.00

	No.	Player	NRMT-MT
□	1	Peter Forsberg, Col.	35.00
□	2	Jim Carey (G), Wsh.	5.00
□	3	Paul Kariya, Ana.	45.00
□	4	Jocelyn Thibault (G), Mtl.	10.00
□	5	Saku Koivu, Mtl.	25.00
□	6	Brian Holzinger, Buf.	5.00
□	7	Todd Harvey, Dal.	5.00
□	8	Jeff O'Neill, Hfd.	8.00
□	9	Oleg Tverdovsky, Ana.	5.00
□	10	Ed Jovanovski, Fla.	8.00

CERTIFIED GOLD TEAM

Insert Set (10 cards): 550.00
Promo Card (Pavel Bure): 5.00

	No.	Player	NRMT-MT
□	1	Eric Lindros, Pha.	75.00
□	2	Wayne Gretzky, L.A.	125.00
□	3	Mario Lemieux, Pgh.	100.00
□	4	Jaromir Jagr, Pgh.	60.00
□	5	Pavel Bure, Van.	40.00
□	6	Brett Hull, Stl.	30.00
□	7	Cam Neely, Bos.	20.00
□	8	Joe Sakic, Col.	50.00
□	9	Martin Brodeur (G), N.J.	40.00
□	10	Patrick Roy (G), Col.	100.00

DOUBLE STRIKE

These cards have two versions: the regular insert (limited to 1,975 copies) and a Gold parallel (limited to 903 copies).

Insert Set (20 cards):			150.00	300.00
	No.	Player	DS	DSG
□□	1	Doug Gilmour, Tor.	8.00	15.00
□□	2	Ron Francis, Pgh.	8.00	15.00
□□	3	Ray Bourque, Bos.	15.00	30.00
□□	4	Chris Chelios, Chi.	10.00	20.00
□□	5	Adam Oates, Bos.	8.00	15.00
□□	6	Mike Ricci, Col.	5.00	10.00
□□	7	Jeremy Roenick, Chi.	8.00	15.00
□□	8	Jason Arnott, Edm.	5.00	10.00
□□	9	Brendan Shanahan, Hfd.	18.00	35.00
□□	10	Joe Nieuwendyk, Dal.	5.00	10.00
□□	11	Trevor Linden, Van.	5.00	10.00
□□	12	Mikael Renberg, Pha.	5.00	10.00
□□	13	Theoren Fleury, Cgy.	8.00	15.00
□□	14	Sergei Fedorov, Det.	15.00	30.00
□□	15	Mark Messier, NYR.	15.00	30.00
□□	16	Keith Primeau, Det.	8.00	15.00
□□	17	Keith Tkachuk, Wpg.	12.00	24.00
□□	18	Scott Stevens, N.J.	5.00	10.00
□□	19	Claude Lemieux, Col.	5.00	10.00
□□	20	Alexei Zhamnov, Wpg.	5.00	10.00

1995 - 96 SIGNATURE ROOKIES HOCKEY DRAFT DAY PROMOS

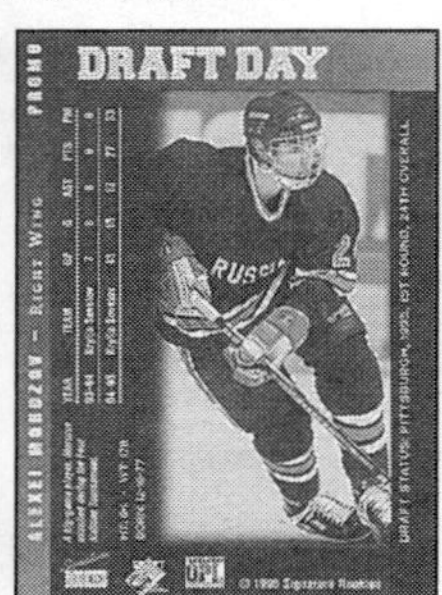

Imprint:

	No.	Player	NRMT-MT
□		Alexei Morozov	3.50
□	FF1	Bryan Berard	2.00
□	JC1	Jim Carey (G)	1.00
□	JC2	Jim Carey (G)	1.00
□	JC3	Jim Carey (G)	1.00
□	JC4	Jim Carey (G)	1.00
□	JC5	Jim Carey (G)	1.00

1995 - 96 SIGNATURE ROOKIES TETRAD

TETRAD PROMO CARD

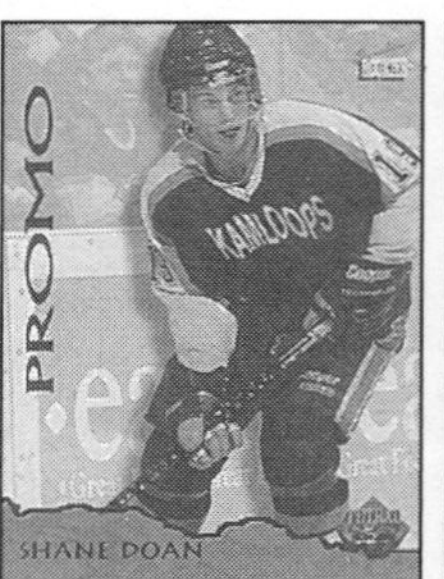

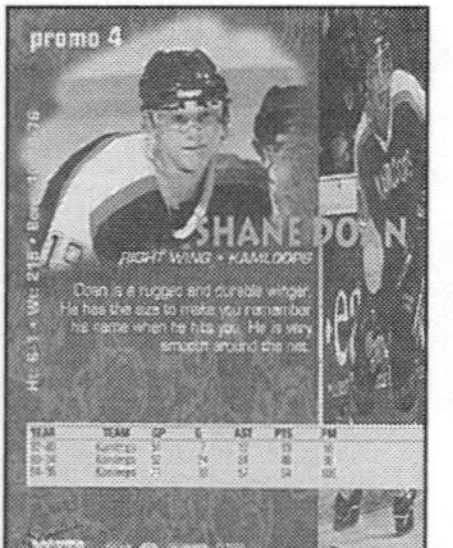

	No.	Player	NRMT-MT
□	4	Shane Doan	.25

SIGNATURE ROOKIES TETRAD

This 76-card four-sport set has only 7 hockey cards.

	No.	Player	NRMT-MT
□	61	Alexei Morozov	3.00
□	62	Radek Dvorak	.50
□	66	Terry Ryan	.25
□	67	Shane Doan	.25
□	68	Brad Church	.25
□	69	Brian Boucher	.25
□	70	Dimitri Nabokov	.20

SR FORCE

This 35-card four-sport insert set has only 10 hockey cards.

	No.	Player	NRMT-MT
□	F1	Nolan Baumgartner	.50
□	F2	Bryan Berard	2.50
□	F3	Aki Berg	.50
□	F4	Daymond Langkow	.50
□	F5	Wade Redden	1.00
□	F6	Martin Brodeur (G)	3.50
□	F7	Jim Carey (G)	.50
□	F8	Jaromir Jagr	5.00
□	F9	Maxim Kuznetsov	.50
□	F10	Terry Ryan	1.00

1995 - 96 SIGNATURE ROOKIES TETRAD AUTOBILIA

PREVIEWS

These cards were inserted in Autobilia basketball packs. Only one hockey player exists.

	No.	Player	NRMT-MT
□	2	Jim Carey (G)	.50

TETRAD AUTOBILIA

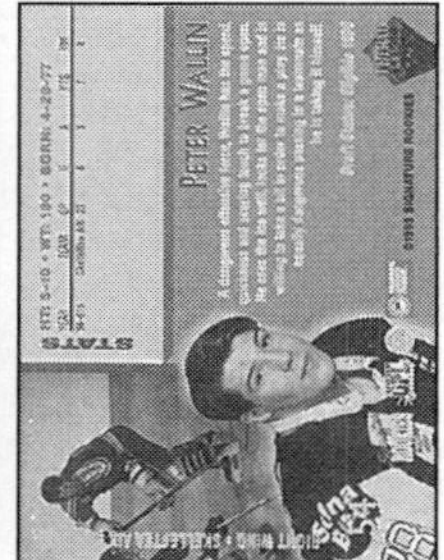

This 100-card four-sport set has only 23 hockey cards.

	No.	Player	NRMT-MT
□	38	Nolan Baumgartner	.25
□	39	Bryan Berard	1.00
□	40	Aki Berg	.25
□	41	Dan Cleary	2.00
□	42	Radek Dvorak	.50
□	43	Patrick Juhlin	.25
□	44	Jan Labraaten	.25
□	45	Daymond Langkow	.50
□	46	Sergei Luchinkin	.25
□	47	Cameron Mann	1.00
□	48	Alexei Morozov	3.00
□	49	Oleg Orekhovski	.25
□	50	Johan Ramstedt	.25
□	51	Wade Redden	1.00
□	52	Sami-Ville Salomaa	.25
□	53	Alexei Vasiljev	.25
□	54	Peter Wallin, Swe.	.25
□	94	Brian Boucher	.50
□	95	Martin Brodeur (G)	3.00
□	96	Brad Church	.25
□	97	Shane Doan	.25
□	98	Terry Ryan	.50
□	99	Ryan Smyth	1.00

1995 - 96 SISU

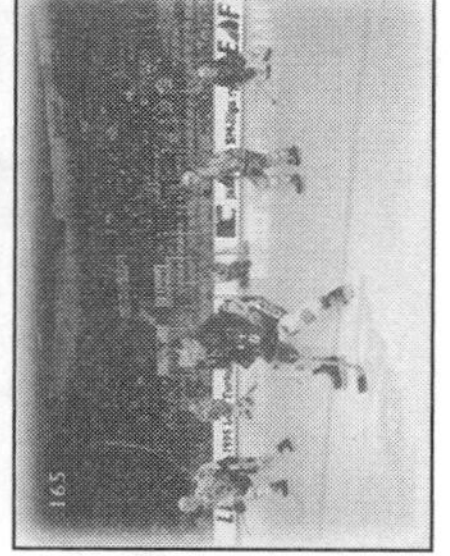

Imprint:

Series One Set (200 cards): 35.00

Series Two Set (200 cards):			35.00
Common Player:			.20
	No.	Player	NRMT-MT
□	1	HIFK Helsinki	.20
□	2	Kimmo Kapanen (G)	.25
□	3	Yuri Kuznetsov	.20
□	4	Simo Saarinen	.20
□	5	Roland Carlsson	.20
□	6	Veli-Pekka Kautonen	.20
□	7	Kristian Fagerstrom	.20
□	8	Mika Kortelainen	.20
□	9	Jari Laukkanen	.20
□	10	Juha Nurminen	.20
□	11	Markku Jurme	.20
□	12	Sami Kapanen	.75
□	13	Darren Boyko	.25
□	14	Marko Ojanen	.20
□	15	HPK Hameenlinna	.20
□	16	Kari Rosenberg (G)	.25
□	17	Petri Engman	.20
□	18	Niko Marttila	.20
□	19	Jari Haapamaki	.20
□	20	Marko Allen	.20
□	21	Erik Kakko	.20
□	22	Mikko Myllykoski	.20
□	23	Jani Hassinen	.20
□	24	Risto Jalo	.20
□	25	Juha Jarvenpaa	.20
□	26	Jari Kauppila	.20
□	27	Toni Makiaho	.20
□	28	Ilves Tampere	.20
□	29	Mika Manninen (G)	.25
□	30	Hannu Henriksson	.20
□	31	Petri Kokko	.20
□	32	Martti Jarventie	.20
□	33	Allan Measures	.20
□	34	Pasi Huura	.20
□	35	Janne Seva	.20
□	36	Tommy Kiviaho	.20
□	37	Reijo Mikkolainen	.20
□	38	Hannu Mattila	.20
□	39	Jari Virtanen	.20
□	40	Sami Ahlberg	.20
□	41	Juha Hautamaa	.20
□	42	Jokerit Helsinki	.20
□	43	Ari Sulander (G)	.50
□	44	Santeri Immonen	.20
□	45	Pasi Sormunen	.20
□	46	Waltteri Immonen	.20
□	47	Mika Stromberg	.20
□	48	Kari Martikainen	.20
□	49	Tommi Sova	.20
□	50	Juha Lind	.20
□	51	Niko Halttunen	.20
□	52	Keijo Sailynoja	.20
□	53	Otakar Janecky	.20
□	54	Timo Saarikoski	.20
□	55	JyP HT Jyvaskyla	.20
□	56	Ari-Pekka Siekkinen (G)	.25
□	57	Vesa Ponto	.20
□	58	Kalle Koskinen	.20
□	59	Jouni Loponen	.20
□	60	Miska Kangasniemi	.20
□	61	Mika Paananen	.20
□	62	Markku Ikonen	.20
□	63	Kimmo Salminen	.20
□	64	Joni Lius	.20
□	65	Lasse Nieminen	.20
□	66	Janne Kurjeniemi	.20
□	67	Marko Virtanen	.20
□	68	KalPa Kuopio	.20
□	69	Jarkko Kortesoja (G)	.25
□	70	Petri Matikainen	.20
□	71	Mika Laaksonen	.20
□	72	Kai Rautio	.20
□	73	Jarno Kaultanen	.20
□	74	Miika Ruokonen	.20
□	75	Jussi Tarvainen	.20
□	76	Mikko Honkonen	.20
□	77	Sami Simonen	.20
□	78	Petr Korinek	.20
□	79	Veli-Pekka Pekkarinen	.20
□	80	Pekka Tirkkonen	.20
□	81	Kiekko-Espoo	.20
□	82	Iiro Itamies (G)	.25

	#	Name	Value
□	83	Tommi Nyyssönen	.20
□	84	Robert Salo	.20
□	85	Sami Nuutinen	.20
□	86	Timo Blomqvist	.20
□	87	Ismo Kuoppala	.20
□	88	Mikko Koivunoro	.20
□	89	Petro Koivunen	.20
□	90	Jarmo Muukkonen	.20
□	91	Sergei Prjahin	.20
□	92	Teemu Riihijarvi	.20
□	93	Juha Ikonen	.20
□	94	Lukko Rauma	.20
□	95	Boris Rousson (G)	.50
□	96	Vesa Salo	.20
□	97	Toni Porkka	.20
□	98	Mika Yli-Maenpaa	.20
□	99	Juha Riihijarvi	.20
□	100	Petri Latti	.20
□	101	Veli-Pekka Ahonen	.20
□	102	Mikko Peltola	.20
□	103	Kalle Sahlstedt	.20
□	104	Jari Torkki	.20
□	105	Jussi Kiuru	.20
□	106	Sakari Palsola	.20
□	107	Tappara Tampere	.20
□	108	Ilpo Kauhanen (G)	.20
□	109	Sami Lehtonen	.20
□	110	Pasi Petrilainen	.20
□	111	Pekka Laksola	.20
□	112	Tommi Haapsaari	.20
□	113	Ville Nieminen	.20
□	114	Arto Kulmala	.20
□	115	Valeri Krykov	.20
□	116	Timo Nurmberg	.20
□	117	Aleksander Barkov	.20
□	118	Miikka Kemppi	.20
□	119	Marko Toivola	.20
□	120	Juha Vuorivirta	.20
□	121	TPS Turku	.20
□	122	Miikka Kiprusoff (G)	.25
□	123	Kimmo Timonen	.20
□	124	Sami Salo	.20
□	125	Kari Harila	.20
□	126	Tuomas Gronman	.25
□	127	Vjatschelav Fandul	.20
□	128	Mika Alatalo	.20
□	129	Jukka Tiilikainen	.20
□	130	Kimmo Rintanen	.20
□	131	Hannes Hyvonen	.20
□	132	Simo Rouvali	.20
□	133	Harri Sillgren	.20
□	134	Harri Suvanto	.20
□	135	TuTo Turku	.20
□	136	Markus Korhonen (G)	.25
□	137	Sebastien Sulku	.20
□	138	Jukka Suomalainen	.20
□	139	Timo Kulonen	.20
□	140	Risto Siltanen	.20
□	141	Sami Leinonen	.20
□	142	Juha Virtanen	.20
□	143	Jari Hirsimaki	.20
□	144	Jouni Tuominen	.20
□	145	Vesa Karjalainen	.20
□	146	Pekka Virta	.20
□	147	Jouko Myrra	.20
□	148	Assat Pori	.20
□	149	Kari Takko (G)	.20
□	150	Timo Nykopp	.20
□	151	Harri Laurila	.20
□	152	Jarno Miikkulainen	.20
□	153	Pasi Peltonen	.20
□	154	Jari Korpisalo	.20
□	155	Teppo Kivela	.20
□	156	Jari Levonen	.20
□	157	Janne Virtanen	.20
□	158	Jarno Makela	.20
□	159	Mikael Kotkaniemi	.20
□	160	Ari Saarinen	.20
□	161	AS: Boris Rousson (G)	.25
□	162	AS: Joni Lehto	.20
□	163	AS: Marko Kiprusoff	.20
□	164	AS: Jere Lehtinen	1.00
□	165	AS: Saku Koivu	4.00
□	166	AS: Kai Nurminen	.20
□	167	AS: Ari Sulander (G)	.25
□	168	AS: Mika Stromberg	.20
□	169	AS: Jarmo Kuusisto	.20
□	170	AS: Tero Arkiomaa	.20
□	171	AS: Otakar Janecky	.20
□	172	AS: Ville Peltonen	.20
□	173	HL: Tony Arima	.20
□	174	HL: Darren Boyko	.20
□	175	HL: Kari-Pekka Friman	.20
□	176	HL: Arto Heiskanen	.20
□	177	HL: Hannu Henriksson	.20
□	178	HL: Erik Hamalainen	.20
□	179	HL: Risto Jalo	.20
□	180	HL: Timo Jutila	.25
□	181	HL: Hannu Jarvenpaa	.20
□	182	HL: Jarmo Kuusisto	.20
□	183	HL: Pekka Laksola	.20
□	184	HL: Harri Laurila	.20
□	185	HL: Pertti Lehtonen	.20
□	186	HL: Jari Lindroos	.20
□	187	HL: Reijo Mikkolainen	.20
□	188	HL: Esa Tommila	.20
□	189	HL: Jari Torkki	.20
□	190	HL: Antti Tuomenoksa	.20
□	191	HL: Ari Vuori	.20
□	192	TPS Turko	.20
□	193	Jokerit Helsinki	.20
□	194	Assat Pori	.20
□	195	Jokerit Helsinki	.20
□	196	TPS Turko	.20
□	197	CL: Kai Nurminen	.20
□	198	CL: Veli-Pekka Kautonen	.20
□	199	CL: Saku Koivu	3.00
□	200	CL: Marko Kiprusoff	.25
□	201	HIFK Helsinki	.20
□	202	Sakari Lindfors (G)	.25
□	203	Lauri Puolanne	.20
□	204	Pertti Lehtonen	.20
□	205	Peter Ahola	.20
□	206	Jere Karalahti	.20
□	207	Kimmo Maki-Kokkila	.20
□	208	Tom Laaksonen	.20
□	209	Tero Hamalainen	.20
□	210	Miro Haapaniemi	.20
□	211	Toni Sihvonen	.20
□	212	Sami Laine	.20
□	213	Iiro Jarvi	.20
□	214	Pekka Tuomisto	.20
□	215	HPK Hameenlinna	.20
□	216	Mika Pietila	.20
□	217	Tom Koivisto	.20
□	218	Tommi Hamalainen	.20
□	219	Kai Rautio	.20
□	220	Jani Nikko	.20
□	221	Mika Kannisto	.20
□	222	Jason Miller	.20
□	223	Niklas Hede	.20
□	224	Tony Virta	.20
□	225	Alexander Andrijevski	.20
□	226	Mika Puhakka	.20
□	227	Timo Peltomaa	.20
□	228	Toni Saarinen	.20
□	229	Ilves Tampere	.20
□	230	Vesa Toskala (G)	.20
□	231	Pekka Kangasalusta	.20
□	232	Juha Lampinen	.20
□	233	Pasi Saarinen	.20
□	234	Teemu Vuorinen	.20
□	235	Jarno Peltonen	.20
□	236	Matti Kaipainen	.20
□	237	Semi Pekki	.20
□	238	Sami Karjalainen	.20
□	239	Jouni Lahtinen	.20
□	240	Pasi Maattanen	.20
□	241	Petri Murtovaara	.20
□	242	Tomi Hirvonen	.20
□	243	Mikko Eloranta	.20
□	244	Mika Arvaja	.20
□	245	Juha Jarvenpaa	.20
□	246	Jokerit Helsinki	.20
□	247	Marko Rantanen	.20
□	248	Marko Tuulola	.20
□	249	Jani-Matti Loikala	.20
□	250	Antti-Jussi Niemi	.20
□	251	Janne Niinimaa	1.00
□	252	Jari Lindroos	.20
□	253	Pasi Saarela	.20
□	254	Yuha Ylonen	.20
□	255	Mika Asikainen	.20
□	256	Eero Somervuori	.20
□	257	Tero Lehtera	.20
□	258	Jukka Penttinen	.20
□	259	Petri Varis	.20
□	260	JyP HT Jyvaskyla	.20
□	261	Marko Leinonen	.20
□	262	Jan Latvala	.20
□	263	Jukka Laamanen	.20
□	264	Pekka Poikilainen	.20
□	265	Thomas Sjogren	.20
□	266	Pasi Kangas	.20
□	267	Toni Koivunen	.20
□	268	Lasse Jansen	.20
□	269	Petri Kujala	.20
□	270	Mikko Inkinen	.20
□	271	KalPa Kuopio	.20
□	272	Pasi Kuivalainen	.20
□	273	Pasi Kolehmainen	.20
□	274	Reijo Ruotsalainen	.50
□	275	Jarkko Glad	.20
□	276	Ivan Vlzek	.20
□	277	Jarno Levonen	.20
□	278	Janne Kekalainen	.20
□	279	Veli-Pekka Nutikka	.20
□	280	Mikko Konttila	.20
□	281	Janne Virtanen	.20
□	282	Pasi Kemppainen	.20
□	283	Kiekko-Espoo	.20
□	284	Mika Rautio	.20
□	285	Teemu Sillanpaa	.20
□	287	Timo Kykopp	.20
□	288	Miikka Teimonen	.20
□	289	Tero Tiainen	.20
□	290	Joonas Jaaskelainen	.20
□	291	Lubomir Kolnik	.20
□	292	Arto Sirvio	.20
□	293	Ilkka Sinisalo	.20
□	294	Timo Hirvonen	.20
□	295	Arto Kuki	.20
□	296	Timo Norppa	.20
□	297	Lukko Rauma	.20
□	298	Timo Kaukanen	.20
□	299	Joni Lehto	.20
□	300	Jarno Miikkulainen	.20
□	301	Kimmo Lotvonen	.20
□	302	Robert Nordmark	.20
□	303	Riku Kallioniemi	.20
□	304	Matti Raunio	.20
□	305	Tommi Turunen	.20
□	306	Jarkko Varvio	.25
□	307	Tero Arkiomaa	.20
□	308	Harri Lonnberg	.20
□	309	Mikko Luovi	.20
□	310	Tappara Tampere	.20
□	311	Jussi Markkanen	.20
□	312	Timo Jutila	.50
□	313	Jukka Ollila	.20
□	314	Antti Rahkonen	.20
□	315	Derek Mayer	.20
□	316	Petri Kalteva	.20
□	317	Jarkko Nikander	.20
□	318	Pauli Jarvinen	.20
□	319	Mikko Helisten	.20
□	320	Ari Haanpaa	.20
□	321	Markus Oijennus	.20
□	322	Janne Ojanen	.20
□	323	TPS Turku	.20
□	324	Fredrik Norrena (G)	.20
□	325	Mika Lehtinen	.20
□	326	Karlis Skrastins	.20
□	327	Manu Laapas	.20
□	328	Antti Aalto	.20
□	329	Teemu Numminen	.20
□	330	Tommi Miettienen	.20
□	331	Lasse Pirjeta	.20
□	332	Miuika Rousu	.20
□	333	Marko Makinen	.20
□	334	Mikko Markkanen	.20
□	335	Tomi Kallio	.20
□	336	Miika Elomo	.50
□	337	Sami Mettovaara	.20
□	338	TuTo Turku	.20

No.	Player	NRMT-MT
339	Jukka Tammi	.20
340	Kari-Pekka Friman	.20
341	Veli-Pekka Hard	.20
342	Antti Tirkkonen	.20
343	Jukka Seppo	.20
344	Kim Ahlroos	.20
345	Marco Poulsen	.20
346	Juha Kuusisaari	.20
347	Mikko Laaksonen	.20
348	Tuomas Jalava	.20
349	Tommi Pullola	.20
350	Tuomas Kalliomaki	.20
351	Assat Pori	.20
352	Karri Kivi	.20
353	Olli Kaski	.20
354	Jouni Vento	.20
355	Tommi Rajamaki	.20
356	Jokke Heinanen	.20
357	Tomas Kapusta	.20
358	Jaroslav Otevrel	.20
359	Timo Salonen	.20
360	Pekka Virta	.20
361	Vesa Goman	.20
362	Pekka Pelktola	.20
363	Rauli Raitainen	.20
364	Pasi Tuominen	.20
365	Kari Syvasalmi	.20
366	Timo Hakanen	.20
367	Aleksander Andrijevski	.20
368	Aleksander Barkov	.20
369	Darren Boyko	.20
370	Vjatschelav Fandul	.20
371	Otakar Janecky	.20
372	Tomas Kapusta	.20
373	Lubomir Kolnik	.20
374	Petr Korinek	.20
375	Derek Mayer	.20
376	Allan Measures	.20
377	Jason Miller	.20
378	Robert Nordmark	.20
379	Jaroslav Otevrel	.20
380	Sergei Prjahin	.20
381	Boris Rousson	.20
382	Thomas Sjogren	.20
383	Karlis Skrastins	.20
384	Ivan Vlzek	.20
385	Vladimir Jursinov	.20
386	Hannu Aravirta	.20
387	Veli-Pekka Ketola	.50
388	Vaclav Sykora	.20
389	Hannu Kapanen	.20
390	Kari Savolainen	.20
391	Harri Rindell	.20
392	Anatoli Bogdanov	.20
393	Sakari Pietila	.20
394	Jukka Rautakorpi	.20
395	Harri Jalava	.20
396	Vladimir Yursinov	.20
397	CL: Jere Lehtinen	.50
398	Checklist 251-300	.20
399	Checklist 301-350	.20
400	CL: Saku Koivu	3.00

PAINKILLERS

Series One Insert Set (8 cards): 25.00

No.	Player	NRMT-MT
1	Jokke Hainanen	3.50
2	Mika Alatalo	3.50
3	Joni Lehto	3.50
4	Harri Lonnberg	3.50
5	Ville Peltonen	5.00
6	Harri Sillgren	3.50
7	Petri Varis	5.00
8	Marko Virtanen	3.50

GOLD CARDS

These are found in both Series One and Series Two packs.

Insert Set (24 cards): 125.00

No.	Player	NRMT-MT
1	Title Card	2.00
2	Jarmo Myllys (G)	10.00
3	Ari Sulander (G)	10.00
4	Jukka Tammi	3.00
5	Erik Hamalainen	3.00
6	Timo Jutila	5.00
7	Marko Kiprusoff	4.00
8	Janne Niinimaa	12.00
9	Petteri Nummelin	3.00
10	Mika Stromberg	3.00
11	Hannu Virta	3.00
12	Raimo Helminen	3.00
13	Sami Kapanen	4.00
14	Esa Keskinen	3.00
15	Saku Koivu	20.00
16	Tero Lehtera	3.00
17	Jere Lehtinen	8.00
18	Mika Nieminen	3.00
19	Janne Ojanen	3.00
20	Marko Palo	3.00
21	Ville Peltonen	6.00
22	Raimo Summanen	3.00
23	Antti Törmänen	4.00
24	Juha Ylonen	3.00

SISU SPECIALS

Series One Insert Set (10 cards): 125.00

No.	Player	NRMT-MT
1	Petri Varis	10.00
2	Boris Rousson (G)	12.00
3	Saku Koivu	30.00
4	Jari Kurri	20.00
5	Jarmo Kuusisto	6.00
6	Janne Ojanen	10.00
7	Jere Lehtinen	15.00
8	Peter Ahola	6.00
9	Jukka Seppo	6.00
10	Michael Nylander	10.00

GHOST GOALIES

Series One Insert Set (10 cards): 100.00

No.	Player	NRMT-MT
1	Sakari Lindfors (G)	10.00
2	Boris Rousson (G)	15.00
3	Ari Sulander (G)	15.00
4	Kari Takko (G)	10.00
5	Fredrik Norrena (G)	10.00
6	Kari Rosenberg (G)	10.00
7	Ari-Pekka Siekkinen (G)	10.00
8	Jukka Tammi (G)	10.00
9	Pasi Kuivalainen (G)	10.00
10	Ilpo Kauhanen (G)	10.00

SUPER CHASE

Player	NRMT-MT
Saku Koivu Golden Helmet	80.00
Janne Niinimaa, Studio Signature	40.00
Saku Koivu	80.00

SPOTLIGHTS

Series Two Insert Set (8 cards): 20.00

No.	Player	NRMT-MT
1	Otakar Janecky	5.00
2	Jari Korpisalo	3.00
3	Juha Riihijarvi	5.00
4	Iiro Jarvi	3.00
5	Thomas Sjogren	3.00
6	Risto Jalo	3.00
7	Jari Hirsimaka	3.00
8	Juha Hautamaa	3.00

DOUBLE TROUBLE

Series Two Insert Set (8 cards): 40.00

No.	Player	NRMT-MT
1	Tuomas Gronman/Kimmo Timonen	5.00
2	Waltteri Immonen/Mika Stromberg	10.00
3	Olli Kaski/Karri Kivi	5.00
4	Joni Lehto/Robert Nordmark	5.00
5	Peter Ahola/Pertti Lehtonen	5.00
6	Timo Blomqvist/Sami Nuutinen	5.00
7	Reijo Ruotsalainen/Ivan Vlzek	5.00
8	Timo Jutila/Pekka Laksola	10.00

NHL DRAFTS

Series Two Insert Set (12 cards): 100.00

No.	Player	NRMT-MT
1	Aki Berg	10.00
2	Teemu Riihijarvi	10.00
3	Miika Elomo	12.00
4	Marko Makinen	8.00
5	Tomi Kallio	8.00
6	Sami Kapanen	10.00
7	Vesa Toskala	15.00
8	Miika Kiprusoff	8.00
9	Timo Hakanen	8.00
10	Juha Vuorivirta	8.00
11	Tomi Hirvonen	8.00
12	Mikko Markkanen	8.00

1995 - 96 SISU LIMITED

The wrappers featured one of three different players: Saku Koivu, Jari Kurri or Teemu Selänne.

Complete Set (108 cards): 60.00
Common Player: .35
Saku Koivu Hologram: 10.00

No.	Player	NRMT-MT
1	Frederik Norrena (G), TPS	.75
2	Hannu Virta, TPS	.35
3	Petteri Nummelin, TPS	.35
4	Tuomas Gronman, TPS	.35
5	Marko Kiprusoff, TPS	.35
6	Saku Koivu, TPS	6.00
7	Raimo Summanen, TPS	.75
8	Esa Keskinen, TPS	1.00
9	Jere Lehtinen, TPS	2.00
10	Ari Sulander (G), Jokent	1.00
11	Waltteri Immonen, Jokent	.35
12	Mika Stromberg, Jokent	.75
13	Janne Niinimaa, Jokent	2.00
14	Otakar Janecky, Jokent	.75
15	Teemu Selänne, Jokent	6.00
16	Jari Kurri, Jokent	3.00
17	Antti Tormanen, Jokent	.75
18	Petri Varis, Jokent	.75
19	Kari Takko (G), Ässät	.75
20	Olli Kaski, Ässät	.35
21	Rauli Raitanen, Ässät	.35
22	Jari Korpisalo, Ässät	.35
23	Teppo Kivela, Ässät	.35
24	Jokka Heinanen, Ässät	.35
25	Arto Javanainen, Ässät	.35
26	Jari Levonen, Ässät	.35
27	Arto Heiskanen, Ässät	.35
28	Jarmo Myllys (G), Lukko	1.00
29	Boris Rousson (G), Lukko	1.00
30	Jarmo Kuusisto, Lukko	.35
31	Joni Lehto, Lukko	.35
32	Robert Nordmark, Lukko	.35
33	Tero Arkiomaa, Lukko	.35
34	Jari Torkki, Lukko	.35
35	Juha Riihijarvi, Lukko	.75
36	Matti Forss, Lukko	.35
37	Sakari Lindfors (G), HIFK	1.00
38	Pertti Lehtonen, HIFK	.35
39	Simo Saarinen, HIFK	.35

	No.	Player	NRMT-MT
☐	40	Esa Tikkanen, HIFK	2.00
☐	41	Ville Peltonen, HIFK	.75
☐	42	Christian Ruuttu, HIFK	.75
☐	43	Mika Kortelainen, HIFK	.35
☐	44	Darren Boyko, HIFK	.35
☐	45	Iiro Jarvi, HIFK	.35
☐	46	Ari-Pekka Siekkinen (G), JyPHT	.35
☐	47	Harri Laurila, JyPHT	.35
☐	48	Jouni Loponen, JyPHT	.35
☐	49	Joni Lius, JyPHT	.35
☐	50	Jari Lindroos, JyPHT	.35
☐	51	Risto Kurkinen, JyPHT	.35
☐	52	Thomas Sjogren, JyPHT	.35
☐	53	Marko Virtanen, JyPHT	.35
☐	54	Michael Nylander, JyPHT	2.00
☐	55	Mika Rautio, Kiekko-Espoo	.35
☐	56	Sami Nuutinen, Kiekko-Espoo	.35
☐	57	Peter Ahola, Kiekko-Espoo	.35
☐	58	Timo Blomqvist, Kiekko-Espoo	.75
☐	59	Ilkka Sinisalo, Kiekko-Espoo	.35
☐	60	Petro Koivunen, Kiekko-Espoo	.35
☐	61	Sergei Prjahin, Kiekko-Espoo	.35
☐	62	Tero Lehtera, Kiekko-Espoo	.35
☐	63	Mariusz Czerkawski, Kiekko-Espoo	.75
☐	64	Pasi Kuivalainen, KalPa	.35
☐	65	Kimmo Timonen, KalPa	.35
☐	66	Reijo Ruotsalainen, KalPa	.75
☐	67	Vesa Salo, KalPa	.35
☐	68	Petr Korinek, KalPa	.35
☐	69	Marko Jantunen, KalPa	.35
☐	70	Pekka Tirkkonen, KalPa	.35
☐	71	Janne Kekalainen, KalPa	.35
☐	72	Sami Kapanen, KalPa	1.00
☐	73	Timo Jutila, Tappara	1.00
☐	74	Pekka Laksola, Tappara	.35
☐	75	Janne Gronvall, Tappara	.35
☐	76	Jiri Kucera, Tappara	.35
☐	77	Janne Ojanen, Tappara	.75
☐	78	Pauli Jarvinen, Tappara	.35
☐	79	Ari Haanpaa, Tappara	.35
☐	80	Aleksander Barkov, Tappara	.35
☐	81	Theoren Fleury, Tappara	4.00
☐	82	Kari Rosenberg (G), HPK	.35
☐	83	Janne Laukkanen, HPK	.35
☐	84	Jani Nikko, HPK	.35
☐	85	Mika Lartama, HPK	.35
☐	86	Kai Nurminen, HPK	.75
☐	87	Tomas Kapusta, HPK	.35
☐	88	Marko Palo, HPK	.35
☐	89	Jarkko Varvio, HPK	1.00
☐	90	Risto Jalo, HPK	.35
☐	91	Jukka Tammi (G), TuTo	.75
☐	92	Risto Siltanen, TuTo	.35
☐	93	Teppo Numminen, TuTo	1.50
☐	94	Marco Poulsen, TuTo	.35
☐	95	Jukka Seppo, TuTo	.35
☐	96	Vesa Karjalainen, TuTo	.35
☐	97	Ted Donato, TuTo	.35
☐	98	Juha Virtanen, TuTo	.35
☐	99	Jari Hirsimaki, TuTo	.35
☐	100	Vesa Toskala (G), Ilves	.75
☐	101	Jyrki Lumme, Ilves	1.50
☐	102	Hannu Henriksson, Ilves	.35
☐	103	Allan Measures, Ilves	.35
☐	104	Timo Peltomaa, Ilves	.35
☐	105	Juha Hautamaa, Ilves	.35
☐	106	Mikko Makela, Ilves	.75
☐	107	Juha Jarvenpaa, Ilves	.35
☐	108	Semi Pekki, Ilves	.35

SIGNED AND SEALED

Insert Set (9 cards): 100.00

	No.	Player	NRMT-MT
☐	1	Sami Kapanen	8.00
☐	2	Christian Ruuttu	8.00
☐	3	Teemu Selänne	30.00
☐	4	Aki Berg	8.00
☐	5	Joni Lehto	6.00
☐	6	Teppo Numminen	8.00
☐	7	Jari Kurri	20.00
☐	8	Esa Tikkanen	10.00
☐	9	Theoren Fleury	20.00

LEAF GALLERY

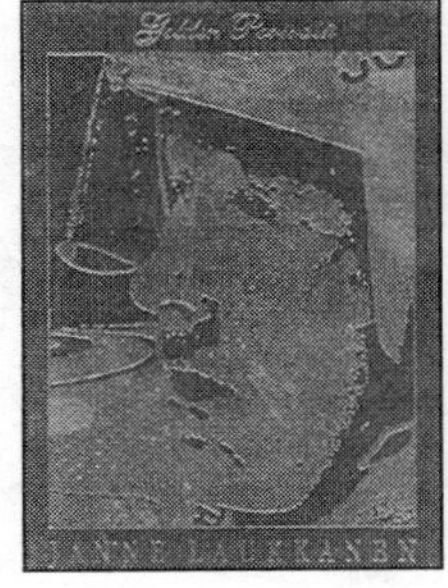

Insert Set (9 cards): 50.00

	No.	Player	NRMT-MT
☐	1	Jyrki Lumme	8.00
☐	2	Janne Laukkanen	4.00
☐	3	Michael Nylander	6.00
☐	4	Janne Ojanen	4.00
☐	5	Peter Ahola	4.00
☐	6	Kari Takko (G)	8.00
☐	7	Hannu Virta	4.00
☐	8	Juha Lind	4.00
☐	9	Sakari Lindfors (G)	8.00

PLATINUM POWER

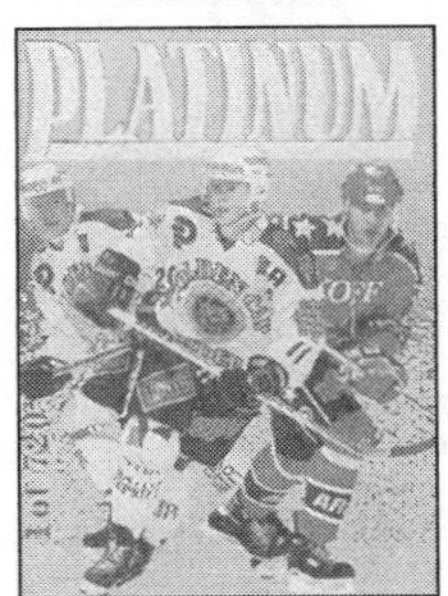

	Player	NRMT-MT
☐	Ville Peltonen/Saku Koivu/Jere Lehtinen	150.00

1995 - 96 SKY BOX EMOTION

Imprint: © 1995 FLEER/SKYBOX INTERNATIONAL
Complete Set (200 cards): 50.00
Common Player: .25
Promo Panel (Jeremy Roenick): 2.00

	No.	Player	NRMT-MT
☐	1	Bobby Dollas Blastin', Ana.	.25
☐	2	Guy Hebert (G) Floored, Ana.	.50
☐	3	Paul Kariya Exulted, Ana.	3.50
☐	4	Oleg Tverdovsky Closin', Ana.	.25
☐	5	Shaun Van Allen Crashin', Ana.	.25
☐	6	Ray Bourque Finesse, Bos.	1.25
☐	7	Al Iafrate Relentless, Bos.	.25
☐	8	Blaine Lacher (G), Magnifique, Bos., Err. (Manifique)	.25
☐	9	Joe Mullen Control, Bos.	.25
☐	10	Cam Neely Bruisin', Bos.	.50
☐	11	Adam Oates Thrashin', Bos.	.75
☐	12	Kevin Stevens Bold, Bos.	.25
☐	13	Don Sweeney Menacing, Bos.	.25
☐	14	Donald Audette Loose, Buf.	.25
☐	15	Garry Galley Glarin', Buf.	.25
☐	16	Dominik Hasek (G), Psyched, Buf.	1.75
☐	**17**	**Brian Holzinger Fluid, Buf., RC**	**.25**
☐	18	Pat LaFontaine Howlin', Buf.	.50
☐	19	Alexei Zhitnik Pressure, Buf.	.25
☐	20	Steve Chiasson Chargin', Cgy.	.25
☐	21	Thereon Fleury Crush, Cgy.	.75
☐	22	Phil Housley Pursuit, Cgy.	.25
☐	23	Trevor Kidd (G), Vision, Cgy.	.50
☐	24	Joe Nieuwendyk Surge, Cgy.	.50
☐	25	Gary Roberts Scorchin', Cgy.	.50
☐	26	Zarley Zalapski Brutal, Cgy.	.25
☐	27	Ed Belfour (G), Tough, Chi.	.75
☐	28	Chris Chelios Swift, Chi.	1.00
☐	29	Sergei Krivokrasov Adrenalized, Chi.	.25
☐	30	Joe Murphy Loose, Chi.	.25
☐	31	Bernie Nicholls Drivin', Chi.	.25
☐	32	Patrick Poulin Winded, Chi.	.25
☐	33	Jeremy Roenick Raw, Chi.	.75
☐	34	Gary Suter Explosive, Chi.	.25
☐	35	René Corbet Burnin', Col.	.25
☐	36	Peter Forsberg Explosive, Col.	2.50
☐	37	Valeri Kamensky Loose, Col.	.50
☐	38	Uwe Krupp Tenacity, Col.	.25
☐	39	Curtis Leschyshyn Fury, Col.	.25
☐	40	Owen Nolan Guts, Col.	.50
☐	41	Mike Ricci Adrenaline, Col.	.25
☐	42	Joe Sakic Control, Col.	2.00
☐	43	Jocelyn Thibault (G), Icy, Col.	.75
☐	44	Bob Bassen Swift, Dal.	.25
☐	45	Dave Gagner Crazed, Dal.	.25
☐	46	Todd Harvey Bumpin', Dal.	.25
☐	47	Derian Hatcher Solid, Dal.	.50
☐	48	Kevin Hatcher Searchin', Dal.	.25
☐	49	Mike Modano Shinin', Dal.	1.25
☐	50	Andy Moog (G), Roarin', Dal.	.50
☐	51	Dino Ciccarelli Wheelin', Det.	.50
☐	52	Paul Coffey Squids!, Det.	.50
☐	53	Sergei Fedorov Deadly, Det.	1.25
☐	54	Vladimir Konstantinov Fearless, Det.	.25
☐	55	Vyacheslav Kozlov Sleek, Det.	.25
☐	56	Nicklas Lidström Stormin', Det.	.50
☐	57	Keith Primeau Primo, Det.	.50
☐	58	Ray Sheppard Hustlin', Det.	.25
☐	59	Mike Vernon (G), Steady, Det.	.50
☐	60	Steve Yzerman Contact, Det.	2.50
☐	61	Jason Arnott Mayhem, Edm.	.50
☐	62	Curtis Joseph Rabid, Edm.	1.50
☐	63	Igor Kravchuk Crucial, Edm.	.25
☐	64	Todd Marchant Focused, Edm.	.25
☐	65	David Oliver Instinct, Edm.	.25
☐	66	Bill Ranford (G), Denied, Edm.	.50
☐	67	Doug Weight Slick, Edm.	.75
☐	68	Stu Barnes Glory, Fla.	.25
☐	69	Jesse Belanger Clawin', Fla.	.25
☐	70	Gord Murphy Slapshot, Fla.	.25
☐	71	Magnus Svensson Grit, Fal.	.25
☐	72	John Vanbiesbrouck (G), Snatched, Fla.	1.50
☐	73	Sean Burke (G), Snag, Hfd.	.50
☐	74	Andrew Cassels Cool, Hfd.	.25
☐	75	Frantisek Kucera Stern, Hfd.	.25
☐	76	Andrei Nikolishin Hungry, Hfd.	.25
☐	77	Geoff Sanderson Burnin', Hfd.	.25
☐	78	Brendan Shanahan Menace, Hfd.	1.50
☐	79	Darren Turcotte Strength, Hfd.	.25
☐	80	Rob Blake Smooth, L.A.	.50
☐	81	Wayne Gretzky King, L.A.	5.00
☐	82	Dimitri Khristich Intense, L.A.	.25
☐	83	Jari Kurri Tenacious, L.A.	.50
☐	84	Jamie Storr (G), Vision, L.A.	.50
☐	85	Darryl Sydor Passion, L.A.	.25
☐	86	Rick Tocchet Bold, L.A.	.25
☐	87	Vincent Damphousse Havoc, Mtl.	.75
☐	88	Vladimir Malakhov Berserk, Mtl.	.25
☐	89	Stéphane Quintal Instinct, Mtl.	.25

	No.	Player	NRMT-MT
☐	90	Mark Recchi Power, Mtl.	.50
☐	91	Patrick Roy (G), Alert, Mtl.	4.00
☐	92	Brian Savage Destroyer, Mtl.	.25
☐	93	Pierre Turgeon Instinct, Mtl.	.50
☐	94	Martin Brodeur (G), Awesome, N.J.	1.75
☐	95	Neal Broten Fiery, N.J.	.25
☐	96	Shawn Chambers Burnin', N.J.	.25
☐	97	Claude Lemieux Wicked, N.J.	.25
☐	98	John MacLean Control. N.J.	.25
☐	99	Randy McKay Possessed, N.J.	.25
☐	100	Scott Niedermayer Venom, N.J.	.50
☐	101	Stéphane Richer Stomp, N.J.	.25
☐	102	Scott Stevens Slam, N.J.	.25
☐	**103**	**Todd Bertuzzi Victory, NYI., RC**	**.75**
☐	104	Patrick Flatley Wild, NYI.	.25
☐	105	Brett Lindros Kickin', NYI.	.25
☐	106	Kirk Muller Tense, NYI.	.25
☐	**107**	**Tommy Salo (G), Shield, NYI., RC**	**.25**
☐	108	Mathieu Schneider Slap, NYI.	.25
☐	109	Alexander Semak Glory, NYI.	.25
☐	110	Dennis Vaske Pressure, NYI.	.25
☐	111	Ray Ferraro Driven, NYR.	.25
☐	112	Adam Graves Iced, NYR.	.25
☐	113	Alexei Kovalev Steady, NYR.	.25
☐	114	Steve Larmer Rough, NYR.	.25
☐	115	Brian Leetch Poundin', NYR.	.75
☐	116	Mark Messier Victory, NYR.	1.25
☐	117	Mike Richter (G), Clutch, NYR.	.75
☐	118	Luc Robitaille Passion, NYR.	.50
☐	119	Ulf Samuelsson Cagey, NYR.	.25
☐	120	Pat Verbeek Pure, NYR.	.25
☐	121	Don Beaupré (G), Force, Ott	.25
☐	122	Radek Bonk Prime, Ott	.25
☐	123	Alexandre Daigle Agile, Ott.	.50
☐	124	Steve Duchesne Hunger, Ott.	.25
☐	125	Steve Larouche Anguish, Ott.	.25
☐	126	Dan Quinn Gliding, Ott.	.25
☐	127	Martin Straka Heart, Ott.	.25
☐	128	Alexei Yashin Style, Ott.	1.00
☐	129	R. Brind'Amour Soarin', Pha.	.50
☐	130	Eric Desjardins Coup!, Pha.	.25
☐	131	Ron Hextall (G), Hexed, Pha.	.50
☐	132	John LeClair Maitre, Pha.	1.25
☐	133	Eric Lindros Pressure, Pha.	3.50
☐	134	Mikael Renberg Courage, Pha.	.25
☐	135	Chris Therien Spirited, Pha.	.25
☐	136	Ron Francis Psyched, Pgh.	.75
☐	137	Jaromir Jagr Lethal, Pgh.	2.50
☐	138	Mario Lemieux Returnin', Pgh.	4.00
☐	139	Dimitri Mironov Absorbed, Pgh.	.25
☐	140	Petr Nedved Fierce, Pgh.	.25
☐	141	Tomas Sandström Tangled, Pgh.	.25
☐	142	Brian Smolinski Clutch, Pgh.	.25
☐	143	Ken Wregget (G), Primed, Pgh.	.25
☐	144	Sergei Zubov Agile, Pgh.	.50
☐	145	Shayne Corson Relentless, Stl.	.50
☐	146	Geoff Courtnall Chillin', Stl.	.25
☐	147	Dale Hawerchuk Rage, Stl.	.50
☐	148	Brett Hull Haulin', Stl.	1.25
☐	149	Ian Laperrière Jazzin', Stl.	.25
☐	150	Al MacInnis Jammin', Stl.	.25
☐	151	Chris Pronger Viscious, Stl.	.25
☐	152	David Roberts Savvy, Stl.	.25
☐	153	Esa Tikkanen Solo, Stl.	.25
☐	154	Ulf Dahlen Poised, S.J.	.25
☐	155	Jeff Friesen Lunge, S.J.	.50
☐	156	Arturs Irbe (G), Thrashin', S.J.	.25
☐	157	Craig Janney Absorbed, S.J.	.25
☐	158	Sergei Makarov Lurking, S.J.	.25
☐	159	Sandis Ozolinsh Hungry, S.J.	.50
☐	160	Mike Rathje Frenzy, S.J.	.25
☐	161	Ray Whitney Jaws, S.J.	.25
☐	162	Brian Bradley Cruisin', T.B.	.25
☐	163	Chris Gratton Electric, T.B.	.50
☐	164	Roman Hamrlik Steady, T.B.	.50
☐	165	Petr Klima Fluid, T.B.	.25
☐	166	Daren Puppa (G), Wall, T.B.	.25
☐	167	Paul Ysebaert Stormin', T.B.	.25
☐	168	Dave Andreychuk Force, Tor.	.25
☐	169	Mike Gartner Pushin', Tor.	.50
☐	170	Todd Gill Crack!, Tor.	.25
☐	171	Doug Gilmour Iced!, Tor.	.75
☐	172	Kenny Jonsson Iced!, Tor.	.25
☐	173	Larry Murphy Bruising, Tor.	.50
☐	174	Félix Potvin (G), Nyet, Tor.	1.25
☐	175	Mats Sundin Bruising, Tor.	1.25
☐	176	Josef Beranek Impact, Van.	.25
☐	177	Jeff Brown Primal, Van., Error (/b: Josef Beranek)	.25
☐	178	Pavel Bure Travail, Van.	1.75
☐	179	Russ Courtnall Aware, Van.	.25
☐	180	Trevor Linden Airborne, Van.	.50
☐	181	Kirk McLean (G), Capture, Van.	.50
☐	182	Alex Mogilny Primed, Van.	.75
☐	183	Roman Oksiuta Deadly, Van.	.25
☐	184	Mike Ridley Electric, Wsh.	.25
☐	185	Jason Allison Breathin', Wsh.	.75
☐	186	Jim Carey (G), Smokin', Wsh.	.25
☐	187	Sergei Gonchar Dynamo, Wsh.	.25
☐	188	Dale Hunter Motorin', Wsh.	.25
☐	189	Calle Johansson Menace, Wsh.	.25
☐	190	Joé Juneau Fury, Wsh.	.25
☐	191	Joe Reekie Power, Wsh.	.25
☐	192	Nelson Emerson Checked, Wpg.	.25
☐	193	Nikola Khabibulin (G), Ready, Wpg.	.75
☐	194	Dave Manson Soaring, Wpg.	.25
☐	195	Teppo Numminen Lightning, Wpg.	.25
☐	196	Teemu Selänne Marauder, Wog.	1.75
☐	197	Keith Tkachuk Thrashin', Wpg.	1.00
☐	198	Alexei Zhamnov Dangerous, Wpg.	.50
☐	199	Checklist	.25
☐	200	Checklist	.25

GENERATIONEXT

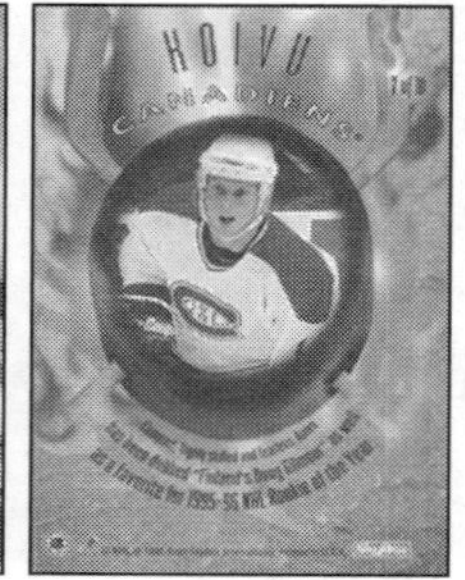

Insert Set (10 cards): 40.00

	No.	Player	NRMT-MT
☐	1	Brian Holzinger, Buf.	2.50
☐	2	Eric Dazé, Chi.	5.00
☐	3	Jason Bonsignore, Edm.	2.50
☐	4	Jamie Storr (G), L.A.	5.00
☐	5	Tommy Salo (G), NYI.	2.50
☐	6	Brendan Wit, Wsh.	2.50
☐	7	Saku Koivu, Mtl.	15.00
☐	8	Todd Bertuzzi, NYI.	5.00
☐	9	Ed Jovanovski, Fla.	5.00
☐	10	Chad Kilger, Ana.	2.50

NTENSE POWER

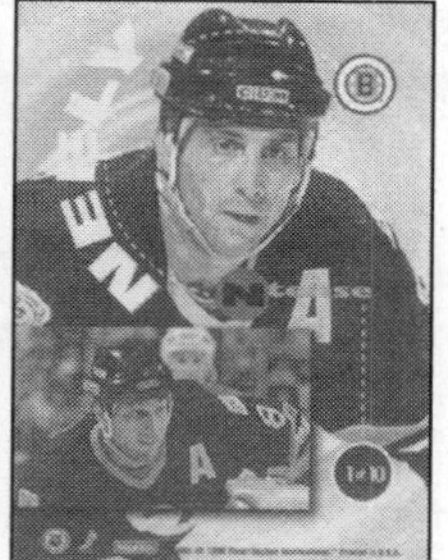

Inset Set (10 cards): 85.00

	No.	Player	NRMT-MT
☐	1	Cam Neely, Bos.	5.00
☐	2	Keith Primeau, Det.	5.00
☐	3	Mark Messier, NYR.	12.00
☐	4	Eric Lindros, Pha.	35.00
☐	5	Mikael Renberg, Pha.	3.00
☐	6	Owen Nolan, Col.	5.00
☐	7	Brendan Shanahan, Hfd.	15.00
☐	8	Kevin Stevens, Bos.	3.00
☐	9	Keith Tkachuk, Wpg.	10.00
☐	10	Rick Tocchet, L.A.	3.00

XCEL

Insert Set (10 cards): 245.00

	No.	Player	NRMT-MT
☐	1	Adam Oates, Bos.	10.00
☐	2	Jeremy Roenick, Chi.	10.00
☐	3	Sergei Fedorov, Det.	18.00
☐	4	Wayne Gretzky, L.A.	75.00
☐	5	Alexei Yashin, Ott.	15.00
☐	6	Eric Lindros, Pha.	50.00
☐	7	Ron Francis, Pgh.	10.00
☐	8	Mario Lemieux, Pgh.	60.00
☐	9	Joe Sakic, Col.	30.00
☐	10	Alexei Zhamnov, Wpg.	6.00

XCITED

Insert Set (20 cards): 50.00

	No.	Player	NRMT-MT
☐	1	Theoren Fleury, Cgy.	1.50
☐	2	Jeremy Roenick, Chi.	1.50
☐	3	Mike Modano, Dal.	2.50
☐	4	Sergei Fedorov, Det.	2.50
☐	5	Wayne Gretzky, L.A.	10.00
☐	6	Brian Leetch, NYR.	1.50
☐	7	Alexei Yashin, Ott.	2.00
☐	8	Brett Hull, Stl.	2.50
☐	9	Jaromir Jagr, Pgh.	5.00
☐	10	Mario Lemieux, Pgh.	8.00
☐	11	Ron Francis, Pgh. (xcx: Ray Bourque)	1.50
☐	12	Keith Primeau, Det.	1.00
☐	13	Joe Sakic, Col.	4.00
☐	14	Peter Forsberg, Col.	5.00
☐	15	Paul Kariya, Ana.	6.00
☐	16	Pavel Bure, Van.	3.50
☐	17	Alexei Zhamnov, Wpg.	1.00
☐	18	Martin Brodeur (G), N.J.	3.50
☐	19	Jim Carey (G), Wsh.	.50
☐	20	Chris Chelios, Chi.	2.00

1995 - 96 SKY BOX IMPACT

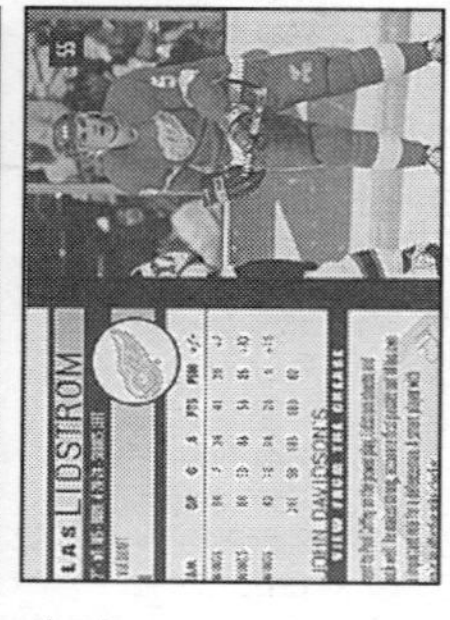

Imprint: © 1996 Fleer/Skybox International

Complete Set (250 cards):	**20.00**
Common Player:	**.10**
Promo Panel (Fleury/Lacher/Lacher/Roenick):	**3.00**

	No.	Player	NRMT-MT
☐	1	Bobby Dollas, Ana.	.10
☐	2	Guy Hebert (G), Ana.	.25
☐	3	Paul Kariya, Ana.	1.25
☐	4	Todd Krygier, Ana.	.10
☐	5	Oleg Tverdovsky, Ana.	.10
☐	6	Shaun Van Allen, Ana.	.10
☐	7	Ray Bourque, Bos.	.50
☐	8	Al Iafrate, Bos.	.10
☐	9	Blaine Lacher (G), Bos.	.10
☐	10	Joe Mullen, Bos.	.10

☐ 11 Cam Neely, Bos. .25
☐ 12 Adam Oates, Bos. .35
☐ 13 Kevin Stevens, Buf. .10
☐ 14 Donald Audette, Buf. .10
☐ 15 Garry Galley, Buf. .10
☐ 16 Dominik Hasek (G), Buf. .75
☐ 17 Pat LaFontaine, Buf. .25
☐ 18 Derek Plante, Buf. .10
☐ 19 Alexei Zhitnik, Buf. .10
☐ 20 Steve Chiasson, Cgy. .10
☐ 21 Theoren Fleury, Cgy. .35
☐ 22 Phil Housley, Cgy. .10
☐ 23 Trevor Kidd (G), Cgy. .25
☐ 24 Joe Nieuwendyk, Cgy. .25
☐ 25 German Titov, Cgy. .10
☐ 26 Zarley Zalapski, Cgy. .10
☐ 27 Ed Belfour (G), Chi. .35
☐ 28 Chris Chelios, Chi. .35
☐ 29 Sergei Krivokrasov, Chi. .10
☐ 30 Joe Murphy, Chi. .10
☐ 31 Bernie Nicholls, Chi. .10
☐ 32 Patrick Poulin, Chi. .10
☐ 33 Jeremy Roenick, Chi. .35
☐ 34 Gary Suter, Chi. .10
☐ 35 Peter Forsberg, Col. 1.00
☐ 36 Valeri Kamensky, Col. .25
☐ 37 Claude Lemieux, Col. .10
☐ 38 Curtis Leschyshyn, Col. .10
☐ 39 Sandis Ozolinsh, Col. .25
☐ 40 Mike Ricci, Col. .10
☐ 41 Joe Sakic, Col. .85
☐ 42 Jocelyn Thibault (G), Col. .35
☐ 43 Bob Bassen, Dal. .10
☐ 44 Dave Gagner, Dal. .10
☐ 45 Todd Harvey, Dal. .10
☐ 46 Derian Hatcher, Dal. .25
☐ 47 Kevin Hatcher, Dal. .10
☐ 48 Mike Modano, Dal. .50
☐ 49 Andy Moog (G), Dal. .25
☐ 50 Dino Ciccarelli, Det. .25
☐ 51 Paul Coffey, Det. .25
☐ 52 Sergei Fedorov, Det. .50
☐ 53 Vladimir Konstantinov, Det. .10
☐ 54 Vyacheslav Kozlov, Det. .10
☐ 55 Nicklas Lidström, Det. .25
☐ 56 Chris Osgood, Det. .35
☐ 57 Keith Primeau, Det. .25
☐ 58 Steve Yzerman, Det. 1.00
☐ 59 Jason Arnott, Edm. .25
☐ 60 Curtis Joseph (G) .60
☐ 61 Igor Kravchuk, Edm. .10
☐ 62 Todd Marchant, Edm. .10
☐ 63 David Oliver, Edm. .10
☐ 64 Bill Ranford, Edm. .25
☐ 65 Doug Weight, Edm. .35
☐ 66 Stu Barnes, Fla. .10
☐ 67 Jesse Belanger, Fla. .10
☐ 68 Gord Murphy, Fla. .10
☐ 69 Magnus Svensson, Fla. .10
☐ 70 John Vanbiesbrouck (G), Fla. .60
☐ 71 Sean Burke (G), Hfd. .25
☐ 72 Andrew Cassels, Hfd. .10
☐ 73 Nelson Emerson, Hfd. .10
☐ 74 Andrei Nikolishin, Hfd. .10
☐ 75 Geoff Sanderson, Hfd. .10
☐ 76 Brendan Shanahan, Hfd. .60
☐ 77 Glen Wesley, Hfd. .10
☐ 78 Rob Blake, L.A. .25
☐ 79 Wayne Gretzky, L.A. 2.00
☐ 80 Dimitri Khristich, L.A. .10
☐ 81 Jari Kurri, L.A. .25
☐ 82 Darryl Sydor, L.A. .10
☐ 83 Rick Tocchet, L.A. .10
☐ 84 Vincent Damphousse, Mtl. .35
☐ 85 Vladimir Malakhov, Mtl. .10
☐ 86 Mark Recchi, Mtl. .25
☐ 87 Patrick Roy (G), Mtl. 1.50
☐ 88 Brian Savage, Mtl. .10
☐ 89 Pierre Turgeon, Mtl. .25
☐ 90 Martin Brodeur (G), N.J. .75
☐ 91 Neal Broten, N.J. .10
☐ 92 Shawn Chambers, N.J. .10
☐ 93 John MacLean, N.J. .10
☐ 94 Randy McKay, N.J. .10
☐ 95 Scott Niedermayer, N.J. .25
☐ 96 Stéphane Richer, N.J. .10
☐ 97 Scott Stevens, N.J. .10
☐ 98 Steve Thomas, N.J. .10
☐ 99 Wendel Clark, NYI. .25
☐ 100 Patrick Flatley, NYI. .10
☐ 101 Scott Lachance, NYI. .10
☐ 102 Brett Lindros, NYI. .10
☐ 103 Kirk Muller, NYI. .10
☐ **104 Tommy Salo (G), NYI., RC .25**
☐ 105 Mathieu Schneider, NYI. .10
☐ 106 Dennis Vaske, NYI. .10
☐ 107 Ray Ferraro, NYR. .10
☐ 108 Adam Graves, NYR. .10
☐ 109 Alexei Kovalev, NYR. .10
☐ 110 Brian Leetch, NYR. .35
☐ 111 Mark Messier, NYR. .50
☐ 112 Mike Richter (G), NYR. .35
☐ 113 Luc Robitaille, NYR. .25
☐ 114 Ulf Samuelsson, NYR. .10
☐ 115 Pat Verbeek, NYR. .10
☐ 116 Don Beaupré (G), Ott. .10
☐ 117 Radek Bonk, Ott. .10
☐ 118 Alexandre Daigle, Ott. .25
☐ 119 Steve Duchesne, Ott. .10
☐ 120 Dan Quinn, Ott. .10
☐ 121 Martin Straka, Ott. .10
☐ 122 Alexei Yashin, Ott. .25
☐ 123 Rod Brind'Amour, Pha. .20
☐ 124 Eric Desjardins, Pha. .10
☐ 125 Ron Hextall (G), Pha. .25
☐ 126 John LeClair, Pha. .50
☐ 127 Eric Lindros, Pha. 1.25
☐ 128 Mikael Renberg, Pha. .10
☐ 129 Chris Therien, Pha. .10
☐ 130 Ron Francis, Pgh. .35
☐ 131 Jaromir Jagr, Pgh. 1.00
☐ 132 Mario Lemieux, Pgh. 1.50
☐ 133 Petr Nedved, Pgh. .10
☐ 134 Tomas Sandström, Pgh. .10
☐ 135 Bryan Smolinski, Pgh. .10
☐ 136 Ken Wregget (G), Pgh. .10
☐ 137 Sergei Zubov, Pgh. .25
☐ 138 Shayne Corson, Stl. .25
☐ 139 Geoff Courtnall, Stl. .10
☐ 140 Dale Hawerchuk, Stl. .25
☐ 141 Brett Hull, Stl. .50
☐ 142 Ian Laperrière, Stl. .10
☐ 143 Al MacInnis, Stl. .10
☐ 144 Chris Pronger, Stl. .25
☐ 145 Esa Tikkanen, Stl. .10
☐ 146 Ulf Dahlen, S.J. .10
☐ 147 Jeff Friesen, S.J. .25
☐ 148 Arturs Irbe (G), S.J. .10
☐ 149 Craig Janney, S.J. .10
☐ 150 Owen Nolan, S.J. .25
☐ 151 Mike Rathje, S.J. .10
☐ 152 Ray Sheppard, S.J. .10
☐ 153 Brian Bradley, T.B. .10
☐ 154 Chris Gratton, T.B. .25
☐ 155 Roman Hamrlik, T.B. .25
☐ 156 Petr Klima, T.B. .10
☐ 157 Daren Puppa (G), T.B. .10
☐ 158 Dave Andreychuk, Tor. .10
☐ 159 Mike Gartner, Tor. .25
☐ 160 Todd Gill, Tor. .10
☐ 161 Doug Gilmour, Tor. .35
☐ 162 Kenny Jonsson, Tor. .10
☐ 163 Larry Murphy, Tor. .50
☐ 164 Félix Potvin (G), Tor. .50
☐ 165 Mats Sundin, Tor. .50
☐ 166 Jeff Brown, Van. .10
☐ 167 Pavel Bure, Van. .75
☐ 168 Russ Courtnall, Van. .10
☐ 169 Trevor Linden, Van. .25
☐ 170 Kirk McLean (G), Van. .25
☐ 171 Alexander Mogilny, Van. .35
☐ 172 Roman Oksiuta, Van. .10
☐ 173 Mike Ridley, Wsh. .10
☐ 174 Peter Bondra, Wsh. .35
☐ 175 Jim Carey (G), , Wsh. .10
☐ 176 Sergei Gonchar, Wsh. .10
☐ 177 Dale Hunter, Wsh. .10
☐ 178 Calle Johansson, Wsh. .10
☐ 179 Joé Juneau, Wsh. .10
☐ 180 Michal Pivonka, Wsh. .10
☐ 181 Nikolai Khabibulin (G), Wpg. .35
☐ 182 Dave Manson, Wpg. .10
☐ 183 Teppo Numminen, Wpg. .10
☐ 184 Teemu Selänne, Wpg. .75
☐ 185 Keith Tkachuk, Wpg. .35
☐ 186 Darren Turcotte, Wpg. .10
☐ 187 Alexei Zhamnov, Wpg. .25
☐ **188 Chad Kilger, Ana., RC .10**
☐ **189 Kyle McLaren, Bos., RC .10**
☐ **190 Brian Holzinger, Buf., RC .25**
☐ **191 Wayne Primeau, Buf., RC .10**
☐ 192 Marty Murray, Cgy. .10
☐ 193 Eric Dazé, Chi. .25
☐ 194 Jon Klemm, Col. .10
☐ 195 Jere Lehtinen, Dal. .25
☐ 196 Jason Bonsignore, Edm. .10
☐ **197 Miroslav Satan, Edm., RC .10**
☐ 198 Ryan Smyth, Edm. .25
☐ 199 Tyler Wright, Edm. .10
☐ 200 Radek Bonk, Ott. .10
☐ 201 Ed Jovanovski, Fla. .25
☐ 202 Jeff O'Neill, Hfd. .10
☐ **203 Aki Berg, L.A, RC. .10**
☐ 204 Jamie Storr (G), L.A. .10
☐ 205 Vitali Yachmenev, L.A. .10
☐ 206 Saku Koivu, Mtl. .75
☐ 207 Denis Pederson, N.J. .10
☐ **208 Todd Bertuzzi, NYI., RC .35**
☐ 209 Bryan McCabe, NYI. .10
☐ 210 Dan Plante, NYI. .10
☐ 211 Peter Ferraro, NYR. .10
☐ **212 Darren Langdon, NYR., RC .10**
☐ 213 Niklas Sundstrom, NYR. .10
☐ **214 Daniel Alfredsson, Ott., RC .60**
☐ 215 Garth Snow, Pha. .10
☐ 216 Ian Moran, Pgh. .10
☐ 217 Richard Park, Pgh. .10
☐ 218 Jamie Rivers, Stl. .10
☐ 219 Roman Vopat, Stl. .10
☐ **220 Marcus Ragnarsson, S.J., RC .10**
☐ 221 Aaron Gavey, T.B. .10
☐ **222 Daymond Langkow, T.B., RC .10**
☐ 223 Darby Hendrickson, Tor. .10
☐ 224 Martin Gendron, Wsh. .10
☐ 225 Brendan Witt, Wsh. .10
☐ 226 Shane Doan, Wpg. .10
☐ 227 Deron Quint, Wpg. .10
☐ 228 Jim Carey (G), Wsh. .10
☐ 229 Peter Forsberg, Col. .50
☐ 230 Paul Kariya, Ana. .60
☐ 231 David Oliver, Edm. .10
☐ 232 Blaine Lacher (G), Bos. .10
☐ 233 Todd Harvey, Dal. .10
☐ 234 Todd Marchant, Edm. .10
☐ 235 Jeff Friesen, S.J. .10
☐ 236 Oleg Tverdovsky, Ana. .10
☐ 237 Jason Arnott, Edm. .25
☐ 238 Cam Neely, Bos. .25
☐ 239 Keith Tkachuk, Wpg. .25
☐ 240 Owen Nolan, Col. .25
☐ 241 Keith Primeau, Det. .25
☐ 242 Peter Bondra, Wsh. .25
☐ 243 Jeremy Roenick, Chi. .25
☐ 244 John LeClair, Pha. .25
☐ 245 Mikael Renberg, Pha. .10
☐ 246 Dave Andreychuk, Tor. .10
☐ 247 Rick Tocchet, Bos. .10
☐ 248 Checklist A .10
☐ 249 Checklist B .10
☐ 250 Checklist C .10

COUNTDOWN TO IMPACT

	No.	Player	NRMT-MT
Insert Set (9 cards):			**150.00**
☐	1	Eric Lindros, Pha.	25.00
☐	2	Jaromir Jagr, Pgh.	20.00
☐	3	Mario Lemieux, Pgh.	30.00
☐	4	Wayne Gretzky, L.A.	40.00
☐	5	Mark Messier, NYR.	10.00
☐	6	Sergei Fedorov, Det.	10.00
☐	7	Paul Kariya, Ana.	25.00
☐	8	Doug Gilmour, Tor.	6.00
☐	9	Pavel Bure, Van.	12.00

DEFLECTORS

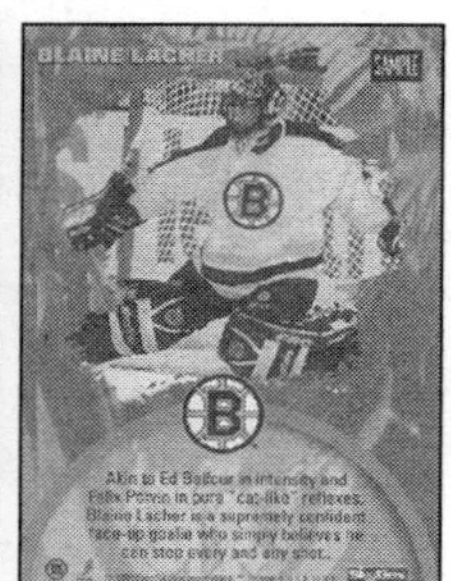

	No.	Player	NRMT-MT
Insert Set (12 cards):			**20.00**
☐	1	Dominik Hasek (G), Buf.	3.00
☐	2	Jim Carey (G), Wsh.	.50
☐	3	Félix Potvin (G), Tor.	2.00
☐	4	Sean Burke (G), Hfd.	1.00
☐	5	Blaine Lacher (G), Bos.	.50
☐	6	John Vanbiesbrouck (G), Fla.	2.50
☐	7	Jocelyn Thibault (G), Col.	1.50
☐	8	Patrick Roy (G), Mtl.	6.00
☐	9	Ed Belfour (G), Chi.	1.50
☐	10	Trevor Kidd (G), Cgy.	1.00
☐	11	Martin Brodeur (G), N.J.	3.00
☐	12	Kirk McLean (G), Van.	1.00

FOX, IT'S A BEAUTIFUL THING

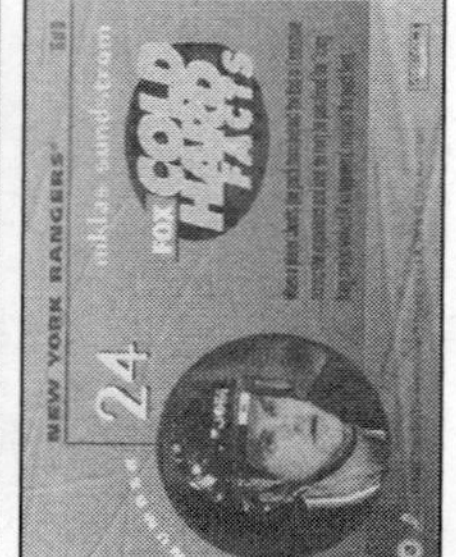

	No.	Player	NRMT-MT
Insert Set (18 cards):			**4.50**
☐	1	Mariusz Czerkawski, Bos.	.25
☐	2	Roman Oksiuta, Van.	.25
☐	3	David Oliver, Edm.	.25
☐	4	Adam Deadmarsh, Col.	.75
☐	5	Denis Chasse, Stl.	.50
☐	6	Sergei Krivokrasov, Chi.	.25
☐	7	Ian Laperrière, Stl.	.25
☐	8	Chris Therien, Pha.	.25
☐	9	Brian Savage, Mtl.	.25
☐	10	Todd Marchant, Edm.	.25
☐	11	Jeff O'Neill, Hfd.	.50
☐	12	Brett Lindros, NYI.	.25
☐	13	Kenny Jonsson, Tor.	.25
☐	14	Manny Fernandez (G), Dal.	.25
☐	15	Brian Holzinger, Buf.	.25
☐	16	Niklas Sundstrom, NYR.	.25
☐	17	Eric Dazé, Chi.	.50
☐	18	Chad Kilger, Ana.	.25

ICEQUAKE

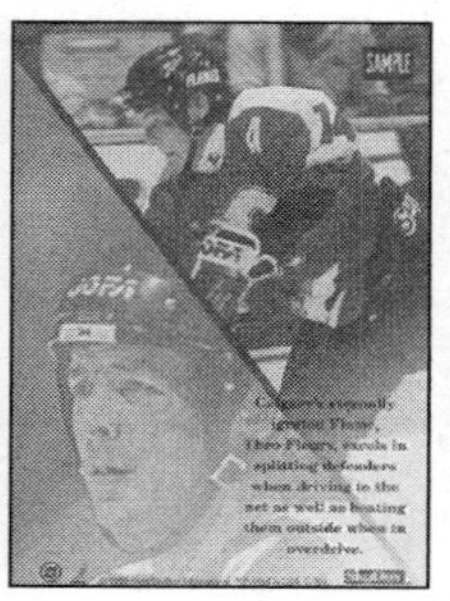

	No.	Player	NRMT-MT
Insert Set (15 cards):			**110.00**
☐	1	Jaromir Jagr, Pgh.	12.00
☐	2	Brett Hull, Stl.	6.00
☐	3	Pavel Bure, Van.	8.00
☐	4	Eric Lindros, Pha.	15.00
☐	5	Mark Messier, NYR.	6.00
☐	6	Wayne Gretzky, L.A.	25.00
☐	7	Mario Lemieux, Pgh.	20.00
☐	8	Peter Forsberg, Col.	12.00
☐	9	Sergei Fedorov, Det.	6.00
☐	10	Cam Neely, Bos.	2.00
☐	11	Owen Nolan, Col.	2.00
☐	12	Alexei Zhamnov, Wpg.	2.00
☐	13	Theoren Fleury, Cgy.	4.00
☐	14	Luc Robitaille, NYR.	2.00
☐	15	Teemu Selänne, Wpg.	8.00

1995 - 96 SKY MINT

This card was available with the redemption of a trade card found in Fleer Metal packs.

Imprint:

	Player	NRMT-MT
☐	Joe Sakic, Col.	50.00

1995 - 96 SKY MOTION

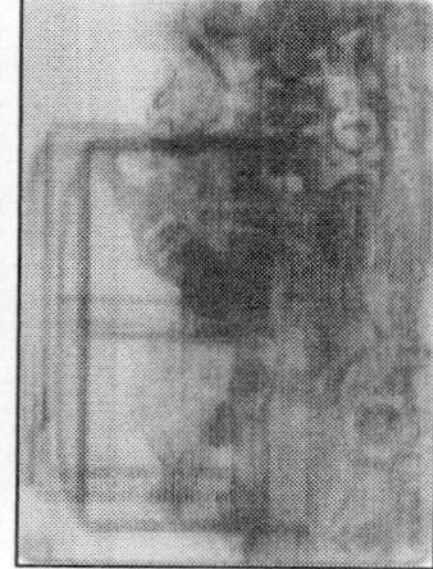

The Jeremy Roenick Sky Motion card was a redemption offer with SkyBox Emotion. The Blaine Lacher Sky Motion card was a redemption in SkyBox Impact packs.

Imprint:

	Player	NRMT-MT
☐	Jeremy Roenick, Chi.	30.00
☐	Blaine Lacher (G), Bos.	15.00

1995 - 96 SLAPSHOT OHL

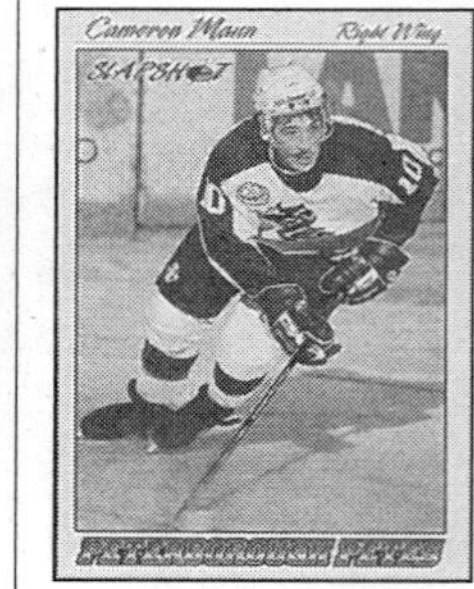

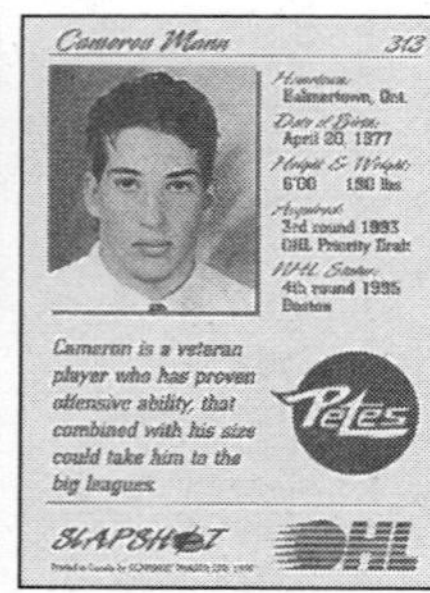

Slapshot: Promotional samples from Toronto Fall Expo.

Imprint: SLAPSHOT IMAGES LTD. 1996 ©

	No.	Player	NRMT-MT
Complete Set (440 cards):			**75.00**
Common Player:			**.15**
		Promo	**NRMT-MT**
☐		Zac Bierk	4.00
☐		Jay McKee	5.00
	No.	**Player**	**NRMT-MT**
☐	01	Title Card/Checklist	.15
☐	02	Checklist Eastern	.15
☐	03	Checklist Central	.15
☐	04	Checklist Western	.15
☐	05	David Branch	.15
☐	06	Bert Templeton, Coach, Barrie	.25
☐	07	Chris George, Barrie	.15
☐	08	Chris Thompson (G), Barrie	.15
☐	09	Quade Lightbody, Barrie	.15
☐	10	Shane Delaronde (G), Barrie	.15
☐	11	Justin Robinson, Barrie	.15
☐	12	Shawn Frappier, Barrie	.15
☐	13	Lucio Nasato, Barrie	.15
☐	14	Jason Payne, Barrie	.15
☐	15	Jason Cannon, Barrie	.15
☐	16	Alexandre Volchkov, Barrie	1.00
☐	17	Daniel Tkaczuk, Barrie	2.75
☐	18	Gerry Lanigan, Barrie	.15
☐	19	Darrell Woodley, Barrie	.15
☐	20	Brian Barker, Barrie	.15
☐	21	Mauricio Alvarez, Barrie	.15
☐	22	Brock Boucher, Barrie	.15
☐	23	Jeff Cowan, Barrie	.15
☐	24	Jan Bulis, Barrie	1.25
☐	25	Jeff Tetzlaff, Barrie	.15
☐	26	Caleb Ward, Barrie	.15
☐	27	Mike White, Barrie	.15
☐	28	Jeremy Miculinic, Barrie	.15
☐	29	Andrew Morrison, Barrie	.15
☐	30	Robert Dubois, Barrie	.15
☐	31	Kory Cooper (G), Belleville	.15
☐	32	Jason Gaggi (G), Belleville	.15
☐	33	Mike Van Volsen, Belleville	.15
☐	34	Paul McInnes, Belleville	.15
☐	35	Harkie Singh, Belleville	.15
☐	36	Robin Lacour, Belleville	.15
☐	37	Jamie Sokolsky, Belleville	.15
☐	38	Marc Dupuis, Belleville	.15
☐	39	Daniel Cleary, Belleville	2.50
☐	40	David Peca, Belleville	.15
☐	41	Adam Robbins, Belleville	.15
☐	42	Steve Tracze, Belleville	.15
☐	43	James Boyd, Belleville	.15
☐	44	Jake Irsag, Belleville	.15
☐	45	Ryan Ready, Belleville	.50
☐	46	Walker McDonald, Belleville	.15
☐	47	Rob Guinn, Belleville	.15
☐	48	Rob Fitzgerald, Belleville	.15
☐	49	Joe Coombs, Belleville	.15
☐	50	Daniel Reja, Belleville	.15
☐	51	Joe Van Volsen, Belleville	.15

☐ 52 Craig Mills, Belleville .25
☐ 53 Murray Hogg, Belleville .15
☐ 54 Andrei Shurupov, Belleville .15
☐ 55 Andrew Williamson, Belleville .15
☐ 56 Mike Minard (G), Detroit .15
☐ 57 Robert Esche (G), Detroit .15
☐ 58 Lee Jinman, Detroit .50
☐ 59 Corey Neilson, Detroit .25
☐ 60 Troy Smith, Detroit .15
☐ 61 Mike Rucinski, Detroit .15
☐ 62 Colin Beardsmore, Detroit .15
☐ 63 Dan Pawlaczyk, Detroit .15
☐ 64 Scott Blair, Detroit .15
☐ 65 Mike Morrone, Detroit .15
☐ 66 Matt Ball, Detroit .15
☐ 67 Steve Dumonski, Detroit .15
☐ 68 Mike Sheehan, Detroit .15
☐ 69 Sean Haggerty, Detroit .50
☐ 70 Andrew Taylor, Detroit .25
☐ 71 Steve Wasylko, Detroit .25
☐ 72 Jan Vodrazka, Detroit .15
☐ 73 Dan Preston, Detroit .15
☐ 74 Jesse Boulerice, Detroit .15
☐ 75 Bryan Berard, Detroit 3.50
☐ 76 Nic Beaudoin, Detroit .25
☐ 77 Tom Buckley, Detroit .15
☐ 78 Mark Cadotte, Detroit .15
☐ 79 Greg Stephan Coach, Detroit .15
☐ 80 Peter DeBoar Coach, Detroit .15
☐ 81 Regan Stocco, Guelph .15
☐ 82 Andy Adams (G), Guelph .15
☐ 83 Brett Thompson (G), Guelph .15
☐ 84 Darryl McArthur, Guelph .15
☐ 85 Ryan Risidore, Guelph .15
☐ 86 Joel Cort, Guelph .15
☐ 87 Chris Hajt, Guelph .50
☐ 88 Bryan McKinney, Guelph .15
☐ 89 Dwayne Hay, Guelph .50
☐ 90 Andrew Clark, Guelph .15
☐ 91 Ryan Robichaud, Guelph .15
☐ 92 Mike Vellinga, Guelph .15
☐ 93 Jamie Wright, Guelph .25
☐ 94 Herbert Vasiljevs, Guelph .15
☐ 95 Dan Cloutier (G), Guelph 2.00
☐ 96 Brian Wesenberg, Guelph .50
☐ 97 Michael Pittman, Guelph .15
☐ 98 Jeff Williams, Guelph .15
☐ 99 Todd Norman, Guelph .50
☐ 100 Brian Willsie, Guelph .15
☐ 101 Jason Jackman, Guelph .15
☐ 102 Mike Lankshear, Guelph .25
☐ 103 Andrew Long, Guelph .15
☐ 104 Nick Bootland, Guelph .15
☐ 105 E.J. McGuire Coach, Guelph .15
☐ 106 Bujar Amidovski (G), Kingston .15
☐ 107 John Hultberg (G), Kingston .15
☐ 108 Eric Olsen, Kingston .15
☐ 109 Chris Allen, Kingston .25
☐ 110 Michael Tilson, Kingston .15
☐ 111 Jeff DaCosta, Kingston .15
☐ 112 Gord Walsh, Kingston .15
☐ 113 Matt Bradley, Kingston .75
☐ 114 Robert Mailloux, Kingston .15
☐ 115 Justin Davis, Kingston .15
☐ 116 Marc Moro, Kingston .25
☐ 117 Cail MacLean, Kingston .15
☐ 118 Jason Sands, Kingston .15
☐ 119 Matt Price, Kingston .15
☐ 120 Zdenek Skorepa, Kingston .15
☐ 121 Jason Morgan, Kingston .15
☐ 122 Mike Oliveira, Kingston .15
☐ 123 Colin Chaulk, Kingston .15
☐ 124 Dylan Taylor, Kingston .15
☐ 125 Kurt Johnston, Kingston .15
☐ 126 Bill Minkhorst, Kingston .15
☐ 127 Wes Swinson, Kingston .15
☐ 128 Adam Fleming, Kingston .15
☐ 129 Chris MacDonald, Coach, Kingston .15
☐ 130 Gary Agnew, Coach, Kingston .15
☐ 131 David Belitski (G), Kitchener .25
☐ 132 Jarrett Rose (G), Kitchener .15
☐ 133 Ryan Mougenel, Kitchener .15
☐ 134 Rob Stanfield, Kitchener .50
☐ 135 Duncan Fader, Kitchener .15
☐ 136 Rob Maric, Kitchener .15
☐ 137 Mark McMahon, Kitchener .15
☐ 138 Serge Payer, Kitchener .15
☐ 139 Paul Traynor, Kitchener .15
☐ 140 Bogdan Rudenko, Kitchener .15
☐ 141 Rob DeCiantis, Kitchener .15
☐ 142 Andrew Dale, Kitchener .25
☐ 143 Jeff Ambrosio, Kitchener .15
☐ 144 Paul Doyle, Kitchener .15
☐ 145 Bryan Duce, Kitchener .15
☐ 146 Jason Byrnes, Kitchener .15
☐ 147 Ryan Pepperall, Kitchener .50
☐ 148 Wes Vander Wal, Kitchener .15
☐ 149 Boyd Devereaux, Kitchener 1.50
☐ 150 Keith Welsh, Kitchener .15
☐ 151 Joe Birch, Kitchener .15
☐ 152 Craig Nelson, Kitchener .15
☐ 153 Brian Hayden, Coach, Kitchener .15
☐ 154 Matt O'Dette, Kitchener .15
☐ 155 Geoff Ward, Coach, Kitchener .15
☐ 156 Frank Ivankovic (G), London .15
☐ 157 Eoin McInerney (G), London .15
☐ 158 Joel Dezainde, London .15
☐ 159 Duncan Dalmad, London .15
☐ 160 Brandon Sugden, London .15
☐ 161 Jamie Wentzell, London .15
☐ 162 Ryan Burgoyne, London .15
☐ 163 Todd Crane, London .15
☐ 164 Chad Cavanagh, London .15
☐ 165 Andrew Fagan, London .15
☐ 166 Ryan Gardner, London .15
☐ 167 Kevin Boyd, London .25
☐ 168 Kevin Barry, London .15
☐ 169 Richard Pitirri, London .15
☐ 170 Adam Colagiacomo, London 1.25
☐ 171 Jason Brooks, London .15
☐ 172 Justin McPolin, London .15
☐ 173 Travis Riggin, London .15
☐ 174 Steve Lowe, London .15
☐ 175 Todd St. Louis, London .15
☐ 176 Kevin Slota, London .15
☐ 177 Ryan McKie, London .15
☐ 178 Corey Isen, London .15
☐ 179 Sasha Cucuz, London .15
☐ 180 Tom Barrett, Coach, London .15
☐ 181 Ken Carroll (G), Niagara Falls .15
☐ 182 Ryan Penney (G), Niagara Falls .15
☐ 183 Jay McKee, Niagara Falls .50
☐ 184 Ryan Taylor, Niagara Falls .15
☐ 185 Jeff Paul, Niagara Falls .25
☐ 186 Jason Ward, Niagara Falls 2.00
☐ 187 Jesse Black, Niagara Falls .15
☐ 188 Steve Nimigon, Niagara Falls .15
☐ 189 Chris Haskett, Niagara Falls .15
☐ 190 Geoff Peters, Niagara Falls .25
☐ 191 Ryan Cirillo, Niagara Falls .15
☐ 192 David Froh, Niagara Falls .15
☐ 193 Jeff Johnstone, Niagara Falls .25
☐ 194 Shane Nash, Niagara Falls .15
☐ 195 Jason Robinson, Niagara Falls .15
☐ 196 Rich Vrataric, Niagara Falls .15
☐ 197 Colin Pepperall, Niagara Falls .50
☐ 198 Craig Jalbert, Niagara Falls .15
☐ 199 Andrew Williamson, Niagara Falls .15
☐ 200 Greg Tymchuk, Niagara Falls .15
☐ 201 Chester Gallant, Niagara Falls .15
☐ 202 Mike Perna, Niagara Falls .15
☐ 203 Adam Nittel, Niagara Falls .15
☐ 204 Dave Burkholder, Coach, Niagara Falls .15
☐ 205 Chris Johnstone, Coach, Niagara Falls .15
☐ 206 Elliott Faust (G), North Bay .15
☐ 207 Scott Roche (G), North Bay .50
☐ 208 Kam White, North Bay .15
☐ 209 Scott Atkins, North Bay .15
☐ 210 Luc Belliveau, North Bay .15
☐ 211 Jamie Vossen, North Bay .15
☐ 212 Ryan MacDonald, North Bay .15
☐ 213 Jim Midgley, North Bay .15
☐ 214 Steven Carpenter, North Bay .15
☐ 215 Jake Martel, North Bay .15
☐ 216 Alex Matvichuk, North Bay .15
☐ 217 Trevor Gallant, North Bay .25
☐ 218 Ryan Gillis, North Bay .15
☐ 219 Kris Cantu, North Bay .15
☐ 220 Mark Provenzano, North Bay .15
☐ 221 Brian Whitley, North Bay .15
☐ 222 Dustin Virag, North Bay .15
☐ 223 Lee Jinman, North Bay .50
☐ 224 Peter McCague, North Bay .15
☐ 225 Herb Bonvie, North Bay .15
☐ 226 Philippe Poirier, North Bay .15
☐ 227 Greg Labenski, North Bay .15
☐ 228 Milan Kostolny, North Bay .15
☐ 229 Ryan Power, North Bay .15
☐ 230 Shane Parker, Coach, North Bay .15
☐ 231 Travis Scott (G), Oshawa .25
☐ 232 Tyrone Garner (G), Oshawa .15
☐ 233 Marty Wilford, Oshawa .25
☐ 234 Ole Anderson, Oshawa .15
☐ 235 Ryan Tocher, Oshawa .15
☐ 236 Nathan Perrott, Oshawa .25
☐ 237 Brandon Coalter, Oshawa .15
☐ 238 John Tripp, Oshawa .50
☐ 239 Jay LeGault, Oshawa .50
☐ 240 Wayne Primeau, Oshawa .50
☐ 241 Trevor Edgar, Oshawa .15
☐ 242 Peter Hogan, Oshawa .25
☐ 243 Warren Holmes, Oshawa .15
☐ 244 Jason Metcalfe, Oshawa .15
☐ 245 Mike Zanutto, Oshawa .15
☐ 246 Jeff Ware, Oshawa .75
☐ 247 Ian MacNeil, Oshawa .15
☐ 248 Jan Snopek, Oshawa .15
☐ 249 Kurt Walsh, Oshawa .25
☐ 250 Marc Savard, Oshawa 1.75
☐ 251 Darcy O'Shea, Oshawa .15
☐ 252 Jason Sweitzer, Oshawa .15
☐ 253 Ryan Lindsay, Oshawa .15
☐ 254 Scott Seiling, Oshawa .15
☐ 255 Stan Butler, Coach, Oshawa .15
☐ 256 Tim Keyes (G), Ottawa .50
☐ 257 Craig Hillier (G), Ottawa .75
☐ 258 Craig Whynot, Ottawa .15
☐ 259 David Bell, Ottawa .15
☐ 260 Rich Bronilla, Ottawa .15
☐ 261 Roy Gray, Ottawa .15
☐ 262 Nick Boynton, Ottawa 1.25
☐ 263 Mike Sim, Ottawa .15
☐ 264 Billy-Jay Johnston, Ottawa .15
☐ 265 Niall Maynard, Ottawa .15
☐ 266 Dan Tudin, Ottawa .15
☐ 267 Jure Kovacevic, Ottawa .15
☐ 268 Ben Gustavson, Ottawa .15
☐ 269 Steve Zoryk, Ottawa .15
☐ 270 Darren Debrie, Ottawa .15
☐ 271 Troy Stonier, Ottawa .15
☐ 272 David Nemirovsky, Ottawa .50
☐ 273 Joel Trottier, Ottawa .50
☐ 274 Mike Lavell, Ottawa .15
☐ 275 Brian Campbell, Ottawa .15
☐ 276 Chris Despatis, Ottawa .15
☐ 277 Sean Blanchard, Ottawa .50
☐ 278 Alyn McCauley, Ottawa 3.00
☐ 279 Chris Pittman, Ottawa .15
☐ 280 Daryl Rivers, Ottawa .15
☐ 281 Brent Johnston (G), Owen Sound .15
☐ 282 Shaun Gallant (G), Owen Sound .15
☐ 283 Shane Kenny, Owen Sound .25
☐ 284 Chris Biagini, Owen Sound .15
☐ 285 Jim Ensom, Owen Sound .15
☐ 286 Marek Babic, Owen Sound .15
☐ 287 Oleg Tsirkounov, Owen Sound .15
☐ 288 Mike Loach, Owen Sound .15
☐ 289 Peter MacKellar, Owen Sound .15
☐ 290 Ryan Davis, Owen Sound .15
☐ 291 John Argiropoulos, Owen Sound .15
☐ 292 Jason Campbell, Owen Sound .15
☐ 293 Ryan Christie, Owen Sound .25
☐ 294 Dan Snyder, Owen Sound .15
☐ 295 Steve Gallace, Owen Sound .15
☐ 296 Scott Seiling, Owen Sound .15
☐ 297 Jeremy Rebek, Owen Sound .15
☐ 298 Adam Mair, Owen Sound .75
☐ 299 Matt Osborne, Owen Sound .15
☐ 300 Mike Galati, Owen Sound .15
☐ 301 Wayne Primeau, Owen Sound .75
☐ 302 Chris Wismer, Owen Sound .15
☐ 303 Larry Paleczny, Owen Sound .15
☐ 304 Kurt Walsh, Owen Sound .25
☐ 305 John Lovell, Coach, Owen Sound .15
☐ 306 Allan Hitchen (G), Peterborough .15

	No.	Player	NRMT-MT
☐	307	Zac Bierk (G), Peterborough	1.25
☐	308	Mike Martone, Peterborough	.15
☐	309	Jonathan Murphy, Peterborough	.15
☐	310	Adrian Murray, Peterborough	.15
☐	311	Rob Giffin, Peterborough	.25
☐	312	Corey Crocker, Peterborough	.15
☐	313	Cameron Mann, Peterborough	2.00
☐	314	Ryan Pawluk, Peterborough	.15
☐	315	Jason MacMillan, Peterborough	.15
☐	316	Shawn Thornton, Peterborough	.15
☐	317	Wade Dawe, Peterborough	.15
☐	318	Eric Landry, Peterborough	.15
☐	319	Steve Hogg, Peterborough	.15
☐	320	Kevin Bolibruck, Peterborough	.25
☐	321	Dave Duerden, Peterborough	.50
☐	322	Mike Williams, Peterborough	.15
☐	323	Andy Johnson, Peterborough	.15
☐	324	Jaret Nixon, Peterborough	.15
☐	325	Evgeny Korolev, Peterborough	.15
☐	326	Matthew Lahey, Peterborough	.15
☐	327	Ryan Schmidt, Peterborough	.15
☐	328	Scott Barney, Peterborough	.75
☐	329	Steve Jones, Peterborough	.15
☐	330	Dave McQueen, Coach, Peterborough	.15
☐	331	Jeff Salajko (G), Sarnia	.15
☐	332	Patrick DesRochers (G), Sarnia	2.00
☐	333	Gerald Moriarity, Sarnia	.15
☐	334	Allan Carr, Sarnia	.15
☐	335	Tom Brown, Sarnia	.15
☐	336	Andy Delmore, Sarnia	.15
☐	337	Darren Mortier, Sarnia	.15
☐	338	Aaron Brand, Sarnia	.25
☐	339	Eric Boulton, Sarnia	.15
☐	340	Jonathan Sim, Sarnia	.50
☐	341	Trevor Letowski, Sarnia	1.00
☐	342	Michael Hanson, Sarnia	.15
☐	343	Todd Miller, Sarnia	.15
☐	344	Brendan Yarema, Sarnia	.15
☐	345	Brad Simms, Sarnia	.15
☐	346	David Nemirovsky, Sarnia	.50
☐	347	Jeff Brown, Sarnia	.50
☐	348	Andrew Proskurnicki, Sarnia	.15
☐	349	Wes Mason, Sarnia	.50
☐	350	Scott Corbett, Sarnia	.15
☐	351	Dave Bourque, Sarnia	.15
☐	352	Sean Brown, Sarnia	.25
☐	353	Marcin Snita, Sarnia	.15
☐	354	Rich Brown, Coach, Sarnia	.15
☐	355	Mark Hunter, Coach, Sarnia	.15
☐	356	Michael Podolka (G), S.S. Marie	.50
☐	357	Dan Cloutier (G), S.S. Marie	2.00
☐	358	Cory Murphy, S.S. Marie	.15
☐	359	Kevin Murnaghan, S.S. Marie	.15
☐	360	André Payette, S.S. Marie	.15
☐	361	Richard Uniacke, S.S. Marie	.65
☐	362	Joe Serosky, S.S. Marie	.15
☐	363	Joe Thornton, S.S. Marie	9.00
☐	364	Ben Schust, S.S. Marie	.15
☐	365	Peter Cava, S.S. Marie	.15
☐	366	Darryl Green, S.S. Marie	.15
☐	367	Trevor Tokarczyk, S.S. Marie	.15
☐	368	Jeff Gies, S.S. Marie	.15
☐	369	Rico Fata, S.S. Marie	3.00
☐	370	Brian Secord, S.S. Marie	.15
☐	371	Scott Cherrey, S.S. Marie	.25
☐	372	Brian Stacey, S.S. Marie	.15
☐	373	Lee Cole, S.S. Marie	.15
☐	374	Richard Jackman, S.S. Marie	.75
☐	375	Jason Doyle, S.S. Marie	.15
☐	376	Brian Stewart, S.S. Marie	.15
☐	377	Blaine Fitzpatrick, S.S. Marie	.15
☐	378	Robert Mulick, S.S. Marie	.15
☐	379	Andy Adams (G), S.S. Marie	.15
☐	380	Joe Paterson, Coach, S.S. Marie	.15
☐	381	Dave MacDonald (G), Sudbury	.15
☐	382	Stephen Valiquette (G), Sudbury	.15
☐	383	Tim Swartz, Sudbury	.15
☐	384	Gregg Lalonde, Sudbury	.15
☐	385	Tyson Flinn, Sudbury	.15
☐	386	Ryan Sly, Sudbury	.15
☐	387	Neal Martin, Sudbury	.15
☐	388	Kevin Hansen, Sudbury	.15
☐	389	Joe Lombardo, Sudbury	.15
☐	390	Darryl Moxam, Sudbury	.15
☐	391	Jeremy Adduono, Sudbury	.15
☐	392	Ryan Shanahan, Sudbury	.15
☐	393	Sean Venedam, Sudbury	.50
☐	394	Andrew Dale, Sudbury	.15
☐	395	Rob Butler, Sudbury	.15
☐	396	Brian Scott, Sudbury	.15
☐	397	Liam MacEachern, Sudbury	.15
☐	398	Luc Gagne, Sudbury	.15
☐	399	Richard Rochefort, Sudbury	.15
☐	400	Noel Burkitt, Sudbury	.15
☐	401	Simon Sherry, Sudbury	.15
☐	402	Brad Domonsky, Sudbury	.15
☐	403	Ron Newhook, Sudbury	.15
☐	404	Serge Dunphy, Sudbury	.15
☐	405	Todd Lalonde, Coach, Sudbury	.15
☐	406	Ryan Gelinas (G), Windsor	.15
☐	407	Terry Joss (G), Windsor	.15
☐	408	Mike Martin, Windsor	.25
☐	409	Chris Van Dyk, Windsor	.25
☐	410	Denis Smith, Windsor	.50
☐	411	Glenn Crawford, Windsor	.50
☐	412	Robert Blain, Windsor	.15
☐	413	Matt Masterson, Windsor	.15
☐	414	Adam Young, Windsor	.15
☐	415	Matt Cooke, Windsor	.50
☐	416	Jeff Zehr, Windsor	.50
☐	417	Wes Ward, Windsor	.15
☐	418	Matt Elich, Windsor	.50
☐	419	Rob Shearer, Windsor	.25
☐	420	Dean Mando, Windsor	.15
☐	421	Chris Kerr, Windsor	.15
☐	422	Vladimir Krechine, Windsor	.15
☐	423	Jeff Martin, Windsor	.50
☐	424	Valery Svoboda, Windsor	.15
☐	425	Dave Geris, Windsor	.25
☐	426	Ryan Pawluk, Windsor	.15
☐	427	Ryan Shaver, Windsor	.15
☐	428	Cameron Kincaid, Windsor	.15
☐	429	Tim Findlay, Windsor	.50
☐	430	Tim Bryan, Windsor	.15
☐	431	Alexandre Volchkov, Barrie	1.00
☐	432	Boyd Devereaux, Kitcherer	1.50
☐	433	Chris Allen, Kingston	.25
☐	434	Jason Doyle, S.S. Marie	.25
☐	435	Wes Mason, Sarnia	.50
☐	436	Chris Hajt, Guelph	.50
☐	437	Kurt Walsh, Owen Sound	.25
☐	438	Glen Crawford, Windsor	.50
☐	439	Jeff Brown, Sarnia	.50
☐	440	Geoff Peters, Niagara Falls	.25

AUTOGRAPHED INSERT

Bierk's autograph has a red hockey stick stamp on the face.

	Player	NRMT-MT
☐	Zac Bierk (G), Autographed	40.00

PROMO INSERTS

These cards were also handed out as promos after the release of product.

	Player	NRMT-MT
☐	Zac Bierk (G), Peterborough	4.00
☐	Nick Boynton, Ottawa	3.00
☐	Adam Colagiacomo, London	8.00
☐	Sean Haggerty, Detroit	6.00
☐	Cameron Mann, Peterborough	6.00
☐	Mike Martin, Windsor	3.00
☐	Jay McKee, Nigara Falls	6.00
☐	Ryan Pepperall, Kitchener	5.00
☐	Scott Roche (G), North Bay	5.00

1995 - 96 SP

Imprint: © 1996 THE UPPER DECK COMPANY

Complete Set (188 cards): 55.00

Common Player: .20

	No.	Player	NRMT-MT
☐	66	Wayne Gretzky, A.S. (L.A.)	12.00

	No.	Player	NRMT-MT
☐	1	Paul Kariya, Ana.	3.50
☐	2	Teemu Selänne, Ana.	1.50
☐	3	Guy Hebert (G), Ana.	.50
☐	4	Steve Rucchin, Ana.	.20
☐	5	Ray Bourque, Bos.	1.25
☐	6	Cam Neely, Bos.	.50
☐	7	Adam Oates, Bos.	.75
☐	**8**	**Kyle McLaren, Bos., RC**	**.20**
☐	9	Bill Ranford (G), Bos.	.50
☐	10	Shawn McEachern, Bos.	.20
☐	11	Don Sweeney, Bos.	.20
☐	12	Pat LaFontaine, Buf.	.50
☐	13	Dominik Hasek (G), Buf.	1.75
☐	**14**	**Brian Holzinger, Buf., RC**	**.20**
☐	15	Alexei Zhitnik, Buf.	.20
☐	16	Theoren Fleury, Cgy.	.75
☐	17	Cory Stillman, Cgy.	.20
☐	18	German Titov, Cgy.	.20
☐	19	Phil Housley, Cgy.	.20
☐	20	Michael Nylander, Cgy.	.20
☐	21	Trevor Kidd (G), Cgy.	.50
☐	22	Eric Dazé, Chi.	.50
☐	23	Chris Chelios, Chi.	1.00
☐	24	Jeremy Roenick, Chi.	.75
☐	25	Gary Suter, Chi.	.20
☐	26	Bernie Nicholls, Chi.	.20
☐	27	Ed Belfour (G), Chi.	.50
☐	28	Tony Amonte, Chi.	.50
☐	29	Peter Forsberg, Col.	2.50
☐	30	Partick Roy (G), Col.	4.00
☐	31	Joe Sakic, Col.	2.00
☐	32	Sandis Ozolinsh, Col.	.50
☐	33	Adam Deadmarsh, Col.	.20
☐	34	Stéphane Fiset (G), Col.	.50
☐	35	Claude Lemieux, Col.	.20
☐	36	Mike Modano, Dal.	1.25
☐	37	Kevin Hatcher, Dal.	.20
☐	38	Joe Nieuwendyk, Dal.	.50
☐	39	Todd Harvey, Dal.	.20
☐	40	Derian Hatcher, Dal.	.50
☐	41	Jere Lehtinen, Dal.	.50
☐	42	Nicklas Lidström, Det.	.50
☐	**43**	**Mathieu Dandenault, Det., RC**	**.20**
☐	44	Sergei Fedorov, Det.	1.25
☐	45	Paul Coffey, Det.	.50
☐	46	Steve Yzerman, Det.	2.50
☐	47	Keith Primeau, Det.	.50
☐	48	Chris Osgood (G), Det.	1.00
☐	49	Vyacheslav Kozlov, Det.	.20
☐	50	Doug Weight, Edm.	.75
☐	51	Jason Arnott, Edm.	.50
☐	**52**	**Miroslav Satan, Edm., RC**	**.20**
☐	53	Zdeno Ciger, Edm.	.20
☐	54	Curtis Joseph (G), Edm.	1.50
☐	55	Scott Mellanby, Fla.	.20
☐	56	John Vanbiesbrouck (G), Fla.	1.50
☐	57	Jody Hull, Fla.	.20
☐	58	Ed Jovanovski, Fla.	.50
☐	**59**	**Radek Dvorak, Fla., RC**	**.20**
☐	60	Rob Niedermayer, Fla.	.20
☐	61	Andrew Cassels, Hfd.	.20
☐	62	Brendan Shanahan, Hfd.	1.50

	No.	Player	Price
☐	63	Nelson Emerson, Hfd.	.20
☐	64	Jeff O'Neill, Hfd.	.50
☐	65	Sean Burke (G), Hfd.	.50
☐	66	Craig Johnson, L.A.	.20
☐	67	Dimitri Khristich, L.A.	.20
☐	68	Vitali Yachmenev, L.A.	.20
☐	**69**	**Aki Berg, L.A., RC**	**.20**
☐	70	Byron Dafoe (G), L.A.	.20
☐	71	Pierre Turgeon, Mtl.	.50
☐	72	Mark Recchi, Mtl.	.50
☐	73	Saku Koivu, Mtl.	1.75
☐	74	Valeri Bure, Mtl.	.20
☐	75	Vincent Damphousse, Mtl.	.75
☐	76	Jocelyn Thibault (G), Mtl.	.75
☐	77	Patrice Brisebois, Mtl.	.20
☐	78	John MacLean, N.J.	.20
☐	79	Martin Brodeur (G), N.J.	1.75
☐	80	Steve Thomas, N.J.	.20
☐	81	Scott Stevens, N.J.	.20
☐	82	Bill Guerin, N.J.	.50
☐	**83**	**Petr Sykora, N.J., RC**	**.20**
☐	84	Scott Niedermayer, N.J.	.50
☐	85	Stéphane Richer, N.J.	.20
☐	86	Zigmund Palffy, NYI.	1.00
☐	87	Travis Green, NYI.	.20
☐	**88**	**Todd Bertuzzi, NYI., RC**	**.75**
☐	89	Mathieu Schneider, NYI.	.20
☐	90	Eric Fichaud (G), NYI.	.20
☐	91	Bryan McCabe, NYI.	.20
☐	92	Mark Messier, NYR.	1.25
☐	93	Pat Verbeek, NYR.	.20
☐	94	Brian Leetch, NYR.	.75
☐	95	Mike Richter (G), NYR.	.75
☐	96	Niklas Sundstrom, NYR.	.20
☐	97	Luc Robitaille, NYR.	.20
☐	98	Adam Graves, NYR.	.20
☐	99	Alexei Kovalev, NYR.	.20
☐	**100**	**Daniel Alfredsson, Ott., RC**	**1.50**
☐	101	Alexei Yashin, Ott.	1.00
☐	102	Radek Bonk, Ott.	.20
☐	103	Alexandre Daigle, Ott.	.50
☐	104	Damian Rhodes (G), Ott.	.20
☐	**105**	**Antti Törmänen, Ott., RC**	.20
☐	106	Eric Lindros, Pha.	3.50
☐	107	Mikael Renberg, Pha.	.20
☐	108	John LeClair, Pha.	1.25
☐	109	Ron Hextall (G), Pha.	.50
☐	110	Rod Brind'Amour, Pha.	.50
☐	111	Joel Otto, Pha.	.20
☐	112	Eric Desjardins, Pha.	.20
☐	113	Mario Lemieux, Pgh.	4.00
☐	114	Jaromir Jagr, Pgh.	2.50
☐	115	Ron Francis, Pgh.	.75
☐	116	Markus Naslund, Pgh.	.20
☐	117	Sergei Zubov, Pgh.	.50
☐	118	Tomas Sandström, Pgh.	.20
☐	119	Tom Barrasso (G), Pgh.	.50
☐	120	Richard Park, Pgh.	.20
☐	121	Brett Hull, Stl.	1.25
☐	122	Shayne Corson, Stl.	.50
☐	123	Dale Hawerchuk, Stl.	.50
☐	124	Chris Pronger, Stl.	.50
☐	125	Al MacInnis, Stl.	.50
☐	126	Grant Fuhr (G), Stl.	.50
☐	127	Wayne Gretzky, Stl.	6.00
☐	128	Geoff Courtnall, Stl.	.20
☐	129	Owen Nolan, S.J.	.50
☐	130	Ray Sheppard, S.J.	.20
☐	131	Chris Terreri (G), S.J.	.20
☐	**132**	**Marcus Ragnarsson, S.J., RC**	**.20**
☐	133	Jeff Friesen, S.J.	.50
☐	134	Doug Bodger, S.J.	.20
☐	135	Roman Hamrlik, T.B.	.50
☐	136	Petr Klima, T.B.	.20
☐	137	Daren Puppa (G), T.B.	.20
☐	138	Aaron Gavey, T.B.	.20
☐	**139**	**Daymond Langkow, T.B., RC**	**.20**
☐	140	Alexander Selivanov, T.B.	.20
☐	141	Mats Sundin, Tor.	1.25
☐	142	Kirk Muller, Tor.	.20
☐	143	Larry Murphy, Tor.	.50
☐	144	Doug Gilmour, Tor.	.75
☐	145	Darby Hendrickson, Tor.	.20
☐	146	Félix Potvin (G), Tor.	1.50
☐	147	Kenny Jonsson, Tor.	.20
☐	148	Alexander Mogilny, Van.	.75
☐	149	Pavel Bure, Van.	1.50
☐	150	Trevor Linden, Van.	.50
☐	151	Corey Hirsch (G), Van.	.20
☐	152	Kirk McLean (G), Van.	.50
☐	153	Esa Tikkanen, Van.	.20
☐	154	Cliff Ronning, Van.	.20
☐	155	Peter Bondra, Wsh.	1.00
☐	156	Jim Carey (G), Wsh.	.20
☐	157	Michal Pivonka, Wsh.	.20
☐	158	Joé Juneau, Wsh.	.20
☐	159	Dale Hunter, Wsh.	.20
☐	160	Steve Konowalchuk, Wsh.	.20
☐	161	Stefan Ustorf, Wsh.	.20
☐	162	Brendan Witt, Wsh.	.20
☐	163	Chad Kilger, Wpg.	.20
☐	164	Keith Tkachuk, Wpg.	1.00
☐	165	Deron Quint, Wpg.	.20
☐	166	Oleg Tverdovsky, Wpg.	.20
☐	167	Alexei Zhamnov, Wpg.	.50
☐	168	Igor Korolev, Wpg.	.20
☐	169	Wade Redden, Cdn.	.50
☐	170	Jarome Iginla, Cdn.	1.25
☐	171	Christian Dubé, Cdn.	.50
☐	172	Jason Podollan, Cdn.	.25
☐	173	Alyn McCauley, Cdn.	1.25
☐	174	Nolan Baumgartner, Cdn.	.25
☐	175	Jason Botterill, Cdn.	.25
☐	**176**	**Chris Phillips, Cdn., RC**	**2.00**
☐	177	Dimitri Nabokov, Rus.	.25
☐	178	Andrei Petrunin, Rus.	.25
☐	179	Alexander Korolyuk, Rus.	.25
☐	180	Sergei Samsonov, Rus.	2.50
☐	**181**	**Ilja Gorokhov, Rus., RC**	**.25**
☐	**182**	**Alexei Kolkunov, Rus., RC**	**.25**
☐	**183**	**Samuel Pahlsson, Swe., RC**	**.25**
☐	184	Mattias Ohlund, Swe.	1.25
☐	**185**	**Markus Nilsson, Swe., RC**	**.50**
☐	**186**	**Daniel Tjarnkvist, Swe., RC**	**.25**
☐	**187**	**Per-Anton Lundstrom, Swe., RC**	**.25**
☐	**188**	**Fredrik Loven, Swe., RC**	**.25**

GREAT CONNECTIONS

Each of these inserts are die-cut.

	No.	Player	NRMT-MT
☐	GC1	Wayne Gretzky	125.00
☐	GC2	Sergei Samsonov	65.00

GRETZKY RECORD COLLECTION

Cards G1-G9 were inserted into Upper Deck Collector's Choice packs, cards G10-G13 were inserted in Upper Deck Series One packs and cards G14-G17 were inserted in Upper Deck Series Two packs.

Insert Set (4 cards): 100.00

	No.	Player	NRMT-MT
☐		Checklist	25.00
☐	G18	Wayne Gretzky, Most Goals	30.00
☐	G19	Wayne Gretzky, Most Assists	30.00
☐	G20	Wayne Gretzky, Most Points	30.00

SP HOLOVIEWS

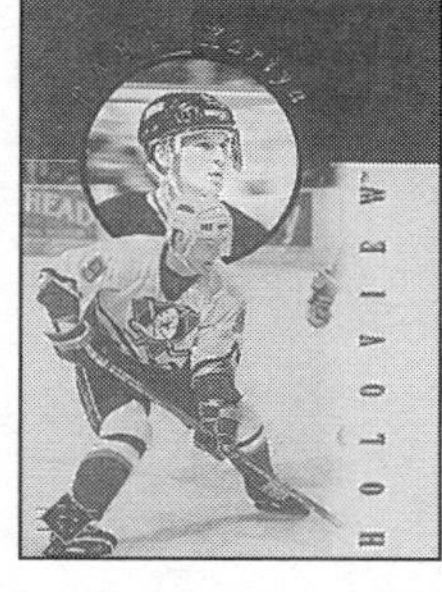

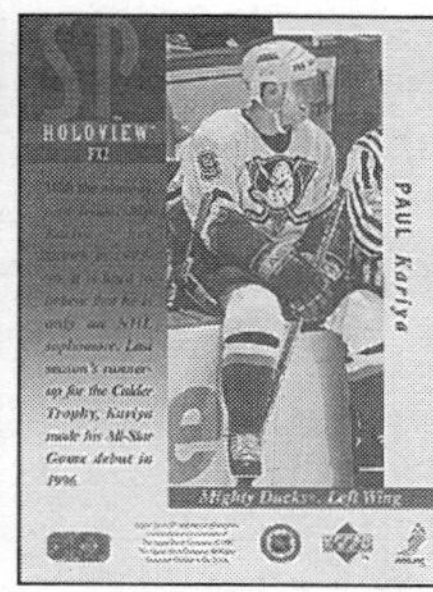

These inserts have two versions: the regular insert and a die-cut Special FX parallel.

Insert Set (20 cards): 120.00 600.00

	No.	Player	Reg.	Die-Cut
☐ ☐	FX1	Teemu Selänne, Ana.	7.00	35.00
☐ ☐	FX2	Paul Kariya, Ana.	12.50	65.00
☐ ☐	FX3	Chris Chelios, Chi.	4.00	20.00
☐ ☐	FX4	Peter Forsberg, Col	10.00	50.00
☐ ☐	FX5	Sergei Fedorov, Det.	5.00	25.00
☐ ☐	FX6	Paul Coffey, Det.	2.00	10.00
☐ ☐	FX7	Steve Yzerman, Det.	10.00	50.00
☐ ☐	FX8	Jason Arnott, Edm.	2.00	10.00
☐ ☐	FX9	Doug Weight, Edm.	3.00	15.00
☐ ☐	FX10	Wayne Gretzky, L.A.	20.00	100.00
☐ ☐	FX11	Vitali Yachmenev, L.A.	1.50	8.00
☐ ☐	FX12	Martin Brodeur (G), N.J.	7.00	35.00
☐ ☐	FX13	Scott Stevens, N.J.	1.50	8.00
☐ ☐	FX14	Mark Messier, NYR.	5.00	125.00
☐ ☐	FX15	Daniel Alfredsson, Ott.	4.00	20.00
☐ ☐	FX16	Eric Lindros, Pha.	12.50	65.00
☐ ☐	FX17	Mario Lemieux, Pgh.	15.00	75.00
☐ ☐	FX18	Jaromir Jagr, Pgh.	10.00	50.00
☐ ☐	FX19	Shayne Corson, Stl.	2.00	10.00
☐ ☐	FX20	Pavel Bure, Van.	7.00	35.00

STARS

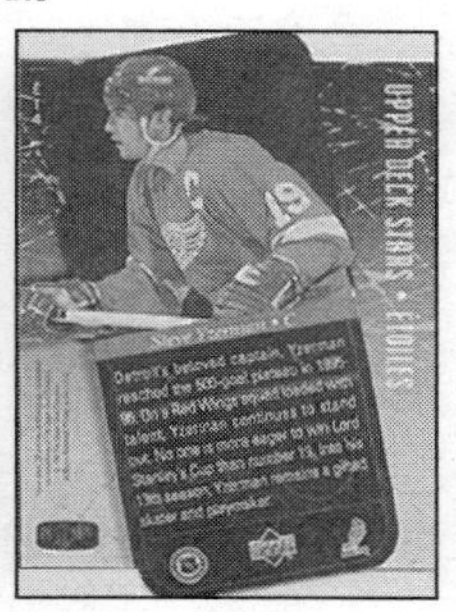

These inserts have two versions: the regular silver insert and a gold parallel. Both versions are die-cut.

Insert Set (30 cards): 85.00 85.00

	No.	Player	Gold	Silver
☐ ☐	E1	Paul Kariya, Ana.	65.00	6.50
☐ ☐	E2	Teemu Selänne, Ana.	35.00	3.50
☐ ☐	E3	Ray Bourque, Bos.	25.00	2.50
☐ ☐	E4	Cam Neely, Bos.	10.00	1.00
☐ ☐	E5	Pat LaFontaine, Buf.	10.00	1.00
☐ ☐	E6	Theoren Fleury, Cgy.	15.00	1.50
☐ ☐	E7	Jeremy Roenick, Chi.	15.00	1.50
☐ ☐	E8	Joe Sakic, Col.	40.00	4.00
☐ ☐	E9	Patrick Roy, Col.	80.00	8.00
☐ ☐	E10	Peter Forsberg, Col.	50.00	5.00
☐ ☐	E11	Mike Modano, Dal.	25.00	2.50
☐ ☐	E12	Sergei Fedorov, Det.	25.00	2.50
☐ ☐	E13	Paul Coffey, Det.	10.00	1.00
☐ ☐	E14	Steve Yzerman, Det.	50.00	5.00
☐ ☐	E15	Pierre Turgeon, Mtl.	10.00	1.00
☐ ☐	E16	Brendan Shanahan, Hfd.	30.00	3.00
☐ ☐	E17	Wayne Gretzky, Stl.	100.00	10.00
☐ ☐	E18	Martin Brodeur, N.J.	35.00	3.50
☐ ☐	E19	Mark Messier, NYR.	25.00	2.50
☐ ☐	E20	Brian Leetch, NYR.	15.00	1.50
☐ ☐	E21	Eric Lindros, Pha.	65.00	6.50
☐ ☐	E22	Mario Lemieux, Pgh.	80.00	8.00
☐ ☐	E23	Jaromir Jagr, Pgh.	50.00	5.00
☐ ☐	E24	Brett Hull, Stl.	25.00	2.50

	No.	Player		
☐☐	E25	Roman Hamrlik, T.B.	10.00	1.00
☐☐	E26	Mats Sundin, Tor.	25.00	2.50
☐☐	E27	Félix Potvin, Tor.	25.00	2.50
☐☐	E28	Alexander Mogilny, Van.	15.00	1.50
☐☐	E29	Pavel Bure, Van.	35.00	3.50
☐☐	E30	Keith Tkachuk, Wpg.	20.00	2.00

1995 - 96 SUPER STICKERS

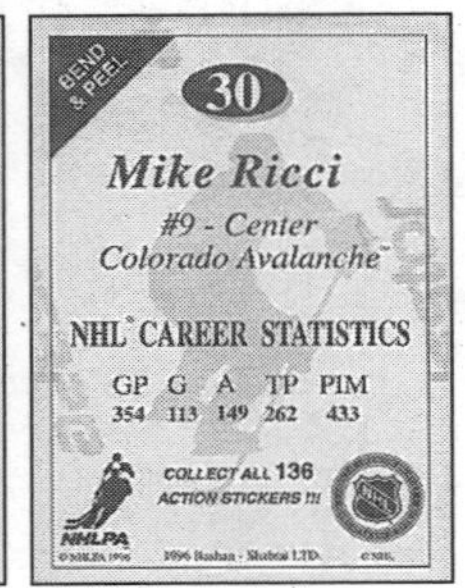

These stickers were issed by Imperial Toy. There is no set album. Team Decals feature a team logo and the facsimile of a player's signature.

Imprint: 1996 Bashan - Shabtai LTD.

Complete Set (136 cards): 35.00

Common Player: .15

	No.	Player	NRMT-MT
☐	1	Anaheim Mighty Ducks/Oleg Tverdovsky	.15
☐	2	Paul Kariya, Ana.	2.00
☐	3	Chad Kilger, Ana.	.15
☐	4	Oleg Tverdovsky, Ana.	.15
☐	5	Boston Bruins/Adam Oates	.25
☐	6	Ray Bourque, Bos.	.75
☐	7	Cam Neely, Bos.	.25
☐	8	Adam Oates, Bos.	.35
☐	9	Kevin Stevens, Bos.	.15
☐	10	Buffalo Sabres/Dominik Hasek	.35
☐	11	Pat LaFontaine, Buf.	.25
☐	12	Dominik Hasek (G), Buf.	.75
☐	13	Alexei Zhitnik, Buf.	.15
☐	14	Calgary Flames/Theoren Fleury	.25
☐	15	Theoren Fleury, Cgy.	.35
☐	16	Phil Housley, Cgy.	.15
☐	17	Trevor Kidd (G), Cgy.	.25
☐	18	Joe Nieuwendyk, Cgy.	.25
☐	19	Zarley Zalapski, Cgy.	.15
☐	20	Chicago Blackhawks/Ed Belfour	.25
☐	21	Jeremy Roenick, Chi.	.35
☐	22	Chris Chelios, Chi.	.50
☐	23	Ed Belfour (G), Chi.	.35
☐	24	Joe Murphy, Chi.	.15
☐	25	Patrick Poulin, Chi.	.15
☐	26	Colorado Avalanche/Peter Forsberg	.75
☐	27	Joe Sakic, Col.	1.25
☐	28	Peter Forsberg, Col.	1.50
☐	29	Sandis Ozolinsh, Col.	.25
☐	30	Mike Ricci, Col.	.15
☐	31	Valeri Kamensky, Col.	.25
☐	32	Dallas Stars/Mike Modano	.35
☐	33	Mike Modano, Dal.	.75
☐	34	Kevin Hatcher, Dal.	.15
☐	35	Andy Moog (G), Dal.	.25
☐	36	Detroit Red Wings/Sergei Fedorov	.25
☐	37	Steve Yzerman, Det.	1.50
☐	38	Sergei Fedorov, Det.	.50
☐	39	Paul Coffey, Det.	.25
☐	40	Keith Primeau, Det.	.25
☐	41	Nicklas Lidström, Det.	.25.15
☐	42	Edmonton Oilers/Bill Ranford	.25
☐	43	Doug Weight, Edm.	.35
☐	44	Jason Arnott, Edm.	.25
☐	45	Bill Ranford (G), Edm.	.25
☐	46	Florida Panthers/John Vanbiesbrouck	.50
☐	47	John Vanbiesbrouck (G), Fla.	.85
☐	48	Stu Barnes, Fla.	.15
☐	49	Scott Mellanby, Fla.	.15
☐	50	Rob Niedermayer, Fla.	.15
☐	51	Hartford Whalers/G.Sanderson	.15
☐	52	Brendan Shanahan, Hfd.	.85
☐	53	Geoff Sanderson, Hfd.	.15
☐	54	Sean Burke (G), Hfd.	.25
☐	55	Jeff O'Neill, Hfd.	.15
☐	56	Los Angeles Kings/Rob Blake	.25
☐	57	Wayne Gretzky, L.A.	3.00
☐	58	Rob Blake, L.A.	.25
☐	59	Rick Tocchet, L.A.	.15
☐	60	Dmitri Khristich, L.A.	.15
☐	61	Kelly Hrudey (G), L.A.	.15
☐	62	Montréal Canadiens/Vincent Damphousse	.25
☐	63	Pierre Turgeon, Mtl.	.25
☐	64	Mark Recchi, Mtl.	.25
☐	65	Saku Koivu, Mtl.	1.00
☐	66	Patrick Roy (G), Mtl.	2.50
☐	67	Vincent Damphousse, Mtl.	.35
☐	68	New Jersey Devils/Scott Stevens	.15
☐	69	Stéphane Richer, N.J.	.15
☐	70	Martin Brodeur (G), N.J.	1.00
☐	71	Scott Niedermayer, N.J.	.25
☐	72	Scott Stevens, N.J.	.15
☐	73	New York Islanders/Mathieu Schneider	.15
☐	74	Kirk Muller, NYI.	.15
☐	75	Mathieu Schneider, NYI.	.15
☐	76	Derek King, NYI.	.15
☐	77	Wendel Clark, NYI.	.25
☐	78	New York Rangers/Mark Messier	.35
☐	79	Brian Leetch, NYR.	.35
☐	80	Mark Messier, NYR.	.75
☐	81	Alexei Kovalev, NYR.	.15
☐	82	Luc Robitaille, NYR.	.25
☐	83	Mike Richter (G), NYR.	.35
☐	84	Ottawa Senators/Radek Bonk	.15
☐	85	Dan Quinn, Ott.	.15
☐	86	Alexandre Daigle, Ott.	.25
☐	87	Steve Duchesne, Ott.	.15
☐	88	Radek Bonk, Ott.	.15
☐	89	Philadelphia Flyers/player signature	.15
☐	90	Eric Lindros, Pha.	2.00
☐	91	Mikael Renberg, Pha.	.15
☐	92	John LeClair, Pha.	.75
☐	93	Eric Desjardins, Pha.	.15
☐	94	Rod Brind'Amour, Pha.	.25
☐	95	Pittsburgh Penguins/Ron Francis	.25
☐	96	Jaromir Jagr, Pgh.	1.50
☐	97	Mario Lemieux, Pgh.	2.50
☐	98	Ron Francis, Pgh.	.35
☐	99	Sergei Zubov, Pgh.	.25
☐	100	St. Louis Blues/Al MacInnis	.25
☐	101	Brett Hull, Stl.	.75
☐	102	Al MacInnis, Stl.	.25
☐	103	Dale Hawerchuk, Stl.	.25
☐	104	Chris Pronger, Stl.	.25
☐	105	San Jose Sharks/Craig Janney	.15
☐	106	Craig Janney, S.J.	.15
☐	107	Pat Falloon, S.J.	.15
☐	108	Arturs Irbe (G), S.J.	.15
☐	109	Ulf Dahlen, S.J.	.15
☐	110	Owen Nolan, S.J.	.25
☐	111	Tampa Bay Lightning/Brian Bradley	.15
☐	112	Roman Hamrlik, T.B.	.25
☐	113	Brian Bradley, T.B.	.15
☐	114	Chris Gratton, T.B.	.25
☐	115	Brian Bellows, T.B.	.15
☐	116	Toronto Maple Leafs/Doug Gilmour	.25
☐	117	Doug Gilmour, Tor.	.35
☐	118	Mats Sundin, Tor.	.75
☐	119	Dave Andreychuk, Tor.	.15
☐	120	Félix Potvin (G), Tor.	.75
☐	121	Larry Murphy, Tor.	.25
☐	122	Vancouver Canucks/Alexander Mogilny	.25
☐	123	Pavel Bure, Van.	1.00
☐	124	Alexander Mogilny, Van.	.50
☐	125	Trevor Linden, Van.	.25
☐	126	Jeff Brown, Van.	.15
☐	127	Kirk McLean (G), Van.	.25
☐	128	Washington Capitals/Jim Carey	.15
☐	129	Joé Juneau, Wsh.	.15
☐	130	Peter Bondra, Wsh.	.50
☐	131	Jim Carey (G), Wsh.	.15
☐	132	Calle Johansson, Wsh.	.15
☐	133	Winnipeg Jets/Teemu Selänne	.50
☐	134	Teemu Selänne, Wpg.	1.00
☐	135	Alexei Zhamnov, Wpg.	.25
☐	136	Keith Tkachuk, Wpg.	.50

DIE-CUT DECALS

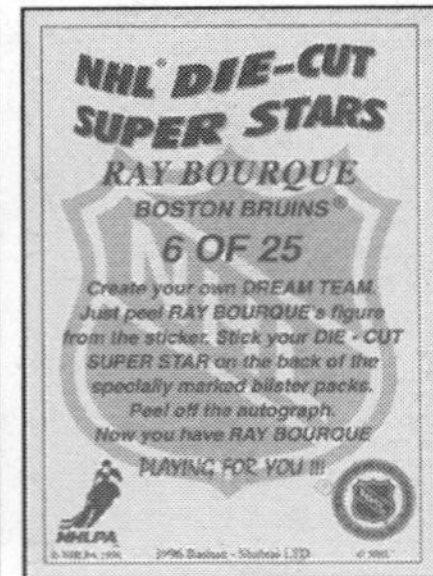

Insert Set (25 cards): 20.00

	No.	Player	NRMT-MT
☐	1	Pierre Turgeon, Mtl.	.50
☐	2	Patrick Roy (G), Mtl.	4.00
☐	3	Pat LaFontaine, Buf.	.50
☐	4	Joe Sakic, Que.	2.00
☐	5	Paul Coffey, Det.	.50
☐	6	Ray Bourque, Bos.	1.25
☐	7	Brian Leetch, NYR.	.75
☐	8	Joé Juneau, Wsh.	.25
☐	9	Jeremy Roenick, Chi.	.75
☐	10	Chris Chelios, Chi.	1.00
☐	11	Brett Hull, Stl.	1.25
☐	12	Paul Kariya, Ana.	3.00
☐	13	Jason Arnott, Edm.	.50
☐	14	Pavel Bure, Van.	1.75
☐	15	Steve Duchesne, Ott.	.25
☐	16	Martin Brodeur (G), N.J.	1.75
☐	17	Eric Lindros, Pha.	3.00
☐	18	Mikael Renberg, Pha.	.25
☐	19	Félix Potvin (G), Tor.	1.25
☐	20	Roman Hamrlik, T.B.	.50
☐	21	Wayne Gretzky, L.A.	5.00
☐	22	Brendan Shanahan, Stl.	1.50
☐	23	Jaromir Jagr, Pgh.	2.50
☐	24	Mario Lemieux, Pgh.	4.00
☐	25	Steve Yzerman, Det.	2.50

1995 - 96 TOPPS

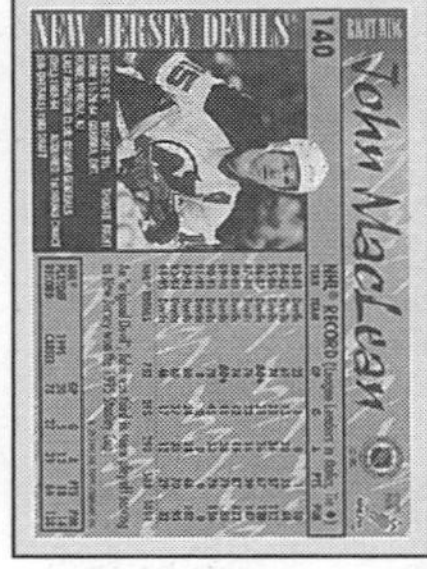

O-Pee-Chee parallel cards for numbers 1-385 were inserted into Series Two packs. O-Pee-Chee cards 257, 326, 333, 351, 359 and 373-385 are short printed.

Marquee Men cards have a third parallel called Power Boosters which were inserted in Series One (1-22) and Series Two (373-383) packs. Power Booster are printed on a thicker card stock.

Imprint: © 1996 THE TOPPS COMPANY, INC.

	PB	Reg.	OPC
Complete Set (385 cards):	.-	30.00	800.00
Series One Power Booster Set (22 cards)	165.00	.-	.-
Series Two Power Booster Set (11 cards)	120.00	.-	.-
Common Player:		.10	.50

	No.	Player	PB	Reg.	OPC
☐☐☐	1	Eric Lindros, Pha.	20.00	1.00	15.00
☐☐☐	2	Dominik Hasek (G), Buf.	10.00	.50	7.50
☐☐☐	3	Jeremy Roenick, Chi.	4.00	.20	1.00
☐☐☐	4	Paul Coffey, Det.	4.00	.25	1.00
☐☐☐	5	Mark Messier, NYI.	8.00	.35	5.00
☐☐☐	6	Peter Bondra, Wsh.	6.00	.25	2.50
☐☐☐	7	Paul Kariya, Ana.	20.00	1.00	15.00
☐☐☐	8	Chris Chelios, Chi.	6.00	.25	2.50
☐☐☐	9	Martin Brodeur (G), N.J.	10.00	.50	7.50
☐☐☐	10	Brett Hull, Stl.	8.00	.35	5.00
☐☐☐	11	Mike Vernon (G), Det.	4.00	.25	1.00
☐☐☐	12	Trevor Linden, Van.	4.00	.25	1.00

	No.	Player			
□□□	13	Pat LaFontaine, Buf.	4.00	.25	1.00
□□□	14	Geoff Sanderson, Hfd.	3.00	.10	.50
□□□	15	Cam Neely, Bos.	4.00	.25	1.00
□□□	16	Brendan Shanahan, Hfd.	9.00	.35	6.00
□□□	17	Jason Arnott, Edm.	3.00	.25	1.00
□□□	18	Mikael Renberg, Pha.	3.00	.10	.50
□□□	19	Mats Sundin, Tor.	8.00	.35	5.00
□□□	20	Pavel Bure, Van.	10.00	.50	7.50
□□□	21	Pierre Turgeon, Mtl.	4.00	.25	1.00
□□□	22	Alexei Zhamnov, Wpg.	4.00	.25	1.00
□□	23	Blaine Lacher (G), Bos.		.10	.50
□□	**24**	**Brian Holzinger, Buf., RC**		**.25**	**.75**
□□	25	Theoren Fleury, Cgy.		.35	2.00
□□	26	Eric Dazé, Chi.		.25	1.00
□□	27	Mike Kennedy, Dal.		.10	.50
□□	28	Darren McCarty, Det.		.10	.50
□□	29	Todd Marchant, Edm.		.10	.50
□□	30	Andrew Cassels, Hfd.		.10	.50
□□	31	Rob Niedermayer, Fla.		.10	.50
□□	32	Eric Lacroix, L.A.		.10	.50
□□	33	Steve Rucchin, Ana.		.10	.50
□□	34	Turner Stevenson, Mtl.		.10	.50
□□	35	Sergei Brylin, N.J.		.10	.50
□□	36	Mathieu Schneider, NYI.		.10	.50
□□	37	Pat Verbeek, NYR.		.10	.50
□□	**38**	**Steve Larouche, Ott., RC**		**.10**	**.50**
□□	39	Rod Brind'Amour, Pha.		.25	1.00
□□	40	Luc Robitaille, Pgh.		.25	1.00
□□	41	Brett Lindros, NYI.		.10	.50
□□	42	Shean Donovan, S.J.		.10	.50
□□	43	David Roberts, Stl.		.10	.50
□□	44	Cory Cross, T.B.		.10	.50
□□	45	Todd Warriner, Tor.		.10	.50
□□	46	John Namestnikov, Van.		.10	.50
□□	47	Sergei Gonchar, Wsh.		.10	.50
□□	48	Nikolai Khabibulin (G), Wpg.		.35	2.00
□□	49	Alexei Zhitnik, Buf.		.10	.50
□□	50	Ray Bourque, Bos.		.50	5.00
□□	51	Paul Kruse, Cgy.		.10	.50
□□	52	Murray Craven, Chi.		.10	.50
□□	53	Andy Moog (G), Dal.		.25	1.00
□□	54	Keith Primeau, Det.		.25	1.00
□□	55	Shayne Corson, Edm.		.25	1.00
□□	56	Johan Garpenlov, Fla.		.10	.50
□□	57	Marek Malik, Hfd.		.10	.50
□□	58	Tony Granato, L.A.		.10	.50
□□	59	Bob Corkum, Ana.		.10	.50
□□	60	Patrick Roy (G), Mtl.		1.50	25.00
□□	**61**	**Chris McAlpine, N.J., RC**		**.10**	**.50**
□□	**62**	**Chris Marinucci, NYI., RC**		**.10**	**.50**
□□	63	Jeff Beukeboom, NYR.		.10	.50
□□	64	Radek Bonk, Ott.		.10	.50
□□	65	John LeClair, Pha.		.50	5.00
□□	66	Len Barrie, Pgh.		.10	.50
□□	67	Teppo Numminen, Pho.		.10	.50
□□	68	Ray Whitney, S.J.		.10	.50
□□	69	Jeff Norton, Stl.		.10	.50
□□	70	Chris Gratton, T.B.		.25	1.00
□□	71	Benoît Hogue, Tor.		.10	.50
□□	72	Bret Hedican, Van.		.10	.50
□□	73	Keith Jones, Wsh.		.10	.50
□□	74	John Cullen, T.B.		.10	.50
□□	75	Brian Leetch, NYR.		.35	2.00
□□	76	Dave Reid, Dal.		.10	.50
□□	77	Dino Ciccarelli, Det.		.25	1.00
□□	78	Gary Roberts, Cgy.		.25	1.00
□□	79	Tony Amonte, Chi.		.25	1.00
□□	80	Mike Modano, Dal.		.50	5.00
□□	81	Doug Brown, Det.		.10	.50
□□	82	Scott Thornton, Edm.		.10	.50
□□	83	Bill Lindsay, Fla.		.10	.50
□□	84	Frantisek Kucera, Hfd.		.10	.50
□□	85	Wayne Gretzky, L.A.		2.00	30.00
□□	86	Joe Sacco, Ana.		.10	.50
□□	87	Benoît Brunet, Mtl.		.10	.50
□□	88	Bill Guerin, N.J.		.25	1.00
□□	89	Travis Green, NYI.		.10	.50
□□	90	Alexei Kovalev, NYR.		.10	.50
□□	91	Stanislav Neckar, Ott.		.10	.50
□□	92	Rob DiMaio, Pha.		.10	.50
□□	93	Chris Joseph, Pgh.		.10	.50
□□	**94**	**Craig Martin, Wpg., RC**		**.10**	**.50**
□□	95	Craig Janney, S.J.		.10	.50
□□	96	Greg Gilbert, Stl.		.10	.50
□□	97	Alexander Semak, T.B.		.10	.50
□□	98	Mike Gartner, Tor.		.25	1.00
□□	99	Cliff Ronning, Van.		.10	.50
□□	100	Mario Lemieux, Pgh.		1.50	25.00
□□	101	Jassen Cullimore, Van.		.10	.50
□□	102	Steve Duchesne, Ott.		.10	.50
□□	103	Derek Plante, Buf.		.10	.50
□□	104	John Gruden, Bos.		.10	.50
□□	105	Michal Sykora, S.J.		.10	.50
□□	106	Trent Klatt, Dal.		.10	.50
□□	107	Nicklas Lidström, Det.		.25	1.00
□□	108	Luke Richardson, Edm.		.10	.50
□□	109	Steven Rice, Hfd.		.10	.50
□□	110	Stu Barnes, Fla.		.10	.50
□□	111	John Druce, L.A.		.10	.50
□□	112	Guy Hebert (G), Ana.		.25	1.00
□□	113	Vladimir Malakhov, Mtl.		.10	.50
□□	114	Claude Lemieux, N.J.		.10	.50
□□	115	Kirk Muller, NYI.		.10	.50
□□	**116**	**Darren Langdon, NYR., RC**		**.10**	**.50**
□□	117	Rob Gaudreau, Ott.		.10	.50
□□	118	Karl Dykhuis, Pha.		.10	.50
□□	119	Richard Park, Pgh.		.10	.50
□□	120	Dave Manson, Pho.		.10	.50
□□	121	Andrei Nazarov, S.J.		.10	.50
□□	122	Bernie Nicholls, S.J.		.10	.50
□□	123	Mikael Andersson, T.B.		.10	.50
□□	124	Todd Gill, Tor.		.10	.50
□□	125	Trevor Linden, Van.		.25	1.00
□□	126	Kelly Miller, Wsh.		.10	.50
□□	127	Don Sweeney, Bos.		.10	.50
□□	128	Jason Dawe, Buf.		.10	.50
□□	129	Steve Chiasson, Cgy.		.10	.50
□□	130	Ed Belfour (G), Chi.		.35	2.00
□□	131	Kerry Huffman, Ott.		.10	.50
□□	132	Tim Taylor, Det.		.10	.50
□□	133	Kirk Maltby, Edm.		.10	.50
□□	134	Jody Hull, Fla.		.10	.50
□□	135	Sean Burke (G), Hfd.		.25	1.00
□□	136	Philippe Boucher, Buf.		.10	.50
□□	137	Valeri Karpov, Ana.		.10	.50
□□	138	Yves Racine, Mtl.		.10	.50
□□	139	Patrick Flatley, NYI.		.10	.50
□□	140	John MacLean, N.J.		.10	.50
□□	141	Sergei Nemchinov, NYR.		.10	.50
□□	142	Don Beaupré (G), Ott.		.10	.50
□□	143	Kevin Dineen, Pha.		.10	.50
□□	144	Ulf Samuelsson, Pgh.		.10	.50
□□	145	Al MacInnis, Stl.		.10	.50
□□	146	Igor Korolev, Stl.		.10	.50
□□	147	Pat Falloon, S.J.		.10	.50
□□	148	Brian Bradley, T.B.		.10	.50
□□	149	Josef Beranek, Van.		.10	.50
□□	150	Mats Sundin, Tor.		.50	5.00
□□	151	Sylvain Côté, Wsh.		.10	.50
□□	152	Keith Tkachuk, Wpg.		.35	3.50
□□	153	Mariusz Czerkawski, Bos.		.10	.50
□□	154	Trevor Kidd (G), Cgy.		.25	1.00
□□	155	Garry Galley, Buf.		.10	.50
□□	156	Gary Suter, Chi.		.10	.50
□□	157	Grant Ledyard, Dal.		.10	.50
□□	158	Doug Weight, Edm.		.35	2.00
□□	159	Jesse Belanger, Fla.		.10	.50
□□	160	Mike Vernon (G), Det.		.25	1.00
□□	161	Robert Kron, Hfd.		.10	.50
□□	162	Marty McSorley, L.A.		.10	.50
□□	163	Todd Krygier, Ana.		.10	.50
□□	164	Scott Niedermayer, N.J.		.25	1.00
□□	165	Mark Recchi, Mtl.		.25	1.00
□□	166	Phil Housley, Cgy.		.10	.50
□□	167	Ron Hextall (G), Pha.		.25	1.00
□□	168	Richard Smehlik, Buf.		.10	.50
□□	169	Chris Tamer, Pgh.		.10	.50
□□	170	Alexei Yashin, Ott.		.35	3.50
□□	171	Sergei Makarov, S.J.		.10	.50
□□	172	Patrice Tardif, Stl.		.10	.50
□□	173	Milos Holan, Ana.		.10	.50
□□	174	J.C. Bergeron (G), T.B.		.10	.50
□□	175	Dave Andreychuk, Tor.		.10	.50
□□	176	Martin Gelinas, Van.		.10	.50
□□	177	Dale Hunter, Wsh.		.10	.50
□□	178	Kevin Haller, Pha.		.10	.50
□□	179	Jeff Shantz, Chi.		.10	.50
□□	180	Adam Oates, Bos.		.35	2.00
□□	181	Ronnie Stern, Cgy.		.10	.50
□□	182	Jamie Langenbrunner, Dal.		.10	.50
□□	183	Mark Fitzpatrick, Fla.		.10	.50
□□	184	Adam Burt, Hfd.		.10	.50
□□	185	Sergei Fedorov, Det.		.50	5.00
□□	186	Robert Lang, L.A.		.10	.50
□□	187	Craig Conroy, Mtl.		.10	.50
□□	188	Ken Danyeko, N.J.		.10	.50
□□	189	Marko Tuomainen, Edm.		.10	.50
□□	190	Ken Wregget (G), Pgh.		.10	.50
□□	191	Mike Rathje, S.J.		.10	.50
□□	192	Dimitri Yushkevich, Pha.		.10	.50
□□	193	Roman Hamrlik, T.B.		.25	1.00
□□	194	Russ Courtnall, Van.		.10	.50
□□	195	Teemu Selänne, Wpg.		.75	10.00
□□	196	Jon Rohloff, Bos.		.10	.50
□□	197	Derian Hatcher, Dal.		.25	1.00
□□	198	Mark Tinordi, Wsh.		.10	.50
□□	199	Patrice Brisebois, Mtl.		.10	.50
□□	200	Jaromir Jagr, Pgh.		1.00	15.00
□□	201	Randy McKay, N.J.		.10	.50
□□	202	Derek King, NYI.		.10	.50
□□	203	Tony Twist, Stl.		.10	.50
□□	204	Jyrki Lumme, Van.		.10	.50
□□	205	Steve Smith, Chi.		.10	.50
□□	206	Bob Rouse, Det.		.10	.50
□□	207	Dave Ellett, Tor.		.10	.50
□□	**208**	**Kevin Dean, N.J., RC**		**.10**	**.50**
□□	**209**	**Rusty Fitzgerald, Pgh., RC**		**.10**	**.50**
□□	210	Jim Carey (G), Wsh.		.10	.50
□□	211	Kenny Jonsson, Tor.		.10	.50
□□	212	Mike Richter (G), NYR.		.35	2.00
□□	213	Glen Wesley, Hfd.		.10	.50
□□	214	Donald Audette, Buf.		.10	.50
□□	215	Curtis Joseph (G), Stl.		.60	8.00
□□	216	Joé Juneau, Wsh.		.10	.50
□□	217	Paul Kariya, Ana.		1.25	20.00
□□	218	Stanley Cup Champions Devils		.10	.50
□□	219	Checklist		.10	.50
□□	220	Checklist		.10	.50
□□	221	Cam Neely, Bos.		.25	1.00
□□	**222**	**Wayne Primeau, Buf., RC**		**.10**	**.50**
□□	223	Yanic Perreault, L.A.		.10	.50
□□	224	Pierre Turgeon, Mtl.		.25	1.00
□□	225	Alexander Mogilny, Van.		.35	2.00
□□	226	Daren Puppa (G), T.B.		.10	.50
□□	227	Ulf Dahlen, S.J.		.10	.50
□□	228	Tomas Sandström, Det.		.10	.50
□□	229	Shayne Corson, Stl.		.25	1.00
□□	230	Chris Chelios, Chi.		.35	2.00
□□	231	Stéphane Richer, N.J.		.10	.50
□□	232	Paul Ranheim, Hfd.		.10	.50
□□	233	Joe Nieuwendyk, Cgy.		.25	1.00
□□	234	Doug Gilmour, Tor.		.35	2.00
□□	235	Jeremy Roenick, Chi.		.35	2.00
□□	236	Joel Otto, Cgy.		.10	.50
□□	237	Steve Yzerman, Det.		1.00	15.00
□□	238	Petr Klima, Edm.		.10	.50
□□	239	Jari Kurri, L.A.		.25	1.00
□□	240	Mark Messier, NYR.		.50	5.00
□□	241	Bill Ranford (G), Edm.		.25	1.00
□□	242	Grant Fuhr (G), Buf.		.25	1.00
□□	243	Brent Severyn, Fla.		.10	.50
□□	244	Ron Francis, Pgh.		.35	2.00
□□	245	Ray Ferraro, NYR.		.10	.50
□□	246	Martin Straka, Ott.		.10	.50
□□	247	Gerald Diduck, Hfd.		.10	.50
□□	248	Dimitri Khristich, L.A.		.10	.50
□□	**249**	**Wayne Flaherty (G), S.J., RC**		**.10**	**.50**
□□	250	Pat LaFontaine, Buf.		.25	1.00
□□	251	Darren Turcotte, Hfd.		.10	.50
□□	252	John Vanbiesbrouck (G), Fla.		.60	8.00
□□	253	Brian Bellows, T.B.		.10	.50
□□	254	Dave Gagner, Dal.		.10	.50
□□	255	Larry Murphy, Tor.		.25	1.00
□□	256	Steve Thomas, N.J.		.10	.50
□□	**257**	**Robert Svehla, Fla., RC**		**.25**	**8.00**
□□	258	Deron Quint, Wpg.		.10	.50
□□	259	Kjell Samuelsson, Pha.		.10	.50
□□	260	Scott Mellanby, Fla.		.10	.50
□□	261	Dan Quinn, Ott.		.10	.50
□□	262	Tom Barrasso (G), Pgh.		.25	1.00
□□	263	Zarley Zalapski, Cgy.		.10	.50
□□	264	Rick Tocchet, L.A.		.10	.50
□□	265	Paul Coffey, Det.		.25	1.00
□□	266	Joe Sakic, Col.		.85	12.00
□□	**267**	**Aki Berg, L.A., RC**		**.10**	**.50**

	No.	Player		
□□	268	Jeff Brown, Hfd.	.10	.50
□□	269	Wendel Clark, Tor.	.25	1.00
□□	270	Vincent Damphousse, Mtl.	.35	2.00
□□	271	Dale Hawerchuk, Stl.	.25	1.00
□□	**272**	**Rhett Warrener, Fla., RC**	**.10**	**.50**
□□	273	Kevin Hatcher, Dal.	.10	.50
□□	274	Calle Johansson, Wsh.	.10	.50
□□	275	Scott Stevens, N.J.	.10	.50
□□	276	Geoff Courtnall, Stl.	.10	.50
□□	277	Kirk McLean (G), Van.	.25	1.00
□□	278	Steve Heinze, Bos.	.10	.50
□□	279	Sylvain Lefebvre, Col	.10	.50
□□	280	Joe Murphy, Chi.	.10	.50
□□	281	Mike Keane, Mtl.	.10	.50
□□	282	Kevin Stevens, Bos.	.10	.50
□□	**283**	**Miroslav Satan, Edm., RC**	**.10**	**.50**
□□	284	Stéphane Fiset (G), Col.	.25	1.00
□□	285	Jeff O'Neill, Hfd.	.25	1.00
□□	**286**	**Denny Lambert, Ott., RC**	**.10**	**.50**
□□	**287**	**Marcus Ragnarsson, S.J., RC**	**.10**	**.50**
□□	288	Adam Deadmarsh, Col.	.10	.50
□□	289	Eric Weinrich, Chi.	.10	.50
□□	290	Eric Desjardins, Pha.	.10	.50
□□	291	Tim Cheveldae (G), Wpg.	.10	.50
□□	292	Glenn Healy (G), NYR.	.10	.50
□□	293	Byron Dafoe (G), L.A.	.10	.50
□□	294	Tom Fitzgerald, Fla.	.10	.50
□□	295	Adam Graves, NYR.	.10	.50
□□	296	Arturs Irbe (G), S.J.	.10	.50
□□	297	Shaun Van Allen, Ana.	.10	.50
□□	298	Kelly Buchberger, Edm.	.10	.50
□□	299	Bob Probert, Chi.	.10	.50
□□	300	Pavel Bure, Van.	.75	10.00
□□	**301**	**Chad Kilger, Ana., RC**	**.10**	**.50**
□□	302	Dominik Hasek (G), Buf.	.75	10.00
□□	303	Bobby Holik, N.J.	.10	.50
□□	304	Petr Nedved, Pgh.	.10	.50
□□	305	Owen Nolan, S.J.	.25	1.00
□□	306	Saku Koivu, Mtl.	.75	10.00
□□	307	Rob Blake, L.A.	.25	1.00
□□	308	Chris Pronger, Stl.	.25	1.00
□□	**309**	**Kyle McLaren, Bos., RC**	**.10**	**.50**
□□	310	Peter Bondra, Wsh.	.35	3.50
□□	311	Nelson Emerson, Hfd.	.10	.50
□□	312	Bryan McCabe, NYI.	.10	.50
□□	313	Darcy Wakaluk (G), Dal.	.10	.50
□□	**314**	**Shane Doan, Wpg., RC**	**.10**	**.50**
□□	315	Félix Potvin (G), Tor.	.50	5.00
□□	316	Jim Dowd, N.J.	.10	.50
□□	317	Roman Oksiuta, Van.	.10	.50
□□	318	Geoff Sanderson, Hfd.	.10	.50
□□	**319**	**Radek Dvorak, Fla., RC**	**.10**	**.50**
□□	320	Paul Ysebaert, T.B.	.10	.50
□□	321	Shawn McEachern, Bos.	.10	.50
□□	322	Vyacheslav Kozlov, Det.	.10	.50
□□	323	Marty McInnis, NYI.	.10	.50
□□	324	Ted Donato, Bos.	.10	.50
□□	325	Martin Brodeur (G), N.J.	.75	10.00
□□	326	Patrick Poulin, T.B.	.10	8.00
□□	327	Eric Lindros, Pha.	1.25	20.00
□□	328	Dallas Drake, Wpg.	.10	.50
□□	329	Sean Hill, Ott.	.10	.50
□□	330	Michal Pivonka, Wsh.	.10	.50
□□	331	Alexei Zhamnov, Wpg.	.25	1.00
□□	332	Cory Stillman, Cgy.	.10	.50
□□	333	Sergei Zubov, Pgh.	.25	8.00
□□	334	Tommy Söderström (G), NYI.	.10	.50
□□	335	Patrik Carnback, Ana.	.10	.50
□□	**336**	**Joe Dziedzic, Pgh., RC**	**.10**	**.50**
□□	337	Steve Duchesne, Ott.	.10	.50
□□	338	Marty Murray, Cgy.	.10	.50
□□	**339**	**Todd Bertuzzi, NYI., RC**	**.35**	**1.00**
□□	340	Jason Arnott, Edm.	.25	1.00
□□	341	Niklas Sundstrom, NYR.	.10	.50
□□	342	Alexandre Daigle, Ott.	.25	1.00
□□	343	Jocelyn Thibault (G), Mtl.	.35	2.00
□□	344	Mikail Shtalenkov (G), Ana.	.10	.50
□□	345	Chris Osgood (G), Det.	.35	3.50
□□	346	Brendan Witt, Wsh.	.10	.50
□□	347	Ian Laperrière, Stl.	.10	.50
□□	348	Zigmund Palffy, NYI.	.35	3.50
□□	349	Brian Savage, Mtl.	.10	.50
□□	350	Michael Peca, Van.	.25	1.00
□□	351	Vitali Yachmenev, L.A.	.10	8.00
□□	352	Luc Robitaille, Pgh.	.25	1.00

	No.	Player			
□□	353	Mikael Renberg, Pha.		.10	.50
□□	354	Ed Jovanovski, Fla.		.25	1.00
□□	355	Jason Doig, Wpg.		.10	.50
□□	356	Todd Harvey, Dal.		.10	.50
□□	357	Viktor Kozlov, S.J.		.10	.50
□□	358	Valeri Bure, Mtl.		.10	.50
□□	359	Peter Forsberg, Col.		1.00	50.00
□□	360	Jeff Friesen, S.J.		.10	.50
□□	361	Andrei Nikolishin, Hfd.		.10	.50
□□	362	Brian Rolston, N.J.		.10	.50
□□	363	Jamie Storr (G), L.A.		.25	1.00
□□	364	Chris Therien, Pha.		.10	.50
□□	365	Oleg Tverdovsky, Ana.		.10	.50
□□	366	David Oliver, Edm.		.10	.50
□□	367	Alexander Selivanov, T.B.		.10	.50
□□	368	Alek Stojanov, Pgh.		.10	.50
□□	**369**	**Daniel Alfredsson, Ott., RC**		**.60**	**5.00**
□□	370	Brendan Shanahan, Det.		.60	8.00
□□	371	Yuri Khmylev, Buf.		.10	.50
□□	372	Brett Hull, Stl.		.50	5.00
□□□	373	Sergei Fedorov, Det.	8.00	.35	25.00
□□□	374	Jaromir Jagr, Pgh.	15.00	.75	50.00
□□□	375	Wayne Gretzky, L.A.	30.00	1.50	140.00
□□□	376	Alexander Mogilny, Van.	5.00	.20	15.00
□□□	377	Patrick Roy (G), Mtl.	25.00	1.25	85.00
□□□	378	Ed Belfour (G), Chi.	5.00	20.00	15.00
□□□	379	Luc Robitaille, Pgh.	4.00	.20	10.00
□□□	380	Peter Forsberg, Col.	15.00	.75	45.00
□□□	381	Adam Oates, Bos.	5.00	.20	15.00
□□□	382	Theoren Fleury, Cgy.	5.00	.20	15.00
□□□	383	Jim Carey (G), Wsh.	3.00	.10	8.00
□□	384	Checklist (201-304)		.10	10.00
□□	385	Checklist (305-385)		.10	10.00

CANADA GOLD

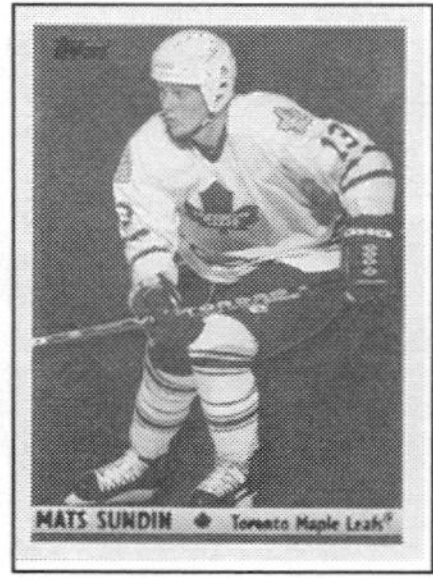

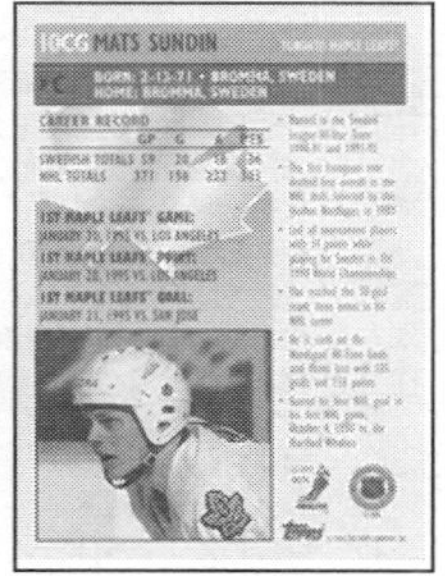

Series One Insert Set (10 cards): 125.00

	No.	Player	NRMT-MT
□	1CG	Patrick Roy (G), Mtl.	50.00
□	2CG	Alexei Yashin, Ott.	10.00
□	3CG	Jason Arnott, Edm.	5.00
□	4CG	Trevor Kidd (G), Cgy.	5.00
□	5CG	Pavel Bure, Van.	20.00
□	6CG	Theoren Fleury, Cgy.	8.00
□	7CG	Pierre Turgeon, Mtl.	5.00
□	8CG	Félix Potvin (G), Tor.	15.00
□	9CG	Teemu Selänne, Wpg.	20.00
□	10CG	Mats Sundin, Tor.	15.00

CANADA JUNIORS

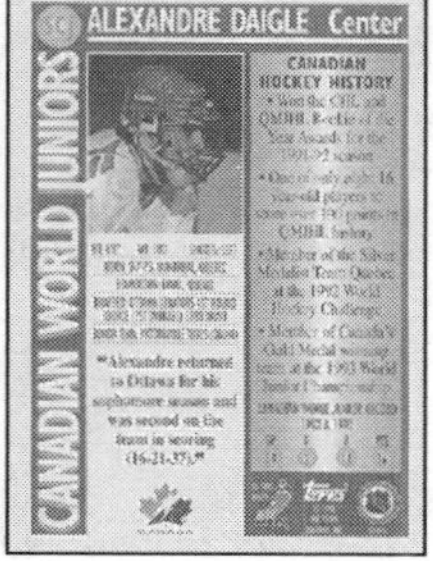

Series One Insert Set (22 cards): 25.00

	No.	Player	NRMT-MT
□	1CJ	Wade Redden, Cdn.	.75
□	2CJ	Jamie Storr (G), Cdn.	1.50
□	3CJ	Larry Courville, Cdn.	.75
□	4CJ	Jason Allison, Cdn.	3.00
□	5CJ	Alexandre Daigle, Cdn.	1.50
□	6CJ	Marty Murray, Cdn.	.75
□	7CJ	Bryan McCabe, Cdn.	.75
□	8CJ	Ryan Smyth, Cdn.	1.50
□	9CJ	Lee Sorochan, Cdn.	.75
□	10CJ	Todd Harvey, Cdn.	.75
□	11CJ	Nolan Baumgartner, Cdn.	.75
□	12CJ	Denis Pederson, Cdn.	.75
□	13CJ	Shean Donovan, Cdn.	.75
□	14CJ	Jason Botterill, Cdn.	.75
□	15CJ	Jeff Friesen, Cdn.	1.50
□	16CJ	Darcy Tucker, Cdn.	.75
□	17CJ	Chad Allan, Cdn.	.75
□	18CJ	Dan Cloutier (G), Cdn.	1.50
□	19CJ	Eric Dazé, Cdn.	1.50
□	20CJ	Jeff O'Neill, Cdn.	1.50
□	21CJ	Jamie Rivers, Cdn.	.75
□	22CJ	Ed Jovanovski, Cdn.	1.50

HIDDEN GEMS

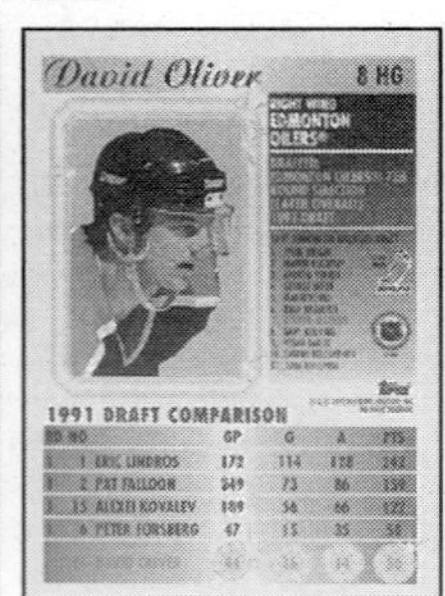

Series One Insert Set (15 cards): 40.00

	No.	Player	NRMT-MT
□	1HG	Theoren Fleury, Cgy.	4.00
□	2HG	Luc Robitaille, Pgh.	2.00
□	3HG	Doug Gilmour, Tor.	4.00
□	4HG	Dominik Hasek (G), Buf.	10.00
□	5HG	Pavel Bure, Van.	10.00
□	6HG	Peter Bondra, Wsh.	6.00
□	7HG	Steve Larmer, NYR.	1.00
□	8HG	David Oliver, Edm.	1.00
□	9HG	Gary Suter, Chi.	1.00
□	10HG	Brett Hull, Stl.	8.00
□	11HG	Kevin Stevens, Pgh.	1.00
□	12HG	Ron Hextall (G), Pha.	2.00
□	13HG	Kirk McLean (G), Van.	2.00
□	14HG	Andy Moog (G), Dal.	2.00
□	15HG	Rick Tocchet, L.A.	1.00

NEW TO GAME

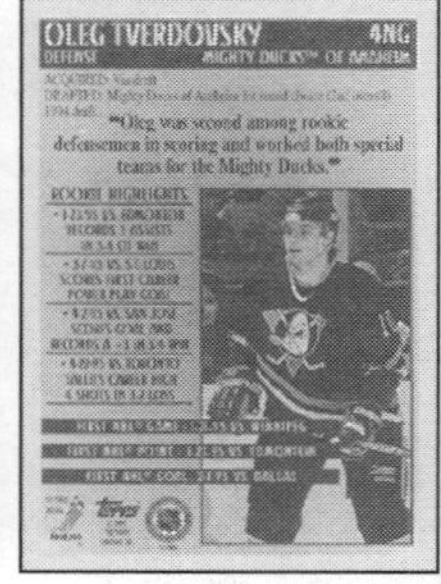

Series One Insert Set (22 cards): 18.00

	No.	Player	NRMT-MT
□	1NG	Jim Carey (G), Wsh.	.50
□	2NG	Sergei Brylin, N.J.	.50
□	3NG	Todd Marchant, Edm.	.50
□	4NG	Oleg Tverdovsky, Ana.	.50
□	5NG	Paul Kariya, Ana.	6.50
□	6NG	Adam Deadmarsh, Col.	.50
□	7NG	Mike Kennedy, Dal.	.50
□	8NG	Roman Oksiuta, Edm.	.50
□	9NG	Kenny Jonsson, Tor.	.50
□	10NG	Peter Forsberg, Col.	5.00
□	11NG	Alexander Selivanov, T.B.	.50
□	12NG	Chris Therien, Pha.	.50
□	13NG	Brian Rolston, N.J.	.50
□	14NG	David Oliver, Edm.	.50
□	15NG	Blaine Lacher (G), Bos.	.50
□	16NG	Sergei Krivokrasov, Chi.	.50

No.	Player	
☐ 17NG	Todd Harvey, Dal.	.50
☐ 18NG	Jeff Friesen, S.J.	1.00
☐ 19NG	Mariusz Czerkawski, Bos.	.50
☐ 20NG	Ian Laperrière, Stl.	.50
☐ 21NG	Brian Savage, Mtl.	.50
☐ 22NG	Andrei Nikolishin, Hfd.	.50

POWER LINES

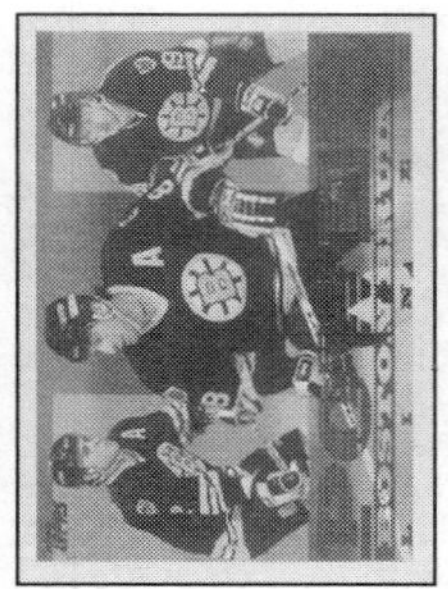
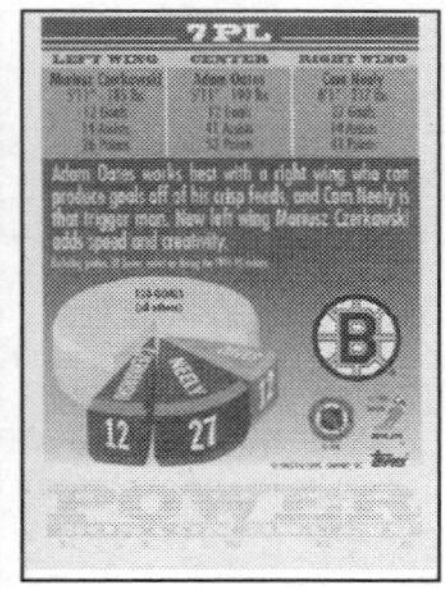

Series One Insert Set (10 cards): 25.00

No.	Player	NRMT-MT
☐ 1PL	John LeClair/Eric Lindros/Mikael Renberg	8.00
☐ 2PL	Keith Tkachuk/Teemu Selänne/Alexei Zhamnov	4.00
☐ 3PL	Adam Graves/Mark Messier/Pat Verbeek	3.50
☐ 4PL	Patrick Poulin/Jeremy Roenick/Tony Amonte	1.50
☐ 5PL	Kevin Stevens/Jaromir Jagr/Ron Francis	5.00
☐ 6PL	Jason Dawe/Pat LaFontaine/Alexander Mogilny	1.50
☐ 7PL	Adam Oates/Cam Neely/Mariusz Czerkawski	1.50
☐ 8PL	Vyacheslav Kozlov/Sergei Fedorov/Doug Brown	3.50
☐ 9PL	Vincent Damphousse/Pierre Turgeon/Mark Recchi	1.00
☐ 10PL	Mike Peluso/Bobby Holik/Randy McKay	.50

MARK MESSIER'S PRO FILES

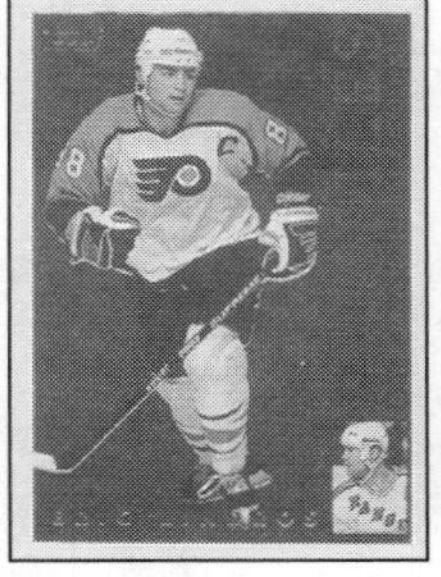
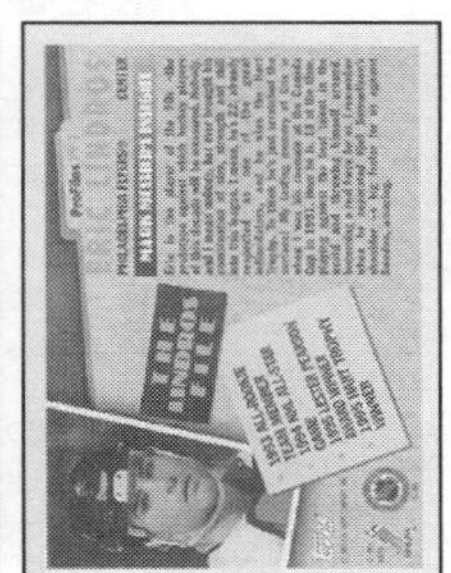

Insert Set (20 cards): 65.00

No.	Player	NRMT-MT
☐ PF1	Wayne Gretzky, L.A.	10.00
☐ PF2	Brian Leetch, NYR.	1.50
☐ PF3	Patrick Roy (G), Mtl.	8.00
☐ PF4	Jaromir Jagr, Pgh.	5.00
☐ PF5	Sergei Fedorov, Det.	2.50
☐ PF6	Martin Brodeur (G), N.J.	3.50
☐ PF7	Eric Lindros, Pha.	6.50
☐ PF8	Jeremy Roenick, Chi.	1.50
☐ PF9	John Vanbiesbrouck (G), Fla.	3.00
☐ PF10	Cam Neely, Bos.	1.00
☐ PF11	Pavel Bure, Van.	3.50
☐ PF12	Paul Coffey, Det.	1.00
☐ PF13	Scott Stevens, N.J.	1.00
☐ PF14	Dominik Hasek (G), Buf.	3.50
☐ PF15	Mario Lemieux, Pgh.	8.00
☐ PF16	Ed Belfour (G), N.J.	1.50
☐ PF17	Doug Gilmour, Tor.	1.50
☐ PF18	Teemu Selänne, Ana.	3.50
☐ PF19	Brett Hull, Stl.	2.50
☐ PF20	Joe Sakic, Col.	4.00

RINK LEADERS

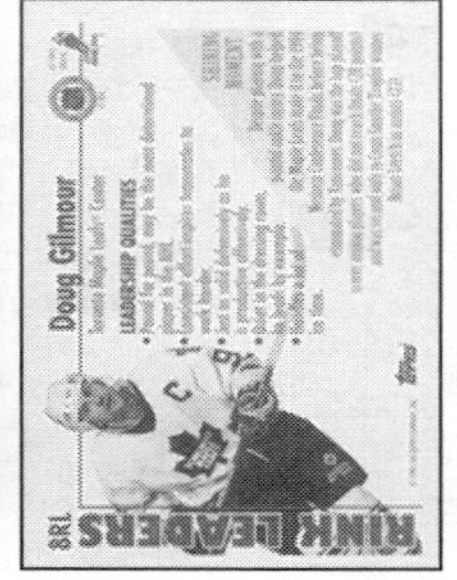

Series One Insert Set (10 cards): 90.00

No.	Player	NRMT-MT
☐ 1RL	Mark Messier, NYR.	8.00
☐ 2RL	Mario Lemieux, Pgh.	30.00
☐ 3RL	Ray Bourque, Bos.	8.00
☐ 4RL	Brett Hull, Stl.	8.00
☐ 5RL	Pat LaFontaine, Buf.	3.00
☐ 6RL	Scott Stevens, N.J.	2.00
☐ 7RL	Keith Tkachuk, Wpg.	6.00
☐ 8RL	Doug Gilmour, Tor.	5.00
☐ 9RL	Chris Chelios, Chi.	6.00
☐ 10RL	Wayne Gretzky, L.A.	35.00

HOME GROWN

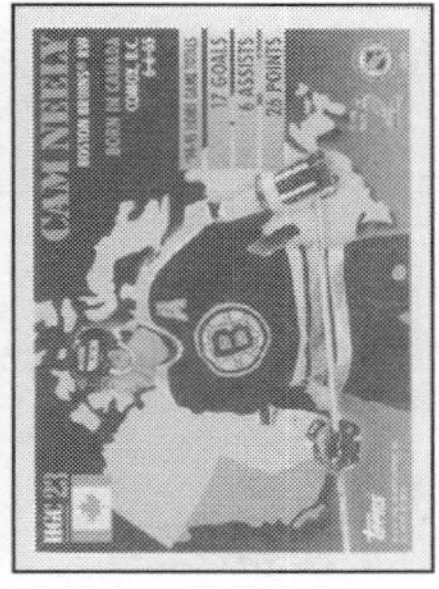

Series One Cdn. Retail Set (15 cards): 150.00
Series Two Cdn. Hobby Set (15 cards): 400.00
U.S. Set (10 cards): 40.00

No.	Player	NRMT-MT
☐ HGC1	Patrick Roy (G), Mtl.	50.00
☐ HGC2	Wendel Clark, NYI.	5.00
☐ HGC3	Pierre Turgeon, Mtl.	5.00
☐ HGC4	Doug Gilmour, Tor.	8.00
☐ HGC5	Theoren Fleury, Cgy.	8.00
☐ HGC6	Eric Lindros, Pha.	40.00
☐ HGC7	Paul Kariya, Ana.	40.00
☐ HGC8	Bill Ranford (G), Edm.	5.00
☐ HGC9	Ray Bourque, Bos.	15.00
☐ HGC10	Brendan Shanahan, Det.	18.00
☐ HGC11	Paul Coffey, Det.	5.00
☐ HGC12	Trevor Linden, Van.	5.00
☐ HGC13	Trevor Kidd (G), Cgy.	5.00
☐ HGC14	Alexandre Daigle, Ott.	5.00
☐ HGC15	Chris Pronger, Stl.	5.00
☐ HGC16	Steve Yzerman, Det.	75.00
☐ HGC17	Todd Harvey, Dal.	8.00
☐ HGC18	Félix Potvin (G), Tor.	35.00
☐ HGC19	Luc Robitaille, Pgh.	10.00
☐ HGC20	Wayne Gretzky, L.A.	175.00
☐ HGC21	Keith Primeau, Det.	10.00
☐ HGC22	Al MacInnis, Stl.	8.00
☐ HGC23	Cam Neely, Bos.	10.00
☐ HGC24	Ed Belfour (G), Chi.	15.00
☐ HGC25	Joé Juneau, Wsh.	8.00
☐ HGC26	Adam Graves, NYI.	8.00
☐ HGC27	Mark Recchi, Mtl.	10.00
☐ HGC28	Stéphane Richer, N.J.	8.00
☐ HGC29	Mark Messier, NYR.	35.00
☐ HGC30	Mario Lemieux, Pgh.	120.00
☐ HGA1	Brian Leetch, NYR.	4.00
☐ HGA2	Jeremy Roenick, Chi.	4.00
☐ HGA3	Mike Modano, Dal.	6.00
☐ HGA4	Pat LaFontaine, Buf.	3.00
☐ HGA5	Keith Tkachuk, Wpg.	5.00
☐ HGA6	Chris Chelios, Chi.	5.00
☐ HGA7	Darren Turcotte, Hfd.	2.00
☐ HGA8	John Vanbiesbrouck (G), Fla.	8.00
☐ HGA9	John LeClair, Pha.	6.00
☐ HGA10	Mike Richter (G), NYR.	4.00

MYSTERY FINEST

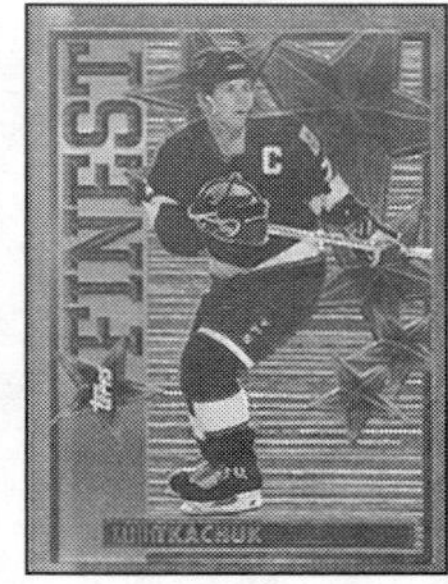

Each card came with a black removable cover on the front. Three players (or four in the case of cards M19-M22) are depicted on the card back. Collectors would remove the black cover to find out which player was depicted on the front and whether the card was a regular insert or a refractor parallel.

Series Two Insert Set (22 cards): 215.00 850.00

No.	Player	Reg.	Ref.
☐☐ M1	Wayne Gretzky, NYR.	30.00	120.00
☐☐ M2	Mario Lemieux, Pgh.	25.00	100.00
☐☐ M3	Mark Messier, NYR.	8.00	30.00
☐☐ M4	Eric Lindros, Pha.	18.00	70.00
☐☐ M5	Sergei Fedorov, Det.	8.00	30.00
☐☐ M6	Joe Sakic, Col.	12.00	45.00
☐☐ M7	Brett Hull, Stl.	8.00	30.00
☐☐ M8	Jaromir Jagr, Pgh.	15.00	60.00
☐☐ M9	Teemu Selänne, Ana.	10.00	40.00
☐☐ M10	Brendan Shanahan, Det.	9.00	35.00
☐☐ M11	Cam Neely, Bos.	4.00	10.00
☐☐ M12	Mikael Renberg, Pha.	3.00	8.00
☐☐ M13	Paul Kariya, Ana.	18.00	70.00
☐☐ M14	Keith Tkachuk, Wpg.	6.00	20.00
☐☐ M15	Pavel Bure, Van.	10.00	35.00
☐☐ M16	Brian Leetch, NYR.	5.00	15.00
☐☐ M17	Scott Stevens, N.J.	3.00	8.00
☐☐ M18	Chris Chelios, Chi.	6.00	20.00
☐☐ M19	Dominik Hasek (G), Buf.	10.00	40.00
☐☐ M20	Patrick Roy (G), Col.	25.00	100.00
☐☐ M21	Martin Brodeur (G), N.J.	10.00	40.00
☐☐ M22	Félix Potvin (G), Tor.	8.00	30.00

YOUNG STARS

Series Two Insert Set (15 cards): 45.00

No.	Player	NRMT-MT
☐ YS1	Paul Kariya, Ana.	10.00
☐ YS2	Martin Brodeur (G), N.J.	5.00
☐ YS3	Mikael Renberg, Pha.	1.50
☐ YS4	Peter Forsberg, Col.	7.50
☐ YS5	Alexei Yashin, Ott.	3.00
☐ YS6	Jeff Friesen, S.J.	2.00
☐ YS7	Oleg Tverdovsky, Ana.	1.50
☐ YS8	Jim Carey (G), Wsh.	1.50
☐ YS9	Alexei Kovalev, NYR.	1.50
☐ YS10	Jason Arnott, Edm.	2.00
☐ YS11	Teemu Selänne, Wpg.	5.00
☐ YS12	Chris Osgood (G), Det.	3.00
☐ YS13	Roman Hamrlik, T.B.	2.00
☐ YS14	Scott Niedermayer, N.J.	2.00
☐ YS15	Jaromir Jagr, Pgh.	7.50

1995 - 96 TOPPS FINEST

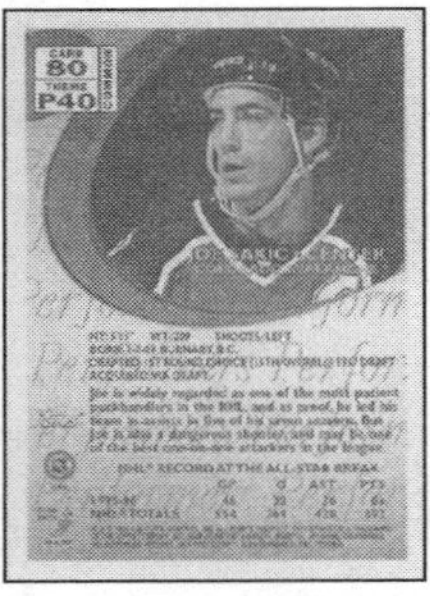

One blank back bronze card was found on the top of every box. There is a blank back card for all 110 bronze cards. All 191 cards have a regular card and refractor parallel. Four basic designs were used: one for "Sterling", one for "Rookies", one for "Performers" and one for "Defenders".

Imprint: © 1996 THE TOPPS COMPANY, INC.

Complete Set (191 cards): 1,100.00 4,200.00

COMMON SERIES - BRONZE

Commons Set (110 cards): 50.00 1,000.00

Common Player: .35 5.00

No.		Player	Box	Com.	Ref.
1	S1	Eric Lindros, Pha.	20.00	5.00	75.00
3	R5	Eric Dazé, Chi.	2.50	.75	8.00
5	P10	Wayne Gretzky, NYR.	30.00	8.00	150.00
6	P7	Dave Andreychuk, Tor.	1.00	.35	5.00
7	D2	Phil Housley, Cgy.	1.00	.35	5.00
8	P26	Mike Gartner, Tor.	2.50	.75	8.00
9	P2	Cam Neely, Bos.	2.50	.75	8.00
10	S7	Brett Hull, Stl.	6.00	2.00	20.00
14	P16	Steve Thomas, N.J.	1.00	.35	5.00
15	S23	Joe Sakic, Col.	12.00	3.50	50.00
17	D4	Steve Duchesne, Ott.	1.00	.35	5.00
20	D13	John Vanbiesbrouck (G), Fla.	8.00	2.50	30.00
21	P3	Randy Burridge, Buf.	1.00	.35	5.00
22	R16	Shane Doan, Wpg.	1.00	.35	5.00
23	P81	Brian Savage, Mtl.	1.00	.35	5.00
24	P82	Luc Robitaille, NYR.	2.50	.75	8.00
26	P91	Peter Forsberg, Col.	15.00	4.00	60.00
33	S8	Scott Stevens, N.J.	1.00	.35	5.00
34	R6	Valeri Bure, Mtl.	1.00	.35	5.00
38	P27	John MacLean, N.J.	1.00	.35	5.00
39	P20	Brendan Shanahan, Hfd.	8.00	2.50	30.00
40	P25	Pat LaFontaine, Buf.	2.50	.75	8.00
42	D15	Larry Murphy, Tor.	2.50	.75	8.00
43	P32	Adam Oates, Bos.	4.00	1.25	12.00
44	P33	Rod Brind'Amour, Pha.	2.50	.75	8.00
46	P6	Pierre Turgeon, Mtl.	2.50	.75	8.00
47	P12	Claude Lemieux, Col.	1.00	.35	5.00
50	P15	Mark Messier, NYR.	6.00	2.00	20.00
51	D9	Bill Ranford (G), Edm.	2.50	.75	8.00
53	R12	Jere Lehtinen, Dal.	2.50	.75	8.00
59	R21	Niklas Sundstrom, NYR.	1.00	.35	5.00
60	S28	John LeClair, Pha.	6.00	2.00	20.00
61	R4	Cory Stillman, Cgy.	1.00	.35	5.00
62	P87	David Oliver, Edm.	1.00	.35	5.00
63	D40	Nikolai Khabibulin (G), Wpg.	4.00	1.25	12.00
64	P89	Steve Rucchin, Ana.	1.00	.35	5.00
66	D42	Jim Carey (G), Wsh.	1.00	.35	5.00
69	D30	Nicklas Lidström, Det.	2.50	.75	8.00
70	P50	Jaromir Jagr, Pgh.	15.00	4.00	60.00
72	D28	Dominik Hasek (G), Buf.	10.00	3.00	40.00
74	P52	Andrew Cassels, Hfd.	1.00	.35	5.00
75	S30	Pavel Bure, Van.	10.00	3.00	40.00
76	R23	Marcus Ragnarsson, S.J.	1.00	.35	5.00
78	P86	Alexei Zhamnov, Wpg.	2.50	.75	8.00
80	P40	Joe Sakic, Col.	12.00	3.50	50.00
81	R14	Chad Kilger, Ana.	1.00	.35	5.00
83	P67	Vyacheslav Kozlov, Det.	1.00	.35	5.00
86	D16	Ron Hextall (G), Pha.	2.50	.75	8.00
89	R9	Richard Park, Pgh.	1.00	.35	5.00
91	P66	Shawn McEachern, Bos.	1.00	.35	5.00
93	D36	Roman Hamrlik, T.B.	2.50	.75	8.00
95	S26	Sergei Fedorov, Det.	6.00	2.00	20.00
98	P74	Rob Niedermayer, Fla.	1.00	.35	5.00
101	R17	Deron Quint, Wpg.	1.00	.35	5.00
103	D31	Scott Niedermayer, N.J.	2.50	.75	8.00
105	D32	Félix Potvin (G), Tor.	6.00	2.00	20.00
106	R8	Brendan Witt, Wsh.	1.00	.35	5.00
107	P53	Zdeno Ciger, Edm.	1.00	.35	5.00
109	P54	Jody Hull, Fla.	1.00	.35	5.00
111	R18	Kyle McLaren, Bos.	1.00	.35	5.00
113	D10	Grant Fuhr (G), Stl.	2.50	.75	8.00
114	P21	Todd Krygier, Wsh.	1.00	.35	5.00
115	S17	Brian Leetch, NYR.	4.00	1.25	12.00
117	P78	Zigmund Palffy, NYI.	5.00	1.50	15.00
118	**R22**	**Antti Törmänen, Ott., RC**	**1.00**	**.35**	**5.00**
119	P46	Mark Recchi, Mtl.	2.50	.75	8.00
120	P90	Mikael Renberg, Pha.	1.00	.35	5.00
121	S3	Chris Chelios, Chi.	5.00	1.50	15.00
122	D33	Guy Hebert (G), Ana.	2.50	.75	8.00
126	D8	Gary Suter, Chi.	1.00	.35	5.00
127	P23	Ron Francis, Pgh.	4.00	1.25	12.00
129	D17	Tom Barrasso (G), Pgh.	2.50	.75	8.00
130	S13	Pat LaFontaine, Buf.	2.50	.75	8.00
131	P22	Pat Verbeek, NYR.	1.00	.35	5.00
133	P29	Rick Tocchet, Bos.	1.00	.35	5.00
134	**R26**	**Petr Sykora, N.J., RC**	**1.00**	**.35**	**5.00**
135	S29	Félix Potvin (G), Tor.	6.00	2.00	20.00
136	P31	Scott Mellanby, Fla.	1.00	.35	5.00
137	D18	Paul Coffey, Det.	2.50	.75	8.00
139	P75	Jason Arnott, Edm.	2.50	.75	8.00
141	D34	Sandis Ozolinsh, Col.	2.50	.75	8.00
143	P38	Brian Bradley, T.B.	1.00	.35	5.00
144	P39	Trevor Linden, Van.	2.50	.75	8.00
145	S24	Patrick Roy (G), Col.	25.00	6.50	100.00
146	**R24**	**Todd Bertuzzi, NYI., RC**	**2.00**	**1.00**	**8.00**
147	P42	Michal Pivonka, Wsh.	1.00	.35	5.00
149	D25	Chris Terreri (G), S.J.	1.00	.35	5.00
150	S10	Mario Lemieux, Pgh.	25.00	6.50	100.00
153	P43	Dale Hawerchuk, Stl.	2.50	.75	8.00
154	P77	Markus Naslund, Pgh.	1.00	.35	5.00
155	P80	Teemu Selänne, Wpg.	10.00	3.00	40.00
157	R25	Vitali Yachmenev, L.A.	1.00	.35	5.00
158	P79	Jason Dawe, Buf.	1.00	.35	5.00
159	D38	Chris Osgood (G), Det.	5.00	1.50	15.00
160	P5	Alexander Mogilny, Van.	4.00	1.25	12.00
163	R11	Shean Donovan, S.J.	1.00	.35	5.00
165	S27	Paul Kariya, Ana.	20.00	5.00	75.00
167	D22	Teppo Numminen, Wpg.	1.00	.35	5.00
170	S4	Doug Gilmour, Tor.	4.00	1.25	12.00
171	D37	Sergei Zubov, Pgh.	2.50	.75	8.00
172	P68	Mikael Nylander, Cgy.	1.00	.35	5.00
173	P71	Geoff Sanderson, Hfd.	1.00	.35	5.00
175	P14	Jeremy Roenick, Chi.	4.00	1.25	12.00
177	P65	Mats Sundin, Tor.	6.00	2.00	20.00
178	D35	Martin Brodeur, N.J.	10.00	3.00	40.00
181	P45	Theoren Fleury, Cgy.	4.00	1.25	12.00
183	**D41**	**Robert Svehla, Fla., RC**	**1.00**	**.50**	**5.00**
186	P85	Sergei Fedorov, Det.	6.00	2.00	20.00
188	S11	John Vanbiesbrouck (G), Fla.	8.00	2.50	30.00
189	P92	Paul Kariya, Ana.	20.00	5.00	75.00

UNCOMMON SERIES - SILVER

Uncommons Set (55 cards): 175.00 725.00

Uncommon Player: 3.00 10.00

No.		Player	Sil.	Ref.
4	P4	Craig Janney, S.J.	3.00	10.00
11	D3	Daren Puppa (G), T.B.	3.00	10.00
12	P9	Tomas Sandström, Pgh.	3.00	10.00
16	P8	Ray Sheppard, Fla.	3.00	10.00
18	P11	Shayne Corson, Stl.	4.00	15.00
27	P85	Jeff Friesen, S.J.	4.00	15.00
28	R3	Aaron Gavey, T.B.	3.00	10.00
29	D39	Kenny Jonsson, Tor.	3.00	10.00
31	P28	Dave Gagner, Dal.	3.00	10.00
32	P88	Alexander Selivanov, T.B.	3.00	10.00
36	P24	Ray Ferraro, NYR.	3.00	10.00
37	D11	Sylvain Côté, Wsh.	3.00	10.00
49	P17	Geoff Courtnall, Stl.	3.00	10.00
48	D7	Al MacInnis, Stl.	3.00	10.00
52	P37	Vincent Damphousse, Mtl.	5.00	20.00
54	R19	Bryan McCabe, NYI.	3.00	10.00
56	D26	Mathieu Schneider, NYI.	3.00	10.00
57	P47	Igor Larionov, S.J.	4.00	15.00
58	P48	Joe Murphy, Chi.	3.00	10.00
65	S19	Brendan Shanahan, Hfd.	12.00	60.00
67	**R7**	**Brian Holzinger, Buf., RC**	**3.00**	**10.00**
68	P58	Stu Barnes, Fla.	3.00	10.00
71	P49	Donald Audette, Buf.	3.00	10.00
73	P51	Peter Bondra, Wsh.	6.00	25.00
77	S2	Ray Bourque, Bos.	8.00	40.00
79	P73	Travis Green, NYI.	3.00	10.00
82	P62	Bill Guerin, N.J.	4.00	15.00
84	P72	Igor Korolev, Wpg.	3.00	10.00
87	P34	Wendel Clark, NYI.	4.00	15.00
90	S6	Dominik Hasek (G), Buf.	15.00	75.00
92	P69	Martin Straka, Ott.	3.00	10.00
94	P76	Roman Oksiuta, Van.	3.00	10.00
96	R2	Jeff O'Neill, Hfd.	4.00	15.00
97	P83	Todd Harvey, Dal.	3.00	10.00
102	P59	Nelson Emerson, Hfd.	3.00	10.00
104	P61	Doug Weight, Edm.	5.00	20.00
108	D27	Ed Belfour (G), Chi.	5.00	20.00
110	S12	Cam Neely, Bos.	4.00	15.00
112	P19	Petr Klima, T.B.	3.00	10.00
116	**R20**	**Daniel Alfredsson, Ott., RC**	**15.00**	**40.00**
124	P64	Joé Juneau, Wsh.	3.00	10.00
125	**R10**	**Radek Dvorak, Fla., RC**	**4.00**	**12.00**
132	D12	Sean Burke (G), Hfd.	4.00	15.00
142	P55	Owen Nolan, S.J.	4.00	15.00
148	D20	Kevin Hatcher, Dal.	3.00	10.00
151	P41	Alexei Yashin, Ott.	6.00	25.00
152	D21	Scott Stevens, N.J.	3.00	10.00
156	D29	Darcy Wakaluk (G), Dal.	3.00	10.00
161	D19	Kirk McLean (G), Van.	4.00	15.00
164	P57	Valeri Kamensky, Col.	4.00	15.00
166	P56	Dmitri Khristich, L.A.	3.00	10.00
168	P44	Joe Nieuwendyk, Dal.	4.00	15.00
169	D24	Mike Richter (G), NYR.	5.00	20.00
174	D23	Eric Desjardins, Pha.	3.00	10.00
182	S21	Pierre Turgeon, Mtl.	4.00	15.00

RARE SERIES - GOLD

Rare Set (26 cards): 1,000.00 2,700.00

No.		Player	Gold	Ref.
2	D1	Ray Bourque, Bos.	30.00	60.00
13	D6	Patrick Roy, Col.	120.00	375.00
19	D5	Chris Chelios, Chi.	25.00	50.00
25	S9	Jeremy Roenick, Chi.	15.00	30.00
30	S16	Theoren Fleury, Cgy.	15.00	30.00
35	S22	Teemu Selänne, Wpg.	40.00	100.00
41	D14	Brian Leetch, NYR.	15.00	30.00
45	S14	Martin Brodeur, N.J.	40.00	100.00
55	P13	Doug Gilmour, Tor.	15.00	30.00
85	R15	Saku Koivu, Mtl.	40.00	100.00
88	P1	Eric Lindros, Pha.	100.00	300.00
99	S15	Mark Messier, NYR.	30.00	60.00
100	S20	Peter Forsberg, Col.	60.00	175.00
123	P63	Keith Tkachuk, Wpg.	25.00	50.00
128	P36	Mike Modano, Dal.	30.00	60.00
138	**R13**	**Aki Berg, L.A., RC**	**12.00**	**25.00**
140	S18	Alexander Mogilny, Van.	15.00	30.00
162	P18	Steve Yzerman, Det.	60.00	175.00
176	R1	Ed Jovanovski, Fla.	12.00	25.00
179	P60	John LeClair, Pha.	30.00	60.00
180	S5	Wayne Gretzky, Stl.	150.00	600.00
184	P35	Brett Hull, Stl.	30.00	60.00
185	S25	Jaromir Jagr, Pgh.	60.00	175.00
187	P70	Pavel Bure, Van.	40.00	100.00
190	P30	Mario Lemieux, Pgh.	120.00	375.00
191		Checklist	12.00	25.00

1995 - 96 TOPPS STADIUM CLUB

These cards have two versions: the regular card and a Members Only mail offer parallel.

Imprint: © 1996 THE TOPPS COMPANY, INC.

Complete Set (225 cards): 60.00

Common Player: .15 .75

No.	Player	Reg.	M.O.
1	Alexander Mogilny, Van.	.35	5.00

	No.	Player	Reg.	M.O.
☐ ☐	2	Ray Bourque, Bos.	.50	10.00
☐ ☐	3	Garry Galley, Buf.	.15	.75
☐ ☐	5	Dave Andreychuk, Tor.	.15	.75
☐ ☐	4	Gary Wesley, Hfd.	.15	.75
☐ ☐	6	Daren Puppa (G), T.B.	.15	.75
☐ ☐	7	Shayne Corson, Stl.	.25	2.00
☐ ☐	8	Kelly Hrudey (G), L.A.	.15	.75
☐ ☐	9	Russ Courtnall, Van.	.15	.75
☐ ☐	10	Chris Chelios, Chi.	.35	8.00
☐ ☐	11	Ulf Samuelsson, Pgh.	.15	.75
☐ ☐	12	Mike Vernon (G), Det.	.25	2.00
☐ ☐	13	Al MacInnis, Stl.	.15	.75
☐ ☐	14	Joel Otto, Cgy.	.15	.75
☐ ☐	15	Patrick Roy (G), Mtl.	2.00	40.00
☐ ☐	16	Steve Thomas, N.J.	.15	.75
☐ ☐	17	Pat Verbeek, NYR.	.15	.75
☐ ☐	18	Joe Nieuwendyk, Dal.	.25	2.00
☐ ☐	19	Todd Krygier, Ana.	.15	.75
☐ ☐	20	Steve Yzerman, Det.	1.25	25.00
☐ ☐	2	Bill Ranford (G), Edm. Error (Card 2)	.25	2.00
☐ ☐	22	Ron Francis, Pgh.	.35	5.00
☐ ☐	23	Sylvain Côté, Wsh.	.15	.75
☐ ☐	24	Grant Fuhr (G), Stl.	.25	2.00
☐ ☐	25	Brendan Shanahan, Hfd.	.60	12.00
☐ ☐	26	John MacLean, N.J.	.15	.75
☐ ☐	27	Darren Turcotte, Wpg.	.15	.75
☐ ☐	28	Bernie Nicholls, Chi.	.15	.75
☐ ☐	29	Sean Burke (G), Hfd.	.25	2.00
☐ ☐	30	Brian Leetch, NYR.	.35	5.00
☐ ☐	31	Dave Gagner, Dal.	.15	.75
☐ ☐	32	Rick Tocchet, Bos.	.15	.75
☐ ☐	33	Ron Hextall (G), Pha.	.25	2.00
☐ ☐	34	Paul Coffey, Det.	.25	2.00
☐ ☐	35	John Vanbiesbrouck (G), Fla.	.60	12.00
☐ ☐	36	Rod Brind'Amour, Pha.	.25	2.000
☐ ☐	37	Brian Savage, Mtl.	.15	.75
☐ ☐	38	Nelson Emerson, Hfd.	.15	.75
☐ ☐	39	Brian Bradley, T.B.	.15	.75
☐ ☐	40	Adam Oates, Bos.	.35	5.00
☐ ☐	41	Kirk McLean (G), Van.	.25	2.00
☐ ☐	42	Kevin Hatcher, Dal.	.15	.75
☐ ☐	43	Mike Keane, Mtl.	.15	.75
☐ ☐	44	Don Beaupré (G), Ott.	.15	.75
☐ ☐	45	Scott Stevens, N.J.	.15	.75
☐ ☐	46	Dale Hawerchuk, Stl.	.25	2.00
☐ ☐	47	Scott Young, Col.	.15	.75
☐ ☐	48	Mark Recchi, Mtl.	.25	2.00
☐ ☐	49	Mike Richter (G), NYR.	.35	5.00
☐ ☐	50	Kevin Stevens, Pgh.	.15	.75
☐ ☐	51	Mike Ridley, Van.	.15	.75
☐ ☐	52	Joe Murphy, Chi.	.15	.75
☐ ☐	53	Stéphane Fiset (G), Col.	.25	2.00
☐ ☐	54	Donald Audette, Buf.	.15	.75
☐ ☐	55	Ed Belfour (G), Chi.	.35	5.00
☐ ☐	56	Rob Blake, L.A.	.25	2.00
☐ ☐	57	Adam Graves, NYR.	.15	.75
☐ ☐	58	Arturs Irbe (G), S.J.	.15	.75
☐ ☐	59	Mathieu Schneider, NYI.	.15	.75
☐ ☐	60	Dominik Hasek (G), Buf.	.75	15.00
☐ ☐	61	Andrew Cassels, Hfd.	.15	.75
☐ ☐	62	Johan Garpenlov, Fla.	.15	.75
☐ ☐	63	Kyle McLaren, Bos.	.15	.75
☐ ☐	64	Petr Nedved, Pgh.	.15	.75
☐ ☐	65	Owen Nolan, S.J.	.25	2.00
☐ ☐	66	Keith Primeau, Det.	.25	2.00
☐ ☐	67	Mark Tinordi, Wsh.	.15	.75
☐ ☐	68	Dimitri Khristich, Wsh.	.15	.75
☐ ☐	69	Chris Pronger, Stl.	.25	2.00
☐ ☐	70	Jaromir Jagr, Pgh.	1.25	25.00
☐ ☐	71	Mike Ricci, Col.	.15	.75
☐ ☐	72	Trevor Kidd (G), Cgy.	.25	2.00
☐ ☐	73	Stu Barnes, Fla.	.15	.75
☐ ☐	74	Doug Weight, Edm.	.35	5.00
☐ ☐	75	Mats Sundin, Tor.	.50	10.00
☐ ☐	76	Scott Niedermayer, N.J.	.25	2.00
☐ ☐	77	John LeClair, Pha.	.50	10.00
☐ ☐	78	Derian Hatcher, Dal.	.25	2.00
☐ ☐	79	Brad May, Duf.	.15	.75
☐ ☐	80	Félix Potvin (G), Tor.	.50	10.00
☐ ☐	81	Derek King, NYI.	.15	.75
☐ ☐	82	Guy Hebert (G), Ana.	.25	2.00
☐ ☐	83	Shawn McEachern, Pgh.	.15	.75
☐ ☐	84	Vyacheslav Kozlov, Det.	.15	.75
☐ ☐	85	Martin Brodeur (G), N.J.	.75	15.00
☐ ☐	86	Ray Whitney, S.J.	.15	.75
☐ ☐	87	Martin Straka, Ott.	.15	.75
☐ ☐	88	Keith Jones, Wsh.	.15	.75
☐ ☐	89	Roman Hamrlik, T.B.	.25	2.00
☐ ☐	90	Keith Tkachuk, Wpg.	.35	8.00
☐ ☐	91	Jim Dowd, N.J.	.15	.75
☐ ☐	92	Sergei Zubov, Pgh.	.25	2.00
☐ ☐	93	Bryan McCabe, NYI.	.15	.75
☐ ☐	94	Rob Niedermayer, Fla.	.15	.75
☐ ☐	95	Alexei Zhamnov, Wpg.	.25	2.00
☐ ☐	96	Zarley Zalapski, Cgy.	.15	.75
☐ ☐	97	Alexandre Daigle, Ott.	.25	2.00
☐ ☐	98	Jocelyn Thibault (G), Col.	.35	5.00
☐ ☐	99	Zigmund Palffy, NYI.	.35	8.00
☐ ☐	100	Luc Robitaille, Pgh.	.25	2.00
☐ ☐	101	Radek Bonk, Ott.	.15	.75
☐ ☐	102	Todd Marchant, Edm.	.15	.75
☐ ☐	103	Todd Harvey, Dal.	.15	.75
☐ ☐	104	Blaine Lacher (G), Bos.	.15	.75
☐ ☐	105	Peter Forsberg, Col.	1.25	25.00
☐ ☐	106	Jeff Friesen, S.J.	.25	2.00
☐ ☐	107	Kenny Jonsson, NYI.	.15	.75
☐ ☐	108	Brett Lindros, NYI.	.15	.75
☐ ☐	109	David Oliver, Edm.	.15	.75
☐ ☐	110	Mikael Renberg, Pha.	.15	.75
☐ ☐	111	Alexander Selivanov, T.B.	.15	.75
☐ ☐	112	Stanislav Neckar, Ott.	.15	.75
☐ ☐	113	Oleg Tverdovsky, Ana.	.15	.75
☐ ☐	114	Shean Donovan, S.J.	.15	.75
☐ ☐	115	Jim Carey (G), Wsh.	.15	.75
☐ ☐	116	Tony Granato, L.A.	.15	.75
☐ ☐	117	Tony Amonte, Chi.	.25	2.00
☐ ☐	118	Tomas Sandström, Pgh.	.15	.75
☐ ☐	119	Rick Tabaracci (G), Cgy.	.15	.75
☐ ☐	120	Ray Ferraro, NYR.	.15	.75
☐ ☐	121	Brian Noonan, Stl.	.15	.75
☐ ☐	122	Miroslav Satan, Edm.	.15	.75
☐ ☐	123	Sergio Momesso, Van.	.15	.75
☐ ☐	124	Gary Suter, Chi.	.15	.75
☐ ☐	125	Eric Desjardins, Pha.	.15	.75
☐ ☐	126	Steve Duchesne, Stl.	.15	.75
☐ ☐	127	Zdeno Ciger, Edm.	.15	.75
☐ ☐	128	Cliff Ronning, Van.	.15	.75
☐ ☐	129	Nicklas Lidström, Det.	.25	2.00
☐ ☐	130	Bill Guerin, N.J.	.25	2.00
☐ ☐	131	Igor Korolev, Wpg.	.15	.75
☐ ☐	132	Roman Oksiuta, Ana.	.15	.75
☐ ☐	133	Jesse Belanger, Fla.	.15	.75
☐ ☐	134	Chris Gratton, T.B.	.25	2.00
☐ ☐	135	Chris Osgood (G), Det.	.35	8.00
☐ ☐	136	Pat Peake, Wsh.	.15	.75
☐ ☐	137	Viktor Kozlov, S.J.	.15	.75
☐ ☐	138	Aaron Gavey, T.B.	.15	.75
☐ ☐	139	Zdenek Nedved, Tor.	.15	.75
☐ ☐	140	Rhett Warrener, Fla.	.15	.75
☐ ☐	141	Marko Kiprusoff, Mtl.	.15	.75
☐ ☐	142	Dan Quinn, Ott.	.15	.75
☐ ☐	143	Alexei Zhitnik, Buf.	.15	.75
☐ ☐	144	Larry Murphy, Tor.	.25	2.00
☐ ☐	145	Phil Housley, Cgy.	.15	.75
☐ ☐	146	Don Sweeney, Bos.	.15	.75
☐ ☐	147	Jason Dawe, Buf.	.15	.75
☐ ☐	148	Marcus Ragnarsson, S.J.	.15	.75
☐ ☐	149	Andrei Nikolishin, Hfd.	.15	.75
☐ ☐	150	Dino Ciccarelli, Det.	.25	2.00
☐ ☐	151	Jari Kurri, L.A.	.25	2.00
☐ ☐	152	Bob Probert, Det.	.15	.75
☐ ☐	153	Randy McKay, N.J.	.15	.75
☐ ☐	154	Michael Nylander, Cgy.	.15	.75
☐ ☐	155	Wendel Clark, NYI.	.25	2.00
☐ ☐	156	Antti Törmänen, Ott.	.15	.75
☐ ☐	157	Nikolai Khabibulin (G), Wpg.	.35	5.00
☐ ☐	158	Tom Barrasso (G), Pgh.	.25	2.00
☐ ☐	159	Vincent Damphousse, Mtl.	.35	5.00
☐ ☐	160	Trevor Linden, Van.	.25	2.00
☐ ☐	161	Valeri Kamensky, Col.	.25	2.00
☐ ☐	162	Mike Gartner, Tor.	.25	2.00
☐ ☐	EC163	Cam Neely, Bos.	.75	2.00
☐ ☐	EC164	Pat LaFontaine, Buf.	.75	2.00
☐ ☐	EC165	Theoren Fleury, Cgy.	1.00	5.00
☐ ☐	EC166	Jeremy Roenick, Chi.	1.00	5.00
☐ ☐	EC167	Joe Sakic, Col.	3.50	20.00
☐ ☐	EC168	Mike Modano, Dal.	2.00	10.00
☐ ☐	EC169	Sergei Fedorov, Det.	2.00	10.00
☐ ☐	EC170	Scott Mellanby, Fla.	.50	1.00
☐ ☐	EC171	Jason Arnott, Edm.	.75	2.00
☐ ☐	EC172	Geoff Sanderson, Hfd.	.50	1.00
☐ ☐	EC173	Wayne Gretzky, L.A.	8.00	50.00
☐ ☐	EC174	Paul Kariya, Ana.	5.00	30.00
☐ ☐	EC175	Pierre Turgeon, Mtl.	.75	2.00
☐ ☐	EC176	Stéphane Richer, N.J.	.50	1.00
☐ ☐	EC177	Kirk Muller, NYI.	.50	1.00
☐ ☐	EC178	Mark Messier, NYR.	2.00	10.00
☐ ☐	EC179	Craig Janney, S.J.	.50	1.00
☐ ☐	EC180	Mario Lemieux, Pgh.	6.50	40.00
☐ ☐	EC181	Eric Lindros, Pha.	5.00	30.00
☐ ☐	EC182	Alexei Yashin, Ott.	1.50	8.00
☐ ☐	EC183	Brett Hull, Stl.	2.00	10.00
☐ ☐	EC184	Doug Gilmour, Tor.	1.00	5.00
☐ ☐	EC185	Petr Klima, T.B.	.50	1.00
☐ ☐	EC186	Pavel Bure, Van.	3.00	15.00
☐ ☐	EC187	Joé Juneau, Wsh.	.50	1.00
☐ ☐	EC188	Teemu Selänne, Wpg.	3.00	15.00
☐ ☐	EC189	Claude Lemieux, N.J.	.50	1.00
☐ ☐	ER190	Vitali Yachmenev, L.A.	.50	1.00
☐ ☐	ER191	Jason Bonsignore, Edm.	.50	1.00
☐ ☐	ER192	Jeff O'Neill, Hfd.	.75	2.00
☐ ☐	ER193	Brendan Witt, Wsh.	.50	1.00
☐ ☐	**ER194**	**Brian Holzinger, Buf., RC**	**.50**	**1.00**
☐ ☐	ER195	Eric Dazé, Chi.	.75	2.00
☐ ☐	ER196	Ed Jovanovski, Fla.	.75	2.00
☐ ☐	ER197	Deron Quint, Wpg.	.50	1.00
☐ ☐	ER198	Marty Murray, Cgy.	.50	1.00
☐ ☐	ER199	Jere Lehtinen, Dal.	.75	2.00
☐ ☐	**ER200**	**Radek Dvorak, Fla., RC**	**.75**	**1.50**
☐ ☐	**ER201**	**Aki Berg, L.A., RC**	**.50**	**1.00**
☐ ☐	**ER202**	**Chad Kilger, Ana., RC**	**.50**	**1.00**
☐ ☐	ER203	Saku Koivu, Mtl.	3.00	15.00
☐ ☐	**ER204**	**Todd Bertuzzi, NYI., RC**	**1.50**	**2.00**
☐ ☐	ER205	Niklas Sundstrom, NYR.	.50	1.00
☐ ☐	**ER206**	**Daniel Alfredsson, Ott., RC**	**2.50**	**10.00**
☐ ☐	**ER207**	**Shane Doan, Wpg., RC**	**.50**	**1.00**
☐ ☐	208	Richard Park, Pgh.	.15	.75
☐ ☐	209	Peter Bondra, Wsh.	.35	8.00
☐ ☐	210	Bryan Smolinski, Pgh.	.15	.75
☐ ☐	**211**	**Tommy Salo (G), NYI., RC**	**.15**	**.75**
☐ ☐	212	Patrick Poulin, Chi.	.15	.75
☐ ☐	**213**	**Mathieu Dandenault, Det., RC**	**.15**	**.75**
☐ ☐	214	Steve Rucchin, Ana.	.15	.75
☐ ☐	215	Ray Sheppard, S.J.	.15	.75
☐ ☐	**216**	**Robert Svehla, Fla., RC**	**.25**	**1.50**
☐ ☐	217	Olaf Kolzig (G), Wsh.	.35	5.00
☐ ☐	218	Alexei Kovalev, NYR.	.15	.75
☐ ☐	219	Ian Moran, Pgh.	.15	.75
☐ ☐	220	Valeri Bure, Mtl.	.15	.75
☐ ☐	221	Dean Malkoc, Van.	.15	.75
☐ ☐	222	Jason Doig, Wpg.	.15	.75
☐ ☐	223	David Nemirovsky, Fla.	.15	.75
☐ ☐	224	Jamie Pushor, Det.	.15	.75
☐ ☐	225	Ricard Persson, N.J.	.15	.75

	No.	Checklists	Reg.
☐	1	Checklist	.10
☐	2	Checklist	.10

EXTREME NORTH

These cards have two versions: the regular card and a Members Only paralell.

	No.	Player	Reg.	M.O.
Insert Set (9 cards):			**85.00**	**45.00**
☐ ☐	EN1	Pavel Bure, Van.	15.00	8.00
☐ ☐	EN2	Teemu Selänne, Wpg.	15.00	8.00
☐ ☐	EN3	Félix Potvin (G), Tor.	10.00	5.00
☐ ☐	EN4	Patrick Roy (G), Mtl.	30.00	20.00
☐ ☐	EN5	Theoren Fleury, Cgy.	6.00	3.00
☐ ☐	EN6	Bill Ranford (G), Edm.	4.00	1.50
☐ ☐	EN7	Pierre Turgeon, Mtl.	4.00	1.50

	No.	Player	Reg.	M.O.
☐ ☐	EN8	Doug Gilmour, Tor.	6.00	3.00
☐ ☐	EN9	Alexander Mogilny, Van.	6.00	3.00

FEARLESS

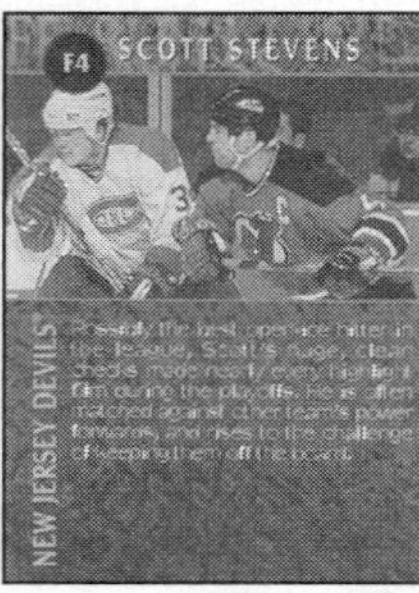

These inserts have two versions: the regular card and a Members Only parallel.

Insert Set (9 cards):			35.00	18.00
	No.	Player	Reg.	M.O.
☐ ☐	F1	Brendan Shanahan, Hfd.	12.00	6.00
☐ ☐	F2	Chris Chelios, Chi.	8.00	4.00
☐ ☐	F3	Keith Primeau, Det.	4.00	1.50
☐ ☐	F4	Scott Stevens, N.J. (vs. Mats Naslund)	2.00	.75
☐ ☐	F5	Rick Tocchet, L.A.	2.00	.75
☐ ☐	F6	Kevin Stevens, Bos.	2.00	.75
☐ ☐	F7	Ulf Samuelsson, NYR. (vs. M. Gartner)	2.00	.75
☐ ☐	F8	Wendel Clark, NYI.	4.00	1.50
☐ ☐	F9	Keith Tkachuk, Wpg.	8.00	4.00

GENERATION TSC

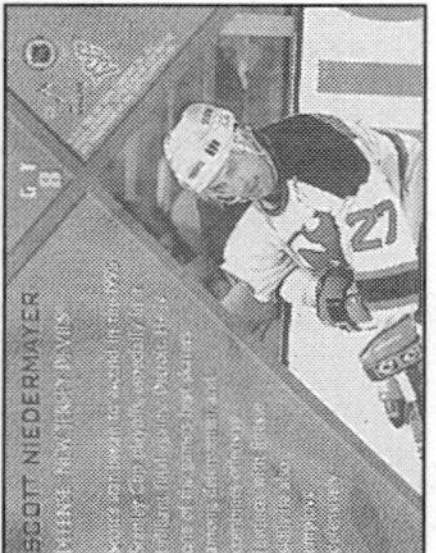

These inserts have two versions: the regular card and a Members Only parallel.

Insert Set (9 cards):			70.00	50.00
	No.	Player	Reg.	M.O.
☐ ☐	GT1	Paul Kariya, Ana.	20.00	15.00
☐ ☐	GT2	Teemu Selänne, Wpg.	10.00	8.00
☐ ☐	GT3	Jaromir Jagr, Pgh.	15.00	12.00
☐ ☐	GT4	Peter Forsberg, Col.	15.00	12.00
☐ ☐	GT5	Martin Brodeur (G), N.J.	10.00	8.00
☐ ☐	GT6	Jim Carey (G), Wsh.	2.00	.75
☐ ☐	GT7	Mikael Renberg, Pha.	2.00	.75
☐ ☐	GT8	Scott Niedermayer, N.J.	4.00	1.50
☐ ☐	GT9	Ed Jovanovski, Fla.	4.00	1.50

METALISTS

These laser-cut cards have two versions: the regular card and a Members Only parallel.

Insert Set (12 cards):			135.00	80.00
	No.	Player	Reg.	M.O.
☐ ☐	M1	Wayne Gretzky, L.A.	40.00	25.00
☐ ☐	M2	Mario Lemieux, Pgh.	30.00	20.00
☐ ☐	M3	Patrick Roy (G), Mtl.	30.00	20.00
☐ ☐	M4	Ray Bourque, Bos.	10.00	5.00
☐ ☐	M5	Ed Belfour (G), Chi.	6.00	3.00
☐ ☐	M6	Tom Barrasso (G), Pgh.	4.00	1.50
☐ ☐	M7	Joe Mullen, Bos.	2.00	.75
☐ ☐	M8	Brian Leetch, NYR.	6.00	3.00
☐ ☐	M9	Mark Messier, NYR.	10.00	5.00
☐ ☐	M10	Dominik Hasek (G), Buf.	15.00	8.00
☐ ☐	M11	Paul Coffey, Det.	4.00	1.50
☐ ☐	M12	Guy Carbonneau, Dal.	2.00	.75

NEMESES

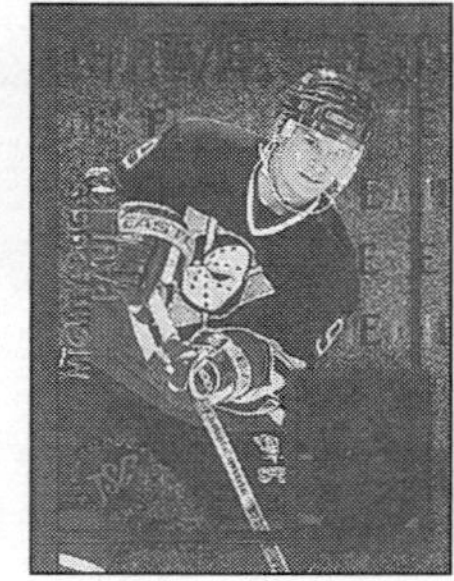

These cards have two versions: the regular card and a Members Only parallel.

Insert Set (9 cards):			160.00	80.00
	No.	Player	Reg.	M.O.
☐ ☐	N1	Eric Lindros/Scott Stevens	30.00	15.00
☐ ☐	N2	Wayne Gretzky/Mario Lemieux	60.00	30.00
☐ ☐	N3	Cam Neely/Claude Lemieux	5.00	2.50
☐ ☐	N4	Pavel Bure/Mike Richter	15.00	7.50
☐ ☐	N5	Brian Leetch/Ray Bourque	10.00	5.00
☐ ☐	N6	Martin Brodeur/Dominik Hasek	20.00	10.00
☐ ☐	N7	Doug Gilmour/Sergei Fedorov	10.00	5.00
☐ ☐	N8	Mark Messier/Joel Otto	10.00	5.00
☐ ☐	N9	Paul Kariya/Peter Forsberg	35.00	18.00

POWER STREAK

These cards have two versions: the regular card and a Members Only parallel.

Insert Set (10 cards):			50.00	30.00
	No.	Player	Reg.	M.O.
☐ ☐	PS1	Pierre Turgeon, Mtl.	4.00	1.50
☐ ☐	PS2	Eric Lindros, Pha.	20.00	15.00
☐ ☐	PS3	Ron Francis, Pgh.	5.00	3.00
☐ ☐	PS4	Paul Coffey, Det.	4.00	1.50
☐ ☐	PS5	Mikael Renberg, Pha.	2.00	.75
☐ ☐	PS6	John LeClair, Pha.	8.00	5.00
☐ ☐	PS7	Dino Ciccarelli, Det.	4.00	1.50
☐ ☐	PS8	Wendel Clark, NYI.	4.00	1.50
☐ ☐	PS9	Brett Hull, Stl.	8.00	5.00
☐ ☐	PS10	Stéphane Richer, N.J.	2.00	.75

MASTER PHOTOS

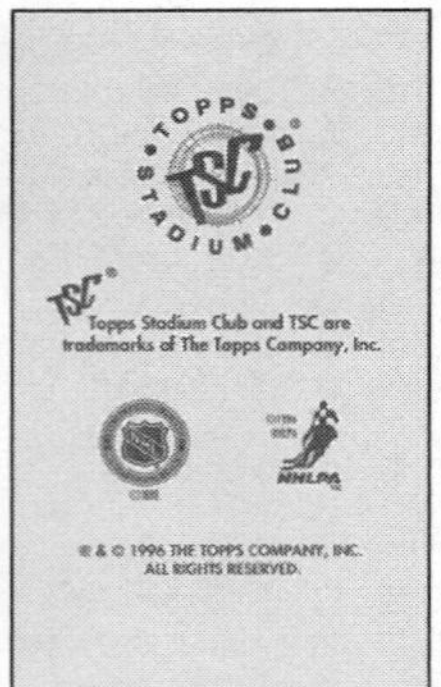

These cards were issued in Topps bubble packs. One 3" x 5" card was issued with a pack of Topps Series One and a Topps team set. Only Canadian team packs are known to exist. Other singles may exist.

	Player	NRMT-MT
☐	Jason Arnott, Edm.	2.00
☐	Theoren Fleury, Cgy.	3.00
☐	Doug Gilmour, Tor.	3.00
☐	Trevor Linden, Van.	2.00
☐	Kirk McLean (G), Van.	2.00
☐	Alexander Mogilny, Van.	3.00
☐	Félix Potvin (G), Tor.	5.00
☐	Mats Sundin, Tor.	5.00
☐	Alexei Yashin, Ott.	4.00

1995 - 96 TOPPS STADIUM CLUB MEMBERS ONLY

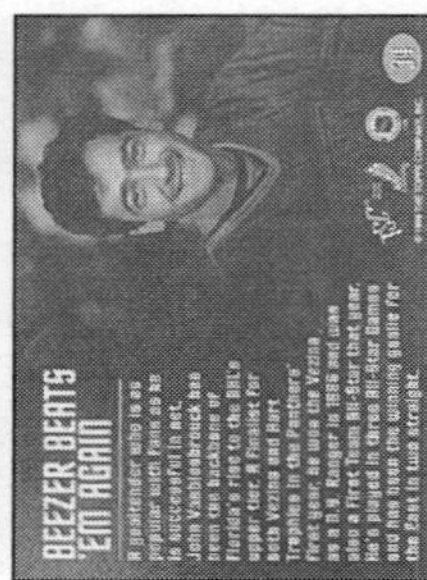

Complete Set (50 cards):			20.00
	No.	Player	NRMT-MT
☐	1	Wayne Gretzky, L.A.	4.00
☐	2	Paul Kariya, Ana.	2.50
☐	3	Brett Hull, Stl.	1.00
☐	4	Chris Chelios, Chi.	.75
☐	5	Paul Coffey, Det.	.35
☐	6	Ed Belfour (G), N.J.	.50
☐	7	Theoren Fleury, Cgy.	.50
☐	8	Owen Nolan, S.J.	.35
☐	9	Al MacInnis, Stl.	.25
☐	10	Alexander Mogilny, Van.	.50
☐	11	Kevin Hatcher, Dal.	.25
☐	12	Doug Weight, Edm.	.50
☐	13	Félix Potvin (G), Tor.	1.00
☐	14	Teemu Selänne, Ana.	1.50
☐	15	Sergei Fedorov, Det.	1.00
☐	16	Larry Murphy, Tor.	.35
☐	17	Joe Sakic, Col.	1.75
☐	18	Mats Sundin, Tor.	1.00
☐	19	Nicklas Lidström, Det.	.35
☐	20	Peter Forsberg, Col.	2.00
☐	21	Chris Osgood (G), Det.	.75
☐	22	Mike Gartner, Tor.	.35
☐	23	Denis Savard/Craig MacTavish	.35
☐	24	Mario Lemieux, Pgh.	3.00
☐	25	Jaromir Jagr, Pgh.	2.00
☐	26	Brendan Shanahan, Hfd.	1.25
☐	27	Scott Stevens, N.J.	.25
☐	28	Ray Bourque, Bos.	1.00
☐	29	Martin Brodeur (G), N.J.	1.50
☐	30	Eric Lindros, Pha.	2.50
☐	31	Peter Bondra, Wsh.	.75

	No.	Player	
☐	32	Scott Mellanby, Fla.	.25
☐	33	Brian Leetch, NYR.	.50
☐	34	John Vanbiesbrouck (G), Fla.	1.25
☐	35	Pat Verbeek, NYR.	.25
☐	36	Cam Neely, Bos.	.35
☐	37	Roman Hamrlik, T.B.	.35
☐	38	Daniel Alfredsson, Ott.	1.00
☐	39	Pierre Turgeon, Mtl.	.35
☐	40	Mark Messier, NYR.	1.00
☐	41	Eric Desjardins, Pha.	.25
☐	42	Dominik Hasek (G), Buf.	1.50
☐	43	John LeClair, Pha.	1.00
☐	44	Mathieu Schneider, NYI.	.25
☐	45	Ron Francis, Pgh.	.50
☐	46	Saku Koivu, Mtl.	1.50
☐	47	Ed Jovanovski, Fla.	.35
☐	48	Vitali Yachmenev, L.A.	.25
☐	49	Petr Sykora, N.J.	.25
☐	50	Eric Dazé, Chi.	.35

1995 - 96 TOPPS SUPER SKILLS

These cards have two versions: the regular card and a Platinum parallel.

Imprint:

		Complete Set (90 cards):	**16.00**	**65.00**
		Common Player:	**.15**	**.50**
	No.	**Player**	**Reg.**	**Plat.**
☐☐	1	Mario Lemieux, Pgh.	1.50	6.00
☐☐	2	Adam Oates, Bos.	.35	1.25
☐☐	3	Donald Audette, Buf.	.15	.50
☐☐	4	Andrew Cassels, Hfd.	.15	.50
☐☐	5	Pat LaFontaine, Buf.	.25	1.00
☐☐	6	Mathieu Schneider, NYI.	.15	.50
☐☐	7	Scott Stevens, N.J.	.15	.50
☐☐	8	Mikael Renberg, Pha.	.15	.50
☐☐	9	Pierre Turgeon, Mtl.	.25	1.00
☐☐	10	Steve Yzerman, Det.	1.00	4.00
☐☐	11	Russ Courtnall, Van.	.15	.50
☐☐	12	Oleg Tverdovsky, Ana.	.15	.50
☐☐	13	Craig Janney, Stl.	.15	.50
☐☐	14	Doug Gilmour, Tor.	.35	1.25
☐☐	15	Wayne Gretzky, L.A.	2.00	8.00
☐☐	16	Paul Kariya, Ana.	1.25	5.00
☐☐	17	Joe Sakic, Que.	.85	3.50
☐☐	18	Peter Forsberg, Que.	1.00	4.00
☐☐	19	Brian Leetch, NYR.	.35	1.25
☐☐	20	Jaromir Jagr, Pgh.	1.00	4.00
☐☐	21	Geoff Sanderson, Hfd.	.15	.50
☐☐	22	Rob Niedermayer, Fla.	.15	.50
☐☐	23	Ray Ferraro, NYI.	.15	.50
☐☐	24	Alexandre Daigle, Ott.	.25	1.00
☐☐	25	Joé Juneau, Wsh.	.15	.50
☐☐	26	Don Sweeney, Bos.	.15	.50
☐☐	27	Scott Niedermayer, N.J.	.25	1.00
☐☐	28	Mike Gartner, Tor.	.25	1.00
☐☐	29	Paul Coffey, Det.	.25	1.00
☐☐	30	Pavel Bure, Van.	.75	3.00
☐☐	31	Teemu Selänne, Wpg.	.75	3.00
☐☐	32	Mats Sundin, Tor.	.50	2.00
☐☐	33	Trevor Linden, Van.	.25	1.00
☐☐	34	Sergei Fedorov, Det.	.50	2.00
☐☐	35	Theoren Fleury, Cgy.	.35	1.25
☐☐	36	Alexander Mogilny, Van.	.35	1.25
☐☐	37	Garry Galley, Buf.	.15	.50
☐☐	38	Stu Barnes, Fla.	.15	.50
☐☐	39	Glen Wesley, Hfd.	.15	.50
☐☐	40	Eric Lindros, Pha.	1.25	5.00
☐☐	41	Stéphane Richer, N.J.	.15	.50
☐☐	42	John LeClair, Pha.	.50	2.00
☐☐	43	Pat Verbeek, NYR.	.15	.50
☐☐	45	Wendel Clark, Tor.	.25	1.00
☐☐	44	Bill Guerin, N.J.	.25	1.00
☐☐	46	Mike Modano, Dal.	.50	2.00
☐☐	47	Keith Primeau, Det.	.25	1.00
☐☐	48	Brett Hull, Stl.	.50	2.00
☐☐	49	Al MacInnis, Stl.	.15	.50
☐☐	50	Chris Chelios, Chi.	.35	1.50
☐☐	51	Keith Tkachuk, Wpg.	.35	1.50
☐☐	52	Dave Andreychuk, Tor.	.15	.50
☐☐	53	Kevin Hatcher, Pgh.	.15	.50
☐☐	54	Chris Pronger, Stl.	.25	1.00
☐☐	55	Brendan Shanahan, Hfd.	.60	2.50
☐☐	56	Luc Robitaille, Pgh.	.25	1.00
☐☐	57	Ray Bourque, Bos.	.50	2.00
☐☐	58	Mark Recchi, Mtl.	.25	1.00
☐☐	59	Brian Bradley, T.B.	.15	.50
☐☐	60	Mark Messier, NYR.	.50	2.00
☐☐	61	Kevin Stevens, Bos.	.15	.50
☐☐	62	John MacLean, N.J.	.15	.50
☐☐	63	Cam Neely, Bos.	.25	1.00
☐☐	64	Rick Tocchet, L.A.	.15	.50
☐☐	65	Jeremy Roenick, Chi.	.35	1.25
☐☐	66	Phil Housley, Cgy.	.15	.50
☐☐	67	Jason Arnott, Edm.	.25	1.00
☐☐	68	Todd Harvey, Dal.	.15	.50
☐☐	69	Jeff Friesen, S.J.	.25	1.00
☐☐	70	Alexei Zhamnov, Wpg.	.25	1.00
☐☐	71	David Oliver, Edm.	.15	.50
☐☐	72	Bernie Nicholls, Chi.	.15	.50
☐☐	73	Jim Carey (G), Wsh.	.15	.50
☐☐	74	Mike Richter (G), NYR.	.35	1.25
☐☐	75	Dominik Hasek (G), Buf.	.75	3.00
☐☐	76	Sean Burke (G), Hfd.	.25	1.00
☐☐	77	Ron Hextall (G), Pha.	.25	1.00
☐☐	78	John Vanbiesbrouck (G), Fla.	.60	2.50
☐☐	79	Tom Barrasso (G), Pgh, Error (/b:Wregget)	.15	.50
☐☐	80	Martin Brodeur (G), N.J.	.75	3.00
☐☐	81	Patrick Roy (G), Mtl.	1.50	6.00
☐☐	82	Trevor Kidd (G), Cgy.	.25	1.00
☐☐	83	Andy Moog (G), Dal.	.25	1.00
☐☐	84	Mike Vernon (G), Det.	.25	1.00
☐☐	85	Félix Potvin (G), Tor.	.50	2.00
☐☐	86	Bill Ranford (G), Edm.	.25	1.00
☐☐	87	Kelly Hrudey (G), L.A.	.15	.50
☐☐	88	Grant Fuhr (G), Stl.	.25	1.00
☐☐	89	Kirk McLean (G), Van.	.25	1.00
☐☐	90	Ed Belfour (G), Chi.	.35	1.25

SUPER ROOKIES

		Insert Set (15 cards)	**6.00**
	No.	**Player**	**NRMT-MT**
☐	SR1	Ed Jovanovski, Fla.	1.00
☐	SR2	Jason Bonsignore, Edm.	.50
☐	SR3	Jeff O'Neill, Hfd.	1.00
☐	SR4	Cory Stillman, Cgy.	.50
☐	SR5	Chad Kilger, Ana.	.50
☐	SR6	Aki Berg, L.A.	.50
☐	SR7	Todd Bertuzzi, NYI.	1.00
☐	SR8	Shane Doan, Wpg.	.50
☐	SR9	Kyle McLaren, Bos.	.50
☐	SR10	Radek Dvorak, Fla.	.75
☐	SR11	Saku Koivu, Mtl.	3.00
☐	SR12	Daniel Alfredsson, Ott.	2.00
☐	SR13	Antti Törmänen, Ana.	.50
☐	SR14	Niklas Sundstrom, NYR.	.50
☐	SR15	Vitali Yachmenev, L.A.	.50

1995 - 96 UPPER DECK

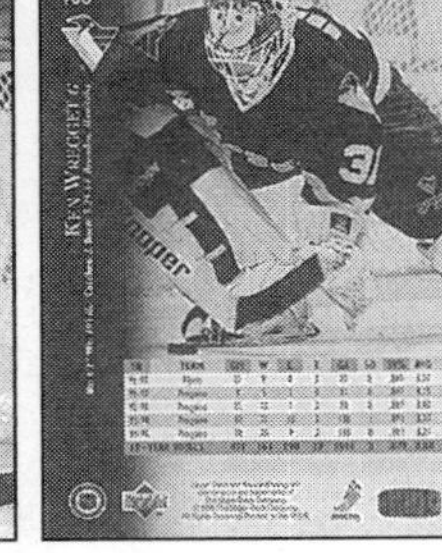

These cards have three versions: the regular card, an Electric Ice parallel and a Electric Ice Gold parallel.

Series One Imprint: © 1995 THE UPPER DECK COMPANY
Series Two Imprint: © 1996 THE UPPER DECK COMPANY

		Series One Set (270 cards):	**28.00**	**160.00**	**2,500.00**
		Series Two Set (300 cards):	**40.00**	**180.00**	**3,500.00**
		Common Player:	**.15**	**.50**	**6.00**
	No.	**Player**	**Reg.**	**Silver**	**Gold**
☐☐☐	1	Cam Neely, Bos.	.25	.75	10.00
☐☐☐	2	Donald Audette, Buf.	.15	.35	6.00
☐☐☐	3	Derian Hatcher, Dal.	.25	.75	10.00
☐☐☐	4	Mike Vernon, Det.	.25	.75	10.00
☐☐☐	5	Daryl Sydor, L.A.	.15	.35	6.00
☐☐☐	6	Patrice Brisebois, Mtl.	.15	.35	6.00
☐☐☐	7	John LeClair, Pha.	.50	5.00	40.00
☐☐☐	8	Luc Robitaille, NYR.	.25	.75	10.00
☐☐☐	9	Todd Krygier, Ana.	.15	.35	6.00
☐☐☐	10	Steve Chiasson, Det.	.15	.35	6.00
☐☐☐	11	Sergei Krivokrasov, Chi.	.15	.35	6.00
☐☐☐	12	Marko Tuomainen, Edm.	.15	.35	6.00
☐☐☐	13	Paul Ranheim, Hfd.	.15	.35	6.00
☐☐☐	14	Brian Rolston, N.J.	.15	.35	6.00
☐☐☐	15	Alexei Yashin, Ott.	.35	3.50	25.00
☐☐☐	16	Joe Mullen, Bos.	.15	.35	6.00
☐☐☐	17	Dallas Drake, Wpg.	.15	.35	6.00
☐☐☐	18	Tony Amonte, Chi.	.25	.75	10.00
☐☐☐	19	Gary Roberts, Cgy.	.25	.75	10.00
☐☐☐	20	Geoff Sanderson, Hfd.	.15	.35	6.00
☐☐☐	21	Gord Murphy, Fla.	.15	.35	6.00
☐☐☐	22	Dean Evason, Cgy.	.15	.35	6.00
☐☐☐	**23**	**Brantt Myhres, T.B., RC**	**.15**	**.35**	**6.00**
☐☐☐	24	Sergei Makarov, S.J.	.15	.35	6.00
☐☐☐	25	Joé Juneau, Wsh.	.15	.35	6.00
☐☐☐	26	Greg Adams, Dal.	.15	.35	6.00
☐☐☐	27	Yuri Khmylev, Buf.	.15	.35	6.00
☐☐☐	28	Yanic Perreault, L.A.	.15	.35	6.00
☐☐☐	29	Jason Arnott, Edm.	.25	.75	10.00
☐☐☐	30	Glen Healy (G), NYR.	.15	.35	6.00
☐☐☐	31	Sergei Brylin, N.J.	.15	.35	6.00
☐☐☐	32	Ian Laperrière, Stl.	.15	.35	6.00
☐☐☐	33	Trevor Linden, Van.	.25	.75	10.00
☐☐☐	34	Nicklas Lidström, Det.	.25	.75	10.00
☐☐☐	35	Don Sweeney, Bos.	.15	.35	6.00
☐☐☐	36	Brian Savage, Mtl.	.15	.35	6.00
☐☐☐	37	Richard Matvichuk, Dal.	.15	.35	6.00
☐☐☐	38	Dale Hawerchuk, Stl.	.25	.75	10.00
☐☐☐	39	Patrick Roy (G), Mtl.	2.00	20.00	200.00
☐☐☐	40	Alexander Semak, N.J.	.15	.35	6.00
☐☐☐	41	Kirk Maltby, Edm.	.15	.35	6.00
☐☐☐	42	Jiri Slegr, Edm.	.15	.35	6.00
☐☐☐	43	Joe Sacco, Ana.	.15	.35	6.00
☐☐☐	44	Claude Lemieux, N.J.	.15	.35	6.00
☐☐☐	45	Eric Weinrich, Chi.	.15	.35	6.00
☐☐☐	46	Ron Francis, Pgh.	.35	1.50	10.00
☐☐☐	47	Jamie Storr (G), L.A.	.25	.75	10.00
☐☐☐	48	Félix Potvin (G), Tor.	.50	5.00	40.00
☐☐☐	49	Steve Duchesne, Ott.	.15	.35	6.00
☐☐☐	50	Jody Hull, Fla.	.15	.35	6.00
☐☐☐	51	Dave Manson, Wpg.	.15	.35	6.00
☐☐☐	52	Marty McInnis, NYI.	.15	.35	6.00
☐☐☐	53	James Patrick, Cgy.	.15	.35	6.00
☐☐☐	54	Joe Sakic, Col.	1.00	10.00	100.00
☐☐☐	55	Andrei Nikolishin, Hfd.	.15	.35	6.00
☐☐☐	56	Adrian Aucoin, Van.	.15	.35	6.00
☐☐☐	**57**	**Wade Flaherty (G), S.J., RC**	**.15**	**.35**	**6.00**
☐☐☐	58	Marek Malik, Hfd.	.15	.35	6.00
☐☐☐	59	Jason Allison, Wsh.	.35	1.50	15.00
☐☐☐	60	Stéphane Matteau, NYR.	.15	.35	6.00
☐☐☐	61	Jason Dawe, Buf.	.15	.35	6.00
☐☐☐	62	Ray Whitney, S.J.	.15	.35	6.00
☐☐☐	63	Bill Lindsay, Fla.	.15	.35	6.00
☐☐☐	64	Alexei Zhamnov, Wpg.	.25	.75	10.00
☐☐☐	65	Adam Deadmarsh, Col.	.25	.75	10.00
☐☐☐	66	Vincent Damphousse, Mtl.	.35	1.50	15.00
☐☐☐	67	Josef Beranek, Van.	.15	.35	6.00
☐☐☐	68	Stanislav Neckar, Ott.	.15	.35	6.00
☐☐☐	69	Alexei Kasatonov, Bos.	.15	.35	6.00
☐☐☐	70	Jim Carey (G), Wsh.	.15	.35	6.00
☐☐☐	71	Todd Marchant, Edm.	.15	.35	6.00
☐☐☐	72	Mike Sillinger, Van.	.15	.35	6.00
☐☐☐	73	Markus Naslund, Pgh.	.15	.35	6.00
☐☐☐	74	John MacLean, N.J.	.15	.35	6.00
☐☐☐	75	Mike Ridley, Van.	.15	.35	6.00
☐☐☐	76	Petr Svoboda, Pha.	.15	.35	6.00
☐☐☐	77	Milos Holan, Ana.	.15	.35	6.00
☐☐☐	78	John Tucker, T.B.	.15	.35	6.00

☐☐☐ 79 Doug Brown, Det. .15 .35 6.00
☐☐☐ 80 Ted Donato, Bos. .15 .35 6.00
☐☐☐ 81 Dmitri Yushkevich, Pha. .15 .35 6.00
☐☐☐ 82 Brett Lindros, NYI. .15 .35 6.00
☐☐☐ 83 Brian Bradley, T.B. .15 .35 6.00
☐☐☐ 84 Mario Lemieux, Pgh. 2.00 20.00 175.00
☐☐☐ 85 Nikolai Khabibulin (G), Wpg. .35 1.50 15.00
☐☐☐ 86 Larry Murphy, Tor. .25 .75 10.00
☐☐☐ 87 Mike Donnelly, L.A. .15 .35 6.00
☐☐☐ **88 Brian Holzinger, Buf., RC .15 .35 6.00**
☐☐☐ **89 Steve Larouche, Ott., RC .15 .35 6.00**
☐☐☐ 90 Ray Ferraro, NYR. .15 .35 6.00
☐☐☐ 91 Mikhail Shtalenkov (G), Ana. .15 .35 6.00
☐☐☐ 92 Viktor Kozlov, S.J. .15 .35 6.00
☐☐☐ 93 Jon Klemm, Col. .15 .35 6.00
☐☐☐ 94 Mark Tinordi, Wsh. .15 .35 6.00
☐☐☐ 95 Bret Hedican, Van. .15 .35 6.00
☐☐☐ 96 Kevin Stevens, Pgh. .15 .35 6.00
☐☐☐ 97 Bernie Nicholls, Chi. .15 .35 6.00
☐☐☐ 98 Pat Verbeek, NYR. .15 .35 6.00
☐☐☐ 99 Wayne Gretzky, L.A. 2.50 25.00 250.00
☐☐☐ 100 René Corbet, Col. .15 .35 6.00
☐☐☐ 101 Shayne Corson, Stl. .25 .75 10.00
☐☐☐ 102 Cliff Ronning, Van. .15 .35 6.00
☐☐☐ 103 Olaf Kolzig (G), Wsh. .35 1.50 15.00
☐☐☐ 104 Dominik Hasek (G), Buf. .75 7.50 75.00
☐☐☐ 105 Corey Millen, Cgy. .15 .35 6.00
☐☐☐ 106 Patrick Flatley, NYI. .15 .35 6.00
☐☐☐ 107 Chris Therien, Pha. .15 .35 6.00
☐☐☐ 108 Ken Wregget (G), Pgh. .15 .35 6.00
☐☐☐ 109 Paul Ysebaert, T.B. .15 .35 6.00
☐☐☐ 110 Mike Gartner, Tor. .25 .75 10.00
☐☐☐ 111 Michal Grosek, Wpg. .15 .35 6.00
☐☐☐ 112 Craig Billington (G), Bos. .15 .35 6.00
☐☐☐ 113 Steve Yzerman, Det. 1.25 12.00 125.00
☐☐☐ 114 Neal Broten, N.J. .15 .35 6.00
☐☐☐ 115 Tom Barrasso (G), Pgh. .25 .75 10.00
☐☐☐ 116 Brent Fedyk, Pha. .15 .35 6.00
☐☐☐ 117 Todd Gill, Tor. .15 .35 6.00
☐☐☐ 118 Petr Klima, T.B. .15 .35 6.00
☐☐☐ 119 Dave Karpa, Ana. .15 .35 6.00
☐☐☐ 120 Geoff Courtnall, Stl. .15 .35 6.00
☐☐☐ 121 Kelly Buchberger, Edm. .15 .35 6.00
☐☐☐ 122 Eric Lacroix, L.A. .15 .35 6.00
☐☐☐ 123 Janne Laukkanen, Col. .15 .35 6.00
☐☐☐ 124 Radek Bonk, Ott. .15 .35 6.00
☐☐☐ 125 Sergio Momesso, Van. .15 .35 6.00
☐☐☐ 126 Esa Tikkanen, Stl. .15 .35 6.00
☐☐☐ 127 Jon Rohloff, Bos. .15 .35 6.00
☐☐☐ **128 Ken Klee, Wsh., RC .15 .35 6.00**
☐☐☐ 129 Johan Garpenlov, Fla. .15 .35 6.00
☐☐☐ 130 Sean Burke (G), Hfd. .25 .75 10.00
☐☐☐ 131 Shean Donovan, S.J. .15 .35 6.00
☐☐☐ 132 Alexei Kovalev, NYR. .15 .35 6.00
☐☐☐ 133 Sylvain Côté, Wsh. .15 .35 6.00
☐☐☐ 134 Jeff Friesen, S.J. .25 .75 10.00
☐☐☐ 135 Scott Pearson, Buf. .15 .35 6.00
☐☐☐ 136 Kirk McLean (G), Van. .25 .75 10.00
☐☐☐ 137 Glen Wesley, Hfd. .15 .35 6.00
☐☐☐ 138 Bob Kudelski, Fla. .15 .35 6.00
☐☐☐ 139 Craig Johnson, Stl. .15 .35 6.00
☐☐☐ 140 Zigmund Palffy, NYI. .35 3.50 25.00
☐☐☐ 141 Kris King, Wpg. .15 .35 6.00
☐☐☐ 142 Rusty Fitzgerald, Pgh. .15 .35 6.00
☐☐☐ 143 Trevor Kidd (G), Cgy. .25 .75 10.00
☐☐☐ 144 Dave Ellett, Tor. .15 .35 6.00
☐☐☐ 145 Kelly Hrudey (G), L.A. .15 .35 6.00
☐☐☐ 146 Igor Kravchuk, Stl. .15 .35 6.00
☐☐☐ 147 Mats Sundin, Tor. .50 5.00 40.00
☐☐☐ 148 Shawn Chambers, N.J. .15 .35 6.00
☐☐☐ 149 Bob Corkum, Ana. .15 .35 6.00
☐☐☐ 150 Shjon Podein, Pha. .15 .35 6.00
☐☐☐ 151 Murray Craven, Chi. .15 .35 6.00
☐☐☐ 152 Roman Hamrlik, T.B. .25 .75 10.00
☐☐☐ 153 Lyle Odelein, Mtl. .15 .35 6.00
☐☐☐ 154 Vyacheslav Kozlov, Det. .15 .35 6.00
☐☐☐ 155 Dave Emma, N.J. .15 .35 6.00
☐☐☐ 156 Benoît Brunet, Mtl. .15 .35 6.00
☐☐☐ 157 Josef Stumpel, Bos. .25 .75 10.00
☐☐☐ 158 Darrin Madeley, Ott. .15 .35 6.00
☐☐☐ 159 Keith Primeau, Det. .25 .75 10.00
☐☐☐ 160 Jeff Norton, Stl. .15 .35 6.00
☐☐☐ 161 Mathieu Schneider, NYI. .15 .35 6.00
☐☐☐ 162 Trent Klatt, Dal. .15 .35 6.00
☐☐☐ 163 Pat Peake, Wsh. .15 .35 6.00
☐☐☐ 164 Rob Gaudreau, Ott. .15 .35 6.00
☐☐☐ 165 Doug Bodger, Buf. .15 .35 6.00
☐☐☐ 166 Sergei Nemchinov, NYR. .15 .35 6.00
☐☐☐ 167 David Oliver, Edm. .15 .35 6.00
☐☐☐ 168 Sandis Ozolinsh, S.J. .25 .75 10.00
☐☐☐ 169 Mark Messier, NYR. .50 5.00 40.00
☐☐☐ 170 Chris Chelios, Chi. .35 3.50 25.00
☐☐☐ 171 Teemu Selänne, Wpg. .75 7.50 75.00
☐☐☐ **172 Robert Svehla, Fla., RC .15 .35 6.00**
☐☐☐ 173 Nikolai Borschevsky, Cgy. .15 .35 6.00
☐☐☐ 174 Chris Pronger, Stl. .25 .75 10.00
☐☐☐ 175 Dave Lowry, Fla. .15 .35 6.00
☐☐☐ 176 Owen Nolan, Col. .25 .75 10.00
☐☐☐ 177 Sylvain Turgeon, Ott. .15 .35 6.00
☐☐☐ 178 Nelson Emerson, Hfd. .15 .35 6.00
☐☐☐ 179 Theoren Fleury, Cgy. .35 1.50 15.00
☐☐☐ 180 Patrick Carnback, Ana. .15 .35 6.00
☐☐☐ 181 Kevin Smyth, Hfd. .15 .35 6.00
☐☐☐ 182 Jeff Shantz, Chi. .15 .35 6.00
☐☐☐ 183 Bob Carpenter, N.J. .15 .35 6.00
☐☐☐ 184 Brendan Shanahan, Hfd. .60 6.00 50.00
☐☐☐ 185 Tomas Sandström, Pgh. .15 .35 6.00
☐☐☐ 186 Eric Desjardins, Pha. .15 .35 6.00
☐☐☐ 187 Alexei Zhitnik, Buf. .15 .35 6.00
☐☐☐ 188 Alexander Mogilny, Van. .35 1.50 15.00
☐☐☐ 189 Mariusz Czerkawski, Bos. .15 .35 6.00
☐☐☐ 190 Vladimir Konstantinov, Det. .15 .35 6.00
☐☐☐ 191 Andy Moog (G), Dal. .25 .75 10.00
☐☐☐ 192 Peter Popovic, Mtl. .15 .35 6.00
☐☐☐ 193 Marty McSorley, L.A. .15 .35 6.00
☐☐☐ 194 Mikael Renberg, Pha. .15 .35 6.00
☐☐☐ 195 Alek Stojanov, Pgh. .15 .35 6.00
☐☐☐ 196 Rick Tabaracci (G), Cgy. .15 .35 6.00
☐☐☐ 197 Adam Oates, Bos. .35 1.50 15.00
☐☐☐ 198 Garry Galley, Buf. .15 .35 6.00
☐☐☐ 199 Todd Harvey, Dal. .15 .35 6.00
☐☐☐ 200 Martin Lapointe, Det. .15 .35 6.00
☐☐☐ 201 Tony Granato, L.A. .15 .35 6.00
☐☐☐ 202 Turner Stevenson, Mtl. .15 .35 6.00
☐☐☐ 203 Jeff Beukeboom, NYR. .15 .35 6.00
☐☐☐ 204 Adam Foote, Col. .25 .75 10.00
☐☐☐ 205 Daren Puppa (G), T.B. .15 .35 6.00
☐☐☐ 206 Paul Kariya, Ana. 1.50 15.00 150.00
☐☐☐ 207 German Titov, Cgy. .15 .35 6.00
☐☐☐ 208 Patrick Poulin, T.B. .15 .35 6.00
☐☐☐ 209 Jesse Belanger, Fla. .15 .35 6.00
☐☐☐ 210 Steven Rice, Hfd. .15 .35 6.00
☐☐☐ 211 Martin Brodeur (G), N.J. .75 7.50 75.00
☐☐☐ 212 Rob Pearson, Tor. .15 .35 6.00
☐☐☐ 213 Igor Larionov, S.J. .25 .75 10.00
☐☐☐ 214 Pavel Bure, Van. .35 3.50 30.00
☐☐☐ 215 Sergei Fedorov, Det. .25 3.00 25.00
☐☐☐ 216 Ed Belfour (G), Chi. .25 .75 10.00
☐☐☐ 217 Mark Messier, NYR. .25 3.00 25.00
☐☐☐ 218 Steve Yzerman, Det. .50 5.00 50.00
☐☐☐ 219 Mats Sundin, Tor. .25 3.00 25.00
☐☐☐ 220 Mike Modano, Dal. .25 3.00 25.00
☐☐☐ 221 Alexander Mogilny, Van. .25 .75 10.00
☐☐☐ 222 Wayne Gretzky, L.A. 1.25 12.00 125.00
☐☐☐ 223 Keith Primeau, Det. .25 .75 10.00
☐☐☐ 224 Adam Graves, NYR. .15 .35 6.00
☐☐☐ 225 Owen Nolan, Col. .25 .75 10.00
☐☐☐ 226 Paul Coffey, Det. .25 .75 10.00
☐☐☐ 227 Jeremy Roenick, Chi. .25 .75 10.00
☐☐☐ 228 Félix Potvin (G), Tor. .25 3.00 25.00
☐☐☐ 229 Trevor Kidd (G), Cgy. .25 .75 10.00
☐☐☐ 230 Ray Bourque, Bos. .25 3.00 25.00
☐☐☐ 231 Mario Lemieux, Pgh. 1.00 10.00 100.00
☐☐☐ 232 Peter Bondra, Wsh. .25 2.00 15.00
☐☐☐ 233 Brett Hull, Stl. .25 3.00 25.00
☐☐☐ 234 Alexei Zhamnov, Wpg. .25 .75 10.00
☐☐☐ 235 Theoren Fleury, Cgy. .25 .75 10.00
☐☐☐ 236 Brian Leetch, NYR. .25 .75 10.00
☐☐☐ 237 Cam Neely, Bos. .25 .75 10.00
☐☐☐ 238 Chris Chelios, Chi. .25 2.00 15.00
☐☐☐ 239 Adam Graves, NYR. .15 .35 6.00
☐☐☐ 240 Doug Gilmour, Tor. .25 .75 10.00
☐☐☐ 241 Jeremy Roenick, Chi. .25 .75 10.00
☐☐☐ 242 Joe Sakic, Col. .50 5.00 50.00
☐☐☐ 243 Keith Tkachuk, Wpg. .25 2.00 15.00
☐☐☐ 244 Luc Robitaille, L.A. .25 .75 10.00
☐☐☐ 245 Paul Kariya, Ana. .75 8.00 75.00
☐☐☐ 246 Owen Nolan, S.J. .25 .75 10.00
☐☐☐ 247 John LeClair, Pha. .25 3.00 25.00
☐☐☐ 248 Paul Coffey, Det. .25 .75 10.00
☐☐☐ 249 Peter Bondra, Wsh. .25 2.00 15.00
☐☐☐ 250 Ray Bourque, Bos. .25 3.00 25.00
☐☐☐ 251 Brett Hull, Stl. .25 3.00 25.00
☐☐☐ 252 Wayne Gretzky, L.A. 1.25 12.00 125.00
☐☐☐ 253 Teemu Selänne, Wpg. .35 3.50 30.00
☐☐☐ 254 Ray Sheppard, Fla. .15 .35 6.00
☐☐☐ 255 Ron Francis, Pgh. .20 .75 8.00
☐☐☐ 256 Kevin Hatcher, Dal. .15 .35 6.00
☐☐☐ 257 Brett Lindros, NYI. .15 .35 6.00
☐☐☐ 258 Claude Lemieux, N.J. .15 .35 6.00
☐☐☐ 259 Saku Koivu, Mtl. .75 7.50 75.00
☐☐☐ **260 Radek Dvorak, Fla., RC .25 .75 8.00**
☐☐☐ 261 Niklas Sundstrom, NYR. .15 .35 6.00
☐☐☐ **262 Chad Kilger, Ana., RC .15 .35 6.00**
☐☐☐ 263 Vitali Yachmenev, L.A. .15 .35 6.00
☐☐☐ 264 Jeff O'Neill, Hfd. .25 .75 10.00
☐☐☐ 265 Brendan Witt, Wsh. .15 .35 6.00
☐☐☐ 266 Jason Bonsignore, Edm. .15 .35 6.00
☐☐☐ **267 Aki Berg, L.A., RC .15 .35 6.00**
☐☐☐ 268 Eric Dazé, Chi. .25 .75 10.00
☐☐☐ **269 Shane Doan, Wpg., RC .15 .35 6.00**
☐☐☐ **270 Daymond Langkow, T.B., RC .15 .35 6.00**
☐☐☐ 271 Alexandre Daigle, Ott. .25 .75 10.00
☐☐☐ 272 Brian Noonan, Stl. .15 .35 6.00
☐☐☐ 273 Guy Carbonneau, Dal. .15 .35 6.00
☐☐☐ 274 Rick Tocchet, L.A. .15 .35 6.00
☐☐☐ 275 Teppo Numminen, Wpg. .15 .35 6.00
☐☐☐ 276 Brian Skrudland, Fla. .15 .35 6.00
☐☐☐ 277 Andrei Trefilov (G), Buf. .15 .35 6.00
☐☐☐ 278 Joe Murphy, Chi. .15 .35 6.00
☐☐☐ 279 Sergei Fedorov, Det. .50 5.00 40.00
☐☐☐ 280 Doug Weight, Edm. .35 1.50 15.00
☐☐☐ 281 Robert Lang, L.A. .15 .35 6.00
☐☐☐ 282 Darryl Shannon, Wpg. .15 .35 6.00
☐☐☐ 283 Cory Stillman, Cgy. .15 .35 6.00
☐☐☐ 284 Gary Suter, Chi. .15 .35 6.00
☐☐☐ 285 Joe Nieuwendyk, Dal. .25 .75 10.00
☐☐☐ 286 Terry Carkner, Fla. .15 .35 6.00
☐☐☐ 287 Dimitri Khristich, L.A. .15 .35 6.00
☐☐☐ 288 Alexander Karpovtsev, NYR. .15 .35 6.00
☐☐☐ 289 Garth Snow (G), Pha. .15 .35 6.00
☐☐☐ 290 Al MacInnis, Stl. .15 .35 6.00
☐☐☐ 291 Doug Gilmour, Tor. .35 1.50 15.00
☐☐☐ 292 Mike Eastwood, Wpg. .15 .35 6.00
☐☐☐ 293 Steve Heinze, Bos. .15 .35 6.00
☐☐☐ 294 Phil Housley, Cgy. .15 .35 6.00
☐☐☐ **295 Tim Taylor, Det., RC .15 .35 6.00**
☐☐☐ 296 Curtis Joseph (G), Edm. .60 6.00 50.00
☐☐☐ 297 Patrick Roy (G), Col. 2.00 20.00 200.00
☐☐☐ 298 Ted Drury, Hfd. .15 .35 6.00
☐☐☐ 299 Igor Korolev, Wpg. .15 .35 6.00
☐☐☐ 300 Ray Bourque, Bos. .50 5.00 40.00
☐☐☐ 301 Darren McCarty, Det. .15 .35 6.00
☐☐☐ **302 Miroslav Satan, Edm., RC .15 .35 6.00**
☐☐☐ 303 Adam Burt, Hfd. .15 .35 6.00
☐☐☐ 304 Valeri Bure, Mtl. .15 .35 6.00
☐☐☐ 305 Sergei Gonchar, Wsh. .15 .35 6.00
☐☐☐ 306 Jason York, Det. .15 .35 6.00
☐☐☐ 307 Brent Grieve, Edm. .15 .35 6.00
☐☐☐ 308 Craig Johnson, Stl. .15 .35 6.00
☐☐☐ 309 Kevin Hatcher, Pgh. .15 .35 6.00
☐☐☐ 310 Rob Niedermayer, Fla. .15 .35 6.00
☐☐☐ 311 Nelson Emerson, Hfd. .15 .35 6.00
☐☐☐ 312 Mark Janssens, Hfd. .15 .35 6.00
☐☐☐ 313 Tommy Söderström (G), NYI. .15 .35 6.00
☐☐☐ 314 Joey Kocur, NYR. .15 .35 6.00
☐☐☐ 315 Craig Janney, S.J. .15 .35 6.00
☐☐☐ 316 Alexander Selivanov, T.B. .15 .35 6.00
☐☐☐ 317 Russ Courtnall, Van. .15 .35 6.00
☐☐☐ **318 Petr Sykora, N.J., RC .15 .35 6.00**
☐☐☐ 319 Rick Zombo, Bos. .15 .35 6.00
☐☐☐ 320 Randy Burridge, Buf. .15 .35 6.00
☐☐☐ 321 John Vanbiesbrouck (G), Fla. .60 6.00 50.00
☐☐☐ 322 Dmitri Mironov, Pgh. .15 .35 6.00
☐☐☐ 323 Sean Hill, Ott. .15 .35 6.00
☐☐☐ 324 Rod Brind'Amour, Pha. .25 .75 10.00
☐☐☐ 325 Wendel Clark, Tor. .25 .75 10.00
☐☐☐ 326 Brent Gilchrist, Dal. .15 .35 6.00
☐☐☐ 327 Tyler Wright, Edm. .15 .35 6.00
☐☐☐ 328 Scott Daniels, Pha. .15 .35 6.00
☐☐☐ 329 Adam Graves, NYR. .15 .35 6.00
☐☐☐ 330 Dean Malkoc, Van. .15 .35 6.00
☐☐☐ 331 Jamie Macoun, Tor. .15 .35 6.00
☐☐☐ **332 Sandy Moger, Bos., RC .15 .35 6.00**
☐☐☐ 333 Michael Peca, Buf. .25 .75 10.00

□□□	334	Greg Johnson, Det.	.15	.35	6.00
□□□	335	Jason Woolley, Fla.	.15	.35	6.00
□□□	336	Rob DiMaio, Pha.	.15	.35	6.00
□□□	337	Damian Rhodes (G), Ott.	.15	.35	6.00
□□□	338	Gino Odjick, Van.	.15	.35	6.00
□□□	339	Peter Bondra, Wsh.	.35	3.50	25.00
□□□	340	Todd Ewen, Ana.	.15	.35	6.00
□□□	341	Matthew Barnaby, Buf.	.15	.35	6.00
□□□	342	Sylvain Lefebvre, Col.	.15	.35	6.00
□□□	343	Oleg Petrov, Mtl.	.15	.35	6.00
□□□	344	Jim Carey (G), Wsh.	.15	.35	6.00
□□□	345	Stu Barnes, Fla.	.15	.35	6.00
□□□	346	Kelly Miller, Wsh.	.15	.35	6.00
□□□	**347**	**Antti Törmänen, Ott., RC**	**.15**	**.35**	**6.00**
□□□	348	Ray Sheppard, S.J.	.15	.35	6.00
□□□	349	Igor Larionov, Det.	.25	.75	10.00
□□□	350	Kjell Samuelsson, Pha.	.15	.35	6.00
□□□	351	Benoît Hogue, Tor.	.15	.35	6.00
□□□	352	Jeff Brown, Van.	.15	.35	6.00
□□□	353	Nolan Baumgartner, Wsh.	.15	.35	6.00
□□□	354	Denis Pederson, N.J.	.15	.35	6.00
□□□	355	Shawn Burr, T.B.	.15	.35	6.00
□□□	356	Jyrki Lumme, Van.	.15	.35	6.00
□□□	357	Kevin Haller, Pha.	.15	.35	6.00
□□□	358	John Cullen, T.B.	.15	.35	6.00
□□□	359	Martin Gelinas, Van.	.15	.35	6.00
□□□	360	Shawn McEachern, Bos.	.15	.35	6.00
□□□	361	Sandy McCarthy, Cgy.	.15	.35	6.00
□□□	362	Grant Marshall, Dal.	.15	.35	6.00
□□□	363	Dean McAmmond, Edm.	.15	.35	6.00
□□□	364	Kevin Todd, L.A.	.15	.35	6.00
□□□	365	Bobby Holik, N.J.	.15	.35	6.00
□□□	366	Joel Otto, Pha.	.15	.35	6.00
□□□	367	Dave Andreychuk, Tor.	.15	.35	6.00
□□□	368	Ron Stern, Cgy.	.15	.35	6.00
□□□	369	Jocelyn Thibault (G), Mtl.	.35	1.50	15.00
□□□	370	Dave Gagner, Dal.	.15	.35	6.00
□□□	371	Bryan Marchment, Edm.	.15	.35	6.00
□□□	372	Jari Kurri, L.A.	.25	.75	10.00
□□□	373	Bill Guerin, N.J.	.25	.75	10.00
□□□	374	Eric Lindros, Pha.	1.50	15.00	150.00
□□□	375	Adam Creighton, Stl.	.15	.35	6.00
□□□	376	Dmitri Yushkevich, Tor.	.15	.35	6.00
□□□	377	Peter Zezel, Stl.	.15	.35	6.00
□□□	378	Valeri Karpov, Ana.	.15	.35	6.00
□□□	379	Mathieu Labrecque (G), Mtl.	.15	.35	6.00
□□□	380	Mick Vukota, NYI.	.15	.35	6.00
□□□	381	Ulf Dahlen, S.J.	.15	.35	6.00
□□□	382	Enrico Ciccone, Chi.	.15	.35	6.00
□□□	383	Scott Niedermayer, N.J.	.25	.75	10.00
□□□	384	Ville Peltonen, S.J.	.15	.35	6.00
□□□	385	Blaine Lacher (G), Bos.	.15	.35	6.00
□□□	386	Pat LaFontaine, Buf.	.25	.75	10.00
□□□	387	Jeff Hackett (G), Chi.	.25	.75	10.00
□□□	388	Mike Keane, Col.	.15	.35	6.00
□□□	389	Pierre Turgeon, Mtl.	.25	.75	10.00
□□□	390	Scott Lachance, NYI.	.15	.35	6.00
□□□	391	Jim Wiemer, T.B.	.15	.35	6.00
□□□	392	Michal Pivonka, Wsh.	.15	.35	6.00
□□□	**393**	**Dennis Bonvie, Edm., RC**	**.15**	**.35**	**6.00**
□□□	394	Glenn Murray, Bos.	.15	.35	6.00
□□□	395	Bobby Dollas, Ana.	.15	.35	6.00
□□□	396	Paul Coffey, Det.	.25	.75	10.00
□□□	397	Stéphane Fiset (G), Col.	.25	.75	10.00
□□□	398	Jere Lehtinen, Dal.	.25	.75	10.00
□□□	399	Scott Mellanby, Fla.	.15	.35	6.00
□□□	400	Robert Kron, Hfd.	.15	.35	6.00
□□□	401	Doug Lidster, NYR.	.15	.35	6.00
□□□	402	Don Beaupré (G), Ott.	.15	.35	6.00
□□□	403	Arturs Irbe (G), S.J.	.15	.35	6.00
□□□	404	Brian Bellows, T.B.	.15	.35	6.00
□□□	405	Corey Hirsch (G), Van.	.15	.35	6.00
□□□	406	Pavel Bure, Van.	.75	7.50	75.00
□□□	407	Chris Gratton, T.B.	.25	.75	10.00
□□□	408	Oleg Tverdovsky, Wpg.	.15	.35	6.00
□□□	409	Derek Plante, Buf.	.15	.35	6.00
□□□	410	Dan Keczmer, Cgy.	.15	.35	6.00
□□□	411	Donald Brashear, Mtl.	.15	.35	6.00
□□□	**412**	**Andrei Vasilyev, NYI., RC**	**.15**	**.35**	**6.00**
□□□	**413**	**Tommy Salo (G), NYI., RC**	**.15**	**.35**	**6.00**
□□□	414	Kevin Lowe, NYR.	.15	.35	6.00
□□□	415	Dody Wood, S.J.	.15	.35	6.00
□□□	416	Denis Chassé, Stl.	.15	.35	6.00
□□□	417	Aaron Gavey, T.B.	.15	.35	6.00
□□□	**418**	**Scott Walker, Van., RC**	**.15**	**.35**	**6.00**
□□□	419	Richard Park, Pgh.	.15	.35	6.00
□□□	420	Mike Modano, Dal.	.50	5.00	40.00
□□□	**421**	**Kyle McLaren, Bos., RC**	**.15**	**.35**	**6.00**
□□□	422	Jeremy Roenick, Chi.	.35	1.50	15.00
□□□	423	Mark Fitzpatrick (G), Fla.	.15	.35	6.00
□□□	**424**	**Landon Wilson, Col., RC**	**.15**	**.35**	**6.00**
□□□	425	Steve Rucchin, Ana.	.15	.35	6.00
□□□	426	Stéphane Richer, N.J.	.15	.35	6.00
□□□	427	Martin Straka, Ott.	.15	.35	6.00
□□□	428	Ron Hextall (G), Pha.	.25	.75	10.00
□□□	**429**	**Joe Dziedzic, Pgh., RC**	**.15**	**.35**	**6.00**
□□□	430	Peter Forsberg, Col.	1.25	12.00	125.00
□□□	431	Dino Ciccarelli, Det.	.25	.75	10.00
□□□	432	Robert Dirk, Ana.	.15	.35	6.00
□□□	**433**	**Wayne Primeau, Buf., RC**	**.15**	**.35**	**6.00**
□□□	434	Denis Savard, Chi.	.25	.75	10.00
□□□	435	Keith Carney, Chi.	.15	.35	6.00
□□□	436	Tom Fitzgerald, Fla.	.15	.35	6.00
□□□	437	Cale Hulse, Cgy.	.15	.35	6.00
□□□	438	Mike Richter (G), NYR.	.35	1.50	15.00
□□□	**439**	**Marcus Ragnarsson, S.J., RC**	**.15**	**.35**	**6.00**
□□□	440	Roman Vopat, Stl.	.15	.35	6.00
□□□	441	Zdenek Nedved, Tor.	.15	.35	6.00
□□□	442	Dale Hunter, Wsh.	.15	.35	6.00
□□□	443	Bob Sweeney, Buf.	.15	.35	6.00
□□□	444	Randy McKay, N.J.	.15	.35	6.00
□□□	445	Chris Osgood (G), Det.	.35	3.50	25.00
□□□	446	Andrei Kovalenko, Edm.	.15	.35	6.00
□□□	447	Darius Kasparaitis, NYI.	.15	.35	6.00
□□□	448	Ulf Samuelsson, Pgh.	.15	.35	6.00
□□□	449	Chris Joseph, T.B.	.15	.35	6.00
□□□	450	Chris Terreri (G), S.J.	.15	.35	6.00
□□□	451	Keith Jones, Wsh.	.15	.35	6.00
□□□	452	Tim Cheveldae (G), Wpg.	.15	.35	6.00
□□□	453	Stephen Leach, Bos.	.15	.35	6.00
□□□	454	Michael Nylander, Cgy.	.15	.35	6.00
□□□	455	Ed Belfour (G), Chi.	.35	1.50	15.00
□□□	456	Claude Lemieux, Col.	.15	.35	6.00
□□□	457	Mike Ricci, Col.	.15	.35	6.00
□□□	458	Shane Churla, Dal.	.15	.35	6.00
□□□	459	Kris Draper, Det.	.15	.35	6.00
□□□	460	Byron Dafoe (G), L.A.	.15	.35	6.00
□□□	461	Troy Mallette, Ott.	.15	.35	6.00
□□□	462	Petr Nedved, Pgh.	.15	.35	6.00
□□□	463	Kenny Jonsson, NYI.	.15	.35	6.00
□□□	464	Keith Tkachuk, Wpg.	.35	3.50	15.00
□□□	465	Jaromir Jagr, Pgh.	1.25	12.00	125.00
□□□	466	Vladimir Malakhov, Mtl.	.15	.35	6.00
□□□	467	Guy Hebert (G), Ana.	.25	.75	10.00
□□□	468	Brad May, Buf.	.15	.35	6.00
□□□	469	Bob Probert, Chi.	.15	.35	6.00
□□□	470	Sandis Ozolinsh, Col.	.25	.75	10.00
□□□	**471**	**Oleg Mikulchik, Ana., RC**	**.15**	**.35**	**6.00**
□□□	472	Steve Thomas, N.J.	.15	.35	6.00
□□□	473	Travis Green, NYI.	.15	.35	6.00
□□□	474	Sergei Zubov, Pgh.	.25	.75	10.00
□□□	475	Bill Houlder, Ana.	.15	.35	6.00
□□□	476	Roman Oksiuta, Van.	.15	.35	6.00
□□□	477	Jamie Rivers, Stl.	.15	.35	6.00
□□□	478	Rob Blake, L.A.	.25	.75	10.00
□□□	479	Todd Elik, Bos.	.15	.35	6.00
□□□	480	Zarley Zalapski, Cgy.	.15	.35	6.00
□□□	481	Darren Turcotte, Wpg.	.15	.35	6.00
□□□	482	Scott Stevens, N.J.	.15	.35	6.00
□□□	483	Pat Falloon, Pha.	.15	.35	6.00
□□□	484	Grant Fuhr (G), Stl.	.25	.75	10.00
□□□	485	Martin Rucinsky, Mtl.	.15	.35	6.00
□□□	486	Brett Hull, Stl.	.50	5.00	40.00
□□□	487	Brian Leetch, NYR.	.35	1.50	15.00
□□□	488	Shaun Van Allen, Ana.	.15	.35	6.00
□□□	489	Valeri Kamensky, Col.	.25	.75	10.00
□□□	490	Mark Recchi, Mtl.	.25	.75	10.00
□□□	491	Jason Muzzatti (G), Hfd.	.15	.35	6.00
□□□	492	Andrew Cassels, Hfd.	.15	.35	6.00
□□□	493	Nick Kypreos, NYR.	.15	.35	6.00
□□□	494	Bryan Smolinski, Pha.	.15	.35	6.00
□□□	495	Owen Nolan, S.J.	.25	.75	10.00
□□□	496	Bryan McCabe, NYI.	.15	.35	6.00
□□□	**497**	**Mathieu Dandenault, Det., RC.**	**.15**	**.35**	**6.00**
□□□	498	Deron Quint, Wpg.	.15	.35	6.00
□□□	499	Jason Doig, Wpg.	.15	.35	6.00
□□□	500	Marty Murray, Cgy.	.15	.35	6.00
□□□	501	Ed Jovanovski, Fla.	.25	.75	10.00
□□□	502	Stefan Ustorf, Wsh.	.15	.35	6.00
□□□	503	Jamie Langenbrunner, Dal.	.25	.75	10.00
□□□	**504**	**Daniel Alfredsson, Ott., RC**	**.75**	**5.00**	**40.00**
□□□	505	Darby Hendrickson, Tor.	.15	.35	6.00
□□□	**506**	**Brett McLean, Cdn., RC**	**.25**	**.75**	**8.00**
□□□	**507**	**Daniel Cleary, Cdn., RC**	**3.00**	**15.00**	**75.00**
□□□	**508**	**Todd Robinson, Cdn., RC**	**.25**	**.75**	**8.00**
□□□	**509**	**Aaron Asham, Cdn., RC**	**.25**	**.75**	**8.00**
□□□	**510**	**Daniel Corso, Cdn., RC**	**.50**	**2.00**	**10.00**
□□□	**511**	**Darren VanOene, Cdn., RC**	**.35**	**1.50**	**8.00**
□□□	**512**	**Trevor Wasyluk, Cdn., RC**	**.25**	**.75**	**8.00**
□□□	**513**	**Josh Holden, Cdn., RC**	**1.00**	**4.00**	**20.00**
□□□	**514**	**Etienne Drapeau, Cdn., RC**	**.25**	**.75**	**8.00**
□□□	**515**	**Matt Osborne, Cdn., RC**	**.25**	**.75**	**8.00**
□□□	**516**	**Zenith Komarniski, Cdn., RC**	**.25**	**.75**	**8.00**
□□□	**517**	**Chris Phillips, Cdn., RC**	**1.25**	**6.00**	**30.00**
□□□	**518**	**Chris Fleury, Cdn., RC**	**.25**	**.75**	**8.00**
□□□	**519**	**Cory Sarich, Cdn., RC**	**.65**	**2.00**	**10.00**
□□□	**520**	**Glenn Crawford, Cdn., RC**	**.25**	**.75**	**8.00**
□□□	**521**	**François Methot, Cdn., RC**	**.25**	**.75**	**8.00**
□□□	**522**	**Geoff Peters, Cdn., RC**	**.25**	**.75**	**8.00**
□□□	**523**	**Joey Tetarenko, Cdn., RC**	**.25**	**.75**	**8.00**
□□□	**524**	**Randy Petruk (G), Cdn., RC**	**.35**	**1.50**	**8.00**
□□□	**525**	**Mathieu Garon (G), Cdn., RC**	**1.25**	**6.00**	**30.00**
□□□	526	Daymond Langkow, Cdn.	.15	.35	6.00
□□□	**527**	**Craig Mills, Cdn., RC**	**.15**	**.35**	**6.00**
□□□	**528**	**Rhett Warrener, Cdn., RC**	**.15**	**.35**	**6.00**
□□□	**529**	**Marc Denis (G), Cdn., RC**	**3.00**	**15.00**	**75.00**
□□□	**530**	**José Théodore (G), Cdn., RC**	**3.00**	**15.00**	**75.00**
□□□	**531**	**Curtis Brown, Cdn., RC**	**.15**	**.35**	**6.00**
□□□	**532**	**Chad Allan, Cdn., RC**	**.15**	**.35**	**6.00**
□□□	**533**	**Denis Gauthier, Cdn., RC**	**.15**	**.35**	**6.00**
□□□	**534**	**Brad Larsen, Cdn., RC**	**.15**	**.35**	**6.00**
□□□	**535**	**Jamie Wright, Cdn., RC**	**.15**	**.35**	**6.00**
□□□	**536**	**Mike Watt, Cdn., RC**	**.15**	**.35**	**6.00**
□□□	**537**	**Jason Holland, Cdn., RC**	**.15**	**.35**	**6.00**
□□□	**538**	**Robb Gordon, Cdn., RC**	**.15**	**.35**	**6.00**
□□□	**539**	**Hnat Domenichelli, Cdn., RC**	**1.00**	**4.00**	**20.00**
□□□	**540**	**Ondrej Kratena, Cze., RC**	**.15**	**.35**	**6.00**
□□□	**541**	**Michal Bros, Cze., RC**	**.15**	**.35**	**6.00**
□□□	**542**	**Marek Posmyk, Cze., RC**	**.15**	**.35**	**6.00**
□□□	**543**	**Mar Melanovsky, Cze., RC**	**.15**	**.35**	**6.00**
□□□	**544**	**Jan Tomajko, Cze., RC**	**.15**	**.35**	**6.00**
□□□	**545**	**Ales Pisa, Cze., RC**	**.15**	**.35**	**6.00**
□□□	546	Miika Elomo, Fin.	.15	.35	6.00
□□□	547	Timo Salonen, Fin.	.15	.35	6.00
□□□	**548**	**Teemu Riihjani, Fin., RC**	**.15**	**.35**	**6.00**
□□□	**549**	**Antti-Jussi Niemi, Fin., RC**	**.15**	**.35**	**6.00**
□□□	**550**	**Petri Petrilainen, Fin., RC**	**.15**	**.35**	**6.00**
□□□	**551**	**Toni Lydman, Fin., RC**	**.15**	**.35**	**6.00**
□□□	552	Dimitri Nabokov, Rus.	.15	.35	6.00
□□□	553	Alexei Morozov, Rus.	.75	5.00	30.00
□□□	554	Sergei Samsonov, Rus.	1.50	10.00	75.00
□□□	**555**	**Alexei Vasilyev, Rus., RC**	**.15**	**.35**	**6.00**
□□□	556	Andrei Petrunin, Rus.	.15	.35	6.00
□□□	557	Dmitri Rjabykin, Rus.	.15	.35	6.00
□□□	**558**	**Sergei Zimakov, Rus., RC**	**.15**	**.35**	**6.00**
□□□	**559**	**Peter Nylander, Swe, RC**	**.15**	**.35**	**6.00**
□□□	**560**	**Markus Nilsson, Swe., RC**	**.25**	**.75**	**8.00**
□□□	**561**	**Niklas Anger, Swe., RC**	**.15**	**.35**	**6.00**
□□□	**562**	**Per Anton Lundstrom, Swe., RC**	**.15**	**.35**	**6.00**
□□□	**563**	**Patrik Wallenberg, Swe., RC**	**.15**	**.35**	**6.00**
□□□	**564**	**Per Ragnar Bergkvist, Swe., RC**	**.15**	**.35**	**6.00**
□□□	**565**	**Mike Sylvia, USA., RC**	**.15**	**.35**	**6.00**
□□□	566	Marty Reasoner, USA.	.15	.35	6.00
□□□	**567**	**Reg Berg, USA., RC**	**.15**	**.35**	**6.00**
□□□	**568**	**Tom Poti, USA., RC**	**.15**	**.35**	**6.00**
□□□	**569**	**Chris Drury, USA., RC**	**.50**	**2.00**	**10.00**
□□□	**570**	**Michael McBain, USA., RC**	**.15**	**.35**	**6.00**

SPECIAL EDITION

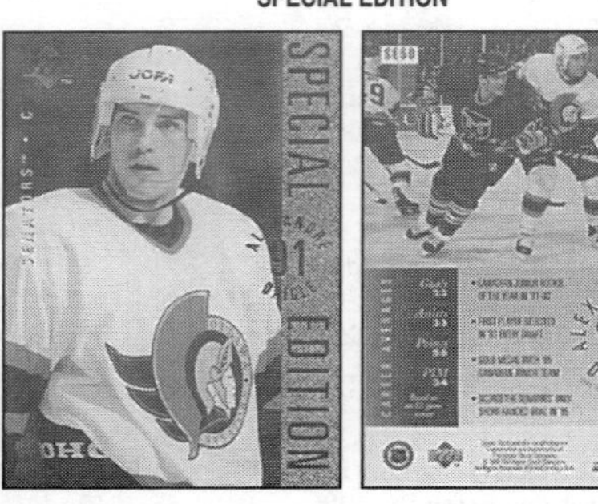

These cards have two versions: the regular insert and a Gold parallel

Series One Set (90 cards):		**50.00**	**350.00**
Series Two Set (90 cards):		**85.00**	**700.00**
Common Player:		**.35**	**3.00**
No.	**Player**	**SE**	**Gold**
☐☐ SE1	Paul Kariya, Ana.	5.00	50.00
☐☐ SE2	Oleg Tverdovsky, Ana.	.35	3.00
☐☐ SE3	Guy Hebert (G), Ana.	.75	5.00
☐☐ SE4	Ray Bourque, Bos.	2.00	20.00
☐☐ SE5	Adam Oates, Bos.	1.25	10.00
☐☐ SE6	Mariusz Czerkawski, Bos.	.35	3.00
☐☐ SE7	Blaine Lacher (G), Bos.	.35	3.00
☐☐ SE8	Doug Bodger, Buf.	.35	3.00
☐☐ SE9	Donald Audette, Buf.	.35	3.00
☐☐ SE10	Pat LaFontaine, Buf.	.75	5.00
☐☐ SE11	Alexei Zhitnik, Buf.	.35	3.00
☐☐ SE12	Joe Nieuwendyk, Cgy.	.75	5.00
☐☐ SE13	Phil Housley, Cgy.	.35	3.00
☐☐ SE14	German Titov, Cgy.	.35	3.00
☐☐ SE15	Trevor Kidd (G), Cgy.	.75	5.00
☐☐ SE16	Bernie Nicholls, Chi.	.35	3.00
☐☐ SE17	Chris Chelios, Chi.	1.50	15.00
☐☐ SE18	Tony Amonte, Chi.	.75	5.00
☐☐ SE19	Ed Belfour (G), Chi.	1.25	10.00
☐☐ SE20	Jon Klemm, Col.	.35	3.00
☐☐ SE21	Peter Forsberg, Col.	4.00	40.00
☐☐ SE22	Adam Deadmarsh, Col.	.35	3.00
☐☐ SE23	Stéphane Fiset (G), Col.	.75	5.00
☐☐ SE24	Dave Gagner, Dal.	.35	3.00
☐☐ SE25	Kevin Hatcher, Dal.	.35	3.00
☐☐ SE26	Mike Modano, Dal.	2.00	20.00
☐☐ SE27	Keith Primeau, Det.	.75	5.00
☐☐ SE28	Dino Ciccarelli, Det.	.75	5.00
☐☐ SE29	Nicklas Lidström, Det.	.75	5.00
☐☐ SE30	Steve Yzerman, Det.	4.00	40.00
☐☐ SE31	Doug Weight, Edm.	1.25	10.00
☐☐ SE32	Bill Ranford (G), Edm.	.75	5.00
☐☐ SE33	Stu Barnes, Fla.	.35	3.00
☐☐ SE34	Bob Kudelski, Fla.	.35	3.00
☐☐ SE35	Rob Niedermayer, Fla.	.35	3.00
☐☐ SE36	Andrew Cassels, Hfd.	.35	3.00
☐☐ SE37	Darren Turcotte, Hfd.	.35	3.00
☐☐ SE38	Andrei Nikolishin, Hfd.	.35	3.00
☐☐ SE39	Sean Burke (G), Hfd.	.75	5.00
☐☐ SE40	Rick Tocchet, L.A.	.35	3.00
☐☐ SE41	Jari Kurri, L.A.	.75	5.00
☐☐ SE42	Rob Blake, L.A.	.75	5.00
☐☐ SE43	Mark Recchi, Mtl.	.75	5.00
☐☐ SE44	Pierre Turgeon, Mtl.	.75	5.00
☐☐ SE45	Vladimir Malakhov, Mtl.	.35	3.00
☐☐ SE46	Valeri Bure, Mtl.	.35	3.00
☐☐ SE47	Stéphane Richer, N.J.	.35	3.00
☐☐ SE48	Bill Guerin, N.J.	.75	5.00
☐☐ SE49	Scott Stevens, N.J.	.35	3.00
☐☐ SE50	Claude Lemieux, N.J.	.35	3.00
☐☐ SE51	Zigmund Palffy, NYI.	1.25	10.00
☐☐ SE52	Kirk Muller, MYI.	.35	3.00
☐☐ SE53	Todd Bertuzzi, NYI.	.75	5.00
☐☐ SE54	Brett Lindros, NYI.	.35	3.00
☐☐ SE55	Brian Leetch, NYR.	1.25	10.00
☐☐ SE56	Alexei Kovalev, NYR.	.35	3.00
☐☐ SE57	Adam Graves, NYR.	.35	3.00
☐☐ SE58	Mike Richter (G), NYR.	1.25	10.00
☐☐ SE59	Alexei Yashin, Ott.	1.50	15.00
☐☐ SE60	Alexandre Daigle, Ott.	.75	5.00
☐☐ SE61	Don Beaupré, Ott.	.35	3.00
☐☐ SE62	Radek Bonk, Ott.	.35	3.00
☐☐ SE63	John LeClair, Pha.	2.00	20.00
☐☐ SE64	Rod Brind'Amour, Pha.	.75	5.00
☐☐ SE65	Ron Hextall (G), Pha.	.75	5.00
☐☐ SE66	Ron Francis, Pgh.	1.25	10.00
☐☐ SE67	Markus Naslund, Pgh.	.35	3.00
☐☐ SE68	Tom Barrasso (G), Pgh.	.75	5.00
☐☐ SE69	Ian Lapperrière, Stl.	.35	3.00
☐☐ SE70	Esa Tikkanen, Stl.	.35	3.00
☐☐ SE71	Al MacInnis, Stl.	.35	3.00
☐☐ SE72	Ulf Dahlen, S.J.	.35	3.00
☐☐ SE73	Craig Janney, S.J.	.35	3.00
☐☐ SE74	Jeff Friesen, S.J.	.75	5.00
☐☐ SE75	Chris Gratton, T.B.	.75	5.00
☐☐ SE76	Roman Hamrlik, T.B.	.75	5.00
☐☐ SE77	Alexander Selivanov, T.B.	.35	3.00
☐☐ SE78	Daren Puppa (G), T.B.	.35	3.00
☐☐ SE79	Dave Andreychuk, Tor.	.35	3.00
☐☐ SE80	Doug Gilmour, Tor.	1.25	10.00
☐☐ SE81	Kenny Jonsson, Tor.	.35	3.00
☐☐ SE82	Trevor Linden, Van.	.75	5.00
☐☐ SE83	Kirk McLean (G), Van.	.75	5.00
☐☐ SE84	Jeff Brown, Van.	.35	3.00
☐☐ SE85	Keith Jones, Wsh.	.35	3.00
☐☐ SE86	José Juneau, Wsh.	.35	3.00
☐☐ SE87	Jim Carey (G), Wsh.	.35	3.00
☐☐ SE88	Keith Tkachuk, Wpg.	1.50	15.00
☐☐ SE89	Teemu Selänne, Wpg.	3.00	30.00
☐☐ SE90	Igor Korolev, Wpg.	.35	3.00
☐☐ SE91	Mike Sillinger, Ana.	.35	3.00
☐☐ SE92	Steve Rucchin, Ana.	.35	3.00
☐☐ SE93	Valeri Karpov, Ana.	.35	3.00
☐☐ SE94	Cam Neely, Bos.	.75	5.00
☐☐ SE95	Shawn McEachern, Bos.	.35	3.00
☐☐ SE96	Kevin Stevens, Bos.	.35	3.00
☐☐ SE97	Ted Donato, Bos.	.35	3.00
☐☐ SE98	Dominik Hasek (G), Buf.	3.00	30.00
☐☐ SE99	Randy Burridge, Buf.	.35	3.00
☐☐ SE100	Jason Dawe, Buf.	.35	3.00
☐☐ SE101	Theoren Fleury, Cgy.	1.25	10.00
☐☐ SE102	Michael Nylander, Cgy.	.35	3.00
☐☐ SE103	Rick Tabaracci (G), Cgy.	.35	3.00
☐☐ SE104	Jermey Roenick, Chi.	1.25	10.00
☐☐ SE105	Bob Probert, Chi.	.35	3.00
☐☐ SE106	Patrick Poulin, Chi.	.35	3.00
☐☐ SE107	Gary Suter, Chi.	.35	3.00
☐☐ SE108	Claude Lemieux, Col.	.35	3.00
☐☐ SE109	Sandis Ozolinsh, Col.	.75	5.00
☐☐ SE110	Patrick Roy (G), Col.	6.50	65.00
☐☐ SE111	Joe Sakic, Col.	3.50	35.00
☐☐ SE112	Derian Hatcher, Dal.	.75	5.00
☐☐ SE113	Greg Adams, Dal.	.35	3.00
☐☐ SE114	Todd Harvey, Dal.	.35	3.00
☐☐ SE115	Sergei Fedorov, Det.	2.00	20.00
☐☐ SE116	Chris Osgood (G), Det.	1.50	15.00
☐☐ SE117	Vyacheslav Kozlov, Det.	.35	3.00
☐☐ SE118	Paul Coffey, Det.	.75	5.00
☐☐ SE119	Jason Arnott, Edm.	.75	5.00
☐☐ SE120	David Oliver, Edm.	.35	3.00
☐☐ SE121	Todd Marchant, Edm.	.35	3.00
☐☐ SE122	John Vanbiesbrouck (G), Fla.	2.50	25.00
☐☐ SE123	Jody Hull, Fla.	.35	3.00
☐☐ SE124	Jason Woolley, Fla.	.35	3.00
☐☐ SE125	Brendan Shanahan, Hfd.	2.50	25.00
☐☐ SE126	Nelson Emerson, Hfd.	.35	3.00
☐☐ SE127	Geoff Sanderson, Hfd.	.35	3.00
☐☐ SE128	Wayne Gretzky, L.A.	8.00	80.00
☐☐ SE129	Marty McSorley, L.A.	.35	3.00
☐☐ SE130	Yanic Perreault, L.A.	.35	3.00
☐☐ SE131	Jocelyn Thibault (G), Mtl.	1.25	10.00
☐☐ SE132	Brian Savage, Mtl.	.35	3.00
☐☐ SE133	Vincent Damphousse, Mtl.	1.25	10.00
☐☐ SE134	John MacLean, N.J.	.35	3.00
☐☐ SE135	Martin Brodeur (G), N.J.	3.00	30.00
☐☐ SE136	Steve Thomas, N.J.	.35	3.00
☐☐ SE137	Scott Niedermayer, N.J.	.75	5.00
☐☐ SE138	Travis Green, NYI.	.35	3.00
☐☐ SE139	Wendel Clark, NYI.	.75	5.00
☐☐ SE140	Tommy Söderström (G), NYI.	.35	3.00
☐☐ SE141	Mark Messier, NYR.	2.00	20.00
☐☐ SE142	Ulf Samuelsson, NYR.	.35	3.00
☐☐ SE143	Ray Ferraro, NYR.	.35	3.00
☐☐ SE144	Luc Robitaille, NYR.	.75	5.00
☐☐ SE145	Daniel Alfredsson, Ott.	1.50	15.00
☐☐ SE146	Martin Straka, Ott.	.35	3.00
☐☐ SE147	Steve Duchesne, Ott.	.35	3.00
☐☐ SE148	Eric Lindros, Pha.	5.00	50.00
☐☐ SE149	Mikael Renberg, Pha.	.35	3.00
☐☐ SE150	Eric Desjardins, Pha.	.35	3.00
☐☐ SE151	Joel Otto, Pha.	.35	3.00
☐☐ SE152	Mario Lemieux, Pgh.	6.50	65.00
☐☐ SE153	Jaromir Jagr, Pgh.	4.00	40.00
☐☐ SE154	Petr Nedved, Pgh.	.35	3.00
☐☐ SE155	Sergei Zubov, Pgh.	.75	5.00
☐☐ SE156	Tomas Sandström, Pgh.	.35	3.00
☐☐ SE157	Brett Hull, Stl.	2.00	20.00
☐☐ SE158	Grant Fuhr (G), Stl.	.75	5.00
☐☐ SE159	Shayne Corson, Stl.	.75	5.00
☐☐ SE160	Chris Pronger, Stl.	.75	5.00
☐☐ SE161	Ray Sheppard, S.J.	.35	3.00
☐☐ SE162	Arturs Irbe (G), S.J.	.35	3.00
☐☐ SE163	Owen Nolan, S.J.	.75	5.00
☐☐ SE164	Andrei Nazarov, S.J.	.35	3.00
☐☐ SE165	Paul Ysebaert, T.B.	.35	3.00
☐☐ SE166	Brian Bradley, T.B.	.35	3.00
☐☐ SE167	Petr Klima, T.B.	.35	3.00
☐☐ SE168	Félix Potvin (G), Tor.	2.00	20.00
☐☐ SE169	Mats Sundin, Tor.	2.00	20.00
☐☐ SE170	Larry Murphy, Tor.	.75	5.00
☐☐ SE171	Benoît Hogue, Tor.	.35	3.00
☐☐ SE172	Pavel Bure, Van.	3.00	30.00
☐☐ SE173	Alexander Mogilny, Van.	1.25	10.00
☐☐ SE174	Cliff Ronning, Van.	.35	3.00
☐☐ SE175	Pat Peake, Wsh.	.35	3.00
☐☐ SE176	Sylvain Côté, Wsh.	.35	3.00
☐☐ SE177	Peter Bondra, Wsh.	1.50	15.00
☐☐ SE178	Dallas Drake, Wpg.	.35	3.00
☐☐ SE179	Tim Cheveldae (G), Wpg.	.35	3.00
☐☐ SE180	Darren Turcotte, Wpg.	.35	3.00

FREEZE FRAME

These cards have two versions: a 5" x 7" box insert and the standard sized insert. The oversize cards were given out as promos.

Series One Insert Set (20 cards):		**85.00**	**175.00**
No.	**Player**	**5"x7"**	**Insert**
☐☐ F1	Peter Forsberg, Col.	7.50	15.00
☐☐ F2	Wayne Gretzky, L.A.	15.00	30.00
☐☐ F3	Eric Lindros, Pha.	10.00	20.00
☐☐ F4	Jaromir Jagr, Pgh.	7.50	15.00
☐☐ F5	Cam Neely, Bos.	1.50	3.00
☐☐ F6	Jeremy Roenick, Chi.	2.25	4.50
☐☐ F7	Mark Messier, NYR.	3.75	7.50
☐☐ F8	Sergei Fedorov, Det.	3.75	7.50
☐☐ F9	Paul Kariya, Ana.	10.00	20.00
☐☐ F10	Pavel Bure, Van.	5.00	10.00
☐☐ F11	Dominik Hasek (G), Buf.	5.00	10.00
☐☐ F12	Theoren Fleury, Cgy.	2.25	4.50
☐☐ F13	Alexei Zhamnov, Wpg.	1.50	3.00
☐☐ F14	Martin Brodeur (G), N.J.	5.00	10.00
☐☐ F15	Brett Hull, Stl.	3.75	7.50
☐☐ F16	Mario Lemieux, Pgh.	12.50	25.00
☐☐ F17	Paul Coffey, Det.	1.50	3.00
☐☐ F18	Brian Leetch, NYR.	2.25	4.50
☐☐ F19	Ray Bourque, Bos.	3.75	7.50
☐☐ F20	Jim Carey (G), Wsh.	1.00	2.00

WAYNE GRETZKY RECORD COLLECTION

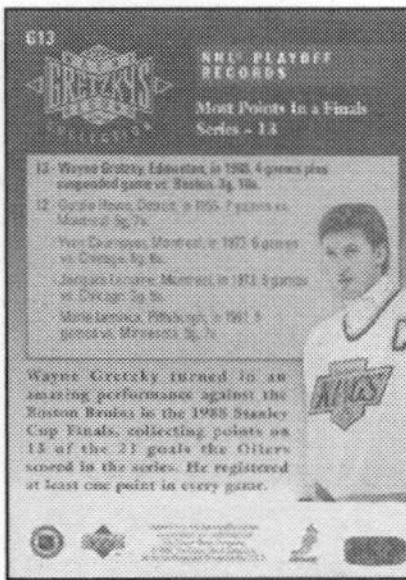

Cards G1-G9 were inserted in U.D. Collector's Choice packs while cards G18-G20 were inserted in SP packs.

Insert Set (10 cards): 100.00

	No.	Player	NRMT-MT
☐		Checklist G10-G13 (© 1995)	10.00
☐	G10	Wayne Gretzky, Most Points - Career	12.00
☐	G11	Wayne Gretzky, Game-Winning Goals/Career	12.00
☐	G12	Wayne Gretzky, Points/One Playoff Year	12.00
☐	G13	Wayne Gretzky [w/Cup], Points/One Final Series	12.00
☐		Checklist G14-G20 (© 1996)	10.00
☐	G14	Wayne Gretzky, Most Goals - Career	12.00
☐	G15	Wayne Gretzky, Most Points - Points	12.00
☐	G16	Wayne Gretzky, Points/One All-Star Game	12.00
☐	G17	Wayne Gretzky, Goals/Period of AS Game	12.00

PREDICTOR SERIES

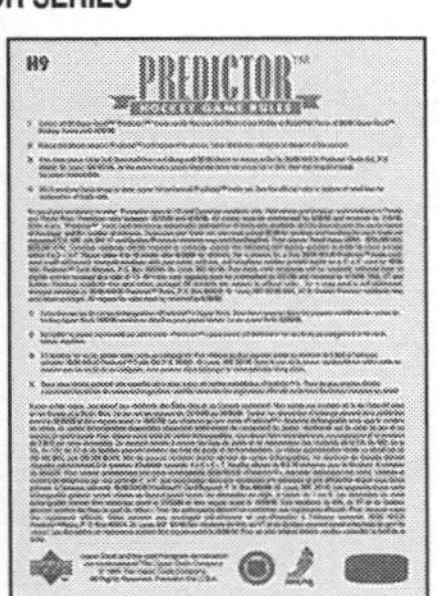

If the depicted player finished first or second in his category, the card could be redeemed for a 10-card gold set. Redeemed Gold cards had the preffix "HR-" or "RR-". Hobby Predictors have bronze foil and a grey background on the card front while Retail Predictors have silver foil and a burgandy background. Redeemed cards have gold foil instead of the bronze or silver.

Hart Set (H1-H10):	**70.00**	**35.00**
Vezina Set (H11-H20):	**40.00**	**20.00**
Calder Set (H21-H30):	**20.00**	**10.00**
Norris Set (H31-H40):	**20.00**	**10.00**
Assists (Goals) Set (R1-R10):	**40.00**	**20.00**
Goals (Assists) Set (R11-R20):	**40.00**	**20.00**
Points Set (R21-R30):	**60.00**	**30.00**
Art Ross Set (R31-R40):	**70.00**	**35.00**
Pearson Set (R41-R50):	**70.00**	**35.00**
Conn Smythe Set (R51-R60):	**80.00**	**40.000**

	No.	Player	Reg.	Gold
☐☐	H1	Eric Lindros, Pha.	12.00	6.00
☐☐	H2	Jaromir Jagr, Pgh.	10.00	5.00
☐☐	H3	Paul Coffey, Det.	2.00	1.00
☐☐	H4	Mario Lemieux, Pgh.	15.00	7.50
☐☐	H5	Martin Brodeur (G), N.J.	7.00	3.50
☐☐	H6	Sergei Fedorov, Det.	5.00	2.50
☐☐	H7	Wayne Gretzky, L.A.	20.00	10.00
☐☐	H8	Peter Forsberg, Col.	10.00	5.00
☐☐	H9	Mark Messier, NYR.	5.00	2.50
☐☐	H10	Long Shot	1.00	.50
☐☐	H11	Martin Brodeur (G), N.J.	7.00	3.50
☐☐	H12	Mike Richter (G), NYR.	3.00	1.50
☐☐	H13	Dominik Hasek (G), Buf.	7.00	3.50
☐☐	H14	Patrick Roy (G), Col.	15.00	7.50
☐☐	H15	Blaine Lacher (G), Bos.	1.50	.75
☐☐	H16	Jim Carey (G), Wsh.	1.50	.75
☐☐	H17	Félix Potvin (G), Tor.	5.00	2.50
☐☐	H18	Ed Belfour, (G), Chi.	3.00	1.50
☐☐	H19	John Vanbiesbrouck (G), Fla.	6.00	3.00
☐☐	H20	Long Shot	1.00	.50
☐☐	H21	Vitali Yachmenev, L.A.	1.50	.75
☐☐	H22	Saku Koivu, Mtl.	7.00	3.50
☐☐	H23	Daniel Alfredsson, Ott.	5.00	2.50
☐☐	H24	Ed Jovanovski, Fla.	2.00	1.00
☐☐	H25	Aki Berg, L.A.	1.50	.75
☐☐	H26	Radek Dvorak, Fla.	1.50	.75
☐☐	H27	Shane Doan, Wpg.	1.50	.75
☐☐	H28	Niklas Sundstrom, NYR.	1.50	.75
☐☐	H29	Eric Dazé, Chi.	2.00	1.00
☐☐	H30	Long Shot	1.00	.50
☐☐	H31	Paul Coffey, Det.	2.00	1.00
☐☐	H32	Ray Bourque, Bos.	5.00	2.50
☐☐	H33	Brian Leetch, NYR.	3.00	1.50
☐☐	H34	Chris Chelios, Chi.	4.00	2.00
☐☐	H35	Scott Stevens, N.J.	1.50	.75
☐☐	H36	Nicklas Lidström, Det.	2.00	1.00
☐☐	H37	Sergei Zubov, Pgh.	2.00	1.00
☐☐	H38	Larry Murphy, Tor.	2.00	1.00
☐☐	H39	Roman Hamrlik, T.B.	2.00	1.00
☐☐	H40	Long Shot	1.00	.50
☐☐	R1	Cam Neely, Bos.	2.00	1.00
☐☐	R2	Eric Lindros, Pha.	12.00	6.00
☐☐	R3	Jaromir Jagr, Pgh.	10.00	5.00
☐☐	R4	Brendan Shanahan, Hfd.	6.00	3.00
☐☐	R5	Brett Hull, Stl.	5.00	2.50
☐☐	R6	Alexander Mogilny, Van.	3.00	1.50
☐☐	R7	Owen Nolan, Col.	2.00	1.00
☐☐	R8	Theoren Fleury, Cgy.	3.00	1.50
☐☐	R9	Pavel Bure, Van.	7.00	3.50
☐☐	R10	Long Shot	1.00	.50
☐☐	R11	Ron Francis, Pgh.	3.00	1.50
☐☐	R12	Paul Coffey, Det.	2.00	1.00
☐☐	R13	Wayne Gretzky, L.A.	20.00	10.00
☐☐	R14	Joe Sakic, Col.	8.00	4.00
☐☐	R15	Steve Yzerman, Det.	10.00	5.00
☐☐	R16	Adam Oates, Bos.	3.00	1.50
☐☐	R17	Joé Juneau, Wsh.	2.00	1.00
☐☐	R18	Brian Leetch, NYR.	3.00	1.50
☐☐	R19	Pat LaFontaine, Buf.	2.00	1.00
☐☐	R20	Long Shot	1.00	.50
☐☐	R21	Eric Lindros, Pha.	12.00	6.00
☐☐	R22	Jaromir Jagr, Pgh.	10.00	5.00
☐☐	R23	Wayne Gretzky, L.A.	20.00	10.00
☐☐	R24	Sergei Fedorov, Det.	5.00	2.50
☐☐	R25	Peter Forsberg, Col.	10.00	5.00
☐☐	R26	Pavel Bure, Van.	7.00	3.50
☐☐	R27	Joe Sakic, Col.	8.00	4.00
☐☐	R28	Alexei Zhamnov, Wpg.	2.00	1.00
☐☐	R29	Pat LaFontaine, Buf.	2.00	1.00
☐☐	R30	Long Shot	1.00	.50
☐☐	R31	Wayne Gretzky, L.A.	20.00	10.00
☐☐	R32	Mario Lemieux, Pgh.	15.00	7.50
☐☐	R33	Eric Lindros, Pha.	12.00	6.00
☐☐	R34	Sergei Fedorov, Det.	5.00	2.50
☐☐	R35	Alexander Mogilny, Van.	3.00	1.50
☐☐	R36	Joe Sakic, Col.	8.00	4.00
☐☐	R37	Peter Forsberg, Col.	10.00	5.00
☐☐	R38	Jaromir Jagr, Pgh.	10.00	5.00
☐☐	R39	Mark Messier, NYR.	5.00	2.50
☐☐	R40	Long Shot	1.00	.50
☐☐	R41	Wayne Gretzky, L.A.	20.00	10.00
☐☐	R42	Mario Lemieux, Pgh.	15.00	7.50
☐☐	R43	Paul Kariya, Ana.	12.00	6.00
☐☐	R44	Sergei Fedorov, Det.	5.00	2.50
☐☐	R45	Joe Sakic, Col.	8.00	4.00
☐☐	R46	Jaromir Jagr, Pgh.	10.00	5.00
☐☐	R47	Jeremy Roenick, Chi.	3.00	1.50
☐☐	R48	Ray Bourque, Bos.	5.00	2.50
☐☐	R49	Teemu Selänne, Wpg.	7.00	3.50
☐☐	R50	Long Shot	1.00	.50
☐☐	R51	Wayne Gretzky, L.A.	20.00	10.00
☐☐	R52	Eric Lindros, Pha.	12.00	6.00
☐☐	R53	Mario Lemieux, Pgh.	15.00	7.50
☐☐	R54	Peter Forsberg, Col.	10.00	5.00
☐☐	R55	Patrick Roy (G), Col.	15.00	7.50
☐☐	R56	Mark Messier, NYR.	5.00	2.50
☐☐	R57	Martin Brodeur (G), N.J.	7.00	3.50
☐☐	R58	Steve Yzerman, Det.	10.00	5.00
☐☐	R59	Ron Francis, Pgh.	3.00	1.50
☐☐	R60	Long Shot	1.00	.50

ALL-STARS

These cards have two versions: a 5" x 7" box insert and the standard size insert.

Series Two Insert Set (20 cards):			**100.00**	**200.00**
	No.	**Player**	**5"x7"**	**Insert**
☐☐	AS1	Ray Bourque/Paul Coffey	4.00	8.00
☐☐	AS2	Scott Stevens/Chris Chelios	3.00	6.00
☐☐	AS3	Jaromir Jagr/Brett Hull	10.00	20.00
☐☐	AS4	Brendan Shanahan/Pavel Bure	8.00	15.00
☐☐	AS5	Mario Lemieux/Wayne Gretzky	30.00	60.00
☐☐	AS6	Martin Brodeur/Ed Belfour (G)	8.00	15.00
☐☐	AS7	Brian Leetch/Nicklas Lidström	3.00	6.00
☐☐	AS8	Roman Hamrlik/Gary Suter	2.00	3.00
☐☐	AS9	Eric Desjardins/Al MacInnis	2.00	3.00
☐☐	AS10	Cam Neely/Andy Moog	2.50	5.00
☐☐	AS11	Peter Bondra/Theoren Fleury	3.00	6.00
☐☐	AS12	Daniel Alfredsson/Teemu Selänne	5.00	10.00
☐☐	AS13	Pat Verbeek/Owen Nolan	2.50	5.00
☐☐	AS14	John LeClair/Paul Kariya	12.00	25.00
☐☐	AS15	Pierre Turgeon/Sergei Fedorov	5.00	10.00
☐☐	AS16	Mark Messier/Doug Weight	5.00	10.00
☐☐	AS17	Eric Lindros/Peter Forsberg	20.00	40.00
☐☐	AS18	Ron Francis/Mats Sundin	5.00	10.00
☐☐	AS19	John Vanbiesbrouck/Chris Osgood (G)	8.00	15.00
☐☐	AS20	Dominik Hasek/Félix Potvin (G)	8.00	15.00

3.5" x 5" ELECTRIC ICE GOLD BLOWUPS

We have little information on this set. Other singles exist.

	No.	Player
☐	48	Félix Potvin (G), Tor.
☐	99	Wayne Gretzky, NYR.
☐	188	Alexander Mogilny, Van.

1995 - 96 UPPER DECK ALL-STAR GAME PREDICTOR

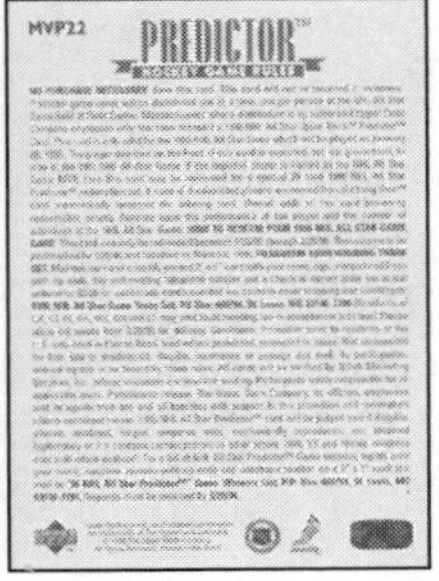

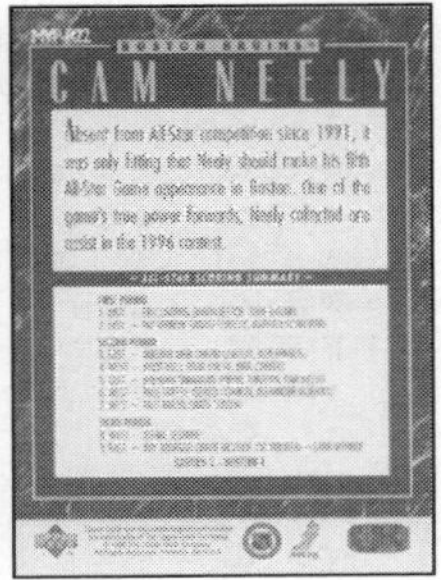

These cards were handed out at the All-Star Game in Boston. Redeemed Gold cards have the prefix "MVP-R". The Silver Adam Oates card has not been confirmed to exist. Ray Bourque's Silver card was the winning card that could be redeemed for a 30-card Gold set.

Imprint: © 1996 THE UPPER DECK COMPANY

	No.	Player	Silver	Gold
Complete Set (29 cards):			**450.00**	**900.00**
□ □	MVP1	Wayne Gretzky, L.A.	50.00	250.00
□ □	MVP2	Sergei Fedorov, Det.	15.00	50.00
□ □	MVP3	Brett Hull, Stl.	15.00	50.00
□ □	MVP4	Alexander Mogilny, Van.	10.00	30.00
□ □	MVP5	Joe Sakic, Col.	25.00	100.00
□ □	MVP6	Paul Kariya, Ana.	35.00	150.00
□ □	MVP7	Teemu Selänne, Wpg.	20.00	80.00
□ □	MVP8	Paul Coffey, Det.	8.00	20.00
□ □	MVP9	Chris Chelios, Chi.	12.00	40.00
□ □	MVP10	Doug Gilmour, Tor.	10.00	30.00
□ □	MVP11	Peter Forsberg, Col.	30.00	120.00
□ □	MVP12	Jeremy Roenick, Chi.	10.00	30.00
□ □	MVP13	Theoren Fleury, Cgy.	10.00	30.00
□ □	MVP14	Mike Modano, Dal.	15.00	50.00
□ □	MVP15	Steve Yzerman, Det.	30.00	120.00
□ □	MVP16	Mario Lemieux, Pgh.	40.00	200.00
□ □	MVP17	Jaromir Jagr, Pgh.	30.00	120.00
□ □	MVP18	Eric Lindros, Ana.	35.00	150.00
□ □	MVP19	Mark Messier, NYR.	15.00	50.00
□ □	MVP20	Brendan Shanahan, Hfd.	18.00	65.00
□ □	MVP21	Ray Bourque, Bos.	15.00	50.00
□ □	MVP22	Cam Neely, Bos.	8.00	20.00
□ □	MVP23	Ron Francis, Pgh.	10.00	30.00
□ □	MVP24	John LeClair, Pha.	15.00	50.00
□ □	MVP25	Brian Leetch, NYR.	10.00	30.00
□ □	MVP26	Peter Bondra, Wsh.	12.00	40.00
□ □	MVP27	Scott Stevens, N.J.	6.00	15.00
□ □	MVP29	Martin Brodeur (G), N.J.	20.00	80.00
□ □	MVP30	Long Shot	2.00	8.00
□	MVP-R28	Adam Oates, Bos.	.–	30.00

1995 - 96 UPPER DECK BE A PLAYER

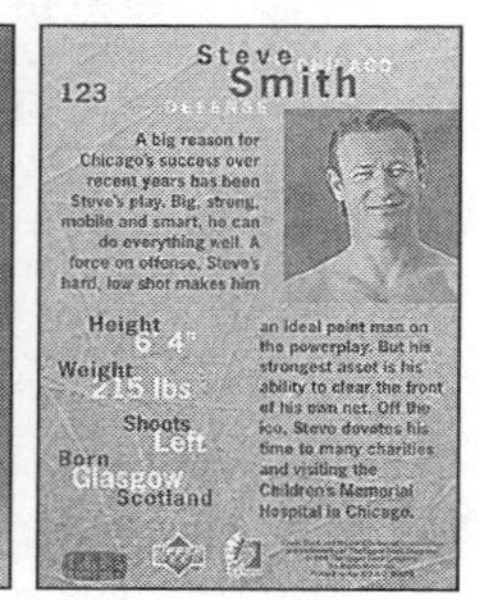

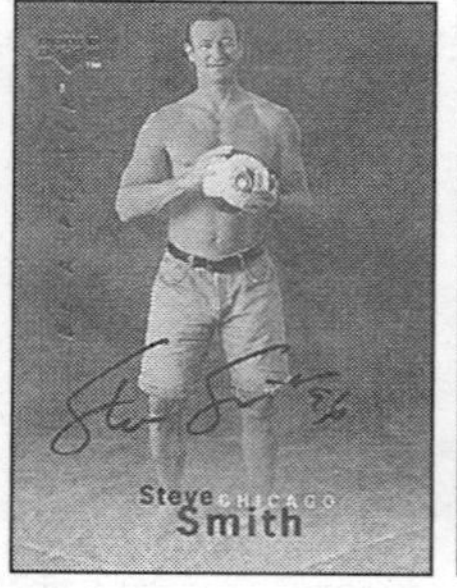

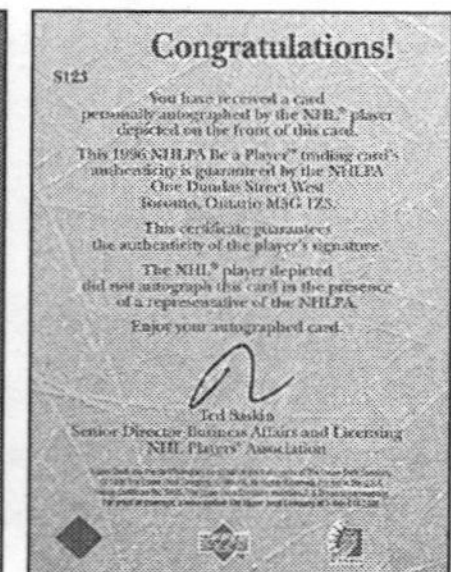

Autograph cards have the prefix "S" and are seeded one per pack. Die-Cut autographs have a gold hologram as opposed to a silver hologram on the card back. Wayne Gretzky signed fewer autographs than any other player: 648 regular cards and 234 Die-Cut cards. Mike Richter's autographs were not inserted into packs. Instead, 3,000 regular autographs and 400 autographed Die-Cut cards were available by mail.

Imprint: © 1996 The Upper Deck Company.

	No.	Player	Reg.	Auto.	Auto. DC
Complete Set (225 cards):			**50.00**	**2,500.00**	
Common Player:			**.25**	**5.00**	**10.00**
□ □ □	1	Brett Hull, Stl.	1.25	40.00	80.00
□ □ □	2	Jyrki Lumme, Van.	.25	5.00	10.00
□ □ □	3	Shean Donovan, S.J.	.25	5.00	10.00
□ □ □	4	Yuri Khmylev, Stl.	.25	5.00	10.00
□ □ □	5	Stéphane Matteau, Stl.	.25	5.00	10.00
□ □ □	6	Basil McRae, Stl.	.25	5.00	10.00
□ □ □	7	Dmitri Yushkevich, Tor.	.25	5.00	10.00
□ □ □	8	Ron Francis, Pgh.	.75	25.00	50.00
□ □ □	9	Keith Carney, Chi.	.25	5.00	10.00
□ □ □	10	Brad Dalgarno, NYI.	.25	5.00	10.00
□ □ □	11	Bob Carpenter, N.J.	.25	5.00	10.00
□ □ □	12	Kevin Stevens, Bos.	.25	8.00	15.00
□ □ □	13	Patrick Flatley, NYI.	.25	5.00	10.00
□ □ □	14	Craig Muni, Buf.	.25	5.00	10.00
□ □ □	15	Travis Green, NYI.	.25	5.00	10.00
□ □ □	16	Derek Plante, Buf.	.25	5.00	10.00
□ □ □	17	Mike Craig, Tor.	.25	5.00	10.00
□ □ □	18	Chris Pronger, Stl.	.50	15.00	30.00
□ □ □	19	Bret Hedican, Van.	.25	5.00	10.00
□ □ □	20	Mathieu Schneider, NYI.	.25	5.00	10.00
□ □ □	21	Chris Therien, Pha.	.25	5.00	10.00
□ □ □	22	Greg Adams, Dal.	.25	8.00	15.00
□ □ □	23	Arturs Irbe (G), S.J.	.25	8.00	15.00
□ □ □	24	Zigmund Palffy, NYI.	1.00	30.00	60.00
□ □ □	25	Peter Douris, Ana.	.25	5.00	10.00
□ □ □	26	Bob Sweeney, Buf.	.25	5.00	10.00
□ □ □	27	Chris Terreri (G), S.J.	.25	5.00	10.00
□ □ □	28	Alexei Zhitnik, Buf.	.25	5.00	10.00
□ □ □	29	Jay Wells, Stl.	.25	5.00	10.00
□ □ □	30	Andrew Cassels, Hfd.	.25	5.00	10.00
□ □ □	31	Radek Bonk, Ott.	.25	5.00	10.00
□ □ □	32	Brian Bellows, T.B.	.25	5.00	10.00
□ □ □	33	Frantisek Kucera, Hfd.	.25	5.00	10.00
□ □ □	34	Valeri Bure, Mtl.	.25	5.00	10.00
□ □ □	35	Randy Wood, Buf.	.25	5.00	10.00
□ □ □	36	Dimitri Khristich, L.A.	.25	5.00	10.00
□ □ □	37	Randy Ladouceur, Ana.	.25	5.00	10.00
□ □ □	38	Nelson Emerson, Hfd.	.25	5.00	10.00
□ □ □	39	Bryan Marchment, Edm.	.25	5.00	10.00
□ □ □	40	Kevin Lowe, NYR.	.25	8.00	15.00
□ □ □	41	Trevor Linden, Van.	.50	15.00	30.00
□ □ □	42	Neal Broten, N.J.	.25	5.00	10.00
□ □ □	43	Tom Chorske, N.J.	.25	5.00	10.00
□ □ □	44	Patrice Brisebois, Mtl.	.25	5.00	10.00
□ □ □	45	Wayne Presley, Stl.	.25	5.00	10.00
□ □ □	46	Murray Craven, Chi.	.25	5.00	10.00
□ □ □	47	Craig Janney, S.J.	.25	5.00	10.00
□ □ □	48	Ken Daneyko, Det.	.25	5.00	10.00
□ □ □	49	Dino Ciccarelli, T.B.	.50	10.00	20.00
□ □ □	50	Jason Dawe, Buf.	.25	5.00	10.00
□ □ □	51	Brad McCrimmon, Hfd.	.25	5.00	10.00
□ □ □	52	Randy McKay, N.J.	.25	5.00	10.00
□ □ □	53	Rudy Poeschek, T.B.	.25	5.00	10.00
□ □ □	54	Calle Johansson, Wsh.	.25	5.00	10.00
□ □ □	55	Wendel Clark, Tor.	.50	12.00	25.00
□ □ □	56	Rob Ray, Buf.	.25	5.00	10.00
□ □ □	57	Garth Snow (G), Pha.	.25	8.00	15.00
□ □ □	58	Joé Juneau, Wsh.	.25	8.00	15.00
□ □ □	59	Craig Wolanin, Col.	.25	5.00	10.00
□ □ □	60	Ray Sheppard, S.J.	.25	8.00	15.00
□ □ □	61	Oleg Tverdovsky, Ana.	.25	8.00	15.00
□ □ □	62	Geoff Sanderson, Hfd.	.25	8.00	15.00
□ □ □	63	Mike Ridley, Van.	.25	5.00	10.00
□ □ □	64	David Oliver, Edm.	.25	5.00	10.00
□ □ □	65	Russ Courtnall, Van.	.25	5.00	10.00
□ □ □	66	Joe Reekie, Wsh.	.25	5.00	10.00
□ □ □	67	Ken Wregget (G), Pgh.	.25	8.00	15.00
□ □ □	68	Teppo Numminen, Wpg.	.25	5.00	10.00
□ □ □	69	Mikhail Shtalenkov (G), Ana.	.25	8.00	15.00
□ □ □	70	Luke Richardson, Edm.	.25	5.00	10.00
□ □ □	71	Brent Gilchrist, Dal.	.25	5.00	10.00
□ □ □	72	Phil Housley, Cgy.	.25	8.00	15.00
□ □ □	73	Greg Johnson, Det.	.25	5.00	10.00
□ □ □	74	Sean Hill, Ana.	.25	5.00	10.00
□ □ □	75	Karl Dykhuis, Pha.	.25	5.00	10.00
□ □ □	76	Tim Cheveldae (G), Wpg.	.25	8.00	15.00
□ □ □	77	Shjon Podein, Edm.	.25	5.00	10.00
□ □ □	78	René Corbet, Col.	.25	5.00	10.00
□ □ □	79	Ronnie Stern, Cgy.	.25	5.00	10.00
□ □ □	80	Mike Donnelly, L.A.	.25	5.00	10.00
□ □ □	81	Randy Cunneyworth, Ott.	.25	5.00	10.00
□ □ □	82	Rick Tocchet, Bos.	.25	8.00	15.00
□ □ □	83	Dallas Drake, Wpg.	.25	5.00	10.00
□ □ □	84	Cam Russell, Chi.	.25	5.00	10.00
□ □ □	85	Daren Puppa (G), T.B.	.25	8.00	15.00
□ □ □	86	Benoît Brunet, Mtl.	.25	5.00	10.00
□ □ □	87	Paul Ranheim, Hfd.	.25	5.00	10.00
□ □ □	88	Bob Rouse, Det.	.25	5.00	10.00
□ □ □	89	Todd Elik, Bos.	.25	5.00	10.00
□ □ □	90	Darcy Wakaluk (G), Dal.	.25	8.00	15.00
□ □ □	91	Cliff Ronning, Van.	.25	5.00	10.00
□ □ □	92	Pat Conacher, L.A.	.25	5.00	10.00
□ □ □	93	Todd Krygier, Ana.	.25	5.00	10.00
□ □ □	94	Dave Babych, Van.	.25	5.00	10.00
□ □ □	95	Pat Falloon, Pha.	.25	5.00	10.00
□ □ □	96	Don Beaupré (G), Ott.	.25	8.00	15.00
□ □ □	97	Wayne Gretzky, L.A.	7.50	900.00	1,600.00
□ □ □	98	Chris Joseph, T.B.	.25	5.00	10.00
□ □ □	99	Vyacheslav Kozlov, Det.	.25	8.00	15.00
□ □ □	100	Brent Fedyk, Dal.	.25	5.00	10.00
□ □ □	101	Tim Taylor, Det.	.25	5.00	10.00
□ □ □	102	Mike Eastwood, Wpg.	.25	5.00	10.00
□ □ □	103	Mike Keane, Col.	.25	5.00	10.00
□ □ □	104	Grant Ledyard, Dal.	.25	5.00	10.00
□ □ □	105	Rob DiMaio, Pha.	.25	5.00	10.00
□ □ □	106	Martin Straka, Ott.	.25	5.00	10.00
□ □ □	107	Scott Young, Col.	.25	5.00	10.00
□ □ □	108	Zarley Zalapski, Cgy.	.25	5.00	10.00
□ □ □	109	Stephen Leach, Bos.	.25	5.00	10.00
□ □ □	110	Jody Hull, Ott.	.25	5.00	10.00
□ □ □	111	Lyle Odelein, N.J.	.25	5.00	10.00
□ □ □	112	Bob Corkum, Ana.	.25	5.00	10.00
□ □ □	113	Rob Blake, L.A.	.50	12.00	25.00
□ □ □	114	Randy Burridge, Buf.	.25	5.00	10.00
□ □ □	115	Keith Primeau, Det.	.50	15.00	30.00
□ □ □	116	Glen Welsey, Hfd.	.25	5.00	10.00
□ □ □	117	Brian Bradley, T.B.	.25	5.00	10.00
□ □ □	118	Steve Konowalchuk, Wsh.	.25	5.00	10.00
□ □ □	119	Patrik Juhlin, Pha.	.25	5.00	10.00
□ □ □	120	John Tucker, T.B.	.25	5.00	10.00
□ □ □	121	Stéphane Fiset (G), Col.	.50	12.00	25.00
□ □ □	122	Mike Hough, Fla.	.25	5.00	10.00
□ □ □	123	Steve Smith, Chi.	.25	10.00	15.00
□ □ □	124	Tom Barrasso (G), Pgh.	.50	25.00	35.00
□ □ □	125	Ray Whitney, S.J.	.25	5.00	10.00
□ □ □	126	Benoît Hogue, Tor.	.25	5.00	10.00
□ □ □	127	Stu Barnes, Fla.	.25	5.00	10.00
□ □ □	128	Craig Ludwig, Dal.	.25	5.00	10.00
□ □ □	129	Curtis Leschyshyn, Col.	.25	5.00	10.00
□ □ □	130	John LeClair, Pha.	1.25	35.00	70.00
□ □ □	131	Dennis Vial, Ott.	.25	5.00	10.00
□ □ □	132	Cory Stillman, Cgy.	.25	5.00	10.00
□ □ □	133	Roman Hamrlik, T.B.	.50	15.00	30.00
□ □ □	134	Al MacInnis, Stl.	.25	12.00	25.00
□ □ □	135	Igor Korolev, Wpg.	.25	5.00	10.00
□ □ □	136	Rick Zombo, Bos.	.25	5.00	10.00
□ □ □	137	Zdeno Ciger, Edm.	.25	5.00	10.00
□ □ □	138	Brian Savage, Mtl.	.25	5.00	10.00
□ □ □	139	Paul Ysebaert, T.B.	.25	5.00	10.00
□ □ □	140	Brent Sutter, Chi.	.25	5.00	10.00
□ □ □	141	Ed Olczyk, Wpg.	.25	5.00	10.00
□ □ □	142	Adam Creighton, T.B.	.25	5.00	10.00
□ □ □	143	Jesse Belanger, Fla.	.25	5.00	10.00
□ □ □	144	Glenn Murray, Pgh.	.25	5.00	10.00
□ □ □	145	Alexander Selivanov, T.B.	.25	5.00	10.00
□ □ □	146	Trent Yawney, Cgy.	.25	5.00	10.00
□ □ □	147	Bruce Driver, NYR.	.25	5.00	10.00
□ □ □	148	Michael Nylander, Cgy.	.25	5.00	10.00
□ □ □	149	Martin Gelinas, Van.	.25	8.00	15.00
□ □ □	150	Yanic Perreault, L.A.	.25	8.00	15.00
□ □ □	151	Craig Billington (G), Bos.	.25	8.00	15.00
□ □ □	152	Pierre Turgeon, Mtl.	.50	15.00	30.00
□ □ □	153	Mike Modano, Dal.	1.25	35.00	70.00
□ □ □	154	Joe Mullen, Bos.	.25	10.00	20.00
□ □ □	155	Todd Ewen, Ana.	.25	5.00	10.00
□ □ □	156	Petr Nedved, Pgh.	.25	10.00	20.00
□ □ □	157	Dominic Roussel (G), Pha.	.25	5.00	10.00
□ □ □	158	Murray Baron, Stl.	.25	5.00	10.00
□ □ □	159	Robert Dirk, Ana.	.25	5.00	10.00
□ □ □	160	Tomas Sandström, Pgh.	.25	8.00	15.00
□ □ □	161	Brian Holzinger, Buf.	.25	5.00	10.00
□ □ □	162	Ken Klee, Wsh.	.25	5.00	10.00
□ □ □	163	Radek Dvorak, Fla.	.50	8.00	15.00
□ □ □	164	Marcus Ragnarsson, S.J.	.25	5.00	10.00
□ □ □	165	Aaron Gavey, T.B.	.25	5.00	10.00
□ □ □	166	Jeff O'Neill, Hfd.	.50	12.00	25.00
□ □ □	167	Chad Kilger, Ana.	.25	5.00	10.00
□ □ □	168	Todd Bertuzzi, NYI.	.25	8.00	15.00
□ □ □	169	Robert Svehla, Fla.	.25	8.00	15.00
□ □ □	170	Eric Dazé, Chi.	.50	20.00	40.00
□ □ □	171	Daniel Alfredsson, Ott.	1.50	30.00	50.00
□ □ □	172	Shane Doan, Wpg.	.25	5.00	10.00
□ □ □	173	Kyle McLaren, Bos.	.25	5.00	10.00
□ □ □	174	Saku Koivu, Mtl.	1.75	60.00	100.00
□ □ □	175	Jere Lehtinen, Dal.	.50	12.00	25.00
□ □ □	176	Nikolai Khabibulin (G), Wpg.	.75	20.00	40.00
□ □ □	177	Niklas Sundstrom, NYR.	.25	8.00	15.00
□ □ □	178	Ed Jovanovski, Fla.	.75	20.00	40.00

	No.	Player			
□□□	179	Jason Bonsignore, Edm.	.25	5.00	10.00
□□□	180	Kenny Jonsson, NYI.	.25	5.00	10.00
□□□	181	Vitali Yachmenev, L.A.	.25	8.00	15.00
□□□	182	Alexei Kovalev, NYR.	.25	8.00	15.00
□□□	183	Sandis Ozolinsh, Col.	.50	10.00	20.00
□□□	184	Rob Niedermayer, Fla.	.25	8.00	15.00
□□□	185	Richard Park, Pgh.	.25	5.00	10.00
□□□	186	Adam Deadmarsh, Col.	.25	15.00	30.00
□□□	187	Sergei Krivokrasov, Chi.	.25	5.00	10.00
□□□	188	Alexandre Daigle, Ott.	.50	10.00	20.00
□□□	189	Jim Carey (G), Wsh.	.25	5.00	10.00
□□□	190	Todd Marchant, Edm.	.25	5.00	10.00
□□□	191	Mike Richter (G), NYR.	1.00	100.00	150.00
□□□	192	Dominik Hasek (G), Buf.	1.75	65.00	125.00
□□□	193	Chris Osgood (G), Det.	1.25	35.00	70.00
□□□	194	Ed Belfour (G), N.J.	1.00	30.00	60.00
□□□	195	Félix Potvin (G), Tor.	1.50	35.00	70.00
□□□	196	Grant Fuhr (G), Stl.	.50	25.00	50.00
□□□	197	Patrick Roy (G), Col.	4.00	150.00	400.00
□□□	198	Ron Hextall (G), Pha.	.50	15.00	30.00
□□□	199	Jocelyn Thibault (G), Mtl.	1.25	30.00	60.00
□□□	200	Kirk McLean (G), Van.	.50	10.00	20.00
□□□	201	Jari Kurri, L.A.	.50	20.00	40.00
□□□	202	Bobby Holik, N.J.	.25	5.00	10.00
□□□	203	Mats Sundin, Tor.	1.00	35.00	70.00
□□□	204	Alexander Mogilny, Van.	1.00	20.00	40.00
□□□	205	Valeri Karpov, Ana.	.25	5.00	10.00
□□□	206	Igor Larionov, Det.	.50	10.00	20.00
□□□	207	Valeri Zelepukin, N.J.	.25	5.00	10.00
□□□	208	Josef Stumpel, Bos.	.50	8.00	15.00
□□□	209	Sergei Nemchinov, Van.	.25	5.00	10.00
□□□	210	Peter Bondra, Wsh.	1.00	25.00	50.0000
□□□	211	Chris Chelios, Chi.	1.00	30.00	60.00
□□□	212	Adam Graves, NYR.	.25	8.00	15.00
□□□	213	Dale Hunter, Wsh.	.25	8.00	15.00
□□□	214	Tony Twist, Stl.	.25	5.00	10.00
□□□	215	Keith Tkachuk, Wpg.	1.00	35.00	70.00
□□□	216	Vladimir Konstantinov, Det.	.25	50.00	80.00
□□□	217	Sandy McCarthy, Cgy.	.25	5.00	10.00
□□□	218	Jamie Macoun, Tor.	.25	5.00	10.00
□□□	219	Scott Stevens, N.J.	.25	8.00	15.00
□□□	220	Mark Tinordi, Wsh.	.25	5.00	10.00
□□□	221	Bob Probert, Chi.	.25	8.00	15.00
□□□	222	Gino Odjick, Van.	.25	5.00	10.00
□□□	223	Ulf Samuelsson, NYR.	.25	5.00	10.00
□□□	224	Stu Grimson, Ana.	.25	5.00	10.00
□□□	225	Marty McSorley, L.A.	.25	8.00	15.00

GREAT MEMORIES

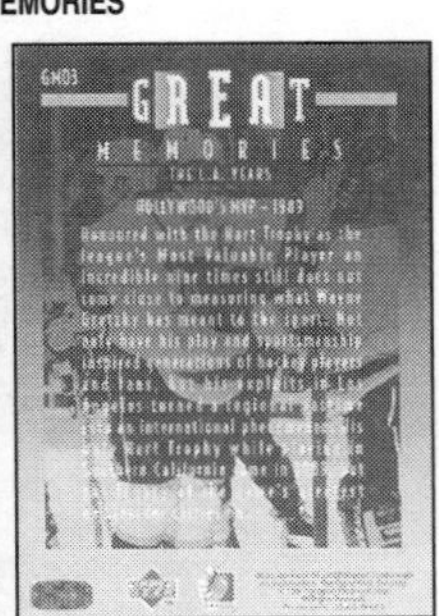

Insert Set (10 cards): 100.00

	No.	Player	NRMT-MT
□	GM01	Wayne Gretzky, The First Game - '88	12.00
□	GM02	Wayne Gretzky, Going Back to Edm. - '88/9	12.00
□	GM03	Wayne Gretzky, Hollywood's MVP - '89	12.00
□	GM04	Wayne Gretzky, Point Number 1851 - '89	12.00
□	GM05	Wayne Gretzky, 23game Assist Streak - '91	12.00
□	GM06	Wayne Gretzky, Goal Number 802 - '94	12.00
□	GM07	Wayne Gretzky, The Tenth Art Ross - '94	12.00
□	GM08	Wayne Gretzky, Conference Champs - '93	12.00
□	GM09	Wayne Gretzky, Stanley Cup Finals - '93	12.00
□	GM10	Wayne Gretzky, 2500 Points - '95	12.00

LETHAL LINES

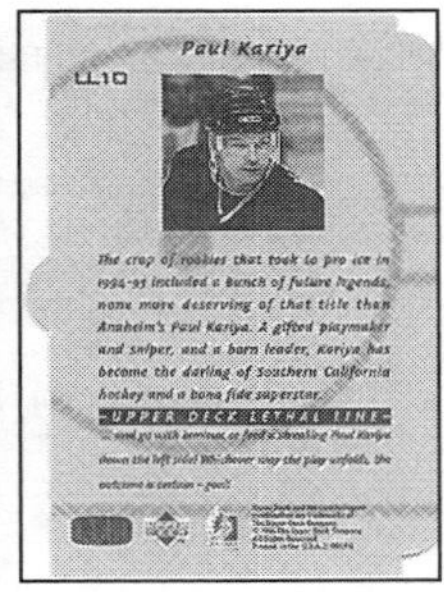

Each set of three cards (LL1-LL3, LL4-LL6, etc.) connect to form a line.

Insert Set (15 cards): 110.00

	No.	Player	NRMT-MT
□	LL1	Keith Tkachuk, Wpg.	5.00
□	LL2	Wayne Gretzky, L.A.	25.00
□	LL3	Brett Hull, Stl.	6.00
□	LL4	Eric Dazé, Chi.	4.00
□	LL5	Saku Koivu, Mtl.	9.00
□	LL6	Daniel Alfredsson, Ott.	5.00
□	LL7	Pavel Bure, Van.	9.00
□	LL8	Sergei Fedorov, Det.	6.00
□	LL9	Alexander Mogilny, Van.	4.00
□	LL10	Paul Kariya, Ana.	15.00
□	LL11	Mario Lemieux, Pgh.	20.00
□	LL12	Jaromir Jagr, Pgh.	12.00
□	LL13	Brendan Shanahan, Hfd.	7.50
□	LL14	Eric Lindros, Pha.	15.00
□	LL15	Alexei Kovalev, NYR.	3.00

1995 - 96 UPPER DECK COLLECTOR'S CHOICE

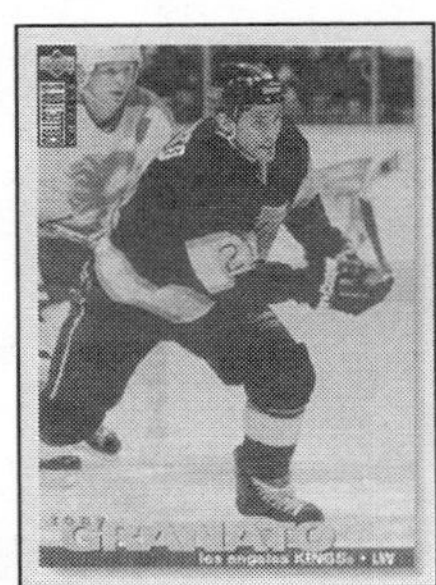

Cards 1-396 have three versions: the regular card, a Player's Club parallel and a Platinum Player's Club parallel. A Young Guns trade card found in packs could be redeemed for a 15-card update set.

Imprint: © 1995 THE UPPER DECK COMPANY

Complete Set (396 cards):	20.00	100.00	140.00
Young Guns Set (15 cards):	12.00		
Young Guns Expired Trade Card:	.50		
Common Player:	.10	.35	3.00

	No.	Player	Reg.	PC	PPC
□□□	1	Wayne Gretzky, L.A.	2.00	15.00	140.00
□□□	2	Darius Kasparaitis, NYI.	.10	.35	3.00
□□□	3	Scott Niedermayer, N.J.	.25	.50	5.00
□□□	4	Brendan Shanahan, Stl.	.60	3.50	35.00
□□□	5	Doug Gilmour, Tor.	.35	1.00	10.00
□□□	6	Lyle Odelein, Mtl.	.10	.35	3.00
□□□	7	Dave Gagner, Dal.	.10	.35	3.00
□□□	8	Gary Suter, Chi.	.10	.35	3.00
□□□	9	Sandis Ozolinsh, S.J.	.25	.50	5.00
□□□	10	Sergei Zubov, NYR.	.10	.35	3.00
□□□	11	Don Beaupré (G), Ott.	.10	.35	3.00
□□□	12	Bill Lindsay, Fla.	.10	.35	3.00
□□□	13	David Oliver, Edm.	.10	.35	3.00
□□□	14	Bob Corkum, Ana.	.10	.35	3.00
□□□	15	German Titov, Cgy.	.10	.35	3.00
□□□	16	Jari Kurri, L.A.	.25	.50	5.00
□□□	17	Cliff Ronning, Van.	.10	.35	3.00
□□□	18	Paul Coffey, Det.	.25	.50	5.00
□□□	19	Ian Laperrière, Stl.	.10	.35	3.00
□□□	20	Dave Andreychuk, Tor.	.10	.35	3.00
□□□	21	Andrei Nikolishin, Hfd.	.10	.35	3.00
□□□	22	Blaine Lacher (G), Bos.	.10	.35	3.00
□□□	23	Yuri Khmylev, Buf.	.10	.35	3.00
□□□	24	Darren Turcotte, Hfd.	.10	.35	3.00
□□□	25	Joe Mullen, Pgh.	.10	.35	3.00
□□□	26	Peter Forsberg, Que.	1.00	8.00	80.00
□□□	27	Paul Ysebaert, T.B.	.10	.35	3.00
□□□	28	Tommy Söderström (G), NYI.	.10	.35	3.00
□□□	29	Rod Brind'Amour, Pha.	.25	.50	5.00
□□□	30	Jim Carey (G), Wsh.	.10	.35	3.00
□□□	31	Geoff Courtnall, Van.	.10	.35	3.00
□□□	32	Vyacheslav Kozlov, Det.	.10	.35	3.00
□□□	33	Ray Ferraro, NYI.	.10	.35	3.00
□□□	34	John MacLean, N.J.	.10	.35	3.00
□□□	35	Benoît Brunet, Mtl.	.10	.35	3.00
□□□	36	Trent Klatt, Dal.	.10	.35	3.00
□□□	37	Chris Chelios, Chi.	.35	2.00	20.00
□□□	38	Tom Pederson, S.J.	.10	.35	3.00
□□□	39	Pat Elynuik, T.B.	.10	.35	3.00
□□□	40	Rob Niedermyer, Fla.	.10	.35	3.00
□□□	41	Jason Arnott, Edm.	.25	.50	5.00
□□□	42	Patrik Carnback, Ana.	.10	.35	3.00
□□□	43	Steve Chiasson, Cgy.	.10	.35	3.00
□□□	44	Marty McSorley, L.A.	.10	.35	3.00
□□□	45	Pavel Bure, Van.	.75	4.00	40.00
□□□	46	Glenn Anderson, Stl.	.10	.35	3.00
□□□	47	Doug Brown, Det.	.10	.35	3.00
□□□	48	Mike Ridley, Van.	.10	.35	3.00
□□□	49	Alexei Zhamnov, Wpg.	.25	.50	5.00
□□□	50	Mariusz Czerkawski, Bos.	.10	.35	3.00
□□□	51	Derek Plante, Buf.	.10	.35	3.00
□□□	52	Andrew Cassels, Hfd.	.10	.35	3.00
□□□	53	Tom Barrasso (G), Pgh.	.25	.50	5.00
□□□	54	Andrei Kovalenko, Que.	.10	.35	3.00
□□□	55	Pat Verbeek, NYR.	.10	.35	3.00
□□□	56	Alexander Semak, N.J.	.10	.35	3.00
□□□	57	Eric Lindros, Pha.	1.25	10.00	100.00
□□□	58	Peter Bondra, Wsh.	.35	2.00	20.00
□□□	59	Marty McInnis, NYI.	.10	.35	3.00
□□□	60	Bill Guerin, N.J.	.25	.50	5.00
□□□	61	Patrice Brisebois, Mtl.	.10	.35	3.00
□□□	62	Andy Moog (G), Dal.	.25	.50	5.00
□□□	63	Eric Weinrich, Chi.	.10	.35	3.00
□□□	64	Arturs Irbe (G), S.J.	.10	.35	3.00
□□□	65	Sean Hill, Ott.	.10	.35	3.00
□□□	66	Jesse Belanger, Fla.	.10	.35	3.00
□□□	67	Bryan Marchment, Edm.	.10	.35	3.00
□□□	68	Joe Sacco, Ana.	.10	.35	3.00
□□□	69	Trevor Kidd (G), Cgy.	.25	.50	5.00
□□□	70	Dan Quinn, L.A. (Ott.)	.10	.35	3.00
□□□	71	Kirk McLean (G), Van.	.10	.35	3.00
□□□	72	Benoît Hogue, Tor.	.10	.35	3.00
□□□	73	Garry Galley, Buf.	.10	.35	3.00
□□□	74	Randy Wood, Tor.	.10	.35	3.00
□□□	75	Nikolai Khabibulin (G), Wpg.	.35	1.00	10.00
□□□	76	Ted Donato, Bos.	.10	.35	3.00
□□□	77	Doug Bodger, Buf.	.10	.35	3.00
□□□	78	Paul Ranheim, Hfd.	.10	.35	3.00
□□□	79	Ulf Samuelsson, Pgh.	.10	.35	3.00
□□□	80	Uwe Krupp, Que.	.10	.35	3.00
□□□	81	Oleg Tverdovsky, Ana.	.10	.35	3.00
□□□	82	Kelly Miller, Wsh.	.10	.35	3.00
□□□	83	Darryl Sydor, L.A.	.10	.35	3.00
□□□	84	Brian Bellows, Mtl.	.10	.35	3.00
□□□	85	Jeremy Roenick, Chi.	.35	1.00	10.00
□□□	86	Phil Bourque, Ott.	.10	.35	3.00
□□□	87	Louie DeBrusk, Edm.	.10	.35	3.00
□□□	88	Joel Otto, Pha.	.10	.35	3.00
□□□	89	Dino Ciccarelli, Det.	.25	.50	5.00
□□□	90	Mats Sundin, Tor.	.50	3.00	30.00
□□□	91	Don Sweeney, Bos.	.10	.35	3.00
□□□	92	Roman Hamrlik, T.B.	.25	.50	5.00
□□□	93	Petr Svoboda, Pha.	.10	.35	3.00
□□□	94	Zigmund Palffy, NYI.	.35	2.00	20.00
□□□	95	Patrick Roy (G), Mtl.	1.50	12.00	120.00
□□□	96	Sergei Krivokrasov, Chi.	.10	.35	3.00
□□□	97	Wade Flaherty (G), S.J.	.10	.35	3.00
□□□	98	Fredrik Olausson, Edm.	.10	.35	3.00
□□□	99	Sergio Momesso, Van.	.10	.35	3.00
□□□	100	Mike Vernon (G), Det.	.25	.50	5.00
□□□	101	Todd Gill, S.J.	.10	.35	3.00
□□□	102	Cam Neely, Bos.	.25	.50	5.00
□□□	103	Wendel Clark, Tor.	.25	.50	5.00
□□□	104	John Tucker, T.B.	.10	.35	3.00
□□□	105	Eric Desjardins, Pha.	.10	.35	3.00
□□□	106	Ed Olczyk, Wpg.	.10	.35	3.00
□□□	107	Bob Beers, T.B.	.10	.35	3.00
□□□	108	Mark Recchi, Mtl.	.25	.50	5.00

☐☐☐ 109 Ed Belfour (G), Chi. .35 1.00 10.00
☐☐☐ 110 Radek Bonk, Ott. .10 .35 3.00
☐☐☐ 111 Cory Stillman, Cgy. .10 .35 3.00
☐☐☐ 112 Jeff Norton, Stl. .10 .35 3.00
☐☐☐ 113 Terry Carkner, Det. .10 .35 3.00
☐☐☐ 114 Félix Potvin (G), Tor. .50 3.00 30.00
☐☐☐ 115 Alexei Kasatonov, Bos. .10 .35 3.00
☐☐☐ 116 Brian Noonan, NYR. .10 .35 3.00
☐☐☐ 117 Daren Puppa (G), T.B. .10 .35 3.00
☐☐☐ 118 Joé Juneau, Wsh. .10 .35 3.00
☐☐☐ 119 Valeri Bure, Mtl. .10 .35 3.00
☐☐☐ 120 Murray Craven, Van. .10 .35 3.00
☐☐☐ 121 Marko Tuomainen, Edm. .10 .35 3.00
☐☐☐ 122 Trevor Linden, Van. .25 .50 5.00
☐☐☐ 123 Zarley Zalapski, Cgy. .10 .35 3.00
☐☐☐ 124 Jeff Shantz, Chi. .10 .35 3.00
☐☐☐ 125 Dmitri Mironov, Tor. .10 .35 3.00
☐☐☐ 126 Jamie Huscroft, Bos. .10 .35 3.00
☐☐☐ 127 Jaromir Jagr, Pgh. 1.00 8.00 80.00
☐☐☐ 128 Brian Bradley, T.B. .10 .35 3.00
☐☐☐ 129 Brett Lindros, NYI. .10 .35 3.00
☐☐☐ 130 Calle Johansson, Wsh. .10 .35 3.00
☐☐☐ 131 Pierre Turgeon, Mtl. .25 .50 5.00
☐☐☐ 132 Denis Savard, Chi. .25 .50 5.00
☐☐☐ 133 Joe Nieuwendyk, Dal. .25 .50 5.00
☐☐☐ 134 Petr Klima, T.B. .10 .35 3.00
☐☐☐ 135 John Druce, L.A. .10 .35 3.00
☐☐☐ 136 Chris Osgood (G), Det. .35 2.00 20.00
☐☐☐ 137 Kenny Jonsson, Tor. .10 .35 3.00
☐☐☐ 138 Jocelyn Lemieux, Hfd. .10 .35 3.00
☐☐☐ 139 Tomas Sandström, Pgh. .10 .35 3.00
☐☐☐ 140 Chris Gratton, T.B. .25 .50 5.00
☐☐☐ 141 Mark Tinordi, Wsh. .10 .35 3.00
☐☐☐ 142 Kirk Muller, NYI. .10 .35 3.00
☐☐☐ 143 Vladimir Malakhov, Mtl. .10 .35 3.00
☐☐☐ 144 Jiri Slegr, Van. .10 .35 3.00
☐☐☐ 145 Shawn McEachern, Bos. .10 .35 3.00
☐☐☐ 146 Shayne Corson, Stl. .25 .50 5.00
☐☐☐ 147 Kelly Hrudey (G), L.A. .10 .35 3.00
☐☐☐ 148 Sergei Fedorov, Det. .50 3.00 30.00
☐☐☐ 149 Mike Gartner, Tor. .25 .50 5.00
☐☐☐ 150 Stéphane Fiset (G), Que. .25 .50 5.00
☐☐☐ 151 Larry Murphy, Tor. .10 .35 3.00
☐☐☐ 152 Enrico Ciccone, T.B. .10 .35 3.00
☐☐☐ 153 Mike Keane, Mtl. .10 .35 3.00
☐☐☐ 154 Steve Larmer, NYR. .10 .35 3.00
☐☐☐ 155 Dale Hunter, Wsh. .10 .35 3.00
☐☐☐ 156 Joe Murphy, Chi. .10 .35 3.00
☐☐☐ 157 Pat LaFontaine, Buf. .25 .50 5.00
☐☐☐ 158 Rob Gaudreau, Ott. .10 .35 3.00
☐☐☐ 159 Paul Kariya, Ana. 1.25 10.00 100.00
☐☐☐ 160 Rob Blake, L.A. .25 .50 1.00
☐☐☐ 161 Keith Primeau, Det. .25 .50 5.00
☐☐☐ 162 Dave Ellett, Tor. .10 .35 3.00
☐☐☐ 163 Alexander Mogilny, Van. .35 1.00 10.00
☐☐☐ 164 Luc Robitaille, Pgh. .25 .50 5.00
☐☐☐ 165 Alexander Selivanov, T.B. .10 .35 3.00
☐☐☐ 166 Keith Jones, Wsh. .10 .35 3.00
☐☐☐ 167 Turner Stevenson, Mtl. .10 .35 3.00
☐☐☐ 168 Keith Tkachuk, Wpg. .35 2.00 20.00
☐☐☐ 169 Bernie Nicholls, S.J. .10 .35 3.00
☐☐☐ 170 Stanislav Neckar, Ott. .10 .35 3.00
☐☐☐ 171 Scott Mellanby, Fla. .10 .35 3.00
☐☐☐ 172 Doug Weight, Edm. .35 1.00 10.00
☐☐☐ 173 Shaun Van Allen, Ana. .25 .50 5.00
☐☐☐ 174 Gary Roberts, Cgy. .10 .35 3.00
☐☐☐ 175 Robert Lang, L.A. .10 .35 3.00
☐☐☐ 176 Martin Gelinas, Van. .10 .35 3.00
☐☐☐ 177 Ray Sheppard, Det. .10 .35 3.00
☐☐☐ 178 Bryan Smolinski, Bos. .10 .35 3.00
☐☐☐ 179 Wayne Presley, Buf. .10 .35 3.00
☐☐☐ 180 Jimmy Carson, Hfd. .10 .35 3.00
☐☐☐ 181 John Cullen, Pgh. .10 .35 3.00
☐☐☐ 182 Mikael Andersson, T.B. .10 .35 3.00
☐☐☐ 183 Dimitri Khristich, L.A. .10 .35 3.00
☐☐☐ 184 Chris Therien, Pha. .10 .35 3.00
☐☐☐ 185 Bobby Holik, N.J. .10 .35 3.00
☐☐☐ 186 Kevin Hatcher, Pgh. .10 .35 3.00
☐☐☐ 187 Patrick Poulin, T.B. .10 .35 3.00
☐☐☐ 188 Pat Falloon, Pha. .10 .35 3.00
☐☐☐ 189 Alexei Yashin, Ott. .35 2.00 20.00
☐☐☐ 190 Gord Murphy, Fla. .10 .35 3.00
☐☐☐ 191 Kirk Maltby, Edm. .10 .35 3.00
☐☐☐ 192 Dave Karpa, Ana. .10 .35 3.00
☐☐☐ 193 Kelly Kisio, Cgy. .10 .35 3.00
☐☐☐ 194 Tony Granato, L.A. .10 .35 3.00
☐☐☐ 195 Al Iafrate, Wsh. .10 .35 3.00
☐☐☐ 196 Nelson Emerson, Hfd. .10 .35 3.00
☐☐☐ 197 Adam Oates, Bos. .35 1.00 10.00
☐☐☐ 198 Rob Ray, Buf. .10 .35 3.00
☐☐☐ 199 Sean Burke (G), Hfd. .25 .50 5.00
☐☐☐ 200 Ron Francis, Pgh. .35 1.00 10.00
☐☐☐ 201 Theoren Fleury, Cgy. .35 1.00 10.00
☐☐☐ 202 Patrick Flatley, NYI. .10 .35 3.00
☐☐☐ 203 Ron Hextall (G), Pha. .25 .50 5.00
☐☐☐ 204 Martin Brodeur (G), N.J. .75 4.00 40.00
☐☐☐ 205 Mike Kennedy, Dal. .10 .35 3.00
☐☐☐ 206 Tony Amonte, Chi. .25 .50 5.00
☐☐☐ 207 Sergei Makarov, S.J. .10 .35 3.00
☐☐☐ 208 Alexandre Daigle, Ott. .25 .50 5.00
☐☐☐ 209 Stu Barnes, Fla. .10 .35 3.00
☐☐☐ 210 Todd Marchant, Edm. .10 .35 3.00
☐☐☐ 211 Valeri Karpov, Ana. .10 .35 3.00
☐☐☐ 212 Phil Housley, Cgy. .10 .35 3.00
☐☐☐ 213 Jamie Storr (G), L.A. .25 .50 5.00
☐☐☐ 214 Brett Hull, Stl. .50 3.00 30.00
☐☐☐ 215 Kris King, Wpg. .10 .35 3.00
☐☐☐ 216 Ray Bourque, Bos. .50 3.00 30.00
☐☐☐ 217 Donald Audette, Buf. .10 .35 3.00
☐☐☐ 218 Steve Rice, Hfd. .10 .35 3.00
☐☐☐ 219 Kevin Stevens, Pgh. .10 .35 3.00
☐☐☐ 220 Mark Messier, NYR. .50 3.00 30.00
☐☐☐ 221 Valeri Kamensky, Que. .25 .50 5.00
☐☐☐ 222 Mikael Renberg, Pha. .10 .35 3.00
☐☐☐ 223 Scott Stevens, N.J. .10 .35 3.00
☐☐☐ 224 Derian Hatcher, Dal. .25 .50 5.00
☐☐☐ 225 Ray Whitney, S.J. .10 .35 3.00
☐☐☐ 226 Bob Kudelski, Fla. .10 .35 3.00
☐☐☐ 227 Mikhail Shtalenkov (G), Ana. .10 .35 3.00
☐☐☐ 228 Nicklas Lidström, Det. .25 .50 5.00
☐☐☐ 229 Adam Creighton, Stl. .10 .35 3.00
☐☐☐ 230 Dave Manson, Wpg. .10 .35 3.00
☐☐☐ 231 Craig Simpson, Buf. .10 .35 3.00
☐☐☐ 232 Chris Pronger, Hfd. .25 .50 5.00
☐☐☐ 233 Adrien Plavsic, Van. .10 .35 3.00
☐☐☐ 234 Alexei Kovalev, NYR. .10 .35 3.00
☐☐☐ **235 Tommy Salo (G), NYI., RC .10 .35 3.00**
☐☐☐ 236 Patrik Juhlin, Pha. .10 .35 3.00
☐☐☐ 237 Tom Chorske, N.J. .10 .35 3.00
☐☐☐ 238 Mike Modano, Dal. .50 3.00 30.00
☐☐☐ 239 Igor Larionov, Det. .25 .50 5.00
☐☐☐ 240 Johan Garpenlov, Fla. .10 .35 3.00
☐☐☐ 241 Todd Krygier, Ana. .10 .35 3.00
☐☐☐ 242 Tie Domi, Tor. .10 .35 3.00
☐☐☐ 243 Bill Houlder, Stl. .10 .35 3.00
☐☐☐ 244 Teemu Selänne, Wpg. .75 4.00 40.00
☐☐☐ 245 Dale Hawerchuk, Stl. .25 .50 5.00
☐☐☐ 246 Bill Ranford (G), Edm. .25 .50 5.00
☐☐☐ 247 Brian Leetch, NYR. .35 1.00 10.00
☐☐☐ 248 Steve Thomas, N.J. .10 .35 3.00
☐☐☐ 249 Dimitri Yushkevich, Tor. .10 .35 3.00
☐☐☐ 250 Stéphane Richer, N.J. .10 .35 3.00
☐☐☐ 251 Todd Harvey, Dal. .10 .35 3.00
☐☐☐ 252 Viktor Kozlov, S.J. .10 .35 3.00
☐☐☐ 253 John Vanbiesbrouck (G), Fla. .60 3.50 35.00
☐☐☐ 254 Rick Tocchet, L.A. .10 .35 3.00
☐☐☐ 255 Bret Hedican, Van. .10 .35 3.00
☐☐☐ 256 Mario Lemieux, Pgh. 1.50 12.00 120.00
☐☐☐ 257 Igor Korolev, Wpg. .10 .35 3.00
☐☐☐ 258 Dominik Hasek (G), Buf. .75 4.00 40.00
☐☐☐ 259 Owen Nolan, S.J. .25 .50 5.00
☐☐☐ 260 Michal Pivonka, Wsh. .10 .35 3.00
☐☐☐ 261 John LeClair, Pha. .50 3.00 30.00
☐☐☐ 262 Claude Lemieux, N.J. .10 .35 3.00
☐☐☐ 263 Mike Donnelly, Dal. .10 .35 3.00
☐☐☐ 264 Craig Janney, S.J. .10 .35 3.00
☐☐☐ 265 Milos Holan, Ana. .10 .35 3.00
☐☐☐ 266 Steve Yzerman, Det. 1.00 8.00 80.00
☐☐☐ 267 Russ Courtnall, Van. .10 .35 3.00
☐☐☐ 268 Esa Tikkanen, NYR. .10 .35 3.00
☐☐☐ 269 Dallas Drake, Wpg. .10 .35 3.00
☐☐☐ 270 Norm Maciver, Wpg. .10 .35 3.00
☐☐☐ 271 Scott Young, Que. .10 .35 3.00
☐☐☐ 272 Glenn Healy (G), NYR. .10 .35 3.00
☐☐☐ 273 Brian Rolston, N.J. .10 .35 3.00
☐☐☐ 274 Corey Millen, Cgy. .10 .35 3.00
☐☐☐ 275 Kevin Miller, S.J. .10 .35 3.00
☐☐☐ 276 Eric Lacroix, L.A. .10 .35 3.00
☐☐☐ 277 Adam Graves, NYR. .10 .35 3.00
☐☐☐ 278 Christian Ruuttu, Chi. .10 .35 3.00
☐☐☐ 279 Steve Duchesne, Stl. .10 .35 3.00
☐☐☐ 280 Stéphane Quintal, Mtl. .10 .35 3.00
☐☐☐ 281 Brent Gretzky, T.B. .10 .35 3.00
☐☐☐ 282 Mike Ricci, Que. .10 .35 3.00
☐☐☐ 283 Sergei Nemchinov, NYR. .10 .35 3.00
☐☐☐ 284 Sylvain Côté, Wsh. .10 .35 3.00
☐☐☐ 285 Neal Broten, N.J. .10 .35 3.00
☐☐☐ 286 Greg Adams, Van. .10 .35 3.00
☐☐☐ 287 Guy Hebert (G), Ana. .25 .50 5.00
☐☐☐ 288 Joe Sakic, Que. .85 6.00 60.00
☐☐☐ 289 Bobby Dollas, Ana. .10 .35 3.00
☐☐☐ 290 Gino Odjick, Van. .10 .35 3.00
☐☐☐ 291 Curtis Joseph (G), Stl. .60 3.50 35.00
☐☐☐ 292 Teppo Numminen, Wpg. .10 .35 3.00
☐☐☐ 293 Geoff Sanderson, Hfd. .10 .35 3.00
☐☐☐ 294 Adam Deadmarsh, Que. .10 .35 3.00
☐☐☐ 295 Kevin Haller, Mtl. .10 .35 3.00
☐☐☐ 296 Sergei Brylin, N.J. .10 .35 3.00
☐☐☐ 297 Ulf Dahlen, S.J. .10 .35 3.00
☐☐☐ 298 Robert Kron, Hfd. .10 .35 3.00
☐☐☐ 299 Dave Lowry, Fla. .10 .35 3.00
☐☐☐ 300 Nikolai Borschevsky, Tor. .10 .35 3.00
☐☐☐ 301 Jeff Brown, Hfd. .10 .35 3.00
☐☐☐ 302 Guy Carbonneau, Dal. .10 .35 3.00
☐☐☐ 303 Alexei Zhitnik, Buf. .10 .35 3.00
☐☐☐ 304 Frantisek Kucera, Chi. .10 .35 3.00
☐☐☐ 305 Curtis Leschyshyn, Que. .10 .35 3.00
☐☐☐ 306 Mike Richter (G), NYR. .35 1.00 10.00
☐☐☐ 307 Dean Evason, Dal. .10 .35 3.00
☐☐☐ 308 Jozef Stumpel, Bos. .25 .50 5.00
☐☐☐ 309 Jeff Friesen, S.J. .25 .50 5.00
☐☐☐ 310 Kelly Buchberger, Edm. .10 .35 3.00
☐☐☐ 311 Michael Nylander, Cgy. .10 .35 3.00
☐☐☐ 312 Josef Beranek, Van. .10 .35 3.00
☐☐☐ 313 Al MacInnis, Stl. .10 .35 3.00
☐☐☐ 314 Ken Wregget (G), Pgh. .10 .35 3.00
☐☐☐ 315 Glen Wesley, Hfd. .10 .35 3.00
☐☐☐ 316 Jocelyn Thibault (G), Que. .35 1.00 10.00
☐☐☐ 317 Jeff Beukeboom, NYR. .10 .35 3.00
☐☐☐ 318 Steve Konowalchuk, Wsh. .10 .35 3.00
☐☐☐ 319 Tim Cheveldae (G), Wpg. .10 .35 3.00
☐☐☐ 320 Vincent Damphousse, Mtl. .35 1.00 10.00
☐☐☐ 321 Mats Naslund, Bos. .10 .35 3.00
☐☐☐ 322 Mathieu Schneider, NYI. .10 .35 3.00
☐☐☐ 323 Petr Nedved, NYR. .10 .35 3.00
☐☐☐ 324 Brent Fedyk, Dal. .10 .35 3.00
☐☐☐ **325 Jussi Tie, Fin., RC .10 .35 3.00**
☐☐☐ **326 Mikko Markkanen, Fin., RC .10 .35 3.00**
☐☐☐ **327 Timo Hakanen, Fin., RC .10 .35 3.00**
☐☐☐ **328 Sami Salonen, Fin., RC .10 .35 3.00**
☐☐☐ **329 Juha Viinikainen, Fin., RC .10 .35 3.00**
☐☐☐ **330 Jani Riihinen, Fin., RC .10 .35 3.00**
☐☐☐ **331 Teemu Riihijarvi, Fin., RC .10 .35 3.00**
☐☐☐ **332 Jaako Niskavaara, Fin., RC .10 .35 3.00**
☐☐☐ **333 Miika Elomo, Fin., RC .10 .35 3.00**
☐☐☐ **334 Tomi Kallio, Fin., RC .10 .35 3.00**
☐☐☐ **335 Vesa Toskala, Fin., RC .10 .35 3.00**
☐☐☐ **336 Tuomas Reijonen, Fin., RC .10 .35 3.00**
☐☐☐ **337 Aki Berg, Fin., RC .10 .35 3.00**
☐☐☐ **338 Tomi Hirvonen, Fin., RC .10 .35 3.00**
☐☐☐ **339 Jussi Salminen, Fin., RC .10 .35 3.00**
☐☐☐ **340 Andreas Sjolund, Swe., RC .10 .35 3.00**
☐☐☐ **341 Johan Ramstedt, Swe., RC .10 .35 3.00**
☐☐☐ **342 Bjorn Danielsson, Swe., RC .10 .35 3.00**
☐☐☐ **343 Per Gustavsson, Swe., RC .10 .35 3.00**
☐☐☐ **344 Niklas Anger, Swe., RC .10 .35 3.00**
☐☐☐ **345 Marcus Nilsson, Swe., RC .25 .50 5.00**
☐☐☐ **346 Per-Anton Lundstrom, Swe., RC .10 .35 3.00**
☐☐☐ **347 Henrik Rehnberg, Swe., RC .10 .35 3.00**
☐☐☐ **348 Robert Borgqvist, Swe., RC .10 .35 3.00**
☐☐☐ **349 Ted Christensen, Swe., RC .10 .35 3.00**
☐☐☐ **350 Samuel Pahlsson, Swe., RC .10 .35 3.00**
Error (Phalsson)
☐☐☐ **351 Fredrik Loven, Swe., RC .10 .35 3.00**
☐☐☐ **352 Patrik Wallenberg, Swe., RC .10 .35 3.00**
☐☐☐ **353 Jan Labraaten, Swe., RC .10 .35 3.00**
☐☐☐ **354 Peter Wallin, Swe., RC .10 .35 3.00**
☐☐☐ 355 Cam Neely, Bos. .25 .50 5.00
☐☐☐ 356 Keith Tkachuk, Wpg. .25 1.00 10.00
☐☐☐ 357 Chris Gratton, T.B. .25 .50 5.00
☐☐☐ 358 Adam Graves, NYR. .10 .35 3.00
☐☐☐ 359 Doug Gilmour, Tor. .25 .50 5.00
☐☐☐ 360 Adam Deadmarsh, Que. .10 .35 3.00
☐☐☐ 361 Wayne Gretzky, L.A. 1.00 8.00 80.00
☐☐☐ 362 Joe Sakic, Que. .50 3.00 30.00

☐☐☐	363	Paul Kariya, Ana.	.75	5.00	50.00
☐☐☐	364	Brett Hull, Stl.	.25	1.50	15.00
☐☐☐	365	Sergei Fedorov, Det.	.25	2.00	20.00
☐☐☐	366	Brian Rolston, N.J.	.10	.35	3.00
☐☐☐	367	Dominik Hasek, Buf.	.35	2.00	20.00
☐☐☐	368	John Vanbiesbrouck (G), Fla.	.35	1.75	18.00
☐☐☐	369	Jim Carey (G), Wsh.	.10	.35	3.00
☐☐☐	370	Paul Kariya, Ana.	.75	5.00	50.00
☐☐☐	371	Peter Forsberg, Que.	.60	4.00	40.00
☐☐☐	372	Jeff Friesen, S.J.	.25	.50	5.00
☐☐☐	373	Kenny Jonsson, Tor.	.10	.35	3.00
☐☐☐	374	Chris Therien, Pha.	.10	.35	3.00
☐☐☐	375	Jim Carey (G), Wsh.	.10.	.35	3.00
☐☐☐	376	John LeClair, Pha.	.25	1.50	15.00
☐☐☐	377	Eric Lindros, Pha.	.75	5.00	50.00
☐☐☐	378	Jaromir Jagr, Pgh.	.60	4.00	40.00
☐☐☐	379	Paul Coffey, Det.	.25	.50	5.00
☐☐☐	380	Chris Chelios, Chi.	.25	1.00	10.00
☐☐☐	381	Dominik Hasek (G), Buf.	.35	2.00	20.00
☐☐☐	382	Keith Tkachuk, Wpg.	.25	1.00	10.00
☐☐☐	383	Alexei Zhamnov, Wpg.	.25	.50	5.00
☐☐☐	384	Theoren Fleury, Cgy.	.25	.50	5.00
☐☐☐	385	Ray Bourque, Bos.	.25	1.50	15.00
☐☐☐	386	Larry Murphy, Tor.	.10	.35	3.00
☐☐☐	387	Ed Belfour (G), Chi.	.25	.50	5.00
☐☐☐	388	Eric Lindros, Pha.	.75	5.00	50.00
☐☐☐	389	Jaromir Jagr, Pgh.	.60	4.00	40.00
☐☐☐	390	Paul Coffey, Det.	.25	.50	5.00
☐☐☐	391	Peter Forsberg, Que.	.60	4.00	40.00
☐☐☐	392	Claude Lemieux, N.J.	.10	.35	3.00
☐☐☐	393	Ron Francis, Pgh.	.25	.50	5.00
☐☐☐	394	Dominik Hasek (G), Buf.	.35	2.00	20.00
☐☐☐	395	Checklist	.20	.50	5.00
☐☐☐	396	Checklist	.20	.50	5.00

	No.	Player	Reg.
☐	397	Saku Koivu, Mtl.	5.00
☐	398	Radek Dvorak, Fla.	.75
☐	399	Ed Jovanovski, Fla.	1.00
☐	400	Brendan Witt, Wsh.	.35
☐	401	Jeff O'Neill, Hfd.	1.00
☐	402	Daymond Langkow, T.B.	.35
☐	403	Shane Doan, Wpg.	.35
☐	404	Bryan McCabe, NYI.	.35
☐	405	Marty Murray, Cgy.	.35
☐	406	Daniel Alfredsson, Ott.	2.50
☐	407	Jason Doig, Wpg.	.35
☐	408	Niklas Sundstrom, NYR.	.35
☐	409	Vitali Yachmenev, L.A.	.35
☐	410	Aki Berg, L.A.	.35
☐	411	Eric Dazé, Chi.	1.00

YOU CRASH THE GAME

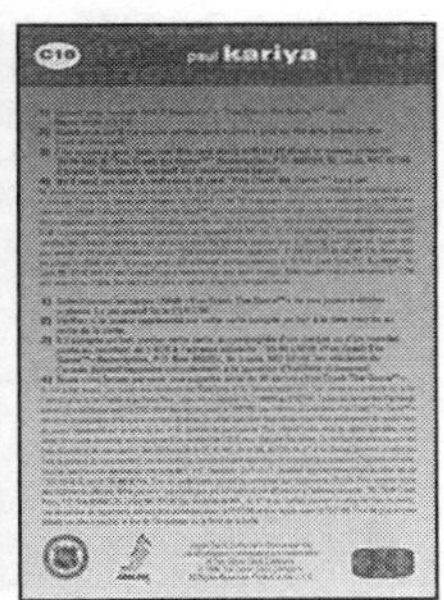

Each gold and silver version have three dates. If the player scored a goal on the specified date, the card could be exchanged for a 50-card "You Crash the Game" set plus a Bonus card of that player.

Insert Set (90 cards): 135.00 700.00

	No.	Player	Silver	Gold
☐☐☐☐☐☐	C1	P. Bure (10-12; 12-17; 3-23)	2.00	10.00
☐☐☐☐☐☐	C2	S. Fedorov (10-19; 12-31; 3-12)	1.50	7.50
☐☐☐☐☐☐	C3	W. Gretzky (10-7; 12-21; 2-10)	6.00	30.00
☐☐☐☐☐☐	C4	E. Lindros (11-12; 1-3; 3-3)	4.00	20.00
☐☐☐☐☐☐	C5	B. Hull (10-10; 12-9; 3-24)	1.50	7.50
☐☐☐☐☐☐	C6	M. Messier (11-8; 1-22; 3-31)	1.50	7.50
☐☐☐☐☐☐	C7	J. Jagr (10-14; 12-17; 3-5)	3.00	15.00
☐☐☐☐☐☐	C8	A. Zhamnov (10-9; 12-28; 2-21)	.75	3.50
☐☐☐☐☐☐	C9	J. Sakic (10-6; 12-9; 2-3)	2.50	12.50
☐☐☐☐☐☐	C10	P. Kariya (10-18; 12-19; 3-17)	4.00	20.00
☐☐☐☐☐☐	C11	T. Fleury (10-27; 12-11; 2-6)	1.00	5.00
☐☐☐☐☐☐	C12	O. Nolan (11-1; 1-4; 3-17)	.75	3.50
☐☐☐☐☐☐	C13	P. Bondra (10-13; 12-2; 3-12)	1.25	6.00
☐☐☐☐☐☐	C14	C. Neely (11-7; 1-11; 3-23)	.75	3.50
☐☐☐☐☐☐	C15	P. Turgeon (10-25; 12-23; 2-21)	.75	3.50
☐☐☐☐☐☐	C16	M. Modano (11-1; 1-5; 2-22)	1.50	7.50
☐☐☐☐☐☐	C17	B. Nicholls (10-10; 12-15; 3-24)	.50	2.50
☐☐☐☐☐☐	C18	A. Yashin (11-4; 12-23; 2-21)	1.25	6.00
☐☐☐☐☐☐	C19	J. Arnott (10-27; 12-18; 2-28)	.75	3.50
☐☐☐☐☐☐	C20	P. Forsberg (11-22; 2-15; 3-27)	3.00	15.00
☐☐☐☐☐☐	C21	D. Gilmour (10-17; 12-16; 2-18)	1.00	5.00
☐☐☐☐☐☐	C22	G. Sanderson (10-11; 12-18; 3-6)	.50	2.50
☐☐☐☐☐☐	C23	J. LeClair (10-15; 12-16; 2-19)	1.50	7.50
☐☐☐☐☐☐	C24	R. Bourque (10-11; 12-16; 2-6)	1.50	7.50
☐☐☐☐☐☐	C25	M. Lemieux (11-1; 12-1; 2-6)	5.00	25.00
☐☐☐☐☐☐	C26	S. Yzerman (11-11; 1-24; 2-27)	3.00	15.00
☐☐☐☐☐☐	C27	P. LaFontaine (10-20; 12-27; 2-17)	.75	3.50
☐☐☐☐☐☐	C28	C. Lemieux (10-7; 12-15; 2-10)	.50	2.50
☐☐☐☐☐☐	C29	P. Coffey (10-15; 12-5; 2-13)	.75	3.50
☐☐☐☐☐☐	C30	M. Sundin (11-7; 1-3; 3-15)	1.50	7.50

YOU CRASH THE GAME - REDEEMED

Winning cards have four versions: the silver winner, a silver bonus card, the gold winner and a gold bonus card. Loser cards do not have bonus versions. Cards C3,C4,C17, C18,C20,C22 and C27 did not win.

Redeemed Set (30 cards): 18.00 35.00 – –
Bonus Set (23 cards): – – 65.00 150.00

	No.	Player	S.W.	G.W.	S.B	G.B.
☐☐☐☐	C1	Pavel Bure, Van.	.75	1.50	4.00	10.00
☐☐☐☐	C2	Sergei Fedorov, Det.	.50	1.00	3.00	7.50
☐☐	C3	Wayne Gretzky, L.A.	2.50	5.00	.–	.–
☐☐	C4	Eric Lindros, Pha.	1.75	3.50	.–	.–
☐☐☐☐	C5	Brett Hull, Stl.	.50	1.00	3.00	7.50
☐☐☐☐	C6	Mark Messier, NYR.	.50	1.00	3.00	7.50
☐☐☐☐	C7	Jaromir Jagr, Pgh.	1.25	2.50	7.00	15.00
☐☐☐☐	C8	Alexei Zhamnov, Wpg.	.25	.50	1.00	3.00
☐☐☐☐	C9	Joe Sakic, Que.	1.00	2.00	6.00	15.00
☐☐☐☐	C10	Paul Kariya, Ana.	1.75	3.50	8.00	20.00
☐☐☐☐	C11	Theoren Fleury, Cgy.	.35	.75	2.00	6.00
☐☐☐☐	C12	Owen Nolan, Que.	.25	.50	1.00	3.00
☐☐☐☐	C13	Peter Bondra, Wsh.	.35	.75	2.00	6.00
☐☐☐☐	C14	Cam Neely, Bos.	.25	.50	1.00	3.00
☐☐☐☐	C15	Pierre Turgeon, Mtl.	.25	.50	1.00	3.00
☐☐☐☐	C16	Mike Modano, Dal.	.50	1.00	3.00	7.50
☐☐	C17	Bernie Nicholls, Chi.	.15	.25	.–	.–
☐☐	C18	Alexei Yashin, Ott.	.35	.75	.–	.–
☐☐☐☐	C19	Jason Arnott, Edm.	.25	.50	1.00	3.00
☐☐	C20	Peter Forsberg, Que.	1.25	2.50	.–	.–
☐☐☐☐	C21	Doug Gilmour, Tor.	.35	.75	2.00	6.00
☐☐	C22	Geoff Sanderson, Hfd.	.15	.25	.–	.–
☐☐☐☐	C23	John LeClair, Pha.	.50	1.00	3.00	7.50
☐☐☐☐	C24	Ray Bourque, Bos.	.50	1.00	3.00	7.50
☐☐☐☐	C25	Mario Lemieux, Pgh.	2.00	4.00	10.00	25.00
☐☐☐☐	C26	Steve Yzerman, Det.	1.25	2.50	7.00	15.00
☐☐	C27	Pat LaFontaine, Buf.	.25	.50	.–	.–
☐☐☐☐	C28	Claude Lemieux, N.J.	.15	.25	1.00	2.50
☐☐☐☐	C29	Paul Coffey, Det.	.35	.75	2.00	6.00
☐☐☐☐	C30	Mats Sundin, Tor.	.50	1.00	3.00	7.50

WAYNE GRETZKY RECORD COLLECTION

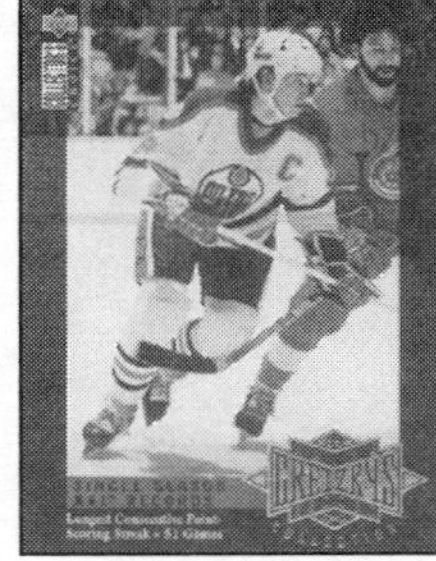

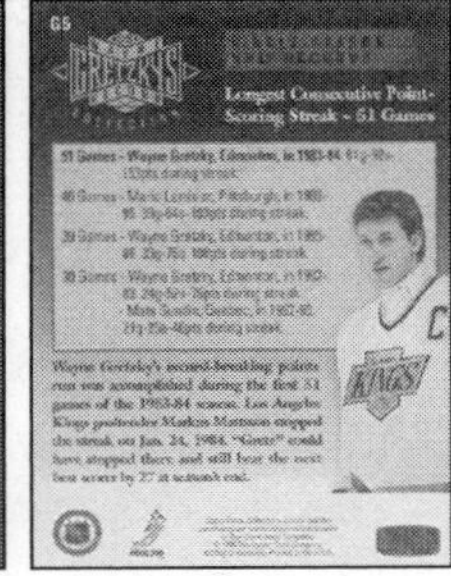

These cards have two versions: a 5" x 7" box insert and the standard size insert. Cards G10-G13 were inserted into Upper Deck Series One, G14-G17 were inserted in Upper Deck Series Two packs and G17-G20 were inserted in SP packs.

Insert Set (10 cards): 45.00

	No.	Player	5"x7"	Insert
☐☐		Checklist [G1-G20], [Wayne Gretzky]	6.00	5.00
☐☐	G1	Wayne Gretzky, Goals/Season	6.00	5.00
☐☐	G2	Wayne Gretzky, Assists/Season	6.00	5.00
☐☐	G3	Wayne Gretzky, Points/Season	6.00	5.00
☐☐	G4	Wayne Gretzky, 3+ Goals/Season	6.00	5.00
☐☐	G5	Wayne Gretzky, Point Streak/Season	6.00	5.00
☐☐	G6	Wayne Gretzky, Assist Streak/Season	6.00	5.00
☐☐	G7	Wayne Gretzky, Assists/Game	6.00	5.00
☐☐	G8	Wayne Gretzky, Goals/inc.Playoffs	6.00	5.00
☐☐	G9	Wayne Gretzky/Jari Kurri	6.00	5.00

1995 - 96 UPPER DECK POST

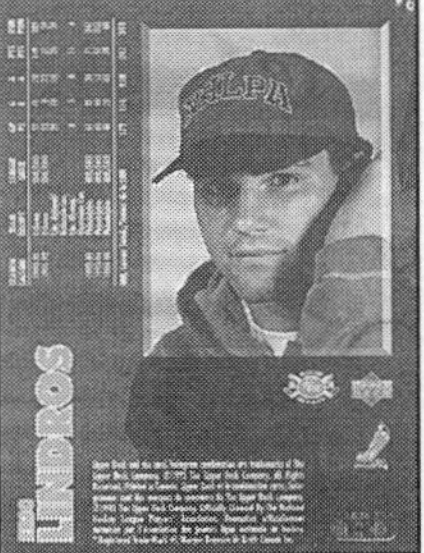

One cellophane wrapped card per Post Honey Combs or Sugar Crisps cereal box.

Imprint:
Complete Set (24 cards): 45.00
Autographed Card (Gretzky, #/500): 1,000.00

	No.	Player	NRMT-MT
☐	1	Ray Bourque	3.00
☐	2	Martin Brodeur (G)	4.00
☐	3	Steve Duchesne	1.00
☐	4	Vincent Damphousse	1.00
☐	5	Eric Desjardins	1.00
☐	6	Eric Lindros	7.50
☐	7	Joé Juneau	1.00
☐	8	Luc Robitaille	1.50
☐	9	Mark Recchi	1.50
☐	10	Patrick Roy (G)	8.50
☐	11	Brendan Shanahan	3.50
☐	12	Scott Stevens	1.00
☐	13	Jason Arnott	1.50
☐	14	Trevor Linden	1.50
☐	15	Chris Chelios	2.50
☐	16	Paul Coffey	1.50
☐	17	Wayne Gretzky	12.00
☐	18	Doug Gilmour	2.00
☐	19	Kelly Hrudey (G)	1.00
☐	20	Paul Kariya	7.50
☐	21	Larry Murphy	1.50
☐	22	Félix Potvin (G)	3.00
☐	23	Keith Tkachuk	2.50
☐	24	Rob Blake	1.50

1995 - 96 UPPER DECK SWEDISH ELITE

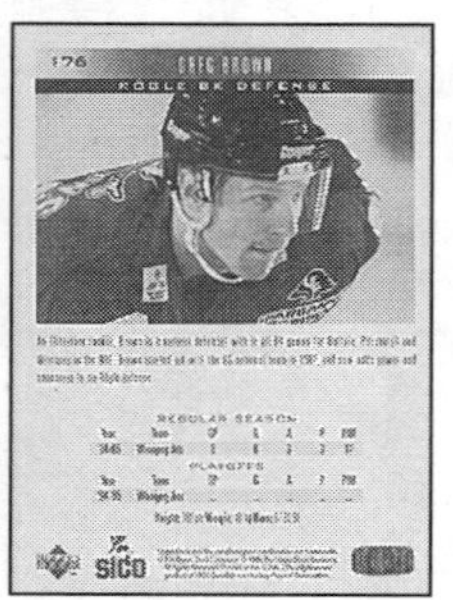

This set is licensed by the Swedish Players' Association, Sico.

Complete Set (260 cards): 40.00
Common Player: .15

	No.	Player	NRMT-MT
☐	1	Joakim Persson, AIK	.25
☐	2	Erik Hamalainen, AIK	.15
☐	3	Dick Tarnstrom, AIK	.15
☐	4	Ricard Franzen, AIK	.15
☐	5	Niclas Havelid, AIK	.15
☐	6	Tony Barthelsson, AIK	.15
☐	7	Tommy Hedlund, AIK	.15
☐	8	Patric Aberg, AIK	.15
☐	9	Stefan Gustavson, AIK	.15
☐	10	Anders Gozzi, AIK	.15
☐	11	David Engblom, AIK	.15
☐	12	Stefan Andersson, AIK	.15
☐	13	Tomas Stranberg, AIK	.15
☐	14	Mats Lindberg, AIK	.15
☐	15	Tommy Lehmann, AIK	.15
☐	16	Bjorn Ahlstrom, AIK	.15
☐	17	Patric Englund, AIK	.15
☐	18	Morgan Samuelsson, AIK	.15
☐	19	Michael Sundlov, Brynas	.25
☐	20	Bedrich Scerban, Brynas	.15
☐	21	Mikael Lindman, Brynas	.15
☐	22	Mikael Wiklander, Brynas	.15
☐	23	Tommy Melkersson, Brynas	.15
☐	24	Stefan Klockare, Brynas	.15
☐	25	Per Lofstrom, Brynas	.15
☐	26	Jonas Johnsson, Brynas	.15
☐	27	Roger Kyro, Brynas	.15
☐	28	Jonas Lofstrom, Brynas	.15
☐	29	Stefan Ketola, Brynas	.15
☐	30	Mikael Wahlberg, Brynas	.15
☐	31	Stefan Polla, Brynas	.15
☐	32	Greg Parks, Brynas	.15
☐	33	Ove Molin, Brynas	.15
☐	34	Peter Larsson, Brynas	.15
☐	35	Fredrik Modin, Brynas	1.00
☐	36	Andreas Dackell, Brynas	.50
☐	37	Thomas Ostlund, Djugarden	.25
☐	38	Tommy Jakobsen, Djugarden	.15
☐	39	Christian Due-Boje, Djugarden	.15
☐	40	Thomas Johansson, Djugarden	.15
☐	41	Joakim Lundberg, Djugarden	.15
☐	42	Bjorn Nord, Djugarden	.15
☐	43	Mikael Magnusson, Djugarden	.15
☐	44	Erik Huusko, Djugarden	.15
☐	45	Anders Kuusko, Djugarden	.15
☐	46	Kristoffer Ottosson, Djugarden	.15
☐	47	Magnus Jansson, Djugarden	.15
☐	48	Niklas Falk, Djugarden	.15
☐	49	Ola Josefsson, Djugarden	.15
☐	50	Per Eklund, Djugarden	.15
☐	51	Espen Knutsen, Djugarden	.75
☐	52	Jens Ohling, Djugarden	.15
☐	53	Patrik Kjellberg, Djugarden	.15
☐	54	Patrik Erickson, Djugarden	.15
☐	55	Jan Viktorsson, Djugarden	.15
☐	56	Markus Ketterer, Farjestad	.25
☐	57	Jesper Duus, Farjestad	.15
☐	58	Sergei Fokin, Farjestad	.15
☐	59	Per Lundell, Farjestad	.15
☐	60	Thomas Rhodin, Farjestad	.15
☐	61	Henrik Rehnberg, Farjestad	.15
☐	62	Roger Johansson, Farjestad	.15
☐	63	Leif Carlsson, Farjestad	.15
☐	64	Hakan Loob, Farjestad	.50
☐	65	Stefan Nilsson, Farjestad	.15
☐	66	Vitali Prokhorov, Farjestad	.15
☐	67	Magnus Arvedsson, Farjestad	.15
☐	68	Jonas Hoglund, Farjestad	.15
☐	69	Mattias Johansson, Farjestad	.15
☐	70	Patrik Wallenberg, Farjestad	.15
☐	71	Clas Eriksson, Farjestad	.15
☐	72	Jorgen Jonsson, Farjestad	.15
☐	73	Peter Nordstrom, Farjestad	.15
☐	74	Peter Ottosson, Farjestad	.15
☐	75	Boo Ahl, HV 71	.25
☐	76	Per Gustafsson, HV 71	.50
☐	77	Niklas Rahm, HV 71	.15
☐	78	Hans Abrahamsson, HV 71	.15
☐	79	Kennth Kennholt, HV 71	.15
☐	80	Daniel Johansson, HV 71	.15
☐	81	Vesa Salo, HV 71	.15
☐	82	Thomas Gustavsson, HV 71	.15
☐	83	Stefan Ornskog, HV 71	.15
☐	84	Stefan Falk, HV 71	.15
☐	85	Peter Hammarstrom, HV 71	.15
☐	86	Johan Davidsson, HV 71	.25
☐	87	Peter Ekelund, HV 71	.15
☐	88	Johan Lindbom, HV 71	.15
☐	89	Esa Keskinen, HV 71	.25
☐	90	Kai Nurminen, HV 71	.25
☐	91	Magnus Eliasson, HV 71	.15
☐	92	Marcus Thuresson, HV 71	.15
☐	93	Johan Brummer, HV 71	.15
☐	94	Johan Hedberg (G), Leksands	.25
☐	95	Tomas Jonsson, Leksands	.25
☐	96	Torbjorn Johansson, Leksands	.15
☐	97	Hans Lodin, Leksands	.15
☐	98	Orjan Lindmark, Leksands	.15
☐	99	Jan Huokko, Leksands	.15
☐	100	Joakim Lidgren, Leksands	.15
☐	101	Per-Erik Eklund, Leksands	.50
☐	102	Anders Carlsson, Leksands	.15
☐	103	Niklas Eriksson, Leksands	.15
☐	104	Michael Karlberg, Leksands	.15
☐	105	Jonas Bergqvist, Leksands	.15
☐	106	Torgny Lowgren, Leksands	.15
☐	107	Stefan Hellqvist, Leksands	.15
☐	108	Markus Akerblom, Leksands	.15
☐	109	Mikael Holmberg, Leksands	.15
☐	110	Andreas Karlsson, Leksands	.15
☐	111	Markus Eriksson, Leksands	.15
☐	112	Tomas Forslund, Leksands	.15
☐	113	Jarmo Myllys, Lulea	.50
☐	114	Lars Modig, Lulea	.15
☐	115	Patrik Hoglund, Lulea	.15
☐	116	Torbjorn Lindberg, Lulea	.15
☐	117	Jan Mertzig, Lulea	.15
☐	118	Petter Nilsson, Lulea	.15
☐	119	Mattias Ohlund, Lulea	3.00
☐	120	Roger Akerstrom, Lulea	.15
☐	121	Stefan Jonsson, Lulea	.15
☐	122	Stefan Nilsson, Lulea	.15
☐	123	Thomas Holmstrom, Lulea	.15
☐	124	Mikael Lindholm, Lulea	.15
☐	125	Johan Stromwall, Lulea	.15
☐	126	Jiri Kucera, Lulea	.15
☐	127	Joakim Backlund, Lulea	.15
☐	128	Robert Nordberg, Lulea	.15
☐	129	Tomas Berglund, Lulea	.15
☐	130	Fredrik Johansson, Lulea	.15
☐	131	Lars Hurtig, Lulea	.15
☐	132	Johan Rosen, Lulea	.15
☐	133	Roger Nordström (G), Malmo	.25
☐	134	Kim Johnsson, Malmo	.15
☐	135	Peter Hasselblad, Malmo	.15
☐	136	Ilja Byakin, Malmo	.15
☐	137	Johan Salle, Malmo	.15
☐	138	Peter Andersson, Malmo	.15
☐	139	Roger Ohman, Malmo	.15
☐	140	Marko Palo, Malmo	.15
☐	141	Raimo Helminen, Malmo	.15
☐	142	Mattias Bosson, Malmo	.15
☐	143	Markus Magnertoft, Malmo	.15
☐	144	Roger Hansson, Malmo	.15
☐	145	Bo Svanberg, Malmo	.15
☐	146	Patrik Sylvegard, Malmo	.15
☐	147	Brian McReynolds, Malmo	.15
☐	148	Hakan Ahlund, Malmo	.15
☐	149	Robert Burakovski, Malmo	.15
☐	150	Stefan Elvenes, Malmo	.15
☐	151	Patrik Boij, Malmo	.15
☐	152	Petter Ronnqvist, MoDo	.25
☐	153	Mattias Timmander, MoDo	.15
☐	154	Lars Jansson, MoDo	.15
☐	155	Frantisek Kaberle, MoDo	.15
☐	156	Hans Jonsson, MoDo	.15
☐	157	Tomas Nanzen, MoDo	.15
☐	158	Marcus Karlsson, MoDo	.15
☐	159	Kristian Gahn, MoDo	.15
☐	160	Magnus Wernblom, MoDo	.15
☐	161	Anders Soderberg, MoDo	.15
☐	162	Martin Hostak, MoDo	.15
☐	163	Kyosti Karjalainen, MoDo	.15
☐	164	Mikael Hakansson, MoDo	.15
☐	165	Jan Larsson, MoDo	.15
☐	166	Per Svartvadet, MoDo	.15
☐	167	Andreas Salomonsson, MoDo	.15
☐	168	Samuel Pahlsson, MoDo	.15
☐	169	Lars Bystrom, MoDo	.15
☐	170	Magnus Swardh, Rogle	.25
☐	171	Anders Berglund, Rogle	.15
☐	172	Pierre Johnsson, Rogle	.15
☐	173	Johan Finnstrom, Rogle	.15
☐	174	Arto Routanen, Rogle	.15
☐	175	Daniel Tjarnqvist, Rogle	.15
☐	176	Greg Brown, Rogle	.15
☐	177	Peter Wallin, Rogle	.15
☐	178	Peter Lundmark, Rogle	.15
☐	179	Roger Elvenes, Rogle	.15
☐	180	Michael Hjalm, Rogle	.15
☐	181	Jens Hemstrom, Rogle	.15
☐	182	Pelle Svensson, Rogle	.15
☐	183	Harjis Vitolins, Rogle	.15
☐	184	Jens Nielsen, Rogle	.15
☐	185	Mats Loov, Rogle	.15
☐	186	Mats Ytter, Västerås	.25
☐	187	Lars Ivarsson, Västerås	.15
☐	188	Edvin Frylen, Västerås	.15
☐	189	Andrei Lyulin, Västerås	.15
☐	190	Johan Tornberg, Västerås	.15
☐	191	Mattias Olsson, Västerås	.15
☐	192	Mats Lusth, Västerås	.15
☐	193	Fredrik Oberg, Västerås	.15
☐	194	Alexei Salomatin, Västerås	.15
☐	195	Mishat Fahrutdinov, Västerås	.15
☐	196	Mikael Pettersson, Västerås	.15
☐	197	Andrei Korolev, Västerås	.15
☐	198	Mattias Loof, Västerås	.15
☐	199	Claes Lindblom, Västerås	.15
☐	200	Paul Andersson, Västerås	.15
☐	201	Roger Rosen, Västerås	.15
☐	202	Hakan Algotsson, Vastra Frolunda	.25
☐	203	Par Djoos, Vastra Frolunda	.15
☐	204	Mikael Sandberg, Vastra Frolunda	.15
☐	205	Joacim Esbjors, Vastra Frolunda	.15
☐	206	Stefan Axelsson, Vastra Frolunda	.15
☐	207	Ronnie Sundin, Vastra Frolunda	.15
☐	208	Stefan Larsson, Vastra Frolunda	.15
☐	209	Petteri Nummelin, Vastra Frolunda	.15
☐	210	Christian Ruuttu, Vastra Frolunda	.25
☐	211	Marko Jantunen, Vastra Frolunda	.15
☐	212	Peter Strom, Vastra Frolunda	.15
☐	213	Peter Berndtsson, Vastra Frolunda	.15
☐	214	Lars Edstrom, Vastra Frolunda	.15
☐	215	Peter Hogardh, Vastra Frolunda	.15
☐	216	Par Edlund, Vastra Frolunda	.15
☐	217	Lars-Goran Wiklander, Vastra Frolunda	.15
☐	218	Henrik Nilsson, Vastra Frolunda	.15
☐	219	Rikard Franzen	.15
☐	220	Fredrik Modin, Brynas	.35
☐	221	Anders Soderberg	.15
☐	222	Per Eklund	.15
☐	223	Hakan Loob	.35
☐	224	Markus Ketterer (G)	.15
☐	225	Esa Keskinen	.25
☐	226	Per Gustafsson, HV71	.35
☐	227	Tomas Jonsson	.25
☐	228	Per-Erik Eklund	.35
☐	229	Mattias Ohlund, Lulea	1.00
☐	230	Jarmo Myllys (G)	.35
☐	231	Peter Andersson	.15
☐	232	Raimo Helminen	.15
☐	233	Christian Ruuttu	.25

	No.	Player	
☐	234	Peter Forsberg	4.00
☐	235	Mikael Renberg	.50
☐	236	Mats Sundin	2.00
☐	237	Michael Nylander	.50
☐	238	Tommy Söderström (G)	.50
☐	239	Nicklas Lidstrom	1.00
☐	240	Kenny Jonsson	.50
☐	241	Patrik Carnback	.50
☐	242	Johan Garpenlov	.50
☐	243	Magnus Svensson	.50
☐	244	Patrik Juhlin	.50
☐	245	Markus Naslund	.50
☐	246	Tommy Salo (G)	.50
☐	247	Fredrik Olausson	.50
☐	248	Tommy Albelin	.50
☐	249	Rikard Franzen	.15
☐	250	Jonas Johnsson	.15
☐	251	Thomas Ostlund	.15
☐	252	Hakan Loob	.75
☐	253	Per Gustafsson, HV71	.50
☐	254	Per-Erik Eklund	.50
☐	255	Tomas Jonsson	.25
☐	256	Mattias Ohlund, Lulea	2.50
☐	257	Peter Andersson	.15
☐	258	Christian Ruuttu	.50
☐	259	Checklist 1-150	.15
☐	260	CL 151-260/inserts	.15

1ST DIVISION STARS

Insert Set (20 cards): 25.00

	No.	Player	NRMT-MT
☐	DS1	Anders Huss	1.50
☐	DS2	Igor Vlasov	1.50
☐	DS3	Ulf Sandstrom	1.50
☐	DS4	Hans Huczkowski	1.50
☐	DS5	Johan Ramstedt	1.50
☐	DS6	Anders Eldebrink	1.50
☐	DS7	Niklas Brannstrom	1.50
☐	DS8	Peter Nilsson	1.50
☐	DS9	Sam Lindstahl	1.50
☐	DS10	Tony Skopac	1.50
☐	DS11	Jonas Eriksson	1.50
☐	DS12	Anders Lonn	1.50
☐	DS13	Peter Hagstrom	1.50
☐	DS14	Magnus Roupe	1.50
☐	DS15	Peter Pettersson	1.50
☐	DS16	Peter Eriksson	1.50
☐	DS17	Fredrik Bergqvist	1.50
☐	DS18	Larry Pilut	1.50
☐	DS19	Peter Olsson	1.50
☐	DS20	Staffan Lundh	1.50

TICKET TO NORTH AMERICA

Insert Set (20 cards): 60.00

	No.	Player	NRMT-MT
☐	NA1	Joakim Persson	2.50
☐	NA2	Dick Tarnstrom	2.50
☐	NA3	Andreas Dackell	4.00
☐	NA4	Fredrik Modin, Brynes	6.00
☐	NA5	Per Eklund	2.50
☐	NA6	Espen Knutsen, Djugarden	4.00
☐	NA7	Fredrik Lindqvist	2.50
☐	NA8	Jonas Hoglund	5.00
☐	NA9	Jorgen Jonsson	2.50
☐	NA10	Johan Davidsson	4.00
☐	NA11	Per Gustafsson, HV71	5.00
☐	NA12	Johan Lindbom, HV71	2.50
☐	NA13	Markus Akerblom	2.50
☐	NA14	Jan Huokko	2.50
☐	NA15	Thomas Holmstrom, Luleo	10.00
☐	NA16	Mattias Ohlund, Lelea	15.00
☐	NA17	Johan Rosen	2.50
☐	NA18	Frantisek Kaberle	2.50
☐	NA19	Mattias Timander, MoDo	4.00
☐	NA20	Magnus Wernblom	2.50

1995 - 96 ZELLER'S MASTERS OF HOCKEY

Each set came with a certificate of authenticity. Each player signed 3,500 cards. Only a Signature Series was available this year.

Imprint:

Complete Set (8 cards):

	Player
☐	Mike Bossy
☐	Ed Giacomin (G)
☐	Gordie Howe
☐	Jacques Laperrière
☐	Gilbert Perreault
☐	Serge Savard
☐	Steve Shutt
☐	Darryl Sittler

1996 METALLIC IMPRESSIONS SUPER MARIO

Each five-card set comes packaged in a tin "Super Mario" container. Imprint: CUI, Inc. Licensed by Mario Lemieux.

Imprint:

Complete Set (5 cards): 30.00

Tin Box (Mario Lemieux): 5.00

	No.	Player	NRMT-MT
☐	1	Mario Lemieux	7.00
☐	2	Mario Lemieux	7.00
☐	3	Mario Lemieux	7.00
☐	4	Mario Lemieux	7.00
☐	5	Mario Lemieux	7.00

1996 TOPPS FINEST BRONZE

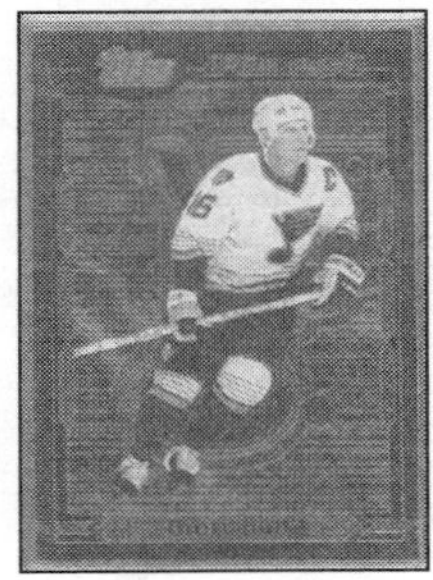

These oversized cards were sold by Topps as a complete set.

Card Size: 2 3/4" x 3 3/4"

Imprint:

Series Three Set (8 cards): 125.00

	No.	Player	NRMT-MT
☐	15	Mark Messier, NYR.	20.00
☐	16	Mario Lemieux, Pgh.	60.00
☐	17	Peter Forsberg, Col.	45.00
☐	18	Félix Potvin (G), Tor.	20.00
☐	19	Alexander Mogilny, Van.	18.00
☐	20	Ray Bourque, Bos.	20.00
☐	21	Ed Jovanovski, Fla.	18.00
☐	22	Mikael Renberg, Pha.	15.00

1996 WIEN

This World Championship set was produced by Semic Sports Cards.

Complete Set (240 cards): 30.00

Common Player: .15

	No.	Player	NRMT-MT
☐	1	Jarmo Myllys (G), Fin.	.25
☐	2	Marko Kiprusoff, Fin.	.15
☐	3	Petteri Nummelin, Fin.	.15
☐	4	Erik Hamalainen, Fin.	.15
☐	5	Timo Jutila, Fin.	.25
☐	6	Janne Niinimaa, Fin.	.50
☐	7	Raimo Summanen, Fin.	.15
☐	8	Janne Ojanen, Fin.	.15
☐	9	Esa Keskinen, Fin.	.15
☐	10	Ari Sulander, Fin.	.15
☐	11	Saku Koivu, Fin.	1.75
☐	12	Jukka Tammi, Fin.	.15
☐	13	Marko Palo, Fin.	.15
☐	14	Raimo Helminen, Fin.	.15
☐	15	Anntti Törmänen, Fin.	.15
☐	16	Ville Peltonen, Fin.	.15
☐	17	Tero Lehterä, Fin.	.15
☐	18	Mika Stromberg, Fin.	.15
☐	19	Sami Kapanen, Fin.	.25
☐	20	Jere Lehtinen, Fin.	.50
☐	21	Juha Ylonen, Fin.	.15
☐	22	Mika Nieminen, Fin.	.15
☐	23	Hannu Virta, Fin.	.15
☐	24	Jari Kurri, Fin.	.50
☐	25	Christian Ruuttu, Fin.	.15
☐	26	Jyrki Lumme, Fin.	.25
☐	27	Teppo Numminen, Fin.	.15
☐	28	Esa Tikkanen, Fin.	.25
☐	29	Janne Laukkanen, Fin.	.15
☐	30	Aki Berg, Fin.	.25
☐	31	Teemu Selänne, Fin.	1.75
☐	32	Markus Ketterer (G), Fin.	.15
☐	33	Joni Lehto, Fin.	.15
☐	34	Juha Riihijarvi, Fin.	.15
☐	35	Sakari Lindfors (G), Fin.	.15
☐	36	Kai Nurminen, Fin.	.15
☐	37	Ville Peltonen/Saku Koivu/Jere Lehtinen	1.00
☐	38	Tommy Söderström (G), Swe.	.25
☐	39	Tommy Salo (G), Swe.	.25
☐	40	Thomas Ostlund, Swe.	.15
☐	41	Boo Ahl, Swe.	.15
☐	42	Calle Johansson, Swe.	.15
☐	43	Tommy Albelin, Swe.	.15
☐	44	Ulf Samuelsson, Swe.	.25
☐	45	Nicklas Lidström, Swe.	.50
☐	46	Magnus Svensson, Swe.	.15
☐	47	Tomas Jonsson, Swe.	.15
☐	48	Tommy Sjodin, Swe.	.15
☐	49	Marcus Ragnarsson, Swe.	.15
☐	50	Christer Olsson, Swe.	.15
☐	51	Rikard Franzen, Swe.	.15
☐	52	Mattias Ohlund, Swe.	.75
☐	53	Kenny Jonsson, Swe.	.25
☐	54	Roger Johansson, Swe.	.15
☐	55	Anders Eriksson, Swe.	.25
☐	56	Mats Sundin, Swe.	1.25
☐	57	Peter Forsberg, Swe.	2.50
☐	58	Mikael Renberg, Swe.	.25
☐	59	Tomas Sandström, Swe.	.25
☐	60	Ulf Dahlen, Swe.	.25
☐	61	Michael Nylander, Swe.	.25
☐	62	Patrik Juhlin, Swe.	.15
☐	63	Patrick Carnback, Swe.	.15
☐	64	Andreas Johansson, Swe.	.15

	No.	Player	NRMT-MT
☐	65	Mikael Johansson, Swe.	.15
☐	66	Per-Erik Eklund, Swe.	.15
☐	67	Tomas Forslund, Swe.	.15
☐	68	Andreas Dackell, Swe.	.15
☐	69	Per Eklund, Swe.	.15
☐	70	Tomas Holmstrom, Swe.	.15
☐	71	Jonas Bergvist, Swe.	.15
☐	72	Daniel Alfredsson, Swe.	1.50
☐	73	Fredrik Modin, Swe.	.50
☐	74	HL: Peter Forsberg, Swe.	1.25
☐	75	Ed Belfour (G), Cdn.	.75
☐	76	Bill Ranford (G), Cdn.	.50
☐	77	Sean Burke (G), Cdn.	.50
☐	78	Ray Bourque, Cdn.	1.25
☐	79	Paul Coffey, Cdn.	.50
☐	80	Scott Stevens, Cdn.	.25
☐	81	Al MacInnis, Cdn.	.25
☐	82	Larry Murphy, Cdn.	.50
☐	83	Eric Desjardins, Cdn.	.25
☐	84	Steve Duchesne, Cdn.	.25
☐	85	Mario Lemieux, Cdn.	4.00
☐	86	Mark Messier, Cdn.	1.25
☐	87	Theoren Fleury, Cdn.	.75
☐	88	Eric Lindros, Cdn.	3.50
☐	89	Rick Tocchet, Cdn.	.25
☐	90	Brendan Shanahan, Cdn.	1.50
☐	91	Claude Lemieux, Cdn.	.25
☐	92	Joé Juneau, Cdn.	.25
☐	93	Luc Robitaille, Cdn.	.50
☐	94	Paul Kariya, Cdn.	3.50
☐	95	Joe Sakic, Cdn.	2.00
☐	96	Mark Recchi, Cdn.	.50
☐	97	Jason Arnott, Cdn.	.50
☐	98	Rod Brind'Amour, Cdn.	.50
☐	99	Wayne Gretzky, Cdn.	5.00
☐	100	Adam Graves, Cdn.	.25
☐	101	Steve Yzerman, Cdn.	2.50
☐	102	Roman Turek (G), Cze.	.50
☐	103	Dominik Hasek (G), Cze.	1.75
☐	104	Petr Briza (G), Cze.	.15
☐	105	Antonin Stavjana, Cze.	.15
☐	106	Frantisek Kucera, Cze.	.15
☐	107	Jiri Vukoukal, Cze.	.15
☐	108	Jan Vopat, Cze.	.15
☐	109	Libor Prochazka, Cze.	.15
☐	110	Petr Kuchyna, Cze.	.15
☐	111	Frantisek Musil, Cze.	.15
☐	112	Leo Gudas, Cze.	.15
☐	113	Jiri Slegr, Cze.	.15
☐	114	Pavel Patera, Cze.	.15
☐	115	Otakar Vejvoda, Cze.	.15
☐	116	Martin Prochazka, Cze.	.15
☐	117	Jiri Kucera, Cze.	.15
☐	118	Pavel Janku, Cze.	.15
☐	119	Roman Meluzin, Cze.	.15
☐	120	Richard Zemlicka, Cze.	.15
☐	121	Martin Hostak, Cze.	.15
☐	122	Jiri Dopita, Cze.	.15
☐	123	Radek Belohlav, Cze.	.15
☐	124	Roman Horak, Cze.	.15
☐	125	Jaromir Jagr, Cze.	2.50
☐	126	Michal Pivonka, Cze.	.25
☐	127	Josef Beranek, Cze.	.15
☐	128	Robert Reichel, Cze.	.25
☐	129	Nikolai Khabibulin (G), Rus.	.75
☐	130	Sergei Abramov, Rus.	.15
☐	131	Yevgeny Tarasov, Rus.	.15
☐	132	Igor Kravchuk, Rus.	.25
☐	133	Dmitri Mironov, Rus.	.25
☐	134	Alexei Zhitnik, Rus.	.25
☐	135	Vladimir Malakhov, Rus.	.25
☐	136	Sergei Zubov, Rus.	.50
☐	137	Dimitri Yushkevich, Rus.	.15
☐	138	Ilya Byakin, Rus.	.15
☐	139	Alexander Smirnov, Rus.	.15
☐	140	Andrei Skopintsev, Rus.	.15
☐	141	Sergei Fedorov, Rus.	1.25
☐	142	Pavel Bure, Rus.	1.75
☐	143	Alexei Zhamnov, Rus.	.50
☐	144	Andrei Kovalenko, Rus.	.25
☐	145	Igor Korolev, Rus.	.25
☐	146	Vyacheslav Kozlov, Rus.	.25
☐	147	Viktor Kozlov , Rus.	.25
☐	148	Alexei Yashin, Rus.	1.00
☐	149	Valeri Kamensky, Rus.	.50
☐	150	Stanislav Romanov, Rus.	.15
☐	151	Vyacheslav Bykov, Rus.	.25
☐	152	Andrei Khomutov, Rus.	.25
☐	153	Sergei Berezin, Rus.	.50
☐	154	German Titov, Rus.	.15
☐	155	Dmitri Denisov, Rus.	.15
☐	156	John Vanbiesbrouck (G), USA.	1.50
☐	157	Jim Carey (G), USA.	.15
☐	158	Mike Richter (G), USA.	.75
☐	159	Chris Chelios, USA.	1.00
☐	160	Brian Leetch, USA.	.75
☐	161	Phil Housley, USA.	.25
☐	162	Gary Suter, USA.	.25
☐	163	Kevin Hatcher, USA.	.25
☐	164	Brett Hull, USA.	1.25
☐	165	Pat LaFontaine, USA.	.50
☐	166	Mike Modano, USA.	1.25
☐	167	Jeremy Roenick, USA.	.75
☐	168	Keith Tkachuk, USA.	1.00
☐	169	Joe Mullen, USA.	.25
☐	170	Craig Janney, USA.	.25
☐	171	Joel Otto, USA.	.25
☐	172	Doug Weight, USA.	.75
☐	173	Scott Young, USA.	.25
☐	174	Michael Rosati, Ita.	.15
☐	175	Bruno Campese, Ita.	.15
☐	176	Robert Oberrauch, Ita.	.15
☐	177	Robert Nardella, Ita.	.15
☐	178	Stefano Figliuzzi, Ita.	.15
☐	179	Maurizio Mansi, Ita.	.15
☐	180	Gaetano Orlando, Ita.	.15
☐	181	Mario Chitarroni, Ita.	.15
☐	182	Martin Pavlu, Ita.	.15
☐	183	Petri Ylonen (G), Fra.	.15
☐	184	Michel Valliere, Fra.	.15
☐	185	Serge Poudrier, Fra.	.15
☐	186	Denis Perez, Fra.	.15
☐	187	Antoine Richer, Fra.	.15
☐	188	Philippe Bozon, Fra.	.15
☐	189	Christian Pouget, Fra.	.15
☐	190	Franck Pajonkowski, Fra.	.15
☐	191	Stephane Barin, Fra.	.15
☐	192	Klaus Merk (G), Ger.	.15
☐	193	Marc Seliger, Ger.	.15
☐	194	Mirco Ludemann, Ger.	.15
☐	195	Jayson Meyer, Ger.	.15
☐	196	Benoît Doucet, Ger.	.15
☐	197	Thomas Brandl, Ger.	.15
☐	198	Dieter Hegen, Ger.	.15
☐	199	Martin Reichel, Ger.	.15
☐	200	Leo Stefan, Ger.	.15
☐	201	Robert Schistad, Nor.	.15
☐	202	Jim Marthinsen, Nor.	.15
☐	203	Tommy Jakobsen, Nor.	.15
☐	204	Petter Salsten, Nor.	.15
☐	205	Svein E. Norstebo, Nor.	.15
☐	206	Espen Knutsen, Nor.	.25
☐	207	Trond Magnussen, Nor.	.15
☐	208	Henrik Aaby, Nor.	.15
☐	209	Marius Rath, Nor.	.15
☐	210	Claus Dalpiaz, Aut.	.15
☐	211	Michael Puschacher, Aut.	.15
☐	212	Robin Doyle, Aut.	.15
☐	213	James Burton, Aut.	.15
☐	214	Herbert Hohenberger, Aut.	.15
☐	215	Andreas Pusnik, Aut.	.15
☐	216	Richard Nascheim, Aut.	.15
☐	217	Dieter Kalt, Aut.	.15
☐	218	Werner Kerth, Aut.	.15
☐	219	Eduard Hartmann, Slo.	.15
☐	220	Jaromir Dragan, Slo.	.15
☐	221	Robert Svehla, Slo.	.25
☐	222	Lubomir Sekeras, Slo.	.15
☐	223	Marian Smerciak, Slo.	.15
☐	224	Jergus Baca, Slo.	.15
☐	225	Stanislav Medrik, Slo.	.15
☐	226	Miroslav Marcinko, Slo.	.15
☐	227	Peter Stastny, Slo.	.50
☐	228	Peter Bondra, Slo.	1.00
☐	229	Zdeno Ciger, Slo.	.15
☐	230	Jozef Stumpel, Slo.	.50
☐	231	Miroslav Satan, Slo.	.15
☐	232	Lubomir Kolnik, Slo.	.15
☐	233	Robert Petrovicky, Slo.	.15
☐	234	Zigmund Palffy, Slo.	1.00
☐	235	Oto Hascak, Slo.	.15
☐	236	Jozef Dano, Slo.	.15
☐	237	CL:Renberg/Koivu	.35
☐	238	CL:Renberg/Koivu	.35
☐	239	CL:Renberg/Koivu	.35
☐	240	CL:Renberg/Koivu	.35
		Super Chase	**NRMT-MT**
☐		Saku Koivu/Mikael Renberg	50.00

HOCKEY LEGENDS

	No.	Player	NRMT-MT
Insert Set (18 cards):			**45.00**
☐	HL1	Ken Dryden (G), Cdn.	8.00
☐	HL2	Guy Lafleur, Cdn.	6.00
☐	HL3	Mike Bossy, Cdn.	4.00
☐	HL4	Valeri Vasiliev, USSR	2.00
☐	HL5	Anatoli Firsov, USSR	2.00
☐	HL6	Alexander Maltsev, USSR	3.00
☐	HL7	Tony Esposito, Cdn.	3.00
☐	HL8	Rod Langway, USA.	2.00
☐	HL9	Bryan Trottier, USA.	3.00
☐	HL10	Lennart Haggroth, Swe.	2.00
☐	HL11	Ulf Nilsson, Swe.	2.00
☐	HL12	Lars-Gunnar Lundberg, Swe.	2.00
☐	HL13	Veli-Pekka Ketola, Fin.	3.00
☐	HL14	Lasse Oksanen, Fin.	2.00
☐	HL15	Pekka Rautakallio, Fin.	2.00
☐	HL16	Jiri Holocek, Cze.	2.00
☐	HL17	Jan Suchy, Cze.	2.00
☐	HL18	Vaclav Nedomansky, Cze.	2.00

NORDIC STARS

	No.	Player	NRMT-MT
Insert Set (6 cards):			**60.00**
☐	NS1	Peter Forsberg, Swe.	20.00
☐	NS2	Teemu Selänne, Fin.	15.00
☐	NS3	Mats Sundin, Swe.	10.00
☐	NS4	Jari Kurri, Fin.	8.00
☐	NS5	Nicklas Lidström, Swe.	8.00
☐	NS6	Esa Tikkanen, Fin.	5.00

SUPER GOALIES

	No.	Player	NRMT-MT
Insert Set (9 cards):			**60.00**
☐	SG1	Dominik Hasek (G), Cze.	10.00
☐	SG2	Ed Belfour (G), Cdn.	7.00
☐	SG3	Jarmo Myllys (G), Fin.	5.00
☐	SG4	Tommy Söderström (G), Swe.	5.00
☐	SG5	Jim Carey (G), USA.	5.00
☐	SG6	Roman Turek (G), Cze.	5.00
☐	SG7	Patrick Roy (G), Cdn.	18.00
☐	SG8	Markus Ketterer (G), Fin.	5.00
☐	SG9	Tommy Salo (G), Swe.	5.00

WORLD CHAMPIONSHIP 1995 ALL-STARS

Insert Set (6 cards): 30.00

	No.	Player	NRMT-MT
☐	AS1	Roman Turek/Jarmo Myllys	5.00
☐	AS2	Timo Jutila/Christer Olsson	4.00
☐	AS3	Tommy Sjodin/Marko Kiprusoff	3.00
☐	AS4	Jere Lehtinen/Sergei Berezin	4.00
☐	AS5	Saku Koivu/Per-Erik Eklund	12.00
☐	AS6	Ville Peltonen/Andrew McKim	3.00

1996 - 97 BICYCLE SPORTS HOCKEY ACES

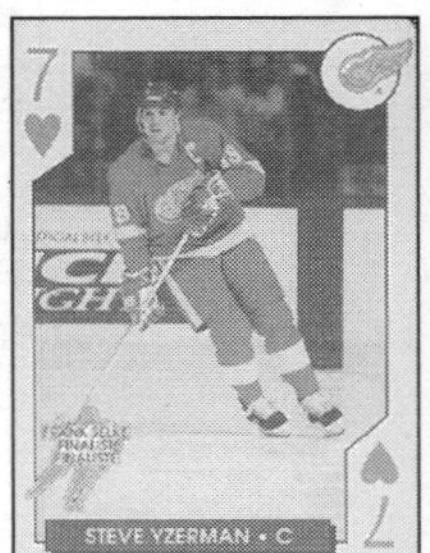

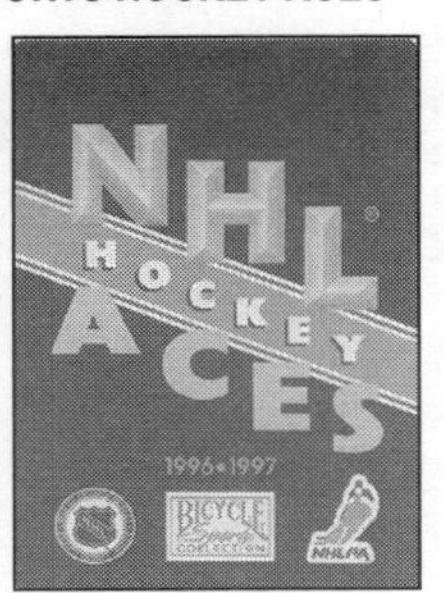

Imprint: 1996-1997 BICYCLE SPORTS COLLECTION

Complete Deck (55 cards): 6.00

	No.	Player	NRMT-MT
☐		Checklist	.15
☐		Eastern Conference logo	.15
☐		Western Conference logo	.15
☐	A♠	Mario Lemieux, Pgh.	1.50
☐	2♠	Travis Green, NYI.	.15
☐	3♠	Roman Hamrlik, T.B.	.25
☐	4♠	Adam Oates, Bos.	.35
☐	5♠	Trevor Linden, Van.	.25
☐	6♠	Daren Puppa (G), T.B.	.15
☐	7♠	Eric Dazé, Chi.	.25
☐	8♠	Rod Brind'Amour, Pha.	.25
☐	9♠	Ron Francis, Pgh.	.35
☐	10♠	Chris Osgood (G), Det.	.35
☐	J♠	Jim Carey (G), Wsh.	.15
☐	Q♠	Ed Jovanovski, Fla.	.25
☐	K♠	Eric Lindros, Pha.	1.50
☐	A♦	Joe Sakic, Col.	1.00
☐	2♦	Alexei Yashin, Ott.	.25
☐	3♦	Jason Arnott, Edm.	.25
☐	4♦	Mike Gartner, Tor.	.25
☐	5♦	Jeremey Roenick, Chi.	.35
☐	6♦	Mike Modano, Dal.	.50
☐	7♦	Pat LaFontaine, Buf.	.25
☐	8♦	Mats Sundin, Tor.	.50
☐	9♦	Brett Hull, Stl.	.50
☐	10♦	Doug Weight, Edm.	.35
☐	J♦	Theoren Fleury, Cgy.	.35
☐	Q♦	Mark Messier, NYR.	.50
☐	K♦	Paul Kariya, Ana.	1.25
☐	A♣	Wayne Gretzky, Stl.	2.00
☐	2♣	Gary Roberts, Cgy.	.25
☐	3♣	Ray Ferraro, L.A.	.15
☐	4♣	Owen Nolan, S.J.	.25
☐	5♣	Chris Chelios, Chi.	.35
☐	6♣	Brendan Shanahan, Hfd.	.60
☐	7♣	Daniel Alfredsson, Ott.	.35
☐	8♣	Brian Leetch, NYR.	.35
☐	9♣	Martin Brodeur (G), N.J.	.75
☐	10♣	Pierre Turgeon, Mtl.	.25
☐	J♣	Alexander Mogilny, Van.	.35
☐	Q♣	John Vanbiesbrouck (G), Fla.	.60
☐	K♣	Jaromir Jagr, Pgh.	1.00
☐	A♥	Patrick Roy (G), Col.	1.50
☐	2♥	Pavel Bure, Van.	.75
☐	3♥	Doug Gilmour, Tor.	.35
☐	4♥	Joe Juneau, Wsh.	.15
☐	5♥	Ray Bourque, Bos.	.50
☐	6♥	Jocelyn Thibault (G), Mtl.	.35
☐	7♥	Steve Yzerman, Det.	1.00
☐	8♥	Grant Fuhr (G), Stl.	.25
☐	9♥	Vincent Damphousse, Mtl.	.35
☐	10♥	Keith Tkachuk, Wpg.	.35
☐	J♥	Teemu Selänne, Ana.	.75
☐	Q♥	Sergei Fedorov, Det.	.50
☐	K♥	Peter Forsberg, Col.	1.00

1996 - 97 CORINTHIAN HEADLINERS

This set is licensed by the NHLPA only.

Imprint:

Complete Set (21 figurines): 150.00

	Player	NRMT-MT
☐	Ray Bourque	8.00
☐	Martin Brodeur (G)	12.00
☐	Pavel Bure	8.00
☐	Chris Chelios	7.50
☐	Sergei Fedorov	8.00
☐	Wayne Gretzky	15.00
☐	Jaromir Jagr	9.00
☐	Jari Kurri	6.50
☐	Brian Leetch	7.50
☐	Claude Lemieux	6.00
☐	Mario Lemieux	12.00
☐	Eric Lindros	10.00
☐	Mark Messier	8.00
☐	Jeremy Roenick	6.50
☐	Patrick Roy (G)	15.00
☐	Joe Sakic	8.00
☐	Teemu Selänne	8.00
☐	Brendan Shanahan	8.00
☐	Mats Sundin	8.00
☐	Keith Tkachuk	7.50
☐	John Vanbiesbrouck (G)	12.00

1996 - 97 DEL EISHOCKEY

Imprint:

Complete Set (360 cards): 50.00

Common Player: .20

	No.	Player	NRMT-MT
☐	1	Gary Prior, Coach	.20
☐	2	Bruno Campese	.20
☐	3	Leonardo Conti	.20
☐	4	Scott Campbell	.20
☐	5	Robert Mendel	.20
☐	6	Serge Poudrier	.20
☐	7	Torsten Fendt	.20
☐	8	Shawn Rivers	.20
☐	9	Stefan Mayer	.20
☐	10	Michael Bakos	.20
☐	11	Tommy Jacobsen	.20
☐	12	Duanne Moeser	.20
☐	13	Tero Arkiomaa	.20
☐	14	Sven Zywitza	.20
☐	15	Craig Streu	.20
☐	16	Terry Campbell	.20
☐	17	Timothy Ferguson	.20
☐	18	Yves Heroux	.20
☐	19	Max Boldt	.20
☐	20	Andre Faust	.20
☐	21	Rochus Schneider	.20
☐	22	Ron Kennedy, Coach	.20
☐	23	Barry Lewis, Asst. Coach	.20
☐	24	Mario Brunetta	.20
☐	25	Udo Dohler	.20
☐	26	Dirk Perschau	.20
☐	27	Darren Durdle	.20
☐	28	Greg Andrusak	.20
☐	29	Leif Carlsson	.20
☐	30	Derek Mayer	.20
☐	31	Rob Leask	.20
☐	32	Chad Biafore	.20
☐	33	Thomas Steen	.20
☐	34	Lorenz Funk	.20
☐	35	Florian Funk	.20
☐	36	Sven Felski	.20
☐	37	Peter Lee	.20
☐	38	Andrew McKim	.50
☐	39	Andrej Lomakin	.20
☐	40	Pelle Svensson	.20
☐	41	Jan Schertz	.20
☐	42	Kraig Nienhuis	.20
☐	43	Niklas Hede	.20
☐	44	Mario Chitarroni	.20
☐	45	Chris Govedaris	.20
☐	46	Pentti Matikainen, Coach	.20
☐	47	Jukka Tammi	.20
☐	48	Rupert Meister	.20
☐	49	Florian Storf	.20
☐	50	Greg Thomson	.20
☐	51	Toni Porkka	.20
☐	52	Sergej Schendelev	.20
☐	53	Kai Rautio	.20
☐	54	Rudi Gorgenlander	.20
☐	55	Petr Kopta	.20
☐	56	Tony Virta	.20
☐	57	Ilja Vorobjev	.20
☐	58	Thomas Popiesch	.20
☐	59	Francois Sills	.20
☐	60	Iiro Jarvi	.20
☐	61	Jurgen Schaal	.20
☐	62	Pavel Vit	.20
☐	63	Timo Peltomaa	.20
☐	64	Igor Schultz	.20
☐	65	Dave Archibald	.20
☐	66	Joni Lehto	.20
☐	67	Brad Jones	.20
☐	68	Miroslav Berek, Coach	.20
☐	69	Karel Lang	.20
☐	70	Peter Franke	.20
☐	71	Markus Krawinkel	.20
☐	72	Zdenek Travnicek	.20
☐	73	Martin Gebel	.20
☐	74	Klaus Micheller	.20
☐	75	Earl Spry	.20
☐	76	Frantisek Frosch	.20
☐	77	Petri Liimatainen	.20
☐	78	Andre Grein	.20
☐	79	Ken Petrash	.20
☐	80	James Hanlon	.20
☐	81	Andrej Kovalev	.20
☐	82	Reemt Pyka	.20
☐	83	Chris Lindberg	.20
☐	84	Jay Luknowsky	.20
☐	85	Peter Ihnacak	.50
☐	86	Marek Strebnicki	.20
☐	87	Johnny Walker	.20
☐	88	Danton Cole	.20
☐	89	Michael Hreus	.20
☐	90	Damian Adamus	.20
☐	91	Bill Lochead, Coach	.20
☐	92	Joakim Persson	.20
☐	93	Ian Wood	.20
☐	94	Pierre Jonsson	.20
☐	95	Juha Lampinen	.20
☐	96	Christian Schmitz	.20
☐	97	Cory Holden	.20
☐	98	Peter Lutter	.20
☐	99	Dieter Bloem	.20
☐	100	Maurizio Catenacci	.20
☐	101	Andrej Fuchs	.20
☐	102	Mark Montanari	.20
☐	103	Boris Fuchs	.20
☐	104	Andreas Salomonsson	.20
☐	105	Robert Reynolds	.20
☐	106	Axel Kammerer	.20
☐	107	Jeff Lazaro	.20
☐	108	Olaf Scholz	.20
☐	109	Tony Cimellaro	.20
☐	110	Kenneth Hodge	.20
☐	111	Gregory Burke	.20
☐	112	Tom Coolen, Coach	.20
☐	113	Marc Pethke	.20
☐	114	Christian Kunast	.20
☐	115	Drahomir Kadlec	.20
☐	116	Florian Kuhn	.20
☐	117	Erich Goldmann	.20
☐	118	Jurgen Simon	.20

	No.	Player	Price
☐	119	Jeff Winstanley	.20
☐	120	Stefano Figliuzzi	.20
☐	121	Maurice Mansi	.20
☐	122	Agostino Casale	.20
☐	123	Hans-Jorg Mayer	.20
☐	124	Dino Felicetti	.20
☐	125	Roland Timoschuk	.20
☐	126	Jim Hoffmann	.20
☐	127	John Porco	.20
☐	128	Rolf Hammer	.20
☐	129	Manuel Hess	.20
☐	130	Andy Rymsha	.20
☐	131	Wolfgang Kummer	.20
☐	132	Trevor Burgess	.20
☐	133	Daniel Kunce	.20
☐	134	Timo Sutinen, Coach	.20
☐	135	Petr Briza (G)	.20
☐	136	Markus Nachtmann	.20
☐	137	Markus Wieland	.20
☐	138	Mike Heidt	.20
☐	139	Peter Gulda	.20
☐	140	Jacek Plachta	.20
☐	141	Georg Franz	.20
☐	142	Stephan Retzer	.20
☐	143	Henry Marcoux	.20
☐	144	Mike Bullard	1.00
☐	145	Jose Charbonneau	.20
☐	146	Wally Schreiber	.20
☐	147	Jorg Handrick	.20
☐	148	Helmut Steiger	.20
☐	149	Marco Sturm	1.50
☐	150	Jonas Jonsson	.20
☐	151	Vesa Salo	.20
☐	152	Gino Cavallini	.20
☐	153	Lars Hurtig	.20
☐	154	Olli Kaski	.20
☐	155	007 Charly??	.20
☐	156	Lance Nethery, Coach	.20
☐	157	Ross Yates, Asst. Coach	.20
☐	158	Joachim Appel	.20
☐	159	Mike Rosati	.20
☐	160	Harold Kreis	.20
☐	161	Paul Stanton	.20
☐	162	Christian Lukes	.20
☐	163	Robert Nardella	.20
☐	164	Alexander Erdmann	.20
☐	165	Stéphane J.G. Richer	.50
☐	166	Martin Ulrich	.20
☐	167	Mike Pellegrims	.20
☐	168	Mario Gehrig	.20
☐	169	Pavel Gross	.20
☐	170	Dave Tomlinson	.20
☐	171	Daniel Korber	.20
☐	172	Francois Guay	.20
☐	173	Jochen Hecht	.20
☐	174	Florian Keller	.20
☐	175	Till Feser	.20
☐	176	Alexander Serikow	.20
☐	177	Christian Pouget	.20
☐	178	Dieter Kalt	.20
☐	179	Paul Beraldo	.20
☐	180	Steven Thornton	.20
☐	181	Robert Cimetta	.20
☐	182	Gary Clark, Coach	.20
☐	183	Bjorn Leonhardt	.20
☐	184	Klaus Dalpiaz	.20
☐	185	Jesper Duus	.20
☐	186	Manuel Hiemer	.20
☐	187	Markus Pottinger	.20
☐	188	Chris Bartolone	.20
☐	189	Christian Gegenfurth	.20
☐	190	Heinrich Schiffl	.20
☐	191	Per Lundel	.20
☐	192	Joel Savage	.20
☐	193	Josef Muller	.20
☐	194	Jari Torkki	.20
☐	195	James Hiller	.20
☐	196	Doud Derraugh	.20
☐	197	Pekka Tirkkonen	.20
☐	198	Martin Reichel	.20
☐	199	Raimond Hilger	.20
☐	200	Michael Schneidawind	.20
☐	201	Scott Beattie	.20
☐	202	Paris Proft	.20
☐	203	Kevin Gaudet, Coach	.20
☐	204	Wayne Cowley	.20
☐	205	Marco Herbst	.20
☐	206	Andreas Schubert	.20
☐	207	Stephan Sinner	.20
☐	208	Heinrich Synowietz	.20
☐	209	Paul Synowietz	.20
☐	210	Dimitri Frolov	.20
☐	211	Andrej Saposhnikov	.20
☐	212	Jedrzej Kasperczyk	.20
☐	213	Joseph West	.20
☐	214	Fabian Ahrens	.20
☐	215	Maurice Lemay	.20
☐	216	Mark Kosturik	.20
☐	217	Mark Jooris	.20
☐	218	Len Soccio	.20
☐	219	Mark Mahon	.20
☐	220	Frank LaScala	.20
☐	221	Jari Pasanen	.20
☐	222	Ralph Vos	.20
☐	223	Anthony Cirelli	.20
☐	224	Emilio Iovio	.20
☐	225	Gerhard Brunner, Coach	.20
☐	226	Pavel Cagas	.20
☐	227	Jonas Eriksson	.20
☐	228	Alexander Engel	.20
☐	229	Gregory Johnston	.20
☐	230	Alexander Wedl	.20
☐	231	Jouni Vento	.20
☐	232	Roger Ohman	.20
☐	233	David Morrison	.20
☐	234	Bruce Eakin	.20
☐	235	Michael Millar	.20
☐	236	Roger Hansson	.20
☐	237	Peter Kwasigroch	.20
☐	238	Branjo Heisig	.20
☐	239	Jukka Seppo	.20
☐	240	Greg Evtushevski	.20
☐	241	Falk Ozellis	.20
☐	242	Daniel Larin	.20
☐	243	Tino Boos	.20
☐	244	Toni Krinner	.20
☐	245	Milan Mokros	.20
☐	246	Peter Ustorf, Coach	.20
☐	247	Klaus Merk	.20
☐	248	David Berge	.20
☐	249	Georg Holzmann	.20
☐	250	Tom O'Regan	.20
☐	251	Jochen Molling	.20
☐	252	Joseph Lehner	.20
☐	253	Marco Rentzsch	.20
☐	254	Pekka Laksola	.20
☐	255	Petri Matikainen	.20
☐	256	Tony Tanti	1.00
☐	257	Gaetan Malo	.20
☐	258	Thomas Schinko	.20
☐	259	Vitali Karamnov	.20
☐	260	Gunther Oswald	.20
☐	261	Christian Brittig	.20
☐	262	Jurgen Rumrich	.20
☐	263	John Chabot	.50
☐	264	Andreas Dimbat	.20
☐	265	Mark Teevens	.20
☐	266	Veli-Pekka Kautonen	.20
☐	267	Jarmo-Sakari Peltonen	.20
☐	268	Hardy Nilsson, Coach	.20
☐	269	Martin Karlsson, Asst. Coach	.20
☐	270	Ake Lilljebjorn	.20
☐	271	Kai Fischer	.20
☐	272	Brad Bergen	.20
☐	273	Andreas Niederberger	.20
☐	274	Sergej Sorokin	.20
☐	275	Robert Sterflinger	.20
☐	276	Peter Andersson	.20
☐	277	Viktor Gordiouk	.50
☐	278	Gordon Sherven	.20
☐	279	Benoît Doucet	.20
☐	280	Bernd Kuhnhauser	.20
☐	281	Dieter Hegen	.20
☐	282	Andreas Brockmann	.20
☐	283	Ernst Kopf	.20
☐	284	Alexej Kudashov	.20
☐	285	Bernd Truntschka	.20
☐	286	Mikko Makela	.20
☐	287	Nikolaus Mondt	.20
☐	288	Boris Lingemann	.20
☐	289	Thomas Brandl	.20
☐	290	Leo Stefan	.20
☐	291	Bob Burns, Coach	.20
☐	292	Carsten Solbach	.20
☐	293	Matthias Hoppe	.20
☐	294	Sascha Goc	.20
☐	295	Gordon Hynes	.20
☐	296	Thomas Gaus	.20
☐	297	Brian Tutt	.20
☐	298	Richard Trojan	.20
☐	299	Daniel Nowak	.20
☐	300	Andreas Renz	.20
☐	301	Sana Hassan	.20
☐	302	Alan Young	.20
☐	303	Mike Bader	.20
☐	304	Robert Brezina	.20
☐	305	Wayne Hynes	.20
☐	306	Mark Bassen	.20
☐	307	Andrew Clark	.20
☐	308	Grant Martin	.20
☐	309	Michael Lay	.20
☐	310	Jackson Penney	.20
☐	311	Rich Chernomaz	.20
☐	312	Mark MacKay	.20
☐	313	Vladimir Fedosov	.20
☐	314	Emanuel Viveiros	.20
☐	315	Jan Eysselt, Coach	.20
☐	316	Michel Valliere	.20
☐	317	Stefan Lahn	.20
☐	318	Christian Gerum	.20
☐	319	Heiko Smazal	.20
☐	320	Christian Curth	.20
☐	321	Miroslav maly	.20
☐	322	Torsten Kienass	.20
☐	323	Thomas Sterflinger	.20
☐	324	Lars Bruggermann	.20
☐	325	Paul Geddes	.20
☐	326	Rolan Ramoser	.20
☐	327	Martin Jiranek	.20
☐	328	Stefan Steinbock	.20
☐	329	Martin Ekrt	.20
☐	330	Jurgen Lechl	.20
☐	331	Dion Del Monte	.20
☐	332	Markus Welz	.20
☐	333	Henrik Holscher	.20
☐	334	Otto Sykora	.20
☐	335	Milos Vanik	.20
☐	336	Robert Murdoch, Coach	.20
☐	337	Bernd Haake, Asst. Coach	.20
☐	338	Joseph Heiss	.20
☐	339	Olaf Grundmann	.20
☐	340	Alexander Genze	.20
☐	341	Jorg Mayr	.20
☐	342	Mirco Ludemann	.20
☐	343	Jayson Meyer	.20
☐	344	Karsten Mende	.20
☐	345	Herbert Hohenberger	.20
☐	346	Joe Cirella	.50
☐	347	Petter Nilsson	.20
☐	348	Jim Montgomery	.20
☐	349	Stefan Mann	.20
☐	350	Luciano Borsato	.20
☐	351	Dwayne Norris	.50
☐	352	Bruno Zarrillo	.20
☐	353	Peter Draisaitl	.20
☐	354	Joe Busillo	.20
☐	355	Andreas Lupzig	.20
☐	356	Rainer Zerwesz	.20
☐	357	Thomas Forslund	.20
☐	358	Tobias Abstreiter	.20
☐	359	Patrick Carnback	.50
☐	360	Franz Demmel	.20

1996 - 97 DONRUSS

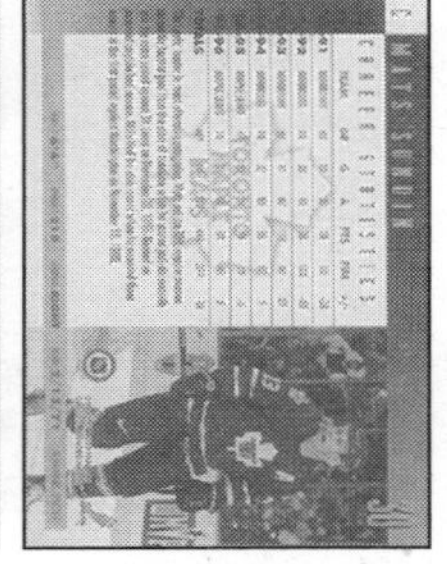

These cards have two versions: the regular card and a Press Proof parallel card.

Imprint: © 1996 DONRUSS TRADING CO.

	No.	Player	Reg.	PP
		Complete Set (240 cards):	**20.00**	**1,100.00**
		Common Player:	**.10**	**3.50**
☐☐	1	Joe Sakic, Col.	.85	40.00
☐☐	2	Jeremy Roenick, Chi.	.35	10.00
☐☐	3	Kirk McLean (G), Van.	.25	5.00
☐☐	4	Zarley Zalapski, Cgy.	.10	3.50
☐☐	5	Jyrki Lumme, Van.	.10	3.50
☐☐	6	Owne Nolan, S.J.	.25	5.00
☐☐	7	Luc Robitaille, NYR.	.25	5.00
☐☐	8	Bob Probert, Chi.	.10	3.50
☐☐	9	Ken Baumgartner, Ana.	.10	3.50
☐☐	10	Rick Tabaracci (G), Cgy.	.10	3.50
☐☐	11	Alexei Zhitnik, Buf.	.10	3.50
☐☐	12	Al MacInnis, Stl.	.10	3.50
☐☐	13	Brain Leetch, NYR.	.35	10.00
☐☐	14	Valeri Kamensky, Col	.25	5.00
☐☐	15	Todd Gill, Tor.	.10	3.50
☐☐	16	Mark Messier, NYR.	.50	20.00
☐☐	17	Pierre Turgeon, Mtl.	.25	5.00
☐☐	18	Mathieu Schneider, Tor.	.10	3.50
☐☐	19	Vyacheslav Kozlov, Det.	.10	3.50
☐☐	20	Milos Holan, Ana.	.10	3.50
☐☐	21	Yanic Perreault, L.A.	.10	3.50
☐☐	22	Mike Modano, Dal.	.50	20.00
☐☐	23	Claude Lemieux, Col.	.10	3.50
☐☐	24	Rob Niedermayer, Fla.	.10	3.50
☐☐	25	Eric Desjardins, Pha.	.10	3.50
☐☐	26	Alexander Semak, NYI.	.10	3.50
☐☐	27	Mark Recchi, Mtl.	.25	5.00
☐☐	28	Viacheslav Fetisov, Det.	.25	5.00
☐☐	29	Kevin Hatcher, Dal.	.10	3.50
☐☐	30	Mats Sundin, Tor.	.50	20.00
☐☐	31	Jeff Reese (G), T.B.	.10	3.50
☐☐	32	Alexander Selivanov, T.B.	.10	3.50
☐☐	33	Jim Carey (G), Wsh.	.10	3.50
☐☐	34	Daren Puppa (G), T.B.	.10	3.50
☐☐	35	Vincent Damphousse, Mtl.	.35	10.00
☐☐	36	John LeClair, Pha.	.50	20.00
☐☐	37	Jon Casey (G), Stl.	.10	3.50
☐☐	38	Chris Terreri (G), S.J.	.10	3.50
☐☐	39	Larry Murphy, Tor.	.25	5.00
☐☐	40	Geoff Sanderson, Hfd.	.10	3.50
☐☐	41	Adam Oates, Bos.	.35	10.00
☐☐	42	Sandy McCarthy, Det.	.10	3.50
☐☐	43	Jaromir Jagr, Pgh.	1.25	50.00
☐☐	44	Roman Oksiuta, Ana.	.10	3.50
☐☐	45	Zigmund Palffy, NYI.	.35	10.00
☐☐	46	Doug Gilmour, Tor.	.35	10.00
☐☐	47	Cliff Ronning, Van.	.10	3.50
☐☐	48	Curtis Leschyshyn, Col.	.10	3.50
☐☐	49	Scott Mellanloy, Fla.	.10	3.50
☐☐	50	Sergei Fedorov, Det.	.50	20.00
☐☐	51	Denis Savard, Chi.	.25	5.00
☐☐	52	Mike Vernon (G), Det.	.25	5.00
☐☐	53	Todd Marchant, Edm.	.10	3.50
☐☐	54	Geoff Courtnall, Stl.	.10	3.50
☐☐	55	Shayne Corson, Stl.	.25	5.00
☐☐	56	Dimitri Khristich, L.A.	.10	3.50
☐☐	57	Scott Stevens, N.J.	.10	3.50
☐☐	58	German Titov, Cgy.	.10	3.50
☐☐	59	Darren Turcotte, S.J.	.10	3.50
☐☐	60	Michal Pivonka, Wsh.	.10	3.50
☐☐	61	Ron Hextall (G), Pha.	.25	5.00
☐☐	62	Ed Belfour (G), Chi.	.35	10.00
☐☐	63	Chris Pronger, Stl.	.25	5.00
☐☐	64	Brian Bellows, T.B.	.10	3.50
☐☐	65	Pavel Bure, Van.	.75	35.00
☐☐	66	Adam Graves, NYR.	.10	3.50
☐☐	67	Tom Barrasso (G), Pgh.	.25	5.00
☐☐	68	Stu Barnes, Fla.	.10	3.50
☐☐	69	Norm Maciver, Wpg.	.10	3.50
☐☐	70	Jesse Belanger, Van.	.10	3.50
☐☐	71	Chris Chelios, Chi.	.35	10.00
☐☐	72	Tommy Söderström (G), NYI.	.10	3.50
☐☐	73	Nelson Emerson, Wpg.	.10	3.50
☐☐	74	Kenny Jonsson, NYI.	.10	3.50
☐☐	75	Bill Lindsay, Fla.	.10	3.50
☐☐	76	Petr Nedved, Pgh.	.10	3.50
☐☐	77	Robert Svehla, Fla.	.10	3.50
☐☐	78	Tomas Sandström, Pgh.	.10	3.50
☐☐	79	Jeff Friesen, S.J.	.25	5.00
☐☐	80	Tony Amonte, Chi.	.25	5.00
☐☐	81	Sylvain Lefebvre, Col.	.10	3.50
☐☐	82	Greg Adams, Dal.	.10	3.50
☐☐	83	Vladimir Konstantinov, Det.	.10	3.50
☐☐	84	Roman Hamrlik, T.B.	.25	5.00
☐☐	85	Doug Weight, Edm.	.35	10.00
☐☐	86	Shaun Van Allen, Ana.	.10	3.50
☐☐	87	Bill Ranford (G), Bos.	.25	5.00
☐☐	88	Jeff Hackett, Chi.	.25	5.00
☐☐	89	Alexei Zhamnov, Wpg.	.25	5.00
☐☐	90	Dale Hawerchuk, Pha.	.25	5.00
☐☐	91	Sergei Zubov, Pgh.	.25	5.00
☐☐	92	Dan Quinn, Pha.	.10	3.50
☐☐	93	Wayne Gretzky, Stl.	2.50	120.00
☐☐	94	Todd Harvey, Dal.	.10	3.50
☐☐	95	Chris Osgood (G), Det.	.35	15.00
☐☐	96	Félix Potvin (G), Tor.	.50	20.00
☐☐	97	Richard Matvichuk, Dal.	.10	3.50
☐☐	98	Wendel Clark, Tor.	.25	5.00
☐☐	99	Bryan Smolinski, Pgh.	.10	3.50
☐☐	100	Rob Blake, L.A.	.50	5.00
☐☐	101	Jocelyn Thibault (G), Mtl.	.35	10.00
☐☐	102	Trevor Linden, Van.	.25	5.00
☐☐	103	Craig MacTavish, Pha.	.10	3.50
☐☐	104	Sandis Ozolinsh, Col.	.25	5.00
☐☐	105	Oleg Tverdovsky, Wpg.	.10	3.50
☐☐	106	Garry Galley, Buf.	.10	3.50
☐☐	107	Derek Plante, Buf.	.10	3.50
☐☐	108	Stéphane Richer, N.J.	.10	3.50
☐☐	109	Dave Andreychuk, N.J.	.10	3.50
☐☐	110	Curtis Joseph (G), Edm.	.60	30.00
☐☐	111	Greg Johnson, Det.	.10	3.50
☐☐	112	Patrick Roy (G), Col.	2.00	80.00
☐☐	113	Pat LaFontaine, Buf.	.10	3.50
☐☐	114	Uwe Krupp, Col.	.10	3.50
☐☐	115	Ulf Dahlen, S.J.	.10	3.50
☐☐	116	Brian Bradley, T.B.	.10	3.50
☐☐	117	Grant Fuhr (G), Stl.	.25	5.00
☐☐	118	Brian Skrudland, Fla.	.10	3.50
☐☐	119	Nicklas Lidström, Det.	.25	5.00
☐☐	120	Steve Chiasson, Cgy.	.10	3.50
☐☐	121	Sean Burke (G), Hfd.	.25	5.00
☐☐	122	Rick Tocchet, Bos.	.10	3.50
☐☐	123	Martin Rucinsky, Mtl.	.10	3.50
☐☐	124	Alexei Yashin, Ott.	.35	15.00
☐☐	125	Mikael Renberg, Pha.	.10	3.50
☐☐	126	Teppo Numminen, Wpg.	.10	3.50
☐☐	127	Randy Burridge, Buf.	.10	3.50
☐☐	128	Radek Bonk, Ott.	.10	3.50
☐☐	129	Scott Young, Col.	.10	3.50
☐☐	130	Gary Suter, Chi.	.10	3.50
☐☐	131	Mario Lemieux, Pgh.	2.00	80.00
☐☐	132	Ray Bourque, Bos.	.50	20.00
☐☐	133	Martin Gelinas, Van.	.10	3.50
☐☐	134	Keith Tkachuk, Wpg.	.35	15.00
☐☐	135	Benoît Hogue, Dal.	.10	3.50
☐☐	136	Ken Wregget (G), Pgh.	.10	3.50
☐☐	137	Eric Lindros, Pha.	1.50	65.00
☐☐	138	Keith Primeau, Det.	.20	5.00
☐☐	139	Peter Forsberg, Col.	1.25	50.00
☐☐	140	Paul Coffey, Det.	.25	5.00
☐☐	141	Mike Ridley, Van.	.10	3.50
☐☐	142	Paul Kariya, Ana.	1.50	65.00
☐☐	143	Jason Arnott, Edm.	.20	5.00
☐☐	144	Joe Murphy, Chi.	.10	3.50
☐☐	145	Adam Deadmarsh, Col.	.10	3.50
☐☐	146	John MacLean, N.J.	.10	3.50
☐☐	147	Peter Bondra, Wsh.	.35	15.00
☐☐	148	Martin Brodeur (G), N.J.	.75	35.00
☐☐	149	Ron Francis, Pgh.	.35	10.00
☐☐	150	Dino Ciccarelli, Det.	.25	5.00
☐☐	151	Joé Juneau, Wsh.	.10	3.50
☐☐	152	Matthew Barnaby, Buf.	.10	3.50
☐☐	153	Mark Tinordi, Wsh.	.10	3.50
☐☐	154	Craig Janney, Wpg.	.10	3.50
☐☐	155	Rod Brind'Amour, Pha.	.25	5.00
☐☐	156	Damian Rhodes (G), Ott.	.10	3.50
☐☐	157	Teemu Selänne, Ana.	.75	35.00
☐☐	158	James Patrick, Cgy.	.10	3.50
☐☐	159	Theoren Fleury, Cgy.	.35	10.00
☐☐	160	Trevor Kidd (G), Cgy.	.25	5.00
☐☐	161	Kirk Muller, Tor.	.10	3.50
☐☐	162	Andrew Cassels, Hfd.	.10	3.50
☐☐	163	Brent Fedyk, Dal.	.10	3.50
☐☐	164	Guy Hebert (G), Ana.	.25	5.00
☐☐	165	Jason Dawe, Buf.	.10	3.50
☐☐	166	Andy Moog (G), Dal.	.25	5.00
☐☐	167	Igor Larionov, Det.	.25	5.00
☐☐	168	Brian Savage, Mtl.	.10	3.50
☐☐	169	Kris Draper, Det.	.10	3.50
☐☐	170	Dave Gagner, Tor.	.10	3.50
☐☐	171	Steve Yzerman, Det.	1.25	50.00
☐☐	172	Nikolai Khabibulin (G), Wpg.	.35	10.00
☐☐	173	Chris Gratton, T.B.	.25	5.00
☐☐	174	Dave Lowry, Fla.	.10	3.50
☐☐	175	Travis Green, NYI.	.10	3.50
☐☐	176	Alexei Kovalev, NYR.	.10	3.50
☐☐	177	Mike Ricci, Col.	.10	3.50
☐☐	178	Brendan Shanahan, Hfd.	.60	30.00
☐☐	179	Corey Hirsch (G), Van.	.10	3.50
☐☐	180	Bill Guerin, N.J.	.25	5.00
☐☐	181	Alexander Mogilny, Van.	.35	10.00
☐☐	182	Steve Duchesne, Ott.	.10	3.50
☐☐	183	Ray Ferraro, L.A.	.10	3.50
☐☐	184	Mike Richter (G), NYR.	.35	10.00
☐☐	185	Yuri Khmylev, Stl.	.10	3.50
☐☐	186	Stéphane Fiset (G), Col.	.25	5.00
☐☐	187	John Vanbiesbrouck (G), Fla.	.60	30.00
☐☐	188	Scott Niedermayer, N.J.	.25	5.00
☐☐	189	Brad May, Buf.	.10	3.50
☐☐	190	Shawn McEachern, Bos.	.10	3.50
☐☐	191	Joe Mullen, Bos.	.10	3.50
☐☐	192	Dominik Hasek, Buf.	.75	35.00
☐☐	193	Steve Thomas, N.J.	.10	3.50
☐☐	194	Russ Courtnall, Van.	.10	3.50
☐☐	195	Joe Nieuwendyk, Dal.	.25	5.00
☐☐	196	Petr Klima, T.B.	.10	3.50
☐☐	197	Brett Hull, Stl.	.50	20.00
☐☐	198	Bernie Nicholls, Chi.	.10	3.50
☐☐	199	Dale Hunter, Wsh.	.10	3.50
☐☐	200	Pat Verkeek, NYR.	.10	3.50
☐☐	201	Phil Housley, N.J.	.10	3.50
☐☐	202	Todd Krygier, Ana.	.10	3.50
☐☐	203	Zdeno Ciger, Edm.	.10	3.50
☐☐	204	Alexandre Daigle, Ott.	.25	5.00
☐☐	205	Cam Neely, Bos.	.25	5.00
☐☐	206	Mike Gartner, Tor.	.25	5.00
☐☐	207	Garth Snow (G), Pha.	.10	3.50
☐☐	208	Pat Falloon, Pha.	.10	3.50
☐☐	209	Kelly Hrudey (G), L.A.	.10	3.50
☐☐	210	Ray Sheppard, Fla.	.10	3.50
☐☐	211	Ted Donato, Bos.	.10	3.50
☐☐	212	Glenn Healy (G), NYR.	.10	3.50
☐☐	213	Radek Dvorak, Fla.	.10	3.50
☐☐	214	Niclas Andersson, NYI.	.10	3.50
☐☐	215	Miroslav Satan, Edm.	.10	3.50
☐☐	216	Roman Vopat, L.A., Err. (Jan Vopat)	.10	3.50
☐☐	217	Bryan McCabe, NYI.	.10	3.50
☐☐	218	Jamie Langenbrunner, Dal.	.10	3.50
☐☐	219	Kyle McLaren, Bos.	.10	3.50
☐☐	220	Stéphane Yelle, Col.	.10	3.50
☐☐	221	Byron Dafoe (G), L.A.	.10	3.50
☐☐	222	Grant Marshall, Dal.	.10	3.50
☐☐	223	Ryan Smyth, Edm.	.25	5.00
☐☐	224	Ville Peltonen, S.J.	.10	3.50
☐☐	225	Deron Quint, Wpg.	.10	3.50
☐☐	226	Brian Holzinger, Buf.	.10	3.50
☐☐	227	José Théodore, Mtl.	.35	5.00
☐☐	228	Ethan Moreau, Chi.	.25	5.00
☐☐	**229**	**Steve Sullivan, N.J., RC**	**.10**	**3.50**
☐☐	230	Kevin Hodson (G), Det.	.25	5.00
☐☐	231	Cory Stillman, Cgy.	.10	3.50
☐☐	232	Ralph Intranuovo, Edm.	.10	3.50

	No.	Player		
□□	233	Vital Yachmenev, L.A.	.10	3.50
□□	234	Marcus Ragnarsson, S.J.	.10	3.50
□□	235	Nolan Baumgartner, Wsh.	.10	3.50
□□	236	Chad Kilger, Wpg.	.10	3.50
□□	237	Niklas Sundstrom, NYR.	.10	3.50
□□	238	CL: 1-120, Paul Coffey, Det.	.25	5.00
□□	239	CL: 121-240, Doug Gilmour, Tor.	.25	5.00
□□	240	CL: Steve Yzerman, Det.	.50	25.00

BETWEEN THE PIPES

These retail pack inserts are serial numbered out of 4,000

Insert Set (10 card): 200.00

	No.	Player	NRMT-MT
□	1	Patrick Roy (G), Col.	65.00
□	2	Martin Brodeur (G), N.J.	30.00
□	3	Jim Carey (G), Wsh.	10.00
□	4	John Vanbiesbrouck (G), Fla.	25.00
□	5	Chris Osgood (G), Det.	15.00
□	6	Ed Belfour (G), Chi.	12.00
□	7	Jocelyn Thibault (G), Mtl.	12.00
□	8	Curtis Joseph (G), Edm.	25.00
□	9	Nikolai Khabibulin (G), Wpg.	12.00
□	10	Félix Potvin (G), Tor.	20.00

DOMINATORS

These hobby pack inserts are serial numbered out of 5,000.

Insert Set (10 cards): 175.00

	No.	Players	NRMT-MT
□	1	Carey/Brodeur/Vanbiesbrouck	15.00
□	2	Khabibulin/Osgood/Thibault	12.00
□	3	Chelios/Coffey/Bourque	12.00
□	4	Lemieux/Jagr/Francis	40.00
□	5	Lindros/Gretzky/Arnott	50.00
□	6	Gilmour/Clark/Turgeon	10.00
□	7	Mogilny/Bure/Linden	15.00
□	8	Kariya/Selänne/Tkachuk	30.00
□	9	Modano/Roenick/Fedorov	15.00
□	10	Dazé/Koivu/Jovanovski	15.00

ELITE SERIES

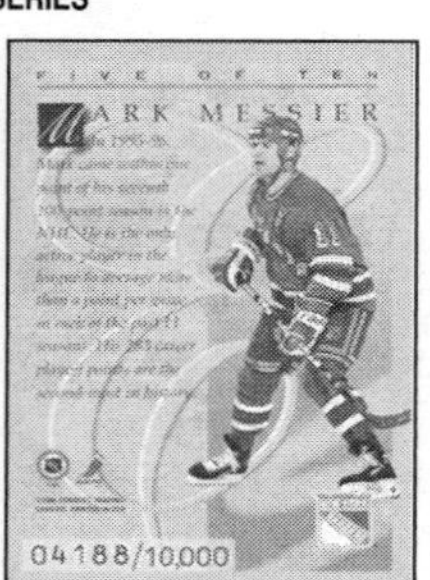

These cards have two versions: a silver card (serial numbered out of 10,000) and a gold card (serial numbered out of 1,500).

Insert Set (10 cards): 125.00 375.00

	No.	Player	Silver	Gold
□□	1	Pavel Bure, Van	12.00	35.00
□□	2	Wayne Gretzky, Stl.	35.00	100.00
□□	3	Doug Weight, Edm.	5.00	15.00
□□	4	Brett Hull, Stl.	8.00	25.00
□□	5	Mark Messier, NYR.	8.00	25.00
□□	6	Brendan Shanahan, Hfd.	10.00	30.00
□□	7	Joe Sakic, Col.	15.00	40.00
□□	8	Sergei Fedorov, Det.	8.00	25.00
□□	9	Eric Lindros, Pha.	20.00	65.00
□□	10	Patrick Roy (G), Col.	28.00	80.00

GO TOP SHELF

These magazine pack inserts are serial numbered out of 2,000

Insert Set (10 cards): 375.00

	No.	Player	NRMT-MT
□	1	Mario Lemieux, Pgh.	80.00
□	2	Teemu Selänne, Ana.	35.00
□	3	Joe Sakic, Col.	40.00
□	4	Alexander Mogilny, Van.	15.00
□	5	Jaromir Jagr, Pgh.	50.00
□	6	Brett Hull, Stl.	25.00
□	7	Mike Modano, Dal.	25.00
□	8	Paul Kariya, Ana.	65.00
□	9	Eric Lindros, Pha.	65.00
□	10	Peter Forsberg, Col.	50.00

HIT LIST

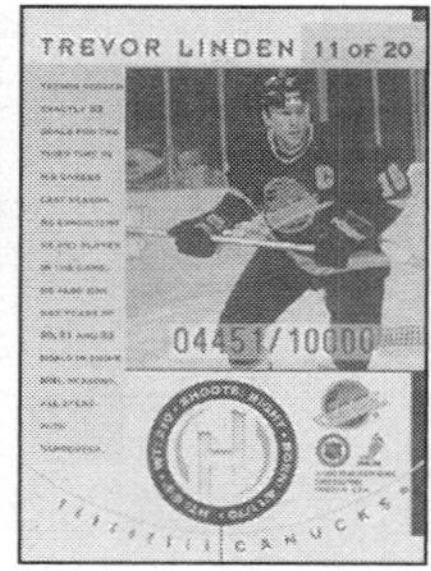

These inserts are serial numbered.

Insert Set (20 cards): 135.00

Promo Card (Eric Lindros, #1): 5.00

	No.	Player	NRMT-MT
□	1	Eric Lindros, Pha.	25.00
□	2	Wendel Clark, Tor.	4.00
□	3	Ed Jovanovski, Fla.	4.00
□	4	Jeremy Roenick, Chi.	6.00
□	5	Doug Weight, Edm.	6.00
□	6	Chris Chelios, Chi.	8.00
□	7	Brendan Shanahan, Hfd.	12.00
□	8	Mark Messier, NYR.	10.00
□	9	Scott Stevens, N.J.	3.00
□	10	Keith Tkachuk, Wpg.	8.00
□	11	Trevor Linden, Van	4.00
□	12	Eric Dazé, Chi.	4.00
□	13	John LeClair, Pha.	10.00
□	14	Peter Forsberg, Col.	20.00
□	15	Doug Gilmour, Tor.	6.00
□	16	Roman Hamrlik, T.B.	4.00
□	17	Owen Nolan, S.J.	4.00
□	18	Claude Lemieux, Col.	3.00
□	19	Saku Koivu, Mtl.	15.00
□	20	Theoren Fleury, Cgy.	6.00

RATED ROOKIES

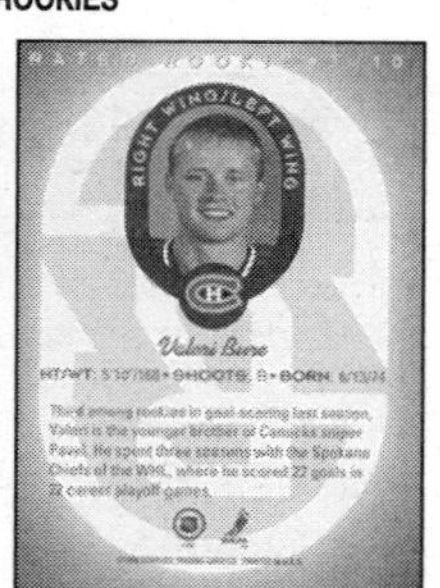

A gold parallel supposedly exists.

Insert Set (10 cards): 40.00

	No.	Player	NRMT-MT
□	1	Eric Dazé, Chi.	4.00
□	2	Petr Sykora, N.J.	3.00
□	3	Valeri Bure, Mtl.	3.00
□	4	Jere Lehtinen, Dal.	4.00
□	5	Jeff O'Neill, Hfd.	4.00
□	6	Saku Koivu, Mtl.	12.00
□	7	Ed Jovanovski, Fla.	4.00
□	8	Eric Fichaud (G), NYI.	4.00
□	9	Todd Bertuzzi, NYI.	4.00
□	10	Daniel Alfredsson, Ott.	4.00

1996 - 97 DONRUSS CANADIAN ICE

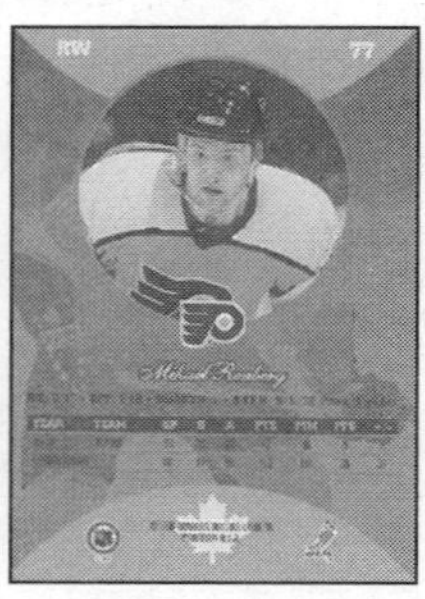

These cards have three versions: the regular card, a Canadian Red parallel (750 of each) and a Canadian Gold parallel (150 of each). Promo cards with clipped corners also exist.

Imprint: © DONRUSS TRADING CARD CO.

Complete Set (150 cards): 1,200.00 35.00

Common Player: .15 3.50 8.00

	No.	Player	Gold	Red	Reg.
□□□	1	Jaromir Jagr, Pgh.	200.00	60.00	2.00
□□□	2	Jocelyn Thibault (G), Mtl.	25.00	8.00	.50
□□□	3	Paul Kariya, Ana.	275.00	85.00	2.50
□□□	4	Derian Hatcher, Dal.	15.00	5.00	.25
□□□	5	Wayne Gretzky, NYR.	450.00	135.00	4.00
□□□	6	Peter Forsberg, Col.	200.00	60.00	2.00
□□□	7	Eric Lindros, Pha.	275.00	85.00	2.50
□□□	8	Adam Oates, Bos.	25.00	8.00	.50
□□□	9	Paul Coffey, Hfd.	15.00	5.00	.25
□□□	10	Chris Osgood (G), Det.	45.00	15.00	.75
□□□	11	Pat LaFontaine, Buf.	15.00	5.00	.25
□□□	12	Mats Sundin, Col.	60.00	20.00	1.00
□□□	13	Rob Niedermayer, Fla.	8.00	3.50	.15
□□□	14	Doug Weight, Edm.	25.00	8.00	.50
□□□	15	Al MacInnis, Stl.	8.00	3.50	.15
□□□	16	Damian Rhodes (G), Ott.	8.00	3.50	.15
□□□	17	Stéphane Fiset (G), L.A.	15.00	5.00	.25
□□□	18	Mike Gartner, Pho.	15.00	5.00	.25
□□□	19	Patrick Roy (G), Col.	300.00	100.00	3.00
□□□	20	Eric Dazé, Chi.	15.00	5.00	.25
□□□	21	Ray Bourque, Bos.	60.00	20.00	1.00
□□□	22	Keith Tkachuk, Pho.	45.00	15.00	.75
□□□	23	Mark Recchi, Mtl.	15.00	5.00	.25
□□□	24	Peter Bondra, Wsh.	45.00	15.00	.75
□□□	25	Mike Modano, Dal.	60.00	20.00	1.00
□□□	26	Mike Richter (G), NYR.	25.00	8.00	.50
□□□	27	Keith Primeau, Hfd.	15.00	5.00	.25
□□□	28	Todd Bertuzzi, NYI.	15.00	8.00	.25
□□□	29	Wendel Clark, Tor.	15.00	5.00	.25
□□□	30	Scott Young, Col.	8.00	3.50	.15
□□□	31	Mario Lemieux, Pgh.	300.00	100.00	3.00
□□□	32	Valeri Kamensky, Col.	15.00	5.00	.25
□□□	33	Kirk McLean (G), Van.	15.00	5.00	.25
□□□	34	Daniel Alfredsson, Ott.	25.00	8.00	.50
□□□	35	Ed Jovanovski, Fla.	15.00	5.00	.25
□□□	36	Kelly Hrudey (G), S.J.	8.00	3.50	.15
□□□	37	Trevor Kidd (G), Cgy.	15.00	5.00	.25
□□□	38	Joé Juneau, Wsh.	8.00	3.50	.15
□□□	39	Steve Yzerman, Det.	200.00	60.00	2.00
□□□	40	Saku Koivu, Mtl.	100.00	35.00	1.50
□□□	41	Alexei Kovalev, NYR.	8.00	3.50	.15
□□□	42	Rob Blake, L.A.	15.00	5.00	.25
□□□	43	Shayne Corson, Stl.	15.00	5.00	.25
□□□	44	Roman Hamrlik, T.B.	15.00	5.00	.25
□□□	45	Stéphane Yelle, Col.	8.00	3.50	.15
□□□	46	Martin Brodeur (G), N.J.	110.00	35.00	1.25
□□□	47	Kirk Muller, Tor.	8.00	3.50	.15
□□□	48	Pat Verbeek, Dal.	8.00	3.50	.15
□□□	49	Jari Kurri, Ana.	15.00	5.00	.25
□□□	50	Michal Pivonka, Wsh.	8.00	3.50	.15
□□□	51	Ron Hextall (G), Pha.	15.00	5.00	.25
□□□	52	Trevor Linden, Van.	15.00	5.00	.25
□□□	53	Vincent Damphousse, Mtl.	25.00	8.00	.50
□□□	54	Owen Nolan, S.J.	15.00	5.00	.25
□□□	55	Sergei Fedorov, Det.	60.00	20.00	1.00
□□□	56	Chris Chelios, Chi.	45.00	15.00	.75
□□□	57	Jeremy Roenick, Pho.	25.00	8.00	.50
□□□	58	Zigmund Palffy, NYI.	45.00	15.00	.75
□□□	59	Pavel Bure, Van.	110.00	35.00	1.50
□□□	60	Dominik Hasek (G), Buf.	110.00	35.00	1.50
□□□	61	Alexei Yashin, Ott.	45.00	15.00	.75

	No.	Player			
☐☐☐	62	Chris Gratton, T.B.	15.00	5.00	.25
☐☐☐	63	Joe Nieuwendyk, Dal.	15.00	5.00	.25
☐☐☐	64	Luc Robitaille, NYR.	15.00	5.00	.25
☐☐☐	65	Brett Hull, Stl.	60.00	20.00	1.00
☐☐☐	66	Sean Burke (G), Hfd.	15.00	5.00	.25
☐☐☐	67	Félix Potvin (G), Tor.	60.00	20.00	1.00
☐☐☐	68	Jason Arnott, Edm.	15.00	5.00	.25
☐☐☐	69	Valeri Bure, Mtl.	8.00	3.50	.15
☐☐☐	70	Tom Barrasso (G), Pgh.	15.00	5.00	.25
☐☐☐	71	Vyacheslav Kozlov, Det.	8.00	3.50	.15
☐☐☐	72	Petr Sykora, N.J.	8.00	3.50	.15
☐☐☐	73	Corey Hirsch (G), Van.	8.00	3.50	.15
☐☐☐	74	Joe Sakic, Col.	165.00	50.00	1.75
☐☐☐	75	Bill Ranford (G), Bos.	15.00	5.00	.25
☐☐☐	76	Yanic Perreault, L.A.	8.00	3.50	.15
☐☐☐	77	Mikael Renberg, Pha.	8.00	3.50	.15
☐☐☐	78	Theoren Fleury, Cgy.	25.00	8.00	.50
☐☐☐	79	Jim Carey (G), Wsh.	8.00	3.50	.15
☐☐☐	80	Vitali Yachmenev, L.A.	8.00	3.50	.15
☐☐☐	81	Martin Rucinsky, Mtl.	8.00	3.50	.15
☐☐☐	82	Jeff O'Neill, Hfd.	15.00	5.00	.25
☐☐☐	83	Marcus Ragnarsson, S.J.	8.00	3.50	.15
☐☐☐	84	John Vanbiesbrouck (G), Fla.	90.00	30.00	1.25
☐☐☐	85	Teemu Selänne, Ana.	110.00	35.00	1.50
☐☐☐	86	Larry Murphy, Tor.	15.00	5.00	.25
☐☐☐	87	Mark Messier, NYR.	60.00	20.00	1.00
☐☐☐	88	Alexei Zhamnov, Chi.	15.00	5.00	.25
☐☐☐	89	Ryan Smith, Edm.	15.00	5.00	.25
☐☐☐	90	Andy Moog (G), Dal.	15.00	5.00	.25
☐☐☐	91	Alexander Mogilny, Van.	25.00	8.00	.35
☐☐☐	92	Kris Draper, Det.	8.00	3.50	.15
☐☐☐	93	Ron Francis, Pgh.	25.00	8.00	.35
☐☐☐	94	Mike Vernon (G), Det.	15.00	5.00	.25
☐☐☐	95	Nikolai Khabibulin (G), Pho.	25.00	8.00	.35
☐☐☐	96	Mariusz Czerkawski, Edm.	8.00	3.50	.15
☐☐☐	97	Mathieu Schneider, Tor.	8.00	3.50	.15
☐☐☐	98	Stéphane Richer, Mtl.	8.00	3.50	.15
☐☐☐	99	Mike Ricci, Col.	8.00	3.50	.15
☐☐☐	100	John LeClair, Pha.	60.00	20.00	.75
☐☐☐	101	Brendan Shanahan, Det.	90.00	30.00	1.25
☐☐☐	102	Daren Puppa (G), T.B.	8.00	3.50	.15
☐☐☐	103	Scott Stevens, N.J.	8.00	3.50	.15
☐☐☐	104	Alexandre Daigle, Ott.	15.00	5.00	.25
☐☐☐	105	Dimitri Khristich, L.A.	8.00	3.50	.15
☐☐☐	106	Bernie Nicholls, S.J.	8.00	3.50	.15
☐☐☐	107	Scott Mellanby, Fla.	8.00	3.50	.15
☐☐☐	108	Brian Leetch, NYR.	25.00	8.00	.50
☐☐☐	109	Grant Fuhr (G), Stl.	15.00	5.00	.25
☐☐☐	110	Pierre Turgeon, Mtl.	15.00	5.00	.25
☐☐☐	111	Jere Lehtinen, Dal	15.00	5.00	.25
☐☐☐	112	Doug Gilmour, Tor.	25.00	8.00	.35
☐☐☐	113	Ed Belfour (G), Chi.	25.00	8.00	.35
☐☐☐	114	Geoff Sanderson, Hfd.	8.00	3.50	.15
☐☐☐	115	Claude Lemieux, Col.	8.00	3.50	.15
☐☐☐	116	Curtis Joseph (G), Edm.	90.00	30.00	1.25
☐☐☐	117	Igor Larionov, Det.	12.00	5.00	.25
☐☐☐	118	Jamie Pushor, Det.	8.00	3.50	.15
☐☐☐	**119**	**Sergei Berezin, Tor., RC**	**25.00**	**10.00**	**1.00**
☐☐☐	120	Eric Fichaud (G), NYI.	15.00	5.00	.25
☐☐☐	121	Wade Redden, Ott.	10.00	4.00	.35
☐☐☐	122	Hnat Domenichelli, Hfd.	10.00	4.00	.35
☐☐☐	**123**	**Rem Murray, Edm., RC**	**10.00**	**4.00**	**.50**
☐☐☐	124	Jarome Iginla, Cgy.	50.00	10.00	.75
☐☐☐	**125**	**Richard Zednik, Wsh., RC**	**20.00**	**8.00**	**.75**
☐☐☐	**126**	**Daniel Goneau, NYR., RC**	**8.00**	**3.50**	**.15**
☐☐☐	127	Ethan Moreau, Chi.	15.00	5.00	.25
☐☐☐	128	Janne Niinimaa, Pha.	15.00	5.00	.50
☐☐☐	**129**	**Tomas Holmstrom, Det., RC**	**20.00**	**8.00**	**.75**
☐☐☐	**130**	**Fredrik Modin, Tor., RC**	**25.00**	**10.00**	**1.00**
☐☐☐	131	Bryan Berard, NYI.	25.00	8.00	.50
☐☐☐	132	Jim Campbell, Stl	15.00	5.00	.25
☐☐☐	133	Chris O'Sullivan, Cgy.	8.00	3.50	.15
☐☐☐	**134**	**Andreas Dackell, Ott., RC**	**8.00**	**3.50**	**.15**
☐☐☐	135	Daymond Langkow, T.B.	8.00	3.50	.15
☐☐☐	136	Kevin Hodson (G),Det.	8.00	3.50	.15
☐☐☐	137	Jamie Langenbrunner, Dal.	15.00	5.00	.25
☐☐☐	138	Mattias Timander, Bos.	8.00	3.50	.15
☐☐☐	139	Tuomas Grönman, Chi.	8.00	3.50	.15
☐☐☐	140	Jonas Hoglund, Cgy.	8.00	3.50	.15
☐☐☐	**141**	**Mike Grier, Edm., RC**	**25.00**	**10.00**	**1.00**
☐☐☐	**142**	**Terry Ryan, Mtl., RC**	**10.00**	**4.00**	**.50**
☐☐☐	143	Darcy Tucker, Mtl.	8.00	3.50	.15
☐☐☐	144	Brandon Convery, Tor.	8.00	3.50	.15
☐☐☐	145	Anders Eriksson, Det.	8.00	3.50	.15
☐☐☐	146	Christian Dubé, NYR.	10.00	4.00	.50
☐☐☐	**147**	**Danius Zubrus, Pha., RC**	**75.00**	**30.00**	**3.00**
☐☐☐	148	CL: Grant Fuhr, Stl.	12.00	5.00	.25
☐☐☐	149	CL: Paul Coffey, Hfd.	12.00	5.00	.25
☐☐☐	150	CL: Ray Bourque, Bos.	30.00	10.00	.35

LES GARDIENS

These cards have two versions; a promo card (xxxx of 1,500) and the insert (serial numbered out of 1,500).

Insert Set (10 cards): **25.00** **275.00**

	No.	Player	Promo	Insert
☐☐	1	Patrick Roy (G), Col.	10.00	100.00
☐☐	2	Jocelyn Thibault (G), Mtl.	2.00	20.00
☐☐	3	Félix Potvin (G), Tor.	3.50	35.00
☐☐	4	Martin Brodeur (G), N.J.	5.00	50.00
☐☐	5	Stéphane Fiset (G), L.A.	2.00	20.00
☐☐	6	Eric Fichaud (G), NYI.	2.00	20.00
☐☐	7	Dominic Roussel (G), Pha.	2.00	15.00
☐☐	8	Manny Fernandez (G), Dal.	2.00	15.00
☐☐	9	Martin Biron (G), Buf.	2.00	20.00
☐☐	10	José Théodore (G), Mtl.	2.00	20.00

MARIO LEMIEUX SCRAPBOOK

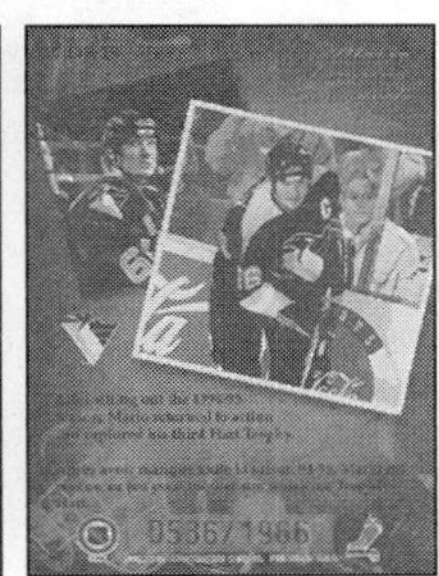

These inserts are serial numbered out of 1,966. One of 500 framed sets was also available through the mail.

Insert Set (25 cards): **250.00**

	No.	Player	NRMT-MT
☐	1	Mario Lemieux, Pgh.	12.00
☐	2	Mario Lemieux, Pgh.	12.00
☐	3	Mario Lemieux, Pgh.	12.00
☐	4	Mario Lemieux, Pgh.	12.00
☐	5	Mario Lemieux, Pgh.	12.00
☐	6	Mario Lemieux, Pgh.	12.00
☐	7	Mario Lemieux, Pgh.	12.00
☐	8	Mario Lemieux, Pgh.	12.00
☐	9	Mario Lemieux, Pgh.	12.00
☐	10	Mario Lemieux, Pgh.	12.00
☐	11	Mario Lemieux, Pgh.	12.00
☐	12	Mario Lemieux, Pgh.	12.00
☐	13	Mario Lemieux, Pgh.	12.00
☐	14	Mario Lemieux, Pgh.	12.00
☐	15	Mario Lemieux, Pgh.	12.00
☐	16	Mario Lemieux, Pgh.	12.00
☐	17	Mario Lemieux, Pgh.	12.00
☐	18	Mario Lemieux, Pgh.	12.00
☐	19	MarioLemieux, Pgh.	12.00
☐	20	Mario Lemieux, Pgh.	12.00
☐	21	Mario Lemieux, Pgh.	12.00
☐	22	Mario Lemieux, Pgh.	12.00
☐	23	Mario Lemieux, Pgh.	12.00
☐	24	Mario Lemieux, Pgh.	12.00
☐	25	Mario Lemieux, Pgh.	12.00
☐		Mario Lemieux Autograph	300.00

O CANADA

These inserts are serial numbered out of 2,000

Insert Set (16 cards): **450.00**

	No.	Player	NRMT-MT
☐	1	Joe Sakic, Col.	40.00
☐	2	Paul Kariya, Ana.	65.00
☐	3	Mark Messier, NYR.	25.00
☐	4	Jarome Iginla, Cgy.	15.00
☐	5	Theoren Fleury, Cgy.	15.00
☐	6	Ed Belfour (G), Chi.	15.00
☐	7	Wayne Gretzky, NYR.	100.00
☐	8	Chris Gratton, T.B.	10.00
☐	9	Doug Gilmour, Tor.	15.00
☐	10	Kirk Muller, Tor.	10.00
☐	11	Eric Lindros, Pha.	65.00
☐	12	Brendan Shanahan, Det.	30.00
☐	13	Mario Lemieux, Pgh.	80.00
☐	14	Eric Dazé, Chi.	10.00
☐	15	Geoff Sanderson, Hfd.	10.00
☐	16	Terry Ryan, Mtl.	10.00

1996 - 97 DONRUSS ELITE

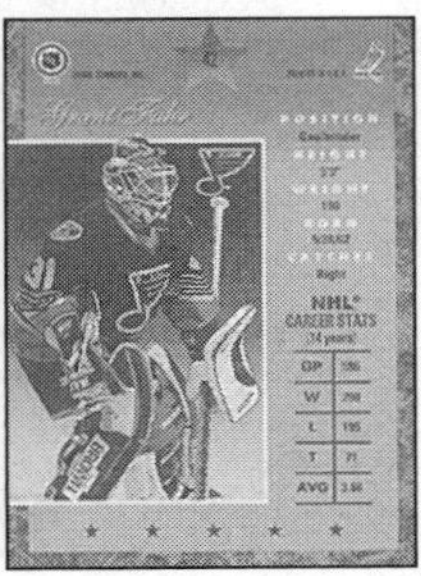

These cards have two versions: the regular card and Die-Cut parallel.

Imprint: © 1997 DONRUSS TRADING CARD CO.

Complete Set (150 cards): **45.00** **1,500.00**

Common Player: **.20** **5.00**

	No.	Player	Reg.	Die-Cut
☐☐	1	Paul Kariya, Ana.	2.50	120.00
☐☐	2	Ron Hextall (G), Pha.	.35	8.00
☐☐	3	Andy Moog (G), Dal.	.35	8.00
☐☐	4	Brett Hull, Stl.	1.00	40.00
☐☐	5	Félix Potvin (G), Tor.	1.00	40.00
☐☐	6	Jocelyn Thibault (G), Mtl.	.50	15.00
☐☐	7	Eric Lindros, Pha.	2.50	120.00
☐☐	8	Jaromir Jagr, Pgh.	2.00	100.00
☐☐	9	Sergei Fedorov, Det.	1.00	40.00
☐☐	10	Wayne Gretzky, NYR.	4.00	200.00
☐☐	11	Peter Bondra, Wsh.	.75	25.00
☐☐	12	Peter Forsberg, Col.	2.00	100.00
☐☐	13	Stéphane Fiset (G), L.A.	.35	8.00
☐☐	14	Owen Nolan, S.J.	.35	8.00
☐☐	15	Rob Niedermayer, Fla.	.20	5.00
☐☐	16	Martin Brodeur (G), N.J.	1.50	60.00
☐☐	17	Ray Bourque, Bos.	1.00	40.00
☐☐	18	Todd Bertuzzi, NYI.	.35	8.00
☐☐	19	Jim Carey (G), Wsh.	.25	5.00
☐☐	20	Chris Chelios, Chi.	.75	25.00
☐☐	21	Chris Osgood (G), Det.	.75	25.00
☐☐	22	Mark Messier, NYR.	1.00	40.00
☐☐	23	Roman Hamrlik, T.B.	.35	8.00
☐☐	24	Kevin Hatcher, Pgh.	.20	5.00
☐☐	25	Doug Weight, Edm.	.50	15.00
☐☐	26	Mark Recchi, Mtl.	.35	8.00
☐☐	27	Jeremy Roenick, Pho.	.50	15.00
☐☐	28	Derian Hatcher, Dal.	.20	5.00
☐☐	29	Grant Fuhr (G), Stl.	.35	8.00
☐☐	30	Scott Stevens, N.J.	.20	5.00
☐☐	31	Adam Oates, Bos.	.50	15.00

	No.	Player		
☐ ☐	32	Scott Mellanby, Fla.	.20	5.00
☐ ☐	33	Mikael Renberg, Pha.	.20	5.00
☐ ☐	34	Corey Hirsch (G), Van.	.20	5.00
☐ ☐	35	Mikael Pivonka, Wsh.	.20	5.00
☐ ☐	36	Stéphane Richer, Mtl.	.20	5.00
☐ ☐	37	Dominik Hasek (G), Buf.	1.50	60.00
☐ ☐	38	Steve Yzerman, Det.	2.00	100.00
☐ ☐	39	Jeff O'Neill, Hfd.	.35	8.00
☐ ☐	40	Ron Francis, Pgh.	.50	15.00
☐ ☐	41	Alexei Yashin, Ott.	.75	25.00
☐ ☐	42	Pat Verbeek, Dal.	.20	5.00
☐ ☐	43	Geoff Courtnall, Stl.	.20	5.00
☐ ☐	44	Doug Gilmour, Tor.	.50	15.00
☐ ☐	45	Trevor Kidd (G), Cgy.	.35	8.00
☐ ☐	46	Jason Arnott, Edm.	.35	8.00
☐ ☐	47	Niklas Sundstrom, NYR.	.20	5.00
☐ ☐	48	Rob Blake, L.A.	.35	8.00
☐ ☐	49	Nikolai Khabibulin (G), Pho.	.50	15.00
☐ ☐	50	Igor Larionov, Det.	.35	8.00
☐ ☐	51	Sean Burke (G), Hfd.	.35	8.00
☐ ☐	52	Zigmund Palffy, NYI.	.75	25.00
☐ ☐	53	Jeff Friesen, S.J.	.35	8.00
☐ ☐	54	Theoren Fleury, Cgy.	.50	15.00
☐ ☐	55	Mats Sundin, Tor.	1.00	40.00
☐ ☐	56	Alexander Mogilny, Van.	.50	15.00
☐ ☐	57	John LeClair, Pha.	1.00	40.00
☐ ☐	58	Shayne Corson, Mtl.	.35	8.00
☐ ☐	59	Teemu Selänne, Ana.	1.50	60.00
☐ ☐	60	Kelly Hrudey (G), S.J.	.20	5.00
☐ ☐	61	Keith Tkachuk, Pho.	.75	25.00
☐ ☐	62	Joe Nieuwendyk, Dal.	.35	8.00
☐ ☐	63	Tom Barrasso (G), Pgh.	.35	8.00
☐ ☐	64	Aaron Gavey, Cgy.	.20	5.00
☐ ☐	65	Alexei Zhamnov, Chi.	.35	8.00
☐ ☐	66	Patrick Roy (G), Col.	3.00	150.00
☐ ☐	67	Al MacInnis, Stl.	.20	5.00
☐ ☐	68	Trevor Linden,Van.	.35	8.00
☐ ☐	69	Bill Guerin, N.J.	.35	8.00
☐ ☐	70	Dimitri Khristich, L.A.	.20	5.00
☐ ☐	71	Eric Dazé, Chi.	.35	8.00
☐ ☐	72	Paul Coffey, Pha.	.35	8.00
☐ ☐	73	Keith Primeau, Hfd.	.35	8.00
☐ ☐	74	John Vanbiesbrouck (G), Fla.	1.25	50.00
☐ ☐	75	Bernie Nicholls, S.J.	.20	5.00
☐ ☐	76	Yanic Perreault, L.A.	.20	5.00
☐ ☐	77	Jere Lehtinen, Dal.	.35	8.00
☐ ☐	78	Luc Robitaille, NYR.	.35	8.00
☐ ☐	79	Todd Gill, S.J.	.20	5.00
☐ ☐	80	Saku Koivu, Mtl.	1.50	60.00
☐ ☐	81	Vyacheslav Kozlov, Det.	.20	5.00
☐ ☐	82	Ed Jovanovski, Fla.	.35	8.00
☐ ☐	83	Brendan Witt, Wsh.	.20	5.00
☐ ☐	84	Alexandre Daigle, Ott.	.35	8.00
☐ ☐	85	Jari Kurri, Ana.	.35	8.00
☐ ☐	86	Mike Vernon (G), Cgy.	.35	8.00
☐ ☐	87	Jeff Beukeboom, NYR.	.20	5.00
☐ ☐	88	Mathieu Schneider, Tor.	.20	5.00
☐ ☐	89	Niclas Andersson, NYI.	.20	5.00
☐ ☐	90	Joé Juneau, Wsh.	.20	5.00
☐ ☐	91	Ed Belfour (G), S.J.	.50	15.00
☐ ☐	92	Curtis Joseph (G), Edm.	1.25	50.00
☐ ☐	93	Rod Brind'Amour, Pha.	.35	8.00
☐ ☐	94	Vitali Yachmenev, L.A.	.20	5.00
☐ ☐	95	Alexander Selivanov, T.B.	.20	5.00
☐ ☐	96	Mike Richter (G), NYR.	.50	15.00
☐ ☐	97	Bill Ranford (G), Bos.	.35	8.00
☐ ☐	98	Wendel Clark,Tor.	.35	8.00
☐ ☐	99	Viacheslav Fetisov, Det.	.35	8.00
☐ ☐	100	Daniel Alfredsson, Ott.	.35	8.00
☐ ☐	101	Pat LaFontaine, Buf.	.35	8.00
☐ ☐	102	Joe Murphy, Stl.	.20	5.00
☐ ☐	103	Pavel Bure, Van.	1.50	60.00
☐ ☐	104	Craig Janney, S.J.	.20	5.00
☐ ☐	105	Radek Dvorak, Fla.	.20	5.00
☐ ☐	106	Cory Stillman, Cgy.	.20	5.00
☐ ☐	107	Adam Graves, NYR.	.20	5.00
☐ ☐	108	Aki Berg, L.A.	.20	5.00
☐ ☐	109	Mario Lemieux, Pgh.	3.00	150.00
☐ ☐	110	Claude Lemieux, Col.	.20	5.00
☐ ☐	111	Sergei Zubov, Dal.	.20	5.00
☐ ☐	112	Pierre Turgeon, Stl.	.35	8.00
☐ ☐	113	Damian Rhodes (G), Ott.	.20	5.00
☐ ☐	114	Daren Puppa, T.B.	.20	5.00
☐ ☐	115	Alexei Zhitnik, Buf.	.20	5.00
☐ ☐	116	Mike Modano, Dal.	1.00	40.00
☐ ☐	117	Kenny Jonsson, NYI.	.20	5.00
☐ ☐	118	Valeri Kamensky, Col.	.35	8.00
☐ ☐	119	Valeri Bure, Mtl.	.20	5.00
☐ ☐	120	Joe Sakic, Col.	1.75	80.00
☐ ☐	121	Kirk McLean (G), Van.	.35	8.00
☐ ☐	122	Petr Sykora, N.J.	.20	5.00
☐ ☐	123	Mike Gartner, Pho.	.35	8.00
☐ ☐	124	Ryan Smyth, Edm.	.35	8.00
☐ ☐	125	Brian Leetch, NYR.	.50	15.00
☐ ☐	126	Brendan Shanahan, Det.	1.25	50.00
☐ ☐	127	Geoff Sanderson, Hfd.	.20	5.00
☐ ☐	128	Corey Schwab (G),T.B.	.20	5.00
☐ ☐	129	Anders Eriksson, Det.	.20	5.00
☐ ☐	**130**	**Harry York, Stl., RC**	**.35**	**8.00**
☐ ☐	131	Jarome Iginla, Cgy.	.75	15.00
☐ ☐	132	Eric Fichaud (G), NYI.	.35	8.00
☐ ☐	**133**	**Patrick Lalime (G), Pgh., RC**	**.20**	**5.00**
☐ ☐	134	Daymond Langkow, T.B.	.20	5.00
☐ ☐	**135**	**Mattias Timander, Bos., RC**	**.20**	**5.00**
☐ ☐	136	Ethan Moreau, Chi.	.35	8.00
☐ ☐	137	Christian Dubé, NYR.	.50	8.00
☐ ☐	**138**	**Sergei Berezin,Tor., RC**	**1.00**	**15.00**
☐ ☐	139	José Théodore (G), Mtl.	.75	15.00
☐ ☐	140	Wade Redden, Ott.	.35	8.00
☐ ☐	**141**	**Danius Zubrus, Pha., RC**	**3.00**	**45.00**
☐ ☐	142	Jim Campbell, Stl.	.35	8.00
☐ ☐	**143**	**Daniel Goneau, NYR., RC**	**.20**	**5.00**
☐ ☐	144	Jamie Langenbrunner, Dal.	.35	8.00
☐ ☐	**145**	**Rem Murray, Edm., RC**	**.50**	**8.00**
☐ ☐	146	Jonas Hoglund, Cgy.	.20	5.00
☐ ☐	147	Bryan Berard, NYI.	.50	15.00
☐ ☐	148	CL: Chris Osgood (G), Det.	.35	8.00
☐ ☐	149	CL: Eric Lindros, Pha.	1.50	60.00
☐ ☐	150	CL: Jason Arnott, Edm.	.35	8.00

	No.	**Hart To Hart Autograph**	**NRMT-MT**
☐	1	Eric Lindros, Pha./ Mario Lemieux, Pgh. (#/500)	550.00

LEMIEUX SERIES

These inserts are serial numbered out of 1,996.

Insert Set (6 cards): 125.00

	No.	**Player**	**NRMT-MT**
☐	1	Mario Lemieux	25.00
☐	2	Mario Lemieux	25.00
☐	3	Mario Lemieux	25.00
☐	4	Mario Lemieux	25.00
☐	5	Mario Lemieux	25.00
☐	6	Mario Lemieux	25.00
☐		Mario Lemieux Autograph	275.00

LINDROS SERIES

These inserts are serial numbered out of 1,995.

Insert Set (6 cards): 110.00

	No.	**Player**	**NRMT-MT**
☐	1	Eric Lindros	20.00
☐	2	Eric Lindros	20.00
☐	3	Eric Lindros	20.00
☐	4	Eric Lindros	20.00
☐	5	Eric Lindros	20.00
☐	6	Eric Lindros	20.00
☐		Eric Lindros Autograph	250.00

ASPIRATIONS

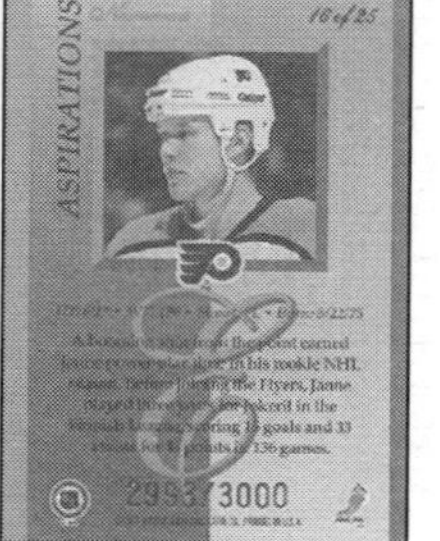

These inserts are serial numbered out of 3,000

Insert Set (25 cards): 150.00

	No.	**Player**	**NRMT-MT**
☐	1	Eric Dazé, Chi.	8.00
☐	2	Daniel Alfredsson, Ott.	8.00
☐	3	Petr Sykora, N.J.	5.00
☐	4	Todd Bertuzzi, NYI.	8.00
☐	5	Saku Koivu, Mtl.	35.00
☐	6	Ed Jovanovski, Fla.	8.00
☐	7	Jim Campbell, Stl.	8.00
☐	8	Valeri Bure, Mtl.	5.00
☐	9	Jeff O'Neill, Hfd.	8.00
☐	10	Jere Lehtinen, Dal.	8.00
☐	11	Terry Ryan, Mtl.	8.00
☐	12	Jonas Hoglund, Cgy.	5.00
☐	13	Daymond Langkow, T.B.	5.00
☐	14	Eric Fichaud (G), NYI.	8.00
☐	15	Danius Zubrus, Pha.	30.00
☐	16	Janne Niinimaa, Pha.	8.00
☐	17	Sergei Berezin, Tor.	8.00
☐	18	Daniel Goneau, NYR.	5.00
☐	19	Jarome Iginla, Pha.	15.00
☐	20	Ethan Moreau, Pha.	8.00
☐	21	Jamie Langenbrunner, Dal.	8.00
☐	22	Rem Murray, Edm.	5.00
☐	23	Bryan Berard, NYI.	15.00
☐	24	Wade Redden, Ott.	5.00
☐	25	Christian Dubé, NYR.	5.00

PAINTED WARRIORS

These cards have two versions: a promo card (xxxx / 2,500) and the insert set (serial numbered out of 2,500).

Insert Set (10 cards): 30.00 250.00

	No.	**Player**	**Promo**	**Insert**
☐ ☐	1	Patrick Roy (G), Col.	10.00	90.00
☐ ☐	2	Mike Richter (G), NYR.	2.00	20.00
☐ ☐	3	Jim Carey (G), Wsh.	1.00	10.00
☐ ☐	4	John Vanbiesbrouck (G), Fla.	4.00	35.00
☐ ☐	5	Jocelyn Thibault (G), Mtl.	2.00	20.00
☐ ☐	6	Félix Potvin (G), Tor.	3.50	30.00
☐ ☐	7	Ed Belfour (G), Chi.	2.00	20.00
☐ ☐	8	Martin Brodeur (G), N.J.	5.00	40.00
☐ ☐	9	Nikolai Khabibulin (G), Pho.	2.00	20.00
☐ ☐	10	Stéphane Fiset (G), L.A.	1.50	15.00

STATUS

These inserts are serial numbered out of 750.

Insert Set (12 cards): 650.00

	No.	**Player**	**NRMT-MT**
☐	1	Pavel Bure, Van.	70.00
☐	2	Keith Tkachuk, Pho.	40.00
☐	3	Sergei Fedorov, Det.	50.00
☐	4	Doug Weight, Edm.	30.00
☐	5	Paul Kariya, Ana.	125.00
☐	6	Owen Nolan, S.J.	20.00
☐	7	Peter Forsberg, Col.	100.00
☐	8	Eric Lindros, Pha.	125.00
☐	9	Alexander Mogilny, Van.	30.00
☐	10	Teemu Selänne, Ana.	70.00
☐	11	Joe Sakic, Col.	80.00
☐	12	Jeremy Roenick, Pho.	30.00

PERSPECTIVES

These inserts are serial numbered out of 500.

Insert Set (12 cards):		**925.00**
No.	**Player**	**NRMT-MT**
☐ 1	Wayne Gretzky, NYR.	250.00
☐ 2	Mark Messier, NYR.	60.00
☐ 3	Steve Yzerman, Det.	125.00
☐ 4	Mario Lemieux, Pgh.	200.00
☐ 5	Paul Coffey, Pha.	30.00
☐ 6	Doug Gilmour, Tor.	35.00
☐ 7	Brendan Shanahan, Det.	75.00
☐ 8	Jaromir Jagr, Pgh.	125.00
☐ 9	Brett Hull, Stl.	60.00
☐ 10	Pat LaFontaine, Buf.	30.00
☐ 11	Chris Chelios,Chi.	50.00
☐ 12	Grant Fuhr, Stl.	30.00

1996 - 97 DURACELL POWER CHECK - PINNACLE

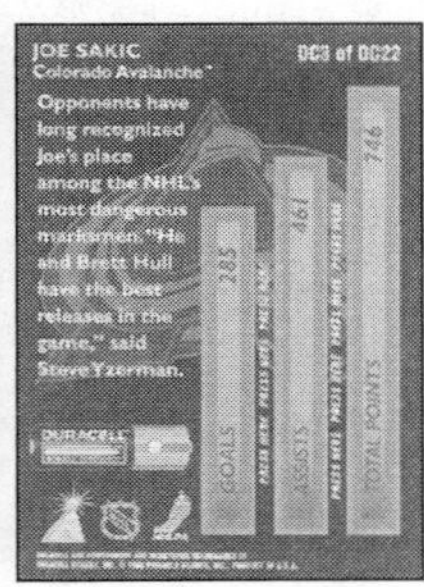

The statistics on the back appear as black bars revealing the stats when heated lightly.

Imprint: © 1996 PINNACLE BRANDS, INC.

Pinnacle All-Cherry Team Set (22 cards):		**25.00**
Pinnacle L'Équipe de Béliveau Set (22 cards):		**25.00**
No.	**All-Cherry Team**	**NRMT-MT**
☐ DC1	Paul Coffey, Det.	.50
☐ DC2	Lyle Odelein, Mtl.	.50
☐ DC3	Joe Sakic, Col.	2.00
☐ DC4	Curtis Joseph, Edm	1.50
☐ DC5	Brett Hull, Stl.	1.25
☐ DC6	Eric Lindros, Pha.	3.50
☐ DC7	Doug Gilmour, Tor.	.75
☐ DC8	Chris Chelios, Chi.	1.00
☐ DC9	Marty McSorley, NYR.	.50
☐ DC10	Kirk Muller, Tor.	.50
☐ DC11	Trevor Linden, Van.	.50
☐ DC12	Brendan Shanahan, Hfd.	1.50
☐ DC13	Tie Domi, Tor.	.50
☐ DC14	Rick Tocchet, Bos.	.50
☐ DC15	Steve Yzerman, Det.	2.50
☐ DC16	Scott Stevens, N.J.	.50
☐ DC17	Patrick Roy, Col.	4.00
☐ DC18	Keith Tkachuk, Wpg.	1.00
☐ DC19	Owen Nolan, S.J.	.50
☐ DC20	Dale Hunter, Wsh.	.50
☐ DC21	Don Cherry, Coach	1.50
☐ DC22	Don Cherry, HNIC (w/ Blue)	1.50
No.	**L'Équipe de Béliveau**	**NRMT-MT**
☐ JB1	Paul Coffey, Det.	.75
☐ JB2	Lyle Odelein, Mtl.	.50
☐ JB3	Joe Sakic, Col.	2.50
☐ JB4	Eric Dazé, Chi.	.75
☐ JB5	Brett Hull, Stl.	1.50
☐ JB6	Martin Brodeur, N.J.	2.00
☐ JB7	Doug Gilmour, Tor.	1.00
☐ JB8	Peter Forsberg, Col.	3.00
☐ JB9	Mike Gartner, Tor.	1.75
☐ JB10	Saku Koivu, Mt.	2.00
☐ JB11	Trevor Linden, Van.	.75
☐ JB12	Félix Potvin, Tor.	1.500
☐ JB13	Mats Sundin, Tor.	1.50
☐ JB14	Pierre Turgeon, Mtl.	.75
☐ JB15	Vincent Damphousse, Mtl.	1.00
☐ JB16	Scott Stevens, N.J.	.50
☐ JB17	Patrick Roy, Col.	4.50
☐ JB18	Keith Tkachuk, Wpg.	1.25
☐ JB19	Ray Bourgue, Bos.	1.50
☐ JB20	Paul Kariya, Ana.	4.00
☐ JB21	Jean Béliveau, Mtl.	1.50
☐ JB22	Jean Béliveau, Mtl.	1.50

1996 - 97 FLAIR

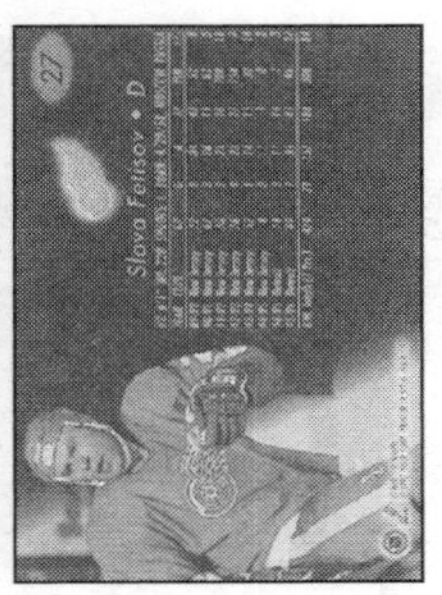

These cards have two versions: the regular card and a Blue Ice parallel (serial numbered out of 250). Blue Ice Cards have the prefix "B" on the card number.

Imprint: © 1997 FLEER CORP.

Complete Set (125 cards):		**150.00**	**3,800.00**
Common Player:		**.35**	**10.00**
Promo Card (Joe Sakic, no #):		**4.00**	
No.	**Player**	**Reg.**	**Blue Ice**
☐☐ 1	Guy Hebert, Ana.	.50	10.00
☐☐ 2	Paul Kariya, Ana.	4.00	225.00
☐☐ 3	Teemu Selänne, Ana.	2.00	100.00
☐☐ 4	Ray Bourque, Bos.	1.50	75.00
☐☐ 5	Adam Oates, Bos.	1.00	25.00
☐☐ 6	Bill Ranford (G), Bos.	.50	10.00
☐☐ 7	Jozef Stumpel, Bos.	.50	10.00
☐☐ 8	Dominik Hasek (G), Buf.	2.00	100.00
☐☐ 9	Pat LaFontaine, Buf.	.50	10.00
☐☐ 10	Alexei Zhitnik, Buf.	.35	6.00
☐☐ 11	Theoren Fleury, Cgy.	1.00	25.00
☐☐ 12	Dave Gagner, Cgy.	.35	6.00
☐☐ 13	Trevor Kidd (G), Cgy.	.50	10.00
☐☐ 14	Tony Amonte, Chi.	.50	10.00
☐☐ 15	Chris Chelios, Chi.	1.25	40.00
☐☐ 16	Eric Dazé, Chi.	.50	10.00
☐☐ 17	Alexei Zhamnov, Chi.	.50	10.00
☐☐ 18	Peter Forsberg, Col.	3.00	150.00
☐☐ 19	Sandis Ozolinsh, Col.	.50	10.00
☐☐ 20	Patrick Roy (G), Col.	5.00	275.00
☐☐ 21	Joe Sakic, Col.	2.50	125.00
☐☐ 22	Derian Hatcher, Dal.	.50	10.00
☐☐ 23	Mike Modano, Dal.	1.50	75.00
☐☐ 24	Andy Moog (G), Dal.	.50	10.00
☐☐ 25	Pat Verbeek, Dal.	.35	6.00
☐☐ 26	Sergei Fedorov, Det.	1.50	75.00
☐☐ 27	Viacheslav Fetisov Det.	.50	10.00
☐☐ 28	Nicklas Lidström, Det.	.50	10.00
☐☐ 29	Chris Osgood (G), Det.	1.25	40.00
☐☐ 30	Brendan Shanahan, Det.	1.75	85.00
☐☐ 31	Steve Yzerman, Det.	3.00	150.00
☐☐ 32	Jason Arnott, Edm.	.50	10.00
☐☐ 33	Curtis Joseph (G), Edm.	1.75	85.00
☐☐ 34	Boris Mironov, Edm.	.35	6.00
☐☐ 35	Ryan Smyth, Edm.	.50	10.00
☐☐ 36	Doug Weight, Edm.	1.00	25.00
☐☐ 37	Ed Jovanovski, Fla.	.50	10.00
☐☐ 38	Ray Sheppard, Fla.	.35	6.00
☐☐ 39	Robert Svehla, Fla.	.35	6.00
☐☐ 40	John Vanbiesbrouck (G), Fla.	1.75	85.00
☐☐ 41	Andrew Cassels, Hfd.	.35	6.00
☐☐ 42	Jason Muzzatti (G), Hfd.	.35	6.00
☐☐ 43	Keith Primeau, Hfd.	.50	10.00
☐☐ 44	Geoff Sanderson, Hfd.	.35	6.00
☐☐ 45	Rob Blake, L.A.	.50	10.00
☐☐ 46	Dimitri Khristich, L.A.	.35	6.00
☐☐ 47	Vincent Damphousse, Mtl.	1.00	25.00
☐☐ 48	Saku Koivu, Mtl.	2.00	100.00
☐☐ 49	Mark Recchi, Mtl.	.50	10.00
☐☐ 50	Martin Rucinsky, Mtl.	.35	6.00
☐☐ 51	Jocelyn Thibault (G), Mtl.	1.00	25.00
☐☐ 52	Martin Brodeur (G), N.J.	2.00	100.00
☐☐ 53	Bill Guerin, N.J.	.50	10.00
☐☐ 54	Scott Stevens, N.J.	.35	6.00
☐☐ 55	Scott Lachance, NYI.	.35	6.00
☐☐ 56	Zigmund Palffy, NYI.	1.25	40.00
☐☐ 57	Tommy Salo (G), NYI.	.35	6.00
☐☐ 58	Brian Smolinski, NYI.	.35	6.00
☐☐ 59	Wayne Gretzky, NYR.	6.00	450.00
☐☐ 60	Brian Leetch, NYR.	1.00	25.00
☐☐ 61	Mark Messier, NYR.	1.50	75.00
☐☐ 62	Mike Richter (G), NYR.	1.00	25.00
☐☐ 63	Daniel Alfredsson, Ott.	.50	10.00
☐☐ 64	Damian Rhodes (G), Ott.	.35	6.00
☐☐ 65	Alexei Yashin, Ott.	1.25	40.00
☐☐ 66	Paul Coffey, Pha.	.50	10.00
☐☐ 67	Dale Hawerchuk, Pha.	.50	10.00
☐☐ 68	Ron Hextall (G), Pha.	.50	10.00
☐☐ 69	John LeClair, Pha.	1.50	75.00
☐☐ 70	Eric Lindros, Pha.	4.00	225.00
☐☐ 71	Nikolai Khabibulin (G), Pho.	1.00	25.00
☐☐ 72	Jeremy Roenick, Pho.	1.00	25.00
☐☐ 73	Keith Tkachuk, Pho.	1.25	40.00
☐☐ 74	Oleg Tverdovsky, Pho.	.35	6.00
☐☐ 75	Ron Francis, Pgh.	1.00	25.00
☐☐ 76	Kevin Hatcher, Pgh.	.35	6.00
☐☐ 77	Jaromir Jagr, Pgh.	3.00	150.00
☐☐ 78	Mario Lemieux, Pgh.	5.00	275.00
☐☐ 79	Peter Nedved, Pgh.	.35	6.00
☐☐ 80	Grant Fuhr (G), Stl.	.50	10.00
☐☐ 81	Brett Hull, Stl.	1.50	75.00
☐☐ 82	Al MacInnis, Stl.	.35	6.00
☐☐ 83	Ed Belfour (G), S.J.	1.00	25.00
☐☐ 84	Tony Granato, S.J.	.35	6.00
☐☐ 85	Owen Nolan, S.J.	.50	10.00
☐☐ 86	Dino Ciccarelli, T.B.	.50	10.00
☐☐ 87	John Cullen, T.B.	.35	6.00
☐☐ 88	Roman Hamrlik, T.B.	.50	10.00
☐☐ 89	Wendel Clark, Tor.	.50	10.00
☐☐ 90	Doug Gilmour, Tor.	1.00	25.00
☐☐ 91	Félix Potvin (G), Tor.	1.50	75.00
☐☐ 92	Mats Sundin, Tor.	1.50	75.00
☐☐ 93	Pavel Bure, Van.	2.00	100.00
☐☐ 94	Corey Hirsch (G), Van.	.35	6.00
☐☐ 95	Trevor Linden, Van.	.50	10.00
☐☐ 96	Alexander Mogilny, Van.	1.00	25.00
☐☐ 97	Peter Bondra, Wsh.	1.25	40.00
☐☐ 98	Jim Carey (G), Wsh.	.35	6.00
☐☐ 99	Dale Hunter, Wsh.	.35	6.00
☐☐ 100	Chris Simon, Wsh.	.35	6.00

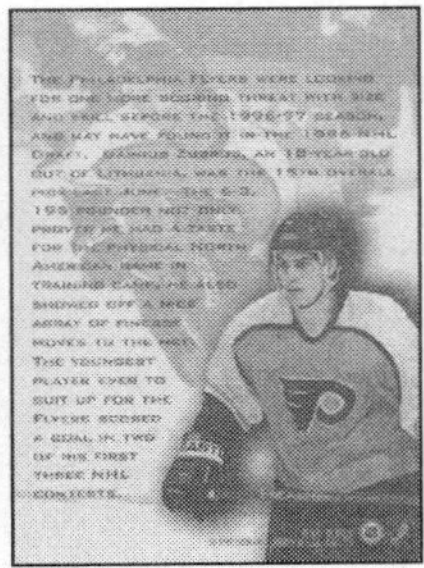

☐☐ **101**	**Mattias Timander, Bos., RC**	**2.00**	**8.00**
☐☐ **102**	**Vaclav Varada, Buf., RC**	**3.00**	**15.00**
☐☐ 103	Jarome Iginla, Cgy.	5.00	20.00
☐☐ 104	Ethan Moreau, Chi.	3.00	10.00
☐☐ 105	Jamie Langenbrunner, Dal.	3.00	10.00
☐☐ **106**	**Roman Turek (G), Dal., RC**	**2.00**	**10.00**
☐☐ **107**	**Tomas Holmstrom, Det., RC**	**5.00**	**20.00**
☐☐ 108	Kevin Hodson (G), Det.	2.00	8.00
☐☐ 109	Mats Lindgren, Edm.	2.00	8.00
☐☐ **110**	**Mike Grier, Edm., RC**	**5.00**	**20.00**
☐☐ **111**	**Rem Murray, Edm., RC**	**4.00**	**8.00**
☐☐ 112	José Théodore (G), Mtl.	6.00	25.00
☐☐ 113	David Wilkie, Mtl.	2.00	8.00
☐☐ 114	Bryan Berard, NYI.	6.00	25.00
☐☐ 115	Eric Fichaud (G), NYI.	3.00	10.00
☐☐ **116**	**Daniel Goneau, NYR., RC**	**2.00**	**8.00**
☐☐ **117**	**Andreas Dackell, Ott., RC**	**2.00**	**8.00**
☐☐ 118	Wade Redden, Ott.	4.00	8.00
☐☐ **119**	**Danius Zubrus, Pha., RC**	**25.00**	**100.00**
☐☐ 120	Janne Niinimaa, Pha.	5.00	20.00
☐☐ **121**	**Patrick Lalime (G), Pgh., RC**	**2.00**	**8.00**
☐☐ **122**	**Harry York, Stl., RC**	**3.00**	**15.00**
☐☐ 123	Jim Campbell, Stl.	3.00	10.00
☐☐ **124**	**Sergei Berezin, Tor., RC**	**4.00**	**20.00**
☐☐ **125**	**Jaroslav Svejkovsky, Wsh., RC**	**10.00**	**40.00**

NOW AND THEN

	No.	Player	NRMT-MT
☐	1	Mark Messier/ Wayne Gretzky/ Mike Gartner	275.00
☐	2	Mario Lemieux/ Patrick Roy/ Kirk Muller	225.00
☐	3	Eric Lindros/ Scott Niedermayer/ Peter Forsberg	175.00

HOT NUMBERS

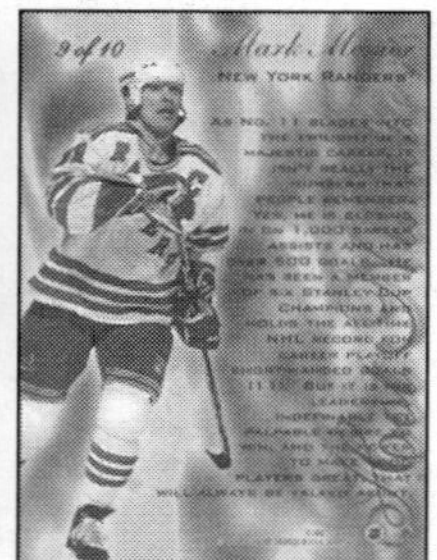

Insert Set (10 cards): 225.00

	No.	Player	NRMT-MT
☐	1	Ray Bourque, Bos.	18.00
☐	2	Paul Coffey, Pha.	10.00
☐	3	Eric Dazé, Chi.	10.00
☐	4	Wayne Gretzky, NYR.	75.00
☐	5	Ed Jovanovski, Fla.	10.00
☐	6	Saku Koivu, Mtl.	25.50
☐	7	Mario Lemieux, Pgh.	60.00
☐	8	Eric Lindros, Pha.	40.00
☐	9	Mark Messier, NYR.	18.00
☐	10	Owen Nolan, S.J.	10.00

CENTRE ICE SPOTLIGHT

Insert Set (10 cards): 140.00

	No.	Player	NRMT-MT
☐	1	Pavel Bure, Van.	15.00
☐	2	Sergei Fedorov, Det.	10.00
☐	3	Peter Forsberg, Col.	20.00
☐	4	Brett Hull, Stl.	10.00
☐	5	Jaromir Jagr, Pgh.	20.00
☐	6	Paul Kariya, Ana.	25.00
☐	7	Joe Sakic, Col.	18.00
☐	8	Teemu Selänne, Ana.	15.00
☐	9	Mats Sundin, Tor.	10.00
☐	10	Steve Yzerman, Det.	20.00

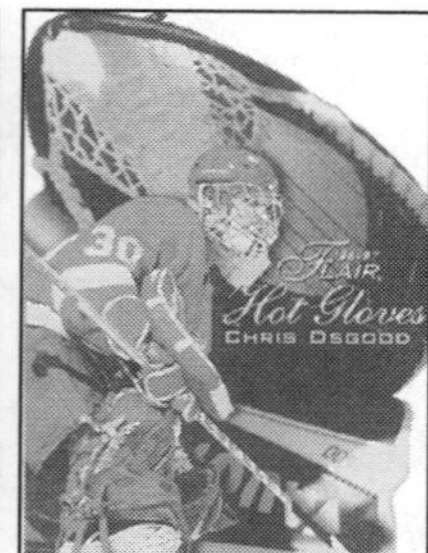

HOT GLOVES

These inserts are die-cut around the glove.

Insert Set (12 cards): 240.00

	No.	Player	NRMT-MT
☐	1	Ed Belfour (G), Chi.	12.00
☐	2	Martin Brodeur (G), N.J.	30.00
☐	3	Jim Carey (G), Wsh.	8.00
☐	4	Dominik Hasek (G), Buf.	30.00
☐	5	Curtis Joseph (G), Edm.	25.00
☐	6	Patrick Lalime (G), Pgh.	8.00
☐	7	Chris Osgood (G), Det.	18.00
☐	8	Félix Potvin (G), Tor.	20.00
☐	9	Mike Richter (G), NYR.	12.00
☐	10	Patrick Roy (G), Col.	175.00
☐	11	Jocelyn Thibault (G), Mtl.	12.00
☐	12	John Vanbiesbrouck (G), Fla.	25.00

1996 - 97 FLEER

Imprint: © 1996 FLEER/SKYBOX INTERNATIONAL
Complete Set (150 cards): 20.00
Common Player: .10

	No.	Player	NRMT-MT
☐	1	Guy Hebert (G), Ana.	.25
☐	2	Paul Kariya, Ana.	1.50
☐	3	Teemu Selänne, Ana.	.75
☐	4	Ray Bourque, Bos.	.50
☐	5	Kyle McLaren, Bos.	.10
☐	6	Adam Oates, Bos.	.35
☐	7	Bill Ranford (G), Bos.	.25
☐	8	Rick Tocchet, Bos.	.10
☐	9	Jason Dawe, Buf.	.10
☐	10	Dominik Hasek (G), Buf.	.75
☐	11	Pat LaFontaine, Buf.	.25
☐	12	Theoren Fleury, Cgy.	.35
☐	13	Trevor Kidd (G), Cgy.	.25
☐	14	German Titov, Cgy.	.10
☐	15	Ed Belfour (G), Chi.	.35
☐	16	Chris Chelios, Chi.	.35
☐	17	Eric Dazé, Chi.	.25
☐	18	Jeremy Roenick, Chi.	.35
☐	19	Gary Suter, Chi.	.10
☐	20	Peter Forsberg, Col.	1.25
☐	21	Valeri Kamensky, Col.	.25
☐	22	Claude Lemieux, Col.	.10
☐	23	Sandis Ozolinsh, Col.	.10
☐	24	Patrick Roy (G), Col.	2.00
☐	25	Joe Sakic, Col.	1.00
☐	26	Derian Hatcher, Dal.	.25
☐	27	Mike Modano, Dal.	.50
☐	28	Sergei Zubov, Pgh. (Dal.)	.25
☐	29	Paul Coffey, Det.	.25
☐	30	Sergei Fedorov, Det.	.50
☐	31	Vladimir Konstantinov, Det.	.10
☐	32	Vyacheslav Kozlov, Det.	.10
☐	33	Chis Osgood (G), Det.	.35
☐	34	Keith Primeau, Det.	.25
☐	35	Steve Yzerman, Det.	1.25
☐	36	Jason Arnott, Edm.	.25
☐	37	Curtis Joseph (G), Edm.	.60
☐	38	Doug Weight, Edm.	.35
☐	39	Ed Jovanovski, Fla.	.25
☐	40	Scott Mellanby, Fla.	.10
☐	41	Rob Niedermayer, Fla.	.10
☐	42	Ray Sheppard, Fla.	.10
☐	43	Robert Svehla, Fla.	.10
☐	44	John Vanbiesbrouck (G), Fla.	.60
☐	45	Sean Burke (G), Hfd.	.25
☐	46	Andrew Cassels, Hfd.	.10
☐	47	Geoff Sanderson, Hfd.	.10
☐	48	Brendan Shanahan, Hfd.	.60
☐	49	Ray Ferraro, L.A.	.10
☐	50	Dimitri Khristich, L.A.	.10
☐	51	Vitali Yachmenev, L.A.	.10
☐	52	Valeri Bure, Mtl.	.10
☐	53	Vincent Damphousse, Mtl.	.35
☐	54	Saku Koivu, Mtl.	.75
☐	55	Mark Recchi, Mtl.	.25
☐	56	Jocelyn Thibault (G), Mtl.	.35
☐	57	Pierre Turgeon, Mtl.	.25
☐	58	Martin Brodeur (G), N.J.	.75
☐	59	Phil Housley, N.J.	.10
☐	60	Scott Niedermayer, N.J.	.25
☐	61	Scott Stevens, N.J.	.10
☐	62	Steve Thomas, N.J.	.10
☐	63	Todd Bertuzzi, NYI.	.25
☐	65	Travis Green, NYI.	.10
☐	65	Kenny Jonsson, NYI.	.10
☐	66	Zigmund Palffy, NYI.	.35
☐	67	Adam Graves, NYR.	.10
☐	68	Wayne Gretzky, NYR.	3.00
☐	69	Alexei Kovalev, NYR.	.10
☐	70	Brian Leetch, NYR.	.35
☐	71	Mark Messier, NYR.	.50
☐	72	Niklas Sundstrom, NYR.	.10
☐	73	Daniel Alfredsson, Ott.	.25
☐	74	Radek Bonk, Ott.	.10
☐	75	Steve Duchesne, Ott.	.10
☐	76	Damian Rhodes (G), Ott.	.10
☐	77	Alexei Yashin, Ott.	.35
☐	78	Rod Brind'Amour, Pha.	.25
☐	79	Eric Desjardins, Pha.	.10
☐	80	Ron Hextall (G), Pha.	.25
☐	81	John LeClair, Pha.	.50
☐	82	Eric Lindros, Pha.	1.25
☐	83	Mikael Renberg, Pha.	.10
☐	84	Tom Barrasso (G), Pgh.	.25
☐	85	Ron Francis, Pgh.	.35
☐	86	Jaromir Jagr, Pgh.	1.25
☐	87	Mario Lemieux, Pgh.	2.00
☐	88	Petr Nedved, Pgh.	.10
☐	89	Bryan Smolinski, Pgh.	.10
☐	90	Nikolai Khabibulin (G), Wpg. (Pho.)	.35
☐	91	Teppo Numminen, Wpg. (Pho.)	.10
☐	92	Keith Tkachuk, Wpg. (Pho.)	.35
☐	93	Oleg Tverdovsky, Wpg. (Pho.)	.10
☐	94	Alexei Zhamnov, Wpg. (Pho.)	.25
☐	95	Shayne Corson, Stl.	.25
☐	96	Grant Fuhr (G), Stl.	.25
☐	97	Brett Hull, Stl.	.50
☐	98	Al MacInnis, Stl.	.10
☐	99	Chris Pronger, Stl.	.25
☐	100	Owen Nolan, S.J.	.25
☐	101	Marcus Ragnarsson, S.J.	.10
☐	102	Chris Terreri (G), S.J.	.10
☐	103	Brian Bradley, T.B.	.10
☐	104	Roman Hamrlik, T.B.	.25
☐	105	Daren Puppa, T.B.	.10
☐	106	Alexander Selivanov, T.B.	.10
☐	107	Doug Gilmour, Tor. Error (Dave Gagner)	.25
☐	108	Larry Murphy, Tor.	.25
☐	109	Félix Potvin (G), Tor.	.50
☐	110	Mats Sundin, Tor.	.50
☐	111	Pavel Bure, Van.	.75
☐	112	Trevor Linden, Van.	.25
☐	113	Kirk McLean (G), Van.	.25
☐	114	Alexander Mogilny, Van.	.35
☐	115	Peter Bondra, Wsh.	.35
☐	116	Jim Carey (G), Wsh.	.10
☐	117	Sergei Gonchar, Wsh.	.10
☐	118	Joé Juneau, Wsh.	.10
☐	119	Michael Pivonka, Wsh.	.10
☐	120	Brendan Witt, Wsh.	.10
☐	121	Nolan Baumgartner, Wsh.	.10
☐	122	Martin Biron (G), Buf.	.10
☐	123	Jason Bonsignore, Edm.	.10
☐	**124**	**Andrew Brunette, Wsh., RC**	**.25**
☐	125	Jason Doig, Wpg.	.10
☐	126	Peter Ferraro, NYR.	.10
☐	127	Eric Fichaud (G), NYI.	.25
☐	128	Ladislav Kohn, Cgy.	.10
☐	129	Jamie Langenbrunner, Dal.	.25
☐	130	Daymond Langkow, T.B.	.10
☐	131	Jay McKee, Buf.	.10
☐	132	Wayne Primeau, Buf.	.10
☐	133	Jamie Storr (G), L.A.	.25
☐	134	José Théodore (G), Mtl.	.35
☐	135	Roman Vopat, L.A.	.10
☐	136	LL: Eric Dazé/Alfredsson/V. Bure/Koivu	.25
☐	137	LL: Mario Lemieux/Jagr/Sakic/Francis	1.00
☐	138	LL: Mario Lemieux/Jagr/Mogilny/Bondra	1.00
☐	139	LL: Ron Francis/Lemieux/Jagr/Forsberg	1.00
☐	140	LL: Brian Leetch/Coffey/Bourque/Chelios	.35
☐	141	LL: Mario Lemieux/Jagr/Kariya/Tkachuk	1.00
☐	142	LL: Jaromir Jagr/Fedorov/LeClair/C. Lemieux	.75
☐	143	LL: Vladimir Konstastinov/Fedorov/Fetisov/Nedved	.25

	No.	Player	NRMT-MT
☐	144	LL: Ron Hextall/Osgood/Carey/Vernon	.20
☐	145	LL: Chris Osgood/Carey/Brodeur/Hextall	.75
☐	146	LL: Jim Carey/Brodeur/Osgood/Puppa	.75
☐	147	LL: Dominik Hasek/Puppa/Hackett, Hebert	.35
☐	148	Checklist	.10
☐	149	Checklist	.10
☐	150	Checklist	.10

ART ROSS TROPHY

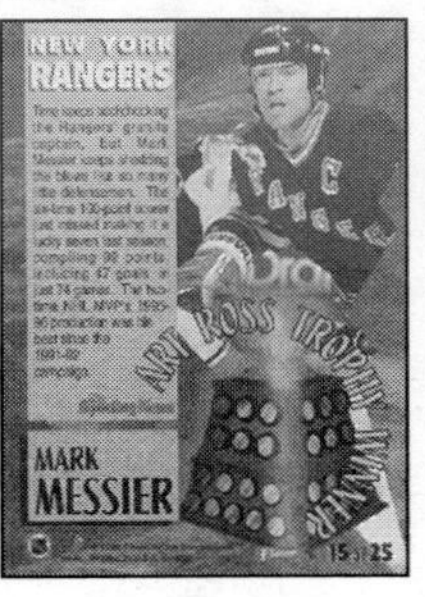

Insert Set (25 cards): **70.00**

	No.	Player	NRMT-MT
☐	1	Pavel Bure, Van.	3.50
☐	2	Sergei Fedorov, Det.	2.50
☐	3	Theoren Fleury, Cgy.	1.50
☐	4	Peter Forsberg, Col.	5.00
☐	5	Ron Francis, Pgh.	1.50
☐	6	Wayne Gretzky, Stl.	10.00
☐	7	Brett Hull, Stl.	2.50
☐	8	Jaromir Jagr, Pgh.	5.00
☐	9	Valeri Kamensky, Col.	1.00
☐	10	Paul Kariya, Ana.	6.50
☐	11	Pal LaFontaine, Buf.	1.00
☐	12	John LeClair, Pha.	2.50
☐	13	Mario Lemieux, Pgh.	8.00
☐	14	Eric Lindros, Pha.	6.50
☐	15	Mark Messier, NYR.	2.50
☐	16	Alexander Mogilny, Van.	1.50
☐	17	Petr Nedved, Pgh.	1.00
☐	18	Adam Oates, Bos.	1.50
☐	19	Jermy Roenick, Chi.	1.50
☐	20	Joe Sakic, Col.	4.00
☐	21	Teemu Selänne, Ana.	3.50
☐	22	Keith Tkachuk, Wpg.	2.00
☐	23	Pierre Turgeon, Mtl.	1.00
☐	24	Doug Weight, Edm.	1.50
☐	25	Steve Yzerman, Det.	5.00

CALDER CANDIDATES

Insert Set (10 cards): **60.00**

	No	Player	NRMT-MT
☐	1	Andrew Brunette, Wsh.	6.00
☐	2	Jason Doig, Wpg.	6.00
☐	3	Peter Ferraro, NYR.	6.00
☐	4	Eric Fichaud (G), NYI.	8.00
☐	5	Ladislav Kohn, Cgy.	6.00
☐	6	Jamie Langenbrunner, Dal.	8.00
☐	7	Daymond Langkow, T.B.	6.00
☐	8	Jamie Storr (G), L.A.	8.00
☐	9	José Théodore (G), Mtl.	12.00
☐	10	Roman Vopat, L.A.	6.00

NORRIS TROPHY

Insert Set (10 cards): **60.00**

	No	Player	NRMT-MT
☐	1	Ray Bourque, Bos.	15.00
☐	2	Chris Chelios, Chi.	12.00
☐	3	Paul Coffey, Det.	6.00
☐	4	Eric Desjardins, Pha.	5.00
☐	5	Phil Housley, N.J.	5.00
☐	6	Vladimir Konstantinov, Det.	5.00
☐	7	Brian Leetch, NYR.	8.00
☐	8	Teppo Numminen, Wpg.	5.00
☐	9	Larry Murphy, Tor.	6.00
☐	10	Sandis Ozolinsh, Col.	6.00

PEARSON AWARD

Insert Set (10 cards): **500.00**

	No	Player	NRMT-MT
☐	1	Pavel Bure, Van.	35.00
☐	2	Sergei Fedorov, Det.	25.00
☐	3	Peter Forsberg, Col.	50.00
☐	4	Wayne Grezky, Stl.	100.00
☐	5	Jaromir Jagr, Pgh.	60.00
☐	6	Paul Kariya, Ana.	65.00
☐	7	Mario Lemieux, Pgh.	80.00
☐	8	Eric Lindros, Pha.	65.00
☐	9	Patrick Roy, Col.	80.00
☐	10	Joe Sakic, Col.	40.00

ROOKIE SENSATIONS

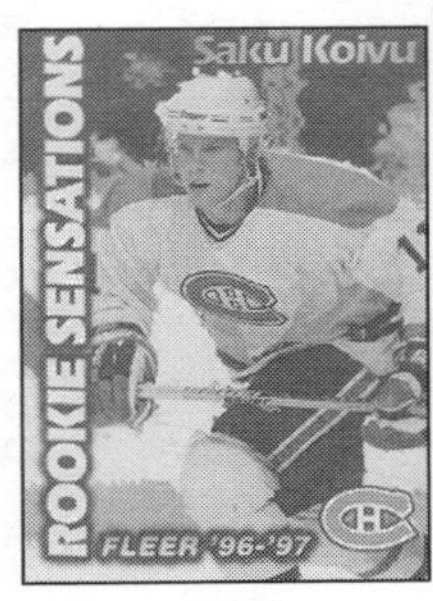

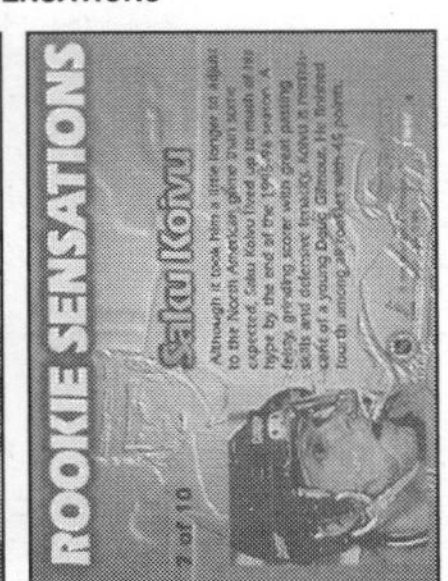

Insert Set (10 cards): **50.00**

	No	Player	NRMT-MT
☐	1	Daniel Alfredsson, Ott.	6.00
☐	2	Todd Bertuzzi, NYI.	6.00
☐	3	Valeri Bure, Mtl.	4.00
☐	4	Eric Dazé, Chi.	6.00
☐	5	Sergei Gonchar, Wsh.	4.00
☐	6	Ed Jovanovski, Fla.	6.00
☐	7	Saku Koivu, Mtl.	18.00
☐	8	Marcus Ragnarsson, S.J.	4.00
☐	9	Petr Sykora, N.J.	4.00
☐	10	Vitali Yachmenev, L.A.	4.00

VEZINA TROPHY

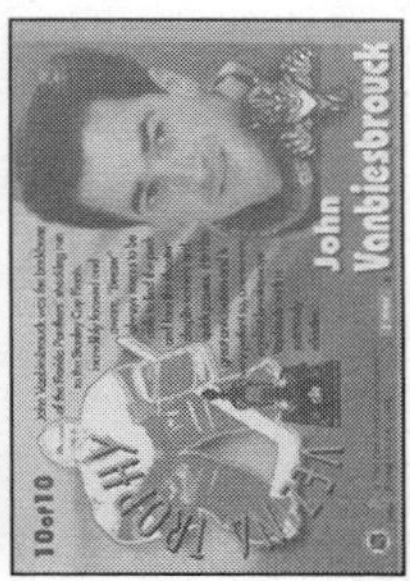

Insert Set (10 cards): **140.00**

	No	Player	NRMT-MT
☐	1	Ed Belfour (G), Chi.	12.00
☐	2	Sean Burke (G), Hfd.	8.00
☐	3	Jim Carey (G), Wsh.	6.00
☐	4	Dominik Hasek (G), Buf.	30.00
☐	5	Ron Hextall (G), Pha.	8.00
☐	6	Chris Osgood (G), Det.	18.00
☐	7	Félix Potvin (G), Tor.	20.00
☐	8	Daren Puppa (G), T.B.	8.00
☐	9	Patrick Roy (G), Col.	60.00
☐	10	John Vanbiesbrouck (G), Fla.	25.00

1996 - 97 FLEER NHL PICKS

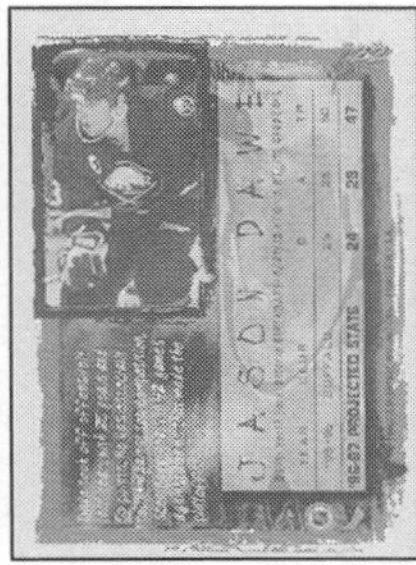

This series features even numbers only. See Topps NHL Picks for corresponding odd numbers.

Imprint: © 1996 FLEER/SKYBOX INTERNATIONAL

Complete Set (92 cards): **15.00**

Common Player: **.10**

	No.	Player	NRMT-MT
☐	2	Joe Sakic, Col.	.85
☐	4	Eric Lindros, Pha.	1.25
☐	6	Paul Kariya, Ana.	1.25
☐	8	Wayne Gretzky, Stl.	3.50
☐	10	Chris Osgood, Det.	.35
☐	12	Brian Leetch, NYR.	.35
☐	14	Ray Bourque, Bos.	.50
☐	16	Ron Francis, Pgh.	.35
☐	18	Keith Tkachuk, Wpg.	.35
☐	20	Paul Coffey, Det.	.25
☐	22	Phil Housley, Wsh.	.10
☐	24	Theoren Fleury, Cgy.	.35
☐	26	Sergei Zubov, Pgh.	.25
☐	28	Adam Oates, Bos.	.35
☐	30	John LeClair, Pha.	.50
☐	32	Pierre Turgeon, Mtl.	.25
☐	34	Nicklas Lidström, Det.	.25
☐	36	Vincent Damphousse, Mtl.	.35
☐	38	Pat LaFontaine, Buf.	.25
☐	40	Brendan Shanahan, Hfd.	.60
☐	42	Robert Svehla, Fla.	.10
☐	44	Peter Bondra, Wsh.	.35
☐	46	Mikael Renberg, Pha.	.10
☐	48	Alexei Yashin, Ott.	.35
☐	50	Zigmund Palffy, NYI.	.35
☐	52	Larry Murphy, Tor.	.25
☐	54	Rod Brind'Amour, Pha.	.25
☐	56	Alexei Zhamnov, Wpg.	.25
☐	58	Jason Arnott, Edm.	.25
☐	60	Craig Janney, Wpg.	.10
☐	62	Jason Woolley, Fla.	.10
☐	64	Jeff Brown, Hfd.	.10
☐	66	Tomas Sandström, Pgh.	.10

	No.	Player	NRMT-MT
☐	68	Doug Gilmour, Tor.	.35
☐	70	Travis Green, NYI.	.10
☐	72	Teppo Numminen, Wpg.	.10
☐	74	Petr Sykora, N.J.	.10
☐	76	Saku Koivu, Mtl.	.75
☐	78	Daniel Alfredsson, Ott.	.25
☐	80	Ron Hextall (G), Pha.	.25
☐	82	Jocelyn Thibault (G), Mtl.	.35
☐	84	Mike Richter (G), NYR.	.35
☐	86	Nikolai Khabibulin (G), Wpg	.35
☐	88	John Vanbiesbrouck (G), Fla.	.60
☐	90	Adam Graves, NYR.	.10
☐	92	Kenny Jonsson, NYI.	.10
☐	94	Jyrki Lumme, Van.	.10
☐	96	Zdeno Ciger, Edm.	.10
☐	98	Ed Jovanovski, Fla.	.25
☐	100	Greg Johnson, Det.	.10
☐	102	Pat Falloon, Pha.	.10
☐	104	Andrew Cassels, Hfd.	.10
☐	106	German Titov, Cgy.	.10
☐	108	Joé Juneau, Wsh.	.10
☐	110	Igor Larionov, Det.	.25
☐	112	Norm Maciver, Wpg.	.10
☐	114	Chris Pronger, Stl.	.25
☐	116	Scott Niedermayer, N.J.	.25
☐	118	Vladimir Malakhov, Mtl.	.10
☐	120	Dale Hawerchuk, Pha.	.25
☐	122	Jason Dawe, Buf.	.10
☐	124	Valeri Bure, Mtl.	.10
☐	126	Marcus Ragnarsson, S.J.	.10
☐	128	Stéphane Richer, N.J.	.10
☐	130	Wendel Clark, Tor.	.25
☐	132	Bryan Smolinski, Pgh.	.10
☐	134	Dmitri Khristich, L.A.	.10
☐	136	Benoît Hogue, Dal.	.10
☐	138	Kirk Muller, Tor.	.10
☐	140	Ray Ferraro, L.A.	.10
☐	142	Vitali Yachmenev, L.A.	.10
☐	144	Jere Lehtinen, Dal.	.25
☐	146	Brandon Convery, Tor.	.10
☐	148	Darcy Tucker, Mtl.	.10
☐	150	Curtis Brown, Buf.	.10
☐	152	Alexei Zhitnik, L.A.	.10
☐	154	John Slaney, L.A.	.10
☐	156	Bruce Driver, N.J.	.10
☐	158	Jeff O'Neill, Hfd.	.25
☐	160	Patrice Brisebois, Mtl.	.10
☐	162	Gord Murphy, Fla.	.10
☐	164	Doug Bodger, S.J.	.10
☐	166	Marty McSorley, NYR.	.10
☐	168	Nolan Baumgartner, Wsh.	.10
☐	170	Mike Gartner, Tor.	.25
☐	172	Alexei Nikolishin, Hfd.	.10
☐	174	Alexei Yegorov, S.J.	.10
☐	176	Dave Reid, Dal.	.10
☐	178	Marty Murray, Cgy.	.10
☐	180	Anders Eriksson, Det.	.10
☐	182	Checklist	.10
☐	184	Checklist	.10

DREAM LINE

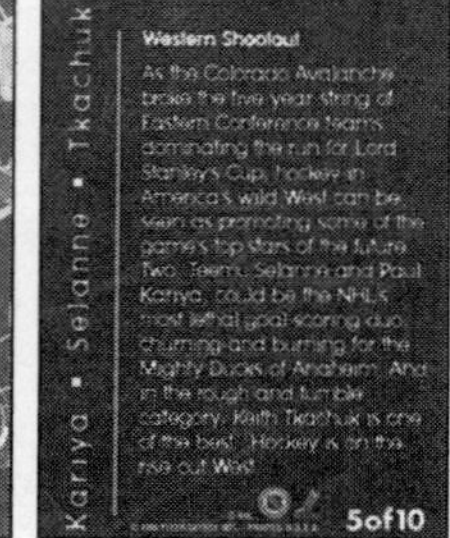

Insert Set (10 cards): 140.00

	No.	Players	NRMT-MT
☐	1	Eric Lindros/Mario Lemieux/Wayne Gretzky	40.00
☐	2	Jeremy Roenick/Chris Chelios/M. Richter	8.00
☐	3	P. Forsberg/Martin Brodeur/D. Alfredsson	15.00
☐	4	Pavel Bure/Alexander Mogilny/Sergei Fedorov	12.00
☐	5	Paul Kariya/Teemu Selänne/Keith Tkachuk	20.00
☐	6	Jaromir Jagr/D. Hasek/R. Hamrlik	15.00
☐	7	John LeClair/Brendan Shanahan/Mike Modano	10.00
☐	8	E. Belfour/J. Vanbiesbrouck/Patrick Roy	30.00
☐	9	V. Kamensky/Joe Sakic/Sandis Ozolinsh	10.00
☐	10	Pat Verbeek/Pat LaFontaine/ Brett Hull	8.00

FABULOUS FIFTY

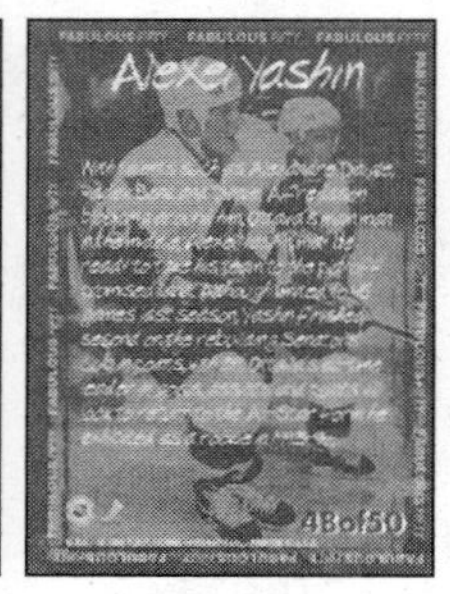

These inserts are seeded one per pack.

Insert Set (50 cards): 30.00

	No.	Player	NRMT-MT
☐	1	Daniel Alfredsson, Ott.	.35
☐	2	Peter Bondra, Wsh.	1.00
☐	3	Ray Bourque, Bos.	1.25
☐	4	Martin Brodeur, N.J.	1.75
☐	5	Pavel Bure, Van.	1.75
☐	6	Jim Carey (G), Wsh.	.20
☐	7	Chris Chelios, Chi.	1.00
☐	8	Paul Coffey, Det.	.35
☐	9	Eric Dazé, Chi.	.35
☐	10	Sergei Fedorov, Det.	1.25
☐	11	Theoren Fleury, Cgy.	.75
☐	12	Peter Forsberg, Col.	2.50
☐	13	Ron Francis, Pgh.	.75
☐	14	Sergei Gonchar, Wsh.	.20
☐	15	Wayne Gretzky, Stl.	5.00
☐	16	Roman Hamrlik, T.B.	.35
☐	17	Kevin Hatcher, Dal.	.20
☐	18	Ron Hextall (G), Pha.	.35
☐	19	Brett Hull, Stl.	1.25
☐	20	Jaromir Jagr, Pgh.	2.50
☐	21	Ed Jovanovski, Fla.	.35
☐	22	Valeri Kamensky, Col.	.35
☐	23	Paul Kariya, Ana.	3.50
☐	24	John LeClair, Pha.	1.25
☐	25	Brian Leetch, NYR.	.75
☐	26	Mario Lemieux, Pgh.	4.00
☐	27	Trevor Linden, Van.	.35
☐	28	Eric Lindros, Pha.	3.50
☐	29	Mark Messier, NYR.	1.25
☐	30	Mike Modano, Dal.	1.25
☐	31	Alexander Mogilny, Van.	.75
☐	32	Petr Nedved, Pgh.	.20
☐	33	Joe Nieuwendyk, Dal.	.35
☐	34	Owen Nolan, S.J.	.35
☐	35	Adam Oates, Bos.	.75
☐	36	Chris Osgood (G), Det.	1.00
☐	37	Sandis Ozolinsh, Col.	.35
☐	38	Zigmund Palffy, NYI.	.75
☐	39	Jeremy Roenick, Chi.	.75
☐	40	Patrick Roy (G), Col.	4.00
☐	41	Joe Sakic, Col.	2.00
☐	42	Teemu Selänne, Ana.	1.75
☐	43	Brendan Shanahan, Hfd.	1.50
☐	44	Keith Tkachuk, Wpg.	1.00
☐	45	Pierre Turgeon, Mtl.	.35
☐	46	John Vanbiesbrouck (G), Fla.	1.50
☐	47	Doug Weight, Edm.	.75
☐	48	Alexei Yashin, Ott.	1.00
☐	49	Steve Yzerman, Det.	2.50
☐	50	Alexei Zhamnov, Wpg.	.35

JAGGED EDGE

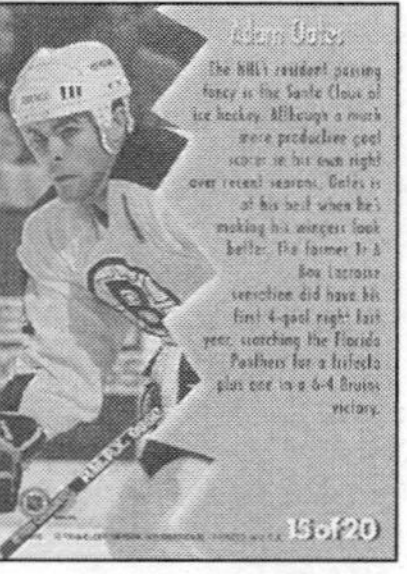

Insert Set (20 cards): 75.00

	No.	Player	NRMT-MT
☐	1	Daniel Alfredsson, Ott.	3.00
☐	2	Theoren Fleury, Cgy.	4.00
☐	3	Alexander Mogilny, Van.	4.00
☐	4	Doug Weight, Edm.	4.00
☐	5	Alexei Yashin, Ott.	5.00
☐	6	Paul Kariya, Ana.	15.00
☐	7	Saku Koivu, Ana.	8.00
☐	8	Sandis Ozolinsh, Col.	3.00
☐	9	Petr Nedved, Pgh.	2.00
☐	10	Jeremy Roenick, Chi.	4.00
☐	11	Mike Modano, Dal.	6.00
☐	12	Jim Carey (G), Wsh.	2.00
☐	13	Ed Jovanovski, Fla.	3.00
☐	14	Alexei Zhamnov, Wpg.	3.00
☐	15	Adam Oates, Bos.	4.00
☐	16	Ron Francis, Pgh.	4.00
☐	17	Brian Leetch, NYR.	4.00
☐	18	Paul Coffey, Det.	3.00
☐	19	Eric Dazé, Chi.	3.00
☐	20	Zigmund Palffy, NYI.	5.00

FANTASY FORCE

Insert Set (10 cards): 100.00

	No.	Player	NRMT-MT
☐	1	John LeClair, Pha.	12.00
☐	2	Chris Osgood (G), Det.	102.00
☐	3	Ron Hextall (G), Pha.	6.00
☐	4	Eric Dazé, Chi.	6.00
☐	5	Jaromir Jagr, Pgh.	25.00
☐	6	Brett Hull, Stl.	12.00
☐	7	Ron Francis, Pgh.	8.00
☐	8	Martin Brodeur (G), N.J.	18.00
☐	9	Sergei Fedorov, Det.	12.00
☐	10	Petr Nedved, Pgh.	4.00

CAPTAIN'S CHOICE

Insert Set (10 cards): 550.00

	No.	Player	NRMT-MT
☐	1	Eric Lindros, Pha.	100.00
☐	2	Steve Yzerman, Det.	75.00
☐	3	Mario Lemieux, Pgh.	120.00
☐	4	Wayne Gretzky, Stl.	150.00
☐	5	Mark Messier, NYR.	35.00
☐	6	Joe Sakic, Col.	60.00
☐	7	Keith Tkachuk, Wpg.	30.00
☐	8	Doug Gilmour, Tor.	20.00
☐	9	Trevor Linden, Van.	15.00
☐	10	Brendan Shanahan, Hfd.	45.00

1996 - 97 FLEER ULTRA

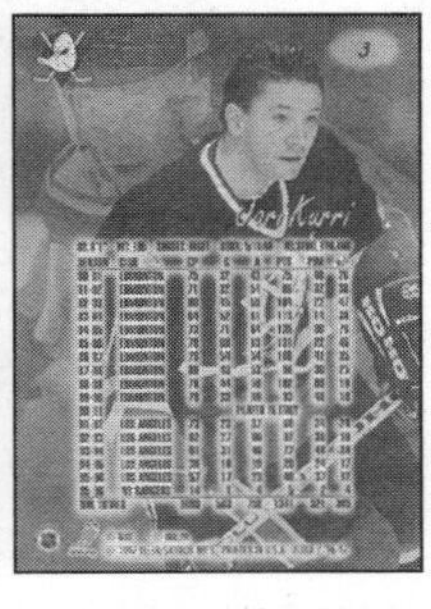

These cards have two versions: a regular card and a Gold Medallion parallel. Gold Medallion cards have the prefix "G" on the card number.

Imprint: © 1997 FLEER/SKYBOX INT'L.

Complete Set (180 cards):			**38.00**	**225.00**
Common Player:			**.15**	**.35**
Promo Card (John LeClair, #S125):			**2.00**	
	No.	**Player**	**Reg.**	**Gold Med.**
□ □	1	Guy Hebert, Ana.	.25	.50
□ □	2	Paul Kariya, Ana.	2.00	15.00
□ □	3	Jari Kurri, Ana.	.25	.50
□ □	4	Roman Oksiuta, Ana.	.15	.35
□ □	5	Ruslan Salei, Ana.	.15	.35
□ □	6	Teemu Selänne, Ana.	1.00	6.00
□ □	7	Darren Van Impe, Ana.	.15	.35
□ □	8	Ray Bourque, Bos.	.50	3.00
□ □	9	Kyle McLaren, Bos.	.15	.35
□ □	10	Adam Oates, Bos.	.25	.50
□ □	11	Bill Ranford (G), Bos.	.25	.50
□ □	12	Rick Tocchet, Bos.	.15	.35
□ □	13	Donald Audette, Buf.	.15	.35
□ □	14	Curtis Brown, Buf.	.15	.35
□ □	15	Jason Dawe, Buf.	.15	.35
□ □	16	Domonik Hasek (G), Buf.	1.00	6.00
□ □	17	Pat LaFontaine, Buf.	.25	.50
□ □	18	Jay McKee, Buf.	.15	.35
□ □	19	Derek Plante, Buf.	.15	.35
□ □	20	Wayne Primeau, Buf.	.15	.35
□ □	21	Theoren Fleury, Cgy.	.25	.75
□ □	22	Dave Gagner, Cgy.	.15	.35
□ □	23	Jonas Hoglund, Cgy.	.15	.35
□ □	24	Jarome Iginla, Cgy.	.50	1.00
□ □	25	Trevor Kidd (G), Cgy.	.25	.50
□ □	26	Robert Reichel, Cgy.	.15	.35
□ □	27	German Titov, Cgy.	.15	.35
□ □	28	Tony Amonte, Chi.	.25	.50
□ □	29	Ed Belfour (G), Chi.	.35	1.00
□ □	30	Chris Chelios, Chi.	.35	2.00
□ □	31	Eric Dazé, Chi.	.25	.50
□ □	32	Ethan Moreau, Chi.	.25	.50
□ □	33	Gary Suter, Chi.	.15	.35
□ □	34	Adam Deadmarsh, Col.	.15	.35
□ □	35	Peter Forsberg, Col.	1.25	10.00
□ □	36	Valeri Kamensky, Col.	.25	.50
□ □	37	Claude Lemieux, Col.	.15	.35
□ □	38	Sandis Ozolinsh, Col.	.25	.50
□ □	39	Patrick Roy (G), Col.	2.00	20.00
□ □	40	Joe Sakic, Col.	1.00	7.50
□ □	41	Landon Wilson, Col.	.15	.35
□ □	42	Derian Hatcher, Dal.	.25	.50
□ □	43	Jamie Langenbrunner, Dal.	.25	.50
□ □	44	Mike Modano, Dal.	.50	3.00
□ □	45	Andy Moog (G), Dal.	.25	.50
□ □	46	Joe Nieuwendyk, Dal.	.25	.50
□ □	47	Pat Verbeek, Dal.	.15	.35
□ □	48	Sergei Zubov, Dal.	.25	.50
□ □	49	Anders Eriksson, Det.	.15	.35
□ □	50	Sergei Fedorov, Det.	.50	3.00
□ □	51	Vladimir Konstantinov, Det.	.15	.35
□ □	52	Vyacheslav Kozlov, Det.	.15	.35
□ □	53	Nicklas Lidström, Det.	.25	.50
□ □	54	Chris Osgood (G), Det.	.35	2.00
□ □	55	Brendan Shanahan, Det.	.60	4.50
□ □	56	Steve Yzerman, Det.	1.25	10.00
□ □	57	Jason Arnott, Edm.	.25	.50
□ □	**58**	**Mike Grier, Edm., RC**	**.75**	**1.00**
□ □	59	Curtis Joseph (G), Edm.	.60	4.50
□ □	**60**	**Rem Murray, Edm., RC**	**.35**	**.50**
□ □	61	Jeff Norton, Edm.	.15	.35
□ □	62	Miroslav Satan, Edm.	.15	.35
□ □	63	Doug Weight, Edm.	.35	1.00
□ □	64	Radek Dvorak, Fla.	.15	.35
□ □	65	Ed Jovanovski, Fla.	.25	.50
□ □	66	Scott Mellanby, Fla.	.15	.35
□ □	67	Rob Niedermayer, Fla.	.15	.35
□ □	68	Ray Sheppard, Fla.	.15	.35
□ □	69	Robert Svehla, Fla.	.15	.35
□ □	70	John Vanbiesbrouck (G), Fla.	.60	4.50
□ □	**71**	**Steve Washburn, Fla., RC**	**.15**	**.35**
□ □	72	Jeff Brown, Hfd.	.15	.35
□ □	73	Sean Burke (G), Hfd.	.25	.50
□ □	74	Hnat Domenichelli, Hfd.	.25	.50
□ □	75	Keith Primeau, Hfd.	.25	.50
□ □	76	Geoff Sanderson, Hfd.	.15	.35
□ □	77	Rob Blake, L.A.	.25	.50
□ □	78	Stéphane Fiset (G), L.A.	.25	.50
□ □	79	Dimitri Khristich, L.A.	.15	.35
□ □	80	Mattias Norstrom, L.A.	.15	.35
□ □	81	Ed Olczyk, L.A.	.15	.35
□ □	82	Jamie Storr (G), L.A.	.25	.50
□ □	83	Jan Vopat, L.A.	.15	.35
□ □	84	Vitali Yachmenev, L.A.	.15	.35
□ □	85	Shayne Corson, Mtl.	.25	.50
□ □	86	Vincent Damphousse, Mtl.	.35	1.00
□ □	87	Saku Koivu, Mtl.	.75	6.00
□ □	88	Mark Recchi, Mtl.	.25	.50
□ □	89	Stéphane Richer, Mtl.	.15	.35
□ □	90	Jocelyn Thibault (G), Mtl.	.35	1.00
□ □	91	David Wilkie, Mtl.	.15	.35
□ □	92	Dave Andreychuk, N.J.	.15	.35
□ □	93	Martin Brodeur (G), N.J.	.75	6.00
□ □	94	Scott Niedermayer, N.J.	.25	.50
□ □	95	Scott Stevens, N.J.	.15	.35
□ □	96	Petr Sykora, N.J.	.15	.35
□ □	97	Steve Thomas, N.J.	.15	.35
□ □	98	Bryan Berard, NYI.	.35	1.50
□ □	99	Todd Bertuzzi, NYI.	.25	.50
□ □	100	Eric Fichaud (G), NYI.	.25	.50
□ □	101	Travis Green, NYI.	.15	.35
□ □	102	Kenny Jonsson, NYI.	.15	.35
□ □	103	Zigmund Palffy, NYI.	.35	2.00
□ □	104	Christian Dubé, NYR.	.25	.50
□ □	**105**	**Daniel Goneau, NYR., RC**	**.15**	**.35**
□ □	106	Wayne Gretzky, NYR.	4.00	25.00
□ □	107	Alexei Kovalev, NYR.	.15	.35
□ □	108	Brian Leetch, NYR.	.35	1.00
□ □	109	Mark Messier, NYR.	.50	3.00
□ □	110	Mike Richter (G), NYR.	.35	1.00
□ □	111	Luc Robitaille, NYR.	.15	.35
□ □	112	Niklas Sundstrom, NYR.	.15	.35
□ □	113	Daniel Alfredsson, Ott.	.25	.50
□ □	114	Radek Bonk, Ott.	.15	.35
□ □	**115**	**Andreas Dackell, Ott., RC**	**.15**	**.35**
□ □	116	Alexandre Daigle, Ott.	.25	.50
□ □	117	Steve Duchesne, Ott.	.15	.35
□ □	118	Wade Redden, Ott.	.25	.50
□ □	119	Damian Rhodes (G), Ott.	.15	.35
□ □	120	Alexei Yashin, Ott.	.35	2.00
□ □	121	Rod Brind'Amour, Pha.	.25	.50
□ □	122	Paul Coffey, Pha.	.25	.50
□ □	123	Eric Desjardins, Pha.	.15	.35
□ □	124	Ron Hextall (G), Pha.	.25	.50
□ □	125	John LeClair, Pha.	.50	3.00
□ □	126	Eric Lindros, Pha.	1.50	15.00
□ □	127	Janne Niinimaa, Pha.	.35	1.00
□ □	128	Mikael Renberg, Pha.	.15	.35
□ □	**129**	**Danius Zubrus, Pha., RC**	**2.50**	**4.00**
□ □	130	Mike Gartner, Pho.	.25	.50
□ □	131	Craig Janney, Pho.	.15	.35
□ □	132	Nikolai Khabibulin (G), Pho.	.35	1.00
□ □	133	Dave Manson, Pho.	.15	.35
□ □	134	Teppo Numminen, Pho.	.15	.35
□ □	135	Jeremy Roenick, Pho.	.35	1.00
□ □	136	Keith Tkachuk, Pho.	.35	2.00
□ □	137	Oleg Tverdovsky, Pho.	.15	.35
□ □	138	Tom Barrasso (G), Pgh.	.25	.50
□ □	139	Ron Francis, Pgh.	.35	1.00
□ □	140	Kevin Hatcher, Pgh.	.15	.35
□ □	141	Jaromir Jagr, Pgh.	1.25	10.00
□ □	**142**	**Patrick Lalime (G), Pgh., RC**	**.15**	**.35**
□ □	143	Mario Lemieux, Pgh.	2.00	20.00
□ □	144	Jim Campbell, Stl.	.25	.50
□ □	145	Grant Fuhr (G), Stl.	.25	.50
□ □	146	Brett Hull, Stl.	.50	3.00
□ □	147	Al MacInnis, Stl.	.15	.35
□ □	148	Pierre Turgeon, Stl.	.15	.35
□ □	**149**	**Harry York, Stl., RC**	**.25**	**.50**
□ □	150	Kelly Hrudey (G), S.J.	.15	.35
□ □	151	Al Iafrate, S.J.	.15	.35
□ □	152	Bernie Nicholls, S.J.	.15	.35
□ □	153	Owen Nolan, S.J.	.25	.50
□ □	154	Darren Turcotte, S.J.	.15	.35
□ □	155	Brian Bradley, T.B.	.15	.35
□ □	156	Dino Ciccarelli, T.B.	.25	.50
□ □	157	Daymond Langkow, T.B.	.15	.35
□ □	159	Daren Puppa (G), T.B.	.15	.35
□ □	160	Alexander Selivanov, T.B.	.15	.35
□ □	**161**	**Sergei Berezin, Tor., RC**	**.75**	**1.00**
□ □	162	Wendel Clark, Tor.	.25	.50
□ □	163	Doug Gilmour, Tor.	.35	1.00
□ □	164	Larry Murphy, Tor.	.25	.50
□ □	165	Félix Potvin (G), Tor.	.50	3.00
□ □	166	Mats Sundin, Tor.	.50	3.00
□ □	167	Pavel Bure, Van.	.75	6.00
□ □	168	Trevor Linden, Van.	.25	.50
□ □	169	Kirk McLean (G), Van.	.25	.50
□ □	170	Alexander Mogilny, Van.	.35	1.00
□ □	171	Esa Tikkanen, Van.	.15	.35
□ □	172	Peter Bondra, Wsh.	.35	2.00
□ □	**173**	**Andrew Brunette, Wsh., RC**	**.25**	**.50**
□ □	174	Jim Carey (G), Wsh.	.15	.35
□ □	175	Sergei Gonchar, Wsh.	.15	.35
□ □	176	Phil Housley, Wsh.	.15	.35
□ □	177	Joé Juneau, Wsh.	.15	.35
□ □	178	Mikael Pivonka, Wsh.	.15	.35
□ □	179	Checklist	.15	.35
□ □	180	Checklist	.15	.35

ULTRA ROOKIES

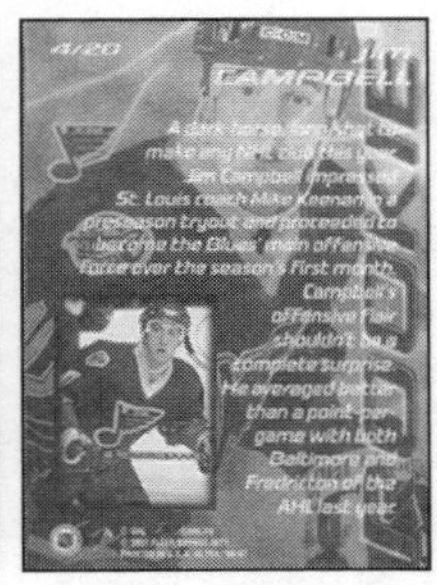

Insert Set (20 cards):			**55.00**
	No.	**Player**	**NRMT-MT**
□	1	Bryan Berard, NYI.	6.00
□	2	Sergei Berezin, Tor.	4.00
□	3	Curtis Brown, Buf.	2.00
□	4	Jim Campbell, Stl.	4.00
□	5	Christian Dubé, NYR.	2.00
□	6	Anders Eriksson, Det.	2.00
□	7	Eric Fichaud (G), NYI.	4.00
□	8	Daniel Goneau, NYR.	2.00
□	9	Mike Grier, Edm.	5.00
□	10	Jarome Iginla, Cgy.	5.00
□	11	Jamie Langenbrunner, Dal.	4.00
□	12	Jay McKee, Buf.	2.00
□	13	Ethan Moreau, Chi.	4.00
□	14	Rem Murray, Edm.	2.00
□	15	Janne Niinimaa, Pha.	5.00
□	16	Wayne Primeau, Buf.	2.00
□	17	Wade Redden, Ott.	2.00
□	18	Jamie Storr (G), L.A.	4.00
□	19	David Wilkie, Mtl.	2.00
□	20	Landon Wilson, Col.	2.00

MR. MOMENTUM

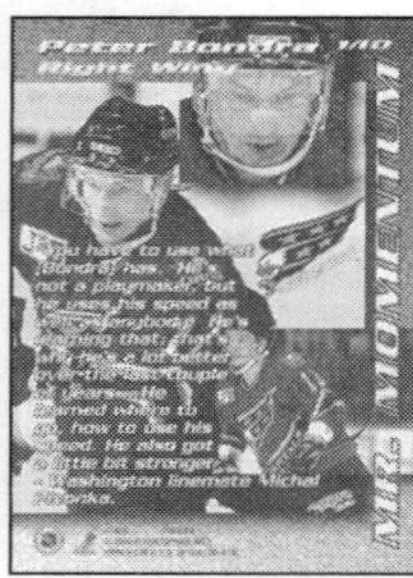

	No.	Player	NRMT-MT
Insert Set (10 cards):			**275.00**
□	1	Peter Bondra, Wsh.	20.00
□	2	Pavel Bure, Van.	35.00
□	3	Ron Francis, Pgh.	15.00
□	4	Brett Hull, Stl.	25.00
□	5	Jaromir Jagr, Pgh.	50.00
□	6	Pat LaFontaine, Buf.	10.00
□	7	Eric Lindros, Pha.	65.00
□	8	Mark Messier, NYR.	25.00
□	9	Mats Sundin, Tor.	25.00
□	10	Steve Yzerman, Det.	50.00

CLEAR THE ICE

	No.	Player	NRMT-MT
Insert Set (10 cards):			**775.00**
□	1	Jim Carey (G), Wsh.	25.00
□	2	Peter Forsberg, Col.	125.00
□	3	Dominik Hasek (G), Buf.	75.00
□	4	Jaromir Jagr, Pgh.	125.00
□	5	John LeClair, Pha.	50.00
□	6	Eric Lindros, Pha.	150.00
□	7	Mark Messier, NYR.	50.00
□	8	Patrick Roy (G), Col.	200.00
□	9	Brendan Shanahan, Det.	65.00
□	10	Keith Tkachuk, Pho.	40.00

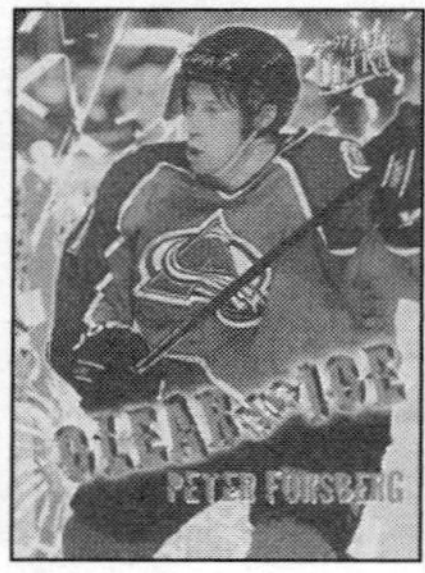

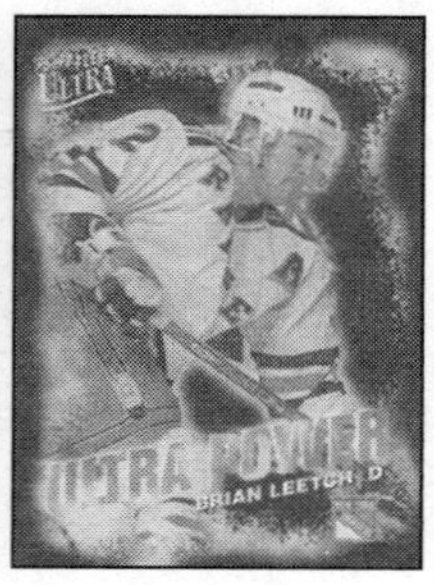

ULTRA POWER

	No.	Player	NRMT-MT
Insert Set (16 cards):			**215.00**
□	1	Ray Bourque, Bos.	12.00
□	2	Chris Chelios, Chi.	10.00
□	3	Paul Coffey, Pha.	6.00
□	4	Sergei Fedorov, Det.	12.00
□	5	Wayne Gretzky, NYR.	50.00
□	6	Roman Hamrlik, T.B.	6.00
□	7	Ed Jovanovski, Fla.	6.00
□	8	Paul Kariya, Ana.	35.00
□	9	Vladimir Konstantinov, Det.	6.00
□	10	Brian Leetch, NYR.	7.50
□	11	Mario Lemieux, Pgh.	40.00
□	12	Nicklas Lidström, Det.	6.00
□	13	Alexander Mogilny, Van.	7.50
□	14	Adam Oates, Bos.	7.50
□	15	Joe Sakic, Col.	20.00
□	16	Teemu Selänne, Ana.	18.00

POWER RED LINE

These inserts are serial numbered out of 1,082.

	No.	Player	NRMT-MT
Insert Set (8 cards):			**400.00**
□	1	Sergei Fedorov, Det.	30.00
□	2	Wayne Gretzky, NYR.	140.00
□	3	Paul Kariya, Ana.	75.00
□	4	Mario Lemieux, Pgh.	100.00
□	5	Alexander Mogilny, Van.	18.00
□	6	Adam Oates, Bos.	18.00
□	7	Joe Sakic, Col.	50.00
□	8	Teemu Selänne, Ana.	40.00

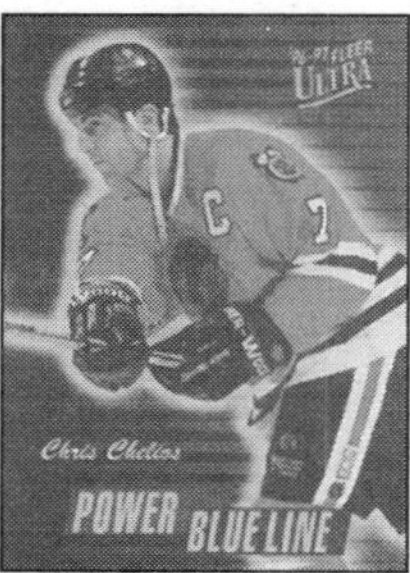

POWER BLUE LINE

These inserts are serial numbered out of 1,082.

	No.	Player	NRMT-MT
Insert Set (8 cards):			**90.00**
□	1	Ray Bourque, Bos.	25.00
□	2	Chris Chelios, Chi.	18.00
□	3	Paul Coffey, Pha.	10.00
□	4	Roman Hamrlik, T.B.	10.00
□	5	Ed Jovanovski, Fla.	10.00
□	6	Vladimir Konstantinov, Det.	10.00
□	7	Brian Leetch, NYR.	15.00
□	8	Nicklas Lidström, Det.	10.00

1996 - 97 GIANT EAGLE MARIO LEMIEUX - PINNACLE

This set was issued in six different three-card packs. An autographed Mario Lemieux was also apparently inserted in the packs.

Imprint:

	No.	Player	NRMT-MT
Complete Set (18 cards):			**25.00**
Album:			**3.00**
□	1	Mario Lemieux	2.00
□	2	Mario Lemieux (w/Cup)	2.00
□	3	Mario Lemieux	2.00
□	4	Mario Lemieux (w/Messier)	3.00
□	5	Mario Lemieux	2.00
□	6	Mario Lemieux	2.00
□	7	Mario Lemieux	2.00
□	8	Mario Lemieux	2.00
□	9	Mario Lemieux	2.00
□	10	Mario Lemieux (w/Jagr)	3.00
□	11	Mario Lemieux	2.00
□	12	Mario Lemieux	2.00
□	13	Mario Lemieux CC'87 (XZX: Gretzky)	3.00
□	14	Mario Lemieux	2.00
□	15	Mario Lemieux	2.00
□	16	Mario Lemieux (w/Gretzky)	3.00
□	17	Mario Lemieux	2.00
□	18	Mario Lemieux	2.00

1996 - 97 GOT-UM HOCKEY GREATS COLLECTION

These coins have two versions: a regular "silver" medallion and a 24 kt. gold-plated parallel. While all 24 kt. gold-plated medallions are supposed to have the engraving "24 kt." on the edge, some gold medallions have come out of the packs without the engraving.

Imprint:

	Player	Silver	Gold
Complete Set (25 coins):			**65.00**
Album:			**4.00**
□□	Ed Belfour (G), Chi.	1.50	40.00
□□	Ray Bourque, Bos.	2.50	75.00
□□	Pavel Bure, Van.	3.50	100.00
□□	Chris Chelios, Chi.	4.00	60.00
□□	Vincent Damphousse, Mtl.	1.50	40.00
□□	Sergei Fedorov, Det.	2.50	75.00
□□	Theoren Fleury, Cgy.	1.50	40.00
□□	Doug Gilmour, Tor.	1.50	40.00
□□	Wayne Gretzky, NYR.	10.00	250.00
□□	Brett Hull, Stl.	3.00	75.00
□□	Jaromir Jagr, Pgh.	2.50	125.00
□□	Paul Kariya, Ana.	5.00	150.00
□□	Mario Lemieux, Pgh.	6.50	175.00
□□	Eric Lindros, Pha.	6.50	150.00
□□	Mark Messier, NYR.	2.50	75.00
□□	Alexander Mogilny, Van.	1.50	40.00
□□	Jeremy Roenick, Pho.	1.50	40.00
□□	Patrick Roy (G), Col.	8.00	175.00
□□	Joe Sakic, Col.	5.00	100.00
□□	Steve Yzerman, Det.	5.00	125.00
□□	Sergei Berezin, Tor.	1.00	30.00
□□	Jim Campbell, Stl.	1.00	35.00
□□	Jarome Iginla, Cgy.	1.50	40.00
□□	Rem Murray, Edm.	1.00	30.00
□□	David Wilkie, Mtl.	1.00	30.00

1996- 97 HOCKEY HALL OF FAME LEGENDS

Artwork by Doug West.

Card Size: 3 1/2" x 5 1/2"

Imprint:

	No.	Player	NRMT-MT
Series Five Set (18 cards):			**135.00**
□	73	Terry Sawchuk (G)	12.00
□	74	Turk Broda (G)	10.00
□	75	Fr. David Bauer	8.00
□	76	George Armstrong	10.00
□	77	Marcel Pronovost	10.00
□	78	Bill Quackenbush	10.00
□	79	Harry Watson	10.00
□	80	Chuck Rayner	10.00
□	81	Keith Allen	8.00
□	82	Art Ross	8.00
□	83	Doug Bentley	8.00
□	84	Max Bentley	8.00
□	85	Charlie Drinkwater	8.00
□	86	Moose Goheen	8.00
□	87	Mike Bossy	13.00
□	88	Glenn Hall (G)	12.00
□	89	Bobby Hull	15.00
□	90	Sam Pollock	8.00

1996 - 97 KELLOGG'S

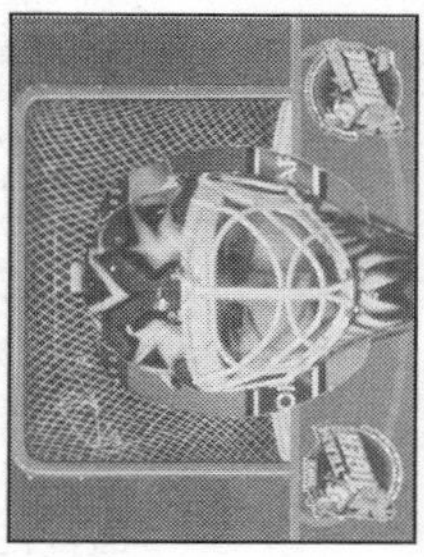
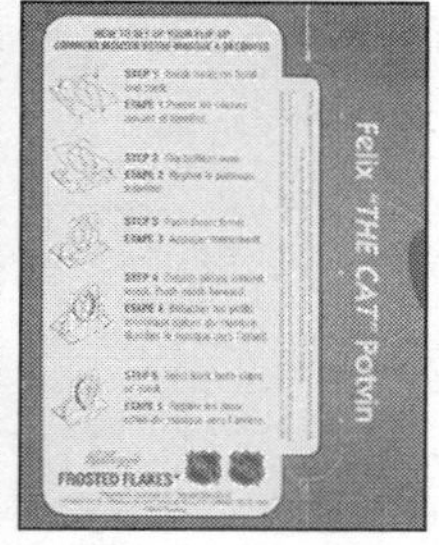

These pop-up cards were issued in specially marked boxes of Kellogg's cereal. The team pop-ups featured a goalie mask with the team logo.

	Player	NRMT-MT
☐	Curtis Joseph (G), Edm.	4.00
☐	Félix Potvin (G), Tor.	3.00
☐	Tony the Tiger	2.00
☐	Calgary Flames	2.00
☐	Montréal Canadiens	2.00
☐	Ottawa Senators	2.00
☐	Vancouver Canucks	2.00

1996 - 97 KENNER STARTING LINEUP

Figurines in both the Canadian and American series are the same.

Imprint:
Canadian Set (15 figurines):
American Set (24 figurines):

	Player	U.S.	Cdn.
☐	Tom Barrasso (G), Pgh.	30.00	.–
☐ ☐	Brian Bradley, T.B.	12.00	12.00
☐ ☐	Jim Carey (G), Wsh.	20.00	20.00
☐	Paul Coffey, Det.	20.00	.–
☐ ☐	Sergei Fedorov, Det.	12.00	12.00
☐ ☐	Ron Francis, Pgh.	12.00	12.00
☐	Dominik Hasek (G), Buf.	35.00	.–
☐ ☐	Paul Kariya, Ana.	30.00	30.00
☐	Pat LaFontaine, Buf.	20.00	.–
☐ ☐	John LeClair, Pha.	20.00	20.00
☐ ☐	Brian Leetch, NYR.	12.00	12.00
☐ ☐	Eric Lindros, Pha.	20.00	20.00
☐ ☐	Al MacInnis, Stl.	12.00	12.00
☐ ☐	Scott Mellanby, Fla.	12.00	12.00
☐ ☐	Mark Messier, NYR.	20.00	20.00
☐	Mike Modano, Dal.	12.00	.–
☐	Adam Oates, Wsh.	12.00	.–
☐ ☐	Mikael Renberg, Pha.	15.00	15.00
☐	Stéphane Richer, Mtl.	12.00	.–
☐	Jeremy Roenick, Chi.	12.00	.–
☐ ☐	Patrick Roy (G), Col.	75.00	75.00
☐ ☐	Joe Sakic, Col.	25.00	25.00
☐	Brendan Shanahan, Det.	15.00	.–
☐ ☐	Mats Sundin, Tor.	15.00	15.00

1996 - 97 KRAFT

Imprint:

Complete Set (72 cards):	**150.00**
Kraft / Upper Deck Album:	**45.00**

TEAM MVP'S

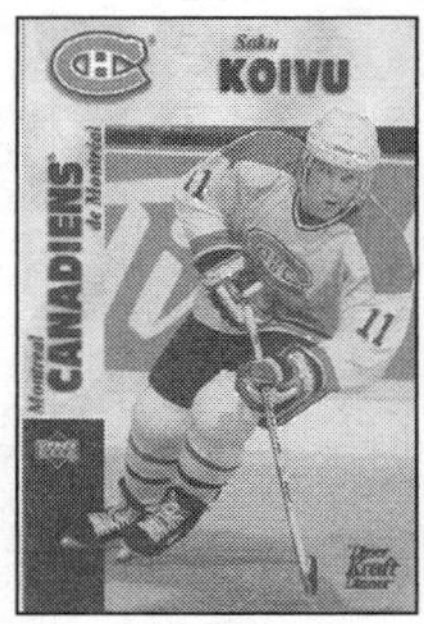

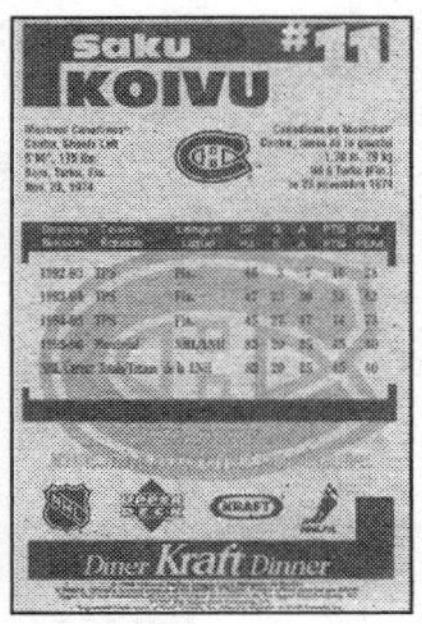

One of 20 different cards was found on the back of specially marked Kraft Dinner Macaroni & Cheese boxes and one of six different cards was found on the back of Kraft Dinner specialty flavours.

Card Size: 3 1/4" x 5"

	Player	NRMT-MT
☐	Guy Hebert (G), Ana.	1.50
☐	Adam Oates, Bos.	1.50
☐	Dominik Hasek (G), Buf.	3.00
☐	Theoren Fleury, Cgy.	1.50
☐	Ed Belfour (G), Chi	1.50
☐	Patrick Roy (G) Col.	5.00
☐	Joe Nieuwendyk, Dal.	1.50
☐	Sergei Fedorov, Det.	2.00
☐	Doug Weight, Edm.	1.50
☐	John Vanbiesbrouck (G), Fla.	2.50
☐	Geoff Sanderson, Hfd.	1.00
☐	Yanic Perreault, L.A.	1.00
☐	Saku Koivu, Mtl.	3.00
☐	Martin Brodeur (G), N.J.	3.00
☐	Zigmund Palffy, NYI.	1.50
☐	Brian Leetch, NYR.	1.50
☐	Alexei Yashin, Ott.	2.00
☐	Eric Lindros, Pha.	4.00
☐	Keith Tkachuk, Pho.	2.00
☐	Mario Lemieux, Pgh.	5.00
☐	Owen Nolan, S.J.	1.50
☐	Daren Puppa (G) T.B.	1.00
☐	Mats Sundin, Tor.	2.00
☐	Alexander Mogilny, Van.	1.50
☐	Michal Pivonka, Wsh.	1.00

FLEX MAGNETS

One of eight different flex magnets was found in specially marked Kraft Dinner 12 box cases.

	Player	NRMT-MT
☐	Theoren Fleury, Cgy.	3.00
☐	Saku Koivu, Mtl.	6.00
☐	Mario Lemieux, Pgh.	12.00
☐	Eric Lindros, Pha.	12.00
☐	Alexander Mogilny, Van.	3.00
☐	Mats Sundin, Tor.	4.00
☐	Doug Weight, Edm.	3.00
☐	Alexei Yashin, Ott.	3.50

ALL-STARS

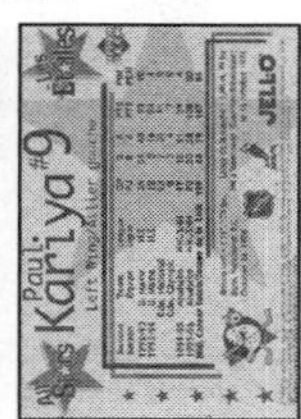

One of six different cards was found on the back of specially marked 102g JELL-O Instant Pudding boxes.

Card Size: 2 3/4" x 4"

	Player	NRMT-MT
☐	Chris Osgood (G), Det.	2.50
☐	Ray Bourque, Bos.	2.50
☐	Chris Chelios, Chi.	2.50
☐	Paul Kariya, Ana.	4.00
☐	Mario Lemieux, Pgh.	5.00
☐	Jaromir Jagr, Pgh.	3.50

NHL MASCOTS / FAVOURITE PLAYER

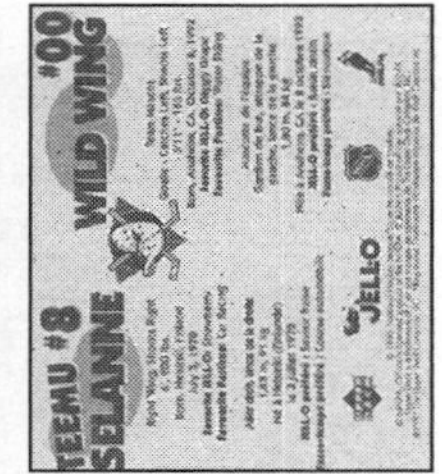

One of five different cards was found on the back of specially marked 85g JELL-O Jelly Powder boxes.

	Player	NRMT-MT
☐	Wild Thing/Teemu Selänne, Ana.	3.00
☐	Harvey Hound/Dave Gagner, Cgy.	1.50
☐	Stanley Panther/R.Niedermayer, Fla.	1.50
☐	S.J. Sharkie/Marty McSorley, S.J.	1.50
☐	Carlton/Félix Potvin (G), Tor.	2.00

TEAM RIVALS

This set of seven disks was available through redemption offer. Details were found on specially marked 500g or 1kg Kraft Peanut Butter jars.

Disk Size: 2 3/4" Diameter

	Player	NRMT-MT
☐	Sakic/Skrudland	5.00
☐	Fleury/Buchberger/etc	2.00
☐	MacInnis/Linden/etc	2.00
☐	Yzerman/Chelios/etc	5.00
☐	M.Lemieux/Lindros/etc	10.00
☐	Kariya/Blake/etc	7.00
☐	Bourque/Graves/etc	2.50

NHL TROPHY TRIUMPHS

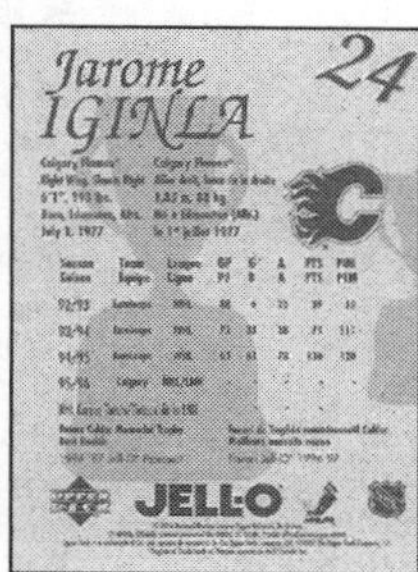

Two of 20 different cards were found on specially marked 4x142g cups of JELL-O Pudding Snacks.

Card Size: 2 1/2" x 3 1/2"

	Player	NRMT-MT
☐	Scotty Bowman (Adams)	1.50
☐	Marc Crawford (Adams)	1.50
☐	Mario Lemieux (Art Ross)	3.50
☐	Peter Forsberg (Art Ross)	2.75
☐	Daniel Alfedsson (Calder)	1.75
☐	Jarome Iginla (Calder)	2.00
☐	Joe Sakic (Conn Smythe)	2.50
☐	LeClair/Jagr/Shanahan (C.Smythe)	2.50
☐	Mario Lemieux (Hart)	3.50
☐	Eric Lindros (Hart)	3.00
☐	Osgood/Vernon (Jennings)	2.25
☐	Mike Richter (Jennings)	1.50
☐	Paul Kariya (Lady Byng)	3.00
☐	Adam Oates (Lady Byng)	1.25
☐	Chris Chelios (Norris)	1.50
☐	Ed Jovanovski (Norris)	1.25
☐	Sergei Fedorov (Selke)	2.25
☐	Ron Francis (Selke)	1.50
☐	Jim Carey (Vezina)	1.00
☐	Jocelyn Thibault (Vezina)	2.00

1996 - 97 LEAF

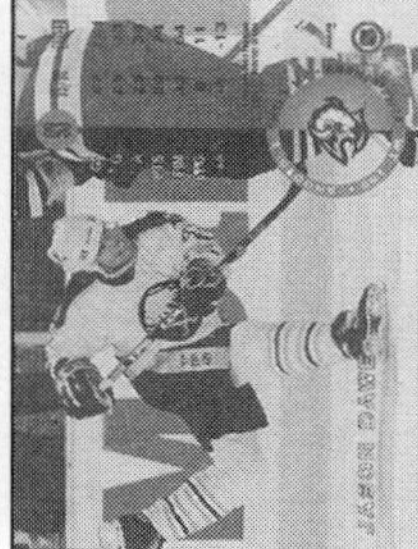

These cards have two versions: the regular card and a die-cut Press Proof parallel.

Imprint: © 1996 DONRUSS TRADING CARD CO.

Complete Set (240 cards):		**35.00**	**1,100.00**
Common Player:		**.15**	**4.00**

	No.	Player	Reg.	PP
☐ ☐	1	Sergei Fedorov, Det	.50	20.00
☐ ☐	2	Bill Ranford (G), Bos.	.50	6.00
☐ ☐	3	Oleg Tverdovsky, Wpg.	.15	4.00
☐ ☐	4	Brad May, Buf.	.15	4.00
☐ ☐	5	Chris Pronger, Stl.	.25	6.00

□□	6	Martin Brodeur, N.J.	.75	40.00
□□	7	Yanic Perreault, L.A.	.15	4.00
□□	8	Garry Galley, Buf.	.15	4.00
□□	9	Shawn McEachern, Bos. (Ott.)	.15	4.00
□□	10	Brian Bellows, T.B.	.15	4.00
□□	11	Ron Francis, Pgh.	.35	10.00
□□	12	Mike Modano, Dal.	.50	20.00
□□	13	Steve Yzerman, Det.	1.25	75.00
□□	14	Joe Mullen, Bos.	.15	4.00
□□	15	Pavel Bure, Van.	.75	40.00
□□	16	Dino Ciccarelli, T.B.	.25	6.00
□□	17	Claude Lemieux, Col.	.15	4.00
□□	18	Stéphane Richer, N.J. (Mtl.)	.15	4.00
□□	19	Dominik Hasek, Buf.	.75	40.00
□□	20	Adam Graves, NYR.	.15	4.00
□□	21	Joé Juneau, Wsh.	.15	4.00
□□	22	Rob Niedermayer, Fla.	.15	4.00
□□	23	Zigmund Palffy, NYI.	.35	10.00
□□	24	Dave Andreychuk, N.J.	.15	4.00
□□	25	Steve Thomas, N.J.	.15	4.00
□□	26	Tom Barrasso (G), Pgh.	.25	6.00
□□	27	Eric Desjardins, Pha.	.15	4.00
□□	28	Curtis Joseph, Edm.	.60	30.00
□□	29	Russ Courtnall, Van.	.15	4.00
□□	30	Stu Barnes, Fla.	.15	4.00
□□	31	Mark Tinordi, Wsh.	.15	4.00
□□	32	Gary Suter, Chi.	.15	4.00
□□	33	Greg Johnson, Det.	.15	4.00
□□	34	Joe Nieuwendyk, Dal.	.25	6.00
□□	35	Norm Maciver, Wpg.	.15	4.00
□□	36	Craig Janney, Wpg.	.15	4.00
□□	37	Mark Recchi, Mtl.	.25	6.00
□□	38	Patrick Roy (G), Col.	2.00	110.00
□□	39	Petr Klima, T.B.	.15	4.00
□□	40	Ken Wregget (G), Pgh.	.15	4.00
□□	41	Rod Brind'Amour, Pha.	.25	6.00
□□	42	Viacheslav Fetisov, Det.	.25	6.00
□□	43	Kirk McLean(G), Van.	.25	6.00
□□	44	Pat LaFontaine, Buf.	.25	6.00
□□	45	Brett Hull, Stl.	.50	20.00
□□	46	Chris Chelios, Chi.	.35	15.00
□□	47	Damian Rhodes (G), Ott.	.15	4.00
□□	48	Kevin Hatcher, Pgh.	.15	4.00
□□	49	Uwe Krupp, Col.	.15	4.00
□□	50	Bernie Nicholls, Chi.	.15	4.00
□□	51	Tommy Söderström (G), NYI.	.15	4.00
□□	52	Teemu Selänne, Ana.	.75	40.00
□□	53	Mats Sundin, Tor.	.50	20.00
□□	54	Jeff Hackett (G), Chi.	.25	6.00
□□	55	Ulf Dahlen, S.J.	.15	4.00
□□	56	Dale Hunter, Wsh.	.15	4.00
□□	57	Robert Kron, Hfd.	.15	4.00
□□	58	Brian Bradley, T.B.	.15	4.00
□□	59	Pat Verbeek, NYR.	.15	4.00
□□	60	Kenny Jonsson, Tor.	.15	4.00
□□	61	Theoren Fleury, Cgy.	.35	10.00
□□	62	Alexander Selivanov, T.B.	.15	4.00
□□	63	Nikolai Khabibulin (G), Wpg.	.35	10.000
□□	64	Grant Fuhr (G), Stl.	.25	6.00
□□	65	Phil Housley, Wsh.	.15	4.00
□□	66	Bill Lindsay, Fla.	.15	4.00
□□	67	Trevor Kidd (G), Cgy.	.25	6.00
□□	68	Jim Carey (G), Wsh.	.15	4.00
□□	69	Brian Skrudland, Fla.	.15	4.00
□□	70	Todd Krygier, Wsh.	.15.	4.00
□□	71	Petr Nedved, Pgh.	.15	4.00
□□	72	Kirk Muller, Tor.	.15	4.00
□□	73	Darren Puppa (G), T.B.	.15	4.00
□□	74	Doug Gilmour, Tor.	.35	10.00
□□	75	Nicklas Lidstrom, Det.	.25	6.00
□□	76	Zdeno Ciger, Edm.	.15	4.00
□□	77	Robert Svehla, Fla.	.15	4.00
□□	78	Andrew Cassels, Hfd.	.15	4.00
□□	79	Vincent Damphousse, Mtl.	.35	10.00
□□	80	Alexandre Daigle, Ott.	.25	6.00
□□	81	Tomas Sandström, Pgh.	.15	4.00
□□	82	Brent Fedyk, Dal.	.15	4.00
□□	83	John LeClair, Pha.	.50	20.00
□□	84	Mario Lemieux, Pgh.	2.00	110.00
□□	85	Sean Burke (G), Hfd.	.25	6.00
□□	86	Cam Neely, Bos.	.25	6.00
□□	87	Jeff Friesen, S.J.	.25.	6.00
□□	88	Guy Hebert (G), Ana.	.25	6.00
□□	89	Jon Casey, Stl.	.15	4.00
□□	90	Rick Tocchet, Bos.	.15	4.00
□□	91	Mike Gartner, Tor. (Pho.)	.25	6.00
□□	92	Tony Amonte, Chi.	.25	6.00
□□	93	Jason Dawe, Buf.	.15	4.00
□□	94	Chris Terreri (G), S.J.	.15	4.00
□□	95	Zarley Zalapski, Cgy.	.15	4.00
□□	96	Martin Rucinsky, Mtl.	.15	4.00
□□	97	Garth Snow (G), Pha.	.15	4.00
□□	98	Sylvain Lefebvre, Tor.	.15	4.00
□□	99	Andy Moog (G), Dal.	.25	6.00
□□	100	Larry Murphy, Tor.	.25	6.00
□□	101	Alexei Yashin, Ott.	.35	15.00
□□	102	Pat Falloon, Pha.	.15	4.00
□□	103	Greg Adams, Dal.	.15	4.00
□□	104	Igor Larionov, Det.	.25	6.00
□□	105	Geoff Sanderson, Hfd.	.15	4.00
□□	106	Jaromir Jagr, Pgh.	1.25	75.00
□□	107	Alexei Zhamnov, Wpg.	.25	6.00
□□	108	Mikael Renberg, Pha.	.15	4.00
□□	109	Kelly Hrudey (G), L.A.	.15	4.00
□□	110	Vladimir Konstantinov, Det.	.15	4.00
□□	111	Brian Savage, Mtl.	.15	4.00
□□	112	Adam Oates, Bos.	.35	10.00
□□	113	Teppo Numminen, Wpg.	.15	4.00
□□	114	Ray Sheppard, Fla.	.15	4.00
□□	115	Michael Nylander, Cgy.	.15	4.00
□□	116	Jozef Stumpel, Bos.	.25	6.00
□□	117	Ed Olczyk, L.A.	.15	4.00
□□	118	Roman Hamrlik, T.B.	.25	6.00
□□	119	Kris Draper, Det.	.15	4.00
□□	120	Chris Gratton, T.B.	.25	6.00
□□	121	Randy Burridge, Wsh.	.15	4.00
□□	122	Ray Bourque, Bos.	.50	20.00
□□	123	Jyrki Lumme, Van.	.15	4.00
□□	124	Dale Hawerchuk, Pha.	.25	6.00
□□	125	Dave Lowry, Fla.	.15	4.00
□□	126	Curtis Leschyshyn, Col.	.15	4.00
□□	127	Martin Gelinas, Van.	.15	4.00
□□	128	Owen Nolan, S.J.	.25	6.00
□□	129	Radek Bonk, Ott.	.15	4.00
□□	130	Sergei Zubov, Pgh.	.25	6.00
□□	131	Travis Green, NYI.	.15	4.00
□□	132	Scott Mellanby, Fla.	.15	4.00
□□	133	Keith Tkachuk, Wpg.	.35	15.00
□□	134	Luc Robitaille, NYR.	.25	6.00
□□	135	Alexei Kovalev, NYR.	.15	4.00
□□	136	Doug Weight, Edm.	.35	10.00
□□	137	Benoît Hogue, Dal.	.15	4.00
□□	138	Cory Stillman, Cgy.	.15	4.00
□□	139	Joe Sakic, Col.	1.00	50.00
□□	140	Wayne Gretzky, Stl. (NYR.)	4.00	150.00
□□	141	Mike Ricci, Col.	.15	4.00
□□	142	Kyle McLaren, Bos.	.15	4.00
□□	143	Deron Quint, Wpg.	.15	4.00
□□	144	Ville Peltonen, S.J.	.15	4.00
□□	145	Todd Harvey, Dal.	.15	4.00
□□	146	Brendan Shanahan, Hfd. (Det.)	.60	30.00
□□	147	Mike Vernon (G), Det.	.25	6.00
□□	148	Eric Lindros, Pha.	1.50	90.00
□□	149	Rick Tabaracci (G), T.B.	.15	4.00
□□	150	Stéphane Yelle, Col.	.15	4.00
□□	151	Chris Osgood (G), Det.	.35	15.00
□□	152	Corey Hirsch (G), Van.	.15	4.00
□□	153	Todd Marchant, Edm.	.15	4.00
□□	154	Keith Primeau, Hfd.	.25	6.00
□□	155	Alexei Zhitnik, L.A.	.15	4.00
□□	156	Félix Potvin (G), Tor.	.50	20.00
□□	157	Vitali Yachmenev, L.A.	.15	4.00
□□	158	Geoff Courtnall, Stl.	.15	4.00
□□	159	Peter Forsberg, Col.	1.25	75.00
□□	160	Radek Dvorak, Fla.	.15	4.00
□□	161	Bryan McCabe, NYI.	.15	4.00
□□	162	Alexander Mogilny, Van.	.35	10.00
□□	163	Shayne Corson, Mtl.	.25	6.00
□□	164	Paul Coffey, Det. (Hfd.)	.25	6.00
□□	165	Brian Leetch, NYR.	.35	10.00
□□	166	Wendel Clark, Tor.	.25	6.00
□□	167	Aaron Gavey, T.B.	.15	4.00
□□	168	Dimitri Khristich, Wsh.	.15	4.00
□□	169	Grant Marshall, Dal.	.15	4.00
□□	170	Valeri Kamensky, Col.	.25	6.00
□□	171	Ryan Smyth, Edm.	.25	6.00
□□	172	Niklas Sundstrom, NYR.	.15	4.00
□□	173	Cliff Ronning, Van. (Pho.)	.15	4.00
□□	174	Al MacInnis, Stl.	.15	4.00
□□	175	Scott Stevens, N.J.	.15	4.00
□□	176	Paul Kariya, Ana.	1.50	90.00
□□	177	Rob Blake, L.A.	.25	6.00
□□	178	Mike Richter (G), NYR.	.35	10.00
□□	179	Jason Arnott, Edm.	.25	6.00
□□	180	Mark Messier, NYR.	.50	20.00
□□	181	Scott Young, Col.	.15	4.00
□□	182	Jocelyn Thibault (G), Mtl.	.35	10.00
□□	183	Marcus Ragnarsson, S.J.	.15	4.00
□□	184	Darren Turcotte, S.J.	.15	4.00
□□	185	Joe Murphy, Stl.	.15	4.00
□□	186	Pierre Turgeon, Stl.	.25	6.00
□□	187	Trevor Linden, Van.	.25	6.00
□□	188	Stéphane Fiset (G), Col.	.25	6.00
□□	189	Miroslav Satan, Edm.	.15	4.00
□□	190	Mathieu Schneider, Tor.	.15	4.00
□□	191	Jeremy Roenick, Chi.	.35	10.00
□□	192	Craig MacTavish, Pha.	.15	4.00
□□	193	John Vanbiesbrouck (G), Fla.	.60	30.00
□□	194	Ron Hextall (G), Pha.	.25	6.00
□□	195	John MacLean, N.J.	.15	4.00
□□	196	Vyacheslav Kozlov, Det.	.15	4.00
□□	197	Sandis Ozolinsh, Col.	.25	6.00
□□	198	Scott Niedermayer, N.J.	.25	6.00
□□	199	Ed Belfour (G), Chi.	.35	10.00
□□	200	Peter Bondra, Wsh.	.35	15.00
□□	201	Jere Lehtinen, Dal.	.25	6.00
□□	202	Eric Dazé, Chi.	.25	6.00
□□	203	Chad Kilger, Wpg.	.15	4.00
□□	204	Saku Koivu, Mtl.	.75	40.00
□□	205	Todd Bertuzzi, NYI.	.25	6.00
□□	206	Petr Sykora, N.J.	.15	4.00
□□	207	Valeri Bure, Mtl.	.15	4.00
□□	208	Ed Jovanovski, Fla.	.25	6.00
□□	209	Jeff O'Neill, Hfd.	.25	6.00
□□	210	Daniel Alfredsson, Ott.	.25	6.00
□□	211	Byron Dafoe (G), L.A.	.15	4.00
□□	212	Brian Holzinger, Buf.	.15	4.00
□□	213	Martin Biron (G), Buf.	.15	4.00
□□	214	Anders Eriksson, Det.	.15	4.00
□□	215	Landon Wilson, Col.	.15	4.00
□□	**216**	**Alexei Yegorov, S.J., RC**	**.15**	**4.00**
□□	**217**	**Jan Caloun, S.J., RC**	**.15**	**4.00**
□□	218	David Sacco, Ana.	.15	4.00
□□	219	David Nemirovsky, Fla.	.15	4.00
□□	220	Anders Myrvold, Col.	.15	4.00
□□	221	Tommy Salo (G), NYI.	.15	4.00
□□	222	Jan Vopat, L.A.	.15	4.00
□□	**223**	**Steve Staios, Bos., RC**	**.15**	**4.00**
□□	224	Patrick Labrecque (G), Mtl.	.15	4.00
□□	225	Jamie Lagenbrunner, Dal.	.15	4.00
□□	226	Denis Pederson, N.J.	.15	4.00
□□	227	Marek Malik, Hfd.	.15	4.00
□□	228	Geoff Sarjeant (G), S.J.	.15	4.00
□□	229	Chris Ferraro, NYR.	.15	4.00
□□	230	Zdenek Nedved, Tor.	.15	4.00
□□	231	Wayne Primeau, Buf.	.15	4.00
□□	232	Daymond Langkow, T.B.	.15	4.00
□□	233	Marko Kiprusoff, Mtl.	.15	4.00
□□	234	Niklas Sundblad, NYR.	.15	4.00
□□	**235**	**Jamie Ram (G), NYR., RC**	**.15**	**4.00**
□□	236	Jamie Rivers, Stl.	.15	4.00
□□	**237**	**Steve Washburn, Fla., RC**	**.15**	**4.00**
□□	238	CL: Teemu Selänne, Ana.	.50	20.00
□□	239	CL: Steve Yzerman, Det.	.65	30.00
□□	240	CL: Eric Lindros, Pha.	.75	50.00

FIRE ON ICE

These retail inserts are serial numbered out of 2,500.

Insert Set (15 cards): 575.00

	No.	Player	NRMT-MT
□	1	Mario Lemieux, Pgh.	100.00
□	2	Alexander Mogilny, Van.	15.00
□	3	Joe Sakic, Col.	50.00
□	4	Paul Kariya, Ana.	75.00
□	5	Wayne Gretzky, NYR.	125.00
□	6	Doug Weight, Edm.	15.00
□	7	Zigmund Palffy, NYI.	25.00
□	8	Eric Lindros, Pha.	75.00
□	9	Teemu Selänne, Ana.	40.00
□	10	Doug Gilmour, Tor.	15.00
□	11	Jeremy Roenick, Chi.	15.00
□	12	Steve Yzerman, Det.	60.00
□	13	Ed Jovanovski, Fla.	10.00
□	14	Mike Modano, Dal.	30.00
□	15	Mark Messier, NYR.	30.00

GOLD LEAF ROOKIES

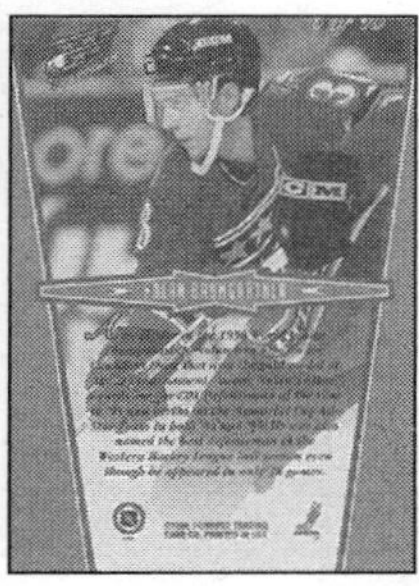

Insert Set (10 cards): 40.00

	No.	Player	NRMT-MT
☐	1	Ethan Moreau, Chi	6.00
☐	2	Kevin Hodson (G), Det.	4.00
☐	3	José Théodore (G), Mtl.	8.00
☐	4	Peter Ferraro, NYR.	4.00
☐	5	Ralph Intranuovo, Tor.	4.00
☐	6	Nolan Baumgartner, Wsh.	4.00
☐	7	Brandon Convery, Tor.	4.00
☐	8	Darcy Tucker, Mtl.	4.00
☐	9	Eric Fichaud (G), NYI.	6.00
☐	10	Steve Sullivan, N.J.	4.00

THE BEST OF...

These magazine pack inserts are serial numbered out of 1,500.

Insert Set (9 cards): 450.00

	No.	Player	NRMT-MT
☐	1	Jaromir Jagr, Pgh.	100.00
☐	2	Eric Dazé, Chi.	20.00
☐	3	Eric Lindros, Pha.	135.00
☐	4	Chris Osgood (G), Det.	40.00
☐	5	Keith Tkachuk, Wpg.	40.00
☐	6	Nikolai Khabibulin (G), Wpg.	30.00
☐	7	Doug Weight, Edm.	30.00
☐	8	Peter Forsberg, Col.	100.00
☐	9	Jocelyn Thibault (G), Mtl.	30.00

LEATHER AND LACES

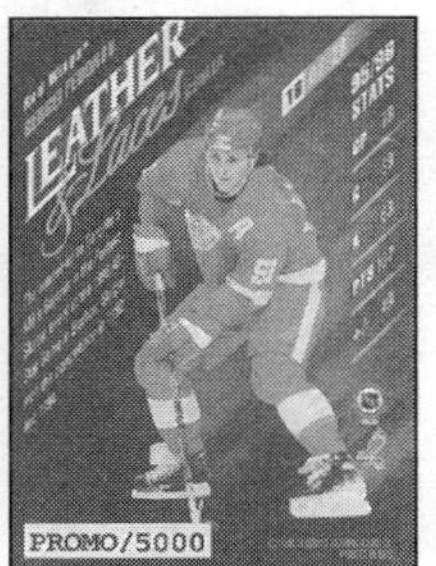

These have two versions: a promo card (PROMO / 5,000) and the insert (serial numbered out of 5,000).

Insert Set (20 cards): 50.00 300.00

	No.	Player	Promo	Insert
☐☐	1	Joe Sakic, Col.	4.00	25.00
☐☐	2	Keith Tkachuk, Wpg.	2.00	12.00
☐☐	3	Brett Hull, Stl.	2.50	15.00
☐☐	4	Paul Coffey, Det.	1.00	5.00
☐☐	5	Jaromir Jagr, Pgh.	5.00	30.00
☐☐	6	Peter Forsberg, Col.	5.00	30.00
☐☐	7	Zigmund Palffy, NYI.	1.50	8.00
☐☐	8	Wayne Gretzky, NYR.	10.00	60.00
☐☐	9	Pavel Bure, Van.	3.50	20.00
☐☐	10	Eric Lindros, Pha.	6.50	40.00
☐☐	11	Alexander Mogilny, Van.	1.50	8.00
☐☐	12	Trevor Linden, Van.	1.00	5.00
☐☐	13	Jeremy Roenick, Chi.	1.50	8.00
☐☐	14	Doug Gilmour, Tor.	1.50	8.00
☐☐	15	Mike Modano, Dal.	2.50	15.00
☐☐	16	Sergei Fedorov, Det.	2.50	15.00
☐☐	17	Brendan Shanahan, Hfd.	3.00	18.00
☐☐	18	Pierre Turgeon, Stl.	1.00	5.00
☐☐	19	Ed Jovanovski, Fla.	1.00	5.00
☐☐	20	Saku Koivu, Mtl.	3.50	20.00

SHUT DOWN

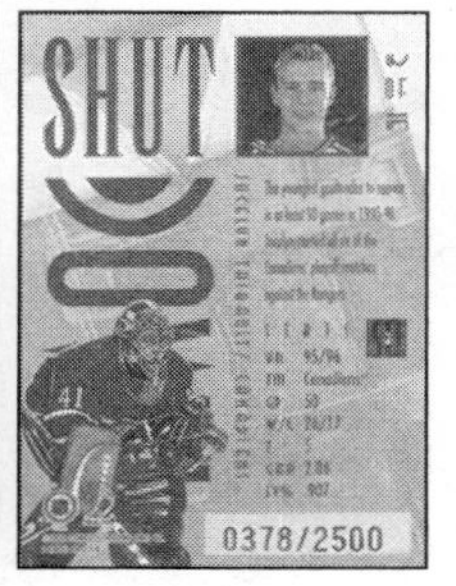

These hobby pack inserts are serial numbered out of 2,500.

Insert Set (15 cards): 375.00

	No.	Player	NRMT-MT
☐	1	Patick Roy (G), Col.	100.00
☐	2	John Vanbiesbrouck (G), Fla.	40.00
☐	3	Jocelyn Thibault (G), Mtl.	20.00
☐	4	Ed Belfour (G), Chi.	20.00
☐	5	Curtis Joseph (G), Edm.	40.00
☐	6	Martin Brodeur (G), N.J.	50.00
☐	7	Damian Rhodes (G), Ott.	15.00
☐	8	Félix Potvin (G), Tor.	35.00
☐	9	Nikolai Khabibulin (G), Wpg.	20.00
☐	10	Jim Carey (G), Wsh.	15.00
☐	11	Mike Richter (G), NYR.	20.00
☐	12	Corey Hirsch (G), Van.	15.00
☐	13	Chris Osgood (G), Det.	25.00
☐	14	Ron Hextall (G), Pha.	15.00
☐	15	Daren Puppa (G), T.B.	15.00

SWEATERS

These cards have two versions: an Away series (serial numbered out of 5,000) and a Home parrallel (serial numbered out of 5,000).

Insert Set (15 cards): 1,500.00 375.00

	No.	Player	Home	Away
☐☐	1	Mario Lemieux, Pgh.	240.00	60.00
☐☐	2	Patrick Roy (G), Col.	240.00	60.00
☐☐	3	Eric Lindros, Pha.	200.00	50.00
☐☐	4	John Vanbiesbrouck (G), Fla.	100.00	25.00
☐☐	5	Paul Kariya, Ana.	200.00	50.00
☐☐	6	Martin Brodeur (G), N.J.	120.00	30.00
☐☐	7	Eric Dazé, Chi.	40.00	10.00
☐☐	8	Mark Messier, NYR.	60.00	15.00
☐☐	9	Jim Carey (G), Wsh.	40.00	10.00
☐☐	10	Brendan Shanahan, Det.	100.00	25.00
☐☐	11	Sergei Fedorov, Det.	60.00	15.00
☐☐	12	Brett Hull, Stl.	60.00	15.00
☐☐	13	Pavel Bure, Van.	120.00	30.00
☐☐	14	Daniel Alfredsson, Ott.	50.00	12.00
☐☐	15	Saku Koivu, Mtl.	120.00	30.00

1996 - 97 LEAF LIMITED

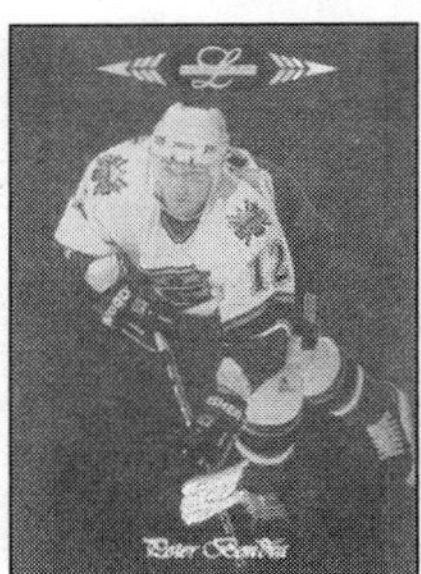

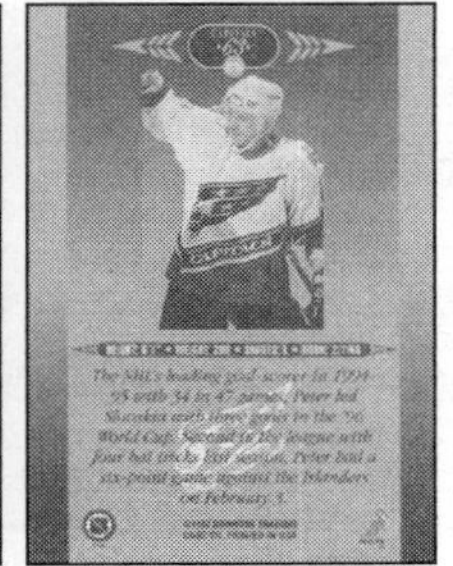

These cards have two versions: the regular card and a Limited Gold parallel set.

Imprint: © 1997 DONRUSS TRADING CARD CO.

Complete Set (90 cards): 70.00 750.00

Common Player: .35 3.50

	No.	Player	Reg.	Gold
☐☐	1	Chris Chelios, Chi.	2.00	20.00
☐☐	2	Brendan Shanahan, Det.	3.00	30.00
☐☐	3	Keith Tkachuk, Pho.	2.00	20.00
☐☐	4	Roman Hamrlik, T.B.	.50	5.00
☐☐	5	Adam Oates, Bos.	1.50	10.00
☐☐	6	Chris Osgood (G), Det.	2.00	20.00
☐☐	7	Wayne Gretzky, NYR.	10.00	125.00
☐☐	8	Alexander Mogilny, Van.	1.50	10.00
☐☐	9	Patrick Roy (G), Col.	8.00	100.00
☐☐	10	Saku Koivu, Mtl.	3.50	35.00
☐☐	11	Jaromir Jagr, Pgh.	5.00	50.00
☐☐	12	Wendel Clark, Tor.	.50	5.00
☐☐	13	Mike Modano, Dal.	2.50	25.00
☐☐	14	Ed Jovanovski, Fla.	.50	3.00
☐☐	15	John LeClair, Pha.	2.50	25.00
☐☐	16	Jim Carey (G), Wsh.	.35	3.50
☐☐	17	Paul Kariya, Ana.	6.50	80.00
☐☐	18	Paul Coffey, Hfd.	.50	5.00
☐☐	19	Todd Bertuzzi, NYI.	.50	5.00
☐☐	20	Owen Nolan, S.J.	.50	5.00
☐☐	21	Dominik Hasek (G), Buf.	3.50	35.00
☐☐	22	Bill Ranford (G), Bos.	.50	5.00
☐☐	23	Scott Stevens, N.J.	.35	3.50
☐☐	24	Brett Hull, Stl.	2.50	25.00
☐☐	25	Trevor Kidd (G), Cgy.	.50	5.00
☐☐	26	Viacheslav Fetisov, Det.	.50	5.00
☐☐	27	Luc Robitaille, NYR.	.50	5.00
☐☐	28	Mats Sundin, Tor.	2.50	25.00
☐☐	29	Peter Forsberg, Col.	5.00	50.00
☐☐	30	John Vanbiesbrouck (G), Fla.	3.00	30.00
☐☐	31	Alexei Yashin, Ott.	2.00	20.00
☐☐	32	Pavel Bure, Van.	3.50	35.00
☐☐	33	Pat Verbeek, Dal.	.35	3.50
☐☐	34	Vitali Yachmenev, L.A.	.35	3.50
☐☐	35	Ron Hextall (G), Pha.	.50	5.00
☐☐	36	Michal Pivonka, Wsh.	.35	3.50
☐☐	37	Eric Dazé, Chi.	.50	5.00
☐☐	38	Pierre Turgeon, Mtl.	.50	4.00
☐☐	39	Petr Nedved, Pgh.	.35	3.50
☐☐	40	Steve Yzerman, Det.	5.00	50.00
☐☐	41	Mike Richter (G), NYR.	1.50	10.00
☐☐	42	Marcus Ragnarsson, S.J.	.35	3.50
☐☐	43	Jason Arnott, Edm.	.50	5.00
☐☐	44	Jocelyn Thibault (G), Mtl.	1.50	10.00
☐☐	45	Alexander Selivanov, T.B.	.35	3.50
☐☐	46	Claude Lemieux, Col.	.35	3.50
☐☐	47	Eric Lindros, Pha.	6.50	80.00
☐☐	48	Grant Fuhr (G), Stl.	.50	5.00
☐☐	49	Ray Bourque, Bos.	2.50	25.00
☐☐	50	Scott Mellanby, Fla.	.35	3.50
☐☐	51	Craig Janney, Pho.	.35	3.50
☐☐	52	Ron Francis, Pgh.	1.50	10.00
☐☐	53	Ed Belfour (G), Chi.	1.50	10.00
☐☐	54	Petr Sykora, N.J.	.35	3.50
☐☐	55	Damian Rhodes (G), Ott.	.35	3.50
☐☐	56	Joe Sakic, Col.	4.00	40.00
☐☐	57	Zigmund Palffy, NYI.	1.50	10.00
☐☐	58	Daren Puppa (G), T.B.	.35	3.50
☐☐	59	Pat LaFontaine, Buf.	.50	5.00
☐☐	60	Nikolai Khabibulin (G), Pho.	1.50	10.00
☐☐	61	Sergei Fedorov, Det.	2.50	25.00
☐☐	62	Valeri Bure, Mtl.	.35	3.50
☐☐	63	Peter Bondra, Wsh.	2.00	20.00
☐☐	64	Teemu Selänne, Ana.	3.50	35.00
☐☐	65	Mark Messier, NYR.	2.50	25.00
☐☐	66	Shayne Corson, Stl.	.50	5.00
☐☐	67	Theoren Fleury, Cgy.	1.50	10.00
☐☐	68	Jeff O'Neill, Hfd.	.50	5.00
☐☐	69	Eric Fichaud, NYI.	.50	5.00
☐☐	70	Doug Gilmour, Tor.	1.50	10.00
☐☐	71	Doug Weight, Edm.	1.50	10.00
☐☐	72	Stéphane Fiset (G), L.A.	.50	5.00
☐☐	73	Daniel Alfredsson, Ott.	.50	5.00
☐☐	74	Trevor Linden, Van.	.50	5.00
☐☐	75	Joe Nieuwendyk, Dal.	.50	5.00
☐☐	76	Brian Bradley, T.B.	.35	3.50
☐☐	77	Jere Lehtinen, Dal.	.50	5.00
☐☐	78	Rob Niedermayer, Fla.	.35	3.50
☐☐	79	Mikael Renberg, Pha.	.35	3.50
☐☐	80	Félix Potvin (G), Tor.	2.50	25.00
☐☐	81	Valeri Kamensky, Col.	.50	5.00
☐☐	82	Brian Leetch, NYR.	1.50	10.00
☐☐	83	Jeff Friesen, S.J.	.50	5.00
☐☐	84	Vincent Damphousse, Mtl.	1.50	10.00
☐☐	85	Mario Lemieux, Pgh.	8.00	100.00
☐☐	86	Jeremy Roenick, Pho.	1.50	10.00
☐☐	87	Martin Brodeur (G), N.J.	3.50	35.00
☐☐	88	Vyacheslav Kozlov, Det.	.35	3.50
☐☐	89	Corey Hirsch (G), Van.	.35	3.50
☐☐	90	Curtis Joseph (G), Edm.	3.00	30.00
☐		CL: Eric Lindros	2.00	.–

BASH THE BOARDS

These cards have three versions: a promo (PROMO / 2,500), the regular insert (serial numbered out of 3,500) and a die-cut limited edition parallel (serial numbered out of 350).

	No.	Player	Promo	L.E.	Reg.
Insert Set (10 cards):			**25.00**	**700.00**	**245.00**
☐☐☐	1	Eric Lindros, Pha.	8.00	250.00	85.00
☐☐☐	2	Mark Messier, NYR.	3.00	75.00	25.00
☐☐☐	3	Owen Nolan, S.J.	1.50	30.00	12.00
☐☐☐	4	Doug Gilmour, Tor.	1.75	40.00	15.00
☐☐☐	5	Keith Tkachuk, Wpg.	2.50	50.00	18.00
☐☐☐	6	Claude Lemieux, Col.	1.50	25.00	10.00
☐☐☐	7	Ed Jovanovski, Fla.	1.50	30.00	12.00
☐☐☐	8	Peter Forsberg, Col.	6.00	175.00	60.00
☐☐☐	9	Brendan Shanahan, Hfd.	3.50	100.00	35.00
☐☐☐	10	Eric Dazé, Chi.	1.50	30.00	12.00

ROOKIES

	No.	Player	NRMT-MT
Insert Set (10 cards):			**110.00**
☐	1	Ethan Moreau, Chi.	12.00
☐	2	Jarome Iginla, Cgy.	15.00
☐	3	Bryan Berard, NYI.	15.00
☐	4	Hnat Domenichelli, Hfd.	12.00
☐	5	Wade Redden, Ott.	8.00
☐	6	Dainius Zubrus, Pha.	25.00
☐	7	Sergei Berezin, Tor.	8.00
☐	8	Jamie Langenbrunner, Dal.	12.00
☐	9	Tomas Holmstrom, Det.	12.00
☐	10	Jonas Hoglund, Cgy.	8.00

STUBBLE

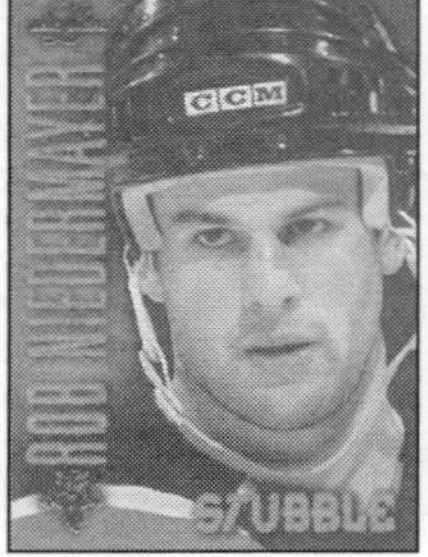

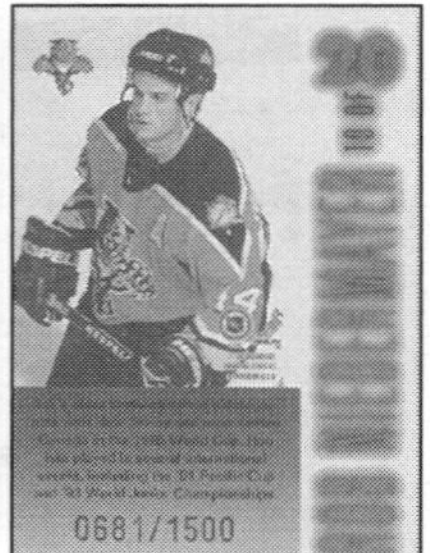

These inserts are serial numbered out of 1,500.

	No.	Player	NRMT-MT
Insert Set (20 cards):			**800.00**
☐	1	Patrick Roy (G), Col.	125.00
☐	2	Eric Lindros, Pha.	100.00
☐	3	Wayne Gretzky, NYR.	160.00
☐	4	Paul Coffey, Det.	20.00
☐	5	Jim Carey (G), Wsh.	15.00
☐	6	Ed Belfour (G), Chi.	25.00
☐	7	Mario Lemieux, Pgh.	125.00
☐	8	Mike Modano, Dal.	35.00
☐	9	Todd Bertuzzi, NYI.	20.00
☐	10	Pavel Bure, Van.	50.00
☐	11	Martin Brodeur, N.J.	50.00
☐	12	Petr Nedved, Pgh.	15.00
☐	13	Alexander Mogilny, Van.	25.00
☐	14	Steve Yzerman, Det.	75.00
☐	15	Brett Hull, Stl.	35.00
☐	16	Joe Sakic, Col.	60.00
☐	17	Scott Mellanby, Fla.	15.00
☐	18	Trevor Linden, Van.	20.00
☐	19	Rob Niedermayer, Fla.	15.00
☐	20	Wendel Clark, Tor.	20.00

1996 - 97 LEAF PREFERRED

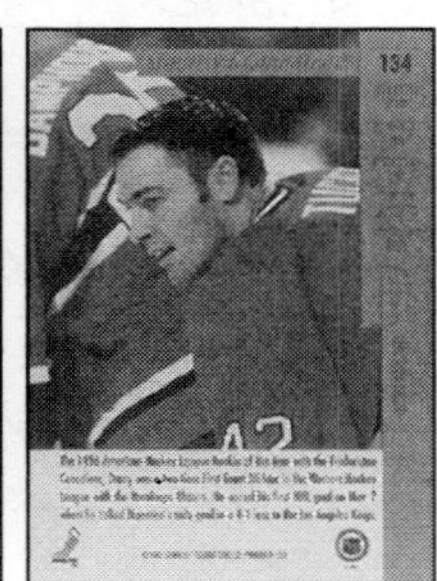

These cards have two versions: the regular card and a Press Proof parallel. The Press Proof cards are limited to 250 copies.

Imprint:

	No.	Player	P.P.	Reg.
Complete Set (150 cards):			**2,500.00**	**35.00**
Common Player:			**5.00**	**.15**
☐☐	1	Patrick Roy (G), Col.	200.00	2.50
☐☐	2	Alexander Mogilny, Van.	15.00	.35
☐☐	3	Bill Ranford, Bos.	10.00	.25
☐☐	4	Jeremy Roenick, Chi.	15.00	.35
☐☐	5	Travis Green, NYI.	5.00	.15
☐☐	6	Owen Nolan, S.J.	10.00	.25
☐☐	7	Paul Kariya, Ana.	160.00	2.00
☐☐	8	Pat Verbeek, NYR.	5.00	.15
☐☐	9	Jeff O'Neill, Hfd.	10.00	.25
☐☐	10	Nikolai Khabibulin (G), Pho.	15.00	.35
☐☐	11	Pat LaFontaine, Buf.	10.00	.25
☐☐	12	Rob Niedermayer, Fla.	5.00	.25
☐☐	13	Luc Robitaille, NYR.	10.00	.25
☐☐	14	Mats Sundin, Tor.	30.00	.75
☐☐	15	Cory Stillman, Cgy.	5.00	.15
☐☐	16	Ray Ferraro, L.A.	5.00	.15
☐☐	17	Alexei Yashin, Ott.	20.00	.50
☐☐	18	Brian Bradley, T.B.	5.00	.15
☐☐	19	Chris Chelios, Chi.	20.00	.50
☐☐	20	Jason Arnott, Edm.	10.00	.25
☐☐	21	Petr Sykora, N.J.	5.00	.15
☐☐	22	Jaromir Jagr, Pgh.	110.00	1.50
☐☐	23	Jim Carey (G), Wsh.	5.00	.15
☐☐	24	Claude Lemieux, Col.	5.00	.15
☐☐	25	Vincent Damphousse, Mtl.	15.00	.35
☐☐	26	Shayne Corson, Mtl.	10.00	.25
☐☐	27	Joe Nieuwendyk, Dal.	10.00	.25
☐☐	28	Kenny Jonsson, NYI.	5.00	.15
☐☐	29	Peter Bondra, Wsh.	20.00	.50
☐☐	30	Ed Belfour (G), Chi.	15.00	.35
☐☐	31	Brendan Shanahan, Det.	60.00	.85
☐☐	32	Eric Desjardins, Pha.	5.00	.15
☐☐	33	Corey Hirsch (G), Van.	5.00	.15
☐☐	34	Viacheslav Fetisov, Det.	10.00	.25
☐☐	35	Craig Janney, S.J.	5.00	.15
☐☐	36	Félix Potvin (G), Tor.	30.00	.75
☐☐	37	Joe Sakic, Col.	90.00	1.25
☐☐	38	Scott Stevens, N.J.	5.00	.15
☐☐	39	Kelly Hrudey (G), L.A.	5.00	.15
☐☐	40	Adam Oates, Bos.	15.00	.35
☐☐	41	John Vanbiesbrouck (G), Fla.	60.00	.85
☐☐	42	Brian Leetch, NYR.	15.00	.35
☐☐	43	Alexander Selivanov, T.B.	5.00	.15
☐☐	44	Mike Modano, Dal.	20.00	.50
☐☐	45	Saku Koivu, Mtl.	50.00	1.00
☐☐	46	Tom Barrasso (G), Pgh.	10.00	.25
☐☐	47	Jere Lehtinen, Dal.	10.00	.25
☐☐	48	Daniel Alfredsson, Ott.	10.00	.25
☐☐	49	Joé Juneau, Wsh.	5.00	.15
☐☐	50	Chris Osgood (G), Det.	20.00	.50
☐☐	51	Dave Andreychuk, N.J.	5.00	.15
☐☐	52	Marcus Ragnarsson, S.J.	5.00	.15
☐☐	53	Valeri Kamensky, Col.	10.00	.25
☐☐	54	Doug Weight, Edm.	15.00	.35
☐☐	55	Mike Richter (G), NYR.	15.00	.35
☐☐	56	Teemu Selänne, Ana.	60.00	1.00
☐☐	57	Stéphane Fiset (G), L.A.	10.00	.25
☐☐	58	Mikael Renberg, Pha.	5.00	.15
☐☐	59	Trevor Linden, Van.	10.00	.25
☐☐	60	Bernie Nicholls, S.J.	5.00	.15
☐☐	61	Eric Dazé, Chi.	10.00	.25
☐☐	62	Ron Francis, Pgh.	15.00	.35
☐☐	63	Sergei Zubov, Dal.	10.00	.25
☐☐	64	Rod Brind'Amour, Pha.	10.00	.25
☐☐	65	Sergei Fedorov, Det.	30.00	.50
☐☐	66	Mark Messier, NYR.	30.00	.50
☐☐	67	Theoren Fleury, Cgy.	15.00	.35
☐☐	68	Ed Jovanovski, Fla.	10.00	.50
☐☐	69	Daren Puppa (G), T.B.	5.00	.15
☐☐	70	Pierre Turgeon, Stl.	10.00	.25
☐☐	71	Oleg Tverdovsky, Pho.	5.00	.15
☐☐	72	Ryan Smyth, Edm.	10.00	.25
☐☐	73	Jocelyn Thibault (G), Mtl.	15.00	.35
☐☐	74	Brendan Witt, Wsh.	5.00	.15
☐☐	75	Igor Larionov, Det.	10.00	.25
☐☐	76	Stéphane Richer, Mtl.	5.00	.15
☐☐	77	Ron Hextall (G), Pha.	10.00	.25
☐☐	78	Mike Ricci, Col.	5.00	.15
☐☐	79	Dimitri Khristich, L.A.	5.00	.15
☐☐	80	Derian Hatcher, Dal.	10.00	.25
☐☐	81	Martin Brodeur, N.J.	60.00	1.00
☐☐	82	Petr Nedved, Pgh.	5.00	.15
☐☐	83	Ray Bourque, Bos.	30.00	.50
☐☐	84	Keith Primeau, Hfd.	10.00	.25
☐☐	85	Sean Burke (G), Hfd.	10.00	.25
☐☐	86	Geoff Sanderson, Hfd.	5.00	.15
☐☐	87	Wendel Clark, Tor.	10.00	.25
☐☐	88	Valeri Bure, Mtl.	5.00	.15
☐☐	89	Keith Tkachuk, Pho.	20.00	.35
☐☐	90	Roman Hamrlik, T.B.	10.00	.25
☐☐	91	Dominik Hasek (G), Buf.	60.00	1.00
☐☐	92	Ray Sheppard, Fla.	5.00	.15
☐☐	93	Todd Bertuzzi, NYI.	10.00	.25
☐☐	94	Pavel Bure, Van.	60.00	1.00
☐☐	95	Alexei Zhamnov, Wpg.	10.00	.25
☐☐	96	Alexei Kovalev, NYR.	5.00	.15
☐☐	97	Jeff Friesen, S.J.	10.00	.25
☐☐	98	Scott Young, Col.	5.00	.15
☐☐	99	Vitali Yachmenev, L.A.	5.00	.15
☐☐	100	Michal Pivonka, Wsh.	5.00	.15
☐☐	101	Paul Coffey, Hfd.	10.00	.25
☐☐	102	Steve Yzerman, Det.	110.00	1.50
☐☐	103	Zigmund Palffy, NYI.	15.00	.35
☐☐	104	Doug Gilmour, Tor.	15.00	.35
☐☐	105	John LeClair, Pha.	30.00	.50
☐☐	106	Brett Hull, Stl.	30.00	.50
☐☐	107	Yanic Perreault, L.A.	5.00	.15
☐☐	108	Bill Guerin, N.J.	10.00	.25
☐☐	109	Damian Rhodes (G), Ott.	5.00	.15
☐☐	110	Peter Forsberg, Col.	110.00	1.50
☐☐	111	Scott Mellanby, Fla.	5.00	.15
☐☐	112	Wayne Gretzky, NYR.	275.00	4.00
☐☐	113	Mario Lemieux, Pgh.	200.00	2.50
☐☐	114	Todd Harvey, Dal.	5.00	.15
☐☐	115	Mark Recchi, Mtl.	10.00	.25
☐☐	116	Trevor Kidd (G), Cgy.	10.00	.25
☐☐	117	Eric Lindros, Pha.	160.00	2.00
☐☐	118	Jarome Iginla, Cgy.	10.00	.75
☐☐	119	Eric Fichaud (G), NYI.	10.00	.25
☐☐	**120**	**Mattias Timander, Bos., RC**	**5.00**	**.15**
☐☐	121	Hnat Domenichelli, Hfd.	10.00	.25
☐☐	122	Chris O'Sullivan, Cgy.	5.00	.15
☐☐	**123**	**Sergei Berezin, Tor., RC**	**15.00**	**1.00**
☐☐	124	Jonas Hoglund, Cgy.	5.00	.15
☐☐	125	Anders Eriksson, Det.	5.00	.15
☐☐	126	Corey Schwab, T.B.	5.00	.15
☐☐	127	Janne Niinimaa, Pha.	10.00	.35
☐☐	**128**	**Dainius Zubrus, Pha., RC**	**85.00**	**2.50**
☐☐	129	Bryan Berard, NYI.	15.00	.35
☐☐	130	Wade Redden, Ott.	10.00	.25
☐☐	131	Wayne Primeau, Buf.	5.00	.15
☐☐	132	Brandon Convery, Tor.	5.00	.15

	No.	Player		
☐☐	**133**	**Richard Zednik, Wsh., RC**	**15.00**	**1.00**
☐☐	134	Darcy Tucker, Mtl.	5.00	.15
☐☐	135	Christian Dubé, NYR.	5.00	.25
☐☐	**136**	**Rem Murray, Edm., RC**	**10.00**	**.35**
☐☐	137	Keven Hodson (G), Det.	8.00	.35
☐☐	**138**	**Steve Washburn, Fla, RC.**	**5.00**	**.15**
☐☐	139	Ethan Moreau, Chi.	10.00	.25
☐☐	140	Daymond Langkow, T.B.	5.00	.15
☐☐	**141**	**Terry Ryan, Mtl., RC**	**10.00**	**.25**
☐☐	142	Curtis Brown, Buf.	5.00	.15
☐☐	**143**	**Steve Sullivan, N.J., RC**	**5.00**	**.15**
☐☐	144	Jamie Langenbrunner, Dal.	5.00	.25
☐☐	**145**	**Daniel Goneau, NYR., RC**	**5.00**	**.15**
☐☐	146	Anson Carter, Wsh.	5.00	.15
☐☐	147	Jim Campbell, Stl.	10.00	.25
☐☐	148	CL: Keith Tkachuk, Pho.	10.00	.25
☐☐	149	CL: Eric Dazé, Chi.	8.00	.25
☐☐	150	CL: Mike Modano, Dal.	10.00	.25

LEAF STEEL

These cards have two versions: the regular steel insert and a gold parallel.

Insert Set (63 cards): 900.00 150.00
Promo Card (Eric Lindros, #77): 6.00 1.50

	No.	Player	Gold	Silver
☐☐	1	Sergei Fedorov, Det.	40.00	5.00
☐☐	2	Martin Brodeur (G), N.J.	55.00	7.00
☐☐	3	Corey Hirsch (G), Van.	6.00	1.00
☐☐	4	Ray Bourque, Bos.	40.00	5.00
☐☐	5	Saku Koivu, Mtl.	55.00	7.00
☐☐	6	Ron Francis, Pgh.	20.00	3.00
☐☐	7	Chris Chelios, Chi.	30.00	4.00
☐☐	8	Scott Mellanby, Fla.	6.00	1.00
☐☐	9	Ron Hextall (G), Pha.	10.00	1.50
☐☐	10	Doug Gilmour, Tor.	20.00	3.00
☐☐	11	Joe Sakic, Col.	60.00	8.00
☐☐	12	Petr Sykora, N.J.	6.00	1.00
☐☐	13	Marcus Ragnarsson, S.J.	6.00	1.00
☐☐	14	Pat Verbeek, NYR.	6.00	1.00
☐☐	15	Stéphane Fiset (G), L.A.	10.00	1.50
☐☐	16	Alexei Yashin, Ott.	30.00	4.00
☐☐	17	Daren Puppa (G), T.B.	6.00	1.00
☐☐	18	Eric Lindros, Pha.	100.00	12.00
☐☐	19	Jason Arnott, Edm.	10.00	1.50
☐☐	20	Todd Bertuzzi, NYI.	10.00	1.50
☐☐	21	Jim Carey (G), Wsh.	6.00	1.00
☐☐	22	Pat LaFontaine, Buf.	10.00	1.50
☐☐	23	Brian Leetch, NYR.	20.00	3.00
☐☐	24	Trevor Linden, Van.	10.00	1.50
☐☐	25	Eric Dazé, Chi.	10.00	1.50
☐☐	26	Pierre Turgeon, Stl.	10.00	1.50
☐☐	27	Tom Barrasso (G), Pgh.	10.00	1.50
☐☐	28	Mike Modano, Dal.	40.00	5.00
☐☐	29	Brendan Shanahan, Det.	45.00	6.00
☐☐	30	Nikolai Khabibulin (G), Pho.	20.00	3.00
☐☐	31	Claude Lemieux, Col.	6.00	1.00
☐☐	32	Zigmund, Palffy, NYI.	20.00	3.00
☐☐	33	Mats Sundin, Tor.	40.00	5.00
☐☐	34	Paul Kariya, Ana.	100.00	12.00
☐☐	35	Daniel Alfredsson, Ott.	10.00	1.50
☐☐	36	Patrick Roy (G), Col.	125.00	15.00
☐☐	37	Jaromir Jagr, Pgh.	80.00	10.00
☐☐	38	Vyacheslav Kozlov, Det.	6.00	1.00
☐☐	39	John LeClair, Pha.	40.00	5.00
☐☐	40	Bill Ranford (G), Bos.	10.00	1.50
☐☐	41	Vitali Yachmenev, L.A.	6.00	1.00
☐☐	42	Mark Messier, NYR.	40.00	5.00
☐☐	43	Valeri Bure, Mtl.	6.00	1.00
☐☐	44	Roman Hamrlik, T.B.	10.00	1.50
☐☐	45	Joe Nieuwendyk, Dal.	10.00	1.50
☐☐	46	Mike Richter (G), NYR.	20.00	3.00
☐☐	47	Theoren Fleury, Cgy.	20.00	3.00
☐☐	48	Wendel Clark, Tor.	10.00	1.50
☐☐	49	Doug Weight, Edm.	20.00	3.00
☐☐	50	Damian Rhodes (G), Ott.	6.00	1.00
☐☐	51	Alexander Mogilny, Van.	20.00	3.00
☐☐	52	Dominik Hasek (G), Buf.	55.00	7.00
☐☐	53	Eric Fichaud (G), NYI.	10.00	1.50
☐☐	54	Adam Oates, Bos.	20.00	3.00
☐☐	55	Jocelyn Thibault (G), Mtl.	20.00	3.00
☐☐	56	Petr Nedved, Pgh.	6.00	1.00
☐☐	57	Mike Vernon (G), Det.	10.00	1.50
☐☐	58	Mikael Renberg, Pha.	6.00	1.00
☐☐	59	Valeri Kamensky, Col.	10.00	1.50
☐☐	60	Peter Forsberg, Col.	80.00	10.00
☐☐	61	Rob Niedermayer, Fla.	6.00	1.00
☐☐	62	Owen Nolan, S.J.	10.00	1.50
☐☐	63	Jere Lehtinen, S.J.	10.00	1.50

MASKED MARAUDERS

These inserts are serial numbered out of 2,500.

Insert Set (12 cards): 325.00

	No.	Player	NRMT-MT
☐	1	Jim Carey (G), Wsh.	15.00
☐	2	Martine Brodeur (G), N.J.	40.00
☐	3	John Vanbiesbrouck (G), Fla.	35.00
☐	4	Patrick Roy (G), Col.	90.00
☐	5	Félix Potvin (G), Tor.	30.00
☐	6	Chris Osgood (G), Det.	25.00
☐	7	Dominik Hasek (G), Buf.	40.00
☐	8	Jocelyn Thibault (G), Mtl.	20.00
☐	9	Nikolai Khabibulin (G), Pho.	20.00
☐	10	Curtis Joseph (G), Edm.	35.00
☐	11	Mike Richter (G), NYR.	20.00
☐	12	Ed Belfour (G), Chi.	20.00

STEEL POWER

These inserts are serial numbered out of 5,000.

Insert Set (12 cards): 450.00

	No.	Player	NRMT-MT
☐	1	Joe Sakic, Col.	35.00
☐	2	Mario Lemieux, Pgh.	75.00
☐	3	Pavel Bure, Van.	30.00
☐	4	Mark Messier, NYR.	20.00
☐	5	Wayne Gretzky, NYR.	90.00
☐	6	Peter Forsberg, Col.	45.00
☐	7	Sergei Fedorov, Det.	20.00
☐	8	Jaromir Jagr, Pgh.	45.00
☐	9	Brett Hull, Stl.	20.00
☐	10	Teemu Selänne, Ana.	30.00
☐	11	Paul Kariya, Ana.	60.00
☐	12	Eric Lindros, Pha.	60.00

VANITY PLATES

These cards have two versions: the regular steel and a gold parallel.

Insert Set (14 cards): 350.00 175.00

	No.	Player	Silver	Gold
☐☐	1	Wayne Gretzky, NYR.	40.00	80.00
☐☐	2	John Vanbiesbrouck (G), Fla.	12.00	25.00
☐☐	3	Chris Osgood (G), Det.	8.00	15.00
☐☐	4	Steve Yzerman, Det.	20.00	40.00
☐☐	5	Brett Hull, Stl.	10.00	20.00
☐☐	6	Mario Lemieux, Pgh.	30.00	60.00
☐☐	7	Eric Lindros, Pha.	25.00	50.00
☐☐	8	Ed Jovanovski, Fla.	5.00	10.00
☐☐	9	Pavel Bure, Van.	15.00	30.00
☐☐	10	Félix Potvin (G), Tor.	10.00	20.00
☐☐	11	Teemu Selänne, Ana.	15.00	30.00
☐☐	12	Keith Tkachuk, Pho.	8.00	15.00
☐☐	13	Curtis Joseph (G), Edm.	12.00	25.00
☐☐	14	Ed Belfour (G), Chi.	6.00	12.00

1996 - 97 MAGGERS

There are no Phoenix Coyotes or Washington Capitals in this set. A second series was probably intended for release but never issued. Supply was based on demand. Singles start at $2.

Magnet Size: 6" x 7 1/2"

Imprint:

	No.	Player
☐	1	Paul Kariya, Ana.
☐	2	Teemu Selänne, Ana.
☐	5	Guy Hebert (G), Ana.
☐	12	Bill Ranford (G), Bos.
☐	13	Adam Oates, Bos.
☐	14	Rick Tocchet, Bos.
☐	15	Cam Neely, Bos.
☐	17	Ray Bourque, Bos.
☐	19	Theoren Fleury, Cgy.
☐	21	Trevor Kidd (G), Cgy.
☐	22	Steve Chiasson, Cgy.
☐	24	German Titov, Cgy.
☐	25	Gary Roberts, Cgy.
☐	26	Ed Belfour (G), Chi.
☐	27	Chris Chelios, Chi.
☐	28	Denis Savard, Chi.
☐	29	Joe Murphy, Chi.
☐	30	Jeremy Roenick, Chi.
☐	31	Gary Suter, Chi.
☐	32	Eric Dazé, Chi.
☐	34	Bernie Nicholls, Chi.
☐	35	Patrick Roy (G), Col.
☐	36	Peter Forsberg, Col.
☐	37	Joe Sakic, Col.
☐	39	Mike Ricci, Col.
☐	40	Claude Lemieux, Col.
☐	42	Alexei Gusarov, Col.
☐	43	Valeri Kamenski, Col.
☐	44	Sandis Ozolinsh, Col.
☐	45	Joe Nieuwendyk, Dal.
☐	47	Derian Hatcher, Dal.
☐	49	Mike Modano, Dal.
☐	50	Andy Moog (G), Dal.
☐	51	Sergei Federov, Det.
☐	53	Vyacheslav Kozlov, Det.
☐	54	Keith Primeau, Det.
☐	55	Steve Yzerman, Det.
☐	57	Dino Ciccarelli, Det.
☐	58	Chris Osgood (G), Det.
☐	60	Mike Vernon (G), Det.
☐	61	Igor Larionov, Det.
☐	62	Paul Coffey, Det.
☐	65	Zdeno Ciger, Edm.
☐	66	Jason Arnott, Edm.
☐	68	John Vanbiesbrouck (G), Fla.
☐	71	Ed Jovanovski, Fla.
☐	73	Sean Burke (G), Hfd.
☐	74	Bendan Shanahan, Hfd.
☐	76	Kelly Hrudey (G), L.A.
☐	78	Kevin Stevens, L.A.
☐	80	Tony Granato, L.A.

	No.	Player
☐	81	Yanic Perreault, L.A.
☐	82	Jocelyn Thibault (G), Mtl.
☐	83	Adrei Kovalenko, Mtl.
☐	84	Benoît Brunet, Mtl.
☐	85	Pierre Turgeon, Mtl.
☐	86	Saku Koivu, Mtl., Error (V. Damphousse)
☐	88	Vincent Damphousse, Mtl., Error (S. Koivu)
☐	91	Martin Brodeur (G), N.J.
☐	92	Scott Stevens, N.J.
☐	93	Phil Housley, N.J.
☐	95	Zigmund Palffy, NYI.
☐	97	Eric Fichaud (G), NYI.
☐	99	Mark Messier, NYR.
☐	101	Mike Richter, NYR.
☐	102	Brian Leetch, NYR.
☐	104	Luc Robitaille, NYR.
☐	105	Pat Verbeek, NYR.
☐	106	Adam Graves, NYR.
☐	109	Alexei Yashin, Ott.
☐	110	Alexandre Daigle, Ott.
☐	111	Eric Lindros, Pha.
☐	113	Ron Hextall (G), Pha.
☐	114	Dale Hawerchuk, Pha.
☐	115	Mikael Renberg, Pha.
☐	117	John LeClair, Pha.
☐	119	Mario Lemieux, Pgh.
☐	122	Tom Barrasso (G), Pgh.
☐	123	Petr Nedved, Pgh.
☐	124	Jaromir Jagr, Pgh.
☐	126	Ron Francis, Pgh.
☐	127	Tomas Sandström, Pgh.
☐	129	Chris Terreri (G), S.J.
☐	131	Owen Nolan, S.J.
☐	133	Jeff Odgers, S.J.
☐	135	Wayne Gretzky, Stl.
☐	137	Brett Hull, Stl.
☐	139	Grant Fuhr (G), Stl.
☐	141	Chris Pronger, Stl.
☐	142	Al MacInnis, Stl.
☐	143	Shayne Corson, Stl.
☐	144	Daren Puppa (G), T.B.
☐	145	Petr Klima, T.B.
☐	146	Félix Potvin, Tor.
☐	149	Doug Gilmour, Tor.
☐	151	Mats Sundin, Tor.
☐	152	Tie Domi, Tor.
☐	153	Wendel Clark, Tor.
☐	155	Cory Hirsch (G), Van.
☐	156	Pavel Bure, Van.
☐	158	Trevor Linden, Van.
☐	159	Alexander Mogilny, Van.
☐	161	Esa Tikkanen, Van.
☐	162	Peter Bondra, Wsh.
☐	164	Joé Juneau, Wsh.
☐	165	Michal Pivonka, Wsh.
☐	166	Sergei Gonchar, Wsh.
☐	167	Jim Carey (G), Wsh.

1996 - 97 McDONALD'S - PINNACLE

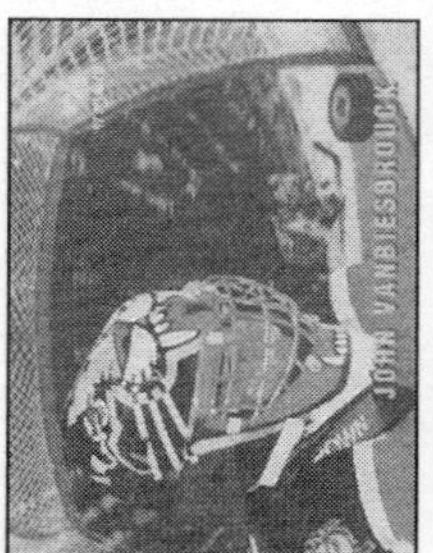

McDonald's Cards 1-20 are called "Ice Breakers" and cards 21-31 are called "Premier Ice Breakers" and cards 32-40 are called Caged "Ice Breakers". Premier Ice Breakers feature full-motion video technology capturing up to 3 seconds of live action.

Imprint:

Complete Set (40 cards): 25.00

	No.	Player	NRMT-MT
☐	McD-1	Paul Coffey, Hfd.	.50
☐	McD-2	Teemu Selänne, Ana.	1.50
☐	McD-3	Eric Dazé, Chi.	.50
☐	McD-4	John LeClair, Pha.	1.00
☐	McD-5	Saku Koivu, Mtl.	1.50
☐	McD-6	Ed Jovanovski, Fla.	.50
☐	McD-7	Chris Osgood (G), Det.	.75
☐	McD-8	Chris Chelios, Chi.	.75
☐	McD-9	Daniel Alfredsson, Ott.	.50
☐	McD-10	Joe Sakic, Col.	1.75
☐	McD-11	Alexander Mogilny, Van.	.50
☐	McD-12	Jeremy Roenick, Pho.	.50
☐	McD-13	Keith Tkachuk, Pho.	.50
☐	McD-14	Doug Gilmour, Tor.	.50
☐	McD-15	Theoren Fleury, Cgy.	.50
☐	McD-16	Doug Weight, Edm.	.50
☐	McD-17	Steve Yzerman, Det.	2.00
☐	McD-18	Zigmund Palffy, NYI.	.50
☐	McD-19	Pierre Turgeon, Mtl.	.50
☐	McD-20	Brian Leetch, NYR.	.50
☐	McD-21	Mario Lemieux, Pgh.	3.00
☐	McD-22	Mark Messier, NYR.	1.00
☐	McD-23	Jaromir Jagr, Pgh.	2.00
☐	McD-24	Brett Hull, Stl.	1.00
☐	McD-25	Eric Lindros, Pha.	2.50
☐	McD-26	Sergei Fedorov, Det.	1.00
☐	McD-27	Pavel Bure, Van.	1.50
☐	McD-28	Peter Forsberg, Col.	2.00
☐	McD-29	Paul Kariya, Ana.	2.50
☐	McD-30	Patrick Roy (G), Col.	3.00
☐	McD-31	Ray Bourque, Bos.	1.00
☐	McD-32	Jim Carey (G), Wsh.	.35
☐	McD-33	Martin Brodeur (G), N.J.	1.50
☐	McD-34	Trevor Kidd (G), Cgy.	.50
☐	McD-35	John Vanbiesbrouck (G), Fla.	1.25
☐	McD-36	Jocelyn Thibault (G), Mtl.	.50
☐	McD-37	Ed Belfour (G), Chi.	.50
☐	McD-38	Félix Potvin (G), Tor.	1.00
☐	McD-39	Damian Rhodes (G), Ott.	.35
☐	McD-40	CL: Curtis Joseph (G)	.50

1996 - 97 MCDONALD'S MASKS

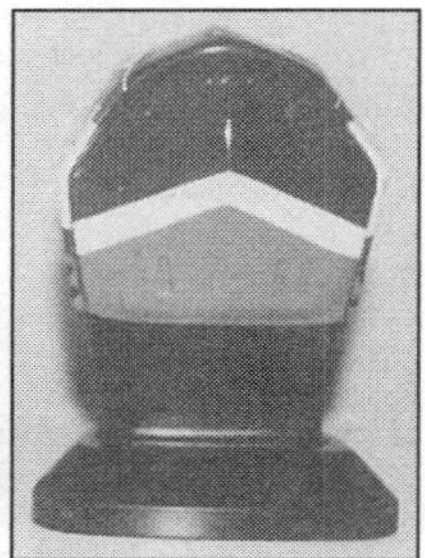

Short Prints (*) were distributed regionally across Canada.

Mask Height: 5"

Imprint:

Complete Set (11 masks): 200.00

	Player	NRMT-MT
☐	Ed Belfour (G), Chi	9.00
☐	Curtis Joseph (G), Edm. (*)	25.00
☐	Trevor Kidd (G), Cgy. (*)	30.00
☐	Kirk McLean (G), Van. (*)	25.00
☐	Félix Potvin (G), Tor.	12.00
☐	Bill Ranford (G), Edm.	9.00
☐	Damian Rhodes (G), Ott. (*)	75.00
☐	Mike Richter (G), NYR.	9.00
☐	Patrick Roy (G), Col.	15.00
☐	Jocelyn Thibault (G), Mtl.	9.00
☐	John Vanbiesbrouck (G), Fla. (*)	15.00

1996 - 97 METAL UNIVERSE

Imprint: © 1997 FLEER/SKYBOX INT'L.

Complete Set (200 cards): 50.00

Common Player: .20

	No.	Player	NRMT-MT
☐	1	Guy Hebert (G), Ana.	.35
☐	2	Paul Kariya, Ana.	2.50
☐	3	Jari Kurri, Ana.	.35
☐	4	Roman Oksiuta, Ana.	.20
☐	5	Steve Rucchin, Ana.	.20
☐	6	Teemu Selänne, Ana.	1.50
☐	7	Ray Bourque, Bos.	1.00
☐	8	Kirk McLaren, Bos.	.20
☐	9	Adam Oates, Bos.	.50
☐	10	Bill Ranford (G), Bos.	.35
☐	11	Rick Tocchet, Bos.	.20
☐	12	Donald Audette, Buf.	.20
☐	13	Jason Dawe, Buf.	.20
☐	14	Dominik Hasek (G), Buf.	1.50
☐	15	Pat LaFontaine, Buf.	.35
☐	16	Derek Plante, Buf.	.20
☐	17	Wayne Primeau, Buf.	.20
☐	18	Theoren Fleury, Cgy.	.50
☐	19	Dave Gagner, Cgy.	.20
☐	20	Trevor Kidd (G), Cgy.	.35
☐	21	James Patrick, Cgy.	.20
☐	22	Robert Reichel, Cgy.	.20
☐	23	German Titov, Cgy.	.20
☐	24	Tony Amonte, Chi.	.35
☐	25	Ed Belfour (G), Chi.	.50
☐	26	Chris Chelios, Chi.	.75
☐	27	Eric Dazé, Chi.	.35
☐	28	Gary Suter, Chi.	.20
☐	29	Alexei Zhamnov, Chi.	.35
☐	30	Adam Deadmarsh, Col.	.20
☐	31	Adam Foote, Col.	.35
☐	32	Peter Forsberg, Col.	2.00
☐	33	Valeri Kamensky, Col.	.35
☐	34	Uwe Krupp, Col.	.20
☐	35	Claude Lemieux, Col.	.20
☐	36	Sandis Ozolinsh, Col.	.35
☐	37	Patrick Roy (G), Col.	3.00
☐	38	Joe Sakic, Col.	1.75
☐	39	Derian Hatcher, Dal.	.35
☐	40	Mike Modano, Dal.	1.00
☐	41	Andy Moog (G), Dal.	.35
☐	42	Joe Nieuwendyk, Dal.	.35
☐	43	Pat Verbeek, Dal.	.20
☐	44	Sergei Zubov, Dal.	.35
☐	45	Sergei Fedorov, Det.	1.00
☐	46	Vladimir Konstantinov, Det.	.20
☐	47	Vyacheslav Kozlov, Det.	.20
☐	48	Nicklas Lidström, Det.	.35
☐	49	Chris Osgood (G), Det.	.75
☐	50	Brendan Shanahan, Det.	1.50
☐	51	Steve Yzerman, Det.	2.00
☐	52	Jason Arnott, Edm.	.35
☐	53	Curtis Joseph (G), Edm.	1.25
☐	54	Andrei Kovalenko, Edm.	.20
☐	55	Miroslav Satan, Edm.	.20
☐	56	Doug Weight, Edm.	.50
☐	57	Radek Dvorak, Fla.	.20
☐	58	Per Gustafsson, Fla.	.20
☐	59	Ed Jovanovski, Fla.	.35
☐	60	Scott Mellanby, Fla.	.20
☐	61	Rob Niedermayer, Fla.	.20
☐	62	Ray Sheppard, Fla.	.20
☐	63	Robert Svehla, Fla.	.20
☐	64	John Vanbiesbrouck (G), Fla.	1.25

☐	65	Jeff Brown, Hfd.	.20
☐	66	Sean Burke (G), Hfd.	.35
☐	67	Paul Coffey, Hfd.	.35
☐	68	Nelson Emerson, Hfd.	.20
☐	69	Jeff O'Neill, Hfd.	.35
☐	70	Keith Primeau, Hfd.	.35
☐	71	Geoff Sanderson, Hfd.	.20
☐	72	Aki Berg, L.A.	.20
☐	73	Rob Blake, L.A.	.35
☐	74	Stéphane Fiset (G), L.A.	.35
☐	75	Dimitri Khristich, L.A.	.20
☐	76	Petr Klima, L.A.	.20
☐	77	Ed Olczyk, L.A.	.20
☐	78	Vitali Yachmenev, L.A.	.20
☐	79	Vincent Damphousse, Mtl.	.50
☐	80	Saku Koivu, Mtl.	1.50
☐	81	Mark Recchi, Mtl.	.35
☐	82	Stéphane Richer, Mtl.	.20
☐	83	Jocelyn Thibault (G), Mtl.	.50
☐	84	Pierre Turgeon, Mtl.	.35
☐	85	Dave Andreychuk, N.J.	.20
☐	86	Martin Brodeur (G), N.J.	1.50
☐	87	Scott Niedermayer, N.J.	.35
☐	88	Scott Stevens, N.J.	.20
☐	89	Petr Sykora, N.J.	.20
☐	90	Steve Thomas, N.J.	.20
☐	91	Todd Bertuzzi, NYI.	.35
☐	92	Travis Green, NYI.	.20
☐	93	Kenny Jonsson, NYI.	.20
☐	94	Bryan McCabe, NYI.	.20
☐	95	Zigmund Palffy, NYI.	.75
☐	96	Wayne Gretzky, NYR.	4.50
☐	97	Alexei Kovalev, NYR.	.20
☐	98	Brian Leetch, NYR.	.75
☐	99	Mark Messier, NYR.	1.00
☐	100	Mike Richter (G), NYR.	.50
☐	101	Luc Robitaille, NYR.	.20
☐	102	Niklas Sundstrom, NYR.	.20
☐	103	Daniel Alfredsson, Ott.	.35
☐	104	Radek Bonk, Ott.	.20
☐	105	Alexandre Daigle, Ott.	.35
☐	106	Steve Duchesne, Ott.	.20
☐	107	Damian Rhodes (G), Ott.	.20
☐	108	Alexei Yashin, Ott.	.75
☐	109	Rod Brind'Amour, Pha.	.35
☐	110	Eric Desjardins, Pha.	.20
☐	111	Dale Hawerchuk, Pha.	.35
☐	112	Ron Hextall (G), Pha.	.35
☐	113	John LeClair, Pha.	1.00
☐	114	Eric Lindros, Pha.	2.50
☐	115	Mikael Renberg, Pha.	.20
☐	116	Mike Gartner, Pho.	.35
☐	117	Craig Janney, Pho.	.20
☐	118	Nikolai Khabibulin (G), Pho.	.50
☐	119	Dave Manson, Pho.	.20
☐	120	Teppo Numminen, Pho.	.20
☐	121	Jeremy Roenick, Pho.	.50
☐	122	Keith Tkachuk, Pho.	.75
☐	123	Oleg Tverdovsky, Pho.	.20
☐	124	Tom Barrasso (G), Pgh.	.35
☐	125	Ron Francis, Pgh.	.50
☐	126	Kevin Hatcher, Pgh.	.20
☐	127	Jaromir Jagr, Pgh.	2.00
☐	128	Mario Lemieux, Pgh.	3.00
☐	129	Peter Nedved, Pgh.	.20
☐	130	Shayne Corson, Stl.	.35
☐	131	Grant Fuhr (G), Stl.	.35
☐	132	Brett Hull, Stl.	1.00
☐	133	Al MacInnis, Stl.	.20
☐	134	Joe Murphy, Stl.	.20
☐	135	Chris Pronger, Stl.	.35
☐	136	Kelly Hrudey (G), S.J.	.20
☐	137	Al Iafrate, S.J.	.20
☐	138	Bernie Nicholls, S.J.	.20
☐	139	Owen Nolan, S.J.	.35
☐	140	Marcus Ragnarsson, S.J.	.20
☐	141	Darren Turcotte, S.J.	.20
☐	142	Bradley Bradley,T.B.	.20
☐	143	Dino Ciccarelli, T.B.	.35
☐	144	Chris Gratton, T.B.	.35
☐	145	Roman Hamrlik, T.B.	.35
☐	146	Daren Puppa (G), T.B.	.20
☐	147	Alexander Selivanov, T.B.	.20
☐	148	Wendel Clark, Tor.	.35
☐	149	Doug Gilmour, Tor.	.50
☐	150	Kirk Muller, Tor.	.20
☐	151	Larry Murphy, Tor.	.35
☐	152	Félix Potvin (G), Tor.	1.00
☐	153	Mathieu Schneider, Tor.	.20
☐	154	Mats Sundin, Tor.	1.00
☐	155	Pavel Bure, Van.	1.50
☐	156	Russ Courtnall, Van.	.20
☐	157	Trevor Linden, Van.	.35
☐	158	Kirk McLean (G), Van.	.35
☐	159	Alexander Mogilny, Van.	.50
☐	160	Esa Tikkanen, Van.	.20
☐	161	Peter Bondra, Wsh.	.75
☐	162	Jim Carey (G), Wsh.	.20
☐	163	Sergei Gonchar, Wsh.	.20
☐	164	Phil Housley, Wsh.	.20
☐	165	Calle Johansson, Wsh.	.20
☐	166	Joé Juneau, Wsh.	.20
☐	167	Mikael Pivonka, Wsh.	.20
☐	168	Brendan Witt, Wsh.	.20
☐	169	Nolan Baumgartner, Wsh.	.20
☐	170	Bryan Berard, NYI.	.75
☐	**171**	**Sergei Berezin, Tor., RC**	**1.00**
☐	172	Curtis Brown, Buf.	.20
☐	**173**	**Jan Caloun, S.J., RC**	**.20**
☐	**174**	**Andreas Dackell, Ott., RC**	.20
☐	175	Hnat Domenichelli, Hfd.	.35
☐	176	Christian Dubé, NYR.	.35
☐	177	Anders Eriksson, Det.	.20
☐	178	Peter Ferraro, NYR.	.20
☐	179	Eric Fichaud (G), NYI.	.35
☐	**180**	**Daniel Goneau, NYR., RC**	.20
☐	**181**	**Mike Grier, Edm., RC**	**1.00**
☐	182	Jarome Iginla, Cgy.	.75
☐	**183**	**Steve Kelly, Edm., RC**	**.35**
☐	184	Jamie Lagenbrunner, Dal.	.35
☐	185	Daymond Langkow, T.B.	.20
☐	**186**	**Jay McKee, Buf., RC**	.20
☐	187	Ethan Moreau, Chi.	.35
☐	**188**	**Rem Murray, Edm., RC**	**.50**
☐	189	Janne Niinimaa, Pha.	.35
☐	190	Wade Redden, Ott.	.35
☐	**191**	**Ruslan Salei, Ana., RC**	**.20**
☐	192	Jamie Storr (G), Ana.	.35
☐	193	Darren Van Impe, L.A.	.20
☐	194	Roman Vopat, Ana.	.20
☐	195	David Wilkie, Mtl.	.20
☐	196	Landon Wilson, Col.	.20
☐	**197**	**Richard Zednik, Wsh., RC**	**1.00**
☐	**198**	**Danius Zubrus, Pha., RC**	**3.00**
☐	199	Checklist	.20
☐	200	Checklist	.20

LETHAL WEAPONS

These inserts have two versions: the regular insert and a Super Power parallel.

	No.	Player	Super	Insert
Insert Set (20 cards):			**400.00**	**100.00**
☐ ☐	1	Peter Bondra, Wsh.	12.00	3.00
☐ ☐	2	Pavel Bure, Van.	20.00	5.00
☐ ☐	3	Sergei Fedorov, Det.	15.00	3.50
☐ ☐	4	Peter Forsberg, Col.	30.00	7.50
☐ ☐	5	Ron Francis, Pgh.	10.00	2.50
☐ ☐	6	Wayne Gretzky, NYR.	60.00	15.00
☐ ☐	7	Brett Hull, Stl.	15.00	3.50
☐ ☐	8	Jaromir Jagr, Pgh.	30.00	7.50
☐ ☐	9	Paul Kariya, Ana.	40.00	10.00
☐ ☐	10	John LeClair, Pha.	15.00	3.50
☐ ☐	11	Mario Lemieux, Pgh.	45.00	12.00
☐ ☐	12	Eric Lindros, Pha.	40.00	10.00
☐ ☐	13	Mark Messier, NYR.	15.00	3.50
☐ ☐	14	Alexander Mogilny, Van.	10.00	2.50
☐ ☐	15	Adam Oates, Bos.	10.00	2.50
☐ ☐	16	Joe Sakic, Col.	25.00	6.00
☐ ☐	17	Teemu Selänne, Ana.	20.00	5.00
☐ ☐	18	Brendan Shanahan, Det.	18.00	4.50
☐ ☐	19	Keith Tkachuk, Pho.	12.00	3.00
☐ ☐	20	Doug Weight, Edm.	10.00	2.50

ICE CRAVINGS

The retail pack inserts have two versions: the regular insert and a Super Power parallel.

	No.	Player	Super	Insert
Insert Set (12 cards):			**400.00**	**100.00**
☐ ☐	1	Martin Brodeur (G), N.J.	40.00	10.00
☐ ☐	2	Pavel Bure, Van.	40.00	10.00
☐ ☐	3	Jim Carey (G), Wsh.	10.00	2.50
☐ ☐	4	Paul Coffey, Hfd.	12.00	3.00
☐ ☐	5	Sergei Fedorov, Det.	30.00	7.50
☐ ☐	6	Jaromir Jagr, Pgh.	60.00	15.00
☐ ☐	7	Paul Kariya, Ana.	60.00	20.00
☐ ☐	8	Pat LaFontaine, Buf.	12.00	3.00
☐ ☐	9	Brian Leetch, NYR.	18.00	4.50
☐ ☐	10	Mario Lemieux, Pgh.	100.00	25.00
☐ ☐	11	Alexander Mogilny, Van.	18.00	4.50
☐ ☐	12	Joe Sakic, Col.	45.00	12.00

COOL STEEL

These hobby pack inserts have two versions: the regular insert and a Super Power parallel.

	No.	Player	Super	Insert
Insert Set (12 cards):			**400.00**	**100.00**
☐ ☐	1	Chris Chelios, Chi.	25.00	6.00
☐ ☐	2	Peter Forsberg, Col.	60.00	15.00
☐ ☐	3	Ron Francis, Pgh.	18.00	4.50
☐ ☐	4	Dominik Hasek (G), Buf.	40.00	10.00
☐ ☐	5	Ed Jovanovski, Fla.	12.00	3.00
☐ ☐	6	Vladimir Konstantinov, Det.	10.00	2.50
☐ ☐	7	Eric Lindros, Pha.	80.00	20.00
☐ ☐	8	Mark Messier, NYR.	40.00	10.00
☐ ☐	9	Patrick Roy (G), Col.	100.00	25.00
☐ ☐	10	Brendan Shanahan, Det.	35.00	9.00
☐ ☐	11	Keith Tkachuk, Pho.	25.00	6.00
☐ ☐	12	John Vanbiesbrouck (G), Fla.	35.00	9.00

ARMOUR PLATE

These inserts have two versions: the regular insert and a Super Power parallel.

	No.	Player	Super	Insert
Insert Set (12 cards):			**600.00**	**150.00**
☐ ☐	1	Ed Belfour (G), Chi.	35.00	9.00
☐ ☐	2	Martin Brodeur (G), N.J.	80.00	20.00
☐ ☐	3	Jim Carey (G), Wsh.	20.00	5.00
☐ ☐	4	Dominik Hasek (G), Buf.	80.00	20.00
☐ ☐	5	Ron Hextall (G), Pha.	25.00	6.00
☐ ☐	6	Chris Osgood (G), Det.	45.00	12.00
☐ ☐	7	Félix Potvin (G), Tor.	60.00	15.00
☐ ☐	8	Daren Puppa (G), T.B.	20.00	5.00
☐ ☐	9	Damian Rhodes (G), Ott.	20.00	5.00
☐ ☐	10	Mike Richter (G), NYR.	35.00	9.00
☐ ☐	11	Patrick Roy (G), Col.	200.00	50.00
☐ ☐	12	John Vanbiesbrouck (G), Fla.	75.00	18.00

1996 - 97 PANINI STICKERS

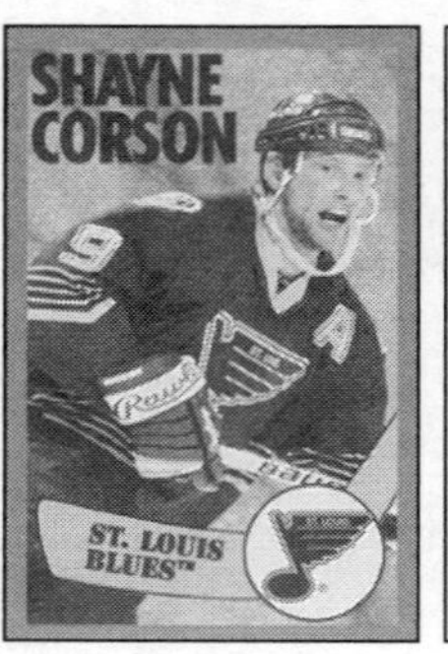

These stickers were released in Europe only and feature many poses from the 1996-97 Fleer set.

Sticker Size: 1 7/8" x 3"
Imprint: Panini S.p.A. - Modena

Complete Set (304 stickers):		**30.00**
Common Player:		**.25**
Album:		**3.00**

No.	Player	NRMT-MT
☐ 1	Ray Bourque, Bos.	1.25
☐ 2	Bill Ranford (G), Bos.	.50
☐ 3	Cam Neely, Bos.	.50
☐ 4	Adam Oates, Bos.	.75
☐ 5	Kyle McLaren, Bos.	.20
☐ 6	Rick Tocchet, Bos.	.20
☐ 7	Shawn McEachern, Bos.	.20
☐ 8	Foil: Boston Bruins Logo	.20
☐ 9	Jozef Stumpel, Bos.	.50
☐ 10	Ted Donato, Bos.	.20
☐ 11	Dave Reid, Bos.	.20
☐ 12	Donald Audette, Buf.	.20
☐ 13	Garry Galley, Buf.	.20
☐ 14	Dominik Hasek (G), Buf.	1.75
☐ 15	Pat LaFontaine, Buf.	.20
☐ 16	Jason Dawe, Buf.	.20
☐ 17	Alexei Zhitnik, Buf.	.20
☐ 18	Brad May, Buf.	.20
☐ 19	Foil: Buffalo Sabres Logo	.20
☐ 20	Matthew Barnaby, Buf.	.20
☐ 21	Darryl Shannon, Buf.	.20
☐ 22	Derek Plante, Buf.	.20
☐ 23	Geoff Sanderson, Hfd.	.20
☐ 24	Sean Burke (G), Hfd.	.50
☐ 25	Nelson Emerson, Hfd.	.20
☐ 26	Brendan Shanahan, Hfd.	1.50
☐ 27	Jeff Brown, Hfd.	.20
☐ 28	Andrew Cassels, Hfd.	.20
☐ 29	Foil: Hartford Whalers Logo	.20
☐ 30	Jeff O'Neill, Hfd.	.50
☐ 31	Robert Kron, Hfd.	.20
☐ 32	Andrei Nikolishin, Hfd.	.20
☐ 33	Brad McCrimmon, Hfd.	.20
☐ 34	Valeri Bure, Mtl.	.20
☐ 35	Vincent Damphousse, Mtl.	.75
☐ 36	Jocelyn Thibault (G), Mtl.	.75
☐ 37	Saku Koivu, Mtl.	1.75
☐ 38	Mark Recchi, Mtl.	.50
☐ 39	Martin Rucinsky, Mtl.	.20
☐ 40	Pierre Turgeon, Mtl.	.50
☐ 41	Foil: Montréal Canadiens, Mtl.	.20
☐ 42	Andrei Kovalenko, Mtl.	.20
☐ 43	Peter Popovic, Mtl.	.20
☐ 44	Vladimir Malakhov, Mtl.	.20
☐ 45	Alexandre Daigle, Ott.	.50
☐ 46	Daniel Alfredsson, Ott.	.50
☐ 47	Damian Rhodes (G), Ott.	.20
☐ 48	Alexei Yashin, Ott.	1.00
☐ 49	Radek Bonk, Ott.	.20
☐ 50	Steve Duchesne, Ott.	.20
☐ 51	Foil: Ottawa Senators Logo	.20
☐ 52	Pavol Demitra, Ott.	.20
☐ 53	Antti Törmänen, Ott.	.20
☐ 54	Stanislav Neckar, Ott.	.20
☐ 55	Randy Cunneyworth, Ott.	.20
☐ 56	Petr Nedved, Pgh.	.20
☐ 57	Ron Francis, Pgh.	.75
☐ 58	Jaromir Jagr, Pgh.	2.50
☐ 59	Mario Lemieux, Pgh.	4.00
☐ 60	Tom Barrasso, Pgh.	.50
☐ 61	Tomas Sandström, Pgh.	.20
☐ 62	Bryan Smolinski, Pgh.	.20
☐ 63	Foil: Pittsburgh Penguins Logo	.50
☐ 64	Sergei Zubov, Pgh. (Dal.)	.20
☐ 65	Dmitri Mironov, Pgh.	.20
☐ 66	Kevin Miller, Pgh.	.20
☐ 67	Scott Mellanby, Fla.	.20
☐ 68	Ed Jovanovski, Fla.	.50
☐ 69	Ray Sheppard, Fla.	.20
☐ 70	John Vanbiesbrouck (G), Fla.	1.50
☐ 71	Radek Dvorak, Fla.	.20
☐ 72	Rob Niedermayer, Fla.	.20
☐ 73	Foil: Florida Panthers Logo	.20
☐ 74	Robert Svehla, Fla.	.20
☐ 75	Johan Garpenlov, Fla.	.20
☐ 76	Martin Straka, Fla.	.20
☐ 77	Paul Laus, Fla.	.20
☐ 78	Steve Thomas, N.J.	.20
☐ 79	Martin Brodeur (G), N.J.	1.75
☐ 80	Scott Stevens, N.J.	.20
☐ 81	Petr Sykora, N.J.	.20
☐ 82	Dave Andreychuk, N.J.	.20
☐ 83	Bill Guerin, N.J.	.50
☐ 84	Foil: New Jersey Devils Logo	.20
☐ 85	Phil Housley, N.J.	.20
☐ 86	Scott Niedermayer, N.J.	.50
☐ 87	Valeri Zelepukin, N.J.	.20
☐ 88	John MacLean, N.J.	.20
☐ 89	Todd Bertuzzi, NYI.	.50
☐ 90	Eric Fichaud (G), NYI.	.50
☐ 91	Zigmund Palffy, NYI.	1.00
☐ 92	Travis Green, NYI.	.20
☐ 93	Kenny Jonsson, NYI.	.20
☐ 94	Bryan McCabe, NYI.	.20
☐ 95	Marty McInnis, NYI.	.20
☐ 96	Foil: New York Islanders Logo	.20
☐ 97	Alexander Semak, NYI.	.20
☐ 98	Niclas Andersson, NYI.	.20
☐ 99	Scott Lachance, NYI.	.20
☐ 100	Adam Graves, NYR.	.20
☐ 101	Mark Messier, NYR.	1.25
☐ 102	Brian Leetch, NYR.	.75
☐ 103	Mike Richter (G), NYR.	.75
☐ 104	Alexei Kovalev, NYR.	.20
☐ 105	Luc Robitaille, NYR.	.20
☐ 106	Foil: New York Rangers Logo	.20
☐ 107	Ulf Samuelsson, NYR.	.20
☐ 108	Niklas Sundstrom, NYR.	.20
☐ 109	Jari Kurri, NYR. (Ana.)	.50
☐ 110	Sergei Nemchinov, NYR.	.20
☐ 111	Rod Brind'Amour, Pha.	.50
☐ 112	John LeClair, Pha.	1.25
☐ 113	Ron Hextall (G), Pha.	.50
☐ 114	Eric Lindros, Pha.	3.50
☐ 115	Eric Desjardins, Pha.	.20
☐ 116	Dale Hawerchuk, Pha.	.50
☐ 117	Foil: Philadelphia Flyers Logo	.20
☐ 118	Mikael Renberg, Pha.	.20
☐ 119	Joel Otto, Pha.	.20
☐ 120	Petr Svoboda, Pha.	.20
☐ 121	Karl Dykhuis, Pha.	.20
☐ 122	Brian Bradley, T.B.	.20
☐ 123	Roman Hamrlik, T.B.	.50
☐ 124	Chris Gratton, T.B.	.50
☐ 125	Daren Puppa (G), T.B.	.20
☐ 126	Petr Klima, T.B.	.20
☐ 127	Alexander Semak, T.B.	.20
☐ 128	Foil: Tampa Bay Lightning Logo	.20
☐ 129	Aaron Gavey, T.B.	.20
☐ 130	Brian Bellows, T.B.	.20
☐ 131	Rob Zamuner, T.B.	.50
☐ 132	Mikael Andersson, T.B.	.20
☐ 133	Peter Bondra, Wsh.	1.00
☐ 134	Jim Carey (G), Wsh.	.20
☐ 135	Sergei Gonchar, Wsh.	.20
☐ 136	Brendan Witt, Wsh.	.20
☐ 137	Sylvain Côté, Wsh.	.20
☐ 138	Joé Juneau, Wsh.	.20
☐ 139	Michal Pivonka, Wsh.	.20
☐ 140	Foil: Washington Capitals Logo	.20
☐ 141	Andrew Brunette, Wsh.	.20
☐ 142	Calle Johansson, Wsh.	.20
☐ 143	Stefan Ustorf, Wsh.	.20
☐ 144	LL: Mario Lemieux, Pgh.	2.00
☐ 145	LL: Ron Francis, Pgh.	.50
☐ 146	LL: Ron Hextall (G), Pha.	.35
☐ 147	LL: Vladimir Konstantinov, Det.	.20
☐ 148	LL: Brian Leetch, NYR.	.35
☐ 149	LL: Gary Roberts, Cgy.	.35
☐ 150	LL: Mario Lemieux, Pgh.	2.00
☐ 151	LL: Chris Chelios, Chi.	.35
☐ 152	LL: Daniel Alfredsson, Ott.	.35
☐ 153	LL: Paul Kariya, Ana.	1.75
☐ 154	LL: Jim Carey (G), Wsh.	.20
☐ 155	LL: Joe Sakic, Col.	1.00
☐ 156	Ed Belfour (G), Chi.	.75
☐ 157	Chris Chelios, Chi.	1.00
☐ 158	Jeremy Roenick, Chi.	.75
☐ 159	Eric Dazé, Chi.	.50
☐ 160	Tony Amonte, Chi.	.50
☐ 161	Bernie Nicholls, Chi.	.20
☐ 162	Foil: Chicago Blackhawks Logo	.20
☐ 163	Gary Suter, Chi.	.20
☐ 164	Denis Savard, Chi.	.50
☐ 165	Brent Sutter, Chi.	.20
☐ 166	Keith Carney, Chi.,	.20
☐ 167	Derian Hatcher, Dal.	.20
☐ 168	Mike Modano, Dal.	1.25
☐ 169	Joe Nieuwendyk, Dal.	.50
☐ 170	Kevin Hatcher, Dal. (Pgh.)	.20
☐ 171	Benoît Hogue, Dal.	.20
☐ 172	Grant Marshall, Dal.	.20
☐ 173	Andy Moog (G), Dal.	.50
☐ 174	Foil: Dallas Stars Logo	.20
☐ 175	Jere Lehtinen, Dal.	.50
☐ 176	Greg Adams, Dal.	.20
☐ 177	Brent Gilchrist, Dal.	.20
☐ 178	Sergei Fedorov, Det.	1.25
☐ 179	Paul Coffey, Det.	.50
☐ 180	Chris Osgood (G), Det.	1.00
☐ 181	Steve Yzerman, Det.	2.50
☐ 182	Vladimir Konstantinov, Det.	.20
☐ 183	Vyacheslav Kozlov, Det.	.20
☐ 184	Foil: Detroit Red Wings Logo	.20
☐ 185	Nicklas Lidstrom, Det.	.50
☐ 186	Keith Primeau, Det.	.50
☐ 187	Viacheslav Fetisov, Det.	.50
☐ 188	Igor Larionov, Det.	.50
☐ 189	Nikolai Khabibulin (G), Wpg. (Pho.)	.75
☐ 190	Chad Kilger, Wpg. (Pho.)	.20
☐ 191	Keith Tkachuk, Wpg. (Pho.)	1.00
☐ 192	Oleg Tverdovsky, Wpg. (Pho.)	.20
☐ 193	Ed Olczyk, Wpg. (Pho.)	.20
☐ 194	Teppo Numminen, Wpg. (Pho.)	.20
☐ 195	Foil: Phoenix Coyotes Logo	.20
☐ 196	Alexei Zhamnov, Wpg. (Pho.)	.50
☐ 197	Dave Manson, Wpg. (Pho.)	.20
☐ 198	Craig Janney, Wpg. (Pho.)	.20
☐ 199	Igor Korolev, Wpg. (Pho.)	.20
☐ 200	Wayne Gretzky, Stl.	6.00
☐ 201	Chris Pronger, Stl.	.50
☐ 202	Brett Hull, Stl.	1.25
☐ 203	Grant Fuhr (G), Stl.	.50
☐ 204	Shayne Corson, Stl.	.50
☐ 205	Geoff Courtnall, Stl.	.20
☐ 206	Foil: St. Louis Blues Logo	.20
☐ 207	Al MacInnis, Stl.	.20
☐ 208	Christer Olsson, Stl.	.20
☐ 209	Adam Creighton, Stl.	.20
☐ 210	Tony Twist, Stl.	.20
☐ 211	Félix Potvin (G), Tor.	1.25
☐ 212	Kirk Muller, Tor.	.20
☐ 213	Wendel Clark, Tor.	.50
☐ 214	Doug Gilmour, Tor.	.75
☐ 215	Mike Gartner, Tor.	.50
☐ 216	Larry Murphy, Tor.	.50
☐ 217	Foil: Toronto Maple Leafs Logo	.20
☐ 218	Mats Sundin, Tor.	1.25
☐ 219	Dave Gagner, Tor.	.20
☐ 220	Mathieu Schneider, Tor.	.20
☐ 221	Tie Domi, Tor.	.20
☐ 222	Paul Kariya, Ana.	3.50
☐ 223	Guy Hebert (G), Ana.	.50
☐ 224	Roman Oksiuta, Ana.	.20
☐ 225	Teemu Selänne, Ana.	1.75
☐ 226	Steve Rucchin, Ana.	.20
☐ 227	Bobby Dollas, Ana.	.20
☐ 228	Foil: Anaheim Mighty Ducks Logo	.20

	No.	Player	Price
☐	229	Darren Van Impe, Ana.	.20
☐	230	Fredrik Olausson, Ana.	.20
☐	231	Shaun Van Allen, Ana.	.20
☐	232	Joe Sacco, Ana.	.20
☐	233	Trevor Kidd (G), Cgy.	.50
☐	234	Theoren Fleury, Cgy.	.75
☐	235	German Titou, Cgy.	.20
☐	236	James Patrick, Cgy.	.20
☐	237	Michael Nylander, Cgy.	.20
☐	238	Cory Stillman, Cgy.	.20
☐	239	Foil: Calgary Flames Logo	.20
☐	240	Gary Roberts, Cgy.	.50
☐	241	Jamie Huscroft, Cgy.	.20
☐	242	Tommy Albelin, Cgy.	.20
☐	243	Zarley Zalapski, Cgy.	.20
☐	244	Peter Forsberg, Col.	2.50
☐	245	Joe Sakic, Col.	2.00
☐	246	Claude Lemieux, Col.	.20
☐	247	Patrick Roy (G), Col.	4.00
☐	248	Valeri Kamensky, Col.	.50
☐	249	Uwe Krupp, Col.	.20
☐	250	Foil: Colorado Avalanche Logo	.20
☐	251	Sandis Ozolinsh, Col.	.50
☐	252	Curtis Leschyshyn, Col.	.20
☐	253	Scott Young, Col.	.20
☐	254	Alexei Gusarov, Col.	.20
☐	255	Curtis Joseph (G), Edm.	1.50
☐	256	Bryan Marchment, Edm.	.20
☐	257	Doug Weight, Edm.	.75
☐	258	Jason Arnott, Edm.	.50
☐	259	Zdeno Ciger, Edm.	.20
☐	260	Miroslav Satan, Edm.	.20
☐	261	Mariusz Czerkawski, Edm.	.20
☐	262	Foil: Edmonton Oilers Logo	.20
☐	263	Jiri Slegr, Edm.	.20
☐	264	Jeff Norton, Edm.	.20
☐	265	Boris Mironov, Edm.	.20
☐	266	Vitali Yachmenev, L.A.	.20
☐	267	Byron Dafoe (G), L.A.	.20
☐	268	Rob Blake, L.A.	.50
☐	269	Ray Ferraro, L.A.	.20
☐	270	Dmitri Khristich, L.A.	.20
☐	271	Kevin Todd, L.A.	.20
☐	272	Yanic Perreault, L.A.	.20
☐	273	Foil: Los Angeles Kings Logo	.20
☐	274	Tony Granato, L.A.	.20
☐	275	Jaroslav Modry, L.A.	.20
☐	276	Mattias Norstrom, L.A.	.20
☐	277	Owen Nolan, S.J.	.50
☐	278	Jeff Friesen, S.J.	.50
☐	279	Marcus Ragnarsson, S.J.	.20
☐	280	Chris Terreri (G), S.J.	.20
☐	281	Darren Turcotte, S.J.	.20
☐	282	Viktor Kozlov, S.J.	.20
☐	283	Ulf Dahlen, S.J.	.20
☐	284	Foil: San Jose Sharks Logo	.20
☐	285	Michal Sykora, S.J.	.20
☐	286	Ray Whitney, S.J.	.20
☐	287	Shean Donovan, S.J.	.20
☐	288	Alexander Mogilny, Van.	.75
☐	289	Pavel Bure, Van.	1.75
☐	290	Trevor Linden, Van.	.50
☐	291	Kirk McLean (G), Van.	.50
☐	292	Russ Courtnall, Van.	.20
☐	293	Jyrki Lumme, Van.	.20
☐	294	Foil: Vancouver Canucks Logo	.20
☐	295	Cliff Ronning, Van.	.20
☐	296	Markus Naslund, Van.	.20
☐	297	Esa Tikkanen, Van.	.20
☐	298	Josef Beranek, Van.	.20
☐	299	Foil: Martin Biron (G), Buf.	.20
☐	300	Foil: Peter Ferraro, NYR.	.20
☐	301	Foil: Jason Bonsignore, Edm.	.20
☐	302	Foil: Jamie Storr (G), L.A.	.50
☐	303	Foil: Eric Fichaud (G), NYI.	.50
☐	304	Foil: Andrew Brunette, Wsh.	.20

1996 - 97 PINNACLE

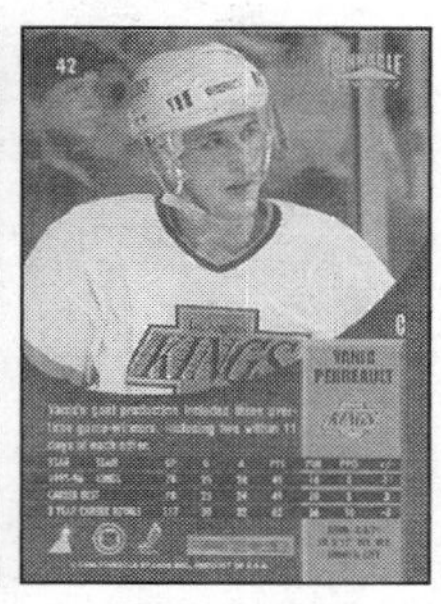

These cards have five versions: the regular card (gold bottom border), a foil card (magazine packs), a premium stock card (silver bottom border), a Rink Collection parallel (dufex technology) and an Artist's Proof parallel.

Imprint: © 1996 PINNACLE BRANDS INC.

Complete Set (250 cards):	**30.00**
Foil/Magazine Set (250 cards):	**40.00**
Premium Stock Set (250 cards):	**75.00**
Rink Collection Set (250 cards):	**450.00**
Artist's Proofs Set (250 cards):	**2,300.00**

	No.	Player	Reg.	Mag.	P.S.	Rink	A.P.
Common Player:			.15	.20	.25	1.75	5.00
☐☐☐☐☐	1	Wayne Gretzky, NYR.	4.00	6.50	9.00	60.00	275.00
☐☐☐☐☐	2	Mark Messier, NYR.	.50	.75	1.50	6.00	35.00
☐☐☐☐☐	3	Kevin Hatcher, Dal.	.15	.20	.25	1.75	5.00
☐☐☐☐☐	4	Scott Stevens, N.J.	.15	.20	.25	1.75	5.00
☐☐☐☐☐	5	Derek Plante, Buf.	.15	.20	.25	1.75	5.00
☐☐☐☐☐	6	Theoren Fleury, Cgy.	.35	.50	1.00	4.00	20.00
☐☐☐☐☐	7	Brian Rolston, N.J.	.15	.20	.25	1.75	5.00
☐☐☐☐☐	8	Teppo Numminen, Wpg.	.15	.20	.25	1.75	5.00
☐☐☐☐☐	9	Adam Graves, NYR.	.15	.20	.25	1.75	5.00
☐☐☐☐☐	10	Jason Dawe, Buf.	.15	.20	.25	1.75	5.00
☐☐☐☐☐	11	Sergei Nemchinov, NYR.	.15	.20	.25	1.75	5.00
☐☐☐☐☐	12	Jeff Brown, Hfd.	.15	.20	.25	1.75	5.00
☐☐☐☐☐	13	Alexei Zhamnov, Wpg.	.25	.35	.75	3.50	10.00
☐☐☐☐☐	14	Paul Coffey, Det.	.25	.35	.75	3.50	10.00
☐☐☐☐☐	15	Kevin Miller, Pgh.	.15	.20	.25	1.75	5.00
☐☐☐☐☐	16	Mike Vernon (G), Det.	.25	.35	.75	3.50	10.00
☐☐☐☐☐	17	Brian Bradley, T.B.	.15	.20	.25	1.75	5.00
☐☐☐☐☐	18	Jeff Friesen, S.J.	.25	.35	.75	3.50	10.00
☐☐☐☐☐	19	Phil Housley, N.J.	.15	.20	.25	1.75	5.00
☐☐☐☐☐	20	Ray Whitney, S.J.	.15	.20	.25	1.75	5.00
☐☐☐☐☐	21	Sergei Fedorov, Det.	.50	.75	1.50	6.00	35.0.0
☐☐☐☐☐	22	Pierre Turgeon, Mtl.	.25	.35	.75	3.50	10.00
☐☐☐☐☐	23	Rick Tocchet, Bos.	.15	.20	.25	1.75	5.00
☐☐☐☐☐	24	Uwe Krupp, Col.	.15	.20	.25	1.75	5.00
☐☐☐☐☐	25	Steve Yzerman, Det.	1.25	2.00	4.00	25.00	125.00
☐☐☐☐☐	26	Tom Chorske, Ott.	.15	.20	.25	1.75	5.00
☐☐☐☐☐	27	Pat LaFontaine, Buf.	.25	.35	.75	3.50	10.00
☐☐☐☐☐	28	Nicklas Lidström, Det.	.25	.35	.75	3.50	10.00
☐☐☐☐☐	29	Ray Ferraro, L.A.	.15	.20	.25	1.75	5.00
☐☐☐☐☐	30	Brian Noonan, Stl.	.15	.20	.25	1.75	5.00
☐☐☐☐☐	31	Dino Ciccarelli, Det.	.25	.35	.75	3.50	10.00
☐☐☐☐☐	32	Rob Niedermayer, Fla.	.15	.20	.25	1.75	5.00
☐☐☐☐☐	33	Stéphane Richer, N.J.	.15	.20	.25	1.75	5.00
☐☐☐☐☐	34	Chris Chelios, Chi.	.35	.50	1.00	5.00	25.00
☐☐☐☐☐	35	Mike Gartner, Tor.	.25	.35	.75	3.50	10.00
☐☐☐☐☐	36	German Titov, Cgy.	.15	.20	.25	1.75	5.00
☐☐☐☐☐	37	Sean Burke (G), Hfd.	.25	.35	.75	3.50	10.00
☐☐☐☐☐	38	Robert Svehla, Fla.	.15	.20	.25	1.75	5.00
☐☐☐☐☐	39	Dave Gagner, Tor.	.15	.20	.25	1.75	5.00
☐☐☐☐☐	40	Sergei Gonchar, Wsh.	.15	.20	.25	1.75	5.00
☐☐☐☐☐	41	Bernie Nicholls, Chi.	.15	.20	.25	1.75	5.00
☐☐☐☐☐	42	Yanic Perreault, L.A.	.15	.20	.25	1.75	5.00
☐☐☐☐☐	43	Adam Deadmarsh, Col.	.15	.20	.25	1.75	5.00
☐☐☐☐☐	44	Dale Hawerchuk, Pha.	.25	.35	.75	3.50	10.00
☐☐☐☐☐	45	Alexei Kovalev, NYR.	.15	.20	.25	1.75	5.00
		Error (Alexander Kapovtsev)					
☐☐☐☐☐	46	Esa Tikkanen, Van.	.15	.20	.25	1.75	5.00
☐☐☐☐☐	47	Valeri Kamensky, Col.	.25	.35	.75	3.50	10.00
☐☐☐☐☐	48	Craig Janney, Wpg.	.15	.20	.25	1.75	5.00
☐☐☐☐☐	49	John LeClair, Pha.	.50	.75	1.50	6.00	35.00
☐☐☐☐☐	50	Radek Bonk, Ott.	.15	.20	.25	1.75	5.00
☐☐☐☐☐	51	David Oliver, Edm.	.15	.20	.25	1.75	5.00
☐☐☐☐☐	52	Todd Harvey, Dal.	.15	.20	.25	1.75	5.00
☐☐☐☐☐	53	Steve Thomas, N.J.	.15	.20	.25	1.75	5.00
☐☐☐☐☐	54	Tony Amonte, Chi.	.25	.35	.75	3.50	10.00
☐☐☐☐☐	55	Mikael Renberg, Pha.	.15	.20	.25	1.75	5.00
☐☐☐☐☐	56	Brendan Shanahan, Hfd.	.60	1.25	1.75	8.00	50.00
☐☐☐☐☐	57	Tom Fitzgerald, Fla.	.15	.20	.25	1.75	5.00
☐☐☐☐☐	58	Chris Pronger, Stl.	.25	.35	.75	3.50	10.00
☐☐☐☐☐	59	Donald Audette, Buf.	.15	.20	.25	1.75	5.00
☐☐☐☐☐	60	Nelson Emerson, Hfd.	.15	.20	.25	1.75	5.00
☐☐☐☐☐	61	Joe Mullen , Bos.	.15	.20	.25	1.75	5.00
☐☐☐☐☐	62	Marty McInnis, NYI.	.15	.20	.25	1.75	5.00
☐☐☐☐☐	63	Martin Rucinsky, Mtl.	.15	.20	.25	1.75	5.00
☐☐☐☐☐	64	Mark Recchi, Mtl.	.25	.35	.75	3.50	10.00
☐☐☐☐☐	65	Vladimir Konstatinov, Det.	.15	.20	.25	1.75	5.00
☐☐☐☐☐	66	Rick Tabaracci (G), Cgy.	.15	.20	.25	1.75	5.00
☐☐☐☐☐	67	Marty McSorley, NYR.	.15	.20	.25	1.75	5.00
☐☐☐☐☐	68	Pat Verbeek, NYR.	.15	.20	.25	1.75	5.00
☐☐☐☐☐	69	Garry Galley, Buf.	.15	.20	.25	1.75	5.00
☐☐☐☐☐	70	Travis Green, NYI.	.15	.20	.25	1.75	5.00
☐☐☐☐☐	71	Chris Tancill, S.J.	.15	.20	.25	1.75	5.00
☐☐☐☐☐	72	Vincent Damphousse, Mtl.	.35	.50	1.00	4.00	20.00
☐☐☐☐☐	73	Benoît Hogue, Dal.	.15	.20	.25	1.75	5.00
☐☐☐☐☐	74	Igor Larionov, Det.	.25	.35	.75	3.50	10.00
☐☐☐☐☐	75	Russ Courtnall, Van.	.15	.20	.25	1.75	5.00
☐☐☐☐☐	76	Mike Hough, Fla.	.15	.20	.25	1.75	5.00
☐☐☐☐☐	77	Alexander Selivanov, T.B.	.15	.20	.25	1.75	5.00
☐☐☐☐☐	78	Peter Forsberg, Col.	1.25	2.00	4.00	25.00	125.0
☐☐☐☐☐	79	Petr Klima, T.B.	.15	.20	.25	1.75	5.00
☐☐☐☐☐	80	Adam Creighton, Stl.	.15	.20	.25	1.75	5.00
☐☐☐☐☐	81	Dave Lowry, Fla.	.15	.20	.25	1.75	5.00
☐☐☐☐☐	82	Andrew Cassels, Hfd.	.15	.20	.25	1.75	5.00
☐☐☐☐☐	83	Martin Gelinas, Van.	.15	.20	.25	1.75	5.00
☐☐☐☐☐	84	Bob Probert, Chi.	.15	.20	.25	1.75	5.00
☐☐☐☐☐	85	Calle Johansson, Wsh.	.15	.20	.25	1.75	5.00
☐☐☐☐☐	86	Mario Lemieux, Pgh.	2.00	4.00	6.50	45.00	200.00
☐☐☐☐☐	87	Alexander Mogilny, Van.	.35	.50	1.00	4.00	20.00
☐☐☐☐☐	88	Guy Hebert (G), Ana.	.25	.35	.75	3.50	10.00
☐☐☐☐☐	89	Bill Ranford (G), Bos.	.25	.35	.75	3.50	10.00
☐☐☐☐☐	90	Kirk McLean (G), Van.	.25	.35	.75	3.50	10.00
☐☐☐☐☐	91	Kenny Jonsson, NYI.	.15	.20	.25	1.75	5.00
☐☐☐☐☐	92	Martin Brodeur (G), N.J.	.75	1.50	3.00	12.00	65.00
☐☐☐☐☐	93	Keith Jones, Wsh.	.15	.20	.25	1.75	5.00
☐☐☐☐☐	94	Ed Belfour (G), Chi.	.35	.50	1.00	4.00	20.00
☐☐☐☐☐	95	Tom Barrasso (G), Pgh.	.25	.35	.75	3.50	10.00
☐☐☐☐☐	96	Félix Potvin (G), Tor.	.50	.75	1.50	6.00	35.00
☐☐☐☐☐	97	Daren Puppa (G), T.B.	.15	.20	.25	1.75	5.00
☐☐☐☐☐	98	Jeremy Roenick, Chi.	.35	.50	1.00	4.00	20.00
☐☐☐☐☐	99	Chris Osgood (G), Det.	.35	.50	1.00	5.00	25.00
☐☐☐☐☐	100	Zigmund Palffy, NYI.	.35	.50	1.00	5.00	25.00
☐☐☐☐☐	101	Ron Hextall (G), Pha.	.25	.35	.75	3.50	10.00
☐☐☐☐☐	102	Jaromir Jagr, Pgh.	1.25	2.00	4.00	25.00	125.0
☐☐☐☐☐	103	Chris Terreri (G), S.J.	.15	.20	.25	1.75	5.00
☐☐☐☐☐	104	Shayne Corson, Stl.	.25	.35	.75	3.50	10.00
☐☐☐☐☐	105	Jim Carey (G), Wsh.	.15	.20	.25	1.75	5.00
☐☐☐☐☐	106	Dominik Hasek (G), Buf.	.75	1.50	3.00	12.00	65.00
☐☐☐☐☐	107	Eric Lindros, Pha.	1.50	3.50	6.00	35.00	175.00
☐☐☐☐☐	108	Petr Nedved, Pgh.	.15	.20	.25	1.75	5.00
☐☐☐☐☐	109	Peter Bondra, Wsh.	.35	.50	1.00	5.00	25.00
☐☐☐☐☐	110	Jeff Hackett (G), Chi.	.25	.35	.75	3.50	10.00
☐☐☐☐☐	111	Trevor Linden, Van.	.25	.35	.75	3.50	10.00
☐☐☐☐☐	112	Mike Richter (G), NYR.	.35	.50	1.00	4.00	20.00
☐☐☐☐☐	113	Claude Lemieux, Col.	.15	.20	.25	1.75	5.00
☐☐☐☐☐	114	Keith Tkachuk, Wpg.	.35	.50	1.00	5.00	25.00
☐☐☐☐☐	115	Pat Falloon, Pha.	.15	.20	.25	1.75	5.00
☐☐☐☐☐	116	Brent Fedyk, Dal.	.15	.20	.25	1.75	5.00
☐☐☐☐☐	117	Todd Marchant, Edm.	.15	.20	.25	1.75	5.00
☐☐☐☐☐	118	Jason Arnott, Edm.	.25	.35	.75	3.50	10.00
☐☐☐☐☐	119	Zarley Zalapski, Cgy.	.15	.20	.25	1.75	5.00
☐☐☐☐☐	120	Kelly Hrudey (G), L.A.	.15	.20	.25	1.75	5.00
☐☐☐☐☐	121	Alexei Yashin, Ott.	.35	.50	1.00	5.00	25.00
☐☐☐☐☐	122	Sergei Zubov, Pgh.	.25	.35	.75	3.50	10.00
☐☐☐☐☐	123	Rod Brind'Amour, Pha.	.25	.35	.75	3.50	10.00
☐☐☐☐☐	124	Mathieu Schneider, Tor.	.15	.20	.25	1.75	5.00
☐☐☐☐☐	125	Bryan Smolinski, Pgh.	.15	.20	.25	1.75	5.00
☐☐☐☐☐	126	Scott Mellanby, Fla.	.15	.20	.25	1.75	5.00
☐☐☐☐☐	127	Doug Gilmour, Tor.	.35	.50	1.00	4.00	20.00
☐☐☐☐☐	128	Brett Hull, Stl.	.50	.75	1.50	6.00	35.00
☐☐☐☐☐	129	Vyacheslav Kozlov, Det.	.15	.20	.25	1.75	5.00
☐☐☐☐☐	130	Adam Oates, Bos.	.35	.50	1.00	4.00	20.00
☐☐☐☐☐	131	Steve Konowalchuk, Wsh.	.15	.20	.25	1.75	5.00
☐☐☐☐☐	132	Robert Kron, Hfd.	.15	.20	.25	1.75	5.00
☐☐☐☐☐	133	Alexandre Daigle, Ott.	.25	.35	.75	3.50	10.00
☐☐☐☐☐	134	Brian Savage, Mtl.	.15	.20	.25	1.75	5.00
☐☐☐☐☐	135	Stu Barnes, Fla.	.15	.20	.25	1.75	5.00
☐☐☐☐☐	136	Cam Neely, Bos.	.25	.35	.75	3.50	10.00
☐☐☐☐☐	137	Steve Rucchin, Ana.	.15	.20	.25	1.75	5.00
☐☐☐☐☐	138	Patrick Roy (G), Col.	2.00	4.00	6.50	45.00	200.00
☐☐☐☐☐	139	Roman Oksiuta, Ana.	.15	.20	.25	1.75	5.00
☐☐☐☐☐	140	Greg Johnson, Det.	.15	.20	.25	1.75	5.00

	No.	Player					
□□□□□	141	Chris Gratton, T.B.	.25	.35	.75	3.50	10.00
□□□□□	142	Jocelyn Thibault, Mtl.	.35	.50	1.00	4.00	20.00
□□□□□	143	Ron Francis, Pgh.	.35	.50	1.00	4.00	20.00
□□□□□	144	Mats Sundin, Tor.	.50	.75	1.50	6.00	35.00
□□□□□	145	Oleg Tverdovsky, Wpg.	.15	.20	.25	1.75	5.00
□□□□□	146	Geoff Courtnall, Stl.	.15	.20	.25	1.75	5.00
□□□□□	147	Kurt Muller, Tor.	.15	.20	.25	1.75	5.00
□□□□□	148	Zdeno Ciger, Edm.	.15	.20	.25	1.75	5.00
□□□□□	149	John MacLean, N.J.	.15	.20	.25	1.75	5.00
□□□□□	150	Damian Rhodes (G), Ott.	.15	.20	.25	1.75	5.00
□□□□□	151	Michael Nylander, Cgy.	.15	.20	.25	1.75	5.00
□□□□□	152	Andrei Kovalenko, Mtl.	.15	.20	.25	1.75	5.00
□□□□□	153	Al MacInnis, Stl.	.15	.20	.25	1.75	5.00
□□□□□	154	Mike Modano, Dal.	.50	.75	1.50	6.00	35.00
□□□□□	155	Teemu Selänne, Ana.	.75	1.50	3.00	12.00	65.00
□□□□□	156	Tomas Sandström, Pgh.	.15	.20	.25	1.75	5.00
□□□□□	157	Bobby Dollas, Ana.	.15	.20	.25	1.75	5.00
□□□□□	158	Doug Weight, Edm.	.35	.50	1.00	4.00	20.00
□□□□□	159	Sandis Ozolinsh, Col.	.25	.35	.75	3.50	10.00
□□□□□	160	Joé Juneau, Wsh.	.15	.20	.25	1.75	5.00
□□□□□	161	Nikolai Khabibulin (G), Wpg.	.35	.50	1.00	4.00	20.00
□□□□□	162	Murray Craven, Chi.	.15	.20	.25	1.75	5.00
□□□□□	163	Cliff Ronning, Van.	.15	.20	.25	1.75	5.00
□□□□□	164	Curtis Joseph (G), Edm.	.60	1.25	1.75	8.00	50.00
□□□□□	165	Darren Turcotte, S.J.	.15	.20	.25	1.75	5.00
□□□□□	166	Andy Moog (G), Dal.	.25	.35	.75	3.50	10.00
□□□□□	167	Mariusz Czerkawski, Edm.	.15	.20	.25	1.75	5.00
□□□□□	168	Keith Primeau, Det.	.25	.35	.75	3.50	10.00
□□□□□	169	Eric Desjardins, Pha.	.15	.20	.25	1.75	5.00
□□□□□	170	Bill Guerin, N.J.	.25	.35	.75	3.50	10.00
□□□□□	171	Glenn Anderson, Stl.	.15	.20	.25	1.75	5.00
□□□□□	172	Mike Ridley, Van.	.15	.20	.25	1.75	5.00
□□□□□	173	Michal Pivonka, Wsh.	.15	.20	.25	1.75	5.00
□□□□□	174	Trevor Kidd (G), Cgy.	.25	.35	.75	3.50	10.00
□□□□□	175	Pavel Bure, Van.	.75	1.50	3.00	12.00	65.00
□□□□□	176	Todd Gill, Tor.	.15	.20	.25	1.75	5.00
□□□□□	177	Dave Andreychuk, N.J.	.15	.20	.25	1.75	5.00
□□□□□	178	Roman Hamrlik, T.B.	.25	.35	.75	3.50	10.00
□□□□□	179	Andrei Nikolishin, Hfd.	.15	.20	.25	1.75	5.00
□□□□□	180	Alexei Zhitnik, Buf.	.15	.20	.25	1.75	5.00
□□□□□	181	Grant Fuhr (G), Stl.	.25	.35	.75	3.50	10.00
□□□□□	182	Dave Reid, Bos.	.15	.20	.25	1.75	5.00
□□□□□	183	Joe Nieuwendyk, Dal.	.25	.35	.75	3.50	10.00
□□□□□	184	Paul Kariya, Ana.	1.50	3.50	6.00	35.00	175.00
□□□□□	185	Jyrki Lumme, Van.	.15	.20	.25	1.75	5.00
□□□□□	186	Owen Nolan, S.J.	.25	.35	.75	3.50	10.00
□□□□□	187	Geoff Sanderson, Hfd.	.15	.20	.25	1.75	5.00
□□□□□	188	Alexander Semak, NYI.	.15	.20	.25	1.75	5.00
□□□□□	189	Larry Murphy, Tor.	.25	.35	.75	3.50	10.00
□□□□□	190	Dimitri Khristich, L.A.	.15	.20	.25	1.75	5.00
□□□□□	191	Shane Churla, Dal.	.15	.20	.25	1.75	5.00
□□□□□	192	Bill Lindsay, Fla.	.15	.20	.25	1.75	5.00
□□□□□	193	Brian Leetch, NYR.	.35	.50	1.00	4.00	20.00
□□□□□	194	Greg Adams, Dal.	.15	.20	.25	1.75	5.00
□□□□□	195	Gary Suter, Chi.	.15	.20	.25	1.75	5.00
□□□□□	196	Wendel Clark, Tor.	.25	.35	.75	3.50	10.00
□□□□□	197	Scott Young, Col.	.15	.20	.25	1.75	5.00
□□□□□	198	Randy Burridge, Buf.	.15	.20	.25	1.75	5.00
□□□□□	199	Ray Bourque, Bos.	.50	.75	1.50	6.00	35.00
□□□□□	200	Joe Murphy, Chi.	.15	.20	.25	1.75	5.00
□□□□□	201	Joe Sakic, Col.	1.00	1.75	3.50	18.00	90.00
□□□□□	202	Saku Koivu, Mtl.	.75	1.50	3.00	12.00	65.00
□□□□□	203	John Vanbiesbrouck (G), Fla.	.60	1.25	1.75	8.00	50.00
□□□□□	204	Ed Jovanovski, Fla.	.25	.35	.75	3.50	10.00
□□□□□	205	Daniel Alfredsson, Ott.	.25	.35	.75	3.50	10.00
□□□□□	206	Vitali Yachmenev, L.A.	.15	.20	.25	1.75	5.00
□□□□□	207	Marcus Ragnarsson, S.J.	.15	.20	.25	1.75	5.00
□□□□□	208	Todd Bertuzzi, NYI.	.25	.35	.75	3.50	10.00
□□□□□	209	Valeri Bure, Mtl.	.15	.20	.25	1.75	5.00
□□□□□	210	Jeff O'Neill, Hfd.	.25	.35	.75	3.50	10.00
□□□□□	211	Corey Hirsch (G), Van.	.15	.20	.25	1.75	5.00
□□□□□	212	Eric Dazé, Chi.	.25	.35	.75	3.50	10.00
□□□□□	213	David Sacco, Ana.	.15	.20	.25	1.75	5.00
□□□□□	214	Jan Vopat, L.A.	.15	.20	.25	1.75	5.00
□□□□□	215	Scott Bailey (G), Bos.	.15	.20	.25	1.75	5.00
□□□□□	216	Jamie Rivers, Stl.	.15	.20	.25	1.75	5.00
□□□□□	217	José Théodore (G), Mtl.	.35	.50	1.00	3.50	15.00
□□□□□	218	Peter Ferraro, NYR.	.15	.20	.25	1.75	5.00
□□□□□	219	Anders Eriksson, Det.	.15	.20	.25	1.75	5.00
□□□□□	220	Wayne Primeau, N.J.	.15	.20	.25	1.75	5.00
□□□□□	221	Denis Pederson, N.J.	.15	.20	.25	1.75	5.00
□□□□□	222	Jay McKee, Buf.	.15	.20	.25	1.75	5.00
□□□□□	223	Sean Pronger, Ana.	.15	.20	.25	1.75	5.00
□□□□□	224	Martin Biron (G), Buf.	.15	.20	.25	1.75	5.00
□□□□□	225	Marek Malik, Hfd.	.15	.20	.25	1.75	5.00
□□□□□	**226**	**Steve Sullivan, N.J., RC**	**.15**	**.20**	**.25**	**1.75**	**5.00**
□□□□□	227	Curtis Brown, Buf.	.15	.20	.25	1.75	5.00
□□□□□	228	Eric Fichaud (G), NYI.	.25	.35	.75	3.50	10.00
□□□□□	**229**	**Jan Caloun, S.J., RC**	**.15**	**.20**	**.25**	**1.75**	**5.00**
□□□□□	230	Miklad Sundblad, Cgy.	.15	.20	.25	1.75	5.00
□□□□□	**231**	**Steve Staios, Bos., RC**	**.15**	**.20**	**.25**	**1.75**	**5.00**
□□□□□	**232**	**Steve Washburn, Fla., RC**	**.15**	**.20**	**.25**	**1.75**	**5.00**
□□□□□	233	Chris Ferraro, NYR.	.15	.20	.25	1.75	5.00
□□□□□	234	Marko Kiprusoff, Mtl.	.15	.20	.25	1.75	5.00
□□□□□	235	Larry Courville, Van.	.15	.20	.25	1.75	5.00
□□□□□	236	David Nemirovsky, Fla.	.15	.20	.25	1.75	5.00
□□□□□	237	Ralph Intranuovo, Edm.	.15	.20	.25	1.75	5.00
□□□□□	238	Kevin Hodson (G), Det.	.15	.20	.25	1.75	5.00
□□□□□	239	Ethan Moreau, Chi.	.25	.35	.75	3.50	10.00
□□□□□	240	Daymond Langkon, T.B.	.15	.20	.25	1.75	5.00
□□□□□	241	Brandon Convery, Tor.	.15	.20	.25	1.75	5.00
□□□□□	242	Cale Hulse, Cgy.	.15	.20	.25	1.75	5.00
□□□□□	243	Zdenek Nedved, Tor.	.15	.20	.25	1.75	5.00
□□□□□	244	Tommy Salo (G), NYI.	.15	.20	.25	1.75	5.00
□□□□□	245	Nolan Baumgartner, Wsh.	.15	.20	.25	1.75	5.00
□□□□□	246	Patrick Labrecque (G), Mtl.	.15	.20	.25	1.75	5.00
□□□□□	247	Jamie Langenbrunner, Dal.	.25	.35	.75	3.50	10.00
□□□□□	248	CL: Pavel Bure, Van.	.35	.75	1.50	6.00	35.00
□□□□□	249	CL: Peter Forsberg, Col.	.75	1.25	2.25	12.00	60.00
□□□□□	250	CL: Teemu Selänne, Ana.	.35	.75	1.50	6.00	35.00

BY THE NUMBERS

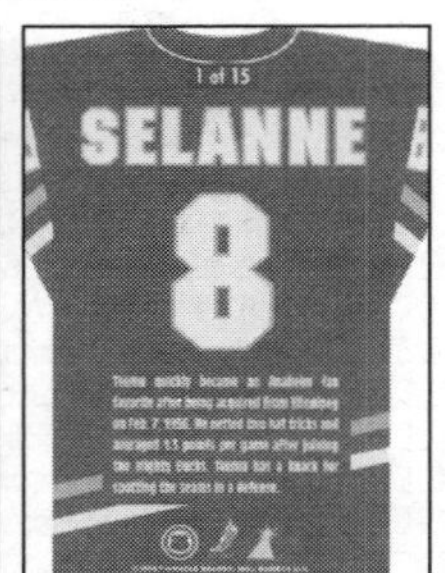

These cards have three versions: a promo card, the die-cut regular insert card and a Premium Stock parallel. The Premium Stock inserts are limited to 903 copies.

Insert Set (15 cards):			85.00	325.00	165.00
	No.	**Player**	**Promo**	**P.S.**	**Die-Cut**
□□□	1	Teemu Selänne, Ana.	3.50	30.00	15.00
□□□	2	Brendan Shanahan, Hfd.	3.00	25.00	12.00
□□□	3	Sergei Fedorov, Det.	2.50	20.00	10.00
□□□	4	Ed Jovanovski, Fla.	1.00	8.00	4.00
□□□	5	Doug Weight, Edm.	1.50	12.00	6.00
□□□	6	Brett Hull, Stl.	2.50	20.00	10.00
□□□	7	Doug Gilmour, Tor.	1.50	12.00	6.00
□□□	8	Jaromir Jagr, Pgh.	5.00	40.00	20.00
□□□	9	Wayne Gretzky, NYR.	10.00	80.00	40.00
□□□	10	Daniel Alfredsson, Ott.	1.50	12.00	6.00
□□□	11	Eric Dazé, Chi.	1.00	8.00	4.00
□□□	12	Mark Messier, NYR.	2.50	20.00	10.00
□□□	13	Jocelyn Thibault (G), Mtl.	1.50	12.00	6.00
□□□	14	Eric Lindros, Pha.	6.50	60.00	30.00
□□□	15	Pavel Bure, Van.	3.50	30.00	15.00

MASKS

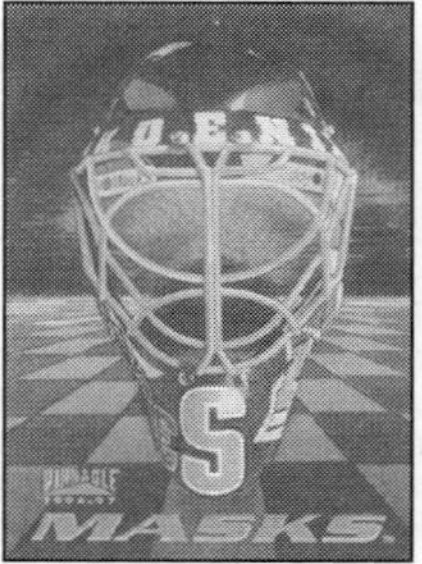

These cards have two versions: the regular insert and a die-cut parallel.

Insert Set (10 cards):			700.00	350.00
	No.	**Player**	**Die-Cut**	**Insert**
□□	1	Patrick Roy (G), Col.	250.00	125.00
□□	2	Mike Richter (G), NYR.	50.00	25.00
□□	3	Curtis Joseph (G), Edm.	100.00	50.00
□□	4	Corey Hirsch (G), Van.	30.00	15.00
□□	5	Martin Brodeur (G), N.J.	120.00	60.00
□□	6	John Vanbiesbrouck (G), Fla.	100.00	50.00
□□	7	Nikolai Khabibulin (G), Wpg.	50.00	25.00
□□	8	Ron Hextall (G), Pha.	40.00	20.00
□□	9	Jocelyn Thibault (G), Mtl.	50.00	25.00
□□	10	Jim Carey (G), Wsh.	30.00	15.00

TEAM PINNACLE

Insert Set (10 cards):			350.00
	No.	**Player**	**NRMT-MT**
□	1	Wayne Gretzky / Joe Sakic	75.00
□	2	Mario Lemieux / Peter Forsberg	60.00
□	3	Eric Lindros / Jeremy Roenick	40.00
□	4	Mark Messier / Doug Weight	20.00
□	5	Brendan Shanahan / Paul Kariya	45.00
□	6	Jaromir Jagr / Brett Hull	35.00
□	7	Ed Jovanovski / Paul Coffey	18.00
□	8	John Vanbiesbrouck / Patrick Roy	60.00
□	9	Martin Brodeur / Chris Osgood	35.00
□	10	Saku Koivu / Eric Dazé	30.00

TROPHIES

Insert Set (10 cards):			275.00
	No.	**Player**	**NRMT-MT**
□	1	Mario Lemieux, Pgh.	80.00
□	2	Paul Kariya, Ana.	65.00
□	3	Sergei Fedorov, Det.	25.00
□	4	Daniel Alfredsson, Ott.	15.00
□	5	Jim Carey, Wsh.	10.00
□	6	Chris Osgood / Mike Vernon, Det.	20.00
□	7	Kris King, Wpg.	10.00
□	8	Chris Chelios, Chi.	20.00
□	9	Joe Sakic, Col.	40.00
□	10	Colorado Avalanche	30.00

1996 - 97 PINNACLE BE A PLAYER

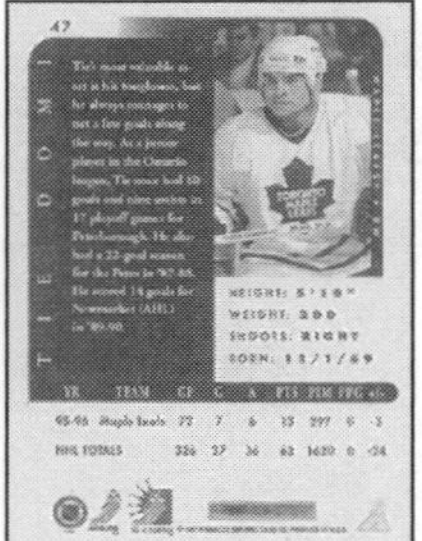

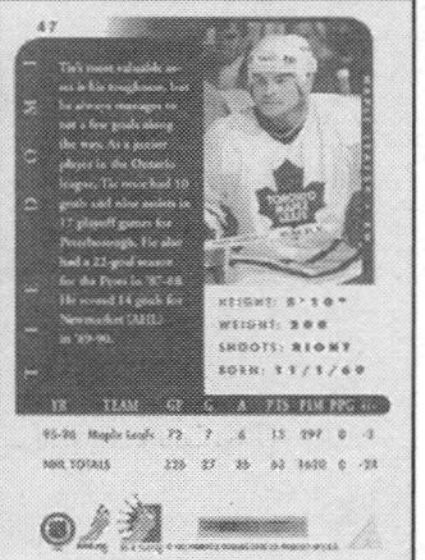

These cards have at least three versions: the regular card, a one per pack autograph insert and an autographed foil card parallel. Promo cards likely exist for all regular cards and Link 2 History cards and have the same value as the regular card. Alexei Zhamnov never returned his cards that were supposed to be signed for this set.

Imprint: © 1997 PINNACLE TRADING CARD CO.

Complete Set (220 cards):				2,000.00	50.00
Common Player:			4.00	8.00	.30
	No.	**Player**	**Auto.**	**Foil Auto.**	**Reg.**
□□□	1	Todd Gill, S.J.	4.00	8.00	.30
□□□	2	Dave Andreychuk, N.J.	6.00	12.00	.30
□□□	3	Igor Kravchuk, Stl.	4.00	8.00	.30
□□□	4	Tom Fitzgerald, Fla.	4.00	8.00	.30
□□□	5	Jeremy Roenick, Pho.	25.00	50.00	1.00
□□□	6	Peter Popovic, Mtl.	4.00	8.00	.30
□□□	7	Andy Moog (G), Dal.	15.00	30.00	.50
□□□	8	Steve Rice, Hfd.	4.00	8.00	.30
□□□	9	Darren Langdon, NYR.	4.00	8.00	.30

□□□	10	Mark Fitzpatrick (G), Fla.	6.00	12.00	.30
□	11	Alexei Zhamnov, Chi.	–	–	.30
□□□	12	Luc Robitaille, NYR.	15.00	30.00	.50
□□□	13	Michal Pivonka, Wsh.	4.00	8.00	.30
□□□	14	Kevin Hatcher, Pgh.	4.00	8.00	.30
□□□	15	Stéphane Yelle, Col.	4.00	8.00	.30
□□□	16	Bill Ranford (G), Bos.	15.00	30.00	.50
□□□	17	Jamie Baker, Tor.	4.00	8.00	.30
□□□	18	Sean Burke (G), Hfd.	10.00	20.00	.50
□□□	19	Al Iafrate, S.J.	4.00	8.00	.30
□□□	20	Mark Recchi, Mtl.	15.00	30.00	.50
□□□	21	Rod Brind'Amour, Pha.	12.00	25.00	.50
□□□	22	Doug Gilmour, N.J.	35.00	60.00	1.50
□□□	23	Mike Wilson, Buf.	4.00	8.00	.30
□□□	**24**	**Barry Potomski, L.A., RC**	**4.00**	**8.00**	**.30**
□□□	25	Mike Gartner, Pho.	15.00	30.00	.50
□□□	26	Jason Wiemer, T.B.	4.00	8.00	.30
□□□	27	Scott Lachance, NYI.	4.00	8.00	.30
□□□	28	Joe Murphy, Chi.	4.00	8.00	.30
□□□	29	Bill Guerin, N.J.	12.00	25.00	.30
□□□	30	Byron Dafoe (G), L.A.	6.00	12.00	.30
□□□	31	Esa Tikkanen, NYR.	4.00	8.00	.30
□□□	32	Ken Baumgartner, Ana.	4.00	8.00	.30
□□□	33	Valeri Kamensky, Col.	12.00	25.00	.50
□□□	34	J.J. Daigneault, Pgh.	4.00	8.00	.30
□□□	35	Ulf Dahlen, Chi.	4.00	8.00	.30
□□□	36	Jason Allison, Wsh.	8.00	15.00	.30
□□□	37	Ted Donato, Bos.	4.00	8.00	.30
□□□	38	Pat Verbeek, Dal.	8.00	15.00	.30
□□□	39	Miroslav Satan, Edm.	6.00	12.00	.30
□□□	40	Eric Desjardins, Pha.	6.00	12.00	.30
□□□	41	Dave Karpa, Col.	4.00	8.00	.30
□□□	42	Jeff Hackett (G), Chi.	10.00	20.00	.30
□□□	43	Doug Brown, Det.	4.00	8.00	.30
□□□	44	Gord Murphy, Fla.	4.00	8.00	.30
□□□	45	Kelly Hrudey (G), S.J.	6.00	12.00	.30
□□□	46	Kelly Miller, Wsh.	4.00	8.00	.30
□□□	47	Tie Domi, Tor.	6.00	12.00	.30
□□□	48	Alexei Yashin, Ott.	20.00	40.00	1.00
□□□	49	German Titov, Cgy.	4.00	8.00	.30
□□□	50	Stéphane Richer, N.J.	6.00	12.00	.30
□□□	51	Corey Hirsch (G), Van.	10.00	20.00	.50
□□□	52	Brad May, Buf.	4.00	8.00	.30
□□□	53	Joe Nieuwendyk, Dal.	12.00	25.00	.30
□□□	54	Sylvain Lefebvre, Tor.	4.00	8.00	.30
□□□□	55	Brian Leetch, NYR.	30.00	60.00	1.00
□□□	56	Petr Svoboda, Pha.	4.00	8.00	.30
□□□	57	Dave Manson, Pho.	4.00	8.00	.30
□□□	58	Jason Woolley, Pgh.	4.00	8.00	.30
□□□	59	Scott Niedermayer, N.J.	6.00	12.00	.30
□□□	60	Kelly Chase, Hfd.	4.00	8.00	.30
□□□	61	Guy Hebert (G), Ana.	12.00	25.00	.50
□□□	62	Shayne Corson, Mtl.	8.00	15.00	.30
□□□	63	Jon Casey (G), Stl.	6.00	12.00	.30
□□□	64	Rob Zettler, Pha.	4.00	8.00	.30
□□□	65	Mikael Andersson, T.B.	4.00	8.00	.30
□□□	66	Tony Amonte, Chi.	20.00	40.00	.50
□□□	67	Johan Garpenlov, Fla.	4.00	8.00	.30
□□□	68	Denny Lambert, Ana.	4.00	8.00	.30
□□□	69	Jim McKenzie, Pho.	4.00	8.00	.30
□□□	70	Darren Turcotte, S.J.	4.00	8.00	.30
□□□	71	Eric Weinrich, Chi.	4.00	8.00	.30
□□□	72	Troy Mallette, Bos.	4.00	8.00	.30
□□□	73	Donald Audette, Buf.	6.00	12.00	.30
□□□	74	Philippe Boucher, L.A.	4.00	8.00	.30
□□□	75	Shawn Chambers, N.J.	4.00	8.00	.30
□□□	76	Joel Otto, Pha.	6.00	12.00	.30
□□□	77	Tommy Salo (G), NYI.	6.00	12.00	.30
□□□	78	Olaf Kolzig (G), Wsh.	20.00	40.00	1.00
□□□	79	Adrian Aucoin, Van.	4.00	8.00	.30
□□□	80	Alek Stojanov, Pgh.	4.00	8.00	.30
□□□	81	Robert Reichel, Cgy.	12.00	25.00	.30
□□□	82	Marc Bureau, Mtl.	4.00	8.00	.30
□□□	83	Alexei Godynyuk, Hfd.	4.00	8.00	.30
□□□	84	Bill Berg, NYR.	4.00	8.00	.30
□□□	85	Marc Bergevin, Det.	4.00	8.00	.30
□□□	86	Kevin Kaminski, Wsh.	4.00	8.00	.30
□□□	87	Uwe Krupp, Col.	4.00	8.00	.30
□□□	88	Boris Mironov, Edm.	4.00	8.00	.30
□□□	89	Bob Bassen, Dal.	4.00	8.00	.30
□□□	90	Darryl Shannon, Pho.	4.00	8.00	.30
□□□	91	Mikael Renberg, Pha.	10.00	20.00	.30
□□□	92	Mike Stapleton, Pho.	4.00	8.00	.30
□□□	93	Dave Roberts, Van.	4.00	8.00	.30
□□□	94	Peter Zezel, N.J.	4.00	8.00	.30
□□□	95	Mathieu Dandenault, Det.	4.00	8.00	.30
□□□	96	Bobby Dollas, Ana.	4.00	8.00	.30
□□□	97	Don Sweeney, Bos.	4.00	8.00	.30
□□□	98	Niclas Andersson, NYI.	4.00	8.00	.30
□□□	99	Pat Jablonski (G), Mtl.	6.00	12.00	.30
□□□	100	John Slaney, L.A.	4.00	8.00	.30
□□□	101	Kevin Todd, L.A.	4.00	8.00	.30
□□□	102	Jamie Pushor, Det.	4.00	8.00	.30
□□□	**103**	**Andreas Johansson, NYI., RC**	**4.00**	**8.00**	**.30**
□□□	104	Corey Schwab (G), T.B.	6.00	12.00	.30
□□□□	**105**	**Todd Simpson, Cgy.**	**4.00**	**8.00**	**.30**
□□□	106	Landon Wilson, Col.	4.00	8.00	.30
□□□	**107**	**Daniel Goneau, NYR., RC**	**4.00**	**8.00**	**.30**
□□□	108	David Wilkie, Mtl.	4.00	8.00	.30
□□□	**109**	**Andreas Dackell, Ott., RC**	**4.00**	**8.00**	**.30**
□□□	110	Marek Malik, Hfd.	4.00	8.00	.30
□□□	111	Mark Messier, NYR.	75.00	150.00	1.50
□□□	112	François Leroux, Pgh.	4.00	8.00	.30
□□□	113	Michal Sykora, N.J.	4.00	8.00	.30
□□□	114	Rob Zamuner, T.B.	8.00	15.00	.30
□□□	115	Craig Berube, Wsh.	4.00	8.00	.30
□□□	116	Mike Ricci, Col.	6.00	12.00	.30
□□□	117	Adam Burt, Hfd.	4.00	8.00	.30
□□□	118	Alexander Karpovtsev, NYR.	4.00	8.00	.30
□□□	119	Shawn McEachern, Ott.	6.00	12.00	.30
□□□	120	Shawn Antoski, Pgh.	4.00	8.00	.30
□□□	121	Dave Reid, Dal.	4.00	8.00	.30
□□□	122	Todd Warriner, Tor.	4.00	8.00	.30
□□□	123	Markus Naslund, Van.	6.00	12.00	.30
□□□	124	Martin Rucinsky, Mtl.	6.00	12.00	.30
□□□	125	Bob Carpenter, N.J.	4.00	8.00	.30
□□□	126	Dean McAmmond, Edm.	4.00	8.00	.30
□□□	127	Trevor Kidd (G), Cgy.	15.00	30.00	.50
□□□	128	Martin Lapointe, Det.	4.00	8.00	.30
□□□	129	Enrico Ciccone, Chi.	4.00	8.00	.30
□□□	130	Dixon Ward, Buf.	4.00	8.00	.30
□□□	131	Jason Muzzatti (G), Hfd.	6.00	12.00	.30
□□□	132	Bryan Smolinski, NYI.	6.00	12.00	.30
□□□	133	Norm Maciver, Pho.	4.00	8.00	.30
□□□	134	Fredrik Olausson, Pho.	4.00	8.00	.30
□□□	135	Daniel Lacroix, Pha.	4.00	8.00	.30
□□□	136	Mike Peluso, Stl.	4.00	8.00	.30
□□□	137	Andrei Nikolishin, Hfd.	4.00	8.00	.30
□□□	138	Rhett Warrener, Fla.	4.00	8.00	.30
□□□	139	Ray Ferraro, L.A.	4.00	8.00	.30
□□□	140	Glen Healy (G), NYR.	8.00	15.00	.30
□□□	141	Steve Duchesne, Ott.	6.00	12.00	.30
□□□	142	Tony Granato, S.J.	6.00	12.00	.30
□□□	143	Cory Cross, T.B.	4.00	8.00	.30
□□□	144	Jon Klemm, Col.	4.00	8.00	.30
□□□	145	Sami Kapanen, Hfd.	6.00	12.00	.30
□□□	146	Grant Marshall, Dal.	4.00	8.00	.30
□□□	147	Matthew Barnaby, Buf.	4.00	8.00	.30
□□□	148	Lyle Odelein, N.J.	4.00	8.00	.30
□□□	149	Joe Dziedzic, Pgh.	4.00	8.00	.30
□□□	150	Sergei Gonchar, Wsh.	4.00	8.00	.30
□□□	151	Doug Zmolek, L.A.	4.00	8.00	.30
□□□	**152**	**Sean O'Donnell, L.A., RC**	**4.00**	**8.00**	**.30**
□□□	153	Scott Thornton, Mtl.	4.00	8.00	.30
□□□	154	Steve Heinze, Bos.	4.00	8.00	.30
□□□	155	Gary Valk, Ana.	4.00	8.00	.30
□□□	156	Jeff Finley, Pho.	4.00	8.00	.30
□□□	157	Trent Klatt, Pha.	4.00	8.00	.30
□□□	158	Jeff Beukeboom, NYR.	4.00	8.00	.30
□□□	159	Theoren Fleury, Cgy.	20.00	40.00	.50
□□□	160	Dana Murzyn, Van.	4.00	8.00	.30
□□□	161	Tommy Albelin, Cgy.	4.00	8.00	.30
□□□	162	Bryan McCabe, NYI.	8.00	15.00	.30
□□□	163	Shaun Van Allen, Ott.	4.00	8.00	.30
□□□	164	Rick Tabaracci (G), T.B.	8.00	15.00	.30
□□□	165	Kevin Miller, Chi.	4.00	8.00	.30
□□□□	166	Mariusz Czerkawski, Edm.	4.00	8.00	.30
□□□	167	Gerald Diduck, Hfd.	4.00	8.00	.30
□□□	168	Brad McCrimmon, Pho.	4.00	8.00	.30
□□□	169	Stéphane Matteau, Stl.	4.00	8.00	.30
□□□	170	Scott Daniels, Pha.	4.00	8.00	.30
□□□	171	Scott Mellanby, Fla.	6.00	12.00	.30
□□□	172	Sandy Moger, Bos.	4.00	8.00	.30
□□□	173	Steve Konowalchuk, Wsh.	4.00	8.00	.30
□□□	174	Doug Weight, Edm.	20.00	40.00	.50
□□□	175	Darren McCarty, Det.	6.00	12.00	.30
□□□	176	Darryl Sydor, Dal.	4.00	8.00	.30
□□□	177	Dave Ellett, Tor. (N.J.)	4.00	8.00	.30
□□□	**178**	**Bob Boughner, Buf., RC**	**4.00**	**8.00**	**.30**
□□□	179	Derek Armstrong, NYI.	4.00	8.00	.30
□□□	180	Gary Suter, Chi.	4.00	8.00	.30
□□□	181	Donald Brashear, Van.	4.00	8.00	.30
□□□	182	Chris Tamer, Pgh.	4.00	8.00	.30
□□□	183	Darrin Shannon, Pho.	4.00	8.00	.30
□□□	184	Stan Neckar, Ott.	4.00	8.00	.30
□□□	185	Brent Severyn, Col.	4.00	8.00	.30
□□□	186	Steve Rucchin, Ana.	6.00	12.00	.30
□□□	187	Jeff Norton, Edm.	4.00	8.00	.30
□□□	188	Steve Finn, L.A.	4.00	8.00	.30
□□□	189	Kjell Samuelsson, Pha.	4.00	8.00	.30
□□□	190	Jeff Friesen, S.J.	8.00	15.00	.30
□□□	191	Shawn Burr, Det.	4.00	8.00	.30
□□□	192	Paul Laus, Fla.	4.00	8.00	.30
□□□	193	Jeff Odgers, S.J.	4.00	8.00	.30
□□□	194	Keith Jones, Col.	4.00	8.00	.30
□□□	195	Rich Matvichuk, Dal.	4.00	8.00	.30
□□□	196	Adam Foote, Col.	6.00	12.00	.30
□□□	197	Bob Errey, Det.	4.00	8.00	.30
□□□	198	Ryan Smyth, Edm.	30.00	60.00	.50
□□□	199	Mark Janssens, Hfd.	4.00	8.00	.30
□□□	200	Claude Lapointe, NYI.	4.00	8.00	.30
□□□	201	Brian Noonan, Van.	4.00	8.00	.30
□□□	202	Damian Rhodes (G), Ott.	8.00	15.00	.30
□□□	203	Dale Hawerchuk, Pha.	15.00	30.00	.50
□□□	204	Bill Lindsay, Fla.	4.00	8.00	.30
□□□	205	Brian Skrudland, Fla.	6.00	12.00	.30
□□□	206	Curtis Joseph, Edm.	25.00	50.00	.75
□□□	207	Jon Rohloff, Bos.	4.00	8.00	.30
□□□	208	Doug Bodger, S.J.	4.00	8.00	.30
□□□	209	Steve Sullivan, N.J.	6.00	12.00	.30
□□□	210	Ricard Persson, N.J.	4.00	8.00	.30
□□□	**211**	**Dwayne Roloson (G), Cgy., RC**	**6.00**	**12.00**	**.30**
□□□	212	Mike Dunham (G), N.J.	6.00	12.00	.30
□□□	**213**	**Marcel Cousineau (G), Tor., RC**	**6.00**	**12.00**	**.50**
□□□	214	Eric Fichaud (G), NYI.	8.00	15.00	.30
□□□	215	Matt Johnson, L.A.	4.00	8.00	.30
□□□	**216**	**Fredrik Modin, Tor., RC**	**6.00**	**12.00**	**.30**
□□□	217	Denis Pederson, N.J.	4.00	8.00	.30
□□□□	218	Kevin Hodson (G), Det.	6.00	12.00	.30
□□□	219	Drew Bannister, T.B.	4.00	8.00	.30
□□□	220	Mike Grier, Edm.	30.00	50.00	2.00

LINK 2 HISTORY

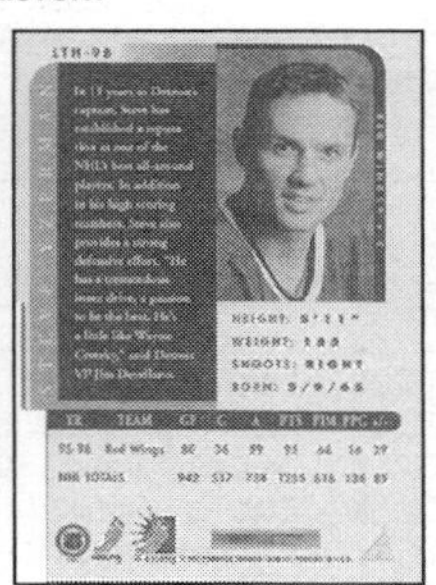

These cards have at least three versions: the regular insert, an autographed insert and an autographed foil card parallel.

Insert Set (20 cards): **35.00**

	No.	Player	Auto.	Foil Auto.	Reg.
□□□	LTH1A	Jarome Iginla, Cgy.	35.00	70.00	1.25
□□□	LTH1B	Teemu Selänne, Ana.	60.00	120.00	2.00
□□□	LTH2A	Harry York, Stl.	15.00	30.00	.75
□□□	LTH2B	Peter Forsberg, Col.	125.00	250.00	3.00
□□□	LTH3A	Sergei Berezin, Tor.	20.00	40.00	1.25
□□□	LTH3B	Brendan Shanahan, Det.	60.00	120.00	2.00
□□□	LTH4A	Ethan Moreau, Chi.	12.00	25.00	.50
□□□	LTH4B	Pavel Bure, Van.	60.00	120.00	2.00
□□□	LTH5A	Jason Arnott, Edm.	25.00	50.00	1.00
□□□	LTH5B	Rem Murray, Edm.	12.00	25.00	.50
□□□	LTH6A	Jamie Langenbrunner, Dal.	15.00	30.00	.50
□□□	LTH6B	Paul Kariya, Ana.	150.00	350.0	3.50
□□□	LTH7A	Jim Campbell, Stl.	20.00	35.00	.50
□□□□	LTH7B	Eric Lindros, Pha.	150.00	350.00	3.50
□□□	LTH8A	Jonas Hoglund, Cgy.	8.00	15.00	.50
□□□	LTH8B	Pat LaFontaine, Buf.	25.00	15.00	1.00
□□□	LTH9A	Wade Redden, Ott.	18.00	35.00	1.00
□□□	LTH9B	Steve Yzerman, Det.	125.00	250.00	2.50
□□□	LTH10A	Patrick Lalime (G), Pgh.	30.00	50.00	2.00
□□□	LTH10B	J. Vanbiesbrouck (G), Fla.	60.00	120.00	2.00

BISCUIT IN THE BASKET

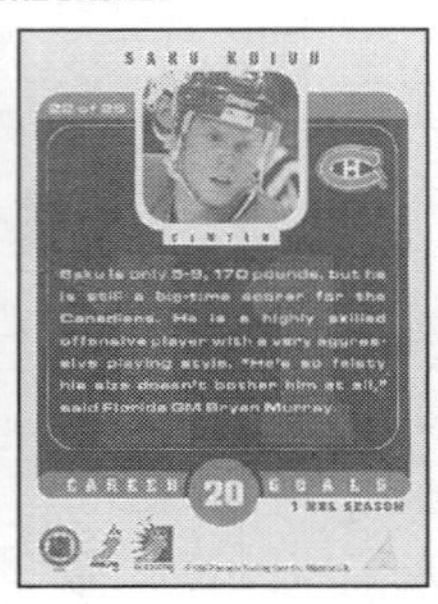

Insert Set (25 cards): 225.00

	No.	Player	NRMT-MT
☐	1	Wayne Gretzky, NYR.	30.00
☐	2	Mario Lemieux, Pgh.	25.00
☐	3	Eric Lindros, Pha.	20.00
☐	4	Theoren Fleury, Cgy.	4.50
☐	5	Peter Forsberg, Col.	15.00
☐	6	Keith Tkachuk, Pho.	6.00
☐	7	Sergei Fedorov, Det.	7.50
☐	8	Mike Modano, Dal.	7.50
☐	9	Jaromir Jagr, Pgh.	15.00
☐	10	Brendan Shanahan, Det.	9.00
☐	11	Teemu Selänne, Ana.	10.00
☐	12	Mats Sundin, Tor.	7.50
☐	13	Steve Yzerman, Det.	15.00
☐	14	Brett Hull, Stl.	7.50
☐	15	Zigmund Palffy, NYI.	6.00
☐	16	Joe Sakic, Col.	12.00
☐	17	John LeClair, Pha.	7.50
☐	18	Pavel Bure, Van.	10.00
☐	19	Mark Messier, NYR.	7.50
☐	20	Paul Kariya, Ana.	20.00
☐	21	Jason Arnott, Edm.	3.00
☐	22	Saku Koivu, Mtl.	10.00
☐	23	Daniel Alfredsson, Ott.	3.00
☐	24	Alexander Mogilny, Van.	4.50
☐	25	Owen Nolan, S.J.	3.00

STACKING THE PADS

Insert Set (15 cards): 250.00

	No.	Player	NRMT-MT
☐	1	Patrick Lalime (G), Pgh.	8.00
☐	2	Chris Osgood (G), Det.	15.00
☐	3	Ron Hextall (G), Pha.	10.00
☐	4	John Vanbiesbrouck (G), Fla.	25.00
☐	5	Martin Brodeur (G), N.J.	30.00
☐	6	Félix Potvin (G), Tor.	20.00
☐	7	Nikolai Khabibulin (G), Pho.	12.00
☐	8	Jim Carey (G), Wsh.	8.00
☐	9	Grant Fuhr (G), Stl.	10.00
☐	10	Mike Richter (G), NYR.	12.00
☐	11	Dominik Hasek (G), Buf.	30.00
☐	12	Andy Moog (G), Dal.	10.00
☐	13	Patrick Roy (G), Col.	50.00
☐	14	Curtis Joseph (G), Edm.	25.00
☐	15	Jocelyn Thibault (G), Mtl.	12.00

DIE-CUT SERIES

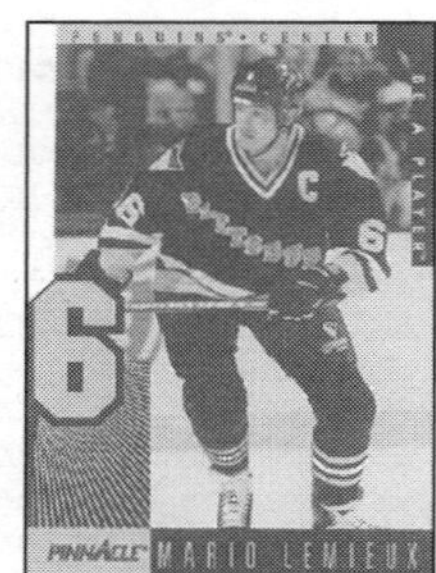

The Lemieux inserts are limited to 66 copies, the Lindros autographs are limited to 88 copies and the Messier autographs are limited to 11 copies.

	No.	Player	NRMT-MT
☐	1	Mario Lemieux, Pgh.	1,300.00
☐	2	Mario Lemieux, Pgh.	1,300.00
☐	1	Mark Messier, Autograph	1,800.00
☐	2	Mark Messier, Autograph	1,800.00
☐	1	Eric Lindros, Autograph	900.00
☐	2	Eric Lindros, Autograph	900.00

1996 - 97 PINNACLE FANtasy

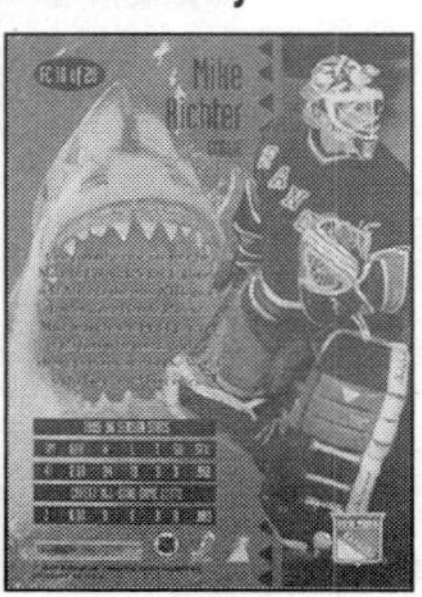

These cards were given out at the 1997 All-Star game Fanfest in San Jose.

Imprint:

CompleteSet (20 cards): 50.00

Promo Card (Eric Lindros): 10.00

	No.	Player	NRMT-MT
☐	1	Ray Bourque, Bos.	2.50
☐	2	Paul Coffey, Hfd.	1.00
☐	3	Eric Lindros, Pha.	6.50
☐	4	Mario Lemieux, Pgh.	8.00
☐	5	Wayne Gretzky, NYR.	10.00
☐	6	Mark Messier, NYR.	2.50
☐	7	Jarome Iginla, Cgy.	1.50
☐	8	Brendan Shanahan, Det.	3.00
☐	9	John Vanbiesbrouck (G), Fla.	3.00
☐	10	Mike Richter (G), NYR.	1.50
☐	11	Chris Chelios, Chi.	2.00
☐	12	Nicklas Lidström, Det.	1.00
☐	13	Sergei Fedorov, Det.	2.50
☐	14	Pavel Bure, Van.	3.50
☐	15	Peter Forsberg, Col.	5.00
☐	16	Brett Hull, Stl.	2.50
☐	17	Joe Sakic, Col.	4.00
☐	18	Owen Nolan, S.J.	1.00
☐	19	Patrick Roy (G), Col.	8.00
☐	20	Ed Belfour (G), Chi.	1.50

MASK

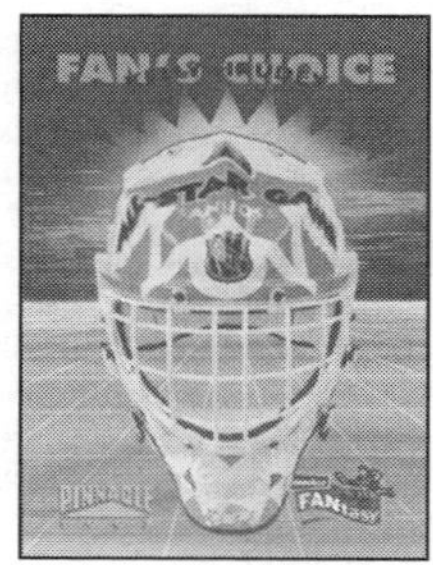

	Player	NRMT-MT
☐	Kelly Hrudey (G), S.J.	20.00

1996 - 97 PINNACLE MINT

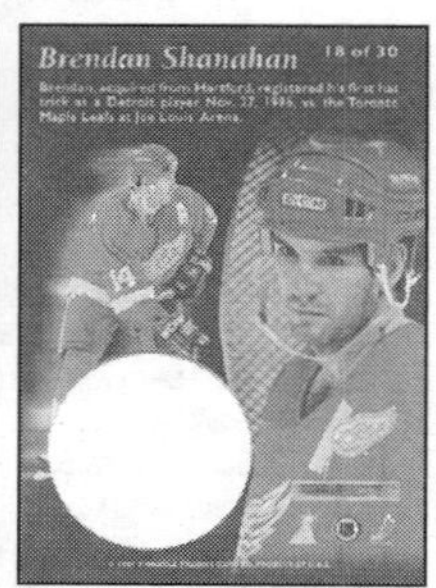

These cards have four versions: a die-cut card (coin holder), a bronze team card, a silver team card and a gold team card (dufex technology).

Imprint:

Complete Card Set (30 cards): 25.00 50.00 300.00 600.00

	No.	Player	Die-Cut	Bronze	Silver	Gold
☐☐☐☐	1	Mario Lemieux, Pgh.	3.00	6.00	30.00	60.00
☐☐☐☐	2	Domink Hasek (G), Buf.	1.50	3.00	15.00	30.00
☐☐☐☐	3	Eric Lindros, Pha.	2.50	5.00	25.00	50.00
☐☐☐☐	4	Jaromir Jagr, Pgh.	2.00	4.00	20.00	40.00
☐☐☐☐	5	Paul Kariya, Ana.	2.50	5.00	25.00	50.00
☐☐☐☐	6	Peter Forsberg, Col.	2.00	4.00	20.00	40.00
☐☐☐☐	7	Pavel Bure, Van.	1.50	3.00	15.00	30.00
☐☐☐☐	8	Sergei Fedorov, Det.	1.00	2.00	10.00	20.00
☐☐☐☐	9	Saku Koivu, Mtl.	1.50	3.00	15.00	30.00
☐☐☐☐	10	Daniel Alfredsson, Ott.	.50	1.00	5.00	10.00
☐☐☐☐	11	Joe Sakic, Col.	1.75	3.50	17.50	35.00
☐☐☐☐	12	Steve Yzerman, Det.	2.00	4.00	20.00	40.00
☐☐☐☐	13	Teemu Selänne, Ana.	1.50	3.00	15.00	30.00
☐☐☐☐	14	Brett Hull, Stl.	1.00	2.00	10.00	20.00
☐☐☐☐	15	Jeremy Roenick, Chi.	.50	1.00	5.00	10.00
☐☐☐☐	16	Mark Messier, NYR.	1.00	2.00	10.00	20.00
☐☐☐☐	17	Mats Sundin, Tor.	1.00	2.00	10.00	20.00
☐☐☐☐	18	Brendan Shanahan, Det.	1.25	2.50	12.00	25.00
☐☐☐☐	19	Keith Tkachuk, Pho.	.75	1.50	7.50	15.00
☐☐☐☐	20	Paul Coffey, Pha.	.35	.75	3.75	7.50
☐☐☐☐	21	Patrick Roy (G), Col.	3.00	6.00	30.00	60.00
☐☐☐☐	22	Chris Chelios, Chi.	.75	1.50	7.50	15.00
☐☐☐☐	23	Martin Brodeur (G), N.J.	1.50	3.00	15.00	30.00
☐☐☐☐	24	Félix Potvin (G), Tor.	1.00	2.00	10.00	20.00
☐☐☐☐	25	Chris Osgood (G), Det.	.75	1.50	7.50	15.00
☐☐☐☐	26	John Vanbiesbrouck (G), Fla	1.25	2.50	12.00	25.00
☐☐☐☐	27	Jocelyn Thibault (G), Mtl.	.50	1.00	5.00	10.00
☐☐☐☐	28	Jim Carey (G), Wsh.	.35	.75	3.75	7.50
☐☐☐☐	29	Jarome Iginla, Cgy.	.50	1.00	5.00	10.00
☐☐☐☐	30	Jim Campbell, Stl.	.35	.75	3.75	7.50

PINNACLE MINT MADALLIONS

These medallions had four versions that were readily available: the brass coin, a nickel-silver coin and a gold plated coin and a fine silver coin. A one of a kind solid gold coin was also available.

Complete Coin Set (30 coins): 75.00 350.00 900.00

	No.	Player	Brass	Nick.-Sil.	Gold-P.	Sil.
☐☐☐☐	01	Mario Lemieux, Pgh.	6.00	30.00	55.00	500.00
☐☐☐☐	02	Dominik Hasek (G), Buf.	2.50	12.00	25.00	200.00
☐☐☐☐	03	Eric Lindros, Pha.	5.00	25.00	45.00	400.00
☐☐☐☐	04	Jaromir Jagr, Pgh.	3.50	17.50	35.00	300.00
☐☐☐☐	05	Paul Kariya, Ana.	5.00	25.00	45.00	400.00
☐☐☐☐	06	Peter Forsberg, Col.	3.50	17.50	35.00	300.00
☐☐☐☐	07	Pavel Bure, Van.	2.50	12.00	25.00	200.00
☐☐☐☐	08	Sergei Fedorov, Det.	1.75	8.75	17.50	125.00
☐☐☐☐	09	Saku Koivu, Mtl.	2.50	12.00	25.00	200.00
☐☐☐☐	10	Daniel Alfredsson, Ott.	1.00	5.00	10.00	60.00
☐☐☐☐	11	Joe Sakic, Col.	3.00	15.00	30.00	250.00
☐☐☐☐	12	Steve Yzerman, Det.	3.50	17.50	35.00	300.00
☐☐☐☐	13	Teemu Selänne, Ana.	2.50	12.00	25.00	200.00
☐☐☐☐	14	Brett Hull, Stl.	1.75	8.75	17.50	125.00
☐☐☐☐	15	Jeremy Roenick, Chi.	1.00	5.00	10.00	60.00
☐☐☐☐	16	Mark Messier, NYR.	1.75	8.75	17.50	125.00
☐☐☐☐	17	Mats Sundin, Tor.	1.75	8.75	17.50	125.00
☐☐☐☐	18	Brendan Shanahan, Det.	2.00	10.00	20.00	150.00
☐☐☐☐	19	Keith Tkachuk, Pho.	1.50	7.50	15.00	100.00
☐☐☐☐	20	Paul Coffey, Pha.	.75	3.75	7.50	40.00
☐☐☐☐	21	Patrick Roy (G), Col.	6.00	30.00	55.00	500.00
☐☐☐☐	22	Chris Chelios, Chi.	1.50	7.50	15.00	100.00
☐☐☐☐	23	Martin Brodeur (G), N.J.	2.50	12.00	25.00	200.00
☐☐☐☐	24	Félix Potvin (G), Tor.	1.75	8.75	17.50	125.00
☐☐☐☐	25	Chris Osgood (G), Det.	1.50	7.50	15.00	100.00
☐☐☐☐	26	John Vanbiesbrouck (G), Fla.	2.00	10.00	20.00	150.00
☐☐☐☐	27	Jocelyn Thibault (G), Mtl.	1.00	5.00	10.00	60.00
☐☐☐☐	28	Jim Carey (G), Wsh.	.75	3.75	7.50	40.00
☐☐☐☐	29	Jarome Iginla, Cgy.	1.00	5.00	10.00	60.00
☐☐☐☐	30	Jim Campbell, Stl.	.75	3.75	7.50	40.00

1996 - 97 PINNACLE SUMMIT

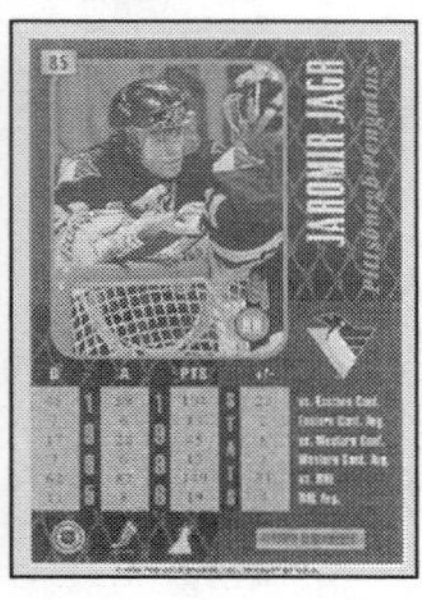

These cards have five versions: the regular card, a metal card (magazine packs), a Premium Stock card, a Summit Ice parallel card and an Artist's Proof parallel. Metal versions have a flat silver face while Premium Stock versions reflect light. Ice parallel cards reflect light on a patterned face and say "Summit Ice" on the back.

Imprint: © 1996 PINNACLE BRANDS, INC.

Complete Set (220 cards): 40.00
Metal/Magazine Set (200 cards): 65.00
Premium Stock Set (200 cards): 150.00
Summit Ice Set (200 cards): 475.00
Artist Proof Set (200 cards): 2,300.00
Common Player: .15 .20 .35 2.00 4.00

	No.	Player	Reg.	Metal	P.S.	Ice	A.P.
□□□□□	1	Joe Sakic, Col.	1.25	2.50	5.00	25.00	85.00
□□□□□	2	Dominik Hasek (G), Buf.	1.00	2.00	4.00	20.00	60.00
□□□□□	3	Paul Coffey, Det.	.25	.35	.50	3.00	8.00
□□□□□	4	Todd Gill, Tor.	.15	.20	.35	2.00	4.00
□□□□□	5	Pat Verbeek, NYR.	.15	.20	.35	2.00	4.00
□□□□□	6	John LeClair, Pha.	.75	1.50	3.00	12.00	30.00
□□□□□	7	Joé Juneau, Wsh.	.15	.20	.35	2.00	4.00
□□□□□	8	Scott Mellanby, Fla.	.15	.20	.35	2.00	4.00
□□□□□	9	Scott Stevens, N.J.	.15	.20	.35	2.00	4.00
□□□□□	10	Ron Francis, Pgh.	.35	.75	1.25	4.00	10.00
□□□□□	11	Larry Murphy, Tor.	.25	.35	.50	3.00	8.00
□□□□□	12	Sandis Ozolinsh, Col.	.25	.35	.50	3.00	8.00
□□□□□	13	Luc Robitaille, NYR.	.25	.35	.50	3.00	8.00
□□□□□	14	Grant Fuhr (G), Stl.	.25	.35	.50	3.00	8.00
□□□□□	15	Adam Oates, Bos.	.35	.75	1.25	4.00	10.00
□□□□□	16	Keith Primeau, Det.	.25	.35	.50	3.00	8.00
□□□□□	17	Mark Recchi, Mtl.	.25	.35	.50	3.00	8.00
□□□□□	18	Brian Bradley, T.B.	.15	.20	.35	2.00	4.00
□□□□□	19	Zdeno Ciger, Edm.	.15	.20	.35	2.00	4.00
□□□□□	20	Zigmund Palffy, NYI.	.35	.75	1.25	4.00	10.00
□□□□□	21	Damian Rhodes (G), Ott.	.15	.20	.35	2.00	4.00
□□□□□	22	Russ Courtnall, Van.	.15	.20	.35	2.00	4.00
□□□□□	23	Mike Modano, Dal.	.75	1.50	3.00	12.00	30.00
□□□□□	24	Geoff Sanderson, Hfd.	.15	.20	.35	2.00	4.00
□□□□□	25	Michal Pivonka, Wsh.	.15	.20	.35	2.00	4.00
□□□□□	26	Randy Burridge, Buf.	.15	.20	.35	2.00	4.00
□□□□□	27	Dimitri Khristich, L.A.	.15	.20	.35	2.00	4.00
□□□□□	28	Mike Gartner, Tor.	.25	.35	.50	3.00	8.00
□□□□□	29	Cam Neely, Bos.	.25	.35	.50	3.00	8.00
□□□□□	30	Mathieu Schneider, Tor.	.15	.20	.35	2.00	4.00
□□□□□	31	Steve Thomas, N.J.	.15	.20	.35	2.00	4.00
□□□□□	32	Mario Lemieux, Pgh.	2.50	6.00	1.00	35.00	200.00
□□□□□	33	Darryl Sydor, Dal	.15	.20	.35	2.00	4.00
□□□□□	34	Alexei Yashin, Ott.	.50	1.00	2.00	8.00	20.00
□□□□□	35	Brett Hull, Stl.	.75	1.50	3.00	12.00	30.00
□□□□□	36	Trevor Kidd (G), Cgy.	.25	.35	.50	3.00	8.00
□□□□□	37	Alexei Zhamnov, Wpg.	.25	.35	.50	3.00	8.00
□□□□□	38	Uwe Krupp, Col.	.15	.20	.35	2.00	4.00
□□□□□	39	Brian Skrudland, Fla.	.15	.20	.35	2.00	4.00
□□□□□	40	Igor Larionov, Det.	.25	.35	.50	3.00	8.00
□□□□□	41	Nikolai Khabibulin (G), Wpg.	.35	.75	1.25	4.00	10.00
□□□□□	42	Pavel Bure, Van.	1.00	2.00	4.00	20.00	60.00
□□□□□	43	Chris Chelios, Chi.	.50	1.00	2.00	8.00	20.00
□□□□□	44	Andrew Cassels, Hfd.	.15	.20	.35	2.00	4.00
□□□□□	45	Owen Nolan, S.J.	.25	.35	.50	3.00	8.00
□□□□□	46	Todd Harvey, Dal.	.15	.20	.35	2.00	4.00
□□□□□	47	Jari Kurri, NYR.	.25	.35	.50	3.00	8.00
□□□□□	48	Olaf Kolzig (G), Wsh.	.35	.75	1.25	4.00	10.00
□□□□□	49	Greg Johnson, Det.	.15	.20	.35	2.00	4.00
□□□□□	50	Dominic Roussel (G), Pha.	.15	.20	.35	2.00	4.00
□□□□□	51	Mats Sundin, Tor.	.75	1.50	3.00	12.00	30.00
□□□□□	52	Robert Svehla, Fla.	.15	.20	.35	2.00	4.00
□□□□□	53	Sandy Moger, Bos.	.15	.20	.35	2.00	4.00
□□□□□	54	Darren Turcotte, S.J.	.15	.20	.35	2.00	4.00
□□□□□	55	Teppo Numminen, Wpg.	.15	.20	.35	2.00	4.00
□□□□□	56	Benoît Hogue, Dal.	.15	.20	.35	2.00	4.00
□□□□□	57	Scott Niedermayer, N.J.	.25	.35	.50	3.00	8.00
□□□□□	58	Alexander Selivanov, T.B.	.15	.20	.35	2.00	4.00
□□□□□	59	Valeri Kamensky, Col.	.25	.35	.50	3.00	8.00
□□□□□	60	Ken Wregget (G), Pgh.	.15	.20	.35	2.00	4.00
□□□□□	61	Travis Green, NYI.	.15	.20	.35	2.00	4.00
□□□□□	62	Peter Bondra, Wsh.	.50	1.00	2.00	8.00	20.00
□□□□□	63	Vladimir Konstantinov, Det.	.15	.20	.35	2.00	4.00
□□□□□	64	Craig Janney, Wpg.	.15	.20	.35	2.00	4.00
□□□□□	65	Joe Nieuwendyk, Fla.	.25	.35	.50	3.00	8.00
□□□□□	66	John Vanbiesbrouck (G), Fla.	.85	1.75	3.50	15.00	40.00
□□□□□	67	Wayne Gretzky, Stl.	4.00	7.50	14.00	45.00	300.00
□□□□□	68	Kirk McLean (G), Van.	.25	.35	.50	3.00	8.00
□□□□□	69	Alexei Zhitnik, Buf.	.15	.20	.35	2.00	4.00
□□□□□	70	Mike Ricci, Col.	.15	.20	.35	2.00	4.00
□□□□□	71	Jeff Beukeboon, NYR.	.15	.20	.35	2.00	4.00
□□□□□	72	Félix Potvin (G), Tor.	1.00	2.00	4.00	20.00	60.00
□□□□□	73	Mikael Renberg, Pha.	.15	.20	.35	2.00	4.00
□□□□□	74	Jamie Baker, S.J. (Tor.)	.15	.20	.35	2.00	4.00
□□□□□	75	Guy Hebert (G), Ana.	.25	.35	.50	3.00	8.00
□□□□□	76	Steve Yzerman, Det.	1.50	3.00	6.00	30.00	125.00
□□□□□	77	Daren Puppa (G), T.B.	.15	.20	.35	2.00	4.00
□□□□□	78	Scott Young, Col.	.15	.20	.35	2.00	4.00
□□□□□	79	Martin Gelinas, Van.	.15	.20	.35	2.00	4.00
□□□□□	80	Dave Gagner, Dal. (Cgy.)	.15	.20	.35	2.00	4.00
□□□□□	81	Tomas Sandström, Pgh.	.15	.20	.35	2.00	4.00
□□□□□	82	Alelexei Kovalev, NYR.	.15	.20	.35	2.00	4.00
□□□□□	83	Ray Whitney, S.J.	.15	.20	.35	2.00	4.00
□□□□□	84	Vyacheslav Kozlov, Det.	.15	.20	.35	2.00	4.00
□□□□□	85	Jaromir Jagr, Pgh.	1.50	3.00	6.00	30.00	125.00
□□□□□	86	Joe Murphy, Chi.	.15	.20	.35	2.00	4.00
□□□□□	87	Patrick Roy (G), Col.	2.50	6.00	10.00	35.00	200.00
□□□□□	88	Ray Sheppard, Fla.	.15	.20	.35	2.00	4.00
□□□□□	89	Chris Terreri (G), S.J.	.15	.20	.35	2.00	4.00
□□□□□	90	Pierre Turgeon, Mtl.	.25	.35	.50	3.00	8.00
□□□□□	91	Theoren Fleury, Cgy.	.35	.75	1.25	4.00	10.00
□□□□□	92	Doug Weight, Edm.	.35	.75	1.25	4.00	10.00
□□□□□	93	Tom Barrasso (G), Pgh.	.25	.35	.50	3.00	8.00
□□□□□	94	Jim Carey (G), Wsh.	.15	.20	.35	2.00	4.00
□□□□□	95	Greg Adams, Dal.	.15	.20	.35	2.00	4.00
□□□□□	96	Brian Leetch, NYR.	.35	.75	1.25	4.00	10.00
□□□□□	97	Ed Belfour (G), Chi.	.35	.75	1.25	4.00	10.00
□□□□□	98	Stéphane Fiset (G), Col.	.25	.35	.50	3.00	8.00
□□□□□	99	Stéphane Richer, N.J.	.15	.20	.35	2.00	4.00
□□□□□	100	Ron Hextall (G), Pgh.	.25	.35	.50	3.00	8.00
□□□□□	101	Mike Vernon (G), Det.	.25	.35	.50	3.00	8.00
□□□□□	102	Jocelyn Thibault (G), Mtl.	.35	.75	1.25	4.00	10.00
□□□□□	103	Joson Arnott, Edm.	.25	.35	.50	3.00	8.00
□□□□□	104	Keith Tkachuk, Wpg.	.50	1.00	2.00	8.00	20.00
□□□□□	105	Sergei Fedorov, Det.	.75	1.50	3.00	12.00	30.00
□□□□□	106	Alexandre Daigle, Ott.	.25	.35	.50	3.00	8.00
□□□□□	107	Alexander Mogilny, Van.	.35	.75	1.25	4.00	10.00
□□□□□	108	German Titov, Cgy.	.15	.20	.35	2.00	4.00
□□□□□	109	Sean Burke (G), Hfd.	.25	.35	.50	3.00	8.00
□□□□□	110	Arturs Irbe (G), S.J.	.15	.20	.35	2.00	4.00
□□□□□	111	Mark Messier, NYR.	.75	1.50	3.00	12.00	30.00
□□□□□	112	Nicklas Lidström, Det.	.25	.35	.50	3.00	8.00
□□□□□	113	Claude Lemieux, Col.	.15	.20	.35	2.00	4.00
□□□□□	114	Martin Brodeur (G), N.J.	1.00	2.00	4.00	20.00	60.00
□□□□□	115	Bernie Nicholls, Chi.	.15	.20	.35	2.00	4.00
□□□□□	116	Paul Kariya, Ana.	2.00	5.00	8.00	28.00	185.00
□□□□□	117	Eric Lindros, Pha.	2.00	5.00	8.00	28.00	185.00
□□□□□	118	Doug Gilmour, Tor.	.35	.75	1.25	4.00	10.00
□□□□□	119	Sergei Zubov, Pgh.	.25	.35	.50	3.00	8.00
□□□□□	120	Adam Graves, NYR.	.15	.20	.35	2.00	4.00
□□□□□	121	Phil Housley, N.J.	.15	.20	.35	2.00	4.00
□□□□□	122	Bob Bassen, Dal.	.15	.20	.35	2.00	4.00
□□□□□	123	Rod Brind'Amour, Pha	.25	.35	.50	3.00	8.00
□□□□□	124	Dave Andreychuk, N.J.	.15	.20	.35	2.00	4.00
□□□□□	125	Corey Hirsch (G), Van.	.15	.20	.35	2.00	4.00
□□□□□	126	Kelly Hrudey (G), L.A.	.15	.20	.35	2.00	4.00
□□□□□	127	Pat LaFontaine, Buf.	.25	.35	.50	3.00	8.00
□□□□□	128	Viacheslav Fetisov, Det.	.25	.35	.50	3.00	8.00
□□□□□	129	OlegTverdovsky, Wpg.	.15	.20	.35	2.00	4.00
□□□□□	130	Andy Moog (G), Dal.	.25	.35	.50	3.00	8.00
□□□□□	131	Stu Barnes, Fla.	.15	.20	.35	2.00	4.00
□□□□□	132	Roman Hamrlik, T.B.	.25	.35	.50	3.00	8.00
□□□□□	133	Teemu Selänne, Ana.	1.00	2.00	4.00	20.00	60.00
□□□□□	134	Trevor Linden, Van.	.50	1.00	2.00	8.00	20.00
□□□□□	135	Chris Osgood (G), Det.	.35	.75	1.25	4.00	18.00
□□□□□	136	Vincent Damphousse, Mtl.	.35	.75	1.25	4.00	10.00
□□□□□	137	Shayne Corson, Stl.	.25	.35	.50	3.00	8.00
□□□□□	138	Jeremy Roenick, Chi.	.35	.75	1.25	4.00	10.00
□□□□□	139	Brendan Shanahan, Hfd.	.85	1.75	3.50	15.00	40.00
□□□□□	140	Wendel Clark, Tor.	.25	.35	.50	3.00	8.00
□□□□□	141	Ray Bourque, Bos.	.75	1.50	3.00	12.00	30.00
□□□□□	142	Peter Forsberg, Col.	1.50	3.00	6.00	30.00	125.00
□□□□□	143	John MacLean, N.J.	.15	.20	.35	2.00	4.00
□□□□□	144	Jeff Friesen, S.J.	.25	.35	.50	3.00	8.00
□□□□□	145	Mike Richter (G), NYR.	.35	.75	1.25	4.00	10.00
□□□□□	146	Dave Reid, Bos.	.15	.20	.35	2.00	4.00
□□□□□	147	Rob Niedermayer, Fla.	.15	.20	.35	2.00	4.00
□□□□□	148	Petr Nedved, Pgh.	.15	.20	.35	2.00	4.00
□□□□□	149	Sylvain Lefebvre, Col.	.15	.20	.35	2.00	4.00
□□□□□	150	Curtis Joseph (G), Edm.	.85	1.75	3.50	15.00	40.00
□□□□□	151	Eric Dazé, Chi.	.25	.35	.50	3.00	8.00
□□□□□	152	Saku Koivu, Mtl.	1.00	2.00	4.00	20.00	60.00
□□□□□	153	Jere Lehtinen, Dal.	.25	.35	.50	3.00	8.00
□□□□□	154	Todd Bertuzzi, NYI.	.25	.35	.50	3.00	8.00
□□□□□	155	Chad Kilger, Wpg.	.15	.20	.35	2.00	4.00
□□□□□	156	Stéphane Yelle, Col.	.15	.20	.35	2.00	4.00
□□□□□	157	Bryan McCabe, NYI.	.15	.20	.35	2.00	4.00
□□□□□	158	Aaron Gavey, T.B.	.15	.20	.35	2.00	4.00
□□□□□	159	Kyle McLaren, Bos.	.15	.20	.35	2.00	4.00
□□□□□	160	Valeri Bure, Mtl.	.15	.20	.35	2.00	4.00
□□□□□	161	Antti Törmänen, Ott.	.15	.20	.35	2.00	4.00
□□□□□	162	Brendan Witt, Wsh.	.15	.20	.35	2.00	4.00
□□□□□	163	Ed Jovanovski, Fla.	.25	.35	.50	3.00	8.00
□□□□□	164	Aki Berg, L.A.	.15	.20	.35	2.00	4.00
□□□□□	165	Marcus Ragnarsson, S.J.	.15	.20	.35	2.00	4.00
□□□□□	166	Miroslav Satan, Edm.	.15	.20	.35	2.00	4.00
□□□□□	167	Daniel Alfredsson, Ott.	.25	.35	.50	3.00	8.00
□□□□□	168	Jeff O'Neill, Hfd.	.25	.35	.50	3.00	8.00
□□□□□	169	Radek Dvorak, Fla.	.15	.20	.35	2.00	4.00
□□□□□	170	Petr Sykora, N.J.	.15	.20	.35	2.00	4.00
□□□□□	171	Vitali Yachmenev, L.A.	.15	.20	.35	2.00	4.00
□□□□□	172	Niklas Andersson, NYI.	.15	.20	.35	2.00	4.00
□□□□□	173	Nolan Baumgartner, Wsh.	.15	.20	.35	2.00	4.00
□□□□□	174	Brandon Convery, Tor.	.15	.20	.35	2.00	4.00
□□□□□	175	Ralph Intranuovo, Edm.	.15	.20	.35	2.00	4.00
□□□□□	176	Niklas Sundblad, Cgy.	.15	.20	.35	2.00	4.00
□□□□□	177	Patrick Labrecque (G), Mtl.	.15	.20	.35	2.00	4.00
□□□□□	178	Eric Fichaud (G), NYI.	.25	.35	.50	3.00	8.00
□□□□□	179	Martin Biron (G), Buf.	.25	.35	.50	3.00	8.00
□□□□□	**180**	**Steve Sullivan, N.J., RC**	**.15**	**.20**	**.35**	**2.00**	**4.00**
□□□□□	181	Peter Ferraro, NYR.	.15	.20	.35	2.00	4.00
□□□□□	182	José Théodore (G), Mtl.	.50	.75	1.50	4.00	10.00
□□□□□	183	Kevin Hodson (G), Det.	.15	.20	.35	2.00	4.00
□□□□□	184	Ethan Moreau, Chi.	.25	.35	.50	3.00	8.00
□□□□□	185	Curtis Brown, Buf.	.15	.20	.35	2.00	4.00
□□□□□	186	Daymond Langkow, T.B.	.15	.20	.35	2.00	4.00
□□□□□	**187**	**Jan Caloun, S.J., RC**	**.15**	**.20**	**.35**	**2.00**	**4.00**
□□□□□	188	Landon Wilson, Col.	.15	.20	.35	2.00	4.00
□□□□□	189	Tommy Salo (G), NYI.	.15	.20	.35	2.00	4.00
□□□□□	190	Anders Eriksson, Det.	.15	.20	.35	2.00	4.00
□□□□□	191	David Nemirovsky, Fla.	.15	.20	.35	2.00	4.00
□□□□□	192	Jamie Langenbrunner, Dal.	.25	.35	.50	3.00	8.00
□□□□□	193	Zdenick Nedved, Tor.	.15	.20	.35	2.00	4.00
□□□□□	194	Todd Hlushko, Cgy.	.15	.20	.35	2.00	4.00
□□□□□	**195**	**Alexei Yegorov, S.J., RC**	**.15**	**.20**	**.35**	**2.00**	**4.00**
□□□□□	196	Jamie Pushor, Det.	.15	.20	.35	2.00	4.00
□□□□□	197	Anders Myrvold, Col.	.15	.20	.35	2.00	4.00
□□□□□	198	CL: Mark Messier, NYR.	.35	.75	1.50	6.00	15.00
□□□□□	199	CL: Brett Hull, Stl.	.35	.75	1.50	6.00	15.00
□□□□□	200	CL: Pavel Bure, Van.	.50	1.00	2.00	10.00	30.00

UNTOUCHABLES

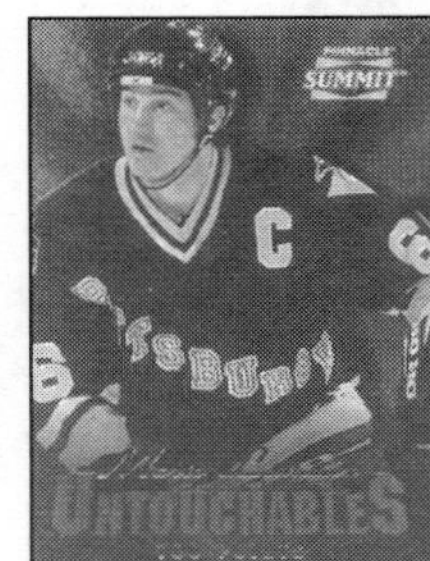

These magazine pack inserts are serial numbered out of 1,000.

Insert Set (18 cards): 950.00
Promo Card (Mario Lemieux, #1): 8.00

	No.	Player	NRMT-MT
□	1	Mario Lemieux, Pgh.	130.00
□	2	Jaromir Jagr, Pgh.	80.00
□	3	Joe Sakic, Col.	65.00

	No.	Player	
☐	4	Ron Francis, Pgh.	20.00
☐	5	Peter Forsberg, Col.	80.00
☐	6	Eric Lindros, Pha.	100.00
☐	7	Paul Kariya, Ana.	100.00
☐	8	Teemu Selänne, Ana.	50.00
☐	9	Alexander Mogilny, Van.	20.00
☐	10	Sergei Fedorov, Det.	35.00
☐	11	Doug Weight, Edm.	20.00
☐	12	Wayne Gretzky, Stl.	160.00
☐	13	Chris Osgood (G), Det.	25.00
☐	14	Jim Carey (G), Wsh.	15.00
☐	15	Patrick Roy (G), Col.	130.00
☐	16	Martin Brodeur (G), N.J.	50.00
☐	17	Félix Potvin (G), Tor.	35.00
☐	18	Ron Hextall (G), Pha.	18.00

IN THE CREASE

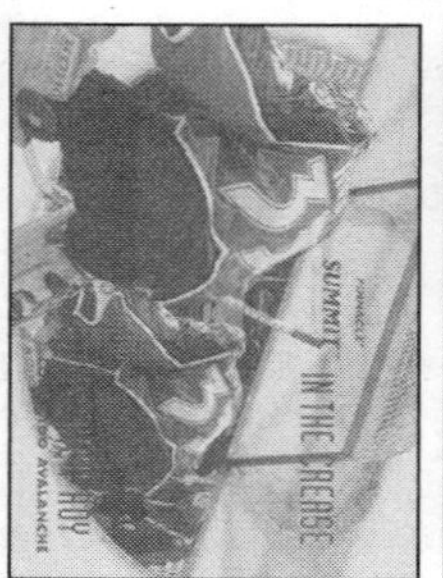
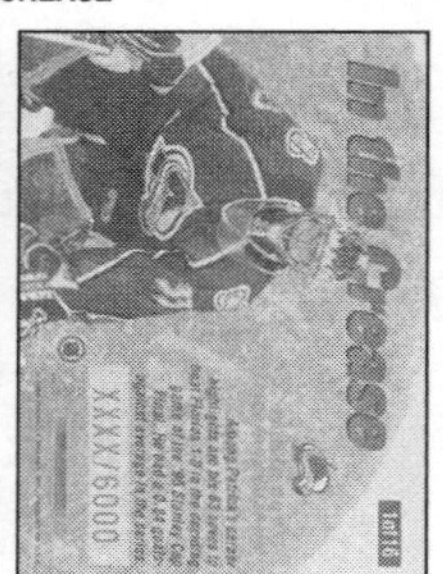

These cards have two versions: the regular insert (serial numbered out of 6,000) and a Premium Stock parallel (prefix PSITC, serial numbered out of 600).

Insert Set (16 cards): 1,000.00 250.00
Promo Card (Patrick Roy, #1): 8.00

	No.	Player	PSITC	Reg.
☐☐	1	Patrick Roy (G), Col.	200.00	50.00
☐☐	2	Mike Richter (G), NYR.	50.00	12.00
☐☐	3	Ed Belfour (G), Chi.	50.00	12.00
☐☐	4	Daren Puppa (G), T.B.	30.00	8.00
☐☐	5	Curtis Joseph (G), Edm.	100.00	25.00
☐☐	6	Jim Carey (G), Wsh.	30.00	8.00
☐☐	7	Damian Rhodes (G), Ott.	30.00	8.00
☐☐	8	Martin Brodeur (G), N.J.	120.00	30.00
☐☐	9	Félix Potvin (G), Tor.	80.00	20.00
☐☐	10	John Vanbiesbrouck (G), Fla.	100.00	25.00
☐☐	11	Jocelyn Thibault (G), Mtl.	50.00	12.00
☐☐	12	Nikolai Khabibulin (G), Wpg.	50.00	12.00
☐☐	13	Chris Osgood (G), Det.	70.00	17.50
☐☐	14	Dominik Hasek (G), Buf.	120.00	30.00
☐☐	15	Corey Hirsch (G), Van.	30.00	8.00
☐☐	16	Ron Hextall (G), Pha.	35.00	10.00

HIGH VOLTAGE

These inserts have two versions: the regular card (serial numbered out of 1,500) and a Mirage parallel (serial numbered out of 600).

Insert Set (16 cards): 1,100.00 550.00
Promo Card (Eric Lindros, #16): 6.00

	No.	Player	Mirage	Reg.
☐☐	1	Mark Messier, NYR.	50.00	25.00
☐☐	2	Joe Sakic, Col.	80.00	40.00
☐☐	3	Paul Kariya, Ana.	130.00	65.00
☐☐	4	Daniel Alfredsson, Ott.	25.00	12.50
☐☐	5	Wayne Gretzky, Stl.	200.00	100.00
☐☐	6	Peter Forsberg, Col.	100.00	50.00
☐☐	7	Eric Dazé, Chi.	25.00	12.50
☐☐	8	Mario Lemieux, Pgh.	160.00	80.00
☐☐	9	Eric Lindros, Pha.	130.00	65.00
☐☐	10	Jeremy Roenick, Chi.	30.00	15.00
☐☐	11	Alexander Mogilny, Van.	30.00	15.00
☐☐	12	Teemu Selänne, Ana.	70.00	35.00
☐☐	13	Sergei Fedorov, Det.	50.00	25.00
☐☐	14	Saku Koivu, Mtl.	70.00	35.00
☐☐	15	Jaromir Jagr, Pgh.	100.00	50.00
☐☐	16	Brett Hull, Stl.	50.00	25.00

1996 - 97 PINNACLE ZENITH

These cards have two versions: the regular card and an Artist's Proof parallel.

Imprint: © 1997 PINNACLE TRADING CARD CO.
Complete Set (150 cards): 60.00 3,000.00
Common Player: .25 5.00

	No.	Player	Reg.	A.P.
☐☐	1	Mike Modano, Dal.	1.50	60.00
☐☐	2	Martin Brodeur (G), N.J.	2.00	85.00
☐☐	3	Pavel Bure, Van.	2.00	85.00
☐☐	4	Ray Bourque, Bos.	1.50	60.00
☐☐	5	Steve Yzerman, Det.	3.00	150.00
☐☐	6	Keith Tkachuk, Pho.	1.25	40.00
☐☐	7	Jim Carey (G), Wsh.	.25	5.00
☐☐	8	Valeri Kamensky, Col.	.50	10.00
☐☐	9	Valeri Bure, Mtl.	.25	5.00
☐☐	10	Ron Francis, Pgh.	1.00	25.00
☐☐	11	Trevor Kidd (G), Cgy.	.50	10.00
☐☐	12	Doug Weight, Edm.	1.00	25.00
☐☐	13	Wayne Gretzky, NYR.	6.00	400.00
☐☐	14	Todd Gill, S.J.	.25	5.00
☐☐	15	Dominik Hasek (G), Buf.	2.00	85.00
☐☐	16	Scott Mellanby, Fla.	.25	5.00
☐☐	17	John LeClair, Pha.	1.50	60.00
☐☐	18	Al MacInnis, Stl.	.25	5.00
☐☐	19	Derian Hatcher, Dal.	.50	10.00
☐☐	20	Stéphane Fiset (G), L.A.	.50	10.00
☐☐	21	Alexander Selivanov, T.B.	.25	5.00
☐☐	22	Vyacheslav Kozlov, Det.	.25	5.00
☐☐	23	Alexei Yashin, Ott.	1.25	40.00
☐☐	24	Wendel Clark, Tor.	.50	10.00
☐☐	25	Ed Belfour (G), Chi.	1.00	25.00
☐☐	26	Travis Green, NYI.	.25	5.00
☐☐	27	Joé Juneau, Wsh.	.25	5.00
☐☐	28	Teemu Selänne, Ana.	2.00	85.00
☐☐	29	Jeff O'Neill, Hfd.	.50	10.00
☐☐	30	Jeremy Roenick, Pho.	1.00	25.00
☐☐	31	Félix Potvin (G), Tor.	1.50	60.00
☐☐	32	Bernie Nicholls, S.J.	.25	5.00
☐☐	33	Steve Thomas, N.J.	.25	5.00
☐☐	34	Alexander Mogilny, Van.	1.00	25.00
☐☐	35	Patrick Roy (G), Col.	5.00	250.00
☐☐	36	Luc Robitaille, NYR.	.50	10.00
☐☐	37	Owen Nolan, S.J.	.50	10.00
☐☐	38	Sergei Zubov, Dal.	.50	10.00
☐☐	39	Pierre Turgeon, Stl.	.50	10.00
☐☐	40	Nikolai Khabibulin (G), Pho.	1.00	25.00
☐☐	41	Adam Oates, Bos.	.50	8.00
☐☐	42	Stéphane Richer, Mtl.	.25	5.00
☐☐	43	Daren Puppa (G), T.B.	.25	5.00
☐☐	44	Joe Sakic, Col.	2.50	125.00
☐☐	45	Ed Jovanovski, Fla.	.50	10.00
☐☐	46	Ron Hextall (G), Pha.	.50	10.00
☐☐	47	Doug Gilmour, Tor.	1.00	25.00
☐☐	48	Paul Coffey, Pha.	.50	10.00
☐☐	49	Craig Janney, Pho.	.25	5.00
☐☐	50	Brendan Witt, Wsh.	.25	5.00
☐☐	51	Jere Lehtinen, Dal.	.50	10.00
☐☐	52	Vitali Yachmenev, L.A.	.25	5.00
☐☐	53	Damian Rhodes (G), Ott.	.25	5.00
☐☐	54	Petr Nedved, Pgh.	.25	5.00
☐☐	55	Theoren Fleury, Cgy.	1.00	25.00
☐☐	56	Petr Sykora, N.J.	.25	5.00
☐☐	57	Kelly Hrudey (G), S.J.	.25	5.00
☐☐	58	Saku Koivu, Mtl.	2.00	85.00
☐☐	59	Brian Bradley, T.B.	.25	5.00
☐☐	60	Arturs Irbe (G), Dal.	.25	5.00
☐☐	61	Eric Lindros, Pha.	4.00	200.00
☐☐	62	Michal Pivonka, Wsh.	.25	5.00
☐☐	63	Joe Nieuwendyk, Dal.	.50	10.00
☐☐	64	Mats Sundin, Tor.	1.50	60.00
☐☐	65	Jason Arnott, Edm.	.50	10.00
☐☐	66	Mike Richter (G), NYR.	1.00	25.00
☐☐	67	Brett Hull, Stl.	1.50	60.00
☐☐	68	Chris Chelios, Chi.	1.25	40.00
☐☐	69	Jocelyn Thibault (G), Mtl.	1.00	25.00
☐☐	70	Oleg Tverdovsky, Pho.	.25	5.00
☐☐	71	Peter Bondra, Wsh.	1.25	40.00
☐☐	72	Bill Ranford (G), Bos.	.50	10.00
☐☐	73	Scott Stevens, N.J.	.25	5.00
☐☐	74	Jaromir Jagr, Pgh.	3.00	150.00
☐☐	75	Corey Hirsch (G), Van.	.25	5.00
☐☐	76	Peter Forsberg, Col.	3.00	150.00
☐☐	77	Brendan Shanahan, Det.	1.75	75.00
☐☐	78	Antii Törmänen, Ott.	.25	5.00
☐☐	79	Marcus Ragnarsson, S.J.	.25	5.00
☐☐	80	Sergei Fedorov, Det.	1.50	60.00
☐☐	81	Todd Bertuzzi, NYI.	.50	10.00
☐☐	82	Grant Fuhr (G), Buf.	.50	10.00
☐☐	83	Pat LaFontaine, Buf.	.50	10.00
☐☐	84	Rob Niedermayer, Fla.	.25	5.00
☐☐	85	Brian Leetch, NYR.	1.00	25.00
☐☐	86	Yanic Perreault, L.A.	.25	5.00
☐☐	87	Dino Ciccarelli, T.B.	.50	10.00
☐☐	88	Dimitri Khristich, L.A.	.25	5.00
☐☐	89	Jeff Friesen, S.J.	.50	10.00
☐☐	90	Paul Kariya, Ana.	4.00	200.00
☐☐	91	John Vanbiesbrouck (G), Fla.	1.75	75.00
☐☐	92	Roman Hamrlik, T.B.	.50	10.00
☐☐	93	Pat Verbeek, Dal.	.25	5.00
☐☐	94	Mark Messier, NYR.	1.50	60.00
☐☐	95	Trevor Linden, Van.	.50	10.00
☐☐	96	Igor Larionov, Det.	.50	10.00
☐☐	97	Zigmund Palffy, NYI.	1.00	25.00
☐☐	98	Tom Barrasso (G), Pgh.	.50	10.00
☐☐	99	Eric Dazé, Chi.	.50	10.00
☐☐	100	Vincent Damphousse, Mtl.	1.00	25.00
☐☐	101	Keith Primeau, Hfd.	.50	10.00
☐☐	102	Claude Lemieux, Col.	.25	5.00
☐☐	103	Daniel Alfredsson, Ott.	.50	10.00
☐☐	104	Ryan Smyth, Edm.	.50	10.00
☐☐	105	Chris Osgood (G), Det.	1.25	40.00
☐☐	106	Bill Guerin, N.J.	.50	10.00
☐☐	107	Shayne Corson, Mtl.	.50	10.00
☐☐	108	Alexei Zhamnov, Chi.	.50	10.00
☐☐	109	Mikael Renberg, Pha.	.25	5.00
☐☐	110	Andy Moog (G), Dal.	.50	10.00
☐☐	111	Larry Murphy, Tor.	.50	10.00
☐☐	112	Curtis Joseph (G), Edm.	1.75	75.00
☐☐	113	Cory Stillman, Cgy.	.25	5.00
☐☐	114	Mario Lemieux, Pgh.	5.00	250.00
☐☐	115	Scott Young, Col.	.25	5.00
☐☐	116	Eric Fichaud (G), NYI.	.50	10.00
☐☐	117	Jonas Hoglund, Cgy.	.25	5.00
☐☐	**118**	**Tomas Holmstrom, Det., RC**	**.25**	**5.00**
☐☐	119	Jarome Iginla, Cgy.	1.50	25.00
☐☐	120	Richard Zednik, Wsh.	1.50	15.00
☐☐	**121**	**Andreas Dackell, Ott., RC**	**.25**	**5.00**
☐☐	122	Anson Carter, Bos.	.25	5.00
☐☐	**123**	**Dainius Zubrus, Pha., RC**	**5.00**	**75.00**
☐☐	124	Janne Niinimaa, Pha.	.50	10.00
☐☐	125	Jason Allison, Wsh.	1.00	25.00
☐☐	126	Bryan Berard, NYI.	1.25	25.00
☐☐	**127**	**Sergei Berezin, Tor., RC**	**1.25**	**15.00**
☐☐	128	Wade Redden, Ott.	.50	8.00
☐☐	129	Jim Campbell, Stl.	.50	10.00
☐☐	130	Darcy Tucker, Mtl.	.25	5.00
☐☐	**131**	**Harry York, Stl., RC**	**.25**	**5.00**
☐☐	132	Brandon Convery, Tor.	.25	5.00
☐☐	133	Ethan Moreau, Chi.	.50	10.00
☐☐	134	Mattias Timander, Bos.	.25	5.00
☐☐	135	Christian Dubé, NYR.	.50	8.00
☐☐	136	Kevin Hodson (G), Det.	.25	5.00
☐☐	137	Anders Eriksson, Det.	.25	5.00
☐☐	138	Chris O'Sullivan, Cgy.	.25	5.00
☐☐	139	Jamie Langenbrunner, Dal.	.50	10.00

	No.	Player		
☐☐	**140**	**Steve Sullivan, N.J., RC**	**.50**	**8.00**
☐☐	141	Daymond Langkow, T.B.	.25	5.00
☐☐	142	Landon Wilson, Bos.	.25	5.00
☐☐	143	Scott Bailey (G), Bos.	.25	5.00
☐☐	**144**	**Terry Ryan, Mtl., RC**	**.50**	**8.00**
☐☐	145	Curtis Brown, Buf.	.25	5.00
☐☐	**146**	**Rem Murray, Edm., RC**	**.50**	**8.00**
☐☐	147	Jamie Pushor, Det.	.25	5.00
☐☐	**148**	**Daniel Goneau, NYR., RC**	**.25**	**5.00**
☐☐	149	Mike Prokopec, Chi.	.25	5.00
☐☐	**150**	**Brad Smyth, L.A., RC**	**.25**	**5.00**

ASSAILANTS

Insert Set (15 cards): **100.00**

	No.	Player	NRMT-MT
☐	1	Alexei Yashin, Ott.	8.00
☐	2	Mike Modano, Dal.	10.00
☐	3	Jason Arnott, Edm.	4.00
☐	4	Mikael Renberg, Pha.	3.00
☐	5	Saku Koivu, Mtl.	15.00
☐	6	Todd Bertuzzi, NYI.	4.00
☐	7	Zigmund Palffy, NYI.	6.00
☐	8	Eric Lindros, Pha.	30.00
☐	9	Pat LaFontaine, Buf.	4.00
☐	10	John LeClair, Pha.	10.00
☐	11	Theoren Fleury, Cgy.	6.00
☐	12	Pierre Turgeon, Stl.	4.00
☐	13	Petr Nedved, Pgh.	3.00
☐	14	Owen Nolan, S.J.	4.00
☐	15	Valeri Bure, Mtl.	3.00

CHAMPION SALUTE

These cards have three versions: a promo, the regular insert and a Diamond Chip parallel.

	No.	Player	Promo	Chip	Insert
Insert Set (15 cards):			**40.00**	**1,400.00**	**250.00**
☐☐☐	1	Mark Messier, NYR.	2.00	75.00	12.50
☐☐☐	2	Wayne Gretzky, NYR.	8.00	325.00	50.00
☐☐☐	3	Grant Fuhr (G), Stl.	1.00	25.00	5.00
☐☐☐	4	Paul Coffey, Det.	1.00	25.00	5.00
☐☐☐	5	Mario Lemieux, Pgh.	6.50	250.00	40.00
☐☐☐	6	Jaromir Jagr, Pgh.	4.00	150.00	25.00
☐☐☐	7	Ron Francis, Pgh.	1.25	35.00	7.50
☐☐☐	8	Joe Sakic, Col.	3.50	120.00	20.00
☐☐☐	9	Peter Forsberg, Col.	4.00	150.00	25.00
☐☐☐	10	Claude Lemieux, Col.	1.00	25.00	5.00
☐☐☐	11	Patrick Roy (G), Col.	6.50	250.00	40.00
☐☐☐	12	Chris Chelios, Chi.	1.75	50.00	10.00
☐☐☐	13	Doug Gilmour, Tor.	1.25	35.00	7.50
☐☐☐	14	Mike Richter (G), NYR.	1.25	35.00	7.50
☐☐☐	15	Martin Brodeur (G), N.J.	3.00	100.00	18.00

Z-TEAM

Insert Set (15 cards): **850.00**

	No.	Player	NRMT-MT
☐	1	Eric LIndros, Pha.	125.00
☐	2	Paul Kariya, Ana.	125.00
☐	3	Teemu Selänne, Ana.	70.00
☐	4	Brendan Shanahan, Det.	60.00
☐	5	Sergei Fedorov, Det.	50.00
☐	6	Steve Yzerman, Det.	100.00
☐	7	Brett Hull, Stl.	50.00
☐	8	Pavel Bure, Van.	70.00
☐	9	Alexander Mogilny, Van.	30.00
☐	10	Jeremy Roenick, Pho.	30.00
☐	11	Jocelyn Thibault (G), Mtl.	30.00
☐	12	Keith Tkachuk, Pho.	40.00
☐	13	Daniel Alfredsson, Ott.	20.00
☐	14	Eric Dazé, Chi.	20.00
☐	15	Jim Carey (G), Wsh.	15.00
☐	16	Félix Potvin (G), Tor.	50.00
☐	17	John Vanbiesbrouck (G), Fla.	60.00
☐	18	Chris Osgood (G), Det.	40.00

1996 - 97 PLAYOFF ONE-ON-ONE HOCKEY CHALLENGE

These cards have an orange border. Cards 405-427 are Rare (silver) and cards 428-440 are Ultra-Rare (gold).

Imprint: © 1996 PLAYOFF CORPORATION

Complete Set (110 cards): **800.00**

Commons (331-367): **.15**

Uncommons (368-404): **.20**

	No.	Player	NRMT-MT
☐	331	Mike Sillinger, Van.	.15
☐	332	Oleg Tverdovsky, Pho.	.15
☐	333	Kevin Stevens, L.A.	.15
☐	334	Joe Nieuwendyk, Dal.	.25
☐	335	Owen Nolan, S.J.	.25
☐	336	Jocelyn Thibault, Mtl.	.35
☐	337	Dave Gagner, Cgy.	.15
☐	338	Ray Sheppard, Fla.	.15
☐	339	Jesse Belanger, Edm.	.15
☐	340	Tony Granato, S.J.	.15
☐	341	Daniel Alfredsson, Ott.	.25
☐	342	Stéphane Richer, Mtl.	.15
☐	343	Mathieu Schneider, Tor.	.15
☐	344	Kirk Muller, Tor.	.15
☐	345	Arturs Irbe (G), Dal.	.15
☐	346	Igor Larionov, Det.	.25
☐	347	Steve Duchesne, Ott.	.15
☐	348	Dave Andreychuk, N.J.	.15
☐	349	Mike Gartner, Pho.	.25
☐	350	Teppo Numminen, Pho.	.15
☐	351	Keith Tkachuk, Pho.	.35
☐	352	Mike Modano, Dal.	.50
☐	353	Paul Kariya, Ana.	2.00
☐	354	German Titov, Cgy.	.15
☐	355	Bernie Nicholls, S.J.	.15
☐	356	Doug Gilmour, Tor.	.35
☐	357	Peter Forsberg, Col.	1.50
☐	358	David Oliver, Edm.	.15
☐	359	Pat Verbeek, Dal.	.15
☐	360	Ron Francis, Pgh.	.35
☐	361	Pat Falloon, Pha.	.15
☐	362	Jeff Friesen, S.J.	.15
☐	363	Todd Krygier, Wsh.	.15
☐	364	Félix Potvin (G), Tor.	.50
☐	365	Shane Churla, NYR.	.15
☐	366	Steve Yzerman, Det.	1.50
☐	367	Kelly Hrudey (G), S.J.	.15
☐	368	Mariusz Czerkawski, Edm.	.20
☐	369	Patrick Poulin, T.B.	.20
☐	370	Chris Chelios, Chi.	.75
☐	371	Ray Bourque, Bos.	1.25
☐	372	Igor Kravchuk, Stl.	.20
☐	373	Kirk Maltby, Det.	.20
☐	374	Bill Ranford (G), Bos.	.50
☐	375	Darryl Sydor, Dal.	.20
☐	376	Rick Tocchet, Bos.	.20
☐	377	J.J. Daigneault, Pgh.	.20
☐	378	Chris Osgood (G), Det.	1.00
☐	379	Zigmund Palffy, NYI.	.75
☐	380	Ray Ferraro, L.A.	.20
☐	381	Don Beaupré (G), Tor.	.25
☐	382	Andy Moog (G), Dal.	.50
☐	383	Sergei Zubov, Dal.	.50
☐	384	Craig Janney, Pho.	.20
☐	385	Sandis Ozolinsh, Col.	.50
☐	386	Dave Reid, Dal.	.20
☐	387	Scott Mellanby, Fla.	.20
☐	388	Saku Koivu, Mtl.	1.75
☐	389	Bryan Smolinski, Pgh.	.20
☐	390	Alexander Selivanov, T.B.	.20
☐	391	Peter Bondra, Wsh.	1.00
☐	392	Esa Tikkanen, Van.	.20
☐	393	Ken Baumgartner, Ana.	.20
☐	394	Ed Belfour (G), Chi.	.75
☐	395	Randy Wood, Dal.	.20
☐	396	Jeff Brown, Hfd.	.20
☐	397	Roman Oksiuta, Ana.	.20
☐	398	Cliff Ronning, Pho.	.20
☐	399	Mike Eastwood, Pho.	.20
☐	400	Nelson Emerson, Hfd.	.20
☐	401	Dave Manson, Pho.	.20
☐	402	Jamie Baker, Tor.	.20
☐	403	Ian Laperrière, L.A.	.20
☐	404	Petr Klima, L.A.	.20
☐	405	Dallas Drake, Pho.	1.00
☐	406	Tim Cheveldae (G), Bos.	1.00
☐	407	Igor Korolev, Pho.	1.00
☐	408	Kevin Hatcher, Pgh.	1.00
☐	409	Dale Hawerchuk, Pha.	2.00
☐	410	Martin Straka, Fla.	1.00
☐	411	Wendel Clark, Tor.	2.00
☐	412	Jari Kurri, Ana.	2.00
☐	413	Darren Turcotte, S.J.	1.00
☐	414	Yuri Khmylev, Stl.	1.00
☐	415	Bob Corkum, Pha.	1.00
☐	416	Roman Hamrlik, T.B.	2.00
☐	417	Jayson More, NYR.	1.00
☐	418	Travis Green, NYI.	1.00
☐	419	Dean McAmmond, Edm.	1.00
☐	420	Valeri Kamensky, Edm.	2.00
☐	421	Jason Dawe, Buf.	1.00
☐	422	Alexander Mogilny, Van.	3.00
☐	423	Keith Jones, Wsh.	1.00
☐	424	Mark Messier, NYR.	5.00
☐	425	John Vanbiesbrouck (G), Fla.	6.00
☐	426	Jim Carey (G), Wsh.	1.00
☐	427	Brett Hull, Stl.	5.00
☐	428	Teemu Selänne, Ana.	65.00
☐	429	Phil Housley, Wsh.	15.00
☐	430	Wayne Gretzky, NYR.	250.00
☐	431	Patrick Roy, Col.	175.00
☐	432	Joe Sakic, Col.	75.00
☐	433	Jaromir Jagr, Pgh.	100.00
☐	434	Doug Weight, Edm.	25.00
☐	435	Rob Niedermayer, Fla.	15.00
☐	436	Mario Lemieux, Pgh.	175.00
☐	437	Sergei Fedorov, Det.	40.00
☐	438	Pavel Bure, Van.	65.00
☐	439	Eric Lindros, Pha.	135.00
☐	440	Martin Brodeur (G), N.J.	65.00

1996 - 97 POST - UPPER DECK

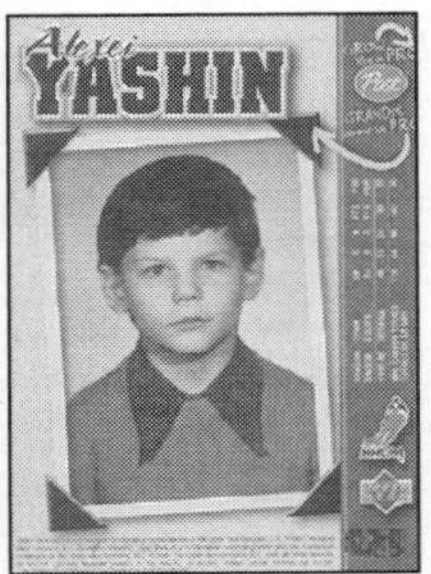

Imprint:

Complete Set (24 cards): **50.00**

	Player	NRMT-MT
☐	Ray Bourque, Bos.	3.00
☐	Chris Chelios, Chi.	2.50
☐	Paul Coffey, Det.	1.50
☐	Vincent Damphousse, Mtl.	2.00
☐	Steve Duchesne, Ott.	1.50
☐	Theoren Fleury, Cgy.	2.00
☐	Doug Gilmour, Tor.	2.00
☐	Wayne Gretzky, NYR.	12.00
☐	Ed Jovanovski, Fla.	1.50
☐	Curtis Joseph (G), Edm.	3.50
☐	Paul Kariya, Ana.	7.50
☐	Eric Lindros, Pha.	7.50

	Player	
☐	Al MacInnis, Stl.	1.50
☐	Félix Potvin (G), Tor.	3.00
☐	Mark Recchi, Mtl.	1.50
☐	Luc Robitaille, NYR.	1.50
☐	Jeremy Roenick, Chi.	2.00
☐	Patrick Roy (G), Col.	9.00
☐	Joe Sakic, Col.	5.00
☐	Mathieu Schneider, Tor.	1.50
☐	Brendan Shanahan, Hfd.	3.50
☐	Scott Stevens, N.J.	1.50
☐	John Vanbiesbrouck (G), Fla.	3.50
☐	Alexei Yashin, Ott.	2.50

STICK UM'S

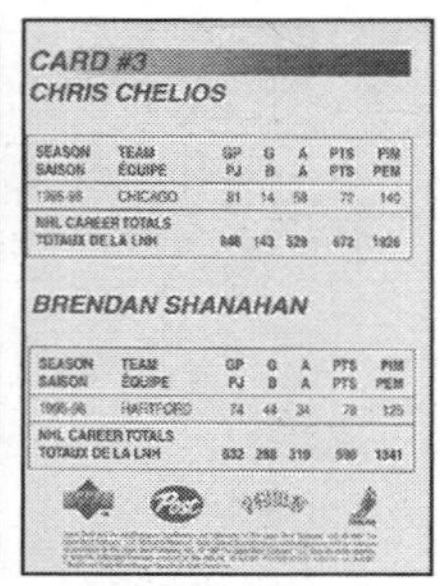

One of four different sticker panels was found in specially marked boxes of Post Pebbles cereals.

Complete Set (4 sticker panels): 20.00

	No.	Player	NRMT-MT
☐	1	Vincent Damphousse/Doug Gilmour	4.00
☐	2	Curtis Joseph/Theoren Fleury	6.00
☐	3	Chris Chelios/Brendan Shanahan	6.00
☐	4	Joe Sakic/Paul Kariya	10.00

1996 - 97 SCORE

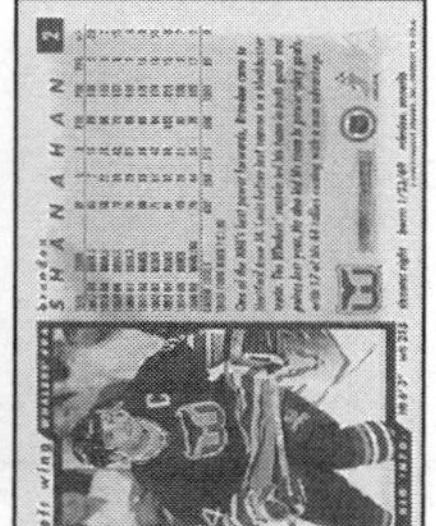

PROMOTIONAL

These Golden Blade promotional cards have two versions: one that deciphers "Sorry, try again" on the back and one that deciphers "Special Artists Proof". Promo cards could not be redeemed.

Promo Set (8 cards): 5.00

	No.	Player	Loser	Winner
☐☐	1	Patrick Roy (G), Col.	3.00	3.00
☐☐	10	Martin Brodeur (G), N.J.	1.25	1.25
☐☐	16	Alexander Mogilny, Van.	.75	.75
☐☐	19	Brett Hull, Stl.	.85	.85
☐☐	63	John Vanbiesbrouck (G), Fla.	1.00	1.00
☐☐	77	Sergei Fedorov, Det.	.85	.85
☐☐	236	Eric Dazé, Chi.	.50	.50
☐☐	238	Saku Koivu, Mtl.	1.25	1.25

SCORE

There are six versions to the Score set. Seeded in packs were regular cards, two different Golden Blades parallels and an Artist's Proof parallel. A shaded area on the back of Golden Blades cards could be decoded to read "Special Artist's Proof" or "Sorry Try Again." The winner card could be redeemed for a special 24 point stock Artist's Proof card (the fifth version). If the cards were sent via a Pinnacle dealer, a "Dealer's Choice" Artist's Proof card was also redeemable (the sixth version).

Golden Blades winners sell at 35-50% more than Golden Blades Losers. Special Artist's Proofs sell at 10% more than Artist's Proofs while Dealer's Choice Artist's Proofs sell at 20% more.

One Golden Blades card (a # 10 Martin Brodeur card) could be decoded for a trip for two to the 1997 NHL All-Star Fanfest Weekend.

Since checklists did not have the decoder bar, there are no Special Artist's Proof, Dealer's Choice Artist's Proof or second Golden Blades versions for cards 271-275.

Imprint: © 1996 PINNACLE BRANDS, INC.

Complete Set (275 cards): 15.00

Golden Blades Set (275 cards): 260.00

Artist's Proof Set (275 cards): 1,700.00

Common Player: .10 .75 4.00

	No.	Player	Reg.	G.B.	A.P.
☐☐☐☐☐☐	1	Patrick Roy (G), Col.	1.50	20.00	125
☐☐☐☐☐☐	2	Brendan Shanahan, Hfd.	.60	5.00	35.00
☐☐☐☐☐☐	3	Rob Niedermayer, Fla.	.10	.75	4.00
☐☐☐☐☐☐	4	Jeff Friesen, S.J.	.25	1.00	6.00
☐☐☐☐☐☐	5	Teppo Numminen, Wpg.	.10	.75	4.00
☐☐☐☐☐☐	6	Mario Lemieux, Pgh.	1.50	20.00	125
☐☐☐☐☐☐	7	Eric Lindros, Pha.	1.25	18.00	100
☐☐☐☐☐☐	8	Paul Kariya, Ana.	1.25	18.00	100
☐☐☐☐☐☐	9	Joe Sakic, Col.	.85	10.00	60.00
☐☐☐☐☐☐	10	Martin Brodeur (G), N.J.	.75	6.00	45.00
☐☐☐☐☐☐	11	Mark Tinordi, Wsh.	.10	.75	4.00
☐☐☐☐☐☐	12	Theroren Fleury, Cgy.	.35	2.00	10.00
☐☐☐☐☐☐	13	Guy Hebert (G), Ana.	.25	1.00	6.00
☐☐☐☐☐☐	14	Dave Gagner, Tor. (Cgy.)	.10	.75	4.00
☐☐☐☐☐☐	15	Travis Green, NYI.	.10	.75	4.00
☐☐☐☐☐☐	16	Alexander Mogilny, Van.	.35	2.00	10.00
☐☐☐☐☐☐	17	Stéphane Fiset (G), Col.	.25	1.00	6.00
☐☐☐☐☐☐	18	Dominik Hasek (G), Buf.	.75	6.00	45.00
☐☐☐☐☐☐	19	Brett Hull, Stl.	.50	4.00	25.00
☐☐☐☐☐☐	20	Zdeno Ciger, Edm.	.10	.75	4.00
☐☐☐☐☐☐	21	Pat Falloon, Pha.	.10	.75	4.00
☐☐☐☐☐☐	22	Jyrki Lumme, Van.	.10	.75	4.00
☐☐☐☐☐☐	23	Rick Tabaracci (G), Cgy.	.10	.75	4.00
☐☐☐☐☐☐	24	Mark Messier, NYR.	.50	4.00	25.00
☐☐☐☐☐☐	25	Yanic Perreault, L.A.	.10	.75	4.00
☐☐☐☐☐☐	26	Mark Recchi, Mtl.	.25	1.00	6.00
☐☐☐☐☐☐	27	Alexander Selivanov, T.B.	.10	.75	4.00
☐☐☐☐☐☐	28	Chris Terreri (G), S.J.	.10	.75	4.00
☐☐☐☐☐☐	29	Jaromir Jagr, Pgh.	1.00	15.00	80.00
☐☐☐☐☐☐	30	Ted Donato, Bos.	.10	.75	4.00
☐☐☐☐☐☐	31	Scott Mellanby, Fla.	.10	.75	4.00
☐☐☐☐☐☐	32	Geoff Courtnall, Stl.	.10	.75	4.00
☐☐☐☐☐☐	33	Michal Pivonka, Wsh.	.10	.75	4.00
☐☐☐☐☐☐	34	Glenn Healy (G), NYR.	.10	.75	4.00
☐☐☐☐☐☐	35	Pavel Bure, Van.	.75	6.00	45.00
☐☐☐☐☐☐	36	Chris Chelios, Chi.	.35	3.00	18.00
☐☐☐☐☐☐	37	Nelson Emerson, Hfd.	.10	.75	4.00
☐☐☐☐☐☐	38	Petr Nedved, Pha.	.10	.75	4.00
☐☐☐☐☐☐	39	Greg Adams, Dal.	.10	.75	4.00
☐☐☐☐☐☐	40	Bill Ranford (G), Edm.	.25	1.00	6.00
☐☐☐☐☐☐	41	Wayne Gretzky, Stl.	2.00	25.00	160
☐☐☐☐☐☐	42	Wendel Clark, Tor.	.25	1.00	6.00
☐☐☐☐☐☐	43	Sandis Ozolinsh, Col.	.25	1.00	6.00
☐☐☐☐☐☐	44	Dave Andreychuk, N.J.	.10	.75	4.00
☐☐☐☐☐☐	45	Brian Bradley, T.B.	.10	.75	4.00
☐☐☐☐☐☐	46	Sean Burke (G), Hfd.	.25	1.00	6.00
☐☐☐☐☐☐	47	Keith Tkachuk, Wpg.	.35	3.00	18.00
☐☐☐☐☐☐	48	Brad May, Buf.	.10	.75	4.00
☐☐☐☐☐☐	49	Brent Gilchrist, Dal.	.10	.75	4.00
☐☐☐☐☐☐	50	Vincent Damphousse, Mtl.	.35	2.00	10.00
☐☐☐☐☐☐	51	Dale Hawerchuk, Pha.	.25	1.00	6.00
☐☐☐☐☐☐	52	Randy Burridge, Buf.	.10	.75	4.00
☐☐☐☐☐☐	53	Ray Bourque, Bos.	.50	4.00	25.00
☐☐☐☐☐☐	54	Keith Primeau, Det.	.25	1.00	6.00
☐☐☐☐☐☐	55	Jason Arnott, Edm.	.25	1.00	6.00
☐☐☐☐☐☐	56	Ron Francis, Pgh.	.35	2.00	10.00
☐☐☐☐☐☐	57	Craig Janney, Wpg.	.10	.75	4.00
☐☐☐☐☐☐	58	Trevor Kidd (G), Cgy.	.25	1.00	6.00
☐☐☐☐☐☐	59	Jason Dawe, Buf.	.10	.75	4.00
☐☐☐☐☐☐	60	Steve Yzerman, Det.	1.00	15.00	80.00
☐☐☐☐☐☐	61	Alexei Kovalev, NYR.	.10	.75	4.00
☐☐☐☐☐☐	62	Steve Duchesne, Ott.	.10	.75	4.00
☐☐☐☐☐☐	63	John Vanbiesbrouck (G), Fla.	.60	5.00	35.00
☐☐☐☐☐☐	64	Steve Thomas, N.J.	.10	.75	4.00
☐☐☐☐☐☐	65	Bernie Nicholls, Chi.	.10	.75	4.00
☐☐☐☐☐☐	66	Alexandre Daigle, Ott.	.25	1.00	6.00
☐☐☐☐☐☐	67	Pat Peake, Wsh.	.10	.75	4.00
☐☐☐☐☐☐	68	Kelly Hrudey (G), L.A.	.10	.75	4.00
☐☐☐☐☐☐	69	Owen Nolan, S.J.	.25	1.00	6.00
☐☐☐☐☐☐	70	Alexei Zhitnik, Buf.	.10	.75	4.00
☐☐☐☐☐☐	71	Pierre Turgeon, Mtl.	.25	1.00	6.00
☐☐☐☐☐☐	72	Mike Modano, Dal.	.50	4.00	25.00
☐☐☐☐☐☐	73	Viacheslav Fetisov, Det.	.25	1.00	6.00
☐☐☐☐☐☐	74	Jim Carey (G), Wsh.	.10	.75	4.00
☐☐☐☐☐☐	75	Larry Murphy, Tor.	.25	1.00	6.00
☐☐☐☐☐☐	76	Roman Oksiuta, Ana.	.10	.75	4.00
☐☐☐☐☐☐	77	Sergei Fedorov, Det.	.50	4.00	25.00
☐☐☐☐☐☐	78	Shayne Corson, Stl.	.25	1.00	6.00
☐☐☐☐☐☐	79	Michael Nylander, Cgy.	.10	.75	4.00
☐☐☐☐☐☐	80	Ron Hextall (G), Pha.	.25	1.00	6.00
☐☐☐☐☐☐	81	Adam Graves, NYR.	.10	.75	4.00
☐☐☐☐☐☐	82	Tommy Söderström (G), NYI.	.10	.75	4.00
☐☐☐☐☐☐	83	Robert Svehla, Fla.	.10	.75	4.00
☐☐☐☐☐☐	84	Vladimir Konstantinov, Det.	.10	.75	4.00
☐☐☐☐☐☐	85	Jeff Hackett (G), Chi.	.25	1.00	6.00
☐☐☐☐☐☐	86	Todd Harvey, Dal.	.10	.75	4.00
☐☐☐☐☐☐	87	Jeff Brown, Hfd.	.10	.75	4.00
☐☐☐☐☐☐	88	Cryan Smolinski, Pgh.	.10	.75	4.00
☐☐☐☐☐☐	89	Oleg Tverdovsky, Wpg.	.10	.75	4.00
☐☐☐☐☐☐	90	Curtis Joseph (G), Edm.	.60	5.00	35.00
☐☐☐☐☐☐	91	Grant Fuhr (G), Stl.	.25	1.00	6.00
☐☐☐☐☐☐	92	Rick Tocchet, Bos.	.10	.75	4.00
☐☐☐☐☐☐	93	Adam Deadmarsh, Col.	.10	.75	4.00
☐☐☐☐☐☐	94	Pat Verbeek, NYR.	.10	.75	4.00
☐☐☐☐☐☐	95	Doug Gilmour, Tor.	.35	2.00	10.00
☐☐☐☐☐☐	96	Jocelyn Thibault (G), Mtl.	.35	2.00	10.00
☐☐☐☐☐☐	97	Radek Bonk, Ott.	.10	.75	4.00
☐☐☐☐☐☐	98	Martin Gelinas, Van.	.10	.75	4.00
☐☐☐☐☐☐	99	Peter Forsberg, Col.	1.00	15.00	80.00
☐☐☐☐☐☐	100	Joe Murphy, Chi.	.10	.75	4.00
☐☐☐☐☐☐	101	Dino Ciccarelli, Det.	.25	1.00	6.00
☐☐☐☐☐☐	102	Rod Brind'Amour, Pha.	.25	1.00	6.00
☐☐☐☐☐☐	103	Kirk Muller, Tor.	.10	.75	4.00
☐☐☐☐☐☐	104	Andy Moog (G), Dal.	.25	1.00	6.00
☐☐☐☐☐☐	105	Nikolai Khabibulin (G), Wpg.	.35	2.00	10.00
☐☐☐☐☐☐	106	Mike Ricci, Col.	.10	.75	4.00
☐☐☐☐☐☐	107	Ray Ferraro, L.A.	.10	.75	4.00
☐☐☐☐☐☐	108	Scott Niedermayer, N.J.	.25	1.00	6.00
☐☐☐☐☐☐	109	Russ Courtnall, Van.	.10	.75	4.00
☐☐☐☐☐☐	110	Dale Hunter, Wsh.	.10	.75	4.00
☐☐☐☐☐☐	111	Cam Neely, Bos.	.25	1.00	6.00
☐☐☐☐☐☐	112	Ray Sheppard, Fla.	.10	.75	4.00
☐☐☐☐☐☐	113	Luc Robitaille, NYR.	.25	1.00	6.00
☐☐☐☐☐☐	114	Al MacInnis, Stl.	.10	.75	4.00
☐☐☐☐☐☐	115	Mathieu Schneider, Tor.	.10	.75	4.00
☐☐☐☐☐☐	116	Claude Lemieux, Col.	.10	.75	4.00
☐☐☐☐☐☐	117	Kevin Hatcher, Dal.	.10	.75	4.00
☐☐☐☐☐☐	118	Daren Puppa (G), T.B.	.10	.75	4.00
☐☐☐☐☐☐	119	Geoff Sanderson, Hfd.	.10	.75	4.00
☐☐☐☐☐☐	120	Zigmund Palffy, NYI.	.35	2.00	10.00
☐☐☐☐☐☐	121	Denis Savard, Chi.	.25	1.00	6.00
☐☐☐☐☐☐	122	Dimitri Khristich, L.A.	.10	.75	4.00
☐☐☐☐☐☐	123	Ed Belfour (G), Chi.	.35	2.00	10.00
☐☐☐☐☐☐	124	Tom Barrasso (G), Pgh.	.25	1.00	6.00
☐☐☐☐☐☐	125	Rob Rouse, Det.	.10	.75	4.00
☐☐☐☐☐☐	126	Tomas Sandström, Pgh.	.10	.75	4.00
☐☐☐☐☐☐	127	Roman Hamrlik, T.B.	.25	1.00	6.00
☐☐☐☐☐☐	128	Alexei Zhamnov, Wpg.	.25	1.00	6.00
☐☐☐☐☐☐	129	Chris Osgood (G), Det.	.35	3.00	18.00
☐☐☐☐☐☐	130	Rob Blake, L.A.	.25	1.00	6.00
☐☐☐☐☐☐	131	Garry Galley, Buf.	.10	.75	4.00
☐☐☐☐☐☐	132	Greg Johnson, Det.	.10	.75	4.00
☐☐☐☐☐☐	133	Brian Skrudland, Fla.	.10	.75	4.00
☐☐☐☐☐☐	134	Martin Rucinsky, Mtl.	.10	.75	4.00
☐☐☐☐☐☐	135	Steve Konowalchuk, Wsh.	.10	.75	4.00
☐☐☐☐☐☐	136	Damian Rhodes (G), Ott.	.10	.75	4.00
☐☐☐☐☐☐	137	Jeremy Roenick, Chi.	.35	2.00	10.00
☐☐☐☐☐☐	139	Scott Stevens, N.J.	.10	.75	4.00
☐☐☐☐☐☐	140	Scott Young, Col.	.10	.75	4.00
☐☐☐☐☐☐	141	Benoît Hogue, Dal.	.10	.75	4.00
☐☐☐☐☐☐	142	Paul Coffey, Det.	.25	1.00	6.00
☐☐☐☐☐☐	143	John MacLean, N.J.	.10	.75	4.00
☐☐☐☐☐☐	144	Joé Juneau, Wsh.	.10	.75	4.00
☐☐☐☐☐☐	145	Teemu Selänne, Ana.	.75	6.00	45.00
☐☐☐☐☐☐	146	Andrew Cassels, Hfd.	.10	.75	4.00
☐☐☐☐☐☐	147	Brian Savage, Mtl.	.10	.75	4.00
☐☐☐☐☐☐	148	Chris Gratton, T.B.	.25	1.00	6.00
☐☐☐☐☐☐	149	Corey Hirsch (G), Van.	.10	.75	4.00
☐☐☐☐☐☐	150	Mike Richter (G), NYR.	.35	2.00	10.00
☐☐☐☐☐☐	151	Shawn McEachern, Bos.	.10	.75	4.00
☐☐☐☐☐☐	152	Joe Nieuwendyk, Dal.	.25	1.00	6.00
☐☐☐☐☐☐	153	Phil Housley, N.J.	.10	.75	4.00
☐☐☐☐☐☐	154	Mike Gartner, Tor. (Pho.)	.25	1.00	6.00-
☐☐☐☐☐☐	155	Kirk McLean (G), Van.	.25	1.00	6.00
☐☐☐☐☐☐	156	Bob Probert, Chi.	.10	.75	4.00
☐☐☐☐☐☐	157	Valeri Kamensky, Col.	.25	1.00	6.00
☐☐☐☐☐☐	158	Vyacheslav Kozlov, Det.	.10	.75	4.00
☐☐☐☐☐☐	159	Eric Desjardins, Pha.	.10	.75	4.00
☐☐☐☐☐☐	160	Mats Sundin, Tor.	.50	4.00	25.00
☐☐☐☐☐☐	161	John LeClair, Pha.	.50	4.00	25.00
☐☐☐☐☐☐	162	Adam Oates, Bos.	.35	2.00	10.00
☐☐☐☐☐☐	163	Cliff Ronning, Van.	.10	.75	4.00

	No.	Player			
□□□□□□	164	Mike Vernon (G), Det.	.25	1.00	6.00
□□□□□□	165	German Titov, Cgy.	.10	.75	4.00
□□□□□□	166	Chris Pronger, Stl.	.25	1.00	6.00
□□□□□□	167	Norm Maciver, Wpg.	.10	.75	4.00
□□□□□□	168	Kenny Jonsson, NYI.	.10	.75	4.00
□□□□□□	169	Tony Amonte, Chi.	.25	1.00	6.00
□□□□□□	170	Doug Weight, Edm.	.35	2.00	10.00
□□□□□□	171	Sergei Zubov, Pgh.	.25	1.00	6.00
□□□□□□	172	Félix Potvin (G), Tor.	.50	4.00	25.00
□□□□□□	173	Trevor Linden, Van.	.25	1.00	6.00
□□□□□□	174	Derek Plante, Buf.	.10	.75	4.00
□□□□□□	175	Uwe Krupp, Col.	.10	.75	4.00
□□□□□□	176	Nicklas Lidström, Det.	.25	1.00	6.00
□□□□□□	177	Mikael Renberg, Pha.	.10	.75	4.00
□□□□□□	178	Igor Larionov, Det.	.25	1.00	6.00
□□□□□□	179	Brian Leetch, NYR.	.35	2.00	10.00
□□□□□□	180	Stu Barnes, Fla.	.10	.75	4.00
□□□□□□	181	Alexei Yashin, Ott.	.35	3.00	18.00
□□□□□□	182	Gary Suter, Chi.	.10	.75	4.00
□□□□□□	183	Ken Wregget (G), Pgh.	.10	.75	4.00
□□□□□□	184	Mike Ridley, Van.	.10	.75	4.00
□□□□□□	185	Peter Bondra, Wsh.	.35	3.00	18.00
□□□□□□	186	Steve Rucchin, Ana.	.10	.75	4.00
□□□□□□	187	Jozef Stumpel, Bos.	.25	1.00	6.00
□□□□□□	188	Matthew Barnaby, Buf.	.10	.75	4.00
□□□□□□	189	James Patrick, Cgy.	.10	.75	4.00
□□□□□□	190	Chris Simon, Col.	.10	.75	4.00
□□□□□□	191	Brent Fedyk, Dal.	.10	.75	4.00
□□□□□□	192	Kris Draper, Det.	.10	.75	4.00
□□□□□□	193	David Oliver, Edm.	.10	.75	4.00
□□□□□□	194	Dave Lowry, Fla.	.10	.75	4.00
□□□□□□	195	Robert Kron, Hfd.	.10	.75	4.00
□□□□□□	196	Andrei Kovalenko, Mtl.	.10	.75	4.00
□□□□□□	197	Bill Guerin, N.J.	.25	1.00	6.00
□□□□□□	198	Ed Olczyk, Wpg.	.10	.75	4.00
□□□□□□	199	Yuri Khmylev, Stl.	.10	.75	4.00
□□□□□□	200	Rob Ray, Buf.	.10	.75	4.00
□□□□□□	201	Joe Mullen, Bos.	.10	.75	4.00
□□□□□□	202	Petr Klima, T.B.	.10	.75	4.00
□□□□□□	203	Todd Krygier, Ana.	.10	.75	4.00
□□□□□□	204	Garth Snow (G), Pha.	.10	.75	4.00
□□□□□□	205	Zarley Zalapski, Cgy.	.10	.75	4.00
□□□□□□	206	Ken Baumgartner, Ana.	.10	.75	4.00
□□□□□□	207	Tony Twist, Stl.	.10	.75	4.00
□□□□□□	208	Todd Gill, Tor. (S.J.)	.10	.75	4.00
□□□□□□	209	Michael Peca, Buf.	.25	1.00	6.00
□□□□□□	210	Darcy Wakaluk (G), Dal.	.10	.75	4.00
□□□□□□	211	Milos Holan, Ana.	.10	.75	4.00
□□□□□□	212	Alexander Semak, NYI.	.10	.75	4.00
□□□□□□	213	Jeff Reese (G), T.B.	.10	.75	4.00
□□□□□□	214	Jon Casey (G), Stl.	.10	.75	4.00
□□□□□□	215	Sandy McCarthy, Cgy.	.10	.75	4.00
□□□□□□	216	Curtis Leschyshyn, Col.	.10	.75	4.00
□□□□□□	217	Todd Marchant, Edm.	.10	.75	4.00
□□□□□□	218	Bob Bassen, Dal.	.10	.75	4.00
□□□□□□	219	Darren Turcotte, S.J.	.10	.75	4.00
□□□□□□	220	David Reid, Bos.	.10	.75	4.00
□□□□□□	221	Brian Bellows, T.B.	.10	.75	4.00
□□□□□□	222	Jesse Belanger, Van.	.10	.75	4.00
□□□□□□	223	Bill Lindsay, Fla.	.10	.75	4.00
□□□□□□	224	Lyle Odelein, Mtl.	.10	.75	4.00
□□□□□□	225	Keith Jones, Wsh.	.10	.75	4.00
□□□□□□	226	Sylvain Lefebvre, Col.	.10	.75	4.00
□□□□□□	227	Shaun Van Allen, Ana.	.10	.75	4.00
□□□□□□	228	Dan Quinn, Pha.	.10	.75	4.00
□□□□□□	229	Richard Matvichuk, Dal.	.10	.75	4.00
□□□□□□	230	Craig MacTavish, Stl.	.10	.75	4.00
□□□□□□	231	Craig Billington (G), Bos.	.10	.75	4.00
□□□□□□	232	Stéphane Richer, N.J.	.10	.75	4.00
□□□□□□	233	Donald Audette, Buf.	.10	.75	4.00
□□□□□□	234	Ulf Dahlen, S.J.	.10	.75	4.00
□□□□□□	235	Steve Chiasson, Cgy.	.10	.75	4.00
□□□□□□	236	Eric Dazé, Chi.	.25	1.00	6.00
□□□□□□	237	Petr Sykora, N.J.	.10	.75	4.00
□□□□□□	238	Saku Koivu, Mtl.	.75	6.00	45.00
□□□□□□	239	Ed Jovanovski, Fla.	.25	1.00	6.00
□□□□□□	240	Daniel Alfredsson, Ott.	.25	1.00	6.00
□□□□□□	241	Vitali Yachmenov, L.A.	.10	.75	4.00
□□□□□□	242	Marcus Ragnarsson, S.J.	.10	.75	4.00
□□□□□□	243	Cory Stillman, Cgy.	.10	.75	4.00
□□□□□□	244	Todd Bertuzzi, NYI.	.25	1.00	6.00
□□□□□□	245	Valeri Bure, Mtl.	.10	.75	4.00
□□□□□□	246	Jere Lehtinen, Dal.	.25	1.00	6.00
□□□□□□	247	Radek Dvorak, Fla.	.10	.75	4.00
□□□□□□	248	Niclas Andersson, NYI.	.10	.75	4.00
□□□□□□	249	Miroslav Satan, Edm.	.10	.75	4.00
□□□□□□	250	Jeff O'Neill, Hfd.	.25	1.00	6.00
□□□□□□	251	Nolan Baumgartner, Wsh.	.10	.75	4.00
□□□□□□	252	Roman Vopat, L.A.	.10	.75	4.00
□□□□□□	253	Bryan McCabe, NYI.	.10	.75	4.00
□□□□□□	254	Jamie Langenbrunner, Dal.	.25	1.00	6.00
□□□□□□	255	Chad Kilger, Wpg. (Pho.)	.10	.75	4.00
□□□□□□	256	Eric Fichaud (G), NYI.	.25	1.00	6.00
□□□□□□	257	Landon Wilson, Col.	.10	.75	4.00
□□□□□□	258	Kyle McLaren, Bos.	.10	.75	4.00
□□□□□□	259	Aaron Gavey, T.B.	.10	.75	4.00
□□□□□□	260	Byron Dafoe (G), L.A.	.10	.75	4.00
□□□□□□	261	Grant Marshall, Dal.	.10	.75	4.00
□□□□□□	262	Shane Doan, Wpg.	.10	.75	4.00
□□□□□□	263	Ralph Intranuovo, Edm.	.10	.75	4.00
□□□□□□	264	Aki Berg, L.A.	.10	.75	4.00
□□□□□□	265	Antti Törmänen, Ott.	.10	.75	4.00
□□□□□□	266	Brian Holzinger, Buf.	.10	.75	4.00
□□□□□□	267	José Théodore (G), Mtl.	.50	2.00	10.00
□□□□□□	268	Ethan Moreau, Chi.	.25	1.00	6.00
□□□□□□	269	Niklas Sundstrom, NYR.	.10	.75	4.00
□□□□□□	270	Brendan Witt, Wsh.	.10	.75	4.00
□□□	271	Checklist 1-70	.10	.75	4.00
□□□	272	Checklist 71-140	.10	.75	4.00
□□□	273	Checklist 141-210	.10	.75	4.00
□□□	274	Checklist 211-275	.10	.75	4.00
□□□	275	Chase Program Checklist	.10	.75	4.00

CHECK IT

Insert Set (16 cards): 285.00

	No.	Player	NRMT-MT
□	1	Eric Lindros, Pha.	65.00
□	2	Peter Forsberg, Col.	50.00
□	3	Keith Tkachuk, Wpg.	20.00
□	4	Cam Neely, Bos.	8.00
□	5	Jeremy Roenick, Chi.	15.00
□	6	Brendan Shanahan, Hfd.	30.00
□	7	Wendel Clark, Tor.	8.00
□	8	Owen Nolan, S.J.	8.00
□	9	Doug Gilmour, Tor.	15.00
□	10	Trevor Linden, Van.	8.00
□	11	Saku Koivu, Mtl.	35.00
□	12	Ed Jovanovski, Fla.	8.00
□	13	Theoren Fleury, Cgy.	15.00
□	14	Doug Weight, Edm.	15.00
□	15	Chris Chelios, Chi.	20.00
□	16	Eric Dazé, Chi.	8.00

DREAM TEAM

Insert Set (12 cards): 160.00

	No.	Player	NRMT-MT
□	1	Eric Lindros, Pha.	20.00
□	2	Paul Kariya, Ana.	20.00
□	3	Joe Sakic, Col.	12.00
□	4	Peter Forsberg, Col.	15.00
□	5	Mark Messier, NYR.	7.50

	No.	Player	NRMT-MT
□	6	Mario Lemieux, Pgh.	25.00
□	7	Jaromir Jagr, Pgh.	15.00
□	8	Wayne Gretzky, Stl.	30.00
□	9	Alexander Mogilny, Van.	4.50
□	10	Pavel Bure, Van.	10.00
□	11	Sergei Fedorov, Det.	7.50
□	12	Patrick Roy (G), Col.	25.00

NET WORTH

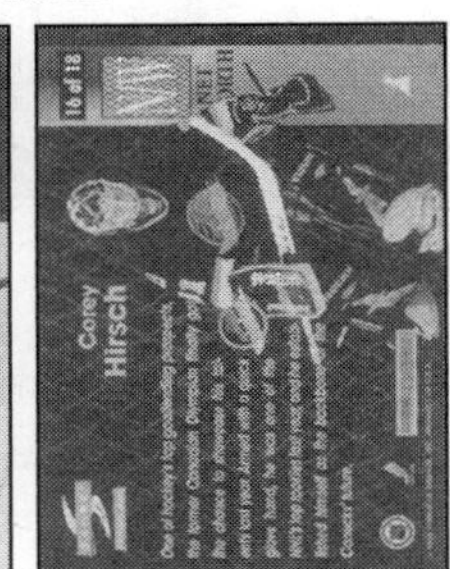

Insert Set (18 cards): 200.00

	No.	Player	NRMT-MT
□	1	Patrick Roy (G), Col.	60.00
□	2	Matrin Brodeur (G), N.J.	25.00
□	3	Jim Carey (G), Wsh.	3.00
□	4	Dominik Hasek (G), Buf.	25.00
□	5	Ed Belfour (G), Chi.	10.00
□	6	Chris Osgood (G), Det.	15.00
□	7	Curtis Joseph (G), Edm.	20.00
□	8	John Vanbiesbrouck (G), Fla.	20.00
□	9	Jocelyn Thibault (G), Mtl.	10.00
□	10	Stéphane Fiset (G), Col.	6.00
□	11	Ron Hextall (G), Pha.	6.00
□	12	Tom Barrasso (G), Pgh.	6.00
□	13	Daren Puppa (G), T.B.	3.00
□	14	Mike Vernon (G), Det.	6.00
□	15	Bill Ranford (G), Edm.	6.00
□	16	Corey Hirsch (G), Van.	3.00
□	17	Damian Rhodes (G), Ott.	3.00
□	18	Nikolai Khabibulin (G), Wpg.	10.00

SUDDEN DEATH

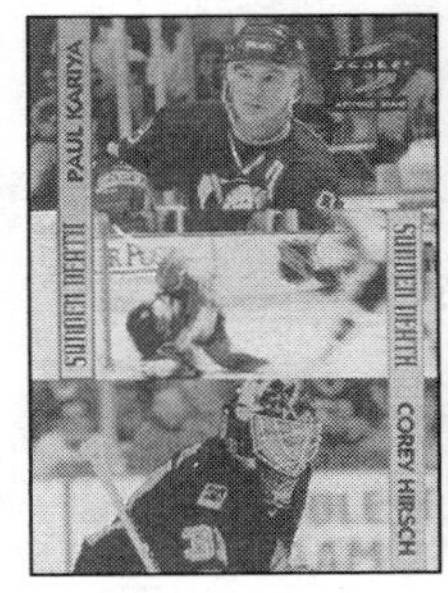

Insert Set (15 cards): 150.00

	No.	Player	NRMT-MT
□	1	M. Brodeur, N.J./P. Turgeon, Mtl.	10.00
□	2	J. Carey, Wsh./S. Yzerman, Det.	12.50
□	3	D. Hasek, Buf./B. Shanahan, Hfd.	12.50
□	4	E. Belfour, Chi./B. Hull, Stl.	6.00
□	5	C. Osgood, Det./J. Roenick, Chi.	6.00
□	6	C. Joseph, Edm./P. Bure, Van.	10.00
□	7	J. Vanbiesbrouck Fla./M. Lemieux, Pgh.	25.00
□	8	J. Thibault, Mtl./A. Mogilny, Van.	6.00
□	9	M. Richter, NYR./J. Jagr, Pgh.	12.50
□	10	T. Barrasso, Pgh./M. Messier, NYR.	6.00
□	11	D. Puppa, T.B./J. Sakic, Col.	10.00
□	12	F. Potvin, Tor./W. Gretzky, Stl.	35.00
□	13	C. Hirsch, Van/ P. Kariya, Ana.	15.00
□	14	R. Hextall, Pha./S. Fedorov, Det.	6.00
□	15	N. Khabibulin, Wpg./T. Selänne, Ana.	10.00

SUPERSTITIONS

Insert Set (13 cards): 25.00

	No.	Player	NRMT-MT
□	1	Teemu Selänne, Ana.	5.00
□	2	Doug Weight, Edm.	2.25
□	3	Mats Sundin, Tor.	3.75
□	4	Mike Modano, Dal.	3.75
□	5	Félix Potvin (G), Tor.	3.75
□	6	Paul Coffey, Det.	1.50
□	7	Ray Bourque, Bos.	3.75
□	8	Chris Chelios, Chi.	3.00
□	9	Ron Hextall (G), Pha.	1.50
□	10	Alexander Selivanov, T.B.	.75
□	11	Brett Hull, Stl.	3.75
□	12	Mike Richter (G), NYR.	2.25
□	13	Scott Mellanby, Fla.	.75

1996 - 97 SCORE BOARD ALL SPORT PAST, PRESENT, FUTURE

This 200-card four-sport set features only 23 hockey cards.These cards have two versions: the regular card and a gold parallel. A 200 card regular set sells at $30.

Imprint:

	No.	Player	Reg.	Gold
□□	71	Ed Jovanovski, Fla.	.50	3.00
□□	72	Chris Phillips	.50	3.00
□□	73	Alexandre Volchkov	.35	1.50
□□	74	Adam Colagiacomo	.25	1.00
□□	75	Jonathan Aitken	.15	.50
□□	76	Rico Fata	1.00	5.00
□□	77	Andrei Zyuzin	.35	1.50
□□	78	Josh Holden	.25	1.00
□□	79	Boyd Devreaux	.25	1.00
□□	97	Bryan Berard	1.00	5.00
□□	98	Dainius Zubrus	.75	4.00
□□	99	Radek Dvorak	.25	1.00
□□	170	Dainius Zubrus	.75	4.00
□□	171	Joe Thornton	2.00	10.00
□□	172	Daniel Brière	.50	3.00
□□	173	Radek Dvorak	.25	1.00
□□	174	Richard Jackman	.15	.50
□□	175	Robert Dome	.25	1.00
□□	176	Serge Samsonov	2.00	10.00
□□	177	Jarome Iginla	.35	1.50
□□	178	Daniel Cleary	.50	3.00
□□	197	Andrei Zyuzin	.35	1.50
□□	198	Ed Jovanovski	.50	3.00

1996 - 97 SCORE BOARD AUTOGRAPH COLLECTION

This 50-card multi-sport set features only six hockey cards. A 50-card set sells at $15.

	No.	Player	NRMT-MT
□	45	Joe Thornton	2.00
□	46	Daniel Cleary	.75
□	47	Robert Dome	.50
□	48	Alexandre Volchkov	.35
□	49	Adam Colagiacomo	.35
□	50	Andrei Zyuzin	.35

GAME BREAKERS

This 30-card set features only two hockey cards. These cards have two versions: the regular insert and a gold version.

	No.	Player	Insert	Gold
□□	GB29	Joe Thornton	15.00	75.00
□□	GB30	Alexandre Volchkov	8.00	25.00

AUTOGRAPHS

Players signed both regular cards and "Gold" autographs. The gold autographs are numbered out of 350.

	Player	Aut.	Gold
□□	Daniel Cleary	20.00	40.00
□□	Adam Colagiacomo	15.00	25.00
□□	Robert Dome	15.00	25.00
□□	Sergei Samsonov	40.00	80.00
□□	Joe Thornton	50.00	100.00
□□	Dainius Zubrus	20.00	40.00
□□	Andrei Zyuzin	15.00	25.00

1996 - 97 SCORE BOARD VISIONS

This 150-card four sport set sells for $50. Other hockey singles exist.

	No.	Player	NRMT-MT
□	94	Manon Rhéaume (G)	4.00

1996 - 97 SCORE BOARD VISIONS SIGNINGS

This 100-card four sport set sell for $50. Other hockey singles exist.

	No.	Player	NRMT-MT
□	78	Manon Rhéaume (G)	4.00

1996 - 97 SISU (FINNISH SM-LIIGA)

This first series was called Sisu Redline. The second series (Sisu Blueline) was never released.

Complete Redline Set (200 cards): 50.00
Common Player: .25

	No.	Player	NRMT-MT
□	1	Checklist 1-50	.25
□	2	Sakari Lindfors (G), HIFK	.50
□	3	Peter Ahola, HIFK	.25
□	4	Jere Karalahti, HIFK	.25
□	5	Pertti Lehtones, HIFK	.25
□	6	Lauri Puolanne, HIFK	.25
□	7	Sami Laine, HIFK	.25
□	8	Tommy Kiviaho, HIFK	.25
□	9	Markku Hurme, HIFK	.25
□	10	Jari Laukkanen, HIFK	.25
□	11	Tero Nyman, HIFK	.25
□	12	Toni Sihvonen, HIFK	.25
□	13	Mika Kortelainen, HIFK	.25
□	14	Tero Hämäläinen, HIFK	.25
□	15	Mika Pietilä (G), HIFK	.25
□	16	Erik Kakko, HIFK	.25
□	17	Tom Koivisto, HIFK	.25
□	18	Jani Nikko, HIFK	.25
□	19	Risto Jalo, HIFK	.25
□	20	Alexsander Andrievski, HIFK	.25
□	21	Jari Kauppila, HIFK	.25
□	22	Jarkko Savijoki, HIFK	.25
□	23	Toni Mäkiaho, HIFK	.25
□	24	Miki Kannisto, HIFK	.25
□	25	Mika Puhakka, HIFK	.25
□	26	Toni Saarinen, HIFK	.25
□	27	Vesa Toskala (G), Ilves	.25
□	28	Teemu Vuorinen, Ilves	.25
□	29	Petri Kokko, Ilves	.25
□	30	Pekka Kangasalusta, Ilves	.25
□	31	Jarno Peltonen, Ilves	.25
□	32	Jarno Peltonen, Ilves	.25
□	33	Mika Arvaja, Ilves	.25
□	34	Matti Kaipainen, Ilves	.25
□	35	Hannu Mattila, Ilves	.25
□	36	Tomi Hirvonen, Ilves	.25
□	37	Jouni Lahtinen, Ilves	.25
□	38	Jari Suorsa, Ilves	.25
□	39	Juha Järvenpää, Ilves	.25
□	40	Semi Pekki, Ilves	.25
□	41	Ari Sulander (G), Jokerit	.50
□	42	Miika Strömberg, Jokerit	.25
□	43	Marko Tuubola, Jokerit	.25
□	44	Pasi Sormunen, Jokerit	.25
□	45	Walteri Immonen, Jokerit	.25
□	46	Jukka Penttinen, Jokerit	.25
□	47	Petri Varis, Jokerit	.25
□	48	Keijo Säilynoja, Jokerit	.25
□	49	Tero Lehterä, Jokerit	.25
□	50	Checklist 51-100	.25
□	51	Jari Lindroos, Jokerit	.25
□	52	Ismo Kuoppala, Jokerit	.25
□	53	Juha Ylönen, Jokerit	.25
□	54	Pasi Saarela, Jokerit	.25
□	55	Marko Leinonen (G), JyPHT	.25
□	56	Kalle Koskinen, JyPHT	.25
□	57	J.P. Laamanen, JyPHT	.25
□	58	Jouni Loponen, JyPHT	.25
□	59	Pekka Poikolainen, JyPHT	.25
□	60	Jan Latvala, JyPHT	.25
□	61	Tino Ahmaoja, JyPHT	.25
□	62	Mika Paananen, JyPHT	.25
□	63	Kimmo Salminen, JyPHT	.25
□	64	Lasse Jämsen, JyPHT	.25
□	65	Thomas Sjögren, JyPHT	.25
□	66	Juha Viinikainen, JyPHT	.25
□	67	Mikko Inkinen, JyPHT	.25
□	68	Toni Koivenen, JyPHT	.25
□	69	Pari Kuivalainen (G), Kiekko	.25
□	70	Tommi Kovanen, Kiekko	.25
□	71	Jermu Pisto, Kiekko	.25
□	72	Ivan Vlzek, Kiekko	.25
□	73	Mika Laaksonen, Kiekko	.25
□	74	Miikka Ruokonen, Kiekko	.25
□	75	Sami Simonen, Kiekko	.25
□	76	Mikko Honkonen, Kiekko	.25
□	77	Veli-Pekka Nutikka, Kiekko	.25
□	78	Arto Sirviö, Kiekko	.25
□	79	Janne Kekäläinen, Kiekko	.25
□	80	Jarno Levonen, Kiekko	.25
□	81	Juss Tarvainen, Kiekko	.25
□	82	Iiro Itämies (G), Kiekko	.25
□	83	Tommi Nyyssönen, Kiekko	.25
□	84	Kari Haakana, Kiekko	.25
□	85	Jarmio Muukkonen, Kiekko	.25
□	86	Tero Nissinen, Kiekko	.25
□	87	Tero Tiainen, Kiekko	.25
□	88	Joonas Jääskeläinen, Kiekko	.25
□	89	Juha Ikonen, Kiekko	.25
□	90	Tomo Norppa, Kiekko	.25
□	91	Teemu Riihijarvi, Kiekko	.25
□	92	Mikko Koivunoro, Kiekko	.25
□	93	Sergei Priakhin, Kiekko	.25
□	94	Timo Hirvonen, Kiekko	.25
□	95	Boris Rousson (G), Lukko	.50
□	96	Kimmo Lotvonen, Lukko	.25
□	97	Riku Kallioniemi, Lukko	.25
□	98	Martti Järventie, Lukko	.25
□	99	Mikko Luori, Lukko	.25
□	100	Checklist 101-150	.25

	No.	Player	Price
☐	101	Kalle Sahlstedt, Lukko	.25
☐	102	Sakari Palsola, Lukko	.25
☐	103	Tommi Turunen, Lukko	.25
☐	104	Petri Lätti, Lukko	.25
☐	105	Jonni Vauhkonea, Lukko	.25
☐	106	Veli Pekka Ahonen, Lukko	.25
☐	107	Jari Torkki, Lukko	.25
☐	108	Jarkko Varvio, Lukko	.25
☐	109	Matti Viitakoski, Lukko	.25
☐	110	Mikko Myllykoski, Lukko	.25
☐	111	Petri Peronmoa, Lukko	.25
☐	112	Vesa Ruotsalainen, Lukko	.25
☐	113	Timo Lohko, Lukko	.25
☐	114	Simo Liukka, Lukko	.25
☐	115	Juha-Pekka Rinkinen, Lukko	.25
☐	116	Timo Mäkinen, Lukko	.25
☐	117	Marko Ek, Lukko	.25
☐	118	Matti Nevalainen, Lukko	.25
☐	119	Ari Santanen, Lukko	.25
☐	120	Jonas Flemming, Lukko	.25
☐	121	Mika Karapuu, Lukko	.25
☐	122	Ilpo Kauhanen (G), Tappara	.25
☐	123	Sami-Ville Salomaa, Tappara	.25
☐	124	Antti Rahkonen, Tappara	.25
☐	125	Harri Laurila, Tappara	.25
☐	126	Sami Lehtonen, Tappara	.25
☐	127	Pasi Petriläinen, Tappara	.25
☐	128	Arto Kulmala, Tappara	.25
☐	129	Jarkko Nikander, Tappara	.25
☐	130	Timo Nurmberg, Tappara	.25
☐	131	Tuomas Reijones, Tappara	.25
☐	132	Aleksander Bartov, Tappara	.25
☐	133	Mika Niittymaki, Tappara	.25
☐	134	Valeri Kryhov, Tappara	.25
☐	135	Fredrik Norrena (G), Tappara	.25
☐	136	Mika Lehtinen, Tappara	.25
☐	137	Sami Salo, Tappara	.25
☐	138	Riku-Petteri Lehtonen, Tappara	.25
☐	139	Mikko Sokka, Tappara	.25
☐	140	Manu Laapas, Tappara	.25
☐	141	Hannes Hyvönea, Tappara	.25
☐	142	Mikka Rousu, Tappara	.25
☐	143	Simo Rouvali, Tappara	.25
☐	144	Tommi Miettinen, Tappara	.25
☐	145	Kimmo Rintanen, Tappara	.25
☐	146	Tommi Kallio, Tappara	.25
☐	147	Antti Aalto, Tappara	.25
☐	148	Miiika Elomo, Tappara	.50
☐	149	Kari Takko (G), Assat	.50
☐	150	Checklist 151-200	.25
☐	151	Tommi Rajamäki, Assat	.25
☐	152	Pasi Peltonen, Assat	.25
☐	153	Karri Kivi, Assat	.25
☐	154	Jokke Heinöne, Assat	.25
☐	155	Teppo Kivelä, Assat	.25
☐	156	Vesa Goman, Assat	.25
☐	157	Pekka Virta, Assat	.25
☐	158	Pasi Tuominen, Assat	.25
☐	159	Tino Hakanen, Assat	.25
☐	160	Jari Levonen, Assat	.25
☐	161	Jari Korpisalo, Assat	.25
☐	162	Timo Salonen, Assat	.25
☐	163	Champions: Jokerit Helsinki	.25
☐	164	Action Card	.25
☐	165	Action Card	.25
☐	166	Action Card	.25
☐	167	Action Card	.25
☐	168	Action Card	.25
☐	169	Action Card	.25
☐	170	Action Card	.25
☐	171	Action Card	.25
☐	172	Action Card	.25
☐	173	Action Card	.25
☐	174	Action Card	.25
☐	175	Ari Sulander (G)	.50
☐	176	Joni Lehto	.25
☐	177	Timo Jutila	1.00
☐	178	Mikko Peltola	.25
☐	179	Juha Riihijärvi	.25
☐	180	Petri Varis	.25
☐	181	Boris Rousson (G)	.50
☐	182	Kimmo Timmonen	.25
☐	183	Mika Strömberg	.25
☐	184	Jari Korpisalo	.25
☐	185	Otakar Janecky	.25
☐	186	Juha Lind	.25
☐	187	Aarne Honkavaara	.25
☐	188	Esko Niemi	.25
☐	189	Raimo Kilpiö	.25
☐	190	Jarmo Wasama	.25
☐	191	Talli Partinen	.25
☐	192	Urpo Ylönen	.25
☐	193	Ilpo Koskela	.25
☐	194	Jorma Vehmanen	.25
☐	195	Pekka Marjamäki	.25
☐	196	Veli-Pekka Ketola	1.00
☐	197	Matti Murto	.25
☐	198	Juhani Tamminen	.25
☐	199	Matti Hagman	.25
☐	200	Checklist	.25

ROOKIE ENERGY

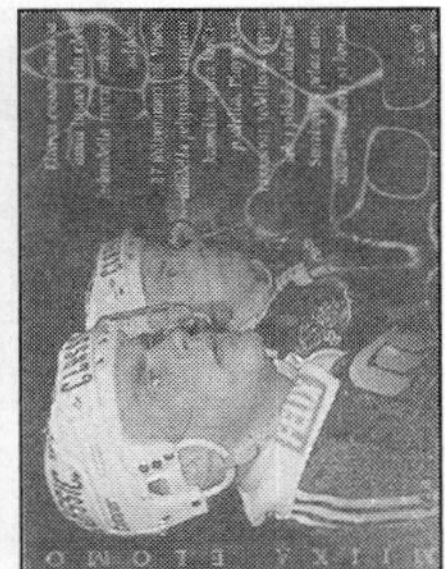

Insert Set (9 cards): 30.00

	No.	Player	NRMT-MT
☐	1	Jani Hurme (G)	8.00
☐	2	Mikko Eloranta	3.00
☐	3	Sami Salo	3.00
☐	4	Tero Hämäläinen	3.00
☐	5	Miika Elomo	5.00
☐	6	Mika Pietilä	3.00
☐	7	Arto Kuki	3.00
☐	8	Vesa Toskalo	4.00
☐	9	Miikka Rousu	3.00

AT THE GALA

Insert Set (8 cards): 25.00

	No.	Player	NRMT-MT
☐	1	Petri Varis	4.00
☐	2	Juha Riihijärvi	6.00
☐	3	Walter Immonen	3.00
☐	4	Jani Hurme (G)	6.00
☐	5	Pasi Kuivalainen	3.00
☐	6	Mika Strömberg	3.00
☐	7	Sakari Pietitä	3.00
☐	8	Ari Sulander (G)	6.00

MIGHTY ADVERSARIES

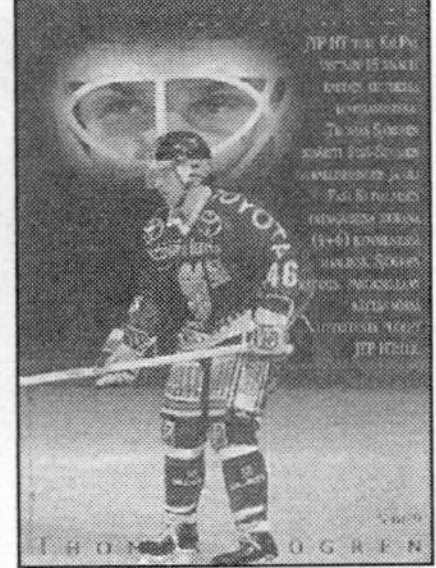

Insert Set (9 cards): 35.00

	No.	Player	NRMT-MT
☐	1	Kari Takko (G)/ Kimmo Rintanen	5.00
☐	2	Boris Rousson (G)/Pasi Saarela	8.00
☐	3	Ilpo Kauhanen (G)/Aleksander Andrijevski	4.00
☐	4	Ari Sulander (G)/Mika Kortelainen	8.00
☐	5	Pasi Kuivalainen (G)/Thomas Sjögren	4.00
☐	6	Vesa Toskela (G)/Janne Ojanen	4.00
☐	7	Fredrik Norrena (G)/Otakar Janecky	5.00
☐	8	Sakari Lindfors (G)/Jari Korpisalo	5.00
☐	9	Ari-Pekka Siekkinen (G)/ Jari Lindroos	4.00

SLEDGEHAMMERS

Insert Set (9 cards): 25.00

	No.	Player	NRMT-MT
☐	1	Hannu Henriksson	3.00
☐	2	Robert Nordmark	3.00
☐	3	Pasi Sormunen	3.00
☐	4	Tuomas Grönman	4.00
☐	5	Derek Mayer	3.00
☐	6	Toni Porkka	3.00
☐	7	Timo Peltomaa	3.00
☐	8	Iiro Järvi	3.00
☐	9	Joni Lehto	3.00

KEEPING IT GREEN

Insert Set (8 cards): 85.00

	No.	Player	NRMT-MT
☐	1	Ari Sulander (G)	30.00
☐	2	Jani Hurme (G)	30.00
☐	3	Boris Rousson (G)	30.00
☐	4	Mika Pietilä (G)	20.00

SUPER BONUS

	Player	NRMT-MT
☐	Juha Riihijärvi, Golden Helmet	75.00
☐	Kari Takko, Sisu Super	40.00

1996 - 97 SELECT CERTIFIED

CORNERSTONES

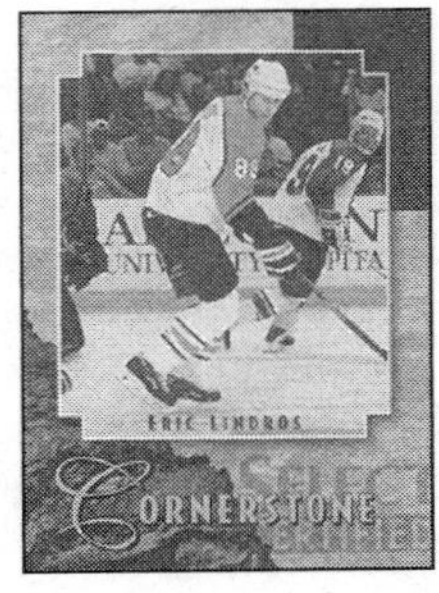

Insert Set (15 cards): 175.00

	No.	Player	NRMT-MT
☐	1	Eric Lindros, Pha.	20.00
☐	2	Mario Lemieux, Pgh.	25.00
☐	3	Jaromir Jagr, Pgh.	15.00
☐	4	Wayne Gretzky, NYR.	30.00
☐	5	Mark Messier, NYR.	7.50
☐	6	Brett Hull, Stl.	7.50
☐	7	Pavel Bure, Van.	10.00
☐	8	Saku Koivu, Mtl.	10.00
☐	9	Joe Sakic, Col.	12.00

1996 - 97 SELECT CERTIFIED EDITION

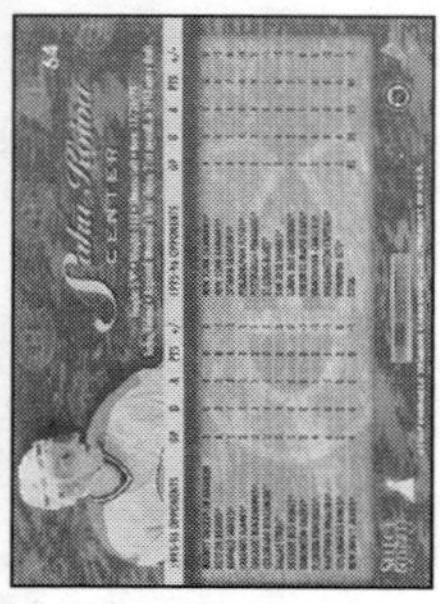

This series has seven versions: the regular card, a Certified Red, a Certifiede Blue, and Artist's Proof, a Mirror Red (60-75 copies), a Mirror Blue (30-40 copies) and a Mirror Gold (19-25 copies). The Certified Blue and the Artist's Proof have the same value. Artist's Proof cards mistakenly say "1 of 500" on the card face; there are in fact only 125-150 copies.

Imprint: © 1997 PINNACLE TRADING CARD COMPANY

Complete Set (120 cards):	**60.00**
Common Player:	**.35**
Promo Card (Wendel Clark, #65):	**.50**

No.	Player	Reg.	Red	Blue A.P.	Mirror Red	Mirror Blue	Mirror Gold
1	Eric Lindros, Pha.	3.50	25.00	150.00	400.00	800.00	2,00.00
2	Mike Modano, Dal.	1.25	10.00	50.00	150.00	300.00	600.00
3	Jocelyn Thibault (G), Mtl.	.75	6.00	25.00	75.00	150.00	300.00
4	Wayne Gretzky, NYR.	5.00	40.00	250.00	700.00	1,400.00	3,600.00
5	Ray Bourque, Bos.	1.25	10.00	50.00	150.00	300.00	600.00
6	Martin Brodeur (G), N.J.	1.75	15.00	80.00	200.00	400.00	850.00
7	Rob Niedermayer, Fla.	.25	2.00	8.00	25.00	50.00	100.00
8	Stéphane Fiset, L.A.	.50	4.00	15.00	45.00	90.00	175.00
9	Pat LaFontaine, Buf.	.50	4.00	15.00	45.00	90.00	175.00
10	Mario Lemieux, Pgh.	4.00	30.00	200.00	500.00	1,00.00	2,600.00
11	Ed Belfour (G), S.J.	.75	6.00	25.00	75.00	150.00	300.00
12	Ron Francis, Pgh.	.75	6.00	25.00	75.00	150.00	300.00
13	Luc Robitaille, NYR.	.50	4.00	15.00	45.00	90.00	175.00
14	Paul Kariya, Ana.	3.50	25.00	150.00	400.00	800.00	2,00.00
15	Doug Gilmour, Tor.	.75	6.00	25.00	75.00	150.00	300.00
16	Joe Sakic, Col.	2.00	18.00	100.00	250.00	500.00	1,100.00
17	Nikolai Khabibulin, Pho.	.75	6.00	25.00	75.00	150.00	300.00
18	Valeri Bure, Mtl.	.25	2.00	8.00	25.00	50.00	100.00
19	Brett Hull, Stl.	1.25	10.00	50.00	150.00	300.00	600.00
20	Chris Osgood (G), Det.	1.00	8.00	35.00	100.00	200.00	400.00
21	Trevor Kidd (G), Cgy.	.50	4.00	15.00	45.00	90.00	175.00
22	Kirk McLean (G), Van.	.50	4.00	15.00	45.00	90.00	175.00
23	Zigmund Palffy, NYI.	.75	6.00	25.00	75.00	150.00	300.00
24	Keith Tkachuk, Pho.	1.00	8.00	35.00	100.00	200.00	400.00
25	Andy Moog (G), Dal.	.50	4.00	15.00	45.00	90.00	175.00
26	Bill Guerin, N.J.	.50	4.00	15.00	45.00	90.00	175.00
27	Chris Chelios, Chi.	1.00	8.00	35.00	100.00	200.00	400.00
28	Damian Rhodes (G), Ott.	.25	2.00	8.00	25.00	50.00	100.00
29	Jim Carey (G), Wsh.	.25	2.00	8.00	25.00	50.00	100.00
30	Ed Jovanovski, Fla.	.50	4.00	15.00	45.00	90.00	175.00
31	Félix Potvin (G), Tor.	1.25	10.00	50.00	150.00	300.00	600.00
32	Teemu Selänne, Ana.	1.75	15.00	80.00	200.00	400.00	850.00
33	John LeClair, Pha.	1.25	10.00	50.00	150.00	300.00	600.00
34	Pavel Bure, Van.	1.75	15.00	80.00	200.00	400.00	850.00
35	Grant Fuhr, Stl.	.50	4.00	15.00	45.00	90.00	175.00
36	Mark Messier, NYR.	1.25	10.00	50.00	150.00	300.00	600.00
37	Vincent Damphousse, Mtl.	.75	6.00	25.00	75.00	150.00	300.00
38	Jason Arnott, Edm.	.50	4.00	15.00	45.00	90.00	175.00
39	Mike Richter (G), NYR.	.75	6.00	25.00	75.00	150.00	300.00
40	Keith Primeau, Hfd.	.50	4.00	15.00	45.00	90.00	175.00
41	Steve Yzerman, Det.	2.50	20.00	125.00	300.00	600.00	1,400.00
42	Trevor Linden, Van.	.50	4.00	15.00	45.00	90.00	175.00
43	Jaromir Jagr, Pgh.	2.50	20.00	125.00	300.00	600.00	1,400.00
44	Sean Burke (G), Hfd.	.50	4.00	15.00	45.00	90.00	175.00
45	Alexei Zhitnik, Buf.	.25	2.00	8.00	25.00	50.00	100.00
46	Dmitri Khristich, L.A.	.25	2.00	8.00	25.00	50.00	100.00
47	Daniel Alfredsson, Ott.	.50	4.00	15.00	45.00	90.00	175.00
48	Roman Hamrlik, T.B.	.50	4.00	15.00	45.00	90.00	175.00
49	Pat Verbeek, Dal.	.25	2.00	8.00	25.00	50.00	100.00
50	Doug Weight, Edm.	.75	6.00	25.00	75.00	150.00	300.00
51	Adam Graves, NYR.	.25	2.00	8.00	25.00	50.00	100.00
52	Michal Pivonka, Wsh.	.25	2.00	8.00	25.00	50.00	100.00
53	Claude Lemieux, Col.	.25	2.00	8.00	25.00	50.00	100.00
54	Scott Stevens, N.J.	.25	2.00	8.00	25.00	50.00	100.00
55	Sergei Fedorov, Det.	1.25	10.00	50.00	150.00	300.00	600.00
56	Owen Nolan, S.J.	.25	2.00	8.00	25.00	50.00	100.00
57	Niclas Andersson, NYI.	1.25	10.00	50.00	150.00	300.00	600.00
58	Cory Stillman, Cgy.	.25	2.00	8.00	25.00	50.00	100.00
59	John Vanbiesbrouck (G), Fla.	1.50	12.00	60.00	175.00	350.00	700.00
60	Craig Janney, S.J.	.25	2.00	8.00	25.00	50.00	100.00
61	Jeff Friesen, S.J.	.50	4.00	15.00	45.00	90.00	175.00
62	Igor Larionov, Det.	.50	4.00	15.00	45.00	90.00	175.00
63	Ron Hextall (G), Pha.	.50	4.00	15.00	45.00	90.00	175.00
64	Saku Koivu, Mtl.	1.75	15.00	80.00	200.00	400.00	850.00
65	Wendel Clark, Tor.	.50	4.00	15.00	45.00	90.00	175.00
66	Curtis Joseph (G), Edm.	1.50	12.00	60.00	175.00	350.00	700.00
67	Valeri Kamensky, Col.	.50	4.00	15.00	45.00	90.00	175.00
68	Adam Oates, Bos.	.75	6.00	25.00	75.00	150.00	300.00
69	Daren Puppa (G), T.B.	.25	2.00	8.00	25.00	50.00	100.00
70	Alexander Mogilny, Van.	.75	6.00	25.00	75.00	150.00	300.00
71	Corey Hirsch (G), Van.	.25	2.00	8.00	25.00	50.00	100.00
72	Brendan Shanahan, Det.	1.50	12.00	60.00	175.00	350.00	700.00
73	Shayne Corson, Mtl.	.50	4.00	15.00	45.00	90.00	175.00
74	Dominik Hasek (G), Buf.	1.75	15.00	80.00	200.00	400.00	850.00
75	Theoren Fleury, Cgy.	.75	6.00	25.00	75.00	150.00	300.00
76	Brian Leetch, NYR.	.75	6.00	25.00	75.00	150.00	300.00
77	Jeremy Roenick, Pho.	.75	6.00	25.00	75.00	150.00	300.00
78	Peter Bondra, Wsh.	1.00	8.00	35.00	100.00	200.00	400.00
79	Eric Dazé, Chi.	.50	4.00	15.00	45.00	90.00	175.00
80	Todd Bertuzzi, NYI.	.50	4.00	15.00	45.00	90.00	175.00
81	Patrick Roy (G), Col.	4.00	30.00	200.00	500.00	1,00.00	2,600.00
82	Pierre Turgeon, Stl.	.50	4.00	15.00	45.00	90.00	175.00
83	Alexei Yashin, Ott.	1.00	8.00	35.00	100.00	200.00	400.00
84	Scott Mellanby, Fla.	.25	2.00	8.00	25.00	50.00	100.00
85	Mats Sundin, Tor.	1.25	10.00	50.00	150.00	300.00	600.00
86	Jari Kurri, Ana.	.50	4.00	15.00	45.00	90.00	175.00
87	Kelly Hrudey (G), S.J.	.25	2.00	8.00	25.00	50.00	100.00
88	Joe Nieuwendyk, Dal.	.50	4.00	15.00	45.00	90.00	175.00
89	Paul Coffey, Pha.	.50	4.00	15.00	45.00	90.00	175.00
90	Jeff O'Neill, Hfd.	.50	4.00	15.00	45.00	90.00	175.00
91	**Kai Nurminen, L.A., RC**	**.25**	**2.00**	**8.00**	**25.00**	**50.00**	**100.00**
92	Anders Eriksson, Det.	.25	2.00	8.00	25.00	50.00	100.00
93	Jarome Iginla, Cgy.	1.00	6.00	20.00	60.00	120.00	225.00
94	Anson Carter, Bos.	.25	2.00	8.00	25.00	50.00	100.00
95	Christian Dubé, NYR.	.75	3.00	10.00	30.00	60.00	120.00
96	**Harry York, Stl., RC**	**.25**	**2.00**	**8.00**	**25.00**	**50.00**	**100.00**
97	**Tomas Holmstrom, Det., RC**	**1.50**	**4.00**	**15.00**	**40.00**	**80.00**	**150.00**
98	**Sergei Berezin, Tor., RC**	**1.50**	**4.00**	**15.00**	**40.00**	**80.00**	**150.00**
99	**Mats Timander, Bos., RC**	**.25**	**2.00**	**8.00**	**25.00**	**50.00**	**100.00**
100	Wade Redden, Ott.	.75	3.00	10.00	30.00	60.00	120.00
101	**Mike Grier, Edm., RC**	**1.50**	**4.00**	**15.00**	**40.00**	**80.00**	**150.00**
102	Jonas Hoglund, Cgy.	.25	2.00	8.00	25.00	50.00	100.00
103	Eric Fichaud (G), NYI.	.50	4.00	15.00	45.00	90.00	175.00
104	Janne Niinimaa, Pha.	.75	3.00	10.00	30.00	60.00	120.00
105	Tomas Grönman, Chi.	.25	2.00	8.00	25.00	50.00	100.00
106	Jim Campbell, Stl.	.50	4.00	15.00	45.00	90.00	175.00
107	**Daniel Goneau, NYR., RC**	**.25**	**2.00**	**8.00**	**25.00**	**50.00**	**100.00**
108	**Patrick Lalime (G), Pgh., RC**	**.25**	**2.00**	**8.00**	**25.00**	**50.00**	**100.00**
109	**Ruslan Salei, Ana., RC**	**.25**	**2.00**	**8.00**	**25.00**	**50.00**	**100.00**
110	**Richard Zednik, Wsh., RC**	**1.50**	**4.00**	**15.00**	**40.00**	**80.00**	**150.00**
111	Chris O'Sullivan, Cgy.	.25	2.00	8.00	25.00	50.00	100.00
112	**Fredrik Modin, Tor., RC**	**1.50**	**4.00**	**15.00**	**40.00**	**80.00**	**150.00**
113	**Brad Smyth, L.A., RC**	**.25**	**2.00**	**8.00**	**25.00**	**50.00**	**100.00**
114	Bryan Berard, NYI.	1.00	6.00	20.00	60.00	120.00	225.00
115	Jamie Langenbrunner, Dal.	.50	4.00	15.00	45.00	90.00	175.00
116	Ethan Moreau, Chi.	.50	4.00	15.00	45.00	90.00	175.00
117	Daymond Langkow, T.B.	.25	2.00	8.00	25.00	50.00	100.00
118	**Andreas Dackell, Ott., RC**	**.25**	**2.00**	**8.00**	**25.00**	**50.00**	**100.00**
119	**Rem Murray, Edm., RC**	**.75**	**3.00**	**10.00**	**30.00**	**60.00**	**120.00**
120	**Dainius Zubrus, Pha., RC**	**5.00**	**10.00**	**40.00**	**100.00**	**250.00**	**400.00**

	No.	Player	NRMT-MT
☐	10	Keith Tkachuk, Pho.	8.00
☐	11	Paul Kariya, Ana.	20.00
☐	12	Teemu Selänne, Ana.	10.00
☐	13	Sergei Fedorov, Det.	7.50
☐	14	Steve Yzerman, Det.	15.00
☐	15	Peter Forsberg, Col.	15.00

FREEZERS

Insert Set (15 cards): 125.00

	No.	Player	NRMT-MT
☐	1	Martin Brodeur (G), N.J.	15.00
☐	2	Patrick Roy (G), Col.	35.00
☐	3	Jim Carey (G), Wsh.	4.00
☐	4	John Vanbiesbrouck (G), Fla.	12.00
☐	5	Dominik Hasek (G), Buf.	15.00
☐	6	Ed Belfour (G), Chi.	6.00
☐	7	Curtis Joseph (G), Edm.	12.00
☐	8	Félix Potvin (G), Tor.	10.00
☐	9	Daren Puppa (G), T.B.	4.00
☐	10	Chris Osgood (G), Det.	8.00
☐	11	Mike Richter (G), NYR.	6.00
☐	12	Jocelyn Thibault (G), Mtl.	6.00
☐	13	Ron Hextall (G), Pha.	5.00
☐	14	Nikolai Khabibulin (G), Pho.	6.00
☐	15	Damian Rhodes (G), Ott.	4.00

1996 - 97 SEVEN ELEVEN PHONE CARDS - SCOREBOARD

Prices are for unused phone cards.

Imprint:

	Den.	Player	Unused
☐	15 min.	Daniel Alfredsson, Ott. (A)	35.00
☐	30 min.	Ray Bourque, Bos.	30.00
☐	30 min.	Pavel Bure, Van.	40.00
☐	15 min.	Paul Coffey, Det.	30.00
☐	15 min.	Vincent Damphousse, Mtl.	20.00
☐	30 min.	Theoren Fleury, Cgy.	35.00
☐	30 min.	Peter Forsberg, Col.	40.00
☐	15 min.	Doug Gilmour, Tor.	30.00
☐	15 min.	Curtis Joseph (G), Edm.	20.00
☐	30 min.	Paul Kariya, Ana.	30.00
☐	30 min.	John LeClair, Pha.	30.00
☐	30 min.	Brian Leetch, NYR.	30.00
☐	15 min.	Trevor Linden, Van.	25.00
☐	30 min.	Eric Lindros, Pha.	30.00
☐	30 min.	Mike Richter (G), NYR.	30.00
☐	15 min.	Joe Sakic, Col.	30.00
☐	15 min.	Brendan Shanahan, Det.	35.00
☐	15 min.	Pierre Turgeon, Mtl.	20.00
☐	15 min.	Doug Weight, Edm.	15.00
☐	30 min.	Steve Yzerman, Det.	40.00

1996 - 97 SKYBOX IMPACT

Imprint: © 1996 FLEER/SKYBOX INTERNATIONAL

Complete Set (175 cards): 20.00

Common Player: .10

Promo Panel (John LeClair): 2.00

Pin Redemption (John LeClair): 35.00

	No.	Player	NRMT-MT
☐	1	Guy Hebert (G), Ana.	.25
☐	2	Paul Kariya, Ana.	1.25
☐	3	Roman Oksiuta, Ana.	.10
☐	4	Teemu Selänne, Ana.	.75
☐	5	Ray Bourque, Bos.	.50
☐	6	Kyle McLaren, Bos.	.10
☐	7	Adam Oates, Bos.	.35
☐	8	Bill Ranford (G), Bos.	.25
☐	9	Rick Tocchet, Bos.	.10
☐	10	Dominik Hasek (G), Buf.	.75
☐	11	Pat LaFontaine, Buf.	.25
☐	12	Michael Peca, Buf.	.25
☐	13	Theoren Fleury, Cgy.	.35
☐	14	Trevor Kidd (G), Cgy.	.25
☐	15	German Titov, Cgy.	.10
☐	16	Tony Amonte, Chi.	.25
☐	17	Ed Belfour (G), Chi.	.35
☐	18	Chris Chelios, Chi.	.35
☐	19	Eric Dazé, Chi.	.10
☐	20	Gary Suter, Chi.	.10
☐	21	Alexei Zhamnov, Chi.	.25
☐	22	Peter Forsberg, Col.	1.00
☐	23	Valeri Kamensky, Col.	.25
☐	24	Uwe Krupp, Col.	.10
☐	25	Claude Lemieux, Col.	.10
☐	26	Sandis Ozolinsh, Col.	.25
☐	27	Patrick Roy (G), Col.	1.50
☐	28	Joe Sakic, Col.	.85
☐	29	Derian Hatcher, Dal.	.25
☐	30	Mike Modano, Dal.	.25
☐	31	Joe Nieuwendyk, Dal.	.25
☐	32	Sergei Zubov, Pgh. (Dal.)	.25
☐	33	Paul Coffey, Det.	.25
☐	34	Sergei Fedorov, Det.	.50
☐	35	Vladimir Konstantinov, Det.	.10
☐	36	Vyacheslav Kozlov, Det.	.10
☐	37	Nicklas Lidström, Det.	.25
☐	38	Chris Osgood (G), Det.	.35
☐	39	Keith Primeau, Det.	.25
☐	40	Steve Yzerman, Det.	1.00
☐	41	Jason Arnott, Edm.	.25
☐	42	Curtis Joseph (G), Edm.	.60
☐	43	Doug Weight, Edm.	.35
☐	44	Radek Dvorak, Fla.	.10
☐	45	Ed Jovanovski, Fla.	.25
☐	46	Scott Mellanby, Fla.	.10
☐	47	Rob Niedermayer, Fla.	.10
☐	48	Ray Sheppard, Fla.	.10
☐	49	Robert Svehla, Fla.	.10
☐	50	John Vanbiesbrouck (G), Fla.	.60
☐	51	Jeff Brown, Hfd.	.10
☐	52	Sean Burke (G), Hfd.	.25
☐	53	Andrew Cassels, Hfd.	.10
☐	54	Geoff Sanderson, Hfd.	.10
☐	55	Brendan Shanahan, Hfd.	.60
☐	56	Byron Dafoe (G), L.A.	.10
☐	57	Ray Ferraro, L.A.	.10
☐	58	Dimitri Khristich, L.A.	.10
☐	59	Vitali Yachmenev, L.A.	.10
☐	60	Valeri Bure, Mtl.	.10
☐	61	Vincent Damphousse, Mtl.	.35
☐	62	Saku Koivu, Mtl.	.75
☐	63	Mark Recchi, Mtl.	.25
☐	64	Martin Rucinsky, Mtl.	.10
☐	65	Jocelyn Thibault (G), Mtl.	.35
☐	66	Pierre Turgeon, Mtl.	.25
☐	67	Dave Andreychuk, N.J.	.10
☐	68	Martin Brodeur (G), N.J.	.75
☐	69	Bill Guerin, N.J.	.25
☐	70	Scott Niedermayer, N.J.	.25
☐	71	Scott Stevens, N.J.	.10
☐	72	Petr Sykora, N.J.	.10
☐	73	Steve Thomas, N.J.	.10
☐	74	Todd Bertuzzi, NYI.	.25
☐	75	Travis Green, NYI.	.10
☐	76	Kenny Jonsson, NYI.	.10
☐	77	Zigmund Palffy, NYI.	.35
☐	78	Adam Graves, NYI.	.10
☐	79	Wayne Gretzky, NYR.	2.50
☐	80	Alexei Kovalev, NYR.	.10
☐	81	Brian Leetch, NYR.	.35
☐	82	Mark Messier, NYR.	.50
☐	83	Mike Richter (G), NYR.	.35
☐	84	Ulf Samuelsson, NYR.	.10
☐	85	Niklas Sundstrom, NYR.	.10
☐	86	Daniel Alfredsson, Ott.	.25
☐	87	Radek Bonk, Ott.	.10
☐	88	Alexandre Daigle, Ott.	.25
☐	89	Steve Duchesne, Ott.	.10
☐	90	Damian Rhodes (G), Ott.	.10
☐	91	Alexei Yashin, Ott.	.35
☐	92	Rod Brind'Amour, Pha.	.25
☐	93	Eric Desjardins, Pha.	.10
☐	94	Dale Hawerchuk, Pha.	.25
☐	95	Ron Hextall (G), Pha.	.25
☐	96	John LeClair, Pha.	.50
☐	97	Eric Lindros, Pha.	1.25
☐	98	Mikael Renberg, Pha.	.10
☐	99	Tom Barrasso (G), Pgh.	.25
☐	100	Ron Francis, Pgh.	.35
☐	101	Jaromir Jagr, Pgh.	1.00
☐	102	Mario Lemieux, Pgh.	1.50
☐	103	Petr Nedved, Pgh.	.10
☐	104	Bryan Smolinski, Pgh.	.10
☐	105	Nikolai Khabibulin (G), Pho.	.35
☐	106	Teppo Numminen, Pho.	.10
☐	107	Keith Tkachuk, Pho.	.35
☐	108	Jeremy Roenick, Chi.	.35
☐	109	Oleg Tverdovsky, Pho.	.10
☐	110	Shayne Corson, Stl.	.25
☐	111	Geoff Courtnall, Stl.	.10
☐	112	Grant Fuhr (G), Stl.	.25
☐	113	Brett Hull, Stl.	.50
☐	114	Al MacInnis, Stl.	.10
☐	115	Chris Pronger, Stl.	.25
☐	116	Jeff Friesen, Stl.	.25
☐	117	Owen Nolan, S.J.	.25
☐	118	Marcus Ragnarsson, S.J.	.10
☐	119	Chris Terreri (G), S.J.	.10
☐	120	Brian Bradley, S.J.	.10
☐	121	Chris Gratton, T.B.	.25
☐	122	Roman Hamrlik, T.B.	.25
☐	123	Daren Puppa (G), T.B.	.10
☐	124	Alexander Selivanov, T.B.	.10
☐	125	Wendel Clark, Tor.	.25
☐	126	Doug Gilmour, Tor.	.25
☐	127	Kirk Muller, Tor.	.10
☐	128	Larry Murphy, Tor.	.25
☐	129	Félix Potvin (G), Tor.	.50
☐	130	Mats Sundin, Tor.	.50
☐	131	Pavel Bure, Van.	.75
☐	132	Russ Courtnall, Van.	.10
☐	133	Trevor Linden, Van.	.25
☐	134	Kirk McLean (G), Van.	.25
☐	135	Alexander Mogilny, Van.	.35
☐	136	Peter Bondra, Wsh.	.25
☐	137	Jim Carey (G), Wsh.	.10
☐	138	Sylvain Côté, Wsh.	.10
☐	139	Sergei Gonchar, Wsh.	.10
☐	140	Phil Housley, Wsh.	.10
☐	141	Joe Juneau, Wsh.	.10
☐	142	Michal Pivonka, Wsh.	.10
☐	143	Brendan Witt, Wsh.	.10
☐	144	Nolan Baumgartner, Wsh.	.10
☐	145	Martin Biron (G), Buf.	.10
☐	146	Jason Bonsignore, Edm.	.10
☐	**147**	**Andrew Brunette, Wsh. RC**	**.25**
☐	148	Jason Doig, Wpg.	.10
☐	149	Peter Ferraro, NYR.	.10
☐	150	Eric Fichaud, NYI.	.25
☐	151	Ladislav Kohn, Cgy.	.10
☐	152	Jamie Langenbrunner, Dal.	.25
☐	153	Daymond Langkow, T.B.	.10
☐	154	Jay McKee, Buf.	.10
☐	155	Marty Murray, Cgy.	.10
☐	156	Wayne Primeau, Buf.	.10
☐	157	Jamie Pushor, Det.	.10
☐	158	Jamie Rivers, Stl.	.10
☐	159	Jamie Storr (G), L.A.	.25
☐	**160**	**Steve Sullivan, N.J., RC**	**.10**
☐	161	José Théodore (G), Mtl.	.35
☐	162	Roman Vopat, L.A.	.10
☐	163	Alexei Yegorov, S.J.	.10
☐	164	Daniel Alfredsson, Ott.	.25
☐	165	Niklas Andersson, NYI.	.10
☐	166	Todd Bertuzzi, NYI.	.25
☐	167	Valeri Bure, Mtl.	.10
☐	168	Eric Dazé, Chi.	.25
☐	169	Saku Koivu, Mtl.	.35
☐	170	Miroslav Satan, Edm.	.10
☐	171	Petr Sykora, N.J.	.10
☐	172	Cory Stillman, N.J.	.10
☐	173	Vitali Yachmenev, L.A.	.10
☐	174	Checklist 1-121	.10
☐	175	Checklist 120-/inserts	.10
☐		Instant Win - Peter Ferraro	.10

BLADE RUNNERS

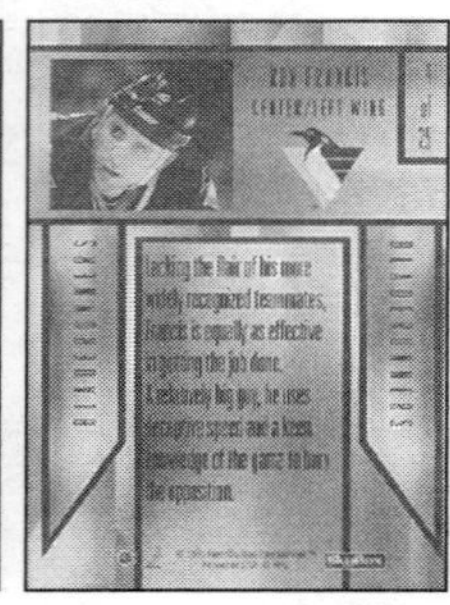

Insert Set (25 cards): 60.00

	No.	Player	NRMT-MT
□	1	Brian Bradley, T.B.	1.50
□	2	Chris Chelios, Chi.	3.00
□	3	Peter Forsberg, Col.	10.00
□	4	Ron Francis, Pgh.	3.00
□	5	Mike Gartner, Tor.	2.00
□	6	Doug Gilmour, Tor.	3.00
□	7	Phil Housley, N.J.	1.50
□	8	Brett Hull, Stl.	5.00
□	9	Valeri Kamensky, Col.	2.00
□	10	Pat LaFontaine, Buf.	2.00
□	11	John LeClair, Pha.	5.00
□	12	Claude Lemieux, Col.	1.50
□	13	Nicklas Lidström, Det.	2.00
□	14	Mark Messier, NYR.	5.00
□	15	Alexander Mogilny, Van.	3.00
□	16	Petr Nedved, Pgh.	1.50
□	17	Adam Oates, Bos.	3.00
□	18	Zigmund Palffy, NYI	3.00
□	19	Jeremy Roenick, Chi.	3.00
□	20	Teemu Selänne, Ana.	7.00
□	21	Brendan Shanahan, Hfd.	6.00
□	22	Keith Tkachuk, Pho.	4.00
□	23	Pierre Turgeon, Mtl.	2.00
□	24	Doug Weight, Edm.	3.00
□	25	Steve Yzerman, Det.	10.00

NHL ON FOX

Insert Set (20 cards): 60.00

	No.	Player	NRMT-MT
□	1	Daniel Alfredsson, Ott.	3.00
□	2	Todd Bertuzzi, NYI	3.00
□	3	Ray Bourque, Bos.	10.00
□	4	Valeri Bure, Mtl.	1.50
□	5	Chris Chelios, Chi.	8.00
□	6	Paul Coffey, Det.	3.00
□	7	Eric Dazé, Chi.	3.00
□	8	Eric Desjardins, Pha.	1.50
□	9	Sergei Gonchar, Wsh.	1.50
□	10	Phil Housley, N.J.	1.50
□	11	Ed Jovanovski, Fla.	3.00
□	12	Vladimir Konstatinov, Det.	1.50
□	13	Saku Koivu, Mtl.	15.00
□	14	Brian Leetch, NYR.	6.00
□	15	Larry Murphy, Tor.	3.00
□	16	Teppo Numminen, Pho.	1.50
□	17	Sandis Ozolinsh, Col.	3.00
□	18	Marcus Ragnarsson, S.J.	1.50
□	19	Petr Sykora, N.J.	1.50
□	20	Vitali Yachmenev, L.A.	1.50

ZERO HEROES

Insert Set (10 cards): 175.00

	No.	Player	NRMT-MT
□	1	Ed Belfour (G), Chi.	12.00
□	2	Sean Burke (G), Hfd.	8.00
□	3	Jim Carey (G), Wsh.	5.00
□	4	Dominik Hasek (G), Buf.	30.00
□	5	Ron Hextall (G), Pha.	8.00
□	6	Chris Osgood (G), Det.	18.00
□	7	Félix Potvin (G), Tor.	20.00
□	8	Daren Puppa (G), T.B.	5.00
□	9	Patrick Roy (G), Col.	70.00
□	10	John Vanbiesbrouck (G), Fla.	25.00

VERSA TEAM

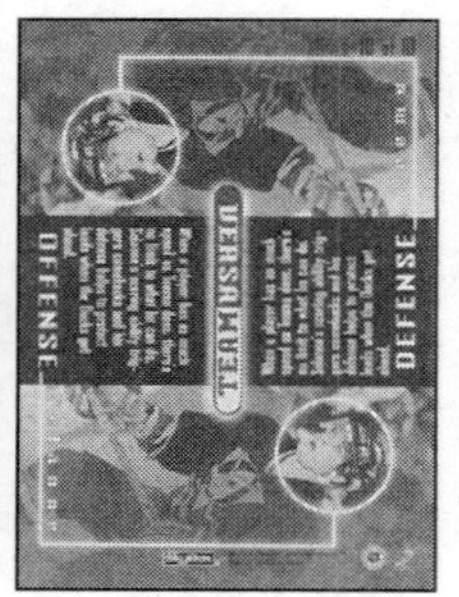

Insert Set (10 cards): 425.00

	No.	Player	NRMT-MT
□	1	Pavel Bure, Van.	30.00
□	2	Sergei Fedorov, Det.	20.00
□	3	Peter Forsberg, Col.	45.00
□	4	Wayne Gretzky, NYR.	90.00
□	5	Jaromir Jagr, Pgh.	45.00
□	6	Paul Kariya, Ana.	60.00
□	7	Mario Lemieux, Pgh.	75.00
□	8	Eric Lindros, Pha.	60.00
□	9	Joe Sakic, Col.	35.00
□	10	Teemu Selänne, Ana.	30.00

COUNTDOWN TO IMPACT

Insert Set (10 cards): 275.00

	No.	Player	NRMT-MT
□	1	Pavel Bure, Van.	20.00
□	2	Sergei Fedorov, Det.	15.00
□	3	Wayne Gretzky, NYR.	60.00
□	4	Jaromir Jagr, Pgh.	30.00
□	5	Ed Jovanovski, Fla.	8.00
□	6	Paul Kariya, Ana.	40.00
□	7	Mario Lemieux, Pgh.	50.00
□	8	Eric Lindros, Pha.	40.00
□	9	Patrick Roy, Col.	50.00
□	10	Joe Sakic, Col.	25.00

1996 - 97 SP

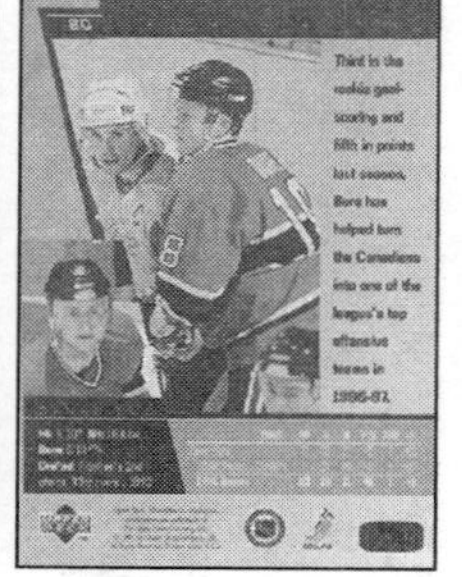

Imprint: © 1997 THE UPPER DECK COMPANY
Complete Set (188 cards): 55.00
Common Player: .20
Promo Card (Wayne Gretzky, #99): 10.00

	No.	Player	NRMT-MT
□	1	Paul Kariya, Ana.	3.50
□	2	Teemu Selänne, Ana.	1.75
□	3	Jari Kurri, Ana.	.50
□	4	Darren Van Impe, Ana.	.20
□	5	Guy Hebert, Ana.	.50
□	6	Steve Rucchin, Ana.	.20
□	7	Ray Bourque, Bos.	1.25
□	8	Kyle McLaren, Bos.	.20
□	9	Bill Ranford (G), Bos.	.50
□	10	Don Sweeney, Bos.	.20
□	11	Adam Oates, Bos.	.75
□	12	Rick Tocchet, Bos.	.20
□	13	Ted Donato, Bos.	.20
□	14	Curtis Brown, Buf.	.20
□	15	Pat LaFontaine, Buf.	.50
□	16	Derek Plante, Buf.	.20
□	17	Dominik Hasek (G), Buf.	1.75
□	18	Brian Holzinger, Buf.	.20
□	19	Alexei Zhitnik, Buf.	.20
□	20	Theoren Fleury, Cgy.	.75
□	21	Trevor Kidd (G), Cgy.	.50
□	22	Steve Chiasson, Cgy.	.20
□	23	Jarome Iginla, Cgy.	1.00
□	24	German Titov, Cgy.	.20
□	25	Zarley Zalapski, Cgy.	.20
□	26	Eric Dazé, Chi.	.50
□	27	Chris Chelios, Chi.	1.00
□	28	Ed Belfour (G), Chi.	.75
□	29	Gary Suter, Chi.	.20
□	30	Alexei Zhamnov, Chi.	.50
□	31	Ethan Moreau, Chi.	.50
□	32	Tony Amonte, Chi.	.50
□	33	Peter Forsberg, Col.	2.50
□	34	Joe Sakic, Col.	2.00
□	35	Patrick Roy (G), Col.	4.00
□	36	Adam Deadmarsh, Col.	.20
□	37	Mike Ricci, Col.	.20
□	38	Adam Foote, Col.	.50
□	39	Claude Lemieux, Col.	.20
□	40	Mike Modano, Dal.	1.25
□	41	Pat Verbeek, Dal.	.20
□	42	Todd Harvey, Dal.	.20
□	43	Sergei Zubov, Dal.	.50
□	44	Andy Moog (G), Dal.	.50
□	45	Derian Hatcher, Dal.	.50
□	46	Jamie Langenbrunner, Dal.	.50
□	47	Steve Yzerman, Det.	2.50
□	48	Sergei Fedorov, Det.	1.25
□	49	Vyacheslav Kozlov, Det.	.20
□	50	Brendan Shanahan, Det.	1.50
□	51	Chris Osgood (G), Det.	1.00
□	52	Nicklas Lidström, Det.	.50
□	53	Vladimir Konstantinov, Det.	.20
□	54	Curtis Joseph (G), Edm.	1.50
□	55	Jason Arnott, Edm.	.50
□	56	Ryan Smyth, Edm.	.50
□	57	Doug Weight, Edm.	.75
□	58	Andrei Kovalenko, Edm.	.20
□	59	Mariusz Czerkawski, Edm.	.20
□	60	Ed Jovanovski, Fla.	.50
□	61	John Vanbiesbrouck (G), Fla.	1.50
□	62	Rob Niedermayer, Fla.	.20
□	63	Robert Svehla, Fla.	.20
□	64	Brian Skrudland, Fla.	.20
□	65	Scott Mellanby, Fla.	.20
□	66	Ray Sheppard, Fla.	.20
□	67	Jeff O'Neill, Hfd.	.50
□	68	Keith Primeau, Hfd.	.50
□	69	Geoff Sanderson, Hfd.	.20
□	70	Sean Burke, Hfd.	.50
□	71	Kevin Dineen, Hfd.	.20
□	72	Andrew Cassels, Hfd.	.20
□	73	Kevin Stevens, L.A.	.20
□	74	Rob Blake, L.A.	.50
□	75	Ed Olczyk, L.A.	.20
□	76	Mattias Norstrom, L.A.	.20
□	77	Syéphane Fiset (G), L.A.	.50
□	78	Vitali Yachmenev, L.A.	.20
□	79	Saku Koivu, Mtl.	1.75
□	80	Valeri Bure, Mtl.	.20
□	81	Jocelyn Thibault (G), Mtl.	.75
□	82	David Wilkie, Mtl.	.20
□	83	Stéphane Richer, Mtl.	.20
□	84	Shayne Corson, Mtl.	.50
□	85	Mark Recchi, Mtl.	.50
□	86	Martin Brodeur (G), N.J.	1.75
□	87	Bobby Holik, N.J.	.20
□	88	Petr Sykora, N.J.	.20
□	89	Scott Stevens, N.J.	.20
□	90	Scott Niedermayer, N.J.	.50
□	91	Bill Guerin, N.J.	.50

	No.	Player	Price
☐	92	Eric Fichaud (G), NYI.	.50
☐	93	Kenny Jonsson, NYI.	.20
☐	94	Travis Green, NYI.	.20
☐	95	Derek King, NYI.	.20
☐	96	Todd Bertuzzi, NYI.	.50
☐	97	Zigmund Palffy, NYI.	.75
☐	98	Mark Messier, NYR.	1.25
☐	99	Wayne Gretzky, NYR.	5.00
☐	100	Mike Richter (G), NYR.	.75
☐	101	Brian Leetch, NYR.	.75
☐	102	Luc Robitaille, NYR.	.50
☐	103	Adam Graves, NYR.	.20
☐	104	Alexei Kovalev, NYR.	.20
☐	105	Radek Bonk, Ott.	.20
☐	106	Alexandre Daigle, Ott.	.50
☐	107	Daniel Alfredsson, Ott.	.20
☐	108	Alexei Yashin, Ott.	1.00
☐	**109**	**Andreas Dackell, Ott., RC**	**.20**
☐	110	Damian Rhodes (G), Ott.	.20
☐	111	Petr Svoboda, Pha.	.20
☐	112	John LeClair, Pha.	1.25
☐	113	Eric Desjardins, Pha.	.20
☐	114	Eric Lindros, Pha.	3.50
☐	115	Mikael Renberg, Pha.	.20
☐	116	Ron Hextall (G), Pha.	.50
☐	**117**	**Danius Zubrus, Pha., RC**	**4.00**
☐	118	Keith Tkachuk, Pho.	1.00
☐	119	Jeremy Roenick, Pho.	.75
☐	120	Nikolai Khabibulin (G), Pho.	.75
☐	121	Oleg Tverdovsky, Pho.	.20
☐	122	Teppo Numminen, Pho.	.20
☐	123	Mike Gartner, Pho.	.50
☐	124	Cliff Ronning, Pho.	.20
☐	125	Mario Lemieux, Pgh.	4.00
☐	126	Jaromir Jagr, Pgh.	2.50
☐	127	Ron Francis, Pgh.	.75
☐	128	Petr Nedved, Pgh.	.20
☐	129	Darius Kasparaitis, Pgh.	.20
☐	130	Kevin Hatcher, Pgh.	.20
☐	131	Joe Mullen, Pgh.	.20
☐	132	Joe Murphy, Stl.	.20
☐	133	Grant Fuhr (G), Stl.	.50
☐	**134**	**Harry York, Stl., RC**	**.20**
☐	135	Chris Pronger, Stl.	.50
☐	136	Brett Hull, Stl.	1.25
☐	137	Pierre Turgeon, Stl.	.50
☐	138	Owen Nolan, S.J.	.50
☐	139	Bernie Nicholls, S.J.	.20
☐	140	Tony Granato, S.J.	.20
☐	141	Kelly Hrudey, S.J.	.20
☐	142	Darren Turcotte, S.J.	.20
☐	143	Jeff Friesen, S.J.	.50
☐	144	Roman Hamrlik, T.B.	.50
☐	145	Chris Gratton, T.B.	.50
☐	146	Daymond Langkow, T.B.	.20
☐	147	Dino Ciccarelli, T.B.	.50
☐	148	Alexander Selivanov, T.B.	.20
☐	149	Brian Bradley, T.B.	.20
☐	150	Wendel Clark, Tor.	.50
☐	151	Mats Sundin, Tor.	1.25
☐	152	Doug Gilmour, Tor.	.75
☐	153	Félix Potvin (G), Tor.	1.25
☐	154	Larry Murphy, Tor.	.20
☐	155	Mathieu Schneider, Tor.	.20
☐	156	Kirk Muller, Tor.	.20
☐	157	Pavel Bure, Van.	1.75
☐	158	Alexander Mogilny, Van.	.75
☐	159	Corey Hirsch (G), Van.	.20
☐	160	Jyrki Lumme, Van.	.20
☐	161	Russ Courtnall, Van.	.20
☐	**162**	**Mike Fountain (G), Van., RC**	**.20**
☐	163	Peter Bondra, Wsh.	1.00
☐	164	Jim Carey (G), Wsh.	.20
☐	165	Sergei Gonchar, Wsh.	.20
☐	166	Joé Juneau, Wsh.	.20
☐	167	Phil Housley, Wsh.	.20
☐	168	Jason Allison, Wsh.	.75
☐	169	Ruslan Salei, Ana.	.20
☐	**170**	**Mattias Timander, Bos., RC**	**.20**
☐	**171**	**Vaclav Varada, Buf., RC**	**.50**
☐	172	Jonas Hoglund, Cgy.	.20
☐	173	Jason Podollan, Fla.	.20
☐	174	José Théodore (G), Mtl.	1.00
☐	**175**	**Roman Turek (G), Dal., RC**	**.35**
☐	176	Anders Eriksson, Det.	.20
☐	**177**	**Mike Grier, Edm., RC**	**1.25**
☐	**178**	**Rem Murray, Edm., RC**	**.50**
☐	179	Per Gustafsson, Fla.	.20
☐	180	Jay Pandolfo, N.J., Error (/b: Patrick Elias)	.50
☐	**181**	**Kai Nurminen, L.A., RC**	**.20**
☐	182	Bryan Berard, NYI.	1.00
☐	183	Christian Dubé, NYR.	.50
☐	**184**	**Daniel Goneau, NYR., RC**	**.20**
☐	185	Wade Redden, Ott.	.50
☐	186	Janne Niinimaa, Pha.	.50
☐	187	Jim Campbell, Stl.	.50
☐	**188**	**Sergei Berezin, Tor., RC**	**1.25**

SP^{X} FORCE

	No.	Player	NRMT-MT
☐	1	E. Lindros, Pha./M. Lemieux, Pgh./ P. Forsberg, Col./W. Gretzky, NYR.	275.00
☐	2	B. Hull, Stl./J. Jagr, Pgh./ P. Bure, Van./T. Selänne, Ana.	200.00
☐	3	C. Osgood, Det./D. Hasek, Buf./ M. Brodeur, N.J./M. Richter, NYR.	175.00
☐	4	A. Eriksson, Det./B. Berard, NYI./ J. Iginla, Cgy./S. Berezin, Tor.	100.00
☐	5	J. Iginla, Cgy./J. Jagr, Pgh./ W. Gretzky, NYR./M. Brodeur, N.J.	250.00

SP^{X} FORCE AUTOGRAPHS

	Player	NRMT-MT
☐	Wayne Gretzky, NYR.	2,200.00
☐	Jaromir Jagr, Pgh.	800.00
☐	Martin Brodeur (G), N.J.	500.00
☐	Jarome Iginla, Cgy.	235.00

INSIDE INFO

These pull-out cards (seeded one per box) have two versions: the regular version and a gold parallel.

	Player	Gold	Reg.
Insert Set (8 cards):		**550.00**	**115.00**
☐ ☐	Wayne Gretzky, NYR.	200.00	40.00
☐ ☐	Keith Tkachuk, Pho.	35.00	8.00
☐ ☐	Brendan Shanahan, Det.	60.00	12.00
☐ ☐	Teemu Selänne, Ana.	75.00	15.00
☐ ☐	Ray Bourque, Bos.	40.00	10.00
☐ ☐	Joe Sakic, Col.	90.00	18.00
☐ ☐	Félix Potvin (G), Tor.	60.00	12.00
☐ ☐	Steve Yzerman, Det.	100.00	20.00

CLEARCUT WINNER

Insert Set (20 cards): **900.00**

	No.	Player	NRMT-MT
☐	CW1	Wayne Gretzky, NYR.	160.00
☐	CW2	Saku Koivu, Mtl.	50.00
☐	CW3	Mario Lemieux, Pgh.	120.00
☐	CW4	Sergei Fedorov, Det.	35.00
☐	CW5	Paul Kariya, Ana.	90.00
☐	CW6	Patrick Roy (G), Col.	120.00
☐	CW7	Jeremy Roenick, Pho.	20.00
☐	CW8	Brendan Shanahan, Det.	45.00
☐	CW9	John Vanbiesbrouck (G), Fla.	45.00
☐	CW10	Doug Weight, Edm.	20.00
☐	CW11	Mark Messier, NYR.	35.00
☐	CW12	Mats Sundin, Tor.	35.00
☐	CW13	Paul Coffey, Pha.	12.00
☐	CW14	Theoren Fleury, Cgy.	20.00
☐	CW15	Steve Yzerman, Det.	75.00
☐	CW16	Pavel Bure, Van.	55.00
☐	CW17	Adam Deadmarsh, Col.	12.00
☐	CW18	Chris Chelios, Chi.	30.00
☐	CW19	Joe Sakic, Col.	60.00
☐	CW20	Eric Dazé, Chi.	12.00

HOLOVIEW COLLECTION

Insert Set (30 cards): **160.00**

	No.	Player	NRMT-MT
☐	HC1	Wayne Gretzky, NYR.	35.00
☐	HC2	Eric Dazé, Chi.	4.00
☐	HC3	Doug Gilmour, Tor.	5.00
☐	HC4	Jason Arnott, Edm.	4.00
☐	HC5	Sergei Fedorov, Det.	8.50
☐	HC6	Chris Chelios, Chi.	7.00
☐	HC7	Alexei Kovalev, NYR.	3.00
☐	HC8	Pat LaFontaine, Buf.	4.00
☐	HC9	Daniel Alfredsson, Ott.	4.00
☐	HC10	Chris Pronger, Stl.	4.00
☐	HC11	Jocelyn Thibault (G), Mtl.	5.00
☐	HC12	Chris Gratton, T.B.	4.00
☐	HC13	Alexei Yashin, Ott.	7.00
☐	HC14	Peter Bondra, Wsh.	7.00
☐	HC15	Saku Koivu, Mtl.	12.00
☐	HC16	Valeri Bure, Mtl.	3.00
☐	HC17	Joé Juneau, Wsh.	3.00
☐	HC18	Tony Amonte, Chi.	4.00
☐	HC19	Brian Holzinger, Buf.	3.00
☐	HC20	Mats Sundin, Tor.	8.50
☐	HC21	Chris Osgood (G), Det.	7.00
☐	HC22	Roman Hamrlik, T.B.	4.00
☐	HC23	Ray Bourque, Bos.	8.50
☐	HC24	Doug Weight, Edm.	5.00
☐	HC25	Mike Modano, Dal.	8.50
☐	HC26	Niklas Sundstrom, NYR.	3.00
☐	HC27	Mike Richter (G), NYR.	5.00
☐	HC28	Zigmund Palffy, NYI.	5.00
☐	HC29	Adam Oates, Bos.	5.00
☐	HC30	Dominik Hasek (G), Buf.	12.00

GAME FILM

Insert Set (20 cards): **375.00**

	No.	Player	NRMT-MT
☐	GF1	Wayne Gretzky, NYR.	75.00
☐	GF2	Peter Forsberg, Col.	35.00
☐	GF3	Patrick Roy (G), Col.	55.00
☐	GF4	Brett Hull, Stl.	17.50
☐	GF5	Keith Tkachuk, Pho.	12.00
☐	GF6	Eric Lindros, Pha.	45.00
☐	GF7	Félix Potvin (G), Tor.	17.50
☐	GF8	John Vanbiesbourck (G), Fla.	20.00
☐	GF9	Paul Kariya, Ana.	45.00
☐	GF10	Mark Messier, NYR.	17.50
☐	GF11	Ed Belfour (G), Chi.	9.00
☐	GF12	Alexander Mogilny, Van.	9.00
☐	GF13	Jim Carey (G), Wsh.	6.00
☐	GF14	Ed Jovanovski, Fla.	8.00
☐	GF15	Theoren Fleury, Cgy.	9.00
☐	GF16	Doug Gilmour, Tor.	9.00
☐	GF17	John LeClair, Pha.	17.50
☐	GF18	Pat LaFontaine, Buf.	8.00
☐	GF19	Paul Coffey, Hfd.	8.00
☐	GF20	Daniel Alfredsson, Ott.	8.00

1996 - 97 SPX

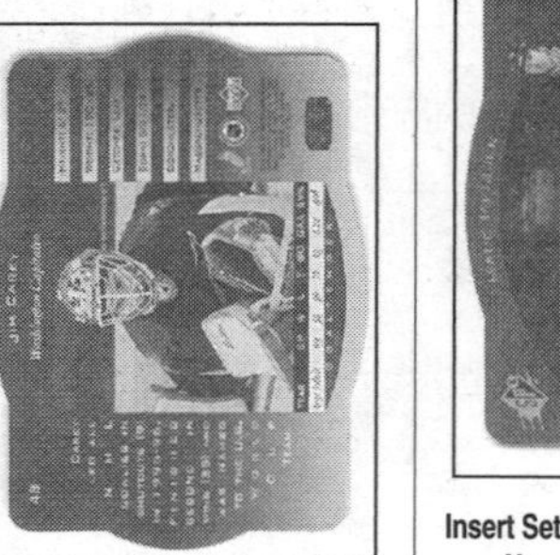

These cards have two versions: the regular card (white lettering on back) and a gold parallel (black lettering on back).

Imprint: © 1996 THE UPPER DECK COMPANY

	No.	Player	Reg.	Gold
Complete Set (50 cards):			110.00	400.00
☐ ☐	1	Paul Kariya, Ana.	7.50	30.00
☐ ☐	2	Teemu Selänne, Ana.	4.00	12.00
☐ ☐	3	Ray Bourque, Bos.	3.00	9.00
☐ ☐	4	Cam Neely, Bos.	1.50	4.00
☐ ☐	5	Theoren Fleury, Cgy.	2.00	5.00
☐ ☐	6	Chris Chelios, Chi.	2.50	7.00
☐ ☐	7	Jeremy Roenick, Chi.	2.00	5.00
☐ ☐	8	Peter Fosberg, Col.	6.00	20.00
☐ ☐	9	Joe Sakic, Col.	5.00	15.00
☐ ☐	10	Patrick Roy, Col.	10.00	45.00
☐ ☐	11	Mike Modano, Dal.	3.00	9.00
☐ ☐	12	Joe Nieuwendyk, Dal.	1.50	4.00
☐ ☐	13	Sergei Fedorov, Det.	3.00	9.00
☐ ☐	14	Steve Yzerman, Det.	6.00	20.00
☐ ☐	15	Paul Coffey, Det.	1.50	4.00
☐ ☐	16	Chris Osgood, Det.	2.50	7.00
☐ ☐	17	Doug Weight, Edm.	2.00	5.00
☐ ☐	18	Pat LaFontaine, Buf.	1.50	4.00
☐ ☐	19	Brendan Shanahan, Hfd.	3.50	10.00
☐ ☐	20	Vitali Yachmenev, L.A.	1.00	2.50
☐ ☐	21	Saku Koivu, Mtl.	4.00	12.00
☐ ☐	22	Pierre Turgeon, Mtl.	1.50	4.00
☐ ☐	23	Petr Sykora, N.J.	1.00	2.50
☐ ☐	24	Scott Stevens, N.J.	1.00	2.50
☐ ☐	25	Martin Brodeur, N.J.	4.00	12.00
☐ ☐	26	Brian Leetch, NYR.	2.00	5.00
☐ ☐	27	Mark Messier, NYR.	3.00	9.00
☐ ☐	28	Mike Richter, NYR.	2.00	5.00
☐ ☐	29	Zigmund Palffy, NYI.	2.00	5.00
☐ ☐	30	Todd Bertuzzi, NYI.	1.50	4.00
☐ ☐	31	Alexei Yashin, Ott.	2.50	7.00
☐ ☐	32	Daniel Alfredsson, Ott.	1.50	7.00
☐ ☐	33	Eric Lindros, Pha.	7.50	30.00
☐ ☐	34	John LeClair, Pha.	3.00	9.00
☐ ☐	35	Keith Tkachuk, Wpg.	2.50	7.00
☐ ☐	36	Alexei Zhamnov, Wpg.	1.50	4.00
☐ ☐	37	Mario Lemieux, Pgh.	10.00	45.00
☐ ☐	38	Jaromir Jagr, Pgh.	6.00	20.00
☐ ☐	39	Wayne Gretzky, NYR.	15.00	50.00
☐ ☐	40	Brett Hull, Stl.	3.00	9.00
☐ ☐	41	Owen Nolan, S.J.	1.50	4.00
☐ ☐	42	Roman Hamrlik, T.B.	1.50	4.00
☐ ☐	43	Mats Sundin, Tor.	3.00	9.00
☐ ☐	44	Félix Potvin, Tor.	3.00	9.00
☐ ☐	45	Doug Gilmour, Tor.	2.00	5.00
☐ ☐	46	Pavel Bure, Van.	4.00	12.00
☐ ☐	47	Alexander Mogilny, Van.	2.00	5.00
☐ ☐	48	Jim Carey, Wsh.	1.00	2.50
☐ ☐	49	Peter Bondra, Wsh.	2.50	7.00
☐ ☐	50	Eric Dazé, Chi.	1.50	4.00

	No.	Inserts	NRMT-MT
☐	GF1	W. Gretzky, NYR./V. Yachmenev, L.A.; E. Dazé, Chi./D. Alfredsson, Ott./S. Koivu, Mtl.	25.00
☐	GT1	Wayne Gretzky, Edm.	30.00
☐		Wayne Gretzky Autograph	450.00

HOLOVIEW

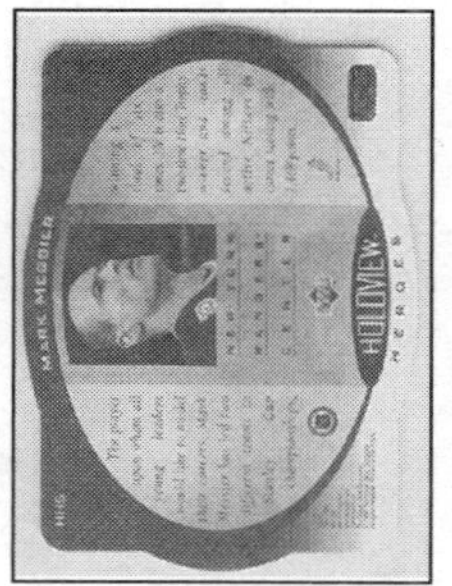

	No.	Player	NRMT-MT
Insert Set (10 cards):			175.00
☐	HH1	Ray Bourque, Bos.	12.00
☐	HH2	Patrick Roy (G), Col.	40.00
☐	HH3	Steve Yzerman, Det.	25.00
☐	HH4	Paul Coffey, Det.	6.00
☐	HH5	Mark Messier, NYR.	12.00
☐	HH6	Mario Lemieux, Pgh.	40.00
☐	HH7	Wayne Gretzky, NYR.	50.00
☐	HH8	Brett Hull, Stl.	12.00
☐	HH9	Doug Gilmour, Tor.	7.50
☐	HH10	Grant Fuhr, Stl.	6.00

1996 - 97 SPORTFX MINI STIX

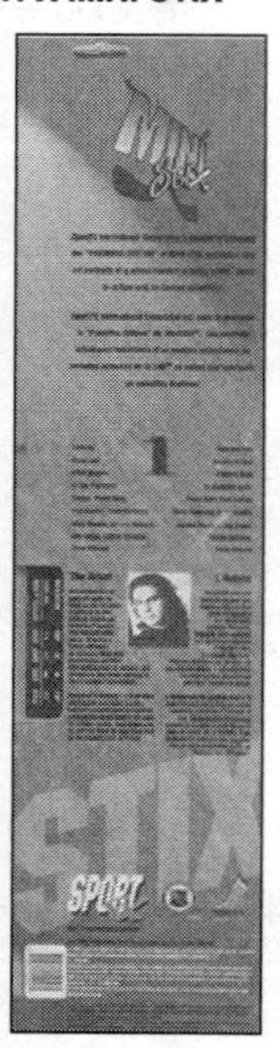

Some sticks were produced in fewer quantities. No more than 6,500 copies were produced of any player. Players portraits are done by Tony Piacente.

Imprint: SPORTS FX INTERNATIONAL CORPORATION

	Player	NRMT-MT
☐	Daniel Alfredsson, Ott.	20.00
☐	Pavel Bure, Van.	20.00
☐	Chris Chelios, Chi.	15.00
☐	Theoren Fleury, Cgy.	20.00
☐	Peter Forsberg, Col.	20.00
☐	Doug Gilmour, Tor.	15.00
☐	Brett Hull, Stl.	15.00
☐	Jaromir Jagr, Pgh.	20.00
☐	Ed Jovanovski, Fla.	15.00
☐	Paul Kariya, Ana.	30.00
☐	Saku Koivu, Mtl.	25.00
☐	Mario Lemieux, Pgh.	30.00
☐	Eric Lindros, Pha.	25.00
☐	Jeremy Roenick, Pho.	15.00
☐	Joe Sakic, Col.	20.00
☐	Teemu Selänne, Ana.	20.00
☐	Mats Sundin, Tor.	20.00
☐	Steve Yzerman, Det.	25.00

1996 - 97 TOPPS NHL PICKS

These cards have two versions: the regular card and an O-Pee-Chee parallel. See Fleer NHL Picks for corresponding even numbers.

Imprint: © 1996 THE TOPPS COMPANY, INC.

	No.	Player	TOPPS	OPC
Complete Set (91 cards):			15.00	120.00
Common Player:			.10	.50
☐ ☐	1	Jaromir Jagr, Pgh.	1.00	10.00
☐ ☐	3	Mario Lemieux, Pgh	1.50	15.00
☐ ☐	5	Peter Forsberg, Col.	1.00	10.00
☐ ☐	7	Teemu Selänne, Ana.	.75	7.50
☐ ☐	9	Alexander Mogilny, Van.	.35	1.50
☐ ☐	11	Patrick Roy (G), Col.	1.50	15.00
☐ ☐	13	Jim Carey (G), Wsh.	.10	.50
☐ ☐	15	Pavel Bure, Van.	.75	7.50
☐ ☐	17	Sergei Fedorov, Det.	.50	4.00
☐ ☐	19	Chris Chelios, Chi.	.35	2.00
☐ ☐	21	Sandis Ozolinsh, Col.	.25	.75
☐ ☐	23	Doug Weight, Edm.	.35	1.50
☐ ☐	25	Mark Messier, NYR.	.50	4.00
☐ ☐	27	Martin Brodeur (G) N.J.	.75	7.50
☐ ☐	29	Brett Hull, Stl.	.50	4.00
☐ ☐	31	Steve Yzerman, Det.	1.00	10.00
☐ ☐	33	Kevin Hatcher, Dal.	.10	.50
☐ ☐	35	Roman Hamrlik, T.B.	.25	.75
☐ ☐	37	Petr Nedved, Pgh.	.10	.50
☐ ☐	39	Valeri Kamensky, Col.	.25	.75
☐ ☐	41	Gary Suter, Chi.	.10	.50
☐ ☐	43	Mats Sundin, Tor.	.50	4.00
☐ ☐	45	Trevor Linden, Van.	.25	.75
☐ ☐	47	Jeremy Roenick, Chi.	.35	1.50
☐ ☐	49	Al MacInnis, Stl.	.10	.50
☐ ☐	51	Mike Modano, Dal.	.50	4.00
☐ ☐	53	Mathieu Schneider, NYI.	.10	.50
☐ ☐	55	Michal Pivonka, Wsh.	.10	.50
☐ ☐	57	Owen Nolan, S.J.	.25	.75
☐ ☐	59	Martin Rucinsky, Mtl.	.10	.50
☐ ☐	61	Joe Nieuwendyk, Dal.	.25	.75
☐ ☐	63	Mark Recchi, Mtl.	.25	.75
☐ ☐	65	Geoff Sanderson, Hfd.	.10	.50
☐ ☐	67	Vyacheslav Koslov, Det.	.10	.50
☐ ☐	69	Pat Verbeek, NYR.	.10	.50
☐ ☐	71	Brian Bradley, T.B.	.10	.50
☐ ☐	73	Steve Duchesne, Ott.	.10	.50
☐ ☐	75	Steve Thomas, N.J.	.10	.50
☐ ☐	77	Eric Dazé, Chi.	.25	.75
☐ ☐	79	Alexei Kovalev, NYR.	.10	.50
☐ ☐	81	Kevin Stevens, L.A.	.10	.50
☐ ☐	83	Curtis Joseph (G), Edm.	.60	5.00
☐ ☐	85	Bill Ranford (G), Bos.	.25	.75
☐ ☐	87	Luc Robitaille, NYR.	.25	.75
☐ ☐	89	Claude Lemieux, Col.	.10	.50
☐ ☐	91	Sergei Gonchar, Wsh.	.10	.50
☐ ☐	93	Eric Desjardins, Pha.	.10	.50
☐ ☐	95	Garry Galley, Pha.	.10	.50
☐ ☐	97	Oleg Tverdovsky, Wpg.	.10	.50
☐ ☐	99	Rob Niedermayer, Fla.	.10	.50
☐ ☐	101	Scott Mellanby, Fla.	.10	.50
☐ ☐	103	Adam Deadmarsh, Col.	.10	.50
☐ ☐	105	Cliff Ronning, Van.	.10	.50
☐ ☐	107	Russ Courtnall, Van.	.10	.50
☐ ☐	109	Keith Primeau, Det.	.25	.75
☐ ☐	111	Rick Tocchet, Bos.	.10	.50
☐ ☐	113	Scott Young, Col.	.10	.50
☐ ☐	115	Scott Stevens, N.J.	.10	.50
☐ ☐	117	Al Iafrate, Bos.	.10	.50
☐ ☐	119	Ray Ferraro, L.A.	.10	.50
☐ ☐	121	Todd Bertuzzi, NYI.	.25	.75

		No.	Player		
☐	☐	123	Alexander Selivanov, T.B.	.10	.50
☐	☐	125	Steve Chiasson, Cgy.	.10	.50
☐	☐	127	Dave Andreychuk, N.J.	.10	.50
☐	☐	129	Ray Sheppard, Fla.	.10	.50
☐	☐	131	Bernie Nicholls, Chi.	.10	.50
☐	☐	133	Tony Amonte, Chi.	.25	.75
☐	☐	135	Nelson Emerson, Hfd.	.10	.50
☐	☐	137	Cam Neely, Bos.	.25	.75
☐	☐	139	Shayne Corson, Stl.	.25	.75
☐	☐	141	Bill Guerin, N.J.	.25	.75
☐	☐	143	Joe Murphy, Chi.	.10	.50
☐	☐	145	Cory Stillman, Cgy.	.10	.50
☐	☐	147	Radik Bonk, Ott.	.10	.50
☐	☐	149	Geoff Courtnall, Stl	.10	.50
☐	☐	151	Chad Kilger, Wpg.	.10	.50
☐	☐	153	Sylvain Côté, Wsh.	.10	.50
☐	☐	155	Glen Wesley, Hfd.	.10	.50
☐	☐	157	Jeff Norton, Edm.	.10	.50
☐	☐	159	Rob Blake, L.A.	.25	.75
☐	☐	161	Calle Johansson, Wsh.	.10	.50
☐	☐	163	Uwe Krupp, Col.	.10	.50
☐	☐	165	James Patrick, Cgy.	.10	.50
☐	☐	167	Dimitri Mironov, Pgh.	.10	.50
☐	☐	169	Vladimir Konstantinov, Det.	.10	.50
☐	☐	171	Mattias Norstrom, NYR.	.10	.50
☐	☐	173	David Wilkie, Mtl.	.10	.50
☐	☐	175	Bryan McCabe, NYI	.10	.50
☐	☐	177	Barry Richter, NYR. (Bos.)	.10	.50
☐	☐	179	Ed Belfour (G), Chi.	.35	1.50
☐	☐		Checklist	.10	.50

ROOKIE STAR

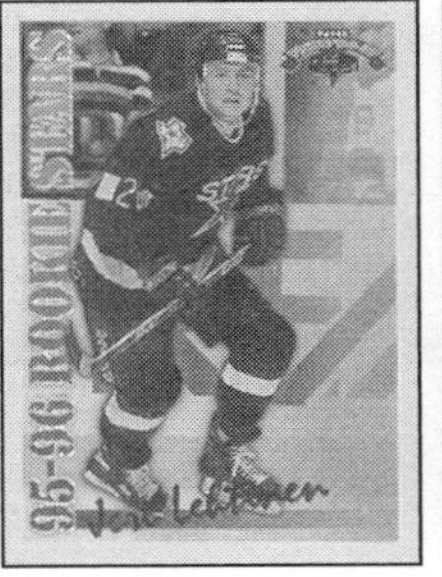

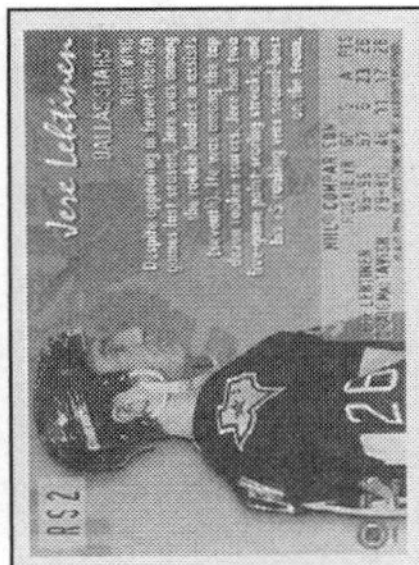

These cards have two versions: the regular card and an O-Pee-Chee parallel.

Insert Set (18 cards): 12.00 TOPPS, 40.00 OPC

		No.	Player	TOPPS	OPC
☐	☐	RS1	Daniel Alfredsson, Ott.	.75	4.00
☐	☐	RS2	Jere Lehtinen, Dal.	.75	4.00
☐	☐	RS3	Vitali Yachmenev, L.A.	.35	2.00
☐	☐	RS4	Eric Dazé, Chi.	.75	4.00
☐	☐	RS5	Saku Koivu, Mtl.	3.00	25.00
☐	☐	RS6	Petr Sykora, N.J.	.35	2.00
☐	☐	RS7	Marcus Ragnarsson, S.J.	.35	2.00
☐	☐	RS8	Valeri Bure, Mtl.	.35	2.00
☐	☐	RS9	Cory Stillman, Cgy.	.35	2.00
☐	☐	RS10	Todd Bertuzzi, NYI.	.75	4.00
☐	☐	RS11	Ed Jovanovski, Fla.	.75	4.00
☐	☐	RS12	Miroslav Satan, Edm.	.35	2.00
☐	☐	RS13	Kyle McLaren, Bos.	.35	2.00
☐	☐	RS14	Bryan Dafoe (G), L.A.	.35	2.00
☐	☐	RS15	Eric Fichaud (G), NYI.	.75	4.00
☐	☐	RS16	Corey Hirsch (G), Van.	.35	2.00
☐	☐	RS17	Jeff O'Neill, Hfd.	.75	4.00
☐	☐	RS18	Niklas Sundstrom, NYR.	.35	2.00

THE FIVE HUNDRED CLUB

Insert Set (8 cards): 80.00

	No.	Player	NRMT-MT
☐	FC1	Wayne Gretzky, Stl.	30.00
☐	FC2	Mike Gartner,Tor.	4.00
☐	FC3	Dino Ciccarelli, Det.	4.00
☐	FC4	Jari Kurri, NYR.	4.00
☐	FC5	Mario Lemieux, Pgh.	25.00
☐	FC6	Mark Messier, NYR.	7.50
☐	FC7	Steve Yzerman, Det.	15.00
☐	FC8	Dale Hawerchuk, Pha.	4.00

FANTASY TEAM

Insert Set (22 cards): 175.00

	No.	Player	NRMT-MT
☐	FT1	Patrick Roy (G), Col.	20.00
☐	FT2	Chris Osgood (G), Det.	5.00
☐	FT3	Martin Brodeur (G), N.J.	8.00
☐	FT4	Ray Bourque, Bos.	6.00
☐	FT5	Brian Leetch, NYR.	4.00
☐	FT6	Chris Chelios, Chi.	5.00
☐	FT7	Paul Coffey, Det.	3.00
☐	FT8	Ed Jovanovski, Fla.	3.00
☐	FT9	Roman Hamrlik, T.B.	3.00
☐	FT10	Wayne Gretzky, Stl.	25.00
☐	FT11	Paul Kariya, Ana.	15.00
☐	FT12	Brett Hull, Stl.	6.00
☐	FT13	Pavel Bure, Van.	8.00
☐	FT14	Jaromir Jagr, Pgh.	12.00
☐	FT15	Mario Lemieux, Pgh.	20.00
☐	FT16	Peter Forsberg, Col.	12.00
☐	FT17	Sergei Fedorov, Det.	8.00
☐	FT18	Jeremy Roenick, Chi.	4.00
☐	FT19	Alexander Mogilny, Van.	4.00
☐	FT20	Joe Sakic, Col.	10.00
☐	FT21	Teemu Selänne, Ana.	8.00
☐	FT22	Eric Lindros, Pha.	15.00

ICE D

Insert Set (15 cards): 125.00

	No.	Player	NRMT-MT
☐	ID1	Brian Leetch, NYR.	6.00
☐	ID2	Ray Bourque, Bos.	10.00
☐	ID3	Chris Chelios, Chi.	8.00
☐	ID4	Scott Stevens, N.J.	3.00
☐	ID5	Ed Jovanovski, Fla.	4.00
☐	ID6	Martin Brodeur (G), N.J.	15.00
☐	ID7	Patrick Roy (G), Col.	35.00
☐	ID8	Chris Osgood (G), Det.	8.00
☐	ID9	Jim Carey (G), Wsh.	3.00
☐	ID10	Dominik Hasek (G), Buf.	15.00
☐	ID11	Ron Hextall (G), Pha.	4.00
☐	ID12	John Vanbiesbrouck (G), Fla.	12.00
☐	ID13	Mike Richter (G), NYR.	6.00
☐	ID14	Félix Potvin (G), Tor.	10.00
☐	ID15	Grant Fuhr (G), Stl.	4.00

TOP SHELF

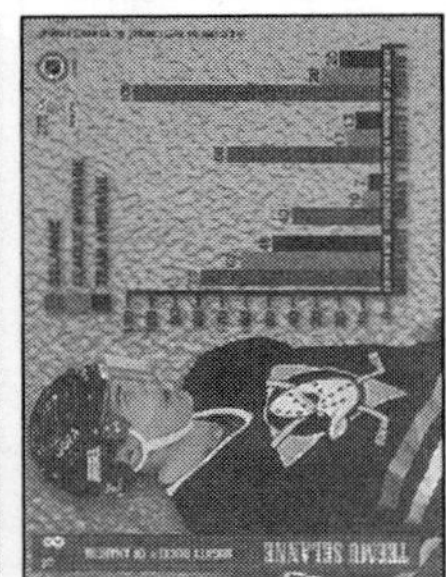

Insert Set (15 cards): 125.00

	No.	Player	NRMT-MT
☐	TS1	John LeClair, Pha.	6.00
☐	TS2	Wayne Gretzky, Stl.	25.00
☐	TS3	Eric Lindros, Pha.	15.00
☐	TS4	Paul Kariya, Ana.	15.00
☐	TS5	Mark Messier, NYR.	6.00
☐	TS6	Jaromir Jagr, Pgh.	12.00
☐	TS7	Peter Forsberg, Col.	12.00
☐	TS8	Teemu Selänne, Ana.	8.00
☐	TS9	Alexander Mogilny, Van.	3.50
☐	TS10	Brett Hull, Stl.	6.00
☐	TS11	Sergei Fedorov, Det.	6.00
☐	TS12	Joe Sakic, Col.	10.00
☐	TS13	Mats Sundin, Tor.	6.00
☐	TS14	Theoren Fleury, Cgy.	3.50
☐	TS15	Steve Yzerman, Det.	12.00

1996 - 97 ULTIMATE LINE-UP TEAM-OUT

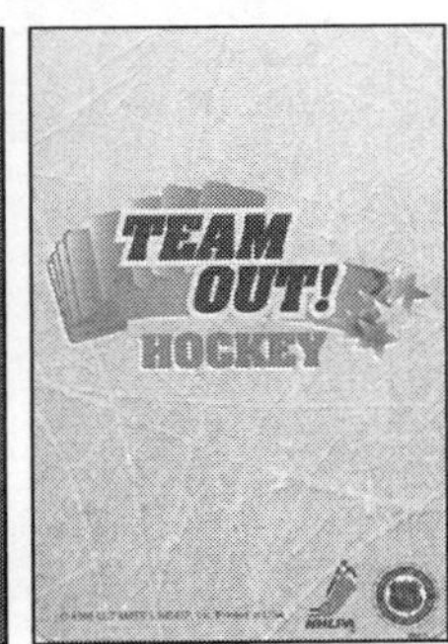

Imprint: © 1996 ULTIMATE LINE-UP, INC.

Complete Set (89 cards): 25.00

Common Player: .15

	Player	NRMT-MT
☐	Daniel Alfredsson, Ott.	.35
☐	Jason Arnott, Edm.	.35
☐	Ed Belfour (G), Chi.	.75
☐	Rob Blake, L.A.	.35
☐	Peter Bondra, Wsh.	1.00
☐	Ray Bourque, Bos.	1.25
☐	Martin Brodeur (G), N.J.	1.75
☐	Jeff Brown, Hfd.	.15
☐	Pavel Bure, Van.	1.75
☐	Jim Carey (G), Wsh.	.15
☐	Chris Chelios, Chi.	1.00
☐	Paul Coffey, Hfd.	.35
☐	Shayne Corson, Stl.	.35
☐	Murray Craven, Chi.	.15
☐	Eric Dazé, Chi.	.35
☐	Eric Desjardins, Pha.	.15
☐	Steve Duchesne, Ott.	.15
☐	Sergei Fedorov, Det.	1.25
☐	Theoren Fleury, Cgy.	.75
☐	Peter Forsberg, Col.	2.50
☐	Grant Fuhr (G), Stl.	.35
☐	Mike Gartner, Pho.	.35
☐	Sergei Gonchar, Wsh.	.15
☐	Chris Gratton, T.B.	.35
☐	Adam Graves, NYR.	.15
☐	Wayne Gretzky, NYR.	6.00
☐	Roman Hamrlik, T.B.	.35
☐	Dominik Hasek (G), Buf.	1.75

	Player	Price
□	Derian Hatcher, Dal.	.35
□	Guy Hebert (G), Ana.	.35
□	Ron Hextall (G), Pha.	.35
□	Brett Hull, Stl.	1.25
□	Jaromir Jagr, Pgh.	2.50
□	Ed Jovanovski, Fla.	.35
□	Joé Juneau, Wsh.	.15
□	Paul Kariya, Ana.	3.50
□	Darius Kasparaitis, NYI.	.15
□	Nikolai Khabibulin (G), Pho.	.75
□	Trevor Kidd (G), Cgy.	.35
□	Saku Koivu, Mtl.	1.75
□	Vyacheslav Kozlov, Det.	.15
□	John LeClair, Pha.	1.25
□	Brian Leetch, NYR.	.75
□	Mario Lemieux, Pgh.	4.00
□	Claude Lemieux, Col.	.15
□	Nicklas Lidström, Det.	.35
□	Eric Lindros, Phi.	3.50
□	Jyrki Lumme, Van.	.15
□	Al MacInnis, Stl.	.15
□	Vladimir Malakhov, Mtl,	.15
□	Kirk McLean (G), Van.	.35
□	Scott Mellanby, Fla.	.15
□	Mark Messier, NYR.	1.25
□	Mike Modano, Dal.	1.25
□	Alexander Mogilny, Van.	.75
□	Larry Murphy, Tor.	.35
□	Scott Niedermayer, N.J.	.35
□	Owen Nolan, S.J.	.35
□	Adam Oates, Bos.	.75
□	Chris Osgood (G), Det.	1.00
□	Sandis Ozolinsh, Col.	.35
□	Zigmund Palffy, NYI.	1.00
□	Félix Potvin (G), Tor.	1.25
□	Stéphane Quintal, Mtl.	.15
□	Marcus Ragnarsson, S.J.	.15
□	Mikael Renberg, Pha.	.15
□	Stéphane Richer, Tor.	.15
□	Mike Richter (G), NYR.	.75
□	Luc Robitaille, NYR.	.35
□	Patrick Roy (G), Col.	4.00
□	Joe Sakic, Col.	2.00
□	Mathieu Schneider, Tor.	.15
□	Teemu Selänne, Ana.	1.75
□	Ryan Smyth, Edm.	.35
□	Scott Stevens, N.J.	.15
□	Keven Stevens, L.A.	.15
□	Mats Sundin, Tor.	1.25
□	Gary Suter, Chi.	.15
□	Robert Svehla, Fla.	.15
□	Esa Tikkanen, Van.	.15
□	Keith Tkachuk, Pho.	1.00
□	Rick Tocchet, Bos.	.15
□	Pierre Turgeon, Mtl.	.35
□	John Vanbiesbrouck (G), Fla.	1.50
□	Glen Wesley, Hfd.	.15
□	Alexei Yashin, Ott.	1.00
□	Steve Yzerman, Det.	2.50
□	Zarley Zalapski, Cgy.	.15
□	Alexei Zhitnik, Buf.	.15

1996 - 97 UPPER DECK

Series One Imprint: © 1996 THE UPPER DECK COMPANY, LLC.
Series Two Imprint: © 1997 THE UPPER DECK COMPANY, LLC.

Series One Set (210 cards):	**35.00**
Series Two Set (180 cards):	**45.00**
Common Player	**.15**

	No.	Player	NRMT-MT
□	1	Paul Kariya, Ana.	2.00
□	2	Guy Hebert (G), Ana.	.25
□	3	J.F. Jomphe, Ana.	.15
□	4	Joe Sacco, Ana.	.15
□	5	Jason York, Ana.	.15
□	6	Alex Hicks, Ana.	.15
□	7	Mikhail Shtalenkov (G), Ana.	.15
□	8	Bill Ranford (G), Bos.	.25
□	9	Kyle McLaren, Bos.	.15
□	10	Rick Tocchet, Bos.	.15
□	11	Jon Rohloff, Bos.	.15
□	12	Jozel Stumpel, Bos.	.25
□	13	Cam Neely, Bos.	.25
□	14	Ray Bourque, Bos.	.75
□	15	Pat LaFontaine, Buf.	.25
□	16	Brian Holzinger, Buf.	.15
□	17	Alexei Zhitnik, Buf.	.15
□	18	Donald Audette, Buf.	.15
□	19	Jason Dawe, Buf.	.15
□	20	Wayne Primeau, Buf.	.15
□	21	Michael Peca, Buf.	.25
□	22	Theoren Fleury, Cgy.	.50
□	23	Sandy McCarthy, Cgy.	.15
□	24	Zarley Zalapski, Cgy.	.15
□	25	Trevor Kidd (G), Cgy.	.25
□	26	Steve Chiasson, Cgy.	.15
□	27	Michael Nylander, Cgy.	.15
□	28	Ronnie Stern, Cgy.	.15
□	29	Eric Dazé, Chi.	.25
□	30	Jeff Hackett (G), Chi.	.25
□	31	Chris Chelios, Chi.	.60
□	32	Tony Amonte, Chi.	.25
□	33	Bob Probert, Chi.	.15
□	34	Eric Weinrich, Chi.	.15
□	35	Jeremy Roenick, Chi.	.50
□	36	Mike Ricci, Col.	.15
□	37	Sandis Ozolinsh, Col.	.25
□	38	Patrick Roy (G), Col.	2.50
□	39	Uwe Krupp, Col.	.15
□	40	Stéphane Yelle, Col.	.15
□	41	Adam Deadmarsh, Col.	.15
□	42	Scott Young, Col.	.15
□	43	Mike Modano, Dal.	.75
□	44	Derian Hatcher, Dal.	.25
□	45	Todd Harvey, Dal.	.15
□	46	Brent Fedyk, Dal.	.15
□	47	Grant Marshall, Dal.	.15
□	48	Jamie Langenbrunner, Dal.	.25
□	49	Jere Lehtinen, Dal.	.25
□	50	Steve Yzerman, Det.	1.50
□	51	Igor Larionov, Det.	.25
□	52	Vladimir Konstantinov, Det.	.15
□	53	Chris Osgood (G), Det.	.60
□	54	Jamie Pushor, Det.	.15
□	55	Darren McCarty, Det.	.15
□	56	Nicklas Lidström, Det.	.25
□	57	Jason Arnott, Edm.	.25
□	58	Doug Weight, Edm.	.50
□	59	Todd Marchant, Edm.	.15
□	60	David Oliver, Edm.	.15
□	61	Luke Richardson, Edm.	.15
□	62	Jason Bonsignore, Edm.	.15
□	63	John Vanbiesbrouck (G), Fla.	.85
□	64	Stu Barnes, Fla.	.15
□	65	Martin Straka, Fla.	.15
□	66	Ed Jovanovski, Fla.	.25
□	67	Robert Svehla, Fla.	.15
□	68	Gord Murphy, Fla.	.15
□	69	Tom Fitzgerald, Fla.	.15
□	70	Jeff O'Neill, Hfd.	.25
□	71	Jason Muzzatti (G), Hfd.	.15
□	72	Sean Burke (G), Hfd.	.25
□	73	Jeff Brown, Hfd.	.15
□	74	Andrew Cassels, Hfd.	.15
□	75	Geoff Sanderson, Hfd.	.15
□	76	Dimitri Khristich, L.A.	.15
□	77	Vitali Yachmenev, L.A.	.15
□	78	Kevin Stevens, L.A.	.15
□	79	Yanic Perreault, L.A.	.15
□	80	Craig Johnson, L.A.	.15
□	81	John Slaney, L.A.	.15
□	82	Saku Koivu, Mtl.	1.00
□	83	Jocelyn Thibault (G), Mtl.	.50
□	84	Vladimir Malakhou, Mtl.	.15
□	85	Turner Stevenson, Mtl.	.15
□	86	Vincent Damphousse, Mtl.	.50
□	87	Mark Recchi, Mtl.	.25
□	88	Patrick Brisebois, Mtl.	.15
□	89	Dave Andreychuk, N.J.	.15
□	90	Bill Guerin, N.J.	.25
□	91	Martin Brodeur (G), N.J.	1.00
□	92	Scott Niedermayer, N.J.	.25
□	93	Petr Sykora, N.J.	.15
□	94	Stéphane Richer, N.J.	.15
□	95	John MacLean, N.J.	.15
□	96	Eric Fichaud (G), NYI.	.25
□	97	Zigmund Palffy, NYI.	.50
□	98	Alexander Semak, NYI.	.15
□	99	Bryan McCabe, NYI.	.15
□	100	Darley Hendrickson, NYI.	.15
□	101	Kenny Jonsson, NYI.	.15
□	102	Marty McInnis, NYI.	.15
□	103	Alexei Kovalev, NYI.	.15
□	104	Ulf Samuelsson, NYR.	.15
□	105	Jeff Beukeboom, NYR.	.15
□	106	Marty McSorley, NYR.	.15
□	107	Niklas Sundstrom, NYR.	.15
□	108	Wayne Gretzky, NYR.	4.00
□	109	Mike Richter, NYR.	.50
□	110	Alexei Yashin, Ott.	.60
□	111	Randy Cunneyworth, Ott.	.15
□	112	Damian Rhodes (G), Ott.	.15
□	113	Daniel Alfredsson, Ott.	.25
□	114	Antti Törmänen, Ott.	.15
□	115	Ted Drury, Ott.	.15
□	116	Janne Laukkanen, Ott.	.15
□	117	Sean Hill, Ott.	.15
□	118	John LeClair, Pha.	.75
□	119	Ron Hextall (G), Pha.	.25
□	120	Dale Hawerchuk, Pha.	.15
□	121	Rod Brind'Amour, Pha.	.25
□	122	Pat Falloon, Pha.	.15
□	123	Eric Desjardins, Pha.	.15
□	124	Joel Otto, Pha.	.15
□	125	Alexei Zhamnov, Wpg.	.25
□	126	Nikolai Khabibulin (G), Wpg.	.50
□	127	Craig Janney, Wpg.	.15
□	128	Deron Quint, Wpg.	.15
□	129	Oleg Tverdovsky, Wpg.	.15
□	130	Chad Kilger, Wpg.	.15
□	131	Teppo Numminen, Wpg.	.15
□	132	Tom Barrasso (G), Wpg.	.25
□	133	Ron Francis, Pgh.	.50
□	134	Petr Nedved, Pgh.	.15
□	135	Ken Wregget, Pgh.	.15
□	136	Joe Dziedgic, Pgh.	.15
□	137	Tomas Sandström, Pgh.	.15
□	138	Dimitri Mironov, Pgh.	.15
□	139	Shayne Corson, Stl.	.25
□	140	Grant Fuhr (G), Stl.	.25
□	141	Al MacInnis, Stl.	.15
□	142	Stephen Leach Stl.	.15
□	143	Murray Baron, Stl.	.15
□	144	Chris Pronger, Stl.	.25
□	145	Jamie Rivers, Stl.	.15
□	146	Owen Nolan, S.J.	.25
□	147	Chris Terreri (G), S.J.	.15
□	148	Marcus Ragnasson, S.J.	.15
□	149	Shean Donovan, S.J.	.15
□	150	Ray Whitney, S.J.	.15
□	151	Michal Sykora, S.J.	.15
□	152	Viktor Kozlov, S.J.	.15
□	153	Roman Hamrlik, T.B.	.25
□	154	Bill Houlder, T.B.	.15
□	155	Mikael Andersson, T.B.	.15
□	156	Petr Klima, T.B.	.15
□	157	Jason Wiemer, T.B.	.15
□	158	Rob Zamuner, T.B.	.25
□	159	Paul Ysebaert, T.B.	.15
□	160	Mats Sundin, Tor.	.75
□	161	Larry Murphy, Tor.	.25
□	162	Doug Gilmour, Tor.	.50
□	163	Todd Warriner, Tor.	.15
□	164	Dimitri Yushkevich, Tor.	.15
□	165	Kirk Muller, Tor.	.15
□	166	Jamie Macoun, Tor.	.15
□	167	Alexander Mogilny, Tor.	.50
□	168	Corey Hirsch (G), Van.	.15
□	169	Trevor Linden, Van.	.25

☐ 170 Markus Naslund, Van. .15
☐ 171 Martin Gelinas, Van. .15
☐ 172 Jyrki Lumme, Van. .15
☐ 173 Bret Hedican, Van. .15
☐ 174 Jim Carey (G), Wsh. .15
☐ 175 Sergei Gonchar, Wsh. .15
☐ 176 Joé Juneau, Wsh. .15
☐ 177 Brendan Witt, Wsh. .15
☐ 178 Dale Hunter, Wsh. .15
☐ 179 Steve Konowalchuk, Wsh. .15
☐ 180 Petr Bondra, Wsh. .60
☐ 181 Jarome Iginla, Cgy. 1.00
☐ 182 Ralph Intranuovo, Edm. .20
☐ 183 Anders Eriksson, Det. .20
☐ **184 Andrew Brunette, Wsh., RC .50**
☐ **185 Steve Sullivan, N.J., RC .20**
☐ 186 Brandon Convery, Tor. .20
☐ 187 Ethan Moreau, Chi. .35
☐ 188 Marko Kiprusoff, Mtl. .20
☐ **189 Jason McBain, Hfd., RC .20**
☐ **190 Mark Kolesar, Tor., RC .20**
☐ **191 Greg DeVries, Edm., RC .20**
☐ **192 Alexei Yegorov, S.J., RC .20**
☐ **193 Sébastien Bordeleau, Mtl., RC .20**
☐ 194 Nick Stajduhar, Edm. .20
☐ **195 Jan Caloun, S.J., RC .20**
☐ 196 Dino Ciccarelli, Det. .25
☐ 197 Ron Hextall, Pha. .25
☐ 198 Murray Baron, Stl. .20
☐ 199 Patrick Roy (G), Col. 1.50
☐ 200 Scott Mellanby, Fla. .20
☐ 201 Tie Domi, Tor. .20
☐ 202 Glenn Healy, NYR. .20
☐ 203 Keith Primeau, Det. .25
☐ 204 Joe Sakic, Col. .75
☐ 205 Jeremy Roenick, Chi. .25
☐ 206 Sergei Fedorov, Det. .35
☐ 207 Claude Lemieux, Col. .20
☐ 208 Theoren Fleury, Cgy. .25
☐ 209 CL: Wayne Gretzky, NYR. .35
☐ 210 CL: Wayne Gretzky, NYR. .35
☐ 211 Teemu Selänne, Ana. 1.00
☐ 212 Jari Kurri, Ana. .25
☐ 213 Darren Van Impe, Ana. .15
☐ 214 Steve Rucchin, Ana. .15
☐ **215 Ruslan Salei, Ana., RC .15**
☐ 216 Adam Oates, Bos. .50
☐ 217 Don Sweeney, Bos. .15
☐ 218 Steve Staios, Bos. .15
☐ 219 Barry Richter, Bos. .15
☐ **220 Mattias Timander, Bos., RC .15**
☐ 221 Ted Donato, Bos. .15
☐ 222 Dominik Hasek (G), Buf. 1.00
☐ 223 Derek Plante, Buf. .15
☐ **224 Vaclav Varada, Buf., RC .35**
☐ 225 Andrei Trefilov (G), Buf. .15
☐ 226 Curtis Brown, Buf. .15
☐ 227 German Titov, Cgy. .15
☐ 228 Robert Reichel, Cgy. .15
☐ 229 Cory Stillman, Cgy. .15
☐ 230 Chris O'Sullivan, Cgy. .15
☐ 231 Corey Millen, Cgy. .15
☐ 232 Jonas Hoglund, Cgy. .15
☐ 233 Alexei Zhamnov, Chi. .25
☐ 234 Ed Belfour (G), Chi. .50
☐ 235 Gary Suter, Chi. .15
☐ 236 Kevin Miller, Chi. .15
☐ 237 Tuomas Grönman, Chi. .15
☐ 238 Enrico Ciccone, Chi. .15
☐ 239 Peter Forsberg, Col. 1.50
☐ 240 Joe Sakic, Col. 1.25
☐ 241 Valeri Kamensky, Col. .25
☐ 242 Landon Wilson, Col. .15
☐ 243 Claude Lemieux, Col. .15
☐ 244 Eric Lacroix, Col. .15
☐ 245 Joe Nieuwendyk, Dal. .25
☐ 246 Sergei Zubov, Dal. .25
☐ 247 Benoît Hogue, Dal. .15
☐ 248 Arturs Irbe (G), Dal. .15
☐ 249 Pat Verbeek, Dal. .15
☐ 250 Sergei Fedorov, Det. .75
☐ 251 Vyacheslav Kozlov, Det. .15
☐ 252 Brendan Shanahan, Det. .85
☐ 253 Kevin Hodson (G), Det. .25
☐ 254 Greg Johnson, Det. .15
☐ **255 Tomas Holmstrom, Det., RC .75**
☐ 256 Curtis Joseph (G), Edm. .85
☐ 257 Dean McAmmond, Edm. .15
☐ 258 Ryan Smyth, Edm. .25
☐ **259 Mike Grier, Edm., RC .75**
☐ 260 Miroslav Satan, Edm. .15
☐ **261 Rem Murray, Edm., RC .25**
☐ 262 Rob Niedermayer, Fla. .15
☐ 263 Ray Sheppard, Fla. .15
☐ 264 Dave Lowry, Fla. .15
☐ 265 Scott Mellanby, Fla. .15
☐ 266 Rhett Warrener, Fla. .15
☐ 267 Per Gustafsson, Fla. .15
☐ 268 Paul Coffey, Hfd. .25
☐ 269 Nelson Emerson, Hfd. .15
☐ 270 Kevin Dineen, Hfd. .15
☐ 271 Keith Primeau, Hfd. .25
☐ 272 Hnat Domenichelli, Hfd. .25
☐ 273 Ray Ferraro, L.A. .15
☐ 274 Stephane Fiset (G), L.A. .25
☐ **275 Kai Nurminen, L.A., RC .15**
☐ **276 Dan Bylsma, L.A., RC .15**
☐ 277 Mattias Norstrom, L.A. .15
☐ 278 Rob Blake, L.A. .25
☐ 279 José Théodore (G), Mtl. .50
☐ 280 Martin Ruchinsky, Mtl. .15
☐ 281 Darcy Tucker, Mtl. .15
☐ 282 David Wilkie, Mtl. .15
☐ 283 Valeri Bure, Mtl. .15
☐ 284 Steve Thomas, N.J. .15
☐ 285 Brian Rolston, N.J. .15
☐ 286 Scott Stevens, N.J. .15
☐ 287 Shawn Chambers, N.J. .15
☐ 288 Denis Pederson, N.J. .15
☐ 289 Lyle Odelein, N.J. .15
☐ 290 Travis Green, NYI. .15
☐ 291 Todd Bertuzzi, NYI. .25
☐ 292 Niklas Andersson, NYI. .15
☐ 293 Darius Kasparaitis, NYI. .15
☐ 294 Bryan Berard, NYI. .50
☐ **295 Daniel Goneau, NYR., RC .15**
☐ 296 Christian Dubé, NYR. .25
☐ 297 Adam Graves, NYR. .15
☐ 298 Sergei Nemchinov, NYR. .15
☐ 299 Mark Messier, NYR. .75
☐ 300 Brian Leetch, NYR. .50
☐ 301 Radek Bonk, Ott. .15
☐ 302 Alexandre Daigle, Ott. .25
☐ **303 Andreas Dackell, Ott., RC .15**
☐ 304 Steve Duchesne, Ott. .15
☐ 305 Wade Redden, Ott. .15
☐ 306 Eric Lindros, Pha. 2.00
☐ 307 Mikael Renberg, Pha. .15
☐ 308 Shjon Podein, Pha. .15
☐ **309 Danius Zubrus, Pha., RC 2.50**
☐ 310 Janne Niinimaa, Pha. .25
☐ 311 Karl Drykhuis, Pha. .15
☐ 312 Jeremy Roenick, Pho. .50
☐ 313 Keith Tkachuk, Pho. .60
☐ 314 Shane Doan, Pho. .15
☐ 315 Cliff Ronning, Pho. .15
☐ 316 Mike Gartner, Pho. .25
☐ 317 Dave Manson, Pho. .15
☐ 318 Shawn Antoski, Pgh. .15
☐ 319 Kevin Hatcher, Pgh. .15
☐ 320 Jaromir Jagr, Pgh. 1.50
☐ 321 Mario Lemieux, Pgh. 2.50
☐ 322 Bryan Smolinski, Pgh. .15
☐ 323 Stefan Bergkvist, Pgh. .15
☐ 324 Brett Hull, Stl. .75
☐ 325 Joe Murphy, Stl. .15
☐ 326 Stéphane Matteau, Stl. .15
☐ 327 Geoff Courtnall, Stl. .15
☐ 328 Jim Campbell, Stl. .25
☐ **329 Harry York, Stl., RC .15**
☐ 330 Kelly Hrudey (G), S.J. .15
☐ 331 Al Iafrate, S.J. .15
☐ 332 Jeff Friesen, S.J. .25
☐ 333 Darren Turcotte, S.J. .15
☐ 334 Bernie Nicholls, S.J. .15
☐ 335 Ville Peltonen, S.J. .15
☐ 336 Dino Ciccarelli, T.B. .25
☐ 337 Chris Gratton, T.B. .25
☐ 338 Daren Puppa (G), T.B. .15
☐ 339 Alexander Selivanov, T.B. .15
☐ 340 Daymond Langkow, T.B. .15
☐ 341 Félix Potvin (G), Tor. .75
☐ 342 Wendel Clark, Tor. .25
☐ 343 Mathieu Schneider, Tor. .15
☐ 344 Dave Ellett, Tor. .15
☐ **345 Fredrik Modin, Tor., RC 1.00**
☐ **346 Sergei Berezin, Tor., RC .50**
☐ 347 Pavel Bure, Van. 1.00
☐ 348 Kirk McLean, Van. .25
☐ 349 Mike Sillinger, Van. .15
☐ 350 Russ Courtnall, Van. .15
☐ 351 Scott Walker, Van. .15
☐ 352 Esa Tikkanen, Van. .15
☐ 353 Pat Peake, Wsh. .15
☐ 354 Olaf Kolzig (G), Wsh. .50
☐ 355 Michal Pivonka, Wsh. .15
☐ **356 Richard Zednik, Wsh., RC .75**
☐ 357 Phil Housley, Wsh. .15
☐ 358 Anson Carter, Wsh. .15
☐ 359 Eric Dazé, Chi. .25
☐ 360 Félix Potvin (G), Tor. .50
☐ 361 Wayne Gretzky, NYR. 2.50
☐ 362 Ed Jovanovski, Fla. .25
☐ 363 Mike Modano, Dal. .35
☐ 364 Peter Bondra, Wsh. .25
☐ 365 Patrick Roy, Col. 1.50
☐ 366 Ray Bourque, Bos. .35
☐ 367 Roman Hamrlik, T.B. .25
☐ 368 John LeClair, Pha. .35
☐ **369 Adam Colagiacomo, Cdn., RC .75**
☐ **370 Joe Thornton, Cdn., RC 8.00**
☐ **371 Patrick Desrochers, Cdn., RC 1.25**
☐ **372 Pierre-Luc Therrien Cdn., RC .25**
☐ **373 Nick Boynton, Cdn., RC 1.00**
☐ **374 Andrew Ference, Cdn., RC .25**
☐ **375 Jean-François Fortin, Cdn., RC .50**
☐ **376 Daniel Tétreault, Cdn., RC .25**
☐ **377 Luc Theoret, Cdn., RC .25**
☐ **378 Mike Van Ryn, Cdn., RC .25**
☐ **379 Scott Barney, Cdn., RC .50**
☐ **380 Harold Druken, Cdn., RC .50**
☐ **381 Dylan Gyori, Cdn., RC .25**
☐ **382 Chris Heron, Cdn., RC .25**
☐ **383 Chad Hinz, Cdn., RC .25**
☐ **384 Patrick Marleau, Cdn., RC 5.00**
☐ **385 Serge Payer, Cdn., RC .25**
☐ **386 Jeremy Reich, Cdn., RC .25**
☐ **387 Daniel Tkaczuk, Cdn., RC 2.75**
☐ **388 Jason Ward, Cdn., RC 1.25**
☐ 389 CL: Wayne Gretzky, NYR. .25
☐ 390 CL: Wayne Gretzky, NYR. .25

LORD STANLEY'S HEROES

The Quarterfinals versions are limited to 500 copies. Semifinals versions are serial numbered out of 1,000 and Finals versions are serial numbered out of 100. These cards were inserted in Series One packs.

Quarterfinals Insert Set (20 cards): 10,000.00 1,400.00 350.00

	No.	Player	Final	SF	QF
☐☐☐	LS1	Wayne Gretzky, NYR.	1,600.00	200.00	50.00
☐☐☐	LS2	Mark Messier, NYR.	275.00	45.00	12.00
☐☐☐	LS3	Mario Lemieux, Pgh.	1,200.00	160.00	40.00
☐☐☐	LS4	Jaromir Jagr, Pgh.	700.00	100.00	25.00
☐☐☐	LS5	Martin Brodeur (G), N.J.	425.00	75.00	18.00
☐☐☐	LS6	Patrick Roy (G), Col.	1,200.00	160.00	40.00
☐☐☐	LS7	Joe Sakic, Col.	500.00	800.00	20.00
☐☐☐	LS8	Peter Forsberg, Col.	700.00	100.00	25.00
☐☐☐	LS9	Theoren Fleury, Cgy.	175.00	30.00	8.00
☐☐☐	LS10	Paul Coffey, Hfd.	125.00	25.00	6.00
☐☐☐	LS11	Doug Gilmour, Tor.	175.00	30.00	8.00
☐☐☐	LS12	Paul Kariya, Ana.	1,00.00	135.00	35.00

□ □ □ LS13 Eric Lindros, Pha.	1,00.00	135.00	35.00
□ □ □ LS14 Sergei Fedorov, Det.	275.00	45.00	12.00
□ □ □ LS15 Eric Dazé, Chi.	125.00	25.00	6.00
□ □ □ LS16 Teemu Selänne, Ana.	425.00	75.00	18.00
□ □ □ LS17 Keith Tkachuk, Pho.	225.00	40.00	10.00
□ □ □ LS18 Pavel Bure, Van.	425.00	75.00	18.00
□ □ □ LS19 Mats Sundin, Tor.	275.00	45.00	12.00
□ □ □ LS20 Saku Koivu, Mtl.	425.00	75.00	18.00

SUPERSTAR SHOWDOWN

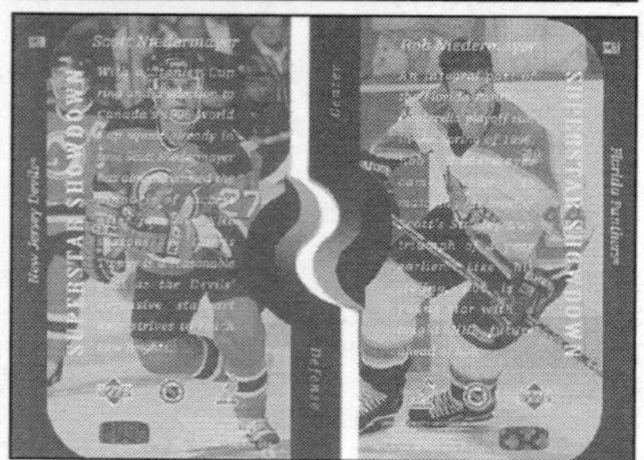

These die-cut cards connect with a matching second card.

Series One Insert Set (60 cards): 165.00

No.	Player	NRMT-MT
□ SS1A	Pavel Bure, Van.	5.00
□ SS1B	Paul Kariya, Ana.	10.00
□ SS2A	Patrick Roy (G), Col.	12.00
□ SS2B	John Vanbiesbrouck (G), Fla.	4.50
□ SS3A	Eric Lindros, Pha.	10.00
□ SS3B	Ed Jovanovski, Fla.	1.00
□ SS4A	Theoren Fleury, Cgy.	2.00
□ SS4B	Doug Gilmour, Tor.	2.00
□ SS5A	Wayne Gretzky, NYR.	15.00
□ SS5B	Mario Lemieux, Pgh.	12.00
□ SS6A	Keith Tkachuk, Pho.	3.00
□ SS6B	Brendan Shanahan, Hfd.	4.50
□ SS7A	Ray Bourque, Bos.	3.75
□ SS7B	Brian Leetch, NYR.	2.00
□ SS8A	Peter Forsberg, Col.	7.50
□ SS8B	Sergei Fedorov, Det.	3.75
□ SS9A	Mark Messier, NYR.	3.75
□ SS9B	Keith Primeau, Hfd.	1.00
□ SS10A	Teemu Selänne, Ana.	5.00
□ SS10B	Alexander Mogilny, Van.	2.00
□ SS11A	Félix Potvin (G), Tor.	3.75
□ SS11B	Jocelyn Thibault (G), Mtl.	2.00
□ SS12A	Martin Brodeur (G), N.J.	5.00
□ SS12B	Eric Fichaud (G), NYI.	1.00
□ SS13A	Roman Hamrlik, T.B.	1.00
□ SS13B	Jaromir Jagr, Pgh.	7.50
□ SS14A	Jim Carey (G), Wsh.	.75
□ SS14B	Saku Koivu, Mtl.	5.00
□ SS15A	Jeremy Roenick, Pho.	2.00
□ SS15B	Brett Hull, Stl.	3.75
□ SS16A	Joe Sakic, Col.	6.00
□ SS16B	Steve Yzerman, Det.	7.50
□ SS17A	Doug Weight, Edm.	2.00
□ SS17B	Pat LaFontaine, Buf.	1.00
□ SS18A	Daniel Alfredsson, Ott.	1.00
□ SS18B	Eric Dazé, Chi.	1.00
□ SS19A	Mike Modano, Dal.	3.75
□ SS19B	Jason Arnott, Edm.	1.00
□ SS20A	Paul Coffey, Hfd.	1.00
□ SS20B	Sandis Ozolinsh, Col.	1.00
□ SS21A	Zigmund Palffy, NYI.	2.00
□ SS21B	Petr Sykora, N.J.	.75
□ SS22A	Ed Belfour (G), Chi.	2.00
□ SS22B	Ron Hextall (G), Pha.	1.00
□ SS23A	Mats Sundin, Tor.	3.75
□ SS23B	Mikael Renberg, Pha.	1.00
□ SS24A	Vitali Yachmenev, L.A.	.75
□ SS24B	Alexei Zhamnov, Wpg.	1.00
□ SS25A	Oleg Tverdovsky, Wpg.	.75
□ SS25B	Kyle McLaren, Bos.	.75
□ SS26A	Dominik Hasek (G), Buf.	5.00
□ SS26B	Petr Nedved, Pgh.	.75
□ SS27A	Chris Chelios, Chi.	3.00
□ SS27B	Chris Pronger, Stl.	1.00
□ SS28A	Scott Niedermayer, N.J.	1.00
□ SS28B	Rob Niedermayer, Fla.	.75
□ SS29A	Marty McSorley, Fla.	.75
□ SS29B	Bob Probert, Det.	.75
□ SS30A	Bill Ranford (G), Edm.	1.00
□ SS30B	Chris Osgood (G), Det.	3.00

GAME JERSEYS

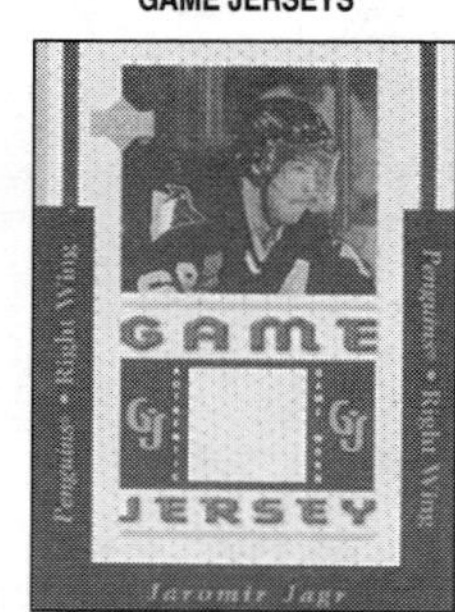

These cards were inserted in both Series One and Series Two packs. An actual piece of the player's hockey jersey is affixed to the card.

Insert Set (13 cards): 4,500.00

No.	Player	NRMT-MT
□ GJ1	Steve Yzerman, Det.	600.00
□ GJ2	Doug Gilmour, Tor.	250.00
□ GJ3	Brett Hull, Stl.	275.00
□ GJ4	Ray Bourque, Bos.	275.00
□ GJ5	Jaromir Jagr, Pgh.	600.00
□ GJ6	Mario Lemieux, Pgh.	800.00
□ GJ7	John Vanbiesbrouck (G), Fla.	350.00
□ GJ8	Eric Lindros, Pha.	700.00
□ GJ9	Mike Modano, Dal.	250.00
□ GJ10	Pavel Bure, Van.	400.00
□ GJ11	Mark Messier, NYR.	300.00
□ GJ12	Theoren Fleury, Cgy.	250.00
□ GJ13	Mats Sundin, Tor.	275.00

GENERATION NEXT

Series Two Insert Set (40 cards): 160.00

No.	Player	NRMT-MT
□ X1	Wayne Gretzky, NYR./Paul Kariya, Ana.	20.00
□ X2	Trevor Linden, Van./Peter Forsberg, Col.	6.00
□ X3	Joe Sakic, Col./Rob Niedermayer, Fla.	5.00
□ X4	Eric Weinrich, Chi./Chris O'Sullivan, Cgy.	1.00
□ X5	Patrick Roy, Col./Jocelyn Thibault, Mtl.	10.00
□ X6	Brett Hull, Stl./Daniel Alfredsson, Ott.	3.00
□ X7	John Vanbiesbrouck, Fla./Chris Osgood, Det.	3.50
□ X8	Ray Bourque, Bos./Roman Hamrlik, T.B.	3.00
□ X9	Paul Coffey, Hfd./Sandis Ozolinsh, Col.	2.00
□ X10	Doug Gilmour, Tor./Sergei Fedorov, Det.	3.00
□ X11	Chris Chelios, Chi./Ed Jovanovski, Fla.	2.00
□ X12	Jeremy Roenick, Pho./Jason Arnott, Edm.	2.00
□ X13	Steve Yzerman, Det./Doug Weight, Edm.	6.00
□ X14	Brendan Shanahan, Det./Todd Bertuzzi, NYI	3.50
□ X15	Wendel Clark, Tor./Keith Tkachuk, Pho.	2.00
□ X16	Teemu Selänne, Ana./Saku Koivu, Mtl.	4.00
□ X17	Jaromir Jagr, Pgh./Zigmund Palffy, NYI.	6.00
□ X18	Ed Belfour, Chi./Martin Brodeur, N.J.	4.00
□ X19	Owen Nolan, S.J./Eric Dazé, Chi.	2.00
□ X20	Valeri Kamensky, Col./Vitali Yachmenev, L.A.	1.00
□ X21	Mike Modano, Dal./Jarome Iginla, Cgy.	3.00
□ X22	Nicklas Lidström, Det./Anders Eriksson, Det.	1.00
□ X23	Brian Leetch, NYR./Bryan Berard, NYI.	2.00
□ X24	Niklas Sundstrom, NYR./Jari Kurri, Ana.	1.00
□ X25	Scott Mellanby, Fla./Adam Deadmarsh, Col.	1.00
□ X26	Peter Bondra, Wsh./Petr Sykora, N.J.	2.00
□ X27	Curtis Joseph, Edm./Eric Fichaud, NYI.	3.50
□ X28	Dominik Hasek, Buf./Roman Turek, Dal.	4.00
□ X29	Alexander Mogilny, Van./Valeri Bure, Cgy.	2.00
□ X30	Theoren Fleury, Cgy./Daymond Langkow, T.B.	2.00
□ X31	Bernie Nicholls, S.J./Sergei Berezin, Tor.	1.00
□ X32	Rick Tocchet, Bos./Chris Gratton, T.B.	1.00
□ X33	Grant Fuhr, Stl./Félix Potvin, Tor.	3.00
□ X34	Kevin Stevens, L.A./Keith Primeau, Hfd.	1.00
□ X35	Rob Blake, L.A./Wade Redden, Ott.	1.00
□ X36	Scott Stevens, N.J./Chris Pronger, Stl.	1.00
□ X37	Ciary Suter, Chi./Kyle McLaren, Bos.	1.00
□ X38	Mats Sundin, Tor./Jonas Hoglund, Cgy.	3.00
□ X39	Larry Murphy, Tor./Sergei Zubov, Dal.	2.00
□ X40	Adam Oates, Bos./Joe Juneau, Wsh.	2.00

POWER PERFORMERS

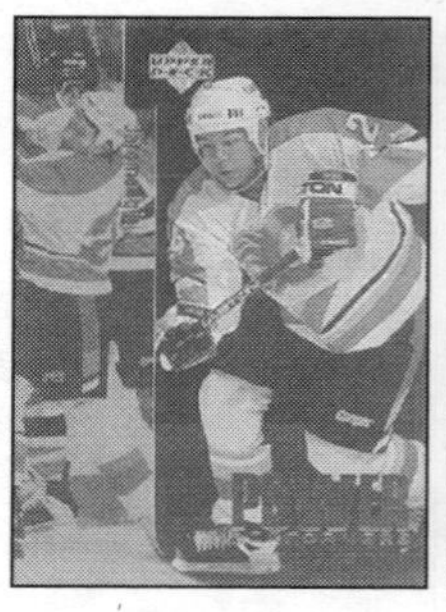

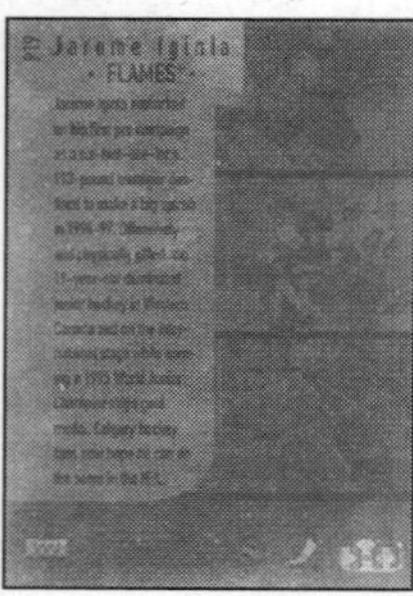

Series Two Insert Set (30 cards): 100.00

No.	Player	NRMT-MT
□ P1	Brendan Shanahan, Det.	12.00
□ P2	Mikael Renberg, Pha.	2.00
□ P3	John LeClair, Pha.	10.00
□ P4	Keith Primeau, Hfd.	4.00
□ P5	Adam Graves, NYR.	2.00
□ P6	Jason Arnott, Edm.	4.00
□ P7	Todd Bertuzzi, NYI.	4.00
□ P8	Ed Jovanovski, Fla.	4.00
□ P9	Scott Stevens, N.J.	2.00
□ P10	Chris Gratton, T.B.	4.00
□ P11	Darius Kasparaitis, Pgh.	2.00
□ P12	Vladimir Konstantinov, Det.	2.00
□ P13	Mike Grier, Edm.	4.00
□ P14	Theoren Fleury, Cgy.	6.00
□ P15	Chris Chelios, Chi.	8.00
□ P16	Trevor Linden, Van.	4.00
□ P17	Claude Lemieux, Col.	2.00
□ P18	Owen Nolan, S.J.	4.00
□ P19	Jarome Iginla, Cgy.	6.00
□ P20	Joe Nieuwendyk, Dal.	4.00
□ P21	Kevin Hatcher, Pgh.	2.00
□ P22	Dino Ciccarelli, T.B.	4.00
□ P23	Adam Deadmarsh, Col.	2.00
□ P24	Chris Pronger, Stl.	4.00
□ P25	Mike Ricci, Col.	2.00
□ P26	Rod Brind'Amour, Pha.	4.00
□ P27	Derian Hatcher, Dal.	4.00
□ P28	Mats Sundin, Tor.	10.00
□ P29	Doug Gilmour, Tor.	6.00
□ P30	Todd Harvey, Dal.	2.00

HART HOPEFULS

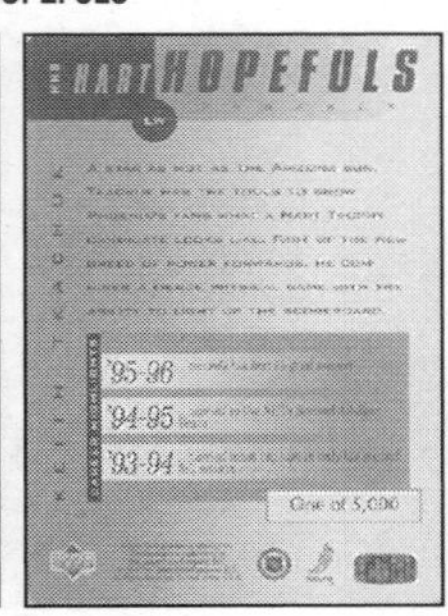

The Bronze inserts are limited to 500 copies. Silver inserts are serial numbered out of 1,000 and Gold inserts are numbered out of 100. These cards were inserted into Series Two packs.

Bronze Inset Set (20 cards): 10,000.001,500.00 375.00

	No.	Player	Gold	Silver	Bronze
□□□	HH1	Wayne Gretzky, NYR.	1,600.00	200.00	50.00
□□□	HH2	Mark Messier, NYR.	275.00	45.00	12.00
□□□	HH3	Eric Lindros, Pha.	1,000.00	135.00	35.00
□□□	HH4	Sergei Fedorov, Det.	275.00	45.00	12.00
□□□	HH5	Saku Koivu, Mtl.	425.00	75.00	18.00
□□□	HH6	John Vanbiesbrouck (G), Fla.	350.00	60.00	15.00
□□□	HH7	Peter Forsberg, Col.	700.00	100.00	25.00
□□□	HH8	Keith Tkachuk, Pho.	225.00	40.00	10.00
□□□	HH9	Paul Kariya, Ana.	1,000.00	135.00	35.00
□□□	HH10	Martin Brodeur, N.J.	425.00	75.00	18.00
□□□	HH11	Patrick Roy (G), Col.	1,200.00	160.00	40.00
□□□	HH12	Alexander Mogilny, Van.	175.00	30.00	8.00
□□□	HH13	Brett Hull, Stl.	275.00	45.00	12.00
□□□	HH14	Pavel Bure, Van.	425.00	75.00	18.00
□□□	HH15	Teemu Selänne, Ana.	425.00	75.00	18.00
□□□	HH16	Mario Lemieux, Pgh.	1,200.00	160.00	40.00
□□□	HH17	Jeremy Roenick, Pho.	175.00	30.00	8.00
□□□	HH18	Jaromir Jagr, Pgh.	700.00	100.00	25.00
□□□	HH19	Steve Yzerman, Det.	700.00	100.00	25.00
□□□	HH20	Joe Sakic, Col.	500.00	80.00	20.00

1996 - 97 UPPER DECK ALL-STAR YOU CRASH THE GAME

Twenty unnumbered blue cards were handed out at the 1996-97 NHL All-Star Game in San Jose. Only 10 Western Conference players, however, are confirmed to have been handed out. If the depicted player scored a goal, that card could be redeemed for a 20-card Gold set. The Gold cards are numbered AR1 to AR20.

Redeemed Gold Set (20 cards): 1,000.00

	No.	Player	Blue	Gold
□	AR1	Tony Amonte, Chi.		20.00
□□	AR2	Paul Kariya, Ana.	150.00	125.00
□□	AR3	Brett Hull, Stl.	50.00	40.00
□□	AR4	Teemu Selänne, Ana.	80.00	60.00
□□	AR5	Steve Yzerman, Det.	125.00	100.00
□□	AR6	Owen Nolan, S.J.	30.00	20.00
□□	AR7	Mats Sundin, Tor.	50.00	40.00
□□	AR8	Pavel Bure, Van.	80.00	60.00
□□	AR9	Brendan Shanahan, Det.	65.00	50.00
□□	AR10	Sandis Ozolinsh, Col.	30.00	20.00
□□	AR11	Keith Tkachuk, Pho.	45.00	30.00
□	AR12	Ray Bourque, Bos.		40.00
□	AR13	Eric Lindros, Pha.		125.00
□	AR14	Mark Messier, NYR.		40.00
□	AR15	John LeClair, Pha.		40.00
□	AR16	Jaromir Jagr, Pgh.		100.00
□	AR17	Dino Ciccarelli, T.B.		20.00
□	AR18	Peter Bondra, Wsh.		30.00
□	AR19	Brian Leetch, NYR.		25.00
□	AR20	Wayne Gretzky, NYR.		200.00

1996 - 97 UPPER DECK COLLECTOR'S CHOICE

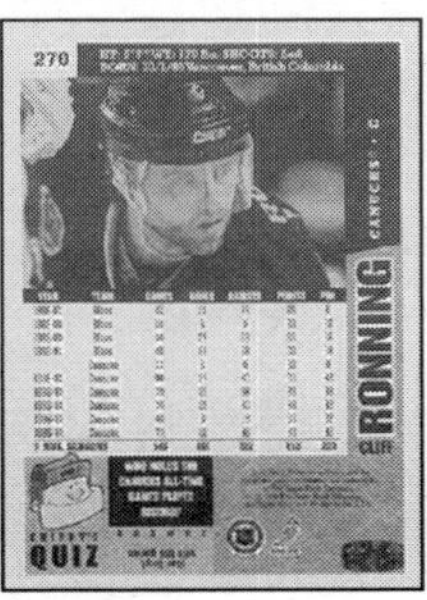

Imprint: © 1996 THE UPPER DECK COMPANY

Complete Set (348 cards):	**30.00**
Young Guns Set (15 cards):	**12.00**
Common Player:	**.10**
Young Guns Trade Card:	**.50**
Promo Card (Wayne Gretzky):	**4.00**

	No.	Player	NRMT-MT
□	1	Paul Kariya, Ana.	1.25
□	2	Teemu Selänne, Ana.	.75
□	3	Steve Rucchin, Ana.	.10
□	4	Mikael Shtalenkov (G), Ana.	.10
□	5	Guy Hebert (G), Ana.	.25
□	6	Shawn Van Allen, Ana.	.10
□	7	Anatoli Semenov, Ana.	.10
□	8	J.F. Jomphe, Ana.	.10
□	9	Alex Hicks, Ana.	.10
□	10	Roman Oskiuta, Ana.	.10
□	11	Todd Ewen, Ana.	.10
□	12	Adam Oates, Bos.	.35
□	13	Ray Bourque, Bos.	.50
□	14	Don Sweeney, Bos.	.10
□	15	Kyle McLaren, Bos.	.10
□	16	Cam Neely, Bos.	.25
□	17	Bill Ranford (G), Bos.	.25
□	18	Rick Tocchet, Bos.	.10
□	19	Ted Donato, Bos.	.10
□	20	Shawn McEachern, Bos. (Ott.)	.10
□	21	Ron Rohloff, Bos.	.10
□	22	Joe Mullen, Bos.	.10
□	23	Pat LaFontaine, Buf.	.25
□	24	Brian Holzinger, Buf.	.10
□	25	Wayne Primeau, Buf.	.10
□	26	Alexei Zhitnik, Buf.	.10
□	27	Derek Plante, Buf.	.10
□	28	Randy Burridge, Buf.	.10
□	29	Brad May, Buf.	.10
□	30	Dominik Hasek (G), Buf.	.75
□	31	Jason Dawe, Buf.	.10
□	32	Michael Peca, Buf.	.25
□	33	Matthew Barnaby, Buf.	.10
□	34	Trevor Kidd (G), Cgy.	.25
□	35	Theoren Fleury, Cgy.	.35
□	36	Cale Hulse, Cgy.	.10
□	37	Bob Sweeney, Cgy.	.10
□	38	Michael Nylander, Cgy.	.10
□	39	German Titov, Cgy.	.10
□	40	Cory Stillman, Cgy	.10
□	41	Zarley Zalapski, Cgy.	.10
□	42	Jocelyn Lemieux, Cgy.	.10
□	43	Sandy McCarthy, Cgy.	.10
□	44	Steve Chiasson, Cgy.	.10
□	45	Eric Dazé, Chi.	.25
□	46	Jeremy Roenick, Chi.	.35
□	47	Chris Chelios, Chi.	.30
□	48	Joe Murphy, Chi. (Stl.)	.10
□	49	Tony Amonte, Chi.	.25
□	50	Bernie Nicholls, Chi.	.10
□	51	Eric Weinrich, Chi.	.10
□	52	Gary Suter, Chi.	.10
□	53	Jeff Shantz, Chi.	.10
□	54	Jeff Hackett (G), Chi.	.25
□	55	Ed Belfour (G), Chi.	.35
□	56	Uwe Krupp, Col.	.10
□	57	Claude Lemieux, Col.	.10
□	58	Adam Deadmarsh, Col.	.10
□	59	Stéphane Fiset (G), Col. (L.A.)	.25
□	60	Sandis Ozolinsh, Col.	.25
□	61	Stéphane Yelle, Col.	.10
□	62	Valeri Kamensky, Col.	.25
□	63	Peter Forsberg, Col.	1.00
□	64	Joe Sakic, Col.	.85
□	65	Patrick Roy (G), Col.	1.50
□	66	Chris Simon, Col.	.10
□	67	Todd Harvey, Dal.	.10
□	68	Joe Nieuwendyk, Dal.	.25
□	69	Mike Modano, Dal.	.50
□	70	Derian Hatcher, Dal.	.25
□	71	Kevin Hatcher, Dal. (Pgh.)	.10
□	72	Benoît Hogue, Dal.	.10
□	73	Guy Carbonneau, Dal.	.10
□	74	Jamie Langenbrunner, Dal.	.25
□	75	Jere Lehtinen, Dal.	.25
□	76	Criag Ludwig, Dal.	.10
□	77	Grant Marshall, Dal.	.10
□	78	Greg Johnson, Det.	.10
□	79	Steve Yzerman, Det.	1.00
□	80	Sergei Fedorov, Det.	.50
□	81	Vyacheslav Kozlov, Det.	.10
□	82	Vladimir Konstantinov, Det.	.10
□	83	Igor Larionov, Det.	.25
□	84	Chris Osgood (G), Det.	.35
□	85	Paul Coffey, Det.	.25
□	86	Nicklas Lidström, Det.	.25
□	87	Keith Primeau, Det.	.25
□	88	Dino Ciccarelli, Det.	.25
□	89	Darren McCarty, Det.	.10
□	90	Curtis Joseph (G), Edm.	.60
□	91	Doug Weight, Edm.	.35
□	92	Jason Arnott, Edm.	.25
□	93	Mariusz Czerkawski, Edm.	.10
□	94	Kelly Buchberger, Edm.	.10
□	95	Zedeno Ciger, Edm.	.10
□	96	David Oliver, Edm.	.10
□	97	Todd Marchant, Edm.	.10
□	98	Miroslav Satan, Edm.	.10
□	99	Bryan Marchment, Edm.	.10
□	100	Louie DeBrusk, Edm.	.10
□	101	John Vanbiesbrouck (G), Fla.	.60
□	102	Scott Mellanby, Fla.	.10
□	103	Rob Niedermayer, Fla.	.10
□	104	Robert Svehla, Fla.	.10
□	105	Ed Jovanovski, Fla.	.25
□	106	Joan Garpenlov, Fla.	.10
□	107	Jody Hull, Fla.	.10
□	108	Bill Lindsay, Fla.	.10
□	109	Terry Carkner, Fla.	.10
□	110	Stu Barnes, Fla.	.10
□	111	Ray Sheppard, Fla.	.10
□	112	Brendan Shanahan, Hfd.	.60
□	113	Geoff Sanderson, Hfd.	.10
□	114	Andrei Nikolishin, Hfd.	.10
□	115	Andrew Cassels, Hfd.	.10
□	116	Nelson Emerson, Hfd.	.10
□	117	Jason Muzzatti (G), Hfd.	.10
□	118	Marek Malik, Hfd.	.10
□	119	Sean Burke (G), Hfd.	.25
□	120	Jeff Brown, Hfd.	.10
□	121	Jeff O'Neill, Hfd.	.25
□	122	Kelly Chase, Hfd.	.10
□	123	Dimitri Khristich, L.A.	.10
□	124	Kevin Stevens, L.A.	.10
□	125	Vitali Yachmenev, L.A.	.10
□	126	Yanic Perreault, L.A.	.10
□	127	Kevin Todd, L.A.	.10
□	128	Aki Berg, L.A.	.10
□	129	Craig Johnson, L.A.	.10
□	130	Mattias Norstrom, L.A.	.10
□	131	Ray Ferraro, L.A.	.10
□	132	Steve Finn, L.A.	.10
□	133	Pierre Turgeon, Mtl.	.25
□	134	Saku Koivu, Mtl.	.75
□	135	Mark Recchi, Mtl.	.25
□	136	Jocelyn Thibault (G), Mtl.	.35
□	137	Andrei Kovalenko, Mtl.	.10
□	138	Vincent Damphousse, Mtl.	.35
□	139	Vladimir Malakhov, Mtl.	.10

	No.	Player	Price
☐	140	Brian Savage, Mtl.	.10
☐	141	Valeri Bure, Mtl.	.10
☐	142	Patrice Brisebois, Mtl.	.10
☐	143	Martin Rucinsky, Mtl.	.10
☐	144	Martin Brodeur (G), N.J.	.75
☐	145	Steve Thomas, N.J.	.10
☐	146	Bill Guerin, N.J.	.25
☐	147	Petr Sykora, N.J.	.10
☐	148	Scott Stevens, N.J.	.10
☐	149	Scott Niedermayer, N.J.	.25
☐	150	Phil Housley, N.J.	.10
☐	151	Brian Rolston, N.J.	.10
☐	152	Neal Broten, N.J.	.10
☐	153	Dave Andreychuk, N.J.	.10
☐	154	Randy McKay, N.J.	.10
☐	155	Eric Fichaud (G), NYI.	.25
☐	156	Zigmund Palffy, NYI.	.35
☐	157	Travis Green, NYI.	.10
☐	158	Darby Hendrickson, NYI.	.10
☐	159	Kenny Jonsson,NYI.	.10
☐	160	Marty McInnis, NYI.	.10
☐	161	Bryan McCabe, NYI.	.10
☐	162	Darius Kasparaitis, NYI.	.10
☐	163	Alexander Semak, NYI.	.10
☐	164	Todd Bertuzzi, NYI.	.25
☐	165	Niclas Andersson, NYI.	.10
☐	166	Mark Messier, NYR.	.50
☐	167	Mike Richter (G), NYR.	.35
☐	168	Nicklas Lidström, NYR.	.25
☐	169	Brian Leetch, NYR.	.25
☐	170	Wayne Gretzky, NYR.	3.50
☐	171	Luc Robitaille, NYR.	.25
☐	172	Marty McSorley, NYR.	.10
☐	173	Jari Kurri, NYR.	.25
☐	174	Adam Graves, NYR.	.10
☐	175	Sergei Nemchinov, NYR.	.10
☐	176	Alexei Kovalev, NYR.	.10
☐	177	Daniel Alfredsson, Ott.	.25
☐	178	Randy Cunneyworth, Ott.	.10
☐	179	Alexei Yashin, Ott.	.35
☐	180	Alexandre Daigle, Ott.	.25
☐	181	Radek Bonk, Ott.	.10
☐	182	Steve Duchesne, Ott.	.10
☐	183	Ted Drury, Ott.	.10
☐	184	Antti Törmänen, Ott.	.10
☐	185	Stanislav Neckar, Ott.	.10
☐	186	Damian Rhodes (G), Ott.	.10
☐	187	Janne Laukkanen, Ott.	.10
☐	188	Eric Lindros, Pha.	1.25
☐	189	Mikael Renberg, Pha.	.10
☐	190	John LeClair, Pha.	.50
☐	191	Ron Hextall (G), Pha.	.25
☐	192	Rod Brind'Amour, Pha.	.25
☐	193	Joel Otto, Pha.	.10
☐	194	Pat Falloon, Pha.	.10
☐	195	Eric Desjardins, Pha.	.10
☐	196	Dale Hawerchuk, Pha.	.25
☐	197	Chris Therien, Pha.	.10
☐	198	Dan Quinn, Pha.	.10
☐	199	Oleg Tverdovsky, Wpg.	.10
☐	200	Chad Kilger, Wpg.	.10
☐	201	Keith Tkachuk, Wpg.	.35
☐	202	Igor Korolev, Wpg.	.10
☐	203	Alexei Zhammov, Wpg.	.25
☐	204	Nikolai Khabibulin (G), Wpg.	.35
☐	205	Shane Doan, Wpg.	.10
☐	206	Deron Quint, Wpg.	.10
☐	207	Craig Janney, Wpg.	.10
☐	208	Norm Maciver, Wpg.	.10
☐	209	Teppo Numminen, Wpg.	.10
☐	210	Mario Lemieux, Pgh.	1.50
☐	211	Jaromir Jagr, Pgh.	1.00
☐	212	Ron Francis, Pgh.	.35
☐	213	Tom Barrasso (G), Pgh.	.25
☐	214	Sergei Zubov, Pgh.	.25
☐	215	Tomas Sandström, Pgh.	.10
☐	216	Joe Dziedzic, Pgh.	.10
☐	217	Richard Park, Pgh.	.10
☐	218	Bryan Smolinski, Pgh.	.10
☐	219	Petr Nedved, Pgh.	.10
☐	220	Ken Wregget (G), Pgh.	.10
☐	221	Dmitri Mironov, Pgh.	.10
☐	222	Peter Zezel, Stl.	.10
☐	223	Brett Hull, Stl.	.50
☐	224	Grant Fuhr (G), Stl.	.25
☐	225	Shayne Corson, Stl.	.25
☐	226	Chris Pronger, Stl.	.25
☐	227	Craig MacTavish, Stl.	.10
☐	228	Al MacInnis, Stl.	.10
☐	229	Geoff Courtnall, Stl.	.10
☐	230	Stéphane Matteau, Stl.	.10
☐	231	Tony Twist, Stl.	.10
☐	232	Brian Noonan, Stl.	.10
☐	233	Owen Nolan, S.J.	.25
☐	234	Shean Donovan, S.J.	.10
☐	235	Darren Turcotte, S.J.	.10
☐	236	Marcus Ragnarsson, S.J.	.10
☐	237	Viktor Kozlov, S.J.	.10
☐	238	Jeff Friesen, S.J.	.25
☐	239	Chris Ferreri (G), S.J.	.10
☐	240	Ray Whitney, S.J.	.10
☐	241	Ville Peltonen, S.J.	.10
☐	242	Andrei Nazarov, S.J.	.10
☐	243	Ulf Dahlen, S.J.	.10
☐	244	Roman Hamrlik, T.B.	.25
☐	245	Chris Gratton, T.B.	.25
☐	246	Petr Klima, T.B.	.10
☐	247	Daren Puppa (G), T.B.	.10
☐	248	Rob Zamuner, T.B.	.25
☐	249	Aaron Gavey, T.B.	.10
☐	250	Brian Bradley, T.B.	.10
☐	251	Paul Ysebaert, T.B.	.10
☐	252	Igor Ulanov, T.B.	.10
☐	253	Alexander Selivanov, T.B.	.10
☐	254	Shawn Burr, T.B.	.10
☐	255	Mats Sundin, Tor.	.50
☐	256	Doug Gilmour, Tor.	.35
☐	257	Félix Potvin, Tor.	.50
☐	258	Wendel Clark, Tor.	.25
☐	259	Kirk Muller, Tor.	.10
☐	260	Dave Gagner, Tor.	.10
☐	261	Tie Domi, Tor.	.10
☐	262	Mathieu Schneider, Tor.	.10
☐	263	Dimitri Yushkevich, Tor.	.10
☐	264	Don Beaupré, Tor.	.10
☐	265	Larry Murphy, Tor.	.25
☐	266	Pavel Bure, Van.	.75
☐	267	Alexander Mogilny, Van.	.35
☐	268	Trevor Linden, Van.	.25
☐	269	Jyrki Lumme, Van.	.10
☐	270	Cliff Ronning, Van.	.10
☐	271	Kirk McLean (G), Van.	.25
☐	272	Corey Hirsch (G), Van.	.10
☐	273	Esa Tikkanen, Van.	.10
☐	274	Gino Odjick, Van.	.10
☐	275	Markus Naslund, Van.	.10
☐	276	Russ Courtnall, Van.	.10
☐	277	Joé Juneau, Wsh.	.10
☐	278	Jim Carey (G), Wsh.	.10
☐	279	Peter Bondra, Wsh.	.35
☐	280	Michal Pivonka, Wsh.	.10
☐	281	Steve Konowalchuk, Wsh.	.10
☐	282	Pat Peake, Wsh.	.10
☐	283	Brendan Witt, Wsh.	.10
☐	284	Stefan Ustorf, Wsh.	.10
☐	285	Keith Jones, Wsh.	.10
☐	286	Sergei Gonchar, Wsh.	.10
☐	287	Sylvain Côté, Wsh.	.10
☐	288	Dale Hunter, Wsh.	.10
☐	289	Paul Kariya, Ana.	.75
☐	290	Wayne Gretzky, NYR.	1.50
☐	291	Eric Lindros, Pha.	.75
☐	292	Steve Yzerman, Det.	.60
☐	293	Mario Lemieux, Pgh.	1.00
☐	294	Jaromir Jagr, Pgh.	.60
☐	295	Keith Tkachuk, Wpg.	.25
☐	296	Mark Messier, NYR.	.35
☐	297	Jeremy Roenick, Chi.	.25
☐	298	Peter Forsberg, Col.	.60
☐	299	Joe Sakic, Col.	.50
☐	300	Theoren Fleury, Cgy.	.25
☐	301	Chris Chelios, Chi.	.25
☐	302	Vladimir Konstantinov, Det.	.10
☐	303	Brian Leetch, NYR.	.25
☐	304	Ray Bourque, Bos.	.35
☐	305	Scott Stevens, N.J.	.10
☐	306	Martin Brodeur (G), N.J.	.50
☐	307	Patrick Roy (G), Col.	1.00
☐	308	Scotty Bowman, Det.	.35
☐	309	P. Kariya, Ana. (G. Hebert/T. Selänne)	.75
☐	310	R. Bourque, Bos. (C. Neely/A. Oates)	.35
☐	311	P. LaFontaine, Buf. (A. Zhitnik/D. Hasek)	.35
☐	312	T. Fleury, Cgy. (T. Kidd/M. Nylander)	.25
☐	313	J. Roenick, Chi. (E. Dazé/C. Chelios)	.25
☐	314	J. Sakic, Col. (P. Roy/P. Forsberg)	1.00
☐	315	M. Modano, Dal. (T. Harvey/J. Nieuwendyk)	.35
☐	316	V. Konstantinov, Det. (P. Coffey/S. Fedorov)	.25
☐	317	D. Weight, Edm. (C. Joseph/J. Arnott)	.25
☐	318	J. Vanbiesbrouck (G), Fla. (R. Niedermayer/E. Jovanovski)	.25
☐	319	B. Shanahan, Hfd. (S. Burke/G. Sanderson)	.25
☐	320	V. Yachmenev, L.A. (D. Khristich/R. Ferraro)	.10
☐	321	S. Koivu, Mtl. (J. ThibaultP. Turgeon)	.50
☐	322	M. Brodeur, N.J. (S. Stevens/S. Thomas)	.50
☐	323	T. Bertuzzi, NYI. (E. Fichaud/Z. Palffy)	.25
☐	324	A. Yashin, Ott. (A. Daigle/D. Rhodes)	.25
☐	325	A. Graves, NYR. (Brian Leetch/M. Richter)	.25
☐	326	J. LeClair, Pha. (M. Renberg/R. Hextall)	.25
☐	327	K. Tkachuk, Wpg. (A. Zhamnov/O. Tverdovsky)	.25
☐	328	J. Jagr, Pgh. (R. Francis/P. Nedved)	.60
☐	329	W. Gretzky, Stl. (B. Hull/A. MacInnis)	1.50
☐	330	O. Nolan, S.J. (C.Terreri/D. Turcotte)	.10
☐	331	R. Hamrlik, T.B. (D. Puppa/C. Gratton)	.10
☐	332	M. Sundin, Tor. (F. Potvin/D. Gilmour)	.35
☐	333	A. Mogilny, Van. (T. Linden/P. Bure)	.25
☐	334	J. Carey (G), Wsh. (Joé Juneau/P. Bondra)	.25
☐	335	E. Lindros, East. (M. Messier/M. Lemieux)	1.00
☐	336	J. Sakic, West. (W. Gretzky/T. Selänne)	1.50
☐	337	Chad Kilger, Wpg.	.10
☐	338	Todd Bertuzzi, NYI.	.25
☐	339	Petr Sykora, N.J.	.10
☐	340	Ed Jovanovski, Fla.	.25
☐	341	Kyle McLaren, Bos.	.10
☐	342	Brian Holzinger, Buf.	.10
☐	343	Jeff O'Neill, Hfd.	.25
☐	344	Daniel Alfredsson, Ott.	.25
☐	345	Brendan Witt, Wsh.	.10
☐	346	Daymond Langkow, T.B.	.10
☐	347	CL: Roy/ C. Lemieux	.25
☐	348	CL: Vanbiesbrouck/ Dvorak	.20

YOUNG GUNS

	No.	Player	Price
☐	349	Jarome Iginla, Cgy.	2.00
☐	350	Sergei Berezin, Tor.	1.50
☐	351	José Théodore, Mtl.	2.00
☐	352	Rem Murray, Edm.	.75
☐	353	Daniel Goneau, NYR.	.50
☐	354	Ethan Moreau, Chi.	.75
☐	355	Jonas Hoglund, Cgy.	.50
☐	356	Anders Eriksson, Det.	.50
☐	357	Christian Dubé, NYR.	.75
☐	358	Roman Turek (G), Dal.	.75
☐	359	Bryan Berard, NYI.	2.00
☐	360	Jim Campbell, Stl.	.75
☐	361	Janne Niinimaa, Pha.	1.00
☐	362	Wade Redden, Ott.	.75
☐	363	Marc Denis, Col.	2.00

OVERSIZE PARALLEL

Card Size: 5" x 7"

Complete Set (18 cards): **35.00**

	No.	Player	NRMT-MT
☐	13	Ray Bourque, Bos.	2.50
☐	23	Pat LaFontaine, Buf.	1.00
☐	35	Theoren Fleury, Cgy.	1.50
☐	62	Valeri Kamensky, Col.	1.00
☐	69	Mike Modano, Dal.	2.50
☐	84	Chris Osgood (G), Det.	2.00
☐	133	Pierre Turgeon, Mtl.	1.00
☐	170	Wayne Gretzky, NYR.	10.00
☐	244	Roman Hamrlik, T.B.	1.00
☐	254	Félix Potvin (G), Tor.	2.50
☐	1	Wayne Gretzky, NYR.	10.00

	No.	Player	Price
□	2	Theoren Fleury, Cgy.	1.50
□	3	Jason Arnott, Edm.	1.00
□	4	Saku Koivu, Tor.	3.50
□	5	Pierre Turgeon, Mtl.	1.00
□	6	Daniel Alfredsson, Ott.	1.00
□	7	Félix Potvin (G), Tor.	2.50
□	8	Alexander Mogilny, Van.	1.50

MVP CARDS

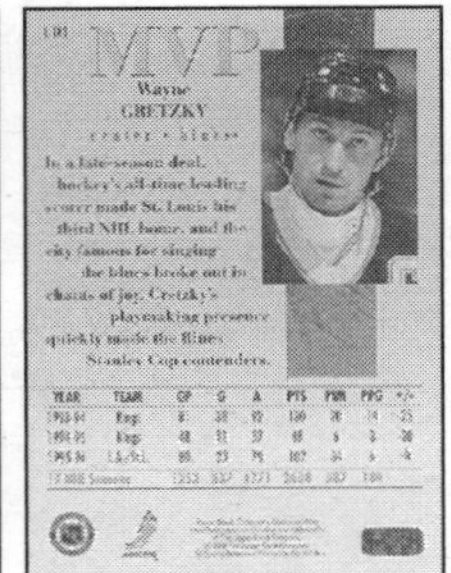

These cards have two versions: the regular insert and a gold parallel.

	No.	Player	Silver	Gold
Insert Set (45 cards):			**25.00**	**250.00**
□ □	UD1	Wayne Gretzky, Stl.	5.00	30.00
□ □	UD2	Ron Francis, Pgh.	.75	4.00
□ □	UD3	Peter Forsberg, Col.	2.50	15.00
□ □	UD4	Alexander Mogilny, Van.	.75	4.00
□ □	UD5	Joe Sakic, Col.	2.00	12.00
□ □	UD6	Claude Lemieux, Col.	.35	2.00
□ □	UD7	Teemu Selänne, Ana.	1.75	10.00
□ □	UD8	John LeClair, Pha.	1.25	6.00
□ □	UD9	Doug Weight, Edm.	.75	4.00
□ □	UD10	Paul Kariya, Ana.	3.00	20.00
□ □	UD11	Theoren Fleury, Cgy.	.75	4.00
□ □	UD12	John Vanbiesbrouck (G), Fla.	1.50	8.00
□ □	UD13	Sergei Fedorov, Det.	1.25	6.00
□ □	UD14	Steve Yzerman, Det.	2.50	15.00
□ □	UD15	Adam Oates, Bos.	.75	4.00
□ □	UD16	Keith Tkachuk, Wpg.	1.00	5.00
□ □	UD17	Mike Modano, Dal.	1.25	6.00
□ □	UD18	Jeremy Roenick, Chi.	.75	4.00
□ □	UD19	Patrick Roy (G), Col.	4.00	25.00
□ □	UD20	Félix Potvin (G), Tor.	1.25	6.00
□ □	UD21	Martin Brodeur (G), N.J.	1.75	10.00
□ □	UD22	Pavel Bure, Van.	1.75	10.00
□ □	UD23	Peter Bondra, Wsh.	1.00	5.00
□ □	UD24	Zigmund Palffy, NYI.	.75	4.00
□ □	UD25	Roman Hamrlik, T.B.	.50	3.00
□ □	UD26	Brendan Shanahan, Hfd.	1.50	8.00
□ □	UD27	Ray Bourque, Bos.	1.25	6.00
□ □	UD28	Paul Coffey, Det.	.50	3.00
□ □	UD29	Brett Hull, Stl.	1.25	6.00
□ □	UD30	Brian Leetch, NYR.	.75	4.00
□ □	UD31	Chris Chelios, Chi.	1.00	5.00
□ □	UD32	Vitali Yachmenev, L.A.	.35	2.00
□ □	UD33	Nicklas Lidström, Det.	.50	3.00
□ □	UD34	Ed Jovanovski, Fla.	.50	3.00
□ □	UD35	Sandis Ozolinsh, Col.	.50	3.00
□ □	UD36	Scott Stevens, N.J.	.35	2.00
□ □	UD37	Eric Dazé, Chi.	.50	3.00
□ □	UD38	Saku Koivu, Mtl.	1.75	10.00
□ □	UD39	Daniel Alfredsson, Ott.	.50	3.00
□ □	UD30	Pat LaFontaine, Buf.	.50	3.00
□ □	UD41	Cam Neely, Bos.	.50	3.00
□ □	UD42	Owen Nolan, S.J.	.50	3.00
□ □	UD43	Jaromir Jagr, Pgh.	2.50	15.00
□ □	UD44	Mats Sundin, Tor.	1.25	6.00
□ □	UD45	Doug Gilmour, Tor.	.75	4.00

STICKUMS

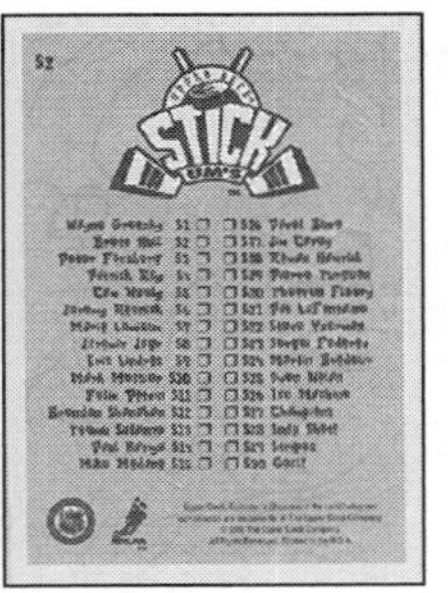

	No.	Player	NRMT-MT
Insert Set (30 stickers):			**35.00**
Poster:			**.50**
□	S1	Wayne Gretzky, Stl.	5.00
□	S2	Brett Hull, Stl.	1.25
□	S3	Peter Forsberg, Col.	2.50
□	S4	Patrick Roy (G), Col.	4.00
□	S5	Cam Neely, Bos.	.50
□	S6	Jeremy Roenick, Chi.	.75
□	S7	Mario Lemieux, Pgh.	4.00
□	S8	Jaromir Jagr, Pgh.	2.50
□	S9	Eric Lindros, Pha.	3.50
□	S10	Mark Messier, NYR.	1.25
□	S11	Félix Potvin (G), Tor.	1.25
□	S12	Brendan Shanahan, Hfd.	1.50
□	S13	Teemu Selänne, Ana.	1.75
□	S14	Paul Kariya, Ana.	3.50
□	S15	Mike Modano, Dal.	1.25
□	S16	Pavel Bure, Van.	1.75
□	S17	Jim Carey (G), Wsh.	.35
□	S18	Roman Hamrlik, T.B.	.50
□	S19	Pierre Turgeon, Stl.	.50
□	S20	Theoren Fleury, Cgy.	.75
□	S21	Pat LaFontaine, Buf.	.50
□	S22	Steve Yzerman, Det.	2.50
□	S23	Sergei Fedorov, Det.	1.25
□	S24	Martin Brodeur (G), N.J.	1.75
□	S25	Owen Nolan, S.J.	.50
□	S26	Ice Machine	.35
□	S27	Champions Stanley Cup	.50
□	S28	Snapshot	.35
□	S29	Stripes	.35
□	S30	Goal!	.35

YOU CRASH THE GAME

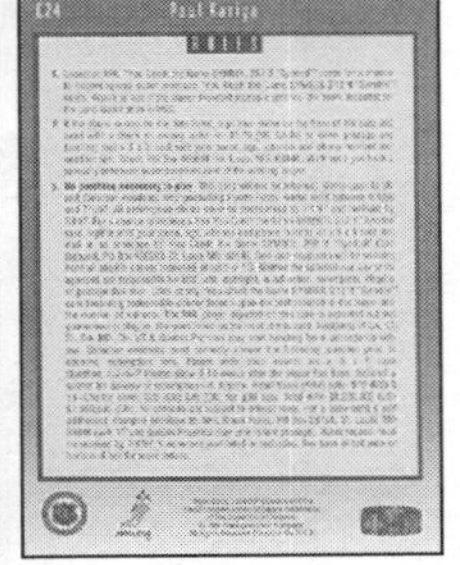

There are three versions for each player except Sakic (7) and Oates (21) for which there are two. Each version has a gold parallel.

	No.	Player	Silver	Gold
Insert Set (88 cards):			**100.00**	**600.00**
□□□□□□	C1	W. Gretzky, NYR. (vs. Ana./L.A./Edm.)	5.00	20.00
□□□□□□	C2	D. Gilmour, Tor. (vs. Pha./Pgh./T.B.)	.75	3.00
□□□□□□	C3	A. Mogilny, Van. (vs. Buf./NYI./Ott.)	.75	3.00
□□□□□□	C4	P. Bondra, Wsh. (vs. Det./L.A./Pho.)	1.00	4.00
□□□□□□	C5	M. Lemieux, Pgh. (vs. Chi./Col.Edm.)	4.00	15.00
□□□□□□	C6	J. Jagr, Pgh. (vs. Cgy./Det./Tor.)	2.50	10.00
□□□□	C7	J. Sakic, Col. (vs. Fla./Pgh.)	2.00	8.00
□□□□□□	C8	V. Yachmenev, L.A. (vs. Hfd./Mtl./N.J.)	.35	1.50
□□□□□□	C9	D. Weight, Edm. (vs. Bos./NYI./NYR.)	.75	3.00
□□□□□□	C10	S. Yzerman, Det. (vs. Bos./Fla./N.J.)	2.50	10.00
□□□□□□	C11	A. Zhamnov, Wpg. (vs. Buf./Hfd./T.B.)	.50	2.00
□□□□□□	C12	J. LeClair, Pha. (vs. Ana./Det./Stl.)	1.25	5.00
□□□□□□	C13	D. Alfredsson, Ott. (vs. Col./L.A./Van.)	.50	2.00
□□□□□□	C14	B. Shanahan, Hfd. (vs. Cgy./Chi./Tor.)	1.50	6.00
□□□□□□	C15	S. Koivu, Mtl. (vs. Ana./L.A./Stl.)	1.75	7.00
□□□□□□	C16	S. Thomas, N.J. (vs. Chi./Pho./Tor.)	.35	1.50
□□□□□□	C17	P. Bure, Van. (vs. Bos./Fla./NYR.)	1.75	7.00
□□□□□□	C18	Vy. Kozlov, Det. (vs. Buf./Ott./T.B.)	.35	1.50
□□□□□□	C19	T. Selänne, Ana. (vs. Hfd./NYI./Pha.)	1.75	7.00
□□□□□□	C20	E. Dazé, Chi. (vs. Bos./Buf./Pgh.)	.50	2.00
□□□□	C21	A. Oates, Bos. (vs. Det./Stl.)	.75	3.00
□□□□□□	C22	R. Bourque, Bos. (vs. Chi./Tor./Van.)	1.25	5.00
□□□□□□	C23	J. Arnott, Edm. (vs. Hfd./Pha./T.B.)	.50	2.00
□□□□□□	C24	P. Kariya, Ana. (vs. Bos./Fla./NYR.)	3.25	13.00
□□□□□□	C25	M. Renberg, Pha. (vs. Det./Pho./S.J.)	.35	1.50
□□□□□□	C26	K. Tkachuk, Wpg. (vs. Mtl./Ott./Pgh.)	1.00	4.00
□□□□□□	C27	B. Leetch, Ana. (vs. Ana./Col./Van.)	.75	3.00
□□□□□□	C28	E. Lindros, Pha. (vs. Cgy./L.A./Stl.)	3.25	13.00
□□□□□□	C29	M. Sundin, Tor. (vs. Buf./Fla./NYI.)	1.25	5.00
□□□□□□	C30	M. Messier, NYR. (vs. Chi./Det./Tor.)	1.25	5.00

YOU CRASH THE GAME REDEEMED

These cards have two versions: the silver redeemed card and a die-cut gold parallel. Numbers 20 and 25 did not win.

	No.	Player	Silver	Gold
Complete Set (28 cards):			**225.00**	**50.00**
□ □	CR1	Wayne Gretzky, NYR.	30.00	75.00
□ □	CR2	Doug Gilmour, Tor.	5.00	10.00
□ □	CR3	Alexander Mogilny, Van.	6.00	15.00
□ □	CR4	Peter Bondra, Wsh.	5.00	15.00
□ □	CR5	Mario Lemieux, Pgh.	25.00	60.00
□ □	CR6	Jaromir Jagr, Pgh.	15.00	35.00
□ □	CR7	Joe Sakic, Col.	12.00	30.00
□ □	CR8	Vitali Yachmenev, L.A.	2.50	5.00
□ □	CR9	Doug Weight, Edm.	5.00	10.00
□ □	CR10	Steve Yzerman, Det.	15.00	35.00
□ □	CR11	Alexei Zhamnov, Wpg.	3.00	6.00
□ □	CR12	John LeClair, Pha.	7.50	18.00
□ □	CR13	Daniel Alfredsson, Ott.	3.00	6.00
□ □	CR14	Brendan Shanahan, Hfd.	9.00	20.00
□ □	CR15	Saku Koivu, Mtl.	10.00	25.00
□ □	CR16	Steve Thomas, N.J.	2.50	5.00
□ □	CR17	Pavel Bure, Van.	10.00	25.00
□ □	CR18	Vyacheslav Kozlov, Det.	2.50	5.00
□ □	CR19	Teemu Selänne, Ana.	10.00	25.00
□ □	CR21	Adam Oates, Bos.	5.00	10.00
□ □	CR22	Ray Bourque, Bos.	7.50	18.00
□ □	CR23	John Arnott, Edm.	3.00	6.00
□ □	CR24	Paul Kariya, Ana.	20.00	50.00
□ □	CR26	Keith Tkachuk, Wpg.	6.00	15.00
□ □	CR27	Brian Leetch, NYR.	5.00	10.00
□ □	CR28	Eric Lindros, Pha.	20.00	50.00
□ □	CR29	Mats Sundin, Tor.	7.50	18.00
□ □	CR30	Mark Messier, NYR.	7.50	18.00

1996 - 97 UPPER DECK BLACK DIAMOND

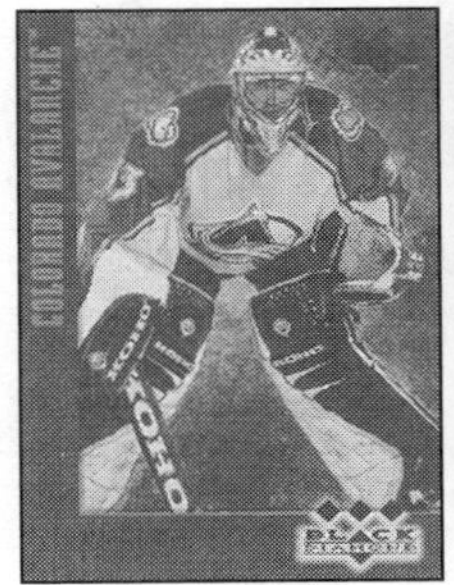

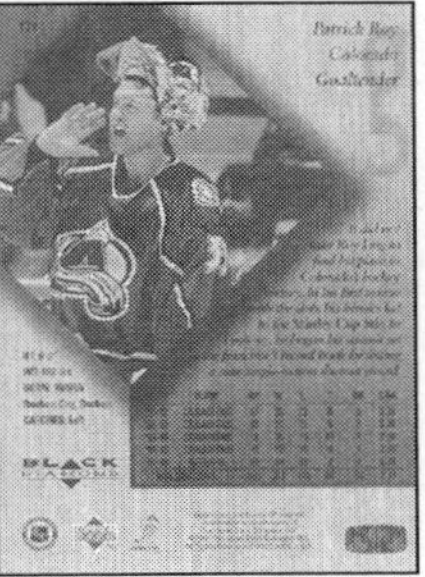

These cards have two versions: the regular card and a gold parallel card. Cards have either one diamond (1-90), two diamonds (91-150) or three diamonds (151-180). There are 50 copies of each Triple Diamond Gold card.

Master Set (180 cards):	**1,000.00**	**6,000.00**
Single Diamond Set (90 cards):	**30.00**	**400.00**
Double Diamond Set (60 cards):	**125.00**	**650.00**
Promo Card (Wayne Gretzky, #180):	**10.00**	
Triple Diamond Set (30 cards):	**900.00**	**5,000.00**

	No.	Player	Single	Gold
□ □	**1**	**Roman Turek (G), Dal., RC**	**.50**	**5.00**
□ □	2	Viacheslav Fetisov, Det.	.50	5.00
□ □	3	Mike Dunham (G), N.J.	.25	4.00
□ □	**4**	**Jean-François Fortin, Cdn., RC**	**.75**	**5.00**
□ □	5	Keith Primeau, Hfd.	.50	5.00
□ □	6	Zigmund Palffy, NYI.	1.00	8.00
□ □	7	Curtis Leschyshyn, Hfd.	.25	4.00
□ □	8	Vladimir Tsyplakov, L.A.	.25	4.00
□ □	9	Adam Graves, NYR.	.25	4.00
□ □	10	Ian Lapperière, L.A.	.25	4.00
□ □	11	Bill Lindsay, Fla.	.25	4.00
□ □	12	Brian Leetch, NYR.	1.00	8.00
□ □	13	Martin Lapointe, Det.	.25	4.00
□ □	**14**	**Scott Barney, Cdn., RC**	**.25**	**4.00**
□ □	**15**	**Mike Grier, Edm., RC**	**2.00**	**12.00**
□ □	16	Vladimir Konstantinov, Det.	.25	4.00
□ □	**17**	**Rem Murray, Edm., RC**	**.75**	**5.00**
□ □	18	Ed Jovanovski, Fla.	.50	5.00
□ □	19	Chris O'Sullivan, Cgy.	.25	4.00
□ □	20	Steve Rucchin, Ana.	.25	4.00
□ □	21	Jay Pandolfo, N.J.	.25	4.00
□ □	**22**	**Nick Boynton, Cdn., RC**	**2.00**	**10.00**
□ □	23	Greg Adams, Dal.	.25	4.00
□ □	**24**	**Adam Colagiacomo, Cdn., RC**	**1.25**	**6.00**
□ □	25	Vincent Damphousse, Mtl.	.75	8.00
□ □	**26**	**Shane Willis, Cdn., RC**	**1.00**	**5.00**
□ □	27	Alexei Kovalev, NYR.	.25	4.00
□ □	28	Doug Gilmour, N.J.	.75	8.00
□ □	29	Joel Otto, Pha.	.25	4.00
□ □	30	Donald Audette, Buf.	.25	4.00
□ □	31	Tommy Salo (G), NYI.	.25	4.00
□ □	32	Rob Ray, Buf.	.25	4.00
□ □	33	Kris Draper, Det.	.25	4.00
□ □	34	Ed Belfour (G), S.J.	.75	8.00
□ □	35	Mike Richter (G), NYR.	.75	8.00
□ □	36	Nikolai Khabibulin (G), Pho.	.75	8.00
□ □	37	Eric Desjardins, Pha.	.25	4.00
□ □	**38**	**Daniel Tkaczuk, Cdn., RC**	**3.50**	**25.00**
□ □	39	Keith Jones, Col.	.25	4.00
□ □	40	Per Gustafsson, Fla.	.25	4.00
□ □	41	Jocelyn Thibault (G), Mtl.	.75	8.00
□ □	42	Mike Gartner, Pho.	.50	5.00
□ □	43	Vitali Yachmenev, L.A.	.25	4.00
□ □	44	Jonas Hoglund, Cgy.	.25	4.00
□ □	45	Craig Janney, Pho.	.25	4.00
□ □	46	Daymond Langkow, T.B.	.25	4.00
□ □	47	Mattias Timander, Bos.	.25	4.00
□ □	48	Scott Young, Col.	.25	4.00
□ □	49	Mikael Renberg, Pha.	.25	4.00
□ □	50	Nicklas Lidström, Det.	.50	5.00
□ □	51	Andrei Kovalenko, Edm.	.50	5.00
□ □	52	Adam Foote, Col.	.50	5.00
□ □	53	Guy Hebert (G), Ana.	.50	5.00
□ □	54	Kevin Hatcher, Pgh	.25	4.00
□ □	55	Rick Tocchet, Wsh	.25	4.00
□ □	56	Sergei Zubov, Dal.	.50	5.00
□ □	57	Chris Phillips, Cdn.	1.25	8.00
□ □	58	Denis Savard, Chi.	.50	5.00
□ □	59	Bernie Nicholls, S.J.	.25	4.00
□ □	60	Jozef Stumpel, Bos.	.50	5.00
□ □	61	Darius Kasparaitis, Pgh.	.25	4.00
□ □	62	Kelly Hrudey, S.J.	.25	4.00
□ □	**63**	**Marcel Cousineau (G), Tor., RC**	**1.00**	**6.00**
□ □	64	Brian Skrudland, Fla.	.25	4.00
□ □	65	Byron Dafoe (G), L.A.	.25	4.00
□ □	66	Ray Sheppard, Fla.	.25	4.00
□ □	67	Chris Simon, Wsh.	.25	4.00
□ □	**68**	**Dainius Zubrus, Pha., RC**	**5.00**	**20.00**
□ □	69	Ethan Moreau, Chi.	.50	5.00
□ □	70	Theoren Fleury, Cgy.	.75	8.00
□ □	71	Damian Rhodes (G), Ott.	.25	4.00
□ □	72	Kevin Dineen, Hfd.	.25	4.00
□ □	73	Kenny Jonsson, NYI.	.25	4.00
□ □	74	Ray Ferraro, L.A.	.25	4.00
□ □	75	Jaromir Jagr, Pgh.	3.00	30.00
□ □	76	Wayne Primeau, Buf.	.25	4.00
□ □	77	Chris Gratton, T.B.	.50	5.00
□ □	78	Alyn McCauley, Cdn.	2.00	8.00
□ □	79	Christian Dubé, NYR.	1.00	5.00
□ □	80	Bill Ranford (G), Wsh.	.50	5.00
□ □	81	Adam Deadmarsh, Col.	.25	4.00
□ □	82	Dale Hunter, Wsh.	.25	4.00
□ □	83	Derek Plante, Buf.	.25	4.00
□ □	84	Todd Bertuzzi, Buf.	.50	5.00
□ □	85	Stéphane Fiset (G), L.A.	.50	5.00
□ □	**86**	**Boyd Devereaux, Cdn., RC**	**1.00**	**6.00**
□ □	87	Jere Lehtinen, Dal.	.50	5.00
□ □	**88**	**Peter Schaefer, Cdn., RC**	**3.00**	**15.00**
□ □	89	Alexander Mogilny, Van.	1.00	8.00
□ □	90	Joé Juneau, Wsh.	.25	4.00

	No.	Player	Double	Gold
□ □	91	Alexandre Daigle, Ott	3.00	12.00
□ □	92	Jeff O'Neill, Hfd.	3.00	12.00
□ □	93	Todd Warriner, Tor.	1.50	6.00
□ □	**94**	**Sergei Berezin, Tor., RC**	**6.00**	**20.00**
□ □	95	Petr Nedved, Pgh.	1.50	6.00
□ □	96	Phil Housley, Wsh.	1.50	6.00
□ □	97	Jason Arnott, Edm.	3.00	12.00
□ □	98	Sandis Ozolinsh, Col.	3.00	12.00
□ □	99	Mike Modano, Dal.	8.00	40.00
□ □	100	Mark Messier, NYR.	8.00	40.00
□ □	101	Ron Francis, Pgh.	4.00	20.00
□ □	102	Oleg Tverdovsky, Pho.	1.50	6.00
□ □	**103**	**Patrick Marleau, Cdn., RC**	**15.00**	**50.00**
□ □	104	Brian Bellows, Ana.	1.50	6.00
□ □	105	Eric Fichaud (G), NYI.	3.00	12.00
□ □	106	Alexei Zhamnov, Chi.	3.00	12.00
□ □	107	Wendel Clark, Tor.	3.00	12.00
□ □	108	Dimitri Khristich, L.A.	1.50	6.00
□ □	109	Mike Ricci, Col.	1.50	6.00
□ □	110	John LeClair, Pha.	8.00	40.00
□ □	111	Owen Nolan, S.J.	3.00	12.00
□ □	112	Bill Guerin, N.J.	3.00	12.00
□ □	113	Vyacheslav Kozlov, Det.	1.50	6.00
□ □	114	Brendan Shanahan, Det.	10.00	50.00
□ □	115	Trevor Linden, Van.	3.00	12.00
□ □	116	José Théodore (G), Mtl.	4.00	15.00
□ □	117	Rod Brind'Amour, Pha.	3.00	12.00
□ □	118	Brian Holzinger, Buf.	1.50	6.00
□ □	119	Shayne Corson, Mtl.	3.00	12.00
□ □	120	Bryan Smolinski, NYI.	1.50	6.00
□ □	121	Tony Granato, S.J.	1.50	6.00
□ □	122	Mariusz Czerkawski, Edm.	1.50	6.00
□ □	123	Andrew Cassels, Hfd.	1.50	6.00
□ □	124	Scott Stevens, N.J.	1.50	6.00
□ □	125	Mike Ridley, Van.	1.50	6.00
□ □	126	Jamie Langenbrunner, Dal.	3.00	12.00
□ □	127	Scott Mellanby, Fla.	1.50	6.00
□ □	128	Grant Fuhr (G), Stl.	3.00	12.00
□ □	129	Félix Potvin (G), Tor.	8.00	40.00
□ □	130	Marc Denis (G), Col.	4.00	15.00
□ □	131	Corey Hirsch (G), Van.	1.50	6.00
□ □	132	Chris Osgood (G), Det.	6.00	30.00
□ □	133	Peter Bondra, Wsh.	6.00	30.00
□ □	134	Martin Brodeur (G), N.J.	12.00	60.00
□ □	135	Pierre Turgeon, Stl.	3.00	12.00
□ □	136	Pat Verbeek, Dal.	1.50	6.00
□ □	137	Scott Niedermayer, N.J.	3.00	12.00
□ □	138	Geoff Sanderson, Hfd.	1.50	6.00
□ □	139	Jason Dawe, Buf.	1.50	6.00
□ □	140	Rob Niedermayer, Fla.	1.50	6.00
□ □	141	Daniel Alfredsson, Ott.	3.00	12.00
□ □	142	Jim Campbell, Stl.	3.00	12.00
□ □	143	Roman Hamrlik, T.B.	3.00	12.00
□ □	144	Rob Blake, L.A.	3.00	12.00
□ □	145	Chris Chelios, Chi.	6.00	30.00
□ □	146	Teemu Selänne, Ana.	12.00	60.00
□ □	147	Jim Carey (G), Bos	1.50	6.00
□ □	148	Dino Ciccarelli, T.B.	3.00	12.00
□ □	149	Mark Recchi, Mtl.	3.00	12.00
□ □	150	Chris Pronger, Stl.	3.00	12.00

	No.	Player	Triple	Gold
□ □	151	Paul Coffey, Pha.	10.00	50.00
□ □	152	Adam Oates, Wsh.	15.00	75.00
□ □	153	Keith Tkachuk, Pho.	20.00	100.00
□ □	154	Janne Niinimaa, Pha.	10.00	50.00
□ □	155	Sergei Fedorov, Det.	25.00	125.00
□ □	156	Dominik Hasek (G), Buf.	35.00	200.00
□ □	157	Eric Lindros, Pha.	65.00	450.00
□ □	158	Curtis Joseph (G), Edm.	30.00	150.00
□ □	159	Alexei Yashin, Ott.	20.00	100.00
□ □	**160**	**Joe Thornton, Cdn., RC**	**50.00**	**300.00**
□ □	161	Bryan Berard, NYI.	15.00	75.00
□ □	162	Steve Yzerman, Det.	50.00	300.00
□ □	163	Mats Sundin, Tor.	25.00	125.00
□ □	164	Jarome Iginla, Cgy.	15.00	75.00
□ □	165	John Vanbiesbrouck (G), Fla.	30.00	150.00
□ □	166	Mario Lemieux, Pgh.	80.00	600.00
□ □	167	Jeremy Roenick, Pho.	15.00	75.00
□ □	**168**	**Patrick Lalime, Pgh., RC**	**10.00**	**50.00**
□ □	169	Joe Sakic, Col.	40.00	225.00
□ □	170	Brett Hull, Stl.	25.00	125.00
□ □	171	Peter Forsberg, Col.	50.00	300.00
□ □	172	Doug Weight, Edm.	15.00	75.00
□ □	173	Tony Amonte, Chi.	10.00	50.00
□ □	174	Patrick Roy (G), Col.	80.00	600.00
□ □	175	Paul Kariya, Ana.	65.00	450.00
□ □	176	Pavel Bure, Van.	35.00	200.00
□ □	177	Ray Bourque, Bos.	25.00	125.00
□ □	178	Saku Koivu, Mtl.	35.00	200.00
□ □	179	Wade Redden, Ott.	10.00	50.00
□ □	180	Wayne Gretzky, NYR.	120.00	900.00

RUN FOR THE CUP

Run For The Cup inserts are serial numbered out of 100.

Insert Set (20 cards): **8,000.00**

	No.	Player	NRMT-MT
□	RC1	Wayne Gretzky, NYR.	1,200.00
□	RC2	Saku Koivu, Mtl.	350.00
□	RC3	Mario Lemieux, Pgh.	800.00
□	RC4	Patrick Roy (G), Col.	800.00
□	RC5	Jaromir Jagr, Pgh.	500.00
□	RC6	John Vanbiesbrouck (G), Fla.	300.00
□	RC7	Peter Forsberg, Col.	500.00
□	RC8	Paul Kariya, Ana.	650.00
□	RC9	Steve Yzerman, Det.	500.00
□	RC10	Joe Sakic, Col.	400.00
□	RC11	Mark Messier, NYR.	250.00
□	RC12	Sergei Fedorov, Det.	250.00
□	RC13	Mats Sundin, Tor.	250.00
□	RC14	Pavel Bure, Van.	350.00
□	RC15	Ed Jovanovski, Fla.	125.00
□	RC16	Mike Modano, Dal.	250.00
□	RC17	Curtis Joseph (G), Edm.	300.00
□	RC18	Teemu Selänne, Ana.	350.00
□	RC19	Jarome Iginla, Cgy.	125.00
□	RC20	Eric Lindros, Pha.	650.00

1996 - 97 UPPER DECK "ICE"

Cards 1-115 have two versions each. Numbers 1-75 have a bronze "Performers" parallel, 76-105 have silver "Phenoms" parallel and 106-115 have a gold "Legends" parallel.

Imprint: © THE UPPER DECK COMPANY, LLC.

Complete Set (150 cards):	**175.00**
Common Player:	**.50**

	No.	Player	Bronze	Reg.
□ □	1	Kevin Todd, Ana.	4.00	.50
□ □	2	Adam Oates, Bos.	10.00	1.50
□ □	3	Bill Ranford (G), Bos.	6.00	1.00
□ □	4	Rick Tocchet, Bos.	4.00	.50
□ □	5	Dominik Hasek (G), Buf.	20.00	3.50
□ □	6	Richard Smehlik, Buf.	4.00	.50
□ □	7	Derek Plante, Buf.	4.00	.50
□ □	8	Joel Bouchard, Cgy.	4.00	.50
□ □	9	Theoren Fleury, Cgy.	10.00	1.50
□ □	10	Chris Chelios, Chi.	15.00	2.00
□ □	11	Ed Belfour (G), Chi.	10.00	1.50
□ □	12	Eric Weinrich, Chi.	4.00	1.00
□ □	13	Tony Amonte, Chi.	6.00	1.00
□ □	14	Greg Adams, Dal.	4.00	.50
□ □	15	Jamie Langenbrunner, Dal.	6.00	1.00
□ □	16	Sergei Zubov, Dal.	6.00	1.00
□ □	17	Pat Verbeek, Dal.	4.00	.50

	No.	Player	Reg.	Silver
☐☐	18	Chris Osgood (G), Det.	15.00	2.00
☐☐	**19**	**Rem Murray, Edm., RC**	**8.00**	**1.50**
☐☐	20	Jason Arnott, Edm.	6.00	1.00
☐☐	21	Curtis Joseph (G), Edm.	18.00	3.00
☐☐	22	Bill Lindsay, Fla.	4.00	.50
☐☐	23	Ray Sheppard, Fla.	4.00	.50
☐☐	24	Martin Straka, Fla.	4.00	.50
☐☐	25	J-S Giguere (G), Hfd.	8.00	1.50
☐☐	26	Sean Burke (G), Hfd.	6.00	1.00
☐☐	27	Keith Primeau, Hfd.	6.00	1.00
☐☐	28	Geoff Sanderson, Hfd.	4.00	.50
☐☐	29	Rob Blake, L.A.	6.00	1.00
☐☐	30	Ian Laperrière, L.A.	4.00	.50
☐☐	31	Byron Dafoe, L.A.	4.00	.50
☐☐	32	Vincent Damphousse, Mtl.	10.00	1.50
☐☐	33	Darcy Tucker, Mtl.	4.00	.50
☐☐	34	Brian Savage, Mtl.	4.00	.50
☐☐	35	Bill Guerin, N.J.	6.00	1.00
☐☐	36	Scott Niedermayer, N.J.	6.00	1.00
☐☐	37	Steve Thomas, N.J.	4.00	.50
☐☐	38	Valeri Zelepukin, N.J.	4.00	.50
☐☐	39	Bryan Smolinski, NYI.	4.00	.50
☐☐	40	Derek King, NYI.	4.00	.50
☐☐	41	Mike Richter, NYR.	10.00	1.50
☐☐	**42**	**Daniel Goneau, NYR., RC**	**4.00**	**.50**
☐☐	43	Brian Leetch, NYR.	10.00	1.50
☐☐	44	Adam Graves, NYR.	4.00	.50
☐☐	45	Damian Rhodes (G), Ott.	4.00	.50
☐☐	46	Mikael Renberg, Pha.	4.00	.50
☐☐	47	Eric Desjardins, Pha.	4.00	.50
☐☐	48	Rod Brind'Amour, Pha.	6.00	1.00
☐☐	49	Janne Niinimaa, Pha.	5.00	1.00
☐☐	50	Dale Hawerchuk, Pha.	4.00	.50
☐☐	51	Jeremy Roenick, Pho.	10.00	1.50
☐☐	52	Mike Gartner, Pho.	6.00	1.00
☐☐	53	Cliff Ronning, Pho.	4.00	.50
☐☐	**54**	**Patrick Lalime (G), Pgh., RC**	**4.00**	**.50**
☐☐	55	Ron Francis, Pgh.	10.00	1.50
☐☐	56	Petr Nedved, Pgh.	4.00	.50
☐☐	57	Bernie Nicholls, S.J.	4.00	.50
☐☐	58	Jeff Friesen, S.J.	6.00	1.00
☐☐	59	Owen Nolan, S.J.	6.00	1.00
☐☐	60	Marty McSorley, S.J.	4.00	.50
☐☐	61	Pierre Turgeon, Stl.	6.00	1.00
☐☐	62	Grant Fuhr (G), Stl.	6.00	1.00
☐☐	63	Chris Pronger, Stl.	6.00	1.00
☐☐	64	Jim Campbell, Stl.	6.00	1.00
☐☐	65	Chris Gratton, T.B.	6.00	1.00
☐☐	66	Dino Ciccarelli, T.B.	6.00	1.00
☐☐	67	Félix Potvin (G), Tor.	15.00	2.50
☐☐	68	Tie Domi, Tor.	4.00	.50
☐☐	69	Doug Gilmour, Tor.	10.00	1.50
☐☐	70	Trevor Linden, Van.	6.00	1.00
☐☐	71	Corey Hirsch (G), Van.	4.00	.50
☐☐	72	Jim Carey (G), Wsh.	4.00	.50
☐☐	73	Chris Simon, Wsh.	4.00	.50
☐☐	74	Mark Tinordi, Wsh.	4.00	.50
☐☐	75	Sergei Gonchar, Wsh.	4.00	.50
	No.	**Player**	**Reg.**	**Silver**
☐☐	76	Paul Kariya, Ana.	100.00	6.50
☐☐	77	Teemu Selänne, Ana.	50.00	3.50
☐☐	78	Jarome Iginla, Cgy.	15.00	1.50
☐☐	79	Eric Dazé, Chi.	15.00	1.00
☐☐	80	Sandis Ozolinsh, Col.	15.00	1.00
☐☐	81	Peter Forsberg, Col.	75.00	5.00
☐☐	82	Mike Modano, Dal.	35.00	2.50
☐☐	83	Anders Eriksson, Det.	8.00	.50
☐☐	84	Sergei Fedorov, Det.	35.00	2.50
☐☐	85	Brendan Shanahan, Det.	45.00	3.00
☐☐	**86**	**Mike Grier Edm., RC**	**20.00**	**2.50**
☐☐	87	Doug Weight, Edm.	20.00	1.50
☐☐	88	Ed Jovanovski, Fla.	15.00	1.00
☐☐	89	Saku Koivu, Mtl.	50.00	3.50
☐☐	90	José Théodore (G), Mtl.	20.00	2.00
☐☐	91	Jocelyn Thibault (G), Mtl.	20.00	1.50
☐☐	92	Martin Brodeur (G), N.J.	50.00	3.50
☐☐	93	Bryan Berard, NYI.	20.00	1.50
☐☐	94	Zigmund Palffy, NYI.	20.00	1.50
☐☐	95	Daniel Alfredsson, Ott.	15.00	1.00
☐☐	96	Alexei Yashin, Ott.	30.00	2.00
☐☐	97	Wade Redden, Ott.	10.00	1.00
☐☐	98	John LeClair, Pha.	35.00	2.50
☐☐	99	Oleg Tverdovsky, Pho.	8.00	.50
☐☐	100	Keith Tkachuk, Pho.	30.00	2.00
☐☐	101	Jaromir Jagr, Pgh.	75.00	5.00
☐☐	102	Roman Hamrlik, Pgh.	15.00	1.00
☐☐	**103**	**Sergei Berezin, Tor., RC**	**12.00**	**2.00**
☐☐	104	Alexander Mogilny, Van.	20.00	1.50
☐☐	105	Pavel Bure, Van.	50.00	3.50
	No.	**Player**	**Reg.**	**Gold**
☐☐	106	Ray Bourque, Bos.	75.00	2.50
☐☐	107	Patrick Roy (G), Col.	350.00	8.00
☐☐	108	Joe Sakic, Col.	185.00	4.00
☐☐	109	Steve Yzerman, Det.	200.00	5.00
☐☐	110	John Vanbiesbrouck (G), Fla.	125.00	3.00
☐☐	111	Mark Messier, NYR.	100.00	2.50
☐☐	112	Wayne Gretzky, NYR.	475.00	12.00
☐☐	113	Eric Lindros, Pha.	300.00	6.50
☐☐	114	Mario Lemieux, Pgh.	350.00	8.00
☐☐	115	Brett Hull, Stl.	90.00	2.50

	No.	Player	Reg.
☐	**116**	**Joe Thornton, Cdn., RC**	**18.00**
☐	117	Marc Denis (G), Cdn.	4.00
☐	118	Martin Biron (G), Cdn.	1.50
☐	119	Jason Doig, Cdn.	.75
☐	120	Daniel Brière, Cdn.	4.00
☐	**121**	**Trevor Letowski, Cdn., RC**	**1.50**
☐	**122**	**Boyd Devereaux, Cdn., RC**	**2.50**
☐	**123**	**Dwayne Hay, Cdn., RC**	**1.50**
☐	124	Hugh Hamilton, Cdn.	.75
☐	**125**	**Brad Isbister, Cdn., RC**	**1.50**
☐	**126**	**Shane Willis, Cdn., RC**	**1.75**
☐	**127**	**Trent Whitfield, Cdn., RC**	**1.50**
☐	**128**	**Jesse Wallin, Cdn., RC**	**2.00**
☐	129	Alyn McCauley, Cdn.	4.00
☐	**130**	**Cameron Mann, Cdn., RC**	**5.00**
☐	131	Jeff Ware, Cdn.	.75
☐	132	Cory Sarich, Cdn.	1.50
☐	**133**	**Rick Jackman, Cdn., RC**	**2.00**
☐	134	Brad Larsen, Cdn.	1.00
☐	**135**	**Peter Schaefer, Cdn., RC**	**3.50**
☐	136	Christian Dubé, Cdn.	1.00
☐	137	Chris Phillips, Cdn.	2.00
☐	138	Sergei Samsonov, Rus.	5.00
☐	139	Alexei Morozov, Rus.	3.50
☐	**140**	**Sergei Fedotov, Rus., RC**	**1.50**
☐	**141**	**Den. Khlopotnov (G), Rus., RC**	**.75**
☐	**142**	**Andrei Markov, Rus., RC**	**1.00**
☐	143	Andrei Petrunin, Rus.	.75
☐	144	Roman Lyasenko, Rus.	.75
☐	**145**	**Joe Corvo, USA., RC**	**1.50**
☐	146	Eric Rasmussen, USA.	1.50
☐	**147**	**Michael York, USA., RC**	**2.00**
☐	148	Brian Boucher (G), USA.	1.75
☐	**149**	**Paul Mara, USA., RC**	**3.00**
☐	150	Marty Reasoner, USA.	1.00

STANLEY CUP FOUNDATIONS

These cards have two versions: the regular insert and a die-cut "Dynasty" parallel.

Insert Set (10 cards): **750.00 3,500.00**

	No.	Player	Reg.	Die-Cut
☐☐	S1	W. Gretzky / M. Messier	150.00	800.00
☐☐	S2	S. Yzerman / B. Shanahan	90.00	450.00
☐☐	S3	J. Vanbiesbrouck / E. Jovanovski	60.00	250.00
☐☐	S4	S. Koivu / J. Thibault	50.00	200.00
☐☐	S5	P. Roy / J. Sakic	120.00	600.00
☐☐	S6	P. Kariya / T. Selänne	90.00	450.00
☐☐	S7	M. Lemieux / J. Jagr	125.00	650.00
☐☐	S8	K. Tkachuk / J. Roenick	30.00	120.00
☐☐	S9	D. Weight / J. Arnott	30.00	120.00
☐☐	S10	E. Lindros / J. LeClair	100.00	500.00

1997 BOWMAN CHL

These cards have two versions: the regular card and an O-Pee-Chee parallel. Cards 121-160 (CHL Prospects) have a thrid "Certified Autograph Issue" parallel. Patrick Marleau and Roberto Luongo had not returned their cards that were supposed to be signed for this set. Prices may vary considerably for regional stars.

Imprint: © THE TOPPS COMPANY, INC.

Complete Set (160 cards): **550.00 35.00**

Common Player: **1.00 .15**

	No.	Player	OPC	Reg.
☐☐	1	Jan Bulis, OHL	3.00	.50
☐☐	2	Daniel Cleary, OHL	12.00	1.50
☐☐	3	Dave Duerden, OHL	1.00	.15
☐☐	4	Cameron Mann, OHL	6.00	.75
☐☐	5	Alyn McCauley, OHL	12.00	1.50
☐☐	6	Tyler Rennette, OHL	1.00	.15
☐☐	7	Marc Savard, OHL	4.00	.75
☐☐	8	Daniel Tkaczuk, OHL	7.50	1.25
☐☐	9	John Tripp, OHL	1.00	.15
☐☐	10	Joel Trottier, OHL	1.00	.15
☐☐	11	Sean Venedam, OHL	1.00	.15
☐☐	12	Alexandre Volchkov, OHL	3.00	.50
☐☐	13	Sean Blanchard, OHL	1.00	.15
☐☐	14	Kevin Bolibruck, OHL	1.00	.15
☐☐	15	Nick Boynton, OHL	1.50	.25
☐☐	16	Paul Mara, OHL	3.00	.50
☐☐	17	Marc Moro, OHL	1.00	.15
☐☐	18	Marty Wilford, OHL	1.00	.15
☐☐	19	Zac Bierk (G), OHL	2.00	.35
☐☐	20	Kory Cooper (G), OHL	1.50	.25
☐☐	21	Richard Rochefort, OHL	1.00	.15
☐☐	22	Matt Cooke, OHL	1.00	.15
☐☐	23	Boyd Devereaux, OHL	4.00	.75
☐☐	24	Rico Fata, OHL	18.00	3.00
☐☐	25	Dwayne Hay, OHL	1.00	.15
☐☐	26	Trevor Letowski, OHL	1.50	.25
☐☐	27	Ryan Mougenel, OHL	1.00	.15
☐☐	28	Todd Norman, OHL	1.50	.25
☐☐	29	Lacy Paleczny, OHL	1.00	.15
☐☐	30	Colin Pepperall, OHL	1.50	.25
☐☐	31	Jonathan Sim, OHL	1.00	.15
☐☐	32	Joe Thornton, OHL	25.00	3.00
☐☐	33	Brian Wesenberg, OHL	1.00	.15
☐☐	34	Andy Delmore, OHL	1.00	.15
☐☐	35	Chris Hajt, OHL	1.00	.15
☐☐	36	Richard Jackman, OHL	1.00	.15
☐☐	37	Denis Smith, OHL	1.00	.15
☐☐	38	Jamie Sokolsky, OHL	1.00	.15
☐☐	39	Paul Traynor, OHL	1.00	.15
☐☐	40	Patrick Desrochers (G), OHL	6.00	1.00
☐☐	41	Robert Esche (G), OHL	2.00	.35
☐☐	42	Roberto Luongo (G), QMJHL	30.00	5.00
☐☐	43	Frédéric Henry (G), QMJHL	1.00	.15
☐☐	44	Marc Olivier Roy, QMJHL	1.00	.15
☐☐	45	Samy Nasreddine, QMJHL	1.00	.15
☐☐	46	J.F. Fortin, QMJHL	1.50	.25
☐☐	47	Martin Ethier, QMJHL	1.00	.15
☐☐	48	Jason Doig, QMJHL	1.00	.15
☐☐	49	Dominic Perna, QMJHL	1.00	.15
☐☐	50	Daniel Brière, QMJHL	15.00	1.75
☐☐	51	Pavel Rosa, QMJHL	4.00	.75
☐☐	52	Philippe Audet, QMJHL	1.00	.15
☐☐	53	Gordie Dwyer, QMJHL	1.00	.15
☐☐	54	Martin Menard, QMJHL	1.00	.15
☐☐	55	Jonathan Delisle, QMJHL	1.00	.15
☐☐	56	Peter Worrell, QMJHL	1.50	.25
☐☐	57	François Methot, QMJHL	1.00	.15
☐☐	58	Steve Bégin, QMJHL	1.00	.15
☐☐	59	Karol Bartanus, QMJHL	1.00	.15
☐☐	60	J.P. Dumont, QMJHL	12.00	1.50
☐☐	61	Marc Denis (G), QMJHL	8.00	1.00
☐☐	62	J.S. Giguère (G), QMJHL	6.00	.75
☐☐	63	Jason Goneau, QMJHL	1.00	.15
☐☐	64	Radoslav Suchy, QMJHL	1.00	.15
☐☐	65	Stéphane Robidas, QMJHL	1.00	.15
☐☐	66	Marc-André Gaudet, QMJHL	1.00	.15
☐☐	67	Eric Drouin, QMJHL	1.00	.15
☐☐	68	Derrick Walser, QMJHL	1.00	.15
☐☐	69	Vincent Lecavalier, QMJHL	60.00	8.00
☐☐	70	Denis Hamel, QMJHL	1.00	.15
☐☐	71	Daniel Corso, QMJHL	3.50	.65
☐☐	72	Martin Moise, QMJHL	1.00	.15
☐☐	73	Eric Belanger, QMJHL	1.00	.15
☐☐	74	Olivier Morin, QMJHL	1.00	.15
☐☐	75	Jerome Tremblay, QMJHL	1.00	.15
☐☐	76	Jody Shelley, QMJHL	1.00	.15

	No.	Player		
□□	77	Eric Normandin, QMJHL	1.00	.15
□□	78	David Thibeault, QMJHL	1.00	.15
□□	79	Christian Daigle, QMJHL	1.00	.15
□□	80	Alexandre Jacques, QMJHL	1.00	.15
□□	81	Brian Boucher (G), WHL	5.00	.75
□□	82	Randy Petruk (G), WHL	1.50	.25
□□	83	Hugh Hamilton, WHL	1.00	.15
□□	84	Joel Kwiatkowski, WHL	1.00	.15
□□	85	Zenith Komarniski, WHL	1.50	.25
□□	86	Joey Tetarenko, WHL	1.00	.15
□□	87	Tyler Willis, WHL	1.00	.15
□□	88	Patrick Marleau, WHL	20.00	2.50
□□	89	Trent Whitfield, WHL	1.00	.15
□□	90	Martin Cerven, WHL	1.00	.15
□□	91	Donnie Kinney, WHL	1.00	.15
□□	92	Brad Isbister, WHL	3.50	.65
□□	93	Todd Robinson, WHL	1.00	.15
□□	94	Greg Leeb, WHL	1.00	.15
□□	95	John Cirjak, WHL	1.00	.15
□□	96	Randy Perry, WHL	1.00	.15
□□	97	Derek Schutz, WHL	1.00	.15
□□	98	Brenden Morrow, WHL	1.50	.25
□□	99	Shawn McNeil, WHL	1.00	.15
□□	100	Brad Ference, WHL	3.00	.50
□□	101	Ryan Hoople (G), WHL	1.50	.25
□□	102	Brian Elder (G), WHL	1.50	.25
□□	103	Mike McBain, WHL	1.00	.15
□□	104	Jesse Wallin, WHL	1.50	.25
□□	105	Chris Phillips, WHL	4.00	.75
□□	106	Kelly Smart, WHL	1.00	.15
□□	107	Arron Asham, WHL	1.00	.15
□□	108	Byron Ritchie, WHL	1.00	.15
□□	109	Derek Morris, WHL	1.50	.25
□□	110	Travis Brigley, WHL	1.00	.15
□□	111	Justin Kurtz, WHL	1.00	.15
□□	112	B.J. Young, WHL	1.00	.15
□□	113	Shane Willis, WHL	3.50	.65
□□	114	Josh Holden, WHL	4.00	.75
□□	115	Cory Sarich, WHL	3.50	.65
□□	116	Brad Larsen, WHL	1.50	.25
□□	117	Stefan Cherneski, WHL	1.50	.25
□□	118	Peter Schaefer, WHL	4.00	.75
□□	119	Dmitri Nabokov, WHL	1.50	.25
□□	120	Sergei Varlamov, WHL	4.00	.75

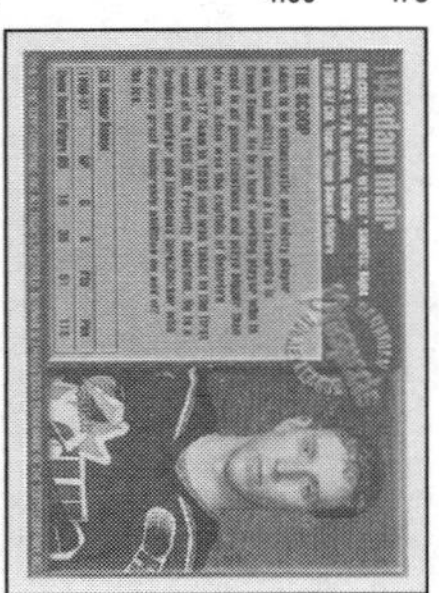

	No.	Player	Aut.	OPC	Reg.
□□□	121	Daniel Cleary, Team Cherry	30.00	12.00	1.50
□□□	122	Jarrett Smith, Team Cherry	12.00	1.00	.15
□□□	123	Alexandre Mathieu, Team Cherry	12.00	1.00	.15
□□□	124	Matt Elich, Team Cherry	12.00	1.00	.15
□□□	125	Joe Thornton, Team Cherry	75.00	25.00	3.00
□□□	126	Mike Brown, Team Cherry	12.00	1.00	.15
□□□	127	Derek Schutz, Team Cherry	12.00	1.00	.15
□□□	128	Benoît Côté, Team Cherry	12.00	1.00	.15
□□□	129	Jason Ward, Team Cherry	25.00	8.00	1.00
□□□	130	Karol Bartanus, Team Cherry	12.00	1.00	.15
□□□	131	Tyler Rennette, Team Cherry	12.00	1.00	.15
□□□	132	Matt Zultek, Team Cherry	15.00	1.50	.25
□□□	133	Brad Ference, Team Cherry	20.00	1.50	.25
□□□	134	Daniel Tetrault, Team Cherry	15.00	1.50	.25
□□□	135	Ray Bonni, Team Cherry	12.00	1.00	.15
□□□	136	Kevin Grimes, Team Cherry	12.00	1.00	.15
□□□	137	Paul Mara, Team Cherry	20.00	3.00	.50
□□□	138	Nikos Tselios, Team Cherry	15.00	1.50	.25
□□□	139	Curtis Cruickshank (G), Team Cherry	12.00	1.00	.15
□□□	140	Pierre-Luc Therrien (G), Team Cherry	12.00	1.00	.15
□□	141	Patrick Marleau, Team Orr	.–	20.00	2.50
□□□	142	Ty Jones, Team Orr	12.00	1.00	.15
□□□	143	Jeremy Reich, Team Orr	12.00	1.00	.15
□□□	144	Adam Mair, Team Orr	12.00	1.00	.15
□□□	145	Adam Colagiacomo, Team Orr	20.00	1.50	.25
□□□	146	Harold Druken, Team Orr	15.00	1.50	.25
□□□	147	Brenden Morrow, Team Orr	15.00	1.50	.25
□□□	148	Jay Legault, Team Orr	20.00	1.50	.25
□□□	149	Jeff Zehr, Team Orr	12.00	1.50	.25
□□□	150	Scott Barney, Team Orr	15.00	1.50	.25
□□□	151	Gregor Baumgartner, Team Orr	12.00	1.50	.25
□□□	152	Daniel Tkaczuk, Team Orr	30.00	10.00	1.25
□□□	153	Eric Brewer, Team Orr	25.00	5.00	.75
□□□	154	Nick Boynton, Team Orr	20.00	1.50	.25
□□□	155	Vratislav Cech, Team Orr	12.00	1.00	.15
□□□	156	Kyle Kos, Team Orr	12.00	1.00	.15
□□□	157	J.F. Fortin, Team Orr	20.00	1.50	.25
□□□	158	Wes Jarvis, Team Orr	12.00	1.50	.15
□□	159	Roberto Luongo (G), Team Orr	.–	30.00	5.00
□□□	160	J.F. Damphousse (G), Team Orr	25.00	5.00	.75

BOWMAN'S BEST

These cards have three versions: the regular insert, a Refractor parallel and an Atomic Refractor parallel. Cards were redeemed via a redemption offer.

Insert Set (20 cards): 300.00 150.00 75.00

	No.	Player	A.R.	Ref.	B.B.
□□□	1	Joe Thornton	50.00	25.00	12.00
□□□	2	Patrick Marleau	30.00	15.00	8.00
□□□	3	Paul Mara	12.00	6.00	3.00
□□□	4	Daniel Tkaczuk	258.00	12.00	6.00
□□□	5	Jason Ward	15.00	8.00	4.00
□□□	6	Nick Boynton	12.00	6.00	3.00
□□□	7	Daniel Cleary	20.00	10.00	5.00
□□□	8	Eric Brewer	15.00	8.00	4.00
□□□	9	Brad Ference	12.00	6.00	3.00
□□□	10	Stefan Cherneski	10.00	5.00	2.50
□□□	11	Ryan Bonni	10.00	5.00	2.50
□□□	12	Adam Colagiacomo	10.00	5.00	2.50
□□□	13	Mike Brown	10.00	5.00	2.50
□□□	14	Scott Barney	12.00	6.00	3.00
□□□	15	Jarrett Smith	10.00	5.00	2.50
□□□	16	Brenden Morrow	10.00	5.00	2.50
□□□	17	J.F. Fortin	10.00	5.00	2.50
□□□	18	Roberto Luongo (G)	50.00	25.00	12.00
□□□	19	Curtis Cruickshank (G)	12.00	6.00	3.00
□□□	20	Pierre-Luc Therrien	10.00	5.00	2.50

1997 - 98 AUTOGRAPHED COLLECTION

This 50-card four-sport set sells for $15. Other hockey singles may exist.

Imprint: © 1998 THE SCORE BOARD, INC.

	No.	Player	NRMT-MT
□	4	Joe Thornton	1.50

ATHLETIC EXCELLENCE

This 12-card insert set features only one hockey player. A 12-card set sells for $65.

	No.	Player	NRMT-MT
□	2	Joe Thornton	6.00

AUTOGRAPHS

Other hockey singles may exist.

	Player	NRMT-MT
□	Joe Thornton (#/1,950)	35.00

1997 MEMORIAL CUP PHONE CARDS

These PowerTel phone cards were issued at the 1997 Memorial Cup in Hull. The Memorial Cup logo phone card has three denominations: a $20 card (gold), a $15 card (silver) and a $10 card (black). The other four $10 phone cards show player action shots.

	Description	$20	$15	$10
□□□	Memorial Cup Logo	25.00	20.00	15.00
□	Hull Olympiques	.–	.–	15.00
□	QMJHL (Moosehead vs. Olympiques)	.–	.–	15.00
□	WHL	.–	.–	15.00
□	OHL (Alyn McCauley)	.–	.–	16.00

1997 OMNITEL CAM NEELY PHONE CARD

This may have been issued a different year. We have little information on this card.

	Player	NRMT-MT
□	Cam Neely	10.00

1997 - 98 BICYCLE SPORTS NHL ACES

Imprint: 1997-1998 BICYCLE SPORTS COLLECTION

Complete Deck (55 cards): 6.00

	No.	Player	NRMT-MT
□		Western Conference Logo Card	.10
□		Eastern Conference Logo Card	.10
□		Checklist	.10
□	A♠	Paul Kariya, Ana.	1.50
□	2♠	Ray Bourque, Bos.	.50
□	3♠	Ryan Smyth, Edm.	.35
□	4♠	Jarome Iginla, Cgy.	.35
□	5♠	Chris Gratton, T.B.	.25
□	6♠	Jeremy Roenick, Chi.	.35
□	7♠	Mike Modano, Dal.	.50
□	8♠	Doug Weight, Edm.	.35
□	9♠	Jim Campbell, Stl.	.15
□	10♠	Sheldon Kennedy, Bos.	.15
□	J♠	Jason Arnott, Edm.	.25
□	Q♠	Peter Forsberg, Col.	1.25
□	K♠	Brian Leetch, NYR.	.35
□	A♦	Bryan Berard, NYI.	.35
□	2♦	Geoff Sanderson, Hfd.	.15
□	3♦	Chris Chelios, Chi.	.35
□	4♦	Félix Potvin (G), Tor.	.50
□	5♦	Adam Oates, Wsh.	.35
□	6♦	Roman Hamrlik, T.B.	.25
□	7♦	Theoren Fleury, Cgy.	.25
□	8♦	Vincent Damphousse, Mtl.	.35
□	9♦	Zigmund Palffy, NYI.	.35
□	10♦	Saku Koivu, Mtl.	.75
□	J♦	Teemu Selänne, Ana.	.75
□	Q♦	John Vanbiesbrouck (G), Fla.	.60
□	K♦	Vladimir Konstantinov, Det.	.15
□	A♣	Michael Peca, Buf.	.25
□	2♣	Jere Lehtinen, Dal.	.25
□	3♣	Trevor Linden, Van.	.25
□	4♣	John LeClair, Pha.	.50
□	5♣	Owen Nolan, S.J.	.25
□	6♣	Pierre Turgeon, Stl.	.25
□	7♣	Tony Amonte, Chi.	.25
□	8♣	Alexei Yashin, Ott.	.35
□	9♣	Mats Sundin, Tor.	.50
□	10♣	Jaromir Jagr, Pgh.	1.25
□	J♣	Wayne Gretzky, NYR.	2.50
□	Q♣	Martin Brodeur (G), N.J.	.75
□	K♣	Tony Granato, S.J.	.15
□	A♥	Dominik Hasek (G), Buf.	.75
□	2♥	Mike Vernon (G), Det.	.25
□	3♥	Doug Gilmour, N.J.	.35
□	4♥	Dimitri Khristich, L.A.	.15
□	5♥	Mark Recchi, Mtl.	.25
□	6♥	Daniel Alfredsson, Ott.	.25
□	7♥	Eric Lindros, Pha.	1.50
□	8♥	Keith Tkachuk, Pho.	.35
□	9♥	Pavel Bure, Van.	.75
□	10♥	Brendan Shanahan, Det.	.60
□	J♥	Sandis Ozolinsh, Col.	.25
□	Q♥	Mark Messier, NYR.	.50
□	K♥	Patrick Roy (G), Col.	2.00

1997 - 98 CORINTHIAN HEADLINERS

Figurine Height: 3"
Package Imprint: © and ™ CORINTHIAN 1997

	Player	**NRMT-MT**
Complete Set (30 figurines):		**175.00**
☐	Martin Brodeur (G), N.J.	10.00
☐	Pavel Bure, Van.	6.00
☐	Chris Chelios, Chi.	6.00
☐	Paul Coffey, Pha.	6.00
☐	Sergei Fedorov, Det.	6.00
☐	Peter Forsberg, Col.	7.50
☐	Grant Fuhr (G), Stl.	8.00
☐	Wayne Gretzky, NYR.	12.00
☐	Brett Hull, Stl.	8.00
☐	Jaromir Jagr, Pgh.	6.00
☐	Paul Kariya, Ana.	8.00
☐	Jari Kurri, Col.	6.00
☐	Pat LaFontaine, Buf.	6.00
☐	Brian Leetch, NYR.	6.00
☐	Claude Lemieux, Col.	6.00
☐	Mario Lemieux, Pgh.	10.00
☐	Eric Lindros, Pha.	8.00
☐	Mark Messier, NYR.	6.00
☐	Félix Potvin (G), Tor.	12.00
☐	Mike Richter (G), NYR.	8.00
☐	Jeremy Roenick, Pho.	6.00
☐	Patrick Roy (G), Col.	12.00
☐	Joe Sakic, Col.	7.50
☐	Teemu Selänne, Ana.	6.00
☐	Brendan Shanahan, Det.	6.00
☐	Mats Sundin, Tor.	6.00
☐	Keith Tkachuk, Pho.	6.00
☐	Pierre Turgeon, Stl.	6.00
☐	John Vanbiesbrouck (G), Fla.	10.00
☐	Steve Yzerman, Det.	7.50

1997 - 98 DONRUSS

These cards have three versions: the regular card, a Press Proof parallel and a die-cut Gold Press Proof.

Imprint: © 1997 DONRUSS TRADING CARD CO.

Complete Set (230 cards):			**25.00**	**140.00**	**2,500**
Common Player:			**.15**	**2.00**	**6.00**
☐☐☐	1	Peter Forsberg, Col.	1.50	50.00	125.00
☐☐☐	2	Steve Yzerman, Det.	1.50	50.00	125.00
☐☐☐	3	Eric Lindros, Pha.	2.00	65.00	150.00
☐☐☐	4	Mark Messier, Van.	.75	20.00	50.00
☐☐☐	5	Patrick Roy (G), Col.	2.50	80.00	175.00
☐☐☐	6	Jeremy Roenick, Pho.	.35	10.00	20.00
☐☐☐	7	Paul Kariya, Ana.	2.00	65.00	150.00
☐☐☐	8	Valeri Bure, Mtl.	.15	2.00	6.00
☐☐☐	9	Dominik Hasek (G), Buf.	1.00	35.00	80.00
☐☐☐	10	Doug Gilmour, N.J.	.35	10.00	20.00
☐☐☐	11	Garth Snow (G), Pha.	.15	2.00	6.00
☐☐☐	12	Todd Bertuzzi, NYI.	.15	2.00	6.00
☐☐☐	13	Chris Osgood (G), Det.	.50	15.00	30.00
☐☐☐	14	Jarome Iginla, Cgy.	.35	10.00	20.00
☐☐☐	15	Lonny Bohonos, Van.	.15	2.00	6.00
☐☐☐	16	Jeff O'Neill, Hfd.	.25	5.00	10.00
☐☐☐	17	Daniel Alfredsson, Ott.	.25	5.00	10.00
☐☐☐	18	Daymond Langkow, T.B.	.15	2.00	6.00
☐☐☐	19	Alexei Yashin, Ott.	.50	15.00	30.00
☐☐☐	20	Byron Dafoe (G), L.A.	.15	2.00	6.00
☐☐☐	21	Michael Peca, Buf.	.25	5.00	10.00
☐☐☐	22	Jim Carey (G), Bos.	.15	2.00	6.00
☐☐☐	23	Pat Verbeek, Dal.	.15	2.00	6.00
☐☐☐	24	Terry Ryan, Mtl.	:15	2.00	6.00
☐☐☐	25	Adam Oates, Wsh.	.35	10.00	20.00
☐☐☐	26	Kevin Hatcher, Pgh.	.15	2.00	6.00
☐☐☐	27	Ken Wregget (G), Pgh.	.15	2.00	6.00
☐☐☐	28	Pierre Turgeon, Stl.	.25	5.00	10.00
☐☐☐	29	John LeClair, Pha.	.75	20.00	50.00
☐☐☐	30	Jere Lehtinen, Dal.	.25	5.00	10.00
☐☐☐	31	Jamie Storr (G), L.A.	.25	5.00	10.00
☐☐☐	32	Doug Weight, Edm.	.35	10.00	20.00
☐☐☐	33	Tommy Salo (G), NYI.	.15	2.00	6.00
☐☐☐	34	Bernie Nicholls, S.J.	.15	2.00	6.00
☐☐☐	35	Jocelyn Thibault, Mtl.	.35	10.00	20.00
☐☐☐	36	Dale Hawerchuk, Pha.	.25	5.00	10.00
☐☐☐	37	Chris Chelios, Chi.	.50	15.00	30.00
☐☐☐	38	Kirk Muller, Fla.	.15	2.00	6.00
☐☐☐	39	Steve Sullivan, Tor.	.15	2.00	6.00
☐☐☐	40	Andy Moog (G), Dal. (Mtl.)	.25	5.00	10.00
☐☐☐	41	Martin Gelinas, Van.	.15	2.00	6.00
☐☐☐	42	Shayne Corson, Mtl.	.25	5.00	10.00
☐☐☐	43	Curtis Joseph, Edm.	.85	28.00	65.00
☐☐☐	44	Donald Audette, Buf.	.15	2.00	6.00
☐☐☐	45	Rick Tocchet, Wsh. (Pho.)	.15	2.00	6.00
☐☐☐	46	Craig Janney, Pho.	.15	2.00	6.00
☐☐☐	47	Geoff Courtnall, Stl.	.15	2.00	6.00
☐☐☐	48	Wade Redden, Ott.	.15	2.00	6.00
☐☐☐	49	Steve Rucchin, Ana.	.15	2.00	6.00
☐☐☐	50	Ethan Moreau, Chi.	.15	2.00	6.00
☐☐☐	**51**	**Steve Shields (G), Buf., RC**	**.25**	**3.00**	**8.00**
☐☐☐	52	Jamie Pushor, Det.	.15	2.00	6.00
☐☐☐	53	Saku Koivu, Mtl.	1.00	35.00	80.00
☐☐☐	54	Oleg Tverdovsky, Pho.	.15	2.00	6.00
☐☐☐	55	Jeff Friesen, S.J.	.25	5.00	10.00
☐☐☐	56	Chris Gratton, T.B. (Pha.)	.25	5.00	10.00
☐☐☐	57	Wendel Clark, Tor.	.25	5.00	10.00
☐☐☐	58	John Vanbiesbrouck (G), Fla.	.85	28.00	65.00
☐☐☐	59	Trevor Kidd (G), Cgy.	.25	5.00	10.00
☐☐☐	60	Sandis Ozolinsh, Col.	.25	5.00	10.00
☐☐☐	61	Dave Andreychuk, N.J.	.15	2.00	6.00
☐☐☐	62	Travis Green, NYI.	.15	2.00	6.00
☐☐☐	63	Paul Coffey, Pha.	.25	5.00	10.00
☐☐☐	64	Roman Turek (G), Dal.	.15	2.00	6.00
☐☐☐	65	Vladimir Konstantinov, Det.	.15	2.00	6.00
☐☐☐	66	Ray Bourque, Bos.	.75	20.00	50.00
☐☐☐	67	Wayne Primeau, Buf.	.15	2.00	6.00
☐☐☐	68	Todd Harvey, Dal.	.15	2.00	6.00
☐☐☐	69	Derek King, Hfd. (Tor.)	.15	2.00	6.00
☐☐☐	70	Adam Graves, NYR.	.15	2.00	6.00
☐☐☐	71	Brett Hull, Stl.	.75	20.00	50.00
☐☐☐	72	Scott Niedermayer, N.J.	.25	5.00	10.00
☐☐☐	73	Mike Vernon (G), Det. (S.J.)	.25	5.00	10.00
☐☐☐	74	Brian Holzinger, Buf.	.15	2.00	6.00
☐☐☐	75	Dainius Zubrus, Pha.	.25	5.00	10.00
☐☐☐	76	Patrick Lalime (G), Pgh.	.15	2.00	6.00
☐☐☐	77	Corey Schwab (G), T.B.	.15	2.00	6.00
☐☐☐	78	Alexandre Daigle, Ott.	.15	2.00	6.00
☐☐☐	79	Geoff Sanderson, Hfd. (Car.)	.15	2.00	6.00
☐☐☐	80	Dave Gagner, Cgy. (Fla.)	.15	3.00	10.00
☐☐☐	81	José Théodore (G), Mtl.	.35	10.00	20.00
☐☐☐	82	Sergei Fedorov, Det.	.75	20.00	50.00
☐☐☐	83	Keith Tkachuk, Pho.	.50	15.00	30.00
☐☐☐	84	Owen Nolan, S.J.	.25	5.00	10.00
☐☐☐	85	Brandon Convery, Tor.	.15	2.00	6.00
☐☐☐	86	Trevor Linden, Van.	.25	5.00	10.00
☐☐☐	87	Landon Wilson, Bos.	.15	2.00	6.00
☐☐☐	88	Claude Lemieux, Col.	.15	2.00	6.00
☐☐☐	89	Dimitri Khristich, L.A.	.15	2.00	6.00
☐☐☐	90	Luc Robitaille, NYR.	.25	5.00	10.00
☐☐☐	91	Todd Warriner, Tor.	.15	2.00	6.00
☐☐☐	92	Kelly Hrudey, S.J.	.15	2.00	6.00
☐☐☐	93	Mike Dunham, N.J.	.15	2.00	6.00
☐☐☐	94	Mike Grier, Edm.	.25	5.00	10.00
☐☐☐	95	Joé Juneau, Wsh.	.15	2.00	6.00
☐☐☐	96	Alexei Zhamnov, Chi.	.15	2.00	6.00
☐☐☐	97	Jamie Langenbrunner, Dal.	.25	5.00	10.00
☐☐☐	98	Sean Pronger, Ana.	.15	2.00	6.00
☐☐☐	99	Janne Niinimaa, Pha.	.25	5.00	10.00
☐☐☐	100	Chris Pronger, Stl.	.25	5.00	10.00
☐☐☐	101	Ray Sheppard, Fla.	.15	2.00	6.00
☐☐☐	102	Tony Amonte, Chi.	.25	5.00	10.00
☐☐☐	103	Ron Tugnutt (G), Ott.	.15	2.00	6.00
☐☐☐	104	Mike Modano, Dal.	.75	20.00	50.00
☐☐☐	**105**	**Dan Trebil, Ana., RC**	**.25**	**3.00**	**8.00**
☐☐☐	106	Alexander Mogilny, Van.	.35	10.00	20.00
☐☐☐	107	Darren McCarty, Det.	.15	2.00	6.00
☐☐☐	108	Ted Donato, Bos.	.15	2.00	6.00
☐☐☐	109	Brian Savage, Mtl.	.15	2.00	6.00
☐☐☐	110	Mike Gartner, Pho.	.25	5.00	10.00
☐☐☐	111	Jim Campbell, Stl.	.15	2.00	6.00
☐☐☐	112	Roman Hamrlik, T.B.	.25	5.00	10.00
☐☐☐	113	Andreas Dackell, Ott.	.15	2.00	6.00
☐☐☐	114	Ron Hextall (G), Pha.	.25	5.00	10.00
☐☐☐	115	Steve Washburn, Fla.	.15	2.00	6.00
☐☐☐	116	Jeff Hackett (G), Chi.	.25	5.00	10.00
☐☐☐	117	Joe Sakic, Col.	1.25	40.00	100.00
☐☐☐	118	Anson Carter, Bos.	.15	2.00	6.00
☐☐☐	119	Vyacheslav Kozlov, Det.	.15	2.00	6.00
☐☐☐	120	Nikolai Khabibulin (G), Pho.	.35	10.00	20.00
☐☐☐	121	Tony Granato, S.J.	.15	2.00	6.00
☐☐☐	122	Al MacInnis, Stl.	.25	5.00	10.00
☐☐☐	123	Daren Puppa (G), T.B.	.15	2.00	6.00
☐☐☐	124	Mike Richter (G), NYR.	.35	10.00	20.00
☐☐☐	125	Zigmund Palffy, NYI.	.35	10.00	20.00
☐☐☐	126	Martin Brodeur (G), N.J.	1.00	35.00	80.00
☐☐☐	127	Rem Murray, Edm.	.15	2.00	6.00
☐☐☐	128	Sean Burke (G), Hfd. (Car.)	.25	5.00	10.00
☐☐☐	129	Aki Berg, L.A.	.15	2.00	6.00
☐☐☐	130	Dmitri Mironov, Pgh.	.15	2.00	6.00
☐☐☐	131	Jamie Allison, Cgy.	.15	2.00	6.00
☐☐☐	132	Valeri Kamensky, Col.	.25	5.00	10.00
☐☐☐	133	Pat LaFontaine, Buf.	.25	5.00	10.00
☐☐☐	134	Jozef Stumpel, Bos.	.25	5.00	10.00
☐☐☐	135	Peter Bondra, Wsh.	.50	15.00	30.00
☐☐☐	136	Mark Recchi, Mtl.	.25	5.00	10.00
☐☐☐	137	Ron Francis, Pgh.	.35	10.00	20.00
☐☐☐	138	Harry York, Stl.	.15	2.00	6.00
☐☐☐	139	Mats Sundin, Tor.	.75	20.00	50.00
☐☐☐	140	Bobby Holik, N.J.	.15	2.00	6.00
☐☐☐	141	Eric Desjardins, Pha.	.15	2.00	6.00
☐☐☐	142	Scott Lachance, NYI.	.15	2.00	6.00
☐☐☐	143	Wayne Gretzky, NYR.	3.00	100.00	250.00
☐☐☐	144	Ed Jovanovski, Fla.	.25	5.00	10.00
☐☐☐	145	Jason Arnott, Edm.	.25	5.00	10.00
☐☐☐	146	Andrew Cassels, Hfd.	.15	2.00	6.00
☐☐☐	147	Roman Vopat, L.A.	.15	2.00	6.00
☐☐☐	148	Dwayne Roloson (G), Cgy.	.15	2.00	6.00
☐☐☐	149	Derek Plante, Buf.	.15	2.00	6.00
☐☐☐	150	Phil Housley, Wsh.	.15	2.00	6.00
☐☐☐	151	Mikael Renberg, Pha.	.15	2.00	6.00
☐☐☐	152	Petr Nedved, Pgh.	.15	2.00	6.00
☐☐☐	153	Grant Fuhr (G), Stl.	.25	5.00	10.00
☐☐☐	154	Félix Potvin (G), Tor.	.75	20.00	50.00
☐☐☐	155	John MacLean, N.J.	.15	2.00	6.00
☐☐☐	156	Brian Leetch, NYR.	.35	10.00	20.00
☐☐☐	157	Rod Brind'Amour, Pha.	.25	5.00	10.00
☐☐☐	158	Ryan Smyth, Edm.	.25	5.00	10.00
☐☐☐	159	Teemu Selänne, Ana.	1.00	35.00	80.00
☐☐☐	160	Theoren Fleury, Cgy.	.35	10.00	20.00
☐☐☐	161	Adam Deadmarsh, Col.	.15	2.00	6.00
☐☐☐	162	Corey Hirsch (G), Van.	.15	2.00	6.00
☐☐☐	163	Bryan Berard, NYI.	.35	10.00	20.00
☐☐☐	164	Ed Belfour (G), Dal.	.35	10.00	20.00
☐☐☐	165	Sergei Berezin, Tor.	.25	5.00	10.00
☐☐☐	166	Damian Rhodes (G), Ott.	.15	2.00	6.00
☐☐☐	167	Guy Hebert (G), Ana.	.25	5.00	10.00
☐☐☐	168	Derian Hatcher, Dal.	.25	5.00	10.00
☐☐☐	169	Jonas Hoglund, Cgy.	.15	2.00	6.00
☐☐☐	170	Matthew Barnaby, Buf.	.15	2.00	6.00
☐☐☐	171	Scott Mellanby, Fla.	.15	2.00	6.00
☐☐☐	172	Bill Ranford, Wsh.	.25	5.00	10.00
☐☐☐	173	Vincent Damphousse, Mtl.	.35	10.00	20.00
☐☐☐	174	Anders Eriksson, Det.	.15	2.00	6.00
☐☐☐	175	Chad Kilger, Pho.	.15	2.00	6.00

	No.	Player			
☐☐☐	176	Darren Turcotte, S.J.	.15	2.00	6.00
☐☐☐	177	Dino Ciccarelli, T.B.	.25	5.00	10.00
☐☐☐	178	Niklas Sundstrom, NYR.	.15	2.00	6.00
☐☐☐	179	Stéphane Fiset (G), L.A.	.25	5.00	10.00
☐☐☐	180	Mike Ricci, Col.	.15	2.00	6.00
☐☐☐	181	Brendan Shanahan, Det.	.85	28.00	65.00
☐☐☐	182	Darcy Tucker, Mtl.	.15	2.00	6.00
☐☐☐	183	Eric Fichaud (G), NYI.	.25	5.00	10.00
☐☐☐	184	Todd Marchant, Edm.	.15	2.00	6.00
☐☐☐	185	Keith Primeau, Hfd. (Car.)	.25	5.00	10.00
☐☐☐	186	Joe Nieuwendyk, Dal.	.25	5.00	10.00
☐☐☐	187	Pavel Bure, Van.	1.00	35.00	80.00
☐☐☐	188	Jaromir Jagr, Pgh.	1.50	50.00	125.00
☐☐☐	189	Kirk McLean (G), Van.	.25	4.00	10.00
☐☐☐	190	Daniel Goneau, NYR.	.15	2.00	6.00
☐☐☐	191	Rob Niedermayer, Fla., Err. (Barnes)	.15	2.00	6.00
☐☐☐	192	Eric Dazé, Chi.	.25	5.00	10.00
☐☐☐	193	Richard Matvichuk, Dal.	.15	2.00	6.00
☐☐☐	194	Scott Stevens, N.J.	.15	2.00	6.00
☐☐☐	195	Dale Hunter, Wsh.	.15	2.00	6.00
☐☐☐	196	Hnat Domenichelli, Cgy.	.25	5.00	10.00
☐☐☐	197	Philippe DeRouville (G), Pgh.	.15	2.00	6.00
☐☐☐	198	Marcel Cousineau (G), Tor.	.15	2.00	6.00
☐☐☐	199	Kevin Hodson (G), Det.	.15	2.00	6.00
☐☐☐	200	J.S. Giguère (G), Hfd. (Car.)	.25	5.00	10.00
☐☐☐	**201**	**Paxton Schafer (G), Bos., RC**	**.25**	**3.00**	**8.00**
☐☐☐	202	Marc Denis (G), Col.	.25	5.00	10.00
☐☐☐	**203**	**Frank Banham, Ana., RC**	**.25**	**3.00**	**8.00**
☐☐☐	204	Vadim Sharifjanov, N.J.	.15	2.00	6.00
☐☐☐	**205**	**Paul Healey, Pha., RC**	**.25**	**3.00**	**8.00**
☐☐☐	**206**	**D.J. Smith, Tor., RC**	**.25**	**3.00**	**8.00**
☐☐☐	**207**	**Christian Matte, Col., RC**	**.25**	**3.00**	**8.00**
☐☐☐	**208**	**Sean Brown, Edm., RC**	**.25**	**3.00**	**8.00**
☐☐☐	**209**	**Tomas Vokoun (G), Mtl., RC**	**.25**	**3.00**	**8.00**
☐☐☐	**210**	**Vladimir Vorobiev, NYR., RC**	**.25**	**3.00**	**8.00**
☐☐☐	**211**	**Jean-Yves Leroux, Chi., RC**	**.25**	**3.00**	**8.00**
☐☐☐	**212**	**Domenic Pittis, Pgh., RC**	**.25**	**3.00**	**8.00**
☐☐☐	**213**	**Derek Wilkinson (G), T.B., RC**	**.25**	**3.00**	**8.00**
☐☐☐	**214**	**Jason Holland, NYI., RC**	**.25**	**3.00**	**8.00**
☐☐☐	**215**	**Pascal Rhéaume, N.J., RC**	**.25**	**3.00**	**8.00**
☐☐☐	216	Steve Kelly, Edm.	.15	2.00	6.00
☐☐☐	217	Vaclav Varada, Buf.	.15	2.00	6.00
☐☐☐	218	Mike Fountain (G), Van.	.15	2.00	6.00
☐☐☐	**219**	**Vaclav Prospal, Pha., RC**	**.75**	**10.00**	**25.00**
☐☐☐	220	Jaroslav Svejkovsky, Wsh.	.25	5.00	10.00
☐☐☐	221	Marty Murray, Cgy.	.15	2.00	6.00
☐☐☐	**222**	**Wade Belak, Col., RC**	**.25**	**3.00**	**8.00**
☐☐☐	**223**	**Jamal Mayers, Stl., RC**	**.25**	**3.00**	**8.00**
☐☐☐	**224**	**Shayne Tororowski, Tor., RC**	**.25**	**3.00**	**8.00**
☐☐☐	**225**	**Mike Knuble, Det., RC**	**.25**	**3.00**	**8.00**
☐☐☐	226	CL: Jarome Iginla, Cgy.	.25	4.00	10.00
☐☐☐	227	CL: Keith Tkachuk, Pho.	.25	5.00	12.00
☐☐☐	228	CL: Adam Oates, Wsh.	.25	4.00	10.00
☐☐☐	229	CL: John LeClair, Pha.	.25	6.00	12.00
☐☐☐	230	CL: Brian Leetch, NYR.	.25	5.00	12.00

BETWEEN THE PIPES

These cards are serial numbered out of 3,000.

Insert Set (10 cards) **250.00**

	No.	Player	NRMT-MT
☐	1	Patrick Roy (G), Col.	75.00
☐	2	Martin Brodeur (G), N.J.	35.00
☐	3	John Vanbiesbrouck (G), Fla.	30.00
☐	4	Dominik Hasek (G), Buf.	35.00
☐	5	Chris Osgood (G), Det.	20.00
☐	6	José Théodore (G), Mtl.	15.00
☐	7	Garth Snow (G), Pha.	12.00
☐	8	Curtis Joseph (G), Edm.	30.00
☐	9	Félix Potvin (G), Tor.	25.00
☐	10	Jocelyn Thibault (G), Mtl.	15.00

ELITE SERIES

These cards are serial numbered out of 2,500.

Insert Set (12 cards): **550.00**

	No.	Player	NRMT-MT
☐	1	Wayne Gretzky, NYR.	110.00
☐	2	Jaromir Jagr, Pgh.	50.00
☐	3	Eric Lindros, Pha.	65.00
☐	4	Paul Kariya, Ana.	65.00
☐	5	Patrick Roy (G), Col.	80.00
☐	6	Steve Yzerman, Det.	50.00
☐	7	Peter Forsberg, Col.	50.00
☐	8	John Vanbiesbrouck (G), Fla.	25.00
☐	9	Brendan Shanahan, Det.	25.00
☐	10	Martin Brodeur (G), N.J.	30.00
☐	11	Dominik Hasek (G), Buf.	30.00
☐	12	Teemu Selänne, Ana.	30.00

LINE 2 LINE

Each Line 2 Line card has a regular insert and a die-cut parallel (serial numbered 1-250). Red cards (forwards) are serial numbered 251-4000 (3,750 total), blue cards (defencemen) are serial numbered 251-2000 (1,750 total) and gold cards are serial numbered 251-1000 (750 total).

Insert Set (24 cards): **725.00 2,100.00**

	No.	Red	Red	Die-Cut
☐☐	2	Teemu Selänne, Ana.	25.00	125.00
☐☐	4	Peter Forsberg, Col.	35.00	175.00
☐☐	5	Steve Yzerman, Det.	35.00	175.00
☐☐	7	Doug Gilmour, N.J.	10.00	40.00
☐☐	10	Brendan Shanahan, Det.	20.00	100.00
☐☐	11	Pavel Bure, Van.	25.00	125.00
☐☐	12	Joe Sakic, Col.	30.00	150.00
☐☐	14	Mike Modano, Dal.	12.00	60.00
☐☐	17	Jarome Iginla, Cgy.	8.00	25.00
☐☐	18	Brett Hull, Stl.	12.00	60.00
☐☐	22	Ryan Smyth, Edm.	8.00	25.00
☐☐	23	Mark Messier, NYR.	12.00	60.00
	No.	**Blue**	**Blue**	**Die-Cut**
☐☐	3	Brian Leetch, NYR.	10.00	35.00
☐☐	6	Oleg Tverdovsky, Pho.	10.00	25.00
☐☐	9	Bryan Berard, NYI.	10.00	35.00
☐☐	13	Chris Chelios, Chi.	15.00	45.00
☐☐	15	Paul Coffey, Pha.	10.00	30.00
☐☐	19	Wade Redden, Ott.	10.00	25.00
☐☐	21	Ray Bourque, Bos.	20.00	60.00
☐☐	24	Sandis Ozolinsh, Col.	10.00	25.00
	No.	**Gold**	**Gold**	**Die-Cut**
☐☐	1	Wayne Gretzky, NYR.	175.00	350.00
☐☐	8	Eric Lindros, Pha.	125.00	250.00
☐☐	16	Jaromir Jagr, Pgh.	90.00	175.00
☐☐	20	Paul Kariya, Ana.	125.00	250.00

RATED ROOKIES

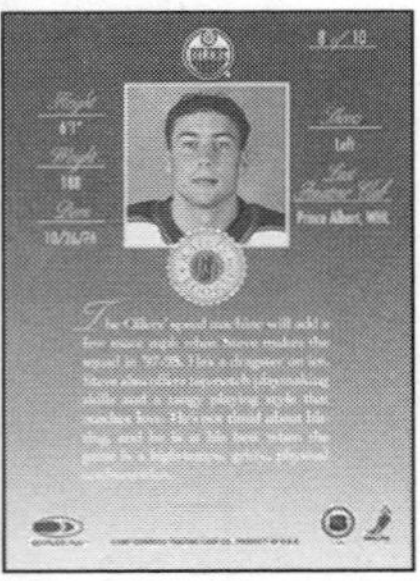

These cards have to versions: the regular insert and a Medalists parallel.

Insert Set (10 cards): **60.00 350.00**

	No.	Player	Insert	Medalist
☐☐	1	Tomas Vokoun (G), Mtl.	4.00	25.00
☐☐	2	Paxton Schafer (G), Bos.	4.00	25.00
☐☐	3	Vaclav Prospal, Pha.	10.00	80.00
☐☐	4	Marc Denis (G), Col.	8.00	60.00
☐☐	5	Domenic Pittis, Pgh.	5.00	35.00
☐☐	6	Christian Matte, Col.	4.00	25.00
☐☐	7	Marcel Cousineau (G), Tor.	4.00	25.00
☐☐	8	Steve Kelly, Edm.	4.00	25.00
☐☐	9	Jaroslav Svejkovsky, Wsh.	10.00	80.00
☐☐	10	J.S. Giguère (G), Hfd. (Car.)	6.00	40.00

RED ALERT

These cards are serial numbered out of 5,000.

Insert Set (10 cards): **100.00**

	No.	Player	NRMT-MT
☐	1	Adam Deadmarsh, Col.	6.00
☐	2	Ryan Smyth, Edm.	8.00
☐	3	Sergei Fedorov, Pgh.	15.00
☐	4	Keith Tkachuk, Pho.	12.00
☐	5	Brett Hull, Stl.	15.00
☐	6	Pavel Bure, Van.	20.00
☐	7	John LeClair, Pha.	15.00
☐	8	Zigmund Palffy, NYI.	10.00
☐	9	Mats Sundin, Tor.	15.00
☐	10	Peter Bondra, Wsh.	12.00

1997 - 98 DONRUSS CANADIAN ICE

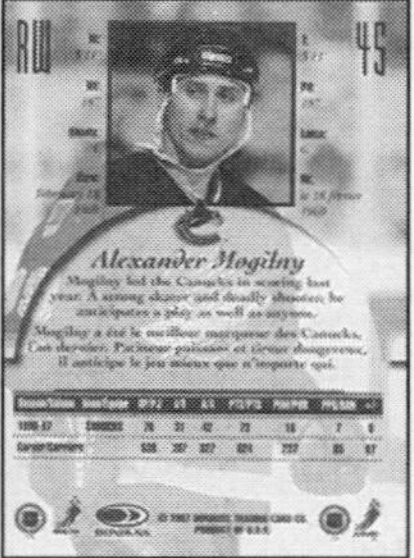

These cards have three versions: the regular card, a Provincial Series (750 copies) and a Dominion Series (150 copies).

Imprint: © 1997 DONRUSS TRADING CARD CO.

Complete Set (150 cards): **35.00**

Provincial Series (150 cards): **1,200.00**

Common Player: **3.50 8.00 .15**

	No.	Player	Prov.	Dom.	Reg.
☐☐☐	1	Patrick Roy (G), Col.	100.00	300.00	2.50

	No.	Player			
□□□	2	Paul Kariya, Ana.	85.00	275.00	2.00
□□□	3	Eric Lindros, Pha.	85.00	275.00	2.00
□□□	4	Steve Yzerman, Det.	60.00	200.00	1.50
□□□	5	Wayne Gretzky, NYR.	135.00	450.00	3.50
□□□	6	Peter Forsberg, Col.	60.00	200.00	1.50
□□□	7	John Vanbiesbrouck (G), Fla.	30.00	100.00	.85
□□□	8	Jaromir Jagr, Pgh.	60.00	200.00	1.50
□□□	9	Jim Campbell, Stl.	3.50	8.00	.15
□□□	10	Dominik Hasek (G), Buf.	35.00	120.00	1.00
□□□	11	Ray Bourque, Bos.	25.00	80.00	.75
□□□	12	Jarome Iginla, Cgy.	12.00	40.00	.35
□□□	13	Mike Modano, Dal.	25.00	80.00	.75
□□□	14	Ed Jovanovski, Fla.	6.00	20.00	.25
□□□	15	Jocelyn Thibault (G), Mtl.	12.00	40.00	.35
□□□	16	Keith Tkachuk, Pho.	20.00	65.00	.50
□□□	17	Brett Hull, Stl.	25.00	80.00	.75
□□□	18	Pavel Bure, Van.	35.00	120.00	1.00
□□□	19	Saku Koivu, Mtl.	35.00	120.00	1.00
□□□	20	Curtis Joseph (G), Edm.	30.00	100.00	.85
□□□	21	Eric Dazé, Chi.	6.00	20.00	.25
□□□	22	Keith Primeau, Hfd. (Car.)	6.00	20.00	.25
□□□	23	Theoren Fleury, Cgy.	12.00	40.00	.35
□□□	24	Pierre Turgeon, Stl.	6.00	20.00	.25
□□□	25	Peter Bondra, Wsh.	20.00	65.00	.50
□□□	26	Ed Belfour (G), S.J.	12.00	40.00	.35
□□□	27	Pat Verbeek, Dal.	3.50	8.00	.15
□□□	28	Chris Osgood, Det.	20.00	65.00	.50
□□□	29	Ray Sheppard, Fla.	3.50	8.00	.15
□□□	30	Stéphane Fiset (G), L.A.	6.00	20.00	.25
□□□	31	Wade Redden, Ott.	3.50	8.00	.15
□□□	32	Trevor Linden, Van.	6.00	20.00	.25
□□□	33	Zigmund Palffy, NYI.	20.00	65.00	.50
□□□	34	Tony Amonte, Chi.	6.00	20.00	.25
□□□	35	Derek Plante, Buf.	3.50	8.00	.15
□□□	36	Jonas Hoglund, Cgy.	3.50	8.00	.15
□□□	37	Guy Hebert (G), Ana.	6.00	20.00	.25
□□□	38	Garth Snow (G), Pha.	3.50	8.00	.15
□□□	39	Chris Gratton, T.B.	6.00	20.00	.25
□□□	40	Mats Sundin, Tor.	25.00	80.00	.75
□□□	41	Geoff Sanderson, Hfd. (Car.)	3.50	8.00	.15
□□□	42	Martin Brodeur (G), N.J.	35.00	120.00	1.00
□□□	43	Jozef Stumpel, Bos.	6.00	20.00	.25
□□□	44	Ron Francis, Pgh.	12.00	40.00	.35
□□□	45	Alexander Mogilny, Van. (w/Bure)	12.00	40.00	.35
□□□	46	Bill Ranford (G), Wsh.	6.00	20.00	.25
□□□	47	Kirk Muller, Fla.	3.50	8.00	.15
□□□	48	Ron Hextall (G), Pha.	6.00	20.00	.25
□□□	49	Doug Gilmour, N.J.	12.00	40.00	.35
□□□	50	Mark Messier, Van.	25.00	80.00	.75
□□□	51	Joe Nieuwendyk, Dal.	6.00	20.00	.25
□□□	52	Ryan Smyth, Edm.	6.00	20.00	.25
□□□	53	Mark Recchi, Mtl.	6.00	20.00	.25
□□□	54	Mike Gartner, Pho.	6.00	20.00	.25
□□□	55	Al MacInnis, Stl.	6.00	20.00	.25
□□□	56	Félix Potvin, Tor.	25.00	80.00	.75
□□□	57	Rob Blake, L.A.	6.00	20.00	.25
□□□	58	Dimitri Khristich, L.A.	3.50	8.00	.15
□□□	59	Jim Carey (G), Bos.	3.50	8.00	.15
□□□	60	Trevor Kidd, Cgy.	6.00	20.00	.25
□□□	61	Martin Gelinas, Van.	3.50	8.00	.15
□□□	62	Oleg Tverdovsky, Pho.	3.50	8.00	.15
□□□	63	Ron Tugnutt (G), Ott.	3.50	8.00	.15
□□□	64	Paul Coffey, Pha.	6.00	20.00	.25
□□□	65	Travis Green, NYI.	3.50	8.00	.15
□□□	66	Andrew Cassels, Hfd. (Car.)	3.50	8.00	.15
□□□	67	Brendan Shanahan, Det.	30.00	100.00	.85
□□□	68	Luc Robitaille, NYR.	6.00	20.00	.25
□□□	69	Pat LaFontaine, Buf.	6.00	20.00	.25
□□□	70	Daymond Langkow, T.B.	3.50	8.00	.15
□□□	71	Petr Nedved, Pgh.	3.50	8.00	.15
□□□	72	Sergei Fedorov, Det.	25.00	80.00	.75
□□□	73	Anson Carter, Bos.	3.50	8.00	.15
□□□	74	Teemu Selänne, Ana.	35.00	120.00	1.00
□□□	75	Nikolai Khabibulin (G), Pho.	12.00	40.00	.35
□□□	76	Ken Wregget (G), Pgh.	3.50	8.00	.15
□□□	77	Dino Ciccarelli, T.B.	6.00	20.00	.25
□□□	78	Adam Oates, Wash.	12.00	40.00	.35
□□□	79	Kirk McLean (G), Van.	6.00	20.00	.25
□□□	80	Wendel Clark, Tor.	6.00	20.00	.25
□□□	81	Jeff Friesen, S.J.	6.00	20.00	.25
□□□	82	Valeri Kamensky, Col.	6.00	20.00	.25
□□□	83	Ethan Moreau, Chi.	3.50	8.00	.15
□□□	84	Matthew Barnaby, Buf.	3.50	8.00	.15
□□□	85	Andy Moog (G), Dal. (Mtl.)	6.00	20.00	.25
□□□	86	Doug Weight, Edm.	12.00	40.00	.35
□□□	87	Mike Dunham (G), N.J.	3.50	8.00	.15
□□□	88	Brian Leetch, NYR.	12.00	40.00	.35
□□□	89	Michael Peca, Buf.	6.00	20.00	.25
□□□	90	Chris Pronger, Stl.	6.00	20.00	.25
□□□	91	Alexei Zhamnov, Chi.	3.50	8.00	.15
□□□	92	Bryan Berard, NYI.	12.00	40.00	.35
□□□	93	John LeClair, Pha.	25.00	80.00	.75
□□□	94	Steve Sullivan, Tor.	3.50	8.00	.15
□□□	95	Grant Fuhr (G), Stl.	6.00	20.00	.25
□□□	96	Mikael Renberg, Pha.	3.50	8.00	.15
□□□	97	Adam Graves, NYR.	3.50	8.00	.15
□□□	98	Ray Ferraro, L.A.	3.50	8.00	.15
□□□	99	Sean Burke, Hfd. (Car.)	6.00	20.00	.25
□□□	100	Jeremy Roenick, Pho.	12.00	40.00	.35
□□□	101	Jeff Hackett (G), Chi.	6.00	20.00	.25
□□□	102	Joe Sakic, Col.	45.00	15.00	1.25
□□□	103	Jamie Langenbrunner, Dal.	6.00	20.00	.25
□□□	104	Stéphane Richer, Mtl.	3.50	8.00	.15
□□□	105	Dave Andreychuk, N.J.	3.50	8.00	.15
□□□	106	Tommy Salo, NYI.	3.50	8.00	.15
□□□	107	Mike Richter (G), NYR.	12.00	40.00	.35
□□□	108	Owen Nolan, S.J.	6.00	20.00	.25
□□□	109	Corey Hirsch (G), Van.	3.50	8.00	.15
□□□	110	Daren Puppa, T.B.	3.50	8.00	.15
□□□	111	Darcy Tucker, Mtl.	3.50	8.00	.15
□□□	112	Daniel Alfredsson, Ott.	6.00	20.00	.25
□□□	113	Rod Brind'Amour, Pha.	6.00	20.00	.25
□□□	114	Scott Stevens, N.J.	3.50	8.00	.15
□□□	115	Vincent Damphousse, Mtl.	12.00	40.00	.35
□□□	116	Mathieu Schneider, Tor.	3.50	8.00	.15
□□□	117	Jason Arnott, Edm.	6.00	20.00	.25
□□□	118	Mike Vernon (G), Det.	6.00	20.00	.25
□□□	119	Sandis Ozolinsh, Col.	6.00	20.00	.25
□□□	120	Chris Chelios, Chi.	20.00	65.00	.50
□□□	121	Mike Grier, Edm.	6.00	20.00	.25
□□□	122	Alexandre Daigle, Ott.	3.50	8.00	.15
□□□	123	Roman Hamrlik, T.B.	6.00	20.00	.25
□□□	124	Derian Hatcher, Dal.	6.00	20.00	.25
□□□	125	Damian Rhodes (G), Ott.	3.50	8.00	.15
□□□	126	Adam Deadmarsh, Col.	3.50	8.00	.15
□□□	127	Alexei Yashin, Ott.	20.00	65.00	.50
□□□	128	Terry Ryan, Mtl.	3.50	8.00	.15
□□□	129	Jeff Ware, Tor.	3.50	8.00	.15
□□□	130	Steve Kelly, Edm.	3.50	8.00	.15
□□□	131	Hnat Domenichelli, Cgy.	6.00	20.00	.25
□□□	**132**	**Steve Shields (G), Buf., RC**	**6.00**	**10.00**	**.35**
□□□	**133**	**Paxton Schafer, Bos., RC**	**3.50**	**8.00**	**.15**
□□□	134	Vadim Sharifjanov, N.J.	3.50	8.00	.15
□□□	**135**	**Vaclav Prospal, Pha., RC**	**1.00**	**20.00**	**40.00**
□□□	136	Mike Fountain (G), Van.	3.50	8.00	.15
□□□	**137**	**Christian Matte, Col., RC**	**3.50**	**8.00**	**.15**
□□□	**138**	**Tomas Vokoun (G), Mtl., RC**	**3.50**	**8.00**	**.15**
□□□	**139**	**Vladimir Vorobiev, NYR., RC**	**3.50**	**8.00**	**.15**
□□□	**140**	**Domenic Pittis, Pgh., RC**	**3.50**	**8.00**	**.25**
□□□	141	Vaclav Varada, Buf.	3.50	8.00	.15
□□□	**142**	**D.J. Smith, Tor., RC**	**3.50**	**8.00**	**.15**
□□□	143	Jaroslav Svejkovsky, Wsh.	3.50	8.00	.15
□□□	144	Jason Holland, NYI.	3.50	8.00	.15
□□□	145	Marc Denis (G), Col.	6.00	20.00	.25
□□□	146	J.S. Giguère (G), Hfd. (Car.)	6.00	20.00	.25
□□□	147	Marcel Cousineau (G), Tor.	3.50	8.00	.15
□□□	148	CL: Dave Andreychuk, N.J.	3.50	8.00	.15
□□□	149	CL: Mike Gartner, Pho.	6.00	20.00	.25
□□□	150	CL: Detroit Red Wings.	6.00	20.00	.25

TREVOR LINDEN AUTOGRAPH

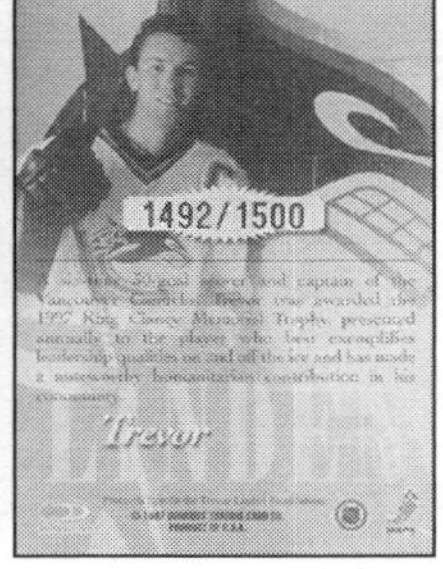

	Player	NRMT-MT
□	T. Linden Autograph	30.00
□	T. Linden Charity Card Offer	.10

LES GARDIENS

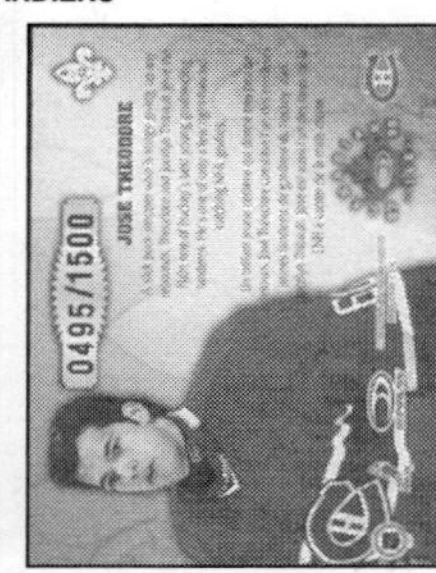

These cards have two versions: a promo card and the insert (serial numbered out of 1,500).

Insert Set (12 cards): **40.00** **325.00**

	No.	Player	Promo	Insert
□□	1	Patrick Roy (G), Col.	10.00	100.00
□□	2	Félix Potvin (G), Tor.	5.00	40.00
□□	3	Martin Brodeur (G), N.J.	6.00	50.00
□□	4	J-S Giguère (G), Hfd. (Car.)	2.50	20.00
□□	5	Stéphane Fiset (G), L.A.	2.50	20.00
□□	6	José Théodore (G), Mtl.	4.00	25.00
□□	7	Jocelyn Thibault (G), Mtl.	4.00	25.00
□□	8	Eric Fichaud (G), NYI.	2.50	25.00
□□	9	Patrick Lalime (G), Pgh.	2.00	18.00
□□	10	Marcel Cousineau (G), Tor.	2.00	18.00
□□	11	Philippe DeRouville (G), Pgh.	2.00	18.00
□□	12	Marc Denis (G), Col.	2.00	20.00

NATIONAL PRIDE

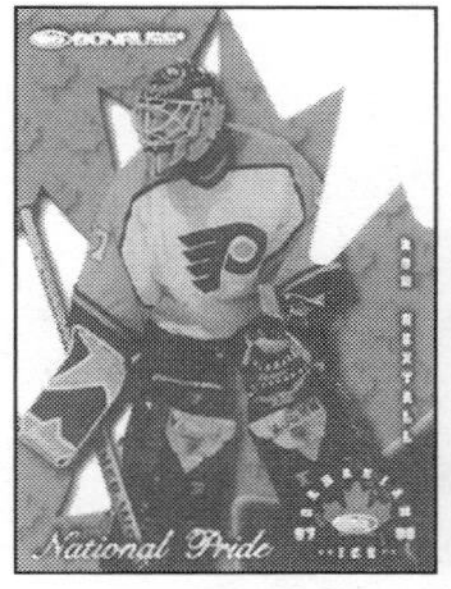

These die-cut inserts are serial numbered out of 1,997.

Insert Set (30 cards): **450.00**

	No.	Player	NRMT-MT
□	1	Wayne Gretzky, NYR.	90.00
□	2	Mark Messier, NYR.	20.00
□	3	Paul Kariya, Ana.	50.00
□	4	Steve Yzerman, Det.	40.00
□	5	Brendan Shanahan, Det.	25.00
□	6	Chris Osgood (G), Det.	15.00
□	7	Adam Oates, Wsh.	10.00
□	8	Eric Lindros, Pha.	50.00
□	9	Doug Gilmour, N.J.	10.00
□	10	Ryan Smyth, Edm.	6.00
□	11	Ray Bourque, Bos.	20.00
□	12	Jason Arnott, Edm.	6.00
□	13	Jarome Iginla, Cgy.	10.00
□	14	Geoff Sanderson, Hfd. (Car.)	6.00
□	15	Alexandre Daigle, Ott.	6.00
□	16	Trevor Linden, Van.	6.00
□	17	Joe Sakic, Col.	35.00
□	18	Mark Recchi, Pha.	6.00
□	19	Theoren Fleury, Cgy.	10.00
□	20	Ron Francis, Pgh.	10.00
□	21	Daymond Langkow, T.B.	6.00
□	22	Ed Belfour (G), S.J.	10.00
□	23	Paul Coffey, Pha.	6.00
□	24	Pierre Turgeon, Stl.	6.00
□	25	Claude Lemieux, Col.	6.00
□	26	Ron Hextall (G), Pha.	6.00
□	27	Curtis Joseph, Edm.	25.00
□	28	Mike Vernon (G), Det.	6.00
□	29	Vincent Damphousse, Mtl.	10.00
□	30	Owen Nolan, S.J.	6.00

STANLEY CUP SCRABOOK

Cards 1-16 (Bronze) are serial numbered out of 2,000; cards 17-24 (Silver) are serial numbered out of 1,500; cards 25-30 (Gold) are serial numbered out of 1,000; cards 31-32 are autographed and serial numbered out of 750; card 33 (Shanahan) is autographed and serial numbered out of 250.

Insert Set (33 cards): 1,400.00

	No.	Player	NRMT-MT
☐	1	Mike Modano, Dal.	18.00
☐	2	Curtis Joseph (G), Edm.	20.00
☐	3	Joe Sakic, Col.	30.00
☐	4	Chris Chelios, Chi.	15.00
☐	5	Chris Osgood (G), Det.	15.00
☐	6	Brett Hull, Stl.	18.00
☐	7	Jeremy Roenick, Pho.	12.00
☐	8	Teemu Selänne, Ana.	25.00
☐	9	Jaromir Jagr, Pgh.	35.00
☐	10	Garth Snow (G), Pha.	8.00
☐	11	Alexei Yashin, Ott.	10.00
☐	12	Steve Shields (G), Buf.	8.00
☐	13	Doug Gilmour, N.J.	10.00
☐	14	José Théodore (G) Mtl.	18.00
☐	15	Mike Richter (G), NYR.	15.00
☐	16	John Vanbiesbrouck (G), Fla.	25.00
☐	17	Ryan Smyth, Edm.	15.00
☐	18	Peter Forsberg, Col.	60.00
☐	19	Steve Yzerman, Det.	50.00
☐	20	Paul Kariya, Ana.	75.00
☐	21	Janne Niinimaa, Pha.	15.00
☐	22	Dominik Hasek (G), Buf.	35.00
☐	23	Mark Messier, NYR.	25.00
☐	24	Martin Brodeur (G), N.J.	35.00
☐	25	Vyacheslav Kozlov, Det.	15.00
☐	26	Sergei Fedorov, Det.	35.00
☐	27	Patrick Roy (G), Col.	150.00
☐	28	Wayne Gretzky, NYR.	175.00
☐	29	John LeClair, Pha.	35.00
☐	30	Paul Coffey, Pha.	30.00
☐	31	Mike Vernon (G), Det.	65.00
☐	32	Eric Lindros, Pha.	200.00
☐	33	Brendan Shanahan, Det.	250.00

1997 - 98 DONRUSS ELITE

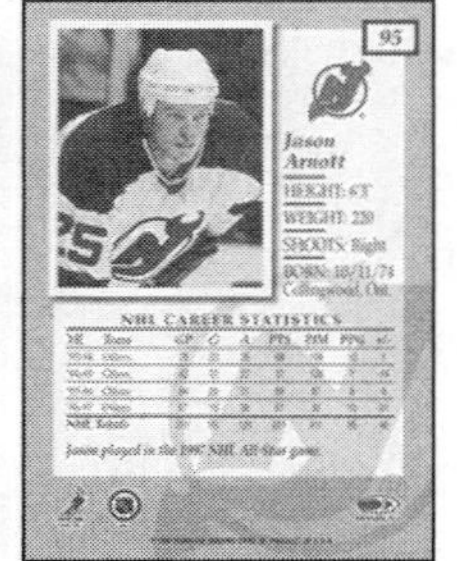

These cards have three versions: the regular card, an Elite Aspirations parallel (750 copies) and an Elite Status parallel (serial numbered out of 100).

Imprint: © 1998 DONRUSS TRADING CARD CO.

Complete Set (150 cards): 5,000.00 1,500.00 40.00

Common Player: 12.00 3.50 .25

	No.	Player	Asp.	Status	Reg.
☐☐☐	1	Peter Forsberg, Col.	250.00	60.00	2.50
☐☐☐	2	Mike Modano, Dal.	80.00	25.00	1.25
☐☐☐	3	John Vanbiesbrouck (G), Fla.	100.00	30.00	1.50
☐☐☐	4	Pavel Bure, Van.	150.00	35.00	1.75
☐☐☐	5	Mark Messier, Van.	80.00	25.00	1.25
☐☐☐	6	Joe Thornton, Bos.	100.00	30.00	1.50
☐☐☐	7	Paul Kariya, Ana.	300.00	85.00	3.50
☐☐☐	8	Martin Brodeur (G), N.J.	150.00	35.00	1.75
☐☐☐	9	Wayne Gretzky, NYR.	500.00	135.00	5.00
☐☐☐	10	Eric Lindros, Pha.	300.00	85.00	3.50
☐☐☐	11	Jaromir Jagr, Pgh.	250.00	60.00	2.50
☐☐☐	12	Brett Hull, Stl.	80.00	25.00	1.25
☐☐☐	13	Jarome Iginla, Cgy.	40.00	12.00	.75
☐☐☐	14	Patrick Roy (G), Col.	400.00	100.00	4.00
☐☐☐	15	Steve Yzerman, Det.	250.00	60.00	2.50
☐☐☐	16	Sergei Samsonov, Bos.	100.00	30.00	1.50
☐☐☐	17	Teemu Selänne, Ana.	150.00	35.00	1.75
☐☐☐	18	Brendan Shanahan, Det.	100.00	30.00	1.50
☐☐☐	19	Curtis Joseph (G), Edm.	100.00	30.00	1.50
☐☐☐	20	Saku Koivu, Mtl.	150.00	35.00	1.75
☐☐☐	21	Ray Bourque, Bos.	80.00	25.00	1.25
☐☐☐	22	Jaroslav Svejkovsky, Wsh.	20.00	8.00	.50
☐☐☐	23	Keith Primeau, Car.	20.00	8.00	.50
☐☐☐	24	Alexandre Daigle, Ott.	12.00	3.50	.20
☐☐☐	25	Vyacheslav Kozlov, Det.	12.00	3.50	.20
☐☐☐	26	Jozef Stumpel, Bos.	20.00	8.00	.50
☐☐☐	27	Alexei Yashin, Ott.	65.00	20.00	1.00
☐☐☐	**28**	**Marian Hossa, Ott., RC**	**175.00**	**40.00**	**4.00**
☐☐☐	29	Bryan Berard, NYI.	40.00	12.00	.75
☐☐☐	30	Dominik Hasek (G), Buf.	150.00	35.00	1.75
☐☐☐	31	Chris Chelios, Chi.	65.00	20.00	1.00
☐☐☐	32	Derian Hatcher, Dal.	20.00	8.00	.50
☐☐☐	33	Ed Jovanovski, Fla.	20.00	8.00	.50
☐☐☐	34	Zigmund Palffy, NYI.	40.00	12.00	.75
☐☐☐	35	Ron Hextall (G), Pha.	20.00	8.00	.50
☐☐☐	36	Daymond Langkow, T.B.	12.00	3.50	.20
☐☐☐	37	Daniel Cleary, Chi.	40.00	12.00	.75
☐☐☐	38	Alyn McCauley, Tor.	80.00	25.00	1.25
☐☐☐	39	Sean Burke (G), Van.	20.00	8.00	.50
☐☐☐	40	Brian Leetch, NYR.	40.00	12.00	.75
☐☐☐	41	Joé Juneau, Wsh.	12.00	3.50	.20
☐☐☐	42	Damian Rhodes (G), Ott.	12.00	3.50	.20
☐☐☐	43	Dino Ciccarelli, Fla.	20.00	8.00	.50
☐☐☐	44	Valeri Kamensky, Col.	20.00	8.00	.50
☐☐☐	45	Guy Hebert (G), Ana.	20.00	8.00	.50
☐☐☐	46	Brad Isbister, Pho.	12.00	3.50	.20
☐☐☐	47	Adam Graves, NYR.	12.00	3.50	.20
☐☐☐	48	Andrew Cassels, Cgy.	12.00	3.50	.20
☐☐☐	49	Joe Sakic, Col.	200.00	45.00	2.00
☐☐☐	50	Dainius Zubrus, Pha.	20.00	8.00	.50
☐☐☐	**51**	**Roberto Luongo (G), NYI., RC**	**200.00**	**50.00**	**5.00**
☐☐☐	52	Ethan Moreau, Chi.	12.00	3.50	.20
☐☐☐	53	Chris Osgood (G), Det.	65.00	20.00	1.00
☐☐☐	54	Stéphane Fiset (G), L.A.	20.00	8.00	.50
☐☐☐	55	Sergei Berezin, Tor.	20.00	8.00	.50
☐☐☐	56	Mike Richter (G), NYR.	40.00	12.00	.75
☐☐☐	57	Valeri Bure, Mtl.	12.00	3.50	.20
☐☐☐	58	Mats Sundin, Tor.	80.00	25.00	1.25
☐☐☐	59	Mike Dunham (G), N.J.	12.00	3.50	.20
☐☐☐	60	Byron Dafoe (G), Bos.	12.00	3.50	.20
☐☐☐	61	Joe Nieuwendyk, Dal.	20.00	8.00	.50
☐☐☐	62	Mike Grier, Edm.	20.00	8.00	.50
☐☐☐	63	Paul Coffey, Pha.	20.00	8.00	.50
☐☐☐	64	Chris Phillips, Ott.	20.00	8.00	.50
☐☐☐	**65**	**Patrik Elias, N.J., RC**	**30.00**	**10.00**	**1.00**
☐☐☐	66	Andy Moog (G), Mtl.	20.00	8.00	.50
☐☐☐	67	Geoff Sanderson, Car.	12.00	3.50	.20
☐☐☐	68	Jere Lehtinen, Dal.	20.00	8.00	.50
☐☐☐	69	Alexander Mogilny, Van.	40.00	12.00	.75
☐☐☐	70	Ryan Smyth, Edm.	20.00	8.00	.50
☐☐☐	71	John LeClair, Pha.	80.00	25.00	1.25
☐☐☐	**72**	**Olli Jokinen, L.A., RC**	**30.00**	**10.00**	**1.00**
☐☐☐	73	Doug Gilmour, N.J.	40.00	12.00	.75
☐☐☐	74	Theoren Fleury, Cgy.	40.00	12.00	.75
☐☐☐	75	Adam Deadmarsh, Col.	12.00	3.50	.20
☐☐☐	76	Scott Mellanby, Fla.	12.00	3.50	.20
☐☐☐	77	Jeremy Roenick, Pho.	40.00	12.00	.75
☐☐☐	78	Jim Campbell, Stl.	12.00	3.50	.20
☐☐☐	79	Daren Puppa (G), T.B.	12.00	3.50	.20
☐☐☐	**80**	**Vaclav Prospal, Pha., RC**	**40.00**	**12.00**	**1.25**
☐☐☐	81	Vincent Damphousse, Mtl.	40.00	12.00	.75
☐☐☐	82	Derek Plante, Buf.	12.00	3.50	.20
☐☐☐	83	Sandis Ozolinsh, Col.	20.00	8.00	.50
☐☐☐	84	Darren McCarty, Det.	12.00	3.50	.20
☐☐☐	85	Luc Robitaille, L.A.	20.00	8.00	.50
☐☐☐	86	Wade Redden, Ott.	12.00	3.50	.20
☐☐☐	87	Eric Fichaud (G), NYI.	20.00	8.00	.50
☐☐☐	88	Jocelyn Thibault (G), Mtl.	40.00	12.00	.75
☐☐☐	89	Trevor Linden, Van.	20.00	8.00	.50
☐☐☐	90	Boyd Devereaux, Edm.	12.00	3.50	.20
☐☐☐	91	Chris Gratton, Pha.	20.00	8.00	.50
☐☐☐	92	Janne Niinimaa, Pha.	20.00	8.00	.50
☐☐☐	93	Jeff Friesen, S.J.	20.00	8.00	.50
☐☐☐	94	Roman Hamrlik, Edm.	20.00	8.00	.50
☐☐☐	95	Jason Arnott, N.J.	20.00	8.00	.50
☐☐☐	96	Sergei Fedorov, Det.	80.00	25.00	1.25
☐☐☐	97	Tony Amonte, Chi.	12.00	3.50	.20
☐☐☐	98	Mattias Ohlund, Van.	40.00	12.00	.75
☐☐☐	99	Patrick Marleau, S.J.	80.00	25.00	1.25
☐☐☐	100	Félix Potvin (G), Tor.	80.00	25.00	1.25
☐☐☐	101	Tommy Salo (G), NYI.	12.00	3.50	.20
☐☐☐	102	Ed Belfour (G), Dal.	40.00	12.00	.75
☐☐☐	103	Doug Weight, Edm.	40.00	12.00	.75
☐☐☐	104	Daniel Alfredsson, Ott.	20.00	8.00	.50
☐☐☐	105	Pierre Turgeon, Mtl.	20.00	8.00	.50
☐☐☐	**106**	**Espen Knutsen, Ana., RC**	**12.00**	**3.50**	**.50**
☐☐☐	107	Trevor Kidd (G), Car.	20.00	8.00	.50
☐☐☐	108	Alexei Morozov, Pgh.	65.00	20.00	1.00
☐☐☐	109	Oleg Tverdovsky, Pho.	12.00	3.50	.20
☐☐☐	110	Grant Fuhr (G), Stl.	20.00	8.00	.50
☐☐☐	111	Pat LaFontaine, NYR.	20.00	8.00	.50
☐☐☐	112	Keith Tkachuk, Pho.	65.00	20.00	1.00
☐☐☐	113	Ron Francis, Pgh.	40.00	12.00	.75
☐☐☐	**114**	**Derek Morris, Cgy., RC**	**15.00**	**5.00**	**.50**
☐☐☐	115	Joe Sakic, Col.	100.00	28.00	1.00
☐☐☐	116	Brian Leetch, NYR.	25.00	10.00	.50
☐☐☐	117	Alyn McCauley, Tor.	40.00	12.00	.65
☐☐☐	118	Pavel Bure, Van.	75.00	18.00	.85
☐☐☐	119	Eric Lindros, Pha.	175.00	45.00	2.00
☐☐☐	120	Teemu Selänne, Ana.	75.00	18.00	.85
☐☐☐	121	Jarome Iginla, Cgy.	25.00	10.00	.50
☐☐☐	122	Steve Yzerman, Det.	125.00	30.00	1.25
☐☐☐	123	Daniel Cleary, Chi.	25.00	10.00	.50
☐☐☐	124	Bryan Berard, NYI.	25.00	10.00	.50
☐☐☐	125	Jaromir Jagr, Pgh.	125.00	30.00	1.25
☐☐☐	126	John Vanbiesbrouck (G), Fla.	50.00	15.00	.75
☐☐☐	127	Mark Messier, Van.	40.00	12.00	.65
☐☐☐	128	Patrick Marleau, S.J.	40.00	12.00	.65
☐☐☐	129	Mike Modano, Dal.	40.00	12.00	.65
☐☐☐	130	Zigmund Palffy, NYI.	25.00	10.00	.50
☐☐☐	131	Félix Potvin (G), Tor.	40.00	12.00	.65
☐☐☐	132	Derek Morris, Cgy.	20.00	8.00	.50
☐☐☐	133	Brendan Shanahan, Det.	50.00	15.00	.75
☐☐☐	134	Sergei Samsonov, Bos.	50.00	15.00	.75
☐☐☐	135	Dainius Zubrus, Pha.	20.00	8.00	.50
☐☐☐	136	Paul Kariya, Ana.	175.00	45.00	2.00
☐☐☐	137	Martin Brodeur (G), N.J.	75.00	18.00	.85
☐☐☐	138	Joe Thornton, Bos.	50.00	15.00	.75
☐☐☐	139	Mattias Ohlund, Van.	20.00	8.00	.50
☐☐☐	140	Ryan Smyth, Edm.	20.00	8.00	.50
☐☐☐	141	Jaroslav Svejkovsky, Wsh.	20.00	8.00	.50
☐☐☐	142	Patrick Roy (G), Col.	250.00	60.00	2.50
☐☐☐	143	Wayne Gretzky, NYR.	300.00	75.00	3.00
☐☐☐	144	Espen Knutsen, Ana.	20.00	8.00	.50
☐☐☐	145	CL: Patrick Marleau, S.J.	40.00	12.00	.65
☐☐☐	146	CL: Pat LaFontaine, NYR.	20.00	8.00	.50
☐☐☐	147	CL: Mike Gartner, Pho.	20.00	8.00	.50
☐☐☐	148	CL: Joe Thornton, Bos.	50.00	15.00	.75
☐☐☐	149	CL: Teemu Selänne, Ana.	75.00	18.00	.85
☐☐☐	150	CL: Mark Messier, Van.	40.00	12.00	.65

BACK TO THE FUTURE

These cards have two versions: the regular card and an autographed parallel.

Insert Set (8 cards): 3,200.00 350.00

	No.	Player	Auto	Reg.
☐☐	1	Eric Lindros/ Joe Thornton	600.00	75.00
☐☐	2	Jocelyn Thibault/ Marc Denis	200.00	20.00
☐☐	3	Teemu Selänne/ Patrick Marleau	275.00	30.00
☐☐	4	Jaromir Jagr/ Daniel Cleary	400.00	40.00
☐☐	5	Sergei Fedorov/ Peter Forsberg	400.00	40.00
☐☐	6	Bobby Hull/ Brett Hull	500.00	50.00
☐☐	7	Martin Brodeur/ Roberto Luongo	400.00	40.00
☐☐	8	Gordie Howe/ Steve Yzerman	900.00	100.00

CRAFTSMEN

These cards have two versions: the regular Craftsmen insert (serial numbered out of 2,400) and a Master Craftsmen parallel (serial numbered out of 100).

Insert Set (30 cards): 2,800.00 350.00

	No.	Player	Master	Reg.
☐☐	1	John Vanbiesbrouck (G), Fla.	10.00	12.00
☐☐	2	Eric Lindros, Pha.	250.00	25.00
☐☐	3	Joe Sakic, Col.	175.00	18.00
☐☐	4	Mark Messier, Van.	80.00	10.00
☐☐	5	Jaroslav Svejkovsky, Wsh.	40.00	5.00
☐☐	6	Dominik Hasek (G), Buf.	135.00	15.00
☐☐	7	Chris Osgood (G), Det.	65.00	8.00
☐☐	8	Martin Brodeur (G), N.J.	135.00	15.00
☐☐	9	Sergei Fedorov, Det.	80.00	10.00
☐☐	10	Daniel Cleary, Chi.	40.00	5.00
☐☐	11	Patrick Marleau, S.J.	80.00	10.00
☐☐	12	Sergei Samsonov, Bos.	100.00	12.00
☐☐	13	Félix Potvin (G), Tor.	80.00	10.00
☐☐	14	Patrick Roy (G), Col.	300.00	30.00
☐☐	15	Teemu Selänne, Ana.	135.00	15.00
☐☐	16	Steve Yzerman, Det.	200.00	20.00
☐☐	17	Jarome Iginla, Cgy.	40.00	5.00
☐☐	18	Mike Modano, Dal.	80.00	10.00
☐☐	19	Wayne Gretzky, NYR.	400.00	40.00
☐☐	20	Pavel Bure, Van.	135.00	15.00
☐☐	21	Ryan Smyth, Edm.	40.00	5.00
☐☐	22	Paul Kariya, Ana.	250.00	25.00
☐☐	23	Peter Forsberg, Col.	200.00	20.00
☐☐	24	Joe Thornton, Bos.	100.00	12.00
☐☐	25	Jaromir Jagr, Pgh.	200.00	20.00
☐☐	26	Bryan Berard, NYI.	40.00	5.00
☐☐	27	Brendan Shanahan, Det.	100.00	12.00
☐☐	28	Keith Tkachuk, Pho.	65.00	8.00
☐☐	29	Curtis Joseph (G), Edm.	100.00	12.00
☐☐	30	Brian Leetch, NYR.	40.00	5.00

PRIME NUMBERS

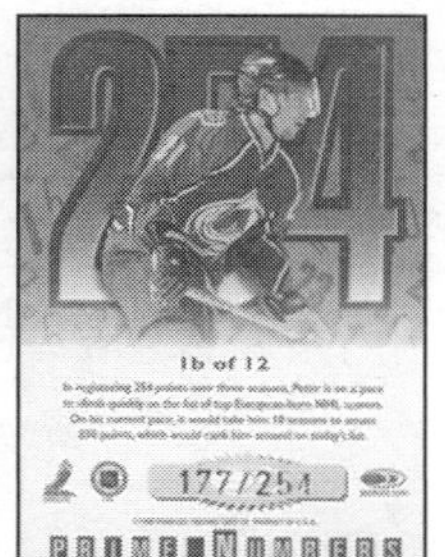

Each player has three different cards each with two versions: a regular insert and a die-cut insert. The three cards link together to highlight a significant statistic for the player (Roy's 349 career wins, for instance) and each card is sequentially numbered to that statistic.

In the case of Roy's die-cut cards, the first 300 of his "3" a-card are die-cut, the first 40 of his "4" b-card are die-cut and the first 9 of his "9" c-card are die-cut. As such, the three toughest versions will always be the uncut a-card, the die-cut b-card and the die-cut c-card.

The print runs for both versions are listed in parantheses after each player. No prices are listed for cards with fewer than 10 cards in existence. In the case of Joe Sakic's "0" b-card, there is no die-cut card available. No price very rare.

	No.	Player	Reg.	Die-Cut
☐☐	1a	Peter Forsberg 2 (54+200)	300.00	120.00
☐☐	1b	Peter Forsberg 5 (204+50)	120.00	300.00
☐☐	1c	Peter Forsberg 4 (250+4)	100.00	
☐☐	2a	Patrick Roy 3 (49+300)	500.00	150.00
☐☐	2b	Patrick Roy 4 (309+40)	160.00	600.00
☐☐	2c	Patrick Roy 9 (340+9)	150.00	
☐☐	3a	Mark Messier 2 (95+200)	120.00	60.00
☐☐	3b	Mark Messier 9 (205+90)	60.00	120.00
☐☐	3c	Mark Messier 5 (290+5)	45.00	
☐☐	4a	Eric Lindros 4 (36+400)	500.00	100.00
☐☐	4b	Eric Lindros 3 (406+30)	100.00	500.00
☐☐	4c	Eric Lindros 6 (430+6)	90.00	
☐☐	5a	Paul Kariya 2 (46+200)	450.00	160.00
☐☐	5b	Paul Kariya 4 (206+40)	160.00	450.00
☐☐	5c	Paul Kariya 6 (240+6)	150.00	
☐☐	6a	Jaromir Jagr 2 (66+200)	275.00	120.00
☐☐	6b	Jaromir Jagr 6 (206+60)	120.00	275.00
☐☐	6c	Jaromir Jagr 6 (260+6)	100.00	
☐☐	7a	Teemu Selänne 2 (37+200)	200.00	85.00
☐☐	7b	Teemu Selänne 3 (207+30)	85.00	225.00
☐☐	7c	Teemu Selänne 7 (230+7)	85.00	
☐☐	8a	John Vanbiesbrouck 2 (88+200)	120.00	75.00
☐☐	8b	John Vanbiesbrouck 8 (208+80)	75.00	120.00
☐☐	8c	John Vanbiesbrouck 8 (280+8)	65.00	
☐☐	9a	Brendan Shanahan 3 (35+300)	175.00	60.00
☐☐	9b	Brendan Shanahan 3 (305+30)	60.00	175.00
☐☐	9c	Brendan Shanahan 5 (330+5)	60.00	
☐☐	10a	Steve Yzerman 5 (39+500)	375.00	70.00
☐☐	10b	Steve Yzerman 3 (509+30)	70.00	400.00
☐☐	10c	Steve Yzerman 9 (530+9)	70.00	
☐☐	11a	Joe Sakic 3 (7+300)	90.00	90.00
☐	11b	Joe Sakic 0 (#/307)	90.00	.–
☐☐	11c	Joe Sakic 7 (300+7)	90.00	
☐☐	12a	Pavel Bure 3 (88+300)	140.00	75.00
☐☐	12b	Pavel Bure 8 (308+80)	75.00	140.00
☐☐	12c	Pavel Bure 8 (380+8)	75.00	

1997 - 98 DONRUSS PREFERRED

This series is divided into four subsets: 100 bronze cards, 60 silver cards, 30 gold cards and 10 platinum cards. Each card has two versions: the regular card and a die-cut Cut To The Chase parallel.

Imprint: © 1997 DONRUSS TRADING CARD CO.

Complete Set (220 cards): 5,000.00 1,250.00

	No.	Sub.	Player	Die-Cut	Reg.
☐☐	1	G	Dominik Hasek (G), Buf.	60.00	20.00
☐☐	2	G	Peter Forsberg, Col.	90.00	30.00
☐☐	3	P	Brendan Shanahan, Det.	60.00	30.00
☐☐	4	P	Wayne Gretzky, NYR.	375.00	120.00
☐☐	5	P	Eric Lindros, Pha.	225.00	75.00
☐☐	6	G	Keith Tkachuk, Pho.	30.00	12.00
☐☐	7	P	Mark Messier, Van.	50.00	25.00
☐☐	8	G	Mike Modano, Dal.	40.00	15.00
☐☐	9	P	John Vanbiesbrouck (G), Fla.	60.00	30.00
☐☐	10	P	Paul Kariya, Ana.	225.00	75.00
☐☐	11	G	Saku Koivu, Mtl.	60.00	20.00
☐☐	12	B	Paul Coffey, Pha.	3.00	.50
☐☐	13	B	Joé Juneau, Wsh.	2.00	.35
☐☐	14	S	Jeff Friesen, S.J.	10.00	3.00
☐☐	15	G	Brett Hull, Stl.	40.00	15.00
☐☐	16	G	Martin Brodeur (G), N.J.	60.00	20.00
☐☐	17	G	Jarome Iginla, Cgy.	20.00	10.00
☐☐	18	S	Keith Primeau, Car.	10.00	3.00
☐☐	19	B	Ed Jovanovski, Fla.	3.00	.50
☐☐	20	B	Jamie Langenbrunner, Dal.	3.00	.50
☐☐	21	S	Derian Hatcher, Dal.	10.00	3.00
☐☐	22	G	Brian Leetch, NYR.	20.00	10.00
☐☐	23	S	Daymond Langkow, T.B.	6.00	2.00
☐☐	24	S	Ray Bourque, Bos.	25.00	8.00
☐☐	25	G	Pavel Bure, Van.	60.00	20.00
☐☐	26	S	Janne Niinimaa, Pha.	10.00	3.00
☐☐	27	S	Jamie Storr (G), L.A.	10.00	3.00
☐☐	28	B	Darcy Tucker, Mtl.	2.00	.35
☐☐	29	B	Anson Carter, Bos.	2.00	.35
☐☐	30	B	Jeff O'Neill, Car.	3.00	.50
☐☐	31	G	Jason Arnott, Edm.	10.00	5.00
☐☐	32	B	Tommy Salo (G), NYI.	2.00	.35
☐☐	33	B	Petr Nedved, Pgh.	2.00	.35
☐☐	34	B	Michael Peca, Buf.	3.00	.50
☐☐	35	S	Ethan Moreau, Chi.	6.00	2.00
☐☐	36	B	Ray Sheppard, Fla.	2.00	.35
☐☐	37	B	Damian Rhodes (G), Ott.	2.00	.35
☐☐	38	S	Mats Sundin, Tor.	25.00	8.00
☐☐	39	G	Alexander Mogilny, Van.	20.00	10.00
☐☐	40	S	Mike Dunham (G), N.J.	6.00	2.00
☐☐	41	P	Steve Yzerman, Det.	150.00	60.00
☐☐	42	S	Alexei Yashin, Ott.	18.00	6.00
☐☐	43	S	Jim Carey (G), Bos.	6.00	2.00
☐☐	44	S	Mike Grier, Edm.	10.00	3.00
☐☐	45	B	Steve Rucchin, Ana.	2.00	.35
☐☐	46	S	Mark Recchi, Mtl.	10.00	3.00
☐☐	47	B	Mike Gartner, Pho.	3.00	.50
☐☐	48	S	Alexandre Daigle, Ott.	6.00	2.00
☐☐	49	G	Eric Fichaud (G), NYI.	10.00	5.00
☐☐	50	B	Harry York, Stl.	2.00	.35
☐☐	51	B	Dino Ciccarelli, Fla.	3.00	.50
☐☐	52	B	Bill Ranford (G), Wsh.	3.00	.50
☐☐	53	G	Adam Deadmarsh, Col.	10.00	5.00
☐☐	54	B	Ed Belfour (G), Dal.	4.00	.50
☐☐	55	S	Jozef Stumpel, L.A.	10.00	3.00
☐☐	56	B	Rem Murray, Edm.	2.00	.35
☐☐	57	B	Pat Verbeek, Dal.	2.00	.35
☐☐	58	B	Pat LaFontaine, NYR.	3.00	.50
☐☐	59	B	Pat Lafontaine	3.00	.50
☐☐	60	B	Grant Fuhr (G), Stl.	3.00	.50
☐☐	61	B	Rob Niedermayer, Fla.	2.00	.35
☐☐	62	B	Brian Savage, Mtl.	2.00	.35
☐☐	63	B	Gary Roberts, Car.	3.00	.50
☐☐	64	B	Tony Amonte, Chi.	3.00	.50
☐☐	65	B	Jere Lehtinen, Dal.	3.00	.50
☐☐	66	B	Dave Andreychuk, N.J.	2.00	.35
☐☐	67	B	Rod Brind'Amour, Pha.	3.00	.50
☐☐	68	B	Mikael Renberg, T.B.	2.00	.35
☐☐	69	S	Doug Gilmour, N.J.	15.00	5.00
☐☐	70	B	Kevin Hatcher, Pgh.	2.00	..35
☐☐	71	B	Byron Dafoe (G), Bos.	2.00	.35
☐☐	72	S	Derek Plante, Buf.	6.00	2.00
☐☐	73	B	Trevor Kidd (G), Car.	3.00	.50
☐☐	74	S	Doug Weight, Edm.	15.00	5.00
☐☐	75	B	Valeri Bure, Mtl.	2.00	.35
☐☐	76	G	John LeClair, Pha.	40.00	15.00
☐☐	77	B	Sergei Berezin, Tor.	3.00	.50
☐☐	78	S	Peter Bondra, Wsh.	18.00	6.00
☐☐	79	G	Bryan Berard, NYI.	20.00	10.00
☐☐	**80**	**B**	**Steve Shields (G), Buf., RC**	**3.00**	**.50**
☐☐	81	G	Chris Osgood (G), Det.	30.00	12.00
☐☐	82	B	Mike Vernon (G), S.J.	3.00	.50
☐☐	83	B	Martin Gelinas, Van.	2.00	.35
☐☐	84	S	Curtis Joseph (G), Edm.	35.00	10.00
☐☐	85	S	Geoff Sanderson, Car.	6.00	2.00
☐☐	86	P	Patrick Roy (G), Col.	300.00	100.00
☐☐	87	G	Jocelyn Thibault (G), Mtl.	20.00	10.00
☐☐	88	S	Jeremy Roenick, Pho.	15.00	5.00
☐☐	89	B	Trevor Linden, Van.	3.00	.50
☐☐	90	S	Daniel Alfredsson, Ott.	10.00	3.00
☐☐	91	B	Sergei Zubov, Dal.	3.00	.50
☐☐	92	S	Dimitri Khristich, Bos.	6.00	2.00
☐☐	93	B	Brian Holzinger, Buf.	2.00	.35
☐☐	94	B	Andrew Cassels, Cgy.	2.00	.35
☐☐	95	G	Teemu Selänne, Ana.	60.00	20.00
☐☐	96	B	Ron Hextall (G), Pha.	3.00	.50
☐☐	97	B	Wade Redden, Ott.	2.00	.35
☐☐	98	B	Jim Campbell, Stl.	2.00	.35
☐☐	99	G	Félix Potvin (G), Tor.	40.00	15.00
☐☐	100	S	Adam Oates, Wsh.	15.00	5.00
☐☐	101	B	Nikolai Khabibulin (G), Pho.	4.00	.50
☐☐	102	S	José Théodore, Mtl.	15.00	5.00
☐☐	103	S	Sandis Ozolinsh, Col.	10.00	3.00
☐☐	104	B	Sean Burke (G), Car.	3.00	.50
☐☐	**105**	**G**	**Vaclav Prospal (G), Pha., RC**	**25.00**	**15.00**
☐☐	106	G	Zigmund Palffy, NYI.	20.00	10.00
☐☐	107	B	Kyle McLaren, Bos.	2.00	.35
☐☐	108	S	Owen Nolan, S.J.	10.00	3.00
☐☐	109	S	Chris Pronger, Stl.	10.00	3.00
☐☐	110	B	Daren Puppa (G), T.B.	2.00	.35
☐☐	111	B	Garth Snow (G), Pha.	2.00	.35
☐☐	112	B	Aki Berg, L.A.	2.00	.35
☐☐	113	B	Andy Moog (G), Mtl.	3.00	.50
☐☐	114	B	Darren McCarty, Det.	2.00	.35
☐☐	115	B	Joe Nieuwendyk, Dal.	3.00	.50
☐☐	116	S	Eric Dazé, Chi.	10.00	3.00

	No.		Player		
☐☐	117	S	Pierre Turgeon, Stl.	10.00	3.00
☐☐	118	B	Ken Wregget (G), Pgh.	2.00	.35
☐☐	119	G	Ryan Smyth, Edm.	10.00	5.00
☐☐	120	B	Kirk Muller, Fla.	2.00	.35
☐☐	121	B	Luc Robitaille, L.A.	3.00	.50
☐☐	122	G	Sergei Fedorov, Det.	40.00	15.00
☐☐	123	B	Sean Pronger, Ana.	2.00	.35
☐☐	124	S	Mike Richter (G), NYR.	15.00	5.00
☐☐	125	P	Jaromir Jagr, Pgh.	150.00	60.00
☐☐	126	B	Claude Lemieux, Col.	2.00	.35
☐☐	127	S	Chris Chelios, Chi.	18.00	6.00
☐☐	128	P	Joe Sakic, Col.	125.00	50.00
☐☐	129	S	Guy Hebert (G), Ana.	10.00	3.00
☐☐	130	S	Chris Gratton, Pha.	10.00	3.00
☐☐	131	B	Steve Sullivan, Tor.	2.00	.35
☐☐	132	B	Al MacInnis, Stl.	3.00	.50
☐☐	133	S	Adam Graves, NYR.	6.00	2.00
☐☐	134	B	Vyacheslav Kozlov, Det.	2.00	.35
☐☐	135	S	Scott Mellanby, Fla.	6.00	2.00
☐☐	136	B	Stéphane Fiset (G), L.A.	3.00	.50
☐☐	137	S	Oleg Tverdovsky, Pho.	6.00	2.00
☐☐	138	S	Theoren Fleury, Cgy.	15.00	5.00
☐☐	139	B	Jeff Hackett (G), Chi.	3.00	.50
☐☐	140	B	Vincent Damphousse, Mtl.	4.00	.50
☐☐	141	S	Roman Hamrlik, T.B.	10.00	3.00
☐☐	142	S	Ron Francis, Pgh.	15.00	5.00
☐☐	143	B	Scott Lachance, NYI.	2.00	.35
☐☐	144	B	Todd Harvey, Dal.	2.00	.35
☐☐	145	S	Marc Denis (G), Col.	10.00	3.00
☐☐	146	G	Jaroslav Svejkovsky, Wsh.	10.00	5.00
☐☐	**147**	**S**	**Olli Jokinen, L.A., RC**	**15.00**	**6.00**
☐☐	148	G	Sergei Samsonov, Bos.	35.00	15.00
☐☐	149	G	Chris Phillips, Ott.	10.00	5.00
☐☐	150	G	Patrick Marleau, S.J.	30.00	12.00
☐☐	151	G	Joe Thornton, Bos.	40.00	18.00
☐☐	152	S	Daniel Cleary, Chi.	10.00	3.00
☐☐	153	G	Alyn McCauley, Tor.	30.00	12.00
☐☐	154	S	Brad Isbister, Pho.	6.00	2.00
☐☐	155	S	Alexei Morozov, Pgh.	25.00	8.00
☐☐	**156**	**B**	**Shawn Bates, Bos., RC**	**2.00**	**.35**
☐☐	**157**	**B**	**Jean-Yves Leroux, Chi., RC**	**2.00**	**.35**
☐☐	158	B	Marcel Cousineau (G), Tor.	2.00	.35
☐☐	159	B	Vaclav Varada, Buf.	2.00	.35
☐☐	160	S	Jean-Sébastien Giguère (G), Cgy.	10.00	3.00
☐☐	**161**	**B**	**Espen Knutsen, Ana., RC**	**3.00**	**.50**
☐☐	**162**	**S**	**Marian Hossa, Ott., RC**	**30.00**	**15.00**
☐☐	**163**	**B**	**Robert Dome, Pgh., RC**	**4.00**	**.75**
☐☐	**164**	**B**	**Juha Lind, Dal., RC**	**3.00**	**.50**
☐☐	165	B	Sergei Fedorov, Det.	8.00	1.00
☐☐	166	B	Jarome Iginla, Cgy.	4.00	.50
☐☐	167	B	Jaroslav Svejkovsky, Wsh.	3.00	.50
☐☐	168	S	Patrick Roy (G), Col.	120.00	30.00
☐☐	169	B	Dominik Hasek (G), Buf.	15.00	1.50
☐☐	170	B	Alexander Mogilny, Van.	4.00	.50
☐☐	171	B	Chris Chelios, Chi.	6.00	.75
☐☐	172	S	Wayne Gretzky, NYR.	150.00	35.00
☐☐	173	B	Peter Forsberg, Col.	25.00	2.50
☐☐	174	B	Ray Bourque, Bos.	8.00	1.00
☐☐	175	S	Joe Sakic, Col.	60.00	15.00
☐☐	176	B	Mike Modano, Dal.	8.00	1.00
☐☐	177	B	Mark Messier, Van.	8.00	1.00
☐☐	178	B	Teemu Selänne, Ana.	15.00	1.50
☐☐	179	S	Steve Yzerman, Det.	75.00	18.00
☐☐	180	S	Eric Lindros, Pha.	100.00	25.00
☐☐	181	B	Doug Weight, Edm.	4.00	.50
☐☐	182	B	John Vanbiesbrouck (G), Fla.	10.00	1.25
☐☐	183	S	Paul Kariya, Ana.	100.00	25.00
☐☐	184	S	Brendan Shanahan, Det.	35.00	10.00
☐☐	185	B	Martin Brodeur (G), N.J.	15.00	1.50
☐☐	186	B	Bryan Berard, NYI.	4.00	.50
☐☐	187	B	Marc Denis (G), Col.	3.00	.50
☐☐	188	B	Brian Leetch, NYR.	4.00	.50
☐☐	189	S	Ryan Smyth, Edm.	15.00	5.00
☐☐	190	B	Dainius Zubrus, Pha.	3.00	.50
☐☐	191	B	Keith Tkachuk, Pho.	6.00	.75
☐☐	192	S	Jaromir Jagr, Pgh.	75.00	18.00
☐☐	193	B	Brett Hull, Stl.	8.00	1.00
☐☐	194	B	Pavel Bure, Van.	15.00	1.50
☐☐	195	B	CL: Sergei Samsonov, Bos.	7.50	1.25
☐☐	196	B	CL: Olli Jokinen, L.A.	3.00	.50
☐☐	197	B	CL: Chris Phillips, Ott.	3.00	.50
☐☐	198	B	CL: Patrick Marleau, S.J.	6.00	1.00
☐☐	199	B	CL: Daniel Cleary, Chi.	3.00	.50
☐☐	200	B	CL: Joe Thornton, Bos.	7.50	1.25

PRECIOUS METALS

These inserts are limited to 100 copies. The cards feature the same photos as the ten platinum cards as well as five gold cards.

Insert Set (15 cards): 5,500.00

	No.		Player	NRMT-MT
☐	1	P	Brendan Shanahan, Det.	250.00
☐	2	G	Joe Thornton, Bos.	200.00
☐	3	P	Wayne Gretzky, NYR.	800.00
☐	4	P	Mark Messier, Van.	200.00
☐	5	P	Patrick Roy (G), Col.	600.00
☐	6	G	Martin Brodeur (G), N.J.	300.00
☐	7	P	Eric Lindros (G), Pha.	500.00
☐	8	P	Paul Kariya (G), Ana.	500.00
☐	9	G	Teemu Selänne, Ana.	300.00
☐	10	P	Jaromir Jagr, Pgh.	400.00
☐	11	P	Joe Sakic, Col.	350.00
☐	12	G	Peter Forsberg, Col.	400.00
☐	13	P	John Vanbiesbrouck (G), Fla.	250.00
☐	14	P	Steve Yzerman, Det.	400.00
☐	15	G	Sergei Samsonov, Bos.	200.00

COLOUR GUARD

These cards are limited to 1,500 copies.

Insert Set (18 cards):			30.00	400.00
	No.	Player	Promo	Insert
☐☐	1	Patrick Roy (G), Col.	8.00	100.00
☐☐	2	Martin Brodeur (G), N.J.	3.50	40.00
☐☐	3	Curtis Joseph (G), Edm.	3.00	35.00
☐☐	4	John Vanbiesbrouck (G), Fla.	3.00	35.00
☐☐	5	Félix Potvin (G), Tor.	2.50	30.00
☐☐	6	Dominik Hasek (G), Buf.	3.50	40.00
☐☐	7	Chris Osgood (G), Det.	2.00	25.00
☐☐	8	Eric Fichaud (G), NYI.	1.00	12.00
☐☐	9	Jocelyn Thibault (G), Mtl.	1.50	20.00
☐☐	10	Marc Denis (G), Col.	1.00	12.00
☐☐	11	José Théodore (G), Mtl.	1.50	20.00
☐☐	12	Mike Vernon (G), S.J.	1.00	12.00
☐☐	13	Jim Carey (G), Bos.	.75	10.00
☐☐	14	Ron Hextall (G), Pha.	1.00	12.00
☐☐	15	Mike Richter (G), NYR.	1.50	20.00
☐☐	16	Ed Belfour (G), Dal.	1.50	20.00
☐☐	17	Mike Dunham (G), N.J.	.75	10.00
☐☐	18	Damian Rhodes (G), Ott.	.75	10.00

LINE OF THE TIMES

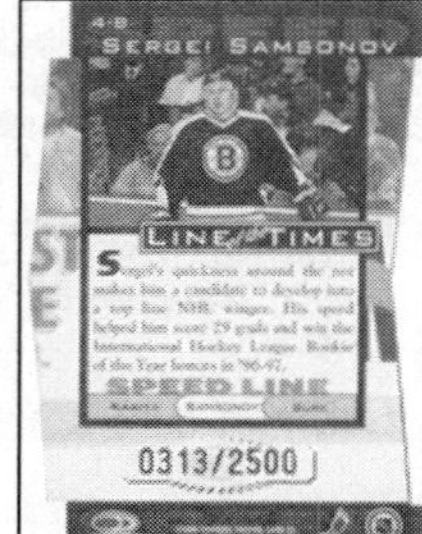

These inserts are limited to 2,500 copies.

Insert Set (24 cards): 700.00

	No.	Player	NRMT-MT
☐	1A	Ryan Smyth, Edm.	10.00
☐	1B	Sergei Fedorov, Det.	25.00
☐	1C	Jaromir Jagr, Pgh.	50.00
☐	2A	Eric Lindros, Pha.	65.00
☐	2B	Joe Thornton, Bos.	30.00
☐	2C	Brendan Shanahan, Det.	30.00
☐	3A	John LeClair, Pha.	25.00
☐	3B	Keith Tkachuk, Pho.	20.00
☐	3C	Brett Hull, Stl.	25.00
☐	4A	Pavel Bure, Van.	35.00
☐	4B	Sergei Samsonov, Bos.	30.00
☐	4C	Paul Kariya, Ana.	65.00
☐	5A	Mike Modano, Dal.	25.00
☐	5B	Teemu Selänne, Ana.	35.00
☐	5C	Patrick Marleau, S.J.	25.00
☐	6A	Wayne Gretzky, NYR.	100.00
☐	6B	Steve Yzerman, Det.	50.00
☐	6C	Daniel Cleary, Chi.	15.00
☐	7A	Jarome Iginla, Cgy.	15.00
☐	7B	Peter Forsberg, Col.	50.00
☐	7C	Mark Messier, Van.	25.00
☐	8A	Joe Sakic, Col.	40.00
☐	8B	Jaroslav Svejkovsky, Wsh.	10.00
☐	8C	Dainius Zubrus, Pha.	10.00

TINS

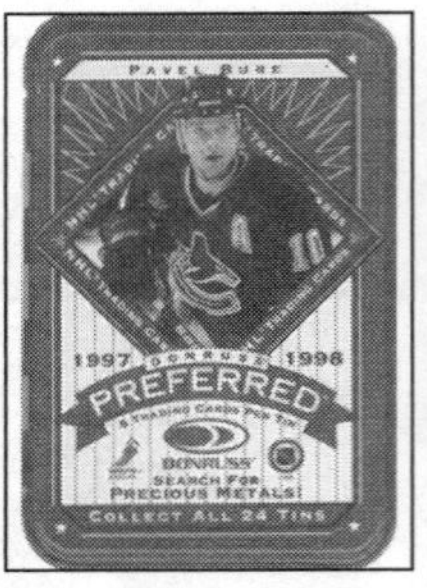

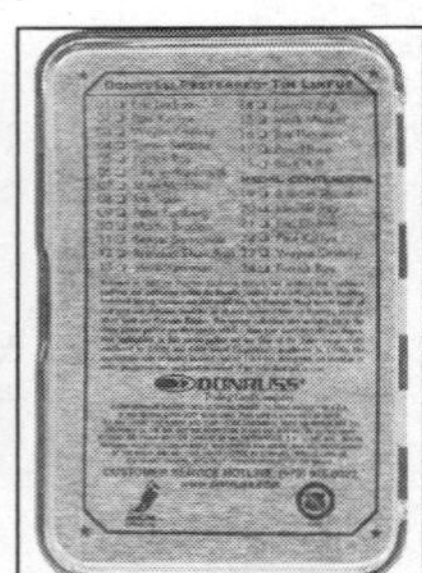

There are four versions to these tins: a blue tin pack, a red tin pack, a blue tin box and a red tin box. Prices are the same for blue and red tins; prices below are for opened tins.

Complete Set (24 tins):

	No.	Player	Box	Pack
☐☐☐☐	1	Eric Lindros, Pha.	15.00	2.50
☐☐☐☐	2	Paul Kariya, Ana.	15.00	2.50
☐☐☐☐	3	Wayne Gretzky, NYR.	25.00	4.00
☐☐☐☐	4	Teemu Selänne, Ana.	8.00	1.50
☐☐☐☐	5	Patrick Roy (G), Col.	20.00	3.00
☐☐☐☐	6	John Vanbiesbrouck (G), Fla.	7.00	1.25
☐☐☐☐	7	Mike Modano, Dal.	6.00	1.00
☐☐☐☐	8	Joe Sakic, Col.	10.00	1.75
☐☐☐☐	9	Peter Forsberg, Col.	12.00	2.00
☐☐☐☐	10	Martin Brodeur (G), N.J.	8.00	1.50
☐☐☐☐	11	Sergei Samsonov, Bos.	7.00	1.25
☐☐☐☐	12	Brendan Shanahan, Det.	7.00	1.25
☐☐☐☐	13	Steve Yzerman, Det.	12.00	2.00
☐☐☐☐	14	Jaromir Jagr, Pgh.	12.00	2.00
☐☐☐☐	15	Mark Messier, Van.	6.00	1.00
☐☐☐☐	16	Joe Thornton, Bos.	7.00	1.25
☐☐☐☐	17	Pavel Bure, Van.	8.00	1.50
☐☐☐☐	18	Brett Hull, Stl.	6.00	1.00
☐☐☐☐	19	Brendan Shanahan, Det.	7.00	1.25
☐☐☐☐	20	Jaromir Jagr, Pgh.	12.00	2.00
☐☐☐☐	21	Eric Lindros, Pha.	15.00	2.50
☐☐☐☐	22	Paul Kariya, Ana.	15.00	2.50
☐☐☐☐	23	Wayne Gretzky, NYR.	25.00	4.00
☐☐☐☐	24	Patrick Roy (G), Col.	20.00	3.00

WIDE TINS

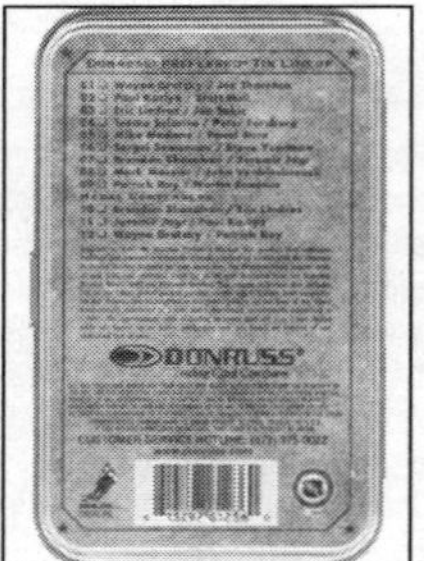

Prices below are for opened this.

Complete Set (12 tins): 45.00

	No.	Player	NRMT-MT
☐	1	Wayne Gretzky/ Joe Thornton	6.00
☐	2	Paul Kariya/ Brett Hull	4.00
☐	3	Eric Lindros/ Joe Sakic	4.50
☐	4	Teemu Selänne/ Peter Forsberg	3.50

☐	5	Pavel Bure/ Mike Modano	2.50
☐	6	Sergei Samsonov/ Steve Yzerman	3.50
☐	7	Jaromir Jagr/ Brendan Shanahan	4.50
☐	8	Mark Messier/ John Vanbiesbrouck (G)	2.50
☐	9	Patrick Roy (G)/ Martin Brodeur (G)	5.00
☐	10	Brendan Shanahan/ Eric Lindros	4.00
☐	11	Jaromir Jagr/ Paul Kariya	5.00
☐	12	Wayne Gretzky/ Patrick Roy (G)	8.00

1997 - 98 DONRUSS PRIORITY

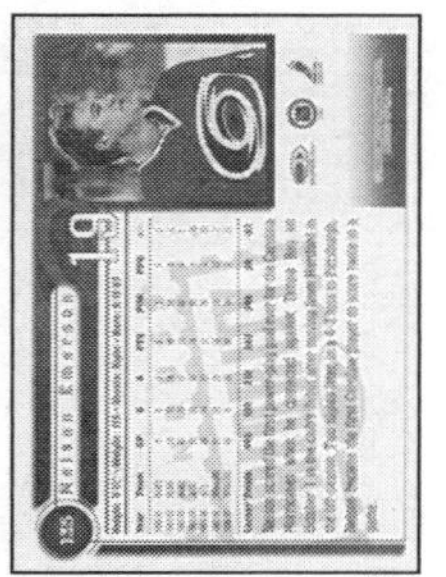

These cards have two versions: the regular card and a Stamp of Approval parallel.

Imprint: © 1997 DONRUSS TRADING CARD CO.

Complete Set (220 cards):		**65.00**
Common Even Number:	**10.00**	**.10**
Common Oldd Number:	**10.00**	**.20**

	No.	Player	Parallel	Reg.
☐☐	1	Patrick Roy (G), Col.	400.00	4.00
☐☐	2	Eric Lindros, Pha.	350.00	2.00
☐☐	3	Keith Tkachuk, Pha.	75.00	1.00
☐☐	4	Steve Yzerman, Det.	250.00	1.50
☐☐	5	John Vanbiesbrouck (G), Fla.	125.00	1.50
☐☐	6	Teemu Selänne, Ana.	150.00	1.00
☐☐	7	Martin Brodeur (G), N.J.	150.00	1.75
☐☐	8	Peter Forsberg, Col.	250.00	1.50
☐☐	9	Brett Hull, Stl.	100.00	1.25
☐☐	10	Wayne Gretzky, NYR.	500.00	3.00
☐☐	11	Mike Modano, Dal.	100.00	1.25
☐☐	12	Sergei Fedorov, Det.	100.00	.75
☐☐	13	Paul Kariya, Ana.	350.00	3.50
☐☐	14	Saku Koivu, Mtl.	150.00	1.00
☐☐	15	Pavel Bure, Van.	150.00	1.75
☐☐	16	Mark Messier, Van.	100.00	.75
☐☐	17	Joe Sakic, Col.	200.00	2.00
☐☐	18	Jaromir Jagr, Pgh.	250.00	1.50
☐☐	19	Brendan Shanahan, Det.	125.00	1.50
☐☐	20	Ray Bourque, Bos.	100.00	.75
☐☐	21	Daymond Langkow, T.B.	10.00	.20
☐☐	22	Alexandre Daigle, Ott. (Pha.)	10.00	.20
☐☐	23	Dainius Zubrus, Pha.	20.00	.50
☐☐	24	Ryan Smyth, Edm.	20.00	.35
☐☐	25	Derek Plante, Buf.	10.00	.20
☐☐	26	Eric Dazé, Chi.	20.00	.35
☐☐	27	Ed Jovanovski, Fla.	20.00	.50
☐☐	28	Sergei Berezin, Tor.	20.00	.35
☐☐	29	Roman Turek (G), Dal.	10.00	.20
☐☐	30	Derian Hatcher, Dal.	20.00	.35
☐☐	31	Jarome Iginla, Cgy.	40.00	.75
☐☐	32	Luc Robitaille, L.A.	20.00	.35
☐☐	33	Rod Brind'Amour, Pha.	20.00	.50
☐☐	34	Mathieu Schneider, Tor.	10.00	.20
☐☐	35	Olaf Kolzig (G), Wsh.	40.00	.75
☐☐	36	Nikolai Khabibulin (G), Pho.	40.00	.35
☐☐	37	Scott Niedermayer, N.J.	10.00	.20
☐☐	38	Keith Primeau, Car.	20.00	.35
☐☐	39	Dimitri Khristich, Bos.	10.00	.20
☐☐	40	Eric Fichaud (G), NYI.	20.00	.35
☐☐	41	Pierre Turgeon, Stl.	20.00	.50
☐☐	42	Kevin Stevens, NYR.	10.00	.20
☐☐	43	Nicklas Lidström, Det.	20.00	.50
☐☐	44	Sean Burke (G), Van.	20.00	.35
☐☐	45	Sandis Ozolinsh, Col.	20.00	.50
☐☐	46	Owen Nolan, S.J.	20.00	.35
☐☐	47	Peter Bondra, Wsh.	75.00	1.00
☐☐	48	Ron Hextall (G), Pha.	20.00	.35
☐☐	49	Geoff Sanderson, Van.	10.00	.20
☐☐	51	Sergei Zubov, Dal.	20.00	.50
☐☐	52	Doug Gilmour, N.J.	40.00	.35
☐☐	53	Oleg Tverdovsky, Pho.	10.00	.20
☐☐	54	Bryan Berard, NYI.	40.00	.35
☐☐	55	Bill Ranford (G), Wsh.	20.00	.50
☐☐	56	Mats Sundin, Tor.	100.00	.75
☐☐	57	Damian Rhodes (G), Ott.	10.00	.20
☐☐	58	Zigmund Palffy, NYI.	40.00	.35
☐☐	59	Mike Grier, Edm.	20.00	.50
☐☐	60	Jozef Stumpel, L.A.	20.00	.35
☐☐	61	Mark Recchi, Mtl.	20.00	.50
☐☐	62	Alexei Zhamnov, Chi.	10.00	.20
☐☐	63	Jere Lehtinen, Dal.	20.00	.50
☐☐	64	Andrew Cassels, Cgy.	10.00	.20
☐☐	65	Kevin Hodson (G), Det.	10.00	.20
☐☐	66	Dino Ciccarelli, Fla.	20.00	.35
☐☐	67	Niklas Sundstrom, NYR.	10.00	.20
☐☐	68	Jeff Hackett (G), Chi.	20.00	.35
☐☐	69	Brian Holzinger, Buf.	10.00	.20
☐☐	70	Jeff Friesen, S.J.	20.00	.35
☐☐	71	Ed Belfour (G), Dal.	40.00	.75
☐☐	72	Wayne Primeau, Buf.	10.00	.20
☐☐	73	Sami Kapanen, Car.	10.00	.20
☐☐	74	Brian Leetch, NYR.	40.00	.35
☐☐	75	Mikael Renberg, T.B.	10.00	.20
☐☐	76	Ron Tugnutt (G), Ott.	10.00	.20
☐☐	77	Ron Francis, Pgh.	40.00	.75
☐☐	78	Jocelyn Thibault (G), Mtl.	40.00	.35
☐☐	79	Jamie Langenbrunner, Dal.	20.00	.50
☐☐	80	Dominik Hasek (G), Buf.	150.00	1.00
☐☐	81	Chris Osgood (G), Det.	75.00	1.00
☐☐	82	Grant Fuhr (G), Stl.	20.00	.35
☐☐	83	Adam Graves, NYR.	10.00	.20
☐☐	84	Janne Niinimaa, Pha.	20.00	.35
☐☐	85	Kelly Hrudey (G), S.J	10.00	.20.
☐☐	86	Mike Dunham (G), N.J.	10.00	.20
☐☐	87	Valeri Kamensky, Col.	20.00	.50
☐☐	88	Cory Stillman, Cgy.	10.00	.20
☐☐	89	Anson Carter, Bos.	10.00	.20
☐☐	90	Igor Larionov, Det.	20.00	.35
☐☐	91	Chris Pronger, Stl.	20.00	.50
☐☐	92	Steve Sullivan, Tor.	10.00	.20
☐☐	93	Mike Gartner, Pho.	20.00	.50
☐☐	94	Jim Campbell, Stl.	10.00	.20
☐☐	95	Valeri Bure, Mtl.	10.00	.20
☐☐	96	Stéphane Fiset (G), L.A.	20.00	.35
☐☐	97	Jason Arnott, Edm.	20.00	.50
☐☐	98	Trevor Kidd (G), Car.	20.00	.35
☐☐	99	Chris Chelios, Chi.	75.00	1.00
☐☐	100	Kevin Hatcher, Pgh.	10.00	.20
☐☐	101	Félix Potvin (G), Tor.	100.00	1.25
☐☐	102	Travis Green, NYI. (Ana.)	10.00	.20
☐☐	103	Dave Gagner, Fla.	10.00	.20
☐☐	104	Byron Dafoe (G), Bos.	10.00	.20
☐☐	105	Rick Tabaracci (G), Cgy.	10.00	.20
☐☐	106	Gary Roberts, Car.	20.00	.35
☐☐	107	Mike Ricci, S.J.	10.00	.20
☐☐	108	Andy Moog (G), Mtl.	20.00	.35
☐☐	109	Sean Pronger, Ana.	10.00	.20
☐☐	110	Paul Coffey, Pha.	20.00	.35
☐☐	111	Trevor Linden, Van.	20.00	.50
☐☐	112	Rob Zamuner, T.B.	20.00	.35
☐☐	113	Daniel Alfredsson, Ott.	20.00	.50
☐☐	114	Ray Sheppard, Fla.	10.00	.20
☐☐	**115**	**Steve Shields (G), Buf., RC**	**20.00**	**.50**
☐☐	116	Ethan Moreau, Chi.	10.00	.20
☐☐	117	Tomas Sandström, Ana.	10.00	.20
☐☐	118	Chris Gratton, Pha.	20.00	.35
☐☐	119	Alexander Mogilny, Van.	40.00	.75
☐☐	120	Roman Hamrlik, Edm.	20.00	.35
☐☐	121	Tommy Salo (G), NYI.	10.00	.20
☐☐	122	Jason Allison, Bos.	40.00	.35
☐☐	123	Curtis Joseph (G), Edm.	125.00	1.50
☐☐	124	Guy Hebert (G), Ana.	20.00	.35
☐☐	125	Jeff O'Neill, Car.	20.00	.50
☐☐	126	Donald Audette, Buf.	10.00	.20
☐☐	127	Claude Lemieux, Col.	10.00	.20
☐☐	128	Brian Savage, Mtl.	10.00	.20
☐☐	129	Scott Mellanby, Fla.	10.00	.20
☐☐	130	Vyacheslav Kozlov, Det.	10.00	.20
☐☐	131	Wade Redden, Ott.	10.00	.20
☐☐	132	John LeClair, Pha.	100.00	.75
☐☐	133	Jeremy Roenick, Pho.	40.00	.75
☐☐	134	Andreas Johansson, Pgh.	10.00	.20
☐☐	135	Nelson Emerson, Car.	10.00	.20
☐☐	136	Daren Puppa (G), T.B.	10.00	.20
☐☐	137	Joé Juneau, Wsh.	10.00	.20
☐☐	138	Garth Snow (G), Pha.	10.00	.20
☐☐	139	Tom Barrasso (G), Pgh.	20.00	.50
☐☐	140	Joe Nieuwendyk, Dal.	20.00	.35
☐☐	141	Theoren Fleury, Cgy.	40.00	.75
☐☐	142	Yanic Perreault, L.A.	10.00	.20
☐☐	143	Mike Richter (G), NYR.	40.00	.75
☐☐	144	Al MacInnis, Stl.	20.00	.35
☐☐	145	Michael Peca, Buf.	20.00	.50
☐☐	146	Darren McCarty, Det.	10.00	.20
☐☐	147	Alexei Yashin, Ott.	75.00	1.00
☐☐	148	Rick Tocchet, Pho.	10.00	.20
☐☐	149	Adam Oates, Wsh.	40.00	.75
☐☐	150	Wendel Clark, Tor.	20.00	.35
☐☐	151	Tony Amonte, Chi.	20.00	.50
☐☐	152	Dave Andreychuk, N.J.	10.00	.20
☐☐	153	Jamie Storr (G), L.A.	20.00	.50
☐☐	154	Craig Janney, Pho.	10.00	.20
☐☐	155	Todd Bertuzzi, NYI.	10.00	.20
☐☐	156	Harry York, Stl.	10.00	.20
☐☐	157	Todd Harvey, Dal.	10.00	.20
☐☐	158	Bobby Holik, N.J.	10.00	.20
☐☐	159	Mike Vernon (G), S.J.	20.00	.50
☐☐	160	Pat LaFontaine, NYR.	20.00	.35
☐☐	161	Doug Weight, Edm.	40.00	.75
☐☐	162	Kirk McLean (G), Car.	20.00	.35
☐☐	163	Adam Deadmarsh, Col.	10.00	.20
☐☐	164	Vincent Damphousse, Mtl.	40.00	.35
☐☐	**165**	**Vaclav Prospal, Pha., RC**	**35.00**	**1.00**
☐☐	166	Daniel Cleary, Chi.	20.00	.35
☐☐	167	Jaroslav Svejkovsky, Wsh.	20.00	.50
☐☐	**168**	**Marco Sturm, S.J., RC**	**20.00**	**.35**
☐☐	**169**	**Robert Dome, Pgh., RC**	**25.00**	**.75**
☐☐	**170**	**Patrik Elias, N.J., RC**	**25.00**	**.50**
☐☐	171	Mattias Ohlund, Van.	40.00	.75
☐☐	**172**	**Espen Knutsen, Ana., RC**	**20.00**	**.35**
☐☐	173	Joe Thornton, Bos.	100.00	1.50
☐☐	**174**	**Jan Bulis, Wsh., RC**	**20.00**	**.35**
☐☐	175	Patrick Marleau, S.J.	75.00	1.25
☐☐	176	Brad Isbister, Pho.	10.00	.20
☐☐	**177**	**Kevin Weekes (G), Fla., RC**	**15.00**	**.50**
☐☐	178	Sergei Samsonov, Bos.	100.00	.85
☐☐	**179**	**Tyler Moss (G), Cgy., RC**	**15.00**	**.50**
☐☐	180	Chris Phillips, Ott.	20.00	.35
☐☐	181	Alyn McCauley, Tor.	75.00	1.25
☐☐	**182**	**Derek Morris, Cgy., RC**	**20.00**	**.35**
☐☐	183	Alexei Morozov, Pgh.	75.00	1.25
☐☐	184	Boyd Devereaux, Edm.	10.00	.20
☐☐	185	Peter Forsberg, Col.	100.00	1.25
☐☐	186	Brendan Shanahan, Det.	60.00	.50
☐☐	187	Teemu Selänne, Ana.	75.00	.85
☐☐	188	Eric Lindros, Pha.	175.00	1.00
☐☐	189	Mark Messier, Van.	50.00	.60
☐☐	190	Vaclav Prospal, Pha.	20.00	.35
☐☐	191	Jarome Iginla, Cgy.	20.00	.50
☐☐	192	Mike Modano, Dal.	50.00	.35
☐☐	193	John Vanbiesbrouck (G), Fla.	60.00	.75
☐☐	194	Bryan Berard, NYI.	20.00	.25
☐☐	195	Patrick Marleau, S.J.	20.00	.50
☐☐	196	Martin Brodeur (G), N.J.	75.00	.50
☐☐	197	Patrick Roy (G), Col.	250.00	2.50
☐☐	198	Félix Potvin (G), Tor.	50.00	.35
☐☐	199	Wayne Gretzky, NYR.	300.00	3.00
☐☐	200	Sergei Samsonov, Bos.	50.00	.50
☐☐	201	Ryan Smyth, Edm.	20.00	.50
☐☐	202	Keith Tkachuk, Pho.	35.00	.25
☐☐	203	Chris Osgood (G), Det.	35.00	.50
☐☐	204	Paul Kariya, Ana.	175.00	1.00
☐☐	205	John LeClair, Pha.	50.00	.60
☐☐	206	Alyn McCauley, Tor.	35.00	.35
☐☐	207	Joe Thornton, Bos.	50.00	.75
☐☐	208	Joe Sakic, Col.	100.00	.75
☐☐	209	Steve Yzerman, Det.	100.00	1.25
☐☐	210	Saku Koivu, Mtl.	75.00	.50
☐☐	211	Pavel Bure, Van.	75.00	.85
☐☐	212	Zigmund Palffy, NYI.	20.00	.25
☐☐	213	Alexei Yashin, Ott.	35.00	.50
☐☐	214	Sergei Fedorov, Det.	50.00	.35
☐☐	215	CL: Joe Thornton, Bos.	40.00	.60
☐☐	216	CL: Patrick Marleau, S.J.	15.00	.25
☐☐	217	CL: Daniel Cleary, Chi.	20.00	.50
☐☐	218	CL: Sergei Samsonov, Det.	40.00	.50
☐☐	219	CL: Jaroslav Svejkovsky, Wsh.	20.00	.50
☐☐	220	CL: Alyn McCauley, Tor.	30.00	.35

DIRECT DEPOSIT

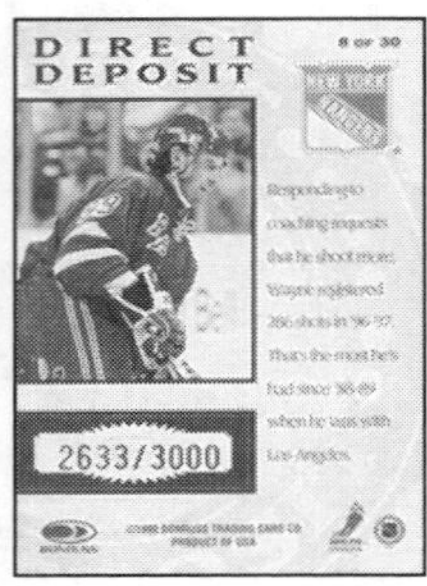

These cards are limited to 3,000 copies.

Insert Set (30 cards): 325.00

	No.	Player	Promo	Insert
☐☐	1	Brendan Shanahan, Det.	30.00	12.00
☐	2	Steve Yzerman, Det.		20.00
☐	3	Pavel Bure, Van.		15.00
☐	4	Jaromir Jagr, Pgh.		20.00
☐	5	Ryan Smyth, Edm.		6.00
☐	6	Sergei Samsonov, Bos.		12.00
☐	7	Mark Messier, Van.		10.00
☐	8	Wayne Gretzky, NYR.		40.00
☐	9	Jarome Iginla, Cgy.		6.00
☐	10	Peter Forsberg, Col.		20.00
☐	11	Joe Sakic, Col.		18.00
☐	12	Sergei Fedorov, Det.		10.00
☐	13	Mike Modano, Dal.		10.00
☐	14	Paul Kariya, Ana.		25.00
☐	15	Teemu Selänne, Ana.		15.00
☐	16	Eric Lindros, Pha.		25.00
☐	17	Keith Tkachuk, Pho.		8.00
☐	18	Patrick Marleau, S.J.		10.00
☐	19	Jaroslav Svejkovsky, Wsh.		6.00
☐	20	Alyn McCauley, Tor.		10.00
☐	21	Saku Koivu, Mtl.		15.00
☐	22	Zigmund Palffy, NYI.		6.00
☐	23	Brett Hull, Stl.		10.00
☐	24	Patrik Elias, N.J.		6.00
☐☐	25	Joe Thornton, Bos.	3.00	12.00
☐☐	26	Espen Knutsen, Ana.	1.00	6.00
☐	27	Daniel Alfredsson, Ott.		6.00
☐	28	John LeClair, Pha.		10.00
☐☐	29	Dainius Zubrus, Pha.	1.00	6.00
☐	30	Jason Arnott, N.J.		6.00

OPENING DAY ISSUES

These cards are limited to 1,000 copies.

Insert Set (30 cards): 800.00

	No.	Player	NRMT-MT
☐	1	Patrick Roy (G), Col.	75.00
☐	2	Eric Lindros, Pha.	60.00
☐	3	Keith Tkachuk, Pha.	18.00
☐	4	Steve Yzerman, Det.	45.00
☐	5	John Vanbiesbrouck (G), Fla.	25.00
☐	6	Teemu Selänne, Ana.	30.00
☐	7	Martin Brodeur (G), N.J.	30.00
☐	8	Peter Forsberg, Col.	45.00
☐	9	Brett Hull, Stl.	30.00
☐	10	Wayne Gretzky, NYR.	100.00
☐	11	Mike Modano, Dal.	20.00
☐	12	Paul Kariya, Ana.	60.00
☐	13	Pavel Bure, Van.	30.00
☐	14	Mark Messier, Van.	20.00
☐	15	Joe Sakic, Col.	35.00
☐	16	Jaromir Jagr, Pgh.	45.00
☐	17	Brendan Shanahan, Det.	25.00
☐	18	Ryan Smyth, Edm.	10.00
☐	19	Jarome Iginla, Cgy.	10.00
☐	20	Bryan Berard, NYI.	15.00
☐	21	Jocelyn Thibault (G), Mtl.	15.00
☐	22	Dominik Hasek (G), Buf.	30.00
☐	23	Chris Osgood (G), Det.	18.0
☐	24	Chris Chelios, Chi.	18.00
☐	25	Félix Potvin (G), Tor.	20.00
☐	26	John LeClair, Pha.	20.00
☐	27	Saku Koivu, Mtl.	30.00
☐	28	Joe Thornton, Bos.	25.00
☐	29	Patrick Marleau, S.J.	20.00
☐	30	Sergei Samsonov, Bos.	25.00

POSTMASTER GENERAL

These cards are limited to 1,500 copies. Promo versions exist for some if not all cards.

Insert Set (20 cards): 325.00

	No.	Player	Promo	Insert
☐	1	Patrick Roy (G), Mtl.		80.00
☐☐	2	John Vanbiesbrouck (G), Fla.	25.00	3.00
☐☐	3	Félix Potvin (G), Tor.	20.00	2.50
☐☐	4	Curtis Joseph (G), Edm.	25.00	3.00
☐☐	5	Mike Richter (G), NYR.	15.00	1.50
☐	6	Jocelyn Thibault (G), Mtl.		15.00
☐	7	Ed Belfour (G), Dal.		15.00
☐	8	Chris Osgood (G), Det.		18.00
☐	9	Ron Hextall (G), Pha.		10.00
☐	10	Martin Brodeur (G), N.J.		30.00
☐	11	Mike Vernon (G), S.J.		10.00
☐	12	Eric Fichaud (G), NYI.		10.00
☐	13	Dominik Hasek (G), Buf.		30.00
☐	14	Byron Dafoe (G), Bos.		10.00
☐	15	Tommy Salo (G), NYI.		10.00
☐	16	Garth Snow (G), Pha.		10.00
☐	17	Tom Barrasso (G), Pgh.		10.00
☐	18	Marc Denis (G), Col.		10.00
☐	19	Grant Fuhr (G), Stl.		10.00
☐	20	Guy Hebert (G), Ana.		10.00

STAMPS AND POSTCARDS

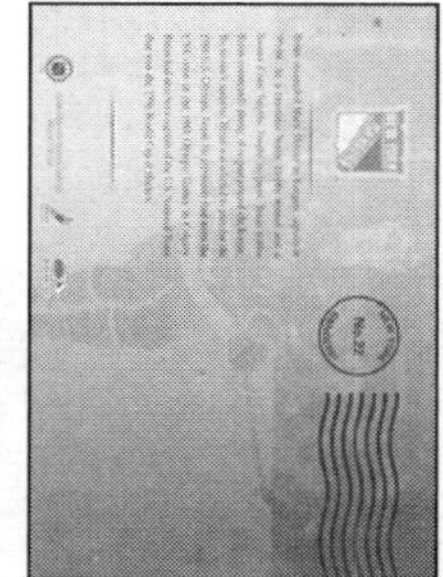

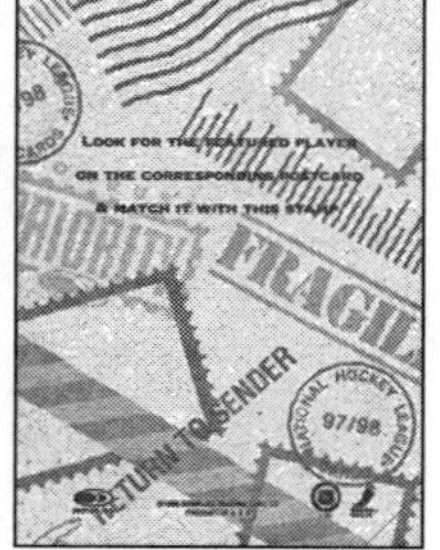

There are four stamp versions for each player in this series: the regular stamp, a bronze stamp, a silver stamp and a gold stamp. Each player also has a 4" x 6" postcard as well. Bronze stamps are valued at 2 times the regular stamp. Silver stamps are valued at 50% of the gold stamp.

Postcard Size: 4" x 6"

Insert Set (36 players):

	No.	Player	Gold	Stamp	4 x 6
☐☐☐☐☐	1	Patrick Roy (G), Col.	80.00	9.00	6.50
☐☐☐☐☐	2	Brendan Shanahan, Det.	30.00	3.75	2.50
☐☐☐☐☐	3	Steve Yzerman, Det.	50.00	6.00	4.00
☐☐☐☐☐	4	Jaromir Jagr, Pgh.	50.00	6.00	4.00
☐☐☐☐☐	5	Pavel Bure, Van.	35.00	4.50	3.00
☐☐☐☐☐	6	Mark Messier, Van.	25.00	3.00	2.00
☐☐☐☐☐	7	Wayne Gretzky, NYR.	100.00	12.00	8.00
☐☐☐☐☐	8	Eric Lindros, Pha.	65.00	7.50	5.00
☐☐☐☐☐	9	Joe Sakic, Col.	40.00	5.00	3.50
☐☐☐☐☐	10	Peter Forsberg, Col.	50.00	6.00	4.00
☐☐☐☐☐	11	John Vanbiesbrouck, Fla.	30.00	3.75	2.50
☐☐☐☐☐	12	Mike Modano, Dal.	25.00	3.00	2.00
☐☐☐☐☐	13	Paul Kariya, Ana.	65.00	7.50	5.00
☐☐☐☐☐	14	Teemu Selänne, Ana.	35.00	4.50	3.00
☐☐☐☐☐	15	Sergei Fedorov, Det.	25.00	3.00	2.00
☐☐☐☐☐	16	Joe Thornton, Bos.	30.00	3.75	2.50
☐☐☐☐☐	17	Sergei Samsonov, Det.	30.00	3.75	2.50
☐☐☐☐☐	18	Patrick Marleau, S.J.	25.00	3.00	2.00
☐☐☐☐☐	19	Ryan Smyth, Edm.	12.00	1.50	1.00
☐☐☐☐☐	20	Jarome Iginla, Cgy.	12.00	1.50	1.00
☐☐☐☐☐	21	John LeClair, Pha.	25.00	3.00	2.00
☐☐☐☐☐	22	Brian Leetch, NYR.	15.00	1.75	1.25
☐☐☐☐☐	23	Chris Chelios, Chi.	20.00	2.25	1.50
☐☐☐☐☐	24	Martin Brodeur (G), N.J.	35.00	4.50	3.00
☐☐☐☐☐	25	Bryan Berard, NYI.	15.00	1.75	1.25
☐☐☐☐☐	26	Keith Tkachuk, Pho.	20.00	2.25	1.50
☐☐☐☐☐	27	Saku Koivu, Mtl.	35.00	4.50	3.00
☐☐☐☐☐	28	Brett Hull, Stl.	25.00	3.00	2.00
☐☐☐☐☐	29	Félix Potvin (G), Tor.	25.00	3.00	2.00
☐☐☐☐☐	30	Chris Osgood (G), Det.	20.00	2.25	1.50
☐☐☐☐☐	31	Dominik Hasek (G), Buf.	35.00	4.50	3.00
☐☐☐☐☐	32	Zigmund Palffy, NYI.	15.00	1.75	1.25
☐☐☐☐☐	33	Jeremy Roenick, Pho.	15.00	1.75	1.25
☐☐☐☐☐	34	Dainius Zubrus, Pha.	12.00	1.50	1.00
☐☐☐☐☐	35	Ray Bourque, Bos.	25.00	3.00	2.00
☐☐☐☐☐	36	Jocelyn Thibault (G), Mtl.	15.00	1.75	1.25

1997 - 98 DONRUSS STUDIO

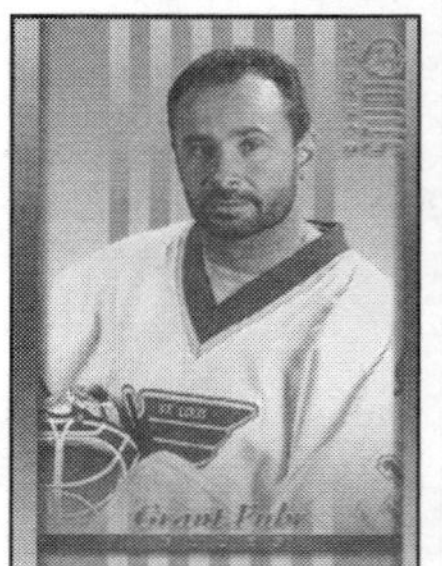

These cards have three versions: the regular card, a "Press Proof" parallel (1000 copies) and a "Gold Press Proof" parallel (250 copies).

Imprint: © 1997 DONRUSS TRADING CARD CO.

Complete Set (110 cards): 2,500.00 1,000.00 40.00

	No.	Player	Gold	P.P.	Reg.
☐☐☐	1	Wayne Gretzky, NYR.	300.00	125.00	4.00
☐☐☐	2	Dominik Hasek (G), Buf.	100.00	45.00	1.50
☐☐☐	3	Eric Lindros, Pha.	175.00	75.00	2.50
☐☐☐	4	Paul Kariya, Ana.	175.00	75.00	2.50
☐☐☐	5	Jaromir Jagr, Pgh.	150.00	60.00	2.00
☐☐☐	6	Brendan Shanahan, Det.	90.00	35.00	1.25
☐☐☐	7	Patrick Roy (G), Col.	250.00	90.00	3.00
☐☐☐	8	Keith Tkachuk, Pho.	50.00	18.00	.75
☐☐☐	9	Mark Messier, Van.	70.00	25.00	1.00
☐☐☐	10	Steve Yzerman, Det.	150.00	60.00	2.00
☐☐☐	11	Brett Hull, Stl.	70.00	25.00	1.00
☐☐☐	12	Jarome Iginla, Cgy.	30.00	12.00	.50
☐☐☐	13	Mike Modano, Dal.	70.00	25.00	1.00
☐☐☐	14	Pavel Bure, Van.	100.00	45.00	1.50
☐☐☐	15	Peter Forsberg, Col.	150.00	60.00	2.00
☐☐☐	16	Ryan Smyth, Edm.	20.00	8.00	.35
☐☐☐	17	John Vanbiesbrouck (G), Fla.	90.00	35.00	1.25
☐☐☐	18	Teemu Selänne, Ana.	100.00	45.00	1.50
☐☐☐	19	Saku Koivu, Mtl.	100.00	45.00	1.50
☐☐☐	20	Martin Brodeur (G), N.J.	100.00	45.00	1.50
☐☐☐	21	Sergei Fedorov, Det.	70.00	25.00	1.00
☐☐☐	22	John LeClair, Pha.	70.00	25.00	1.00
☐☐☐	23	Joe Sakic, Col.	120.00	50.00	1.75
☐☐☐	24	José Théodore (G), Mtl.	30.00	12.00	.50
☐☐☐	25	Marc Denis (G), Col.	20.00	8.00	.35
☐☐☐	26	Dainius Zubrus, Pha.	20.00	8.00	.35
☐☐☐	27	Bryan Berard, NYI.	30.00	12.00	.50
☐☐☐	28	Ray Bourque, Bos.	70.00	25.00	1.00
☐☐☐	29	Curtis Joseph (G), Edm.	90.00	35.00	1.25
☐☐☐	30	Chris Chelios, Chi.	50.00	18.00	.75
☐☐☐	31	Alexei Yashin, Ott.	50.00	18.00	.75
☐☐☐	32	Adam Oates, Wsh.	30.00	12.00	.50
☐☐☐	33	Anson Carter, Bos.	10.00	4.00	.20

	No.	Player			
□□□	34	Jim Campbell, Stl.	10.00	4.00	.20
□□□	35	Jason Arnott, Edm.	20.00	8.00	.35
□□□	36	Derek Plante, Buf.	10.00	4.00	.20
□□□	37	Guy Hebert (G), Ana.	20.00	8.00	.35
□□□	38	Oleg Tverdovsky, Pho.	10.00	4.00	.20
□□□	39	Ed Jovanovski, Fla.	20.00	8.00	.35
□□□	40	Jeremy Roenick, Pho.	30.00	12.00	.50
□□□	41	Scott Mellanby, Fla.	10.00	4.00	.20
□□□	42	Keith Primeau, Car.	20.00	8.00	.35
□□□	43	Ron Hextall (G), Pha.	20.00	8.00	.35
□□□	44	Daren Puppa (G), T.B.	10.00	4.00	.20
□□□	45	Jim Carey (G), Bos.	10.00	4.00	.20
□□□	46	Zigmund Palffy, NYI.	30.00	12.00	.50
□□□	47	Jaroslav Svejkovsky, Wsh.	20.00	8.00	.35
□□□	48	Daymond Langkow, T.B.	10.00	4.00	.20
□□□	49	Mikael Renberg, T.B.	10.00	4.00	.20
□□□	50	Pat LaFontaine, NYR.	20.00	8.00	.35
□□□	51	Mike Grier, Edm.	20.00	8.00	.35
□□□	52	Stéphane Fiset (G), L.A.	20.00	8.00	.35
□□□	53	Luc Robitaille, L.A.	20.00	8.00	.35
□□□	54	Joe Thornton, Bos.	90.00	35.00	1.25
□□□	55	Joe Nieuwendyk, Das.	20.00	8.00	.35
□□□	56	Mike Dunham (G), N.J.	10.00	4.00	.20
□□□	57	Mark Recchi, Mtl.	20.00	8.00	.35
□□□	58	Ed Belfour (G), Dal.	30.00	12.00	.50
□□□	59	Mike Richter (G), NYR.	30.00	12.00	.50
□□□	60	Peter Bondra, Wsh.	50.00	18.00	.75
□□□	61	Trevor Kidd (G), Car.	20.00	8.00	.35
□□□	62	Sean Burke (G), Car.	20.00	8.00	.35
□□□	63	Nikolai Khabibulin (G), Pho.	30.00	12.00	.50
□□□	64	Pierre Turgeon, Stl.	20.00	8.00	.35
□□□	65	Dino Ciccarelli, T.B.	20.00	8.00	.35
□□□	66	Félix Potvin (G), Tor.	70.00	25.00	1.00
□□□	67	Mats Sundin, Tor.	70.00	25.00	1.00
□□□	68	Joé Juneau, Wsh.	10.00	4.00	.20
□□□	69	Mike Vernon (G), S.J.	20.00	8.00	.35
□□□	70	Adam Deadmarsh, Col.	10.00	4.00	.20
□□□	71	Damian Rhodes (G), Ott.	10.00	4.00	.20
□□□	72	Michael Peca, Buf.	20.00	8.00	.35
□□□	73	Jean-Sébastien Giguère (G), Cgy.	20.00	8.00	.35
□□□	74	Ron Francis, Pgh.	30.00	12.00	.50
□□□	75	Roman Hamrlik, T.B.	20.00	8.00	.35
□□□	76	Vincent Damphousse, Mtl.	30.00	12.00	.50
□□□	77	Jocelyn Thibault (G), Mtl.	30.00	12.00	.50
□□□	78	Claude Lemieux, Col.	10.00	4.00	.20
□□□	**79**	**Steve Shields (G), Buf., RC**	**20.00**	**8.00**	**.35**
□□□	80	Dimitri Khristich, Bos.	10.00	4.00	.20
□□□	81	Theoren Fleury, Cgy.	30.00	12.00	.50
□□□	82	Sandis Ozolinsh, Col.	20.00	8.00	.35
□□□	83	Ethan Moreau, Chi.	10.00	4.00	.20
□□□	84	Geoff Sanderson, Car.	10.00	4.00	.20
□□□	85	Paul Coffey, Pha.	20.00	8.00	.35
□□□	86	Brian Leetch, NYR.	30.00	12.00	.50
□□□	87	Chris Osgood (G), Det.	50.00	18.00	.75
□□□	88	Kirk McLean (G), Van.	20.00	8.00	.35
□□□	89	Mike Gartner, Pho.	20.00	8.00	.35
□□□	90	Chris Gratton, Pha.	20.00	8.00	.35
□□□	91	Eric Fichaud (G), NYI.	20.00	8.00	.35
□□□	92	Alexandre Daigle, Ott.	10.00	4.00	.20
□□□	93	Doug Gilmour, N.J.	30.00	12.00	.50
□□□	94	Daniel Alfredsson, Ott.	20.00	8.00	.35
□□□	95	Doug Weight, Edm.	30.00	12.00	.50
□□□	96	Derian Hatcher, Dal.	20.00	8.00	.35
□□□	97	Wade Redden, Ott.	10.00	4.00	.20
□□□	98	Jeff Friesen, S.J.	20.00	8.00	.35
□□□	99	Tony Amonte, Chi.	20.00	8.00	.35
□□□	100	Janne Niinimaa, Pha.	20.00	8.00	.35
□□□	101	Trevor Linden, Van.	20.00	8.00	.35
□□□	102	Grant Fuhr (G), Stl.	20.00	8.00	.35
□□□	103	Chris Phillips, Ott.	20.00	8.00	.35
□□□	104	Sergei Berezin, Tor.	20.00	8.00	.35
□□□	105	CL: Brendan Shanahan, Det.	45.00	15.00	.60
□□□	106	CL: Steve Yzerman, Det.	75.00	30.00	1.00
□□□	107	CL: Teemu Selänne, Ana.	50.00	20.00	.75
□□□	108	CL: Eric Lindros, Pha.	85.00	35.00	1.25
□□□	109	CL: Wayne Gretzky, NYR.	150.00	60.00	2.00
□□□	110	CL: Patrick Roy (G), Col.	120.00	45.00	1.50

STUDIO PORTRAITS

These cards actually parallel the regular standard-sized card except for their different numbering system.

Photo Size: 8" x 10"

Portraits Set (36 photos): 60.00

	No.	Player	NRMT-MT
□	1	Wayne Gretzky, NYR.	6.00
□	2	Dominik Hasek (G), Buf.	2.00
□	3	Eric Lindros, Pha.	4.00
□	4	Paul Kariya, Ana.	4.00
□	5	Jaromir Jagr, Pgh.	3.00
□	6	Brendan Shanahan, Det.	1.75
□	7	Patrick Roy (G), Col.	5.00
□	8	Keith Tkachuk, Pho.	1.25
□	9	Mark Messier, Van.	1.50
□	10	Steve Yzerman, Det.	3.00
□	11	Brett Hull, Stl.	1.50
□	12	Jarome Iginla, Cgy.	1.00
□	13	Mike Modano, Dal.	1.50
□	14	Pavel Bure, Van.	2.00
□	15	Peter Forsberg, Col.	3.00
□	16	Ryan Smyth, Edm.	1.00
□	17	John Vanbiesbrouck (G), Fla.	1.75
□	18	Teemu Selänne, Ana.	2.00
□	19	Saku Koivu, Mtl.	2.00
□	20	Martin Brodeur (G), N.J.	2.00
□	21	Sergei Fedorov, Det.	1.50
□	22	Joe Thornton, Bos.	1.75
□	23	Joe Sakic, Col.	2.50
□	24	Bryan Berard, NYI.	1.00
□	25	John LeClair, Pha.	1.50
□	26	Marc Denis (G), Col.	1.00
□	27	Dainius Zubrus, Pha.	1.00
□	28	Crhis Chelios, Chi.	1.25
□	29	Jason Arnott, Edm.	1.00
□	30	Jermey Roenick, Pho.	1.00
□	31	Zigmund Palffy, NYI.	1.00
□	32	Jaroslav Svejkovsky, Wsh.	1.00
□	33	Mike Richter (G), NYR.	1.0
□	34	Félix Potvin (G), Tor.	1.50
□	35	Brian Leetch, NYR.	1.00
□	36	Chris Osgood (G), Det.	1.25

HARD HATS

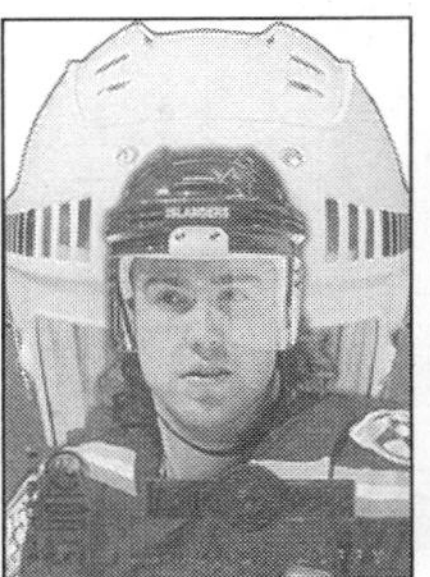

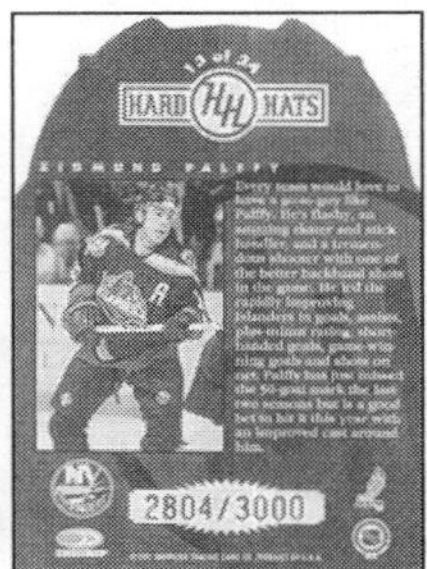

These die-cut inserts are serial numbered out of 3000.

Insert Set (24 cards): 375.00

	No.	Player	NRMT-MT
□	1	Wayne Gretzky, NYR.	65.00
□	2	Eric Lindros, Pha.	40.00
□	3	Paul Kariya, Ana.	40.00
□	4	Bryan Berard, NYI.	8.00
□	5	Dainius Zubrus, Pha.	6.00
□	6	Daymond Langkow, T.B.	6.00
□	7	Keith Tkachuk, Pho.	10.00
□	8	Ryan Smyth, Edm.	6.00
□	9	Brendan Shanahan, Det.	15.00
□	10	Steve Yzerman, Det.	30.00
□	11	Teemu Selänne, Ana.	20.00
□	12	Jarome Iginla, Cgy.	8.00
□	13	Zigmund Palffy, NYI.	8.00
□	14	Sergei Berezin, Tor.	6.00
□	15	Saku Koivu, Mtl.	20.00
□	16	Peter Forsberg, Col.	30.00
□	17	Joe Sakic, Col.	25.00
□	18	Pavel Bure, Van.	20.00
□	19	Jaromir Jagr, Pgh.	30.00
□	20	Brett Hull, Stl.	12.00
□	21	Sergei Fedorov, Det.	6.00
□	22	Mike Grier, Edm.	6.00
□	23	Ethan Moreau, Chi.	12.00
□	24	Mats Sundin, Tor.	

SILHOUETTES

These laser-cut cards have two versions: the standard-sized insert (serial numbered out 1500) and 8" x 10" parallels (serial numbered out of 3000).

Insert Set (24 cards): 675.00 475.00

	No.	Player	8 x 10	Reg.
□□	1	Wayne Gretzky, NYR.	100.00	65.00
□□	2	Eric Lindros, Pha.	60.00	40.00
□□	3	Patrick Roy (G), Col.	75.00	50.00
□□	4	Martin Brodeur (G), N.J.	30.00	20.00
□□	5	Paul Kariya, Ana.	60.00	40.00
□□	6	Mark Messier, Van.	18.00	12.00
□□	7	Dominik Hasek (G), Buf.	30.00	20.00
□□	8	Brett Hull, Stl.	18.00	12.00
□□	9	Pavel Bure, Van.	30.00	20.00
□□	10	Steve Yzerman, Det.	45.00	30.00
□□	11	Brendan Shanahan, Det.	25.00	15.00
□□	12	Joe Sakic, Col.	35.00	25.00
□□	13	Peter Forsberg, Col.	45.00	30.00
□□	14	Sergei Fedorov, Det.	18.00	12.00
□□	15	John LeClair, Pha.	18.00	12.00
□□	16	John Vanbiesbrouck (G), Fla.	25.00	15.00
□□	17	Teemu Selänne, Ana.	30.00	20.00
□□	18	Keith Tkachuk, Pho.	15.00	10.00
□□	19	Mike Modano, Dal.	18.00	12.00
□□	20	Félix Potvin (G), Tor.	18.00	12.00
□□	21	Ryan Smyth, Edm.	12.00	8.00
□□	22	Jaromir Jagr, Pgh.	45.00	30.00
□□	23	Brian Leetch, NYR.	12.00	8.00
□□	24	Jarome Iginla, Cgy.	12.00	8.00

1997 - 98 ESSO OLYMPIC HOCKEY HEROES

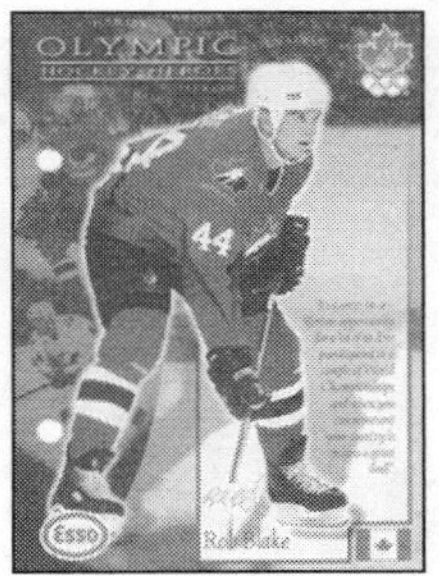

One of six different 10-card packs was available each week for six weeks at Esso gas stations for only $2.99. An album and eight page dividers came with the first week's pack. There is both an English and French version available. Twenty Canadian players also signed 500 sheets each.

Page Size: 4 3/4" x 6 5/8"

Imprint: *TRADEMARK OF IMPERIAL OIL LIMITED. IMPERIAL OIL, LICENSEE.

Complete Set (60 pages): 40.00

Album: 4.00

	No.	Player	Aut.	Sheet
□□	1	Brian Fischer address/ Table of Contents		.50

	No.	Player		
☐☐	2	Nagano Winter Games		.50
☐☐	3	CBC Olympic Hockey/ Schedule		.50
☐☐	4	Schedule		.50
☐☐	5	Team Canada (XCX: Eric Lindros)		2.00
☐☐☐	6	Eric Lindros, Cdn.	425.00	5.00
☐☐☐	7	Joe Sakic, Cdn.	275.00	3.50
☐☐☐	8	Trevor Linden, Cdn.	50.00	1.00
☐☐☐	9	Paul Kariya, Cdn.	425.00	5.00
☐☐☐	10	Brendan Shanahan, Cdn.	185.00	2.50
☐☐☐	11	Rod Brind'Amour, Cdn.	50.00	1.00
☐☐☐	12	Theoren Fleury, Cdn.	75.00	1.25
☐☐☐	13	Eric Desjardins, Cdn.	35.00	1.00
☐☐☐	14	Scott Niedermayer, Cdn.	50.00	1.00
☐☐☐	15	Chris Pronger, Cdn.	50.00	1.00
☐☐☐	16	Rob Blake, Cdn.	50.00	1.00
☐☐☐	17	Patrick Roy (G), Cdn.	550.00	6.00
☐☐☐	18	Curtis Joseph (G), Cdn.	175.00	2.50
☐☐☐	19	Keith Primeau, Cdn.	50.00	1.00
☐☐	20	Mark Messier, Cdn.		2.00
☐☐☐	21	Adam Foote, Cdn.	35.00	1.00
☐☐	22	Team U.S.A. (XCX: Brian Leetch)		.75
☐☐	23	Keith Tkachuk, USA.		1.50
☐☐	24	Mike Modano, USA.		2.00
☐☐	25	John LeClair, USA.		2.00
☐☐	26	Doug Weight, USA.		1.25
☐☐	27	Brett Hull, USA.		2.00
☐☐	28	Jeremy Roenick, USA.		1.25
☐☐	29	Brian Leetch, USA.		1.25
☐☐	30	Chris Chelios, USA.		1.50
☐☐	31	Kevin Hatcher, USA.		.75
☐☐	32	Derian Hatcher, USA.		1.00
☐☐	33	Mike Richter (G), USA.		1.25
☐☐	34	John Vanbiesbrouck (G), USA.		2.50
☐☐	35	Team Russia (XCX: Sergei Fedorov)		1.25
☐☐	36	Sergei Fedorov, Rus.		2.00
☐☐	37	Alexei Yashin, Rus.		1.50
☐☐	38	Pavel Bure, Rus.		3.00
☐☐	39	Alexander Mogilny, Rus.		1.25
☐☐	40	Nikolai Khabibulin (G), Rus.		1.25
☐☐	41	Team Sweden (XCX: Mats Sundin)		1.25
☐☐	42	Mats Sundin, Swe.		2.00
☐☐	43	Peter Forsberg, Swe.		4.00
☐☐	44	Daniel Alfredsson, Swe.		1.00
☐☐	45	Nicklas Lidström, Swe.		1.00
☐☐	46	Kenny Jonsson, Swe.		.75
☐☐	47	Team Finland		.75
☐☐	48	Saku Koivu, Fin.		3.00
☐☐	49	Esa Tikkanen, Fin.		.75
☐☐	50	Teemu Selänne, Fin.		3.00
☐☐	51	Team Czech Rep. (XCX: D. Hasek/ J.Jagr)		2.00
☐☐	52	Jaromir Jagr, Cze.		4.00
☐☐	53	Roman Hamrlik, Cze.		1.00
☐☐	54	Dominik Hasek (G), Cze.		3.00
☐☐	55	Women's Team Canada		.75
☐☐☐	56	Nancy Drolet, Cdn.	35.00	1.00
☐☐☐	57	Geraldine Heaney, Cdn.	35.00	1.00
☐☐☐	58	Hayley Wickenheiser, Cdn.	70.00	2.00
☐☐☐	59	Cassie Campbell, Cdn.	50.00	1.50
☐☐☐	60	Stacy Wilson, Cdn.	35.00	1.00

1997 - 98 GAME OF HER LIFE

This eight-card set features players from the 1998 Canadian Olympic women's hockey team.

Complete Set (8 cards): **20.00**

	Player	NRMT-MT
☐	Cassie Campbell, Cdn.	4.00
☐	Angela James, Cdn.	2.50
☐	Luce Letendre, Cdn.	2.50
☐	Shannon Miller, Coach, Cdn.	2.00
☐	Manon Rhéaume (G), Cdn.	6.00
☐	France St. Louis, Cdn.	2.50
☐	Vicky Sunhohara, Cdn.	2.50
☐	Hayley Wickenheiser, Cdn.	4.00

1997 - 98 GENERAL MILLS OLYMPICS

This 9-card multi-sport set features six hockey players. The most expensive single in the set is Elvis Stojko at $15. A complete 9-card set sells at $35.

	Player	NRMT-MT
☐	Cassie Campbell, Cdn.	4.00
☐	Eric Desjardins, Cdn.	2.50
☐	Nancy Drolet, Cdn.	2.50
☐	Geraldine Heaney, Cdn.	2.50
☐	Brendan Shanahan, Cdn.	6.00
☐	Vicky Sunhohara, Cdn.	2.50

1997 - 98 KATCH MEDALLIONS

Medallion Diameter: 2 3/8"
Imprint:

		Gold	Sil.	Reg.
Complete Set (168 medallions):		**1,500.00**	**600.00**	**150.00**
Common Player:		**8.00**	**3.00**	**.50**

No.	Player	Gold	Sil.	Reg.
☐ 1	Guy Hebert (G), Ana.	12.00	5.00	.60
☐ 2	Paul Kariya, Ana.	80.00	35.00	3.50
☐ 3	Espen Knutsen, Ana.	8.00	3.00	.50
☐ 4	Tomas Sandström, Ana.	8.00	3.00	.50
☐ 5	Teemu Selänne, Ana.	40.00	18.00	1.75
☐ 6	Scott Young, Ana.	8.00	3.00	.50
☐ 7	Per-Johan Axelsson, Bos.	8.00	3.00	.50
☐ 8	Ray Bourque, Bos.	30.00	12.00	1.25
☐ 9	Jim Carey (G), Bos.	8.00	3.00	.50
☐ 10	Ted Donato, Bos.	8.00	3.00	.50
☐ 11	Dimitri Khristich, Bos.	8.00	3.00	.50
☐ 12	Sergei Samsonov, Bos.	35.00	15.00	1.50
☐ 13	Matthew Barnaby, Buf.	8.00	3.00	.50
☐ 14	Jason Dawe, Buf.	8.00	3.00	.50
☐ 15	Dominik Hasek (G), Buf.	40.00	18.00	1.75
☐ 16	Michael Peca, Buf.	12.00	5.00	.60
☐ 17	Rob Ray, Buf.	8.00	3.00	.50
☐ 18	Alexei Zhitnik, Buf.	8.00	3.00	.50
☐ 19	Andrew Cassels, Buf.	8.00	3.00	.50
☐ 20	Theoren Fleury, Cgy.	18.00	7.50	.75
☐ 21	Jarome Iginla, Cgy.	18.00	7.50	.75
☐ 22	Sandy McCarthy, Cgy.	8.00	3.00	.50
☐ 23	Tyler Moss (G), Cgy.	8.00	3.00	.50
☐ 24	Cory Stillman, Cgy.	8.00	3.00	.50
☐ 25	Sean Burke (G), Car.	12.00	5.00	.60
☐ 26	Kevin Dineen, Car.	8.00	3.00	.50
☐ 27	Stu Grimson, Car.	8.00	3.00	.50
☐ 28	Steven Rice, Car.	8.00	3.00	.50
☐ 29	Keith Primeau, Car.	12.00	5.00	.60
☐ 30	Geoff Sanderson, Car.	8.00	3.00	.50
☐ 31	Tony Amonte, Chi.	12.00	5.00	.60
☐ 32	Chris Chelios, Chi.	25.00	10.00	1.00
☐ 33	Daniel Cleary, Chi.	18.00	7.50	.75
☐ 34	Jeff Hackett (G), Chi.	12.00	5.00	.60
☐ 35	Ethan Moreau, Chi.	8.00	3.00	.50
☐ 36	Bob Probert, Chi.	8.00	3.00	.50
☐ 37	Adam Deadmarsh, Col.	8.00	3.00	.50
☐ 38	Peter Forsberg, Col.	60.00	25.00	2.50
☐ 39	Claude Lemieux, Col.	8.00	3.00	.50
☐ 40	Sandis Ozolinsh, Col.	12.00	5.00	.60
☐ 41	Patrick Roy (G), Col.	90.00	40.00	4.00
☐ 42	Joe Sakic, Col.	50.00	20.00	2.00
☐ 43	Ed Belfour (G), Dal.	18.00	7.50	.75
☐ 44	Derian Hatcher, Dal.	12.00	5.00	.60
☐ 45	Jere Lehtinen, Dal.	12.00	5.00	.60
☐ 46	Mike Modano, Dal.	30.00	12.00	1.25
☐ 47	Joe Nieuwendyk, Dal.	12.00	5.00	.60
☐ 48	Darryl Sydor, Dal.	8.00	3.00	.50
☐ 49	Sergei Fedorov, Det.	30.00	12.00	1.25
☐ 50	Vyacheslav Kozlov, Det.	8.00	3.00	.50
☐ 51	Darren McCarty, Det.	8.00	3.00	.50
☐ 52	Chris Osgood (G), Det.	25.00	10.00	1.00
☐ 53	Brendan Shanahan, Det.	35.00	15.00	1.50
☐ 54	Steve Yzerman, Det.	60.00	25.00	2.50
☐ 55	Jason Arnott, Edm.	12.00	5.00	.60
☐ 56	Boyd Devereaux, Edm.	8.00	3.00	.50
☐ 57	Curtis Joseph (G), Edm.	35.00	15.00	1.50
☐ 58	Alexei Kovalenko, Edm.	8.00	3.00	.50
☐ 59	Ryan Smyth, Edm.	12.00	5.00	.60
☐ 60	Doug Weight, Edm.	18.00	7.50	.75
☐ 61	Ed Jovanovski, Fla.	12.00	5.00	.60
☐ 62	Scott Mellanby, Fla.	8.00	3.00	.50
☐ 63	David Nemirovsky, Fla.	8.00	3.00	.50
☐ 64	Rob Niedermayer, Fla.	8.00	3.00	.50
☐ 65	Ray Sheppard, Fla.	8.00	3.00	.50
☐ 66	John Vanbiesbrouck (G), Fla.	35.00	15.00	1.50
☐ 67	Aki Berg, L.A.	8.00	3.00	.50
☐ 68	Rob Blake, L.A.	12.00	5.00	.60
☐ 69	Stéphane Fiset (G), L.A.	12.00	5.00	.60
☐ 70	Donald MacLean, L.A.	8.00	3.00	.50
☐ 71	Yanic Perreault, L.A.	8.00	3.00	.50
☐ 72	Luc Robitaille, L.A.	12.00	5.00	.60
☐ 73	Valeri Bure, Mtl.	8.00	3.00	.50
☐ 74	Vincent Damphousse, Mtl.	18.00	7.50	.75
☐ 75	Saku Koivu, Mtl.	40.00	18.00	1.75
☐ 76	Vladimir Malakhov, Mtl.	8.00	3.00	.50
☐ 77	Mark Recchi, Mtl.	12.00	5.00	.60
☐ 78	Jocelyn Thibault (G), Mtl.	18.00	7.50	.75
☐ 79	Martin Brodeur (G), N.J.	40.00	18.00	1.75
☐ 80	Patrik Elias, N.J.	12.00	5.00	.60
☐ 81	Doug Gilmour, N.J.	18.00	7.50	.75
☐ 82	Bill Guerin, N.J.	12.00	5.00	.60
☐ 83	Scott Niedermayer, N.J.	12.00	5.00	.60
☐ 84	Scott Stevens, N.J.	8.00	3.00	.50
☐ 85	Bryan Berard, NYI.	18.00	7.50	.75
☐ 86	Eric Fichaud (G), NYI.	12.00	5.00	.60
☐ 87	Travis Green, NYI.	8.00	3.00	.50
☐ 88	Kenny Jonsson, NYI.	8.00	3.00	.50
☐ 89	Bryan McCabe, NYI.	8.00	3.00	.50
☐ 90	Zigmund Palffy, NYI.	18.00	7.50	.75
☐ 91	Adam Graves, NYR.	8.00	3.00	.50
☐ 92	Wayne Gretzky, NYR.	150.00	60.00	6.00
☐ 93	Pat LaFontaine, NYR.	12.00	5.00	.60
☐ 94	Brian Leetch, NYR.	18.00	7.50	.75
☐ 95	Mike Richter (G), NYR.	18.00	7.50	.75
☐ 96	Kevin Stevens, NYR.	8.00	3.00	.50
☐ 97	Daniel Alfredsson, Ott.	12.00	5.00	.60
☐ 98	Alexandre Daigle, Ott.	8.00	3.00	.50
☐ 99	Chris Phillips, Ott.	12.00	5.00	.60
☐ 100	Wade Redden, Ott.	8.00	3.00	.50
☐ 101	Damian Rhodes, Ott.	8.00	3.00	.50
☐ 102	Alexei Yashin, Ott.	25.00	10.00	1.00
☐ 103	Paul Coffey, Pha.	12.00	5.00	.60
☐ 104	Chris Gratton, Pha.	12.00	5.00	.60
☐ 105	Ron Hextall (G), Pha.	12.00	5.00	.60
☐ 106	John LeClair, Pha.	30.00	12.00	1.25
☐ 107	Eric Lindros, Pha.	80.00	35.00	3.50
☐ 108	Dainius Zubrus, Pha.	12.00	5.00	.60
☐ 109	Mike Gartner, Pho.	12.00	5.00	.60
☐ 110	Brad Isbister, Pho.	8.00	3.00	.50
☐ 111	Nikolai Khabibulin (G), Pho.	18.00	7.50	.75
☐ 112	Jeremy Roenick, Pho.	18.00	7.50	.75
☐ 113	Keith Tkachuk, Pho.	25.00	10.00	1.00
☐ 114	Oleg Tverdovsky, Pho.	8.00	3.00	.50
☐ 115	Tom Barrasso (G), Pgh.	12.00	5.00	.60
☐ 116	Ron Francis, Pgh.	18.00	7.50	.75
☐ 117	Kevin Hatcher, Pgh.	8.00	3.00	.50
☐ 118	Jaromir Jagr, Pgh.	60.00	25.00	2.50
☐ 119	Alexei Morozov, Pgh.	25.00	10.00	1.00
☐ 120	Petr Nedved, Pgh.	8.00	3.00	.50
☐ 121	Patrick Marleau, S.J.	25.00	10.00	1.00
☐ 122	Marty McSorley, S.J.	8.00	3.00	.50
☐ 123	Bernie Nicholls, S.J.	8.00	3.00	.50
☐ 124	Owen Nolan, S.J.	12.00	5.00	.60
☐ 125	Marco Sturm, S.J.	8.00	3.00	.50
☐ 126	Mike Vernon (G), S.J.	12.00	5.00	.60
☐ 127	Jim Campbell, Stl.	8.00	3.00	.50
☐ 128	Grant Fuhr (G), Stl.	12.00	5.00	.60
☐ 129	Brett Hull, Stl.	30.00	12.00	1.25
☐ 130	Al MacInnis, Stl.	12.00	5.00	.60
☐ 131	Pierre Turgeon, Stl.	12.00	5.00	.60
☐ 132	Tony Twist, Stl.	8.00	3.00	.50
☐ 133	Brian Bradley, T.B.	8.00	3.00	.50
☐ 134	Dino Ciccarelli, T.B.	12.00	5.00	.60
☐ 135	Roman Hamrlik, T.B.	12.00	5.00	.60
☐ 136	Daymond Langkow, T.B.	8.00	3.00	.50
☐ 137	Daren Puppa (G), T.B.	8.00	3.00	.50
☐ 138	Mikael Renberg, T.B.	8.00	3.00	.50
☐ 139	Wendel Clark, Tor.	12.00	5.00	.60
☐ 140	Tie Domi, Tor.	8.00	3.00	.50
☐ 141	Alyn McCauley, Tor.	25.00	10.00	1.00
☐ 142	Félix Potvin (G), Tor.	30.00	12.00	1.25
☐ 143	Mathieu Schneider, Tor.	8.00	3.00	.50
☐ 144	Mats Sundin, Tor.	30.00	12.00	1.25
☐ 145	Pavel Bure, Van.	40.00	18.00	1.75
☐ 146	Trevor Linden, Van.	12.00	5.00	.60

	No.	Player			
☐	147	Kirk McLean (G), Van.	12.00	5.00	.60
☐	148	Mark Messier, Van.	30.00	12.00	1.25
☐	149	Alexander Mogilny, Van.	18.00	7.50	.75
☐	150	Mattias Ohlund, Van.	18.00	7.50	.75
☐	151	Peter Bondra, Wsh.	25.00	10.00	1.00
☐	152	Joé Juneau, Wsh.	8.00	3.00	.50
☐	153	Adam Oates, Wsh.	18.00	7.50	.75
☐	154	Bill Ranford (G), Wsh.	12.00	5.00	.60
☐	155	Jaroslav Svejkovsky, Wsh.	12.00	5.00	.60
☐	156	Richard Zednik, Wsh.	8.00	3.00	.50
☐	157	TL: Wayne Gretzky, NYR.	75.00	30.00	3.00
☐	158	TL: Eric Lindros, Pha.	40.00	17.50	1.75
☐	159	TL: Paul Kariya, Ana.	40.00	17.50	1.75
☐	160	TL: Patrick Roy (G), Col.	45.00	20.00	2.00
☐	161	TL: Steve Yzerman, Det.	30.00	12.00	1.25
☐	162	TL: Jaromir Jagr, Pgh.	30.00	12.00	1.25
☐	163	TL: Brett Hull, Stl.	15.00	6.00	.60
☐	164	Joe Thornton, Bos.	35.00	15.00	1.50
☐	165	Vaclav Prospal, Pha.	18.00	7.50	.75
☐	166	Mike Johnson, Tor.	30.00	12.00	1.25
☐	167	Eric Messier, Col.	8.00	3.00	.50
☐	168	Jan Bulis, Wsh.	8.00	3.00	.50

1997 - 98 KENNER STARTING LINEUP

Figurines in both the American and Canadian series are the same.

Canadian Set (19 figurines): 325.00 –

American Set (21 figurines): – 350.00

	Player	Cdn.	U.S.
☐ ☐	Daniel Alfredsson, Ott.	20.00	20.00
☐ ☐	Jason Arnott, Edm.	15.00	15.00
☐ ☐	Peter Bondra, Wsh.	15.00	15.00
☐ ☐	Martin Brodeur (G), N.J.	25.00	25.00
☐ ☐	Chris Chelios, Chi.	15.00	15.00
☐	Paul Coffey, Pha.	20.00	.–
☐ ☐	Peter Forsberg, Col.	20.00	30.00
☐ ☐	Wayne Gretzky, NYR.	55.00	55.00
☐ ☐	Ron Hextall (G), Pha.	25.00	25.00
☐ ☐	Jaromir Jagr, Pgh.	20.00	20.00
☐	Patrick Lalime (G), Pgh.	25.00	.–
☐ ☐	Eric Lindros, Pha.	20.00	20.00
☐ ☐	Mark Messier, Van.	15.00	15.00
☐ ☐	Chris Osgood (G), Det.	25.00	25.00
☐ ☐	Sandis Ozolinsh, Col.	15.00	15.00
☐ ☐	Zigmund Palffy, NYI.	15.00	15.00
☐ ☐	Daren Puppa (G), T.B.	35.00	25.00
☐ ☐	Mark Recchi, Mtl.	15.00	15.00
☐ ☐	Teemu Selänne, Ana.	20.00	20.00
☐ ☐	Keith Tkachuk, Pho.	15.00	15.00
☐ ☐	John Vanbiesbrouck (G), Fla.	30.00	30.00
	Lemieux retirement special		
☐	Mario Lemieux, Pgh.		35.00

1997 - 98 KENNER STARTING LINEUP ONE ON ONE

Figurines in both the American and Canadian series are the same.

Canadian Set (5 figurine pairs): 200.00 –

American Set (7 figurine pairs): – 250.00

	Player	Cdn.	U.S.
☐ ☐	R.Bourque/ M.Sundin	30.00	30.00
☐ ☐	W.Gretzky/ D.Hasek (G)	75.00	75.00
☐ ☐	J.Jagr/ P.Roy (G)	60.00	60.00
☐ ☐	P.Kariya/ E.Lindros	45.00	45.00
☐ ☐	O.Nolan/ C.Osgood (G)	35.00	35.00
☐	M.Richter (G)/ J.Sakic	30.00	–
☐	J.Roenick/ S.Yzerman	30.00	–

1997 - 98 KENNER STARTING LINEUP TIMELESS LEGENDS

This nine figurine multi-sport set features two hockey players.

	Player	NRMT-MT
☐	Tony Esposito (G), Chi.	20.00
☐	Maurice Richard, Mtl.	15.00

1997 - 98 KENNER STARTING LINEUP CANADIAN TIMELESS LEGENDS

Complete Set (5 figurines): 75.00

	Player	NRMT-MT
☐	Jean Béliveau, Mtl.	15.00
☐	Mike Bossy, NYI.	15.00
☐	Marcel Dionne, L.A.	15.00
☐	Glenn Hall (G), Chi.	25.00
☐	Bernie Parent (G), Pha.	25.00

1997 - 98 KENNER STARTING LINEUP 12" FIGURINES

This multi-sport set features only one hockey players.

	Player	NRMT-MT
☐	Bobby Orr, Bos.	50.00

1997 - 98 KRAFT

Imprint: * REGISTERED TRADE-MARK OF KRAFT CANADA INC. THE PINNACLE LOGO IS USED WITH PERMISSION OF PINNACLE TRADING CARD COMPANY.

Master Set (50 cards):

Album:

WORLD'S BEST PLAYERS

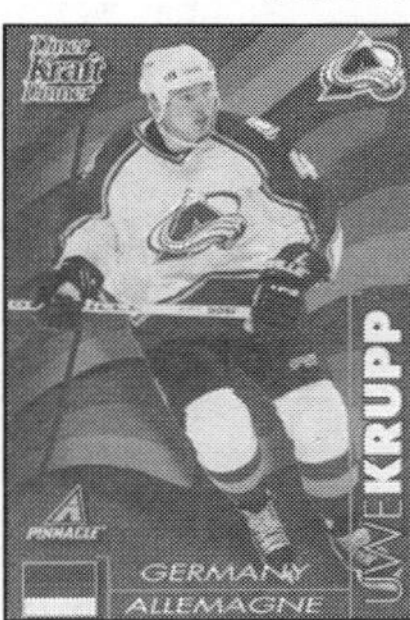

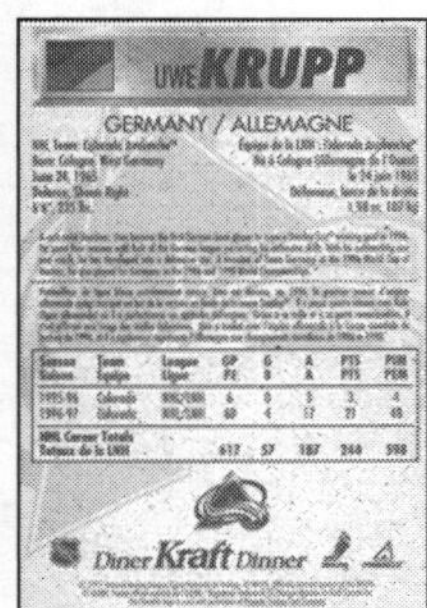

One of 26 different cards was found on the back of Kraft Dinner boxes.

Card Size:

		Player	NRMT-MT
☐	Cdn.	Vincent Damphousse, Mtl.	1.00
☐	Cdn.	Theoren Fleury, Cgy.	1.00
☐	Cdn.	Ron Francis, Pgh.	1.00
☐	Cdn.	Wayne Gretzky, NYR.	4.00
☐	Cdn.	Paul Kariya, Ana.	2.00
☐	Cdn.	Eric Lindros, Pha.	2.00
☐	Cdn.	Mark Messier, Van.	1.25
☐	Cdn.	Adam Oates, Wsh.	1.00
☐	Cdn.	Steve Yzerman, Det.	1.50
☐	Cze.	Jaromir Jagr, Pgh.	1.50
☐	Fin.	Saku Koivu, Mtl.	1.25
☐	Fin.	Teemu Selänne, Ana.	1.25
☐	Ger.	Uwe Krupp, Col.	1.00
☐	Rus.	Sergei Fedorov, Det.	1.25
☐	Rus.	Alexei Yashin, Ott.	1.00
☐	Slo.	Peter Bondra, Wsh.	1.00
☐	Slo.	Zigmund Palffy, NYI.	1.00
☐	Slo.	Jozef Stumpel, L.A.	1.00
☐	Swe.	Peter Forsberg, Col.	1.50
☐	Swe.	Mikael Renberg, T.B.	1.00
☐	Swe.	Mats Sundin, Tor.	1.25
☐	USA.	Brett Hull, Stl.	1.25
☐	USA.	John LeClair, Pha.	1.25
☐	USA.	Mike Modano, Dal.	1.25
☐	USA.	Keith Tkachuk, Pho.	1.00
☐	USA.	Doug Weight, Edm.	1.00

JUNIORS TO PROS OF CANADA

One of six different cards was found on specially marked boxes of JELL-O Instant Pudding (4 serve size).

Card Size:

	Player	NRMT-MT
☐	Wayne Gretzky, NYR.	2.50
☐	Paul Kariya, Ana.	1.50
☐	Eric Lindros, Pha.	1.50
☐	Mark Messier, Van.	1.00
☐	Patrick Roy (G), Col.	2.00
☐	Joe Sakic, Col.	1.00

JUNIORS TO PROS OF THE WORLD

One of six different cards was found on specially marked boxes of JELL-O Jelly Powder (85g).

Card Size:

	Player	NRMT-MT
☐	Chris Chelios, Chi.	.75
☐	Sergei Fedorov, Det.	.75
☐	Jaromir Jagr, Pgh.	1.00
☐	Saku Koivu, Mtl.	.75
☐	Zigmund Palffy, NYI.	.75
☐	Mats Sundin, Tor.	.75

ROAD TO JAPAN

A set of 12 disks was available through redemption offer.

Disk Diametre:

1997 - 98 KRAFT CASE CARDS

One of eight different cards was found in specially marked 12-box cases of Kraft Dinner.

Card Size:

Complete Set (8 cards): 35.00

	Player	NRMT-MT
☐	Vincent Damphousse, Mtl.	4.00
☐	Theoren Fleury, Cgy.	4.00
☐	Paul Kariya, Ana.	12.00
☐	Saku Koivu, Mtl.	6.00
☐	Mark Messier, Van.	5.00
☐	Mats Sundin, Tor.	5.00
☐	Doug Weight, Edm.	4.00
☐	Alexei Yashin, Ott.	4.00

1997 - 98 KRAFT SPOON STICKERS

Each package of four spoons and an eight-player sticker panel was available the with purchase of two JELL-O Pudding Snacks and/or JELL-O Gel Snacks.

Sticker Panel Size:

	Player	NRMT-MT
☐	R.Brind'Amour/ E.Lindros/ T.Fleury/ P.Roy/ Team Canada/ Cu.Joseph P.Kariya/ J.Sakic/ W.Gretzky	

1997 - 98 LEAF

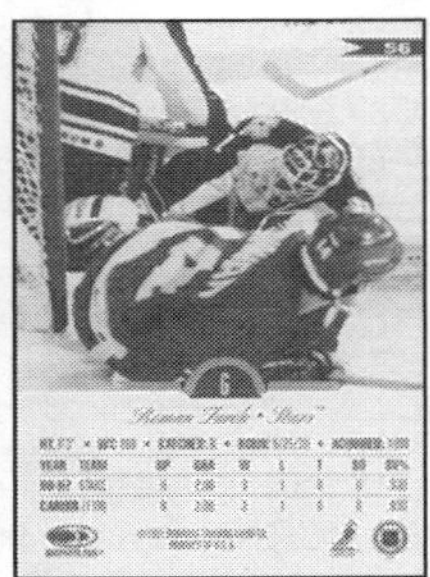

Each card has three versions in the regular packaging: the regular card, a coloured parallel (Bronze, Silver or Gold) and a coloured die-cut parallel (X-Axis, Y-Axis or Z-Axis). Cards 148-197 in the regular series are short printed.

Bronze cards are limited to 1800 copies: 73 players are bronze-X (1400 uncut, 400 die-cut), 20 players are bronze-Y (1600, 200) and 5 players are bronze-Z (1700, 100).

Silver cards are limited to 900 copies: 19 players are silver-X (500, 400), 33 players are silver-Y (700, 200) and 11 players are silver-Z (800, 100).

Gold cards are limited to 450 copies: 4 players are gold-X (50, 400), 25 players are gold-Y (250, 200) and 10 players are gold-Z (350, 100).

Two additional parallels for cards 1-147 and 198-200 are found in Leaf International: a regular card and a Universal Ice parallel (250 copies). Cards 198-200 are renumbered 148-150 in this series.

International cards are valued at 1.5 times the regular Leaf issue. A 150-card Leaf International set sells for $70.

Imprint: © 1997 DONRUSS TRADING CARD CO.

Complete Set (200 cards): 160.00

	No.	Player	U.I.	DC	FM	Reg.
☐☐☐☐☐	GX 1	Eric Lindros, Pha.	225.00	125.00	550.00	2.50
☐☐☐☐☐	GZ 2	Dominik Hasek (G), Buf.	100.00	200.00	80.00	1.50
☐☐☐☐☐	GZ 3	Peter Forsberg, Col.	150.00	300.00	120.00	2.00
☐☐☐☐☐	GZ 4	Steve Yzerman, Det.	150.00	300.00	120.00	2.00
☐☐☐☐☐	GZ 5	John Vanbiesbrouck (G), Fla.	90.00	175.00	70.00	1.25
☐☐☐☐☐	GX 6	Paul Kariya, Ana.	225.00	125.00	550.00	2.50

□□□□□	GZ 7	Martin Brodeur (G), N.J.	100.00	200.00	80.00	1.50
□□□□□	GX 8	Wayne Gretzky, NYR.	400.00	200.00	900.00	4.00
□□□□□	GY 9	Mark Messier, Van.	75.00	80.00	65.00	1.00
□□□□□	GZ 10	Jaromir Jagr, Pgh.	150.00	300.00	120.00	2.00
□□□□□	GY 11	Brett Hull, Stl.	75.00	80.00	65.00	1.00
□□□□□	GZ 12	Brendan Shanahan, Det.	90.00	175.00	70.00	1.25
□□□□□	GY 13	Ray Bourque, Bos.	75.00	80.00	65.00	1.00
□□□□□	GY 14	Jarome Iginla, Cgy.	25.00	35.00	20.00	.50
□□□□□	GY 15	Mike Modano, Dal.	75.00	80.00	65.00	1.00
□□□□□	GY 16	Curtis Joseph (G), Edm.	90.00	100.00	80.00	1.25
□□□□□	SX 17	Ed Jovanovski, Fla.	18.00	10.00	6.00	.35
□□□□□	GZ 18	Teemu Selänne, Ana.	100.00	200.00	80.00	1.50
□□□□□	GY 19	Saku Koivu, Mtl.	100.00	110.00	90.00	1.50
□□□□□	SZ 20	Eric Fichaud (G), NYI.	18.00	35.00	7.50	.35
□□□□□	SX 21	Paul Coffey, Pha.	18.00	10.00	6.00	.35
□□□□□	SX 22	Jeremy Roenick, Pho.	25.00	15.00	10.00	.50
□□□□□	BX 23	Owen Nolan, S.J.	18.00	10.00	3.00	.35
□□□□□	GY 24	Félix Potvin (G), Tor.	75.00	80.00	65.00	1.00
□□□□□	SZ 25	Alexander Mogilny, Van.	25.00	75.00	15.00	.50
□□□□□	SX 26	Alexandre Daigle, Ott.	10.00	6.00	4.00	.15
□□□□□	SX 27	Chris Gratton, Pha.	18.00	10.00	6.00	.35
□□□□□	SX 28	Geoff Sanderson, Car.	10.00	6.00	4.00	.15
□□□□□	SX 29	Dimitri Khristich, Bos.	10.00	6.00	4.00	.15
□□□□□	GY 30	Bryan Berard, NYI.	25.00	35.00	20.00	.50
□□□□□	BX 31	Vyachesiav Kozlov, Det.	10.00	6.00	2.00	.15
□□□□□	BY 32	Jeff Hackett (G), Chi.	18.00	20.00	4.00	.35
□□□□□	BY 33	Bill Ranford (G), Wsh.	18.00	20.00	4.00	.35
□□□□□	SY 34	Pat LaFontaine, NYR.	18.00	20.00	10.00	.35
□□□□□	GY 35	Joe Sakic, Col.	135.00	150.00	120.00	1.75
□□□□□	BX 36	Niklas Sundstrom, NYR.	10.00	6.00	2.00	.15
□□□□□	BX 37	Martin Gelinas, Van.	10.00	6.00	2.00	.15
□□□□□	BX 38	Mikael Renberg, T.B.	10.00	6.00	2.00	.15
□□□□□	BX 39	Trevor Linden, Van.	18.00	10.00	3.00	.35
□□□□□	BY 40	Jozef Stumpel, L.A.	18.00	20.00	4.00	.35
□□□□□	SZ 41	CL: Joe Thornton, Bos.	50.00	125.00	25.00	.75
□□□□□	GY 42	Jocelyn Thibault (G), Mtl.	25.00	35.00	20.00	.50
□□□□□	BX 43	Pierre Turgeon, Mtl.	18.00	10.00	3.00	.35
□□□□□	BX 44	Ron Francis, Pgh.	25.00	15.00	4.00	.50
□□□□□	SY 45	Damian Rhodes (G), Ott.	10.00	12.00	6.00	.15
□□□□□	SY 46	Jamie Langenbrunner, Dal.	18.00	20.00	10.00	.35
□□□□□	SZ 47	Chris Osgood (G), Det.	50.00	125.00	25.00	.75
□□□□□	SY 48	Vaclav Varada, Buf.	10.00	12.00	6.00	.15
□□□□□	GZ 49	Ryan Smyth, Edm.	18.00	35.00	15.00	.35
□□□□□	BX 50	Daren Puppa (G), T.B.	10.00	6.00	2.00	.15
□□□□□	BX 51	Petr Nedved, Pgh.	10.00	6.00	2.00	.15
□□□□□	BX 52	Ron Hextall (G), Pha.	18.00	10.00	3.00	.35
□□□□□	BX 53	Joé Juneau, Wsh.	10.00	6.00	2.00	.15
□□□□□	SY 54	Jim Campbell, Stl.	10.00	12.00	6.00	.15
□□□□□	SZ 55	Zigmund Palffy, NYI.	25.00	75.00	15.00	.50
□□□□□	BX 56	Roman Turek (G), Dal.	10.00	6.00	2.00	.15
□□□□□	GY 57	Adam Deadmarsh, Col.	10.00	12.00	8.00	.4
□□□□□	BX 58	Rob Niedermayer, Fla.	10.00	6.00	2.00	.15
□□□□□	GY 59	Alexei Yashin, Ott.	50.00	60.00	45.00	.75
□□□□□	GY 60	Pavel Bure, Van.	100.00	110.00	90.00	1.50
□□□□□	GY 61	Jason Arnott, Edm.	18.00	20.00	15.00	.35
□□□□□	SY 62	Nikolai Khabibulin (G), Pho.	25.00	35.00	18.00	.50
□□□□□	SY 63	Sean Burke (G), Car.	18.00	20.00	10.00	.35
□□□□□	SX 64	Chris Chelios, Chi.	50.00	30.00	20.00	.75
□□□□□	BX 65	Mike Ricci, Col.	10.00	6.00	2.00	.15
□□□□□	SY 66	Sergei Berezin, Tor.	18.00	20.00	10.00	.35
□□□□□	GY 67	Jaroslav Svejkovsky, Wsh.	18.00	20.00	15.00	.35
□□□□□	BX 68	Brian Savage, Mtl.	10.00	6.00	2.00	.15
□□□□□	BX 69	Roman Vopat, L.A.	10.00	6.00	2.00	.15
□□□□□	SX 70	Mike Richter (G), NYR.	25.00	15.00	10.00	.50
□□□□□	SY 71	Jim Carey (G), Bos.	10.00	12.00	6.00	.15
□□□□□	BY 72	Guy Hebert (G), Ana.	18.00	20.00	4.00	.35
□□□□□	GY 73	Keith Tkachuk, Pho.	50.00	60.00	45.00	.75
□□□□□	BX 74	Kirk McLean (G), Van.	18.00	10.00	3.00	.35
□□□□□	SY 75	Janne Niinimaa, Pha.	18.00	20.00	10.00	.35
□□□□□	SY 76	Roman Hamrlik, T.B.	18.00	20.00	10.00	.35
□□□□□	SY 77	Darcy Tucker, Mtl.	10.00	12.00	6.00	.15
□□□□□	BX 78	Pat Verbeek, Dal.	10.00	6.00	2.00	.15
□□□□□	BX 79	Hnat Domenichelli, Cgy.	18.00	10.00	3.00	.35
□□□□□	SY 80	Doug Gilmour, N.J.	25.00	35.00	18.00	.50
□□□□□	GY 81	Mike Grier, Edm.	18.00	20.00	15.00	.35
□□□□□	BX 82	Ken Wregget (G), Pgh.	10.00	6.00	2.00	.15
□□□□□	BX 83	Dlno Ciccarelli, T.B.	18.00	10.00	3.00	.35
□□□□□	BX 84	Steve Sullivan, Tor.	10.00	6.00	2.00	.15
□□□□□	SX 85	Anson Carter, Bos.	10.00	6.00	4.00	.15
□□□□□	**BY 86**	**Steve Shields (G), Buf., RC**	**18.00**	**20.00**	**4.00**	**.35**
□□□□□	SY 87	Ed Belfour (G), Dal.	25.00	35.00	18.00	.50
□□□□□	BX 88	Darren McCarty, Det.	10.00	6.00	2.00	.15
□□□□□	BX 89	Adam Graves, NYR.	10.00	6.00	2.00	.15
□□□□□	BX 90	Chris Pronger, Stl.	18.00	10.00	3.00	.35
□□□□□	SY 91	Peter Bondra, Wsh.	50.00	60.00	30.00	.75
□□□□□	SY 92	Oleg Tverdovsky, Pho.	10.00	12.00	6.00	.15
□□□□□	BX 93	Stéphane Fiset (G), L.A.	18.00	10.00	3.00	.35
□□□□□	BY 94	Mike Vernon (G), S.J.	18.00	20.00	4.00	.35
□□□□□	BX 95	Scott Lachance, NYI.	10.00	6.00	2.00	.15
□□□□□	BX 96	Corey Schwab (G), T.B.	10.00	6.00	2.00	.15
□□□□□	BY 97	Eric Dazé, Chi.	18.00	20.00	4.00	.35
□□□□□	BX 98	Jere Lehtinen, Dal.	18.00	10.00	3.00	.35
□□□□□	BX 99	Donald Audette, Buf.	10.00	6.00	2.00	.15
□□□□□	GY 100	John LeClair, Pha.	75.00	80.00	65.00	1.00
□□□□□	BX 101	Steve Rucchin, Ana.	10.00	6.00	2.00	.15
□□□□□	SX 102	Jeff Friesen, S.J.	18.00	10.00	6.00	.35
□□□□□	SX 103	Daymond Langkow, T.B.	10.00	6.00	4.00	.15
□□□□□	SY 104	Mike Dunham (G), N.J.	10.00	12.00	6.00	.15
□□□□□	BZ 105	CL: Marc Denis (G), Col.	18.00	35.00	3.50	.35
□□□□□	BX 106	Andrew Cassels, Cgy.	10.00	6.00	2.00	.15
□□□□□	BX 107	Michael Peca, Buf.	18.00	10.00	3.00	.35
□□□□□	BX 108	Joe Nieuwendyk, Dal.	18.00	10.00	3.00	.35
□□□□□	BX 109	Vincent Damphousse, Mtl.	25.00	15.00	4.00	.50
□□□□□	BX 110	Scott Mellanby, Fla.	10.00	6.00	2.00	.15
□□□□□	BX 111	Patrick Lalime (G), Pgh.	10.00	6.00	2.00	.15
□□□□□	SY 112	Derek Plante, Buf.	10.00	12.00	6.00	.15
□□□□□	SY 113	Wade Redden, Ott.	10.00	12.00	6.00	.15
□□□□□	SY 114	Marcel Cousineau (G), Tor.	10.00	12.00	6.00	.15
□□□□□	BX 115	Ray Sheppard, Fla.	10.00	6.00	2.00	.15
□□□□□	BX 116	Dave Andreychuk, N.J.	10.00	6.00	2.00	.15
□□□□□	GY 117	Brian Leetch, NYR.	25.00	35.00	20.00	.50
□□□□□	BY 118	Sandis Ozolinsh, Col.	18.00	20.00	4.00	.35
□□□□□	BX 119	Keith Primeau, Car.	18.00	10.00	3.00	.35
□□□□□	BX 120	Brian Holzinger, Buf.	10.00	6.00	2.00	.15
□□□□□	BX 121	Luc Robitaille, L.A.	18.00	10.00	3.00	.35
□□□□□	SX 122	José Théodore (G), Mtl.	25.00	15.00	10.00	.50
□□□□□	SY 123	Grant Fuhr (G), Stl.	18.00	20.00	10.00	.35
□□□□□	GY 124	Dainius Zubrus, Pha.	18.00	20.00	15.00	.35
□□□□□	BZ 125	Rod Brind'Amour, Pha.	18.00	35.00	3.50	.35
□□□□□	SY 126	Trevor Kidd (G), Car.	18.00	20.00	10.00	.35
□□□□□	BX 127	Mark Recchi, Mtl.	18.00	10.00	3.00	.35
□□□□□	GY 128	Patrick Roy (G), Col.	250.00	275.00	225.00	3.00
□□□□□	BX 129	Kevin Hatcher, Dal.	10.00	6.00	2.00	.15
□□□□□	SY 130	Adam Oates, Wsh.	25.00	35.00	18.00	.50
□□□□□	SX 131	Doug Weight, Edm.	25.00	15.00	10.00	.50
□□□□□	**SX 132**	**Vaclav Prospal, Pha., RC**	**25.00**	**15.00**	**10.00**	**1.00**
□□□□□	SY 133	Harry York, Stl.	18.00	20.00	10.00	.35
□□□□□	BX 134	Todd Bertuzzi, NYI.	10.00	6.00	2.00	.15
□□□□□	GY 135	Sergei Fedorov, Det.	75.00	80.00	65.00	1.00
□□□□□	SX 136	Theoren Fleury, Cgy.	50.00	30.00	20.00	.75
□□□□□	BY 137	Chad Kilger, Pho.	10.00	12.00	2.50	.15
□□□□□	SX 138	Jamie Storr (G), L.A.	18.00	10.00	3.00	.35
□□□□□	BY 139	Tony Amonte, Chi.	18.00	20.00	4.00	.35
□□□□□	BY 140	Rem Murray, Edm.	10.00	12.00	2.50	.15
□□□□□	BX 141	Chris O'Sullivan, Cgy.	10.00	6.00	2.00	.15
□□□□□	SZ 142	Mats Sundin, Tor.	75.00	150.00	30.00	1.00
□□□□□	SZ 143	Ethan Moreau, Chi.	10.00	25.00	5.00	.15
□□□□□	SY 144	Derian Hatcher, Dal.	18.00	20.00	10.00	.35
□□□□□	SY 145	Daniel Alfredsson, Ott.	18.00	20.00	10.00	.35
□□□□□	BX 146	Corey Hirsch (G), Van.	10.00	6.00	2.00	.15
□□□□□	BX 147	Landon Wilson, Bos.	10.00	6.00	2.00	.15

□□□	GY 148	Marc Denis (G), Col.	20.00	15.00	1.50
□□□	BX 149	Boyd Devereaux, Edm.	6.00	2.00	1.00
□□□	GX 150	Joe Thornton, Bos.	50.00	275.00	6.00
□□□	GZ 151	Sergei Samsonov, Bos.	125.00	50.00	6.00
□□□	SY 152	Alyn McCauley, Tor.	60.00	30.00	4.00
□□□	SZ 153	Erik Rasmussen, Buf.	25.00	5.00	1.00
□□□	SX 154	Patrick Marleau, S.J.	30.00	20.00	4.00
□□□	**SY 155**	**Olli Jokinen, L.A., RC**	**50.00**	**25.00**	**4.00**
□□□	SZ 156	Chris Phillips, Ott.	35.00	7.50	1.50
□□□	**SZ 157**	**Tomas Vokoun, Mtl., RC**	**25.00**	**5.00**	**1.00**
□□□	**SZ 158**	**Chris Dingman, Cgy., RC**	**25.00**	**5.00**	**1.00**
□□□	GY 159	Daniel Cleary, Chi.	20.00	15.00	1.50
□□□	**BX 160**	**Juha Lind, Dal., RC**	**6.00**	**2.00**	**1.00**
□□□	**BY 161**	**Jean-Yves Leroux, Chi., RC**	**12.00**	**2.50**	**1.00**
□□□	SY 162	Brad Isbister, Pho.	12.00	6.00	1.00
□□□	BX 163	Vadim Sharifjanov, N.J.	6.00	2.00	1.00
□□□	SX 164	Alexei Morozov, Pgh.	30.00	20.00	4.00
□□□	BX 165	Vaclav Prospal, Pha.	18.00	6.00	3.00
□□□	BY 166	Vaclav Varada, Buf.	12.00	2.50	1.00
□□□	BZ 167	Jaroslav Svejkovsky, Wsh.	35.00	3.50	.35
□□□	SY 168	Eric Lindros, Pha.	200.00	100.00	10.00
□□□	BY 169	Dominik Hasek (G), Buf.	100.00	20.00	5.00
□□□	BY 170	Peter Forsberg, Col.	150.00	30.00	7.50
□□□	SY 171	Steve Yzerman, Det.	150.00	75.00	7.50
□□□	BX 172	John Vanbiesbrouck (G), Fla.	50.00	15.00	4.50
□□□	SY 173	Paul Kariya, Ana.	200.00	100.00	10.00
□□□	BZ 174	Martin Brodeur (G), N.J.	175.00	18.00	5.00
□□□	SY 175	Wayne Gretzky, NYR.	325.00	160.00	15.00
□□□	BX 176	Mark Messier, Van.	35.00	10.00	4.00
□□□	BZ 177	Jaromir Jagr, Pgh.	275.00	28.00	7.50
□□□	BX 178	Brett Hull, Stl.	35.00	10.00	4.00
□□□	BY 179	Brendan Shanahan, Det.	90.00	18.00	4.50
□□□	BX 180	Jarome Iginla, Cgy.	12.00	3.50	2.00
□□□	BY 181	Mike Modano, Dal.	75.00	15.00	4.00
□□□	BY 182	Teemu Selänne, Ana.	12.00	2.50	1.00
□□□	BY 183	Bryan Berard, NYI.	30.00	6.00	2.00
□□□	SY 184	Ryan Smyth, Edm.	20.00	10.00	1.50
□□□	BX 185	Keith Tkachuk, Pho.	25.00	6.50	3.00
□□□	BX 186	Dainius Zubrus, Pha.	10.00	3.00	1.50
□□□	BX 187	Patrick Roy (G), Col.	160.00	50.00	12.00
□□□	BX 188	Trevor Linden, Van.	10.00	3.00	.75
□□□	BX 189	Trevor Linden, Van.	10.00	3.00	.75
□□□	BX 190	Trevor Linden, Van.	10.00	3.00	.75
□□□	BX 191	Trevor Linden, Van.	10.00	3.00	.75
□□□	BX 192	Trevor Linden, Van.	10.00	3.00	.75
□□□	BX 193	Trevor Linden, Van.	10.00	3.00	.75
□□□	BX 194	Trevor Linden, Van.	10.00	3.00	.75
□□□	BX 195	Trevor Linden, Van.	10.00	3.00	.75
□□□	BX 196	Trevor Linden, Van.	10.00	3.00	.75
□□□	BX 197	Trevor Linden, Van.	10.00	3.00	.75

□□□□□	BX 198	CL: Chris Phillips, Ott. (#148)	18.00	10.00	3.00	.35
□□□□□	BX 199	CL: Sergei Samsonov, Bos. (#149)	75.00	45.00	12.00	1.25
□□□□□	BX 200	CL: Daniel Cleary, Chi. (#150)	18.00	10.00	3.00	.35

BANNER SEASON

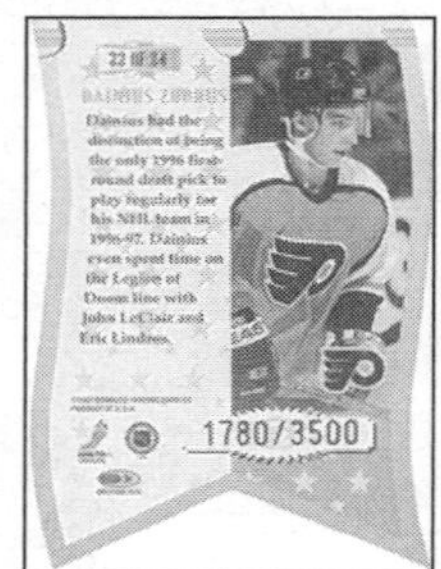

These die-cut inserts are limited to 3,500 copies.

Insert Set (24 cards): 300.00

	No.	Player	NRMT-MT
□	1	Paul Kariya, Ana.	30.00
□	2	Eric Lindros, Pha.	30.00
□	3	Wayne Gretzky, NYR.	50.00
□	4	Jaromir Jagr, Pgh.	25.00
□	5	Steve Yzerman, Det.	25.00
□	6	Brendan Shanahan, Det.	12.00
□	7	John LeClair, Pha.	10.00
□	8	Teemu Selänne, Ana.	15.00
□	9	Mike Modano, Dal.	10.00
□	10	Ryan Smyth, Edm.	5.00
□	11	Brett Hull, Stl.	10.00
□	12	Zigmund Palffy, NYI.	6.00
□	13	Peter Forsberg, Col.	25.00
□	14	Keith Tkachuk, Pho.	8.00
□	15	Saku Koivu, Mtl.	15.00
□	16	Sergei Fedorov, Det.	10.00
□	17	Brian Leetch, NYR.	6.00
□	18	Bryan Berard, NYI.	6.00
□	19	Mats Sundin, Tor.	10.00
□	20	Jarome Iginla, Cgy.	6.00
□	21	Sergei Berezin, Tor.	5.00
□	22	Dainius Zubrus, Pha.	5.00
□	23	Mike Grier, Edm.	5.00
□	24	Joe Sakic, Col.	20.00

FIRE ON ICE

These inserts are limited to 1,000 copies.

Insert Set (16 cards): 825.00

	No.	Player	NRMT-MT
☐	1	Wayne Gretzky, NYR.	150.00
☐	2	Eric Lindros, Pha.	100.00
☐	3	Jaromir Jagr, Pgh.	75.00
☐	4	Steve Yzerman, Det.	75.00
☐	5	Brendan Shanahan, Det.	40.00
☐	6	Mike Modano, Dal.	35.00
☐	7	Joe Sakic, Col.	65.00
☐	8	Pavel Bure, Van.	50.00
☐	9	Ryan Smyth, Edm.	20.00
☐	10	Teemu Selänne, Ana.	50.00
☐	11	Mark Messier, Van.	35.00
☐	12	Peter Forsberg, Col.	75.00
☐	13	Dainius Zubrus, Pha.	20.00
☐	14	Joe Thornton, Bos.	35.00
☐	15	Sergei Samsonov, Bos.	35.00
☐	16	Paul Kariya, Ana.	100.00

PIPE DREAMS

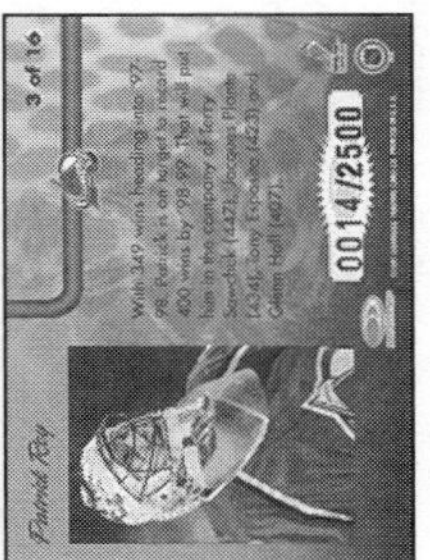

These inserts are limited to 2,500 copies. Promo versions exist for some, if not all, singles.

Insert Set (16 cards): 325.00

	No.	Player	Promo	Insert
☐	1	Dominik Hasek (G), Buf.		40.00
☐	2	John Vanbiesbrouck (G), Fla.		30.00
☐	3	Patrick Roy (G), Col.		90.00
☐	4	Curtis Joseph (G), Edm.		30.00
☐☐	5	Félix Potvin (G), Tor.	2.50	25.00
☐☐	6	Martin Brodeur (G), N.J.	3.50	40.00
☐	7	Guy Hebert (G), Ana.		12.00
☐☐	8	Mike Richter (G), NYR.	1.50	15.00
☐	9	José Théodore (G), Mtl.		15.00
☐	10	Jim Carey (G), Bos.		12.00
☐	11	Damian Rhodes (G), Ott.		12.00
☐	12	Jocelyn Thibault (G), Mtl.		15.00
☐	13	Nikolai Khabibulin (G), Pho.		15.00
☐	14	Chris Osgood (G), Det.		20.00
☐	15	Eric Fichaud (G), NYI.		12.00
☐	16	Mike Dunham (G), N.J.		12.00

ERIC LINDROS COLLECTION

These inserts are limited to 100 copies. Each card features a piece of Eric Lindros's equipment.

	Player	NRMT-MT
☐	Eric Lindros (Home Jersey)	600.00
☐	Eric Lindros (Away Jersey)	600.00
☐	Eric Lindros (Stick)	500.00
☐	Eric Lindros (Gloves)	500.00
☐	Eric Lindros (Stirrups)	500.00

1997 - 98 LIMITED

This 200-card set contains four levels of difficulty: Counterparts, Double Team, Unlimited Potential/Talent and Star Factor (less than 600 copies of each card). Each card has two versions: a regular card and a Limited Exposure parallel. There is less than 25 copies of each Limited Exposure Star Factor card.

Imprint: © 1997 DONRUSS TRADING CARD CO.

Master Set (200 cards): 20,000.00 2,500.00

Promo Card (Eric Lindros, #183): 5.00

	No.	Player	L.E.	Reg.
☐☐	1	B. Shanahan/ H.York	25.00	2.00
☐☐	2	P. Forsberg/ M. Knuble	40.00	3.50
☐☐	3	C. Osgood (G)/ K. McLean (G)	18.00	1.50
☐☐	6	P. Coffey/ D. Sydor	6.00	.50
☐☐	7	P. Bure/ V. Bure	30.00	2.50
☐☐	9	S. Koivu/ M. Sundin	30.00	2.50
☐☐	10	T. Kidd (G)/ C. Hirsch (G)	6.00	.50
☐☐	12	Z. Palffy/ R. Bonk	12.00	1.00
☐☐	14	J. Carey (G)/ B. Ranford (G)	6.00	.50
☐☐	15	J. LeClair/ C. Lemieux	20.00	1.75
☐☐	18	A. Graves/ K. Jones	4.00	.35
☐☐	19	M. Modano/ T. Linden	20.00	1.75
☐☐	21	D. Hatcher/ K. Hatcher	6.00	.50
☐☐	22	D. Alfredsson/ D. Andreychuk	6.00	.50
☐☐	24	T. Fleury/ G. Courtnall	12.00	1.00
☐☐	25	M. Messier/ D. Ciccarelli	20.00	1.75
☐☐	28	E. Belfour (G)/ A. Moog (G)	12.00	1.00
☐☐	30	E. Lindros/ T. Bertuzzi	60.00	5.00
☐☐	31	D. Langkow/ D. Roberts	4.00	.35
☐☐	32	M. Richter (G)/ G. Fuhr (G)	12.00	1.00
☐☐	36	J. Sakic/ B. Nicholls	35.00	3.00
☐☐	37	E. Jovanovski/ D.J. Smith	6.00	.50
☐☐	39	M. Peca/ M. Murray	6.00	.50
☐☐	40	M. Gartner/ W. Clark	6.00	.50
☐☐	43	J. Nieuwendyk/ J. Iginla	6.00	.50
☐☐	44	P. Roy/ J. Thibault	75.00	6.00
☐☐	45	H. Domenichelli/ A. Cassels	6.00	.50
☐☐	46	C. Dubé/ S. Sullivan	4.00	.35
☐☐	49	Der. Plante/ T. Harvey	4.00	.35
☐☐	52	M. Recchi/ L. Wilson	6.00	.50
☐☐	53	D. Tucker/ P. Rhéaume	4.00	.35
☐☐	54	C. O'Sullivan/ A. Eriksson	4.00	.35
☐☐	57	F. Potvin (G)/ D. Rhodes (G)	20.00	1.75
☐☐	58	B. Holzinger/ M. Ricci	4.00	.35
☐☐	60	E. Moreau/ J. MacLean	4.00	.35
☐☐	61	J. Juneau/ J. O'Neill	6.00	.50
☐☐	63	B. Dafoe (G)/ S. Shields (G)	6.00	.50
☐☐	64	M. Renberg/ N. Sundstrom	4.00	.35
☐☐	65	R. Smyth/ E. Dazé	6.00	.50
☐☐	67	J. Campbell/ C. Janney	4.00	.35
☐☐	68	A. Mogilny/ M. Barnaby	12.00	1.00
☐☐	71	A. Yashin/ B. Savage	18.00	1.50
☐☐	72	J. Friesen/ D. McCarty	6.00	.50
☐☐	73	D. Khristich/ C. Kilger	4.00	.35
☐☐	75	L. Robitaille/ P. Verbeek	6.00	.50
☐☐	76	D. Hasek (G)/ J. Storr (G)	30.00	2.50
☐☐	79	J. Arnott/ R. Niedermayer	6.00	.50
☐☐	80	E. Desjardins/ C. Phillips	6.00	.50
☐☐	81	Cu. Joseph (G)/ J. Théodore (G)	25.00	2.00
☐☐	82	D. Gilmour/ R. Brind'Amour	12.00	1.00
☐☐	83	K. Tkachuk/ R. Tocchet	18.00	1.50
☐☐	85	C. Pronger/ A. Berg	6.00	.50
☐☐	88	J. Hoglund/ R. Zamuner	6.00	.50
☐☐	89	R. Hextall (G)/ K. Hodson (G)	6.00	.50
☐☐	91	V. Prospal/ Vya. Kozlov	10.00	.75
☐☐	93	O. Tverdovsky/ S. Zubov	6.00	.50
☐☐	96	J. Svejkovsky/ J. Stumpel	6.00	.50
☐☐	101	W. Primeau/ S. Pronger	4.00	.35
☐☐	102	J.S. Giguère (G)/ G. Hebert (G)	6.00	.50
☐☐	105	J. Roenick/ T. Amonte	12.00	1.00
☐☐	106	S. Ozolinsh/ K. McLaren	6.00	.50
☐☐	107	A. Carter/ S. Kelly	4.00	.35
☐☐	110	T. Green/ S. Mellanby	4.00	.35
☐☐	111	P. LaFontaine/ V. Kamensky	6.00	.50
☐☐	113	J. Vanbiesbrouck (G)/ R. Turek (G)	25.00	2.00
☐☐	117	O. Nolan/ S. Rucchin	6.00	.50
☐☐	118	D. Audette/ T. Donato	4.00	.35
☐☐	121	V. Vorobiev/ A. Johansson	4.00	.35
☐☐	124	E. Fichaud (G)/ N. Khabibulin (G)	12.00	1.00
☐☐	125	R. Bourque/ E. Messier	20.00	1.75
☐☐	126	S. Fedorov/ K. Primeau	20.00	1.75
☐☐	129	P. Bondra/ R. Vopat	18.00	1.50
☐☐	130	T. Salo (G)/ C. Schwab (G)	6.00	.50
☐☐	135	G. Sanderson/ J. Lehtinen	6.00	.50
☐☐	136	J. Niinimaa/ J. Pushor	6.00	.50
☐☐	137	A. Dackell/ V. Damphousse	12.00	1.00
☐☐	141	R. Murray/ R. Sheppard	4.00	.35
☐☐	142	P. Schafer (G)/ P. Lalime (G)	6.00	.50
☐☐	144	T. Marchant/ T. Granato	4.00	.35
☐☐	146	R. Hamrlik/ N. Lidström	6.00	.50
☐☐	148	C. Gratton/ D. Goneau	6.00	.50
☐☐	150	M. Brodeur (G)/ S. Fiset (G)	30.00	2.50
☐☐	154	S. Berezin/ D. Pederson	6.00	.50
☐☐	156	P. Nedved/ K. Muller	4.00	.35
☐☐	160	M. Cousineau (G)/ J. Hackett (G)	6.00	.50
☐☐	161	A. Deadmarsh/ A. Daigle	4.00	.35
☐☐	162	A. Oates/ T. Warriner	12.00	1.00
☐☐	166	C. Chelios/ S. Lachance	18.00	1.50
☐☐	167	J. Langenbrunner/ B. Convery	6.00	.50
☐☐	170	D. Puppa (G)/ G. Snow (G)	6.00	.50
☐☐	172	P. Turgeon/ S. Corson	6.00	.50
☐☐	176	W. Redden/ S. Stevens	4.00	.35
☐☐	178	V. Varada/ I. Larionov	6.00	.50
☐☐	182	B. Berard/ B. Leetch	12.00	1.00
☐☐	185	B. Hull/ M. Gelinas	20.00	1.75
☐☐	188	M. Vernon (G)/ K. Wregget (G)	6.00	.50
☐☐	191	D. Weight/ D. Turcotte	12.00	1.00
☐☐	194	S. Burke (G)/ M. Dunham (G)	6.00	.50
☐☐	195	D. Zubrus/ S. Bordeleau	6.00	.50
☐☐	199	M. Grier/ R. Francis	12.00	1.00

DOUBLE TEAM

	No.	Player	L.E.	Reg.
☐☐	5	Fla.: J. Vanbiesbrouck (G)/ E. Jovanovski	150.00	15.00
☐☐	13	Tor.: M. Sundin/ S. Berezin	100.00	10.00
☐☐	17	Det.: K. Hodson (G)/ M. Knuble	12.00	2.00
☐☐	23	Buf.: S. Shields (G)/ V. Varada	12.00	2.00
☐☐	27	Edm.: M. Grier/ J. Arnott	25.00	4.00
☐☐	33	Wsh.: A. Oates/ J. Svejkovsky	75.00	7.50
☐☐	34	Mtl.: S. Koivu/ D. Tucker	150.00	15.00
☐☐	42	Dal.: M. Modano/ R. Turek (G)	100.00	10.00
☐☐	47	Col.: M. Denis (G)/ V. Kamensky	25.00	4.00
☐☐	51	Stl.: B. Hull/ J. Campbell	125.00	12.50
☐☐	56	Ana.: P. Kariya/ T. Selänne	350.00	35.00
☐☐	59	NYI.: E. Fichaud (G)/ T. Green	25.00	4.00
☐☐	66	N.J.: D. Gilmour/ P. Rhéaume	50.00	6.00
☐☐	74	N.J.: M. Brodeur (G)/ D. Andreychuk	175.00	17.50
☐☐	78	N.J.: M. Dunham (G)/ V. Sharifjanov	12.00	2.00
☐☐	87	Chi.: E. Moreau/ C. Chelios	75.00	7.50
☐☐	92	Bos.: R. Bourque/ J. Thornton	150.00	15.00
☐☐	97	NYR.: W. Gretzky/ V. Vorobiev	500.00	50.00
☐☐	100	Pha.: V. Prospal/ P. Coffey	20.00	5.00
☐☐	104	Van.: P. Bure/ A. Mogilny	175.00	17.50
☐☐	115	Det.: S. Yzerman/ C. Osgood (G)	250.00	25.00
☐☐	116	Tor.: M. Cousineau (G)/ S. Sullivan	12.00	2.00
☐☐	119	Hfd.: G. Sanderson/ S. Burke (G)	25.00	4.00
☐☐	123	Mtl.: J. Thibault (G)/ T. Ryan	75.00	7.50
☐☐	131	Bos.: S. Samsonov/ J. Carey (G)	125.00	12.50
☐☐	132	Col.: A. Deadmarsh/ J. Sakic	175.00	17.50
☐☐	140	Pho.: K. Tkachuk/ J. Roenick	100.00	10.00
☐☐	152	Mtl.: J. Théodore (G)/ M. Recchi	75.00	7.50
☐☐	158	Stl.: H. York/ P. Turgeon	25.00	4.00
☐☐	159	Pgh.: A. Johansson/ P. Lalime (G)	12.00	2.00
☐☐	168	Pha.: J. Niinimaa/ J. LeClair	125.0	12.50
☐☐	173	Edm.: D. Weight/ R. Murray	75.00	7.50
☐☐	177	Cgy.: J. Iginla/ T. Fleury	75.00	7.50
☐☐	180	L.A.: R. Vopat/ S. Fiset (G)	25.00	4.00
☐☐	181	NYI.: Z. Palffy/ B. Berard	75.00	7.50
☐☐	184	Buf.: Der. Plante/ B. Holzinger	12.00	2.00
☐☐	186	Ott.: D. Alfredsson/ D. Rhodes (G)	25.00	4.00
☐☐	189	Ott.: A. Yashin/ W. Redden	75.00	7.50
☐☐	192	T.B.: D. Langkow/ D. Puppa (G)	12.00	2.00
☐☐	196	S.J.: O. Nolan/ J. Friesen	25.00	4.00

UNLIMITED POTENTIAL/TALENT

	No.	Player	L.E.	Reg.
☐☐	8	S. Berezin/ J. Jagr	500.00	60.00
☐☐	16	J. Niinimaa/ C. Chelios	150.00	25.00
☐☐	29	J. S. Giguère (G)/ F. Potvin (G)	200.00	30.00
☐☐	38	V. Prospal/ B. Shanahan	300.00	40.00
☐☐	50	M. Grier/ E. Lindros	650.00	80.00
☐☐	70	B. Berard/ B. Leetch	100.00	18.00
☐☐	86	M. Cousineau (G)/ D. Hasek (G)	350.00	45.00
☐☐	94	E. Moreau/ J. LeClair	200.00	30.00
☐☐	99	J. Campbell/ R. Smyth	40.00	12.00
☐☐	109	D. Zubrus/ P. Forsberg	500.00	60.00
☐☐	114	J. Iginla/ P. Kariya	650.00	80.00
☐☐	127	M. Denis (G)/ M. Brodeur (G)	350.00	45.00
☐☐	133	D. Langkow/ K. Tkachuk	150.00	25.00
☐☐	143	J. Svejkovsky/ T. Selänne	350.00	45.00
☐☐	151	J. Théodore (G)/ P. Roy (G)	800.00	100.00
☐☐	165	S. Koivu/ S. Yzerman	500.00	60.00
☐☐	174	E. Fichaud (G)/ Cu. Joseph (G)	300.00	40.00
☐☐	187	J. Thornton/ M. Messier	200.00	30.00
☐☐	197	V. Vorobiev/ S. Fedorov	200.00	30.00
☐☐	200	P. Marleau/ W. Gretzky	1,200.00	125.00

STAR FACTOR

	No.	Player		
□□	4	Wayne Gretzky, NYR.	1,650.00	150.00
□□	11	Teemu Selänne, Ana.	400.00	50.00
□□	20	Brett Hull, Stl.	25.00	35.00
□□	26	Ryan Smyth, Edm.	60.00	10.00
□□	35	Paul Kariya, Ana.	900.00	90.00
□□	41	Steve Yzerman, Det.	700.00	75.00
□□	48	Peter Forsberg, Col.	700.00	75.00
□□	55	Jaromir Jagr, Pgh.	700.00	75.00
□□	62	John Vanbiesbrouck (G), Fla.	350.00	45.00
□□	69	Alexei Yashin, Ott.	200.00	30.00
□□	77	Félix Potvin (G), Tor.	250.00	35.00
□□	84	Mark Messier, NYR.	250.00	35.00
□□	90	John LeClair, Pha.	250.00	35.00
□□	95	Adam Deadmarsh, Col.	60.00	10.00
□□	98	Sergei Fedorov, Det.	250.00	35.00
□□	103	Curtis Joseph (G), Edm.	350.00	45.00
□□	108	Paul Coffey, Pha.	75.00	12.00
□□	112	Adam Oates, Wsh.	135.00	20.00
□□	120	Jeremy Roenick, Pho.	135.00	30.00
□□	122	Alexander Mogilny, Van.	135.00	20.00
□□	128	Mats Sundin, Tor.	250.00	35.00
□□	134	Mike Richter (G), NYR.	135.00	20.00
□□	138	Keith Tkachuk, Pho.	200.00	30.00
□□	139	Ray Bourque, Bos.	250.00	35.00
□□	145	Sandis Ozolinsh, Col.	75.00	12.00
□□	147	Dominik Hasek (G), Buf.	400.00	50.00
□□	149	Martin Brodeur (G), N.J.	400.00	50.00
□□	153	Pavel Bure (G), Van.	400.00	50.00
□□	155	Doug Gilmour, N.J.	135.00	20.00
□□	157	Theoren Fleury, Cgy.	135.00	20.00
□□	163	Zigmund Palffy, NYI.	135.00	20.00
□□	164	Ed Belfour, Dal.	135.00	20.00
□□	169	Brendan Shanahan, Det.	350.00	45.00
□□	171	Chris Osgood (G), Det.	200.00	30.00
□□	175	Chris Chelios, Chi.	200.00	30.00
□□	179	Brian Leetch, NYR.	135.00	20.00
□□	183	Eric Lindros, Pha.	900.00	90.00
□□	190	Joe Sakic, Col.	550.00	60.00
□□	193	Mike Modano, Dal.	250.00	35.00
□□	198	Patrick Roy (G), Col.	1,250.00	125.00

FABRIC OF THE GAME

This 72-card set contains five levels of difficulty: Major Material (21 cards, sequentially numbered to 1000), Star Material (18 cards, sequentially numbered to 750), Superstar Material (12 cards, sequentially numbered to 500), Hall of Fame material (12 cards, sequentially numbered to 250) and Legendary Material (9 cards, sequentially numbered to 100). Each level is divided into three subsets featuring a different fabric: Goals-Nylon, Wins-Canvas and Assists-Wood.

Insert Set (72 cards):

	No.	Player	NRMT-MT
□	1	Wayne Gretzky, NYR., Goals (#/250)	350.00
□	2	Martin Brodeur (G), N.J. (#/750)	60.00
□	3	Dainius Zubrus, Pha., Goals (#/1000)	10.00
□	4	Joe Sakic, Col., Assists (#/500)	110.00
□	5	Joe Sakic, Col., Goals (#/250)	125.00
□	6	Sergei Fedorov, Det., Assists (#/750)	35.00
□	7	John Vanbiesbrouck (G), Fla. (#/250)	100.00
□	8	Saku Koivu, Mtl., Assists (#/1000)	35.00
□	9	J.S. Giguère (G), Cgy. (#/1000)	10.00
□	10	Paul Kariya, Ana., Goals (#/750)	125.00
□	11	Mike Richter (G), NYR. (#/500)	25.00
□	12	Paul Coffey, Pha., Assists (#/100)	75.00
□	13	Brendan Shanahan, Det., Goals (#/100)	250.00
□	14	Jaromir Jagr, Pgh., Assists (#/500)	135.00
□	15	Félix Potvin (G), Tor. (#/500)	45.00
□	16	Mats Sundin, Tor., Goals (#/500)	45.00
□	17	Mike Vernon (G), S.J. (#/250)	35.00
□	18	Keith Tkachuk, Pho., Goals (#/750)	25.00
□	19	Doug Gilmour, N.J., Assists (#/250)	40.00
□	20	Patrick Roy (G), Col. (#/100)	600.00
□	21	Sergei Samsonov, Bos., Goals (#/1000)	30.00
□	22	Mike Grier, Edm., Assists (#/1000)	30.00
□	23	Curtis Joseph, Edm. (#/500)	60.00
□	24	Zigmund Palffy, NYI., Goals (#/750)	20.00
□	25	Chris Osgood (G), Det. (#/750)	25.00
□	26	Mats Sundin, Tor., Assists (#/750)	35.00
□	27	Kelly Hrudey (G), S.J. (#/250)	35.00
□	28	Brett Hull, Stl., Assists (#/500)	45.00
□	29	Ray Bourque, Bos., Assists (#/250)	75.00
□	30	Nikolai Khabibulin (G), Pho. (#/750)	20.00
□	31	Bryan Berard, NYI., Assists (#/1000)	15.00
□	32	Jaroslav Svejkovsky, Wsh., Goals (#/1000)	10.00
□	33	Ed Belfour, Dal. (#/500)	25.00
□	34	Wayne Gretzky, NYR., Assists (#/100)	800.00
□	35	Jeremy Roenick, Pho., Goals (#/500)	25.00
□	36	Andy Moog, Mtl. (#/100)	75.00
□	37	Eric Lindros, Pha., Goals (#/750)	125.00
□	38	Brett Hull, Stl., Goals (#/100)	200.00
□	39	Marcel Cousineau (G), Tor. (#/1000)	8.00
□	40	Paul Kariya, Ana., Assists (#/1000)	70.00
□	41	Mike Dunham (G), N.J. (#/1000)	8.00
□	42	Chris Phillips, Ott., Assists (#/1000)	8.00
□	43	Teemu Selänne, Ana., Goals (#/500)	75.00
□	44	Mark Messier, Van., Assists (#/100)	200.00
□	45	Grant Fuhr (G), Stl. (#/100)	75.00
□	46	Daniel Alfredsson, Ott., Goals (#/1000)	10.00
□	47	Marc Denis (G), Col. (#/1000)	10.00
□	48	Daymond Langkow, T.B., Goals (#/1000)	5.00
□	49	Steve Yzerman, Det., Assists (#/250)	160.00
□	50	Ryan Smyth, Edm., Goals (#/750)	15.00
□	51	Alexander Mogilny, Van., Goals (#/250)	40.00
□	52	Ron Hextall (G), Pha. (#/250)	35.00
□	53	Brendan Shanahan, Det., Assists (#/750)	50.00
□	54	Jim Carey (G), Bos. (#/750)	12.00
□	55	Eric Lindros, Pha., Assists (#/750)	125.00
□	56	Eric Fichaud (G), NYI. (#/1000)	8.00
□	57	Sergei Berezin, Tor., Goals (#/1000)	5.00
□	58	Chris Chelios, Chi., Assists (#/250)	50.00
□	59	Mark Messier, Van., Goals (#/250)	75.00
□	60	Damian Rhodes, Ott. (#/1000)	8.00
□	61	Jarome Iginla, Cgy., Assists (#/1000)	15.00
□	62	Jocelyn Thibault (G), Mtl. (#/750)	20.00
□	63	John LeClair, Pha., Goals (#/750)	34.00
□	64	Brian Leetch, NYR., Assists (#/500)	35.00
□	65	Dominik Hasek (G), Buf. (#/750)	60.00
□	66	Pavel Bure, Van., Goals (#/500)	75.00
□	67	Mike Modano, Dal., Assists (#/750)	35.00
□	68	Daniel Cleary, Chi., Goals (#/1000)	15.00
□	69	Janne Niinimaa, Pha., Assists (#/1000)	10.00
□	70	Steve Yzerman, Det., Goals (#/100)	400.00
□	71	José Théodore (G), Mtl. (#/1000)	15.00
□	72	Peter Forsberg, Col., Assists (#/750)	90.00

1997 - 98 MCDONALD'S - UPPER DECK ICE

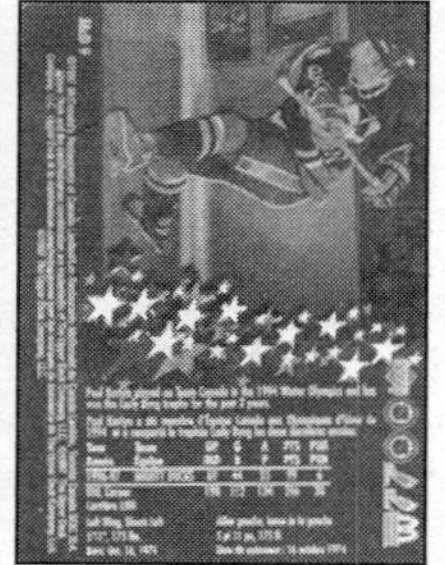

Cards McD23-McD32 are "Caged Ice" subsets and cards McD33-McD40 are "Ice Breakers" subsets. McDonald's was released in late December, 1997.

Imprint: © 1997 MCDONALD'S RESTAURANTS OF CANADA LIMITED. © 1997 THE UPPER DECK COMPANY.

Complete Set (40 cards): 30.00

	No.	Player	NRMT-MT
□	McD1	Wayne Gretzky, NYR.	4.50
□	McD2	Theoren Fleury, Cgy.	.50
□	McD3	Pavel Bure, Van.	1.50
□	McD4	Saku Koivu, Mtl.	1.50
□	McD5	Joe Sakic, Col.	1.75
□	McD6	Wade Redden, Ott.	.35
□	McD7	Keith Tkachuk, Pho.	.75
□	McD8	Eric Lindros, Pha.	2.50
□	McD9	Paul Kariya, Ana.	2.50
□	McD10	Bryan Berard, NYI.	.50
□	McD11	Teemu Selänne, Ana.	1.50
□	McD12	Jarome Iginla, Cgy.	.50
□	McD13	Mats Sundin, Tor.	1.00
□	McD14	Brendan Shanahan, Det.	1.25
□	McD15	Peter Forsberg, Col.	2.00
□	McD16	Brett Hull, Stl.	1.00
□	McD17	Ray Bourque, Bos.	1.00
□	McD18	Doug Weight, Edm.	.50
□	McD19	Steve Yzerman, Det.	2.00
□	McD20	Jaromir Jagr, Pgh.	2.00
□	McD21	Vincent Damphousse, Mtl.	.50
□	McD22	Trevor Linden, Van.	.35
□	McD23	Patrick Roy (G), Col.	3.00
□	McD24	John Vanbiesbrouck (G), Fla.	1.25
□	McD25	Martin Brodeur (G), N.J.	1.50
□	McD26	Dominik Hasek (G), Buf.	1.50
□	McD27	Curtis Joseph (G), Edm.	1.25
□	McD28	Andy Moog (G), Mtl.	.35
□	McD29	Mike Richter (G), NYR.	.50
□	McD30	Damian Rhodes (G), Ott.	.35
□	McD31	Félix Potvin (G), Tor.	1.00
□	McD32	Chris Osgood (G), Det.	.75
□	McD33	Joe Thornton, Bos.	1.25
□	McD34	Patrick Marleau, S.J.	1.00
□	McD35	Jaroslav Svejkovsky, Wsh.	.35
□	McD36	Daniel Cleary, Chi.	.50
□	McD37	Chris Phillips, Ott.	.35
□	McD38	Alexei Morozov, Pgh.	1.00
□	McD39	Vaclav Prospal, Pha.	.35
□	McD40	Sergei Samsonov, Bos.	1.25

GAME FILM

Insert Set (10 cards): 125.00

	No.	Player	NRMT-MT
□	F1	Wayne Gretzky, NYR.	30.00
□	F2	Alexander Mogilny, Van.	5.00
□	F3	Steve Yzerman, Det.	15.00
□	F4	Eric Lindros, Pha.	20.00
□	F5	Patrick Roy (G), Col.	25.00
□	F6	Paul Kariya, Ana.	20.00
□	F7	Ray Bourque, Bos.	7.50
□	F8	Saku Koivu, Mtl.	10.00
□	F9	Theoren Fleury, Cgy.	5.00
□	F10	Mats Sundin, Tor.	7.50

WAYNE GRETZKY PRIZES

	Player	NRMT-MT
□	Wayne Gretzky 5" x 7" card	30.00
□	Wayne Gretzky Game Film (100 copies)	1,200.00

1997 - 98 MCDONALD'S MEDALLIONS

These medallions were sold at McDonald's Restaurants in Canada and feature members of the 1998 Canadian Olympic team.

Imprint: none - McDonald's logo.

Complete Set (12 medallions): 20.00

Medallion Holder: 3.00

	Player	NRMT-MT
□	Team Canada/ Patrick Roy	3.50
□	Curtis Joseph/ Martin Brodeur	2.00
□	Rob Blake/ Al MacInnis	1.00
□	Adam Foote/ Eric Desjardins	1.00
□	Chris Pronger/ Ray Bourque	1.50
□	Scott Stevens/ Rob Zamuner	1.00
□	Wayne Gretzky/ Joe Sakic	5.00
□	Paul Kariya/ Theoren Fleury	3.00
□	Trevor Linden/ Rod Brind'Amour	1.00
□	Eric Lindros/ Joe Nieuwendyk	3.00
□	Brendan Shanahan/ Shayne Corson	2.00
□	Steve Yzerman/ Keith Primeau	3.00

1997 - 98 OMEGA

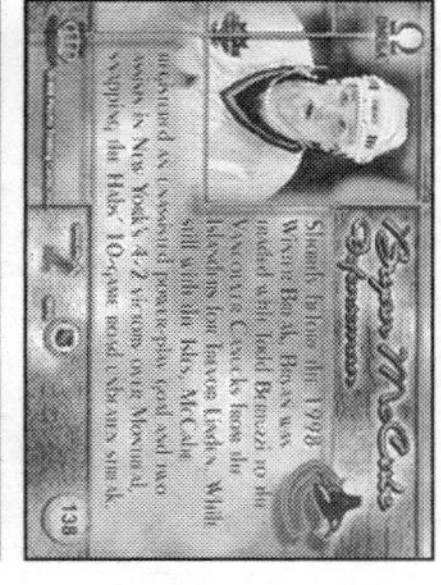

These cards have six versions: the regular silver card, a Gold parallel (retail), a Dark Grey parallel, a Copper parallel (hobby), an Emerald Green parallel (Canadian packs) and an Ice Blue parallel (limited to 67 copies). The Gold, Copper and Emerald Green parallels sell at approximately the same value. The Dark Grey parallel sells at two times the regular parallels. A Dark Grey set sells at $400.

Imprint: © 1997 PACIFIC TRADING CARDS, INC.

	Ice Blue	Par.	Reg.
Complete Set (250 cards):		**250.00**	**40.00**
Common Player:	**15.00**	**.50**	**.15**
Sample Card (Mike Modano):			**1.00**

No.	Player	Ice Blue	Par.	Reg.
1	**Matt Cullen, Ana., RC**	**15.00**	**.50**	**.15**
2	Guy Hebert (G), Ana.	25.00	1.50	.35
3	Paul Kariya, Ana.	250.00	10.00	2.00
4	Dmitri Mironov, Ana.	15.00	.50	.15
5	Steve Rucchin, Ana.	15.00	.50	.15
6	Tomas Sandström, Ana.	15.00	.50	.15
7	Teemu Selänne, Ana.	125.00	5.00	1.00
8	Mikhail Shtalenkov (G), Ana.	15.00	.50	.15
9	**Pavel Trnka, Ana., RC**	**15.00**	**.50**	**.15**
10	Jason Allison, Bos.	40.00	2.25	.50
11	Per-Johan Axelsson, Bos.	15.00	.50	.15
12	Ray Bourque, Bos.	80.00	3.75	.75
13	Anson Carter, Bos.	15.00	.50	.15
14	Byron Dafoe (G), Bos.	15.00	.50	.15
15	Ted Donato, Bos.	15.00	.50	.15
16	**Hal Gill, Bos., RC**	**15.00**	**.50**	**.15**
17	Dimitri Khristich, Bos.	15.00	.50	.15
18	Sergei Samsonov, Bos.	80.00	4.00	.85
19	Joe Thornton, Bos.	80.00	4.00	.85
20	Jason Dawe, Buf.	15.00	.50	.15
21	Michal Grosek, Buf.	15.00	.50	.15
22	Dominik Hasek (G), Buf.	125.00	5.00	1.00
23	Brian Holzinger, Buf.	15.00	.50	.15
24	Michael Peca, Buf.	25.00	1.50	.35
25	Derek Plante, Buf.	15.00	.50	.15
26	Miroslav Satan, Buf.	15.00	.50	.15
27	**Steve Shields (G), Buf., RC**	**25.00**	**1.50**	**.35**
28	Andrew Cassels, Cgy.	15.00	.50	.15
29	Theoren Fleury, Cgy.	40.00	2.25	.50
30	Jarome Iginla, Cgy.	40.00	2.25	.50
31	**Derek Morris, Cgy., RC**	**25.00**	**1.50**	**.35**
32	**Tyler Moss (G), Cgy., RC**	**25.00**	**1.50**	**.35**
33	Michael Nylander, Cgy.	15.00	.50	.15
34	Dwayne Roloson (G), Cgy.	15.00	.50	.15
35	Cory Stillman, Cgy.	15.00	.50	.15
36	Rick Tabaracci (G), Cgy.	15.00	.50	.15
37	German Titov, Cgy.	15.00	.50	.15
38	**Jon Battaglia, Cgy., RC**	**15.00**	**.50**	**.15**
39	Nelson Emerson, Car.	15.00	.50	.15
40	Martin Gelinas, Car.	15.00	.50	.15
41	Sami Kapanen, Car.	15.00	.50	.15
42	Trevor Kidd (G), Car.	25.00	1.50	.35
43	Kirk McLean (G), Car.	25.00	1.50	.35
44	Keith Primeau, Car.	25.00	1.50	.35
45	Gary Roberts, Car.	25.00	1.50	.35
46	Tony Amonte, Chi.	25.00	1.50	.35
47	Keith Carney, Chi.	15.00	.50	.15
48	Chris Chelios, Chi.	60.00	3.00	.60
49	Eric Dazé, Chi.	25.00	1.50	.35
50	**Brian Felsner, Chi., RC**	**15.00**	**.50**	**.15**
51	Jeff Hackett (G), Chi.	25.00	1.50	.35
52	**Christian Laflamme, Chi., RC**	**15.00**	**.50**	**.15**
53	Alexei Zhamnov, Chi.	15.00	.50	.15
54	Craig Billington (G), Col.	15.00	.50	.15
55	Adam Deadmarsh, Col.	15.00	.50	.15
56	Peter Forsberg, Col.	200.00	7.50	1.50
57	Valeri Kamensky, Col.	25.00	1.50	.35
58	Uwe Krupp, Col.	15.00	.50	.15
59	Jari Kurri, Col.	25.00	1.50	.35
60	Claude Lemieux, Col.	15.00	.50	.15
61	**Eric Messier, Col., RC**	**15.00**	**.50**	**.15**
62	Jeff Odgers, Col.	15.00	.50	.15
63	Sandis Ozolinsh, Col.	25.00	1.50	.35
64	Patrick Roy (G), Col.	300.00	12.00	2.50
65	Joe Sakic, Col.	150.00	6.00	1.25
66	Greg Adams, Dal.	15.00	.50	.15
67	Ed Belfour (G), Dal.	40.00	2.25	.50
68	Manny Fernandez (G), Dal.	15.00	.50	.15
69	Derian Hatcher, Dal.	25.00	1.50	.35
70	Jamie Langenbrunner, Dal.	25.00	1.50	.35
71	Jere Lehtinen, Dal.	25.00	1.50	.35
72	**Juha Lind, Dal., RC**	**15.00**	**.50**	**.15**
73	Mike Modano, Dal.	80.00	3.75	.75
74	Joe Nieuwendyk, Dal.	25.00	1.50	.35
75	Darryl Sydor, Dal.	15.00	.50	.15
76	Pat Verbeek, Dal.	15.00	.50	.15
77	Sergei Zubov, Dal.	25.00	1.50	.35
78	Viacheslav Fetisov, Det.	25.00	1.50	.35
79	Brent Gilchrist, Det.	15.00	.50	.15
80	Kevin Hodson (G), Det.	15.00	.50	.15
81	Vyacheslav Kozlov, Det.	15.00	.50	.15
82	Igor Larionov, Det.	25.00	1.50	.35
83	Nicklas Lidström, Det.	25.00	1.50	.35
84	Darren McCarty, Det.	15.00	.50	.15
85	Larry Murphy, Det.	25.00	1.50	.35
86	Chris Osgood (G), Det.	60.00	3.00	.60
87	Brendan Shanahan, Det.	100.00	4.50	.85
88	Steve Yzerman, Det.	200.00	7.50	1.50
89	Kelly Buchberger, Edm.	15.00	.50	.15
90	Mike Grier, Edm.	25.00	1.50	.35
91	Bill Guerin, Edm.	25.00	1.50	.35
92	Roman Hamrlik, Edm.	25.00	1.50	.35
93	Curtis Joseph (G), Edm.	100.00	4.50	.85
94	Boris Mironov, Edm.	15.00	.50	.15
95	Ryan Smyth, Edm.	25.00	1.50	.35
96	Doug Weight, Edm.	40.00	2.25	.50
97	Dino Ciccarelli, Fla.	25.00	1.50	.35
98	Dave Gagner, Fla.	15.00	.50	.15
99	Ed Jovanovski, Fla.	25.00	1.50	.35
100	Scott Mellanby, Fla.	15.00	.50	.15
101	Robert Svehla, Fla.	15.00	.50	.15
102	John Vanbiesbrouck (G), Fla.	100.00	4.50	.85
103	Steve Washburn, Fla.	15.00	.50	.15
104	**Kevin Weekes (G), Fla., RC**	**25.00**	**1.50**	**.35**
105	Ray Whitney, Fla.	15.00	.50	.15
106	Rob Blake, L.A.	25.00	1.50	.35
107	Stéphane Fiset (G), L.A.	25.00	1.50	.35
108	Garry Galley, L.A.	40.00	2.50	.75
109	**Steve McKenna, L.A., RC**	**15.00**	**.50**	**.15**
110	Glen Murray, L.A.	15.00	.50	.15
111	Yanic Perreault, L.A.	15.00	.50	.15
112	Luc Robitaille, L.A.	25.00	1.50	.35
113	Jamie Storr (G), L.A.	25.00	1.50	.35
114	Jozef Stumpel, L.A.	25.00	1.50	.35
115	Vladimir Tsyplakov, L.A.	15.00	.50	.15
116	Shayne Corson, Mtl.	25.00	1.50	.35
117	Vincent Damphousse, Mtl.	40.00	2.25	.50
118	Saku Koivu, Mtl.	125.00	5.00	1.00
119	Vladimir Malakhov, Mtl.	15.00	.50	.15
120	Andy Moog (G), Mtl.	25.00	1.50	.35
121	Mark Recchi, Mtl.	25.00	1.50	.35
122	Martin Rucinsky, Mtl.	15.00	.50	.15
123	Brian Savage, Mtl.	15.00	.50	.15
124	Jocelyn Thibault (G), Mtl.	40.00	2.25	.50
125	Jason Arnott, N.J.	25.00	1.50	.35
126	**Brad Bombardir, N.J., RC**	**15.00**	**.50**	**.15**
127	Martin Brodeur (G), N.J.	125.00	5.00	1.00
128	**Patrik Elias, N.J., RC**	**25.00**	**1.50**	**.50**
129	Doug Gilmour, N.J.	40.00	2.25	.50
130	Bobby Holik, N.J.	15.00	.50	.15
131	Randy McKay, N.J.	15.00	.50	.15
132	Scott Niedermayer, N.J.	25.00	1.50	.35
133	**Krzysztof Oliwa, N.J., RC**	**15.00**	**.50**	**.15**
134	Scott Stevens, N.J.	15.00	.50	.15
135	Petr Sykora, N.J.	15.00	.50	.15
136	Bryan Berard, NYI.	40.00	2.25	.50
137	Travis Green, NYI.	15.00	.50	.15
138	Bryan McCabe, NYI.	15.00	.50	.15
139	Sergei Nemchinov, NYI.	15.00	.50	.15
140	Zigmund Palffy, NYI.	40.00	2.25	.50
141	Robert Reichel, NYI.	15.00	.50	.15
142	Tommy Salo (G), NYI.	15.00	.50	.15
143	Bryan Smolinski, NYI.	15.00	.50	.15
144	Adam Graves, NYR.	15.00	.50	.15
145	Wayne Gretzky, NYR.	400.00	15.00	3.00
146	Pat LaFontaine, NYR.	25.00	1.50	.35
147	Brian Leetch, NYR.	40.00	2.25	.50
148	Mike Richter (G), NYR.	25.00	1.50	.35
149	Kevin Stevens, NYR.	15.00	.50	.15
150	Niklas Sundstrom, NYR.	15.00	.50	.15
151	Tim Sweeney, NYR.	15.00	.50	.15
152	Daniel Alfredsson, Ott.	25.00	1.50	.35
153	**Magnus Arvedsson, Ott., RC**	**15.00**	**.50**	**.15**
154	Andreas Dackell, Ott.	15.00	.50	.15
155	Igor Kravchuk, Ott.	15.00	.50	.15
156	Shawn McEachern, Ott.	15.00	.50	.15
157	Damian Rhodes (G), Ott.	15.00	.50	.15
158	Ron Tugnutt (G), Ott.	15.00	.50	.15
159	Alexei Yashin, Ott.	60.00	3.00	.60
160	Rod Brind'Amour, Pha.	25.00	1.50	.35
161	Paul Coffey, Pha.	25.00	1.50	.35
162	Eric Desjardins, Pha.	25.00	1.50	.35
163	**Colin Forbes, Pha., RC**	**15.00**	**.50**	**.15**
164	Chris Gratton, Pha.	25.00	1.50	.35
165	Ron Hextall (G), Pha.	25.00	1.50	.35
166	Trent Klatt, Pha.	15.00	.50	.15
167	John LeClair, Pha.	80.00	3.75	.75
168	Eric Lindros, Pha.	250.00	10.00	2.00
169	Joel Otto, Pha.	15.00	.50	.15
170	Garth Snow (G), Pha.	15.00	.50	.15
171	Dainius Zubrus, Pha.	25.00	1.50	.35
172	Dallas Drake, Pho.	15.00	.50	.15
173	Mike Gartner, Pho.	25.00	1.50	.35
174	Nikolai Khabibulin (G), Pho.	40.00	2.25	.50
175	Teppo Numminen, Pho.	15.00	.50	.15
176	Jeremy Roenick, Pho.	40.00	2.25	.50
177	Keith Tkachuk, Pho.	60.00	3.00	.60
178	Rick Tocchet, Pho.	15.00	.50	.15
179	Oleg Tverdovsky, Pho.	15.00	.50	.15
180	Juha Ylönen, Pho.	15.00	.50	.15
181	Stu Barnes, Pgh.	15.00	.50	.15
182	Tom Barrasso (G), Pgh.	25.00	1.50	.35
183	Rob Brown, Pgh.	15.00	.50	.15
184	Ron Francis, Pgh.	40.00	2.25	.50
185	Kevin Hatcher, Pgh.	15.00	.50	.15
186	Jaromir Jagr, Pgh.	200.00	7.50	1.50
187	Alexei Morozov, Pgh.	50.00	3.00	.75
188	Ed Olczyk, Pgh.	15.00	.50	.15
189	Jim Campbell, Stl.	15.00	.50	.15
190	Geoff Courtnall, Stl.	15.00	.50	.15
191	Pavol Demitra, Stl.	15.00	.50	.15
192	Steve Duchesne, Stl.	15.00	.50	.15
193	Grant Fuhr (G), Stl.	25.00	1.50	.35
194	Brett Hull, Stl.	80.00	3.75	.75
195	Al MacInnis, Stl.	25.00	1.50	.35
196	Chris Pronger, Stl.	25.00	1.50	.35
197	**Pascal Rhéaume, Stl., RC**	**15.00**	**.50**	**.15**
198	Jamie Rivers, Stl.	15.00	.50	.15
199	Pierre Turgeon, Stl.	25.00	1.50	.35
200	Jeff Friesen, S.J.	25.00	1.50	.35
201	Tony Granato, S.J.	15.00	.50	.15
202	John MacLean, S.J.	15.00	.50	.15
203	Patrick Marleau, S.J.	50.00	3.00	.75
204	Marty McSorley, S.J.	15.00	.50	.15
205	Owen Nolan, S.J.	25.00	1.50	.35
206	**Marco Sturm, S.J., RC**	**25.00**	**1.50**	**.35**
207	Mike Vernon (G), S.J.	25.00	1.50	.35
208	**Andrei Zyuzin, S.J., RC**	**15.00**	**.50**	**.15**
209	Karl Dykhuis, T.B.	15.00	.50	.15
210	Daymond Langkow, T.B.	15.00	.50	.15
211	Bryan Marchment, T.B.	15.00	.50	.15
212	Daren Puppa (G), T.B.	15.00	.50	.15
213	Mikael Renberg, T.B.	15.00	.50	.15
214	Alexander Selivanov, T.B.	15.00	.50	.15
215	Paul Ysebaert, T.B.	15.00	.50	.15
216	Rob Zamuner, T.B.	25.00	1.50	.35
217	Sergei Berezin, Tor.	25.00	1.50	.35
218	Wendel Clark, Tor.	25.00	1.50	.35
219	Marcel Cousineau (G), Tor.	15.00	.50	.15
220	Tie Domi, Tor.	15.00	.50	.15
221	**Mike Johnson, Tor., RC**	**60.00**	**5.00**	**2.00**
222	Igor Korolev, Tor.	15.00	.50	.15
223	Félix Potvin (G), Tor.	80.00	3.75	.75
224	Mathieu Schneider, Tor.	15.00	.50	.15
225	Mats Sundin, Tor.	15.00	.50	.15
226	**Yannick Tremblay, Tor., RC**	**15.00**	**.50**	**.15**
227	Donald Brashear, Van.	15.00	.50	.15

	No.	Player			
□□□□□□	228	Pavel Bure, Van.	125.00	5.00	1.00
□□□□□□	229	Sean Burke (G), Van.	25.00	1.50	.35
□□□□□□	230	Trevor Linden, Van.	25.00	1.50	.35
□□□□□□	231	Mark Messier, Van.	80.00	3.75	.75
□□□□□□	232	Alexander Mogilny, Van.	40.00	2.25	.50
□□□□□□	233	Markus Naslund, Van.	15.00	.50	.15
□□□□□□	234	Mattias Ohlund, Van.	30.00	2.50	.50
□□□□□□	**235**	**Dave Scatchard, Van., RC**	**15.00**	**.50**	**.15**
□□□□□□	236	Peter Bondra, Wsh.	60.00	3.00	.60
□□□□□□	237	Andrew Brunette, Wsh.	15.00	.50	.15
□□□□□□	238	Phil Housley, Wsh.	15.00	.50	.15
□□□□□□	239	Dale Hunter, Wsh.	15.00	.50	.15
□□□□□□	240	Calle Johansson, Wsh.	15.00	.50	.15
□□□□□□	241	Joé Juneau, Wsh.	15.00	.50	.15
□□□□□□	242	Olaf Kolzig (G), Wsh.	40.00	2.25	.50
□□□□□□	243	Adam Oates, Wsh.	40.00	2.25	.50
□□□□□□	244	Richard Zednik, Wsh.	15.00	.50	.15
□□□□□□	245	Chris Chelios/ Keith Tkachuk	25.00	1.50	.35
□□□□□□	246	Mike Modano/ Ed Belfour	25.00	1.50	.35
□□□□□□	247	Teemu Selänne/ Saku Koivu	40.00	2.25	.50
□□□□□□	248	Eric Lindros/ Shayne Corson	125.00	5.00	1.00
□□□□□□	249	Patrick Roy (G)/ Martin Brodeur (G)	150.00	6.00	1.25
□□□□□□	250	Wayne Gretzky/ Mark Messier	250.00	7.50	1.50

NO SCORING ZONE

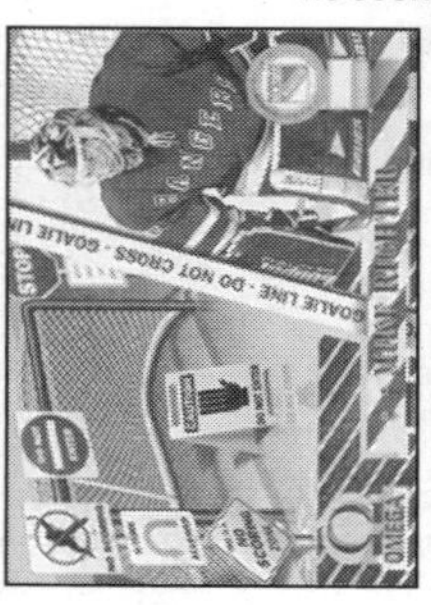

Insert Set (10 cards): 75.00

	No.	Player	NRMT-MT
□	1	Dominik Hasek (G), Buf.	12.00
□	2	Patrick Roy (G), Col.	20.00
□	3	Ed Belfour (G), Dal.	6.00
□	4	Chris Osgood (G), Det.	6.00
□	5	John Vanbiesbrouck (G), Fla.	8.00
□	6	Andy Moog (G), Mtl.	5.00
□	7	Martin Brodeur (G), N.J.	12.00
□	8	Mike Richter (G), NYR.	6.00
□	9	Ron Hextall (G), Pha.	5.00
□	10	Félix Potvin (G), Tor.	7.00

SILKS

Insert Set (12 cards): 300.00

	No.	Player	NRMT-MT
□	1	Paul Kariya, Ana.	40.00
□	2	Teemu Selänne, Ana.	20.00
□	3	Peter Forsberg, Col.	30.00
□	4	Patrick Roy (G), Col.	50.00
□	5	Joe Sakic, Col.	25.00
□	6	Steve Yzerman, Det.	30.00
□	7	Martin Brodeur (G), N.J.	20.00
□	8	Wayne Gretzky, NYR.	60.00
□	9	Eric Lindros, Pha.	40.00
□	10	Jaromir Jagr, Pgh.	30.00
□	11	Pavel Bure, Van.	20.00
□	12	Mark Messier, Van.	15.00

GAME FACE

Insert Set (20 cards): 300.00

	No.	Player	NRMT-MT
□	1	Paul Kariya, Ana.	25.00
□	2	Teemu Selänne, Ana.	15.00
□	3	Peter Forsberg, Col.	20.00
□	4	Joe Sakic, Col.	18.00
□	5	Mike Modano, Dal.	10.00
□	6	Nicklas Lidström, Det.	6.00
□	7	Brendan Shanahan, Det.	12.00
□	8	Steve Yzerman, Det.	20.00
□	9	Ryan Smyth, Edm.	6.00
□	10	Saku Koivu, Mtl.	15.00
□	11	Wayne Gretzky, NYR.	40.00
□	12	John LeClair, Pha.	10.00
□	13	Eric Lindros, Pha.	25.00
□	14	Dainius Zubrus, Pha.	6.00
□	15	Keith Tkachuk, Pho.	8.00
□	16	Jaromir Jagr, Pgh.	20.00
□	17	Brett Hull, Stl.	10.00
□	18	Pavel Bure, Van.	15.00
□	19	Mark Messier, Van.	10.00
□	20	Peter Bondra, Wsh.	8.00

STICK HANDLE

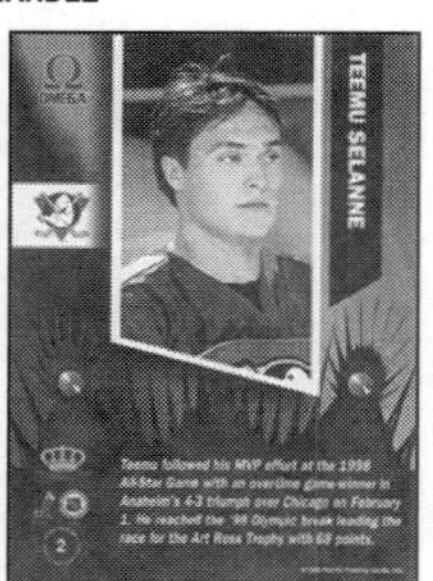

Insert Set (20 cards): 600.00

	No.	Player	NRMT-MT
□	1	Paul Kariya, Ana.	65.00
□	2	Teemu Selänne, Ana.	35.00
□	3	Theoren Fleury, Cgy.	15.00
□	4	Chris Chelios, Chi.	20.00
□	5	Peter Forsberg, Col.	50.00
□	6	Joe Sakic, Col.	40.00
□	7	Mike Modano, Dal.	25.00
□	8	Brendan Shanahan, Det.	30.00
□	9	Steve Yzerman, Det.	50.00
□	10	Saku Koivu, Mtl.	35.00
□	11	Doug Gilmour, N.J.	15.00
□	12	Zigmund Palffy, NYI.	15.00
□	13	Wayne Gretzky, NYR.	100.00
□	14	Pat LaFontaine, NYR.	12.00
□	15	John LeClair, Pha.	25.00
□	16	Eric Lindros, Pha.	50.00
□	17	Jaromir Jagr, Pgh.	25.00
□	18	Mats Sundin, Tor.	35.00
□	19	Pavel Bure, Van.	35.00
□	20	Mark Messier, Van.	25.00

1997 - 98 PACIFIC CROWN COLLECTION

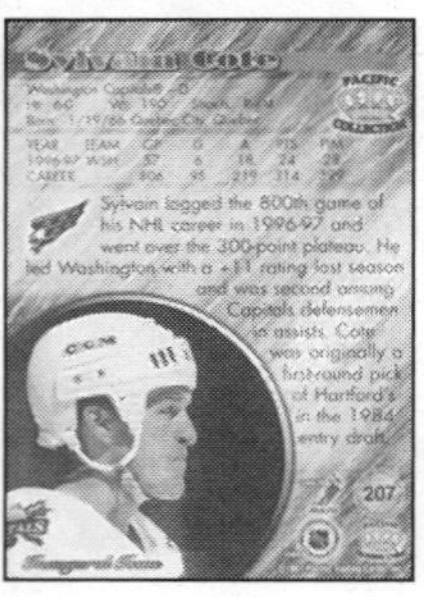

These cards have six versions: the regular card, an Emerald Green (Canadian) parallel, a Copper (Hobby) parallel, a Silver (Retail) parallel, a Red parallel and an Ice Blue (limited to 67 copies) parallel. The Green, Copper and Silver parallels all sell at approximately the same price. The Red parallel sells at two times the regular parallels. A Red set sells at $600. There is no card #66 in this set. It was retired in recognition of Mario Lemieux.

Imprint: © 1997 PACIFIC TRADING CARDS, INC.

Complete Set (350 cards): 350.00 40.00

Common Player: 20.00 .50 .15

	No.	Player	Ice Blue	Par.	Reg.
□□□□□□	1	Ray Bourque, Bos.	85.00	3.00	.75
□□□□□□	2	Brian Leetch, NYR.	45.00	2.00	.50
□□□□□□	3	Claude Lemieux, Col.	20.00	.60	.15
□□□□□□	4	Mike Modano, Dal.	85.00	3.00	.75
□□□□□□	5	Zigmund Palffy, NYI.	45.00	2.00	.50
□□□□□□	6	Nikolai Khabibulin (G), Pho.	45.00	2.00	.50
□□□□□□	7	Chris Chelios, Chi.	65.00	2.50	.60
□□□□□□	8	Teemu Selänne, Ana.	150.00	6.00	1.00
□□□□□□	9	Paul Kariya, Ana.	375.00	12.00	2.00
□□□□□□	10	John LeClair, Pha.	85.00	3.00	.75
□□□□□□	11	Mark Messier, NYR.	85.00	3.00	.75
□□□□□□	12	Jarome Iginla, Cgy.	45.00	2.00	.50
□□□□□□	13	Petr Nedved, Pgh.	20.00	.60	.15
□□□□□□	14	Brendan Shanahan, Det.	110.00	4.00	.85
□□□□□□	15	Dino Ciccarelli, T.B.	30.00	1.50	.35
□□□□□□	16	Brett Hull, Stl.	85.00	3.00	.75
□□□□□□	17	Wendel Clark, Tor.	30.00	1.50	.35
□□□□□□	18	Peter Bondra, Wsh.	65.00	2.50	.60
□□□□□□	19	Steve Yzerman, Det.	300.00	10.00	1.50
□□□□□□	20	Ed Belfour (G), S.J.	45.00	2.00	.50
□□□□□□	21	Peter Forsberg, Col.	300.00	10.00	1.50
□□□□□□	22	Mike Gartner, Pho.	30.00	1.50	.35
□□□□□□	23	Jim Carey (G), Bos.	20.00	.60	.15
□□□□□□	24	Mike Vernon (G), Det.	30.00	1.50	.35
□□□□□□	25	Vincent Damphousse, Mtl.	45.00	2.00	.50
□□□□□□	26	Adam Graves, NYR.	20.00	.60	.15
□□□□□□	27	Ron Hextall (G), Pha.	30.00	1.50	.35
□□□□□□	28	Keith Tkachuk, Pho.	65.00	2.50	.60
□□□□□□	29	Félix Potvin (G), Tor.	85.00	3.00	.75
□□□□□□	30	Martin Brodeur (G), N.J.	150.00	6.00	1.00
□□□□□□	31	Rod Brind'Amour, Pha.	30.00	1.50	.35
□□□□□□	32	Pierre Turgeon, Stl.	30.00	1.50	.35
□□□□□□	33	Patrick Roy (G), Col.	450.00	16.00	2.50
□□□□□□	34	John Vanbiesbrouck (G), Fla.	110.00	4.00	.85
□□□□□□	35	Andy Moog (G), Dal.	30.00	1.50	.35
□□□□□□	36	Sergei Berezin, Tor.	30.00	1.50	.35
□□□□□□	37	Adam Oates, Wsh.	45.00	2.00	.50
□□□□□□	38	Joe Sakic, Col.	200.00	8.00	1.25
□□□□□□	39	Dominik Hasek (G), Buf.	150.00	6.00	1.00
□□□□□□	40	Patrick Lalime (G), Pgh.	20.00	.60	.15
□□□□□□	41	Bobby Dollas, Ana.	20.00	.60	.15
□□□□□□	42	Kyle McLaren, Bos.	20.00	.60	.15
□□□□□□	43	Wayne Primeau, Buf.	20.00	.60	.15
□□□□□□	44	Stéphane Richer, Mtl.	20.00	.60	.15
□□□□□□	45	Theoren Fleury, Cgy.	45.00	2.00	.50
□□□□□□	46	Kevin Miller, Chi.	20.00	.60	.15
□□□□□□	47	Adam Deadmarsh, Col.	20.00	.60	.15
□□□□□□	48	Darryl Sydor, Dal.	20.00	.60	.15
□□□□□□	49	Igor Larionov, Det.	30.00	1.50	.35
□□□□□□	50	Radek Dvorak, Fla.	20.00	.60	.15
□□□□□□	51	Andrei Kovalenko, Edm.	20.00	.60	.15
□□□□□□	52	Keith Primeau, Hfd.	30.00	1.50	.35
□□□□□□	53	Ray Ferraro, L.A.	20.00	.60	.15
□□□□□□	54	David Wilkie, Mtl.	20.00	.60	.15
□□□□□□	55	Bobby Holik, N.J.	20.00	.60	.15
□□□□□□	56	Tommy Salo (G), NYI.	20.00	.60	.15
□□□□□□	57	Jeff Beukeboom, NYR.	20.00	.60	.15

58	Daniel Alfredsson, Ott.	30.00	1.50	.35
59	Mikael Renberg, Pha.	20.00	.60	.15
60	Norm Maciver, Pho.	20.00	.60	.15
61	Darius Kasparaitis, Pgh.	20.00	.60	.15
62	Geoff Courtnall, Stl.	20.00	.60	.15
63	Jeff Friesen, S.J.	30.00	1.50	.35
64	Brian Bradley, T.B.	20.00	.60	.15
65	Tie Domi, Tor.	20.00	.60	.15
67	Martin Gelinas, Van.	20.00	.60	.15
68	Jaromir Jagr, Pgh.	300.00	10.00	1.50
69	Steve Konowalchuk, Wsh.	20.00	.60	.15
70	Brian Bellows, Ana.	20.00	.60	.15
71	Jozef Stumpel, Bos.	30.00	1.50	.35
72	Darryl Shannon, Buf.	20.00	.60	.15
73	Todd Simpson, Cgy.	20.00	.60	.15
74	Ulf Dahlen, Chi.	20.00	.60	.15
75	Sandis Ozolinsh, Col.	30.00	1.50	.35
76	Sergei Zubov, Dal.	30.00	1.50	.35
77	Paul Coffey, Pha.	30.00	1.50	.35
78	Nicklas Lidström, Det.	30.00	1.50	.35
79	Jason Arnott, Edm.	30.00	1.50	.35
80	Ray Sheppard, Fla.	20.00	.60	.15
81	Sean Burke (G), Hfd.	30.00	1.50	.35
82	Vladimir Tsyplakov, L.A.	20.00	.60	.15
83	Darcy Tucker, Mtl.	20.00	.60	.15
84	Dave Andreychuk, N.J.	20.00	.60	.15
85	Scott Lachance, NYI.	20.00	.60	.15
86	Niklas Sundstrom, NYR.	20.00	.60	.15
87	Ron Tugnutt (G), Ott.	20.00	.60	.15
88	Eric Lindros, Pha.	375.00	12.00	2.00
89	Alexander Mogilny, Van.	45.00	2.00	.50
90	Kris King, Pho.	20.00	.60	.15
91	Sergei Fedorov, Det.	85.00	3.00	.75
92	Ed Olczyk, Pgh.	20.00	.60	.15
93	Doug Gilmour, N.J.	45.00	2.00	.50
94	Ryan Smyth, Edm.	30.00	1.50	.35
95	Scott Pellerin, Stl.	20.00	.60	.15
96	Pavel Bure, Van.	150.00	6.00	1.00
97	Jeremy Roenick, Pho.	45.00	2.00	.50
98	Todd Gill, S.J.	20.00	.60	.15
99	Wayne Gretzky, NYR.	600.00	20.00	3.50
100	Roman Hamrlik, T.B.	30.00	1.50	.35
101	Rob Zettler, Tor.	20.00	.60	.15
102	Sergei Nemchinov, Van.	20.00	.60	.15
103	Sergei Gonchar, Wsh.	20.00	.60	.15
104	Steve Rucchin, Ana.	20.00	.60	.15
105	Landon Wilson, Bos.	20.00	.60	.15
106	Anatoli Semenov, Buf.	20.00	.60	.15
107	Corey Millen, Cgy.	20.00	.60	.15
108	Eric Dazé, Chi.	30.00	1.50	.35
109	Mike Ricci, Col.	20.00	.60	.15
110	Jamie Langenbrunner, Dal.	30.00	1.50	.35
111	Viacheslav Fetisov, Det.	30.00	1.50	.35
112	Rem Murray, Edm.	20.00	.60	.15
113	Tom Fitzgerald, Fla.	20.00	.60	.15
114	Robert Kron, Hfd.	20.00	.60	.15
115	Kevin Stevens, L.A.	20.00	.60	.15
116	Valeri Bure, Mtl.	20.00	.60	.15
117	Bill Guerin, N.J.	30.00	1.50	.35
118	Bryan McCabe, NYI.	20.00	.60	.15
119	Alexei Kovalev, NYR.	20.00	.60	.15
120	Alexei Yashin, Ott.	65.00	2.50	.60
121	Eric Desjardins, Pha.	30.00	1.50	.35
122	Teppo Numminen, Pho.	20.00	.60	.15
123	Ron Francis, Pgh.	45.00	2.00	.50
124	Chris Pronger, Stl.	30.00	1.50	.35
125	Viktor Kozlov, S.J.	20.00	.60	.15
126	Corey Schwab (G), T.B.	20.00	.60	.15
127	Fredrik Modin, Tor.	20.00	.60	.15
128	Markus Naslund, Van.	20.00	.60	.15
129	Dale Hunter, Wsh.	20.00	.60	.15
130	Warren Rychel, Ana.	20.00	.60	.15
131	Anson Carter, Bos.	20.00	.60	.15
132	Miroslav Satan, Buf.	20.00	.60	.15
133	Trevor Kidd (G), Cgy.	30.00	1.50	.35
134	Sergei Krivokrasov, Chi.	20.00	.60	.15
135	Adam Foote, Col.	30.00	1.50	.35
136	Brent Gilchrist, Dal.	20.00	.60	.15
137	Chris Osgood (G), Det.	65.00	2.50	.60
138	Doug Weight, Edm.	45.00	2.00	.50
139	Martin Straka, Fla.	20.00	.60	.15
140	Jeff O'Neill, Hfd.	30.00	1.50	.35
141	Byron Dafoe, L.A.	20.00	.60	.15
142	Brian Savage, Mtl.	20.00	.60	.15
143	Lyle Odelein, N.J.	20.00	.60	.15
144	Niklas Andersson, NYI.	20.00	.60	.15
145	Luc Robitaille, NYR.	30.00	1.50	.35
146	Damian Rhodes (G), Ott.	20.00	.60	.15
147	Garth Snow (G), Pha.	20.00	.60	.15
148	Craig Janney, Pho.	20.00	.60	.15
149	Fredrik Olausson, Pgh.	20.00	.60	.15
150	Joe Murphy, Stl.	20.00	.60	.15
151	Owen Nolan, S.J.	30.00	1.50	.35
152	Shawn Burr, T.B.	20.00	.60	.15
153	Dimitri Yushkevich, Tor.	20.00	.60	.15
154	Trevor Linden, Van.	30.00	1.50	.35
155	Joé Juneau, Wsh.	20.00	.60	.15
156	Sean Pronger, Ana.	20.00	.60	.15
157	Jeff Odgers, Bos.	20.00	.60	.15
158	Brian Holzinger, Buf.	20.00	.60	.15
159	Dave Gagner, Cgy.	20.00	.60	.15
160	Jeff Hackett (G), Chi.	30.00	1.50	.35
161	Eric Lacroix, Col.	20.00	.60	.15
162	Pat Verbeek, Dal.	20.00	.60	.15
163	Darren McCarty, Det.	20.00	.60	.15
164	Mike Grier, Edm.	30.00	1.50	.35
165	Per Gustafsson, Fla.	20.00	.60	.15
166	Andrew Cassels, Hfd.	20.00	.60	.15
167	Vitali Yachmenev, L.A.	20.00	.60	.15
168	Jocelyn Thibault (G), Mtl.	45.00	2.00	.50
169	John MacLean, N.J.	20.00	.60	.15
170	Travis Green, NYI.	20.00	.60	.15
171	Ulf Samuelsson, NYR.	20.00	.60	.15
172	**Bruce Gardiner, Ott., RC**	**20.00**	**.60**	**.15**
173	Janne Niinimaa, Pha.	30.00	1.50	.35
174	Jim Johnson, Pho.	20.00	.60	.15
175	Stu Barnes, Pgh.	20.00	.60	.15
176	Harry York, Stl.	20.00	.60	.15
177	Al Iafrate, S.J.	20.00	.60	.15
178	Paul Ysebaert, T.B.	20.00	.60	.15
179	Mathieu Schneider, Tor.	20.00	.60	.15
180	Corey Hirsch (G), Van.	20.00	.60	.15
181	Mark Tinordi, Wsh.	20.00	.60	.15
182	Kevin Todd, Ana.	20.00	.60	.15
183	Tim Sweeney, Bos.	20.00	.60	.15
184	Donald Audette, Buf.	20.00	.60	.15
185	Jonas Hoglund, Cgy.	20.00	.60	.15
186	Brent Sutter, Chi.	20.00	.60	.15
187	Scott Young, Col.	20.00	.60	.15
188	Arturs Irbe (G), Dal.	20.00	.60	.15
189	Vladimir Konstantinov, Det.	20.00	.60	.15
190	Mats Lindgren, Edm.	20.00	.60	.15
191	Dave Nemirovsky, Fla.	20.00	.60	.15
192	Sami Kapanen, Hfd.	20.00	.60	.15
193	Rob Blake, L.A.	30.00	1.50	.35
194	Sébastien Bordeleau, Mtl.	20.00	.60	.15
195	Steve Thomas, N.J.	20.00	.60	.15
196	Bryan Smolinski, NYI.	20.00	.60	.15
197	Mike Richter (G), NYR.	45.00	2.00	.50
198	Randy Cunneyworth, Ott.	20.00	.60	.15
199	Pat Falloon, Pha.	20.00	.60	.15
200	Cliff Ronning, Pho.	20.00	.60	.15
201	Ken Wregget (G), Pgh.	20.00	.60	.15
202	Al MacInnis, Stl.	30.00	1.50	.35
203	Tony Granato, S.J.	20.00	.60	.15
204	Rob Zamuner, T.B.	30.00	1.50	.35
205	Mats Sundin, Tor.	85.00	3.00	.75
206	Mike Ridley, Van.	20.00	.60	.15
207	Sylvain Côté, Wsh.	20.00	.60	.15
208	Joe Sacco, Ana.	20.00	.60	.15
209	Ted Donato, Bos.	20.00	.60	.15
210	Matthew Barnaby, Buf.	20.00	.60	.15
211	Cory Stillman, Cgy.	20.00	.60	.15
212	Gary Suter, Chi.	20.00	.60	.15
213	Valeri Kamensky, Col.	30.00	1.50	.35
214	Derian Hatcher, Dal.	30.00	1.50	.35
215	Jamie Pushor, Det.	20.00	.60	.15
216	Mariusz Czerkawski, Edm.	20.00	.60	.15
217	Kirk Muller, Fla.	20.00	.60	.15
218	Kevin Dineen, Hfd.	20.00	.60	.15
219	Dimitri Khristich, L.A.	20.00	.60	.15
220	Martin Rucinsky, Mtl.	20.00	.60	.15
221	Denis Pederson, N.J.	20.00	.60	.15
222	Bryan Berard, NYI.	20.00	.60	.15
223	Alexander Karpovtsev, NYR.	20.00	.60	.15
224	Shawn McEachern, Ott.	20.00	.60	.15
225	Dale Hawerchuk, Pha.	30.00	1.50	.35
226	Bob Corkum, Pho.	20.00	.60	.15
227	Kevin Hatcher, Pgh.	20.00	.60	.15
229	Darren Turcotte, S.J.	20.00	.60	.15
230	Patrick Poulin, T.B.	20.00	.60	.15
231	Jamie Macoun, Tor.	20.00	.60	.15
232	Jyrki Lumme, Van.	20.00	.60	.15
233	Bill Ranford (G), Wsh.	30.00	1.50	.35
234	Dmitri Mironov, Ana.	20.00	.60	.15
235	Mattias Timander, Bos.	20.00	.60	.15
236	Alexei Zhitnik, Buf.	20.00	.60	.15
237	Hnat Domenichelli, Cgy.	30.00	1.50	.35
238	Murray Craven, Chi.	20.00	.60	.15
239	Mike Keane, Col.	20.00	.60	.15
240	Benoît Hogue, Dal.	20.00	.60	.15
241	Martin Lapointe, Det.	20.00	.60	.15
242	Curtis Joseph (G), Edm.	110.00	4.00	.85
243	Robert Svehla, Fla.	20.00	.60	.15
244	Glen Wesley, Hfd.	20.00	.60	.15
245	Stéphane Fiset (G), L.A.	30.00	1.50	.35
246	Shayne Corson, Mtl.	30.00	1.50	.35
247	Scott Niedermayer, N.J.	30.00	1.50	.35
248	**Steve Webb, NYI., RC**	**20.00**	**.60**	**.15**
249	Esa Tikkanen, NYR.	20.00	.60	.15
250	Alexandre Daigle, Ott.	20.00	.60	.15
251	Trent Klatt, Pha.	20.00	.60	.15
252	Oleg Tverdovsky, Pho.	20.00	.60	.15
253	Dave Roche, Pgh.	20.00	.60	.15
254	Tony Twist, Stl.	20.00	.60	.15
255	Bernie Nicholls, S.J.	20.00	.60	.15
256	Rick Tabaracci (G), T.B.	20.00	.60	.15
258	Kirk McLean (G), Van.	30.00	1.50	.35
257	Todd Warriner, Tor.	20.00	.60	.15
259	Phil Housley, Wsh.	20.00	.60	.15
260	Guy Hebert (G), Ana.	30.00	1.50	.35
261	Steve Heinze, Bos.	20.00	.60	.15
262	Derek Plante, Buf.	20.00	.60	.15
263	German Titov, Cgy.	20.00	.60	.15
264	Tony Amonte, Chi.	30.00	1.50	.35
265	Uwe Krupp, Col.	20.00	.60	.15
266	Joe Nieuwendyk, Dal.	30.00	1.50	.35
267	Vyacheslav Kozlov, Det.	20.00	.60	.15
268	Kelly Buchberger, Edm.	20.00	.60	.15
269	Rob Niedermayer, Fla.	20.00	.60	.15
270	Geoff Sanderson, Hfd.	20.00	.60	.15
271	Jan Vopat, L.A.	20.00	.60	.15
272	Saku Koivu, Mtl.	150.00	6.00	1.00
273	Scott Stevens, N.J.	20.00	.60	.15
274	Eric Fichaud (G), NYI.	30.00	1.50	.35
275	Russ Courtnall, NYR.	20.00	.60	.15
276	Wade Redden, Ott.	20.00	.60	.15
277	Petr Svoboda, Pha.	20.00	.60	.15
278	Andreas Dackell, Ott.	20.00	.60	.15
279	Jason Woolley, Pgh.	20.00	.60	.15
280	Stéphane Matteau, Stl.	20.00	.60	.15
281	**Stephen Guolla, S.J., RC**	**20.00**	**.60**	**.15**
282	John Cullen, T.B.	20.00	.60	.15
283	Steve Sullivan, Tor.	20.00	.60	.15
284	Bret Hedican, Van.	20.00	.60	.15
285	Michal Pivonka, Wsh.	20.00	.60	.15
286	Darren Van Impe, Ana.	20.00	.60	.15
287	Rob DiMaio, Bos.	20.00	.60	.15
288	Garry Galley, Buf.	20.00	.60	.15
289	Kent Manderville, Cgy.	20.00	.60	.15
290	Bob Probert, Chi.	20.00	.60	.15
291	Keith Jones, Col.	20.00	.60	.15
292	Guy Carbonneau, Dal.	20.00	.60	.15
293	Tomas Sandström, Det.	20.00	.60	.15
294	**Daniel McGillis, Edm., RC**	**20.00**	**.60**	**.15**
295	Brian Skrudland, Fla.	20.00	.60	.15
296	Stu Grimson, Hfd.	20.00	.60	.15
297	Doug Zmolek, Bos.	20.00	.60	.15
298	Mark Recchi, Mtl.	30.00	1.50	.35
299	Valeri Zelepukin, N.J.	20.00	.60	.15
300	Derek Armstrong, NYI.	20.00	.60	.15
301	**Eric Cairns, NYR., RC**	**20.00**	**.60**	**.15**
302	Steve Duchesne, Ott.	20.00	.60	.15
303	Dainius Zubrus, Pha.	30.00	1.50	.35
304	Deron Quint, Pho.	20.00	.60	.15
305	Joe Dziedzic, Pgh.	20.00	.60	.15
306	Mike Peluso, Stl.	20.00	.60	.15
307	Andrei Nazarov, S.J.	20.00	.60	.15
308	Chris Gratton, T.B.	30.00	1.50	.35
309	Mike Craig, Tor.	20.00	.60	.15
310	Lonny Bohonos, Van.	20.00	.60	.15
311	Rick Tocchet, Wsh.	20.00	.60	.15
312	Ted Drury, Ana.	20.00	.60	.15
313	Jean-Yves Roy, Bos.	20.00	.60	.15
314	Jason Dawe, Buf.	20.00	.60	.15

☐☐☐☐☐☐	315	Jamie Allison, Cgy.	20.00	.60	.15
☐☐☐☐☐☐	316	Alexei Zhamnov, Chi.	20.00	.60	.15
☐☐☐☐☐☐	317	Aaron Miller, Col.	20.00	.60	.15
☐☐☐☐☐☐	318	Todd Krygier, Wsh.	20.00	.60	.15
☐☐☐☐☐☐	319	Tomas Holmström, Det.	30.00	1.50	.35
☐☐☐☐☐☐	320	Todd Marchant, Edm.	20.00	.60	.15
☐☐☐☐☐☐	321	Scott Mellanby, Fla.	20.00	.60	.15
☐☐☐☐☐☐	322	Marek Malik, Hfd.	20.00	.60	.15
☐☐☐☐☐☐	323	Dan Bylsma, L.A.	20.00	.60	.15
☐☐☐☐☐☐	324	Stéphane Quintal, Mtl.	20.00	.60	.15
☐☐☐☐☐☐	325	Ken Daneyko, N.J.	20.00	.60	.15
☐☐☐☐☐☐	326	Robert Reichel, NYI.	20.00	.60	.15
☐☐☐☐☐☐	327	Daniel Goneau, NYR.	20.00	.60	.15
☐☐☐☐☐☐	328	Sergei Zholtok, Ott.	20.00	.60	.15
☐☐☐☐☐☐	329	Kjell Samuelsson, Pha.	20.00	.60	.15
☐☐☐☐☐☐	330	Shane Doan, Pho.	20.00	.60	.15
☐☐☐☐☐☐	331	Radek Bonk, Ott.	20.00	.60	.15
☐☐☐☐☐☐	332	Jim Campbell, Stl.	20.00	.60	.15
☐☐☐☐☐☐	333	Marty McSorley, S.J.	20.00	.60	.15
☐☐☐☐☐☐	334	Brantt Myhres, T.B.	20.00	.60	.15
☐☐☐☐☐☐	**335**	**Mike Johnson, Tor., RC**	**65.00**	**6.00**	**3.00**
☐☐☐☐☐☐	336	Mike Sillinger, Van.	20.00	.60	.15
☐☐☐☐☐☐	337	Kelly Hrudey (G), S.J.	20.00	.60	.15
☐☐☐☐☐☐	338	Joel Bouchard, Cgy.	20.00	.60	.15
☐☐☐☐☐☐	339	Brian Noonan, Van.	20.00	.60	.15
☐☐☐☐☐☐	340	Dean Chynoweth, Bos.	20.00	.60	.15
☐☐☐☐☐☐	341	Michael Peca, Buf.	30.00	1.50	.35
☐☐☐☐☐☐	**342**	**Jeff Toms, T.B., RC**	**20.00**	**.60**	**.15**
☐☐☐☐☐☐	343	Denis Savard, Chi.	30.00	1.50	.35
☐☐☐☐☐☐	344	Stéphane Yelle, Col.	20.00	.60	.15
☐☐☐☐☐☐	345	Grant Ledyard, Dal.	20.00	.60	.15
☐☐☐☐☐☐	346	Ronnie Stern, Cgy.	20.00	.60	.15
☐☐☐☐☐☐	347	Petr Klima, Edm.	20.00	.60	.15
☐☐☐☐☐☐	348	Johan Garpenlov, Fla.	20.00	.60	.15
☐☐☐☐☐☐	349	Nelson Emerson, Hfd.	20.00	.60	.15
☐☐☐☐☐☐	350	Matt Johnson, L.A.	20.00	.60	.15
☐☐☐☐☐☐	**351**	**Ken Belanger, NYI., RC**	**20.00**	**.60**	**.15**

CARD-SUPIALS

Insert Set (20 mini + 20 standard-sized cards): 400.00

	No.	Player	Mini	Reg.
☐☐	1	Paul Kariya, Ana.	15.00	30.00
☐☐	2	Teemu Selänne, Ana.	7.50	15.00
☐☐	3	Jarome Iginla, Cgy.	3.00	6.00
☐☐	4	Peter Forsberg, Col.	12.00	25.00
☐☐	5	Mike Modano, Dal.	6.00	12.00
☐☐	6	Sergei Fedorov, Det.	6.00	12.00
☐☐	7	Vladimir Konstantinov, Det.	2.50	5.00
☐☐	8	Steve Yzerman, Det.	12.00	25.00
☐☐	9	John Vanbiesbrouck (G), Fla.	7.50	15.00
☐☐	10	Martin Brodeur (G), N.J.	9.00	18.00
☐☐	11	Doug Gilmour, N.J.	3.00	6.00
☐☐	12	Wayne Gretzky, NYR.	25.00	45.00
☐☐	13	Mark Messier, NYR.	6.00	12.00
☐☐	14	John LeClair, Pha.	6.00	12.00
☐☐	15	Eric Lindros, Pha.	15.00	30.00
☐☐	16	Jeremy Roenick, Pho.	3.00	6.00
☐☐	17	Keith Tkachuk, Pho.	4.00	8.00
☐☐	18	Brett Hull, Stl.	6.00	12.00
☐☐	19	Félix Potvin (G), Tor.	6.00	12.00
☐☐	20	Pavel Bure, Van.	9.00	18.00

CRAMER'S CHOICE AWARDS

Insert Set (10 cards): 1,400.00

	No.	Player	NRMT-MT
☐	1	Paul Kariya, Ana.	200.00
☐	2	Dominik Hasek (G), Buf.	100.00
☐	3	Jarome Iginla, Cgy.	50.00
☐	4	Peter Forsberg, Col.	160.00
☐	5	Patrick Roy (G), Col.	250.00
☐	6	Steve Yzerman, Det.	160.00
☐	7	Wayne Gretzky, NYR.	325.00
☐	8	Mark Messier, NYR.	80.00
☐	9	Eric Lindros, Pha.	200.00
☐	10	Jaromir Jagr, Pgh.	160.00

GOLD CROWN DIE-CUTS

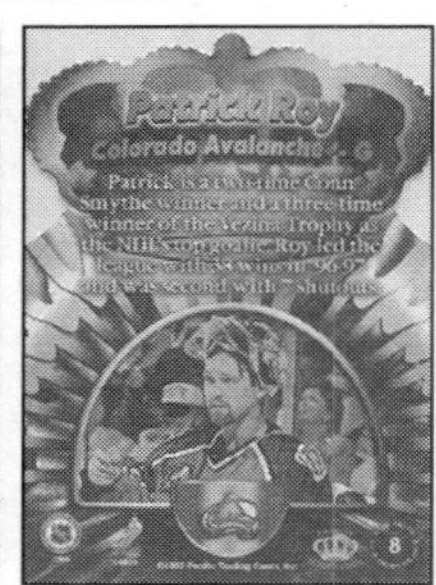

Insert Set (20 cards): 325.00

	No.	Player	NRMT-MT
☐	1	Paul Kariya, Ana.	35.00
☐	2	Teemu Selänne, Ana.	18.00
☐	3	Dominik Hasek (G), Buf.	18.00
☐	4	Michael Peca, Buf.	6.00
☐	5	Jarome Iginla, Cgy.	6.00
☐	6	Chris Chelios, Chi.	8.00
☐	7	Peter Forsberg, Col.	25.00
☐	8	Patrick Roy (G), Col.	40.00
☐	9	Joe Sakic, Col.	20.00
☐	10	Brendan Shanahan, Det.	15.00
☐	11	Steve Yzerman, Det.	25.00
☐	12	Ryan Smyth, Edm.	8.00
☐	13	John Vanbiesbrouck (G), Fla.	15.00
☐	14	Martin Brodeur (G), N.J.	20.00
☐	15	Wayne Gretzky, NYR.	50.00
☐	16	Mark Messier, NYR.	12.00
☐	17	Eric Lindros, Pha.	35.00
☐	18	Jaromir Jagr, Pgh.	25.00
☐	19	Brett Hull, Stl.	12.00
☐	20	Pavel Bure, Van.	18.00

IN THE CAGE LASER-CUTS

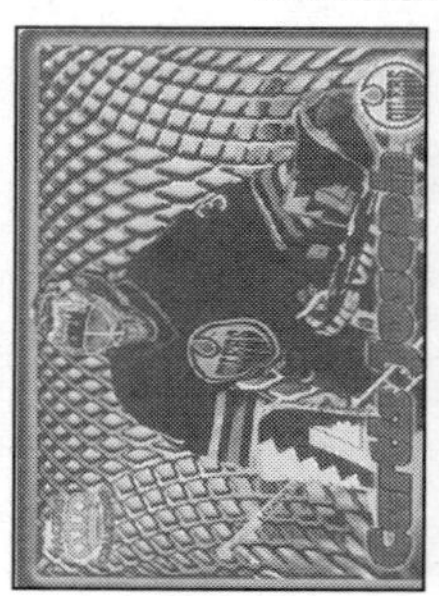

Insert Set (20 cards): 550.00

	No.	Player	NRMT-MT
☐	1	Guy Hebert (G), Ana.	20.00
☐	2	Dominik Hasek (G), Buf.	50.00
☐	3	Trevor Kidd (G), Cgy.	20.00
☐	4	Jeff Hackett (G), Chi.	20.00
☐	5	Patrick Roy (G), Col.	150.00
☐	6	Andy Moog (G), Dal.	20.00
☐	7	Chris Osgood (G), Det.	30.00
☐	8	Mike Vernon (G), Det.	20.00
☐	9	Curtis Joseph (G), Edm.	40.00
☐	10	John Vanbiesbrouck (G), Fla.	40.00
☐	11	Jocelyn Thibault (G), Mtl.	25.00
☐	12	Martin Brodeur (G), N.J.	50.00
☐	13	Mike Richter (G), NYR.	25.00
☐	14	Ron Hextall (G), Pha.	20.00
☐	15	Garth Snow (G), Pha.	20.00
☐	16	Nikolai Khabibulin (G), Pho.	25.00
☐	17	Patrick Lalime (G), Pgh.	20.00
☐	18	Grant Fuhr (G), Stl.	20.00
☐	19	Ed Belfour (G), S.J.	25.00
☐	20	Félix Potvin (G), Tor.	35.00

SLAP SHOTS DIE-CUTS

Insert Set (36 cards): 550.00

	No.	Player	NRMT-MT
☐	1A	Paul Kariya, Ana.	50.00
☐	1B	Jari Kurri, Ana.	8.00
☐	1C	Teemu Selänne, Ana.	25.00
☐	2A	Peter Forsberg, Col.	40.00
☐	2B	Joe Sakic, Col.	35.00
☐	2C	Claude Lemieux, Col.	6.00
☐	3A	Brendan Shanahan, Det.	20.00
☐	3B	Sergei Fedorov, Det.	15.00
☐	3C	Steve Yzerman, Det.	40.00
☐	4A	Mark Recchi, Mtl.	6.00
☐	4B	Vincent Damphousse, Mtl.	8.00
☐	4C	Stéphane Richer, Mtl.	6.00
☐	5A	Wayne Gretzky, NYR.	85.00
☐	5B	Mark Messier, NYR.	15.00
☐	5C	Brian Leetch, NYR.	8.00
☐	6A	Rod Brind'Amour, Pha.	6.00
☐	6B	Eric Lindros, Pha.	50.00
☐	6C	John LeClair, Pha.	15.00
☐	7A	Keith Tkachuk, Pho.	10.00
☐	7B	Jeremy Roenick, Pho.	8.00
☐	7C	Mike Gartner, Pho.	6.00
☐	8A	Petr Nedved, Pgh.	6.00
☐	8B	Ron Francis, Pgh.	8.00
☐	8C	Jaromir Jagr, Pgh	40.00
☐	9A	Geoff Courtnall, Stl.	6.00
☐	9B	Pierre Turgeon, Stl.	6.00
☐	9C	Brett Hull, Stl.	15.00
☐	10A	Wendel Clark, Tor.	6.00
☐	10B	Mats Sundin, Tor.	15.00
☐	10C	Sergei Berezin, Tor.	6.00
☐	11A	Pavel Bure, Van.	25.00
☐	11B	Trevor Linden, Van.	6.00
☐	11C	Alexander Mogilny, Can.	8.00
☐	12A	Joé Juneau, Wsh.	6.00
☐	12B	Adam Oates, Wsh.	8.00
☐	12C	Peter Bondra, Wsh.	10.00

TEAM CHECKLISTS CEL CARDS

Insert Set (26 cards): 425.00

	No.	Player	NRMT-MT
☐	1	Teemu Selänne, Ana.	20.00
☐	2	Ray Bourque, Bos.	12.00
☐	3	Dominik Hasek (G), Buf.	20.00
☐	4	Jarome Iginla, Cgy.	8.00
☐	5	Keith Primeau, Hfd. (Car.)	5.00
☐	6	Chris Chelios, Chi.	10.00
☐	7	Patrick Roy (G), Col.	60.00
☐	8	Mike Modano, Dal.	12.00
☐	9	Steve Yzerman, Det.	30.00
☐	10	Curtis Joseph (G), Edm.	18.00
☐	11	John Vanbiesbrouck (G), Fla.	18.00
☐	12	Rob Blake, L.A.	5.00
☐	13	Stéphane Richer, Mtl.	5.00
☐	14	Martin Brodeur (G), N.J.	30.00
☐	15	Zigmund Palffy, NYI.	8.00
☐	16	Wayne Gretzky, NYR.	75.00
☐	17	Alexandre Daigle, Ott.	5.00
☐	18	Eric Lindros, Pha.	40.00
☐	19	Jeremy Roenick, Pho.	8.00
☐	20	Jaromir Jagr, Pgh.	30.00
☐	21	Brett Hull, Stl.	12.00
☐	22	Owen Nolan, S.J.	5.00

	No.	Player	NRMT-MT
□	23	Dino Ciccarelli, T.B.	5.00
□	24	Félix Potvin (G), Tor.	12.00
□	25	Pavel Bure, Van.	20.00
□	26	Peter Bondra, Wsh.	10.00

1997 - 98 PACIFIC CROWN ROYALE

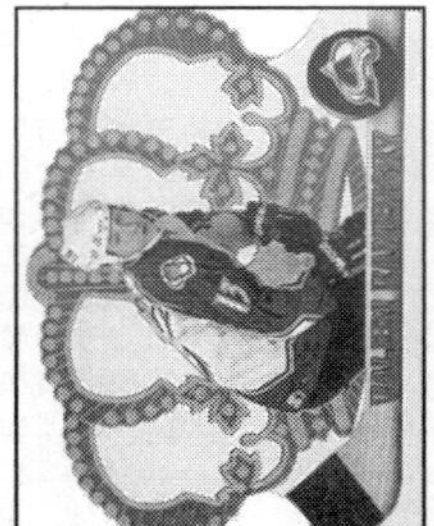

These die-cut cards have four versions: the regular card, a Silver parallel (U.S packs), an Emerald Green parallel (Canadian packs) and an Ice Blue parallel.

Imprint: © 1997 PACIFIC TRADING CARDS, INC.

Complete Set (144 cards): – 900.00 150.00

Common Player: 15.00 3.00 .50

Sample Card (Mike Modano): 2.00

	No.	Player	Ice Blue	Par.	Reg.
□□□□	1	Guy Hebert (G), Ana.	25.00	6.00	1.00
□□□□	2	Paul Kariya, Ana.	250.00	35.00	6.50
□□□□	3	Steve Rucchin, Ana.	15.00	3.00	.50
□□□□	4	Tomas Sandström, Ana.	15.00	3.00	.50
□□□□	5	Teemu Selänne, Ana.	15.00	3.00	.50
□□□□	6	Jason Allison, Bos.	40.00	8.00	1.50
□□□□	7	Ray Bourque, Bos.	80.00	12.50	2.50
□□□□	8	Anson Carter, Bos.	15.00	3.00	.50
□□□□	9	Byron Dafoe (G), Bos.	15.00	3.00	.50
□□□□	10	Ted Donato, Bos.	15.00	3.00	.50
□□□□	11	Joe Thornton, Bos.	80.00	12.50	3.00
□□□□	12	Jason Dawe, Buf.	15.00	3.00	.50
□□□□	13	Michal Grosek, Buf.	15.00	3.00	.50
□□□□	14	Dominik Hasek (G), Buf.	125.00	17.50	3.50
□□□□	15	Michael Peca, Buf.	25.00	6.00	1.00
□□□□	16	Miroslav Satan, Buf.	15.00	3.00	.50
□□□□	**17**	**Chris Dingman, Cgy., RC**	**15.00**	**3.00**	**.50**
□□□□	18	Theoren Fleury, Cgy.	40.00	8.00	1.50
□□□□	19	Jarome Iginla, Cgy.	40.00	8.00	1.50
□□□□	**20**	**Tyler Moss (G), Cgy., RC**	**25.00**	**6.00**	**1.00**
□□□□	21	Cory Stillman, Cgy.	15.00	3.00	.50
□□□□	22	Kevin Dineen, Car.	15.00	3.00	.50
□□□□	23	Nelson Emerson, Car.	15.00	3.00	.50
□□□□	24	Trevor Kidd (G), Car.	25.00	6.00	1.00
□□□□	25	Keith Primeau, Car.	25.00	6.00	1.00
□□□□	26	Geoff Sanderson, Car.	15.00	3.00	.50
□□□□	27	Tony Amonte, Chi.	25.00	6.00	1.00
□□□□	28	Chris Chelios, Chi.	60.00	10.00	2.00
□□□□	29	Eric Dazé, Chi.	25.00	6.00	1.00
□□□□	30	Jeff Hackett (G), Chi.	25.00	6.00	1.00
□□□□	31	Chris Terreri (G), Chi.	15.00	3.00	.50
□□□□	32	Adam Deadmarsh, Col.	15.00	3.00	.50
□□□□	33	Peter Forsberg, Col.	200.00	25.00	5.00
□□□□	34	Valeri Kamensky, Col.	25.00	6.00	1.00
□□□□	35	Jari Kurri, Col.	25.00	6.00	1.00
□□□□	36	Claude Lemieux, Col.	15.00	3.00	.50
□□□□	37	Patrick Roy (G), Col.	300.00	40.00	8.00
□□□□	38	Joe Sakic, Col.	150.00	20.00	4.00
□□□□	39	Ed Belfour (G), Dal.	40.00	8.00	1.50
□□□□	40	Derian Hatcher, Dal.	25.00	6.00	1.00
□□□□	41	Mike Modano, Dal.	80.00	12.50	2.50
□□□□	42	Joe Nieuwendyk, Dal.	25.00	6.00	1.00
□□□□	43	Pat Verbeek, Dal.	15.00	3.00	.50
□□□□	44	Sergei Zubov, Dal.	25.00	6.00	1.00
□□□□	45	Sergei Fedorov, Det.	80.00	12.50	2.50
□□□□	46	Vyacheslav Kozlov, Det.	15.00	3.00	.50
□□□□	47	Nicklas Lidström, Det.	25.00	6.00	1.00
□□□□	48	Darren McCarty, Det.	15.00	3.00	.50
□□□□	49	Chris Osgood (G), Det.	60.00	10.00	2.00
□□□□	50	Brendan Shanahan, Det.	100.00	15.00	3.00
□□□□	51	Steve Yzerman, Det.	200.00	25.00	5.00
□□□□	52	Jason Arnott, Edm.	25.00	6.00	1.00
□□□□	53	Curtis Joseph (G), Edm.	100.00	15.00	3.00
□□□□	54	Ryan Smyth, Edm.	25.00	6.00	1.00
□□□□	55	Doug Weight, Edm.	40.00	8.00	1.50
□□□□	56	Dave Gagner, Fla.	15.00	3.00	.50
□□□□	57	Ed Jovanovski, Fla.	25.00	6.00	1.00
□□□□	58	Viktor Kozlov, Fla.	15.00	3.00	.50
□□□□	59	Scott Mellanby, Fla.	15.00	3.00	.50
□□□□	60	John Vanbiesbrouck (G), Fla.	100.00	15.00	3.00
□□□□	**61**	**Kevin Weekes (G), Fla., RC**	**25.00**	**6.00**	**1.00**
□□□□	62	Rob Blake, L.A.	25.00	6.00	1.00
□□□□	**63**	**Donald MacLean, L.A., RC**	**15.00**	**3.00**	**.50**
□□□□	64	Yanic Perreault, L.A.	15.00	3.00	.50
□□□□	65	Luc Robitaille, L.A.	25.00	6.00	1.00
□□□□	66	Jozef Stumpel, L.A.	25.00	6.00	1.00
□□□□	67	Shayne Corson, Mtl.	25.00	6.00	1.00
□□□□	68	Vincent Damphousse, Mtl.	40.00	8.00	1.50
□□□□	69	Saku Koivu, Mtl.	125.00	17.50	3.50
□□□□	70	Andy Moog (G), Mtl.	25.00	6.00	1.00
□□□□	71	Mark Recchi, Mtl.	25.00	6.00	1.00
□□□□	72	Stéphane Richer, Mtl.	15.00	3.00	.50
□□□□	73	Martin Brodeur (G), N.J.	125.00	17.50	3.50
□□□□	**74**	**Patrik Elias, N.J., RC**	**25.00**	**6.00**	**2.00**
□□□□	75	Doug Gilmour, N.J.	40.00	8.00	1.50
□□□□	76	Bobby Holik, N.J.	15.00	3.00	.50
□□□□	77	Scott Stevens, N.J.	15.00	3.00	.50
□□□□	78	Bryan Berard, NYI.	40.00	8.00	1.50
□□□□	79	Zigmund Palffy, NYI.	40.00	8.00	1.50
□□□□	80	Robert Reichel, NYI.	15.00	3.00	.50
□□□□	81	Tommy Salo (G), NYI.	15.00	3.00	.50
□□□□	82	Bryan Smolinski, NYI.	15.00	3.00	.50
□□□□	83	Adam Graves, NYR.	15.00	3.00	.50
□□□□	84	Wayne Gretzky, NYR.	400.00	50.00	10.00
□□□□	85	Pat LaFontaine, NYR.	25.00	6.00	1.00
□□□□	86	Brian Leetch, NYR.	40.00	8.00	1.50
□□□□	87	Mike Richter (G), NYR.	40.00	8.00	1.50
□□□□	88	Niklas Sundstrom, NYR.	15.00	3.00	.50
□□□□	89	Daniel Alfredsson, Ott.	25.00	6.00	1.00
□□□□	90	Alexandre Daigle, Ott.	15.00	3.00	.50
□□□□	91	Shawn McEachern, Ott.	15.00	3.00	.50
□□□□	92	Chris Phillips, Ott.	25.00	6.00	2.00
□□□□	93	Ron Tugnutt (G), Ott.	15.00	3.00	.50
□□□□	94	Alexei Yashin, Ott.	60.00	10.00	2.00
□□□□	95	Rod Brind'Amour, Pha.	25.00	6.00	1.00
□□□□	96	Chris Gratton, Pha.	25.00	6.00	1.00
□□□□	97	Ron Hextall (G), Pha.	25.00	6.00	1.00
□□□□	98	John LeClair, Pha.	80.00	12.50	2.50
□□□□	99	Eric Lindros, Pha.	250.00	35.00	6.50
□□□□	**100**	**Vaclav Prospal, Pha., RC**	**35.00**	**7.00**	**2.50**
□□□□	101	Dainius Zubrus, Pha.	25.00	6.00	1.00
□□□□	102	Mike Gartner, Pho.	25.00	6.00	1.00
□□□□	103	Brad Isbister, Pho.	15.00	3.00	.50
□□□□	104	Nikolai Khabibulin (G), Pho.	40.00	8.00	1.50
□□□□	105	Jeremy Roenick, Pho.	40.00	8.00	1.50
□□□□	106	Cliff Ronning, Pho.	15.00	3.00	.50
□□□□	107	Keith Tkachuk, Pho.	60.00	10.00	2.00
□□□□	108	Tom Barrasso (G), Pgh.	25.00	6.00	1.00
□□□□	109	Ron Francis, Pgh.	40.00	8.00	1.50
□□□□	110	Jaromir Jagr, Pgh.	200.00	25.00	5.00
□□□□	111	Alexei Morozov, Pgh.	50.00	10.00	2.50
□□□□	112	Ed Olczyk, Pgh.	15.00	3.00	.50
□□□□	113	Jim Campbell, Stl.	15.00	3.00	.50
□□□□	114	Pavol Demitra, Stl.	15.00	3.00	.50
□□□□	115	Steve Duchesne, Stl.	15.00	3.00	.50
□□□□	116	Grant Fuhr (G), Stl.	25.00	6.00	1.00
□□□□	117	Brett Hull, Stl.	80.00	12.50	2.50
□□□□	118	Pierre Turgeon, Stl.	25.00	6.00	1.00
□□□□	119	Jeff Friesen, S.J.	25.00	6.00	1.00
□□□□	120	Patrick Marleau, S.J.	50.00	10.00	2.50
□□□□	121	Owen Nolan, S.J.	25.00	6.00	1.00
□□□□	**122**	**Marco Sturm, S.J., RC**	**15.00**	**3.00**	**.50**
□□□□	123	Mike Vernon, S.J.	25.00	6.00	1.00
□□□□	124	Dino Ciccarelli, T.B.	25.00	6.00	1.00
□□□□	125	Roman Hamrlik, T.B.	25.00	6.00	1.00
□□□□	126	Daren Puppa (G), T.B.	15.00	3.00	.50
□□□□	127	Paul Ysebaert, T.B.	15.00	3.00	.50
□□□□	128	Sergei Berezin, Tor.	25.00	6.00	1.00
□□□□	129	Wendel Clark, Tor.	25.00	6.00	1.00
□□□□	130	Alyn McCauley, Tor.	50.00	10.00	2.50
□□□□	131	Félix Potvin (G), Tor.	80.00	12.50	2.50
□□□□	132	Mats Sundin, Tor.	80.00	12.50	2.50
□□□□	133	Pavel Bure, Van.	125.00	17.50	3.50
□□□□	134	Martin Gelinas, Van.	15.00	3.00	.50
□□□□	135	Trevor Linden, Van.	25.00	6.00	1.00
□□□□	136	Mark Messier, Van.	80.00	12.50	2.50
□□□□	137	Alexander Mogilny, Van.	40.00	8.00	1.50
□□□□	138	Peter Bondra, Wsh.	60.00	10.00	2.00
□□□□	139	Dale Hunter, Wsh.	15.00	3.00	.50
□□□□	140	Joé Juneau, Wsh.	15.00	3.00	.50
□□□□	141	Olaf Kolzig, Wsh.	40.00	8.00	1.50
□□□□	142	Adam Oates, Wsh.	40.00	8.00	1.50
□□□□	143	Jaroslav Svejkovsky, Wsh.	25.00	6.00	1.00
□□□□	144	Richard Zednik, Wsh.	15.00	3.00	.50

HAT TRICKS

Hat Tricks insertion ratio is [1:25].

Insert Set (20 cards): 300.00

	No.	Player	NRMT-MT
□	1	Paul Kariya, Ana.	35.00
□	2	Teemu Selänne, Ana.	18.00
□	3	Joe Thornton, Bos.	15.00
□	4	Peter Forsberg, Col.	25.00
□	5	Joe Sakic, Col.	20.00
□	6	Mike Modano, Dal.	12.00
□	7	Brendan Shanahan, Det.	15.00
□	8	Steve Yzerman, Det.	25.00
□	9	Ryan Smyth, Edm.	6.00
□	10	Zigmund Palffy, NYI.	10.00
□	11	Wayne Gretzky, NYR.	60.00
□	12	John LeClair, Pha.	12.00
□	13	Eric Lindros, Pha.	35.00
□	14	Keith Tkachuk, Pho.	8.00
□	15	Jaromir Jagr, Pgh.	25.00
□	16	Brett Hull, Stl.	12.00
□	17	Mats Sundin, Tor.	12.00
□	18	Pavel Bure, Van.	18.00
□	19	Mark Messier, Van.	12.00
□	20	Peter Bondra, Wsh.	8.00

LAMPLIGHTERS

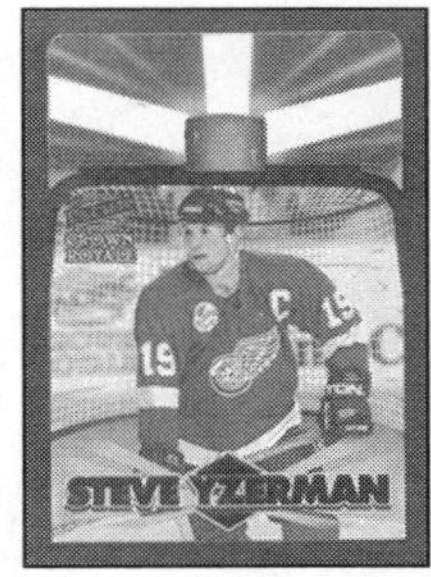

These laser-cut cards have an insertion ratio of [1:73].

Insert Set (20 cards): 750.00

	No.	Player	NRMT-MT
□	1	Paul Kariya, Ana.	80.00
□	2	Teemu Selänne, Ana.	40.00
□	3	Joe Thornton, Bos.	30.00
□	4	Michael Peca, Buf.	10.00
□	5	Peter Forsberg, Col.	60.00
□	6	Joe Sakic, Col.	50.00
□	7	Mike Modano, Dal.	25.00
□	8	Brendan Shanahan, Det.	35.00
□	9	Steve Yzerman, Det.	60.00
□	10	Saku Koivu, Mtl.	40.00
□	11	Wayne Gretzky, NYR.	125.00
□	12	Pat LaFontaine, NYR.	10.00
□	13	John LeClair, Pha.	25.00
□	14	Eric Lindros, Pha.	80.00
□	15	Dainius Zubrus, Pha.	10.00
□	16	Keith Tkachuk, Pho.	20.00
□	17	Jaromir Jagr, Pgh.	60.00
□	18	Brett Hull, Stl.	25.00
□	19	Pavel Bure, Van.	40.00
□	20	Mark Messier, Van.	25.00

BLADES OF STEEL

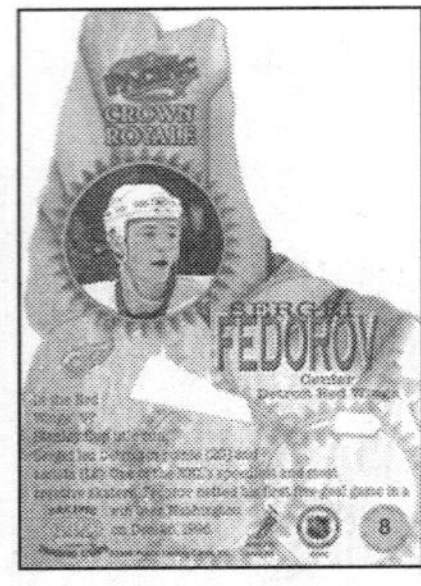

Blades of Steel insertion ratio is [1:49].

Insert Set (20 cards): 550.00

	No.	Player	NRMT-MT
☐	1	Paul Kariya, Ana.	50.00
☐	2	Teemu Selänne, Ana.	30.00
☐	3	Joe Thornton, Bos.	25.00
☐	4	Chris Chelios, Chi.	15.00
☐	5	Peter Forsberg, Col.	40.00
☐	6	Patrick Roy (G), Col.	60.00
☐	7	Mike Modano, Dal.	20.00
☐	8	Sergei Fedorov, Det.	20.00
☐	9	Brendan Shanahan, Det.	25.00
☐	10	Steve Yzerman, Det.	40.00
☐	11	Ryan Smyth, Edm.	12.00
☐	12	Saku Koivu, Mtl.	30.00
☐	13	Bryan Berard, NYI.	12.00
☐	14	Wayne Gretzky, NYR.	75.00
☐	15	Brian Leetch, NYR.	12.00
☐	16	Eric Lindros, Pha.	50.00
☐	17	Jaromir Jagr, Pgh.	40.00
☐	18	Brett Hull, Stl.	20.00
☐	19	Pavel Bure, Van.	30.00
☐	20	Mark Messier, Van.	20.00

FREEZE OUT

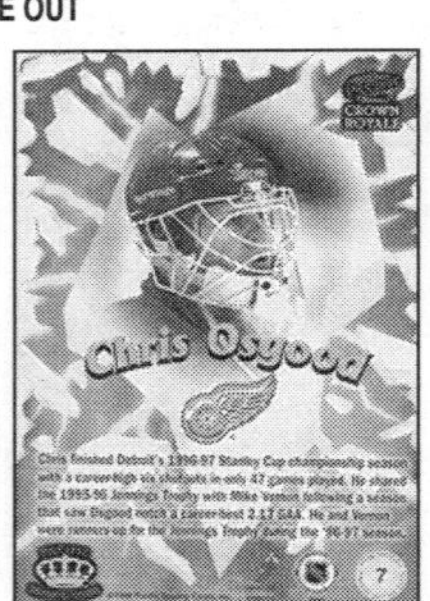

Freeze Out insertion ratio is [1:25].

Insert Set (20 cards): 300.00

	No.	Player	NRMT-MT
☐	1	Guy Hebert (G), Ana.	12.00
☐	2	Byron Dafoe (G), Bos.	10.00
☐	3	Dominik Hasek (G), Buf.	30.00
☐	4	Tyler Moss (G), Cgy.	10.00
☐	5	Patrick Roy (G), Col.	65.00
☐	6	Ed Belfour (G), Dal.	15.00
☐	7	Chris Osgood (G), Det.	15.00
☐	8	Curtis Joseph (G), Edm.	20.00
☐	9	John Vanbiesbrouck (G), Fla.	20.00
☐	10	Andy Moog (G), Mtl.	12.00
☐	11	Martin Brodeur (G), N.J.	30.00
☐	12	Mike Richter (G), NYR.	15.00
☐	13	Ron Hextall (G), Pha.	10.00
☐	14	Garth Snow (G), Pha.	10.00
☐	15	Nikolai Khabibulin (G), Pho.	15.00
☐	16	Tom Barrasso (G), Pgh.	10.00
☐	17	Grant Fuhr (G), Stl.	10.00
☐	18	Mike Vernon (G), S.J.	10.00
☐	19	Félix Potvin (G), Tor.	18.00
☐	20	Olaf Kolzig (G), Wsh.	15.00

CRAMER'S CHOICE AWARDS

Cramer's Choice Awards oversized cards are inserted one per box.

Card Size:

Insert Set (10 cards): 110.00

	No.	Player	NRMT-MT
☐☐	1	Paul Kariya, Ana.	15.00
☐☐	2	Teemu Selänne, Ana.	8.00
☐☐	3	Joe Thornton, Bos.	6.00
☐☐	4	Peter Forsberg, Col.	12.00
☐☐	5	Patrick Roy (G), Col.	20.00
☐☐	6	Steve Yzerman, Det.	12.00
☐☐	7	Wayne Gretzky, NYR.	25.00
☐☐	8	Eric Lindros, Pha.	15.00
☐☐	9	Jaromir Jagr, Pgh.	12.00
☐☐	10	Pavel Bure, Van.	8.00

1997 - 98 PACIFIC DYNAGON

These cards have six versions: the regular Gold card, an Emerald Green parallel (Canadian), a Copper parallel (Hobby), a Silver parallel (Retail), a Red parallel and an Ice Blue parallel. The Copper, Silver and Emerald Green parallels sell at approximately the same value. The Red parallel sells at two times the regular parallel. A Red set sells at $2,800.

Imprint: © 1997 PACIFIC TRADING CARDS, INC.

Complete Set (156 cards): – 1,500.00 150.00

Common Player: 15.00 6.00 .50

Sample Card (Mike Modano):

	No.	Player	Ice Blue	Par.	Reg.
☐☐☐☐☐☐	1	Brian Bellows, Ana.	15.00	6.00	.50
☐☐☐☐☐☐	2	Guy Hebert (G), Ana.	25.00	10.00	1.00
☐☐☐☐☐☐	3	Paul Kariya, Ana.	250.00	65.00	6.50
☐☐☐☐☐☐	4	Steve Rucchin, Ana.	15.00	6.00	.50
☐☐☐☐☐☐	5	Teemu Selänne, Ana.	125.00	35.00	3.50
☐☐☐☐☐☐	6	Jason Allison, Bos.	40.00	15.00	1.50
☐☐☐☐☐☐	7	Ray Bourque, Bos.	80.00	25.00	2.50
☐☐☐☐☐☐	8	Jim Carey (G), Bos.	15.00	6.00	.50
☐☐☐☐☐☐	9	Jozef Stumpel, Bos.	25.00	10.00	1.00
☐☐☐☐☐☐	10	Dominik Hasek (G), Buf.	125.00	35.00	3.50
☐☐☐☐☐☐	11	Brian Holzinger, Buf.	15.00	6.00	.50
☐☐☐☐☐☐	12	Michael Peca, Buf.	25.00	10.00	1.00
☐☐☐☐☐☐	13	Derek Plante, Buf.	15.00	6.00	.50
☐☐☐☐☐☐	14	Miroslav Satan, Buf.	15.00	6.00	.50
☐☐☐☐☐☐	15	Theoren Fleury, Cgy.	40.00	15.00	1.50
☐☐☐☐☐☐	16	Jonas Hoglund, Cgy.	15.00	6.00	.50
☐☐☐☐☐☐	17	Jarome Iginla, Cgy.	40.00	15.00	1.50
☐☐☐☐☐☐	18	Trevor Kidd (G), Cgy.	25.00	10.00	1.00
☐☐☐☐☐☐	19	German Titov, Cgy.	15.00	6.00	.50
☐☐☐☐☐☐	20	Sean Burke (G), Hfd. (Car.)	25.00	10.00	1.00
☐☐☐☐☐☐	21	Andrew Cassels, Hfd. (Car.)	15.00	6.00	.50
☐☐☐☐☐☐	22	Keith Primeau, Hfd. (Car.)	25.00	10.00	1.00
☐☐☐☐☐☐	23	Geoff Sanderson, Hfd. (Car.)	15.00	6.00	.50
☐☐☐☐☐☐	24	Tony Amonte, Chi.	25.00	10.00	1.00
☐☐☐☐☐☐	25	Chris Chelios, Chi.	60.00	20.00	2.00
☐☐☐☐☐☐	26	Eric Dazé, Chi.	25.00	10.00	1.00
☐☐☐☐☐☐	27	Jeff Hackett (G), Chi.	25.00	10.00	1.00
☐☐☐☐☐☐	28	Ethan Moreau, Chi.	15.00	6.00	.50
☐☐☐☐☐☐	29	Peter Forsberg, Col.	200.00	50.00	5.00
☐☐☐☐☐☐	30	Valeri Kamensky, Col.	25.00	10.00	1.00
☐☐☐☐☐☐	31	Claude Lemieux, Col.	15.00	6.00	.50
☐☐☐☐☐☐	32	Sandis Ozolinsh, Col.	25.00	10.00	1.00
☐☐☐☐☐☐	33	Patrick Roy (G), Col.	300.00	80.00	8.00
☐☐☐☐☐☐	34	Joe Sakic, Col.	150.00	40.00	4.00
☐☐☐☐☐☐	35	Derian Hatcher, Dal.	25.00	10.00	1.00
☐☐☐☐☐☐	36	Jamie Langenbrunner, Dal.	25.00	10.00	1.00
☐☐☐☐☐☐	37	Mike Modano, Dal.	80.00	25.00	2.50
☐☐☐☐☐☐	38	Joe Nieuwendyk, Dal.	25.00	10.00	1.00
☐☐☐☐☐☐	39	Darryl Sydor, Dal.	15.00	6.00	.50
☐☐☐☐☐☐	40	Sergei Zubov, Dal.	25.00	10.00	1.00
☐☐☐☐☐☐	41	Sergei Fedorov, Det.	80.00	25.00	2.50
☐☐☐☐☐☐	42	Vladimir Konstantinov, Det.	15.00	6.00	.50
☐☐☐☐☐☐	43	Chris Osgood (G), Det.	60.00	20.00	2.00
☐☐☐☐☐☐	44	Brendan Shanahan, Det.	100.00	30.00	3.00
☐☐☐☐☐☐	45	Mike Vernon (G), Det.	25.00	10.00	1.00
☐☐☐☐☐☐	46	Steve Yzerman, Det.	200.00	50.00	5.00
☐☐☐☐☐☐	47	Kelly Buchberger, Edm.	15.00	6.00	.50
☐☐☐☐☐☐	48	Mike Grier, Edm.	25.00	10.00	1.00
☐☐☐☐☐☐	49	Curtis Joseph (G), Edm.	100.00	30.00	3.00
☐☐☐☐☐☐	50	Rem Murray, Edm.	15.00	6.00	.50
☐☐☐☐☐☐	51	Ryan Smyth, Edm.	25.00	10.00	1.00
☐☐☐☐☐☐	52	Doug Weight, Edm.	40.00	15.00	1.50
☐☐☐☐☐☐	53	Ed Jovanovski, Fla.	25.00	10.00	1.00
☐☐☐☐☐☐	54	Scott Mellanby, Fla.	15.00	6.00	.50
☐☐☐☐☐☐	55	Ray Sheppard, Fla.	15.00	6.00	.50
☐☐☐☐☐☐	56	Robert Svehla, Fla.	15.00	6.00	.50
☐☐☐☐☐☐	57	John Vanbiesbrouck (G), Fla.	100.00	30.00	3.00
☐☐☐☐☐☐	58	Rob Blake, L.A.	25.00	10.00	1.00
☐☐☐☐☐☐	59	Ray Ferraro, L.A.	15.00	6.00	.50
☐☐☐☐☐☐	60	Dimitri Khristich, L.A.	15.00	6.00	.50
☐☐☐☐☐☐	61	Vladimir Tsyplakov, L.A.	15.00	6.00	.50
☐☐☐☐☐☐	62	Vincent Damphousse, Mtl.	40.00	15.00	1.50
☐☐☐☐☐☐	63	Saku Koivu, Mtl.	40.00	15.00	1.50
☐☐☐☐☐☐	64	Mark Recchi, Mtl.	25.00	10.00	1.00
☐☐☐☐☐☐	65	Stéphane Richer, Mtl.	15.00	6.00	.50
☐☐☐☐☐☐	66	Jocelyn Thibault (G), Mtl.	40.00	15.00	1.50
☐☐☐☐☐☐	67	Dave Andreychuk, N.J.	15.00	6.00	.50
☐☐☐☐☐☐	68	Martin Brodeur (G), N.J.	125.00	35.00	3.50
☐☐☐☐☐☐	69	Doug Gilmour, N.J.	40.00	15.00	1.50
☐☐☐☐☐☐	70	Bobby Holik, N.J.	15.00	6.00	.50
☐☐☐☐☐☐	71	John MacLean, N.J.	15.00	6.00	.50
☐☐☐☐☐☐	72	Bryan Berard, NYI.	40.00	15.00	1.50
☐☐☐☐☐☐	73	Travis Green, NYI.	15.00	6.00	.50
☐☐☐☐☐☐	74	Zigmund Palffy, NYI.	40.00	15.00	1.50
☐☐☐☐☐☐	75	Tommy Salo (G), NYI.	15.00	6.00	.50
☐☐☐☐☐☐	76	Bryan Smolinski, NYI.	15.00	6.00	.50
☐☐☐☐☐☐	77	Adam Graves, NYR.	15.00	6.00	.50
☐☐☐☐☐☐	78	Wayne Gretzky, NYR.	400.00	100.00	10.00
☐☐☐☐☐☐	79	Alexei Kovalev, NYR.	15.00	6.00	.50
☐☐☐☐☐☐	80	Brian Leetch, NYR.	40.00	15.00	1.50
☐☐☐☐☐☐	81	Mark Messier, NYR.	80.00	25.00	2.50
☐☐☐☐☐☐	82	Mike Richter (G), NYR.	40.00	15.00	1.50
☐☐☐☐☐☐	83	Daniel Alfredsson, Ott.	25.00	10.00	1.00
☐☐☐☐☐☐	84	Alexandre Daigle, Ott.	15.00	6.00	.50
☐☐☐☐☐☐	85	Wade Redden, Ott.	15.00	6.00	.50
☐☐☐☐☐☐	86	Damian Rhodes (G), Ott.	15.00	6.00	.50
☐☐☐☐☐☐	87	Alexei Yashin, Ott.	60.00	20.00	2.00
☐☐☐☐☐☐	88	Rod Brind'Amour, Pha.	25.00	10.00	1.00
☐☐☐☐☐☐	89	Ron Hextall (G), Pha.	25.00	10.00	1.00
☐☐☐☐☐☐	90	John LeClair, Pha.	80.00	25.00	2.50
☐☐☐☐☐☐	91	Eric Lindros, Pha.	250.00	65.00	6.50
☐☐☐☐☐☐	92	Janne Niinimaa, Pha.	25.00	10.00	1.00
☐☐☐☐☐☐	93	Garth Snow (G), Pha.	15.00	6.00	.50
☐☐☐☐☐☐	94	Dainius Zubrus, Pha.	25.00	10.00	1.00
☐☐☐☐☐☐	95	Mike Gartner, Pho.	25.00	10.00	1.00
☐☐☐☐☐☐	96	Nikolai Khabibulin (G), Pho.	40.00	15.00	1.50
☐☐☐☐☐☐	97	Jeremy Roenick, Pho.	40.00	15.00	1.50
☐☐☐☐☐☐	98	Keith Tkachuk, Pho.	60.00	20.00	2.00
☐☐☐☐☐☐	99	Oleg Tverdovsky, Pho.	15.00	6.00	.50
☐☐☐☐☐☐	100	Ron Francis, Pgh.	40.00	15.00	1.50
☐☐☐☐☐☐	101	Kevin Hatcher, Pgh.	15.00	6.00	.50
☐☐☐☐☐☐	102	Jaromir Jagr, Pgh.	200.00	50.00	5.00
☐☐☐☐☐☐	103	Patrick Lalime (G), Pgh.	15.00	6.00	.50
☐☐☐☐☐☐	104	Petr Nedved, Pgh.	15.00	6.00	.50
☐☐☐☐☐☐	105	Jim Campbell, Stl.	15.00	6.00	.50
☐☐☐☐☐☐	106	Grant Fuhr (G), Stl.	25.00	10.00	1.00
☐☐☐☐☐☐	107	Brett Hull, Stl.	80.00	25.00	2.50
☐☐☐☐☐☐	108	Pierre Turgeon, Stl.	25.00	10.00	1.00
☐☐☐☐☐☐	109	Harry York, Stl.	15.00	6.00	.50
☐☐☐☐☐☐	110	Jeff Friesen, S.J.	25.00	10.00	1.00
☐☐☐☐☐☐	111	Tony Granato, S.J.	15.00	6.00	.50
☐☐☐☐☐☐	**112**	**Stephen Guolla, S.J., RC**	**15.00**	**6.00**	**.50**

	No.	Player	Ice Blue	Par.	Reg.
☐☐☐☐☐☐	113	Viktor Kozlov, S.J.	15.00	6.00	.50
☐☐☐☐☐☐	114	Owen Nolan, S.J.	25.00	10.00	1.00
☐☐☐☐☐☐	115	Dino Ciccarelli, T.B.	25.00	10.00	1.00
☐☐☐☐☐☐	116	John Cullen, T.B.	15.00	6.00	.50
☐☐☐☐☐☐	117	Chris Gratton, T.B.	25.00	10.00	1.00
☐☐☐☐☐☐	118	Roman Hamrlik, T.B.	25.00	10.00	1.00
☐☐☐☐☐☐	119	Daymond Langkow, T.B.	15.00	6.00	.50
☐☐☐☐☐☐	120	Sergei Berezin, Tor.	25.00	10.00	1.00
☐☐☐☐☐☐	121	Wendel Clark, Tor.	25.00	10.00	1.00
☐☐☐☐☐☐	122	Félix Potvin (G), Tor.	80.00	25.00	2.50
☐☐☐☐☐☐	123	Steve Sullivan, Tor.	15.00	6.00	.50
☐☐☐☐☐☐	124	Mats Sundin, Tor.	80.00	25.00	2.50
☐☐☐☐☐☐	125	Pavel Bure, Van.	125.00	35.00	3.50
☐☐☐☐☐☐	126	Martin Gelinas, Van.	15.00	6.00	.50
☐☐☐☐☐☐	127	Trevor Linden, Van.	25.00	10.00	1.00
☐☐☐☐☐☐	128	Kirk McLean (G), Van.	25.00	10.00	1.00
☐☐☐☐☐☐	129	Alexander Mogilny, Van.	40.00	15.00	1.50
☐☐☐☐☐☐	130	Peter Bondra, Wsh.	60.00	20.00	2.00
☐☐☐☐☐☐	131	Joé Juneau, Wsh.	15.00	6.00	.50
☐☐☐☐☐☐	132	Steve Konowalchuk, Wsh.	15.00	6.00	.50
☐☐☐☐☐☐	133	Adam Oates, Wsh.	40.00	15.00	1.50
☐☐☐☐☐☐	134	Bill Ranford (G), Wsh.	15.00	6.00	.50
☐☐☐☐☐☐	135	P. Kariya/ T. Selänne	125.00	35.00	3.50
☐☐☐☐☐☐	136	D. Hasek (G)/ M. Peca	80.00	25.00	2.50
☐☐☐☐☐☐	137	T. Fleury/ J. Iginla	25.00	10.00	1.00
☐☐☐☐☐☐	138	P. Forsberg/ P. Roy	150.00	40.00	4.00
☐☐☐☐☐☐	139	B. Shanahan/ S. Yzerman	100.00	30.00	3.00
☐☐☐☐☐☐	140	W. Gretzky/ M. Messier	200.00	50.00	5.00
☐☐☐☐☐☐	141	J. LeClair/ E. Lindros	125.00	35.00	3.50
☐☐☐☐☐☐	142	J. Jagr/ P. Lalime (G)	100.00	30.00	3.00
☐☐☐☐☐☐	143	J. Campbell/ B. Hull	25.00	10.00	1.00
☐☐☐☐☐☐	144	S. Berezin/ M. Sundin	25.00	10.00	1.00
		Rookies	**Ice Blue**	**Par.**	**Reg.**
☐☐☐☐☐☐		Joe Thornton, Bos.	80.00	25.00	3.00
☐☐☐☐☐☐		Sergei Samsonov, Bos.	80.00	25.00	3.00
☐☐☐☐☐☐		**Shawn Bates, Bos., RC**	**15.00**	**6.00**	**1.00**
☐☐☐☐☐☐		Patrick Marleau, S.J.	50.00	20.00	2.50
☐☐☐☐☐☐		Alyn McCauley, Tor.	50.00	20.00	2.50
☐☐☐☐☐☐		Mattias Ohlund, Van.	25.00	10.00	1.50
☐☐☐☐☐☐		**Espen Knutsen, Ana., RC**	**15.00**	**6.00**	**1.00**
☐☐☐☐☐☐		Chris Phillips, Ott.	25.00	10.00	1.50
☐☐☐☐☐☐		Erik Rasmussen, Buf.	15.00	6.00	1.00
☐☐☐☐☐☐		Dan Cleary, Chi.	25.00	10.00	1.50
☐☐☐☐☐☐		**Olli Jokinen, L.A., RC**	**25.00**	**10.00**	**1.50**
☐☐☐☐☐☐		**Marian Hossa, Ott., RC**	**75.00**	**30.00**	**6.00**

TANDEMS

These double-sided cards parallel the front of each regular card. Tandems insertion ratio is [1:37]

Insert Set (72 cards): **2,000.00**
Common Player: **10.00**

	No.	Player	NRMT-MT
☐	1	Wayne Gretzky/ Eric Lindros	175.00
☐	2	Joe Sakic/ Paul Kariya	115.00
☐	3	Jarome Iginla/ Mark Messier	40.00
☐	4	Patrick Roy (G)/ Dominik Hasek (G)	125.00
☐	5	Peter Forsberg/ Jaromir Jagr	85.00
☐	6	Brendan Shanahan/ Keith Tkachuk	50.00
☐	7	Steve Yzerman/ Teemu Selänne	80.00
☐	8	Sergei Fedorov/ Brett Hull	45.00
☐	9	Dainius Zubrus/ Patrick Lalime (G)	18.00
☐	10	Sergei Berezin/ Mike Grier	18.00
☐	11	Zigmund Palffy/ Curtis Joseph (G)	50.00
☐	12	Chris Osgood (G)/ Martin Brodeur (G)	60.00
☐	13	J. Vanbiesbrouck (G)/ J. Thibault (G)	50.00
☐	14	Saku Koivu/ Pavel Bure	60.00
☐	15	John LeClair/ Peter Bondra	40.00
☐	16	Mats Sundin/ Janne Niinimaa	40.00
☐	17	Félix Potvin (G)/ Jim Carey (G)	40.00
☐	18	Grant Fuhr/ B. Hull & J. Campbell	20.00
☐	19	W. Gretzky & A. Kovalev/ B. Leetch	100.00
☐	20	E. Lindros & J. LeClair/ R. Brind'Amour	75.00
☐	21	D. Hasek (G) & M. Peca/ Miroslav Satan	35.00
☐	22	J. Jagr & P. Lalime (G)/ Petr Nedved	60.00
☐	23	J. Iginla & T. Fleury/ Trevor Kidd (G)	20.00
☐	24	P. Kariya & T. Selänne/ G. Hebert (G)	100.00
☐	25	P. Forsberg & P. Roy (G)/ C. Lemieux	125.00
☐	26	S. Yzerman & B. Shanahan/ V. Konstantinov	70.00
☐	27	M. Sundin & S. Berezin/ W. Clark	25.00
☐	28	Ray Bourque/ Derek Plante	40.00
☐	29	Brian Bellows/ Jason Allison	25.00
☐	30	Steve Rucchin/ Keith Primeau	18.00
☐	31	Jozef Stumpel/ Eric Dazé	18.00
☐	32	Brian Holzinger/ Jamie Langenbrunner	18.00
☐	33	Michael Peca/ Tony Amonte	18.00
☐	34	German Titov/ Darryl Sydor	10.00
☐	35	Theoren Fleury/ Chris Chelios	25.00
☐	36	Jonas Hoglund/ Dimitri Khristich	10.00
☐	37	Sean Burke (G)/ Dave Andreychuk	18.00
☐	38	Geoff Sanderson/ Derian Hatcher	18.00
☐	39	Andrew Cassels/ Jeff Hackett (G)	18.00
☐	40	Ethan Moreau/ Ray Ferraro	10.00
☐	41	Sandis Ozolinsh/ Doug Gilmour	25.00
☐	42	Valeri Kamensky/ Mike Modano	40.00
☐	43	Joe Nieuwendyk/ Vladimir Tsyplakov	18.00
☐	44	Sergei Zubov/ Mike Vernon (G)	18.00
☐	45	Rob Blake/ Bobby Holik	18.00
☐	46	Vincent Damphousse/ Doug Weight	25.00
☐	47	Mark Recchi/ Ryan Smyth	18.00
☐	48	Stéphane Richer/ John MacLean	10.00
☐	49	Kelly Buchberger/ Ed Jovanovski	18.00
☐	50	Rem Murray/ Owen Nolan	18.00
☐	51	Robert Svehla/ Bill Ranford (G)	18.00
☐	52	Ray Sheppard/ Steve Sullivan	10.00
☐	53	Scott Mellanby/ John Cullen	10.00
☐	54	Garth Snow (G)/ Alexandre Daigle	10.00
☐	55	Ron Hextall (G)/ Alexander Mogilny	25.00
☐	56	Kirk McLean (G)/ Adam Oates	25.00
☐	57	Joé Juneau/ Dino Ciccarelli	18.00
☐	58	Steve Konowalchuk/ Jim Campbell	10.00
☐	59	Trevor Linden/ Pierre Turgeon	18.00
☐	60	Martin Gelinas/ Jeff Friesen	18.00
☐	61	Roman Hamrlik/ Harry York	18.00
☐	62	Kevin Hatcher/ Chris Gratton	18.00
☐	63	Ron Francis/ Jeremy Roenick	25.00
☐	64	Nikolai Khabibulin (G)/ Viktor Kozlov	25.00
☐	65	Daymond Langkow/ Mike Gartner	18.00
☐	66	Oleg Tverdovsky/ Stephen Guolla	10.00
☐	67	Tony Granato/ Tommy Salo (G)	10.00
☐	68	Bryan Smolinski/ Wade Redden	10.00
☐	69	Adam Graves/ Damian Rhodes (G)	10.00
☐	70	Mike Richter (G)/ Alexei Yashin	25.00
☐	71	Daniel Alfredsson/ Bryan Berard	25.00
☐	72	Travis Green/ Alexei Kovalev	10.00

BEST-KEPT SECRETS

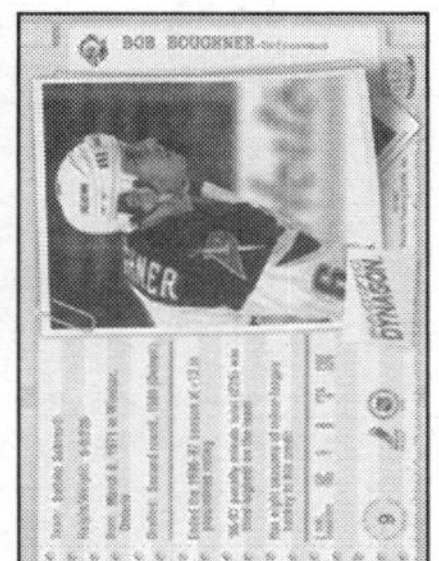

Bonus Set (110 cards): **25.00**
Common Player: **.20**

	No.	Player	NRMT-MT
☐	1	J.J. Daigneault, Ana.	.20
☐	2	Paul Kariya, Ana.	2.00
☐	3	Dave Karpa, Ana.	.20
☐	4	Teemu Selänne, Ana.	1.00
☐	5	Ray Bourque, Bos.	.60
☐	6	Jim Carey (G), Bos.	.20
☐	**7**	**Davis Payne, Bos., RC**	**.35**
☐	**8**	**Paxton Schafer (G), Bos., RC**	**.35**
☐	9	Bob Boughner, Buf.	.20
☐	10	Dominik Hasek (G), Buf.	1.00
☐	11	Brad May, Buf.	.20
☐	12	Cale Hulse, Cgy.	.20
☐	13	Jarome Iginla, Cgy.	.35
☐	14	James Patrick, Cgy.	.20
☐	15	Zarley Zalapski, Cgy.	.20
☐	16	Jeff Brown, Hfd. (Car.)	.20
☐	17	Keith Primeau, Hfd. (Car.)	.35
☐	18	Steven Rice, Hfd. (Car.)	.20
☐	19	James Black, Chi.	.20
☐	20	Chris Chelios, Chi.	.50
☐	21	Steve Dubinsky, Chi.	.20
☐	22	Steve Smith, Chi.	.20
☐	23	Craig Billington (G), Col.	.20
☐	24	Peter Forsberg, Col.	1.50
☐	25	Jon Klemm, Col.	.20
☐	26	Patrick Roy (G), Col.	2.50
☐	27	Joe Sakic, Col.	1.25
☐	28	Neal Broten, Dal.	.20
☐	29	Richard Matvichuk, Dal.	.20
☐	30	Mike Modano, Dal.	.60
☐	31	Andy Moog (G), Dal.	.35
☐	32	Sergei Fedorov, Det.	.60
☐	33	Kirk Maltby, Det.	.20
☐	34	Brendan Shanahan, Det.	.75
☐	35	Tim Taylor, Det.	.20
☐	36	Steve Yzerman, Det.	1.50
☐	37	Louie DeBrusk, Edm.	.20
☐	**38**	**Joe Hulbig, Edm., RC**	**.20**
☐	39	Ryan Smyth, Edm.	.35
☐	40	Mike Hough, Fla.	.20
☐	41	Jody Hull, Fla.	.20
☐	42	Paul Laus, Fla.	.20
☐	43	John Vanbiesbrouck (G), Fla.	.75
☐	44	Aki Berg, L.A.	.20
☐	45	Ray Ferraro, L.A.	.20
☐	46	Craig Johnson, L.A.	.20
☐	47	Ian Laperrière, L.A.	.20
☐	48	Vincent Damphousse, Mtl.	.50
☐	49	Dave Manson, Mtl.	.20
☐	50	Stéphane Richer, Mtl.	.20
☐	51	Craig Rivet, Mtl.	.20
☐	52	Martin Brodeur (G), N.J.	1.00
☐	53	Jay Pandolfo, N.J.	.20
☐	54	Brian Rolston, N.J.	.20
☐	55	Doug Houda, NYI.	.20
☐	56	Brent Hughes, NYI.	.20
☐	57	Zigmund Palffy, NYI.	.50
☐	58	Adam Graves, NYR.	.20
☐	59	Wayne Gretzky, NYR.	4.00
☐	60	Chris Ferraro, NYR.	.20
☐	61	Glenn Healy (G), NYR.	.20
☐	62	Brian Leetch, NYR.	.35
☐	63	Mark Messier, NYR.	.60
☐	64	Radim Bicanek, Ott.	.20
☐	65	Philip Crowe, Ott.	.20
☐	**66**	**Christer Olsson, Ott., RC**	**.20**
☐	67	Jason York, Ott.	.20
☐	68	Rod Brind'Amour, Pha.	.35
☐	69	John Druce, Pha.	.20
☐	70	Daniel Lacroix, Pha.	.20
☐	71	John LeClair, Pha.	.60
☐	72	Eric Lindros, Pha.	2.00
☐	73	Murray Baron, Pho.	.20
☐	74	Mike Gartner, Pho.	.35
☐	75	Brad McCrimmon, Pho.	.20
☐	76	Keith Tkachuk, Pho.	.50
☐	77	Jaromir Jagr, Pgh.	1.50
☐	78	Patrick Lalime (G), Pgh.	.20
☐	79	Ian Moran, Pgh.	.20
☐	80	Petr Nedved, Pgh.	.20
☐	81	Brett Hull, Stl.	.60
☐	82	Robert Petrovicky, Stl.	.20
☐	83	Pierre Turgeon, Stl.	.35
☐	84	Trent Yawney, Stl.	.20
☐	85	Tim Hunter, S.J.	.20
☐	86	Marcus Ragnarsson, S.J.	.20
☐	87	Dody Wood, S.J.	.20
☐	88	Dino Ciccarelli, T.B.	.35
☐	89	Alexander Selivanov, T.B.	.20
☐	90	Jason Wiemer, T.B.	.20
☐	91	Sergei Berezin, Tor.	.35
☐	92	Félix Potvin (G), Tor.	.60
☐	93	Mats Sundin, Tor.	.60
☐	94	Craig Wolanin, Tor.	.20
☐	95	Pavel Bure, Van.	1.00
☐	96	Troy Crowder, Van.	.20
☐	97	Dana Murzyn, Van.	.20
☐	98	Gino Odjick, Van.	.20
☐	99	Craig Berube, Wsh.	.20
☐	100	Peter Bondra, Wsh.	.50
☐	101	Mike Eagles, Wsh.	.20
☐	102	Andrei Nikolishin, Wsh.	.20
☐	103	AW: Paul Kariya, Ana.	1.25
☐	104	AW: Dominik Hasek (G), Buf.	.60
☐	105	AW: Michael Peca, Buf.	.35
☐	106	AW: M. Brodeur (G)/ M. Dunham (G)	.60
☐	107	AW: Bryan Berard, NYI.	.35
☐	108	AW: Brian Leetch, NYR.	.35
☐	109	AW: Tony Granato, S.J.	.20
☐	110	AW: Trevor Linden, Van.	.35

DYNAMIC DUOS

Dynamic Duos insertion ratio is [1:37].

Insert Set (30 cards): 425.00

	No.	Player	NRMT-MT
☐	1A	Paul Kariya, Ana.	35.00
☐	1B	Teemu Selänne, Ana.	18.00
☐	2A	Ray Bourque, Bos.	12.00
☐	2B	Jim Carey (G), Bos.	4.00
☐	3A	Dominik Hasek (G), Buf.	18.00
☐	3B	Michael Peca, Buf.	5.00
☐	4A	Theoren Fleury, Cgy.	10.00
☐	4B	Jarome Iginla, Cgy.	10.00
☐	5A	Peter Forsberg, Col.	30.00
☐	5B	Claude Lemieux, Col.	6.00
☐	6A	Patrick Roy (G), Col.	45.00
☐	6B	Joe Sakic, Col.	25.00
☐	7A	Sergei Fedorov, Det.	12.00
☐	7B	Vladimir Konstantinov, Det.	4.00
☐	8A	Brendan Shanahan, Det.	15.00
☐	8B	Steve Yzerman, Det.	30.00
☐	9A	Bryan Berard, NYI.	6.00
☐	9B	Zigmund Palffy, NYI.	10.00
☐	10A	Wayne Gretzky, NYR.	60.00
☐	10B	Brian Leetch, NYR.	10.00
☐	11A	Eric Lindros, Pha.	35.00
☐	11B	Dainius Zubrus, Pha.	5.00
☐	12A	Jeremy Roenick, Pho.	5.00
☐	12B	Keith Tkachuk, Pho.	10.00
☐	13A	Jaromir Jagr, Pgh.	30.00
☐	13B	Patrick Lalime (G), Pgh.	4.00
☐	14A	Jim Campbell, Stl.	4.00
☐	14B	Brett Hull, Stl.	12.00
☐	15A	Pavel Bure, Van.	18.00
☐	15B	Alexander Mogilny, Van.	6.00

STONEWALLERS

Stonewallers insertion ratio is [1:73].

Insert Set (20 cards): 300.00

	No.	Player	NRMT-MT
☐	1	Guy Hebert (G), Ana.	12.00
☐	2	Jim Carey (G), Bos.	10.00
☐	3	Dominik Hasek (G), Buf.	35.00
☐	4	Trevor Kidd (G), Cgy.	12.00
☐	5	Jeff Hackett (G), Chi.	12.00
☐	6	Patrick Roy (G), Col.	85.00
☐	7	Chris Osgood (G), Det.	15.00
☐	8	Mike Vernon (G), Det.	12.00
☐	9	Curtis Joseph (G), Edm.	25.00
☐	10	John Vanbiesbrouck (G), Fla.	25.00
☐	11	Jocelyn Thibault (G), Mtl.	15.00
☐	12	Martin Brodeur (G), N.J.	35.00
☐	13	Tommy Salo (G), NYI.	10.00
☐	14	Mike Richter (G), NYR.	15.00
☐	15	Ron Hextall (G), Pha.	12.00
☐	16	Garth Snow (G), Pha.	10.00
☐	17	Nikolai Khabibulin (G), Pho.	15.00
☐	18	Patrick Lalime (G), Pgh.	10.00
☐	19	Grant Fuhr (G), Stl.	12.00
☐	20	Félix Potvin (G), Tor.	20.00

KINGS OF THE NHL

Kings of the NHL insertion ratio is [1:361].

Insert Set (10 cards): 1,200.00

	No.	Player	NRMT-MT
☐	1	Paul Kariya, Ana.	175.00
☐	2	Peter Forsberg, Col.	150.00
☐	3	Patrick Roy (G), Col.	225.00
☐	4	Joe Sakic, Col.	100.00
☐	5	John Vanbiesbrouck (G), Fla.	70.00
☐	6	Wayne Gretzky, NYR.	275.00
☐	7	Mark Messier, NYR.	65.00
☐	8	Eric Lindros, Pha.	175.00
☐	9	Jaromir Jagr, Pgh.	150.00
☐	10	Pavel Bure, Van.	75.00

1997 - 98 PACIFIC INVINCIBLE

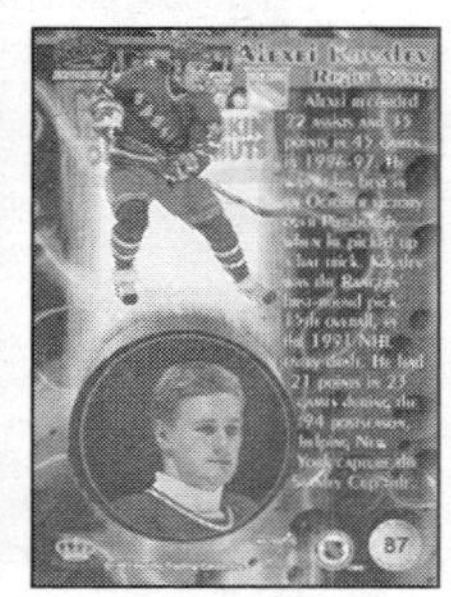

These cards have six versions: a one-per-pack regular card, an Emerald Green (Canadian) parallel, a Copper (Hobby) parallel, a Silver (Retail) parallel, a Red parallel and an Ice Blue parallel. The Green, Copper and Silver parallels all sell at approximately the same price. The Red parallel sells at two times the regular parallels. A Red set sells at $3,200.

Imprint: © 1997 PACIFIC TRADING CARDS, INC.

Complete Set (150 cards): 175.00

Common Player: .75 6.00 20.00

	No.	Player	Ice Blue	Par.	Reg.
☐☐☐☐☐☐	1	Brian Bellows, Ana.	20.00	6.00	.75
☐☐☐☐☐☐	2	Guy Hebert (G), Ana.	30.00	10.00	1.50
☐☐☐☐☐☐	3	Paul Kariya, Ana.	275.00	80.00	10.00
☐☐☐☐☐☐	4	Teemu Selänne, Ana.	150.00	40.00	5.00
☐☐☐☐☐☐	5	Darren Van Impe, Ana.	20.00	6.00	.75
☐☐☐☐☐☐	6	Jason Allison, Bos.	45.00	15.00	2.25
☐☐☐☐☐☐	7	Ray Bourque, Bos.	85.00	28.00	3.75
☐☐☐☐☐☐	8	Jim Carey (G), Bos.	20.00	6.00	.75
☐☐☐☐☐☐	9	Ted Donato, Bos.	20.00	6.00	.75
☐☐☐☐☐☐	10	Jozef Stumpel, Bos.	30.00	10.00	1.50
☐☐☐☐☐☐	11	Jason Dawe, Buf.	20.00	6.00	.75
☐☐☐☐☐☐	12	Dominik Hasek (G), Buf.	150.00	40.00	5.00
☐☐☐☐☐☐	13	Michael Peca, Buf.	30.00	10.00	1.50
☐☐☐☐☐☐	14	Derek Plante, Buf.	20.00	6.00	.75
☐☐☐☐☐☐	15	Miroslav Satan, Buf.	20.00	6.00	.75
☐☐☐☐☐☐	16	Theoren Fleury, Cgy.	45.00	15.00	2.25
☐☐☐☐☐☐	17	Dave Gagner, Cgy.	20.00	6.00	.75
☐☐☐☐☐☐	18	Jonas Hoglund, Cgy.	20.00	6.00	.75
☐☐☐☐☐☐	19	Jarome Iginla, Cgy.	45.00	15.00	2.25
☐☐☐☐☐☐	20	Trevor Kidd (G), Cgy.	30.00	10.00	1.50
☐☐☐☐☐☐	21	German Titov, Cgy.	20.00	6.00	.75
☐☐☐☐☐☐	22	Sean Burke (G), Hfd. (Car.)	30.00	10.00	1.50
☐☐☐☐☐☐	23	Andrew Cassels, Hfd. (Car.)	20.00	6.00	.75
☐☐☐☐☐☐	24	Derek King, Hfd. (Tor.)	20.00	6.00	.75
☐☐☐☐☐☐	25	Keith Primeau, Hfd. (Car.)	30.00	10.00	1.50
☐☐☐☐☐☐	26	Geoff Sanderson, Hfd. (Car.)	20.00	6.00	.75
☐☐☐☐☐☐	27	Tony Amonte, Chi.	30.00	10.00	1.50
☐☐☐☐☐☐	28	Chris Chelios, Chi.	65.00	20.00	3.00
☐☐☐☐☐☐	29	Eric Dazé, Chi.	30.00	10.00	1.50
☐☐☐☐☐☐	30	Jeff Hackett (G), Chi.	30.00	10.00	1.50
☐☐☐☐☐☐	31	Ethan Moreau, Chi.	20.00	6.00	.75
☐☐☐☐☐☐	32	Alexei Zhamnov, Chi.	20.00	6.00	.75
☐☐☐☐☐☐	33	Adam Deadmarsh, Col.	20.00	6.00	.75
☐☐☐☐☐☐	34	Peter Forsberg, Col.	225.00	60.00	7.50
☐☐☐☐☐☐	35	Valeri Kamensky, Col.	30.00	10.00	1.50
☐☐☐☐☐☐	36	Claude Lemieux, Col.	20.00	6.00	.75
☐☐☐☐☐☐	37	Sandis Ozolinsh, Col.	30.00	10.00	1.50
☐☐☐☐☐☐	38	Patrick Roy (G), Col.	350.00	100.00	12.00
☐☐☐☐☐☐	39	Joe Sakic, Col.	175.00	50.00	6.00
☐☐☐☐☐☐	40	Jamie Langenbrunner, Dal.	30.00	10.00	1.50
☐☐☐☐☐☐	41	Mike Modano, Dal.	85.00	28.00	3.75
☐☐☐☐☐☐	42	Andy Moog (G), Dal.	30.00	10.00	1.50
☐☐☐☐☐☐	43	Joe Nieuwendyk, Dal.	30.00	10.00	1.50
☐☐☐☐☐☐	44	Pat Verbeek, Dal.	20.00	6.00	.75
☐☐☐☐☐☐	45	Sergei Zubov, Dal.	30.00	10.00	1.50
☐☐☐☐☐☐	46	Sergei Fedorov, Det.	85.00	28.00	3.75
☐☐☐☐☐☐	47	Vladimir Konstantinov, Det.	20.00	6.00	.75
☐☐☐☐☐☐	48	Vyacheslav Kozlov, Det.	20.00	6.00	.75
☐☐☐☐☐☐	49	Nicklas Lidström, Det.	30.00	10.00	1.50
☐☐☐☐☐☐	50	Chris Osgood (G), Det.	65.00	20.00	3.00
☐☐☐☐☐☐	51	Brendan Shanahan, Det.	110.00	35.00	4.50
☐☐☐☐☐☐	52	Mike Vernon (G), Det.	30.00	10.00	1.50
☐☐☐☐☐☐	53	Steve Yzerman, Det.	225.00	60.00	7.50
☐☐☐☐☐☐	54	Jason Arnott, Edm.	30.00	10.00	1.50
☐☐☐☐☐☐	55	Mike Grier, Edm.	30.00	10.00	1.50
☐☐☐☐☐☐	56	Curtis Joseph (G), Edm.	150.00	40.00	5.00
☐☐☐☐☐☐	57	Rem Murray, Edm.	20.00	6.00	.75
☐☐☐☐☐☐	58	Ryan Smyth, Edm.	30.00	10.00	1.50
☐☐☐☐☐☐	59	Doug Weight, Edm.	45.00	15.00	2.25
☐☐☐☐☐☐	60	Ed Jovanovski, Fla.	30.00	10.00	1.50
☐☐☐☐☐☐	61	Scott Mellanby, Fla.	20.00	6.00	.75
☐☐☐☐☐☐	62	Kirk Muller, Fla.	20.00	6.00	.75
☐☐☐☐☐☐	63	Ray Sheppard, Fla.	20.00	6.00	.75
☐☐☐☐☐☐	64	John Vanbiesbrouck (G), Fla.	110.00	35.00	4.50
☐☐☐☐☐☐	65	Rob Blake, L.A.	30.00	10.00	1.50
☐☐☐☐☐☐	66	Ray Ferraro, L.A.	20.00	6.00	.75
☐☐☐☐☐☐	67	Stéphane Fiset (G), L.A.	30.00	10.00	1.50
☐☐☐☐☐☐	68	Dimitri Khristich, L.A.	20.00	6.00	.75
☐☐☐☐☐☐	69	Vladimir Tsyplakov, L.A.	20.00	6.00	.75
☐☐☐☐☐☐	70	Vincent Damphousse, Mtl.	45.00	15.00	2.25
☐☐☐☐☐☐	71	Saku Koivu, Mtl.	150.00	40.00	5.00
☐☐☐☐☐☐	72	Mark Recchi, Mtl.	30.00	10.00	1.50
☐☐☐☐☐☐	73	Stéphane Richer, Mtl.	20.00	6.00	.75
☐☐☐☐☐☐	74	Jocelyn Thibault (G), Mtl.	45.00	15.00	2.25
☐☐☐☐☐☐	75	Dave Andreychuk, N.J.	20.00	6.00	.75
☐☐☐☐☐☐	76	Martin Brodeur (G), N.J.	150.00	40.00	5.00
☐☐☐☐☐☐	77	Doug Gilmour, N.J.	45.00	15.00	2.25
☐☐☐☐☐☐	78	Bobby Holik, N.J.	20.00	6.00	.75
☐☐☐☐☐☐	79	Denis Pederson, N.J.	20.00	6.00	.75
☐☐☐☐☐☐	80	Bryan Berard, NYI.	45.00	15.00	2.25
☐☐☐☐☐☐	81	Travis Green, NYI.	20.00	6.00	.75
☐☐☐☐☐☐	82	Zigmund Palffy, NYI.	45.00	15.00	2.25
☐☐☐☐☐☐	83	Tommy Salo (G), NYI.	20.00	6.00	.75
☐☐☐☐☐☐	84	Bryan Smolinski, NYI.	20.00	6.00	.75
☐☐☐☐☐☐	85	Adam Graves, NYR.	20.00	6.00	.75
☐☐☐☐☐☐	86	Wayne Gretzky, NYR.	500.00	125.00	15.00
☐☐☐☐☐☐	87	Alexei Kovalev, NYR.	20.00	6.00	.75
☐☐☐☐☐☐	88	Brian Leetch, NYR.	45.00	15.00	2.25
☐☐☐☐☐☐	89	Mark Messier, NYR.	85.00	28.00	3.75
☐☐☐☐☐☐	90	Mike Richter (G), NYR.	45.00	15.00	2.25
☐☐☐☐☐☐	91	Luc Robitaille, NYR.	30.00	10.00	1.50
☐☐☐☐☐☐	92	Daniel Alfredsson, Ott.	30.00	10.00	1.50
☐☐☐☐☐☐	93	Alexandre Daigle, Ott.	20.00	6.00	.75
☐☐☐☐☐☐	94	Steve Duchesne, Ott.	20.00	6.00	.75
☐☐☐☐☐☐	95	Wade Redden, Ott.	1.00	8.00	25.00
☐☐☐☐☐☐	96	Ron Tugnutt (G), Ott.	20.00	6.00	.75
☐☐☐☐☐☐	97	Alexei Yashin, Ott.	65.00	20.00	3.00
☐☐☐☐☐☐	98	Rod Brind'Amour, Pha.	30.00	10.00	1.50
☐☐☐☐☐☐	99	Paul Coffey, Pha.	30.00	10.00	1.50
☐☐☐☐☐☐	100	Ron Hextall (G), Pha.	30.00	10.00	1.50
☐☐☐☐☐☐	101	John LeClair, Pha.	85.00	28.00	3.75
☐☐☐☐☐☐	102	Eric Lindros, Pha.	275.00	80.00	10.00
☐☐☐☐☐☐	103	Janne Niinimaa, Pha.	30.00	10.00	1.50
☐☐☐☐☐☐	104	Mikael Renberg, Pha.	20.00	6.00	.75
☐☐☐☐☐☐	105	Dainius Zubrus, Pha.	30.00	10.00	1.50
☐☐☐☐☐☐	106	Mike Gartner, Pho.	30.00	10.00	1.50
☐☐☐☐☐☐	107	Nikolai Khabibulin (G), Pho.	45.00	15.00	2.25
☐☐☐☐☐☐	108	Jeremy Roenick, Pho.	45.00	15.00	2.25
☐☐☐☐☐☐	109	Keith Tkachuk, Pho.	65.00	20.00	3.00
☐☐☐☐☐☐	110	Oleg Tverdovsky, Pho.	20.00	6.00	.75
☐☐☐☐☐☐	111	Ron Francis, Pgh.	45.00	15.00	2.25
☐☐☐☐☐☐	112	Kevin Hatcher, Pgh.	20.00	6.00	.75
☐☐☐☐☐☐	113	Jaromir Jagr, Pgh.	225.00	60.00	7.50
☐☐☐☐☐☐	114	Patrick Lalime (G), Pgh.	20.00	6.00	.75
☐☐☐☐☐☐	115	Petr Nedved, Pgh.	20.00	6.00	.75
☐☐☐☐☐☐	116	Ed Olczyk, Pgh.	20.00	6.00	.75
☐☐☐☐☐☐	117	Jim Campbell, Stl.	20.00	6.00	.75
☐☐☐☐☐☐	118	Geoff Courtnall, Stl.	20.00	6.00	.75
☐☐☐☐☐☐	119	Grant Fuhr (G), Stl.	30.00	10.00	1.50
☐☐☐☐☐☐	120	Brett Hull, Stl.	85.00	28.00	3.75
☐☐☐☐☐☐	121	Sergio Momesso, Stl.	20.00	6.00	.75
☐☐☐☐☐☐	122	Pierre Turgeon, Stl.	30.00	10.00	1.50
☐☐☐☐☐☐	123	Ed Belfour (G), S.J.	45.00	15.00	2.25
☐☐☐☐☐☐	124	Jeff Friesen, S.J.	30.00	10.00	1.50
☐☐☐☐☐☐	125	Tony Granato, S.J.	20.00	6.00	.75
☐☐☐☐☐☐	126	Stephen Guolla, S.J.	20.00	6.00	.75
☐☐☐☐☐☐	127	Bernie Nicholls, S.J.	20.00	6.00	.75
☐☐☐☐☐☐	128	Owen Nolan, S.J.	30.00	10.00	1.50
☐☐☐☐☐☐	129	Dino Ciccarelli, T.B.	30.00	10.00	1.50
☐☐☐☐☐☐	130	John Cullen, T.B.	20.00	6.00	.75
☐☐☐☐☐☐	131	Chris Gratton, T.B.	30.00	10.00	1.50
☐☐☐☐☐☐	132	Roman Hamrlik, T.B.	30.00	10.00	1.50
☐☐☐☐☐☐	133	Daymond Langkow, T.B.	20.00	6.00	.75
☐☐☐☐☐☐	134	Paul Ysebaert, T.B.	20.00	6.00	.75
☐☐☐☐☐☐	135	Sergei Berezin, Tor.	30.00	10.00	1.50
☐☐☐☐☐☐	136	Wendel Clark, Tor.	30.00	10.00	1.50
☐☐☐☐☐☐	137	Félix Potvin (G), Tor.	85.00	28.00	3.75
☐☐☐☐☐☐	138	Steve Sullivan, Tor.	20.00	6.00	.75
☐☐☐☐☐☐	139	Mats Sundin, Tor.	85.00	28.00	3.75
☐☐☐☐☐☐	140	Pavel Bure, Van.	150.00	40.00	5.00
☐☐☐☐☐☐	141	Martin Gelinas, Van.	20.00	6.00	.75
☐☐☐☐☐☐	142	Trevor Linden, Van.	30.00	10.00	1.50
☐☐☐☐☐☐	143	Kirk McLean (G), Van.	30.00	10.00	1.50
☐☐☐☐☐☐	144	Alexander Mogilny, Van.	45.00	15.00	2.25

	No.	Player			
□□□□□□	145	Peter Bondra, Wsh.	65.00	20.00	3.00
□□□□□□	146	Dale Hunter, Wsh.	20.00	6.00	.75
□□□□□□	147	Joé Juneau, Wsh.	20.00	6.00	.75
□□□□□□	148	Steve Konowalchuk, Wsh.	20.00	6.00	.75
□□□□□□	149	Adam Oates, Wsh.	45.00	15.00	2.25
□□□□□□	150	Bill Ranford (G), Wsh.	30.00	10.00	1.50

ATTACK ZONE

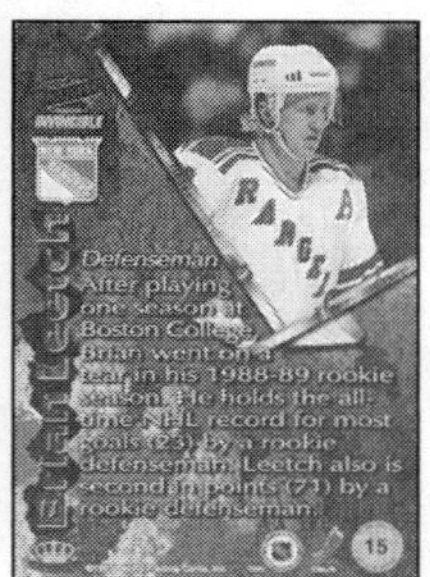

Insert Set (24 cards): **350.00**

	No.	Player	NRMT-MT
□	1	Paul Kariya, Ana.	35.00
□	2	Teemu Selänne, Ana.	20.00
□	3	Michael Peca, Buf.	5.00
□	4	Jarome Iginla, Cgy.	8.00
□	5	Peter Forsberg, Col.	30.00
□	6	Claude Lemieux, Col.	4.00
□	7	Joe Sakic, Col.	25.00
□	8	Mike Modano, Dal.	81200
□	9	Sergei Fedorov, Det.	12.00
□	10	Brendan Shanahan, Det.	18.00
□	11	Steve Yzerman, Det.	30.00
□	12	Bryan Berard, NYI.	8.00
□	13	Zigmund Palffy, NYI.	8.00
□	14	Wayne Gretzky, NYR.	60.00
□	15	Brian Leetch, NYR.	8.00
□	16	Mark Messier, NYR.	12.00
□	17	John LeClair, Pha.	12.00
□	18	Eric Lindros, Pha.	35.00
□	19	Ron Francis, Pgh.	8.00
□	20	Jaromir Jagr, Pgh.	30.00
□	21	Brett Hull, Stl.	12.00
□	22	Dino Ciccarelli, T.B.	5.00
□	23	Pavel Bure, Van.	18.00
□	24	Alexander Mogilny, Van.	8.00

FEATURE PERFORMERS

Insert Set (36 cards): **375.00**

	No.	Player	NRMT-MT
□	1	Paul Kariya, Ana.	25.00
□	2	Teemu Selänne, Ana.	15.00
□	3	Ray Bourque, Bos.	10.00
□	4	Dominik Hasek (G), Buf.	15.00
□	5	Jarome Iginla, Cgy.	6.00
□	6	Chris Chelios, Chi.	8.00
□	7	Peter Forsberg, Col.	20.00
□	8	Claude Lemieux, Col.	3.00
□	9	Patrick Roy (G), Col.	30.00
□	10	Joe Sakic, Col.	18.00
□	11	Mike Modano, Dal.	10.00
□	12	Sergei Fedorov, Det.	10.00
□	13	Vladimir Konstantinov, Det.	3.00
□	14	Brendan Shanahan, Det.	12.00
□	15	Mike Vernon (G), Det.	4.00
□	16	Steve Yzerman, Det.	20.00
□	17	John Vanbiesbrouck (G), Fla.	12.00
□	18	Saku Koivu, Mtl.	15.00
□	19	Martin Brodeur (G), N.J.	15.00
□	20	Zigmund Palffy, NYI.	6.00
□	21	Wayne Gretzky, NYR.	40.00
□	22	Mark Messier, NYR.	10.00
□	23	Alexandre Daigle, Ott.	4.00
□	24	John LeClair, Pha.	10.00
□	25	Eric Lindros, Pha.	25.00
□	26	Janne Niinimaa, Pha.	4.00
□	27	Jeremy Roenick, Pho.	6.00
□	28	Jaromir Jagr, Pgh.	20.00
□	29	Patrick Lalime (G), Pgh.	3.00
□	30	Jim Campbell, Stl.	3.00
□	31	Brett Hull, Stl.	10.00
□	32	Sergei Berezin, Tor.	4.00
□	33	Félix Potvin (G), Tor.	10.00
□	34	Mats Sundin, Tor.	10.00
□	35	Alexander Mogilny, Van.	6.00
□	36	Peter Bondra, Wsh.	8.00

REGIME

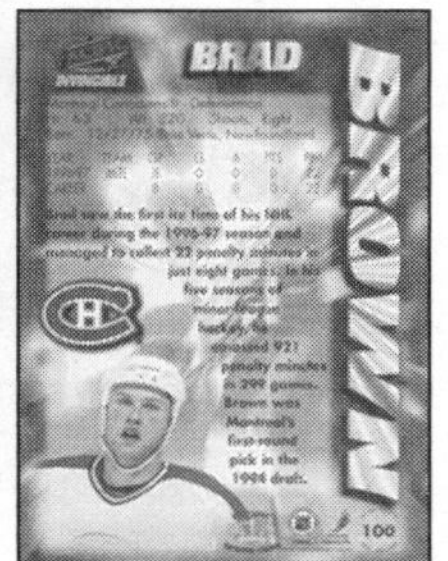

Bonus Set (220 cards): **40.00**
Common Player: **.20**

	No.	Player	NRMT-MT
□	1	Ken Baumgartner, Ana.	.20
□	2	Mark Janssens, Ana.	.20
□	3	Jean-François Jomphe, Ana.	.20
□	4	Paul Kariya, Ana.	2.00
□	5	Jason Marshall, Ana.	.20
□	6	Richard Park, Ana.	.20
□	7	Teemu Selänne, Ana.	1.00
□	8	Mikhail Shtalenkov (G), Ana.	.20
□	9	Bob Beers, Bos.	.20
□	10	Ray Bourque, Bos.	.60
□	11	Jim Carey (G), Bos.	.20
□	12	Brett Harkins, Bos.	.20
□	13	Sheldon Kennedy, Bos.	.20
□	14	Troy Mallette, Bos.	.20
□	15	Sandy Moger, Bos.	.20
□	16	Jon Rohloff, Bos.	.20
□	17	Don Sweeney, Bos.	.20
□	18	Randy Burridge, Buf.	.20
□	19	Michal Grosek, Buf.	.20
□	20	Dominik Hasek (G), Buf.	1.00
□	21	Rob Ray, Buf.	.20
□	**22**	**Steve Shields (G), Buf., RC**	**.35**
□	23	Richard Smehlik, Buf.	.20
□	24	Dixon Ward, Buf.	.20
□	25	Mike Wilson, Buf.	.20
□	26	Tommy Albelin, Cgy.	.20
□	27	Aaron Gavey, Cgy.	.20
□	28	Todd Hlushko, Cgy.	.20
□	29	Jarome Iginla, Cgy.	.35
□	30	Yves Racine, Cgy.	.20
□	31	Dwayne Roloson (G), Cgy.	.20
□	32	Mike Sullivan, Cgy.	.20
□	33	Ed Ward, Cgy.	.20
□	34	Adam Burt, Hfd. (Car.)	.20
□	35	Nelson Emerson, Hfd. (Car.)	.20
□	36	Kevin Haller, Hfd. (Car.)	.20
□	37	Derek King, Hfd. (Car.)	.20
□	38	Curtis Leschyshyn, Hfd. (Car.)	.20
□	39	Chris Murray, Hfd. (Car.)	.20
□	40	Jason Muzzatti (G), Hfd. (Car.)	.20
□	41	Keith Carney, Chi.	.20
□	42	Chris Chelios, Chi.	.50
□	43	Enrico Ciccone, Chi.	.20
□	44	Jim Cummins, Chi.	.20
□	45	Cam Russell, Chi.	.20
□	46	Jeff Shantz, Chi.	.20
□	47	Michal Sykora, Chi.	.20
□	48	Chris Terreri, Chi.	.20
□	49	Eric Weinrich, Chi.	.20
□	50	René Corbet, Col.	.20
□	51	Peter Forsberg, Col.	1.50
□	52	Alexei Gusarov, Col.	.20
□	53	Uwe Krupp, Col.	.20
□	54	Sylvain Lefebvre, Col.	.20
□	55	Eric Messier, Col.	.20
□	56	Patrick Roy (G), Col.	2.50
□	57	Joe Sakic, Col.	1.25
□	58	Brent Severyn, Col.	.20
□	59	Greg Adams, Dal.	.20
□	60	Todd Harvey, Dal.	.20
□	61	Jere Lehtinen, Dal.	.35
□	62	Craig Ludwig, Dal.	.20
□	63	Mike Modano, Dal.	.60
□	64	Andy Moog (G), Dal.	.35
□	65	Dave Reid, Dal.	.20
□	66	Roman Turek (G), Dal.	.20
□	67	Doug Brown, Det.	.20
□	68	Kris Draper, Det.	.20
□	69	Sergei Fedorov, Det.	.60
□	70	Joey Kocur, Det.	.20
□	71	Kirk Maltby, Det.	.20
□	72	Bob Rouse, Det.	.20
□	73	Brendan Shanahan, Det.	.75
□	74	Aaron Ward, Det.	.20
□	75	Steve Yzerman, Det.	1.50
□	76	Greg de Vries, Edm.	.20
□	77	Bob Essensa (G), Edm.	.20
□	78	Kevin Lowe, Edm.	.20
□	79	Bryan Marchment, Edm.	.20
□	80	Dean McAmmond, Edm.	.20
□	81	Boris Mironov, Edm.	.20
□	82	Luke Richardson, Edm.	.20
□	83	Ryan Smyth, Edm.	.35
□	84	Terry Carkner, Fla.	.20
□	85	Ed Jovanovski, Fla.	.35
□	86	Bill Lindsay, Fla.	.20
□	87	Dave Lowry, Fla.	.20
□	88	Gord Murphy, Fla.	.20
□	89	John Vanbiesbrouck (G), Fla.	.75
□	90	Steve Washburn, Fla.	.20
□	91	Chris Wells, Fla.	.20
□	92	Philippe Boucher, L.A.	.20
□	93	Steve Finn, L.A.	.20
□	94	Mattias Norstrom, L.A.	.20
□	95	Kai Nurminen, L.A.	.20
□	96	Sean O'Donnell, L.A.	.20
□	97	Yanic Perreault, L.A.	.20
□	98	Jeff Shevalier, L.A.	.20
□	99	Brad Smyth, L.A.	.20
□	100	Brad Brown, Mtl.	.20
□	101	Jassen Cullimore, Mtl.	.20
□	102	Vincent Damphousse, Mtl.	.35
□	103	Vladimir Malakhov, Mtl.	.20
□	104	Peter Popovic, Mtl.	.20
□	105	Stéphane Richer, Mtl.	.20
□	106	Turner Stevenson, Mtl.	.20
□	107	José Théodore (G), Mtl.	.35
□	108	Martin Brodeur (G), N.J.	1.00
□	109	Bob Carpenter, N.J.	.20
□	110	Mike Dunham (G), N.J.	.20
□	**111**	**Patrik Elias, N.J., RC**	**.50**
□	112	Dave Ellett, N.J.	.20
□	113	Doug Gilmour, N.J.	.35
□	114	Randy McKay, N.J.	.20
□	115	Todd Bertuzzi, NYI.	.20
□	116	Kenny Jonsson, NYI.	.20
□	117	Paul Kruse, NYI.	.20
□	118	Claude Lapointe, NYI.	.20
□	119	Zigmund Palffy, NYI.	.35
□	120	Richard Pilon, NYI.	.20
□	121	Dan Plante, NYI.	.20
□	122	Dennis Vaske, NYI.	.20
□	123	Shane Churla, NYR.	.20
□	124	Bruce Driver, NYR.	.20
□	125	Mike Eastwood, NYR.	.20
□	126	Patrick Flatley, NYR.	.20
□	127	Adam Graves, NYR.	.20
□	128	Wayne Gretzky, NYR.	4.00
□	129	Brian Leetch, NYR.	.35
□	130	Doug Lidster, NYR.	.20
□	131	Mark Messier, NYR.	.60
□	132	Tom Chorske, Ott.	.20
□	133	Sean Hill, Ott.	.20

	No.	Player	Price
☐	134	Denny Lambert, Ott.	.20
☐	135	Janne Laukkanen, Ott.	.20
☐	136	Frank Musil, Ott.	.20
☐	137	Lance Pitlick, Ott.	.20
☐	138	Shaun VanAllen, Ott.	.20
☐	139	Rod Brind'Amour, Pha.	.35
☐	140	Paul Coffey, Pha.	.35
☐	141	Karl Dykhuis, Pha.	.20
☐	142	Dan Kordic, Pha.	.20
☐	143	Daniel Lacroix, Pha.	.20
☐	144	John LeClair, Pha.	.60
☐	145	Eric Lindros, Pha.	2.00
☐	146	Joel Otto, Pha.	.20
☐	147	Shjon Podein, Pha.	.20
☐	148	Chris Therien, Pha.	.20
☐	149	Shane Doan, Pho.	.20
☐	150	Dallas Drake, Pho.	.20
☐	151	Jeff Finley, Pho.	.20
☐	152	Mike Gartner, Pho.	.35
☐	153	Nikolai Khabibulin, Pho.	.35
☐	154	Darrin Shannon, Pho.	.20
☐	155	Mike Stapleton, Pho.	.20
☐	156	Keith Tkachuk, Pho.	.50
☐	157	Tom Barrasso (G), Pgh.	.35
☐	158	Josef Beranek, Pgh.	.20
☐	159	Alex Hicks, Pgh.	.20
☐	160	Jaromir Jagr, Pgh.	1.50
☐	161	Patrick Lalime (G), Pgh.	.20
☐	162	François Leroux, Pgh.	.20
☐	163	Petr Nedved, Pgh.	.20
☐	164	Roman Oksiuta, Pgh.	.20
☐	165	Chris Tamer, Pgh.	.20
☐	166	Marc Bergevin, Stl.	.20
☐	167	Jon Casey, Stl.	.20
☐	168	Craig Conroy, Stl.	.20
☐	169	Brett Hull, Stl.	.60
☐	170	Igor Kravchuk, Stl.	.20
☐	171	Stephen Leach, Stl.	.20
☐	172	Ricard Persson, Stl.	.20
☐	173	Pierre Turgeon, Stl.	.35
☐	174	Ed Belfour (G), S.J.	.35
☐	175	Doug Bodger, S.J.	.20
☐	176	Shean Donovan, S.J.	.20
☐	177	Bob Errey, S.J.	.20
☐	178	Todd Ewen, S.J.	.20
☐	179	Wade Flaherty (G), S.J.	.20
☐	180	Mike Rathje, S.J.	.20
☐	181	Ron Sutter, S.J.	.20
☐	182	Mikael Andersson, T.B.	.20
☐	183	Dino Ciccarelli, T.B.	.35
☐	184	Cory Cross, T.B.	.20
☐	185	Jamie Huscroft, T.B.	.20
☐	186	Rudy Poeschek, T.B.	.20
☐	187	Daren Puppa, T.B.	.20
☐	188	David Shaw, T.B.	.20
☐	189	Jay Wells, T.B.	.20
☐	190	Jamie Baker, Tor.	.20
☐	191	Sergei Berezin, Tor.	.35
☐	192	Brandon Convery, Tor.	.20
☐	193	Darby Hendrickson, Tor.	.20
☐	194	Matt Martin, Tor.	.20
☐	195	Félix Potvin (G), Tor.	.60
☐	196	Jason Smith, Tor.	.20
☐	197	Craig Wolanin, Tor.	.20
☐	198	Adrian Aucoin, Van.	.20
☐	199	Dave Babych, Van.	.20
☐	200	Donald Brashear, Van.	.20
☐	201	Pavel Bure, Van.	1.00
☐	202	Chris Joseph, Van.	.20
☐	203	Alexander Mogilny, Van.	.35
☐	204	David Roberts, Van.	.20
☐	205	Scott Walker, Van.	.20
☐	206	Peter Bondra, Wsh.	.50
☐	207	Andrew Brunette, Wsh.	.20
☐	208	Calle Johansson, Wsh.	.20
☐	209	Ken Klee, Wsh.	.20
☐	210	Olaf Kolzig (G), Wsh.	.35
☐	211	Kelly Miller, Wsh.	.20
☐	212	Joe Reekie, Wsh.	.20
☐	213	Chris Simon, Wsh.	.20
☐	214	Brendan Witt, Wsh.	.20
☐	215	Paul Kariya, Ana.	1.50
☐	216	Peter Forsberg, Col.	1.25
☐	217	Patrick Roy (G), Col.	1.75
☐	218	Wayne Gretzky, NYR.	3.00
☐	219	Eric Lindros, Pha.	1.50
☐	220	Jaromir Jagr, Pgh.	1.25

OFF THE GLASS CEL-FUSIONS

Insert Set (20 cards): 450.00

	No.	Player	NRMT-MT
☐	1	Paul Kariya, Ana.	50.00
☐	2	Teemu Selänne, Ana.	30.00
☐	3	Michael Peca, Buf.	6.00
☐	4	Jarome Iginla, Cgy.	6.00
☐	5	Peter Forsberg, Col.	40.00
☐	6	Joe Sakic, Col.	35.00
☐	7	Sergei Fedorov, Det.	18.00
☐	8	Brendan Shanahan, Det.	25.00
☐	9	Steve Yzerman, Det.	40.00
☐	10	Mike Grier, Edm.	6.00
☐	11	Saku Koivu, Mtl.	30.00
☐	12	Wayne Gretzky, NYR.	90.00
☐	13	Mark Messier, NYR.	18.00
☐	14	Eric Lindros, Pha.	50.00
☐	15	Dainius Zubrus, Pha.	8.00
☐	16	Keith Tkachuk, Pho.	12.00
☐	17	Jaromir Jagr, Pgh.	40.00
☐	18	Brett Hull, Stl.	18.00
☐	19	Sergei Berezin, Tor.	6.00
☐	20	Pavel Bure, Van.	30.00

1997 - 98 PACIFIC PARAMOUNT

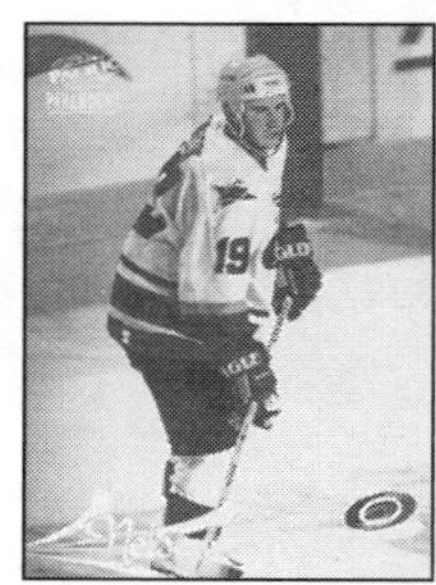

These cards have six versions: the regular card, an Emerald Green parallel (Canadian), a Copper parallel (Hobby), a Silver parallel (Retail), a Dark Grey parallel and an Ice Blue parallel. The Copper, Silver and Emerald Green parallels sell at approximately the same value. The Dark Grey parallel sells at two times the regular parallels. A Dark Grey set sells at $400.

Imprint: © 1997 PACIFIC TRADING CARDS, INC.

Complete Set (200 cards): – 250.00 35.00

Common Player: 15.00 .50 .15

Sample Card (Mike Modano): 1.00

	No.	Player	Ice Blue	Par.	Reg.
☐☐☐☐☐☐	1	Guy Hebert (G), Ana.	25.00	1.50	.35
☐☐☐☐☐☐	2	Paul Kariya, Ana.	250.00	10.00	2.00
☐☐☐☐☐☐	**3**	**Espen Knutsen, Ana., RC**	**15.00**	**.50**	**.15**
☐☐☐☐☐☐	4	Dmitri Mironov, Ana.	15.00	.50	.15
☐☐☐☐☐☐	5	Steve Rucchin, Ana.	300.00	12.00	2.50
☐☐☐☐☐☐	6	Tomas Sandström, Ana.	15.00	.50	.15
☐☐☐☐☐☐	7	Teemu Selänne, Ana.	125.00	5.00	1.00
☐☐☐☐☐☐	8	Scott Young, Ana.	15.00	.50	.15
☐☐☐☐☐☐	9	Ray Bourque, Bos.	80.00	3.75	.75
☐☐☐☐☐☐	10	Jim Carey (G), Bos.	15.00	.50	.15
☐☐☐☐☐☐	11	Anson Carter, Bos.	15.00	.50	.15
☐☐☐☐☐☐	12	Ted Donato, Bos.	15.00	.50	.15
☐☐☐☐☐☐	13	Dave Ellett, Bos.	15.00	.50	.15
☐☐☐☐☐☐	14	Dimitri Khristich, Bos.	15.00	.50	.15
☐☐☐☐☐☐	15	Sergei Samsonov, Bos.	80.00	4.00	.85
☐☐☐☐☐☐	16	Joe Thornton, Bos.	80.00	4.00	.85
☐☐☐☐☐☐	17	Matthew Barnaby, Buf.	15.00	.50	.15
☐☐☐☐☐☐	18	Jason Dawe, Buf.	15.00	.50	.15
☐☐☐☐☐☐	19	Dominik Hasek (G), Buf.	125.00	5.00	1.00
☐☐☐☐☐☐	20	Brian Holzinger, Buf.	15.00	.50	.15
☐☐☐☐☐☐	21	Michael Peca, Buf.	25.00	1.50	.35
☐☐☐☐☐☐	22	Derek Plante, Buf.	15.00	.50	.15
☐☐☐☐☐☐	23	Erik Rasmussen, Buf.	15.00	.50	.15
☐☐☐☐☐☐	24	Miroslav Satan, Buf.	15.00	.50	.15
☐☐☐☐☐☐	**25**	**Steve Bégin, Cgy., RC**	**15.00**	**.50**	**.15**
☐☐☐☐☐☐	26	Andrew Cassels, Cgy.	15.00	.50	.15
☐☐☐☐☐☐	27	Chris Dingman, Cgy.	15.00	.50	.15
☐☐☐☐☐☐	28	Theoren Fleury, Cgy.	40.00	2.25	.50
☐☐☐☐☐☐	29	Jonas Hoglund, Cgy.	15.00	.50	.15
☐☐☐☐☐☐	30	Jarome Iginla, Cgy.	40.00	2.25	.50
☐☐☐☐☐☐	31	Rick Tabaracci (G), Cgy.	15.00	.50	.15
☐☐☐☐☐☐	32	German Titov, Cgy.	15.00	.50	.15
☐☐☐☐☐☐	33	Kevin Dineen, Car.	15.00	.50	.15
☐☐☐☐☐☐	34	Nelson Emerson, Car.	15.00	.50	.15
☐☐☐☐☐☐	35	Trevor Kidd (G), Car.	25.00	1.50	.35
☐☐☐☐☐☐	36	Stephen Leach, Car.	15.00	.50	.15
☐☐☐☐☐☐	37	Keith Primeau, Car.	25.00	1.50	.35
☐☐☐☐☐☐	38	Steven Rice, Car.	15.00	.50	.15
☐☐☐☐☐☐	39	Gary Roberts, Car.	25.00	1.50	.35
☐☐☐☐☐☐	40	Tony Amonte, Chi.	25.00	1.50	.35
☐☐☐☐☐☐	41	Chris Chelios, Chi.	60.00	3.00	.60
☐☐☐☐☐☐	42	Dan Cleary, Chi.	35.00	2.00	.50
☐☐☐☐☐☐	43	Eric Dazé, Chi.	25.00	1.50	.35
☐☐☐☐☐☐	44	Jeff Hackett (G), Chi.	25.00	1.50	.35
☐☐☐☐☐☐	45	Sergei Krivokrasov, Chi.	15.00	.50	.15
☐☐☐☐☐☐	46	Ethan Moreau, Chi.	15.00	.50	.15
☐☐☐☐☐☐	47	Alexei Zhamnov, Chi.	15.00	.50	.15
☐☐☐☐☐☐	48	Adam Deadmarsh, Col.	15.00	.50	.15
☐☐☐☐☐☐	49	Peter Forsberg, Col.	200.00	7.50	1.50
☐☐☐☐☐☐	50	Valeri Kamensky, Col.	25.00	1.50	.35
☐☐☐☐☐☐	51	Jari Kurri, Col.	25.00	1.50	.35
☐☐☐☐☐☐	52	Claude Lemieux, Col.	15.00	.50	.15
☐☐☐☐☐☐	53	Sandis Ozolinsh, Col.	25.00	1.50	.35
☐☐☐☐☐☐	54	Patrick Roy (G), Col.	300.00	12.00	2.50
☐☐☐☐☐☐	55	Joe Sakic, Col.	150.00	6.00	1.25
☐☐☐☐☐☐	56	Ed Belfour (G), Dal.	15.00	.50	.15
☐☐☐☐☐☐	57	Derian Hatcher, Dal.	25.00	1.50	.35
☐☐☐☐☐☐	58	Jamie Langenbrunner, Dal.	25.00	1.50	.35
☐☐☐☐☐☐	59	Jere Lehtinen, Dal.	25.00	1.50	.35
☐☐☐☐☐☐	60	Mike Modano, Dal.	80.00	3.75	.75
☐☐☐☐☐☐	61	Joe Nieuwendyk, Dal.	25.00	1.50	.35
☐☐☐☐☐☐	62	Darryl Sydor, Dal.	15.00	.50	.15
☐☐☐☐☐☐	63	Pat Verbeek, Dal.	15.00	.50	.15
☐☐☐☐☐☐	64	Anders Eriksson, Det.	15.00	.50	.15
☐☐☐☐☐☐	65	Sergei Fedorov, Det.	80.00	3.75	.75
☐☐☐☐☐☐	66	Vyacheslav Kozlov, Det.	15.00	.50	.15
☐☐☐☐☐☐	67	Nicklas Lidström, Det.	25.00	1.50	.35
☐☐☐☐☐☐	68	Darren McCarty, Det.	15.00	.50	.15
☐☐☐☐☐☐	69	Chris Osgood (G), Det.	60.00	3.00	.60
☐☐☐☐☐☐	70	Brendan Shanahan, Det.	100.00	4.50	.85
☐☐☐☐☐☐	71	Steve Yzerman, Det.	200.00	7.50	1.50
☐☐☐☐☐☐	72	Jason Arnott, Edm.	25.00	1.50	.35
☐☐☐☐☐☐	73	Boyd Devereaux, Edm.	15.00	.50	.15
☐☐☐☐☐☐	74	Mike Grier, Edm.	25.00	1.50	.35
☐☐☐☐☐☐	75	Curtis Joseph (G), Edm.	100.00	4.50	.85
☐☐☐☐☐☐	76	Andrei Kovalenko, Edm.	15.00	.50	.15
☐☐☐☐☐☐	77	Ryan Smyth, Edm.	25.00	1.50	.35
☐☐☐☐☐☐	78	Doug Weight, Edm.	40.00	2.25	.50
☐☐☐☐☐☐	79	Dave Gagner, Fla.	15.00	.50	.15
☐☐☐☐☐☐	80	Ed Jovanovski, Fla.	25.00	1.50	.35
☐☐☐☐☐☐	81	Scott Mellanby, Fla.	15.00	.50	.15
☐☐☐☐☐☐	82	Kirk Muller, Fla.	15.00	.50	.15
☐☐☐☐☐☐	83	Rob Niedermayer, Fla.	15.00	.50	.15
☐☐☐☐☐☐	84	Ray Sheppard, Fla.	15.00	.50	.15
☐☐☐☐☐☐	85	Esa Tikkanen, Fla.	15.00	.50	.15
☐☐☐☐☐☐	86	John Vanbiesbrouck (G), Fla.	100.00	4.50	.85
☐☐☐☐☐☐	87	Rob Blake, L.A.	25.00	1.50	.35
☐☐☐☐☐☐	88	Stéphane Fiset (G), L.A.	25.00	1.50	.35
☐☐☐☐☐☐	89	Garry Galley, L.A.	15.00	.50	.15
☐☐☐☐☐☐	**90**	**Olli Jokinen, L.A., RC**	**25.00**	**1.50**	**.60**
☐☐☐☐☐☐	91	Luc Robitaille, L.A.	25.00	1.50	.35
☐☐☐☐☐☐	92	Jozef Stumpel, L.A.	25.00	1.50	.35
☐☐☐☐☐☐	93	Shayne Corson, Mtl.	25.00	1.50	.35
☐☐☐☐☐☐	94	Vincent Damphousse, Mtl.	40.00	2.25	.50
☐☐☐☐☐☐	95	Saku Koivu, Mtl.	125.00	5.00	1.00
☐☐☐☐☐☐	96	Andy Moog (G), Mtl.	25.00	1.50	.35
☐☐☐☐☐☐	97	Mark Recchi, Mtl.	25.00	1.50	.35
☐☐☐☐☐☐	98	Stéphane Richer (G), Mtl.	15.00	.50	.15
☐☐☐☐☐☐	99	Brian Savage, Mtl.	15.00	.50	.15
☐☐☐☐☐☐	100	Dave Andreychuk, N.J.	15.00	.50	.15
☐☐☐☐☐☐	101	Martin Brodeur (G), N.J.	125.00	5.00	1.00
☐☐☐☐☐☐	102	Doug Gilmour, N.J.	40.00	2.25	.50
☐☐☐☐☐☐	103	Bobby Holik, N.J.	15.00	.50	.15
☐☐☐☐☐☐	104	John MacLean, N.J.	15.00	.50	.15
☐☐☐☐☐☐	105	Brian Rolston, N.J.	15.00	.50	.15
☐☐☐☐☐☐	106	Bryan Berard, NYI.	40.00	2.25	.50
☐☐☐☐☐☐	107	Todd Bertuzzi, NYI.	25.00	1.50	.35
☐☐☐☐☐☐	108	Travis Green, NYI.	15.00	.50	.15
☐☐☐☐☐☐	109	Zigmund Palffy, NYI.	40.00	2.25	.50
☐☐☐☐☐☐	110	Robert Reichel, NYI.	15.00	.50	.15
☐☐☐☐☐☐	111	Tommy Salo (G), NYI.	15.00	.50	.15
☐☐☐☐☐☐	112	Bryan Smolinski, NYI.	15.00	.50	.15
☐☐☐☐☐☐	113	Christian Dubé, NYR.	15.00	.50	.15
☐☐☐☐☐☐	114	Adam Graves, NYR.	15.00	.50	.15
☐☐☐☐☐☐	115	Wayne Gretzky, NYR.	400.00	15.00	3.00

	No.	Player			
☐☐☐☐☐☐	116	Alexei Kovalev, NYR.	15.00	.50	.15
☐☐☐☐☐☐	117	Pat LaFontaine, NYR.	25.00	1.50	.35
☐☐☐☐☐☐	118	Brian Leetch, NYR.	40.00	2.25	.50
☐☐☐☐☐☐	119	Mike Richter, NYR.	40.00	2.25	.50
☐☐☐☐☐☐	120	Brian Skrudland, NYR.	15.00	.50	.15
☐☐☐☐☐☐	121	Kevin Stevens, NYR.	15.00	.50	.15
☐☐☐☐☐☐	122	Daniel Alfredsson, Ott.	25.00	1.50	.35
☐☐☐☐☐☐	123	Radek Bonk, Ott.	15.00	.50	.15
☐☐☐☐☐☐	124	Alexandre Daigle, Ott.	15.00	.50	.15
☐☐☐☐☐☐	**125**	**Marian Hossa, Ott., RC**	**75.00**	**6.00**	**2.50**
☐☐☐☐☐☐	126	Igor Kravchuk, Ott.	15.00	.50	.15
☐☐☐☐☐☐	127	Chris Phillips, Ott.	25.00	1.50	.50
☐☐☐☐☐☐	128	Damian Rhodes, Ott.	15.00	.50	.15
☐☐☐☐☐☐	129	Alexei Yashin, Ott.	60.00	3.00	.60
☐☐☐☐☐☐	130	Rod Brind'Amour, Pha.	25.00	1.50	.35
☐☐☐☐☐☐	131	Chris Gratton, Pha.	25.00	1.50	.35
☐☐☐☐☐☐	132	Ron Hextall (G), Pha.	25.00	1.50	.35
☐☐☐☐☐☐	133	John LeClair, Pha.	80.00	3.75	.75
☐☐☐☐☐☐	134	Eric Lindros, Pha.	250.00	10.00	2.00
☐☐☐☐☐☐	135	Janne Niinimaa, Pha.	25.00	1.50	.35
☐☐☐☐☐☐	**136**	**Vaclav Prospal, Pha., RC**	**35.00**	**2.00**	**.75**
☐☐☐☐☐☐	137	Garth Snow (G), Pha.	15.00	.50	.15
☐☐☐☐☐☐	138	Dainius Zubrus, Pha.	25.00	1.50	.35
☐☐☐☐☐☐	139	Mike Gartner, Pho.	25.00	1.50	.35
☐☐☐☐☐☐	140	Brad Isbister, Pho.	15.00	.50	.15
☐☐☐☐☐☐	141	Nikolai Khabibulin, Pho.	40.00	2.25	.50
☐☐☐☐☐☐	142	Jeremy Roenick, Pho.	40.00	2.25	.50
☐☐☐☐☐☐	143	Cliff Ronning, Pho.	15.00	.50	.15
☐☐☐☐☐☐	144	Keith Tkachuk, Pho.	60.00	3.00	.60
☐☐☐☐☐☐	145	Rick Tocchet, Pho.	15.00	.50	.15
☐☐☐☐☐☐	146	Oleg Tverdovsky, Pho.	15.00	.50	.15
☐☐☐☐☐☐	147	Tom Barrasso (G), Pho.	25.00	1.50	.35
☐☐☐☐☐☐	148	Ron Francis, Pgh.	40.00	2.25	.50
☐☐☐☐☐☐	149	Kevin Hatcher, Pgh.	15.00	.50	.15
☐☐☐☐☐☐	150	Jaromir Jagr, Pgh.	200.00	7.50	1.50
☐☐☐☐☐☐	151	Darius Kasparaitis, Pgh.	15.00	.50	.15
☐☐☐☐☐☐	152	Alexei Morozov, Pgh.	50.00	3.00	.75
☐☐☐☐☐☐	153	Petr Nedved, Pgh.	15.00	.50	.15
☐☐☐☐☐☐	154	Ed Olczyk, Pgh.	15.00	.50	.15
☐☐☐☐☐☐	155	Jim Campbell, Stl.	15.00	.50	.15
☐☐☐☐☐☐	156	Kelly Chase, Stl.	15.00	.50	.15
☐☐☐☐☐☐	157	Geoff Courtnall, Stl.	15.00	.50	.15
☐☐☐☐☐☐	158	Grant Fuhr (G), Stl.	25.00	1.50	.35
☐☐☐☐☐☐	159	Brett Hull, Stl.	80.00	3.75	.75
☐☐☐☐☐☐	160	Joe Murphy, Stl.	15.00	.50	.15
☐☐☐☐☐☐	161	Pierre Turgeon, Stl.	25.00	1.50	.35
☐☐☐☐☐☐	162	Tony Twist, Stl.	15.00	.50	.15
☐☐☐☐☐☐	163	Shawn Burr, S.J.	15.00	.50	.15
☐☐☐☐☐☐	164	Jeff Friesen, S.J.	25.00	1.50	.35
☐☐☐☐☐☐	165	Tony Granato, S.J.	15.00	.50	.15
☐☐☐☐☐☐	166	Viktor Kozlov, S.J.	15.00	.50	.15
☐☐☐☐☐☐	167	Patrick Marleau, S.J.	50.00	3.00	.75
☐☐☐☐☐☐	168	Stéphane Matteau, S.J.	15.00	.50	.15
☐☐☐☐☐☐	169	Owen Nolan, S.J.	25.00	1.50	.35
☐☐☐☐☐☐	170	Mike Vernon (G), S.J.	25.00	1.50	.35
☐☐☐☐☐☐	171	Dino Ciccarelli, T.B.	25.00	1.50	.35
☐☐☐☐☐☐	172	Karl Dykhuis, T.B.	15.00	.50	.15
☐☐☐☐☐☐	173	Roman Hamrlik, T.B.	25.00	1.50	.35
☐☐☐☐☐☐	174	Daymond Langkow, T.B.	15.00	.50	.15
☐☐☐☐☐☐	175	Mikael Renberg, T.B.	15.00	.50	.15
☐☐☐☐☐☐	176	Alexander Selivanov, T.B.	15.00	.50	.15
☐☐☐☐☐☐	177	Paul Ysebaert, T.B.	15.00	.50	.15
☐☐☐☐☐☐	178	Sergei Berezin, Tor.	25.00	1.50	.35
☐☐☐☐☐☐	179	Wendel Clark, Tor.	25.00	1.50	.35
☐☐☐☐☐☐	180	Glenn Healy (G), Tor.	15.00	.50	.15
☐☐☐☐☐☐	181	Derek King, Tor.	15.00	.50	.15
☐☐☐☐☐☐	182	Alyn McCauley, Tor.	50.00	3.00	.75
☐☐☐☐☐☐	183	Félix Potvin (G), Tor.	80.00	3.75	.75
☐☐☐☐☐☐	184	Martin Prochazka, Tor.	15.00	.50	.15
☐☐☐☐☐☐	185	Mats Sundin, Tor.	80.00	3.75	.75
☐☐☐☐☐☐	186	Pavel Bure, Van.	125.00	5.00	1.00
☐☐☐☐☐☐	187	Martin Gelinas, Van.	15.00	.50	.15
☐☐☐☐☐☐	188	Trevor Linden, Van.	25.00	1.50	.35
☐☐☐☐☐☐	189	Kirk McLean (G), Van.	25.00	1.50	.35
☐☐☐☐☐☐	190	Mark Messier, Van.	80.00	3.75	.75
☐☐☐☐☐☐	**191**	**Lubomir Vaic, Van., RC**	**15.00**	**.50**	**.15**
☐☐☐☐☐☐	192	Mattias Ohlund, Van.	30.00	2.50	.50
☐☐☐☐☐☐	193	Peter Bondra, Wsh.	60.00	3.00	.60
☐☐☐☐☐☐	194	Dale Hunter, Wsh.	15.00	.50	.15
☐☐☐☐☐☐	195	Joé Juneau, Wsh.	15.00	.50	.15
☐☐☐☐☐☐	196	Olaf Kolzig (G), Wsh.	40.00	2.25	.50
☐☐☐☐☐☐	197	Steve Konowalchuk, Wsh.	15.00	.50	.15
☐☐☐☐☐☐	198	Adam Oates, Wsh.	40.00	2.25	.50
☐☐☐☐☐☐	199	Bill Ranford (G), Wsh.	25.00	1.50	.35
☐☐☐☐☐☐	200	Jaroslav Svejkovsky, Wsh.	25.00	1.50	.35

CANADIAN GREATS

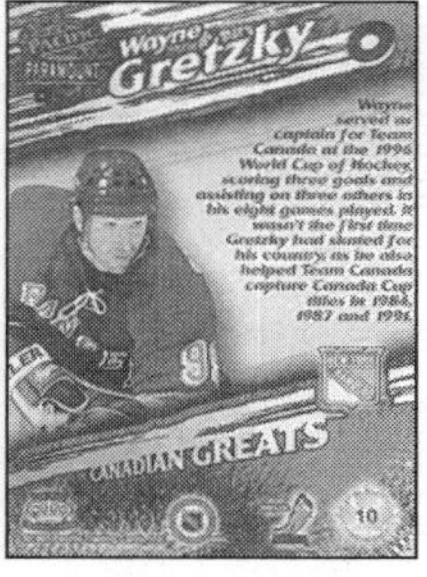

Canadian Greats insertion ratio in Canadian packs is [2:48].

Insert Set (12 cards): 175.00

	No.	Player	NRMT-MT
☐	1	Paul Kariya, Ana.	25.00
☐	2	Joe Thornton, Bos.	10.00
☐	3	Jarome Iginla, Cgy.	4.00
☐	4	Patrick Roy (G), Col.	30.00
☐	5	Joe Sakic, Col.	15.00
☐	6	Brendan Shanahan, Det.	10.00
☐	7	Steve Yzerman, Det.	20.00
☐	8	Ryan Smyth, Edm.	4.00
☐	9	Martin Brodeur (G), N.J.	12.00
☐	10	Wayne Gretzky, NYR.	35.00
☐	11	Eric Lindros, Pha.	25.00
☐	12	Mark Messier, Van.	8.00

PHOTOENGRAVINGS

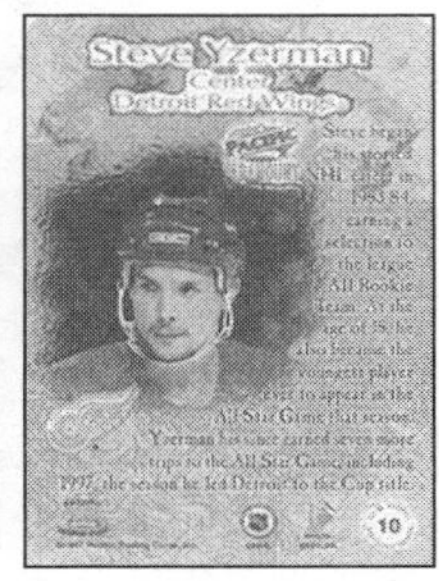

Photoengravings insertion ratio is [2:37].

Insert Set (20 cards): 250.00

	No.	Player	NRMT-MT
☐	1	Paul Kariya, Ana.	20.00
☐	2	Teemu Selänne, Ana.	12.00
☐	3	Joe Thornton, Bos.	10.00
☐	4	Dominik Hasek (G), Buf.	12.00
☐	5	Peter Forsberg, Col.	18.00
☐	6	Patrick Roy (G), Col.	25.00
☐	7	Joe Sakic, Col.	15.00
☐	8	Mike Modano, Dal.	8.00
☐	9	Brendan Shanahan, Det.	10.00
☐	10	Steve Yzerman, Det.	18.00
☐	11	John Vanbiesbrouck (G), Fla.	10.00
☐	12	Saku Koivu, Mtl.	12.00
☐	13	Wayne Gretzky, NYR.	35.00
☐	14	John LeClair, Pha.	8.00
☐	15	Eric Lindros, Pha.	20.00
☐	16	Keith Tkachuk, Pho.	6.00
☐	17	Jaromir Jagr, Pgh.	18.00
☐	18	Brett Hull, Stl.	8.00
☐	19	Pavel Bure, Van.	12.00
☐	20	Mark Messier, Van.	8.00

BIG NUMBERS

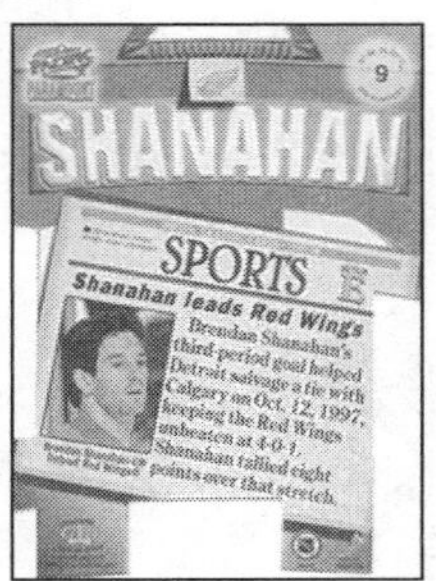

Big Numbers Die-Cuts insertion ratio is [1:37].

Insert Set (20 cards): 350.00

	No.	Player	NRMT-MT
☐	1	Paul Kariya, Ana.	35.00
☐	2	Teemu Selänne, Ana.	15.00
☐	3	Joe Thornton, Bos.	12.00
☐	4	Dominik Hasek, Buf.	15.00
☐	5	Peter Forsberg, Col.	25.00
☐	6	Patrick Roy, Col.	40.00
☐	7	Joe Sakic, Col.	20.00
☐	8	Sergei Fedorov, Det.	10.00
☐	9	Brendan Shanahan, Det.	12.00
☐	10	Steve Yzerman, Det.	25.00
☐	11	John Vanbiesbrouck, Fla.	12.00
☐	12	Martin Brodeur, N.J.	15.00
☐	13	Doug Gilmour, N.J.	6.00
☐	14	Wayne Gretzky, NYR.	50.00
☐	15	Eric Lindros, Pha.	35.00
☐	16	Keith Tkachuk, Pho.	8.00
☐	17	Jaromir Jagr, Pgh.	25.00
☐	18	Brett Hull, Stl.	10.00
☐	19	Pavel Bure, Van.	15.00
☐	20	Mark Messier, Van.	10.00

GLOVE SIDE

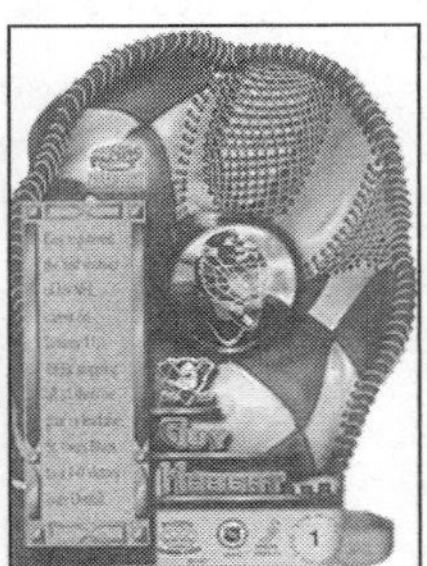

Glove Side Laser-Cuts insertion ratio is [1:73].

Insert Set (20 cards): 400.00

	No.	Player	NRMT-MT
☐	1	Guy Hebert (G), Ana.	12.00
☐	2	Dominik Hasek (G), Buf.	40.00
☐	3	Trevor Kidd (G), Car.	12.00
☐	4	Jeff Hackett (G), Chi.	12.00
☐	5	Patrick Roy (G), Col.	90.00
☐	6	Ed Belfour (G), Dal.	15.00
☐	7	Chris Osgood (G), Det.	20.00
☐	8	Curtis Joseph (G), Edm.	30.00
☐	9	John Vanbiesbrouck (G), Fla.	30.00
☐	10	Andy Moog (G), Mtl.	12.00
☐	11	Martin Brodeur (G), N.J.	40.00
☐	12	Tommy Salo (G), NYI.	10.00
☐	13	Mike Richter (G), NYR.	15.00
☐	14	Ron Hextall (G), Pha.	12.00
☐	15	Garth Snow (G), Pha.	10.00
☐	16	Nikolai Khabibulin (G), Pho.	15.00
☐	17	Tom Barrasso (G), Pgh.	12.00
☐	18	Grant Fuhr (G), Stl.	12.00
☐	19	Mike Vernon (G), S.J.	12.00
☐	20	Félix Potvin (G), Tor.	25.00

1997 - 98 PACIFIC REVOLUTION

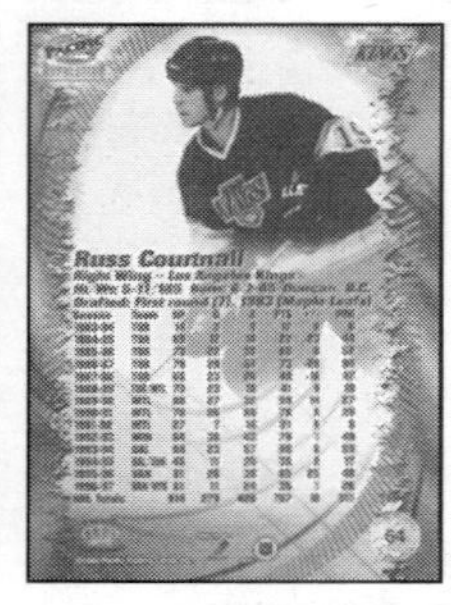

These cards have five versions: the regular card, an Emerald Green parallel (Canadian), a Copper parallel (Hobby), a Silver parallel (Retail) and an Ice Blue parallel.

Imprint: © 1997 PACIFIC TRADING CARDS, INC.

Complete Set (150 cards):		–	**1,000.00**	**150.00**
Common Player:		**15.00**	**6.00**	**.50**
Sample Card (Mike Modano):				**2.00**

	No.	Player	Ice Blue	Par.	Reg.
☐☐☐☐☐	1	Guy Hebert (G), Ana.	25.00	10.00	1.00
☐☐☐☐☐	2	Paul Kariya, Ana.	250.00	65.00	6.50
☐☐☐☐☐	3	Dmitri Mironov, Ana.	15.00	6.00	.50
☐☐☐☐☐	4	Ruslan Salei, Ana.	15.00	6.00	.50
☐☐☐☐☐	5	Teemu Selänne, Ana.	125.00	35.00	3.50
☐☐☐☐☐	6	Jason Allison, Bos.	40.00	15.00	1.50
☐☐☐☐☐	7	Ray Bourque, Bos.	80.00	25.00	2.50
☐☐☐☐☐	8	Byron Dafoe (G), Bos.	15.00	6.00	.50
☐☐☐☐☐	9	Ted Donato, Bos.	15.00	6.00	.50
☐☐☐☐☐	10	Dimitri Khristich, Bos.	15.00	6.00	.50
☐☐☐☐☐	11	Joe Thornton, Bos.	80.00	25.00	3.00
☐☐☐☐☐	12	Matthew Barnaby, Buf.	15.00	6.00	.50
☐☐☐☐☐	13	Jason Dawe, Buf.	15.00	6.00	.50
☐☐☐☐☐	14	Dominik Hasek (G), Buf.	125.00	35.00	3.50
☐☐☐☐☐	15	Michael Peca, Buf.	25.00	10.00	1.00
☐☐☐☐☐	16	Miroslav Satan, Buf.	15.00	6.00	.50
☐☐☐☐☐	17	Theoren Fleury, Cgy.	40.00	15.00	1.50
☐☐☐☐☐	18	Jarome Iginla, Cgy.	40.00	15.00	1.50
☐☐☐☐☐	19	Marty McInnis, Cgy.	15.00	6.00	.50
☐☐☐☐☐	20	Cory Stillman, Cgy.	15.00	6.00	.50
☐☐☐☐☐	21	Rick Tabaracci (G), Cgy.	15.00	6.00	.50
☐☐☐☐☐	22	Martin Gelinas, Car.	15.00	6.00	.50
☐☐☐☐☐	23	Sami Kapanen, Car.	15.00	6.00	.50
☐☐☐☐☐	24	Trevor Kidd (G), Car.	25.00	10.00	1.00
☐☐☐☐☐	25	Keith Primeau, Car.	15.00	6.00	.50
☐☐☐☐☐	26	Gary Roberts, Car.	25.00	10.00	1.00
☐☐☐☐☐	27	Tony Amonte, Chi.	25.00	10.00	1.00
☐☐☐☐☐	28	Chris Chelios, Chi.	60.00	20.00	2.00
☐☐☐☐☐	29	Eric Dazé, Chi.	25.00	10.00	1.00
☐☐☐☐☐	30	Jeff Hackett (G), Chi.	25.00	10.00	1.00
☐☐☐☐☐	31	Dimitri Nabokov, Chi.	25.00	10.00	1.00
☐☐☐☐☐	32	Peter Forsberg, Col.	200.00	50.00	5.00
☐☐☐☐☐	33	Valeri Kamensky, Col.	15.00	6.00	.50
☐☐☐☐☐	34	Jari Kurri, Col.	25.00	10.00	1.00
☐☐☐☐☐	35	Claude Lemieux, Col.	15.00	6.00	.50
☐☐☐☐☐	**36**	**Eric Messier, Col., RC**	**15.00**	**6.00**	**.50**
☐☐☐☐☐	37	Sandis Ozolinsh, Col.	25.00	10.00	1.00
☐☐☐☐☐	38	Patrick Roy (G), Col.	300.00	80.00	8.00
☐☐☐☐☐	39	Joe Sakic, Col.	150.00	40.00	4.00
☐☐☐☐☐	40	Ed Belfour (G), Dal.	40.00	15.00	1.50
☐☐☐☐☐	41	Jamie Langenbrunner, Dal.	25.00	10.00	1.00
☐☐☐☐☐	42	Jere Lehtinen, Dal.	25.00	10.00	1.00
☐☐☐☐☐	43	Mike Modano, Dal.	80.00	25.00	2.50
☐☐☐☐☐	44	Joe Nieuwendyk, Dal.	25.00	10.00	1.00
☐☐☐☐☐	45	Sergei Zubov, Dal.	25.00	10.00	1.00
☐☐☐☐☐	46	Viacheslav Fetisov, Det.	25.00	10.00	1.00
☐☐☐☐☐	47	Nicklas Lidström, Det.	25.00	10.00	1.00
☐☐☐☐☐	48	Darren McCarty, Det.	15.00	6.00	.50
☐☐☐☐☐	49	Larry Murphy, Det.	25.00	10.00	1.00
☐☐☐☐☐	50	Chris Osgood (G), Det.	60.00	20.00	2.00
☐☐☐☐☐	51	Brendan Shanahan, Det.	100.00	30.00	3.00
☐☐☐☐☐	52	Steve Yzerman, Det.	200.00	50.00	5.00
☐☐☐☐☐	53	Roman Hamrlik, Edm.	25.00	10.00	1.00
☐☐☐☐☐	54	Bill Guerin, Edm.	25.00	10.00	1.00
☐☐☐☐☐	55	Curtis Joseph (G), Edm.	100.00	30.00	3.00
☐☐☐☐☐	56	Ryan Smyth, Edm.	25.00	10.00	1.00
☐☐☐☐☐	57	Doug Weight, Edm.	40.00	15.00	1.50
☐☐☐☐☐	58	Dino Ciccarelli, Fla.	25.00	10.00	1.00
☐☐☐☐☐	59	Dave Gagner, Fla.	15.00	6.00	.50
☐☐☐☐☐	60	Ed Jovanovski, Fla.	25.00	10.00	1.00
☐☐☐☐☐	61	Paul Laus, Fla.	15.00	6.00	.50
☐☐☐☐☐	62	John Vanbiesbrouck (G), Fla.	100.00	30.00	3.00
☐☐☐☐☐	63	Ray Whitney, Fla.	15.00	6.00	.50
☐☐☐☐☐	64	Russ Courtnall, L.A.	15.00	6.00	.50
☐☐☐☐☐	65	Yanic Perreault, L.A.	15.00	6.00	.50
☐☐☐☐☐	66	Luc Robitaille, L.A.	25.00	10.00	1.00
☐☐☐☐☐	67	Jozef Stumpel, L.A.	25.00	10.00	1.00
☐☐☐☐☐	68	Vladimir Tsyplakov, L.A.	15.00	6.00	.50
☐☐☐☐☐	69	Shayne Corson, Mtl.	25.00	10.00	1.00
☐☐☐☐☐	70	Vincent Damphousse, Mtl.	40.00	15.00	1.50
☐☐☐☐☐	71	Saku Koivu, Mtl.	125.00	35.00	3.50
☐☐☐☐☐	72	Andy Moog (G), Mtl.	25.00	10.00	1.00
☐☐☐☐☐	73	Mark Recchi, Mtl.	25.00	10.00	1.00
☐☐☐☐☐	74	Jocelyn Thibault (G), Mtl.	40.00	15.00	1.50
☐☐☐☐☐	75	Martin Brodeur (G), N.J.	15.00	6.00	.50
☐☐☐☐☐	**76**	**Patrik Elias, N.J., RC**	**25.00**	**10.00**	**2.00**
☐☐☐☐☐	77	Doug Gilmour, N.J.	40.00	15.00	1.50
☐☐☐☐☐	78	Bobby Holik, N.J.	15.00	6.00	.50
☐☐☐☐☐	79	Scott Niedermayer, N.J.	25.00	10.00	1.00
☐☐☐☐☐	80	Bryan Berard, NYI.	40.00	15.00	1.50
☐☐☐☐☐	81	Travis Green, NYI.	15.00	6.00	.50
☐☐☐☐☐	82	Zigmund Palffy, NYI.	40.00	15.00	1.50
☐☐☐☐☐	83	Robert Reichel, NYI.	15.00	6.00	.50
☐☐☐☐☐	84	Tommy Salo (G), NYI.	15.00	6.00	.50
☐☐☐☐☐	85	Dan Cloutier (G), NYR.	25.00	10.00	1.00
☐☐☐☐☐	86	Adam Graves, NYR.	15.00	6.00	.50
☐☐☐☐☐	87	Wayne Gretzky, NYR.	400.00	100.00	10.00
☐☐☐☐☐	88	Pat LaFontaine, NYR.	25.00	10.00	1.00
☐☐☐☐☐	89	Brian Leetch, NYR.	40.00	15.00	1.50
☐☐☐☐☐	90	Mike Richter (G), NYR	40.00	15.00	1.50
☐☐☐☐☐	91	Kevin Stevens, NYR.	15.00	6.00	.50
☐☐☐☐☐	92	Daniel Alfredsson, Ott.	25.00	10.00	1.00
☐☐☐☐☐	93	Shawn McEachern, Ott.	15.00	6.00	.50
☐☐☐☐☐	94	Damian Rhodes (G), Ott.	15.00	6.00	.50
☐☐☐☐☐	95	Ron Tugnutt (G), Ott.	15.00	6.00	.50
☐☐☐☐☐	96	Alexei Yashin, Ott.	60.00	20.00	2.00
☐☐☐☐☐	97	Rod Brind'Amour, Pha.	25.00	10.00	1.00
☐☐☐☐☐	98	Paul Coffey, Pha.	25.00	10.00	1.00
☐☐☐☐☐	99	Alexandre Daigle, Pha.	15.00	6.00	.50
☐☐☐☐☐	100	Chris Gratton, Pha.	25.00	10.00	1.00
☐☐☐☐☐	101	Ron Hextall (G), Pha.	15.00	6.00	.50
☐☐☐☐☐	102	John LeClair, Pha.	80.00	25.00	2.50
☐☐☐☐☐	103	Eric Lindros, Pha.	250.00	65.00	6.50
☐☐☐☐☐	104	Dainius Zubrus, Pha.	25.00	10.00	1.00
☐☐☐☐☐	105	Mike Gartner, Pho.	25.00	10.00	1.00
☐☐☐☐☐	106	Craig Janney, Pho.	15.00	6.00	.50
☐☐☐☐☐	107	Nikolai Khabibulin (G), Pho.	40.00	15.00	1.50
☐☐☐☐☐	108	Jeremy Roenick, Pho.	40.00	15.00	1.50
☐☐☐☐☐	109	Keith Tkachuk, Pho.	60.00	20.00	2.00
☐☐☐☐☐	110	Stu Barnes, Pgh.	15.00	6.00	.50
☐☐☐☐☐	111	Tom Barrasso (G), Pgh.	25.00	10.00	1.00
☐☐☐☐☐	112	Ron Francis, Pgh.	40.00	15.00	1.50
☐☐☐☐☐	113	Jaromir Jagr, Pgh.	200.00	50.00	5.00
☐☐☐☐☐	**114**	**Peter Skudra (G), Pgh., RC**	**15.00**	**6.00**	**.50**
☐☐☐☐☐	115	Martin Straka, Pgh.	15.00	6.00	.50
☐☐☐☐☐	**116**	**Blair Atcheynum, Stl., RC**	**15.00**	**6.00**	**.50**
☐☐☐☐☐	117	Jim Campbell, Stl.	15.00	6.00	.50
☐☐☐☐☐	118	Geoff Courtnall, Stl.	15.00	6.00	.50
☐☐☐☐☐	119	Steve Duchesne, Stl.	15.00	6.00	.50
☐☐☐☐☐	120	Grant Fuhr (G), Stl.	25.00	10.00	1.00
☐☐☐☐☐	121	Brett Hull, Stl.	80.00	25.00	2.50
☐☐☐☐☐	122	Pierre Turgeon, Stl.	25.00	10.00	1.00
☐☐☐☐☐	123	Jeff Friesen, S.J.	15.00	6.00	.50
☐☐☐☐☐	124	John MacLean, S.J.	15.00	6.00	.50
☐☐☐☐☐	125	Patrick Marleau, S.J.	50.00	20.00	2.50
☐☐☐☐☐	126	Owen Nolan, S.J.	25.00	10.00	1.00
☐☐☐☐☐	**127**	**Marco Sturm, S.J., RC**	**15.00**	**6.00**	**.50**
☐☐☐☐☐	128	Mike Vernon (G), S.J.	25.00	10.00	1.00
☐☐☐☐☐	129	Daren Puppa (G), T.B.	15.00	6.00	.50
☐☐☐☐☐	130	Mikael Renberg, T.B.	15.00	6.00	.50
☐☐☐☐☐	131	Paul Ysebaert, T.B.	15.00	6.00	.50
☐☐☐☐☐	132	Rob Zamuner, T.B.	25.00	10.00	1.00
☐☐☐☐☐	133	Wendel Clark, Tor.	25.00	10.00	1.00
☐☐☐☐☐	134	Tie Domi, Tor.	15.00	6.00	.50
☐☐☐☐☐	135	Igor Korolev, Tor.	15.00	6.00	.50
☐☐☐☐☐	136	Félix Potvin (G), Tor.	80.00	25.00	2.50
☐☐☐☐☐	137	Mats Sundin, Tor.	80.00	25.00	2.50
☐☐☐☐☐	138	Donald Brashear, Van.	15.00	6.00	.50
☐☐☐☐☐	139	Pavel Bure, Van.	125.00	35.00	3.50
☐☐☐☐☐	140	Sean Burke (G), Van.	25.00	10.00	1.00
☐☐☐☐☐	141	Trevor Linden, Van.	25.00	10.00	1.00
☐☐☐☐☐	142	Mark Messier, Van.	80.00	25.00	2.50
☐☐☐☐☐	143	Alexander Mogilny, Van.	40.00	15.00	1.50
☐☐☐☐☐	144	Mattias Ohlund, Van.	30.00	15.00	1.50
☐☐☐☐☐	145	Peter Bondra, Wsh.	60.00	20.00	2.00
☐☐☐☐☐	146	Phil Housley, Wsh.	15.00	6.00	.50
☐☐☐☐☐	147	Dale Hunter, Wsh.	15.00	6.00	.50
☐☐☐☐☐	148	Joé Juneau, Wsh.	15.00	6.00	.50
☐☐☐☐☐	149	Olaf Kolzig (G), Wsh.	40.00	15.00	1.50
☐☐☐☐☐	150	Adam Oates, Wsh.	40.00	15.00	1.50

TEAM CHECKLIST

Insertion ratio for these laser-cut cards is [1:25].

	No.	Player	NRMT-MT
Insert Set (26 cards):			**350.00**
☐	1	Paul Kariya, Ana.	35.00
☐	2	Joe Thornton, Bos.	15.00
☐	3	Michael Peca, Buf.	6.00
☐	4	Theoren Fleury, Cgy.	8.00
☐	5	Keith Primeau, Car.	6.00
☐	6	Chris Chelios, Chi.	10.00
☐	7	Patrick Roy (G), Col.	40.00
☐	8	Mike Modano, Dal.	12.00
☐	9	Steve Yzerman, Det.	25.00
☐	10	Ryan Smyth, Edm.	6.00
☐	11	John Vanbiesbrouck (G), Fla.	15.00
☐	12	Jozef Stumpel, L.A.	6.00
☐	13	Saku Koivu, Mtl.	18.00
☐	14	Martin Brodeur (G), N.J.	18.00
☐	15	Zigmund Palffy, NYI.	8.00
☐	16	Wayne Gretzky, NYR.	50.00
☐	17	Daniel Alfredsson, Ott.	6.00
☐	18	Eric Lindros, Pha.	35.00
☐	19	Keith Tkachuk, Pho.	10.00
☐	20	Jaromir Jagr, Pgh.	25.00
☐	21	Brett Hull, Stl.	12.00
☐	22	Mike Vernon (G), S.J.	6.00
☐	23	Rob Zamuner, T.B.	6.00
☐	24	Mats Sundin, Tor.	12.00
☐	25	Pavel Bure, Van.	18.00
☐	26	Peter Bondra, Wsh.	10.00

RETURN TO SENDER

Insertion ratio for these die-cut cards is [1:25].

	No.	Player	NRMT-MT
Insert Set (20 cards):			**275.00**
☐	1	Guy Hebert (G), Ana.	8.00
☐	2	Byron Dafoe (G), Bos.	8.00
☐	3	Dominik Hasek (G), Buf.	30.00
☐	4	Jeff Hackett (G), Chi.	8.00
☐	5	Patrick Roy (G), Col.	65.00
☐	6	Ed Belfour (G), Dal.	12.00
☐	7	Chris Osgood (G), Det.	15.00
☐	8	Curtis Joseph (G), Edm.	20.00
☐	9	John Vanbiesbrouck (G), Fla.	20.00
☐	10	Andy Moog (G), Mtl.	8.00
☐	11	Martin Brodeur (G), N.J.	30.00
☐	12	Tommy Salo (G), NYI.	8.00
☐	13	Mike Richter (G), NYR.	12.00
☐	14	Ron Hextall (G), Pha.	8.00
☐	15	Nikolai Khabibulin (G), Pho.	12.00

	No.	Player	NRMT-MT
☐	16	Tom Barrasso (G), Pgh.	8.00
☐	17	Grant Fuhr (G), Stl.	8.00
☐	18	Mike Vernon (G), S.J.	8.00
☐	19	Félix Potvin (G), Tor.	18.00
☐	20	Olaf Kolzig (G), Wsh.	12.00

1998 ALL STAR GAME

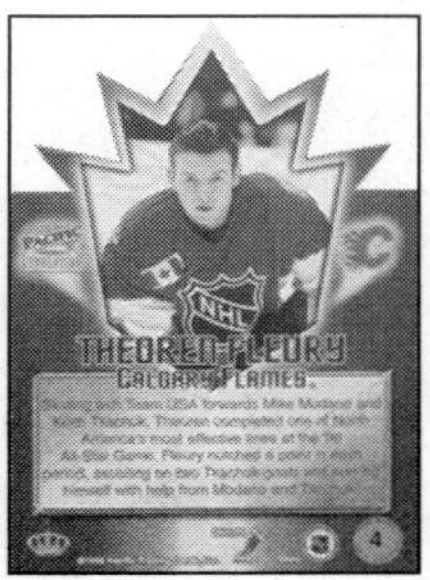

Insertion ratio for these die-cut cards is [1:49].

Insert Set (20 cards): 475.00

	No.	Player	NRMT-MT
☐	1	Teemu Selänne, Ana.	25.00
☐	2	Ray Bourque, Bos.	18.00
☐	3	Dominik Hasek (G), Buf.	25.00
☐	4	Theoren Fleury, Cgy.	12.00
☐	5	Chris Chelios, Chi.	15.00
☐	6	Peter Forsberg, Col.	35.00
☐	7	Patrick Roy (G), Col.	60.00
☐	8	Joe Sakic, Col.	30.00
☐	9	Ed Belfour (G), Dal.	12.00
☐	10	Mike Modano, Dal.	18.00
☐	11	Brendan Shanahan, Det.	20.00
☐	12	Saku Koivu, Mtl.	25.00
☐	13	Martin Brodeur (G), N.J.	25.00
☐	14	Wayne Gretzky, NYR.	75.00
☐	15	John LeClair, Pha.	18.00
☐	16	Eric Lindros, Pha.	50.00
☐	17	Jaromir Jagr, Pgh.	35.00
☐	18	Pavel Bure, Van.	25.00
☐	19	Mark Messier, Van.	18.00
☐	20	Peter Bondra, Wsh.	15.00

NHL ICONS

Insertion ratio for these die-cut cards is [1:121].

Insert Set (10 cards): 700.00

	No.	Player	NRMT-MT
☐	1	Paul Kariya, Ana.	100.00
☐	2	Teemu Selänne, Ana.	40.00
☐	3	Peter Forsberg, Col.	75.00
☐	4	Patrick Roy (G), Col.	120.00
☐	5	Steve Yzerman, Det.	75.00
☐	6	Martin Brodeur (G), N.J.	40.00
☐	7	Wayne Gretzky, NYR.	150.00
☐	8	Eric Lindros, Pha.	100.00
☐	9	Jaromir Jagr, Pgh.	75.00
☐	10	Pavel Bure, Van.	40.00

1997 - 98 PANINI STICKERS

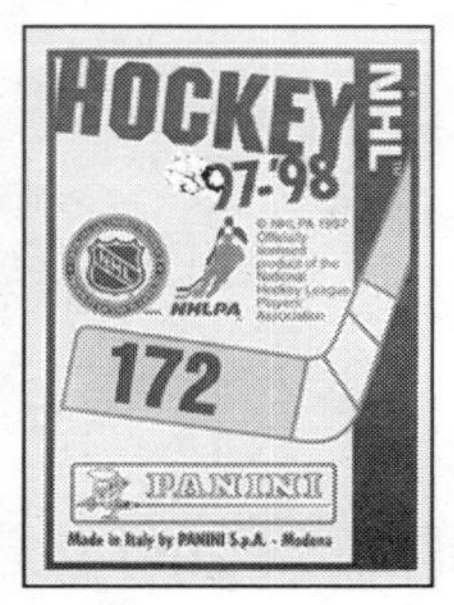

This series was issued for European distribution only.

Sticker Size: 2 1/8" x 3"

Imprint: Panini S.p.A.

Complete Set (252 stickers): 25.00

	No.	Player	NRMT-MT
☐	1	Rob DiMaio, Bos.	.20
☐	2	Jeff Odgers, Bos.	.20
☐	3	Jozef Stumpel, Bos.	.20
☐	4	Ted Donato, Bos.	.20
☐	5	Mattias Timander, Bos.	.20
☐	6	Boston Bruins logo	.20
☐	7	Don Sweeney, Bos.	.20
☐	8	Jim Carey (G), Bos.	.20
☐	9	Ray Bourque, Bos.	1.25
☐	10	Dominik Hasek (G), Buf.	1.75
☐	11	Alexei Zhitnik, Buf.	.20
☐	12	Derek Plante, Buf.	.20
☐	13	Michael Peca, Buf.	.50
☐	14	Darryl Shannon, Buf.	.20
☐	15	Buffalo Sabres logo	.20
☐	16	Donald Audette, Buf.	.20
☐	17	Michal Grosek, Buf.	.20
☐	18	Miroslav Satan, Buf.	.20
☐	19	Robert Kron, Car.	.20
☐	20	Geoff Sanderson, Car.	.20
☐	21	Andrew Cassels, Car.	.20
☐	22	Marek Malik, Car.	.20
☐	23	Derek King, Car.	.20
☐	24	Carolina Hurricanes logo	.20
☐	25	Sami Kapanen, Car.	.20
☐	26	Alexander Godynyuk, Car.	.20
☐	27	Keith Primeau, Car.	.50
☐	28	Saku Koivu, Mtl.	1.75
☐	29	Vincent Damphousse, Mtl.	.75
☐	30	Brian Savage, Mtl.	.20
☐	31	Valeri Bure, Mtl.	.20
☐	32	Mark Recchi, Mtl.	.50
☐	33	Montréal Canadiens logo	.20
☐	34	Vladimir Malakhov, Mtl.	.20
☐	35	Peter Popovic, Mtl.	.20
☐	36	Martin Rucinsky, Mtl.	.20
☐	37	Radek Bonk, Ott.	.20
☐	38	Alexandre Daigle, Ott.	.50
☐	39	Sergei Zholtok, Ott.	.20
☐	40	Janne Laukkanen, Ott.	.20
☐	41	Daniel Alfredsson, Ott.	.20
☐	42	Ottawa Senators logo	.20
☐	43	Alexei Yashin, Ott.	.20
☐	44	Frank Musil, Ott.	.20
☐	45	Steve Duchesne, Ott.	.20
☐	46	Darius Kasparaitis, Pgh.	.20
☐	47	Jaromir Jagr, Pgh.	2.50
☐	48	Roman Oksiuta, Pgh.	.20
☐	49	Kevin Hatcher, Pgh.	.20
☐	50	Ron Francis, Pgh.	.75
☐	51	Pittsburgh Penguins logo	.20
☐	52	Petr Nedved, Pgh.	.20
☐	53	Andreas Johansson, Pgh.	.20
☐	54	Fredrik Olausson, Pgh.	.20
☐	55	Robert Svehla, Fla.	.20
☐	56	Radek Dvorak, Fla.	.20
☐	57	Martin Straka, Fla.	.20
☐	58	Kirk Muller, Fla.	.20
☐	59	Per Gustafsson, Fla.	.20
☐	60	Florida Panthers logo	.20
☐	61	Ray Sheppard, Fla.	.20
☐	62	Johan Garpenlov, Fla.	.20
☐	63	Scott Mellanby, Fla.	.20
☐	64	Martin Brodeur (G), N.J.	1.75
☐	65	Bobby Holik, N.J.	.20
☐	66	Doug Gilmour, N.J.	.75
☐	67	Valeri Zelepukin, N.J.	.20
☐	68	Petr Sykora, N.J.	.20
☐	69	New Jersey logo	.20
☐	70	John MacLean, N.J.	.20
☐	71	Dave Andreychuk, N.J.	.20
☐	72	Scott Niedermayer, N.J.	.50
☐	73	Zigmund Palffy, N.Y.I.	.75
☐	74	Tommy Salo (G), N.Y.I.	.20
☐	75	Niklas Andersson, N.Y.I.	.20
☐	76	Kenny Jonsson, N.Y.I.	.20
☐	77	Robert Reichel, N.Y.I.	.20
☐	78	New York Islanders logo	.20
☐	79	Travis Green, N.Y.I.	.20
☐	80	Bryan Berard, N.Y.I.	.75
☐	81	Bryan Smolinski, N.Y.I.	.20
☐	82	Wayne Gretzky, N.Y.R.	5.00
☐	83	Mark Messier, N.Y.R.	.20
☐	84	Brian Leetch, N.Y.R.	.20
☐	85	Alexei Kovalev, N.Y.R.	.20
☐	86	Esa Tikkanen, N.Y.R.	.20
☐	87	New York Rangers logo	.20
☐	88	Ulf Samuelsson, N.Y.R.	.20
☐	89	Niklas Sundstrom, N.Y.R.	.20
☐	90	Alexander Karpovtsev, N.Y.R.	.20
☐	91	Ron Hextall (G), Pha.	.50
☐	92	Eric Lindros, Pha.	3.50
☐	93	Rod Brind'Amour, Pha.	.50
☐	94	Janne Niinimaa, Pha.	.20
☐	95	Dainius Zubrus, Pha.	.50
☐	96	Philadelphia Flyers logo	.20
☐	97	Petr Svoboda, Pha.	.20
☐	98	John LeClair, Pha.	1.25
☐	99	Mikael Renberg, Pha.	.20
☐	100	Dino Ciccarelli, T.B.	.50
☐	101	Roman Hamrlik, T.B.	.50
☐	102	Alexander Selivanov, T.B.	.20
☐	103	Chris Gratton, T.B.	.50
☐	104	Mikael Andersson, T.B.	.20
☐	105	Tampa Bay Lightning logo	.20
☐	106	Igor Ulanov, T.B.	.20
☐	107	John Cullen, T.B.	.20
☐	108	Rob Zamuner, T.B.	.50
☐	109	Peter Bondra, Wsh.	1.00
☐	110	Bill Ranford (G), Wsh.	.50
☐	111	Michal Pivonka, Wsh.	.20
☐	112	Sergei Gonchar, Wsh.	.20
☐	113	Calle Johansson, Wsh.	.20
☐	114	Washington Capitals logo	.20
☐	115	Dale Hunter, Wsh.	.20
☐	116	Adam Oates, Wsh.	.75
☐	117	Andrei Nikolishin, Wsh.	.20
☐	118	LL: Dominik Hasek (G), Buf.	1.00
☐	119	LL: Bryan Berard, N.Y.I.	.50
☐	120	LL: Brian Leetch, N.Y.R.	.50
☐	121	LL: Paul Kariya, Ana.	2.00
☐	122	LL: Michael Peca, Buf.	.50
☐	123	LL: Keith Tkachuk, Pho..	.50
☐	124	LL: Martin Brodeur (G), N.J.	1.00
☐	125	LL: John LeClair, Pha.	.75
☐	126	LL: Miroslav Satan, Buf.	.20
☐	127	LL: Patrick Roy (G), Col.	2.50
☐	128	Alexei Zhamnov, Chi.	.50
☐	129	Chris Chelios, Chi.	1.00
☐	130	Ulf Dahlen, Chi.	.20
☐	131	Tony Amonte, Chi.	.50
☐	132	Michal Sykora, Chi.	.20
☐	133	Chicago Black Hawks logo	.20
☐	134	Eric Weinrich, Chi.	.20
☐	135	Sergei Krivokrasov, Chi.	.20
☐	136	Eric Dazé, Chi.	.50
☐	137	Pat Verbeek, Dal.	.20
☐	138	Sergei Zubov, Dal.	.50
☐	139	Mike Modano, Dal.	1.25
☐	140	Darryl Sydor, Dal.	.20
☐	141	Dave Reid, Dal.	.20
☐	142	Dallas Stars logo	.20
☐	143	Benoît Hogue, Dal.	.20
☐	144	Joe Nieuwendyk, Dal.	.50
☐	145	Jere Lehtinen, Dal.	.50
☐	146	Nicklas Lidström, Det.	.50
☐	147	Vladimir Konstantinov, Det.	.20
☐	148	Sergei Fedorov, Det.	1.25

No.	Player	Price
149	Steve Yzerman, Det.	2.50
150	Tomas Sandström, Det.	.20
151	Detroit Red Wings logo	.20
152	Igor Larionov, Det.	.50
153	Vyacheslav Kozlov, Det.	.20
154	Brendan Shanahan, Det.	1.50
155	Nikolai Khabibulin (G), Pho.	.75
156	Teppo Numminen, Pho.	.20
157	Jeremy Roenick, Pho.	.75
158	Mike Gartner, Pho.	.50
159	Igor Korolev, Pho.	.20
160	Phoenix Coyotes logo	.20
161	Craig Janney, Pho.	.20
162	Keith Tkachuk, Pho.	1.00
163	Oleg Tverdovsky, Pho.	.20
164	Pierre Turgeon, Stl.	.50
165	Igor Kravchuk, Stl.	.20
166	Robert Petrovicky, Stl.	.20
167	Geoff Courtnall, Stl.	.20
168	Brett Hull, Stl.	1.25
169	St. Louis Blues logo	.20
170	Chris Pronger, Stl.	.50
171	Joe Murphy, Stl.	.20
172	Grant Fuhr (G), Stl.	.50
173	Dimitri Yushkevich, Tor.	.20
174	Wendel Clark, Tor.	.50
175	Steve Sullivan, Tor.	.20
176	Tie Domi, Tor.	.20
177	Todd Warriner, Tor.	.20
178	Toronto Maple Leafs logo	.20
179	Mats Sundin, Tor.	1.25
180	Sergei Berezin, Tor.	.20
181	Fredrik Modin, Tor.	.20
182	Dimitri Mironov, Ana.	.20
183	Paul Kariya, Ana.	3.50
184	Steve Rucchin, Ana.	.20
185	Darren Van Impe, Ana.	.20
186	Joe Sacco, Ana.	.20
187	Anaheim Mighty Ducks logo	.20
188	Teemu Selänne, Ana.	1.75
189	Jari Kurri, Ana.	.50
190	Brian Bellows, Ana.	.20
191	Dave Gagner, Cgy.	.20
192	German Titov, Cgy.	.20
193	Marty McInnis, Cgy.	.20
194	Jarome Iginla, Cgy.	.20
195	Tommy Albelin, Cgy.	.20
196	Calgary Flames logo	.20
197	Joel Bouchard, Cgy.	.20
198	Jonas Hoglund, Cgy.	.20
199	Theoren Fleury, Cgy.	.75
200	Uwe Krupp, Col.	.20
201	Peter Forsberg, Col.	2.50
202	Adam Foote, Col.	.50
203	Valeri Kamensky, Col.	.50
204	Joe Sakic, Col.	2.00
205	Colorado Avalanche logo	.20
206	Sandis Ozolinsh, Col.	.50
207	Alexei Gusarov, Col.	.20
208	Patrick Roy (G), Col.	4.00
209	Andrei Kovalenko, Edm.	.20
210	Jason Arnott, Edm.	.50
211	Mariusz Czerkawski, Edm.	.20
212	Ryan Smyth, Edm.	.20
213	Mats Lindgren, Edm.	.20
214	Edmonton Oilers logo	.20
215	Doug Weight, Edm.	.75
216	Boris Mironov, Edm.	.20
217	Petr Klima, Edm.	.20
218	Vladimir Tsyplakov, L.A.	.20
219	Mattias Norstrom, L.A.	.20
220	Rob Blake, L.A.	.50
221	Kai Nurminen, L.A.	.20
222	Vitali Yachmenev, L.A.	.20
223	Los Angeles Kings logo.	.20
224	Ray Ferraro, L.A.	.20
225	Kevin Stevens, L.A.	.20
226	Dimitri Khristich, L.A.	.20
227	Tony Granato, S.J.	.20
228	Bernie Nicholls, S.J.	.20
229	Doug Bodger, S.J.	.20
230	Owen Nolan, S.J.	.50
231	Viktor Kozlov, S.J.	.20
232	San Jose Sharks	.20
233	Jeff Friesen, S.J.	.50
234	Marcus Ragnarsson, S.J.	.20
235	Andrei Nazarov, S.J.	.20
236	Pavel Bure, Van.	1.75
237	Alexander Mogilny, Van.	.75
238	Martin Gelinas, Van.	.20
239	Markus Naslund, Van.	.20
240	David Roberts, Van.	.20
241	Vancouver Canucks logo	.20
242	Trevor Linden, Van.	.50
243	Mike Ridley, Van.	.20
244	Jyrki Lumme, Van.	.20
245	Janne Niinimaa, Pha.	.20
246	Patrick Lalime (G), Pgh.	.20
247	Bryan Berard, N.Y.I.	.50
248	Jim Campbell, Stl.	.50
249	Dainius Zubrus, Pha.	.50
250	Sergei Berezin, Tor.	.20
251	Jarome Iginla, Cgy.	.50
252	Jarome Iginla, Cgy.	.50

1997 - 98 PINNACLE

Cards 1-100 have a second Rink Collection parallel and a third Artist's Proof parallel.

Imprint: © 1997 PINNACLE TRADING CARD CO.

	A.P.	R.C.	Reg.
Complete Set (200 cards):	–.	–.	30.00
Parallel Set (100 cards):	1,500.00	300.00	–.
Common Player:	5.00	2.00	.15

No.	Player	A.P.	R.C.	Reg.
1	**Espen Knutsen, Ana., RC**	**5.00**	**2.00**	**.15**
2	**Juha Lind, Dal., RC**	**5.00**	**2.00**	**.15**
3	Erik Rasmussen, Buf.	5.00	2.00	.15
4	**Olli Jokinen, L.A., RC**	**10.00**	**3.00**	**.75**
5	Chris Phillips, Ott.	10.00	3.00	.50
6	Alexei Morozov, Pgh.	20.00	6.00	1.00
7	Chris Dingman, Cgy.	5.00	2.00	.15
8	Mattias Ohlund, Van.	10.00	3.00	.50
9	Sergei Samsonov, Bos.	40.00	10.00	1.25
10	Daniel Cleary, Chi.	10.00	3.00	.50
11	Terry Ryan, Mtl.	5.00	2.00	.15
12	Patrick Marleau, S.J.	20.00	6.00	1.00
13	Boyd Devereaux, Edm.	5.00	2.00	.15
14	**Donald MacLean, L.A., RC**	**5.00**	**2.00**	**.15**
15	Marc Savard, NYR.	5.00	2.00	.15
16	**Magnus Arvedson, Ott., RC**	**5.00**	**2.00**	**.15**
17	**Marian Hossa, Ott., RC**	**40.00**	**10.00**	**3.00**
18	Alyn McCauley, Tor.	20.00	6.00	1.00
19	**Vaclav Prospal, Pha., RC**	**15.00**	**4.00**	**1.00**
20	Brad Isbister, Pho.	5.00	2.00	.15
21	**Robert Dome, Pgh., RC**	**10.00**	**3.00**	**.50**
22	Kevyn Adams, Tor.	5.00	2.00	.15
23	Joe Thornton, Bos.	40.00	10.00	1.25
24	**Jan Bulis, Wsh., RC**	**10.00**	**3.00**	**.50**
25	Jaroslav Svejkovsky, Wsh.	10.00	3.00	.50
26	Saku Koivu, Mtl.	70.00	18.00	1.50
27	Mark Messier, Van.	50.00	12.00	1.00
28	Dominik Hasek (G), Buf.	70.00	18.00	1.50
29	Patrick Roy (G), Col.	160.00	40.00	3.00
30	Jaromir Jagr, Pgh.	100.00	25.00	2.00
31	Jarome Iginla, Cgy.	20.00	6.00	.50
32	Joe Sakic, Col.	80.00	20.00	1.75
33	Jeremy Roenick, Pho.	20.00	6.00	.50
34	Chris Osgood (G), Det.	35.00	10.00	.75
35	Brett Hull, Stl.	50.00	12.00	1.00
36	Mike Vernon (G), S.J.	10.00	3.00	.25
37	John Vanbiesbrouck (G), Fla.	60.00	15.00	1.25
38	Ray Bourque, Bos.	50.00	12.00	1.00
39	Doug Gilmour, N.J.	20.00	6.00	.50
40	Keith Tkachuk, Pho.	35.00	10.00	.75
41	Pavel Bure, Van.	70.00	18.00	1.50
42	Sean Burke (G), Hfd.	10.00	3.00	.25
43	Martin Brodeur (G), N.J.	70.00	18.00	1.50
44	Damian Rhodes, Ott.	5.00	2.00	.15
45	Geoff Sanderson, Car.	5.00	2.00	.15
46	Bill Ranford (G), Wsh.	10.00	3.00	.25
47	Kevin Hodson (G), Det.	5.00	2.00	.15
48	Eric Lindros, Pha.	125.00	35.00	2.50
49	Owen Nolan, S.J.	10.00	3.00	.25
50	Mats Sundin, Tor.	50.00	12.00	1.00
51	Ed Belfour (G), S.J.	20.00	6.00	.50
52	Stéphane Fiset (G), L.A.	10.00	3.00	.25
53	Paul Kariya, Ana.	125.00	35.00	2.50
54	Doug Weight, Edm.	20.00	6.00	.50
55	Mike Richter (G), NYR.	20.00	6.00	.50
56	Zigmund Palffy, NYI.	20.00	6.00	.50
57	John LeClair, Pha.	50.00	12.00	1.00
58	Alexander Mogilny, Van.	20.00	6.00	.50
59	Tommy Salo (G), NYI.	5.00	2.00	.15
60	Trevor Kidd (G), Car.	10.00	3.00	.25
61	Jason Arnott, Edm.	10.00	3.00	.25
62	Adam Oates, Wsh.	20.00	6.00	.50
63	Garth Snow (G), Pha.	5.00	2.00	.15
64	Rob Blake, L.A.	10.00	3.00	.25
65	Chris Chelios, Chi.	35.00	10.00	.75
66	Eric Fichaud (G), NYI.	10.00	3.00	.25
67	Wayne Gretzky, NYR.	225.00	50.00	4.00
68	Dino Ciccarelli, T.B.	10.00	3.00	.25
69	Pat LaFontaine, NYR.	10.00	3.00	.25
70	Andy Moog (G), Mtl.	10.00	3.00	.25
71	Steve Yzerman, Det.	100.00	25.00	2.00
72	Jeff Hackett (G), Chi.	10.00	3.00	.25
73	Peter Forsberg, Col.	100.00	25.00	2.00
74	Arturs Irbe (G), Van.	5.00	2.00	.15
75	Pierre Turgeon, Mtl.	10.00	3.00	.25
76	Tom Barrasso (G), Pgh.	10.00	3.00	.25
77	Sergei Fedorov, Det.	50.00	12.00	1.00
78	Ron Francis, Pgh.	20.00	6.00	.50
79	Mike Dunham (G), N.J.	5.00	2.00	.15
80	Brendan Shanahan, Det.	60.00	15.00	1.25
81	Grant Fuhr (G), Stl.	10.00	7.00	.25
82	Jamie Storr (G), L.A.	10.00	3.00	.25
83	Jim Carey (G), Bos.	5.00	2.00	.15
84	Daren Puppa (G), T.B.	5.00	2.00	.15
85	Vincent Damphousse, Mtl.	20.00	6.00	.50
86	Teemu Selänne, Ana.	70.00	18.00	1.50
87	Dwayne Roloson (G), Cgy.	5.00	2.00	.15
88	Kirk McLean (G), Van.	10.00	3.00	.25
89	Olaf Kolzig (G), Wsh.	20.00	6.00	.50
90	Guy Hebert (G), Ana.	10.00	3.00	.25
91	Mike Modano, Dal.	50.00	12.00	1.00
92	Brian Leetch, NYR.	20.00	6.00	.50
93	Curtis Joseph (G), Edm.	60.00	15.00	1.25
94	Nikolai Khabibulin (G), Pho.	20.00	6.00	.50
95	Félix Potvin (G), Tor.	50.00	12.00	1.00
96	Ken Wregget (G), Pgh.	5.00	2.00	.15
97	**Steve Shields (G), Buf., RC**	**10.00**	**3.00**	**.25**
98	Jocelyn Thibault (G), Mtl.	20.00	6.00	.50
99	Ron Tugnutt (G), Ott.	5.00	2.00	.15
100	Ron Hextall (G), Pha.	10.00	3.00	.25
101	Michael Peca, Buf.			.25
102	Donald Audette, Buf.			.15
103	Theoren Fleury, Cgy.			.50
104	Mark Recchi, Mtl.			.25
105	Dainius Zubrus, Pha.			.25
106	Trevor Linden, Van.			.25
107	Joé Juneau, Wsh.			.15
108	Matthew Barnaby, Buf.			.15
109	Keith Primeau, Car.			.25
110	Joe Nieuwendyk, Dal.			.25
111	Rod Brind'Amour, Pha.			.25
112	Daymond Langkow, T.B.			.15
113	Ed Jovanovski, Fla.			.25
114	Adam Deadmarsh, Col.			.15
115	Scott Niedermayer, N.J.			.25
116	Al MacInnis, Stl.			.25
117	Vyacheslav Kozlov, Det.			.15
118	Jere Lehtinen, Dal.			.25
119	Jeff Friesen, S.J.			.25
120	Alexei Kovalev, NYR.			.15
121	Eric Dazé, Chi.			.25
122	Mariusz Czerkawski, Edm.			.15
123	Alexei Zhamnov, Chi.			.15
124	Petr Nedved, Pgh.			.15
125	Dmitri Mironov, Ana.			.15
126	Alexei Yashin, Ott.			.75

	No.	Player	Price
☐	127	Todd Marchant, Edm.	.15
☐	128	Sandis Ozolinsh, Col.	.25
☐	129	Igor Larionov, Det.	.25
☐	130	Jim Campbell, Stl.	.15
☐	131	Dave Andreychuk, N.J.	.15
☐	132	Glen Wesley, Car.	.15
☐	133	Rem Murray, Edm.	.15
☐	134	Steve Sullivan, Tor.	.15
☐	135	Miroslav Satan, Buf.	.15
☐	136	Bill Guerin, N.J.	.25
☐	137	Mike Gartner, Pho.	.25
☐	138	Jozef Stumpel, L.A.	.25
☐	139	Darryl Sydor, Dal.	.15
☐	140	Darcy Tucker, Mtl.	.15
☐	141	Robert Svehla, Fla.	.15
☐	142	Steve Duchesne, Ott.	.15
☐	143	Kevin Stevens, NYR.	.15
☐	144	Mikael Renberg, T.B.	.15
☐	145	Bryan Berard, NYI.	.50
☐	146	Ray Ferraro, L.A.	.15
☐	147	Jason Allison, Bos.	.50
☐	148	Tony Amonte, Chi.	.25
☐	149	Luc Robitaille, L.A.	.25
☐	150	Mathieu Schneider, Tor.	.15
☐	151	Steve Rucchin, Ana.	.15
☐	152	Brian Savage, Mtl..	.15
☐	153	Paul Coffey, Pha.	.25
☐	154	Jeff O'Neill, Car.	.25
☐	155	Daniel Alfredsson, Ott.	.25
☐	156	Dave Gagner, Fla.	.15
☐	157	Rob Niedermayer, Fla.	.15
☐	158	Scott Stevens, N.J.	.15
☐	159	Alexandre Daigle, Ott.	.15
☐	160	Stéphane Richer, Mtl.	.15
☐	161	Harry York, Stl.	.15
☐	162	Sergei Berezin, Tor.	.25
☐	163	Claude Lemieux, Col.	.15
☐	164	Ray Sheppard, Fla.	.15
☐	165	Bernie Nicholls, S.J.	.15
☐	166	Oleg Tverdovsky, Pho.	.15
☐	167	Travis Green, NYI.	.15
☐	168	Martin Gelinas, Van.	.15
☐	169	Derek Plante, Buf.	.15
☐	170	Gary Roberts, Car.	.25
☐	171	Kevin Hatcher, Pgh.	.15
☐	172	Martin Rucinsky, Mtl.	.15
☐	173	Pat Verbeek, Dal.	.15
☐	174	Adam Graves, NYR.	.15
☐	175	Roman Hamrlik, T.B.	.25
☐	176	Darren McCarty, Det.	.15
☐	177	Mike Grier, Edm.	.25
☐	178	Andrew Cassels, Cgy.	.15
☐	179	Dimitri Khristich, L.A.	.15
☐	180	Tomas Sandström, Ana.	.15
☐	181	Peter Bondra, Wsh.	.75
☐	182	Derian Hatcher, Dal.	.25
☐	183	Chris Gratton, Pha.	.25
☐	184	John MacLean, N.J.	.15
☐	185	Wendel Clark, Tor.	.25
☐	186	Valeri Kamensky, Col.	.25
☐	187	Tony Granato, S.J.	.15
☐	**188**	**Vladimir Vorobiev, NYR., RC**	**.15**
☐	189	Ethan Moreau, Chi.	.15
☐	190	Kirk Muller, Fla.	.15
☐	191	Peter Forsberg, Col.	1.00
☐	192	Wayne Gretzky, NYR.	2.00
☐	193	Jaromir Jagr, Pgh.	1.00
☐	194	Mark Messier, Van.	.50
☐	195	Brian Leetch, NYR.	.25
☐	196	John LeClair, Pha.	.50
☐	197	Jeremy Roenick, Pho.	.25
☐	198	Checklist	.15
☐	199	Checklist	.15
☐	200	Checklist	.15

OVERSIZE CARDS

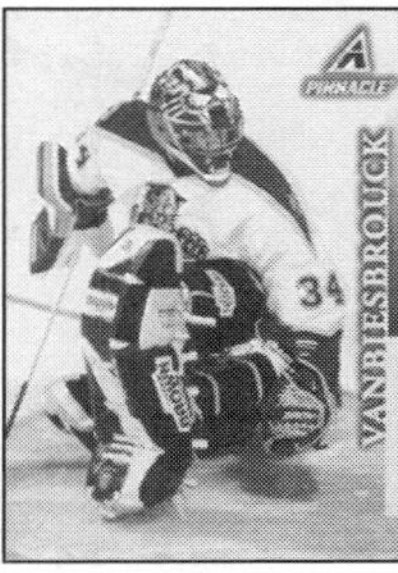

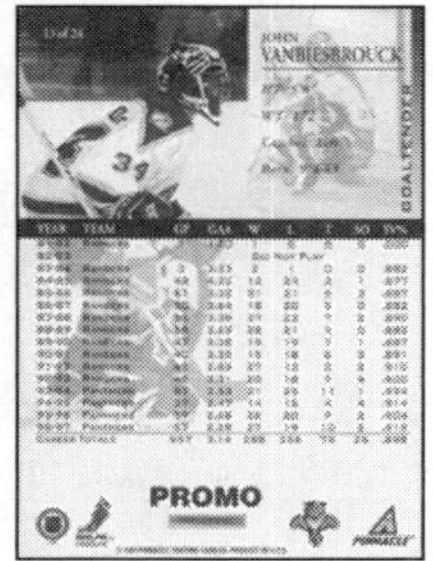

These cards parallel the regular cards.

Card Size:

Complete Set (24 cards): 45.00

	No.	Player	NRMT-MT
☐	1	Eric Lindros, Pha.	4.00
☐	2	Paul Kariya, Ana.	4.00
☐	3	Joe Thornton, Bos.	1.75
☐	4	Dominik Hasek (G), Buf.	2.00
☐	5	Patrick Roy (G), Col.	5.00
☐	6	Keith Tkachuk, Pho.	1.00
☐	7	Martin Brodeur (G), N.J.	2.00
☐	8	Brett Hull, Stl.	1.50
☐	9	Mark Messier, Van.	1.50
☐	10	Saku Koivu, Mtl.	2.00
☐	11	Jaromir Jagr, Pgh.	3.00
☐	12	Joe Sakic	2.50
☐	13	John Vanbiesbrouck (G), Fla.	1.75
☐	14	Pavel Bure, Van.	2.00
☐	15	Jarome Iginla, Cgy.	1.00
☐	16	Mats Sundin, Tor.	1.50
☐	17	Wayne Gretzky, NYR.	6.00
☐	18	Steve Yzerman, Det.	3.00
☐	19	Peter Forsberg, Col.	3.00
☐	20	Brendan Shanahan, Det.	2.50
☐	21	Sergei Fedorov, Det.	1.50
☐	22	Curtis Joseph (G), Edm.	1.75
☐	23	John LeClair, Pha.	1.50
☐	24	Teemu Selänne, Ana.	2.00

MASKS

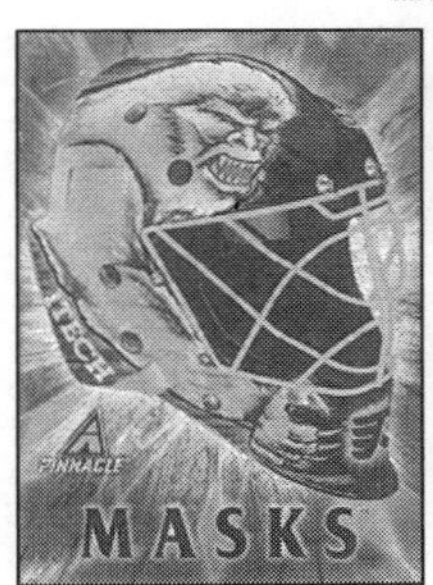

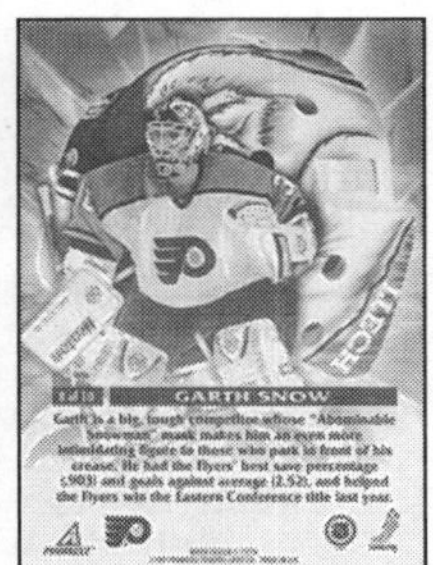

These inserts have two versions: the regular card and a die-cut parallel.

	No.	Player	Die-Cut	Reg.
Insert Set (10 cards):			**650.00**	**325.00**
☐☐	1	John Vanbiesbrouck, Fla.	80.00	40.00
☐☐	2	Mike Richter (G), NYR.	50.00	25.00
☐☐	3	Martin Brodeur (G), N.J.	100.00	50.00
☐☐	4	Curtis Joseph (G), Edm.	80.00	40.00
☐☐	5	Patrick Roy (G), Col.	250.00	125.00
☐☐	6	Guy Hebert (G), Ana.	40.00	20.00
☐☐	7	Jeff Hackett (G), Chi.	40.00	20.00
☐☐	8	Garth Snow (G), Pha.	30.00	20.00
☐☐	9	Nikolai Khabibulin, Pho.	50.00	25.00
☐☐	10	Grant Fuhr (G), Stl.	40.00	20.00

TEAM PINNACLE

Insert Set (10 cards): 325.00

	No.	Player	NRMT-MT
☐	1	M. Brodeur (G)/ P. Roy (G)	60.00
☐	2	D. Hasek (G)/ Cu. Joseph (G)	25.00
☐	3	B.Leetch/ C.Chelios	20.00
☐	4	W.Gretzky/ P.Kariya	80.00
☐	5	E.Lindros/ M.Messier	45.00
☐	6	J.Jagr/ K.Tkachuk	35.00
☐	7	S.Koivu/ P.Forsberg	40.00
☐	8	J.LeClair/ B.Shanahan	25.00
☐	9	D.Gilmour/ S.Yzerman	30.00
☐	10	J.Vanbiesbrouck (G)/ C.Osgood (G)	20.00

GOALIE TINS

Prices below are for opened tins.

Tin Size:

Complete Set (10 tins): 15.00

	No.	Player	NRMT-MT
☐	1	Martin Brodeur (G), N.J.	2.50
☐	2	Grant Fuhr (G), Stl.	1.25
☐	3	Jeff Hackett (G), Chi.	1.25
☐	4	Guy Hebert (G), Ana.	1.25
☐	5	Curtis Joseph (G), Edm.	2.00
☐	6	Nikolai Khabibulin (G), Pho.	1.50
☐	7	Mike Richter (G), NYR.	1.50
☐	8	Patrick Roy (G), Col.	5.00
☐	9	Garth Snow (G), Pha.	1.00
☐	10	John Vanbiesbrouck (G), Fla.	2.00

1997 - 98 PINNACLE BE A PLAYER

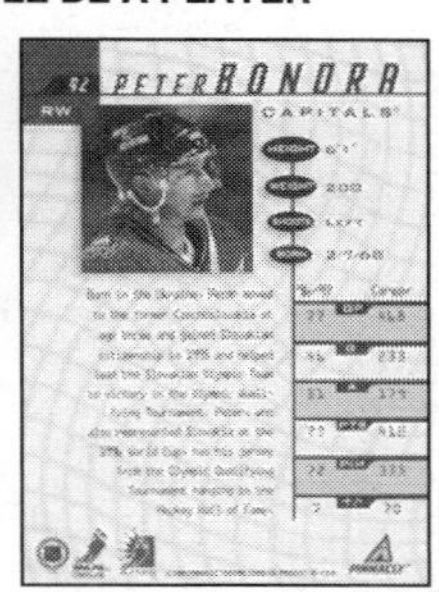

These cards have four versions: the regular card, an autographed card (3500 copies), a foil die-cut autographed card (400 copies) and a foil-prismatic die-cut autographed card (100 copies). Eight cards are short-printed (*) in the autographed foil die-cut autographed and prismatic die-cut autographed parallel versions. There are no Eric Lindros regular autographs, only foil die-cut (44 copies) and prismatic die-cut (44 copies) autographs. There are no Bryan Berard autographed cards.

Imprint: © 1998 PINNACLE TRADING CARD CO.

Complete Set (250 cards): 40.00

Autographed Set (248 cards): 2,700.00

	No.	Player	Prism.	Die-Cut	Aut.	Reg.
Common Player:			**25.00**	**8.00**	**4.00**	**.25**
☐☐☐☐	1	Eric Lindros, Pha. (**)			–.	3.50
☐☐☐☐	2	Martin Brodeur (G), N.J. (*)	900.00	450.00	225.00	2.00
☐☐☐☐	3	Saku Koivu, Mtl.	250.00	100.00	50.00	2.00
☐☐☐☐	4	Félix Potvin (G), Tor.	200.00	80.00	40.00	1.50
☐☐☐☐	5	Adam Oates, Wsh.	125.00	50.00	25.00	1.00
☐☐☐☐	6	Rob DiMaio, Bos.	25.00	8.00	4.00	.25
☐☐☐☐	7	Jari Kurri, Col.	50.00	20.00	10.00	.50
☐☐☐☐	8	Andrew Cassels, Cgy.	25.00	8.00	4.00	.25
☐☐☐☐	9	Trevor Linden, Van.	40.00	15.00	8.00	.50
☐☐☐☐	10	Jocelyn Thibault (G), Mtl.	125.00	50.00	25.00	1.00
☐☐☐☐	11	Chris Chelios, Chi.	125.00	50.00	25.00	1.25
☐☐☐☐	12	Paul Coffey, Pha.	100.00	40.00	20.00	.50
☐☐☐☐	13	Nikolai Khabibulin (G), Pho.	75.00	30.00	15.00	1.00
☐☐☐☐	14	Robert Lang, Pgh.	25.00	8.00	4.00	.25
☐☐☐☐	15	Brett Hull, Stl. (*)	400.00	200.00	100.00	1.50
☐☐☐☐	16	Mike Sillinger, Van.	25.00	8.00	4.00	.25
☐☐☐☐	17	Lyle Odelein, N.J.	25.00	8.00	4.00	.25
☐	18	Bryan Berard, NYI.	–.	–.	–.	1.00
☐☐☐☐	19	Craig Muni, Dal.	25.00	8.00	4.00	.25
☐☐☐☐	20	Kris Draper, Det.	25.00	8.00	4.00	.25
☐☐☐☐	21	Ed Jovanovski, Fla.	75.00	30.00	15.00	.50
☐☐☐☐	22	Keith Tkachuk, Pho.	100.00	40.00	20.00	1.25

No.	Player				
23	Dean Malkoc, Bos.	25.00	8.00	4.00	.25
24	Cory Stillman, Cgy.	25.00	8.00	4.00	.25
25	Chris Osgood (G), Det.	150.00	60.00	30.00	1.25
26	Dainius Zubrus, Pha.	100.00	40.00	25.00	.50
27	Yves Racine, T.B.	25.00	8.00	4.00	.25
28	**Eric Cairns, NYR., RC**	**25.00**	**8.00**	**4.00**	**.25**
29	Dan Bylsma, L.A.	25.00	8.00	4.00	.25
30	Chris Terreri (G), Chi.	40.00	15.00	8.00	.25
31	Bill Huard, Edm.	25.00	8.00	4.00	.25
32	Warren Rychel, Ana.	25.00	8.00	4.00	.25
33	Scott Walker, Van.	25.00	8.00	4.00	.25
34	Brian Holzinger, Buf.	25.00	8.00	4.00	.25
35	Roman Turek (G), Dal.	40.00	15.00	8.00	.25
36	Ron Tugnutt (G), Ott.	40.00	15.00	8.00	.25
37	Mike Richter (G), NYR.	125.00	50.00	25.00	1.00
38	Mattias Norstrom, L.A.	25.00	8.00	4.00	.25
39	Joe Sacco, Ana.	25.00	8.00	4.00	.25
40	Derek King, Tor.	25.00	8.00	4.00	.25
41	Brad Werenka, Pgh.	25.00	8.00	4.00	.25
42	Paul Kruse, NYI.	25.00	8.00	4.00	.25
43	**Mike Knuble, Det., RC**	**25.00**	**8.00**	**4.00**	**.25**
44	Michael Peca, Buf.	25.00	8.00	4.00	.25
45	**Jean-Yves Leroux, Chi., RC**	**50.00**	**20.00**	**10.00**	**.50**
46	Ray Sheppard, Fla.	25.00	8.00	4.00	.25
47	**Reid Simpson, N.J., RC**	**25.00**	**8.00**	**4.00**	**.25**
48	Rob Brown, Pgh.	25.00	8.00	4.00	.25
49	Dave Babych, Van.	25.00	8.00	4.00	.25
50	Scott Pellerin, Stl.	25.00	8.00	4.00	.25
51	**Bruce Gardiner, Ott., RC**	**25.00**	**8.00**	**4.00**	**.25**
52	Adam Deadmarsh, Col.	40.00	15.00	8.00	.25
53	Curtis Brown, Buf.	25.00	8.00	4.00	.25
54	Jason Marshall, Ana.	25.00	8.00	4.00	.25
55	Gerald Diduck, Pho.	25.00	8.00	4.00	.25
56	Mick Vukota, T.B.	25.00	8.00	4.00	.25
57	Kevin Dean, N.J.	25.00	8.00	4.00	.25
58	Adam Graves, NYR.	40.00	15.00	8.00	.25
59	Craig Conroy, Stl.	25.00	8.00	4.00	.25
60	Cale Hulse, Cgy.	25.00	8.00	4.00	.25
61	Dimitri Khristich, Bos.	25.00	8.00	4.00	.25
62	Chris Wells, Fla.	25.00	8.00	4.00	.25
63	Travis Green, NYI.	25.00	8.00	4.00	.25
64	Tyler Wright, Pgh.	25.00	8.00	4.00	.25
65	Chris Simon, Wsh.	25.00	8.00	4.00	.25
66	Mikhail Shtalenkov (G), Ana.	40.00	15.00	8.00	.25
67	Anson Carter, Bos.	40.00	15.00	8.00	.25
68	Zarley Zalapski, Cgy.	25.00	8.00	4.00	.25
69	Per Gustafsson, Tor.	25.00	8.00	4.00	.25
70	Jayson More, Pho.	25.00	8.00	4.00	.25
71	Steve Thomas, N.J.	25.00	8.00	4.00	.25
72	Todd Marchant, Edm.	25.00	8.00	4.00	.25
73	Gary Roberts, Car.	40.00	15.00	8.00	.50
74	Richard Smehlik, Buf.	25.00	8.00	4.00	.25
75	**Aaron Miller, Col., RC**	**25.00**	**8.00**	**4.00**	**.25**
76	Daren Puppa (G), T.B.	40.00	15.00	8.00	.25
77	Garth Snow (G), Pha.	40.00	15.00	8.00	.25
78	Greg deVries, Edm.	25.00	8.00	4.00	.25
79	Randy Burridge, Buf.	25.00	8.00	4.00	.25
80	Jim Cummins, Chi.	25.00	8.00	4.00	.25
81	Richard Pilon, NYI.	25.00	8.00	4.00	.25
82	Chris McAlpine, Stl.	25.00	8.00	4.00	.25
83	Joe Sakic, Col. (*)	1,000.00	500.00	250.00	2.50
84	Ted Drury, Ana.	25.00	8.00	4.00	.25
85	Brent Gilchrist, Dal.	25.00	8.00	4.00	.25
86	**Dallas Eakins, Fla., RC**	25.00	8.00	4.00	.25
87	Bruce Driver, NYR.	25.00	8.00	4.00	.25
88	Jamie Huscroft, T.B.	25.00	8.00	4.00	.25
89	Jeff Brown, Tor.	25.00	8.00	4.00	.25
90	Janne Laukkanen, Ott.	25.00	8.00	4.00	.25
91	Ken Klee, Wsh.	25.00	8.00	4.00	.25
92	Peter Bondra, Wsh.	125.00	50.00	25.00	1.25
93	Ian Moran, Pgh.	25.00	8.00	4.00	.25
94	Stéphane Quintal, Mtl.	25.00	8.00	4.00	.25
95	Jason York, Ott.	25.00	8.00	4.00	.25
96	Todd Harvey, Dal.	25.00	8.00	4.00	.25
97	Vyacheslav Kozlov, Det.	40.00	15.00	8.00	.25
98	Kevin Haller, Car.	25.00	8.00	4.00	.25
99	Alexei Zhamnov, Chi.	40.00	15.00	8.00	.25
100	Craig Johnson, L.A.	25.00	8.00	4.00	.25
101	Mike Keane, NYR.	25.00	8.00	4.00	.25
102	Craig Rivet, Mtl.	25.00	8.00	4.00	.25
103	Roman Vopat, L.A.	25.00	8.00	4.00	.25
104	Jim Johnson, Pho.	25.00	8.00	4.00	.25
105	Ray Whitney, Fla.	40.00	15.00	8.00	.25
106	Ron Sutter, S.J.	25.00	8.00	4.00	.25
107	Jamie McLennan (G), Stl.	500.00	20.00	10.00	.25
108	Kris King, Tor.	25.00	8.00	4.00	.25
109	**Lance Pitlick, Ott., RC**	**25.00**	**8.00**	**4.00**	**.25**
110	Mike Dunham (G), N.J.	40.00	15.00	8.00	.25
111	Jim Dowd, Cgy.	25.00	8.00	4.00	.25
112	Geoff Sanderson, Hfd.	40.00	15.00	8.00	.25
113	Vladimir Vujtek, T.B.	25.00	8.00	4.00	.25
114	Tim Taylor, Bos.	25.00	8.00	4.00	.25
115	Sandis Ozolinsh, Col.	50.00	20.00	10.00	.50
116	Scott Daniels, N.J.	25.00	8.00	4.00	.25
117	Bob Corkum, Pho.	25.00	8.00	4.00	.25
118	Kirk McLean (G), Car.	50.00	20.00	10.00	.50
119	Darcy Tucker, Mtl.	25.00	8.00	4.00	.25
120	Dennis Vaske, NYI.	25.00	8.00	4.00	.25
121	Kirk Muller, Fla.	40.00	15.00	8.00	.25
122	Jay McKee, Buf.	25.00	8.00	4.00	.25
123	Jere Lehtinen, Dal.	40.00	15.00	8.00	.25
124	Ruslan Salei, Ana.	25.00	8.00	4.00	.25
125	Al MacInnis, Stl. (*)	250.00	120.00	60.00	.50
126	Ulf Samuelsson, NYR.	25.00	8.00	4.00	.25
127	Rick Tocchet, Pho.	40.00	15.00	8.00	.25
128	Nick Kypreos, Tor.	25.00	8.00	4.00	.25
129	Joel Bouchard, Cgy.	25.00	8.00	4.00	.25
130	Jeff O'Neill, Car.	40.00	15.00	8.00	.50
131	**Daniel McGillis, Edm., RC**	**25.00**	**8.00**	**4.00**	**.25**
132	Sean Pronger, Ana.	25.00	8.00	4.00	.25
133	Vladimir Malakhov, Mtl.	25.00	8.00	4.00	.25
134	Petr Sykora, N.J.	25.00	8.00	4.00	.25
135	Zigmund Palffy, NYI.	75.00	30.00	15.00	1.00
136	Joe Reekie, Wsh.	25.00	8.00	4.00	.25
137	Chris Gratton, Pha.	50.00	20.00	10.00	.50
138	Craig Billington (G), Col.	40.00	15.00	8.00	.25
139	Steve Washburn, Fla.	25.00	8.00	4.00	.25
140	Robert Kron, Car.	25.00	8.00	4.00	.25
141	Larry Murphy, Det.	40.00	15.00	8.00	.50
142	Shean Donovan, Col.	25.00	8.00	4.00	.25
143	Scott Young, Col.	25.00	8.00	4.00	.25
144	Janne Niinimaa, Pha.	40.00	15.00	8.00	.50
145	**Ken Belanger, NYI., RC**	**25.00**	**8.00**	**4.00**	**.25**
146	Pavol Demitra, Stl.	25.00	8.00	4.00	.25
147	Roman Hamrlik, Edm.	40.00	15.00	8.00	.50
148	Lonny Bohonos, Van.	25.00	8.00	4.00	.25
149	Mike Eagles, Wsh.	25.00	8.00	4.00	.25
150	Kelly Buchberger, Edm.	25.00	8.00	4.00	.25
151	Mattias Timander, Bos.	25.00	8.00	4.00	.25
152	Benoît Hogue, Dal.	25.00	8.00	4.00	.25
153	Joey Kocur, Det.	25.00	8.00	4.00	.25
154	Mats Lindgren, Edm.	25.00	8.00	4.00	.25
155	Aki Berg, L.A.	25.00	8.00	4.00	.25
156	Tim Sweeney, NYR.	25.00	8.00	4.00	.25
157	Vincent Damphousse, Mtl.	75.00	30.00	15.00	1.00
158	Dan Kordic, Pha.	25.00	8.00	4.00	.25
159	Darius Kasparaitis, Pgh.	25.00	8.00	4.00	.25
160	Randy McKay, N.J.	25.00	8.00	4.00	.25
161	Steve Staios, Van.	25.00	8.00	4.00	.25
162	Brendan Witt, Wsh.	25.00	8.00	4.00	.25
163	Paul Ysebaert, T.B.	25.00	8.00	4.00	.25
164	Greg Adams, Dal.	25.00	8.00	4.00	.25
165	Kent Manderville, Car.	25.00	8.00	4.00	.25
166	Steve Dubinsky, Chi.	25.00	8.00	4.00	.25
167	David Nemirovsky, Fla.	25.00	8.00	4.00	.25
168	Todd Bertuzzi, NYI.	40.00	15.00	8.00	.25
169	**Frédéric Chabot, L.A., RC**	**25.00**	**8.00**	**4.00**	**.25**
170	Dmitri Mironov, Ana.	25.00	8.00	4.00	.25
171	Pat Peake, Wsh.	25.00	8.00	4.00	.25
172	Ed Ward, Cgy.	25.00	8.00	4.00	.25
173	Jeff Shantz, Chi.	25.00	8.00	4.00	.25
174	Dave Gagner, Fla.	25.00	8.00	4.00	.25
175	Randy Cunneyworth, Ott.	25.00	8.00	4.00	.25
176	Daymond Langkow, T.B.	25.00	8.00	4.00	.25
177	Alex Hicks, Pgh.	25.00	8.00	4.00	.25
178	Darby Hendrickson, Tor.	25.00	8.00	4.00	.25
179	Mike Sullivan, Bos.	25.00	8.00	4.00	.25
180	Anders Eriksson, Det.	25.00	8.00	4.00	.25
181	Turner Stevenson, Mtl.	25.00	8.00	4.00	.25
182	Shane Churla, NYR.	25.00	8.00	4.00	.25
183	Dave Lowry, S.J.	25.00	8.00	4.00	.25
184	Joé Juneau, Wsh.	40.00	15.00	8.00	.25
185	Bob Essensa, Edm.	25.00	8.00	4.00	.25
186	James Black, Chi.	25.00	8.00	4.00	.25
187	Michal Grosek, Buf.	25.00	8.00	4.00	.25
188	Tomas Holmstrom, Det.	40.00	15.00	8.00	.50
189	Ian Laperrière, L.A.	25.00	8.00	4.00	.25
190	Terry Yake, Stl.	25.00	8.00	4.00	.25
191	Jason Smith, Tor.	25.00	8.00	4.00	.25
192	Sergei Zholtok, Ott.	25.00	8.00	4.00	.25
193	Doug Houda, NYI.	25.00	8.00	4.00	.25
194	Guy Carbonneau, Mtl.	40.00	15.00	8.00	.25
195	Terry Carkner, Fla.	25.00	8.00	4.00	.25
196	Alexei Gusarov, Col.	25.00	8.00	4.00	.25
197	Vladimir Tsyplakov, L.A.	25.00	8.00	4.00	.25
198	Jarrod Skalde, Chi.	25.00	8.00	4.00	.25
199	Marty Murray, Cgy.	25.00	8.00	4.00	.25
200	Aaron Ward, Det.	25.00	8.00	4.00	.25
201	Bobby Holik, N.J.	40.00	15.00	8.00	.25
202	Steve Chiasson, Car.	25.00	8.00	4.00	.25
203	Brantt Myhres, Pha.	25.00	8.00	4.00	.25
204	**Eric Messier, Col., RC**	**25.00**	**8.00**	**4.00**	**.25**
205	René Corbet, Col.	25.00	8.00	4.00	.25
206	Mathieu Schneider, Tor.	25.00	8.00	4.00	.25
207	Tom Chorske, NYI.	25.00	8.00	4.00	.25
208	Doug Lidster, NYR.	25.00	8.00	4.00	.25
209	Igor Ulanov, T.B.	25.00	8.00	4.00	.25
210	**Blair Atcheynum, Stl., RC**	**25.00**	**8.00**	**4.00**	**.25**
211	Sébastien Bordeleau, Mtl.	25.00	8.00	4.00	.25
212	Alexei Morozov, Pgh.	100.00	40.00	25.00	1.50
213	**Vaclav Prospal, Pha., RC**	**80.00**	**30.00**	**20.00**	**1.50**
214	**Brad Bombardir, N.J., RC**	**25.00**	**8.00**	**4.00**	**.25**
215	Mattias Ohlund, Van.	100.00	40.00	25.00	.50
216	**Chris Dingman, Cgy., RC**	**25.00**	**8.00**	**4.00**	**.25**
217	Erik Rasmussen, Buf.	25.00	8.00	4.00	.25
218	Mike Johnson, Tor.	120.00	50.00	30.00	3.00
219	Chris Phillips, Ott.	60.00	25.00	15.00	.50
220	Sergei Samsonov, Bos.	200.00	80.00	50.00	1.75
221	Patrick Marleau, S.J.	120.00	50.00	30.00	1.50
222	Alyn McCauley, Tor.	100.00	40.00	25.00	1.50
223	**Ryan Vandenbussche, NYR., RC**	**25.00**	**8.00**	**4.00**	**.25**
224	Daniel Cleary, Chi.	100.00	40.00	25.00	.75
225	**Magnus Arvedsson, Ott., RC**	**25.00**	**8.00**	**4.00**	**.25**
226	Brad Isbister, Pho.	25.00	8.00	4.00	.25
227	**Pascal Rhéaume, S.H., RC**	**25.00**	**8.00**	**4.00**	**.25**
228	**Patrik Elias, N.J., RC**	**80.00**	**30.00**	**20.00**	**1.00**
229	**Krzysztof Oliwa, N.J., RC**	**40.00**	**15.00**	**8.00**	**.50**
230	**Tyler Moss (G), Cgy., RC**	**40.00**	**20.00**	**15.00**	**1.00**
231	Jamie Rivers, Stl.	25.00	8.00	4.00	.25
232	Joe Thornton, Bos.	200.00	80.00	50.00	1.75
233	**Steve Shields (G), Buf., RC**	**40.00**	**20.00**	**15.00**	**1.00**
234	**Dave Scatchard, Van., RC**	**25.00**	**8.00**	**4.00**	**.25**
235	**Patrick Côté, Dal., RC**	**25.00**	**8.00**	**4.00**	**.25**
236	**Rich Brennan, S.J., RC**	**25.00**	**8.00**	**4.00**	**.25**
237	Boyd Devereaux, Edm.	40.00	15.00	8.00	.25
238	Per-Johan Axelsson, Bos.	25.00	8.00	4.00	.25
239	**Craig Millar, Edm., RC**	**25.00**	**8.00**	**4.00**	**.25**
240	Juha Ylönen, Pho.	25.00	8.00	4.00	.25
241	**Donald MacLean, L.A., RC**	**25.00**	**8.00**	**4.00**	**.25**
242	Jaroslav Svejkovsky, Wsh.	40.00	15.00	8.00	.25
243	**Marco Sturm, S.J., RC**	**25.00**	**8.00**	**4.00**	**.25**
244	**Steve McKenna, L.A., RC**	**25.00**	**8.00**	**4.00**	**.25**
245	**Derek Morris, Cgy., RC**	**40.00**	**15.00**	**8.00**	**.50**
246	Dean Chynoweth, Bos.	25.00	8.00	4.00	.25
247	Alexander Mogilny, Van. (*)	300.00	150.00	75.00	1.00
248	Ray Bourque, Bos. (*)	500.00	250.00	125.00	1.50
249	Ed Belfour (G), Dal. (*)	325.00	160.00	80.00	1.00
250	John LeClair, Pha. (*)	600.00	300.00	150.00	1.50

ONE TIMERS

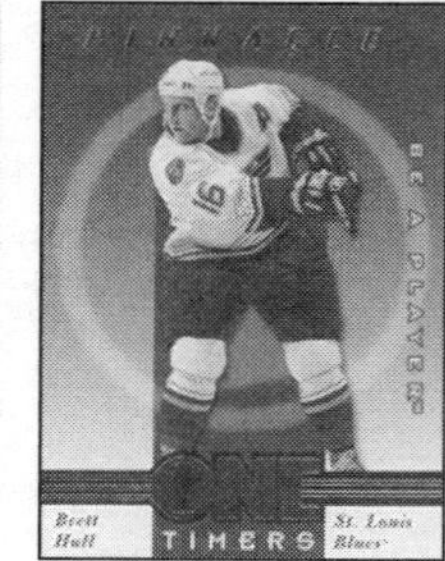

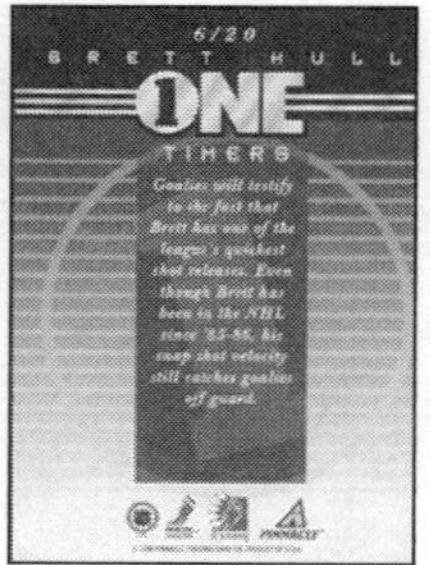

Insert Set (20 cards): 100.00

No.	Player	NRMT-MT
1	Wayne Gretzky, NYR.	25.00
2	Keith Tkachuk, Pho.	4.00
3	Eric Lindros, Pha.	15.00
4	Brendan Shanahan, Det.	6.00
5	Paul Kariya, Ana.	15.00
6	Brett Hull, Stl.	5.00
7	Jaromir Jagr, Pgh.	10.00
8	Teemu Selänne, Ana.	7.00
9	John LeClair, Pha.	5.00
10	Mike Modano, Dal.	5.00

	No.	Player	Price
☐	11	Peter Forsberg, Col.	10.00
☐	12	Pavel Bure, Van.	7.00
☐	13	Peter Bondra, Wsh.	4.00
☐	14	Saku Koivu, Mtl.	7.00
☐	15	Pat LaFontaine, NYR.	3.00
☐	16	Patrik Elias, N.J.	3.00
☐	17	Richard Zednick, Wsh.	3.00
☐	18	Mike Johnson, Tor.	4.00
☐	19	Marco Sturm, S.J.	2.00
☐	20	Joe Thornton, Bos.	6.00

STACKING THE PADS

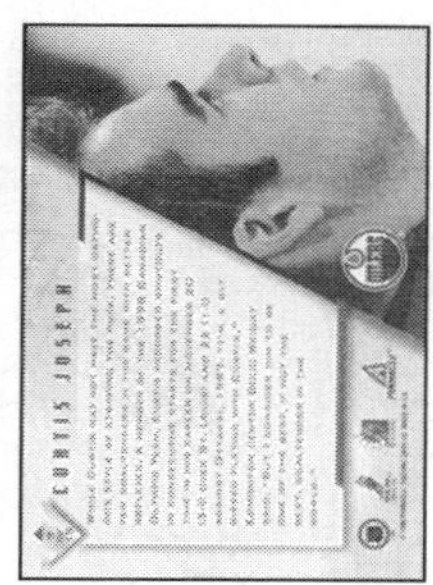

Insert Set (15 cards): 100.00

	No.	Player	NRMT-MT
☐	1	Guy Hebert (G), Ana.	5.00
☐	2	Dominik Hasek (G), Buf.	15.00
☐	3	Félix Potvin (G), Tor.	8.00
☐	4	Patrick Roy (G), Col.	30.00
☐	5	Ed Belfour (G), Dal.	6.00
☐	6	Chris Osgood (G), Det.	7.00
☐	7	Curtis Joseph (G), Edm.	10.00
☐	8	John Vanbiesbrouck (G), Fla.	10.00
☐	9	Jocelyn Thibault (G), Mtl.	6.00
☐	10	Mike Richter (G), NYR.	6.00
☐	11	Martin Brodeur (G), N.J.	15.00
☐	12	Garth Snow (G), Pha.	5.00
☐	13	Nikolai Khabibulin (G), Pho.	6.00
☐	14	Tommy Salo (G), NYI.	5.00
☐	15	Byron Dafoe (G), Bos.	5.00

TAKE A NUMBER

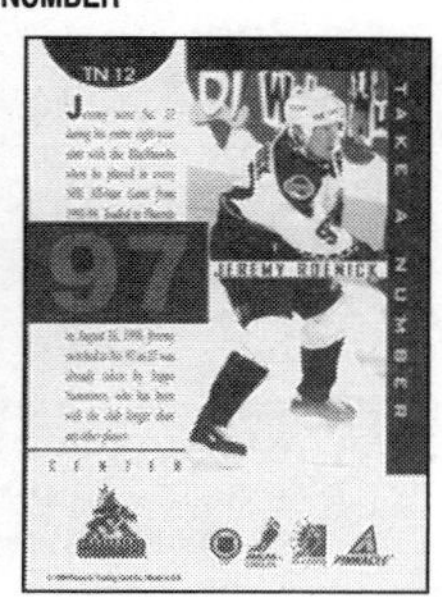

Insert Set (20 cards): 150.00

	No.	Player	NRMT-MT
☐	1	Ray Bourque, Bos.	10.00
☐	2	Eric Dazé, Chi.	5.00
☐	3	Ed Belfour (G), Dal.	6.00
☐	4	Patrick Roy (G), Col.	30.00
☐	5	Sergei Fedorov, Det.	10.00
☐	6	John Vanbiesbrouck (G), Fla.	12.00
☐	7	Doug Gilmour, N.J.	6.00
☐	8	Wayne Gretzky, NYR.	50.00
☐	9	Bryan Berard, NYI.	6.00
☐	10	Eric Lindros, Pha.	25.00
☐	11	Paul Coffey, Pha.	5.00
☐	12	Jeremy Roenick, Pho.	6.00
☐	13	Brett Hull, Stl.	10.00
☐	14	Pierre Turgeon, Stl.	5.00
☐	15	Keith Primeau, Car.	5.00
☐	16	Daren Puppa, T.B.	5.00
☐	17	Mark Messier, Van.	10.00
☐	18	Alexander Mogilny, Van.	6.00
☐	19	Joe Sakic, Col.	18.00
☐	20	Jaromir Jagr, Pgh.	20.00

1997 - 98 PINNACLE BEEHIVES

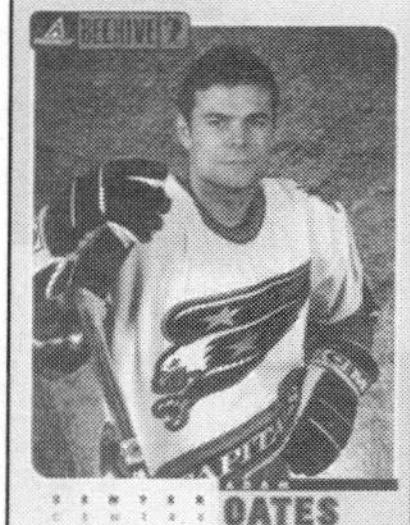

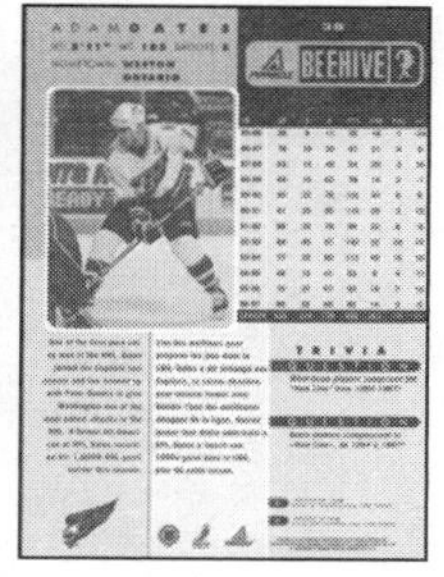

These cards have two versions: the regular card and a Golden Portraits parallel [1:3]. Cards 51-75 have a third autographed parallel. Autographed cards 54 and 55 were available through a redemption offer only.

Imprint: © 1998 PINNACLE TRADING CARD CO.

Complete Set (75 cards): 125.00 75.00
Common Player: 1.00 .50
Promo Card (Eric Lindros, #1): 4.00

	No.	Player	Aut.	Golden	Reg.
☐☐	1	Eric Lindros, Pha.		6.00	4.00
☐☐	2	Teemu Selänne, Ana.		4.00	2.00
☐☐	3	Brendan Shanahan, Det.		3.25	1.75
☐☐	4	Joe Sakic, Col.		5.00	2.50
☐☐	5	John LeClair, Pha.		3.00	1.50
☐☐	6	Brett Hull, Stl.		3.00	1.50
☐☐	7	Jaromir Jagr, Pgh.		6.00	3.00
☐☐	8	Bryan Berard, NYI.		2.00	1.00
☐☐	9	Peter Forsberg, Col.		6.00	3.00
☐☐	10	Ed Belfour (G), Dal.		2.00	1.00
☐☐	11	Steve Yzerman, Det.		5.00	2.50
☐☐	12	Curtis Joseph (G), Edm.		3.25	1.75
☐☐	13	Saku Koivu, Mtl.		4.00	2.00
☐☐	14	Keith Tkachuk, Pho.		2.50	1.25
☐☐	15	Pavel Bure, Van.		4.00	2.00
☐☐	16	Félix Potvin (G), Tor.		3.00	1.50
☐☐	17	Ray Bourque, Bos.		3.00	1.50
☐☐	18	Theoren Fleury, Cgy.		2.00	1.00
☐☐	19	Patrick Roy (G), Col.		10.00	5.00
☐☐	20	Joe Nieuwendyk, Dal.		1.50	.75
☐☐	21	Alexei Yashin, Ott.		2.50	1.25
☐☐	22	Owen Nolan, S.J.		1.50	.75
☐☐	23	Mark Recchi, Mtl.		1.50	.75
☐☐	24	Dominik Hasek (G), Buf.		4.00	2.00
☐☐	25	Chris Chelios, Chi.		2.50	1.25
☐☐	26	Mike Modano, Dal.		3.00	1.50
☐☐	27	John Vanbiesbrouck (G), Fla.		3.25	1.75
☐☐	28	Brian Leetch, NYR.		2.00	1.00
☐☐	29	Dino Ciccarelli, Fla.		3.00	.75
☐☐	30	Mark Messier, Van.		3.00	1.50
☐☐	31	Paul Kariya, Ana.		8.00	4.00
☐☐	32	Jocelyn Thibault (G), Mtl.		2.00	1.00
☐☐	33	Wayne Gretzky, NYR.		12.00	6.00
☐☐	34	Doug Weight, Edm.		2.00	1.00
☐☐	35	Yanic Perreault, L.A.		1.00	.50
☐☐	36	Luc Robitaille, L.A.		1.50	.75
☐☐	37	Chris Osgood (G), Det.		2.50	1.25
☐☐	38	Adam Oates, Wsh.		2.00	1.00
☐☐	39	Mats Sundin, Tor.		3.00	1.50
☐☐	40	Trevor Linden, Van.		1.50	.75
☐☐	41	Mike Richter (G), NYR.		2.00	1.00
☐☐	42	Zigmund Palffy, NYI.		2.00	1.00
☐☐	43	Pat LaFontaine, NYR.		1.50	.75
☐☐	44	Grant Fuhr (G), Stl.		1.50	.75
☐☐	45	Martin Brodeur (G), N.J.		4.00	2.00
☐☐	46	Sergei Fedorov, Det.		3.00	1.50
☐☐	47	Doug Gilmour, N.J.		2.00	1.00
☐☐	48	Daniel Alfredsson, Ott.		1.50	.75
☐☐	49	Ron Francis, Pgh.		2.00	1.00
☐☐	50	Geoff Sanderson, Van.		1.00	.50
☐☐☐	51	Joe Thornton, Bos.	35.00	3.00	1.75
☐☐☐	**52**	**Vaclav Prospal, Pha. (Ott.), RC**	**20.00**	**2.00**	**1.00**
☐☐☐	**53**	**Patrik Elias, N.J., RC**	**20.00**	**2.00**	**1.00**
☐☐☐	**54**	**Mike Johnson, Tor., RC**	**30.00**	**7.00**	**5.00**
☐☐☐	55	Alyn McCauley, Tor.	25.00	2.00	1.50
☐☐☐	**56**	**Brendan Morrison, N.J., RC**	**30.00**	**5.00**	**3.50**
☐☐☐	57	Johnny Bower (G), Tor.	30.00	4.00	2.00
☐☐☐	58	John Bucyk, Bos.	25.00	3.50	1.75
☐☐☐	59	Stan Mikita, Chi.	40.00	5.00	2.50
☐☐☐	60	Ted Lindsay, Det.	20.00	3.00	1.50
☐☐☐	61	Maurice Richard, Mtl.	100.00	10.00	5.00
☐☐☐	62	Andy Bathgate, NYR.	20.00	3.00	1.50
☐☐☐	**63**	**Stefan Cherneski, Brandon, RC**	**20.00**	**2.00**	**1.50**
☐☐☐	**64**	**Craig Hillier (G), Ottawa-OHL, RC**	**20.00**	**2.00**	**1.50**
☐☐☐	65	Daniel Tkaczuk, Barrie	25.00	3.00	1.75
☐☐☐	66	Josh Holden, Regina	20.00	2.00	1.50
☐☐☐	**67**	**Marian Cisar, Spokane, RC**	**20.00**	**2.00**	**1.50**
☐☐☐	**68**	**J.P. Dumont, Val d'or, RC**	**30.00**	**6.00**	**4.00**
☐☐☐	**69**	**Roberto Luongo (G), Val d'or, RC**	**50.00**	**10.00**	**6.00**
☐☐☐	**70**	**Aren Miller (G), Spokane, RC**	**20.00**	**2.00**	**1.50**
☐☐☐	71	Mathieu Garon (G), Victoriaville	25.00	2.00	1.50
☐☐☐	**72**	**Charlie Stephens, Toronto, RC**	**25.00**	**3.50**	**2.50**
☐☐☐	**73**	**Sergei Varlamov, Swift Current, RC**	**20.00**	**2.00**	**1.50**
☐☐☐	**74**	**Pierre Dagenais, Rouyn-Noranda, RC**	**20.00**	**2.00**	**1.50**
☐☐☐	75	Willie O'Ree, Bos.	40.00	6.00	3.00

BEEHIVE TEAM

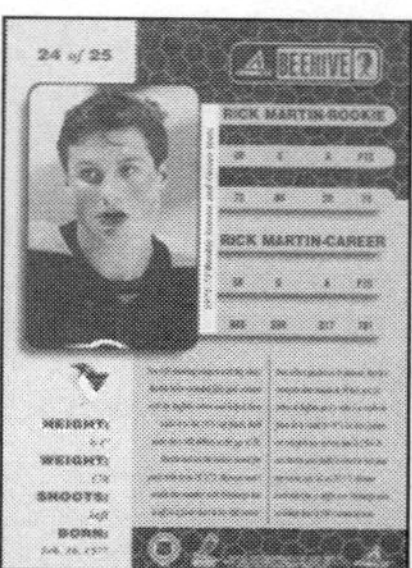

These cards have two versions: the regular insert [1:11] and a Golden parallel [1:49].

Insert Set (25 cards): 700.00 350.00

	No.	Player	Golden	Reg.
☐☐	1	Paul Kariya, Ana.	60.00	30.00
☐☐	2	Mark Messier, Van.	20.00	10.00
☐☐	3	Mike Modano, Dal.	20.00	10.00
☐☐	4	Brendan Shanahan, Det.	24.00	12.00
☐☐	5	John Vanbiesbrouck, Fla.	24.00	12.00
☐☐	6	Martin Brodeur (G), N.J.	30.00	15.00
☐☐	7	Wayne Gretzky, NYR.	100.00	50.00
☐☐	8	Eric Lindros, Pha.	60.00	30.00
☐☐	9	Peter Forsberg, Col.	50.00	25.00
☐☐	10	Jaromir Jagr, Pgh.	50.00	25.00
☐☐	11	Teemu Selänne, Ana.	30.00	15.00
☐☐	12	John LeClair, Pha.	20.00	10.00
☐☐	13	Saku Koivu, Mtl.	30.00	15.00
☐☐	14	Brett Hull, Stl.	20.00	10.00
☐☐	15	Patrick Roy (G), Col.	80.00	40.00
☐☐	16	Steve Yzerman, Det.	40.00	20.00
☐☐	17	Keith Tkachuk, Pho.	16.00	8.00
☐☐	18	Pat LaFontaine, NYR.	12.00	6.00
☐☐	19	Joe Sakic, Col.	40.00	20.00
☐☐	20	Patrik Elias, N.J.	16.00	8.00
☐☐	21	Vaclav Prospal, Pha.	20.00	10.00
☐☐	22	Joe Thornton, Bos.	24.00	12.00
☐☐	23	Sergei Samsonov, Bos.	24.00	12.00
☐☐	24	Alexei Morozov, Pgh.	20.00	10.00
☐☐	25	Marco Sturm, S.J.	12.00	6.00

1997 - 98 PINNACLE CBC SPORTS

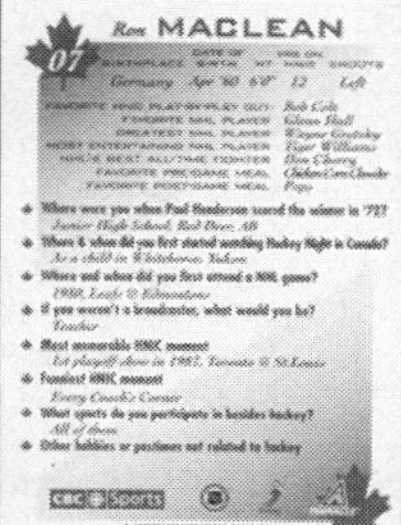

We have no pricing information on these singles.

Imprint: © 1997 PINNACLE TRADING CARD CO.

	No.	Player
☐	1	Steve Armitage
☐	2	Don Cherry
☐	3	Bob Cole
☐	4	Chris Cuthbert

	No.	Player
☐	5	John Garrett
☐	6	Dick Irvin
☐	7	Ron Maclean
☐	8	Greg Millen
☐	9	Harry Neale
☐	10	Scott Oake
☐	11	Scott Russell
☐	12	John Shannon
☐	13	Don Whittman

1997 - 98 PINNACLE CERTIFIED

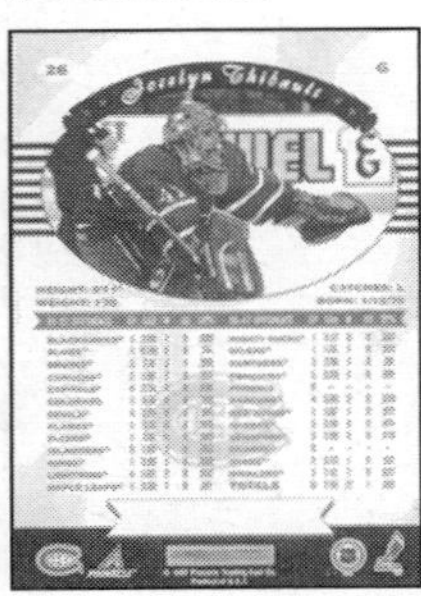

These cards have five versions: the regular card, a Certified Red parallel, a Mirror Red parallel, a Mirror Blue parallel and a Mirror Gold parallel. Regular card goalies (1-30) are short printed and inserted one per pack.

Imprint: © 1997 Pinnacle Trading Card Co.

Complete Set (130 cards): 75.00
Certified Red Set (130 cards): 650.00
Common Player: 100.00 50.00 25.00 2.00 .35
Unnumbered Checklists: .10

	No.	Player	MG	MB	MR	Red	Reg.
☐☐☐☐☐	1	Dominik Hasek (G), Buf.	600.	300.	150.	15.00	3.00
☐☐☐☐☐	2	Patrick Roy (G), Col.	2,000.	1,000.	475.	40.00	7.00
☐☐☐☐☐	3	Martin Brodeur (G), N.J.	600.	300.	150.	15.00	3.00
☐☐☐☐☐	4	Chris Osgood (G), Det.	300.	150.	80.	8.00	1.50
☐☐☐☐☐	5	Andy Moog (G), Dal.	150.	75.	40.	5.00	1.00
☐☐☐☐☐	6	J. Vanbiesbrouck (G), Fla.	500.	250.	125.	12.00	2.50
☐☐☐☐☐	**7**	**Steve Shields (G), Buf., RC**	**125.**	**60.**	**30.**	**4.00**	**1.00**
☐☐☐☐☐	8	Mike Vernon (G), Det.	125.	60.	30.	4.00	1.00
☐☐☐☐☐	9	Ed Belfour (G), S.J.	250.	150.	80.	8.00	1.50
☐☐☐☐☐	10	Grant Fuhr (G), Stl.	150.	75.	40.	5.00	1.00
☐☐☐☐☐	11	Félix Potvin (G), Tor.	400.	200.	100.	10.00	2.00
☐☐☐☐☐	12	Bill Ranford (G), Wsh.	150.	75.	40.	5.00	1.00
☐☐☐☐☐	13	Mike Richter (G), NYR.	250.	150.	80.	8.00	1.50
☐☐☐☐☐	14	Stéphane Fiset (G), L.A.	150.	75.	40.	5.00	1.00
☐☐☐☐☐	15	Jim Carey (G), Bos.	125.	60.	30.	3.00	.75
☐☐☐☐☐	16	Nikolai Khabibulin (G), Pho.	250.	125.	60.	6.00	1.25
☐☐☐☐☐	17	Ken Wregget (G), Pgh.	125.	60.	30.	3.00	.75
☐☐☐☐☐	18	Curtis Joseph (G), Edm.	250.	125.	60.	6.00	1.25
☐☐☐☐☐	19	Guy Hebert (G), Ana.	150.	75.	40.	5.00	1.00
☐☐☐☐☐	20	Damian Rhodes (G), Ott.	125.	60.	30.	3.00	.75
☐☐☐☐☐	21	Trevor Kidd (G), Cgy.	150.	75.	40.	5.00	1.00
☐☐☐☐☐	22	Daren Puppa (G), T.B.	125.	60.	30.	3.00	.75
☐☐☐☐☐	23	Patrick Lalime (G), Pgh.	125.	60.	30.	3.00	.75
☐☐☐☐☐	24	Tommy Salo (G), NYI.	125.	60.	30.	3.00.	.75
☐☐☐☐☐	25	Sean Burke (G), Hfd.	150.	75.	40.	5.00	1.00
☐☐☐☐☐	26	Jocelyn Thibault (G), Mtl.	250.	125.	60.	6.00	1.25
☐☐☐☐☐	27	Kirk McLean (G), Van.	150.	75.	40.	5.00	1.00
☐☐☐☐☐	28	Garth Snow (G), Pha.	125.	60.	30.	3.00	.75
☐☐☐☐☐	29	Ron Tugnutt (G), Ott.	125.	60.	30	3.00	.75
☐☐☐☐☐	30	Jeff Hackett (G), Chi.	150.	75.	40.	5.00	1.00
☐☐☐☐☐	31	Eric Lindros, Pha.	1,400.	600.	300.	30.00	4.50
☐☐☐☐☐	32	Peter Forsberg, Col.	900.	450.	225.	20.00	3.50
☐☐☐☐☐	33	Mike Modano, Dal.	400.	200.	100.	10.00	1.50
☐☐☐☐☐	34	Paul Kariya, Ana.	1,400.	600.	300.	30.00	4.50
☐☐☐☐☐	35	Jaromir Jagr, Pgh.	900.	450.	225.	22.00	3.50
☐☐☐☐☐	36	Brian Leetch, NYR.	250.	125.	60.	6.00	.75
☐☐☐☐☐	37	Keith Tkachuk, Pho.	300.	150.	80.	8.00	1.00
☐☐☐☐☐	38	Steve Yzerman, Det.	900.	450.	225.	22.00	3.50
☐☐☐☐☐	39	Teemu Selänne, Ana.	600.	300.	150.	15.00	2.50
☐☐☐☐☐	40	Bryan Berard, NYI.	250.	125.	60.	6.00	.75
☐☐☐☐☐	41	Ray Bourque, Bos.	400.	200.	100.	10.00	1.50
☐☐☐☐☐	42	Theoren Fleury, Cgy.	250.	125.	60.	6.00	.75
☐☐☐☐☐	43	Mark Messier, NYR.	400.	200.	100.	10.00	1.50
☐☐☐☐☐	44	Saku Koivu, Mtl.	600.	300.	150.	15.00	2.50
☐☐☐☐☐	45	Pavel Bure, Van.	600.	300.	150.	15.00	2.50
☐☐☐☐☐	46	Peter Bondra, Wsh.	300.	150.	80.	8.00	1.00
☐☐☐☐☐	47	Dave Gagner, Cgy.	100.	50.	25.	2.00	.35
☐☐☐☐☐	48	Ed Jovanovski, Fla.	150.	75.	40.	4.00	.50
☐☐☐☐☐	49	Adam Oates, Wsh.	250.	125.	60.	6.00	.75
☐☐☐☐☐	50	Joe Sakic, Col.	700.	350	180.	18.00	3.00
☐☐☐☐☐	51	Doug Gilmour, N.J.	250.	125.	60.	6.00	.75
☐☐☐☐☐	52	Jim Campbell, Stl.	100.	50.	25.	2.00	.35
☐☐☐☐☐	53	Mats Sundin, Tor.	400.	200.	100.	10.00	1.50
☐☐☐☐☐	54	Derian Hatcher, Dal.	150.	75.	40.	4.00	.50
☐☐☐☐☐	55	Jarome Iginla, Cgy.	200.	100.	50.	6.00	.75
☐☐☐☐☐	56	Sergei Fedorov, Det.	400.	200.	100.	10.00	1.50
☐☐☐☐☐	57	Keith Primeau, Hfd.	150.	75.	40.	4.00	.50
☐☐☐☐☐	58	Mark Recchi, Mtl.	150.	75.	40.	4.00	.50
☐☐☐☐☐	59	Owen Nolan, S.J.	150.	75.	40.	4.00	.50
☐☐☐☐☐	60	Alexander Mogilny, Van.	250.	125.	60.	6.00	.75
☐☐☐☐☐	61	Brendan Shanahan, Det.	500.	250.	125.	12.00	1.75
☐☐☐☐☐	62	Pierre Turgeon, Stl.	150.	75.	40.	4.00	.50
☐☐☐☐☐	63	Joe Juneau, Wsh.	100.	50.	25.	2.00	.35
☐☐☐☐☐	64	Steve Rucchin, Ana.	100.	50.	25.	2.00	.35
☐☐☐☐☐	65	Jeremy Roenick, Pho.	250.	125.	60.	6.00	.75
☐☐☐☐☐	66	Doug Weight, Edm.	250.	125.	60.	6.00	.75
☐☐☐☐☐	67	Valeri Kamensky, Col.	150.	75.	40.	4.00	.50
☐☐☐☐☐	68	Tony Amonte, Chi.	150.	75.	40.	4.00	.50
☐☐☐☐☐	69	Dave Andreychuk, N.J.	100.	50.	25.	2.00	.35
☐☐☐☐☐	70	Brett Hull, Stl.	400.	200.	100.	10.00	1.50
☐☐☐☐☐	71	Wendel Clark, Tor.	150.	75.	40.	4.00	.50
☐☐☐☐☐	72	Vincent Damphousse, Mtl.	250.	125.	60.	6.00	.75
☐☐☐☐☐	73	Mike Grier, Edm.	150.	75.	40.	4.00	.50
☐☐☐☐☐	74	Chris Chelios, Chi.	300.	150.	80.	8.00	1.00
☐☐☐☐☐	75	Nicklas Lidström, Det.	150.	75.	40.	4.00	.50
☐☐☐☐☐	76	Joe Nieuwendyk, Dal.	150.	75.	40.	4.00	.50
☐☐☐☐☐	77	Rob Blake, L.A.	150.	75.	40.	4.00	.50
☐☐☐☐☐	78	Alexei Yashin, Ott.	300.	150.	75.	7.50	1.00
☐☐☐☐☐	79	Ryan Smyth, Edm.	150.	75.	40.	4.00	.50
☐☐☐☐☐	80	Pat LaFontaine, Buf.	150.	75.	40.	4.00	.50
☐☐☐☐☐	81	Jeff Friesen, S.J.	150.	75.	40.	4.00	.50
☐☐☐☐☐	82	Ray Ferraro, L.A.	100.	50.	25.	2.00	.35
☐☐☐☐☐	83	Steve Sullivan, Tor.	100.	50.	25.	2.00	.35
☐☐☐☐☐	84	Chris Gratton, T.B.	150.	75.	40.	4.00	.50
☐☐☐☐☐	85	Mike Gartner, Pho.	150.	75.	40.	4.00	.50
☐☐☐☐☐	86	Kevin Hatcher, Pgh.	100.	50.	25.	2.00	.35
☐☐☐☐☐	87	Ted Donato, Bos.	100.	50.	25.	2.00	.35
☐☐☐☐☐	88	German Titov, Cgy.	100.	50.	25.	2.00	.35
☐☐☐☐☐	89	Sandis Ozolinsh, Col.	150.	75.	40.	4.00	.50
☐☐☐☐☐	90	Ray Sheppard, Fla.	100.	50.	25.	2.00	.35
☐☐☐☐☐	91	John MacLean, N.J.	100.	50.	25.	2.00	.35
☐☐☐☐☐	92	Luc Robitaille, L.A.	150.	75.	40.	4.00	.50
☐☐☐☐☐	93	Rod Brind'Amour, Pha.	150.	75.	40.	4.00	.50
☐☐☐☐☐	94	Zigmund Palffy, NYI.	250.	125.	60.	6.00	.75
☐☐☐☐☐	95	Peter Nedved, Pgh.	100.	50.	25.	2.00	.35
☐☐☐☐☐	96	Adam Graves, NYR.	100.	50.	25.	2.00	.35
☐☐☐☐☐	97	Jozef Stumpel, Bos.	150.	75.	40.	4.00	.50
☐☐☐☐☐	98	Alexandre Daigle, Ott.	100.	50.	25.	2.00	.35
☐☐☐☐☐	99	Michael Peca, Buf.	150.	80.	40.	4.00	.50
☐☐☐☐☐	100	Wayne Gretzky, NYR.	2,800.	1,200.	550.	45.00	7.00
☐☐☐☐☐	101	Alexei Zhamnov, Chi.	100.	50.	25.	2.00	.35
☐☐☐☐☐	102	Paul Coffey, Pha.	150.	75.	40.	4.00	.50
☐☐☐☐☐	103	Oleg Tverdovsky, Pho.	100.	50.	25.	2.00	.35
☐☐☐☐☐	104	Trevor Linden, Van.	150.	75.	40.	4.00	.50
☐☐☐☐☐	105	Dino Ciccarelli, T.B.	150.	75.	40.	4.00	.50
☐☐☐☐☐	106	Andrei Kovalenko, Edm.	100.	50.	25.	2.00	.35
☐☐☐☐☐	107	Scott Mellanby, Fla.	100.	50.	25.	2.00	.35
☐☐☐☐☐	108	Bryan Smolinski, NYI.	100.	50.	25.	2.00	.35
☐☐☐☐☐	109	Bernie Nicholls, S.J.	100.	50.	25.	2.00	.35
☐☐☐☐☐	110	Derek Plante, Buf.	100.	50.	25.	2.00	.35
☐☐☐☐☐	111	Pat Verbeek, Dal.	100.	50.	25.	2.00	.35
☐☐☐☐☐	112	Adam Deadmarsh, Col.	100.	50.	25.	2.00	.35
☐☐☐☐☐	113	Martin Gelinas, Van.	100.	50.	25.	2.00	.35
☐☐☐☐☐	114	Daniel Alfredsson, Ott.	150.	75.	40.	4.00	.50
☐☐☐☐☐	115	Scott Stevens, N.J.	150.	75.	40.	4.00	.50
☐☐☐☐☐	116	Dainius Zubrus, Pha.	150.	75.	40.	4.00	.50
☐☐☐☐☐	117	Kirk Muller, Fla.	100.	50.	25.	2.00	.35
☐☐☐☐☐	118	Brian Holzinger, Buf.	100.	50.	25	2.00	.35
☐☐☐☐☐	119	John LeClair, Pha.	400.	200.	100.	1.00	1.50
☐☐☐☐☐	120	Al MacInnis, Stl.	150.	75.	40.	4.00	.50
☐☐☐☐☐	121	Ron Francis, Pgh.	250.	125.	60.	6.00	.75
☐☐☐☐☐	122	Eric Dazé, Chi.	150.	75.	40.	4.00	.50
☐☐☐☐☐	123	Travis Green, NYI.	100.	50.	25.	2.00	.35
☐☐☐☐☐	124	Jason Arnott, Edm.	150.	75.	40.	4.00	.50
☐☐☐☐☐	125	Geoff Sanderson, Hfd.	100.	50.	25.	2.00	.35
☐☐☐☐☐	126	Dimitri Khristich, L.A.	100.	50.	25.	2.00	.35
☐☐☐☐☐	127	Sergei Berezin, Tor.	150.	75.	40.	4.00	.50
☐☐☐☐☐	128	Jeff O'Neill, Hfd.	150.	75.	40.	4.00	.50
☐☐☐☐☐	129	Claude Lemieux, Col.	100.	50.	25.	2.00	.35
☐☐☐☐☐	130	Andrew Cassels, Hfd.	100.	50.	25.	2.00	.35

CERTIFIED TEAM

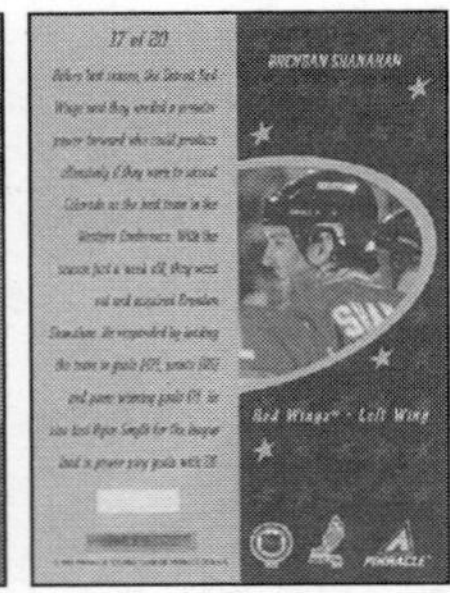

These cards have two versions: the regular insert and a Gold (serial numbered out of 300) parallel. A third Mirror Gold version also exists.

Insert Set (20 cards): 300.00
Promo Card (Steve Yzerman, #13): 3.00

	No.	Player	Gold	Reg.
☐☐☐	1	Martin Brodeur (G), N.J.	50.00	15.00
☐☐☐	2	Patrick Roy (G), Col.	150.00	30.00
☐☐☐	3	John Vanbiesbrouck (G), Fla.	45.00	12.00
☐☐☐	4	Dominik Hasek (G), Buf.	50.00	15.00
☐☐☐	5	Chris Chelios, Chi.	18.00	6.00
☐☐☐	6	Brian Leetch, NYR.	18.00	6.00
☐☐☐	7	Wayne Gretzky, NYR.	200.00	40.00
☐☐☐	8	Eric Lindros, Pha.	100.00	25.00
☐☐☐	9	Paul Kariya, Ana.	100.00	25.00
☐☐☐	10	Peter Forsberg, Col.	75.00	20.00
☐☐☐	11	Keith Tkachuk, Pho.	25.00	8.00
☐☐☐	12	Mark Messier, Van.	30.00	10.00
☐☐☐	13	Steve Yzerman, Det.	75.00	20.00
☐☐☐	14	Jaromir Jagr, Pgh.	75.00	20.00
☐☐☐	15	Mats Sundin, Tor.	30.00	10.00
☐☐☐	16	Teemu Selänne, Ana.	50.00	15.00
☐☐☐	17	Brendan Shanahan, Det.	45.00	12.00
☐☐☐	18	Saku Koivu, Mtl.	50.00	15.00
☐☐☐	19	Brett Hull, Stl.	30.00	10.00
☐☐☐	20	John LeClair, Pha.	30.00	10.00

ROOKIE TEAM

These cards have two versions: the regular card and a gold parallel. A third Mirror Gold version also exists.

Insert Set (12 cards):

	No.	Player	Gold	Reg.
☐☐☐	A	Joe Thornton, Bos.	75.00	15.00
☐☐☐	B	Chris Phillips, Ott.	25.00	6.00
☐☐☐	C	Patrick Marleau, S.J.	60.00	12.00
☐☐☐	D	Sergei Samsonov, Bos.	75.00	15.00
☐☐☐	E	Daniel Cleary, Chi.	25.00	6.00
☐☐☐	F	Olli Jokinen, L.A.	25.00	6.00
☐☐☐	G	Alyn McCauley, Tor.	40.00	10.00
☐☐☐	H	Alexei Morozov, Pgh.	40.00	10.00
☐☐☐	I	Brad Isbister, Pha.	20.00	5.00
☐☐☐	J	Boyd Devereaux, Edm.	20.00	5.00
☐☐☐	K	Espen Krutsen, Ana.	20.00	5.00
☐☐☐	L	Marc Savard, NYR.	20.00	5.00

SUMMIT

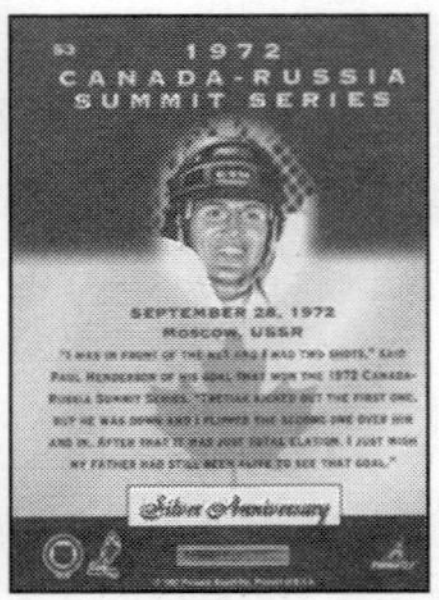

The autographed has three versions: one signed in black (limited to 700 copies), one signed in silver (limited to 200) and one signed in gold (limited to 100).

Insert Set (4 cards): 40.00

	No.	Player	NRMT-MT
☐	S1	Paul Henderson	12.00
☐	S2	Paul Henderson	12.00
☐	S3	Paul Henderson	12.00
☐	S4	Paul Henderson	12.00
☐	S5	Paul Henderson (Black Ink Autograph)	80.00

☐	S5	Paul Henderson (Silver Ink Autograph)	175.00
☐	S5	Paul Henderson (Gold Ink Autograph)	375.00

1997 - 98 PINNACLE EPIX

This 24-player set was inserted into 1997-98 Pinnacle products: Pinnacle Certified, Score, Pinnacle and Pinnacle Zenith. Each player has one of four cards (Game, Season, Moment or Play) inserted into each product. In turn, each card (Game, Season, Moment or Play) is available in three colours: emerald, orange or violet. So while Gretzky has a total of 12 Epix cards, only three Epix cards are available in any one product.

EPIX PLAY

Play cards E1-E6 were available in Pinnacle Certified, E7-E12 were available in Score, E13-E18 were available in Pinnacle and E19-E24 were available in Pinnacle Zenith.

Imprint:

	No.	Player	Emerald	Orange	Violet
☐☐☐	E1	Wayne Gretzky, NYR.	120.00	60.00	30.00
☐☐☐	E2	John Vanbiesbrouck (G), Fla.	35.00	17.50	8.75
☐☐☐	E3	Joe Sakic, Col.	50.00	25.00	12.50
☐☐☐	E4	Alexei Yashin, Ott.	24.00	12.00	6.00
☐☐☐	E5	Sergei Fedorov, Det.	30.00	15.00	7.50
☐☐☐	E6	Keith Tkachuk, Pho.	24.00	12.00	6.00
☐☐☐	E7	Patrick Roy (G), Col.	100.00	50.00	25.00
☐☐☐	E8	Martin Brodeur (G), N.J.	40.00	20.00	10.00
☐☐☐	E9	Steve Yzerman, Det.	60.00	30.00	15.00
☐☐☐	E10	Saku Koivu, Mtl.	40.00	20.00	10.00
☐☐☐	E11	Félix Potvin (G), Tor.	30.00	15.00	7.50
☐☐☐	E12	Mark Messier, Van.	30.00	15.00	7.50
☐☐☐	E13	Eric Lindros, Pha.	80.00	40.00	20.00
☐☐☐	E14	Peter Forsberg, Col.	60.00	30.00	15.00
☐☐☐	E15	Teemu Selänne, Ana.	40.00	20.00	10.00
☐☐☐	E16	Brendan Shanahan, Det.	35.00	17.50	8.75
☐☐☐	E17	Curtis Joseph (G), Edm.	35.00	17.50	8.75
☐☐☐	E18	Brett Hull, Stl.	30.00	15.00	7.50
☐☐☐	E19	Paul Kariya, Ana.	80.00	40.00	20.00
☐☐☐	E20	Jaromir Jagr, Pgh.	60.00	30.00	15.00
☐☐☐	E21	Pavel Bure, Van.	40.00	20.00	10.00
☐☐☐	E22	Dominik Hasek (G), Buf.	40.00	20.00	10.00
☐☐☐	E23	John LeClair, Pha.	30.00	15.00	7.50
☐☐☐	E24	Doug Gilmour, N.J.	20.00	10.00	5.00

EPIX GAME

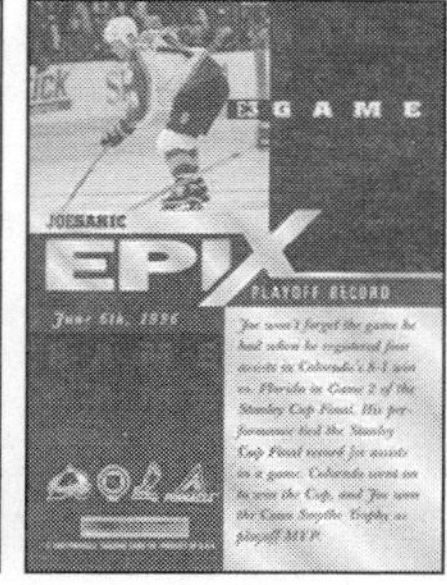

Game cards E1-E6 were available in Score, E7-E12 were available in Pinnacle, E13-E18 were available in Zenith and E19-E24 were available in Pinancle Certified.

	No.	Player	Emerald	Orange	Violet
☐☐☐	E1	Wayne Gretzky, NYR.	250.00	100.00	50.00
☐☐☐	E2	John Vanbiesbrouck (G), Fla.	75.00	30.00	15.00
☐☐☐	E3	Joe Sakic, Col.	100.00	40.00	20.00
☐☐☐	E4	Alexei Yashin, Ott.	50.00	20.00	10.00
☐☐☐	E5	Sergei Fedorov, Det.	65.00	25.00	12.50
☐☐☐	E6	Keith Tkachuk, Pho.	50.00	20.00	10.00
☐☐☐	E7	Patrick Roy (G), Col.	200.00	80.00	40.00
☐☐☐	E8	Martin Brodeur (G), N.J.	85.00	35.00	17.50
☐☐☐	E9	Steve Yzerman, Det.	125.00	50.00	25.00
☐☐☐	E10	Saku Koivu, Mtl.	85.00	35.00	17.50
☐☐☐	E11	Félix Potvin (G), Tor.	65.00	25.00	12.50
☐☐☐	E12	Mark Messier, Van.	65.00	25.00	12.50
☐☐☐	E13	Eric Lindros, Pha.	165.00	65.00	35.00
☐☐☐	E14	Peter Forsberg, Col.	125.00	50.00	25.00
☐☐☐	E15	Teemu Selänne, Ana.	85.00	35.00	17.50
☐☐☐	E16	Brendan Shanahan, Det.	75.00	30.00	15.00
☐☐☐	E17	Curtis Joseph (G), Edm.	75.00	30.00	15.00
☐☐☐	E18	Brett Hull, Stl.	65.00	25.00	12.50
☐☐☐	E19	Paul Kariya, Ana.	165.00	65.00	35.00
☐☐☐	E20	Jaromir Jagr, Pgh.	125.00	50.00	25.00
☐☐☐	E21	Pavel Bure, Van.	85.00	35.00	17.50
☐☐☐	E22	Dominik Hasek (G), Buf.	85.00	35.00	17.50
☐☐☐	E23	John LeClair, Pha.	65.00	25.00	12.50
☐☐☐	E24	Doug Gilmour, N.J.	45.00	15.00	7.50

EPIX SEASON

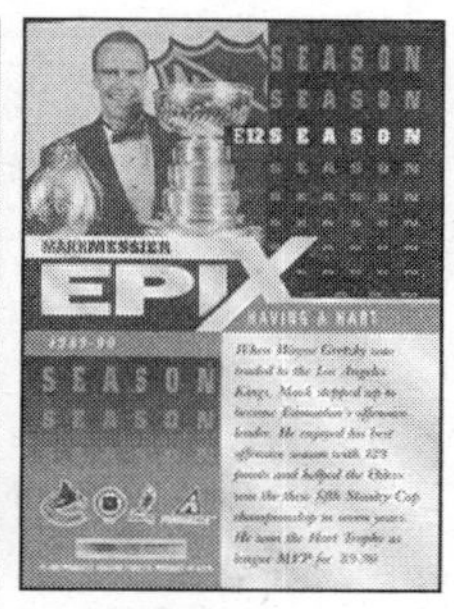

Season cards E1-E6 were available in Pinnacle, E7-E12 were available in Zenith, E13-E18 were available in Pinancle Certified and E19-E24 were available in Score.

	No.	Player	Emerald	Orange	Violet
☐☐☐	E1	Wayne Gretzky, NYR.	500.00	200.00	100.00
☐☐☐	E2	John Vanbiesbrouck (G), Fla.	150.00	60.00	30.00
☐☐☐	E3	Joe Sakic, Col.	200.00	80.00	40.00
☐☐☐	E4	Alexei Yashin, Ott.	100.00	40.00	20.00
☐☐☐	E5	Sergei Fedorov, Det.	125.00	50.00	25.00
☐☐☐	E6	Keith Tkachuk, Pho.	100.00	40.00	20.00
☐☐☐	E7	Patrick Roy (G), Col.	400.00	160.00	80.00
☐☐☐	E8	Martin Brodeur (G), N.J.	175.00	70.00	35.00
☐☐☐	E9	Steve Yzerman, Det.	250.00	100.00	50.00
☐☐☐	E10	Saku Koivu, Mtl.	175.00	70.00	35.00
☐☐☐	E11	Félix Potvin (G), Tor.	125.00	50.00	25.00
☐☐☐	E12	Mark Messier, Van.	125.00	50.00	25.00
☐☐☐	E13	Eric Lindros, Pha.	325.00	130.00	65.00
☐☐☐	E14	Peter Forsberg, Col.	250.00	100.00	50.00
☐☐☐	E15	Teemu Selänne, Ana.	175.00	70.00	35.00
☐☐☐	E16	Brendan Shanahan, Det.	150.00	60.00	30.00
☐☐☐	E17	Curtis Joseph (G), Edm.	150.00	60.00	30.00
☐☐☐	E18	Brett Hull, Stl.	125.00	50.00	25.00
☐☐☐	E19	Paul Kariya, Ana.	325.00	130.00	65.00
☐☐☐	E20	Jaromir Jagr, Pgh.	250.00	100.00	50.00
☐☐☐	E21	Pavel Bure, Van.	175.00	70.00	35.00
☐☐☐	E22	Dominik Hasek (G), Buf.	175.00	70.00	35.00
☐☐☐	E23	John LeClair, Pha.	125.00	50.00	25.00
☐☐☐	E24	Doug Gilmour, N.J.	85.00	30.00	15.00

EPIX MOMENT

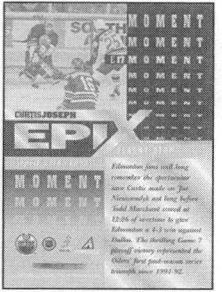

Moment cards E1-E6 were available in Zenith, E7-E12 were available in Pinnacle Certified, E13-E18 were available in Score and E19-E24 were available in Pinnacle.

Insert Set (24 cards):

	No.	Player	Emerald	Orange	Violet
☐☐☐	E1	Wayne Gretzky, NYR.	1,500.00	500.00	250.00
☐☐☐	E2	John Vanbiesbrouck (G), Fla.	450.00	150.00	75.00
☐☐☐	E3	Joe Sakic, Col.	600.00	200.00	100.00
☐☐☐	E4	Alexei Yashin, Ott.	300.00	100.00	50.00
☐☐☐	E5	Sergei Fedorov, Det.	375.00	125.00	65.00
☐☐☐	E6	Keith Tkachuk, Pho.	300.00	100.00	50.00
☐☐☐	E7	Patrick Roy (G), Col.	1,200.00	400.00	200.00
☐☐☐	E8	Martin Brodeur (G), N.J.	500.00	175.00	85.00
☐☐☐	E9	Steve Yzerman, Det.	750.00	250.00	125.00
☐☐☐	E10	Saku Koivu, Mtl.	500.00	175.00	85.00
☐☐☐	E11	Félix Potvin (G), Tor.	375.00	125.00	65.00
☐☐☐	E12	Mark Messier, Van.	375.00	125.00	65.00
☐☐☐	E13	Eric Lindros, Pha.	1,000.00	325.00	165.00
☐☐☐	E14	Peter Forsberg, Col.	750.00	250.00	125.00
☐☐☐	E15	Teemu Selänne, Ana.	500.00	175.00	85.00
☐☐☐	E16	Brendan Shanahan, Det.	450.00	150.00	75.00
☐☐☐	E17	Curtis Joseph (G), Edm.	450.00	150.00	75.00
☐☐☐	E18	Brett Hull, Stl.	375.00	125.00	65.00
☐☐☐	E19	Paul Kariya, Ana.	1,000.00	325.00	165.00
☐☐☐	E20	Jaromir Jagr, Pgh.	750.00	250.00	125.00
☐☐☐	E21	Pavel Bure, Van.	500.00	175.00	85.00
☐☐☐	E22	Dominik Hasek (G), Buf.	500.00	175.00	85.00
☐☐☐	E23	John LeClair, Pha.	375.00	125.00	65.00
☐☐☐	E24	Doug Gilmour, N.J.	250.00	85.00	45.00

1997 - 98 PINNACLE INSIDE

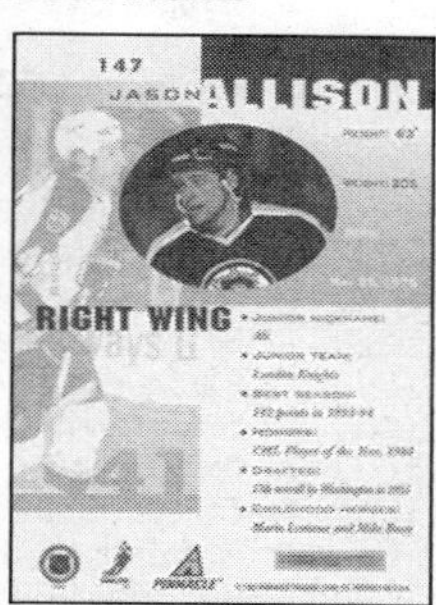

Cards 1-90 have three versions: the regular card, a Coach's Collection parallel and an Executive Collection parallel. A fourth promo version also exist; promo cards have the same value as the regular card.

Imprint: © 1997 PINNACLE TRADING CARD CO.

Complete Set (190 cards): 50.00

Parallel Set (100 cards): 600.00

	No.	Player	E.C.	C.C.	Reg.
Common Player:			20.00	1.50	.25
☐☐☐	1	Brendan Shanahan, Det.	125.00	15.00	1.75
☐☐☐	2	Dominik Hasek (G), Buf.	150.00	17.50	2.00
☐☐☐	3	Wayne Gretzky, NYR.	500.00	50.00	6.00
☐☐☐	4	Eric Lindros, Pha.	350.00	35.00	4.00
☐☐☐	5	Keith Tkachuk, Pho.	75.00	10.00	1.25
☐☐☐	6	Jaromir Jagr, Pgh.	250.00	25.00	3.00
☐☐☐	7	Martin Brodeur (G), N.J.	150.00	17.50	2.00
☐☐☐☐	8	Peter Forsberg, Col.	250.00	25.00	3.00
☐☐☐	9	Chris Osgood (G), Det.	75.00	10.00	1.25
☐☐☐☐	10	Paul Kariya, Ana.	350.00	35.00	4.00
☐☐☐	11	Pavel Bure, Van.	150.00	17.50	2.00
☐☐☐	12	Brett Hull, Stl.	100.00	12.50	1.50
☐☐☐	13	Saku Koivu, Mtl.	150.00	17.50	2.00
☐☐☐	14	Zigmund Palffy, NYI.	50.00	7.00	1.00
☐☐☐	15	Mike Modano, Dal.	100.00	12.50	1.50
☐☐☐	16	Ray Bourque, Bos.	100.00	12.50	1.50
☐☐☐	17	Jarome Iginla, Cgy.	50.00	7.00	1.00
☐☐☐	18	Chris Chelios, Chi.	75.00	10.00	1.25
☐☐☐	19	John Vanbiesbrouck (G), Fla.	125.00	15.00	1.75
☐☐☐	20	Brian Leetch, NYR.	50.00	7.00	1.00
☐☐☐	21	Mats Sundin, Tor.	100.00	12.50	1.50
☐☐☐	22	Ron Hextall (G), Pha.	30.00	3.00	.50
☐☐☐	23	Stéphane Fiset (G), L.A.	30.00	3.00	.50
☐☐☐	24	Steve Yzerman, Det.	250.00	25.00	3.00
☐☐☐	25	Curtis Joseph (G), Edm.	125.00	15.00	1.75
☐☐☐	26	Daniel Alfredsson, Ott.	30.00	3.00	.50
☐☐☐	27	Owen Nolan, S.J.	30.00	3.00	.50
☐☐☐	28	Adam Oates, Wsh.	50.00	7.00	1.00
☐☐☐	29	Corey Hirsch (G), Van.	20.00	1.50	.25
☐☐☐	30	Sean Burke (G), Hfd.	30.00	3.00	.50
☐☐☐	31	Eric Fichaud (G), NYI.	30.00	3.00	.50
☐☐☐	32	Ken Wregget (G), Pgh.	20.00	1.50	.25
☐☐☐	33	Dainius Zubrus, Pha.	30.00	3.00	.50
☐☐☐	34	Alexander Mogilny, Van.	50.00	7.00	1.00
☐☐☐	35	Bill Ranford (G), Wsh.	30.00	3.00	.50
☐☐☐	36	Vincent Damphousse, Mtl.	50.00	7.00	1.00
☐☐☐	37	Patrick Roy (G), Col.	400.00	40.00	5.00
☐☐☐	38	Teemu Selänne, Ana.	150.00	17.50	2.00
☐☐☐	39	Pat LaFontaine, Buf.	30.00	3.00	.50
☐☐☐	40	Theoren Fleury, Cgy.	50.00	7.00	1.00
☐☐☐	41	Jeff Hackett (G), Chi.	30.00	3.00	.50
☐☐☐	42	Sergei Fedorov, Det.	100.00	12.50	1.50
☐☐☐	43	Jocelyn Thibault (G), Mtl.	50.00	7.00	1.00
☐☐☐	44	Nikolai Khabibulin (G), Pho.	50.00	7.00	1.00
☐☐☐	45	Daren Puppa (G), T.B.	20.00	1.50	.25
☐☐☐	46	Félix Potvin (G), Tor.	100.00	12.50	1.50
☐☐☐	47	Andy Moog (G), Dal.	30.00	3.00	.50
☐☐☐	48	Doug Weight, Edm.	50.00	7.00	1.00
☐☐☐	49	Tommy Salo (G), NYI.	20.00	1.50	.25
☐☐☐	50	Mark Messier, NYR.	100.00	12.50	1.50

	No.	Player			
☐☐☐	51	Grant Fuhr (G), Stl.	30.00	3.00	.50
☐☐☐	52	Ron Francis, Pgh.	50.00	7.00	1.00
☐☐☐	53	Tony Amonte, Chi.	30.00	3.00	.50
☐☐☐	54	Joe Sakic, Col.	175.00	20.00	2.50
☐☐☐	55	Jason Arnott, Edm.	30.00	3.00	.50
☐☐☐	56	José Théodore (G), Mtl.	20.00	1.50	.25
☐☐☐	57	Alexei Yashin, Ott.	75.00	10.00	1.25
☐☐☐	58	John LeClair, Pha.	100.00	12.50	1.50
☐☐☐	59	Jeremy Roenick, Pho.	50.00	7.00	1.00
☐☐☐	60	Kirk McLean (G), Van.	30.00	3.00	.50
☐☐☐	61	Arturs Irbe (G), Dal.	20.00	1.50	.25
☐☐☐	62	Jim Carey (G), Bos.	30.00	3.00	.50
☐☐☐	63	J.S. Giguère (G), Hfd.	20.00	1.50	.25
☐☐☐	64	Marc Denis (G), Col.	30.00	3.00	.50
☐☐☐	65	Damian Rhodes (G), Ott.	20.00	1.50	.25
☐☐☐	66	Jim Campbell, Stl.	20.00	1.50	.25
☐☐☐	67	Patrick Lalime (G), Pgh.	10.00	75.00	1.00
☐☐☐	68	Garth Snow (G), Pha.	20.00	1.50	.25
☐☐☐	69	Marcel Cousineau (G), Tor.	20.00	1.50	.25
☐☐☐☐	70	Guy Hebert (G), Ana.	30.00	3.00	.50
☐☐☐	71	Rob Blake, L.A.	30.00	3.00	.50
☐☐☐	**72**	**Tomas Vokoun (G), Mtl., RC**	**20.00**	**1.50**	**.25**
☐☐☐	73	Doug Gilmour, Tor.	50.00	7.00	1.00
☐☐☐	74	Ed Belfour (G), S.J.	50.00	7.00	1.00
☐☐☐	**75**	**Parris Duffus (G), Pho., RC**	**20.00**	**1.50**	**.25**
☐☐☐	76	Mike Fountain (G), Van.	20.00	1.50	.25
☐☐☐	**77**	**Steve Shields (G), Buf., RC**	**30.00**	**3.00**	**.50**
☐☐☐	78	Geoff Sanderson, Hfd.	20.00	1.50	.25
☐☐☐	79	Roman Turek (G), Dal.	20.00	1.50	.25
☐☐☐	80	Bryan Berard, NYI.	50.00	7.00	1.00
☐☐☐	81	Mike Richter (G), NYR.	50.00	7.00	1.00
☐☐☐	82	Ron Tugnutt (G), Ott.	20.00	1.50	.25
☐☐☐	83	Peter Bondra, Wsh.	75.00	10.00	1.25
☐☐☐	84	Mike Vernon (G), Det.	30.00	3.00	.50
☐☐☐	85	Mike Grier, Edm.	30.00	3.00	.50
☐☐☐	86	Ed Jovanovski, Fla.	30.00	3.00	.50
☐☐☐	87	Trevor Kidd (G), Cgy.	30.00	3.00	.50
☐☐☐	88	Eric Dazé, Chi.	30.00	3.00	.50
☐☐☐	89	Wendel Clark, Tor.	30.00	3.00	.50
☐☐☐	90	Checklist	20.00	1.50	.25
☐	91	Nicklas Lidström, Det.			.50
☐	92	Rod Brind'Amour, Pha.			.50
☐	93	Hnat Domenichelli, Cgy.			.50
☐	94	Rem Murray, Edm.			.25
☐	95	Scott Niedermayer, N.J.			.25
☐	96	Martin Rucinsky, Mtl.			.25
☐	97	Mike Gartner, Pho.			.50
☐	98	Kevin Hatcher, Pgh.			.25
☐	99	Daymond Langkow, T.B.			.25
☐	100	Jamie Langenbrunner, Dal.			.50
☐	101	Ted Donato, Bos.			.25
☐	102	Steve Sullivan, Tor.			.25
☐	103	Martin Gelinas, Van.			.25
☐	104	Adam Graves, NYR.			.25
☐	105	Donald Audette, Buf.			.25
☐	106	Andrew Cassels, Hfd.			.25
☐	107	Alexei Zhamnov, Chi.			.25
☐	108	Kirk Muller, Fla.			.25
☐	109	Alexandre Daigle, Ott.			.25
☐	110	Chris Gratton, T.B.			.50
☐	111	Andrew Brunette, Wsh.			.25
☐	112	Mark Recchi, Mtl.			.50
☐	113	Jari Kurri, Ana.			.50
☐	114	Valeri Kamensky, Col.			.50
☐	115	Joe Nieuwendyk, Dal.			.50
☐	116	Vyacheslav Kozlov, Det.			.25
☐	117	Steve Kelly, Edm.			.25
☐	118	Dave Andreychuk, N.J.			.25
☐	119	Mikael Renberg, Pha.			.25
☐	120	Sergei Berezin, Tor.			.50
☐	121	Jeff Friesen, S.J.			.50
☐	122	Pierre Turgeon, Stl.			.50
☐	**123**	**Vladimir Vorobiev, NYR., RC**			**.25**
☐	124	Dimitri Khristich, L.A.			.25
☐	125	Jaroslav Svejkovsky, Wsh.			.50
☐	126	Vladimir Konstantinov, Det.			.25
☐	127	Jozef Stumpel, Bos.			.50
☐	128	Michael Peca, Buf.			.50
☐	129	Jonas Hoglund, Cgy.			.25
☐	130	Travis Green, NYI.			.25
☐	131	Bill Guerin, N.J.			.50
☐	132	Oleg Tverdovsky, Pho.			.25
☐	133	Petr Nedved, Pgh.			.25
☐	134	Dino Ciccarelli, T.B.			.50
☐	135	Brian Savage, Mtl.			.25
☐	136	Steve Duchesne, Ott.			.25
☐	137	Sandis Ozolinsh, Col.			.50
☐	138	Derian Hatcher, Dal.			.50
☐	139	Ray Sheppard, Fla.			.25
☐	140	Brian Bellows, Ana.			.25
☐	**141**	**Paul Brousseau, T.B., RC**			**.35**
☐	142	Tony Granato, L.A.			.25
☐	**143**	**Vaclav Prospal, Pha., RC**			**1.50**
☐	144	Vitali Yachmenev, L.A.			.25
☐	145	John MacLean, N.J.			.25
☐	146	Igor Larionov, Det.			.50
☐	147	Jason Allison, Bos.			1.00
☐	148	Derek Plante, Buf.			.25
☐	149	Jeff O'Neill, Hfd.			.50
☐	150	Trevor Linden, Van.			.50
☐	151	Joé Juneau, Wsh.			.25
☐	152	Brandon Convery, Tor.			.25
☐	153	Kevin Stevens, L.A.			.25
☐	154	Scott Stevens, N.J.			.25
☐	155	Niklas Sundstrom, NYR.			.25
☐	156	Claude Lemieux, Col.			.25
☐	157	Pat Verbeek, Dal.			.25
☐	158	Mariusz Czerkawski, Edm.			.25
☐	159	Robert Svehla, Fla.			.25
☐	160	Paul Coffey, Pha.			.50
☐	161	Al MacInnis, Stl.			.50
☐	162	Roman Hamrlik, T.B.			.50
☐	163	Brian Holzinger, Buf.			.25
☐	164	Cory Stillman, Det.			.25
☐	165	Scott Mellanby, Fla.			.25
☐	166	Todd Warriner, Tor.			.25
☐	167	Terry Ryan, Mtl.			.25
☐	168	Luc Robitaille, NYR.			.50
☐	169	Ed Olczyk, Pgh.			.25
☐	170	Adam Deadmarsh, Col.			.25
☐	171	Anson Carter, Bos.			.25
☐	**172**	**Mike Knuble, Det., RC**			**.25**
☐	173	Cliff Ronning, Pho.			.25
☐	174	Rick Tocchet, Wsh.			.25
☐	175	Chris Pronger, Stl.			.50
☐	176	Matthew Barnaby, Buf.			.25
☐	177	Andrei Kovalenko, Edm.			.25
☐	178	Bryan Smolinski, NYI.			.25
☐	179	Janne Niinimaa, Pha.			.50
☐	180	Ray Ferraro, L.A.			.25
☐	181	Dave Gagner, Cgy.			.25
☐	182	Rob Niedermayer, Fla.			.25
☐	183	Vadim Sharifjanov, N.J.			.25
☐	184	Ethan Moreau, Chi.			.25
☐	185	Bernie Nicholls, S.J.			.25
☐	**186**	**Jean-Yves Leroux, Chi., RC**			**.25**
☐	187	Jere Lehtinen, Dal.			.50
☐	188	Steve Rucchin, Ana.			.25
☐	189	Keith Primeau, Hfd.			.50
☐	190	Checklist			.25

INSIDE TRACK

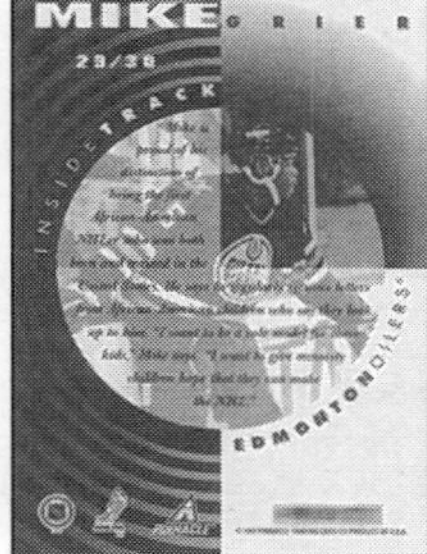

Insert Set (30 cards): 650.00

	No.	Player	NRMT-MT
☐	1	Wayne Gretzky, NYR.	75.00
☐	2	Patrick Roy (G), Col.	60.00
☐	3	Eric Lindros, Pha.	50.00
☐	4	Paul Kariya, Ana.	50.00
☐	5	Peter Forsberg, Col.	35.00
☐	6	Martin Brodeur (G), N.J.	25.00
☐	7	John Vanbiesbrouck (G), Fla.	20.00
☐	8	Joe Sakic, Col.	30.00
☐	9	Steve Yzerman, Det.	35.00
☐	10	Jaromir Jagr, Pgh.	35.00
☐	11	Teemu Selänne, Ana.	25.00
☐	12	Pavel Bure, Van.	25.00
☐	13	Sergei Fedorov, Det.	18.00
☐	14	Brendan Shanahan, Det.	20.00
☐	15	Dominik Hasek (G), Buf.	25.00
☐	16	Saku Koivu, Mtl.	25.00
☐	17	Jocelyn Thibault (G), Mtl.	10.00
☐	18	Mark Messier, NYR.	18.00
☐	19	Brett Hull, Stl.	18.00
☐	20	Félix Potvin (G), Tor.	18.00
☐	21	Curtis Joseph (G), Edm.	20.00
☐	22	Zigmund Palffy, NYI.	10.00
☐	23	Mats Sundin, Tor.	18.00
☐	24	Keith Tkachuk, Pho.	12.00
☐	25	John LeClair, Pha.	18.00
☐	26	Mike Richter (G), NYR.	10.00
☐	27	Alexander Mogilny, Van.	10.00
☐	28	Jarome Iginla, Cgy.	10.00
☐	29	Mike Grier, Edm	8.00
☐	30	Dainius Zubrus, Pha.	8.00

STOPPERS

Disk Diameter: 2 1/2"

Insert Set (24 cards): 150.00

	No.	Player	NRMT-MT
☐	1	Patrick Roy (G), Col.	35.00
☐	2	John Vanbiesbrouck (G), Fla.	10.00
☐	3	Dominik Hasek (G), Buf.	15.00
☐	4	Martin Brodeur (G), N.J.	15.00
☐	5	Mike Richter (G), NYR.	6.00
☐	6	Guy Hebert (G), Ana.	4.00
☐	7	Jim Carey (G), Bos.	3.00
☐	8	Jeff Hackett (G), Chi.	4.00
☐	9	Roman Turek (G), Dal.	3.00
☐	10	Kevin Hodson (G), Det.	3.00
☐	11	Mike Vernon (G), Det.	4.00
☐	12	Curtis Joseph (G), Edm.	10.00
☐	13	J.S. Giguère (G), Hfd.	5.00
☐	14	José Théodore (G), Mtl.	5.00
☐	15	Jocelyn Thibault (G), Mtl.	6.00
☐	16	Nikolai Khabibulin (G), Pho.	6.00
☐	17	Garth Snow (G), Pha.	3.00
☐	18	Ron Hextall (G), Pha.	4.00
☐	19	Steve Shields (G), Buf.	3.00
☐	20	Grant Fuhr (G), Buf.	4.00
☐	21	Félix Potvin (G), Tor.	8.00
☐	22	Marcel Cousineau (G), Tor.	3.00
☐	23	Bill Ranford (G), Wsh.	4.00
☐	24	Ed Belfour (G), S.J.	6.00

STAND-UP GUYS

One Stand-Up Guy was inserted into each large can.

Insert Set (20 cards): 30.00

	No.	Player	NRMT-MT
☐	1A/B	T. Barrasso/M. Vernon	1.50
☐	1C/D	T. Barrasso/M. Vernon	1.50
☐	2A/B	Bordeur/Vanbiesbrouck	5.00
☐	2C/D	Brodeur/Vanbiesbrouck	5.00
☐	3A/B	J. Thibault/J. Carey	2.00
☐	3C/D	J. Thibault/J. Carey	2.00

	No.	Player	
☐	4A/B	G. Snow/M. Cousineau	1.50
☐	4C/D	G. Snow/M. Consineau	1.50
☐	5A/B	P. Roy/E. Fichaud	6.00
☐	5C/D	P. Roy/E.Fichaud	6.00
☐	6A/B	P. Lalime/G. Fuhr	1.50
☐	6C/D	P. Lalime/G. Fuhr	1.50
☐	7A/B	J. Hackett/O. Kolzig	2.00
☐	7CD	J. Hackett/O. Kolzig	2.00
☐	8A/B	T. Kidd/G. Hebert	1.50
☐	8C/D	T. Kidd/G. Hebert	1.50
☐	9A/B	N. Khabibulin/C. Hirsch	2.00
☐	9C/D	N. Khabibulin/C. Hirsch	2.00
☐	10A/B	K. Hrudey/Cu. Joseph	4.00
☐	10C/D	K. Hrudey/Cu. Joseph	4.00

CANS

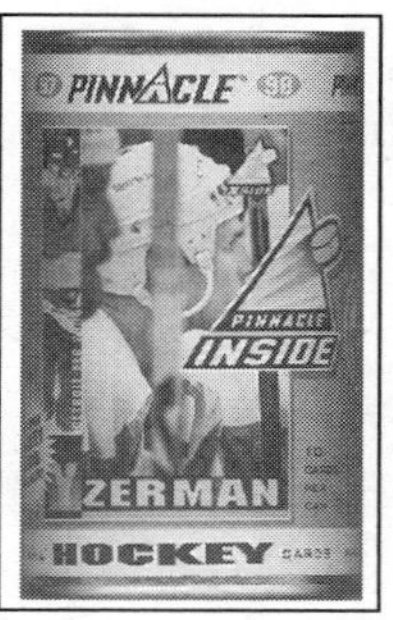

There are two versions for each can: the regular can and a gold parallel can. Prices below are for opened cans.

Complete Set (24 cans): 150.00 30.00

	No.	Player	Gold	Reg.
☐☐	1	Patrick Roy (G), Col.	15.00	3.00
☐☐	2	Martin Brodeur (G), N.J.	7.00	1.50
☐☐	3	John Vanbiesbrouck (G), Fla.	6.00	1.25
☐☐	4	Curtis Joseph (G), Edm.	6.00	1.25
☐☐	5	Mike Richter (G), NYR.	3.00	.75
☐☐	6	Jocelyn Thibault (G), Mtl.	3.00	.75
☐☐	7	Guy Hebert (G), Ana.	2.50	.50
☐☐	8	Mike Vernon (G), Det.	2.50	.50
☐☐	9	Wayne Gretzky, NYR.	20.00	4.00
☐☐	10	Paul Kariya, Ana.	12.50	2.50
☐☐	11	Peter Forsberg, Col.	10.00	2.00
☐☐	12	Eric Lindros, Pha.	12.50	2.50
☐☐	13	Jaromir Jagr, Pgh.	10.00	2.00
☐☐	14	Steve Yzerman, Det.	10.00	2.00
☐☐	15	Joe Sakic, Col.	8.00	1.75
☐☐	16	Saku Koivu, Mtl.	7.00	1.50
☐☐	17	John LeClair, Pha.	5.00	1.00
☐☐	18	Keith Tkachuk, Pho.	4.00	.85
☐☐	19	Teemu Selänne, Wpg.	7.00	1.50
☐☐	20	Pavel Bure, Van.	7.00	1.50
☐☐	21	Brendan Shanahan, Det.	6.00	1.25
☐☐	22	Mark Messier, NYR.	5.00	1.00
☐☐	23	Mats Sundin, Tor.	5.00	1.00
☐☐	24	Brett Hull, Stl.	5.00	1.00

LARGE CANS

These oversize cans feature goaltenders and their masks. Prices are for opened cans.

Complete Set (8 cans): 65.00 12.00

	No.	Player	Gold	Reg.
☐☐	2	John Vanbiesbrouck (G), Fla	10.00	2.00
☐☐		Patrick Roy (G), Col.	25.00	5.00
☐☐		Curtis Joseph (G), Edm.	10.00	2.00
☐☐		Guy Hebert (G), Ana.	4.00	.75
☐☐		Garth Snow (G), Pha.	4.00	.75
☐☐		Jocelyn Thibault (G), Mtl.	5.00	1.00
☐☐		Martin Brodeur (G), N.J.	12.50	2.50
☐☐		Mike Richter (G), NYR.	5.00	1.00

1997 - 98 PINNACLE MINI MASKS

Mask Height:

	Player	NRMT-MT
☐	Martin Brodeur (G), N.J.	35.00
☐	Guy Hebert (G), Ana.	35.00
☐	Curtis Joseph (G), Edm.	35.00
☐	Mike Richter (G), NYR.	35.00
☐	Patrick Roy (G), Col.	40.00
☐	John Vanbiesbrouck (G), Fla.	35.00

1997 - 98 PINNACLE MINT

There are four versions for each card: a die-cut coin-holder card, a Bronze Mint Team card, a Silver Mint Team card and a Gold Mint Team card.

Imprint: © 1998 PINNACLE TRADING CARD CO.

Complete Set (30 cards):

	No.	Player	Gold	Silver	Bronze	D-C
☐☐☐☐	1	Eric Lindros, Pha.	40.00	20.00	4.00	2.00
☐☐☐☐	2	Paul Kariya, Ana.	40.00	20.00	4.00	2.00
☐☐☐☐	3	Peter Forsberg, Col.	30.00	15.00	3.00	1.50
☐☐☐☐	4	John Vanbiesbrouck (G), Fla.	17.50	8.50	1.75	.85
☐☐☐☐	5	Steve Yzerman, Det.	30.00	15.00	3.00	1.50
☐☐☐☐	6	Brendan Shanahan, Det.	17.50	8.50	1.75	.85
☐☐☐☐	7	Teemu Selänne, Ana.	20.00	10.00	2.00	1.00
☐☐☐☐	8	Dominik Hasek (G), Buf.	20.00	10.00	2.00	1.00
☐☐☐☐	9	Jarome Iginla, Cgy.	10.00	5.00	1.00	.50
☐☐☐☐	10	Mats Sundin, Tor.	15.00	7.50	1.50	.75
☐☐☐☐	11	Patrick Roy (G), Col.	50.00	25.00	5.00	2.50
☐☐☐☐	12	Joe Sakic, Col.	25.00	12.50	2.50	1.25
☐☐☐☐	13	Mark Messier, Van.	15.00	7.50	1.50	.75
☐☐☐☐	14	Sergei Fedorov, Det.	15.00	7.50	1.50	.75
☐☐☐☐	15	Saku Koivu, Mtl.	20.00	10.00	2.00	1.00
☐☐☐☐	16	Martin Brodeur (G), N.J.	20.00	10.00	2.00	1.00
☐☐☐☐	17	Pavel Bure, Van.	20.00	10.00	2.00	1.00
☐☐☐☐	18	Wayne Gretzky, NYR.	60.00	30.00	6.00	3.00
☐☐☐☐	19	Brian Leetch, NYR.	10.00	5.00	1.00	.50
☐☐☐☐	20	John LeClair, Pha.	15.00	7.50	1.50	.75
☐☐☐☐	21	Keith Tkachuk, Pho.	12.50	6.00	1.25	.60
☐☐☐☐	22	Jaromir Jagr, Pgh.	30.00	15.00	3.00	1.50
☐☐☐☐	23	Brett Hull, Stl.	15.00	7.50	1.50	.75
☐☐☐☐	24	Curtis Joseph (G), Edm.	17.50	8.50	1.75	.85
☐☐☐☐	25	Jaroslav Svejkovsky, Wsh.	8.00	5.00	1.00	.50
☐☐☐☐	26	Sergei Samsonov, Bos.	15.00	7.50	1.75	.85
☐☐☐☐	27	Alexei Morozov, Pgh.	12.50	6.00	1.50	.75
☐☐☐☐	28	Alyn McCauley, Tor.	12.50	6.00	1.50	.75
☐☐☐☐	29	Joe Thornton, Bos.	15.00	7.50	1.75	.85
☐☐☐☐	30	Vaclav Prospal, Pha.	8.00	5.00	1.00	.50

PINNACLE MINT MEDALLIONS

There are six versions of each medallion: a brass medallion, a brass Artist's Proof medallion, a nickel medallion, a nickel Artist's Proof medallion, a gold-plated medallion and a gold-plated Artist's Proof medallion (100 copies).

Imprint: © 1998 PINNACLE TRADING CARD CO.

	No.	Player	Gold	Nick.	Brass
☐☐☐	1	Eric Lindros, Pha.	100.00	20.00	4.00
☐☐☐	2	Paul Kariya, Ana.	100.00	20.00	4.00
☐☐☐	3	Peter Forsberg, Col.	75.00	15.00	3.00
☐☐☐	4	John Vanbiesbrouck (G), Fla.	40.00	8.50	1.75
☐☐☐	5	Steve Yzerman, Det.	75.00	15.00	3.00
☐☐☐	6	Brendan Shanahan, Det.	40.00	8.50	1.75
☐☐☐	7	Teemu Selänne, Ana.	50.00	10.00	2.00
☐☐☐	8	Dominik Hasek (G), Buf.	50.00	10.00	2.00
☐☐☐	9	Jarome Iginla, Cgy.	25.00	5.00	1.00
☐☐☐	10	Mats Sundin, Tor.	35.00	7.50	1.50
☐☐☐	11	Patrick Roy (G), Col.	125.00	25.00	5.00
☐☐☐	12	Joe Sakic, Col.	60.00	12.50	2.50
☐☐☐	13	Mark Messier, Van.	35.00	7.50	1.50
☐☐☐	14	Sergei Fedorov, Det.	35.00	7.50	1.50
☐☐☐	15	Saku Koivu, Mtl.	50.00	10.00	2.00
☐☐☐	16	Martin Brodeur, N.J.	50.00	10.00	2.00
☐☐☐	17	Pavel Bure, Van.	50.00	10.00	2.00
☐☐☐	18	Wayne Gretzky, NYR.	150.00	30.00	6.00
☐☐☐	19	Brian Leetch, NYR.	25.00	5.00	1.00
☐☐☐	20	John LeClair, Pha.	35.00	7.50	1.50
☐☐☐	21	Keith Tkachuk, Pho.	30.00	6.00	1.25
☐☐☐	22	Jaromir Jagr, Pgh.	75.00	15.00	3.00
☐☐☐	23	Brett Hull, Stl.	35.00	7.50	1.50
☐☐☐	24	Curtis Joseph (G), Edm.	40.00	8.50	1.75
☐☐☐	25	Jaroslav Svejkovsky, Wsh.	20.00	5.00	1.00
☐☐☐	26	Sergei Samsonov, Bos.	35.00	7.50	1.75
☐☐☐	27	Alexei Morozov, Pgh.	30.00	6.00	1.50
☐☐☐	28	Alyn McCauley, Tor.	30.00	6.00	1.50
☐☐☐	29	Joe Thornton, Bos.	35.00	7.50	1.75
☐☐☐	30	Vaclav Prospal, Pha.	20.00	5.00	1.00

	No.	Artist's Proof	Gold	Nick.	Brass
☐☐☐	1	Eric Lindros, Pha.	250.00	100.00	65.00
☐☐☐	2	Paul Kariya, Ana.	250.00	100.00	65.00
☐☐☐	3	Peter Forsberg, Col.	200.00	75.00	50.00
☐☐☐	4	John Vanbiesbrouck (G), Fla.	125.00	45.00	30.00
☐☐☐	5	Steve Yzerman, Det.	200.00	75.00	50.00
☐☐☐	6	Brendan Shanahan, Det.	125.00	45.00	30.00
☐☐☐	7	Teemu Selänne, Ana.	150.00	50.00	35.00
☐☐☐	8	Dominik Hasek (G), Buf.	150.00	50.00	35.00
☐☐☐	9	Jarome Iginla, Cgy.	60.00	20.00	15.00
☐☐☐	10	Mats Sundin, Tor.	100.00	40.00	25.00
☐☐☐	11	Patrick Roy (G), Col.	300.00	120.00	80.00
☐☐☐	12	Joe Sakic, Col.	175.00	60.00	40.00
☐☐☐	13	Mark Messier, Van.	100.00	40.00	25.00
☐☐☐	14	Sergei Fedorov, Det.	100.00	40.00	25.00
☐☐☐	15	Saku Koivu, Mtl.	150.00	50.00	35.00
☐☐☐	16	Martin Brodeur, N.J.	150.00	50.00	35.00
☐☐☐	17	Pavel Bure, Van.	150.00	50.00	35.00
☐☐☐	18	Wayne Gretzky, NYR.	400.00	150.00	100.00
☐☐☐	19	Brian Leetch, NYR.	60.00	20.00	15.00
☐☐☐	20	John LeClair, Pha.	100.00	40.00	25.00
☐☐☐	21	Keith Tkachuk, Pho.	80.00	30.00	20.00
☐☐☐	22	Jaromir Jagr, Pgh.	200.00	75.00	50.00
☐☐☐	23	Brett Hull, Stl.	100.00	40.00	25.00
☐☐☐	24	Curtis Joseph (G), Edm.	125.00	45.00	30.00
☐☐☐	25	Jaroslav Svejkovsky, Wsh.	40.00	15.00	10.00
☐☐☐	26	Sergei Samsonov, Bos.	100.00	35.00	25.00
☐☐☐	27	Alexei Morozov, Pgh.	80.00	30.00	20.00
☐☐☐	28	Alyn McCauley, Tor.	80.00	30.00	20.00
☐☐☐	29	Joe Thornton, Bos.	100.00	35.00	25.00
☐☐☐	30	Vaclav Prospal, Pha.	40.00	15.00	10.00

MINTERNATIONAL

Each player in this series has both a card and an oversized medallion.

Medallion Size:

Insert Set (6 medallions): 100.00 80.00

	No.	Player	Coin	Card
☐☐	1	Eric Lindros, Pha.	30.00	25.00
☐☐	2	Peter Forsberg, Col.	25.00	20.0
☐☐	3	Brett Hull, Stl.	12.00	10.00
☐☐	4	Teemu Selänne, Ana.	18.00	15.00
☐☐	5	Dominik Hasek, Buf.	18.00	15.00
☐☐	6	Pavel Bure, Van.	18.00	15.00

1997 - 98 PINNACLE TOTALLY CERTIFIED

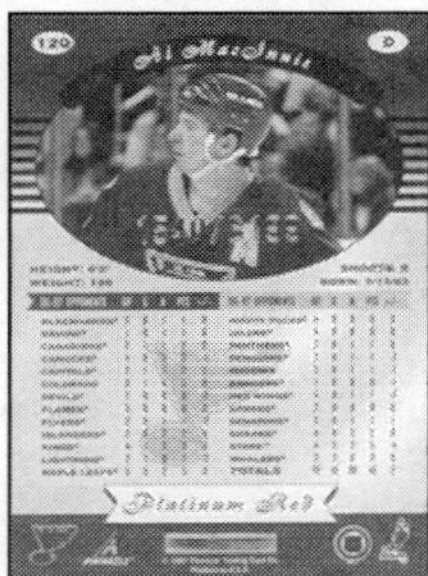

While these cards have the same checklist as Pinnacle Certified, they have different photography and are all serial numbered on the card back. Goalies (1-30) are shortprinted throughout the set. The four versions are Platinum Red (goalies numbered out 4,299, skaters numbered out of 6,199), Platinum Blue (goalies numbered out of 2,599, skaters numbered out of 3,099), Platinum Gold (goalies numbered out of 59, skaters numbered out of 69) and Platinum Mirror Gold (skaters numbered out of 30, goalies numbered out of 25). The Platinum Mirror Gold cards were available with the redemption of a Mirror Gold card only. Promo cards for this series also exist.

Imprint: © 1997 PINNACLE TRADING CARD, CO.

	No.	Player	Gold	Blue	Red
		Complete Set (130 cards):	**400.00**	**800.00**	**–**
		Common Player	**50.00**	**3.50**	**2.50**
□□□□	1	Dominik Hasek (G), Buf.	400.00	30.00	12.00
□□□□	2	Patrick Roy (G), Col.	1,000.00	70.00	30.00
□□□□	3	Martin Brodeur (G), N.J.	400.00	30.00	12.00
□□□□	4	Chris Osgood (G), Det.	250.00	18.00	6.00
□□□□	5	Andy Moog (G), Dal.	100.00	10.00	4.00
□□□□	6	J. Vanbiesbrouck (G), Fla.	350.00	25.00	10.00
□□□□	7	Steve Shields (G), Buf.	100.00	10.00	4.00
□□□□	8	Mike Vernon (G), Det.	100.00	10.00	4.00
□□□□	9	Ed Belfour (G), S.J.	100.00	10.00	4.00
□□□□	10	Grant Fuhr (G), Stl.	100.00	10.00	4.00
□□□□	11	Félix Potvin (G), Tor.	300.00	20.00	8.00
□□□□	12	Bill Ranford (G), Wsh.	100.00	10.00	4.00
□□□□	13	Mike Richter (G), NYR.	175.00	15.00	5.00
□□□□	14	Stéphane Fiset (G), L.A.	100.00	10.00	4.00
□□□□	15	Jim Carey (G), Bos.	60.00	5.00	3.00
□□□□	16	Nikolai Khabibulin (G), Pho.	175.00	15.00	5.00
□□□□	17	Ken Wregget (G), Pgh.	60.00	5.00	3.00
□□□□	18	Curtis Joseph (G), Edm.	350.00	25.00	10.00
□□□□	19	Guy Hebert (G), Ana.	100.00	10.00	4.00
□□□□	20	Damian Rhodes (G), Ott.	60.00	5.00	3.00
□□□□	21	Trevor Kidd (G), Cgy.	100.00	10.00	4.00
□□□□	22	Daren Puppa (G), T.B.	60.00	5.00	3.00
□□□□	23	Patrick Lalime (G), Pgh.	60.00	5.00	3.00
□□□□	24	Tommy Salo (G), NYI.	60.00	5.00	3.00
□□□□	25	Sean Burke (G), Hfd.	100.00	10.00	4.00
□□□□	26	Jocelyn Thibault (G), Mtl.	175.00	15.00	5.00
□□□□	27	Kirk McLean (G), Van.	100.00	10.00	4.00
□□□□	28	Garth Snow (G), Pha.	60.00	5.00	3.00
□□□□	29	Ron Tugnutt (G), Ott.	60.00	5.00	3.00
□□□□	30	Jeff Hackett (G), Chi.	100.00	10.00	4.00
□□□□	31	Eric Lindros, Pha.	600.00	40.00	20.00
□□□□	32	Peter Forsberg, Col.	450.00	35.00	15.00
□□□□	33	Mike Modano, Dal.	250.00	18.00	6.00
□□□□	34	Paul Kariya, Ana.	600.00	40.00	20.00
□□□□	35	Jaromir Jagr, Pgh.	450.00	35.00	15.00
□□□□	36	Brian Leetch, NYR.	125.00	10.00	4.00
□□□□	37	Keith Tkachuk, Pho.	200.00	15.00	5.00
□□□□	38	Steve Yzerman, Det.	450.00	35.00	15.00
□□□□	39	Teemu Selänne, Ana.	350.00	25.00	10.00
□□□□	40	Bryan Berard, NYI.	125.00	10.00	4.00
□□□□	41	Ray Bourque, Bos.	250.00	18.00	6.00
□□□□	42	Theoren Fleury, Cgy.	125.00	10.00	4.00
□□□□	43	Mark Messier, NYR.	250.00	18.00	6.00
□□□□	44	Saku Koivu, Mtl.	350.00	25.00	10.00
□□□□	45	Pavel Bure, Van.	350.00	25.00	10.00
□□□□	46	Peter Bondra, Wsh.	200.00	15.00	5.00
□□□□	47	Dave Gagner, Cgy. (Fla.)	50.00	3.50	2.00
□□□□	48	Ed Jovanovski, Fla.	75.00	6.00	3.00
□□□□	49	Adam Oates, Wsh.	125.00	10.00	4.00
□□□□	50	Joe Sakic, Col.	400.00	30.00	12.00
□□□□	51	Doug Gilmour, N.J.	125.00	10.00	4.00
□□□□	52	Jim Campbell, Stl.	50.00	3.50	2.00
□□□□	53	Mats Sundin, Tor.	250.00	18.00	6.00
□□□□	54	Derian Hatcher, Dal.	75.00	6.00	3.00
□□□□	55	Jarome Iginla, Cgy.	125.00	10.00	4.00
□□□□	56	Sergei Fedorov, Det.	250.00	18.00	6.00
□□□□	57	Keith Primeau, Hfd.	75.00	6.00	3.00
□□□□	58	Mark Recchi, Mtl.	75.00	6.00	3.00
□□□□	59	Owen Nolan, S.J.	75.00	6.00	3.00
□□□□	60	Alexander Mogilny, Van.	125.00	10.00	4.00
□□□□	61	Brendan Shanahan, Det.	300.00	20.00	8.00
□□□□	62	Pierre Turgeon, Stl.	75.00	6.00	3.00
□□□□	63	Joé Juneau, Wsh.	50.00	3.50	2.00
□□□□	64	Steve Rucchin, Ana.	50.00	3.50	2.00
□□□□	65	Jeremy Roenick, Pho.	125.00	10.00	4.00
□□□□	66	Doug Weight, Edm.	125.00	10.00	4.00
□□□□	67	Valeri Kamensky, Col.	75.00	6.00	3.00
□□□□	68	Tony Amonte, Chi.	75.00	6.00	3.00
□□□□	69	Dave Andreychuk, N.J.	50.00	3.50	2.00
□□□□	70	Brett Hull, Stl.	250.00	18.00	6.00
□□□□	71	Wendel Clark, Tor.	75.00	6.00	3.00
□□□□	72	Vincent Damphousse, Mtl.	125.00	10.00	4.00
□□□□	73	Mike Grier, Edm.	75.00	6.00	3.00
□□□□	74	Chris Chelios, Chi.	200.00	15.00	5.00
□□□□	75	Nicklas Lidström, Det.	75.00	6.00	3.00
□□□□	76	Joe Nieuwendyk, Dal.	75.00	6.00	3.00
□□□□	77	Rob Blake, L.A.	75.00	6.00	3.00
□□□□	78	Alexei Yashin, Ott.	200.00	15.00	5.00
□□□□	79	Ryan Smyth, Edm.	75.00	6.00	3.00
□□□□	80	Pat LaFontaine, Buf.	75.00	6.00	3.00
□□□□	81	Jeff Friesen, S.J.	75.00	6.00	3.00
□□□□	82	Ray Ferraro, L.A.	50.00	3.50	2.00
□□□□	83	Steve Sullivan, Tor.	50.00	3.50	2.00
□□□□	84	Chris Gratton, T.B.	75.00	6.00	3.00
□□□□	85	Mike Gartner, Pho.	75.00	6.00	3.00
□□□□	86	Kevin Hatcher, Pgh.	50.00	3.50	2.00
□□□□	87	Ted Donato, Bos.	50.00	3.50	2.00
□□□□	88	German Titov, Cgy.	50.00	3.50	2.00
□□□□	89	Sandis Ozolinsh, Col.	75.00	6.00	3.00
□□□□	90	Ray Sheppard, Fla.	50.00	3.50	2.00
□□□□	91	John MacLean, N.J.	50.00	3.50	2.00
□□□□	92	Luc Robitaille, L.A.	75.00	6.00	3.00
□□□□	93	Rod Brind'Amour, Pha.	75.00	6.00	3.00
□□□□	94	Zigmund Palffy, NYI.	125.00	10.00	4.00
□□□□	95	Peter Nedved, Pgh.	50.00	3.50	2.00
□□□□	96	Adam Graves, NYR.	50.00	3.50	2.00
□□□□	97	Jozef Stumpel, Bos.	75.00	6.00	3.00
□□□□	98	Alexandre Daigle, Ott.	50.00	3.50	2.00
□□□□	99	Michael Peca, Buf.	75.00	6.00	3.00
□□□□	100	Wayne Gretzky, NYR.	1,300.00	70.00	30.00
□□□□	101	Alexei Zhamnov, Chi.	50.00	3.50	2.00
□□□□	102	Paul Coffey, Pha.	75.00	6.00	3.00
□□□□	103	Oleg Tverdovsky, Pho.	50.00	3.50	2.00
□□□□	104	Trevor Linden, Van.	75.00	6.00	3.00
□□□□	105	Dino Ciccarelli, T.B.	75.00	6.00	3.00
□□□□	106	Andrei Kovalenko, Edm.	50.00	3.50	2.00
□□□□	107	Scott Mellanby, Fla.	50.00	3.50	2.00
□□□□	108	Bryan Smolinski, NYI.	50.00	3.50	2.00
□□□□	109	Bernie Nicholls, S.J.	50.00	3.50	2.00
□□□□	110	Derek Plante, Buf.	50.00	3.50	2.00
□□□□	111	Pat Verbeek, Dal.	50.00	3.50	2.00
□□□□	112	Adam Deadmarsh, Col.	50.00	3.50	2.00
□□□□	113	Martin Gelinas, Van.	50.00	3.50	2.00
□□□□	114	Daniel Alfredsson, Ott.	75.00	6.00	3.00
□□□□	115	Scott Stevens, N.J.	50.00	3.50	2.00
□□□□	116	Dainius Zubrus, Pha.	75.00	6.00	3.00
□□□□	117	Kirk Muller, Fla.	50.00	3.50	2.00
□□□□	118	Brian Holzinger, Buf.	50.00	3.50	2.00
□□□□	119	John LeClair, Pha.	250.00	18.00	6.00
□□□□	120	Al MacInnis, Stl.	75.00	6.00	3.00
□□□□	121	Ron Francis, Pgh.	125.00	10.00	4.00
□□□□	122	Eric Dazé, Chi.	75.00	6.00	3.00
□□□□	123	Travis Green, NYI.	50.00	3.50	2.00
□□□□	124	Jason Arnott, Edm.	75.00	6.00	3.00
□□□□	125	Geoff Sanderson, Hfd.	50.00	3.50	2.00
□□□□	126	Dimitri Khristich, L.A.	50.00	3.50	2.00
□□□□	127	Sergei Berezin, Tor.	75.00	6.00	3.00
□□□□	128	Jeff O'Neill, Hfd.	75.00	6.00	3.00
□□□□	129	Claude Lemieux, Col.	50.00	3.50	2.00
□□□□	130	Andrew Cassels, Hfd.	50.00	3.50	2.00

1997 - 98 PINNACLE UNCUT

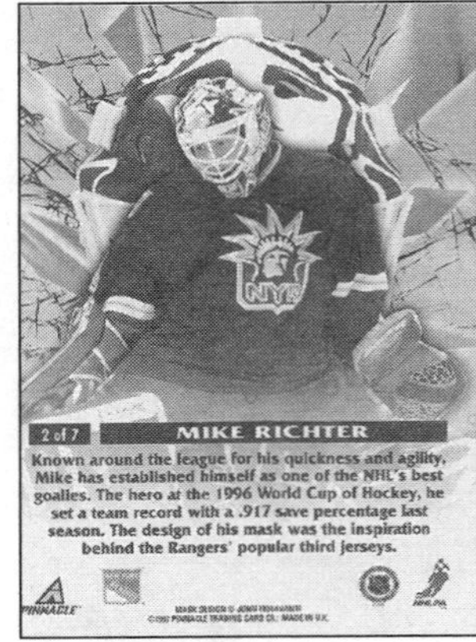

Card Size: 13 3/8" x 18 3/4"
Imprint: © 1997 PINNACLE TRADING CARD CO.
Complete Set (7 cards):

	No.	Player	NRMT-MT
□		Martin Brodeur (G), N.J.	
□	2	Mike Richter (G), NYR.	
□		Guy Hebert (G), Ana.	
□		Curtis Joseph (G), Edm.	
□	5	Patrick Roy (G), Col.	
□		John Vanbiesbrouck (G), Fla.	
□		Garth Snow (G), Pha.	

1997 - 98 PLAYMATE PRO ZONE

Complete Set (6 figurines):

	Player	NRMT-MT
□	Jaromir Jagr, Pgh.	
□	Eric Lindros, Pha.	
□	Patrick Roy (G), Col.	
□	Sergei Fedorov, Det.	
□	Paul Kariya, Ana.	
□	John Vanbiesbrouck (G), Fla.	

1997 - 98 POST

These cards were produced by Pinnacle and issued in specially marked boxes of Post Honey Comb and Sugar Crisps. This series was released in early December, 1997.

Imprint: © 1997 PINNACLE TRADING CARD CO.

	No.	Player	NRMT-MT
		Complete Set (24 cards):	**75.00**
		Eric Lindros Autograph:	**500.00**
□	1	Eric Lindros, Pha.	8.00
□	2	Patrick Roy (G), Col.	10.00
□	3	Joe Sakic, Col.	5.00
□	4	Brian Leetch, NYR.	2.50
□	5	Mark Messier, Van.	3.00
□	6	Jason Arnott, Edm.	1.50
□	7	Paul Kariya, Ana.	8.00
□	8	Martin Brodeur (G), N.J.	4.50
□	9	Vincent Damphousse, Mtl.	2.00
□	10	Steve Yzerman, Det.	6.50
□	11	Brett Hull, Stl.	3.00
□	12	Chris Chelios, Chi.	2.50
□	13	Sergei Fedorov, Det.	3.00
□	14	Nicklas Lidström, Det.	1.50
□	15	Sergei Berezin, Tor.	1.50
□	16	Dominik Hasek (G), Buf.	4.50
□	17	Pavel Bure, Van.	4.50

	No.	Player	Price
□	18	Saku Koivu, Mtl.	4.50
□	19	Teemu Selänne, Ana.	4.50
□	20	Peter Forsberg, Col.	6.50
□	21	Jaromir Jagr, Pgh.	6.50
□	22	Peter Bondra, Wsh.	2.50
□	23	Alexei Yashin, Ott.	2.50
□	24	Viacheslav Fetisov, Det.	1.50

POST FOIL CARDS

Two cards were available in specially marked three-pack cases of Post cereal.

Complete Set (6 cards): **30.00**

	No.	Player	NRMT-MT
□	F1	Eric Lindros, Pha.	10.00
□	F2	Patrick Roy (G), Col.	12.00
□	F3	Mark Messier, Van.	4.00
□	F4	Jason Arnott, Edm.	3.00
□	F5	Joe Sakic, Col.	6.00
□	F6	Paul Kariya, Ana.	10.00

1997 - 98 SCORE

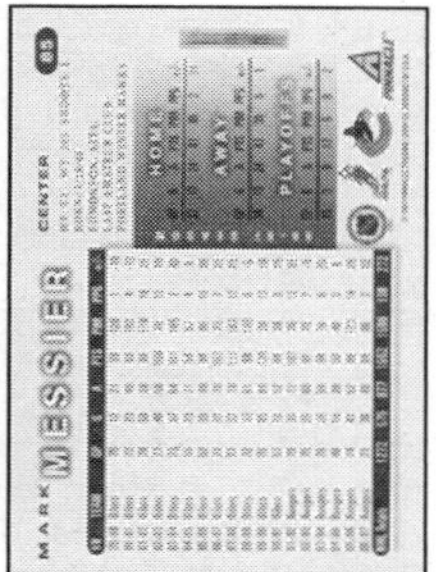

Cards 1-160 have three versions: the regular card, a Golden Blades parallel (1:7) and an Artist's Proofs (1:35) parallel. Six players also have a promo card.

Imprint: © 1997 PINNACLE TRADING CARD CO.

Complete Set (270 cards): **18.00**

Parallel Set (160 cards): **600.00 100.00 .–**

Common Player: **3.50 .75 1.00**

	No.	Player	A.P.	G.B.	Reg.
□□□	1	Sean Burke (G), Car.	7.00	2.00	.25
□□□	2	Chris Osgood (G), Det.	15.00	5.00	.50
□□□	3	Garth Snow (G), Pha.	3.50	.75	.10
□□□	4	Mike Vernon (G), S.J.	7.00	2.00	.25
□□□	5	Grant Fuhr (G), Stl.	7.00	2.00	.25
□□□	6	Guy Hebert (G), Ana.	7.00	2.00	.25
□□□	7	Arturs Irbe (G), Van.	3.50	.75	.10
□□□	8	Andy Moog (G), Mtl.	7.00	2.00	.25
□□□	9	Tommy Salo (G), NYI.	3.50	.75	.10
□□□	10	Nikolai Khabibulin (G), Pho.	10.00	3.50	.35
□□□	11	Mike Richter (G), NYR.	10.00	3.50	.35
□□□	12	Corey Hirsch (G), Van.	3.50	.75	.10
□□□	13	Bill Ranford (G), Wsh.	7.00	2.00	.25
□□□	14	Jim Carey (G), Bos.	3.50	.75	.10
□□□	15	Jeff Hackett (G), Chi.	7.00	2.00	.25
□□□	16	Damian Rhodes (G), Ott.	3.50	.75	.10
□□□	17	Tom Barrasso (G), Pgh.	7.00	2.00	.25
□□□	18	Daren Puppa (G), T.B.	3.50	.75	.10
□□□	19	Craig Billington (G), Col.	3.50	.75	.10
□□□	20	Ed Belfour (G), Dal.	10.00	3.50	.35
□□□	21	Mikhail Shtalenkov (G), Ana.	3.50	.75	.10
□□□	22	Glenn Healy (G), Tor.	3.50	.75	.10
□□□	23	Marcel Cousineau (G), Tor.	3.50	.75	.10
□□□	24	Kevin Hodson (G), Det.	3.50	.75	.10
□□□	25	Olaf Kolzig (G), Wsh.	10.00	3.50	.35
□□□	26	Eric Fichaud (G), NYI.	7.00	2.00	.25
□□□	27	Ron Hextall (G), Pha.	7.00	2.00	.25
□□□	28	Rick Tabaracci (G), Cgy.	3.50	.75	.10
□□□	29	Félix Potvin (G), Tor.	20.00	6.00	.60
□□□	30	Martin Brodeur (G), N.J.	40.00	8.50	.85
□□□	31	Curtis Joseph (G), Edm.	30.00	7.50	.75
□□□	32	Ken Wregget (G), Pgh.	3.50	.75	.10
□□□	33	Patrick Roy (G), Col.	100.00	20.00	2.00
□□□□	34	John Vanbiesbrouck (G), Fla.	30.00	7.50	.75
□□□	35	Stéphane Fiset (G), L.A.	7.00	2.00	.25
□□□	36	Roman Turek (G), Dal.	3.50	.75	.10
□□□	37	Trevor Kidd (G), Car.	7.00	2.00	.25
□□□	38	Dwayne Roloson (G), Cgy.	3.50	.75	.10
□□□	39	Dominik Hasek (G), Buf.	40.00	8.50	.85
□□□	40	Patrick Lalime (G), Pgh.	3.50	.75	.10
□□□	41	Jocelyn Thibault (G), Mtl.	10.00	3.50	.35
□□□	42	José Théodore (G), Mtl.	10.00	3.50	.35
□□□	43	Kirk McLean (G), Van.	7.00	2.00	.25
□□□	**44**	**Steve Shields (G), Buf., RC**	**7.00**	**2.00**	**.25**
□□□	45	Mike Dunham (G), N.J.	3.50	.75	.10
□□□	46	Jamie Storr (G), L.A.	7.00	2.00	.25
□□□	47	Byron Dafoe (G), Bos.	3.50	.75	.10
□□□	48	Chris Terreri (G), Chi.	3.50	.75	.10
□□□	49	Ron Tugnutt (G), Ott.	3.50	.75	.10
□□□	50	Kelly Hrudey (G), S.J.	3.50	.75	.10
□□□	**51**	**Vaclav Prospal, Pha., RC**	**8.00**	**2.50**	**.60**
□□□	52	Alyn McCauley, Tor.	15.00	5.00	.50
□□□	53	Jaroslav Svejkovsky, Bos.	7.00	2.00	.25
□□□	54	Joe Thornton, Bos.	20.00	6.00	.75
□□□	**55**	**Chris Dingman, Cgy., RC**	**3.50**	**.75**	**.10**
□□□	56	Vadim Sharifjanov, N.J.	3.50	.75	.10
□□□	57	Larry Courville, Van.	3.50	.75	.10
□□□	58	Erik Rasmussen, Buf.	3.50	.75	.10
□□□	59	Sergei Samsonov, Bos.	20.00	6.00	.75
□□□	60	Kevyn Adams, Tor.	3.50	.75	.10
□□□	61	Daniel Cleary, Chi.	7.00	2.00	.35
□□□	**62**	**Martin Prochazka, Tor., RC**	**3.50**	**.75**	**.10**
□□□	63	Mattias Ohlund, Van.	7.00	2.00	.35
□□□	**64**	**Juha Lind, Dal., RC**	**3.50**	**.75**	**.10**
□□□	**65**	**Olli Jokinen, L.A., RC**	**7.00**	**2.00**	**.60**
□□□	**66**	**Espen Knutsen, Ana., RC**	**3.50**	**.75**	**.10**
□□□	67	Marc Savard, NYR.	3.50	.75	.10
□□□	68	Hnat Domenichelli, Cgy.	7.00	2.00	.25
□□□	**69**	**Warren Luhning, NYI., RC**	**3.50**	**.75**	**.10**
□□□	**70**	**Magnus Arvedsson, Ott., RC**	**3.50**	**.75**	**.10**
□□□	71	Chris Phillips, Ott.	7.00	2.00	.35
□□□	72	Brad Isbister, Pho.	3.50	.75	.10
□□□	73	Boyd Devereaux, Edm.	3.50	.75	.10
□□□	74	Alexei Morozov, Pgh.	15.00	5.00	.50
□□□	**75**	**Vladimir Vorobiev, NYR., RC**	**3.50**	**.75**	**.10**
□□□	76	Steve Rice, Car.	3.50	.75	.10
□□□	77	Tony Granato, S.J.	3.50	.75	.10
□□□	78	Lonny Bohonos, Van.	3.50	.75	.10
□□□	79	Dave Gagner, Fla.	3.50	.75	.10
□□□	80	Brendan Shanahan, Det.	30.00	7.50	.75
□□□	81	Brett Hull, Stl.	20.00	6.00	.60
□□□□	82	Jaromir Jagr, Pgh.	60.00	12.50	1.25
□□□□	83	Peter Forsberg, Col.	60.00	12.50	1.25
□□□□	84	Paul Kariya, Ana.	75.00	15.00	1.50
□□□	85	Mark Messier, Van.	20.00	6.00	.60
□□□□	86	Steve Yzerman, Det.	60.00	12.50	1.25
□□□	87	Keith Tkachuk, Pho.	15.00	5.00	.50
□□□□	88	Eric Lindros, Pha.	75.00	15.00	1.50
□□□	89	Ray Bourque, Bos.	15.00	5.00	.50
□□□	90	Chris Chelios, Chi.	10.00	3.50	.35
□□□	91	Sergei Fedorov, Det.	20.00	6.00	.60
□□□	92	Mike Modano, Dal.	20.00	6.00	.60
□□□	93	Doug Gilmour, N.J.	10.00	3.50	.35
□□□	94	Saku Koivu, Mtl.	40.00	8.50	.85
□□□	95	Mats Sundin, Tor.	20.00	6.00	.60
□□□	96	Pavel Bure, Van.	40.00	8.50	.85
□□□	97	Theoren Fleury, Cgy.	10.00	3.50	.35
□□□	98	Keith Primeau, Car.	7.00	2.00	.25
□□□	99	Wayne Gretzky, NYR.	125.00	25.00	2.50
□□□	100	Doug Weight, Edm.	10.00	3.50	.35
□□□	101	Alexandre Daigle, Ott.	3.50	.75	.10
□□□	102	Owen Nolan, S.J.	7.00	2.00	.25
□□□	103	Peter Bondra, Wsh.	15.00	5.00	.50
□□□	104	Pat LaFontaine, NYR.	7.00	2.00	.25
□□□	105	Kirk Muller, Fla.	10.00	3.50	.35
□□□	106	Zigmund Palffy, NYI.	3.50	.75	.10
□□□	107	Jeremy Roenick, Pho.	10.00	3.50	.35
□□□	108	John LeClair, Pha.	20.00	6.00	.60
□□□	109	Derek Plante, Buf.	3.50	.75	.10
□□□	110	Geoff Sanderson, Car.	3.50	.75	.10
□□□	111	Dimitri Khristich, Bos.	3.50	.75	.10
□□□	112	Vincent Damphousse, Mtl.	10.00	3.50	.35
□□□	113	Teemu Selänne, Ana.	40.00	8.50	.85
□□□	114	Tony Amonte, Chi.	3.50	.75	.10
□□□	115	Dave Andreychuk, N.J.	3.50	.75	.10
□□□	116	Alexei Yashin, Ott.	15.00	5.00	.50
□□□	117	Adam Oates, Wsh.	10.00	3.50	.35
□□□	118	Pierre Turgeon, Stl.	7.00	2.00	.25
□□□	119	Dino Ciccarelli, T.B.	7.00	2.00	.25
□□□	120	Ryan Smyth, Edm.	7.00	2.00	.25
□□□	121	Ray Sheppard, Fla.	3.50	.75	.10
□□□	122	Jozef Stumpel, L.A.	7.00	2.00	.25
□□□	123	Jarome Iginla, Cgy.	3.50	.75	.10
□□□	124	Pat Verbeek, Dal.	3.50	.75	.10
□□□	125	Joe Sakic, Col.	50.00	10.00	1.00
□□□	126	Brian Leetch, NYR.	10.00	3.50	.35
□□□	127	Rod Brind'Amour, Pha.	7.00	2.00	.25
□□□	128	Wendel Clark, Tor.	7.00	2.00	.25
□□□	129	Alexander Mogilny, Van.	10.00	3.50	.35
□□□	130	Mark Recchi, Pha.	7.00	2.00	.25
□□□	131	Daniel Alfredsson, Ott.	7.00	2.00	.25
□□□	132	Ron Francis, Pgh.	10.00	3.50	.35
□□□	133	Martin Gelinas, Van.	3.50	.75	.10
□□□	134	Andrew Cassels, Car.	3.50	.75	.10
□□□	135	Joe Nieuwendyk, Dal.	7.00	2.00	.25
□□□	136	Jason Arnott, Edm.	7.00	2.00	.25
□□□	137	Bryan Berard, NYI.	10.00	3.50	.35
□□□	138	Mikael Renberg, T.B.	3.50	.75	.10
□□□	139	Mike Gartner, Pho.	7.00	2.00	.25
□□□	140	Joé Juneau, Wsh.	3.50	.75	.10
□□□	141	John MacLean, N.J.	3.50	.75	.10
□□□	142	Adam Graves, NYR.	3.50	.75	.10
□□□	143	Petr Nedved, Pgh.	3.50	.75	.10
□□□	144	Trevor Linden, Van.	7.00	2.00	.25
□□□	145	Sergei Berezin, Tor.	7.00	2.00	.25
□□□	146	Adam Deadmarsh, Col.	3.50	.75	.10
□□□	147	Jeff O'Neill, Hfd.	7.00	2.00	.25
□□□	148	Rob Blake, L.A.	7.00	2.00	.25
□□□	149	Luc Robitaille, NYR. (L.A.)	3.50	.75	.10
□□□	150	Markus Naslund, Van.	3.50	.75	.10
□□□	151	Ethan Moreau, Chi.	3.50	.75	.10
□□□	152	Martin Rucinsky, Mtl.	3.50	.75	.10
□□□	153	Mike Grier, Edm.	7.00	2.00	.25
□□□	154	Craig Janney, Pho.	3.50	.75	.10
□□□	155	John Cullen, T.B.	3.50	.75	.10
□□□	156	Alexei Kovalev, NYR.	3.50	.75	.10
□□□	157	Tony Twist, Stl.	3.50	.75	.10
□□□	158	Claude Lemieux, Col.	3.50	.75	.10
□□□	159	Kevin Stevens, NYR.	3.50	.75	.10
□□□	160	Mathieu Schneider, Tor.	3.50	.75	.10
□	161	Randy Cunneyworth, Ott.			.10
□	162	Darius Kasparaitis, Pgh.			.10
□	163	Joe Murphy, Stl.			.10
□	164	Brandon Convery, Tor.			.10
□	165	Janne Niinimaa, Pha.			.25
□	166	Paul Coffey, Pha.			.25
□	167	Daymond Langkow, T.B.			.10
□	168	Chris Gratton, Pha.			.25
□	169	Ray Ferraro, L.A.			.10
□	170	Jeff Friesen, S.J.			.25
□	171	Ted Donato, Bos.			.10
□	172	Brian Holzinger, Buf.			.10
□	173	Travis Green, NYI.			.10
□	174	Sandis Ozolinsh, Col.			.25
□	175	Alexei Zhamnov, Chi.			.10
□	176	Steve Rucchin, Ana.			.10
□	177	Scott Mellanby, Fla.			.10
□	178	Andrei Kovalenko, Edm.			.10
□	179	Donald Audette, Buf.			.10
□	180	Bernie Nicholls, S.J.			.10
□	181	Jonas Hoglund, Cgy.			.10
□	182	Nicklas Lidström, Det.			.25
□	183	Bobby Holik, N.J.			.10
□	184	Geoff Courtnall, Stl.			.10
□	185	Steve Sullivan, Tor.			.10
□	186	Valeri Kamensky, Col.			.25
□	187	Michael Peca, Buf.			.25
□	188	Jere Lehtinen, Dal.			.25
□	189	Robert Svehla, Fla.			.10
□	190	Darren McCarty, Det.			.10
□	191	Brian Savage, Mtl.			.10
□	192	Harry York, Stl.			.10
□	193	Eric Dazé, Chi.			.25
□	194	Niklas Sundstrom, NYR.			.10
□	195	Oleg Tverdovsky, Pho.			.10
□	196	Eric Desjardins, Pha.			.10
□	197	German Titov, Cgy.			.10
□	198	Derian Hatcher, Dal.			.25
□	199	Bill Guerin, N.J.			.25
□	200	Rob Zamuner, T.B.			.25
□	201	Dale Hunter, Wsh.			.10
□	202	Darcy Tucker, Mtl.			.10
□	203	Andreas Dackell, Ott.			.10
□	204	Jason Dawe, Buf.			.10
□	205	Brian Rolston, N.J.			.10
□	206	Ed Olczyk, Pgh.			.10
□	207	Todd Warriner, Tor.			.10
□	208	Mariusz Czerkawski, NYI.			.10
□	209	Vyacheslav Kozlov, Det.			.10
□	210	Marty MacInnis, Cgy.			.10

	No.	Player	NRMT-MT
☐	211	Jamie Langenbrunner, Dal.	.25
☐	212	Vitali Yachmenev, L.A.	.10
☐	213	Stéphane Richer, Mtl.	.10
☐	214	Roman Hamrlik, T.B.	.25
☐	215	Jim Campbell, Stl.	.10
☐	216	Matthew Barnaby, Buf.	.10
☐	217	Benoît Hogue, Dal.	.10
☐	218	Robert Reichel, NYI.	.10
☐	219	Tie Domi, Tor.	.10
☐	220	Steve Konowalchuk, Wsh.	.10
☐	221	Radek Dvorak, Fla.	.10
☐	222	Kevin Hatcher, Pgh.	.10
☐	223	Viktor Kozlov, S.J.	.10
☐	224	Scott Stevens, N.J.	.10
☐	225	Cory Stillman, Cgy.	.10
☐	226	Anson Carter, Bos.	.10
☐	227	Rem Murray, Edm.	.10
☐	228	Vladimir Konstantinov, Det.	.10
☐	229	Scott Niedermayer, N.J.	.25
☐	230	Steve Duchesne, Stl.	.10
☐	231	Valeri Bure, Mtl.	.10
☐	232	Miroslav Satan, Buf.	.10
☐	233	Jason Allison, Bos.	.35
☐	234	Mark Fitzpatrick (G), Fla.	.10
☐	235	Ed Jovanovski, Fla.	.25
☐	236	Esa Tikkanen, Fla.	.10
☐	237	Stu Barnes, Pgh.	.10
☐	238	Darryl Sydor, Dal.	.10
☐	239	Ulf Samuelsson, NYR.	.10
☐	240	Dmitri Mironov, Ana.	.10
☐	241	Bryan Smolinski, NYI.	.10
☐	242	Rob Ray, Buf.	.10
☐	243	Todd Marchant, Edm.	.10
☐	244	Cliff Ronning, Pho.	.10
☐	245	Alexander Selivanov, T.B.	.10
☐	246	Rick Tocchet, Pho.	.10
☐	247	Vladimir Malakhov, Mtl.	.10
☐	248	Al MacInnis, Stl.	.25
☐	249	Dainius Zubrus, Pha.	.25
☐	250	Keith Jones, Col.	.10
☐	251	Darren Turcotte, Stl.	.10
☐	252	Ulf Dahlen, Chi.	.10
☐	253	Rob Niedermayer, Fla.	.10
☐	254	J.J. Daigneault, Ana.	.10
☐	255	Michal Grosek, Buf.	.10
☐	256	Chris Therien, Pha.	.10
☐	257	Adam Foote, Col.	.25
☐	258	Tomas Sandström, Ana.	.10
☐	259	Scott Lachance, NYI.	.10
☐	260	Paul Kariya, Ana.	.75
☐	261	Pavel Bure, Van.	.35
☐	262	Mike Modano, Dal.	.25
☐	263	Steve Yzerman, Det.	.50
☐	264	Sergei Fedorov, Det.	.25
☐	265	Eric Lindros, Pha.	.75
☐	266	CL: Dominik Hasek, Buf.	.35
☐	267	CL: Bryan Berard, NYI.	.25
☐	268	CL: Michael Peca, Buf.	.25
☐	269	CL: M.Brodeur (G)/ M. Dunham (G)	.35
☐	270	CL: Paul Kariya, Ana.	.75

CHECK-IT

Check-It insertion ratio is [1:19].

	No.	Player	NRMT-MT
Insert Set (30 cards):			**75.00**
☐	1	Eric Lindros, Pha. (vs. Jay McKee)	12.00
☐	2	Mark Recchi, Mtl.	2.00
☐	3	Brendan Shanahan, Det. (vs. R.Dvorak)	5.00
☐	4	Keith Tkachuk, Pho.	3.00
☐	5	John LeClair, Pha. (vs. Dana Murzyn)	4.00
☐	6	Doug Gilmour, N.J. (vs. Travis Green)	2.50
☐	7	Jarome Iginla, Cgy.	2.50
☐	8	Ryan Smyth, Edm.	2.00
☐	9	Chris Chelios, Chi. (vs. Bobby Holik)	3.00
☐	10	Mike Grier, Edm.	2.00
☐	11	Vincent Damphousse, Mtl. (vs. D.Gagner)	2.50
☐	12	Bryan Berard, NYI. (vs. Jason Dawe)	2.50
☐	13	Jaromir Jagr, Pgh. (vs. Travis Green)	7.00
☐	14	Michael Peca, Buf. (vs. Eric Desjardins)	2.00
☐	15	Dino Ciccarelli, T.B.	2.00
☐	16	Rod Brind'Amour, Pha. (vs. Bobby Holik)	2.00
☐	17	Owen Nolan, S.J. (vs. Ian Moran)	2.00
☐	18	Pat Verbeek, Dal. (vs. Dan McGillis)	2.00

NET WORTH

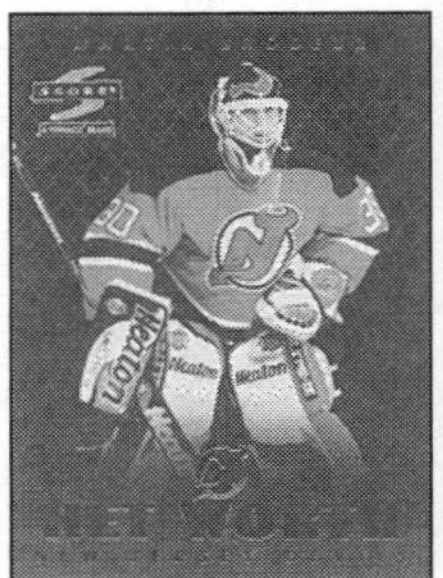

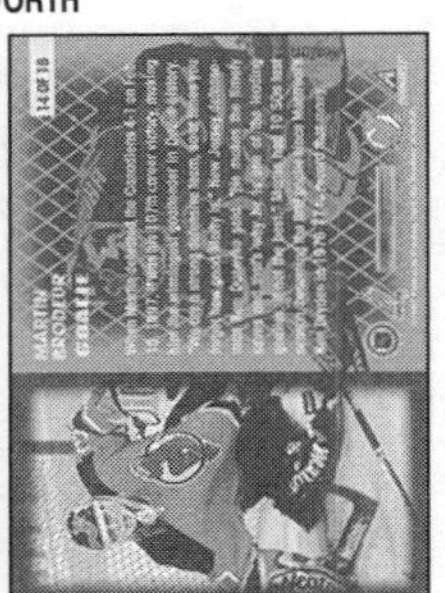

Net Worth insertion ratio is [1:35].

	No.	Player	NRMT-MT
Insert Set (18 cards):			**150.00**
☐	1	Guy Hebert (G), Ana.	6.00
☐	2	Jim Carey (G), Bos.	5.00
☐	3	Trevor Kidd (G), Car.	6.00
☐	4	Chris Osgood (G), Det.	9.00
☐	5	Curtis Joseph (G), Edm.	12.00
☐	6	Mike Richter (G), NYR.	8.00
☐	7	Damian Rhodes (G), Ott.	5.00
☐	8	Garth Snow (G), Pha.	5.00
☐	9	Nikolai Khabibulin (G), Pho.	8.00
☐	10	Grant Fuhr (G), Stl.	6.00
☐	11	Jocelyn Thibault (G), Mtl.	8.00
☐	12	Tommy Salo (G), NYI.	5.00
☐	13	Patrick Roy (G), Col.	45.00
☐	14	Martin Brodeur (G), N.J.	18.00
☐	15	John Vanbiesbrouck (G), Fla.	12.00
☐	16	Félix Potvin (G), Tor.	10.00
☐	17	Dominik Hasek (G), Buf.	18.00
☐	18	Ed Belfour (G), Dal.	8.00

1997 - 98 SCORE TEAM SETS

These cards have three versions: a regular card, a Platinum Team parallel [1:6] and a Premiere Club parallel [1:31].

	No.	Player	P.C.	Plat.	Reg.
Anaheim Mighty Ducks (20 cards):			**125.00**	**30.00**	**15.00**
☐☐☐	1	Paul Kariya, Ana.	65.00	13.00	6.50
☐☐☐	2	Teemu Selänne, Ana.	35.00	7.00	3.50
☐☐☐	3	Steve Rucchin, Ana.	5.00	1.00	.50
☐☐☐	4	Dmitri Mironov, Ana.	5.00	1.00	.50
☐☐☐	5	Matt Cullen, Ana.	5.00	1.00	.50
☐☐☐	6	Kevin Todd, Ana.	5.00	1.00	.50
☐☐☐	7	Joe Sacco, Ana.	5.00	1.00	.50
☐☐☐	8	J.J. Daigneault, Ana.	5.00	1.00	.50
☐☐☐	9	Darren Van Impe, Ana.	5.00	1.00	.50
☐☐☐	10	Scott Young, Ana.	5.00	1.00	.50
☐☐☐	11	Ted Drury, Ana.	5.00	1.00	.50
☐☐☐	12	Tomas Sandström, Ana.	5.00	1.00	.50
☐☐☐	13	Warren Rychel, Ana.	5.00	1.00	.50
☐☐☐	14	Guy Hebert (G), Ana.	10.00	2.00	1.00
☐☐☐	15	Shawn Antoski, Ana.	5.00	1.00	.50
☐☐☐	16	Mikhail Shtalenkov (G), Ana.	5.00	1.00	.50
☐☐☐	17	Peter LeBoutilier, Ana.	5.00	1.50	.75
☐☐☐	18	Sean Pronger, Ana.	5.00	1.00	.50
☐☐☐	19	Dave Karpa, Ana.	5.00	1.00	.50
☐☐☐	20	Espen Knutsen, Ana.	5.00	1.00	.50
Boston Bruins (20 cards):			**125.00**	**30.00**	**15.00**
☐☐☐	1	Shawn Bates, Bos.	5.00	1.00	.50
☐☐☐	2	Jim Carey (G), Bos.	5.00	1.00	.50
☐☐☐	3	Rob Tallas (G), Bos.	5.00	1.00	.50
☐☐☐	4	Ray Bourque, Bos.	25.00	5.00	2.50
☐☐☐	5	Dimitri Khristich, Bos.	5.00	1.00	.50
☐☐☐	6	Ted Donato, Bos.	5.00	1.00	.50
☐☐☐	7	Jason Allison, Bos.	15.00	3.00	1.50
☐☐☐	8	Anson Carter, Bos.	5.00	1.00	.50
☐☐☐	9	Rob DiMaio, Bos.	5.00	1.00	.50
☐☐☐	10	Steve Heinze, Bos.	5.00	1.00	.50
☐☐☐	11	Jean-Yves Roy, Bos.	5.00	1.00	.50
☐☐☐	12	Randy Robitaille, Bos.	5.00	1.50	.75
☐☐☐	13	Byron Dafoe (G), Bos.	5.00	1.00	.50
☐☐☐	14	Sergei Samsonov, Bos.	25.00	5.00	3.00
☐☐☐	15	Ken Baumgartner, Bos.	5.00	1.00	.50
☐☐☐	16	Dave Ellett, Bos.	5.00	1.00	.50
☐☐☐	17	Joe Thornton, Bos.	25.00	5.00	3.00
☐☐☐	18	Jeff Odgers, Bos.	5.00	1.00	.50
☐☐☐	19	Kyle McLaren, Bos.	5.00	1.00	.50
☐☐☐	20	Don Sweeney, Bos.	5.00	1.00	.50
Buffalo Sabres (20 cards):			**100.00**	**25.00**	**12.00**
☐☐☐	1	Dominik Hasek (G), Buf.	35.00	7.00	3.50
☐☐☐	2	Steve Shields (G), Buf.	5.00	1.00	.50
☐☐☐	3	Dixon Ward, Buf.	5.00	1.00	.50
☐☐☐	4	Donald Audette, Buf.	5.00	1.00	.50
☐☐☐	5	Matthew Barnaby, Buf.	5.00	1.00	.50
☐☐☐	6	Randy Burridge, Buf.	5.00	1.00	.50
☐☐☐	7	Jason Dawe, Buf.	5.00	1.00	.50
☐☐☐	8	Michal Grosek, Buf.	5.00	1.00	.50
☐☐☐	9	Brian Holzinger, Buf.	5.00	1.00	.50
☐☐☐	10	Brad May, Buf.	5.00	1.00	.50
☐☐☐	11	Michael Peca, Buf.	10.00	2.00	1.00
☐☐☐	12	Derek Plante, Buf.	5.00	1.00	.50
☐☐☐	13	Wayne Primeau, Buf.	5.00	1.00	.50
☐☐☐	14	Rob Ray, Buf.	5.00	1.00	.50
☐☐☐	15	Miroslav Satan, Buf.	5.00	1.00	.50
☐☐☐	16	Erik Rasmussen, Buf.	5.00	1.00	.50
☐☐☐	17	Jason Woolley, Buf.	5.00	1.00	.50
☐☐☐	18	Alexei Zhitnik, Buf.	5.00	1.00	.50
☐☐☐	19	Darryl Shannon, Buf.	5.00	1.00	.50
☐☐☐	20	Mike Wilson, Buf.	5.00	1.00	.50
Colorado Avalanche (20 cards):			**150.00**	**40.00**	**20.00**
☐☐☐	1	Patrick Roy (G), Col.	75.00	15.00	7.50
☐☐☐	2	Craig Billington (G), Col.	5.00	1.00	.50
☐☐☐	3	Marc Denis (G), Col.	10.00	2.00	1.00
☐☐☐	4	Peter Forsberg, Col.	50.00	10.00	5.00
☐☐☐	5	Jari Kurri, Col.	10.00	2.00	1.00
☐☐☐	6	Sandis Ozolinsh, Col.	10.00	2.00	1.00
☐☐☐	7	Valeri Kamensky, Col.	10.00	2.00	1.00
☐☐☐	8	Adam Deadmarsh, Col.	5.00	1.00	.50
☐☐☐	9	Keith Jones, Col.	5.00	1.00	.50
☐☐☐	10	Josef Marha, Col.	5.00	1.00	.50
☐☐☐	11	Claude Lemieux, Col.	5.00	1.00	.50
☐☐☐	12	Adam Foote, Col.	10.00	2.00	1.00
☐☐☐	13	Eric Lacroix, Col.	5.00	1.00	.50
☐☐☐	14	René Corbet, Col.	5.00	1.00	.50
☐☐☐	15	Uwe Krupp, Col.	5.00	1.00	.50
☐☐☐	16	Sylvain Lefebvre, Col.	5.00	1.00	.50
☐☐☐	17	Mike Ricci, Col.	5.00	1.00	.50
☐☐☐	18	Joe Sakic, Col.	40.00	8.00	4.00
☐☐☐	19	Stéphane Yelle, Col.	5.00	1.00	.50
☐☐☐	20	Yves Sarault, Col.	5.00	1.00	.50
Detroit Red Wings (20 cards):			**150.00**	**40.00**	**20.00**
☐☐☐	1	Brendan Shanahan, Det.	30.00	6.00	3.00
☐☐☐	2	Steve Yzerman, Det.	50.00	10.00	5.00
☐☐☐	3	Sergei Fedorov, Det.	25.00	5.00	2.50
☐☐☐	4	Nicklas Lidström, Det.	10.00	2.00	1.00
☐☐☐	5	Igor Larionov, Det.	10.00	2.00	1.00
☐☐☐	6	Darren McCarty, Det.	5.00	1.00	.50
☐☐☐	7	Vyacheslav Kozlov, Det.	5.00	1.00	.50
☐☐☐	8	Larry Murphy, Det.	10.00	2.00	1.00
☐☐☐	9	Vladimir Konstantinov, Det.	5.00	1.00	.50
☐☐☐	10	Martin Lapointe, Det.	5.00	1.00	.50
☐☐☐	11	Vyacheslav Fetisov, Det.	10.00	2.00	1.00
☐☐☐	12	Kris Draper, Det.	5.00	1.00	.50
☐☐☐	13	Doug Brown, Det.	5.00	1.00	.50
☐☐☐	14	Brent Gilchrist, Det.	5.00	1.00	.50
☐☐☐	15	Kirk Maltby, Det.	5.00	1.00	.50
☐☐☐	16	Tomas Holmstrom, Det.	10.00	2.00	1.00
☐☐☐	17	Chris Osgood (G), Det.	20.00	4.0	2.00
☐☐☐	18	Kevin Hodson (G), Det.	5.00	1.00	.50
☐☐☐	19	Jamie Pushor, Det.	5.00	1.00	.50
☐☐☐	20	Mike Knuble, Det.	5.00	1.00	.50
Montréal Canadiens (20 cards):			**125.00**	**30.00**	**15.00**
☐☐☐	1	Andy Moog (G), Mtl.	10.00	2.00	1.00
☐☐☐	2	Jocelyn Thibault (G), Mtl.	15.00	3.00	1.50
☐☐☐	3	José Théodore (G), Mtl.	15.00	3.00	1.50
☐☐☐	4	Vincent Damphousse, Mtl.	15.00	3.00	1.50
☐☐☐	5	Mark Recchi, Mtl.	10.00	2.00	1.00
☐☐☐	6	Brian Savage, Mtl.	5.00	1.00	.50
☐☐☐	7	Saku Koivu, Mtl.	35.00	7.00	3.50

	No.	Player			
□□□	8	Stéphane Richer, Mtl.	5.00	1.00	.50
□□□	9	Martin Rucinsky, Mtl.	5.00	1.00	.50
□□□	10	Valeri Bure, Mtl.	5.00	1.00	.50
□□□	11	Vladimir Malakhov, Mtl.	5.00	1.00	.50
□□□	12	Shayne Corson, Mtl.	10.00	2.00	1.00
□□□	13	Darcy Tucker, Mtl.	5.00	1.00	.50
□□□	14	Sébastien Bordeleau, Mtl.	5.00	1.00	.50
□□□	15	Terry Ryan, Mtl.	5.00	1.00	.50
□□□	16	David Ling, Mtl.	5.00	1.50	.75
□□□	17	Dave Manson, Mtl.	5.00	1.00	.50
□□□	18	Benoît Brunet, Mtl.	5.00	1.00	.50
□□□	19	Marc Bureau, Mtl.	5.00	1.00	.50
□□□	20	Patrice Brisebois, Mtl.	5.00	1.00	.50
New Jersey Devils (20 cards):			**100.00**	**25.00**	**12.00**
□□□	1	Doug Gilmour, N.J.	15.00	3.00	1.50
□□□	2	Bobby Holik, N.J.	5.00	1.00	.50
□□□	3	Dave Andreychuk, N.J.	5.00	1.00	.50
□□□	4	John MacLean, N.J.	5.00	1.00	.50
□□□	5	Bill Guerin, N.J.	10.00	2.00	1.00
□□□	6	Brian Rolston, N.J.	5.00	1.00	.50
□□□	7	Scott Niedermayer, N.J.	10.00	2.00	1.00
□□□	8	Scott Stevens, N.J.	5.00	1.00	.50
□□□	9	Valeri Zelepukin, N.J.	5.00	1.00	.50
□□□	10	Steve Thomas, N.J.	5.00	1.00	.50
□□□	11	Denis Pederson, N.J.	5.00	1.00	.50
□□□	12	Randy McKay, N.J.	5.00	1.00	.50
□□□	13	Mike Dunham, N.J.	5.00	1.00	.50
□□□	14	Petr Sykora, N.J.	5.00	1.00	.50
□□□	15	Lyle Odelein, N.J.	5.00	1.00	.50
□□□	16	Martin Brodeur (G), N.J.	35.00	7.00	3.50
□□□	17	Vadim Sharifjanov, N.J.	5.00	1.00	.50
□□□	18	Bob Carpenter, N.J.	5.00	1.00	.50
□□□	19	Sergei Brylin, N.J.	5.00	1.00	.50
□□□	20	Ken Daneyko, N.J.	5.00	1.00	.50
New York Rangers (20 cards):			**150.00**	**40.00**	**20.00**
□□□	1	Wayne Gretzky, NYR.	100.00	50.00	10.00
□□□	2	Brian Leetch, NYR.	15.00	3.00	1.50
□□□	3	Mike Keane, NYR.	5.00	1.00	.50
□□□	4	Adam Graves, NYR.	5.00	1.00	.50
□□□	5	Niklas Sundstrom, NYR.	5.00	1.00	.50
□□□	6	Kevin Stevens, NYR.	5.00	1.00	.50
□□□	7	Alexei Kovalev, NYR.	5.00	1.00	.50
□□□	8	Alexander Karpovtsev, NYR.	5.00	1.00	.50
□□□	9	Bill Berg, NYR.	5.00	1.00	.50
□□□	10	Pat LaFontaine, NYR.	5.00	1.00	.50
□□□	11	Bruce Driver, NYR.	5.00	1.00	.50
□□□	12	Pat Flatley, NYR.	5.00	1.00	.50
□□□	13	Vladimir Vorobiev, NYR.	5.00	1.00	.50
□□□	14	Christian Dubé, NYR.	5.00	1.00	.50
□□□	15	Ulf Samuelsson, NYR.	5.00	1.00	.50
□□□	16	Mike Richter (G), NYR.	15.00	3.00	1.50
□□□	17	Jason Muzzatti (G), NYR.	5.00	1.00	.50
□□□	18	Daniel Goneau, NYR.	5.00	1.00	.50
□□□	19	Marc Savard, NYR.	5.00	1.50	.75
□□□	20	Jeff Beukeboom, NYR.	5.00	1.00	.50
Philadelphia Flyers (20 cards):			**125.00**	**30.00**	**15.00**
□□□	1	Ron Hextall (G), Pha.	10.00	2.00	1.00
□□□	2	Garth Snow (G), Pha.	5.00	1.00	.50
□□□	3	Eric Lindros, Pha.	65.00	13.00	6.50
□□□	4	John LeClair, Pha.	25.00	5.00	2.50
□□□	5	Rod Brind'Amour, Pha.	10.00	2.00	1.00
□□□	6	Chris Gratton, Pha.	10.00	2.00	1.00
□□□	7	Eric Desjardins, Pha.	5.00	1.00	.50
□□□	8	Trent Klatt, Pha.	5.00	1.00	.50
□□□	9	Janne Niinimaa, Pha.	10.00	2.00	1.00
□□□	10	Luke Richardson, Pha.	5.00	1.00	.50
□□□	11	Paul Coffey, Pha.	10.00	2.00	1.00
□□□	12	Dainius Zubrus, Pha.	10.00	2.00	1.00
□□□	13	Shjon Podein, Pha.	5.00	1.00	.50
□□□	14	Joel Otto, Pha.	5.00	1.00	.50
□□□	15	Chris Therien, Pha.	5.00	1.00	.50
□□□	16	Pat Falloon, Pha.	5.00	1.00	.50
□□□	17	Petr Svoboda, Pha.	5.00	1.00	.50
□□□	18	Vaclav Prospal, Pha.	15.00	1.50	.75
□□□	19	John Druce, Pha.	5.00	1.00	.50
□□□	20	Daniel Lacroix, Pha.	5.00	1.00	.50
Pittsburgh Penguins (20 cards):			**125.0**	**30.00**	**15.00**
□□□	1	Tom Barrasso (G), Pgh.	10.00	2.00	1.00
□□□	2	Ken Wregget (G), Pgh.	5.00	1.00	.50
□□□	3	Patrick Lalime (G), Pgh.	5.00	1.00	.50
□□□	4	Jaromir Jagr, Pgh.	50.00	10.00	5.00
□□□	5	Ron Francis, Pgh.	15.00	3.00	1.50
□□□	6	Petr Nedved, Pgh.	5.00	1.00	.50
□□□	7	Ed Olczyk, Pgh.	5.00	1.00	.50
□□□	8	Kevin Hatcher, Pgh.	5.00	1.00	.50
□□□	9	Stu Barnes, Pgh.	5.00	1.00	.50
□□□	10	Darius Kasparaitis, Pgh.	5.00	1.00	.50
□□□	11	Greg Johnson, Pgh.	5.00	1.00	.50
□□□	12	Garry Valk, Pgh.	5.00	1.00	.50
□□□	13	Roman Oksiuta, Pgh.	5.00	1.00	.50
□□□	14	Dan Quinn, Pgh.	5.00	1.00	.50
□□□	15	Alex Hicks, Pgh.	5.00	1.00	.50
□□□	16	Robert Dome, Pgh.	5.00	1.00	.50
□□□	17	Dave Roche, Pgh.	5.00	1.00	.50
□□□	18	Alexei Morozov, Pgh.	20.00	4.00	2.50
□□□	19	Rob Brown, Pgh.	5.00	1.00	.50
□□□	20	Domenic Pittis, Pgh.	5.00	1.00	.50
St. Louis Blues (20 cards):			**100.00**	**25.00**	**12.00**
□□□	1	Brett Hull, Stl.	25.00	5.00	2.50
□□□	2	Pierre Turgeon, Stl.	10.00	2.00	1.00
□□□	3	Joe Murphy, Stl.	5.00	1.00	.50
□□□	4	Jim Campbell, Stl.	5.00	1.00	.50
□□□	5	Harry York, Stl.	5.00	1.00	.50
□□□	6	Al MacInnis, Stl.	10.00	2.00	1.00
□□□	7	Chris Pronger, Stl.	10.00	2.00	1.00
□□□	8	Darren Turcotte, Stl.	5.00	1.00	.50
□□□	9	Robert Petrovicky, Stl.	5.00	1.00	.50
□□□	10	Tony Twist, Stl.	5.00	1.00	.50
□□□	11	Grant Fuhr (G), Stl.	10.00	2.00	1.00
□□□	12	Scott Pellerin, Stl.	5.00	1.00	.50
□□□	13	Jamie Rivers, Stl.	5.00	1.00	.50
□□□	14	Chris McAlpine, Stl.	5.00	1.00	.50
□□□	15	Geoff Courtnall, Stl.	5.00	1.00	.50
□□□	16	Steve Duchesne, Stl.	5.00	1.00	.50
□□□	17	Libor Zabransky, Stl.	5.00	1.00	.50
□□□	18	Pavol Demitra, Stl.	5.00	1.00	.50
□□□	19	Marc Bergevin, Stl.	5.00	1.00	.50
□□□	20	Jamie McLennan (G), Stl.	10.00	2.00	1.00
Toronto Maple Leafs (20 cards):			**125.00**	**30.00**	**15.00**
□□□	1	Félix Potvin (G), Tor.	25.00	5.00	2.50
□□□	2	Glenn Healy (G), Tor.	5.00	1.00	.50
□□□	3	Marcel Cousineau (G), Tor.	5.00	1.00	.50
□□□	4	Mats Sundin, Tor.	25.00	5.00	2.50
□□□	5	Wendel Clark, Tor.	10.00	2.00	1.00
□□□	6	Sergei Berezin, Tor.	10.00	2.00	1.00
□□□	7	Steve Sullivan, Tor.	5.00	1.00	.50
□□□	8	Tie Domi, Tor.	5.00	1.00	.50
□□□	9	Todd Warriner, Tor.	5.00	1.00	.50
□□□	10	Mathieu Schneider, Tor.	5.00	1.00	.50
□□□	11	Mike Craig, Tor.	5.00	1.00	.50
□□□	12	Darby Hendrickson, Tor.	5.00	1.00	.50
□□□	13	Fredrik Modin, Tor.	5.00	1.00	.50
□□□	14	Brandon Convery, Tor.	5.00	1.00	.50
□□□	15	Kevyn Adams, Tor.	5.00	1.00	.50
□□□	16	Dimitri Yushkevich, Tor.	5.00	1.00	.50
□□□	17	Alyn McCauley, Tor.	20.00	4.00	2.50
□□□	18	Derek King, Tor.	5.00	1.00	.50
□□□	19	Jamie Baker, Tor.	5.00	1.00	.50
□□□	20	Martin Prochazka, Tor.	5.00	1.00	.50
Vancouver Canucks (20 cards):			**125.00**	**30.00**	**15.00**
□□□	1	Pavel Bure, Van.	35.00	7.00	3.50
□□□	2	Alexander Mogilny, Van.	15.00	3.00	1.50
□□□	3	Mark Messier, Van.	25.00	5.00	2.50
□□□	4	Trevor Linden, Van.	10.00	2.00	1.00
□□□	5	Martin Gelinas, Van.	5.00	1.00	.50
□□□	6	Mattias Ohlund, Van.	10.00	2.00	1.00
□□□	7	Markus Naslund, Van.	5.00	1.00	.50
□□□	8	Jyrki Lumme, Van.	5.00	1.00	.50
□□□	9	Lonny Bohonos, Van.	5.00	1.00	.50
□□□	10	Kirk McLean (G), Van.	10.00	2.00	1.00
□□□	11	Corey Hirsch (G), Van.	5.00	1.00	.50
□□□	12	Arturs Irbe (G), Van.	5.00	1.00	.50
□□□	13	Larry Courville, Van.	5.00	1.00	.50
□□□	14	Adrian Aucoin, Van.	5.00	1.00	.50
□□□	15	Grant Ledyard, Van.	5.00	1.00	.50
□□□	16	Gino Odjick, Van.	5.00	1.00	.50
□□□	17	Donald Brashear, Van.	5.00	1.00	.50
□□□	18	Brian Noonan, Van.	5.00	1.00	.50
□□□	19	David Roberts, Van.	5.00	1.00	.50
□□□	20	Dave Babych, Van.	5.00	1.00	.50

1997 - 98 SP AUTHENTIC

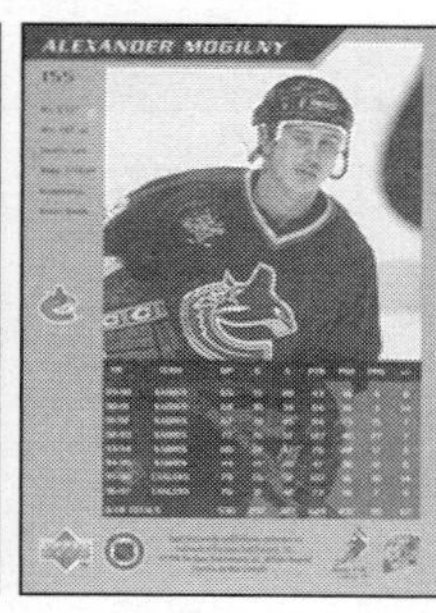

Imprint: © 1998 THE UPPER DECK COMPANY

Complete Set (198 cards): 75.00

Common Player: .20

	No.	Player	NRMT-MT
□	1	Teemu Selänne, Ana.	1.75
□	2	Sean Pronger, Ana.	.20
□	3	Joe Sacco, Ana.	.20
□	4	Tomas Sandström, Ana.	.20
□	5	Steve Rucchin, Ana.	.20
□	6	Paul Kariya, Ana.	3.50
□	7	Ted Donato, Ana.	.20
□	8	Ray Bourque, Bos.	1.25
□	9	Tim Taylor, Bos.	.20
□	10	Jason Allison, Bos.	.75
□	11	Kyle McLaren, Bos.	.20
□	12	Dimitri Khristich, Bos.	.20
□	13	Jason Dawe, Buf.	.20
□	14	Dominik Hasek (G), Buf.	1.75
□	15	Miroslav Satan, Buf.	.20
□	16	Brian Holzinger, Buf.	.20
□	17	Alexei Zhitnik, Buf.	.20
□	18	Theoren Fleury, Cgy.	.75
□	19	Cory Stillman, Cgy.	.20
□	20	Jarome Iginla, Cgy.	.75
□	21	Sandy McCarthy, Cgy.	.20
□	22	German Titov, Cgy.	.20
□	23	Glen Wesley, Car.	.20
□	24	Keith Primeau, Car.	.50
□	25	Geoff Sanderson, Car.	.20
□	26	Gary Roberts, Car.	.50
□	27	Sami Kapanen, Car.	.20
□	28	Jeff O'Neill, Car.	.50
□	29	Tony Amonte, Chi.	.50
□	30	Chris Chelios, Chi.	1.00
□	31	Eric Dazé, Chi.	.50
□	32	Alexei Zhamnov, Chi.	.20
□	33	Chris Terreri (G), Chi.	.20
□	34	Sergei Krivokrasov, Chi.	.20
□	35	Joe Sakic, Col.	2.00
□	36	Peter Forsberg, Col.	2.50
□	37	Patrick Roy (G), Col.	4.00
□	38	Claude Lemieux, Col.	.20
□	39	Valeri Kamensky, Col.	.50
□	40	Adam Deadmarsh, Col.	.20
□	41	Sandis Ozolinsh, Col.	.50
□	42	Jari Kurri, Col.	.50
□	43	Mike Modano, Dal.	1.25
□	44	Ed Belfour, Dal.	.75
□	45	Derian Hatcher, Dal.	.50
□	46	Sergei Zubov, Dal.	.50
□	47	Jamie Langenbrunner, Dal.	.50
□	48	Jere Lehtinen, Dal.	.50
□	49	Joe Nieuwendyk, Dal.	.50
□	50	Vyacheslav Kozlov, Det.	.20
□	51	Chris Osgood (G), Det.	1.00
□	52	Steve Yzerman, Det.	2.50
□	53	Nicklas Lidström, Det.	.50
□	54	Igor Larionov, Det.	.50
□	55	Brendan Shanahan, Det.	1.50
□	56	Anders Eriksson, Det.	.20
□	57	Darren McCarty, Det.	.20
□	58	Doug Weight, Edm.	.75
□	59	Jason Arnott, Edm.	.50
□	60	Curtis Joseph (G), Edm.	1.50
□	61	Ryan Smyth, Edm.	.50
□	62	Dean McAmmond, Edm.	.20
□	63	Mike Grier, Edm.	.50
□	64	Kelly Buchberger, Edm.	.20

☐ 65 Ed Jovanovski, Fla. .50
☐ 66 Ray Whitney, Fla. .20
☐ 67 Rob Niedermayer, Fla. .20
☐ 68 Scott Mellanby, Fla. .20
☐ 69 John Vanbiesbrouck (G), Fla. 1.50
☐ 70 Viktor Kozlov, Fla. .20
☐ 71 Jozef Stumpel, L.A. .50
☐ 72 Rob Blake, L.A. .50
☐ 73 Garry Galley, L.A. .20
☐ 74 Vladimir Tsyplakov, L.A. .20
☐ 75 Yanic Perreault, L.A. .20
☐ 76 Stéphane Fiset (G), L.A. .50
☐ 77 Luc Robitaille, L.A. .50
☐ 78 Valeri Bure, Mtl. .20
☐ 79 Mark Recchi, Mtl. .50
☐ 80 Saku Koivu, Mtl. 1.75
☐ 81 Andy Moog, Mtl. .50
☐ 82 Vincent Damphousse, Mtl. .50
☐ 83 Vladmir Malakhov, Mtl. .20
☐ 84 Shayne Corson, Mtl. .50
☐ 85 Scott Stevens, N.J. .20
☐ 86 Bill Guerin, N.J. .50
☐ 87 Martin Brodeur (G), N.J. 1.75
☐ 88 Doug Gilmour, N.J. .75
☐ 89 Bobby Holik, N.J. .20
☐ 90 Petr Sykora, N.J. .20
☐ 91 Zigmund Palffy, NYI. .75
☐ 92 Bryan Berard, NYI. .75
☐ 93 Tommy Salo, NYI. .20
☐ 94 Travis Green, NYI. .20
☐ 95 Kenny Jonsson, NYI. .20
☐ 96 Todd Bertuzzi, NYI. .20
☐ 97 Robert Reichel, NYI. .20
☐ 98 Pat LaFontaine, NYR. .50
☐ 99 Wayne Gretzky, NYR. 5.00
☐ 100 Brian Leetch, NYR. .75
☐ 101 Mike Richter (G), NYR. .75
☐ 102 Alexei Kovalev, NYR. .20
☐ 103 Adam Graves, NYR. .20
☐ 104 Niklas Sundstrom, NYR. .20
☐ 105 Alexei Yashin, Ott. 1.00
☐ 106 Daniel Alfredsson, Ott. .50
☐ 107 Alexandre Daigle, Ott. .20
☐ 108 Wade Redden, Ott. .20
☐ 109 Andreas Dackell, Ott. .20
☐ 110 Shawn McEachern, Ott. .20
☐ 111 Eric Lindros, Pha. 3.50
☐ 112 Chris Gratton, Pha. .50
☐ 113 Paul Coffey, Pha. .50
☐ 114 John LeClair, Pha. 1.25
☐ 115 Rod Brind'Amour, Pha. .50
☐ 116 Ron Hextall (G), Pha. .50
☐ 117 Dainius Zubrus, Pha. .50
☐ 118 Jeremy Roenick, Pho. .75
☐ 119 Keith Tkachuk, Pho. 1.00
☐ 120 Nikolai Khabibulin (G), Pho. .75
☐ 121 Rick Tocchet, Pho. .20
☐ 122 Teppo Numminen, Pho. .20
☐ 123 Craig Janney, Pho. .20
☐ 124 Mike Gartner, Pho. .50
☐ 125 Jaromir Jagr, Pgh. 2.50
☐ 126 Ron Francis, Pgh. .75
☐ 127 Kevin Hatcher, Pgh. .20
☐ **128 Robert Dome, Pgh., RC .20**
☐ 129 Martin Straka, Pgh. .20
☐ **130 Petr Skudra (G), Pgh., RC .50**
☐ 131 Owen Nolan, S.J. .50
☐ 132 Bernie Nicholls, S.J. .20
☐ 133 Mike Vernon (G), S.J. .50
☐ 134 Jeff Friesen, S.J. .50
☐ 135 Tony Granato, S.J. .20
☐ 136 Mike Ricci, S.J. .20
☐ 137 Jim Campbell, Stl. .20
☐ 138 Brett Hull, Stl. 1.25
☐ 139 Chris Pronger, Stl. .50
☐ 140 Al MacInnis, Stl. .50
☐ 141 Pierre Turgeon, Stl. .50
☐ 142 Pavol Demitra, Stl. .20
☐ 143 Grant Fuhr (G), Stl. .50
☐ 144 Steve Duchesne, Stl. .20
☐ 145 Daymond Langkow, T.B. .20
☐ 146 Alexander Selivanov, T.B. .20
☐ 147 Daren Puppa (G), T.B. .20
☐ 148 Dino Ciccarelli, T.B. .50
☐ 149 Roman Hamrlik, T.B. .50
☐ 150 Mats Sundin, Tor. 1.25
☐ 151 Félix Potvin (G), Tor. 1.25
☐ 152 Wendel Clark, Tor. .50
☐ 153 Sergei Berezin, Tor. .50
☐ 154 Steve Sullivan, Tor. .20
☐ 155 Alexander Mogilny, Van. .75
☐ 156 Pavel Bure, Van. 1.75
☐ 157 Mark Messier, Van. 1.25
☐ 158 Bret Hedican, Van. .20
☐ 159 Kirk McLean (G), Van. .50
☐ 160 Trevor Linden, Van. .50
☐ **161 Dave Scatchard, Van., RC .50**
☐ 162 Adam Oates, Wsh. .75
☐ 163 Joé Juneau, Wsh. .20
☐ 164 Peter Bondra, Wsh. 1.00
☐ 165 Bill Ranford (G), Wsh. .50
☐ 166 Sergei Gonchar, Wsh. .20
☐ 167 Calle Johansson, Wsh. .20
☐ 168 Phil Housley, Wsh. .20
☐ **169 Espen Knutsen, Ana., RC .50**
☐ **170 Pavel Trnka, Ana., RC .50**
☐ 171 Joe Thornton, Bos. 1.25
☐ 172 Sergei Samsonov, Bos. 1.25
☐ 173 Erik Rasmussen, Buf. .20
☐ **174 Tyler Moss (G), Cgy., RC .75**
☐ **175 Derek Morris, Cgy., RC 1.00**
☐ 176 Craig Mills, Chi. .20
☐ 177 Daniel Cleary, Chi. .50
☐ **178 Eric Messier, Col., RC .50**
☐ 179 Kevin Hodson (G), Det. .20
☐ **180 Mike Knuble, Det., RC .50**
☐ 181 Boyd Devereaux, Edm. .20
☐ **182 Craig Millar, Edm., RC .50**
☐ **183 Kevin Weekes (G), Fla, RC .75**
☐ **184 Donald MacLean, L.A., RC .50**
☐ **185 Patrik Elias, N.J., RC 1.25**
☐ **186 Zdeno Chara, NYI., RC 1.00**
☐ 187 Chris Phillips, Ott. .50
☐ **188 Vaclav Prospal, Pha., RC 1.25**
☐ 189 Brad Isbister, Pho. .20
☐ 190 Alexei Morozov, Pgh. 1.00
☐ 191 Patrick Marleau, S.J. 1.00
☐ **192 Marco Sturm, S.J., RC .50**
☐ **193 Brendan Morrison, N.J., RC 4.00**
☐ **194 Mike Johnson, Tor., RC 5.00**
☐ 195 Alyn McCauley, Tor. 1.00
☐ 196 Mattias Ohlund, Van. .50
☐ 197 Richard Zednik, Wsh. .20
☐ **198 Jan Bulis, Wsh., RC .50**

ICONS

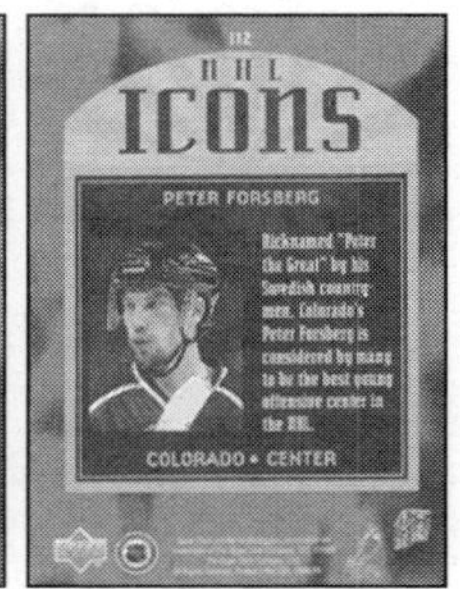

These inserts have three versions. The regular insert, an embossed insert and a die-cut insert (100 copies).

	No.	Player	D.C.	Emb.	Reg.
Insert Set (40 cards):			**7,000.00**	**550.00**	**275.00**
☐☐☐	I1	Pat LaFontaine, Buf.	65.00	6.00	3.00
☐☐☐	I2	Brett Hull, Stl.	175.00	12.00	6.00
☐☐☐	I3	Chris Chelios, Chi.	125.00	10.00	5.00
☐☐☐	I4	Joe Sakic, Col.	300.00	25.00	12.00
☐☐☐	I5	John Vanbiesbrouck, Fla.	200.00	16.00	8.00
☐☐☐	I6	Patrik Elias, N.J.	65.00	6.00	3.00
☐☐☐	I7	Eric Lindros, Pha.	500.00	40.00	20.00
☐☐☐	I8	Jaromir Jagr, Pgh.	375.00	30.00	15.00
☐☐☐	I9	Joe Thornton, Bos.	175.00	15.00	8.00
☐☐☐	I10	Brendan Shanahan, Det.	200.00	16.00	8.00
☐☐☐	I11	Paul Kariya, Ana.	500.00	40.00	20.00
☐☐☐	I12	Peter Forsberg, Col.	375.00	30.00	15.00
☐☐☐	I13	Ed Belfour (G), Dal.	100.00	8.00	4.00
☐☐☐	I14	Martin Brodeur (G), N.J.	250.00	20.00	10.00
☐☐☐	I15	Alexei Morozov, Pgh.	125.00	10.00	6.00
☐☐☐	I16	Mark Messier, Van.	175.00	12.00	6.00
☐☐☐	I17	John LeClair, Pha.	175.00	12.00	6.00
☐☐☐	I18	Luc Robitaille, L.A.	65.00	6.00	3.00
☐☐☐	I19	Teemu Selänne, Ana.	250.00	20.00	10.00
☐☐☐	I20	Theoren Fleury, Cgy.	100.00	8.00	4.00
☐☐☐	I21	Steve Yzerman, Det.	375.00	30.00	15.00
☐☐☐	I22	Chris Phillips, Ott.	65.00	6.00	3.00
☐☐☐	I23	Keith Tkachuk, Pho.	125.00	10.00	5.00
☐☐☐	I24	Patrick Roy (G), Col.	600.00	50.00	25.00
☐☐☐	I25	Mark Recchi, Mtl.	65.00	6.00	3.00
☐☐☐	I26	Wayne Gretzky, NYR.	750.00	60.00	30.00
☐☐☐	I27	Dino Ciccarelli, T.B.	65.00	6.00	3.00
☐☐☐	I28	Ray Bourque, Bos.	175.00	12.00	6.00
☐☐☐	I29	Tony Amonte, Chi.	65.00	6.00	3.00
☐☐☐	I30	Daniel Alfredsson, Ott.	65.00	6.00	3.00
☐☐☐	I31	Saku Koivu, Mtl.	250.00	20.00	10.00
☐☐☐	I32	Doug Weight, Edm.	100.00	8.00	4.00
☐☐☐	I33	Mats Sundin, Tor.	250.00	20.00	10.00
☐☐☐	I34	Dominik Hasek (G), Buf.	250.00	20.00	10.00
☐☐☐	I35	Scott Stevens, N.J.	65.00	6.00	3.00
☐☐☐	I36	Pavel Bure, Van.	250.00	20.00	10.00
☐☐☐	I37	Mike Modano, Dal.	175.00	12.00	6.00
☐☐☐	I38	Zigmund Palffy, NYI.	100.00	8.00	4.00
☐☐☐	I39	Brian Leetch, NYR.	100.00	8.00	4.00
☐☐☐	I40	Marco Sturm, S.J.	65.00	6.00	3.00

SIGN OF THE TIMES AUTOGRAPHS

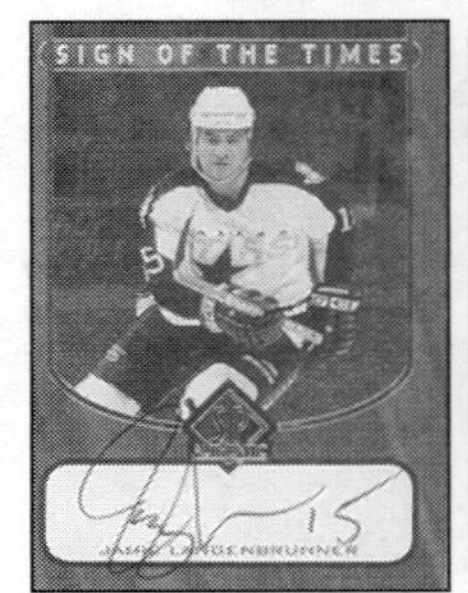

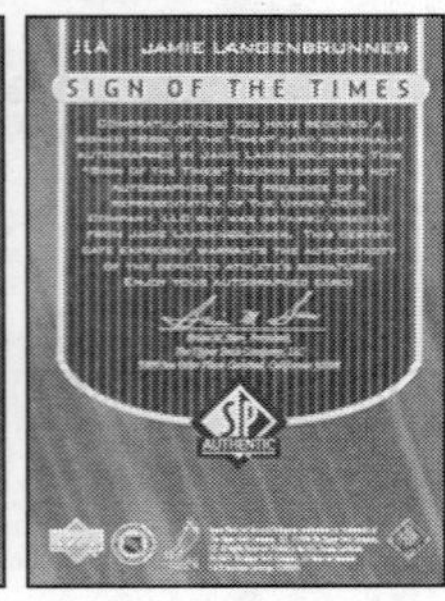

	No.	Player	NRMT-MT
Insert Set (29 cards):			**1,400.00**
☐	S1	Wayne Gretzky, NYR.	400.00
☐	S2	Patrick Roy (G), Col.	250.00
☐	S3	Steve Yzerman, Det.	185.00
☐	S4	Sergei Samsonov, Bos.	65.00
☐	S5	Brett Hull, Stl.	55.00
☐	S6	Ray Bourque, Bos.	55.00
☐	S7	Joe Thornton, Bos.	65.00
☐	S8	Yanic Perreault, L.A.	15.00
☐	S9	Chris Chelios, Chi.	40.00
☐	S10	Tony Amonte, Chi.	20.00
☐	S11	Jamie Langenbrunner, Dal.	20.00
☐	S12	Mats Sundin, Tor.	55.00
☐	S13	Grant Fuhr (G), Stl.	25.00
☐	S14	Doug Weight, Edm.	30.00
☐	S15	Martin Brodeur (G), N.J.	125.00
☐	S16	Bryan Berard, NYI.	30.00
☐	S17	Peter Bondra, Wsh.	40.00
☐	S18	Nicklas Lidström, Det.	20.00
☐	S19	Rob Niedermayer, Fla.	20.00
☐	S20	Nikolai Khabibulin (G), Pho.	30.00
☐	S21	José Théodore (G), Mtl.	20.00
☐	S22	Darren McCarty, Det.	15.00
☐	S23	Guy Hebert (G), Ana.	20.00
☐	S24	Jarome Iginla, Cgy.	30.00
☐	S25	Dainius Zubrus, Pha.	25.00
☐	S26	Jaroslav Svejkovsky, Wsh.	30.00
☐	S27	Sergei Berezin, Tor.	20.00
☐	S28	Mike Grier, Edm.	20.00
☐	S29	Brian Holzinger, Buf.	15.00

MARK OF A LEGEND AUTOGRAPHS

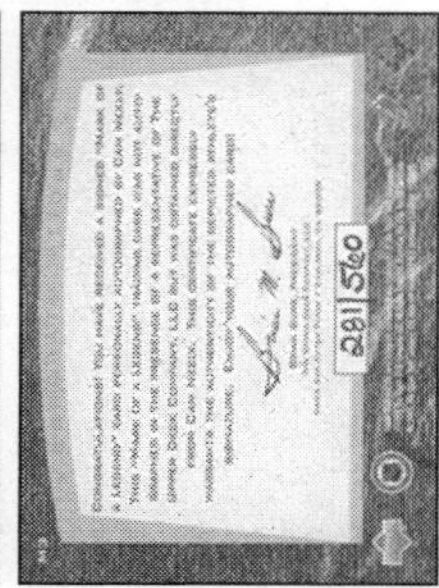

Insert Set (6 cards):			1,000.00
	No.	Player	NRMT-MT
☐	M1	Gordie Howe, Det.	500.00
☐	M2	Billy Smith (G), NYI.	50.00
☐	M3	Cam Neely, Bos.	75.00
☐	M4	Bryan Trottier, NYI.	75.00
☐	M5	Bobby Hull, Chi.	100.00
☐	M6	Wayne Gretzky, NYR.	450.00

TRADITION AUTOGRAPHS

Insert Set (6 cards):			2,350.00
	No.	Player	NRMT-MT
☐	T1	Wayne Gretzky/ Gordie Howe	1,400.00
☐	T2	Patrick Roy (G)/ Billy Smith (G)	400.00
☐	T3	Joe Thornton/ Cam Neely	200.00
☐	T4	Bryan Berard/ Bryan Trottier	100.00
☐	T5	Brett Hull/ Bobby Hull	300.00
☐	T6	Ray Bourque/ Cam Neely	300.00

1997 - 98 SP^X

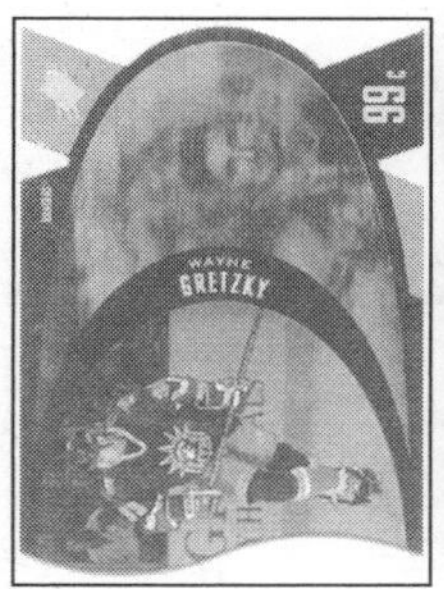

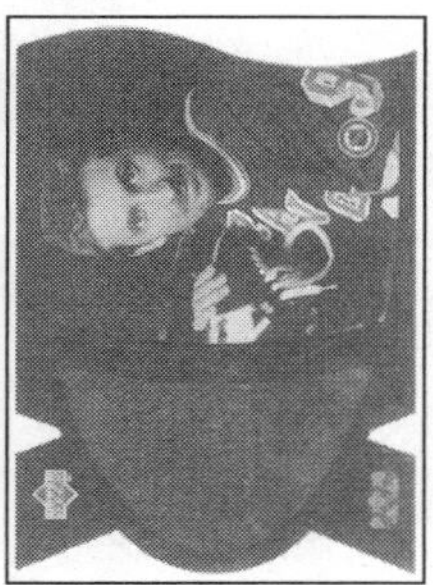

These cards have six versions: the regular card, a Steel parallel, a Bronze parallel, a Silver parallel, a Gold parallel and a Grand Finale parallel (50 copies). The Steel parallel is valued at 2 times the regular card; the Silver parallel is valued at 50% of the Gold parallel. A Steel set sells at $100; a Silver set sells $200.

Imprint: © 1997 THE UPPER DECK COMPANY, LLC.

Complete Set (50 cards):

Common Player:			80.00	4.00	1.50	.50
	No.	Player	G.F.	Gold	Bronze	Reg.
☐☐☐☐☐☐	1	Paul Kariya, Ana.	650.00	-.	15.00	6.00
☐☐☐☐☐☐	2	Teemu Selänne, Ana.	350.00	20.00	8.00	3.00
☐☐☐☐☐☐	3	Ray Bourque, Bos.	250.00	15.00	6.00	2.00
☐☐☐☐☐☐	4	Dominik Hasek (G), Buf.	350.00	20.00	8.00	3.00
☐☐☐☐☐☐	5	Pat LaFontaine, Buf.	100.00	6.00	2.50	.75
☐☐☐☐☐☐	6	Theoren Fleury, Cgy.	150.00	9.00	3.50	1.25
☐☐☐☐☐☐	7	Jarome Iginla, Cgy.	150.00	9.00	3.50	1.25
☐☐☐☐☐☐	8	Tony Amonte, Chi.	100.00	6.00	2.50	.75
☐☐☐☐☐☐	9	Chris Chelios, Chi.	200.00	12.00	5.00	1.50
☐☐☐☐☐☐	10	Patrick Roy (G), Col.	750.00	50.00	18.00	6.00
☐☐☐☐☐☐	11	Peter Forsberg, Col.	500.00	30.00	12.00	5.00
☐☐☐☐☐☐	12	Joe Sakic, Col.	400.00	25.00	10.00	3.50
☐☐☐☐☐☐	13	Mike Modano, Dal.	250.00	15.00	6.00	2.00
☐☐☐☐☐☐	14	Steve Yzerman, Det.	500.00	30.00	12.00	5.00
☐☐☐☐☐☐	15	Sergei Fedorov, Det.	250.00	15.00	6.00	2.00
☐☐☐☐☐☐	16	Brendan Shanahan, Det.	300.00	18.00	7.00	2.50
☐☐☐☐☐☐	17	Doug Weight, Edm.	150.00	9.00	3.50	1.25
☐☐☐☐☐☐	18	Jason Arnott, Edm.	100.00	6.00	2.50	.75
☐☐☐☐☐☐	19	Curtis Joseph (G), Edm.	300.00	18.00	7.00	2.50
☐☐☐☐☐☐	20	J.Vanbiesbrouck (G), Fla.	300.00	18.00	7.00	2.50
☐☐☐☐☐☐	21	Ed Jovanovski, Fla.	100.00	6.00	2.50	.75
☐☐☐☐☐☐	22	Geoff Sanderson, Hfd.	80.00	4.00	1.50	.50
☐☐☐☐☐☐	23	Rob Blake, L.A.	100.00	6.00	2.50	.75
☐☐☐☐☐☐	24	Saku Koivu, Mtl.	350.00	20.00	8.00	3.00
☐☐☐☐☐☐	25	Doug Gilmour, N.J.	150.00	9.00	3.50	1.25
☐☐☐☐☐☐	26	Scott Stevens, N.J.	80.00	4.00	1.50	.50
☐☐☐☐☐☐	27	Martin Brodeur (G), N.J.	350.00	20.00	8.00	3.00
☐☐☐☐☐☐	28	Zigmund Palffy, NYI.	150.00	9.00	3.50	1.25
☐☐☐☐☐☐	29	Bryan Berard, NYI.	150.00	9.00	3.50	1.25
☐☐☐☐☐☐	30	Wayne Gretzky, NYR.	1,000.00	65.00	25.00	8.00
☐☐☐☐☐☐	31	Mike Richter (G), NYR.	150.00	9.00	3.50	1.25
☐☐☐☐☐☐	32	Mark Messier, NYR.	250.00	15.00	6.00	2.00
☐☐☐☐☐☐	33	Brian Leetch, NYR.	150.00	9.00	3.50	1.25
☐☐☐☐☐☐	34	Daniel Alfredsson, Ott.	100.00	6.00	2.50	.75
☐☐☐☐☐☐	35	Alexei Yashin, Ott.	200.00	12.00	5.00	1.50
☐☐☐☐☐☐	36	Eric Lindros, Pha.	50.00	-.	15.00	5.00
☐☐☐☐☐☐	37	Janne Niinimaa, Pha.	100.00	6.00	2.50	.75
☐☐☐☐☐☐	38	John LeClair, Pha.	250.00	15.00	6.00	2.00
☐☐☐☐☐☐	39	Jeremy Roenick, Pho.	150.00	9.00	3.50	1.25
☐☐☐☐☐☐	40	Keith Tkachuk, Pho.	200.00	12.00	5.00	1.50
☐☐☐☐☐☐	41	Ron Francis, Pgh.	150.00	9.00	3.50	1.25
☐☐☐☐☐☐	42	Jaromir Jagr, Pgh.	500.00	30.00	12.00	5.00
☐☐☐☐☐☐	43	Brett Hull, Stl.	250.00	15.00	6.00	2.00
☐☐☐☐☐☐	44	Owen Nolan, S.J.	100.00	6.00	2.50	.75
☐☐☐☐☐☐	45	Chris Gratton, T.B.	100.00	6.00	2.50	.75
☐☐☐☐☐☐	46	Mats Sundin, Tor.	250.00	15.00	6.00	2.00
☐☐☐☐☐☐	47	Pavel Bure, Van.	350.00	20.00	8.00	3.00
☐☐☐☐☐☐	48	Adam Oates, Wsh.	150.00	9.00	3.50	1.25
☐☐☐☐☐☐	49	Joé Juneau, Wsh.	80.00	4.00	1.50	.50
☐☐☐☐☐☐	50	Peter Bondra, Wsh.	200.00	12.00	5.00	1.50

SP^X DIMENSION

Insert Set (20 cards):			1,200.00
	No.	Player	NRMT-MT
☐	SPX1	Wayne Gretzky, NYR.	250.00
☐	SPX2	Jeremy Roenick, Pho.	25.00
☐	SPX3	Mark Messier, NYR.	50.00
☐	SPX4	Eric Lindros, Pha.	150.00
☐	SPX5	Doug Gilmour, N.J.	30.00
☐	SPX6	Pavel Bure, Van.	75.00
☐	SPX7	Brendan Shanahan, Det.	60.00
☐	SPX8	Bryan Berard, NYI.	30.00
☐	SPX9	Curtis Joseph (G), Edm.	30.00
☐	SPX10	Chris Chelios, Chi.	40.00
☐	SPX11	Sergei Fedorov, Det.	50.00
☐	SPX12	Adam Oates, Wsh.	30.00
☐	SPX13	Zigmund Palffy, NYI.	40.00
☐	SPX14	Theoren Fleury, Cgy.	30.00
☐	SPX15	Keith Tkachuk, Pho.	40.00
☐	SPX16	Peter Forsberg, Col.	125.00
☐	SPX17	Mats Sundin, Tor.	50.00
☐	SPX18	Teemu Selänne, Ana.	75.00
☐	SPX19	Paul Kariya, Ana.	150.00
☐	SPX20	Brett Hull, Stl.	50.00

DUOVIEW

Six cards have a second autographed version.

Insert Set (10 cards):

	Player	Auto.	Insert
☐☐	Wayne Gretzky, NYR.	1,800.00	350.00
☐☐	Jaromir Jagr, Pgh.	750.00	200.00
☐☐	Martin Brodeur (G), N.J.	350.00	125.00
☐☐	Jarome Iginla, Cgy.	175.00	50.00
☐☐	Steve Yzerman, Det.	.-	200.00
☐☐	Patrick Roy (G), Col.	1,200.00	300.00
☐☐	Doug Weight, Edm.	175.00	50.00
☐☐	John Vanbiesbrouck (G), Fla.	.-	100.00
☐☐	Dominik Hasek (G), Buf.	.-	125.00
☐☐	Joe Sakic, Col.	.-	175.00

1997 - 98 SPORT FX MINI STIX

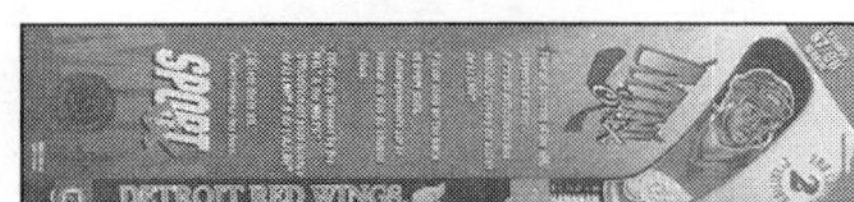

Artwork by Tony Piacente. No more than 6,500 copies of any player will be produced.

Stick Length: 22 3/4"

Imprint:

	Player	NRMT-MT
☐	Peter Bondra, Wsh.	15.00
☐	Ray Bourque, Bos.	15.00
☐	Pavel Bure, Van.	15.00
☐	Chris Chelios, Chi.	15.00
☐	Sergei Fedorov, Det.	15.00
☐	Peter Forsberg, Col.	15.00
☐	Doug Gilmour, N.J.	15.00
☐	Brett Hull, Stl.	15.00
☐	Jarome Iginla, Cgy.	15.00
☐	Jaromir Jagr, Pgh.	15.00
☐	Paul Kariya, Ana.	20.00
☐	Saku Koivu, Mtl.	15.00
☐	Pat LaFontaine, NYR.	15.00
☐	John LeClair, Pha.	15.00
☐	Brian Leetch, NYR.	15.00
☐	Eric Lindros, Pha.	20.00
☐	Mike Modano, Dal.	15.00
☐	Owen Nolan, S.J.	15.00
☐	Zigmund Palffy, NYI.	15.00
☐	Jeremy Roenick, Pho.	15.00
☐	Joe Sakic, Col.	15.00
☐	Geoff Sanderson, Car.	15.00
☐	Brendan Shanahan, Det.	15.00
☐	Mats Sundin, Tor.	15.00
☐	Alexei Yashin, Ott.	15.00

1997 - 98 SPORTS ILLUSTRATED FOR KIDS

GREAT PLAYOFF MOMENTS

This four-card insert set was in addition to S.I. For Kids' regular issue. Two cards were hockey players, the other two were basketball players. The panel was inserted in the May 1998 issue.

	Player
☐	May 10, 197-: Bobby Orr, Bos.
☐	May 25, 1985: Wayne Gretzky, Edm.

1997 - 98 TOPPS STICKERS

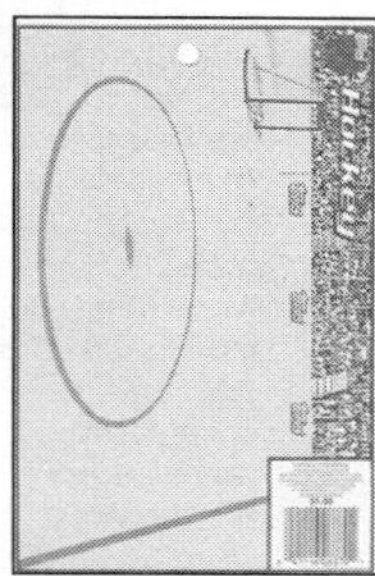

This five-panel set features 12 players on each panel.

Imprint: THE TOPPS CO., INC.

Complete Set (5 panels):			10.00
	No.	Player	NRMT-MT
☐	1	R.Bourque/ A.Daigle/ T.Domi/ P.Forsberg/ D.Gilmour/ D.Hasek/ M.Messier/ F.Potvin/ J.Roenick/ B.Shanahan/ P.Turgeon/ O.Tverdovsky	2.00
☐	2	T.Amonte/ J.Arnott/ P.Bondra/ W.Clark/ V.Damphousse/ T.Fleury/ R.Hamrlik/ E.Lindros/ O.Nolan/ J.Sakic/ J.Thibault/ J.Vanbiesbrouck	2.00
☐	3	D.Alfredsson/ B.Berard/ R.Blake/ P.Bure/ J.Iginla/ S.Koivu/ B.Leetch/ M.Modano/ M.Peca/ D.Rhodes/ P.Roy/ K.Tkachuk	2.00
☐	4	R.Brind'Amour/ S.Fedorov/ W.Gretzky/ B.Hull/ K.McLean/ A.Oates/ K.Primeau/ M.Recchi/ T.Selänne/ R.Smyth/ R.Tabaracci/ D.Weight	2.00
☐	5	C.Chelios/ J.Jagr/ Cu. Joseph/ P.Kariya/ J.LeClair/ T.Linden/ Z.Palffy/ M.Richter/ M.Sundin/ J.Thornton/ A.Yashin/ S.Yzerman	2.00

1997 - 98 UPPER DECK

30 cards from each series have a Game-Dated foil parallel (seeded 1:1,500 packs).
The Willie O'Ree promo card was handed out at the 1998 NHL All-Star Fanfest in Vancouver.

Imprint: © 1997 THE UPPER DECK COMPANY, LLC.

Series One Set (210 cards):	**35.00**
Series Two Set (210 cards):	**35.00**
Common Player:	**.15**
Promo Card (Willie O'Ree, #22):	**3.00**

	No.	Player	Foil	Reg.
☐☐	1	4/9/97: Teemu Selänne, Ana.	300.00	1.00
☐	2	Steve Rucchin, Ana.		.15
☐	3	Kevin Todd, Ana.		.15
☐	4	Darren Van Impe, Ana.		.15
☐	5	Mark Janssens, Ana.		.15
☐	6	Guy Hebert (G), Ana.		.25
☐	7	Sean Pronger, Ana.		.15
☐	8	Jason Allison, Bos.		.50
☐☐	9	3/27/97: Ray Bourque, Bos.	200.00	.75
☐	10	Landon Wilson, Bos.		.15
☐	11	Anson Carter, Bos.		.15
☐	12	Jean-Yves Roy, Bos.		.15
☐	13	Kyle McLaren, Bos.		.15
☐	14	Don Sweeney, Bos.		.15
☐	15	Brian Holzinger, Buf.		.15
☐	16	Matthew Barnaby, Buf.		.15
☐	17	Wayne Primeau, Buf.		.15
☐	**18**	**Steve Shields (G), Buf., RC**		**.25**
☐	19	Jason Dawe, Buf.		.15
☐	20	Donald Audette, Buf.		.15
☐	21	Dixon Ward, Buf.		.15
☐	22	Hnat Domenichelli, Cgy.		.25
☐	23	Trevor Kidd (G), Cgy.		.25
☐	24	Jarome Iginla, Cgy.		.50
☐	25	Sandy McCarthy, Cgy.		.15
☐	26	Marty McInnis, Cgy.		.15
☐	27	Jonas Hoglund, Cgy.		.15
☐	28	Aaron Gavey, Cgy.		.15
☐	29	Keith Primeau, Hfd. (Car.)		.25
☐☐	30	1/18/97: Geoff Sanderson, Hfd. (Car.)	75.00	.15
☐	31	Sean Burke (G), Hfd. (Car.)		.25
☐	32	Steve Rice, Hfd. (Car.)		.15
☐	33	Stu Grimson, Hfd. (Car.)		.15
☐	34	Jeff O'Neill, Hfd. (Car.)		.25
☐	35	Curtis Leschyshyn, Hfd.		.15
☐	36	Chris Chelios, Chi.		.50
☐	37	Sergei Krivokrasov, Chi.		.15
☐	38	Jeff Hackett (G), Chi.		.25
☐	39	Bob Probert, Chi.		.15
☐	40	Chris Terreri (G), Chi.		.15
☐	41	Eric Dazé, Chi.		.25
☐	42	Alexei Zhamnov, Chi.		.15
☐☐	43	5/24/97: Patrick Roy (G), Col.	700.00	2.50
☐	44	Sandis Ozolinsh, Col.		.25
☐	**45**	**Eric Messier, Col., RC**		**.15**
☐	46	Adam Deadmarsh, Col.		.15
☐☐	47	5/24/97: Claude Lemieux, Col.	75.00	.15
☐	48	Mike Ricci, Col.		.15
☐	49	Stéphane Yelle, Col.		.15
☐	50	Joe Nieuwendyk, Dal.		.25
☐	51	Derian Hatcher, Dal.		.25
☐	52	Jere Lehtinen, Dal.		.25
☐	53	Roman Turek (G), Dal.		.15
☐	54	Darryl Sydor, Dal.		.15
☐	55	Todd Harvey, Dal.		.15
☐	56	Mike Modano, Dal.		.75
☐☐	57	6/7/97: Steve Yzerman, Det.	450.00	1.50
☐	58	Martin Lapointe, Det.		.15
☐☐	59	6/7/97: Darren McCarty, Det.	75.00	.15
☐☐	60	6/7/97: Mike Vernon (G), Det.	100.00	.25
☐	61	Kirk Maltby, Det.		.15
☐	62	Kris Draper, Det.		.15
☐☐	63	6/7/97: Vladimir Konstantinov, Det.	75.00	.15
☐☐	64	4/29/97: Todd Marchant, Edm.	75.00	.15
☐	65	Doug Weight, Edm.		.50
☐	66	Jason Arnott, Edm.		.25
☐	67	Mike Grier, Edm.		.25
☐	68	Mats Lindgren, Edm.		.15
☐	69	Bryan Marchment, Edm.		.15
☐	70	Rem Murray, Edm.		.15
☐	71	Radek Dvorak, Fla.		.15
☐☐	72	4/17/97: John Vanbiesbrouck (G), Fla.	250.00	.85
☐	73	Robert Svehla, Fla.		.15
☐	74	Bill Lindsay, Fla.		.15
☐	75	Paul Laus, Fla.		.15
☐	76	Kirk Muller, Fla.		.15
☐	77	Dave Nemirovsky, Fla.		.15
☐	78	Roman Vopat, L.A.		.15
☐	79	Jan Vopat, L.A.		.15
☐	80	Dimitri Khristich, L.A.		.15
☐	81	Glen Murray, L.A.		.15
☐	82	Mattias Norstrom, L.A.		.15
☐	83	Ian Laperrière, L.A.		.15
☐☐	84	1/18/97: Mark Recchi, Mtl.	100.00	.25
☐☐	85	11/6/96: José Théodore (G), Mtl.	100.00	.50
☐	86	Vincent Damphousse, Mtl.		.50
☐	87	Sébastien Bordeleau, Mtl.		.15
☐	88	Darcy Tucker, Mtl.		.15
☐	89	Martin Rucinsky, Mtl.		.15
☐	90	Jocelyn Thibault (G), Mtl.		.50
☐☐	91	2/26/97: Doug Gilmour, N.J.	125.00	.50
☐	92	Brian Rolston, N.J.		.15
☐	93	Jay Pandolfo, N.J.		.15
☐	94	John MacLean, N.J.		.15
☐	95	Scott Stevens, N.J.		.15
☐	96	Dave Andreychuk, N.J.		.15
☐	97	Denis Pederson, N.J.		.15
☐☐	98	6/19/97: Bryan Berard, NYI.	125.00	.50
☐	99	Zigmund Palffy, NYI.		.50
☐	100	Bryan McCabe, NYI.		.15
☐	101	Rich Pilon, NYI.		.15
☐	102	Eric Fichaud (G), NYI.		.25
☐	103	Todd Bertuzzi, NYI.		.15
☐	104	Robert Reichel, NYI.		.15
☐☐	105	10/16/96: Christian Dubé, NYR.	75.00	.15
☐	106	Niklas Sundstrom, NYR.		.15
☐☐	107	5/4/97: Mike Richter (G), NYR.	125.00	.50
☐	108	Adam Graves, NYR.		.15
☐☐	109	5/18/97: Wayne Gretzky, NYR.	1,000.00	3.00
☐	110	Bruce Driver, NYR.		.15
☐	111	Esa Tikkanen, NYR.		.15
☐☐	112	4/17/97: Daniel Alfredsson, Ott.	100.00	.25
☐	113	Ron Tugnutt (G), Ott.		.15
☐	114	Steve Duchesne, Ott.		.15
☐	115	Bruce Gardiner, Ott.		.15
☐	116	Sergei Zholtok, Ott.		.15
☐	117	Alexandre Daigle, Ott.		.15
☐☐	118	4/11/97: Wade Redden, Ott.	75.00	.15
☐	119	Mikael Renberg, Pha.		.15
☐	120	Trent Klatt, Pha.		.15
☐☐	121	5/25/97: Rod Brind'Amour, Pha.	100.00	.25
☐	122	Dainius Zubrus, Pha.		.25
☐	123	John LeClair, Pha.		.75
☐☐	124	5/16/97: Janne Niinimaa, Pha.	100.00	.25
☐	**125**	**Vaclav Prospal, Pha., RC**		**.75**
☐☐	126	1/18/97: Keith Tkachuk, Pho.	150.00	.60
☐	127	Jeremy Roenick, Pho.		.50
☐	128	Mike Gartner, Pho.		.25
☐	129	Nikolai Khabibulin (G), Pho.		.50
☐	130	Chad Kilger, Pho.		.15
☐	131	Shane Doan, Pho.		.15
☐	132	Cliff Ronning, Pho.		.15
☐☐	133	1/15/97: Patrick Lalime (G), Pgh.	75.00	.15
☐	134	Greg Johnson, Pgh.		.15
☐☐	135	11/30/96: Ron Francis, Pgh.	125.00	.50
☐	136	Darius Kasparaitis, Pgh.		.15
☐	137	Petr Nedved, Pgh.		.15
☐	138	Jason Woolley, Pgh.		.15
☐	139	Fredrik Olausson, Pgh.		.15
☐	140	Harry York, Stl.		.15
☐☐	141	12/22/96: Brett Hull, Stl.	200.00	.75
☐	142	Chris Pronger, Stl.		.25
☐☐	143	11/1/96: Jim Campbell, Stl.	75.00	.15
☐	**144**	**Libor Zabransky, Stl., RC**		**.15**
☐	145	Grant Fuhr (G), Stl.		.25
☐	146	Pavol Demitra, Stl.		.15
☐☐	147	1/18/97: Owen Nolan, S.J.	100.00	.25
☐	148	Stephen Guolla, S.J.		.15
☐	149	Marcus Ragnarsson, S.J.		.15
☐	150	Bernie Nicholls, S.J.		.15
☐	151	Todd Gill, S.J.		.15
☐	152	Shean Donovan, S.J.		.15
☐	153	Corey Schwab (G), T.B.		.15
☐☐	154	2/20/97: Dino Ciccarelli, T.B.	100.00	.25
☐	155	Chris Gratton, T.B.		.25
☐	156	Alexander Selivanov, T.B.		.15
☐	157	Roman Hamrlik, T.B.		.25
☐	158	Daymond Langkow, T.B.		.15
☐	159	Paul Ysebaert, T.B.		.15
☐	160	Steve Sullivan, Tor.		.15
☐	161	Sergei Berezin, Tor.		.25
☐	162	Fredrik Modin, Tor.		.15
☐	163	Todd Warriner, Tor.		.15
☐	164	Wendel Clark, Tor.		.25
☐	165	Jason Podollan, Tor.		.15
☐	166	Darby Hendrickson, Tor.		.15
☐	167	Martin Gelinas, Van.		.15
☐☐	168	1/18/97: Pavel Bure, Van.	300.00	1.00
☐	169	Trevor Linden, Van.		.25
☐	170	Mike Sillinger, Van.		.15
☐	171	Corey Hirsch (G), Van.		.15
☐	**172**	**Lonny Bohonos, Van., RC**		**.15**
☐	173	Markus Naslund, Van.		.15
☐	174	Steve Konowalchuk, Wsh.		.15
☐	175	Dale Hunter, Wsh.		.15
☐	176	Joé Juneau, Wsh.		.15
☐	177	Adam Oates, Wsh.		.50
☐	178	Bill Ranford (G), Wsh.		.25
☐	179	Pat Peake, Wsh.		.15
☐	180	Sergei Gonchar, Wsh.		.15
☐	**181**	**Mike Leclerc, Ana., RC**		**.15**
☐	**182**	**Randy Robitaille, Bos., RC**		**.25**
☐	**183**	**Paxton Schafer (G), Bos., RC**		**.15**
☐	**184**	**Rumun Ndur, Buf., RC**		**.15**
☐	**185**	**Christian Laflamme, Chi., RC**		**.15**
☐	**186**	**Wade Belak, Col., RC**		**.15**
☐	**187**	**Mike Knuble, Det., RC**		**.15**
☐	188	Steve Kelly, Edm.		.15
☐	**189**	**Patrik Elias, N.J., RC**		**.50**
☐	**190**	**Ken Belanger, NYI., RC**		**.15**
☐	**191**	**Colin Forbes, Pha., RC**		**.15**
☐	192	Juha Ylönen, Pho.		.15
☐	**193**	**David Cooper, Tor., RC**		**.15**
☐	**194**	**D.J. Smith, Tor., RC**		**.15**
☐	195	Jaroslav Svejkovsky, Wsh.		.25
☐	196	Tie Domi, Tor.		.15
☐	197	Bob Probert, Chi.		.15
☐	198	Doug Gilmour, N.J.		.25
☐	199	Dino Ciccarelli, T.B.		.25
☐	200	Martin Gelinas, Van.		.15
☐	201	Tony Twist, Stl.		.15
☐	202	Claude Lemieux, Col.		.15
☐	203	Vladimir Konstantinov, Det.		.15
☐	204	Ulf Samuelsson, NYR.		.15
☐	205	Chris Simon, Wsh.		.15
☐	206	Gino Odjick, Van.		.15
☐	207	Mike Grier, Edm.		.25
☐	208	Tony Amonte, Chi.		.25
☐	209	CL: Wayne Gretzky, NYR.		.50
☐	210	CL: Patrick Roy (G), Col.		.35
☐☐	211	4/16/97: Paul Kariya, Ana.	600.00	2.00
☐	212	J.J. Daigneault, Ana.		.15
☐	213	Dmitri Mironov, Ana.		.15
☐	214	Joe Sacco, Ana.		.15
☐	215	Richard Park, Ana.		.15
☐	**216**	**Espen Knutsen, Ana., RC**		**.15**
☐	217	Dave Karpa, Ana.		.15
☐☐	218	6/21/97: Joe Thornton, Bos.	200.00	1.00
☐☐	219	6/21/97: Sergei Samsonov, Bos.	200.00	1.00
☐	220	P.J. Axerlsson, Bos.		.15
☐	221	Ted Donato, Bos.		.15
☐	222	Dean Chynoweth, Bos.		.15
☐	**223**	**Rob Tallas (G), Bos., RC**		**.15**
☐	224	Mattias Timander, Bos.		.15
☐☐	225	Dominik Hasek (G), Buf.	300.00	1.00
☐	226	Erik Rasmussen, Buf.		.15
☐☐	227	6/19/97: Michael Peca, Buf.	100.00	.25

☐ 228 Rob Ray, Buf. .15
☐ 229 Vaclav Varada, Buf. .15
☐ 230 Curtis Brown, Buf. .15
☐ 231 Jay McKee, Buf. .15
☐☐ 232 2/3/97: Theoren Fleury, Cgy. 125.00 .50
☐ **233 Derek Morris, Cgy., RC .50**
☐ 234 Chris Dingman, Cgy. .15
☐ 235 Chris O'Sullivan, Cgy. .15
☐ 236 Rick Tabaracci (G), Cgy. .15
☐ 237 Tommy Albelin, Cgy. .15
☐ 238 Todd Simpson, Cgy. .15
☐ 239 Sami Kapanen, Car. .15
☐☐ 240 10/1/97: Gary Roberts, Car. 100.00 .25
☐ 241 Kevin Dineen, Car. .15
☐ 242 Kevin Haller, Car. .15
☐ 243 Nelson Emerson, Car. .15
☐ 244 Glen Wesley, Car. .15
☐☐ 245 1/18/97: Tony Amonte, Chi. 100.00 .25
☐ 246 Eric Weinrich, Chi. .15
☐ 247 Daniel Cleary, Chi. .50
☐ 248 Jeff Shantz, Chi. .15
☐ 249 Jean-Yves Leroux, Chi. .15
☐ 250 Ethan Moreau, Chi. .15
☐ 251 Craig Mills, Chi. .15
☐☐ 252 5/2/97: Peter Forsberg, Col. 450.00 1.50
☐☐ 253 10/15/96: Joe Sakic, Col. 350.00 1.25
☐ 254 Valeri Kamensky, Col. .25
☐ 255 Adam Foote, Col. .25
☐ 256 Josef Marha, Col. .15
☐ **257 Christian Matte, Col., RC .15**
☐ 258 Aaron Miller, Col. .15
☐ 259 Ed Belfour (G), Dal. .50
☐ 260 Jamie Langenbrunner, Dal. .25
☐ **261 Juha Lind, Dal., RC .15**
☐ 262 Pat Verbeek, Dal. .15
☐ 263 Sergei Zubov, Dal. .25
☐ 264 Dave Reid, Dal. .15
☐ 265 Greg Adams, Dal. .15
☐☐ 266 6/7/97: Sergei Fedorov, Det. 200.00 .75
☐☐ 267 6/7/97: Nicklas Lidström, Det. 100.00 .25
☐☐ 268 Brendan Shanahan, Det. 250.00 .85
☐ 269 Chris Osgood (G), Det. .60
☐ 270 Aaron Ward, Det. .15
☐☐ 271 6/7/97: Vyacheslav Kozlov, Det. 75.00 .15
☐ 272 Kevin Hodson (G), Det. .15
☐☐ 273 4/29/97: Curtis Joseph (G), Edm. 250.00 .82
☐☐ 274 4/25/97: Ryan Smyth, Edm. 100.00 .25
☐ 275 Dean McAmmond, Edm. .15
☐ 276 Boris Mironov, Edm. .15
☐ 277 Dennis Bonvie, Edm. .15
☐ 278 Kelly Buchberger, Edm. .15
☐ 279 Kevin Lowe, Edm. .15
☐ 280 Ray Sheppard, Fla. .15
☐ 281 Rob Niedermayer, Fla. .15
☐☐ 282 10/27/96: Scott Mellanby, Fla. 75.00 .15
☐ 283 Terry Carkner, Fla. .15
☐ 284 Ed Jovanovski, Fla. .25
☐ 285 Gord Murphy, Fla. .15
☐ 286 Tom Fitzgerald, Fla. .15
☐ 287 Jamie Storr (G), L.A. .25
☐ **288 Olli Jokinen, L.A., RC .50**
☐ 289 Vladimir Tsyplakov, L.A. .15
☐☐ 290 10/12/97: Luc Robitaille, L.A. 100.00 .25
☐ 291 Vitali Yachmenev, L.A. .15
☐ **292 Donald MacLean, L.A., RC .15**
☐ 293 Saku Koivu, Mtl. 1.00
☐ 294 Andy Moog (G), Mtl. .25
☐ 295 Patrice Brisebois, Mtl. .15
☐ 296 Brad Brown, Mtl. .15
☐ 297 Turner Stevenson, Mtl. .15
☐ 298 Shayne Corson, Mtl. .25
☐ 299 Brian Savage, Mtl. .15
☐☐ 300 4/497: Martin Brodeur (G), N.J. 300.00 1.00
☐ 301 Scott Niedermayer, N.J. .25
☐ **302 Krzysztof Oliwa, N.J., RC .50**
☐ 303 Valeri Zelepukin, N.J. .15
☐ 304 Bobby Holik, N.J. .15
☐ 305 Ken Daneyko, N.J. .15
☐ 306 Lyle Odelein, N.J. .15
☐ 307 Travis Green, NYI. .15
☐ **308 Steve Webb, NYI., RC .15**
☐ 309 Dan Plante, NYI. .15
☐ 310 Bryan Smolinski, NYI. .15
☐ 311 Claude Lapointe, NYI. .15
☐ 312 Kenny Jonsson, NYI. .15
☐ 313 Ulf Samuelsson, NYR. .15
☐ 314 Jeff Beukeboom, NYR. .15
☐ 315 Mike Keane, NYR. .15
☐☐ 316 1/27/97: Brian Leetch, NYR. 125.00 .50
☐ 317 Shane Churla, NYR. .15
☐ 318 Pat LaFontaine, NYR. .25
☐ 319 Alexei Kovalev, NYR. .15
☐ 320 Radek Bonk, Ott. .15
☐ 321 Alexei Yashin, Ott. .60
☐ 322 Damian Rhodes (G), Ott. .15
☐ 323 Andreas Dackell, Ott. .15
☐ **324 Magnus Arvedsson, Ott., RC .15**
☐☐ 325 6/22/96: Chris Phillips, Ott. 100.00 .25
☐ **326 Marian Hossa, Ott., RC 3.00**
☐ 327 Chris Gratton, Pha. .25
☐ 328 Shjon Podein, Pha. .15
☐☐ 329 12/19/96: Paul Coffey, Pha. 100.00 .25
☐ 330 Luke Richardson, Pha. .15
☐☐ 331 1/18/97: Eric Lindros, Pha. 600.00 2.00
☐ 332 Eric Desjardins, Pha. .15
☐ 333 Joel Otto, Pha. .15
☐ 334 Craig Janney, Pho. .15
☐☐ 335 1/18/97: Oleg Tverdovsky, Pho. 75.00 .15
☐ 336 Teppo Numminen, Pho. .15
☐ 337 Jim McKenzie, Pho. .15
☐ 338 Dallas Drake, Pho. .15
☐ 339 Rick Tocchet, Pho. .15
☐ 340 Brad Isbister, Pho. .15
☐ 341 Alexei Morozov, Pgh. .75
☐☐ 342 11/30/96: Jaromir Jagr, Pgh. 450.00 1.50
☐ 343 Kevin Hatcher, Pgh. .15
☐ 344 Ken Wregget (G), Pgh. .15
☐ 345 Chris Tamer, Pgh. .15
☐ **346 Robert Dome, Pgh., RC .50**
☐ 347 Neil Wilkinson, Pgh. .15
☐ 348 Chris McAlpine, Stl. .15
☐ 349 Joe Murphy, Stl. .15
☐ 350 Robert Petrovicky, Stl. .15
☐ 351 Marc Bergevin, Stl. .15
☐ 352 Al MacInnis, Stl. .25
☐☐ 353 12/22/96: Pierre Turgeon, Stl. 100.00 .25
☐☐ 354 6/21/97: Patrick Marleau, S.J. 150.00 .75
☐ **355 Marco Sturm, S.J., RC .25**
☐ 356 Mike Vernon (G), S.J. .25
☐ 357 Al Iafrate, S.J. .15
☐ 358 Jeff Friesen, S.J. .25
☐ 359 Viktor Kozlov, S.J. .15
☐☐ 360 1/18/97: Tony Granato, S.J. 75.00 .15
☐ 361 Mikael Renberg, T.B. .15
☐ 362 Daren Puppa, T.B. .15
☐ 363 Roman Hamrlik, T.B. .25
☐ 364 Rob Zamuner, T.B. .25
☐ 365 Cory Cross, T.B. .15
☐ 366 Patrick Poulin, T.B. .15
☐ 367 Félix Potvin (G), Tor. .75
☐ 368 Tie Domi, Tor. .15
☐☐ 369 10/31/96: Mats Sundin, Tor. 200.00 .75
☐ 370 Jeff Ware, Tor. .15
☐ 371 Alyn McCauley, Tor. .75
☐ 372 Mathieu Schneider, Tor. .15
☐ 373 Craig Wolanin, Tor. .15
☐☐ 374 7/28/97: Mark Messier, Van. 200.00 .75
☐ 375 Kirk McLean (G), Van. .25
☐ 376 Donald Brashear, Van. .15
☐ 377 Arturs Irbe (G), Van. .15
☐ 378 Jyrki Lumme, Van. .15
☐ 379 Gino Odjick, Van. .15
☐ 380 Mattias Ohlund, Van. .50
☐ **381 Jan Bulis, Wsh., RC .25**
☐ 382 Andrew Brunette, Wsh. .15
☐ 383 Calle Johansson, Wsh. .15
☐ 384 Brendan Witt, Wsh. .15
☐ 385 Mark Tinordi, Wsh. .15
☐ 386 Ken Klee, Wsh. .15
☐ 387 Chris Simon, Wsh. .15
☐ 388 Richard Zednick, Wsh. .15
☐ 389 Ed Jovanovski, Fla. .25
☐ 390 Darren McCarty, Det. .15
☐ 391 Darius Kasparaitis, Pgh. .15
☐ 392 Bryan Marchment, Edm. .15
☐ 393 Matthew Barnaby, Buf. .15
☐ 394 Chris Chelios, Chi. .25
☐ 395 Ulf Samuelsson, NYR. .15
☐ 396 Scott Stevens, N.J. .15
☐ 397 Derian Hatcher, Dal. .25
☐ 398 Chris Pronger, Stl. .25
☐ **399 Mathieu Chouinard (G), Cdn., RC 1.00**
☐ **400 Jake McCraken (G), Cdn., RC 1.00**
☐ **401 Bryan Allen, Cdn., RC .75**
☐ **402 Christian Chartier, Cdn., RC .35**
☐ **403 Jonathan Girard, Cdn., RC .35**
☐ **404 Abe Hearst, Cdn., RC .35**
☐ **405 Stephen Peat, Cdn., RC .50**
☐ **406 Robyn Regehr, Cdn., RC .50**
☐ **407 Blair Betts, Cdn., RC .35**
☐ **408 Eric Chouinard (G), Cdn., RC .50**
☐ **409 Brett DeCecco, Cdn., RC .35**
☐ **410 Rico Fata, Cdn., RC 3.50**
☐ **411 Simon Gagné, Cdn., RC .75**
☐ **412 Vincent Lecavalier, Cdn., RC 10.00**
☐ **413 Manny Malhotra, Cdn., RC 3.50**
☐ **414 Norm Milley, Cdn., RC .50**
☐ **415 Justin Papineau, Cdn., RC .75**
☐ **416 Garrett Prosofsky, Cdn., RC .50**
☐ **417 Mike Ribeiro, Cdn., RC 2.00**
☐ **418 Brad Richards, Cdn., RC .50**
☐ 419 CL: Wayne Gretzky, NYR. .50
☐ 420 CL: Patrick Roy (G), Col. .35

THE SPECIALISTS

These cards have two versions: a Level 1 insert (limited to 4,000 copies) and a Level 2 parallel (serial numbered from 1 to 100).

Insert Set (30 cards): 450.00

	No.	Player	Level 2	Level 1
☐☐	S1	Wayne Gretzky, NYR.	1,300.00	50.00
☐☐	S2	Patrick Roy (G), Col.	1,000.00	40.00
☐☐	S3	Jaromir Jagr, Pgh.	550.00	25.00
☐☐	S4	Joe Sakic, Col.	400.00	20.00
☐☐	S5	Mark Messier, NYR.	250.00	12.00
☐☐	S6	Eric Lindros, Pha.	750.00	35.00
☐☐	S7	John Vanbiesbrouck (G), Fla.	300.00	15.00
☐☐	S8	Teemu Selänne, Ana.	350.00	18.00
☐☐	S9	Paul Kariya, Ana.	750.00	35.00
☐☐	S10	Pavel Bure, Van.	350.00	18.00
☐☐	S11	Sergei Fedorov, Det.	250.00	12.00
☐☐	S12	Peter Bondra, Wsh.	200.00	10.00
☐☐	S13	Mats Sundin, Tor.	250.00	12.00
☐☐	S14	Brendan Shanahan, Det.	300.00	15.00
☐☐	S15	Keith Tkachuk, Pho.	200.00	10.00
☐☐	S16	Brett Hull, Stl.	250.00	12.00
☐☐	S17	Jeremy Roenick, Pho.	150.00	8.00
☐☐	S18	Dominik Hasek (G), Buf.	350.00	18.00
☐☐	S19	Steve Yzerman, Det.	550.00	25.00
☐☐	S20	John LeClair, Pha.	250.00	12.00
☐☐	S21	Peter Forsberg, Col.	550.00	25.00
☐☐	S22	Zigmund Palffy, NYI.	150.00	8.00
☐☐	S23	Tony Amonte, Chi.	100.00	6.00
☐☐	S24	Jarome Iginla, Cgy.	150.00	8.00
☐☐	S25	Curtis Joseph (G), Edm.	300.00	15.00
☐☐	S26	Mike Modano, Dal.	250.00	12.00
☐☐	S27	Ray Bourque, Bos.	250.00	12.00
☐☐	S28	Brian Leetch, NYR.	150.00	8.00
☐☐	S29	Bryan Berard, NYI.	150.00	8.00
☐☐	S30	Martin Brodeur (G), N.J.	350.00	18.00

3 STAR SELECTIONS

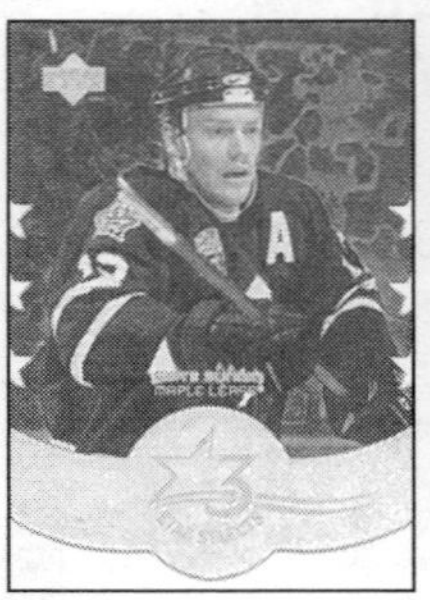

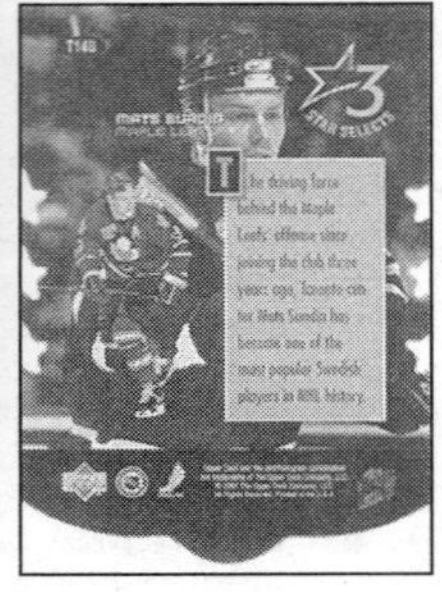

Series One insertion ratio is [1:4].

Insert Set (60 cards): 120.00

	No.	Player	NRMT-MT
☐	T1A	Eric Lindros, Pha.	8.00
☐	T1B	Wayne Gretzky, NYR.	12.00
☐	T1C	Peter Forsberg, Col.	6.00
☐	T2A	Dominik Hasek (G), Chi.	4.00
☐	T2B	Patrick Roy (G), Col.	10.00
☐	T2C	John Vanbiesbrouck (G), Fla.	3.50
☐	T3A	Joe Sakic, Col.	5.00
☐	T3B	Steve Yzerman, Det.	6.00
☐	T4A	Bryan Berard, NYI.	1.75
☐	T4B	Brian Leetch, NYR.	1.75
☐	T4C	Chris Chelios, Chi.	2.50
☐	T5A	Teemu Selänne, Ana.	4.00
☐	T5B	Jaromir Jagr, Pgh.	6.00
☐	T5C	Pavel Bure, Van.	4.00
☐	T6A	Owen Nolan, S.J.	1.25
☐	T6B	Brendan Shanahan, Det.	3.50
☐	T6C	Keith Tkachuk, Pho.	2.50
☐	T7A	Sergei Fedorov, Det.	3.00
☐	T7B	Niklas Sundstrom, NYR.	1.25
☐	T7C	Michael Peca, Buf.	1.25
☐	T8A	Janne Niinimaa, Pha.	1.25
☐	T8B	Saku Koivu, Mtl.	4.00
☐	T8C	Jere Lehtinen, Dal.	1.25
☐	T9A	Tony Amonte, Chi.	1.25
☐	T9B	John LeClair, Pha.	3.00
☐	T9C	Brett Hull, Stl.	3.00
☐	T10A	Martin Brodeur (G), N.J.	4.00
☐	T10B	Curtis Joseph (G), Edm.	3.50
☐	T10C	Mike Richter (G), NYR.	1.75
☐	T11A	Ray Bourque, Bos.	3.00
☐	T11B	Mark Messier, Van.	3.00
☐	T11C	Scott Stevens, N.J.	1.00
☐	T12A	Patrick Lalime (G), Pgh.	1.00
☐	T12B	Marc Denis (G), Col.	1.50
☐	T12C	José Théodore (G), Mtl.	1.75
☐	T13A	Adam Deadmarsh, Col.	1.00
☐	T13B	Doug Weight, Edm.	1.75
☐	T13C	Bill Guerin, N.J.	1.50
☐	T14A	Daniel Alfredsson, Ott.	1.50
☐	T14B	Mats Sundin, Tor.	3.00
☐	T14C	Nicklas Lidström, Det.	1.50
☐	T15A	Jim Campbell, Stl.	1.00
☐	T15B	Dainius Zubrus, Pha.	1.50
☐	T15C	Daymond Langkow, T.B.	1.00
☐	T16A	Mike Grier, Edm.	1.50
☐	T16B	Mike Modano, Dal.	3.00
☐	T16C	Jeremy Roenick, Pho.	1.75
☐	T17A	Jason Arnott, Edm.	1.50
☐	T17B	Trevor Linden, Van.	1.50
☐	T17C	Rod Brind'Amour, Pha.	1.50
☐	T18A	Adam Oates, Wsh.	1.75
☐	T18B	Doug Gilmour, N.J.	1.75
☐	T18C	Joé Juneau, Wsh.	1.00
☐	T19A	Sergei Berezin, Tor.	1.50
☐	T19B	Alexander Mogilny, Van.	1.75
☐	T19C	Alexei Zhamnov, Chi.	1.00
☐	T20A	Derian Hatcher, Dal.	1.50
☐	T20B	Wade Redden, Ott.	1.00
☐	T20C	Sandis Ozolinsh, Col.	1.50

GAME JERSEYS

Series One insertion ratio is [1:2,500]. The Roy autograph is limited to 33 copies while the Gretzky autograph is limited to 99 copies. Card GJ10 does not exist.

Series 1 Insert Set (7 cards):
Series 2 Insert Set (6 cards):

	No.	Player	NRMT-MT
☐	GJ1	Patrick Roy (G), Col.-Home	750.00
☐	GJ2	Patrick Roy (G), Col.-Away	750.00
☐	GJ3	Dominik Hasek (G), Buf.	400.00
☐	GJ4	Jarome Iginla, Cgy.	200.00
☐	GJ5	Sergei Fedorov, Det.	300.00
☐	GJ6	Tony Amonte, Chi.	200.00
☐	GJ7	Joe Sakic, Que. (Col.)	450.00
☐	GJ8	Wayne Gretzky, NYR.	1,000.00
☐	GJ9	Saku Koivu, Mtl.	400.00
☐	GJ11	Mike Richter (G), NYR.	250.00
☐	GJ12	Doug Weight, Edm.	200.00
☐	GJ13	Brendan Shanahan, N.J. (Det.)	350.00
☐	GJ14	Brian Leetch, NYR.	250.00
		Autograph	**NRMT-MT**
☐		Patrick Roy Autograph	3,000.00
☐		Wayne Gretzky Autograph	4,000.00

SIXTH SENSE

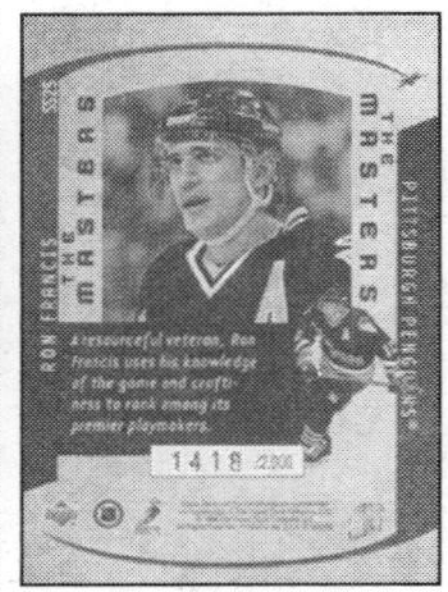

These Series Two cards have two versions: a Masters insert (#/2000) and a Wizards insert (#/100).

Insert Set (30 cards): 600.00

	No.	Player	Wiz.	Master
☐ ☐	SS1	Wayne Gretzky, NYR.	1,000.00	75.00
☐ ☐	SS2	Jaromir Jagr, Pgh.	500.00	35.00
☐ ☐	SS3	Sergei Fedorov, Det.	250.00	18.00
☐ ☐	SS4	Brett Hull, Stl.	250.00	18.00
☐ ☐	SS5	Brian Leetch, NYR.	150.00	15.00
☐ ☐	SS6	Joe Thornton, Bos.	250.00	20.00
☐ ☐	SS7	Ray Bourque, Bos.	250.00	18.00
☐ ☐	SS8	Teemu Selänne, Ana.	350.00	25.00
☐ ☐	SS9	Paul Kariya, Ana.	650.00	50.00
☐ ☐	SS10	Doug Weight, Edm.	150.00	12.00
☐ ☐	SS11	Mark Messier, Van.	250.00	18.00
☐ ☐	SS12	Adam Oates, Wsh.	150.00	12.00
☐ ☐	SS13	Mats Sundin, Tor.	250.00	18.00
☐ ☐	SS14	Brendan Shanahan, Det.	300.00	20.00
☐ ☐	SS15	Saku Koivu, Mtl.	350.00	25.00
☐ ☐	SS16	Doug Gilmour, N.J.	150.00	12.00
☐ ☐	SS17	Eric Lindros, Pha.	650.00	50.00
☐ ☐	SS18	Tony Amonte, Chi.	100.00	10.00
☐ ☐	SS19	Joe Sakic, Col.	400.00	30.00
☐ ☐	SS20	Steve Yzerman, Det.	500.00	35.00
☐ ☐	SS21	Peter Forsberg, Col.	500.00	35.00
☐ ☐	SS22	Geoff Sanderson, Hfd.	100.00	10.00
☐ ☐	SS23	Keith Tkachuk, Pho.	200.00	15.00
☐ ☐	SS24	Pavel Bure, Van.	350.00	25.00
☐ ☐	SS25	Ron Francis, Pgh.	150.00	12.00
☐ ☐	SS26	Zigmund Palffy, NYI.	150.00	12.00
☐ ☐	SS27	Daniel Alfredsson, Ott.	100.00	10.00
☐ ☐	SS28	Bryan Berard, NYI.	150.00	12.00
☐ ☐	SS29	Mike Modano, Dal.	250.00	18.00
☐ ☐	SS30	Patrick Roy (G), Col.	800.00	60.00

SMOOTH GROOVES

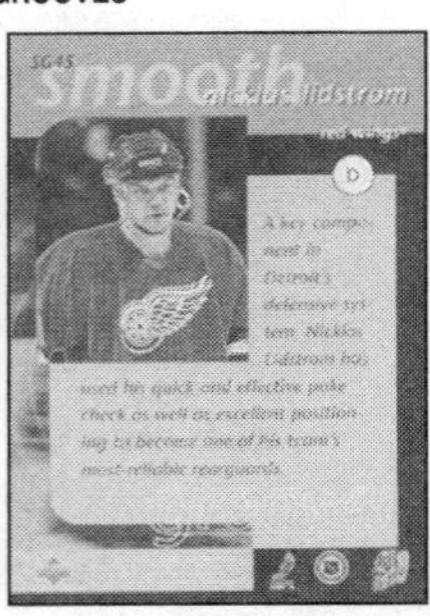

Insert Set (60 cards): 120.00

	No.	Player	NRMT-MT
☐	SG1	Wayne Gretzky, NYR.	12.00
☐	SG2	Patrick Roy (G), Col.	10.00
☐	SG3	Patrick Marleau, S.J.	2.50
☐	SG4	Martin Brodeur (G), N.J.	4.00
☐	SG5	Zigmund Palffy, NYI.	2.00
☐	SG6	Joe Thornton, Bos.	3.50
☐	SG7	Chris Chelios, Chi.	2.50
☐	SG8	Teemu Selänne, Ana.	4.00
☐	SG9	Paul Kariya, Ana.	8.00
☐	SG10	Tony Amonte, Chi.	1.50
☐	SG11	Mark Messier, Van.	3.00
☐	SG12	Jarome Iginla, Cgy.	2.00
☐	SG13	Mats Sundin, Tor.	3.00
☐	SG14	Brendan Shanahan,Det.	3.50
☐	SG15	Ed Jovanovski, Fla.	1.50
☐	SG16	Brett Hull, Stl.	3.00
☐	SG17	Brian Rolston, N.J.	1.00
☐	SG18	Saku Koivu, Mtl.	4.00
☐	SG19	Steve Yzerman, Det.	6.00
☐	SG20	Doug Weight, Edm.	2.00
☐	SG21	Peter Forsberg, Col.	6.00
☐	SG22	Brian Leetch, NYR.	2.00
☐	SG23	Alexei Yashin, Ott.	2.50
☐	SG24	Owen Nolan, S.J.	1.50
☐	SG25	Mike Grier, Edm.	1.50
☐	SG26	Jere Lehtinen, Dal.	1.50
☐	SG27	Vaclav Prospal, Pha.	2.00
☐	SG28	Sandis Ozolinsh, Col.	1.50
☐	SG29	Mike Modano, Dal.	3.00
☐	SG30	Sergei Samsonov, Bos.	2.50
☐	SG31	Curtis Joseph (G), Edm.	3.50
☐	SG32	Daymond Langkow, T.B.	1.00
☐	SG33	Doug Gilmour, N.J.	2.00
☐	SG34	Bryan Berard, NYI.	2.00
☐	SG35	Joe Sakic, Col.	5.00
☐	SG36	Wade Redden, Ott.	1.00
☐	SG37	Keith Tkachuk, Pho.	2.50
☐	SG38	Jaromir Jagr, Pgh.	6.00
☐	SG39	Dominik Hasek (G), Buf.	4.00
☐	SG40	Patrick Lalime (G), Pgh.	1.00
☐	SG41	Janne Niinimaa, Pha.	1.50
☐	SG42	Oleg Tverdovsky, Pho.	1.00
☐	SG43	Vitali Yachmenev, L.A.	1.00
☐	SG44	Rob Niedermayer, Fla.	1.00
☐	SG45	Nicklas Lidström, Det.	1.50
☐	SG46	Jim Campbell, Stl.	1.00
☐	SG47	Roman Hamrlik, T.B.	1.50
☐	SG48	Eric Lindros, Pha.	8.00
☐	SG49	Brian Holzinger, Buf.	1.00
☐	SG50	John LeClair, Pha.	3.00
☐	SG51	Sergei Berezin, Tor.	1.50
☐	SG52	Jaroslav Svejkovsky, Wsh.	1.50
☐	SG53	Mike Richter (G), NYR.	2.00
☐	SG54	John Vanbiesbrouck (G), Fla.	3.50
☐	SG55	Keith Primeau, Car.	1.50
☐	SG56	Adam Oates, Wsh.	2.00
☐	SG57	Jeremy Roenick, Pho.	2.00
☐	SG58	Pavel Bure, Van.	4.00
☐	SG59	Dainius Zubrus, Pha.	1.50
☐	SG60	José Théodore (G), Mtl.	2.00

1997 - 98 UPPER DECK BLACK DIAMOND

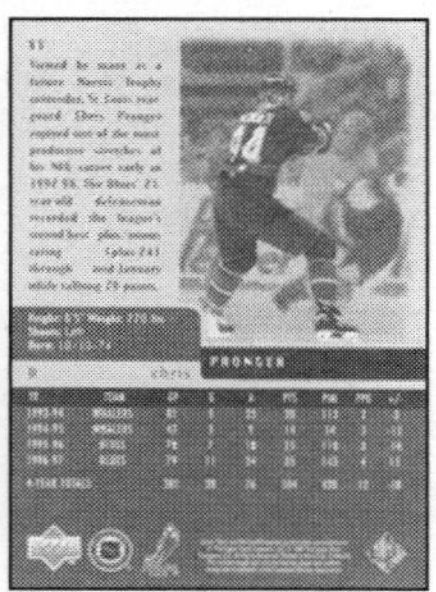

These cards have four versions: a Single diamond, a Double diamond parallel, a Triple diamond parallel and a Quadruple diamond parallel. The Quadruple Diamond parallel is limited to 50 copies.

Imprint: © 1998 THE UPPER DECK COMPANY, LLC.

Complete Set (150 cards): 300.00 150.00 125.00

Common Player: 20.00 1.00 .35 .20

	No.	Player	Quad.	Triple	Double	Single
□□□□	1	Alexei Zhitnik, Buf.	20.00	1.00	.35	.20
□□□□	2	Adam Graves, NYR.	20.00	1.00	.35	.20
□□□□	3	Keith Primeau, Car.	30.00	2.50	1.00	.50
□□□□	4	Mike Richter (G), NYR.	50.00	5.00	1.75	.85
□□□□	5	Félix Potvin (G), Tor.	100.00	10.00	3.00	1.50
□□□□	6	Valeri Bure, Mtl.	20.00	1.00	.35	.20
□□□□	7	Mark Messier, Van.	100.00	10.00	3.00	1.50
□□□□	8	Dainius Zubrus, Pha.	30.00	2.50	1.00	.50
□□□□	9	Owen Nolan, S.J.	30.00	2.50	1.00	.50
□□□□	10	Kenny Jonsson, NYI.	20.00	1.00	.35	.20
□□□□	11	Ron Francis, Pgh.	50.00	5.00	1.75	.85
□□□□	12	Bryan Berard, NYI.	50.00	5.00	1.75	.85
□□□□	**13**	**Eric Messier, Col., RC**	**20.00**	**1.50**	**.75**	**.50**
□□□□	14	Paul Kariya, Ana.	400.00	25.00	8.00	4.00
□□□□	**15**	**Teemu Elomo, Fin., RC**	**30.00**	**2.50**	**1.25**	**1.00**
□□□□	16	Joe Nieuwendyk, Dal.	30.00	2.50	1.00	.50
□□□□	17	Scott Stevens, N.J.	20.00	1.00	.35	.20
□□□□	18	Zigmund Palffy, NYI.	50.00	5.00	1.75	.85
□□□□	19	Brett Hull, Stl.	100.00	10.00	3.00	1.50
□□□□	20	Dominik Hasek, Buf.	175.00	15.00	4.00	2.00
□□□□	21	Dino Ciccarelli, Fla.	30.00	2.50	1.00	.50
□□□□	22	Rob Niedermayer, Fla.	20.00	1.00	.35	.20
□□□□	23	Mark Recchi, Mtl.	30.00	2.50	1.00	.50
□□□□	24	Brad Isbister, Pho.	20.00	1.00	.35	.20
□□□□	**25**	**Timo Vertala, Fin., RC**	**25.00**	**2.00**	**1.00**	**.75**
□□□□	**26**	**Mika Noronen (G), Fin., RC**	**40.00**	**5.00**	**2.50**	**2..00**
□□□□	27	Sandis Ozolinsh, Col.	30.00	2.50	1.00	.50
□□□□	28	Chris Phillips, Ott.	30.00	2.50	1.00	.50
□□□□	29	Chris Chelios, Chi.	75.00	7.50	2.50	1.25
□□□□	30	Jason Dawe, Buf.	20.00	1.00	.35	.20
□□□□	31	Kirk McLean (G), Car.	30.00	2.50	1.00	.50
□□□□	32	Jason Allison, Bos.	20.00	1.00	.35	.20
		(xcx: D.Weight)	50.00	5.00	1.75	.85
□□□□	33	Brian Leetch, NYR.	50.00	5.00	1.75	.85
□□□□	34	Guy Hebert (G), Ana.	30.00	2.50	1.00	.50
□□□□	**35**	**David Legwand, USA., RC**	**350.00**	**25.00**	**15.00**	**12.00**
□□□□	**36**	**Pierre Hedin, Swe., RC**	**20.00**	**1.50**	**.75**	**.50**
□□□□	37	Sergei Samsonov, Bos.	125.00	12.00	3.50	2.00
□□□□	38	Bill Guerin, Edm.	30.00	2.50	1.00	.50
□□□□	39	Chris Osgood (G), Det.	75.00	7.50	2.50	1.25
□□□□	40	Jere Lehtinen, Dal.	30.00	2.50	1.00	.50
□□□□	41	Patrick Roy (G), Col.	450.00	30.00	10.00	5.00
□□□□	42	John Vanbiesbrouck (G), Fla.	135.00	12.00	3.50	1.75
□□□□	**43**	**Maxim Afinogenov, Rus., RC**	**25.00**	**2.00**	**1.00**	**.75**
□□□□	**44**	**Patrik Elias, N.J., RC**	**35.00**	**4.00**	**2.00**	**1.50**
□□□□	45	Josh Holden, Cdn.	30.00	2.50	1.50	.75
□□□□	46	Saku Koivu, Mtl.	175.00	15.00	4.00	2.00
□□□□	**47**	**Maxim Balmockhnykh, Rus., RC**	**20.00**	**1.50**	**.75**	**.50**
□□□□	48	Pasi Petriläinen, Fin.	30.00	2.50	1.50	.75
□□□□	49	Robert Reichel, NYI.	20.00	1.00	.35	.20
□□□□	50	Wade Redden, Ott.	20.00	1.00	.35	.20
□□□□	51	Richard Zednik, Wsh.	20.00	1.00	.35	.20
□□□□	**52**	**Ty Jones, USA., RC**	**25.00**	**2.00**	**1.00**	**.75**
□□□□	53	Nikolai Khabibulin (G), Pho.	50.00	5.00	1.75	.85
□□□□	54	Kyle McLaren, Bos.	20.00	1.00	.35	.20
□□□□	55	Daniel Tkaczuk, Cdn.	35.00	3.00	2.00	1.00
□□□□	56	Alexei Zhamnov, Chi.	20.00	1.00	.35	.20
□□□□	**57**	**Donald MacLean, L.A., RC**	**20.00**	**1.50**	**.75**	**.50**
□□□□	58	Dave Gagner, Fla.	20.00	1.00	.35	.20
□□□□	59	Jeremy Roenick, Pho.	50.00	5.00	1.75	.85
□□□□	60	Ray Bourque, Bos.	100.00	10.00	3.00	1.50
□□□□	61	Rod Brind'Amour, Pha.	30.00	2.50	1.00	.50
□□□□	62	Miroslav Satan, Buf.	20.00	1.00	.35	.20
□□□□	63	Eric Dazé, Chi.	30.00	2.50	1.00	.50
□□□□	64	Mike Ricci, Col.	20.00	1.00	.35	.20
□□□□	65	John LeClair, Pha.	100.00	10.00	3.00	1.50
□□□□	66	Bryan Marchment, T.B.	20.00	1.00	.35	.20
□□□□	**67**	**Henrik Petré, Swe., RC**	**20.00**	**1.50**	**.75**	**.50**
□□□□	68	John MacLean, S.J.	20.00	1.00	.35	.20
□□□□	**69**	**Artem Chubarov, Rus., RC**	**20.00**	**1.50**	**.75**	**.50**
□□□□	70	Doug Gilmour, N.J.	50.00	5.00	1.75	.85
□□□□	**71**	**Marco Sturm, S.J., RC**	**30.00**	**2.50**	**1.25**	**1.00**
□□□□	72	Jaromir Jagr, Pgh.	300.00	20.00	6.00	3.00
□□□□	73	Daniel Alfredsson, Ott.	30.00	2.50	1.00	.50
□□□□	74	Daren Puppa (G), T.B.	20.00	1.00	.35	.20
□□□□	75	Adam Deadmarsh, Col.	20.00	1.00	.35	.20
□□□□	76	Luc Robitaille, L.A.	30.00	2.50	1.00	.50
		(xcx: G. Murray)				
□□□□	77	Mats Sundin, Tor.	100.00	10.00	3.00	1.50
□□□□	78	Dan Cloutier (G), NYR.	30.00	2.50	1.00	.50
□□□□	**79**	**Manny Malhotra, Cdn., RC**	**100.00**	**10.00**	**5.00**	**4.00**
□□□□	80	Mike Modano, Dal.	100.00	10.00	3.00	1.50
□□□□	**81**	**Espen Knutsen, Ana., RC**	**20.00**	**1.50**	**.75**	**.50**
□□□□	82	Sergei Fedorov, Det.	100.00	10.00	3.00	1.50
□□□□	83	Chris Pronger, Stl.	30.00	2.50	1.00	.50
□□□□	84	Doug Weight, Edm.	50.00	5.00	1.75	.85
□□□□	85	Dmitri Nabakov, Chi.	20.00	1.00	.35	.20
□□□□	86	Gary Roberts, Car.	30.00	2.50	1.00	.50
□□□□	87	Peter Bondra, Wsh.	75.00	7.50	2.50	1.25
□□□□	**88**	**Robert Dome, Pgh., RC**	**30.00**	**2.50**	**1.25**	**1.00**
□□□□	**89**	**Jan Bulis, Wsh., RC**	**20.00**	**1.50**	**.75**	**.50**
□□□□	**90**	**Eric Brewer, Cdn., RC**	**65.00**	**8.00**	**4.00**	**3.00**
□□□□	**91**	**Nikos Tselios, USA., RC**	**35.00**	**4.00**	**2.00**	**1.50**
□□□□	92	Scott Mellanby, Fla.	20.00	1.00	.35	.20
□□□□	**93**	**Vitali Vishnevsky, Rus., RC**	**20.00**	**1.50**	**.75**	**.50**
□□□□	94	Derian Hatcher, Dal.	30.00	2.50	1.00	.50
□□□□	95	Teemu Selänne, Ana.	175.00	15.00	4.00	2.00
□□□□	96	Joe Sakic, Col.	225.00	18.00	5.00	2.50
□□□□	97	Alexander Mogilny, Van.	50.00	5.00	1.75	.85
□□□□	**98**	**Jesse Boulerice, USA., RC**	**20.00**	**1.50**	**.75**	**.50**
□□□□	**99**	**Johan Forsander, Swe., RC**	**20.00**	**1.50**	**.75**	**.50**
□□□□	100	Pierre Turgeon, Stl.	30.00	2.50	1.00	.50
		(xcx: T. Harvey)				
□□□□	101	Tony Amonte, Chi.	30.00	2.50	1.00	.50
□□□□	**102**	**Timo Ahmaoja, Fin., RC**	**20.00**	**1.50**	**.75**	**.50**
□□□□	103	Rob Blake, L.A.	30.00	2.50	1.00	.50
□□□□	**104**	**Derek Morris, Cgy., RC**	**30.00**	**2.50**	**1.25**	**1.00**
□□□□	**105**	**Alex Tanguay, Cdn., RC**	**65.00**	**8.00**	**4.00**	**3.00**
□□□□	106	Peter Forsberg, Col.	300.00	20.00	6.00	3.00
□□□□	107	Shayne Corson, Mtl.	30.00	2.50	1.00	.50
□□□□	**108**	**Tyler Moss (G), Cgy., RC**	**25.00**	**2.00**	**1.00**	**.75**
□□□□	109	Adam Oates, Wsh.	50.00	5.00	1.75	.85
□□□□	110	Keith Tkachuk, Pho.	75.00	7.50	2.50	1.25
□□□□	111	Alexei Yashin, Ott.	75.00	7.50	2.50	1.25
□□□□	112	Joe Thornton, Bos.	125.00	12.00	3.50	2.00
□□□□	113	Andy Moog (G), Mtl.	30.00	2.50	1.00	.50
□□□□	**114**	**Daniel Sedin, Swe., RC**	**100.00**	**10.00**	**6.00**	**5.00**
□□□□	115	Pavel Bure, Van.	175.00	15.00	4.00	2.00
□□□□	**116**	**Denis Shvidky, Rus., RC**	**65.00**	**8.00**	**4.00**	**3.00**
□□□□	117	Jason Arnott, N.J.	30.00	2.50	1.00	.50
□□□□	**118**	**Mike Johnson, Tor., RC**	**100.00**	**10.00**	**6.00**	**5.00**
□□□□	119	Nicklas Lidström, Det.	30.00	2.50	1.00	.50
□□□□	120	Mattias Ohlund, Van.	30.00	2.50	1.50	.75
□□□□	121	Alexander Selivanov, T.B.	20.00	1.00	.35	.20
□□□□	122	Martin Brodeur (G), N.J.	175.00	15.00	4.00	2.00
□□□□	123	Steve Yzerman, Det.	300.00	20.00	6.00	3.00
□□□□	**124**	**Dmitri Vlassenkov, Rus., RC**	**20.00**	**1.50**	**.75**	**.50**
□□□□	**125**	**Jeff Farkas, USA., RC**	**30.00**	**2.50**	**1.25**	**1.00**
□□□□	126	Curtis Joseph (G), Edm.	135.00	12.00	3.50	1.75
□□□□	127	Yanic Perreault, L.A.	20.00	1.00	.35	.20
□□□□	128	Alyn McCauley, Tor.	65.00	6.50	3.00	1.50
□□□□	129	Vyacheslav Kozlov, Det.	20.00	1.00	.35	.20
□□□□	130	Alexei Morozov, Pgh.	65.00	6.50	3.00	1.50
□□□□	**131**	**Roberto Luongo (G), Cdn., RC**	**250.00**	**20.00**	**10.00**	**8.00**
□□□□	132	Jarome Iginla, Cgy.	50.00	5.00	1.75	.85
□□□□	133	Pat LaFontaine, NYR.	30.00	2.50	1.00	.50
□□□□	134	Ed Belfour (G), Dal.	50.00	5.00	1.75	.85
□□□□	**135**	**Toby Peterson, USA., RC**	**20.00**	**1.50**	**.75**	**.50**
□□□□	**136**	**Henrik Sedin, Swe., RC**	**100.00**	**10.00**	**6.00**	**5.00**
□□□□	137	Marcus Nilsson, Swe.	20.00	1.00	.35	.20
□□□□	138	Cameron Mann, Cdn.	30.00	2.50	1.50	.75
□□□□	**139**	**Eero Somervuori, Fin., RC**	**30.00**	**2.50**	**1.25**	**1.00**
□□□□	140	Patrick Marleau, S.J.	65.00	6.50	3.00	1.50
□□□□	141	Ed Jovanovski, Fla.	30.00	2.50	1.00	.50
□□□□	142	Roman Hamrlik, T.B.	30.00	2.50	1.00	.50
□□□□	143	Theoren Fleury, Cgy.	50.00	5.00	1.75	.85
□□□□	144	Wayne Gretzky, NYR.	600.00	40.00	12.00	6.00
□□□□	145	Eric Lindros, Pha.	400.00	25.00	8.00	4.00
□□□□	146	Boyd Devereaux, Edm.	20.00	1.00	.35	.20
□□□□	147	Sami Kapanen, Car.	20.00	1.00	.35	.20
□□□□	148	Grant Fuhr (G), Stl.	30.00	2.50	1.00	.50
□□□□	149	Brendan Shanahan, Det.	135.00	12.00	3.50	1.75
□□□□	**150**	**Vincent Lecavalier, Cdn., RC**	**400.00**	**30.00**	**15.00**	**12.00**

PREMIUM CUT

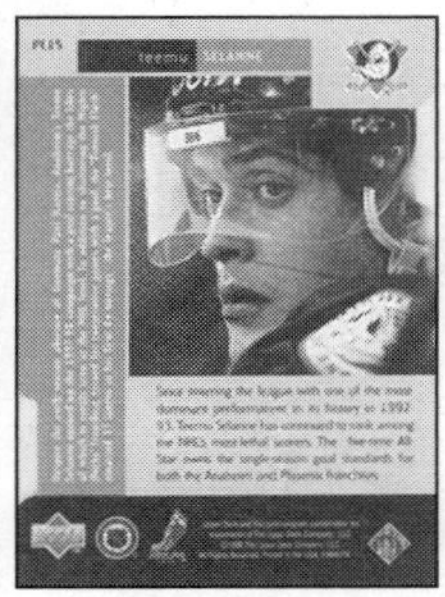

These cards have four versions: a Single diamond, a Double diamond parallel, a Triple diamond parallel and a Quadruple diamond parallel.

Insert Set (30 cards): 600.00 300.00 250.00

	No.	Player	Quad.	Triple	Double	Single
□□□□	PC1	Wayne Gretzky, NYR.	350.00	100.00	45.00	30.00
□□□□	PC2	Patrick Roy (G), Col.	250.00	75.00	35.00	25.00
□□□□	PC3	Brendan Shanahan, Det.	75.00	30.00	12.00	8.00
□□□□	PC4	Ray Bourque, Bos.	60.00	25.00	9.00	6.00
□□□□	PC5	Alexei Morozov, Pgh.	50.00	20.00	7.50	5.00
□□□□	PC6	John LeClair, Pha.	60.00	25.00	9.00	6.00
□□□□	PC7	Steve Yzerman, Det.	150.00	50.00	22.00	15.00
□□□□	PC8	Patrik Elias, N.J.	30.00	10.00	4.50	3.00
□□□□	PC9	Pavel Bure, Van.	100.00	35.00	15.00	10.00
□□□□	PC10	Brian Leetch, NYR.	40.00	15.00	6.00	4.00
□□□□	PC11	Peter Forsberg, Col.	150.00	50.00	22.00	15.00
□□□□	PC12	Marco Sturm, S.J.	30.00	10.00	4.50	3.00
□□□□	PC13	Eric Lindros, Pha.	200.00	65.00	30.00	20.00
□□□□	PC14	Keith Tkachuk, Pho.	50.00	20.00	7.50	5.00
□□□□	PC15	Teemu Selänne, Ana.	100.00	35.00	15.00	10.00
□□□□	PC16	Bryan Berard, NYI.	40.00	15.00	6.00	4.00
□□□□	PC17	Joe Thornton, Bos.	60.00	25.00	9.00	6.00
□□□□	PC18	Brett Hull, Stl.	60.00	25.00	9.00	6.00
□□□□	PC19	Nicklas Lidström, Det.	30.00	10.00	4.50	3.00
□□□□	PC20	Jaromir Jagr, Pgh.	150.00	50.00	22.00	15.00
□□□□	PC21	Vaclav Prospal, Pha.	40.00	15.00	6.00	4.00
□□□□	PC22	Pat LaFontaine, NYR.	30.00	10.00	4.50	3.00
□□□□	PC23	Mark Messier, Van.	60.00	25.00	9.00	6.00
□□□□	PC24	Martin Brodeur (G), N.J.	100.00	35.00	15.00	10.00
□□□□	PC25	Mike Modano, Dal.	60.00	25.00	9.00	6.00
□□□□	PC26	Paul Kariya, Ana.	200.00	65.00	30.00	20.00
□□□□	PC27	Mike Johnson, Tor.	60.00	25.00	9.00	6.00
□□□□	PC28	Sergei Samsonov, Bos.	60.00	25.00	9.00	6.00
□□□□	PC29	Joe Sakic, Col.	125.00	40.00	18.00	12.00
□□□□	PC30	Mats Sundin, Tor.	60.00	25.00	9.00	6.00

PREMIUM CUT MYSTERY HORIZONTAL

These cards are all quadruple diamond horzontals.

	No.	Player	NRMT-MT
□	PC1	Wayne Gretzky, NYR. (1 of 10)	Very Rare
□	PC2	Patrick Roy (G), Col. (1 of 10)	Very Rare
□	PC3	Brendan Shanahan, Det. [1:15,000]	Very Rare
□	PC4	Ray Bourque, Bos. [1:90]	25.00
□	PC5	Alexei Morozov, Pgh. [1:90]	20.00
□	PC6	John LeClair, Pha. [1:2,000]	125.00
□	PC7	Steve Yzerman, Det. [1:90]	50.00
□	PC8	Patrik Elias, N.J. [1:30]	10.00
□	PC9	Pavel Bure, Van. [1:2,000]	175.00
□	PC10	Brian Leetch, NYR. [1:30]	15.00
□	PC11	Peter Forsberg, Col. [1:2,000]	250.00
□	PC12	Marco Sturm, S.J. [1:90]	15.00
□	PC13	Eric Lindros, Pha. [1:15,000]	Very Rare
□	PC14	Keith Tkachuk, Pho. [1:90]	20.00
□	PC15	Teemu Selänne, Ana. [1:90]	40.00
□	PC16	Bryan Berard, NYI. [1:30]	12.00
□	PC17	Joe Thornton, Bos. [1:30]	20.00
□	PC18	Brett Hull, Stl. [1:30]	18.00
□	PC19	Nicklas Lidström, Det. [1:30]	10.00
□	PC20	Jaromir Jagr, Pgh. [1:2,000]	250.00
□	PC21	Vaclav Prospal, Pha. [1:90]	20.00
□	PC22	Pat LaFontaine, NYR. [1:90]	15.00

	No.	Player	Price
☐	PC23	Mark Messier, Van. [1:30]	18.00
☐	PC24	Martin Brodeur (G), N.J. [1:2,000]	175.00
☐	PC25	Mike Modano, Dal. [1:90]	25.00
☐	PC26	Paul Kariya, Ana. [1:90]	75.00
☐	PC27	Mike Johnson, Tor. [1:30]	15.00
☐	PC28	Sergei Samsonov, Bos. [1:2,000]	150.00
☐	PC29	Joe Sakic, Col. [1:30]	35.00
☐	PC30	Mats Sundin, Tor. [1:30]	18.00

1997 - 98 UPPER DECK COLLECTOR'S CHOICE

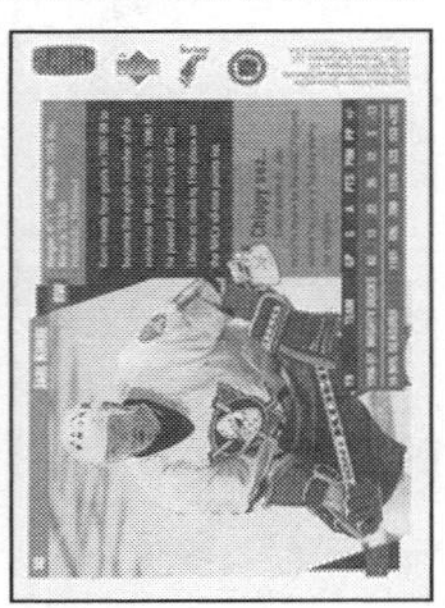

Imprint: © 1997 THE UPPER DECK COMPANY, LLC.

Complete Set (320 cards): 25.00

Common Player: .10

	No.	Player	NRMT-MT
☐	1	Guy Hebert (G), Ana.	.20
☐	2	Sean Pronger, Ana.	.10
☐	3	Dmitri Mironov, Ana.	.10
☐	4	Darren Van Impe, Ana.	.10
☐	5	Joe Sacco, Ana.	.10
☐	6	Ted Drury, Ana.	.10
☐	7	Steve Rucchin, Ana.	.10
☐	8	Teemu Selänne, Ana.	.75
☐	9	Paul Kariya, Ana.	1.50
☐	10	Jari Kurri, Ana.	.25
☐	11	Kevin Todd, Ana.	.10
☐	12	Ray Bourque, Bos.	.50
☐	13	Anson Carter, Bos.	.10
☐	14	Ted Donato, Bos.	.10
☐	15	Kyle McLaren, Bos.	.10
☐	16	Jason Allison, Bos.	.35
☐	17	Jim Carey (G), Bos.	.10
☐	18	Jozef Stumpel, Bos.	.10
☐	19	Jean-Yves Roy, Bos.	.10
☐	20	Steve Heinze, Bos.	.10
☐	21	Sheldon Kennedy, Bos.	.10
☐	22	Dominik Hasek (G), Buf.	.75
☐	23	Rob Ray, Buf.	.10
☐	24	Derek Plante, Buf.	.10
☐	25	Brian Holzinger, Buf.	.10
☐	26	Michael Peca, Buf.	.25
☐	27	Matthew Barnaby, Buf.	.10
☐	28	Donald Audette, Buf.	.10
☐	29	Alexei Zhitnik, Buf.	.10
☐	30	Garry Galley, Buf.	.10
☐	31	Pat LaFontaine, Buf.	.25
☐	32	Jason Dawe, Buf.	.10
☐	33	Hnat Domenichelli, Cgy.	.25
☐	34	Jarome Iginla, Cgy.	.35
☐	35	Chris O'Sullivan, Cgy.	.10
☐	36	Todd Simpson, Cgy.	.10
☐	37	Trevor Kidd (G), Cgy.	.25
☐	38	Dave Gagner, Cgy.	.10
☐	39	German Titov, Cgy.	.10
☐	40	Theoren Fleury, Cgy.	.35
☐	41	Dwayne Roloson, Cgy.	.10
☐	42	Marty McInnis, Cgy.	.10
☐	43	Jonas Hoglund, Cgy.	.10
☐	44	Tony Amonte, Chi.	.25
☐	45	Gary Suter, Chi.	.10
☐	46	Chris Chelios, Chi.	.35
☐	47	Jeff Hackett (G), Chi.	.25
☐	48	Ulf Dahlen, Chi.	.10
☐	49	Bob Probert, Chi.	.10
☐	50	Kevin Miller, Chi.	.10
☐	51	Ethan Moreau, Chi.	.10
☐	52	Eric Weinrich, Chi.	.10
☐	53	Eric Dazé, Chi.	.25
☐	54	Peter Forsberg, Col.	1.25
☐	55	Joe Sakic, Col.	1.00
☐	56	Patrick Roy (G), Col.	2.00
☐	57	Adam Deadmarsh, Col.	.10
☐	58	Valeri Kamensky, Col.	.25
☐	59	Keith Jones, Col.	.10
☐	60	Sandis Ozolinsh, Col.	.25
☐	61	Mike Ricci, Col.	.10
☐	62	Claude Lemieux, Col.	.10
☐	63	Mike Keane, Col.	.10
☐	64	Adam Foote, Col.	.25
☐	65	Mike Modano, Dal.	.50
☐	66	Pat Verbeek, Dal.	.10
☐	67	Andy Moog (G), Dal.	.25
☐	68	Joe Nieuwendyk, Dal.	.25
☐	69	Jamie Langenbrunner, Dal.	.25
☐	70	Derian Hatcher, Dal.	.25
☐	71	Greg Adams, Dal.	.10
☐	72	Darryl Sydor, Dal.	.10
☐	73	Dave Reid, Dal.	.10
☐	74	Jere Lehtinen, Dal.	.25
☐	75	Todd Harvey, Dal.	.10
☐	76	Brendan Shanahan, Det.	.60
☐	77	Mike Vernon, Det.	.25
☐	78	Steve Yzerman, Det.	1.25
☐	79	Sergei Fedorov, Det.	.50
☐	80	Chris Osgood (G), Det.	.35
☐	81	Nicklas Lidström, Det.	.25
☐	82	Vladimir Konstantinov, Det.	.10
☐	83	Darren McCarty, Det.	.10
☐	84	Kirk Maltby, Det.	.10
☐	85	Vyacheslav Kozlov, Det.	.10
☐	86	Martin Lapointe, Det.	.10
☐	87	Doug Weight, Edm.	.35
☐	88	Mike Grier, Edm.	.25
☐	89	Curtis Joseph (G), Edm.	.60
☐	90	Andrei Kovalenko, Edm.	.10
☐	91	Rem Murray, Edm.	.10
☐	92	Ryan Smyth, Edm.	.25
☐	93	Mariusz Czerkawski, Edm.	.10
☐	**94**	**Drew Bannister, Edm., RC**	**.10**
☐	95	Jason Arnott, Edm.	.25
☐	96	Luke Richardson, Edm.	.10
☐	97	Dean McAmmond, Edm.	.10
☐	98	Kirk Muller, Fla.	.10
☐	99	Ray Sheppard, Fla.	.10
☐	100	Scott Mellanby, Fla.	.10
☐	101	Ed Jovanovski, Fla.	.25
☐	102	John Vanbiesbrouck (G), Fla.	.60
☐	103	Radek Dvorak, Fla.	.10
☐	104	Robert Svehla, Fla.	.10
☐	105	Rob Niedermayer, Fla.	.10
☐	106	Dave Nemirovsky, Fla.	.10
☐	107	Steve Washburn, Fla.	.10
☐	108	Bill Lindsay, Fla.	.10
☐	109	Kevin Dineen, Hfd.	.10
☐	110	Keith Primeau, Hfd.	.25
☐	111	Sean Burke (G), Hfd.	.25
☐	112	Derek King, Hfd.	.10
☐	113	Andrew Cassels, Hfd.	.10
☐	114	Glen Wesley, Hfd.	.10
☐	115	Nelson Emerson, Hfd.	.10
☐	116	Geoff Sanderson, Hfd.	.10
☐	117	Jeff O'Neill, Hfd.	.25
☐	118	Kent Manderville, Hfd.	.10
☐	119	Dimitri Khristich, L.A.	.10
☐	120	Ian Laperrière, L.A.	.10
☐	121	Aki Berg, L.A.	.10
☐	122	Vladimir Tsyplakov, L.A.	.10
☐	123	Vitali Yachmenev, L.A.	.10
☐	124	Roman Vopat, L.A.	.10
☐	125	Rob Blake, L.A.	.25
☐	126	Jan Vopat, L.A.	.10
☐	127	Byron Dafoe (G), L.A.	.10
☐	**128**	**Jeff Shevalier, L.A., RC**	**.10**
☐	129	Saku Koivu, Mtl.	.75
☐	130	Vincent Damphousse, Mtl.	.35
☐	131	Brian Savage, Mtl.	.10
☐	132	Valeri Bure, Mtl.	.10
☐	133	Mark Recchi, Mtl.	.25
☐	134	Jocelyn Thibault (G), Mtl.	.35
☐	135	José Théodore (G), Mtl.	.35
☐	136	Dave Manson, Mtl.	.10
☐	137	Shayne Corson, Mtl.	.25
☐	138	Stéphane Richer, Mtl.	.10
☐	139	Doug Gilmour, N.J.	.35
☐	140	Scott Stevens, N.J.	.10
☐	141	Martin Brodeur (G), N.J.	.75
☐	142	Dave Andreychuk, N.J.	.10
☐	143	Bobby Holik, N.J.	.10
☐	144	Brian Rolston, N.J.	.10
☐	145	Jay Pandolfo, N.J.	.10
☐	146	John MacLean, N.J.	.10
☐	147	Bill Guerin, N.J.	.25
☐	148	Scott Niedermayer, N.J.	.25
☐	149	Denis Pederson, N.J.	.10
☐	150	Zigmund Palffy, NYI.	.35
☐	151	Robert Reichel, NYI.	.10
☐	152	Bryan Smolinski, NYI.	.10
☐	153	Eric Fichaud (G), NYI.	.25
☐	154	Todd Bertuzzi, NYI.	.10
☐	155	Bryan Berard, NYI.	.35
☐	156	Niklas Andersson, NYI.	.10
☐	157	Bryan McCabe, NYI.	.10
☐	158	Tommy Salo, NYI.	.10
☐	159	Kenny Jonsson, NYI.	.10
☐	160	Travis Green, NYI.	.10
☐	161	Mike Richter (G), NYR.	.25
☐	162	Brian Leetch, NYR.	.35
☐	163	Adam Graves, NYR.	.10
☐	**164**	**Vladimir Vorobiev, NYR., RC**	**.10**
☐	165	Niklas Sundstrom, NYR.	.10
☐	166	Russ Courtnall, NYR.	.10
☐	167	Wayne Gretzky, NYR.	3.00
☐	168	Mark Messier, NYR.	.50
☐	169	Alexander Karpovtsev, NYR.	.10
☐	170	Luc Robitaille, NYR.	.25
☐	171	Ulf Samuelsson, NYR.	.10
☐	172	Daniel Alfredsson, Ott.	.25
☐	173	Alexei Yashin, Ott.	.35
☐	174	Alexandre Daigle, Ott.	.10
☐	175	Andreas Dackell, Ott.	.10
☐	176	Wade Redden, Ott.	.10
☐	177	Sergei Zholtok, Ott.	.10
☐	178	Damian Rhodes (G), Ott.	.10
☐	179	Steve Duchesne, Ott.	.10
☐	180	Shawn McEachern, Ott.	.10
☐	181	Ron Tugnutt (G), Ott.	.10
☐	182	John LeClair, Pha.	.50
☐	183	Janne Niinimaa, Pha.	.25
☐	184	Mikael Renberg, Pha.	.10
☐	**185**	**Vaclav Prospal, Pha., RC**	**.50**
☐	186	Eric Lindros, Pha.	1.50
☐	187	Dainius Zubrus, Pha.	.25
☐	188	Ron Hextall (G), Pha.	.25
☐	189	Paul Coffey, Pha.	.25
☐	190	Dale Hawerchuk, Pha.	.25
☐	191	Trent Klatt, Pha.	.10
☐	192	Rod Brind'Amour, Pha.	.25
☐	193	Nikolai Khabibulin (G), Pho.	.35
☐	194	Keith Tkachuk, Pho.	.35
☐	195	Jeremy Roenick, Pho.	.35
☐	196	Mike Gartner, Pho.	.25
☐	197	Dallas Drake, Pho.	.10
☐	198	Oleg Tverdovsky, Pho.	.10
☐	199	Cliff Ronning, Pho.	.10
☐	200	Teppo Numminen, Pho.	.10
☐	201	Craig Janney, Pho.	.10
☐	202	Deron Quint, Pho.	.10
☐	203	Jason Woolley, Pgh.	.10
☐	204	Ron Francis, Pgh.	.35
☐	205	Jaromir Jagr, Pgh.	1.25
☐	206	Greg Johnson, Pgh.	.10
☐	207	Kevin Hatcher, Pgh.	.10
☐	208	Patrick Lalime (G), Pgh.	.10
☐	209	Petr Nedved, Pgh.	.10
☐	210	Ken Wregget (G), Pgh.	.10
☐	211	Darius Kasparaitis, Pgh.	.10
☐	212	Stu Barnes, Pgh.	.10
☐	213	Joe Dziedzic, Pgh.	.10
☐	214	Owen Nolan, S.J.	.25
☐	215	Jeff Friesen, S.J.	.25
☐	216	Ed Belfour (G), S.J.	.35
☐	217	Viktor Kozlov, S.J.	.10
☐	218	Tony Granato, S.J.	.10
☐	219	Darren Turcotte, S.J.	.10
☐	**220**	**Stephen Guolla, S.J., RC**	**.10**
☐	221	Marty McSorley, S.J.	.10
☐	222	Marcus Ragnarsson, S.J.	.10
☐	223	Al Iafrate, S.J.	.10
☐	224	Brett Hull, Stl.	.50

- ☐ 225 Grant Fuhr (G), Stl. .25
- ☐ 226 Pierre Turgeon, Stl. .25
- ☐ 227 Geoff Courtnall, Stl. .10
- ☐ 228 Jim Campbell, Stl. .10
- ☐ 229 Harry York, Stl. .10
- ☐ 230 Tony Twist, Stl. .10
- ☐ 231 Joe Murphy, Stl. .10
- ☐ 232 Pavol Demitra, Stl. .10
- ☐ 233 Chris Pronger, Stl. .25
- ☐ 234 Al MacInnis, Stl. .25
- ☐ 235 Daren Puppa (G), T.B. .10
- ☐ 236 Chris Gratton, T.B. .25
- ☐ 237 Dino Ciccarelli, T.B. .25
- ☐ 238 Rob Zamuner, T.B. .25
- ☐ 239 Igor Ulanov, T.B. .10
- ☐ 240 Roman Hamrlik, T.B. .25
- ☐ 241 Alexander Selivanov, T.B. .10
- ☐ 242 Patrick Poulin, T.B. .10
- ☐ 243 Daymond Langkow, T.B. .10
- ☐ 244 Corey Schwab (G), T.B. .10
- ☐ 245 Mats Sundin, Tor. .50
- ☐ 246 Wendel Clark, Tor. .25
- ☐ 247 Sergei Berezin, Tor. .25
- ☐ 248 Steve Sullivan, Tor. .10
- ☐ 249 Fredrik Modin, Tor. .10
- ☐ 250 Darby Hendrickson, Tor. .10
- ☐ 251 Jason Podollan, Tor. .10
- ☐ 252 Félix Potvin (G), Tor. .50
- ☐ 253 Tie Domi, Tor. .10
- ☐ 254 Todd Warriner, Tor. .10
- ☐ 255 Pavel Bure, Van. .75
- ☐ 256 Alexander Mogilny, Van. .35
- ☐ 257 Martin Gelinas, Van. .10
- ☐ 258 Corey Hirsch (G), Van. .10
- ☐ 259 Trevor Linden, Van. .25
- ☐ 260 Mike Sillinger, Van. .10
- ☐ 261 Markus Naslund, Van. .10
- ☐ 262 Jyrki Lumme, Van. .10
- ☐ 263 Gino Odjick, Van. .10
- ☐ 264 Mike Ridley, Van. .10
- ☐ 265 Dave Roberts, Van. .10
- ☐ 266 Adam Oates, Wsh. .35
- ☐ 267 Bill Ranford (G), Wsh. .25
- ☐ 268 Joé Juneau, Wsh. .10
- ☐ 269 Chris Simon, Wsh. .10
- ☐ 270 Peter Bondra, Wsh. .35
- ☐ 271 Dale Hunter, Wsh. .10
- ☐ 272 Jaroslav Svejkovsky, Wsh. .25
- ☐ 273 Sergei Gonchar, Wsh. .10
- ☐ 274 Steve Konowalchuk, Wsh. .10
- ☐ 275 Phil Housley, Wsh. .10
- ☐ **276 Angela James, Cdn., RC .25**
- ☐ **277 Nancy Drolet, Cdn., RC .25**
- ☐ **278 Lesley Reddon (G), Cdn., RC .25**
- ☐ **279 Hayley Wickenheiser, Cdn., RC .50**
- ☐ **280 Vicki Sunohara, Cdn., RC .35**
- ☐ **281 Cassie Campbell, Cdn., RC .35**
- ☐ **282 Geraldine Heaney, Cdn., RC .25**
- ☐ **283 Judy Diduck, Cdn., RC .25**
- ☐ **284 France St.Louis, Cdn., RC .25**
- ☐ **285 Danielle Goyette, Cdn., RC .25**
- ☐ **286 Thérèse Brisson, Cdn., RC .25**
- ☐ **287 Stacy Wilson, Cdn., RC .25**
- ☐ **288 Danielle Dubé, Cdn., RC .25**
- ☐ **289 Jayna Hefford, Cdn., RC .35**
- ☐ **290 Luce Letendre, Cdn., RC .25**
- ☐ **291 Lori Dupuis, Cdn., RC .25**
- ☐ **292 Rebecca Fahey, Cdn., RC .25**
- ☐ **293 Fiona Smith, Cdn., RC .25**
- ☐ **294 Laura Schuler, Cdn., RC .25**
- ☐ **295 Karen Nystrom, Cdn., RC .25**
- ☐ 296 Joe Thornton, Cdn. .60
- ☐ 297 Peter Schaefer, Cdn. .25
- ☐ 298 Daniel Tkaczuk, Cdn. .25
- ☐ 299 Alyn McCauley, Cdn. .50
- ☐ 300 Shane Willis, Cdn. .15
- ☐ 301 Chris Phillips, Cdn. .25
- ☐ 302 Marc Denis (G), Cdn. .25
- ☐ 303 Jason Ward, Cdn. .25
- ☐ 304 Patrick Marleau, Cdn. .50
- ☐ 305 Brad Isbister, Cdn. .15
- ☐ 306 Cameron Mann, Cdn. .25
- ☐ 307 Dan Cleary, Cdn. .25
- ☐ 308 Brad Larsen, Cdn. .15
- ☐ 309 Nick Boynton, Cdn. .15
- ☐ 310 Scott Barney, Cdn. .15
- ☐ 311 Boyd Devereaux, Cdn. .15
- ☐ 312 CL: Wayne Gretzky, NYR. 1.50
- ☐ 313 CL: Steve Yzerman, Det. .50
- ☐ 314 CL: Jaromir Jagr, Pgh. .50
- ☐ 315 CL: Jarome Iginla, Cgy. .25
- ☐ 316 CL: Patrick Roy (G), Col. 1.25
- ☐ 317 CL: John Vanbiesbrouck (G), Fla. .35
- ☐ 318 CL: Paul Kariya, Ana. 1.00
- ☐ 319 CL: Doug Weight, Edm. .25
- ☐ 320 CL: Mats Sundin, Tor. .25

YOU CRASH THE GAME

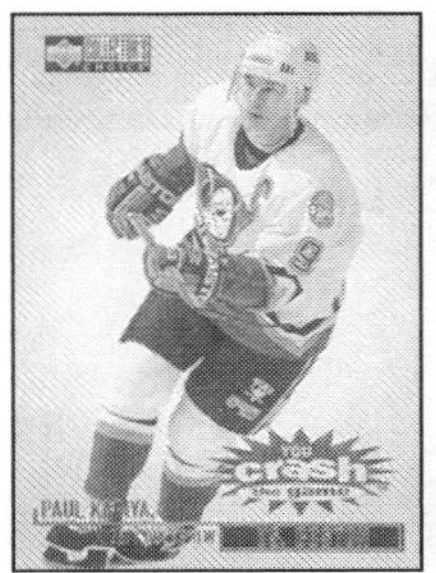

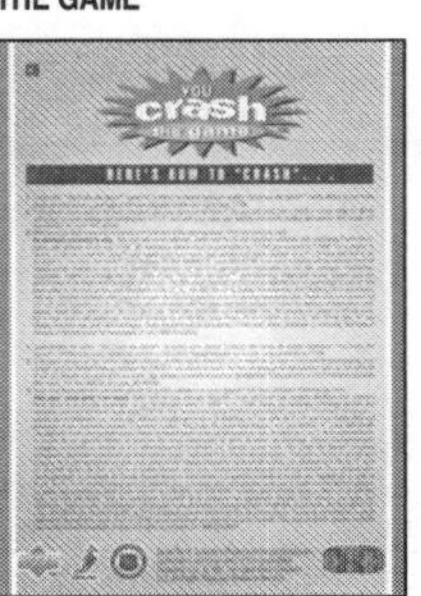

Each player has three different opponents. If the player scores against that opponent during the 1997-98 season, that card can be redeemed for a "specially enhanced premium card of that player". Cards C23, C27, C29 and C30 did not win.

Insert Set (90 cards): 125.00

	No.	Player	NRMT-MT
☐☐☐	C1	W. Gretzky, NYR. (vs. Col./Det./Edm.)	5.00
☐☐☐	C2	M. Modano, Dal. (vs. Fla./NYI./NYR.)	1.25
☐☐☐	C3	D. Weight, Edm. (vs. Buf./NYR./Ott.)	.75
☐☐☐	C4	B. Shanahan, Det. (vs. Mtl./Pha./Pgh.)	1.50
☐☐☐	C5	R.Sheppard, Fla. (vs. Ana./Det./Pho.)	.50
☐☐☐	C6	K. Primeau, Hfd. (vs. Cgy./Det./Tor.)	.50
☐☐☐	C7	R. Bourque, Bos. (vs. Chi./L.A./Van.)	1.25
☐☐☐	C8	T. Selänne, Ana. (vs. N.J./NYI./Wsh.)	1.75
☐☐☐	C9	P. Kariya, Ana. (vs. Bos./Pgh./T.B.)	3.50
☐☐☐	C10	T. Amonte, Chi. (vs. Mtl./NYR./Pha.)	.50
☐☐☐	C11	S. Koivu, Mtl. (vs. Cgy./Pho./S.J.)	1.75
☐☐☐	C12	D. Audette, Buf. (vs. Ana./Edm./Stl.)	.50
☐☐☐	C13	D. Gilmour, N.J. (vs. Cgy./Stl./Tor.)	.75
☐☐☐	C14	T. Fleury, Cgy. (vs. Buf./Fla./Pha.)	.75
☐☐☐	C15	A. Yashin, Ott. (vs. Col./L.A./Tor.)	1.00
☐☐☐	C16	Z.Palffy, NYI. (vs. Chi./Det./S.J.)	.75
☐☐☐	C17	D. Khristich, L.A. (vs. Ott./T.B./Wsh.)	.50
☐☐☐	C18	J.Sakic, Col. (vs. N.J./NYR./Pha.)	2.00
☐☐☐	C19	S. Yzerman, Det. (vs. Buf./Mtl./Pha.)	2.50
☐☐☐	C20	E. Lindros, Pha. (vs. Ana./Pho./Tor.)	3.50
☐☐☐	C21	P. Forsberg, Col. (vs. Fla./Pha./Wsh.)	2.50
☐☐☐	C22	D. Ciccarelli, T.B. (vs. Dal./Det./Edm.)	.50
☐☐☐	C23	M. Sundin, Tor. (vs. Buf./Mtl./Ott.)	1.25
☐☐☐	C24	P. Bure, Van. (vs. NYR./NYI./Pgh.)	1.75
☐☐☐	C25	P. Bondra, Wsh. (vs. Chi./L.A./Van.)	1.00
☐☐☐	C26	B. Hull, Stl. (vs. Bos./NYR./Wsh.)	1.25
☐☐☐	C27	K. Tkachuk, Pho. (vs. Bos./N.J./T.B.)	1.00
☐☐☐	C28	J. Jagr, Pgh. (vs. Det./Edm./Stl.)	2.50
☐☐☐	C29	J. Iginla, Cgy. (vs. Mtl./Ott./Wsh.)	.75
☐☐☐	C30	O. Nolan, S.J. (vs. Buf./Fla./NYI.)	.50

STICK UM'S

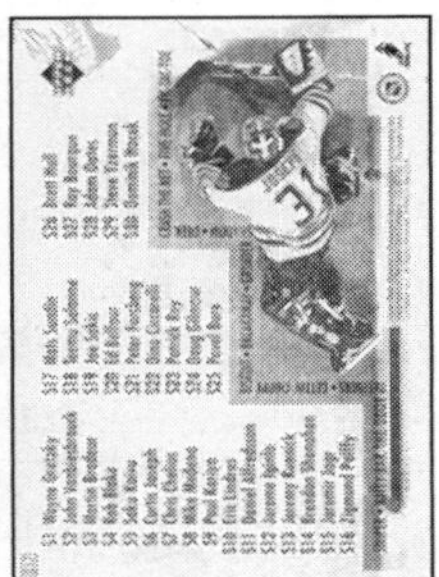

Insert Set (30 stickers): 35.00

	No.	Player	NRMT-MT
☐	S1	Wayne Gretzky, NYR.	5.00
☐	S2	John Vanbiesbrouck (G), Fla.	1.50
☐	S3	Martin Brodeur (G), N.J.	1.75
☐	S4	Rob Blake, L.A.	.50
☐	S5	Saku Koivu, Mtl.	1.75
☐	S6	Curtis Joseph (G), Edm.	1.50
☐	S7	Chris Chelios, Chi.	1.00
☐	S8	Mike Modano, Dal.	1.25
☐	S9	Paul Kariya, Ana.	3.50
☐	S10	Eric Lindros, Pha.	3.50
☐	S11	Daniel Alfredsson, Ott.	.50
☐	S12	Jarome Iginla, Cgy.	.75
☐	S13	Jeremy Roenick, Pho.	.75
☐	S14	Brendan Shanahan, Det.	1.50
☐	S15	Jaromir Jagr, Pgh.	2.50
☐	S16	Zigmund Palffy, NYI.	.75
☐	S17	Mats Sundin, Tor.	1.25
☐	S18	Teemu Selänne, Ana.	1.75
☐	S19	Joe Sakic, Col.	2.00
☐	S20	Ed Belfour (G), S.J.	.75
☐	S21	Peter Forsberg, Col.	2.50
☐	S22	Dino Ciccarelli, T.B.	.50
☐	S23	Patrick Roy (G), Col.	4.00
☐	S24	Doug Gilmour, N.J.	.75
☐	S25	Pavel Bure, Van.	1.75
☐	S26	Brett Hull, Stl.	1.25
☐	S27	Ray Bourque, Bos.	1.25
☐	S28	Adam Oates, Wsh.	.75
☐	S29	Steve Yzerman, Det.	2.50
☐	S30	Dominik Hasek (G), Buf.	1.75

MAGIC MEN

Insert Set (10 cards): 50.00

	No.	Player	NRMT-MT
☐	MM1	Wayne Gretzky, NYR.	8.00
☐	MM2	Wayne Gretzky, NYR.	8.00
☐	MM3	Wayne Gretzky, NYR.	8.00
☐	MM4	Wayne Gretzky, NYR.	8.00
☐	MM5	Wayne Gretzky, NYR.	8.00
☐	MM6	Patrick Roy (G), Col.	6.00
☐	MM7	Patrick Roy (G), Col.	6.00
☐	MM8	Patrick Roy (G), Col.	6.00
☐	MM9	Patrick Roy (G), Col.	6.00
☐	MM10	Patrick Roy (G), Col.	6.00

STAR QUEST

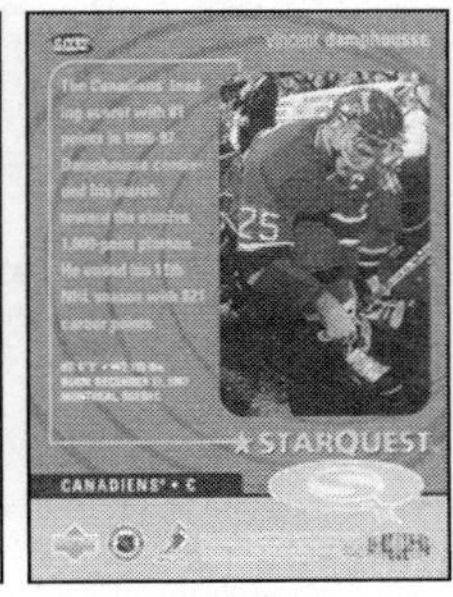

Star Quest cards are inserted at four levels of difficulty: Star Quest 1 cards (1-45) are inserted one per pack; Star Quest 2 cards (46-65) are inserted one per 21 packs; Star Quest 3 cards (66-80) are inserted one per 71 packs; and Star Quest 4 (81-90) are inserted one per 145 packs.

Star Quest 1 Set (45 cards): 10.00
Star Quest 2 Set (20 cards): 50.00
Star Quest 3 Set (15 cards): 100.00
Star Quest 4 Set (10 cards): 425.00

	No.	Player	NRMT-MT
	STAR QUEST 1		
☐	SQ1	Bryan Berard, NYI.	.50
☐	SQ2	Robert Svehla, Fla.	.20
☐	SQ3	Peter Nedved, Pgh.	.20
☐	SQ4	Steve Sullivan, Tor.	.20
☐	SQ5	Nicklas Lidström, Det.	.35
☐	SQ6	Wade Redden, Ott.	.20
☐	SQ7	Jason Arnott, Edm.	.35
☐	SQ8	Martin Gelinas, Van.	.20
☐	SQ9	Mikael Renberg, Pha.	.20
☐	SQ10	Jeff Friesen, S.J.	.35
☐	SQ11	Chris Chelios, Chi.	.60
☐	SQ12	Jarome Iginla, Cgy.	.50
☐	SQ13	Vyacheslav Kozlov, Det.	.20
☐	SQ14	Brian Holzinger, Buf.	.20
☐	SQ15	Eric Dazé, Chi.	.35
☐	SQ16	Pat Verbeek, Dal.	.20
☐	SQ17	Jozef Stumpel, Bos.	.35

	No.	Player	Price
☐	SQ18	Rob Niedermayer, Fla.	.20
☐	SQ19	Sergei Fedorov, Det.	.75
☐	SQ20	Brian Leetch, NYR.	.50
☐	SQ21	Bill Guerin, N.J.	.35
☐	SQ22	Dino Ciccarelli, T.B.	.35
☐	SQ23	Adam Oates, Wsh.	.50
☐	SQ24	Mike Grier, Edm.	.35
☐	SQ25	Alexandre Daigle, Ott.	.20
☐	SQ26	Janne Niinimaa, Pha.	.35
☐	SQ27	Dimitri Khristich, L.A.	.20
☐	SQ28	Oleg Tverdovsky, Pho.	.20
☐	SQ29	Félix Potvin (G), Tor.	.75
☐	SQ30	Mike Richter (G), NYR.	.50
☐	SQ31	Curtis Joseph (G), Edm.	1.00
☐	SQ32	Vincent Damphousse, Mtl.	.50
☐	SQ33	Vladimir Konstantinov, Det.	.20
☐	SQ34	Andy Moog (G), Dal.	.35
☐	SQ35	Nikolai Khabibulin (G), Pho.	.50
☐	SQ36	Ed Belfour (G), S.J.	.50
☐	SQ37	Scott Mellanby, Fla.	.20
☐	SQ38	Sandis Ozolinsh, Col.	.35
☐	SQ38	Travis Green, NYI.	.20
☐	SQ40	Patrick Lalime (G), Pgh.	.20
☐	SQ41	Niklas Sundstrom, NYR.	.20
☐	SQ42	Guy Hebert (G), Ana.	.35
☐	SQ43	Vitali Yachmenev, L.A.	.20
☐	SQ44	Roman Hamrlik, T.B.	.35
☐	SQ45	Adam Deadmarsh, Col.	.20

STAR QUEST 2

	No.	Player	Price
☐	SQ46	Alexei Zhamnov, Chi.	1.00
☐	SQ47	Saku Koivu, Mtl.	5.00
☐	SQ48	Sergei Berezin, Tor.	1.50
☐	SQ49	Mark Messier, NYR.	3.50
☐	SQ50	Martin Brodeur (G), N.J.	5.00
☐	SQ51	Daniel Alfredsson, Ott.	1.50
☐	SQ52	John LeClair, Pha.	3.50
☐	SQ53	Mike Vernon (G), Det.	1.50
☐	SQ54	Ron Francis, Pgh.	2.00
☐	SQ55	Keith Primeau, Hfd.	1.50
☐	SQ56	Pierre Turgeon, Stl.	1.50
☐	SQ57	Jim Carey (G), Bos.	1.00
☐	SQ58	Peter Bondra, Wsh.	2.50
☐	SQ59	Pavel Bure, Van.	5.00
☐	SQ60	Ray Sheppard, Fla.	1.00
☐	SQ61	Chris Gratton, T.B.	1.50
☐	SQ62	Derek Plante, Buf.	1.00
☐	SQ63	Joe Sakic, Col.	6.00
☐	SQ64	Theoren Fleury, Cgy.	2.00
☐	SQ65	Tony Amonte, Chi.	1.50

STAR QUEST 3

	No.	Player	Price
☐	SQ66	Zigmund Palffy, NYI.	8.00
☐	SQ67	Steve Yzerman, Det.	25.00
☐	SQ68	Doug Weight, Edm.	8.00
☐	SQ69	Alexander Mogilny, Van.	8.00
☐	SQ70	Doug Gilmour, N.J.	8.00
☐	SQ71	Peter Forsberg, Col.	25.00
☐	SQ72	Alexei Yashin, Ott.	6.00
☐	SQ73	Geoff Sanderson, Hfd.	6.00
☐	SQ74	Brendan Shanahan, Det.	15.00
☐	SQ75	Mark Recchi, Mtl.	6.00
☐	SQ76	Brett Hull, Stl.	12.00
☐	SQ77	Ray Bourque, Bos.	12.00
☐	SQ78	Owen Nolan, S.J.	6.00
☐	SQ79	Jeremy Roenick, Pho.	8.00
☐	SQ80	Teemu Selänne, Ana.	18.00

STAR QUEST 4

	No.	Player	Price
☐	SQ81	Dominik Hasek (G), Buf.	35.00
☐	SQ82	Mike Modano, Dal.	25.00
☐	SQ83	Mats Sundin, Tor.	25.00
☐	SQ84	John Vanbiesbrouck (G), Fla.	30.00
☐	SQ85	Paul Kariya, Ana.	65.00
☐	SQ86	Patrick Roy (G), Col.	80.00
☐	SQ87	Keith Tkachuk, Pho.	20.00
☐	SQ88	Eric Lindros, Pha.	65.00
☐	SQ89	Jaromir Jagr, Pgh.	50.00
☐	SQ90	Wayne Gretzky, NYR.	100.00

WORLD DOMINATION

	No.	Player	NRMT-MT
Insert Set (20 cards):			**65.00**
☐	W1	Wayne Gretzky, NYR.	10.00
☐	W2	Mark Messier, Van.	2.50
☐	W3	Steve Yzerman, Det.	5.00
☐	W4	Brandan Shanahan, Det.	3.00
☐	W5	Paul Kariya, Ana.	6.50
☐	W6	Joe Sakic, Col.	4.00
☐	W7	Eric Lindros, Pha.	6.50
☐	W8	Rod Brind'Armour, Pha.	1.50
☐	W9	Keith Primeau, Car.	1.50
☐	W10	Trevor Linden, Van.	1.50
☐	W11	Theoren Fleury, Cgy.	2.00
☐	W12	Scott Niedermayer, N.J.	1.50
☐	W13	Rob Blake, L.A.	1.50
☐	W14	Chris Pronger, Stl.	1.50
☐	W15	Eric Desjardins, Pha.	1.50
☐	W16	Adam Foote, Col.	1.50
☐	W17	Scott Stevens, N.J.	1.50
☐	W18	Patrick Roy (G), Col.	8.00
☐	W19	Curtis Joseph (G), Edm.	3.00
☐	W20	Martin Brodeur (G), N.J.	3.50

1997 - 98 UPPER DECK DIAMOND VISION

These cards have two versions: the regular card and a Signature Moves [1:5] parallel.

Imprint:

	No.	Player	Sign.	Reg.
Complete Set (25 cards):			**350.00**	**175.00**
☐☐	1	Wayne Gretzky, NYR.	60.00	30.00
☐☐	2	Patrick Roy (G), Col.	50.00	25.00
☐☐	3	Jaromir Jagr, Pgh.	30.00	15.00
☐☐	4	Steve Yzerman, Det.	30.00	15.00
☐☐	5	Martin Brodeur (G), N.J.	20.00	10.00
☐☐	6	Paul Kariya, Ana.	40.00	20.00
☐☐	7	John Vanbiesbrouck (G), Fla.	15.00	7.50
☐☐	8	Ray Bourque, Bos.	12.00	6.00
☐☐	9	Theoren Fleury, Cgy.	8.00	4.00
☐☐	10	Pavel Bure, Van.	20.00	10.00
☐☐	11	Brendan Shanahan, Det.	15.00	7.50
☐☐	12	Brian Leetch, NYR.	8.00	4.00
☐☐	13	Owen Nolan, S.J.	6.00	3.00
☐☐	14	Peter Forsberg, Col.	30.00	15.00
☐☐	15	Doug Weight, Edm.	8.00	4.00
☐☐	16	Teemu Selänne, Ana.	20.00	10.00
☐☐	17	Mats Sundin, Tor.	12.00	6.00
☐☐	18	Keith Tkachuk, Pho.	10.00	5.00
☐☐	19	Tony Amonte, Chi.	6.00	3.00
☐☐	20	Joe Sakic, Col.	25.00	12.50
☐☐	21	Zigmund Palffy, NYI.	8.00	4.00
☐☐	22	Eric Lindros, Pha.	40.00	20.00
☐☐	23	Sergei Fedorov, Det.	12.00	6.00
☐☐	24	Dominik Hasek (G), Buf.	20.00	10.00
☐☐	25	Brett Hull, Stl.	12.00	6.00

DEFINING MOMENTS

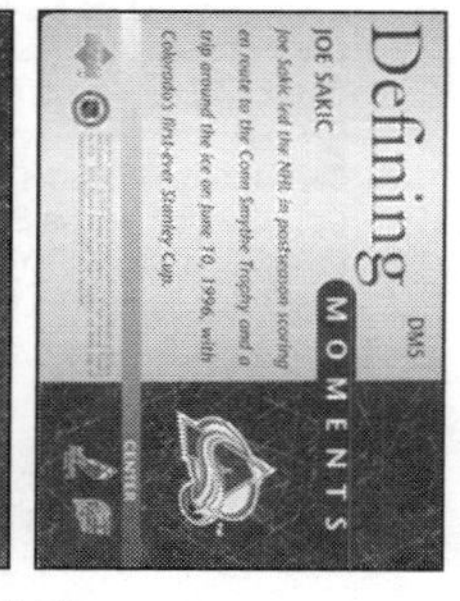

Defining Moments insertion ratio is [1:40].

	No.	Player	NRMT-MT
Insert Set (6 cards):			**375.00**
☐	DM1	Wayne Gretzky, NYR.	125.00
☐	DM2	Patrick Roy (G), Col.	100.00
☐	DM3	Steve Yzerman, Det.	65.00
☐	DM4	Jaromir Jagr, Pgh.	65.00
☐	DM5	Joe Sakic, Col.	55.00
☐	DM6	Brendan Shanahan, Det.	40.00

REEL TIME

Reel Time insertion ratio is [1:500].

	Player	NRMT-MT
☐	Wayne Gretzky, NYR.	300.00

1997 - 98 UPPER DECK ICE

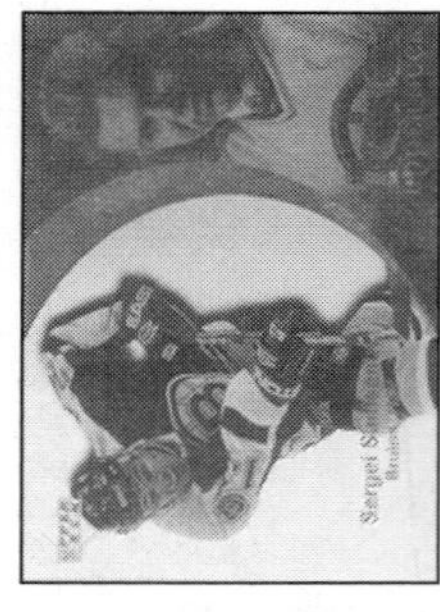

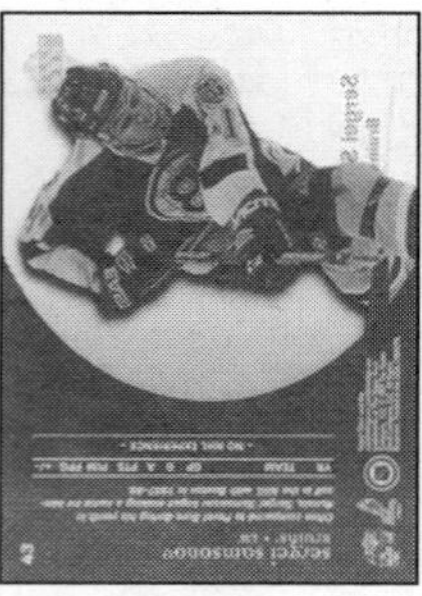

Each card has three versions: the regular card, a gold Power Shift parallel [1:23] and a third coloured parallel.

Cards 1-30 have a red Ice Performers parallel [1:2], cards 31-60 have a blue Ice Phenoms parallel [1:3] and cards 61-90 have a green Ice Legends parallel [1:11].

Imprint: © 1997 THE UPPER DECK COMPANY.

	No.	Player	Gold	Colour	Reg.
Complete Set (90 cards):			**1,200.00**	**-.**	**100.00**
Ice Performers Set (30 cards):				**60.00**	
Ice Phenoms Set (30 cards):				**90.00**	
Ice Legends Set (30 cards):				**450.00**	
Common Player:			**5.00**	**-.**	**.50**
☐☐☐	1	Nelson Emerson (G), Car.	5.00	1.00	.50
☐☐☐	2	Derian Hatcher, Dal.	10.00	2.00	1.00
☐☐☐	3	Mike Richter (G), NYR.	18.00	3.00	1.50
☐☐☐	4	Sergei Berezin, Tor.	10.00	2.00	1.00
☐☐☐	5	Nicklas Lidström, Det.	10.00	2.00	1.00
☐☐☐	6	Ryan Smyth, Edm.	10.00	2.00	1.00
☐☐☐	7	Martin Brodeur (G), N.J.	55.00	7.00	3.50
☐☐☐	8	Geoff Sanderson, Car.	5.00	1.00	.50
☐☐☐	9	Doug Weight, Edm.	18.00	3.00	1.50
☐☐☐	10	Owen Nolan, S.J.	10.00	2.00	1.00
☐☐☐	11	Daniel Alfredsson, Ott.	10.00	2.00	1.00
☐☐☐	12	Peter Bondra, Wsh.	25.00	4.00	2.00
☐☐☐	13	Jim Campbell, Stl.	5.00	1.00	.50
☐☐☐	14	Rob Niedermayer, Fla.	5.00	1.00	.50
☐☐☐	15	Daymond Langkow, T.B.	5.00	1.00	.50
☐☐☐	16	Zigmund Palffy, NYI.	18.00	3.00	1.50
☐☐☐	17	Adam Oates, Wsh.	18.00	3.00	1.50
☐☐☐	18	Adam Deadmarsh, Col.	5.00	1.00	.50
☐☐☐	19	Brian Holzinger, Buf.	5.00	1.00	.50
☐☐☐	20	Jarome Iginla, Cgy.	18.00	3.00	1.50
☐☐☐	21	Janne Niinimaa, Pha.	10.00	2.00	1.00
☐☐☐	22	Dino Ciccarelli, Fla.	10.00	2.00	1.00
☐☐☐	23	Mark Recchi, Mtl.	10.00	2.00	1.00
☐☐☐	24	Sandis Ozolinsh, Col.	10.00	2.00	1.00
☐☐☐	25	Keith Primeau, Car.	10.00	2.00	1.00
☐☐☐	26	Ed Jovanovski, Fla.	10.00	2.00	1.00
☐☐☐	27	Jeremy Roenick, Pho.	18.00	3.00	1.50
☐☐☐	28	Alexei Yashin, Ott.	25.00	4.00	2.00
☐☐☐	29	Félix Potvin (G), Tor.	35.00	5.00	2.50
☐☐☐	30	Chris Osgood (G), Det.	25.00	4.00	2.00
☐☐☐	31	Marc Denis (G), Col.	10.00	3.00	1.00
☐☐☐	**32**	**Tyler Moss (G), Cgy., RC**	**10.00**	**3.00**	**1.50**
☐☐☐	33	Kevin Hodson (G), Det.	5.00	1.50	.50
☐☐☐	34	Jamie Storr (G), L.A.	10.00	3.00	1.00
☐☐☐	35	Roman Turek (G), Dal.	5.00	1.50	.50
☐☐☐	36	José Théodore (G), Mtl.	18.00	4.50	1.50
☐☐☐	**37**	**Magnus Arvedsson, Ott., RC**	**5.00**	**1.50**	**.75**
☐☐☐	38	Daniel Cleary, Chi.	10.00	3.00	1.50
☐☐☐	**39**	**Mike Knuble, Det., RC**	**5.00**	**1.50**	**.75**
☐☐☐	40	Jaroslav Svejkovsky, Wsh.	10.00	3.00	1.00
☐☐☐	41	Patrick Marleau, S.J.	25.00	6.00	2.50
☐☐☐	42	Mattias Ohlund, Van.	10.00	3.00	1.50
☐☐☐	43	Sergei Samsonov, Bos.	35.00	8.00	3.00
☐☐☐	**44**	**Espen Knutsen, Ana., RC**	**5.00**	**1.50**	**.75**
☐☐☐	**45**	**Vaclav Prospal, Pha., RC**	**15.00**	**5.00**	**2.50**
☐☐☐	46	Joe Thornton, Bos.	35.00	8.00	3.00
☐☐☐	47	Chris Phillips, Ott.	10.00	3.00	1.50
☐☐☐	**48**	**Mike Johnson, Tor., RC**	**30.00**	**10.00**	**6.00**
☐☐☐	49	Dainius Zubrus, Pha.	10.00	3.00	1.00
☐☐☐	50	Wade Redden, Ott.	5.00	1.50	.50
☐☐☐	**51**	**Derek Morris, Cgy., RC**	**10.00**	**3.00**	**1.50**
☐☐☐	**52**	**Marco Sturm, S.J., RC**	**10.00**	**3.00**	**1.50**
☐☐☐	**53**	**Donald MacLean, L.A., RC**	**5.00**	**1.50**	**.75**
☐☐☐	54	Bryan Berard, NYI.	18.00	4.50	1.50
☐☐☐	55	Richard Zednik, Wsh.	5.00	1.50	.50

	No.	Player			
□□□	56	Alexei Morozov, Pgh..	25.00	6.00	2.50
□□□	57	Erik Rasmussen, Buf.	5.00	1.50	.50
□□□	**58**	**Olli Jokinen, L.A., RC**	**15.00**	**5.00**	**2.00**
□□□	**59**	**Jan Bulis, Wsh., RC**	**10.00**	**3.00**	**1.50**
□□□	**60**	**Patrik Elias, N.J., RC**	**15.00**	**5.00**	**2.00**
□□□	61	Peter Forsberg, Col.	75.00	25.00	5.00
□□□	62	Mike Modano, Dal.	35.00	12.50	2.50
□□□	63	Tony Amonte, Chi.	10.00	5.00	1.00
□□□	64	Theoren Fleury, Cgy.	18.00	7.50	1.50
□□□	65	Ron Francis, Pgh.	18.00	7.50	1.50
□□□	66	Brett Hull, Stl.	35.00	12.50	2.50
□□□	67	Chris Chelios, Chi.	25.00	10.00	2.00
□□□	68	Jaromir Jagr, Pgh.	75.00	25.00	5.00
□□□	69	Sergei Fedorov, Det.	35.00	12.50	2.50
□□□	70	Keith Tkachuk, Pho.	25.00	10.00	2.00
□□□	71	Mark Messier, Van.	35.00	12.50	2.50
□□□	72	Pat LaFontaine, NYR.	10.00	5.00	1.00
□□□	73	Mats Sundin, Tor.	35.00	12.50	2.50
□□□	74	John Vanbiesbrouck (G), Fla.	45.00	15.00	3.00
□□□	75	John LeClair, Pha.	35.00	12.50	2.50
□□□	76	Brian Leetch, NYR.	18.00	7.50	1.50
□□□	77	Ray Bourque, Bos.	35.00	12.50	2.50
□□□	78	Saku Koivu, Mtl.	55.00	17.50	3.50
□□□	79	Joe Sakic, Col.	65.00	20.00	4.00
□□□	80	Teemu Selänne, Ana.	55.00	17.50	3.50
□□□	81	Curtis Joseph (G), Edm.	45.00	15.00	3.00
□□□	82	Doug Gilmour, N.J.	18.00	7.50	1.50
□□□	83	Patrick Roy (G), Col.	125.00	40.00	8.00
□□□	84	Brendan Shanahan, Det.	45.00	15.00	3.00
□□□	85	Paul Kariya, Ana.	100.00	35.00	6.50
□□□	86	Pavel Bure, Van.	55.00	17.50	3.50
□□□	87	Dominik Hasek (G), Buf.	55.00	17.50	3.50
□□□	88	Eric Lindros, Pha.	100.00	35.00	6.50
□□□	89	Steve Yzerman, Det.	75.00	25.00	5.00
□□□	90	Wayne Gretzky, NYR.	150.00	50.00	10.00

ICE CHAMPIONS

These cards have two versions: the regular insert [1:47] and a Ice Champions 2 parallel (serial numbered out of 100).

Insert Set (20 cards): **500.00**

	No.	Player	Ice	Reg.
□□	IC1	Wayne Gretzky, NYR.	900.00	75.00
□□	IC2	Patrick Roy (G), Col.	700.00	60.00
□□	IC3	Eric Lindros, Pha.	550.00	45.00
□□	IC4	Saku Koivu, Mtl.	300.00	25.00
□□	IC5	Dominik Hasek (G), Buf.	300.00	25.00
□□	IC6	Joe Thornton, Bos.	175.00	18.00
□□	IC7	Martin Brodeur (G), N.J.	300.00	25.00
□□	IC8	Teemu Selänne, Ana.	300.00	25.00
□□	IC9	Paul Kariya, Ana.	550.00	45.00
□□	IC10	Joe Sakic, Col.	350.00	30.00
□□	IC11	Mark Messier, Van.	175.00	15.00
□□	IC12	Peter Forsberg, Col.	475.00	35.00
□□	IC13	Mats Sundin, Tor.	175.00	15.00
□□	IC14	Brendan Shanahan, Det.	225.00	20.00
□□	IC15	Keith Tkachuk, Pho.	150.00	10.00
□□	IC16	Brett Hull, Stl.	175.00	15.00
□□	IC17	John Vanbiesbrouck (G), Fla.	225.00	20.00
□□	IC18	Jaromir Jagr, Pgh.	425.00	35.00
□□	IC19	Steve Yzerman, Det.	425.00	35.00
□□	IC20	Sergei Samsonov, Bos.	175.00	18.00

LETHAL LINES

Lethal Lines insertion ratio is [1:18].

Insert Set (30 cards): **250.00**

	No.	Player	NRMT-MT
□	L1A	Paul Kariya, Ana.	20.00
□	L1B	Wayne Gretzky, NYR.	35.00
□	L1C	Joe Thornton, Bos.	7.50
□	L2A	Brendan Shanahan, Det.	9.00
□	L2B	Eric Lindros, Pha.	20.00
□	L2C	Jaromir Jagr, Pgh.	15.00
□	L3A	Keith Tkachuk, Pho.	6.00
□	L3B	Mark Messier, Van.	7.50
□	L3C	Owen Nolan, S.J.	3.50
□	L4A	Daniel Alfredsson, Ott.	3.50
□	L4B	Peter Forsberg, Col.	15.00
□	L4C	Mats Sundin, Tor.	7.50
□	L5A	Ryan Smyth, Edm.	3.50
□	L5B	Steve Yzerman, Det.	15.00
□	L5C	Jarome Iginla, Cgy.	3.50
□	L6A	Sergei Samsonov, Bos.	7.50
□	L6B	Igor Larionov, Det.	3.50
□	L6C	Sergei Fedorov, Det.	7.50
□	L7A	Patrik Elias, N.J.	4.00
□	L7B	Alexei Morozov, Pgh.	6.00
□	L7C	Vaclav Prospal, Pha.	5.00
□	L8A	John LeClair, Pha.	7.50
□	L8B	Mike Modano, Dal.	7.50
□	L8C	Brett Hull, Stl.	7.50
□	L9A	Olli Jokinen, L.A.	5.00
□	L9B	Saku Koivu, Mtl.	10.00
□	L9C	Teemu Selänne, Ana.	10.00
□	L10A	Brian Leetch, NYR.	5.00
□	L10B	Patrick Roy (G), Col.	25.00
□	L10C	Nicklas Lidström, Det.	3.50

1997 - 98 UPPER DECK SWEDISH

Imprint:

Complete Set (200 cards): **45.00**

Common Player: **.20**

	No.	Player	NRMT-MT
□	1	Miikka Kiprusoff (G), AIK	.35
□	2	Karri Kivi, AIK	.20
□	3	Erik Hamalainen, AIK	.20
□	4	Libor Prochazka, AIK	.20
□	5	Dick Ternstrom, AIK	.20
□	6	Niclas Havelid, AIK	.20
□	7	Tomas Strandberg, AIK	.20
□	8	Stefan Gustavsson, AIK	.20
□	9	Anders Gozzi, AIK	.20
□	10	Pavel Patera, AIK	.20
□	11	David Engblom, AIK	.20
□	12	Peter Hammarstrom, AIK	.20
□	13	Mats Lindberg, AIK	.20
□	14	Fredrik Krekula, AIK	.20
□	15	Otakar Vejboda, AIK	.20
□	16	Bjorn Ahlstrom, AIK	.20
□	17	Michael Sundlov (G), Brynäs	.20
□	18	Par Djoos, Brynäs	.20
□	19	Tommy Melkersson, Brynäs	.20
□	20	Stefan Klockare, Brynäs	.20
□	21	Johan Hansson, Brynäs	.20
□	22	Per Lofstrom, Brynäs	.20
□	23	Tommy Westlund, Brynäs	.20
□	24	Teppo Kivela, Brynäs	.20
□	25	Niclas Wallin, Brynäs	.20
□	26	Roger Kyro, Brynäs	.20
□	27	Ove Molin, Brynäs	.20
□	28	Mikko Luovi, Brynäs	.20
□	29	Evgeny Davydov, Brynäs	.35
□	30	Anders Huss, Brynäs	.20
□	31	Peter Nylander, Brynäs	.20
□	32	Jan Larsson, Brynäs	.20
□	33	Tommy Söderström (G), Djurgårdens	.75
□	34	Marcus Matthiason, Djurgårdens	.20
□	35	Daniel Carlsson, Djurgårdens	.20
□	36	Ronnie Pettersson, Djurgårdens	.20
□	37	Kenneth Kennholt, Djurgårdens	.20
□	38	Bjorn Nord, Djurgårdens	.20
□	39	Mikael Johansson, Djurgårdens	.20
□	40	Daniel Tjarnqvist, Djurgårdens	.20
□	41	Charles Berglund, Djurgårdens	.20
□	42	Mikael Johansson, Djurgårdens	.20
□	43	Marcus Nilsson, Djurgårdens	.20
□	44	Nichlas Falk, Djurgårdens	.20
□	45	Fredrik Lindqvist, Djurgårdens	.20
□	46	Patric Kjellberg, Djurgårdens	.20
□	47	Patrik Erickson, Djurgårdens	.20
□	48	Jan Viktorsson, Djurgårdens	.20
□	49	Niklas Anger, Djurgårdens	.35
□	50	Boris Rousson (G), Färjestad	.50
□	51	Peter Jakobsson, Färjestad	.20
□	52	Peter Nordstrom, Färjestad	.20
□	53	Sergei Fokin, Färjestad	.20
□	54	Niklas Sjokvist, Färjestad	.20
□	55	Jaroslav Sprachek, Färjestad	.20
□	56	Greger Artursson, Färjestad	.20
□	57	Roger Johansson, Färjestad	.20
□	58	Stefan Nilsson, Färjestad	.20
□	59	Pelle Prestberg, Färjestad	.20
□	60	Kristian Huselius, Färjestad	.20
□	61	Mathias Johansson, Färjestad	.20
□	62	Trond Magnussen, Färjestad	.20
□	63	Claes Eriksson, Färjestad	.20
□	64	Jörgen Jönsson, Färjestad	.20
□	65	Atle Olson, Färjestad	.20
□	66	Patrik Wallenberg, Färjestad	.20
□	67	Lars-Goran Wiklander, Frölunda	.20
□	68	Mikael Sandberg (G), Frölunda	.35
□	69	Christer Olsson, Frölunda	.20
□	70	Joachim Esbjors, Frölunda	.20
□	71	Henrik Nilsson, Frölunda	.20
□	72	Arto Blomsten, Frölunda	.20
□	73	Magnus Johansson, Frölunda	.20
□	74	Stefan Larsson, Frölunda	.20
□	75	Par Edlund, Frölunda	.20
□	76	Marko Jantunen, Frölunda	.20
□	77	Joni Lius, Frölunda	.20
□	78	Patrik Carnback, Frölunda	.20
□	79	Ville Peltonen, Frölunda	.20
□	80	Peter Berndtsson, Frölunda	.20
□	81	Kai Nurminen, Frölunda	.35
□	82	Jonas Esbjors, Frölunda	.20
□	83	Peter Strom, Frölunda	.20
□	84	Kari Takko (G), HV 71	.50
□	85	Johan Forsander, HV 71	.20
□	86	Jouni Loponen, HV 71	.20
□	87	David Petrasek, HV 71	.20
□	88	Daniel Johansson, HV 71	.20
□	89	Fredrik Stillman, HV 71	.20
□	90	Anatoli Fedotov, HV 71	.20
□	91	Stefan Örnskog, HV 71	.20
□	92	Stafan Falk, HV 71	.20
□	93	Peter Ekelund, HV 71	.20
□	94	Esa Keskinen, HV 71	.50
□	95	Patrik Lundback, HV 71	.20
□	96	Anders Huusko, HV 71	.20
□	97	Magnus Svensson, HV 71	.20
□	98	Alexei Salomatin, HV 71	.20
□	99	Patrik Englund, HV 71	.20
□	100	Åke Liljebjorn (G), Leksands	.35
□	101	Tomas Jonsson, Leksands	.35
□	102	Torbjorn Johansson, Leksands	.20
□	103	Hans Lodin, Leksands	.20
□	104	Magnus Svensson, Leksands	.20
□	105	Andreas Karlsson, Leksands	.20
□	106	Joakim Lidgren, Leksands	.20
□	107	Fredrik Jonsson, Leksands	.20
□	108	Per-Erik Eklund, Leksands	.50
□	109	Anders Carlsson, Leksands	.20
□	110	Johan Witehall, Leksands	.20
□	111	Jens Nielsen, Leksands	.20
□	112	Niklas Eriksson, Leksands	.20
□	113	Jonas Bergqvist, Leksands	.20
□	114	Stefan Hellqvist, Leksands	.20
□	115	Markus Akerblom, Leksands	.20
□	116	Anders Lonn, Leksands	.20
□	117	Jarmo Myllys (G), Luleå	.50
□	118	Johan Finnstrom, Luleå	.20
□	119	Sergei Bautin, Luleå	.35
□	120	Jan Mertzig, Luleå	.20
□	121	Osmo Soutokorva, Luleå	.20

	No.	Player	Price
☐	122	Roger Åkerstrom, Luleå	.20
☐	123	Stefan Jonsson, Luleå	.20
☐	124	Stefan Nilsson, Luleå	.20
☐	125	Jonas Ronnqvist, Luleå	.20
☐	126	Joakim Backlund, Luleå	.20
☐	127	Robert Nordberg, Luleå	.20
☐	128	Mikael Lovgren, Luleå	.20
☐	129	Anders Burstrom, Luleå	.20
☐	130	Fredrik Johansson, Luleå	.20
☐	131	Mika Alatalo, Luleå	.20
☐	132	Fredrik Nilsson, Luleå	.20
☐	133	Roger Nordstrom (G), Malmö	.50
☐	134	Andrew Verner (G), Malmö	.50
☐	135	Marko Kiprusoff, Malmö	.35
☐	136	Kim Johnsson, Malmö	.20
☐	137	Magnus Nilsson, Malmö	.20
☐	138	Jaspar Damgaardr, Malmö	.20
☐	139	Marek Malik, Malmö	.20
☐	140	Mats Lusth, Malmö	.20
☐	141	Janne Ojanen, Malmö	.50
☐	142	Mikko Peltola, Malmö	.20
☐	143	Mathias Bosson, Malmö	.20
☐	144	Daniel Rydmark, Malmö	.20
☐	145	Patrik Sylvegård, Malmö	.20
☐	146	Juha Riihijarvi, Malmö	.35
☐	147	Fredrik Oberg, Malmö	.20
☐	148	Mikael Burakovsky, Malmö	.20
☐	149	Petter Ronnqvist (G), MoDo	.20
☐	150	Pierre Hedin, MoDo	.35
☐	151	Jan-Axel Alavaara, MoDo	.20
☐	152	Frantisek Kaberle, MoDo	.20
☐	153	Hans Jonsson, MoDo	.20
☐	154	Jonas Junkka, MoDo	.20
☐	155	Marcus Karlsson, MoDo	.20
☐	156	Kristian Gahn, MoDo	.20
☐	157	Magnus Wernblom, MoDo	.20
☐	158	Anders Soderberg, MoDo	.20
☐	159	Daniel Sedin, MoDo	2.00
☐	160	Henrik Sedin, MoDo	2.00
☐	161	Samuel Påhlsson, MoDo	.20
☐	162	Per Svartvadet, MoDo	.20
☐	163	Andreas Salomonsson, MoDo	.20
☐	164	Ravil Yakubov, MoDo	.20
☐	165	David Vyborny, MoDo	.20
☐	166	Magnus Lindvist (G), Södertälje	.20
☐	167	Anders Eldebrink, Södertälje	.20
☐	168	Johan Nordgren, Södertälje	.20
☐	169	Christian Due-Boje, Södertälje	.20
☐	170	Jonas Heed, Södertälje	.20
☐	171	Josef Boumedienne, Södertälje	.20
☐	172	Marko Virtanen, Södertälje	.20
☐	173	Kyosti Karjalainen, Södertälje	.20
☐	174	Jorgen Bemstrom, Södertälje	.20
☐	175	Joakim Eriksson, Södertälje	.20
☐	176	Jens Ohlinng, Södertälje	.20
☐	177	Martin Hostak, Södertälje	.20
☐	178	Lars Dahlstrom, Södertälje	.20
☐	179	Niklas Brannstrom, Södertälje	.20
☐	180	Mikko Mäkelä, Södertälje	.50
☐	181	Petr Korinek, Södertälje	.20
☐	182	Joakim Persson (G), Vasterås	.20
☐	183	Tobias Lilja, Vasterås	.20
☐	184	Edvin Frylen, Vasterås	.20
☐	185	Jakob Karlsson, Vasterås	.20
☐	186	Johan Tornberg, Vasterås	.20
☐	187	Patrik Hoglund, Vasterås	.20
☐	188	Mattias Loof, Vasterås	.20
☐	189	Mikael Pettersson, Vasterås	.20
☐	190	Johan Modin, Vasterås	.20
☐	191	Fredrik Eriksson, Vasterås	.20
☐	192	Henrik Nordfeldt, Vasterås	.20
☐	193	Jonas Olsson, Vasterås	.20
☐	194	Roger Jonsson, Vasterås	.20
☐	195	Roger Rosen, Vasterås	.20
☐	196	Henric Bjorkman, Vasterås	.20
☐	197	Harri Sillgren, Vasterås	.20
☐	198	Paul Anderson Everberg, Vasterås	.20
☐	199	Tommy Söderström (G), Djurgårdens	.75
☐	200	Stefan Nilsson, Luleå	.20
☐	201	Tomas Jonsson, Leksands	.35
☐	202	Jonas Bergqvist, Leksands	.20
☐	203	Christer Olsson, Frölunda	.35
☐	204	Per Svartvadet, MoDo	.20
☐	205	Anders Huss, Brynäs	.20
☐	206	Roger Johansson, Färjestad	.20
☐	207	Stefan Örnskog, HV 71	.20
☐	208	Anders Eldebrink, Södertälje	.20
☐	209	Niclas Havelid, AIK	.20
☐	210	Charles Berglund, Djurgårdens	.20
☐	211	Kai Nurminen, Frölunda	.20
☐	212	Stefan Nilsson, Luleå	.35
☐	213	Per-Erik Eklund, Leksands	.50
☐	214	Janne Ojanen, Malmö	.50
☐	215	Per Svartvadet, MoDo	.20
☐	216	Michael Sundlöv (G), Brynäs	.20
☐	217	Roger Johansson, Färjestad	.20
☐	218	Stefan Örnskog, HV 71	.20
☐	219	Kyosti Karjalainen, Södertälje	.20
☐	220	Roger Rosen, Västerås	.20
☐	221	Jonas Bergvist, Leksands	.20
☐	222	Esa Keskinen, HV 71	.50
☐	223	Christer Olsson, Frölunda	.35
☐	224	Checklist	.20
☐	225	Checklist	.20

STICK-UM'S

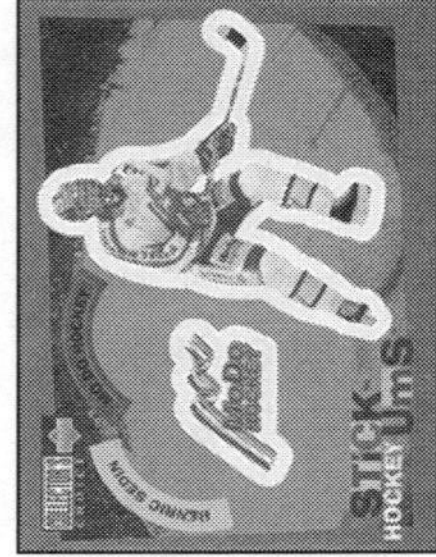

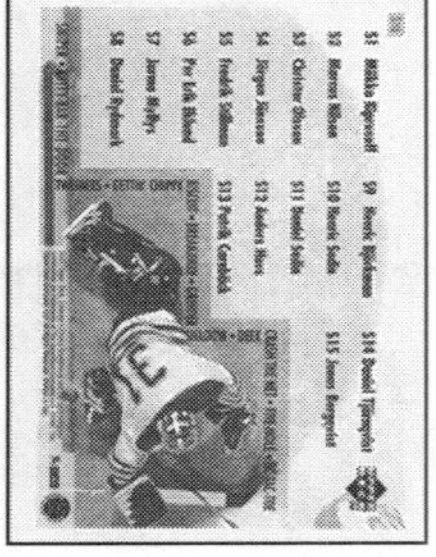

Stick-Um's insertion ratio is [1:3].

Insert Set (15 stickers): 35.00

Poster: 3.00

	No.	Player	NRMT-MT
☐	S1	Miika Kiprusoff (G), AIK	4.00
☐	S2	Marcus Nilsson, Djurgårdens	2.00
☐	S3	Christer Olsson, Frölunda	2.00
☐	S4	Jörgen Jönsson, Färjestad	2.00
☐	S5	Fredrik Stillman, HV 71	2.00
☐	S6	Per-Erik Eklund, Leksands	2.00
☐	S7	Jarmo Myllys (G), Luleå	4.00
☐	S8	Daniel Rydmark, Malmö	2.00
☐	S9	Henric Bjorkman, Vasteras	2.00
☐	S10	Henrik Sedin, MoDo	6.00
☐	S11	Daniel Sedin, MoDo	6.00
☐	S12	Anders Huss, Brynäs	2.00
☐	S13	Patrik Carnback, Frölunda	2.00
☐	S14	Daniel Tjarnqvist, Djurgårdens	2.00
☐	S15	Jonas Bergqvist, Leksands	2.00

UPPER DECK SELECTS

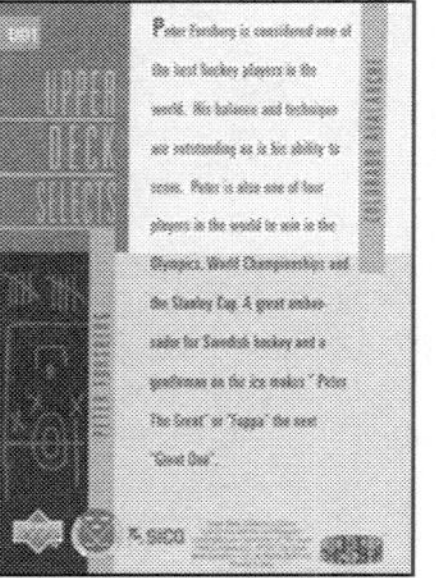

UD Selects insertion ratio is [1:8].

Insert Set (15 cards): 65.00

	No.	Player	NRMT-MT
☐	UDS1	Peter Forsberg, Col.	12.00
☐	UDS2	Daniel Sedin, MoDo	8.00
☐	UDS3	Niklas Falk, Djurgårdens	4.00
☐	UDS4	Marko Jantunen, Frölunda	4.00
☐	UDS5	Ville Peltonen, Frölunda	4.00
☐	UDS6	Jörgen Jönsson, Färjestad	4.00
☐	UDS7	Roger Johansson, Färjestad	4.00
☐	UDS8	Stefan Ornskog, HV 71	4.00
☐	UDS9	Henrik Sedin, MoDo	8.00
☐	UDS10	Jonas Bergqvist, Leksands	4.00
☐	UDS11	Tomas Jonsson, Leksands	6.00
☐	UDS12	Stefan Nilsson, Luleå	4.00
☐	UDS13	Janne Ojanen, Malmö	6.00
☐	UDS14	Magnus Wernblom, MoDo	4.00
☐	UDS15	Edvin Frylen, Västerås	4.00

YOU CRASH THE GAME

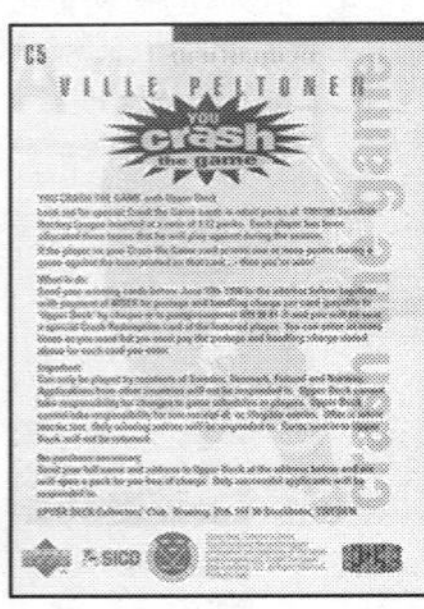

Insertion ratio is [1:12].

Insert Set (30 cards): 150.00

	No.	Player	NRMT-MT
☐	C1	Patric Kjellberg, Djurgårdens	6.00
☐	C2	Mikael Johansson, Djurgårdens	6.00
☐	C3	Daniel Tjärnqvist, Djugårdens	6.00
☐	C4	Christer Olsson, Frölunda	6.00
☐	C5	Ville Peltonen, Frölunda	6.00
☐	C6	Kai Nurminen, Frölunda	6.00
☐	C7	Stefan Nilsson, Luleå	6.00
☐	C8	Jan Mertzig, Luleå	6.00
☐	C9	Anders Carlsson, Leksands	6.00
☐	C10	Jonas Bergqvist, Leksands	6.00
☐	C11	Magnus Svensson, Leksands	6.00
☐	C12	Janne Ojanen, Malmö	8.00
☐	C13	Marko Kiprusoff, Malmö	6.00
☐	C14	Juha Riihijärvi, Malmö	6.00
☐	C15	Daniel Sedin, MoDo	12.00
☐	C16	Henrik Sedin, MoDo	12.00
☐	C17	Evgeny Davydov, Brynäs	6.00
☐	C18	Anders Hussm Brynäs	6.00
☐	C19	Janne Larsson, Brynäs	6.00
☐	C20	Roger Johansson, Färjestad	6.00
☐	C21	Jörgen Jönsson, Färjestad	6.00
☐	C22	Kristian Huselius, Färjestad	6.00
☐	C23	Stefan Örnskog, HV 71	6.00
☐	C24	Anders Huusko, HV 71	6.00
☐	C25	Esa Keskinen, HV 71	8.00
☐	C26	Joakim Eriksson, Södertälje	6.00
☐	C27	Anders Eldebrink, Södertälje	6.00
☐	C28	Mikko Mäkelä, Södertälje	8.00
☐	C29	Henric Bjorkman, Västerås	6.00
☐	C30	Roger Rosen, Västerås	6.00

1997 - 98 VALU-NET

These phone cards have up to four versions. Each card is a $5 phone card (sold individually at Shoppers Drug Mart and Pharmaprix in Canada). A number of promo cards were available as well as "Ask Me About Valu-Net" badges in both French and English.

Imprint: © VALU-NET TELECOMMUNICATIONS INC.

Complete Set (24 cards):

	Player	NRMT-MT
☐	Marc Crawford, Coach, Cdn.	5.00
☐	Martin Brodeur (G), Cdn.	6.00
☐	Curtis Joseph (G), Cdn.	5.00
☐☐☐	Patrick Roy (G), Cdn.	12.00
☐	Rob Blake, Cdn.	5.00
☐	Ray Bourque, Cdn.	5.00
☐☐☐	Eric Desjardins, Cdn.	5.00
☐	Adam Foote, Cdn.	5.00
☐	Al MacInnis, Cdn.	5.00
☐	Chris Pronger, Cdn.	5.00
☐	Scott Stevens, Cdn.	5.00
☐	Rod Brind'Amour, Cdn.	5.00
☐	Shayne Corson, Cdn.	5.00
☐	Theoren Fleury, Cdn.	5.00
☐	Wayne Gretzky, Cdn.	15.00
☐☐☐	Paul Kariya, Cdn.	10.00
☐	Trevor Linden, Cdn.	5.00
☐☐☐	Eric Lindros, Cdn.	10.00
☐	Joe Nieuwendyk, Cdn.	5.00
☐	Keith Primeau, Cdn.	5.00
☐☐☐	Joe Sakic, Cdn.	8.00
☐☐☐	Brendan Shanahan, Cdn.	5.00
☐	Steve Yzerman, Cdn.	8.00
☐	Rob Zamuner, Cdn.	5.00

PLAYERS, PREMIUM AND SIGNAUTURE SERIES

These three series were sold as complete sets. Except for one or two poses, photos are different for all three series. Players Series cards (10 phone time units) were limited to 25,000 copies, Premium Series cards (12 phone time units) were limited to 8,000 copies and Signature Series cards (15 phone time units) were autographed and limited to 999 copies. We have no pricing information on these series.

Complete Set (24 cards):

Album:

	Player
□□□	Marc Crawford, Coach, Cdn.
□□□	Martin Brodeur (G), Cdn.
□□□	Curtis Joseph (G), Cdn.
□□□	Patrick Roy (G), Cdn.
□□□	Rob Blake, Cdn.
□□□	Ray Bourque, Cdn.
□□□	Eric Desjardins, Cdn.
□□□	Adam Foote, Cdn.
□□□	Al MacInnis, Cdn.
□□□	Chris Pronger, Cdn.
□□□	Scott Stevens, Cdn.
□□□	Rod Brind'Amour, Cdn.
□□□	Shayne Corson, Cdn.
□□□	Theoren Fleury, Cdn.
□□□	Wayne Gretzky, Cdn.
□□□	Paul Kariya, Cdn.
□□□	Trevor Linden, Cdn.
□□□	Eric Lindros, Cdn.
□□□	Joe Nieuwendyk, Cdn.
□□□	Keith Primeau, Cdn.
□□□	Mark Recchi, Cdn.
□□□	Joe Sakic, Cdn.
□□□	Brendan Shanahan, Cdn.
□□□	Steve Yzerman, Cdn.
□□□	Rob Zamuner, Cdn.
□□	Team Canada
□□	Team Canada
□□	Team Canada
□□	Team Canada
□□	Team Canada

1997 - 98 VISIONS SIGNINGS

These cards have two versions: the regular card and a gold parallel. There are only four hockey players in this 50-card four-sport set. A 50-card regular set sells for $20 and a 50-card gold set sells for $60.

Imprint: © 1997 THE SCORE BOARD, INC.

	No.	Player	Reg.	Gold
□□	40	Dainius Zubrus	.75	2.00
□□	41	Joe Thornton	1.50	4.50
□□	42	Daniel Cleary	.75	2.00
□□	43	Sergei Samsonov, Detroit-IHL	1.50	4.50

AUTOGRAPHS

Other hockey singles may exist.

	Player	NRMT-MT
□	Sergei Samsonov	35.00
□	Joe Thornton	35.00
□	Dainius Zubrus	25.00

ARTISTRY

These cards have two versions: the regular card and an autographed parallel. There is only one hockey player in this 20-card set. A 20-card set sells for $125.

	No.	Player	Auto.	Reg.
□□	A20	Dainius Zubrus	6.00	50.00

1997 - 98 ZENITH

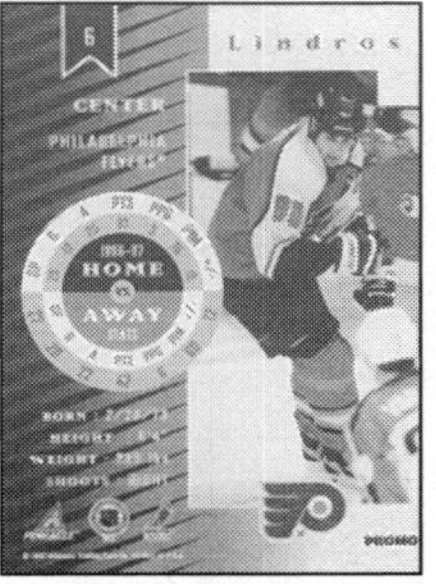

These cards have three versions: the regular card, a Silver parallel and a Gold parallel. At least four cards also have a promo version.

Imprint: © 1998 PINNACLE TRADING CARD CO.

	No.	Player	Gold	Sil.	Reg.
		Complete Set (100 cards):	15.00	3.00	.50
□□□	1	Jarome Iginla, Cgy.	50.00	7.50	1.50
□□□	2	Peter Forsberg, Col.	225.00	25.00	5.00
□□□	3	Brendan Shanahan, Det.	125.00	15.00	3.00
□□□	4	Wayne Gretzky, NYR.	500.00	50.00	10.00
□□□	5	Steve Yzerman, Det.	225.00	25.00	5.00
□□□□	6	Eric Lindros, Pha.	300.00	35.00	6.50
□□□	7	Keith Tkachuk, Pho.	70.00	10.00	2.00
□□□	8	John LeClair, Pha.	100.00	12.50	2.50
□□□□	9	John Vanbiesbrouck (G), Fla.	125.00	15.00	3.00
□□□	10	Patrick Roy (G), Col.	350.00	40.00	8.00
□□□	11	Ray Bourque, Bos.	100.00	12.50	2.50
□□□	12	Theoren Fleury, Cgy.	50.00	7.50	1.50
□□□	13	Brian Leetch, NYR.	50.00	7.50	1.50
□□□	14	Chris Chelios, Chi.	70.00	10.00	2.00
□□□	15	Paul Kariya, Ana.	300.00	35.00	6.50
□□□	16	Mark Messier, Van.	100.00	12.50	2.50
□□□	17	Curtis Joseph (G), Edm.	125.00	15.00	3.00
□□□	18	Mike Richter (G), NYR.	50.00	7.50	1.50
□□□	19	Jeremy Roenick, Pho.	50.00	7.50	1.50
□□□	20	Dominik Hasek (G), Buf.	150.00	17.50	3.50
□□□	21	Martin Brodeur (G), N.J.	150.00	17.50	3.50
□□□	22	Sergei Fedorov, Det.	100.00	12.50	2.50
□□□	23	Pierre Turgeon, Stl.	30.00	5.00	1.00
□□□	24	Teemu Selänne, Ana.	150.00	17.50	3.50
□□□	25	Brett Hull, Stl.	100.00	12.50	2.50
□□□□	26	Saku Koivu, Mtl.	150.00	17.50	3.50
□□□	27	Owen Nolan, S.J.	30.00	5.00	1.00
□□□	28	Jozef Stumpel, L.A.	30.00	5.00	1.00
□□□	29	Joe Sakic, Col.	175.00	20.00	4.00
□□□	30	Zigmund Palffy, NYI.	50.00	7.50	1.50
□□□	31	Jaromir Jagr, Pgh.	225.00	25.00	5.00
□□□	32	Adam Oates, Wsh.	50.00	7.50	1.50
□□□	33	Jeff Friesen, S.J.	30.00	5.00	1.00
□□□	34	Pavel Bure, Van.	150.00	17.50	3.50
□□□	35	Chris Osgood (G), Det.	70.00	10.00	2.00
□□□	36	Mark Recchi, Mtl.	30.00	5.00	1.00
□□□	37	Mike Modano, Dal.	100.00	12.50	2.50
□□□	38	Félix Potvin (G), Tor.	100.00	12.50	2.50
□□□	39	Vincent Damphousse, Mtl.	50.00	7.50	1.50
□□□	40	Byron Dafoe (G), Bos.	15.00	3.00	.50
□□□	41	Luc Robitaille, L.A.	30.00	5.00	1.00
□□□	42	Peter Bondra, Wsh.	70.00	10.00	2.00
□□□	43	Daniel Alfredsson, Ott.	30.00	5.00	1.00
□□□□	44	Pat LaFontaine, NYR.	30.00	5.00	1.00
□□□	45	Mikael Renberg, T.B.	15.00	3.00	.50
□□□	46	Doug Gilmour, N.J.	50.00	7.50	1.50
□□□	47	Dino Ciccarelli, Fla.	30.00	5.00	1.00
□□□	48	Mats Sundin, Tor.	100.00	12.50	2.50
□□□	49	Ed Belfour (G), Dal.	50.00	7.50	1.50
□□□	50	Ron Francis, Pgh.	50.00	7.50	1.50
□□□	51	Miroslav Satan, Buf.	15.00	3.00	.50
□□□	52	Cory Stillman, Cgy.	15.00	3.00	.50
□□□	53	Bryan Berard, NYI.	50.00	7.50	1.50
□□□	54	Keith Primeau, Car.	30.00	5.00	1.00
□□□	55	Eric Dazé, Chi.	30.00	5.00	1.00
□□□	56	Chris Gratton, Pha.	30.00	5.00	1.00
□□□	57	Claude Lemieux, Col.	30.00	5.00	1.00
□□□	58	Nicklas Lidström, Det.	30.00	5.00	1.00
□□□	59	Olaf Kolzig (G), Wsh.	50.00	7.50	1.50
□□□	60	Grant Fuhr (G), Stl.	30.00	5.00	1.00
□□□	61	Jamie Langenbrunner, Dal.	30.00	5.00	1.00
□□□	62	Doug Weight, Edm.	50.00	7.50	1.50
□□□	63	Joe Nieuwendyk, Dal.	30.00	5.00	1.00
□□□	64	Yanic Perreault, L.A.	15.00	3.00	.50
□□□	65	Jocelyn Thibault (G), Mtl.	50.00	7.50	1.50
□□□	66	Guy Hebert (G), Ana.	30.00	5.00	1.00
□□□	67	Shayne Corson, Mtl.	30.00	5.00	1.00
□□□	68	Bobby Holik, N.J.	15.00	3.00	.50
□□□	69	Sami Kapanen, Car.	15.00	3.00	.50
□□□	70	Robert Reichel, NYI.	15.00	3.00	.50
□□□	71	Ryan Smyth, Edm.	30.00	5.00	1.00
□□□	72	Alexei Yashin, Ott.	70.00	10.00	2.00
□□□	73	Trevor Linden, Van.	30.00	5.00	1.00
□□□	74	Rod Brind'Amour, Pha.	30.00	5.00	1.00
□□□	75	Dave Gagner, Fla.	15.00	3.00	.50
□□□	76	Nikolai Khabibulin (G), Pho.	50.00	7.50	1.50
□□□	77	Tom Barrasso (G), Pgh.	30.00	5.00	1.00
□□□	78	Tony Amonte, Chi.	30.00	5.00	1.00
□□□	79	Alexander Mogilny, Van.	50.00	7.50	1.50
□□□	80	Jason Allison, Bos.	50.00	7.50	1.50
□□□	**81**	**Patrik Elias, N.J., RC**	**30.00**	**5.00**	**1.50**
□□□	**82**	**Mike Johnson, Tor., RC**	**80.00**	**12.00**	**5.00**
□□□	83	Richard Zednik, Wsh.	15.00	3.00	1.00
□□□	84	Patrick Marleau, S.J.	60.00	9.00	2.50
□□□	85	Mattias Ohlund, Van.	20.00	4.00	1.50
□□□	86	Sergei Samsonov, Bos.	90.00	12.00	3.00
□□□	**87**	**Marco Sturm, S.J., RC**	**20.00**	**4.00**	**1.00**
□□□	88	Alyn McCauley, Tor.	60.00	9.00	2.50
□□□	89	Chris Phillips, Ott.	20.00	4.00	1.50
□□□	**90**	**Bredan Morrison, N.J., RC**	**90.00**	**15.00**	**6.00**
□□□	**91**	**Vaclav Prospal, Pha., RC**	**35.00**	**7.00**	**2.00**
□□□	92	Joe Thornton, Bos.	90.00	12.00	3.00
□□□	93	Boyd Devereaux, Edm.	15.00	3.00	1.00
□□□	94	Alexei Morozov, Pgh.	60.00	9.00	2.50
□□□	**95**	**Vincent Lecavalier, Cdn., RC**	**350.00**	**40.00**	**15.00**
□□□	**96**	**Manny Malhotra, Cdn., RC, Err. (Maholtra)**	**80.00**	**12.00**	**4.00**
□□□	**97**	**Roberto Luongo (G), Cdn., RC**	**200.00**	**25.00**	**8.00**
□□□	98	Mathieu Garon (G), Cdn.	25.00	5.00	2.00
□□□	**99**	**Alex Tanguay, Cdn., RC**	**55.00**	**10.00**	**3.00**
□□□	100	Josh Holden, Cdn.	25.00	5.00	2.00

OVERSIZE 5" x 7" CARDS

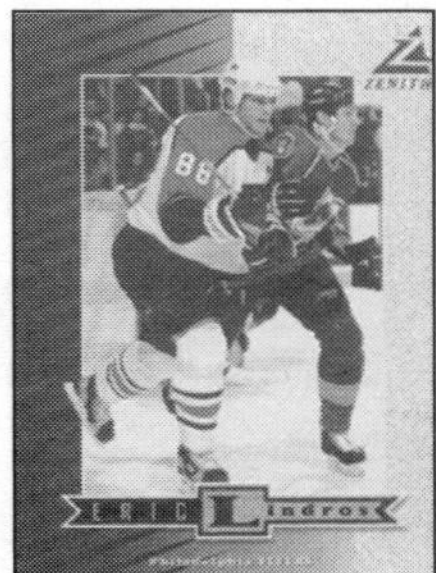

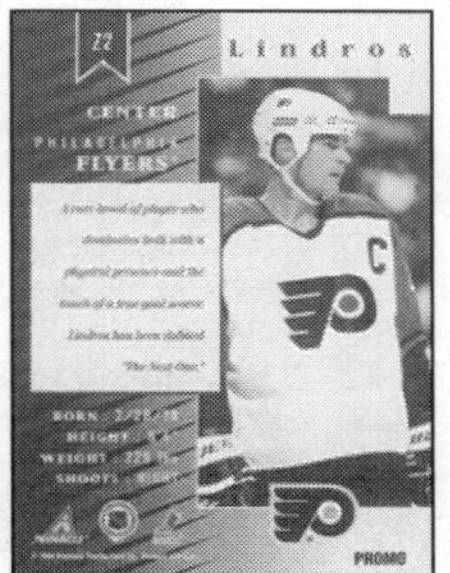

These cards have three versions: the regular card, an Impulse parallel and a Golden Impulse parallel (serial numbered out of 100). One standard-sized card came packaged inside each 5" x 7" card. Collectors could either keep the 5" x 7" card or tear the oversized card to see which card was inside. Oversize cards do not have the same photos as the smaller cards. Nine different 5" x 7" promo cards exist; each promo card has the same value as the regular card.

Card Size: 5" x 7"

Complete Set (80 cards):

	No.	Player	Gold	Sil.	Reg.
□□□	Z1	Wayne Gretzky, NYR.	500.00	50.00	10.00
□□□□	Z2	Eric Lindros, Pha.	300.00	35.00	6.50
□□□	Z3	Patrick Roy (G), Col.	350.00	40.00	8.00
□□□□	Z4	John Vanbiesbrouck (G), Fla.	125.00	15.00	3.00
□□□	Z5	Martin Brodeur (G), N.J.	150.00	15.00	3.50
□□□□	Z6	Teemu Selänne, Ana.	150.00	15.00	3.50
□□□□	Z7	Joe Sakic, Col.	175.00	20.00	4.00
□□□	Z8	Jaromir Jagr, Pgh.	225.00	25.00	5.00
□□□	Z9	Brendan Shanahan, Det.	125.00	15.00	3.00
□□□	Z10	Ed Belfour (G), Dal.	50.00	7.50	1.50
□□□	Z11	Guy Hebert (G), Ana.	30.00	5.00	1.00
□□□	Z12	Doug Gilmour, N.J.	50.00	7.50	1.50
□□□	Z13	Keith Primeau, Car.	30.00	5.00	1.00
□□□	Z14	Grant Fuhr (G), Stl.	30.00	5.00	1.00
□□□	Z15	Joe Nieuwendyk, Dal.	30.00	5.00	1.00
□□□	Z16	Ryan Smyth, Edm.	30.00	5.00	1.00
□□□	Z17	Chris Osgood (G), Det.	70.00	10.00	2.00
□□□	Z18	Keith Tkachuk, Pho.	70.00	10.00	2.00
□□□	Z19	Peter Forsberg, Col.	225.00	25.00	5.00

□□□	Z20	Jarome Iginla, Cgy.	50.00	7.50	1.50
□□□□	Z21	Steve Yzerman, Det.	225.00	25.00	5.00
□□□	Z22	Jeremy Roenick, Pho.	50.00	7.50	1.50
□□□	Z23	Jozef Stumpel, L.A.	30.00	5.00	1.00
□□□	Z24	Mark Recchi, Mtl.	30.00	5.00	1.00
□□□	Z25	Daniel Alfredsson, Ott.	30.00	5.00	1.00
□□□□	Z26	Pat LaFontaine, NYR.	30.00	5.00	1.00
□□□	Z27	Zigmund Palffy, NYI.	50.00	7.50	1.50
□□□	Z28	Jason Allison, Bos.	50.00	7.50	1.50
□□□	Z29	Yanic Perreault, L.A.	15.00	3.00	.50
□□□	Z30	Olaf Kolzig (G), Wsh.	50.00	7.50	1.50
□□□	Z31	Mikael Renberg, T.B.	15.00	3.00	.50
□□□	Z32	Bryan Berard, NYI.	50.00	7.50	1.50
□□□	Z33	Jocelyn Thibault (G), Mtl.	50.00	7.50	1.50
□□□	Z34	Shayne Corson, Mtl.	30.00	5.00	1.00
□□□	Z35	Dave Gagner, Fla.	15.00	3.00	.50
□□□	Z36	Claude Lemieux, Col.	15.00	3.00	.50
□□□□	Z37	Saku Koivu, Mtl.	150.00	17.50	3.50
□□□□	Z38	Curtis Joseph (G), Edm.	125.00	15.00	3.00
□□□	Z39	Chris Chelios, Chi.	70.00	10.00	2.00
□□□	Z40	Ray Bourque, Bos.	100.00	12.50	2.50
□□□	Z41	Adam Oates, Wsh.	50.00	7.50	1.50
□□□	Z42	Félix Potvin (G), Tor.	100.00	12.50	2.50
□□□	Z43	Peter Bondra, Wsh.	70.00	10.00	2.00
□□□	Z44	Sergei Fedorov, Det.	100.00	12.50	2.50
□□□□	Z45	Paul Kariya, Ana.	300.00	35.00	6.50
□□□	Z46	Theoren Fleury, Cgy.	50.00	7.50	1.50
□□□	Z47	John LeClair, Pha.	100.00	12.50	2.50
□□□	Z48	Brett Hull, Stl.	100.00	12.50	2.50
□□□	Z49	Rod Brind'Amour, Pha.	30.00	5.00	1.00
□□□	Z50	Doug Weight, Edm.	50.00	7.50	1.50
□□□	Z51	Jamie Langenbrunner, Dal.	30.00	5.00	1.00
□□□	Z52	Mats Sundin, Tor.	100.00	12.50	2.50
□□□	Z53	Ron Francis, Pgh.	50.00	7.50	1.50
□□□	Z54	Eric Dazé, Chi.	30.00	5.00	1.00
□□□	Z55	Nicklas Lidström, Det.	30.00	5.00	1.00
□□□	Z56	Luc Robitaille, L.A.	30.00	5.00	1.00
□□□	Z57	Vincent Damphousse, Mtl.	50.00	7.50	1.50
□□□	Z58	Mike Modano, Dal.	100.00	12.50	2.50
□□□	Z59	Pavel Bure, Van.	150.00	17.50	3.50
□□□	Z60	Owen Nolan, S.J.	30.00	5.00	1.00
□□□	Z61	Pierre Turgeon, Mtl.	30.00	5.00	1.00
□□□	Z62	Dominik Hasek (G), Buf.	150.00	17.50	3.50
□□□	Z63	Mike Richter (G), NYR.	50.00	7.50	1.50
□□□	Z64	Mark Messier, Van.	100.00	12.50	2.50
□□□	Z65	Brian Leetch, NYR.	50.00	7.50	1.50
□□□	Z66	Sergei Samsonov, Bos.	90.00	12.00	3.00
□□□	Z67	Alexei Morozov, Pgh.	60.00	9.00	2.50
□□□	Z68	Marco Sturm, S.J.	20.00	4.00	1.00
□□□	Z69	Patrik Elias, N.J.	30.00	5.00	1.00
□□□	Z70	Alyn McCauley, Tor.	60.00	9.00	2.50
□□□	Z71	Mike Johnson, Tor.	80.00	12.00	3.00
□□□	Z72	Richard Zednik, Wsh.	15.00	3.00	1.00
□□□	Z73	Mattias Ohlund, Van.	20.00	4.00	1.50
□□□	Z74	Joe Thornton, Bos.	90.00	12.00	3.00
□□□	Z75	Vincent Lecavalier, Cdn.	350.00	40.00	12.00
□□□	Z76	Manny Malhotra, Cdn.	80.00	12.00	3.00
□□□	Z77	Roberto Luongo (G), Cdn.	200.00	25.00	7.00
□□□	Z78	Mathieu Garon (G), Cdn.	25.00	5.00	2.00
□□□	Z79	Alex Tanguay, Cdn.	55.00	10.00	2.50
□□□	Z80	Josh Holden, Cdn.	25.00	5.00	2.00

CHASING THE CUP

Insertion ratio is [1:25].

Insert Set (15 cards): 300.00

	No.	Player	NRMT-MT
□	1	Patrick Roy (G), Col.	50.00
□	2	Wayne Gretzky, NYR.	60.00
□	3	Jaromir Jagr, Pgh.	30.00
□	4	Eric Lindros, Pha.	40.00
□	5	Mike Modano, Dal.	15.00
□	6	Brendan Shanahan, Det.	18.00
□	7	Brett Hull, Stl.	15.00
□	8	John LeClair, Pha.	15.00
□	9	Jocelyn Thibault (G), Mtl.	10.00
□	10	Ed Belfour (G), S.J.	10.00
□	11	Martin Brodeur (G), N.J.	20.00
□	12	Peter Forsberg, Col.	30.00
□	13	Saku Koivu, Mtl.	20.00
□	14	Pat LaFontaine, NYR.	8.00
□	15	Steve Yzerman, Det.	25.00

ROOKIE REIGN

Insertion ratio is [1:25].

Insert Set (15 cards): 300.00

	No.	Player	NRMT-MT
□	1	Sergei Samsonov, Bos.	35.00
□	2	Joe Thornton, Bos.	35.00
□	3	Erik Rasmussen, Buf.	10.00
□	4	Brendan Morrison, N.J.	30.00
□	5	Magnus Arvedsson, Ott.	10.00
□	6	Vaclav Prospal, Pha.	25.00
□	7	Brad Isbister, Pho.	10.00
□	8	Alexei Morozov, Pgh.	30.00
□	9	Marco Sturm, S.J.	10.00
□	10	Patrick Marleau, S.J.	30.00
□	11	Alyn McCauley, Tor.	30.00
□	12	Mike Johnson, Tor.	30.00
□	13	Mattias Ohlund, Van.	20.00
□	14	Patrik Elias, N.J.	25.00
□	15	Richard Zednik, Wsh.	10.00

Z-TEAM

These cards have three versions: the regular insert, a gold parallel insert and a 5" x 7" card.

Insert Set (9 cards): 1,600.00 425.00 425.00

	No.	Player	Gold	5x7	Reg.
□□□	1	Teemu Selänne, Ana.	150.00	35.00	35.00
□□□	2	Wayne Gretzky, NYR.	400.00	100.00	100.00
□□□	3	Patrick Roy (G), Col.	300.00	80.00	80.00
□□□	4	Eric Lindros, Pha.	250.00	65.00	65.00
□□□	5	Peter Forsberg, Col.	200.00	50.00	50.00
□□□	6	Paul Kariya, Ana.	250.00	65.00	65.00
□□□	7	John LeClair, Pha.	100.00	25.00	25.00
□□□	8	Martin Brodeur, N.J.	150.00	35.00	35.00
□□□	9	Brendan Shanahan, Det.	125.00	30.00	30.00

ROOKIE Z-TEAM

These cards have two versions: the regular card and a gold parallel.

Insert Set (9 cards): 625.00 240.00

	No.	Player	Gold	Reg.
□□	10	Joe Thornton, Bos.	125.00	50.00
□□	11	Mattias Ohlund, Van.	65.00	25.00
□□	12	Mike Johnson, Tor.	100.00	40.00
□□	13	Vaclav Prospal, Pha.	65.00	25.00
□□	14	Sergei Samsonov, Bos.	125.00	50.00
□□	15	Marco Sturm, S.J.	50.00	15.00
□□	16	Patrik Elias, N.J.	65.00	25.00
□□	17	Richard Zednik, Wsh.	50.00	15.00
□□	18	Alexei Morozov, Pgh.	85.00	35.00

1998 BOWMAN

These cards have three versions: the regular card, an O-Pee-Chee parallel and a 50th Anniversary parallel (50 copies of each). Topps also had plans to release BowmanChrome cards for numbers 1-164. There would be six versions to BowmanChrome: BowmanChrome, BowmanChrome Refractor, BowmanChrome O-Pee-Chee, BowmanChrome O-Pee-Chee Refractor, BowmanChrome 50th Anniversary and BowmanChrome 50th Anniversary Refractor. Prices may vary considerably for regional stars.

Complete Set (165 cards):

	No.	Player	50th	OPC	Reg.
□□□	1	Robert Esche (G), OHL	20.00	.75	.35
□□□	2	Chris Hajt, OHL	15.00	.35	.15
□□□	3	Mark McMahon, OHL	15.00	.35	.15
□□□	4	Jeff Brown, OHL	15.00	.35	.15
□□□	5	Richard Jackman, OHL	30.00	1.25	.65
□□□	6	Greg Labenski, OHL	15.00	.35	.15
□□□	7	Marek Pasmyk, OHL	15.00	.35	.15
□□□	8	Brian Willsie, OHL	15.00	.35	.15
□□□	9	Jason Ward, OHL	50.00	2.00	1.00
□□□	10	Manny Malhotra, OHL	100.00	4.00	2.00
□□□	11	Matt Cooke, OHL	15.00	.35	.15
□□□	12	Mike Gorman (G), OHL	20.00	.50	.25
□□□	13	Rodney Richard, OHL	15.00	.35	.15
□□□	14	David Legwand, OHL	250.00	10.00	5.00
□□□	15	Jon Sim, OHL	15.00	.50	.25
□□□	16	Peter Sarno, OHL	15.00	.50	.25
□□□	17	Andrew Long, OHL	15.00	.35	.15
□□□	18	Peter Cava, OHL	15.00	.35	.15
□□□	19	Colin Pepperall, OHL	15.00	.50	.25
□□□	20	Jay Legault, OHL	15.00	.50	.25
□□□	21	Brian Finley (G), OHL	20.00	.50	.25
□□□	22	Martin Skoula, OHL	15.00	.35	.15
□□□	23	Brian Campbell, OHL	15.00	.35	.15
□□□	24	Sean Blanchard, OHL	15.00	.35	.15
□□□	25	Bryan Allen, OHL	35.00	1.50	.75
□□□	26	Peter Hogan, OHL	15.00	.35	.15
□□□	27	Nick Boynton, OHL	20.00	.75	.35
□□□	28	Matt Bradley, OHL	25.00	1.00	.50
□□□	29	Jeremy Adduono, OHL	15.00	.50	.25
□□□	30	Mike Henrich, OHL	35.00	1.50	.75
□□□	31	Justin Papineau, OHL	30.00	1.25	.65
□□□	32	Bujar Amidovski, OHL	15.00	.35	.15
□□□	33	Robert Mailloux, OHL	15.00	.35	.15
□□□	34	Daniel Tkaczuk, OHL	60.00	2.50	1.25
□□□	35	Sean Avery, OHL	15.00	.35	.15
□□□	36	Mark Bell, OHL	15.00	.50	.25
□□□	37	Kevin Colley, OHL	15.00	.35	.15
□□□	38	Norm Milley, OHL	20.00	.75	.35
□□□	39	Scott Barney, OHL	20.00	.75	.35
□□□	40	Joel Trottier, OHL	15.00	.35	.15
□□□	41	Brent Belecki (G), WHL	20.00	.50	.25
□□□	42	Randy Petruk (G), WHL	20.00	.50	.25
□□□	43	Brad Ference, WHL	20.00	.75	.35
□□□	44	Perry Johnson, WHL	15.00	.35	.15
□□□	45	Joel Kwiatkowski, WHL	15.00	.35	.15
□□□	46	Zenith Komarniski, WHL	15.00	.50	.25
□□□	47	Greg Kuznik, WHL	15.00	.35	.15
□□□	48	Andrew Ference, WHL	15.00	.35	.15
□□□	49	Jason Deleurme, WHL	15.00	.50	.25
□□□	50	Trent Whitfield, WHL	15.00	.35	.15
□□□	51	Dylan Gyori, WHL	15.00	.35	.15
□□□	52	Todd Robinson, WHL	25.00	1.00	.50
□□□	53	Marian Hossa, WHL	150.00	6.00	3.00
□□□	54	Mike Hurley, WHL	15.00	.35	.15
□□□	55	Greg Leeb, WHL	20.00	.75	.35
□□□	56	Andrej Podkonicky, WHL	15.00	.35	.15
□□□	57	Quinn Hancock, WHL	15.00	.50	.25
□□□	58	Marian Cisar, WHL	20.00	.75	.35
□□□	59	Bret DeCecco, WHL	15.00	.35	.15
□□□	60	Brenden Morrow, WHL	15.00	.50	.25
□□□	61	Evan Lindsay (G), WHL	20.00	.50	.25
□□□	62	Terry Friesen (G), WHL	20.00	.50	.25
□□□	63	Ryan Shannon, WHL	15.00	.35	.15
□□□	64	Michal Rozsival, WHL	15.00	.35	.15
□□□	65	Luc Theoret, WHL	15.00	.35	.15
□□□	66	Brad Stuart, WHL	50.00	2.00	1.00
□□□	67	Burke Henry, WHL	15.00	.35	.15
□□□	68	Cory Sarich, WHL	25.00	1.00	.50
□□□	69	Martin Sonnenberg, WHL	15.00	.35	.15
□□□	70	Mark Smith, WHL	15.00	.50	.25
□□□	71	Shawn McNeil, WHL	15.00	.50	.25
□□□	72	Brad Moran, WHL	15.00	.50	.25
□□□	73	Josh Holden, WHL	25.00	1.00	.50
□□□	74	Cory Cyrenne, WHL	15.00	.50	.25
□□□	75	Shane Willis, WHL	25.00	1.00	.50
□□□	76	Stefan Cherneski, WHL	15.00	.50	.25
□□□	77	Jay Henderson, WHL	15.00	.35	.15
□□□	78	Ronald Petrovicky, WHL	15.00	.50	.25
□□□	79	Sergei Varlamov, WHL	35.00	1.50	.75
□□□	80	Chad Hinz, WHL	15.00	.35	.15
□□□	81	Mathieu Garon (G), QMJHL	50.00	2.00	1.00
□□□	82	Mathieu Chouinard (G), QMJHL	20.00	.75	.35
□□□	83	Dominic Perna, QMJHL	25.00	1.00	.50
□□□	84	Didier Tremblay, QMJHL	15.00	.35	.15
□□□	85	Mike Ribiero, QMJHL	75.00	3.00	1.50
□□□	86	Marty Johnston, QMJHL	15.00	.50	.25
□□□	87	Remi Royer, QMJHL	15.00	.35	.15
□□□	88	Patrick Pelchat, QMJHL	15.00	.35	.15
□□□	89	Daniel Corso, QMJHL	20.00	.75	.35
□□□	90	François Fortier, QMJHL	15.00	.35	.15
□□□	91	Marc-André Gaudet, QMJHL	15.00	.35	.15
□□□	92	François Beauchemin, QMJHL	15.00	.35	.15
□□□	93	Michel Tremblay, QMJHL	15.00	.35	.15
□□□	94	Jean-Philippe Pare, QMJHL	15.00	.35	.15
□□□	95	François Methot, QMJHL	15.00	.50	.25
□□□	96	David Thibeault, QMJHL	15.00	.50	.25
□□□	97	Jonathan Girard, Jr., QMJHL	15.00	.35	.15
□□□	98	Karol Bartanus, QMJHL	15.00	.35	.15
□□□	99	Peter Ratchuk, QMJHL	15.00	.35	.15
□□□	100	Pierre Dagenais, QMJHL	25.00	1.00	.50
□□□	101	Philippe Sauvé (G), QMJHL	35.00	1.50	.75
□□□	102	Rémi Bergeron (G), QMJHL	20.00	.50	.25
□□□	103	Vincent Lecavalier, QMJHL	300.00	12.00	6.00
□□□	104	Eric Chouinard, QMJHL	20.00	.75	.35
□□□	105	Oleg Timchenko, QMJHL	15.00	.35	.15
□□□	106	Sébastien Roger, QMJHL	15.00	.35	.15
□□□	107	Simon Gagné, QMJHL	20.00	.75	.35
□□□	108	Alex Tanguay, QMJHL	35.00	1.50	.75
□□□	109	David Gosselin, QMJHL	15.00	.35	.15

	No.	Player			
☐☐☐	110	Ramzi Abid, QMJHL	35.00	1.50	.75
☐☐☐	111	Eric Drouin, QMJHL	15.00	.35	.15
☐☐☐	112	Dominic Auger, QMJHL	15.00	.35	.15
☐☐☐	113	Martin Moise, QMJHL	15.00	.35	.15
☐☐☐	114	Randy Cooper, QMJHL	15.00	.35	.15
☐☐☐	115	Alexandre Mathieu, QMJHL	20.00	.75	.35
☐☐☐	116	Brad Richards, QMJHL	15.00	.35	.15
☐☐☐	117	Dmitri Tolkunov, QMJHL	15.00	.35	.15
☐☐☐	118	Alexei Tezikov, QMJHL	15.00	.35	.15
☐☐☐	119	Derrick Walser, QMJHL	15.00	.50	.25
☐☐☐	120	Adam Borzecki, QMJHL	15.00	.35	.15
☐☐☐	121	Ramzi Abid, CHL	35.00	1.50	.75
☐☐☐	122	Brett Allan, CHL	15.00	.35	.15
☐☐☐	123	Mark Bell, CHL	15.00	.50	.25
☐☐☐	124	Blair Betts, CHL	15.00	.35	.15
☐☐☐	125	Randy Copley, CHL	15.00	.35	.15
☐☐☐	126	Simon Gagné, CHL	20.00	.75	.35
☐☐☐	127	Michael Henrich, CHL	35.00	1.50	.75
☐☐☐	128	Vincent Lecavalier, CHL	300.00	12.00	6.00
☐☐☐	129	Norm Milley, CHL	20.00	.75	.35
☐☐☐	130	Chris Nielsen, CHL	15.00	.35	.15
☐☐☐	131	Rico Fata, CHL	100.00	4.00	2.00
☐☐☐	132	Mike Ribeiro, CHL	75.00	3.00	1.50
☐☐☐	133	Bryan Allen, CHL	35.00	1.50	.75
☐☐☐	134	John Erksine, CHL	15.00	.35	.15
☐☐☐	135	Jonathan Girard, Jr., CHL	15.00	.35	.15
☐☐☐	136	Stephen Peat, CHL	20.00	.75	.35
☐☐☐	137	Robyn Regehr, CHL	20.00	.75	.35
☐☐☐	138	Brad Stuart, CHL	50.00	2.00	1.00
☐☐☐	139	Patrick DesRochers (G), CHL	35.00	1.50	.75
☐☐☐	140	Jason Labarbera (G), CHL	25.00	1.00	.50
☐☐☐	141	David Cameron, CHL	15.00	.35	.15
☐☐☐	142	Jonathan Cheechoo, CHL	50.00	2.00	1.00
☐☐☐	143	Eric Chouinard, CHL	20.00	.75	.35
☐☐☐	144	Brent Gauvreau, CHL	15.00	.35	.15
☐☐☐	145	Scott Gomez, CHL	25.00	1.00	.50
☐☐☐	146	Jeff Heerema, CHL	35.00	1.50	.75
☐☐☐	147	David Legwand, CHL	250.00	10.00	5.00
☐☐☐	148	Manny Malhotra, CHL	100.00	4.00	2.00
☐☐☐	149	Justin Papineau, CHL	30.00	1.25	.65
☐☐☐	150	Andrew Peters, CHL	15.00	.35	.15
☐☐☐	151	Michael Rupp, CHL	35.00	1.50	.75
☐☐☐	152	Alex Tanguay, CHL	35.00	1.50	.75
☐☐☐	153	François Beauchemin, CHL	15.00	.35	.15
☐☐☐	154	Mathieu Biron, CHL	20.00	.75	.35
☐☐☐	155	Jiri Fischer, CHL	20.00	.75	.35
☐☐☐	156	Alex Henry, CHL	15.00	.35	.15
☐☐☐	157	Kyle Rossiter, CHL	15.00	.35	.15
☐☐☐	158	Martin Skoula, CHL	15.00	.35	.15
☐☐☐	159	Mathieu Chouinard (G), CHL	20.00	.75	.35
☐☐☐	160	Philippe Sauvé (G), CHL	35.00	1.50	.75
☐☐☐	161	MVP: Brian Finley (G), OHL	20.00	.50	.25
☐☐☐	162	MVP: Brent Belecki (G), WHL	20.00	.50	.25
☐☐☐	163	MVP: Dominic Perna, WHL	25.00	1.00	.50
☐☐☐	164	MVP: Jonathan Cheechoo, CHL	50.00	2.00	1.00
☐☐☐	165	Checklist	15.00	.35	.15

SCOUT'S CHOICE

Insert Set (21 cards): 65.00

	No.	Player	NRMT-MT
☐	SC1	Bryan Allen	3.00
☐	SC2	Manny Malhotra	6.00
☐	SC3	Daniel Tkaczuk	4.00
☐	SC4	Bujar Amidovski	2.00
☐	SC5	Patrick DesRochers (G)	3.00
☐	SC6	Brad Ference	2.00
☐	SC7	Marian Hossa	6.00
☐	SC8	Brad Stuart	3.00
☐	SC9	Sergei Varlamov	3.00
☐	SC10	Randy Petruk (G)	2.00
☐	SC11	Karol Bartanus	2.00
☐	SC12	Vincent Lecavalier	12.00
☐	SC13	Jonathan Girard	2.00
☐	SC14	Peter Ratchuk	2.00
☐	SC15	Alex Tanguay	3.00
☐	SC16	Rico Fata	6.00
☐	SC17	Brian Finley	2.00
☐	SC18	Jonathan Cheechoo	4.00
☐	SC19	Scott Gomez	2.00
☐	SC20	Michal Rozsival	2.00
☐	SC21	Mathieu Garon (G)	4.00

CERTIFIED AUTOGRAPHS

These cards have three versions: a blue foil card, a silver foil card and a gold foil card. There is believed to be fewer than 25 copies of each autographed gold foil card. Prices may vary for regional stars.

	No.	Player	Gold	Silver	Blue
☐☐☐	A1	Justin Papineau	80.00	30.00	20.00
☐☐☐	A2	Jason Labarbera (G)	75.00	25.00	18.00
☐☐☐	A3	Michael Rupp	80.00	30.00	20.00
☐☐☐	A4	Stephen Peat	60.00	20.00	15.00
☐☐☐	A5	Manny Malhotra	160.00	60.00	40.00
☐☐☐	A6	Michael Henrich	100.00	40.00	25.00
☐☐☐	A7	Kyle Rossiter	50.00	15.00	12.00
☐☐☐	A8	Mark Bell	50.00	15.00	12.00
☐☐☐	A9	Mathieu Chouinard (G)	75.00	25.00	18.00
☐☐☐	A10	Vincent Lecavalier	400.00	150.00	100.00
☐☐☐	A11	David Legwand	325.00	120.00	80.00
☐☐☐	A12	Bryan Allen	80.00	30.00	20.00
☐☐☐	A13	François Beauchemin	50.00	15.00	12.00
☐☐☐	A14	Robyn Regehr	50.00	15.00	12.00
☐☐☐	A15	Eric Chouinard	60.00	20.00	15.00
☐☐☐	A16	Norm Milley	60.00	20.00	15.00
☐☐☐	A17	Alex Henry	50.00	15.00	12.00
☐☐☐	A18	Ramzi Abid	80.00	30.00	20.00
☐☐☐	A19	Jiri Fischer	60.00	20.00	15.00
☐☐☐	A20	Patrick DesRochers (G)	100.00	40.00	25.00
☐☐☐	A21	Mathieu Biron	60.00	20.00	15.00
☐☐☐	A22	Brad Stuart	100.00	40.00	25.00
☐☐☐	A23	Philippe Sauvé (G)	100.00	40.00	25.00
☐☐☐	A24	John Erskine	50.00	15.00	12.00
☐☐☐	A25	Jonathan Cheechoo	120.00	45.00	30.00
☐☐☐	A26	Brett Allan	50.00	15.00	12.00
☐☐☐	A27	Scott Gomez	75.00	25.00	18.00
☐☐☐	A28	Chris Neilsen	50.00	15.00	12.00
☐☐☐	A29	David Cameron	50.00	15.00	12.00
☐☐☐	A30	Jonathan Girard, Jr.	50.00	15.00	12.00
☐☐☐	A31	Jeff Heerema	80.00	30.00	20.00
☐☐☐	A32	Blair Betts	50.00	15.00	12.00
☐☐☐	A33	Andrew Peters	50.00	15.00	12.00
☐☐☐	A34	Randy Copley	50.00	15.00	12.00
☐☐☐	A35	Alex Tanguay	80.00	30.00	20.00
☐☐☐	A36	Simon Gagné	75.00	25.00	18.00
☐☐☐	A37	Brent Gauvreau	50.00	15.00	12.00
☐☐☐	A38	Mike Ribeiro	120.00	45.00	30.00
☐☐☐	A39	Martin Skoula	50.00	15.00	12.00
☐☐☐	A40	Rico Fata	160.00	60.00	40.00

1998 MCDONALD'S NAGANO WAYNE GRETZKY

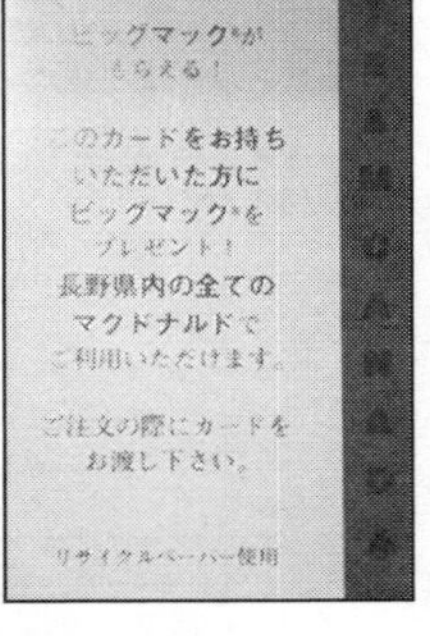

We have little information on this advertising card. It was issued during the 1998 Winter Olympics in Nagano, Japan.

	Player
☐	Wayne Gretzky, Cdn.

1998 - 99 DONRUSS PROMO

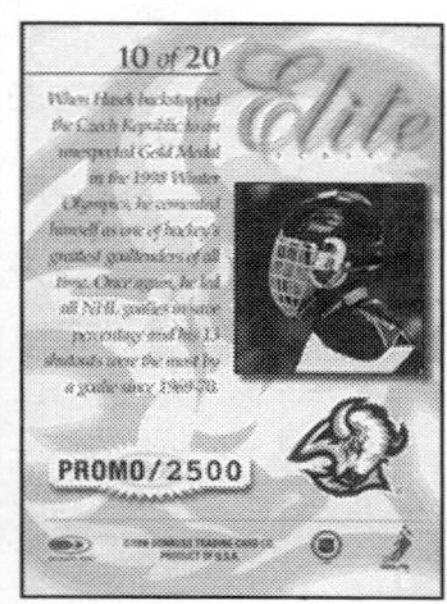

This series was terminated when Pinnacle Brands and Donruss Trading Company went bankrupt and lost their hockey license for 1998-99. This promo was for one of the "Elite Series" inserts. Other singles may exist.

	No.	Player
☐	10	Dominik Hasek (G), Buf.

1998 - 99 PACIFIC

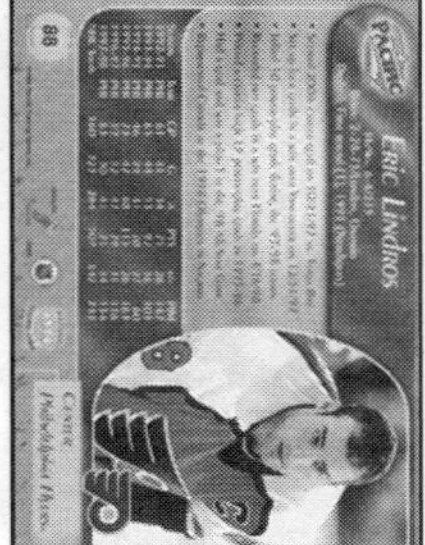

These cards have three versions: the regular card, a Red parallel and an Ice Blue parallel. Only the regular cards and Ice Blue parallels are priced for this edition. There is no card #66; the number was retired in recognition of Mario Lemieux.

Imprint: © 1998 Pacific Trading Cards, Inc.

Complete Set (450 cards):

Common Player: 15.00 .15

	No.	Player	Ice Blue	Reg.
☐☐☐	1	Damian Rhodes (G), Ott.	15.00	.15
☐☐☐	2	Mattias Ohlund, Van.	30.00	.25
☐☐☐	3	Craig Ludwig, Dal.	15.00	.15
☐☐☐	4	Rob Blake, L.A.	25.00	.35
☐☐☐	5	Nicklas Lidström, Det.	25.00	.35
☐☐☐	6	Calle Johansson, Wsh.	15.00	.15
☐☐☐	7	Chris Chelios, Chi.	50.00	.75
☐☐☐	8	Teemu Selänne, Ana.	100.00	1.50
☐☐☐	9	Paul Kariya, Ana.	250.00	2.50
☐☐☐	10	Pavel Bure, Van.	100.00	1.50
☐☐☐	11	Mark Messier, Van.	65.00	1.00
☐☐☐	12	Peter Bondra, Wsh.	50.00	.75
☐☐☐	13	Mats Sundin, Tor.	65.00	1.00
☐☐☐	14	Brendan Shanahan, Det.	75.00	1.25
☐☐☐	15	Jamie Langenbrunner, Dal.	25.00	.35
☐☐☐	16	Brett Hull, Stl.	65.00	1.00
☐☐☐	17	Rod Brind'Amour, Pha.	25.00	.35
☐☐☐	18	Adam Deadmarsh, Col.	15.00	.15
☐☐☐	19	Steve Yzerman, Det.	175.00	2.00
☐☐☐	20	Ed Belfour (G), Dal.	35.00	.50
☐☐☐	21	Peter Forsberg, Col.	175.00	2.00
☐☐☐	22	Dino Ciccarelli, Det.	25.00	.35
☐☐☐	23	Brian Bellows, Wsh.	15.00	.15
☐☐☐	24	Janne Niinimaa, Edm.	25.00	.35
☐☐☐	25	Joe Nieuwendyk, Dal.	25.00	.35
☐☐☐	26	Patrik Elias, N.J.	15.00	.15
☐☐☐	27	Michael Peca, Buf.	25.00	.35
☐☐☐	28	Tie Domi, Tor.	15.00	.15
☐☐☐	29	Félix Potvin (G), Tor.	65.00	1.00
☐☐☐	30	Martin Brodeur (G), N.J.	100.00	1.50
☐☐☐	31	Grant Fuhr (G), Stl.	25.00	.35
☐☐☐	32	Trevor Linden, NYI.	25.00	.35
☐☐☐	33	Patrick Roy (G), Col.	300.00	3.00
☐☐☐	34	John Vanbiesbrouck (G), Fla.	75.00	1.25
☐☐☐	35	Tom Barrasso (G), Pgh.	25.00	.35
☐☐☐	36	Matthew Barnaby, Buf.	15.00	.15

□□□	37	Olaf Kolzig (G), Wsh.	35.00	.50
□□□	38	Pavol Demitra, Stl.	15.00	.15
□□□	39	Dominik Hasek (G), Buf.	100.00	1.50
□□□	40	Chris Terreri (G), S.J.	15.00	.15
□□□	41	Jason Allison, Bos.	35.00	.50
□□□	42	Richard Smehik, Buf.	15.00	.15
□□□	43	Frank Banham, Ana.	15.00	.15
□□□	44	Chris Pronger, Stl.	25.00	.35
□□□	45	Matt Cullen, Ana.	15.00	.15
□□□	46	Mike Rucinski, Ana.	15.00	.15
□□□	47	Mike Crowley, Ana.	15.00	.15
□□□	48	Scott Young, Ana.	15.00	.15
□□□	49	Brian Savage, Mtl.	15.00	.15
□□□	50	Travis Green, Ana.	15.00	.15
□□□	51	John LeClair, Pha.	65.00	1.00
□□□	52	Adam Foote, Col.	15.00	.15
□□□	53	Derek Morris, Cgy.	15.00	.15
□□□	54	Guy Hebert (G), Ana.	25.00	.35
□□□	55	Chris Gratton, Pha.	25.00	.35
□□□	56	Sergei Zubov, Dal.	25.00	.35
□□□	57	Dave Karpa, Ana.	15.00	.15
□□□	58	Sergei Varlamov, Cgy.	15.00	.15
□□□	59	Josef Marha, Ana.	15.00	.15
□□□	60	Jason Marshall, Dal.	15.00	.15
□□□	61	Jeff Nielsen, Ana.	15.00	.15
□□□	62	Steve Rucchin, Ana.	15.00	.15
□□□	63	Tomas Sandström, Ana.	15.00	.15
□□□	64	Jason Bonsignore, T.B.	15.00	.15
□□□	65	Mikhael Shtalenkov (G), Ana.	15.00	.15
□□□	67	Tom Askey, Ana.	15.00	.15
□□□	68	Jaromir Jagr, Pgh.	175.00	2.00
□□□	69	Per Axelsson, Bos.	15.00	.15
□□□	70	Ken Baumgartner, Bos.	15.00	.15
□□□	71	Jiri Slegr, Pgh.	15.00	.15
□□□	72	Mathieu Schneider, Tor.	15.00	.15
□□□	73	Anson Carter, Bos.	15.00	.15
□□□	74	Byron Dafoe (G), Bos.	15.00	.15
□□□	75	Rob DiMaio, Bos.	15.00	.15
□□□	76	Ted Donato, Bos.	15.00	.15
□□□	77	Ray Bourque, Bos.	65.00	1.00
□□□	78	Dave Ellett, Bos.	15.00	.15
□□□	79	Steve Heinze, Bos.	15.00	.15
□□□	80	Geoff Sanderson, Buf.	15.00	.15
□□□	81	Miroslav Satan, Buf.	15.00	.15
□□□	82	Martin Straka, Fla.	15.00	.15
□□□	83	Dimitri Khristich, Bos.	15.00	.15
□□□	84	Grant Ledyard, Bos.	15.00	.15
□□□	85	Cameron Mann, Bos.	20.00	.35
□□□	86	Kyle McLaren, Bos.	15.00	.15
□□□	87	Sergei Samsonov, Bos.	60.00	1.25
□□□	88	Eric Lindros, Pha.	250.00	2.50
□□□	89	Alexander Mogilny, Van.	35.00	.50
□□□	90	Joé Juneau, Wsh.	15.00	.15
□□□	91	Sergei Fedorov, Det.	65.00	1.00
□□□	92	Rick Tocchet, Pho.	15.00	.15
□□□	93	Doug Gilmour, N.J.	35.00	.50
□□□	94	Ryan Smyth, Edm.	25.00	.35
□□□	95	Alexei Morozov, Pgh.	35.00	1.00
□□□	96	Phil Housley, Wsh.	15.00	.15
□□□	97	Jeremy Roenick, Pho.	35.00	.35
□□□	98	Jay More, Pho.	15.00	.15
□□□	99	Wayne Gretzky, NYR.	400.00	4.00
□□□	100	Robbie Tallas (G), Bos.	15.00	.15
□□□	101	Tim Taylor, Bos.	15.00	.15
□□□	102	Joe Thornton, Bos.	60.00	1.25
□□□	103	Donald Audette, Buf.	15.00	.15
□□□	104	Curtis Brown, Buf.	15.00	.15
□□□	105	Michal Grosek, Buf.	15.00	.15
□□□	106	Brian Holzinger, Buf.	15.00	.15
□□□	107	Derek Plante, Buf.	15.00	.15
□□□	108	Rob Ray, Buf.	15.00	.15
□□□	109	Darryl Shannon, Buf.	15.00	.15
□□□	110	Steve Shields (G), Buf.	15.00	.15
□□□	111	Vaclav Varada, Buf.	15.00	.15
□□□	112	Dixon Ward, Buf.	15.00	.15
□□□	113	Jason Woolley, Buf.	15.00	.15
□□□	114	Alexei Zhitnik, Buf.	15.00	.15
□□□	115	Andrew Cassels, Cgy..	15.00	.15
□□□	116	Hnat Domenichelli, Cgy.	25.00	.35
□□□	117	Theoren Fleury, Cgy.	35.00	.50
□□□	118	Denis Gauthier, Cgy.	15.00	.15
□□□	119	Cale Hulse, Cgy.	15.00	.15
□□□	120	Jarome Iginla, Cgy.	35.00	.50
□□□	121	Marty McInnis, Cgy.	15.00	.15
□□□	122	Tyler Moss (G), Cgy.	25.00	.35
□□□	123	Michael Nylander, Cgy.	15.00	.15
□□□	124	Dwayne Roloson (G), Cgy.	15.00	.15
□□□	125	Cory Stillman, Cgy.	15.00	.15
□□□	126	Rick Tabaracci (G), Cgy.	15.00	.15
□□□	127	German Titov, Cgy.	15.00	.15
□□□	128	Jason Wiemer, Cgy.	15.00	.15
□□□	129	Steve Chaisson, Cgy.	15.00	.15
□□□	130	Kevin Dineen, Car.	15.00	.15
□□□	131	Nelson Emerson, Car.	15.00	.15
□□□	132	Martin Gelinas, Car.	15.00	.15
□□□	133	Stu Grimson, Car.	15.00	.15
□□□	134	Sami Kapanen, Car.	15.00	.15
□□□	135	Trevor Kidd (G), Car.	25.00	.35
□□□	136	Robert Kron, Car.	15.00	.15
□□□	137	Jeff O'Neill, Car.	25.00	.35
□□□	138	Keith Primeau, Car.	25.00	.35
□□□	139	Paul Ranheim, Car.	15.00	.15
□□□	140	Gary Roberts, Car.	25.00	.35
□□□	141	Glen Wesley, Car.	15.00	.15
□□□	142	Tony Amonte, Chi.	25.00	.35
□□□	143	Eric Dazé, Chi.	25.00	.35
□□□	144	Jeff Hackett (G), Chi.	25.00	.35
□□□	145	Greg Johnson, Chi.	15.00	.15
□□□	146	Chad Kilger, Chi.	15.00	.15
□□□	147	Sergei Krivokrasov, Chi.	15.00	.15
□□□	148	Christian LaFlamme, Chi.	15.00	.15
□□□	149	Jean-Yves Leroux, Chi.	15.00	.15
□□□	150	Dmitri Nabokov, Chi.	15.00	.15
□□□	151	Jeff Shantz, Chi.	15.00	.15
□□□	152	Gary Suter, Chi.	15.00	.15
□□□	153	Eric Weinrich, Chi.	15.00	.15
□□□	154	Todd White, Chi.	15.00	.15
□□□	155	Alexei Zhamnov, Chi.	15.00	.15
□□□	158	Wade Belak, Col.	15.00	.15
□□□	157	Craig Billington (G), Col.	15.00	.15
□□□	158	René Corbet, Col.	15.00	.15
□□□	159	Shean Donovan, Col.	15.00	.15
□□□	160	Valeri Kamensky, Col.	25.00	.35
□□□	161	Uwe Krupp, Col.	15.00	.15
□□□	162	Jari Kurri, Col.	25.00	.35
□□□	163	Eric Lacroix, Col.	15.00	.15
□□□	164	Claude Lemieux, Col.	15.00	.15
□□□	165	Eric Messier, Col.	15.00	.15
□□□	166	Jeff Odgers, Col.	15.00	.15
□□□	167	Sandis Ozolinsh, Col.	25.00	.35
□□□	168	Warren Rychel, Col.	15.00	.15
□□□	169	Joe Sakic, Col.	135.00	1.75
□□□	170	Stéphane Yelle, Col.	15.00	.15
□□□	171	Greg Adams, Dal.	15.00	.15
□□□	172	Jason Botterill, Dal.	15.00	.15
□□□	173	Guy Carbonneau, Dal.	15.00	.15
□□□	174	Shawn Chambers, Dal.	15.00	.15
□□□	175	Manny Fernandez (G), Dal.	15.00	.15
□□□	176	Derian Hatcher, Dal.	25.00	.35
□□□	177	Benoît Hogue, Dal.	15.00	.15
□□□	178	Mike Keane, Dal.	15.00	.15
□□□	179	Jere Lehtinen, Dal.	25.00	.35
□□□	180	Juha Lind, Dal.	15.00	.15
□□□	181	Mike Modano, Dal.	65.00	1.00
□□□	182	Brian Skurdland, Dal.	15.00	.15
□□□	183	Darryl Sydor, Dal.	15.00	.15
□□□	184	Roman Turek (G), Dal.	15.00	.15
□□□	185	Pat Verbeek, Dal.	15.00	.15
□□□	186	Jamie Wright, Dal.	15.00	.15
□□□	187	Doug Brown, Det.	15.00	.15
□□□	188	Kris Draper, Det.	15.00	.15
□□□	189	Anders Eriksson, Det.	15.00	.15
□□□	190	Viacheslav Fetisov, Det.	15.00	.15
□□□	191	Brent Gilchrist, Det.	15.00	.15
□□□	192	Kevin Hodson (G), Det.	15.00	.15
□□□	193	Tomas Holmstrom, Det.	15.00	.15
□□□	194	Mike Knuble, Det.	15.00	.15
□□□	195	Joey Kocur, Det.	15.00	.15
□□□	196	Vyacheslav Kozlov, Det.	15.00	.15
□□□	197	Martin Lapointe, Det.	15.00	.15
□□□	198	Igor Larionov, Det.	25.00	.35
□□□	199	Kirk Maltby, Det.	15.00	.15
□□□	200	Norm Maracle (G), Det.	15.00	.15
□□□	201	Darren McCarty, Det.	15.00	.15
□□□	202	Dmitri Mironov, Det.	15.00	.15
□□□	203	Larry Murphy, Det.	25.00	.35
□□□	204	Chris Osgood (G), Det.	50.00	.75
□□□	205	Kelly Buchberger, Edm.	15.00	.15
□□□	206	Bob Essensa (G), Edm.	15.00	.15
□□□	207	Scott Fraser, Edm.	15.00	.15
□□□	208	Mike Grier, Edm.	25.00	.35
□□□	209	Bill Guerin, Edm.	25.00	.35
□□□	210	Tony Hrkac, Edm.	15.00	.15
□□□	211	Curtis Joseph (G), Edm.	75.00	1.25
□□□	212	Mats Lindgren, Edm.	15.00	.15
□□□	213	Todd Marchant, Edm.	15.00	.15
□□□	214	Dean McAmmond, Edm.	15.00	.15
□□□	215	Craig Millar, Edm.	15.00	.15
□□□	216	Boris Mironov, Edm.	15.00	.15
□□□	217	Doug Weight, Edm.	35.00	.50
□□□	218	Valeri Zelepukin, Edm.	15.00	.15
□□□	219	Roman Hamrlik, Edm.	25.00	.35
□□□	220	Radek Dvorak, Fla.	15.00	.15
□□□	221	Dave Gagner, Fla.	15.00	.15
□□□	222	Ed Jovanovski, Fla.	25.00	.35
□□□	223	Viktor Kozlov, Fla.	15.00	.15
□□□	224	Paul Laus, Fla.	15.00	.15
□□□	225	Kirk McLean (G), Fla.	25.00	.35
□□□	226	Scott Mellanby, Fla.	15.00	.15
□□□	227	Kirk Muller, Fla.	15.00	.15
□□□	228	Robert Svehla, Fla.	15.00	.15
□□□	229	Steve Washburn, Fla.	15.00	.15
□□□	230	Kevin Weekes (G), Fla.	15.00	.15
□□□	231	Ray Whitney, Fla.	15.00	.15
□□□	232	Peter Worrell, Fla.	15.00	.15
□□□	233	Russ Courtnall, L.A.	15.00	.15
□□□	234	Stéphane Fiset (G), L.A.	25.00	.35
□□□	235	Garry Galley, L.A.	15.00	.15
□□□	236	Craig Johnson, L.A.	15.00	.15
□□□	237	Ian Laperrière, L.A.	15.00	.15
□□□	238	Donald MacLean, L.A.	15.00	.15
□□□	239	Steve McKenna, L.A.	15.00	.15
□□□	240	Sandy Moger, L.A.	15.00	.15
□□□	241	Glen Murray, L.A.	15.00	.15
□□□	242	Sean O'Donnell, L.A.	15.00	.15
□□□	243	Yanic Perreault, L.A.	15.00	.15
□□□	244	Luc Robitaille, L.A.	25.00	.35
□□□	245	Jamie Storr (G), L.A.	25.00	.35
□□□	246	Jozef Stumpel, L.A.	25.00	.35
□□□	247	Vladimir Tsyplakov, L.A.	15.00	.15
□□□	248	Benoît Brunet, Mtl.	15.00	.15
□□□	249	Shayne Corson, Mtl.	25.00	.35
□□□	250	Vincent Damphousse, Mtl.	35.00	.50
□□□	251	Eric Houde, Mtl.	15.00	.15
□□□	252	Saku Koivu, Mtl.	100.00	1.50
□□□	253	Vladimir Malakhov, Mtl.	15.00	.15
□□□	254	Dave Manson, Mtl.	15.00	.15
□□□	255	Andy Moog (G), Mtl.	25.00	.35
□□□	256	Mark Recchi, Mtl.	25.00	.35
□□□	257	Martin Rucinsky, Mtl.	15.00	.15
□□□	258	Jocelyn Thibault (G), Mtl.	35.00	.50
□□□	259	Mick Vukota, Mtl.	15.00	.15
□□□	260	Dave Andreychuck, N.J.	15.00	.15
□□□	261	Jason Arnott, N.J.	25.00	.35
□□□	262	Mike Dunham (G), N.J.	15.00	.15
□□□	263	Bobby Holik, N.J.	15.00	.15
□□□	264	Randy McKay, N.J.	15.00	.15
□□□	265	Brendan Morrison, N.J.	60.00	1.25
□□□	266	Scott Niedermayer, N.J.	25.00	.35
□□□	267	Lyle Odelein, N.J.	15.00	.15
□□□	268	Krzysztof Oliwa, N.J.	15.00	.15
□□□	269	Denis Pederson, N.J.	15.00	.15
□□□	270	Brian Rolston, N.J.	15.00	.15
□□□	271	Sheldon Souray, N.J.	15.00	.15
□□□	272	Scott Stevens, N.J.	15.00	.15
□□□	273	Petr Sykora, N.J.	15.00	.15
□□□	274	Steve Thomas, N.J.	15.00	.15
□□□	275	Bryan Berard, NYI.	35.00	.50
□□□	276	Zdeno Chara, NYI.	15.00	.15
□□□	277	Vladimir Chebaturkin, NYI.	15.00	.15
□□□	278	Tom Chorske, NYI.	15.00	.15
□□□	279	Mariusz Czerkawski, NYI.	15.00	.15
□□□	280	Jason Dawe, NYI.	15.00	.15
□□□	281	Wade Flaherty (G), NYI.	15.00	.15
□□□	282	Kenny Jonsson, NYI.	15.00	.15
□□□	283	Sergei Nemchinov, NYI.	15.00	.15
□□□	284	Zigmund Palffy, NYI.	35.00	.50
□□□	285	Richard Pilon, NYI.	15.00	.15
□□□	286	Robert Reichel, NYI.	15.00	.15
□□□	287	Joe Sacco, NYI.	15.00	.15
□□□	288	Tommy Salo (G), NYI.	15.00	.15
□□□	289	Bryan Smolinski, NYI.	15.00	.15
□□□	290	Jeff Beukeboom, NYR.	15.00	.15
□□□	291	Dan Cloutier (G), NYR.	25.00	.35
□□□	292	Bruce Driver, NYR.	15.00	.15

	No.	Player		
☐☐☐	293	Adam Graves, NYR.	15.00	.15
☐☐☐	294	Alexei Kovalev, NYR.	15.00	.15
☐☐☐	295	Pat LaFontaine, NYR.	15.00	.15
☐☐☐	296	Darren Langdon, NYR.	15.00	.15
☐☐☐	297	Brian Leetch, NYR.	35.00	.50
☐☐☐	298	Mike Richter (G), NYR.	35.00	.50
☐☐☐	299	Ulf Samuelsson, NYR.	15.00	.15
☐☐☐	300	Marc Savard, NYR.	15.00	.15
☐☐☐	301	Kevin Stevens, NYR.	15.00	.15
☐☐☐	302	Niklas Sundstrom, NYR.	15.00	.15
☐☐☐	303	Tim Sweeney, NYR.	15.00	.15
☐☐☐	304	Vladimir Vorobiev, NYR.	15.00	.15
☐☐☐	305	Daniel Alfredsson, Ott.	25.00	.35
☐☐☐	306	Magnus Arvedson, Ott.	15.00	.15
☐☐☐	307	Radek Bonk, Ott.	15.00	.15
☐☐☐	308	Andreas Dackell, Ott.	15.00	.15
☐☐☐	309	Bruce Gardiner, Ott.	15.00	.15
☐☐☐	310	Igor Kravchuk, Ott.	15.00	.15
☐☐☐	311	Denny Lambert, Ott.	15.00	.15
☐☐☐	312	Janne Laukkanen, Ott.	15.00	.15
☐☐☐	313	Shawn McEachern, Ott.	15.00	.15
☐☐☐	314	Chris Phillips, Ott.	15.00	.15
☐☐☐	315	Wade Redden, Ott.	15.00	.15
☐☐☐	316	Ron Tugnutt (G), Ott.	15.00	.15
☐☐☐	317	Shaun Van Allen, Ott.	15.00	.15
☐☐☐	318	Alexei Yashin, Ott.	50.00	.75
☐☐☐	319	Jason York, Ott.	15.00	.15
☐☐☐	320	Sergei Zholtok, Ott.	15.00	.15
☐☐☐	321	Sean Burke (G), Pha.	25.00	.35
☐☐☐	322	Paul Coffey, Pha.	25.00	.35
☐☐☐	323	Alexandre Daigle, Pha.	25.00	.35
☐☐☐	324	Eric Desjardins, Pha.	15.00	.15
☐☐☐	325	Colin Forbes, Pha.	15.00	.15
☐☐☐	326	Ron Hextall (G), Pha.	25.00	.35
☐☐☐	327	Trent Klatt, Pha.	15.00	.15
☐☐☐	328	Dan McGillis, Pha.	15.00	.15
☐☐☐	329	Joel Otto, Pha.	15.00	.15
☐☐☐	330	Shjon Podein, Pha.	15.00	.15
☐☐☐	331	Mike Sillinger, Pha.	15.00	.15
☐☐☐	332	Chris Therien, Pha.	15.00	.15
☐☐☐	333	Dainius Zubrus, Pha.	25.00	.35
☐☐☐	334	Bob Corkum, Pho.	15.00	.15
☐☐☐	335	Jim Cummins, Pho.	15.00	.15
☐☐☐	336	Jason Doig, Pho.	15.00	.15
☐☐☐	337	Dallas Drake, Pho.	15.00	.15
☐☐☐	338	Mike Gartner, Pho.	25.00	.35
☐☐☐	339	Brad Isbister, Pho.	15.00	.15
☐☐☐	340	Craig Janney, Pho.	15.00	.15
☐☐☐	341	Nikolai Khabibulin (G), Pho.	35.00	.50
☐☐☐	342	Teppo Numminen, Pho.	15.00	.15
☐☐☐	343	Cliff Ronning, Pho.	15.00	.15
☐☐☐	344	Keith Tkachuk, Pho.	50.00	.75
☐☐☐	345	Oleg Tverdovsky, Pho.	15.00	.15
☐☐☐	346	Jim Waite (G), Pho.	15.00	.15
☐☐☐	347	Juha Ylönen, Pho.	15.00	.15
☐☐☐	348	Stu Barnes, Pgh.	15.00	.15
☐☐☐	349	Rob Brown, Pgh.	15.00	.15
☐☐☐	350	Robert Dome, Pgh.	15.00	.15
☐☐☐	351	Ron Francis, Pgh.	35.00	.50
☐☐☐	352	Kevin Hatcher, Pgh.	15.00	.15
☐☐☐	353	Alex Hicks, Pgh.	15.00	.15
☐☐☐	354	Darius Kasparaitis, Pgh.	15.00	.15
☐☐☐	355	Robert Lang, Pgh.	15.00	.15
☐☐☐	356	Fredrik Olausson, Pgh.	15.00	.15
☐☐☐	357	Ed Olczyk, Pgh.	15.00	.15
☐☐☐	358	Petr Skudra (G), Pgh.	15.00	.15
☐☐☐	359	Chris Tamer, Pgh.	15.00	.15
☐☐☐	360	Ken Wregget (G), Pgh.	15.00	.15
☐☐☐	361	Blair Atcheynum, Stl.	15.00	.15
☐☐☐	362	Jim Campbell, Stl.	15.00	.15
☐☐☐	363	Kelly Chase, Stl.	15.00	.15
☐☐☐	364	Craig Conroy, Stl.	15.00	.15
☐☐☐	365	Geoff Courtnall, Stl.	15.00	.15
☐☐☐	366	Steve Duchesne, Stl.	15.00	.15
☐☐☐	367	Todd Gill, Stl.	15.00	.15
☐☐☐	368	Al MacInnis, Stl.	25.00	.35
☐☐☐	369	Jamie McLennan (G), Stl.	25.00	.35
☐☐☐	370	Scott Pellerin, Stl.	15.00	.15
☐☐☐	371	Pascal Rhéaume, Stl.	15.00	.15
☐☐☐	372	Jamie Rivers, Stl.	15.00	.15
☐☐☐	373	Darren Turcotte, Stl.	15.00	.15
☐☐☐	374	Pierre Turgeon, Stl.	25.00	.35
☐☐☐	375	Tony Twist, Stl.	15.00	.15
☐☐☐	376	Terry Yake, Stl.	15.00	.15
☐☐☐	377	Richard Brennan, S.J.	15.00	.15
☐☐☐	378	Murray Craven, S.J.	15.00	.15
☐☐☐	379	Jeff Friesen, S.J.	25.00	.35
☐☐☐	380	Tony Granato, S.J.	15.00	.15
☐☐☐	381	Bill Houlder, S.J.	15.00	.15
☐☐☐	382	Kelly Hrudey (G), S.J.	15.00	.15
☐☐☐	383	Alexander Korolyuk, S.J.	15.00	.15
☐☐☐	384	John MacLean, S.J.	15.00	.15
☐☐☐	385	Bryan Marchment, S.J.	15.00	.15
☐☐☐	386	Patrick Marleau, S.J.	35.00	1.00
☐☐☐	387	Stéphane Matteau, S.J.	15.00	.15
☐☐☐	388	Marty McSorley, S.J.	15.00	.15
☐☐☐	389	Bernie Nicholls, S.J.	15.00	.15
☐☐☐	390	Owen Nolan, S.J.	25.00	.35
☐☐☐	391	Mike Ricci, S.J.	15.00	.15
☐☐☐	392	Marco Sturm, S.J.	15.00	.15
☐☐☐	393	Mike Vernon (G), S.J.	25.00	.35
☐☐☐	394	Andrei Zyuzin, S.J.	25.00	.35
☐☐☐	395	Mikael Andersson, T.B.	15.00	.15
☐☐☐	396	Zac Bierk (G), T.B.	25.00	.35
☐☐☐	397	Enrico Ciccone, T.B.	15.00	.15
☐☐☐	398	Louis DeBrusk, T.B.	15.00	.15
☐☐☐	399	Karl Dykhuis, T.B.	15.00	.15
☐☐☐	400	Daymond Langkow, T.B.	15.00	.15
☐☐☐	401	Mike McBain, T.B.	15.00	.15
☐☐☐	402	Sandy McCarthy, T.B.	15.00	.15
☐☐☐	403	Daren Puppa (G), T.B.	15.00	.15
☐☐☐	404	Mikael Renberg, T.B.	15.00	.15
☐☐☐	405	Stéphane Richer, T.B.	15.00	.15
☐☐☐	406	Alexander Selivanov, T.B.	15.00	.15
☐☐☐	407	Darcy Tucker, T.B.	15.00	.15
☐☐☐	408	Paul Ysebaert, T.B.	15.00	.15
☐☐☐	409	Rob Zamuner, T.B.	25.00	.35
☐☐☐	410	Sergei Berezin, Tor.	15.00	.15
☐☐☐	411	Wendal Clark, Tor.	25.00	.35
☐☐☐	412	Sylvain Côté, Tor.	15.00	.15
☐☐☐	413	Mike Johnson, Tor.	35.00	1.00
☐☐☐	414	Derek King, Tor.	15.00	.15
☐☐☐	415	Kris King, Tor.	15.00	.15
☐☐☐	416	Igor Korolev, Tor.	15.00	.15
☐☐☐	417	Daniil Markov, Tor.	15.00	.15
☐☐☐	418	Alyn McCauley, Tor.	35.00	1.00
☐☐☐	419	Fredrik Modin, Tor.	15.00	.15
☐☐☐	420	Martin Prochazka, Tor.	15.00	.15
☐☐☐	421	Jason Smith, Tor.	15.00	.15
☐☐☐	422	Steve Sullivan, Tor.	15.00	.15
☐☐☐	423	Yannick Tremblay, Tor.	15.00	.15
☐☐☐	424	Todd Bertuzzi, Van.	15.00	.15
☐☐☐	425	Donald Brashear, Van.	15.00	.15
☐☐☐	426	Bret Hedican, Van.	15.00	.15
☐☐☐	427	Arturs Irbe (G), Van.	15.00	.15
☐☐☐	428	Jyrki Lumme, Van.	15.00	.15
☐☐☐	429	Brad May, Van.	15.00	.15
☐☐☐	430	Bryan McCabe, Van.	15.00	.15
☐☐☐	431	Markus Naslund, Van.	15.00	.15
☐☐☐	432	Brian Noonan, Van.	15.00	.15
☐☐☐	433	Dave Scatchard, Van.	15.00	.15
☐☐☐	434	Garth Snow (G), Van.	15.00	.15
☐☐☐	435	Lubomir Vaic, Van.	15.00	.15
☐☐☐	436	Peter Zezel, Van.	15.00	.15
☐☐☐	437	Craig Berube, Wsh.	15.00	.15
☐☐☐	438	Jeff Brown, Wsh.	15.00	.15
☐☐☐	439	Andrew Brunette, Wsh	15.00	.15.
☐☐☐	440	Jan Bulis, Wsh.	15.00	.15
☐☐☐	441	Sergei Gonchar, Wsh.	15.00	.15
☐☐☐	442	Dale Hunter, Wsh.	15.00	.15
☐☐☐	443	Steve Konowalchuk, Wsh.	15.00	.15
☐☐☐	444	Kelly Miller, Wsh.	15.00	.15
☐☐☐	445	Adam Oates, Wsh.	35.00	.50
☐☐☐	446	Bill Ranford (G), Wsh.	25.00	.35
☐☐☐	447	Jaroslav Svejkovsky, Wsh.	25.00	.35
☐☐☐	448	Esa Tikkanen, Wsh.	15.00	.15
☐☐☐	449	Mark Tinordi, Wsh.	15.00	.15
☐☐☐	450	Brendan Witt, Wsh.	15.00	.15
☐☐☐	451	Richard Zednik, Wsh.	15.00	.15

CRAMER'S CHOICE AWARDS

Insert Set (10 cards): **1,300.00**

	No.	Player	NRMT-MT
☐	1	Sergei Samsonov, Bos.	85.00
☐	2	Dominik Hasek (G), Buf.	100.00
☐	3	Peter Forsberg, Col.	150.00
☐	4	Patrick Roy (G), Col.	250.00
☐	5	Mike Modano, Dal.	75.00
☐	6	Martin Brodeur (G), N.J.	100.00
☐	7	Wayne Gretzky, NYR.	300.00
☐	8	Eric Lindros, Pha.	200.00
☐	9	Jaromir Jagr, Pgh.	150.00
☐	10	Pavel Bure, Van.	100.00

DYNAGON ICE

This series has two versions: an insert card and a Titanium parallel (99 copies).

Insert Set (20 cards):

	No.	Player	Tit.	Reg.
☐☐	1	Paul Kariya, Ana.	250.00	5.00
☐☐	2	Teemu Selänne, Ana.	150.00	3.00
☐☐	3	Sergei Samsonov, Bos.	70.00	2.50
☐☐	4	Dominik Hasek (G), Buf.	150.00	3.00
☐☐	5	Peter Forsberg, Col.	200.00	4.00
☐☐	6	Patrick Roy (G), Col.	300.00	6.00
☐☐	7	Joe Sakic, Col.	175.00	3.50
☐☐	8	Mike Modano, Dal.	80.00	2.00
☐☐	9	Sergei Fedorov, Det.	80.00	2.00
☐☐	10	Steve Yzerman, Det.	200.00	4.00
☐☐	11	Saku Koivu, Mtl.	150.00	3.00
☐☐	12	Martin Brodeur (G), N.J.	150.00	3.00
☐☐	13	Wayne Gretzky, NYR.	400.00	8.00
☐☐	14	John LeClair, Pha.	80.00	2.00
☐☐	15	Eric Lindros, Pha.	250.00	5.00
☐☐	16	Jaromir Jagr, Pgh.	200.00	4.00
☐☐	17	Pavel Bure, Van.	150.00	3.00
☐☐	18	Mark Messier, Van.	80.00	2.00
☐☐	19	Peter Bondra, Wsh.	60.00	1.50
☐☐	20	Olaf Kolzig (G), Wsh.	45.00	1.50

GOLD CROWN DIE-CUTS

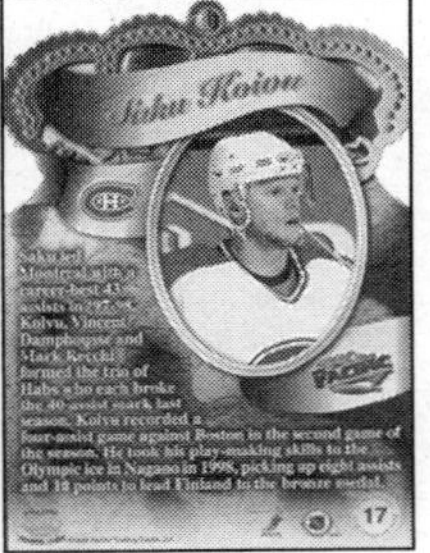

Insert Set (36 cards): **400.00**

	No.	Player	NRMT-MT
☐	1	Paul Kariya, Ana.	30.00
☐	2	Teemu Selänne, Ana.	15.00
☐	3	Sergei Samsonov, Bos.	12.00
☐	4	Dominik Hasek (G), Buf.	15.00
☐	5	Michael Peca, Buf.	6.00
☐	6	Theoren Fleury, Cgy.	6.00
☐	7	Chris Chelios, Chi.	8.00
☐	8	Peter Forsberg, Col.	20.00
☐	9	Patrick Roy (G), Col.	35.00
☐	10	Joe Sakic, Col.	18.00
☐	11	Ed Belfour (G), Dal.	6.00
☐	12	Mike Modano, Dal.	10.00
☐	13	Sergei Fedorov, Det.	10.00
☐	14	Chris Osgood (G), Det.	9.00
☐	15	Brendan Shanahan, Det.	12.00
☐	16	Steve Yzerman, Det.	20.00
☐	17	Saku Koivu, Mtl.	12.00
☐	18	Martin Brodeur (G), N.J.	15.00
☐	19	Patrik Elias, N.J.	6.00
☐	20	Doug Gilmour, N.J.	6.00
☐	21	Trevor Linden, NYI.	6.00
☐	22	Zigmund Palffy, NYI.	8.00
☐	23	Wayne Gretzky, NYR.	45.00
☐	24	John LeClair, Pha.	10.00
☐	25	Eric Lindros, Pha.	30.00
☐	26	Dainius Zubrus, Pha.	6.00
☐	27	Keith Tkachuk, Pho.	9.00
☐	28	Tom Barrasso (G), Pgh.	6.00
☐	29	Jaromir Jagr, Pgh.	20.00
☐	30	Brett Hull, Stl.	10.00
☐	31	Félix Potvin (G), Tor.	12.00
☐	32	Mats Sundin, Tor.	10.00
☐	33	Pavel Bure, Van.	15.00
☐	34	Mark Messier, Van.	10.00
☐	35	Peter Bondra, Wsh.	9.00
☐	36	Olaf Kolzig (G), Wsh.	6.00

TEAM CHECKLISTS

Insert Set (30 cards): 200.00

	No.	Player	NRMT-MT
☐	1	Paul Kariya, Ana.	15.00
☐	2	Sergei Samsonov, Bos.	7.50
☐	3	Dominik Hasek (G), Buf.	9.00
☐	4	Theoren Fleury, Cgy.	4.00
☐	5	Keith Primeau, Car.	3.50
☐	6	Chris Chelios, Chi.	4.50
☐	7	Patrick Roy (G), Col.	18.00
☐	8	Mike Modano, Dal.	6.00
☐	9	Steve Yzerman, Det.	12.00
☐	10	Ryan Smyth, Edm.	3.50
☐	11	John Vanbiesbrouck (G), Fla.	7.50
☐	12	Jozef Stumpel, L.A.	3.50
☐	13	Saku Koivu, Mtl.	7.50
☐	14	Nashville Predators	5.00
☐	15	Martin Brodeur (G), N.J.	9.00
☐	16	Zigmund Palffy, NYI.	4.50
☐	17	Wayne Gretzky, NYR.	25.00
☐	18	Alexei Yashin, Ott.	4.50
☐	19	Eric Lindros, Pha.	15.00
☐	20	Keith Tkachuk, Pho.	4.50
☐	21	Jaromir Jagr, Pgh.	12.00
☐	22	Brett Hull, Stl.	6.00
☐	23	Patrick Marleau, S.J.	5.00
☐	24	Rob Zamuner, T.B.	3.50
☐	25	Mats Sundin, Tor.	6.00
☐	26	Pavel Bure, Van.	9.00
☐	27	Olaf Kolzig (G), Wsh.	4.00
☐	28	Atlanta Thrashers	5.00
☐	29	Minnesota Wild	5.00
☐	30	Columbus Blue Jackets	5.00

1998 - 99 PACIFIC PARAMOUNT

These cards have five versions: the regular card, an Emerald Green parallel, a Silver parallel, a Copper parallel and an Ice Blue parallel. These cards were not released at press time.

Imprint: © 1998 Pacific Trading Cards, Inc.

	No.	Player
☐☐☐☐☐	1	Travis Green
☐☐☐☐☐	2	Buy Hebert
☐☐☐☐☐	3	Paul Kariya
☐☐☐☐☐	4	Josef Marha
☐☐☐☐☐	5	Steve Rucchin
☐☐☐☐☐	6	Tomas Sandström
☐☐☐☐☐	7	Teemu Selänne
☐☐☐☐☐	8	Jason Allison
☐☐☐☐☐	9	Per Axelsson
☐☐☐☐☐	10	Ray Bourque
☐☐☐☐☐	11	Anson Carter
☐☐☐☐☐	12	Byron Dafoe
☐☐☐☐☐	13	Ted Donato
☐☐☐☐☐	14	Dave Ellett
☐☐☐☐☐	15	Dimitri Khristich
☐☐☐☐☐	16	Sergei Samsonov
☐☐☐☐☐	17	Matthew Barnaby
☐☐☐☐☐	18	Michal Grosek
☐☐☐☐☐	19	Dominik Hasek
☐☐☐☐☐	20	Brian Holzinger
☐☐☐☐☐	21	Michael Peca
☐☐☐☐☐	22	Miroslav Satan
☐☐☐☐☐	23	Vaclav Varada
☐☐☐☐☐	24	Dixon Ward
☐☐☐☐☐	25	Alexei Zhitnik
☐☐☐☐☐	26	Andrew Cassels
☐☐☐☐☐	27	Theoren Fleury
☐☐☐☐☐	28	Jarome Iginla
☐☐☐☐☐	29	Marty McInnis
☐☐☐☐☐	30	Derek Morris
☐☐☐☐☐	31	Michael Nylander
☐☐☐☐☐	32	Cory Stillman
☐☐☐☐☐	33	Rick Tabaracci
☐☐☐☐☐	34	Kevin Dineen
☐☐☐☐☐	35	Nelson Emerson
☐☐☐☐☐	36	Martin Gelinas
☐☐☐☐☐	37	Sami Kapanen
☐☐☐☐☐	38	Trevor Kidd
☐☐☐☐☐	39	Robert Kron
☐☐☐☐☐	40	Jeff O'Neill
☐☐☐☐☐	41	Keith Primeau
☐☐☐☐☐	42	Gary Roberts
☐☐☐☐☐	43	Tony Amonte
☐☐☐☐☐	44	Chris Chelios
☐☐☐☐☐	45	Paul Coffey
☐☐☐☐☐	46	Eric Dazé
☐☐☐☐☐	47	Doug Gilmour
☐☐☐☐☐	48	Jeff Hackett
☐☐☐☐☐	49	Jean-Yves Leroux
☐☐☐☐☐	50	Eric Weinrich
☐☐☐☐☐	51	Alexei Zhamnov
☐☐☐☐☐	52	Craig Billington
☐☐☐☐☐	53	Adam Deadmarsh
☐☐☐☐☐	54	Adam Foote
☐☐☐☐☐	55	Peter Forsberg
☐☐☐☐☐	56	Valeri Kamensky
☐☐☐☐☐	57	Claude Lemieux
☐☐☐☐☐	58	Eric Messier
☐☐☐☐☐	59	Sandis Ozolinsh
☐☐☐☐☐	60	Patrick Roy
☐☐☐☐☐	61	Joe Sakic
☐☐☐☐☐	62	Ed Belfour
☐☐☐☐☐	63	Derian Hatcher
☐☐☐☐☐	64	Brett Hull
☐☐☐☐☐	65	Jamie Langenbrunner
☐☐☐☐☐	66	Jere Lehtinen
☐☐☐☐☐	67	Juha Lind
☐☐☐☐☐	68	Mike Modano
☐☐☐☐☐	69	Joe Nieuwendyk
☐☐☐☐☐	70	Darryl Sydor
☐☐☐☐☐	71	Roman Turek
☐☐☐☐☐	72	Sergei Zubov
☐☐☐☐☐	73	Anders Eriksson
☐☐☐☐☐	74	Sergei Eriksson
☐☐☐☐☐	75	Kevin Hodson
☐☐☐☐☐	76	Vyacheslav Kozlov
☐☐☐☐☐	77	Igor Larionov
☐☐☐☐☐	78	Nicklas Lidström
☐☐☐☐☐	79	Darren McCarty
☐☐☐☐☐	80	Larry Murphy
☐☐☐☐☐	81	Chris Osgood
☐☐☐☐☐	82	Brendan Shanahan
☐☐☐☐☐	83	Steve Yzerman
☐☐☐☐☐	84	Kelly Buchberger
☐☐☐☐☐	85	Mike Grier
☐☐☐☐☐	86	Bill Guerin
☐☐☐☐☐	87	RomanHamrlik
☐☐☐☐☐	88	Todd Marchant
☐☐☐☐☐	89	Dean McAmmond
☐☐☐☐☐	90	Boris Mironov
☐☐☐☐☐	91	Janne Niinimaa
☐☐☐☐☐	92	Ryan Smyth
☐☐☐☐☐	93	Doug Weight
☐☐☐☐☐	94	Dino Ciccarelli
☐☐☐☐☐	95	Dave Gagner
☐☐☐☐☐	96	Ed Jovanovski
☐☐☐☐☐	97	Viktor Kozlov
☐☐☐☐☐	98	Paul Laus
☐☐☐☐☐	99	Scott Mellanby
☐☐☐☐☐	100	Robert Svehla
☐☐☐☐☐	101	Ray Whitney
☐☐☐☐☐	102	Rob Blake
☐☐☐☐☐	103	Russ Courtnall
☐☐☐☐☐	104	Stéphane Fiset
☐☐☐☐☐	105	Glen Murray
☐☐☐☐☐	106	Yanic Perreault
☐☐☐☐☐	107	Luc Robitaille
☐☐☐☐☐	108	Jamie Storr
☐☐☐☐☐	109	Jozef Stumpel
☐☐☐☐☐	110	Vladimir Tsyplakov
☐☐☐☐☐	111	Shayne Corson
☐☐☐☐☐	112	Vincent Damphousse
☐☐☐☐☐	113	Saku Koivu
☐☐☐☐☐	114	Vladimir Malakhov
☐☐☐☐☐	115	Dave Manson
☐☐☐☐☐	116	Mark Recchi
☐☐☐☐☐	117	Martin Rucinsky
☐☐☐☐☐	118	Brian Savage
☐☐☐☐☐	119	Jocelyn Thibault
☐☐☐☐☐	120	Blair Atcheynum
☐☐☐☐☐	121	Andrew Brunette
☐☐☐☐☐	122	Mike Dunham
☐☐☐☐☐	123	Tom Fitzgerald
☐☐☐☐☐	124	Sergei Krivokrasov
☐☐☐☐☐	125	Denny Lambert
☐☐☐☐☐	126	Jay More
☐☐☐☐☐	127	Mikhail Shtalenkov
☐☐☐☐☐	128	Darren Turcotte
☐☐☐☐☐	129	Scott Walker
☐☐☐☐☐	130	Dave Andreychuk
☐☐☐☐☐	131	Jason Arnott
☐☐☐☐☐	132	Martin Brodeur
☐☐☐☐☐	133	Patrik Elias
☐☐☐☐☐	134	Bobby Holik
☐☐☐☐☐	135	Randy McKay
☐☐☐☐☐	136	Scott Niedermayer
☐☐☐☐☐	137	Krzysztof Oliwa
☐☐☐☐☐	138	Sheldon Souray
☐☐☐☐☐	139	Scott Stevens
☐☐☐☐☐	140	Bryan Berard
☐☐☐☐☐	141	Mariusz Czerkawski
☐☐☐☐☐	142	Jason Dawe
☐☐☐☐☐	143	Kenny Jonsson
☐☐☐☐☐	144	Trevor Linden
☐☐☐☐☐	145	Zigmund Palffy
☐☐☐☐☐	146	Richard Pilon
☐☐☐☐☐	147	Robert Reichel
☐☐☐☐☐	148	Tommy Salo

149 Bryan Smolinski
150 Dan Cloutier
151 Adam Graves
152 Wayne Gretzky
153 Alexei Kovalev
154 Pat LaFontaine
155 Brain Leetch
156 Mike Richter
157 Ulf Samuelsson
158 Kevin Stevens
159 Niklas Sundstrom
160 Daniel Alfredsson
161 Magnus Arvedson
162 Andreas Dackell
163 Igor Kravchuk
164 Shawn McEaschern
165 Chris Phillips
166 Damian Rhodes
167 Ron Tugnutt
168 Alexei Yashin
169 Ron Brind'Amour
170 Alexandre Daigle
171 Eric Desjardins
172 Colin Forbes
173 Chris Gratton
174 Ron Hextall
175 Trent Klatt
176 John LeClair
177 Eric Lindros
178 John Vanbiesbrouck
179 Dainius Zubrus
180 Dallas Drake
181 Brad Isbister
182 Nikolai Khabibulin
183 Teppo Nemminen
184 Jeremy Roenick
185 Cliff Ronning
186 Keith Tkachuk
187 Rick Tocchet
188 Oleg Tverdovsky
189 Stu Barnes
190 Tom Barrasso
191 Kevin Hatcher
192 Jaromir Jagr
193 Darius Kasparaitis
194 Alexei Morozov
195 Fredrik Olausson
196 Jiri Slegr
197 Martin Straka
198 Jim Campbell
199 Kelly Chase
200 Craig Conroy
201 Geoff Courtnall
202 Pavol Demitra
203 Grant Fuhr
204 Al MacInnis
205 Jamie McLennan
206 Chris Pronger
207 Pierre Turgeon
208 Tony Twist
209 Jeff Friesen
210 Tony Granato
211 Patrick Marleau
212 Stéphane Matteau
213 Marty McSorley
214 Owen Nolan
215 Marco Sturm
216 Mike Vernon
217 Karl Dykhuis
218 Sandy McCarthy
219 Mikael Renberg
220 Stéphane Richer
221 Alexander Selivanov
222 Paul Ysebaert
223 Rob Zamuner
224 Sergei Berezin
225 Tie Domi
226 Mike Johnson
227 Curtis Joseph
228 Derek King
229 Igor Korolev
230 Mathieu Schneider
231 Mats Sundin
232 Todd Bertuzzi
233 Donald Brashear
234 Pavel Bure
235 Arturs Irbe
236 Mark Messier
237 Alexander Mogilny
238 Mattias Ohlund
239 Dave Scatchard
240 Garth Snow
241 Brian Bellows
242 Peter Bondra
243 Jeff Brown
244 Sergei Gonchar
245 Calle Johansson
246 Joe Juneau
247 Olaf Kolzig
248 Steve Konowalchuk
249 Adam Oates
250 Richard Zednik

GLOVE SIDE LASER-CUTS

No.	Player
1	Guy Hebert (G)
2	Byron Dafoe (G)
3	Dominik Hasek (G)
4	Trevor Kidd (G)
5	Jeff Hackett (G)
6	Patrick Roy (G)
7	Ed Belfour (G)
8	Chris Osgood (G)
9	Mike Dunham (G)
10	Martin Brodeur (G)
11	Tommy Salo (G)
12	Mike Richter (G)
13	Damian Rhodes (G)
14	Ron Hextall (G)
15	Nikolai Khabibulin (G)
16	Tom Barrasso (G)
17	Grant Fuhr (G)
18	Mike Vernon (G)
19	Curtis Joseph (G)
20	Olaf Kolzig (G)

HALL OF FAME BOUND

No.	Player
1	Teemu Selänne
2	Dominik Hasek
3	Peter Forsberg
4	Patrick Roy
5	Steve Yzerman
6	Martin Brodeur
7	Wayne Gretzky
8	Eric Lindros
9	Jaromir Jagr
10	Mark Messier

SPECIAL DELIVERY DIE-CUTS

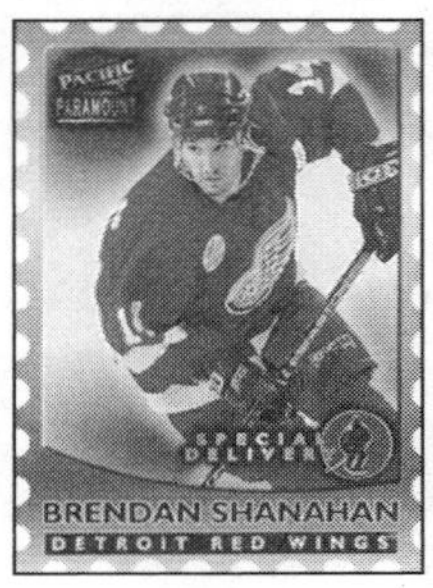

No.	Player
1	Paul Kariya
2	Teemu Selänne
3	Sergei Samsonov
4	Peter Forsberg
5	Joe Sakic
6	Mike Modano
7	Sergei Fedorov
8	Brendan Shanahan
9	Steve Yzerman
10	Saku Koivu
11	Zigmund Palffy
12	Wayne Gretzky
13	John LeClair
14	Eric Lindros
15	Keith Tkachuk
16	Jaromir Jagr
17	Mats Sundin
18	Pavel Bure
19	Mark Messier
20	Peter Bondra

TEAM CHECKLISTS DIE-CUTS

No.	Player
1	Teemu Selänne, Ana
2	Sergei Samsonov, Bos.
3	Dominik Hasek, Buf.
4	Theoren Fleury, Cal.
5	Keith Primeau, Car.
6	Chris Chelios, Chi.
7	Patrick Roy, Col.
8	Mike Modano, Dal.
9	Steve Yzerman, Det.
10	Ryan Smith, Edm.
11	Dino Ciccarelli, Fla.
12	Rob Blake, L.A.
13	Saku Koivu, Mtl.
14	Tom Fitzgerald, Nas.
15	Martin Brodeur, N.J.
16	Zigmund Palffy, N.Y.
17	Wayne Gretzky, N.Y.
18	Alexei Yashin, Ott.
19	Eric Lindros, Pha.
20	Keith Tkachuk, Phe.
21	Jaromir Jagr, Pgh.
22	Grant Fuhr, Stl.
23	Patrick Marleau, S.J.
24	Rob Zamuner, T.B.
25	Mats Sundin, Tor.
26	Mark Messier, Van.
27	Peter Bondra, Wsh.

1998 - 99 SPORT FX MINI STIX

Artwork by Tony Piacente. Each stick has a regular version and a Gold Rush parallel (maximum 250 copies). This series was released just before press time.

Stick Length: 23"

Player Sticks

☐☐ Jason Allison, Bos.
☐☐ Pavel Bure, Van.
☐☐ Sergei Fedorov, Det.
☐☐ Theoren Fleury, Cgy.
☐☐ Peter Forsberg, Col.
☐☐ Ron Francis, Car.
☐☐ Doug Gilmour, Chi.
☐☐ Brett Hull, Stl.
☐☐ Jaromir Jagr, Pgh.
☐☐ Paul Kariya, Ana.
☐☐ Saku Koivu, Mtl.
☐☐ Brian Leetch, NYR.
☐☐ Eric Lindros, Pha.
☐☐ Adam Oates, Wsh.
☐☐ Zigmund Palffy, NYI.
☐☐ Michael Peca, Buf.
☐☐ Joe Sakic, Col.
☐☐ Sergei Samsonov, Bos.
☐☐ Teemu Selänne, Ana.
☐☐ Scott Stevens, N.J.
☐☐ Mats Sundin, Tor.
☐☐ Doug Weight, Edm.
☐☐ Alexei Yashin, Ott.
☐☐ Steve Yzerman, Det.

Goalie Sticks

☐☐ Ed Belfour (G), Dal.
☐☐ Martin Brodeur (G), N.J.
☐☐ Dominik Hasek (G), Buf.
☐☐ Curtis Joseph (G), Tor.
☐☐ Olaf Kolzig (G), Wsh.
☐☐ Chris Osgood (G), Det.
☐☐ Mike Richter (G), NYR.
☐☐ Patrick Roy (G), Col.
☐☐ John Vanbiesbrouck (G), Pha.

1998 - 99 SP^X "FINITE"

Each card has three versions: the regular card, a Radiance parallel and a Spectrum parallel. This series was not yet released at press time.

Imprint: © 1998 The Upper Deck Company, LLC.

Promo

☐ Wayne Gretzky, NYR.

No. Player

☐☐☐ 1 Teemu Selänne, Ana.
☐☐☐ 2 Guy Hebert (G), Ana.
☐☐☐ 3 Josef Marha, Ana.
☐☐☐ 4 Travis Green, Ana.
☐☐☐ 5 Sergei Samsonov, Bos.
☐☐☐ 6 Jason Allison, Bos.
☐☐☐ 7 Byron Dafoe (G), Bos.
☐☐☐ 8 Dominik Hasek (G), Buf.
☐☐☐ 9 Michael Peca, Buf.
☐☐☐ 10 Erik Rasmussen, Buf.
☐☐☐ 11 Matthew Barnaby, Buf.
☐☐☐ 12 Theoren Fleury, Cgy.
☐☐☐ 13 Derek Morris, Cgy.
☐☐☐ 14 Valeri Bure, Cgy.
☐☐☐ 15 Trevor Kidd (G), Car.
☐☐☐ 16 Sami Kapanen, Car.
☐☐☐ 17 Bates Battaglia, Car.
☐☐☐ 18 Tony Amonte, Chi.
☐☐☐ 19 Dmitri Nabokov, Chi.
☐☐☐ 20 Daniel Cleary, Chi.
☐☐☐ 21 Jeff Hackett (G), Chi.
☐☐☐ 22 Joe Sakic, Col.
☐☐☐ 23 Valeri Kamensky, Col.
☐☐☐ 24 Patrick Roy (G), Col.
☐☐☐ 25 Wade Belak, Col.
☐☐☐ 26 Joe Nieuwendyk, Dal.
☐☐☐ 27 Mike Keane, Dal.
☐☐☐ 28 Jere Lehtinen, Dal.
☐☐☐ 29 Ed Belfour (G), Dal.
☐☐☐ 30 Steve Yzerman, Det.
☐☐☐ 31 Dmitri Mironov, Det.
☐☐☐ 32 Brendan Shanahan, Det.
☐☐☐ 33 Nicklas Lidström, Det.
☐☐☐ 34 Doug Weight, Edm.
☐☐☐ 35 Janne Niinimaa, Edm.
☐☐☐ 36 Bill Guerin, Edm.
☐☐☐ 37 Ray Whitney, Fla.
☐☐☐ 38 Robert Svehla, Fla.
☐☐☐ 39 Ed Jovanovski, Fla.
☐☐☐ 40 Vladimir Tsyplakov, L.A.
☐☐☐ 41 Jozef Stumpel, L.A.
☐☐☐ 42 Rob Blake, L.A.
☐☐☐ 43 Mark Recchi, Mtl.
☐☐☐ 44 Andy Moog (G), Mtl.
☐☐☐ 45 Matt Higgins, Mtl.
☐☐☐ 46 Martin Brodeur (G), N.J.
☐☐☐ 47 Doug Gilmour, N.J.
☐☐☐ 48 Brendan Morrison, N.J.
☐☐☐ 49 Patrik Elias, N.J.
☐☐☐ 50 Trevor Linden, NYI
☐☐☐ 51 Bryan Berard, NYI
☐☐☐ 52 Zdeno Chara, NYI
☐☐☐ 53 Wayne Gretzky, NYR
☐☐☐ 54 Marc Savard, NYR
☐☐☐ 55 Daniel Goneau, NYR
☐☐☐ 56 Pat LaFontaine, NYR
☐☐☐ 57 Alexei Yashin, Ott.
☐☐☐ 58 Marian Hossa, Ott.
☐☐☐ 59 Wade Redden, Ott.
☐☐☐ 60 John LeClair, Pha.
☐☐☐ 61 Alexandre Daigle, Pha.
☐☐☐ 62 Rod Brind'Amour, Pha.
☐☐☐ 63 Chris Therien, Pha.
☐☐☐ 64 Keith Tkachuk, Pho.
☐☐☐ 65 Brad Isbister, Pho.
☐☐☐ 66 Nikolai Khabibulin (G), Pho.
☐☐☐ 67 Robert Dome, Pgh.
☐☐☐ 68 Alexei Morozov, Pgh.
☐☐☐ 69 Stu Barnes, Pgh.
☐☐☐ 70 Tom Barrasso (G), Pgh.
☐☐☐ 71 Owen Nolan, S.J.
☐☐☐ 72 Marco Sturm, S.J.
☐☐☐ 73 Patrick Marleau, S.J.
☐☐☐ 74 Pierre Turgeon, Stl.
☐☐☐ 75 Chris Pronger, Stl.
☐☐☐ 76 Pavol Demitra, Stl.
☐☐☐ 77 Grant Fuhr (G), Stl.
☐☐☐ 78 Stéphane Richer, T.B.
☐☐☐ 79 Zac Bierk (G), T.B.
☐☐☐ 80 Alexander Selivanov, T.B.
☐☐☐ 81 Mike Johnson, Tor.
☐☐☐ 82 Mats Sundin, Tor.
☐☐☐ 83 Alyn McAuley, Tor.
☐☐☐ 84 Pavel Bure, Van.
☐☐☐ 85 Todd Bertuzzi, Van.
☐☐☐ 86 Garth Snow (G), Van.
☐☐☐ 87 Peter Bondra, Wsh.
☐☐☐ 88 Olaf Kolzig (G) Wsh.
☐☐☐ 89 Jan Bulis, Wsh.
☐☐☐ 90 Sergei Gonchar, Wsh.
☐☐☐ 91 Pavel Bure, Van.
☐☐☐ 92 Joe Sakic, Col.
☐☐☐ 93 Steve Yzerman, Det.
☐☐☐ 94 Jaromir Jagr, Pgh.
☐☐☐ 95 Peter Forsberg, Col.
☐☐☐ 96 Brendan Shanahan, Det.
☐☐☐ 97 Brett Hull, Stl.
☐☐☐ 98 Alexei Yashin, Ott.
☐☐☐ 99 Wayne Gretzky, NYR
☐☐☐ 100 Eric Lindros, Pha.
☐☐☐ 101 Sergei Samsonov, Bos.
☐☐☐ 102 John LeClair, Pha.
☐☐☐ 103 Diminik Hasek (G), Buf.
☐☐☐ 104 Teemu Selänne, Ana.
☐☐☐ 105 Martin Brodeur (G), N.J.
☐☐☐ 106 Tony Amonte, Chi.
☐☐☐ 107 Theoren Fleury, Cgy.
☐☐☐ 108 Rob Blake, L.A.
☐☐☐ 109 Mike Modano, Dal.
☐☐☐ 110 Peter Bondra, Wsh.
☐☐☐ 111 Brian Leetch, NYR.
☐☐☐ 112 Nicklas Lidström, Det.
☐☐☐ 113 Doug Weight, Edm.
☐☐☐ 114 Zigmund Palffy, NYI.
☐☐☐ 115 Saku Koivu, Mtl.
☐☐☐ 116 Paul Kariya, Ana.
☐☐☐ 117 Ray Bourque, Bos.
☐☐☐ 118 Mats Sundin, Tor.
☐☐☐ 119 Patrick Roy (G), Col.
☐☐☐ 120 Chris Chelios, Chi.
☐☐☐ 121 Sergei Samsonov, Bos.
☐☐☐ 122 Mike Johnson, Tor.
☐☐☐ 123 Patrik Elias, N.J.
☐☐☐ 124 Josef Marha, Ana.
☐☐☐ 125 Dan Cloutier (G), NYR.
☐☐☐ 126 Cameron Mann, Bos.
☐☐☐ 127 Mattias Ohlund, Van.
☐☐☐ 128 Daniel Cleary, Chi.
☐☐☐ 129 Anders Eriksson, Det.
☐☐☐ 130 Patrick Marleau, S.J.
☐☐☐ 131 Jan Bulis, Wsh.
☐☐☐ 132 Alyn McAuley, Tor.
☐☐☐ 133 Joe Thornton, Bos.
☐☐☐ 134 Andrei Zyuzin, S.J.
☐☐☐ 135 Richard Zednik, Wsh.
☐☐☐ 136 Derek Morris, Cgy.
☐☐☐ 137 Bates Battaglia, Car.
☐☐☐ 138 Mike Watt, Edm.
☐☐☐ 139 Dmitri Nabokov, Chi.
☐☐☐ 140 Marian Hossa, Ott.
☐☐☐ 141 Daniel Goneau, NYR.
☐☐☐ 142 Erik Rasmussen, Buf.
☐☐☐ 143 Daniel Brière, Pho.
☐☐☐ 144 Norm Maracle (G), Det.
☐☐☐ 145 Brendan Morrison, N.J.
☐☐☐ 146 Brad Isbister, Pho.
☐☐☐ 147 Brian Boucher (G), Pha.
☐☐☐ 148 Zac Bierk (G), T.B.
☐☐☐ 149 Alexei Morozov, Pgh.
☐☐☐ 150 Marco Sturm, S.J.
☐☐☐ 151 Wayne Gretzky, NYR.
☐☐☐ 152 Eric Lindros, Pha.
☐☐☐ 153 Paul Kariya, Ana.
☐☐☐ 154 Patrick Roy (G), Col.
☐☐☐ 155 Sergei Samsonov, Bos.
☐☐☐ 156 Steve Yzerman, Det.
☐☐☐ 157 Teemu Selänne, Ana.
☐☐☐ 158 Brendan Shanahan, Det.
☐☐☐ 159 Dominik Hasek (G), Buf.
☐☐☐ 160 Mark Messier, Van.
☐☐☐ 161 Martin Brodeur (G), N.J.
☐☐☐ 162 Mats Sundin, Tor.
☐☐☐ 163 Joe Sakic, Col.
☐☐☐ 164 John LeClair, Pha.
☐☐☐ 165 Jaromir Jagr, Pgh.
☐☐☐ 166 Peter Forsberg, Col.
☐☐☐ 167 Theoren Fleury, Cgy.
☐☐☐ 168 Peter Bondra, Wsh.
☐☐☐ 169 Mike Modano, Dal.
☐☐☐ 170 Pavel Bure, Van.
☐☐☐ 171 Patrick Roy (G), Col.
☐☐☐ 172 Eric Lindros, Pha.
☐☐☐ 173 Dominik Hasek (G), Buf.
☐☐☐ 174 Jaromir Jagr, Pgh.
☐☐☐ 175 Steve Yzerman, Det.
☐☐☐ 176 Martin Brodeur (G), N.J.
☐☐☐ 177 Ray Bourque, Bos.
☐☐☐ 178 Peter Forsberg, Col.
☐☐☐ 179 Paul Kariya, Ana.
☐☐☐ 180 Wayne Gretzky, NYR.

1998 - 99 TOPPS

This 165-card series was not yet released at press time. Each card will have two versions: the regular Topps card and an O-Pee-Chee parallel.

	No.	Player
□ □	1	Peter Forsberg, Col.
□ □	2	Petr Sykora, N.J.
□ □	3	Byron Dafoe (G), Bos.
□ □	4	Ron Francis, Car.
□ □	5	Alexei Yashin, Ott.
□ □	6	Dave Ellett, Bos.
□ □	7	Jamie Langenbrunner, Dal.
□ □	8	Doug Weight, Edm.
□ □	9	Jason Woolley, Buf.
□ □	10	Paul Coffey, Chi.
□ □	11	Uwe Krupp, Det.
□ □	12	Tomas Sandström, Ana.
□ □	13	Scott Mellanby, Fla.
□ □	14	Vladimir Tsyplakov, L.A.
□ □	15	Martin Rucinsky, Mtl.
□ □	16	Mikael Renberg, T.B.
□ □	17	Marco Sturm, S.J.
□ □	18	Eric Lindros, Pha.
□ □	19	Sean Burke, Pha.
□ □	20	Martin Brodeur (G), N.J.
□ □	21	Boyd Devereaux, Edm.
□ □	22	Kelly Buchberger, Edm.
□ □	23	Scott Stevens, N.J.
□ □	24	Jamie Storr (G), L.A.
□ □	25	Anders Eriksson, Det.
□ □	26	Gary Suter, S.J.
□ □	27	Theoren Fleury, Cgy.
□ □	28	Steve Leach, Car.
□ □	29	Félix Potvin (G), Tor.
□ □	30	Brett Hull, Dal.
□ □	31	Mike Grier, Edm.
□ □	32	Cale Hulse, Cgy.
□ □	33	Larry Murphy, Det.
□ □	34	Rick Tocchet, Pho.
□ □	35	Eric Desjardins, Pha.
□ □	36	Igor Kravchuk, Ott.
□ □	37	Rob Niedermayer, Fla.
□ □	38	Bryan Smolinski, NYI.
□ □	39	Valeri Kamensky, Col.
□ □	40	Ryan Smyth, Edm.
□ □	41	Bruce Driver, NYR.
□ □	42	Mike Johnson, Tor.
□ □	43	Rob Zamuner, T.B.
□ □	44	Steve Duchesne, L.A.
□ □	45	Martin Straka, Pgh.
□ □	46	Bill Houlder, S.J.
□ □	47	Craig Conroy, Stl.
□ □	48	Guy Hebert (G), Ana.
□ □	49	Colin Forbes, Pha.
□ □	50	Mike Modano, Dal.
□ □	51	Jamie Pushor, Ana.
□ □	52	Jarome Iginla, Cgy.
□ □	53	Paul Kariya, Ana.
□ □	54	Mattias Ohlund, Van.
□ □	55	Sergei Berezin, Tor.
□ □	56	Peter Zezel, Van.
□ □	57	Teppo Numminen, Pho.
□ □	58	Dale Hunter, Wsh.
□ □	59	Sandy Moger, L.A.
□ □	60	John LeClair, Pha.
□ □	61	Wade Redden, Ott.
□ □	62	Patrik Elias, N.J.
□ □	63	Rob Blake, L.A.
□ □	64	Todd Marchant, Edm.
□ □	65	Claude Lemieux, Col.
□ □	66	Trevor Kidd (G), Car.
□ □	67	Sergei Fedorov, Det.
□ □	68	Joe Sakic, Col.
□ □	69	Derek Morris, Cgy.
□ □	70	Alexei Morozov, Pgh.
□ □	71	Mats Sundin, Tor.
□ □	72	Daymond Langkow, T.B.
□ □	73	Kevin Hatcher, Pgh.
□ □	74	Damian Rhodes (G), Ott.
□ □	75	Brian Leetch, NYR.
□ □	76	Saku Koivu, Mtl.
□ □	77	Rick Tabaracci (G), Wsh.
□ □	78	Bernie Nicholls, S.J.
□ □	79	Alyn McCauley, Tor.
□ □	80	Patrice Brisebois, Mtl.
□ □	81	Bret Hedican, Van.
□ □	82	Sandy McCarthy, T.B.
□ □	83	Viktor Kozlov, Fla.
□ □	84	Derek King, Tor.
□ □	85	Alexander Selivanov, T.B.
□ □	86	Mike Vernon (G), S.J.
□ □	87	Jeff Beukeboom, NYR.
□ □	88	Tommy Salo (G), NYI.
□ □	89	Adam Graves, NYR.
□ □	90	Randy McKay, N.J.
□ □	91	Richard Pilon, NYI.
□ □	92	Richard Zednik, Wsh.
□ □	93	Jeff Hackett (G), Chi.
□ □	94	Michael Peca, Buf.
□ □	95	Brent Gilchrist, Det.
□ □	96	Stu Grimson, Ana.
□ □	97	Bob Probert, Chi.
□ □	98	Stu Barnes, Pgh.
□ □	99	Ruslan Salei, Ana.
□ □	100	Al MacInnis, Stl.
□ □	101	Ken Daneyko, N.J.
□ □	102	Paul Ranheim, Car.
□ □	103	Marty McInnis, Cgy.
□ □	104	Marian Hossa, Ott.
□ □	105	Darren McCarty, Det.
□ □	106	Guy Carbonneau, Dal.
□ □	107	Dallas Drake, Pho.
□ □	108	Sergei Samsonov, Bos.
□ □	109	Teemu Selänne, Ana.
□ □	110	Checklist
□ □	111	Jaromir Jagr, Pgh.
□ □	112	Joe Thornton, Bos.
□ □	113	Jon Klemm, Col.
□ □	114	Grant Fuhr (G), Stl.
□ □	115	Nikolai Khabibulin (G), Pho.
□ □	116	Rod Brind'Amour, Pha.
□ □	117	Trevor Linden, NYI.
□ □	118	Vincent Damphousse, Mtl.
□ □	119	Dino Ciccarelli, Fla.
□ □	120	Pat Verbeek, Dal.
□ □	121	Sandis Ozolinsh, Col.
□ □	122	Garth Snow (G), Van.
□ □	123	Ed Belfour (G), Dal.
□ □	124	Keith Primeau, Car.
□ □	125	Jason Allison, Bos.
□ □	126	Peter Bondra, Wsh.
□ □	127	Ulf Samuelsson, NYR.
□ □	128	Jeff Friesen, S.J.
□ □	129	Jason Bonsignore, T.B.
□ □	130	Daniel Alfredsson, Ott.
□ □	131	Bobby Holik, N.J.
□ □	132	Jozef Stumpel, L.A.
□ □	133	Brian Bellows, Wsh.
□ □	134	Chris Osgood (G), Det.
□ □	135	Alexei Zhamnov, Chi.
□ □	136	Mattias Norstrom, L.A.
□ □	137	Drake Berehowsky, Edm.
□ □	138	Mark Messier, Van.
□ □	139	Geoff Courtnall, Stl.
□ □	140	Marc Bureau, Pha.
□ □	141	Don Sweeney, Bos.
□ □	142	Wendel Clark, T.B.
□ □	143	Scott Niedermayer, N.J.
□ □	144	Chris Therien, Pha.
□ □	145	Kirk Muller, Fla.
□ □	146	Wayne Primeau, Buf.
□ □	147	Tony Granato, S.J.
□ □	148	Derian Hatcher, Dal.
□ □	149	Daniel Brière, Pho.
□ □	150	Fredrik Olausson, Pgh.
□ □	151	Joé Juneau, Wsh.
□ □	152	Michal Grosek, Buf.
□ □	153	Janne Laukkanen, Ott.
□ □	154	Keith Tkachuk, Pho.
□ □	155	Marty McSorley, S.J.
□ □	156	Owen Nolan, S.J.
□ □	157	Mark Tinordi, Wsh.
□ □	158	Steve Washburn, Fla.
□ □	159	Luke Richardson, Pha.
□ □	160	Kris King, Tor.
□ □	161	Joe Nieuwendyk, Dal.
□ □	162	Travis Green, Ana.
□ □	163	Dominik Hasek (G), Buf.
□ □	164	Dimitri Khristich, Bos.
□ □	165	Dave Manson, Mtl.
□ □	166	Chris Chelios, Chi.
□ □	167	Claude Lapointe, NYI.
□ □	168	Kris Draper, Det.
□ □	169	Brad Isbister, Pho.
□ □	170	Patrick Marleau, S.J.
□ □	171	Jeremy Roenick, Pho.
□ □	172	Darren Langdon, NYR.
□ □	173	Kevin Dineen, Car.
□ □	174	Luc Robitaille, L.A.
□ □	175	Steve Yzerman, Det.
□ □	176	Sergei Zubov, Dal.
□ □	177	Ed Jovanovski, Fla.
□ □	178	Sami Kapanen, Car.
□ □	179	Adam Oates, Wsh.
□ □	180	Pavel Bure, Van.
□ □	181	Chris Pronger, Stl.
□ □	182	Pat Falloon, Ott.
□ □	183	Darcy Tucker, T.B.
□ □	184	Zigmund Palffy, NYI.
□ □	185	Curtis Brown, Buf.
□ □	186	Curtis Joseph (G), Tor.
□ □	187	Valeri Zelepukin, Edm.
□ □	188	Russ Courtnall, L.A.
□ □	189	Adam Foote, Col.
□ □	190	Patrick Roy (G), Col.
□ □	191	Cory Stillman, Cgy.
□ □	192	Alexei Zhitnik, Buf.
□ □	193	Olaf Kolzig (G), Wsh.
□ □	194	Mark Fitzpatrick (G), Chi.
□ □	195	Eric Dazé, Chi.
□ □	196	Zarley Zalapski, Mtl.
□ □	197	Niklas Sundstrom, NYR.
□ □	198	Bryan Berard, NYI.
□ □	199	Jason Arnott, N.J.
□ □	200	Mike Richter, NYR.
□ □	201	Ken Baumgartner, Bos,
□ □	202	Jason Dawe, NYI.
□ □	203	Nicklas Lidström, Det.
□ □	204	Tony Amonte, Chi.
□ □	205	Kjell Samuelsson, Pha.
□ □	206	Ray Bourque, Bos.
□ □	207	Alexander Mogilny, Van.
□ □	208	Pierre Turgeon, Stl.
□ □	209	Tom Barrasso (G), Pgh.
□ □	210	Richard Matvichuk, Dal.
□ □	211	Sergei Krivokrasov, Nas.
□ □	212	Ted Drury, Ana.
□ □	213	Matthew Barnaby, Buf.
□ □	214	Denis Pederson, N.J.
□ □	215	John Vanbiesbrouck (G), Pha.
□ □	216	Brendan Shanahan, Det.
□ □	217	Jocelyn Thibault (G), Mtl.
□ □	218	Nelson Emerson, Car.
□ □	219	Wayne Gretzky, NYR.
□ □	220	Checklist
□ □	221	Ramzi Abid, Col.
□ □	222	Mark Bell, Chi.
□ □	223	Michael Henrich,Edm.
□ □	224	Vincent Lecavalier, T.B.
□ □	225	Rico Fata, Cgy.
□ □	226	Bryan Allen, Van.
□ □	227	Daniel Tkaczuk, Cgy.
□ □	228	Brad Stuart, S.J.
□ □	229	Derrick Walser, Rimouski
□ □	230	Jonathan Cheechoo, S.J.
□ □	231	Sergei Varlamov, Cgy.
□ □	232	Scott Gomez, N.J.
□ □	233	Jeff Heerema, Car.
□ □	234	David Legwand, Nas.
□ □	235	Manny Malhotra, NYR.
□ □	236	Michael Rupp, NYI.
□ □	237	Alex Tanguay, Col.
□ □	238	Mathieu Biron, L.A.
□ □	239	Bujar Amidovski, Toronto (OHL)

☐☐ 240 Brian Finley (G), Barrie
☐☐ 241 Philippe Sauvé (G), Col.
☐☐ 242 Jiri Fischer, Det.

CERTIFIED AUTOGRAPHS

There are nine cards in this series.

	No.	Player
☐	A1	Jason Allison, Bos.
☐	A2	Sergei Samsonov, Bos.
☐	A3	John LeClair, Pha.
☐	A4	Mattias Ohlund, Van.
☐	A5	Jaromir Jagr, Pgh.
☐	A6	Keith Tkachuk, Pho.
☐	A7	Patrik Elias, N.J.
☐	A8	Dominik Hasek (G), Buf.
☐	A9	Brian Leetch, NYR.

BLAST FROM THE PAST

This 10-card set features reprinted versions of Topps rookie cards.

	No.	Player
☐	1	Wayne Gretzky
☐	2	Mark Messier
☐	3	Ray Bourque
☐	4	Patrick Roy (G),
☐	5	Grant Fuhr (G),
☐	6	Brett Hull
☐	7	Gordie Howe
☐	8	Stan Mikita
☐	9	Bobby Hull
☐	10	Phil Esposito

BOARD MEMBERS

There are 15 cards in this series.

	No.	Player
☐	B1	Chris Pronger, Stl.
☐	B2	Chris Chelios, Chi.
☐	B3	Brian Leetch, NYR.
☐	B4	Ray Bourque, Bos.
☐	B5	Mattias Ohlund, Van.
☐	B6	Nicklas Lidström, Det.
☐	B7	Sergei Zubov, Dal.
☐	B8	Scott Niedermayer, N.J.
☐	B9	Larry Murphy, Det.
☐	B10	Sandis Ozolinsh, Col.
☐	B11	Rob Blake, L.A.
☐	B12	Scott Stevens, N.J.
☐	B13	Derian Hatcher, Dal.
☐	B14	Kevin Hatcher, Pgh.
☐	B15	Wade Redden, Ott.

ICE AGE 2000

There are 15 cards in this series.

	No.	Player
☐	I1	Paul Kariya, Ana.
☐	I2	Marco Sturm, S.J.
☐	I3	Jarome Iginla, Cgy.
☐	I4	Denis Pederson, N.J.
☐	I5	Wade Redden, Ott.
☐	I6	Jason Allison, Bos.
☐	I7	Chris Pronger, Stl.
☐	I8	Peter Forsberg, Col.
☐	I9	Saku Koivu, Mtl.
☐	I10	Eric Lindros, Pha.
☐	I11	Sergei Samsonov, Bos.
☐	I12	Mattias Ohlund, Van.
☐	I13	Joe Thornton, Bos.
☐	I14	Mike Johnson, Tor.
☐	I15	Nikolai Khabibulin (G), Pho.

LOCAL LEGENDS

There are 15 cards in this series.

	No.	Player
☐	L1	Peter Forsberg, Col.
☐	L2	Mats Sundin, Tor.
☐	L3	Zigmund Palffy, NYI.
☐	L4	Jaromir Jagr, Pgh.
☐	L5	Dominik Hasek (G), Buf.
☐	L6	Martin Brodeur (G), N.J.
☐	L7	Wayne Gretzky, NYR.
☐	L8	Patrick Roy (G), Col.
☐	L9	Eric Lindros, Pha.
☐	L10	Joe Sakic, Col.
☐	L11	Mark Messier, Van.
☐	L12	Mike Modano, Dal.
☐	L13	Sergei Fedorov, Det.
☐	L14	Pavel Bure, Van.
☐	L15	Teemu Selänne, Ana.

MYSTERY FINEST

This 20-card set will have two versions: a Finest insert and a Refractor parallel.

	No.	Player
☐☐	M1	Teemu Selänne, Ana.
☐☐	M2	Olaf Kolzig (G), Wsh.
☐☐	M3	Pavel Bure, Van.
☐☐	M4	Wayne Gretzky, NYR.
☐☐	M5	Mike Modano, Dal.
☐☐	M6	Jaromir Jagr, Pgh.
☐☐	M7	Dominik Hasek (G), Buf.
☐☐	M8	Peter Forsberg, Col.
☐☐	M9	Eric Lindros, Pha.
☐☐	M10	John LeClair, Pha.
☐☐	M11	Zigmund Palffy, NYI.
☐☐	M12	Martin Brodeur (G), N.J.
☐☐	M13	Keith Tkachuk, Pho.
☐☐	M14	Peter Bondra, Wsh.
☐☐	M15	Nicklas Lidström, Det.
☐☐	M16	Patrick Roy (G), Col.
☐☐	M17	Chris Chelios, Chi.
☐☐	M18	Saku Koivu, Mtl.
☐☐	M19	Mark Messier, Van.
☐☐	M20	Joe Sakic, Col.

SEASON'S BEST

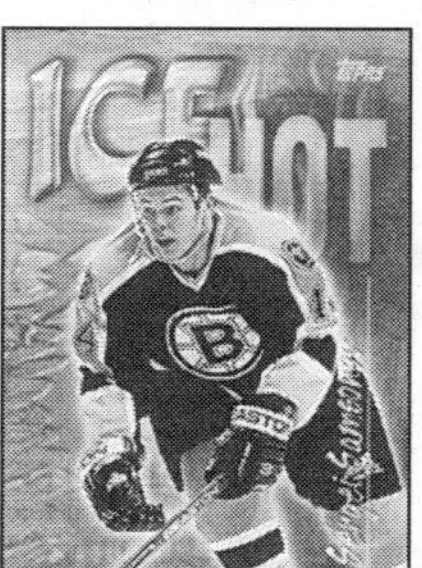

There are 30 cards in this series.

	No.	Player
☐	SB1	Dominik Hasek (G), Buf.
☐	SB2	Martin Brodeur (G), N.J.
☐	SB3	Ed Belfour (G), Dal.
☐	SB4	Curtis Joseph (G), Edm.
☐	SB5	Jeff Hackett (G), Chi.
☐	SB6	Tom Barrasso (G), Pgh.
☐	SB7	Mike Johnson, Tor.
☐	SB8	Sergei Samsonov, Bos.
☐	SB9	Patrik Elias, N.J.
☐	SB10	Patrick Marleau, S.J.
☐	SB11	Mattias Ohlund, Van.
☐	SB12	Marco Sturm, S.J.
☐	SB13	Teemu Selänne, Ana.
☐	SB14	Peter Bondra, Wsh.
☐	SB15	Pavel Bure, Van.
☐	SB16	John LeClair, Pha.
☐	SB17	Zigmund Palffy, NYI.
☐	SB18	Keith Tkachuk, Pho.
☐	SB19	Jaromir Jagr, Pgh.
☐	SB20	Wayne Gretzky, NYR.
☐	SB21	Peter Forsberg, Col.
☐	SB22	Ron Francis, Pgh.
☐	SB23	Adam Oates, Wsh.
☐	SB24	Jozef Stumpel, L.A.
☐	SB25	Chris Pronger, Stl.
☐	SB26	Larry Murphy, Det.
☐	SB27	Jason Allison, Bos.
☐	SB28	John LeClair, Pha.
☐	SB29	Randy McKay, N.J.
☐	SB30	Dainius Zubrus, Pha.

1998 - 99 UPPER DECK

This 210-card set will be released in November.There will be three versions of each card: the regular card a UD Exclusive parallel (sequentially numbered out of 100) and a one-of-one parallel.

FANTASTIC FINISHERS

There are 30 cards in this insert set. These inserts will have three versions: the regular insert, a Tier 2 insert (squentially numbered out of 1500) and a one-of-one parallel.

FROZEN IN TIME

There are 30 cards in this insert set. These inserts will have three versions: the regular insert, a Tier 2 insert (squentially numbered out of 1000) and a one-of-one parallel.

GAME JERSEYS

There are 30 cards in this insert set.

LORD STANLEY'S HEROES

There are 30 cards in this insert set. These inserts will have three versions: the regular insert, a Tier 2 insert (sequentially numbered out of 2000) and a one-of-one parallel.

1998 - 99 UD CHOICE

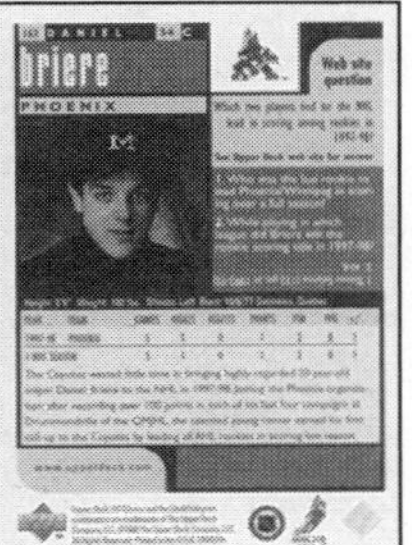

These cards have three versions: the regular card, a Choice Reserve parallel and a Prime Choice Reserve oarakkek (sequentially numbered out of 100).

Imprint: © 1998 The Upper Deck Company, LLC.

Complete Set (310 cards):

No.	Player	Prime	C.R.	Reg.
	Common Player:	**10.00**	**.50**	**.10**
1	Guy Hebert (G), Ana.	20.00	1.50	.25
2	Mikail Shtalenkov (G), Ana.	10.00	.50	.10
3	Josef Marha, Ana.	10.00	.50	.10
4	Paul Kariya, Ana.	200.00	12.50	1.25
5	Travis Green, Ana.	10.00	.50	.10
6	Steve Rucchin, Ana.	10.00	.50	.10
7	Matt Cullen, Ana.	10.00	.50	.10
8	Teemu Selänne, Ana.	90.00	7.00	.75
9	Antti Aalto, Ana.	10.00	.50	.10
10	Byron Dafoe (G), Bos.	10.00	.50	.10
11	Ted Donato, Bos.	10.00	.50	.10
12	Dimitri Khristich, Bos.	10.00	.50	.10
13	Sergei Samsonov, Bos.	60.00	6.00	.60
14	Jason Allison, Bos.	30.00	3.00	.35
15	Ray Bourque, Bos.	60.00	5.00	.50
16	Kyle McLaren, Bos.	10.00	.50	.10
17	Cameron Mann, Bos.	10.00	.50	.10
18	Shawn Bates, Bos.	10.00	.50	.10
19	Joe Thornton, Bos.	60.00	6.00	.60
20	Vaclav Varada, Buf.	10.00	.50	.10
21	Brian Holzinger, Buf.	10.00	.50	.10
22	Miroslav Satan, Buf.	10.00	.50	.10
23	Dominik Hasek (G), Buf.	90.00	7.00	.75
24	Michael Peca, Buf.	20.00	1.50	.25
25	Erik Rasmussen, Buf.	10.00	.50	.10
26	Alexei Zhitnik, Buf.	10.00	.50	.10
27	Geoff Sanderson, Buf.	10.00	.50	.10
28	Donald Audette, Buf.	10.00	.50	.10
29	Derek Morris, Cgy.	10.00	.50	.10
30	German Titov, Cgy.	10.00	.50	.10
31	Valeri Bure, Cgy.	10.00	.50	.10
32	Michael Nylander, Cgy.	10.00	.50	.10
33	Cory Stillman, Cgy.	10.00	.50	.10
34	Theoren Fleury, Cgy.	30.00	3.00	.35
35	Jarome Iginla, Cgy.	20.00	1.50	.25
36	Gary Roberts, Car.	20.00	1.50	.25
37	Jeff O'Neill, Car.	20.00	1.50	.25
38	Bates Battaglia, Car.	10.00	.50	.10
39	Keith Primeau, Car.	20.00	1.50	.25
40	Sami Kapanen, Car.	10.00	.50	.10
41	Glen Wesley, Car.	10.00	.50	.10
42	Trevor Kidd (G), Car.	20.00	1.50	.25
43	Nelson Emerson, Car.	10.00	.50	.10
44	Daniel Cleary, Chi.	20.00	1.50	.25
45	Eric Dazé, Chi.	20.00	1.50	.25
46	Chris Chelios, Chi.	45.00	4.00	.35
47	Gary Suter, Chi.	10.00	.50	.10
48	Alexei Zhamnov, Chi.	10.00	.50	.10
49	Jeff Hackett (G), Chi.	20.00	1.50	.25
50	Dimitri Nabokov, Chi.	10.00	.50	.10
51	Tony Amonte, Chi.	20.00	1.50	.25
52	Jean-Yves Leroux, Chi.	10.00	.50	.10
53	Eric Messier, Col.	10.00	.50	.10
54	Patrick Roy (G), Col	275.00	15.00	1.50
55	Claude Lemieux, Col.	10.00	.50	.10
56	Peter Forsberg, Col.	150.00	10.00	1.00
57	Adam Deadmarsh, Col.	10.00	.50	.10
58	Valeri Kamensky, Col.	20.00	1.50	.25
59	Joe Sakic, Col.	10.00	.50	.10
60	Sandis Ozolinsh, Col.	20.00	1.50	.25
61	Jamie Langenbrunner, Dal.	20.00	1.50	.25
62	Joe Nieuwendyk, Dal.	20.00	1.50	.25
63	Ed Belfour (G), Dal.	30.00	3.00	.35
64	Juha Lind, Dal.	10.00	.50	.10
65	Derian Hatcher, Dal.	20.00	1.50	.25
66	Sergei Zubov, Dal.	20.00	1.50	.25
67	Darryl Sydor, Dal.	10.00	.50	.10
68	Jere Lehtinen, Dal.	20.00	1.50	.25
69	Mike Modano, Dal.	60.00	5.00	.50
70	Larry Murphy, Det.	20.00	1.50	.25
71	Igor Larionov, Det.	20.00	1.50	.25
72	Darren McCarty, Det.	10.00	.50	.10
73	Steve Yzerman, Det.	150.00	10.00	1.00
74	Chris Osgood (G), Det.	45.00	4.00	.35
75	Sergei Fedorov, Det.	60.00	5.00	.50
76	Brendan Shanahan, Det.	75.00	6.00	.60
77	Nicklas Lidström, Det.	20.00	1.50	.25
78	Vyacheslav Kozlov, Det.	10.00	.50	.10
79	Dean McAmmond, Edm.	10.00	.50	.10
80	Roman Hamrlik, Edm.	20.00	1.50	.25
81	Curtis Joseph (G), Edm.	75.00	6.00	.60
82	Ryan Smyth, Edm.	20.00	1.50	.25
83	Boris Mironov, Edm.	10.00	.50	.10
84	Bill Guerin, Edm.	20.00	1.50	.25
85	Doug Weight, Edm.	30.00	3.00	.35
86	Janne Niinimaa, Edm.	10.00	.50	.10
87	Ray Whitney, Fla.	10.00	.50	.10
88	Robert Svehla, Fla.	10.00	.50	.10
89	John Vanbiesbrouck (G), Fla.	75.00	6.00	.60
90	Scott Mellanby, Fla.	10.00	.50	.10
91	Ed Jovanovski, Fla.	20.00	1.50	.25
92	Dave Gagner, Fla.	10.00	.50	.10
93	Dino Ciccarelli, Fla.	20.00	1.50	.25
94	Rob Niedermayer, Fla.	10.00	.50	.10
95	Rob Blake, L.A.	20.00	1.50	.25
96	Yanic Perrault, L.A.	10.00	.50	.10
97	Stéphane Fiset (G), L.A.	20.00	1.50	.25
98	Luc Robitaille, L.A.	20.00	1.50	.25
99	Glen Murray, L.A.	10.00	.50	.10
100	Jozef Stumpel, L.A.	20.00	1.50	.25
101	Vladimir Tsyplakov, L.A.	10.00	.50	.10
102	Donald MacLean, L.A.	10.00	.50	.10
103	Shayne Corson, Mtl.	20.00	1.50	.25
104	Vladimir Malakhov, Mtl.	10.00	.50	.10
105	Saku Koivu, Mtl.	90.00	7.00	.75
106	Andy Moog (G), Mtl.	20.00	1.50	.25
107	Matt Higgins, Mtl.	10.00	.50	.10
108	Dave Manson, Mtl.	10.00	.50	.10
109	Mark Recchi, Mtl.	20.00	1.50	.25
110	Vincent Damphousse, Mtl.	30.00	3.00	.35
111	Brian Savage, Mtl.	10.00	.50	.10
112	Petr Sykora, N.J.	10.00	.50	.10
113	Scott Stevens, N.J.	10.00	.50	.10
114	Patrik Elias, N.J.	10.00	.50	.10
115	Bobby Holik, N.J.	10.00	.50	.10
116	Martin Brodeur (G), N.J.	90.00	7.00	.75
117	Doug Gilmour, N.J.	35.00	3.00	.35
118	Jason Arnott, N.J.	25.00	1.50	.25
119	Scott Niedermayer, N.J.	25.00	1.50	.25
120	Brendan Morrison, N.J.	40.00	6.00	.60
121	Zigmund Palffy, NYI.	35.00	3.00	.35
122	Trevor Linden, NYI.	25.00	1.50	.25
123	Bryan Berard, NYI.	35.00	3.00	.35
124	Zdeno Chara, NYI.	10.00	.50	.10
125	Kenny Jonsson, NYI.	10.00	.50	.10
126	Robert Reichel, NYI.	10.00	.50	.10
127	Bryan Smolinski, NYI.	10.00	.50	.10
128	Wayne Gretzky, NYR.	350.00	20.00	2.00
129	Brian Leetch, NYR.	35.00	3.00	.35
130	Pat LaFontaine, NYR.	25.00	1.50	.25
131	Dan Cloutier (G), NYR.	25.00	1.50	.25
132	Nicklas Sundstrom, NYR.	10.00	.50	.10
133	Marc Savard, NYR.	10.00	.50	.10
134	Adam Graves, NYR.	10.00	.50	.10
135	Mike Richter (G), NYR.	35.00	3.00	.35
136	Jeff Beukeboom, NYR.	10.00	.50	.10
137	Daniel Goneau, NYR.	10.00	.50	.10
138	Shawn McEachern, Ott.	10.00	.50	.10
139	Damian Rhodes (G), Ott.	10.00	.50	.10
140	Wade Redden, Ott.	10.00	.50	.10
141	Alexei Yashin, Ott.	45.00	4.00	.35
142	Marian Hossa, Ott.	30.00	5.00	.50
143	Chris Phillips, Ott.	10.00	.50	.10
144	Daniel Alfredsson, Ott.	25.00	1.50	.25
145	Vaclav Prospal, Ott.	25.00	1.50	.25
146	Andreas Dackell, Ott.	10.00	.50	.10
147	Sean Burke (G), Pha.	25.00	1.50	.25
148	Alexandre Daigle, Pha.	25.00	1.50	.25
149	Rod Brind'Amour, Pha.	25.00	1.50	.25
150	Chris Gratton, Pha.	25.00	1.50	.25
151	Paul Coffey, Pha.	25.00	1.50	.25
152	Eric Lindros, Pha.	200.00	12.50	1.25
153	John LeClair, Pha.	60.00	5.00	.50
154	Chris Therien, Pha.	10.00	.50	.10
155	Keith Carney, Pho.	10.00	.50	.10
156	Craig Janney, Pho.	10.00	.50	.10
157	Teppo Numminen, Pho.	10.00	.50	.10
158	Jeremy Roenick, Pho.	35.00	3.00	.35
159	Oleg Tverdovsky, Pho.	25.00	1.50	.25
160	Keith Tkachuk, Pho.	45.00	4.00	.35
161	Brad Isbister, Pho.	10.00	.50	.10
162	Nikolai Khabibulin (G), Pho.	35.00	3.00	.35
163	Daniel Brière, Pho.	25.00	1.50	.25
164	Juha Ylönen, Pho.	10.00	.50	.10
165	Tom Barrasso (G), Pgh.	25.00	1.50	.25
166	Alexei Morozov, Pgh.	35.00	3.00	.50
167	Stu Barnes, Pgh.	10.00	.50	.10
168	Jaromir Jagr, Pgh.	150.00	10.00	1.00
169	Ron Francis, Pgh.	35.00	3.00	.35
170	Peter Skudra (G), Pgh.	10.00	.50	.10
171	Robert Dome, Pgh.	10.00	.50	.10
172	Kevin Hatcher, Pgh.	10.00	.50	.10

	No.	Player			
□□□	173	Patrick Marleau, S.J.	35.00	3.00	.50
□□□	174	Jeff Friesen, S.J.	25.00	1.50	.25
□□□	175	Owen Nolan, S.J.	25.00	1.50	.25
□□□	176	John MacLean, S.J.	10.00	.50	.10
□□□	177	Mike Vernon (G), S.J.	25.00	1.50	.25
□□□	178	Marcus Ragnarsson, S.J.	10.00	.50	.10
□□□	179	Andrei Zyuzin, S.J.	25.00	1.50	.25
□□□	180	Mike Ricci, S.J.	10.00	.50	.10
□□□	181	Marco Sturm, S.J.	10.00	.50	.10
□□□	182	Steve Duchesne, Stl.	10.00	.50	.10
□□□	183	Brett Hull, Stl.	60.00	5.00	.50
□□□	184	Pierre Turgeon, Stl.	25.00	1.50	.25
□□□	185	Chris Pronger, Stl.	25.00	1.50	.25
□□□	186	Pavol Demitra, Stl.	10.00	.50	.10
□□□	187	Jamie McLennan (G), Stl.	25.00	1.50	.25
□□□	188	Al MacInnis, Stl.	25.00	1.50	.25
□□□	189	Jim Campbell, Stl.	10.00	.50	.10
□□□	190	Geoff Courtnall, Stl.	10.00	.50	.10
□□□	191	Daren Puppa (G), T.B.	10.00	.50	.10
□□□	192	Daymond Langkow, T.B.	10.00	.50	.10
□□□	193	Stéphane Richer, T.B.	10.00	.50	.10
□□□	194	Paul Ysebaert, T.B.	10.00	.50	.10
□□□	195	Alexander Selivanov, T.B.	10.00	.50	.10
□□□	196	Rob Zamuner, T.B.	25.00	1.50	.25
□□□	197	Mikael Renberg, T.B.	10.00	.50	.10
□□□	198	Mathieu Schneider, Tor.	10.00	.50	.10
□□□	199	Mike Johnson, Tor.	35.00	3.00	.50
□□□	200	Alyn McAuley, Tor.	35.00	3.00	.50
□□□	201	Sergei Berezin, Tor.	10.00	.50	.10
□□□	202	Wendel Clark, Tor.	25.00	1.50	.25
□□□	203	Mats Sundin, Tor.	60.00	5.00	.50
□□□	204	Tie Domi, Tor.	10.00	.50	.10
□□□	205	Jyrki Lumme, Van.	10.00	.50	.10
□□□	206	Mattias Ohlund, Van.	25.00	1.50	.25
□□□	207	Garth Snow (G), Van.	10.00	.50	.10
□□□	208	Pavel Bure, Van.	90.00	7.00	.75
□□□	209	Dave Scatchard, Van.	10.00	.50	.10
□□□	210	Alexander Mogilny, Van.	35.00	3.00	.35
□□□	211	Mark Messier, Van.	60.00	5.00	.50
□□□	212	Todd Bertuzzi, Van.	10.00	.50	.10
□□□	213	Peter Bondra, Wsh.	45.00	4.00	.35
□□□	214	Joé Juneau, Wsh.	10.00	.50	.10
□□□	215	Olaf Kolzig (G), Wsh.	35.00	3.00	.35
□□□	216	Jan Bulis, Wsh,.	10.00	.50	.10
□□□	217	Adam Oates, Wsh.	35.00	3.00	.35
□□□	218	Richard Zednik, Wsh.	10.00	.50	.10
□□□	219	Calle Johansson, Wsh.	10.00	.50	.10
□□□	220	Phil Housley, Wsh.	10.00	.50	.10
□□□	221	Dominik Hasek (G), Buf.	45.00	3.50	.35
□□□	222	Ray Bourque, Bos.	30.00	2.50	.25
□□□	223	Chris Chelios, Chi.	25.00	1.50	.25
□□□	224	Paul Kariya, Ana.	100.00	6.50	.65
□□□	225	Wayne Gretzky, NYR.	200.00	10.00	1.00
□□□	226	Jaromir Jagr, Pgh.	75.00	5.00	.50
□□□	227	Rob Blake, L.A.	20.00	1.00	.25
□□□	228	Adam Foote, Col.	20.00	1.00	.25
□□□	229	Peter Forsberg, Col.	75.00	5.00	.50
□□□	230	Joe Sakic, Col.	55.00	4.00	.35
□□□	231	Mark Recchi, Mtl.	20.00	1.00	.25
□□□	232	Patrick Roy (G), Col.	135.00	7.50	.75
□□□	233	Nicklas Lidström, Det.	20.00	1.00	.25
□□□	234	Rob Blake, L.A.	20.00	1.00	.25
□□□	235	John LeClair, Pha.	30.00	2.50	.25
□□□	236	Wayne Gretzky, NYR.	200.00	10.00	1.00
□□□	237	Eric Lindros, Pha.	100.00	6.50	.65
□□□	238	Brian Leetch, NYR.	25.00	1.50	.25
□□□	239	Scott Stevens, N.J.	10.00	.50	.10
□□□	240	Paul Kariya, Ana.	100.00	6.50	.65
□□□	241	Peter Forsberg, Col.	75.00	5.00	.50
□□□	242	Teemu Selänne, Ana.	45.00	3.50	.35
□□□	243	Patrick Roy (G), Col.	135.00	7.50	.75
□□□	244	Dominik Hasek (G), Buf.	45.00	3.50	.35
□□□	245	Martin Brodeur (G), N.J.	45.00	3.50	.35
□□□	246	Mike Richter (G), NYR.	25.00	1.50	.25
□□□	247	John Vanbiesbrouck (G), Fla.	35.00	3.00	.25
□□□	248	Chris Osgood (G), Det.	25.00	1.50	.25
□□□	249	Ed Belfour (G), Dal.	25.00	1.50	.25
□□□	250	Tom Barrasso (G), Pgh.	20.00	1.00	.25
□□□	251	Curtis Joseph (G), Edm.	35.00	3.00	.25
□□□	252	Sean Burke (G), Pha.	20.00	1.00	.25
□□□	253	Josh Holden, Cdn.	20.00	1.00	.25
□□□	254	Daniel Tkaczuk, Cdn.	25.00	1.50	.35
□□□	255	Manny Malhotra, Cdn.	25.00	1.50	.35
□□□	256	Eric Brewer, Cdn.	25.00	1.50	.35
□□□	257	Alex Tanguay, Cdn.	25.00	1.50	.35
□□□	258	Roberto Luongo (G), Cdn.	35.00	3.00	.50
□□□	259	Vincent Lecavalier, Cdn.	50.00	6.00	.60
□□□	260	Mathieu Garon (G), Cdn.	20.00	1.00	.25
□□□	261	Brad Ference, Cdn.	20.00	1.00	.25
□□□	262	Jesse Wallin, Cdn.	20.00	1.00	.25
□□□	263	Zenith Komarniski, Cdn.	20.00	1.00	.25
□□□	264	Sean Blanchard, Cdn.	20.00	1.00	.25
□□□	265	Cory Sarich, Cdn.	20.00	1.00	.25
□□□	266	Mike Van Ryn, Cdn.	20.00	1.00	.25
□□□	267	Steve Bégin, Cdn.	20.00	1.00	.25
□□□	268	Matt Cooke, Cdn.	20.00	1.00	.25
□□□	269	Daniel Corso, Cdn.	20.00	1.00	.25
□□□	270	Brett McLean, Cdn.	20.00	1.00	.25
□□□	271	Jean-Pierre Dumont, Cdn.	25.00	1.50	.35
□□□	272	Jason Ward, Cdn.	20.00	1.00	.25
□□□	273	Brian Willsie, Cdn.	20.00	1.00	.25
□□□	274	Matt Bradley, Cdn.	20.00	1.00	.25
□□□	275	Olli Jokinen, Fin.	20.00	1.00	.25
□□□	276	Teemu Elomo, Fin.	15.00	.75	.25
□□□	277	Timo Vertala, Fin.	15.00	.75	.25
□□□	278	Mika Noronen (G), Fin.	20.00	1.00	.25
□□□	279	Pasi Petrilainen, Fin.	15.00	.75	.25
□□□	280	Timo Ahmaoja, Fin.	15.00	.75	.25
□□□	281	Eero Somervuori, Fin.	15.00	.75	.25
□□□	282	Maxim Afinogenov, Rus.	15.00	.75	.25
□□□	283	Maxim Balmochnykh, Rus.	15.00	.75	.25
□□□	284	Artem Chubarov, Rus.	15.00	.75	.25
□□□	285	Vitali Vishnevsky, Rus.	15.00	.75	.25
□□□	286	Denis Shvidky, Rus.	20.00	1.00	.25
□□□	287	Dmitri Vlassenkov, Rus.	15.00	.75	.25
□□□	288	Magnus Nilsson, Swe.	15.00	.75	.25
□□□	289	Mikael Homqvist, Swe.	15.00	.75	.25
□□□	290	Mattias Karlin, Swe.	15.00	.75	.25
□□□	291	Pierre Hedin, Swe.	15.00	.75	.25
□□□	292	Henrik Petré, Swe.	15.00	.75	.25
□□□	293	Johan Forsander, Swe.	15.00	.75	.25
□□□	294	Daniel Sedin, Swe.	35.00	3.00	.50
□□□	295	Henrik Sedin, Swe.	35.00	3.00	.50
□□□	296	Markus Nilsson, Swe.	15.00	.75	.25
□□□	297	Paul Mara, USA.	20.00	1.00	.25
□□□	298	Brian Gionta, USA.	20.00	1.00	.25
□□□	299	Chris Hajt, USA.	20.00	1.00	.25
□□□	300	Mike Mottau, USA.	20.00	1.00	.25
□□□	301	Jean-Marc Pelletier, USA.	20.00	1.00	.25
□□□	302	David Legwand, USA.	50.00	6.00	.60
□□□	303	Ty Jones, USA.	20.00	1.00	.25
□□□	304	Nikos Tselios, USA.	20.00	1.00	.25
□□□	305	Jesse Boulerice, USA.	20.00	1.00	.25
□□□	306	Jeff Farkas, USA.	20.00	1.00	.25
□□□	307	Toby Peterson, USA.	20.00	1.00	.25
□□□	308	CL: Wayne Gretzky, NYR.	175.00	10.00	1.00
□□□	309	CL: Patrick Roy (G), Col.	135.00	7.50	.75
□□□	310	CL: Steve Yzerman, Det.	75.00	5.00	.50

BOBBING HEADS

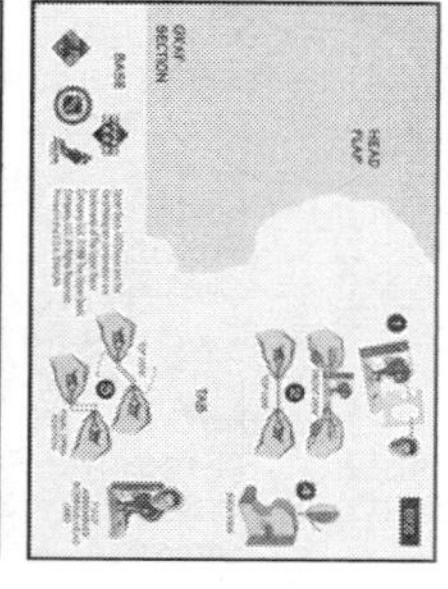

Insert Set (30 cards):			20.00
	No.	Player	NRMT-MT
□	BH1	Wayne Gretzky	5.00
□	BH2	Keith Tkachuk	1.00
□	BH3	Ray Bourque	1.25
□	BH4	Brett Hull	1.25
□	BH5	Jaromir Jagr	2.00
□	BH6	John LeClair	1.25
□	BH7	Martin Brodeur	1.75
□	BH8	Eric Lindros	3.50
□	BH9	Mark Messier	1.25
□	BH10	John Vanbiesbrouck	1.50
□	BH11	Paul Kariya	3.50
□	BH12	Luc Robitaille	.50
□	BH13	Zigmund Palffy	1.00
□	BH14	Peter Forsberg	2.50
□	BH15	Teemu Selänne	1.75
□	BH16	Mike Modano	1.25
□	BH17	Mats Sundin	1.25
□	BH18	Dominik Hasek	1.75
□	BH19	Joe Sakic	2.00
□	BH20	Rob Blake	.50
□	BH21	Patrick Roy	4.00
□	BH22	Sergei Samsonov	1.50
□	BH23	Chris Chelios	1.00
□	BH24	Brendan Shanahan	1.50
□	BH25	Theoren Fleury	.75
□	BH26	Ed Belfour	.75
□	BH27	Steve Yzerman	2.50
□	BH28	Saku Koivu	1.75
□	BH29	Brian Leetch	.75
□	BH30	Pavel Bure	1.75

DRAW YOUR OWN

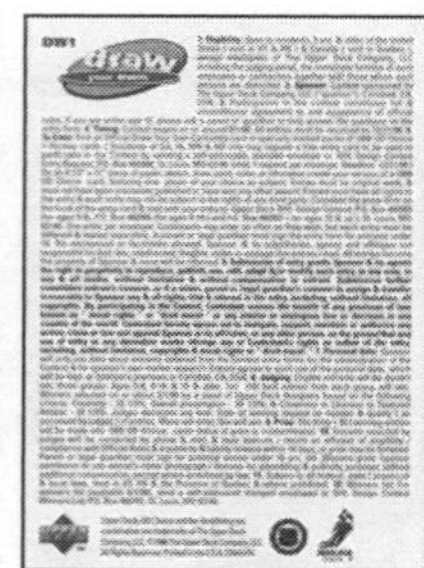

	Player	NRMT-MT
□	Wayne Gretzky	.10

STAR QUEST

This series has four versions: a Blue insert, a Green insert, a Red insert and a Gold insert (sequentially numbered out of 100).

Insert Set (30 cards):			2,500.00	150.00	40.00	15.00
	No.	Player	Gold	Red	Green	Blue
□□□□	SQ1	Wayne Gretzky	350.00	40.00	10.00	4.00
□□□□	SQ2	Pavel Bure	90.00	15.00	3.50	1.50
□□□□	SQ3	Patrick Roy	275.00	30.00	8.00	3.00
□□□□	SQ4	Dominik Hasek	90.00	15.00	3.50	1.50
□□□□	SQ5	Teemu Selänne	90.00	15.00	3.50	1.50
□□□□	SQ6	Sergei Samsonov	60.00	10.00	3.00	1.25
□□□□	SQ7	Brian Leetch	30.00	5.00	1.50	.50
□□□□	SQ8	Saku Koivu	90.00	15.00	3.50	1.50
□□□□	SQ9	Brendan Shanahan	75.00	12.50	3.00	1.25
□□□□	SQ10	Alexei Yashin	45.00	7.50	2.00	.75
□□□□	SQ11	Joe Sakic	115.00	17.50	4.00	1.75
□□□□	SQ12	Patrik Elias	10.00	4.00	1.00	.50
□□□□	SQ13	Theoren Fleury	30.00	5.00	1.50	.50
□□□□	SQ14	Peter Bondra	45.00	7.50	2.00	.75
□□□□	SQ15	John LeClair	60.00	10.00	2.50	1.00
□□□□	SQ16	Jaromir Jagr	150.00	20.00	5.00	2.00
□□□□	SQ17	Ed Belfour	45.00	5.00	1.50	.50
□□□□	SQ18	Steve Yzerman	150.00	20.00	5.00	2.00
□□□□	SQ19	Mats Sundin	60.00	10.00	2.50	1.00
□□□□	SQ20	Peter Forsberg	150.00	20.00	5.00	2.00
□□□□	SQ21	Ray Bourque	60.00	10.00	2.50	1.00
□□□□	SQ22	Brett Hull	60.00	10.00	2.50	1.00
□□□□	SQ23	Martin Brodeur	90.00	15.00	3.50	1.50
□□□□	SQ24	Mike Modano	60.00	10.00	2.50	1.00
□□□□	SQ25	Paul Kariya	200.00	25.00	6.50	2.50
□□□□	SQ26	Tony Amonte	20.00	5.00	1.00	.50
□□□□	SQ27	Mike Johnson	40.00	7.50	2.50	1.00
□□□□	SQ28	Eric Lindros	200.00	25.00	6.50	2.50
□□□□	SQ29	Mark Messier	60.00	10.00	2.50	1.00
□□□□	SQ30	Keith Tkachuk	45.00	7.50	2.00	.75

CHAPTER THREE

NHL TEAM SETS

NHL TEAM SETS

ANAHEIM MIGHTY DUCKS

1993 - 94 MIGHTY DUCKS CAPS

These blank-back caps are limited to 15,000 copies. Singles start at $1.00.
Cap diameter: 1 1/2"
Sponsor: none
Complete Set (6 caps): 6.00

- ☐ Mighty Ducks
- ☐ 1 Tim Sweeney
- ☐ 2 Bobby Dollas
- ☐ 3 Stu Grimson
- ☐ 4 Terry Yake
- ☐ 5 Bob Corkum

1994 - 95 MIGHTY DUCKS CARL'S JR.

Paul Kariya is the most expensive single at $10-12. Singles start at 50¢.
Card Size: 2 1/2" x 3 1/2"
Sponsor: CarlÆs Jr.
Complete Set (28 cards): 20.00

- ☐ 1 Patrick Carnback
- ☐ 2 Bob Corkum
- ☐ 3 Robert Dirk
- ☐ 4 Bobby Dollas
- ☐ 5 Peter Douris
- ☐ 6 Todd Ewen
- ☐ 7 Shaun Van Allen
- ☐ 8 Garry Valk
- ☐ 9 Guy Hebert (G)
- ☐ 10 Paul Kariya
- ☐ 11 Valeri Karpov
- ☐ 12 Steven King
- ☐ 13 Todd Krygier
- ☐ 14 Tom Kurvers
- ☐ 15 Randy Ladouceur
- ☐ 16 Stéphan Lebeau
- ☐ 17 John Lilley
- ☐ 18 Don McSween
- ☐ 19 Steve Rucchin
- ☐ 20 David Sacco
- ☐ 21 Joe Sacco
- ☐ 22 Mikhail Shtalenkov (G)
- ☐ 23 Jim Thomson
- ☐ 24 Olef Tverdovsky
- ☐ 25 David Williams
- ☐ 26 Mascot Wild Wing
- ☐ 27 Sponsor Carl Karcher
- ☐ 28 Sponsor Logo Happy Star

1995 - 96 MIGHTY DUCKS PHOTOS

We have little information on this set. Other singles exist.
Photo Size: 5" x 7"
Sponsor: none

- ☐ Bobby Dollas
- ☐ Paul Kariya
- ☐ David Karpa
- ☐ Steve Rucchin
- ☐ Mikhail Shtalenkov (G)
- ☐ Garry Valk

1996 - 97 MIGHTY DUCKS UP FRONT SPORTS

The most expenive singles are Paul Kariya at $6-8 and Teemu Selänne at $3-4. Regular singles start at 50¢ while pop-up singles (21-24) start at $1.50. Card number 9 (Garry Valk) is unconfirmed. A 26-card set sells for $25.
Card Size: 2 1/2" x 3 1/2"
Sponsor: Southland Micro Systems

- ☐ 1 Mikhail Shtalenkov (G)
- ☐ 2 Bobby Dollas
- ☐ 3 Roman Oksiuta
- ☐ 4 Kevin Todd
- ☐ 5 Ted Drury
- ☐ 6 Joe Sacco
- ☐ 7 Dmitri Mironov
- ☐ 8 Warren Rychel
- ☐ 10 Shawn Antoski
- ☐ 11 Steve Rucchin
- ☐ 12 Ken Baumgartner
- ☐ 13 Brian Bellows
- ☐ 14 Nikolai Tsulygin
- ☐ 15 Jason Marshall
- ☐ 16 Darren Van Impe
- ☐ 17 David Karpa
- ☐ 18 Mascot Wild Wing
- ☐ 19 J.F. Jomphe
- ☐ 20 Sean Pronger
- ☐ 21 Guy Hebert (G)
- ☐ 22 Paul Kariya
- ☐ 23 Jari Kurri
- ☐ 24 Teemu Selänne
- ☐ 25 Sponsor Southland
- ☐ 26 Sponsor Southland
- ☐ 27 Ron Wilson, Coach

ATLANTA FLAMES

1972 - 73 FLAMES COCA-COLA

Bernie Geoffrion and Pat Quinn are the most expensive singles at $8-10 in NRMT. Singles start at $2.
Card Size: 3 1/2" x 5 1/2"
Sponsors: none
Complete Set (20 cards): 60.00

- ☐ Curt Bennett
- ☐ Dan Bouchard (G)
- ☐ Rey Comeau
- ☐ Bernie Geoffrion
- ☐ Bob Leiter
- ☐ Kerry Ketter
- ☐ Billy MacMillan
- ☐ Randy Manery
- ☐ Keith McCreary
- ☐ Lew Morrison
- ☐ Phil Myre (G)
- ☐ Bob Paradise
- ☐ Noel Picard
- ☐ Bill Plager
- ☐ Noel Price
- ☐ Pat Quinn
- ☐ Jacques Richard
- ☐ Leon Rochefort
- ☐ Larry Romanchych
- ☐ John Stewart

1974 - 75 FLAMES

These cards feature colour photographs and a facsimile signature on the card front. Dan Bouchard is the most expensive single at $5-6. Singles start at $1.50. Other singles may exist.
Card Size:
Sponsors: none

- ☐ Curt Bennett
- ☐ Dan Bouchard (G)
- ☐ Rey Comeau
- ☐ Tim Ecclestone
- ☐ Hilliard Graves
- ☐ Buster Harvey
- ☐ Bob Leiter
- ☐ Tom Lysiak
- ☐ Randy Manery
- ☐ Phil Myre (G)
- ☐ Pat Quinn
- ☐ Larry Romanchych
- ☐ Eric Vail

1977 - 78 FLAMES

These cards feature colour photographs and a facsimile signature on the card front. Dan Bouchard is the most expensive single at $3-4. Singles start at $1.00. Other singles may exist.
Card Size:
Sponsors: none

- ☐ Dan Bouchard (G)
- ☐ Guy Chouinard
- ☐ Bill Clement
- ☐ Rey Comeau
- ☐ Tim Ecclestone
- ☐ John Gould
- ☐ Ken Houston
- ☐ Ed Kea
- ☐ Tom Lysiak
- ☐ Richard Mulhern
- ☐ Harold Phillipoff
- ☐ Willi Plett
- ☐ Pat Ribble
- ☐ Dave Shand
- ☐ Eric Vail

1978 - 79 FLAMES

Dan Bouchard and Réjean Lemelin are the most expensive singles at $3-4 in NRMT. Singles start at $1.00.
Card Size: 3 1/2" x 5 1/2"
Sponsor: Coca-Cola, WLTA Radio
Complete Set (20 cards): 35.00

- ☐ Dan Bouchard (G)
- ☐ Guy Chouinard
- ☐ Bill Clement
- ☐ Greg Fox
- ☐ Ken Houston
- ☐ Ed Kea
- ☐ Bobby Lalonde
- ☐ Red Laurence
- ☐ Réjean Lemelin (G)
- ☐ Tom Lysiak
- ☐ Bob MacMillan
- ☐ Brad Marsh
- ☐ Bob Murdoch
- ☐ Harold Phillipof
- ☐ Willi Plett
- ☐ Jean Pronovost
- ☐ Pat Ribble
- ☐ Rod Seiling
- ☐ Dave Shand
- ☐ Eric Vail

1979 - 80 FLAMES

These cards feature colour photography. Kent Nilsson is the most expensive card at $4-5 in NRMT. Singles start at $1.00
Card Size: 3 1/2" x 5 1/2"
Sponsors: Coca-Cola, WLTA Radio, Winn Dixie.
Complete Set (20 cards): 35.00

- ☐ Curt Bennett
- ☐ Dan Bouchard (G)
- ☐ Guy Chouinard
- ☐ Bill Clement
- ☐ Jim Craig (G)
- ☐ Ken Houston
- ☐ Don Lever
- ☐ Bob MacMillan
- ☐ Brad Marsh
- ☐ Bob Murdoch
- ☐ Kent Nilsson
- ☐ Willi Plett
- ☐ Jean Pronovost
- ☐ Pekka Rautakallio
- ☐ Paul Reinhart
- ☐ Pat Riggin
- ☐ Phil Russell
- ☐ David Shand
- ☐ Garry Unger
- ☐ Eric Vail

1979 - 80 FLAMES BLACK AND WHITE

These postcards feature black and white photos and a facsimile signature on the card front. Kent Nilsson is the most expensive single at $4-5. Singles start at $1.00.
Card Size: 3 3/4" x 5 1/4"
Sponsors: none
Complete Set (20 cards): 35.00

- ☐ Curt Bennett
- ☐ Ivan Boldirev
- ☐ Dan Bouchard (G)
- ☐ Guy Chouinard
- ☐ Bill Clement
- ☐ Ken Houston
- ☐ Bob MacMillan
- ☐ Al MacNeil, Coach
- ☐ Brad Marsh
- ☐ Bob Murdoch
- ☐ Kent Nilsson
- ☐ Willi Plett
- ☐ Jean Pronovost
- ☐ Pekka Rautakallio
- ☐ Phil Russell
- ☐ Paul Reinhart
- ☐ Darcy Rota
- ☐ Dave Shand
- ☐ Garry Unger
- ☐ Eric Vail

BOSTON BRUINS

1957 - 58 BRUINS

Milt Schmidt is the most expensive single at $15 in NRMT. Singles start at $6. Other singles may exist.
Photo Size: 6 5/8" x 8 1/8"
Sponsors: none

- ☐ Bob Armstrong
- ☐ Jack Bionda
- ☐ Léo Boivin
- ☐ Real Chevrefils
- ☐ Fern Flaman
- ☐ Léo Labine
- ☐ Fleming Mackell
- ☐ Don McKenney
- ☐ Doug Mohns
- ☐ Johnny Peirson
- ☐ Larry Regan
- ☐ Milt Schmidt
- ☐ Vic Stasiuk
- ☐ Jerry Toppazzini

1970 - 71 BRUINS ASHTRAYS

These ashtrays were sold at the Boston Garden. Other singles may exist.
Ashtray Size: 5 1/2"
Sponsor: none

- ☐ Johnny Bucyk
- ☐ Ted Green
- ☐ Ken Hodge
- ☐ Reggie Leach
- ☐ Derek Sanderson

1970 - 71 BRUINS STANLEY CUP CHAMPIONS

This series was issued in two nine-photo packs. The most expensive singles are Bobby Orr at $30-35 and Phil Esposito at $8-10 in NRMT. Commons start at $2
Card Size: 6" x 8"
Sponsors: none
Complete Set (18 cards): 85.00

- ☐ Don Awrey
- ☐ Garnet Bailey
- ☐ Johnny Bucyk
- ☐ Wayne Carleton
- ☐ Wayne Cashman
- ☐ Gerry Cheevers (G)
- ☐ Gary Doak
- ☐ Phil Esposito
- ☐ Ken Hodge
- ☐ Ed Johnston (G)
- ☐ Don Marcotte
- ☐ John McKenzie
- ☐ Bobby Orr
- ☐ Derek Sanderson
- ☐ Dallas Smith
- ☐ Rick Smith
- ☐ Fred Stanfield
- ☐ Ed Westfall

1971 - 72 BRUINS

This series was originally issued in booklet form. The most expensive singles are Bobby Orr at $30-35 and Phil Esposito at $8-10 in NRMT. Singles start at $2.
Card Size: 3 1/2" x 5 1/2"
Sponsors: none
Complete Set (20 cards): 65.00

- ☐ Don Awrey
- ☐ Ace Bailey
- ☐ John Bucyk
- ☐ Wayne Cashman
- ☐ Gerry Cheevers (G)
- ☐ Phil Esposito
- ☐ Ted Green
- ☐ Ken Hodge
- ☐ Ed Johnston (G)
- ☐ Reggie Leach
- ☐ Don Marcotte
- ☐ John McKenzie
- ☐ Bobby Orr
- ☐ Garry Peters
- ☐ Derek Sanderson
- ☐ Rick Smith
- ☐ Dallas Smith
- ☐ Fred Stanfield
- ☐ Mike Walton
- ☐ Ed Westfall

1983 - 84 BRUINS

Photos are black and white. Ray Bourque is the most expensive single at $10-12. Singles start $1.00.

Card Size: 3 1/8" x 4 1/8"

Sponsors: none

Complete Set (17 cards): 35.00

- ☐ Ray Bourque
- ☐ Bruce Crowder
- ☐ Keith Crowder
- ☐ Luc Dufour
- ☐ Tom Fergus
- ☐ Randy Hillier
- ☐ Steve Kasper
- ☐ Gord Kluzak
- ☐ Mike Krushelnyski
- ☐ Peter McNab
- ☐ Rick Middleton
- ☐ Mike Milbury
- ☐ Mike O'Connell
- ☐ Terry O'Reilly
- ☐ Brad Palmer
- ☐ Barry Pederson
- ☐ Pete Peeters (G)

1984 - 85 BRUINS

Ray Bourque is the most expensive single at $10-12. Singles start $1.00.

Card Size: 3 5/8" x 5 5/8"

Sponsors: none

Complete Set (20 cards): 35.00

- ☐ Ray Bourque
- ☐ Lyndon Byers
- ☐ Geoff Courtnall
- ☐ Keith Crowder
- ☐ Tom Fergus
- ☐ Mike Gillis
- ☐ Steve Kasper
- ☐ Doug Keans (G)
- ☐ Gord Kluzak
- ☐ Ken Linseman
- ☐ Nevin Markwart
- ☐ Rick Middleton
- ☐ Mike Milbury
- ☐ Mike O'Connell
- ☐ Terry O'Reilly
- ☐ Barry Pederson
- ☐ Pete Peeters (G)
- ☐ Charlie Simmer
- ☐ Louis Sleigher
- ☐ Mats Thelin

1988 - 89 BRUINS SPORTS ACTION

Ray Bourque is the most expensive single at $3-4. Singles start at 75¢.

Card Size: 2 1/2" x 3 1/2"

Sponsor: Bruins Pro Shop

Complete Set (24 cards): 15.00

- ☐ Ray Bourque
- ☐ Randy Burridge
- ☐ Lyndon Byers
- ☐ Keith Crowder
- ☐ Craig Janney
- ☐ Bob Joyce
- ☐ Steve Kasper
- ☐ Gord Kluzak
- ☐ Reed Larson
- ☐ Réjean Lemelin (G)
- ☐ Ken Linseman
- ☐ Tom McCarthy
- ☐ Rick Middleton
- ☐ Jay Miller
- ☐ Andy Moog (G)
- ☐ Cam Neely
- ☐ Terry O'Reilly
- ☐ Allen Pederson
- ☐ Willi Plett
- ☐ Bob Sweeney
- ☐ Michael Thelvin
- ☐ Glen Wesley
- ☐ Janney/Joyce
- ☐ Bourque/Neely

1989 - 90 BRUINS SPORTS ACTION

Ray Bourque is the most expensive single at $3-4. Singles start at 75¢.

Card Size: 2 1/2" x 3 1/2"

Sponsor: Bruins Pro Shop

Complete Set (24 cards): 15.00

- ☐ Ray Bourque
- ☐ Andy Brickley
- ☐ Randy Burridge
- ☐ Lyndon Byers
- ☐ Bob Carpenter
- ☐ John Carter
- ☐ Rob Cimetta
- ☐ Garry Galley
- ☐ Bob Gould
- ☐ Greg Hawgood
- ☐ Craig Janney
- ☐ Bob Joyce
- ☐ Réjean Lemelin (G)
- ☐ Ken Linseman
- ☐ Andy Moog (G)
- ☐ Nevin Markwart
- ☐ Cam Neely
- ☐ Allen Pederson
- ☐ Stéphane Quintal
- ☐ Bob Sweeney
- ☐ Michael Thelvin
- ☐ Glen Wesley
- ☐ Bruins Scorers
- ☐ Bruins Champions

1989 - 90 BRUINS SPORTS ACTION UPDATE

Ray Bourque is the most expensive single at $3-4. Singles start at 75¢.

Card Size: 2 1/2" x 3 1/2"

Sponsor: Bruins Pro Shop

Complete Set (12 cards): 10.00

- ☐ Ray Bourque
- ☐ Dave Christian
- ☐ Peter Douris
- ☐ Gord Kluzak
- ☐ Brian Lawton
- ☐ Mike Millar
- ☐ Dave Poulin
- ☐ Brian Propp
- ☐ Don Sweeney
- ☐ Graeme Townshend
- ☐ Jim Wiemer
- ☐ Bourque/Lemelin/Neely

1990 - 91 BRUINS SPORTS ACTION

Ray Bourque is the most expensive single at $3-4. Singles start at 75¢. Nevin Markwart and Stéphane Quintal are considered short prints and sell at $2-3.

Card Size: 2 1/2" x 3 1/2"

Sponsor: Bruins Pro Shop

Complete Set (26 cards): 25.00

- ☐ Bob Beers
- ☐ Ray Bourque
- ☐ Andy Brickley
- ☐ Randy Burridge
- ☐ John Byce
- ☐ Lyndon Byers
- ☐ Bob Carpenter
- ☐ John Carter
- ☐ Dave Christian
- ☐ Peter Douris
- ☐ Garry Galley
- ☐ Ken Hodge, Jr.
- ☐ Craig Janney
- ☐ Réjean Lemelin
- ☐ Nevin Markwart
- ☐ Andy Moog (G)
- ☐ Cam Neely
- ☐ Chris Nilan
- ☐ Allen Pederson
- ☐ Dave Poulin
- ☐ Stéphane Quintal
- ☐ Bob Sweeney
- ☐ Don Sweeney
- ☐ Wes Walz
- ☐ Glen Wesley
- ☐ Lemelin/Moog

1991 - 92 BRUINS SPORTS ACTION

Ray Bourque is the most expensive single at $2-3. Singles start at 50¢.

Card Size: 2 1/2" x 3 1/2"

Sponsor: Bruins Pro Shop

Complete Set (24 cards): 15.00

- ☐ Brent Ashton
- ☐ Bob Beers
- ☐ Daniel Berthiaume (G)
- ☐ Ray Bourque
- ☐ Bob Carpenter
- ☐ Peter Douris
- ☐ Glen Featherstone
- ☐ Ken Hodge, Jr.
- ☐ Jeff Lazaro
- ☐ Stephen Leach
- ☐ Andy Moog (G)
- ☐ Gord Murphy
- ☐ Cam Neely
- ☐ Adam Oates
- ☐ Dave Poulin
- ☐ Dave Reid
- ☐ Vladimir Ruzicka
- ☐ Bob Sweeney
- ☐ Don Sweeney
- ☐ Jim Vesey
- ☐ Glen Wesley
- ☐ Jim Wiemer
- ☐ Chris Winnes
- ☐ Moog/Bourque/Neely

1991 - 92 BRUINS SPORTS ACTION LEGENDS

The most expensive singles are Bobby Orr at $3-4 and Ray Bourque at $2-3. Singles start at 50¢.

Card Size: 2 1/2" x 3 1/2"

Sponsor: Bruins Pro Shop

Complete Set (36 cards): 15.00

- ☐ Bob Armstrong
- ☐ Léo Boivin
- ☐ Ray Bourque
- ☐ Frank Brimsek (G)
- ☐ Johnny Bucyk
- ☐ Wayne Cashman
- ☐ Gerry Cheevers (G)
- ☐ Dit Clapper
- ☐ Bill Cowley
- ☐ Phil Esposito
- ☐ Fern Flaman
- ☐ Lionel Hitchman
- ☐ Fleming Mackell
- ☐ Don Marcotte
- ☐ Don McKenney
- ☐ Rick Middleton
- ☐ Doug Mohns
- ☐ Terry O'Reilly
- ☐ Bobby Orr
- ☐ Brad Park
- ☐ John Pierson
- ☐ Bill Quackenbush
- ☐ Jean Ratelle
- ☐ Art Ross
- ☐ Ed Sandford
- ☐ Terry Sawchuk (G)
- ☐ Milt Schmidt
- ☐ Eddie Shore
- ☐ Harry Sinden
- ☐ Tiny Thompson (G)
- ☐ Cooney Weiland
- ☐ Ed Westfall
- ☐ M.Hill/B.Cowley/R.Conacher
- ☐ Schmidt/Weiland/B.Cowley
- ☐ Quackenbush/Flaman/Sawchuk/Armstrong/Boivin
- ☐ Schmidt/W.Dumart/B.Bauer

1992 - 93 BRUINS

Ray Bourque is the most expensive single at $3-4. Singles start at 50¢.

Card Size: 3 1/2" x 5 1/2"

Sponsors: none

Complete Set (12 cards): 15.00

- ☐ Ray Bourque
- ☐ Ted Donato
- ☐ Joé Juneau
- ☐ Dimitri Kvartalnov
- ☐ Stephen Leach
- ☐ Andy Moog (G)
- ☐ Adam Oates
- ☐ Dave Poulin
- ☐ Gordie Roberts
- ☐ Vladimir Ruzicka
- ☐ Don Sweeney
- ☐ Glen Wesley

BUFFALO SABRES

1972 - 73 SABRES

Photos by Robert Shaver. The most expensive singles are Gilbert Perreault at $10-12 and Tim Horton at $6-8. Singles start at $2.

Card Size: 3 1/2" x 5 1/2"

Sponsors: none

Complete Set (20 cards): 40.00

- ☐ Steve Atkinson
- ☐ Larry Carriere
- ☐ Roger Crozier (G)
- ☐ Butch Deadmarsh
- ☐ Dave Dryden (G)
- ☐ Larry Hillman
- ☐ Tim Horton
- ☐ Jim Lorentz
- ☐ Don Luce
- ☐ Richard Martin
- ☐ Gerry Meehan
- ☐ Larry Mickey
- ☐ Gilbert Perreault
- ☐ Tracy Pratt
- ☐ Craig Ramsay
- ☐ René Robert
- ☐ Mike Robitaille
- ☐ Jim Schoenfeld
- ☐ Paul Terbenche
- ☐ Randy Wyrozub

1973 - 74 SABRES

Photos by Robert Shaver. The most expensive singles in NRMT are Gilbert Perreault at $10-12 and Tim Horton at $6-8. Singles start at $2.

Card Size: 3 1/2" x 5 1/2"

Sponsors: none

Complete Set (23 cards): 45.00

- ☐ Steve Atkinson
- ☐ Larry Carriere
- ☐ Frank Christie, Trainer
- ☐ Joe Crozier
- ☐ Roger Crozier (G)
- ☐ Dave Dryden (G)
- ☐ Rick Dudley
- ☐ John Gould
- ☐ Tim Horton
- ☐ Jim Lorentz
- ☐ Don Luce
- ☐ Richard Martin
- ☐ Gerry Meehan
- ☐ Larry Mickey
- ☐ Joe Noris
- ☐ Gilbert Perreault
- ☐ Tracy Pratt
- ☐ Craig Ramsay
- ☐ René Robert
- ☐ Mike Robitaille
- ☐ Doug Rombough
- ☐ Jim Schoenfeld
- ☐ Paul Terbenche

1973 - 74 SABRES BELLS MARKET

The most expensive single is Gilbert Perreault at $12-15 in NRMT. Singles start at $5.

Card Size: 3 15/16" x 5 1/2"
Sponsor: Bells Markets
Complete Set (4 cards): 30.00

- ☐ Roger Crozier (G)
- ☐ Jim Lorentz
- ☐ Richard Martin
- ☐ Gilbert Perreault

1974 - 75 SABRES

The most expensive single is Gilbert Perreault at $10-12 in NRMT. Singles start at $2.

Card Size: 3 1/2" x 5 1/2"
Sponsors: none
Complete Set (21 cards): 35.00

- ☐ Gary Bromley (G)
- ☐ Larry Carriere
- ☐ Roger Crozier (G)
- ☐ Rick Dudley
- ☐ Rocky Farr (G)
- ☐ Lee Fogolin
- ☐ Danny Gare
- ☐ Norm Gratton
- ☐ Jocelyn Guevremont
- ☐ Bill Hajt
- ☐ Jerry Korab
- ☐ Jim Lorentz
- ☐ Don Luce
- ☐ Richard Martin
- ☐ Peter McNab
- ☐ Larry Mickey
- ☐ Gilbert Perreault
- ☐ Craig Ramsay
- ☐ René Robert
- ☐ Jim Schoenfeld
- ☐ Brian Spencer

1975 - 76 SABRES CHARLES LINNETT STUDIOS

There are supposedly 12 cards in this series. The most expensive single is Gilbert Perreault at $10-12 in NRMT. Singles start at $3.

Photo Size: 8 1/2" x 11"
Sponsor: Charles Linnett Studios
Complete Set (12 cards):

- ☐ Roger Crozier (G)
- ☐ Gerry Desjardins (G)
- ☐ Dave Dryden (G)
- ☐ Jim Lorentz
- ☐ Don Luce
- ☐ Richard Martin
- ☐ Peter McNab
- ☐ Gerry Meehan
- ☐ Gilbert Perreault
- ☐ René Robert
- ☐ Jim Schoenfeld
- ☐ Fred Stanfield

1979 - 80 SABRES BELLS MARKET

The most expensive single is Richard Martin at $3-4 in NRMT. Singles start at $2.

Photo Size: 7 1/2" x 10"
Sponsor: Bells Market
Complete Set (9 cards): 25.00

- ☐ Don Edwards (G)
- ☐ Danny Gare
- ☐ Jerry Korab
- ☐ Richard Martin
- ☐ Tony McKegney
- ☐ Craig Ramsay
- ☐ Bob Sauvé (G)
- ☐ Jim Schoenfeld
- ☐ John Van Boxmeer

1980 - 81 SABRES WENDT'S

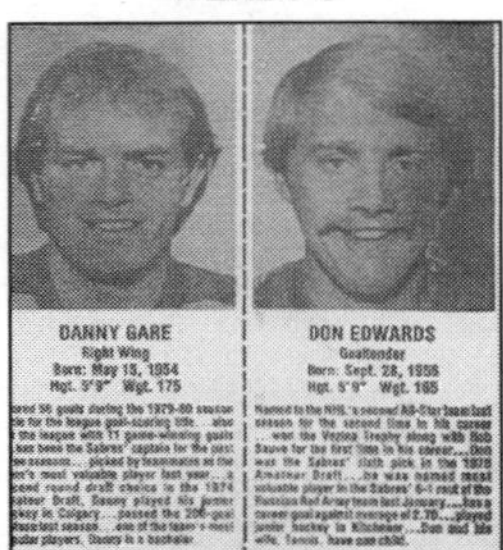

These two card panels were issued in as many as five different colour tints: Light Blue (1-2, 5-8), Dark Blue (1-8), Red (1-8), Green (1, 3), and Magenta (3). Panels may exist for each colour.

Panel Size: 3 3/4" x 5 1/2"
Sponsor: Wendt

- ☐ 1 Craig Ramsay/Jim Schoenfeld
- ☐ 2 Derek Smith/John VanBoxmeer
- ☐ 3 Don Edwards/Danny Gare
- ☐ 4 Gilbert Perreault/Ric Seiling
- ☐ 5 Don Luce/André Savard
- ☐ 6 Rick Dudley/Richie Dunn
- ☐ 7 Bill Hajt/Tony MacKegney
- ☐ 8 Bob Sauvé/Richard Martin

1981 - 82 SABRES WENDT'S

This series was issued on the backs of milk cartons. Gilbert Perreault is the the most expensive single at $15-20 in NRMT. Singles start at $10.

Card Size: 3 3/4" x 7 1/2"
Sponsor: Wendt
Complete Set (16 panels): 150.00

- ☐ 1 Craig Ramsay
- ☐ 2 John Van Boxmeer
- ☐ 3 Don Edwards (G)
- ☐ 4 Gilbert Perreault
- ☐ 5 Alan Haworth
- ☐ 6 Jim Schoenfeld
- ☐ 7 Richie Dunn
- ☐ 8 Bob Sauvé (G)
- ☐ 9 Bill Hajt
- ☐ 10 Larry Playfair
- ☐ 11 Tony McKegney
- ☐ 12 Mike Ramsey
- ☐ 13 André Savard
- ☐ 14 Dale McCourt
- ☐ 15 Ric Seiling
- ☐ 16 Yvon Lambert

1982 - 83 SABRES WENDT'S

This series was issued on the backs of milk cartons. Scotty Bowman, Phil Housley and Gilbert Perreault are the most expensive singles at $15-20. Singles start at $10.

Card Size: 3 3/4" x 7 1/2"
Sponsor: Wendt
Complete Set (17 panels): 150.00

- ☐ 2 Home Schedule
- ☐ 3 Craig Ramsay
- ☐ 4 John Van Boxmeer
- ☐ 5 Lindy Ruff
- ☐ 6 Bob Sauvé (G)
- ☐ 7 Gilbert Perreault
- ☐ 8 Ric Seiling
- ☐ 9 Jacques Cloutier (G)
- ☐ 10 Larry Playfair
- ☐ 11 Phil Housley
- ☐ 12 Mike Foligno
- ☐ 13 Tony McKegney
- ☐ 14 Dale McCourt
- ☐ 15 Mike Ramsey
- ☐ 16 Hannu Virta
- ☐ 17 Brent Peterson
- ☐ 18 Scotty Bowman

1984 - 85 SABRES BLUE SHIELD

There were supposedly only 500 sets issued. The most expensive singles are Dave Andreychuk and Tom Barrasso at $20-25. Singles start at $3.

Card Size: 2 1/2" x 3 3/4"
Sponsor: Blue Shield
Complete Set (21 cards): 125.00

- ☐ Dave Andreychuk
- ☐ Tom Barrasso (G)
- ☐ Adam Creighton
- ☐ Paul Cyr
- ☐ Mal Davis
- ☐ Mike Foligno
- ☐ Bill Hajt
- ☐ Gilles Hamel
- ☐ Phil Housley
- ☐ Sean McKenna
- ☐ Mike Moler
- ☐ Gilbert Perreault
- ☐ Brent Peterson
- ☐ Larry Playfair
- ☐ Craig Ramsay
- ☐ Mike Ramsey
- ☐ Lindy Ruff
- ☐ Bob Sauvé (G)
- ☐ Ric Seiling
- ☐ John Tucker
- ☐ Hannu Virta

1985 - 86 SABRES BLUE SHIELD

This series was issued in two forms: standard-size cards and postcards. Pricing is the same for both sets. Daren Puppa is the most expensive card at $6-8. Singles start at $1.00. The Jim Schoenfeld card was removed from the set and sells at $15-20. Sets sold without the Schoenfeld are $40

Postcard Size: 4" x 6"
Card Size: 2 1/2" x 3 1/2"
Sponsor: Blue Shield
Complete Set (28 cards): 50.00

- ☐☐ Mikael Andersson
- ☐☐ Dave Andreychuk
- ☐☐ Tom Barrasso (G)
- ☐☐ Adam Creighton
- ☐☐ Paul Cyr
- ☐☐ Mal Davis
- ☐☐ Steve Dykstra
- ☐☐ Dave Fenyves
- ☐☐ Mike Foligno
- ☐☐ Bill Hajt
- ☐☐ Bob Halkidis
- ☐☐ Gilles Hamel
- ☐☐ Phil Housley
- ☐☐ Pat Hughes
- ☐☐ Normand Lacombe
- ☐☐ Chris Langevin
- ☐☐ Sean McKenna
- ☐☐ Gaetano Orlando
- ☐☐ Gilbert Perreault
- ☐☐ Larry Playfair
- ☐☐ Daren Puppa (G)
- ☐☐ Craig Ramsay
- ☐☐ Mike Ramsey
- ☐☐ Lindy Ruff
- ☐☐ Ric Seiling
- ☐☐ John Tucker
- ☐☐ Hannu Virta
- ☐☐ Jim Schoenfeld, Coach

1986 - 87 SABRES BLUE SHIELD

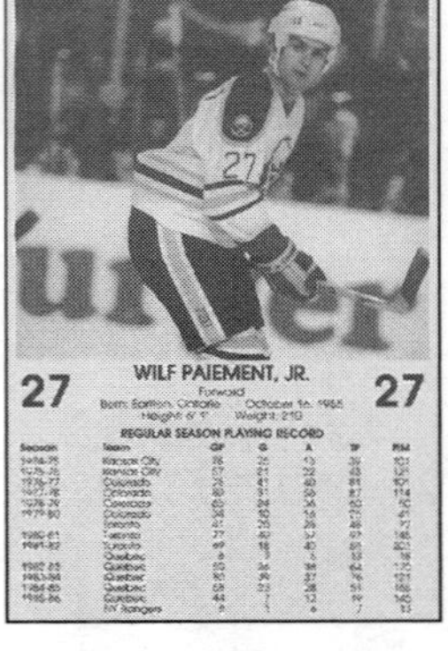

27
WILF PAIEMENT, JR.
Forward
27
REGULAR SEASON PLAYING RECORD

Gilbert Perreault is the the most expensive single at $5-6. Singles start at $1.00.

Postcard Size: 4" x 6"
Sponsor: Blue Shield
Complete Set (28 cards): 35.00

- ☐ Shawn Anderson
- ☐ Dave Andreychuk
- ☐ Scott Arniel
- ☐ Tom Barrasso (G)
- ☐ Jacques Cloutier (G)
- ☐ Adam Creighton
- ☐ Paul Cyr
- ☐ Steve Dykstra
- ☐ Dave Fenyves
- ☐ Mike Foligno
- ☐ Clark Gillies
- ☐ Bill Hajt
- ☐ Bob Halkidis
- ☐ Jim Hofford
- ☐ Phil Housley
- ☐ Jim Korn
- ☐ Uwe Krupp
- ☐ Tom Kurvers
- ☐ Normand Lacombe
- ☐ Gaetano Orlando
- ☐ Wilf Paiement
- ☐ Gilbert Perreault
- ☐ Daren Puppa (G)
- ☐ Mike Ramsey
- ☐ Lindy Ruff
- ☐ Christian Ruuttu
- ☐ Doug Smith
- ☐ John Tucker

1987 - 88 SABRES BLUE SHIELD

Gilbert Perreault is the the most expensive single at $5-6. Singles start at $1.00.

Postcard Size: 4" x 5"
Sponsor: Blue Shield
Complete Set (28 cards): 30.00

- ☐ Mikael Andersson
- ☐ Dave Andreychuk
- ☐ Scott Arniel
- ☐ Tom Barrasso
- ☐ Jacques Cloutier
- ☐ Adam Creighton
- ☐ Mike Donnelly
- ☐ Mike Foligno
- ☐ Clark Gillies
- ☐ Bob Halkidis
- ☐ Mike Hartman
- ☐ Ed Hospodar
- ☐ Phil Housley
- ☐ Calle Johansson
- ☐ Uwe Krupp
- ☐ Jan Ludvig
- ☐ Kevin Maguire
- ☐ Mark Napier
- ☐ Ken Priestlay
- ☐ Daren Puppa
- ☐ Mike Ramsey
- ☐ Joe Reekie
- ☐ Lindy Ruff
- ☐ Christian Ruuttu
- ☐ Ray Sheppard
- ☐ Doug Smith
- ☐ John Tucker
- ☐ Pierre Turgeon

1987 - 88 SABRES WONDER BREAD/HOSTESS

This set was issued as a three panel album. The first panel is a Sabres team photo. The other two panels can be cut out into 15 cards each measuring 2 5/8" x 3 15/16". The most expensive single is Pierre Turgeon at $6-8 while other singles start at 50¢. An uncut, 3-panel set sells at $30.

Panel Size: 10 3/4" x 13 1/2"
Sponsor: Wonder Bread, Hostess
Complete Set (30 cards): 25.00

- ☐ 1987-88 Team Photo
- ☐ Ted Sator
- ☐ Barry Smith
- ☐ Don Lever
- ☐ Jacques Cloutier #1 (G)
- ☐ Calle Johansson #3
- ☐ Steve Dykstra #4
- ☐ Mike Ramsey #5
- ☐ Phil Housley #6
- ☐ John Tucker #7
- ☐ Scott Arniel #9
- ☐ Mikael Andersson #14
- ☐ Doug Smith #15
- ☐ Mike Foligno #17
- ☐ Kevin Maguire #19
- ☐ Christian Ruuttu #21
- ☐ Lindy Ruff #22
- ☐ Ray Sheppard #23
- ☐ Ed Hospodar #24
- ☐ Dave Andreychuk #25
- ☐ Bob Logan #26
- ☐ Joe Reekie #27
- ☐ Tom Barrasso #30 (G)
- ☐ Daren Puppa #31 (G)
- ☐ Jan Ludvig #36
- ☐ Shawn Anderson #37
- ☐ Adam Creighton #38
- ☐ Uwe Krupp #40
- ☐ Mark Napier #65
- ☐ Pierre Turgeon #77
- ☐ Clark Gillies #90

1988-89 SABRES BLUE SHIELD

Pierre Turgeon is the the most expensive single at $6-8. Singles start at 75¢. Benoît Hogue, Jan Ludvig, Mark Napier and Joe Reekie were added late to the set and sell at $2-3. A 24-card set without these four players is $30.

Postcard Size: 4" x 6"
Sponsor: Blue Shield
Complete Set (28 cards): 35.00

☐ Mikael Andersson #14
☐ Dave Andreychuk #25
☐ Scott Arniel #9
☐ Doug Bodger #8
☐ Jacques Cloutier #1 (G)
☐ Mike Donnelly #16
☐ Mike Foligno #17
☐ Bob Halkidis #18
☐ Mike Hartman #20
☐ Phil Housley #6
☐ Calle Johansson #3
☐ Uwe Krupp #4
☐ Kevin Maguire #19
☐ Jeff Parker #29
☐ Larry Playfair #27
☐ Daren Puppa #31 (G)
☐ Mike Ramsey #5
☐ Lindy Ruff #22
☐ Christian Ruuttu #21
☐ Ray Sheppard #23
☐ John Tucker #7
☐ Pierre Turgeon #77
☐ Rick Vaive #12
☐ Mascot Sabretooth
☐ Benoît Hogue #33
☐ Jan Ludvig #36
☐ Mark Napier #65
☐ Joe Reekie #55

1988 - 89 SABRES WONDER BREAD/HOSTESS

This set was issued as a three panel album. The first panel is a Sabres team photo. The other two panels can be cut out into 15 cards each measuring 2 3/4" x 3 3/8". The most expensive single is Pierre Turgeon at $6-8 while other singles start at 50¢. An uncut, 3-panel set sells at $30.

Panel Size: 10 3/4" x 13 1/2"
Sponsor: Wonder Bread, Hostess
Complete Set (30 cards): 25.00

☐ 1988-89 Team Photo
☐ Ted Sator
☐ Barry Smith
☐ Don Lever
☐ Jacques Cloutier #1 (G)
☐ Calle Johansson #3
☐ Uwe Krupp #4
☐ Mike Ramsey #5
☐ Phil Housley #6
☐ John Tucker #7
☐ Doug Bodger #8
☐ Scott Arniel #9
☐ Mikael Andersson #14
☐ Mike Foligno #17
☐ Bob Halkidis #18
☐ Kevin Maguire #19
☐ Mike Hartman #20
☐ Christian Ruuttu #21
☐ Lindy Ruff #22
☐ Ray Sheppard #23
☐ Dave Andreychuk #25
☐ Larry Playfair #27
☐ Jeff Parker #29
☐ Daren Puppa #31 (G)
☐ Benoît Hogue #33
☐ Jan Ludvig #36
☐ Adam Creighton #38
☐ Brad Miller #44
☐ Joe Reekie #55
☐ Mark Napier #65
☐ Pierre Turgeon #77

1989 - 90 SABRES BLUE SHIELD

Alexander Mogilny is the most expensive single at $5-7. Singles start at 50¢.

Postcard Size: 4" x 6"
Sponsor: Blue Shield
Complete Set (24 cards): 25.00

☐ Dave Andreychuk #25
☐ Scott Arniel #9
☐ Doug Bodger #8
☐ Mike Foligno #17
☐ Mike Hartman #20
☐ Benoît Hogue #33
☐ Phil Housley #6
☐ Dean Kennedy #26
☐ Uwe Krupp #4
☐ Grant Ledyard #3
☐ Kevin Maguire #19
☐ Clint Malarchuk #39 (G)
☐ Alexander Mogilny #89
☐ Jeff Parker #29
☐ Larry Playfair #27
☐ Ken Priestlay #56
☐ Daren Puppa #31 (G)
☐ Mike Ramsey #5
☐ Christian Ruuttu #21
☐ Ray Sheppard #23
☐ Dave Snuggerud #18
☐ Pierre Turgeon #77
☐ Rick Vaive #12
☐ Mascot Sabretooth

1989 - 90 SABRES CAMPBELL'S

This set was issued as a three panel album. The first panel super-imposes three modern day colour photos over a black and white 1970 photo. The other two panels can be cut out into 16 and 12 cards each measuring 2 1/2" x 3 3/8". The most expensive single is Alexander Mogilny at $5-7 while other singles start at 75¢. An uncut, 3-panel set sells at $30.

Panel Size: 10" x 13 1/2"; 7 1/2" x 13 1/2"
Sponsor: Campbell's Chunky Soup
Complete Set (28 cards): 25.00

☐ 20th Anniversary Photo
☐ Rick Dudley
☐ Don Lever
☐ John Tortorella
☐ Grant Ledyard #3
☐ Uwe Krupp #4
☐ Mike Ramsey #5
☐ Phil Housley #6
☐ Doug Bodger #8
☐ Scott Arniel #9
☐ Mike Foligno #17
☐ Dave Snuggerud #18
☐ Kevin Maguire #19
☐ Mike Hartman #20
☐ Christian Ruuttu #21
☐ Rick Vaive #22
☐ Ray Sheppard #23
☐ Dave Andreychuk #25
☐ Dean Kennedy #26
☐ Larry Playfair #28
☐ Jeff Parker #29
☐ Clint Malarchuk #30 (G)
☐ Daren Puppa #31 (G)
☐ Robert Ray #32
☐ Benoît Hogue #33
☐ Shawn Anderson #37
☐ Pierre Turgeon #77
☐ Alexander Mogilny #89
☐ 20th Anniversary Sabres Logo

1990 - 91 SABRES BLUE SHIELD

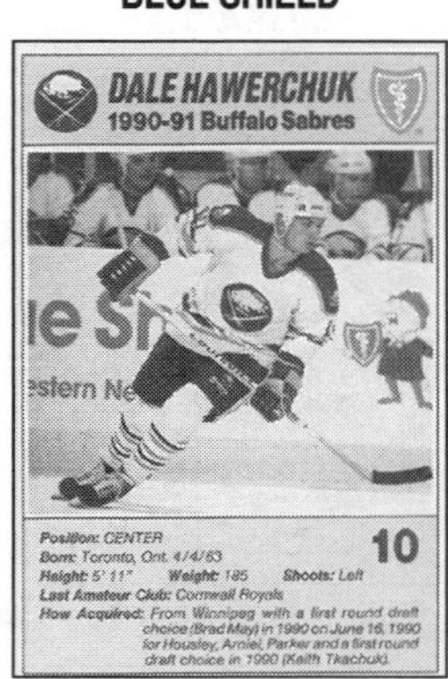

Alexander Mogilny is the most expensive single at $3-4. Singles start at 50¢.

Postcard Size: 4" x 6"
Sponsor: Blue Shield
Complete Set (26 cards): 20.00

☐ Dave Andreychuk #25
☐ Donald Audette #28
☐ Doug Bodger #8
☐ Greg Brown #9
☐ Brian Curran #39
☐ Lou Franceschetti #15
☐ Mike Hartman #20
☐ Dale Hawerchuk #10
☐ Benoît Hogue #33
☐ Dean Kennedy #26
☐ Uwe Krupp #4
☐ Grant Ledyard #3
☐ Mikko Mäkelä #42
☐ Clint Malarchuk #30 (G)
☐ Alexander Mogilny #89
☐ Daren Puppa #31 (G)
☐ Mike Ramsey #5
☐ Rob Ray #32
☐ Christian Ruuttu #21
☐ Jiri Sejba #23
☐ Dave Snuggerud #18
☐ John Tucker #7
☐ Pierre Turgeon #77
☐ Rick Vaive #22
☐ Jay Wells #24
☐ Mascot Sabretooth

1990 - 91 SABRES CAMPBELL'S

This set was issued as a three panel album. The first panel is a Sabres team photo with a photo of Mikko Makelä on the reverse. The other two panels can be cut out into 16 cards each measuring 2 1/2" x 3 3/8". The most expensive single is Alexander Mogilny at $3-4 while singles start at 75¢. An uncut, 3-panel set sells at $25.

Panel Size: 10" x 13 1/2"
Sponsor: Campbell's
Complete Set (32 cards): 20.00

☐ Team Photo/Mikko Mäkelä
☐ Grant Ledyard #3
☐ Uwe Krupp #4
☐ Mike Ramsey #5
☐ John Tucker #7
☐ Doug Bodger #8
☐ Greg Brown #9
☐ Dale Hawerchuk #10
☐ Sabres Logo
☐ Darrin Shannon #16
☐ Mike Foligno #17
☐ Dave Snuggerud #18
☐ Bob Corkum #19
☐ Mike Hartman #20
☐ Christian Ruuttu #21
☐ Rick Vaive #22
☐ Jiri Sejba #23
☐ Jay Wells #24
☐ Dave Andreychuk #25
☐ Dean Kennedy #26
☐ Donald Audette #28
☐ Clint Malarchuk #30 (G)
☐ Daren Puppa #31 (G)
☐ Rob Ray #32
☐ Benoît Hogue #33
☐ Darcy Loewen #36
☐ Mikko Makelä #42
☐ Brad Miller #44
☐ Pierre Turgeon #77
☐ Alexander Mogilny #89
☐ Rick Dudley
☐ John Van Boxmeer
☐ John Tortorella

1991 - 92 SABRES BLUE SHIELD

Alexander Mogilny is the most expensive single at $3-4. Singles start at 50¢.

Postcard Size: 4" x 6"
Sponsor: Blue Shield
Complete Set (26 cards): 20.00

☐ Dave Andreychuk #25
☐ Donald Audette #28
☐ Doug Bodger #8
☐ Mike Donnelly #34
☐ Tom Draper #35
☐ Kevin Haller #7
☐ Dale Hawerchuk #10
☐ Randy Hillier #23
☐ Pat LaFontaine #16
☐ Grant Ledyard #3
☐ Clint Malarchuk #30 (G)
☐ Brad May #27
☐ Brad Miller #44
☐ Alexander Mogilny #89
☐ Colin Patterson #17
☐ Daren Puppa #31 (G)
☐ Mike Ramsey #5
☐ Rob Ray #32
☐ Christian Ruuttu #21
☐ Dave Snuggerud #18
☐ Ken Sutton #41
☐ Tony Tanti #19
☐ Rick Vaive #22
☐ Jay Wells #24
☐ Randy Wood #15
☐ Mascot Sabretooth

1991 - 92 SABRES CAMPBELL'S/PEPSI

This set was issued as a three panel album. The first panel is a Sabres team photo. The other two panels can be cut out into 16 and 12 cards each measuring 2 1/2" x 3 3/8". Two versions exist: one with the Campbell's Chunky Soup logo and one with the Pepsi logo. Both versions have the same value. The most expensive single is Alexander Mogilny at $3-4 while singles start at 50¢. An uncut, 3-panel set sells at $25.

Panel Size: 10" x 13 1/2"; 7 1/2" x 13 1/2"
Sponsor: Campbell's Chunky Soup or Pepsi
Complete Set (28 cards): 20.00

☐☐ Team Photo
☐☐ Grant Ledyard #3
☐☐ Mike Ramsey #5
☐☐ Kevin Haller #7
☐☐ Doug Bodger #8
☐☐ Dale Hawerchuk #10
☐☐ Randy Wood #15
☐☐ Pat LaFontaine #16
☐☐ Colin Patterson #17
☐☐ Dave Snuggerud #18
☐☐ Tony Tanti #19
☐☐ Christian Ruuttu #21
☐☐ Rick Vaive #22
☐☐ Randy Hillier #23
☐☐ Jay Wells #24
☐☐ Dave Andreychuk #25
☐☐ Brad May #27
☐☐ Donald Audette #28
☐☐ Clint Malarchuk #30 (G)
☐☐ Daren Puppa #31 (G)
☐☐ Rob Ray #32
☐☐ Mike Donnelly #34
☐☐ Tom Draper #35
☐☐ Ken Sutton #41
☐☐ Brad Miller #44
☐☐ Alexander Mogilny #89
☐☐ Mascot Sabretooth
☐☐ Sabres Logo
☐☐ NHL 75th Anniversary Logo

1992 - 93 SABRES BLUE SHIELD

Dominik Hasek is the most expensive single at $5-7. Singles start at 50¢.
Postcard Size: 4" x 6"
Sponsor: Blue Shield
Complete Set (26 cards): 20.00

☐ 1 Dave Andreychuk #25
☐ 2 Donald Audette #28
☐ 3 Doug Bodger #8
☐ 41 Bob Corkum
☐ 5 Mike Donnelly #34
☐ 6 Dave Hannan
☐ 7 Dominik Hasek #39 (G)
☐ 8 Dale Hawerchuk #10
☐ 9 Yuri Khmylev
☐ 10 Pat LaFontaine #16
☐ 11 Grant Ledyard #3
☐ 12 Brad May #27
☐ 13 Alexander Mogilny #89
☐ 14 Randy Moller
☐ 15 John Muckler
☐ 16 Colin Patterson #17
☐ 17 Wayne Presley
☐ 18 Daren Puppa #31 (G)
☐ 19 Mike Ramsey #5
☐ 20 Rob Ray #32
☐ 21 Richard Smehlik
☐ 22 Ken Sutton #41
☐ 23 Petr Svoboda
☐ 24 Bob Sweeney
☐ 25 Randy Wood #15
☐ 26 Mascot Sabretooth

1992 - 93 SABRES JUBILEE

The most expensive single is the Hasek/Puppa card at $4-5. Singles start at 75¢.
Postcard Size: 4" x 7"
Sponsor: Jubilee
Complete Set (16 cards): 20.00

☐ Dave Andreychuk
☐ Doug Bodger
☐ Gord Donnelly/Rob Ray
☐ Dominik Hasek /Daren Puppa (G)
☐ Dale Hawerchuk
☐ Yuri Khmylev/Viktor Gordiouk
☐ Pat LaFontaine
☐ Brad May
☐ Alexander Mogilny
☐ Randy Moller/Ken Sutton
☐ Wayne Presley
☐ Donald Audette
☐ Mike Ramsey
☐ Richard Smehlik/Bob Corkum
☐ Petr Svoboda
☐ Bob Sweeney
☐ Randy Wood

1993 - 94 SABRES NOCO EXPRESS SHOP

Dominik Hasek is the most expensive single at $4-5. Singles start at 50¢.
Postcard Size: 2 1/2" x 3 1/2"
Sponsor: Noco Express Shop
Complete Set (20 cards): 15.00

☐ Roger Crozier (G)
☐ Rick Dudley
☐ Mike Foligno
☐ Grant Fuhr (G)
☐ Danny Gare
☐ Dominik Hasek (G)
☐ Dale Hawerchuk
☐ Tim Horton
☐ Pat LaFontaine
☐ Don Luce
☐ Richard Martin
☐ Brad May
☐ Alexander Mogilny
☐ Gilbert Perreault
☐ Craig Ramsay
☐ Mike Ramsey
☐ René Robert
☐ Jim Schoenfeld
☐ Mascot Sabretooth
☐ Seymour Knox/Punch Imlach/ Northrup Knox

CALGARY FLAMES

1980 - 81 FLAMES

Kent Nilsson is the most expensive single at $3-4. Singles start at $1.00.
Postcard Size: 3 3/4" x 5"
Sponsors: none
Complete Set (24 cards): 35.00

☐ Dan Bouchard (G)
☐ Guy Chouinard
☐ Bill Clement
☐ Denis Cyr
☐ Randy Holt
☐ Ken Houston
☐ Kevin Lavallee
☐ Réjean Lemelin
☐ Don Lever
☐ Bob MacMillan
☐ Brad Marsh
☐ Bob Murdoch
☐ Kent Nilsson
☐ Jim Peplinski
☐ Willi Plett
☐ Pekka Rautakalio
☐ Paul Reinhardt
☐ Pat Riggin (G)
☐ Phil Russell
☐ Brad Smith
☐ Jay Soleway
☐ Eric Vail
☐ Bert Wilson
☐ Team Photo

1981-82 FLAMES

Lanny McDonald is the most expensive single at $3-4. Singles start at $1.00.
Postcard Size: 3 3/4" x 5"
Sponsors: none
Complete Set (21 cards): 30.00

☐ Charlie Bourgeois
☐ Mel Bridgman
☐ Guy Chouinard
☐ Bill Clement
☐ Denis Cyr
☐ Jamie Hislop
☐ Ken Houston
☐ Steve Konroyd
☐ Dan Labraaten
☐ Kevin Lavallee
☐ Réjean Lemelin (G)
☐ Lanny McDonald
☐ Gary McAdam
☐ Bob Murdoch
☐ Kent Nilsson
☐ Jim Peplinski
☐ Willi Plett
☐ Pekka Rautakallio
☐ Paul Reinhart
☐ Pat Riggin (G)
☐ Phil Russell

1982 - 83 FLAMES

Al MacInnis is the most expensive single at $6-8. Singles start at 75¢.
Postcard Size: 4" x 5 3/4"
Sponsors: none
Complete Set (24 cards): 30.00

☐ Charlie Bourgeois
☐ Mel Bridgman
☐ Guy Chouinard
☐ Steve Christoff
☐ Richie Dunn
☐ Don Edwards (G)
☐ Kari Eloranta
☐ David Hindmarsh
☐ Jamie Hislop
☐ Tim Hunter
☐ Kari Jalonen
☐ Bob Johnson
☐ Steve Konroyd
☐ Kevin Lavallee
☐ Réjean Lemelin (G)
☐ Al MacInnis
☐ Lanny McDonald
☐ Carl Mokosak
☐ Kent Nilsson
☐ Jim Peplinski
☐ Paul Reinhardt
☐ Pat Ribble
☐ Doug Risebrough
☐ Phil Russell

1985 - 86 FLAMES RED ROOSTER

This set was issued as a six panel set. Panels can be cut out into five cards each measuring 2 3/4" x 3 5/8". Al MacInnis and Mike Vernon are the most expensive singles at $5-6. Singles start at 50¢. A cut-out 30-card set sells at $20.
Panel Size: 2 3/4" x 18 1/8"
Sponsors: Red Rooster, Old Dutch, Post
Complete Set (6 panels): 25.00

☐ Bob Johnson
☐ Bob Murdoch
☐ Pierre Pagé
☐ Colin Patterson
☐ Dan Quinn
☐ Paul Baxter
☐ Perry Berezan
☐ Mark D'Amour (G)
☐ Richard Kromm
☐ Al MacInnis
☐ Ed Beers
☐ Charlie Bourgeois
☐ Réjean Lemelin (G)
☐ Joel Otto
☐ Carey Wilson
☐ Steve Bozek
☐ Tim Hunter
☐ Lanny McDonald
☐ Lanny McDonald
☐ Doug Risebrough
☐ Gino Cavallini
☐ Steve Konroyd
☐ Jim Peplinski
☐ Paul Reinhart
☐ Neil Sheehy
☐ Hakan Loob
☐ Jamie Macoun
☐ Doug Risebrough
☐ Gary Suter
☐ Mike Vernon (G)

1986 - 87 FLAMES RED ROOSTER

This set was issued as a six panel set. Panels can be cut out into five cards each measuring 2 3/4" x 3 5/8". The most expensive singles are Gary Roberts and Mike Vernon at $4-5. Singles start at 50¢ A cut-out 30-card set sells at $20.
Panel Size: 2 3/4" x 18 1/8"
Sponsors: Red Rooster, Old Dutch
Complete Set (6 panels): 25.00

☐ Paul Baxter
☐ Perry Berezan
☐ Steve Bozek
☐ Brian Bradley
☐ Brian Engblom
☐ Nick Fotiu
☐ Tim Hunter
☐ Bob Johnson
☐ Réjean Lemelin (G)
☐ Hakan Loob
☐ Al MacInnis
☐ Jamie Macoun
☐ Lanny McDonald
☐ Lanny McDonald
☐ Joe Mullen
☐ Joe Mullen
☐ Bob Murdoch
☐ Joel Otto
☐ Pierre Pagé
☐ Colin Patterson
☐ Jim Peplinski
☐ Paul Reinhart
☐ Paul Reinhart
☐ Doug Risebrough
☐ Gary Roberts
☐ Neil Sheehy
☐ Gary Suter
☐ John Tonelli
☐ Mike Vernon (G)
☐ Carey Wilson

1987 - 88 FLAMES RED ROOSTER

This set was issued as a six panel set. Panels can be cut out into five cards each measuring 2 3/4" x 3 5/8". Brett Hull is the most expensive single at $15-20. Singles start at 50¢. A cut-out 30-card set sells at $40.
Panel Size: 2 3/4" x 18 1/8"
Sponsor: Red Rooster
Complete Set (6 panels): 50.00

☐ Perry Berezan
☐ Steve Bozek
☐ Mike Bullard
☐ Shane Churla
☐ Doug Dadswell
☐ Brian Glynn
☐ Brett Hull
☐ Tim Hunter
☐ Hakan Loob
☐ Hakan Loob
☐ Al MacInnis
☐ Brad McCrimmon
☐ Lanny McDonald
☐ Joe Mullen
☐ Dana Murzyn
☐ Ric Nattress
☐ Joe Nieuwendyk
☐ Joe Nieuwendyk
☐ Joel Otto
☐ Colin Patterson
☐ Jim Peplinski
☐ Paul Reinhart
☐ Gary Roberts
☐ Gary Suter
☐ John Tonelli
☐ Mike Vernon (G)
☐ Terry Crisp, Coach
☐ Pierre Pagé, Coach
☐ Doug Risebrough, Coach

1990 - 91 FLAMES IGA

Theoren Fleury and Doug Gilmour are the most expensive singles at $3-4. Singles start at 50¢. Paul Baxter, Guy Charron, Doug Risebrough and the checklist card are supposedly short printed and sell at $2-3. A 26-card set sells for $25
Card Size: 2 1/2" x 3 1/2"
Sponsors: IGA, McGavin's
Complete Set (30 cards): 30.00

☐ Theoren Fleury
☐ Doug Gilmour
☐ Jiri Hrdina
☐ Mark Hunter
☐ Tim Hunter
☐ Roger Johansson
☐ Jamie Macoun
☐ Al MacInnis
☐ Brian MacLellan
☐ Sergei Makarov
☐ Stéphane Matteau

- ☐ Dana Murzyn
- ☐ Frank Musil
- ☐ Ric Nattress
- ☐ Joe Nieuwendyk
- ☐ Joel Otto
- ☐ Colin Patterson
- ☐ Sergei Priakin
- ☐ Paul Ranheim
- ☐ Robert Reichel
- ☐ Gary Roberts
- ☐ Gary Suter
- ☐ Tim Sweeney
- ☐ Mike Vernon (G)
- ☐ Rick Wamsley (G)
- ☐ MacInnis/Makarov
- ☐ Paul Baxter
- ☐ Guy Charron
- ☐ Doug Risebrough
- ☐ Checklist

1991 - 92 FLAMES IGA

Theoren Fleury and Doug Gilmour are the most expensive singles at $2-3. Singles start at 50¢. Paul Baxter, Guy Charron, Doug Risebrough and the checklist card are supposedly short printed and sell at $2-3. A 26-card set sells for $20.
Card Size: 2 1/2" x 3 1/2"
Sponsor: IGA
Complete Set (30 cards): 25.00

- ☐ Theoren Fleury
- ☐ Tomas Forslund
- ☐ Doug Gilmour
- ☐ Marc Habscheid
- ☐ Tim Hunter
- ☐ Jim Kyte
- ☐ Al MacInnis
- ☐ Jamie Macoun
- ☐ Sergei Makarov
- ☐ Stéphane Matteau
- ☐ Frank Musil
- ☐ Ric Nattress
- ☐ Joe Nieuwendyk
- ☐ Mark Osiecki
- ☐ Joel Otto
- ☐ Paul Ranheim
- ☐ Robert Reichel
- ☐ Gary Roberts
- ☐ Neil Sheehy
- ☐ Martin Simard
- ☐ Ronnie Stern
- ☐ Gary Suter
- ☐ Tim Sweeney
- ☐ Mike Vernon (G)
- ☐ Rick Wamsley (G)
- ☐ Carey Wilson
- ☐ Paul Baxter
- ☐ Guy Charron
- ☐ Doug Risebrough
- ☐ Checklist

1992 - 93 FLAMES IGA

Theoren Fleury is the most expensive single at $2-3. Singles start at 50¢.
Card Size: 2 1/2" x 3 1/2"
Sponsor: IGA
Complete Set (30 cards): 20.00

- ☐ 001 Checklist
- ☐ 002 Craig Berube
- ☐ 003 Gary Leeman
- ☐ 004 Joel Otto
- ☐ 005 Robert Reichel
- ☐ 006 Gary Roberts
- ☐ 007 Greg Smyth
- ☐ 008 Gary Suter
- ☐ 009 Jeff Reese (G)
- ☐ 010 Mike Vernon (G)
- ☐ 011 Carey Wilson
- ☐ 012 Trent Yawney
- ☐ 013 Michel Petit
- ☐ 014 Paul Ranheim
- ☐ 015 Sergei Makarov
- ☐ 016 Frank Musil
- ☐ 017 Joe Nieuwendyk
- ☐ 018 Alexander Godynyuk
- ☐ 019 Roger Johansson
- ☐ 020 Theoren Fleury
- ☐ 021 Chris Lindberg
- ☐ 022 Al MacInnis
- ☐ 023 Kevin Dahl
- ☐ 024 Chris Dahlquist
- ☐ 025 Ronnie Stern
- ☐ 026 Dave King
- ☐ 027 Guy Charron
- ☐ 028 Slavomir Lener
- ☐ 029 Jamie Hislop
- ☐ 030 Franchise History

1997 - 98 FLAMES FAMOUS FLAMES

These photos were issued with each game program. Other singles exist.
Photo Size: 6" x 9"

- ☐ 28 Brett Hull

CALIFORNIA GOLDEN SEALS

No sets known.

CAROLINA HURRICANES

1997 - 98 HURRICANES SPRINT

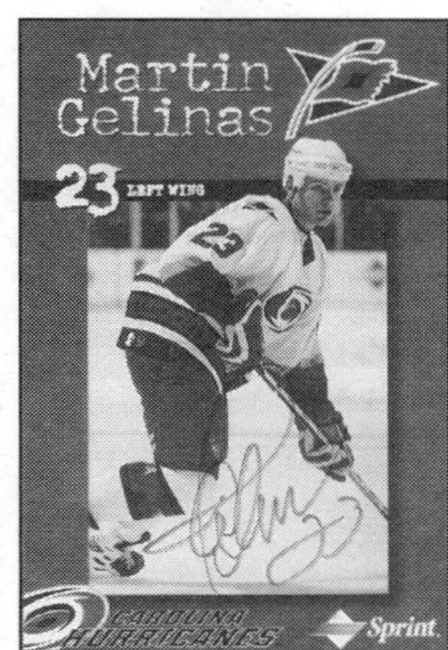

We have little information on this set. Other singles exist.
Card Size: 4" x 6"
Sponsor: Sprint

- ☐ Martin Gelinas

CHICAGO BLACKHAWKS

1968 - 69 BLACKHAWKS

Stan Mikita is the most expensive single at $15-20. Singles start at $5.
Card Size: 4" x 6"
Sponsors: none

- ☐ Dennis Hull
- ☐ Doug Jarrett
- ☐ Chico Maki
- ☐ Gilles Marotte
- ☐ Stan Mikita
- ☐ Jim Pappin
- ☐ Pat Stapleton
- ☐ Ken Wharram

1970 - 71 BLACKHAWKS

The Hull/Mikita/Wirtz card is the most expensive single at $15-20. Singles start at $3.
Card Size: 4" x 6"
Sponsors: none

- ☐ Lou Angotti
- ☐ Bryan Campbell
- ☐ B.Hull/B.Wirtz/S. Mikta
- ☐ Dennis Hull
- ☐ T.Ivan/B.Reay
- ☐ Doug Jarrett
- ☐ Keith Magnuson
- ☐ Hubert Martin
- ☐ Stan Mikita
- ☐ Eric Nesterenko
- ☐ Jim Pappin
- ☐ Allan Pinder
- ☐ Paul Schmyr
- ☐ Bill White

1979 - 80 BLACKHAWKS

We have little information on this set. Singles start at $1.00 in NRMT. Other singles may exist. There are likely earlier team issued sets as well.
Card Size: 4" x 6"
Sponsors: none

- ☐ Keith Brown
- ☐ J.P. Bordeleau
- ☐ Ted Bulley
- ☐ Alain Daigle
- ☐ Tony Esposito (G)
- ☐ Greg Fox
- ☐ Tim Higgins
- ☐ Reg Kerr
- ☐ Cliff Koroll
- ☐ Tom Lysiak
- ☐ Keith Magnuson
- ☐ John Marks
- ☐ Stan Mikita
- ☐ Grant Mulvey
- ☐ Bob Murray
- ☐ Mike O'Connell
- ☐ Rich Preston
- ☐ Bob Pulford
- ☐ Terry Ruskowski
- ☐ Mark Veisor (G)
- ☐ Doug Wilson

1980 - 81 BLACKHAWKS

These cards have a brown background. Denis Savard is the most expensive single at $5-6 in NRMT. Singles start at $1.00.
Card Size: 4" x 6"
Sponsors: none
Complete Set (25 cards): 35.00

- ☐ Murray Bannerman (G)
- ☐ J.P. Bordeleau
- ☐ Keith Brown
- ☐ Ted Bulley
- ☐ Tony Esposito (G)
- ☐ Greg Fox
- ☐ Tim Higgins
- ☐ Dave Hutchinson
- ☐ Reg Kerr
- ☐ Cliff Koroll
- ☐ Doug Lecuyer
- ☐ Tom Lysiak
- ☐ Keith Magnuson
- ☐ John Marks
- ☐ Grant Mulvey
- ☐ Bob Murray
- ☐ Mike O'Connell
- ☐ Rick Paterson
- ☐ Rich Preston
- ☐ Terry Ruskowski
- ☐ Denis Savard
- ☐ Rod Sedlbauer
- ☐ Darryl Sutter
- ☐ Tim Trimper
- ☐ Doug Wilson

1980 - 81 BLACKHAWKS

These cards have a white border. Denis Savard is the most expensive single at $5-6 in NRMT. Singles start at $1.50.
Photo Size: 5 1/2" x 8 1/2"
Sponsors: none
Complete Set (14 cards): 25.00

- ☐ Murray Bannerman (G)
- ☐ J.P. Bordeleau
- ☐ Keith Brown
- ☐ Tony Esposito (G)
- ☐ Greg Fox
- ☐ Tim Higgins
- ☐ Doug Lecuyer
- ☐ John Marks
- ☐ Grant Mulvey
- ☐ Rich Preston
- ☐ Terry Ruskowski
- ☐ Denis Savard
- ☐ Darryl Sutter
- ☐ Tim Trimper

1981 - 82 BLACKHAWKS

Denis Savard is the most expensive single at $5-6. Singles start at $1.00.
Card Size: 3 1/2" x 5 1/2"
Sponsors: none
Complete Set (26 cards): 35.00

- ☐ Murray Bannerman (G)
- ☐ Keith Brown
- ☐ Ted Bulley
- ☐ Doug Crossman
- ☐ Jerome Dupont
- ☐ Tony Esposito (G)
- ☐ Greg Fox
- ☐ Bill Gardner
- ☐ Tim Higgins
- ☐ Dave Hutchinson
- ☐ Reg Kerr
- ☐ Tom Lysiak
- ☐ John Marks
- ☐ Peter Marsh
- ☐ Grant Mulvey
- ☐ Bob Murray
- ☐ Rick Paterson
- ☐ Rich Preston
- ☐ Bob Pulford
- ☐ Terry Ruskowski
- ☐ Denis Savard
- ☐ Al Secord
- ☐ Glen Sharpley
- ☐ Darryl Sutter
- ☐ Tony Tanti
- ☐ Doug Wilson

1982 - 83 BLACKHAWKS

Steve Larmer is the most expensive single at $5-6. Singles start at $1.00.
Card Size: 3 1/2" x 5 1/2"
Sponsors: none
Complete Set (23 cards): 30.00

- ☐ Murray Bannerman (G)
- ☐ Keith Brown
- ☐ Doug Crossman
- ☐ Dennis Cyr
- ☐ Tony Esposito (G)
- ☐ Dave Feamster
- ☐ Bill Gardner
- ☐ Greg Fox
- ☐ Tim Higgins
- ☐ Steve Larmer
- ☐ Steve Ludzik
- ☐ Tom Lysiak
- ☐ Peter Marsh
- ☐ Grant Mulvey
- ☐ Bob Murray
- ☐ Troy Murray
- ☐ Rick Paterson
- ☐ Rich Preston
- ☐ Denis Savard
- ☐ Al Secord
- ☐ Darryl Sutter
- ☐ Orval Tessier
- ☐ Doug Wilson

1983 - 84 BLACKHAWKS

Steve Larmer is the most expensive single at $5-6. Singles start at $1.00. Other singles may exist.
Card Size: 3 1/2" x 5 1/2"
Sponsors: none

- ☐ Murray Bannerman (G)
- ☐ Keith Brown
- ☐ Doug Crossman
- ☐ Dennis Cyr
- ☐ Tony Esposito (G)
- ☐ Dave Feamster
- ☐ Steve Larmer
- ☐ Steve Ludzik
- ☐ Bob Murray
- ☐ Troy Murray
- ☐ Rich Preston
- ☐ Denis Savard
- ☐ Al Secord
- ☐ Orval Tessier

1986 - 87 BLACKHAWKS COKE

Steve Larmer and Denis Savard are the most expensive singles at $3-4. Singles start $1.00.

Card Size: 3 1/2" x 6 1/2"
Sponsor: Coke
Complete Set (24 cards): 25.00

- ☐ Murray Bannerman (G)
- ☐ Marc Bergevin
- ☐ Keith Brown
- ☐ Dave Donnelly
- ☐ Curt Fraser
- ☐ Steve Larmer
- ☐ Steve Ludzik
- ☐ Dave Manson
- ☐ Bob Murray
- ☐ Troy Murray
- ☐ Gary Nylund
- ☐ Jack O'Callahan
- ☐ Ed Olczyk
- ☐ Rick Paterson
- ☐ Wayne Presley
- ☐ Rich Preston
- ☐ Bob Sauvé (G)
- ☐ Denis Savard
- ☐ Al Secord
- ☐ Mike Stapleton
- ☐ Darryl Sutter
- ☐ Bill Watson
- ☐ Behn Wilson
- ☐ Doug Wilson

1987 - 88 BLACKHAWKS COKE

Steve Larmer and Denis Savard are the most expensive singles at $3-4. Singles start at $1.00.
Card Size: 3 1/2" x 6 1/2"
Sponsor: Coke
Complete Set (30 cards): 25.00

- ☐ Murray Bannerman (G)
- ☐ Marc Bergevin (G)
- ☐ Keith Brown
- ☐ Glen Cochrane
- ☐ Curt Fraser
- ☐ Steve Larmer
- ☐ Mark LaVarre
- ☐ Steve Ludzik
- ☐ Dave Manson
- ☐ Bob Mason (G)
- ☐ Bob McGill
- ☐ Bob Murdoch
- ☐ Bob Murray
- ☐ Troy Murray
- ☐ Brian Noonan
- ☐ Gary Nylund
- ☐ Darren Pang (G)
- ☐ Wayne Presley
- ☐ Everett Sanipass
- ☐ Denis Savard
- ☐ Mike Stapleton
- ☐ Darryl Sutter
- ☐ Duane Sutter
- ☐ Steve Thomas
- ☐ Wayne Thomas
- ☐ Rick Vaive
- ☐ Dan Vincelette
- ☐ Bill Watson
- ☐ Behn Wilson
- ☐ Doug Wilson

1988 - 89 BLACKHAWKS COKE

Ed Belfour is the most expensive single at $6-8. Singles start at 75¢.
Card Size: 3 1/2" x 6 1/2"
Sponsor: Coke
Complete Set (25 cards): 25.00

- ☐ Ed Belfour (G)
- ☐ Keith Brown
- ☐ Bruce Cassidy
- ☐ Mike Eagles
- ☐ Dirk Graham
- ☐ Mike Hudson
- ☐ Steve Larmer
- ☐ Dave Manson
- ☐ Jacques Martin
- ☐ Bob McGill
- ☐ E.J. Maguire
- ☐ Troy Murray
- ☐ Brian Noonan
- ☐ Darren Pang (G)
- ☐ Wayne Presley
- ☐ Everett Sanipass
- ☐ Denis Savard
- ☐ Duane Sutter
- ☐ Steve Thomas
- ☐ Rick Vaive
- ☐ Dan Vincelette
- ☐ Jimmy Waite (G)
- ☐ Doug Wilson
- ☐ Trent Yawney
- ☐ Mike Keenan, Coach

1989 - 90 BLACKHAWKS COKE

These cards were originally issued in panels. Jeremy Roenick is the most expensive single at $6-8. Singles start at 75¢.
Card Size: 4" x 6"
Sponsor: Coke
Complete Set (27 cards): 25.00

- ☐ Bob Bassen
- ☐ Keith Brown
- ☐ Alain Chevrier (G)
- ☐ Jacques Cloutier (G)
- ☐ Adam Creighton
- ☐ Greg Gilbert
- ☐ Dirk Graham
- ☐ Mike Hudson
- ☐ Steve Konroyd
- ☐ Steve Larmer
- ☐ E.J. Maguire
- ☐ Dave Manson
- ☐ Jacques Martin
- ☐ Bob McGill
- ☐ Bob Murray
- ☐ Troy Murray
- ☐ Wayne Presley
- ☐ Jeremy Roenick
- ☐ Everett Sanipass
- ☐ Denis Savard
- ☐ Al Secord
- ☐ Duane Sutter
- ☐ Steve Thomas
- ☐ Wayne Van Dorp
- ☐ Doug Wilson
- ☐ Trent Yawney
- ☐ Mike Keenan, Coach

1990 - 91 BLACKHAWKS COKE

This set was originally issued in panels. Chris Chelios is the most expensive single at $3-4. Singles start at 50¢.
Card Size: 3 1/2" x 6"
Sponsor: Coke
Complete Set (28 cards): 20.00

- ☐ Ed Belfour (G)
- ☐ Keith Brown
- ☐ Chris Chelios
- ☐ Jacques Cloutier (G)
- ☐ Adam Creighton
- ☐ Greg Gilbert
- ☐ Michel Goulet
- ☐ Dirk Graham
- ☐ Stu Grimson
- ☐ Mike Hudson
- ☐ Steve Konroyd
- ☐ Steve Larmer
- ☐ Jocelyn Lemieux
- ☐ E.J. Maguire
- ☐ Dave Manson
- ☐ Bob McGill
- ☐ Mike McNeill
- ☐ Greg Millen (G)
- ☐ Troy Murray
- ☐ Mike Peluso
- ☐ Wayne Presley
- ☐ Jeremy Roenick
- ☐ Darryl Sutter
- ☐ Steve Thomas
- ☐ Vladislav Tretiak
- ☐ Doug Wilson
- ☐ Trent Yawney
- ☐ Mike Keenan, Coach

1991 - 92 BLACKHAWKS COKE

This set was originally issued in panels. Chris Chelios is the most expensive single at $2-3. Singles start at 50¢.
Card Size: 3 1/2" x 6"
Sponsor: Coke
Complete Set (28 cards): 20.00

- ☐ Ed Belfour (G)
- ☐ Keith Brown
- ☐ Rod Buskas
- ☐ Chris Chelios
- ☐ Karl Dykhuis
- ☐ Greg Gilbert
- ☐ Michel Goulet
- ☐ Dirk Graham
- ☐ Stu Grimson
- ☐ Mike Hudson
- ☐ Steve Konroyd
- ☐ Frank Kucera
- ☐ Steve Larmer
- ☐ Brad Lauer
- ☐ Jocelyn Lemieux
- ☐ Bryan Marchment
- ☐ Dave McDowall
- ☐ Brian Noonan
- ☐ Mike Peluso
- ☐ Rich Preston
- ☐ Jeremy Roenick
- ☐ Steve Smith
- ☐ Mike Stapleton
- ☐ Brent Sutter
- ☐ Darryl Sutter
- ☐ John Tonelli
- ☐ Jimmy Waite (G)
- ☐ Mike Keenan, Coach

1993 - 94 BLACKHAWKS COKE

This set was originally issued in panels. Chris Chelios is the most expensive single at $2-3. Singles start at 50¢.
Card Size: 3 1/2" x 6"
Sponsor: Coke
Complete Set (30 cards): 20.00

- ☐ Paul Baxter
- ☐ Ed Belfour (G)
- ☐ Keith Carney
- ☐ Chris Chelios
- ☐ Dave Christian
- ☐ Michel Goulet
- ☐ Dirk Graham
- ☐ Jeff Hackett (G)
- ☐ Darin Kimble
- ☐ Frank Kucera
- ☐ Jocelyn Lemieux
- ☐ Stéphane Matteau
- ☐ Joe Murphy
- ☐ Troy Murray
- ☐ Phil Myre
- ☐ Brian Noonan
- ☐ Patrick Poulin
- ☐ Rich Preston
- ☐ Bob Pulford
- ☐ Jeremy Roenick
- ☐ Cam Russell
- ☐ Christian Ruuttu
- ☐ Jeff Shantz
- ☐ Steve Smith
- ☐ Darryl Sutter
- ☐ Rich Sutter
- ☐ Brent Sutter
- ☐ Kevin Todd
- ☐ Eric Weinrich
- ☐ Neil Wilkinson

COLORADO AVALANCHE

1996 - 97 AVALANCHE POSTCARDS

We have little information on this set. Other singles exist.
Card Size: 3 1/2" x 5 1/2"
Sponsor: none

- ☐ Peter Forsberg
- ☐ Patrick Roy (G)

1996 - 97 AVALANCHE BURGER KING PHOTO PUCKS

We have little information on this set. Four Photo Pucks feature two players while the last one is a team puck.
Sponsor: Burger King
Complete Set (5 pucks): 35.00

- ☐ P. Roy (G)/ A. Foote
- ☐ J. Sakic/ A. Deadmarsh
- ☐ C. Lemieux/ P. Forsberg
- ☐ V. Kamensky/ M. Ricci
- ☐ Avalanche

1997 - 98 AVALANCHE DENVER POST PINS

We have little information on this set. Other singles exist.
Sponsor: Denver Post

- ☐ 3 Patrick Roy (G)
- ☐ 4 Marc Crawford, Coach

COLORADO ROCKIES

1976 - 77 ROCKIES HOCKEY TALK

These cards were originally issued as two-card panels. Colin Campbell is the most expensive single at $4-5 in NRMT. Singles start at $2.
Card Size: 2 9/16" x 2 1/8"
Sponsors: none
Complete Set (20 cards): 75.00

- ☐ Ron Andruff
- ☐ Chuck Arnason
- ☐ Henry Boucha
- ☐ Colin Campbell
- ☐ Gary Croteau
- ☐ Guy Delparte
- ☐ Steve Durbano
- ☐ Tom Edur
- ☐ Doug Favell (G)
- ☐ Dave Hudson
- ☐ Bryan Lefley
- ☐ Roger Lemelin
- ☐ Simon Nolet
- ☐ Wilf Paiement
- ☐ Michel Plasse (G)
- ☐ Tracy Pratt
- ☐ Nelson Pyatt
- ☐ Phil Roberto
- ☐ Sean Shanahan
- ☐ Larry Skinner

1976 - 77 ROCKIES COCA-COLA CANS

These cans feature player drawings with a line that reads "Meet the Colorado Rockies Hockey Team".
Can Size: 4 1/4" x 1 3/4"
Sponsor: Coca-Cola

- ☐ Ron Andruff
- ☐ Chuck Arnason
- ☐ Colin Campbell
- ☐ Gary Croteau
- ☐ Barry Dean
- ☐ Guy Delparte
- ☐ Denis Dupère
- ☐ Tom Edur
- ☐ Doug Favell (G)
- ☐ Paul Gardner
- ☐ Dave Hudson
- ☐ Mike Kitchen
- ☐ Bryan Lefley
- ☐ Simon Nolet
- ☐ Wilf Paiement
- ☐ Michel Plasse (G)
- ☐ Tracy Pratt
- ☐ Nelson Pyatt
- ☐ Sean Shanahan
- ☐ John Van Boxmeer
- ☐ Johnny Wilson
- ☐ Cheerleader Krazy George

1977 - 78 ROCKIES COCA-COLA CANS

These cans are similar to the 1976-77 cans except that the print is in red instead of black and the player drawing is on the opposite side.

Can Size: 4 1/4" x 1 3/4"
Sponsor: Coca-Cola

- ☐ Ron Andruff
- ☐ Barry Beck
- ☐ Gary Croteau
- ☐ Ron Delorme
- ☐ Denis Dupère
- ☐ Tom Edur
- ☐ Doug Favell (G)
- ☐ Paul Gardner
- ☐ Dave Hudson
- ☐ Rick Jodzio
- ☐ Mike Kitchen
- ☐ Bryan Lefley
- ☐ Wilf Paiement
- ☐ Michel Plasse (G)
- ☐ Nelson Pyatt
- ☐ Andy Spruce
- ☐ Mark Suzor
- ☐ John Van Boxmeer
- ☐ Pat Kelly, Coach
- ☐ Cheerleader Krazy George

1979 - 80 ROCKIES

Lanny McDonald is the most expensive single at $5-7 in NRMT. Singles start at $2.

Card Size: 4" x 6"
Sponsors: none
Complete Set (23 cards): 50.00

- ☐ Hardy Astrom (G)
- ☐ Doug Berry
- ☐ Nick Beverley
- ☐ Mike Christie
- ☐ Gary Croteau
- ☐ Lucien DeBlois
- ☐ Ron Delorme
- ☐ Mike Gillis
- ☐ Trevor Johansen
- ☐ Mike Kitchen
- ☐ Lanny McDonald
- ☐ Mike McEwen
- ☐ Bill McKenzie (G)
- ☐ Kevin Morrison
- ☐ Bill Oleschuk (G)
- ☐ Randy Pierce
- ☐ Michel Plasse (G)
- ☐ Joel Quenneville
- ☐ Rob Ramage
- ☐ René Robert
- ☐ Don Saleski
- ☐ Barry Smith
- ☐ Jack Valiquette

1981 - 82 ROCKIES

The most expensive singles are Rob Ramage and Glenn Resch at $2-3. Singles start $1.00.

Postcard Size: 3 1/2" x 5 1/2"
Sponsors: none
Complete Set (30 cards): 35.00

- ☐ Brent Ashton
- ☐ Aaron Broten
- ☐ Dave Cameron
- ☐ Joe Cirella
- ☐ Dwight Foster
- ☐ Paul Gagné
- ☐ Marshall Johnston
- ☐ Veli-Pekka Ketola
- ☐ Mike Kitchen
- ☐ Rick Laferriere (G)
- ☐ Don Lever
- ☐ Tapio Levo
- ☐ Bob Lorimer
- ☐ Bill MacMillan
- ☐ Bob MacMillan
- ☐ Merlin Malinowski
- ☐ Bert Marshall
- ☐ Kevin Maxwell
- ☐ Joe Micheletti
- ☐ Bobby Miller
- ☐ Phil Myre (G)
- ☐ Graeme Nicolson
- ☐ Jukka Porvari
- ☐ Joel Quenneville
- ☐ Rob Ramage
- ☐ Glenn Resch (G)
- ☐ Steve Tambellini
- ☐ Yvon Vautour
- ☐ John Wensink
- ☐ Team Logo

DALLAS STARS

DALLAS STARS.

1993 - 94 STARS SOUTHWEST AIRLINES

We have very little information on this set. Photos are in black and white. Other singles exist.

Card Size: 3" x 5"
Sponsors: Southwest Airlines

- ☐ Russ Courtnall

1994 - 95 STARS CAPS

Mike Modano is the most expensive single at $2 in NRMT. Singles start at 50¢.

Diametre: 1 3/4"
Sponsors: none
Complete Set (25 caps): 12.00

- ☐ Dave Barr
- ☐ Brad Berry
- ☐ Neal Broten
- ☐ Paul Broten
- ☐ Paul Cavallini
- ☐ Shane Churla
- ☐ Russ Courtnall
- ☐ Mike Craig
- ☐ Ulf Dahlen
- ☐ Dean Evason
- ☐ Dave Gagner
- ☐ Bob Gainey
- ☐ Brent Gilchrist
- ☐ Derian Hatcher
- ☐ Doug Jarvis
- ☐ Jim Johnson
- ☐ Trent Klatt
- ☐ Grant Ledyard
- ☐ Craig Ludwig
- ☐ Mike McPhee
- ☐ Mike Modano
- ☐ Andy Moog (G)
- ☐ Mark Tinordi
- ☐ Darcy Wakaluk (G)
- ☐ Rick Wilson

1994 - 95 STARS SOUTHWEST AIRLINES

Mike Modano is the most expensive single at $3-4. Singles start at 75¢.

Postcard Size:
Sponsor: Southwest Airlines
Complete Set (23 cards): 20.00

- ☐ Paul Broten
- ☐ Paul Cavallini
- ☐ Shane Churla
- ☐ Gord Donnelly
- ☐ Mike Donnelly
- ☐ Dean Evason
- ☐ Dave Gagner
- ☐ Brent Gilchrist
- ☐ Todd Harvey
- ☐ Derian Hatcher
- ☐ Kevin Hatcher
- ☐ Mike Kennedy
- ☐ Trent Klatt
- ☐ Mike Lalor
- ☐ Grant Ledyard
- ☐ Craig Ludwig
- ☐ Richard Matvichuk
- ☐ Corey Millen
- ☐ Mike Modano
- ☐ Andy Moog (G)
- ☐ Darcy Wakaluk (G)
- ☐ Peter Zezel
- ☐ Doug Zmolek

1996 - 97 STARS SOUTHWEST AIRLINES

Mike Modano is the most expensive single at $2-3. Singles start at 75¢.

Postcard Size:
Sponsor: Southwest Airlines
Complete Set (27 cards): 20.00

- ☐ Greg Adams
- ☐ Bob Bassen
- ☐ Neal Broten
- ☐ Guy Carbonneau
- ☐ Brent Gilchrist
- ☐ Todd Harvey
- ☐ Derian Hatcher
- ☐ Benoît Hogue
- ☐ Bill Huard
- ☐ Arturs Irbe (G)
- ☐ Mike Kennedy
- ☐ Mike Lalor
- ☐ Jamie Langenbrunner
- ☐ Grant Ledyard
- ☐ Jere Lehtinen
- ☐ Craig Ludwig
- ☐ Grant Marshall
- ☐ Richard Matvichuk
- ☐ Mike Modano
- ☐ Joe Nieuwendyk
- ☐ Andy Moog
- ☐ Dave Reid
- ☐ Darryl Sydor
- ☐ Pat Verbeek
- ☐ Sergei Zubov
- ☐ Bob Gainey, G.M.
- ☐ Ken Hitchcock, Coach

DETROIT RED WINGS

1970 - 71 RED WINGS MARATHON OIL

We have little information on this set. The most expensive singles are Gordie Howe at $40-50 in NRMT and Frank Mahovlich and Alex Delvecchio at $10-15. Singles start at $4. Other singles may exist.

Photo Size: 7 1/2" x 14"
Sponsor: Marathon Oil

- ☐ Gary Bergman
- ☐ Wayne Connelly
- ☐ Alex Delvecchio
- ☐ Roy Edwards (G)
- ☐ Gordie Howe
- ☐ Bruce MacGregor
- ☐ Frank Mahovlich
- ☐ Dale Rolfe
- ☐ Jim Rutherford (G)
- ☐ Garry Unger
- ☐ Tom Webster

1976 RED WINGS

We have little information on this black and white photo set. Singles start at $3. Other singles may exist.

Card Size: 2 1/2" x 3 1/2"
Sponsors: none

- ☐ Gerry Abel
- ☐ Sid Abel
- ☐ Doug Barkley
- ☐ Joe Carveth
- ☐ Alex Delvecchio
- ☐ Bill Gadsby
- ☐ Hal Jackson
- ☐ Joe Klukay
- ☐ Ted Lindsay
- ☐ Jim Orlando
- ☐ Marty Pavelich
- ☐ Marcel Pronovost
- ☐ Marc Reaume
- ☐ Leo Reise
- ☐ Glen Skov
- ☐ Jack Stewart

1979 - 80 RED WINGS

Rogatien Vachon is the most expensive card at $3-4 in NRMT. Singles start at $1.50.

Card Size: 4" x 5"
Sponsors: none
Complete Set (19 cards): 40.00

- ☐ Tommy Bergman
- ☐ Dan Bolduc
- ☐ Mike Foligno
- ☐ Jean Hamel
- ☐ Glen Hicks
- ☐ Bill Hogaboam
- ☐ Greg Joly
- ☐ Willie Huber
- ☐ Jim Korn
- ☐ Dan Labraaten
- ☐ Barry Long
- ☐ Reed Larson
- ☐ Dale McCourt
- ☐ Vaclav Nedomansky
- ☐ Jim Rutherford (G)
- ☐ Dennis Polonich
- ☐ Errol Thompson
- ☐ Roggie Vachon (G)
- ☐ Paul Woods

1980-81 RED WINGS

We have little information on this set. Ted Lindsay is the most expensive single at $3-4 in NRMT. Singles start at $1.50.

Photo Size: 8" x 10 1/2"
Sponsors: none
Complete Set (32 photos): 40.00

- ☐ Mike Blaisdell
- ☐ Réjean Cloutier
- ☐ Mike Foligno
- ☐ Jody Gage
- ☐ Gilles Gilbert (G)
- ☐ Jean Hamel
- ☐ Glenn Hicks
- ☐ Bill Hogaboam
- ☐ Willie Huber
- ☐ Al Jensen (G)
- ☐ Greg Joly
- ☐ Jim Korn
- ☐ Dan Labraaten
- ☐ Reed Larson
- ☐ Ted Lindsay
- ☐ George Lyle
- ☐ Peter Mahovlich
- ☐ Dale McCourt
- ☐ Perry Miller
- ☐ Vaclav Nedomansky
- ☐ Dan Olesevich
- ☐ John Ogrodnick
- ☐ Joe Paterson
- ☐ Brent Peterson
- ☐ Dennis Polonich
- ☐ Marcel Pronovost
- ☐ Jim Rutherford (G)
- ☐ Jim Skinner
- ☐ Errol Thompson
- ☐ Rick Vasko
- ☐ Russ Wilson
- ☐ Paul Woods

1984 - 85 RED WINGS

These photos are printed on thin stock and do not mention the photographer's name on the card front. We have no pricing information on this set.

Card Size: 3 3/4" x 6"
Sponsor: Little Caesars Pizza

- ☐ Pierre Aubry
- ☐ John Barrett
- ☐ Ivan Boldirev
- ☐ Colin Campbell
- ☐ Frank Cernik
- ☐ Milan Chalupa
- ☐ Ron Duguay
- ☐ Dwight Foster
- ☐ Danny Gare
- ☐ Kelly Kisio
- ☐ Randy Ladouceur
- ☐ Lane Lambert
- ☐ Reed Larson
- ☐ Bob Manno
- ☐ Corrado Micalef (G)
- ☐ Eddy Mio (G)
- ☐ John Ogrodnick
- ☐ Brad Park

- ☐ Nick Polano, Coach
- ☐ Darryl Sittler
- ☐ Greg Smith
- ☐ Larry Trader
- ☐ Dave Williams
- ☐ Steve Yzerman

1985 - 86 RED WINGS

These photos are printed on a heavier stock than the 1984-85 photos and do mention the photographer's name to the right of the photo. Seven cards feature the same pose (†) as the 1984-85 card. We have no pricing information on this set.

Card Size: 3 3/4" x 6"
Sponsor: Little Caesars Pizza

- ☐ John Barrett
- ☐ Chris Cichocki
- ☐ Jim Devellano
- ☐ Ron Duguay
- ☐ Dwight Foster
- ☐ Tim Friday
- ☐ Gerard Gallant
- ☐ (†) Danny Gare
- ☐ Doug Houda
- ☐ Kelly Kisio
- ☐ Petr Klima
- ☐ Joey Kocur
- ☐ (†) Randy Ladouceur
- ☐ (†) Lane Lambert
- ☐ (†) Reed Larson
- ☐ Claude Loiselle
- ☐ Adam Oates
- ☐ (†) John Ogrodnick
- ☐ (†) Brad Park
- ☐ Bob Probert
- ☐ (†) Greg Smith
- ☐ Harold Snepsts
- ☐ Ray Staszak
- ☐ Greg Stefan (G)
- ☐ Warren Young
- ☐ Steve Yzerman

1986 - 87 RED WINGS

These photos are printed on the same stock as the 1985-86 cards but mention the photographer's name to the left of the photo. Nine cards feature the same pose (†) as the 1984-85 or 1985-86 card. We have no pricing information on this set.

Card Size: 3 3/4" x 6"
Sponsor: Little Caesars Pizza

- ☐ Brent Ashton
- ☐ Dave Barr
- ☐ (†) Shawn Burr
- ☐ Billy Carroll
- ☐ Steve Chiasson
- ☐ Gilbert Delorme
- ☐ Jacques Demers, Coach
- ☐ (†) Gerard Gallant
- ☐ Doug Halward
- ☐ Glen Hanlon (G)
- ☐ Tim Higgins
- ☐ (†) Petr Klima
- ☐ (†) Joey Kocur
- ☐ Mark Kumpel
- ☐ Dave Lewis
- ☐ Basil McRae
- ☐ Lee Norwood
- ☐ Adam Oates
- ☐ Mike O'Connell
- ☐ (†) John Ogrodnick
- ☐ (†) Bob Probert
- ☐ Sam St. Laurent (G)
- ☐ Ric Seiling
- ☐ Doug Shedden
- ☐ (†) Harold Snepsts
- ☐ (†) Greg Stefan (G)
- ☐ Darren Veitch
- ☐ (†) Steve Yzerman
- ☐ Rick Zombo

1987 - 88 RED WINGS LITTLE CAESARS

These cards are similar to the 1986-87 cards. The most expensive singles are Steve Yzerman at $12-15 and Adam Oates at $5-7. Singles start $1.00.

Card Size: 3 3/4" x 6"
Sponsor: Little Caesars Pizza

- ☐ Brent Ashton
- ☐ Dave Barr
- ☐ Mel Bridgman
- ☐ Shawn Burr
- ☐ John Chabot
- ☐ Steve Chiasson
- ☐ Gilbert Delorme
- ☐ Jacques Demers, Coach
- ☐ Gerard Gallant
- ☐ Adam Graves
- ☐ Doug Halward
- ☐ Glen Hanlon (G)
- ☐ Tim Higgins
- ☐ Petr Klima
- ☐ Joe Kocur
- ☐ Joe Murphy
- ☐ Lee Norwood
- ☐ Adam Oates
- ☐ Mike O'Connell
- ☐ Bob Probert
- ☐ Jeff Sharples
- ☐ Greg Stefan (G)
- ☐ Darren Veitch
- ☐ Steve Yzerman
- ☐ Rick Zombo

1988 - 89 RED WINGS

These cards are similar to previous Little Caesars issues. Once again, numerous poses from earlier sets were reused in this set. We have little pricing information on this set.

Card Size: 3 3/4" x 6"
Sponsor: Little Caesars Pizza

- ☐ Dave Barr
- ☐ Shawn Burr
- ☐ John Chabot
- ☐ Steve Chiasson
- ☐ Gilbert Delorme
- ☐ Jacques Demers, Coach
- ☐ Miroslav Frycer
- ☐ Gerard Gallant
- ☐ Adam Graves
- ☐ Doug Halward
- ☐ Glen Hanlon (G)
- ☐ Tim Higgins
- ☐ Doug Houda
- ☐ Kris King
- ☐ Petr Klima
- ☐ Joey Kocur
- ☐ Paul MacLean
- ☐ Joe Murphy
- ☐ Jim Nill
- ☐ Lee Norwood
- ☐ Adam Oates
- ☐ Mike O'Connell
- ☐ Jim Pavese
- ☐ Bob Probert
- ☐ Jeff Sharples
- ☐ Greg Stefan (G)
- ☐ Steve Yzerman
- ☐ Rick Zombo

1988 - 89 RED WINGS

Steve Yzerman is the most expensive single at $10-12. Singles start $1.00.

Card Size: 3 5/8" x 5 1/2"
Sponsor: S.A.M.
Complete Set (10 cards): 20.00

- ☐ Shawn Burr
- ☐ John Chabot
- ☐ Jacques Demers
- ☐ Gerard Gallant
- ☐ Glen Hanlon (G)
- ☐ Lee Norwood
- ☐ Mike O'Connell
- ☐ Jeff Sharples
- ☐ Steve Yzerman
- ☐ Rick Zombo

1989 - 90 RED WINGS LITTLE CAESARS

These cards feature two photos on the front. We have no pricing information on this set.

Card Size: 3 3/4" x 8 1/2"
Sponsor: Little Caesars Pizza

- ☐ Dave Barr
- ☐ Shawn Burr
- ☐ Jimmy Carson
- ☐ John Chabot
- ☐ Steve Chiasson
- ☐ Bernie Federko
- ☐ Gerard Gallant
- ☐ Marc Habscheid
- ☐ Glen Hanlon (G)
- ☐ Doug Houda
- ☐ Joey Kocur
- ☐ Kevin McClelland
- ☐ Lee Norwood
- ☐ Mike O'Connell
- ☐ Borje Salming
- ☐ Greg Stefan (G)
- ☐ Steve Yzerman
- ☐ Rick Zombo
- ☐ Jacques Demers, Coach
- ☐ D.Lewis/ P.Myre/ J.Demers/ C.Campbell
- ☐ Team Photo (blank back)

1990 - 91 RED WINGS LITTLE CAESARS

These cards feature two photos on the front like the 1989-90 series, but have blank backs instead. We have no pricing information on this set.

Card Size: 3 3/4" x 8 1/2"
Sponsor: Little Caesars Pizza

- ☐ Dave Barr
- ☐ Shawn Burr
- ☐ John Chabot
- ☐ Tim Cheveldae (G)
- ☐ Per Djoos
- ☐ Bobby Dollas
- ☐ Sergei Fedorov
- ☐ Brent Fedyk
- ☐ Johan Garpenlov
- ☐ Rick Green
- ☐ Sheldon Kennedy
- ☐ Kevin McClelland
- ☐ Brad McCrimmon
- ☐ Randy McKay
- ☐ Keith Primeau
- ☐ Bob Probert
- ☐ Steve Yzerman
- ☐ Rick Zombo
- ☐ Mickey Redmond
- ☐ Bryan Murray, Coach
- ☐ Team Photo

1991 - 92 RED WINGS LITTLE CAESARS

The most expensive singles are Steve Yzerman at $8-10 and Sergei Fedorov at $5-7. Singles start at $1.00.

Card Size: 8 1/2" x 3 5/8"
Sponsor: Little Caesars Pizza
Complete Set (19 cards): 35.00

- ☐ Shawn Burr
- ☐ Jimmy Carson
- ☐ Steve Chiasson
- ☐ Sergei Fedorov
- ☐ Gerard Gallant
- ☐ Johan Garpenlov
- ☐ Rick Green
- ☐ Marc Habscheid
- ☐ Sheldon Kennedy
- ☐ Martin Lapointe
- ☐ Nicklas Lidström
- ☐ Brad McCrimmon
- ☐ Bryan Murray, Coach
- ☐ Keith Primeau
- ☐ Bob Probert
- ☐ Dennis Vial
- ☐ Paul Ysebaert
- ☐ Steve Yzerman
- ☐ Red Wings

1996 - 97 RED WINGS HOCKEYTOWN PUCKS

We have little information on this series of pucks.

- ☐ Alex Delvecchio
- ☐ Mickey Redmond
- ☐ Brendan Shanahan
- ☐ Steve Yzerman

1996 - 97 RED WINGS PHOTO PUCKS

Four PhotoPucks feature two players while the last one is a team puck.

Sponsor: Burger King
Complete Set (5 pucks): 40.00

- ☐ C. Osgood (G)/ M. Vernon (G)
- ☐ V. Konstantinov/ N. Lidström
- ☐ B. Shanahan/ S. Fedorov
- ☐ S. Yzerman/ Vy. Kozlov
- ☐ Red Wings

EDMONTON OILERS

1979 - 80 OILERS

The most expensive singles in NRMT are Wayne Gretzky at $60-70 and Mark Messier at $20-25. Singles start at $1.50. Andy Moog has a variation card with the wrong birthdate. Both the error card and the corrected version have the same value.

Card Size: 3 1/2" x 5 1/4"
Sponsors: none
Complete Set (23 cards): 90.00

- ☐ Brett Callighen
- ☐ Colin Campbell
- ☐ Ron Chipperfield
- ☐ Cam Connor
- ☐ Peter Driscoll
- ☐ Dave Dryden (G)
- ☐ Bill Flett
- ☐ Lee Fogolin
- ☐ Wayne Gretzky
- ☐ Al Hamilton
- ☐ Doug Hicks
- ☐ Dave Hunter
- ☐ Kevin Lowe
- ☐ Dave Lumley
- ☐ Blair MacDonald
- ☐ Kari Makkonen
- ☐ Mark Messier
- ☐☐ Ed Mio (G)
- ☐ Pat Price
- ☐ Dave Semenko
- ☐ Bobby Schmautz
- ☐ Risto Siltanen
- ☐ Stan Weir

1980 - 81 OILERS ZELLERS

We have little information on this set. Singles were given out during practices in West Edmonton Mall. Other singles may exist.

Card Size: 5" x 7"
Sponsor: Zellers

- ☐ Curt Brackenbury
- ☐ Brett Callighen
- ☐ Wayne Gretzky
- ☐ Matti Hagman
- ☐ Billy Harris
- ☐ Doug Hicks
- ☐ John Hughes
- ☐ Dave Hunter
- ☐ Jari Kurri
- ☐ Ron Low (G)
- ☐ Dave Lumley
- ☐ Mark Messier

☐ Ed Mio (G)
☐ Don Murdoch
☐ Dave Semenko
☐ Risto Siltanen
☐ Bryan Watson
☐ Stan Weir

1981 - 82 OILERS RED ROOSTER

This set was originally issued in panels. Single card prices are listed below. Regional stars may carry a premium.

Card Size: 2 3/4" x 3 5/8"
Sponsors: Red Rooster, Post
Complete Set (23 cards): 75.00

☐	Glenn Anderson #9	3.00
☐	Curt Brackenbury #15	.75
☐	Brett Callighen #18	.75
☐	Paul Coffey #7	8.00
☐	Lee Fogolin #2	.75
☐	Mike Forbes #26	.75
☐	Grant Fuhr #1 (G)	6.00
☐	Ted Green	.75
☐	Wayne Gretzky #99	12.00
☐	Wayne Gretzky #99	12.00
☐	Wayne Gretzky #99	12.00
☐	Wayne Gretzky #99	12.00
☐	Matti Hagman #10	.75
☐	Billy Harris	.75
☐	Doug Hicks #5	.75
☐	Pat Hughes #16	.75
☐	Dave Hunter #12	.75
☐	Jari Kurri #17	6.00
☐	Garry Lariviere #6	.75
☐	Ron Low #30 (G)	1.00
☐	Kevin Lowe #4	3.00
☐	Dave Lumley #20	.75
☐	Mark Messier #11	10.00
☐	Andy Moog #35 (G)	5.00
☐	Glen Sather	2.00
☐	Dave Semenko #27	.75
☐	Risto Siltanen #8	.75
☐	Garry Unger #77	.75
☐	Stan Weir #21	.75

1981 - 82 OILERS WEST EDMONTON MALL

Single card prices are listed below. Regional stars may carry a premium. Other singles may exist.

Photo Size: 5" x 7"
Sponsors: West Edmonton Mall

☐	Paul Coffey	20.00
☐	Lee Fogolin	4.00
☐	Grant Fuhr (G)	12.00
☐	Wayne Gretzky	90.00
☐	Billy Harris	4.00
☐	Charlie Huddy	6.00
☐	Gary Lariviere	4.00
☐	Dave Lumley	4.00
☐	Risto Siltanen	4.00
☐	Stan Weir	4.00

1982 - 83 OILERS RED ROOSTER

This set was originally issued in panels. Single card prices are listed below. Regional stars may carry a premium.

Card Size: 2 3/4" x 3 5/8"
Sponsors: Red Rooster, Post
Complete Set (23 cards): 40.00

☐	Glenn Anderson #9	2.00
☐	Laurie Boschman #14	.75
☐	Paul Coffey #7	6.00
☐	Lee Fogolin #2	.75
☐	Grant Fuhr #31 (G)	5.00
☐	Ted Green	.75
☐	Randy Gregg #21	1.00
☐	Wayne Gretzky #99	10.00
☐	Wayne Gretzky #99	10.00
☐	Wayne Gretzky #99	10.00
☐	Wayne Gretzky #99	10.00
☐	Marc Habscheid #23	.75
☐	Charlie Huddy #22	1.00
☐	Pat Hughes #16	.75
☐	Dave Hunter #12	.75
☐	Don Jackson #29	.75
☐	Jari Kurri #17	5.00
☐	Garry Lariviere #6	.75
☐	Ken Linseman #13	.75
☐	Ron Low #30 (G)	1.00
☐	Kevin Lowe #4	2.00
☐	Dave Lumley #20	.75
☐	Mark Messier #11	8.00
☐	Andy Moog #35	4.00
☐	John Muckler	1.00
☐	Jaroslav Pouzar #10	.75
☐	Tom Roulston #24	.75
☐	Glen Sather	2.00
☐	Dave Semenko #27	.75
☐	Garry Unger #77	.75

1983 - 84 OILERS

There are two versions of this set: a postcard-sized set that was issued in complete sets and a longer size photo edition issued during practices in West Edmonton Mall. We have little pricing information on singles. The longer-sized cards are likely valued at 2-3 times the regular card.

Card Size: 4 1/2" x 6 1/2"
Photo Size Length: 7 1/2"
Sponsor: none
Complete Set (21 cards): 100.00

☐☐ Glenn Anderson #9
☐☐ Rick Chartraw #6
☐☐ Paul Coffey #7
☐☐ Lee Fogolin #2
☐☐ Grant Fuhr (G) #31
☐☐ Randy Gregg #21
☐☐ Wayne Gretzky #99
☐☐ Charlie Huddy #22
☐☐ Pat Hughes #16
☐☐ Dave Hunter #12
☐☐ Don Jackson #29
☐☐ Jari Kurri #17
☐☐ Willy Lindstrom #19
☐☐ Ken Linseman #13
☐☐ Kevin Lowe #4
☐☐ Dave Lumley #20
☐☐ Kevin McClelland #24
☐☐ Mark Messier #11
☐☐ Andy Moog (G) #35
☐☐ Jaroslav Pouzar #10
☐☐ Dave Semenko #27

1983 - 84 OILERS MCDONALD'S STICKERS

This set was originally issued in panels. The Gretzky panel sells at $12-15. Single panels start at 75¢. Regular stickers measure 1 9/16" x 2 1/2" while the coaches and two goalie stickers measure 3" x 2 1/2".

Panel Size: 3" x 5"
Sponsor: McDonald's
Complete Set (7 panels): 35.00
Album: 5.00

☐ Glenn Anderson #9
Jaroslav Pouzar #10
Green/Sather/Muckler

☐ Rick Chartraw #6
Wayne Gretzky #99
Dave Lumley #20
Willy Lindstrom #19

☐ Paul Coffey #7
Raimo Summanen #25
Andy Moog #35 (G)

☐ Pat Conacher #15
Lee Fogolin #2
Don Jackson #29
Mark Messier #11

☐ Randy Gregg #21
Charle Huddy #22
Kevin Lowe #4
Emery Edge Award

☐ Pat Hughes #16
Kevin McClelland #24
Grant Fuhr #31 (G)

☐ Dave Hunter #12
Jari Kurri #17
Ken Linseman #13
Dave Semenko #27

1983 - 84 OILERS MCDONALD'S BUTTONS

There are two versions of this set: buttons sponsored by Ronald McDonald House and buttons issued by the Oilers. Kevin Lowe has a photo variation in the McDonald's series; he is shown with or without his helmet. Lowe is only pictured with a helmet in the Oilers series. Photos are the same in each series except for Randy Gregg's. The most expensive single is Wayne Gretzky at $20-25 while singles start at $4. Team issued buttons may be valued at 2-3x the McDonald's photo.

Button Diametre: 2 1/4"

Sponsor: Ronald McDonald House
Complete Set (25 buttons): 100.00

☐☐ Glenn Anderson
☐☐ Ken Berry
☐☐ Paul Coffey
☐☐ Pat Conacher
☐☐ Lee Fogolin
☐☐ Grant Fuhr (G)
☐☐ Ted Green
☐☐ Randy Gregg
☐☐ Wayne Gretzky
☐☐ Charlie Huddy
☐☐ Pat Hughes
☐☐ Dave Hunter
☐☐ Don Jackson
☐☐ Jari Kurri
☐☐ Willy Lindstrom
☐☐ Ken Linseman
☐☐☐ Kevin Lowe
☐☐ Dave Lumley
☐☐ Kevin McClelland
☐☐ Mark Messier
☐☐ Andy Moog (G)
☐☐ John Muckler
☐☐ Jaroslav Pouzar
☐☐ Glen Sather
☐☐ Dave Semenko

1984 - 85 OILERS

The most expensive singles are Wayne Gretzky at $10-15 and Mark Messier at $5-7. Singles start at 75¢.

Card Size: 4 1/2" x 6 1/2"
Sponsors: none
Complete Set (23 cards): 40.00

☐ Glenn Anderson
☐ Bill Carroll
☐ Paul Coffey
☐ Lee Fogolin
☐ Grant Fuhr (G)
☐ Randy Gregg
☐ Wayne Gretzky
☐ Charlie Huddy
☐ Pat Hughes
☐ Dave Hunter
☐ Don Jackson
☐ Mike Krushelnyski
☐ Jari Kurri
☐ Willy Lindstrom
☐ Kevin Lowe
☐ Dave Lumley
☐ Kevin McClelland
☐ Larry Melnyk
☐ Mark Messier
☐ Andy Moog (G)
☐ Mark Napier
☐ Jaroslav Pouzar
☐ Dave Semenko

1984 - 85 OILERS RED ROOSTER

This series was originally issued in panels. There are four Wayne Gretzky cards each valued at $8-10. Mark Messier sells at $4-5 and singles start at 50¢.

Card Size: 2 3/4" x 3 5/8"
Sponsors: Red Rooster, Old Dutch, Post
Complete Set (30 cards): 45.00

☐ Glenn Anderson
☐ Billy Carroll
☐ Paul Coffey
☐ Lee Fogolin
☐ Grant Fuhr (G)
☐ Ted Green
☐ Randy Gregg
☐ Wayne Gretzky
☐ Wayne Gretzky
☐ Wayne Gretzky
☐ Wayne Gretzky
☐ Marc Habscheid
☐ Charlie Huddy
☐ Pat Hughes
☐ Dave Hunter
☐ Don Jackson
☐ Mike Krushelnyski
☐ Jari Kurri
☐ Willy Lindstrom
☐ Kevin Lowe
☐ Dave Lumley
☐ Kevin McClelland
☐ Larry Melnyk
☐ Mark Messier
☐ Andy Moog (G)
☐ John Muckler
☐ Mark Napier
☐ Jaroslav Pouzar
☐ Glen Sather
☐ Dave Semenko

1985 - 86 OILERS RED ROOSTER

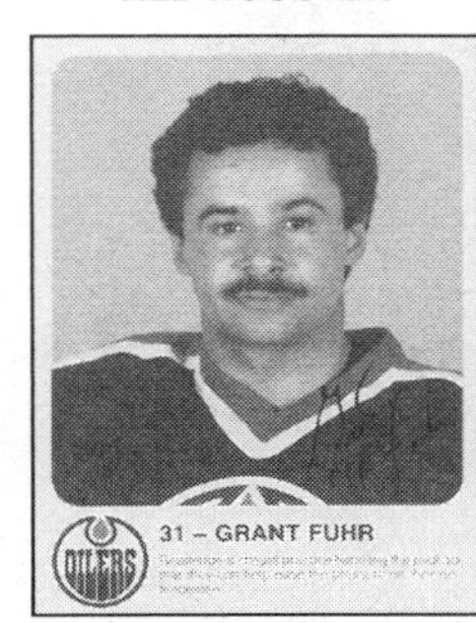

This series was originally issued in panels. There are three Wayne Gretzky cards each valued at $8-10. Mark Messier sells at $4-5 and singles start at 50¢.

Card Size: 2 3/4" x 3 5/8"
Sponsors: Red Rooster, Old Dutch, Post
Complete Set (30 cards): 40.00

☐ Glenn Anderson
☐ Paul Coffey

☐ Lee Fogolin
☐ Grant Fuhr (G)
☐ Randy Gregg
☐ Wayne Gretzky
☐ Wayne Gretzky
☐ Wayne Gretzky
☐ Charlie Huddy
☐ Dave Hunter
☐ Don Jackson
☐ Mike Krushelnyski
☐ Jari Kurri
☐ Kevin Lowe
☐ Dave Lumley
☐ Craig MacTavish
☐ Bob McCammon
☐ Kevin McClelland
☐ Marty McSorley
☐ Mark Messier
☐ Andy Moog (G)
☐ John Muckler
☐ Mark Napier
☐ Mike Rogers
☐ Glen Sather
☐ Dave Semenko
☐ Gord Shervan
☐ Steve Smith
☐ Raimo Summanen
☐ Esa Tikkanen

1986 - 87 OILERS

The most expensive singles are Wayne Gretzky at $15-20 and Mark Messier at $5-7. Singles start at 75¢.

Card Size: 3 3/4" x 6 5/8"
Sponsors: none
Complete Set (24 cards): 40.00

☐ Glenn Anderson
☐ Jeff Beukeboom
☐ Paul Coffey
☐ Lee Fogolin
☐ Grant Fuhr (G)
☐ Randy Gregg
☐ Wayne Gretzky
☐ Charlie Huddy
☐ Dave Hunter
☐ Mike Krushelnyski
☐ Stu Kulak
☐ Jari Kurri
☐ Kevin Lowe
☐ Craig MacTavish
☐ Kevin McClelland
☐ Marty McSorley
☐ Mark Messier
☐ Andy Moog (G)
☐ Craig Muni
☐ Mark Napier
☐ Jaroslav Pouzar
☐ Steve Smith
☐ Raimo Summanen
☐ Esa Tikkanen

1986 - 87 OILERS RED ROOSTER

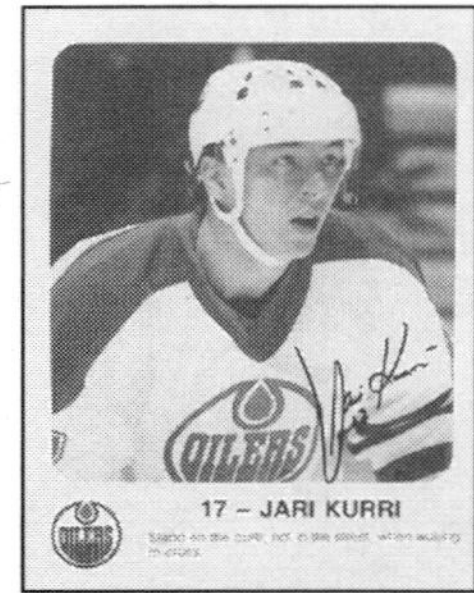

This series was originally issued in panels. There are two Wayne Gretzky cards each valued at $8-10. Mark Messier sells at $4-5 and singles start at 50¢.

Card Size: 2 3/4" x 3 5/8"
Sponsors: Red Rooster, Old Dutch
Complete Set (30 cards): 35.00

☐ Glenn Anderson
☐ Jeff Beukeboom
☐ Paul Coffey
☐ Lee Fogolin
☐ Grant Fuhr (G)
☐ Danny Gare
☐ Steve Graves
☐ Ted Green
☐ Randy Gregg
☐ Wayne Gretzky
☐ Wayne Gretzky
☐ Charlie Huddy
☐ Dave Hunter
☐ Mike Krushelnyski
☐ Stu Kulak
☐ Jari Kurri
☐ Kevin Lowe
☐ Craig MacTavish
☐ Kevin McClelland
☐ Marty McSorley
☐ Mark Messier
☐ Andy Moog (G)
☐ Andy Moog (G)
☐ John Muckler
☐ Craig Muni
☐ Mark Napier
☐ Glen Sather
☐ Steve Smith
☐ Raimo Summanen
☐ Esa Tikkanen

1987 - 88 OILERS

The most expensive singles are Wayne Gretzky at $15-20 and Mark Messier at $5-7. Singles start at 75¢.

Card Size: 3 3/4" x 6 5/8"
Sponsors: none
Complete Set (22 cards): 35.00

☐ Keith Acton
☐ Glenn Anderson
☐ Jeff Beukeboom
☐ Grant Fuhr (G)
☐ Wayne Gretzky
☐ Dave Hannan
☐ Charlie Huddy
☐ Mike Krushelnyski
☐ Jari Kurri
☐ Normand Lacombe
☐ Kevin Lowe
☐ Craig MacTavish
☐ Kevin McClelland
☐ Marty McSorley
☐ Mark Messier
☐ Craig Muni
☐ Selmar Odelein
☐ Daryl Reaugh (G)
☐ Craig Simpson
☐ Warren Skorodenski (G)
☐ Steve Smith
☐ Esa Tikkanen

1988 - 89 OILERS

Mark Messier is the most expensive single at $4-5. Singles start at 75¢.

Card Size: 3 3/4" x 6 5/8"
Sponsors: none
Complete Set (27 cards): 25.00

☐ Glenn Anderson
☐ Jeff Beukeboom
☐ Dave Brown
☐ Kelly Buchberger
☐ Jimmy Carson
☐ Miroslav Frycer
☐ Grant Fuhr (G)
☐ Randy Gregg
☐ Doug Halward
☐ Charlie Huddy
☐ Dave Hunter
☐ Tomas Jonsson
☐ Chris Joseph
☐ Jari Kurri
☐ Normand Lacombe
☐ Mark Lamb
☐ John LeBlanc
☐ Kevin Lowe
☐ Craig MacTavish
☐ Kevin McClelland
☐ Mark Messier
☐ Craig Muni
☐ Bill Ranford (G)
☐ Craig Redmond
☐ Craig Simpson
☐ Steve Smith
☐ Esa Tikkanen

1988 - 89 OILERS ACTION MAGAZINE

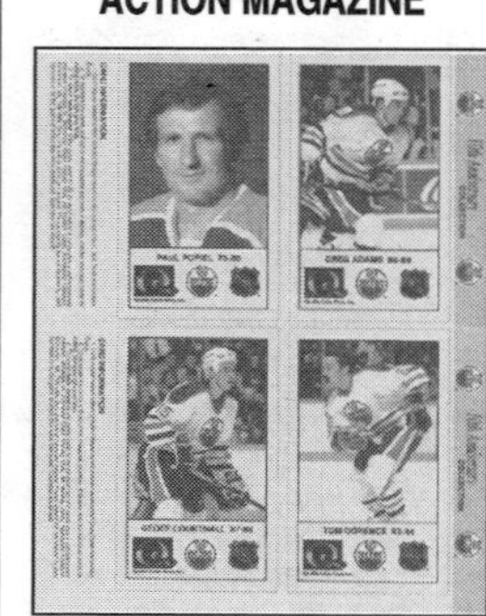

These cards were issued as four-card panels inserted into game programs. Wayne Gretzky's first panel (cards 45-48) sells at $30-35 while his second panel (cards 53-56) sells at $15-20. Gretzky is also pictured on a third panel with the 1988 Stanley Cup (cards 137-140) which is valued at $10-15. Mark Messier's panel (cards 89-92) sells at $8-10 and single panels start $3. Cut out cards measure 2 9/16" x 4 5/16"

Card Size: 9 1/4" x 7 7/16"
Sponsor: Action Magazine
Complete Set (41 panels): 35.00

☐ 1 Garry Unger
2 Chris Joseph
3 Raimo Summanen
4 Mike Zanier (G)
☐ 5 Kevin Lowe
6 Dave Semenko
7 Pete Driscoll
8 Ken Solheim
☐ 9 Glenn Anderson
10 Curt Brackenbury
11 Ron Shudra
12 Gord Shervan
☐ 13 Randy Gregg
14 Larry Melnyk
15 Tom Roulston
16 Billy Carroll
☐ 17 Jeff Beukeboom
18 Jaroslav Pouzar
19 Jeff Brubaker
20 Danny Gare
☐ 21 Craig MacTavish
22 Reijo Ruotsalainen
23 Willy Lindstrom
24 Pat Hughes
☐ 25 Jim Wiemer
26 Selmar Odelein
27 Kent Nilsson
28 Mark Napier
☐ 29 Esa Tikkanen
30 John Miner
31 Tom McMurchy
32 Steve Graves
☐ 33 Craig Muni
34 Moe Mantha
35 Dave Lumley
36 Ron Low (G)
☐ 37 Marty McSorley
38 Steve Dykstra
39 Risto Jalo
40 Dave Hunter
☐ 41 Jari Kurri
42 Lee Fogolin
43 Moe Lemay
44 Stu Kulak
☐ 45 Charlie Huddy
46 Wayne Gretzky
47 Ken Linseman
48 Risto Siltanen
☐ 49 Glen Sather
50 Brett Callighen
51 Eddy Mio (G)
52 Ken Hammond
☐ 53 Jimmy Carson
54 Paul Coffey
55 HL: Wayne Gretzky
56 Reed Larson
☐ 57 Ted Green
58 Matti Hagman
59 Marc Habscheid
60 Bill Ranford (G)
☐ 61 Mark Lamb
62 Daryl Reaugh (G)
63 Al Hamilton
64 HL: Paul Coffey
☐ 65 Grant Fuhr (G)
66 Stan Weir
67 Ken Berry
68 John Muckler
☐ 69 Doug Smith
70 Lance Nethery
71 Bill Flett
72 Mike Forbes
☐ 73 Martin Gelinas
74 Ron Chipperfield
75 Reg Kerr
76 Don Jackson
☐ 77 Keith Acton
78 Gary Edwards (G)
79 Mike Krushelnyski
80 L.Kulchisky/P.Millar/B.Stafford
☐ 81 Normand Lacombe
82 Pat Price
83 Dave Hannan
84 Garry Lariviere
☐ 85 Greg C. Adams
86 Poul Popeil
87 Tom Gorence
88 Geoff Courtnall
☐ 89 Mark Messier
90 Dave Dryden (G)
91 Andy Moog (G)
92 Jim Ennis
☐ 93 Craig Simpson
94 Laurie Boschman
95 Doug Hicks
96 Rick Chartraw
☐ 97 '84 Cup Champions
98 Ron Carter
99 Blair MacDonald
100 Dean Clark
☐ 101 Glen Cochrane
102 Lindsay Middlebrook (G)
103 Ron Areshenkoff
104 Billy Harris
☐ 105 Mark Messier
106 John Blum
107 Wayne Bianchin
108 Tom Bladon
☐ 109 Kevin McClelland
110 Roy Sommer
111 Mike Toal
112 Don Ashby
☐ 113 Donald Nachbaur
114 '85 Cup Champions
115 Jim Corsi (G)
116 John Hughes
☐ 117 HL: Glen Sather
118 Bob Dupuis
119 Jim Harrison
120 Don Murdoch
☐ 121 Steve Smith
122 Pete LoPresti (G)
123 Colin Campbell
124 Bryan Watson
☐ 125 John Bednarski
126 '87 Cup Champions
127 Scott Metcalfe
128 Mike Rogers
☐ 129 Dan Newman
130 HL: Grant Fuhr (G)
131 Warren Skorodenski (G)
132 Todd Strueby
☐ 133 Kelly Buchberger
134 Cam Connor
135 Dean Hopkins
136 Mike Moller
☐ 137 '88 Cup Champions
138 Byron Baltimore
139 Pat Conacher
140 Ray Cote
☐ 141 Walt Poddubny
142 Jim Playfair
143 Nick Fotiu
144 Kari Makkonen
☐ 145 Dave Brown
146 Terry Martin
147 François Leroux
148 Kari Jalonen
☐ 149 Tomas Jonsson
150 Dave Donnelly
151 Mike Ware
152 Don Cutts (G)
☐ 153 Miroslav Frycer
154 Bruce MacGregor
155 Kim Issel
156 Marco Baron (G)
☐ 157 Doug Halward
158 Barry Fraser
159 Alan May
160 Bobby Schmautz
☐ 161 Craig Redmond
162 '89 All-Star Game
163 Alex Tidey
164 Wayne Van Dorp

1990 - 91 OILERS IGA

Mark Messier is the most expensive single at $5-6. Singles start at 50¢. Ted Green, Ron Low, John Muckler and the checklist card are supposedly short printed and sell at $2-3. A 26-card set sells at $25..

Card Size: 2 1/2" x 3 1/2"
Sponsors: McGavin's, IGA
Complete Set (30 cards): 30.00

- ☐ Glenn Anderson
- ☐ Dave Brown
- ☐ Jeff Beukeboom
- ☐ Kelly Buchberger
- ☐ Martin Gelinas
- ☐ Adam Graves
- ☐ Charlie Huddy
- ☐ Chris Joseph
- ☐ Petr Klima
- ☐ Mark Lamb
- ☐ Ken Linseman
- ☐ Kevin Lowe
- ☐ Craig MacTavish
- ☐ Mark Messier
- ☐ Joey Moss
- ☐ Craig Muni
- ☐ Joe Murphy
- ☐ Bill Ranford (G)
- ☐ Anatoli Semenov
- ☐ Craig Simpson
- ☐ Geoff Smith
- ☐ Steve Smith
- ☐ Kari Takko (G)
- ☐ Esa Tikkanen
- ☐ K.Low/L.Kulchisky/ B.Stafford/S.Poirier
- ☐ HL: Mark Messier
- ☐ Ted Green
- ☐ Ron Low
- ☐ John Muckler
- ☐ Checklist

1991 - 92 OILERS IGA

Bill Ranford is the most expensive single at $2-3. Singles start at 50¢. Ted Green, Ron Low, Keith Primeau and the checklist card are supposedly short printed and sell at $2-3. A 26-card set sells at $15.

Card Size: 2 1/2" x 3 1/2"
Sponsor: IGA
Complete Set (30 cards): 20.00

- ☐ Josef Beranek
- ☐ Kelly Buchberger
- ☐ Vincent Damphousse
- ☐ Louie DeBrusk
- ☐ Martin Gelinas
- ☐ Peter Ing (G)
- ☐ Petr Klima
- ☐ Mark Lamb
- ☐ Kevin Lowe
- ☐ Norm Maciver
- ☐ Craig MacTavish
- ☐ Troy Mallette
- ☐ Dave Manson
- ☐ Scott Mellanby
- ☐ Craig Muni
- ☐ Joe Murphy
- ☐ Bill Ranford (G)
- ☐ Steve Rice
- ☐ Luke Richardson
- ☐ Anatoli Semenov
- ☐ David Shaw
- ☐ Craig Simpson
- ☐ Geoff Smith
- ☐ Scott Thornton
- ☐ Esa Tikkanen
- ☐ IGA logo
- ☐ Ted Green
- ☐ Ron Low
- ☐ Kevin Primeau
- ☐ Checklist

1992 - 93 OILERS

Doug Weight is the most expensive card at $2-3. Singles start at 75¢.

Card Size: 3 3/4" x 6 7/8"
Sponsors: none
Complete Set (22 cards): 15.00

- ☐ Kelly Buchberger
- ☐ Zdeno Ciger
- ☐ Shayne Corson
- ☐ Louie DeBrusk
- ☐ Todd Elik
- ☐ Brian Glynn
- ☐ Mike Hudson
- ☐ Chris Joseph
- ☐ Igor Kravchuk
- ☐ Francois Leroux
- ☐ Craig MacTavish
- ☐ Dave Manson
- ☐ Shjon Podein
- ☐ Bill Ranford (G)
- ☐ Steve Rice
- ☐ Luke Richardson
- ☐ Craig Simpson
- ☐ Geoff Smith
- ☐ Kevin Todd
- ☐ Vladimir Vujtek
- ☐ Doug Weight
- ☐ Brad Werenka

1992 - 93 OILERS IGA

Bill Ranford is the most expensive single at $2-3. Singles start at 50¢.

Card Size: 2 1/2" x 3 1/2"
Sponsor: IGA
Complete Set (30 cards): 15.00

- ☐ 001 Checklist
- ☐ 002 Josef Beranek
- ☐ 003 Kelly Buchberger
- ☐ 004 Shayne Corson
- ☐ 005 Dan Currie
- ☐ 006 Louie DeBrusk
- ☐ 007 Martin Gelinas
- ☐ 008 Brent Gilchrist
- ☐ 009 Brian Glynn
- ☐ 010 Greg Hawgood
- ☐ 011 Chris Joseph
- ☐ 012 Petr Klima
- ☐ 013 Craig MacTavish
- ☐ 014 Dave Manson
- ☐ 015 Scott Mellanby
- ☐ 016 Craig Muni
- ☐ 017 Bernie Nicholls
- ☐ 018 Bill Ranford (G)
- ☐ 019 Luke Richardson
- ☐ 020 Craig Simpson
- ☐ 021 Geoff Smith
- ☐ 022 Vladimir Vujtek
- ☐ 023 Esa Tikkanen
- ☐ 024 Ron Tugnutt (G)
- ☐ 025 Shaun Van Allen
- ☐ 026 Glen Sather
- ☐ 027 Ted Green
- ☐ 028 Ron Low
- ☐ 029 Kevin Primeau
- ☐ 030 Oilers

1993 - 94 OILERS STARTER PHOTOS

These photos were issued with game programs. Jason Arnott is the most expensive photo at $10-15. Singles start at $5. Each card is numbered out of 5000.

Photo Size: 8" x 10"
Sponsor: Starter
Complete Set (41 cards): 225.00

- ☐ 06OCT Todd Elik
- ☐ 08OCT Igor Kravchuk
- ☐ 16OCT Dave Manson
- ☐ 20OCT Kelly Buchberger
- ☐ 22OCT Bill Ranford (G)
- ☐ 24OCT Craig MacTavish
- ☐ 29OCT Alexander Kerch
- ☐ 03NOV Chris Joseph
- ☐ 20NOV Geoff Smith
- ☐ 21NOV Ian Herbers
- ☐ 24NOV Fred Brathwaite (G)
- ☐ 27NOV Doug Weight
- ☐ 29NOV Ilya Byakin
- ☐ 01DEC Luke Richardson
- ☐ 15DEC Scott Pearson
- ☐ 17DEC Adam Bennett
- ☐ 22DEC Louie DeBrusk
- ☐ 27DEC Brad Werenka
- ☐ 29DEC Shayne Corson
- ☐ 02JAN Steve Rice
- ☐ 07JAN Kirk Maltby
- ☐ 26JAN Shjon Podein
- ☐ 28JAN Peter White
- ☐ 29JAN Vladimir Vujtek
- ☐ 02FEB Scott Thornton
- ☐ 04FEB Roman Oksiuta
- ☐ 06FEB Bob Beers
- ☐ 09FEB Fred Olausson
- ☐ 12FEB Wayne Cowley
- ☐ 13FEB Dean McAmmond
- ☐ 23FEB Jason Arnott
- ☐ 25FEB Ron Low
- ☐ 27FEB Tyler Wright
- ☐ 09MAR Kevin Primeau
- ☐ 11MAR Jozef Cierny
- ☐ 23MAR Gordon Mark
- ☐ 25MAR Brent Grieve
- ☐ 27MAR Brad Zavisha
- ☐ 08APR Mike Stapleton
- ☐ 10APR Glen Sather

1995 - 96 OILERS

We have little information on this blank-back series. Other singles exist.

Card Size: 3 3/4" x 7 1/8"

- ☐ Curtis Joseph

1996 - 97 OILERS

This Oilers series can be distringuished from previous years by the new Oilers' shoulder logo. The photos on these blank-back cards were taken by Gerry Thomas. Curtis Joseph is the most expensive single at $3-4. Singles start at 75¢.

Card Size: 3 3/4" x 7 1/8"
Complete Set (27 cards): 20.00

- ☐ Jason Arnott #7
- ☐ Sean Brown #8
- ☐ Kelly Buchberger #16
- ☐ Mariusz Czerkawsi #21
- ☐ Louie DeBrusk #29
- ☐ Boyd Devereaux #19
- ☐ Greg de Vries #5
- ☐ Donald Dufresne #34
- ☐ Bob Essensa (G) #30
- ☐ Mike Grier #25
- ☐ Curtis Joseph (G) #31
- ☐ Steve Kelly #10
- ☐ Petr Klima #85
- ☐ Andrei Kovalenko #51
- ☐ Mats Lindgren #14
- ☐ Kevin Lowe #4
- ☐ Todd Marchant #26
- ☐ Bryan Marchment #24
- ☐ Daniel McGillis #23
- ☐ Boris Mironov #2
- ☐ Rem Murray #17
- ☐ Jeff Norton #6
- ☐ Dean McAmmond #37
- ☐ Luke Richardson #22
- ☐ Miroslav Satan #18
- ☐ Ryan Smyth #94
- ☐ Doug Weight #39

1997 - 98 OILERS

The photos on these blank-back cards were taken by Gerry Thomas. Curtis Joseph is the most expensive single at $3-4. Singles start at 75¢.

Card Size: 3 3/4" x 7 1/8"
Complete Set (27 cards): 20.00

- ☐ Jason Arnott #7
- ☐ Drew Bannister #55
- ☐ Sean Brown #23
- ☐ Kelly Buchberger #16
- ☐ Boyd Devereaux #19
- ☐ Greg de Vries #5
- ☐ Bob Essensa (G) #30
- ☐ Doug Friedman #8
- ☐ Mike Grier #25
- ☐ Bill Huard #28
- ☐ Curtis Joseph (G) #31
- ☐ Joe Hulbig #12
- ☐ Steve Kelly #10
- ☐ Andrei Kovalenko #51
- ☐ Georges Laraque #27
- ☐ Mats Lindgren #14
- ☐ Kevin Lowe #4
- ☐ Todd Marchant #26
- ☐ Bryan Marchment #24
- ☐ Dean McAmmond #37
- ☐ Daniel McGillis #33
- ☐ Boris Mironov #2
- ☐ Bryan Muir #6
- ☐ Rem Murray #17
- ☐ Ryan Smyth #94
- ☐ Mike Watt #9
- ☐ Doug Weight #39

1997 - 98 OILERS SEASON TICKET CARD

This "Let Yourself Go!" card has season ticket information on the card back.

Card Size: 5" x 6 1/2"
Sponsors: Edmonton Oilers Ticket Office

- ☐ Curtis Joseph (G)

FLORIDA PANTHERS

1993 - 94 PANTHERS

Scott Mellanby is the most expensive single at $3. Singles start at $1.00. Other cards may exist.

Card Size: 3 3/4" x 7"

Sponsors: none

- ☐ Joe Cirella
- ☐ Tom Fitzgerald
- ☐ Mike Foligno
- ☐ Paul Laus
- ☐ Bill Lindsay
- ☐ Andrei Lomakin
- ☐ Scott Mellanby
- ☐ Brent Severyn

1994 - 95 PANTHERS HEALTH PLAN

We have no pricing information on this set.

Card Size: 4" x 10"

Sponsor: Health Plan of Florida

- ☐ Brian Skrudland
- ☐ John Vanbiesbrouck (G)
- ☐ Scott Mellanby
- ☐ Stu Barnes
- ☐ Jesse Belanger

1994 - 95 PANTHERS BOSTON ROTISSERIE

We have no pricing information on this set. Other singles may exist.

Card Size: 2 1/2" x 3"

Sponsor: Boston Rotisserie Chicken

- ☐ Dave Lowry
- ☐ Gord Murphy
- ☐ John Vanbiesbrouck (G)
- ☐ Mascot Panther

1996 - 97 PANTHERS WINN-DIXIE CARD ALBUM

This set was issued as a four panel album. The first panel features a collage of Panthers' photos. The next two panels can be cut out into 12 cards while the last panel can be cut out into 6 cards plus one Winn-Dixie ad card. The most expensive cut-out single is John Vanbiesbrouck at $3-4. Singles start at 50¢. An uncut album sells at $20.

Panel Sizes: 7 1/2" x 12 1/2"; 5" x 12 1/2"

Card Size: 2 1/2" x 3 1/8"

Sponsor: Winn-Dixie

Complete Set (30 cards): 15.00

- ☐ Terry Carkner #2
- ☐ Paul Laus #3
- ☐ Per Gustafsson #4
- ☐ Gord Murphy #5
- ☐ Rhett Warrener #7
- ☐ Dave Lowry #10
- ☐ Bill Lindsay #11
- ☐ Jody Hull #12
- ☐ David Nemirovsky #15
- ☐ Jason Podollan #17
- ☐ Mike Hough #18
- ☐ Radek Dvorak #19
- ☐ Brian Skrudland #20
- ☐ Tom Fitzgerald #21
- ☐ Chris Wells #23
- ☐ Robert Svehla #24
- ☐ Ray Sheppard #26
- ☐ Scott Mellanby #27
- ☐ Martin Straka #28
- ☐ Johan Garpenlov #29
- ☐ Mark Fitzpatrick (G) #30
- ☐ John Vanbiesbrouck (G) #34
- ☐ Rob Niedermayer #44
- ☐ Ed Jovanovski #55
- ☐ Doug MacLean, Coach
- ☐ Lindy Ruff, Asst. Coach
- ☐ Duane Sutter, Asst. Coach
- ☐ Billy Smith, Goal Coach
- ☐ Mascot Stanley C. Panther
- ☐ Prince of Wales Trophy

1997 - 98 PANTHERS WINN-DIXIE CARD ALBUM

This set was issued as a four panel album. The first panel features a collage of Panthers' photos. The next two panels can be cut out into 12 cards while the last panel can be cut out into 6 cards plus one Winn-Dixie/ Broward County Arena ad card. The most expensive cut-out single is John Vanbiesbrouck at $3-4. Singles start at 50¢. An uncut album sells at $20.

Panel Sizes: 7 1/2" x 12 1/2"

Card Size: 2 1/2" x 3 1/8"

Sponsor: Winn-Dixie

Complete Set (30 cards): 15.00

- ☐ Kevin Weekes (G) #1
- ☐ John Vanbiesbrouck (G) #34
- ☐ Terry Carkner #2
- ☐ Paul Laus #3
- ☐ Gord Murphy #5
- ☐ Jeff Norton #6
- ☐ Rhett Warrener #7
- ☐ Dallas Eakins #8
- ☐ Kirk Muller #9
- ☐ Esa Tikkanen #10
- ☐ Bill Lindsay #11
- ☐ Ray Whitney #14
- ☐ Dave Gagner #15
- ☐ Steve Washburn #17
- ☐ Radek Dvorak #19
- ☐ Tom Fitzgerald #21
- ☐ Dino Ciccarelli #22
- ☐ Chris Wells #23
- ☐ Robert Svehla #24
- ☐ Viktor Kozlov #25
- ☐ Ray Sheppard #26
- ☐ Scott Mellanby #27
- ☐ Johan Garpenlov #29
- ☐ Rob Niedermayer #44
- ☐ Ed Jovanovski #55
- ☐ Bryan Murray, Coach
- ☐ Duane Sutter, Asst. Coach
- ☐ Joe Cirella, Asst. Coach
- ☐ Billy Smith, Goal Coach
- ☐ Mascot Stanley C. Panther

HARTFORD WHALERS

1982 - 83 WHALERS JUNIOR WHALERS

Ron Francis is the most expensive single at $20-25. Singles start at $1.50.

Card Size: 3 1/4" x 6 3/8"

Sponsors: Hartford Courant, Junior Whalers Fan Club

Complete Set (22 cards): 50.00

- ☐ Greg C. Adams
- ☐ Russ Anderson
- ☐ Ron Francis
- ☐ Michel Galarneau
- ☐ Dan Fridgen
- ☐ Archie Henderson
- ☐ Ed Hospodar
- ☐ Mark Johnson
- ☐ Chris Kotsopoulos
- ☐ Pierre Larouche
- ☐ George Lyle
- ☐ Greg Millen (G)
- ☐ Warren Miller
- ☐ Ray Neufeld
- ☐ Mark Renaud
- ☐ Risto Siltanen
- ☐ Stuart Smith
- ☐ Blaine Stoughton
- ☐ Doug Sulliman
- ☐ Bob Sullivan
- ☐ Mike Veisor (G)
- ☐ Mickey Volcan
- ☐ Blake Wesley

1983 - 84 WHALERS JUNIOR WHALERS

Ron Francis is the most expensive single at $8-10. Singles start at $1.50.

Card Size: 3 3/4" x 8 1/4"

Sponsors: Hartford Courant, Junior Whalers Fan Club

Complete Set (22 cards): 40.00

- ☐ Bob Crawford
- ☐ Mike Crombeen
- ☐ Richie Dunn
- ☐ Normand Dupont
- ☐ Ron Francis
- ☐ Ed Hospodar
- ☐ Marty Howe
- ☐ Mark Johnson
- ☐ Chris Kotsopoulos
- ☐ Pierre Lacroix
- ☐ Greg Malone
- ☐ Greg Millen (G)
- ☐ Ray Neufeld
- ☐ Joel Quenneville
- ☐ Torrie Robertson
- ☐ Risto Siltanen
- ☐ Blaine Stoughton
- ☐ Steve Stoyanovich
- ☐ Doug Sulliman
- ☐ Sylvain Turgeon
- ☐ Mike Veisor (G)
- ☐ Mike Zuke

1984 - 85 WHALERS JUNIOR WHALERS

Ron Francis is the most expensive single at $6-8. Singles start at $1.50.

Card Size: 3 3/4" x 8 1/4"

Sponsors: Wendy's, Junior Whalers Fan Club

Complete Set (22 cards): 35.00

- ☐ Jack Brownschidle
- ☐ Sylvain Côté
- ☐ Bob Crawford
- ☐ Mike Crombeen
- ☐ Tony Currie
- ☐ Ron Francis
- ☐ Mark Fusco
- ☐ Dave Jensen
- ☐ Mark Johnson
- ☐ Chris Kotsopoulos
- ☐ Greg Malone
- ☐ Greg Millen (G)
- ☐ Ray Neufeld
- ☐ Randy Pierce
- ☐ Joel Quenneville
- ☐ Torrie Robertson
- ☐ Ulf Samuelsson
- ☐ Risto Siltanen
- ☐ Dave Tippett
- ☐ Sylvain Turgeon
- ☐ Steve Weeks (G)
- ☐ Mike Zuke

1985 - 86 WHALERS JUNIOR WHALERS

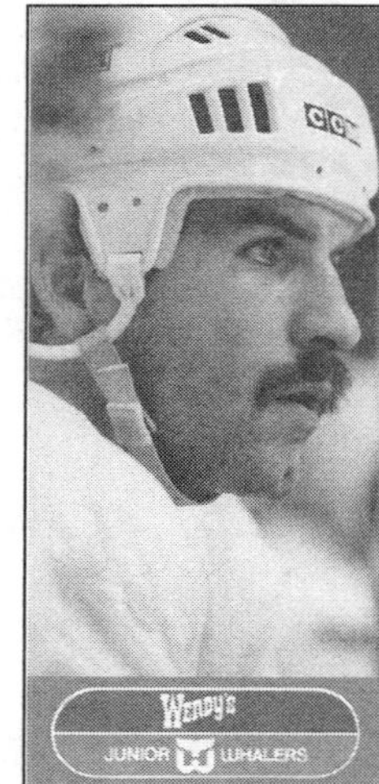

Ron Francis is the most expensive single at $5-7. Singles start at $1.50.

Card Size: 3 3/4" x 8 1/4"

Sponsors: Wendy's, Junior Whalers Fan Club

Complete Set (23 cards): 35.00

- ☐ Jack Brownschidle
- ☐ Sylvain Côté
- ☐ Bob Crawford
- ☐ Kevin Dineen
- ☐ Paul Fenton
- ☐ Ray Ferraro
- ☐ Ron Francis
- ☐ Scott Kleinendorst
- ☐ Paul Lawless
- ☐ Mike Liut (G)
- ☐ Paul MacDermid
- ☐ Greg Malone
- ☐ Dana Murzyn
- ☐ Ray Neufeld
- ☐ Jorgen Pettersson
- ☐ Joel Quenneville
- ☐ Torrie Robertson
- ☐ Ulf Samuelsson
- ☐ Risto Siltanen
- ☐ Dave Tippett
- ☐ Sylvain Turgeon
- ☐ Steve Weeks (G)
- ☐ Mike Zuke

1986 - 87 WHALERS JUNIOR WHALERS

Ron Francis is the most expensive single at $5-7. Singles start at $1.50.

Card Size: 3 3/4" x 8 1/4"

Sponsors: Thomas', Junior Whalers Fan Club

Complete Set (23 cards): 30.00

- ☐ John Anderson
- ☐ Dave Babych
- ☐ Wayne Babych
- ☐ Sylvain Côté
- ☐ Kevin Dineen
- ☐ Dean Evason
- ☐ Ray Ferraro
- ☐ Ron Francis
- ☐ Bill Gardner
- ☐ Stewart Gavin
- ☐ Doug Jarvis
- ☐ Scott Kleinendorst
- ☐ Paul Lawless
- ☐ Mike Liut (G)
- ☐ Paul MacDermid
- ☐ Mike McEwen
- ☐ Dana Murzyn
- ☐ Joel Quenneville
- ☐ Torrie Robertson
- ☐ Ulf Samuelsson
- ☐ Dave Tippett
- ☐ Sylvain Turgeon
- ☐ Steve Weeks (G)

1987 - 88 WHALERS JUNIOR WHALERS

Ron Francis is the most expensive single at $4-6. Singles start at $1.50.

Card Size: 3 3/4" x 8 1/4"

Sponsors: Burger King, Pepsi, Junior Whalers Fan Club

Complete Set (21 cards): 25.00

- ☐ John Anderson
- ☐ Dave Babych
- ☐ Sylvain Côté
- ☐ Kevin Dineen
- ☐ Dean Evason
- ☐ Ray Ferraro
- ☐ Ron Francis
- ☐ Stewart Gavin
- ☐ Doug Jarvis
- ☐ Scott Kleinendorst
- ☐ Randy Ladouceur
- ☐ Paul Lawless
- ☐ Mike Liut (G)
- ☐ Paul MacDermid
- ☐ Dana Murzyn
- ☐ Joel Quenneville
- ☐ Torrie Robertson

- ☐ Ulf Samuelsson
- ☐ Dave Tippett
- ☐ Sylvain Turgeon
- ☐ Steve Weeks (G)

1988-89 WHALERS JUNIOR WHALERS

Ron Francis is the most expensive single at $4-5. Singles start $1.00.

Card Size: 3 11/16" x 8 1/4"

Sponsors: Ground Round, Pepsi, Junior Whalers Fan Club

Complete Set (18 cards): 20.00

- ☐ John Anderson
- ☐ Dave Babych
- ☐ Sylvain Côté
- ☐ Kevin Dineen
- ☐ Dean Evason
- ☐ Ray Ferraro
- ☐ Ron Francis
- ☐ Scott Kleinendorst
- ☐ Randy Ladouceur
- ☐ Mike Liut (G)
- ☐ Paul MacDermid
- ☐ Brent Peterson
- ☐ Joel Quenneville
- ☐ Torrie Robertson
- ☐ Ulf Samuelsson
- ☐ Dave Tippett
- ☐ Sylvain Turgeon
- ☐ Carey Wilson

1989 - 90 WHALERS JUNIOR WHALERS

Ron Francis is the most expensive single at $4-5. Singles start at $1.00. Ed Kastelic, Todd Krygier and Mike Tomlak were added late in the season and sell at $2-3. A 21-card set without the three update players sells at $20.

Card Size: 3 11/16" x 8 1/4"

Sponsors: Milk, Junior Whalers Fan Club

Complete Set (24 cards): 25.00

- ☐ Mikael Andersson
- ☐ Dave Babych
- ☐ Sylvain Côté
- ☐ Randy Cunneyworth
- ☐ Kevin Dineen
- ☐ Dean Evason
- ☐ Ray Ferraro
- ☐ Ron Francis
- ☐ Jody Hull
- ☐ Grant Jennings
- ☐ Randy Ladouceur
- ☐ Brian Lawton
- ☐ Mike Liut (G)
- ☐ Paul MacDermid
- ☐ Joel Quenneville
- ☐ Ulf Samuelsson
- ☐ Brad Shaw
- ☐ Peter Sidorkiewicz (G)
- ☐ Dave Tippett
- ☐ Pat Verbeek
- ☐ Scott Young
- ☐ Ed Kastelic
- ☐ Todd Krygier
- ☐ Mike Tomlak

1990 - 91 WHALERS JUNIOR WHALERS

Gordie Howe is the most expensive single at $6-8. Singles start at $75¢. Rob Brown, Chris Goverdaris, Jim McKenzie and Daryl Reaugh are short printed and sell at $2-3. A 23-card set sells at $15.

Card Size: 3 3/4" x 8 1/4"

Sponsors: 7-Eleven, Junior Whalers Fan Club

Complete Set (27 cards): 20.00

- ☐ Mikael Andersson
- ☐ Dave Babych
- ☐ Yvon Corriveau
- ☐ Sylvain Côté
- ☐ Doug Crossman
- ☐ Randy Cunneyworth
- ☐ Paul Cyr
- ☐ Kevin Dineen
- ☐ Dean Evason
- ☐ Ron Francis
- ☐ Bobby Holik
- ☐ Gordie Howe
- ☐ Grant Jennings
- ☐ Ed Kastelic
- ☐ Todd Krygier
- ☐ Randy Ladouceur
- ☐ Ulf Samuelsson
- ☐ Brad Shaw
- ☐ Peter Sidorkiewicz (G)
- ☐ Mike Tomlak
- ☐ Pat Verbeek
- ☐ Carey Wilson
- ☐ Scott Young
- ☐ Rob Brown
- ☐ Chris Govedaris
- ☐ Jim McKenzie
- ☐ Daryl Reaugh (G)

1991 - 92 WHALERS JUNIOR WHALERS

Geoff Sanderson is the most expensive single at $4-6. Singles start at 75¢. James Black, Paul Cyr, Paul Gillis, Dan Keczmer, and Steve Konroyd are shortprinted and sell at $2-3. Andrew Cassels is also short printed and sells at $3-4. A 22-card set sells at $15.

Card Size: 3 3/4" x 8 1/4"

Sponsors: 7-Eleven, Junior Whalers Fan Club

Complete Set (28 cards): 25.00

- ☐ Mikael Andersson
- ☐ Marc Bergevin
- ☐ Rob Brown
- ☐ Adam Burt
- ☐ Murray Craven
- ☐ John Cullen
- ☐ Randy Cunneyworth
- ☐ Joe Day
- ☐ Mark Greig
- ☐ Bobby Holik
- ☐ Doug Houda
- ☐ Mark Hunter
- ☐ Ed Kastelic
- ☐ Randy Ladouceur
- ☐ Jim McKenzie
- ☐ Michel Picard
- ☐ Geoff Sanderson
- ☐ Brad Shaw
- ☐ Peter Sidorkiewicz (G)
- ☐ Pat Verbeek
- ☐ Kay Whitmore (G)
- ☐ Zarley Zalapski
- ☐ James Black
- ☐ Andrew Cassels
- ☐ Paul Cyr
- ☐ Paul Gillis
- ☐ Dan Keczmer
- ☐ Steve Konroyd

1992 - 93 WHALERS DAIRY MART

Sean Burke and Geoff Sanderson are the most expensive singles at $3-4. Singles start at 75¢.

Card Size: 2 3/8" x 3 1/2"

Sponsors: Dairy Mart, Junior Whalers Fan Club

Complete Set (26 cards): 25.00

- ☐ Jim Agnew
- ☐ Sean Burke (G)
- ☐ Adam Burt
- ☐ Andrew Cassels
- ☐ Murray Craven
- ☐ Randy Cunneyworth
- ☐ Paul Gillis
- ☐ Paul Holmgren
- ☐ Doug Houda
- ☐ Mark Janssens
- ☐ Tim Kerr
- ☐ Steve Konroyd
- ☐ Nick Kypreos
- ☐ Randy Ladouceur
- ☐ Jim McKenzie
- ☐ Michael Nylander
- ☐ Allen Pedersen
- ☐ Robert Petrovicky
- ☐ Frank Pietrangelo (G)
- ☐ Patrick Poulin
- ☐ Geoff Sanderson
- ☐ Pat Verbeek
- ☐ Eric Weinrich
- ☐ Terry Yake
- ☐ Zarley Zalapski

1993 - 94 WHALERS COCA-COLA

Chris Pronger is the most expensive single at $4-5. Singles start at 75¢.

Card Size: 2 3/8" x 3 1/2"

Sponsor: Coca-Cola

Complete Set (24 cards): 25.00

- ☐ Sean Burke (G)
- ☐ Adam Burt
- ☐ Andrew Cassels
- ☐ Randy Cunneyworth
- ☐ Alexander Godynyuk
- ☐ Mark Greig
- ☐ Mark Janssens
- ☐ Robert Kron
- ☐ Bryan Marchment
- ☐ Brad McCrimmon
- ☐ Pierre McGuire
- ☐ Michael Nylander
- ☐ James Patrick
- ☐ Frank Pietrangelo (G)
- ☐ Marc Potvin
- ☐ Chris Pronger
- ☐ Brian Propp
- ☐ Jeff Reese (G)
- ☐ Geoff Sanderson
- ☐ Jim Sandlak
- ☐ Jim Storm
- ☐ Darren Turcotte
- ☐ Pat Verbeek
- ☐ Zarley Zalapski

KANSAS CITY SCOUTS

No sets known.

LOS ANGELES KINGS

1980 - 81 KINGS

Marcel Dionne is the most expensive single at $6-8. Singles start at $1.00. 5000 sets were given away at Kings' "Card Night".

Card Size: 2 1/2" x 3 1/2"

Sponsors: none

Complete Set (14 cards): 20.00

- ☐ 1 Marcel Dionne
- ☐ 2 Glenn Goldup
- ☐ 3 Doug Halward
- ☐ 4 Billy Harris
- ☐ 5 Steve Jensen
- ☐ 6 Jerry Korab
- ☐ 7 Mario Lessard (G)
- ☐ 8 Dave Lewis
- ☐ 9 Mike Murphy
- ☐ 10 Rob Palmer
- ☐ 11 Charlie Simmer
- ☐ 12 Dave Taylor
- ☐ 13 Garry Unger
- ☐ 14 Jay Wells

1984 - 85 KINGS SMOKEY THE BEAR

Marcel Dionne is the most expensive single at $5-6. Singles start at 75¢.
Card Size: 2 15/16" x 4 3/8"
Sponsor: Smokey The Bear
Complete Set (23 cards): 20.00

☐ 1 Russ Anderson
☐ 2 Marcel Dionne
☐ 3 Brian Engblom
☐ 4 Daryl Evans
☐ 5 Jim Fox
☐ 6 Garry Galley
☐ 7 Anders Hakansson
☐ 8 Mark Hardy
☐ 9 Bob Janecyk (G)
☐ 10 John P. Kelly
☐ 11 Brian MacLellan
☐ 12 Bernie Nicholls
☐ 13 Craig Redmond
☐ 14 Terry Ruskowski
☐ 15 Doug Smith
☐ 16 Dave Taylor
☐ 17 Jay Wells
☐ 18 Daren Eliot (G)
☐ 19 Rick Lapointe
☐ 20 Bob Miller
☐ 21 Steve Seguin
☐ 22 Phil Sykes
☐ 23 Pat Quinn, Coach

1987 - 88 KINGS

Luc Robitaille is the most expensive player at $10-12. Singles start $1.00.
Card Size: 4" x 6"
Sponsors: none
Complete Set (23 cards): 30.00

☐ Bob Bourne
☐ Jimmy Carson
☐ Steve Duchesne
☐ Darren Eliot (G)
☐ Bryan Erickson
☐ Jim Fox
☐ Garry Galley
☐ Paul Guay
☐ Mark Hardy
☐ Bob Janecyk (G)
☐ Dean Kennedy
☐ Grant Ledyard
☐ Morris Lukowich
☐ Sean McKenna
☐ Roland Melanson (G)
☐ Bernie Nicholls
☐ Joe Paterson
☐ Larry Playfair
☐ Luc Robitaille
☐ Phil Sykes
☐ Dave Taylor
☐ Jay Wells
☐ Dave Williams

1988 - 89 KINGS SMOKEY THE BEAR

The most expensive singles are Wayne Gretzky at $15-20 and Luc Robitaille at $4-5. Singles start at 75¢.
Card Size: 2 1/2" x 3 1/2"
Sponsor: Smokey The Bear
Complete Set (25 cards): 25.00

☐ Mike Allison
☐ Ken Baumgartner
☐ Bob Carpenter
☐ Doug Crossman
☐ Dale DeGray
☐ Steve Duchesne
☐ Ron Duguay
☐ Mark Fitzpatrick (G)
☐ Jim Fox
☐ Robbie Ftorek
☐ Wayne Gretzky
☐ Gilles Hamel
☐ Glenn Healy (G)
☐ Mike Krushelnyski
☐ Tom Laidlaw
☐ Bryan Maxwell
☐ Wayne McBean
☐ Marty McSorley
☐ Bernie Nicholls
☐ Cap Raedar
☐ Luc Robitaille
☐ Dave Taylor
☐ John Tonelli
☐ Tim Watters
☐ Checklist

1989 - 90 KINGS SMOKEY THE BEAR

The most expensive singles are Wayne Gretzky at $12-15 and Luc Robitaille at $3-4. Singles start at 75¢.
Card Size: 2 1/2" x 3 1/2"
Sponsor: Smokey The Bear
Complete Set (25 cards): 25.00

☐ 1 Wayne Gretzky
☐ 2 Tim Watters
☐ 3 Mikael Lindholm
☐ 4 Mike Allison
☐ 5 Steve Kasper
☐ 6 Dave Taylor
☐ 7 Larry Robinson
☐ 8 Luc Robitaille
☐ 9 Barry Beck
☐ 10 Keith Crowder
☐ 11 Petr Prajsler
☐ 12 Mike Krushelnyski
☐ 13 John Tonelli
☐ 14 Steve Duchesne
☐ 15 Jay Miller
☐ 16 Kelly Hrudey
☐ 17 Marty McSorley
☐ 18 Mario Gosselin (G)
☐ 19 Craig Duncanson
☐ 20 Bob Kudelski
☐ 21 Brian Benning
☐ 22 Mikko Mäkelä
☐ 23 Tom Laidlaw
☐ 24 Checklist

1990 - 91 KINGS SMOKEY THE BEAR

The most expensive singles are Wayne Gretzky at $10-12 and Luc Robitaille at $2-3. Singles start at 75¢.
Card Size: 2 1/2" x 3 1/2"
Sponsor: Smokey The Bear
Complete Set (25 cards): 25.00

☐ 1 Wayne Gretzky
☐ 2 Brian Benning
☐ 3 Rob Blake
☐ 4 Tim Watters
☐ 5 Todd Elik
☐ 6 Tomas Sandstrom
☐ 7 Steve Kasper
☐ 8 Dave Taylor
☐ 9 Larry Robinson
☐ 10 Luc Robitaille
☐ 11 Tony Granato
☐ 12 Tom Laidlaw
☐ 13 François Breault
☐ 14 John Tonelli
☐ 15 Steve Duchesne
☐ 16 Jay Miller
☐ 17 Kelly Hrudey (G)
☐ 18 Marty McSorley
☐ 19 Daniel Berthiaume (G)
☐ 20 Bob Kudelski
☐ 21 Brad Jones
☐ 22 John McIntyre
☐ 23 Rod Buskas
☐ 24 Mascot Kingston
☐ Kings/RC challenge

1991 - 92 KINGS

This 25th Anniversary Great Western Forum set features only three hockey players. Wayne Gretzky sells at $15-20, Rogatien Vachon sells at $3-4 and Marcel Dionne sells at $4-5.
Sponsors: none

☐ Marcel Dionne
☐ Wayne Gretzky
☐ Rogatien Vachon

MINNESOTA NORTH STARS

1970-71 NORTH STARS

We have no pricing information on this set. Other singles may exist.
Card Size: 3 1/2" x 5 1/2"
Sponsor: none

☐ Barry Gibbs
☐ Bill Goldsworthy
☐ Danny Grant
☐ Ted Harris
☐ Césare Maniago (G)
☐ Jean-Paul Parise
☐ Tom Reid
☐ Bobby Rousseau
☐ Tom Williams
☐ Gump Worsley (G)

1973 - 74 NORTH STARS

Gump Worsley is the most expensive single at $8-10 in NRMT. Singles start at $2.
Card Size: 3 5/8" x 5"
Sponsors: none
Complete Set (20 cards): 40.00

☐ Fred Barrett
☐ Gary Bergman
☐ Jude Drouin
☐ Tony Featherstone
☐ Barry Gibbs
☐ Bill Goldsworthy
☐ Danny Grant
☐ Buster Harvey
☐ Dennis Hextall
☐ Parker MacDonald
☐ Césare Maniago (G)
☐ Lou Nanne
☐ Rod Norrish
☐ Dennis O'Brien
☐ Murray Oliver
☐ Jean-Paul Parise
☐ Dean Prentice
☐ Tom Reid
☐ Fred Stanfield
☐ Gump Worsley (G)

1978 - 79 NORTH STARS CLOVERLEAF DAIRY

These two-card panels were found on the backs of milk cartons and are available with either a red or purple tint. The Bobby Smith/Gary Edwards panel is the most expensive at $20-25 in NRMT. Singles start at $12.
Panel Size: 3 3/4" x 7 5/8"
Sponsors: Cloverleaf Dairy
Complete Set (9 panels): 150.00

☐ 1 Gilles Meloche (G)/Gary Sargent
☐ 2 Fred Barrett/Per-Olov Brasar
☐ 3 J.P. Parise/Greg Smith
☐ 4 Al MacAdam/K.A. Andersson
☐ 5 Gary Edwards(G)/Bobby Smith
☐ 6 Mike Polich/Brad Maxwell
☐ 7 Steve Payne/Glen Sharpley
☐ 8 Tim Young/Kris Manery
☐ 9 Ron Zanussi/Tom Younghams

1979-80 NORTH STARS

Bobby Smith is the most expensive single at $5-6 in NRMT. Singles start at $1.00. Other singles may exist.
Postcard Size: 3 1/2" x 5 1/2"
Sponsors: none

☐ Kent-Erik Andersson
☐ Fred Barrett
☐ Gary Edwards (G)
☐ Mike Fidler
☐ Craig Hartsburg
☐ Al MacAdam
☐ Kris Manery
☐ Brad Maxwell
☐ Tom McCarthy
☐ Gilles Meloche (G)
☐ Steve Payne
☐ Mike Polich
☐ Gary Sargent
☐ Paul Schmyr
☐ Bobby Smith
☐ Greg Smith
☐ Glen Sonmor
☐ Tim Young
☐ Tom Younghams
☐ Ron Zanussi

1980 - 81 NORTH STARS

The most expensive players are Bobby Smith and Jack Carlson ('70s movie Slap Shot) sell at $3-4. Singles start at $1.00.
Postcard Size: 3 1/2" x 5 1/2"
Sponsors: none
Complete Set (24 cards): 25.00

☐ Kent-Erik Andersson
☐ Fred Barrett
☐ Don Beaupré (G)
☐ Jack Carlson
☐ Steve Christoff
☐ Mike Eaves
☐ Gary Edwards (G)
☐ Curt Giles
☐ Craig Hartsburg
☐ Al MacAdam
☐ Brad Maxwell
☐ Tom McCarthy
☐ Gilles Meloche (G)
☐ Steve Payne
☐ Mike Polich
☐ Gary Sargent
☐ Glen Sharpley
☐ Paul Schmyr
☐ Bobby Smith
☐ Greg Smith
☐ Tim Young
☐ Tom Younghams
☐ Ron Zanussi
☐ M.Oliver/J.P. Parise/G.Somner

1981-82 NORTH STARS

The most expensive singles are Dino Ciccarelli at $6-8 and Neal Broten at $4-5 Singles start at $1.00.

Postcard Size: 3 1/2" x 5 1/2"
Sponsors: none
Complete Set (24 cards): 25.00

☐ Kent-Erik Andersson
☐ Fred Barrett
☐ Don Beaupré (G)
☐ Neal Broten
☐ Jack Carlson
☐ Steve Christoff
☐ Dino Ciccarelli
☐ Mike Eaves
☐ Anders Hakansson
☐ Craig Hartsburg
☐ Al MacAdam
☐ Brad Maxwell
☐ Kevin Maxwell
☐ Tom McCarthy
☐ Gilles Meloche (G)
☐ Bill Nyrop
☐ Steve Payne
☐ Brad Palmer
☐ Gordie Roberts
☐ Gary Sargent
☐ Bobby Smith
☐ Tim Young
☐ M.Oliver/J.P. Parise/G.Somner

1982 - 83 NORTH STARS

Dino Ciccarelli is the most expensive single at $4-5. Singles start $1.00.

Postcard Size: 3 1/2" x 5 1/2"
Sponsors: none
Complete Set (24 cards): 25.00

☐ Fred Barrett
☐ Don Beaupré (G)
☐ Brian Bellows
☐ Neal Broten
☐ Dino Ciccarelli
☐ Jordy Douglas
☐ Mike Eaves
☐ George Ferguson
☐ Ron Friest
☐ Curt Giles
☐ Craig Hartsburg
☐ Al MacAdam
☐ Dan Mandich
☐ Brad Maxwell
☐ Tom McCarthy
☐ Gilles Meloche (G)
☐ Steve Payne
☐ Willi Plett
☐ Gordie Roberts
☐ Gary Sargent
☐ Bobby Smith
☐ Ken Solheim
☐ Tim Young
☐ D.Ciccarelli/B.Bellows
☐ Team Photo

1983 - 84 NORTH STARS

Dino Ciccarelli is the most expensive single at $3-4. Singles start $1.00.

Postcard Size: 3 1/2" x 5 1/2"
Sponsors: none
Complete Set (27 cards): 25.00

☐ Keith Acton
☐ Brent Ashton
☐ Don Beaupré (G)
☐ Brian Bellows
☐ Neal Broten
☐ Dino Ciccarelli
☐ Jordy Douglas
☐ George Ferguson
☐ Curt Giles
☐ Craig Hartsburg
☐ Brian Lawton
☐ Craig Levie
☐ Lars Lindgren
☐ Al MacAdam
☐ Bill Mahoney, Coach
☐ Dan Mandich
☐ Dennis Maruk
☐ Brad Maxwell
☐ Tom McCarthy
☐ Gilles Meloche (G)
☐ Mark Napier
☐ Steve Payne
☐ Willi Plett
☐ Dave Richter
☐ Gordie Roberts
☐ Randy Velischek
☐ Team Photo

1984 - 85 NORTH STARS

Dino Ciccarelli is the most expensive single at $2-3. Singles start at 75¢.

Postcard Size: 3 1/2" x 5 1/2"
Sponsors: none
Complete Set (25 cards): 20.00

☐ Keith Acton
☐ Don Beaupré (G)
☐ Brian Bellows
☐ Scott Bjugstad
☐ Neal Broten
☐ Dino Ciccarelli
☐ Curt Giles
☐ Craig Hartsburg
☐ Tom Hirsch
☐ Paul Holmgren
☐ Brian Lawton
☐ Dan Mandich
☐ Dennis Maruk
☐ Brad Maxwell
☐ Tom McCarthy
☐ Rollie Melanson (G)
☐ Gilles Meloche (G)
☐ Mark Napier
☐ Steve Payne
☐ Willi Plett
☐ Dave Richter
☐ Gordie Roberts
☐ Bob Rouse
☐ Harold Snepts
☐ Ken Solheim

1984 - 85 NORTH STARS 7-ELEVEN

Dino Ciccarelli is the most expensive single at $2-3. Singles start at 75¢.

Card Size: 2 5/8" x 4 1/4"
Sponsor: 7-Eleven
Complete Set (12 cards): 12.00

☐ 1 Neal Broten
☐ 2 Willi Plett
☐ 3 Craig Hartsburg
☐ 4 Brian Bellows
☐ 5 Gordie Roberts
☐ 6 Keith Acton
☐ 7 Paul Holmgren
☐ 8 Gilles Meloche (G)
☐ 9 Dennis Maruk
☐ 10 Tom McCarthy
☐ 11 Steve Payne
☐ 12 Dino Ciccarelli

1985 - 86 NORTH STARS

Dino Ciccarelli is the most expensive single at $2-3. Singles start at 75¢.

Postcard Size: 3 1/2" x 5 1/2"
Sponsors: none
Complete Set (27 cards): 20.00

☐ Keith Acton
☐ Don Beaupré (G)
☐ Brian Bellows
☐ Bo Berglund
☐ Scott Bjugstad
☐ Neal Broten
☐ Jon Casey (G)
☐ Dino Ciccarelli
☐ Tim Coulis
☐ Curt Giles
☐ Craig Hartsburg
☐ Dirk Graham
☐ Mats Hallin
☐ Craig Hartsburg
☐ Tom Hirsch
☐ Dave Langevin
☐ Brian Lawton
☐ Craig Levie
☐ Dan Mandich
☐ Dennis Maruk
☐ Tom McCarthy
☐ Tony McKegney
☐ Rollie Melanson (G)
☐ Steve Payne
☐ Gordie Roberts
☐ Bob Rouse
☐ Gord Shervan

1985 - 86 NORTH STARS 7-ELEVEN

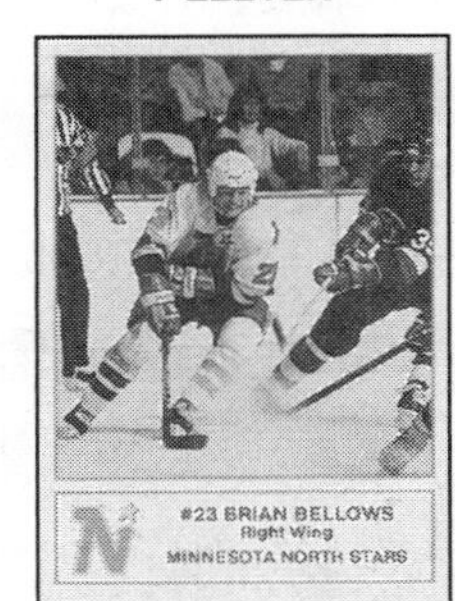

Dino Ciccarelli is the most expensive single at $2-3. Singles start at 75¢.

Card Size: 2 1/2" x 3 1/2"
Sponsor: 7-Eleven
Complete Set (12 cards): 12.00

☐ 1 Dino Ciccarelli
☐ 2 Scott Bjugstad
☐ 3 Curt Giles
☐ 4 Don Beaupré (G)
☐ 5 Tony McKegney
☐ 6 Neal Broten
☐ 7 Willi Plett
☐ 8 Craig Hartsburg
☐ 9 Brian Bellows
☐ 10 Keith Acton
☐ 11 Dave Langevin
☐ 12 Dirk Graham

1986 - 87 NORTH STARS 7-ELEVEN

Dino Ciccarelli is the most expensive single at $2-3. Singles start at 75¢.

Card Size: 2 1/2" x 3 1/2"
Sponsor: 7-Eleven
Complete Set (12 cards): 12.00

☐ 1 Neal Broten
☐ 2 Brian MacLellan
☐ 3 Willi Plett
☐ 4 Scott Bjugstad
☐ 5 Don Beaupré (G)
☐ 6 Dino Ciccarelli
☐ 7 Craig Hartsburg
☐ 8 Dennis Maruk
☐ 9 Bob Rouse
☐ 10 Gordie Roberts
☐ 11 Bob Brooke
☐ 12 Brian Bellows

1987 - 88 NORTH STARS

The most expensive singles are Dino Ciccarelli and Dave Gagner at $2-3. Singles start at 75¢.

Postcard Size: 3 1/2" x 5 1/2"
Sponsors: none
Complete Set (31 cards): 20.00

☐ Keith Acton
☐ Dave Archibald
☐ Warren Babe
☐ Don Beaupré (G)
☐ Brian Bellows
☐ Mike Berger
☐ Scott Bjugstad
☐ Bob Brooke
☐ Herb Brooks
☐ Neal Broten
☐ Dino Ciccarelli
☐ Larry DePalma
☐ Dave Gagner
☐ Curt Giles
☐ Dirk Graham
☐ Craig Hartsburg
☐ Tom Hirsch
☐ Brian Lawton
☐ Brian MacLellan
☐ Dennis Maruk
☐ Basil McRae
☐ Frank Musil
☐ Steve Payne
☐ Pat Price
☐ Chris Pryor
☐ Gordie Roberts
☐ Bob Rouse
☐ Terry Ruskowski
☐ Kari Takko (G)
☐ Ron Wilson
☐ Richard Zemlak

1988 - 89 NORTH STARS AMERICAN DAIRY

We have no pricing information on this set.

Card Size: 3 1/2" x 7 1/8"
Sponsor: American Dairy Assoc.

☐ Brian Bellows
☐ Bob Brooke
☐ Neal Broten
☐ Jon Casey (G)
☐ Shawn Chambers
☐ Dino Ciccarelli
☐ Larry DePalma
☐ Curt Fraser
☐ Link Gaetz
☐ Dave Gagner
☐ Stewart Gavin
☐ Curt Giles
☐ Marc Habscheid
☐ Mark Hardy
☐ Craig Hartsburg
☐ Brian MacLellan
☐ Moe Mantha
☐ Basil McRae
☐ Frank Musil
☐ Dusan Pasek
☐ Bob Rouse
☐ Terry Ruskowski
☐ Kari Takko (G)

MONTRÉAL CANADIENS

1966-67 CANADIENS IGA STAMPS

Prices are in NRMT. Stamps in EX sell at 50% of NRMT pricing.

Stamp Size: 3/4" x 3/4"
Sponsors: IGA

Complete Set (10 stamps):	300.00
☐ Ralph Backstrom #6	25.00
☐ Dick Duff #8	35.00
☐ John Ferguson #22	35.00
☐ Terry Harper #19	25.00
☐ Ted Harris #10	25.00
☐ Claude Larose #11	25.00
☐ Gilles Tremblay #21	25.00
☐ J.C. Tremblay #3	40.00
☐ Bobby Rousseau #15	25.00
☐ Gump Worsley #30 (G)	100.00

1967 - 68 CANADIENS

These photos are in black and white. Prices are in NRMT. Regional stars do carry a premium.

Postcard Size: 3 1/2" x 5 3/8"
Sponsors: none

Complete Set (28 cards):	110.00
☐ Toe Blake	8.00
☐ Ralph Backstrom	3.00
☐ Dave Balon	3.00
☐ Jean Béliveau	25.00
☐ Yvan Cournoyer	10.00
☐ Dick Duff	5.00
☐ John Ferguson	5.00
☐ Danny Grant	5.00
☐ Terry Harper	3.00
☐ Ted Harris	3.00
☐ Charlie Hodge (G)	5.00

- ☐ Jacques Laperrière 5.00
- ☐ Claude Larose 3.00
- ☐ Jacques Lemaire 8.00
- ☐ Gary Monahan 3.00
- ☐ Claude Provost 3.00
- ☐ Mickey Redmond 3.00
- ☐ Henri Richard 8.00
- ☐ Jim Roberts 3.00
- ☐ Léon Rochefort 3.00
- ☐ Bobby Rousseau 3.00
- ☐ Jean-Guy Talbot 3.00
- ☐ Gilles Tremblay 3.00
- ☐ J.C. Tremblay 5.00
- ☐ Rogatien Vachon (G) 10.00
- ☐ Carol Vadnais 5.00
- ☐ Bryan Watson 3.00
- ☐ Gump Worsley (G) 8.00

1967 - 68 CANADIENS IGA CARDS

Prices are in NRMT. Regional stars do carry a premium.

Card Size: 1 5/8" x 1 7/8"
Sponsors: IGA
Complete Set (23 cards): 600.00

- ☐ Ralph Backstrom #6 20.00
- ☐ Jean Béliveau #4 90.00
- ☐ Toe Blake 30.00
- ☐ Yvan Cournoyer #12 50.00
- ☐ Dick Duff #8 30.00
- ☐ John Ferguson #22 30.00
- ☐ Danny Grant #23 30.00
- ☐ Terry Harper #19 20.00
- ☐ Ted Harris #10 20.00
- ☐ Jacques Laperrière #2 35.00
- ☐ Claude Larose #11 20.00
- ☐ Jacques Lemaire #25 45.00
- ☐ Garry Monahan #20 20.00
- ☐ Claude Provost #14 20.00
- ☐ Mickey Redmond #24 30.00
- ☐ Henri Richard #16 45.00
- ☐ Bobby Rousseau #15 20.00
- ☐ Serge Savard #18 40.00
- ☐ Gilles Tremblay #5 20.00
- ☐ J.C. Tremblay #3 30.00
- ☐ Rogatien Vachon #30 (G) 50.00
- ☐ Carol Vadnais #17 30.00
- ☐ Gump Worsley #1 (G) 45.00

1968 - 69 CANADIENS IGA CARDS

Prices are in NRMT. Regional stars do carry a premium.

Card Size: 1 1/4" x 2 1/4"
Sponsors: IGA
Complete Set (19 cards): 500.00

- ☐ Ralph Backstrom 20.00
- ☐ Jean Béliveau 90.00
- ☐ Yvan Cournoyer 45.00
- ☐ Dick Duff 30.00
- ☐ John Ferguson 30 00
- ☐ Terry Harper 20.00
- ☐ Ted Harris 20.00
- ☐ Jacques Laperrière 30.00
- ☐ Jacques Lemaire 40.00
- ☐ Garry Monahan 20.00
- ☐ Claude Provost 20.00
- ☐ Mickey Redmond 30.00
- ☐ Henri Richard 45.00
- ☐ Bobby Rousseau 20.00
- ☐ Serge Savard 35.00
- ☐ Gilles Tremblay 20.00
- ☐ J.C. Tremblay 30.00
- ☐ Rogatien Vachon (G) 45.00
- ☐ Gump Worsley (G) 40.00

1969 - 70 CANADIENS PROSTAR PROMOTIONS

Cards have a facsimile autograph on the front. There are numerous variations in this set. Prices are in NRMT. Regional stars do carry a premium.

Postcard Size: 3 1/2" x 5 1/2"
Sponsor: ProStar Promotions
Complete Set (31 cards): 110.00

- ☐ Ralph Backstrom 3.00
- ☐ Jean Béliveau 20.00
- ☐ Christian Bordeleau 3.00
- ☐ Pierre Bouchard 3.00
- ☐ Guy Charron 3.00
- ☐ Bill Collins 3.00
- ☐ Yvan Cournoyer 8.00
- ☐ John Ferguson 5.00
- ☐ Terry Harper 3.00
- ☐ Ted Harris 3.00
- ☐ Réjean Houle 5.00
- ☐ Jacques Laperrière 6.00
- ☐ Guy Lapointe 8.00
- ☐ Claude Larose 3.00
- ☐ Jacques Lemaire 7.00
- ☐ Frank Mahovlich 10.00
- ☐ Peter Mahovlich 5.00
- ☐ Phil Myre (G) 5.00
- ☐ Larry Pleau 3.00
- ☐ Claude Provost 3.00
- ☐ Mickey Redmond 5.00
- ☐ Henri Richard 8.00
- ☐ Phil Roberto 3.00
- ☐ Jim Roberts 3.00
- ☐ Bobby Rousseau 3.00
- ☐ Claude Ruel 3.00
- ☐ Serge Savard 6.00
- ☐ Marc Tardif 5.00
- ☐ Gilles Tremblay 3.00
- ☐ J.C. Tremblay 5.00
- ☐ Rogatien Vachon (G) 8.00

1970 - 71 CANADIENS

Prices are in NRMT. Regional stars do carry a premium.

Postcard Size: 3 1/2" x 5 1/2"
Sponsors: none
Complete Set (23 cards): 90.00

- ☐ Ralph Backstrom 3.00
- ☐ Jean Béliveau 18.00
- ☐ Pierre Bouchard 3.00
- ☐ Guy Charron 3.00
- ☐ Bill Collins 3.00
- ☐ Yvan Cournoyer 8.00
- ☐ John Ferguson 5.00
- ☐ Terry Harper 3.00
- ☐ Réjean Houle 5.00
- ☐ Jacques Laperrière 5.00
- ☐ Guy Lapointe 6.00
- ☐ Claude Larose 3.00
- ☐ Jacques Lemaire 7.00
- ☐ Frank Mahovlich 10.00
- ☐ Peter Mahovlich 3.00
- ☐ Phil Myre (G) 5.00
- ☐ Larry Pleau 3.00
- ☐ Mickey Redmond 5.00
- ☐ Henri Richard 8.00
- ☐ Serge Savard 6.00
- ☐ Marc Tardif 5.00
- ☐ J.C. Tremblay 5.00
- ☐ Rogatien Vachon (G) 6.00

1971 CANADIENS PINS

Prices are in NRMT. Regional stars do carry a premium.

Pin Diametre: 1 3/4"
Sponsors: none
Complete Set (22 pins): 150.00

- ☐ Ralph Backstrom 3.00
- ☐ Jean Béliveau 15.00
- ☐ Yvan Cournoyer 7.00
- ☐ Ken Dryden (G) 50.00
- ☐ John Ferguson 5.00
- ☐ Terry Harper 3.00
- ☐ Ted Harris 3.00
- ☐ Guy Lafleur 40.00
- ☐ Jacques Laperrière 5.00
- ☐ Guy Lapointe 5.00
- ☐ Jacques Lemaire 7.00
- ☐ Frank Mahovlich 10.00
- ☐ Peter Mahovlich 3.00
- ☐ Claude Provost 3.00
- ☐ Mickey Redmond 5.00
- ☐ Henri Richard 8.00
- ☐ Bobby Rousseau 3.00
- ☐ Claude Ruel 3.00
- ☐ Serge Savard 5.00
- ☐ J.C. Tremblay 5.00
- ☐ Rogatien Vachon (G) 7.00
- ☐ Gump Worsley (G) 8.00

1971 - 72 CANADIENS PROSTAR PROMOTIONS

Prices are in NRMT. Regional stars do carry a premium.

Card Size: 3 1/2" x 5 1/2"
Sponsor: ProStar Promotions
Complete Set (25 cards): 100.00

- ☐ Pierre Bouchard 2.00
- ☐ Scotty Bowman 5.00
- ☐ Yvan Cournoyer 5.00
- ☐ Denis DeJordy (G) 3.00
- ☐ Ken Dryden (G) 40.00
- ☐ Terry Harper 2.00
- ☐ Dale Hoganson 2.00
- ☐ Réjean Houle 3.00
- ☐ Guy Lafleur 35.00
- ☐ Jacques Laperrière 4.00
- ☐ Guy Lapointe 4.00
- ☐ Claude Larose 2.00
- ☐ Jacques Lemaire 6.00
- ☐ Frank Mahovlich 8.00
- ☐ Peter Mahovlich 2.00
- ☐ Al MacNeil 2.00
- ☐ Phil Myre 3.00
- ☐ Larry Pleau 2.00
- ☐ Henri Richard 6.00
- ☐ Phil Roberto 2.00
- ☐ Jim Roberts 2.00
- ☐ Serge Savard 4.00
- ☐ Marc Tardif 3.00
- ☐ J.C. Tremblay 3.00
- ☐ Rogatien Vachon (G) 5.00

1971 - 72 CANADIENS PROSTAR PROM. UPDATE

Prices are in NRMT. Regional stars do carry a premium. Bobby Sheehan is considered shortprinted.

Card Size: 3 1/2" x 5 1/2"
Sponsor: ProStar Promotions
Complete Set (8 cards): 90.00

- ☐ Jean Béliveau 20.00
- ☐ Yvan Cournoyer 10.00
- ☐ Ken Dryden (G) 50.00
- ☐ Frank Mahovlich 15.00
- ☐ Phil Roberto 5.00
- ☐ Léon Rochefort 5.00
- ☐ Bobby Sheehan 15.00
- ☐ Rogatien Vachon (G) 10.00

1972 - 73 CANADIENS PROSTAR PROMOTIONS

Prices are in NRMT. Regional stars do carry a premium.

Card Size: 3 1/2" x 5 1/2"
Sponsor: ProStar Promotions
Complete Set (22 cards): 100.00

- ☐ Chuck Arnason 2.00
- ☐ Pierre Bouchard 2.00
- ☐ Scotty Bowman 4.00
- ☐ Yvan Cournoyer 5.00
- ☐ Ken Dryden (G) 30.00
- ☐ Réjean Houle 3.00
- ☐ Guy Lafleur 30.00
- ☐ Jacques Laperrière 4.00
- ☐ Guy Lapointe 4.00
- ☐ Claude Larose 2.00
- ☐ Chuck Lefley 2.00
- ☐ Jacques Lemaire 5.00
- ☐ Frank Mahovlich 7.00
- ☐ Peter Mahovlich 2.00
- ☐ Bob Murdoch 2.00
- ☐ Michel Plasse (G) 3.00
- ☐ Henri Richard 5.00
- ☐ Jim Roberts 2.00
- ☐ Serge Savard 4.00
- ☐ Steve Shutt 20.00
- ☐ Marc Tardif 3.00
- ☐ Murray Wilson 2.00

1973 - 74 CANADIENS PROSTAR PROMOTIONS

Prices are in NRMT. Regional stars do carry a premium.

Card Size: 3 1/2" x 5 1/2"
Sponsor: ProStar Promotions
Complete Set (22 cards): 100.00

- ☐ Jean Béliveau 10.00
- ☐ Pierre Bouchard 2.00
- ☐ Scotty Bowman 4.00
- ☐ Yvan Cournoyer 5.00
- ☐ Bob Gainey 10.00
- ☐ Dave Gardner 2.00
- ☐ Guy Lafleur 20.00
- ☐ Yvon Lambert 5.00
- ☐ Jacques Laperrière 4.00
- ☐ Guy Lapointe 4.00
- ☐ Michel Laroque (G) 3.00
- ☐ Claude Larose 2.00
- ☐ Check Lefley 2.00
- ☐ Jacques Lemaire 5.00
- ☐ Frank Mahovlich 7.00
- ☐ Peter Mahovlich 2.00
- ☐ Michel Plasse (G) 3.00
- ☐ Henri Richard 5.00
- ☐ Jim Roberts 2.00
- ☐ Larry Robinson 30.00
- ☐ Serge Savard 4.00
- ☐ Steve Shutt 8.00
- ☐ Wayne Thomas (G) 4.00
- ☐ Murray Wilson 2.00

1974 - 75 CANADIENS

Cards fronts either do or do not have a facsimile signature on the card front. Pierre Bouchard and Yvon Lambert both have variations with and without an autograph. Prices are in NRMT. Regional stars do carry a premium.

Card Size: 3 1/2" x 5 1/2"
Sponsors: none
Complete Set (27 cards): 100.00

- ☐☐ Pierre Bouchard 2.00
- ☐ Scotty Bowman 4.00
- ☐ Rick Chartraw 2.00
- ☐ Yvan Cournoyer 5.00
- ☐ Ken Dryden (G) 20.00
- ☐ Bob Gainey 6.00
- ☐ Glenn Goldup 2.00
- ☐ Guy Lafleur 20.00
- ☐☐ Yvon Lambert 2.00
- ☐ Jacques Laperrière 4.00
- ☐ Guy Lapointe 4.00
- ☐ Michel Larocque (G) 4.00
- ☐ Chuck Lefley 2.00
- ☐ Jacques Lemaire 5.00
- ☐ Peter Mahovlich 2.00
- ☐ Henri Richard 5.00
- ☐ Doug Risebrough 4.00
- ☐ Jim Roberts 2.00
- ☐ Larry Robinson 15.00
- ☐ Glen Sather 4.00
- ☐ Serge Savard 4.00
- ☐ Steve Shutt 6.00
- ☐ Wayne Thomas (G) 4.00
- ☐ Mario Tremblay 6.00
- ☐ John Van Boxmeer 2.00
- ☐ Murray Wilson 2.00

1975 - 76 CANADIENS

Prices are in NRMT. Regional stars do carry a premium.

Card Size: 3 1/2" x 5 1/2"
Sponsors: none
Complete Set (20 cards): 70.00

- ☐ Don Awrey 2.00
- ☐ Pierre Bouchard 2.00
- ☐ Scotty Bowman 4.00
- ☐ Yvan Cournoyer 5.00
- ☐ Ken Dryden (G) 18.00
- ☐ Bob Gainey 6.00
- ☐ Doug Jarvis 5.00
- ☐ Guy Lafleur 18.00
- ☐ Yvon Lambert 2.00
- ☐ Guy Lapointe 4.00
- ☐ Michel Larocque (G) 5.00
- ☐ Jacques Lemaire 5.00
- ☐ Peter Mahovlich 2.00
- ☐ Doug Risebrough 2.00
- ☐ Jim Roberts 2.00
- ☐ Larry Robinson 10.00
- ☐ Serge Savard 4.00
- ☐ Steve Shutt 5.00
- ☐ Mario Tremblay 4.00
- ☐ Murray Wilson 2.00

1976-77 CANADIENS

Prices are in NRMT. Regional stars do carry a premium.
Card Size: 3 1/2" x 5 1/2"
Sponsors: none
Complete Set (23 cards): 70.00

- ☐ Pierre Bouchard 2.00
- ☐ Scotty Bowman 4.00
- ☐ Rick Chartraw 2.00
- ☐ Yvan Cournoyer 5.00
- ☐ Ken Dryden (G) 15.00
- ☐ Bob Gainey 5.00
- ☐ Réjean Houle 4.00
- ☐ Doug Jarvis 2.00
- ☐ Yvon Lambert 2.00
- ☐ Guy Lafleur 15.00
- ☐ Guy Lapointe 4.00
- ☐ Michel Larocque (G) 4.00
- ☐ Jacques Lemaire 5.00
- ☐ Peter Mahovlich 2.00
- ☐ Bill Nyrop 2.00
- ☐ Doug Risebrough 2.00
- ☐ Jim Roberts 2.00
- ☐ Larry Robinson 7.00
- ☐ Claude Ruel 2.00
- ☐ Serge Savard 4.00
- ☐ Steve Shutt 5.00
- ☐ Mario Tremblay 4.00
- ☐ Murray Wilson 2.00

1977 - 78 CANADIENS

Prices are in NRMT. Regional stars do carry a premium.
Card Size: 3 1/2" x 5 1/2"
Sponsors: none
Complete Set (25 cards): 70.00

- ☐ Pierre Bouchard 2.00
- ☐ Scotty Bowman 4.00
- ☐ Rick Chartraw 2.00
- ☐ Yvan Cournoyer 5.00
- ☐ Ken Dryden (G) 12.00
- ☐ Brian Engblom 2.00
- ☐ Bob Gainey 5.00
- ☐ Réjean Houle 4.00
- ☐ Doug Jarvis 2.00
- ☐ Guy Lafleur 12.00
- ☐ Yvon Lambert 2.00
- ☐ Guy Lapointe 4.00
- ☐ Michel Larocque (G) 4.00
- ☐ Pierre Larouche 4.00
- ☐ Jacques Lemaire 5.00
- ☐ Gilles Lupien 2.00
- ☐ Pierre Mondou 4.00
- ☐ Bill Nyrop 2.00
- ☐ Doug Risebrough 2.00
- ☐ Larry Robinson 6.00
- ☐ Claude Ruel 2.00
- ☐ Serge Savard 4.00
- ☐ Steve Shutt 5.00
- ☐ Mario Tremblay 4.00
- ☐ Murray Wilson 2.00

1978 - 79 CANADIENS

Prices are in NRMT. Regional stars do carry a premium.
Card Size: 3 1/2" x 5 1/2"
Sponsors: none
Complete Set (26 cards): 70.00

- ☐ Scotty Bowman 4.00
- ☐ Rick Chartraw 2.00
- ☐ Cam Conner 2.00
- ☐ Yvan Cournoyer 5.00
- ☐ Ken Dryden (G) 10.00
- ☐ Brian Engblom 2.00
- ☐ Bob Gainey 4.00
- ☐ Réjean Houle 4.00
- ☐ Pat Hughes 2/.00
- ☐ Doug Jarvis 2.00
- ☐ Guy Lafleur 10.00
- ☐ Yvon Lambert 2.00
- ☐ Rod Langway 8.00
- ☐ Guy Lapointe 4.00
- ☐ Michel Larocque (G) 4.00
- ☐ Pierre Larouche 4.00
- ☐ Jacques Lemaire 5.00
- ☐ Gilles Lupien 2.00
- ☐ Pierre Mondou 2.00
- ☐ Mark Napier 2.00
- ☐ Doug Risebrough 2.00
- ☐ Larry Robinson 5.00
- ☐ Claude Ruel 2.00
- ☐ Serge Savard 4.00
- ☐ Steve Shutt 5.00
- ☐ Mario Tremblay 4.00

1979 - 80 CANADIENS

Guy Lafleur is the most expensive single at $6-8 in NRMT. Singles start at $1.00. Two cards are supposedly shortprinted and sell at a premium: Bernie Geoffrion at $5-7 and Richard Sévigny at $2-4.
Card Size: 3 1/2" x 5 1/2"
Sponsors: none
Complete Set (25 cards): 40.00

- ☐ Rick Chartraw
- ☐ Normand Dupont
- ☐ Brian Engblom
- ☐ Bob Gainey
- ☐ Bernie Geoffrion
- ☐ Danny Geoffrion
- ☐ Denis Herron (G)
- ☐ Réjean Houle
- ☐ Doug Jarvis
- ☐ Guy Lafleur
- ☐ Yvon Lambert
- ☐ Rod Langway
- ☐ Guy Lapointe
- ☐ Michel Larocque (G)
- ☐ Pierre Larouche
- ☐ Gilles Lupien
- ☐ Pierre Mondou
- ☐ Mark Napier
- ☐ Doug Risebrough
- ☐ Larry Robinson
- ☐ Claude Ruel
- ☐ Serge Savard
- ☐ Richard Sévigny (G)
- ☐ Steve Shutt
- ☐ Mario Tremblay

1980 - 81 CANADIENS

Guy Lafleur is the most expensive single at $6-8. Singles start at $1.50.
Card Size: 3 1/2" x 5 1/2"
Sponsors: none
Complete Set (26 cards): 40.00

- ☐ Keith Acton
- ☐ Bill Baker
- ☐ Rick Chartraw
- ☐ Brian Engblom
- ☐ Bob Gainey
- ☐ Gaston Gingras
- ☐ Denis Herron (G)
- ☐ Réjean Houle
- ☐ Doug Jarvis
- ☐ Guy Lafleur
- ☐ Yvon Lambert
- ☐ Rod Langway
- ☐ Guy Lapointe
- ☐ Michel Larocque (G)
- ☐ Pierre Larouche
- ☐ Pierre Mondou
- ☐ Mark Napier
- ☐ Chris Nilan
- ☐ Doug Risebrough
- ☐ Larry Robinson
- ☐ Claude Ruel
- ☐ Serge Savard
- ☐ Richard Sévigny (G)
- ☐ Steve Shutt
- ☐ Mario Tremblay
- ☐ Doug Wickenheiser

1981 - 82 CANADIENS

Sixteen cards (†) feature the same card photo as the 1980-81 set. Guy Lafleur is the most expensive single at $5-7. Singles start at $1.50.
Card Size: 3 1/2" x 5 1/2"
Sponsors: none
Complete Set (28 cards): 35.00

- ☐ (†) Keith Acton
- ☐ Bob Berry
- ☐ Jeff Brubaker
- ☐ Gilbert Delorme
- ☐ Brian Engblom
- ☐ (†) Bob Gainey
- ☐ (†) Gaston Gingras
- ☐ (†) Denis Herron (G)
- ☐ Réjean Houle
- ☐ Mark Hunter
- ☐ (†) Doug Jarvis
- ☐ (†) Guy Lafleur
- ☐ Rod Langway
- ☐ Jacques Laperrière
- ☐ (†) Guy Lapointe
- ☐ Craig Laughlin
- ☐ (†) Pierre Mondou
- ☐ (†) Mark Napier
- ☐ (†) Chris Nilan
- ☐ Robert Picard
- ☐ (†) Doug Risebrough
- ☐ (†) Larry Robinson
- ☐ (†) Richard Sévigny (G)
- ☐ (†) Steve Shutt
- ☐ (†) Mario Tremblay
- ☐ Rick Wamsley (G)
- ☐ (†) Doug Wickenheiser
- ☐ Team Photo

1982-83 CANADIENS

Guy Lafleur is the most expensive single at $5-7. Singles start at $1.00.
Card Size: 3 1/2" x 5 1/2"
Sponsors: none
Complete Set (28 cards): 30.00

- ☐ Keith Acton
- ☐ Bob Berry
- ☐ Guy Carbonneau
- ☐ Dan Daoust
- ☐ Gilbert Delorme
- ☐ Bob Gainey
- ☐ Gaston Gingras
- ☐ Rick Green
- ☐ Réjean Houle
- ☐ Mark Hunter
- ☐ Guy Lafleur
- ☐ Jacques Laperrière
- ☐ Craig Ludwig
- ☐ Pierre Mondou
- ☐ Mark Napier
- ☐ Mats Naslund
- ☐ Ric Nattress
- ☐ Chris Nilan
- ☐ Robert Picard
- ☐ Henri Richard
- ☐ Larry Robinson
- ☐ Bill Root
- ☐ Richard Sévigny (G)
- ☐ Steve Shutt
- ☐ Mario Tremblay
- ☐ Ryan Walter
- ☐ Rick Wamsley (G)
- ☐ Doug Wickenheiser

1982-83 CANADIENS STEINBERG

Cards originally measured 3 1/2" x 7 1/2" with a coupon. Guy Lafleur is the most expensive single at $4-6. Singles start at 75¢. A cut-out set sells at $20.
Card Size: 3 1/2" x 5 1/2"
Sponsor: Steinberg
Complete Set (24 cards): 25.00
Album: 5.00

- ☐ Keith Acton
- ☐ Guy Carbonneau
- ☐ Gilbert Delorme
- ☐ Bob Gainey
- ☐ Rick Green
- ☐ Réjean Houle
- ☐ Mark Hunter
- ☐ Guy Lafleur
- ☐ Craig Ludwig
- ☐ Pierre Mondou
- ☐ Mark Napier
- ☐ Mats Naslund
- ☐ Ric Nattress
- ☐ Chris Nilan
- ☐ Robert Picard
- ☐ Larry Robinson
- ☐ Bill Root
- ☐ Richard Sévigny (G)
- ☐ Steve Shutt
- ☐ Mario Tremblay
- ☐ Ryan Walter
- ☐ Rick Wamsley (G)
- ☐ Doug Wickenheiser
- ☐ Montréal Canadiens

1983 - 84 CANADIENS

Chris Chelios is the most expensive single at $8-10. Singles start $1.00.
Card Size: 3 1/2" x 5 1/2"
Sponsors: none
Complete Set (32 cards): 30.00

- ☐ Jean Béliveau
- ☐ Bob Berry
- ☐ Guy Carbonneau
- ☐ Kent Carlsson
- ☐ John Chabot
- ☐ Chris Chelios
- ☐ Gilbert Delorme
- ☐ Bob Gainey
- ☐ Rick Green
- ☐ Jean Hamel
- ☐ Mark Hunter
- ☐ Guy Lafleur
- ☐ Jacques Lemaire
- ☐ Jacques Laperrière
- ☐ Craig Ludwig
- ☐ Pierre Mondou
- ☐ Mats Naslund

☐ Ric Nattress
☐ Chris Nilan
☐ Steve Penney (G)
☐ Jacques Plante
☐ Larry Robinson
☐ Bill Root
☐ Richard Sévigny (G)
☐ Steve Shutt
☐ Bobby Smith
☐ Mario Tremblay
☐ Alfie Turcotte
☐ Perry Turnbull
☐ Ryan Walter
☐ Rick Wamsley (G)
☐ Doug Wickenheiser

1984 - 85 CANADIENS

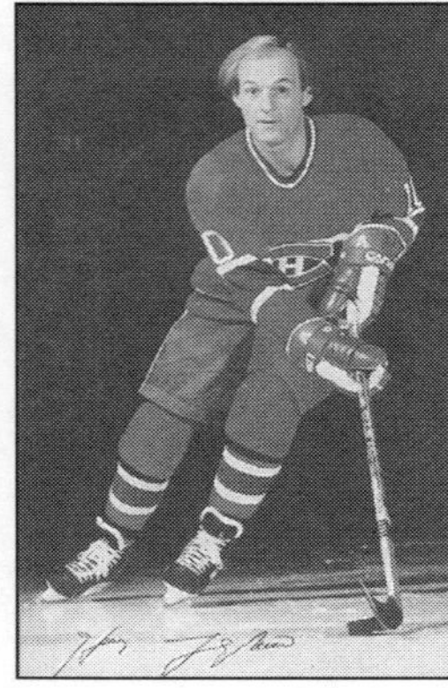

The most expensive players are at Chris Chelios and Guy Lafleur at $4-6. Singles start $1.00.

Card Size: 3 1/2" x 5 1/2"
Sponsors: none
Complete Set (28 cards): 30.00

☐ Guy Carbonneau
☐ Kent Carlsson
☐ Chris Chelios
☐ Lucien DeBlois
☐ Ron Flockhart
☐ Bob Gainey
☐ Rick Green
☐ Jean Hamel
☐ Mark Hunter
☐ Tom Kurvers
☐ Guy Lafleur
☐ Jacques Laperrière
☐ Jacques Lemaire
☐ Craig Ludwig
☐ Pierre Mondou
☐ Mats Naslund
☐ Ric Nattress
☐ Chris Nilan
☐ Mike McPhee
☐ Steve Penney (G)
☐ Jean Perron
☐ Larry Robinson
☐ Bobby Smith
☐ Doug Soetaert (G)
☐ Petr Svoboda
☐ Mario Tremblay
☐ Alfie Turcotte
☐ Ryan Walter

1985 - 86 CANADIENS

Patrick Roy is the most expensive single at $40-50. Claude Lemieux and Stéphane Richer sell at $6-8. Singles start $1.00.

Card Size: 3 1/2" x 5 1/2"
Sponsors: none
Complete Set (28 cards): 100.00

☐ Serge Boisvert
☐ Randy Bucyk
☐ Guy Carbonneau
☐ Chris Chelios
☐ Kjell Dahlin
☐ Bob Gainey
☐ Gaston Gingras
☐ Rick Green
☐ John Kordic
☐ Tom Kurvers
☐ Mike Lalor
☐ Claude Lemieux
☐ Craig Ludwig
☐ David Maley
☐ Mike McPhee
☐ Sergio Momesso
☐ Mats Naslund
☐ Chris Nilan
☐ Steve Penney (G)
☐ Jean Perron
☐ Stéphane Richer
☐ Larry Robinson
☐ Steve Rooney
☐ Patrick Roy (G)
☐ Brian Skrudland
☐ Bobby Smith
☐ Doug Soetaert (G)
☐ Petr Svoboda
☐ Mario Tremblay
☐ Ryan Walter

1985-86 CANADIENS PROVIGO STICKERS

Patrick Roy is the most expensive single at $25-30. Singles start $1.00.

Sticker Size: 1 1/8" x 2 1/4"
Sponsor: Provigo
Complete Set (25 cards): 65.00
Team Binder: 5.00

☐ Guy Carbonneau
☐ Chris Chelios
☐ Kjell Dahlin
☐ Lucien DeBlois
☐ Bob Gainey
☐ Rick Green
☐ Tom Kurvers
☐ Mike Lalor
☐ Craig Ludwig
☐ Mike McPhee
☐ Sergio Momesso
☐ Mats Naslund
☐ Chris Nilan
☐ Steve Penney (G)
☐ Jean Perron
☐ Stéphane Richer
☐ Larry Robinson
☐ Steve Rooney
☐ Patrick Roy (G)
☐ Brian Skrudland
☐ Bobby Smith
☐ Doug Soetaert (G)
☐ Petr Svoboda
☐ Mario Tremblay
☐ Ryan Walter

1985 - 86 CANADIENS PROVIGO/COKE PLACEMATS

The Patrick Roy placemat is the most expensive at $15-20. Single placemats start at $3.

Placemat Size: 10" x 16"
Sponsors: Provigo, Coke, CJMS 128, La Presse
Complete Set (8 placemats): 40.00

☐ Carbonneau/Rooney/McPhee
☐ Chelios/Roy (G)/Momesso
☐ DeBlois/Kurvers/Ludwig
☐ Green/Smith/Lalor
☐ Naslund/Dahlin/Svoboda
☐ Nilan/Soetaert (G)/Robinson
☐ Richer/Walter/Skrudland
☐ Tremblay/Penney (G)/Gainey

1985-86 CANADIENS PROVIGO/PEPSI PLACEMATS

The Chelios/Penney placemat is the most expensive single at $6-8. Single placemats start at $3. The team placemat shows the 12 players in the set.

Placemat Size: 11" x 17"
Sponsors: Provigo, Pepsi
Complete Set (7 placemats): 25.00

☐ Gainey/Carbonneau
☐ Naslund/Kurvers
☐ Nilan/Svoboda
☐ Penney (G)/Chelios
☐ Robinson/Boisvert
☐ Tremblay/Smith
☐ Canadiens

1985-86 CANADIENS PROVIGO/PEPSI PENNANTS

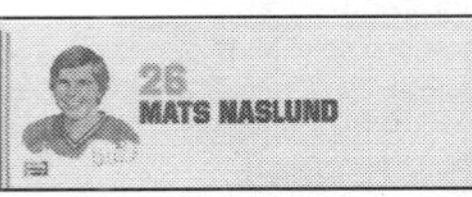

This set features the same artwork as the Provigo/Pepsi placemats. Chris Chelios is the most expensive single at $4-6. Singles start at $2.

Pennant Size: 9 1/2" x 26"
Sponsors: Provigo, Pepsi
Complete Set (12 pennants): 20.00

☐ Serge Boisvert
☐ Guy Carbonneau
☐ Chris Chelios
☐ Bob Gainey
☐ Tom Kurvers
☐ Mats Naslund
☐ Chris Nilan
☐ Steve Penney (G)
☐ Larry Robinson
☐ Bobby Smith
☐ Petr Svoboda
☐ Mario Tremblay

1986 - 87 CANADIENS

Patrick Roy is the most expensive single at $20-25. Singles start $1.00.

Card Size: 3 1/2" x 5 1/2"
Sponsors: none
Complete Set (27 cards): 40.00

☐ Guy Carbonneau
☐ Chris Chelios
☐ Shayne Corson
☐ Kjell Dahlin
☐ Bob Gainey
☐ Gaston Gingras
☐ Rick Green
☐ Brian Hayward (G)
☐ John Kordic
☐ Mike Lalor
☐ Jacques Laperrière
☐ Claude Lemieux
☐ Craig Ludwig
☐ David Maley
☐ Mike McPhee
☐ Sergio Momesso
☐ Mats Naslund
☐ Chris Nilan
☐ Jean Perron
☐ Stéphane Richer
☐ Larry Robinson
☐ Steve Rooney
☐ Patrick Roy (G)
☐ Brian Skrudland
☐ Bobby Smith
☐ Petr Svoboda
☐ Ryan Walter

1987 - 88 CANADIENS

Patrick Roy is the most expensive single at $15-20. Singles start at $1.00. Stéphane Richer has a version with a moustache as well as without.

Card Size: 3 1/2" x 5 1/2"
Sponsors: none
Complete Set (33 cards): 35.00

☐ François Allaire
☐ Guy Carbonneau
☐ Jose Charbonneau
☐ Shayne Corson
☐ Kjell Dahlin
☐ Bob Gainey
☐ Gaston Gingras
☐ Rick Green
☐ Brian Hayward (G)
☐ John Kordic
☐ Mike Lalor
☐ Jacques Laperrière
☐ Claude Lemieux
☐ Craig Ludwig
☐ David Maley
☐ Mike McPhee
☐ Sergio Momesso
☐ Claude Mouton
☐ Mats Naslund
☐ Chris Nilan
☐ Jean Perron
☐ ☐ Stéphane Richer
☐ Larry Robinson
☐ Steve Rooney
☐ Patrick Roy (G)
☐ Scott Sandelin
☐ Serge Savard
☐ Brian Skrudland
☐ Bobby Smith
☐ Petr Svoboda
☐ Gilles Thibodeau
☐ Larry Trader
☐ Ryan Walter

1987 - 88 CANADIENS KODAK PHOTOS

We have no pricing information on this set. These photos may have been issued at an earlier date.

Photo Size: 3 1/2" x 5 1/2"
Sponsors: Kodak

☐ Guy Carbonneau
☐ Bob Gainey
☐ Rick Green
☐ Mike McPhee
☐ Mats Naslund
☐ Chris Nilan
☐ Larry Robinson
☐ Bobby Smith

1987 - 88 CANADIENS VACHON STICKERS

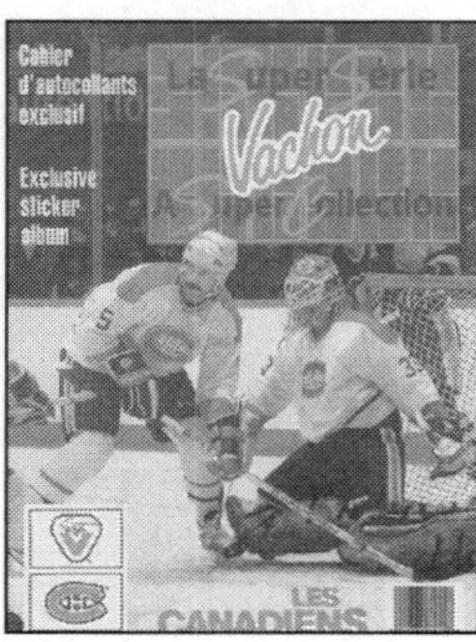

There are 88 stickers in this set. Stickers appear on more than one panel. Other panels may exist. There are sticker variations with or without the sticker number. Panels with Patrick Roy sell at $5-6 while panels with two or more Patrick Roy stickers sells at $6-8. Single panels sell at $1.00.

Panel Size: 2 7/8" x 5 9/16"
Sponsor: Vachon
Album: 5.00

☐ 1 Team Photo TL
7 Jean Perron
28 Bobby Smith
38 Mike McPhee
57 John Kordic
☐ 1 Team Photo TL
38 Mike McPhee
41 Bobby Smith
67 Brian Hayward (G)
Vachon Logo
☐ 2 Team Photo TC
12 Bob Gainey
40 Kjell Dahlin
43 Patrick Roy (G)
70 Rick Green
☐ 2 Team Photo TC
24 Ryan Walter
40 Kjell Dahlin
53 Bob Gainey
82 Chris Chelios
☐ 3 Team Photo TR
7 Jean Perron
28 Bobby Smith
44 Larry Trader
57 John Kordic
☐ 3 Team Photo TR
10 Jean Perron
34 Brian Skrudland
44 Larry Trader
62 Guy Carbonneau
☐ 3 Team Photo TR
41 Bobby Smith
44 Larry Trader
67 Brian Hayward (G)
Vachon
☐ 4 Team Photo BL
12 Bob Gainey
43 Patrick Roy (G)
48 Mats Naslund
70 Rick Green
☐ 4 Team Photo BL
24 Ryan Walter
48 Mats Naslund
53 Bob Gainey
82 Chris Chelios
☐ 5 Team Photo BC
7 Jean Perron
28 Bobby Smith
50 Shayne Corson
57 John Kordic
☐ 5 Team Photo BC
41 Bobby Smith
50 Shayne Corson
67 Brian Hayward (G)
Vachon
☐ 6 Team Photo BR
16 Guy Carbonneau
47 Mats Naslund
52 Stéphane Richer
76 Patrick Roy (G)
☐ 6 Team Photo BR
24 Ryan Walter
52 Stéphane Richer
53 Bob Gainey
82 Chris Chelios
☐ 8 Jacques Laperrière
20 Chris Nilan
29 Mike McPhee
59 Mike Lalor
65 Rick Green
☐ 8 Jacques Laperrière
23 Roy/Carbonneau
29 Mike McPhee
59 Mike Lalor
71 Patrick Roy (G)
☐ 9 François Allaire
25 Ryan Walter
31 Claude Lemieux
61 Brian Hayward (G)
73 Larry Robinson
☐ 9 François Allaire
30 Bobby Smith
31 Claude Lemieux
61 Brian Hayward (G)
77 Petr Svoboda
☐ 9 François Allaire
31 Claude Lemieux
36 Brian Skrudland
61 Brian Hayward (G)
85 Bobby Smith
☐ 9 François Allaire
31 Claude Lemieux
61 Brian Hayward (G)
77 Petr Svoboda
86 Bobby Smith
☐ 10 Jean Perron
34 Brian Skrudland
54 Stéphane Richer
62 Guy Carbonneau
86 Bobby Smith
☐ 11 Jacques Laperrière
23 Roy/Carbonneau
37 Mike McPhee
63 Guy Carbonneau
71 Patrick Roy (G)
☐ 11 Jacques Laperrière
37 Mike McPhee
56 Sergio Momesso
63 Guy Carbonneau
87 Mats Naslund
☐ 13 Bob Gainey
14 Guy Carbonneau
45 Mats Naslund
58 John Kordic
72 Larry Robinson
☐ 13 Bob Gainey
18 Bob Gainey
45 Mats Naslund
64 Brian Hayward (G)
72 Larry Robinson
☐ 13 Bob Gainey
22 Mike Lalor
45 Mats Naslund
68 Rick Green
72 Larry Robinson
☐ 14 Guy Carbonneau
26 Bobby Smith
55 Sergio Momesso
58 John Kordic
83 Chris Chelios
☐ 14 Guy Carbonneau
19 Chris Nilan
49 Shayne Corson
58 John Kordic
78 Chris Chelios
☐ 15 Guy Carbonneau
35 Craig Ludwig
46 Mats Naslund
75 Petr Svoboda
84 Brian Hayward (G)
☐ 17 Mike McPhee
42 Patrick Roy G()
60 Mike Lalor
69 Patrick Roy (G)
88 Bob Gainey
☐ 19 Chris Nilan
22 Mike Lalor
49 Shayne Corson
68 Rick Green
78 Chris Chelios
☐ 20 Chris Nilan
42 Patrick Roy (G)
65 Rick Green
69 Patrick Roy (G)
88 Bob Gainey
☐ 21 Guy Carbonneau
27 Mats Naslund
51 Stéphane Richer
74 Patrick Roy (G)
80 Craig Ludwig
☐ 21 Guy Carbonneau
32 Bobby Smith
51 Stéphane Richer
79 Chris Chelios
80 Craig Ludwig
☐ 21 Guy Carbonneau
35 Craig Ludwig
51 Stéphane Richer
80 Craig Ludwig
84 Brian Hayward (G)
☐ 22 Mike Lalor
26 Bobby Smith
55 Sergio Momesso
68 Rick Green
83 Chris Chelios
☐ 23 Roy/Carbonneau
42 Patrick Roy (G)
69 Patrick Roy (G)
71 Patrick Roy (G)
88 Bob Gainey
☐ 30 Bobby Smith
39 Kjell Dahlin
66 Rick Green
77 Petr Svoboda
Vachon
☐ 33 Claude Lemieux
39 Kjell Dahlin
66 Rick Green
81 Craig Ludwig
Vachon
☐ 42 Patrick Roy (G)
56 Sergio Momesso
69 Patrick Roy (G)
87 Mats Naslund
88 Bob Gainey

1988 - 89 CANADIENS

Patrick Roy is the most expensive single at $12-15. Singles start $1.00.

Card Size: 3 1/2" x 5 1/2"
Sponsors: none
Complete Set (30 cards): 30.00

☐ François Allaire
☐ Pat Burns
☐ Guy Carbonneau
☐ José Charbonneau
☐ Chris Chelios
☐ Ronald Corey
☐ Shayne Corson
☐ Russ Courtnall
☐ Eric Desjardins
☐ Bob Gainey
☐ Brent Gilchrist
☐ Rick Green
☐ Brian Hayward (G)
☐ Mike Keane
☐ Mike Lalor
☐ Jacques Laperrière
☐ Claude Lemieux
☐ Craig Ludwig
☐ Steve Martinson
☐ Mike McPhee
☐ Mats Naslund
☐ Stéphane Richer
☐ Larry Robinson
☐ Patrick Roy (G)
☐ Serge Savard
☐ Brian Skrudland
☐ Bobby Smith
☐ Petr Svoboda
☐ Gilles Thibodeau
☐ Ryan Walter

1989 - 90 CANADIENS

Patrick Roy is the most expensive single at $8-10. Singles start $1.00.

Card Size: 3 1/2" x 5 1/2"
Sponsors: none
Complete Set (32 cards): 30.00

☐ François Allaire
☐ Pat Burns
☐ Guy Carbonneau
☐ Chris Chelios
☐ Tom Chorske
☐ Ronald Corey
☐ Shayne Corson
☐ Russ Courtnall
☐ J.J. Daigneault
☐ Eric Desjardins
☐ Martin Desjardins
☐ Donald Dufresne
☐ Brent Gilchrist
☐ Brian Hayward (G)
☐ Mike Keane
☐ Jacques Laperrière
☐ Stéphan Lebeau
☐ Sylvain Lefebvre
☐ Claude Lemieux
☐ Jocelyn Lemieux
☐ Craig Ludwig
☐ Jyrki Lumme
☐ Steve Martinson
☐ Mike McPhee
☐ Mats Naslund
☐ Stéphane Richer
☐ Patrick Roy (G)
☐ Serge Savard
☐ Brian Skrudland
☐ Bobby Smith
☐ Petr Svoboda
☐ Ryan Walter

1989 - 90 CANADIENS KRAFT/LE JOURNAL

This set was originally issued in panels. Patrick Roy is the most expensive single at $8-10. Cut out singles start at 75¢.

Card Size: 3 3/4" x 5 1/2"
Sponsors: Kraft, Le Journal
Complete Set (24 cards): 25.00

☐ Pat Burns
☐ Guy Carbonneau #21
☐ Chris Chelios #24
☐ Shayne Corson #27
☐ Russ Courtnall #6
☐ J.J. Daigneault #48
☐ Eric Desjardins #28
☐ Todd Ewen #36
☐ Brent Gilchrist #41
☐ Brian Hayward #1 (G)
☐ Mike Keane #12
☐ Stephane Lebeau #47
☐ Sylvain Lefebvre #3
☐ Claude Lemieux #32
☐ Craig Ludwig #17
☐ Mike McPhee #35
☐ Mats Naslund #26
☐ Stéphane Richer #44
☐ Patrick Roy #33 (G)
☐ Mathieu Schneider #18
☐ Brian Skrudland #39
☐ Bobby Smith #15
☐ Petr Svoboda #25
☐ Ryan Walter #11

1989-90 CANADIENS PROVIGO FIGURINES

Patrick Roy is the most expensive figurine at $35-40. Singles start at $5.

Figurine height: 3"

Sponsor: Provigo

Complete Set (13 figurines): 80.00

- ☐ Guy Carbonneau #21
- ☐ Chris Chelios #24
- ☐ Shayne Corson #27
- ☐ Russ Courtnall #6
- ☐ Bob Gainey #23
- ☐ Craig Ludwig #17
- ☐ Mike McPhee #35
- ☐ Mats Naslund #26
- ☐ Stéphane Richer #44
- ☐ Patrick Roy #33 (G)
- ☐ Brian Skrudland #39
- ☐ Bobby Smith #15
- ☐ Petr Svoboda #25

1990 - 91 CANADIENS

Patrick Roy is the most expensive single at $6-8. Singles start $1.00.

Card Size: 3 1/2" x 5 1/2"

Sponsors: none

Complete Set (33 cards): 25.00

- ☐ François Allaire
- ☐ Jean-Claude Bergeron (G)
- ☐ Benoît Brunet
- ☐ Pat Burns
- ☐ Guy Carbonneau
- ☐ Andrew Cassels
- ☐ Tom Chorske
- ☐ Ronald Corey
- ☐ Shayne Corson
- ☐ Russ Courtnall
- ☐ J.J. Daigneault
- ☐ Eric Desjardins
- ☐ Gerald Diduck
- ☐ Don Dufresne
- ☐ Todd Ewen
- ☐ Brent Gilchrist
- ☐ Mike Keane
- ☐ Jacques Laperrière
- ☐ Stéphan Lebeau
- ☐ Sylvain Lefebvre
- ☐ Mike McPhee
- ☐ Lyle Odelein
- ☐ Mark Pederson
- ☐ Stephane Richer
- ☐ Patrick Roy (G)
- ☐ Denis Savard
- ☐ Serge Savard
- ☐ Mathieu Schneider
- ☐ Brian Skrudland
- ☐ Petr Svoboda
- ☐ Charles Thiffault
- ☐ Sylvain Turgeon
- ☐ Ryan Walter

1991 - 92 CANADIENS

Patrick Roy and John LeClair are the most expensive singles at $5-7. Singles start at $1.00.

Card Size: 3 1/2" x 5 1/2"

Sponsors: none

Complete Set (31 cards): 30.00

- ☐ François Allaire
- ☐ Patrice Brisebois
- ☐ Pat Burns
- ☐ Guy Carbonneau
- ☐ Ron Corey
- ☐ Shayne Corson
- ☐ Alain Côté
- ☐ Russ Courtnall
- ☐ J.J. Daigneault
- ☐ Eric Desjardins
- ☐ Don Dufresne
- ☐ Todd Ewen
- ☐ Brent Gilchrist
- ☐ Mike Keane
- ☐ Jacques Laperrière
- ☐ Stéphan Lebeau
- ☐ John LeClair
- ☐ Sylvain Lefebvre
- ☐ Mike McPhee
- ☐ Kirk Muller
- ☐ Lyle Odelein
- ☐ André Racicot (G)
- ☐ Mario Roberge
- ☐ Patrick Roy (G)
- ☐ Denis Savard
- ☐ Serge Savard
- ☐ Mathieu Schneider
- ☐ Brian Skrudland
- ☐ Petr Svoboda
- ☐ Charles Thiffault
- ☐ Sylvain Turgeon

1992 - 93 CANADIENS

The most expensive singles are Patrick Roy at $5-7 and John LeClair at $4-6. Singles start $1.00.00.

Card Size: 3 1/2" x 5 1/2"

Sponsors: none

Complete Set (27 cards): 25.00

- ☐ Brian Bellows
- ☐ Patrice Brisebois
- ☐ Benoît Brunet
- ☐ Guy Carbonneau
- ☐ J.J. Daigneault
- ☐ Vincent Damphousse
- ☐ Eric Desjardins
- ☐ Jacques Demers
- ☐ Gilbert Dionne
- ☐ Don Dufresne
- ☐ Todd Ewen
- ☐ Kevin Haller
- ☐ Sean Hill
- ☐ Mike Keane
- ☐ Patric Kjellberg
- ☐ Stephan Lebeau
- ☐ John LeClair
- ☐ Kirk Muller
- ☐ Lyle Odelein
- ☐ Oleg Petrov
- ☐ André Racicot (G)
- ☐ Mario Roberge
- ☐ Ed Ronan
- ☐ Patrick Roy (G)
- ☐ Denis Savard
- ☐ Mathieu Schneider
- ☐ Brian Skrudland

1992 - 93 CANADIENS O-PEE-CHEE FANFEST

This set was issued in a puck-shaped box for the 1993 All-Star Fanfest in Montréal. 5000 sets were made. The promo panel features Henri Richard, Jean Béliveau, Yvan Cournoyer and Maurice Richard.

Card Size: 3 1/2" x 5 1/2"

Sponsor: O-Pee-Chee

Complete Set (66 cards): 75.00

Promo Panel: 5.00

	No.	Player	Price
☐	1	Montréal Forum	.50
☐	2	Butch Bouchard	1.00
☐	3	Henri Richard	1.75
☐	4	Serge Savard	.75
☐	5	HL:Toe Blake	1.75
☐	6	HL:Maurice Richard	6.00
☐	7	Stéphan Lebeau	.50
☐	8	Kevin Haller	.50
☐	9	Guy Carbonneau	.50
☐	10	Jacques Demers	.50
☐	11	Serge Savard	.75
☐	12	Montréal Forum	.50
☐	13	Howie Morenz	4.00
☐	14	Jean Béliveau	4.00
☐	15	Jacques Laperrière	1.00
☐	16	Bob Gainey	1.50
☐	17	HL: Guy Lafleur	4.00
☐	18	Jacques Raymond	.50
☐	19	Sean Hill	.50
☐	20	Eric Desjardins	.50
☐	21	Aurèle Joliat	3.00
☐	22	Doug Harvey	2.00
☐	23	Yvan Cournoyer	2.00
☐	24	HL: Frank Mahovlich	2.00
☐	25	J.J. Daigneault	.50
☐	26	Kirk Muller	.50
☐	27	Jean Béliveau	4.00
☐	28	Georges Vézina (G)	3.50
☐	29	Maurice Richard	6.00
☐	30	Patrick Roy (G)	6.00
☐	31	Benoît Brunet	.50
☐	32	HL: Jacques Plante	3.00
☐	33	Ralph Backstrom	.50
☐	34	Elmer Lach	1.50
☐	35	Stanley Cup Winners	1.00
☐	36	Jacques Laperrière	1.00
☐	37	Statistics	.50
☐	38	Vincent Damphousse	1.00
☐	39	Frank Mahovlich	2.00
☐	40	Jacques Plante (G)	3.00
☐	41	Stanley Cup Winners	1.00
☐	42	Kenny Reardon	1.00
☐	43	Claude Provost	.50
☐	44	HL: Jean Béliveau	4.00
☐	45	Ed Ronan	.50
☐	46	Statistics	.50
☐	47	Bill Durnan	1.75
☐	48	Stanley Cup	1.25
☐	49	Patrice Brisebois	.50
☐	50	Denis Savard	.75
☐	51	Ken Dryden (G)	4.50
☐	52	Lou Fontinato	.50
☐	53	Jean-Guy Talbot	.50
☐	54	Bernie Geoffrion	2.25
☐	55	Joe Malone	1.25
☐	56	Oleg Petrov	.50
☐	57	Guy Lafleur	4.00
☐	58	Bert Olmstead	1.00
☐	59	Dream Team	2.00
☐	60	Brian Bellows	.50
☐	61	HL: Henri Richard	2.00
☐	62	Jacques Lemaire	2.00
☐	63	Dickie Moore	1.50
☐	64	Gump Worsley (G)	2.25
☐	65	Toe Blake	2.00
☐	66	Checklist	.50

1993 - 94 CANADIENS

Patrick Roy is the most expensive single at $4-6. Singles start $1.00.

Card Size: 3 1/2" x 5 1/2"

Sponsors: none

Complete Set (26 cards): 20.00

- ☐ Brian Bellows
- ☐ Patrice Brisebois
- ☐ Benoît Brunet
- ☐ Guy Carbonneau
- ☐ J.J. Daigneault
- ☐ Vincent Damphousse
- ☐ Jacques Demers
- ☐ Eric Desjardins
- ☐ Gilbert Dionne
- ☐ Paul DiPietro
- ☐ Kevin Haller
- ☐ Mike Keane
- ☐ Stephan Lebeau
- ☐ John LeClair
- ☐ Gary Leeman
- ☐ Kirk Muller
- ☐ Lyle Odelein
- ☐ Peter Popovic
- ☐ André Racicot (G)
- ☐ Rob Ramage
- ☐ Mario Roberge
- ☐ Ed Ronan
- ☐ Patrick Roy (G)
- ☐ Matheiu Schneider
- ☐ Pierre Sévigny
- ☐ Ron Wilson

1993 - 94 CANADIENS MOLSON EXPORT

Singles start at $4. Photos were given out on game nights. Other singles may exist.

Photo Size: 8" x 10 1/2"

Sponsor: Molson

- ☐ 16OCT93 Guy Carbonneau
- ☐ 03NOV93 Mike Keane
- ☐ 20NOV93 Kirk Muller
- ☐ 12JAN94 Brian Bellows
- ☐ 17JAN94 Benoît Brunet
- ☐ 30JAN94 Mathieu Schneider
- ☐ 23FEB94 Kevin Haller
- ☐ 16MAR94 Peter Popovic
- ☐ 21APR94 Mario Roberge

1994 - 95 CANADIENS

Patrick Roy is the most expensive single at $4-6. Singles start at $1.00.

Card Size: 3 1/2" x 5 1/2"

Sponsor: none

Complete Set (27 cards): 20.00

- ☐ Brian Bellows
- ☐ Donald Brashear
- ☐ Patrice Brisebois
- ☐ Benoît Brunet
- ☐ J.J. Daigneault
- ☐ Vincent Damphousse
- ☐ Jacques Demers
- ☐ Eric Desjardins
- ☐ Gilbert Dionne
- ☐ Paul DiPietro
- ☐ Gerry Fleming
- ☐ Bryan Fogarty
- ☐ Mike Keane
- ☐ John LeClair
- ☐ Jim Montgomery
- ☐ Kirk Muller
- ☐ Lyle Odelein
- ☐ Oleg Petrov
- ☐ Peter Popovic
- ☐ Yves Racine
- ☐ Ed Ronan
- ☐ Patrick Roy (G)
- ☐ Brian Savage
- ☐ Mathieu Schneider
- ☐ Pierre Sévigny
- ☐ Turner Stevenson
- ☐ Ron Tugnutt (G)

1994 - 95 CANADIENS MOLSON EXPORT

Photos were given out on game nights. Singles start at $4. Other singles exist.

Photo Size: 8" x 10 1/2"

Sponsor: Molson

- ☐ 18SEP94 Ron Tugnutt
- ☐ 29JAN95 Patrice Brisebois
- ☐ 20FEB95 Lyle Odelein
- ☐ 25MAR95 Pierre Sévigny
- ☐ 08APR95 Bryan Fogarty
- ☐ 29APR95 Yves Racine

1995 - 96 CANADIENS

Patrick Roy and Saku Koivu are the most expensive singles at $4-5. Singles start at $1.00.

Card Size: 3 1/2" x 5 1/2"

Sponsors: none

Complete Set (20 cards): 20.00

- ☐ Donald Brashear
- ☐ Patrice Brisebois
- ☐ Benoît Brunet
- ☐ Valeri Bure
- ☐ Marc Bureau
- ☐ Vincent Damphousse
- ☐ Mike Keane
- ☐ Saku Koivu
- ☐ Vladimir Malakhov
- ☐ Lyle Odelein
- ☐ Oleg Petrov
- ☐ Petr Popovic
- ☐ Stéphane Quintal
- ☐ Yves Racine
- ☐ Mark Recchi
- ☐ Patrick Roy (G)
- ☐ Brian Savage
- ☐ Turner Stevenson
- ☐ Mario Tremblay
- ☐ Pierre Turgeon

1995 - 96 CANADIENS FORUM TICKETS

Prices reflect red seat tickets.

Card Size: 2 7/8" x 7 1/2"

Sponsors: none

Complete Set (47 cards): 650.00

	Date	Player	Price
☐	18SEP	Montréal Forum	10.00
☐	20SEP	Jack Laviolette	10.00
☐	23SEP	Edouard Lalonde	10.00
☐	27SEP	Didier Pitre	10.00
☐	30SEP	Georges Vézina (G)	30.00
☐	07OCT	Joe Malone	15.00
☐	14OCT	Joe Hall	10.00
☐	21OCT	Sprague Cleghorn	10.00

☐ 23OCT Aurèle Joliat 25.00
☐ 25OCT Sylvio Mantha 15.00
☐ 28OCT Howie Morenz 40.00
☐ 04NOV Herb Gardiner 10.00
☐ 08NOV George Hainsworth (G) 20.00
☐ 18NOV Toe Blake 10.00
☐ 20NOV Albert Siebert 10.00
☐ 25NOV Kenneth Reardon 10.00
☐ 02DEC Elmer Lach 10.00
☐ 06DEC Herbert O'Conner 10.00
☐ 09DEC Emile Bouchard 10.00
☐ 16DEC M.Richard/B.Durnan 50.00
☐ 23DEC Doug Harvey 25.00
☐ 06JAN Bert Olmstead 10.00
☐ 08JAN Tom Johnson 10.00
☐ 10JAN Dickie Moore 15.00
☐ 13JAN Bernie Geoffrion 25.00
☐ 22JAN Jean Béliveau 40.00
☐ 27JAN Jacques Plante (G) 40.00
☐ 28JAN Henri Richard 30.00
☐ 31JAN Gump Worsley (G) 25.00
☐ 10FEB Jacques Laperrière 10.00
☐ 12FEB Yvan Cournoyer 20.00
☐ 17FEB Jacques Lemaire 20.00
☐ 24FEB Serge Savard 15.00
☐ 09MAR Guy Lapointe 15.00
☐ 11MAR Frank Mahovlich 25.00
☐ 16MAR Ken Dryden (G) 50.00
☐ 18MAR Guy Lafleur 50.00
☐ 20MAR Steve Shutt 20.00
☐ 23MAR Bob Gainey 20.00
☐ 25MAR Molson/Raymond 10.00
☐ 27MAR F.Selke/J.A.O'Brien 10.00
☐ 01APR Dandurand/Gorman 10.00
☐ 03APR Cattarinch/Northey 10.00
☐ 06APR S.Pollock/S.Bowman 15.00
☐ 13APR Montréal Forum 10.00

1995 - 96 CANADIENS MOLSON EXPORT

Singles start at $4. Photos were given out on game nights. Other singles may exist.
Photo Size: 8" x 11"
Sponsor: Molson

☐ 07OCT95 Benoît Brunet
☐ 25OCT95 Vladimir Malakhov
☐ 20NOV95 Stéphane Quintal
☐ 16DEC95 Brian Savage
☐ 10JAN96 Patrice Brisebois
☐ 13JAN96 Mark Recchi
☐ 31JAN96 Vincent Damphousse
☐ 24FEB96 Pierre Turgeon
☐ 09MAR96 Lyle Odelein
☐ 25MAR96 Turner Stevenson
☐ 01APR96 Peter Popovic
☐ 13APR96 Saku Koivu
☐ 28APR96 Valeri Bure

1995-96 CANADIENS MCDONALD'S

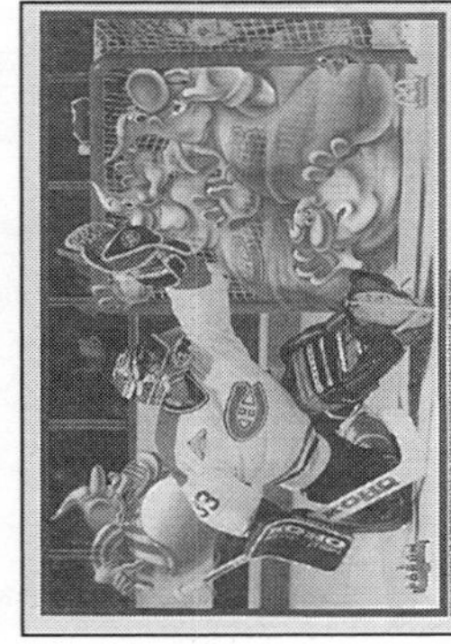

Placemat sell at $10-12.
Placemat Size:11" x 17"
Sponsor: McDonald's
Complete Set (4 placemats): 35.00

☐ Jean Béliveau
☐ Guy Lafleur
☐ Patrick Roy
☐ M.Richard/G.Lafleur/J.Béliveau

1996 - 97 CANADIENS MOLSON EXPORT

Photos were given out on game nights. Singles start at $4. Other singles exist.
Photo Size: 8" x 11"
Sponsor: Molson

☐ 16SEP96 Peter Popovic
☐ 22SEP96 Mark Recchi
☐ 04DEC96 Vladimir Malakhov
☐ 11DEC96 David Wilkie
☐ 21DEC96 Stéphane Quintal
☐ 04JAN97 Scott Thornton
☐ 11JAN97 Turner Stevenson
☐ 20JAN97 Saku Koivu
☐ 05APR97 Dave Manson
☐ 07APR97 Jassen Cullimore

1996 - 98 CANADIENS

This new series of Canadiens' postcards started with the 1996-97 season. Photos are taken by Robert Laberge.
Team sets were available at the Molson Centre as well as through the Canadiens' fan club.
12 cards were the same in both the 1996-97 and 1997-98 sets. Players were added or removed from the team set when they were traded.
Team sets sell at $12-15. Saku Koivu is the most expensive single at $3-4 while singles start at 75¢.
Card Size: 3" x 5 1/2"
Sponsors: none

☐ 96/7 Murray Baron #36
☐ 97/8 Sébastien Bordeleau #71
☐ 96-8 Patrice Brisebois #43
☐ 96-8 Benoît Brunet #17
☐ 96/7 Valeri Bure #18
☐ 97/8 Valeri Bure #20
☐ 96-8 Marc Bureau #28
☐ 97/8 Brett Clark #29
☐ 96-8 Shayne Corson #27
☐ 96/7 Jassen Cullimore #35
☐ 96-8 Vincent Damphousse #25
☐ 97/8 Jonas Hoglund #44
☐ 96/7 Pat Jablonski (G) #39
☐ 96/7 Saku Koivu #11 (Cooper equip.)
☐ 97/8 Saku Koivu #11 (Nike equip.)
☐ 96-8 Vladimir Malakhov #18
☐ 97/8 Dave Manson #22
☐ 97/8 Andy Moog (G) #35
☐ 96/7 Chris Murray #22
☐ 96-8 Peter Popovic #34
☐ 97/8 Patrick Poulin #37
☐ 96/7 Stéphane Quintal #5 (Home)
☐ 97/8 Stéphane Quintal #5 (Away)
☐ 96-8 Mark Recchi #8
☐ 96/7 Stéphane Richer #44
☐ 97/8 Craig Rivet #52
☐ 96-8 Martin Rucinsky #26
☐ 96-8 Brian Savage #49
☐ 96/7 Turner Stevenson #30
☐ 97/8 Turner Stevenson #23
☐ 96-8 Jocelyn Thibault (G) #41
☐ 96-8 Scott Thornton #24
☐ 96/7 Darcy Tucker #42
☐ 97/8 Igor Ulanov #55
☐ 97/8 Mick Vukota #21
☐ 96/7 David Wilkie #3
☐ 97/8 Zarley Zalapski #3
☐ 96/7 Mario Tremblay, Coach
☐ 97/8 Alain Vigneault, Coach

NASHVILLE PREDATORS

No sets known.

NEW JERSEY DEVILS

1983 - 84 DEVILS

The most expensive singles are John MacLean at $6-8 and Pat Verbeek at $5-6. Singles start at 75¢.
Card Size: 3 1/2" x 6"
Sponsors: none
Complete Set (25 cards): 25.00

☐ Mike Antonovich
☐ Mel Bridgman
☐ Aaron Broten
☐ Murray Bromwell
☐ Dave Cameron
☐ Rich Chernomaz
☐ Joe Cirella
☐ Ken Daneyko
☐ Larry Floyd
☐ Paul Gagné
☐ Mike Kitchen
☐ Jeff Larmer
☐ Don Lever
☐ Dave Lewis
☐ Bob Lorimer
☐ Ron Low (G)
☐ Jan Ludvig
☐ John MacLean
☐ Bob MacMillan
☐ Hector Marini
☐ Rick Meagher
☐ Grant Mulvey
☐ Glenn Resch (G)
☐ Phil Russell
☐ Pat Verbeek

1984 - 85 DEVILS

Kirk Muller is the most expensive single at $5-7. Singles start at 75¢.
Card Size: 3 1/2" x 6"
Sponsors: none
Complete Set (25 cards): 20.00

☐ Mel Bridgman #18
☐ Aaron Broten #10
☐ Doug Carpenter
☐ Rich Chernomaz #14
☐ Joe Cirella #2
☐ Bruce Driver #23
☐ Paul Gagne #17
☐ Uli Hiemer #28
☐ Tim Higgins #20
☐ Bob Hoffmeyer #21
☐ Hannu Kamppurri #33 (G)
☐ Don Lever #9
☐ Dave Lewis #25
☐ Bob Lorimer #4
☐ Ron Low #30 (G)
☐ Jan Ludvig #29
☐ John MacLean #15
☐ Rick Meagher #16
☐ Kirk Muller #27
☐ Dave Pichette #8
☐ Rich Preston #19
☐ Glenn Resch #1 (G)
☐ Phil Russell #5
☐ Doug Sulliman #22
☐ Pat Verbeek #12

1985 - 86 DEVILS

Reportedly 3,000 sets were produced. Kirk Muller is the most expensive single at $6-8. Singles start at $1.50.
Card Size: 3 5/8" x 5 1/2"
Sponsors: none
Complete Set (10 cards): 18.00

☐ 1 Mark Johnson
☐ 2 Craig Billington (G)
☐ 3 Alain Chevrier (G)
☐ 4 Paul Gagné
☐ 5 Greg Adams
☐ 6 Glenn Resch (G)
☐ 7 Craig Wolanin
☐ 8 Perry Anderson
☐ 9 Kirk Muller
☐ 10 Randy Velischek

1986 - 87 DEVILS S.O.B.E.R.

Kirk Muller is the most expensive single at $4-5. Singles start at 75¢.
Card Size: 2 1/2" x 3 1/2"
Sponsors: S.O.B.E.R., Howard Bank, Independant Insurance Agents of Bergun County
Complete Set (20 cards): 25.00

☐ Greg Adams #24
☐ Perry Anderson #25
☐ Timo Blomqvist #5
☐ Andy Brickley #26
☐ Mel Bridgman #18
☐ Aaron Broten #10
☐ Alain Chevrier #30 (G)
☐ Joe Cirella #2
☐ Ken Daneyko #3
☐ Bruce Driver #23
☐ Uli Hiemer #28
☐ Mark Johnson #12
☐ Jan Ludvig #29
☐ John MacLean #15
☐ Peter McNab #7
☐ Kirk Muller #9
☐ Doug Sulliman #22
☐ Randy Velischek #27
☐ Pat Verbeek #16
☐ Craig Wolanin #16

1987 - 88 DEVILS

We have little information on this set. Other singles exist.
Card Size: 3 3/4" x 4 3/4"
Sponsors: none

☐ Bob Sauvé #28 (G)

1988 - 89 DEVILS CARETTA TRUCKING

The most expensive singles are Brendan Shanahan at $12-15 and Sean Burke at $4-5. Singles start at $75¢.
Card Size: 2 7/8" x 4 1/4"
Sponsor: Caretta Trucking
Complete Set (30 cards): 35.00

☐ Perry Anderson #25
☐ Bob Bellemore
☐ Aaron Broten #10
☐ Doug Brown #24
☐ Sean Burke #1 (G)
☐ Anders Carlsson #20
☐ Joe Cirella #2
☐ Pat Conacher #32
☐ Ken Daneyko #3
☐ Bruce Driver #23
☐ Bob Hoffmeyer
☐ Jamie Huscroft #4
☐ Mark Johnson #12
☐ Jim Korn #14
☐ Tom Kurvers #5
☐ Lou Lamoriello
☐ Claude Loiselle #19
☐ John MacLean #15
☐ David Maley #8
☐ Doug McKay
☐ Kirk Muller #9
☐ Jack O'Callahan #7
☐ Steve Rooney #18
☐ Bob Sauvé #28 (G)
☐ Jim Schoenfeld
☐ Brendan Shanahan #11
☐ Patrik Sundstrom #17
☐ Randy Velischek #27
☐ Pat Verbeek #16
☐ Craig Wolanin #6

1989 - 90 DEVILS CARETTA TRUCKING

There are two variations: cards with the Caretta Trucking logo and cards without the logo. Brendan Shanahan is the most expensive single at $8-10. Singles start at $75¢.

Card Size: 2 7/8" x 4 1/4"
Sponsor: Caretta Trucking
Complete Set (29 cards): 25.00

☐ ☐ Tommy Albelin #26
☐ ☐ Bob Bellemore
☐ ☐ Neil Brady #19
☐ ☐ Aaron Broten #10
☐ ☐ Doug Brown #24
☐ ☐ Sean Burke #1 (G)
☐ ☐ Pat Conacher #32
☐ ☐ John Cunniff
☐ ☐ Ken Daneyko #3
☐ ☐ Bruce Driver #23
☐ ☐ Viacheslav Fetisov #2
☐ ☐ Mark Johnson #12
☐ ☐ Jim Korn #14
☐ ☐ Lou Lamoriello
☐ ☐ John MacLean #15
☐ ☐ David Maley #8
☐ ☐ Kirk Muller #9
☐ ☐ Janne Ojanen #22
☐ ☐ Walt Poddubny #21
☐ ☐ Reijo Ruotsalainen #29
☐ ☐ Brendan Shanahan #11
☐ ☐ Sergei Starikov #4
☐ ☐ Patrik Sundstrom #17
☐ ☐ Peter Sundstrom #20
☐ ☐ Chris Terreri #31 (G)
☐ ☐ Sylvain Turgeon #16
☐ ☐ Randy Velischek #27
☐ ☐ Eric Weinrich #7
☐ ☐ Craig Wolanin #6

1990 - 91 DEVILS

Brendan Shanahan is the most expensive single at $6-8. Singles start at 75¢.

Card Size: 2 1/2" x 3 1/2"
Sponsors: none
Complete Set (20 cards): 20.00

☐ Tommy Albelin
☐ Laurie Boschman
☐ Doug Brown
☐ Sean Burke (G)
☐ Tim Burke
☐ Zdeno Ciger
☐ Pat Conacher
☐ Troy Crowder
☐ John Cunniff
☐ Ken Daneyko
☐ Bruce Driver
☐ Viacheslav Fetisov
☐ Alexei Kasatonov
☐ Lou Lamoriello
☐ Claude Lemieux
☐ David Maley
☐ John MacLean
☐ Jon Morris
☐ Kirk Muller
☐ Lee Norwood
☐ Myles O'Connor
☐ Walt Poddubny
☐ Brendan Shanahan
☐ Peter Stastny
☐ Alan Stewart
☐ Warren Strelow
☐ Doug Sulliman
☐ Patrik Sundstrom
☐ Chris Terreri (G)
☐ Eric Weinrich

1991 - 92 DEVILS

Singles start at $3.

Card Size: 2 1/2" x 6"
Sponsors: none
Complete Set (10 cards): 20.00

☐ 82-83 Devils Photo
☐ 83-84 Devils Photo
☐ 84-85 Devils Photo
☐ 85-86 Devils Photo
☐ 86-87 Devils Photo
☐ 87-88 Devils Photo
☐ 88-89 Devils Photo
☐ 89-90 Devils Photo
☐ 90-91 Devils Photo
☐ 91-92 Devils Photo

1996 - 97 DEVILS SHARP ELECTRONICS

Martin Brodeur is the most expensive single at $2-3. Singles start at 50¢.

Card Size: 2 1/2" x 3 1/2"
Sponsor: Sharp Electronics
Complete Set (30 cards): 20.00

☐ Mike Dunham (G) #1
☐ Ken Daneyko #3
☐ Scott Stevens #4
☐ Denis Pederson #10
☐ Steve Sullivan #11
☐ Bill Guerin #12
☐ Brian Rolston #14
☐ John MacLean #15
☐ Bobby Holik #16
☐ Petr Sykora #17
☐ Sergei Brylin #18
☐ Bob Carpenter #19
☐ Jay Pandolfo #20
☐ Randy McKay #21
☐ Patrik Elias #22
☐ Dave Andreychuk #23
☐ Lyle Odelein #24
☐ Valeri Zelepukin #25
☐ Jason Smith #26
☐ Scott Niedermayer #27
☐ Kevin Dean #28
☐ Shawn Chambers #29
☐ Martin Brodeur (G) #30
☐ Steve Thomas #32
☐ Reid Simpson #33
☐ Lou Lamoriello, G.M.
☐ Jacques Lemaire, Coach
☐ Jacques Caron, Asst. Coach
☐ Robbie Ftorek, Asst. Coach
☐ John H. McMullen, Owner

NEW YORK ISLANDERS

1979 - 80 ISLANDERS

Prices are in NRMT. Regional stars do carry a premium.

Card Size: 3" x 5"
Sponsors: none
Complete Set (22 cards): 60.00

☐ Mike Bossy 12.00
☐ Bob Bourne 2.00
☐ Curt Giles 2.00
☐ Billy Harris 2.00
☐ Lorne Henning 2.00
☐ Gary Howatt 2.00
☐ Anders Kallur 2.00
☐ Mike Kaszycki 2.00
☐ Dave Langevin 2.00
☐ Dave Lewis 2.00
☐ Bob Lorimer 2.00
☐ Wayne Merrick 2.00
☐ Bob Nystrom 4.00
☐ Stefan Persson 2.00
☐ Denis Potvin 7.50
☐ Jean Potvin 2.00
☐ Glenn Resch (G) 5.00
☐ Billy Smith (G) 6.50
☐ Steve Tambellini 2.00
☐ John Tonelli 5.00
☐ Bryan Trottier 8.50
☐ Islanders logo 2.00

1983 - 84 ISLANDERS

Mike Bossy is the most expensive single at $6-8. Singles start at $1.50.

Card Size: 2 1/2" x 3 1/2"
Sponsors: none
Complete Set (19 cards): 35.00

☐ Mike Bossy
☐ Bob Bourne
☐ Billy Carroll
☐ Clark Gillies
☐ Mats Hallin
☐ Kelly Hrudey (G)
☐ Tomas Jonsson
☐ Dave Langevin
☐ Rollie Melanson (G)
☐ Wayne Merrick
☐ Ken Morrow
☐ Bob Nystrom
☐ Denis Potvin
☐ Billy Smith (G)
☐ Brent Sutter
☐ Duane Sutter
☐ John Tonelli
☐ Bryan Trottier
☐ Team Photo

1983 - 84 ISLANDERS ISLANDER NEWS

Mike Bossy (card #2) is the most expensive single at $5-6. Singles start at 75¢.

Card Size: 2 1/2" x 3 1/2"
Sponsor: Islander News
Complete Set (38 cards): 30.00

☐ 1 Checklist
☐ 2 Mike Bossy
☐ 3 Bob Bourne
☐ 4 Billy Carroll
☐ 5 Greg Gilbert
☐ 6 Clark Gillies
☐ 7 Butch Goring
☐ 8 Mats Hallin
☐ 9 Anders Kallur
☐ 10 Wayne Merrick
☐ 11 Bob Nystrom
☐ 12 Brent Sutter
☐ 13 Duane Sutter
☐ 14 John Tonelli
☐ 15 Bryan Trottier
☐ 16 Tomas Jonsson
☐ 17 Gordie Lane
☐ 18 Dave Langevin
☐ 19 Ken Morrow
☐ 20 Stefan Persson
☐ 21 Denis Potvin
☐ 22 Rollie Melanson (G)
☐ 23 Billy Smith (G)
☐ 24 Stanley Cup
☐ 25 Stanley Cup
☐ 26 Stanley Cup
☐ 27 Lorne Henning
☐ 28 Bill Torrey
☐ 29 Al Arbour
☐ 30 Ron Waske/Jim Pickard
☐ 31 '79-80 Team Photo
☐ 32 '80-81 Team Photo
☐ 33 '81-82 Team Photo
☐ 34 '82-83 Team Photo
☐ 35 Mike Bossy
☐ 36 Billy Smith (G)
☐ 37 Bryan Trottier
☐ 38 Butch Goring

1984 - 85 ISLANDERS ISLANDER NEWS

Pat LaFontaine (card #11) is the most expensive single at $10-12. Singles start at 75¢.

Card Size: 2 1/2" x 3 1/2"
Sponsor: Islander News
Complete Set (37 cards): 40.00

☐ 1 Checklist
☐ 2 Mike Bossy
☐ 3 Bob Bourne
☐ 4 Pat Flatley
☐ 5 Greg Gilbert
☐ 6 Clark Gillies
☐ 7 Mats Hallin
☐ 8 Anders Kallur
☐ 9 Alan Kerr
☐ 10 Roger Kortko
☐ 11 Pat LaFontaine
☐ 12 Bob Nystrom
☐ 13 Brent Sutter
☐ 14 Duane Sutter
☐ 15 John Tonelli
☐ 16 Bryan Trottier
☐ 17 Paul Boutilier
☐ 18 Gerald Diduck
☐ 19 Gord Dineen
☐ 20 Tomas Jonsson
☐ 21 Gordie Lane
☐ 22 Dave Langevin
☐ 23 Ken Morrow
☐ 24 Stefan Persson
☐ 25 Denis Potvin
☐ 26 Kelly Hrudey
☐ 27 Billy Smith (G)
☐ 28 Bill Torrey
☐ 29 Al Arbour
☐ 30 Brian Kilrea
☐ 31 Ron Wiske/Jim Pickard
☐ 32 HL: Mike Bossy
☐ 33 HL: Denis Potvin
☐ 34 HL: Billy Smith (G)
☐ 35 HL: Bryan Trottier
☐ 36 '84-85 Team Photo
☐ 37 Wales Conf. Champs

1989 - 90 ISLANDERS

Pat LaFontaine is the most expensive single at $3-4. Singles start at 75¢.

Card Size: 3 7/8" x 7 1/4"
Sponsors: none
Complete Set (22 cards): 30.00

☐ Al Arbour
☐ Dean Chynoweth
☐ Dave Chyzowski
☐ Doug Crossman
☐ Gerald Diduck
☐ Tom Fitzgerald
☐ Mark Fitzpatrick (G)
☐ Patrick Flatley
☐ Glenn Healy (G)
☐ Alan Kerr
☐ Pat LaFontaine
☐ Mikko Mäkelä
☐ Don Maloney
☐ Jeff Norton
☐ Gary Nylund
☐ Rich Pilon
☐ Brent Sutter
☐ Gilles Thibaudeau
☐ Bryan Trottier
☐ David Volek
☐ Mick Vukota
☐ Randy Wood

1993 - 94 ISLANDERS CHEMICAL

Mike Bossy is the most expensive single at $3-4. Singles start at 75¢.

Card Size: 2 1/2" x 3 1/2"
Sponsor: Chemical Business Bank
Complete Set (10 cards): 12.00

☐ Mike Bossy
☐ Clark Gillies
☐ Gerry Hart
☐ Wayne Merrick
☐ Bob Nystrom
☐ Denis Potvin
☐ Billy Smith (G)
☐ John Tonelli
☐ Ed Westfall
☐ Islanders

1996 - 97 ISLANDERS 25TH ANNIVERSARY

These postcards feature black and white photos. Zigmund Palffy is the most expensive single at $2-3. Singles start at 75¢.

Postcard Size:
Sponsor: none
Complete Set (23 cards): 20.00

☐ Niclas Andersson
☐ Derek Armstrong
☐ Todd Bertuzzi
☐ Eric Fichaud (G)
☐ Travis Green
☐ Doug Houda
☐ Brent Hughes
☐ Kenny Jonssön
☐ Derek King
☐ Paul Kruse
☐ Claude Lapointe
☐ Scott Lachance
☐ Bryan McCabe
☐ Marty McInnis
☐ Zigmund Palffy
☐ Dan Plante
☐ Richard Pilon
☐ Tommy Salo (G)
☐ Bryan Smolinski
☐ Dennis Vaske
☐ Mick Vukota
☐ Randy Wood
☐ Mike Milbury, Coach

NEW YORK RANGERS

1981 - 82 RANGERS

We have little information on this series. Other singles exist.
Postcard Size: 3 1/2" x 5 1/2"
Sponsors: none
☐ Mark Pavelich #40

1987 - 88 RANGERS

We have little information on this series. Other singles exist.
Card Size: 4 1/2" x 6 1/2"
Sponsors: none
☐ Marcel Dionne

1989 - 90 RANGERS MARINE MIDLAND

The most expensive singles are Brian Leetch, John Vanbiesbrouck at $6-8 and Mike Richter at $5-6. Singles start at 75¢.
Card Size: 2 5/8" x 3 5/6"
Sponsor: Marine Midland Bank
Complete Set (30 cards): 30.00
☐ Jeff Bloemberg #38
☐ Paul Broten #37
☐ Ulf Dahlen #16
☐ Jan Erixon #20
☐ Bob Froese #33 (G)
☐ Ron Greschner #4
☐ Mark Hardy #14
☐ Miloslav Horava #6
☐ Mark Janssens #15
☐ Kris King #12
☐ Kelly Kisio #11
☐ Brian Leetch #2
☐ Troy Mallette #26
☐ Corey Millen #23
☐ Randy Moller #24
☐ Brian Mullen #19
☐ Roger Neilson
☐ Bernie Nicholls #9
☐ Chris Nilan #30
☐ John Ogrodnick #25
☐ James Patrick #3
☐ Rudy Poeschek #29
☐ Mike Richter #35 (G)
☐ Normand Rochefort #5
☐ Lindy Ruff #44
☐ David Shaw #21
☐ Darren Turcotte #8
☐ John Vanbiesbrouck #34 (G)
☐ Carey Wilson #17
☐ Rangers/MasterCard

1992 - 93 RANGERS

We have little information on this series. Other singles exist.
Postcard Size: 3 1/2" x 5 1/2"
Sponsors: none
☐ Brian Leetch
☐ Mark Messier

1996 - 97 RANGERS

We have very little information on this set. Gretzky was the first in a series of 41 cards. Cards were given out with Rangers game programs.
Card Size: 8" x 10"
Sponsors: none
☐ 1 Wayne Gretzky

1997 - 98 RANGERS WELSH FARMS SHEETS

Singles start at $5. These sheets are sequentially numbered out of 2,250. There are 41 sheets in the series.
Sheet Size: 8 1/2" x 11"
Sponsor: Welsh Farms
☐ 27 Brian Skrudland

OTTAWA SENATORS

1992 - 93 SENATORS 580 CFRA RADIO

Singles start at $1.00
Card Size: 4" x 6"
Sponsors: 580 CFRA, Today's Colonial Furniture
Complete Set (21 cards): 15.00
☐ Dave Archibald
☐ Jamie Baker
☐ Daniel Berthiaume (G)
☐ Laurie Boschman
☐ Neil Brady
☐ Mark Freer
☐ Radek Hamr
☐ Jody Hull
☐ Tomas Jelinek
☐ Bob Kudelski
☐ Mark Lamb
☐ Jeff Lazaro
☐ Chris Luongo
☐ Darcy Loewen
☐ Norm Maciver
☐ Andrew McBain
☐ Mike Peluso
☐ Brad Shaw
☐ Doug Smail
☐ Sylvain Turgeon
☐ Steve Weeks (G)

1993 - 94 SENATORS KRAFT PHOTOS

Alexei Yashin is the most expensive single at $5-7. Singles start at $3. 13 of the 26 players are short printed (*) and start at $4.
Photo Size: 8 1/2" x 11"
Sponsors: Kraft
Complete Set (27 photos): 50.00
Album: 15.00
☐ Dave Archibald
☐ Craig Billington
☐ Rick Bowness
☐ Robert Burakovsky (*)
☐ Alexandre Daigle
☐ Pavol Demitra (*)
☐ Gord Dineen
☐ Dmitri Filimonov (*)
☐ Brian Glynn (*)
☐ Bill Huard (*)
☐ Jarmo Kekäläinen (*)
☐ Bob Kudelski (*)
☐ Mark Lamb (*)
☐ Darcy Loewen
☐ Norm Maciver
☐ Darrin Madeley (G) (*)
☐ Troy Mallette
☐ Brad Marsh
☐ Dave McLlwain
☐ Darren Rumble (*)
☐ Vladimir Ruzicka (*)
☐ Brad Shaw
☐ Graeme Townshend (*)
☐ Sylvain Turgeon
☐ Dennis Vial (*)
☐ Alexei Yashin
☐ Team Photo

1994 - 95 SENATORS BELL MOBILITY

Alexei Yashin is the most expensive single at $3-4. Singles start at 75¢.
Card Size: 4" x 6"
Sponsor: Bell Mobility
Complete Set (28 cards): 20.00
☐ Dave Archibald
☐ Don Beaupré (G)
☐ Radim Bicanek
☐ Craig Billington (G)
☐ Claude Boivin
☐ Radek Bonk
☐ Phil Bourque
☐ Rick Bowness
☐ Randy Cunneyworth
☐ Chris Dahlquist
☐ Alexandre Daigle
☐ Pat Elynuik
☐ Rob Gaudreau
☐ Sean Hill
☐ Bill Huard
☐ Kerry Huffman
☐ Scott Levins
☐ Norm Maciver
☐ Darrin Madeley (G)
☐ Troy Mallette
☐ Brad Marsh
☐ Dave McLlwain
☐ Troy Murray
☐ Stanislav Neckar
☐ Jim Paek
☐ Sylvain Turgeon
☐ Dennis Vial
☐ Alexei Yashin

1995 - 96 SENATORS

Daniel Alfredsson is the most expensive single at $4-5. Singles start at 75¢.
Card Size: 4" x 6"
Sponsors: none
Complete Set (27 cards): 20.00
☐ Daniel Alfredsson
☐ Dave Archibald
☐ Mike Bales (G)
☐ Don Beaupré (G)
☐ Radek Bonk
☐ Phil Bourque
☐ Tom Chorske
☐ Joe Cirella
☐ Randy Cunnyworth
☐ Alexandre Daigle
☐ Ted Drury
☐ Steve Duchesne
☐ Rob Gaudreau
☐ Sean Hill
☐ Kerry Huffman
☐ Scott Levins
☐ Troy Mallette
☐ Brad Marsh
☐ Trent McCleary
☐ Jaroslav Modry
☐ Frank Musil
☐ Stanislav Neckar
☐ Dan Quinn
☐ Martin Straka
☐ Antti Törmänen
☐ Dennis Vial
☐ Alexei Yashin

1996 - 97 SENATORS PIZZA HUT

Daniel Alfredsson and Alexei Yashin are the most expensive singles at $3-4. Singles start at 75¢.

Card Size: 4" x 6"
Sponsor: Pizza Hut
Complete Set (30 cards): 20.00

- ☐ Daniel Alfredsson
- ☐ Radek Bonk
- ☐ Tom Chorske
- ☐ Randy Cunneyworth
- ☐ Andreas Dackell
- ☐ Alexandre Daigle
- ☐ Steve Duchesne
- ☐ Bruce Gardiner
- ☐ Dave Hannan
- ☐ Sean Hill
- ☐ Denny Lambert
- ☐ Janne Laukkanen
- ☐ Jacques Martin
- ☐ Shawn McEachern
- ☐ Frank Musil
- ☐ Phil Myre
- ☐ Stanislav Neckar
- ☐ Christer Olsson
- ☐ Perry Pearn
- ☐ Lance Pitlick
- ☐ Craig Ramsay
- ☐ Wade Redden
- ☐ Damian Rhodes (G)
- ☐ Ron Tugnutt (G)
- ☐ Shaun Van Allen
- ☐ Dennis Vial
- ☐ Alexei Yashin
- ☐ Jason York
- ☐ Jason Zent
- ☐ Sergei Zholtok

1997 - 98 SENATORS

The most expensive single is Alexei Yashin at $3-4. Singles start at 50¢.

Card Size: 3" x 4 1/2"
Sponsors: none
Complete Set (25 cards): 15.00

- ☐ Daniel Alfredsson #11
- ☐ Magnus Arvedsson #20
- ☐ Radek Bonk #14
- ☐ Randy Cunneyworth #7
- ☐ Andreas Dackell #10
- ☐ Alexandre Daigle #9
- ☐ Bruce Gardiner #25
- ☐ Igor Kravchuk #29
- ☐ Denny Lambert #28
- ☐ Janne Laukkanen #27
- ☐ Shawn McEachern #15
- ☐ Stan Neckar #24
- ☐ Chris Phillips #5
- ☐ Lance Pitlick #2
- ☐ Wade Redden #6
- ☐ Damian Rhodes (G) #1
- ☐ Ron Tugnutt #31
- ☐ Shaun Van Allen #22
- ☐ Dennis Vial #21
- ☐ Alexei Yashin #19
- ☐ Jason York #33
- ☐ Sergei Zholtok #16
- ☐ Jacques Martin, Coach
- ☐ Perry Pearn, Asst. Coach
- ☐ Craig Ramsay, Asst. Coach

PHILADELPHIA FLYERS

1970 - 71 FLYERS

Doug Favell is the most expensive single at $5-7. Singles start at $2. Other singles may exist.

Card Size: 3 1/2" x 5 1/2"
Sponsors: none

- ☐ Barry Ashbee
- ☐ Gary Dornhoefer
- ☐ W.Elliott/ F.Leurs
- ☐ Doug Favell (G)
- ☐ Earl Heiskala
- ☐ Larry Hillman
- ☐ André Lacroix
- ☐ Lew Morrison
- ☐ Simon Nolet
- ☐ Garry Peters
- ☐ Vic Stasiuk
- ☐ George Swarbrick

1972 - 73 FLYERS MIGHTY MILK HOCKEY STARS

These cards were issued on the backs of milk cartons. Other singles may exist. Bobby Clarke is the most expensive single at $60-70 in NRMT. Singles start at $12.

Card Size: 3 5/8" x 7 1/2"
Sponsors: Mighty Milk, Channel 29

- ☐ Serge Bernier
- ☐ Bobby Clarke
- ☐ Gary Dornhoefer
- ☐ Doug Favell (G)
- ☐ Jean-Guy Gendron
- ☐ Bill Lesuk
- ☐ Lew Morrison
- ☐ Ed Van Impe

1975 - 76 FLYERS GINGER ALE CANS

Super-imposed player photos are in black and white. We have little information on these "Stanley Cup Champions" cans. Other singles may exist.

Sponsor: Canada Dry Ginger Ale

- ☐ Bill Barber
- ☐ Tom Bladon
- ☐ Mel Bridgman
- ☐ Bobby Clarke
- ☐ Terry Crisp
- ☐ Gary Dornhoefer
- ☐ André Dupont
- ☐ Larry Goodenough
- ☐ Bob Kelly
- ☐ Orest Kindrachuk
- ☐ Reggie Leach
- ☐ Ross Lonsberry
- ☐ Rick MacLeish
- ☐ Jack McIlhargey
- ☐ Don Saleski
- ☐ Dave Schultz
- ☐ Wayne Stephenson (G)
- ☐ Bobby Taylor (G)
- ☐ Ed Van Impe
- ☐ Jimmy Watson
- ☐ Joe Watson

1981 - 82 FLYERS DELAWARE GROUP TICKETS

These cards look like game tickets and were issued in strips. Other singles exist.

Ticket Size: 1 5/8" x 4"
Sponsor: The Delaware Group

- ☐ 9 Paul Holmgren
- ☐ 10 Behn Wilson
- ☐ 11 Ken Linseman
- ☐ 12 Brian Propp
- ☐ 13 Reggie Leach
- ☐ 14 Flyers #22
- ☐ 15 Bill Barber
- ☐ 16 Flyers #2

1983 - 84 FLYERS J.C. PENNEY

The most expensive singles are Pelle Lindberg at $10-12 and Bobby Clarke at $6-8. Singles start at $1.50.

Card Size: 4" x 6"
Sponsor: J.C. Penney
Complete Set (22 cards): 40.00

- ☐ Ray Allison
- ☐ Bill Barber
- ☐ Frank Bathe
- ☐ Lindsay Carson
- ☐ Bobby Clarke
- ☐ Glen Cochrane
- ☐ Doug Crossman
- ☐ Miroslav Dvorak
- ☐ Thomas Eriksson
- ☐ Bob Froese (G)
- ☐ Randy Holt
- ☐ Mark Howe
- ☐ Tim Kerr
- ☐ Pelle Lindberg (G)
- ☐ Brad Marsh
- ☐ Brad McCrimmon
- ☐ Dave Poulin
- ☐ Brian Propp
- ☐ Ilkka Sinisalo
- ☐ Darryl Sittler
- ☐ Rich Sutter
- ☐ Ron Sutter

1986 - 87 FLYERS

The most expensive singles are Ron Hextall and Rick Tocchet at $5-7. Mike Keenan is at $3-4. Singles start at $1.00. Bob Froese is short printed and sells at $3-5. A 29-card sets sell at $30.

Card Size: 4 1/8" x 6"
Sponsors: none
Complete Set (30 cards): 35.00

- ☐ Bill Barber
- ☐ Dave Brown
- ☐ Lindsay Carson
- ☐ Murray Craven
- ☐ Pat Croce
- ☐ Doug Crossman
- ☐ J.J. Daigneault
- ☐ Per-Erik Eklund
- ☐ Bob Froese (G)
- ☐ Ron Hextall (G)
- ☐ Paul Holmgren
- ☐ Ed Hospodar
- ☐ Mark Howe
- ☐ Mike Keenan
- ☐ Tim Kerr
- ☐ Brad Marsh
- ☐ Brad McCrimmon
- ☐ E.J. Maguire
- ☐ Scott Mellanby
- ☐ Bernie Parent
- ☐ Dave Poulin
- ☐ Brian Propp
- ☐ Glenn Resch (G)
- ☐ Ilkka Sinisalo
- ☐ Derrick Smith
- ☐ Daryl Stanley
- ☐ Ron Sutter
- ☐ Rick Tocchet
- ☐ Peter Zezel
- ☐ Team Photo

1989 - 90 FLYERS

Bobby Clarke is the most expensive single at $3-4. Singles start at $1.00.

Card Size: 4 1/8" x 6"
Sponsors: none
Complete Set (29 cards): 25.00

- ☐ Keith Acton
- ☐ Craig Berube
- ☐ Mike Bullard
- ☐ Terry Carkner
- ☐ Jeff Chychrun
- ☐ Bob Clarke
- ☐ Murray Craven
- ☐ Mike Eaves
- ☐ Per-Erik Eklund
- ☐ Ron Hextall (G)
- ☐ Paul Holmgren
- ☐ Mark Howe
- ☐ Kerry Huffman
- ☐ Tim Kerr
- ☐ Scott Mellanby
- ☐ Gord Murphy
- ☐ Andy Murray
- ☐ Pete Peeters (G)
- ☐ Dave Poulin
- ☐ Brian Propp
- ☐ Kjell Samuelsson
- ☐ Ilkka Sinisalo
- ☐ Derrick Smith
- ☐ Doug Sulliman
- ☐ Ron Sutter
- ☐ Rick Tocchet
- ☐ Jay Wells
- ☐ Ken Wregget (G)
- ☐ Team Photo

1990 - 91 FLYERS

Mike Ricci is the most expensive single at $2-3. Singles start at 75¢.

Card Size: 4 1/8" x 6"
Sponsors: none
Complete Set (26 cards): 20.00

- ☐ Keith Acton
- ☐ Murray Baron
- ☐ Craig Berube
- ☐ Terry Carkner
- ☐ Jeff Chychrun
- ☐ Murray Craven
- ☐ Per-Erik Eklund
- ☐ Ron Hextall (G)
- ☐ Tony Horacek
- ☐ Martin Hostak
- ☐ Mark Howe
- ☐ Kerry Huffman
- ☐ Tim Kerr
- ☐ Dale Kushner
- ☐ Norman Lacombe
- ☐ Jiri Latal
- ☐ Scott Mellanby
- ☐ Gord Murphy
- ☐ Pete Peeters (G)
- ☐ Mike Ricci
- ☐ Kjell Samuelsson
- ☐ Derrick Smith
- ☐ Ron Sutter
- ☐ Rick Tocchet
- ☐ Ken Wregget (G)
- ☐ Team Photo

1991 - 92 FLYERS J.C. PENNEY

Rod Brind'Amour is the most expensive single at $2-3. Singles start at 75¢.

Card Size: 4 1/8" x 6"
Sponsors: J.C. Penney
Complete Set (26 cards): 20.00

- ☐ Keith Acton
- ☐ Rod Brind'Amour
- ☐ Dave Brown
- ☐ Terry Carkner
- ☐ Kimbi Daniels
- ☐ Kevin Dineen
- ☐ Steve Duchesne
- ☐ Per-Erik Eklund
- ☐ Corey Foster
- ☐ Ron Hextall (G)
- ☐ Tony Horacek
- ☐ Mark Howe
- ☐ Kerry Huffman
- ☐ Brad Jones
- ☐ Steve Kasper
- ☐ Dan Kordic
- ☐ Jiri Latal
- ☐ Andrei Lomakin
- ☐ Gord Murphy
- ☐ Mark Pederson
- ☐ Dan Quinn
- ☐ Mike Ricci
- ☐ Kjell Samuelsson
- ☐ Rick Tocchet
- ☐ Ken Wregget (G)
- ☐ Team Photo

1992 - 93 FLYERS J.C. PENNEY

Eric Lindros is the most expensive single at $10-12. Singles start at 75¢.

Card Size: 4 1/8" x 6"

Sponsor: J.C. Penney

Complete Set (23 cards): 25.00

- ☐ Keith Acton
- ☐ Stéphane Beauregard (G)
- ☐ Brian Benning
- ☐ Rod Brind'Amour
- ☐ Claude Boivin
- ☐ Dave Brown
- ☐ Terry Carkner
- ☐ Shawn Cronin
- ☐ Kevin Dineen
- ☐ Per-Erik Eklund
- ☐ Doug Evans
- ☐ Brent Fedyk
- ☐ Garry Galley
- ☐ Gord Hynes
- ☐ Eric Lindros
- ☐ Andrei Lomakin
- ☐ Ryan McGill
- ☐ Ric Nattress
- ☐ Greg Paslawski
- ☐ Mark Recchi
- ☐ Dominic Roussel (G)
- ☐ Dimitri Yushkevich
- ☐ Team Photo

1992 - 93 FLYERS UPPER DECK SHEETS

Eric Lindros (15/11/92) is the most expensive sheet at $30-35. Lindros' second and third sheet sell at $15-20. Singles start at $4..

Photo Size: 8 1/2" x 11"

Sponsors: Upper Deck

Complete Set (44 photos): 250.00

- ☐ 19SEP Kevin Dineen
- ☐ 24SEP Brian Benning
- ☐ 03OCT Mark Recchi
- ☐ 09OCT Keith Acton
- ☐ 15OCT Rod Brind'Amour
- ☐ 18OCT Dave Brown
- ☐ 22OCT Dominic Roussel (G)
- ☐ 24OCT Gord Hynes
- ☐ 07NOV Claude Boivin
- ☐ 12NOV Dimitri Yushkevich
- ☐ 15NOV Eric Lindros
- ☐ 19NOV Steve Kasper
- ☐ 22NOV Team Photo
- ☐ 27NOV Greg Paslawski
- ☐ 03DEC Terry Carkner
- ☐ 06DEV Shawn Cronin
- ☐ 12DEC Brent Fedyk
- ☐ 17DEC Garry Galley
- ☐ 19DEC Andrei Lomakin
- ☐ 23DEC B.Dineen/K.Dineen
- ☐ 07JAN Stéphane Beauregard (G)
- ☐ 09JAN Mark Recchi
- ☐ 10JAN Ryan McGill
- ☐ 14JAN Doug Evans
- ☐ 17JAN Dineen/Acton/Carkner
- ☐ 21JAN Ric Nattress
- ☐ 24JAN Rod Brind'Amour
- ☐ 26JAN Tommy Soderstrom (G)
- ☐ 28JAN Per-Erik Eklund
- ☐ 09FEB Dave Brown
- ☐ 11FEB Soderstrom/Yushkevich Roussel/McGill/Lindros
- ☐ 14FEB Josef Beranek
- ☐ 25FEB Greg Paslawski
- ☐ 27FEB Hartsburg/B.Dineen/ Hitchcock
- ☐ 02MAR Keith Acton
- ☐ 11MAR Mark Recchi
- ☐ 13MAR Garry Galley
- ☐ 13MAR Team Photo
- ☐ 16MAR Terry Carkner
- ☐ 21MAR Dominic Roussel (G)
- ☐ 25MAR Greg Hawgood
- ☐ 03APR Viacheslav Butsayev
- ☐ 04APR Recchi/Lindros/Fedyk
- ☐ 08APR Lomakin/Yushkevich/ Butsayev
- ☐ 12APR Clarke/E.Snider/ B.Barber/B.Parent/K.Allen

1993 - 94 FLYERS J.C. PENNEY

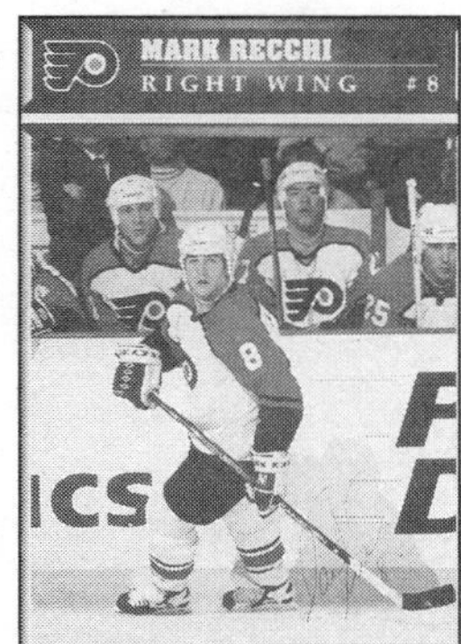

Eric Lindros is the most expensive single at $8-10. Singles start at 75¢.

Card Size: 4 1/8" x 6"

Sponsor: J.C. Penney

Complete Set (24 cards): 25.00

- ☐ Josef Beranek
- ☐ Claude Boivin
- ☐ Jason Bowen
- ☐ Rod Brind'Amour
- ☐ Viacheslav Butsayev
- ☐ Dave Brown
- ☐ Al Conroy
- ☐ Kevin Dineen
- ☐ Per-Erik Eklund
- ☐ Brent Fedyk
- ☐ Jeff Finley
- ☐ Garry Galley
- ☐ Eric Lindros
- ☐ Stewart Malgunas
- ☐ Ryan McGill
- ☐ Rob Ramage
- ☐ Mark Recchi
- ☐ Mikael Renberg
- ☐ Dominic Roussel (G)
- ☐ Yves Racine
- ☐ Tommy Soderstrom (G)
- ☐ Dave Tippett
- ☐ Dimitri Yushkevich
- ☐ Team Photo

1993 - 94 FLYERS GAME SHEETS

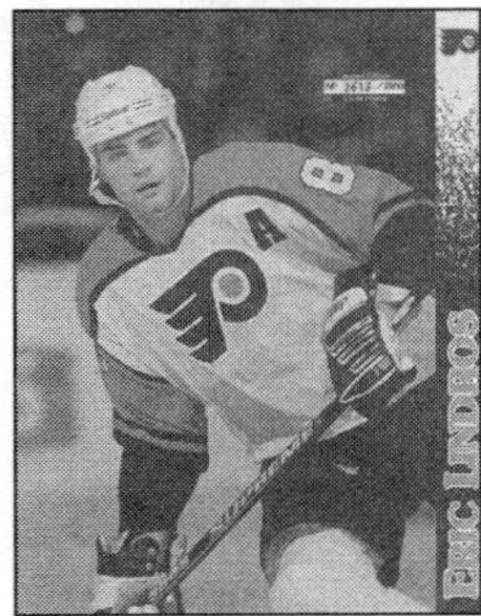

Eric Lindros is the most expensive sheet at $20-25. Singles start at $4.

Photo Size: 8 1/2" x 11"

Sponsors: none

Complete Set (44 photos): 200.00

- ☐ 16SEP Greg Hawgood
- ☐ 21SEP Brent Fedyk
- ☐ 26SEP Terry Carkner
- ☐ 05OCT Mark Recchi
- ☐ 10OCT Dave Brown
- ☐ 12OCT Jason Bowen
- ☐ 16OCT Kevin Dineen
- ☐ 21OCT Per-Erik Eklund
- ☐ 23OCT Eric Lindros
- ☐ 04NOV Mikael Renberg
- ☐ 07NOV Ryan McGill
- ☐ 11NOV Garry Galley
- ☐ 13NOV Yves Racine
- ☐ 18NOV Stewart Malgunas
- ☐ 21NOV Rod Brind'Amour
- ☐ 24NOV Coaches
- ☐ 26NOV Al Conroy
- ☐ 09DEC Dominic Roussel (G)
- ☐ 12DEC Dmitri Yushkevich
- ☐ 16DEC Team Photo
- ☐ 18DEC Mark Recchi
- ☐ 21DEC Viacheslav Butsayev
- ☐ 23DEC Rookies
- ☐ 11JAN Josef Beranek
- ☐ 13JAN Captains
- ☐ 16JAN Dave Tippett
- ☐ 19JAN Tommy Soderstrom (G)
- ☐ 29JAN Eric Lindros
- ☐ 03JAN Claude Boivin
- ☐ 10FEB Dimitri Yushkevich
- ☐ 13FEB Jeff Finley
- ☐ 21FEB Rob Ramage
- ☐ 24FEB Rob Zettler
- ☐ 08MAR Tim Kerr
- ☐ 10MAR Kevin Dineen
- ☐ 13MAR All-Stars
- ☐ 19MAR Dominic Roussel (G)
- ☐ 24MAR André Faust
- ☐ 27MAR Rod Brind'Amour
- ☐ 29MAR Brent Fedyk
- ☐ 31MAR Mark Lamb
- ☐ 07APR '73-74 Team Photo
- ☐ 10APR Eric Lindros
- ☐ 12APR Players Thanks

1994 - 95 FLYERS GAME SHEETS

We have little information on this set. Sheets are similar to the 1992-93 and 1993-94 sets. 1995-96 and 1996-97 game sheets were also likely released.

Size: 8 1/2" x 11"

Sponsors: none

Complete Set (35 cards)

- ☐ Garry Galley
- ☐ Kevin Dineen
- ☐ Mark Lamb
- ☐ Stewart Malgunas
- ☐ Eric Lindros
- ☐ Shjon Podein
- ☐ Rod Brind'Amour
- ☐ Dominic Roussel (G)
- ☐ Ron Hextall (G)
- ☐ Patrik Juhlin
- ☐ T. Murray/K.Acton/T. Webster
- ☐ Mikael Renberg
- ☐ Kevin Haller
- ☐ Rob Zettler
- ☐ Chris Therien
- ☐ Craig MacTavish
- ☐ John LeClair
- ☐ Eric Desjardins
- ☐ Rob DiMaio
- ☐ Dimitri Yushkevich
- ☐ Lindros/Leclair/Renberg
- ☐ Anatoli Semenov
- ☐ Y.Dupré/Therien/Juhlin
- ☐ Karl Dykhuis
- ☐ Gilbert Dionne
- ☐ Shawn Antoski
- ☐ Dave Brown
- ☐ Lindros/MacTavish/Brind'Amour
- ☐ Team Photo
- ☐ Eric Lindros
- ☐ Brent Fedyk
- ☐ Ron Hextall (G)
- ☐ Petr Svoboda
- ☐ Lindros/LeClair/Renberg
- ☐ John LeClair

1996 - 97 FLYERS OCEAN SPRAY

Eric Lindros is the most expensive single at $5-7. Singles start at 75¢ Other players exist.

Card Size: 4 1/8" x 6"

Sponsors: Ocean Spray Cranberries

Complete Set (24 cards): 20.00

- ☐ Rod Brind'Amour
- ☐ Paul Coffey
- ☐ Scott Daniels
- ☐ Eric Desjardins
- ☐ John Druce
- ☐ Karl Dykhuis
- ☐ Pat Falloon
- ☐ Dale Hawerchuk
- ☐ Ron Hextall (G)
- ☐ Trent Klatt
- ☐ Dan Kordic
- ☐ Daniel Lacroix
- ☐ John LeClair
- ☐ Eric Lindros
- ☐ Janne Niinimaa
- ☐ Joel Otto
- ☐ Shjon Podein
- ☐ Mikael Renberg
- ☐ Kjell Samuelsson
- ☐ Garth Snow
- ☐ Petr Svoboda
- ☐ Chris Therien
- ☐ Dainius Zubrus
- ☐ Team Photo

1997 - 98 FLYERS COMCAST CALLING CARDS

We have little information on these 15-min. phone cards. Other singles exist.

Sponsor: Comcast

- ☐ Alexandre Daigle
- ☐ Chris Gratton
- ☐ John LeClair

PHOENIX COYOTES

1996 - 97 COYOTES COCA-COLA

The most expensive singles are Keith Tkachuk at $3-4 and Jeremy Roenick at $2-3. Singles start at 50¢. The backs of each player's two (or three) cards are identical.

Card Size: 3 1/2" x 6 1/2"

Sponsor: Coca-Cola

Complete Set (35 cards): 20.00

- ☐ Bob Corkum #21
- ☐ Shane Doan #19
- ☐ Dallas Drake #11
- ☐ Dallas Eakins #6
- ☐ Mike Eastwood #32
- ☐ Jeff Finley #26
- ☐ Mike Gartner #22 (looking right)
- ☐ Mike Gartner #22 (facing forward)
- ☐ Mike Hudson #28
- ☐ Craig Janney #15
- ☐ Jim Johnson #8
- ☐ Nikolai Khabibulin (G) #35 (facing right)
- ☐ Nikolai Khabibulin (G) #35 (facing left)
- ☐ Chad Kilger #18
- ☐ Kris King #17 (skating right)
- ☐ Kris King #17 (facing right)
- ☐ Igor Korolev #23
- ☐ Norm Maciver #44
- ☐ Dave Manson #4
- ☐ Brad McCrimmon #10
- ☐ Jim McKenzie #33
- ☐ Teppo Numminen #27
- ☐ Deron Quint #5
- ☐ Jeremy Roenick #97 (referee in background)
- ☐ Jeremy Roenick #97 (skating forward)
- ☐ Jeremy Roenick #97 (looking left)
- ☐ Cliff Ronning #77
- ☐ Darrin Shannon #34
- ☐ Mike Stapleton #14
- ☐ Keith Tkachuk #7 (looking left)
- ☐ Keith Tkachuk #7 (looking right)
- ☐ Oleg Tverdovsky #20
- ☐ Darcy Wakaluk (G) #43
- ☐ Paul MacLean/ Don Hay/ Zinetula Bilyaletdinov
- ☐ Coyotes Team Photo

1997 - 98 COYOTES COCA-COLA

The most expensive singles are Keith Tkachuk at $3-4 and Jeremy Roenick at $2-3. Singles start at 50¢. The backs of each player's two or three cards are identical.

Card Size: 3 3/8" x 6 3/8"
Sponsor: Coca-Cola
Complete Set (35 cards): 20.00

- ☐ Benoît Allaire, Goalie Coach
- ☐ Murray Baron #2
- ☐ Bob Corkum #21
- ☐ Gerald Diduck #4
- ☐ Shane Doan #19
- ☐ Jason Doig #55
- ☐ Dallas Drake #11
- ☐ Mike Gartner #22
- ☐ Brad Isbister #16
- ☐ Craig Janney #15
- ☐ Jim Johnson #8
- ☐ Nikolai Khabibulin (G) #35
- ☐ Chad Kilger #18
- ☐ Norm Maciver #44
- ☐ Jocelyn Lemieux #32
- ☐ Jim McKenzie #33 (helmet)
- ☐ Jim McKenzie #33 (no helmet)
- ☐ Jayson More #6
- ☐ Teppo Numminen #27
- ☐ Deron Quint #5
- ☐ Gordie Roberts, Asst.Coach
- ☐ Jeremy Roenick #97 (facing right)
- ☐ Jeremy Roenick #97 (facing front)
- ☐ Jeremy Roenick #97 (skating)
- ☐ Cliff Ronning #77
- ☐ Jim Schoenfeld, Coach
- ☐ Darrin Shannon #34
- ☐ John Slaney #26
- ☐ Mike Stapleton #14
- ☐ Keith Tkachuk #7
- ☐ Rick Tocchet #92
- ☐ John Tortorella, Asst.Coach
- ☐ Jimmy Waite (G) #28
- ☐ Darcy Wakaluk (G) #43
- ☐ Juha Ylönen #36

PITTSBURGH PENGUINS

1971 - 72 PENGUINS

Red Kelly is the most expensive single at $3-4 in NRMT. Singles start at $2.00

Card Size: 3 1/2" x 6"
Sponsor: Sportcolor
Complete Set (21 cards): 45.00

- ☐ Syl Apps
- ☐ Les Binkley (G)
- ☐ Dave Burrows
- ☐ Darryl Edestrand
- ☐ Roy Edwards (G)
- ☐ Val Fonteyne
- ☐ Nick Harbaruk
- ☐ Bryan Hextall
- ☐ Sheldon Kannegeiser
- ☐ Red Kelly
- ☐ Bob Leiter
- ☐ Keith McCreary
- ☐ Joe Noris
- ☐ Greg Polis
- ☐ Jean Pronovost
- ☐ René Robert
- ☐ Jim Rutherford (G)
- ☐ Ken Schinkel
- ☐ Ron Schock
- ☐ Bryan Watson
- ☐ Bob Woytowich

1974 - 75 PENGUINS

Pierre Larouche is the most expensive single at $5-6 in NRMT. Singles start at $2.00

Postcard Size: 3 1/2" x 5 1/2"
Sponsors: none
Complete Set (22 cards): 35.00

- ☐ Syl Apps
- ☐ Chuck Arnason
- ☐ Dave Burrows
- ☐ Colin Campbell
- ☐ Nelson Debenedet
- ☐ Steve Durbano
- ☐ Vic Hadfield
- ☐ Gary Inness (G)
- ☐ B.J. Johnson(G)
- ☐ Rick Kehoe
- ☐ Bob Kelly
- ☐ Jean-Guy Lagace
- ☐ Ron Lalonde
- ☐ Pierre Larouche
- ☐ Lowell MacDonald
- ☐ Dennis Owchar
- ☐ Bob Paradise
- ☐ Kelly Pratt
- ☐ Jean Pronovost
- ☐ Ron Schock
- ☐ Ron Stackhouse
- ☐ Barry Williams

1977 - 78 PENGUINS MCDONALD'S PUCK BUCKS

Pierre Larouche is the most expensive single at $3-4 in NRMT. Singles start at $1.50.

Card Size: 2" x 3 1/2"
Sponsors: McDonald's
Complete Set (18 cards): 30.00

- ☐ Russ Anderson
- ☐ Syl Apps
- ☐ Wayne Biachin
- ☐ Dave Burrows
- ☐ Colin Campbell
- ☐ Blair Chapman
- ☐ Mike Corrigan
- ☐ Jim Hamilton
- ☐ Denis Herron (G)
- ☐ Rick Kehoe
- ☐ Pierre Larouche
- ☐ Lowell MacDonald
- ☐ Greg Malone
- ☐ Dennis Owchar
- ☐ Jean Pronovost
- ☐ Ron Stackhouse
- ☐ Dunc Wilson (G)
- ☐ Johnny Wilson

1983 - 84 PENGUINS COKE IS IT!

Marty McSorley is the most expensive single at $6-8. Singles start at $1.00

Card Size: 5" x 7"
Sponsor: Coke
Complete Set (19 cards): 45.00

- ☐ Pat Boutette
- ☐ Andy Brickley
- ☐ Mike Bullard
- ☐ Ted Bulley
- ☐ Rod Buskas
- ☐ Randy Carlyle
- ☐ Michel Dion (G)
- ☐ Bob Errey
- ☐ Ron Flockhart
- ☐ Steve Gatzos
- ☐ Jim Hamilton
- ☐ Dave Hannan
- ☐ Denis Herron (G)
- ☐ Troy Loney
- ☐ Bryan Maxwell
- ☐ Marty McSorley
- ☐ Norm Schmidt
- ☐ Mark Taylor
- ☐ Greg Tebbutt

1983 - 84 PENGUINS HEINZ

Rick Kehoe is the most expensive single at $3-4. Singles start at $1.50.

Card Size: 6" x 9"
Sponsor: Heinz
Complete Set (22 cards): 35.00

- ☐ Paul Baxter
- ☐ Pat Boutette
- ☐ Randy Boyd
- ☐ Mike Bullard
- ☐ Randy Carlyle
- ☐ Marc Chorney
- ☐ Michel Dion (G)
- ☐ Bill Gardner
- ☐ Pat Graham
- ☐ Anders Hakansson
- ☐ Dave Hannan
- ☐ Denis Herron (G)
- ☐ Greg Hotham
- ☐ Stan Jonathan
- ☐ Rick Kehoe
- ☐ Peter Lee
- ☐ Greg Malone
- ☐ Kevin McClelland
- ☐ Ron Meighan
- ☐ Doug Shedden
- ☐ André St. Laurent
- ☐ Rich Sutter

1984 - 85 PENGUINS HEINZ

Marty McSorley is the most expensive single at $5-7. Singles start at $1.50.

Card Size: 6" x 9"
Sponsor: Heinz
Complete Set (22 cards): 35.00

- ☐ Pat Boutette
- ☐ Andy Brickley
- ☐ Mike Bullard
- ☐ Rod Buskas
- ☐ Randy Carlyle
- ☐ Michel Dion (G)
- ☐ Bob Errey
- ☐ Ron Flockhart
- ☐ Greg Fox
- ☐ Steve Gatzos
- ☐ Denis Herron (G)
- ☐ Greg Hotham
- ☐ Rick Kehoe
- ☐ Bryan Maxwell
- ☐ Marty McSorley
- ☐ Tom O'Regan
- ☐ Gary Rissling
- ☐ Roberto Romano (G)
- ☐ Tom Roulston
- ☐ Rocky Saganiuk
- ☐ Doug Shedden
- ☐ Mark Taylor

1986 - 87 PENGUINS KODAK

Mario Lemieux is the most expensive single at $35-40. Singles start at $1.00.

Card Size: 2 3/16" x 2 1/2"
Sponsor: Kodak
Complete Set (26 cards): 50.00

- ☐ Bob Berry
- ☐ Mike Blaisdell
- ☐ Doug Bodger
- ☐ Rod Buskas
- ☐ John Chabot
- ☐ Randy Cunneyworth
- ☐ Ron Duguay
- ☐ Bob Errey
- ☐ Dan Frawley
- ☐ David Hannan
- ☐ Randy Hillier
- ☐ Jim Johnson
- ☐ Kevin LaVallée
- ☐ Mario Lemieux
- ☐ Willy Lindstrom
- ☐ Moe Mantha
- ☐ Gilles Meloche (G)
- ☐ Dan Quinn
- ☐ Jim Roberts
- ☐ Roberto Romano (G)
- ☐ Terry Ruskowski
- ☐ Norm Schmidt
- ☐ Craig Simpson
- ☐ Ville Siren
- ☐ Warren Young (G)
- ☐ Team Photo

1987 - 88 PENGUINS KODAK

Mario Lemieux is the most expensive single at $25-30. Singles start at $1.00.

Card Size: 2 3/16" x 2 1/2"
Sponsor: Kodak
Complete Set (26 cards): 40.00

- ☐ Doug Bodger
- ☐ Rob Brown
- ☐ Rod Buskas
- ☐ Jock Callander
- ☐ Paul Coffey
- ☐ Randy Cunneyworth
- ☐ Chris Dahlquist
- ☐ Bob Errey
- ☐ Dan Frawley
- ☐ Steve Guenette (G)
- ☐ Randy Hillier
- ☐ Dave Hunter
- ☐ Jim Johnson
- ☐ Mike Kachowski
- ☐ Chris Kontos
- ☐ Mario Lemieux
- ☐ Troy Loney
- ☐ Dwight Mathiasen
- ☐ Dave McLlwain
- ☐ Gilles Meloche (G)
- ☐ Dan Quinn
- ☐ Pat Riggin (G)
- ☐ Charlie Simmer
- ☐ Ville Siren
- ☐ Wayne Van Dorp
- ☐ Team Photo

1989 - 90 PENGUINS ELBY'S BIG BOY

Mario Lemieux is the most expensive single at $10-12. Singles start at $1.00. Other singles exist.

Card Size: 4" x 6"
Sponsors: Elby's, Coke

- ☐ Phil Bourque
- ☐ Rob Brown
- ☐ Mario Lemieux
- ☐ Kevin Stevens
- ☐ Zarley Zalapski

1989 - 90 PENGUINS FOODLAND

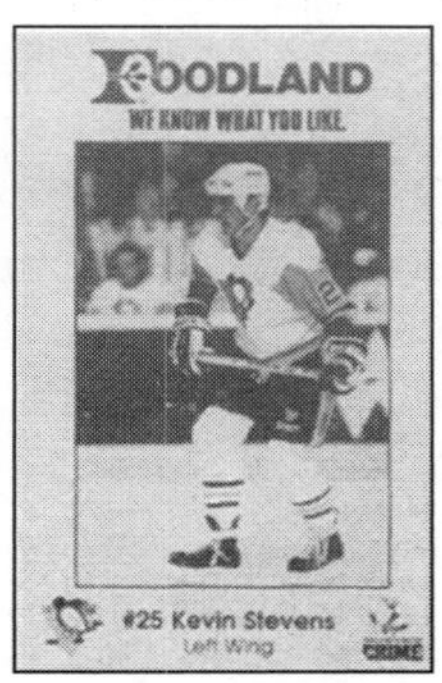

Mario Lemieux is the most expensive single at $10-12. Singles start at $1.00. Gilbert Delorme and Troy Loney were late additions and sell at $3-4. A 15-card set sells at $20.

Card Size: 2 5/8" x 4 1/8"
Sponsor: Foodland
Complete Set (17 cards): 25.00

- ☐ 1 Rob Brown
- ☐ 2 Jim Johnson
- ☐ 3 Zarley Zalapski
- ☐ 4 Paul Coffey
- ☐ 5 Phil Bourque
- ☐ 6 Dan Quinn
- ☐ 6 Gilbert Delorme
- ☐ 7 Kevin Stevens
- ☐ 8 Bob Errey
- ☐ 9 John Cullen
- ☐ 10 Mario Lemieux
- ☐ 11 Randy Hillier
- ☐ 12 Jay Caufield
- ☐ 13 Andrew McBain
- ☐ 13 Troy Loney
- ☐ 14 Wendell Young (G)
- ☐ 15 Tom Barrasso (G)

1990 - 91 PENGUINS

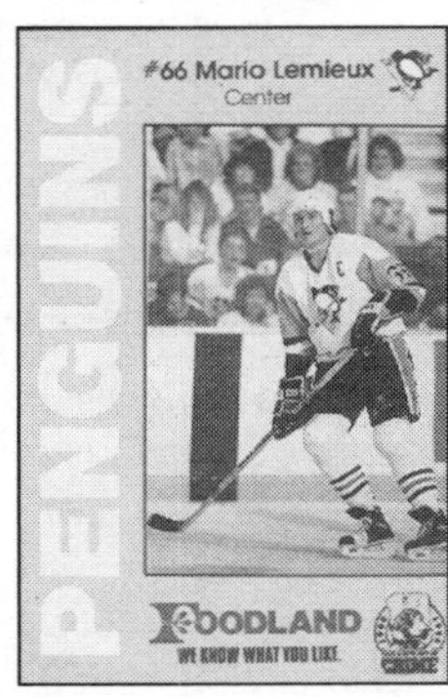

The most expensive singles are Jaromir Jagr at $8-10 and Mario Lemieux at $6-8. Singles start at $1.00.

Card Size: 2 11/16" x 4 1/8"
Sponsor: Foodland
Complete Set (15 cards): 20.00

- ☐ 1 Phil Bourque
- ☐ 2 Paul Coffey
- ☐ 3 Randy Hillier
- ☐ 4 Barry Pederson
- ☐ 5 Tom Barrasso (G)
- ☐ 6 Mark Recchi
- ☐ 7 Bob Johnson
- ☐ 8 Joe Mullen
- ☐ 9 Kevin Stevens
- ☐ 10 John Cullen
- ☐ 11 Jaromir Jagr
- ☐ 12 Zarley Zalapski
- ☐ 13 Mario Lemieux
- ☐ 14 Tony Tanti
- ☐ 15 Bryan Trottier

1991 - 92 PENGUINS ELBY'S BIG BOY

Jaromir Jagr and Mario Lemieux are the most expensive singles at $6-8. Singles start at $1.00.

Card Size: 4" x 6"
Sponsors: Elby's, Coke
Complete Set (23 cards): 35.00

- ☐ Phil Bourque #29
- ☐ Scotty Bowman
- ☐ Jay Caufield #16
- ☐ Jeff Daniels #43
- ☐ Ron Francis #10
- ☐ Jaromir Jagr #68
- ☐ Grant Jennings #3
- ☐ Jamie Leach #20
- ☐ Mario Lemieux #66
- ☐ Troy Loney #24
- ☐ Joe Mullen #7
- ☐ Larry Murphy #55
- ☐ Jim Paek #2
- ☐ Frank Pietrangelo #40 (G)
- ☐ Ken Priestlay #18
- ☐ Mark Recchi #8
- ☐ Gord Roberts #28
- ☐ Ulf Samuelsson #5
- ☐ Paul Stanton #22
- ☐ Kevin Stevens #25
- ☐ Peter Taglianetti #32
- ☐ Rick Tocchet #92
- ☐ Bryan Trottier #19
- ☐ Wendell Young #1 (G)

1991 - 92 PENGUINS FOODLAND

Jaromir Jagr and Mario Lemieux are the most expensive singles at $6-8. Singles start at $1.00.

Card Size: 2 1/2" x 3 1/2"
Sponsor: Foodland
Complete Set (15 cards): 20.00

- ☐ 1 Jim Paek
- ☐ 2 Ulf Samuelsson
- ☐ 3 Ron Francis
- ☐ 4 Mario Lemieux
- ☐ 5 Rick Tocchet
- ☐ 6 Joe Mullen
- ☐ 7 Troy Loney
- ☐ 8 Kevin Stevens
- ☐ 9 Tom Barrasso (G)
- ☐ 10 Larry Murphy
- ☐ 11 Jaromir Jagr
- ☐ 12 Bryan Trottier
- ☐ 13 Paul Stanton
- ☐ 14 Peter Taglianetti
- ☐ 15 Phil Bourque

1991 - 92 PENGUINS FOODLAND STICKERS

This series was issued in three-sticker panels. The stickers have the same photos as the 1991-92 Topps set. The Lemieux/Jagr panel sells at $8-10. Single panels start at $3.

Panel Size: 2 1/2" x 10 1/2"
Sponsors: Topps, Foodland
Complete Set (4 panels): 20.00

- ☐ Bryan Trottier / Joe Mullen / Larry Murphy
- ☐ Tom Barrasso (G) / Ron Francis / Ulf Samuelsson
- ☐ Jaromir Jagr / Mario Lemieux / Kevin Stevens
- ☐ Mark Recchi / Paul Coffey / Frank Pietrangelo (G)

1992 - 93 PENGUINS COKE/CLARK

The most expensive singles are Mario Lemieux at $6-8 and Jaromir Jagr at $5-7. Singles start at 75¢.

Card Size: 2 1/2" x 3 1/2"
Sponsors: Coke, Clark
Complete Set (26 cards): 30.00

- ☐ Tom Barrasso (G)
- ☐ Scotty Bowman
- ☐ Jay Caufield
- ☐ Jeff Daniels
- ☐ Bob Errey
- ☐ Bryan Fogarty
- ☐ Ron Francis
- ☐ Jaromir Jagr
- ☐ Grant Jennings
- ☐ Mario Lemieux
- ☐ Troy Loney
- ☐ Shawn McEachern
- ☐ Joe Mullen
- ☐ Larry Murphy
- ☐ Mike Needham
- ☐ Jim Paek
- ☐ Kjell Samuelsson
- ☐ Ulf Samuelsson
- ☐ Paul Stanton
- ☐ Mike Stapleton
- ☐ Kevin Stevens
- ☐ Martin Straka
- ☐ Dave Tippett
- ☐ Rick Tocchet
- ☐ Ken Wregget (G)
- ☐ Mascot Penguins

1992 - 93 PENGUINS FOODLAND

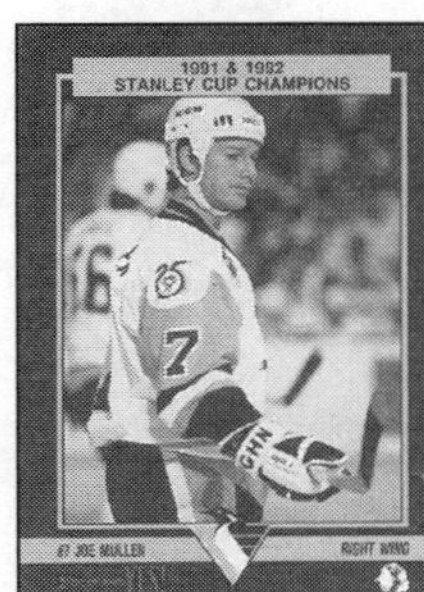

The most expensive singles are Mario Lemieux at $6-8 and Jaromir Jagr at $5-7. Singles start at 75¢.

Card Size: 2 1/2" x 3 1/2"
Sponsor: Foodland
Complete Set (18 cards): 20.00

- ☐ 1 Mario Lemieux
- ☐ 2 Bob Errey
- ☐ 3 Jaromir Jagr
- ☐ 4 Rick Tocchet
- ☐ 5 Tom Barrasso (G)
- ☐ 6 Joe Mullen
- ☐ 7 Ron Francis
- ☐ 8 Troy Loney
- ☐ 9 Shawn McEachern
- ☐ 10 Larry Murphy
- ☐ 11 Jim Paek
- ☐ 12 Ulf Samuelsson
- ☐ 13 Paul Stanton
- ☐ 14 Kjell Samuelsson
- ☐ 15 Kevin Stevens
- ☐ 16 Dave Tippett
- ☐ 17 Martin Straka
- ☐ 18 Mascot Penguins

1992 - 93 PENGUINS FOODLAND STICKERS

This series was issued in three-sticker panels. The Lemieux panel sells at $6-8. Single panels start at $3.

Panel Size: 2 1/2" x 10 1/2"
Sponsor: Foodland
Complete Set (4 panels): 15.00

- ☐ Ron Francis / Jim Paek / Kevin Stevens
- ☐ Tom Barrasso (G) / Mario Lemieux / Troy Loney
- ☐ Joe Mullen / Ulf Samuelsson / Rick Tocchet
- ☐ Jaromir Jagr / Shawn McEachern / Larry Murphy

1993 - 94 PENGUINS FOODLAND

Mario Lemieux is the most expensive single at $4-5. Singles start at 75¢.

Card Size: 2 1/2" x 3 1/2"
Sponsor: Foodland
Complete Set (25 cards): 20.00

- ☐ 1 Mario Lemieux
- ☐ 2 Grant Jennings
- ☐ 3 Ulf Samuelsson
- ☐ 4 Rick Tocchet
- ☐ 5 Marty McSorley
- ☐ 6 Rick Kehoe
- ☐ 7 Doug Brown
- ☐ 8 Martin Straka
- ☐ 9 Jim Paek
- ☐ 10 Ken Wregget (G)
- ☐ 11 Jeff Daniels
- ☐ 12 Bryan Trottier
- ☐ 13 Larry Murphy
- ☐ 14 Ron Francis
- ☐ 15 Mike Needham
- ☐ 16 Mike Ramsey
- ☐ 17 Kevin Stevens
- ☐ 18 Kjell Samuelsson
- ☐ 19 Ed Johnston
- ☐ 20 Markus Naslund
- ☐ 21 Mike Stapleton
- ☐ 22 Peter Taglianetti
- ☐ 23 Jaromir Jagr
- ☐ 24 Tom Barrasso (G)
- ☐ 25 Joe Mullen

1994 - 95 PENGUINS FOODLAND

Jaromir Jagr is the most expensive single at $4-5. Singles start at 75¢.

Card Size: 2 1/2" x 3 1/2"
Sponsor: Foodland
Complete Set (25 cards): 20.00

- ☐ 1 Grant Jennings
- ☐ 2 Greg Hawgood
- ☐ 3 Shawn McEachern
- ☐ 4 Len Barrie
- ☐ 5 Ulf Samuelsson
- ☐ 6 Joe Mullen
- ☐ 7 John Cullen
- ☐ 8 Mike Hudson
- ☐ 9 Ron Francis
- ☐ 10 Tomas Sandstrom
- ☐ 11 Eddie Johnston
- ☐ 12 Chris Tamer
- ☐ 13 François Leroux
- ☐ 14 Luc Robitaille
- ☐ 15 Markus Naslund
- ☐ 16 Ken Wregget (G)
- ☐ 17 Chris Joseph
- ☐ 18 Peter Taglianetti
- ☐ 19 Kevin Stevens
- ☐ 20 Jim McKenzie
- ☐ 21 Kjell Samuelsson
- ☐ 22 Tom Barrasso (G)
- ☐ 23 Jaromir Jagr
- ☐ 24 Larry Murphy
- ☐ 25 Martin Straka

1995 - 96 PENGUINS FOODLAND

Mario Lemieux is the most expensive single at $4-5. Singles start at 50¢.

Card Size: 2 1/2" x 3 1/2"
Sponsor: Foodland
Complete Set (24 cards): 15.00

- ☐ 1 Ron Francis
- ☐ 2 Glen Murray
- ☐ 3 Chris Wells
- ☐ 4 Markus Naslund
- ☐ 5 Jaromir Jagr
- ☐ 6 François Leroux
- ☐ 7 Richard Park
- ☐ 8 Norm Maciver
- ☐ 9 Ken Wregget (G)
- ☐ 10 Tom Barrasso (G)
- ☐ 11 Rick Kehoe, Asst. Coach
- ☐ 12 Sergei Zubov
- ☐ 13 Joe Dziedzic
- ☐ 14 Ed Patterson
- ☐ 15 Tomas Sandström
- ☐ 16 Dave Roche
- ☐ 17 Petr Nedved
- ☐ 18 Chris Tamer
- ☐ 19 Chris Joseph
- ☐ 20 Ian Moran
- ☐ 21 Mascot Iceburgh
- ☐ 22 Ed Johnston, Coach
- ☐ 23 Mario Lemieux
- ☐ 24 Bryan Smolinski, Error (Ian Moran)
- ☐ 25 Dmitri Mironov

1996 - 97 PENGUINS BURGER KING PHOTO PUCKS

Four PhotoPucks feature two players while the last one is a team puck.

Sponsor: Burger King

Complete Set (5 pucks): 35.00

☐ Patrick Lalime (G)
  Ken Wregget (G)
☐ Kevin Hatcher
  Darius Kasparaitis
☐ Jaromir Jagr
  Ron Francis
☐ Mario Lemieux
  Petr Nedved
☐ Penguins

1996 - 97 PENGUINS TRIBUNE REVIEW

Mario Lemieux is the most expensive single at $10-12. Singles start at $2.

Card Size: 4" x 5 1/2"

Sponsor: Tribune Review

Complete Set (8 cards): 35.00

☐ Tom Barrasso (G)
☐ Ron Francis
☐ Jaromir Jagr
☐ Mario Lemieux
☐ Joe Mullen
☐ Ulf Samuelsson
☐ Kevin Stevens
☐ Bryan Trottier

QUÉBEC NORDIQUES

1980 - 81 NORDIQUES

The most expensive players are Michel Goulet and Peter Stastny at $6-8. Singles start at $1.50. Michel Bergeron, Ron Grahame, Dave Pichette and Wally Weir are considered short prints and sell at $2-3 each. A 24-card set sells at $35.

Postcard Size: 3 1/2" x 5 1/2"

Sponsors: none

Complete Set (28 cards): 45.00

☐ Michel Bergeron
☐ Serge Bernier
☐ Ron Chipperfield
☐ Kim Clackson
☐ Réal Cloutier
☐ Alain Côté
☐ Michel Dion (G)
☐ André Dupont
☐ Robbie Ftorek
☐ Michel Goulet
☐ Ron Grahame (G)
☐ Jamie Hislop
☐ Dale Hoganson
☐ Dale Hunter
☐ Pierre Lacroix
☐ Garry Larivière
☐ Richard Leduc
☐ Lee Norwood
☐ John Paddock
☐ Dave Pichette
☐ Michel Plasse (G)
☐ Jacques Richard
☐ Normand Rochefort
☐ Anton Stastny
☐ Peter Stastny
☐ Marc Tardif
☐ Wally Weir
☐ John Wensink

1981 - 82 NORDIQUES

The most expensive players are Michel Goulet and Peter Stastny at $4-5. Singles start at $1.00.

Postcard Size: 3 1/2" x 5 1/2"

Sponsors: none

Complete Set (21 cards): 30.00

☐ Pierre Aubry
☐ Michel Bergeron
☐ Dan Bouchard (G)
☐ Réal Cloutier
☐ Alain Côté
☐ André Dupont
☐ Miroslav Frycer
☐ Michel Goulet
☐ Dale Hunter
☐ Pierre Lacroix
☐ Mario Marois
☐ Dave Pichette
☐ Michel Plasse (G)
☐ Jacques Richard
☐ Normand Rochefort
☐ Anton Stastny
☐ Marian Stastny
☐ Peter Stastny
☐ Marc Tardif
☐ Charles Thiffault
☐ Wally Weir

1982 - 83 NORDIQUES

The most expensive players are Michel Goulet and Peter Stastny at $4-5. Singles start at $1.00.

Postcard Size: 3 1/2" x 5 1/2"

Sponsors: none

Complete Set (26 cards): 30.00

☐ Pierre Aubry
☐ Michel Bergeron
☐ Dan Bouchard (G)
☐ Réal Cloutier
☐ Alain Côté
☐ André Dupont
☐ John Garrett (G)
☐ Michel Goulet
☐ Jean Hamel
☐ Dale Hunter
☐ Rick Lapointe
☐ Clint Malarchuk (G)
☐ Mario Marois
☐ Randy Moller
☐ Wilf Paiement
☐ Dave Pichette
☐ Jacques Richard
☐ Normand Rochefort
☐ Louis Sleigher
☐ Anton Stastny
☐ Marian Stastny
☐ Peter Stastny
☐ Marc Tardif
☐ Charles Thiffault
☐ Wally Weir
☐ Title Card

1983 - 84 NORDIQUES

The most expensive players are Michel Goulet and Peter Stastny at $3-4. Singles start at $1.00.

Postcard Size: 3 1/2" x 5 1/2"

Sponsors: none

Complete Set (32 cards): 30.00

☐ Pierre Aubry
☐ Michel Bergeron
☐ Dan Bouchard (G)
☐ Réal Cloutier
☐ Alain Côté
☐ André Doré
☐ André Dupont
☐ John Garrett (G)
☐ Paul Gillis
☐ Mario Gosselin (G)
☐ Michel Goulet
☐ Jean Hamel
☐ Dale Hunter
☐ Rick Lapointe
☐ Clint Malarchuk (G)
☐ Jimmy Mann
☐ Mario Marois
☐ Randy Moller
☐ Wilf Paiement
☐ Dave Pichette
☐ Pat Price
☐ Jacques Richard
☐ Normand Rochefort
☐ Jean-François Sauvé
☐ André Savard
☐ Louis Sleigher
☐ Anton Stastny
☐ Marian Stastny
☐ Peter Stastny
☐ Marc Tardif
☐ Wally Weir
☐ Blake Wesley

1984 - 85 NORDIQUES

The most expensive players are Michel Goulet and Peter Stastny at $3-4. Singles start at $1.00.

Postcard Size: 3 1/2" x 5 1/2"

Sponsors: none

Complete Set (27 cards): 25.00

☐ Brent Ashton
☐ Bruce Bell
☐ Michel Bergeron
☐ Dan Bouchard (G)
☐ Alain Côté
☐ Gord Donnelly
☐ Luc Dufour
☐ Jean-Marc Gaulin
☐ Paul Gillis
☐ Mario Gosselin (G)
☐ Michel Goulet
☐ Dale Hunter
☐ Guy Lapointe, Asst. Coach
☐ Jimmy Mann
☐ Mario Marois
☐ Brad Maxwell
☐ Randy Moller
☐ Simon Nolet, Asst. Coach
☐ Wilf Paiement
☐ Pat Price
☐ Normand Rochefort
☐ Jean-François Sauvé
☐ André Savard
☐ Richard Sévigny (G)
☐ Anton Stastny
☐ Marian Stastny
☐ Peter Stastny

1985 - 86 NORDIQUES GENERAL FOODS

There are two versions of these cards: cards with a Nordiques logo or cards with a General Foods logo. Pricing for both versions is identical. Photos are credited to André Pichette. The most expensive players are Michel Goulet and Peter Stastny at $3-4. Singles start at $1.00.

Card Size: 3 1/2" x 5 1/2"

Sponsor: General Foods

Complete Set (29): 25.00

☐ ☐ Peter Andersson
☐ ☐ Brent Ashton
☐ ☐ Michel Bergeron
☐ ☐ Jeff Brown
☐ ☐ Alain Côté
☐ ☐ Gilbert Delorme
☐ ☐ Gord Donnelly
☐ ☐ Mike Eagles
☐ ☐ Paul Gillis
☐ ☐ Mario Gosselin (G)
☐ ☐ Michel Goulet
☐ ☐ Ron Harris
☐ ☐ Dale Hunter
☐ ☐ Mark Kumpel
☐ ☐ Jason Lafrenière
☐ ☐ Clint Malarchuk (G)
☐ ☐ Randy Moller
☐ ☐ Simon Nolet
☐ ☐ Robert Picard
☐ ☐ Pat Price
☐ ☐ Ken Quinney
☐ ☐ Normand Rochefort
☐ ☐ Richard Sévigny (G)
☐ ☐ David Shaw
☐ ☐ Risto Siltanen
☐ ☐ Anton Stastny
☐ ☐ Peter Stastny
☐ ☐ Charles Thiffault
☐ ☐ Richard Zemlak

1985 - 86 NORDIQUES MCDONALD'S

The most expensive players are Michel Goulet and Peter Stastny at $3-4. Singles start at $1.00.

Postcard Size: 3 1/2" x 5 1/2"

Sponsors: McDonald's, Le Soleil, CHRC80

Complete Set (22 cards): 25.00

☐ Brent Ashton
☐ Jeff Brown
☐ Alain Côté
☐ Gilbert Delorme
☐ Gord Donnelly
☐ Mike Eagles
☐ Paul Gillis
☐ Mario Gosselin (G)
☐ Michel Goulet
☐ Dale Hunter
☐ Mark Kumpel
☐ Jason Lafrenière
☐ Clint Malarchuk (G)
☐ Randy Moller
☐ Robert Picard
☐ Pat Price
☐ Normand Rochefort
☐ Richard Sévigny (G)
☐ David Shaw
☐ Risto Siltanen
☐ Anton Stastny
☐ Peter Stastny

1985 - 86 NORDIQUES PROVIGO/PEPSI PLACEMATS

The Goulet/Hunter placemat is the most expensive single at $5-6. Single placemats start at $3. The team placemat shows the 12 players in the set.

Placemat Size: 11" x 17"

Sponsors: Provigo, Pepsi

Complete Set (7 placemats): 25.00

☐ B.Ashton/R.Moller
☐ M.Gosselin (G)/C.Malarchuk (G)
☐ D.Hunter/M.Goulet
☐ P.Price/R.Picard
☐ P.Stastny/A.Stastny
☐ A.Côté/J.Anderson
☐ Nordiques

1985 - 86 NORDIQUES PEPSI PENNANTS

This set features the same artwork as the Provigo/Pepsi placemats. The most expensive singles are Michel Goulet and Peter Stastny at $3-4. Singles start at $2.

Pennant Size: 9 1/2" x 26"

Sponsors: Provigo, Pepsi

Complete Set (12 pennants): 20.00

☐ John Anderson
☐ Brent Ashton
☐ Alain Côté
☐ Mario Gosselin (G)
☐ Michel Goulet
☐ Dale Hunter
☐ Clint Malarchuk (G)
☐ Randy Moller
☐ Robert Picard
☐ Pat Price
☐ Anton Stastny
☐ Peter Stastny

1985 - 86 NORDIQUES PROVIGO STICKERS

Michel Goulet and Peter Stastny are the most expensive singles at $3-4. Singles start at $1.00.

Sticker Size: 1 1/8" x 2 1/4"
Sponsor: Provigo
Complete Set (25 cards): 30.00
Team Binder: 5.00

☐ John Anderson
☐ Brent Ashton
☐ Wayne Babych
☐ Michel Bergeron
☐ Alain Côté
☐ Gilbert Delorme
☐ Mike Eagles
☐ Steve Finn
☐ Paul Gillis
☐ Mario Gosselin (G)
☐ Michel Goulet
☐ Dale Hunter
☐ Mark Kumpel
☐ Clint Malarchuk (G)
☐ Jimmy Mann
☐ Mario Marois
☐ Randy Moller
☐ Wilf Paiement
☐ Pat Price
☐ Jean-François Sauvé
☐ Richard Sévigny (G)
☐ David Shaw
☐ Anton Stastny
☐ Peter Stastny

1986 - 87 NORDIQUES

The most expensive singles are Michel Goulet and Peter Stastny at $3-4. Singles start at $1.00.

Card Size: 3 1/2" x 5 1/2"
Sponsors: none
Complete Set (30 cards): 25.00

☐ Michel Bergeron
☐ Jeff Brown
☐ Alain Côté
☐ Bill Derlago
☐ Gord Donnelly
☐ Mike Eagles
☐ Steve Finn
☐ Paul Gillis
☐ Mario Gosselin (G)
☐ Michel Goulet
☐ Mike Hough
☐ Dale Hunter
☐ Jason Lafrenière
☐ Clint Malarchuk (G)
☐ Basil McRae
☐ Randy Moller
☐ Simon Nolet
☐ John Ogrodnick
☐ Robert Picard
☐ Pat Price
☐ Normand Rochefort
☐ Richard Sévigny (G)
☐ David Shaw
☐ Doug Shedden
☐ Risto Siltanen
☐ Anton Stastny
☐ Peter Stastny
☐ Charles Thiffault
☐ Richard Zemlak
☐ Team Photo

1986 - 87 NORDIQUES GENERAL FOODS

These cards have blank backs. Photos are credited to André Pichette. The most expensive singles are Michel Goulet and Peter Stastny at $3-4. Singles start at $1.00.

Card Size: 3 1/2" x 5 1/2"
Sponsor: General Foods
Complete Set (26 cards): 25.00

☐ Brent Ashton
☐ Michel Bergeron
☐ Jeff Brown
☐ Alain Côté
☐ Gilbert Delorme
☐ Gord Donnelly
☐ Mike Eagles
☐ Paul Gillis
☐ Mario Gosselin (G)
☐ Mike Hough
☐ Dale Hunter
☐ Mark Kumpel
☐ Jason Lafrenière
☐ Clint Malarchuk (G)
☐ Randy Moller
☐ Simon Nolet
☐ Robert Picard
☐ Ken Quinney
☐ Normand Rochefort
☐ Richard Sévigny (G)
☐ David Shaw
☐ Risto Siltanen
☐ Anton Stastny
☐ Peter Stastny
☐ Charles Thiffault
☐ Richard Zemlak

1986 - 87 NORDIQUES MCDONALD'S

The most expensive singles are Michel Goulet and Peter Stastny at $3-4. Singles start at $1.00.

Card Size: 3 1/2" x 5 1/2"
Sponsor: McDonald's, Le Soleil, CHRC80
Complete Set (25 cards): 25.00

☐ John Anderson
☐ Brent Ashton
☐ Jeff Brown
☐ Alain Côté
☐ Gilbert Delorme
☐ Mike Eagles
☐ Steve Finn
☐ Paul Gillis
☐ Mario Gosselin (G)
☐ Michel Goulet
☐ Mike Hough
☐ Dale Hunter
☐ Mark Kumpel
☐ Alain Lemieux
☐ Clint Malarchuk (G)
☐ Jimmy Mann
☐ Randy Moller
☐ Wilf Paiement
☐ Pat Price
☐ Normand Rochefort
☐ Jean-François Sauvé
☐ Richard Sévigny (G)
☐ David Shaw
☐ Anton Stastny
☐ Peter Stastny

1986 - 87 NORDIQUES YUM YUM

The most expensive players are Michel Goulet and Peter Stastny at $4-5. Singles start at $2.

Card Size: 2" x 2 1/2"
Sponsors: none
Complete Set (10 cards): 20.00

☐ Alain Côté
☐ Gilbert Delorme
☐ Paul Gillis
☐ Michel Goulet
☐ Dale Hunter
☐ Clint Malarchuk (G)
☐ Robert Picard
☐ Normand Rochefort
☐ Anton Stastny
☐ Peter Stastny

1987 - 88 NORDIQUES GENERAL FOODS

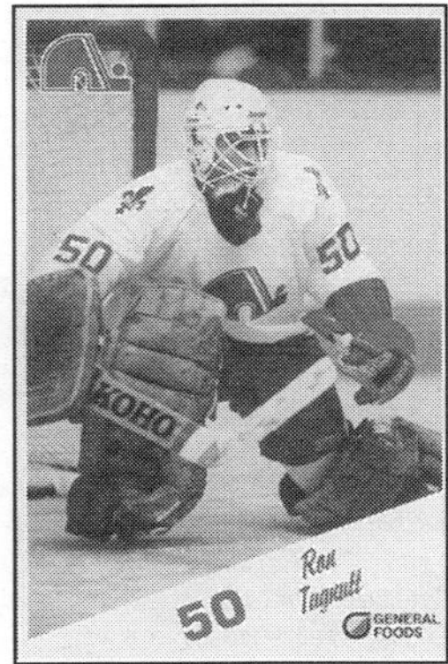

These cards have blank backs. The most expensive singles are Michel Goulet and Peter Stastny at $3-4. Singles start at $1.00.

Card Size: 3 3/4" x 5 5/8"
Sponsor: General Foods
Complete Set (32 cards): 25.00

☐ Tommy Albelin
☐ Jeff Brown
☐ Mario Brunetta (G)
☐ Terry Carkner
☐ Alain Côté
☐ Gord Donnelly
☐ Gaetan Duchesne
☐ Mike Eagles
☐ Steve Finn
☐ Paul Gillis
☐ Mario Gosselin (G)
☐ Michel Goulet
☐ Stéphane Guerard
☐ Alan Haworth
☐ Mike Hough
☐ Jeff Jackson
☐ Stu Kulak
☐ Jason Lafrenière
☐ Lane Lambert
☐ David Latta
☐ Max Middendorf
☐ Randy Moller
☐ Robert Picard
☐ Daniel Poudrier
☐ Ken Quinney
☐ Normand Rochefort
☐ Richard Sévigny (G)
☐ Anton Stastny
☐ Peter Stastny
☐ Ron Tugnutt (G)
☐ A.Chainey/A.Savard/G.Lapointe
☐ Mascot Badaboum

1987 - 88 NORDIQUES YUM YUM

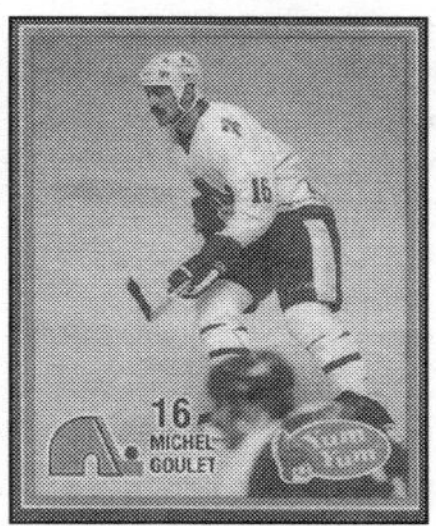

The most expensive singles are Michel Goulet and Peter Stastny at $4-5. Singles start at $2. Mario Gosselin has a variation with the uniform number 83 on the back and one with the proper uniform number 33.

Card Size: 2" x 2 1/2"
Sponsors: none
Complete Set (10 cards): 20.00

☐ Alain Côté
☐ Paul Gillis
☐☐ Mario Gosselin (G)
☐ Michel Goulet
☐ Alan Haworth
☐ Jason Lafrenière
☐ Robert Picard
☐ Normand Rochefort
☐ Anton Stastny
☐ Peter Stastny

1988 - 89 NORDIQUES GENERAL FOODS

There are two versions of this set: cards with the sponsors' logos and cards without the sponsors' logos. Card backs are blank. Pricing for both versions is identical. Joe Sakic is the most expensive single at $12-15. Singles start at $1.00.

Card Size: 3 3/4" x 5 5/8"
Sponsors: General Foods, Le Journal, CHRC80
Complete Set (33 cards): 35.00

☐☐ Tommy Albelin #28
☐☐ Joel Baillargeon #38
☐☐ Jeff Brown #22
☐☐ Mario Brunetta (G) #30
☐☐ Alain Côté #19
☐☐ Gord Donnelly #34
☐☐ Daniel Doré #15
☐☐ Gaetan Duchesne #14
☐☐ Steve Finn #29
☐☐ Marc Fortier #9
☐☐ Paul Gillis #23
☐☐ Mario Gosselin (G) #33
☐☐ Michel Goulet #16
☐☐ Jari Grönstrand #5
☐☐ Stéphane Guérard #6
☐☐ Jeff Jackson #25
☐☐ Iiro Jarvi #11
☐☐ Lane Lambert #7
☐☐ David Latta #27
☐☐ Curtis Leschyshyn #46
☐☐ Bob Mason (G) #1
☐☐ Randy Moller #21
☐☐ Robert Picard #24
☐☐ Walt Poddubny #75
☐☐ Joe Sakic #88
☐☐ Greg Smyth #4
☐☐ Anton Stastny #20
☐☐ Peter Stastny #26
☐☐ Trevor Stienburg #17
☐☐ Mark Vermette #10
☐☐ S.Aubry/A.Chainey/G.Lapointe/R.Lapointe
☐☐ Mascot Badaboum
☐☐ Team Photo
☐☐ Mascot Badaboum

1989 - 90 NORDIQUES GENERAL FOODS

Horizontal photos are used in this set. There are two versions of this set: cards with the General Foods logo and cards without the logo. Pricing for both versions is identical. Joe Sakic is the most expensive single at $8-10. Guy Lafleur sells at $4-5 and Stéphane Fiset sells at $3-4. Singles start at $1.00. There are nine players who are not in the General Foods set. A 30-card General Foods set sells at $25.

Card Size: 3 3/4" x 5 5/8"
Sponsor: General Foods
Complete Set (39): 30.00

☐ Serge Aubry
☐☐ Michel Bergeron, Coach
☐☐ Jeff Brown
☐ Alain Chainey
☐☐ Joe Cirella
☐☐ Lucien DeBlois
☐☐ Daniel Doré
☐☐ Steve Finn
☐☐ Stéphane Fiset (G)
☐ Bryan Fogarty
☐☐ Marc Fortier
☐☐ Paul Gillis
☐☐ Michel Goulet
☐☐ Jari Grödstrand
☐☐ Stéphane Guérard
☐☐ Mike Hough
☐ Tony Hrkac
☐☐ Jeff Jackson
☐☐ Iiro Jarvi
☐☐ Kevin Kaminski
☐☐ Darin Kimble
☐☐ Guy Lafleur
☐ Guy Lapointe
☐☐ David Latta
☐ Brian Lawton
☐☐ Curtis Leschyshyn
☐☐ Claude Loiselle
☐☐ Mario Marois
☐ Tony McKegney
☐☐ Ken McRae
☐ Greg Millen (G)
☐ Randy Moller
☐☐ Sergei Mylnikov (G)
☐☐ Michel Petit
☐☐ Robert Picard
☐☐ Joe Sakic
☐ Peter Stastny
☐☐ Ron Tugnutt (G)
☐☐ Team Photo

1989 - 90 NORDIQUES POLICE

Horizontal photos are used in this set. Joe Sakic is the most expensive single at $8-10. Singles start at $1.00.

Card Size: 2 3/4" x 4"
Sponsor: ville de Vanier
Complete Set (27 cards): 25.00

☐ Jeff Brown
☐ Joe Cirella
☐ Lucien Deblois
☐ Daniel Doré
☐ Steve Finn
☐ Stéphane Fiset (G)
☐ Marc Fortier
☐ Paul Gillis
☐ Michel Goulet
☐ Stéphane Guérard
☐ Mike Hough
☐ Jeff Jackson
☐ Iiro Jarvi
☐ Darin Kimble
☐ Guy Lafleur
☐ David Latta
☐ Curtis Leschyshyn
☐ Claude Loiselle
☐ Mario Marois
☐ Ken McRae
☐ Sergei Mylnikov (G)
☐ Michel Petit
☐ Robert Picard
☐ Jean-Marc Routhier
☐ Joe Sakic
☐ Peter Stastny
☐ Ron Tugnutt (G)

1990 - 91 NORDIQUES

Horizontal photos are used in this set. Joe Sakic is the most expensive single at $6-8. Singles start at $1.00.

Card Size: 3 3/4" x 5 5/8"
Sponsors: none
Complete Set (26 cards): 20.00

☐ Joe Cirella
☐ Lucien DeBlois
☐ Daniel Doré
☐ Steve Finn
☐ Stéphane Fiset (G)
☐ Bryan Fogarty
☐ Marc Fortier
☐ Paul Gillis
☐ Michel Goulet
☐ Stéphane Guérard
☐ Mike Hough
☐ Tony Hrkac
☐ Jeff Jackson
☐ Iiro Jarvi
☐ Kevin Kaminski
☐ Darin Kimble
☐ David Latta
☐ Curtis Leschyshyn
☐ Claude Loiselle
☐ Mario Marois
☐ Tony McKegney
☐ Ken McRae
☐ Michel Petit
☐ Joe Sakic
☐ Peter Stastny
☐ Ron Tugnutt (G)

1990 - 91 NORDIQUES PETRO-CANADA

Joe Sakic and Mats Sundin are the most expensive singles at $6-8. Singles start at $1.00.

Card Size: 3 3/4" x 5 5/8"
Sponsor: Petro-Canada
Complete Set (28 cards): 25.00

☐ Aaron Broten
☐ Dave Chambers
☐ Joe Cirella
☐ Lucien DeBlois
☐ Steve Finn
☐ Bryan Fogarty
☐ Marc Fortier
☐ Robbie Ftorek
☐ Paul Gillis
☐ Scott Gordon (G)
☐ Mike Hough
☐ Tony Hrkac
☐ Darin Kimble
☐ Guy Lafleur
☐ Curtis Leschyshyn
☐ Claude Loiselle
☐ Jacques Martin
☐ Tony McKegney
☐ Owen Nolan
☐ Michel Petit
☐ Joe Sakic
☐ Everett Sanipass
☐ Mats Sundin
☐ John Tanner (G)
☐ Ron Tugnutt (G)
☐ Dan Vincelette
☐ Craig Wolanin
☐ Team Photo

1991 - 92 NORDIQUES PETRO-CANADA

The most expensive singles are Joe Sakic at $5-6 and Mats Sundin at $4-5. Singles start at $1.00.

Card Size: 3 3/4" x 5 5/8"
Sponsor: Petro-Canada
Complete Set (35 cards): 25.00

☐ Don Barber
☐ Jacques Cloutier (G)
☐ Steve Finn
☐ Stéphane Fiset (G)
☐ Bryan Fogarty
☐ Adam Foote
☐ Marc Fortier
☐ Alexei Gusarov
☐ Mike Hough
☐ Don Jackson
☐ Valeri Kamensky
☐ John Kordic
☐ Claude Lapointe
☐ Curtis Leschyshyn
☐ Jacques Martin
☐ Mike McNeill
☐ Ken McRae
☐ Kip Miller
☐ Stéphane Morin
☐ Owen Nolan
☐ Pierre Pagé
☐ Greg Paslawski
☐ Herb Raglan
☐ Joe Sakic
☐ Doug Smail
☐ Greg Smyth
☐ Mats Sundin
☐ Mikhail Tatarinov
☐ Ron Tugnutt (G)
☐ Tony Twist
☐ Wayne Van Dorp
☐ Randy Velischek
☐ Mark Vermette
☐ Craig Wolanin
☐ Mascot Badaboum

1992 - 93 NORDIQUES PETRO-CANADA

Joe Sakic is the most expensive single at $4-5. Singles start at 75¢.

Card Size: 3 1/2" x 5 5/8"
Sponsor: Petro-Canada
Complete Set (39 cards): 20.00

☐ Dan Bouchard
☐ Gino Cavallini
☐ Jacques Cloutier (G)
☐ Steve Duchesne
☐ Steve Finn
☐ Stéphane Fiset (G)
☐ Adam Foote
☐ Alexei Gusarov
☐ Ron Hextall (G)
☐ Mike Hough
☐ Kerry Huffman
☐ Tim Hunter
☐ Don Jackson
☐ Valeri Kamensky
☐ David Karpa
☐ Andrei Kovalenko
☐ Claude Lapointe
☐ Curtis Leschyshyn
☐ Bill Lindsay
☐ Jacques Martin
☐ Owen Nolan
☐ Pierre Pagé
☐ Scott Pearson
☐ Herb Raglan
☐ Mike Ricci
☐ Martin Rucinsky
☐ Joe Sakic
☐ André Savard
☐ Chris Simon
☐ Mats Sundin
☐ John Tanner (G)
☐ Mikhail Tatarinov
☐ Tony Twist
☐ Wayne Van Dorp
☐ Mark Vermette
☐ Craig Wolanin
☐ Scott Young
☐ Mascot Badaboum
☐ Team Photo

1994 - 95 NORDIQUES BURGER KING

Joe Sakic is the most expensive single at $3-4. Singles start at 75¢.

Card Size: 3 1/2" x 6"
Sponsor: Burger King
Complete Set (24 cards): 20.00

☐ Bob Bassen
☐ Wendel Clark
☐ Adam Deadmarsh
☐ Steve Finn
☐ Stéphane Fiset (G)
☐ Adam Foote
☐ Peter Forsberg
☐ Alexei Gusarov
☐ Valeri Kamensky
☐ Andrei Kovalenko
☐ Uwe Krupp
☐ Claude Lapointe
☐ Janne Laukkanen
☐ Sylvain Lefebvre
☐ Paul MacDermid
☐ Owen Nolan
☐ Mike Ricci
☐ Martin Rucinsky
☐ Joe Sakic
☐ Chris Simon
☐ Jocelyn Thibault (G)
☐ Craig Wolanin
☐ Scott Young

ST. LOUIS BLUES

1971 - 72 BLUES

Al Arbour is the most expensive single at $4-5. Singles start at $2.

Card Size: 3 1/2" x 5 1/2"
Sponsors: none
Complete Set (25 cards): 50.00

☐ Al Arbour
☐ John Arbour
☐ Carl Brewer
☐ Jacques Caron (G)
☐ Terry Crisp
☐ André Dupont
☐ Jack Egers
☐ Larry Hornung
☐ Brian Lavender
☐ Mike Murphy
☐ Gerry Odrowski
☐ Danny O'Shea
☐ Mike Parizeau
☐ Noel Picard
☐ Barclay Plager
☐ Bill Plager
☐ Bob Plager
☐ Phil Roberto
☐ Gary Sabourin
☐ Frank St. Marseille
☐ Floyd Thomson
☐ Garry Unger
☐ Ernie Wakely (G)
☐ Tom Woodcock
☐ G.Marchant/A.McPherson

1972 - 73 BLUES

Bob Johnson is the most expensive single at $3-4. Singles start at $2.

Card Size: 6 7/8" x 8 3/4"
Sponsors: none
Complete Set (22 cards): 40.00

☐ Jacques Caron (G)
☐ Steve Durbano
☐ Jack Egers
☐ Chris Evans
☐ Jean Hamel
☐ Fran Huck
☐ Brent Hughes
☐ Bob Johnson
☐ Mike Lampman
☐ Bob McCord
☐ Wayne Merrick
☐ Mike Murphy
☐ Danny O'Shea
☐ Barclay Plager
☐ Bob Plager
☐ Pierre Plante
☐ Phil Roberto
☐ Gary Sabourin
☐ Wayne Stephenson (G)
☐ Jean-Guy Talbot
☐ Floyd Thomson
☐ Garry Unger

1972 - 73 BLUES

Photos are in black and white. Al Arbour is the most expensive single at $4-5. Singles start at $2.

Card Size: 8" x 10"

Sponsors: none

Complete Set (25 cards): 50.00

☐ Al Arbour
☐ Jacques Caron (G)
☐ André Dupont
☐ Steve Durbano
☐ Jack Egers
☐ Chris Evans
☐ Fran Huck
☐ Bob Johnson (G)
☐ Mike Lampman
☐ Wayne Merrick
☐ Mike Murphy
☐ Danny O'Shea
☐ Kevin O'Shea
☐ Noel Picard
☐ Barclay Plager
☐ Bob Plager
☐ Phil Roberto
☐ Gary Sabourin
☐ Frank St. Marseille
☐ Wayne Stephenson (G)
☐ Floyd Thomson
☐ Garry Unger
☐ Sid Solomon/Sid Soloman Jr.
☐ B. McCreary/ J.G. Probstein/G.Kyle GT. Woocock/ A. Solomon/T.Madden
☐ Lynn Patrick/Sid Abel

1973 - 74 BLUES

John Davidson is the most expensive single at $5-6. Singles start at $2. Gary Unger has two cards.

Card Size: 6 7/8" x 8 3/4"

Sponsors: none

Complete Set (24 cards): 50.00

☐ Lou Angotti
☐ Don Awrey
☐ John Davidson (G)
☐ Ab DeMarco
☐ Steve Durbano
☐ Chris Evans
☐ Larry Giroux
☐ Jean Hamel
☐ Nick Harbaruk
☐ J. Bob Kelly
☐ Mike Lampman
☐ Wayne Merrick
☐ Barclay Plager
☐ Bob Plager
☐ Pierre Plante
☐ Phil Roberto
☐ Gary Sabourin
☐ Glen Sather
☐ Wayne Stephenson (G)
☐ Jean-Guy Talbot
☐ Floyd Thomson
☐ Garry Unger
☐ Garry Unger
☐ Team Photo

1978 - 79 BLUES

Bernie Federko and Brian Sutter are the most expensive singles at $4-6 in NRMT. Singles start at $1.50.

Postcard Size: 6 7/8" x 8 3/4"

Sponsors: none

Complete Set (21 cards): 35.00

☐ Wayne Babych
☐ Curt Bennett
☐ Harvey Bennett
☐ Jack Brownschidle
☐ Mike Crombeen
☐ Tony Currie
☐ Bernie Federko
☐ Barry Gibbs
☐ Larry Giroux
☐ Inge Hammarstrom
☐ Phil Myre (G)
☐ Larry Patey
☐ Barclay Plager
☐ Rick Shinske
☐ John Smrke
☐ Ed Staniowski (G)
☐ Bob Stewart
☐ Brian Sutter
☐ Garry Unger
☐ Blue Angels
☐ Fan Van

1986 - 87 BLUES

Singles sell at $1.50-2.00.

Photo Size: 8 1/2" x 11"

Sponsors: none

Complete Set (20 photos): 20.00

☐ 1967-68 Blues
☐ 1968-69 Blues
☐ 1969-70 Blues
☐ 1970-71 Blues
☐ 1971-72 Blues
☐ 1972-73 Blues
☐ 1973-74 Blues
☐ 1974-75 Blues
☐ 1975-76 Blues
☐ 1976-77 Blues
☐ 1977-78 Blues
☐ 1978-79 Blues
☐ 1979-80 Blues
☐ 1980-81 Blues
☐ 1981-82 Blues
☐ 1982-83 Blues
☐ 1983-84 Blues
☐ 1984-85 Blues
☐ 1985-86 Blues
☐ 1986-87 Blues

1987 - 88 BLUES

Brett Hull is the most expensive single at $12-15. Singles start at $1.00.

Card Size: 3 1/2" x 5 1/2"

Sponsors: none

Complete Set (24 cards): 35.00

☐ Brian Benning
☐ Mike Bullard
☐ Gino Cavallini
☐ Paul Cavallini
☐ Craig Coxe
☐ Robert Dirk
☐ Doug Evans
☐ Todd Ewen
☐ Bernie Federko
☐ Gaston Gingras
☐ Tony Hrkac
☐ Brett Hull
☐ Tony McKegney
☐ Rick Meagher
☐ Greg Millen (G)
☐ Sergio Momesso
☐ Greg Paslawski
☐ Herb Raglan
☐ Dave Richter
☐ Vincent Riendeau (G)
☐ Gordie Roberts
☐ Brian Sutter
☐ Tom Tilley
☐ Steve Tuttle

1987 - 88 BLUES KODAK

Doug Gilmour is the most expensive single at $6-8. Singles start at $1.00.

Card Size: 2 3/16" x 3"

Sponsor: Kodak

Complete Set (26 cards): 25.00

☐ Brian Benning #2
☐ Tim Bothwell #6
☐ Charlie Bourgeois #4
☐ Paul Cavallini #14
☐ Gino Cavallini #17
☐ Michael Dark #26
☐ Doug Evans #32
☐ Todd Ewen #21
☐ Bernie Federko #24
☐ Ron Flockhart #12
☐ Doug Gilmour #9
☐ Gaston Gingras #23
☐ Tony Hrkac #18
☐ Mark Hunter #20
☐ Jocelyn Lemieux #16
☐ Tony McKegney #10
☐ Rick Meagher #22
☐ Greg Millen #29 (G)
☐ Robert Nordmark #27
☐ Greg Paslawski #28
☐ Herb Raglan #25
☐ Rob Ramage #5
☐ Cliff Ronning #7
☐ Brian Sutter #11
☐ Perry Turnbull #19
☐ Rick Wamsley #30 (G)

1988 - 89 BLUES KODAK

Brett Hull is the most expensive single at $10-12. Singles start at $1.00.

Card Size: 3 1/2" x 4 1/4"

Sponsor: Kodak

Complete Set (24 cards): 30.00

☐ Brian Benning #2
☐ Mike Bullard
☐ Gino Cavallini #17
☐ Paul Cavallini #14
☐ Craig Coxe #15
☐ Robert Dirk
☐ Doug Evans #32
☐ Todd Ewen #21
☐ Bernie Federko #24
☐ Gaston Gingras #23
☐ Tony Hrkac #18
☐ Brett Hull #16
☐ Tony McKegney #10
☐ Rick Meagher #22
☐ Greg Millen #29 (G)
☐ Sergio Momesso #27
☐ Greg Paslawski #28
☐ Herb Raglan #25
☐ Dave Richter #5
☐ Vincent Riendeau #30 (G)
☐ Gordie Roberts #4
☐ Brian Sutter #11
☐ Tom Tilley #20
☐ Steve Tuttle #35

1988 - 89 BLUES KODAK

Brett Hull is the most expensive single at $8-10. Singles start at $1.00.

Card Size: 2 3/16" x 3"

Sponsor: Kodak

Complete Set (25 cards): 25.00

☐ Brian Benning #2
☐ Tim Bothwell #6
☐ Paul Cavallini #14
☐ Gino Cavallini #17
☐ Craig Coxe #15
☐ Doug Evans #32
☐ Todd Ewen #21
☐ Bernie Federko #24
☐ Gaston Gingras #23
☐ Tony Hrkac #18
☐ Brett Hull #16
☐ Mike Lalor #26
☐ Tony McKegney #10
☐ Rick Meagher #22
☐ Greg Millen #29 (G)
☐ Sergio Momesso #27
☐ Greg Paslawski #28
☐ Herb Raglan #25
☐ Dave Richter #5
☐ Vincent Riendeau #30 (G)
☐ Gordie Roberts #4
☐ Cliff Ronning #7
☐ Tom Tilley #20
☐ Steve Tuttle #35
☐ Peter Zezel #9

1989 - 90 BLUES KODAK

Brett Hull is the most expensive single at $6-8. Rod Brind'Amour, Adam Oates and Curtis Joseph sell at $4-6. Singles start at $1.00.

Card Size: 2 3/8" x 3"

Sponsor: Kodak

Complete Set (25 cards): 25.00

☐ Rod Brind'Amour #19
☐ Jeff Brown #21
☐ Paul Cavallini #14
☐ Gino Cavallini #17
☐ Kelly Chase #39
☐ Brett Hull #16
☐ Pat Jablonski #1 (G)
☐ Curtis Joseph #31 (G)
☐ Mike Lalor #26
☐ Dominic Lavoie #38
☐ Dave Lowry #10
☐ Paul MacLean #15
☐ Rick Meagher #22
☐ Sergio Momesso #27
☐ Adam Oates #12
☐ Adrien Plavsic #23
☐ Herb Raglan #25
☐ Vincent Riendeau #30 (G)
☐ Gordie Roberts #4
☐ Brian Sutter
☐ Dave Thomlinson #40
☐ Tom Tilley #20
☐ Steve Tuttle #35
☐ Tony Twist #6
☐ Peter Zezel #9

1990 - 91 BLUES KODAK

Brett Hull is the most expensive single at $8-10. Singles start at $1.00.

Card Size: 2 1/2" x 3 1/2"

Sponsor: Kodak

Complete Set (25 cards): 25.00

☐ Bob Bassen
☐ Rod Brind'Amour
☐ Jeff Brown
☐ Dave Bruce
☐ Gino Cavallini
☐ Paul Cavallini
☐ Geoff Courtnall
☐ Robert Dirk
☐ Glen Featherstone
☐ Brett Hull
☐ Curtis Joseph (G)
☐ Dave Lowry
☐ Paul MacLean
☐ Mario Marois
☐ Rick Meagher
☐ Sergio Momesso
☐ Adam Oates
☐ Vincent Riendeau (G)
☐ Cliff Ronning
☐ Harold Snepsts
☐ Scott Stevens
☐ Brian Sutter
☐ Rich Sutter
☐ Steve Tuttle
☐ Ron Wilson

1991 - 92 BLUES

Brendan Shanahan is the most expensive single at $6-8. Singles start at $1.00.

Postcard Size: 3 1/2" x 5 1/2"

Sponsors: none

Complete Set (22 cards): 25.00

☐ Murray Baron
☐ Bob Bassen
☐ Jeff Brown
☐ Garth Butcher
☐ Gino Cavallini
☐ Paul Cavallini
☐ Kelly Chase
☐ Dave Christian
☐ Nelson Emerson
☐ Brett Hull
☐ Pat Jablonski (G)
☐ Curtis Joseph (G)
☐ Darin Kimble
☐ Dave Lowry
☐ Michel Mongeau
☐ Adam Oates
☐ Rob Robinson
☐ Brendan Shanahan
☐ Rich Sutter
☐ Ron Sutter
☐ Ron Wilson
☐ Rick Zombo

1992 - 93 BLUES UPPER DECK/ MCDONALD'S BEST OF THE BLUES

This series was available at McDonald's in six-card packs. Stars sell at $4-5. Singles start at 50¢. Brett Hull signed 100 cards that were inserted into packs. The Hull autograph sells at $200-225.

Card Size: 2 1/2" x 3 1/2"

Sponsor: Upper Deck, McDonald's

Complete Set (28 cards): 25.00

Album: 10.00

☐ 1 Glenn Hall (G)
☐ 2 Doug Gilmour
☐ 3 Al Arbour
☐ 4 Mike Liut (G)
☐ 5 Blake Dunlop
☐ 6 Noel Picard
☐ 7 Bob Plager

☐ 8 Ab McDonald
☐ 9 Curtis Joseph (G)
☐ 10 Wayne Babych
☐ 11 Red Berenson
☐ 12 Brett Hull
☐ 13 Bob Gassoff
☐ 14 Bernie Federko
☐ 15 Gary Sabourin
☐ 16 Joe Mullen
☐ 17 Adam Oates
☐ 18 Jorgen Pettersson
☐ 19 Frank St. Marseille
☐ 20 Scott Stevens
☐ 21 Rob Ramage
☐ 22 Jacques Plante (G)
☐ 23 Rick Meagher
☐ 24 Barclay Plager
☐ 25 Brian Sutter
☐ 26 Perry Turnbull
☐ 27 Garry Unger
☐ 28 Checklist
☐ Brett Hull autograph

1996 - 97 BLUES ST. LOUIS DISPATCH 30TH ANNIVERSARY SERIES

We have no pricing information on this set.
Photo Size: 8 1/2" x 11"
Sponsor: St. Louis Dispatch

☐ 1 Brett Hull
☐ 2 Al MacInnis
☐ 3 Grant Fuhr (G)
☐ 4 Tony Twist
☐ 5 Chris Pronger

SAN JOSE SHARKS

1991 - 92 SHARKS SPORTS ACTION

Jeff Hackett is the most expensive single at $1.50. Singles start at 50¢.
Card Size: 2 1/2" x 3 1/2"
Sponsors: Sports Action
Complete Set (22 cards): 15.00

☐ Perry Anderson
☐ Perry Berezan
☐ Steve Bozek
☐ Dean Evason
☐ Pat Falloon
☐ Paul Fenton
☐ Link Gaetz
☐ Jeff Hackett (G)
☐ Ken Hammond
☐ Brian Hayward (G)
☐ Tony Hrkac
☐ Kelly Kisio
☐ Brian Lawton
☐ Pat McLeod
☐ Bob McGill
☐ Brian Mullen
☐ Jarmo Myllys (G)
☐ Wayne Presley
☐ Neil Wilkinson
☐ Doug Wilson
☐ Rob Zettler
☐ Sharks game action

1992 - 93 SHARKS PACIFIC BELL SHEETS

These sheets are limited to 4,500 copies. Sandis Ozolinsh is the most expensive single at $6-8. Singles start at $4.
Photo Size: 8 1/2" x 11"
Sponsor: Pacific Bell
Complete Set (40 photos): 150.00

☐ Jamie Baker
☐ Mark Beaufait
☐ Viatcheslav Butsayev
☐ Dale Craigwell
☐ Shawn Cronin
☐ Gaetan Duchesne
☐ Todd Elik
☐ Pat Falloon
☐ Wade Flaherty (G)
☐ Johan Garpenlov
☐ Rob Gaudreau
☐ Arturs Irbe (G)
☐ AS: Arturs Irbe (G)
☐ Viktor Kozlov
☐ Vlastimil Kroupa
☐ Mike Lalor
☐ Igor Larionov
☐ Sergei Makarov
☐ David Maley
☐ Jason More
☐ Jeff Norton
☐ Jeff Odgers
☐ AS: Sandis Ozolinsh
☐ Tom Pederson
☐ Pete Stemkowski
☐ Mike Sullivan
☐ Michal Sykora
☐ Ray Whitney
☐ Dody Wood
☐ Jimmy Waite (G)
☐ Doug Zmolek
☐ Kevin Constantine
Duane Sutter/ Vasily Tikhonov
☐ B.Errey/R.Zettler
☐ M.Rathje/A.Nazarov
☐ R.Whitney/P.Falloon
☐ San Jose Arena
☐ Sharks Faceoff
☐ Sharks Photo
☐ Air Shark
☐ Zamboni with Fin

1993 - 94 SHARKS IL PORNAIO SHEETS

Singles start at $3.50. These sheets are sequentially numbered out of 12,000. Other singles exist.
Sheet Size: 8 1/2" x 11"
Sponsor: Il Pornaio

☐ 14OCT Arturs Irbe (G)

1994 - 95 SHARKS PACIFIC BELL SHEETS

Singles start at $4. These sheets are sequentially numbered out of 7,700. Other singles exist.
Sheet Size: 8 1/2" x 11"
Sponsor: Pacific Bell

☐ 1OCT94 Arturs Irbe (G)

1995 - 96 SHARKS PACIFIC BELL SHEETS

Singles start at $5. These sheets are sequentially numbered out of 3,100. Other singles exist.
Sheet Size: 8 1/2" x 11"
Sponsor: Pacific Bell

☐ 12OCT Ray Whitney (XZX: P. Falloon)
☐ 11NOV Mascot S.J. Sharkie
☐ 7DEC S.J. Sharkie Van
☐ 9DEC Sharks head tunne (XZX: A. Irbe)
☐ 8JAN 1996 All Star Game logo
☐ 1MAR 5th year anniversary logo
☐ 6MAR Zamboni

1996 - 97 SHARKS PACIFIC BELL SHEETS

Ed Belfour is the most expensive single at $10-12. Singles start at $5.
Sheet Size: 8 1/2" x 11"
Sponsor: Pacific Bell
Complete Set (40 cards): 185.00

☐ 5OCT Owen Nolan
☐ 12OCT Ulf Dahlen
☐ 16OCT Chris Terreri
☐ 30OCT Doug Bodger
☐ 2NOV Todd Gill
☐ 6NOV Kelly Hrudey (G)
☐ 8NOV Michal Sykora
☐ 12NOV Ron Sutter
☐ 21NOV Darren Turcotte
☐ 23NOV Al Iafrate
☐ 27NOV Bernie Nicholls
☐ 7DEC Chris Tancill
☐ 11DEC Andrei Nazarov
☐ 13DEC Viktor Kozlov
☐ 17DEC Todd Ewen
☐ 26DEC Owen Nolan
☐ 2JAN Jeff Friesen
☐ 4JAN Ville Peltonen
☐ 7JAN Doug Bodger
☐ 9JAN Mike Rathje
☐ 13JAN Dody Wood
☐ 22JAN Tim Hunter
☐ 24JAN Marty McSorley
☐ 1FEB Greg Hawgood
☐ 3FEB Shean Donovan
☐ 5FEB W. Cashman/ A. Sims/ R. Sommer
☐ 18FEB Kelly Hrudey (G)
☐ 20FEB Todd Ewen
☐ 6MAR Darren Turcotte
☐ 9MAR Vlastimil Kroupa
☐ 11MAR Marcus Ragnarsson (XCX: K. Todd)
☐ 14MAR Tony Granato
☐ 15MAR Todd Gill
☐ 234MAR Marty McSorley
☐ 26MAR Ed Belfour (G)
☐ 28MAR Bob Errey
☐ 2APR T. Granata/ T. Gill/ O. Nolan
☐ 4APR AS: O. Nolan/ T. Granato
☐ 7APR Stephen Guolla
☐ 11APR Jeff Friesen (XCX: J. Roenick)

1997 - 98 SHARKS PACIFIC BELL SHEETS

Patrick Marleau is the most expensive single at $10-15. Singles start at $5.
Sheet Size: 8 1/2" x 11"
Sponsor: Pacific Bell
Complete Set (44 sheets): 200.00

☐ 1OCT AW: Tony Granato
☐ 4OCT Kelly Hrudey (G)
☐ 7OCT Viktor Kozlov
☐ 11OCT Marcus Ragnarsson
☐ 13OCT Mike Rathje (XCX: J. Garpenlov)
☐ 16OCT Doug Bodger
☐ 22OCT Shean Donovan (XCX: Ryan Smyth)
☐ 4NOV Bill Houlder
☐ 7NOV Bernie Nicholls
☐ 8NOV Jeff Friesen (XCX: G. Snow)
☐ 12NOV Mike Vernon (G)
☐ 15NOV Marco Sturm
☐ 18NOV Stephane Matteau
☐ 27NOV Andrei Nazarov
☐ 10DEC Marty McSorley
☐ 16DEC Andrei Zyuzin (XCX: T. Donato)
☐ 18DEC Patrick Marleau
☐ 26DEC Tony Granato (XCX: S. Thornton)
☐ 6JAN Murray Craven
☐ 10JAN Shawn Burr (XCX: P. Coffey)
☐ 12JAN Owen Nolan
☐ 14JAN Ron Sutter
☐ 21JAN Todd Gill
☐ 23JAN Jeff Friesen
☐ 24JAN Andrei Zyuzin
☐ 27JAN Dave Lowry
☐ 29JAN John MacLean
☐ 31JAN Mike Ricci
☐ 2FEB M. Sturm, Ger./ M. Ragnarsson, Swe.
☐ 26FEB Alexandre Korolyuk
☐ 2MAR Patrick Marleau
☐ 5MAR Darryl Sutter (XCX: B. Nicholls)
☐ 9MAR Bernie Nicholls
☐ 16MAR Owen Nolan (XCX: Cu. Joseph)
☐ 18MAR Al Iafrate
☐ 21MAR Rich Brennan (XCX: R. Corbet)
☐ 24MAR Mike Vernon (G)
☐ 7APR Marco Sturm
☐ 9APR Mike Ricci
☐ 11APR Joe Murphy
☐ 18APR Bryan Marchment (XCX: G. Murray)
☐ 26APR Team Photo
☐ 28APR Mike Vernon (G)
☐ 2MAY Owen Nolan

TAMPA BAY LIGHTNING

1992 - 93 LIGHTNING SHERATON INN

These cards were originally issued as a panel. Roman Hamrlik is the most expensive single at $3-4. Singles start at 75¢.
Card Size: 2 1/2" x 3 1/2"
Sponsor: Sheraton Inn
Complete Set (28 cards): 25.00

☐ Mikael Andersson
☐ Bob Beers
☐ J.C. Bergeron (G)
☐ Marc Bergevin
☐ Tim Bergland
☐ Brian Bradley
☐ Marc Bureau
☐ Wayne Cashman
☐ Shawn Chambers
☐ Danton Cole
☐ Adam Creighton
☐ Terry Crisp
☐ Rob DiMaio
☐ Phil Esposito
☐ Tony Esposito
☐ Roman Hamrlik
☐ Pat Jablonski (G)
☐ Steve Kasper
☐ Chris Kontos
☐ Steve Maltais
☐ Joe Reekie
☐ John Tucker
☐ Wendell Young (G)
☐ Rob Zamuner
☐ Mascot Thunderbug
☐ Lightning card
☐ Inaugural season
☐ Sheraton logo

1993 - 94 LIGHTNING KASH N'CARRY

Chris Gratton is the most expensive single at $6-8. Singles start at $1.00. Other singles may exist.
Card Size: 5" x 7"
Sponsor: Kash n' Karry

☐ Brian Bradley
☐ Shawn Chambers
☐ Chris Gratton
☐ Adam Creighton
☐ Rob DiMaio
☐ Wendell Young (G)

1994 - 95 LIGHTNING SKY BOX SPORTS CAFÉ

This set was originally issued as a panel. Chris Gratton is the most expensive single at $2-3. Singles start at 75¢.
Card Size: 2 1/2" x 3 1/4"
Sponsor: SkyBox Sports Café
Complete Set (28 cards): 20.00

☐ Mikael Andersson
☐ Marc Bergevin
☐ Brian Bradley
☐ Marc Bureau
☐ Wayne Cashman
☐ Shawn Chambers
☐ Enrico Ciccone
☐ Danton Cole
☐ Adam Creighton
☐ Terry Crisp

☐ Jim Cummins
☐ Pat Elynuik
☐ Phil Esposito
☐ Tony Esposito
☐ Gerard Gallant
☐ Danny Gare
☐ Chris Gratton
☐ Roman Hamrlik
☐ Chris Joseph
☐ Petr Klima
☐ Chris LiPuma
☐ Rudy Poeschek
☐ Daren Puppa (G)
☐ Denis Savard
☐ John Tucker
☐ Wendell Young (G)
☐ Rob Zamuner
☐ Mascot Thunderbug

1994 - 95 LIGHTNING HEALTH PLAN

We have little information on this set. Other singles may exist.
Card Size: 4" x 5"
Sponsor: Florida Health Plan
☐ Daren Puppa (G)
☐ Chris Gratton

1995 - 96 LIGHTNING SKYBOX SPORTS CAFÉ

Chris Gratton is the most expensive single at $4-5. Singles start at $1.00.
Card Size: 3 3/4" x 9"
Sponsors: Sky Box Sports Café, others
Complete Set (21 cards): 25.00
☐ Mikael Andersson
☐ Brian Bellows
☐ J.C. Bergeron (G)
☐ Brian Bradley
☐ Shawn Burr
☐ Enrico Ciccone
☐ Cory Cross
☐ John Cullen
☐ Aaron Gavey
☐ Chris Gratton
☐ Roman Hamrlik
☐ Bill Houlder
☐ Petr Klima
☐ Rudy Poeschek
☐ Daren Puppa (G)
☐ Alexander Selivanov
☐ David Shaw
☐ John Tucker
☐ Jason Wiemer
☐ Paul Ysebaert
☐ Rob Zamuner

1995 - 96 LIGHTNING SKYBOX SPORTS CAFÉ

These cards were originally issued as a panel. Chris Gratton is the most expensive single at $3-4. Singles start at 75¢.
Card Size: 2 1/2" x 3 1/2"
Sponsor: SkyBox Sports Café
Complete Set (29 cards): 15.00
☐ Mikael Andersson
☐ J.C. Bergeron (G)
☐ Marc Bergevin
☐ Brian Bradley
☐ Marc Bureau
☐ Wayne Cashman
☐ Eric Charron
☐ Enrico Ciccone
☐ Terry Crisp
☐ Cory Cross
☐ Phil Esposito
☐ Tony Esposito
☐ Danny Gare
☐ Chris Gratton
☐ Bob Halkidis
☐ Roman Hamrlik
☐ Ben Hankinson
☐ Petr Klima
☐ Brantt Myhres
☐ Adrien Plavsic
☐ Rudy Poeschek
☐ Daren Puppa (G)
☐ Alexander Selivanov
☐ Alexander Semak
☐ John Tucker
☐ Jason Wiemer
☐ Paul Ysebaert
☐ Rob Zamuner
☐ Team Photo

TORONTO MAPLE LEAFS

1964 - 65 MAPLE LEAFS

Prices are in NRMT.
Card Size: 3 1/2" x 5 1/2"
Sponsors: none
Complete Set (23 cards): 125.00
☐ George Amstrong 10.00
☐ Andy Bathgate 7.50
☐ Bob Baun 4.00
☐ Johnny Bower (G) 12.00
☐ Carl Brewer 4.00
☐ Kent Douglas 4.00
☐ Dick Duff 6.00
☐ Ron Ellis 4.00
☐ Billy Harris 4.00
☐ Tim Horton 18.00
☐ Punch Imlach 6.00
☐ Red Kelly 10.00
☐ Dave Keon 12.00
☐ Frank Mahovlich 15.00
☐ Don McKenney 4.00
☐ Dickie Moore 10.00
☐ Jim Pappn 4.00
☐ Bob Pulford 7.50
☐ Terry Sawchuk (G) 20.00
☐ Eddie Shack 10.00
☐ Don Simmons (G) 6.00
☐ Allan Stanley 7.50
☐ Ron Stewart 4.00

1966 - 67 MAPLE LEAFS ESSO COASTERS

Prices are in NRMT.
Coaster Diametre: 8"
Sponsor: Esso
Complete Set (10 coasters): 200.00
☐ George Armstrong 25.00
☐ Johnny Bower (G) 30.00
☐ Ron Ellis 10.00
☐ Tim Horton 60.00
☐ Punch Imlach 20.00
☐ Dave Keon 30.00
☐ Frank Mahovlich 50.00
☐ Bob Pulford 25.00
☐ Brit Selby 10.00
☐ Eddie Shack 30.00

1968 - 69 MAPLE LEAFS

Tim Horton is the most expensive single at $10-12 in NRMT. Singles start at $2. We have no pricing information on complete sets.
Card Size: 3 1/2" x 5 1/2"
Sponsors: none
☐ George Armstrong
☐ Bob Baun
☐ Johnny Bower (G)
☐ John Brenneman
☐ Brian Conacher
☐ Jim Dorey
☐ Ron Ellis
☐ Bruce Gamble (G)
☐ Paul Henderson
☐ Larry Hillman
☐ Tim Horton
☐ Larry Jeffrey
☐ Red Kelly
☐ Dave Keon
☐ Orland Kurtenbach
☐ Rick Ley
☐ Murray Oliver
☐ Jim Pappin
☐ Mike Pelyk
☐ Pierre Pilote
☐ Marcel Pronovost
☐ Eddie Shack
☐ Darryl Sly
☐ Floyd Smith
☐ Allan Stanley
☐ Bill Sutherland

1969 - 70 MAPLE LEAFS

Tim Horton is the most expensive single at $10-12 in NRMT. Singles start at $2. We have no pricing information on complete sets.
Card Size: 3 1/2" x 5 1/2"
Sponsors: none
☐ George Armstrong
☐ Johnny Bower (G)
☐ Wayne Carleton
☐ King Clancy
☐ Terry Clancy
☐ Brian Conacher
☐ Marv Edwards (G)
☐ Ron Ellis
☐ Bruce Gamble (G)
☐ Brian Glennie
☐ Jim Harrison
☐ Larry Hillman
☐ Tim Horton
☐ Dave Keon
☐ Rick Ley
☐ Frank Mahovlich
☐ Jim McKenny
☐ Larry Mickey
☐ Murray Oliver
☐ Jim Pappin
☐ Mike Pelyk
☐ Marcel Pronovost
☐ Bob Pulford
☐ Pat Quinn
☐ Brit Selby
☐ Al Smith
☐ Floyd Smith
☐ Allan Stanley
☐ Norm Ullman
☐ Mike Walton
☐ Ron Ward

1970 - 71 MAPLE LEAFS

Darryl Sittler is the most expensive single at $25-30 in NRMT. Singles start at $2. Other singles may exist.
Card Size: 3 1/2" x 5 1/2"
Sponsors: none
☐ Jim Dorey
☐ Ron Ellis
☐ Bruce Gamble (G)
☐ Jim Harrison
☐ Paul Henderson
☐ Rick Ley
☐ Bob Liddington
☐ Jim McKenny
☐ Garry Monahan
☐ Mike Pelyk
☐ Jacques Plante (G)
☐ Brad Selwood
☐ Darryl Sittler
☐ Guy Trottier
☐ Mike Walton

1971 - 72 MAPLE LEAFS

The most expensive singles are Jacques Plante and Darryl Sittler at $12-15 in NRMT. Singles start at $2. Other singles may exist.
Card Size: 3 1/2" x 5 1/2"
Sponsors: none
☐ Bob Baun
☐ Jim Dorey
☐ Denis Dupère
☐ Ron Ellis
☐ Brian Glennie
☐ Jim Harrison
☐ Paul Henderson
☐ Dave Keon
☐ Rick Ley
☐ Billy MacMillan
☐ Don Marshall
☐ Jim McKenny
☐ Garry Monahan
☐ Bernie Parent (G)
☐ Mike Pelyk
☐ Jacques Plante (G)
☐ Brad Selwood
☐ Darryl Sittler
☐ Brian Spencer
☐ Guy Trottier
☐ Norm Ullman

1972 - 73 MAPLE LEAFS

There are several variations in this set. Jacques Plante is the most expensive single at $12-15 in NRMT. Singles start at $2. We have no pricing information on complete sets.
Card Size: 3 1/2" x 5 1/2"
Sponsors: none
☐ Bob Baun
☐ Terry Clancy
☐ Denis Dupère
☐ Ron Ellis
☐ George Ferguson
☐ Brian Glennie
☐ John Grisdale
☐ Paul Henderson
☐ Pierre Jary
☐ Rick Kehoe
☐ Dave Keon
☐ Ron Low (G)
☐ Joe Lundrigan
☐ Larry McIntyre
☐ Jim McKenny
☐ Garry Monahan
☐ Randy Osburn
☐ Mike Pelyk
☐ Jacques Plante (G)
☐ Darryl Sittler
☐ Errol Thompson
☐ Norm Ullman

1973 - 74 MAPLE LEAFS

The most expensive singles in NRMT are Lanny McDonald at $10-12 and Borje Salming at $8-10. Singles start at $2. Variations may exist.
Card Size: 3 1/2" x 5 1/2"
Sponsors: none
Complete Set (25 cards): 75.00
☐ Johnny Bower
☐ Willie Brossart
☐ Denis Dupère
☐ Ron Ellis
☐ Doug Favell (G)
☐ Brian Glennie
☐ Jim Gregory
☐ Inge Hammarstrom
☐ Paul Henderson
☐ Eddie Johnston (G)
☐ Rick Kehoe
☐ Red Kelly
☐ Dave Keon
☐ Lanny McDonald
☐ Jim McKenny
☐ Garry Monahan
☐ Bob Neely
☐ Mike Pelyk
☐ Borje Salming
☐ Eddie Shack
☐ Darryl Sittler
☐ Errol Thompson
☐ Ian Turnbull
☐ Norm Ullman
☐ Dunc Wilson (G)

1974 - 75 MAPLE LEAFS

Lanny McDonald is the most expensive single at $6-8 in NRMT. Singles start at $2. Variations may exist.
Card Size: 3 1/2" x 5 1/2"
Sponsors: none
Complete Set (24 cards): 65.00
☐ Claire Alexander
☐ Dave Dunn
☐ Ron Ellis
☐ George Ferguson
☐ Bill Flett
☐ Brian Glennie
☐ Inge Hammarstrom
☐ Dave Keon
☐ Lanny McDonald
☐ Jim McKenny
☐ Gord McRae (G)
☐ Lyle Moffat
☐ Bob Neely
☐ Gary Sabourin
☐ Borje Salming
☐ Rod Seiling
☐ Eddie Shack
☐ Darryl Sittler
☐ Blaine Stoughton
☐ Errol Thompson
☐ Ian Turnbull
☐ Norm Ullman
☐ Dave Williams
☐ Dunc Wilson (G)

1975 - 76 MAPLE LEAFS

Lanny McDonald and Darryl Sittler are the most expensive single at $4-6 in NRMT. Singles start at $2. Variations may exist.
Card Size: 3 1/2" x 5 1/2"
Sponsors: none
Complete Set (21 cards): 60.00
☐ Don Ashby
☐ Pat Boutette
☐ Dave Dunn
☐ Doug Favell (G)
☐ George Ferguson
☐ Brian Glennie
☐ Inge Hammarstrom
☐ Greg Hubick
☐ Lanny McDonald
☐ Jim McKenny
☐ Gord McRae (G)
☐ Bob Neely
☐ Borje Salming
☐ Rod Seiling
☐ Darryl Sittler
☐ Blaine Stoughton
☐ Wayne Thomas (G)
☐ Ian Turnbull
☐ Stan Weir
☐ Dave Williams
☐ Ian Turnbull

1976 - 77 MAPLE LEAFS

Lanny McDonald and Darryl Sittler are the most expensive singles at $5-6 in NRMT. Singles start at $1.50.

Card Size: 3 1/2" x 5 1/2"
Sponsors: none
Complete Set (23 cards): 40.00

☐ Claire Alexander
☐ Don Ashby
☐ Pat Boutette
☐ Randy Carlyle
☐ George Ferguson
☐ Scott Garland
☐ Brian Glennie
☐ Inge Hammarstrom
☐ Lanny McDonald
☐ Jim McKenny
☐ Gord McRae (G)
☐ Bob Neely
☐ Mike Palmateer (G)
☐ Mike Pelyk
☐ Borje Salming
☐ Darryl Sittler
☐ Wayne Thomas (G)
☐ Errol Thompson
☐ Ian Turnbull
☐ Jack Valiquette
☐ Kurt Walker
☐ Stan Weir
☐ Dave Williams

1977 - 78 MAPLE LEAFS

Lanny McDonald and Darryl Sittler are the most expensive singles at $4-6 in NRMT. Singles start at $1.50.
Card Size: 3 1/2" x 5 1/2"
Sponsors: none
Complete Set (21 cards): 35.00

☐ Don Ashby
☐ Pat Boutette
☐ Randy Carlyle
☐ Ron Ellis
☐ George Ferguson
☐ Brian Glennie
☐ Inge Hammarstrom
☐ Trevor Johansen
☐ Jim Jones
☐ Lanny McDonald
☐ Jim McKenny
☐ Gord McRae (G)
☐ Bob Neely
☐ Mike Palmateer (G)
☐ Borje Salming
☐ Darryl Sittler
☐ Errol Thompson
☐ Ian Turnbull
☐ Jack Valiquette
☐ Kurt Walker
☐ Dave Williams

1978 - 79 MAPLE LEAFS

Lanny McDonald and Darryl Sittler are the most expensive singles at $4-5 in NRMT. Singles start at $1.50.
Card Size: 3 1/2" x 5 1/2"
Sponsors: none
Complete Set (23 cards): 35.00

☐ John Anderson
☐ Bruce Boudreau
☐ Dave Burrows
☐ Jerry Butler
☐ Ron Ellis
☐ Paul Harrison
☐ Dave Hutchison
☐ Trevor Johansen
☐ Jimmy Jones
☐ Dan Maloney
☐ Lanny McDonald
☐ Walt McKechnie
☐ Garry Monahan
☐ Roger Neilson
☐ Mike Palmateer (G)
☐ Borje Salming
☐ Darryl Sittler
☐ Lorne Stamler
☐ Ian Turnbull
☐ Dave Williams
☐ Ron Wilson
☐ H.Ballard/K.Clancy
☐ Maple Leaf Gardens

1979 - 80 MAPLE LEAFS

Darryl Sittler is the most expensive single at $4-5 in NRMT. Singles start at $1.50. Variations may exist.
Card Size: 3 1/2" x 5 1/2"
Sponsors: none
Complete Set (30 cards): 35.00

☐ John Anderson
☐ Harold Ballard
☐ Laurie Boschman
☐ Pat Boutette
☐ Carl Brewer
☐ Dave Burrows
☐ Jiri Crha (G)
☐ Ron Ellis
☐ Paul Gardner
☐ Paul Harrison (G)
☐ Pat Hickey
☐ Greg Hotham
☐ Dave Hutchison
☐ Punch Imlach
☐ Jimmy Jones
☐ Mark Kirton
☐ Dan Maloney
☐ Terry Martin
☐ Lanny McDonald
☐ Walt McKechnie
☐ Wilf Paiement
☐ Mike Palmateer (G)
☐ Joel Quenneville
☐ Rocky Saganiuk
☐ Borje Salming
☐ Darryl Sittler
☐ Floyd Smith
☐ Bob Stephenson
☐ Ian Turnbull
☐ Ron Wilson

1980 - 81 MAPLE LEAFS

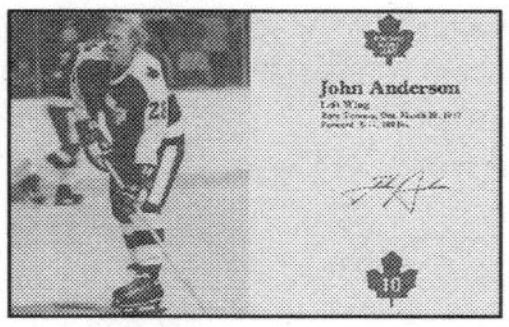

Darryl Sittler is the most expensive single at $3-4 in NRMT. Singles start at $1.00. Variations may exist.
Card Size: 3 1/2" x 5 1/2"
Sponsors: none
Complete Set (26 cards): 25.00

☐ John Anderson
☐ Harold Ballard
☐ Laurie Boschman
☐ Johnny Bower
☐ King Clancy
☐ Jiri Crha (G)
☐ Joe Crozier
☐ Bill Derlago
☐ Dick Duff
☐ Viteslav Duris
☐ Dave Farrish
☐ Stewart Gavin
☐ Paul Harrison (G)
☐ Pat Hickey
☐ Mark Kirton
☐ Terry Martin
☐ Gerry McNamara
☐ Wilf Paiement
☐ Robert Picard
☐ Curt Ridley (G)
☐ Rocky Saganiuk
☐ Borje Salming
☐ Dave Shand
☐ Darryl Sittler
☐ Ian Turnbull
☐ Rick Vaive

1981 - 82 MAPLE LEAFS

Darryl Sittler is the most expensive single at $3-4. Singles start at $1.00. Variations may exist.
Postcard Size: 3 1/2" x 5 1/2"
Sponsors: none
Complete Set (26 cards): 25.00

☐ John Anderson
☐ Harold Ballard
☐ Jim Benning
☐ Fred Boimistruck
☐ Laurie Boschman
☐ Bill Derlago
☐ Stewart Gavin
☐ Michel Larocque (G)
☐ Don Luce
☐ Bob McGill
☐ Dan Maloney
☐ Bob Manno
☐ Paul Marshall
☐ Terry Martin
☐ Barry Melrose
☐ Mike Nykoluk
☐ Wilf Paiement
☐ René Robert
☐ Rocky Saganiuk
☐ Borje Salming
☐ Darryl Sittler
☐ Vincent Tremblay (G)
☐ Rick Vaive
☐ Gary Yaremchuk
☐ Ron Zanussi
☐ H.Ballard/F.Selke

1982 - 83 MAPLE LEAFS

Borje Salming is the most expensive single at $3-4. Singles start at $1.00. Variations may exist.
Postcard Size: 3 1/2" x 5 1/2"
Sponsors: none
Complete Set (27 cards): 25.00

☐ Russ Adams
☐ John Anderson
☐ Normand Aubin
☐ Harold Ballard
☐ Jim Benning
☐ Serge Boisvert
☐ Dan Daoust
☐ Bill Derlago
☐ Miroslav Frycer
☐ Stewart Gavin
☐ Gaston Gingras
☐ Billy Harris
☐ Paul Higgins
☐ Peter Ihnacak
☐ Jim Korn
☐ Dan Maloney
☐ Terry Martin
☐ Frank Nigro
☐ Mike Nykoluk
☐ Gary Nylund
☐ Mike Palmateer (G)
☐ Walt Poddubny
☐ Rick St. Croix (G)
☐ Borje Salming
☐ Greg Terrion
☐ Vincent Tremblay (G)
☐ Rick Vaive

1983 - 84 MAPLE LEAFS

Borje Salming is the most expensive single at $3-4. Singles start at $1.00.
Postcard Size: 3 1/2" x 5 1/2"
Sponsors: none
Complete Set (26 cards): 25.00

☐ John Anderson
☐ Jim Benning
☐ Dan Daoust
☐ Bill Derlago
☐ Dave Farrish
☐ Miroslav Frycer
☐ Stewart Gavin
☐ Gaston Gingras
☐ Pat Graham
☐ Billy Harris
☐ Peter Ihnacak
☐ Jim Korn
☐ Gary Leeman
☐ Dan Maloney
☐ Terry Martin
☐ Basil McRae
☐ Frank Nigro
☐ Mike Nykoluk
☐ Gary Nylund
☐ Mike Palmateer (G)
☐ Walt Poddubny
☐ Rick St. Croix (G)
☐ Borje Salming
☐ Bill Stewart
☐ Greg Terrion
☐ Rick Vaive

1984 - 85 MAPLE LEAFS

Russ Courtnall and Al Iafrate are the most expensive singles at $4-5. Singles start at $1.00.
Postcard Size: 3 1/2" x 5 1/2"
Sponsors: none
Complete Set (24 cards): 25.00

☐ John Anderson
☐ Jim Benning
☐ Allan Bester (G)
☐ John Brophy
☐ Jeff Brubaker
☐ Russ Courtnall
☐ Dan Daoust
☐ Bill Derlago
☐ Miroslav Frycer
☐ Stewart Gavin
☐ Al Iafrate
☐ Peter Ihnacak
☐ Jeff Jackson
☐ Jim Korn
☐ Gary Leeman
☐ Dan Maloney
☐ Bob McGill
☐ Gary Nylund
☐ Walt Poddubny
☐ Bill Root
☐ Borje Salming
☐ Greg Terrion
☐ Rick Vaive
☐ Ken Wregget (G)

1985 - 86 MAPLE LEAFS

Wendel Clark is the most expensive single at $10-12. Singles start at $1.00.
Postcard Size: 3 1/2" x 5 1/2"
Sponsors: none
Complete Set (28 cards): 30.00

☐ Harold Ballard
☐ Jim Benning
☐ Tim Bernhardt (G)
☐ Johnny Bower
☐ Jeff Brubaker
☐ Wendel Clark
☐ Russ Courtnall
☐ Dan Daoust
☐ Don Edwards (G)
☐ Tom Fergus
☐ Miroslav Frycer
☐ Al Iafrate
☐ Peter Ihnacak
☐ Jeff Jackson
☐ Jim Korn
☐ Chris Kotsopoulos
☐ Gary Leeman
☐ Brad Maxwell
☐ Bob McGill
☐ Gary Nylund
☐ Walt Poddubny
☐ Borje Salming
☐ Marian Stastny
☐ Greg Terrion
☐ Steve Thomas
☐ Rick Vaive
☐ Blake Wesley
☐ Ken Wregget (G)

1986 - 87 MAPLE LEAFS

This series has two versions: one regular series and one with the player's name in caps. Wendel Clark and Vincent Damphousse are the most expensive singles at $6-8. Singles start at $1.00.

Postcard Size: 3 1/2" x 5 1/2"

Sponsors: none

Complete Set (24 cards): 25.00

☐☐ Mike Allison
☐☐ Wendel Clark
☐☐ Russ Courtnall
☐☐ Vincent Damphousse
☐☐ Dan Daoust
☐☐ Jerome Dupont
☐☐ Tom Fergus
☐☐ Miroslav Frycer
☐☐ Todd Gill
☐☐ Dan Hoganson
☐☐ Al Iafrate
☐☐ Miroslav Ihnacak
☐☐ Peter Ihnacak
☐☐ Terry Johnson
☐☐ Chris Kotsopoulos
☐☐ Gary Leeman
☐☐ Bob McGill
☐☐ Bill Root
☐☐ Borje Salming
☐☐ Brad Smith
☐☐ Greg Terrion
☐☐ Steve Thomas
☐☐ Rick Vaive
☐☐ Ken Wregget (G)

1987 - 88 MAPLE LEAFS 5" x 8"

Wendel Clark and Vincent Damphousse are the most expensive singles at $4-5. Singles start at $1.00.

Postcard Size: 5" x 8"

Sponsors: none

Complete Set (23 cards): 25.00

☐ Allan Bester (G)
☐ Wendel Clark
☐ Russ Courtnall
☐ Vincent Damphousse
☐ Dan Daoust
☐ Dale DeGray
☐ Tom Fergus
☐ Miroslav Frycer
☐ Al Iafrate
☐ Peter Ihnacak
☐ Chris Kotsopoulos
☐ Rick Lanz
☐ Gary Leeman
☐ Ed Olczyk
☐ Mark Osborne
☐ Luke Richardson
☐ Borje Salming
☐ Al Secord
☐ Dave Semenko
☐ Brad Smith
☐ Greg Terrion
☐ Ken Wregget (G)
☐ Team Photo

1987 - 88 MAPLE LEAFS 3 1/2" x 5 1/2"

We have little information on this set. Other singles may exist.

Card Size: 3 1/2" x 5 1/2"

Sponsors: none

☐ Russ Courtnall

1987 - 88 MAPLE LEAFS KELLOGGS P.L.A.Y.

Wendel Clark and Vincent Damphousse are the most expensive singles at $2-3. Singles start at 75¢.

Card Size: 2 3/4" x 3 1/4"

Sponsors: Kelloggs, Salada

Complete Set (30 cards): 20.00

☐ 1 N. LaVerne Shipley
☐ 2 Tom Gosnell
☐ 3 Checklist
☐ 4 Harold Ballard
☐ 5 Superintendent D. Almond
☐ 6 Wendel Clark
☐ 7 Tom Fergus
☐ 8 Borje Salming
☐ 9 Ed Olczyk
☐ 10 Gary Leeman
☐ 11 Rick Lanz
☐ 12 Allan Bester (G)
☐ 13 Todd Gill
☐ 14 Al Secord
☐ 15 Miroslav Frycer
☐ 16 Chris Kotsopoulos
☐ 17 Vincent Damphousse
☐ 18 Mike Allison
☐ 19 Al Iafrate
☐ 20 Dan Daoust
☐ 21 Greg Terrion
☐ 22 Brad Smith
☐ 23 Mark Osborne
☐ 24 Peter Ihnacak
☐ 25 Dale DeGray
☐ 26 Dave Semenko
☐ 27 Luke Richardson
☐ 28 John Brophy
☐ 29 Ken Wregget (G)
☐ 30 Russ Courtnall

1988 - 89 MAPLE LEAFS KELLOGGS P.L.A.Y.

Wendel Clark and Vincent Damphousse are the most expensive singles at $2-3. Singles start at 75¢.

Card Size: 2 3/4" x 3 1/2"

Sponsor: Kelloggs

Complete Set (30 cards): 20.00

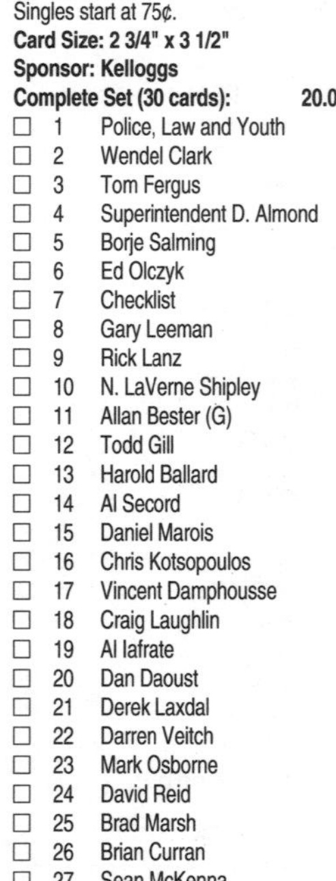
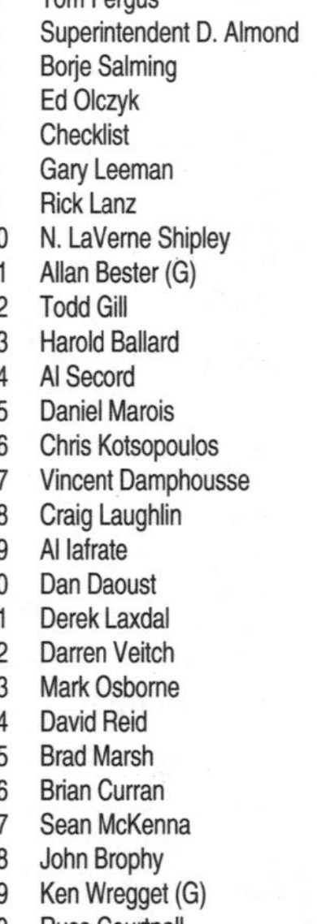

☐ 1 Police, Law and Youth
☐ 2 Wendel Clark
☐ 3 Tom Fergus
☐ 4 Superintendent D. Almond
☐ 5 Borje Salming
☐ 6 Ed Olczyk
☐ 7 Checklist
☐ 8 Gary Leeman
☐ 9 Rick Lanz
☐ 10 N. LaVerne Shipley
☐ 11 Allan Bester (G)
☐ 12 Todd Gill
☐ 13 Harold Ballard
☐ 14 Al Secord
☐ 15 Daniel Marois
☐ 16 Chris Kotsopoulos
☐ 17 Vincent Damphousse
☐ 18 Craig Laughlin
☐ 19 Al Iafrate
☐ 20 Dan Daoust
☐ 21 Derek Laxdal
☐ 22 Darren Veitch
☐ 23 Mark Osborne
☐ 24 David Reid
☐ 25 Brad Marsh
☐ 26 Brian Curran
☐ 27 Sean McKenna
☐ 28 John Brophy
☐ 29 Ken Wregget (G)
☐ 30 Russ Courtnall

1990 - 91 MAPLE LEAFS

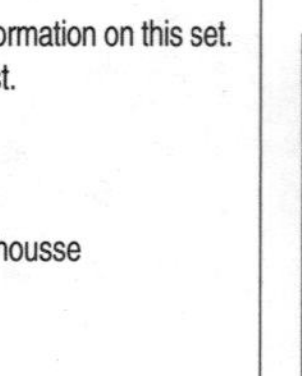

We have no pricing information on this set. Other singles may exist.

Card Size: 4" x 6"

Sponsors: none

☐ Aaron Broten
☐ Vincent Damphousse
☐ Dave Ellett
☐ Paul Fenton
☐ Tom Fergus
☐ Lou Franceschetti
☐ Al Iafrate
☐ Peter Ing (G)
☐ Mike Krushelnyski
☐ Tom Kurvers
☐ Gary Leeman
☐ Kevin Maguire
☐ Brad Marsh
☐ Scott Pearson
☐ Michel Petit
☐ Rob Ramage
☐ Dave Reid
☐ Luke Richardson
☐ Joe Sacco
☐ Doug Shedden
☐ Scott Thornton

1990 - 91 MAPLE LEAFS KELLOGGS P.L.A.Y.

Wendel Clark and Grant Fuhr are the most expensive singles at $2-3. Singles start at 75¢.

Card Size:

Sponsor: Kelloggs

Complete Set (30 cards): 20.00

☐ 1 Chief Don Hillock
☐ 2 Dep. Chief B. Cousineau
☐ 3 Lanny the Police Dog
☐ 4 Cliff Fletcher
☐ 5 Tom Watt
☐ 6 Bob Rouse
☐ 7 Dave Ellett
☐ 8 Dave Hannan
☐ 9 Glenn Anderson
☐ 10 Gary Leeman
☐ 11 Rob Pearson
☐ 12 Claude Loiselle
☐ 13 Craig Berube
☐ 14 Wendel Clark
☐ 15 Tom Fergus
☐ 16 Mike Bullard
☐ 17 Todd Gill
☐ 18 Michel Petit
☐ 19 Peter Zezel
☐ 20 Mike Krushelnyski
☐ 21 Lucien DeBlois
☐ 22 Darryl Shannon
☐ 23 Grant Fuhr (G)
☐ 24 Daniel Marois
☐ 25 Rob Cimetta
☐ 26 Jeff Reese (G)
☐ 27 Bob Halkidis
☐ 28 Brian Bradley
☐ 29 Mike Foligno
☐ 30 Alexander Godynyuk

1992 - 93 MAPLE LEAFS KODAK

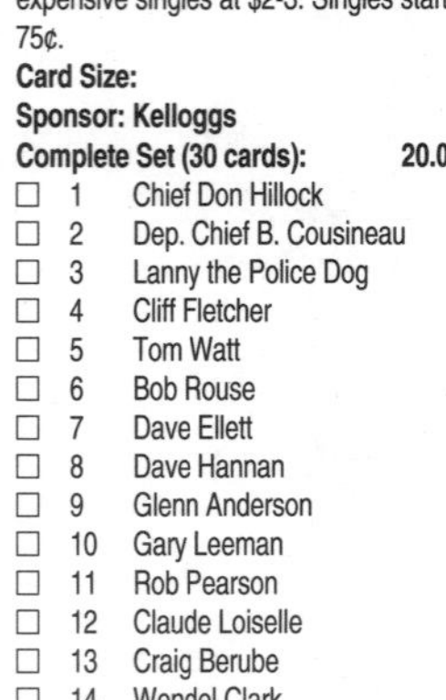

These photos are printed on Kodak paper. The most expensive singles are Félix Potvin at $3-4 and Doug Gilmour at $2-3. Singles start at 75¢.

Card Size: 4" x 6 1/8"

Sponsor: Kodak

Complete Set (21 cards): 20.00

☐ Glenn Anderson
☐ Dave Andreychuk
☐ Ken Baumgartner
☐ Drake Berehowsky
☐ Bill Berg
☐ Nikolai Borschevsky
☐ Wendel Clark
☐ John Cullen
☐ Mike Eastwood
☐ Dave Ellett
☐ Doug Gilmour
☐ Sylvain Lefebvre
☐ Jamie Macoun
☐ Kent Manderville
☐ Dave McLlwain
☐ Dmitri Mironov
☐ Mark Osborne
☐ Rob Pearson
☐ Félix Potvin (G)
☐ Bob Rouse
☐ Peter Zezel

1993 - 94 MAPLE LEAFS ABALENE PHOTOS

These singles start at $1.00. Other singles exist.

Card Size:
Sponsor: Albalene

- ☐ Dave Andreychuk
- ☐ Bill Berg
- ☐ Nikolai Borschevsky
- ☐ Wendel Clark
- ☐ John Cullen
- ☐ Mike Eastwood
- ☐ Dave Ellett
- ☐ Mike Gartner
- ☐ Todd Gill
- ☐ Doug Gilmour
- ☐ Mike Krushelnyski
- ☐ Alexei Kudashov
- ☐ Sylvain Lefebvre
- ☐ Jamie Macoun
- ☐ Kent Manderville
- ☐ Dmitri Mironov
- ☐ Mark Osborne
- ☐ Rob Pearson
- ☐ Félix Potvin (G)
- ☐ Damian Rhodes (G)
- ☐ Bob Rouse
- ☐ Peter Zezel

1993 - 94 MAPLE LEAFS BLACK'S POP UPS

The most expensive single is Félix Potvin at $2-3. Singles start at 50¢.

Card Size: 2 1/2" x 3 1/2"
Sponsors: Black's, Score
Complete Set (24 cards): 15.00
Album: 5.00

- ☐ 1 Wendel Clark
- ☐ 2 Doug Gilmour
- ☐ 3 Glenn Anderson
- ☐ 4 Peter Zezel
- ☐ 5 Bob Rouse
- ☐ 6 Rob Pearson
- ☐ 7 Mark Osborne
- ☐ 8 Dmitri Mironov
- ☐ 9 Dave McLlwain
- ☐ 10 Kent Manderville
- ☐ 11 Jamie Macoun
- ☐ 12 Sylvain Lefebvre
- ☐ 13 Dave Andreychuk
- ☐ 14 Drake Berehowsky
- ☐ 15 Bill Berg
- ☐ 16 John Cullen
- ☐ 17 Ken Baumgartner
- ☐ 18 Nikolai Borschevsky
- ☐ 19 Mike Eastwood
- ☐ 20 Dave Ellett
- ☐ 21 Mike Foligno
- ☐ 22 Todd Gill
- ☐ 23 Mike Krushelnyski
- ☐ 24 Félix Potvin (G)

1993 - 94 MAPLE LEAFS KODAK

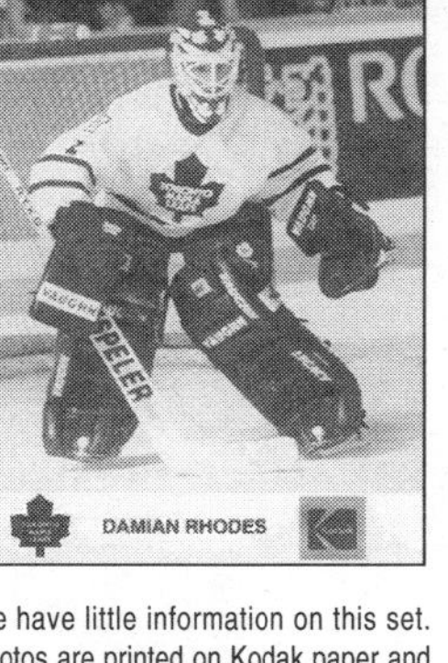

We have little information on this set. Photos are printed on Kodak paper and are practically identical in style to the 1992-93 series. Other singles exist.

Card Size: 4" x 6"
Sponsor: Kodak

- ☐ Damian Rhodes (G)

1994 - 95 MAPLE LEAFS COKE

Félix Potvin is the most expensive single at $3-4. Singles start at 75¢.

Card Size: 4 3/4" x 7"
Sponsors:Coca Cola
Complete Set (17 cards): 20.00

- ☐ Dave Andreychuk
- ☐ Ken Baumgartner
- ☐ Bill Berg
- ☐ Nikolai Borschevsky
- ☐ Mike Eastwood
- ☐ Dave Ellett
- ☐ Mike Gartner
- ☐ Todd Gill
- ☐ Doug Gilmour
- ☐ Alexei Kudashov
- ☐ Jamie Macoun
- ☐ Kent Manderville
- ☐ Dmitri Mironov
- ☐ Mark Osborne
- ☐ Félix Potvin (G)
- ☐ Damian Rhodes (G)
- ☐ Maple Leafs card

VANCOUVER CANUCKS

1970 - 71 CANUCKS LEO LEADERS PLAYER OF THE WEEK

Photos are in black and white on these blank-back cards. Pat Quinn is the most expensive single at $8-10 in NRMT. Singles start at $4.

Card Size: 5" x 7"
Sponsor: Royal Bank
Complete Set (20 cards): 80.00

- ☐ André Boudrias
- ☐ Mike Corrigan
- ☐ Ray Cullen
- ☐ Gary Doak
- ☐ George Gardner (G)
- ☐ Murray Hall
- ☐ Charlie Hodge (G)
- ☐ Dan Johnson
- ☐ Orland Kurtenbach
- ☐ Wayne Maki
- ☐ Rosaire Paiement
- ☐ Paul Popiel
- ☐ Pat Quinn
- ☐ Marc Reaume
- ☐ Darryl Sly
- ☐ Dale Tallon
- ☐ Ted Taylor
- ☐ Barry Wilkins
- ☐ Dunc Wilson (G)
- ☐ Jim Wiste

1971 - 72 CANUCKS LEO LEADERS PLAYER OF THE WEEK

Photos are in black and white on these blank back cards. Pat Quinn is the most expensive single at $6-8 in NRMT. Singles start at $3. Card #10 was supposedly never issued.

Card Size: 5" x 7"
Sponsor: Royal Bank
Complete Set (20 cards): 60.00

- ☐ 1 Bobby Lalonde
- ☐ 2 Mike Corrigan
- ☐ 3 Murray Hall
- ☐ 4 Jocelyn Guevremont
- ☐ 5 Pat Quinn
- ☐ 6 Orland Kurtenbach
- ☐ 7 Paul Popiel
- ☐ 8 Ron Ward
- ☐ 9 Rosaire Paiement
- ☐ 11 Dale Tallon
- ☐ 12 Bobby Schmautz
- ☐ 13 Dennis Kearns
- ☐ 14 Barry Wilkins
- ☐ 15 Dunc Wilson (G)
- ☐ 16 André Boudrias
- ☐ 17 Ted Taylor
- ☐ 18 George Gardner (G)
- ☐ 19 John Schella
- ☐ 20 Wayne Maki
- ☐ 21 Gary Doak

1972 - 73 CANUCKS LEO LEADERS PLAYER OF THE WEEK

These photos are in full colour. Orland Kurtenbach is the most expensive single at $3-5 in NRMT. Singles start at $3.

Card Size: 5" x 7"
Sponsor: Royal Bank
Complete Set (21 cards): 50.00

- ☐ Dale Balon
- ☐ Gregg Boddy
- ☐ Larry Bolonchuk
- ☐ André Boudrias
- ☐ Ed Dyck
- ☐ Jocelyn Guevremont
- ☐ Jim Hargraves
- ☐ Dennis Kearns
- ☐ Orland Kurtenbach
- ☐ Bobby Lalonde
- ☐ Richard Lemieux
- ☐ Don Lever
- ☐ Bryan McSheffrey
- ☐ Wayne Maki
- ☐ Gerry O'Flaherty
- ☐ Bobby Schmautz
- ☐ Dale Tallon
- ☐ Don Tannahill
- ☐ Barry Wilkins
- ☐ Dunc Wilson (G)
- ☐ John Wright

1972 - 73 CANUCKS NALLEY'S

These singles were issued on the backs of Nalley's Potato Chip triple packs. Pat Quinn is the most expensive single at $30-35 in NRMT. Singles start at $20.

Card Size: 6 3/4" x 5 3/8"
Sponsor: Nalley's Potato Chips
Complete Set (6 cards): 150.00

- ☐ André Boudrias
- ☐ George Gardner (G)
- ☐ Wayne Maki
- ☐ Rosaire Paiement
- ☐ Pat Quinn
- ☐ Barry Wilkins

1973 - 74 CANUCKS PLAYER OF THE WEEK

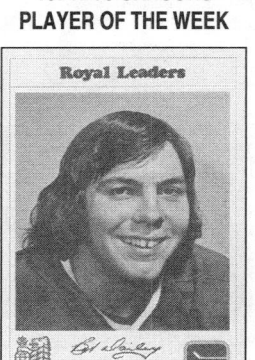

Orland Kurtenbach is the most expensive single at $3-5 in NRMT. Singles start at $3.

Card Size: 5" x 7"
Sponsor: Royal Bank
Complete Set (21 cards): 50.00

- ☐ Paulin Bordeleau
- ☐ André Boudrias
- ☐ Jacques Caron (G)
- ☐ Bob Dailey
- ☐ Dave Dunn
- ☐ Jocelyn Guevremont
- ☐ Dennis Kearns
- ☐ Jerry Korab
- ☐ Orland Kurtenbach
- ☐ Bobby Lalonde
- ☐ Richard Lemieux
- ☐ Don Lever
- ☐ Bill McCreary
- ☐ Bryan McSheffrey
- ☐ Gerry O'Flaherty
- ☐ Bobby Schmautz
- ☐ Gary Smith (G)
- ☐ Don Tannahill
- ☐ Dennis Ververgaert
- ☐ Barry Wilkins
- ☐ John Wright

1974 - 75 CANUCKS PLAYER OF THE WEEK

Singles start at $3 in NRMT.

Card Size: 5" x 7"
Sponsor: Royal Bank
Complete Set (21 cards): 50.00

- ☐ Gregg Boddy

☐ Paulin Bordeleau
☐ André Boudrias
☐ Bob Dailey
☐ Ab DeMarco
☐ John Gould
☐ John Grisdale
☐ Dennis Kearns
☐ Bobby Lalonde
☐ Don Lever
☐ Ken Lockett (G)
☐ Gerry Meehan
☐ Garry Monahan
☐ Chris Oddleifson
☐ Gerry O'Flaherty
☐ Tracy Pratt
☐ Mike Robitaille
☐ Léon Rochefort
☐ Gary Smith (G)
☐ Dennis Ververgaert
☐ Jim Wiley

1975 - 76 CANUCKS PLAYER OF THE WEEK

Harold Snepts is the most expensive single at $4-5 in NRMT. Singles start at $2.
Card Size: 4 3/4" x 7 1/4"
Sponsor: Royal Bank
Complete Set (22 cards): 40.00

☐ Rick Blight
☐ Gregg Boddy
☐ Paulin Bordeleau
☐ André Boudrias
☐ Bob Dailey
☐ Ab DeMarco
☐ John Gould
☐ John Grisdale
☐ Dennis Kearns
☐ Bobby Lalonde
☐ Don Lever
☐ Ken Lockett (G)
☐ Garry Monahan
☐ Bob Murray
☐ Chris Oddleifson
☐ Gerry O'Flaherty
☐ Tracy Pratt
☐ Mike Robitaille
☐ Ron Sedlbauer
☐ Gary Smith (G)
☐ Harold Snepsts
☐ Dennis Ververgaert

1976 - 77 CANUCKS PLAYER OF THE WEEK

Césare Maniago and Harold Snepsts are the most expensive singles at $3-5 in NRMT. Singles start at $2.
Card Size: 4 3/4" x 7 1/4"
Sponsor: Royal Bank
Complete Set (23 cards): 40.00

☐ Rick Blight
☐ Bob Dailey
☐ Dave Fortier
☐ Brad Gassoff
☐ John Gould
☐ John Grisdale
☐ Dennis Kearns
☐ Bobby Lalonde
☐ Don Lever
☐ Césare Maniago (G)
☐ Garry Monahan
☐ Bob Murray
☐ Chris Oddleifson
☐ Gerry O'Flaherty
☐ Curt Ridley (G)
☐ Mike Robitaille
☐ Ron Sedlbauer
☐ Harold Snepsts
☐ Andy Spruce
☐ Ralph Stewart
☐ Dennis Ververgaert
☐ Mike Walton
☐ Jim Wiley

1977 - 78 CANUCKS PLAYER OF THE WEEK

Césare Maniago and Harold Snepsts are the most expensive singles at $3-4 in NRMT. Singles start at $2.
Card Size: 4 1/4" x 5 1/2"
Sponsor: Royal Bank
Complete Set (21 cards): 35.00

☐ Rick Blight
☐ Larry Carrière
☐ Ron Flockhart
☐ Brad Gassoff
☐ Jere Gillis
☐ Larry Goodenough
☐ Hilliard Graves
☐ John Grisdale
☐ Dennis Kearns
☐ Don Lever
☐ Césare Maniago (G)
☐ Bob Manno
☐ Jack McIlhargey
☐ Garry Monahan
☐ Chris Oddleifson
☐ Gerry O'Flaherty
☐ Curt Ridley (G)
☐ Ron Sedlbauer
☐ Harold Snepsts
☐ Dennis Ververgaert
☐ Mike Walton

1977- 78 CANUCKS GINGER ALE CANS

Super-imposed player photos are in black and white. We have no pricing information on these cans. Other singles may exist.
Can: 16 oz.
Sponsors: Canada Dry Ginger Ale

☐ Rick Blight
☐ Brad Gassoff
☐ Jere Gillis
☐ Larry Goodenough
☐ Hilliard Graves
☐ Dennis Kearns
☐ Don Lever
☐ Césare Maniago (G)
☐ Jack McIlhargey
☐ Garry Monahan
☐ Chris Oddleifson
☐ Curt Ridley (G)
☐ Derek Sanderson
☐ Harold Snepsts
☐ Dennis Ververgaert
☐ Mike Walton

1978 - 79 CANUCKS PLAYER OF THE WEEK

The most expensive singles in NRMT are Stan Smyl at $4-5 and Glen Hanlon at $3-4. Singles start at $1.50.
Card Size: 4 1/4" x 5 1/2"
Sponsor: Royal Bank
Complete Set (23 cards): 35.00

☐ Rick Blight
☐ Gary Bromley (G)
☐ Bill Derlago
☐ Roland Eriksson
☐ Curt Fraser
☐ Jere Gillis
☐ Thomas Gradin
☐ Hilliard Graves
☐ John Grisdale
☐ Glen Hanlon (G)
☐ Randy Holt
☐ Dennis Kearns
☐ Don Lever
☐ Lars Lindgren
☐ Bob Manno
☐ Pit Martin
☐ Jack McIlhargey
☐ Chris Oddleifson
☐ Ron Sedlbauer
☐ Stan Smyl
☐ Harold Snepsts
☐ Dennis Ververgaert
☐ Lars Zetterstrom

1979 - 80 CANUCKS ROYAL BANK

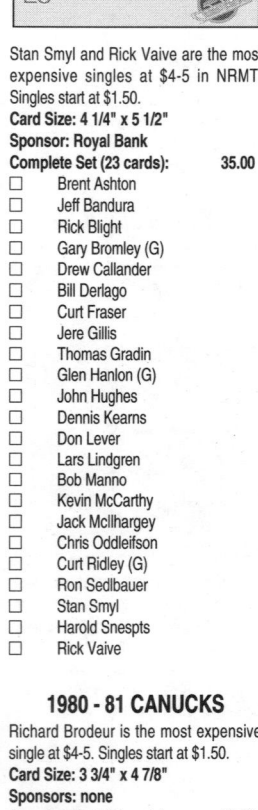

Stan Smyl and Rick Vaive are the most expensive singles at $4-5 in NRMT. Singles start at $1.50.
Card Size: 4 1/4" x 5 1/2"
Sponsor: Royal Bank
Complete Set (23 cards): 35.00

☐ Brent Ashton
☐ Jeff Bandura
☐ Rick Blight
☐ Gary Bromley (G)
☐ Drew Callander
☐ Bill Derlago
☐ Curt Fraser
☐ Jere Gillis
☐ Thomas Gradin
☐ Glen Hanlon (G)
☐ John Hughes
☐ Dennis Kearns
☐ Don Lever
☐ Lars Lindgren
☐ Bob Manno
☐ Kevin McCarthy
☐ Jack McIlhargey
☐ Chris Oddleifson
☐ Curt Ridley (G)
☐ Ron Sedlbauer
☐ Stan Smyl
☐ Harold Snepsts
☐ Rick Vaive

1980 - 81 CANUCKS

Richard Brodeur is the most expensive single at $4-5. Singles start at $1.50.
Card Size: 3 3/4" x 4 7/8"
Sponsors: none
Complete Set (22 cards): 35.00

☐ Brent Ashton
☐ Ivan Boldirev
☐ Per-Olov Brasar
☐ Richard Brodeur (G)
☐ Gary Bromley (G)
☐ Jerry Butler
☐ Colin Campbell
☐ Curt Fraser
☐ Thomas Gradin
☐ Glen Hanlon (G)
☐ Dennis Kearns
☐ Rick Lanz
☐ Lars Lindgren
☐ Dave Logan
☐ Gary Lupul
☐ Kevin McCarthy
☐ Gerry Minor
☐ Darcy Rota
☐ Bobby Schmautz
☐ Stan Smyl
☐ Harold Snepsts
☐ Tiger Williams

1980 - 81 CANUCKS SILVERWOOD DAIRIES

One three-card panel was found in 4L bags of Silverwood Dairies milk. The Hanlon/Brasar/Campbell panel is the most expensive at $5-7. Single panels start at $3. Cut-out singles measure 2 7/16" x 4 1/8" and start at $1.50. A cut-out 24-card set sells at $40.
Panel Size: 4 1/8" x 7 3/8"
Sponsor: Silverwood Dairies
Complete Set (8 panels): 50.00

☐ Thomas Gradin
Dennis Kearns
Brent Ashton
☐ Glen Hanlon (G)
Per-Olov Brasar
Colin Campbell
☐ Rick Lanz
Darcy Rota
Gerry Minor
☐ Kevin McCarthy
Richard Brodeur (G)
Gary Lupul
☐ Bobby Schmautz
Curt Fraser
Dave Logan
☐ Stan Smyl
Jerry Butler
Bob Manno
☐ Harold Snepsts
Ivan Boldirev
Gary Bromley (G)
☐ David Williams
Lars Lindgren
Kevin Primeau

1981 - 82 CANUCKS

Richard Brodeur is the most expensive single at $3-4. Singles start at $1.50.
Card Size: 3 3/4" x 4 7/8"
Sponsors: none
Complete Set (20 cards): 30.00

☐ Ivan Boldirev
☐ Per-Olov Brasar
☐ Richard Brodeur (G)
☐ Jiri Bubla
☐ Jerry Butler
☐ Colin Campbell
☐ Anders Eldebrink
☐ Curt Fraser
☐ Thomas Gradin
☐ Doug Halward
☐ Glen Hanlon (G)
☐ Rick Lanz
☐ Gary Lupul
☐ Blair MacDonald
☐ Kevin McCarthy
☐ Gerry Minor
☐ Lars Molin
☐ Darcy Rota
☐ Stan Smyl
☐ Tiger Williams

1981 - 82 CANUCKS SILVERWOOD DAIRIES

One three-card panel was found in 4L bags of Silverwood Dairies milk. The Lanz/Fraser/Crawford panel is the most expensive at $6-8. Single panels start at $3. Cut-out singles measure 2 7/16" x 4 1/8" and start at $1.00. A cut-out 24-card set sells at $35.

Panel Size: 4 1/4" x 7 3/8"
Sponsor: Silverwood Dairies
Complete Set (8 panels): 35.00

☐ Richard Brodeur (G)
Lars Lindgren
Darcy Rota
☐ Thomas Gradin
Jiri Bubla
Blair MacDonald
☐ Glen Hanlon (G)
Harold Snepsts
Gerry Minor
☐ Ivan Hlinka
Jerry Butler
Doug Halward
☐ Rick Lanz
Curt Fraser
Marc Crawford
☐ Kevin McCarthy
Ivan Boldirev
Lars Molin
☐ Stan Smyl
Colin Campbell
Per-Olov Brasar
☐ Dave Williams
Anders Eldebrink
Gary Lupul

1982 - 83 CANUCKS

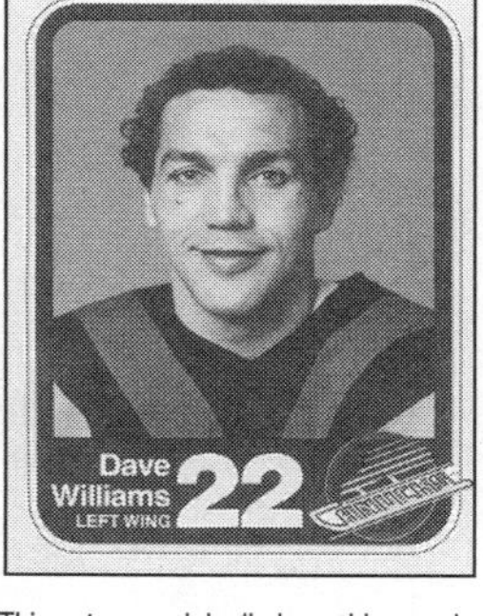

This set was originally issued in panels. Three panels have six cards while the team photo panel has five cards. The team photo measures 4 7/8" x 7 1/2". Richard Brodeur is the most expensive cut-out single at $3-4. Singles start at $1.50.

Card Size: 4 7/8" x 3 3/4"
Sponsors: none
Complete Set (23 cards): 25.00

☐ Ivan Boldirev
☐ Richard Brodeur (G)
☐ Jiri Bubla
☐ Garth Butcher
☐ Ron Delorme
☐ Ken Ellacott (G)
☐ Curt Fraser
☐ Thomas Gradin
☐ Doug Halward
☐ Ivan Hlinka
☐ Rick Lanz
☐ Moe Lemay
☐ Lars Lindgren
☐ Kevin McCarthy
☐ Gerry Minor
☐ Lars Molin
☐ Jim Nill
☐ Darcy Rota
☐ Stan Smyl
☐ Harold Snepsts
☐ Patrik Sundstrom
☐ Dave Williams
☐ Team Photo

1983 - 84 CANUCKS

This set was originally issued in panels. Three panels have six cards while the team photo panel has five cards. The team photo measures 4 7/8" x 7 1/2". Marc Crawford is the most expensive cut-out single at $6-8. Singles start at $1.00.

Card Size: 4 7/8" x 3 3/4"
Sponsors: none
Complete Set (23 cards): 25.00

☐ Richard Brodeur #35 (G)
☐ Jiri Bubla #29
☐ Garth Butcher #5
☐ Marc Crawford #28
☐ Ron Delorme #19
☐ John Garrett #31(G)
☐ Jere Gillis #4
☐ Thomas Gradin #23
☐ Doug Halward #2
☐ Mark Kirton #16
☐ Rick Lanz #4
☐ Gary Lupul #7
☐ Kevin McCarthy #25
☐ Lars Molin #26
☐ Jim Nill #8
☐ Michel Petit #3
☐ Darcy Rota #18
☐ Stan Smyl #12
☐ Harold Snepsts #27
☐ Patrik Sundstrom #17
☐ Tony Tanti #9
☐ Dave Williams #22
☐ Team Photo

1984 - 85 CANUCKS

This set was originally issued in panels. Four panels have six player cards while the last panel features two 4 3/4" x7" photos. Cam Neely is the most expensive cut-out single at $10-15. Singles start at $1.00. A cut-out 24-card set sells for $25.

Card Size: 4 1/4" x 3 1/4"
Sponsors: none
Complete Set (26 cards): 30.00

☐ Neil Belland
☐ Richard Brodeur (G)
☐ Jiri Bubla
☐ Garth Butcher
☐ Frank Caprice (G)
☐ J.J. Daigneault
☐ Ron Delorme
☐ John Garrett (G)
☐ Thomas Gradin
☐ Taylor Hall
☐ Doug Halward
☐ Rick Lanz
☐ Moe Lemay
☐ Doug Lidster
☐ Gary Lupul
☐ Al MacAdam
☐ Peter McNab
☐ Cam Neely
☐ Michel Petit
☐ Darcy Rota
☐ Petri Skriko
☐ Stan Smyl
☐ Patrik Sundstrom
☐ Tony Tanti
☐ Air Canucks
☐ Team Photo

1985 - 86 CANUCKS

This set was originally issued in panels. Four panels have six player cards while the last panel features a team photo measuring 4 5/8" x 7". Cam Neely is the most expensive cut-out single at $8-10. Singles start at $1.00.

Card Size: 4 1/4" x 3 3/8"
Sponsors: none
Complete Set (25 cards): 25.00

☐ Richard Brodeur (G)
☐ Jiri Bubla
☐ Garth Butcher
☐ Frank Caprice (G)
☐ Glen Cochrane
☐ Craig Coxe
☐ J.J. Daigneault
☐ Thomas Gradin
☐ Taylor Hall
☐ Doug Halward
☐ Jean-Marc Lanthier
☐ Rick Lanz
☐ Moe Lemay
☐ Doug Lidster
☐ Dave Lowry
☐ Gary Lupul
☐ Cam Neely
☐ Brent Peterson
☐ Jim Sandlak
☐ Petri Skriko
☐ Stan Smyl
☐ Patrik Sundstrom
☐ Steve Tambellini
☐ Tony Tanti
☐ Team Photo

1986 - 87 CANUCKS

This set was originally issued in six-card panels. Singles start at 75¢.

Card Size: 2 1/2" x 3 1/2"
Sponsors: none
Complete Set (24 cards): 20.00

☐ Richard Brodeur #35 (G)
☐ Garth Butcher #5
☐ Frank Caprice #30 (G)
☐ Glen Cochrane #29
☐ Craig Coxe #32
☐ Taylor Hall #8
☐ Stu Kulak #16
☐ Rick Lanz #4
☐ Moe Lemay #14
☐ Doug Lidster #3
☐ Dave Lowry #22
☐ Brad Maxwell #27
☐ Barry Pederson #7
☐ Brent Peterson #10
☐ Michel Petit #24
☐ Dave Richter #6
☐ Jim Sandlak #33
☐ Petri Skriko #26
☐ Stan Smyl #12
☐ Patrik Sundstrom #17
☐ Rich Sutter #15
☐ Steve Tambellini #20
☐ Tony Tanti #9
☐ Wendell Young #1 (G)

1987-88 CANUCKS FORMULA SHELL

This set was originally issued in four-card panels. One card from each panel was an advertisement card. An eight-panel (32 cards) set sells at $18. Kirk McLean is the most expensive cut-out single at $3-4. Singles start at 75¢.

Card Size: 2 1/2" x 3 1/2"
Sponsor: Formula Shell
Complete Set (24 cards): 15.00

☐ Greg Adams
☐ Jim Benning
☐ Randy Boyd
☐ Richard Brodeur (G)
☐ David Bruce
☐ Garth Butcher
☐ Frank Caprice (G)
☐ Craig Coxe
☐ Willie Huber
☐ Doug Lidster
☐ Dave Lowry
☐ Kirk McLean (G)
☐ Larry Melnyk
☐ Barry Pederson
☐ Dave Richter
☐ Jim Sandlak
☐ Dave Saunders
☐ Petri Skriko
☐ Stan Smyl
☐ Daryl Stanley
☐ Rich Sutter
☐ Steve Tambellini
☐ Tony Tanti
☐ Doug Wickenheiser

1989-89 CANUCKS MOHAWK

This set was originally issued in four-card panels. Trevor Linden is the most expensive single at $5-6. Singles start at 75¢.

Card Size: 2 1/2" x 3 1/2"
Sponsor: Mohawk
Complete Set (24 cards): 15.00

☐ Greg Adams #8
☐ Jim Benning #4
☐ Ken Berry #18
☐ Randy Boyd # 29
☐ Steve Bozek #14
☐ Brian Bradley #10
☐ David Bruce #25
☐ Garth Butcher #5
☐ Kevan Guy #2
☐ Doug Lidster #3
☐ Trevor Linden #16
☐ Kirk McLean #1 (G)
☐ Larry Melnyk #24
☐ Robert Nordmark #6
☐ Barry Pederson #7
☐ Paul Reinhart #23
☐ Jim Sandlak #19
☐ Petri Skriko #26
☐ Stan Smyl #12
☐ Harold Snepsts #27
☐ Ronnie Stern #20
☐ Rich Sutter #15
☐ Tony Tanti #9
☐ Steve Weeks #31 (G)

1989 - 90 CANUCKS

This set was originally issued in four-card panels. Trevor Linden is the most expensive single at $5-6. Singles start at 75¢.

Card Size: 2 1/2" x 3 1/2"
Sponsor: Mohawk
Complete Set (24 cards): 15.00

☐ Greg Adams #8
☐ Jim Benning #4
☐ Steve Bozek #14
☐ Brian Bradley #10
☐ Garth Butcher #5
☐ Craig Coxe #22
☐ Igor Larionov #18
☐ Doug Lidster #3

☐ Trevor Linden #16
☐ Kirk McLean #1 (G)
☐ Larry Melnyk #24
☐ Robert Nordmark #6
☐ Barry Pederson #7
☐ Paul Reinhart #23
☐ Jim Sandlak #19
☐ Petri Skriko #26
☐ Doug Smith
☐ Stan Smyl #12
☐ Harold Snepsts #27
☐ Daryl Stanley #29
☐ Rich Sutter #15
☐ Tony Tanti #9
☐ Steve Weeks #31 (G)

1990 - 91 CANUCKS MOHAWK

Trevor Linden and Petr Nedved are the most expensive singles at $3-4. Singles start at 75¢.
Card Size: 2 1/2" x 3 1/2"
Sponsor: Mohawk
Complete Set (29 cards): 15.00
☐ Greg Adams
☐ Jim Agnew
☐ Steve Bozek
☐ Garth Butcher
☐ Dave Capuano
☐ Craig Coxe
☐ Gerald Diduck
☐ Troy Gamble
☐ Don Gibson
☐ Kevan Guy
☐ Robert Kron
☐ Tom Kurvers
☐ Igor Larionov
☐ Doug Lidster
☐ Trevor Linden
☐ Jyrki Lumme
☐ Jay Mazur
☐ Andrew McBain
☐ Kirk MlcLean (G)
☐ Rob Murphy
☐ Petr Nedved
☐ Robert Nordmark
☐ Gino Odjick
☐ Adrien Plavsic
☐ Dan Quinn
☐ Jim Sandlak
☐ Stan Smyl
☐ Ronnie Stern
☐ Garry Valk

1990 - 91 CANUCKS PLAYER OF THE MONTH

Trevor Linden is the most expensive single at $8-10. Singles start at $4. Kirk McLean has two photos.
Photo Size: 8" x 10"
Sponsor: Molson Canadian
Complete Set (6 photos): 35.00
☐ Brian Bradley
☐ Troy Gamble
☐ Doug Lidster
☐ Trevor Linden
☐ Kirk McLean (G)
☐ Kirk McLean (G)

1991 - 92 CANUCKS

These cards have blank backs. Pavel Bure is the most expensive single at $10-12. Singles start at $1.00.
Card Size: 3 3/4" x 8 1/2"
Sponsor: none
Complete Set (23 cards): 30.00
☐ Greg Adams
☐ Pavel Bure
☐ Dave Babych
☐ Geoff Courtnall
☐ Gerald Diduck
☐ Robert Dirk
☐ Troy Gamble (G)
☐ Randy Gregg
☐ Robert Kron
☐ Igor Larionov
☐ Doug Lidster
☐ Trevor Linden
☐ Jyrki Lumme
☐ Kirk McLean (G)
☐ Sergio Momesso
☐ Rob Murphy
☐ Dana Murzyn
☐ Petr Nedved
☐ Gino Odjick
☐ Adrien Plavsic
☐ Cliff Ronning
☐ Jim Sandlak
☐ Ryan Walter

1991 - 92 CANUCKS

These cards have player bios on the back. Pavel Bure is the most expensive single at $12-15. Singles start at $2.
Photo Size: 8" x 10"
Sponsor: none
Complete Set (23 cards): 40.00
☐ Greg Adams
☐ Pavel Bure
☐ Dave Babych
☐ Geoff Courtnall
☐ Gerald Diduck
☐ Robert Dirk
☐ Troy Gamble (G)
☐ Randy Gregg
☐ Robert Kron
☐ Igor Larionov
☐ Doug Lidster
☐ Trevor Linden
☐ Jyrki Lumme
☐ Kirk McLean (G)
☐ Sergio Momesso
☐ Rob Murphy
☐ Dana Murzyn
☐ Petr Nedved
☐ Gino Odjick
☐ Adrien Plavsic
☐ Cliff Ronning
☐ Jim Sandlak
☐ Ryan Walter

1991 - 92 CANUCKS PLAYER OF THE MONTH

Pavel Bure has two photos each selling at $15-20. Singles start at $4.
Photo Size: 8" x 10"
Sponsor: Molson Canadian
Complete Set (6 photos): 50.00
☐ Greg Adams
☐ Pavel Bure
☐ Pavel Bure
☐ Igor Larionov
☐ Trevor Linden
☐ Kirk McLean (G)
☐ Cliff Ronning

1992 - 93 CANUCKS ROAD TRIP

Pavel Bure is the most expensive single at $6-8. Singles start at $1.
Card Size: 4 3/4" x 7"
Sponsor: Abalene
Complete Set (25 cards): 25.00
☐ Greg Adams
☐ Shawn Antoski
☐ Dave Babych
☐ Pavel Bure
☐ Geoff Courtnall
☐ Gerald Diduck
☐ Robert Dirk
☐ Tom Fergus
☐ Robert Kron
☐ Doug Lidster
☐ Trevor Linden
☐ Jyrki Lumme
☐ Kirk McLean (G)
☐ Sergio Momesso
☐ Dana Murzyn
☐ Petr Nedved
☐ Gino Odjick
☐ Adrien Plavsic
☐ Cliff Ronning
☐ Jim Sandlak
☐ Jiri Slegr
☐ Garry Valk
☐ Ryan Walter
☐ Dixon Ward
☐ Kay Whitmore (G)

1993 - 94 CANUCKS GOT-UM COINS

These coins were issued one per pack. We have little pricing information on this series. Pavel Bure is the most expensive single at $6-8. Singles start at $2. Some short prints may exist. 22 kt. gold-plated coins were also available.
Coin Diameter: 1 1/4"
Sponsor: Got-Um Coins
Complete Set (23 coins):
Album: 5.00
☐ Pat Quinn
☐ Trevor Linden
☐ Pavel Bure
☐ Kirk McLean (G)
☐ Adrien Plavsic
☐ Cliff Ronning
☐ Dana Murzyn
☐ Dave Babch
☐ Dixon Ward
☐ Geoff Courtnall
☐ Gerald Diduck
☐ Gino Odjick
☐ Greg Adams
☐ Jiri Slegr
☐ John McIntyre
☐ José Charbonneau
☐ Kay Whitmore (G)
☐ Jyrki Lumme
☐ Murray Craven
☐ Robert Dirk
☐ Sergio Momesso
☐ Shawn Antoski
☐ Tim Hunter

1994 - 95 CANUCKS COLLECTOR SERIES

Pavel Bure is the most expensive single at $12-15. Singles start at $3. Other singles may exist. This may, in fact, be a 1993-94 set.
Photo Size: 8" x 10 1/2"
Sponsor: none
☐ Greg Adams
☐ Shawn Antoski
☐ Dave Babych
☐ Jeff Brown
☐ Pavel Bure
☐ Geoff Courtnall
☐ Gerald Diduck
☐ Martin Gelinas
☐ Brian Glynn
☐ Tim Hunter
☐ Nathan Lafayette
☐ Trevor Linden
☐ Jyrki Lumme
☐ Kirk McLean (G)
☐ Dana Murzyn
☐ Gino Odjick
☐ Adrien Plavsic
☐ Cliff Ronning
☐ Jiri Slegr
☐ Kay Whitmore (G)

1995 - 96 CANUCKS BUILDING THE DREAM

Pavel Bure is the most expensive single at $6-8. Singles start at $1.
Card Size: 5" x 7"
Sponsor: Abalene
Complete Set (18 cards): 20.00
☐ 1 Kirk McLean (G)
☐ 2 Kay Whitmore (G)
☐ 3 Bret Hedican
☐ 4 Tim Hunter
☐ 5 Dana Murzyn
☐ 6 Jyrki Lumme
☐ 7 Cliff Ronning
☐ 8 Jeff Brown
☐ 9 Martin Gelinas
☐ 10 Pavel Bure
☐ 11 Jiri Slegr
☐ 12 Sergio Momesso
☐ 13 Gino Odjick
☐ 14 Geoff Courtnall
☐ 15 John McIntyre
☐ 16 Trevor Linden
☐ 17 Michael Peca
☐ 18 Dave Babych

1996 - 97 CANUCKS

Pavel Bure is the most expensive single at $4-6. Singles start at 50¢.
Card Size:
Sponsor: IGA
Complete Set (27 cards):
☐ Adrian Aucoin #6
☐ Dave Babych #44
☐ Donald Brashear #8
☐ Pavel Bure #96
☐ Russ Courtnall #9
☐ Troy Crowder #18
☐ Mike Foutain (G) #30
☐ Martin Gelinas #23
☐ Bret Hedican #3
☐ Corey Hirsch (G) #31
☐ Chris Joseph #32
☐ Trevor Linden #16
☐ Jyrki Lumme #21
☐ Kirk McLean (G) #1
☐ Alexander Mogilny #89
☐ Dana Murzyn #5
☐ Markus Naslund #19
☐ Gino Odjick #29
☐ Mike Ridley #17
☐ David Roberts #7
☐ Leif Rohlin #27
☐ Alexander Semak #20
☐ Mike Sillinger #26
☐ Esa Tikkanen #10
☐ Scott Walker #24
☐ Mark Wotton #4
☐ Team Photo

1997 - 98 CANUCKS COKE

We have little information on this set. Other singles exist.
Card Size: 3 3/4" x 5 1/2"
Sponsor: Coke
☐ Mark Messier

WASHINGTON CAPITALS

1974 - 75 CAPITALS

These photos are in black and white. Yvon Labre is the most expensive single at $2-4 in NRMT. Singles start at $2.
Card Size: 5" x 7"
Sponsors: none
Complete Set (24 cards): 50.00
☐ John Adams (G)
☐ Jim Anderson, Coach
☐ Ron Anderson
☐ Steve Atkinson
☐ Michel Belhumeur (G)
☐ Mike Bloom
☐ Gord Brooks
☐ Bruce Cowick
☐ Denis Dupère
☐ Jack Egers
☐ Jim Hrycuik

☐ Greg Joly
☐ Dave Kryskow
☐ Yvon Labre
☐ Pete Laframboise
☐ Bill Lesuk
☐ Ron Low (G)
☐ Joe Lundrigan
☐ Mike Marson
☐ Bill Mikkelson
☐ Doug Mohns
☐ André Peloffy
☐ Milt Schmidt, G.M.
☐ Gord Smith

1978 - 79 CAPITALS

We have no pricing information on this set.
Card Size: 5" x 7"
Sponsors: none

☐ Jim Bedard (G)
☐ Michel Bergeron
☐ Greg Carroll
☐ Guy Charron
☐ Rolf Edberg
☐ Rick Green
☐ Gord Lane
☐ Mark Lofthouse
☐ Jack Lynch
☐ Dennis Maruk
☐ Paul Mulvey
☐ Robert Picard
☐ Bill Riley
☐ Tom Rowe
☐ Bob Sirois
☐ Gord Smith
☐ Leif Svensson
☐ Ryan Walter
☐ Bernie Wolfe

1979 - 80 CAPITALS

Photos are in black and white. Mike Gartner is the most expensive single at $20-25 in NRMT. Singles start at $1.50.
Card Size: 5 1/4" x 7 7/8"
Sponsors: none
Complete Set (23 cards): 50.00

☐ Pierre Bouchard
☐ Guy Charron
☐ Rolf Edberg
☐ Mike Gartner
☐ Rick Green
☐ Bengt Gustafsson
☐ Dennis Hextall
☐ Gary Inness (G)
☐ Yvon Labre
☐ Antero Lehtonen
☐ Mark Lofthouse
☐ Paul McKinnon
☐ Dennis Maruk
☐ Paul Mulvey
☐ Robert Picard
☐ Greg Polis
☐ Errol Rausse
☐ Tom Rowe
☐ Peter Scamurra
☐ Bob Sirois
☐ Wayne Stephenson (G)
☐ Leif Svensson
☐ Ryan Walter

1980 - 81 CAPITALS

Mike Gartner is the most expensive single at $15-20 in NRMT. Singles start at $1.50.
Card Size: 5" x 7"
Sponsors: none
Complete Set (24 cards): 45.00

☐ Pierre Bouchard
☐ Guy Charron
☐ Rolf Edberg
☐ Mike Gartner
☐ Gary Green
☐ Rick Green
☐ Bengt Gustafsson
☐ Alan Hangsleben
☐ Wes Jarvis
☐ Bob Kelly
☐ Yvon Labre
☐ Bill Mahoney
☐ Dennis Maruk
☐ Paul McKinnon
☐ Paul Mulvey
☐ Mike Palmateer (G)
☐ Jean Pronovost
☐ Pat Ribble
☐ Rick Smith
☐ Wayne Stephenson (G)
☐ Darren Veitch
☐ Dennis Ververgaert
☐ Howard Walker
☐ Ryan Walter

1981 - 82 CAPITALS

Mike Gartner is the most expensive single at $12-15. Singles start at $1.50.
Card Size: 5" x 7"
Sponsors: none
Complete Set (22 cards): 40.00

☐ Timo Blomqvist
☐ Bobby Carpenter
☐ Glen Currie
☐ Gaetan Duchesne
☐ Mike Gartner
☐ Bob Gould
☐ Rick Green
☐ Doug Hicks
☐ Randy Holt
☐ Wes Jarvis
☐ Al Jensen (G)
☐ Dennis Maruk
☐ Terry Murray
☐ Lee Norwood
☐ Mike Palmateer (G)
☐ Dave Parro (G)
☐ Torrie Robertson
☐ Greg Theberge
☐ Chris Valentine
☐ Darren Veitch
☐ Howard Walker
☐ Ryan Walter

1982 - 83 CAPITALS

The most expensive singles are Scott Stevens at $12-15 and Mike Gartner at $10-12. Singles start at $1.50.
Card Size: 5" x 7"
Sponsors: none
Complete Set (25 cards): 45.00

☐ Timo Blomqvist
☐ Ted Bulley
☐ Bob Carpenter
☐ Glen Currie
☐ Brian Engblom
☐ Mike Gartner
☐ Bob Gould
☐ Bengt Gustafsson
☐ Alan Haworth
☐ Randy Holt
☐ Ken Houston
☐ Doug Jarvis
☐ Rod Langway
☐ Craig Laughlin
☐ Dennis Maruk
☐ Bryan Murray
☐ Terry Murray
☐ Lee Norwood
☐ Milan Novy
☐ Dave Parro (G)
☐ David Poile
☐ Pat Riggin (G)
☐ Scott Stevens
☐ Chris Valentine
☐ Darren Veitch

1984 - 85 CAPITALS

Mike Gartner and Scott Stevens are the most expensive singles at $8-10. Singles start at $1.50.
Card Size: 4 1/2" x 6"
Sponsor: Pizza Hut
Complete Set (15 cards): 40.00

☐ Bob Carpenter
☐ Dave Christian
☐ Glen Currie
☐ Gaetan Duchesne
☐ Mike Gartner
☐ Bob Gould
☐ Bengt Gustafsson
☐ Alan Haworth
☐ Doug Jarvis
☐ Al Jensen (G)
☐ Rod Langway
☐ Craig Laughlin
☐ Larry Murphy
☐ Pat Riggin (G)
☐ Scott Stevens

1985 - 86 CAPITALS

Mike Gartner and Scott Stevens are the most expensive singles at $6-8. Singles start at $1.50.
Card Size: 4 1/2" x 6"
Sponsor: Pizza Hut
Complete Set (15 cards): 35.00

☐ Bob Carpenter
☐ Dave Christian
☐ Gaetan Duchesne
☐ Mike Gartner
☐ Bob Gould
☐ Bengt Gustafsson
☐ Alan Haworth
☐ Doug Jarvis
☐ Al Jensen (G)
☐ Rod Langway
☐ Craig Laughlin
☐ Larry Murphy
☐ Pat Riggin (G)
☐ Scott Stevens
☐ Darren Veitch

1986 - 87 CAPITALS POLICE SET

These cards were issued in two-card panels. The Gartner/Gould panel is the most expensive at $5-6. Single panels sell at $1.50. Cut-out cards measure 2 5/8" x 3 3/4" and start at 75¢. A cut-out 24-card set sells at $15.
Panel Size: 2 5/8" x 7 1/2"
Sponsor: Police
Complete Set (12 panels): 20.00

☐ Greg Adams #22
John Barrett #6
☐ Bob Carpenter #10
Dave Christian #27
☐ Yvon Corriveau #26
Gaetan Duchesne #14
☐ Lou Franceschetti #32
Mike Gartner #11
☐ Bob Gould #23
Kevin Hatcher #4
☐ Alan Haworth #15
Al Jensen #35 (G)
☐ David Jensen #9
Rod Langway #5
☐ Craig Laughlin #18
Stephen Leach #21
☐ Larry Murphy #8
Bryan Murray
☐ Pete Peeters #1 (G)
Jorgen Pettersson #12
☐ Michal Pivonka #17
David Poile
☐ Greg Smith #19
Scott Stevens #3

1986 - 87 CAPITALS KODAK

These cards were originally issued in panels. The team photo measures 8" x 10". Mike Gartner is the most expensive single at $6-8. Singles start at $1.00.
Card Size: 2" x 2 5/8"
Sponsor: Kodak
Complete Set (26 cards): 30.00

☐ Greg Adams
☐ John Barrett
☐ John Blum
☐ Dave Christian
☐ Bob Crawford
☐ Gaetan Duchesne
☐ Lou Franceschetti
☐ Mike Gartner
☐ Bob Gould
☐ Jeff Greenlaw
☐ Kevin Hatcher
☐ Alan Haworth
☐ David Jensen
☐ Rod Langway
☐ Craig Laughlin
☐ Bob Mason (G)
☐ Kelly Miller
☐ Larry Murphy
☐ Bryan Murray
☐ Pete Peeters (G)
☐ Michal Pivonka
☐ Mike Ridley
☐ Gary Sampson
☐ Greg Smith
☐ Scott Stevens
☐ Team Photo

1987 - 88 CAPITALS

Mike Gartner is the most expensive single at $4-5. Singles start at $1.00.
Panel Size: 5 1/4" x 8"
Sponsors: none
Complete Set (23 cards): 25.00

☐ Greg Adams
☐ John Barrett
☐ Dave Christian
☐ Lou Franceschetti
☐ Garry Galley
☐ Mike Gartner
☐ Bob Gould
☐ Bengt Gustafsson
☐ Kevin Hatcher
☐ Dale Hunter
☐ David Jensen
☐ Ed Kastelic
☐ Rod Langway
☐ Craig Laughlin
☐ Clint Malarchuk (G)
☐ Kelly Miller
☐ Larry Murphy
☐ Pete Peeters (G)
☐ Michal Pivonka
☐ Mike Ridley
☐ Greg Smith
☐ Scott Stevens
☐ Peter Sundstrom

1987 - 88 CAPITALS KODAK

These cards were originally issued in panels. The team photo measures 8 1/4" x 11". Mike Gartner is the most expensive single at $5-6. Singles start at $1.00.
Card Size: 2 3/16" x 2 15/16"
Sponsor: Kodak
Complete Set (26 cards): 25.00

☐ Greg Adams #22
☐ John Barrett #6
☐ Dave Christian #27
☐ Lou Franceschetti #25
☐ Garry Galley #2
☐ Mike Gartner #11
☐ Bob Gould #23
☐ Bengt Gustafsson #16
☐ Kevin Hatcher #4
☐ Bill Houlder #34
☐ Dale Hunter #32
☐ Ed Kastelic #29
☐ Rod Langway #5
☐ Craig Laughlin #18
☐ Clint Malarchuk #30 (G)
☐ Kelly Miller #10
☐ Larry Murphy #8
☐ Bryan Murray
☐ Pete Peeters #1 (G)
☐ Michal Pivonka #20
☐ David Poile
☐ Mike Ridley #17
☐ Greg Smith #19
☐ Scott Stevens #3
☐ Peter Sundstrom #12
☐ Team Photo

1988 - 89 CAPITALS

Mike Gartner is the most expensive single at $4-5. Singles start at $1.00.
Card Size: 5" x 7"
Sponsors: none
Complete Set (21 cards): 20.00

☐ Dave Christian
☐ Yvon Corriveau
☐ Geoff Courtnall
☐ Lou Franceschetti
☐ Mike Gartner
☐ Bob Gould
☐ Bengt Gustafsson
☐ Kevin Hatcher
☐ Dale Hunter
☐ Rod Langway
☐ Stephen Leach
☐ Grant Ledyard

- ☐ Clint Malarchuk (G)
- ☐ Kelly Miller
- ☐ Larry Murphy
- ☐ Pete Peeters (G)
- ☐ Michal Pivonka
- ☐ Mike Ridley
- ☐ Neil Sheehy
- ☐ Scott Stevens
- ☐ Peter Sundstrom

1988 - 89 CAPITALS SMOKEY THE BEAR

Mike Gartner is the most expensive single at $3-4. Singles start at 75¢.

Card Size: 2 5/8" x 3 3/4"
Sponsors: Smokey The Bear
Complete Set (24 cards): 15.00

- ☐ Dave Christian #27
- ☐ Yvon Corriveau #26
- ☐ Geoff Courtnall #14
- ☐ Lou Franceschetti #25
- ☐ Mike Gartner #11
- ☐ Bob Gould #23
- ☐ Bengt Gustafsson #16
- ☐ Kevin Hatcher #4
- ☐ Dale Hunter #32
- ☐ Rod Langway #5
- ☐ Stephen Leach #21
- ☐ Grant Ledyard #6
- ☐ Clint Malarchuk #30 (G)
- ☐ Kelly Miller #10
- ☐ Larry Murphy #8
- ☐ Bryan Murray
- ☐ Pete Peeters #1 (G)
- ☐ Michal Pivonka #20
- ☐ David Poile
- ☐ Mike Ridley #17
- ☐ Neil Sheehy #15
- ☐ Scott Stevens #3
- ☐ Peter Sundstrom #12
- ☐ Smokey the Bear

1989 - 90 CAPITALS

Dino Ciccarelli is the most expensive single at $2-3. Singles start at $1.00.

Card Size: 5" x 7"
Sponsors: none
Complete Set (23 cards): 20.00

- ☐ Don Beaupré (G)
- ☐ Dave Christian
- ☐ Dino Ciccarelli
- ☐ Yvon Corriveau
- ☐ Geoff Courtnall
- ☐ Kevin Hatcher
- ☐ Bill Houlder
- ☐ Dale Hunter
- ☐ Calle Johansson
- ☐ Dimitri Khristich
- ☐ Scot Kleinendorst
- ☐ Nick Kypreos
- ☐ Rod Langway
- ☐ Stephen Leach
- ☐ Bob Mason (G)
- ☐ Alan May
- ☐ Kelly Miller
- ☐ Michal Pivonka
- ☐ Mike Ridley
- ☐ Bob Rouse
- ☐ Neil Sheehy
- ☐ Scott Stevens
- ☐ Doug Wickenheiser

1989 - 90 CAPITALS KODAK

This set was originally issued in panels. Dino Ciccarelli is the most expensive single at $2-3. Singles start at $1.00.

Card Size: 2 3/16" x 2 1/2"
Sponsors: Kodak
Complete Set (25 cards): 20.00

- ☐ Don Beaupré #33 (G)
- ☐ Tim Berglund #11
- ☐ Dino Ciccarelli #22
- ☐ Geoff Courtnall #14
- ☐ John Druce #19
- ☐ Kevin Hatcher #4
- ☐ Dale Hunter #32
- ☐ Calle Johansson #6
- ☐ Bob Joyce #27
- ☐ Scot Kleinendorst #29
- ☐ Rob Laird
- ☐ Rod Langway #5
- ☐ Stephen Leach #21
- ☐ Mike Liut #1 (G)
- ☐ Steve Maltais #26
- ☐ Alan May #16
- ☐ Kelly Miller #10
- ☐ Terry Murray
- ☐ Michal Pivonka #20
- ☐ David Poile
- ☐ Mike Ridley #17
- ☐ Bob Rouse #8
- ☐ Neil Sheehy #15
- ☐ Scott Stevens #3
- ☐ John Tucker #12

1990 - 91 CAPITALS KODAK

This set was originally issued as a three-panel set. Peter Bondra is the most expensive single at $6-8. Singles start at 75¢.

Card Size: 2" x 2 5/8"
Sponsor: Kodak
Complete Set (25 cards): 20.00

- ☐ Don Beaupré (G)
- ☐ Tim Bergland
- ☐ Peter Bondra
- ☐ Dino Ciccarelli
- ☐ John Druce
- ☐ Kevin Hatcher
- ☐ Dale Hunter
- ☐ Al Iafrate
- ☐ Calle Johansson
- ☐ Dimitri Khristich
- ☐ Nick Kypreos
- ☐ Mike Lalor
- ☐ Rod Langway
- ☐ Stephen Leach
- ☐ Mike Liut (G)
- ☐ Alan May
- ☐ Kelly Miller
- ☐ Terry Murray
- ☐ John Perpich
- ☐ Michal Pivonka
- ☐ David Poile
- ☐ Mike Ridley
- ☐ Ken Sabourin
- ☐ Mikhail Tatarinov
- ☐ Dave Tippett

1990 - 91 CAPITALS SMOKEY THE BEAR

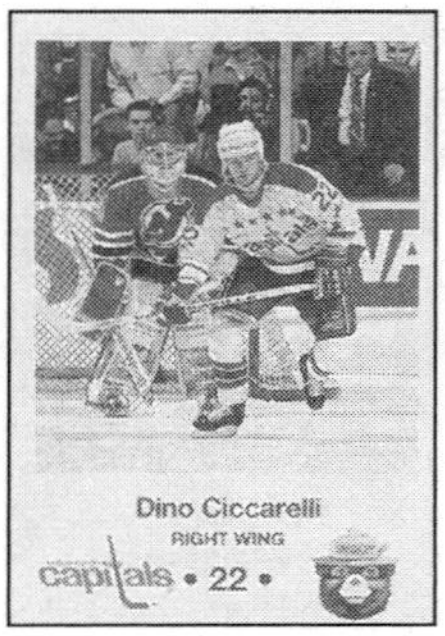

Peter Bondra is the most expensive single at $6-8. Singles start at 75¢.

Card Size: 2 5/8" x 3 3/4"
Sponsors: Smokey The Bear
Complete Set (22 cards): 15.00

- ☐ Don Beaupré (G)
- ☐ Tim Bergland
- ☐ Peter Bondra
- ☐ Dino Ciccarelli
- ☐ John Druce
- ☐ Kevin Hatcher
- ☐ Jim Hrivnak (G)
- ☐ Dale Hunter
- ☐ Calle Johansson
- ☐ Nick Kypreos
- ☐ Mike Lalor
- ☐ Rod Langway
- ☐ Stephen Leach
- ☐ Mike Liut (G)
- ☐ Alan May
- ☐ Kelly Miller
- ☐ Rob Murray
- ☐ Michal Pivonka
- ☐ Mike Ridley
- ☐ Neil Sheehy
- ☐ Mikhail Tatarinov
- ☐ Dave Tippett

1991 - 92 CAPITALS SMOKEY THE BEAR

Peter Bondra is the most expensive single at $5-6. Singles start at 75¢.

Card Size: 5" x 7"
Sponsors: Smokey The Bear
Complete Set (25 cards): 20.00

- ☐ Don Beaupré (G)
- ☐ Tim Bergland
- ☐ Peter Bondra
- ☐ Randy Burridge
- ☐ Shawn Chambers
- ☐ Dino Ciccarelli
- ☐ Sylvain Côté
- ☐ John Druce
- ☐ Jeff Greenlaw
- ☐ Kevin Hatcher
- ☐ Dale Hunter
- ☐ Al Iafrate
- ☐ Calle Johansson
- ☐ Dimitri Khristich
- ☐ Todd Krygier
- ☐ Nick Kypreos
- ☐ Mike Lalor
- ☐ Rod Langway
- ☐ Mike Liut (G)
- ☐ Alan May
- ☐ Kelly Miller
- ☐ Michal Pivonka
- ☐ Mike Ridley
- ☐ Ken Sabourin
- ☐ Dave Tippett

1991 - 92 CAPITALS KODAK

This set was originally issued as a three-panel set. Each panel measures 11" x 8". The first panel ("Red Hot and Blue") has space for autographs. The second panel has 15 player cards while the third panel has ten player cards plus a Kodak coupon. Peter Bondra is the most expensive cut-out single at $5-6. Singles start at 75¢.

Card Size: 2 3/16" x 2 3/4"
Sponsor: Kodak
Complete Set (25 cards): 20.00

- ☐ Don Beaupré (G)
- ☐ Tim Bergland
- ☐ Peter Bondra
- ☐ Randy Burridge
- ☐ Shawn Chambers
- ☐ Dino Ciccarelli
- ☐ Sylvain Côté
- ☐ John Druce
- ☐ Kevin Hatcher
- ☐ Jim Hrivnak (G)
- ☐ Dale Hunter
- ☐ Al Iafrate
- ☐ Calle Johansson
- ☐ Dimitri Khristich
- ☐ Todd Krygier
- ☐ Nick Kypreos
- ☐ Rod Langway
- ☐ Mike Liut (G)
- ☐ Paul MacDermid
- ☐ Alan May
- ☐ Kelly Miller
- ☐ Michal Pivonka
- ☐ Mike Ridley
- ☐ Brad Schlegel
- ☐ Dave Tippett

1992 - 93 CAPITALS KODAK

This set was originally issued as a three-panel set. Each panel measures 11" x 8". The first panel has room for autographs. The second panel has 15 player cards and the third panel has ten player cards plus a Kodak coupon. Peter Bondra is the most expensive cut-out single at $2-3. Singles start at 75¢.

Card Size: 2 3/16" x 2 3/4"
Sponsor: Kodak
Complete Set (25 cards): 15.00

- ☐ Shawn Anderson
- ☐ Don Beaupré (G)
- ☐ Peter Bondra
- ☐ Randy Burridge
- ☐ Bob Carpenter
- ☐ Paul Cavallini
- ☐ Sylvain Côté
- ☐ Pat Elynuik
- ☐ Kevin Hatcher
- ☐ Jim Hrivnak (G)
- ☐ Dale Hunter
- ☐ Al Iafrate
- ☐ Calle Johansson
- ☐ Keith Jones
- ☐ Dimitri Khristich
- ☐ Steve Konowalchuk
- ☐ Todd Krygier
- ☐ Rod Langway
- ☐ Paul MacDermid
- ☐ Alan May
- ☐ Kelly Miller
- ☐ Michal Pivonka
- ☐ Mike Ridley
- ☐ Reggie Savage
- ☐ Jason Woolley

1995 - 96 CAPITALS

This series was issued as an album. Peter Bondra is the most expensive single at $2-3. Singles start at 50¢.

Card Size:
Sponsors: none
Complete Set (28 cards): 15.00

- ☐ Jason Allison
- ☐ Craig Berube
- ☐ Peter Bondra
- ☐ Jim Carey (G)
- ☐ Sylvain Côté
- ☐ Mike Eagles
- ☐ Martin Gendron
- ☐ Sergei Gonchar
- ☐ Dale Hunter
- ☐ Calle Johansson
- ☐ Jim Johnson
- ☐ Keith Jones
- ☐ Joé Juneau
- ☐ Kevin Kaminski
- ☐ Ken Klee
- ☐ Olaf Kolzig (G)
- ☐ Steve Konowalchuk
- ☐ Kelly Miller
- ☐ Jeff Nelson
- ☐ Pat Peake
- ☐ Michal Pivonka
- ☐ Joe Reekie
- ☐ Mark Tinordi
- ☐ Stefan Ustorf
- ☐ Brendan Witt
- ☐ Jim Schoenfeld, Coach
- ☐ Mascot Slapshot
- ☐ Mascot Slapshot

WINNIPEG JETS

1979 - 80 JETS

Bobby Hull is the most expensive single at $8-10 in NRMT. Singles start at $1.00.

Postcard Size: 3 1/2" x 5 1/2"
Sponsors: none
Complete Set (28 cards): 30.00

- ☐ Mike Amodeo
- ☐ Al Cameron
- ☐ Scott Campbell
- ☐ Wayne Dillon
- ☐ Jude Drouin
- ☐ John Ferguson
- ☐ Hillard Graves
- ☐ Pierre Hamel (G)
- ☐ Dave Hoyda
- ☐ Bobby Hull
- ☐ Bill Lesuk
- ☐ Willy Lindstrom
- ☐ Morris Lukowich
- ☐ Jimmy Mann
- ☐ Peter Marsh
- ☐ Gord McTavish
- ☐ Tom McVie
- ☐ Barry Melrose
- ☐ Lyle Moffat
- ☐ Craig Norwich
- ☐ Lars-Erik Sjoberg
- ☐ Gary Smith (G)
- ☐ Gordon Smith
- ☐ Lorne Stamler
- ☐ Peter Sullivan
- ☐ Bill Sutherland
- ☐ Ron Wilson
- ☐ Jets card

1980 - 81 JETS

Dave Babych is the most expensive single at $3-4. Singles start at $1.00.
Card Size: 3 1/2" x 5 1/2"
Sponsors: none
Complete Set (23 cards): 20.00

- ☐ Dave Babych
- ☐ Al Cameron
- ☐ Scott Campbell
- ☐ Dave Christian
- ☐ Jude Drouin
- ☐ Norm Dupont
- ☐ Danny Geoffrion
- ☐ Pierre Hamel (G)
- ☐ Barry Legge
- ☐ Willy Lindstrom
- ☐ Barry Long
- ☐ Morris Lukowich
- ☐ Kris Manery
- ☐ Jimmy Mann
- ☐ Moe Mantha
- ☐ Markus Mattsson (G)
- ☐ Richard Mulhern
- ☐ Doug Smail
- ☐ Don Spring
- ☐ Anders Steen
- ☐ Peter Sullivan
- ☐ Tim Trimper
- ☐ Ron Wilson

1981 - 82 JETS

Photos are in black and white on these blank-back cards. Dale Hawerchuk is the most expensive single at $12-15. Singles start at $1.00.
Card Size: 3 1/2" x 5 1/2"
Sponsors: none
Complete Set (24 cards): 35.00

- ☐ Scott Arniel
- ☐ Dave Babych
- ☐ Dave Christian
- ☐ Lucien DeBlois
- ☐ Norm Dupont
- ☐ Larry Hopkins
- ☐ Dale Hawerchuk
- ☐ Craig Levie
- ☐ Willy Lindstrom
- ☐ Morris Lukowich
- ☐ Bengt Lundholm
- ☐ Paul MacLean
- ☐ Jimmy Mann
- ☐ Bryan Maxwell
- ☐ Serge Savard
- ☐ Doug Smail
- ☐ Doug Soetaert (G)
- ☐ Don Spring
- ☐ Ed Staniowski (G)
- ☐ Thomas Steen
- ☐ Bill Sutherland
- ☐ Tim Trimper
- ☐ Tim Watters
- ☐ Tom Watt

1982 - 83 JETS

Dale Hawerchuk has two singles each selling at $8-10. Singles start at $1.00.
Card Size: 3 1/2" x 5 1/2"
Sponsors: none
Complete Set (28 cards): 35.00

- ☐ Scott Arniel
- ☐ Dave Babych
- ☐ Jerry Butler
- ☐ Wade Campbell
- ☐ Dave Christian
- ☐ Lucien DeBlois
- ☐ Norm Dupont
- ☐ Dale Hawerchuk
- ☐ Dale Hawerchuk
- ☐ Jim Kyte
- ☐ Craig Levie
- ☐ Willy Lindstrom
- ☐ Morris Lukowich
- ☐ Bengt Lundholm
- ☐ Paul MacLean
- ☐ Jimmy Mann
- ☐ Bryan Maxwell
- ☐ Brian Mullen
- ☐ Serge Savard
- ☐ Doug Smail
- ☐ Doug Soetaert (G)
- ☐ Don Spring
- ☐ Ed Staniowski (G)
- ☐ Thomas Steen
- ☐ Bill Sutherland
- ☐ Tom Watt
- ☐ Tim Watters
- ☐ Team Photo

1983 - 84 JETS

Dale Hawerchuk is the most expensive single at $6-8. Singles start at $1.00.
Card Size: 3 1/4" x 5 1/4"
Sponsors: none
Complete Set (25 cards): 25.00

- ☐ Scott Arniel
- ☐ Dave Babych
- ☐ Laurie Boschman
- ☐ Wade Campbell
- ☐ Lucien DeBlois
- ☐ John Ferguson
- ☐ John Gibson
- ☐ Dale Hawerchuk
- ☐ Brian Hayward (G)
- ☐ Jim Kyte
- ☐ Barry Long
- ☐ Morris Lukowich
- ☐ Bengt Lundholm
- ☐ Paul MacLean
- ☐ Jimmy Mann
- ☐ Moe Mantha
- ☐ Andrew McBain
- ☐ Brian Mullen
- ☐ Robert Picard
- ☐ Doug Smail
- ☐ Doug Soetaert (G)
- ☐ Thomas Steen
- ☐ Tim Watters
- ☐ Ron Wilson
- ☐ Tim Young

1984 - 85 JETS SAFETY TIPS

This set was issued in two-card panels. The Hawerchuk/Arniel panel sells at $3-4. Single panels start at $1.00. Cut-out singles measure 2 5/8" x 3 3/4" and start at 50¢. A cut-out 24-card set sells at $10.
Panel Size: 2 5/8" x 7 1/2"
Sponsor: Police
Complete Set (12 panels): 15.00

- ☐ Laurie Boschman #16 / Paul Pooley #23
- ☐ Randy Carlyle #8 / Jim Kyte #6
- ☐ Dave Ellett #2 / Dave Babych #44
- ☐ Dale Hawerchuk #10 / Scott Arniel #11
- ☐ Brian Hayward #1 (G) / Marc Behrend #29 (G)
- ☐ Bengt Lundholm #22 / Ron Wilson #24
- ☐ Andrew McBain #20 / Brian Mullen #19
- ☐ Robert Picard #3 / Tim Watters #7
- ☐ Doug Smail #29 / Paul MacLean #15
- ☐ Perry Turnbull #27 / Morris Lukowich #12
- ☐ B.Sutherland/B.Long/R.Bowness / Thomas Steen #25
- ☐ John Ferguson / Team Photo

1985 - 86 JETS

11. Scott Arniel

These cards have blank backs. Dale Hawerchuk is the most expensive single at $4-5. Singles start at $1.00.
Card Size: 3 1/4" x 5 1/4"
Sponsors: none
Complete Set (22 cards): 20.00

- ☐ Scott Arniel
- ☐ Laurie Boschman
- ☐ Dan Bouchard (G)
- ☐ Randy Carlyle
- ☐ Dave Ellett
- ☐ Dale Hawerchuk
- ☐ Brian Hayward (G)
- ☐ Jim Kyte
- ☐ Paul MacLean
- ☐ Andrew McBain
- ☐ Anssi Melametsa
- ☐ Brian Mullen
- ☐ Jim Nill
- ☐ Dave Silk
- ☐ Doug Smail
- ☐ Thomas Steen
- ☐ Perry Turnbull
- ☐ Tim Watters
- ☐ Ron Wilson
- ☐ John B. Ferguson
- ☐ B.Sutherland/B.Long/R.Bowness
- ☐ Team Photo

1985 - 86 JETS POLICE SAFETY TIPS

This set was issued in two-card panels. The Hawerchuk/Arniel panel sells at $3-4. Single panels start at $1.00. cut-out singles measure 2 5/8" x 3 3/4" and start at 50¢. A cut-out 24-card set sells at $10.
Panel Size: 2 5/8" x 7 1/2"
Sponsor: Police
Complete Set (12 panels): 15.00

- ☐ Laurie Boschman #16 / Jim Nill #17
- ☐ Randy Carlyle #8 / Jim Kyte #6
- ☐ Dave Ellett #2 / Dave Silk #34
- ☐ Dale Hawerchuk #10 / Scott Arniel #11
- ☐ Brian Hayward #1 (G) / Dan Bouchard #35 (G)
- ☐ Mario Marois #22 / Ron Wilson #24
- ☐ Andrew McBain #20 / Brian Mullen #19
- ☐ Anssi Melametsa #14 / Tim Watters #7
- ☐ Doug Smail #9 / Paul MacLean #15
- ☐ Perry Turnbull #27 / Ray Neufeld #28
- ☐ B.Sutherland/B.Long/R.Bowness / Thomas Steen #25
- ☐ John Ferguson / Team Photo

1985 - 86 JETS GAME OF THE MONTH

This series was issued on the backs of milk cartons. Dale Hawerchuk is the most expensive panel at $25-30. Singles start at $10.
Panel Size:
Sponsor: Silverwood Dairies
Complete Set (6 panels): 65.00

- ☐ Laurie Boschman
- ☐ Randy Carlyle
- ☐ Dave Ellett
- ☐ Dale Hawerchuk
- ☐ Paul MacLean
- ☐ Brian Mullen

1986 - 87 JETS

These cards have blank backs. Dale Hawerchuk is the most expensive single at $4-5. Singles start at $1.00.
Card Size: 3 1/4" x 5 1/4"
Sponsors: none
Complete Set (26 cards): 20.00

- ☐ Brad Berry
- ☐ Laurie Boschman
- ☐ Randy Carlyle
- ☐ Bill Derlago
- ☐ Dave Ellett
- ☐ Gilles Hamel
- ☐ Dale Hawerchuk
- ☐ Hannu Jarvenpaa
- ☐ Jim Kyte
- ☐ Paul MacLean
- ☐ Andrew McBain
- ☐ Mario Marois
- ☐ Brian Mullen
- ☐ Ray Neufeld
- ☐ Jim Nill
- ☐ Fredrik Olausson
- ☐ Steve Penney (G)
- ☐ Eldon Reddick (G)
- ☐ Doug Smail
- ☐ Thomas Steen
- ☐ Perry Turnbull
- ☐ Tim Watters
- ☐ Ron Wilson
- ☐ John Ferguson
- ☐ Bill Sutherland/ Dan Maloney/R.Bowness
- ☐ Team Photo

1987 - 88 JETS

Dale Hawerchuk is the most expensive single at $3-4. Singles start at 75¢.
Card Size: 3 1/4" x 5 1/4"
Sponsors: none
Complete Set (24 cards): 15.00

- ☐ Brad Berry
- ☐ Daniel Berthiaume (G)
- ☐ Laurie Boschman
- ☐ Randy Carlyle
- ☐ Iain Duncan
- ☐ Dave Ellett
- ☐ Pat Elynuik
- ☐ Gilles Hamel
- ☐ Dale Hawerchuk
- ☐ Hannu Jarvenpaa
- ☐ Jim Kyte
- ☐ Paul MacLean
- ☐ Mario Marois
- ☐ Andrew McBain
- ☐ Ray Neufeld
- ☐ Fredrik Olausson

☐ Eldon Reddick (G)
☐ Steve Rooney
☐ Doug Smail
☐ Thomas Steen
☐ Peter Taglianetti
☐ Tim Watters
☐ Ron Wilson
☐ Team Photo

1988 - 89 JETS POLICE SAFETY TIPS

This set was issued in two-card panels. The Hawerchuk/Kyte panel sells at $3-4. Single panels start at $1.00. cut-out singles measure 2 5/8" x 3 3/46" and start 50¢. A cut-out 24-card set sells at $10.
Panel Size: 2 5/8" x 7 1/2"
Sponsor: Police
Complete Set (12 panels): 15.00

☐ Brent Ashton
Randy Carlyle
☐ Laurie Boschman
Andrew McBain
☐ Alain Chevrier (G)
Eldon Redddick (G)
☐ Iain Duncan
Mario Marois
☐ Dave Ellett
Pat Elynuik
☐ Randy Gilhen
Sutherland/B.Southern/St.Croix
☐ Dale Hawerchuk
Jim Kyte
☐ Dave Hunter
Doug Smail
☐ Hannu Jarvenpaa
Fredrik Olausson
☐ Ray Neufeld
Teppo Numminen
☐ Thomas Steen
Peter Taglianetti
☐ Dan Maloney
Team Photo

1989 - 90 JETS SAFEWAY

Dale Hawerchuk is the most expensive single at $2-3. Singles start at 50¢.
Card Size: 3 3/4" x 6 5/8"
Sponsor: Safeway
Complete Set (30 cards): 15.00

☐ Brent Ashton #7
☐ Stu Barnes #14
☐ Brad Berry #29
☐ Daniel Berthiaume #30 (G)
☐ Laurie Boschman #16
☐ Randy Carlyle #8
☐ Shawn Cronin #44
☐ Randy Cunneyworth #18
☐ Gord Donnelly #34
☐ Tom Draper #37 (G)
☐ Iain Duncan #19
☐ Dave Ellett #2
☐ Pat Elynuik #15
☐ Bob Essensa #35 (G)
☐ Paul Fenton #11
☐ Dale Hawerchuk #10
☐ Brent Hughes #46
☐ Mark Kumpel #21
☐ Moe Mantha #22
☐ Dave McLlwain #20
☐ Brian McReynolds #26
☐ Teppo Numminen #27
☐ Fredrik Olausson #4
☐ Greg Paslawski #28
☐ Doug Smail #12
☐ Thomas Steen #25
☐ Peter Taglianetti #32
☐ B.Murdoch/A.Suhonen/C.Drake
☐ Mascot Benny
☐ Team Photo

1990 - 91 JETS IGA

Singles start at 50¢.
Card Size: 3 1/2" x 6 1/2"
Sponsor: IGA
Complete Set (35 cards): 15.00

☐ Scott Arniel
☐ Brent Ashton
☐ Don Barber
☐ Stéphane Beauregard (G)
☐ Randy Carlyle
☐ Danton Cole
☐ Shawn Cronin
☐ Gord Donnelly
☐ Clare Drake
☐ Kris Draper
☐ Iain Duncan
☐ Pat Elynuik
☐ Bob Essensa (G)
☐ Doug Evans
☐ Phil Housley
☐ Sergei Kharin
☐ Mark Kumpel
☐ Guy Larose
☐ Paul MacDermid
☐ Moe Mantha
☐ Bryan Marchment
☐ Dave McLlwain
☐ Bob Murdoch
☐ Teppo Numminen
☐ Fredrik Olausson
☐ Ed Olczyk
☐ Mark Osborne
☐ Greg Paslawski
☐ Terry Simpson
☐ Thomas Steen
☐ Phil Sykes
☐ Rick Tabaracci (G)
☐ Simon Wheeldon
☐ Mascot Benny
☐ Team Photo

1991 - 92 JETS IGA/CARAMILK

Singles start at 50¢.
Card Size: 3 1/2" x 6 1/2"
Sponsors: IGA, Caramilk
Complete Set (35 cards): 15.00

☐ Stu Barnes
☐ Stéphane Beauregard (G)
☐ Luciano Borsato
☐ Randy Carlyle
☐ Danton Cole
☐ Shawn Cronin
☐ Burton Cummings
☐ Mike Eagles
☐ Pat Elynuik
☐ Bryan Erickson
☐ Bob Essensa (G)
☐ Doug Evans
☐ Mike Hartman
☐ Phil Housley
☐ Dean Kennedy
☐ Paul MacDermid
☐ Moe Mantha
☐ Rob Murray
☐ Troy Murray
☐ Teppo Numminen
☐ Fredrik Olausson
☐ Ed Olczyk
☐ Mark Osborne
☐ John Paddock
☐ Kent Paynter
☐ Dave Prior
☐ Russ Romaniuk
☐ Darrin Shannon
☐ Terry Simpson
☐ Thomas Steen
☐ Phil Sykes
☐ Rick Tabaracci (G)
☐ Glen Williamson
☐ Mascot Benny
☐ '90-91 Team Photo

1993 - 94 JETS RUFFLES

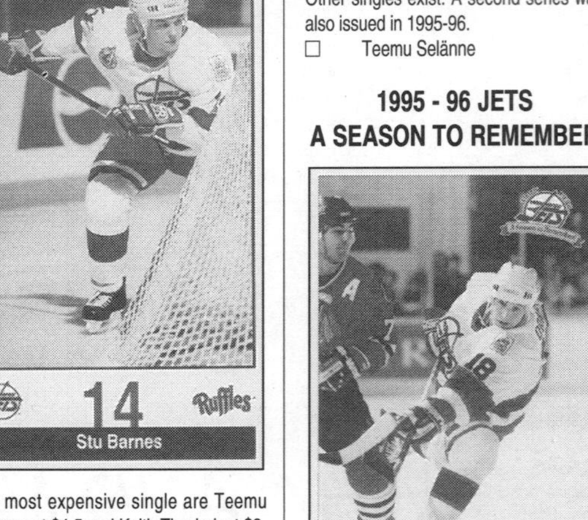

The most expensive single are Teemu Selänne at $4-5 and Keith Tkachuk at $3-4. Singles start at 50¢.
Card Size: 3 1/2" x 6 1/2"
Sponsor: Ruffles
Complete Set (29 cards): 20.00

☐ Stu Barnes
☐ Sergei Bautin
☐ Stéphane Beauregard (G)
☐ Zinetula Bilyaletdinov
☐ Arto Blomsten
☐ Luciano Borsato
☐ Tie Domi
☐ Mike Eagles
☐ Nelson Emerson
☐ Bryan Erickson
☐ Bob Essensa (G)
☐ Yan Kaminsky
☐ Dean Kennedy
☐ Kris King
☐ Boris Mironov
☐ Andy Murray
☐ Teppo Numminen
☐ Stéphane Quintal
☐ Fredrik Olausson
☐ John Paddock
☐ Teemu Selänne
☐ Darrin Shannon
☐ Thomas Steen
☐ Keith Tkachuk
☐ Igor Ulanov
☐ Paul Ysebaert
☐ Alexei Zhamnov
☐ Mascot Benny
☐ Team Photo

1994 - 95 JETS BOOK MARKS

We have little information on this set. Other singles exist. A second series was also issued in 1995-96.

☐ Teemu Selänne

1995 - 96 JETS A SEASON TO REMEMBER

The most expensive singles are Teemu Selänne at $4-5 and Keith Tkachuk at $3-4. Singles start at 50¢.
Card Size: 3 1/4" x 6 1/2"
Sponsors: none
Complete Set (26 cards): 20.00

☐ Tim Cheveldae (G) #27
☐ Shane Doan #19
☐ Jason Doig #55
☐ Dallas Drake #18
☐ Mike Eastwood #32
☐ Randy Gilhen #15
☐ Nikolai Khabibulin (G) #35
☐ Kris King #17
☐ Igor Korolev #23
☐ Stewart Malgunas #36
☐ Dave Manson #4
☐ Jim McKenzie #33
☐ Teppo Numminen #27
☐ Ed Olczyk #16
☐ Deron Quint #5
☐ Ed Ronan #30
☐ Teemu Selänne #8
☐ Darrin Shannon #34
☐ Darryl Shannon #24
☐ Mike Stapleton #14
☐ Keith Tkachuk #7
☐ Darren Turcotte #89
☐ Alexei Zhamnov #10
☐ R.Carlyle/ P.Pearn/ T.Simpson
☐ Team Photo
☐ Benny the Mascot

CHAPTER FOUR

WHA AND MISCELLANEOUS TEAM SETS

WHA TEAM SETS

CINCINATTI STINGERS

1975 - 76 STINGERS

We have little information on this set. Each hot dog wrapper featured one player. A 1976-77 set apparently also exists.
Size: 1 5/8" x 2 3/4"
Sponsor: Kahn's weiners

☐ Serge Aubry
☐ Bryan Campbell
☐ Rick Dudley
☐ Pierre Guite
☐ John Hughes
☐ Claude Larose
☐ Jacques Locas
☐ Bernie MacNeil
☐ Mike Pelyk
☐ Ron Plumb
☐ Dale Smedso
☐ Dennis Sobchuk
☐ Gene Sobchuk
☐ Gary Veneruzzo

CLEVELAND CRUSADERS

1972 - 73 CRUSADERS

Gerry Cheevers is the most expensive single at $15-18 in NRMT. Singles start at $2.
Card Size: 3 1/2" x 5 1/2"
Sponsors: none
Complete Set (19 cards): 50.00

☐ Paul Andrea
☐ Doug Brindley
☐ Ron Buchanan
☐ Gerry Cheevers (G)
☐ Ray Clearwater
☐ Bob Dillabough
☐ John Hanna
☐ Joe Hardy
☐ Ted Hodgson
☐ Ralph Hopiavuori
☐ Bill Horton
☐ Gary Jarrett
☐ Skip Krake
☐ Jim McMasters
☐ Wayne Muloin
☐ Gerry Pinder
☐ Richard Pumple
☐ Paul Schmyr
☐ Bob Whidden (G)

1972 - 73 CRUSADERS CHARLES LINNETT PHOTOS

We have little information on this set. Other singles may exist.
Photo Size: 8 1/2" x 11"
Sponsor: Charles Linnett

☐ Ron Buchanan
☐ Ray Clearwater
☐ Bob Dillabough
☐ Grant Erickson
☐ Ted Hodgson
☐ Ralph Hopiavouri
☐ Billb Horton
☐ Ralph Hopramon
☐ Gary Jarrett
☐ Skip Krake
☐ Jim McMasters
☐ Wayne Muloin
☐ Bill Needham, Coach
☐ Rick Pumple
☐ Paul Shmyr
☐ Robert Whidden (G)
☐ Jim Wiste

HOUSTON AEROS

1975 - 76 AEROS

Gordie Howe is the most expensive single at $15-20 in NRMT. Mark Howe sells at $8-10 and John Tonelli sells at $6-8. Singles start at $2.
Card Size: 3 1/2" x 5 1/2"
Sponsors: none
Complete Set (19 cards): 50.00

☐ Ron Grahaeme (G)
☐ Larry Hale
☐ Murray Hall
☐ Gordie Howe
☐ Mark Howe
☐ Marty Howe
☐ André Hinse
☐ Frank Hughes
☐ Glen Irwin
☐ Gordon Labossiere
☐ Don Larway
☐ Larry Lund
☐ Poul Popeil
☐ Rich Preston
☐ Terry Ruskowski
☐ Wayne Rutledge (G)
☐ John Schella
☐ Ted Taylor
☐ John Tonelli

LOS ANGELES SHARKS

1972 - 73 SHARKS

GEORGE GARDNER

Photos are in black and white. Singles sell at $3-5.
Card Size: 2 5/8" x 3 9/16"
Sponsors: none
Complete Set (19 cards): 50.00

☐ Mike Byers
☐ Bart Crashley
☐ George Gardner (G)
☐ Russ Gillow (G)
☐ Tom Gilmore
☐ Earl Heiskala
☐ J.P. LeBlanc
☐ Ralph MacSweyn
☐ Ted McCaskill
☐ Jim Niekamp
☐ Gerry Odrowski
☐ Tom Serviss
☐ Peter Slater
☐ Steve Sutherland
☐ Joe Szura
☐ Gary Veneruzzo
☐ Jim Watson
☐ Alton White
☐ Bill Young

MINNESOTA FIGHTING SAINTS

1972 - 73 FIGHTING SAINTS

We have little information on this set. Other singles likely exist.
Size: 3 1/2" x 5 1/2"
Sponsors: none
Complete Set (25 cards):

☐ Mike Antonovich #12
☐ John Arbour #17
☐ Terry Ball #21
☐ Keith Christiansen #6
☐ Wayne Connelly #7
☐ Mike Curran (G) #1
☐ Craig Falkman #16
☐ Ted Hampson #10
☐ Jimmy Johnson #20
☐ Bill Klatt #8
☐ George Konik #19
☐ Leonard Lilyholm #15
☐ Bob MacMillan #14
☐ Jack McCartan (G) #30
☐ Mike McMahon #23
☐ George Morrison #9
☐ Dick Paradise #2
☐ Mel Pearson #26
☐ Terry Ryan #18
☐ Blaine Rydman #22
☐ Frank Sanders #4
☐ Glen Sonmor, Coach
☐ Fred Speck #11
☐ Carl Wetzel (G) #35
☐ Bill Young #24

1974 - 75 FIGHTING SAINTS

We have little information on this set. Other singles likely exist.
Size: 3 1/2" x 5 1/2"
Sponsors: none

☐ Mike Antonovich
☐ John Arbour
☐ Ron Busniuk
☐ Wayne Connelly
☐ Mike Curran (G)
☐ Gord Gallant
☐ Ary Gambucci
☐ John Garrett (G)
☐ Ted Hampson
☐ Murray Heatley
☐ Fran Huck
☐ Jim Johnson
☐ Mike McMahon
☐ Rick Smith
☐ Mike Walton

NEW ENGLAND WHALERS

1972 - 73 WHALERS

Photos are in black and white. Singles sell at $4-5 in NRMT.
Card Size: 4 7/8" x 4 5/8"
Sponsors: none
Complete Set (17 cards): 65.00

☐ Mike Byers
☐ Terry Caffery
☐ John Cunniff
☐ John Danby
☐ Jim Dorey
☐ Tom Earl
☐ John French
☐ Ted Green
☐ Ric Jordan
☐ Bruce Landon
☐ Rick Ley
☐ Larry Pleau
☐ Brad Selwood
☐ Tim Sheehy
☐ Al Smith (G)
☐ Tom Webster
☐ Tom Williams

OTTAWA NATIONALS

1972 - 73 NATIONALS

Photos are in black and white. Singles sell at $2-4 in NRMT.
Card Size: 4 1/8" x 4 3/4"
Sponsors: none
Complete Set (23 cards): 40.00

☐ Mike Amodeo
☐ Les Binkley (G)
☐ Mike Boland
☐ Wayne Carleton
☐ Bob Charlebois
☐ Ron Climie
☐ Brian Conacher
☐ Rick Cunningham
☐ John Donnelly
☐ Brian Gibbons
☐ Jack Gibson
☐ Gilles Gratton (G)
☐ Steve King
☐ Gavin Kirk
☐ Bob Leduc
☐ Tom Martin
☐ Chris Meloff
☐ Ron Riley
☐ Rick Sentes
☐ Tom Simpson
☐ Ken Stephenson
☐ Guy Trottier
☐ Steve Warr

PHOENIX ROADRUNNERS

1975 - 76 ROADRUNNERS

Photos are in black and white. Robbie Ftorek is the most expensive single at $4-5 in NRMT. Singles start at $1.50.
Card Size: 3" x 4"
Sponsors: none
Complete Set (22 cards): 25.00

☐ Serge Beaudoin
☐ Jim Boyd
☐ Jim Clarke
☐ Cam Connor
☐ Mike Cormier
☐ Barry Dean
☐ Robbie Ftorek
☐ Dave Gorman
☐ John Gray
☐ Del Hall
☐ Ron Huston
☐ Murray Keogan
☐ Gary Kurt (G)
☐ Garry Lariviere
☐ Al McLeod
☐ Peter McNamee
☐ John Migneault
☐ Lauri Mononen
☐ Jim Niekamp
☐ Jack Norris (G)
☐ Pekka Rautakallio
☐ Ron Serafini

1976 - 77 ROADRUNNERS

Robbie Ftorek is the most expensive single at $3-4 in NRMT. Singles start at $1.50.

Card Size: 3 7/16" x 4 3/8"
Sponsors: none
Complete Set (18 cards): 20.00

☐ Serge Beaudoin
☐ Mike Cormier
☐ Robbie Ftorek
☐ Del Hall
☐ Clay Hebenton (G)
☐ André Hinse
☐ Mike Hobin
☐ Frank Hughes
☐ Ron Huston
☐ Gary Kurt (G)
☐ Garry Lariviere
☐ Bob Liddington
☐ Lauri Mononen
☐ Jim Niekamp
☐ Pekka Rautakallio
☐ Seppo Repo
☐ Jerry Rollins
☐ Juhani Tamminen

QUÉBEC NORDIQUES

1973 - 74 NORDIQUES PROSTAR PROMOTIONS

Richard Brodeur is the most expensive single at $6-8 in NRMT. Singles start at $1.50.

Card Size: 3 1/2" x 5 1/2"
Sponsor: Pro Star Promotions
Complete Set (29 cards): 40.00

☐ Mike Archambault
☐ Serge Aubry
☐ Alain Beaule
☐ Yves Bergeron
☐ Serge Bernier
☐ Jacques Blain
☐ Richard Brodeur (G)
☐ Alain Caron
☐ Michel Deguise
☐ Ken Desjardins
☐ Guy Dufour
☐ Maurice Filion, Coach
☐ André Gaudette
☐ Jean-Guy Gendron
☐ Jeannot Gilbert
☐ Réjean Giroux
☐ Frank Golembrosky
☐ Bob Guindon
☐ Pierre Guite
☐ Dale Hoganson
☐ Réjean Houle
☐ François Lacombe
☐ Paul Larose
☐ Rénald Leclerc
☐ Michel Parizeau
☐ Jean Payette
☐ Michel Rouleau
☐ Pierre Roy
☐ Jean-Claude Tremblay

1976 - 77 NORDIQUES

Richard Brodeur is the most expensive single at $5-6 in NRMT. Singles start at $1.50.

Postcard Size: 3 1/2" x 5 1/2"
Sponsors: none
Complete Set (20 cards): 35.00

☐ Serge Aubry
☐ Paul Baxter
☐ Jean Bernier
☐ Serge Bernier
☐ Christian Bordeleau
☐ Paulin Bordeleau
☐ André Boudrias
☐ Curt Brackenbury
☐ Richard Brodeur (G)
☐ Réal Cloutier
☐ Charles Constantin
☐ Jim Dorey
☐ Bob Fitchner
☐ Richard Grenier
☐ François Lacombe
☐ Pierre Roy
☐ Steve Sutherland
☐ Marc Tardif
☐ Jean-Claude Tremblay
☐ Wally Weir

1976 - 77 NORDIQUES MARIE ANTOINETTE

Artwork is credited to Claude Laroche. Richard Brodeur is the most expensive single at $8-10 in NRMT. Singles start at $5.

Photo Size: 8" x 10 1/2"
Sponsor: Marie Antoinette
Complete Set (14 cards): 75.00

☐ Paul Baxter
☐ Serge Bernier
☐ Paulin Bordeleau
☐ André Boudrias
☐ Curt Brackenbury
☐ Richard Brodeur (G)
☐ Réal Cloutier
☐ Charles Constantin
☐ Bob Fitchner
☐ Richard Grenier
☐ Marc Tardif
☐ Jean-Claude Tremblay
☐ Steve Sutherland
☐ Wally Weir

SAN DIEGO MARINERS

1976 - 77 MARINERS

We have no pricing information on this set.

Size: 5" x 8"
Sponsor: Dean's Photo Services
Complete Set (14 cards):

☐ Kevin Devine
☐ Bob Dobek
☐ Norm Ferguson
☐ Brent Hughes
☐ Randy Legge
☐ Ken Lockett (G)
☐ Kevin Morrison
☐ Joe Noris
☐ Gerry Pinder
☐ Brad Rhines
☐ Wayne Rivers
☐ Paul Shmyr
☐ Gary Venneruzzo
☐ Ernie Wakely (G)

VANCOUVER BLAZERS

1973 - 74 BLAZERS

Colin Campbell is the most expensive single at $4-5 in NRMT. Singles sell at $2.

Card Size: 3 1/2" x 5"
Sponsors: none
Complete Set (19 cards): 40.00

☐ Jim Adair
☐ Don Burgess
☐ Bryan Campbell
☐ Colin Campbell
☐ Mike Chernoff
☐ Peter Donnelly
☐ George Gardner (G)
☐ Sam Gellard
☐ Ed Hatoum
☐ Dave Hutchison
☐ Danny Lawton
☐ Ralph MacSweyn
☐ Denis Meloche
☐ John Micneault
☐ Murray Myers
☐ Michel Plante
☐ Ron Plumb
☐ Claude St. Sauveur
☐ Irvin Spencer

WINNIPEG JETS

1978 - 79 JETS

Kent Nilsson is the most expensive single at $6-8 in NRMT. Singles start at $1.50.

Postcard Size: 3 1/2" x 5 1/2"
Sponsor: Baker & Sons Ltd.
Complete Set (23 cards): 30.00

☐ Mike Amodeo
☐ Scott Campbell
☐ Kim Clackson
☐ Joe Daley (G)
☐ John Gray
☐ Ted Green
☐ Robert Guindon
☐ Glenn Hicks
☐ Larry Hillman
☐ Bill Lesuk
☐ Willy Lindstrom
☐ Barry Long
☐ Morris Lukowich
☐ Paul MacKinnon
☐ Markus Mattsson (G)
☐ Lyle Moffat
☐ Kent Nilsson
☐ Rich Preston
☐ Terry Ruskowski
☐ Lars-Erik Sjoberg
☐ Peter Sullivan
☐ Paul Terbenche
☐ Steve West

BRITISH ELITE LEAGUE

1995 - 96 STEELERS

We have no pricing information on this 24-card set. An album was also available. The arena and team photo cards measure 3 5/8" x 5 1/4" while the trophy card measures 2 3/4" x 5 1/4".

Card Size: 2 3/8" x 3 1/2"
Sponsors: Sheffield Police

☐ Neil Abel
☐ Nicky Chinn
☐ Tim Cranston
☐ Alex Dampier

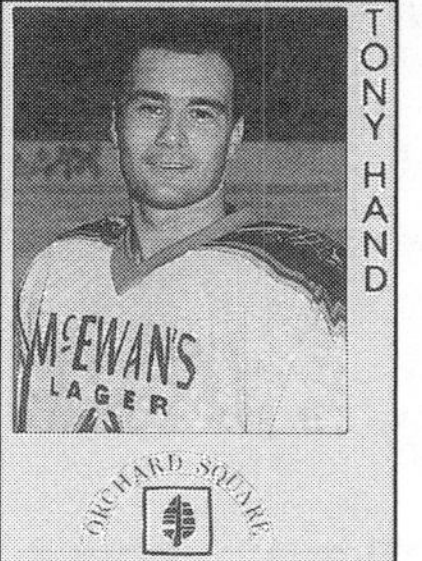

☐ Perry Doyle
☐ Tony Hand
☐ Scott Heaton
☐ Chris Kelland
☐ Andre Malo
☐ Martin McKay
☐ Les Millie
☐ Scott Neil
☐ Steve Nemeth
☐ Mike O'Connor
☐ Tommy Plummer
☐ Ken Priestlay
☐ Ron Shudra
☐ Clyde Tuyl
☐ Mark Wright
☐ Sharon Lawley/Anne Weston/ Hayley Roach/Andy Akers
☐ Mascot Foggy Dan
☐ Arena
☐ Team Photo
☐ Trophies

1997 - 98 STEELERS

We have no pricing information on this 24-card set. An album was also available.

Card Sizes: 2 3/8" x 3 1/2"; 3 5/8" x 5 3/16"
Sponsor: South Yorkshire Police, Tinsley Wire Limited, British Steel Engineering Steels

☐ Scott Allison
☐ Corey Beaulieu
☐ Nicky Chinn
☐ Ed Courtenay
☐ Tim Cranston
☐ Dion Del Monte
☐ Piero Greco (G)
☐ Tony Hand
☐ James Hibbert (G)
☐ Chris Kelland
☐ Frank Kovacs
☐ David Longstaff
☐ André Malo
☐ Tom Plommer
☐ Ken Priestlay
☐ Ron Shudra
☐ Jamie Van der Horst
☐ Mike Ware
☐ Rob Wilson
☐ Alex Dampier, Mgr.
☐ Clyde Tuyl, Coach
☐ Mascot Steeler Foggy Dan
☐ Sheffield Arena (3 5/8" x 5 3/16")
☐ Team Photo (3 5/8" x 5 3/16")

CHAPTER FIVE

MINOR LEAGUE TEAM SETS

MINOR LEAGUE TEAM SETS

ADIRONDACK RED WINGS
(AHL)

1995 - 96 RED WINGS

Anders Eriksson and Kevin Hodson are the most expensive singles at $1.00-1.50. Singles start at 50¢.
Card Size: 2 1/2" x 3 1/2"
Sponsor: Split Second
Complete Set (24 cards): 12.00

☐ Jeff Bloemberg
☐ Curtis Bowen
☐ Dave Chyzowski
☐ Sylvain Cloutier
☐ Ryan Duthie
☐ Anders Eriksson
☐ Yan Golubovsky
☐ Ben Hankinson
☐ Kevin Hodson (G)
☐ Scott Hollis
☐ Mike Knuble
☐ Jason MacDonald
☐ Mark Major
☐ Norm Maracle
☐ Kurt Miller
☐ Mike Needham
☐ Troy Neumeier
☐ Mark Ouimet
☐ Jamie Pushor
☐ Stacy Roest
☐ Brandon Smith
☐ Kerry Toporowski
☐ Wes Walz
☐ Aaron Ward
☐ Macot Hockeye

ATLANTA KNIGHTS (IHL)

1992 - 93 KNIGHTS

Manon Rhéaume is the most expensive single at $5.00. Singles sell at 50¢.
Size: 2 1/2" x 3 1/2"
Sponsor: Sport Print
Complete Set (24 cards): 12.00

☐ Manon Rhéaume (G)
☐ J.C. Bergeron (G)
☐ Tim Bergeron
☐ Jean Blouin
☐ Scott Boston
☐ Jeff Buchanan
☐ Don Burke
☐ Jock Callander
☐ Christian Campeau
☐ Brent Gretzky
☐ Matt Hervey
☐ Jason Lafrenière
☐ Rick Lanz
☐ Chris LiPuma
☐ David Littman (G)
☐ Steve Maltais
☐ Colin Miller
☐ Keith Osborne
☐ Sergei Ossipov
☐ Shawn Rivers
☐ Shayne Stevenson
☐ Dan Vincelette
☐ Gene Ubriaco, Coach
☐ Knights/ Checklist

1993 - 94 KNIGHTS

Manon Rhéaume is the most expensive single at $6.00. Singles sell at 50¢.
Size: 2 1/2" x 3 1/2"
Sponsor: Sport Print
Complete Set (24 cards): 12.00

☐ J.C. Bergeron
☐ Jeff Buchanan
☐ Christian Campeau
☐ Eric Charron
☐ Cory Cross
☐ Stan Drulia
☐ Eric Dubois
☐ Devin Edgerton
☐ Mike Greenlay (G)
☐ Brent Gretzky
☐ Steve Larouche
☐ Chris LiPuma
☐ Jeff Madill
☐ Bill McDougall
☐ Colin Miller
☐ Manon Rhéaume (G)
☐ Shawn Rivers
☐ Normand Rochefort
☐ Jason Ruff
☐ Martin Tanguay
☐ Marc Tardif
☐ Gene Ubriaco, Coach
☐ Knights/ Checklist

BALTIMORE SKIPJACKS
(AHL)

1991 - 92 SKIPJACKS

Olaf Kolzig is the most expensive single at $1.00-1.50. Singles start at 50¢.
Card Size: 2 1/2" x 3 1/2"
Sponsors: Wendy's, Coke
Complete Set (15 cards): 10.00

☐ 1 Tim Taylor
☐ 2 Brent Hughes
☐ 3 Trevor Halverson
☐ 4 Bobby Reynolds
☐ 5 Ken Lovsin
☐ 6 Olaf Kolzig (G)
☐ 7 Reggie Savage
☐ 8 Jim Mathieson
☐ 9 Todd Hlushko
☐ 10 Mark Ferner
☐ 11 John Purves
☐ 12 Steve Seftel
☐ 13 Craig Duncanson
☐ 14 Simon Wheeldon
☐ 15 Bob Babcock

BINGHAMPTON RANGERS
(AHL)

1992 - 93 RANGERS

Corey Hirsch and Sergei Zubov are the most expensive singles at $1.00-1.50. Singles start at 50¢.
Card Size: 2 1/2" x 3 1/2"
Sponsors: none
Complete Set (24 cards): 10.00

☐ 1 Rangers card
☐ 2 Mike Hurlbut
☐ 3 Michael Stewart
☐ 4 Craig Duncanson
☐ 5 Rick Bennett
☐ 6 Dave Thomlinson
☐ 7 Mike Stevens
☐ 8 Rob Kenny
☐ 9 Chris Cichocki
☐ 10 Sergei Zubov
☐ 11 Don Biggs
☐ 12 Joby Messier
☐ 13 Steven King
☐ 14 Dave Archibald
☐ 15 Brian McReynolds
☐ 16 Dave Marcinyshyn
☐ 17 Jean-Yves Roy
☐ 18 Peter Fiorentino
☐ 19 Daniel Lacroix
☐ 20 Per Djoos
☐ 21 Boris Rousson (G)
☐ 22 Corey Hirsch (G)
☐ 23 Mascot Rockey Ranger
☐ 24 Rangers card

1994 - 95 RANGERS

Corey Hirsch is the most expensive single at $1.00-1.50. Singles start at 50¢.
Card Size: 2 1/2" x 3 1/2"
Sponsor: Classic
Complete Set (24 cards): 10.00

☐ Eric Cairns
☐ Craig Duncanson
☐ Peter Fiorentino
☐ Ken Gernander
☐ Jim Hiller
☐ Corey Hirsch (G)
☐ Rob Kenny
☐ Andrei Kudinov
☐ Darren Langdon
☐ Scott Malone
☐ Shawn McCosh
☐ Mike McLaughlin
☐ Joby Messier
☐ Jeff Nielson
☐ Mattias Norstrom
☐ Jamie Ram (G)
☐ Barry Richter
☐ Jean-Yves Roy
☐ Brad Rubachuk
☐ Dave Smith
☐ Dmitri Starostenko
☐ Michael Stewart
☐ Darcy Werenka

1995 - 96 RANGERS

Singles start at 50¢.
Card Size: 2 1/2" x 3 1/2"
Sponsor: Split Second
Complete Set (25 cards): 10.00

☐ Sylvain Blouin
☐ Eric Cairns
☐ Chris Ferraro
☐ Peter Ferraro
☐ Maxim Galanov
☐ Ken Gernander
☐ Brad Jones
☐ Pavel Komarov
☐ Andrei Kudinov
☐ Daniel Lacroix
☐ Steve Larouche
☐ Jon Hillebrandt
☐ Scott Malone
☐ Cal McGowan
☐ Jeff Nielsen
☐ Jamie Ram (G)
☐ Shawn Reid
☐ Barry Richter
☐ Andy Silverman
☐ Lee Sorochan
☐ Dmitri Starostenko
☐ Ryan Vandenbussche
☐ Rick Willis
☐ George Burnett, Coach
☐ Mike Busniuk, Coach

1996 - 97 RANGERS

Dan Cloutier is the most expensive single at $2-3. Singles start at 50¢.
Card Size: 2 1/2" x 3 1/2"
Sponsor: Split Second
Complete Set (24 cards): 10.00

☐ Micah Aivazoff
☐ Sylvain Blouin
☐ Ed Campbell
☐ Dan Cloutier (G)
☐ Chris Ferraro
☐ Peter Ferraro
☐ Peter Fiorentino
☐ Eric Flinton
☐ Maxim Golanov
☐ Ken Gernander
☐ Mike Martin
☐ Bob Maudie
☐ Jeff Nielsen
☐ Rocky Raccoon
☐ Ken Shepard
☐ Andy Silverman
☐ Adam Smith
☐ Lee Sorochan
☐ Ryan VandenBussche
☐ Vladimir Vorobiev
☐ Rick Willis
☐ George Burnett, Coach
☐ Mike Busniak, Coach
☐ AHL Card

BIRMINGHAM BULLS
(ECHL)

1993 - 94 BULLS

Singles start at 50¢.
Card Size: 2 5/8" x 3 5/8"
Sponsors: Fox 21, WJOX 690, Coke
Complete Set (23 cards): 10.00

☐ 1 Bulls card
☐ 2 Jim Larkin
☐ 3 Brett Barnett
☐ 4 Joe Flanagan
☐ 5 Butch Kaebel
☐ 6 Scott Matusovich
☐ 7 Chuck E. Hughes
☐ 8 Dave Craievich
☐ 9 Alexander Havanov
☐ 10 Paul Marshall
☐ 11 Jim Peters
☐ 12 Chris Marshall
☐ 13 Jerome Bechard
☐ 14 Jean-Alain Schneider
☐ 15 Kevin Kerr
☐ 16 Rob Krauss
☐ 17 Greg Burke
☐ 18 Mark Romaine
☐ 19 Bruce Garber
☐ 20 Phil Roberto
☐ 21 Dave Cavaliere
☐ 22 Tim Woodburn
☐ Checklist

1994 - 95 BULLS

Brad Smyth is the most expensive single at $1.00-1.50. Singles start at 50¢.
Card Size: 2 3/4" x 3 3/4"
Sponsors: 94.5 FM, WBMG 45
Complete Set (23 cards): 10.00

☐ Greg Bailey
☐ Norm Bazin
☐ Jerome Bechard
☐ Dave Boyd
☐ David Craievich
☐ Rob Donovan
☐ Jon Duval
☐ Sandy Galuppo
☐ Todd Harris
☐ Ian Hebert
☐ Craig Johnson
☐ John Joyce
☐ Chris Kerber
☐ Olaf Kjenstad
☐ Mike Krassner
☐ Jim Larkin
☐ Craig Lutes
☐ Mark Michaud
☐ Jean-Marc Plante
☐ Phil Roberto
☐ Brad Smyth
☐ Checklist

1995 - 96 BULLS

Singles start at 50¢.
Card Size: 2 3/4" x 3 3/4"
Sponsors: Chevron, WJOX
Complete Set (23 cards): 10.00

☐ Phil Roberto
☐ Lancy Brady
☐ Jeff Wells
☐ Brad Prefontaine
☐ Mark Raiter
☐ Rob Donovan
☐ Chris Grenville
☐ Colin Gregor
☐ Mike Latendresse
☐ John Morabito
☐ Brendan Creagh
☐ Chris Bergeron
☐ Jerome Bechard
☐ Craig Lutes
☐ Ian Herbert
☐ John Joyce
☐ Jeff Callinan
☐ Jason Dexter
☐ Olaf Kjenstad
☐ Chad Erickson
☐ Ray Pack
☐ Mascot Toro The Bull
☐ Chris Kerber
☐ M.Coulter/S.Giffin
☐ Doug Laxton
☐ Randy Armstrong
☐ Lee Davis
☐ Herb Winches
☐ Ben Cook

CAPE BRETON OILERS
(AHL)

1994 - 95 OILERS

Todd Marchant and David Oliver are the most expensive singles at $1-1.50. Singles start at 50¢.
Card Size: 2 1/2" x 3 1/2"
Sponsor: Classic
Complete Set (23 cards): 10.00

☐ Scott Allison
☐ Martin Bakula
☐ Ladislav Benysek
☐ Dennis Bonvie
☐ Jozef Cierny
☐ Duane Dennis
☐ Greg DeVries
☐ Joaquin Gage (G)
☐ Ian Herbers
☐ Ralph Intranuovo
☐ Claude Jurtras
☐ Marc LaForge
☐ Todd Marchant
☐ Darcy Martini
☐ Roman Oksiuta
☐ David Oliver
☐ Steve Passmore (G)
☐ Nick Stajduhar
☐ John Van Kessel
☐ David Vyborny
☐ Peter White
☐ Tyler Wright
☐ Brad Zavisha

CINCINNATI CYCLONES
(ECHL/IHL)

1991 - 92 CYCLONES

Singles start at 50¢.
Card Size: 2 3/8" x 3 1/2"
Sponsors: 19 Fox, Bell
Complete Set (25 cards): 10.00

☐ Dan Beaudette
☐ Steve Benoît, Trainer
☐ Steve Cadieux
☐ Craig Charron
☐ David Craievich
☐ Doug Dadswell (G)
☐ Dennis Desrosiers, Coach
☐ Terry Ficorelli, Announcer
☐ Jeff Hogden
☐ Kevin Kerr
☐ Jaan Luik
☐ Scott Luik
☐ Chris Marshall
☐ Daryn McBride
☐ Doug Melnyk
☐ David Moore
☐ Tom Neziol
☐ Mark Romaine
☐ Jay Rose
☐ Martin St. Amour
☐ Kevin Scott
☐ Peter Schure
☐ Steve Shaunessy
☐ Blaine Stoughton, Asst. Coach
☐ Bobby Wallwork

1992 - 93 CYCLONES

Singles start at 50¢.
Size: 2 1/2" x 3 1/2"
Sponsor: Bell Telephone
Complete Set (30 cards): 12.00

☐ Bill Armstrong #27
☐ Ralph Barahona #16
☐ Steve Benoît, Trainer
☐ Mike Bodarchuk #14
☐ Craig Charron #7
☐ Todd Copeland #33
☐ Doug Dadswell (G) #35
☐ Mike Dagenais #6
☐ Kevin Dean #20
☐ Dennis Desrosiers, Coach
☐ Chad Erickson (G) #34
☐ Todd Flichel #3
☐ Alan Hepple #23
☐ Dennis Holland #18
☐ Sergei Kharin #15
☐ David Latta #29
☐ Jeff Madill #12
☐ Jon Morris #10
☐ Dean Morton #21
☐ Chris Nelson #2
☐ Darcy Norton #25
☐ Alex Ochoa, Trainer
☐ Howie Rosenblatt #24
☐ Scott Shaunessy #5
☐ Blaine Stoughton,Asst.Coach
☐ Mario Thyer #28
☐ Al Tuer #4
☐ Terry Ficorelli, Announcer
☐ Wildman Walker, Announcer
☐ Mascot Mr. Cyclone

1996 - 97 CYCLONES

Singles start at 50¢.
Size: 2 1/2" x 3 1/2"
Sponsor: Split Second
Complete Set (25 cards): 10.00

☐ Don Biggs #22
☐ Mike Casselman #17
☐ Chris Cichocki #33
☐ Ted Crowley #4
☐ Eric Dandenault #37
☐ Dale DeGray #51
☐ Jeff Greenlaw #29
☐ Todd Hawkins #12
☐ Al Hill, Asst.Coach
☐ Tony Horacek #24
☐ Duane Joyce #3
☐ Nick Kenney, Trainer
☐ Marc Laniel #26
☐ Paul Lawless #13
☐ Doug MacDonald #44
☐ Todd MacDonald (G) #1
☐ Dave Marcinyshyn #27
☐ Mark Mills, Equipment
☐ Scott Morrow #28
☐ Myles O'Connor #6
☐ Geoff Sarjeant (G) #31
☐ Ron Smith, Coach
☐ Scott Thomas #19
☐ Jeff Wells #5
☐ Mascot Snowbird

CLEVELAND BARONS
(AHL)

1951 - 52 BARONS

We have no pricing information on this 20-photo set.
Photo Size: 6" x 9"
Sponsors: none

☐ Bob Bailey
☐ Johnny Bower (G)
☐ Joe Carveth
☐ Ray Ceresino
☐ Bob Chrystal
☐ Bun Cook
☐ Paul Gladu
☐ Jack Gordon
☐ Ike Hildebrand
☐ Joe Lund
☐ Eddie Olson
☐ Fern Perreault
☐ Jerry Reid
☐ Ed Reigle
☐ Phil Samis
☐ Ken Schultz
☐ Fred Shero
☐ Fred Thurier
☐ Tom Williams
☐ Steve Wochy

1960 - 61 BARONS

We have no pricing information on this 19-card set.
Card Size: 5 3/8" x 6 3/4"
Sponsors: none

☐ Ron Attwell
☐ Les Binkley
☐ Bill Dineen
☐ John Ferguson
☐ Cal Gardner
☐ Fred Glover
☐ Jack Godron
☐ Aldo Guidolin
☐ Greg Hicks
☐ Wayne Larkin
☐ Moe Mantha
☐ Gil Mayer
☐ Eddie Mazur
☐ Jim Mikol
☐ Bill Needham
☐ Cal Stearns
☐ Bill Sutherland
☐ Tom Williams
☐ Team Photo

CLEVELAND LUMBERJACKS
(IHL)

1992 - 93 LUMBERJACKS

Singles start at 50¢.
Card Size: 2 3/8" x 3 1/2"
Sponsors: WKNR, Rusterminator
Complete Set (25 cards): 10.00

☐ 1 Lumberjacks
☐ 2 Larry Gordon, G.M.
☐ 3 Paul Laus
☐ 4 Travis Thiessen
☐ 5 Phil Russell, Coach
☐ 6 Gilbert Delorme
☐ 7 Jamie Heward
☐ 8 Greg Andrusak
☐ 9 David Quinn
☐ 10 Perry Ganchar
☐ 11 George Zajankala
☐ 12 Todd Nelson
☐ 13 Dave Michayluk
☐ 14 Bruce Racine (G)
☐ 15 Rob Dopson (G)
☐ 16 Bert Godin (G)
☐ 17 Ed Patterson
☐ 18 Justin Duberman
☐ 19 Sandy Smith
☐ 20 Jason Smart
☐ 21 Ken Priestlay
☐ 22 Daniel Gauthier
☐ 23 Robert Melanson
☐ 24 Mark Major
☐ 25 Paul Dyck

1993 - 94 LUMBERJACKS

Singles start at 50¢.
Card Size: 2 3/8" x 3 1/2"
Sponsors: WMMS, Peak
Complete Set (21 cards): 10.00

☐ Greg Andrusak
☐ Steve Bancroft
☐ Jamie Black
☐ Jock Callander
☐ Mike Dagenais
☐ Gilbert Delorme
☐ Rob Dopson (G)
☐ Justin Duberman
☐ Paul Dyck
☐ Perry Ganchar
☐ Todd Hawkins
☐ Jamie Heward
☐ Ladislav Karabin
☐ Dave Michayluk
☐ Pat Neaton
☐ Rick Paterson, Coach
☐ Ed Patterson
☐ Olie Sundstrom (G)
☐ Chris Tamer
☐ Travis Thiessen
☐ Leonid Toropchenko

1995 - 96 LUMBERJACKS

Patrick Lalime is the most expensive at $2-3. Singles start at 50¢.
Card Size: 2 3/8" x 3 1/2"
Sponsors: Huntington Bank, WKNR
Complete Set (24 cards): 12.00

☐ Peter Allen
☐ Bill Armstrong
☐ Len Barrie
☐ Dave Baseggio
☐ Oleg Belov
☐ Drake Berehowsky
☐ Stefan Bergkvist
☐ Jock Callander
☐ Jeff Christian
☐ Philippe DeRouville (G)
☐ Corey Foster
☐ Perry Ganchar
☐ Victor Gervais
☐ Rick Hayward
☐ Patrick Lalime (G)
☐ Brad Laur
☐ Dave McLlwain
☐ Dave Michayluk
☐ Mark Osborne
☐ Rick Paterson
☐ Domenic Pittis
☐ Ryan Savoia
☐ Mike Stevens
☐ Lumberjacks cards

COLUMBUS CHECKERS
(IHL)

1967 - 68 CHECKERS

These cards feature black and white photography and a facsimile signature. We have no pricing information on this set.
Size: 8 3/4" x 10 3/4"
Sponsors: none
Complete Set (16 cards)

☐ Moe Bartoli
☐ Bill Bond
☐ Serge Boudreault
☐ Gord Dibley (G)
☐ Bret Fizzell
☐ Chuck Kelly
☐ Ted Leboda
☐ Nelson Leclair
☐ R. Paquette
☐ Dick Proceviat
☐ Hartley Stakowski
☐ Ken Sutvla
☐ Nelson Tremblay
☐ Jack Turner
☐ Al White
☐ Team Photo

1969 CHECKERS

These cards feature black and white photography and the player's name at the bottom of the photo. We have no pricing information on this set.
Size: 4" x 7 1/4"
Sponsors: none
Complete Set (16 cards)

☐ John Bailey
☐ Moe Bartoli
☐ Kerry Bond
☐ André Daoust (G)
☐ Bert Fizzell
☐ Marcel Goudreau
☐ Jim Graham
☐ Paul Jackson
☐ Ken Laidlaw
☐ Noel Lirette
☐ Gary Longman
☐ Garry MacMillan
☐ Gary Mork
☐ Matt Thorp (G)
☐ Jack Turner
☐ Al White

DAYTON BOMBERS
(ECHL)

1992 - 93 BOMBERS

Singles start at 50¢.
Card Size: 2 1/2" x 3 1/2"
Sponsor: WTVE 104.7
Complete Set (21 cards): 8.00

☐ Steve Bogoyevac
☐ Darren Colbourne
☐ Derek Crawford
☐ Derek Donald
☐ Ray Edwards
☐ Doug Evans
☐ Sandy Galuppo
☐ Shayne Green
☐ Rod Houck
☐ Peter Kasowski
☐ Steve Kerrigan
☐ Frank Kovacs
☐ Darren Langdon
☐ Denis Larocque
☐ Darwin MacPherson
☐ Tom Nemeth
☐ Claude Noel
☐ Tony Peters
☐ Marshall Phillip
☐ Mike Reier
☐ Steve Wilson

1993 - 94 BOMBERS

Singles start at 50¢.
Card Size: 2 1/2" x 3 1/2"
Sponsor: WTVE 104.7
Complete Set (18 cards): 8.00

☐ 1 Checklist
☐ 2 Jeff Levy
☐ 3 Steve Wilson
☐ 4 Jason Downey
☐ 5 Jim Peters
☐ 6 Ondrej Kriz
☐ 7 Steve Bogoyevac
☐ 8 Jason Disiewich
☐ 9 Marc Savard
☐ 10 Dan O'Shea
☐ 11 Tom Nemeth
☐ 12 Guy Prince
☐ 13 Ray Edwards
☐ 14 Sergei Kharin
☐ 15 Derek Donald
☐ 16 Darwin McPherson
☐ 17 Jeff Stolp
☐ 18 Mascot Adam Bomber

1994 - 95 BOMBERS

Singles start at 50¢.
Card Size: 2 1/2" x 3 1/2"
Sponsors: none
Complete Set (24 cards): 10.00

- ☐ 1 Checklist
- ☐ 2 Paul Taylor
- ☐ 3 Steve Wilson
- ☐ 4 Jason Downey
- ☐ 5 Craig Charron
- ☐ 6 Jim Lessard
- ☐ 7 Karson Karbel
- ☐ 8 Jamie Steer
- ☐ 9 Rob Hartnell
- ☐ 10 Mike Doers
- ☐ 11 Sean Gagnon
- ☐ 12 Kevin Brown
- ☐ 13 John Brill
- ☐ 14 Dean Fedorchuk
- ☐ 15 Tony Gruba
- ☐ 16 Steve Lingren
- ☐ 17 Brandon Smith
- ☐ 18 Jeff Stolp
- ☐ 19 Mike Vandeberghe
- ☐ 20 Jim Playfair
- ☐ 21 Action card
- ☐ 22 Jamie Steer
- ☐ 23 Steve Wilson
- ☐ 24 Jeff Stolp

1995 - 96 BOMBERS

Singles start at 50¢.
Card Size: 5" x 7"
Sponsors: none
Complete Set (18 cards): 8.00

- ☐ Paul Andrea
- ☐ Brent Brekke
- ☐ John Brill
- ☐ Kevin Brown
- ☐ Jeff Buckley
- ☐ Greg Burke
- ☐ Jason Downey
- ☐ Sean Gagnon
- ☐ Dwayne Gylywoychuk
- ☐ Derek Herlofsky
- ☐ Chris Johnston
- ☐ Sergei Kharin
- ☐ Steve Lingren
- ☐ Matt McElwee
- ☐ Colin Miller
- ☐ Mike Murray
- ☐ Mike Naylor
- ☐ Sean Ortiz
- ☐ Rob Peters
- ☐ Jeff Petric
- ☐ Jim Playfair
- ☐ Nick Poole
- ☐ Brian Renfrew
- ☐ Steve Roberts
- ☐ Ted Russell
- ☐ Jeremy Stasiuk
- ☐ George Zajankala
- ☐ Mascot Adam Bomber
- ☐ AS: Steve Lingren
- ☐ AS: Jim Playfair
- ☐ Sean Gagnon
- ☐ Sergei Kharin

ERIE PANTHERS
(ECHL)

1994 - 95 PANTHERS

Singles start at 50¢.
Card Size: 2 1/2" x 3 1/2"
Sponsor: C&J Sports
Complete Set (20 cards): 8.00

- ☐ Cam Brown #9
- ☐ Scott Burfoot #17
- ☐ Stéphane Charbonneau #19
- ☐ Ian DeCorby #20
- ☐ Vassili Demin #6
- ☐ Larry Empey #5
- ☐ Vern Guetens (G) #16
- ☐ Ron Hansis, Coach #2
- ☐ Brad Harrison #8
- ☐ Andrei Kozlov #11
- ☐ Patrick Laughlin, Trainer #4
- ☐ Kevin McKinnon #10
- ☐ Francis Ouellette (G) #15
- ☐ Justin Peca #14
- ☐ Vyacheslav Polikarkin #18
- ☐ Barry Smith, Coach #3
- ☐ Jason Smith #13
- ☐ Sergei Stas #7
- ☐ Chris Tschupp #12
- ☐ Panthers card/Checklist #1

FLINT SPIRITS
(IHL)

1987 - 88 SPIRITS

John Cullen is the most expensive single at $2-3. Singles start at 50¢.
Card Size: 2 1/2" x 3 1/2"
Sponsors: none
Complete Set (20 cards): 10.00

- ☐ Mark Chitaroni
- ☐ John Cullen
- ☐ Bob Fleming
- ☐ Keith Gretzky
- ☐ Todd Hawkins
- ☐ Mike Hoffman
- ☐ Curtis Hunt
- ☐ Dwaine Hutton
- ☐ Trent Kaese
- ☐ Tom Karalis
- ☐ Ray LeBlanc (G)
- ☐ Darren Lowe
- ☐ Brett MacDonald
- ☐ Chris McSorley
- ☐ Mike Mersch
- ☐ Victor Posa
- ☐ Kevin Schamehorn
- ☐ Ron Stern
- ☐ Don Waddell
- ☐ Dan Woodley

1988 - 89 SPIRITS

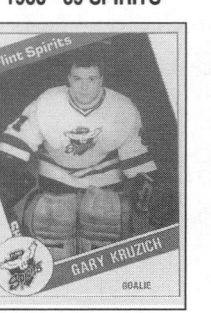

John Cullen is the most expensive single at $2-3. Singles start at 50¢.
Card Size: 2 1/2" x 3 1/2"
Sponsors: none
Complete Set (22 cards): 10.00

- ☐ Dean Anderson
- ☐ Rob Bryden
- ☐ John Devereaux
- ☐ Stéphane Giguère
- ☐ Steve Harrison
- ☐ Yves Heroux
- ☐ Mike Hoffman
- ☐ Peter Horachek
- ☐ Guy Jacob
- ☐ Bob Kennedy
- ☐ Gary Kruzich
- ☐ Lonnie Loach
- ☐ Brett MacDonald
- ☐ Mike MacWilliam
- ☐ Moe Mansi
- ☐ Mike Mersch
- ☐ Michel Mongeau
- ☐ Ken Spangler
- ☐ Mark Vichorek
- ☐ Troy Vollhoffer
- ☐ Don Waddell
- ☐ S.Harrison/M/Mersch/M.Hoffman

FREDERICTON CANADIENS
(AHL)

1992 - 93 CANADIENS

Jesse Belanger, Donald Brashear and Turner Stevenson are the most expensive singles at $1-1.50. Singles start at 50¢.
Card Size: 2 1/2" x 3 3/4"
Sponsors: Ben's Bakery, Village, Pepsi
Complete Set (28 cards): 15.00

- ☐ Jesse Belanger
- ☐ Paulin Bordeleau
- ☐ Donald Brashear
- ☐ Patrik Carnback
- ☐ Frédéric Chabot (G)
- ☐ Eric Charron
- ☐ Alain Côté
- ☐ Paul DiPietro
- ☐ Craig Ferguson
- ☐ Gerry Fleming
- ☐ Luc Gauthier
- ☐ Robert Guillet
- ☐ Patric Kjellberg
- ☐ Les Kuntar (G)
- ☐ Patrick Langois
- ☐ Ryan Kuwabara
- ☐ Steve Larouche
- ☐ Jacques Parent
- ☐ Charles Paulin
- ☐ Oleg Petrov
- ☐ Yves Sarault
- ☐ Pierre Sévigny
- ☐ Darcy Simon
- ☐ Turner Stevenson
- ☐ Lindsay Vallis
- ☐ Steve Veilleux
- ☐ Mascot Tricolo
- ☐ Fredericton card

1993 - 94 CANADIENS

Donald Brashear and Turner Stevenson are the most expensive singles at $1-1.50. Singles start at 50¢.
Card Size: 2 1/2" x 3 1/2"
Sponsors: Ben's Bakery, Village, Pepsi
Complete Set (30 cards): 15.00

- ☐ Brent Bilodeau #5
- ☐ Paulin Bordeleau, Coach
- ☐ Donald Brashear #24
- ☐ Martin Brochu (G) #1
- ☐ Craig Darby#10
- ☐ Kevin Darby #20
- ☐ Mario Doyon #19
- ☐ Craig Ferguson #11
- ☐ Craig Fiander (G) #30
- ☐ Gerry Fleming #28
- ☐ Luc Gauthier, Asst. Coach
- ☐ Robert Guillet #12
- ☐ Les Kuntar (G) #29
- ☐ Ryan Kuwabara #21
- ☐ Patrick Langlois, Equipment
- ☐ Marc Laniel #26
- ☐ Christian Larivière #8
- ☐ Kevin O'Sullivan #32
- ☐ Denis Ouellete, Trainer
- ☐ Jacques Parent, Therapist
- ☐ Oleg Petrov #6
- ☐ Charles Poulin #16
- ☐ Christian Proulx #3
- ☐ Tony Prpic #27
- ☐ Yves Sarault #22
- ☐ Turner Stevenson #23
- ☐ Lindsay Vallis #18
- ☐ Mascot Tricolo
- ☐ Fredericton card
- ☐ Donald Brashear (fighting)

1994 - 95 CANADIENS

Valeri Bure and Jim Campbell are the most expensive singles at $1.50-2. Singles start at 50¢.
Card Size: 2 1/2" x 3 1/2"
Sponsors: Ben's Bakery, President's Choice, Max
Complete Set (30 cards): 15.00

- ☐ Louis Bernard
- ☐ Brent Bilodeau
- ☐ Paulin Bordeleau, Coach
- ☐ Donald Brashear
- ☐ Martin Brochu (G)
- ☐ Valeri Bure
- ☐ Jim Campbell
- ☐ Paul Chagnon
- ☐ Craig Conroy
- ☐ Craig Darby
- ☐ Dion Darling
- ☐ Craig Ferguson
- ☐ Scott Fraser
- ☐ Luc Gauthier
- ☐ Patrick Labrecque (G)
- ☐ Marc Lamothe
- ☐ Patrick Langlois
- ☐ Brad Layzelle
- ☐ Derek Maguire
- ☐ Chris Murray
- ☐ Kevin O'Sullivan
- ☐ Jacques Parent
- ☐ Christian Proulx
- ☐ Craig Rivet
- ☐ Yves Sarault
- ☐ Turner Stevenson
- ☐ Martin Sychra
- ☐ Tim Tisdale
- ☐ David Wilkie
- ☐ Mascot Tricolo

1995 - 96 CANADIENS

Jim Campbell is the most expensive singles at $1.50-2. Singles start at 50¢.
Card Size: 2 1/2" x 3 1/2"
Sponsors: Ben's Bakery, President's Choice, Max
Complete Set (29 cards): 15.00

- ☐ Louis Bernard
- ☐ Paulin Bordeleau, Coach
- ☐ Sébastien Bordeleau
- ☐ Martin Brochu (G)
- ☐ Jim Campbell
- ☐ Paul Chagnon
- ☐ Craig Conroy
- ☐ Keli Corpse
- ☐ Dion Darling
- ☐ Rory Fitzpatrick
- ☐ Scott Fraser
- ☐ Luc Gauthier
- ☐ Gaston Gingras
- ☐ David Grenier
- ☐ Harold Hersh
- ☐ Patrick Labrecque (G)
- ☐ Marc Lamothe
- ☐ Patrick Langlois
- ☐ Alan Letang
- ☐ Alexei Lojkin
- ☐ Xavier Majic
- ☐ Chris Murray
- ☐ Jacques Parent
- ☐ Craig Rivet
- ☐ Mario Roberge
- ☐ Pierre Sévigny
- ☐ Darcy Tucker
- ☐ Adam Wiesel
- ☐ Mascot Tricolo

1996 - 97 CANADIENS

José Théodore is the most expensive singles at $3-4. Singles start at 50¢.
Card Size: 2 1/2" x 3 1/2"
Sponsors: Jolly Rancher, Leaf, Chrysler
Complete Set (29 cards): 15.00

- ☐ Paulin Bordeleau, Coach
- ☐ Sébastien Bordeleau #17
- ☐ Brad Brown #24
- ☐ Paul Chagnon
- ☐ Earl Cronan #40
- ☐ Dion Darling #4
- ☐ Jimmy Drolet #8
- ☐ Gerry Fleming #28
- ☐ Scott Fraser #21
- ☐ Luc Gauthier
- ☐ François Groleau #38
- ☐ Miloslav Guren #19
- ☐ Harold Hersh #22
- ☐ Eric Houde #32
- ☐ Patrick Langlois
- ☐ Alan Letang #31

- ☐ David Ling #27
- ☐ Alexei Lojkin #23
- ☐ Boyd Olson #10
- ☐ Jacques Parent
- ☐ Tony Prpic #12
- ☐ Jessie Rezansoff #14
- ☐ Craig Rivet #26
- ☐ Pierre Sévigny #25
- ☐ Todd Sparks #41
- ☐ José Théodore #1 (G)
- ☐ Tomas Vokoun #29 (G)
- ☐ Adam Wiesel #5
- ☐ Mascot Tricolo

FREDERICTON EXPRESS
(AHL)

1982 - 83 EXPRESS

Marc Crawford is the most expensive single at $4-5. Sylvain Côté, Jacques Demers and Clint Malarchuk sell at $2-3. Singles start at 50¢.
Card Size: 2 1/2" x 3 3/4"
Sponsors: Police, CFNB, Pepsi
Complete Set (26 cards): 20.00

- ☐ 1 Team Photo
- ☐ 2 B.J. MacDonald
- ☐ 3 Sylvain Côté
- ☐ 4 Michel Bolduc
- ☐ 5 Gary Lupul
- ☐ 6 Clint Malarchuk (G)
- ☐ 7 Tony Currie
- ☐ 8 Tim Tookey
- ☐ 9 Anders Eldebrink
- ☐ 10 Basil McRae
- ☐ 11 Kelly Elcombe
- ☐ 12 Jacques Demers
- ☐ 13 Frank Caprice (G)
- ☐ 14 Terry Johnson
- ☐ 15 Grant Martin
- ☐ 16 André Chartrain
- ☐ 17 Marc Crawford
- ☐ 18 Gaston Therrien
- ☐ 19 Andy Schliebener
- ☐ 20 Christian Tanguay
- ☐ 21 Art Rutland
- ☐ 22 Jean Marc Gaulin
- ☐ 23 Neil Belland
- ☐ 24 André Côté
- ☐ 25 Jim McRae
- ☐ 26 S.Beckingham/M.Flynn

1983 - 84 EXPRESS

Mike Hough is the most expensive single at $2-3. Singles start at 50¢.
Card Size: 2 1/2" x 3 3/4"
Sponsors: Police, CFNB, Pepsi
Complete Set (27 cards): 15.00

- ☐ 1 Team Photo
- ☐ 2 Frank Caprice (G)
- ☐ 3 Michael Dufour (G)
- ☐ 4 Brian Ford (G)
- ☐ 5 Jean-Marc Lanthier
- ☐ 6 Jim Dobson
- ☐ 7 Mike Hough
- ☐ 8 Rick Lapointe
- ☐ 9 Michel Bolduc
- ☐ 10 Christian Tanguay
- ☐ 11 Tony Currie
- ☐ 12 Moe Lemay
- ☐ 13 Bruce Halloway
- ☐ 14 Neil Belland
- ☐ 15 Richard Turmel
- ☐ 16 Claude Julien
- ☐ 17 André Chartrain
- ☐ 18 Grant Martin
- ☐ 19 Réjean Vignola
- ☐ 20 André Côté
- ☐ 21 Jean-Marc Gaulin
- ☐ 22 Andy Schliebener
- ☐ 23 Stu Kulak
- ☐ 24 Mike Eagles
- ☐ 25 Earl Jessiman
- ☐ 26 Marty Flynn/S.Beckingham
- ☐ Checklist

1984 - 85 EXPRESS

Marc Crawford is the most expensive single at $3-4. Mike Hough and Clint Malarchuk sell at $2-3. Singles start at 50¢.
Card Size: 2 1/2" x 3 3/4"
Sponsors: Police, CFNB, Pepsi
Complete Set (28 cards): 18.00

- ☐ 1 Dave Morrison
- ☐ 2 David Shaw
- ☐ 3 Bruce Halloway
- ☐ 4 Roger Haegglund
- ☐ 5 Neil Belland
- ☐ 6 Gord Donnelly
- ☐ 7 David Bruce
- ☐ 8 Claude Julien
- ☐ 9 Dan Wood
- ☐ 10 Clint Malarchuk (G)
- ☐ 11 Jere Gillis
- ☐ 12 Mike Hough
- ☐ 13 Michel Bolduc
- ☐ 14 Peter Loob
- ☐ 15 Steve Driscoll
- ☐ 16 Newll Brown
- ☐ 17 Jim Dobson
- ☐ 18 Wendell Young (G)
- ☐ 19 Mark Kumpel
- ☐ 20 Mike Eagles
- ☐ 21 Tom Thornbury
- ☐ 22 Grant Martin
- ☐ 23 Marc Crawford
- ☐ 24 Andy Schliebener
- ☐ 25 Earl Jeesiman
- ☐ 26 Yvon Vautour
- ☐ 27 Craig Coxe
- ☐ 28 Blake Wesley

1985 - 86 EXPRESS

Marc Crawford is the most expensive single at $3-4. Singles start at 50¢.
Card Size: 2 1/2" x 3 3/4"
Sponsors: Police, CFNB, Pepsi
Complete Set (28 cards): 15.00

- ☐ 1 Scott Tottle
- ☐ 2 David Bruce
- ☐ 3 Team Photo
- ☐ 4 Marc Crawford
- ☐ 5 Mike Stevens
- ☐ 6 Gary Lupul
- ☐ 7 Alain Lemieux
- ☐ 8 Mike Hough
- ☐ 9 Tony Currie
- ☐ 10 Dunc MacIntyre
- ☐ 11 Jere Gillis
- ☐ 12 Wendell Young (G)
- ☐ 13 Jean-Marc Lanthier
- ☐ 14 Ken Quinney
- ☐ 15 Claude Julien
- ☐ 16 Michel Petit
- ☐ 17 Luc Guenette
- ☐ 18 Andy Schliebener
- ☐ 19 Mark Kirton
- ☐ 20 Gord Donnelly
- ☐ 21 Tom Karalis
- ☐ 22 Daniel Poudrier
- ☐ 23 Neil Belland
- ☐ 24 Dale Dunbar
- ☐ 25 Marty Flynn/S.Beckingham
- ☐ 26 Jean-Marc Gaulin
- ☐ 27 Al MacAdam
- ☐ 28 André Savard

1986 - 87 EXPRESS

Marc Crawford is the most expensive single at $3-4. Singles start at 50¢.
Card Size: 2 1/2" x 3 3/4"
Sponsors: Police, CFNB, Pepsi
Complete Set (26 cards): 15.00

- ☐ Jim Agnew
- ☐ Brian Bertuzzi
- ☐ David Bruce
- ☐ Frank Caprice (G)
- ☐ Marc Crawford
- ☐ Steven Finn
- ☐ Jean-Marc Gaulin
- ☐ Scott Gordon (G)
- ☐ Taylor Hall
- ☐ Yves Heroux
- ☐ Mike Hough
- ☐ Tom Karalis
- ☐ Mark Kirton
- ☐ Jean-Marc Lanthier
- ☐ Jean LeBlanc
- ☐ Brett MacDonald
- ☐ Duncan MacIntyre
- ☐ Greg Malone
- ☐ Terry Perkins
- ☐ Daniel Poudrier
- ☐ Jeff Rohlicek
- ☐ André Savard
- ☐ Mike Stevens
- ☐ Trevor Stienburg
- ☐ M.Flynn/S.Beckingham
- ☐ Team Photo

GREENSBORO MONARCHS
(ECHL)

1991 - 92 MONARCHS

Singles start at 50¢.
Card Size: 2 1/2" x 3 1/2"
Sponsors: none
Complete Set (19 cards): 8.00

- ☐ Rob Bateman
- ☐ Phil Berger
- ☐ Mike Butters
- ☐ John Devereaux
- ☐ Eric Dubois
- ☐ Todd Gordon
- ☐ Chris Laganas
- ☐ Eric LeMarque
- ☐ Timo Makela
- ☐ Greg Menges
- ☐ Daryl Noren
- ☐ Peter Sentner
- ☐ Boyd Sutton
- ☐ Nick Vitucci
- ☐ Shawn Wheeler
- ☐ Scott White
- ☐ Chris Wolanin
- ☐ Dean Zayonce
- ☐ Team Photo

1992 - 93 MONARCHS

Singles start at 50¢.
Card Size: 2 1/2" x 3 1/2"
Sponsors: none
Complete Set (19 cards): 8.00

- ☐ 1 Team Photo
- ☐ 2 Chris Wolanin
- ☐ 3 Bill Horn
- ☐ 4 Brock Woods
- ☐ 5 Phil Berger
- ☐ 6 Dan Bylsma
- ☐ 7 Davis Payne
- ☐ 8 Wayne Muir
- ☐ 9 Andrei Iakovenko
- ☐ 10 Roger Larche
- ☐ 11 Jamie Nicholls
- ☐ 12 Darryl Noren
- ☐ 13 Todd Gordon
- ☐ 14 Claude Maillet
- ☐ 15 Dave Burke
- ☐ 16 Jamie Steer
- ☐ 17 Greg Capson
- ☐ 18 Chris Lappin
- ☐ 19 Greg Menges

1993 - 94 MONARCHS

Singles start at 50¢.
Card Size: 2 1/2" x 3 1/2"
Sponsors: none
Complete Set (16 cards): 7.00

- ☐ Phil Berger
- ☐ Trevor Burgess
- ☐ Dan Bylsma
- ☐ Greg Capson
- ☐ Brendan Creagh
- ☐ Dan Gravelle
- ☐ Sébastien LaPlante
- ☐ Savo Mitrovic
- ☐ Tom Newman
- ☐ Jamie Nicolls
- ☐ Davis Payne
- ☐ Stig Salomonsson
- ☐ Sverre Sears
- ☐ Chris Valicevic
- ☐ John Young
- ☐ Dean Zayonce

1994 - 95 MONARCHS

Singles start at 50¢.
Card Size: 2 1/2" x 3 1/2"
Sponsors: none
Complete Set (20 cards): 7.00

- ☐ Phil Berger
- ☐ Brendan Creagh
- ☐ Mark DeSantis
- ☐ Doug Evans
- ☐ Jeff Gabriel
- ☐ Dwayne Gylywoychuk
- ☐ Bill Horn
- ☐ Artur Kupacs
- ☐ Scott McKay
- ☐ Ron Pasco
- ☐ David Payne
- ☐ Hugo Proulx
- ☐ Howie Rosenblatt
- ☐ Sverre Sears
- ☐ Chad Seibel
- ☐ Peter Skudra
- ☐ Jeremy Stevenson
- ☐ Glenn Stewart
- ☐ Dean Zayonce
- ☐ Mascot Monte

HALIFAX CITADELS
(AHL)

1989 - 90 CITADELS

Robbie Ftorek is the most expensive single at $1-1.50. Singles start at 50¢.
Card Size: 2 1/2" x 4 1/2"
Sponsors: Farmers Co-Op Dairy, 92 CJCH
Complete Set (26 cards): 12.00

- ☐ Jason Baillargeon
- ☐ Jamie Baker
- ☐ Mario Brunetta
- ☐ Gerald Bzdel
- ☐ David Espe
- ☐ Bryan Fogarty
- ☐ Robbie Ftorek
- ☐ Scott Gordon (G)
- ☐ Dean Hopkins
- ☐ Miroslav Ihnacak
- ☐ Claude Julien
- ☐ Kevin Kaminski
- ☐ Claude Lapointe
- ☐ Max Middendorf
- ☐ Stéphane Morin
- ☐ Dave Pichette
- ☐ Ken Quinney
- ☐ Jean-Marc Richard
- ☐ Jean-Marc Routhier
- ☐ Jaroslav Sevcik
- ☐ Brent Severyn
- ☐ Greg Smyth
- ☐ Trevor Stienburg
- ☐ Mark Vermette
- ☐ Ladislav Tresl
- ☐ C.McQuaid/Brent Smith

1990 - 91 CITADELS

Stéphane Fiset is the most expensive single at $3-4. Singles start at 50¢.
Card Size: 2 3/4" x 4 1/4"
Sponsors: Farmers Co-Op Dairy, 92 CJCH
Complete Set (28 cards): 15.00

- ☐ Jamie Baker
- ☐ Mike Bishop (G)
- ☐ Gerald Bzdel
- ☐ Daniel Doré
- ☐ Mario Doyon
- ☐ David Espe
- ☐ Stéphane Fiset (G)
- ☐ Scott Gordon (G)
- ☐ Stéphane Guérard
- ☐ Dean Hopkins
- ☐ Miroslav Ihnacak
- ☐ Jeff Jackson
- ☐ Clement Jodoin
- ☐ Claude Lapointe
- ☐ Dave Latta
- ☐ Chris McQuaid
- ☐ Kip Miller
- ☐ Stéphane Morin
- ☐ Ken Quinney
- ☐ Jean-Marc Richard
- ☐ Serge Roberge

☐ Jaroslav Sevcik
☐ Brent Severyn
☐ Mike Shuman
☐ Greg Smyth
☐ Jim Sprott
☐ Trevor Stienburg
☐ Mark Vermette

HAMILTON CANUCKS
(AHL)

1992 - 93 CANUCKS

Singles start at 50¢.
Card Size: 2 1/2" x 3 1/2"
Sponsors: Y95 Radio, Diamond Memories Sportscards
Complete Set (30 cards): 12.00

☐ Shawn Antoski
☐ Robin Bawa
☐ Jamie Carlson
☐ Jassen Cullimore
☐ Alain Deeks
☐ Neil Eisenhut
☐ Mike Fountain (G)
☐ Troy Gamble (G)
☐ Jason Herter
☐ Pat Hickey
☐ Dane Jackson
☐ Dan Kesa
☐ Mario Marois, Error (Marios)
☐ Bob Mason (G)
☐ Mike Maurice
☐ Jay Mazur
☐ Jack McIlhargey
☐ Sandy Moger
☐ Stéphane Morin
☐ Eric Murano
☐ Troy Neumeier
☐ Matt Newson
☐ Libor Polasek
☐ Phil von Stefenelli
☐ Doug Torrel
☐ Doug Tretiak
☐ Rick Vaive
☐ Mario Marois/Pat Hickey
☐ Jeff Lumby
☐ Team Photo

HAMPTON ROAD ADMIRALS
(ECHL)

1992 - 93 ADMIRALS

Singles start at 50¢.
Card Size: 2 1/2" x 3 1/2"
Sponsors: Ward's Sporting Goods, Ogden Services, WCMS
Complete Set (20 cards): 8.00

☐ Claude Barthe
☐ Mark Bernard
☐ John Brophy
☐ Trevor Duhaime
☐ Victor Gervais
☐ Kurt Kabat
☐ Paul Krepelka
☐ Al MacIsaac
☐ Steve Martell
☐ Brian Martin
☐ Harry Mews
☐ Steve Mirabile
☐ Dave Morisette
☐ Steve Poapst
☐ Jason Rathbone
☐ Chris Scarlata
☐ Shawn Snesar
☐ Kelly Sorenson
☐ Rod Taylor
☐ Nick Vitucci

1993 - 94 ADMIRALS

Singles start at 50¢.
Card Size: 2 1/2" x 3 1/2"
Sponsors: Ward's Sporting Goods, Ogden Services, WCMS
Complete Set (20 cards): 8.00

☐ John Brophy
☐ Rick Burrell
☐ Daniel Chaput
☐ Brendan Curley
☐ Victor Gervais
☐ Brian Goudie
☐ Shamus Gregga
☐ Al MacIsaac
☐ Kevin Malgunas
☐ Dennis McEwen
☐ Jason McIntyre
☐ Mark Michaud
☐ Ron Pascucci
☐ Darren Perkins
☐ Steven Perkovic
☐ Shawn Snesar
☐ Kelly Sorenson
☐ Rod Taylor
☐ Richie Walcott
☐ Shawn Wheeler

1994 - 95 ADMIRALS

Patrick Lalime is the most expensive single at $4-5. Singles start at 50¢.
Card Size: 2 1/2" x 3 1/2"
Sponsors: none
Complete Set (22 cards): 10.00

☐ 1 John Brophy
☐ 2 Al MacIsaac
☐ 3 Patrick Lalime (G)
☐ 4 Colin Gregor
☐ 5 Ron Pascucci
☐ 6 John Porco
☐ 7 Trevor Halverson
☐ 8 Rod Taylor
☐ 9 Brian Goudie
☐ 10 Chris Phelps
☐ 11 Tom Menicci
☐ 12 Anthony MacAulay
☐ 13 Rick Kowalsky
☐ 14 Dennis McEwen
☐ 15 Kelly Sorenson
☐ 16 Brendan Curely
☐ 17 Jason MacIntyre
☐ 18 Jim Brown
☐ 19 Matt Mallgrave
☐ 20 Ron Majic
☐ 21 Corwin Saurdiff
☐ 22 Team Photo

1995 - 96 ADMIRALS

Singles start at 50¢.
Card Size: 2 1/2" x 3 1/2"
Sponsors: Ward's Sporting Goods
Complete Set (25 cards): 10.00

☐ HRA-1 Team Photo
☐ HRA-2 John Brophy
☐ HRA-3 Al MacIsaac
☐ HRA-4 Darryl Paquette
☐ HRA-5 Mark Bernard
☐ HRA-6 Ron Pascucci
☐ HRA-7 Dominic Maltais
☐ HRA-8 Jason MacIntyre
☐ HRA-9 Serge Aubin
☐ HRA-10 Rick Kowalsky
☐ HRA-11 Claude Fillion
☐ HRA-12 Rod Taylor
☐ HRA-13 Al. Krivchenkov
☐ HRA-14 David St. Pierre
☐ HRA-15 Steve Richards
☐ HRA-16 Trevor Halverson
☐ HRA-17 Chris Phelps
☐ HRA-18 Jeff Kostuch
☐ HRA-19 Sean Selmser
☐ HRA-20 Aaron Downey
☐ HRA-21 Bob Woods
☐ HRA-22 Sergei Voronov
☐ HRA-23 Corwin Saurdiff
☐ HRA-24 Rick Burrell
☐ HRA-25 Gary Mansfield

HUNTINGTON BLIZZARD
(ECHL)

1993 - 94 BLIZZARD

2500 sets were available. Singles start at 50¢.
Card Size: 2 1/2" x 3 1/2"
Sponsors: WCHS
Complete Set (27 cards): 12.00

☐ Ray Alcindor
☐ Shayne Antoski
☐ Greg Bailey
☐ Jared Bednar
☐ Andy Borggaard
☐ Malcolm Cameron
☐ Dave Dimitri
☐ Mark Franks
☐ Ray Gallagher
☐ Murray Garbutt
☐ Brad Harrison
☐ Todd Huyber
☐ Ron Majic
☐ Bob May
☐ Jim Mill
☐ Jim Mirabello
☐ Dave Persigehl
☐ Paul Pickard
☐ Scott Roberts
☐ Greg Scott
☐ Geoff Simpson
☐ Doug Stromback
☐ Dave Weekley
☐ Misty Zambito
☐ Mascot Klondike Bear
☐ Blizzard Babes
☐ Blizzards Card

1994 - 95 BLIZZARD

Singles start at 50¢.
Card Size: 2 1/2" x 3 1/2"
Sponsors: WSAZ, 93RVC Radio
Complete Set (26 cards): 12.00

☐ 1 Checklist
☐ 2 Steve Barnes
☐ 3 Jared Bednar
☐ 4 Jim Bermingham
☐ 5 Todd Brost
☐ 6 Andy Brown
☐ 7 Ray Edwards
☐ 8 Trent Eigner
☐ 9 Dan Fournel
☐ 10 Mark Franks
☐ 11 Gord Frantti
☐ 12 Chris Gordon
☐ 13 Kelly Harper
☐ 14 J.C. Ihrig
☐ 15 Mitch Kean
☐ 16 Jeff Levy
☐ 17 Chris Morque
☐ 18 Derek Schooley
☐ 19 Jim Solly
☐ 20 Mike Stone
☐ 21 Jason Weinrich
☐ 22 Mark Woolf
☐ 23 Paul Pickard
☐ 24 Mascot Klondike Bear
☐ 25 Blizzard Babes
☐ 32 Blizzards card

INDIANAPOLIS CHECKERS
(CHL)

1981 - 82 CHECKERS

Kelly Hrudey is the most expensive single at $12-15. Singles start at 75¢.
Card Size: 2 3/8" x 3 1/2"
Sponsor: Pizza Hut
Complete Set (20 cards): 25.00

☐ 1 Mike Hordy
☐ 2 Randy Johnston
☐ 3 John Marks
☐ 4 Tim Lockridge
☐ 5 Darcey Regier
☐ 6 Garth MacGuigan
☐ 7 Charlie Skjodt
☐ 8 Mats Hallin
☐ 9 Frank Beaton
☐ 10 Kevin Devine
☐ 11 Steve Stoyanovich
☐ 12 Lorne Stamler
☐ 13 Red Laurence
☐ 14 Monty Trottier
☐ 15 Neil Hawryliw
☐ 16 Kelly Davis
☐ 17 Glen Duncan
☐ 18 Kelly Hrudey (G)
☐ 19 Bob Holland
☐ 20 Bruce Andres

1982 - 83 CHECKERS

Kelly Hrudey is the most expensive single at $10-12. Singles start at 75¢.
Card Size: 2 3/8" x 3 1/2"
Sponsor: Pizza Hut
Complete Set (21 cards): 20.00

☐ Kelly Davis
☐ Kevin Devine
☐ Gord Dineen
☐ Glen Duncan
☐ Greg Gilbert
☐ Mike Greeder
☐ Mats Hallin
☐ Dave Hanson
☐ Rob Holland
☐ Scott Howson
☐ Kelly Hrudey (G)
☐ Randy Johnston
☐ Red Laurence
☐ Tim Lockridge
☐ Garth MacGuigan
☐ Darcy Regier
☐ Dan Revell
☐ Dave Simpson
☐ Lorne Stamler
☐ Steve Stoyanovich
☐ Monty Trottier

INDIANAPOLIS ICE
(IHL)

1992 - 93 ICE

Singles start at 50¢.
Card Size: 2 1/2" x 3 1/2"
Sponsors: none
Complete Set (26 cards): 12.00

☐ Alexander Andrijevski
☐ Steve Bancroft
☐ Zac Boyer
☐ Rod Buskas
☐ Shawn Byram
☐ Joe Cleary
☐ Ron Conn
☐ Joe Cowley
☐ Trevor Dam
☐ Ivan Droppa
☐ Tracy Egeland
☐ Dave Hakstol
☐ Kevin Hodson
☐ Tony Horacek
☐ Tony Hrkac
☐ Sergei Krivokrasov
☐ Brad Lauer
☐ Ray LeBlanc
☐ Owen Lessard
☐ Kevin St. Jacques
☐ Mike Speer
☐ Milan Tichy
☐ Kerry Toporowski
☐ Sean Williams
☐ Craig Woodcroft
☐ Jim Playfair/J.Marks

1994 - 95 ICE

Singles start at 50¢.
Card Size: 2 1/2" x 3 1/2"
Sponsor: Classic
Complete Set (26 cards): 12.00

☐ Hugo Belanger
☐ Bruce Cassidy
☐ Rob Conn
☐ Ivan Droppa
☐ Steve Dubinsky
☐ Karl Dykhuis
☐ Craig Fisher
☐ Daniel Gauthier
☐ Tony Horacek
☐ Bobby House
☐ Bob Kellogg
☐ Sergei Klimovich
☐ Sergei Krivokrasov
☐ Andy MacIntyre
☐ Dean Malkoc
☐ Matt Oates
☐ Mike Pomichter
☐ Mike Prokopec
☐ Jeff Ricciardi
☐ Chris Rogles
☐ Bogdan Savenko
☐ Jeff Shantz
☐ Christian Soucy
☐ Duane Sutter
☐ Travis Thiessen
☐ Team Photo

JOHNSTOWN CHIEFS
(ECHL)

1989 - 90 CHIEFS

Singles start at 50¢. Cards 1-18 were likely part of a 1988-89 issue.
Card Size: 2 1/2" x 3 1/2"
Sponsors: Sheetz, 850 WJAC
Complete Set (18 cards): 8.00

☐ 19 Rick Burchill
☐ 20 Bob Goulet
☐ 21 John Messuri
☐ 22 Darren Servatius
☐ 23 Rick Boyd
☐ 24 Bob Kennedy
☐ 25 Mike Rossetti
☐ 26 Dan Williams
☐ 27 Mark Bogoslowski
☐ 28 Dean Hall
☐ 29 Mitch Molloy
☐ 30 Darren Schwartz
☐ 31 Doug Weiss
☐ 32 Marc Vachon
☐ 33 Mike Jeffrey
☐ 34 Frank Dell
☐ 35 Sean Finn
☐ 36 Steve Carlson

1993 - 94 CHIEFS

Singles start at 50¢.
Card Size: 2 1/2" x 3 1/2"
Sponsors: Ponderosa Steakhouse, K.B. Card Company
Complete Set (23 cards): 10.00

☐ 1 John Bradley

☐ 2 Campbell Blair
☐ 3 François Bourdeau
☐ 4 Bob Woods
☐ 5 Ted Dent
☐ 6 Matt Hoffman
☐ 7 Gord Christian
☐ 8 Tim Hanus
☐ 9 Phil Soukoroff
☐ 10 Jason Jennings
☐ 11 Dusty McLellan
☐ 12 Dennis Purdie
☐ 13 Chuck Wiegand
☐ 14 Jamie Adams
☐ 15 Jan Beran
☐ 16 Rob Laurie
☐ 17 Cory Banika
☐ 18 Perry Florio
☐ 19 Rob Leask
☐ 20 Ed Johnstone
☐ 21 John Daley
☐ 22 Matt Koeck
☐ Chiefs card

1994 - 95 CHIEFS

Singles start at 50¢.
Card Size: 2 1/2" x 3 1/2"
Sponsors: Ponderosa Steakhouse, WHMTZ Radio
Complete Set (24 cards): 10.00

☐ 1 Checklist
☐ 2 Jason Brousseau
☐ 3 Brandon Christian
☐ 4 Gord Christian
☐ 5 Bruce Coles
☐ 6 Ted Dent
☐ 7 Martin D'Orsonnens
☐ 8 Perry Florio
☐ 9 Rod Hinks
☐ 10 Matt Hoffman
☐ 11 Aaron Israel
☐ 12 Jason Jennings
☐ 13 Rob Laurie
☐ 14 Rob Leask
☐ 15 Dennis Purdie
☐ 16 Kevin Quinn
☐ 17 Jason Richard
☐ 18 Dan Sawyer
☐ 19 Ben Wyzansky
☐ 20 Matt Yingst
☐ 21 Trainers
☐ 22 Ed Johnstone
☐ 23 WHMTZ-FM
☐ 24 WHMTZ-FM

KALAMAZOO WINGS (IHL)

1977 - 78 WINGS

These cards feature black and white photography. We have no pricing information on this set. Other singles may exist although the set is believed to be complete at 15 cards.
Size: 2 1/2" x 3 1/2"
Sponsor: ISB Bank
Complete Set (15 cards)

☐ 1 George Klasons
☐ 2 Ron Wilson
☐ 3 Bob Lemieux, Coach
☐ 4 Len Ircandia
☐ 5 Ron Kennedy
☐ 6 Daniel Poulin
☐ 7 Terry Ryan
☐ 8 Yvon Dupuis
☐ 9 Tom Milani
☐ 10 Mike Wanchuk
☐ 11 Steve Lee
☐ 12 Yves Guilmette (G)
☐ 13 Al Genovy
☐ 15 Jim Baxter (G)
☐ 18 Alvin White

KANSAS CITY BLADES (IHL)

1990 - 91 BLADES

Singles start at 50¢.
Card Size: 2 1/2" x 3 1/2"
Sponsor: The Jones Store Co.
Complete Set (20 cards): 8.00

☐ 1 Claudio Scremin
☐ 2 Jeff Odgers
☐ 3 Wade Flaherty (G)
☐ 4 Rick Barkovich
☐ 5 Ron Handy
☐ 6 Kevin Sullivan
☐ 7 Randy Exelby
☐ 8 Darin Smith
☐ 9 Stu Kulak
☐ 10 Andrew Akervik
☐ 11 Scott White
☐ 12 Claude Julien
☐ 13 Mike Hitner
☐ 14 Michael Colman
☐ 15 Kury Semandel
☐ 16 Mike Kelfer
☐ 17 Mark Karpen
☐ 18 Lee Giffin
☐ 19 Cam Plante
☐ 20 Jim Latos

KNOXVILLE CHEROKEES (ECHL)

1991 - 92 CHEROKEES

Singles start at 50¢.
Card Size: 2 1/2" x 3 1/2"
Sponsor: The News-Sentinel
Complete Set (20 cards): 8.00

☐ Dean Anderson
☐ Karl Clauss
☐ Jamie Dabanovich
☐ Trevor Forsythe
☐ Joel Gardner
☐ Mike Gober
☐ Mike Greenlay
☐ Galen Head
☐ Roman Hubalek
☐ Brett Lawrence
☐ Shawn Lillie
☐ Dean McDonald
☐ Robert Melanson
☐ Troy Mick
☐ Bill Nyrop
☐ Greg Pankewicz
☐ Steve Ryding
☐ David Shute
☐ Chad Thompson
☐ Bruno Villeneuve

1993 - 94 CHEROKEES

Manon Rhéaume is the most expensive single at $4-5. Singles start at 50¢.
Card Size: 2 1/2" x 3 1/2"
Sponsors: none
Complete Set (20 cards): 12.00

☐ Scott Boston
☐ Cory Cadden
☐ Tim Chase
☐ Steven Flomenhoft
☐ Scott Gordon (G)
☐ Jon Larson
☐ Carl LeBlanc
☐ Kim Maier
☐ Wes McCauley
☐ Scott Mercalfe
☐ Mike Murray
☐ Hayden O'Rear
☐ Jeff Reid
☐ Manon Rhéaume (G)
☐ Marc Rodgers

☐ Doug Searle
☐ Barry Smith
☐ Martin Tanguay
☐ Nicholas Vachon
☐ Bruno Villeneuve

1994 - 95 CHEROKEES

Singles start at 50¢.
Card Size: 2 1/2" x 3 1/2"
Sponsors: American Clothing
Complete Set (24 cards): 10.00

☐ 1 Checklist
☐ 2 Barry Smith
☐ 3 Aaron Fackler
☐ 4 Andy Davis
☐ 5 Stéphane Ménard
☐ 6 Doug Searle
☐ 7 Hayden O'Rear
☐ 8 Sean Brown
☐ 9 Mike Murray
☐ 10 Jon Jenkins
☐ 11 Sean Pronger
☐ 12 Steven Flomenhoft
☐ 13 David Neilson
☐ 14 Jack Callahan
☐ 15 Carl LeBlanc
☐ 16 Alain Deeks
☐ 17 George Zajankala
☐ 18 Chris Fess
☐ 19 Michel Gaul
☐ 20 Pat Murray
☐ 21 Robb McIntyre
☐ 22 Vaclav Nedomansky, Jr
☐ 23 Cory Cadden
☐ 24 Michael Burman

LAS VEGAS THUNDER (IHL)

1993 - 94 THUNDER

Singles start at 50¢.
Card Size: 2 1/2" x 3 1/2"
Sponsor: Saturn
Complete Set (32 cards): 10.00

☐ Brent Ashton
☐ Bob Bourne
☐ Rod Buskas
☐ Lyndon Byers
☐ Rich Campbell
☐ Colin Cowherd
☐ Butch Goring
☐ Steve Gotaas
☐ Marc Habscheid
☐ Brett Hauer
☐ Shawn Heaphy
☐ Scott Hollis
☐ Peter Ing (G)
☐ Steve Jaques
☐ Bob Joyce
☐ Jim Kyte
☐ Patrice Lefebvre
☐ Clint Malarchuk (G)
☐ Ken Quinney
☐ Jean-Marc Richard
☐ Todd Richards
☐ Marc Rodgers
☐ Jeff Sharples
☐ Randy Smith
☐ Greg Spenrath
☐ Bob Strumm
☐ Kirk Tomlinson
☐ Kerry Toporowski
☐ Mark Vermette
☐ Steve Wissman
☐ Thunder card
☐ Mascot Boom Boom

1994 - 95 THUNDER

Radek Bonk is the most expensive single at $2-3. Singles start at 50¢.
Card Size: 2 1/2" x 3 1/2"
Sponsor: Chevrolet
Complete Set (29 cards): 15.00

☐ James Black
☐ Radek Bonk
☐ Rich Campbell
☐ Frank Evans
☐ Marc Habscheid
☐ Alex Hicks
☐ Bob Joyce
☐ Jim Kyte
☐ Patrice Lefebvre
☐ Darcy Loewen
☐ Sal Lombardi
☐ Clint Malarchuk (G)
☐ Andrew McBain
☐ Chris McSorley
☐ David Neilson
☐ Jerry Olenyn
☐ Ken Quinney
☐ Eldon Reddick (G)
☐ Jeff Reid
☐ Manon Rhéaume (G)
☐ Jean-Marc Richard
☐ Todd Richards
☐ Marc Rodgers
☐ Jeff Sharples
☐ Jarrod Skalde
☐ Bob Strumm
☐ Kerry Toporowski
☐ Morning Radio
☐ Mascot Boom Boom

1995 - 96 THUNDER

Singles start at 50¢.
Card Size: 2 1/2" x 3 1/2"
Sponsor: Edge Ice
Complete Set (25 cards): 12.00

☐ Bill Bowler
☐ Peter Fiorentino
☐ Greg Hawgood
☐ Sasha Lakovic
☐ Patrice Lefebvre
☐ Darcy Loewen
☐ Clint Malarchuk (G)
☐ Gord Marx
☐ Chris McSorley
☐ Blaine Moore
☐ Vaclav Nedomansky, Jr
☐ Eldon Reddick (G)
☐ Jeff Roccoardo
☐ Jean-Marc Richard
☐ Marc Rodgers
☐ Ken Quinney
☐ Ruslan Salei
☐ Jeff Sharples
☐ Daniel Shank
☐ Todd Simon
☐ Bob Strumm
☐ Rhett Trombley
☐ Vladimir Tsyplakov
☐ Sergei Zholtok
☐ Mascot Boom Boom

1996 - 97 THUNDER

Singles start at 50¢.
Card Size: 2 1/2" x 3 1/2"
Sponsors: Heinekin, etc.
Complete Set (24 cards): 10.00

☐ Igor Bashkatov
☐ Kevin Dahl
☐ Chris Dahlquist
☐ Pavol Demitra
☐ Parris Duffus (G)
☐ Martin Gendron
☐ Brent Gretzky
☐ Kerry Huffman
☐ Igor Karpenko
☐ Don Larner
☐ Patrice Lefebvre

☐ Darcy Loewen
☐ Blaine Moore
☐ Ken Quinney
☐ Jeff Serowik
☐ Jason Simon
☐ Rhett Trombley
☐ Sergei Yerkowich
☐ Sergei Zholtok
☐ Bob Strumm, G.M.
☐ Clint Malarchuk, A.G.M.
☐ Chris McSorley, Coach
☐ Mascot Boom Boom
☐ IHL Card

LOUISIANA ICE GATORS (ECHL)

1995 - 96 ICE GATORS

Singles start at 50¢.
Card Size: 2 1/2" x 3 1/2
Sponsors: none
Complete Set (21 cards): 8.00

☐ Bob Berg
☐ John Depourcq
☐ Wade Fournier
☐ Fred Goltz
☐ Ron Handy
☐ Mike Heany
☐ Dean Hulett
☐ Jim Latos
☐ George Maneluk
☐ Rob McCaig
☐ Jason McQuat
☐ Rod Pasma
☐ Sean Rowe
☐ Bryan Schoen
☐ Darryl Shedden
☐ Doug Shedden
☐ Fred Spoltore
☐ Chris Valicevic
☐ Rob Valicevic
☐ John Vary
☐ Marty Yewchuk

1995 - 96 ICE GATORS PLAYOFFS

Singles start at 50¢.
Card Size: 2 1/2" x 3 1/2"
Sponsor: Chevrolet
Complete Set (21 cards): 8.00

☐ Bob Berg
☐ Aaron Boh
☐ Eric Cloutier
☐ John DePourcq
☐ Wade Fournier
☐ Ron Handy
☐ Mike Heaney
☐ Dean Hulett
☐ Jim Latos
☐ George Maneluk
☐ Rob McCaig
☐ Jason McQuat
☐ Chad Nelson
☐ Dan O'Rourke
☐ Rod Pasma
☐ Darryl Shedden
☐ Doug Shedden
☐ John Spoltore
☐ Chuck Thuss
☐ C.Valicevic/R.Valicevic
☐ John Vary

MILWAUKEE ADMIRALS
(AHL)

1981 - 82 ADMIRALS

These cards feature black and white photography. Singles start at $1.00.
Card Size: 2 1/2" x 3 1/2"
Imprint: TCMA Ltd.
Sponsors: none
Complete Set (15 cards): 12.00

☐ 1 Pat Rabbitt
☐ 2 Réal Paiement
☐ 3 Fred Berry
☐ 4 Blaine Peerless
☐ 5 John Flesch
☐ 6 Yves Preston
☐ 7 Bruce McKay
☐ 8 Dale Yakiwchuk
☐ 9 Lorne Bokshowan
☐ 10 Danny Lecours
☐ 11 Sheldon Currie
☐ 12 Doug Robb
☐ 13 Rob Polman Tuin (G)
☐ 14 Bob Collyard
☐ 15 Tim Ringler

1994 - 95 ADMIRALS

Singles start at 50¢.
Card Size: 2 1/2" x 3 1/2"
Sponsor: Classic
Complete Set (28 cards): 12.00

☐ Doug Agnew
☐ Peter Bakovic
☐ Matt Block
☐ Gino Cavallini
☐ Sylvain Couturier
☐ Brian Dobbin
☐ Shawn Evans
☐ Chris Govedaris
☐ Jim Hrivnak (G)
☐ Tony Hrkac
☐ Fabian Joseph
☐ Mark LaForest (G)
☐ Don MacAdam
☐ Dave Mackey
☐ Pat MacLeod
☐ Dave Marcinyshyn
☐ Bob Mason (G)
☐ Mike McNeill
☐ Kent Paynter
☐ Ken Sabourin
☐ Trevor Sim
☐ Martin Simard
☐ Mike Tomlak
☐ Steve Tuttle
☐ Randy Velischek
☐ Brad Werenka
☐ Phil Wittliff
☐ Fabulous Fritz

MONCTON ALPINES
(AHL)

1983 - 84 ALPINES

Steve Smith is the most expensive single at $4-5. Singles start at 75¢.
Card Size: 2 1/2" x 3 3/4"
Sponsors: Police, CKCW, Coke, Hostess
Complete Set (27 cards): 20.00

☐ 1 Doug Messier
☐ 2 Chris Smith (G)
☐ 3 Marc Baron (G)
☐ 4 Mark Zanier (G)
☐ 5 Dwayne Boettger
☐ 6 Lowell Loveday
☐ 7 Joe McDonnell
☐ 8 Peter Dineen
☐ 9 John Blum
☐ 10 Steve Smith
☐ 11 Reg Kerr
☐ 12 Tom Rowe
☐ 13 Ross Lambert
☐ 14 Pat Conacher
☐ 15 Paul Miller
☐ 16 Bert Yachimel
☐ 17 Tom Gorence
☐ 18 Jeff Crawford
☐ 19 Serge Boisvert
☐ 20 Todd Strueby
☐ 21 Todd Bidner
☐ 22 Dean Dachyshyn
☐ 23 Ray Cote
☐ 24 Shawn Babcock
☐ 25 Shawn Dineen
☐ 26 Marc Habscheid
☐ Checklist

MONCTON GOLDEN FLAMES
(AHL)

1984 - 85 GOLDEN FLAMES

Mike Vernon is the most expensive single at $10-12. Singles start at 75¢.
Card Size: 2 12" x 3 3/4"
Sponsors: Police, CKCW, Coke, Hostess
Complete Set (26 cards): 25.00

☐ 1 Brian Patafie
☐ 2 Mike Bianni
☐ 3 Pierre Pagé
☐ 4 Neil Sheehy
☐ 5 George White
☐ 6 Mark Lamb
☐ 7 Dan Kane
☐ 8 Dan Bolduc
☐ 9 Lou Kiriakou
☐ 10 Joel Otto
☐ 11 Dale DeGray
☐ 12 Mike Clayton
☐ 13 Mickey Volcan
☐ 14 Ted Pearson
☐ 15 Mario Simioni
☐ 16 Keith Hanson
☐ 17 Yves Courteau
☐ 18 Dan Cormier
☐ 19 Todd Hooey
☐ 20 Mike Vernon (G)
☐ 21 Dave Meszaros (G)
☐ 22 Bruce Eakin
☐ 23 Tony Stiles
☐ 24 Ed Kastelic
☐ 25 Pierre Rioux
☐ 26 Gino Cavallini

1985 - 86 GOLDEN FLAMES

Brian Bradley and Geoff Courtnall are the most expensive singles at $4-5. Singles start at 75¢.
Card Size: 2 12" x 3 3/4"
Sponsors: Police, CKCW, Coke, Hostess
Complete Set (28 cards): 20.00

☐ 1 Terry Crisp
☐ 2 Dan Bolduc
☐ 3 Terry Crisp/Dan Bolduc
☐ 4 Al Pedersen
☐ 5 Dave Meszaros (G)
☐ 6 George White
☐ 7 Mark Lamb
☐ 8 Doug Kostynski
☐ 9 Brian Bradley
☐ 10 Ron Kivell
☐ 11 Geoff Courtnall
☐ 12 Tony Stiles
☐ 13 Jim Buettgen
☐ 14 Cleon Dasklakis (G)
☐ 15 Rick Kosti (G)
☐ 16 Kevan Guy
☐ 17 John Blum
☐ 18 B.Patafie/M.Bianni/J.Druet
☐ 19 Greg Johnston
☐ 20 Dale DeGray
☐ 21 John Meulenbroeks
☐ 22 Dave Reid
☐ 23 Jay Miller
☐ 24 Yves Courteau
☐ 25 Robin Bartel
☐ 26 Benoît Doucet
☐ 27 Pete Bakovic
☐ 28 Team Photo

1986 - 87 GOLDEN FLAMES

Brett Hull is the most expensive single at $30-35. Bill Ranford sells at $6-8 and Gary Roberts sells at $6-8. Singles start at 75¢.
Card Size: 2 12" x 3 3/4"
Sponsors: Police, CKCW, Coke, McDonald's
Complete Set (28 cards): 60.00

☐ 1 Terry Crisp
☐ 2 Danny Bolduc
☐ 3 Doug Dadswell (G)
☐ 4 Doug Kostynski
☐ 5 Bill Ranford (G)
☐ 6 Brian Patafie
☐ 7 Dave Pasin
☐ 8 Darwin McCutcheon
☐ 9 Team Photo
☐ 10 Kevan Guy
☐ 11 Kraig Nienhuis
☐ 12 Gary Roberts
☐ 13 Ken Sabourin
☐ 14 Marc D'Amour (G)
☐ 15 Don Mercier
☐ 16 Wade Campbell
☐ 17 Mark Peterson
☐ 18 Cleon Daskalakis (G)
☐ 19 Lyndon Byers
☐ 20 Brett Hull
☐ 21 Bob Sweeney
☐ 22 Gord Hynes
☐ 23 Peter Bakovic
☐ 24 Dave Reid
☐ 25 Mike Rucinski
☐ 26 Ray Podloski
☐ 27 Bob Bodak
☐ 28 John Carter

MONCTON HAWKS
(AHL)

1987 - 88 HAWKS

Rick Bowness is the most expensive single at $1.50-2. Singles start at 75¢.
Card Size: 2 1/2" x 3 5/8"
Sponsors: Police, CKCW, Coke, Shoppers Drug Mart
Complete Set (25 cards): 15.00

☐ Joel Baillargeon
☐ Rick Bowness
☐ Bobby Dollas
☐ Peter Douris
☐ Iain Duncan
☐ Bob Essensa (G)
☐ Todd Flichel
☐ Rob Fowler
☐ Randy Gilhen
☐ Matt Hervey
☐ Brent Hughes
☐ Jamie Husgen
☐ Mike Jeffrey
☐ Guy Larose
☐ Chris Levasseur
☐ Len Nielson
☐ Roger Ohman
☐ Dave Quigley (G)
☐ Ron Pesetti
☐ Steve Penney (G)
☐ Scott Schneider
☐ Ryan Stewart
☐ Gord Whitaker
☐ Team Photo
☐ Rick Carrano/Wayne Flemming

1989 - 90 HAWKS

Singles start at 75¢. Other singles exist.
Card Size: 2 1/2" x 3 5/8"
Sponsors: Police

☐ Iain Duncan
☐ Matt Hervey
☐ Sergei Kharin
☐ Denis Laroque
☐ Tyler Larter
☐ Chris Norton

1990 - 91 HAWKS

Rick Tabaracci is the most expensive single at $2-3. Singles start at 75¢.
Card Size: 2 1/2" x 3 5/8"
Sponsors: Police, CKCW, Hostess Frito Lay
Complete Set (25 cards): 15.00

☐ Larry Bernard
☐ Lee Davidson
☐ Iain Duncan
☐ Craig Duncanson
☐ Dallas Eakins
☐ Dave Farrish
☐ Wayne Flemming
☐ Todd Flichel
☐ Peter Hankinson
☐ Matt Hervey
☐ Brent Hughes
☐ Anthony Joseph
☐ Sergei Kharin
☐ Denis Larocque
☐ Guy Larose
☐ Tyler Larter
☐ Scott Levins
☐ Bryan Marchment
☐ Chris Norton
☐ Mike O'Neill
☐ Grant Richison
☐ Scott Schneider
☐ Rob Snitzer
☐ Rick Tabaracci (G)
☐ Simon Wheeldon
☐ Team Card

1991 - 92 HAWKS

Rick Tabaracci is the most expensive single at $2-3. Singles start at 75¢.
Card Size: 2 1/2" x 3 5/8"
Sponsors: Police, CKCW, Hostess Frito Lay
Complete Set (28 cards): 18.00

☐ Luciano Borsato
☐ Jason Cirone
☐ Rob Cowie
☐ Lee Davidson
☐ Kris Draper
☐ Dallas Eakins
☐ Dave Farrish
☐ Wayne Flemming
☐ Sean Gauthier
☐ Ken Gernander
☐ Tod Hartje
☐ Bob Joyce
☐ Claude Julien
☐ Chris Kiene
☐ Mark Kumpel

☐ Derek Langille
☐ Tyler Larter
☐ John LeBlanc
☐ Scott Levins
☐ Rob Murray
☐ Kent Paynter
☐ Rudy Poeschek
☐ Dave Prior
☐ Warren Rychel
☐ Rob Snitzer
☐ Rick Tabaracci (G)
☐ Darren Veitch
☐ Mascot The Hawk

NASHVILLE KNIGHTS
(CHL)

1989 - 90 KNIGHTS

Singles sell at 50¢.
Card Size: 2 1/2" x 3 1/2"
Sponsor: Lee's Country Chicken
Complete Set (23 cards): 10.00

☐ Pat Bingham
☐ André Brassard
☐ Mike Bukta
☐ Chris Cambio
☐ Glen Engevik
☐ Archie Henderson
☐ Billy Huard
☐ Todd Jenkins
☐ Brock Kelly
☐ Eddie Krayer
☐ Garth Lamb
☐ Rob Levasseur
☐ Dan O'Brien
☐ John Reid (G)
☐ John Reid (G)
☐ Jeff Salzbrunn
☐ Mike Schwalb
☐ Ron Servatius
☐ Jason Simon
☐ Dave Cavaliere/Craig Jenkins
☐ Matt Gallagher/Scott Greer
☐ Rob Polk/Ron Fuller
☐ Chick-E-Lee

NEW HAVEN NIGHTHAWKS
(AHL)

1989 - 90 NIGHTHAWKS

Singles sell at 50¢.
Card Size: 2 1/2" x 3 1/2"
Sponsor: Casio
Complete Set (15 cards): 7.00

☐ Ken Baumgartner
☐ Jon Bednarski
☐ Tom Colley
☐ Rick Dudley
☐ Daryl Evans
☐ Ed Johnstone
☐ Alain Langlais
☐ Mark Lofthouse
☐ Parker McDonald
☐ Hubie McDonough
☐ Bill Plager
☐ Ron Scott
☐ Bobby Sheehan
☐ Doug Soetaert (G)
☐ Jim Wiemer

NEWMARKET SAINTS
(AHL)

1990 - 91 SAINTS

Damian Rhodes is the most expensive single at $3-4. Singles start at 75¢.
Card Size: 2 1/2" x 3 3/4"
Sponsor: Police
Complete Set (26 cards): 18.00

☐ Frank Anzalone
☐ Tim Bean
☐ Brian Blad
☐ Alan Hepple
☐ Robert Horyna
☐ Kent Hulst
☐ Mike Jackson
☐ Greg Johnston
☐ Derek Langille
☐ Mike Millar
☐ Mike Moes
☐ Bill Purcell
☐ Bobby Reynolds
☐ Damian Rhodes (G)
☐ Bill Root
☐ Joe Sacco
☐ Darryl Shannon
☐ Doug Shedden
☐ Mike Stevens
☐ Darren Veitch
☐ Greg Walters
☐ Bryan Cousineau
☐ Donald Hillock
☐ Eldred King
☐ Frank Kovacs
☐ Police Dog Lanny

NOVA SCOTIA OILERS
(AHL)

1984 - 85 OILERS

Steve Smith is the most expensive single at $5-6. Singles start at 75¢.
Card Size: 2 1/2" x 3 5/8"
Sponsors: Police, Q104, Coke, Hostess
Complete Set (26 cards): 20.00

☐ 1 Mark Holden (G)
☐ 2 Dave Allison
☐ 3 Dwayne Boettger
☐ 4 Lowell Loveday
☐ 5 Réjean Cloutier
☐ 6 Ray Cote
☐ 7 Pat Conacher
☐ 8 Ken Berry
☐ 9 Steve Graves
☐ 10 Todd Strueby
☐ 11 Steve Smith
☐ 12 Archie Henderson
☐ 13 Dean Dachyshyn
☐ 14 Marc Habscheid
☐ 15 Larry Melnyk
☐ 16 Raimo Summanen
☐ 17 Jim Playfair
☐ 18 Mike Zanier (G)
☐ 19 Ian Wood (G)
☐ 20 Dean Hopkins
☐ 21 Norm Aubin
☐ 22 Tony Currie
☐ 23 Ross Lambert
☐ 24 Terry Martin
☐ 25 E.Chadwick/L.Kish/B.Boucher
☐ 26 Lou Christian/Kevin Farris

1985 - 86 OILERS

Jeff Beukeboom is the most expensive single at $4-5. Singles start at 75¢.
Card Size: 2 1/2" x 3 5/8"
Sponsors: Police, Q104, Coke, IGA, Hostess
Complete Set (28 cards): 20.00

☐ 1 Dean Hopkins
☐ 2 Jeff Larmer
☐ 3 Mike Moller
☐ 4 Dean Dachyshyn
☐ 5 Bruce Boudreau
☐ 6 Ken Solheim
☐ 7 Jeff Beukeboom
☐ 8 Mark Lavarre
☐ 9 John Ollson
☐ 10 Lou Crawford
☐ 11 Warren Skorodenski (G)
☐ 12 Dwayne Boettger
☐ 13 Daryl Reaugh (G)
☐ 14 John Miner
☐ 15 Jim Ralph (G)
☐ 16 Wayne Presley
☐ 17 Steve Graves
☐ 18 Tom McMurchy
☐ 19 Darin Sceviour
☐ 20 Kent Paynter
☐ 21 Larry Kish
☐ 22 Jim Playfair
☐ 23 Kevin Farris/Ralph Mosher
☐ 24 Mickey Volcan
☐ 25 Ron Low
☐ 26 Don Biggs
☐ 27 Bruce Eakin
☐ 28 Team Photo

NOVA SCOTIA VOYAGEURS
(AHL)

1977 - 78 VOYAGEURS

Pat Hughes and Rick Meagher are the most expensive singles at $2-3. Singles start at $1.00.
Card Size: 2 1/8" x 4 1/2"
Sponsor: Farmers Co-Op Dairy
Complete Set (24 cards): 25.00

☐ Bruce Baker
☐ Maurice Barrette
☐ Barry Borrett
☐ Tim Burke
☐ Jim Cahoon
☐ Norm Dupont
☐ Greg Fox
☐ Mike Hobin
☐ Bob Holland
☐ Don Howse
☐ Pat Hughes
☐ Chuck Luksa
☐ Dave Lumley
☐ Al MacNeil
☐ Gord MacTavish
☐ Rick Meagher
☐ Mike Polich
☐ Moe Robinson
☐ Gaeton Rochette
☐ Pierre Roy
☐ Frank St. Marseille
☐ Derrick St. Marseille
☐ Rod Schutt
☐ Ron Wilson

1983 - 84 VOYAGEURS

Brian Skrudland and Mike McPhee are the most expensive singles at $3-4. Singles start at 75¢.
Card Size: 2 1/8" x 4 1/2"
Sponsors: Police, Q104, Coke, Hostess
Complete Set (24 cards): 20.00

☐ 1 Mark Holden (G)
☐ 2 Bill Kitchen
☐ 3 Dave Allison
☐ 4 Stéphane Lefebvre
☐ 5 Stan Hennigar
☐ 6 Steve Marengère
☐ 7 John Goodwin
☐ 8 John Newberry
☐ 9 Bill Rilay
☐ 10 Norman Baron
☐ 11 Brian Skrudland
☐ 12 Mike Lalor
☐ 13 Blair Barnes
☐ 14 Rémi Gagné
☐ 15 Steve Penney (G)
☐ 16 Michel Therrien
☐ 17 Dave Stoyanovich
☐ 18 Brian Patafie/Lou Christian
☐ 19 Mike McPhee
☐ 20 Wayne Thompson
☐ 21 Ted Fauss
☐ 22 Jeff Teal
☐ 23 Larry Landon
☐ 24 Greg Moffett

OKLAHOMA CITY BLAZERS

1992 - 93 BLAZERS

Singles start at 50¢.
Card Size: 2 1/2" x 3 1/2"
Sponsors: TD Sports Cards, Planters Nuts & Snacks
Complete Set (18 cards): 8.00

☐ Carl Boudreau
☐ Joel Burton
☐ Sylvain Fleury
☐ Brendan Garvey
☐ Guy Girouard
☐ Sean Gorman
☐ Jamie Hearn
☐ Craig Johnson
☐ Paul Krake
☐ Chris Laganas
☐ Daniel Larin
☐ Mark McGinn
☐ Alan Perry
☐ Steve Simoni
☐ Jim Solly
☐ Boyd Sutton
☐ Team Photo
☐ Blazers card

PENSACOLA ICE PILOTS
(ECHL)

1996 - 97 ICE PILOTS

2,000 sets were produced. Brent Gretzky is the most expensive single at $1-1.50. Singles start at 50¢.
Card Size: 2 1/2" x 3 1/2"
Sponsors: DLUX Printing
Complete Set (24 cards): 12.00

☐ 1 Craig Brown
☐ 2 Stéphane Julien
☐ 3 David Barozzino
☐ 4 Jeremy Mylymok
☐ 5 Patrik Allvin
☐ 6 Rostislav Saglo
☐ 7 Glen Metropolit
☐ 8 Chad Quenneville
☐ 9 Trevor Buchanan
☐ 10 Brandon Gray
☐ 11 Jon Pirrong
☐ 12 Brent Gretzky
☐ 13 Martin LaChaine
☐ 14 Brian Secord
☐ 15 Hugo Belanger
☐ 16 Christian Sbrocca
☐ 17 Tony Prpic
☐ 18 Shane Calder
☐ 19 Nick Stajduhar
☐ 20 Brendan Concannon
☐ 21 Sean Gauthier
☐ 22 Al Pederson
☐ 23 George Kozak
☐ Information Card

PEORIA RIVERMEN
(IHL)

1992 - 93 RIVERMEN

Singles start at 50¢.
Card Size: 2 1/2" x 3 1/2"
Sponsors: Coke, Kroger
Complete Set (30 cards): 15.00

☐ Jeff Batters
☐ Parris Duffus (G)
☐ Greg Eberle
☐ John Faginkrantz
☐ Denny Felsner
☐ Derek Frenette
☐ Ron Handy
☐ Joe Hawley
☐ Terry Hollinger
☐ Ron Hoover
☐ Dan Laperrière
☐ Lee J. Leslie
☐ Dave Mackey
☐ Jason Marshall
☐ Brian McKee
☐ Rick Meagher
☐ Kevin Miehm
☐ Brian Pellerin
☐ Richard Pion
☐ Mark Reeds
☐ Kyle Reeves
☐ Rob Robinson
☐ Jason Ruff

☐ Geoff Sarjeant (G)
☐ Darren Veitch
☐ Doug Wickenheiser
☐ Shawn Wheeler
☐ Coke Coupon
☐ Rivermen card
☐ Checklist

1993 - 94 RIVERMEN

Singles start at 50¢.
Card Size: 2 1/2" x 3 1/2"
Sponsors: Hat Tricks
Complete Set (31 cards): 15.00

☐ Mark Bassen
☐ Jeff Batters
☐ René Chapdelaine
☐ Doug Crossman
☐ Parris Duffus (G)
☐ Greg Eberle
☐ Doug Evans
☐ Kevin Evans
☐ John Faginkrantz
☐ Denny Felsner
☐ Derek Frenette
☐ Terry Hollinger
☐ Ron Hoover
☐ Butch Kaebel
☐ Nathan Lafayette
☐ Dan Laperrière
☐ Dave Mackey
☐ Paul MacLean
☐ Michel Mongeau
☐ Brian Pellerin
☐ Richard Pion
☐ Vitali Prokhorov
☐ Mark Reeds
☐ John Roderick
☐ Geoff Sarjeant (G)
☐ Steve Staios
☐ Darren Veitch
☐ Nick Vitucci
☐ Rivermen card
☐ Alcohol awareness
☐ Checklist

PHOENIX ROADRUNNERS
(IHL)

1992 - 93 ROADRUNNERS

Singles start at 50¢.
Card Size: 2 1/2" x 3 1/2"
Sponsor: Safeway
Complete Set (28 cards): 12.00

☐ Tim Bothwell
☐ François Breault
☐ Tim Bresliun
☐ René Chapdelaine
☐ Sylvain Couturier
☐ Phil Crowe
☐ Darryl Gilmour (G)
☐ David Goverde
☐ Ed Kastelic
☐ Rick Kozuback
☐ Ted Kramer
☐ Robert Lang
☐ Guy Lévêque
☐ Jim Maher
☐ Brad McCaughey
☐ Shawn McCosh
☐ John Mokosak
☐ Keith Redmond
☐ Mike Ruark
☐ Brandy Semchuk
☐ Dave Stewart
☐ Brad Tiley
☐ Dave Tretowicz
☐ Mike Vukonich
☐ Tim Watters
☐ Sean Whyte
☐ Darryl Williams
☐ Mascot Rocky Roadrunner

1993 - 94 ROADRUNNERS

Singles start at 50¢.
Card Size: 2 1/2" x 3 1/2"
Sponsor: Jessen
Complete Set (25 cards): 10.00

☐ Tim Breslin
☐ Brian Chapman
☐ Stéphane Charbonneau
☐ Dan Currie
☐ Rick Dudley
☐ Marc Fortier
☐ David Goverde
☐ Kevin Grant
☐ Mark Hardy
☐ Dean Hulett
☐ Pauli Jaks (G)
☐ Bob Jay
☐ Rick Knickle (G)
☐ Guy Lévêque
☐ Eric Lavigne
☐ Dominic Lavoie
☐ Jim Maher
☐ Brian McReynolds
☐ Rob Murphy
☐ Keith Redmond
☐ Dave Stewart
☐ Dave Tomlinson
☐ Brad Tiley
☐ Jim Vesey
☐ Darryl Williams

1995 - 96 ROADRUNNERS

Jamie Storr is the most expensive single at $2-3. Singles start at 50¢.
Card Size: 2 1/2" x 3 1/2"
Sponsor: Safeway
Complete Set (24 cards): 12.00

☐ Ruslan Batyrshin
☐ Frederik Beaubien
☐ John Blue
☐ Mike Boback
☐ Kevin Brown
☐ Jim Burton
☐ Dan Bylsma
☐ Brian Chapman
☐ Rob Cowie
☐ Devin Edgerton
☐ Rob Laird
☐ Ken McRae
☐ Barry Potomski
☐ Daniel Rydmark
☐ Jeff Shevalier
☐ Gary Shuchuk
☐ Chris Snell
☐ Jamie Storr (G)
☐ Dave Thomlinson
☐ Nicholas Vachon
☐ Jan Vopat
☐ Steve Wilson
☐ Phoenix Trainers
☐ Mascot Rocky Roadrunner

PORTLAND PIRATES
(AHL)

1993 - 94 PIRATES

Olaf Kolzig is the most expensive single at $3-4. Singles start at 50¢.
Card Size: 2 1/2" x 3 1/2"
Sponsor: Pepsi
Complete Set (25 cards): 12.00

☐ Mike Boback
☐ Kerry Clark
☐ Byron Dafoe (G)
☐ Eric Fenton
☐ Paul Gardner
☐ Kent Hulst
☐ Chris Jensen
☐ Martin Jiranek
☐ Kevin Kaminski
☐ Ken Klee
☐ Olaf Kolzig (G)
☐ Chris Longo
☐ Jim Mathieson
☐ Darren McAusland
☐ Todd Nelson
☐ Jeff Nelson
☐ Randy Pearce
☐ Michel Picard
☐ Steve Poapst
☐ Jeff Sirkka
☐ John Slaney
☐ Barry Trotz
☐ Jason Woolley
☐ Mascot Checkers
☐ Pirates card

1994 - 95 PIRATES

Singles start at 50¢.
Card Size: 2 1/2" x 3 1/2"
Sponsor: Classic
Complete Set (23 cards): 10.00

☐ Norm Batherson
☐ Mike Boback
☐ Andrew Brunette
☐ Jim Carey (G)
☐ Jason Christie
☐ Kerry Clark
☐ Brian Curran
☐ Martin Gendron
☐ Sergei Gonchar
☐ Kent Hulst
☐ Chris Jensen
☐ Kevin Kaminski
☐ Ken Klee
☐ Chris Longo
☐ Jim Mathieson
☐ Darren McAusland
☐ Jeff Nelson
☐ Todd Nelson
☐ Mike Parson
☐ Steve Poapst
☐ André Racicot (G)
☐ Sergei Tertyshny
☐ Stefan Ustorf

1995 - 96 PIRATES

Jason Allison is the most expensive single at $2-3. Singles start at 50¢.
Card Size: 2 1/2" x 3 1/2"
Sponsor: Dunkin' Donuts
Complete Set (24 cards): 12.00

☐ Alexander Alexeyev
☐ Jason Allison
☐ Norm Batherson
☐ Frank Bialowas
☐ Patrick Boileau
☐ Andrew Brunette
☐ Stéphane Charbonneau
☐ Jason Christie
☐ Brian Curran
☐ Martin Gendron
☐ Kent Hulst
☐ Alexander Kharlamov
☐ Jim Mathieson
☐ Darren McAusland
☐ Jeff Nelson
☐ Darryl Paquette
☐ Rob Pearson
☐ Steve Poapst
☐ Joel Poirier
☐ Sergei Tertyshny
☐ Ron Tugnutt (G)
☐ Stefan Ustorf
☐ Barry Trotz, Coach
☐ Mascot Crackers

1996 - 97 PIRATES

Jaroslav Svejkovsky is the most expensive single at $1.50-2. Singles start at 50¢.
Card Size: 2 1/2" x 3 1/2"
Sponsor: Split Second
Complete Set (25 cards): 10.00

☐ Stewart Malguna #4
☐ Norm Batherson #7
☐ Nolan Baumgartner #5
☐ Patrick Boileau #27
☐ Martin Brochu (G) #30
☐ Andrew Brunette #19
☐ Anson Carter #33
☐ Jason Christie #21
☐ Brad Church #12
☐ Miika Elomo #20
☐ Benoît Gratton #25
☐ Trevor Halverson #28
☐ Kent Hulst #10
☐ Alexander Kharlamov #22
☐ Daniel Laperriere #24
☐ Darren McAusland #16
☐ Ron Pascucci #6
☐ Steve Poapst #3
☐ Marc Potvin #9
☐ Robb Stauber (G) #1
☐ Jaroslav Svejkovsk #15y
☐ Richard Zednik #14
☐ Barry Trotz, Coach
☐ Paul Gardner, Asst. Coach
☐ AHL Card

QUÉBEC ACES

1963-64 ACES

Photos are in black and white. Gump Worsley is the most expensive single at $40-50 in NRMT. Doug Harvey sells at $25-30. Singles start at $4.
Card Size: 3 1/2" x 5 1/2"
Sponsors: none
Complete Set (22 cards): 125.00

☐ Don Blackburn
☐ Skippy Burchell
☐ Billy Carter
☐ Floyd Curry
☐ Bill Dineen
☐ Wayne Freitag
☐ Jean Gauthier
☐ Terry Gray
☐ John Hanna
☐ Doug Harvey
☐ Wayne Hicks
☐ Charlie Hodge (G)
☐ Charlie Hodge (G)
☐ Ed Hoekstra
☐ Frank Martin
☐ Jim Morrison
☐ Cleveland Mortson
☐ Gerry O'Drowski
☐ Rino Robazza
☐ Léon Rochefort
☐ Bill Sutherland
☐ Gump Worsley (G)

1965-66 ACES

Photos are in black and white. Bernie Geoffrion is the most expensive single at $20-25 in NRMT. Singles start at $4.
Card Size: 3 1/2" x 5 1/2"
Sponsors: none
Complete Set (18 cards): 80.00

☐ Gilles Banville (G)
☐ Gary Bauman (G)
☐ Don Blackburn
☐ Jean-Guy Gendron
☐ Bernie Geoffrion
☐ Terry Gray
☐ John Hanna
☐ Wayne Hicks
☐ Ed Hoekstra
☐ Don Johns
☐ Gordon Labossière
☐ Yvon Lacoste
☐ Jimmy Morrison
☐ Cleveland Mortson
☐ Simon Nolet
☐ Noel Price
☐ Rino Robazza
☐ Bill Sutherland

RALEIGH ICECAPS
(ECHL)

1993 - 94 ICECAPS

Singles start at 50¢.
Card Size: 2 1/2" x 3 1/2"
Sponsors: none
Complete Set (20 cards): 8.00

☐ Ralph Barahona
☐ Rick Barkovich
☐ Matt Delguidice
☐ Martin d'Orsonnens
☐ Jamie Erb
☐ Chad Erickson
☐ Donevan Hextall
☐ Shaune Kane
☐ Al Leggett
☐ Derek Linnell
☐ Joe McCarthy
☐ Chris Nelson
☐ Barry Nieckar
☐ Jim Powers
☐ Stan Reddick
☐ Kevin Riehl
☐ Jeff Robison
☐ David Shute
☐ Lyle Wildgoose
☐ Kurt Kleinendorst

1994 - 95 ICECAPS

Singles start at 50¢.
Card Size: 2 1/2" x 3 1/2"
Sponsors: none
Complete Set (19 cards): 8.00

☐ Jon Blessman
☐ Rick Barkovich

☐ Alexander Chunchukov
☐ Frank Cirone
☐ Brett Duncan
☐ Anton Fedorov
☐ Todd Hunter
☐ Rodrigo Lavinsh
☐ Derek Linnell
☐ Eric Long
☐ Scott MacNair
☐ Brad Mullahy
☐ Lenny Pereira
☐ Jimmy Powers
☐ Chris Pojar
☐ Kevin Riehl
☐ Todd Reirden
☐ Justin Tomlinson
☐ Lyle Wildgoose

RICHMOND RENEGADES
(ECHL)

1991 - 92 RENEGADES
Singles start at 50¢.
Card Size: 2 1/2" x 3 1/2"
Sponsor: Domino's Pizza
Complete Set (20 cards): 8.00
☐ 1 Rob Vanderydt
☐ 2 Larry Rooney
☐ 3 Brendan Flynn
☐ 4 Scott Drevitch
☐ 5 Jouni Lehto
☐ 6 Todd Drevitch
☐ 7 Paul Rutherford
☐ 8 Dave Aiken
☐ 9 Pat Bingham
☐ 10 Trevor Jobe
☐ 11 Bob Berg
☐ 12 Mark Kuntz
☐ 13 Joe Capprini
☐ 14 Trevor Converse
☐ 15 Steve Scheifele
☐ 16 Jon Gustafson
☐ 17 Marco Fuster
☐ 18 Guy Gadowsky
☐ 19 Dave Allison
☐ 20 Jamie McLennan (G)

1992 - 93 RENEGADES
Singles start at 50¢.
Card Size: 2 1/2" x 3 1/2"
Sponsor: Kellogg's
Complete Set (20 cards): 8.00
☐ Will Averill
☐ Frank Bialowas
☐ Scott Drevitch
☐ Brendan Flynn
☐ Guy Gadowsky
☐ Jon Gustafson
☐ Phil Huber
☐ Mike James
☐ Jeffrey Kampersal
☐ Mark Kuntz
☐ Sean LeBrun
☐ Kevin Malgunas
☐ Jim McGeough
☐ Ed Sabo
☐ Jeff Saterdalen
☐ Alan Schuler
☐ Martin Smith
☐ Roy Sommer
☐ Jeff Torrey
☐ Ben Wyzansky

1993 - 94 RENEGADES
Singles start at 50¢.
Card Size: 2 1/2" x 3 1/2"
Sponsor: XL 102 Radio
Complete Set (20 cards): 8.00
☐ 1 Ken Weiss
☐ 2 Guy Phillips
☐ 3 Alexander Zhdan
☐ 4 Alan Schuler
☐ 5 John Craighead
☐ 6 Colin Gregor
☐ 7 Rob MacInnis
☐ 8 Devin Derksen
☐ 9 John Renard
☐ 10 Peter Allen
☐ 11 Roy Sommer
☐ 12 Milan Hnilicka
☐ 13 Oleg Santurian
☐ 14 Brendan Flynn
☐ 15 Ken Blum
☐ 16 Steve Bogoyevac
☐ 17 Eric Germain
☐ 18 Chris Foy
☐ 19 Darren Colbourne
☐ 20 Jon Gustafson

1994 - 95 RENEGADES
Jan Benda is the most expensive single at $1-1.50. Singles start at 50¢.
Card Size: 2 1/2" x 3 1/2"
Sponsor: Q94
Complete Set (20 cards): 8.00
☐ Jan Benda
☐ Lou Body
☐ Steve Bogoyevac
☐ Jason Currie
☐ Chris Foy
☐ Scott Gruhl
☐ Shane Henry
☐ Don Lester
☐ Garrett MacDonald
☐ Kurt Mallett
☐ Blaine Moore
☐ Jay Murphy
☐ Sean O'Brien
☐ Andrew Shier
☐ Grant Sjervin
☐ Shawn Snesar
☐ Roy Sommer
☐ Mike Taylor
☐ Chris Tucker
☐ Darren Wetherill

1995 - 96 RENEGADES
Singles start at 50¢.
Card Size: 2 1/2" x 3 1/2"
Sponsor: Bleacher Bum, Q94
Complete Set (25 cards): 10.00
☐ Sandy Allan (G)
☐ Lou Body
☐ Michael Burman
☐ Steve Carpenter
☐ Andy Davis
☐ Brendan Flynn
☐ Brian Goudie
☐ Scott Gruhl
☐ Greg Hadden
☐ Rob Jones
☐ Garrett MacDonald
☐ Kurt Mallett
☐ Jason Mallon
☐ Mike Morin
☐ Jay Murphy
☐ Dmitri Pankov
☐ Martin Roy
☐ Trevor Senn
☐ Grant Sjervin
☐ Roy Sommer
☐ Todd Sparks
☐ Mike Taylor
☐ Darren Wetherill
☐ C. Laughlin/H.Feuerstein
☐ Mascot The Gade

ROANOKE EXPRESS
(ECHL)

1993 - 94 EXPRESS
Singles start at 50¢.
Card Size: 2 1/2" x 3 1/2"
Sponsors: Virginia Bank, Advance Auto Parts, J93.5 FM, WJPRTV 27
Complete Set (25 cards): 10.00
☐ Frank Anzalone
☐ Will Averill
☐ Claude Barthe
☐ Lev Berdichevsky
☐ Hughes Bouchard
☐ Reggie Brezeault
☐ Ilja Dubkov
☐ Pat Ferschweller
☐ Kyle Galloway
☐ Jeff Jestadt
☐ Roger Larche
☐ Dana McGuane
☐ Jim Mill
☐ Dave Morissette
☐ HL: Dave Morissette
☐ Chris Potter
☐ Dan Ryder
☐ Gairin Smith
☐ Michael Smith
☐ Tony Szabo
☐ Stephen Tepper
☐ Oleg Yashin
☐ Team Photo
☐ Sponsor logo
☐ Sponsor logo

1994 - 95 EXPRESS
Singles start at 50¢.
Card Size: 2 1/2" x 3 1/2"
Sponsors: Rally's, J93.5FM, WJPR TV 27
Complete Set (23 cards): 10.00
☐ Frank Anzalone
☐ Robin Bouchard
☐ Jason Clarke
☐ Stéphane Desjardins
☐ Ilja Dubukov
☐ Pat Ferschwiler
☐ Carl Fleury
☐ Dave Gagnon
☐ Jeff Jestadt
☐ Jon Larson
☐ Derek Laxdal
☐ Mark Luger
☐ Dana McGuane
☐ Chris Potter
☐ Dan Ryder
☐ Marty Schriner
☐ Michael Smith
☐ Dave Stewart
☐ Rouslan Toujikov
☐ Oleg Yashin
☐ Mascot Loco
☐ Team Photo
☐ Board of Directors

1995 - 96 EXPRESS
Singles start at 50¢.
Card Size: 2 1/2" x 3 1/2"
Sponsors: none
Complete Set (25 cards): 10.00
☐ Frank Anzalone
☐ Daniel Berthiaume
☐ L.P. Charbonneau
☐ Ted Christian
☐ Jason Clarke
☐ Paul Crôteau
☐ Matt DelGuidice (G)
☐ Ilja Dubukov
☐ Brian Gallentine
☐ Tim Hanley
☐ Duane Harmer
☐ Craig Herr
☐ Dave Holum
☐ Jeff Jablonski
☐ Jeff Jestadt
☐ Nick Jones
☐ Jon Larson
☐ Chris Pollack
☐ Chris Potter
☐ Marty Schriner
☐ Michael Smith
☐ Mike Stacchi
☐ Dave Stewart
☐ Mascot Loco
☐ Team Photo

ROCHESTER AMERICANS
(AHL)

1991 - 92 AMERICANS DUNKIN' DONUTS
Lindy Ruff is the most expensive single at $1-1.50. Singles start at 50¢.
Card Size: 2 1/2" x 3 1/2"
Sponsor: Dunkin' Donuts
Complete Set (16 cards): 8.00
☐ Greg Brown
☐ Peter Ciavaglia
☐ Bob Corkum
☐ Brian Curren
☐ David DiVita
☐ Tom Draper (G)
☐ Jody Gage
☐ Dan Frawley
☐ Dave Littman (G)
☐ Darcy Loewen
☐ Don McSween
☐ Brad Rubachuk
☐ Lindy Ruff
☐ Joel Savage
☐ Jiri Sejba
☐ Chris Snell

1991 - 92 AMERICANS KODAK/WEGMONS PHOTO
Lindy Ruff is the most expensive single at $1-1.50. Singles start at 50¢.
Card Size: 2 1/4" x 3 1/8"
Sponsors: Wegmons Photo Centre, Kodak
Complete Set (26 cards): 12.00
☐ Ian Boyce
☐ John Bradley
☐ Greg Brown
☐ Keith Carney
☐ Peter Ciavaglia
☐ Bob Corkum
☐ Brian Curran
☐ David DiVita
☐ Lou Franceschetti
☐ Dan Frawley
☐ Jody Gage
☐ Kevin Haller
☐ Don Lever
☐ Dave Littman (G)
☐ Darcy Loewen
☐ Steve Ludzik
☐ Terry Martin
☐ Don McSween
☐ Brad Miller
☐ Sean O'Donnell
☐ Brad Rubachuk
☐ Lindy Ruff
☐ Joel Savage
☐ Jiri Sejba
☐ Chris Snell
☐ Jason Winch

1991 - 92 AMERICANS GENNY LIGHT POSTCARDS
Lindy Ruff is the most expensive single at $1-1.50. Singles start at 50¢.
Postcard Size: 3 1/2" x 5 1/2"
Sponsors: Genny Light
Complete Set (21 cards): 10.00
☐ Dave Baseggio
☐ John Bradley
☐ Greg Brown
☐ Keith Carney
☐ Peter Ciavaglia
☐ Bob Corkum
☐ David DiVita
☐ Tom Draper (G)
☐ Lou Franceschetti
☐ Dan Frawley
☐ Bill Houlder
☐ Don Lever
☐ David Littman (G)
☐ Terry Martin
☐ Don McSween
☐ Sean O'Donnell
☐ Lindy Ruff
☐ Joel Savage
☐ Jiri Sejba
☐ Chris Snell
☐ Ed Zawatsky

1992 - 93 AMERICANS DUNKIN' DONUTS
Olaf Kolzig is the most expensive single at $1-1.50. Singles start at 50¢.
Card Size: 2 1/2" x 3 1/2"
Sponsor: Dunkin' Donuts
Complete Set (20 cards): 10.00
☐ Peter Ambroziak
☐ Greg Brown
☐ Peter Ciavaglia
☐ Jozef Cierny
☐ David DiVita
☐ Dan Frawley
☐ Jody Gage
☐ Andrei Jakovenko
☐ Olaf Kolzig (G)
☐ Doug MacDonald
☐ Mike McLaughin
☐ Sean O'Donnell
☐ Bill Pye
☐ Brad Rubachuk
☐ Bruce Shoebottom
☐ Todd Simon
☐ Jeff Sirkka
☐ Chris Snell
☐ Scott Thomas
☐ Jason Young

1992 - 93 AMERICANS KODAK/WEGMONS PHOTO
Olaf Kolzig is the most expensive single at $1-1.50. Singles start at 50¢.
Card Size: 2 1/4" x 3 1/8"
Sponsors: Wegmons Photo Centre, Kodak
Complete Set (26 cards): 12.00
☐ Peter Ambroziak
☐ Greg Brown
☐ Peter Ciavaglia
☐ Jozef Cierny
☐ David DiVita
☐ Dan Frawley
☐ Jody Gage
☐ Tony Iob
☐ Olaf Kolzig (G)
☐ Doug MacDonald
☐ Terry Martin
☐ Mike McLaughlin
☐ Sean O'Donnell
☐ Brad Pascall
☐ Bill Pye
☐ Brad Rubachuk

☐ Joel Savage
☐ Bruce Shoebottom
☐ Todd Simon
☐ Jeff Sirkka
☐ Chris Snell
☐ Scott Thomas
☐ John Van Boxmeer
☐ Jason Winch
☐ Jason Young
☐ Mascot The Moose

1993 - 94 AMERICANS KODAK/WEGMONS PHOTO

Singles start at 50¢.
Card Size: 2 1/2" x 3 1/2"
Sponsors: Wegmons Photo Centre, Kodak
Complete Set (25 cards): 10.00

☐ Peter Ambroziak
☐ Mike Bavis
☐ James Black
☐ Derek Booth
☐ Philippe Boucher
☐ David Cooper
☐ Todd Flichel
☐ Jody Gage
☐ Viktor Gordiouk
☐ Bill Horn
☐ Markus Ketterer (G)
☐ Mark Krys
☐ Doug MacDonald
☐ Terry Martin
☐ Dean Melanson
☐ Sean O'Donnell
☐ Brad Pascall
☐ Sergei Petrenko
☐ Brad Rubachuk
☐ Todd Simon
☐ Scott Thomas
☐ John Van Boxmeer
☐ Mikhail Volkov
☐ Jason Young
☐ Mascot The Moose

1995 - 96 AMERICANS

Steve Shields is the most expensive single at $1.50-2. Singles start at 50¢.
Card Size: 2 1/2" x 3 1/2"
Sponsors: Split Second
Complete Set (25 cards): 12.00

☐ Craig Charron
☐ David Cooper
☐ Dan Frawley
☐ Jody Gage
☐ Terry Hollinger
☐ Dane Jackson
☐ Ladislav Karabin
☐ Sergei Klimentiev
☐ Jamie Leach
☐ Jay Mazur
☐ Dean Melanson
☐ Scott Metcalfe
☐ Barrie Moore
☐ Scott Nichol
☐ Roman Ndur
☐ Scott Pearson
☐ Serge Roberge
☐ Steve Shields (G)
☐ Robb Stauber (G)
☐ John Tortorella
☐ Mikhail Volkov
☐ Dixon Ward
☐ Bob Westerby
☐ Mike Wilson
☐ Shayne Wright

SAGINAW GEARS
(IHL)

1978 - 79 GEARS

Photos are in black and white. Bob Froese is the most expensive single at $4-5. Singles start at $1.00.
Card Size: 2 1/2" x 3 1/2"
Sponsors: none
Complete Set (20 cards): 25.00

☐ Wren Blair
☐ Marcel Comeau
☐ Dennis Desrosiers
☐ Jon Fontas
☐ Bob Froese (G)
☐ Gunner Garrett
☐ Bob Gladney
☐ Warren Holmes
☐ Larry Hopkins
☐ Stu Irving
☐ Scott Jesse
☐ Lynn Jorgenson
☐ Doug Keans (G)
☐ Claude Larochelle
☐ Paul McIntosh
☐ Don Perry
☐ Greg Steel
☐ Mark Suzor
☐ Mark Toffolo
☐ Dave Westner

SAINT JOHN FLAMES
(AHL)

1994 - 95 FLAMES

Singles start at 50¢.
Card Size: 2 1/2" x 3 1/2"
Sponsor: Classic
Complete Set (25 cards): 12.00

☐ Joel Bouchard
☐ Rick Carrière
☐ Ryan Duthie
☐ Neil Eisenhut
☐ Léonard Esau
☐ Bob Francis
☐ Mark Greig
☐ François Groleau
☐ Sami Helenius
☐ Todd Hlushko
☐ Dan Kushner
☐ Bobby Maxwell
☐ Scott Morrow
☐ Mike Murray
☐ Jason Muzzatti (G)
☐ Barry Nieckar
☐ Nicolas Perreault
☐ Jeff Perry
☐ Dwayne Roloson
☐ Todd Simpson
☐ Cory Stillman
☐ David Struch
☐ Niklas Sundbald
☐ Andrei Trefilov (G)
☐ Vesa Viitakoski
☐ Harbour Station

1995 - 96 FLAMES

Singles start at 50¢.
Card Size: 2 1/2" x 3 1/2"
Sponsors: none
Complete Set (25 cards): 12.00

☐ Jamie Allison
☐ Paul Baxter
☐ Joel Bouchard
☐ Tom Coolen
☐ Brett Duncan
☐ Ian Gordon
☐ Sami Helenius
☐ Todd Hlushko
☐ Marc Hussey
☐ Ladislav Kohn
☐ Frank Kovacs
☐ David Ling
☐ Jesper Mattson
☐ Keith McCambridge
☐ Marty Murray
☐ Mike Murray
☐ David Neilson
☐ Jeff Perry
☐ Darren Ritchie
☐ Dwayne Roloson (G)
☐ Todd Simpson
☐ Jarrod Skalde
☐ David Struch
☐ Niklas Sundblad
☐ Vesa Viitakoski

ST. JOHN'S MAPLE LEAFS
(AHL)

1992 - 93 MAPLE LEAFS

Marc Crawford is the most expensive single at $2-3. Singles start at 50¢.
Card Size: 2 1/2" x 3 3/4"
Sponsors: none
Complete Set (25 cards): 12.00

☐ Patrik Augusta
☐ Drake Berehowsky
☐ Robert Cimetta
☐ Marc Crawford
☐ Ted Crowley
☐ Mike Eastwood
☐ Todd Hawkins
☐ Curtis Hunt
☐ Eric Lacroix
☐ Guy Lehoux
☐ Kent Manderville
☐ Kevin McClelland
☐ Ken McRae
☐ Brad Miller
☐ Yanic Perreault
☐ Rudy Poeschek
☐ Joel Quenneville
☐ Damian Rhodes (G)
☐ Joe Sacco
☐ Jeff Serowik
☐ Scott Sharples (G)
☐ Dave Tomlinson
☐ Nick Wohlers
☐ Mascot Buddy
☐ Team Photo

1993 - 94 MAPLE LEAFS

Marc Crawford is the most expensive single at $2-3. Singles start at 50¢.
Card Size: 2 1/2" x 3 3/4"
Sponsors: none
Complete Set (25 cards): 12.00

☐ Patrik Augusta
☐ Frank Bialowas
☐ Rich Chernomaz
☐ Terry Chitaroni
☐ Marcel Cousineau (G)
☐ Marc Crawford
☐ Todd Gillingham
☐ Chris Govedaris
☐ Paul Holden
☐ Curtis Hunt
☐ Alexei Kudashov
☐ Eric Lacroix
☐ Guy Lehoux
☐ Matt Mallgrave
☐ Grant Marshall
☐ Ken McRae
☐ Yanic Perreault
☐ Bruce Racine (G)
☐ Damian Rhodes (G)
☐ Chris Snell
☐ Dan Stiver
☐ Andy Sullivan
☐ Ryan Vandenbussche
☐ Steffon Walby
☐ Mascot Buddy

1994 - 95 MAPLE LEAFS

Kenny Jonsson is the most expensive single at $1.50-2. Singles start at 50¢.
Card Size: 2 1/2" x 3 3/4"
Sponsor: Classic
Complete Set (24 cards): 10.00

☐ Patrik Augusta
☐ Ken Belanger
☐ Frank Bialowas
☐ Rich Chernomaz
☐ Brandon Convery
☐ Marcel Cousineau (G)
☐ Trent Cull
☐ Nathan Dempsey
☐ Kelly Fairchild
☐ Janne Gronvall
☐ David Harlock
☐ Darby Hendrickson
☐ Marc Hussey
☐ Kenny Jonsson
☐ Mark Kolesar
☐ Alexei Kudashov
☐ Guy Lehoux
☐ Guy Lévèque
☐ Matt Martin
☐ Robb McIntyre
☐ Bruce Racine (G)
☐ Ryan Vandenbussche
☐ Steffon Walby
☐ Todd Warriner

1995 - 96 MAPLE LEAFS

Brent Gretzky is the most expensive single at $1-1.50. Singles start at 50¢.
Card Size: 2 1/2" x 3 3/4"
Sponsor: Classic
Complete Set (25 cards): 10.00

☐ Ken Belanger
☐ Rob Butz
☐ Brandon Convery
☐ Marcel Cousineau (G)
☐ Trent Cull
☐ Nathan Dempsey
☐ Kelly Fairchild
☐ Mike Foligno
☐ Brent Gretzky
☐ Janne Gronvall
☐ David Harlock
☐ Jamie Heward
☐ Mark Kolesar
☐ Guy Lehoux
☐ Kent Manderville
☐ Kory Mullin
☐ Jason Saal (G)
☐ Shayne Toporowski
☐ Paul Vincent
☐ Steffon Walby
☐ Mike Ware
☐ Todd Warriner
☐ Tom Watt
☐ Mascot Buddy
☐ Team Photo

SALT LAKE GOLDEN EAGLES
(IHL)

1988 - 89 GOLDEN EAGLES

Theoren Fleury is the most expensive single at $8-10. Singles start at 50¢.
Card Size: 2 1/2" x 3 1/2"
Sponsor: Smokey The Bear
Complete Set (24 cards): 20.00

☐ 1 Rick Barkovich
☐ 2 Michael Dark
☐ 3 Terry Perkins
☐ 4 Peter Lappin
☐ 5 Wayne Cowley
☐ 6 Rich Chernomaz
☐ 7 Steve Smith
☐ 8 Theoren Fleury
☐ 9 Dave Reierson
☐ Smokey The Bear (no#)
☐ 11 Martin Simard
☐ 12 Stu Grimson
☐ 13 Darwin McCutcheon
☐ 14 Doug Clarke
☐ 15 Doug Pickell
☐ 16 Randy Bucyk
☐ 17 Jim Johannson
☐ 18 Rick Lessard
☐ 19 Ken Sabourin
☐ 20 Chris Biotti
☐ 21 Jeff Wenaas
☐ 22 Mark Holmes
☐ 23 Bob Bodak
☐ 24 Marc Bureau

SAN DIEGO GULLS
(IHL)

1992 - 93 GULLS

Singles start at 50¢.
Card Size: 2 1/2" x 3 1/2"
Sponsors: none
Complete Set (24 cards): 10.00

☐ John Anderson
☐ Perry Anderson
☐ Scott Arniel
☐ Michael Brewer
☐ Dale DeGray
☐ Gord Dineen
☐ Rick Dudley
☐ Larry Floyd
☐ Keith Gretzky
☐ Peter Hankinson
☐ Bill Houlder
☐ Andrei Jakovenko
☐ Rick Knickle (G)
☐ Denny Lambert
☐ Mitch Lamoureux
☐ Clint Malarchuk (G)
☐ Steve Martinson
☐ Hubie McDonough
☐ Don McSween
☐ Mitch Molloy
☐ Robbie Nichols
☐ Lindy Ruff
☐ Daniel Shank
☐ Sergei Starikov

SIOUX CITY MUSKETEERS (IHL)

1974 - 75 MUSKETEERS

These cards are printed on yellow stock with green ink. Singles start at $1.00.
Size: 2 1/2" x 3 3/4"
Sponsors: none
Complete Set (20 cards): 15.00

☐ Steve Boyle #8
☐ Dave Davies #12
☐ Steve Desloges #6
☐ Greg Gilbert #5
☐ Barry Head #9
☐ Steve Heathwood #16
☐ Dave Kartio #7
☐ Ralph Kloiber (G) #30
☐ Pete Maxwell (G) #27
☐ Randy McDonald #19
☐ Terry Mulroy (G) #1
☐ Sam Nelligan #11
☐ Julian Nixon #15
☐ Mike Noel #20
☐ Jim Peck #3
☐ Bogdan Podwysocki #18
☐ John Saville #10
☐ Alex Shibicky #17
☐ Bob Thomerson #4
☐ Jim White #2

SPRINGFIELD INDIANS

(AHL)

1983 - 84 INDIANS

Singles start at 50¢.
Card Size: 2 1/2" x 3 1/2"
Sponsors: none
Complete Set (25 cards): 12.00

☐ 1 Gil Hudon (G)
☐ 2 Jim Ralph (G)
☐ 3 Todd Bergen
☐ 4 Len Hachborn
☐ 5 John Olsson
☐ 6 Steve Tsujira
☐ 7 Gordie Williams
☐ 8 Dave Brown
☐ 9 Dan Frawley
☐ 10 Tom McMurchy
☐ 11 Dave Michayluk
☐ 12 Bob Mormina
☐ 13 Perry Pelensky
☐ 14 Andy Brickley
☐ 15 Ross Fitzpatrick
☐ 16 Florent Robidoux
☐ 17 Jeff Smith
☐ 18 Rod Willard
☐ 19 Darrell Anholt
☐ 20 Steve Blyth
☐ 21 Don Dietrich
☐ 22 Steve Smith
☐ 23 Daryl Stanley
☐ 24 Taras Zytynsky
☐ 25 Doug Sauter

1984 - 85 INDIANS

Singles start at 50¢.
Card Size: 2 1/2" x 3 1/2"
Sponsors: none
Complete Set (25 cards): 12.00

☐ 1 Mike Sandis (G)
☐ 2 Lorne Molleken (G)
☐ 3 Todd Lumbard (G)
☐ 4 Randy Velischek
☐ 5 David Jensen
☐ 6 Ken Leiter
☐ 7 Vern Smith
☐ 8 Alan Kerr
☐ 9 Scott Howson
☐ 10 Tim Coulis
☐ 11 Terry Tait
☐ 12 Tim Trimper
☐ 13 Ron Flockhart
☐ 14 Ron Handy
☐ 15 Jim Poner
☐ 16 Chris Pryor
☐ 17 Dale Henry
☐ 18 Mark Hamway
☐ 19 Monty Trottier
☐ 20 Miroslav Mally
☐ 21 Dirk Graham
☐ 22 Roger Kortko
☐ 23 Bob Bodak
☐ 24 Lorne Henning
☐ 25 Checklist

TALLAHASSEE TIGER SHARKS

(ECHL)

1995 - 96 TIGER SHARKS

Singles start at 50¢.
Card Size: 2 1/2" x 3 1/2"
Sponsor: Burger King
Complete Set (27 cards): 12.00

☐ 1 Rodrigo Lavinsh
☐ 2 Jon Engfer
☐ 3 Rod Aldoff
☐ 4 Aaron Kriss
☐ 5 Ron Pasco
☐ 6 Mark Deazley
☐ 7 Sean O'Brien
☐ 8 Kevin Paden
☐ 9 Darren Schwartz
☐ 10 Jim Paradise
☐ 11 John Uniac
☐ 12 Cal Ingraham
☐ 13 Matt Osiecki
☐ 14 Greg Geldart
☐ 15 Alexander Savchenkov
☐ 16 Casey Hungle
☐ 17 Mark Richards
☐ 18 Bob Bell
☐ 19 Mascot Frenzy
☐ 20 Jim Mirabello
☐ 21 Mark Richards/Bob Bell
☐ 22 Terry Christensen
☐ 23 Jack Capuano
☐ 24 Jerry Hilker
☐ 25 Walter Edwards
☐ 26 Tony Mancuso
☐ 27 John Summers

THUNDER BAY SENATORS

(CHL)

1993 - 94 SENATORS

Trent McLeary is the most expensive single at $1-1.50. Singles start at 50¢.
Card Size: 2 1/2" x 3 1/2"
Sponsors: 580 CKPR, Rising Star Promotions
Complete Set (19 cards): 8.00

☐ Mel Angelstad
☐ Richard Borgo
☐ Brian Downey
☐ Jamie Hayden
☐ Tommi Hietalal
☐ Todd Howarth
☐ Chris Hynnes
☐ Jean-François Labbé (G)
☐ Trent McCleary
☐ Barry McKinley
☐ Terry Menard
☐ Llew NcWana
☐ Don Osborne
☐ Bruce Ramsay
☐ Vern Ray
☐ Gerry St. Cyr
☐ Ron Talakowki
☐ Tom Warden
☐ Bryan Wells

1994 - 95 SENATORS

Singles start at 50¢.
Card Size: 2 1/2" x 3 1/2"
Sponsors: Rising Star Promotions
Complete Set (19 cards): 8.00

☐ Mel Angelstad
☐ Jean Blouin
☐ Alain Côté
☐ Jason Firth
☐ Rival Fullum
☐ Jake Grimes
☐ Todd Howarth
☐ Lance Leslie
☐ Mike McCourt
☐ Barry McKinley
☐ Llew NcWana
☐ Don Osborne
☐ Steve Parson
☐ Darren Perkins
☐ Neal Purdon
☐ Bruce Ramsay
☐ Chris Rowland
☐ Derek Scanlan
☐ Pat Szturm

1995 - 96 BAY SENATORS

Singles start at 50¢.
Card Size: 2 1/2" x 3 1/2"
Sponsors: Shoppers Drug Mart, Rising Star Promotions
Complete Set (20 cards): 8.00

☐ Mel Angelstad
☐ Omer Belisle
☐ Frédéric Cassivi (G)
☐ Brandon Christian
☐ Jason Disher
☐ Jason Firth
☐ Rival Fullum
☐ Todd Howarth
☐ Chris Hynnes
☐ Barry McKinley
☐ Terry Menard
☐ Derek Nicolson
☐ Llew NcWana
☐ Steve Parson
☐ Darren Perkins
☐ Dan Poirier
☐ Neal Purdon
☐ Bruce Ramsay
☐ Pat Szturm
☐ Team Photo

TOLEDO STORM

(ECHL)

1992 - 93 STORM

Singles start at 50¢.
Card Size: 2 3/8" x 3 1/2"
Sponsor: WIOT 104, The Distillery
Series One Set (30 cards): 12.00

☐ Wade Bartley
☐ Derek Booth
☐ Rick Corriveau
☐ Mark Deazeley
☐ Iain Duncan
☐ Jeff Gibbons
☐ Alex Hicks
☐ Jeff Jablonski
☐ Rick Judson
☐ Scott King (G)
☐ Scott Luhrmann
☐ Bruce MacDonald
☐ Chris McSorley
☐ Tim Mouser
☐ Greg Puhalski
☐ Pat Pylypuik
☐ Alex Roberts
☐ Brent Sapergia
☐ Barry Soskin
☐ Jason Stos
☐ Andy Suhy
☐ Mike Williams
☐ Distillery Crew
☐ Checklist
☐ Beth Daniels
☐ Don Davis
☐ Dennis O'Brien
☐ Becky Shock
☐ Wil Worster
☐ The Dawbusters

Series Two Set (24 cards): 10.00

☐ Derek Booth #23
☐ Rick Corriveau #24
☐ Mark Deazeley #12
☐ Iain Duncan #19
☐ Jeff Gibbons, P.R. #6
☐ Alex Hicks #21
☐ Jeff Jablonski #16
☐ John Johnson #13
☐ Rick Judson #20
☐ Scott King (G) #8
☐ Scott Luhrmann, Equipment #3
☐ Bruce MacDonald #18
☐ Chris McSorley, Coach #2
☐ Tim Mouser, P.R. #5
☐ Barry Potomskin #22
☐ Greg Puhalski #17
☐ Pat Pylypuik #10
☐ Alex Roberts #11
☐ Jeff Rohlicek #14
☐ Claude Scott, Fan #7
☐ Barry Soskin, G.M. #4
☐ Andy Suhy #9
☐ Dan Wiebe #15
☐ Checklist #1
☐ Mark Richards #25

1993 - 94 STORM

Singles start at 50¢.
Card Size: 2 3/8" x 3 1/2"
Sponsors: none
Complete Set (29 cards): 12.00

☐ 1 Checklist
☐ 2 Chris McSorley, Coach
☐ 3 Barry Soskin, G.M.
☐ 4 Tim Mouser, P.R.
☐ 5 Jeff Gibbons, P.R.
☐ 6 Scott Luhrmann
☐ 7 Nick Vitucci
☐ 8 Andy Suhy
☐ 9 Pat Pylypuik
☐ 10 Chris Belanger
☐ 11 Mike Markovich
☐ 12 Darren Perkins
☐ 13 Dennis Snedden
☐ 14 Mark Deazeley
☐ 15 Mark McCreary
☐ 16 Jeff Rohlicek
☐ 17 Chris Bergeron
☐ 18 John Hendry
☐ 19 Greg Puhalski
☐ 20 Bruce MacDonald
☐ 21 Marc Lyons
☐ 22 Rick Judson
☐ 23 Alex Hicks
☐ 24 Barry Potomski
☐ 25 Rick Corriveau
☐ 26 Kyle Reeves
☐ 27 Erin Whitten (G)
☐ 28 Brian Schoen
☐ 29 Riley Cup Champs

1994 - 95 STORM

Singles start at 50¢.
Card Size: 2 1/2" x 3 1/2"
Sponsors: none
Complete Set (24 cards): 10.00

☐ Dave Bankoske
☐ Wyatt Buckland
☐ Rick Corriveau
☐ Norm Dezainde
☐ Iain Duncon
☐ Jeff Gibbons
☐ Alain Harvey
☐ John Hendry
☐ Ed Henrich
☐ Rick Judson
☐ Mike Latendress
☐ Scott Luhrmann
☐ B.J. MacPherson
☐ Jim Maher
☐ Jay Neal
☐ Marquis Mathieu
☐ Shawn Penn
☐ Darren Perkins
☐ Greg Puhalski
☐ Gerry St. Cyr
☐ Barry Soskin
☐ Rhett Trombley
☐ Nick Vitucci
☐ Riley Cup Champions

1995 - 96 STORM

Singles start at 50¢.
Card Size: 2 1/2" x 3 1/2"
Sponsors: Frito Lay
Complete Set (26 cards): 12.00

☐ Wade Bartley
☐ Brandon Carper
☐ Dan Carter
☐ Norman Dezainde
☐ Jason Gladney
☐ Patrick Gladu
☐ David Goverde
☐ Chuck Imburgia
☐ Rick Judson
☐ Mark Kelly
☐ Paul Koch
☐ Mike Kolenda
☐ Rob Laurie
☐ Scott Luhrmann
☐ B.J. MacPherson
☐ Glen Mears
☐ Shawn Penn
☐ Nicolas Perreault
☐ Greg Puhalski
☐ Dennis Purdie
☐ Jason Smart
☐ Barry Soskin
☐ Mark Stitt
☐ Todd Wetzel
☐ Mike Whitton
☐ Frito Lay

WHEELING THUNDERBIRDS
(ECHL)

1992 - 93 THUNDERBIRDS

Singles start at 50¢.
Card Size: 2 1/2" x 3 1/2"
Sponsor: Those Guys Productions
Complete Set (24 cards): 10.00

☐ 1 Thunderbirds card
☐ 2 Claude Barthe
☐ 3 Joel Blain
☐ 4 Derek DeCosty
☐ 5 Marc Deschamps
☐ 6 Tom Dion
☐ 7 Devin Edgerton
☐ 8 Pete Heine
☐ 9 Kim Maier
☐ 10 Mike Millham (G)
☐ 11 Cory Paterson
☐ 12 Trevor Pochipinski
☐ 13 Tim Roberts
☐ 14 Mark Rodgers
☐ 15 Darren Schwartz
☐ 16 Trevor Senn
☐ 17 Tim Tisdale
☐ 18 John Uniac
☐ 19 Denny Magruder
☐ 20 Chuck Greenwood/Jim Smith
☐ 21 Larry Kish
☐ 22 Doug Sauter
☐ 23 Mascot T-Bird
☐ 24 Doug Bacon

1993 - 94 THUNDERBIRDS

Singles start at 50¢.
Card Size: 2 1/2" x 3 1/2"
Sponsor: Those Guys Productions
Complete Set (21 cards): 8.00

☐ 1 Checklist
☐ 2 Darren Schwartz
☐ 3 Cory Paterson
☐ 4 Derek DeCosty
☐ 5 Jim Bermingham
☐ 6 Brock Woods
☐ 7 Tim Roberts
☐ 8 Eric Raymond
☐ 9 Brett Abel
☐ 10 Sébastien Fortier
☐ 11 John Johnson
☐ 12 Brent Pope
☐ 13 Marquis Mathieu
☐ 14 Terry Virtue
☐ 15 Vadim Silvchenko
☐ 16 Clayton Gainer
☐ 17 Sylvain Lapointe
☐ 18 Douig Sauter
☐ 19 Larry Kish
☐ 20 Denny Magruder
☐ 21 Bill Cordery

1994 - 95 THUNDERBIRDS

Singles start at 50¢.
Card Size: 2 1/2" x 3 1/2"
Sponsor: Those Guys Productions
Complete Set (12 cards): 5.00

☐ 1 Checklist
☐ 2 Tim Tisdale
☐ 3 Brock Woods
☐ 4 Vadim Silvchenko
☐ 5 Tim Roberts
☐ 6 Derek DeCosty
☐ 7 Steve Gibson
☐ 8 Xavier Majic
☐ 9 Peter Marek
☐ 10 Greg Loder
☐ 11 Gairin Smith
☐ 12 Darren McAusland

CHAPTER SIX

JUNIOR & COLLEGE TEAM SETS

U. ARIZONA ICE CATS

1985 - 86 ICECATS

These cards were originally issued as a sheet. Glenn Hall is the most expensive single at $4-5. Singles start at 50¢.

Card Size: 2 5/8" x 4 1/8"
Sponsors: none
Complete Set (20 cards): 12.00

- ☐ Arizona Icecats
- ☐ Dan Anderson
- ☐ Don Carlson (G)
- ☐ Dan Divjak
- ☐ Shane Fausel
- ☐ Flavio Gentile
- ☐ Leo Golembiewski
- ☐ Jeremy Goltz
- ☐ Glenn Hall
- ☐ Stvee Hutchings
- ☐ Aaron Joffe
- ☐ Greg Mithcell
- ☐ Cory Oleson
- ☐ Ricky Rope
- ☐ Drew Sibr
- ☐ Dean Sives
- ☐ Tommy Smith
- ☐ Nate Soules
- ☐ Kelly Walker
- ☐ Icecat Leaders

BELLEVILLE BULLS

(OHL)

1983 - 84 BULLS

Team owner Wayne Gretzky is the most expensive single at $60-70. Al Iafrate sells at $8-10 while Craig Billington and Dan Quinn sell at $2-4. Singles start at 75¢.

Card Size: 2 5/8" x 4 1/8"
Sponsors: Police, McDonald's, Canadian Tire, Bert Jones GM, Kiwanis International, CJBQ
Complete Set (30 cards): 90.00

- ☐ 1 Bulls Logo
- ☐ 2 Quinte Sports Centre
- ☐ 3 Dan Quinn
- ☐ 4 Dave MacLean
- ☐ 5 Scott Gardiner
- ☐ 6 Mike Knuude
- ☐ 7 Brian Martin
- ☐ 8 Dr. R. Vaughn
- ☐ 9 John MacDonald (G)
- ☐ 10 Brian Small
- ☐ 11 Mike Savage
- ☐ 12 Dunc MacIntyre
- ☐ 13 Charlie Moore
- ☐ 14 Jim Andanoff
- ☐ 15 Mario Martini
- ☐ 16 Rick Adolfi
- ☐ 17 Mike Vellucci
- ☐ 18 Scott McMichael
- ☐ 19 Ali Butorac
- ☐ 20 Al Iafrate
- ☐ 21 Rob Crocock
- ☐ 22 Craig Coxe
- ☐ 23 Grant Robertson
- ☐ 24 Craig Billington (G)
- ☐ 25 Darren Gani
- ☐ 26 Tim Bean
- ☐ 27 Wayne Gretzky
- ☐ 28 Russ Soule
- ☐ 29 Larry Mavety
- ☐ 30 Team Photo

1984 - 85 BULLS

Craig Billington is the most expensive single at $2-3. Singles start at 75¢.

Card Size: 2 5/8" x 4 1/8"
Sponsors: Police, McDonald's, Canadian Tire, Coke, Bert Jones GM, Vaughan Sports, Richard Ellis Printing, Kiwanis International
Complete Set (31 cards): 25.00

- ☐ 1 Team Photo
- ☐ 2 Dr. R. Vaughan
- ☐ 3 Larry Mavety
- ☐ 4 Dunc MacIntyre
- ☐ 5 Bulls Logo
- ☐ 6 Mike Knuude
- ☐ 7 John Purves
- ☐ 8 Charlie Moore
- ☐ 9 Stan Drulia
- ☐ 10 Craig Billington (G)
- ☐ 11 Dave MacLean
- ☐ 12 Darren Moxam
- ☐ 13 Shane Doyle
- ☐ 14 Larry Vanherzele
- ☐ 15 Tim Bean
- ☐ 16 Kent Brimmer
- ☐ 17 Angelo Catenaro
- ☐ 18 Steve Linesman
- ☐ 19 Grant Robertson
- ☐ 20 John Reid
- ☐ 21 Dean Whyte
- ☐ 22 Darren Gani
- ☐ 23 Roger Robertson
- ☐ 24 Gary Callaghan
- ☐ 25 John Tamer
- ☐ 26 Todd Hawkins
- ☐ 27 Jim Andanoff
- ☐ 28 Chris Rutledge
- ☐ 29 Matt Taylor
- ☐ 30 Mike Hartman

BRANDON WHEAT KINGS

(WHL)

1982 - 83 WHEAT KINGS

Ron Hextall is the most expensive single at $15-20. Singles start at 75¢.

Card Size: 2 3/8" x 4"
Sponsors: Police, Safeway
Complete Set (24 cards): 25.00

- ☐ 1 Wheat King Logo
- ☐ 2 Kevin Pylypow
- ☐ 3 Dean Kennedy
- ☐ 4 Sonny Sodke
- ☐ 5 Darren Schmidt
- ☐ 6 Cam Plante
- ☐ 7 Sid Cranston
- ☐ 8 Brue Thomson
- ☐ 9 Dave McDowall
- ☐ 10 Bill Vince
- ☐ 11 Kelly Glowa
- ☐ 12 Tom McMurchy
- ☐ 13 Ed Palichuk
- ☐ 14 Roy Caswell
- ☐ 15 Allan Tarasuk
- ☐ 16 Brent Jessiman
- ☐ 17 Randy Slawson
- ☐ 18 Gord Smith
- ☐ 19 Mike Sturgeon
- ☐ 20 Larry Blumstead
- ☐ 21 Kirk Blomquist
- ☐ 22 Ron Loustel
- ☐ 23 Ron Hextall (G)
- ☐ 24 Brandon Police

1983 - 84 WHEAT KINGS

Ron Hextall is the most expensive single at $10-12. Ray Ferraro sells at $6-8. Singles start at 75¢.

Card Size: 2 1/4" x 4"
Sponsors: Police, Lions International, Optimist Club
Complete Set (24 cards): 25.00

- ☐ 1 Brian Wells
- ☐ 2 Jim Agnew
- ☐ 3 Gord Paddock
- ☐ 4 John Dzikowski
- ☐ 5 Kelly Kozack
- ☐ 6 Brian Lomow
- ☐ 7 Pat Loyer
- ☐ 8 Rob Ordman
- ☐ 9 Brad Wells
- ☐ 10 Dave Thomlinson
- ☐ 11 Cam Plante
- ☐ 12 Jay Palmer (G)
- ☐ 13 Boyd Lomow
- ☐ 14 Brent Jessiman
- ☐ 15 Paul More
- ☐ 16 Stacy Prtt
- ☐ 17 Brandon Police
- ☐ 18 Jack Sangster
- ☐ 19 Derek Laxdal
- ☐ 20 Ray Ferraro
- ☐ 21 Allan Tarasuk
- ☐ 22 Randy Cameron
- ☐ 23 Dave Curry
- ☐ 24 Ron Hextall (G)

1984 - 85 WHEAT KINGS

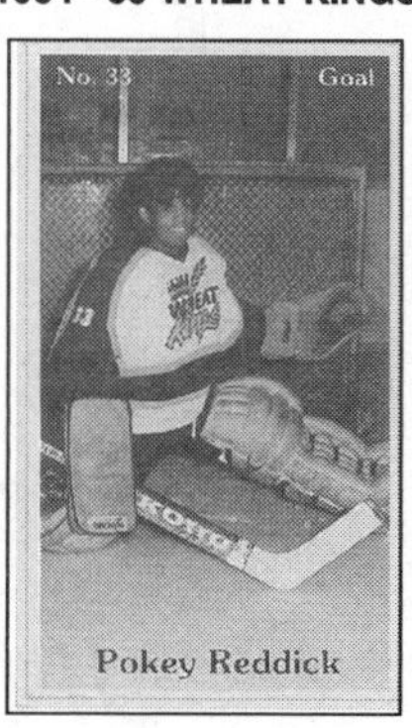

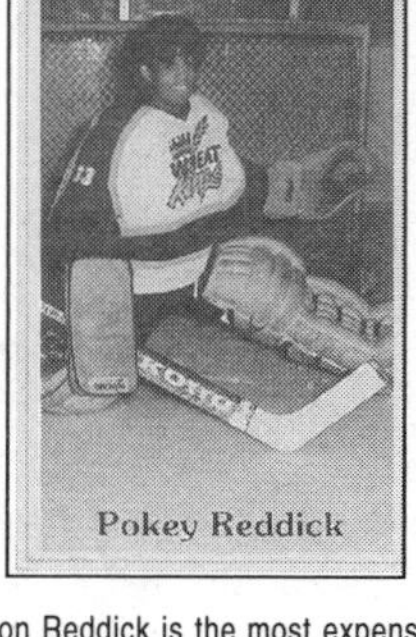
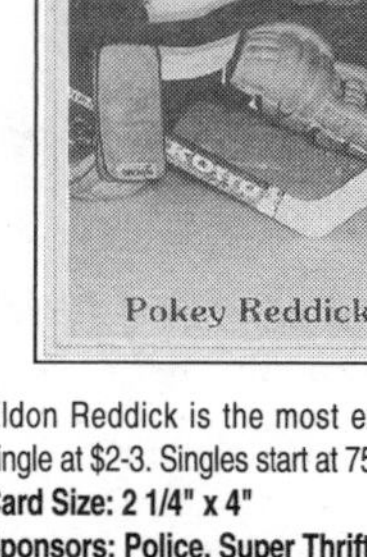

Eldon Reddick is the most expensive single at $2-3. Singles start at 75¢.

Card Size: 2 1/4" x 4"
Sponsors: Police, Super Thrifty Drugs
Complete Set (24 cards): 15.00

- ☐ 1 Garnet Kazuik
- ☐ 2 Brent Mireau
- ☐ 3 Bryan Lomow
- ☐ 4 Dean Shaw (G)
- ☐ 5 Dean Sexsmith
- ☐ 6 Brad Mueller
- ☐ 7 John Dzikowski
- ☐ 8 Artie Feher (G)
- ☐ 9 Pat Loyer
- ☐ 10 Murray Rice
- ☐ 11 Derek Laxdal
- ☐ 12 Perry Fafard
- ☐ 13 Lee Trim
- ☐ 14 Dan Hart
- ☐ 15 Trent Ciprick
- ☐ 16 Jeff Waver
- ☐ 17 Brandon Police
- ☐ 18 Jack Sangster
- ☐ 19 Darwin MacPherson
- ☐ 20 Eldon Reddick (G)
- ☐ 21 Boyd Lomow
- ☐ 22 Dave Thomlinson
- ☐ 23 Paul More
- ☐ 24 Brent Severyn

1985 - 86 WHEAT KINGS

Singles start at 75¢.

Card Size: 2 1/4" x 4"
Sponsors: Police, Lions International, Optimist Club
Complete Set (24 cards): 15.00

- ☐ 1 Kelly Hitchins
- ☐ 2 Brent Mireau
- ☐ 3 Byron Lomow
- ☐ 4 Bob Heeney
- ☐ 5 Dean Sexsmith
- ☐ 6 Dave Curry
- ☐ 7 John Dzikowski
- ☐ 8 Artie Feher (G)
- ☐ 9 Kevin Mayo
- ☐ 10 Murray Rice
- ☐ 11 Derek Laxdal
- ☐ 12 Al Cherniwchan
- ☐ 13 Lee Trim
- ☐ 14 Terry Yake
- ☐ 15 Trent Ciprick
- ☐ 16 Jeff Waver
- ☐ 17 Team Photo
- ☐ 18 Jack Sangster
- ☐ 19 Mike Morin
- ☐ 20 Jason Phillips
- ☐ 21 Rod Williams
- ☐ 22 Dave Thomlinson
- ☐ 23 Shane Eirickson
- ☐ 24 Randy Hoffart

1988 - 89 WHEAT KINGS

Trevor Kidd is the most expensive single at $3-4. Singles start at 75¢.

Card Size: 2 1/4" x 4"
Sponsors: Police, 7-Eleven
Complete Set (24 cards): 15.00

- ☐ 1 Kevin Cheveldayoff
- ☐ 2 Bob Woods
- ☐ 3 Dwayne Newman
- ☐ 4 Mike Vandenberghe
- ☐ 5 Brad Woods
- ☐ 6 Gary Audette
- ☐ 7 Mark Bassen
- ☐ 8 Troy Frederick
- ☐ 9 Troy Kennedy
- ☐ 10 Barry Dreger
- ☐ 11 Bill Whistle
- ☐ 12 Jeff Odgers
- ☐ 13 Sheldon Kowalchuk
- ☐ 14 Chris Robertson
- ☐ 15 Don Laurin
- ☐ 16 Curtis Folkett
- ☐ 17 Team Photo
- ☐ 18 Kelly McCrimmon
- ☐ 19 Doug Sauter
- ☐ 20 Kelly Hitchins
- ☐ 21 Trevor Kidd (G)
- ☐ 22 Pryce Wood
- ☐ 23 Cam Brown
- ☐ 24 Greg Hutchings

1989 - 90 WHEAT KINGS

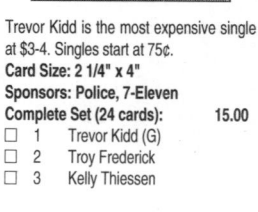

Trevor Kidd is the most expensive single at $3-4. Singles start at 75¢.

Card Size: 2 1/4" x 4"
Sponsors: Police, 7-Eleven
Complete Set (24 cards): 15.00

- ☐ 1 Trevor Kidd (G)
- ☐ 2 Troy Frederick
- ☐ 3 Kelly Thiessen

☐ 4 Pryce Wood
☐ 5 Mike Vandenberghe
☐ 6 Chris Constant
☐ 7 Hardy Sauter
☐ 8 Cam Brown
☐ 9 Bart Cote
☐ 10 Jeff Hoad
☐ 11 Kevin Robertson
☐ 12 Dwayne Newman
☐ 13 Calvin Flint
☐ 14 Glen Webster
☐ 15 Greg Hutchings
☐ 16 Rob Puchniak
☐ 17 Gary Audette
☐ 18 Kevin Schmalz
☐ 19 Dwayne Gylywoychuk
☐ 20 Jeff Odgers
☐ 21 Brian Purdy
☐ 22 Merv Priest
☐ 23 Doug Sauter
☐ 24 Team Photo

1990 - 91 WHEAT KINGS

Trevor Kidd is the most expensive single at $3-4. Singles start at 75¢.
Card Size: 2 1/4" x 4"
Sponsors: Police, 7-Eleven
Complete Set (24 cards): 15.00

☐ 1 Jeff Hoad
☐ 2 Merv Priest
☐ 3 Mike Vandenberghe
☐ 4 Bart Côté
☐ 5 Hardy Sauter
☐ 6 Mark Johnston
☐ 7 Kelly McCrimmon
☐ 8 Team Photo
☐ 9 Kevin Robertson
☐ 10 Glen Webster
☐ 11 Greg Hutchings
☐ 12 Dan Kopec
☐ 13 Dwayne Gylywoychuk
☐ 14 Brian Purdy
☐ 15 Trevor Kidd (G)
☐ 16 Johan Skillgard
☐ 17 Stu Scantlebury
☐ 18 Byron Penstock
☐ 19 Rob Puchniak
☐ 20 Gary Audette
☐ 21 Calvin Flint
☐ 22 Jason White
☐ 23 Chris Constant
☐ 24 Glen Gulutzan

1992 - 93 WHEAT KINGS

Dan Cloutier is the most expensive single at $2-3. Singles start at 75¢.
Card Size: 2 1/4" x 4"
Sponsors: Police, 7-Eleven, UCT
Complete Set (24 cards): 15.00

☐ Aris Brimanis
☐ Colin Cloutier (G)
☐ Chris Dingman
☐ Mike Dubinsky
☐ Todd Dutiaume
☐ Mark Franks
☐ Craig Geekie
☐ Dwayne Gylywoychuk
☐ Scott Hlady
☐ Jeff Hoad
☐ Bobby House
☐ Chris Johnston
☐ Mark Kolesar
☐ Scott Laluk
☐ Mike Maneluk
☐ Sean McFatridge
☐ Marty Murray
☐ Byron Penstock
☐ Darren Ritchie
☐ Trevor Robins
☐ Ryan Smith
☐ Jeff Staples
☐ Darcy Werenka
☐ Mascot Willie

BRANTFORD ALEXANDERS

(OHL)

1983 - 84 ALEXANDERS

Bob Probert is the most expensive single at $8-10. Shayne Corson sells at $6-8. Singles start at 75¢.
Card Size: 2 3/4" x 3 1/2"
Sponsors: Police
Complete Set (30 cards): 40.00

☐ 1 Ken Gratton
☐ 2 Shayne Corson
☐ 3 Bob Probert
☐ 4 Bruce Bell
☐ 5 Warren Bechard
☐ 6 Jason Lafrenière
☐ 7 Ron Moffat
☐ 8 Jack Calbeck
☐ 9 Marc West
☐ 10 Larry Van Herzele
☐ 11 Doug Stewart
☐ 12 Brian MacDonald
☐ 13 Dave Draper
☐ 14 Jeff Jackson
☐ 15 Steve Linseman
☐ 16 Steve Short
☐ 17 Allan Bester (G)
☐ 18 John Weir
☐ 19 Chris Pusey
☐ 20 Mike Millar
☐ 21 Chris Glover
☐ 22 Bob Pierson
☐ 23 Phil Priddle
☐ 24 Grant Anderson
☐ 25 Ken Gagner
☐ 26 Andy Alway
☐ 27 Todd Francis
☐ 28 John Meulenbroeks
☐ 29 Mike Chettleburgh
☐ 30 Bill Dynes

BROCKVILLE BRAVES

1987 - 88 BRAVES

Singles start at 75¢.
Card Size: 2 5/8" x 3 5/8"
Sponsors: Police, Pepsi, Black & Decker, IGA
Complete Set (25 cards): 15.00

☐ 1 Police logo
☐ 2 Steve Harper
☐ 3 Peter Kelly
☐ 4 Mac MacLean
☐ 5 Mike McCourt
☐ 6 Paul MacLean
☐ 7 Mark Michaud (G)
☐ 8 Alain Marchessault
☐ 9 Tom Roman
☐ 10 Darren Burns
☐ 11 Scott Halpenny (G)
☐ 12 Ray Gallagher
☐ 13 Bob Lindsay
☐ 14 Brett Harkins
☐ 15 Dave Hyrsky
☐ 16 Richard Marchessault
☐ 17 Scott Boston
☐ 18 Steve Hogg (G)
☐ 19 Chris Webster
☐ 20 Stuart Birnie
☐ 21 Brett Dunk
☐ 22 Charles Cusson
☐ 23 Pat Gooley
☐ 24 Andy Rodman
☐ 25 Peter Radlein

1988 - 89 BRAVES

Singles start at 75¢.
Card Size: 2 5/8" x 3 5/8"
Sponsors: Police, Pepsi, Black & Decker, IGA
Complete Set (25 cards): 15.00

☐ 1 Ray Gallagher
☐ 2 Peter Kelly
☐ 3 Steve Harper
☐ 4 Winston Jones
☐ 5 Mac MacLean
☐ 6 Kevin Doherty
☐ 7 Stuart Birnie
☐ 8 Charles Cusson
☐ 9 Paul MacLean
☐ 10 Bob Lindsay
☐ 11 Darren Burns
☐ 12 Rick Pracey (G)
☐ 13 Mike Malloy
☐ 14 Dave Hyrsky
☐ 15 Rob Percival
☐ 16 Jarrett Eligh
☐ 17 Pat Gooley
☐ 18 Michael Bracco (G)
☐ 19 Ken Crook
☐ 20 Brad Osborne
☐ 21 Todd Reynolds
☐ 22 Mike McCourt
☐ 23 Chris Webster
☐ 24 Kevin Lune
☐ 25 Police logo

CHICOUTIMI SAGUENÉENS

(QMJHL)

1984 - 85 SAGUENÉENS

Stéphane Richer is the most expensive single at $5-6. Singles start at $1.50.
Photo Size: 8 1/2" x 11"
Sponsors: none
Complete Set (24 photos): 30.00

☐ Mario Barbe
☐ Mario Bazinet
☐ Daniel Berthiaume (G)
☐ Francis Breault
☐ Gregg Choules
☐ Christian Duperron
☐ Luc Dufour
☐ Luc Duval
☐ Patrick Emond
☐ Marc Fortier
☐ Steve Gauthier
☐ Yves Heroux
☐ Daniel Jomphe
☐ Gilles Laberge
☐ Claude Lajoie
☐ Serge Lauzon
☐ Roch Marinier
☐ Pierre Millier
☐ Marc Morin
☐ Scott Rettew
☐ Jean-Marc Richard
☐ Stéphane Richer
☐ Pierre Sévigny
☐ D.Bedard/M.Boivin/G.Byatt
☐ J.M.Couture/P.Gosselin/
☐ J.Y.Laberge/R.Riverin

CLARKSON GOLDEN KNIGHTS

(ECAC)

1992 - 93 KNIGHTS

Todd Marchant is the most expensive single at $2-3. Singles start at 50¢.
Card Size: 2 1/2" x 3 1/2"
Sponsors: none
Complete Set (24 cards): 15.00

☐ Josh Bartell
☐ Hugo Belanger
☐ Craig Conroy
☐ Jason Currie
☐ Steve Dubinsky
☐ Shawn Fotheringham
☐ Dave Green
☐ Ed Henrihc
☐ Chris Lipsett
☐ Todd Marchant
☐ Brian Mueller
☐ Kevin Murphy
☐ Martin d'Orsonnens
☐ Steve Palmer
☐ Patrice Robitaille
☐ Chris Rogles
☐ Jerry Rosenheck
☐ Chris de Ruiter
☐ Guy Sanderson
☐ David Seitz
☐ Mikko Tavi
☐ Patrick Theriault
☐ Marko Tuomainen
☐ M.d'Orsonnens/S.Dubinsky

CORNWALL ROYALS

(OHL)

1991 - 92 ROYALS

Singles start at 50¢.
Card Size: 2 5/8" x 3 3/4"
Sponsors: Police
Complete Set (29 cards): 15.00

☐ 1 Jason Meloche
☐ 2 Mark DeSantis
☐ 3 Richard Raymond
☐ 4 Gord Pell
☐ 5 Dave Lemay
☐ 6 John Lovell
☐ 7 Ryan Vandenbussche
☐ 8 David Babcock
☐ 9 Sam Oliveira
☐ 10 Jeremy Stevenson
☐ 11 Todd Walker
☐ 12 Jean-Alain Schneider
☐ 13 Ilpo Kauhanen (G)
☐ 14 Guy Lévêque
☐ 15 Shayne Gaffar
☐ 16 Rival Fullum
☐ 17 Mike Prokopec
☐ 18 Nathan Lafayette
☐ 19 Larry Courville
☐ 20 Chris Clancy
☐ 21 Tom Nemeth
☐ 22 Jeff Reid
☐ 23 Paul Andrea
☐ 24 John Slaney
☐ 25 Alan Letang
☐ 26 Rob Dykeman (G)
☐ 27 P.Fixter/B.O'Leary
☐ 28 Chief Claude Shaver
☐ 29 Checklist

FERRIS STATE BULLDOGS

(CCHA)

1991 - 92 BULLDOGS

Singles start at 50¢.
Card Size: 2 1/2" x 3 1/2"
Sponsors: none
Complete Set (30 cards): 12.00

☐ Aaron Asp
☐ Seth Appert
☐ J.J. Bamberger
☐ Kevin Beals
☐ Scott Bell
☐ Brad Burnham
☐ Dan Chaput
☐ Tim Christian
☐ Bob Daniels
☐ Colin Dodunski
☐ Mick Dolan
☐ John Duff
☐ Daryl Filipek
☐ John Gruden
☐ Luke Harvey
☐ Jeff Jestadt
☐ Dave Karpa
☐ Gary Kitching
☐ Mike Kolenda
☐ Craig Lisko
☐ Mike May
☐ Pat Mazzoli
☐ Robb McIntyre
☐ Kevin Moore
☐ Greg Paine
☐ Dwight Parrish
☐ Val Passarelli
☐ Keith Sergott
☐ Doug Smith
☐ Mascot The Bulldog

GUELPH STORM

(OHL)

1995 - 96 STORM

Dan Cloutier is the most expensive single at $1.50-2. Singles start at 50¢.

Card Size: 2 1/2" x 3 1/2"

Sponsor: Axiom Communications, Burger King, Domino's Pizza

Complete Set (30 cards): 10.00

- ☐ 1 Checklist
- ☐ 2 Andrew Clark
- ☐ 3 Dwayne Hay
- ☐ 4 Jason Jackman
- ☐ 5 Burger King ad
- ☐ 6 Nick Bootland
- ☐ 7 Andrew Long
- ☐ 8 Todd Norman
- ☐ 9 Michael Pittman
- ☐ 10 Herbert Vasilijevs
- ☐ 11 Jeff Williams
- ☐ 12 Joel Cort
- ☐ 13 Chris Hajt
- ☐ 14 Brian Willsie
- ☐ 15 Brian Wesenberg
- ☐ 16 Mike Lankshear
- ☐ 17 Darryl McArthur
- ☐ 18 Bryan McKinney
- ☐ 19 Regan Stocco
- ☐ 20 Ryan Risidore
- ☐ 21 Mike Vellinga
- ☐ 22 Dan Cloutier (G)
- ☐ 23 Bryan McMullen
- ☐ 24 Brett Thompson
- ☐ 25 Ryan Robichaud
- ☐ 26 Kid's Club
- ☐ 27 Jamie Wright
- ☐ 28 Guelph Police
- ☐ 29 Mike Galati
- ☐ 30 Domino's Pizza

1996 - 97 STORM

Manny Malhotra is the most expensive single at $2-3. Singles start at 50¢.

Card Size: 2 1/2" x 3 1/2"

Sponsors: Burger King, Domino's Pizza

Complete Set (36 cards): 15.00

- ☐ 1 Checklist
- ☐ 2 Brett Thompson
- ☐ 3 David MacDonald
- ☐ 4 John Zubyck
- ☐ 5 Denis Ivanov
- ☐ 6 Joel Cort
- ☐ 7 Chris Hajt
- ☐ 8 Manny Malhotra
- ☐ 9 Mike Dombkiewicz
- ☐ 10 Ryan Robichaud
- ☐ 11 Kent McDonell
- ☐ 12 Joe Gerbe
- ☐ 13 Mike Christian
- ☐ 14 Brian Wesenberg
- ☐ 15 Todd Norman
- ☐ 16 Darryl McArthur
- ☐ 17 Richard Irwin
- ☐ 18 Brian Willsie
- ☐ 19 Mike Vellinga
- ☐ 20 Jason Jackman
- ☐ 21 Chris Madden
- ☐ 22 Dwayne Hay
- ☐ 23 Joey Bartley
- ☐ 24 Mike Lankshear
- ☐ 25 Andrew Long
- ☐ 26 Matt Bell
- ☐ 27 Nick Bootland
- ☐ 28 E.J. McGuire
- ☐ 29 Rick Allain
- ☐ 30 Burger King
- ☐ 31 Kid's Club
- ☐ 32 M.Malhotra/ T.Norman
- ☐ 33 Domino's Pizza
- ☐ 34 Domino's Pizza
- ☐ 35 C.Hajt/ D.Hay
- ☐ 36 Team Photo

HALIFAX MOOSEHEAD

(QMJHL)

1995 - 96 MOOSEHEAD

This was the first year that Halifax produced a team set. As with later series, the team set could be bought at Halifax's home arena, the MetroCentre, or at Moosehead Cold Beer Stores. Jean-Sébastien Giguère is the most expensive single at $2-3. Singles sell at 50¢.

Size: 2 1/2" x 3 1/2"

Sponsors: Sobeys

Complete Set (26 cards): 15.00

- ☐ Elias Abrahamsson #6
- ☐ Frédéric Belanger #22
- ☐ Jamie Brown #7
- ☐ David Carson #20
- ☐ Étienne Drapeau #9
- ☐ Jean-Sébastien Giguère (G) #47
- ☐ Chris Halverson #5
- ☐ Harlin Hayes (G) #31
- ☐ Eric Houde #33
- ☐ Patrick Lafleur #27
- ☐ Mark Lynk #10
- ☐ Nicolas Maheux #19
- ☐ Billy Manley #16
- ☐ Jan Melichercik #18
- ☐ Steve Mongrain #15
- ☐ Danielle Payette #26
- ☐ Chris Peyton #23
- ☐ Derrick Pyke #11
- ☐ Jody Shelley #25
- ☐ Brian Surette #12
- ☐ Joel Theriault #53
- ☐ Didier Tremblay #4
- ☐ Clement Jodoin, Head Coach
- ☐ Shawn MacKenzie, Asst. Coach
- ☐ Chris McQuaid, Athletic Trainer
- ☐ Title Card

1996 - 97 MOOSEHEAD

Jean-Sébastien Giguère is the most expensive single at $2-3. Singles start at 50¢. The first edition features players in their home uniforms, while the second edition features players in their away uniforms.

Card Size: 2 1/2" x 3 1/2"

Sponsors: Sobeys

Series One Set (28 cards): 15.00

- ☐ Elias Abrahamsson #6
- ☐ Frédéric Belanger #22
- ☐ Martin Bilodeau (G) #1
- ☐ Jamie Brown #7
- ☐ Marc Chouinard #55
- ☐ Benoît Dusbalon #19
- ☐ Jean-Sébastien Giguère (G) #47
- ☐ Andrew Gilby #26
- ☐ Clement Jodoin
- ☐ Alex Johnstone #34
- ☐ Eric Laplante #11
- ☐ Jean-Simon Lemay #44
- ☐ Mark Lynk #10
- ☐ Shawn Mackenzie
- ☐ Billy Manley #16
- ☐ Alexandre Mathieu #15
- ☐ Chris McQuaid
- ☐ Todd Row #9
- ☐ Ryan Rowell #23
- ☐ François Sasseville #40
- ☐ Jody Shelley #25
- ☐ Jeffrey Sullivan #27
- ☐ Alex Tanguay #18
- ☐ Didier Tremblay #4
- ☐ Jason Troini #33
- ☐ Clark Udle #19
- ☐ Team Photo
- ☐ Checklist

Series Two Set (28 cards): 15.00

- ☐ Elias Abrahamsson #6
- ☐ Frédéric Bélanger #22
- ☐ Martin Bilodeau (G) #1
- ☐ Jamie Brown #7
- ☐ Marc Chouinard #55
- ☐ Benoît Dusbalon #19
- ☐ Jean-Sébastien Giguère (G) #47
- ☐ Andrew Gilby #26
- ☐ Clement Jodoin
- ☐ Alex Johnstone #34
- ☐ Eric Laplante #11
- ☐ Jean-Simon Lemay #44
- ☐ Mark Lynk #10
- ☐ Shawn Mackenzie
- ☐ Billy Manley #16
- ☐ Alexandre Mathieu #15
- ☐ Chris McQuaid
- ☐ Martin Pouiot
- ☐ Todd Row #9
- ☐ Ryan Rowell #23
- ☐ François Sasseville #40
- ☐ Jody Shelley #25
- ☐ Jeffrey Sullivan #27
- ☐ Alex Tanguay #18
- ☐ Didier Tremblay #4
- ☐ Jason Troini #33
- ☐ J.Shelley/J.S. Giguère (G)
- ☐ Checklist

1997 - 98 MOOSEHEAD

Alex Tanguay is the most expensive single at 75¢-$1.50. Singles sell at 50¢. The first edition features players in their home uniforms while the second edition feature players in their away uniforms.

Size: 2 1/2" x 3 1/2"

Sponsors: Sobeys

Series One Set (28 cards): 10.00

- ☐ Frédéric Belanger #22
- ☐ Martin Bilodeau (G) #1
- ☐ Marc-André Binette #17
- ☐ Alexandre Couture #41
- ☐ Andrew Gilby #2
- ☐ Alex Johnstone #34
- ☐ Eric Laplante #11
- ☐ P.J. Lynch #44
- ☐ Mark Lynk #77
- ☐ Joey MacDonald (G)
- ☐ Ali MacEachern #36
- ☐ Billy Manley #16
- ☐ Alexandre Mathieu #32
- ☐ Steve Mongrain (G) #31
- ☐ Ryan Power #19
- ☐ Brandon Reid #55
- ☐ Todd Row #20
- ☐ Dean Stock #10
- ☐ Jeff Sullivan #27
- ☐ Alex Tanguay #18
- ☐ Didier Tremblay #4
- ☐ Jason Troini #33
- ☐ Dwight Wolfe #23
- ☐ Danny Grant, Coach
- ☐ Shawn MacKenzie, Asst. Coach
- ☐ Chris McQuaid, Athletic Trainer
- ☐ Team Photo
- ☐ Checklist

Series Two Set (28 cards): 10.00

- ☐ Frédéric Belanger #22
- ☐ Martin Bilodeau (G) #1
- ☐ Marc-André Binette #17
- ☐ Alexandre Couture #41
- ☐ Mauro Di Paolo #45
- ☐ Alex Johnstone #34
- ☐ P.J. Lynch #44
- ☐ Joey MacDonald (G) #31
- ☐ Al MacEachern #36
- ☐ Boris Majesky #5
- ☐ Bill Manley #16
- ☐ Alexandre Mathieu #32
- ☐ Ryan Power #19
- ☐ Stephen Quirk #20
- ☐ Brandon Reid #55
- ☐ A.J. Rivers #7
- ☐ Dean Stock #10
- ☐ Jeffrey Sullivan #27
- ☐ Alex Tanguay #18
- ☐ Alex Tanguay (Team Canada)
- ☐ Jason Troini #33
- ☐ Andrew Warr #40
- ☐ Dwight Wolfe #23
- ☐ Danny Grant, Head Coach
- ☐ Shawn MacKenzie, Asst. Coach
- ☐ Chris McQuaid, Athletic Trainer
- ☐ Mascot Hal Moosemaniac
- ☐ Checklist

HAMILTON FINCUPS

(OHA)

1975 - 76 FINCUPS

Dale McCourt is the most expensive single at $4-5. Singles start at $1.00.

Card Size: 2 1/2" x 3 1/2"

Sponsors: none

Complete Set (18 cards): 20.00

- ☐ Jack Anderson
- ☐ Mike Clarke
- ☐ Greg Clause
- ☐ Joe Contini
- ☐ Mike Fedorko
- ☐ Paul Foley
- ☐ Greg Hickey
- ☐ Tony Harvath
- ☐ Mike Keating
- ☐ Archie King
- ☐ Ted Long
- ☐ Dale McCourt
- ☐ Dave Norris
- ☐ Greg Redquest
- ☐ Glenn Richardson
- ☐ Ron Roscoe
- ☐ Ric Seiling
- ☐ Danny Shearer

HULL OLYMPIQUES

(QMJHL)

1987 - 88 OLYMPIQUES

Team President Wayne Gretzky is the most expensive single at $60-70. Singles start at $1.00

Card Size: 2 3/4" x 4"

Sponsors: Police, CJRC 1150

Complete Set (24 cards): 90.00

- ☐ Joe Aloi
- ☐ Joel Bain
- ☐ Christian Breton

- ☐ Benoît Brunet
- ☐ Guy Dupuis
- ☐ Martin Gelinas
- ☐ Jason Glickman (G)
- ☐ Wayne Gretzky, Edm.
- ☐ Denis Heon
- ☐ Herbie Hohenberger
- ☐ Ken MacDermid
- ☐ Craig Martin
- ☐ Mark McLane
- ☐ Stéphane Matteau
- ☐ Kelly Nester
- ☐ Jacques Parent
- ☐ Marc Saumier
- ☐ Claude-Charles Sauriol
- ☐ Joe Suk
- ☐ Alain Vigneault
- ☐ George Wilcox
- ☐ Olympiques card
- ☐ Olympiques card
- ☐ Olympiques card

KAMLOOPS BLAZERS

(WHL)

1984 - 85 BLAZERS

Rob Brown is the most expensive single at $4-5. Singles start at $1.00.

Card Size: 2 3/4" x 4"

Sponsors: Police, NL Radio, Thompson Valley Savings

Complete Set (24 cards): 25.00

- ☐ Will Anderson
- ☐ Brian Benning
- ☐ Brian Bertuzzi
- ☐ Rob Brown
- ☐ Todd Carnelley
- ☐ Dean Clark
- ☐ Rob DiMaio
- ☐ Greg Evtuschevski
- ☐ Mark Ferner
- ☐ Greg Hawgood
- ☐ Ken Hitchcock
- ☐ Mark Kachowski
- ☐ Bob Labrier
- ☐ Pat Mangold
- ☐ Gord Mark
- ☐ Len Mark
- ☐ Rob McKinley (G)
- ☐ Mike Nottingham
- ☐ Neil Pilon
- ☐ Rudy Poeschek
- ☐ Daryl Reaugh (G)
- ☐ Ryan Stewart
- ☐ Mark Thietke
- ☐ Gord Walker

1985 - 86 BLAZERS

Rob Brown is the most expensive single at $3-4. Singles start at $1.00.

Card Size: 2 3/4" x 4"

Sponsor: Police

Complete Set (26 cards): 25.00

- ☐ Robin Bawa
- ☐ Craig Berube
- ☐ Rob Brown
- ☐ Pat Bingham
- ☐ Todd Carnelly
- ☐ Randy Hansch (G)
- ☐ Greg Hawgood
- ☐ Ken Hitchcock
- ☐ Mark Kachowski
- ☐ Troy Kennedy
- ☐ R.T. Labrier
- ☐ Dave Marcinyshyn
- ☐ Len Mark
- ☐ Rob McKinley (G)
- ☐ Ken Morrison
- ☐ Pat Nogier (G)
- ☐ Mike Nottingham
- ☐ Doug Pickell
- ☐ Rudy Poeschek
- ☐ Mike Ragot
- ☐ Don Schmidt
- ☐ Ron Shudra
- ☐ Peter Soberlak
- ☐ Lonnie Spink
- ☐ Chris Tarnowski
- ☐ Greg Wallace

1986 - 87 BLAZERS

Cards were originally issued in panels. Mark Recchi is the most expensive single at $25-30. Singles start at $1.00.

Card Size: 2 1/2" x 4"

Sponsors: Police, NL Radio

Complete Set (24 cards): 45.00

- ☐ Warren Babe
- ☐ Robin Bawa
- ☐ Rob Brown
- ☐ Dean Cook
- ☐ Scott Daniels
- ☐ Mario Desjardins
- ☐ Bill Harrington
- ☐ Greg Hawgood
- ☐ Serge Lajoie
- ☐ Dave Marcinyshyn
- ☐ Len Mark
- ☐ Rob McKinley
- ☐ Casey McMillan
- ☐ Darcy Norton
- ☐ Kelly Para
- ☐ Doug Pickell
- ☐ Rudy Poeschek
- ☐ Mark Recchi
- ☐ Don Schmidt
- ☐ Ron Shudra
- ☐ Chris Tarnowski
- ☐ Steve Wienke
- ☐ Rich Wiest
- ☐ Team Photo

1987 - 88 BLAZERS

Mark Recchi is the most expensive single at $15-20. Singles start at $1.00.

Card Size: 2 1/2" x 3 1/2"

Sponsors: Police, NL Radio

Complete Set (24 cards): 35.00

- ☐ Warren Babe
- ☐ Paul Checknita
- ☐ Dave Chyzowski
- ☐ Dean Cook (G)
- ☐ Greg Davies
- ☐ Kim Deck
- ☐ Todd Decker
- ☐ Bill Harrington
- ☐ Greg Hawgood
- ☐ Phil Huber
- ☐ Steve Kloepzig
- ☐ Willie MacDonald (G)
- ☐ Pat MacLeod
- ☐ Casey McMillan
- ☐ Glenn Mulvenna
- ☐ Mike Needham
- ☐ Darcy Norton
- ☐ Devon Oleniuk
- ☐ Doug Pickell
- ☐ Garth Premak
- ☐ Mark Recchi
- ☐ Don Schmidt
- ☐ Alec Shelfo
- ☐ Team Photo

1988 - 89 BLAZERS

Cards were originally issued in panels. Corey Hirsch is the most expensive single at $4-5. Singles start at 75¢. There are also 12 ad cards that came with the panels.

Card Size: 2 1/2" x 3 1/2"

Sponsors: Police, NL Radio

Complete Set (24 cards): 20.00

- ☐ Cory Anderson
- ☐ Pat Bingham
- ☐ Ed Bertuzzi
- ☐ Zac Boyer
- ☐ Trevor Buchanan
- ☐ Dave Chyzowski
- ☐ Dean Cook (G)
- ☐ Cory Crichton
- ☐ Kim Deck
- ☐ Ryan Harrison
- ☐ Brad Heschuk
- ☐ Corey Hirsch (G)
- ☐ Phil Huber
- ☐ Len Jorgenson
- ☐ Paul Kruse
- ☐ Dave Linford
- ☐ Pat MacLeod
- ☐ Darwin McClelland
- ☐ Cal McGowan
- ☐ Mike Needham
- ☐ Don Schmidt
- ☐ Brian Shantz
- ☐ Darryl Sydor
- ☐ Steve Yule

1989 - 90 BLAZERS

Scott Niedermayer is the most expensive single at $5-6. Singles start at 75¢.

Card Size: 2 1/2" x 3 1/2"

Sponsor: Police

Complete Set (24 cards): 20.00

- ☐ Len Barrie
- ☐ Craig Bonner
- ☐ Jarrett Bousquet
- ☐ Zac Boyer
- ☐ Murray Duval
- ☐ Shea Esselmont
- ☐ Todd Essolmont
- ☐ Todd Harris
- ☐ Corey Hirsch (G)
- ☐ Phil Huber
- ☐ Lance Johnson
- ☐ Paul Kruse
- ☐ Dean Malkoc
- ☐ Dale Mason
- ☐ Cal McGowan
- ☐ Joey Mittelsteadt
- ☐ Mike Needham
- ☐ Scott Niedermayer
- ☐ Brian Shantz
- ☐ Trevor Sim
- ☐ Darryl Sydor
- ☐ Jeff Waatchorn
- ☐ Clayton Young
- ☐ Steve Yule

1993 - 94 BLAZERS

Jarome Iginla is the most expensive single at $4-5. Singles start at 75¢.

Card Size: 2 1/2" x 3 1/2"

Sponsors: Police, NL Radio

Complete Set (24 cards): 20.00

- ☐ Nolan Baumgartner
- ☐ Rod Branch
- ☐ Jarret Deuling
- ☐ Shane Doan
- ☐ Hnat Domenichelli
- ☐ Scott Ferguson
- ☐ Greg Hart
- ☐ Jason Holland
- ☐ Ryan Huska
- ☐ Jarome Iginla
- ☐ Mike Josephson
- ☐ Aaron Keller
- ☐ Mike Krooshoop
- ☐ Scott Loucks
- ☐ Brad Lukowich
- ☐ Bob Maudie
- ☐ Chris Murray
- ☐ Tyson Nash
- ☐ Steve Passmore
- ☐ Rod Stevens
- ☐ Jason Strudwick
- ☐ Darcy Tucker
- ☐ Bob Westerby
- ☐ David Wilkie

KELOWNA WINGS

(WHL)

1983 - 84 WINGS

Brent Gilchrist is the most expensive single at $2-3. Singles start at $1.00.

Photo Size: 8" x 10 3/4"

Sponsor: Esso

Complete Set (23 cards): 25.00

- ☐ Craig Butz
- ☐ Bruno Campese
- ☐ Grant Delcourt
- ☐ R.J. Dundas
- ☐ Rocky Dundas
- ☐ Jeff Fenton
- ☐ Mark Fioretti
- ☐ Brent Gilchrist
- ☐ Mikael Jonsson
- ☐ Cam Lozoruk
- ☐ Dave MacDonald
- ☐ Dave McLay
- ☐ Darwein Moeller
- ☐ Ed Palichuk
- ☐ Jeff Sharples
- ☐ Bob Shaw
- ☐ Shawn Vincent
- ☐ Tod Voshell
- ☐ Darcy Wakaluk
- ☐ Chad Walker
- ☐ Stuart Wenaas
- ☐ Terry Zaporkan
- ☐ Greg Zuk

KINGSTON CANADIANS

(OHL)

1981 - 82 CANADIANS

Kirk Muller is the most expensive single at $15-20. Singles start at $1.00.

Card Size: 2 5/8" x 4"

Sponsors: Police, McDonald's, Independant Insurance Brokers, LaSalle Sports

Complete Set (25 cards): 35.00

- ☐ 1 Canadians Logo
- ☐ 2 Scott MacLellan
- ☐ 3 Dave Courtemanche
- ☐ 4 Mark Reade
- ☐ 5 Shawn Babcock
- ☐ 6 Phil Bourque
- ☐ 7 Ian MacInnis
- ☐ 8 Neail Trineer
- ☐ 9 Syl Grandmaitre
- ☐ 10 Carmine Vani
- ☐ 11 Chuck Brimmer
- ☐ 12 Mike Linseman
- ☐ 13 Steve Seguin
- ☐ 14 Dan Wood
- ☐ 15 Kirk Muller
- ☐ 16 Jim Aldred
- ☐ 17 Rick Wilson
- ☐ 18 Mike Siltala
- ☐ 19 Howie Scruton
- ☐ 20 Mike Stothers
- ☐ 21 Dennis Smith
- ☐ 22 Steve Richey (G)
- ☐ 23 Mike Moffat (G)
- ☐ 24 Jim Morrison
- ☐ 25 Randy Plumb

1982 - 83 CANADIANS

Singles start at 75¢.

Card Size: 2 5/8" x 4"

Imprint: Fourway Graphics

Sponsor: Police, Beatrice, Coke, Empire Life, Independant Insurance Brokers

Complete Set (27 cards): 15.00

- ☐ 1 Jim Morrison
- ☐ 2 Dennis Smith
- ☐ 3 Curtis Collin
- ☐ 4 Joel Brown
- ☐ 5 Ron Handy
- ☐ 6 Carmine Vani
- ☐ 7 Al Andrews (G)
- ☐ 8 Mike Siltala
- ☐ 9 Syl Grandmaitre
- ☐ 10 Steve Seguin
- ☐ 11 Brian Dobbin
- ☐ 12 Mark Reade
- ☐ 13 John Kemp (G)
- ☐ 14 Dan Mahon
- ☐ 15 Keith Knight
- ☐ 16 Ron Sanko
- ☐ 17 John Landry
- ☐ 18 Chris Brant
- ☐ 19 Dave Simurda
- ☐ 20 Mike Lafoy
- ☐ 21 Scott MacLellan
- ☐ 22 Brad Walcot
- ☐ 23 Steve Richey (G)
- ☐ 24 Rod Graham
- ☐ 25 Ben Levesque
- ☐ 26 Checklist/Logo
- ☐ 27 Int. Hall of Fame

1983 - 84 CANADIANS

Singles start at 75¢.
Card Size: 2 5/8" x 3 5/8"
Sponsor: Police, Beatrice, Bennett Foods, Dacon Corp., Swiss Chalet, Coke, Empire Life, Independant Insurance Brokers, Graham Stein Funeral Homes
Complete Set (30 cards): 15.00

- ☐ 1 Checklist
- ☐ 2 Dennis Smith
- ☐ 3 Ben Lévesque
- ☐ 4 Constable Arie Moraal
- ☐ 5 Tom Allen
- ☐ 6 Mike Plesh
- ☐ 7 Roger Belanger
- ☐ 8 Jeff Chychrun
- ☐ 9 Mike King
- ☐ 10 Scott Metcalfe
- ☐ 11 David Lundmark
- ☐ 12 Tim Salmon
- ☐ 13 Ted Linesman
- ☐ 14 Chris Clifford (G)
- ☐ 15 Todd Elik
- ☐ 16 Kevin Conway
- ☐ 17 Barry Burkholder
- ☐ 18 Joel Brown
- ☐ 19 Steve King
- ☐ 20 Craig Kales
- ☐ 21 John Humphries
- ☐ 22 David James
- ☐ 23 Dave Simurda
- ☐ 24 Allen Bishop
- ☐ 25 Jeff Hogg (G)
- ☐ 26 Rick Cornacchia
- ☐ 27 Ken Slater
- ☐ 28 Constable Bill Dextater
- ☐ 29 Checklist/Logo
- ☐ 30 Int. Hall of Fame

1984 - 85 CANADIANS

Singles start at 75¢.
Card Size: 2 5/8" x 3 5/8"
Sponsor: Police, Beatrice, Bennett Foods, Coke, Dacon Corp, Empire Life, Independant Insurance Brokers, Swiss Chalet, Gurnsey Prealty, Pratt Murray Realty
Complete Set (30 cards): 15.00

- ☐ 1 Kington Police logo
- ☐ 2 Rick Cornaccia
- ☐ 3 Constable Arie Moraal
- ☐ 4 Ken Slater
- ☐ 5 Checklist/Logo
- ☐ 6 Scott Metcalfe
- ☐ 7 Chris Clifford (G)
- ☐ 8 Todd Elik
- ☐ 9 Len Spratt (G)
- ☐ 10 Mike Plesh
- ☐ 11 Marc Lyons
- ☐ 12 Barry Burkholder
- ☐ 13 Rick Fera
- ☐ 14 David Hoover
- ☐ 15 Andy Rivers
- ☐ 16 Marc Laforge
- ☐ 17 Peter Viscovich
- ☐ 18 Jeff Chychrun
- ☐ 19 Wayne Erskine
- ☐ 20 Todd Clarke
- ☐ 21 Darren Wright
- ☐ 22 Tony Rocca
- ☐ 23 Brian Verbeek
- ☐ 24 Herb Raglan
- ☐ 25 Daril Holmes
- ☐ 26 Len Coyle
- ☐ 27 Ted Linseman
- ☐ 28 Int. Hall of Fame
- ☐ 29 Troy MacNevin
- ☐ 30 Peter Campbell

1985 - 86 CANADIANS

Singles start at 75¢.
Card Size: 2 5/8" x 3 5/8"
Sponsor: Police, Beatrice, Bennett Foods, Coke, Dacon Corp, Empire Life, K96 Country Radio, Mac's Milk, Swiss Chalet, Gurnsey Realty, Pratt Murray Realty, O'Tooles
Complete Set (30 cards): 15.00

- ☐ 1 Kingston Police
- ☐ 2 Dale Sandles
- ☐ 3 Constable Arie Moraal
- ☐ 4 Fred O'Donnell
- ☐ 5 Checklist/Logo
- ☐ 6 Scott Metcalfe
- ☐ 7 Chris Clifford (G)
- ☐ 8 Steve Seftel
- ☐ 9 Andy Pearson (G)
- ☐ 10 Jeff Cornelius
- ☐ 11 Marc Lyons
- ☐ 12 Barry Burkholder
- ☐ 13 Bryan Fogarty
- ☐ 14 Jeff Sirkka
- ☐ 15 Scott Pearson
- ☐ 16 Marc Laforge
- ☐ 17 Peter Viscovich
- ☐ 18 Jeff Chychrun, Error (Chycren)
- ☐ 19 Wayne Erskine
- ☐ 20 Todd Clarke
- ☐ 21 Darren Wright
- ☐ 22 Mike Maurice
- ☐ 23 Brian Verbeek
- ☐ 24 Mike Fiset
- ☐ 25 Daril Holmes
- ☐ 26 Len Coyle
- ☐ 27 Ted Linseman
- ☐ 28 Int. Hall of Fame
- ☐ 29 Troy MacNevin
- ☐ 30 Peter Campbell

1986 - 87 CANADIANS

Singles start at 50¢.
Card Size: 2 5/8" x 3 5/8"
Sponsor: Police, Bennett Foods, Coke, Dacon Corp, Empire Life, F96 Country Radio, Mac's Milk, McDonald's, Swiss Chalet
Complete Set (30 cards): 12.00

- ☐ 1 Checklist/Logo
- ☐ 2 Fred O'Donnell
- ☐ 3 Constable Arie Moraal
- ☐ 4 Dale Sandles
- ☐ 5 Kingston Police
- ☐ 6 Brian Tessier (G)
- ☐ 7 Franco Giammarco (G)
- ☐ 8 Peter Liptrott
- ☐ 9 Chris Clifford (G)
- ☐ 10 Scott Metcalfe
- ☐ 11 Scott Pearson
- ☐ 12 Bryan Fogarty
- ☐ 13 Daril Holmes
- ☐ 14 Andy Rivers
- ☐ 15 Troy MacNevin
- ☐ 16 Marc Laforge
- ☐ 17 Wayne Erskine
- ☐ 18 Peter Viskovich
- ☐ 19 Mike Maurice
- ☐ 20 Steve Seftel
- ☐ 21 Chad Badaway
- ☐ 22 Marc Lyons
- ☐ 23 Jeff Sirkka
- ☐ 24 Mike Fiset
- ☐ 25 John Battice
- ☐ 26 Len Coyle
- ☐ 27 Sloan Torti
- ☐ 28 Alain Laforge
- ☐ 29 Ted Linseman
- ☐ 30 Peter Campbell

1987 - 88 CANADIANS

Singles start at 50¢.
Card Size: 2 5/8" x 3 5/8"
Sponsor: Police, Beatrice, Bennett Foods, Coke, Dacon Corp, Empire Life, Mac's Milk, Gurnsey Realty, Shopsy's, Pratt Murray Realty, Ambassador Hotel, 96.3 CFMK
Complete Set (30 cards): 12.00

- ☐ 1 Constable Arie Moraal
- ☐ 2 Gord Wood
- ☐ 3 Kingston Police
- ☐ 4 Jacques Tremblay
- ☐ 5 Rhonda Sheridan
- ☐ 6 Jeff Wilson (G)
- ☐ 7 Franco Giammarco (G)
- ☐ 8 Peter Liptrott
- ☐ 9 David Weiss (G)
- ☐ 10 Joel Morin
- ☐ 11 Mark Turner
- ☐ 12 Jeff Sirkka
- ☐ 13 James Henckle
- ☐ 14 Mike Bodnarchuk
- ☐ 15 Mike Cavanaugh
- ☐ 16 Darcy Cahill
- ☐ 17 Kevin Falesy
- ☐ 18 Dean Pella
- ☐ 19 Brad Gratton
- ☐ 20 Steve Seftel
- ☐ 21 Bryan Fogarty
- ☐ 22 Scott Pearson
- ☐ 23 Tyler Pella
- ☐ 24 Mike Fiset
- ☐ 25 John Baddice
- ☐ 26 Len Coyle
- ☐ 27 Geoff Schneider
- ☐ 28 Chris Lukey
- ☐ 29 Trevor Smith
- ☐ 30 Peter Campbell

KITCHENER RANGERS

(OHL)

1982 - 83 RANGERS

Al MacInnis is the most expensive single at $15-18. Singles start at 75¢.
Card Size: 2 3/4" x 3 1/2"
Sponsors: Police, CKKW 1090, Dutch Boy, Schneider's, Cober Printing Ltd.
Complete Set (30 cards): 35.00

- ☐ 1 Waterloo Police
- ☐ 2 Chief Harold Basse
- ☐ 3 Sponsor Logo
- ☐ 4 Joe Crozier
- ☐ 5 Checklist/Logo
- ☐ 6 Kerry Kerch (G)
- ☐ 7 Tom St. James
- ☐ 8 Wendell Young (G)
- ☐ 9 David Shaw
- ☐ 10 Darryl Boudreau (G)
- ☐ 11 David Bruce
- ☐ 12 Wayne Presley
- ☐ 13 Garnet McKechney
- ☐ 14 Kevin Petendra
- ☐ 15 Brian Wilks
- ☐ 16 Jim Quinn
- ☐ 17 Al MacInnis
- ☐ 18 Dave Nicholls
- ☐ 19 Mike Eagles
- ☐ 20 Mike Hough
- ☐ 21 Greg Puhalski
- ☐ 22 Darren Wright
- ☐ 23 Todd Steffan
- ☐ 24 John Tucker
- ☐ 25 Kent Paynter
- ☐ 26 Andy O'Brien
- ☐ 27 Les Bradley
- ☐ 28 Scott Biggs
- ☐ 29 Chris Martin
- ☐ 30 Dave Webster

1983 - 84 RANGERS

Singles start at 75¢.
Card Size: 2 3/4" x 3 1/2"
Sponsors: Police, CKKW 1090, Dutch Boy, Schneider's, Cober Printing Ltd., Maple Leaf
Complete Set (30 cards): 15.00

- ☐ 1 Joe Mantione (G)
- ☐ 2 Jim Quinn
- ☐ 3 Checklist/Logo
- ☐ 4 Rob MacInnis
- ☐ 5 Louie Berardicurti
- ☐ 6 Neil Sandilands
- ☐ 7 Darren Wright
- ☐ 8 Tom Barrett
- ☐ 9 Brian Wilks
- ☐ 10 Garnet McKechney
- ☐ 11 David Bruce
- ☐ 12 Kent Paynter
- ☐ 13 Sponsor Logos
- ☐ 14 Scott Kerr
- ☐ 15 Greg Puhalski
- ☐ 16 Wayne Presley
- ☐ 17 Carmine Vani
- ☐ 18 Shawn Burr
- ☐ 19 Dave Latta
- ☐ 20 John Tucker
- ☐ 21 Mike Stevens
- ☐ 22 Chief Harold Basse
- ☐ 23 Waterloo Police
- ☐ 24 Peter Bakovic
- ☐ 25 Brian Ross
- ☐ 26 Brad Balshin
- ☐ 27 David Shaw
- ☐ 28 Chris Trainer
- ☐ 29 Les Bradley
- ☐ 30 Ray LeBlanc (G)

1984 - 85 RANGERS

Singles start at 75¢.
Card Size: 2 3/4" x 3 1/2"
Sponsors: Police, CKKW 1090, Schneider's, Cober Printing Ltd.
Complete Set (30 cards): 15.00

- ☐ 1 Waterloo Police
- ☐ 2 Chief Harold Basse
- ☐ 3 Garnet McKechney
- ☐ 4 Tom Barrett
- ☐ 5 Checklist/Logo
- ☐ 6 Mike Bishop (G)
- ☐ 7 Craig Wolanin
- ☐ 8 Steve Marcolini
- ☐ 9 Peter Langlois
- ☐ 10 Dave Weiss (G)

- ☐ 11 Ken Alexander
- ☐ 12 Ian Pound
- ☐ 13 Doug Stromback
- ☐ 14 Joel Brown
- ☐ 15 Brian Wilks
- ☐ 16 Robert Rubic
- ☐ 17 Kent Paynter
- ☐ 18 Jon Helsinki
- ☐ 19 Greg Puhalski
- ☐ 20 Wayne Presley
- ☐ 21 Dave McLlwain
- ☐ 22 Shawn Burr
- ☐ 23 Dave Latta
- ☐ 24 John Keller
- ☐ 25 Mike Stevens
- ☐ 26 Sponsor Logos
- ☐ 27 Richard Adolfi
- ☐ 28 Grant Sanders
- ☐ 29 Les Bradley
- ☐ 30 Sponsor Logos

1985 - 86 RANGERS

Singles start at 75¢.
Card Size: 2 3/4" x 3 1/2"
Sponsors: Police, CKKW 1090, Zehrs, Maple Leaf, Cober Printing Ltd.
Complete Set (30 cards): 15.00

- ☐ 1 Waterloo Police
- ☐ 2 Chief Harold Basse
- ☐ 3 Sponsor Logo
- ☐ 4 Tom Barrett
- ☐ 5 Checklist/Logo
- ☐ 6 Dave Weiss (G)
- ☐ 7 Steve Marcolini
- ☐ 8 Kevin Grant
- ☐ 9 Ken Alexander
- ☐ 10 Mike Volpe (G)
- ☐ 11 Ian Pound
- ☐ 12 Brett MacDonald
- ☐ 13 Scott Taylor
- ☐ 14 Greg Hankkio
- ☐ 15 Mike Morrison
- ☐ 16 Mike Wolak
- ☐ 17 Craig Booker
- ☐ 18 Jeff Noble
- ☐ 19 Shawn Tyers
- ☐ 20 Peter Lisy
- ☐ 21 Shawn Burr
- ☐ 22 David Latta
- ☐ 23 Ron Sanko
- ☐ 24 Doug Jones
- ☐ 25 Paul Penelton
- ☐ 26 Blair MacPherson
- ☐ 27 Richard Hawkins
- ☐ 28 Brad Sparkes
- ☐ 29 Ron Goodall
- ☐ 30 Kevin Duguay

1986 - 87 RANGERS

17 JEFF NOBLE

Singles start at 75¢.
Card Size: 2 3/4" x 3 1/2"
Sponsors: Police, CKKW 1090, Zehrs, Schneiders, Cober Printing Ltd.
Complete Set (30 cards): 15.00

- ☐ 1 Waterloo Police
- ☐ 2 Chief Harold Basse
- ☐ 3 Sponsor Logo
- ☐ 4 Tom Barrett
- ☐ 5 Checklist/Logo
- ☐ 6 Dave Weiss (G)
- ☐ 7 Darren Rumble
- ☐ 8 Kevin Garnett
- ☐ 9 Len Fawcett
- ☐ 10 Darren Beals (G)
- ☐ 11 Ed Kister
- ☐ 12 Scott Taylor
- ☐ 13 Darren Moxam
- ☐ 14 Paul Epoch
- ☐ 15 Richard Borgo
- ☐ 16 Allan Lake
- ☐ 17 Jeff Noble
- ☐ 18 Mark Montanari
- ☐ 19 Jim Hutton
- ☐ 20 Kelly Cain
- ☐ 21 Craig Booker
- ☐ 22 David Latta
- ☐ 23 Doug Jones
- ☐ 24 Gary Callahan
- ☐ 25 Bruno Lapensee
- ☐ 26 Scott Montgomery
- ☐ 27 Ron Goodall
- ☐ 28 Discount Card
- ☐ 29 Steve Ewing
- ☐ 30 Joe McDonnell

1987 - 88 RANGERS

24—Darren Rumble—1987-88

Singles start at 75¢.
Card Size: 2 3/4" x 3 1/2"
Imprint: Cober Printing Ltd.
Sponsors: Police, Optimists Club
Complete Set (30 cards): 15.00

- ☐ 1 Waterloo Police
- ☐ 2 Chief Harold Basse
- ☐ 3 Children's Bonus Card
- ☐ 4 Joe McDonnell
- ☐ 5 Checklist/Logo
- ☐ 6 Gus Morschauser (G)
- ☐ 7 Rick Allen
- ☐ 8 Kevin Grant
- ☐ 9 Rob Thiel
- ☐ 10 Darren Beals (G)
- ☐ 11 Cory Keenan
- ☐ 12 Rival Fullum
- ☐ 13 Tony Crisp
- ☐ 14 Tyler Ertel
- ☐ 15 Richard Borgo
- ☐ 16 Steven Rice
- ☐ 17 Rob Sangster
- ☐ 18 Jeff Noble
- ☐ 19 Mark Montanari
- ☐ 20 Jim Mutton
- ☐ 21 Craig Booker
- ☐ 22 Doug Jones
- ☐ 23 Randy Pearce
- ☐ 24 Darren Rumble
- ☐ 25 Joe Ranger
- ☐ 26 Sponsor
- ☐ 27 Ron Goodall
- ☐ 28 Allan Lake
- ☐ 29 Scott Montgomery
- ☐ 30 Sponsor Card

1988 - 89 RANGERS

16 — Steven Rice — 1988-89

Singles start at 50¢.
Card Size: 2 3/4" x 3 1/2"
Imprint: Cober Printing Ltd.
Sponsors: Police, Optimists Club
Complete Set (30 cards): 12.00

- ☐ 1 Waterloo Police
- ☐ 2 Chief Harold Basse
- ☐ 3 Bonus Card
- ☐ 4 Joe McDonnell
- ☐ 5 Checklist/Logo
- ☐ 6 Mike Torchia (G)
- ☐ 7 Rick Allain
- ☐ 8 John Uniac
- ☐ 9 Rob Thiel
- ☐ 10 Gus Morschauser (G)
- ☐ 11 Cory Keenan
- ☐ 12 Rival Fullum
- ☐ 13 Jason Firth
- ☐ 14 Joey St. Aubin
- ☐ 15 Richard Borgo
- ☐ 16 Steven Rice
- ☐ 17 Rob Sangster
- ☐ 18 Gilbert Dionne
- ☐ 19 Mark Montanari
- ☐ 20 Shayne Stevenson
- ☐ 21 Pierre Gagnon
- ☐ 22 Kirk Tomlinson
- ☐ 23 Randy Pearce
- ☐ 24 Brad Barton
- ☐ 25 Chris LiPuma
- ☐ 26 Sponsor Logo
- ☐ 27 Steve Herniman
- ☐ 28 Darren Rumble
- ☐ 29 Rick Chambers
- ☐ 30 Sponsor Logo

1989 - 90 RANGERS

10 — Dave Schill — 1989-90

Singles start at 50¢.
Card Size: 2 3/4" x 3 1/2"
Imprint: Cober Printing Ltd.
Sponsors: Police, Optimists Club
Complete Set (30 cards): 12.00

- ☐ 1 Waterloo Police
- ☐ 2 Chief Harold Basse
- ☐ 3 Children's Bonus Card
- ☐ 4 Joe McDonnell
- ☐ 5 Checklist/Logo
- ☐ 6 Mike Torchia (G)
- ☐ 7 Rick Allain
- ☐ 8 John Uniac
- ☐ 9 Jack Williams
- ☐ 10 Dave Schill (G)
- ☐ 11 John Copley
- ☐ 12 Cory Keenan
- ☐ 13 Rival Fullum
- ☐ 14 Jason Firth
- ☐ 15 Joey St. Aubin
- ☐ 16 Richard Borgo
- ☐ 17 Steven Rice
- ☐ 18 Rob Sangster
- ☐ 19 Gilbert Dionne
- ☐ 20 Jamie Israel
- ☐ 21 Shayne Stevenson
- ☐ 22 Gib Tucker
- ☐ 23 Randy Pearce
- ☐ 24 Brad Barton
- ☐ 25 Chris LiPuma
- ☐ 26 Sponsor Logos
- ☐ 27 Kevin Falesy
- ☐ 28 Steve Smith
- ☐ 29 Rick Chambers
- ☐ 30 Sponsor Logos

1990 - 91 RANGERS

Steve Smith — 1990-91

Singles start at 50¢.
Card Size: 2 3/4" x 3 1/2"
Imprint: Cober Printing Ltd.
Sponsors: Police, Optimists Club
Complete Set (30 cards): 12.00

- ☐ 1 Waterloo Police
- ☐ 2 Chief Harold Basse
- ☐ 3 Joe McDonnell
- ☐ 4 Rick Chambers
- ☐ 5 Checklist
- ☐ 6 Mike Torchia (G)
- ☐ 7 Len DeVuono
- ☐ 8 John Uniac
- ☐ 9 Steve Smith
- ☐ 10 Rob Stopar (G)
- ☐ 11 Tony McCabe
- ☐ 12 Jason Firth
- ☐ 13 Joey St. Aubin
- ☐ 14 Richard Borgo
- ☐ 15 Norm Dezainde
- ☐ 16 Jeff Szeryk
- ☐ 17 Derek Gauthier
- ☐ 18 Jamie Israel
- ☐ 19 Shayne McCosh
- ☐ 20 Gib Tucker
- ☐ 21 Paul McCallion
- ☐ 22 Mike Allen
- ☐ 23 Brad Barton
- ☐ 24 Chris LiPuma
- ☐ 25 Justin Cullen
- ☐ 26 Sponsor Logos
- ☐ 27 Rob Saarinen
- ☐ 28 Jack Williams
- ☐ 29 Steve Rice
- ☐ 30 Sponsor Logos

LAKE SUPERIOR STATE LAKERS

(CCHA)

1991 - 92 LAKERS

Brian Rolston is the most expensive single at $2-3. Singles start at 50¢.
Card Size: 2 1/2" x 3 1/2"
Sponsors: none
Complete Set (33 cards): 15.00

- ☐ Keith Aldridge
- ☐ Dan Angelelli
- ☐ Mark Astley
- ☐ Mike Bachusz
- ☐ Steve Barnes
- ☐ Clayton Beddoes
- ☐ David Gartshore
- ☐ Tim Hanley
- ☐ Matt Hanson
- ☐ John Hendry
- ☐ Dean Hulett
- ☐ Jeff Jackson
- ☐ Blaine Lacher (G)
- ☐ Darrin Madeley (G)
- ☐ Mike Matteucci
- ☐ Scott McCabe
- ☐ Kurt Miller
- ☐ Mike Morin
- ☐ Jay Ness
- ☐ Gino Pulente
- ☐ Brian Rolston
- ☐ Paul Sass
- ☐ Michael Smith
- ☐ Wayne Strachan
- ☐ Sean Tallaire
- ☐ Adam Thompson
- ☐ Jason Trzcinski
- ☐ Rob Valicevic
- ☐ Jason Welch
- ☐ Darren Wetherill
- ☐ Brad Willner
- ☐ Team Photo
- ☐ Team Photo

LETHBRIDGE HURRICANES

(WHL)

1988 - 89 HURRICANES

This set was originally issued in three-card panels. One card from each panel was an ad/coupon card. Singles start at 50¢.
Card Size: 2 1/2" x 3 1/2"
Sponsors: Police, CJOC
Complete Set (24 cards): 10.00

- ☐ Mark Bassen
- ☐ Pete Berthelsen
- ☐ Bryan Bosch
- ☐ Paul Checknita
- ☐ Kelly Ens
- ☐ Jeff Ferguson (G)
- ☐ Scott Fukami
- ☐ Colin Gregor
- ☐ Mark Greig
- ☐ Rob Hale
- ☐ Ted Hutchings
- ☐ Dusty Imoo (G)
- ☐ Ivan Jessey
- ☐ Mark Kuntz
- ☐ Corey Lyons
- ☐ Shane Mazutinec
- ☐ Casey McMillan
- ☐ Pat Pylypuik
- ☐ Brad Rubachuk
- ☐ Jason Ruff
- ☐ Chad Seibel
- ☐ Wes Walz
- ☐ Jim Wheatcroft
- ☐ Team Photo

1989 - 90 HURRICANES

This set was originally issued in three-card panels. One card from each panel was an ad/coupon card. Singles start at 50¢.
Card Size: 2 1/2" x 3 1/2"
Sponsors: Police, CJOC
Complete Set (24 cards): 10.00

- ☐ Doug Barrault
- ☐ Pete Berthelsen
- ☐ Bryan Bosch
- ☐ Kelly Ens
- ☐ Mark Greig
- ☐ Ron Gunville
- ☐ Rob Hale
- ☐ Neil Hawryluk
- ☐ David Holzer
- ☐ Dusty Imoo (G)
- ☐ Darcy Kaminski
- ☐ Bob Loucks
- ☐ Corey Lyons
- ☐ Duane Maruschak
- ☐ Jamie McLennan (G)
- ☐ Shane Peacock
- ☐ Pat Pylypuik
- ☐ Gary Reilly
- ☐ Brad Rubachuk
- ☐ Jason Ruff
- ☐ Kevin St. Jacques
- ☐ Wes Walz
- ☐ Darcy Werenka
- ☐ Brad Zimmer

1993 - 94 HURRICANES

This set was originally issued in three-card panels. One card from each panel was an ad/coupon card. Singles start at 50¢.
Card Size: 2 1/2" x 3 1/2"
Sponsors: Police, CJOC
Complete Set (24 cards): 10.00

- ☐ Rob Daun
- ☐ Derek Diener
- ☐ Kirk DeWalle
- ☐ Scott Giuco
- ☐ David Jesiolowski
- ☐ Todd MacIsaac
- ☐ Stanm Matwijiw
- ☐ Larry McMorran
- ☐ Brad Mehalko
- ☐ Shane Peacock
- ☐ Randy Perry
- ☐ Byron Ritchie
- ☐ Domenic Rittis
- ☐ Bryce Salvador
- ☐ Lee Sorochan
- ☐ Ryan Smith
- ☐ Mark Szoke
- ☐ Scott Townsend
- ☐ David Trofimenkofl
- ☐ Ivan Vologjaninov
- ☐ Jason Widmer
- ☐ Derek Wood
- ☐ Aaron Zarowny
- ☐ Mascot Twister

LONDON KNIGHTS

(OHL)

1985 - 86 KNIGHTS

Brendan Shanahan is the most expensive single at $30-40. Singles start at 75¢.
Card Size: 2 3/4" x 3 1/2"
Sponsors: Police, Kellogg's/Salada
Complete Set (30 cards): 50.00
Album: 5.00

- ☐ 1 Chief LaVerne Shipley
- ☐ 2 Joe Ranger
- ☐ 3 Checklist/Logo
- ☐ 4 Don Boyd
- ☐ 5 Harry E. Sparling
- ☐ 6 Murray Nystrom
- ☐ 7 Bob Halkidis
- ☐ 8 Morgan Watts
- ☐ 9 Brendan Shanahan
- ☐ 10 Brian Dobbin
- ☐ 11 Ed Kister
- ☐ 12 Darin Smith
- ☐ 13 Greg Puhalski
- ☐ 14 Dave Haas
- ☐ 15 Pete McLeod
- ☐ 16 Frank Tremblay
- ☐ 17 Matthew Smyth
- ☐ 18 Glen Leslie
- ☐ 19 Mike Zombo
- ☐ 20 Jamie Groke
- ☐ 21 Brad Schlegel
- ☐ 22 Kelly Cain
- ☐ 23 Tom Allen
- ☐ 24 Rod Gerow
- ☐ 25 Pat Vachon
- ☐ 26 Paul Cook
- ☐ 27 Jeff Reese (G)
- ☐ 28 Fred Kean
- ☐ 29 Scott Cumming (G)
- ☐ 30 John Williams

1986 - 87 KNIGHTS

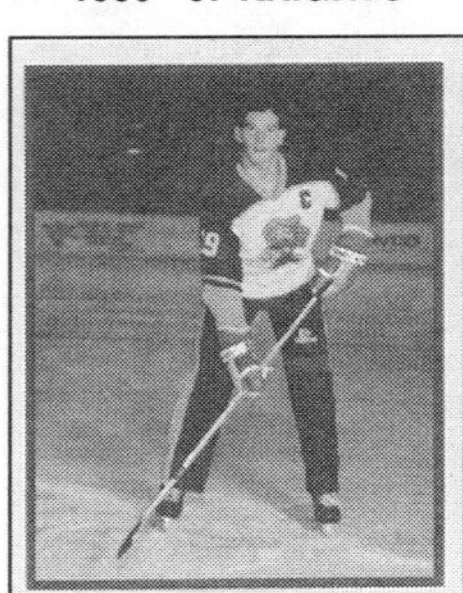

Brendan Shanahan is the most expensive single at $20-30. Singles start at 75¢.
Card Size: 2 3/4" x 3 1/2"
Sponsors: Police, Kellogg's/Salada
Complete Set (30 cards): 40.00
Album: 5.00

- ☐ 1 Chief LaVerne Shipley
- ☐ 2 Mayor Tom Gosnell
- ☐ 3 Checklist/Logo
- ☐ 4 Wayne Maxner
- ☐ 5 Harry E. Sparling
- ☐ 6 Brendan Shanahan
- ☐ 7 Pat Vachon
- ☐ 8 Brad Schlegel
- ☐ 9 Barry Earhart
- ☐ 10 Jean Marc MacKenzie
- ☐ 11 Jason Simon
- ☐ 12 Jim Sprott
- ☐ 13 Bill Long
- ☐ 14 Murray Nystrom
- ☐ 15 Shayne Stevenson
- ☐ 16 Don Martin
- ☐ 17 Ian Pound
- ☐ 18 Peter Lisy
- ☐ 19 Steve Marcolini
- ☐ 20 Craig Majaury
- ☐ 21 Trevor Dam
- ☐ 22 Dave Akey
- ☐ 23 Dennis McEwen
- ☐ 24 Shane Whelan
- ☐ 25 Greg Hankkio
- ☐ 26 Pat Kelly
- ☐ 27 Stephen Titus (G)
- ☐ 28 Fred Kean
- ☐ 29 Chris Somers (G)
- ☐ 30 Gord Clark

MAINE BLACK BEARS

(Hockey East)

1992 - 93 BLACK BEARS

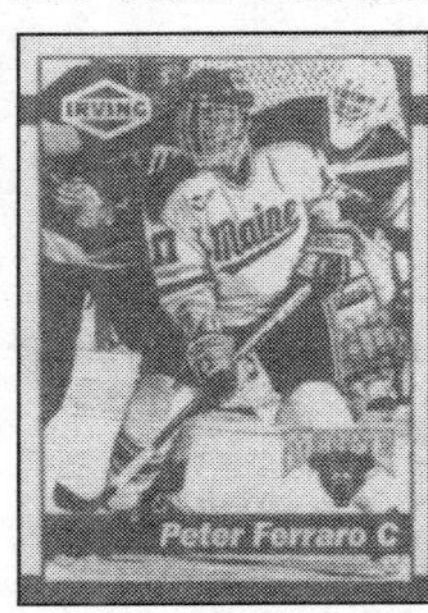

Paul Kariya is the most expensive single at $20-25. Garth Snow has two cards each at $2-3. Singles start at 50¢.
Card Size: 2 1/2" x 3 1/2"
Sponsors: Irving
Series One Set (1-16): 10.00
Series Two Set (17-36): 30.00

- ☐ 1 Black Bears card
- ☐ 2 Mike Dunham (G)
- ☐ 3 Andy Silverman
- ☐ 4 Matt Martin
- ☐ 5 Chris Imes
- ☐ 6 Jason Weinrich
- ☐ 7 Scott Pellerin
- ☐ 8 Dan Murphy
- ☐ 9 Dave LaCouture
- ☐ 10 Patrice Tardif
- ☐ 11 Eric Fenton
- ☐ 12 Jim Montgomery
- ☐ 13 Kent Salfi
- ☐ 14 Jean-Yves Roy
- ☐ 15 Garth Snow (G)
- ☐ 16 Cal Ingram
- ☐ 17 Black Bears card
- ☐ 18 Mike Dunham (G)
- ☐ 19 Chris Imes
- ☐ 20 Paul Kariya
- ☐ 21 Mike Latendresse
- ☐ 22 Dan Murphy
- ☐ 23 Dave MacIsaac
- ☐ 24 Dave LaCouture
- ☐ 25 Chris Ferraro
- ☐ 26 Peter Ferraro
- ☐ 27 Jim Montgomery
- ☐ 28 Brad Purdie
- ☐ 29 Lee Saunders
- ☐ 30 Justin Tomberlin
- ☐ 31 Chuck Texeira
- ☐ 32 Martin Mercier
- ☐ 33 Garth Snow (G)
- ☐ 34 Cal Ingraham
- ☐ 35 Greg Hirsch
- ☐ 36 Jamie Thompson

1993 - 94 BLACK BEARS

Paul Kariya has two cards (#s 41, 60) at $10-12. Kariya also has two multiple single cards (#s 37, 61) at $4-6. Singles start at 50¢.
Card Size: 2 1/2" x 3 1/2"
Sponsors: Irving
Series Three Set (37-61): 35.00

- ☐ 37 P. Kariya/L.Wlasow
- ☐ 38 Andy Silverman
- ☐ 39 Jason Weinrich
- ☐ 40 Jason Mansoff
- ☐ 41 Paul Kariya
- ☐ 42 Mike Latendresse
- ☐ 43 Barry Clukey
- ☐ 44 Wayne Conlan
- ☐ 45 Dave MacIsaac
- ☐ 46 Patrice Tardif
- ☐ 47 Brad Purdie
- ☐ 48 Dan Shermerhorn
- ☐ 49 Lee Saunders
- ☐ 50 Justin Tomberlin
- ☐ 51 Chuck Texeira
- ☐ 52 Tim Lovell
- ☐ 53 Cal Ingraham
- ☐ 54 Leo Wlasow
- ☐ 55 Blair Allison
- ☐ 56 Blair Marsh
- ☐ 57 Marcel Pineau
- ☐ 58 Trevor Roenick
- ☐ 59 Reg Cardinal
- ☐ 60 Paul Kariya
- ☐ 61 J.Montgomery/P.Kariya

MEDICINE HAT TIGERS

(WHL)

1982 - 83 TIGERS

Murray Craven is the most expensive single at $5-6. Singles start at $1.00.
Card Size: 3" x 4"
Sponsors: none
Complete Set (21 cards): 20.00

- ☐ Al Conroy
- ☐ Murray Craven
- ☐ Mark Frank
- ☐ Kevan Guy
- ☐ Jim Hougen
- ☐ Ken Jorgenson
- ☐ Matt Kabayama
- ☐ Brent Kisilivich
- ☐ Mark Lamb
- ☐ Mike Lay
- ☐ Dean McArthur
- ☐ Brent Meckling
- ☐ Shawn Nagurny
- ☐ Kodie Nelson
- ☐ Al Pedersen
- ☐ Todd Pederson
- ☐ Jay Reid
- ☐ Gord Shmyrko
- ☐ Brent Steblyk
- ☐ Rocky Trottier
- ☐ Dan Turner

1983 - 84 TIGERS

Murray Craven is the most expensive single at $4-5. Singles start at $1.00.
Card Size: 2 3/4" x 5"
Sponsors: Police, McDonald's
Complete Set (23 cards): 20.00

- ☐ 1 Murray Craven
- ☐ 2 Shane Churla
- ☐ 3 Don Herczeg
- ☐ 4 Gary Johnson
- ☐ 5 Brent Kisilivich
- ☐ 6 Blair MacDonald
- ☐ 7 Terry Knight
- ☐ 8 Mark Lamb

☐ 9 Al Pedersen
☐ 10 Trevor Semeniuk
☐ 11 Dan Turner
☐ 12 Brent Steblyk
☐ 13 Rocky Trottier
☐ 14 Kevan Guy
☐ 15 Bobby Bassen
☐ 16 Brent Meckling
☐ 17 Matt Kabayama
☐ 18 Gord Hynes
☐ 19 Daryl Henry
☐ 20 Jim Kambeitz
☐ 21 Mike Lay
☐ 22 Gord Shmyrko
☐ 23 Al Conroy

1985 - 86 TIGERS

Mark Fitzpatrick is the most expensive single at $4-5. Singles start at $1.00.
Card Size: 2 1/4" x 4"
Sponsors: Police, McDonald's
Complete Set (24 cards): 20.00

☐ 1 MikeClaringbull
☐ 2 Doug Houda
☐ 3 Mark Kuntz
☐ 4 Guy Phillips
☐ 5 Rob DiMaio
☐ 6 Al Conroy
☐ 7 Craig Berube
☐ 8 Doug Sauter
☐ 9 Dean Chynoweth
☐ 10 Scott McCrady
☐ 11 Neil Brady
☐ 12 Dale Kushner
☐ 13 Jeff Wenaas
☐ 14 Wayne Hynes
☐ 15 Troy Gamble
☐ 16 Bryan Maxwell
☐ 17 Gord Hynes
☐ 18 Wayne McBean
☐ 19 Mark Pederson
☐ 20 Darren Cota
☐ 21 Randy Siska
☐ 22 Dave Mackey
☐ 23 Mark Fitzpatrick (G)
☐ 24 Doug Ball

MICHIGAN STATE SPARTANS
(CCHA)

1993 - 94 SPARTANS

Bryan Smolinski is the most expensive single at $4-5. Anson Carter sells at $2-3. Singles start at 50¢.
Card Size: 2 1/2" x 3 1/2"
Sponsors: none
Complete Set (32 cards): 20.00

☐ Matt Abers
☐ Michael Burkett
☐ Mike Buzak
☐ Anson Carter
☐ Brian Clifford
☐ Brian Crane
☐ Steve Ferranti
☐ Ryan Fleming
☐ Steve Guolla
☐ Kelly Harper
☐ Eric Kruse
☐ Ron Mason
☐ Mike Mattis
☐ Rem Murray
☐ Steve Norton
☐ Nicolas Perreault
☐ Tom Ross
☐ Chris Slater
☐ Chris Smith
☐ Bryan Smolinski
☐ Chris Sullivan
☐ Steve Suk
☐ Bart Turner
☐ Tony Tuzzolino
☐ Bart Vanstaalduinen
☐ Mike Ware
☐ John Weidenbach
☐ John Wiegand
☐ Scott Worden
☐ Mascot Sparty
☐ Spartans Arena
☐ Spartans Logo

MICHIGAN TECH HUSKIES
(WCHA)

1990 - 91 HUSKIES

Singles start at 50¢.
Card Size: 2 1/2" x 3 1/2"
Sponsor: The Daily Mining Gazette
Complete Set (31 cards): 12.00

☐ Jim Bonner
☐ Newell Brown
☐ Dwight DeGiacomo
☐ Rod Ewacha
☐ Peter Grant
☐ Tim Hartnett
☐ Mike Hauswirth
☐ Kelly Hurd
☐ Kelly Hurd
☐ Randy Lewis
☐ Jay Luknowsky
☐ Darcy Martini
☐ Reid MacDonald
☐ Don Osborne
☐ Greg Parnell
☐ Davis Payne
☐ Kent Plaquin
☐ Damian Rhodes (G)
☐ Geoff Sarjeant (G)
☐ Jamie Steer
☐ Rob Tustian
☐ Tim Watters
☐ John Young
☐ Layne Lebel/Jeff Hill
☐ Ken Martel/Mark Leach
☐ H.McEwen/J.Storm/K.Manninen
☐ K.Perreault/D.Brkic
☐ Scott Vetteraino/Jamie Ram
☐ John Young/Kelly Hurd
☐ Huskies Photo
☐ Huskies Photo

1991 - 92 HUSKIES

Singles start at 50¢.
Card Size: 2 1/2" x 3 1/2"
Sponsors: none
Complete Set (36 cards): 15.00

☐ Jim Bonner
☐ Darren Brkic
☐ Rod Ewacha
☐ Tim Hartnett
☐ Mike Hauswirth
☐ Jeff Hill
☐ Layne Lebel
☐ Randy Lewis
☐ AS: Randy Lewis
☐ John MacInnes
☐ Darcy Martini
☐ AS: Darcy Martini
☐ Reid MacDonald
☐ Hugh McEwen
☐ Bob Olson
☐ Don Osborne
☐ Greg Parnell
☐ Davis Payne
☐ Kirby Perreault
☐ Ken Plaquin
☐ Jamie Ram (G)
☐ Geoff Sarjeant (G)
☐ AS: Geoff Sarjeant (G)
☐ Jamie Steer
☐ AS: Jamie Steer
☐ Jim Sotrm
☐ Scott Vettraino
☐ John Young
☐ Justin Peca/L.Gavey/R.Stevens B.Peterson/T.Seale
☐ D.Martini/D.Payne/G.Sarjeant K.Plaquin/J.Storm/J.Ram J.Steer/J.Bonner
☐ Team Photo
☐ Huskies players
☐ Huskies players
☐ Huskies players
☐ Huskies players
☐ Huskies players

MINNESOTA GOLDEN GOPHERS
(WCHA)

1991 - 92 GOLDEN GOPHERS

Trent Klatt is the most expensive single at $1.50-2. Singles start at 50¢.
Card Size: 2 1/2" x 3 1/2"
Sponsor: MCI
Complete Set (26 cards): 15.00

☐ Scott Bell
☐ Tony Bianchi
☐ John Brill
☐ Jeff Callinan (G)
☐ Joe Dziedzic
☐ Sean Fabian
☐ Jed Fiebelkorn
☐ Nick Gerebi
☐ Darby Hendrickson
☐ Craig Johnson
☐ Trent Klatt
☐ Cory Laylin
☐ Steve Magnusson
☐ Chris McAlpine
☐ Justin McHugh
☐ Eric Means
☐ Mike Muller
☐ Tom Newman (G)
☐ Jeff Nielsen
☐ John O'Connell
☐ Larry Olimb
☐ Travis Richards
☐ Brandon Steege
☐ Jeff Stolp
☐ Todd Westlund
☐ Doug Zmolek

1992 - 93 GOLDEN GOPHERS

Singles start at 50¢.
Card Size: 2 1/2" x 3 1/2"
Sponsors: none
Complete Set (25 cards): 10.00

☐ Scott Bell
☐ Tony Bianchi
☐ John Brill
☐ Jeff Callinan (G)
☐ Joe Dziedzic
☐ Jed Fiebelkorn
☐ Darby Hendrickson
☐ Craig Johnson
☐ Steve Magnusson
☐ Chris McAlpine
☐ Justin McHugh
☐ Eric Means
☐ Jeff Moen (G)
☐ Tom Newman (G)
☐ Jeff Nielsen
☐ Travis Richards
☐ Brandon Steege
☐ Todd Westlund
☐ Doug Woog
☐ Jesse Bertogliat/Brian Bonin
☐ Bobby Dustin/Dave Larson
☐ Matt Stelljes/Ryan Alstead
☐ Dan Trebil/Greg Zwakman
☐ Charlie Wasley/Mike McAlpine
☐ Dan Woog/Jim Hillman

1993 - 94 GOLDEN GOPHERS

Singles start at 50¢.
Card Size: 2 1/2" x 3 1/2"
Sponsors: none
Complete Set (30 cards): 12.00

☐ Brett Abrahamson
☐ Jesse Bertogliat
☐ Tony Bianchi
☐ Brian Bonin
☐ Andy Brink
☐ Jeff Callinan (G)
☐ Nick Checco
☐ Bobby Dustin
☐ Joe Dziedzic
☐ Jed Fiebelkorn
☐ Brent Godbout
☐ Dan Hendrickson
☐ Jim Hillman
☐ John Hillman
☐ Brian LaFleur
☐ Dave Larson
☐ Steve Magnusson
☐ Chris McAlpine
☐ Mike McAlpiune
☐ Justin McHugh
☐ Eric Means
☐ Jeff Moen (G)
☐ Jeff Nielsen
☐ Brandon Steege
☐ Dan Trebil
☐ Charlie Wasley
☐ Dan Woog
☐ Doug Woog
☐ Greg Zwakman
☐ Golden Gophers card

1994 - 95 GOLDEN GOPHERS

The Broten brothers card is the most expensive single at $1.50-2. Singles start at 50¢.
Card Size: 2 1/2" x 3 1/2"
Sponsors: none
Complete Set (30 cards): 12.00

☐ Will Anderson
☐ Scott Bell
☐ Jesse Bertogliat
☐ Brian Bonin
☐ Andy Brink
☐ Jeff Callinan (G)
☐ Nick Checco
☐ Mike Crowley
☐ Steve DeBus
☐ Bobby Dustin
☐ Jed Fiebelkorn
☐ Brent Godbout
☐ Jason Godbout
☐ Casey Hankinson
☐ Dan Hendrickson
☐ Ryan Kraft
☐ Brian LaFleur
☐ Dave Larson
☐ Justin McHugh
☐ Jeff Moen (G)
☐ Jay Moser
☐ Lou Nanne
☐ Joe Pakratz
☐ Jason Seils
☐ Brandon Steege
☐ Dan Trebil
☐ Charlie Wasley
☐ Dan Woog
☐ Doug Woog
☐ Greg Zwakman
☐ A.Broten/N.Broten/P.Broten

MINN.-DULUTH BULLDOGS
(WCHA)

1985 - 86 BULLDOGS

Brett Hull is the most expensive single at $20-25. Singles start at 50¢.
Card Size: 2 1/2" x 3 1/5"
Sponsor: Tim & Larry's Sportscards
Complete Set (36 cards): 35.00

☐ 1 Skeeter Moore
☐ 2 Terry Shold
☐ 3 Mike DeAngelis
☐ 4 Rob Pallin
☐ 5 Norm Maciver
☐ 6 Wayne Smith
☐ 7 Dave Cowan
☐ 8 Darin Illikainen
☐ 9 Rick Hayko (G)
☐ 10 Guy Gosselin
☐ 11 Paul Roff
☐ 12 Jim Toninato
☐ 13 Tom Hanson
☐ 14 Mike Cortes (G)
☐ 15 Matt Christensen
☐ 16 Bruce Fishback
☐ 17 Mark Odnokon
☐ 18 Brian Johnson
☐ 19 Bob Alexander
☐ 20 Tom Lorentz
☐ 21 Roman Sindelar
☐ 22 Jim Spregner
☐ 23 Dan Tousigant
☐ 24 Sean Toomey
☐ 25 Brian Durand
☐ 26 John Hyduke (G)
☐ 27 Brian Nelson
☐ 28 Brett Hull
☐ 29 John DeLisle
☐ 30 Pat Janostin
☐ 31 Ben Duffy
☐ 32 Sean Krakiwsky
☐ 33 Mike Sertich
☐ 34 Jim Knapp/G.Kulyk/R.Menz/ T.McDonald/M.Valesano/ D.Hoganson/B.Feissner
☐ 35 Cheerleaders
☐ 36 Mascot Maroon Loon

1993 - 94 BULLDOGS

Singles start at 50¢.
Card Size: 2 1/2" x 3 1/5"
Sponsors: none
Complete Set (30 cards): 12.00

☐ Rod Aldoff
☐ Niklas Axelson
☐ David Buck
☐ Jermoe Butler
☐ Brian Caruso
☐ Marc Christian
☐ Joe Ciccarello
☐ Brad Federenko
☐ Rusty Fitzgerald
☐ Jason Garatti
☐ Greg Hanson
☐ Don Jablonic
☐ Kraig Karakas
☐ Brett Larson
☐ Taras Lendzyk
☐ Derek Locker
☐ Chris Marinucci
☐ Rod Miller
☐ Rick Mrozik
☐ Aaron Novak
☐ Corey Osmak
☐ Sergei Petrov
☐ Jeff Romfo
☐ Mike Sertich
☐ Chris Sittlow
☐ Joe Tamminen
☐ M.Christian/C.Culic
☐ Kyle Erickson/A.Roy
☐ T.Mickolajak/C.Snell
☐ Bulldogs card

MONTRÉAL JUNIORS

(QMJHL)

1979 - 80 JUNIORS BLACK & WHITE

Photos are in black and white. Denis Savard is the most expensive single at $20-25. Mike Krushelnyski sells at $3-4. Singles start at 75¢.
Card Size: 3 3/4" x 5 5/8"
Sponsor: Paul Sauvé Studios
Complete Set (30 cards): 40.00

☐ Jeff Barratt
☐ André Bégin
☐ Denis Champagne
☐ Denis Cyr
☐ Ghyslain Cyr
☐ Roland Diotte
☐ Pierre Dubois
☐ Sylvaine Gagné
☐ Guy Jacob
☐ Mike Krushelnyski
☐ Ron Lapointe
☐ Richard Lavallée
☐ Daniel Laxton
☐ François Laxton
☐ François Lecompte
☐ Eikke Leime
☐ Pierre Martin
☐ Bill Mulcahy
☐ Gaetano Orlando
☐ Patrice Pare
☐ Mario Patry
☐ Fabian Pavlin
☐ Roger Poitras
☐ Constant Priondolo
☐ Denis Savard
☐ Eric Taylor
☐ Denis Tremblay
☐ J. Jacques Vézina
☐ Taras Zytysky

1979 - 80 JUNIORS COLOUR

Photos are in colour. Denis Savard is the most expensive single at $20-25. Mike Krushelnyski sells at $3-4. Singles start at 75¢.
Card Size: 3 3/4" x 5 5/8"
Sponsor: Paul Sauvé Studios
Complete Set (25 cards): 35.00

☐ Jeff Barratt
☐ André Bégin
☐ Alain Bouchard
☐ Denis Champagne
☐ Denis Cyr
☐ Roland Diotte
☐ Pierre Dubois
☐ Sylvain Gagné
☐ Guy Jacob
☐ Mike Klassen
☐ Mike Krushelnyski
☐ Richard Lavallée
☐ François Lecompte
☐ Eikke Leime
☐ Pierre Martin
☐ Eric Morin
☐ Bill Mulcahy
☐ Gaetano Orlando
☐ Patrice Pare
☐ Constant Priondolo
☐ Denis Savard
☐ Jacques St. Jean
☐ J. Jacques Vézina
☐ Taras Zytysky

NANAIMO CLIPPERS

(BCJHL)

1991 - 92 CLIPPERS

Singles start at 50¢.
Card Size: 3 3/8" x 4 7/8"
Sponsor: DEC Productions
Complete Set (22 cards): 10.00

☐ Glenn Calder
☐ Wade Dayley
☐ Jason Disiewich
☐ Andy Faulkener
☐ Darren Holme
☐ Casey Hungle
☐ Jim Ingram
☐ Chris Jones
☐ Ryan Keller
☐ Jade Kersey
☐ Scott Kowalski
☐ Sean Krause
☐ Jim Lessard
☐ Ryan Loxam
☐ Mickey McGuire
☐ Dan Murphy (G)
☐ Jason Northard
☐ Trevor Pest
☐ Brian Schiebel (G)
☐ Sjon Wynia
☐ Shawn York
☐ Geordie Young

NIAGARA FALLS THUNDER

(OHL)

1988 - 89 THUNDER

Keith Primeau is the most expensive single at $8-10. Singles start at 75¢.
Card Size: 2 5/8" x 4 1/8"
Sponsors: Police, CJRN 710
Complete Set (25 cards): 25.00

☐ 1 Thunder Logo
☐ 2 Brad May
☐ 3 Paul Wolanski
☐ 4 Keith Primeau
☐ 5 Mark Lawrence
☐ 6 Mike Rosati
☐ 7 Dennis Vial
☐ 8 Shawn McCosh
☐ 9 Jason Soules
☐ 10 Rob Fournier
☐ 11 Scott Pearson
☐ 12 Jamie Leach
☐ 13 Colin Millar
☐ 14 Bryan Fogarty
☐ 15 Keith Osborne
☐ 16 Stan Drulia
☐ 17 Paul Laus
☐ 18 Adrian Vanderslot
☐ 19 Greg Allen
☐ 20 Don Pancoe
☐ 21 Alain LaForge
☐ 22 Bill LaForge
☐ 23 Steve Locke
☐ 24 Benny Rogano
☐ 25 Heavy Evason

1989 - 90 THUNDER

BRAD MAY

Keith Primeau is the most expensive single at $6-8. Singles start at 75¢.
Card Size: 2 5/8" x 4 1/8"
Sponsors: Arby's, Pizza Pizza
Complete Set (25 cards): 20.00

☐ Greg Allen
☐ Roch Belley (G)
☐ David Benn
☐ Andy Bezeau
☐ George Burnett
☐ Rodd Coopman
☐ Randy Hall
☐ John Johnson
☐ Paul Laus
☐ Mark Lawrence
☐ Brad May
☐ Don McConnell
☐ Brian Mueggler
☐ Don Pancoe
☐ Keith Primeau
☐ Geoff Rawson
☐ Ken Ruddick
☐ Greg Suchan
☐ Steve Udvari (G)
☐ Jeff Walker
☐ Jason Winch
☐ Paul Wolanski
☐ P.Bruneau/D.Scott
☐ Thunder Logo
☐ Checklist

NORTH BAY CENTENNIALS

(OHL)

1982 - 83 CENTENNIALS

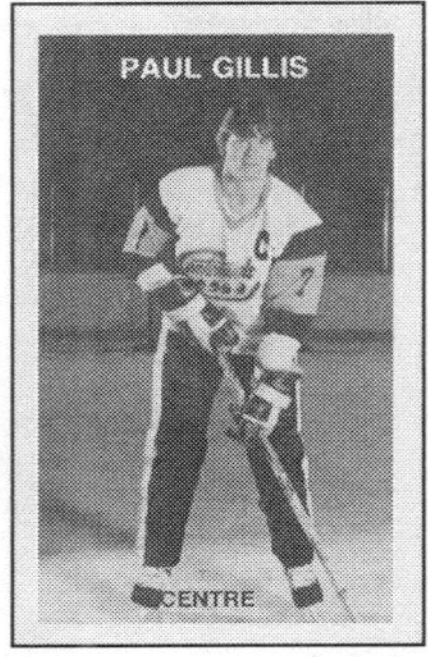

Andrew McBain is the most expensive single at $2-3. Singles start at $1.00.
Card Size: 2 1/2" x 3 3/8"
Sponsors: Aunt May's City Bakery, CFCH-600
Complete Set (24 cards): 20.00

☐ Allen Bishop
☐ John Capel
☐ Rob Degagne
☐ Phil Drouillard
☐ Jeff Eatough
☐ Tony Gillard
☐ Paul Gillis
☐ Pete Handley
☐ Mark Hatcher
☐ Tim Helmer
☐ Craig Kales
☐ Bob Laforest
☐ Mark Laforest (G)
☐ Bill Maguire
☐ Andrew McBain
☐ Ron Meighan
☐ Rick Morocco
☐ Alain Raymond
☐ Joe Reekie
☐ Joel Smith (G)
☐ Bert Templeton
☐ Kevin Vescio
☐ Peter Woodgate
☐ Don Young

1983 - 84 CENTENNIALS

Kevin Hatcher is the most expensive single at $5-6. Singles start at $1.00.
Card Size: 2 1/2" x 3 3/8"
Sponsors: Aunt May's City Bakery, CFCG-600
Complete Set (25 cards): 25.00

☐ Peter Abric
☐ Richard Benoit
☐ Scott Birnie
☐ John Capel
☐ Curtis Collin
☐ Ron Degagne
☐ Kevin Hatcher
☐ Mark Hatcher
☐ Tim Helmer
☐ Jim Hunter
☐ Kevin Kerr
☐ Nick Kypreos
☐ Mike Larouche
☐ Greg Larsen
☐ Mark Lavarre
☐ Brett MacDonald
☐ Wayne Macphee
☐ Peter McGrath
☐ Rob Nichols
☐ Ron Sanko
☐ Bert Templeton
☐ Kevin Vescio
☐ Mike Webber
☐ Peter Woodgate
☐ Sponsor Logos

OSHAWA GENERALS

(OHL)

1980 - 81 GENERALS

RICK LANZ - EX-GENERAL
VANCOUVER CANUCKS

Bobby Orr is the most expensive single at $90-100. Dave Andreychuk sells at $20-25. Singles start at $1.50.
Card Size: 2 5/8" x 4 1/8"
Sponsors: Police, McDonald's, CKAR 1350
Complete Set (25 cards): 135.00

☐ 1 Generals Logo
☐ 2 Ray Flaherty
☐ 3 Craig Kitchener
☐ 4 Dan Revell
☐ 5 Bob Kucheran
☐ 6 Pat Poulin
☐ 7 Dave Andreychuk
☐ 8 Barry Tabobondung
☐ 9 Steve Konroyd
☐ 10 Paul Edwards
☐ 11 Dale DeGray
☐ 12 Joe Cirella
☐ 13 Norm Schmidt
☐ 14 Markus Lehto
☐ 15 Mitch Lamoureux
☐ 16 Tony Tanti
☐ 17 Bill Laforge
☐ 18 Greg Gravel
☐ 19 Mike Lekum
☐ 20 Chris Smith (G)
☐ 21 Peter Sidorkiewicz (G)
☐ 22 Greg Stefan (G)
☐ 23 Tom McCarthy
☐ 24 Rick Lanz
☐ 25 Bobby Orr

1981 - 82 GENERALS

Dave Andreychuk is the most expensive single at $15-20. John MacLean sells at $10-15. Singles start at $1.50.
Card Size: 2 5/8" x 4 1/8"
Sponsors: Police, McDonald's, CKAR 1350
Complete Set (25 cards): 55.00

☐ 1 Generals Logo
☐ 2 Chris Smith (G)
☐ 3 Peter Sidorkiewicz (G)
☐ 4 Ali Butorac
☐ 5 Dan Revell
☐ 6 Mitch Lamoureux
☐ 7 Norm Schmidt
☐ 8 Paul Edwards
☐ 9 Dan Nicholson
☐ 10 John Hutchings
☐ 11 Dave Gans
☐ 12 Dave Andreychuk
☐ 13 Mike Stern
☐ 14 Dale DeGray
☐ 15 Mike Lekun
☐ 16 Greg Gravel
☐ 17 Dave MacLean
☐ 18 Tony Tanti
☐ 19 John MacLean
☐ 20 Jim Uens
☐ 21 Guy Jacob
☐ 22 Jeff Steffan
☐ 23 Paul Theriault
☐ 24 Sherry Bassinb
☐ 25 Durham Police

1982 - 83 GENERALS

John MacLean is the most expensive single at $8-10. Singles start at $1.00.
Card Size: 2 5/8" x 4 1/8"
Sponsors: Police, McDonald's, CKAR 1350
Complete Set (25 cards): 30.00

☐ 1 Generals Logo
☐ 2 Jeff Hogg (G)
☐ 3 Peter Sidorkiewicz (G)
☐ 4 Dale DeGray
☐ 5 Joe Cirella
☐ 6 Todd Smith
☐ 7 Scott Brydges
☐ 8 Jeff Steffan
☐ 9 Don Biggs
☐ 10 Todd Hooey
☐ 11 Tony Tanti
☐ 12 Danny Gratton
☐ 13 Steve King
☐ 14 Dan Defazio
☐ 15 John MacLean
☐ 16 Tim Burgess
☐ 17 Mike Stern
☐ 18 Dan Nicholson
☐ 19 David Gans
☐ 20 John Hutchings
☐ 21 Norm Schmidt
☐ 22 Todd Charlesworth
☐ 23 Paul Theriault
☐ 24 Sherry Bassin
☐ 25 Durham Police

1983 - 84 GENERALS

Kirk McLean is the most expensive single at $15-20. Singles start at $1.00.
Card Size: 2 5/8" x 4 1/8"
Sponsors: Police, McDonald's, CKAR 1350
Complete Set (30 cards): 35.00

☐ 1 Peter Sidorkiewicz (G)
☐ 2 Kirk McLean (G)
☐ 3 Todd Charlesworth
☐ 4 Ian Ferguson
☐ 5 John Hutchings
☐ 6 Generals Logo
☐ 7 Mark Haarmann
☐ 8 Joel Curtis
☐ 9 Dan Gratton
☐ 10 Steve Hedington
☐ 11 Scott Brydges
☐ 12 CKAR Radio
☐ 13 Brad Walcot
☐ 14 Paul Theriault
☐ 15 Jon Jenkins
☐ 16 Sherry Bassin
☐ 17 Craig Morrison
☐ 18 Sponsor Logo
☐ 19 Bruce Melanson
☐ 20 Mike Stern
☐ 21 Gary McColgan
☐ 22 Lee Giffin
☐ 23 Brent Maki
☐ 24 Ronald McDonald
☐ 25 Jeff Steffan
☐ 26 John Stevens
☐ 27 David Gans
☐ 28 Don Biggs
☐ 29 Chris Crandall
☐ 30 Durham Police

1989 - 90 GENERALS

Eric Lindros is the most expensive single at $40-50. Singles start at 75¢.
Card Size: 2 5/8" x 4 1/8"
Sponsor: Police
Complete Set (35 cards): 60.00

☐ 1 Cory Banika
☐ 2 David Craievich
☐ 3 Scott Hollis
☐ 4 Mike Decoff
☐ 5 Joe Busillo
☐ 6 Matt Hoffman
☐ 7 Craig Donaldson
☐ 8 Jason Denomme
☐ 9 Brian Grieve
☐ 10 Wade Simpson
☐ 11 Dale Craigwell
☐ 12 Mike Lenarduzzi
☐ 13 Rick Cornaccia
☐ 14 Dan Edwards
☐ 15 Kevin Butt (G)
☐ 16 Oshawa Generals
☐ 17 Clair Cornish
☐ 18 Jarrod Skalde
☐ 19 Mark Deazeley
☐ 20 Jean-Paul Davis
☐ 21 Todd Coopman
☐ 22 Trevor McIvor
☐ 23 Mike Craig
☐ 24 Paul O'Hagan
☐ 25 Iain Fraser
☐ 26 Sponsor Logo
☐ 27 Sponsor Logo
☐ 28 Sponsor Logo
☐ 29 Durham Police
☐ 30 Generals Logo
☐ 31 Eric Lindros
☐ 32 Bill Armstrong
☐ 33 Chris Vanclief
☐ 34 Scott Luik
☐ 35 Fred Brathwaite (G)

1990 - 91 GENERALS

Eric Lindros is the most expensive single at $35-40. Singles start at 75¢.
Card Size: 2 5/8" x 3 3/4"
Sponsor: Police
Complete Set (30 cards): 50.00

☐ 1 Sponsor Logo
☐ 2 Mike Côté
☐ 3 Fred Brathwaite (G)
☐ 4 Scott Luik
☐ 5 Sponsor Logo
☐ 6 Mike Fountain (G)
☐ 7 Rick Cornacchia
☐ 8 David Edwards
☐ 9 Tony Sweet
☐ 10 Jan Benda
☐ 11 David Dorosh
☐ 12 Craig Lutes
☐ 13 Eric Lindros
☐ 14 David Craievich
☐ 15 Wade Simpson
☐ 16 Dale Craigwell
☐ 17 Generals Logo
☐ 18 Matt Hoffman
☐ 19 Rob Pearson
☐ 20 Paul O'Hagan
☐ 21 Brent Grieve
☐ 22 Mark Deazeley
☐ 23 Clair Cornish
☐ 24 B.J. MacPherson
☐ 25 Jason Weaver
☐ 26 Markus Brunner
☐ 27 Trevor Burgess
☐ 28 Jean-Paul Davis
☐ 29 Durham Police
☐ 30 Scott Hollis

1991 - 92 GENERALS DOMINO'S PIZZA

Eric Lindros is the most expensive single at $12-15. Jason Arnott sells at $6-8. Singles start at 50¢.
Card Size: 2 1/2" x 3 1/2"
Sponsors: Domino's Pizza, Coke
Complete Set (31 cards): 30.00

☐ 1 Mike Fountain (G)
☐ 2 Brian Grieve
☐ 3 Trevor Burgess
☐ 4 Wade Simpson
☐ 5 Ken Sheppard
☐ 6 Stéphane Yelle
☐ 7 Matt Hoffman
☐ 8 Neil Iserhoff
☐ 9 Rob Leask
☐ 10 Kevin Spero
☐ 11 Scott Hollis
☐ 12 Sean Brown
☐ 13 Todd Bradley
☐ 14 Darryl LaFrance
☐ 15 Markus Brunner
☐ 16 B.J. MacPherson
☐ 17 Jason Campeau
☐ 18 Jason Weaver
☐ 19 Jan Benda
☐ 20 Jason Arnott
☐ 21 Eric Lindros
☐ 22 Wayne Daniels
☐ 23 Joe Cook
☐ 24 Coke Sponsor
☐ 25 Domino's Pizza
☐ 26 Mark Deazeley
☐ 27 Jean-Paul Davis
☐ 28 Brian Grieve
☐ 29 Team Photo
☐ 30 I.Young/L.Marson/Cornacchia
☐ 31 Prosport's Action

1991 - 92 GENERALS

This set was originally issued as a 26-card sheet. Eric Lindros is the most expensive single at $10-12. Jason Arnott sells at $5-6. Singles start at 50¢.
Card Size: 2 1/2" x 3 1/2"
Sponsors: none
Complete Set (26 cards): 20.00

☐ David Anderson
☐ Jason Arnott
☐ Jan Benda
☐ Todd Bradley
☐ Fred Brathwaite (G)
☐ Markus Brunner
☐ Trevor Burgess
☐ Jason Campeau
☐ Joe Cook
☐ Mike Côté
☐ Jean-Paul Davis
☐ Mark Deazeley
☐ Mike Fountain (G)
☐ Brian Grieve
☐ Matt Hoffman
☐ Scott Hollis
☐ Neil Iserhoff
☐ Darryl LaFrance
☐ Eric Lindros
☐ Craig Lutes
☐ B.J. MacPherson
☐ Wade Simpson
☐ Kevin Spero
☐ Troy Sweet
☐ Jason Weaver
☐ Stéphane Yelle

1992 - 93 GENERALS

This set was originally issued as a 26-card sheet. Jason Arnott is the most expensive single at $4-5. Singles start at 50¢.
Card Size: 2 1/2" x 3 1/2"
Sponsors: none
Complete Set (26 cards): 15.00

☐ Aaron Albright
☐ Jason Arnott
☐ Todd Bradley
☐ Mark Brooks
☐ Sean Brown
☐ Trevor Burgess
☐ Jason Campeau
☐ Joe Cook
☐ Serge Dunphy
☐ Joel Gagnon
☐ Steve Haight
☐ Chris Hall
☐ Scott Hollis
☐ Neil Iserhoff
☐ Billy-Jay Johnston
☐ Jason Julian
☐ Brian Kent
☐ Jamie Kress
☐ Darryl Lafrance
☐ B.J. MacPherson
☐ Jason McQuat
☐ Rob McQuat
☐ Wade Simpson
☐ Stéphane Soullière
☐ Kevin Spero
☐ Stéphane Yelle

OTTAWA 67'S

(OHL)

1981 - 82 67'S

Brian Kilrea is the most expensive single at $3-4. Singles start at $2.
Card Size: 5 1/2" x 8 1/2"
Sponsors: none
Complete Set (25 cards): 50.00

☐ James Allison
☐ John Boland
☐ Randy Boyd
☐ Adam Creighton
☐ Bill Dowd
☐ Dwayne Davison
☐ Alan Hepple
☐ Mike James
☐ Brian Kilrea
☐ Moe Lemay
☐ Banny Longe
☐ Paul Louttit
☐ Don MacLaren
☐ John Ollson
☐ Brian Patafie
☐ Mark Paterson
☐ Phil Patterson
☐ Larry Power
☐ Jim Ralph (G)
☐ Darcy Roy
☐ Brad Shaw
☐ Brian Small
☐ Doug Stewart
☐ Jeff Vaive
☐ Fraser Wood

1982 - 83 67'S

Darren Pang and Brian Kilrea are the most expensive singles at $3-4. Singles start at $1.00.

Card Size: 2 5/8" x 4 1/8"
Sponsors: M.O.M. Printing, Coke, Channel 12
Complete Set (25 cards): 30.00

- ☐ Bruce Cassidy
- ☐ Greg Coram (G)
- ☐ Adam Creighton
- ☐ Bill Dowd
- ☐ Gord Hamilton
- ☐ Scott Hammond
- ☐ Alan Hepple
- ☐ Alan Hepple
- ☐ Jim Jackson
- ☐ Mike James
- ☐ Brian Kilrea
- ☐ Paul Louttit
- ☐ Brian McKinnon
- ☐ Don MacLaren
- ☐ John Ollson
- ☐ Darren Pang (G)
- ☐ Mark Paterson
- ☐ Phil Patterson
- ☐ Larry Power
- ☐ Gary Roberts
- ☐ Brian Rome
- ☐ Darcy Roy
- ☐ Brad Shaw
- ☐ Doug Stewart
- ☐ Jeff Vaive

1983 - 84 67'S

Gary Roberts is the most expensive single at $10-15. Singles start at $1.00.

Card Size: 2 5/8" x 4 1/8"
Sponsors: M.O.M. Printing, Coke, Channel 12
Complete Set (27 cards): 35.00

- ☐ Richard Adolfi
- ☐ Bill Bennett
- ☐ Bruce Cassidy
- ☐ Todd Clarke
- ☐ Greg Coram (G)
- ☐ Adam Creighton
- ☐ Bob Giffin
- ☐ Gord Hamilton
- ☐ Gord Hamilton Jr
- ☐ Scott Hammond
- ☐ John Hanna
- ☐ Tim Helmer
- ☐ Steve Hrynewich
- ☐ Jim Jackson
- ☐ Mike James
- ☐ Brian Kilrea
- ☐ Larry MacAndrew
- ☐ Brian McKinnon
- ☐ Don McLaren
- ☐ Ron Myllari
- ☐ Darren Pang (G)
- ☐ Mark Paterson
- ☐ Phil Patterson
- ☐ Gary Roberts
- ☐ Darcy Roy
- ☐ Brad Shaw
- ☐ Steve Simoni

1984 - 85 67'S

Gary Roberts is the most expensive single at $8-10. Singles start at $1.00.

Card Size: 2 5/8" x 4 1/8"
Sponsors: FOCUS Photographic Services, Coke
Complete Set (28 cards): 30.00

- ☐ Tom Allen
- ☐ Graydon Almstedt
- ☐ Bill Bennett
- ☐ Bruce Cassidy
- ☐ Greg Coram (G)
- ☐ Bob Ellett
- ☐ Tony Geesink
- ☐ Bob Giffin
- ☐ John Hanna
- ☐ Tim Helmer
- ☐ Andy Helmuth
- ☐ Steve Hrynewich
- ☐ Rob Hudson
- ☐ Jim Jackson
- ☐ Steve Kayser
- ☐ Bill Kuchma
- ☐ Mike Larouche
- ☐ Tom Lawson
- ☐ Rick Lessard
- ☐ Gary Roberts
- ☐ Jerry Scott
- ☐ John Sheppard
- ☐ Steve Simoni
- ☐ Greg Sliz
- ☐ Gord Thomas
- ☐ Chris Vickers
- ☐ Bert Weir
- ☐ Dennis Wigle

1992 - 93 67'S

This set was originally issued as a sheet. Michael Peca is the most expensive single at $3-4. Singles start at 50¢.

Card Size: 2 1/2" x 3 1/2"
Sponsor: Ottawa Citizen
Complete Set (24 cards): 12.00

- ☐ Ken Belanger
- ☐ Curt Bowen
- ☐ Rich Bronilla
- ☐ Mathew Burnett
- ☐ Shawn Caplice
- ☐ Mike Carr
- ☐ Chris Coveny
- ☐ Howard Darwin
- ☐ Shean Donovan
- ☐ Mark Edmundson
- ☐ Billy Hall
- ☐ Mike Johnson
- ☐ Brian Kilrea
- ☐ Grayson Lafoley
- ☐ Grant Marshall
- ☐ Cory Murphy
- ☐ Michael Peca
- ☐ Greg Ryan
- ☐ Jeff Salajko (G)
- ☐ Gerry Skrypec
- ☐ Sean Spencer
- ☐ Steve Washburn
- ☐ Mark Yakabuski
- ☐ 67's card

OWEN SOUND PLATERS

(OHL)

1993 - 94 PLATERS

Jamie Storr has three singles each selling at $2-3. Singles start at 50¢.

Card Size: 2 1/2" x 3 1/2"
Sponsors: The Eastwood Network, Carrick, The Sport Stop, Domino's Pizza
Complete Set (36 cards): 15.00

- ☐ Craig Binns
- ☐ Jim Brown
- ☐ Andrew Brunette
- ☐ Luigi Calce
- ☐ Jason Campbell
- ☐ Paddy Flynn
- ☐ Kirk Furey
- ☐ Jerry Harrigan
- ☐ Joe Harris
- ☐ Rod Hinks
- ☐ Marian Kacir
- ☐ Shane Kenny
- ☐ Jeff Kostuch
- ☐ Dave Lemay
- ☐ Jason MacDonald
- ☐ Rick Mancini
- ☐ Kirk Maltby
- ☐ Brian Medeiros
- ☐ Mike Morrone
- ☐ Ryan Mougenel
- ☐ Scott Penton
- ☐ Wayne Primeau
- ☐ Jeremy Rebek
- ☐ Rob Schweyer
- ☐ Willie Skilliter
- ☐ Jamie Storr (G)
- ☐ Jamie Storr (G) (Gold)
- ☐ Jamie Storr (Mask)
- ☐ Scott Walker
- ☐ Kevin Weekes (G)
- ☐ Kevin Weekes (Mask)
- ☐ Shayne Wright
- ☐ R.Hinks/J.MacDonald K.Weekes/M.Kacir
- ☐ Jamie Storr/K.Primeau
- ☐ Domino's Ad
- ☐ Eastwood Ad

PETERBOROUGH PETES

(OHL)

1988 - 89 PETES COKE

We have little information on this set. Other singles exist.

Sponsor: Coke

- ☐ Tie Domi

1991 - 92 PETES

Chris Pronger is the most expensive single at $3-4. Singles start at 75¢.

Card Size: 2 1/2" x 3 3/4"
Imprint: C.P. Graphics
Sponsors: Police, Quaker, Kiwanis International
Complete Set (30 cards): 20.00

- ☐ 1 Jason Dawe
- ☐ 2 Chris Pronger
- ☐ 3 Scott Turner
- ☐ 4 Chad Grills
- ☐ 5 Brent Tully
- ☐ 6 Mike Harding
- ☐ 7 Chris Longo
- ☐ 8 Mascot Slapshot
- ☐ 9 Doug Searle
- ☐ 10 Mike Tomlinson
- ☐ 11 Bryan Gendron
- ☐ 12 Andrew Verner (G)
- ☐ 13 Ryan Black
- ☐ 14 Don O'Neill
- ☐ 15 Jeff Twohey
- ☐ 16 Dale McTavish
- ☐ 17 Jeff Walker
- ☐ 18 Matt St. Germain
- ☐ 19 Dave Roche
- ☐ 20 Colin Wilson
- ☐ 21 Jassen Cullimore Err. (Jason)
- ☐ 22 Chad Lang
- ☐ 23 Dick Todd
- ☐ 24 Geordie Kinnear
- ☐ 25 Shawn Heins
- ☐ 26 Jay Johnson
- ☐ 27 Kelly Vipond
- ☐ Kiwanis Sponsor
- ☐ Quaker Sponsor
- ☐ Peterborough Police

PORTLAND WINTER HAWKS

(WHL)

1986 - 87 WINTER HAWKS

Glen Wesley is the most expensive single at $4-5. Singles start at 75¢.

Card Size: 2 1/2" x 3 1/2"
Sponsor: AM/PM Mini Market
Complete Set (24 cards): 20.00

- ☐ Dave Archibald
- ☐ Bruce Basken
- ☐ Thomas Bjuhr
- ☐ Shawn Clouston
- ☐ Jeff Finley
- ☐ Bob Foglietta
- ☐ Brian Gerrits
- ☐ Darryl Gilmour (G)
- ☐ Dennis Holland
- ☐ Steve Kloepzig
- ☐ Jim Latos
- ☐ Dave McLay
- ☐ Scott Melnyk
- ☐ Troy Mick
- ☐ Roy Mitchell
- ☐ Jamie Nicolls
- ☐ Trevor Pohl
- ☐ Troy Pohl
- ☐ Glen Seymour (G)
- ☐ Jeff Sharples
- ☐ Jay Stark
- ☐ Jim Swan
- ☐ Glen Wesley
- ☐ Dan Woodley

1988 - 89 WINTER HAWKS

Byron Dafoe is the most expensive single at $5-6. Singles start at 75¢.

Card Size: 2 1/2" x 3 1/2"
Sponsors: Fred Meyer, Pepsi
Complete Set (21 cards): 15.00

- ☐ Wayne Anchikoski
- ☐ Eric Badzgon (G)
- ☐ Chad Biafore
- ☐ James Black
- ☐ Terry Black
- ☐ Shaun Clouston
- ☐ Byron Dafoe (G)
- ☐ Brent Fleetwood
- ☐ Rob Flintoft
- ☐ Bryan Gourdie
- ☐ Mark Greyeyes
- ☐ Dennis Holland
- ☐ Kevin Jorgenson
- ☐ Greg Leahy
- ☐ Troy Mick
- ☐ Roy Mitchell
- ☐ Joey Mittelsteadt
- ☐ Mike Moore
- ☐ Scott Mydan
- ☐ Calvin Thudiun
- ☐ Sponsor Pepsi

1989 - 90 WINTER HAWKS

Byron Dafoe is the most expensive single at $3-5. Singles start at 75¢.

Card Size: 2 1/2" x 3 1/2"
Sponsors: Fred Meyer, Pepsi
Complete Set (21 cards): 15.00

- ☐ James Black
- ☐ Vince Cocciolo
- ☐ Byron Dafoe (G)
- ☐ Cam Danyluk

- ☐ Kim Deck
- ☐ Dean Dorchak
- ☐ Brent Fleetwood
- ☐ Rick Fry
- ☐ Bryan Gourlie
- ☐ Brad Harrison
- ☐ Juson Innes
- ☐ Dean Intwert (G)
- ☐ Kevin Jorgenson
- ☐ Todd Kinniburgh
- ☐ Greg Leahy
- ☐ Jamie Linden
- ☐ Scott Mydan
- ☐ Mike Ruark
- ☐ Jeff Sebastian
- ☐ Brandon Smith
- ☐ Steve Young

1993 - 94 WINTER HAWKS

Adam Deadmarsh is the most expensive single at $4-5. Singles start at 50¢.
Card Size: 2 1/2" x 3 1/2"
Sponsors: Fred Meyer, Pepsi
Complete Set (24 cards): 15.00

- ☐ Mike Arbulic
- ☐ Lonny Bohonos
- ☐ Shannon Briske
- ☐ Dave Cammock
- ☐ Shawn Collins
- ☐ Matt Davidson
- ☐ Adam Deadmarsh
- ☐ Jake Deadmarsh
- ☐ Brett Fizzell
- ☐ Colin Foley
- ☐ Brad Isbister
- ☐ Scott Langkow (G)
- ☐ Mike Little
- ☐ Dmitri Markovsky
- ☐ Jason McBain
- ☐ Scott Nichol
- ☐ Brent Peterson
- ☐ Nolan Pratt
- ☐ Scott Rideout (G)
- ☐ Layne Roland
- ☐ Dave Scratchard
- ☐ Brandon Smith
- ☐ Brad Swanson
- ☐ Brad Symes
- ☐ Jason Wiemer
- ☐ Mike Williamson
- ☐ Hawks Action
- ☐ Hawks Action
- ☐ Hawks Action
- ☐ Hawks Action

PRINCE ALBERT RAIDERS

(WHL)

1984 - 85 RAIDERS

Photos are in black and white. Ken Baumgartner is the most expensive single at $10-12. Singles start at $1.00.
Sticker Size: 2" x 1 3/4"
Sponsors: Police, Burger King
Complete Set (20 stickers): 20.00

- ☐ Ken Baumgartner
- ☐ Brad Bennett
- ☐ Dean Braham
- ☐ Rod Dallman
- ☐ Neil Davey
- ☐ Pat Elynuik
- ☐ Collin Feser
- ☐ Dave Goertz
- ☐ Steve Gotaas
- ☐ Tony Grenier
- ☐ Roydon Gunn
- ☐ Doug Hobson
- ☐ Dan Hodgson
- ☐ Curtis Hunt
- ☐ Kim Issel
- ☐ Ward Komonosky
- ☐ David Manson
- ☐ Dale McFee
- ☐ Ken Morrison
- ☐ Dave Pasin
- ☐ Don Schmidt
- ☐ Emanuel Viveiros

1990 - 91 RAIDERS

Singles start at 50¢.
Card Size: 2 1/2" x 3 1/2"
Sponsor: High Noon Optimist Club
Complete Set (22 cards): 10.00

- ☐ Scott Allison
- ☐ Laurie Billeck
- ☐ Jeff Gorman
- ☐ Donevan Hextall
- ☐ Troy Hjertaas
- ☐ Don Kesa
- ☐ Jason Kwiatkowski
- ☐ Travis Laycock
- ☐ Lee J. Leslie
- ☐ Jamie Linden
- ☐ Dean McAmmond
- ☐ Dave Nelson
- ☐ Troy Neumeier
- ☐ Pat Odnokon
- ☐ Brian Pellerin
- ☐ Darren Perkins
- ☐ Curt Regnier
- ☐ Chad Seibel
- ☐ Mark Stowe
- ☐ Darren Van Impe
- ☐ Shane Zulyniak
- ☐ Raiders card

1991 - 92 RAIDERS

Singles start at 50¢.
Card Size: 2 1/2" x 3 1/2"
Sponsor: High Noon Optimist Club
Complete Set (23 cards): 10.00

- ☐ Mike Fedorko
- ☐ Jeff Gorman
- ☐ Merv Haney
- ☐ Donevan Hextall
- ☐ Troy Hjertaas
- ☐ Dan Kesa
- ☐ Jason Klassen
- ☐ Jason Kwiatkowski
- ☐ Jeff Lank
- ☐ Travis Laycock
- ☐ Lee J. Leslie
- ☐ Stan Matwijiw
- ☐ Dean McAmmond
- ☐ David Nelson
- ☐ Mark Odnokon
- ☐ Darren Perkins
- ☐ Ryan Pisiak
- ☐ Nick Polychronopoulos
- ☐ Curt Regnier
- ☐ Jason Renard
- ☐ Barkley Swenson
- ☐ Darren Van Impe
- ☐ Shane Zulyniak

1993 - 94 RAIDERS

Singles start at 50¢.
Card Size: 2 1/2" x 3 1/2"
Sponsor: High Noon Optimist Club
Complete Set (21 cards): 10.00

- ☐ Ryan Bast
- ☐ Rodney Bowers
- ☐ Van Burgess
- ☐ Brad Church
- ☐ Joaquin Gage (G)
- ☐ Jeff Gorman
- ☐ Merv Haney
- ☐ Greg Harvey
- ☐ Paul Healey
- ☐ Shane Hnidy
- ☐ Russell Hogue
- ☐ Jason Issel
- ☐ Steve Kelly
- ☐ Jeff Lank
- ☐ Mike McGhan
- ☐ Denis Pederson
- ☐ Mitch Shawara
- ☐ Shayne Toporowski
- ☐ Dean Whitney
- ☐ Darren Wright
- ☐ Shane Zulyniak

1995 - 96 RAIDERS

Shane Willis is the most expensive single at $1.50-2. Singles start at 50¢.
Card Size: 2 1/2" x 3 1/2"
Sponsor: High Noon Optimist Club
Complete Set (22 cards): 10.00

- ☐ Rod Branch
- ☐ Curtis Brown
- ☐ Brad Church
- ☐ Kris Fizzell
- ☐ Dallas Flaman
- ☐ Don Halverson
- ☐ Shane Hnidy
- ☐ Russell Hogue
- ☐ Jason Issel
- ☐ Garnet Jacobson
- ☐ Kevin Kellett
- ☐ Steve Kelly
- ☐ Dylan Kemp
- ☐ Michael McGhan
- ☐ Marian Menhart
- ☐ Chris Phillips
- ☐ Blaine Russell
- ☐ Mitch Shawara
- ☐ Dave Van Drunen
- ☐ Roman Vopat
- ☐ Shane Willis
- ☐ Darren Wright

QUÉBEC RAMPARTS

(QMJHL)

1980 - 81 RAMPARTS

Singles start at $1.00.
Card Size: 2" x 3"
Sponsors: None
Complete Set (22 cards): 20.00

- ☐ Marc Bertrand
- ☐ Jacques Chouinard
- ☐ Roger Côté
- ☐ Gaston Drapeau
- ☐ Claude Drouin
- ☐ Gaetan Duchesne
- ☐ Scott Fraser
- ☐ Jean-Paul Larivière
- ☐ André Larocque
- ☐ Roberto Lavoie
- ☐ Stéphane Lessard
- ☐ Marc Lemay
- ☐ Paul Lévesque
- ☐ Richard Linteau
- ☐ Patrice Massé
- ☐ Jean-Marc Lanthier
- ☐ David Pretty
- ☐ Guy Riel
- ☐ Daniel Rioux
- ☐ Roberto Romano (G)
- ☐ Michel Therrien
- ☐ Gilles Tremblay

RAYSIDE-BALFOUR JR. CANADIANS

1989 - 90 JUNIOR CANADIANS

Singles start at 50¢.
Card Size: 2 3/8" x 3 3/8"
Sponsor: Loeb IGA
Complete Set (20 cards): 10.00

- ☐ Dave Barrett
- ☐ Dan Baston
- ☐ Rick Chartrand
- ☐ Simon Chartrand
- ☐ Ron Clark
- ☐ Brian Dickison
- ☐ Trevor Duncan
- ☐ Don Gauthier
- ☐ Shawn Hawkins
- ☐ Roy Hildebrandt
- ☐ Al Laginski
- ☐ Eric Lanteigne
- ☐ Mike Leblanc
- ☐ Kevin MacDonald
- ☐ Mike Mooney
- ☐ Rick Potvin
- ☐ Rick Poulin
- ☐ Steve Prior
- ☐ Scott Sutton
- ☐ Team Photo

1990 - 91 JUNIOR CANADIANS

Troy Mallette is the most expensive single at $1.00. Singles start at 50¢.
Card Size: 2 3/8" x 3 3/8"
Sponsor: Belanger Construction Ltd.
Complete Set (23 cards): 10.00

- ☐ Dan Baston
- ☐ Jon Boeve (G)
- ☐ Jordan Boyle
- ☐ Serge Coulombe
- ☐ Mike Dore
- ☐ Denis Gosselin
- ☐ Mike Gratton
- ☐ Jason Hall
- ☐ Grant Healey
- ☐ Marc Lafrenière
- ☐ Alain Leclair
- ☐ Mike Longo
- ☐ Matthew Mooney
- ☐ Virgil Nose
- ☐ Trevor Oystrick (G)
- ☐ Steve Proceviat
- ☐ Chris Puskas
- ☐ Yvon Quenneville
- ☐ Michael Sullivan
- ☐ Trevor Tremblay
- ☐ Sean Van Amburg
- ☐ Troy Mallette
- ☐ Canadians card

1991 - 92 JUNIOR CANADIANS

Singles start at 50¢.
Card Size: 2 3/8" x 3 3/8"
Imprint: Acme Printers
Sponsor: K.L.S. Erectors Ltd.
Complete Set (23 cards): 10.00

- ☐ Dan Baston
- ☐ Don Cucksey
- ☐ Dean Cull
- ☐ Mike Dore
- ☐ Denis Gosselin
- ☐ Jason Hall (G)
- ☐ Grant Healey
- ☐ Marc Lafrenière
- ☐ Mike Longo
- ☐ Scott Maclellan
- ☐ Matt Mooney
- ☐ Rob Moxness (G)
- ☐ Virgil Nose
- ☐ Trent Oystrick
- ☐ Jon Stewart
- ☐ Jon Stos
- ☐ Dave Sutton
- ☐ Scott Sutton
- ☐ Trevor Tremblay
- ☐ Jaak Valiots
- ☐ Sean Van Amburg
- ☐ Jason Young, Stickboy
- ☐ Canadians card

RED DEER REBELS

(WHL)

1993 - 94 REBELS

Singles start at 50¢.
Card Size: 2 1/2" x 3 1/2"
Sponsors: none
Complete Set (30 cards): 12.00

- ☐ Peter Anholt
- ☐ Byron Briske
- ☐ Curtis Cardinal
- ☐ Jason Clague
- ☐ Dale Donaldson
- ☐ Dave Greenway
- ☐ Scott Grimwood
- ☐ Sean Halifax
- ☐ Chris Kibermanis

☐ Pete LeBoutilier
☐ Pete LeBoutilier (Action)
☐ Terry Lindgren
☐ Chris Maillet
☐ Eddie Marchant
☐ Mike McBain
☐ Mike Moller
☐ Andy Nowicki
☐ Berkley Pennock
☐ Tyler Quiring
☐ Craig Reichert
☐ Ken Richardson
☐ Sean Selmser
☐ Vaclav Slansky
☐ Mark Toljanich
☐ Darren Van Impe
☐ Pete Vandermeer
☐ Chris Wickenheiser
☐ Brad Zimmer
☐ Jonathan Zukiwsky
☐ Rebels Arena

1995 - 96 REBELS

Singles start at 50¢.
Card Size: 2 1/2" x 3 1/2"
Sponsors: none
Complete Set (24 cards): 10.00

☐ Aaron Asham
☐ Bryan Boorman
☐ Aleksei Boudaev
☐ Mike Broda
☐ Mike Brown
☐ Jay Henderson
☐ David Hruska
☐ Chris Kibermanis
☐ Brad Leeb
☐ Terry Lindgren
☐ Mike McBain
☐ Brent McDonald
☐ Ken MacKay
☐ Harlan Pratt
☐ Greg Schmidt
☐ Pete Vendermeer
☐ Jesse Wallin
☐ Lance Ward
☐ Mike Whitney (G)
☐ Chris Wickenheiser
☐ B.J. Young
☐ Jonathan Zukiwsky
☐ Team Photo

REGINA PATS

(WHL)

1981 - 82 PATS

Garth Butcher is the most expensive single at $4-5. Gary Leeman sells at $3-4. Singles start at 75¢.
Card Size: 2 5/8" x 4 1/8"
Sponsors: Police, CKRM 80, Safeway
Complete Set (25 cards): 15.00

☐ 1 Pats Logo
☐ 2 Garth Butcher
☐ 3 Lyndon Byers
☐ 4 Jock Callander
☐ 5 Marc Centrone
☐ 6 Dave Goertz
☐ 7 Evans Dobni
☐ 8 Dale Derkatch
☐ 9 Jeff Crawford
☐ 10 Jim Clarke
☐ 11 Jason Meyer
☐ 12 Gary Leeman
☐ 13 Bruce Holloway
☐ 14 Ken Heppner
☐ 15 Taylor Hall
☐ 16 Wally Schrieber
☐ 17 Kevin Pylypow
☐ 18 Ray Plamondon
☐ 19 Brent Pascal
☐ 20 Dave Michayluk
☐ 21 Barry Trotz
☐ 22 Al Tuer
☐ 23 Tony Vogel
☐ 24 Marty Wood
☐ 25 Regina Police Logo

1982 - 83 PATS

Gary Leeman and Stu Grimson are the most expensive singles at $2-3. Singles start at 75¢.
Card Size: 2 5/8" x 4 1/8"
Sponsors: Police, CKRM 80, Safeway, Cornwall Centre, Seven Oaks Motor Inn
Complete Set (25 cards): 15.00

☐ 1 Regina Police
☐ 2 Todd Lumbard (G)
☐ 3 Jamie Reeve (G)
☐ 4 Dave Goertz
☐ 5 John Miner
☐ 6 Doug Trapp
☐ 7 R.J. Dundas
☐ 8 Stu Grimson
☐ 9 Al Tuer
☐ 10 Rick Herbert
☐ 11 Tony Vogel
☐ 12 John Bekkers
☐ 13 Dale Derkatch
☐ 14 Gary Leeman
☐ 15 Nevin Markwart
☐ 16 Kurt Wickenheiser
☐ 17 Jeff Frank
☐ 18 Marc Centrone
☐ 19 Taylor Hall
☐ 20 Lyndon Byers
☐ 21 Jason Meyer
☐ 22 Jeff Crawford
☐ 23 Don Boyd
☐ 24 Barry Trapp
☐ 25 Mascot K-9 Blue

1983 - 84 PATS

Gary Leeman is the most expensive single at $2-3. Singles start at 75¢.
Card Size: 2 5/8" x 4 1/8"
Sponsors: Police, CKRM 980, Safeway, Cornwall Centre, Seven Oaks Motor Inn, Royal Studios
Complete Set (25 cards): 15.00

☐ 1 Regina Pats Logo
☐ 2 Todd Lumbard (G)
☐ 3 Jamie Reeve (G)
☐ 4 Dave Goertz
☐ 5 John Miner
☐ 6 Doug Trapp
☐ 7 R.J. Dundas
☐ 8 Stu Grimson
☐ 9 Al Tuer
☐ 10 Rick Herbert
☐ 11 Tony Vogel
☐ 12 John Bekkers
☐ 13 Dale Derkatch
☐ 14 Gary Leeman
☐ 15 Nevin Markwart
☐ 16 Kurt Wickenheiser
☐ 17 Jeff Frank
☐ 18 Marc Centrone
☐ 19 Taylor Hall
☐ 20 Lyndon Byers
☐ 21 Jayson Meyer
☐ 22 Jeff Crawford
☐ 23 Don Boyd
☐ 24 Barry Trapp
☐ 25 Mascot K-9 Big Blue

1986 - 87 PATS

Mark Janssens is the most expensive single at $1.00. Singles start at 50¢.
Card Size: 2 1/2" x 3 1/2"
Sponsors: Royal Studios, Forbes-Anderson Press
Complete Set (30 cards): 12.00

☐ Troy Bakogeorge
☐ Grant Chorney
☐ Gary Dickie
☐ Milan Dragicevic
☐ Mike Dyck
☐ Craig Endean
☐ Mike Gibson
☐ Erin Ginnell
☐ Brad Hornung
☐ Mark Janssens
☐ Trent Kachur
☐ Craig Kalawsky
☐ Dan Logan
☐ Jim Mathieson
☐ Darin McInnes
☐ Darrin McKechnie
☐ Rob McKinley (G)
☐ Brad Miller
☐ Stacy Nickel
☐ Cregg Nicol
☐ Len Nielsen
☐ Darren Parsons
☐ Doug Sauter
☐ Ray Savard
☐ Dennis Sobchuk
☐ Chris Tarnowski
☐ Mike Van Slooten
☐ Brian Wilkie
☐ Rod Williams
☐ Mascot K-9 Big Blue

1987 - 88 PATS

Mike Sillinger is the most expensive single at $1.00. Singles start at 50¢.
Card Size: 2 1/2" x 3 1/2"
Imprint: Forbes-Anderson Press ltd.
Sponsors: Royal Studios
Complete Set (28 cards): 12.00

☐ Kevin Clemens
☐ Gary Dickie
☐ Milan Dragicevic
☐ Mike Dyck
☐ Craig Endean
☐ Kevin Gallant
☐ Jamie Heward
☐ Rod Houk (G)
☐ Mark Janssens
☐ Trent Kachur
☐ Craig Kalawsky
☐ Frank Kovacs
☐ Darren Kwiatkowski
☐ Brian Leibel
☐ Tim Logan
☐ Jim Mathieson
☐ Darrin McKechnie
☐ Rob McKinely
☐ Brad Miller
☐ Cregg Nicol
☐ Doug Sauter
☐ Dan Sexton
☐ Mike Sillinger
☐ Dennis Sobchuk
☐ Stanley Szumlak
☐ Mike Van Slooten
☐ Mascot K-9 Big Blue
☐ Team Photo

1988 - 89 PATS

Mike Sillinger is the most expensive single at $1.00. Singles start at 50¢.
Card Size: 2 1/2" x 3 1/2"
Imprint: Forbes-Anderson Press Ltd.
Sponsors: Royal Studios
Complete Set (22 cards): 10.00

☐ Shane Bogden
☐ Cam Braver
☐ Scott Daniels
☐ Gary Dickie
☐ Mike Dyck
☐ Dave Gerse
☐ Kevin Haller
☐ Rod Houck
☐ Frank Kovacs
☐ Brian Leibel
☐ Bernie Lynch
☐ Kelly Markwart
☐ Jim Mathieson
☐ Brad Miller
☐ Dwayne Monteith
☐ Curtis Nykyforuk
☐ Darren Parsons
☐ Cory Paterson
☐ Jeff Sebastian
☐ Mike Sillinger
☐ Chad Silver
☐ Jamie Splett

1989 - 90 PATS

Mike Sillinger is the most expensive single at $1.00. Singles start at 50¢.
Card Size: 2 1/2" x 3 1/2"
Sponsor: Mr. Lube
Complete Set (19 cards): 10.00

☐ Kelly Chotowetz
☐ Hal Christiansen
☐ Scott Daniels
☐ Wade Fennig
☐ Jason Glickman
☐ Jamie Heward
☐ Terry Hollinger
☐ Frank Kovacs
☐ Kelly Markwart
☐ Jim Mathieson
☐ Cam McLellan
☐ Troy Mick
☐ Greg Pankewicz
☐ Cory Paterson
☐ Garry Pearce
☐ Mike Risdale
☐ Colin Ruck
☐ Mike Sillinger
☐ Jamie Splett

RICHELIEU RIVERAINS

1984 - 85 RIVERAINS

Stéphane Quintal is the most expensive single at $4-5. Singles start at $1.00.
Card Size: 4" x 5 1/2"
Sponsors: none
Complete Set (19 cards): 20.00

☐ Miguel Baldris
☐ Nicolas Beaulieu
☐ Martin Côté
☐ Sylvain Coutourier
☐ Dominic Edmond
☐ Yves Gaucher
☐ Eric Gobel
☐ Carl Lemieux
☐ Michel Lévesque
☐ Brad Loi
☐ Eric Primeau
☐ Stéphane Quintal
☐ Jean-Michel Ray
☐ Serge Richard
☐ Stéphane Robinson
☐ Danny Rochefort
☐ Martin Savaria
☐ Sylvain Senecal
☐ Eric Charron

1988 - 89 RIVERAINS

Singles start at 50¢.
Card Size: 2 7/8" x 4"
Sponsors: none
Complete Set (30 cards): 12.00

☐ Marc Beaurivage
☐ Denis Benoît
☐ Jonathan Black
☐ Richard Boisvert
☐ Hughes Bouchard
☐ François Bourdeau
☐ Guy Caplette
☐ Bertrand Cournoyer
☐ Yves Cournoyer
☐ Michel Deguise
☐ Patrick Grise
☐ Robert Guillet
☐ Jimmy Lachance
☐ Roger Laporte
☐ Frédéric Lefebvre
☐ Frédéric Maltais
☐ André Millette
☐ Joseph Napolitano
☐ Rémy Patoine
☐ Jean Plamondon
☐ Steve Plasse
☐ Jean-François Poirier
☐ Jacques Provencal
☐ Alain Rancourt
☐ Frédéric Savard
☐ François St-Germain
☐ Martin Tanguay
☐ Richard Valois
☐ Stéphane Valois
☐ Team Photo

RIMOUSKI OCÉANIC

(QMJHL)

1996-97 OCÉANIC

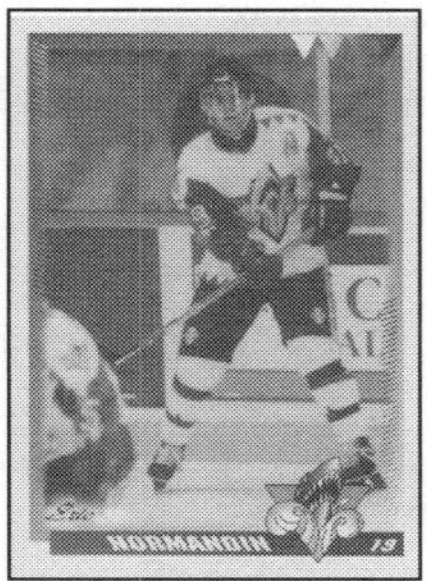

Vincent Lecavalier is the most expensive single at $6-8. Singles start at 50¢.
Card Size: 2 1/2" x 3 1/2"
Sponsors: none
Series One Set (28 cards): 15.00

- ☐ Jonathan Beaulieu
- ☐ Martin Bédard
- ☐ Eric Belzile
- ☐ Denis Boily
- ☐ Dave Bolduc
- ☐ Yan Bouchard
- ☐ Nicolas Chabot
- ☐ Eryc Collin
- ☐ Eric Drouin
- ☐ Yannick Dupont
- ☐ Frédéric Girard
- ☐ Jimmy Grondin
- ☐ Vincent Lecavalier
- ☐ Frédéric Levac
- ☐ François Lévesque
- ☐ Philippe Lord
- ☐ David Malenfant
- ☐ Eric Normandin
- ☐ Mathieu Normandin
- ☐ Philippe Plante
- ☐ Martin Poitras
- ☐ David St. Onge
- ☐ Philippe Sauvé
- ☐ Sébastien Simard
- ☐ Mathieu Sunderland
- ☐ Bobby Lebel
- ☐ Gaston Thérien
- ☐ Team Photo

Series Two Set (10 cards): 4.00

- ☐ Eric Bélanger
- ☐ Eric Bélanger
- ☐ Philippe Grondin
- ☐ Jason Lehoux
- ☐ Jonathan Lévesque
- ☐ Guillaume Rodrigue
- ☐ Joé Rullier
- ☐ Russell Smith
- ☐ Derrick Walser
- ☐ Mascot Louky

SASKATOON BLADES

(WHL)

1981 - 82 BLADES

Brian Skrudland is the most expensive single at $3-4. Singles start at 75¢.
Card Size: 2 1/2" x 3 7/8"
Sponsors: Police, McDonald's
Complete Set (25 cards): 20.00

- ☐ 1 Team Photo
- ☐ 2 Daryl Stanley
- ☐ 3 Leroy Gorski
- ☐ 4 Donn Clark
- ☐ 5 Brad Duggen
- ☐ 6 Dave Chartier
- ☐ 7 Dave Brown
- ☐ 8 Adam Thompson
- ☐ 9 Bruce Eakin
- ☐ 10 Brian Skrudland
- ☐ 11 Roger Kortko
- ☐ 12 Ron Dreger
- ☐ 13 Daryl Lubiniecki
- ☐ 14 Marc Habscheid
- ☐ 15 Saskatoon Police
- ☐ 16 Todd Strueby
- ☐ 17 Craig Hurley
- ☐ 18 Bill Hlynsky
- ☐ 19 Lane Lambert
- ☐ 20 Mike Bloski
- ☐ 21 Bruce Gordon
- ☐ 22 Perry Ganchar
- ☐ 23 Ron Loustel
- ☐ 24 Blades Logo
- ☐ 25 Checklist

1983 - 84 BLADES

Wendel Clark is the most expensive single at $10-15. Singles start at 75¢.
Card Size: 2 1/2"x 3 3/4"
Sponsors: Police, Burger King
Complete Set (24 cards): 25.00

- ☐ 1 Team Photo
- ☐ 2 Trent Yawney
- ☐ 3 Grant Jennings
- ☐ 4 Duncan MacPherson
- ☐ 5 Greg Holtby
- ☐ 6 Dan Leier
- ☐ 7 Dwaine Hutton
- ☐ 8 Wendel Clark
- ☐ 9 Kerry Laviolette
- ☐ 10 Dave Chartier
- ☐ 11 Dale Henry
- ☐ 12 Randy Smith
- ☐ 13 Kevin Kowalchuk
- ☐ 14 Todd MacLellan
- ☐ 15 Saskatoon Police
- ☐ 16 Larry Korchinski
- ☐ 17 Curtis Chamberlain
- ☐ 18 Greg Lebsack
- ☐ 19 Ron Dreger
- ☐ 20 Doug Kyle
- ☐ 21 Rick Smith
- ☐ 22 Joey Kocur
- ☐ 23 Allan Larouchelle
- ☐ 24 Mark Thietke

1984 - 85 BLADES

Photos are in black and white. Wendel Clark is the most expensive single at $10-12. Singles start at $1.00.
Sticker Size: 2" x 1 3/4"
Sponsors: Police, Burger King
Complete Set (20 stickers): 25.00

- ☐ Jack Bowkus
- ☐ Curtis Chamberlain
- ☐ Wendel Clark
- ☐ Ron Dreger
- ☐ Randy Hoffart
- ☐ Mark Holick
- ☐ Greg Holtby
- ☐ Grant Jennings
- ☐ Kevin Kowalchuk
- ☐ Bryan Larkin
- ☐ James Latos
- ☐ Duncan MacPherson
- ☐ Rod Matechuk
- ☐ Todd McLellan
- ☐ Darren Moren
- ☐ Mike Morin
- ☐ Devon Oleniuk
- ☐ Grant Tkachuk
- ☐ Troy Vollhoffer
- ☐ Trent Yawney

1986 - 87 BLADES

Singles start at $2.
Photo Size: 8 1/2" x 11"
Sponsor: Shell Oil
Complete Set (25 photos): 35.00

- ☐ Blair Atcheynum
- ☐ Colin Bayer
- ☐ Jack Bowkus
- ☐ Mike Butka
- ☐ Kelly Chase
- ☐ Tim Cheveldae (G)
- ☐ Blaine Chrest
- ☐ Kerry Clark
- ☐ Brian Glynn
- ☐ Mark Holick
- ☐ Kevin Kaminski
- ☐ Tracy Katelnikoff
- ☐ Kory Kocur
- ☐ Brian Larkin
- ☐ Curtis Leschyshyn
- ☐ Dan Logan
- ☐ Todd MacLellan
- ☐ Devon Oleniuk
- ☐ Marty Prazma
- ☐ Mary Reimer
- ☐ Walter Shutter
- ☐ Grant Tkachuk
- ☐ Tony Twist
- ☐ Shaun Van Allen

1989 - 90 BLADES

Singles start at 75¢.
Card Size: 2 3/4" x 4"
Sponsor: Saskatoon Police
Complete Set (25 cards): 18.00

- ☐ 1 Chief Joe Penkala
- ☐ 2 Saskatoon Police Logo
- ☐ 3 Marcel Comeau
- ☐ 4 Dean Kuntz
- ☐ 5 Mike Greenlay
- ☐ 6 Jody Praznik
- ☐ 7 Ken Sutton
- ☐ 8 Shawn Snesar
- ☐ 9 Shane Langager
- ☐ 10 Dean Holoien
- ☐ 11 Rob Lelacheur
- ☐ 12 David Struch
- ☐ 13 Collin Bauer
- ☐ 14 Kevin Yellowaga
- ☐ 15 Drew Sawtell
- ☐ 16 Brian Gerrits
- ☐ 17 Kirk Roworth
- ☐ 18 Tracey Katelnikoff
- ☐ 19 Scott Scissons
- ☐ 20 Jason Smart
- ☐ 21 Jason Christie
- ☐ 22 Darin Bader
- ☐ 23 Kevin Kaminsky
- ☐ 24 Kory Kocur
- ☐ 25 Darwin MacPherson

1990 - 91 BLADES

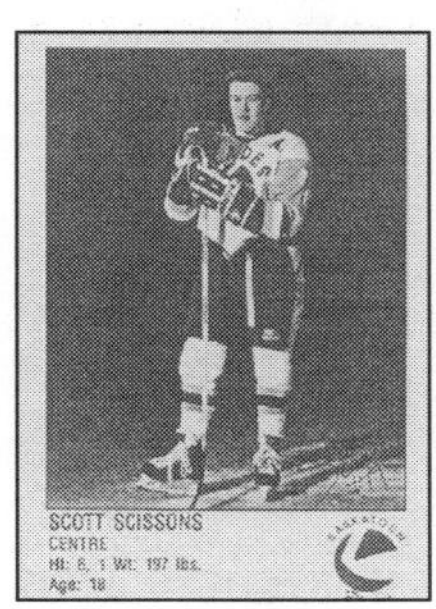

Singles start at 75¢.
Card Size: 2 1/2" x 3 1/2"
Sponsor: Saskatoon Police
Complete Set (27 cards): 15.00

- ☐ 1 Terry Ruskowski
- ☐ 2 Trevor Robins
- ☐ 3 Cam Moon
- ☐ 4 Jeff Buchanan
- ☐ 5 Mark Raiter
- ☐ 6 Trevor Sherban
- ☐ 7 Jason Knox
- ☐ 8 Dean Rambo
- ☐ 9 Rob LeCacheur
- ☐ 10 David Struch
- ☐ 11 Greg Leahy
- ☐ 12 Derek Tibbatts
- ☐ 13 Shane Calder
- ☐ 14 Richard Matvichuk
- ☐ 15 Trent Coghill
- ☐ 16 Mark Wotton
- ☐ 17 Kelly Markwart
- ☐ 18 Mark Franks
- ☐ 19 Scott Scissons
- ☐ 20 Tim Cox
- ☐ 21 Gaetan Blouin
- ☐ 22 Darin Bader
- ☐ 23 Shawn Yakimishyn
- ☐ 24 Ryan Strain
- ☐ 25 Jason Peters
- ☐ 26 Blades card
- ☐ 27 Blades card

1991 - 92 BLADES

Singles start at 50¢.
Card Size: 2 1/2" x 3 1/2"
Sponsor: Saskatoon Police
Complete Set (25 cards): 10.00

- ☐ 1 Lorne Molleken
- ☐ 2 Trevor Robins (G)
- ☐ 3 Norm Maracle
- ☐ 4 Jeff Buchanan
- ☐ 5 Mark Raiter
- ☐ 6 Bryce Goebel
- ☐ 7 Rhett Trombley
- ☐ 8 Chad Rusnak
- ☐ 9 Jason Knight
- ☐ 10 David Struch
- ☐ 11 Shane Calder
- ☐ 12 Derek Tibbatts
- ☐ 13 Glen Gulutzan
- ☐ 14 Richard Matvichuk
- ☐ 15 Chad Michalchuk
- ☐ 16 Mark Wotton
- ☐ 17 Mark Franks
- ☐ 18 Andy McIntyre
- ☐ 19 Ryan Fujita
- ☐ 20 Sean McFatridge
- ☐ 21 Jason Becker
- ☐ 22 Shawn Yakimishyn
- ☐ 23 James Startup
- ☐ 24 Paul Buczkowski
- ☐ Crime Dog McGruff

1993 - 94 BLADES

Singles start at 75¢.
Card Size: 5 1/2" x 8 1/2"
Sponsor: Coca-Cola
Complete Set (25 cards): 15.00

- ☐ Chad Allan
- ☐ Frank Banham
- ☐ Wade Belak
- ☐ Paul Buczkowski
- ☐ Shane Calder
- ☐ Mark Deyell
- ☐ Jason Duda
- ☐ Trevor Ethier
- ☐ Mike Gray
- ☐ Trevor Hanas
- ☐ Devon Hanson
- ☐ Andrew Kemper
- ☐ Kirby Law
- ☐ Andy Macintyre
- ☐ Norm Maracle
- ☐ Ivan Salon
- ☐ Todd Simpson
- ☐ Derek Tibbatts
- ☐ Rhett Warrener
- ☐ Clark Wilm
- ☐ Mark Wotton
- ☐ F.Banham/M.Deyell/I.Salon
- ☐ F.Tibbatts/C.Wilm/A.Macintyre
- ☐ Team Photo

SAULT SAINTE MARIE GREYHOUNDS

(OHL)

1980 - 81 GREYHOUNDS

John Vanbiesbrouck is the most expensive single at $40-45. Ron Francis sells at $25-30. Singles start at $1.00.
Card Size: 2 1/2" x 4"
Sponsor: 920 CKCY
Complete Set (25 cards): 80.00

- ☐ Tony Butorac
- ☐ Tony Cella
- ☐ Terry Crisp
- ☐ Marc D'Amour (G)
- ☐ Gord Dineen
- ☐ Ron Francis
- ☐ Steve Gatzos
- ☐ John Goodwin
- ☐ Ron Handy
- ☐ Huey Larkin
- ☐ Ken Latta
- ☐ Vic Morin
- ☐ Rick Morocco
- ☐ Jim Pavese
- ☐ Brian Petterle

☐ Ken Porteous
☐ Dirk Rueter
☐ Doug Shedden
☐ Steve Smith
☐ Terry Tait
☐ John Vanbiesbrouck (G)
☐ Tim Zwijack
☐ S.S. Marie Police
☐ OMJHL Logo
☐ Greyhounds Logo

1981 - 82 GREYHOUNDS

John Vanbiesbrouck is the most expensive single at $30-35. Ron Francis sells at $20-25 and Rick Tocchet sells at $15-20. Singles start at $1.00.

Card Size: 2 1/2" x 4"
Sponsors: 920 CKCY, Bluebird Bakery, Coke, Canadian Tire
Complete Set (28 cards): 75.00

☐ Jim Alfred
☐ Dave Andreoli
☐ Richard Beaulne
☐ Bruce Bell
☐ Chuck Brimmer
☐ Tony Cella
☐ Kevin Conway
☐ Terry Crisp
☐ Marc D'Amour (G)
☐ Gord Dineen
☐ Chris Felix
☐ Ron Francis
☐ Steve Graves
☐ Wayne Groulx
☐ Huey Larkin
☐ Ken Latta
☐ Mike Lococo
☐ Jim Pavese
☐ Dirk Rueter
☐ Steve Smith
☐ Terry Tait
☐ Rick Tocchet
☐ John Vanbiesbrouck (G)
☐ Harry Wolfe
☐ J.D. Yari
☐ Bluebird Bakery Logo
☐ Canadian Tire Logo
☐ Coke Logo

1982 - 83 GREYHOUNDS

John Vanbiesbrouck is the most expensive single at $20-25. Rick Tocchet sells at $10-12 and Jeff Beukeboom sells at $2-3. Singles start at $1.00.

Card Size: 2 1/2" x 4"
Sponsors: 920 CKCY, Bluebird Bakery, Station Mall
Complete Set (25 cards): 35.00

☐ Jim Aldred
☐ John Armelin
☐ Richard Beaulne
☐ Jeff Beukeboom
☐ Tony Cella
☐ Kevin Conway
☐ Terry Crisp
☐ Chris Felix
☐ Steve Graves
☐ Gus Greco
☐ Wayne Groulx
☐ Sam Haidy
☐ Tim Hoover
☐ Pat Lahey
☐ Huey Larkin
☐ Mike Lococo
☐ Mike Neill
☐ Ken Sabourin
☐ Steve Smith
☐ Terry Tait
☐ Rick Tocchet
☐ John Vanbiesbrouck (G)
☐ Harry Wolfe
☐ Bluebird Bakery Logo
☐ Station Mall Logo

1983 - 84 GREYHOUNDS

Rick Tocchet is the most expensive single at $8-10. Singles start at $1.00.

Card Size: 2 1/2" x 4"
Sponsors: 920 CKCY, Coke, IGA
Complete Set (25 cards): 25.00

☐ Jeff Beukeboom
☐ Grame Bonar
☐ Chris Brant
☐ John English
☐ Chris Felix
☐ Rick Fera
☐ Marc Fournier
☐ Steve Graves
☐ Gus Greco
☐ Wayne Groulx
☐ Sam Haidy
☐ Tim Hoover
☐ Jerry Iuliano
☐ Pat Lahey
☐ Mike Lococo
☐ Jean-Marc MacKenzie
☐ Mike Oliverio
☐ Brit Peer
☐ Joey Rampton
☐ Ken Sabourin
☐ Jim Samec
☐ Rick Tocchet
☐ Harry Wolfe
☐ Coke Logo
☐ IGA Logo

1984 - 85 GREYHOUNDS

Bob Probert is the most expensive single at $6-8. Derek King sells at $3-4. Singles start at $1.00.

Card Size: 2 1/2" x 4"
Sponsors: 920 CKCY, Coke, IGA
Complete Set (25 cards): 25.00

☐ Marty Abrams
☐ Jeff Beukeboom
☐ Chris Brant
☐ Terry Crisp
☐ Chris Felix
☐ Scott Green
☐ Wayne Groulx
☐ Steve Hollett
☐ Tim Hoover
☐ Derek King
☐ Tyler Larter
☐ Jean-Marc MacKenzie
☐ Scott Mosey
☐ Mike Oliverio
☐ Grit Peer
☐ Wayne Presley
☐ Bob Probert
☐ Brian Rome
☐ Ken Sabourin
☐ Ron Veccia
☐ Harry Wolfe
☐ Coke Logo
☐ IGA Logo

1987 - 88 GREYHOUNDS

Regional stars do carry a premium.

Card Size: 2 1/2" x 4"
Sponsors: Police, 920 CKCY, Coke, IGA, Canadian Tire, McDonald's
Complete Set (35 cards): 120.00

	No.	Player	Price
☐	1	Chief Barry King	1.00
☐	2	Dan Currie	1.00
☐	3	Mike Glover	1.00
☐	4	Tyler Larter	1.00
☐	5	Bob Jones	1.00
☐	6	Singer Lyndon Slewidge	1.00
☐	7	Brad Jones	1.00
☐	8	Ron Francis	10.00
☐	9	Dale Turnbull	1.00
☐	10	Don McConnell	1.00
☐	11	Chris Felix	1.00
☐	12	Steve Udvari	1.00
☐	13	Shawn Simpson	1.00
☐	14	Rob Zettler	2.00
☐	15	Phil Esposito	10.00
☐	16	J. Vanbiesbrouck (G)	12.00
☐	17	Mike Oliverio	1.00
☐	18	Colin Ford	1.00
☐	19	Steve Herniman	1.00
☐	20	Troy Mallette	2.00
☐	21	Craig Hartsburg	4.00
☐	22	Don Boyd	1.00
☐	23	Peter Fiorentino	1.00
☐	24	Jeff Columbus	1.00
☐	25	Brad Stepan	1.00
☐	26	Rick Tocchet	6.00
☐	27	Shane Sargant	1.00
☐	28	Wayne Muir	1.00
☐	29	Wayne Gretzky	90.00
☐	30	Gary Luther	1.00
☐	31	Harry Wolfe	1.00
☐	32	Rod Thacker	1.00
☐	33	Terry Tait	1.00
☐	34	Brian Howard	1.00
☐	35	Greg Johnston	1.00

1989 - 90 GREYHOUNDS

Ron Francis is the most expensive single at $6-8. Adam Foote sells at 2-3. Singles start at 75¢.

Card Size: 2 3/4" x 3 1/2"
Sponsors: Police, McDonald's, Canadian Tire, Classic Hits
Complete Set (30 cards): 25.00

☐ 1 CL: Chief Barry King
☐ 2 S.S. Marie Police
☐ 3 Ted Nolan
☐ 4 Greyhounds Logo
☐ 5 Sherry Bassin
☐ 6 Jim Ritchie
☐ 7 Bob Boughner
☐ 8 Denny Lambert
☐ 9 Doug Minor
☐ 10 Rick Pracey
☐ 11 Colin Miller
☐ 12 Kevin King
☐ 13 Ron Francis
☐ 14 Rick Kowalsky
☐ 15 Adam Foote
☐ 16 Wade Whitten
☐ 17 Dale Turnbull
☐ 18 Bob Jones
☐ 19 David Carrie
☐ 20 Brad Tuley
☐ 21 Wayne Muir
☐ 22 Dave Babcock
☐ 23 David Matsos
☐ 24 Dan Ferguson
☐ 25 Jeff Szeryk
☐ 26 Mike Zuke
☐ 27 Dave Doucette
☐ 28 John Campbell
☐ 29 Graeme Harvey
☐ 30 John Fuselli

1993 - 94 GREYHOUNDS

The most expensive singles are Dan Cloutier and Kevin Hodson at $2-3. Singles start at 75¢.

Card Size: 2 1/2" x 3 1/2"
Sponsors: Precision Litho, Toronto Dominion Bank, Pepsi
Complete Set (32 cards): 25.00

☐ 1 Memorial Cup
☐ 2 Dan Tanevski
☐ 3 Mark Matier
☐ 4 Oliver Pastinsky
☐ 5 Peter MacKeller
☐ 6 Drew Bannister
☐ 7 Sean Gagnon
☐ 8 Joe Clarke
☐ 9 Chad Penney
☐ 10 Neal Martin
☐ 11 Perry Pappas
☐ 12 David Matsos
☐ 13 Rick Kowalsky
☐ 14 Gary Roach
☐ 15 Jarret Reid
☐ 16 Steve Sullivan
☐ 17 Tom MacDonald
☐ 18 Jodie Murphy
☐ 19 Ralph Intranuovo
☐ 20 Brad Baber
☐ 21 Blaine Thompson
☐ 22 Aaron Gavey
☐ 23 Wade Gibson
☐ 24 Kiley Hill
☐ 25 Jeff Toms
☐ 26 Joe Van Volsen
☐ 27 Dan Cloutier (G)
☐ 28 Kevin Hodson (G)
☐ 29 D.Mayville/S.Bassin
☐ 30 Ted Nolan/D.Flynn
☐ 31 Greyhounds Staff
☐ 32 M.Zuke/F.Varcoe/J.Mayne/M.Sicard

1996 - 97 GREYHOUNDS

Joe Thornton has two cards each at $5-6. Singles start at 50¢. An autographed set was also available.

Card Size: 2 1/2" x 3 1/2"
Sponsors: Steelworkers, Toronto Dominion Bank and Trust
Complete Set (28 cards): 25.00

☐ Wes Booker #24
☐ Bill Browne #3
☐ Peter Cava #14
☐ Justin Davis #15
☐ J.J. Dickie #26
☐ Oak Hewer #7
☐ Richard Jackman #23
☐ Richard Jackman
☐ Matt Lahey #22
☐ David Mayville
☐ Jake McCracken #30 (G)
☐ Marc Moro #21
☐ Robert Mulick #28
☐ Daniel Passero #5
☐ Joe Paterson
☐ Nathan Perrot #18
☐ Michal Podolka #33 (G)
☐ Nick Robinson #6
☐ Ben Schust #12
☐ Joe Seroski #11
☐ Chad Spurr #25
☐ Brian Stewart #29
☐ Joe Thornton #19
☐ Joe Thornton
☐ Trevor Tokarczyk #16
☐ Richard Uniacke #9
☐ David Wight #20
☐ Chad Woollard #17
☐ Bob Jones/Mike Zuke
☐ Team Photo

SEATTLE THUNDERBIRDS

(WHL)

SEATTLE

1993 - 94 THUNDERBIRDS

Brendan Witt and Deron Quint are the most expensive singles at $1.50-2. Singles start at 50¢.

Card Size: 2 1/2"x 3 1/2"
Sponsors: none
Complete Set (30 cards): 15.00

☐ Mike Barrie
☐ Doug Bonner
☐ David Carson
☐ Jeff Dewar
☐ Brett Duncan
☐ Shawn Gervais
☐ Chris Herperger
☐ Troy Hyatt
☐ Curt Kamp
☐ Olaf Kjenstadt
☐ Walt Kyle
☐ Milt Mastad
☐ Alexandre Matvichuk
☐ Larry McMorran
☐ Jim McTaggart
☐ Regan Mueller
☐ Kevin Mylander
☐ Drew Palmer
☐ Jeff Peddigrew
☐ Darryl Plandowski
☐ Deron Quint
☐ Darrell Sandback
☐ Chris Schmidt
☐ Lloyd Shaw
☐ Darcy Smith
☐ Rob Tallas (G)
☐ Paul Vincent
☐ Chris Wells
☐ Brendan Witt
☐ Team Photo

SPOKANE CHIEFS

(WHL)

1989 - 90 CHIEFS

Pat Falloon and Travis Green are the most expensive singles at $3-4. Ray Whitney and Jon Klemm sell at $1-2. Singles start at 75¢.

Card Size: 2 1/2" x 3 1/2"

Sponsor: Teachers Credit Union

Complete Set (20 cards): 15.00

- ☐ Mike Chrun
- ☐ Shawn Dietrich
- ☐ Milan Dragicevic
- ☐ Frank Evans
- ☐ Pat Falloon
- ☐ Jeff Ferguson
- ☐ Travis Green
- ☐ Bobby House
- ☐ Mick Jickling
- ☐ Jon Klemm
- ☐ Steve Junker
- ☐ Chris Rowland
- ☐ Dennis Saharchuk
- ☐ Kerry Toporowski
- ☐ Trevor Tovell
- ☐ Bram Vanderkracht
- ☐ Ray Whitney

1995 - 96 CHIEFS

Jason Podollan is the most expensive single at $1-1.50. Singles start at 50¢.

Card Size: 2 1/2" x 3 1/2"

Sponsors: None

Complete Set (30 cards): 15.00

- ☐ 1 David Lemanowicz
- ☐ 2 Scott Fletcher
- ☐ 3 Hugh Hamilton
- ☐ 4 Chris Lane
- ☐ 5 Dmitri Leonov
- ☐ 6 Darren Sinclair
- ☐ 7 Ty Jones
- ☐ 8 Kris Graf
- ☐ 9 Trent Whitfield
- ☐ 10 Martin Cerven
- ☐ 11 Randy Favaro
- ☐ 12 Jason Podollan
- ☐ 13 Joel Boschman
- ☐ 14 Jared Hope
- ☐ 15 Greg Leeb
- ☐ 16 John Cirjak
- ☐ 17 Mike Haley
- ☐ 18 Ryan Berry
- ☐ 19 Sean Gillam
- ☐ 20 Derek Schutz
- ☐ 21 Joe Cardarelli
- ☐ 22 Adam Magarrell
- ☐ 23 Jay Bertsch
- ☐ 24 John Shockey
- ☐ 25 Mike Babcock
- ☐ 26 Parry Shockey
- ☐ 27 T.D. Forss
- ☐ 28 Ted Schott
- ☐ 29 Dan Mitchell
- ☐ 30 Aren Miller

SUDBURY WOLVES

(OHL)

1984 - 85 WOLVES

Jeff Brown is the most expensive single at $5-6. Singles start at 75¢.

Card Size: 3 1/2" x 6"

Sponsors: Pepsi, Burger King, Hires, CKSO 79

Complete Set (16 cards): 15.00

- ☐ 1 Andy Spruce
- ☐ 2 Sean Envoy (G)
- ☐ 3 Mario Martini
- ☐ 4 Brent Daugherty
- ☐ 5 Mario Chitaroni
- ☐ 6 Dan Chiasson
- ☐ 7 Jeff Brown
- ☐ 8 Todd Sepkowski
- ☐ 9 Brad Belland
- ☐ 10 Glenn Greenough
- ☐ 11 John Landry
- ☐ 12 Max Middendorf
- ☐ 13 David Moylan
- ☐ 14 Jamie Nadjiwan
- ☐ 15 Warren Rychel
- ☐ 16 Ed Smith

1985 - 86 WOLVES

Jeff Brown is the most expensive single at $4-5. Singles start at 75¢.

Card Size: 2 3/4" x 4"

Imprint: Journal Printing

Sponsors: Police, Burger King, IGA, Rotary International, United Steelworkers

Complete Set (16 cards): 15.00

- ☐ 1 Sudbury Police
- ☐ 2 Sponsor Logos
- ☐ 3 Checklist
- ☐ 4 Chief R. Zanibbi
- ☐ 5 Wayne Maxner
- ☐ 6 Sean Envoy (G)
- ☐ 7 Todd Lalonde
- ☐ 8 Costa Papista
- ☐ 9 Robin Rubic
- ☐ 10 David Moylan
- ☐ 11 Brent Daugherty
- ☐ 12 Glenn Greenough
- ☐ 13 Mario Chitaroni
- ☐ 14 Ken McRae
- ☐ 15 Mike Hudson
- ☐ 16 Andy Paquette
- ☐ 17 Ed Lemaire
- ☐ 18 Mark Turner
- ☐ 19 Craig Duncanson
- ☐ 20 Jeff Brown
- ☐ 21 Team Photo
- ☐ 22 Max Middendorf
- ☐ 23 Keith Van Rooyen
- ☐ 24 Brad Walcot
- ☐ 25 Ron Wilson
- ☐ 26 Bill White

1986 - 87 WOLVES

Photos are credited to Rigo Peloso. Singles start at 75¢.

Card Size: 3" x 4 1/8"

Sponsors: Police, INCO, IGA, Rotary International, Burger King, United Steelworkers, Journal Printing

Complete Set (16 cards): 15.00

- ☐ 1 Anders Hoberg (G)
- ☐ 1 Ted Mielczarek (G)
- ☐ 2 Todd Lalonde
- ☐ 3 Costa Papista
- ☐ 4 Justin Corbeil
- ☐ 5 Dave Moylan
- ☐ 6 Brent Daugherty
- ☐ 8 Mario Chitaroni
- ☐ 9 Jim Way
- ☐ 10 Dean Jalbert
- ☐ 11 President J. Drago
- ☐ 12 Ken McRae
- ☐ 14 Steve Hedington
- ☐ 15 Mike Hudson
- ☐ 16 Pierre Gagnon
- ☐ 17 Peter Hughes
- ☐ 18 Mark Turner
- ☐ 19 Sudbury Police
- ☐ 20 Wayne Doucet
- ☐ 21 Paul DiPietro
- ☐ 22 Max Middendorf
- ☐ 23 Phil Paquette
- ☐ 25 Rob Wilson
- ☐ 26 Checklst
- ☐ 27 Chief R. Zanibbi
- ☐ 28 Claude D'Amour
- ☐ 29 Guy Blanchard
- ☐ 30 Joe Desrosiers
- ☐ 31 Jake Bisschops
- ☐ 33 Bill White

1987 - 88 WOLVES

Singles start at 75¢.

Card Size: 3" x 4 1/8"

Sponsors: Police, INCO, Air Canada, Rotary International, Pure Springs Ginger Ale, United Steelworkers, Journal Printing

Complete Set (26 cards): 15.00

- ☐ 1 Checklist
- ☐ 2 Ted Mielczarek (G)
- ☐ 3 Dan Gatenby
- ☐ 4 Todd Lalonde
- ☐ 5 Justin Corbeil
- ☐ 6 Jordan Fois
- ☐ 7 Rodney Lapointe
- ☐ 8 Dave Akey
- ☐ 9 Jim Smith
- ☐ 10 Fred Pennell
- ☐ 11 Joey Simon
- ☐ 12 Luciano Fagioli
- ☐ 13 Robb Graham
- ☐ 14 John Uniac
- ☐ 15 Dave Carrie
- ☐ 16 Pierre Gagnon
- ☐ 17 Peter Hughes
- ☐ 18 Scott McCullough
- ☐ 19 Dean Guitard
- ☐ 20 Pat Holley
- ☐ 21 Chad Bradaway
- ☐ 22 Paul DiPietro
- ☐ 23 Derek Thompson
- ☐ 24 Scott Luce
- ☐ 25 Rob Wilson
- ☐ 26 Chief R. Zanibbi

1988 - 89 WOLVES

Singles start at 75¢.

Card Size: 3" x 4 1/8"

Imprint: Journal Printing

Sponsors: Police, INCO, Loeb IGA, Air Canada, Rotary International, Pizza Hut, United Steelworkers

Complete Set (26 cards): 15.00

- ☐ 1 Checklist
- ☐ 2 David Goverde (G)
- ☐ 3 Ted Mielczarek (G)
- ☐ 4 Adam Bennett
- ☐ 5 Kevin Grant
- ☐ 6 Jordan Fois
- ☐ 7 Sean O'Donnell
- ☐ 8 Kevin Meisner
- ☐ 9 Jim Smith
- ☐ 10 Fred Pennell
- ☐ 11 Tyler Pella
- ☐ 12 Dean Pella
- ☐ 13 Darren Bell
- ☐ 14 Derek Thompson
- ☐ 15 Terry Chitaroni
- ☐ 16 Sean Stansfield
- ☐ 17 Alastair Still
- ☐ 18 Jim Sonmez
- ☐ 19 Shannon Bolton
- ☐ 20 Andy Paquette
- ☐ 21 Mark Turner
- ☐ 22 Paul DiPietro
- ☐ 23 Robert Knesaurek
- ☐ 24 Todd Lalonde
- ☐ 25 Scott Herniman
- ☐ 26 Chief R. Zanibbi

1989 - 90 WOLVES

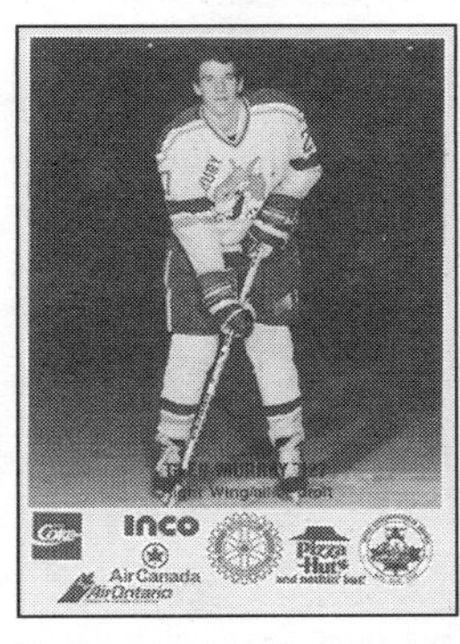

Glen Murray is the most expensive single at $1.50-2. Singles start at 75¢.

Card Size: 3" x 4 1/8"

Imprint: Journal Printing

Sponsors: Police, Coke, INCO, Air Canada, Pizza Hut, United Steelworkers, Rotary International

Complete Set (25 cards): 15.00

- ☐ 1 Checklist
- ☐ 2 Alastair Still
- ☐ 3 Bill Kovacs
- ☐ 4 Darren Bell
- ☐ 5 Scott Mahoney
- ☐ 6 Glen Murray
- ☐ 7 Alain Laforge
- ☐ 8 Jamie Matthews
- ☐ 9 Jon Boeve (G)
- ☐ 10 Adam Bennett
- ☐ 11 Derek Etches
- ☐ 12 Marcus Middleton
- ☐ 13 Jim Sonmez
- ☐ 14 Leonard MacDonald
- ☐ 15 Paul DiPietro
- ☐ 16 Neil Ethier
- ☐ 17 Sean O'Donnell
- ☐ 18 Andy MacVicar
- ☐ 19 David Goverde (G)
- ☐ 20 Jason Young
- ☐ 21 Wade Bartley
- ☐ 22 Barry Young
- ☐ 23 Chief R. Zanibbi
- ☐ 24 Terry Chitaroni
- ☐ 25 Rob Knesaurek

1990 - 91 WOLVES

Michael Peca is the most expensive single at $3-4. Singles start at 75¢.

Card Size: 3" x 4 1/8"

Sponsors: Police, INCO, Air Canada, Pizza Hut, United Steelworkers, Rotary International, Journal Printing

Complete Set (25 cards): 15.00

- ☐ 1 Darryl Paquette
- ☐ 2 Adam Bennett
- ☐ 3 Barry Young
- ☐ 4 Jon Boeve
- ☐ 5 Kyle Blacklock
- ☐ 6 Sean O'Donnell
- ☐ 7 Dan Ryder
- ☐ 8 Wade Bartley
- ☐ 9 Jamie Matthews
- ☐ 10 Rod Hinks
- ☐ 11 Derek Etches

- ☐ 12 Brandon Convery
- ☐ 13 Glen Murray
- ☐ 14 Bill Kovacs
- ☐ 15 Terry Chitaroni
- ☐ 16 Jason Young
- ☐ 17 Alastair Still
- ☐ 18 Shawn Rivers
- ☐ 19 Alain Laforge
- ☐ 20 J.D. Eaton
- ☐ 21 Michael Peca
- ☐ 22 Mascot Howler
- ☐ 23 Mike Yeo
- ☐ 24 Checklist
- ☐ 25 Chief R. Zanibbi

1991 - 92 WOLVES

Michael Peca is the most expensive single at $3-4. Singles start at 75¢.
Card Size: 3" x 4 1/8"
Imprint: Acme Printing
Sponsors: Police, INCO, Air Ontario, Pizza Hut, United Steelworkers, Coke, The Westbury
Complete Set (25 cards): 15.00

- ☐ 1 Chief R. Zanibbi
- ☐ 2 Mascot Howler
- ☐ 3 Team Photo
- ☐ 4 Kyle Blacklock
- ☐ 5 Sean Gagnon
- ☐ 6 Bernie John
- ☐ 7 Bob MacIsaac
- ☐ 8 Jamie Rivers
- ☐ 9 Shawn Rivers
- ☐ 10 Joel Sandie
- ☐ 11 Barry Young
- ☐ 12 George Dourian (G)
- ☐ 13 Dan Ryder
- ☐ 14 Derek Armstrong
- ☐ 15 Terry Chitaroni
- ☐ 16 Brandon Convery
- ☐ 17 Tim Favot
- ☐ 18 Rod Hinks
- ☐ 19 Jamie Matthews
- ☐ 20 Barrie Moore
- ☐ 21 Glen Murray
- ☐ 22 Michael Peca
- ☐ 23 Michael Yeo
- ☐ 24 Jason Young
- ☐ 25 Jason Zohil

1992 - 93 WOLVES

Singles start at 75¢.
Card Size: 3" x 4 1/8"
Sponsors: Police, INCO, Air Canada, Pizza Hut, United Steelworkers, Westbury Hotel, Journal Printing
Complete Set (27 cards): 15.00

- ☐ 1 Mascot Howler
- ☐ 2 Chief R. Zanibbi
- ☐ 3 Bob MacIsaac
- ☐ 4 Joel Sandie
- ☐ 5 Rory Fitzpatrick
- ☐ 6 Mike Wilson
- ☐ 7 Shawn Frappier
- ☐ 8 Bernie John
- ☐ 9 Jamie Rivers
- ☐ 10 Jamie Matthews
- ☐ 11 Zdenek Nedved
- ☐ 12 Ryan Shanahan
- ☐ 13 Corey Crane
- ☐ 14 Matt Kiereck
- ☐ 15 Rick Bodkin
- ☐ 16 Derek Armstrong
- ☐ 17 Barrie Moore
- ☐ 18 Rod Hinks
- ☐ 19 Kayle Short
- ☐ 20 Michael Yeo
- ☐ 21 Gary Coupal
- ☐ 22 Dennis Maxwell
- ☐ 23 Steve Potvin
- ☐ 24 Joel Poirier
- ☐ 25 Greg Dreveng (G)
- ☐ 26 Mark Gowan
- ☐ 27 Steve Staios

1993 - 94 WOLVES

Singles start at 75¢.
Card Size: 3" x 4 1/8"
Imprint: Acme Printing
Sponsors: Police, INCO, Air Canada, Pizza Hut, United Steelworkers, Coke, The Westbury
Complete Set (26 cards): 15.00

- ☐ 1 Chief R. Zanibbi
- ☐ 2 Mascot The Howler
- ☐ 3 Jay McKee
- ☐ 4 Chris McMurtry
- ☐ 5 Rory Fitzpatrick
- ☐ 6 Mike Wilson
- ☐ 7 Shawn Frappier
- ☐ 8 Jamie Rivers
- ☐ 9 Jamie Matthews
- ☐ 10 Zdenek Nedved
- ☐ 11 Ryan Shanahan
- ☐ 12 Andrew Dole
- ☐ 13 Mark Giannetti
- ☐ 14 Rick Bodkin
- ☐ 15 Barrie Moore
- ☐ 16 Gary Coupal
- ☐ 17 Ilya Lysenko
- ☐ 18 Simon Sherry
- ☐ 19 Steve Potvin
- ☐ 20 Joel Poirier
- ☐ 21 Shawn Silver (G)
- ☐ 22 Michael Yeo
- ☐ 23 Jeff Melnechuk (G)
- ☐ 24 Sean Venedam
- ☐ 25 Bob MacIsaac
- ☐ 26 Sponsors Logos

1996 - 97 WOLVES

Paul Mara is the most expensive single at $4-5. Singles start at 75¢.
Card Size: 3" x 4 1/8"
Sponsors: Police, Coke, INCO, Air Ontario, Westbury Howard Johnson, United Steelworkers, Rotary International
Complete Set (25 cards): 15.00

- ☐ 1 Alex McCauley
- ☐ 2 Mascot The Howler
- ☐ 3 Wolves Logo
- ☐ 4 Jeremy Adduono #10
- ☐ 5 Louie Blackbird #21
- ☐ 6 Tom Brown #23
- ☐ 7 Peter Campbell #14
- ☐ 8 Brad Domonsky #27
- ☐ 9 Tyson Flinn #4
- ☐ 10 Jason Gaggi #30 (G)
- ☐ 11 Luc Gagne #18
- ☐ 12 Kevin Hansen #7
- ☐ 13 Kon. Kalmikov #96
- ☐ 14 Robin Lacour #25
- ☐ 15 Joe Lombardo #8
- ☐ 16 Paul Mara #2
- ☐ 17 Norm Milley #9
- ☐ 18 Scott Page #24
- ☐ 19 Richard Rochefort #19
- ☐ 20 Brian Scott #20
- ☐ 21 Chris Shanahan #11
- ☐ 22 Ryan Sly #5
- ☐ 23 Jonas Soling #15
- ☐ 24 Tim Swartz #3
- ☐ 25 Steve Valiquette #1 (G)

SWIFT CURRENT BRONCOS

(WHL)

1995 - 96 BRONCOS

Singles start at 75¢.
Card Size: 2 1/2" x 3 1/2"
Sponsors: Zellers, Creative Video, Dairy Producers, Forbes Anderson Press
Complete Set (20 cards): 12.00

- ☐ Aaron MacDonald
- ☐ Brad Larsen
- ☐ Brent Sopel
- ☐ Chad Beagle
- ☐ Chris Szysky
- ☐ Colin O'Hara
- ☐ Craig Millar
- ☐ Derek Arbez
- ☐ Jaroslav Obsut
- ☐ Jeff Kirwan
- ☐ Jeff Schaeffer
- ☐ Jeff Henkelman
- ☐ Jeremy Rondeau
- ☐ Jesse Rezansoff
- ☐ Josh St. Louis
- ☐ Kurt Drummond
- ☐ Ryan Gernemia
- ☐ Sergei Varlamov
- ☐ Terry Friesen
- ☐ Tyler Willis

TACOMA ROCKETS

(WHL)

1992 - 93 ROCKETS

Singles start at 75¢.
Card Size: 2 1/2" x 3 1/2"
Sponsors: none
Complete Set (30 cards): 15.00

- ☐ Alexander Alexeev
- ☐ Jamie Black
- ☐ Jamie Butt
- ☐ Jeff Calvert
- ☐ Don Clark
- ☐ Marcel Comeau
- ☐ Duane Crouse
- ☐ Allan Egeland
- ☐ Marty Flichel
- ☐ Trever Fraser
- ☐ Jason Kwiatkowski
- ☐ Todd MacDonald
- ☐ Dave McMillen
- ☐ Tony Penchthalt
- ☐ Ryan Phillips
- ☐ Mike Piersol
- ☐ Dennis Pinfold
- ☐ Kevin Powell
- ☐ Tyler Prosofsky
- ☐ Stu Scantlebury
- ☐ Drew Schoneck
- ☐ Adam Smith
- ☐ Corey Stock
- ☐ Barkley Swenson
- ☐ Michal Sykora
- ☐ Dallas Thompson
- ☐ John Varga
- ☐ Toby Weishaar
- ☐ Michal Sykora (Action)
- ☐ Rockets Logo

1993 - 94 ROCKETS

Kyle McLaren is the most expensive single at $1.50-2. Singles start at 75¢.
Card Size: 2 1/2" x 3 1/2"
Sponsors: none
Complete Set (30 cards): 15.00

- ☐ Alexander Alexeev
- ☐ Jamie Butt
- ☐ Trevor Cairns
- ☐ Jeff Calvert (G)
- ☐ Marcel Comeau
- ☐ Jason Deleurme
- ☐ Allan Egeland
- ☐ Marty Flichel
- ☐ Trever Fraser
- ☐ Lada Hampeis
- ☐ Tavis Hansen
- ☐ Burt Henderson
- ☐ Jeff Jubenville
- ☐ Todd MacDonald
- ☐ Kyle McLaren
- ☐ Kory Mullin
- ☐ Steve Oviatt
- ☐ Ryan Phillips
- ☐ Mike Piersol
- ☐ Dennis Pinfold
- ☐ Tyler Prosfsky
- ☐ Jamie Reeve
- ☐ Adam Smith
- ☐ Corey Stock
- ☐ Michal Sykora
- ☐ Dallas Thompson
- ☐ John Varga
- ☐ Team Photo
- ☐ Tacoma Dome
- ☐ Tacome Rockets

VICTORIA COUGARS

(WHL)

1981 - 82 COUGARS

Geoff Courtnall is the most expensive single at $6-8. Singles start at $1.00.
Card Size: 3" x 5"
Sponsors: Police, Westcoast Savings Credit Union
Complete Set (16 cards): 20.00

- ☐ Bob Bales
- ☐ Greg Barber
- ☐ Ray Benik
- ☐ Rich Chernomaz
- ☐ Daryl Coldwell
- ☐ Geoff Courtnall
- ☐ Paul Cyr
- ☐ Wade Jenson (G)
- ☐ Stu Kulak
- ☐ Peter Martin
- ☐ John Mokosak
- ☐ Mark Morrison
- ☐ Bryant Seaton
- ☐ Jack Shupe
- ☐ Eric Thurston
- ☐ Randy Wickware

1982 - 83 COUGARS

Grant Fuhr is the most expensive single at $15-20. Russ Courtnall sells at $6-8 and Geoff Courtnall sells at $4-6. Singles start at $1.00.
Card Size: 3" x 5"
Sponsors: Police, Westcoast Savings Credit Union, CFAX 1070
Complete Set (23 cards): 30.00

- ☐ Steve Bayliss
- ☐ Ray Beink
- ☐ Rich Chernomaz
- ☐ Geoff Courtnall
- ☐ Russ Courtnall
- ☐ Paul Cyr
- ☐ Shawn Green
- ☐ Fabian Joseph
- ☐ Stu Kulak
- ☐ Brenn Leach
- ☐ Jack MacKeigan
- ☐ Dave Mackey
- ☐ Mark McLeary
- ☐ Dan Moberg
- ☐ John Mokosak
- ☐ Mark Morrison
- ☐ Eric Thurston
- ☐ Ron Viglasi
- ☐ Curt Fraser

- ☐ Grant Fuhr (G)
- ☐ Gary Lupul
- ☐ Brad Palmer
- ☐ Barry Pederson

1983 - 84 COUGARS

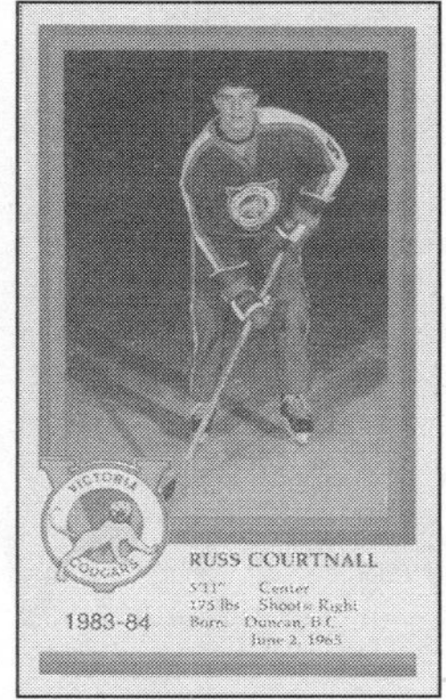

Russ Courtnall is the most expensive single at $4-6. Singles start at $1.00.
Card Size: 3" x 5"
Sponsors: Police, Westcoast Savings Credit Union, CFAX 1070
Complete Set (24 cards): 20.00

- ☐ Misko Antisin
- ☐ Steve Baylis
- ☐ Paul Bifano
- ☐ Russ Courtnall
- ☐ Greg Davies
- ☐ Dean Drozdiak
- ☐ Jim Gunn
- ☐ Richard Hajdu
- ☐ Randy Hansch (G)
- ☐ Matt Hervey
- ☐ Fabian Joseph
- ☐ Ron Kivell
- ☐ Brenn Leach
- ☐ Jack Mackeigan
- ☐ Dave Mackey
- ☐ Tom Martin
- ☐ Darren Moren (G)
- ☐ Adam Morrison
- ☐ Dan Sexton
- ☐ Randy Siska
- ☐ Eric Thurston
- ☐ Simon Wheeldon
- ☐ Murray Bannerman (G)
- ☐ Gord Roberts

1984 - 85 COUGARS

The most expensive singles are Russ and Geoff Courtnall at $3-5. Singles start at $1.00.
Card Size: 3" x 5"
Sponsors: Police, Westcoast Savings Credit Union, CFAX 1070
Complete Set (24 cards): 20.00

- ☐ Misko Antisin
- ☐ Greg Batters
- ☐ Chris Calverly
- ☐ Darin Choquette
- ☐ Russ Courtnall
- ☐ Rick Davidson
- ☐ Bill Gregoir
- ☐ Richard Hajdu
- ☐ Randy Hansch (G)
- ☐ Rob Kivell
- ☐ Brad Melin
- ☐ Jim Mentis
- ☐ Adam Morrison
- ☐ Mark Morrison
- ☐ Kodie Nelson
- ☐ Ken Priestlay
- ☐ Bruce Pritchard
- ☐ Trevor Semeniuk
- ☐ Dan Sexton
- ☐ Randy Siska
- ☐ Chris Tarnowski
- ☐ Mel Bridgman
- ☐ Geoff Courtnall
- ☐ Torrie Robertson

1989 - 90 COUGARS

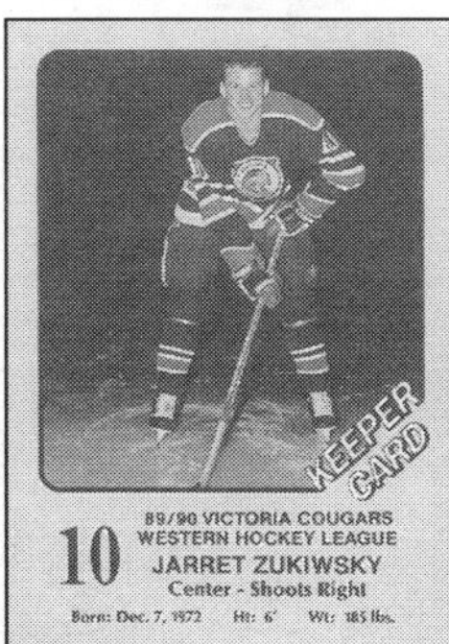

Singles start at 75¢.
Card Size: 2 3/4" x 4"
Sponsors: Flynn Printing, Safeway, Romeo's
Complete Set (21 cards): 15.00

- ☐ John Badduke
- ☐ Terry Bendera
- ☐ Trevor Buchanan
- ☐ Jarret Burgoyne (G)
- ☐ Dino Caputo
- ☐ Chris Catellier
- ☐ Mark Cipriano
- ☐ Milan Drag
- ☐ Dean Dyer
- ☐ Shayne Green
- ☐ Ryan Harrison
- ☐ Corey Jones (G)
- ☐ Terry Klapstein
- ☐ Jason Knox
- ☐ Curtis Nykyforuk
- ☐ Jason Peters
- ☐ Blair Scott
- ☐ Mike Seaton
- ☐ Rob Sumner
- ☐ Larry Woo
- ☐ Jarret Zukiwsky

WESTERN MICHIGAN BRONCOS

(CCHA)

1992 - 93 BRONCOS

Singles start at 50¢.
Card Size: 2 1/2" x 3 1/2"
Sponsors: none
Complete Set (30 cards): 12.00

- ☐ Chris Belanger
- ☐ Joe Bonnett
- ☐ Brent Brekke
- ☐ Chris Brooks
- ☐ Jeremy Brown
- ☐ Tom Carriere
- ☐ Scott Chartier
- ☐ Ryan D'Arcy
- ☐ Pat Ferschweiler
- ☐ Brian Gallentine
- ☐ Jim Holman
- ☐ Derek Innanen
- ☐ Jason Jennings
- ☐ Mikail Lapin
- ☐ François Leroux
- ☐ Jamal Mayers
- ☐ Kevin McCaffrey
- ☐ Dave Mitchell
- ☐ Brian Renfrew
- ☐ Mike Schafer
- ☐ Derek Schooley
- ☐ Neil Smith
- ☐ Colin Ward
- ☐ Dave Weaver
- ☐ Mike Whitton
- ☐ Bill Wilkinson
- ☐ Peter Wilkinson
- ☐ Byron Witkowski
- ☐ Lawson Arena

1993 - 94 BRONCOS

Singles start at 50¢.
Card Size: 2 1/2" x 3 1/2"
Sponsors: none
Complete Set (30 cards): 12.00

- ☐ David Agnew
- ☐ Brent Brekke
- ☐ Chris Brooks
- ☐ Craig Brown
- ☐ Jeremy Brown
- ☐ Justin Caldwell
- ☐ Tom Carriere
- ☐ Tony Code
- ☐ Matt Cressman
- ☐ Jim Culhane
- ☐ Ryan D'Arcy
- ☐ Brian Gallentine
- ☐ Matt Greene
- ☐ Rob Hodge
- ☐ Jim Holman
- ☐ Derek Innanen
- ☐ Mark Jodoin
- ☐ Brendan Kenny
- ☐ Misha Lapin
- ☐ Darren Maloney
- ☐ Jamal Mayers
- ☐ Dave Mitchell
- ☐ Brian Renfrew
- ☐ Mike Schafer
- ☐ Derek Schooley
- ☐ Colin Ward
- ☐ Mike Whitton
- ☐ Bill Wilkinson
- ☐ Peter Wilkinson
- ☐ Shawn Zimmerman

WINDSOR SPITFIRES

(OHL)

1989 - 90 SPITFIRES

Singles start at 50¢.
Card Size: 2 1/2" x 3 1/2"
Sponsors: none
Complete Set (22 cards): 10.00

- ☐ Sean Burns
- ☐ Glen Craig
- ☐ Brian Forestell
- ☐ Chris Fraser
- ☐ Trent Gleason
- ☐ Jon Hartley
- ☐ Ron Jones
- ☐ Bob Leeming
- ☐ Kevin MacKay
- ☐ Kevin McDougall
- ☐ Ryan Merritt
- ☐ David Myles
- ☐ Sean O'Hagan (G)
- ☐ Mike Polano
- ☐ Jason Snow
- ☐ Brad Smith
- ☐ Jason Stos
- ☐ Jon Stos
- ☐ Jamie Vargo
- ☐ Trevor Walsh
- ☐ K.J. White
- ☐ Jason Zohil

1992 - 93 SPITFIRES

Photos are credited to Sean Murphy. Adam Graves is the most expensive single at $2-3. Singles start at 50¢.
Card Size: 2 5/8" x 3 5/8"
Sponsor: Devonshire Mall
Complete Set (31 cards): 15.00

- ☐ 1 Checklist
- ☐ 2 Matt Martin
- ☐ 3 Luke Clowes
- ☐ 4 Jason Haelzle
- ☐ 5 Adam Graves
- ☐ 6 Craig Lutes
- ☐ 7 David Pluck
- ☐ 8 Colin Wilson
- ☐ 9 Bill Bowler
- ☐ 10 Ryan O'Neill
- ☐ 11 Adam Young
- ☐ 12 Gerrard Masse
- ☐ 13 Daryl Lavoie
- ☐ 14 Peter Allison
- ☐ 15 Ernie Godden
- ☐ 16 Brady Blain
- ☐ 17 Todd Warriner
- ☐ 18 Rick Marshall
- ☐ 19 Craig Johnson
- ☐ 20 Kelly Vipond
- ☐ 21 Mascot Devy Bear
- ☐ 22 Stephen Webb
- ☐ 23 Scott Miller
- ☐ 24 Dennis Purdie
- ☐ 25 Steve Gibson
- ☐ 26 Mike Hartwick
- ☐ 27 Shawn Heins
- ☐ 28 David Benn
- ☐ 29 Matt Mullin
- ☐ 30 David Mitchell
- ☐ 31 T.Warriner/C.Stillman

CHAPTER SEVEN
ALPHABETICAL INDEX

This alphabetical index cross-references player cards in chapters one through five. Chapter one sets are listed first in alphabetical order by brand, then NHL team issued sets (chapter two) are listed and lastly all other team issued sets (chapters three through five).

There is a series of abbreviations throughout this text. Some key abbreviations include: **Aut.** (Autograph), **BAP** (Be A Player), **FU** (Fleer Ultra), **OPC** (O-Pee-Chee), **PacificInv**. (Pacific Invincible), **PCC** (Pacific Crown Collection), **PH** (Parkhurst), **Prmr** (Premier), **SB** (ScoreBoard), **SkBx** (SkyBox), **SLU** (Starting Line Up), **SR** (Signature Rookies), **T.** (Topps), **TSC** (Topps Stadium Club), **UD** (Upper Deck) and **UDCC** (Upper Deck Collector's Choice). Please see the glossary for a list of other abbreviations.

Topps cards from 1968-69 through 1991-92 are listed with O-Pee-Chee cards. Take notice that Bicycle Sports NHL Hockey Aces are listed under "Aces", Pinnacle Be A Player and Upper Deck Be A Player cards are listed under "BeAPlayer", Funmate Puffy Stickers are listed under "Puffy Stickers", Seventh Inning Sketch cards are listed under "Sketch", Pinnacle Summit cards are listed under "Summit", Future Trends cards are listed under "Trends".

A

AIVAZOFF, MICAH
93/4 ClassicProspects 72
93/4 Donruss 421
93/4 FleerUltra 303
93/4 Parkhurst 253
93/4 PowerPlay 303
93/4 Premier 345
94/5 Premier 104
89/90 ProCards(AHL) 6
90/1 ProCards 417
91/2 ProCards 131
93/4 ToppsStadiumClub 263
93/4 UpperDeck 432
94/5 UDBeAPlayer-Aut. 173
96/7 Binghampton

AKERBLOM, BENGT
89/90 SemicElitserien 70

AKERBLOM, BJORN
89/90 SemicElitserien 258
90/1 SemicElitserien 168

AKERBLOM, MARKUS
94/5 ElitSet 53
95/6 ElitSet 240, -FaceTo 15
90/1 SemicElitserien 216
91/2 SemicElitserien 144
92/3 SemicElitserien 169
95/6 udElite 108, NA13
97/8 udSwedish 115

AKERMAN, JOHAN
94/5 ElitSet 240
95/6 ElitSet 8

ÅKERSTROM, ROGER
94/5 ElitSet 278
95/6 ElitSet 78, -FaceToFace 8
89/90 SemicElitserien 153
90/1 SemicElitserien 233
91/2 SemicElitserien 258
92/3 SemicElitserien 294
95/6 udElite 120
97/8 udSwedish 122

AKERVIK, ANDY
88/9 ProCards(Kalamazoo)
90/1 ProCards 593
91/2 ProCards 526
90/1 KansasCity 10

AKEY, DAVE
86/7 London 22
87/8 Sudbury 8

AKULININ, IGOR
90/1 O-Pee-Chee 491

ALAIN, GABRIEL
52/3 AnonymousOHL 71

ALATALO, ILKKA
78/9 SM-Liiga 149

ALATALO, MIKA
94/5 AutoPhonex 1
94/5 Classic T76
92/3 Jyvas-Hyva 126
93/4 Jyvas-Hyva 234
95 PaniniWorlds 177
94 Semic 21
95 Semic 15
93 SemicSticker 62
93/4 Sisu 202
94/5 Sisu 165,-Spec 1,-Horos 20
95/6 Sisu 128, -Painkiller 2
97/8 udSwedish 131

ALAVAARA, JAN-AXEL
95/6 ElitSet 278, -Rookies 2
97/8 udSwedish 151

ALBELIN, TOMMY
95 Globe 10
88/9 O-Pee-Chee 210
89/90 O-Pee-Chee 241
90/1 OPC/Topps 323
88/9 opcSticker 184/53
97/8 PacificRegime 26
88/9 PaniniSticker 348
89/90 PaniniSticker 257
90/1 PaniniSticker 76
96/7 PaniniSticker 242
97/8 PaniniSticker 195
95/6 Parkhurst 126
94/5 Pinnacle 508
96/7 PinnacleBeAPlayer 161
94/5 Premier 251
90/1 ProSet 162
90/1 Score 378
91/2 Score(CDN) 393
89 SemicSticker 6
93 SemicSticker 28
94 Semic 60
95/6 udElite 248
90/1 UpperDeck 88
97/8 UpperDeck 237
96 Wien 43
89/90 N.J.
90/1 N.J.
87/8 QUE/GeneralFoods
88/9 QUE
88/9 QUE/GeneralFoods

ALBRIGHT, AARON
92/3 Oshawa

ALBRIGHT, CLINT
45-64 BeeHives(NYR)

ALCINDOR, RAY
93/4 Huntington

ALDCORN, GARY
45-64 BeeHives(TOR)
57/8 Parkhurst(TOR) 24
58/9 Parkhurst 18
60/1 Parkhurst 33
93/4 Parkie(56/7) 122
60/1 ShirriffCoin 53

ALDOFF, ROD
93/4 Minn-Duluth
95/6 Tallahassee 3

ALDRED, JIM
81/2 Kingston 16
82/3 SSMarie

ALDRIDGE, KEITH
91/2 LakeSuperior

ALENIUS, ANTTI
66/7 Champion 147

ALEXANDER, BOB
85/6 Minn-Duluth 19

ALEXANDER, CLAIRE
76/7 OPC 321
74/5 TOR
75/6 TOR
76/7 TOR

ALEXANDER, KEN
84/5 Kitchener 11
85/6 Kitchener 9

ALEXANDRE, ARTHUR
27-32 LaPresse 31/2

ALEXANDROV, BORIS
92/3 Trends(76) 150

ALEXANDROV, IGOR
92/3 UpperDeck 611

ALEXEEV, ALEXANDER
92/3 Classic 54
95/6 Portland
92/3 Tacoma (x3)
93/4 Tacoma

ALFORS, PEKKA
65/6 Hellas 120

ALFRED, JIM
81/2 SSMarie

ALFREDSSON, DANIEL
96/7 Aces 7 (Clubs)
97/8 Aces 6 (Hearts)
95/6 Bowman 110, BB16
95/6 Donruss 299, -Rated 14
96/7 Donruss-Rated 10
97/8 Donruss 17
96/7 DonrussCanadianIce 34
97/8 DonrussCanadianIce 112
95/6 DonrussElite 25, -Rookie 3
96/7 D.Elite 100, -Aspirations 2
97/8 DonrussElite 104
97/8 DonrussPreferred 90
97/8 D.Priority 113,-DirDep 27
97/8 DonrussStudio 94
94/5 ElitSet 82, -NHLDraft 6
97/8 EssoOlympic 44
96/7 Flair 63
96/7 Fleer 136
96/7 Fleer 73, -Rookie 1
95/6 FleerMetal 169
96/7 FleerNHLPicks 78, -Fab 1
96/7 F.Picks-Dream 3, Jagged 1
95/6 FleerUltra 329,-High 1
96/7 FleerUltra 113
95 Globe 47
97/8 KatchMedallion 97
97/8 KennerSLU
96/7 Kraft-Trophy
96/7 Leaf 210, -Sweaters 14
97/8 Leaf 145
95/6 LeafLimited 25, -Rookie 2
96/7 LeafLimited 73
96/7 LeafPreferred 48, -Steel 35
97/8 Limited 22, 186, -fabric 46
96/7 McDonalds McD9
96/7 MetalUniverse 103
97/8 Omega 152
98/9 Pacific 305
97/8 PacificCrown 58
97/8 PacificCrownRoyale 89
97/8 PcfcDynagon! 83,-Tand 71
97/8 PacificInvincible 92
97/8 PacificParamount 122
98/9 PacificParamount 160
97/8 PcfcRevolutn 92,-TmCL 17
96/7 PaniniStickers 46,152
97/8 PaniniStickers 41
95 PaniniWorlds 160
95/6 Parkhurst 257, 507, PP38
95/6 Parkie-Crown(2) 15
96/7 Pinnacle 205, -ByThe 10
97/8 Pinnacle 155
96/7 Pinn.BeAPlayer-Biscuit 23
97/8 PinnacleBeehive 48
97/8 PinnacleCertified 114
97/8 PinnacleInside 26
95/6 P.Zenith 149,-RookRoll 10
96/7 P.Zenith 103, -ZTeam 13
96/7 Playoff 341
96/7 PinnacleMint! 10
96/7 SB'7Eleven
96/7 Score 240
97/8 Score 131
95/6 SelectCertified 122
96/7 SelectCertified 47
92/3 SemicElitserien 319
95/6 SkyBoxImpact 214
96/7 SkBxImpact 86, 164, -Fox 1
95/6 SP 100, FX15
96/7 SP 107, GF20, HC9
97/8 SPAuthentic 106, 130
96/7 SportFX MiniStix
96/7 SPx 32, GF1
97/8 SPx 34
95/6 Summit 182
96/7 Summit 167, -HiVoltage 4
96/7 TeamOut
95/6 ToppsFinest 116
95/6 Topps 369
98/9 Topps 130
96/7 ToppsNHLPicks RS1
95/6 ToppsStadiumClub ER206
95/6 TSC-Members 38
97/8 ToppsStickers 3
95/6 ToppsSuperSkills SR12
95/6 UD 504, AS12, H23, SE145
96/7 UpperDeck 113, X6, SS18A
97/8 UD 112, SS27, T14A
95/6 UDBeAPlayer 171, LL6
96/7 UDBlackDiamond 141
97/8 UDBlackDiamond 73
98/8 UDChoice 144
95/6 UDCollChoice 406
96/7 UDCC 177, 344,C13, UD39
96/7 UDCollChoice-Oversize 6/8
97/8 UDCC 172, SQ51, S11
96/7 UpperDeck"Ice" 95
97/8 UpperDeckIce 11, L4A
96 Wien 72
97/8 Zenith 43, Z25
95/6 OTT
96/7 OTT/PizzaHut
97/8 OTT

ALGOTSSON, HAKAN
94/5 ElitSet 2, -Gold 7, -Clean 10
95/6 ElitSet 137, -Spidermen
95 Globe 4
94 Semic 51
89/90 SemicElitserien 264
90/1 SemicElitserien 28
91/2 SemicElitserien 278
92/3 SemicElitserien 300
93 SemicSticker 2
95/6 udElite 202

ALHO, RISTO
66/7 Champion 140

ALINIC, JAN
94/5 APS 224
95/6 APS 171, 376
95 Semic 164

ALKULA, JUKKA
66/7 Champion 205
74 Hellas 3
78/9 SM-Liiga 184
71/2 WilliamsFIN 128
72/3 WilliamsFIN 191
73/4 WilliamsFIN 149

ALKUNEN, KAUKO
71/2 WilliamsFIN 277

ALLAIN, RICK
90/1 ProCards 139
91/2 ProCards 51
89/90 SketchMEM 41
88/9 Kitchener 7
89/90 Kitchener 7

ALLAIN, RICK
96/7 Guelph 29

ALLAIRE, BENOÎT
97/8 PHO

ALLAIRE, FRANÇOIS
87/8 MTL
87/8 MTL/Stickers 9
88/9 MTL/Stickers
89/90 MTL
90/1 MTL/Figurine
91/2 MTL

ALLAN, BRETT
98 BowmanCHL 122, A26

ALLAN, BRYAN
98 BowmanCHL25,133,SC1,A12

ALLAN, CHAD
94/5 AutoPhonex 2
95/6 Donruss-CanadaJr 4
95/6 DonrussElite-WorldJrs 3
95/6 Topps 17CJ
94/5 ToppsFinest 147
94/5 UpperDeck 499
95/6 UpperDeck 532
93/4 Saskatoon

ALLAN, MONTAGU
83&87 HallOfFame 123
83 HHOF Postcard (I)

ALLAN, SANDY
92/3 Classic 19
92/3 ClassicFourSport 168
91/2 SketchOHL 51
93/4 Slapshot(NorthBay) 2
95/6 Richmond

ALLAN, SIR MONTAGUE
94/5 HHOFLegends 52

ALLARD, ANDRÉ
79 PaniniSticker 381

ALLARD, PIERRE
90/1 SketchQMJHL 227
91/2 SketchQMJHL 14

ALLEN, BRYAN
98/9 Topps 226
97/8 UpperDeck 401

ALLEN, CHRIS
95/6 Bowman P2
95/6 FutureLegends-SSD 2
95/6 Slapshot 109, 433

ALLEN, GEORGE
34-43 BeeHives(CHI)
39/40 OPC (V301-1) 79
43-47 ParadeSportiv e
45-54 QuakerOats

ALLEN, GREG
90/1 SketchOHL 251
89/90 SketchOHL 145
88/9 NiagaraFalls 19
89/90 NiagaraFalls

ALLEN, JASON
97/8 PacificCrownRoyale 6
97/8 Pinnacle 147
94/5 Slapshot(Sudbury) 25

ALLEN, KEITH
96/7 HHOFLegends 81
54/5 Parkhurst 47
92/3 PHA/UD12APR93

ALLEN, MARKO
93/4 Jyvas-Hyva 55
92/3 Jyvas-Hyva 25
93/4 Sisu 236
94/5 Sisu 4
95/6 Sisu 20

ALLEN, MIKE
90/1 SketchOHL 226
90/1 Kitchener 22

ALLEN, PETER
95/6 Cleveland
93/4 Richmond 10

ALLEN, RICK
87/8 Kitchener 7

ALLEN, SCOTT
91/2 ProCards 444

ALLEN, SQUEE
34-43 BeeHives(NYA)

ALLEN, TOM
83/4 Kingston 5
85/6 London 23
84/5 Ottawa67s

ALLISON, BLAIR
92/3 MPSPhotoSJHL 4
93/4 Maine 55

ALLISON, DAVE
88/9 ProCards(Indianapolis)
93/4 Slapshot(Kingston) 24
83/4 NovaScotia 3
84/5 NovaScotia 2
91/2 Richmond 19

ALLISON, JAMIE
97/8 Donruss 131
95/6 EdgeIce 75
97/8 PacificCrown 315
91/2 SketchOHL 189
93/4 Slapshot(Detroit) 15
94/5 Slapshot(Detroit) 17
94/5 Slapshot(MEM) 91
98/9 Topps 125, A1, I6, SB27
94/5 UpperDeck 464
95/6 SaintJohn

ALLISON, JASON
93/4 Classic 13
94/5 Classic 110, C1, CP14, R1
94/5 Classic T73
93/4 ClassicFourSport 200
94/5 ClassicFourSport 160
94/5 C4'Images 114
93/4 Donruss CAN1
95/6 Donruss 75, -CanadaJr. 12
97/8 DonrussPriority 122
94/5 Flair 195
94/5 Fleer 231
94/5 FleerUltra 386
94/5 Leaf 511, -GoldL.Rookie 13
95/6 Leaf 103
94/5 LeafLimited 98
95/6 LeafLimited 5
97/8 Omega 10
98/9 Pacific 41
97/8 PacificDynagon! 6,-Tand 29
97/8 PacificInvincible 6
98/9 PacificParamount 8
97/8 PacificRevolution 6
95/6 Parkhurst 494
94/5 ParkieSE 194, 208
93/4 Pinnacle 466
94/5 Pinn. 247, 474, 530, RTP7
96/7 PinnacleBeAPlayer 36
97/8 PinnacleInside 147
96/7 PinnacleZenith 125
95/6 Playoff 106
94/5 Premier 467
95/6 ProMagnet 29
94/5 Score 206, 231
95/6 Score 128
97/8 Score 233
97/8 Score(BOS) 7
94/5 Select 193, YE8
91/2 SketchOHL 381
95/6 SkyBoxEmotion 185
94/5 SP 151
96/7 SP 168
97/8 SPAuthentic 10
98/9 SPx "Finite" 6
95/6 Topps 4CJ
94/5 ToppsFinest 55, 154
94/5 ToppsStadiumClub 118
93/4 UpperDeck 537
94/5 UD 242, 535, C4, SP174
94/5 UDBeAPlayer R155
95/6 UpperDeck 59
97/8 UpperDeck 8
97/8 UDBlackDiamond 32
98/9 UDChoice 14
97/8 UDCollChoice 16
97/8 Zenith 80, Z28
95/6 WSH
95/6 Portland

ALLISON, MICHAEL
93/4 Slapshot(Kingston) 24

ALLISON, MIKE
81/2 OPC 221, Topps(E) 94
89/90 OPC/Topps 141
90/1 O-Pee-Chee 417
88/9 PaniniSticker 73
82/3 Post
88/9 L.A/Smokeys
89/90 L.A/Smokeys 4
86/7 TOR
87/8 TOR/P.L.A.Y. 18

ALLISON, PETER
92/3 Windsor 14

ALLISON, RAY
83/4 O-Pee-Chee 259
80/1 OPC/Topps 126
89/90 ProCards(AHL) 338
84/5 KelownaWings&WHL 52
83/4 PHA

ALLISON, SCOTT
90/1 Score 424
90/1 SketchWHL 273
91/2 SketchWHL 276
94/5 CapeBreton
90/1 PrinceAlbert
97/8 SheffieldSteelers

ALLMAN, STEVE
92 SemicSticker 28

ALLSON, JAMES
81/2 Ottawa67s

ALLVIN, PATRICK
96/7 Penascola 5

ALMASY, PETER
92 SemicSticker 239

ALMSTEDT, GRAYDON
84/5 Ottawa67s

ALOI, JOE
87/8 Hull

ALSTEAD, RYAN
92/3 Minnesota

ALTHOFF, CHRISTIAN
94/5 DEL 357

ALTRICHTER, MARTIN
94/5 APS 250
95/6 APS 125

ALVAREZ, MAURICIO
95/6 Slapshot 21

ALWAY, ANDY
83/4 Brantford 26

AMADIO, DAVE
68/9 O-Pee-Chee 157
70/1 OPC/Topps 33
68/9 ShirriffCoin LA10

AMADIO, LEO
52/3 AnonymousOHL 75

AMANN, RICH
95 Globe 219
94 Semic 273
93 SemicSticker 155

AMBROSIO, JEFF
94/5 ParkieSE 266
95/6 Slapshot 143
94/5 SigRookies FF1

AMROZIAK, PETER
89/90 SketchOHL 60
90/1 SketchOHL 76
91/2 SketchOHL 291
92/3 Rochester/Kodak
93/4 Rochester
92/3 Rochester/Dunkin'Donuts

AMIDOVSKI, BUJAR
95/6 Slapshot 106
98 BowmanCHL 32, SC4
98/9 Topps 239

AMODEO, DOMINIC
92/3 CanadaNats

AMODEO, MIKE
72/3 O-Pee-Chee 291
79/80 O-Pee-Chee 268
82 SemicSticker 126
72/3 OttawaNationals
78/9 Winnipeg
79/80 WPG

AMONTE, TONY
97/8 Aces 7 (Clubs)
92/3 Bowman 389
93/4 Donruss 217, 411
94/5 Donruss 107
95/6 Donruss 121
96/7 Donruss 80
97/8 Donruss 102
97/8 DonrussCanadianIce 34
97/8 DonrussElite 97
97/8 DonrussPreferred 64
97/8 DonrussPriority 151
97/8 DonrussStudio 99
96/7 Flair 14
94/5 Fleer 37
92/3 FleerUltra 133, -Rookie 1
93/4 FleerUltra 202
94/5 FleerUltra 273
95/6 FleerUltra 216
96/7 FleerUltra 28
95 Globe 121
93/4 HockeyWit 2
97/8 KatchMedallion 31
93/4 Leaf 17
94/5 Leaf 2
95/6 Leaf 17
96/7 Leaf 92
97/8 Leaf 139
97/8 Limited 105
96/7 MetalUniverse 24
97/8 Omega 46
91/2 OPC/Topps 26
92/3 OPC 155, 255, -25Years 24
91/2 opcPremier 11
98/9 Pacific 142
97/8 PacificCrown 264
97/8 PacificCrownRoyale 27
97/8 PcfcDynagon! 24,-Tand 33
97/8 PacificInvincible 27
97/8 PacificParamount 40
98/9 PacificParamount 43
97/8 PacificRevolution 27
92/3 PaniniSticker 270, T
93/4 PaniniSticker 90
94/5 PaniniSticker 128
95/6 PaniniSticker 160
96/7 PaniniSticker 160
97/8 PaniniSticker 131
91/2 Parkhurst 114, 443
92/3 Parkhurst 107, 235
93/4 Parkhurst 132
94/5 ParkieSE 36
94/5 Parkhurst V56
95/6 Parkhurst 311
91/2 Pinnacle 301, 390
92/3 Pinnacle 55, -Team2000 4
93/4 Pinnacle 6, -Tm2001 19
94/5 Pinnacle 16
96/7 Pinnacle 54
97/8 Pinnacle 148
96/7 PinnacleBeAPlayer 66
97/8 PinnacleCertified 68
97/8 PinnacleInside 53
95/6 Playoff 235
94/5 POG 65
95/6 POG 63
94/5 Post
93/4 PowerPlay 156
93/4 Premier 70
94/5 Premier 5
91/2 ProSet 550
92/3 ProSet 118, -Rookie 1
91/2 PSPlatinum 262
91/2 Score(CND) 288, (U.S) 398
92/3 Score 389, 415, 506
92/3 Score-YoungStar 2
93/4 Score 215
94/5 Score 92
95/6 Score 133
96/7 Score 169
97/8 Score 114
92/3 SeasonsPatch 27

94/5 Select 115
93 SemicSticker 188
96/7 SkyBoxImpact 16
94/5 SP 26
95/6 SP 28
96/7 SP 32, HC18
97/8 SPAuthentic 29, I29, S10
97/8 SPx 8
98/8 SPx"Finite" 18, 106
95/6 Summit 165
92/3 Topps 6, 229
95/6 Topps 79, 4PL
98/9 Topps 204
96/7 ToppsNHLPicks 133
92/3 ToppsStadiumClub 32, 250
93/4 ToppsStadiumClub 458
95/6 ToppsStadiumClub 117
97/8 ToppsSticker 2
91/2 UpperDeck 440, 450
92/3 UD 13, 138, 359, 453, 635
92/3 UD AR1,AR7,-LockerAS 51
93/4 UpperDeck 64, SP-97
94/5 UpperDeck 4, SP105
95/6 UpperDeck 18, SE18
96/7 UD 32, -AllStarYCTG AR1
97/8 UD 208, 245, GJ6
97/8 UD S23, SG10, SS18, T9A
93/4 UDBeAPlayer 1
94/5 UDBeAPlayer R17, -Aut. 97
96/7 UDBlackDiamond 173
97/8 UDBlackDiamond 101
98/9 UDChoice 51, SQ26
95/6 UDCollChoice 206
96/7 UDCollChoice 49
97/8 UDCC 44, C10, SQ65
97/8 udDiamondVision 19
96/7 UpperDeck"Ice" 13
97/8 UpperDeckIce 63
97/8 Zenith 78

AMORE, ANGELO
91/2 SketchOHL 358

ANCHIKOSKI, WAYNE
91/2 AvantGardeBC 156, 167
87/8 Portland
88/9 Portland

ANCICKA, MARTIN
94/5 APS 55
95/6 APS 347

ANDANOFF, JIM
83/4 Belleville 14
84/5 Belleville 27

ANDELMIN, TEUVO
66/7 Champion 81

ANDERSEN, CATO TOM
95 Globe 192
94 Semic 253
95 Semic 181
92 SemicSticker 34
93 SemicSticker 232

ANDERSEN, RICHARD
79 PaniniSticker 364

ANDERSON, CORY
88/9 Kamloops

ANDERSON, DAN
85/6 Arizona

ANDERSON, DAVE
90/1 SketchOHL 126
89/90 SketchOHL 39
91/2 Oshawa

ANDERSON, DEAN
89/90 ProCards(AHL) 105
90/1 ProCards 166
88/9 Flint
91/2 Knoxville

ANDERSON, EARL
82? JDMcCarthy
77/8 OPC/Topps 114

ANDERSON, ERNIE
23/4 PaulinsCandy 66

ANDERSON, EVAN
91/2 AirCanadaSJHL A45, 28

ANDERSON, GLENN
90/1 Bowman 195
91/2 Bowman 116
92/3 Bowman 104
95/6 DEL 441
93/4 Donruss 340, 460
94/5 Donruss 254
83/4 Esso
92/3 FleerUltra 207
93/4 FleerUltra 9
94/5 FleerUltra 135
88/9 FritoLay
93/4 HockeyWit 50
86/7 Kraft Sports 11
89/90 Kraft 10
93/4 Leaf 41
94/5 Leaf 14
81/2 O-Pee-Chee 108
82/3 O-Pee-Chee 100
83/4 O-Pee-Chee 24
84/5 O-Pee-Chee 238
85/6 O-Pee-Chee 168
86/7 OPC/Topps 80
87/8 O-Pee-Chee 199
88/9 OPC/Topps 189
89/90 O-Pee-Chee 226, 303
90/1 OPC/Topps 145
91/2 OPC/Topps 124
92/3 O-Pee-Chee 134
91/2 opcPremier 10
87/8 opcStars 1
81/2 opcSticker 217
82/3 opcSticker 99-100
83/4 opcSticker 92-93, 158
84/5 opcSticker 247-48
85/6 opcSticker 227/94
86/7 opcSticker 78
87/8 opcSticker 95
88/9 opcSticker 229
89/90 opcSticker 218
90/1 Panini(EDM) 1
87/8 PaniniSticker 265
88/9 PaniniSticker 57
89/90 PaniniSticker 77
90/1 PaniniSticker 227
91/2 PaniniSticker 120
92/3 PaniniSticker 76
93/4 PaniniSticker 225
91/2 Parkhurst 177
92/3 Parkhurst 178
93/4 Parkhurst 201
80/1 Pepsi Cap
91/2 Pinnacle 12
92/3 Pinnacle 355
93/4 Pinnacle 398
96/7 Pinnacle 171
82/3 Post
93/4 PowerPlay 237
93/4 Premier 104
94/5 Premier 270
90/1 ProSet 81
91/2 ProSet 75
92/3 ProSet 185
83/4 PuffySticker 2
90/1 Score 114, -HotCards 54
91/2 Score(CDN) 47, 611
91/2 Score(US) 47, 61T
92/3 Score 241
93/4 Score 180, 449
83/4 7ElevenCokeCup
84/5 7ElevenDisk
83/4 SouhaitsRen.KeyChain
92/3 Topps 162
91/2 ToppsStadiumClub 116
92/3 ToppsStadiumClub 124
93/4 ToppsStadiumClub 168
90/1 UpperDeck 284
91/2 UpperDeck 250
95/6 UDCollChoice 46
83/4 Vachon 21
81/2 EDM/RedRooster
82/3 EDM/RedRooster
83/4 EDM
83/4 EDM/Buttons
83/4 EDM/McDonald
84/5 EDM
84/5 EDM/RedRooster
85/6 EDM/RedRooster
86/7 EDM
86/7 EDM/RedRooster
87/8 EDM
88/9 EDM
88/9 EDM/ActionMagazine 9
90/1 EDM/McGavins
90/1 TOR/P.L.A.Y. 9
92/3 TOR/Kodak
93/4 TOR/Blacks 3

ANDERSON, GRANT
83/4 Brantford 24

ANDERSON, JACK
75/6 Hamilton

ANDERSON, JIM
74/5 OPC/Topps 118
74/5 WSH

ANDERSON, JOHN
83/4 Esso
84/5 Kelloggs Disk
80/1 OPC/Topps 79
81/2 O-Pee-Chee 313
82/3 O-Pee-Chee 315
83/4 O-Pee-Chee 325
84/5 OPC 295, Topps 136
85/6 OPC/Topps 20
86/7 OPC/Topps 13
87/8 OPC/Topps 45
88/9 OPC/Topps 190
89/90 OPC/Topps 124
81/2 opcSticker 107
82/3 opcSticker 73, 74
83/4 opcSticker 30, 31
84/5 opcSticker 18
85/6 opcSticker 10 /138
87/8 opcSticker 204/63
86/7 opcSticker 54 /192
88/9 opcSticker270 /134
87/8 PaniniSticker 45
88/9 PaniniSticker 239
80/1 Pepsi Cap
82/3 Post
90/1 ProCards 543
91/2 ProCards 361
83/4 PuffySticker 4
83/4 7ElevenCokeCup
84/5 7ElevenDisk
83/4 Vachon 81
86/7 HFD/JuniorWhalers
87/8 HFD/JuniorWhalers
88/9 HFD/JuniorWhalers
85/6 QUE/GeneralFoods
85/6 QUE/Pennant
85/6 QUE/Placemat
85/6 QUE/Provigo
86/7 QUE/McDonald
78/9 TOR
79/80 TOR
80/1 TOR
81/2 TOR
82/3 TOR
83/4 TOR
84/5 TOR
92/3 SanDiego

ANDERSON, OLE
95/6 Slapshot 234

ANDERSON, PERRY
91/2 OPC/Topps 501
92/3 O-Pee-Chee 38
91/2 Parkhurst 164
89/90 ProCards(AHL) 216
90/1 ProCards 561
91/2 ProSet 481
91/2 Score(CDN) 649, (U.S) 99T
92/3 Topps 286
92/3 ToppsStadiumClub 89
85/6 N.J
86/7 N.J/SOBER
88/9 N.J/Caretta
91/2 S.J.
92/3 SanDiego

ANDERSON, RON C.
70/1 Colgate Stamp 48
70/1 EddieSargent 18
71/2 EddieSargent 18
70/1 Esso Stamp
69/70 O-Pee-Chee 14
71/2 OPC/Topps 163

ANDERSON, RON F.
72/3 O-Pee-Chee 298

ANDERSON, RON H.
74/5 Loblaws
74/5 OPC 314
74/5 WSH

ANDERSON, RUSS
78/9 OPC/Topps 156
79/80 OPC/Topps 264
82/3 HFD/JuniorWhalers
84/5 L.A/Smokeys
77/8 PGH/PuckBuck

ANDERSON, SHAWN
91/2 Bowman 147
94/5 Leaf 346
88/9 ProCards(Rochester)
90/1 ProSet 513
91/2 ToppsStadiumClub 358
86/7 BUF
87/8 BUF/WonderBread
89/90 BUF/Campbell
92/3 WSH/Kodak

ANDERSON, TOM
34-43 BeeHives(NYA)
36-39 DiamondMatch (2), (3)
39/40 OPC (V301-1) 61

ANDERSON, VERN
91/2 AirCanadaSJHL C13

ANDERSON, WILL
84/5 Kamloops
94/5 Minnesota

ANDERSSON, BO MIKAEL
91/2 Bowman 11
92/3 Bowman 158
93/4 Donruss 322
94/5 Donruss 14
93/4 EASports 130
92/3 FleerUltra 406
93/4 FleerUltra 421
94/5 FleerUltra 370
95 Globe 42
93/4 Leaf 285
94/5 Leaf 347
92/3 O-Pee-Chee 214
90/1 OPC/Topps 35
91/2 OPC/Topps 197
92/3 opcPremier 55
98/9 Pacific 395
97/8 PacificRegime 182
90/1 PaniniSticker 47
92/3 PaniniSticker 258
93/4 PaniniSticker 216
94/5 PaniniSticker 186
96/7 PaniniSticker 132
97/8 PaniniSticker 104
91/2 Parkhurst 63
92/3 Parkhurst 169
93/4 Parkhurst 198
94/5 Parkhurst 226
95/6 Parkhurst 196
92/3 Pinnacle 384
93/4 Pinnacle 329
94/5 Pinnacle 451
96/7 PinnacleBeAPlayer 65
94/5 POG 220
93/4 PowerPlay 440
93/4 Premier 150
94/5 Premier 287
88/9 ProCards(Rochester)
90/1 ProSet 98
91/2 ProSet 394
92/3 ProSet 65
91/2 PSPlatinum 180
92/3 Score 215
93/4 Score 427
95 Semic 72
89/90 SemicElitserien 274
90/1 SemicElitserien 45
91/2 SemicElitserien 290
93 SemicSticker 37
92/3 Topps 151
95/6 Topps 123
91/2 ToppsStadiumClub 39
92/3 ToppsStadiumClub 348
93/4 ToppsStadiumClub 97, 427
94/5 ToppsStadiumClub 75
91/2 UpperDeck 238
92/3 UpperDeck 103
94/5 UpperDeck 297
96/7 UpperDeck 155
95/6 UDCollChoice 182
85/6 BUF
87/8 BUF/BlueShield
87/8 BUF/WonderBread
88/9 BUF/BlueShield
88/9 BUF/WonderBread
89/90 HFD/JuniorWhalers
90/1 HFD/JuniorWhalers
91/2 HFD/JuniorWhalers
92/3 T.B/Sheraton
94/5 T.B/SkyBoxSportsCafe
95/6 T.B.
95/6 T.B/SkyBoxSportsCafe

ANDERSSON, CHRISTER
72 SemicSticker 44

ANDERSSON, DICK
89/90 SemicElitserien 193

ANDERSSON, ERIK
90/1 SemicElitserien 97
91/2 SemicElitserien 25

ANDERSSON, FREDRIK
94/5 ElitSet 17, -Clean 9
95/6 ElitSet 271
89/90 SemicElitserien 169, 215
90/1 SemicElitserien 3
91/2 SemicElitserien 201
92/3 SemicElitserien 223
92 SemicSticker 52

ANDERSSON, GUNNAR
72 SemicSticker 59

ANDERSSON, HENRIK
89/90 SemicElitserien 246
90/1 SemicElitserien 156

ANDERSSON, J.A.
91/2 SemicElitserien 310

ANDERSSON, JON
90/1 SemicElitserien 47

ANDERSSON, KENT-ERIK
80/1 O-Pee-Chee 383
81/2 OPC 158, Topps(W) 102
82/3 O-Pee-Chee 218
78/9 OPC/Topps 17
79 PaniniSticker 200
78/9 MIN/Cloverleaf 4
79/80 MIN
80/1 MIN
81/2 MIN

ANDERSSON, KENNETH
90/1 SemicElitserien 196

ANDERSSON, MATTIAS
89/90 SemicElitserien 81
90/1 SemicElitserien 206
91/2 SemicElitserien 134
92/3 SemicElitserien 155

ANDERSSON, MIKAEL
see Bo Mikael Andersson

ANDERSSON, NIKLAS
95/6 Bowman 126
92/3 ClassicProspects 120
96/7 Donruss 214
96/7 DonrussElite 89
95/6 FutureLegends 2
95 Globe 51
97/8 PacificCrown 144
96/7 PaniniSticker 98
97/8 PaniniSticker 75
95/6 Parkhurst 398
96/7 PinnacleBeAPlayer 98
91/2 ProCards 533
96/7 Score 248
93/4 Score 460
96/7 SelectCertified 57
89/90 SemicElitserien 281
90/1 SemicElitserien 39
91/2 SemicElitserien 317
93 SemicSticker 44
96/7 SkyBoxImpact 165
96/7 Summit 172
91/2 UpperDeck 29
93/4 UpperDeck 239
96/7 UpperDeck 292
96/7 UDCollChoice 165
97/8 UDCollChoice 156

ANDERSSON, OLA
89/90 SemicElitserien 68
90/1 SemicElitserien 66
91/2 SemicElitserien 246

ANDERSSON, PAUL
94/5 ElitSet 107
95/6 ElitSet 131
89/90 SemicElitserien 283
91/2 SemicElitserien 265
92/3 SemicElitserien 298
95/6 udElite 200

ANDERSSON, PENTTI
66/7 Champion 119

ANDERSSON, PETER
96/7 DEL 276
94/5 ElitSet 267
95/6 ElitSet 87, 307, -Face 14
95 Globe 11
94/5 Parkhurst 88
94/5 Premier 212
95 Semic 60
90/1 SemicElitserien 128
91/2 SemicElitserien 180, 343
92/3 SemicElitserien 345
91 SemicSticker 36
92 SemicSticker 55
93 SemicSticker 27
95/6 udElite 138, 231, 257
92/3 UpperDeck 481
93/4 UpperDeck 71

ANDERSSON, PETER
82 SemicSticker 12
89 SemicSticker 11
91 SemicSticker 35
92 SemicSticker 54
85/6 QUE

ANDERSSON, SHAWN
95/6 ElitSet 155
95/6 udElite 12

ANDERSSON-JUNKKA, JONAS
94/5 AutoPhonex
94/5 ElitSet 184, -Rookie 2
95/6 ElitSet 138
94/5 ParkieSE 238

ANDREA, PAUL
70/1 Esso Stamp
70/1 OPC/Topps 77
68/9 ShirriffCoin Pi8
91/2 SketchOHL 24
72/3 Cleveland
91/2 Cornwall 23
95/6 Dayton

ANDREOLI, DAVE
81/2 SSMarie

ANDRES, BRUCE
81/2 Indianapolis 20

ANDREWS, AL
82/3 Kingston 7

ANDREWS, JEFF
93/4 Slapshot(Oshawa) 9

ANDREWS, LLOYD
24/5 Champs (C144)
23/4 (V145-1) 21
24/5 (V145-2) 59

ANDREYCHUK, DAVE
90/1 Bowman 246
91/2 Bowman 22
92/3 Bowman 44
95/6 Bowman 7
83 CanadaJuniors
93/4 Donruss 342
94/5 Donruss 323
95/6 Donruss 98
96/7 Donruss 109
97/8 Donruss 61
97/8 DonrussPreferred 66
97/8 DonrussPriority 152
97/8 D.CanadianIce 105, 148
93/4 EASports 136
94/5 Flair 177
94/5 Fleer 212
95/6 FleerMetal 141
92/3 FleerUltra 12
93/4 FleerUltra 57, -Red 1
94/5 FU 211,-Red 1,-Power 1
95/6 FleerUltra 158
96/7 FleerUltra 92
95/6 Hoyle'WEST 2 (Hearts)
94/5 Kraft'HockeyH
93/4 Leaf 63, -GoldL.AS 4
94/5 Leaf 72
95/6 Leaf 270
96/7 Leaf 24
97/8 Leaf 116
94/5 LeafLimited 34
95/6 LeafLimited 21
96/7 LeafPreferred 51
97/8 Limited 22, 74
94/5 McDonalds 18
96/7 MetalUniverse 85
84/5 OPC 17, 353, Topps 13
85/6 OPC/Topps 143
86/7 OPC/Topps 16
87/8 OPC/Topps 3
88/9 OPC/Topps 163, M
89/90 OPC/Topps 106, OPC 299
90/1 OPC/Topps 169
91/2 OPC/Topps 38
92/3 O-Pee-Chee 141
84/5 opcSticker 209, 210
85/6 opcSticker 187/61
86/7 opcSticker 49
87/8 opcSticker 147/8
88/9 opcSticker 261
89/90 opcSticker 258/137
98/9 Pacific 260
97/8 PacificCrown 84
97/8 PcfcDynagon! 67,-Tand 37
97/8 PacificInvincible 75
97/8 PacificParamount 100
98/9 PacificParamount 130
87/8 PaniniSticker 19, 27
88/9 PaniniSticker 223
89/90 PaniniSticker 215
90/1 PaniniSticker 29
91/2 PaniniSticker 309
92/3 PaniniSticker 249
93/4 PaniniSticker 223
94/5 PaniniSticker 194, 236, JJ
95/6 PaniniSticker 203
96/7 PaniniSticker 82
97/8 PaniniSticker 71
91/2 Parkhurst 17, 437
92/3 Parkhurst 10, 409
93/4 Parkhurst 200
94/5 Parkhurst 303, V89
95/6 Parkhurst 470
94/5 ParkieSE 182
91/2 Pinnacle 122
92/3 Pinnacle 58
93/4 Pinnacle 42,-NiftyFifty 1, 11
94/5 Pinnacle 5, Promo 5
95/6 Pinnacle 31
96/7 Pinnacle 177
96/7 PinnacleBeAPlayer 2
97/8 Pinnacle 131
97/8 PinnacleCertified 69
97/8 PinnacleInside 118
95/6 Pinn.Zenith 41, -Gifted 13
95/6 Playoff 93
96/7 Playoff 348
94/5 POG 229
95/6 POG 260
93/4 PowerPlay 238, -Slap 1
93/4 Premier 235
94/5 Premier 38, 510
94/5 Premier-Finest(Topps) 4
95/6 ProMagnet 71
90/1 ProSet 17, 363
91/2 ProSet 23
92/3 ProSet 15, 249
91/2 PSPlatinum 8
90/1 Score 189, -Hot 87
91/2 Score(CDN) 497, (U.S) 277
92/3 Score 204
93/4 Score 343, 481, DD1
94/5 Score DT11, NP10
95/6 Score 109
96/7 Score 44
97/8 Score 115
97/8 Score(N.J.) 3
94/5 Select 99
95/6 SelectCertified 28
95/6 SkyBoxEmotion 168
95/6 SkyBoxImpact 158, 246
96/7 SkyBoxImpact 66
94/5 SP 119
95/6 Summit 36
96/7 Summit 124
95/6 SuperSkills 52
95/6 SuperSticker 119
92/3 Topps 164
95/6 Topps 175
94/5 ToppsFinest 39
95/6 ToppsFinest 6
96/7 ToppsNHLPicks 127
91/2 ToppsStadiumClub 93
92/3 ToppsStadiumClub 132
93/4 ToppsStadiumClub 23
93/4 TSC-MembersOnly 13
94/5 T.StadiumClub 58, 140
95/6 ToppsStadiumClub 5

90/1 UpperDeck 41
91/2 UpperDeck 124
92/3 UpperDeck 269, 456
93/4 UpperDeck 86, SP-155
93/4 UDBeAPlayer-Roots 18
94/5 UD 313, R6, R35, SP77
95/6 UpperDeck 367, SE79
96/7 UpperDeck 89
97/8 UpperDeck 96
94/5 UDBeAPlayer R33, -Aut. 52
95/6 UDCollChoice 20
96/7 UDCollChoice 153
97/8 UDCollChoice 142
84/5 BUF/BlueShield
85/6 BUF
86/7 BUF
87/8 BUF/BlueShield
87/8 BUF/WonderBread
88/9 BUF/BlueShield
88/9 BUF/WonderBread
89/90 BUF/BlueShield
89/90 BUF/Campbell
90/1 BUF/BlueShield
90/1 BUF/Campbell
91/2 BUF/BlueShield
91/2 BUF/Campbell
92/3 BUF/BlueShield
92/3 BUF/Jubilee
96/7 N.J/Sharp
92/3 TOR/Kodak
93/4 TOR/Abalene
93/4 TOR/Blacks 13
94/5 TOR
80/1 Oshawa 7
81/2 Oshawa 12

ANDRIJEVSKI, ALEXANDER
92/3 ClassicProspects 75
91/2 OPC 31R
95/6 Sisu 225, 367
96/7 Sisu 20, -MightyAdv. 3
92/3 UpperDeck 333, 342
93/4 UpperDeck 26
92/3 Indianapolis

ANDRUFF, RON
77/8 O-Pee-Chee 288
78/9 O-Pee-Chee 315
76/7 COL.R/CokeCans
77/8 COL.R/CokeCans
93/4 COL.R

ANDRUSAK, GREG
90/1 CanadaNats
94/5 Classic T52
94/5 ClassicFourSport 156
92/3 ClassicProspects 110
93/4 ClassicProspects 156
96/7 DEL 28
92/3 ClevelandLumberjacks 8
93/4 ClevelandLumberjacks

ANGELELLI, DAN
91/2 LakeSuperior

ANGELSTAD, MEL
93/4 ThunderBay
94/5 ThunderBay
95/6 ThunderBay

ANGER, NIKLAS
95/6 UpperDeck 561
95/6 UDCollChoice 344
97/8 udSwedish 49

ANGLEHART, SERGE
90/1 ProCards 485
91/2 ProCards 124
89/90 SketchMEM 74

ANGNEL, BENJAMIN
95 PaniniWorlds 106

ANGOTTI, LOU
64-67 BeeHives(CHI, NYR)
64/5 CokeCap NYR17
70/1 Colgate Stamp 8
70/1 DadsCookies
70/1 EddieSargent 40
71/2 EddieSargent 38
72/3 EddieSargent 65
70/1 Esso Stamp
72/3 Letraset 16
68/9 OPC/T. 103, -Puck 11
69/70 O-Pee-Chee 134
70/1 OPC/Topps 12
71/2 OPC/Topps 212
72/3 O-Pee-Chee 243
73/4 O-Pee-Chee 224
74/5 OPC/Topps 63
94/5 Parkie(64/5) 96
95/6 Parkie(66/7) 28
68/9 ShirriffCoin PGH11
71/2 TheTorontoSun
64/5 Topps 66
66/7 Topps 116
70/1 CHI
73/4 STL

ANHOLT, DARRELL
83/4 Springfield 19

ANHOLT, PETER
90/1 SketchWHL 22
91/2 SketchWHL 140
93/4 RedDeer

ANISIN, VYACHESLAV
72 Hellas 73
74 Hellas 42
73/4 Soviet Stars 14
74/5 Soviet Stars 18
91/2 Trends72 90
72/3 WilliamsFIN 21
73/4 WilliamsFIN 1

ANKEN, OLIVIER
79 PaniniSticker 258

ANNECK, DORIAN
94/5 SigRookies 45

ANNING, LES
49 TurfCigarette s 44

ANSAKORPI, PERTTI
66/7 Champion 157
65/6 Hellas 157
70/1 Kuvajulkaisut 208
71/2 WilliamsFIN 129
72/3 WilliamsFIN 192
73/4 WilliamsFIN 150

ANTAL, ELOD
79 PaniniSticker 313

ANTISIN, MISKO
95 PaniniWorlds 125
83/4 Victoria
84/5 Victoria

ANTONIK, MIKI
92/3 BCJHL 127

ANTONIN, JIRI
95/6 APS 322

ANTONOVICH, JEFF
94/5 Slapshot(MEM) 16

ANTONOVICH, MIKE
79/80 O-Pee-Chee 349
74/5 opcWHA 37
75/6 opcWHA 111
76/7 opcWHA 23
77/8 opcWHA 34
83/4 N.J.
72/3 Minnesota
74/5 Minnesota

ANTOS, DEAN
91/2 ProCards 232

ANTOS, MILAN
94/5 APS 269
95/6 APS 140

ANTOSKI, SHAWN
93/4 Donruss 498
93/4 FleerUltra 437
94/5 FleerUltra 381
93/4 Leaf 368
91/2 OPC/Topps 98
92/3 opcPremier 10
93/4 Parkhurst 479
94/5 Parkhurst 248
96/7 PinnacleBeAPlayer 120
93/4 Premier 31
94/5 Premier 226
91/2 ProCards 595
90/1 Score 429
91/2 Score(CDN) 353, (U.S) 323
97/8 Score(ANA) 15
89/90 SketchOHL 152
93/4 ToppsStadiumClub 288
91/2 UpperDeck 351
92/3 UpperDeck 81
93/4 UpperDeck 325
96/7 UpperDeck 318
96/7 ANA/UpFrontSports
94/5 PHA
92/3 VAN/RoadTrip
93/4 VAN/Coins
94/5 VAN
92/3 Hamilton

ANTOSKI, SHAYNE
89/90 SketchOHL 161
90/1 SketchMEM 118
90/1 SketchOHL 301
91/2 SketchOHL 120
93/4 Huntington

ANTTI, PETTER
89/90 SemicElitserien 167

ANTTILA, KARI
70/1 Kuvajulkaisut 327

ANTTILA, PEKKA
70/1 Kuvajulkaisut 365

ANZALONE, FRANK
90/1 Newmarket
93/4 Roanoke
94/5 Roanoke
95/6 Roanoke

APPEL, JOACHIM
94/5 DEL 273
95/6 DEL 264
96/7 DEL 158

APPERT, SETH
91/2 FerrisState

APPLETON, JOEL
91/2 AirCanadaSJHL D2

APPS, J. SYL (SR.)
34-43 BeeHives(TOR)
45-64 BeeHives(TOR)
83&87 HallOfFame 212
83 HHOF Postcard (O)
36/7 OPC (V304D) 101
37/8 OPC (V304E) 141
39/40 OPC (V301-1) 6
40/1 OPC (V301-2) 118, 146
55/6 Parkhurst 28
93/4 Parkie(56/7) P5
38/9 QuakerOats
45-54 QuakerOats
36/7 WWGum (V356) 23

APPS, SYL M. (JR.)
77/8 Coke Mini
70/1 Colgate Stamp 26
70/1 EddieSargent 113
71/2 EddieSargent 161
72/3 EddieSargent 169
91/2 Kraft 50, 83
74/5 LiptonSoup 49
74/5 Loblaws
71/2 OPC/Topps 77
72/3 OPC 115, Topps 11
73/4 OPC 76, Topps 160
74/5 OPC/Topps 13, 183
75/6 OPC/Topps 130
76/7 OPC/Topps 50, 218
76/7 OPC 392, T-Glossy 13
77/8 OPC/Topps 248
78/9 OPC/Topps 56
79/80 O-Pee-Chee 366
80/1 O-Pee-Chee 362
72/3 Post Transfers 8
71/2 TheTorontoSun
71/2 PGH
74/5 PGH
77/8 PGH/PuckBuck

ARABSKI, ROB
94/5 Slapshot(Brantford) 7

ARAVIRTA, HANNU
92/3 Jyvas-Hyva 69
95/6 Sisu 386

ARBELIUS, PEKKA
80/1 Mallasjuoma 110
82 SemicSticker 46
82 Skopbank
71/2 WilliamsFIN 297

ARBEZ, DEREK
95/6 SwiftCurrent

ARBOUR, AL
52/3 AnonymousOHL 5
45-64 BeeHives(CHI,DET,TOR)
62 CeramicTiles
82? JDMcCarthy
93/4 Kraft-Coach
68/9 O-Pee-Chee 128
69/70 OPC 178, -Sticker
74/5 OPC/Topps 91
53/4 Parkhurst 37
93/4 Parkie(56/7) 61
90/1 ProSet 671
60/1 ShirriffCoin 67
61/2 ShirriffCoin 60
62/3 ShirriffCoin 20
68/9 ShirriffCoin STL3
71/2 TheTorontoSun
57/8 Topps 38
58/9 Topps 64
59/60 Topps 35
60/1 Topps 64
61/2 York 33
83/4 NYI/Islander 29
84/5 NYI 29
89/90 NYI
71/2 STL
72/3 STL/8"x10"
92/3 STL/UpperDeck 3

ARBOUR, AMOS
23/4 (V145-1) 20

ARBOUR, JOHN
68/9 O-Pee-Chee 189
75/6 opcWHA 54
71/2 TheTorontoSun
71/2 STL
72/3 Minnesota
74/5 Minnesota

ARBOUR, TY
23/4 PaulinsCandy 44

ARBULIC, MIKE
93/4 Portland

ARCAND, BILLY
51/2 LavalDairy 54
52/3 StLawrence 99

ARCANGELONI, STÉPHANE
95 PaniniWorlds 107
94 Semic 222

ARCELLA, GERRY
91/2 SketchOHL 379

ARCHAMBAULT, MICHEL
72/3 O-Pee-Chee 320
73/4 QuébecNordiques

ARCHIBAL, GEORGES
51/2 LacStJean 47

ARCHIBALD, DAVE
90/1 CanadaNats
91/2 CanadaNats
92 CanadaWinterOlympics 180
96/7 DEL 65
93/4 Donruss 231
94/5 Leaf 432
88/9 OPC/Topps 112
89/90 OPC/Topps 10
89/90 opcSticker 201/59
88/9 opcStickFS 1
88/9 PaniniSticker 88
94/5 PaniniSticker 102
94/5 ParkieSE 118
93/4 PowerPlay 168
93/4 Premier 458
90/1 Score 162
92/3 Score-CndOlympic 3
94/5 Score 133
93/4 ToppsStadiumClub 399
92/3 UpperDeck 473
93/4 UpperDeck 105
94/5 UpperDeck 383
87/8 MIN
92/3 OTT
93/4 OTT/Kraft
94/5 OTT/Bell
95/6 OTT
92/3 Binghampton
86/7 Portland

ARCHIBALD, DENNIS
91/2 AvantGardeBCJHL 130
92/3 BCJHL 44

ARÈS, STEVE
90/1 SketchQMJHL 75
91/2 SketchQMJHL 109

ARESHENKOFF, RON
88/9 EDM/ActionMagazine 103

ARGENTOS, GIUSEPPE
91/2 SketchQMJHL 41

ARGIROPOULOS, JOHN
95/6 Slapshot 291

ARIAL, SIMON
91/2 SketchQMJHL 150

ARIMA, TONY
80/1 Mallasjuoma 54
95/6 Sisu 173

ARKIOMAA, TERO
96/7 DEL 13
92/3 Jyvas-Hyva 136
93/4 Jyvas-Hyva 232
95 PaniniWorlds 184
94 Semic 23
95 Semic 31
93/4 Sisu 198
94/5 Sisu 85, 173, -Fire 1
95/6 Sisu 170, 307
95/6 SisuLimited 33

ARMELIN, JOHN
82/3 SSMarie

ARMITAGE, STEVE
97/8 Pinnacle-CBC Sports 1

ARMSTRONG, BILL C.
90/1 ProCards 45
91/2 ProCards 280
89/90 SketchMEM 82
89/90 SketchOHL 20, 199
89/90 Oshawa 32

ARMSTRONG, BILL H.
91/2 OPC/Topps 36
89/90 ProCards(AHL) 349
90/1 ProCards 50
91/2 ProCards 266
92/3 Cincinnati

ARMSTRONG, BOB
45-64 BeeHives(BOS)
52/3 Parkhurst 84
54/5 Parkhurst 55
93/4 Parkie(56/7) 7
23/4 PaulinsCandy 56
60/1 ShirriffCoin 118
61/2 ShirriffCoin 12
54/5 Topps 7
57/8 Topps 3
58/9 Topps 1
59/60 Topps 39
60/1 Topps 56
61/2 Topps 13
56-66 TorontoStar 2FEB60
57/8 BOS
91/2 BOS/Legends (x2)

ARMSTRONG, CHRIS
94/5 Classic 32, T25
93/4 Donruss CAN2
95/6 EdgeIce 22
93/4 Pinnacle 459
93/4 UpperDeck 546

ARMSTRONG, DEREK
93/4 ClassicProspects 178
94/5 Leaf 51
97/8 PacificCrown 300
96/7 PinnacleBeAPlayer 179
91/2 SketchOHL 246
91/2 Sudbury 14
92/3 Sudbury 16

ARMSTRONG, GEORGE
45-64 BeeHives(TORx3)
64-67 BeeHives(TOR)
62 CeramicTiles
63-5 ChexPhoto
64/5 CokeCap TOR-9
65/6 CocaCola
83&87 HallOfFame 197
83 HHOF Postcard (N)
96/7 HHOFLegends 76
70/1 OPC/Topps 113
52/3 Parkhurst 51
53/4 Parkhurst 11
54/5 Parkhurst 24
55/6 Parkhurst 4
57/8 Parkhurst(TOR) 1
58/9 Parkhurst 7, 48
59/60 Parkhurst 7
60/1 Parkhurst 17
61/2 Parkhurst 17
62/3 Parkhurst 13
63/4 Parkhurst 13, 73
92/3 Parkhurst 17
93/4 Parkhurst 38
93/4 Parkie(56/7) 125
94/5 Parkie(64/5) 122
95/6 Parkie(66/7) 116, 139, 146
67/8 PostFlipBooks
45-54 QuakerOats
60/1 ShirriffCoin 9
61/2 ShirriffCoin 51
62/3 ShirriffCoin 10
68/9 ShirriffCoin TOR1
63/4 TheTorontoStar
64/5 Topps 69
65/6 Topps 19
66/7 Topps 84, -USATest 17
67/8 Topps 83
54-67 TorontoStar V8
56-66 Tor.Star 57/8,58/9,63/4
60/1 York, -Glasses
61/2 York 37
62/3 YorkTransfer 17
63/4 York 16
67/8 York [x2]
64/5 TOR
66/7 TOR/Coaster
68/9 TOR
69/70 TOR

ARMSTRONG, JACK
52/3 AnonymousOHL 91
51/2 BasDuFleuve 6

ARMSTRONG, MURRAY
34-43 BeeHives(TOR)
37/8 OPC (V304E) 146
39/40 OPC (V301-1) 19

ARMSTRONG, NEIL
91/2 ProSet-HOF 5

ARMSTRONG, RANDY
95/6 Birmingham

ARMSTRONG, TIM
88/9 ProCards(Newmarket)
89/90 ProCards(AHL) 114

ARNASON, CHUCK
72-84 Dernière 72/3
74/5 Loblaws
74/5 O-Pee-Chee 385
75/6 OPC/Topps 57
76/7 OPC/Topps 92
77/8 O-Pee-Chee 379
78/9 O-Pee-Chee 389
76/7 COL.R
76/7 COL.R/CokeCans
72/3 MTL
74/5 PGH

ARNHOLT, P.M.
96/7 DEL 333

ARNIEL, SCOTT
90/1 Bowman 243
91/2 Bowman 206
95/6 EdgeIce 129
83/4 O-Pee-Chee 379
84/5 O-Pee-Chee 333
86/7 OPC/Topps 194
87/8 OPC/Topps 137
88/9 OPC/Topps 90
89/90 OPC/Topps 187
90/1 OPC/Topps 324
91/2 OPC/Topps 137
90/1 opcPremier 1
84/5 opcSticker 286
86/7 opcSticker 58
88/9 opcSticker258 /126
90/1 Panini(WPG) 1
88/9 PaniniSticker 224
89/90 PaniniSticker 213
90/1 PaniniSticker 30
91/2 PaniniSticker 74
82/3 Post
90/1 ProSet 18, 557
83/4 PuffySticker 2
90/1 Score 251, 68T
91/2 Score(CDN) 256
83/4 SouhaitsRen.KeyChain
83/4 7ElevenCokeCup
84/5 7ElevenDisk
91/2 ToppsStadiumClub 30
90/1 UpperDeck 397
83/4 Vachon 121
86/7 BUF
87/8 BUF/BlueShield
87/8 BUF/WonderBread
88/9 BUF/BlueShield
88/9 BUF/WonderBread
89/90 BUF/BlueShield
89/90 BUF/Campbell
81/2 WPG
82/3 WPG
82/3 WPG
84/5 WPG/Police
85/6 WPG
85/6 WPG/Police
90/1 WPG/IGA
92/3 SanDiego

ARNMARK, GORAN
89/90 SemicElitserien 170
90/1 SemicElitserien 4
91/2 SemicElitserien 202

ARNOST, TOM
94/5 APS 258
95/6 APS 155

ARNOTT, JASON
95/6 Aces 6 (Diamond)
96/7 Aces 3 (Diamond)
97/8 Aces J (Spades)
93/4 Classic 7, DP7
94/5 Classic AR2, TC1, -Promo
93/4 ClassicFourSport 191
93/4 C4'Images 62, 142
94/5 C.Prospects 11,-ROY 1
93/4 Donruss120, H, -Rated 12
94/5 Donruss 25, -Elite 1
95/6 Donruss 44
96/7 Donruss 143, -Dominator 5
97/8 Donruss 145
96/7 DonrussCanadianIce 68
97/8 D.CdnIce 117, -National 12
95/6 DonrussElite 101
96/7 DonrussElite 46, 150
97/8 DonrussElite 95
97/8 DonrussPreferred 31
97/8 DonrussPriority 97
97/8 D.Studio 35,-Portraits 29
94/5 Flair 56, -Centre 1
96/7 Flair 32
94/5 Fleer 68, -Franchise 1
96/7 Fleer 36
95/6 FleerMetal 52, -Iron 1
96/7 FleerNHLPicks 58
93/4 FleerUltra 312, -Wave 1
94/5 FleerUltra 68, -AllRook 1
94/5 FleerUltra-Pivots1,-Power 1
95/6 FleerUltra 52, -Crease 1
95/6 FleerUltra-High 2, -Rising 1
96/7 FleerUltra 57
95 Globe 95
95/6 Hoyle'WEST 3 (Hearts)
97/8 KatchMedallion 55
97/8 KennerSLU
93/4 KraftGold
94/5 Kraft-Sharpshooter
95/6 Kraft-Tickets
93/4 Leaf 382, -Freshman 7
94/5 Leaf 133, -GoldL.Rook 2
94/5 Leaf-GoldStar 10, -Ltd. 8
95/6 Leaf 119
96/7 Leaf 179
97/8 Leaf 61
94/5 LeafLimited 66
95/6 LeafLimited 22
96/7 LeafLimited 43
96/7 LeafPreferd 20,-L.Steel 19
97/8 Limited 27, 79
96/7 Maggers 66
94/5 McDonalds 37
95/6 McDonalds 14
96/7 MetalUniverse 52
97/8 Omega 125
98/9 Pacific 261
97/8 PacificCrown 79
97/8 PacificCrownRoyale 52
97/8 PacificInvincible 54
97/8 PacificParamount 72
98/9 PacificParamount 131
94/5 PaniniSticker W
95/6 PaniniSticker 255
96/7 PaniniSticker 258
97/8 PaniniSticker 210
95 PaniniWorlds 11
93/4 Parkhurst 261, C6, W8
94/5 Parkhurst 271, V84, C8

95/6 Parkhurst 73
94/5 ParkieSE 59
93/4 Pinnacle 441, SR7
94/5 Pinnacle 124, 463, NL14
95/6 Pinnacle 16
96/7 Pinnacle 118
97/8 Pinnacle 61
96/7 PinnBAP LTH5A,-Biscuit 21
97/8 PinnacleCertified 124
95/6 PinnacleFANtasy 22
97/8 PinnacleInside 55
95/6 P.Zenith 23,-GiftedGrind 15
96/7 P.Zenith 65, -Assailants 3
95/6 Playoff 37
94/5 POG 97
95/6 POG 106
94/5 Post
97/8 Post, F4
93/4 PowerPlay 337, -Rookie 1
94/5 Premier 193, 530
94/5 Premier-Finest(OPC) 10
95/6 ProMagnet 81
93/4 Score 594, (CDN) DD7
94/5 Score 254, TF8
95/6 Score 8, -GoldenBlades 20
96/7 Score 55
97/8 Score 136
94/5 Select 87
95/6 SelectCert. 9, -Double 8
96/7 SelectCertified 38
91/2 SketchOHL 148
95/6 SkyBoxEmotion 61
95/6 SkyBoxImpact 59, 237
96/7 SkyBoxImpact 41
94/5 SP 40
95/6 SP 51, FX8
96/7 SP 55, HC4
97/8 SPAuthentic 59
97/8 SPx 18
95/6 Summit 18, -MadHatter 6
96/7 Summit 103
95/6 SuperSticker 44, Die-Cut 13
96/7 TeamOut
95/6 Topps 17, 340, 3CG, YS10
98/9 Topps 199
94/5 ToppsFinest 21
95/6 ToppsFinest 139
93/4 ToppsStadiumClub 345
93/4 TSC-MembersOnly 49
94/5 ToppsStadiumClub 7, 115
94/5 TSC-MembersOnly 31
95/6 ToppsStadiumClub 171
97/8 ToppsSticker 2
95/6 SuperSkills 67
93/4 UpperDeck 423, SP-48, R9
94/5 UpperDeck 305, IG2, SP26
95/6 UpperDeck 29, SE119
96/7 UD 57, P6, SS19B, X12
97/8 UpperDeck 66, T17A
93/4 UDBeAPlayer 19
94/5 UDBAP R34, R93, R134
94/5 UDBAP-Aut. 110
96/7 UDBlackDiamond 97
97/8 UDBlackDiamond 117
98/9 UDChoice 118
95/6 UDCollChoice 41, C19
96/7 UDCollChoice 92, 317, C23
96/7 UDCC'Oversize 3of8
97/8 UDCollChoice 95, SQ7
96/7 UpperDeck"Ice" 20, S9
96 Wien 97
93/4 EDM23FEB94
96/7 EDM
97/8 EDM
91/2 Oshawa
91/2 Oshawa/Domino 20
92/3 Oshawa

ARNOULD, PATRICK
79 PaniniSticker 343

ARO, JORMA
74 Hellas 4
70/1 Kuvajulkaisut 119
80/1 Mallasjuoma 25
72 Panda
78/9 SM-Liiga 46
71/2 WilliamsFIN 169
72/3 WilliamsFIN 120
73/4 WilliamsFIN 174

ARO, KARI
65/6 Hellas 7

ARO, SEPPO
70/1 Kuvajulkaisut 309
72/3 WilliamsFIN 322

AROMAKI, JUHANI
66/7 Champion 204

ARSENAULT, DAN
89/90 SketchMEM 72

ARSENAULT, YAN
90/1 SketchQMJHL 237
91/2 SketchQMJHL 142

ARTHUR, FRED
82/3 O-Pee-Chee 245
82/3 Post

ARTURSSON, GREGER
95/6 ElitSet 216
89/90 SemicElitserien 83
90/1 SemicElitserien 256
91/2 SemicElitserien 89
97/8 udSwedish 56

ARUNDEL, JOHN
52/3 LavalDairy 99
52/3 StLawrence 63

ARVAJA, MIKA
92/3 Jyvas-Hyva 45
93/4 Jyvas-Hyva 144
93/4 Sisu 149
94/5 Sisu 133
95/6 Sisu 244
96/7 Sisu 33

ARVAJA, PERTTI
71/2 WilliamsFIN 97
72/3 WilliamsFIN 138
73/4 WilliamsFIN 105

ARVANITIS, PETER
92/3 BCJHL 57

ARVEDSSON, MAGNUS
94/5 ElitSet 196
95/6 ElitSet 43
97/8 Omega 153
98/9 Pacific 306
98/9 PacificParamount 161
97/8 Pinnacle 16
97/8 PinnacleBeAPlayer 225
97/8 Score 70
93/4 SemicElitserien 86
97/8 UpperDeck 324
95/6 udElite 67
97/8 UpperDeckIce 37
97/8 Zenith 89,-RookRgn 5, Z67
97/8 OTT

ARVSELL, HENRIK
94/5 Elit-CleanSweep 8

ASBERG, MAGNUS
89/90 SemicElitserien 48

ASHAM, AARON
97/8 Bowman 107
95/6 UpperDeck 509
95/6 RedDeer

ASHBEE, BARRY
65/6 CocaCola
70/1 Esso Stamp
72/3 Letraset 21
71/2 O-Pee-Chee 104
72/3 O-Pee-Chee 206
71/2 TheTorontoSun
70/1 PHA

ASHBY, DON
77/8 O-Pee-Chee 365
78/9 O-Pee-Chee 351
88/9 EDM/ActionMagazine 112
75/6 TOR
76/7 TOR
77/8 TOR

ASHLEY, JOHN
83&87 HallOfFame 213
83 HHOF Postcard (O)

ASHTON, BRENT
90/1 Bowman 130
91/2 Bowman 211
92/3 Bowman 357
92/3 FleerUltra 1
89/90 Kraft 46
86/7 Kraft Sports 42
82/3 O-Pee-Chee 135
83/4 O-Pee-Chee 225
85/6 O-Pee-Chee 170
86/7 OPC/Topps 181
87/8 OPC/Topps 100
88/9 OPC/Topps 128
89/90 OPC/Topps 181
90/1 OPC/Topps 24
91/2 OPC/Topps 240
82/3 opcSticker 227
85/6 opcSticker 153/24
86/7 opcSticker 25
87/8 opcSticker 108
88/9 opcSticker250/120
89/90 opcSticker 138
90/1 Panini(WPG) 2
87/8 PaniniSticker 244
88/9 PaniniSticker 40
89/90 PaniniSticker 164
90/1 PaniniSticker 321
91/2 PaniniSticker 70
92/3 Parkhurst 258
80/1 Pepsi Cap
91/2 Pinnacle 280
82/3 Post
90/1 ProSet 323
91/2 ProSet 272, 352
91/2 PSPlatinum 155
90/1 Score 31
91/2 Score(CDN) 78
91/2 Score(U.S) 78, 22T
92/3 Score 164
93/4 Score 434
83/4 SouhaitsRen.KeyChain
92/3 Topps 191
91/2 ToppsStadiumClub 90
92/3 ToppsStadiumClub 146
93/4 ToppsStadiumClub 51
90/1 UpperDeck 220
91/2 UpperDeck 303
91/2 BOS/SportsAction
81/2 COL.R
86/7 DET/Caesars
87/8 DET
83/4 MIN
84/5 QUE
85/6 QUE
85/6 QUE/GeneralFoods
85/6 QUE/McDonald
85/6 QUE/Pennant
85/6 QUE/Placemats
85/6 QUE/Provigo
86/7 QUE/GeneralFoods
86/7 QUE/McDonald
79/80 VAN
80/1 VAN
80/1 VAN/Silverwood
88/9 WPG/Police
89/90 WPG/Safeway
90/1 WPG/IGA
93/4 LasVegas

ASIKAINEN, MIKA
95/6 Sisu 255

ASKEY, TOM
98/9 Pacific 67

ASLIN, PETER
94/5 ElitSet 54, -CleanSweep 5
89/90 SemicElitserien 121
90/1 SemicElitserien 100
91/2 SemicElitserien 104
92/3 SemicElitserien 125
93 SemicSticker 1

ASP, AARON
91/2 FerrisState

ASSELSTINE, RON
90/1 ProSet 681

ASSELTINE, JACK
23/4 PaulinsCandy 25

AST, DOUG
91/2 AvantGardeBCJHL 135
92/3 BCJHL 24

ASTLEY, MARK
92/3 CanadaNats
94/5 ClassicImages 68
93/4 Donruss 44
95/6 EdgeIce 62
95/6 FleerUltra 209
93/4 Parkhurst 295
93/4 Premier 342
94/5 Score CT13
93/4 ToppsStadiumClub 311
93/4 UpperDeck 494
91/2 LakeSuperior

ASTRAHANTSEV, KONSTANTIN
94 Semic 149
93 SemicSticker 138

ASTROM, HARDY
80/1 O-Pee-Chee 269
79 PaniniSticker 185
79/80 COL.R

ATANASOV, IVAN
79 PaniniSticker 350

ATCHEYNUM, BLAIR
98/9 Pacific 361
98/9 PacificParamount 120
97/8 PacificRevolution 116
97/8 PinnacleBeAPlayer 210
89/90 ProCards(AHL) 288
90/1 ProCards 178
91/2 ProCards 107
86/7 Saskatoon

ATCHINSON, A.
1912-13 Imperial(C57) 4

ATKINS, SCOTT
95/6 Slapshot 209

ATKINSON, STEVE
72/3 EddieSargent 40
70/1 Esso Stamp
74/5 Loblaws
71/2 OPC/Topps 162
72/3 O-Pee-Chee 40, Topps 47
73/4 O-Pee-Chee 245
74/5 OPC/Topps 192
72/3 BUF
73/4 BUF
74/5 WSH

ATTERSLEY, BOB
52/3 AnonymousOHL 84

ATTWELL, RON
51/2 Cleveland

AUBIN, NORMAND
82/3 O-Pee-Chee 316
82/3 Post
82/3 TOR
84/5 NovaScotia 21

AUBIN, SERGE
94/5 AutoPhonex 4
95/6 HamptonHRA-9

AUBRY, PIERRE
72-84 Dernière 81/2
82/3 O-Pee-Chee 277
83/4 O-Pee-Chee 289
83/4 SouhaitsRen.KeyChain
91/2 SketchQMJHL 273
84/5 DET/Caesars
81/2 QUE
82/3 QUE
83/4 QUE

AUBRY, SERGE
75/6 opcWHA 3
88/9 QUE
88/9 QUE/GeneralFoods
89/90 QUE
73/4 QuébecNordiques
76/7 QuébecNordiques
75/6 Cincinnati

AUCOIN, ADRIAN
92/3 CanadaNats
93/4 CanadaNats
93/4 ClassicProspects LP11
93/4 FleerUltra 458
97/8 PacificRegime 198
96/7 PinnacleBeAPlayer 79
93/4 PowerPlay 478
93/4 Premier-TmCanada 3
94/5 Score CT14
97/8 Score(VAN) 14
93/4 UpperDeck 251
95/6 UpperDeck 56
96/7 VAN
96/7 VAN/IGA

AUDET, GÉRARD
51/2 LacStJean 23

AUDET, PHILIPPE
97/8 Bowman 52
95/6 Classic 44

AUDETTE, DONALD
92/3 Bowman 288
93/4 Donruss 32
94/5 Donruss 304
95/6 Donruss 141
97/8 Donruss 44
95/6 DonrussElite 49
97/8 DonrussPriority 126
94/5 Flair 15
94/5 Fleer 19
95/6 FleerMetal 12
92/3 FleerUltra-Rookie 2
93/4 FleerUltra 273
94/5 FleerUltra 19
95/6 FleerUltra 15
96/7 FleerUltra 13
93/4 Leaf 272
94/5 Leaf 64
95/6 Leaf 274
97/8 Leaf 99
95/6 LeafLimited 12
97/8 Limited 118
96/7 MetalUniverse 12
91/2 OPC/Topps 273
92/3 O-Pee-Chee 117
98/9 Pacific 103
97/8 PacificCrown 184
92/3 PaniniSticker U
93/4 PaniniSticker 103
94/5 PaniniSticker 93
95/6 PaniniSticker 19
96/7 PaniniSticker 12
97/8 PaniniSticker 16
91/2 Parkhurst 11
92/3 Parkhurst 18, 231
93/4 Parkhurst 26
94/5 Parkhurst 23
95/6 Parkhurst 292
91/2 Pinnacle 330
92/3 Pinnacle 38
93/4 Pinnacle 274
94/5 Pinnacle 244
95/6 Pinnacle 104
96/7 Pinnacle 59
97/8 Pinnacle 102
96/7 PinnacleBeAPlayer 73
97/8 PinnacleInside 105
95/6 Playoff 11
94/5 POG 48
93/4 PowerPlay 295
93/4 Premier 61
94/5 Premier 289
89/90 ProCards(AHL) 265
90/1 ProCards 289
95/6 ProMagnet 110
91/2 ProSet 524
92/3 ProSet 18, -Rookie 3
91/2 PSPlatinum 249
91/2 Score(CDN) 279, (U.S) 389
92/3 Score 393,-Sharpshooter19
93/4 Score 77
94/5 Score 157
95/6 Score 101
96/7 Score 233
97/8 Score 179
97/8 Score(BUF) 4
92/3 SeasonsPatch 43
94/5 Select 26
95/6 SkyBoxEmotion 14
95/6 SkyBoxImpact 14
92/3 Topps 12, 206
95/6 Topps 214
95/6 ToppsFinest 71
92/3 ToppsStadiumClub 112
93/4 ToppsStadiumClub 213
94/5 ToppsStadiumClub 87
95/6 ToppsStadiumClub 54
95/6 ToppsSuperSkills 3
90/1 UpperDeck 519
91/2 UpperDeck 585
92/3 UpperDeck 2, 306
93/4 UpperDeck 5
94/5 UpperDeck 30, SP97
95/6 UpperDeck 2, SE9
96/7 UpperDeck 18
97/8 UpperDeck 20
94/5 UDBeAPlayer-Aut. 31
96/7 UDBlackDiamond 30
98/9 UDChoice 28
95/6 UDCollChoice 217
97/8 UDCollChoice 28, C12
90/1 BUF/BlueShield
90/1 BUF/Campbell
91/2 BUF/BlueShield
91/2 BUF/Campbell
92/3 BUF/BlueShield
92/3 BUF/Jubillee

AUDETTE, GARY
91/2 AvantGardeBCJ 20
90/1 SketchWHL 235
88/9 Brandon 6
89/90 Brandon 17
90/1 Brandon 20

AUGER, DOMINIC
98 BowmanCHL 112

AUGUSTA, JOSEF
94/5 APS 276
95/6 APS 98
92/3 Trends(76) 136

AUGUSTA, PATRIK
92/3 ClassicProspects 36
95/6 EdgeIce 148
92/3 StJohn's
93/4 StJohn's
94/5 StJohn's

AUGUSTA, PAVEL
94/5 APS 231
95/6 APS 25

AUHUBER, KLAUS
79 PaniniSticker 101

AURIE, LARRY
33/4 Anonymous(V129) 19
34-43 BeeHives(DET)
33/4 CndGum (V252)
33/4 Hamilton (V288) 44
34/5 OPC (V304B) 51
36/7 OPC (V304D) 131
34/5 SweetCaporal
33/4 WWGum (V357) 59

AUSTIN, COLIN
89/90 SketchOHL 163

AUSTIN, DARCY
90/1 SketchWHL 121
91/2 SketchWHL 336

AUSTMAN, J.
24/5 Holland 10

AUTERE, ANTTI
91/2 ProCards 448

AUVINEN, HANNU
70/1 Kuvajulkaisut 278
71/2 WilliamsFIN 149

AVDEJEV, IVAN
89/90 SemicElitserien 111

AVERILL, WILL
92/3 Richmond
93/4 Roanoke

AWREY, DON
65/6 CocaCola
70/1 DadsCookies
70/1 EddieSargent 2
71/2 EddieSargent 13
72/3 EddieSargent 23
70/1 Esso Stamp
72/3 Letraset 8
74/5 Loblaws, -Update
68/9 OPC/Topps 3
69/70 O-Pee-Chee 203
70/1 OPC/Topps 4
71/2 OPC 3
72/3 OPC 170, -Tm.Canada
73/4 OPC 240
74/5 OPC/Topps 80
75/6 OPC 344
76/7 OPC 311
77/8 OPC/Topps 137
78/9 O-Pee-Chee 383
94/5 Parkie(64/5) 19
95/6 Parkie(66/7) 12
68/9 ShirriffCoin BOS3
71/2 TheTorontoSun
65/6 Topps 99
67/8 Topps 37
91/2 Trends(72) 17, -Aut.
70/1 BOS
71/2 BOS
75/6 MTL
73/4 STL

AVERY, SEAN
98 BowmanCHL 35

AXELSON, NIKLAS
93/4 Minn-Duluth

AXELSSON, MAGNUS
92/3 SemicElitserien 146

AXELSSON, PER-JOHAN
94/5 ElitSet 248
95/6 ElitSet 204
97/8 KatchMedallion 7
97/8 Omega 11
98/9 Pacific 69
98/9 PacificParamount 9
94/5 ParkieSE 240
97/8 PinnacleBeAPlayer 238
97/8 UpperDeck 220

AXELSSON, STEFAN
94/5 ElitSet 130
95/6 ElitSet 201
89/90 SemicElitserien 269
90/1 SemicElitserien 33
91/2 SemicElitserien 283
92/3 SemicElitserien 306
95/6 udElite 206

AXINTE, DIMITRU
79 PaniniSticker 316

AYERS, VERNON
34/5 OPC (V304B) 65
33/4 WWGum (V357) 51
36-39 DiamondMatch (1), (2), (3)

B

BABANDO, PETE
45-64 BeeHives(BOS,CHI,DET)
51/2 Parkhurst 51
52/3 Parkhurst 16

BABCOCK, BOB
92/3 opcPremier 56
89/90 ProCards(AHL) 84
90/1 ProCards 209
91/2 ProCards 569
91/2 Baltimore 15

BABCOCK, DAVID
90/1 SketchOHL 151
91/2 SketchOHL 197
91/2 Cornwall 8
89/90 SSMarie 22

BABCOCK, MIKE
95/6 Spokane 25
91/2 SketchWHL 275

BABCOCK, SHAWN
81/2 Kingston 5
83/4 Moncton 24

BABE, WARREN
88/9 ProCards(Kalamazoo)
90/1 ProCards 101
87/8 MIN
86/7 Kamloops
87/8 Kamloops

BABER, BRAD
91/2 SketchOHL 338
93/4 Slapshot(SSMarie) 12
93/4 SSMarie 20

BABIC, MAREK
95/6 Slapshot 286

BABIN, MICHAEL
95 PaniniWorlds 105
94 Semic 226
92 SemicSticker 228
93 SemicSticker 257

BABINOV, SERGEI
82 SemicSticker 54
83/4 SovietStars

BABY, JOHN
78/9 O-Pee-Chee 366
79/80 O-Pee-Chee 357

BABYCH, DAVE
90/1 Bowman 256
92/3 Bowman 119
83/4 Esso
92/3 FleerUltra 218
95/6 FleerUltra 315
84/5 Kelloggs Disk
90/1 Kraft 1
94/5 Leaf 430
81/2 O-Pee-Chee 358
82/3 O-Pee-Chee 375, 376

83/4 O-Pee-Chee 380
84/5 O-Pee-Chee 334
85/6 OPC/Topps 10
86/7 OPC/Topps 73, 144
87/8 OPC/Topps 5
88/9 OPC/Topps 164
89/90 OPC/Topps 46
90/1 OPC/Topps 328
89/90 O-Pee-Chee 304
92/3 O-Pee-Chee 213
81/2 opcSticker 137
82/3 opcSticker 207
83/4 opcSticker 163, 285, 286
84/5 opcSticker 287
85/6 opcSticker 249/129
86/7 opcSticker 50
87/8 opcSticker 208/75
88/9 opcSticker 267/131
89/90 opcSticker 265/146
97/8 PacificRegime 199
87/8 PaniniSticker 40
88/9 PaniniSticker 236
89/90 PaniniSticker 225
90/1 PaniniSticker 40
92/3 PaniniSticker 35
91/2 Parkhurst 187
92/3 Parkhurst 424
93/4 Parkhurst 481
80/1 Pepsi Cap
91/2 Pinnacle 270
92/3 Pinnacle 201
94/5 Pinnacle 353
97/8 PinnacleBeAPlayer 49
81/2 Post PopUp 26
82/3 Post
93/4 PowerPlay 456
93/4 Premier 428
94/5 Premier 256
90/1 ProSet 99
91/2 ProSet 503
92/3 ProSet 200
83/4 PuffySticker 1
90/1 Score 172
91/2 Score(CDN) 584, (U.S) 34T
92/3 Score 212
97/8 Score(VAN) 20
83/4 7ElevenCokeCup
84/5 7ElevenDisk
83/4 SouhaitsRen.KeyChain
83/4 StaterMint H8
81/2 Topps 1
84/5 Topps 150
92/3 Topps 138
92/3 ToppsStadiumClub 120
90/1 UpperDeck 194
93/4 UpperDeck 376
95/6 UDBeAPlayer 94
83/4 Vachon 122
86/7 HFD/JuniorWhalers
87/8 HFD/JuniorWhalers
88/9 HFD/JuniorWhalers
89/90 HFD/JuniorWhalers
90/1 HFD/JuniorWhalers
91/2 VAN
93/4 VAN/Coins
94/5 VAN
95/6 VAN/Building 18
96/7 VAN
96/7 VAN/IGA
80/1 WPG
81/2 WPG
82/3 WPG
83/4 WPG
84/5 WPG/Police

BABYCH, WAYNE
79/80 OPC/Topps 142
80/1 O-Pee-Chee 281
81/2 OPC 290, Topps(W) 114
82/3 O-Pee-Chee 299
83/4 O-Pee-Chee 310
84/5 O-Pee-Chee 181
85/6 OPC/Topps 108
86/7 O-Pee-Chee 213
81/2 opcSticker 130
82/3 opcSticker 201
85/6 opcSticker 103/236
82/3 Post
86/7 HFD/JuniorWhalers
85/6 QUE/Provigo
78/9 STL
92/3 STL/UpperDeck 10

BACA, JERGUS
94/5 ElitSet 168, -ForeignAff 9
91/2 OPC/Topps 131
90/1 opcPremier 2
91/2 ProCards 94
90/1 ScoreTraded 101
94 Semic 199
89 SemicSticker 185
92 SemicSticker 130
92/3 Topps 64
91/2 UpperDeck 425
96 Wien 224

BACARI, AL
52/3 StLawrence 44
52/3 LavalDairy 10

BACH, RYAN
91/2 AirCanadaSJHL B28

BACHUSZ, MIKE
91/2 LakeSuperior

BACIK, TIM
91/2 SketchOHL 331

BACKLUND, JOAKIM
89/90 SemicElitserien 144
95/6 udElite 127
97/8 udSwedish 126

BACKLUND, PATRICK
95/6 ElitSet 282

BACKMAN, GUNNAR
70/1 Kuvajulkaisut 22

BACKSTROM, RALPH
71/2 Bazooka Panel 22
45-64 BeeHives(MTL)
64-67 BeeHives(MTL)
62 CeramicTiles
63-5 ChexPhoto
64/5 CokeCap MTL-6
65/6 CocaCola
70/1 Colgate Stamp 21
71/2 EddieSargent 79
72/3 EddieSargent 88
69/70 O-Pee-Chee 166
68/9 OPC/Topps 60
70/1 OPC/Topps 54
71/2 OPC/Topps 108
72/3 OPC 131, Topps 133
74/5 opcWHA 47
75/6 opcWHA 23
76/7 opcWHA 124
58/9 Parkhurst 16
59/60 Parkhurst 29
60/1 Parkhurst 41, 56
61/2 Parkhurst 39
62/3 Parkhurst 44
63/4 Parkhurst 24, 83
92/3 Parkhurst58 PR18
93/4 Parkie(56/7) 77
94/5 Parkie(64/5) 73
95/6 Parkie(66/7) 64
67 Post FlipBook
68/9 Post Marble
90/1 ProCards 367
91/2 ProCards 405
60/1 ShirriffCoin 31
61/2 ShirriffCoin 114
62/3 ShirriffCoin 26
68/9 ShirriffCoin MTL8
64/5 Topps 78
65/6 Topps 73
66/7 Topps 75, -USATest 6
67/8 Topps 67
54-67 TorontoStar V7
56-66 TorontoStar 60/1
71/2 TheTorontoSun
91/2 Ultimate06 7, -Aut. 7
60/1 York
61/2 York 24
67/8 York 14, 27, 34
62/3 YorkTransfer 16
67/8 MTL
67/8 MTL/IGA
68/9 MTL/IGA
69/70 MTL/ProStar
70/1 MTL
71 MTL/Pins
92/3 MTL/OPC 33

BACON, DOUG
92/3 Wheeling 24

BADAL, ALES
94/5 APS 129

BADAWAY, CHAD
86/7 Kingston 21

BADDICE, JOHN
87/8 Kingston 25

BADDUKE, JOHN
94/5 Classic E4
90/1 SketchWHL 241
91/2 SketchWHL 49
89/90 Victoria

BADER, DARIN
90/1 SketchWHL 94
89/90 Saskatoon 22
90/1 Saskatoon 22

BADER, MIKE
94/5 DEL 431
95/6 DEL 398
96/7 DEL 303

BADZGON, ERIC
87/8 Portland
88/9 Portland

BAGU, BRAD
92/3 MPSPhotoSJHL 48
90/1 SketchWHL 243
91/2 SketchWHL 239

BAIANI, MIKE
85/6 Moncton 18

BAILEY, BOB
45-64 BeeHives(TOR)
54/5 Parkhurst 28
57/8 Topps 19
51/2 Cleveland

BAILEY, CHRISTINA
94/5 Classic W38

BAILEY, GARNET (ACE)
70/1 EddieSargent 13
72/3 EddieSargent 28
70/1 Esso Stamp
82? JDMcCarthy
74/5 Loblaws
70/1 OPC/Topps 10
72/3 OPC 191
74/5 OPC 332
75/6 OPC/Topps 284, 330
76/7 OPC 304
77/8 OPC/Topps 196
78/9 O-Pee-Chee 276
71/2 TheTorontoSun
70/1 BOS
71/2 BOS

BAILEY, GREG
90/1 SketchOHL 351
91/2 SketchOHL 121
94/5 Birmingham
93/4 Huntington

BAILEY, I.W. (ACE)
33/4 Anonymous (V129) 3
33/4 CndGum (V252)
35-40 CrownBrand 66
33 GoudeySport 29
33/4 Hamilton (V288) 11
83&87 HallOfFame 198
83 HHOF Postcard (N)
93/4 HHOFLegends 32
33/4 OPC (V304A) 13
55/6 Parkhurst 30
94/5 Parkie(64/5)-Greats 1
33/4 WWGum (V357) 22
32/3 TOR/OKeefe 6

BAILEY, JOHN
69 ColumbusCheckers

BAILEY, R
82/3 Post

BAILEY, SCOTT
95/6 Bowman 158
95/6 EdgeIce 58
95/6 Parkhurst 524
96/7 Pinnacle 215
96/7 PinnacleZenith 143
90/1 SketchMEM 73
90/1 SketchWHL 202
91/2 SketchWHL 4

BAILLARGEON, JASON
89/90 Halifax

BAILLARGEON, JOE
88/9 ProCards(Halifax)
89/90 ProCards(AHL) 178

88/9 QUE
88/9 QUE/GeneralFoods
87/8 Moncton

BAIN, DON
83&87 HallOfFame 227
83 HHOF Postcard (B)

BAIN, JOE
87/8 Hull

BAIRD, BOB
94/5 Slapshot(Brantford) 21

BAIRD, KEN
75/6 opcWHA 37
77/8 opcWHA 46

BAIRD, MARK
91/2 AirCanadaSJHL B11

BAKER, BILL
94/5 MiracleOnIce 1,2
83/4 O-Pee-Chee 240
82/3 Post
80/1 MTL

BAKER, BRUCE
77/8 NovaScotia

BAKER, DARIN
88/9 ProCards(Kalamazoo)

BAKER, HOBEY
83&87 HallOfFame 17
83 HHOF Postcard (B)
92/3 HHOFLegends 6

BAKER, JAMIE
91/2 Bowman 136
92/3 Bowman 436
93/4 EASports 93
92/3 FleerUltra 360
93/4 FleerUltra 6
93/4 Leaf 134
94/5 Leaf 421
92/3 O-Pee-Chee 41
97/8 PacificRegime 190
93/4 PaniniSticker 113
92/3 Parkhurst 353
93/4 Parkhurst 459
91/2 Pinnacle 348
93/4 Pinnacle 378
94/5 Pinnacle 502
96/7 PinnacleBeAPlayer 17
95/6 Playoff 301
96/7 Playoff 402
95/6 POG 232
93/4 Premier 22
89/90 ProCards(AHL) 156
90/1 ProCards 449
91/2 ProCards 541
93/4 Score 57, 546
97/8 Score(TOR) 19
96/7 Summit 74
92/3 Topps 506
92/3 ToppsStadiumClub 136
93/4 ToppsStadiumClub 461
94/5 ToppsStadiumClub 249
92/3 UpperDeck 130, 464
94/5 UpperDeck 439
92/3 OTT
93/4 S.J/Pacific Bell
89/90 Halifax
90/1 Halifax

BAKER, STEVE
80/1 O-Pee-Chee 346
81/2 O-Pee-Chee 231

BAKOGEORGE, TROY
86/7 Regina

BAKOS, MICHAEL
96/7 DEL 10

BAKOVIC, PETER
89/90 ProCards(IHL) 168
90/1 ProCards 330
91/2 ProCards 596
83/4 Kitchener 24
94/5 Milwaukee
85/6 Moncton 27
86/7 Moncton 23

BAKULA, MARTIN
95/6 APS 110
93/4 ClassicProspects 158
94/5 CapeBreton

BAL, JAG
91/2 AvantGardeBCJHL 144
92/3 BCJHL 37

BALASZ, DAVID
94/5 APS 227
95/6 APS 162

BALAZ, RADOSLAV
91/2 SketchQMJHL 196

BALCOMBE, DARREN
92/3 MPSPhotoSJHL 59

BALDERIS, HELMUT
79 PaniniSticker 152
82 SemicSticker 70
78 SovietChamps
83/4 SovietStars
77-80 Sportscaster 47-1113
92/3 Trends(76) 130

BALDRIS, MIGUEL
84/5 Richelieu

BALDWIN, DOUG
45-54 QuakerOats

BALES, BOB
81/2 Victoria

BALES, MIKE
92/3 Classic 73
93/4 Classic 126
95/6 Parkhurst 419
95/6 OTT

BALFOUR, EARL
45-64 BeeHives(CHI,TOR)
54/5 Parkhurst 25
60/1 ShirriffCoin 68
58/9 Topps 37
59/60 Topps 50
61/2 Topps 3, 21

BALFOUR, MURRAY
45-64 BeeHives(CHI)
64-67 BeeHives(BOS)
62 CeramicTiles
64/5 CokeCap BOS-12
94/5 Parkie(64/5) 17
60/1 ShirriffCoin 65
61/2 ShirriffCoin 30
59/60 Topps 33
60/1 Topps 12
61/2 Topps 33, -Stamp
62/3 Topps 36
63/4 Topps 35
64/5 Topps 90

BALKOVEC, MACO
92/3 BCJHL 236

BALL, DOUG
85/6 MedicineHat 24

BALL, MATT
93/4 Slapshot(Detroit) 8
94/5 Slapshot(Detroit) 7
94/5 Slapshot(MEM) 81
95/6 Slapshot 66

BALL, TERRY
78/9 SM-Liiga 28
72/3 Minnesota

BALLARD, HAROLD
83&87 HallOfFame 63
83 HHOF Postcard (E)
78/9 TOR
79/80 TOR
80/1 TOR
81/2 TOR
82/3 TOR
85/6 TOR
87/8 TOR/P.L.A.Y. 4
88/9 TOR/P.L.A.Y. 13

BALLEUX, MARTIN
90/1 SketchQMJHL 63
91/2 SketchQMJHL 37

BALMOCKHNYKH, MAXIM
97/8 UDBlackDiamond 47
98/9 UDChoice 283

BALOG, TYSON
91/2 AirCanadaSJHL A3
92/3 MPSPhotoSJHL 143

BALOGH, JANOS
79 PaniniSticker 267

BALON, DAVE
45-64 BeeHives(MTL, NYRx2)
64-67 BeeHives(MTL)
62 CeramicTiles
63-5 ChexPhoto
64/5 CokeCap MTL-20

70/1 Colgate Stamp 33
70/1 EddieSargent 119
71/2 EddieSargent 125
72/3 EddieSargent 220
70/1 Esso Stamp
68/9 O-Pee-Chee 169
69/70 O-Pee-Chee 191
70/1 OPC/Topps 61
71/2 OPC/Topps 229
72/3 OPC 162, Topps 117
63/4 Parkhurst 38, 97
94/5 Parkie(64/5) 68
95/6 Parkie(66/7) 62
60/1 ShirriffCoin 94
68/9 ShirriffCoin NYR15
54-67 TorontoStar V11
64/5 TheTorontoStar
71/2 TorontoSun
62/3 Topps 56, -Buck
64/5 Topps 37
65/6 Topps 72
66/7 Topps 74
63/4 York 33
67/8 MTL

BALSHIN, BRAD
83/4 Kitchener 26

BALTIMORE, BYRON
75/6 opcWHA 9
88/9 EDM/ActionMagazine 138

BAMBERGER, J.J.
91/2 FerrisState

BANCROFT, STEVE
92/3 ClassicProspects 48
90/1 ProCards 159
91/2 ProCards 49
89/90 SketchOHL 85
93/4 ClevelandLumberjacks
92/3 Indianapolis

BANDURA, JEFF
79/80 VAN

BANHAM, FRANK
97/8 Donruss 203
98/9 Pacific 43
93/4 Saskatoon

BANIKA, COREY
89/90 SketchMEM 87
89/90 SketchOHL 17
93/4 Johnstown 17
89/90 Oshawa 1

BANKOSKE, DAVE
94/5 Toledo

BANKS, DARREN
92/3 opcPremier 118
93/4 Parkhurst 286
90/1 ProCards 622
91/2 ProCards 582

BANNERMAN, MURRAY
81/2 O-Pee-Chee 68
82/3 O-Pee-Chee 61
83/4 O-Pee-Chee 97
84/5 O-Pee-Chee 32
85/6 OPC/Topps 27
86/7 OPC/Topps 180
83/4 opcSticker 113, 164
84/5 opcSticker 32, 135
85/6 opcSticker 27/155
87/8 PaniniSticker 218, 221
84/5 Topps 27
80/1 CHI/4x6
80/1 CHI/5.5x8.5
81/2 CHI
82/3 CHI
83/4 CHI
86/7 CHI/Coke
87/8 CHI/Coke
83/4 Victoria

BANNISTER, DARIN
90/1 ProCards 298
91/2 ProCards 136

BANNISTER, DREW
95/6 Bowman 104
94/5 Classic 64
93/4 Donruss CAN3
95/6 EdgeIce 99
95/6 Parkhurst 467
93/4 Pinnacle 460
96/7 PinnacleBeAPlayer 219
90/1 SketchOHL 152

91/2 SketchOHL 327
93/4 Slapshot(SSMarie) 6
97/8 UDCollChoice 94
97/8 EDM
93/4 SSMarie 6

BANVILLE, GILLES
65/6 QuébecAces

BARAHONA, RALPH
90/1 ProCards 132
91/2 UpperDeck 496
92/3 Cincinnati
93/4 Raleigh

BARBE, MARLO
88/9 ProCards(CapeBreton)
89/90 ProCards(AHL) 132
84/5 Chicoutimi

BARBER, BILL
95/6 HHOFLegends 55
93/4 HockeyWit 13
74/5 LiptonSoup 31
74/5 Loblaws
82/3 McDonalds 11
73/4 OPC/Topps 81
74/5 OPC/Topps 8
75/6 OPC/Topps 226
76/7 OPC/Topps 178, 215
76/7 OPC 391, T-Glossy 12
77/8 OPC/Topps 227
78/9 OPC/Topps 69, 176
79/80 OPC/Topps 140
80/1 OPC/Topps 200
81/2 O-Pee-Chee 238, 247, 253
81/2 Topps 2, 59, (East) 123
82/3 O-Pee-Chee 244, 246, 247
83/4 O-Pee-Chee 260
84/5 O-Pee-Chee 156
81/2 opcSticker 155, 174
82/3 opcSticker 110, 170
83/4 opcSticker 5, 194
92/3 Parkhurst 469
82/3 Post
83/4 PuffySticker 9
90/1 Score 356
83/4 SouhaitsRen.KeyChain
92/3 Trends(76) 169
75/6 PHA/GingerAle
81/2 PHA/Tickets 15
83/4 PHA
86/7 PHA
92/3 PHA/UD 12APR93

BARBER, DON
90/1 Bowman 179
90/1 OPC/Topps 53
90/1 PaniniSticker 259
90/1 ProSet 558
91/2 ProSet 464
90/1 Score 284, 14T
90/1 UpperDeck 28
91/2 QUE/PetroCanada
90/1 WPG/IGA

BARBER, GREG
81/2 Victoria

BARIL, TONY
24/5 Crescent Selkirks 3

BARILKO, BILL
45-64 BeeHives(TOR)
48-52 Exhibits
51/2 Parkhurst 52
93/4 Parkhurst PR35
45-54 QuakerOats
91/2 ProSet 340

BARIN, STÉPHANE
94 Semic 228
92 SemicSticker 229
93 SemicSticker 258
96 Wien 191

BARKER, BRIAN
95/6 Slapshot 20

BARKER, ELDON
92/3 MPSPhotoSJHL 93

BARKER, RANDY
92/3 BCJHL 223

BARKLEY, DOUG
45-64 BeeHives(DETx2)
64-67 BeeHives(DET)
62 CeramicTiles
64/5 CokeCap DET-5
65/6 CocaCola

63/4 Parkhurst 60
94/5 Parkie(64/5) 49
64/5 Topps 9
65/6 Topps 43
62/3 YorkTransfer 24
63/4 York 46
76 DET

BARLUND, NIKLAS
91/2 SketchWHL 231

BARKOV, ALEKSANDER
95/6 Sisu 117, 368
96/7 Sisu 132
95/6 SisuLimited 80

BARKOVICH, RICH
88/9 ProCards(Indianapolis)
89/90 ProCards(IHL) 193
90/1 ProCards 588
90/1 KansasCity 4
93/4 Raleigh
94/5 Raleigh
88/9 SaltLake 1

BARLIE, VEGAR
94 Semic 267

BARLOW, BOB
70/1 EddieSargent 93
69/70 O-Pee-Chee 196
70/1 OPC/Topps 45

BARLOW, HUGH
52/3 AnonymousOHL 33

BARNABY, MATTHEW
93/4 ClassicProspects 179
93/4 Donruss 42
94/5 Donruss 289
95/6 Donruss 383
96/7 Donruss 152
97/8 Donruss 170
97/8 DonrussCanadianIce 84
93/4 FleerUltra 13
97/8 KatchMedallion 13
93/4 Leaf 362
94/5 Leaf 285
97/8 Limited 68
98/9 Pacific 36
97/8 PacificCrown 210
97/8 PacificParamount 17
98/9 PacificParamount 17
97/8 PacificRevolution 12
96/7 PaniniSticker 20
92/3 Parkhurst 483
93/4 Parkhurst 296
93/4 Pinnacle 216
97/8 Pinnacle 108
96/7 PinnacleBeAPlayer 147
97/8 PinnacleInside 176
93/4 Premier 346
96/7 Score 188
97/8 Score 216
97/8 Score(BUF) 5
91/2 SketchQMJHL 189
96/7 SkyBoxImpact 124
98/9 Topps 213
93/4 ToppsStadiumClub 321
93/4 UpperDeck 439, SP-13
95/6 UpperDeck 341
97/8 UpperDeck 16, 393
96/7 UDCollChoice 33
97/8 UDCollChoice 27

BARNES, BLAIR
83/4 NovaScotia 13

BARNES, BRIAN
91/2 AvantGardeBCJHL 102
92/3 BCJHL 121

BARNES, JAMIE
90/1 SketchWHL 303
91/2 SketchWHL 293

BARNES, NORM
80/1 O-Pee-Chee 308
81/2 opcSticker 67

BARNES, ROB
78/9 SM-Liiga 72

BARNES, STEVE
94/5 Huntington 2
91/2 LakeSuperior

BARNES, STU
92/3 Bowman 26
90/1 CanadaNats
93/4 Donruss 377, 432
94/5 Donruss 306
95/6 Donruss 132
96/7 Donruss 68
97/8 Donruss 191
94/5 Fleer 76
95/6 FleerMetal 58
94/5 FleerUltra 78
95/6 FleerUltra 59
93/4 Leaf 350
94/5 Leaf 73
95/6 Leaf 36
96/7 Leaf 30, 90
97/8 Omega 181
92/3 O-Pee-Chee 39
91/2 opcPremier 109
98/9 Pacific 348
97/8 PacificCrown 175
98/9 PacificParamount 189
97/8 PacificRevolution 110
95/6 PaniniSticker 69
91/2 Parkhurst 419
93/4 Parkhurst 226
95/6 Parkhurst 86
94/5 ParkieSE 66
91/2 Pinnacle 319
93/4 Pinnacle 426
94/5 Pinnacle 47
95/6 Pinnacle 40
96/7 Pinnacle 135
95/6 Playoff 152
94/5 POG 104
95/6 POG 115
93/4 PowerPlay 345
93/4 Premier 351
94/5 Premier 458
91/2 ProSet 566
91/2 PSPlatinum 273
90/1 Score 391
91/2 Score(CDN) 630, 80T
92/3 Score 319
93/4 Score 380, 644
94/5 Score 138
95/6 Score 22
96/7 Score 180
97/8 Score 237
97/8 Score(PGH) 9
95/6 SkyBoxEmotion 68
95/6 SkyBoxImpact 66
94/5 SP 43
98/9 SPx"Finite" 69
95/6 Summit 47
96/7 Summit 131
95/6 SuperSticker 48
92/3 Topps 210
95/6 Topps 110
98/9 Topps 98
94/5 ToppsFinest 66
95/6 ToppsFinest 68
92/3 ToppsStadiumClub 285
94/5 ToppsStadiumClub 261
95/6 ToppsStadiumClub 73
95/6 ToppsSuperSkills 38
91/2 UpperDeck 53
92/3 UpperDeck 426
93/4 UpperDeck 94
94/5 UpperDeck 493
95/6 UpperDeck 345, SE33
96/7 UpperDeck 64
95/6 UDBeAPlayer 127
98/9 UDChoice 167
95/6 UDCollChoice 209
96/7 UDCollChoice 110
97/8 UDCollChoice 212
94/5 FLA/HealthPlan
89/90 WPG/Safeway
91/2 WPG/IGA
93/4 WPG/Ruffles

BARNETT, BRETT
89/90 ProCards(IHL) 92
90/1 ProCards 107
93/4 Birmingham 3

BARNEY, SCOTT
97/8 Bowman 150, BB14
98 BowmanCHL 39
95/6 Slapshot 328
96/7 UpperDeck 379
96/7 UDBlackDiamond 14
97/8 UDCollChoice 310

BARNSTABLE, SCOTT
90/1 SketchWHL 153

BARON, MARC
88/9 EDM/ActionMagazine 156
83/4 Moncton 3

BARON, MURRAY
91/2 Bowman 243
92/3 Bowman 409
93/4 FleerUltra 407
91/2 OPC/Topps 373
97/8 PacificD-BestKept 73
91/2 Pinnacle 204
92/3 Pinnacle 144
89/90 ProCards(AHL) 334
90/1 ProCards 35
91/2 ProSet 472
90/1 Score 399
91/2 Score(CDN) 183, 616
91/2 Score(U.S) 183, 66T
91/2 Score-YoungStar 27
92/3 Score 176
93/4 Score 294
92/3 Topps 354
91/2 ToppsStadiumClub 334
92/3 ToppsStadiumClub 194
94/5 ToppsStadiumClub 168
90/1 UpperDeck 275
91/2 UpperDeck 497
96/7 UpperDeck 143, 198
95/6 UDBeAPlayer 158
96/7 MTL
90/1 PHA
97/8 PHO
91/2 STL

BARON, NORMAN
83/4 NovaScotia 10

BAROZZINO, DAVID
96/7 Penascola 3

BARR, DAVID
90/1 Bowman 231
91/2 Bowman 49
86/7 O-Pee-Chee 237
89/90 OPC/Topps 13
90/1 OPC/Topps 308
91/2 OPC/Topps 147
91/2 opcPremier 54
89/90 opcSticker 250/113
89/90 PaniniSticker 60
93/4 PowerPlay 320
90/1 ProSet 65
91/2 ProSet 65
91/2 Score(CDN) 187, 597
91/2 Score(U.S) 187, 47T
92/3 Score 315
92/3 Topps 197
91/2 ToppsStadiumClub 141
92/3 ToppsStadiumClub 291
90/1 UpperDeck 257
94/5 DAL
86/7 DET/Caesars
87/8 DET/Caesars
88/9 DET/Caesars
89/90 DET/Caesars
90/1 DET/Caesars

BARR, DON
92/3 BCJHL 4, 18

BARRASSO, TOM
90/1 Bowman 209
91/2 Bowman 80,419-20, 423-24
92/3 Bowman 250
95/6 Bowman 47
93/4 Donruss 260
94/5 Donruss 208
95/6 Donruss 291
96/7 Donruss 67
96/7 DonrussCanadianIce 70
96/7 DonrussElite 63
97/8 D.Priority 139,-PostGen 17
93/4 EASports 108
94/5 Flair 133
96/7 Fleer 84
95/6 FleerMetal 115
92/3 FleerUltra 162
93/4 FleerUltra 26
94/5 FleerUltra 162
95/6 FleerUltra 364
96/7 FleerUltra 138
88/9 FritoLay
95 Globe 102
93/4 HighLiner 6
93/4 HockeyWit 25
97/8 KatchMedallion 115
94/5 KennerSLU (U.S)
95/6 KennerSLU (CDN)
96/7 KennerSLU (U.S)
92/3 Kraft-Disk
93/4 Kraft-Cutout
94/5 Kraft-Dinner
95/6 Kraft-Crease
93/4 Leaf 196, -GoldLeafAS 5
93/4 Leaf-PaintedWarrior 9
94/5 Leaf 103
96/7 Leaf 26
96/7 LeafPreferred 46, -Steel 27
96/7 Maggers 122
96/7 MetalUniverse 124
97/8 Omega 182
84/5 OPC 18, 212, 375, 379
85/6 OPC/Topps 105
85/6 OPC/T.-AS 12, OPC 263
86/7 OPC/Topps 91
87/8 OPC/Topps 78
88/9 OPC/Topps 107
89/90 OPC/Topps 36
90/1 OPC/Topps 65
91/2 OPC/Topps 372, 402
92/3 O-Pee-Chee 340
91/2 opcPremier 103
88/9 opcStars 1
84/5 opcSticker 205, 206
84/5 opcStickr 227/226, 228/229
85/6 opcSticker 114, 179
85/6 opcSticker 55/203, 189/62
86/7 opcSticker 45/186
88/9 opcSticker 259/127
89/90 opcSticker 235/98
98/9 Pacific 35, -GoldCrown 28
97/8 PacificCrownRoyale 108
97/8 PacificCR-FreezeOut 16
97/8 PcfcParamnt 147,-Glove 17
98/9 PcfcParamnt 190,-Glove 16
97/8 PacificRegime 157
97/8 PcfcRevolutn 111,-Retrn 16
87/8 PaniniSticker 22
88/9 PaniniSticker 219
89/90 PaniniSticker 312
90/1 PaniniSticker 134
91/2 PaniniSticker 271
92/3 PaniniSticker 219
93/4 PaniniSticker 88, 141
94/5 PaniniSticker 81
96/7 PaniniSticker 60
91/2 Parkhurst 139
92/3 Parkhurst 134
93/4 Parkhurst 157
95/6 Parkhurst 435
91/2 Pinnacle 44
92/3 Pinnacle 298
93/4 Pinnacle 3, -TeamP 7
94/5 Pinnacle 20, GT17
95/6 Pinnacle 97
96/7 Pinnacle 95
97/8 Pinnacle 76
97/8 PinnInside - StandUp 1
95/6 PinnacleZenith 90
96/7 PinnacleZenith 98
94/5 POG 291
95/6 POG 221
93/4 PowerPlay 187, -Net 1
93/4 Premier 175, 204, 446, 501
93/4 Prmr-Black(OPC) 9, (T) 11
94/5 Premier 84, 206, 311
90/1 ProSet 227, -P1
91/2 ProSet 186
91/2 PS-ThePuck 22
92/3 ProSet 145
91/2 PSPlatinum 96, PC3
90/1 Score 121
91/2 Score(CDN) 225, (U.S) 225
92/3 Score 70
93/4 Score 225, 483, -Dream 1
94/5 Score 31
95/6 Score 152
96/7 Score 124,-Net 12,-Sddn 10
97/8 Score 17
97/8 Score(PGH) 1
92/3 SeasonsPatch 36
94/5 Select 88
95/6 SelectCertified 95
89 SemicSticker 153
93 SemicSticker 169
95 Semic 215
84/5 7ElevenDisk
85/6 7Eleven 2
96/7 SkyBoxImpact 99
95/6 SP 119
98/9 SPx"Finite" 70
95/6 Summit 88
96/7 Summit 93
84/5 Topps 14, 158
92/3 Topps 503
95/6 Topps 262
98/9 Topps 209, SB6
94/5 ToppsFinest-Ring 19
95/6 ToppsFinest 129
91/2 T.StadiumClub 155
92/3 T.StadiumClub 416
93/4 TSC 79, -Master (1) 12
94/5 T.StadiumClub-Dynasty 1
95/6 T.StadiumClub 158, M6
95/6 ToppsSuperSkills 79
90/1 UpperDeck 121
91/2 UpperDeck 116
92/3 UpperDeck 243
93/4 UpperDeck 45, SP-120
94/5 UpperDeck 70
95/6 UpperDeck 115, SE68
96/7 UpperDeck 132
95/6 UDBeAPlayer 124
98/9 UDChoice 165, 250
95/6 UDCollChoice 53
96/7 UDCollChoice 213
97/8 Zenith 77
84/5 BUF/BlueShield
85/6 BUF
86/7 BUF
87/8 BUF/BlueShield
87/8 BUF/WonderBread
89/90 PGH/Foodland 15
90/1 PGH/Foodland 5
91/2 PGH/Foodland 9
91/2 PGH/Topps
92/3 PGH/Coke
92/3 PGH/Foodland 5
92/3 PGH/FoodSticker
93/4 PGH/Foodland 24
94/5 PGH 22
95/6 PGH/Foodland
96/7 PGH/Tribune

BARRATT, JEFF
79/80 Montréal, -B&W

BARRAULT, DOUG
92/3 ClassicProspects 61
94/5 FleerUltra 294
93/4 PowerPlay 88
91/2 ProCards 155
93/4 Score 457
89/90 Lethbridge

BARRETT, DAVE
89/90 Rayside

BARRETT, FRED
70/1 Esso Stamp
74/5 Loblaws
71/2 OPC 128
73/4 OPC 264
74/5 OPC/Topps 234
75/6 OPC/Topps 124
76/7 OPC/Topps 249
77/8 OPC 291
78/9 OPC/Topps 185, OPC 308
80/1 OPC/Topps 253
83/4 SouhaitsRen.KeyChain
71/2 TheTorontoSun
73/4 MIN
78/9 MIN/Cloverleaf 2
79/80 MIN
80/1 MIN
81/2 MIN
82/3 MIN

BARRETT, JOHN
82/3 O-Pee-Chee 80
83/4 O-Pee-Chee 117
84/5 O-Pee-Chee 49
82/3 Post
84/5 DET/Caesars
85/6 DET/Caesars
86/7 WSH/Kodak
86/7 WSH/Police
87/8 WSH
87/8 WSH/Kodak

BARRETT, TOM
95/6 Slapshot 180
83/4 Kitchener 8
84/5 Kitchener 4
85/6 Kitchener 4
86/7 Kitchener 4

BARRETTE, MAURICE
77/8 NovaScotia

BARRIE, DOUG
71/2 EddieSargent 28
70/1 Esso Stamp
71/2 OPC/Topps 22
75/6 opcWHA 117
76/7 opcWHA 119
71/2 TheTorontoSun

BARRIE, LEN
92/3 ClassicProspects 53
94/5 Fleer 161
94/5 Leaf 491
93/4 Parkhurst 351
90/1 ProCards 49
91/2 ProCards 274
89/90 SketchMEM 1
95/6 Topps 66
91/2 UpperDeck 459
94/5 PGH 4
95/6 ClevelandLumberjacks
89/90 Kamloops

BARRIE, MIKE
94/5 SigRookies 40
91/2 SketchWHL 60
93/4 Seattle

BARRY, KEVIN
95/6 Slapshot 168

BARRY, MARTIN
33/4 Anonymous (V129) 38
34-43 BeeHives(DET, MTL)
35/6 Champion
35-40 CrownBrand 62, 195
33-35 DiamondMatch
83&87 HallOfFame 214
83 HHOF Postcard (O)
35/6 OPC (V304C) 81
39/40 OPC (V301-1) 57
33/4 WWGum (V357) 27
36/7 WWGum (V356) 4

BARRY, RAY
45-64 BeeHives(BOS)
51/2 Parkhurst 32

BARTA, LIBOR
95/6 APS 200

BARTANUS, KAROL
97 BowmanCHL 59, 130
98 BowmanCHL 98, SC11

BARTEL, ROB
85/6 Moncton 25

BARTELL, JOSH
92/3 Clarkson

BARTH, TODD
92/3 MPSPhotoSJHL 112

BARTHE, CLAUDE
90/1 SketchQMJHL 268
92/3 Hampton
93/4 Roanoke
92/3 Wheeling 2

BARTHELSON, TONY
94/5 ElitSet 204
95/6 ElitSet 6
89/90 SemicElitserien 198
95/6 udElite 6

BARTLETT, JIM
60/1 ShirriffCoin 113
58/9 Topps 26
59/60 Topps 51

BARTLEY, JOEY
96/7 Guelph 23

BARTLEY, WADE
89/90 Sudbury 21
90/1 Sudbury 8
92/3 Toledo 1
95/6 Toledo

BARTMAN, J.
95/6 DEL 316

BARTOLI, MOE
67/8 ColumbusCheckers
69 ColumbusCheckers

BARTOLONE, CHRIS
96/7 DEL 188

BARTON, BRAD
89/90 SketchMEM 45
90/1 SketchOHL 227
91/2 SketchOHL 93
94/5 Slapshot(Brantford) 10
88/9 Kitchener 24
89/90 Kitchener 24
90/1 Kitchener 23

BARTON, PAT
91/2 SketchOHL 71
94/5 Slapshot(Guelph) 14

BARTUS, MIROSLAV
94/5 APS 247
95/6 APS 12

BASALGIN, ANDREI
91/2 OPC 49R

BASANTA, MARK
91/2 AvantGardeBC 41, 122
92/3 BCJHL 221

BASEGGIO, DAVE
90/1 ProCards 270
91/2 ProCards 9
95/6 Cleveland
91/2 Rochester/Genny

BASHKATOV, IGOR
96/7 LasVegas

BASILIO, SEAN
89/90 SketchOHL 31, 177
90/1 SketchOHL 127
91/2 SketchOHL 271

BASKEN, BRUCE
86/7 Portland

BASQUE, CLAUDE
51/2 LacStJean 48

BASSE, HAROLD
82/3 Kitchener 2
83/4 Kitchener 22
84/5 Kitchener 2
85/6 Kitchener 2
86/7 Kitchener 2
87/8 Kitchener 2
88/9 Kitchener 2
89/90 Kitchener 2
90/1 Kitchener 2

BASSEGGIO, DAVE
89/90 ProCards(AHL) 277

BASSEN, BOB
91/2 Bowman 379
92/3 Bowman 378
93/4 Donruss 476
94/5 Donruss 257
92/3 FleerUltra 182
93/4 FleerUltra 408
91/2 OPC/Topps 51
92/3 O-Pee-Chee 139
91/2 PaniniSticker 29
93/4 PaniniSticker 163
91/2 Parkhurst 379
93/4 Parkhurst 445
94/5 Parkhurst 184
92/3 Pinnacle 203
93/4 Pinnacle 169
94/5 Pinnacle 327
96/7 PinnacleBeAPlayer 89
95/6 Playoff 245
95/6 POG 83
89/90 ProCards(IHL) 53
90/1 ProSet 520
91/2 ProSet 221
91/2 Score(CDN) 179, (U.S) 179
92/3 Score 132
93/4 Score 279
95/6 Score 216
96/7 Score 218
95/6 SkyBoxEmotion 44
95/6 SkyBoxImpact 43
96/7 Summit 122
92/3 Topps 454
91/2 ToppsStadiumClub 367
92/3 ToppsStadiumClub 176
91/2 UpperDeck 319
92/3 UpperDeck 181
93/4 UpperDeck 2
94/5 UpperDeck 481
89/90 CHI/Coke
96/7 DAL/Southwest

94/5 QUE/BurgerKing
90/1 STL/Kodak
91/2 STL
83/4 MedicineHat 15

BASSEN, HAROLD (HANK)
45-64 BeeHives(DET)
64-67 BeeHives(DET)
65/6 CocaCola
62/3 Parkhurst 19
61/2 ShirriffCoin 80
65/6 Topps 106
66/7 Topps 107

BASSEN, MARK
92/3 CanadaNats
94/5 DEL 364, 366
95/6 DEL 239
96/7 DEL 306
89/90 ProCards(AHL) 355
90/1 ProCards 43
91/2 ProCards 33
88/9 Brandon 7
88/9 Lethbridge
93/4 Peoria

BASSEN, SHERWOOD
91/2 SketchAwards 9
81/2 Oshawa 24
82/3 Oshawa 24
83/4 Oshawa 16
89/90 SSMarie 5
93/4 SSMarie 29

BAST, RYAN
93/4 PrinceAlbert

BASTIEN, BAZ
43-47 ParadeSportive
45-54 QuakerOats

BASTIEN, MORRIS
36/7 WWGum (V356) 131

BASTON, DAN
89/90 Rayside
90/1 Rayside
91/2 Rayside

BATCHVAROV, MARIN
79 PaniniSticker 352

BATEMAN, ROB
91/2 Greensboro

BATES, L.
37 BritishSporting 36

BATES, SHAWN
97/8 DonrussPreferred 156
97/8 PacificDynagon -Rookies
97/8 Score(BOS) 1
98/9 UDChoice 18

BATHE, FRANK
80/1 O-Pee-Chee 389
91/2 ProCards 68
83/4 PHA

BATHERSON, NORM
93/4 ClassicProspects 157
94/5 Portland
95/6 Portland
96/7 Portland

BATHGATE, ANDY
68/9 Bauer
45-64 BeeHives(NYRx2, TOR)
64-67 BeeHives(DET, TOR)
62 CeramicTiles
64/5 CokeCap TOR-9, TOR-10
65/6 CocaCola
70/1 EddieSargent 173
70/1 Esso Stamp
83&87 HallOfFame 215
83 HHOF Postcard (O)
70/1 OPC 207
68/9 OPC/Topps 104
53/4 Parkhurst 56
92/3 Parkhurst PR22
93/4 Parkie(56/7) 90, 173
94/5 Parkie(64/5) 124, 174
95/6 Parkie(66/7) 44
97/8 PinnacleBeehive 62
60/1 ShirriffCoin 89
61/2 ShirriffCoin 88
62/3 ShirriffCoin 48
68/9 ShirriffCoin PGH5
81/2 TCMA 8
54/5 Topps 11
57/8 Topps 60
58/9 Topps 21
59/60 Topps 34
60/1 Topps 45
61/2 Topps 22, 53, -Stamp
62/3 Topps 52, -Buck
63/4 Topps 52
64/5 Topps 48, 86
66/7 Topps 44
54-67 TorontoStar V6, V10
56-66 Tor.Star 58/9, 60/1, 63/4
63/4 TheTorontoStar
64/5 TheTorontoStar
91/2 Ultimate(O6) 18, 74, -Aut.
93/4 Zellers
64/5 TOR

BATHGATE, FRANK
52/3 LavalDairy 89

BATIANI, ALESSANDRO
92 SemicSticker 251

BATKIEWICZ, JOSEF
74 Hellas 92
73/4 WilliamsFIN 85
79 PaniniSticker 126

BATTAGLIA, JON (BATES)
97/8 Omega 38
98/9 SPx"Finite" 17, 137
98/9 UDChoice 38

BATTERS, GREG
84/5 Victoria

BATTERS, JEFF
92/3 Peoria
93/4 Peoria

BATTERSBY, BROOKE
92/3 MPSPhotoSJHL 10

BATTICE, JOHN
89/90 SketchOHL 29
86/7 Kingston 25

BATYRSHIN, RUSLAN
95/6 Phoenix

BAUER, BOB
34-43 BeeHives(BOS)
39/40 OPC (V301-1) 99
43-47 ParadeSportive
91/2 BOS/Legends

BAUER, COLLIN
90/1 ProCards 238
91/2 ProCards 220
89/90 Saskatoon 13

BAUER, DAVID
96/7 HHOFLegends 75

BAUER, REINHOLD
72 SemicSticker 113

BAUER, STEPHAN
94/5 DEL 340
95/6 DEL 296

BAUMAN, GARY
68/9 O-Pee-Chee 145
65/6 Québec

BAUMGARTNER, GREGOR
97/8 Bowman 151

BAUMGARTNER, KEN
94/5 Donruss 288
96/7 Donruss 9
92/3 FleerUltra 416
93/4 FleerUltra 429
94/5 FleerUltra 212
90/1 O-Pee-Chee 414
91/2 OPC/Topps 316
98/9 Pacific 70
97/8 PacificRegime 1
92/3 PaniniSticker 85
92/3 Parkhurst 413
93/4 Parkhurst 207
95/6 Parkhurst 476
91/2 Pinnacle 239
96/7 PinnacleBeAPlayer 32
95/6 Playoff 201, 314
96/7 Playoff 393
93/4 PowerPlay 448
88/9 ProCards(NewHaven)
90/1 ProSet 178
91/2 ProSet 432
90/1 Score 265
91/2 Score(CDN) 148, (U.S) 148
92/3 Score 35
96/7 Score 206
97/8 Score(BOS) 15
92/3 Topps 217
98/9 Topps 201
92/3 ToppsStadiumClub 103
94/5 ToppsStadiumClub 98
90/1 UpperDeck 439
91/2 UpperDeck 402
93/4 UDBAP-Roots 29
94/5 UDBAP R140,R166,-Aut. 149
96/7 ANA/UpFrontSports 12
88/9 L.A/Smokeys
92/3 TOR/Kodak
93/4 TOR/Blacks 17
94/5 TOR
89/90 NewHaven
84/5 PrinceAlbert

BAUMGARTNER, NOLAN
94/5 AutoPhonex B4
94/5 Classic 9, CP6
95/6 Classic AS1, BK20
94/5 ClassicFourSport 124
95/6 ClassicFiveSport 126, -Aut.
95/6 C'5Sport-Sig 73, -Strive 10
94/5 C4'Images 102
95/6 Donruss -CanadaJr. 3
96/7 Donruss 235
95/6 DonrussElite-WorldJrs 4
96/7 Fleer 121
96/7 FleerNHLPicks 168
96/7 Leaf-Rookie 6
94/5 LeafLimited-CanadaJrs 1
96/7 MetalUniverse 169
95/6 Parkhurst 491
94/5 Pinnacle 525
96/7 Pinnacle 245
96/7 Score 251
94/5 SigRookies 25
96/7 SkyBoxImpact 144
94/5 Slapshot(MEM) 4
95/6 SP 174
94/5 SRGoldStandard 76, GS2
96/7 Summit 173
95/6 Tetrad F1
95/6 TetAutobilia 38
95/6 Topps 11CJ
94/5 ToppsFinest 148
94/5 UpperDeck 505
95/6 UpperDeck 353
93/4 Kamloops
96/7 Portland

BAUN, BOB
45-64 BeeHives(TOR)
64-67 BeeHives(TORx2)
62 CeramicTiles
63-5 ChexPhoto
64/5 CokeCap TOR-21
65/6 CocaCola
70/1 Colgate Stamp 66
70/1 DadsCookies
70/1 EddieSargent 64
71/2 EddieSargent 196
72/3 EddieSargent 199
70/1 Esso Stamp
71/2 FritoLay
91/2 Kraft 28
72/3 Letraset 9
68/9 OPC/Topps 24
69/70 OPC/T. 57, OPC-Sticker
70/1 OPC 223, Topps 24
71/2 OPC/Topps 196
72/3 OPC 66, Topps 134
57/8 Parkhurst (TOR) 20
58/9 Parkhurst 15
59/60 Parkhurst 21
60/1 Parkhurst 11
61/2 Parkhurst 11
62/3 Parkhurst 3
63/4 Parkhurst 18, 78
92/3 Parkhurst59 PR12
93/4 Parkie(56/7) 123
94/5 Parkie(64/5) 120
95/6 Parkie(66/7) 117
60/1 ShirriffCoin 7
61/2 ShirriffCoin 50
62/3 ShirriffCoin 19
68/9 ShirriffCoin DET13
64/5 Topps 57
65/6 Topps 13
66/7 Topps 83
56-66 TorontoStar 63/4, 65/6
63/4 TheTorontoStar
64/5 TheTorontoStar
71/2 TheTorontoSun
91/2 Ultimate(O6) 30, 93
60/1 York
61/2 York 1
63/4 York 7
64/5 TOR
68/9 TOR
71/2 TOR
72/3 TOR

BAUTIN, SERGEI
93/4 Donruss 378
92/3 FleerUltra 440
93/4 FleerUltra 10
93/4 Leaf 242
92/3 opcPremier 84
92/3 Parkhurst 435
93/4 Pinnacle 197
93/4 PowerPlay 268
93/4 Premier 332
92/3 RedAce(Blue) 16,(Violet) 16
93/4 Score 351
92/3 UpperDeck 337, 499
93/4 UpperDeck 514
97/8 udSwedish 119
93/4 WPG/Ruffles

BAVAUDIN, DENIS
73/4 WilliamsFIN 304

BAVIS, MARK
93/4 Classic 60

BAVIS, MIKE
93/4 Classic 60
94/5 Classic-Autograph
93/4 ClassicProspects 66
93/4 Rochester

BAWA, ROBIN
95/6 EdgeIce 187
88/9 ProCards(Baltimore)
89/90 ProCards(AHL) 99
90/1 ProCards 536
91/2 ProCards 597
93/4 ToppsStadiumClub 445
92/3 Hamilton
85/6 Kamloops
86/7 Kamloops

BAWLF, NICK
1910-11 Imperial (C56) 18

BAXTER, JIM
77/8 Kalamazoo 15

BAXTER, PAUL
72-84 Dernière 78/9
79/80 O-Pee-Chee 372
82/3 O-Pee-Chee 238
82/3 Post
83/4 Vachon 1
85/6 CGY/RedRooster
86/7 CGY/RedRooster
90/1 CGY/McGavins
91/2 CGY/IGA
93/4 CHI/Coke
83/4 PGH/Heinz
76/7 QuébecNordiques
76/7 QuébecNordiques/MA
95/6 SaintJohn

BAYER, COLIN
86/7 Saskatoon

BAYER, MARCO
95 PaniniWorlds 118

BAYLIS, STEVE
82/3 Victoria
83/4 Victoria

BAZIN, NORM
94/5 Birmingham

BAZINET, MARIO
84/5 Chicoutimi

BAZINET, MICHAEL
90/1 SketchQMJHL 217

BEACH, GEORGE
30s? ABC ChewingGum 40

BEADLE, STEVE
90/1 ProCards 37

BEAGAN, BETH
94/5 Classic W36

BEAGLE, CHAD
95/6 SwiftCurrent

BEALS, DARREN
88/9 ProCards(CapeBreton)
86/7 Kitchener 10
87/8 Kitchener 10

BEALS, KEVIN
91/2 FerrisState

BEAMIN, RYAN
92/3 BCJHL 92

BEAMIN, TIM
89/90 ProCards(AHL) 116
90/1 ProCards 163
83/4 Belleville 26
84/5 Belleville 15
90/1 Newmarket

BEAR, ROB
91/2 AirCanadaSJHL D24

BEADSMORE, COLIN
95/6 Slapshot 62

BEATON, FRANK
81/2 Indianapolis 9

BEATON, JASON
89/90 SketchOHL 168
90/1 SketchOHL 302

BEATON, JOE
37 BritishSportng 37

BEATTIE, DONALD
52/3 AnonymousOHL 56

BEATTIE, JACK
33-35 DiamondMatch

BEATTIE, JOHN "RED"
33/4 Anonymous (V129) 35
34-43 BeeHives(BOS)
28/9 PaulinsCandy 46
33/4 WWGum (V357) 29
38/9 BruinsMagazine

BEATTIE, SCOTT
91/2 AirCanadaSJHL B25
96/7 DEL 201

BEAUBIEN, FREDERICK
95/6 EdgeIce 181
95/6 Phoenix

BEAUCAGE, MARC
90/1 SketchQMJHL 47
91/2 SketchQMJHL 231

BEAUCHAMP, DENIS
90/1 SketchQMJHL 261
91/2 SketchQMJHL 263

BEAUCHEMIN, FRANÇOIS
98 BowmanCHL 92, 153, A13

BEAUCHESNE, SERGE
92/3 BCJHL 197

BEAUDETTE, DAN
91/2 Cincinnati

BEAUDIN, NORM
70/1 OPC/Topps 48
72/3 OPC 290
74/5 opcWHA 11
73/4 QuakerOats 9
72/3 7ElevenCups

BEAUDOIN, CARL
94/5 Slapshot(MEM) 60

BEAUDOIN, NICOLAS
95/6 Classic 43
93/4 Slapshot(Detroit) 22
94/5 Slapshot(Detroit) 24
94/5 Slapshot(MEM) 98
95/6 Slapshot 76

BEAUDOIN, ROGER
51/2 LacStJean 46

BEAUDOIN, SERGE
75/6 Phoenix
76/7 Phoenix

BEAUFAIT, MARK
92/3 ClassicProspects 24
93/4 FleerUltra 478
95 PaniniWorlds 234
93/4 Pinnacle 206
93/4 PowerPlay 498
93/4 Prmr-TeamUSA 6
93/4 T.StadiumClub-TmUSA 1
93/4 S.J/Pacific Bell

BEAULE, ALAIN
73/4 Québec

BEAULIEU, COREY
89/90 ProCards(AHL) 286
97/8 SheffieldSteelers

BEAULIEU, JONATHAN
96/7 Rimouski

BEAULIEU, NIC
89/90 ProCards(CapeBreton)
89/90 ProCards(IHL) 109
90/1 ProCards 521
84/5 Richelieu

BEAULNE, RICHARD
81/2 SSMarie
82/3 SSMarie

BEAUPRÉ, CLAUDE
52/3 AnonymousOHL 166

BEAUPRÉ, DON
90/1 Bowman 72
91/2 Bowman 304
92/3 Bowman 222, 297
95/6 Donruss 246
93/4 EASports 156
94/5 Fleer 141
95/6 FleerMetal 103
92/3 FleerUltra 229
93/4 FleerUltra 28
94/5 FleerUltra 387
95/6 FleerUltra 109
92/3 Kraft'Disk
94/5 KraftDinner
95/6 Kraft-Crease
95/6 Leaf 52
92/3 McDonalds McD15
81/2 OPC 159, Topps(W) 103
82/3 O-Pee-Chee 163
83/4 O-Pee-Chee 122
84/5 O-Pee-Chee 94, Topps 70
85/6 OPC/Topps 142
86/7 OPC/Topps 89
87/8 OPC/Topps 132
88/9 OPC/Topps 42
90/1 OPC/Topps 253, O
91/2 OPC/Topps 505
92/3 O-Pee-Chee 28
81/2 opcSticker 89, 146
82/3 opcSticker 193
83/4 opcSticker 121
87/8 opcSticker 51/190
88/9 opcSticker 197/61
87/8 PaniniSticker 289
88/9 PaniniSticker 84
90/1 PaniniSticker 158
91/2 PaniniSticker 201
92/3 PaniniSticker 159
93/4 PaniniSticker 33
94/5 PaniniSticker 27
95/6 PaniniSticker 57
91/2 Parkhurst 416
92/3 Parkhurst 197
93/4 Parkhurst 225
95/6 Parkhurst 152
91/2 Pinnacle 148
92/3 Pinnacle 48, 268
93/4 Pinnacle 292
94/5 Pinnacle 355
95/6 Pinnacle 87
95/6 Playoff 177
96/7 Playoff 381
94/5 POG 298
95/6 POG 200
93/4 PowerPlay 463
93/4 Premier 304
90/1 ProSet 307
91/2 ProSet 257, 601
92/3 ProSet 206
91/2 PSPlatinum 139
90/1 Score 215
91/2 Score(CDN) 185, (U.S) 185
92/3 Score 320
93/4 Score 58
95/6 Score 246
92/3 SeasonsPatch 49
94/5 Select 12
95/6 SelectCertified 104
95/6 SkyBoxEmotion 121
95/6 SkyBoxImpact 116
83/4 SouhaitsRen.KeyChain
94/5 SP 82
95/6 Summit 35
84/5 Topps 70
92/3 Topps 195
95/6 Topps 142
91/2 ToppsStadiumClub 246
92/3 ToppsStadiumClub 270
93/4 ToppsStadiumClub 71
95/6 ToppsStadiumClub 44
90/1 UpperDeck 217
91/2 UpperDeck 197
92/3 UpperDeck 23, 310
93/4 UpperDeck 123
94/5 UpperDeck 389, SP143
95/6 UpperDeck 402, SE61
95/6 UDBeAPlayer 96
95/6 UDCollChoice 11
96/7 UDCollChoice 264
80/1 MIN
81/2 MIN
82/3 MIN
83/4 MIN
84/5 MIN
85/6 MIN
85/6 MIN/7Eleven 4
86/7 MIN/7Eleven 5
87/8 MIN
94/5 OTT/Bell
95/6 OTT
89/90 WSH
89/90 WSH/Kodak
90/1 WSH/Kodak
90/1 WSH/Smokey
91/2 WSH/Kodak
91/2 WSH/Smokey
92/3 WSH/Kodak

BEAUPRÉ, MARTIN
90/1 SketchMEM 44
90/1 SketchQMJHL 41
91/2 SketchQMJHL 94

BEAUREGARD, DANNY
90/1 SketchMEM 39
90/1 SketchQMJHL 31
91/2 SketchQMJHL 89

BEAUREGARD, STÉPHANE
92/3 Bowman 405
95/6 EdgeIce 188
92/3 FleerUltra 369
93/4 FleerUltra 451
95/6 FutureLegends 26
92/3 opcPremier 88
90/1 OPC/Topps 223
90/1 Panini(WPG) 3
91/2 Parkhurst 426
88/9 ProCards(Moncton)
89/90 ProCards(IHL) 139
90/1 ProSet 648
90/1 Score 282
91/2 Score(CDN) 638
92/3 Score 402
92/3 Topps 62
92/3 ToppsStadiumClub 304
90/1 UpperDeck 415
92/3 UpperDeck 536
92/3 PHA/JCPenney
92/3 PHA/UD 07JAN93
90/1 WPG/IGA
91/2 WPG/IGA
93/4 WPG/Ruffles

BEAURIVAGE, MARC
88/9 Richelieu

BEAUVAIS, ERIC
90/1 SketchQMJHL 112, 188
91/2 SketchQMJHL 57

BEAZLEY, PAUL
94/5 Slapshot(Windsor) 4

BECHARD, JEROME
93/4 ClassicProspects 229
90/1 ProCards 356
91/2 ProCards 363
93/4 Birmingham 13
94/5 Birmingham
95/6 Birmingham

BECHARD, WARREN
83/4 Brantford 5

BECK, BARRY
84/5 Kelloggs Disk
82/3 McDonalds 27
78/9 OPC/Topps 121
79/80 OPC/Topps 35
80/1 OPC/Topps 90, 170
81/2 O-Pee-Chee 220, 230

82/3 O-Pee-Chee 219, 220
83/4 O-Pee-Chee 241
84/5 OPC 140, Topps 105
85/6 OPC/Topps 138
81/2 opcSticker 168
82/3 opcSticker 135
83/4 opcSticker 210
84/5 opcSticker 100
85/6 opcSticker 82/213
81/2 Post PopUp 14
82/3 Post
83/4 PuffySticker 20
84/5 7ElevenDisk
85/6 7Eleven 13
83/4 SouhaitsRen.KeyChain
81/2 Topps 3, (East) 124
77/8 COL.R/CokeCans
89/90 L.A/Smokeys 9

BECK, BRAD
88/9 ProCards(Indianapolis)
91/2 ProCards 429

BECK, ROB
91/2 AirCanadaSJHL 13, A40
92/3 MPSPhotoSJHL 22

BECKER, BARRY
91/2 SketchWHL 228

BECKER, JASON
91/2 SketchWHL 118
91/2 Saskatoon 21

BECKER, TROY
91/2 AvantGardeBCJHL 10

BECKETT, BOB
93/4 Parkie(56/7) 13

BECKINGHAM, SCOTT
82/3 Fredericton 26
83/4 Fredericton 26
85/6 Fredericton 25
86/7 Fredericton

BEDARD, CAM
52/3 AnonymousOHL 41

BEDARD, DAN
84/5 Chicoutimi

BEDARD, JIM
45-64 BeeHives(CHI)

BEDARD, JIM
80/1 Mallasjuoma 198
78/9 OPC/Topps 243
79/80 OPC/Topps 62
77/8 WSH
78/9 WSH

BEDARD, MARTIN
96/7 Rimouski

BEDARD, ROGER
52/3 LavalDairy 115
52/3 StLawrence 105

BEDDOES, CLAYTON
95/6 Bowman 102
94/5 Classic 50
95/6 EdgeIce 59
95/6 Parkhurst 286
91/2 LakeSuperior

BEDNAR, JAROSLAV
95/6 APS 145
91/2 SketchWHL 11
93/4 Huntington
94/5 Huntington 3

BEDNAR, VLADIMIR
72 Hellas 97
74 Hellas 66
70/1 Kuvajulkaisut 41
69/70 MästerSerien 9
72 SemicSticker 41
74 SemicSticker 68
72/3 WilliamsFIN 1

BEDNARSKI, JOHN
76/7 OPC/Topps 231
88/9 EDM/ActionMagazine 125
89/90 NewHaven

BEERS, BOB
90/1 Bowman 34
93/4 Donruss 426
93/4 EASports 127
92/3 FleerUltra 407
93/4 FleerUltra 18
94/5 FleerUltra 69
94/5 Leaf 43, 537
90/1 OPC/Topps 113
97/8 PacificRegime 9
93/4 PaniniSticker 217
95 PaniniWorlds 220
92/3 Parkhurst 401
91/2 Pinnacle 326
93/4 Pinnacle 186
94/5 Pinnacle 419
93/4 PowerPlay 227, 338
93/4 Premier 44
94/5 Premier 41
89/90 ProCards(AHL) 68
90/1 ProCards 140
91/2 ProSet 520
90/1 Score 385
93/4 Score 369, 575
94/5 Score 7
90/1 UpperDeck 125
91/2 UpperDeck 490
95/6 UDCollChoice 107
90/1 BOS/SportsAction
91/2 BOS/SportsAction
93/4 EDM 06FEB94
92/3 T.B/Sheraton

BEERS, ED
83/4 O-Pee-Chee 76
84/5 OPC 219, 354, Topps 24
85/6 OPC/Topps 144
86/7 O-Pee-Chee 238
83/4 opcSticker 141
84/5 opcSticker 243
85/6 opcSticker 214/83
83/4 Vachon 2
85/6 CGY/RedRooster

BEGG, GARY
69/70 MästarSerien 16

BEGIN, ANDRÉ
79/80 Montréal, -B&W

BEGIN, STEVE
97/8 Bowman 58
97/8 PacificParamount 25
98/9 UDChoice 267

BEHM, DANIEL
91/2 SemicElitserien 162

BEHREND, MARC
84/5 WPG/Police

BEINK, RAY
82/3 Victoria

BEKKERS, JOHN
82/3 Regina 12
83/4 Regina 12

BELAK, WADE
94/5 Classic 11
94/5 ClassicFourSport 126
94/5 C4'Images 104
94/5 ClassicImages 20
97/8 Donruss 222
98/9 Pacific 158
94/5 SigRookies 18
94/5 SRGoldStandard 77
98/9 SPx"Finite" 25
97/8 UpperDeck 186
93/4 Saskatoon

BELANGER, CHRIS
93/4 ClassicProspects 246
93/4 Toledo 10
92/3 WestMich. (x2)

BELANGER, DOMINIC
91/2 SketchOHL 107

BELANGER, ERIC
96/7 Rimouski
97/8 Bowman 73

BELANGER, FRANÇOIS
90/1 SketchMEM 40
90/1 SketchQMJHL 32

BELANGER, FRÉDÉRIC
95/6 Halifax
96/7 Halifax (1), (2)
97/8 Halifax (1), (2)

BELANGER, HUGO
93/4 C'Prospects 147
96/7 Penascola 15
92/3 Clarkson
93/4 Indianapolis

BELANGER, JESSE
93 C4'Images 32
92/3 C'Prospects 115, BC11
93/4 Donruss 123
94/5 Donruss 321
95/6 Donruss 204
96/7 Donruss 70
94/5 Flair 63
94/5 Fleer 77
93/4 FleerUltra 320
94/5 FleerUltra 79
95/6 FleerUltra 60
95/6 KraftDinner
93/4 Leaf 278
94/5 Leaf 145
95/6 Leaf 62
94/5 LeafLimited 19
95/6 PaniniSticker 70
92/3 Parkhurst 488
93/4 Parkhurst 346, C15
94/5 Parkhurst 86, 284, V31
95/6 Parkhurst 87
94/5 Pinnacle 122
95/6 Pinnacle 18
95/6 Playoff 40, 153
96/7 Playoff 339
94/5 POG 368
95/6 POG 114
93/4 PowerPlay 89, -Rookie 2
93/4 Premier 451
94/5 Premier 197, 544
94/5 Prmr-Finest(OPC) 12
90/1 ProCards 71
91/2 ProCards 85
93/4 Score 454, 585
94/5 Score 257
95/6 Score 155
96/7 Score 222
95/6 SkyBoxEmotion 69
95/6 SkyBoxImpact 67
95/6 Summit 20
95/6 Topps 159
94/5 ToppsStadiumClub 63
95/6 ToppsStadiumClub 133
94/5 UpperDeck 72, SP119
95/6 UpperDeck 209
95/6 UDBeAPlayer 143
95/6 UDCollChoice 66
94/5 FLA/HealthPlan
92/3 Fredericton

BELANGER, KEN
97/8 PacificCrown 351
97/8 PinnacleBeAPlayer 145
91/2 SketchOHL 312
93/4 Slapshot(Guelph) 14
97/8 UpperDeck 190
92/3 Ottawa67s
94/5 StJohns
95/6 StJohns

BELANGER, RAY
27-32 LaPresse 29/30

BELANGER, ROGER
83/4 Kingston 7

BELANGER, YVES
76/7 OPC/Topps 168
77/8 OPC 367
78/9 OPC/Topps 44

BELECKI, BRENT
98 BowmanCHL 41, 162

BELFOUR, ED
95/6 Aces 5 (Clubs)
90/1 Bowman 7
91/2 Bowman 390
92/3 Bowman 90, 199
95/6 Bowman 53
93/4 Donruss 64
94/5 Donruss 275, -IceMaster 1
94/5 Donruss-Masked 1, -Dom 7
95/6 Don. 108,-Bet 10,-Dom 8
96/7 Donruss 62, -Between 6
97/8 Donruss 164
96/7 D.CdnIce 113, -OCanada 6
97/8 D.CdnIce 26, -National 22
95/6 DonrussElite 20, -Painted 4
96/7 DonrussElite 91, -Painted 7
97/8 DonrussElite 102
97/8 D.Preferred 54,-ColGrd 16
97/8 D.Priority 71,-PostGen 7
97/8 DonrussStudio 68
93/4 EASports 30, 187
94/5 Flair 31
96/7 Flair 83, -HotGloves 1
94/5 Fleer 38, -Netminder 1
96/7 Fleer 15, -Vezina 1
95/6 FleerMetal 23, -Iron 2
96/7 FleerNHLPicks-Dream 8
92/3 FleerUltra 32, -AS 9
93/4 FleerUltra 22, -AS 10,-AW 1
94/5 FleerUltra 39
95/6 F.Ultra 30, 365, -PrmrPad 1
96/7 FleerUltra 29
91/2 Gillette 18
95 Globe 74
96/7 Got-Um HockeyGreats Coin
92/3 HighFive P6
93/4 HighLiner 2
93/4 HockeyWit 18
95/6 Hoyle'WEST 4 (Hearts)
97/8 KatchMedallion 43
93 KennerSLU
92/3 Kraft-Disk
93/4 KraftDinner
94/5 KraftDinner, -Masks
95/6 Kraft'Disk, -Crease
96/7 KraftDinner
93/4 Leaf 62, -AS 10, -Painted 6
94/5 Leaf 296, -Gold 7,-Crease 2
95/6 Leaf 329
96/7 Leaf 199, -ShutDown 4
97/8 Leaf 87
94/5 LeafLimited 3
95/6 LeafLimited 15, -Stick 8
96/7 LeafLimited 53, -Stubble 6
96/7 LeafPreferred 30
96/7 LP-Masked 12, -Vanity 14
97/8 Limited 28, 164, -fabric 33
96/7 Maggers 26
92/3 McDonalds McD01
93/4 McDonalds McH6
95/6 McDonalds McD29
96/7 McDonalds McD37, 'Masks
96/7 MetalUniv. 25, -Armour 1
97/8 Omega 67, 246,-NoScor 3
91/2 OPC/Topps 4, 20, 263, 271
91/2 OPC/T. 288, 425, 518-19
92/3 O-Pee-Chee 81
91/2 opcPremier 19
98/9 Pacific 20, -GoldCrown 11
97/8 PacificCrown 20, -InThe 19
97/8 PacificCrownRoyale 39
97/8 PacificCR-FreezeOut 6
97/8 PacificInvincible 123
97/8 PcfcParamount 56,-Glove 6
98/9 PcfcParamount 62,-Glove 7
97/8 PacificRegime 174
97/8 PacificRevolution 40
97/8 PcfcRev-ASGame 9,-Rtrn 6
91/2 PaniniSticker 9, 337
92/3 PaniniSticker 3, 284
93/4 PaniniSticker 140, 155
94/5 PaniniSticker 135
95/6 PaniniSticker 166
96/7 PaniniStickers 156
91/2 Parkhurst 30, 218
92/3 Parkhurst 28, 461
93/4 Parkhurst 44
94/5 Parkhurst 41
95/6 Parkhurst 41,-AS 6, -Goal 6
94/5 ParkieSE seV14
95 PH'Inconnet
91/2 Pinnacle 127, 388, 400
92/3 Pinnacle 118, 265, -Team 1
93/4 Pinn. 224,227,255, -Team 1
94/5 Pinnacle 42, GT4
95/6 Pinnacle 153, -First 7
96/7 Pinnacle 94
97/8 Pinnacle 51
97/8 PinnacleBeAPlayer 249
97/8 P.BAP-Stack/Pad 5,-Take 3
97/8 PinnacleBeehive 10
97/8 PinnacleCertified 9
97/8 PinnacleFANtasy 20
97/8 PinnacleInside 74, -Stop 24
95/6 PinnacleZenith 95
96/7 PinnacleZenith 25
95/6 Playoff 21
96/7 Playoff 394
94/5 POG 276
95/6 POG 71, 020
93/4 PowerPlay 46,-Netminder 2
93/4 Premier 60, 95
93/4 Prmr-Black(OPC) 16, (T) 14
94/5 Premier 285
88/9 ProCards(Saginaw)
95/6 ProMagnet 1, MAG2, IC01
90/1 ProSet 598
91/2 ProSet 43, 321, 600
92/3 ProSet 33
91/2 PSPlatinum 26
90/1 ScoreTraded 103T
91/2 Score(CDN) 300-01,320-21
91/2 Score(CDN) 323, 378, 510
91/2 Score(U.S) 290,348,410-11
91/2 Score(U.S) 430-31, 433
91/2 Score-Hot 9, -Young 32
92/3 Score 178, -Young 25
93/4 Score 70, 485, -AS 42
94/5 Score 149
95/6 Score 87, 318
96/7 Score 123,-Net 5,-Sudden 4
97/8 Score 20, -Networth 18
92/3 SeasonsPatch 3
93/4 SeasonsPatch 1
94/5 Select 53
95/6 SelectCertified 93
96/7 SelectCertif. 11,-Freezers 6
95 Semic 78
91 SemicSticker 53
92 SemicSticker 76
95/6 SkyBoxEmotion 27
95/6 SkBx.Impact 27, -Deflect 9
96/7 SkBx.Impact 17, -Zero 1
94/5 SP 24
95/6 SP 27
96/7 SP 28, GF11
97/8 SPAuthentic 44, I13
98/9 SPx 29
91/2 StarPics 20
95/6 Summit 120, -InThe 4
96/7 Summit 97, -InThe 3
95/6 SuperSticker 20, 23
96/7 TeamOut
92/3 Topps 22
95/6 Topps 130, 378
95/6 Topps HGC24, PF16
98/9 Topps 123, SB3
94/5 ToppsFinest 51, -Div. 11
95/6 ToppsFinest 108
96/7 ToppsNHLPicks 179
91/2 ToppsStadiumClub 333
92/3 T.StadiumClub 243, 333
93/4 TSC 99, 144, 150, -AS
94/5 T.StadiumClub 155, 180
95/6 T.StadiumClub 55, M5
91/2 TSC-MembersOnly [x2]
94/5 TSC-MembersOnly 35
95/6 TSC-MembersOnly 6
95/6 ToppsSuperSkills 90
90/1 UpperDeck 55
91/2 UpperDeck 39, 81,164,625
91/2 UpperDeck AW2,AW4,AW7
92/3 UpperDeck 203, -Locker 19
93/4 UD 147, SP-27, AW3
94/5 UpperDeck 290, SP15, H27
95/6 UD 216,455,AS6,SE19,H18
96/7 UD 234, SS22A, X18
97/8 UpperDeck 259
95/6 UDBeAPlayer 194
96/7 UDBlackDiamond 34
97/8 UDBlackDiamond 134
98/9 UDChoice 63, 249, SQ17
95/6 UDCollChoice 109, 387
96/7 UDCollChoice 55
97/8 UDCC 216, S20, SQ36
96/7 UpperDeck"Ice" 11
96 Wien 75, SG2
97/8 Zenith 49,Z10,-ChasCup 10
88/9 CHI/Coke
90/1 CHI/Coke
91/2 CHI/Coke
93/4 CHI/Coke
96/7 S.J/PacificBellSheet 26Mar

BELHUMEUR, MICHEL
72/3 OPC 273
74/5 OPC/Topps 153
75/6 OPC/Topps 232
76/7 OPC 296
74/5 WSH

BELIAVSKI, ALEXANDER
94/5 ElitSet 274
95/6 ElitSet 145

BELISLE, OMER
95/6 ThunderBay

BELISLE, PATRICK
91/2 SketchQMJHL 9

BELITSKI, DAVID
94/5 AutoPhonex 5
95/6 Classic 86
94/5 ParkieSE 251
93/4 Slapshot(Kitchener) 2, 27
94/5 Slapshot(Kitchener) 2
94/5 SlapshotPromo
95/6 Slapshot 131

BÉLIVEAU, JEAN
45-64 BeeHives(MTL)
64-67 BeeHives(MTL)
63-5 ChexPhoto
64/5 CokeCap MTL-4
65/6 CocaCola
70/1 DadsCookies
72-84 Dernière 72/3, 77/8
96/7 Duracell JB2 1,22
70/1 EddieSargent 108
62/3 ElProductoDisk
70/1 Esso Stamp
88/9 Esso Sticker
48-52 Exhibits (x2)
83&87 HallOfFame 31
83 HHOF Postcard (C)
94/5 HHOFLegends 46
93/4 HockeyWit 23
96/7 KennerLegend
91/2 Kraft 68
51-54 LaPatrie 15Jan52
51/2 LavalDairy 1
68/9 O-Pee-Chee 166
69/70 O-Pee-Chee 220
69/70 opcMiniStckr, -Stamp
69/70 OPC/Topps 10
70/1 OPC/Topps 55
70/1 opc/t-Deckle 21, -Sticker
71/2 OPC/Topps 263
53/4 Parkhurst 27
54/5 Parkhurst 3
55/6 Parkhurst 44, 74, 77
57/8 Parkhurst (MTL) 3
58/9 Parkhurst 34
59/60 Parkhurst 6
60/1 Parkhurst 49, 59
61/2 Parkhurst 45
62/3 Parkhurst 39
63/4 Parkhurst 30, 89
92/3 Parkhurst PR30
93/4 Parkie(56/7) 64, 138, 149
93/4 Parkie(56/7) 150, 172, A5
94/5 Parkie(64/5)85,142,146,172
95/6 Parkie(66/7) 73, 125
67/8 PostFlipBook
68/9 Post Marble
45-54 QuakerOats
72 SemicSticker 207
60/1 ShirriffCoin 30
61/2 ShirriffCoin 102
62/3 ShirriffCoin 32
68/9 ShirriffCoin Mo6
77-9 Sportscaster 10-14, 33-785
91/2 StarPics 4
52/3 StLawrence 39
81/2 TCMA 11
64/5 Topps 33
65/6 Topps 6
66/7 Topps 73,127,-USATest 31
67/8 Topps 74
68/9 Topps 61
54-67 TorontoStar 66/7, V8
56-66 TorontoStar 57/8, 58/9
56-66 Tor.Star 63/4, 64/5, 65/6
63/4 TheTorontoStar
64/5 TheTorontoStar
71/2 WilliamsFIN 379
60/1 York, -Glasses
61/2 York 10
62/3 YorkTransfer 8
63/4 York 26
67/8 York 23, 25, 28, (no#)
94/5 Zellers
67/8 MTL
67/8 MTL/IGA
68/9 MTL
69/70 MTL/ProStar
70/1 MTL
71 MTL/Pins
71/2 MTL
73/4 MTL
83/4 MTL
92/3 MTL/OPC 14, 27, 44
95/6 MTL/Forum 22Jan96

BELL, BOB
91/2 AvantGardeBC 118
95/6 Tallahassee 18, 21

BELL, BRUCE
85/6 O-Pee-Chee 231
85/6 opcSticker 142
87/8 PaniniSticker 308
89/90 ProCards(AHL) 135
90/1 ProCards 234
91/2 ProCards 338
84/5 QUE
83/4 Brantford 4
81/2 SSMarie

BELL, DARREN
90/1 SketchOHL 26
88/9 Sudbury 13
89/90 Sudbury 4

BELL, DAVID
95/6 Slapshot 259

BELL, GORDIE
45-54 QuakerOats

BELL, MARK
98 BowmanCHL 36, 123, A8
98/9 Topps 222

BELL, MATT
96/7 Guelph 26

BELL, SCOTT
91/2 FerrisState
91/2 Minnesota
92/3 Minnesota
94/5 Minnesota

BELL, TIM
92/3 BCJHL 11

BELL, TONY
90/1 SketchOHL 51
91/2 SketchOHL 222

BELLAND, BRAD
84/5 Sudbury 9

BELLAND, NEIL
84/5 VAN
82/3 Fredericton 23
83/4 Fredericton 14
84/5 Fredericton 5
85/6 Fredericton 23

BELLAVANCE, J.R.
51/2 BasDuFleuve 33

BELLAVANCE, NORMAND
51/2 BasDuFleuve 40
52/3 BasDuFleuve 11

BELLEFEUILLE, BLAKE
95/6 Classic 57

BELLEFEUILLE, PETE
25-27 Anonymous 61

BELLEFONTAINE, SCOTT
91/2 AirCanadaSJHL 42, C41
90/1 SketchWHL 20

BELLEMORE, BOB
88/9 N.J/Caretta
89/90 N.J

BELLEROSE, ERIC
92/3 CanadaNats
90/1 SketchQMJHL 135
91/2 SketchQMJHL 118

BELLEY, ROCH
89/90 SketchOHL 139
90/1 SketchOHL 252
89/90 NiagaraFalls
91/2 ProCards 497

BELLIO, JOHN
82 SemicSticker 127

BELLIVEAU, DAVE
90/1 SketchQMJHL 207
91/2 SketchQMJHL 164

BELLIVEAU, LUC
95/6 Slapshot 210

BELLIVEAU, RADEK
90/1 SketchQMJHL 78

BELLOWS, BRIAN
90/1 Bowman 182
91/2 Bowman 129
92/3 Bowman 200, 260
93/4 Donruss 170
94/5 Donruss 203
95/6 Donruss 341

96/7 Donruss 64
93/4 EASports 71
94/5 Flair 84
94/5 Fleer 101
92/3 FleerUltra 100, 324
93/4 FleerUltra 4
94/5 FleerUltra 105
95/6 FleerUltra 307
88/9 FritoLay
93/4 HockeyWit 11
90/1 Kraft 2
91/2 Kraft 38
93/4 Leaf 76
94/5 Leaf 301
96/7 Leaf 10
92/3 McDonalds McD-02
83/4 O-Pee-Chee 165, 167
84/5 O-Pee-Chee 95, 359, T. 71
85/6 OPC/Topps 50, A
86/7 OPC/Topps 75
87/8 OPC/Topps 94
88/9 OPC/Topps 95
89/90 OPC/Topps 177
90/1 OPC/Topps 70,200,T-TL 15
91/2 OPC/Topps 44, 110
92/3 O-Pee-Chee 384
90/1 opcPremier 3
92/3 opcPremier 75
83/4 opcSticker 142
84/5 opcSticker 44, 45
85/6 opcSticker 41
86/7 opcSticker 167/28
87/8 opcSticker 53/194
88/9 opcSticker 203
89/90 opcSticker 200/58
98/9 Pacific 23
97/8 PacificCrown 70
97/8 PcfcDynagon! 1,-Tandm 29
97/8 PacificInvincible 1
98/9 PacificParamount 241
87/8 PaniniSticker 286, 296
88/9 PaniniSticker 89
89/90 PaniniSticker 105
90/1 PaniniSticker 257
91/2 PaniniSticker 108
92/3 PaniniSticker 88
93/4 PaniniSticker 15
95/6 PaniniSticker 128
96/7 PaniniSticker 130
97/8 PaniniSticker 190
91/2 Parkhurst 79
92/3 Parkhurst 87
93/4 Parkhurst 371
94/5 Parkhurst 112
95/6 Parkhurst 466
91/2 Pinnacle 129
92/3 Pinnacle 325
93/4 Pinnacle 22
94/5 Pinnacle 290
97/8 PinnacleInside 140
95/6 Playoff 91
94/5 POG 132
95/6 POG 253
93/4 PowerPlay 124
93/4 Premier 202
94/5 Premier 219
90/1 ProSet 130
91/2 ProSet 109, -The Puck 13
91/2 PSPlatinum 59
83/4 PuffySticker 17
90/1 Score 7, 322, -HotCards 3
91/2 Score(CDN) 160, (U.S) 160
92/3 Score 335
93/4 Score 4, (CDN) DD6
94/5 Score 73
95/6 Score 231
96/7 Score 221
94/5 Select 91
84/5 7ElevenDisk
85/6 7Eleven 9
83/4 SouhaitsRen.KeyChain
95/6 Summit 11
95/6 SuperSticker 115
92/3 Topps 240
95/6 Topps 253
98/9 Topps 133
94/5 ToppsFinest 105
91/2 ToppsStadiumClub 87
92/3 ToppsStadiumClub 293
93/4 ToppsStadiumClub 156
90/1 UpperDeck 126, 308
91/2 UpperDeck 236
92/3 UD 172, 471, 636, G1
93/4 UpperDeck 390, SP-76
94/5 UpperDeck 309, SP130
95/6 UpperDeck 404
95/6 UDBeAPlayer 32
96/7 UDBlackDiamond 104
95/6 UDCollChoice 84
96/7 ANA/UpFrontSports
82/3 MIN
83/4 MIN
84/5 MIN
84/5 MIN/7Eleven 4
85/6 MIN
85/6 MIN/7Eleven 9
86/7 MIN/7Eleven 12
87/8 MIN
88/9 MIN/American
92/3 MTL
92/3 MTL/OPC 60
93/4 MTL
93/4 MTL/Molson
94/5 MTL/Molson
95/6 T.B.

BELLRINGER, DON
51/2 BasDuFleuve 50

BELOHLAV, RADEK
94/5 APS 110
95/6 APS 64, 374
96 Wien 123

BELOSHEIKIN, EVGENY
89 SemicSticker 78
91/2 ProCards 223
87/8 SovietStars

BELOV, OLEG
95 PaniniWorlds 41
93/4 UpperDeck 274
95/6 ClevelandLumberjacks

BELZILE, ERIC
96/7 Rimouski

BEMSTROM, JORGEN
97/8 udSwedish 174

BENAK, JAROSLAV
94/5 APS 168

BENAQUEZ, FERNAND
51/2 LacStJean 17

BENARD, LEO
23/4 Crescent Selkirks 2
24/5 Crescent Selkirks 11
23/4 PaulinsCandy 10

BENAZIC, CAL
92/3 BCJHL 185

BENDA, JAN
95/6 APS 399
95/6 DEL 435
95 PaniniWorlds 62
90/1 SketchOHL 326
91/2 SketchOHL 149
90/1 Oshawa 10
91/2 Oshawa
91/2 Oshawa/Dominos 19
94/5 Richmond

BENDELIN, TORGNY
94/5 ElitSet 295

BENDERA, TERRY
90/1 SketchWHL 170
91/2 SketchWHL 224
89/90 Victoria

BENEDICT, CLINT
25-27 Anonymous 95
24/5 Champs (C144)
83&87 HallOfFame 107
83 HHOF Postcard (H)
1912-13 Imperial C57 3
27-32 LaPresse 28/9
24/5 MapleCrispettes (V130) 2
23/4 (V145-1) 7
24/5 (V145-2) 32

BENES, STANISLAV
94/5 APS 141
95/6 APS 250

BENIC, GEOFF
88/9 ProCards(Indianapolis)

BENIK, RAY
81/2 Victoria

BENN, DAVID
89/90 SketchOHL 126
90/1 SketchOHL 123
91/2 SketchOHL 39
89/90 NiagaraFalls
92/3 Windsor 28

BENNETT, ADAM
94/5 Leaf 389
93/4 Parkhurst 334
94/5 Parkhurst 77
91/2 ProCards 501
90/1 SketchOHL 378
93/4 UpperDeck 237
94/5 UpperDeck 202
93/4 EDM 17DEC93
88/9 Sudbury 4
89/90 Sudbury 10
90/1 Sudbury 2

BENNETT, BILL
83/4 Ottawa67s
84/5 Ottawa67s

BENNETT, BRAD
90/1 CanadaNats
84/5 PrinceAlbert

BENNETT, CURT
74/5 Loblaws
73/4 OPC 149, Topps 152
74/5 OPC/Topps 33
75/6 OPC/Topps 8
76/7 OPC/Topps 202, OPC 379
77/8 OPC/Topps 97
78/9 OPC/Topps 31
79/80 O-Pee-Chee 344
79 PaniniSticker 214
72/3 ATL
74/5 ATL
79/80 ATL
79/80 ATL/B&W
78/9 STL

BENNETT, HARVEY
77/8 OPC 282
78/9 OPC/Topps 163
79 PaniniSticker 219
78/9 STL

BENNETT, RICK
90/1 OPC/Topps 252
90/1 ProCards 21
91/2 ProCards 198
90/1 Score 400
90/1 UpperDeck 540
92/3 Binghampton

BENNING, BRIAN
92/3 Bowman 39
93/4 Donruss 129
92/3 FleerUltra 151
93/4 FleerUltra 3, 321
93/4 Leaf 328
94/5 Leaf 379
87/8 OPC/Topps 122
88/9 OPC/Topps 174
89/90 OPC/Topps 86
90/1 OPC/Topps 365
91/2 OPC/Topps 283, 359
92/3 O-Pee-Chee 68
87/8 opcStars 2
87/8 opcSticker 124/112
88/9 opcSticker 18/151
89/90 opcSticker 120, 24/162
88/9 PaniniSticker 101
89/90 PaniniSticker 124
92/3 Parkhurst 125, 284
93/4 Parkhurst 343
94/5 ParkieSE 65
91/2 Pinnacle 402
92/3 Pinnacle 45
93/4 Pinnacle 341
94/5 Pinnacle 414
94/5 POG 111
93/4 PowerPlay 90
94/5 Premier 389
90/1 ProSet 114
91/2 ProSet 398
92/3 ProSet 135
91/2 PSPlatinum 182
90/1 Score(U.S) 306
91/2 Score(CDN) 186, (U.S) 186
92/3 Score 133
93/4 Score 64, 512
92/3 Topps 250
92/3 ToppsStadiumClub 91
94/5 ToppsStadiumClub 157
91/2 UpperDeck 415
92/3 UpperDeck 301
93/4 UpperDeck 496
94/5 UpperDeck 217
84/5 Kamloops
89/90 L.A./Smokeys 21
90/1 L.A./Smokeys 2
92/3 PHA/JCPenney
92/3 PHA/UD 24SEP92
87/8 STL
87/8 STL/Kodak
88/9 STL
88/9 STL/Kodak

BENNING, JIM
82/3 O-Pee-Chee 317
83/4 O-Pee-Chee 326
84/5 O-Pee-Chee 296
85/6 O-Pee-Chee 250
87/8 O-Pee-Chee 260
90/1 O-Pee-Chee 455
82/3 opcSticker 64
84/5 opcSticker 21
85/6 opcSticker 16/146
88/9 opcSticker 58/191
88/9 PaniniSticker 133
82/3 Post
90/1 ProCards 329
90/1 ProSet 292
92/3 ProSet 181
83/4 Vachon 82
84/5 KelownaWings&WHL 51
81/2 TOR
82/3 TOR
83/4 TOR
84/5 TOR
85/6 TOR
87/8 VAN/Shell
88/9 VAN/Mohawk
89/90 VAN

BENOÎT, DENIS
88/9 Richelieu

BENOÎT, JOE
34-43 BeeHives(MTL.C)
40/1 OPC (V301-2) 121
43-47 ParadeSportive
45-54 QuakerOats

BENOÎT, MAURICE
51/2 BasDuFleuve 19
52/3 BasDuFleuve 21

BENOÎT, RICHARD
83/4 NorthBay

BENOÎT, STEVE
91/2 Cincinnati
92/3 Cincinnati

BENSON, BILL
34-43 BeeHives(NYA)
40/1 OPC (V301-2) 135

BENSON, BOB
23/4 PaulinsCandy 65

BENSON, R.J.
24/5 Holland 6

BENTHAM
91/2 AvantGardeBC 160

BENTLEY, DOUG
34-43 BeeHives(CHIx2)
45-64 BeeHives(CHI)
48-52 Exhibits
83&87 HallOfFame 77
83 HHOF Postcard (F)
96/7 HHOFLegends 83
43-47 ParadeSportive
51/2 Parkhurst 48
93/4 Parkie(56/7) P11

BENTLEY, MAX
34-43 BeeHives(CHI)
45-64 BeeHives(NYR, TOR)
48-52 Exhibits
83&87 HallOfFame 32
83 HHOF Postcard (C)
96/7 HHOFLegends 84
40/1 OPC (V301-2) 131
43-47 ParadeSportive
51/2 Parkhurst 81
52/3 Parkhurst 95
53/4 Parkhurst 55
45-54 QuakerOats

BENYSEK, LADISLAV
95/6 APS 342
94/5 CapeBreton

BERALDO, PAUL
95/6 DEL 321
96/7 DEL 179
89/90 ProCards(AHL) 55
88/9 ProCards(Maine)

BERAN, JAN
93/4 Johnstown 15

BERAN, KAREL
95/6 APS 203

BERANEK, JIRI
94/5 APS 157
95/6 APS 87
91/2 SketchWHL 39

BERANEK, JOSEF
94/5 APS 243
95/6 APS 148
92/3 Bowman 100
92/3 ClassicProspects 81
93/4 Donruss 247
94/5 Donruss 13
95/6 Donruss 356
94/5 Fleer 221
92/3 FleerUltra 56
93/4 FleerUltra 17
94/5 FleerUltra 153
95 Globe 158
93/4 Leaf 103
94/5 Leaf 31
95/6 Leaf 232
92/3 O-Pee-Chee 178
91/2 opcPremier 149
97/8 PacificRegime 158
92/3 PaniniSticker I
95/6 PaniniSticker 291
96/7 PaniniSticker 298
95 PaniniWorlds 203
91/2 Parkhurst 47
92/3 Parkhurst 360
93/4 Parkhurst 153
94/5 Parkhurst 166
95/6 Parkhurst 208
91/2 Pinnacle 303
92/3 Pinnacle 208
93/4 Pinnacle 424
94/5 Pinnacle 148
95/6 Pinnacle 140
94/5 POG 356
93/4 PowerPlay 177
93/4 Premier 467
94/5 Premier 141
91/2 ProSet 534
91/2 PSPlatinum 255
92/3 Score 105
93/4 Score 439
94/5 Score 77
95/6 Score 118
94 Semic 176
95 Semic 154
92 SemicSticker 137
93 SemicSticker 105
95/6 SkyBoxEmotion 176
92/3 Topps 177
95/6 Topps 149
92/3 ToppsStadiumClub 214
93/4 ToppsStadiumClub 69
91/2 UpperDeck 17, 595
92/3 UpperDeck 196, E11
93/4 UpperDeck 15, SP-113
94/5 UpperDeck 117, SP56
95/6 UpperDeck 67
95/6 UDCollChoice 312
96 Wien 127
91/2 EDM/IGA
92/3 EDM/IGA 2
92/3 PHA/UD 14FEB93
93/4 PHA 11JAN94
93/4 PHA/JCPenney

BERANEK, MILAN
95/6 APS 324

BERARD, BRYAN
97/8 Aces A (Diamonds)
96/7 AllSportPPF 97
94/5 AutoPhonex 29, P1
94/5 C'Images 1, CE1, PD1
95/6 Classic 1, 84, 99, AS8, BK1
95/6 C'FiveSport 123, CS5, FT5
95/6 C5-Preview, -Sig 70
97/8 Donruss 163, -Line 9
96/7 D.CanadianIce 131
97/8 D.CanadianIce 92
95/6 DonrussElite-WorldJrs 25
96/7 DonrussElite 147, -Aspir 23
97/8 D.Elite 29, 124,-Craftsm 26
97/8 DonrussPreferred 79, 186
97/8 D.Priority 54,194,-OpD 20
97/8 D.Priority-Post 25,-Stmp 25
97/8 D.Studio 27,-Hard 4,-Por 24
96/7 Flair 114
96/7 FleerUltra 98, -Rookie 1
97/8 KatchMedallion 85
97/8 Leaf 30, 183, -BanrSea 18
94/5 LeafLimited-USAJrs 1
96/7 LeafLimited-Rookies 3
96/7 LeafPreferred 129
97/8 Limited 70, 181, 182
97/8 Limited-fabric 31
97/8 McDonald's McD10
96/7 MetalUniverse 170
97/8 Omega 136
98/9 Pacific 275
97/8 PacificCrown 222
97/8 PacificCrownRoyale 78
97/8 PacificCR-BladeOfSteel 13
97/8 PcfcDynag! 72,-BstKpt 107
97/8 PcfcD -Dyn 9A,-Tand 71
97/8 PacificInv. 80, -Attack 12
97/8 PacificParamount 106
98/9 PacificParamount 140
97/8 PacificRevolution 80
97/8 PaniniSticker 80, 119, 247
94/5 ParkieSE 250
97/8 Pinnacle 145
97/8 P.BAP 18,-TakeANum 9
97/8 PinnacleBeehive 8
97/8 PinnacleCertified 40
97/8 PinnacleInside 80
96/7 PinnacleZenith 126
97/8 Score 137, 267, -checkit 12
94/5 Select 149
96/7 SelectCertified 114
94/5 SigRookies 60
94/5 Slapshot(Detroit) 18
94/5 Slapshot(MEM) 92
95/6 Slapshot 75
94/5 SP 174
96/7 SP 182
96/7 SP-SPxForce 4
97/8 SPAuthentic 92, S16, T4
97/8 SPx 29, SPX8
98/9 SPx"Finite" 51
95 Tetrad SR2
95/6 Tetrad F2
95/6 TetradAutobilia 39
98/9 Topps 198
94/5 ToppsFinest 114
97/8 ToppsSticker 3
94/5 UpperDeck 522
96/7 UpperDeck 294, X23
97/8 UD98,S29,SG34,SS28,T4A
96/7 UDBlackDiamond 161
97/8 UDBlackDiamond 12, PC16
98/9 UDChoice 123
96/7 UDCollChoice 359
97/8 UDCollChoice 155, SQ1
96/7 UpperDeck"Ice" 93
97/8 UpperDeckIce 54
97/8 Zenith 53, Z32

BERARDICURTI, LOUIE
83/4 Kitchener 5

BERDICHEVSKY, LEV
92/3 RedAce(Blue) 32,(Violet) 32
91/2 O-Pee-Chee 50R
93/4 Roanoke

BEREHOWSKY, DRAKE
92/3 ClassicProspects 59
93/4 Donruss 336
92/3 FleerUltra 417
93/4 FleerUltra 90
92/3 HumptyDumpty (2)
94/5 Leaf 410
91/2 OPC/Topps 70
92/3 opcPremier 131
90/1 Panini(TOR) 1
93/4 Parkhurst 199
94/5 Parkhurst 231
94/5 ParkieSE 177
92/3 Pinnacle 231
95/6 POG 218
93/4 PowerPlay 239
93/4 Premier 69
90/1 Score 434
91/2 Score(CDN) 275, (U.S) 385
93/4 Score 355
90/1 SketchOHL 52
91/2 SketchOHL 70
98/9 Topps 137
93/4 ToppsStadiumClub 331
90/1 UpperDeck 361
92/3 UpperDeck 415
93/4 UpperDeck 20
94/5 UpperDeck 458
94/5 UDBeAPlayer-Aut. 55
93/4 TOR/Blacks 14
92/3 TOR/Kodak
95/6 ClevelandLumberjacks
92/3 StJohns

BEREK, MIROSLAV
94/5 DEL 415
95/6 DEL 218
96/7 DEL 68

BERENSON, GORDON (RED)
45-64 BeeHives(MTLx2)
64-67 BeeHives(MTL)
62 CeramicTiles
63-5 ChexPhoto
70/1 Colgate Stamp 24
70/1 DadsCookies
70/1 EddieSargent 177
71/2 EddieSargent 51
72/3 EddieSargent 73
70/1 Esso Stamp
82? JDMcCarthy
74/5 LiptonSoup 25
74/5 Loblaws, Update
69/70 opcMiniSticker, Stamp
70/1 opc/t-Deckle 25, -Sticker
71/2 opcPoster 10
68/9 OPC/Topps 114
69/70 OPC/Topps 20
70/1 OPC/Topps 103
71/2 OPC/Topps 91
72/3 OPC 123, -Topps 95
72/3 opc-Crests 7, -TmCanada
73/4 OPC 10, Topps 174
74/5 OPC/Topps 19
75/6 OPC/Topps 22
76/7 OPC/Topps 236
77/8 OPC/Topps 107
78/9 OPC/Topps 218
63/4 Parkhurst 26, 85
94/5 Parkie(64/5) 80
95/6 Parkie(66/7) 92
72/3 Post Transfers 2
72 SemicSticker 183
62/3 ShirriffCoin 42
68/9 ShirriffCoin STL4
64/5 TheTorontoStar
71/2 TheTorontoSun
64/5 Topps 61
65/6 Topps 9
66/7 Topps 92, -USATest 10
67/8 Topps 24
91/2 Trends(72) 48, -Aut
63/4 York 36
92/3 STL/UpperDeck 11

BERENZWEIG, ANDREW (BUBBA)
94/5 Classic DP1
94/5 Select 151

BEREZAN, PERRY
92/3 Bowman 105
90/1 OPC/Topps 357
91/2 OPC/Topps 485
92/3 O-Pee-Chee 182
89/90 PaniniSticker 110
91/2 Parkhurst 381
91/2 Pinnacle 287
92/3 Pinnacle 148
90/1 ProSet 459
91/2 ProSet 487
90/1 Score 379
91/2 Score(CDN) 527
91/2 ScoreTraded 94T
92/3 Score 169
92/3 Topps 342
91/2 ToppsStadiumClub 227
92/3 ToppsStadiumClub 441
92/3 UpperDeck 451
85/6 CGY/RedRooster
86/7 CGY/RedRooster
87/8 CGY/RedRooster
91/2 S.J

BEREZIN, SERGEI
94/5 Classic 67
94/5 DEL 221
95/6 DEL 217
97/8 Donruss 165
96/7 DonrussCanadianIce 119
96/7 D.Elite 138, -Aspirations 17
97/8 DonrussElite 55
97/8 Donruss Preferred 77
97/8 DonrussPriority 28
97/8 D.Studio 104, -HardHats 14
96/7 Flair 124
96/7 FleerUltra 161, -Rookie 2
96/7 Got-UmHockeyGreatsCoin
97/8 Leaf 66, -BannerSeason 21
96/7 LeafLimited-Rookies 7
96/7 LeafPreferred 123
97/8 Limited 8, 13,154, -fabric 57
96/7 MetalUniverse 171
97/8 Omega 217
97/8 Pacific-OffTheGlass 19
98/9 Pacific 410
97/8 PacificC 36, -Slap10C
97/8 PacificCrownRoyale 128
97/8 PacificDynagon! 120, 144
97/8 PcfcD-BstKt 91,-Tand 10,27
97/8 PacificInv. 135, -Feature 32
97/8 PacificParamount 178
98/9 PacificParamount 224
97/8 PacificRegime 191
97/8 PaniniSticker 180, 250
97/8 Pinnacle 162
96/7 PinnacleBeAPlayer LTH3A
97/8 PinnacleCertified 127
97/8 PinnacleInside 120
96/7 PinnacleZenith 127
97/8 Post
97/8 Score 145
97/8 Score(TOR) 6
96/7 SelectCertified 98
95 Semic 135
96/7 SP 188, -SPxForce
97/8 SPAuthentic 153, S27
98/9 Topps 55
96/7 UpperDeck 346, X31
97/8 UD 161, SG51, T19A,
96/7 UDBlackDiamond 94
98/9 UDChoice 201
96/7 UDCollChoice 350
97/8 UDCollChoice 247, SQ48
96/7 UpperDeck"Ice" 103
97/8 UpperDeckIce 4
96 Wien 153, AS4

BEREZNIUK, CHAD
90/1 SketchWHL 305

BERG, AKI
94/5 AutoPhonex 6, P4
95/6 Bowman 146
94/5 Classic DP2
95/6 Classic 3, BK3
95/6 ClassicFiveSport 125
95/6 C'5Sport-Sig 72, -Strive Q
95/6 Donruss 325
97/8 Donruss 129
96/7 DonrussElite 108
97/8 DonrussPreferred 112
95/6 FleerMetal 170
95/6 FleerUltra 330
95/6 FutureLegends 27
97/8 KatchMedallion 67
95/6 LeafLimited 20
97/8 Limited 85
96/7 MetalUniverse 72
97/8 PacificD-BestKept 44
95/6 Parkhurst 253, 510
97/8 PinnacleBeAPlayer 155
95/6 P.Zenith 146, -RookieRoll 6
96/7 Score 264
95/6 SelectCertified 127
93/4 Sisu 38
95/6 Sisu-NHLDraft 1
95/6 SisuLimited-S&S 4
95/6 SkyBoxImpact 203
95/6 SP 69
95/6 Summit 175
96/7 Summit 164
95/6 Tetrad F3
95/6 TetradAutobilia 40
95/6 Topps 267
95/6 ToppsFinest 138
95/6 ToppsStadiumClub 201
95/6 ToppsSuperSkills SR6
95/6 UpperDeck 267, H25
95/6 UDCollChoice 337, 407
96/7 UDCollChoice 128
97/8 UDCollChoice 121
96 Wien 30

BERG, BILL
91/2 Bowman 216
93/4 Leaf 287
91/2 OPC/Topps 122
93/4 Parkhurst 472
94/5 ParkieSE 181
94/5 Pinnacle 57
96/7 PinnacleBeAPlayer 84
94/5 Premier 136
88/9 ProCards(Springfield)
89/90 ProCards(AHL) 232
91/2 ProSet 145
91/2 Score(CDN) 541
97/8 Score(NYR) 9
91/2 ToppsStadiumClub 385
94/5 UDBeAPlayer-Aut. 57
92/3 TOR/Kodak
93/4 TOR/Abalene
93/4 TOR/Blacks 15
94/5 TOR

BERG, BOB
90/1 ProCards 432
91/2 ProCards 384
89/90 SketchOHL 72
90/1 SketchOHL 400
95/6 Louisiana, -Playoffs
91/2 Richmond 11

BERG, REG
95/6 DonrussElite-WorldJrs 32
95/6 UpperDeck 567

BERGE, DAVID
96/7 DEL 248

BERGEN, BRAD
94/5 DEL 234
95/6 DEL 81
96/7 DEL 272

BERGEN, TODD
83/4 Springfield 3

BERGENHEIM, CHRISTER
72/3 WilliamsFIN 139

BERGER, JURG
79 PaniniSticker 264

BERGER, MIKE
88/9 ProCards(Kalamazoo)
89/90 ProCards(AHL) 285
87/8 MIN

BERGER, PHIL
91/2 Greensboro
92/3 Greensboro 5
93/4 Greensboro
94/5 Greensboro

BERGER, STANISLAV
94/5 APS 284
95/6 APS 268

BERGERON, CHRIS
95/6 Birmingham
93/4 Toledo 17

BERGERON, DAVID
91/2 SketchQMJHL 172

BERGERON, GERMAIN
52/3 AnonymousOHL 37
51/2 LacStJean 44

BERGERON, J.C.
95/6 Donruss 241
90/1 opcPremier 4
90/1 Panini(MTL) 1
93/4 PaniniSticker 220
95/6 Parkhurst 465
89/90 ProCards(AHL) 181
91/2 ProCards 77
90/1 ProSet 614
95/6 Topps 174
90/1 UpperDeck 408
90/1 MTL
92/3 T.B./Sheraton
95/6 T.B.
95/6 T.B./SkyBoxSportsCafe
92/3 AtlantaKnights
93/4 AtlantaKnights

BERGERON, J. MICHEL
72-84 Dernière 81/2
80/1 QUE
81/2 QUE
82/3 QUE
83/4 QUE
84/5 QUE
85/6 QUE
85/6 QUE/GeneralFoods
85/6 QUE/Provigo
86/7 QUE
86/7 QUE/GeneralFoods
89/90 QUE
89/90 QUE/GeneralFoods

BERGERON, MARTIN
90/1 ProCards 17

BERGERON, MICHEL
76/7 OPC/Topps 71, OPC 385
77/8 OPC/Topps 159
78/9 O-Pee-Chee 273
78/9 WSH

BERGERON, MICHEL
see J. Michel Bergeron

BERGERON, RÉMI
98 BowmanCHL 102

BERGERON, TIM
92/3 AtlantaKnights

BERGERON, YVAN
90/1 SketchQMJHL 101
73/4 QuébecNordiques

BERGEVIN, MARC
92/3 Durivage 30
92/3 FleerUltra 200
94/5 Leaf 384
89/90 O-Pee-Chee 249
97/8 PacificRegime 166
95 PaniniWorlds 9
92/3 Pinnacle 385
93/4 Pinnacle 304, CA22
94/5 Pinnacle 183
96/7 PinnacleBeAPlayer 85
93/4 Premier 373
94/5 Premier 507
89/90 ProCards(AHL) 251
91/2 ProSet 397
91/2 PSPlatinum 176
92/3 Score 404
93/4 Score 363
97/8 Score(STL) 19
92/3 Topps 61
92/3 ToppsStadiumClub 174
93/4 ToppsStadiumClub 154
94/5 ToppsStadiumClub 101
97/8 UpperDeck 351
94/5 UDBeAPlayer-Aut. 10
86/7 CHI/Coke
87/8 CHI/Coke
91/2 HFD/JuniorWhalers
92/3 T.B./Sheraton
94/5 T.B./SkyBoxSportsCafe
95/6 T.B./SkyBoxSportsCafe

BERGGREN, BO
74 SemicSticker 22

BERGIN, TONY
92/3 MPSPhotoSJHL 109

BERGKVIST, JONAS
95 PaniniWorlds 154
94 Semic 73
95 Semic 63
89 SemicSticker 17
97/8 udSwedish 113, 202, 221
97/8 udSwed. C10,S15,UDS10

BERGKVIST, P.R.
95/6 ElitSet 235
95/6 UpperDeck 564

BERGKVIST, STEFAN
94/5 Classic 28
95/6 Classic 88
96/7 UpperDeck 323
95/6 ClevelandLumberjacks

BERGLAND, CHARLES
95 PaniniWorlds 149
97/8 udSwedish 41, 210

BERGLAND, TIM
91/2 Bowman 297
90/1 O-Pee-Chee 507
91/2 OPC/Topps 34
91/2 Parkhurst 409
88/9 ProCards(Baltimore)
89/90 ProCards(AHL) 95
90/1 ProSet 550
91/2 ProSet 507
91/2 ToppsStadiumClub 351
92/3 ToppsStadiumClub 127
92/3 T.B/Sheraton
90/1 WSH
90/1 WSH/Kodak
91/2 WSH
91/2 WSH/Kodak

BERGLUND, ANDERS
94/5 ElitSet 9
95/6 ElitSet 284
89/90 SemicElitserien 80, 255
90/1 SemicElitserien 6, 163
91/2 SemicElitserien 208, 268
92/3 SemicElitserien 225, 294
95/6 udElite 171

BERGLUND, ART
89 SemicSticker 152

BERGLUND, BO
84/5 O-Pee-Chee 276
89/90 SemicElitserien 14
89 SemicSticker 14
83/4 Vachon 61
85/6 MIN

BERGLUND, CHARLES
94/5 ElitSet 183, -GoldCard 3
95 Globe 37
95 Semic 67
89/90 SemicElitserien 65
90/1 SemicElitserien 284
91/2 SemicElitserien 66, 351
92/3 SemicElitserien 86
91 SemicSticker 42

BERGLAND, TIM
92/3 Topps 244
89/90 WSH/Kodak
90/1 WSH

BERGLUND, TOMAS
94/5 ElitSet 78
95/6 ElitSet 81
89/90 SemicElitserien 165
90/1 SemicElitserien 239
91/2 SemicElitserien 169
92/3 SemicElitserien 189
95/6 udElite 129

BERGMAN, ANDERS
89/90 SemicElitserien 74
90/1 SemicElitserien 248
91/2 SemicElitserien 79
92/3 SemicElitserien 101

BERGMAN, GARY
68/9 Bauer
64-67 BeeHives(DET)
64/5 CokeCap DET-18
65/6 CocaCola
70/1 Colgate Stamp 73
70/1 DadsCookies
70/1 EddieSargent 49
71/2 EddieSargent 54
72/3 EddieSargent 79
70/1 Esso Stamp
82? JDMcCarthy
72/3 Letraset 19
74/5 Loblaws, -Update
73/4 MacsMilk Disk
68/9 OPC/Topps 25
69/70 OPC/Topps 58
70/1 OPC 154
71/2 OPC/Topps 119
72/3 OPC 164, Topps 49
72/3 OPC-Crests 8, -TmCanada
73/4 OPC/Topps 65
75/6 OPC/Topps 236
76/7 OPC/Topps 159
94/5 Parkie(64/5) 57
95/6 Parkie(66/7) 41, 136
72/3 Post Transfers 9
68/9 ShirriffCoin DET1
64/5 Topps 8
65/6 Topps 107
66/7 Topps 47
66/7 Topps-USATest 47
67/8 Topps 47
71/2 TheTorontoSun
91/2 Trends(72) 87, -Aut
91/2 Ultimate(O6) 67, -Aut 67
70/1 DET/Marathon
73/4 MIN

BERGMAN, JAN
89/90 SemicElitserien 223
90/1 SemicElitserien 57
91/2 SemicElitserien 230

BERGMAN, SUNE
94/5 ElitSet 299

BERGMAN, THOMAS
72 Hellas 25
74 Hellas 23
82? JDMcCarthy
74/5 Loblaws
73/4 OPC 204
74/5 OPC 365
79/80 OPC/Topps 148
75/6 opcWHA 29
76/7 opcWHA 51
72 SemicSticker 55
71/2 WilliamsFIN 42
72/3 WilliamsFIN 43
79/80 DET

BERGQVIST, FREDRIK
94/5 ElitSet 294
91/2 SemicElitserien 211
92/3 SemicElitserien 234
95/6 udElite DS17

BERQVIST, JONAS
95 Globe 34
94/5 ElitSet 250,-Gold9,-Studio 6
95/6 ElitSet 69, -Mega 2
91/2 SemicElitserien 149, 356
92/3 SemicElitserien 167
95/6 udElite 105
96 Wien 71

BERGSTROM, ERIK
94/5 ElitSet 169
95/6 ElitSet 127
92/3 SemicElitserien 276

BERGSTROM, LARS
94/5 ElitSet 301

BERLINQUETTE, LOUIS
25-27 Anonymous 47
24/5 Champs (C144)
24/5 MapleCrispettes (V130) 30
23/4 PaulinsCandy 32
24/5 (V145-2) 41

BERMINGHAM, JIM
90/1 SketchQMJHL 49
91/2 SketchQMJHL 226
94/5 Huntington 4
93/4 Wheeling 5

BERNAQUEZ, BERNIE
51/2 BasDuFleuve 46

BERNAQUEZ, FERNAND
52/3 BasDuFleuve 26

BERNARD, LARRY
89/90 ProCards(AHL) 32
90/1 ProCards 245
90/1 Moncton

BERNARD, LOUIS
91/2 SketchQMJHL 276
93/4 Slapshot(Drum.) 11
94/5 Fredericton
95/6 Fredericton

BERNARD, MARK
92/3 Hampton
95/6 Hampton HRA-5

BERNDANER, IGNAZ
79 PaniniSticker 98

BERNDTSSON, PETER
94/5 ElitSet 70
95/6 ElitSet 143
89/90 SemicElitserien 279
90/1 SemicElitserien 44
91/2 SemicElitserien 295
95/6 udElite 213
97/8 udSwedish 80

BERNHARDT, TIM
85/6 O-Pee-Chee 166
85/6 opcSticker 9/137
88/9 ProCards(Newmarket)
89/90 ProCards(AHL) 110
85/6 TOR

BERNIE, JOHN
90/1 SketchOHL 61

BERNIER, ART
91 C55 Reprint 37
1911-12 Imperial (C55) 37
1910-11 Imperial (C56) 25
1912-13 Imperial (C57) 6
1910-11 Imperial Post 37

BERNIER, JEAN
77/8 opcWHA 2
76/7 QuébecNordiques

BERNIER, PASCAL
91/2 SketchQMJHL 265

BERNIER, SERGE
71/2 Bazooka Panel 24
72-84 Dernière 77/8, 78/9
71/2 EddieSargent 155
72/3 EddieSargent 97
70/1 Esso Stamp
71/2 OPC/Topps 19
72/3 OPC 152, Topps 36
79/80 OPC/Topps 47
80/1 O-Pee-Chee 309
74/5 opcWHA 5
75/6 opcWHA 60, 70
76/7 opcWHA 109
77/8 opcWHA 60
80/1 Pepsi Cap
71/2 TheTorontoSun
72/3 PHA/MightyMilk
80/1 QUE
73/4 QuébecNordiques
76 QuébecNordiques/MA
76/7 QuébecNordiques

BERRA, ANDRE
72 SemicSticker 142

BERRY, BOB
72/3 EddieSargent 98
70/1 Esso Stamp
93/4 Kraft-Coach
74/5 Loblaws
71/2 OPC/Topps 76
72/3 OPC 9, Topps 21
73/4 OPC 175, Topps 172
74/5 OPC/Topps 18
75/6 OPC/Topps 196, 320
76/7 OPC 300
77/8 OPC 268
92/3 Parkhurst 312
81/2 MTL
82/3 MTL
83/4 MTL
86/7 PGH/Kodak

BERRY, BRAD
91/2 ProCards 144
90/1 SemicElitserien 178
94/5 DAL
86/7 WPG
87/8 WPG
89/90 WPG/Safeway

BERRY, BRENT
92/3 BCJHL 156

BERRY, DOUG
79/80 COL.R

BERRY, FRED
81/2 Milwaukee 3

BERRY, KEN
83/4 EDM/Buttons
88/9 EDM/ActionMagazine 67
88/9 VAN/Mohawk
84/5 NovaScotia 8

BERRY, ROB
71/2 TheTorontoSun

BERRY, RYAN
95/6 Spokane 18

BERTAGGIA, SANDRO
95 Globe 213
95 PaniniWorlds 119
91 SemicSticker 184
92 SemicSticker 200
93 SemicSticker 116

BERTELL, KRISTEN
66/7 Champion 112

BERTHELSON, PETE
88/9 Lethbridge
89/90 Lethbridge

BERTHIAUME, DANIEL
91/2 Bowman 190
92/3 Bowman 140
92/3 FleerUltra 361
93/4 FleerUltra 54
87/8 O-Pee-Chee 217
88/9 OPC/Topps 142
89/90 O-Pee-Chee 296
90/1 OPC/Topps 180, 247
91/2 OPC/Topps 313
90/1 opcPremier 5
87/8 opcStars 3
87/8 opcSticker 249/139
88/9 opcSticker 149
87/8 PaniniSticker 356
88/9 PaniniSticker 148
92/3 Parkhurst 359
91/2 Pinnacle 165
90/1 ProSet 454, 73T
91/2 Score(CDN) 132, (U.S) 132
91 SemicSticker 54
92/3 Topps 505
91/2 ToppsStadiumClub 290
92/3 ToppsStadiumClub 101
90/1 UpperDeck 381, 412
91/2 UpperDeck 150
91/2 BOS/SportsAction
90/1 L.A/Smokeys 19
92/3 OTT
87/8 WPG
89/90 WPG/Safeway
84/5 Chicoutimi
95/6 Roanoke

BERTOGLIAT, JESSE
92/3 Minnesota
93/4 Minnesota
94/5 Minnesota

BERTRAND, MARC
80/1 QuébecRamparts

BERTRAND, RON
89/90 SketchOHL 172
90/1 SketchOHL 303
91/2 SketchOHL 52

BERTSCH, JAY
95/6 Spokane 23

BERTUZZI, BRIAN
84/5 Kamloops
86/7 Fredericton

BERTUZZI, ED
88/9 Kamloops

BERTUZZI, TODD
95/6 Bowman 156, BB30
93/4 Classic 14
94/5 Classic 103, T40
95/6 Classic 85
93/4 ClassicFourSport 204
94/5 ClassicImages 37
95/6 Donruss 346, -RatedRook 2
96/7 Donruss-RatedRook 9
97/8 Donruss 12
96/7 DonrussCanadianIce 28
95/6 DonrussElite 57, -Rookie 4
96/7 DonrussElite 18, -Aspir 4
97/8 DonrussPriority 155
96/7 Fleer 63, -Rookie 2
95/6 FleerMetal 171
95/6 FleerUltra 331, -High 3
96/7 FleerUltra 99
96/7 Leaf 205
97/8 Leaf 134
95/6 LeafLimited 19, -Rookie 10
96/7 LeafLimited 19, -Stubble 9
96/7 LeafPreferred 93, -Steel 20
97/8 Limited 30
96/7 MetalUniverse 91
98/9 Pacific 424
97/8 PacificParamount 107
98/9 PacificParamount 232
97/8 PacificRegime 115
96/7 PaniniSticker 89
95/6 Parkhurst 264, PP44
96/7 Pinnacle 208
97/8 PinnacleBeAPlayer 168
95/6 P.Zenith 140, -RookieRoll 9
96/7 Pinn.Zenith 81, -Assailant 6
96/7 Score 244
95/6 SelectCertified 123
96/7 SelectCertified 80
91/2 SketchOHL 357
95/6 SkBxEmotion 103, -Next 8

95/6 SkyBoxImpact 208
96/7 SkBxImpact 74, 166, -Fox 2
93/4 Slapshot(Guelph) 23
94/5 Slapshot(Guelph) 22
95/6 SP 88
96/7 SP 96
96/7 SPx 30
98/9 SPx"Finite" 85
95/6 Summit 193
96/7 Summit 154
95/6 Topps 339
95/6 ToppsFinest 146
96/7 ToppsNHLPicks 121, RS10
95/6 ToppsStadiumClub 204
95/6 ToppsSuperSkills SR7
95/6 UpperDeck SE53
96/7 UpperDeck 291, P7, X14
97/8 UpperDeck 103
95/6 UpperDeckBeAPlayer 168
96/7 UDBlackDiamond 84
98/9 UDChoice 212
96/7 UDCollChoice 164,323, 338
97/8 UDCollChoice 154

BERUBE, CRAIG
93/4 Leaf 314
90/1 O-Pee-Chee 448
92/3 O-Pee-Chee 147
91/2 opcPremier 47
97/8 PacificD-BestKept 99
98/9 Pacific 437
91/2 Parkhurst 246
96/7 PinnacleBeAPlayer 115
90/1 ProSet 450
91/2 ProSet 495
91/2 Score(CDN) 578, (U.S) 28T
92/3 Score 258
92/3 Topps 208
92/3 ToppsStadiumClub 458
90/1 UpperDeck 498
94/5 UDBeAPlayer-Aut. 64
92/3 CGY/IGA 2
89/90 PHA
90/1 PHA
90/1 TOR/P.L.A.Y. 13
95/6 WSH
85/6 Kamloops
85/6 MedicineHat 7

BERUBE, SÉBASTIEN
91/2 SketchQMJHL 6

BERWANGER, MARKUS
94/5 DEL 259
95/6 DEL 345

BES, JEFF
93/4 ClassicProspects 144
90/1 SketchOHL 201
91/2 SketchOHL 346
93/4 UpperDeck 255

BESETTE, ROGER
52/3 StLawrence 78

BESETTE, MARCEL
51/2 LavalDairy 68

BESETTE, ROGER
51/2 LavalDairy 48

BESSEY, B.
93/4 Waterloo

BESTER, ALLAN
90/1 Bowman 154
95/6 EdgeIce 170
84/5 O-Pee-Chee 297
87/8 O-Pee-Chee 236
89/90 O-Pee-Chee 271
90/1 OPC/Topps 32
84/5 opcSticker 20
87/8 opcSticker 162
89/90 opcSticker 169
90/1 Panini(TOR) 2, 5
87/8 PaniniSticker 323
88/9 PaniniSticker 116
89/90 PaniniSticker 139
91/2 ProCards 118
90/1 ProSet 275
90/1 Score 27
90/1 UpperDeck 241
84/5 TOR
87/8 TOR
87/8 TOR/P.L.A.Y. 12
88/9 TOR/P.L.A.Y. 11
83/4 Brantford 17

BETS, MAXIM
93/4 Classic 15
93/4 ClassicFourSport 208
94/5 Parkhurst V37
93/4 Pinnacle 502
94/5 Pinnacle RTP6
94/5 UpperDeck SP1

BETTIOL, FRANK
52/3 AnonymousOHL 53

BETTS, BLAIR
98 BowmanCHL 124, A32
97/8 UpperDeck 407

BETY, SÉBASTIEN
93/4 Slapshot(Drum.) 4

BEUKEBOOM, JEFF
91/2 Bowman 110
92/3 Bowman 347
96/7 DonrussElite 87
92/3 FleerUltra 351
90/1 O-Pee-Chee 471
92/3 O-Pee-Chee 237
91/2 OPC/Topps 284
98/9 Pacific 290
97/8 PacificCrown 57
90/1 Panini(EDM) 2
88/9 PaniniSticker 56
91/2 Parkhurst 341
95/6 Parkhurst 410
91/2 Pinnacle 229
92/3 Pinnacle 112
93/4 Pinnacle 309
95/6 Pinnacle 112
96/7 PinnacleBeAPlayer 158
95/6 POG 185
93/4 PowerPlay 389
93/4 Premier 54
90/1 ProSet 439
91/2 ProSet 444
91/2 PSPlatinum 206
91/2 Score(CDN) 253
92/3 Score 137
93/4 Score 94
97/8 Score(NYR) 20
93 SemicSticker 112
96/7 Summit 71
92/3 Topps 57
95/6 Topps 63
98/9 Topps 87
94/5 ToppsFinest-Ring 9
91/2 ToppsStadiumClub 350
92/3 ToppsStadiumClub 129
93/4 ToppsStadiumClub 7
91/2 UpperDeck 394
92/3 UpperDeck 161
95/6 UpperDeck 203
96/7 UpperDeck 105
97/8 UpperDeck 314
94/5 UDBeAPlayer-Aut. 107
98/9 UDChoice 136
95/6 UDCollChoice 317
86/7 EDM
86/7 EDM/RedRooster
87/8 EDM
88/9 EDM
88/9 EDM/ActionMagazine 17
90/1 EDM/McGavins
85/6 NovaScotia 7
82/3 SSMarie
83/4 SSMarie
84/5 SSMarie

BEVERIDGE, BILL
33/4 Anonymous V12 9 25
34-43 BeeHives(MTL.M)
35-40 CrownBrand 122
36-39 DiamondMatch (1)
34/5 OPC (V304B) 54
37/8 OPC (V304E) 161
33/4 WWGum (V357) 60
36/7 WWGum (V356) 82

BEVERLEY, NICK
72/3 OPC 281
73/4 OPC 239
75/6 OPC/Topps 279
76/7 OPC/Topps 41
77/8 OPC/Topps 198
78/9 OPC/Topps 111
79/80 COL.R

BEZEAU, ANDY
95/6 EdgeIce 125
89/90 SketchOHL 147

90/1 SketchOHL 253
89/90 NiagaraFalls

BIACHIN, WAYNE
78/9 OPC/Topps 103
77/8 PGH/PuckBuck

BIAFORE, CHAD
96/7 DEL 32
87/8 Portland
88/9 Portland

BIAGINI, CHRIS
95/6 Slapshot 284

BIALOWAS, DWIGHT
74/5 OPC 372
75/6 OPC/Topps 106
76/7 OPC/Topps 198
77/8 OPC 271

BIALOWAS, FRANK
95/6 Portland
92/3 Richmond
93/4 StJohns
94/5 StJohns

BIALYNICKI, KRZYSZTOF
73/4 WilliamsFIN 86

BIANCHI, TONY
91/2 Minnesota
92/3 Minnesota
93/4 Minnesota

BIANCHIN, WAYNE
74/5 Loblaws
77/8 OPC/Topps 188
79/80 O-Pee-Chee 290
88/9 EDM/ActionMagazine 107

BIANNI, MIKE
84/5 Moncton 2
85/6 Moncton 18

BIBEAULT, PAUL
34-43 BeeHives
43-47 ParadeSportive

BICANEK, RADIM
93/4 Classic 36
94/5 Classic 111, T46
95/6 Classic 83
95/6 Donruss 15
95/6 Leaf 69
97/8 PacificD-BestKept 64
95/6 Pinnacle 217
95/6 Score 306
93/4 UpperDeck 262
94/5 OTT/Bell

BICKELL, J.P.
83&87 HallOfFame 184
83 HHOF Postcard (J)

BIDNER, TODD
83/4 Moncton 21

BIEGL, RADOVAN
94/5 APS 24
95/6 APS 316

BIEIKE, RENÉ
94/5 DEL 245
95/6 DEL 220

BIELAS, ROLF
74 Hellas 119
70/1 Kuvajulkaisut 81
79 PaniniSticker 253

BIERK, ZAC
97/8 Bowman 19
98/9 Pacific 396
93/4 Slapshot(Peterborough) 10
95/6 Slapshot 307, -Aut. -Promo
98/9 SPx"Finite" 79, 148

BIETTE, K.
91/2 SketchWHL 227

BIFANO, PAUL
83/4 Victoria

BIGGS, DON
93/4 ClassicProspects 83
95/6 EdgeIce 110
88/9 ProCards(Hershey)
89/90 ProCards(AHL) 331
91/2 ProCards 205
92/3 Binghampton
96/7 Cincinnati
85/6 NovaScotia 26
82/3 Oshawa 9
83/4 Oshawa 28

BIGGS, KENNETH
51/2 LavalDairy 40

BIGGS, SCOTT
82/3 Kitchener 28

BIGNELL, GREG
89/90 SketchOHL 86

BILES, C.
28/9 PaulinsCandy 59

BILL, ROB
88/9 ProCards(Utica)
89/90 ProCards(AHL) 228

BILLECK, LAURIE
90/1 SketchWHL 261
91/2 SketchWHL 152
90/1 PrinceAlbert

BILLINGTON, CRAIG
92/3 Bowman 102
90/1 CanadaNats
93/4 Donruss 226
95/6 Donruss 381
94/5 Flair 119
92/3 FleerUltra 334
93/4 FleerUltra 378
94/5 FleerUltra 145
94/5 KraftDinner
93/4 Leaf 354
94/5 Leaf 84
97/8 Omega 54
92/3 O-Pee-Chee 372
98/9 Pacific 157
97/8 PacificD-BestKept 23
98/9 PacificParamount 52
87/8 PaniniSticker 72
94/5 PaniniSticker 108
91/2 Parkhurst 320
92/3 Parkhurst 330
93/4 Parkhurst 138
94/5 Parkhurst 158
95/6 Parkhurst 285
93/4 Pinnacle 352
94/5 Pinnacle 320
97/8 PinnacleBeAPlayer 138
94/5 POG 289
93/4 PowerPlay 169
93/4 Premier 374
94/5 Premier 482
88/9 ProCards(Utica)
89/90 ProCards(AHL) 224
91/2 PSPlatinum 197
92/3 Score 228
93/4 Score 207, 521, -P.AS 1
94/5 Score 167
96/7 Score 231
97/8 Score19
97/8 Score(COL) 2
94/5 Select 49
92/3 Topps 48
92/3 ToppsStadiumClub 343
93/4 TSC-AllStar
91/2 UpperDeck 559
92/3 UpperDeck 315
93/4 UpperDeck 424, Sp-105
94/5 UpperDeck 370, SP53
95/6 UpperDeck 112
95/6 UDBeAPlayer 151
85/6 N.J
93/4 OTT/Kraft
94/5 OTT/Bell
83/4 Belleville 24
84/5 Belleville 10

BILLKVAM, ARNE
94 Semic 268
92 SemicSticker 35
93 SemicSticker 245

BILODEAU, BRENT
91/2 Arena 13
91/2 Classic 14
91/2 ClassicFourSport 14, -Aut
93/4 ClassicProspects 58
90/1 SketchMEM 99
90/1 SketchWHL 1, 346
91/2 SketchWHL 180
91/2 StarPics 53
91/2 UltimateDP 14, -Aut 14, 70
91/2 UD 694, 'CzechWJC 81
93/4 Fredericton
94/5 Fredericton

BILODEAU, MARTIN
96/7 Halifax (1), (2)
97/8 Halifax (1), (2)

BILODEAU, ROLAND
51/2 BasDuFleuve 17
52/3 BasDuFleuve 56

BILOUS, JASON
91/2 AvantGardeBCJ 136

BILYALETDINOV, ZINETULA
82 SemicSticker 58
79/80 SovietStars
83/4 SovietStars
87/8 SovietStars
96/7 PHO
93/4 WPG/Ruffles

BINETTE, MARC-ANDRÉ
97/8 Halifax (1), (2)

BINGHAM, PAT
85/6 Kamloops
88/9 Kamloops
89/90 Nashville
91/2 Richmond 9

BINKLEY, LES
52/3 AnonymousOHL 174
70/1 Colgate Stamp 75
70/1 DadsCookies
70/1 EddieSargent 175
71/2 EddieSargent 166
70/1 Esso Stamp
68/9 OPC/Topps 100
69/70 OPC/Topps 110
69/70 OPC-Sticker, -Stamp
70/1 OPC/T.-Deckle10,OPC 200
71/2 OPC/Topps 192
72/3 OPC 300
72 SemicSticker 215
68/9 ShirriffCoin PIT6
71/2 TheTorontoSun
71/2 PGH
72/3 OttawaNationals
60/1 Cleveland

BINNIE, TROY
89/90 SketchOHL 52
90/1 SketchOHL 77

BINNS, CRAIG
91/2 SketchOHL 179

BIONDA, JACK
45-64 BeeHives(TOR)
93/4 Parkie(56/7) 14
57/8 Topps 2
57/8 BOS

BIOTTI, CHRIS
89/90 ProCards(IHL) 202
88/9 SaltLake 20

BIRCH, JOE
95/6 Slapshot 151

BIRD, JAMIE
91/2 SketchQMJHL 178
94/5 Slapshot(MEM) 56

BIRK, HARALD
94/5 DEL 318
95/6 DEL 23

BIRK, KLAUS
94/5 DEL 328
95/6 DEL 324

BIRMINGHAM, JIM
89/90 SketchMEM 71

BIRNIE, SCOTT
83/4 NorthBay

BIRNIE, STUART
87/8 Brockville 20
88/9 Brockville 7

BIRON, MARTIN
95/6 Classic 16, BK13
96/7 DonrussCdnIce-Gardiens 9
96/7 Fleer 122
96/7 Leaf 213
96/7 PaniniSticker 299
95/6 Parkhurst 295
96/7 Pinnacle 224
96/7 SkyBoxImpact 145
96/7 Summit 179
98/9 Topps 238
96/7 UpperDeck"Ice" 118

BIRON, MATHIEU
98 BowmanCHL 154, A21

BISAILLON, J.P.
51/2 LavalDairy 71
52/3 StLawrence 30

BISAILLON, PATRICK
90/1 SketchMEM 32
90/1 SketchQMJHL 34
91/2 SketchQMJHL 264

BISHOP, ALLEN
83/4 Kingston 24
82/3 NorthBay

BISHOP, MIKE
90/1 ProCards 465
90/1 Halifax
84/5 Kitchener 6

BISSCHOPS, JAKE
89/90 Sudbury 31

BISSETT, THOMAS
95 PaniniWorlds 232
90/1 ProCards 480
91/2 SemicElitserien 52
92/3 SemicElitserien 63

BISSON, STEVE
88/9 ProCards(Sherbrooke)
89/90 ProCards(IHL) 130

BISSONETTE, ERIC
90/1 SketchQMJHL 166, 205
89/90 SketchMEM 60

BJORK, ANDERS
92/3 SemicElitserien 41

BJORK, STEFAN
92/3 SemicElitserien 350

BJORKMAN, HENRIC
89/90 SemicElitserien 131
90/1 SemicElitserien 207
91/2 SemicElitserien 135
92/3 SemicElitserien 154
97/8 udSwedish 196, C29, S9

BJORNOFT, NIKLAS
92/3 SemicElitserien 179

BJUGSTAD, SCOTT
86/7 OPC/Topps 23
86/7 opcSticker 168/29
88/9 PaniniSticker 90
88/9 ProCards(Kalamazoo)
89/90 ProCards (AHL) 15
91/2 ProCards 404
90/1 ProSet 455
84/5 MIN
85/6 MIN
85/6 MIN/7Eleven 2
86/7 MIN/7Eleven 4
87/8 MIN

BJUHR, THOMAS
86/7 Portland
89/90 SemicElitserien 20
90/1 SemicElitserien 87
91/2 SemicElitserien 16
92/3 SemicElitserien 37

BLACK, CLINT
91/2 AvantGardeBCJHL 133
92/3 BCJHL 27

BLACK, JAMIE
93/4 ClassicProspects 122
90/1 SketchWHL 318
91/2 SketchWHL 172
93/4 ClevelandLumberjacks
92/3 Tacoma

BLACK, JAMIE H.
92/3 Bowman 252
93/4 Donruss 85
95/6 FutureLegends 48
92/3 O-Pee-Chee 388
97/8 PacificD-BestKept 19
97/8 PinnacleBeAPlayer 186
89/90 ProCards(AHL) 292
90/1 ProCards 191
91/2 ProCards 101
92/3 Topps 232
92/3 ToppsStadiumClub 303
91/2 UpperDeck 580
92/3 UpperDeck 323
93/4 UpperDeck 517
91/2 HFD/JuniorWhalers
94/5 LasVegas
87/8 Portland
88/9 Portland
89/90 Portland
93/4 Rochester

BLACK, JESSE
95/6 Slapshot 187

BLACK, JONATHAN
88/9 Richelieu

BLACK, RYAN
90/1 SketchOHL 352
91/2 Peterborough 13
91/2 SketchOHL 144

BLACK, STEVE
45-64 BeeHives(DET)

BLACK, TERRY
87/8 Portland
88/9 Portland

BLACKBIRD, LOU
96/7 Sudbury 5

BLACKBURN, BOB
70/1 Esso Stamp
69/70 O-Pee-Chee 113

BLACKBURN, DON
68/9 ShirriffCoin Ph8
63/4 QuébecAces
65/6 QuébecAces

BLACKLOCK, KYLE
90/1 SketchOHL 379
91/2 SketchOHL 254
90/1 Sudbury 5
91/2 Sudbury 4

BLACKNED, BRANT
91/2 SketchQMJHL 244

BLAD, BRIAN
88/9 ProCards(Newmarket)
89/90 ProCards(AHL) 107
90/1 ProCards 164
91/2 ProCards 608
94/5 Slapshot(Brantford) 14
90/1 Newmarket

BLADON, TOM
74/5 Loblaws
74/5 OPC 396
75/6 OPC/Topps 74
76/7 OPC/Topps 164
77/8 OPC/Topps 131
78/9 OPC/Topps 152
79/80 OPC/Topps 204
80/1 OPC/Topps 135
88/9 EDM/ActionMagazine 108
75/6 PHA/GingerAle

BLAHA, JAN
94/5 APS 60

BLAHA, MICHAEL
91/2 UD 669, 'CzechWJC 30

BLAHA, PAVEL
94/5 APS 255

BLAIN, BRADY
93/4 Slapshot(Windsor) 12
92/3 Windsor 16
91/2 SketchOHL 194

BLAIN, JACQUES
73/4 QuébecNordiques

BLAIN, JOEL
90/1 SketchQMJHL 149
91/2 SketchQMJHL 212
92/3 Wheeling 3

BLAIN, ROB
95/6 Slapshot 412

BLAIR, ANDY
33/4 Anonymous (V129) 11
34-43 BeeHives(TOR)
36-39 DiamondMatch (4)
33/4 Hamilton V288 9
27-32 LaPresse 29/30
34/5 OPC (V304B) 70
33/4 WWGum (V357) 4
36/7 WWGum (V356) 56
32/3 TOR/OKeefe 5

BLAIR, CAM
93/4 Johnstown 2

BLAIR, DAN
52/3 AnonymousOHL 50

BLAIR, SCOTT
94/5 Slapshot(Detroit) 14
94/5 Slapshot(MEM) 88
95/6 Slapshot 64

BLAIR, WREN
78/9 Saginaw

BLAISDELL, MIKE
82/3 O-Pee-Chee 81
83/4 O-Pee-Chee 242
82/3 Post
88/9 ProCards(Newmarket)
83/4 SouhaitsRen.KeyChain
80/1 DET
86/7 PGH/Kodak

BLAKE, JEFF
93/4 Waterloo

BLAKE, HECTOR (TOE)
34-43 BeeHives(MTL)
63-5 ChexPhoto
35-40 CrownBrand 108
72-84 Dernière 77/8
48-52 Exhibits
83&87 HallOfFame 92
83 HHOF Postcard (G)
51/2 LavalDairy 76
37/8 OPC (V304E) 160
40/1 OPC (V301-2) 101
43-47 ParadeSportive
55/6 Parkhurst 67
57/8 Parkhurst (MTL) 16
58/9 Parkhurst 9
59/60 Parkhurst 27
63/4 Parkhurst 34, 93
93/4 Parkhurst PR47
93/4 Parkie(56/7) 84
94/5 Parkie(64/5) 87
91/2 ProSet 337
38/9 QuakerOats
45-54 QuakerOats
60/1 ShirriffCoin 40
61/2 ShirriffCoin 101
62/3 ShirriffCoin 31
64/5 Topps 43
65/6 Topps 1
66/7 Topps 1
61/2 York 22
67/8 MTL
67/8 MTL/IGA
92/3 MTL/OPC 5, 65
95/6 MTL/Forum 18Nov95

BLAKE, ROB
90/1 Bowman 142
91/2 Bowman 182
92/3 Bowman 367
93/4 Donruss 158
95/6 Donruss 22
96/7 Donruss 100
96/7 DonrussCanadianIce 42
97/8 DonrussCanadianIce 57
96/7 DonrussElite 48
93/4 EASports 61
97/8 EssoOlympic 16
94/5 Flair 77
96/7 Flair 45
94/5 Fleer 93, -FranchiseFu 2
95/6 FleerMetal 69
92/3 FleerUltra 79
93/4 FleerUltra 24
94/5 FleerUltra 96
95/6 FleerUltra 73
96/7 FleerUltra 77
91/2 Gillette 6
95 Globe 82
95/6 Hoyle'WEST 5 (Hearts)
97/8 KatchMedallion 68
91/2 Kelloggs 22
95/6 KennerSLU
96/7 Kraft'Disk
97/8 Kraft - RoadToNagano
93/4 Leaf 172
94/5 Leaf 12, -GoldLeafStar 12
95/6 Leaf 148
96/7 Leaf 177
94/5 LeafLimited 32
95/6 LeafLimited 71
97/8 McDonalds - Medallions
96/7 MetalUniverse 73
97/8 Omega 106
92/3 O-Pee-Chee 243
91/2 OPC/Topps 6, 112
90/1 opcPremier 6
91/2 opcPremier 44
98/9 Pacific 4
97/8 PacificCrown193,-TmCL 12
97/8 PacificCrownRoyale 62
97/8 PcfcDynagon! 58,-Tand 45
97/8 PacificInvincible 65
97/8 PacificParamount 87
98/9 PcfcParamnt 102,-TmCL 12
91/2 PaniniSticker 86, 339
92/3 PaniniSticker 71
93/4 PaniniSticker 209
94/5 PaniniSticker 177
95/6 PaniniSticker 272
96/7 PaniniSticker 268
97/8 PaniniSticker 220
95 PaniniWorlds 8
91/2 Parkhurst 293
92/3 Parkhurst 302
93/4 Parkhurst 94
94/5 Parkhurst 105, V85
95/6 Parkhurst 106
91/2 Pinnacle 201
92/3 Pinnacle 32, -Tm2000 16
93/4 Pinnacle 46
94/5 Pinnacle 9, BR10, TP4
95/6 Pinnacle 198
97/8 Pinnacle 64
97/8 PinnacleCertified 77
97/8 PinnacleInside 71
95/6 PinnacleZenith 88
95/6 Playoff 48
94/5 POG 129
95/6 POG 138
93/4 PowerPlay 113
93/4 Premier 56
94/5 Premier 498
95/6 ProMagnet 61
90/1 ProSet 611
91/2 ProSet 92
92/3 ProSet 67
91/2 PSPlatinum 51, PC8
90/1 Score 421
91/2 Score(CDN) 27, 379
91/2 Score(U.S) 27, 349
91/2 Score-YoungStar 8
92/3 Score 177, -Young 38
93/4 Score 236
94/5 Score 47
95/6 Score 11, -CheckIt 9
96/7 Score 130
97/8 Score 148
94/5 Select 98
95/6 SelectCertified 74
95 Semic 79
95/6 SkyBoxEmotion 80
95/6 SkyBoxImpact 78
94/5 SP 53
96/7 SP 74
97/8 SPAuthentic 72
97/8 SPx 23
98/9 SPx "Finite" 42, 108
95/6 Summit 86
95/6 SuperSticker 56, 58
96/7 TeamOut
92/3 Topps 211
95/6 Topps 307
98/9 Topps 63, B11
94/5 ToppsFinest 45
96/7 ToppsNHLPicks 159
91/2 ToppsStadiumClub 348
92/3 ToppsStadiumClub 23
93/4 ToppsStadiumClub 246
94/5 ToppsStadiumClub 135
95/6 ToppsStadiumClub 56
93/4 TSC-MembersOnly 8
97/8 ToppsStickers 3
97/8 ValuNet
90/1 UpperDeck 45
91/2 UpperDeck 43, 148
92/3 UpperDeck 140
93/4 UpperDeck 317, SP-68
94/5 UD 488, 564, C32, SP35
95/6 UpperDeck 478, SE42
96/7 UpperDeck 278, X35
93/4 UDBeAPlayer-Roots 20
94/5 UDBeAPlayer R40, G3
95/6 UDBeAPlayer 113
96/7 UDBlackDiamond 144
97/8 UDBlackDiamond 103
98/9 UDChoice 95, 227
98/9 UDChoice 234, BH20
95/6 UDCollChoice 160
97/8 UDCollChoice 125, S4
96/7 UpperDeck"Ice" 29
90/1 L.A/Smokeys 3

BLANCHARD, GUY
89/90 Sudbury 29

BLANCHARD, SEAN
97/8 Bowman 13
98 BowmanCHL 24
95/6 Slapshot 277
98/9 UDChoice 264

BLASKO, DAN
91/2 AvantGardeBCJHL 19
92/3 BCJHL 81

BLAZEK, LADISLAV
94/5 APS 2
95/6 APS 102

BLAZEK, ROMAN
94/5 APS 264
95/6 APS 141

BLAZEK, TOMAS
94/5 APS 41
95/6 APS 331
93/4 Parkhurst 517
94/5 SP 156

BLEICHER, MARCUS
94/5 DEL 149
95/6 DEL 143

BLESSMAN, JOHN
88/9 ProCards(Utica)
94/5 Raleigh

BLIGHT, RICK
76/7 OPC/Topps 238
77/8 OPC/Topps 259
78/9 OPC/Topps 7
79/80 O-Pee-Chee 395
80/1 O-Pee-Chee 372
75/6 VAN/RoyalBank
76/7 VAN/RoyalBank
77/8 VAN/GingerAle
77/8 VAN/RoyalBank
78/9 VAN/RoyalBank
79/80 VAN

BLINCO, RUSS
34-43 BeeHives(MTL.M)
35-40 CrownBrand 53
35/6 OPC (V304C) 75
36/7 OPC (V304D) 127
37/8 OPC (V304E) 169
34/5 SweetCaporal
36/7 WWGum (V356) 30

BLINOV, YURI
72 Hellas 69
74 Hellas 62
91/2 Trends72 34
72/3 WilliamsFIN 22

BLISHEN, DON
90/1 SketchWHL 116

BLOCK, KEN
73/4 QuakerOats 37

BLOCK, MATT
94/5 Milwaukee

BLOEM, DIETER
95/6 DEL 249
96/7 DEL 99

BLOEMBERG, JEFF
90/1 O-Pee-Chee 483
89/90 ProCards(IHL) 38
90/1 ProCards 10
91/2 ProCards 210
90/1 UpperDeck 370
89/90 NYR/MarineMidland
95/6 Adirondack

BLOMQUIST, KIRK
82/3 Brandon 21

BLOMQVIST, ARI
80/1 Mallasjuoma 64
78/9 SM-Liiga 83

BLOMQVIST, TIMO
80/1 Mallasjuoma 70
89/90 SemicElitserien 171
90/1 SemicElitserien 127
91/2 SemicElitserien 179
92/3 SemicElitserien 203
89 SemicSticker 32
95/6 Sisu 86, -Double 6
95/6 SisuLimited 58
78/9 SM-Liiga 67
86/7 N.J./SOBER
81/2 WSH
82/3 WSH

BLOMSTEN, ARTO
93/4 Donruss 506
95 Globe 20
94/5 Leaf 125
93/4 Parkhurst 232
95/6 Parkhurst 373
93/4 Premier 453
89/90 SemicElitserien 53
90/1 SemicElitserien 276
91/2 SemicElitserien 59
92/3 SemicElitserien 78
93 SemicSticker 4
92/3 UpperDeck 369, 376
93/4 UpperDeck 505, SP-174
97/8 udSwedish 72
93/4 WPG/Ruffles

BLONDIN, CARL
91/2 SketchQMJHL 99

BLOOM, MIKE
74/5 Loblaws
74/5 OPC 369
75/6 OPC 376
77/8 OPC 375
76/7 OPC/Topps 56
74/5 WSH
81/2 Saskatoon 20

BLOUIN, GAETAN
90/1 SketchWHL 95
90/1 Saskatoon 21

BLOUIN, JACQUES
91/2 SketchQMJHL 136

BLOUIN, JEAN
91/2 ProCards 290
90/1 SketchQMJHL 56
92/3 AtlantaKnights
94/5 ThunderBay

BLOUIN, SYLVAIN
94/5 SigRookies 59
91/2 SketchQMJHL 238
95/6 Binghampton
96/7 Binghampton

BLOYE, DAM
93/4 Slapshot(NorthBay) 16
94/5 Slapshot(NorthBay) 19

BLUE, CHRIS
92/3 BCJHL 107

BLUE, JOHN
92/3 Parkhurst 245, CP19
93/4 Pinnacle 335
94/5 POG 271
93/4 PowerPlay 287
93/4 Premier 209
90/1 ProCards 103
91/2 ProCards 50
93/4 Score 399
93/4 ToppsStadiumClub 334
93/4 UpperDeck 74
95/6 Phoenix

BLUM, JOHN
88/9 ProCards(Adirondack)
89/90 ProCards(AHL) 73
90/1 ProCards 128
88/9 EDM/ActionMagazine 106
86/7 WSH/Kodak
83/4 Moncton 9
85/6 Moncton 17

BLUM, KEN
90/1 SketchOHL 202
93/4 Richmond 15

BLUMSTEAD, LARRY
82/3 Brandon 20

BLYTH, STEVE
83/4 Springfield 20

BOAKE, PETER
91/2 AirCanadaSJHL B8

BOBACK, MIKE
92/3 Classic 83
93/4 ClasicProspects 46
93/4 Portland
94/5 Portland
95/6 Phoenix

BOBILLIER, FRÉDY
95 PaniniWorlds 120

BOBROV, VSEVOLD
73/4 Soviet Stars 23
74/5 Soviet Stars 22
91/2 Trends72 10

BOCHENSKY, BRETISLAV
94/5 APS 288

BODAK, BOB
89/90 ProCards(AHL) 295
86/7 Moncton 27
88/9 SaltLake 23
84/5 Springfield 23

BODAK, MIKE
90/1 ProCards 3

BODARCHUK, MIKE
92/3 Cincinnati

BODDY, GREG
72/3 EddieSargent 223
74/5 Loblaws
73/4 OPC 235
74/5 OPC 349
75/6 OPC/Topps 285
72/3 VAN/RoyalBank
74/5 VAN/RoyalBank
75/6 VAN/RoyalBank

BODGER, DOUG
90/1 Bowman 245
91/2 Bowman 21
92/3 Bowman 13
93/4 Donruss 33
95/6 Donruss 226
93/4 EASports 13
94/5 Flair 16
96/7 FleerPicks 164
92/3 FleerUltra 258
93/4 FleerUltra 31
94/5 FleerUltra 20
93/4 Leaf 19
94/5 Leaf 357
96/7 Leaf 132
85/6 OPC/Topps 38
86/7 OPC/Topps 24
87/8 OPC/Topps 125
88/9 OPC/Topps 96
89/90 OPC/Topps 154
90/1 OPC/Topps 282
91/2 OPC/Topps 207
92/3 O-Pee-Chee 146
85/6 opcSticker 99/230
86/7 opcSticker 232/103
88/9 opcSticker 234/102
89/90 opcSticker 257/136
97/8 PacificRegime 175
87/8 PaniniSticker 141
88/9 PaniniSticker 332
89/90 PaniniSticker 209
90/1 PaniniSticker 33
91/2 PaniniSticker 307
92/3 PaniniSticker 245
93/4 PaniniSticker 109
97/8 PaniniSticker 229
91/2 Parkhurst 15
92/3 Parkhurst 253
95/6 Parkhurst 454
91/2 Pinnacle 8
93/4 Pinnacle 82
94/5 Pinnacle 357
92/3 Pinnacle 97
96/7 PinnacleBeAPlayer 208
94/5 POG 49
93/4 PowerPlay 26
93/4 Premier 29
90/1 ProSet 19
91/2 ProSet 19, -The Puck 3
92/3 ProSet 17
91/2 PSPlatinum 12
90/1 Score 211
91/2 Score(CDN) 517, (U.S) 297
92/3 Score 226
93/4 Score 21
94/5 Score 198
95/6 Score 171
96/7 SkyBoxImpact 104
95/6 SP 134
92/3 Topps 247
91/2 ToppsStadiumClub 114
92/3 ToppsStadiumClub 147
93/4 ToppsStadiumClub 354
94/5 ToppsStadiumClub 148
90/1 UpperDeck 50
91/2 UpperDeck 477
92/3 UpperDeck 207
93/4 UpperDeck 187
94/5 UpperDeck 494
95/6 UpperDeck SE8
94/5 UDBeAPlayer-Aut. 39
95/6 UDCollChoice 77
88/9 BUF/BlueShield
88/9 BUF/WonderBread
89/90 BUF/BlueShield
89/90 BUF/Campbell
90/1 BUF/BlueShield
90/1 BUF/Campbell
91/2 BUF/BlueShield
91/2 BUF/Campbell
92/3 BUF/BlueShield
92/3 BUF/Jubillee
86/7 PGH/Kodak
87/8 PGH/Kodak
96/7 S.J/PacificBellSheet (x2)
97/8 S.J/PacificBellSheet

BODKIN, RICK
94/5 Slapshot(Sudbury) 12
92/3 Sudbury 15
93/4 Sudbury 14

BODNAR, GUS
45-64 BeeHives(BOS, CHI)
51/2 Parkhurst 40
52/3 Parkhurst 37
53/4 Parkhurst 75
54/5 Parkhurst 62
45-54 QuakerOats
91/2 Ultimate(O6) 31, -Aut. 31

BODNARCHUK, MIKE
90/1 ProCards 574
91/2 ProCards 419
87/8 Kingston 14

BODUNOV, ALEKSANDR
74 Hellas 43
74 SemicSticker 41
73/4 Soviet Stars 16
74/5 Soviet Stars 19
91/2 Trends72 32
73/4 WilliamsFIN 2

BODY, LOU
94/5 AutoPhonex 8
94/5 Richmond
95/6 Richmond

BODYCK, BRENT
90/1 ProCards 59

BOE, VINCE
90/1 SketchWHL 15

BØE ANDERSON, CARL OSCAR
95 PaniniWorlds 240

BOEHM, RICK
94/5 DEL 374

BOESCH, GARTH
45-64 BeeHives(TOR)
45-54 QuakerOats

BOETTGER, DWAYNE
83/4 Moncton 5
84/5 NovaScotia 3
85/6 NovaScotia 12

BOEVE, JON
90/1 Rayside
89/90 Sudbury 9
90/1 Sudbury 4

BOGAS, CHRIS
95/6 DonrussElite-WorldJrs 26

BOGDANOV, ANATOLI
92/3 Jyvas-Hyva 35
95/6 Sisu 392

BOGDEN, SHANE
88/9 Regina

BOGELSACK, FRIEDHELM
94/5 DEL 132
95/6 DEL 124
79 PaniniSticker 255

BOGOSLOWSKI, MARK
89/90 Johnstown 27

BOGOYEVAC, STEVE
92/3 Dayton
93/4 Dayton 7
93/4 Richmond 16
94/5 Richmond

BOH, AARON
91/2 SketchWHL 16
95/6 Louisiana Playoffs

BOHACEK, JAN
94/5 APS 72
95/6 APS 180

BOHM, RICHARD
95/6 DEL 371
95 Semic 170

BOHONOS, LONNY
95/6 Bowman 93
94/5 ClassicImages 69
95/6 EdgeIce 87
97/8 Donruss 15
97/8 PacificCrown 310
97/8 PinnacleBeAPlayer 148
97/8 Score 78
97/8 Score(VAN) 9
93/4 PortlandWinterHawks

BOHUN, BRYAN
91/2 AirCanadaSJHL 14, A6

BOIGER, ELMAR
94/5 DEL 178
95/6 DEL 180

BOIJ, PATRICK
95/6 udElite 151

BOILEAU, CLAUDE
52/3 AnonymousOHL 136

BOILEAU, MARC
52/3 AnonymousOHL 116
62/3 Parkhurst 29
74/5 OPC/Topps 49

BOILEAU, PATRICK
95/6 EdgeIce 51
95/6 Portland
96/7 Portland

BOILY, DENIS
96/7 Rimouski

BOIMSTRUCK, FRED
82/3 O-Pee-Chee 318
82/3 Post
81/2 TOR

BOISVERT, ANDRÉ
51/2 LacStJean 18

BOISVERT, GILLES
52/3 AnonymousOHL 118

BOISVERT, RICHARD
88/9 Richelieu

BOISVERT, SERGE
89/90 SemicElitserien 277
90/1 SemicElitserien 40
91/2 SemicElitserien 288
92/3 SemicElitserien 310
85/6 MTL
85/6 MTL/Pennant
85/6 MTL/PepsiPlacemats
82/3 TOR
83/4 Moncton 19

BOITEAU, J.S.
91/2 SketchQMJHL 50

BOIVIN, CLAUDE
93/4 Parkhurst 146
94/5 Parkhurst 159
90/1 ProCards 48
91/2 ProCards 273
92/3 ProSet 130
91/2 PSPlatinum 264
92/3 Score 352
89/90 SketchMEM 69
92/3 Topps 427
92/3 ToppsStadiumClub 16
91/2 UpperDeck 475
92/3 UpperDeck 57
94/5 UpperDeck 146
94/5 OTT/Bell
93/4 PHA 03JAN94
92/3 PHA/JCPenney
93/4 PHA/JCPenney
92/3 PHA/UD 07NOV92

BOIVIN, FRÉDÉRIC
90/1 SketchQMJHL 140
91/2 SketchQMJHL 220

BOIVIN, LÉO JOSEPH
45-64 BeeHives(BOS, TOR)
64-67 BeeHives(BOS, DET)
64/5 CokeCap BOS-20
65/6 CocaCola
62 CeramicTiles
87 HallOfFame 252

68/9 OPC/Topps 101
69/70 OPC/T. 122, -Sticker
70/1 OPC/Topps 42, -Deckle 15
52/3 Parkhurst 34
53/4 Parkhurst 6
54/5 Parkhurst 26
93/4 Parkie(56/7) 11
94/5 Parkie(64/5) 9
95/6 Parkie(66/7) 48
45-54 QuakerOats
60/1 ShirriffCoin 107
61/2 ShirriffCoin 5
68/9 ShirriffCoin PGH7
57/8 Topps 18
58/9 Topps 20
59/60 Topps 26
60/1 Topps 62
61/2 Topps 7, -Stamp
62/3 Topps 5, -Buck
63/4 Topps 5
64/5 Topps 50
65/6 Topps 32
66/7 Topps 50
54-67 TorontoStar V7
56-66 TorontoStar 62/3
63/4 TheTorontoStar
64/5 TheTorontoStar
57/8 BOS
91/2 BOS/Legends (x2)

BOIVIN, M.
84/5 Chicoutimi

BOJCUN, T.
89/90 SketchOHL 122
90/1 SketchOHL 353

BOKENFOHR, MURRAY
90/1 SketchWHL 325

BOKSHOWAN, LORNE
81/2 Milwaukee 9

BOLAN, EDDY
51/2 BasDuFleuve 52

BOLAND, JOHN
81/2 Ottawa67s

BOLAND, MIKE
72/3 OttawaNational

BOLDIN, IGOR
92/3 RedAce(Blue) 12,(Violet) 12
94/5 Sisu 32, 167, -FireOnIce 2

BOLDIREV, IVAN
72/3 EddieSargent 51
74/5 Loblaws
72/3 OPC 41, Topps 146
73/4 OPC/Topps 68
74/5 OPC/Topps 16
75/6 OPC/Topps 12
76/7 OPC/Topps 251
77/8 OPC/Topps 61
78/9 OPC/Topps 135
79/80 OPC/Topps 127
80/1 OPC/Topps 52
81/2 O-Pee-Chee 329
82/3 O-Pee-Chee 338
83/4 O-Pee-Chee 118
84/5 O-Pee-Chee 50, Topps 38
85/6 OPC/Topps 92
82/3 opcSticker 241
83/4 opcSticker 132
84/5 opcSticker 39
85/6 opcSticker 34/164
80/1 Pepsi Cap
82/3 Post
71/2 TheTorontoSun
78/9 ATL/B&W
84/5 DET/Caesars
80/1 VAN
80/1 VAN/Silverwood
81/2 VAN
81/2 VAN/Silverwood
82/3 VAN

BOLDT, MAX
96/7 DEL 19

BOLDUC, ALEX
36/7 WWGum (V356) 119

BOLDUC, DAN
79/80 OPC/Topps 173
79/80 DET
84/5 Moncton 8
85/6 Moncton 2, 3
86/7Moncton 2

BOLDUC, DAVE
96/7 Rimouski

BOLDUC, MICHEL
82/3 Fredericton 4
83/4 Fredericton 9
84/5 Fredericton 13

BOLIBRUCK, KEVIN
94/5 AutoPhonex 9
97/8 Bowman 14
95/6 Classic 94
95/6 Slapshot 320

BOLL, FRANK (BUZZ)
33/4 Anonymous (V129) 4
34-43 BeeHives(TOR)
35/6 OPC (V304C) 90
36/7 OPC (V304D) 119
37/8 OPC (V304E) 140
39/40 OPC (V301-1) 21
38/9 QuakerOats
36/7 WWGum (V356) 40

BOLONCHUK, LARRY
76/7 O-Pee-Chee 322
78/9 OPC/Topps 129, OPC 387
72/3 VAN/RoyalBank

BOLTON, HUGH
45-64 BeeHives(TOR)
51/2 Parkhurst 79
55/6 Parkhurst 14, 69
57/8 Parkhurst(TOR) 13
93/4 Parkie(56/7) 124
45-54 QuakerOats

BOLTON, SHANNON
88/9 Sudbury 19

BOMBARDIR, BRAD
94/5 ClassicImages 51
95/6 FutureLegends 1
97/8 Omega 126
97/8 PinnacleBeAPlayer 214
94/5 SigRookies 66
91/2 UpperDeck'CzechWJC 55

BONAR, DAN
82/3 O-Pee-Chee 150

BONAR, GRAHAM
88/9 ProCards(Indianapolis)
83/4SSMarie

BOND, BILL
67/8 ColumbusCheckers

BOND, KERRY
69 ColumbusCheckers

BOND, ROLAND
74 Hellas 24
74 SemicSticker 15
73/4 WilliamsFIN 24

BONDRA, PETER
95/6 Aces 7 (Diamonds)
91/2 Bowman 299
92/3 Bowman 248
95/6 Bowman 55
93/4 Donruss 366
94/5 Donruss 31
95/6 Donruss 19, -Marksmen 1
96/7 Donruss 147
97/8 Donruss 135, -RedAlert 10
96/7 DonrussCanadianIce 24
97/8 DonrussCanadianIce 25
95/6 DonrussElite 48
96/7 DonrussElite 11
97/8 DonrussPreferred 78
97/8 DonrussPriority 47
97/8 DonrussStudio 60
93/4 EASports 155
95/6 EdgeIce 120, C15
94/5 Flair 196
96/7 Flair 97
94/5 Fleer 232
96/7 Fleer 115, 138
95/6 FleerMetal 156
96/7 FleerNHLPicks 44, -Fab 2
92/3 FleerUltra 230
93/4 FleerUltra 46
94/5 FleerUltra 231
95/6 FleerUltra 172, 319,-Extra 1
95/6 FU-RedLightSpecials 1
96/7 FleerUltra 172, -Mr.Mom.
95/6 Hoyle'EAST 2 (Hearts)
97/8 KatchMedallion 151
97/8 KennerSLU
95/6 KraftDinner
96/7 Kraft-Disk
97/8 Kraft - WorldsBest
93/4 Leaf 79
94/5 Leaf 277
95/6 Leaf 136
96/7 Leaf 200
97/8 Leaf 91
95/6 LeafLimited 30
96/7 LeafLimited 63
96/7 LeafPreferred 29
97/8 Limited 129
96/7 Maggers 162
96/7 MetalUniv. 161, -Lethal 1
97/8 Omega 236,-GameFace 20
91/2 OPC/Topps 362
92/3 O-Pee-Chee 106
90/1 opcPremier 7
98/9 Pacific 12
98/9 Pcfc-DynaIce 19,-GldCr 35
97/8 PacificCrown 18
97/8 PCC-Slap 12C, TeamCL 26
97/8 PacificCrownRoyale 138
97/8 PacificCR -HatTricks 20
97/8 PacificDynagon! 130
97/8 PcfcD-BstKpt 100,-Tand 15
97/8 PacificInv. 145, -Feature 36
97/8 PacificParamount 193
98/9 PacificParamount 242
98/9 PcfcP-SpeDel 20,-TmCL 27
97/8 PacificRegime 206
97/8 PacificRevolution 145
97/8 PcfcRev-ASG 20,-TmCL 26
92/3 PaniniSticker 164
93/4 PaniniSticker 24
95/6 PaniniSticker 139, 151
96/7 PaniniSticker 133
97/8 PacificSticker 109
91/2 Parkhurst 188
92/3 Parkhurst 204
93/4 Parkhurst 222
94/5 Parkhurst 251
95/6 Parkhurst 490
94/5 ParkieSE seV13
91/2 Pinnacle 87
92/3 Pinnacle 82
93/4 Pinnacle 164
94/5 Pinnacle 281
95/6 Pinnacle -Roaring20s 14
96/7 Pinnacle 109
97/8 Pinnacle 181
97/8 PinnacleCertified 46
97/8 PinnacleInside 83
95/6 PinnacleZenith 49
96/7 PinnacleZenith 71
95/6 Playoff 212, 320
96/7 Playoff 391
95/6 POG 281
97/8 Post
93/4 PowerPlay 258
93/4 Premier 12
94/5 Premier 283
90/1 ProSet 645
91/2 ProSet 511
92/3 ProSet 209
91/2 PSPlatinum 244
90/1 ScoreTraded 71T
91/2 Score(CDN) 216, (U.S) 216
92/3 Score 165
93/4 Score 344, -P.AS 12
93/4 Score-International 4
94/5 Score 12
95/6 Score 53, -Lamplighter 7
95/6 Score-GoldenBlades 4
96/7 Score 185
97/8 Score 103
94/5 Select 89
95/6 SelectCertified 51
96/7 SelectCertified 78
95/6 SkyBoxImpact 174, 242
96/7 SkyBoxImpact 136
94/5 SP 129
95/6 SP 155
96/7 SP 163, HC14
97/8 SPAuthentic 164, S17
96/7 SPx 49
97/8 SPx 50
98/9 SPx"Finite" 87, 110, 168
97/8 SportFX MiniStix
95/6 Summit 63, -MadHatter 11
96/7 Summit 62
95/6 SuperSticker 130
96/7 TeamOut
92/3 Topps 294
95/6 Topps 6, 310, 6HG
98/9 Topps 126, M14, SB14
95/6 ToppsFinest 73
91/2 ToppsStadiumClub 37
92/3 ToppsStadiumClub 286
93/4 T.StadiumClub 82, -AllStar
94/5 ToppsStadiumClub 247
95/6 ToppsStadiumClub 209
95/6 TSC-MembersOnly 31
97/8 ToppsSticker 2
90/1 UpperDeck 536
91/2 UpperDeck 131, E12
92/3 UD 115, -LockerAS 1
93/4 UpperDeck 95,308,SP-168
94/5 UpperDeck 135, SP85
95/6 UD 232, 249, 339, SE177
95/6 UD AS11,-ASPredicMVP26
96/7 UpperDeck 180, 364, X26
96/7 UD-AllStarYCTG AR18
97/8 UpperDeck S12
95/6 UDBeAPlayer 210
96/7 UDBlackDiamond 133
97/8 UDBlackDiamond 87
98/9 UDChoice 213, SQ14
95/6 UDCollChoice 58, C13
96/7 UDCC 279, 334, C4, UD23
97/8 UDCC 270, C25, SQ58
97/8 UpperDeckIce 12
96 Wien 228
97/8 Zenith 42,, Z43
90/1 WSH/Kodak
90/1 WSH/Smokey
91/2 WSH
91/2 WSH/Kodak
92/3 WSH/Kodak
95/6 WSH

BONELLO, FRANK
52/3 AnonymousOHL 172

BONIN, BRIAN
95/6 FutureLegends-SS&D 3
92/3 Minnesota
93/4 Minnesota
94/5 Minnesota

BONIN, MARCEL
45-64 BeeHives(DET, MTL)
82? JDMcCarthy
51/2 LavalDairy 15
57/8 Parkhurst(MTL) 18
58/9 Parkhurst 32
59/60 Parkhurst 12
60/1 Parkhurst 51
61/2 Parkhurst 47
62/3 Parkhurst 45
93/4 Parkie(56/7) 19
60/1 ShirriffCoin 29
61/2 ShirriffCoin 115
62/3 ShirriffCoin 27
54/5 Topps 59
54-67 TorontoStar V9
60/1 York
61/2 York 29
60/1 YorkGlasses

BONK, RADEK
94/5 Asset 20, 45
93/4 Classic 98, N10, CL4
94/5 Classic 3, CP13, R2, T47
94/5 Classic-Aut., -Preview
94/5 C'4Sport 117, BC14
94/5 C'4Sport HV12, &C4
94/5 C'Images 25, CE13, PR6
93/4 C4'Images CC16
93/4 C'Prospects 1-3,100,200
93/4 C'Prospects LP21
95/6 Donruss 194
96/7 Donruss 128
95/6 DonrussElite 62
95/6 EdgeIce 158
94/5 Fleer 142, -Rookie 1
96/7 Fleer 74
95/6 FleerMetal 102
95/6 FleerUltra 110, -High 4
96/7 FleerUltra 114
95/6 Hoyle'EAST 3 (Hearts)
95/6 Leaf 263, -StudioRookie 20
96/7 Leaf 129
96/7 MetalUniverse 104
98/9 Pacific 307
97/8 PacificCrown 331
97/8 PacificParamount 123
95/6 PaniniSticker 50
96/7 PaniniSticker 49
97/8 PaniniSticker 37
95/6 Parkhurst 147
95/6 Pinnacle 43
96/7 Pinnacle 50
95/6 Playoff 72
95/6 POG 194
95/6 ProMagnet 111
95/6 Score 190
96/7 Score 97
94/5 Select 186
95/6 SkyBoxEmotion 122
95/6 SkyBoxImpact 117
96/7 SkyBoxImpact 87
94/5 SP 80, -Premier 9
95/6 SP 102
96/7 SP 105
94/5 SigRookies CF1
94/5 SRGoldStandard 78, GS3
95/6 Summit 123
95/6 SuperSticker 84, 88
95/6 Topps 64
94/5 ToppsFinest 3
94/5 T.Finest-BBest 3, (R) 11
96/7 ToppsNHLPicks 147
95/6 ToppsStadiumClub 101
94/5 TSC-MembersOnly 48
94/5 UD 304, 538, 542, SP144
95/6 UpperDeck 124, SE62
96/7 UpperDeck 301
97/8 UpperDeck 320
95/6 UDBeAPlayer 31
95/6 UDCollChoice 110
96/7 UDCollChoice 181
94/5 OTT/Bell
95/6 OTT
96/7 OTT/PizzaHut
97/8 OTT
94/5 LasVegas

BONNER, CRAIG
89/90 SketchMEM 23
90/1 SketchWHL 298
91/2 SketchWHL 91
89/90 Kamloops

BONNER, DOUG
94/5 LeafLimited-USAJrs 2
94/5 ToppsFinest 113
93/4 Seattle

BONNER, JIM
90/1 Mich.Tech
91/2 Mich.Tech

BONNEY, WAYNE
90/1 ProSet 682

BONNEYMAN, ART
28/9 PaulinsCandy 41

BONNEYT, JOE
92/3 WestMich.

BONNI, RYAN
97/8 Bowman 135, BB11

BONSIGNORE, JASON
95/6 Bowman 101
93/4 Classic 99, N4, CL2
94/5 Classic 4, R3, T22, -Aut.
95/6 Classic 97, BK17
94/5 C'FourSport 118, HV16
95/6 C'FiveSport 127, -Sig. 74
95/6 C'FiveSport-Strive 6 (H)
94/5 C4'Images 97
94/5 ClassicImages 45
93/4 C'Prospects 201, -Aut.
93/4 Donruss USA2
95/6 Donruss 249, -Pointer 3
96/7 Fleer 123
95/6 FleerMetal 172
95/6 FleerUltra 332
95/6 Leaf 229, -Studio 12
94/5 LeafLimited-USAJrs 3
95/6 LeafLimited 59
98/9 Pacific 64
95/6 PaniniSticker 256
96/7 PaniniSticker 301
93/4 Parkhurst 510
95/6 Parkhurst 80
93/4 Pinnacle 489
95/6 Pinnacle 207
95/6 PinnacleZenith 136
95/6 Playoff 256
95/6 ProMagnet 82
94/5 Score 209
95/6 Score 308
95/6 SelectCertified 113
95/6 SkyBoxEmotion-Next 3
95/6 SkyBoxImpact 196
96/7 SkyBoxImpact 146
93/4 Slapshot(N.Falls) 23, 28
94/5 Slapshot(Sudbury) 17
94/5 SP 173
98/9 Topps 129
94/5 ToppsFinest 117
95/6 ToppsStadiumClub ER191
95/6 ToppsSuperSkills SR2
93/4 UpperDeck 560
94/5 UpperDeck 523
95/6 UpperDeck 266
96/7 UpperDeck 62
95/6 UDBeAPlayer 179

BONVIE, DENNIS
95/6 Leaf 306
91/2 SketchOHL 54
95/6 UpperDeck 393
97/8 UpperDeck 277
94/5 CapeBreton

BONVIE, HERB
95/6 Slapshot 225

BOOKER, CRAIG
85/6 Kitchener 17
86/7 Kitchener 21
87/8 Kitchener 21

BOOKER, WES
96/7 SSMarie

BOOMER, RON
52/3 AnonymousOHL 180

BOON, DICKIE
83&87 HallOfFame 108
83 HHOF Postcard (H)
60/1 Topps 17
61/2 Topps -Stamp

BOONE, KEN
93/4 Slapshot(Kingston) 11

BOORK, LEIF
94/5 ElitSet 303
91/2 SemicElitserien 313
92/3 SemicElitserien 335

BOORMAN, BRYAN
95/6 RedDeer

BOOS, TINO
95/6 DEL 167
96/7 DEL 243

BOOTH, DEREK
90/1 SketchOHL 254
93/4 Rochester
92/3 Toledo (1), (2)

BOOTHMAN, GEORGE
34-43 BeeHives(TOR)

BOOTLAND, NICK
95/6 Slapshot 104
95/6 Guelph 6
96/7 Guelph 27

BORDELEAU, CHRISTIAN
72-84 Dernière
70/1 EddieSargent 185
71/2 EddieSargent 187
70/1 Esso Stamp
72/3 Letraset 24
71/2 OPC/Topps 51
72/3 OPC 299
73/4 opc-Posters 17
75/6 opcWHA 116
76/7 opcWHA 49
73/4 QuakerOats 15
72/3 7ElevenCups
71/2 TheTorontoSun
69/70 MTL/ProStar
76/7 QuébecNordiques

BORDELEAU, J.P.
72-84 Dernière 79/80
74/5 Loblaws
73/4 OPC 258
74/5 OPC/Topps 69, OPC 309
75/6 OPC 369
76/7 OPC/Topps 208
77/8 OPC/Topps 156
78/9 OPC/Topps 101
79/80 OPC/Topps 212
80/1 O-Pee-Chee 339
79/80 CHI
80/1 CHI/4x6
80/1 CHI/5.5x8.5

BORDELEAU, PAULIN
74/5 Loblaws
74/5 O-Pee-Chee 340
75/6 OPC/Topps 151
76/7 opcWHA 98
77/8 opcWHA 32
90/1 ProCards 74
91/2 ProCards 91
76/7 QuébecNordiques
76 QuébecNordiques/MA
73/4 VAN/RoyalBank
74/5 VAN/RoyalBank
75/6 Fredericton
93/4 Fredericton
94/5 Fredericton
95/6 Fredericton
96/7 Fredericton

BORDELEAU, SÉBASTIEN
95/6 EdgeIce 38
97/8 Limited 195
97/8 PacificCrown 194
97/8 PinnacleBeAPlayer 211
97/8 Score 14
91/2 SketchQMJHL 210
94/5 Slapshot(MEM) 69
96/7 UpperDeck 193
97/8 UpperDeck 87
97/8 MTL
95/6 Fredericton
96/7 Fredericton

BORGGAARD, ANDY
93/4 Huntington

BORGO, RICHARD
92/3 ClassicProspects 103
89/90 SketchMEM 35
90/1 SketchOHL 228
86/7 Kitchener 15
87/8 Kitchener 15
88/9 Kitchener 15
89/90 Kitchener 16
90/1 Kitchener 14
93/4 ThunderBay

BORGQVIST, ROBERT
95/6 UDCollChoice 348

BORGSTROM, JORMA
65/6 Hellas 52
70/1 Kuvajulkaisut 279
71/2 WilliamsFIN 150
72/3 WilliamsFIN 140

BORLAND, BILL
24/5 Crescent Selkirks 14
23/4 PaulinsCandy 1
28/9 PaulinsCandy 77

BORRETT, BARRY
77/8 NovaScotia

BORSATO, LUCIANO
92/3 Bowman 52
95/6 DEL 207
96/7 DEL 350
92/3 FleerUltra 239
93/4 FleerUltra 452
92/3 O-Pee-Chee 149
92/3 PaniniSticker E
93/4 PaniniSticker 195
91/2 Parkhurst 425
92/3 Parkhurst 439
93/4 Parkhurst 501
94/5 ParkieSE 200
91/2 Pinnacle 353
92/3 Pinnacle 218
93/4 PowerPlay 471
93/4 Premier 234
94/5 Premier 148
89/90 ProCards(AHL) 35
91/2 ProCards 186
92/3 PS-RookG.Ldr 8,-TmLdr 15
91/2 PSPlatinum 275
92/3 Score 256
93/4 Score 401
92/3 Topps 239
92/3 ToppsStadiumClub 81
93/4 ToppsStadiumClub 317
91/2 UpperDeck 599
92/3 UpperDeck 77
91/2 WPG/IGA

93/4 WPG/Ruffles
91/2 Moncton

BORSCHEVSKY, NIKOLAI
92/3 Classic 52
93/4 Donruss 332
93/4 EASports 137, 220
92/3 FleerUltra 418, -Imports 1
93/4 FleerUltra 99
94/5 FleerUltra 375
93/4 Leaf 137
94/5 Leaf 279
92/3 opcPremier 100
93/4 PaniniSticker 224
94/5 PaniniSticker 192
92/3 Parkhurst 186, 216
93/4 Parkhurst 203
92/3 Pinnacle 397
93/4 Pinnacle 12
94/5 Pinnacle 160
94/5 POG 230
93/4 PowerPlay 240
93/4 Premier 107
92/3 RedAce(Blue) 11,(Violet) 11
93/4 Score 41, -International 12
94/5 Score 30
93/4 ToppsStadiumClub 375
94/5 ToppsStadiumClub 209
92/3 UpperDeck 572
93/4 UpperDeck 164, SP-156
94/5 UpperDeck 405
95/6 UpperDeck 173
95/6 UDCollChoice 300
92/3 TOR/Kodak
93/4 TOR/Abalene
93/4 TOR/Blacks 18
94/5 TOR

BORYS, CORY
91/2 AirCanadaSJHL D35

BORZECKI, ADAM
98 BowmanCHL 120

BOSCH, BRYAN
88/9 Lethbridge
89/90 Lethbridge

BOSCHER, RICHARD
91/2 AirCanadaSJHL B1
92/3 MPSPhotoSJHL 130

BOSCHMAN, JOE
95/6 Spokane 13

BOSCHMAN, LAURIE
91/2 Bowman 282
86/7 Kraft Sports 72
80/1 OPC/Topps 179
81/2 O-Pee-Chee 314
83/4 O-Pee-Chee 381
84/5 OPC 335, Topps 151
85/6 O-Pee-Chee 251
86/7 OPC/Topps 184
87/8 O-Pee-Chee 222
88/9 O-Pee-Chee 200
90/1 OPC/Topps 39
91/2 OPC/Topps 202
90/1 opcPremier 8
81/2 opcSticker 103
84/5 opcSticker 288
85/6 opcSticker 254, 134
86/7 opcSticker 111
88/9 opcSticker 139/10
89/90 opcSticker 147, 266
87/8 PaniniSticker 368
88/9 PaniniSticker 153
89/90 PaniniSticker 169
90/1 PaniniSticker 320
91/2 PaniniSticker 215
91/2 Parkhurst 316
92/3 Parkhurst 122
80/1 Pepsi Cap
92/3 Pinnacle 375
90/1 ProSet 324, 476
91/2 ProSet 426
90/1 Score 63T
91/2 Score(CDN) 436
92/3 Score 374, 513
93/4 Score 289
84/5 7ElevenDisk
92/3 Topps 246
91/2 ToppsStadiumClub 292
92/3 ToppsStadiumClub 310
93/4 ToppsStadiumClub 3
90/1 UpperDeck 103
91/2 UpperDeck 279
83/4 Vachon 123
82/3 EDM/RedRooster
88/9 EDM/ActionMagazine 94
90/1 N.J
92/3 OTT
79/80 TOR
81/2 TOR
80/1 TOR
83/4 WPG
84/5 WPG/Police
85/6 WPG
85/6 WPG/Police
85/6 WPG/Silverwood
86/7 WPG
87/8 WPG
88/9 WPG/Police
89/90 WPG/Safeway

BOSSON, MATHIAS
94/5 ElitSet 252
95/6 ElitSet 94
95/6 udElite 142
97/8 udSwedish 143

BOSSY, MIKE
93/4 Classic 116, -Autograph
72-84 Dernière 77/8 80/1, 82/3
88/9 EssoAllStar
96/7 HHOFLegends 87
84/5 Kelloggs Disk
82/3 McDonalds 6, 21
78/9 OPC/Topps 1, 63, 67, 115
79/80 OPC/T. 1, 5, 7, 161, 230
80/1 OPC/Topps 25, 204, 262
81/2 OPC 198, 208, 219, 382
81/2 OPC 386, 388, 390
82/3 OPC 2, 197, 199
83/4 OPC 1, 3, 205, 210
84/5 OPC 122, 209, 362, 376
85/6 OPC/Topps 130, T-AS 9
86/7 OPC/Topps 90, B, T-AS 4
87/8 OPC/Topps 105
92/3 OPC 391, -25Years 11
81/2 opcSticker 150, 158, 253
82/3 opcSticker 1, 50, 51, 165
83/4 opcSticker 10, 78, 79, 176
83/4 opcSticker 306, 321, 322
84/5 opcSticker 82, 83, 235/234
85/6 opcSticker 66, 118
86/7 opcSticker 217, 194/56
86/7 opcSticker 117/131
87/8 opcSticker 244
80/1 opcSuperCard 12
87/8 PaniniSticker 97
81/2 Post PopUp 6
82/3 Post
90/1 ProSet 650
91/2 PS-HOF 1
87/8 ProSportWatch CW6
83/4 PuffySticker 19
85/6 7Eleven 12
84/5 7ElevenDisk
83/4 SouhaitsRen.KeyChain
77-9 Sportscaster 47-16
81/2 Topps 4, 57, 91, (E) 125
84/5 Topps 91, 155
96 Wien HL3
95/6 Zellers
79/80 NYI
83/4 NYI
84/5 NYI 32
83/4 NYI/Islander 2, 35
84/5 NYI/Islander 2
93/4 NYI/Chemical

BOSTON, SCOTT
89/90 SketchOHL 87
90/1 SketchOHL 340
91/2 SketchOHL 115
92/3 AtlantaKnights
87/8 Brockville 17
93/4 Knoxville

BOSTROM, HELGE
33/4 CndGum (V252)

BOSTROM, JUHANI
70/1 Kuvajulkaisut 101
72 Panda
78/9 SM-Liiga 38
71/2 WilliamsFIN 111
72/3 WilliamsFIN 81
73/4 WilliamsFIN 126

BOTHWELL, TIM
84/5 O-Pee-Chee 182
85/6 OPC/Topps 161
87/8 OPC/Topps 29
87/8 opcSticker 26/167
85/6 opcSticker 49/180
88/9 ProCards(Peoria)
89/90 ProCards(AHL) 23
90/1 SketchWHL 42
91/2 SketchWHL 328
87/8 STL/Kodak
88/9 STL/Kodak
92/3 Phoenix

BOTTERI, STÉPHANE
94 Semic 217
92 SemicSticker 221
93 SemicSticker 251

BOTTERILL, JASON
93/4 Donruss CAN4
95/6 Donruss-CanadaJr 18
95/6 DonrussElite-WorldJrs 10
98/9 Pacific 172
93/4 Pinnacle 467
94/5 Score 202
94/5 SP 143
95/6 SP 175
95/6 Topps 14CJ
94/5 ToppsFinest 144
93/4 UpperDeck 534

BOUCHA, HENRY
72/3 EddieSargent 84
82? JDMcCarthy
74/5 LiptonSoup 32
74/5 Loblaws
73/4 OPC/Topps 33
74/5 OPC/Topps 38
76/7 OPC/Topps 209
75/6 opcWHA 79
72 SemicSticker 126
76/7 COL.R

BOUCHARD, ALAIN
79/80 Montréal

BOUCHARD, DAN
72-84 Dernière 79/80, 81/2
72/3 EddieSargent 14
74/5 LiptonSoup 44
74/5 Loblaws
82/3 McDonalds 1
72/3 OPC 203
73/4 OPC/Topps 45
74/5 OPC/Topps 15
75/6 OPC/Topps 268
76/7 OPC/Topps 111
77/8 OPC/Topps 37
78/9 OPC/Topps 169
79/80 OPC/Topps 28
80/1 OPC/Topps 68
81/2 O-Pee-Chee 270, 277
82/3 O-Pee-Chee 278, 279
83/4 O-Pee-Chee 290
84/5 OPC 277, Topps 128
85/6 O-Pee-Chee 246
81/2 opcSticker 73, 84
82/3 opcSticker 27
83/4 opcSticker 245
84/5 opcSticker 172, 173
85/6 opcSticker 143/13
79 PaniniSticker 53
80/1 Pepsi Cap
83/4 PuffySticker 18
83/4 SouhaitsRen.KeyChain
83/4 Vachon 62
72/3 ATL
74/5 ATL
77/8 ATL
78/9 ATL/Coke
79/80 ATL
79/80 ATL/B&W
80/1 CGY
81/2 QUE
82/3 QUE
83/4 QUE
84/5 QUE
92/3 QUE/PetroCanada
85/6 WPG
85/6 WPG/Police

BOUCHARD, EDMOND
24/5 Champs (C144)
23/4 (V145-1) 37
24/5 (V145-2) 19

BOUCHARD, EMILE (BUTCH)
34-43 BeeHives(MTL.C)
45-64 BeeHives(MTL)
72-84 Dernière 77/8
48-52 Exhibits
83&87 HallOfFame 228
83 HHOF Postcard (M)
51/2 LaPatrie 9-Dec
43-47 ParadeSportive (x3)
51/2 Parkhurst 3
52/3 Parkhurst 13
53/4 Parkhurst 32
54/5 Parkhurst 6, 97
55/6 Parkhurst 46, 71
45-54 QuakerOats
91/2 Ultimate(O6) 8, -Aut 8
92/3 MTL/OPC 2
95/6 MTL/Forum 9Dec95

BOUCHARD, ERIC
91/2 SketchWHL 137

BOUCHARD, GILLES
90/1 SketchMEM 34
90/1 SketchQMJHL 38

BOUCHARD, HUGHES
91/2 SketchQMJHL 152
88/9 Richelieu
93/4 Roanoke

BOUCHARD, JOEL
93/4 Donruss CAN5
97/8 PacificCrown 338
97/8 PaniniSticker 197
93/4 Pinnacle 461
97/8 PinnacleBeAPlayer 129
90/1 SketchQMJHL 244
91/2 SketchQMJHL 143
93/4 UpperDeck 541
96/7 UpperDeck"Ice" 8
94/5 SaintJohn
95/6 SaintJohn

BOUCHARD, LÉO
52/3 BasDuFleuve 57
52/3 LavalDairy 25
52/3 StLawrence 41

BOUCHARD, PIERRE
71/2 Bazooka Panel 20
72-84 Dernière 72/3, 73/4, 79/80
71/2 EddieSargent 111
72/3 EddieSargent 116
74/5 Loblaws
71/2 OPC 2
72/3 OPC 165
73/4 OPC 261
74/5 OPC/Topps 254
75/6 OPC/Topps 304
76/7 OPC/Topps 177
77/8 OPC/Topps 20
78/9 OPC/Topps 116
79/80 O-Pee-Chee 289
80/1 O-Pee-Chee 373
71/2 TheTorontoSun
69/70 MTL/ProStar
70/1 MTL
71/2 MTL
72/3 MTL
73/4 MTL
74/5 MTL
75/6 MTL
76/7 MTL
77/8 MTL
79/80 WSH
80/1 WSH

BOUCHARD, ROB
91/2 SketchQMJHL 48
94/5 Roanoke
96/7 Rimouski

BOUCHER, BILLY
25-27 Anonymous 1, 2, 19
24/5 Champs (C144)
24/5 MapleCrispettes(V130) 11
23/4 (V145-1) 16
24/5 (V145-2) 46

BOUCHER, BOB
84/5 NovaScotia 25

BOUCHER, BRIAN
94/5 AutoPhonex 10
97 BowmanCHL 81
95/6 DonrussElite-WorldJrs 23
94/5 Select 155
98/9 SPx"Finite" SS27
95/6 Tetrad 69
95/6 TetradAutobilia95
96/7 UpperDeck"Ice" 148

BOUCHER, BROCK
95/6 Slapshot 22

BOUCHER, CHARLIE
91/2 SketchQMJHL 174

BOUCHER, DENIS
52/3 AnonymousOHL 135

BOUCHER, FRANK
34-43 BeeHives(NYR)
35-40 CrownBrand 68
33-35 DiamondMatch
36-39 DiamondMatch (2), (2), (3)
83&87 HallOfFame 93
83 HHOF Postcard (G)
27-32 LaPresse 28/9
60/1 Topps 29
61/2 Topps-Stamp
36/7 WWGum (V356) 16

BOUCHER, GEORGE
83&87 HallOfFame 229
83 HHOF Postcard (L)
27-32 LaPresse 28/9
23/4 (V145-1) 6
24/5 (V145-2) 2

BOUCHER, PHILIPPE
91/2 Arena 10
91/2 Classic 11
91/2 ClassicFourSport 11, -Aut.
92/3 ClassicProspects 68
93/4 Durivage 4
93/4 FleerUltra 70, -Rookies 1
94/5 Leaf 539
92/3 opcPremier 72
97/8 PacificRegime 92
92/3 Parkhurst 16
93/4 Parkhurst 24, C11
94/5 ParkieSE 16
93/4 Pinnacle 213
96/7 PinnacleBeAPlayer 74
93/4 PowerPlay 296
94/5 Premier 371
93/4 Score 455
91/2 SketchAwards 21, 25
90/1 SketchMEM 103
90/1 SketchQMJHL 50
91/2 SketchQMJHL 43
91/2 StarPics 28, 36
95/6 Topps 136
94/5 ToppsStadiumClub 64
91/2 UltimateDP 11, 67, 75
91/2 UltimateDP 82, 89, -Aut 67
91/2 UpperDeck 68
92/3 UpperDeck 484
93/4 UpperDeck 82, SP-14
94/5 UpperDeck 71
93/4 Rochester

BOUCHER, ROB
24/5 Champs (C144)

BOUCHER, SCOTT
92/3 BCJHL 167

BOUCHER, TYLER
91/2 AvantGardeBC 90, 159
92/3 BCJHL 119

BOUDAEV, ALEKSEI
95/6 RedDeer

BOUDREAU, BRUCE
78/9 O-Pee-Chee 280
79/80 O-Pee-Chee 354
88/9 ProCards(Springfield)
89/90 ProCards(IHL) 108
90/1 ProCards 541
91/2 ProCards 260
78/9 TOR
85/6 NovaScotia 5

BOUDREAU, CARL
89/90 SketchMEM 56
90/1 SketchQMJHL 97
91/2 SketchQMJHL 116
92/3 Oklahoma

BOUDREAU, DARRYL
82/3 Kitchener 10

BOUDREAU, RENÉ
36/7 WWGum (V356) 117

BOUDREAU, DAVE
90/1 SketchQMJHL 119
91/2 SketchQMJHL 117

BOUDREAULT, SERGE
67/8 ColumbusCheckers

BOUDRIAS, ANDRÉ
71/2 Bazooka Panel 16
70/1 DadsCookies
70/1 EddieSargent 219
71/2 EddieSargent 215
72/3 EddieSargent 214
70/1 Esso Stamp
74/5 LiptonSoup 14
74/5 Loblaws
68/9 OPC/Topps 53
69/70 OPC/Topps 16
70/1 OPC/Topps 121
71/2 OPC/Topps 12
72/3 OPC 93, Topps 158
73/4 OPC/Topps 19
74/5 OPC/Topps 117, 191
75/6 OPC/Topps 60, 329
76/7 opcWHA 87
72 SemicSticker 210
68/9 ShirriffCoin MIN3
71/2 TheTorontoSun
70/1 VAN/RoyalBank
71/2 VAN/RoyalBank 16
72/3 VAN/Nalleys
72/3 VAN/RoyalBank
73/4 VAN/RoyalBank
74/5 VAN/RoyalBank
75/6 VAN/RoyalBank
76/7 QuébecNordiques
76 QuébecNordiques/MA

BOUGHNER, BOB
97/8 PacificD-BestKept 9
96/7 PinnacleBeAPlayer 178
90/1 SketchMEM 4
90/1 SketchOHL 153
89/90 SSMarie 7

BOUGIE, GEORGE
51/2 LavalDairy 77
52/3 StLawrence 32

BOULANGER, BOB
88/9 ProCards(Sherbrooke)
97/8 UDBlackDiamond 98

BOULERICE, JESSE
95/6 Slapshot 74
98/9 UDChoice 305

BOULIANE, ANDRÉ
90/1 SketchQMJHL 264
91/2 SketchQMJHL 149

BOULIN, VLADISLAV
94/5 Flair 125
94/5 FleerUltra 342
94/5 Leaf 456
94/5 ParkieSE 125
94/5 Premier 434
94/5 UpperDeck 266

BOULTON, ERIC
93/4 Slapshot(Oshawa) 21
95/6 Slapshot 339

BOUMEDIENNE, JOSEF
97/8 udSwedish 171

BOURASSA, BERTRAND
51/2 LavalDairy 81

BOURBONNAIS, RICK
77/8 O-Pee-Chee 312

BOURBONNAIS, ROGER
69/70 MästarSerien 36

BOURDEAU, FRANÇOIS
90/1 SketchQMJHL 104
91/2 SketchQMJHL 68
93/4 Johnstown 3
88/9 Richelieu

BOURDON, ARMAND
51/2 LacStJean 9

BOURGEAULT, LEO
27-32 LaPresse 29/30
33/4 OPC (V304A) 28

BOURGEOIS, CHARLIE
86/7 O-Pee-Chee 239
86/7 opcSticker 178/41
87/8 PaniniSticker 309
88/9 ProCards(Binghampton)
81/2 CGY
82/3 CGY
85/6 CGY/RedRooster
87/8 STL/Kodak

BOURGEOIS, SHAWN
91/2 AvantGardeBC 15
92/3 BCJHL 202

BOURGET, STÉPHANE
90/1 SketchQMJHL 99

BOURNE, BOB
75/6 OPC/Topps 163
77/8 OPC/Topps 93
78/9 OPC/Topps 69
78/9 OPC/Topps 126
79/80 OPC/Topps 56
80/1 O-Pee-Chee 276
81/2 OPC 201, Topps(E) 87
82/3 O-Pee-Chee 198
83/4 O-Pee-Chee 4
84/5 OPC 123, Topps 92
85/6 OPC/Topps 97
86/7 OPC/Topps 14
87/8 OPC/Topps 167
88/9 OPC/Topps 101
88/9 opcStars 2
81/2 opcSticker 163
82/3 opcSticker 53
83/4 opcSticker 80, 174
84/5 opcSticker 89
85/6 opcSticker 67/191
86/7 opcSticker 208/82
88/9 opcSticker 213/84
88/9 PaniniSticker 399
82/3 Post
83/4 SouhaitsRen.KeyChain
84/5 KelownaWingsWHL 42
87/8 L.A.
79/80 NYI
83/4 NYI
83/4 NYI/Islander 3
84/5 NYI 3
93/4 LasVegas

BOURQUE, CLAUDE
34-43 BeeHives(MTL)
35-40 CrownBrand 199
39/40 OPC (V301-1) 28

BOURQUE, DAVE
95/6 Slapshot 351

BOURQUE, PHIL
90/1 Bowman 205
91/2 Bowman 94
92/3 Bowman 293
92/3 FleerUltra 352
95 Globe 126
89/90 OPC/Topps 19
90/1 OPC/Topps 41
91/2 OPC/Topps 33
92/3 opcPremier 73
89/90 PaniniSticker 317
90/1 PaniniSticker 129
91/2 PaniniSticker 272
92/3 PaniniSticker 225
95 PaniniWorlds 223
91/2 Parkhurst 136
91/2 Pinnacle 227
92/3 Pinnacle 353
93/4 Pinnacle 331
94/5 Pinnacle 112
91/2 ProSet 189
90/1 ProSet 228
90/1 Score 234
91/2 Score(CDN) 69, (U.S) 69
92/3 Score 223
93/4 Score 308
92/3 Topps 442
91/2 ToppsStadiumClub 168
92/3 ToppsStadiumClub 282
90/1 UpperDeck 31
91/2 UpperDeck 398
92/3 UpperDeck 141, 452
95/6 UDCollChoice 86
94/5 OTT/Bell
95/6 OTT
89/90 PGH/Elbys
89/90 PGH/Foodland 5
90/1 PGH/Foodland 1
91/2 PGH/Elbys
91/2 PGH/Foodland 15
81/2 Kingston 6

BOURQUE, RAY
95/6 Aces 8 (Diamonds)
96/7 Aces 5 (Hearts)
97/8 Aces 2 (Spades)
90/1 Bowman 31

91/2 Bowman 356, -Promo
92/3 Bowman 3, 223
95/6 Bowman 2
96/7 CorinthianHeadliner
72-84 Dernière 79/80, 82/3
93/4 Donruss 24
94/5 Donruss 68, -Dom. 2
95/6 Donruss 127, -Dom. 3
96/7 Donruss 132, -Dom. 3
97/8 Donruss 66, -Line 21
96/7 D.CanadianIce 21, 150
97/8 D.CdnIce 11, -National 11
95/6 DonrussElite 9
96/7 DonrussElite 17
97/8 DonrussElite 21
97/8 DonrussPreferred 24, 174
97/8 DPriority 20,-Stamps 35
97/8 D.Priority -Postcards 35
97/8 DonrussStudio 28
96/7 Duracell JB19
92/3 Durivage 31
93/4 Durivage 26
93/4 EASports 7, 122, 185
88/9 Esso Sticker
94/5 Flair 8
96/7 Flair 4, -HotNumber 1
94/5 Fleer 9
96/7 Fleer 4, 140, -Norris 1
95/6 FleerMetal 6
96/7 FleerNHLPicks 14, -Fab 3
92/3 FleerUltra 2, -AS 2, -AW 8
93/4 FleerUltra 1, -AS 2
94/5 FleerUltra 10, -AS 1, -AW 1
95/6 FleerUltra 8
96/7 F.Ultra 8, -Blue 1, -Power 1
88/9 FritoLay
91/2 Gillette 26
95 Globe 77
96/7 Got-UmHockeyGreatsCoin
92/3 HighFive 1
93/4 HockeyWit 77
95/6 Hoyle'EAST 4 (Hearts)
92/3 HumptyDumpty (1)
97/8 KatchMedallion 8
93/4 KennerSLU
94/5 KennerSLU (U.S)
97/8 KennerSLU - 1on1
94 Koululainen
89/90 Kraft 52, -Sticker 4
90/1 Kraft 3, 80
91/2 Kraft 57
92/3 Kraft'AllStar
93/4 Kraft-Captain
94/5 Kraft-AS, -AW
95/6 Kraft-Disk
96/7 Kraft-AS, -Disk
97/8 Kraft -RoadToNagano
93/4 Leaf 215, -GoldAS 7
94/5 Leaf 77, GoldStar 6
95/6 Leaf 106, -Gold 3
96/7 Leaf 122
97/8 Leaf 13
94/5 LeafLimited 84
95/6 LeafLimited 16
96/7 LeafLimited 49
96/7 LeafPreferred 83, -Steel 4
97/8 Limited 92, 125, 139
97/8 Limited -fabric 29
96/7 Maggers 17
82/3 McDonalds 28
91/2 McDonalds McH-3, McD10
92/3 McDonalds McH-05
93/4 McDonalds McH4
94/5 McDonalds McD5
96/7 McDonalds McD31
97/8 McDonalds McD17, F7
97/8 McDonalds -Medallions
96/7 MetalUniverse 7
97/8 Omega 12
80/1 OPC/Topps 2, 140
81/2 OPC 1, 17,Topps 5, (E) 126
82/3 O-Pee-Chee 7, 24
83/4 O-Pee-Chee 45
84/5 OPC 1, 211, T. 1, 157
85/6 OPC/Topps 40, B, -AS 5
86/7 OPC/Topps 1, T-AS 11
87/8 OPC/Topps 87, F, T-AS 1
88/9 OPC/Topps I, 73, T-AS 5
89/90 OPC/Topps 110
89/90 OPC 316, Topps-AS 7
90/1 OPC/Topps I, 43, 165, 196
90/1 O-Pee-Chee 475
91/2 OPC/T. 66, 170, 261, 517
92/3 O-Pee-Chee 126, 348
90/1 opcPremier 9
91/2 opcPremier 119, 192
87/8 opcStars 4
88/9 opcStars 3
81/2 opcSticker 49
82/3 opcSticker 86, 87, 166
83/4 opcSticker 46, 47, 173
84/5 opcSticker 143, 183
85/6 opcSticker 115, 157
86/7 opcSticker 34, 119/133
87/8 opcSticker 67, 140
87/8 opcSticker 178/33, 116/128
88/9 opcStick 23,208/79,117/247
89/90 opcSticker 32, 162/24
89/90 opcStickFS 33
98/9 Pacific 77
97/8 PacificCrown 1, -TeamCL 2
97/8 PacificCrownRoyale 7
97/8 PcfcDynagon! 7,-BstKpt 5
97/8 PcfcD-Dyn 2A,-Tandem 28
97/8 PacificInv. 7, -Feature 3
97/8 PacificParamount 9
98/9 PacificParamount 10
97/8 PacificRegime 10
97/8 PcfcRevolution 7,-ASGm 2
87/8 PaniniSticker 6, 381
88/9 PaniniSticker 204, 405
89/90 PaniniSticker 187, 201
90/1 PaniniSticker 17, 322
91/2 PaniniSticker 171, 335
92/3 PaniniSticker 144, 279
93/4 PaniniSticker 10
94/5 PaniniSticker 8
95/6 PaniniSticker 9
96/7 PaniniSticker 1
97/8 PaniniSticker 9
91/2 Parkhurst 9, 221, 469, 472
92/3 Parkhurst 1, 464
93/4 Parkhurst 14
94/5 Parkhurst 13, 304, C2
95/6 Parkhurst 11, PP22, -AS 5
95/6 Parkie-Crown(2) 9
94/5 ParkieSe seV18
91/2 Pinnacle15, 368, B2
92/3 Pinnacle 2, -TeamP 2
93/4 Pinnacle 250, CA2, -TmP 8
94/5 Pinnacle 190, BR7, TP3
95/6 Pinnacle 56
96/7 Pinnacle 199
97/8 Pinnacle 38
97/8 P.BAP 248,-TakeANum 1
97/8 PinnacleBeehive 17
97/8 PinnacleCertified 41
95/6 PinnacleFANtasy 2
96/7 PinnacleFANtasy 1
97/8 PinnacleInside 16
95/6 PinnacleZenith 29
96/7 PinnacleZenith 4
95/6 Playoff 5, 116, 226
96/7 Playoff 371
94/5 POG 42, 263, 327
95/6 POG 4, 18, 36
94/5 Post
96/7 Post
81/2 Post PopUp 1
93/4 PowerPlay 16, -Salp 2
93/4 Premier 93, 350, 383
93/4 Prmr-Black(OPC) 21, (T) 15
94/5 Premier 36, 420, 454, 490
95/6 ProMagnet 11
90/1 ProSet 1,357, 384
91/2 ProSet 9, 296, 322, 567
91/2 PS-ThePuck 1
92/3 ProSet 4, 261
91/2 PSPlatinum 2, 278
83/4 PuffySticker 11
96/7 SB'7Eleven
90/1 Score 200, 313, 363, 368
90/1 Score-HotCards 35
91/2 ScoreCDN 50,319,331,374
91/2 ScoreUS 50, 344, 415, 429
92/3 Score 100,419,447,490,520
93/4 Score 29, -Franchise 1
93/4 Score-Dream 7,-P.AS 21,48
94/5 Score 180, DT3, NP21
95/6 Score 199
96/7 Score 53, -Superstition 7
97/8 Score 89
97/8 Score(BOS) 4
92/3 SeasonsPatch 17
94/5 Select 18, FL2
95/6 SelectCert. 34, -Double 3
96/7 SelectCertified 5
89 SemicSticker 57
91 SemicSticker 55
92 SemicSticker 80
93 SemicSticker 192
84/5 7ElevenDisk
85/6 7Eleven 1
95/6 SkyBoxEmotion 6
95/6 SkyBoxImpact 7
96/7 SkyBoxImpact 5, -Fox 3
83/4 SouhaitsRen.KeyChain
94/5 SP 6, -Premier 20
95/6 SP 5, E3
96/7 SP 7, HC23, -Inside
97/8 SPAuthentic 8, I28, S6, T6
96/7 SPx 3, HHI
97/8 SPx 3
98/9 SPx"Finite" 117, 177
97/8 SportFX MiniStix
95/6 Summit 33, -GM 13
96/7 Summit 141
95/6 SuperSticker 6, -DieCut 6
96/7 TeamOut
91/2 Topps-TeamLdr. 19
92/3 Topps 221, 262
95/6 Topps 50, HGC9, RL3
98/9 Topps 206, B4,-RookRep 3
94/5 ToppsFinest 35, -Div. 2
94/5 T.Finest-BBest(Blue) 1
95/6 ToppsFinest 2, 77
96 ToppsFinestBronze 20
96/7 T.Picks 94, ID2, FT4
91/2 T.StadiumClub 233
92/3 T.StadiumClub 249, 267
93/4 TSC 160, -Finest 12
93/4 TSC-Master(1) 3, -AS
94/5 TSC 77, 267, -Finest 8
95/6 T.StadiumClub 2, M4, N6
91/2 TSC-MembersOnly
93/4 TSC-MembersOnly 25
94/5 TSC-MembersOnly 2
95/6 TSC-MembersOnly 28
97/8 ToppsSticker 1
95/6 ToppsSuperSkills 57
90/1 UD 64, 240, 320, 489
91/2 UpperDeck 255, 633, AW5
92/3 UpperDeck 265, 626
92/3 UD-LockerAS 39
93/4 UpperDeck116, NL4, SP-7
94/5 UD 296, C26, R14, SP4
95/6 UD 230, 250, 300, AS1
95/6 UD F19, H32, R48, SE4
95/6 UD-All-StarPredict MVP21
96/7 UD 14, 366, GJ4, SS7A
96/7 UD X8, -AllStarYCTG AR12
97/8 UD 9, S27, SS7, T11A
94/5 UDBeAPlayer R32, -Aut. 32
96/7 UDBlackDiamond 177
97/8 UDBlackDiamond 60, PC4
98/9 UDChoice 15, 222
98/9 UDChoice BH3, SQ21
95/6 UDCC 216, 385, C24
96/7 UDCC 13, 304, 310, C22
96/7 UDCC UD27, -Oversize 13
97/8 UDCC 12, C7, S27, SQ77
97/8 udDiamondVision 8
96/7 UpperDeck"Ice" 106
97/8 UpperDeckIce 77
97/8 ValuNet
96 Wien 78
97/8 Zenith 11, Z40
83/4 BOS
84/5 BOS
88/9 BOS/SportsAction
88/9 BOS/SportsAction
89/90 BOS/SportsAction (x3)
90/1 BOS/SportsAction
91/2 BOS/Legends
91/2 BOS/SportsAction (x2)
92/3 BOS

BOUSQUET, JARRET
89/90 SketchMEM 14
90/1 SketchWHL 285
91/2 SketchWHL 80
89/90 Kamloops

BOUSTEDT, TOM
94/5 ElitSet 297

BOUTETTE, PAT
76/7 O-Pee-Chee 367
77/8 O-Pee-Chee 284
78/9 O-Pee-Chee 374
79/80 O-Pee-Chee 319
80/1 OPC/Topps 14
81/2 OPC 255, Topps(E) 81
82/3 O-Pee-Chee 263
83/4 O-Pee-Chee 276
84/5 O-Pee-Chee 171
82/3 opcSticker 148
83/4 opcSticker 233
82/3 Post
83/4 SouhaitsRen. KeyChain
83/4 PGH
83/4 PGH/Heinz
84/5 PGH/Heinz
75/6 TOR
76/7 TOR
77/8 TOR
78/9 TOR
79/80 TOR

BOUTILIER, PAUL
84/5 NYI 17

BOUVRETTE, LIONEL
43-47 ParadeSportive

BOVAIR
89/90 SketchOHL 118

BOWEN, CURTIS
92/3 Classic 12, LP8
93/4 Classic 16
94/5 Classic 26, T19
92/3 ClassicFourSport 161
93/4 Donruss CAN6
95/6 EdgeIce 1
95/6 FleerUltra 333
93/4 Pinnacle 468
90/1 SketchOHL 78
91/2 SketchOHL 305
93/4 UpperDeck 547
95/6 Adirondack
92/3 Ottawa67s

BOWEN, JASON
92/3 Classic 9
92/3 ClassicFourSport 158, -Aut.
93/4 Donruss 241
94/5 Donruss 32
93/4 FleerUltra 35
94/5 FleerUltra 154
94/5 Leaf 248
93/4 Parkhurst 418
93/4 Pinnacle 215
94/5 Pinnacle 111
93/4 PowerPlay 404
94/5 Premier 234
93/4 Score 471
90/1 SketchWHL 97
91/2 SketchWHL 288
93/4 UpperDeck 240
93/4 PHA 12OCT93
93/4 PHA/JCPenney

BOWER, JOHNNY
45-64 BeeHives(NYR, TOR)
64-67 BeeHives(TORx2)
62 CeramicTiles
63-5 ChexPhoto
64/5 CokeCap TOR-1
65/6 CocaCola, -Book A, W
88/9 EssoAllStar
83&87 HallOfFame 211
83 HHOF Postcard (O)
93/4 HHOFLegends 23
93/4 HighLiner 9
68/9 OPC/Topps 122, -Puck 17
69/70 O-Pee-Chee 187
54/5 Parkhurst 65
58/9 Parkhurst 46
59/60 Parkhurst 25, 32
60/1 Parkhurst 3
61/2 Parkhurst 3
62/3 Parkhurst 16
63/4 Parkhurst 5, 65
92/3 Parkhurst PR3
93/4 Parkhurst DPR8
93/4 Parkie(56/7) 103
94/5 Parkie(64/5) 129, TW4
95/6 Parkie(66/7) 119
97/8 PinnacleBeeHive 57
67/8 PostFlipBook
68/9 Post Marble
60/1 ShirriffCoin 1
61/2 ShirriffCoin 41
62/3 ShirriffCoin 1
68/9 ShirriffCoin TOR6
63/4 TheTorontoStar
64/5 Topps 40
65/6 Topps 77
66/7 Topps 12, -USATest 12
67/8 Topps 76
54-67 TorontoStar V9
56-66 TorontoStar 59/60
91/2 Ultimate(O6) 32,80,-Aut. 80
60/1 York, -Glasses
61/2 York 8
62/3 York Transfer
63/4 York 2
67/8 York 16, 23, 25, 26, 27
67/8 York 29, 30, 34, 36
92/3 Zellers (x2)
64/5 TOR
66/7 TOR/Coaster
68/9 TOR
69/70 TOR
73/4 TOR
80/1 TOR
85/6 TOR
51/2 ClevelandBarons

BOWERS, RODNEY
93/4 PrinceAlbert

BOWIE, RUSSELL
83&87 HallOfFame 48
83 HHOF Postcard (D)

BOWKUS, JACK
84/5 Saskatoon
86/7 Saskatoon

BOWLER, BILL
91/2 SketchOHL 188
93/4 Slapshot(Windsor) 8
94/5 Slapshot(Windsor) 10
95/6 LasVegas
92/3 Windsor 9

BOWMAN, BILL
24/5 Crescent Selkirks 4

BOWMAN, KIRK
77/8 O-Pee-Chee 309
78/9 OPC/Topps 61

BOWMAN, RALPH
34-43 BeeHives(DET)
36-39 DiamondMatch (1)

BOWMAN, SCOTTY
72-84 Dernière 72/3
93/4 HockeyWit 49
93/4 Kraft'Coach
96/7 Kraft-Trophy
74/5 OPC/Topps 261
84/5 opcSticker 213
91/2 ProSet-HOF 4
77-9 Sportscastr 82-05, 91-2162
96/7 UDCollChoice 308
82/3 BUF/Wendt 18
71/2 MTL
72/3 MTL
73/4 MTL
74/5 MTL
75/6 MTL
76/7 MTL
77/8 MTL
78/9 MTL
95/6 MTL/Forum 6Apr96
91/2 PGH/Elbys
92/3 PGH/Coke

BOWNASS, JACK
51/2 LavalDairy 61
52/3 StLawrence 98

BOWNESS, RICK
77/8 O-Pee-Chee 265
78/9 OPC/Topps 173
81/2 O-Pee-Chee 361
88/9 ProCards(Moncton)
89/90 ProCards(AHL) 75
90/1 ProCards 143
94/5 OTT/Bell
93/4 OTT/Kraft
84/5 WPG/Police
85/6 WPG
85/6 WPG/Police
86/7 WPG
87/8 Moncton

BOYCE, ARTHUR
1912-13 Imperial (C57) 40

BOYCE, IAN
90/1 ProCards 268
91/2 ProCards 249
91/2 Rochester/Kodak

BOYD, DAVE
94/5 Birmingham

BOYD, DON
85/6 London 4
82/3 Regina 23
83/4 Regina 23
87/8 SSMarie 22

BOYD, IRVIN (YANK)
34-43 BeeHives(BOS)

BOYD, JAMES
93/4 Slapshot(Kitchener) 14
95/6 Slapshot 43

BOYD, JIM
75/6 Phoenix

BOYD, KEVIN
95/6 Slapshot 167

BOYD, RANDY
83/4 O-Pee-Chee 283
91/2 ProCards 609
83/4 PGH/Heinz
87/8 VAN/Shell
88/9 VAN/Mohawk
81/2 Ottawa

BOYD, RICK
88/9 ProCards(Indianapolis)
89/90 Johnstown 23

BOYD, STEVE
94/5 Classic W33
89/90 SketchOHL 37

BOYER, WALLY
64-67 BeeHives(CHI, TOR)
70/1 DadsCookies
70/1 EddieSargent 171
70/1 Esso Stamp
68/9 OPC/Topps 105
69/70 OPC/Topps 118
70/1 O-Pee-Chee 203
72/3 O-Pee-Chee 308
68/9 ShirriffCoin PGH12
71/2 TheTorontoSun
66/7 Topps 55

BOYER, ZAC
93/4 ClassicProspects 114
89/90 SketchMEM 2
90/1 SketchWHL 284
91/2 SketchWHL 84
92/3 Indianapolis
88/9 Kamloops
89/90 Kamloops

BOYKO, DARREN
92/3 Jyvas-Hyva 7
93/4 Sisu 96
94/5 Sisu 10
95/6 Sisu 13, 174, 369
95/6 SisuLimited 44

BOYKO, R.
95/6 Classic 82

BOYLE, JORDAN
90/1 Rayside

BOYLE, STEVE
74/5 SiouxCity

BOYNTON, NICK
97/8 Bowman 15, 154, BB6
98 BowmanCHL 27
95/6 Classic 92
95/6 Slapshot 262, -Promo
96/7 UpperDeck 373
96/7 UDBlackDiamond 22
97/8 UDCollChoice 309

BOZEK, DARWIN
89/90 ProCards(AHL) 11

BOZEK, ROMAN
94/5 APS 112
95/6 APS 70

BOZEK, STEVE
90/1 Bowman 64
91/2 Bowman 325
82/3 O-Pee-Chee 151
83/4 O-Pee-Chee 77
84/5 O-Pee-Chee 220
87/8 O-Pee-Chee 216
90/1 OPC/Topps 76
91/2 OPC/Topps 242, 397
82/3 opcSticker 233
89/90 opcSticker 67/207
90/1 Panini(VAN) 3
90/1 PaniniSticker 301
91/2 PaniniSticker 48
91/2 Pinnacle 61
90/1 ProSet 293
91/2 ProSet 486
90/1 ScoreTraded 89T
91/2 Score(CDN) 252, 556
91/2 Score(U.S) 6T
92/3 Score 37
91/2 ToppsStadiumClub 28
83/4 Vachon 3
85/6 CGY/RedRooster
86/7 CGY/RedRooster
87/8 CGY/RedRooster
91/2 S.J
88/9 VAN/Mohawk
89/90 VAN
90/1 VAN/Mohawk

BOZIK, MOJMIR
89 SemicSticker 188

BOZON, PHILIPPE
94/5 Donruss 261
92/3 FleerUltra 392
93/4 FleerUltra 210
95 Globe 205
94/5 Leaf 321
92/3 O-Pee-Chee 257
92/3 opcPremier 25
95 PaniniWorlds 112
91/2 Parkhurst 375
92/3 Parkhurst 159, 452
93/4 Parkhurst 179
94/5 ParkieSE 153
93/4 Premier 68
92 SemicSticker 230
92/3 Topps 433
92/3 ToppsStadiumClub 8
93/4 ToppsStadiumClub 214
94/5 ToppsStadiumClub 233
92/3 UpperDeck 283
93/4 UpperDeck 113, SP-134
96 Wien 188

BRABEC, JAROSLAV
94/5 APS 105
95/6 APS 71, 266

BRACCO, JON
92/3 MPSPhotoSJHL 102

BRACCO, MICHAEL
88/9 Brockville 18

BRACKENBURY, CURT
72-84 Dernière 78/9
79/80 O-Pee-Chee 308
81/2 O-Pee-Chee 109
76/7 opcWHA 4
80/1 Pepsi Cap
80/1 EDM/Zellers
81/2 EDM/RedRooster
88/9 EDM/ActionMagazine 10
76 QuébecNordiques/MA
76/7 QuébecNordiques

BRADWAY, CHAD
87/8 Sudbury 21

BRADFORD, BRENT
92/3 BCJHL 63

BRADLEY, BRIAN
95/6 Aces 4 (Clubs)
90/1 Bowman 58
91/2 Bowman 159
92/3 Bowman 283
93/4 Donruss 324
94/5 Donruss 40
95/6 Donruss 139
96/7 Donruss 116
95/6 DonrussElite 82
93/4 EASports 129
94/5 Flair 170
94/5 Fleer 203
96/7 Fleer 103
95/6 FleerMetal 135
92/3 FleerUltra 408
93/4 FleerUltra 36
94/5 FleerUltra 202
95/6 FleerUltra 308

96/7 FleerUltra 155
95/6 Hoyle'EAST 5 (Hearts)
97/8 KatchMedallion 133
96/7 KennerSLU
93/4 KraftDinner
95/6 KraftDinner
93/4 Leaf 209
94/5 Leaf 42
95/6 Leaf 159
96/7 Leaf 58
96/7 LeafLimited 76
96/7 LeafPreferred 18
93/4 McDonalds MCD01
96/7 MetalUniverse 142
89/90 O-Pee-Chee 287
90/1 OPC/Topps 59, 115
91/2 OPC/Topps 234
92/3 O-Pee-Chee 27
91/2 opcPremier 185, 190
89/90 opcSticker 63 /205
97/8 PacificCrown 64
90/1 Panini(VAN) 4
89/90 PaniniSticker 152
90/1 PaniniSticker 302
91/2 PaniniSticker 93
93/4 PaniniSticker S
94/5 PaniniSticker 182
95/6 PaniniSticker 124
96/7 PaniniSticker 122
91/2 Parkhurst 171
92/3 Parkhurst 174
93/4 Parkhurst 465
94/5 Parkhurst 221, V71
95/6 Parkhurst 190
91/2 Pinnacle 90
93/4 Pinnacle 60
94/5 Pinnacle 278
96/7 Pinnacle 17
92/3 Pinnacle 387
96/7 PinnacleZenith 59
95/6 Playoff 197
94/5 POG 221
95/6 POG 246
93/4 PowerPlay 228
93/4 Premier 117
94/5 Premier 247
95/6 ProMagnet 66
90/1 ProSet 294
91/2 ProSet 489
92/3 ProSet 174
91/2 PSPlatinum 231
90/1 Score 198
91/2 Score(CDN) 255
92/3 Score 259
93/4 Score 230, -P.AS 33, 50
93/4 Score-Franchise 20
94/5 Score 179
95/6 Score 232
96/7 Score 45
94/5 Select 43
95/6 SelectCertified 83
95/6 SkyBoxEmotion 162
95/6 SkyBoxImpact 153
96/7 SkyBoxImpact 120,-Blade 1
94/5 SP 114
96/7 SP 149
95/6 Summit 146
96/7 Summit 18
95/6 SuperSticker 111, 113
92/3 Topps 291
95/6 Topps 148
95/6 ToppsFinest 143
96/7 ToppsNHLPicks 71
91/2 ToppsStadiumClub 257
92/3 ToppsStadiumClub 163
93/4 T.StadiumClub 212, -AllStar
95/6 ToppsStadiumClub 39
93/4 TSC-MembersOnly 41
95/6 ToppsSuperSkills 59
90/1 UpperDeck 79
92/3 UD 544, -LockerAS 20
93/4 UD 121, 305, SP-148
94/5 UpperDeck 118, SP74
95/6 UpperDeck 83, SE166
95/6 UDBeAPlayer 117
95/6 UDCollChoice 128
96/7 UDCollChoice 250
86/7 CGY/RedRooster
92/3 T.B/Sheraton
93/4 T.B/KashNKarry
94/5 T.B/SkyBoxSportsCafe
95/6 T.B
95/6 T.B/SkyBoxSportsCafe
90/1 TOR/P.L.A.Y. 28
88/9 VAN/Mohawk
89/90 VAN
90/1 VAN/Molson
85/6 Moncton 9

BRADLEY, JOHN
93/4 Johnstown 1
91/2 Rochester/Genny
91/2 Rochester/Kodak

BRADLEY, LES
82/3 Kitchener 27
83/4 Kitchener 29
84/5 Kitchener 29

BRADLEY, MATT
95/6 Bowman P3
98 BowmanCHL 28
95/6 Slapshot 113
98/9 UDChoice 274

BRADLEY, TODD
91/2 SketchOHL 150
93/4 Slapshot(Oshawa) 13
91/2 Oshawa
91/2 Oshawa/Domino13
92/3 Oshawa

BRADY, FRED
52/3 AnonymousOHL 60

BRADY, LANCY
95/6 Birmingham

BRADY, NEIL
90/1 Bowman 88
92/3 opcPremier 82
93/4 PaniniSticker 119
92/3 Parkhurst 124
93/4 Premier 17
88/9 ProCards(Utica)
90/1 ProCards 568
93/4 Score 293
93/4 ToppsStadiumClub 199
92/3 TSC-MembersOnly
93/4 UpperDeck 81
89/90 N.J
92/3 OTT
85/6 MedicineHat 11

BRAGNALO, RICHARD
77/8 O-Pee-Chee 296
78/9 O-Pee-Chee 308
82 SemicSticker 134

BRAHAM, DEAN
84/5 PrinceAlbert

BRANCH, DAVID
90/1 SketchOHL 300
95/6 Slapshot 5

BRANDCH, ROD
94/5 Slapshot(MEM) 1
93/4 Kamloops
95/6 PrinceAlbert

BRANCIK, RICHARD
94/5 APS 21
95/6 APS 118

BRAND, AARON
95/6 Classic 96
95/6 Slapshot 338
94/5 Slapshot(Sar) 9

BRAND, SCOTT
93/4 Waterloo

BRANDL, THOMAS
94/5 DEL 202
95/6 DEL 205, 430
96/7 DEL 289
95 Globe 221
95 PaniniWorlds 63
94 Semic 280
91 SemicSticker 165
93 SemicSticker 166
96 Wien 197

BRANDNER, CHRISTOPH
95 PaniniWorlds 275

BRANDOW, HOWARD
23/4 Crescent Selkirks 4
24/5 Crescent Selkirks 1
23/4 PaulinsCandy 7

BRANNARE, STEFAN
92/3 BCJHL 154

BRANNSTROM, FABIAN
94/5 DEL 74
95/6 DEL 71

BRANNSTROM, NIKLAS
94/5 ElitSet 275
89/90 SemicElitserien 210
91/2 SemicElitserien 98
92/3 SemicElitserien 120
95/6 udElite DS7
97/8 udSwedish 179

BRANT, CHRIS
88/9 ProCards(Binghampton)
82/3 Kingston 18
83/4 SSMarie
84/5 SSMarie

BRASAR, PER-OLOV
78/9 OPC/Topps 99
79/80 OPC/Topps 192
80/1 O-Pee-Chee 291
81/2 O-Pee-Chee 330
81/2 opcSticker 244
79 PaniniSticker 195
80/1 Pepsi Cap
78/9 MIN/Cloverleaf 2
80/1 VAN
80/1 VAN/Silverwood
81/2 VAN
81/2 VAN/Silverwood

BRASEY, PAT
91 SemicSticker 182
92 SemicSticker 198
93 SemicSticker 113

BRASHEAR, DONALD
94/5 Classic E1
93/4 ClassicProspects 146
94/5 Donruss 146
94/5 FleerUltra 310
94/5 Leaf 227
97/8 Omega 227
98/9 Pacific 425
98/9 PacificParamount 233
97/8 PacificRegime 200
97/8 PacificRevolution 138
96/7 PinnacleBeAPlayer 181
97/8 Score(VAN) 17
90/1 SketchQMJHL 245
91/2 SketchQMJHL 139
95/6 UpperDeck 411
97/8 UpperDeck 376
94/5 MTL
95/6 MTL
96/7 VAN
96/7 VAN/IGA
92/3 Fredericton
93/4 Fredericton
94/5 Fredericton

BRESAGK, MICHAEL
95 PaniniWorlds 59

BRASSARD, CHRIS
94/5 Slapshot(Kitchener) 19

BRASSARD, JOEL
91/2 SketchQMJHL 38

BRATASH, OLEG
90/1 O-Pee-Chee 525

BRATHWAITE, FRED
93/4 Donruss 119
94/5 Donruss 320
95/6 EdgeIce 31
93/4 FleerUltra 313
94/5 FleerUltra 289
94/5 Leaf 26
93/4 PowerPlay 339
93/4 Score 618
89/90 SketchMEM 77
90/1 SketchMEM 3
89/90 SketchOHL 23
90/1 SketchOHL 327
91/2 SketchOHL 169
93/4 UpperDeck 435
93/4 EDM 24NOV93
89/90 Oshawa 35
90/1 Oshawa 3
91/2 Oshawa

BRAUER, CAM
90/1 ProCards 173
91/2 ProCards 98
88/9 Regina

BRAULT, BOB
52/3 BasDuFleuve 61

BRAUN, FRANK
74 Hellas 113
70/1 Kuvajulkaisut 82

BRAZDA, RADOMIR
94/5 APS 256
95/6 APS 320

BREARLEY, PETER
93/4 Slapshot(Kitchener) 17

BREAULT, FRANÇOIS
91/2 OPC/Topps 496
88/9 ProCards(NewHaven)
89/90 ProCards(AHL) 2
90/1 ProSet 612
91/2 ProSet 541
90/1 L.A/Smokeys 13
84/5 Chicoutimi
92/3 Phoenix

BREEN, GEORGE
95/6 Classic 70, -Aut.
95/6 ClassicFiveSport 129, 189

BREILIN, MATTI
66/7 Champion 69

BREISTROFF, MICHEL
94 Semic 218

BREITENBACH, KEN
77/8 O-Pee-Chee 279

BREKKE, BRENT
95/6 Dayton
92/3 WestMich.
93/4 WestMich.

BRENNAN, DOUG
33-35 DiamondMatch
33/4 WWGum (V357) 45

BRENNAN, LES
36/7 WWGum (V356) 106

BRENNAN, MICHAEL
91/2 AirCanadaSJHL B50

BRENNAN, RICHARD
98/9 Pacific 377
97/8 PinnacleBeAPlayer 236
91/2 UpperDeck'CzechWJC 76
97/8 S.J/PacificBellSheets

BRENNEMAN, JOHN
64-67 BeeHives(TOR)
64/5 CokeCap CHI-12
68/9 OPC/Topps 83
68/9 ShirriffCoin OAK2
68/9 TOR

BRENT, STEVE
91/2 AirCanadaSJHL D42
92/3 MPSPhotoSJHL 6

BRESAGK, MICHAEL
94/5 DEL 249
95/6 DEL 244

BRESAGK, THOMAS
94/5 DEL 409
95/6 DEL 407

BRESLIN, TIM
91/2 ProCards 395
92/3 Phoenix
93/4 Phoenix

BRETON, CHRIS
87/8 Hull

BREWER, CARL
45-64 BeeHives(TOR)
64-67 BeeHives(TOR)
62 CeramicTiles
64/5 CokeCap TOR-2
69/70 OPC/T. 59, OPC-Sticker
70/1 OPC 243
71/2 OPC/Topps 222
59/60 Parkhurst 3
60/1 Parkhurst 18
61/2 Parkhurst 18
62/3 Parkhurst 8
63/4 Parkhurst 8, 68
92/3 Parkhurst 62 PR13
93/4 Parkie(56/7) FS1
94/5 Parkie(64/5) 114
97/8 7ElevenCups
60/1 ShirriffCoin 3
61/2 ShirriffCoin 45
62/3 ShirriffCoin 5, 51
64/5 Topps 75
65/6 Topps 78
54-67 TorontoStarV7, V11
56-66 TorontoStar 61/2
63/4 TheTorontoStar
64/5 TheTorontoStar
71/2 TheTorontoSun
60/1 York -Glasses
61/2 York 13
62/3 YorkTransfer 5
63/4 York 17
71/2 STL
64/5 TOR
79/80 TOR

BREWER, ERIC
97/8 Bowman 153, BB8
97/8 UDBlackDiamond 90
98/9 UDChoice 256

BREWER, MICHAEL
92/3 SanDiego
92/3 CanadaNats

BREZEAULT, RÉGINALD
90/1 SketchQMJHL 182
91/2 SketchQMJHL 157
93/4 Roanoke

BREZGUNOV, VADIM
91/2 O-Pee-Chee 11R

BREZINA, ROBERT
94/5 DEL 426
95/6 DEL 395
96/7 DEL 304

BRIAND, AMAULD
94 Semic 229
92 SemicSticker 231
93 SemicSticker 259

BRICKER, HARRY
89/90 ProCards(AHL) 357
90/1 ProCards 52

BRICKLEY, ANDY
90/1 Bowman 27
92/3 Bowman 17
89/90 OPC/Topps 29
90/1 OPC/Topps 88
87/8 PaniniSticker 86
89/90 PaniniSticker 194
90/1 PaniniSticker 16
90/1 ProSet 406
92/3 Score 296
92/3 Topps 109
92/3 ToppsStadiumClub 208
90/1 UpperDeck 84
89/90 BOS/SportsAction
90/1 BOS/SportsAction
86/7 N.J/SOBER
83/4 PGH
84/5 PGH/Heinz
83/4 Springfield 14

BRICKNELL, COREY
93/4 Slapshot(NiagarFalls) 20

BRIDGMAN, MEL
84/5 KelownaWings&WHL 30
76/7 OPC/Topps 26
77/8 OPC/Topps 121
78/9 OPC/Topps 26
79/80 OPC/Topps 201
80/1 OPC/Topps 189, 263
81/2 O-Pee-Chee 248
82/3 O-Pee-Chee 39, 40
83/4 O-Pee-Chee 226
84/5 OPC 109, 361, Topps 84
85/6 OPC/Topps 42
86/7 OPC/Topps 136
87/8 OPC/Topps 17
88/9 OPC/Topps 36
82/3 opcSticker 213
83/4 opcSticker 265
84/5 opcSticker 71
85/6 opcSticker 57
86/7 opcSticker 203
87/8 PaniniSticker 249
82/3 Post
84/5 7ElevenDisk
85/6 7Eleven 11
83/4 SouhaitsRen.KeyChain
82/3 StaterMint
81/2 CGY
82/3 CGY
87/8 DET/Caesars
83/4 N.J
84/5 N.J
86/7 N.J/SOBER
75/6 PHA/GingerAle
84/5 Victoria

BRIÈRE, DANIEL
96/7 AllSportPPF 172
95/6 Bowman P4
97/8 Bowman 50
95/6 Classic 58, AS17
94/5 ParkieSE 261
98/9 SPx"Finite" 143
98/9 Topps 149
98/9 UDChoice 163
96/7 UpperDeck"Ice" 120

BRIGHT, CHRIS
93/4 ClassicProspects 245
90/1 ProCards 188
91/2 ProCards 110

BRIGLEY, TRAVIS
97/8 Bowman 110

BRILL, JOHN
93/4 ClassicProspects 232
94/5 Dayton 13
95/6 Dayton
91/2 Minnesota
92/3 Minnesota

BRILLANT, PIERRE
51/2 BasDuFleuve 36
52/3 LavalDairy 13
52/3 StLawrence 50

BRIMANIS, ARIS
94/5 ClassicImages 76
93/4 ClassicProspects 138
94/5 Donruss 65
94/5 Leaf 123
92/3 Brandon 1

BRIMMAR, CHUCK
81/2 Kingston 11
81/2 SSMarie

BRIMMER, KEN
84/5 Belleville 16

BRIMSEK, FRANK
34-43 BeeHives(BOS)
45-64 BeeHives(BOS, CHI)
83&87 HallOfFame 124
83 HHOF Postcard (I)
39/40 OPC (V301-1) 97
43-47 ParadeSportive
94/5 Parkhurst 64-Greats 7
91/2 BOS/Legends

BRIND'AMOUR, ROD
96/7 Aces 8 (Spades)
91/2 AirCanadaSJHL D51
90/1 Bowman 23
91/2 Bowman 374
92/3 Bowman 224, 268
93/4 Donruss 248
94/5 Donruss 80
95/6 Donruss 188
96/7 Donruss 155
97/8 Donruss 157
97/8 CanadianIce 113
95/6 DonrussElite 91
96/7 DonrussElite 93
97/8 DonrussPreferred 67
97/8 DonrussPriority 33
93/4 EASports 100
97/8 EssoOlympic 11
94/5 Flair 126
94/5 Fleer 150
96/7 Fleer 78
95/6 FleerMetal 108
96/7 FleerNHLPicks 54
92/3 FleerUltra 152
93/4 FleerUltra 74
94/5 FleerUltra 155
95/6 FleerUltra 115, -Crease 2
96/7 FleerUltra 121
93/4 HockeyWit 59
95/6 Hoyle'EAST 6 Hearts
92/3 HumptyDumpty (1)
97/8 Kraft -RoadToNagano
97/8 Kraft-Sticker
93/4 Leaf 26
94/5 Leaf 150
95/6 Leaf 154
96/7 Leaf 41
97/8 Leaf 125
94/5 LeafLimited 78
95/6 LeafLimited 69
96/7 LeafPreferred 64
97/8 Limited 82
92/3 McDonalds Mc D-16
97/8 McDonalds-Medallions
96/7 MetalUniverse 109
97/8 Omega 160
90/1 OPC/Topps 332
91/2 OPC/Topps 490
92/3 O-Pee-Chee 49
91/2 opcPremier 94
92/3 opcPremier-Star 9
98/9 Pacific 17
97/8 PacificCrown 31, -Slap 6A
97/8 PacificCrownRoyale 95
97/8 PacificDynagon! 88
97/8 PcfcD-BstKpt 68,-Tand 20
97/8 PacificInvincible 98
97/8 PacificParamount 130
98/9 PacificParamount 169
97/8 PacificRegime 139
97/8 PacificRevolution 97
90/1 PaniniSticker 266, 343
91/2 PaniniSticker 30
92/3 PaniniSticker 187
93/4 PaniniSticker 47
94/5 PaniniSticker 37
95/6 PaniniSticker 114
96/7 PaniniSticker 111
97/8 PaniniSticker 93
95 PaniniWorlds 19
91/2 Parkhurst 124
92/3 Parkhurst 126
93/4 Parkhurst 152
94/5 Parkhurst 167
95/6 Parkhurst 158
94/5 ParkieSE seV25
91/2 Pinnacle 9
92/3 Pinnacle 26, -Team2000 18
93/4 Pinnacle 170, -Tm2001 11
94/5 Pinnacle 273
95/6 Pinnacle 109
96/7 Pinnacle 123
97/8 Pinnacle111
96/7 PinnacleBeAPlayer 21
97/8 PinnacleCertified 93
97/8 PinnacleInside 92
95/6 PinnacleZenith 68
95/6 Playoff 291
94/5 POG 373
95/6 POG 202
93/4 PowerPlay 178
93/4 Premier 115
94/5 Premier 17
95/6 ProMagnet 46
90/1 ProSet 259
91/2 ProSet 211, 453
91/2 PS-ThePuck 20
92/3 ProSet 132
91/2 PSPlatinum 90
90/1 Score 131, 328, -Hot 98
90/1 Score-YoungStar 31
91/2 Score(CDN) 85, 618
91/2 Score(U.S) 85, 68T
92/3 Score 324, -Young 26
93/4 Score 45
94/5 Score 132, NP13
95/6 Score 244
96/7 Score 102
97/8 Score 127, -CheckIt 16
97/8 Score(PHA) 5
92/3 SeasonsPatch 39
94/5 Select 119
95/6 SelectCertified 59
95 Semic 90
95/6 SkyBoxEmotion 129
95/6 SkyBoxImpact 123
96/7 SkyBoxImpact 92
94/5 SP 86
95/6 SP 110
98/9 SPx"Finite") 62
97/8 SPAuthentic 115
95/6 Summit 79
96/7 Summit 123
95/6 SuperSticker 94
92/3 Topps 90
95/6 Topps 39
98/9 Topps 116
94/5 ToppsFinest 85
95/6 ToppsFinest 44
91/2 ToppsStadiumClub 184

92/3 ToppsStadiumClub 202
93/4 ToppsStadiumClub 78
95/6 ToppsStadiumClub 36
97/8 ToppsSticker 4
90/1 UpperDeck 36, 347
91/2 UpperDeck 189, 547
92/3 UpperDeck 15, 264
93/4 UpperDeck 361, SP-114
94/5 UpperDeck 111, SP57
95/6 UpperDeck 324, SE64
96/7 UpperDeck 121, P26
97/8 UpperDeck 121, T17C
94/5 UDBeAPlayer -Aut. 175
96/7 UDBlackDiamond 117
97/8 UDBlackDiamond 61
98/9 UDChoice 149
95/6 UDCollChoice 29
96/7 UDCollChoice 192
97/8 UDCollChoice 192
96/7 UpperDeck"Ice" 48
97/8 ValuNet
96 Wien 98
97/8 Zenith 74, Z49
91/2 PHA/JCPenney
92/3 PHA/JCPenney
92/3 PHA/UD 15OCT92
92/3 PHA/UD 24JAN93
93/4 PHA 21NOV93
93/4 PHA 27MAR94
93/4 PHA/JCPenney
94/5 PHA
96/7 PHA/OceanSpray
89/90 STL/Kodak
90/1 STL/Kodak

BRINDLEY, DOUG
72/3 ClevelandCrusaders

BRINK, ANDY
93/4 Donruss USA3
93/4 Pinnacle 490
93/4 Minnesota
94/5 Minnesota

BRISEBOIS, PATRICE
92/3 Bowman 435
93/4 Donruss 171
94/5 Donruss 250
92/3 Durivage 32
93/4 Durivage 7
94/5 Flair 85
94/5 Fleer 102
96/7 FleerNHLPicks 160
92/3 FleerUltra 325
93/4 FleerUltra 52
94/5 FleerUltra 106
95/6 FleerUltra 254
93/4 Leaf 191
94/5 Leaf 325
92/3 O-Pee-Chee 239
92/3 PaniniSticker 155
95/6 PaniniSticker 44
91/2 Parkhurst 309
92/3 Parkhurst 320
93/4 Parkhurst 105
94/5 Parkhurst 116
95/6 Parkhurst 380
92/3 Pinnacle 153
93/4 Pinnacle 253
94/5 Pinnacle 191
95/6 Playoff 272
95/6 POG 152
93/4 PowerPlay 125
93/4 Premier 59
91/2 ProCards 80
91/2 Score(CDN) 272, (U.S) 382
92/3 Score 388
93/4 Score 163
95/6 Score 148
97/8 Score(MTL) 20
91/2 SketchAwards 24
89/90 SketchMEM 59
90/1 SketchMEM 62
90/1 SketchQMJHL 8
95/6 SP 77
92/3 Topps 189
95/6 Topps 199
98/9 Topps 80
92/3 ToppsStadiumClub 238
93/4 ToppsStadiumClub 27
90/1 UpperDeck 454
91/2 UpperDeck 442
92/3 UpperDeck 277
93/4 UpperDeck 318
94/5 UpperDeck 193
95/6 UpperDeck 6
96/7 UpperDeck 88
97/8 UpperDeck 295
95/6 UDBeAPlayer 44
95/6 UDCollChoice 61
96/7 UDCollChoice 142
91/2 MTL
92/3 MTL
92/3 MTL/OPC 49
93/4 MTL
94/5 MTL
94/5 MTL/MolsonExport
95/6 MTL
95/6 MTL/Molson
96-98 MTL

BRISKE, BYRON
94/5 SigRookies 58
93/4 RedDeer

BRISKE, SHANNON
93/4 Portland

BRISSON, SYLVAIN
91/2 SketchQMJHL 42

BRISSON, THÉRÈSE
94/5 Classic W4
97/8 UDCollChoice 286

BRISTOW, CAM
91/2 AirCanadaSJHL D41
90/1 SketchWHL 246

BRITTIG, CHRISTIAN
94/5 DEL 307
95/6 DEL 65
96/7 DEL 261

BRIZA, PETR
95/6 APS 355
94/5 DEL 260
95/6 DEL 242
96/7 DEL 135
95 Globe 146
91/2 Jyvas-Hyva 43
92/3 Jyvas-Hyva 121
95 PaniniWorlds 186
94 Semic 165
95 Semic 140, 213
89 SemicSticker 180
91 SemicSticker 102
93 SemicSticker 89
93/4 Sisu 366
96 Wien 104

BRKIC, DARREN
90/1 Mich.Tech
91/2 Mich.Tech

BRKLACICH, STEVE
52/3 LavalDairy 61

BROADBENT, DAVE
52/3 AnonymousOHL 163

BROADBENT, HARRY
24/5 Champs (C144)
83&87 HallOfFame 3
83 HHOF Postcard (A)
3-Dec Imperial (C57) 2
24/5 MapleCrispettes (V130) 18
23/4 (V145-1) 9
24/5 (V145-2) 39

BROCHU, MARTIN
93/4 ClassicProspects 94
95/6 EdgeIce 39, -Quantum 11
90/1 SketchQMJHL 67
91/2 SketchQMJHL 44
93/4 Fredericton
94/5 Fredericton
95/6 Fredericton
96/7 Portland

BROCHU, STÉPHANE
90/1 ProCards 546
91/2 ProCards 445

BROCKLEHURST, CRAIG
90/1 SketchOHL 27

BROCKMANN, ANDREAS
94/5 DEL 93
95/6 DEL 95, 436
96/7 DEL 282
91 SemicSticker 167
93 SemicSticker 156

BRODA, MIKE
95/6 RedDeer

BRODA, WALTER (TURK)
34-43 BeeHives(TOR)
45-64 BeeHives(TOR)
64-67 BeeHives(TOR)
48-52 Exhibits
83&87 HallOfFame 94
83 HHOF Postcard (G)
96/7 HHOFLegends 74
91/2 Kraft 37
36/7 OPC (V304D) 97
37/8 OPC (V304E) 133
39/40 OPC V301-1 2
40/1 OPC (V301-2) 108, 130
43-47 ParadeSportive
51/2 Parkhurst 75
55/6 Parkhurst 23
92/3 Parkhurst PR6
93/4 Parkie(56/7) P6
38/9 QuakerOats
45-54 QuakerOats

BRODDEN, CONNELL
93/4 Parkie(56/7) 82

BRODERICK, KEN
69/70 O-Pee-Chee 197
75/6 O-Pee-Chee 340
76/7 opcWHA 44
77/8 opcWHA 4

BRODERICK, LEN
57/8 Parkhurst(MTL) 21, 23

BRODEUR, DENIS
51/2 BasDuFleuve 2
52/3 BasDuFleuve 17

BRODEUR, MARTIN
95/6 Aces 9 (Clubs)
96/7 Aces 9 (Clubs)
97/8 Aces Q (Clubs)
95/6 Bowman 70, BB8
94/5 Classic AR1
93/4 C4'Images 101
93/4 ClassicProspects 12
96/7 CorinthianHeadliners
97/8 CorinthianHeadliners
93/4 Donruss 195, -Rated 10
94/5 Donruss 24, -Masked 2
94/5 Donruss-Elite 2
95/6 Donruss 149, -Dominator 4
95/6 Donruss-Between 5
96/7 Donruss 148, -Dom 1,-Bet 2
97/8 Donruss 126,-Elit 10,-Bet 2
96/7 D.CdnIce 46, -Gardiens 4
97/8 DCI 42,-Gard 3, -Scrap 24
95/6 DonrussElite 43, -Painted 3
96/7 DonrussElite 16, -Painted 8
97/8 DonrussElite 8, 137
97/8 DE -BackTo 7, -Craftsmn 8
97/8 DonrussPreferred 16, 185
97/8 D.Pref.-ColGrd 2,-PrecM 6
97/8 D.Pref.-WideTins 9, Tins 10
97/8 DonrussPriority 7, 196
97/8 D.Prio. -OpDay 7,-PostG 10
97/8 D.Prio.-Pstcrd 24,-Stamp24
97/8 D.Studio 20,-Portr 20,-Sil 4
96/7 Duracell JB6
93/4 Durivage 5
95/6 EdgeIce L11
94/5 Flair 92
96/7 Flair 52, -HotGlove 2
94/5 Fleer 111, -Netminder 2
96/7 Fleer 58, 145, 146
95/6 FleerMetal 81
96/7 F.Picks-Dream 3, -Fab 4
96/7 F.Picks-FantasyForce 8
93/4 FleerUltra 357, -Wave 2
94/5 FU 115, -AW 2,-AllRook 2
95/6 FleerUltra 86, 186, 366
95/6 FU-High 5, -PadMen 3
96/7 FleerUltra 93
95/6 Hoyle'EAST 7 Hearts
97/8 KatchMedallion 79
95/6 KennerSLU
97/8 KennerSLU
94/5 KraftDinner, -AW
95/6 Kraft'Crease
96/7 KraftDinner
97/8 Kraft -RoadToNagano
93/4 Leaf 345
94/5 Leaf 56, -Crease 9, -Gold 8
94/5 Leaf-GoldRook 1, -Ltd. 13
95/6 Leaf 66, -Road 2
96/7 Leaf 6, -Shut 6, -Sweater 6
97/8 Leaf 7, 174 -PipeDreams 6
94/5 LeafLimited 70
95/6 LeafLimited 18, -Stick 2
96/7 LeafLimited 87, -Stubble 11
96/7 LeafPreferred 81,-Steel 2
96/7 LeafPreferred-Masked 2
97/8 Limited 74, 127, 149, 150
97/8 Limited -fabric 2
96/7 Maggers 91
94/5 McDonalds 35
95/6 McDonalds 27
96/7 McDonalds McD33
97/8 McD' McD25, -Medallions
96/7 MetalUniv. 86, -Armour 2
96/7 MU-IceCarvings 1
97/8 Omega 127, 249, -Silks 7
97/8 Omega -NoScoringZone 7
92/3 O-Pee-Chee 59
98/9 Pacific 30,-Cram 6,-T.CL 15
98/9 Pcfc-DynIce 12, -GoldC 18
97/8 PacificCrown 30
97/8 PCC-Supial 10, -Gold 14
97/8 PCC-InThe 12, -TmCL 14
97/8 PacificCrownRoyale 73
97/8 PacificCR -FreezeOut 11
97/8 PacificDynagon! 68
97/8 PacificD-BestKept 52, 106
97/8 Pcfc.D-Stone 12,-Tandm 12
97/8 PacificInv. 76, -Feature 19
97/8 PcfcParamnt 101,-BigN 12
97/8 PcfcP -CdnGrts 9,-Glove 11
98/9 PcfcParamnt 132,-TmCL 15
98/9 PcfcP-Glove 10,-HOF 6
97/8 PacificRegime 108
97/8 PcfcRevolutn 75,-TmCL 14
97/8 PcfcRev -AllStarGame 13
97/8 PcfcRev-Icons 6,-Return 11
94/5 PaniniSticker 35
95/6 PaniniSticker 90
96/7 PaniniSticker 79
93/4 Parkhurst 380
94/5 Parkhurst 126, 278
95/6 Parkhurst 122, PP32, -AS 6
95/6 PH-Crown(1) 11, -Goal 1
94/5 ParkieSE seV8
94/5 Pinnacle 145, 462, GT7
95/6 Pinnacle-Masks 2, -Clear 1
95/6 Pinnacle-Roaring20s 3
96/7 Pinn. 92,-Mask 5, -TmP 9
97/8 Pinnacle 43, -Masks 3
97/8 Pinnacle-TmP 1,-GoalTin 1
97/8 P.BAP 2,-Stacking/Pads 11
97/8 P.BeeHive 45,-TeamBH 6
97/8 PinnacleCertified 3,-Team 1
97/8 Pinnacle-EPIX 8
95/6 PinnacleFANtasy 19
97/8 PinnacleInside 7, -Cans 2
97/8 P.Inside -BigCans, -Stop 5
97/8 P.Inside-StndUp 2,-Track 6
97/8 PinnacleMask
96/7 PinnacleMint 23
97/8 PinnacleMint 16
97/8 PinnacleUncut
95/6 Pinn.Zenith 12, -ZTeam 2
96/7 Pinn.Zenith 2,-Champion 15
95/6 Playoff 57, 275
96/7 Playoff 440
94/5 POG 167, 284, 326
94/5 Post
97/8 Post
93/4 PowerPlay 374
93/4 Premier 401
94/5 Premier 83, 190, 380, 470
94/5 Premier-Finest(OPC) 14
95/6 ProMagnet 31, IC02
90/1 Score 439
92/3 Score 480
93/4 Score 648
95/6 Score 25, 323
96/7 Score 10, -Net 2, -Sudden 1
97/8 Score 30, 269, -NetWrth 14
97/8 Score(N.J.) 16
94/5 Select 78
95/6 SelectCertified 24, -Gold 9
96/7 SelectCertified 6, -Freez 1
90/1 SketchQMJHL 222
91/2 SketchQMJHL 1
95/6 SkBxEmotion 94, -Xcited 18
95/6 SkBxImpact 90, -Deflect 11
96/7 SkyBoxImpact 67
94/5 SP 63
95/6 SP 79, E18, FX12
96/7 SP 86, -SPxForce 3, 5
97/8 SPAuthentic 87, I14, S15
96/7 SPx 25
97/8 SPx 27, -DuoView
98/9 SPx"Finite" 46,105,161,176
95/6 Summit 27, -GM 2, -InThe 1
96/7 Summit 114, -Unt 8,-InCr 8
95/6 SuperSticker 70, DieCut 6
98/9 Topps 20, L6, M12, SB2
92/3 ToppsStadiumClub 233
93/4 ToppsStadiumClub 352
94/5 TSC 119, 186, 264
95/6 T.StadiumClub 85, G5
96/7 TeamOut
95/6 Tetrad F6, -SR 6
95/6 TetradAutobilia96
92/3 Topps 513
95/6 Topps 9,325,M21,PF6,YS2
94/5 ToppsFinest 71
95/6 ToppsFinest 178, 45
95 ToppsFinestBronz e 12
96/7 T.Picks 27, ID6, FT3
93/4 TSC-MembersOnly 46
95/6 TSC-MembersOnly 29
95/6 ToppsSuperSkills 80
92/3 UpperDeck 408
93/4 UpperDeck 334
94/5 UD 96,IG11,H12,H29,SP43
95/6 UD 211, AS6, F14, H5, H11
95/6 UpperDeck R57, SE135
95/6 UD-AllStarPredict MVP29
96/7 UpperDeck 91, HH10
96/7 UD LS05, SS12A, X18
97/8 UD 300, GJ10, S30, SG4
97/8 UD T10A, -BlowUp
94/5 UDBAP R58, R130, -Aut. 3
96/7 BeAPlayer-Stacking 5
96/7 UDBlackDiamond 134
97/8 UDBlackD. 122, PC24
98/9 UDChoice 116, 245
98/9 UDChoice BH7, SQ23
95/6 UDCollChoice 204
96/7 UDCollChoice 144, 306
96/7 UDCC 322, S24, UD21
97/8 UDCC 141, S3, SQ50
97/8 udDiamondVision 5
96/7 UpperDeck"Ice" 92
97/8 UpperDeckIce 7, IC7
97/8 ValueNet
97/8 Zenith 21, Z5, -ZTeam 8
96/7 N.J/Sharp

BRODEUR, RICHARD
72-84 Dernière 78/9, 82/3
83/4 Esso
84/5 Kelloggs Disk
86/7 Kraft Sports 62
82/3 McDonalds 2
79/80 OPC/Topps 176
81/2 O-Pee-Chee 331
82/3 O-Pee-Chee 339, 340
83/4 O-Pee-Chee 346
84/5 O-Pee-Chee 314
85/6 O-Pee-Chee 180
86/7 O-Pee-Chee 246
87/8 O-Pee-Chee 257
82/3 opcSticker 7, 247
83/4 opcSticker 276, 277
84/5 opcSticker 277
86/7 opcSticker 98/228
87/8 opcSticker 189/50
75/6 opcWHA 44
76/7 opcWHA 12
77/8 opcWHA 38
87/8 PaniniSticker 340
80/1 Pepsi Cap
82/3 Post
88/9 ProCards(Binghampton)
83/4 PuffySticker 1
84/5 7ElevenDisk
83/4 SouhaitsRen.KeyChain
83/4 Vachon 101
80/1 VAN
80/1 VAN/Silverwood
81/2 VAN
81/2 VAN/Silverwood
82/3 VAN
83/4 VAN
84/5 VAN
85/6 VAN
86/7 VAN
87/8 VAN/Shell
73/4 QuébecNordiques
76/7 QuébecNordiques
76 QuébecNordiques/MA

BRODIE, ANDREW
89/90 SketchOHL 68
90/1 SketchOHL 79

BRODMAN, MARIO
93 SemicSticker 120

BRODNICKE, RICHARD
94/5 DEL 350

BROMLEY, GARY
74/5 Loblaws
74/5 OPC/Topps 7
75/6 O-Pee-Chee 368
79/80 OPC/Topps 167
80/1 O-Pee-Chee 330
77/8 opcWHA 45
74/5 BUF/BellsMarket
78/9 VAN/RoyalBank
79/80 VAN
80/1 VAN
80/1 VAN/Silverwood

BROMS, ANDERS
89/90 SemicElitserien 143

BRONILLA, RICH
95/6 Slapshot 260
92/3 Ottawa67s

BROOKBANK, LEIGH
91/2 AirCanadaSJHL B30
92/3 MPSPhotoSJHL 157

BROOKE, BOB
90/1 Bowman 79
85/6 O-Pee-Chee 202
86/7 OPC/Topps 48
87/8 OPC/Topps 64
88/9 OPC/Topps 61
89/90 O-Pee-Chee 215
90/1 OPC/Topps 105
86/7 opcSticker 219/89
87/8 PaniniSticker 301
88/9 PaniniSticker 91
89 SemicSticker 171
86/7 MIN/7Eleven 11
87/8 MIN
88/9 MIN/American

BROOKS, CHRIS
92/3 WestMich.
93/4 WestMich.

BROOKS, GORD
74/5 Loblaws
74/5 WSH

BROOKS, HERB
94/5 MiracleOnIce 41, 42
79/80 USAOlympicTea m 15
87/8 MIN

BROOKS, JASON
95/6 Slapshot 171

BROOKS, MARK
92/3 Oshawa

BROOKS, ROSS
74/5 Loblaws
74/5 O-Pee-Chee 376

BROOKS, W.
28/9 PaulinsCandy 80

BROPHY, JOHN
84/5 TOR
87/8 TOR/P.L.A.Y. 28
88/9 TOR/P.L.A.Y. 28
92/3 Hampton
93/4 Hampton
94/5 Hampton 1
95/6 Hampton HR A-2

BROS, MICHAL
95/6 APS 120
95/6 UpperDeck 541

BROSSART, WILLIE
74/5 Loblaws, -Update
73/4 TOR

BROST, TOD
90/1 CanadaNats
91/2 CanadaNats
93/4 CanadaNats
92 CanadaWinterOlympics 191
93/4 FleerUltra 459
93/4 PowerPlay 479
93/4 Premier-TmCanada 8
94/5 Huntington 5

BROTEN, AARON
90/1 Bowman 185
91/2 Bowman 162
82/3 O-Pee-Chee 136
83/4 O-Pee-Chee 227
85/6 O-Pee-Chee 249
87/8 OPC/Topps 46
88/9 OPC/Topps 138
89/90 OPC/Topps 180, OPC 308
90/1 OPC/Topps 118
90/1 opcPremier 10
83/4 opcSticker 226
85/6 opcSticker 62/189
87/8 opcSticker 62
88/9 opcSticker 76
89/90 opcSticker 88/229
87/8 PaniniSticker 78
88/9 PaniniSticker 271
89/90 PaniniSticker 254
90/1 PaniniSticker 247
91/2 PaniniSticker 105
90/1 ProSet 131, 530
90/1 Score 162, -Hot 72
91/2 Score(CDN) 250, 337
91/2 Score(U.S) 307, 21T
90/1 UpperDeck 210
81/2 COL.R
83/4 N.J
84/5 N.J
89/90 N.J
88/9 N.J/Caretta
86/7 N.J/SOBER
90/1 QUE/PetroCanada
90/1 TOR
94/5 Minnesota

BROTEN, NEAL
90/1 Bowman 178
91/2 Bowman 121, 420
92/3 Bowman 81
94/5 Donruss 67
95/6 Donruss 259
94/5 Flair 39
95/6 FleerMetal 82
92/3 FleerUltra 89
93/4 FleerUltra 296
94/5 FleerUltra 48
95/6 FleerUltra 87, 187
88/9 FritoLay
94/5 Leaf 246
95/6 Leaf 286, -Road 7
94/5 MiracleOnIce 3-4, 49
82/3 O-Pee-Chee 164
83/4 O-Pee-Chee 168
84/5 OPC 96, Topps 72
85/6 OPC/Topps 124
86/7 OPC/Topps 99
87/8 OPC/Topps 11
88/9 OPC/Topps 144
89/90 OPC/Topps 87, OPC 306
90/1 O-Pee-Chee 90
91/2 OPC/Topps 420
92/3 O-Pee-Chee 62
82/3 opcSticker 190
83/4 opcSticker 120
84/5 opcSticker 46
85/6 opcSticker 40/169
86/7 opcSticker 166
87/8 opcSticker 52/193
88/9 opcSticker 201/72
89/90 opcSticker 202
97/8 PacificDynag-BestKept 28
87/8 PaniniSticker 297
88/9 PaniniSticker 92
89/90 PaniniSticker 107
90/1 PaniniSticker 261
91/2 PaniniSticker 107
92/3 PaniniSticker 89
93/4 PaniniSticker 272
95/6 PaniniSticker 80
91/2 Parkhurst 80
92/3 Parkhurst 313
93/4 Parkhurst 54
94/5 Parkhurst 53
95/6 Parkhurst 120
91/2 Pinnacle 161
92/3 Pinnacle 209
93/4 Pinnacle 334
94/5 Pinnacle 293
95/6 Pinnacle 117
95/6 Playoff 276
94/5 POG 76
95/6 POG 157

93/4 PowerPlay 57
93/4 Premier 131
94/5 Premier 74
90/1 ProSet 132
91/2 ProSet 112
91/2 PSPlatinum 188
83/4 PuffySticker 13
90/1 Score 144
91/2 Score(CDN) 337, 500
91/2 Score(U.S) 280, 307
92/3 Score 32
93/4 Score 166
94/5 Score 113
95/6 Score 265
89 SemicSticker 165
91 SemicSticker 140
95/6 SkyBoxEmotion 95
95/6 SkyBoxImpact 91
91/2 ToppsStadiumClub 99
92/3 ToppsStadiumClub 90
93/4 ToppsStadiumClub 28
92/3 Topps 309
90/1 UpperDeck 48
91/2 UpperDeck 232
92/3 UpperDeck 206
93/4 UpperDeck 109, SP-34
94/5 UpperDeck 273, SP18
95/6 UpperDeck 114
95/6 UDBeAPlayer 42
95/6 UDCollChoice 285
96/7 UDCollChoice 152
94/5 DAL
96/7 DAL/Southwest
81/2 MIN
82/3 MIN
83/4 MIN
84/5 MIN
84/5 MIN/7Eleven 1
85/6 MIN
85/6 MIN/7Eleven 6
86/7 MIN/7Eleven 1
87/8 MIN
88/9 MIN/American
94/5 Minnesota

BROTEN, PAUL
90/1 Bowman 224
92/3 Bowman 265
92/3 FleerUltra 134, 353
94/5 Leaf 409
91/2 OPC/Topps 215
92/3 O-Pee-Chee 364
91/2 Parkhurst 336
93/4 Parkhurst 324
94/5 Parkhurst 60
92/3 Pinnacle 212
94/5 Pinnacle 433
94/5 Premier 261
89/90 ProCards(IHL) 28
90/1 ScoreTraded 41T
92/3 Score 353
93/4 Score 297, 658
92/3 Topps 355
91/2 ToppsStadiumClub 376
92/3 ToppsStadiumClub 109
91/2 UpperDeck 550
92/3 UpperDeck 148
93/4 UpperDeck 468
94/5 UpperDeck 15
94/5 DAL
94/5 DAL/Southwest
89/90 NYR/MarineMidland
94/5 Minnesota

BROUGHTON, GEORGE
1912-13 Imperial (C57) 39

BROUSSEAU, JASON
89/90 SketchMEM 67
90/1 SketchQMJHL 57
91/2 SketchQMJHL 230
94/5 Johnstown 2

BROUSSEAU, PAUL
93/4 ClassicProspects 152
97/8 PinnacleInside 141
90/1 SketchQMJHL 177
91/2 SketchQMJHL 206

BROWER, SCOTT
89/90 ProCards(IHL) 36
90/1 ProCards 302
93/4 Sisu 256

BROWN, ADAM
34-43 BeeHives(DET)
45-64 BeeHives(CHI)
51/2 Parkhurst 30

BROWN, ANDY
72/3 EddieSargent 83
74/5 opcWHA 58
94/5 Huntington 6

BROWN, ARNIE
see Stewart A. Brown

BROWN, BOB (SR.)
52/3 AnonymousOHL 15
91/2 SketchAwards 19
94/5 Slapshot(MEM) 36

BROWN, BRAD
94/5 ClassicFourSport 132
94/5 C4'Images 109
93/4 Classic 100
94/5 Classic 16
95/6 Classic 90
97/8 PacificRegime 100
94/5 SigRookies FF2
91/2 SketchOHL 53
93/4 Slapshot(NorthBay) 1, 25
94/5 Slapshot(NorthBay) 4
94/5 SRGoldStandard 79
97/8 UpperDeck 296
96/7 Fredericton

BROWN, CAL
90/1 ProCards 171

BROWN, CAM
90/1 ProCards 336
91/2 ProCards 598
88/9 Brandon 23
89/90 Brandon 8
94/5 Erie

BROWN, CONNY
see Patrick C. Brown

BROWN, CRAIG
93/4 WestMich.
96/7 Penascola 1

BROWN, CURTIS
95/6 DonrussElite -WorldJrs. 11
96/7 FleerNHLPicks 150
96/7 FleerUltra 14, -Rookies 3
96/7 LeafPreferred 142
96/7 MetalUniverse 172
98/9 Pacific 104
96/7 Pinnacle 227
97/8 PinnacleBeAPlayer 53
96/7 PinnacleZenith 145
94/5 SigRookies 63
96/7 SP 14
96/7 Summit 185
98/9 Topps 185
95/6 UpperDeck 531
96/7 UpperDeck 226
97/8 UpperDeck 230
95/6 PrinceAlbert

BROWN, DAN
89/90 SketchOHL 99

BROWN, DAVE
94/5 Leaf 428
90/1 Panini(EDM) 3
88/9 PaniniSticker 319
90/1 ProSet 440
91/2 ProSet 452
91/2 Score(CDN) 634, (U.S) 84T
93/4 UpperDeck 459
88/9 EDM
88/9 EDM/ActionMagazine 145
90/1 EDM/McGavins
86/7 PHA
93/4 PHA 10OCT93
91/2 PHA/JCPenney
92/3 PHA/JCPenney
92/3 PHA/UD 09FEB93
92/3 PHA/UD 18OCT92
93/4 PHA/JCPenney
94/5 PHA
81/2 Saskatoon 7
83/4 Springfield 8

BROWN, DOUG
91/2 Bowman 285
92/3 Bowman 126
93/4 Donruss 258
94/5 Donruss 213
95 Globe 114
93/4 FleerUltra 393
93/4 Leaf 378
94/5 Leaf 116
89/90 O-Pee-Chee 242
88/9 OPC/Topps 115
90/1 OPC/Topps 117
91/2 OPC/Topps 42, 191
92/3 O-Pee-Chee 333
88/9 opcSticker 80/209
88/9 opcStickFS 2
98/9 Pacific 187
97/8 PacificRegime 67
88/9 PaniniSticker 272
90/1 PaniniSticker 67
93/4 Parkhurst 424
94/5 ParkieSE 135
91/2 Pinnacle 363
94/5 Pinnacle 197
96/7 PinnacleBeAPlayer 43
93/4 PowerPlay 411
94/5 Premier 263
90/1 ProSet 163
91/2 ProSet 138
91/2 Score(CDN) 163, (U.S) 163
92/3 Score 118
93/4 Score 582
94/5 Score 15
95/6 Score 193
97/8 Score(DET) 13
94 Semic 117
92 SemicSticker 165
92/3 Topps 139
95/6 Topps 81, 8PL
91/2 ToppsStadiumClub 47
92/3 ToppsStadiumClub 331
90/1 UpperDeck 159
91/2 UpperDeck 214
94/5 UpperDeck 422
95/6 UpperDeck 79
94/5 UDBeAPlayer-Aut. 28
95/6 UDCollChoice 47
88/9 N.J/Caretta
89/90 N.J
90/1 N.J
93/4 PGH/Foodland 7

BROWN, ERIC
93/4 Waterloo

BROWN, GEORGE ALLAN
34-43 BeeHives(MTL)
37/8 OPC (V304E) 157

BROWN, GEORGE V.
83&87 HallOfFame 152
83 HHOF Postcard (L)

BROWN, GERRY
34-43 BeeHives(DET)

BROWN, GREG
95/6 EliteSet 287
90/1 opcPremier 11
91/2 ProCards 18
90/1 ProSet 590
90/1 ScoreTraded 96T
91/2 Score(CDN) 518
95/6 udElite 176
90/1 BUF/BlueShield
90/1 BUF/Campbell
91/2 Rochester/Genny
91/2 Rochester/Kodak
92/3 Rochester/Kodak
91/2 Rochestr/Dunkin'Donuts
92/3 Rochestr/Dunkin'Donuts

BROWN, JAMIE
95/6 Halifax
96/7 Halifax (1), (2)

BROWN, JASON
91/2 AirCanadaSJHL B46
92/3 MPSPhotoSJHL 18

BROWN, JEFF
90/1 Bowman 25
91/2 Bowman 385
92/3 Bowman 247
93/4 Donruss 293, 499
94/5 Donruss 109
95/6 Donruss 183
95/6 DonrussElite 78
93/4 EASports 121
94/5 Flair 188
94/5 Fleer 222
95/6 FleerMetal 148
96/7 FleerNHLPicks 64
92/3 FleerUltra 183
93/4 FleerUltra 223
94/5 FleerUltra 221
95/6 FleerUltra 165
96/7 FleerUltra 72
95/6 Hoyle'WEST 6 Hearts
89/90 Kraft 28
93/4 Leaf 29
94/5 Leaf 247
95/6 Leaf 245
94/5 LeafLimited 18
96/7 MetalUniverse 65
88/9 O-Pee-Chee 201
89/90 OPC/Topps 28
90/1 OPC/Topps 295
91/2 OPC/Topps 222
88/9 opcSticker 192
89/90 opcSticker 193
98/9 Pacific 438
97/8 PacificD-BestKept 16
98/9 PacificParamount 243
88/9 PaniniSticker 325
89/90 PaniniSticker 325
90/1 PaniniSticker 274
91/2 PaniniSticker 23
92/3 PaniniSticker 25
93/4 PaniniSticker 165
94/5 PaniniSticker 152
95/6 PaniniSticker 297
96/7 PaniniSticker 27
91/2 Parkhurst 156
93/4 Parkhurst 173
94/5 Parkhurst 244, V45
95/6 Parkhurst 365
91/2 Pinnacle 72
92/3 Pinnacle 13
93/4 Pinnacle 39
94/5 Pinnacle 34
95/6 Pinnacle 29
96/7 Pinnacle 12
97/8 PinnacleBeAPlayer 89
95/6 Playoff 206
96/7 Playoff 396
94/5 POG 313
95/6 POG 276
93/4 PowerPlay 207
93/4 Premier 363, 381
94/5 Premier 272, 487
90/1 ProSet 260
91/2 ProSet 212
92/3 ProSet 158
91/2 PSPlatinum 114
90/1 Score 41
91/2 Score(CDN) 496, (U.S) 276
92/3 Score 220
93/4 Score 194
95/6 Score 23
96/7 Score 87
94/5 Select 110
95/6 SkyBoxEmotion 177
95/6 SkyBoxImpact 166
96/7 SkyBoxImpact 51
94/5 SP 123
95/6 SuperSticker 126
96/7 TeamOut
92/3 Topps 174
95/6 Topps 268
91/2 ToppsStadiumClub 148
92/3 ToppsStadiumClub 263
93/4 T.StadiumClub 188, -Fin. 2
94/5 TSC-MembersOnly 23
90/1 UpperDeck 191
91/2 UpperDeck 211
93/4 UpperDeck 130, SP-135
94/5 UpperDeck 34, SP81
95/6 UpperDeck 352, SE84
96/7 UpperDeck 73
95/6 UDCollChoice 301
96/7 UDCollChoice 120
85/6 QUE
85/6 QUE/McDonald
86/7 QUE
86/7 QUE/GeneralFoods
86/7 QUE/McDonald
87/8 QUE/GeneralFoods
88/9 QUE
88/9 QUE/GeneralFoods
89/90 QUE
89/90 QUE/GeneralFoods
89/90 QUE/Police
89/90 STL/Kodak
90/1 STL/Kodak
91/2 STL
94/5 VAN
95/6 VAN/Building 8
84/5 Sudbury 7
85/6 Sudbury 20

BROWN, JEFF
95/6 Bowman P5
98 BowmanCHL 4
95/6 Classic 96
94/5 Slapshot(Sarnia) 21
95/6 Slapshot 347, 439

BROWN, JEREMY
92/3 WestMich.
93/4 WestMich.

BROWN, JERRY
34-43 BeeHives(DET)

BROWN, JIM
90/1 SketchOHL 298
91/2 SketchOHL 288
94/5 Hampton 18
93/4 OwenSound

BROWN, JOE
82/3 Kingston 4
83/4 Kingston 18
84/5 Kitchener 14

BROWN, KEITH
90/1 Bowman 10
92/3 Bowman 4
94/5 Fleer 78
93/4 FleerUltra 322
94/5 FleerUltra 295
81/2 OPC 55, Topps(W) 67
82/3 O-Pee-Chee 62
83/4 O-Pee-Chee 98
84/5 OPC 33, Topps 28
86/7 O-Pee-Chee 206
92/3 O-Pee-Chee 48
80/1 OPC/Topps 98
85/6 OPC/Topps 59
87/8 OPC/Topps 47
90/1 OPC/Topps 276
81/2 opcSticker 115
84/5 opcSticker 28
87/8 PaniniSticker 233
90/1 PaniniSticker 192
91/2 PaniniSticker 21
92/3 PaniniSticker 13
91/2 Parkhurst 261
92/3 Parkhurst 274
91/2 Pinnacle 154, 370
92/3 Pinnacle 92
93/4 Pinnacle 422
94/5 Pinnacle 368
90/1 ProSet 49
91/2 ProSet 371
90/1 Score 161
91/2 Score(CDN) 76, (U.S) 76
92/3 Score 68
93/4 Score 384, 569
92/3 Topps 52
92/3 ToppsStadiumClub 274
93/4 ToppsStadiumClub 58, 281
79/80 CHI
80/1 CHI/4x6
80/1 CHI/5.5x8.5
81/2 CHI
82/3 CHI
83/4 CHI
86/7 CHI/Coke
87/8 CHI/Coke
88/9 CHI/Coke
89/90 CHI/Coke
90/1 CHI/Coke
91/2 CHI/Coke

BROWN, KEVIN
93/4 Classic 17, 33
94/5 Classic 36, T31
94/5 ClassicImages 28
95/6 Donruss 168
95/6 EdgeIce 182
94/5 Leaf 457
95/6 Leaf 38
94/5 LeafLimited 7
94/5 ParkieSE 77
95/6 Pinnacle 215
95/6 Score 301
93/4 Slapshot(Detroit) 17
94/5 ToppsFinest 15
94/5 UpperDeck 249
95/6 Phoenix

BROWN, KEVIN A.
90/1 SketchOHL 255
91/2 SketchOHL 108, 218
94/5 Dayton 12
95/6 Dayton

BROWN, LARRY
71/2 EddieSargent 159
72/3 EddieSargent 95
70/1 Esso Stamp
74/5 O-Pee-Chee 271
75/6 O-Pee-Chee 377
76/7 O-Pee-Chee 355
77/8 O-Pee-Chee 289
78/9 O-Pee-Chee 361
79/80 O-Pee-Chee 323
71/2 TheTorontoSun

BROWN, LISA
94/5 Classic W24

BROWN, MIKE
97/8 Bowman 126, BB13
95/6 RedDeer

BROWN, NEWELL
84/5 Fredericton 16
90/1 Mich.Tech

BROWN, PATRICK CORNELIUS (CONNY)
34-43 BeeHives(DET)

BROWN, RICH
94/5 Slapshot(Sarnia) 27
95/6 Slapshot 354

BROWN, ROB (JR.)
90/1 Bowmam 202, -HatTrick 3
91/2 Bowman 16
92/3 Bowman 168
95/6 EdgeIce 104, -Quantum 4
92/3 FleerUltra 33
94/5 FleerUltra 304
95/6 FutureLegends 13
94/5 Leaf 540
97/8 Omega 183
88/9 OPC/Topps 109
89/90 OPC/Topps 193
89/90 OPC 309, Topps-AS 8
90/1 OPC/Topps 19
91/2 OPC/Topps 83
92/3 O-Pee-Chee 170
88/9 opcSticker 131/267,237/107
89/90 opcSticker 163/25, 236/99
88/9 opcStickFS 3
89/90 opcStickFS 31
98/9 Pacific 349
88/9 PaniniSticker 336
89/90 PaniniSticker 186, 310
90/1 PaniniSticker 128
91/2 PaniniSticker 315
92/3 PaniniSticker 10
91/2 Parkhurst 60, 258
91/2 Pinnacle 141
92/3 Pinnacle 331
97/8 PinnacleBeAPlayer 48
90/1 ProSet 229
91/2 ProSet 80, 606
91/2 PSPlatinum 42
90/1 Score 105,-Hot 51,-Young 5
91/2 Score(CDN) 466, (U.S) 246
92/3 Score 244,-Sharpshooter22
97/8 Score(PGH) 19
92/3 Topps 72
91/2 ToppsStadiumClub 200
92/3 ToppsStadiumClub 295
90/1 UpperDeck 142
91/2 UpperDeck 198
92/3 UpperDeck 387
94/5 UpperDeck 403
90/1 HFD/JuniorWhalers
91/2 HFD/JuniorWhalers
84/5 Kamloops
85/6 Kamloops
87/8 PGH/Kodak
89/90 PGH/Elbys
89/90 PGH/Foodland 1
86/7 Kamloops

BROWN, RYAN
91/2 SketchWHL 127

BROWN, SEAN
95/6 Classic 20, 83
97/8 Donruss 208
90/1 SketchOHL 203
93/4 Slapshot(Oshawa) 8
95/6 Slapshot 352
96/7 EDM
97/8 EDM
94/5 Knoxville 8
91/2 Oshawa/Domino 12
92/3 Oshawa

BROWN, STEWART ARNOLD (ARNIE)
64-67 BeeHives(NYR)
64/5 CokeCap NYR-4
65/6 CocaCola
70/1 Colgate Stamp 76
70/1 DadsCookies
70/1 EddieSargent 116
71/2 EddieSargent 57
72/3 EddieSargent 72
70/1 Esso Stamp
74/5 Loblaws
68/9 OPC/Topps 68
69/70 OPC/Topps 34
70/1 OPC/Topps 66
71/2 OPC/Topps 14
72/3 OPC 144, Topps 111
73/4 OPC 225
94/5 Parkie(64/5) 97
95/6 Parkie(66/7) 86
68/9 ShirriffCoin NY6
71/2 TheTorontoSun
64/5 Topps 34
65/6 Topps 90
66/7 Topps 90, -USATest 48
67/8 Topps 89

BROWN, TOM
94/5 Slapshot(Sarnia) 6
95/6 Slapshot 335
96/7 Sudbury 6

BROWN, WALTER
83&87 HallOfFame 78
83 HHOF Postcard (F)

BROWNE, BILL
96/7 SSMarie

BROWNE, CECIL
23/4 Crescent Selkirks 7
24/5 Crescent Selkirks 6
25 Dominion 103
23/4 PaulinsCandy 5
28/9 PaulinsCandy 63

BROWNLEE, BRENT
91/2 SketchOHL 364
90/1 SketchWHL 128

BROWNSCHIDLE, JACK
78/9 O-Pee-Chee 379
79/80 O-Pee-Chee 278
80/1 OPC/Topps 101
81/2 O-Pee-Chee 302
82/3 O-Pee-Chee 300
83/4 O-Pee-Chee 311
82/3 Post
84/5 HFD/JuniorWhalers
85/6 HFD/JuniorWhalers
78/9 STL

BRUBAKER, JEFF
88/9 ProCards(Adirondack)
88/9 EDM/ActionMagazine 19
81/2 MTL
84/5 TOR
85/6 TOR

BRUCE, DAVID
92/3 Bowman 358
92/3 FleerUltra 191
92/3 O-Pee-Chee 246
88/9 PaniniSticker 137
92/3 PaniniSticker 126
91/2 Parkhurst 384
92/3 Pinnacle 159
89/90 ProCards(IHL) 173
90/1 ProCards 86
91/2 ProSet 485
92/3 ProSet 170
91/2 PSPlatinum 227
91/2 Score(CDN) 644
92/3 Score 301
92/3 Topps 448
92/3 ToppsStadiumClub 284
92/3 UpperDeck 102
90/1 STL/Kodak
87/8 VAN/Shell
88/9 VAN/Mohawk
84/5 Fredericton 7

85/6 Fredericton 2
86/7 Fredericton
82/3 Kitchener 11
83/4 Kitchener 11

BRUGGEMANN, LARS
94/5 DEL 284
95/6 DEL 297
96/8 DEL 324

BRUK, DAVID
94/5 APS 86
95/6 APS 44

BRULÉ, ERIC
91/2 ProCards 302
90/1 SketchMEM 28
90/1 SketchQMJHL 26

BRUMMER, JOHAN
94/5 ElitSet 95
95/6 ElitSet 229
89/90 SemicElitserien 44
90/1 SemicElitserien 194
92/3 SemicElitserien 296
95/6 udElite 93

BRUMWELL, MURRAY
83/4 O-Pee-Chee 228
83/4 opcSticker 179
88/9 ProCards(Utica)
89/90 ProCards(AHL) 9
90/1 ProCards 435
83/4 N.J

BRUNA, MIROSLAV
95/6 APS 197

BRUNCHK, BEDRICH
72 SemicSticker 35
74 SemicSticker 74
71/2 WilliamsFIN 21

BRUNEAU, PAUL
89/90 SketchOHL 141
89/90 NiagaraFalls

BRUNET, BENOÎT
92/3 Bowman 414
93/4 Donruss 166
95/6 Donruss 367
92/3 Durivage 19
93/4 Durivage 8
95/6 FleerMetal 75
92/3 FleerUltra 101
93/4 FleerUltra 349
95/6 FleerUltra 255
93/4 Leaf 363
94/5 Leaf 401
96/7 Maggers 84
92/3 O-Pee-Chee 352
98/9 Pacific 248
93/4 PaniniSticker 20
95/6 PaniniSticker 39
93/4 Parkhurst 375
95/6 Parkhurst 116
94/5 Pinnacle 452
95/6 Playoff 162
95/6 POG 146
93/4 PowerPlay 366
93/4 Premier 84
94/5 Premier 94
88/9 ProCards(Sherbrooke)
89/90 ProCards(AHL) 186
97/8 Score(MTL) 18
92/3 Topps 137
95/6 Topps 87
92/3 ToppsStadiumClub 134
93/4 ToppsStadiumClub 422
94/5 ToppsStadiumClub 227
91/2 UpperDeck 469
92/3 UpperDeck 80
93/4 UpperDeck 415
95/6 UpperDeck 156
95/6 UDBeAPlayer 86
95/6 UDCollChoice 35
90/1 MTL
92/3 MTL
92/3 MTL/OPC 31
93/4 MTL
93/4 MTL/Molson
94/5 MTL
95/6 MTL
95/6 MTL/Molson
96-98 MTL
87/8 Hull

BRUNET, GERRY
51/2 LacStJean 58

BRUNET, LUC
27-32 LaPresse 28/9

BRUNETEAU, EDDIE
43-47 ParadeSportive

BRUNETEAU, MODERE (MUD)
34-43 BeeHives(DET)
39/40 OPC (V301-1) 43
40/1 OPC (V301-2) 138
43-47 ParadeSportive
36/7 WWGum (V356) 47

BRUNETTA, MARIO
96/7 DEL 24
90/1 PaniniSticker 152
89/90 ProCards(AHL) 159
87/8 QUE/GeneralFoods
88/9 QUE
88/9 QUE/GeneralFoods
89/90 Halifax

BRUNETTE, ANDREW
96/7 Fleer 124, -Calder 1
96/7 FleerUltra 173
95/6 FutureLegends 47
97/8 Omega 237
98/9 Pacific 439
98/9 PacificParamount 121
97/8 PacificRegime 207
96/7 PaniniSticker 141, 304
97/8 PinnacleInside 111
90/1 SketchOHL 277
91/2 SketchOHL 284
96/7 SkyBoxImpact 147
96/7 UpperDeck 184
97/8 UpperDeck 382
93/4 OwenSound
94/5 Portland
95/6 Portland
96/7 Portland

BRUNNER, GERHARD
96/7 DEL 225

BRUNNER, MARKUS
90/1 SketchOHL 328
91/2 SketchOHL 151
90/1 Oshawa 26
91/2 Oshawa
91/2 Oshawa/Dominos 15

BRUNS, ROGER
94/5 DEL 437

BRUNSING, FRANK
94/5 DEL 224

BRUS, KJELL
72 SemicSticker 63

BRUSELINCK, DEREK
92/3 MPSPhotoSJHL 151

BRUX, ARNO
94/5 DEL 333
95/6 DEL 237

BRYAN, TIM
95/6 Slapshot 430

BRYDEN, ROB
88/9 ProCards(Sherbrooke)
88/9 Flint

BRYDGE, BILL
33/4 Anonymous (V129) 22
33/4 CndGum (V252)
33-35 DiamondMatch
36-39 DiamondMatch (1), (2), (3)
25 Dominion 101
23/4 PaulinsCandy 19
33/4 WWGum (V357) 2

BRYDGES, PAUL
88/9 ProCards(Rochester)
89/90 ProCards(AHL) 27
93/4 Slapshot(Guelph) 27
94/5 Slapshot(Guelph) 28

BRYDGES, SCOTT
82/3 Oshawa 7
83/4 Oshawa 11

BRYDSON, GLENN
34-43 BeeHives(CHI)
33/4 CndGum V252
36-39 DiamondMatch -1, 4, 5, 6
34/5 OPC V304B 64
33/4 WWGum V357 39

BRYLIN, SERGEI
92/3 Classic 47
92/3 ClassicFourSport 188

95/6 Donruss 52
95/6 FleerUltra 88
95/6 Leaf 40
95/6 Parkhurst 119
93/4 Pinnacle 509
95/6 Pinnacle 120
95/6 Playoff 277
92/3 RedAce(Blue) 23,(Violet) 23
95/6 Score 274
97/8 Score(N.J.) 19
95/6 Topps 35, 2NG
93/4 UpperDeck 276
94/5 UpperDeck 329
95/6 UpperDeck 31
95/6 UDCollChoice 296
96/7 N.J/Sharp

BUBLA, JIRI
72 Hellas 95
74 Hellas 67
83/4 O-Pee-Chee 347
84/5 O-Pee-Chee 315
83/4 opcSticker 143
79 PaniniSticker 76
72 SemicSticker 38
74 SemicSticker 53
83/4 SouhaitsRen.KeyChain
83/4 Vachon 102
71/2 WilliamsFIN 22
72/3 WilliamsFIN 2
73/4 WilliamsFIN 44
81/2 VAN
81/2 VAN/Silverwood
82/3 VAN
83/4 VAN
84/5 VAN
85/6 VAN

BUBOLA, ADRIAN
91/2 AvantGardeBCJ 9

BUCCIARELLI, BRIAN
88/9 ProCards(Hershey)

BUCHAL, JAROSLAV
95/6 APS 164

BUCHANAN, BUCKY
51/2 LavalDairy 56
52/3 LavalDairy 29

BUCHANAN, GREG
91/2 AvantGardeBCJHL 6
92/3 BCJHL 211

BUCHANAN, JEFF
90/1 SketchWHL 89
91/2 SketchWHL 102
92/3 AtlantaKnights
93/4 AtlantaKnights
90/1 Saskatoon 4
91/2 Saskatoon 4

BUCHANAN, KIRK
92/3 BCJHL 188

BUCHANAN, ROB
74/5 opcWHA 23
73/4 QuakerOats 36
75/6 opcWHA 39
72/3 ClevelandCrusaders
72/3 ClevelandCrusaders/Linnet

BUCHANAN, TREVOR
88/9 Kamloops
96/7 Penascola 9
89/90 Victoria

BUCHBERGER, KELLY
92/3 Bowman 393
94/5 Donruss 18
92/3 FleerUltra 291
93/4 FleerUltra 314
94/5 FleerUltra 290
96/7 Kraft'Disk
94/5 Leaf 333
97/8 Omega 89
92/3 O-Pee-Chee 125
98/9 Pacific 205
97/8 PacificCrown 268
97/8 PcfcDynag! 47,-Tandem 49
98/9 PacificParamount 84
90/1 Panini(EDM) 4
93/4 PaniniSticker 241
94/5 PaniniSticker 201
95/6 PaniniSticker 261
95 PaniniWorlds 15
91/2 Parkhurst 275
95/6 Parkhurst 77

92/3 Pinnacle 95
93/4 Pinnacle 58
94/5 Pinnacle 332
97/8 PinnacleBeAPlayer 150
94/5 POG 98
95/6 POG 111
93/4 PowerPlay 340
94/5 Premier 404
90/1 ProSet 441
91/2 ProSet 385
92/3 ProSet 48
91/2 Score(CDN) 429
92/3 Score 126, -Sharp 11
93/4 Score 317
97/8 SPAuthentic 64
92/3 Topps 455
95/6 Topps 298
98/9 Topps 22
92/3 ToppsStadiumClub 235
94/5 ToppsStadiumClub 121
92/3 UpperDeck 123
93/4 UpperDeck 197
94/5 UpperDeck 134
95/6 UpperDeck 121
97/8 UpperDeck 278
95/6 UDCollChoice 310
96/7 UDCollChoice 94
88/9 EDM
88/9 EDM/ActionMagazine 133
90/1 EDM/McGavins
91/2 EDM/IGA
92/3 EDM
92/3 EDM/IGA 3
93/4 EDM 20OCT93
96/7 EDM
97/8 EDM

BUCHER, LAURENT
91/2 UD 668, 'CzechWJC 29

BUCHWEISER, H.
95/6 DEL 352

BUCK, DAVE
93/4 Minn-Duluth

BUCKBERGER, ASHLEY
91/2 SketchWHL 193
94/5 Slapshot(MEM) 18

BUCKLAND, FRANK
83&87 HallOfFame 216
83 HHOF Postcard (O)

BUCKLAND, WYATT
90/1 SketchOHL 278
91/2 SketchOHL 287
94/5 Toledo

BUCKLE, CHAD
92/3 BCJHL 196

BUCKLEY, JEFF
95/6 Dayton

BUCKLEY, TOM
94/5 Slapshot(Detroit) 10
94/5 Slapshot(MEM) 84
95/6 Slapshot 77

BUCKMAN, CHRIS
92/3 BCJHL 139

BUCYK, JOHNNY
45-64 BeeHives(BOS), (DET)
64-67 BeeHives(BOS)
62 CeramicTiles
64/5 CokeCap BOS-9
65/6 CocaCola
70/1 Colgate Stamp 46
70/1 DadsCookies
70/1 EddieSargent 8
71/2 EddieSargent 9
72/3 EddieSargent 16
70/1 Esso Stamp
83&87 HallOfFame 181
83 HHOF Postcard (J)
74/5 Loblaws
73/4 MacsMilk Disk
68/9 OPC/Topps 5, OPC 210
69/70 OPC/Topps 26
70/1 OPC/Topps 2
71/2 OPC/T. 35, 249,255, T.1-3
72/3 OPC 1, Topps 60
73/4 OPC 147, Topps 26
74/5 OPC/Topps 28, 239, 245
75/6 OPC/Topps 9
76/7 OPC/Topps 95
76/7 OPC 381, T-Glossy 14

77/8 OPC/Topps 155
93/4 Parkie(56/7) 56
94/5 Parkie(64/5) 1, SL1
95/6 Parkie(66/7) 5, SL1
97/8 PinnacleBeeHive 58
70/1 PostShooters
60/1 ShirriffCoin 104
61/2 ShirriffCoin 7
68/9 ShirriffCoin BOS6
81/2 TCMA 5
57/8 Topps 10
58/9 Topps 40
59/60 Topps 23
60/1 Topps 11
61/2 Topps 8, -Stamp
62/3 Topps 11, -Buck
63/4 Topps 11
64/5 Topps 100
65/6 Topps 101
66/7 Topps 39, -USATest 39
67/8 Topps 42
54-67 TorontoStar V8
56-66 TorontoStar 63/4
63/4 TheTorontoStar
71/2 TheTorontoSun
70/1 BOS
70/1 BOS/Ashtray
71/2 BOS
91/2 BOS/Legends
93/4 Zellers

BUCYK, RANDY
89/90 ProCards(IHL) 205
90/1 ProCards 608
85/6 MTL
88/9 SaltLake 16

BUCZKOWSKI, PAUL
91/2 SketchWHL 105
91/2 Saskatoon 24
93/4 Saskatoon

BUDA, DAVE
89/90 ProCards(AHL) 54

BUDAI, JEFF
91/2 SketchWHL 269

BUDEAU, DENNIS
91/2 AirCanadaSJHL D18

BUDKIN, RICK
93/4 Slapshot(Sudbury) 14

BUDY, TIM
89/90 ProCards(AHL) 226

BUETOW, JASON
90/1 SketchOHL 279
91/2 SketchOHL 286

BUETTGEN, JIM
85/6 Moncton 13

BUJAR, KRZYSZTOF
89 SemicSticker 142
92 SemicSticker 280

BUKAC, LUDEK
95/6 APS 351
94/5 DEL 369
92 SemicSticker 170

BULIS, JAN
95/6 Bowman P6
97/8 Bowman 1
97/8 DonrussPriority 174
97/8 KatchMedallion 168
98/9 Pacific 440
97/8 Pinnacle 24
95/6 Slapshot 24
97/8 SPAuthentic 198
98/9 SPx"Finite" 89, 131
97/8 UpperDeck 381
97/8 UDBlackDiamond 89
98/9 UDChoice 216
97/8 UpperDeckIce 59

BULJIN, VLADISLAV
91/2 UD'CzechWJC 2

BULLARD, MIKE
90/1 Bowman 114
94/5 DEL 258
95/6 DEL 256
96/7 DEL 144
82/3 O-Pee-Chee 262, 264
83/4 O-Pee-Chee 277
84/5 OPC 172, 365, Topps 123
85/6 OPC/Topps 67
86/7 OPC/Topps 83

87/8 O-Pee-Chee 210
88/9 OPC/Topps 152
89/90 OPC/Topps 21
90/1 OPC/Topps 274
82/3 opcSticker 149
83/4 opcSticker 235
84/5 opcSticker 118
85/6 opcSticker 104/237
86/7 opcSticker 228/98
87/8 opcSticker 37/180
88/9 opcSticker 93, 119/249
89/90 opcSticker 104/241
88/9 PaniniSticker 8
90/1 PaniniSticker 119
91/2 Parkhurst 397
91/2 Pinnacle 69
82/3 Post
90/1 ProSet 211
91/2 ProSet 496
91/2 PSPlatinum 233
83/4 PuffySticker 9
92/3 Score 218
91/2 Score(CDN) 590, (U.S) 40T
84/5 7ElevenDisk
85/6 7Eleven 15
83/4 SouhaitsRen.KeyChain
92/3 Topps 146
92/3 ToppsStadiumClub 494
90/1 UpperDeck 230
87/8 CGY/RedRooster
83/4 PGH
83/4 PGH/Heinz
84/5 PGH/Heinz
89/90 PHA
87/8 STL
88/9 STL
90/1 TOR/P.L.A.Y. 16

BULLER, HY
45-64 BeeHives(NYR)
51/2 Parkhurst 91
52/3 Parkhurst 98
53/4 Parkhurst 58

BULLEY, TED
78/9 OPC/Topps 217
79/80 OPC/Topps 7, 128
80/1 OPC/Topps 229
81/2 OPC 56, Topps(W) 68
82/3 O-Pee-Chee 360
82/3 Post
79/80 CHI
80/1 CHI/4x6
81/2 CHI
83/4 PGH
82/3 WSH

BULLOCK, GREG
95/6 Classic 71, -Aut.
95/6 ClassicFiveSport 131
97/8 udSwedish 148

BURAKOVSKY, MIKE
95/6 ElitSet 263, -Rookies 7

BURAKOVSKY, ROBERT
93/4 ClassicProspects 166
95/6 ElitSet 262, -FaceToFace 9
93/4 FleerUltra 379
93/4 Leaf 429
93/4 Parkhurst 144
89/90 SemicElitserien 16
90/1 SemicElitserien 85
91/2 SemicElitserien 189
92/3 SemicElitserien 221
91 SemicSticker 44
93/4 UpperDeck 498, SP-106
95/6 udElite 149
93/4 OTT/Kraft

BURCH, BILL
25-27 Anonymous 79
24/5 Champs (C144)
83&87 HallOfFame 64
83 HHOF Postcard (E)
24/5 MapleCrispettes (V130) 21
23/4 (V145-1) 35
24/5 (V145-2) 13

BURCHELL, FREDERICK (SKIPPY)
51-54 LaPatrie 15Feb53
52/3 StLawrence 6
63/4 QuébecAces

BURCHILL, RICK
89/90 Johnstown 19

BURDA, VACLAV
95/6 APS 272

BURE, PAVEL
95/6 Aces 9 (Diamonds)
96/7 Aces 2 (Hearts)
97/8 Aces 9 (Hearts)
92/3 Bowman 154
95/6 Bowman 65, BB13
92/3 Classic-Autograph
93/4 Classic 117, N6, -Aut.
94/5 ClassicImages 10, 100
94/5 ClassicImages CE10, PL1
93/4 ClassicProspects LP22
96/7 CorinthianHeadliners
97/8 CorinthianHeadliners
95/6 DEL 442
93/4 Donruss 351, X, -IceKing 8
94/5 Donruss 19,-Dom 8, -Elite 3
95/6 Donruss 170, -Dominator 6
96/7 Donruss 65,-Dom 7, -Elite 1
97/8 Don. 187, -Line 11, -Red 6
96/7 D.CanadianIce 59
97/8 D.CanadianIce 18
95/6 DonrussElite 77
96/7 DonrussElite 103, -Status 1
97/8 D.Elite 4, 118,-Craftsmn 20
97/8 DE -Primenumbers 12
97/8 D.Preferd 25, 194,-Line 4A
97/8 D.Pref -Wide Tins5,-Tins 17
97/8 DonrussPriority 15, 211
97/8 D.Prio -DirDep3,-OpDay 13
97/9 D.Prio -Postcrd 5, -Stamp 5
97/8 D.Studio 14,-HardHats 18
97/8 D.Studio-Portr 14,-Sil 9
93/4 EASports 143
97/8 EssoOlympic 38
94/5 Flair 189, -Hot 1, -Scoring 1
96/7 Flair 93, -Centre 1
94/5 Fleer 223, -Headliner 1
96/7 Fleer 111, -Art 1,-Pearson 1
95/6 FleerMetal 149, -Heavy 1
95/6 FleerMetal-International 2
92/3 FleerUltra 219, -AW 9
92/3 FU-Import 2, -Rookie 3
93/4 FleerUltra 37, -AS 17
93/4 FU-Red 2, -Speed 1
94/5 FleerUltra 222,-AS 7,-Red 2
94/5 FU-Scoring 1, -Speed 1
95/6 FleerUltra 166, 379
96/7 FleerUltra 167, -MrMom. 2
96/7 F.Picks-Dream 4, -Fab 5
91/2 Gillette 10
95 Globe 174
96/7 Got-UmHockeyGreatsCoin
93/4 HockeyWit 7
95/6 Hoyle'WEST A (Diamonds)
97/8 KatchMedallion 145
94/5 KennerSLU
95/6 KennerSLU (U.S.)
93/4 KraftDinner, -CutOut
94/5 Kraft'AllStar
95/6 KraftDinner
93/4 Leaf 10, -GoldAS 8
94/5 Leaf 10,-Gld 4,-Fir 3,-Ltd 24
95/6 Leaf 135, -Fire 1
96/7 Leaf 15,-Leathr 9,-Sweatr13
97/8 Leaf 60, -FireOnIce 8
94/5 LeafLimited 100, -Gold 10
95/6 LeafLimited 17
96/7 LeafLimited 32, -Stubble 10
96/7 LeafPref. 94,-Steel 3,-Van 9
97/8 Limited 7,104,153,-fabric 66
96/7 Maggers 156
93/4 McDonalds McD02
94/5 McDonalds McD23
95/6 McDonalds McD8
96/7 McDonalds McD27
97/8 McDonalds McD3
96/7 MetalUniverse 155
96/7 MU-IceCarving 2, -Lethal 2
97/8 Omega 228,-GameFace 18
97/8 Omega -Silk 11, -StickH 19
92/3 O-Pee-Chee 25, 324
92/3 OPC-25Years 25, -Box
91/2 opcPremier 67, -Star 10
98/9 Pacific 10,-Cram 10,-Tm 26
98/9 Pcfc-DynIce 17,-GoldC 33
97/8 PacificCrown 96
97/8 PCC-Supial 20, -Gold 20

97/8 PCC-Slap 11A,-TeamCL 25
97/8 PacificCrownRoyale 133
97/8 PCR -Blade 19, -Cramer 10
97/8 PCR -HatTrick 18,-Lamp 19
97/8 PacificDynagon! 125
97/8 PcfcD-BestKpt 95,-Dyn 15A
97/8 PcfcD-Kings 10,-Tandm 14
97/8 PacificInvincible 140
97/8 Pcfc.Inv.-Attack 23, -Off 20
97/8 PacificParamount 186
97/8 PcfcP-BigN 19,-Photo 19
98/9 PcfcParamnt 234,-Spec 18
97/8 PacificRegime 201
97/8 PacificRevolution 139
97/8 PcfcRev -AllStarGame 18
97/8 PcfcRev -Icon 10,-TmCL 25
92/3 PaniniSticker 271, 290, C
93/4 PaniniSticker O
94/5 PaniniSticker 146, 235a,GG
95/6 PaniniSticker 293
96/7 PaniniSticker 289
98/9 PaniniSticker 236
95 PaniniWorlds 281
91/2 Parkhurst 404, 446, 462
92/3 PH 188, 234, 460, 506
93/4 Parkhurst 211, G7, W2
94/5 Parkhurst 297, V18, C24
95/6 Parkhurst 248, 482, -AS 3
95/6 PH-AS, -Crown(1) 5
94/5 ParkieSE 187, ES15
91/2 Pinnacle 315
92/3 Pinnacle 110, -TeamP 4
92/3 Pinnacle-Tm2000 8
93/4 Pinnacle 320, -Tm2001 3
93/4 P-Nifty 1, 6, -TeamP 10
94/5 Pinnacle 140, MVPC, BR13
94/5 Pinnacle GR4, NL17, TP12
95/6 Pinnacle 1,-Clr 12,-Roar 8
96/7 Pinnacle 175,248,-Numb 15
97/8 Pinnacle 41
96/7 P.BAP LTH4B, -Biscuit 18
97/8 PinnacleBAP -OneTimer 12
97/8 PinnacleBeeHive 15
97/8 PinnacleCertified 45
97/8 Pinnacle- EPIX 21
95/6 PinnacleFANtasy 12
96/7 PinnacleFANtasy 14
97/8 PinnacleInside 11,-Can 20
97/8 PinnacleInside-Track 12
96/7 PinnacleMint 7
97/8 PinnacleMint 17,-Minterntl 6
95/6 PinnZenith 9, -ZTeam 12
96/7 PinnacleZenith 3, -ZTeam 8
95/6 Playoff 100, 207, 316
96/7 Playoff 438
94/5 POG 266, 341, 376
95/6 POG 21, 274
94/5 Post
97/8 Post
93/4 PowerPlay 248, -Point 1
93/4 PowerPlay-GlobalGreat 1
93/4 Premier 260, 440
93/4 Premier-Black(OPC) 7
94/5 Premier 39, 151, 325, 415
94/5 Prmr-Finest(T) 1, -GoTo 5
95/6 ProMagnet 21
91/2 ProSet 564
92/3 ProSet 192, CC3
92/3 PS-Rookie 2, -TL 13
91/2 PSPlatinum 272
91/2 RedAce
91/2 ScoreTraded 49T
92/3 Score 14, -Promo(CDN) 14
92/3 Score 504, 523, -YS 30
93/4 Score 333, -P.AS 31, -Int. 1
93/4 S-Dream 19, -Franchise 22
94/5 Score 190,DT24, NP5,TF24
95/6 Score 135, -Border 11
95/6 Score-Dream 10, -Lamp 2
96/7 Score 35,-Drm 10,-Sddn 6
97/8 Score 96, 261
97/8 Score(VAN) 1
96/7 SB'7Eleven
92/3 SeasonsPatch 31
93/4 SeasonsPatch 2
94/5 Select 92, FL6
95/6 SelectCertified 16, -Gold 5
96/7 SelectCertified 34, -Corn 7
91 SemicSticker 89
92 SemicSticker 116
95/6 SkBxEmotion 178,-Xcited16
95/6 SkyBoxImpact 167, -Ice 3
95/6 SkBxImpact-Countdown 9
96/7 SBI 131,-Versa 6,-Count 1
94/5 SP 121, -Premier 16
95/6 SP 149, E29, FX20
96/7 SP 157, CW16, -Force 2
97/8 SPAuthentic 156, I36
96/7 SPx 46
97/8 SPx 47, SPX 6
98/9 SPx"Finite" 84, 91, 170
96/7 SportFX MiniStix
97/8 SportFX MiniStix
91/2 StarPics 25
95/6 Summit 7, -GM 7, -Mad 7
96/7 Summit 42, 200
95/6 SuperSticker 123, -DC 14
96/7 TeamOut
92/3 Topps 8, 353
95/6 Topps 20, 300, 5CG
95/6 Topps 5HG, M15, PF11
98/9 Topps 180, L14, M3, SB15
94/5 ToppsFinest 24, -Div. 20
94/5 TF-BBest (Blue) 11
95/6 ToppsFinest 75, 187
94 ToppsFinestBronze 4
96/7 ToppsNHLPicks 15, FT13
91/2 TriGlobe 5,6
91/2 TriGlobeMagFive 6-10
92/3 T.StadiumClub 246, 489
93/4 T.StadiumClub 480, -AS
94/5 T.StadiumClub 10
94/5 TSC-Dynasty 3, -Finest 5
95/6 TSC EC186, EN1, N4
91/2 TSC-MembersOnly
94/5 TSC-MembersOnly 4
95/6 TSC-MembersOnly 41
97/8 ToppsSticker 3
95/6 ToppsSuperSkills 30
90/1 UpperDeck 524
91/2 UpperDeck 54, 555, 647
92/3 UpperDeck 156, 362, 431
92/3 UD E2, ERT1, WG5, SP2
92/3 UD-LockerAS 21
93/4 UpperDeck 35, 307, H2
93/4 UD HB5, SP-162, -Hero 30
94/5 UD 227, 469, H2, H19, R25
94/5 UD R31, R53, SP171
95/6 UpperDeck 214, 406, AS4
95/6 UD F10, R9, R26, SE172
96/7 UD 347, GJ10, HH14, LS18
96/7 UD SS1A, -AllStarYCTG A8
97/8 UD 168, S10, SG58
97/8 UD SS24, T5C
93/4 UDBeAPlayer 20, -Roots 15
94/5 UDBAP R35, R177, UC3
96/7 UDBlckDiamond 176, RC14
97/8 UDBlackDiamond 115, PC9
98/9 UDChoice 208, BH30, SQ2
95/6 UDCollChoice 45, C1
96/7 UDCollChoice 266, 333
96/7 UDCC C17, S16, UD22
97/8 UDCC 255, C24,S25,SQ59
97/8 udDiamondVision 10
96/7 UpperDeck"Ice" 105
97/8 UpperDeckIce 86
96 Wien 142
97/8 Zenith 34, Z59
91/2 VAN
91/2 VAN/Molson
93/4 VAN/Coins
94/5 VAN
95/6 VAN/Building 10
96/7 VAN
96/7 VAN/IGA

BURE, VALERI
95/6 Bowman 160, BB28
92/3 Classic 14, LP9, -Aut.
93/4 Classic 18
94/5 Classic 30, R4, T34
92/3 C'FourSport 163, BC8,LP24
94/5 ClassicImages 77
95/6 Donruss 102
96/7 Donruss-Rated 3
97/8 Donruss 8
96/7 DonrussCanadianIce 69
96/7 DonrussElite 119, -Asp. 8
97/8 DonrussElite 57
97/8 DonrussPreferred 75
97/8 DonrussPriority 95
95/6 EdgeIce 40, C11,-Quant 10
94/5 Flair 86
96/7 Fleer 52, 136, -Rookie 3
96/7 FleerNHLPicks 124
94/5 FleerUltra 311
95/6 FleerUltra 256
97/8 KatchMedallion 73
94/5 Leaf 471
95/6 Leaf 39
96/7 Leaf 207
96/7 LeafLimited 62
96/7 LeafPreferred 88, -Steel 43
97/8 Limited 7
95/6 McDonalds McD34
97/8 PacificCrown 116
96/7 PaniniSticker 34
97/8 PaniniSticker 31
93/4 Parkhurst 509, 528
95/6 Parkhurst 114, 511
94/5 ParkieSE 87
93/4 Pinnacle 501
94/5 Pinnacle 492
95/6 Pinnacle 174
96/7 Pinnacle 209
95/6 PinnacleZenith 125
96/7 PinnZenith 9, -Assialants 15
95/6 POG 147
94/5 Premier 337
95/6 ProMagnet 20
94/5 Score 215
95/6 Score 138
96/7 Score 245
97/8 Score 96
97/8 Score(MTL) 10
94/5 Select 187
95/6 SelectCertified 131
96/7 SelectCertified 18
95 Semic 134
91/2 SketchWHL 1
96/7 SkBxImpact 60,167,-Fox 4
94/5 SP-Premier 11
95/6 SP 74
96/7 SP 80, HC16
97/8 SPAuthentic 78
98/9 SPx"Finite" 14
95/6 Summit 197
96/7 Summit 160
95/6 Topps 358
95/6 ToppsStadiumClub 220
94/5 ToppsFinest 48
95/6 ToppsFinest 34
96/7 ToppsNHLPicks RS8
91/2 UpperDeck 647
93/4 UpperDeck 571
94/5 UpperDeck 255, C8, SP131
95/6 UpperDeck 304, SE46
96/7 UpperDeck 283, X29
94/5 UDBeAPlayer R159
95/6 UDBeAPlayer 34
97/8 UDBlackDiamond 6
98/9 UDChoice 31
95/6 UDCollChoice 119
96/7 UDCollChoice 141
97/8 UDCollChoice 132
95/6 MTL
95/6 MTL/Molson
96/7 MTL
97/8 MTL
94/5 Fredericton

BUREAU, MARC
91/2 Bowman 126, 417
92/3 Bowman 382
92/3 O-Pee-Chee 78
91/2 OPC/Topps 93
91/2 Parkhurst 302
92/3 Parkhurst 400
93/4 Parkhurst 461
91/2 Pinnacle 335
93/4 Pinnacle 321
96/7 PinnacleBeAPlayer 82
93/4 Premier 344
89/90 ProCards(IHL) 208
90/1 ProCards 603
91/2 ProSet 544
90/1 Score 423
91/2 Score(CDN) 476
97/8 Score(MTL) 19
92/3 Topps 179
98/9 Topps 140
91/2 ToppsStadiumClub 322
92/3 ToppsStadiumClub 30
93/4 ToppsStadiumClub 134
91/2 UpperDeck 274
95/6 MTL
96-98 MTL
92/3 T.B/Sheraton
94/5 T.B/SkyBoxSportsCafe
95/6 T.B/SkyBoxSportsCafe
88/9 SaltLake 24

BURFOOT, SCOTT
94/5 Erie

BURGER, JIRI
95/6 APS 88

BURGESS, DON
74/5 opcWHA 32
77/8 opcWHA 66
73/4 VancouverBlazers

BURGESS, TIM
82/3 Oshawa 16

BURGESS, TREVOR
96/7 DEL 132
90/1 SketchOHL 329
91/2 SketchOHL 162
93/4Greensboro
90/1 Oshawa 27
91/2 Oshawa
91/2 Oshawa/Dominos 3
92/3 Oshawa

BURGESS, VAN
90/1 SketchWHL 45
91/2 SketchWHL 170
93/4 PrinceAlbert

BURGOYNE, JARRET
89/90 Victoria

BURGOYNE, RYAN
95/6 Slapshot 162

BURKE, CLAUDE
36/7 WWGum (V356) 112

BURKE, DAVE
92/3 Greensboro 15

BURKE, DON
92/3 AtlantaKnights

BURKE, ED
33-35 DiamondMatch
36-39 DiamondMatch (1)

BURKE, GREG
96/7 DEL 111
93/4 Birmingham 17
95/6 Dayton

BURKE, JIM
90/1 ProCards 174
91/2 ProCards 111

BURKE, JUSTIN
90/1 SketchWHL 63

BURKE, MARTIN
34-43 BeeHives(CHI)
33/4 CndGum (V252)
35-40 CrownBrand 69
33-35 DiamondMatch
36-39 DiamondMatch (1), (2), (3)
36-39 DiamondMatch (4), (5), (6)
33/4 Hamilton (V288) 3
27-32 LaPresse 28/9
33/4 WWGum (V357) 14
36/7 WWGum (V356) 72
28/9 MTL/LaPatrie 11

BURKE, SEAN
91/2 Bowman 275
95/6 Bowman 26
91/2 CanadaNats
92 CanadaWinterOlympics 185
92/3 Classic 117
93/4 Donruss 141
94/5 Donruss 158
95/6 Donruss 28, -Between 8
96/7 Donruss 121
97/8 Donruss 128
96/7 DonrussCanadianIce 66
97/8 DonrussCanadianIce 99
95/6 DonrussElite 107
96/7 DonrussElite 51
97/8 DonrussElite 39
97/8 DonrussPreferred 104
97/8 DonrussPriority 44
97/8 DonrussStudio 62
93/4 EASports 60
94/5 Flair 70
94/5 Fleer 84
96/7 Fleer 45, -Vezina 2
95/6 FleerMetal 63
92/3 FleerUltra 68
93/4 FleerUltra 15
94/5 FleerUltra 87
95/6 FleerUltra 65, 367, -Pad 2
96/7 FleerUltra 73
88/9 FritoLay
97/8 KatchMedallion 25
89/90 Kraft 53, -Sticker 6
90/1 Kraft 4
92/3 Kraft-Disk
94/5 Kraft-Dinner
95/6 Kraft-Crease
93/4 Leaf 132
94/5 Leaf 85
95/6 Leaf 63
96/7 Leaf 85
97/8 Leaf 63
95/6 LeafLimited 14
96/7 LeafPreferred 85
97/8 Limited 119, 194
96/7 Maggers 73
96/7 MetalUniverse 66
97/8 Omega 229
88/9 OPC/Topps 94
89/90 OPC/Topps 92
90/1 OPC/Topps 140
91/2 OPC/Topps 67
92/3 opcPremier 92
88/9 opcSticker 82/211
89/90 opcSticker 86, 34/174
88/9 opcStickFS 4
89/90 opcStickFS 8
98/9 Pacific 321
97/8 PacificCrown 81
97/8 PcfcDynag! 20,-Tandem 37
97/8 PacificInvincible 22
97/8 PacificRevolution 140
88/9 PaniniSticker 267
89/90 PaniniSticker 185, 256
90/1 PaniniSticker 77
91/2 PaniniSticker 212
93/4 PaniniSticker 131
94/5 PaniniSticker 117
95/6 PaniniSticker 35
96/7 PaniniSticker 24
92/3 Parkhurst 57
95/6 Parkhurst 96
94/5 ParkieSE 71
92/3 Pinnacle 295
93/4 Pinnacle 31
94/5 Pinnacle 114, GT12
95/6 Pinnacle 124, -Masks 9
96/7 Pinnacle 37, 60
97/8 Pinnacle 42
96/7 PinnacleBeAPlayer 18
97/8 PinnacleCertified 25
97/8 PinnacleInside 30
95/6 PinnacleZenith 100
95/6 Playoff 45
94/5 POG 281
95/6 POG 131
93/4 PowerPlay 103
93/4 Premier 241
94/5 Premier 542
95/6 ProMagnet 126
90/1 ProSet 164
91/2 ProSet 132
92/3 ProSet PV2
90/1 Score 34,-Hot 17,-Young11
91/2 Score(CDN) 465, (U.S) 245
92/3 Score-CdnOlympicHero 13
93/4 Score 126, -Franchise 8
94/5 Score 84
95/6 Score 32, 320
96/7 Score 46
97/8 Score 1
94/5 Select 127
95/6 SelectCertified 100
96/7 SelectCertified 44
95/6 SkyBoxEmotion 73
95/6 SkBxImpact 71, -Deflect 4
96/7 SkyBoxImpact 52, -Zero 2
94/5 SP 51
95/6 SP 65
96/7 SP 70
95/6 Summit 125, -InThe 13
96/7 Summit 109
95/6 SuperSkills 76
95/6 SuperSticker 54
95/6 Topps 135
98/9 Topps 19
95/6 ToppsFinest 132
91/2 ToppsStadiumClub 76
93/4 ToppsStadiumClub 207
94/5 ToppsStadiumClub 171
95/6 ToppsStadiumClub 29
90/1 UpperDeck 66
91/2 UpperDeck 183
92/3 UpperDeck 518
94/5 UpperDeck 158
95/6 UpperDeck 130, SE39
96/7 UpperDeck 72
97/8 UpperDeck 31
94/5 UDBeAPlayer-Aut. 53
98/9 UDChoice 147, 252
95/6 UDCollChoice 199
96/7 UDCollChoice 119, 319
97/8 UDCollChoice 111
96/7 UpperDeck"Ice" 26
96 Wien 77
92/3 HFD/DairyMart
93/4 HFD/Coke
88/9 N.J/Caretta
89/90 N.J
90/1 N.J

BURKE, TIM
90/1 N.J
77/8 NovaScotia

BURKETT, MICHAEL
93/4 Mich.State

BURKHARD, ALFRED
94/5 DEL 25

BURKHOLDER, BARRY
83/4 Kingston 17
84/5 Kingston 12
85/6 Kingston 12

BURKHOLDER, DAVE
95/6 Slapshot 204

BURKITT, NOEL
95/6 Slapshot 400

BURKITT, TOBY
90/1 SketchOHL 354
91/2 SketchOHL 356

BURLIN, DICK
89/90 SemicElitserien 201

BURMAN, MICHAEL
90/1 SketchOHL 304
91/2 SketchOHL 62
93/4 Slapshot(NorthBay) 11
94/5 Knoxville 24
95/6 Richmond

BURNETT, GEORGE
91/2 SketchAwards 7
89/90 SketchOHL 124
91/2 SketchOHL 203
94/5 Slapshot(Kitchener) 35
95/6 Binghampton
96/7 Binghampton
89/90 NiagaraFalls

BURNETT, MATTHEW
92/3 Ottawa67s

BURNHAM, BRAD
91/2 FerrisState

BURNIE, STU
88/9 ProCards(Springfield)
90/1 ProCards 531

BURNS
91/2 AvantGardeBCJHL 159

BURNS, BOB
94/5 DEL 416
96/7 DEL 291

BURNS, CHARLES
68/9 Bauer
45-64 BeeHives(BOS)
62 CeramicTiles
70/1 Colgate Stamp 19
70/1 DadsCookies
70/1 EddieSargent 87
71/2 EddieSargent 87
72/3 EddieSargent 106
70/1 Esso Stamp
82? JDMcCarthy
68/9 OPC/Topps 108
69/70 OPC/Topps 129
70/1 OPC/Topps 44, -Deckle 13
71/2 OPC/Topps 238, Topps 21
72/3 OPC 178
61/2 ShirriffCoin 4
58/9 Topps 43
59/60 Topps 40
60/1 Topps 24
61/2 Topps 11, -Stamp
62/3 Topps 15
63/4 Topps 9
56-66 TorontoStar 62/3
71/2 TheTorontoSun

BURNS, DARREN
87/8 Brockville 10
88/9 Brockville 11

BURNS, LANCE
90/1 SketchWHL 130
91/2 SketchWHL 346

BURNS, NORMAN
34-43 BeeHives(NYR)

BURNS, PAT
93/4 Kraft-Coach
90/1 ProSet 669
88/9 MTL
89/90 MTL
89/90 MTL/Kraft
90/1 MTL
91/2 MTL

BURNS, R.R.
95/6 DEL 383

BURNS, ROB
74/5 Loblaws
75/6 OPC/Topps 104

BURNS, SEAN
90/1 SketchOHL 177
89/90 Windsor

BURR, SHAWN
90/1 Bowman 232
91/2 Bowman 43
92/3 Bowman 122
92/3 FleerUltra 44
93/4 Leaf 296
94/5 Leaf 368
87/8 OPC/Topps 164
88/9 OPC/Topps 78
89/90 OPC/Topps 101
90/1 OPC/Topps 74
91/2 OPC/Topps 184
92/3 O-Pee-Chee 24
87/8 opcStars 5
87/8 opcSticker 125/113
89/90 opcSticker 252/115
97/8 PacificCrown 152
97/8 PacificParamount 163
87/8 PaniniSticker 247
88/9 PaniniSticker 41
89/90 PaniniSticker 63
90/1 PaniniSticker 213
91/2 PaniniSticker 135
91/2 Parkhurst 45
93/4 Parkhurst 328
94/5 Parkhurst 62
95/6 Parkhurst 461
91/2 Pinnacle 86
92/3 Pinnacle 171
93/4 Pinnacle 93
94/5 Pinnacle 318
96/7 PinnacleBeAPlayer 191
93/4 Premier 83
90/1 ProSet 66
91/2 ProSet 58
92/3 ProSet 45
90/1 Score 49, -Hot 21
91/2 Score(CDN) 54, (U.S) 54
92/3 Score 207
93/4 Score 175
95/6 Score 13
94/5 Slapshot(Sarnia) 29
92/3 Topps 178
91/2 ToppsStadiumClub 101
92/3 ToppsStadiumClub 126
93/4 ToppsStadiumClub 313
90/1 UpperDeck 111
91/2 UpperDeck 315
93/4 UpperDeck 91
94/5 UpperDeck 484
95/6 UpperDeck 355
94/5 UDBeAPlayer-Aut. 93
96/7 UDCollChoice 254
86/7 DET/Caesars
87/8 DET/Caesars
88/9 DET/Caesars
88/9 DET/S.A.M.
89/90 DET/Caesars
90/1 DET/Caesars
91/2 DET/Caesars

97/8 S.J/PacificBellSheet
95/6 T.B.
83/4 Kitchener 18
84/5 Kitchener 22
85/6 Kitchener 21

BURRELL, RICK
93/4 Hampton
95/6 Hampton HRA -24

BURRIDGE, RANDY
91/2 Bowman 349, 410
92/3 Bowman 29, 225
93/4 Donruss 503
94/5 Donruss 66
96/7 Donruss 127
94/5 Flair 197
95/6 FleerMetal 13
93/4 FleerUltra 444
95/6 FleerUltra 210
94/5 Leaf 291
96/7 Leaf 121
86/7 OPC/Topps 70
88/9 OPC/Topps 33
89/90 OPC/Topps 121, OPC 303
90/1 OPC/Topps 190
91/2 OPC/Topps 358
92/3 O-Pee-Chee 370
91/2 opcPremier 43
88/9 opcSticker 159, 29/169
89/90 opcSticker 95, 144, 28/166
97/8 PacificRegime 18
88/9 PaniniSticker 208
89/90 PaniniSticker 197
91/2 PaniniSticker 174
92/3 PaniniSticker 163
91/2 Parkhurst 190
93/4 Parkhurst 492
95/6 Parkhurst 293
91/2 Pinnacle 55
92/3 Pinnacle 115
93/4 Pinnacle 418
94/5 Pinnacle 110
96/7 Pinnacle 198
97/8 PinnacleBeAPlayer 79
94/5 POG 243
93/4 PowerPlay 464
90/1 ProSet 2
91/2 ProSet 4, 510
92/3 ProSet 207
91/2 PSPlatinum 241
90/1 Score 72
91/2 Score(CDN) 102, 564
91/2 Score(U.S) 102, 14T
92/3 Score 297
93/4 Score 370
94/5 Score 90
95/6 Score 164
96/7 Score 52
97/8 Score(BUF) 6
96/7 Summit 26
92/3 Topps 83
95/6 ToppsFinest 21
91/2 ToppsStadiumClub 119
92/3 ToppsStadiumClub 61
93/4 ToppsStadiumClub 416
94/5 ToppsStadiumClub 163
90/1 UpperDeck 196
91/2 UpperDeck 567
92/3 UpperDeck 153
93/4 UpperDeck 504
95/6 UpperDeck 320, SE99
95/6 UDBeAPlayer 114
96/7 UDCollChoice 28
88/9 BOS/SportsAction
89/90 BOS/SportsAction
90/1 BOS/SportsAction
91/2 WSH
91/2 WSH/Kodak
92/3 WSH/Kodak

BURROWS, DAVE
77/8 Coke Mini
72/3 EddieSargent 182
74/5 Loblaws
72/3 OPC 133, Topps 82
73/4 OPC 140, Topps 27
74/5 OPC/Topps 137, 241
75/6 OPC/Topps 186
76/7 OPC/Topps 83
77/8 OPC/Topps 66
78/9 OPC/Topps 254
80/1 OPC/Topps 147
71/2 PGH
74/5 PGH
77/8 PGH/PuckBuck
78/9 TOR
79/80 TOR

BURSTROM, ANDERS
94/5 ElitSet 173
95/6 ElitSet 250
97/8 udSwedish 129

BURT, ADAM
90/1 Bowman 252
93/4 Donruss 139
92/3 FleerUltra 69
93/4 Leaf 280
90/1 O-Pee-Chee 431
97/8 PacificRegime 34
91/2 PaniniSticker 318
92/3 PaniniSticker 264
91/2 Parkhurst 291
91/2 Pinnacle 77
93/4 Pinnacle 313
94/5 Pinnacle 356
95/6 Pinnacle 200
96/7 PinnacleBeAPlayer 117
95/6 Playoff 155
90/1 ProSet 447
90/1 Score 370
91/2 Score(CDN) 449
92/3 Score 261
93/4 Score 307
92/3 Topps 283
95/6 Topps 184
92/3 ToppsStadiumClub 139
90/1 UpperDeck 324
95/6 UpperDeck 303
91/2 HFD/JuniorWhalers
92/3 HFD/DairyMart
93/4 HFD/Coke

BURTON, ARCHIE
52/3 AnonymousOHL 16

BURTON, CUMMING
52/3 AnonymousOHL 8

BURTON, JAMES
95 Globe 188
95 Semic 184
96 Wien 213

BURTON, JOE
92/3 Oklahoma

BURTON, JIM
95/6 Phoenix

BUSCH, R.
95/6 DEL 238

BUSCHAN, ANDREI
94/5 ClassicFourSport 152

BUSH, ED
34-43 BeeHives(DET)

BUSILLO, JOE
96/7 DEL 354
89/90 SketchMEM 86
89/90 SketchOHL 3
90/1 SketchMEM 16
90/1 SketchOHL 154
89/90 Oshawa 5

BUSKAS, ROD
90/1 O-Pee-Chee 509
87/8 PaniniSticker 144
91/2 Pinnacle 417
90/1 ProSet 456
90/1 ScoreTraded 12T
91/2 Score(CDN) 427
91/2 CHI/Coke
90/1 L.A/Smokeys 23
83/4 PGH
84/5 PGH/Heinz
86/7 PGH/Kodak
87/8 PGH/Kodak
92/3 Indianapolis
93/4 LasVegas

BUSNIUK, MIKE
80/1 O-Pee-Chee 326
81/2 O-Pee-Chee 249
91/2 SketchWHL 306
95/6 Binghampton
96/7 Binghampton

BUSNIUK, RON
74/5 Minnesota

BUSWELL, WALTER
34-43 BeeHives(MTL)
35-40 CrownBrand 113
36-39 DiamondMatch (3)
37/8 OPC (V304E) 174
39/40 OPC (V301-1) 32
38/9 QuakerOats
36/7 WWGum (V356) 32

BUTCHER, GARTH
91/2 Bowman 383
92/3 Bowman 124
93/4 Donruss 289, 477
93/4 EASports 122
92/3 FleerUltra 184
93/4 FleerUltra 27
84/5 KelownaWings&WHL 49
93/4 Leaf 239
94/5 Leaf 466
88/9 O-Pee-Chee 202
89/90 O-Pee-Chee 314
90/1 OPC/Topps 150
91/2 OPC/Topps 204
92/3 O-Pee-Chee 280
87/8 opcSticker 20 0/59
88/9 opcSticker 54 /185
89/90 opcSticker 72 /210
90/1 Panini(VAN) 5
87/8 PaniniSticker 343
88/9 PaniniSticker 134
89/90 PaniniSticker 158
91/2 PaniniSticker 28
92/3 PaniniSticker 24
93/4 PaniniSticker 164
91/2 Parkhurst 374
92/3 Parkhurst 390
93/4 Parkhurst 449
94/5 Parkhurst 188
91/2 Pinnacle 85, 409
92/3 Pinnacle 72
93/4 Pinnacle 66
94/5 Pinnacle 394
95/6 Pinnacle 53
93/4 PowerPlay 208
93/4 Premier 316
94/5 Premier 441
90/1 ProSet 295
91/2 ProSet 210, 583
92/3 ProSet 160
91/2 PSPlatinum 223
90/1 Score 18
91/2 Score(CDN) 24, (U.S) 24
92/3 Score 65
93/4 Score 173, -P.AS 24
94/5 Score 13
92/3 Topps 281
91/2 ToppsStadiumClub 223
92/3 ToppsStadiumClub 287
93/4 T.StadiumClub 21, -AllStar
90/1 UpperDeck 98
91/2 UpperDeck 397
83/4 Vachon 103
91/2 STL
82/3 VAN
83/4 VAN
84/5 VAN
85/6 VAN
86/7 VAN
87/8 VAN/Shell
88/9 VAN/Mohawk
89/90 VAN
90/1 VAN/Mohawk
81/2 Regina 2

BUTENSCHON, SVEN
94/5 Slapshot(MEM) 33
94/5 SRTetrad CIV

BUTKA, MIKE
89/90 Nashville
86/7 Saskatoon

BUTKO, SERGEJ
95/6 APS 158

BUTLER, JERRY
74/5 Loblaws
74/5 OPC 393
75/6 OPC/Topps 167
76/7 OPC 336
77/8 OPC 349
78/9 O-Pee-Chee 304
79/80 O-Pee-Chee 393
80/1 O-Pee-Chee 351
81/2 O-Pee-Chee 332
80/1 Pepsi Cap
78/9 TOR
80/1 VAN
80/1 VAN/Silverwood
81/2 VAN
81/2 VAN/Silverwood
82/3 WPG

BUTLER, JEROME
93/4 Minn-Duluth

BUTLER, ROB
95/6 Slapshot 395

BUTLER, ROD
93/4 Waterloo

BUTLER, STAN
95/6 Slapshot 255

BUTORAC, ALI
83/4 Belleville 19
81/2 Oshawa 4

BUTORAC, TONY
80/1 SSMarie

BUTSAYEV, VYACHESLAV
93/4 Classic 87
92/3 ClassicProspects 131
92/3 ClassicProspects BC14
92/3 FleerUltra 153
93/4 FleerUltra 385
93/4 Leaf 307
91/2 O-Pee-Chee 12R
92/3 opcPremier 31
92/3 Parkhurst 363
93/4 Parkhurst 151
94/5 Parkhurst 213
94/5 Pinnacle 498
93/4 Premier 79
92/3 RedAce(Blue) 14,(Violet) 14
93/4 Score 656
94 Semic 148
91 SemicSticker 90
92 SemicSticker 114
93/4 ToppsStadiumClub 94
92/3 UpperDeck 503
93/4 UpperDeck 406
94/5 UpperDeck 417
92/3 PHA/UD 03APR93
92/3 PHA/UD 08APR93
93/4 PHA 21DEC93
93/4 PHA/JCPenney
93/4 S.J/Gameline

BUTT, JAMIE
92/3 Tacoma
93/4 Tacoma

BUTT, KEVIN
89/90 SketchMEM 76
89/90 SketchOHL 18
90/1 SketchOHL 101
89/90 Oshawa 15

BUTTERFIELD, JACK
83&87 HallOfFame 167
83 HHOF Postcard (M)

BUTTERS, MIKE
90/1 ProCards 551
91/2 Greensboro

BUTZ, CRAIG
83/4 KelownaWings

BUTZ, ROB
95/6 StJohns
71/2 OPC/Topps 249, Topps 2

BUZAK, MIKE
95/6 EdgeIce 91
93/4 Mich.State

BUZAS, GYORGY
79 PaniniSticker 273

BUZEK, PETR
94/5 APS 167
95/6 Classic 52, -Aut.
95/6 ClassicFiveSport 133
94/5 SP 155

BYAKIN, ILYA
93/4 Donruss 427
95/6 ElitSet 261
94/5 FleerUltra 70
90/1 O-Pee-Chee 1R
91/2 O-Pee-Chee 13R
93/4 Parkhurst 341
93/4 PowerPlay 341
94/5 Premier 223
93/4 Score 619
95 Semic 124
91 SemicSticker 83
93 SemicSticker 131
89/90 SovietNats
95/6 udElite 136
96 Wien 138
93/4 EDM 29NOV94

BYATT, GUY
84/5 Chicoutimi

BYCE, JOHN
90/1 Bowman 38
91/2 ProCards 59
90/1 ScoreTraded 62T
90/1 UpperDeck 25
90/1 BOS/SportsAction

BUE, CARLOS
91/2 SketchWHL 217

BYE, KAREN
94/5 Classic W27

BYERS, JERRY
74/5 Loblaws
74/5 O-Pee-Chee 273

BYERS, LYNDON
90/1 O-Pee-Chee 464
90/1 ProSet 3
84/5 BOS
88/9 BOS/SportsAction
89/90 BOS/SportsAction
90/1 BOS/SportsAction
93/4 LasVegas
86/7 Moncton 19
81/2 Regina 3
82/3 Regina 20
83/4 Regina 20

BYERS, MIKE
68/9 ShirriffCoin TOR-17
70/1 Colgate Stamp 55
71/2 EddieSargent 80
70/1 Esso Stamp
70/1 OPC 160
71/2 OPC/Topps 34
71/2 TheTorontoSun
72/3 LosAngelesSharks
72/3 NewEngland

BYFUGLIEN, JAMIE
91/2 AirCanadaSJHL C21

BYKOV, VYACHESLAV (SLAVA)
95 Globe 180
90/1 O-Pee-Chee 10R
95 PaniniWorlds 49
94 Semic 145
95 Semic 138
89 SemicSticker 92
91 SemicSticker 100
93 SemicSticker 147
89/90 SovietNats
83/4 SovietStars
87/8 SovietStars
96 Wien 151

BYLSMA, DAN
97/8 PacificCrown 323
97/8 PinnacleBeAPlayer 29
96/7 UpperDeck 276
92/3 Greensboro 6
93/4 Greensboro
95/6 Phoenix

BYLSMA, SHELDON
91/2 AirCanadaSJHL D29
92/3 MPSPhotoSJHL 167

BYRAM, SHAWN
88/9 ProCards(Springfield)
89/90 ProCards(AHL) 235
90/1 ProCards 496
91/2 ProCards 482
92/3 Indianapolis

BYRNES, JASON
94/5 Slapshot(Kitchener) 7
95/6 Slapshot 146

BYRON, J.W.
24/5 Crescent Falcons 2
24/5 Holland 8

BYSTROM, LARS
94/5 ElitSet 92, -Studio 9
95/6 ElitSet 109
89/90 SemicElitserien 182
90/1 SemicElitserien 17
91/2 SemicElitserien 216
92/3 SemicElitserien 245
95/6 udElite 169

BZDEL, GERALD
88/9 ProCards(Haifaxl)
89/90 ProCards(AHL) 174
90/1 ProCards 444
91/2 ProCards 529
89/90 Halifax
90/1 Halifax

BZDEL, MIKE
92/3 BCJHL 150

C

CABANA, CHADDEN
91/2 SketchWHL 298

CADDEN, CORY
93/4 Knoxville
94/5 Knoxville 23

CADIEUX, STEVE
91/2 Cincinnati

CADOTTS, MARK
95/6 Slapshot 78

CAFFERY, JACK
52/3 AnonymousOHL 154
45-64 BeeHives(BOS)
55/6 Parkhurst 19
93/4 Parkie(56/7) 12
57/8 Topps 8

CAFFERY, TERRY
69/70 O-Pee-Chee 135
72/3 NewEngland

CAGAS, PAVEL
94/5 APS 1
95/6 APS 101
96/7 DEL 226

CAHAN, LARRY
45-64 BeeHives(NYRx3), (TOR)
64-67 BeeHives(NYR)
62 CeramicTiles
70/1 DadsCookies
70/1 EddieSargent 79
70/1 Esso Stamp
70/1 OPC 164
72/3 OPC 307
68/9 OPC/Topps 35
55/6 Parkhurst 16
93/4 Parkie(56/7) 87
61/2 ShirriffCoin 95
71/2 TheTorontoSun
57/8 Topps 59
58/9 Topps 23
61/2 Topps 52
62/3 Topps 48
63/4 Topps 51

CAHILL, DARCY
90/1 SketchOHL 204

CAHOON, JIM
77/8 NovaScotia

CAHTINEN, TIMO
92/3 SemicElitserien 331

CAIN, AARON
91/2 AirCanadaSJHL A39
92/3 MPSPhotoSJHL 23

CAIN, HERBERT
34-43 BeeHives(MTL.M)
35-40 CrownBrand 78, 152
35/6 OPC(V304C) 77
36/7 OPC(V304D) 110
37/8 OPC(V304E) 172
39/40 OPC(V301-1) 42
38/9 QuakerOats
34/5 SweetCaporal
36/7 WWGum(V356) 46

CAIN, JIM (DUTCH)
25-27 Anonymous 91
24/5 Champs(C144)
24/5 MapleCrispette(V130) 16
24/5 (V145-2) 35

CAIRNS, ERIC
97/8 PacificCrown 301
97/8 PinnacleBeAPlayer 28
91/2 SketchOHL 31
93/4 Slapshot(Detroit) 7
94/5 Binghampton
95/6 Binghampton

CAIRNS, TREVOR
93/4 Tacoma

CAISSIE, JEREMY
91/2 SketchQMJHL 279

CAJANEK, PETR
94/5 APS 202
95/6 APS 46
94/5 ParkieSE 214
94/5 UpperDeck 507

CALCE, LUIGI
91/2 SketchOHL 282
93/4 OwenSound

CALDER, FRANK
83&87 HallOfFame 18
83 HHOF Postcard (B)
93/4 HHOFLegends 36

CALDER, GLENN
91/2 AvantGardeBCJHL 79
92/3 BCJHL 98

CALDER, PIERRE
90/1 SketchQMJHL 61

CALDER, SHANE
90/1 SketchWHL 73
91/2 SketchWHL 109
96/7 Penascola 18
90/1 Saskatoon 13
91/2 Saskatoon 11
93/4 Saskatoon

CALDR, VLADIMIR
94/5 APS 286
95/6 APS 51

CALDWELL, JUSTIN
93/4 WestMichigan

CALLAHAN, GARY
88/9 ProCards(Binghampton)

CALLAHAN, JACK
94/5 AutoPhonex 11
94/5 Knoxville 14

CALLANDER, DREW
79/80 VAN

CALLANDER, JOCK
95/6 EdgeIce 115
88/9 ProCards(Mus)
90/1 ProCards 371
91/2 ProCards 291
92/3 ProSet 175
93/4 UpperDeck 10
87/8 PGH/Kodak
92/3 AtlantaKnights
93/4 Cleveland
95/6 Cleveland
81/2 Regina 4

CALLIGHEN, BRETT
79/80 O-Pee-Chee 315
81/2 O-Pee-Chee 110
82/3 O-Pee-Chee 103
80/1 OPC/Topps 114
81/2 opcSticker 212
80/1 Pepsi Cap
81/2 Post PopUp 20
82/3 Post
79/80 EDM
80/1 EDM/Zellers
81/2 EDM/RedRooster
88/9 EDM/ActionMagazine 50

CALLINAN, JEFF
95/6 Birmingham

CALOUN, JAN
92/3 Classic 38
92/3 C'FourSport-Aut.
94/5 ClassicImages 23, PR10
95/6 EdgeIce 144
95/6 FutureLegends 16
96/7 Leaf 217
96/7 MetalUniverse 173
96/7 Pinnacle 229
95 Semic 159
96/7 Summit 187
91/2 UD'CzechWJC 91
96/7 UpperDeck 195

CALVANESE, RALPH
88/9 ProCards(Springfield)

CALVERLY, CHRIS
84/5 Victoria

CALVERT, JEFF
90/1 SketchWHL 159
91/2 SketchWHL 153
92/3 Tacoma
93/4 Tacoma

CAMAZZOLA, JIMMY
95 Globe 234
92 SemicSticker
93 SemicSticker 212

CAMERON, AL
77/8 OPC/Topps 48
78/9 O-Pee-Chee 396
80/1 Pepsi Cap
79/80 WPG
80/1 WPG

CAMERON, CRAIG
74/5 Loblaws, -Update
72/3 OPC 13, Topps 22
73/4 OPC 42, Topps 147
74/5 OPC/Topps 263
75/6 OPC/Topps 239
76/7 OPC 327

CAMERON, DAVE
82/3 Post
81/2 COL.R
83/4 N.J

CAMERON, DAVID
98 BowmanCHL 141, A29

CAMERON, DON
26 Dominion 25

CAMERON, HARRY
83&87 HallOfFame 95
83 HHOF Postcard (G)

CAMERON, J
25 Dominion 70

CAMERON, JULIAN
89/90 SketchMEM 52

CAMERON, MALCOLM
93/4 Huntington

CAMERON, RANDY
84/5 KelownaWings 7

CAMMOCK, DAVE
91/2 SketchWHL 36
93/4 Portland

CAMPBELL, AARON
91/2 AirCanadaSJHL A33

CAMPBELL, ANGUS
83&87 HallOfFame 125
83 HHOF Postcard (I)
1910-11 Imperial (C56) 9

CAMPBELL, BRIAN
98 BowmanCHL 23
95/6 Slapshot 275

CAMPBELL, BRYAN
70/1 Esso Stamp
69/70 O-Pee-Chee 106
71/2 OPC/Topps 214
73/4 OPC-Posters 19
74/5 OPCWHA 6
75/6 OPCWHA 31
76/7 OPCWHA 16
77/8 OPCWHA 22
73/4 QuakerOats 13
71/2 TheTorontoSun
70/1 CHI
75/6 Cincinnati
73/4 VancouverBlazers

CAMPBELL, CAMERON
92/3 BCJHL 28

CAMPBELL, CASSIE
94/5 Classic W5
97/8 EssoOlympic 59
97/8 GameOfHerLife
97/8 General Mills
97/8 UDCollChoice 281

CAMPBELL, CLARENCE
83&87 HallOfFame 4
83 HHOF Postcard (A)

CAMPBELL, COLIN
75/6 O-Pee-Chee 346
76/7 O-Pee-Chee 372
78/9 O-Pee-Chee 269
79/80 O-Pee-Chee 339
80/1 O-Pee-Chee 380
81/2 O-Pee-Chee 333
82/3 O-Pee-Chee 82
83/4 O-Pee-Chee 119
84/5 O-Pee-Chee 51, Topps 39
80/1 Pepsi Cap
83/4 SouhaitsRen.KeyChains
76/7 COL.R
76/7 COL.R/CokeCans
84/5 DET/Caesars
89/90 DET/Caesars
79/80 EDM
88/9 EDM/ActionMagazine 123
74/5 PGH
77/8 PGH/PuckBuck
80/1 VAN
80/1 VAN/Silverwood
81/2 VAN
81/2 VAN/Silverwood
73/4 VancouverBlazers

CAMPBELL, DUKE
49 TurfCigarette s 37

CAMPBELL, ED
96/7 Binghampton

CAMPBELL, JASON
95/6 Slapshot 292
93/4 OwenSound

CAMPBELL, JIM
97/8 Aces 9 (Spades)
91/2 Arena 21
91/2 Classic 25
91/2 ClassicFourSport 25, -Aut.
93/4 C4'Images 46
93/4 ClassicProspects LP1
97/8 Donruss 111
96/7 D.CanadianIce 132
97/8 D.CanadianIce 9
96/7 D.Elite 142, -Aspirations 7
97/8 DonrussElite 78
97/8 DonrussPreferred 98
97/8 DonrussPriority 94
97/8 DonrussStudio 34
96/7 Flair 123
93/4 FleerUltra 479
96/7 FleerUltra 144, -Rookies 4
96/7 Got-UmHockeyGreatsCoin
97/8 KatchMedallion 127
97/8 Leaf 54
96/7 LeafPreferred 147
97/8 Limited 51, 67, 99
97/8 Omega 189
98/9 Pacific 362
97/8 PacificCrown 332
97/8 PacificCrownRoyale 113
97/8 PacificDynagon! 105, 143
97/8 PcfcD-Dyn14A,-Tand 18,58
97/8 PcfcInvincible 117,-Feat 30
97/8 PacificParamount 155
98/9 PacificParamount 198
97/8 PacificRevolution 117
98/9 PaniniSticker 248
95 PaniniWorlds 233
97/8 Pinnacle 130
96/7 PinnacleBeAPlayer LTH7A
97/8 PinnacleCertified 52
97/8 PinnacleInside 66
96/7 PinnacleMint 30
96/7 PinnacleZenith 129
93/4 PowerPlay 499
93/4 Premier-TeamUSA 17
97/8 Score 215
97/8 Score(STL) 4
96/7 SelectCertified 106
91/2 SketchQMJHL 209
96/7 SP 187
97/8 SPAuthentic 137
91/2 StarPics 62
93/4 T.StadiumClub-TmUSA 2
91/2 UltimateDP 19, -Aut 19
91/2 UD'CzechWJC 71
92/3 UpperDeck 605
96/7 UpperDeck 328
97/8 UD 143, SG46, T15A
98/9 UDChoice 189
96/7 UDCollChoice 360
97/8 UDCollChoice 228
96/7 UDBlackDiamond 142
96/7 UpperDeck"Ice" 64
97/8 UpperDeckIce 13
94/5 Fredericton
95/6 Fredericton

CAMPBELL, JOHN
89/90 SSMarie 28

CAMPBELL, PETER
96/7 Sudbury 7

CAMPBELL, RICH
93/4 LasVegas
94/5 LasVegas

CAMPBELL, SCOTT
94/5 DEL 7
95/6 DEL 4
96/7 DEL 4
89/90 SketchOHL 103
90/1 SketchOHL 355
91/2 SketchOHL 201

CAMPBELL, SCOTT
80/1 Pepsi Cap
79/80 WPG
80/1 WPG
77/8 WinnipegJets

CAMPBELL, SPIFF
24/5 Champs (C144)
24/5 (V145-2) 8

CAMPBELL, TERRY
94/5 DEL 407
96/7 DEL 16

CAMPBELL, WADE
83/4 O-Pee-Chee 382
84/5 O-Pee-Chee 336
89/90 ProCards'AHL 130
90/1 ProCards 221
83/4 Vachon 124
82/3 WPG
83/4 WPG
86/7 Moncton 16

CAMPEAU, BERT
25-27 Anonymous 64

CAMPEAU, CHRISTIAN
90/1 SketchQMJHL 72
91/2 SketchQMJHL 35
92/3 AtlantaKnights
93/4 AtlantaKnights

CAMPEAU, JASON
93/4 Slapshot(NorthBay) 7
94/5 Slapshot(NorthBay) 8
91/2 SketchOHL 152

CAMPEAU, J.C. (TOD)
45-64 BeeHives(MTL)
51-54 LaPatrie 29Mar53
51/2 LavalDairy 43
43-47 ParadeSportive
45-54 QuakerOats
52/3 StLawrence 77

CAMPESE, BRUNO
96/7 DEL 2
95 Globe 227
95 PaniniWorlds 76
96 Wien 175
83/4 KelownaWings

CANALE, JOE
91/2 SketchAwards 27
90/1 SketchMEM 46
90/1 SketchQMJHL 43
91/2 SketchQMJHL 97

CANIELSSON, MARTIN
92/3 SemicElitserien 134

CANNON, JASON
95/6 Slapshot 15

CANTU, KRIS
94/5 Slapshot(NorthBay) 13
95/6 Slapshot 219

CAPEK, IVO
94/5 APS 71
95/6 APS 269

CAPELLO, JEFF
88/9 ProCards(Rochester)

CAPILLAS, ANTONIO
79 PaniniSticker 375

CAPLA, BORIS
94/5 DEL 391

CAPLETTE, GUY
88/9 Richelieu

CAPLICE, SHAWN
90/1 SketchOHL 28
91/2 SketchOHL 223
92/3 Ottawa

CAPRICE, FRANK
87/8 PaniniSticker 339
89/90 ProCards'AHL 72
84/5 VAN
85/6 VAN
86/7 VAN
87/8 VAN/Shell
82/3 Fredericton 13
83/4 Fredericton 2
86/7 Fredericton

CAPSON, GREG
92/3 Greensboro 17
93/4 Greensboro

CAPUANO, DAVE
91/2 Bowman 323
90/1 OPC/Topps 170
91/2 OPC/Topps 318
90/1 Panini(VAN) 6
91/2 PaniniSticker 41
89/90 ProCards'IHL 145
90/1 ProSet 543
91/2 ProSet 237
90/1 ScoreTraded 105T
91/2 Score(CDN) 86, (U.S) 86
91/2 ToppsStadiumClub 53
91/2 UpperDeck 202
90/1 VAN/Mohawk

CAPUANO, JACK
88/9 ProCards(Newmarket)
91/2 ProCards 55

CAPUTO, DINO
90/1 SketchWHL 245
89/90 Victoria

CARBONNEAU, GUY
90/1 Bowman 44
91/2 Bowman 338
92/3 Bowman 38
93/4 Donruss 450
92/3 Durivage 1
93/4 Durivage 9
92/3 FleerUltra 102, -AW 3
93/4 FleerUltra 350
95/6 FleerUltra 228
86/7 Kraft Sports 21
89/90 Kraft 19
91/2 Kraft 79
93/4 Kraft-Captain
94/5 Leaf 23
96/7 Leaf 35
83/4 O-Pee-Chee 185
84/5 O-Pee-Chee 257
85/6 O-Pee-Chee 233
86/7 OPC/Topps 176
87/8 O-Pee-Chee 232
88/9 O-Pee-Chee 203
89/90 OPC/Topps 53, OPC 329
90/1 OPC/Topps 93
91/2 OPC/Topps 54
92/3 O-Pee-Chee 206
91/2 opcPremier 152
88/9 opcStars 4
83/4 opcSticker 180
84/5 opcSticker 160
85/6 opcSticker135 /255
86/7 opcSticker 7/152
87/8 opcSticker 7/146
88/9 opcSticker 41/172, 209/80
89/90 opcSticker 213/74, 48/194
98/9 Pacific 173
97/8 PacificCrown 292
90/1 Panini(MTL) 2
87/8 PaniniSticker 64
88/9 PaniniSticker 256, 407
89/90 PaniniSticker 241, 381
90/1 PaniniSticker 58
91/2 PaniniSticker 197
92/3 PaniniSticker 149
93/4 PaniniSticker 19
94/5 PaniniSticker 10
91/2 Parkhurst 92, 466
92/3 Parkhurst 485, 508
93/4 Parkhurst 372
95/6 Parkhurst 332
94/5 ParkieSE 155
91/2 Pinnacle 130, 374
92/3 Pinnacle 43
93/4 Pinnacle 280, -Promo 280
93/4 Pinnacle CA12
94/5 Pinnacle 372
95/6 Pinnacle 144
97/8 PinnacleBeAPlayer 194
93/4 PowerPlay 126
93/4 Premier 250
94/5 Premier 282
90/1 ProSet 146
91/2 ProSet 130, 345, 576
92/3 ProSet 88, CC5
91/2 ProSet -ThePuck 15
91/2 PSPlatinum 63
87/8 ProSportWatch CW2
90/1 Score 91, -HotCards 43
91/2 Score(CDN) 19, (U.S) 19
92/3 Score 269, 524
93/4 Score 51
94/5 Score 46
95/6 Score 280
85/6 7Eleven 10
92/3 Topps 125
98/9 Topps 106
91/2 ToppsStadiumClub 31
92/3 T.StadiumClub 260, 289
93/4 ToppsStadiumClub 1
94/5 ToppsStadiumClub 174
95/6 ToppsStadiumClub M12
91/2 TSC-MembersOnly
90/1 UpperDeck 188
91/2 UpperDeck 265
92/3 UpperDeck 260, 439
94/5 UpperDeck 122
95/6 UpperDeck 273
93/4 UDBeAPlayer'Roots 9
94/5 UDBAP R67, -Aut. 106
95/6 UDCollChoice 302
96/7 UDCollChoice 73
83/4 Vachon 41
96/7 DAL/Southwest
82/3 MTL
82/3 MTL/Steinber
83/4 MTL
84/5 MTL
85/6 MTL
85/6 MTL/Pennant
85/6 MTL/PepsiPlacemats
85/6 MTL/ProvPlacemats
85/6 MTL/ProvStickers
87/8 MTL
87/8 MTL/Kodak
87/8 MTL/Stickers 14, 15, 16, 21
87/8 MTL/Stickers 23, 62, 63
88/9 MTL
89/90 MTL
89/90 MTL/Figurine
89/90 MTL/Kraft
90/1 MTL
91/2 MTL
92/3 MTL
92/3 MTL/OPC 9
93/4 MTL
93/4 MTL/Molson

CARDARELLI, JOE
95/6 Spokane 21

CARDIFF, JIM
73/4 QuakerOats 31

CARDIFF, MARK
90/1 SketchOHL 256
91/2 SketchOHL 207

CARDINAL, C.
92/3 MPSPhotoSJHL 13

CARDINAL, CURTIS
93/4 RedDeer

CARDINAL, ERIC
90/1 SketchQMJHL 110
91/2 SketchQMJHL 232

CARDINAL, SYLVAIN
91/2 SketchQMJHL 93

CAREY, J.
91/2 SketchWHL 285

CAREY, JIM
95/6 Aces 6 (Spades)
96/7 Aces J (Spades)
95/6 Bowman 74
94/5 ClassicImages 4, 99
94/5 ClassicImages CE4, PR2
95/6 Donruss 189, -Dominator 6
95/6 D-Between 6, -Rookie 1
96/7 Donruss 33, -Dom 1, -Bet 3
97/8 Donruss 22
96/7 DonrussCanadianIce 79
97/8 DonrussCanadianIce 59
95/6 Don.Elite 69, -Painted 10
96/7 DonrussElite 19, -Painted 3
97/8 D.Preferred 43,-ColGrd 13
97/8 DonrussStudio 45
95/6 EdgeIce 52, C5, TW7
95/6 EdgeIce-Quantum 8
96/7 Flair 98, -HotGloves 3
94/5 Fleer 233
96/7 Fleer 116,144-46, -Vezina 3
95/6 FleerMetal 157
95/6 FleerUltra 173, 320, 368
95/6 FU-AllRookie 1, -PrmrPad 4
96/7 FleerUltra 174, -Clear 1
96/7 F.Picks-Fab 6, -Jagged 12
97/8 KatchMedallion 9
96/7 KennerSLU
95/6 Kraft-CreaseKeeper
96/7 Kraft-TrophyTriumph
95/6 Leaf 78, -Freeze 1, -Gold 1
95/6 Leaf-StudioRookie 1
96/7 Leaf 68, -Shut 10, -Sweat 9
97/8 Leaf 71, -PipeDreams 10
95/6 LeafLimited 55, -Stick 1
96/7 LeafLimited 16, -Stubble 5
96/7 L.Pref. 23,-Mask 1,-Steel 21
97/8 Limited 14, 131, -fabric 54
96/7 Maggers 167
95/6 McDonalds McD40
96/7 McDonalds M cD32
96/7 MetalUniverse 162
96/7 MU-Armour 3, -IceCarv 3
97/8 PacificCrown 23
97/8 PacificDynagon! 8
97/8 PcfcD-BstKpt 6,-Dynam 2B
97/8 PcfcD-Stone 2,-Tandem 17
97/8 PacificInvincible 8
97/8 PacificParamount 10
97/8 PacificRegime 11
95/6 PaniniSticker 145, 303
96/7 PaniniSticker 134, 154
97/8 PaniniSticker 8
95/6 Parkhurst 492, PP36
95/6 PH-Crown(1) 16, -Goal 5
95/6 Pinnacle 138, -Masks 3
95/6 Pinnacle-Roaring20s 9
96/7 Pinnacle 105, -Masks 10
97/8 Pinnacle 83
96/7 PinnacleBAP-Stacking 8
97/8 PinnacleCertified 15
95/6 PinnacleFANtasy 20
97/8 P.Inside 62, -Stand Up 3
97/8 P.Inside -Stop 7
96/7 PinnacleMint 28
95/6 PinnZenith 5, -ZTeam 18
96/7 PinnZenith 7, -ZTeam 15
95/6 Playoff 104, 213
96/7 Playoff 426
95/6 POG 287, 027
95/6 ProMagnet 26
95/6 Score 78, 317, -Dream 12
96/7 Score 74, -Net 3, -Sudden 2
97/8 Score 14, -NetWorth 2
97/8 Score(BOS) 2
95/6 SelectCert. 12, -Future 2
96/7 SelectCert. 29, -Freezer 3
94/5 Sig.Rookies 44
95/6 SRDraftDay JC1-JC5
95/6 SkBxEmotion 186,-Xcited19
95/6 SkyBoxImpact 175, 228
95/6 SkyBoxImpact-Deflect 2
96/7 SkyBoxImpact 137, -Zero 3
94/5 SP 128
95/6 SP 156
96/7 SP 164, GF13
96/7 SPx 48
95/6 Summit 51, -InTheCrease 6
96/7 Summit 94,-InCr 6,-Unt 14
95/6 SuperSticker 128, 131
96/7 TeamOut
95/6 Tetrad F7, -Aut'Promo 2
95/6 Topps 210, 383, 1NG, YS8
95/6 ToppsFinest 66
96/7 ToppsPicks 13, ID9
95/6 T.StadiumClub 115, G6
95/6 ToppsSuperSkills 73
95/6 UD 344, F20, H16, SE87
96/7 UpperDeck 174, SS14A
95/6 UDBeAPlayer 189
96/7 UDBlackDiamond 147
95/6 UDCC 30, 369, 375
96/7 UDCC 278, 334, S17
97/8 UDCC 17, SQ57
96/7 UpperDeck"Ice" 72
96 Wien 157, SG5
95/6 WSH

CARIGNAN, PATRICK
91/2 SketchQMJHL 160

CARKNER, TERRY
91/2 Bowman 232
92/3 Bowman 129
93/4 Donruss 422
92/3 FleerUltra 370
93/4 FleerUltra 304
89/90 OPC/Topps 3
90/1 OPC/Topps 381
91/2 OPC/Topps 291, 329
92/3 O-Pee-Chee 180
97/8 PacificRegime 84
89/90 PaniniSticker 297
90/1 PaniniSticker 114
91/2 PaniniSticker 235
92/3 PaniniSticker 190
93/4 PaniniSticker 54
91/2 Parkhurst 342
92/3 Parkhurst 362
93/4 Parkhurst 332
94/5 Parkhurst 69
95/6 Parkhurst 354
91/2 Pinnacle 51
92/3 Pinnacle 63
93/4 Pinnacle 286
94/5 Pinnacle 221
97/8 PinnacleBeAPlayer 195
93/4 PowerPlay 328
93/4 Premier 152
94/5 Premier 359
90/1 ProSet 212
91/2 ProSet 173
92/3 ProSet 269
91/2 PSPlatinum 212
90/1 Score 47
91/2 Score(CDN) 64, (U.S) 64
92/3 Score 66
93/4 Score 233, 508
92/3 Topps 465
91/2 ToppsStadiumClub 219
92/3 ToppsStadiumClub 463
93/4 ToppsStadiumClub 252
90/1 UpperDeck 398
91/2 UpperDeck 204
94/5 UpperDeck 467
95/6 UpperDeck 286
97/8 UpperDeck 283
94/5 UDBAP R167, -Aut. 144
95/6 UDCollChoice 113
96/7 UDCollChoice 109
96/7 FLA/WinnDixie
97/8 FLA/WinnDixie
89/90 PHA
90/1 PHA
91/2 PHA/JCPenney
92/3 PHA/JCPenney
92/3 PHA/UD 03DEC92
92/3 PHA/UD 16MAR93
92/3 PHA/UD 17JAN93
93/4 PHA 26S EP93
87/8 QUE/GeneralFoods

CARLETON, WAYNE
70/1 EddieSargent 6
71/2 EddieSargent 131
70/1 Esso Stamp
72/3 Letraset 18
69/70 O-Pee-Chee 184
70/1 OPC/Topps 9, -Sticker
71/2 OPC/Topps 178
72/3 O-Pee-Chee 337
73/4 OPC-Posters 8
74/5 opcWHA 45
75/6 opcWHA 43
68/9 Post Marble
72/3 7ElevenCups
68/9 ShirriffCoin(TOR) 2
71/2 TheTorontoSun
67/8 Topps 77
91/2 Ultimate06 47, -Aut. 47
70/1 BOS
69/70 TOR
72/3 OttawaNationals

CARLSSON, ANDERS
94/5 ElitSet 210
95/6 ElitSet 236, -Champs 5
88/9 ProCards(Utica)
89/90 SemicElitserien 38

90/1 SemicElitserien 185
91/2 SemicElitserien 354
92/3 SemicElitserien 61
91 SemicSticker 48
95/6 udElite 102
97/8 udSwedish 109, C9
88/9 N.J./Caretta

CARLSSON, ARNE
70/1 Kuvajulkaisut 23
72 Panda
72 SemicSticker 50
74 SemicSticker 3
71/2 WilliamsFIN 43
73/4 WilliamsFIN 25

CARLSSON, BJORN
89/90 SemicElitserien 228
90/1 SemicElitserien 65
91/2 SemicElitserien 240

CARLSSON, CALLE
92/3 UpperDeck 228

CARLSON, DON
85/6 ArizonaIceCats

CARLSON, JACK
80/1 MIN
81/2 MIN

CARLSON, JAMIE
92/3 Hamilton

CARLSSON, DANIEL
97/8 udSwedish 35

CARLSSON, KEN
83/4 Vachon 42
83/4 MTL
84/5 MTL

CARLSSON, LEIF
96/7 DEL 29
95/6 ElitSet 219
89/90 SemicElitserien 268
90/1 SemicElitserien 29
91/2 SemicElitserien 84
92/3 SemicElitserien 106
95/6 udElite 63

CARLSSON, PER-OLOF
89/90 SemicElitserien 133
90/1 SemicElitserien 212
91/2 SemicElitserien 141
92/3 SemicElitserien 168

CARLSSON, ROLAND
95/6 Sisu 5

CARLSON, STEVE
89/90 Johnstown 36

CARLSSON, THOMAS
94/5 ElitSet 129
89/90 SemicElitserien 224
91/2 SemicElitserien 233

CARLYLE, RANDY
91/2 Bowman 199
92/3 Bowman 287
86/7 Kraft Sports 73
89/90 Kraft 47
78/9 O-Pee-Chee 312
79/80 OPC/Topps 124
80/1 O-Pee-Chee 367
81/2 OPC 256, Topps(E) 112
82/3 O-Pee-Chee 265-66
83/4 O-Pee-Chee 278
84/5 O-Pee-Chee 337
85/6 OPC/Topps 57
86/7 OPC/Topps 144
87/8 OPC/Topps 9
88/9 O-Pee-Chee 204
89/90 O-Pee-Chee 291
90/1 OPC/Topps 51
91/2 OPC/Topps 72
92/3 O-Pee-Chee 12
81/2 opcSticker 183, 255
82/3 opcSticker 144
83/4 opcSticker 227
84/5 opcSticker 291
85/6 opcSticker 251
86/7 opcSticker 107/237
87/8 opcSticker 248/138
88/9 opcSticker 148
89/90 opcSticker 143/264
90/1 Panini(WPG) 4
87/8 PaniniSticker 360
88/9 PaniniSticker 149
89/90 PaniniSticker 168
90/1 PaniniSticker 314
91/2 PaniniSticker 76
91/2 Parkhurst 418
91/2 Pinnacle 288
92/3 Pinnacle 87
81/2 Post PopUp 8
82/3 Post (PGH)
93/4 Premier 86
90/1 ProSet 325
91/2 ProSet 273
92/3 ProSet 265
83/4 FunmatePuffySticker 12
90/1 Score 136
91/2 Score(CDN) 125, (U.S) 125
92/3 Score 167
93/4 Score-PinnacleAS 27
83/4 SouhaitsRen.KeyChain
92/3 Topps 147
91/2 ToppsStadiumClub 94
92/3 ToppsStadiumClub 332
93/4 T.StadiumClub-AllStar
90/1 UpperDeck 331
83/4 PGH
83/4 PGH/Heinz
84/5 PGH/Heinz
76/7 TOR
77/8 TOR
84/5 WPG/Police
85/6 WPG
85/6 WPG/Police
85/6 WPG/Silverwood
86/7 WPG
87/8 WPG
88/9 WPG
89/90 WPG/Safeway
90/1 WPG/IGA
91/2 WPG/IGA
95/6 WPG

CARNBACK, PATRIK
92/3 ClassicProspects 105
96/7 DEL 359
93/4 Donruss 6
94/5 Donruss 29
94/5 ElitSet 270
94/5 Fleer 1
93/4 FleerUltra 251
95 Globe 41
95/6 Hoyle'WEST 7 (Hearts)
94/5 Leaf 102
94/5 PaniniSticker N
95/6 PaniniSticker 224
95 PaniniWorlds 152
93/4 Parkhurst 8
94/5 Parkhurst 7, V28
95/6 Parkhurst 1
94/5 Pinnacle 189
95/6 Playoff 111
93/4 PowerPlay 281
93/4 Premier 379
94/5 Premier-Finest(OPC) 1
95/6 ProMagnet 36
93/4 Score 615
95 Semic 74
89/90 SemicElitserien 276
90/1 SemicElitserien 37
91/2 SemicElitserien 287
91 SemicSticker 46
93 SemicSticker 43
95/6 Topps 335
93/4 ToppsStadiumClub 434
94/5 ToppsStadiumClub 53
93/4 UpperDeck 463
94/5 UpperDeck 475
95/6 UpperDeck 180
95/6 UDCollChoice 42
95/6 udElite 241
97/8 udSwedish S13
96 Wien 63
94/5 ANA/Carl'sJr.
92/3 Fredericton

CARNEGIE, HERBIE
51-54 LaPatrie 01Mar53
51/2 LavalDairy 16
52/3 StLawrence 53

CARNEGIE, OSSIE
51/2 BasDuFleuve 13

CARNELLEY, TODD
84/5 Kamloops
85/6 Kamloops

CARNEY, KEITH
92/3 Classic 102
93/4 Donruss 412
92/3 FleerUltra 13
94/5 Leaf 359
97/8 Omega 47
92/3 opcPremier 81
97/8 PacificRegime 41
96/7 PaniniSticker 166
92/3 Parkhurst 15
92/3 Pinnacle 229
92/3 ProSet 223
92/3 Score 461
92/3 UpperDeck 402
93/4 UpperDeck 516
94/5 UpperDeck 449
95/6 UpperDeck 435
95/6 UDBeAPlayer 9
98/9 UDChoice 155
93/4 CHI/Coke

CARON, ALAIN
72/3 O-Pee-Chee 324
73/4 QuakerOats 38
73/4 QuebecNordiques

CARON, CHRISTIAN
91/2 SketchQMJHL 92

CARON, JACQUES
72/3 EddieSargent 193
72/3 OPC 140,-Crests 18,T. 86
89/90 ProCards(AHL) 301
96/7 N.J/Sharp
71/2 STL
72/3 STL
72/3 STL/8"x10"
73/4 VAN/RoyalBank

CARON, MARTIN
90/1 SketchQMJHL 203

CARON, PAT
89/90 SketchMEM 64

CARPANO, ANDREA
93/4 Slapshot(SSMaire) 1

CARPENTER, BOB
90/1 Bowman 30
92/3 Bowman 10
95/6 FleerUltra 188
93/4 Leaf 421
94/5 Leaf 436
82/3 O-Pee-Chee 361
83/4 O-Pee-Chee 366
84/5 O-Pee-Chee 194
85/6 OPC/Topps 26, C
86/7 OPC/Topps 150
87/8 OPC/Topps 30
88/9 OPC/Topps 72
89/90 OPC/Topps 167
90/1 OPC/Topps 139
91/2 OPC/Topps 404
92/3 O-Pee-Chee 131
91/2 opcPremier 148
92/3 opcPremier 78
82/3 opcSticker 154
83/4 opcSticker 206
84/5 opcSticker 132
85/6 opcSticker 112
86/7 opcSticker250/140
87/8 opcSticker 252
88/9 opcSticker 153/24
97/8 PacificRegime 109
88/9 PaniniSticker 74
89/90 PaniniSticker 196
90/1 PaniniSticker 7
91/2 PaniniSticker 181
92/3 PaniniSticker 140
91/2 Parkhurst 226
94/5 ParkieSE 96
91/2 Pinnacle 99, 396
92/3 Pinnacle 315
94/5 Pinnacle 201
96/7 PinnacleBeAPlayer 125
95/6 POG 156
82/3 Post
93/4 Premier 413
90/1 ProSet 4
91/2 ProSet 349
91/2 PSPlatinum 154
83/4 FunmatePuffySticker 20
90/1 Score 16
91/2 Score(CDN) 162, (U.S) 162
92/3 Score 142
93/4 Score 267, 578
97/8 Score(N.J.) 18
89 SemicSticker 168
83/4 SouhaitsRen.KeyChain
92/3 Topps 378
91/2 ToppsStadiumClub 161
92/3 ToppsStadiumClub 122
93/4 ToppsStadiumClub 175
94/5 ToppsStadiumClub 158
90/1 UpperDeck 158
92/3 UpperDeck 478
95/6 UpperDeck 183
95/6 UDBeAPlayer 11
89/90 BOS/SportsAction
90/1 BOS/SportsAction
91/2 BOS/SportsAction
88/9 L.A/Smokeys
96/7 N.J/Sharp
81/2 WSH
82/3 WSH
84/5 WSH/PizzaHut
85/6 WSH/PizzaHut
86/7 WSH/Police
92/3 WSH/Kodak

CARPENTER, DOUG
88/9 ProCards(Halifax)
91/2 ProCards 382
84/5 N.J.

CARPENTER, STEVEN
94/5 Slapshot(NorthBay) 9
95/6 Slapshot 214

CARR, ALLAN
95/6 Slapshot 334

CARR, GENE
74/5 Loblaws
74/5 O-Pee-Chee 320
75/6 O-Pee-Chee 343
76/7 O-Pee-Chee 290
77/8 O-Pee-Chee 298
78/9 OPC/Topps 14
71/2 TheTorontoSun

CARR, LORNE
34-43 BeeHives(NYA, TOR)
36-39 DiamondMatch (1), (2), (3)
39/40 OPC (V301-1) 62
45-54 QuakerOats
36/7 WWGum (V356) 26

CARR, MIKE
92/3 Ottawa67s

CARRANO, RICK
87/8 Moncton

CARRIE, DAVE
89/90 SSMarie 19
87/8 Sudbury 15

CARRIER, MARIO
93/4 Slapshot(Drum.) 26

CARRIERE, LARRY
74/5 Loblaws
72/3 O-Pee-Chee 282
73/4 O-Pee-Chee 260
74/5 OPC/Topps 43
75/6 OPC/Topps 154
76/7 O-Pee-Chee 297
77/8 O-Pee-Chee 304
78/9 O-Pee-Chee 272
72/3 BUF
73/4 BUF
74/5 BUF
77/8 VAN/RoyalBank

CARRIERE, TOM
92/3 WestMich
93/4 WestMich

CARROL, LORNE
24/5 Crescent Falcons 9

CARROLL, BILLY
83/4 O-Pee-Chee 5
85/6 O-Pee-Chee 203
85/6 opcSticker 224/91
84/5 EDM
84/5 EDM/RedRooster
88/9 EDM/ActionMagazine 16
86/7 DET/Caesars
83/4 NYI
83/4 NYI/Islander 4

CARROLL, GEORGE
24/5 Champs (C144)
24/5 MapleCrispette (V130) 20
24/5 (V145-2) 42

CARROLL, GREG
79/80 OPC/Topps 184
78/9 WSH

CARROLL, KEN
94/5 Slapshot(Sarnia) 2
95/6 Slapshot 181

CARROL, LORNE
24/5 Crescent Falcons 9

CARSE, BILL ALLISON
34-43 BeeHives(CHI)
39/40 OPC (V301-1) 80

CARSE, BOB ALEXANDER
34-43 BeeHives(BOS), (CHI)
43-47 ParadeSportive
45-54 QuakerOats

CARSON, DAVIE
95/6 Halifax
93/4 Seattle

CARSON, GERALD (STUB)
34-43 BeeHives(MTL.M)
33/4 CndGum (V252)
33-35 DiamondMatch
36-39 DiamondMatch (1)
34/5 SweetCaporal
33/4 WWGum (V357) 24

CARSON, JIMMY
90/1 Bowman 229
91/2 Bowman 52
92/3 Bowman 108
93/4 Donruss 159, 500
95/6 Donruss 359
94/5 Fleer 85
92/3 FleerUltra 45
93/4 FleerUltra 42, 250
94/5 FleerUltra 299
93/4 HockeyWit 62
90/1 Kraft 5
93/4 Leaf 149
95/6 Leaf 308
92/3 O-Pee-Chee 152
87/8 OPC/Topps 92
88/9 OPC/Topps 9
89/90 OPC/Topps 127
90/1 OPC/Topps 231
91/2 OPC/Topps 104
88/9 opcMini 5
90/1 opcPremier 12
91/2 opcPremier 167
87/8 opcSticker 210/76, 126/114
88/9 opcSticker 158
89/90 opcSticker 221, 222
87/8 opcStars 6
87/8 PaniniSticker 279
88/9 PaniniSticker 75
89/90 PaniniSticker 72
90/1 PaniniSticker 214
91/2 PaniniSticker 139
92/3 PaniniSticker 114
93/4 PaniniSticker 204
95/6 PaniniSticker 26
91/2 Parkhurst 43
92/3 Parkhurst 308
93/4 Parkhurst 368
94/5 Parkhurst 239
94/5 ParkieSE 69
91/2 Pinnacle 173
92/3 Pinnacle 329
93/4 Pinnacle 285
94/5 Pinnacle 436
93/4 PowerPlay 114
93/4 Premier 376
94/5 Premier 326
90/1 ProSet 67
91/2 ProSet 55
91/2 PSPlatinum 33
90/1 Score 64, -HotCards 28
91/2 Score(CDN) 224, (U.S) 224
92/3 Score 9, -Sharpshooter 9
93/4 Score 109, 572
89 SemicSticker 163
91 SemicSticker 150
93 SemicSticker 187
92/3 Topps 398
91/2 ToppsStadiumClub 121
92/3 ToppsStadiumClub 277
93/4 ToppsStadiumClub 118
90/1 UpperDeck 132
91/2 UpperDeck 161
92/3 UpperDeck 253
94/5 UpperDeck 198
95/6 UDCollChoice 180
89/90 DET/Caesars
91/2 DET/Caesars
88/9 EDM
88/9 EDM/ActionMagazine 53
88/9 L.A

CARSON, LINDSAY
83/4 O-Pee-Chee 261
83/4 opcSticker 181
88/9 ProCards(Binghampton)
83/4 PHA
86/7 PHA

CARTER, ANSON
93/4 Donruss CAN7
97/8 Donruss 118
97/8 DonrussCanadianIce 73
97/8 DonrussPreferred 29
97/8 DonrussPriority 89
97/8 DonrussStudio 33
97/8 Leaf 85
96/7 LeafPreferd 146
97/8 Limited 107
97/8 Omega 13
98/9 Pacific 73
97/8 PacificCC 131
97/8 PacificCrownRoyale 8
97/8 PacificParamount 11
98/9 PacificParamount 11
93/4 Pinnacle 469
97/8 PinnacleBeAPlayer 67
97/8 PinnacleInside 171
96/7 PinnacleZenith 122
97/8 Score 226
97/8 Score(BOS) 8
96/7 SelectCert 94
93/4 UpperDeck 531
96/7 UpperDeck 358
97/8 UpperDeck 11
97/8 UDCollChoice 13
96/7 Portland

CARTER, BILLY
60/1 ShirriffCoin 115
63/4 QuébecAces

CARTER, JOHN
90/1 Bowman 39
92/3 FleerUltra 399
91/2 OPC/Topps 300
90/1 PaniniSticker 8
88/9 ProCards(Maine)
90/1 ProSet 5
90/1 Score 283
91/2 Score(CDN) 557, (U.S) 7T
90/1 UpperDeck 211
89/90 BOS/SportsAction
90/1 BOS/SportsAction
86/7 Moncton 28

CARTER, LYLE
71/2 TheTorontoSun

CARTER, RON
88/9 EDM/ActionMagazine 98

CARTER, SHAWN
91/2 AvantGardeBCJHL 97

CARUSO, JAMES
89/90 SketchOHL 156
90/1 SketchOHL 305
91/2 SketchOHL 88

CARVER, ORRIN
52/3 AnonymousOHL 97

CARVETH, JOE
34-43 BeeHives(DET)
45-64 BeeHives(MTL)
40/1 (OPC V301-2) 123
43-47 ParadeSportive
45-54 QuakerOats
76 DET
51/2 ClevelandCrusaders

CASALE, AGOSTINO
96/7 DEL 122

CASAVANT, DENYS
43-47 ParadeSportive

CASEY, DAVE
88/9 ProCards(Adirondack)
89/90 ProCards(AHL) 316

CASEY, GERALD
52/3 AnonymousOHL 95

CASEY, JON
90/1 Bowman 183
91/2 Bowman 119
92/3 Bowman 269
93/4 Donruss 16
96/7 Donruss 37
93/4 EASports 36
95/6 EdgeIce 176
92/3 FleerUltra 90
93/4 FleerUltra 91, 266
91/2 Kraft 75
92/3 Kraft-Disk
93/4 Leaf 322
96/7 Leaf 89
93/4 McDonalds McD03
89/90 OPC/Topps 48
90/1 OPC/Topps 269, B
91/2 OPC/Topps 237
92/3 O-Pee-Chee 16
91/2 opcPremier 112
92/3 opcPremier-Star 7
89/90 opcSticker 197/53
97/8 PacificRegime 167
89/90 PaniniSticker 114
90/1 PaniniSticker 254
91/2 PaniniSticker 118
92/3 PaniniSticker 87
93/4 PaniniSticker 276
95/6 PaniniSticker 199
91/2 Parkhurst 77
92/3 Parkhurst 73
93/4 Parkhurst 12
95/6 Parkhurst 177
94/5 ParkieSE 158
91/2 Pinnacle 144
92/3 Pinnacle 42
93/4 Pinnacle 357
94/5 Pinnacle 393
96/7 PinnacleBeAPlayer 63
93/4 PowerPlay 17
93/4 Premier 437
94/5 Premier 229
90/1 ProSet 133
91/2 ProSet 111
92/3 ProSet 82
91/2 PSPlatinum 56
90/1 Score 182, -HotCards 80
91/2 Score(CDN) 191, (U.S) 191
92/3 Score 249
93/4 Score 193,526, -P.AS 41,49
94/5 Score 111
95/6 Score 290
96/7 Score 214
92/3 SeasonsPatch 64
92/3 Topps 379
91/2 ToppsStadiumClub 138
92/3 ToppsStadiumClub 198
93/4 TSC 303, 456, -AllStar
94/5 ToppsStadiumClub 184
90/1 UpperDeck 385
91/2 UpperDeck 205
92/3 UD 190, -LockerAS 40
93/4 UpperDeck 507, SP-8
94/5 UpperDeck 206
95/6 UpperDeck 70
85/6 MIN
88/9 MIN/American

CASHMAN, WAYNE
71/2 EddieSargent 14
72/3 EddieSargent 18
70/1 Esso Stamp
74/5 LiptonSoup 9
74/5 Loblaws
73/4 MacsMilk Disk
70/1 OPC/Topps 7, OPC 233
71/2 OPC/Topps 129
72/3 OPC 68,-TmCdn, Topps 29
73/4 OPC 85, Topps 166
74/5 OPC/Topps 206
75/6 OPC/Topps 63
76/7 OPC/Topps 165
77/8 OPC/Topps 234, -Glossy 1
78/9 OPC/Topps 124
79/80 OPC/Topps 79
80/1 O-Pee-Chee 318
81/2 O-Pee-Chee 11
82/3 O-Pee-Chee 8
94/5 Parkie(64/5) 18
72/3 Post Transfers 3

82/3 Post
71/2 TheTorontoSun
91/2 Trends(72) 25, -Aut.
70/1 BOS
71/2 BOS
91/2 BOS/Legends
96/7 S.J/PacificBellSheets
92/3 T.B/Sheraton
94/5 T.B/SkyBoxSportsCafe
95/6 T.B/SkyBoxSportsCafe

CASSELMAN, MIKE
96/7 Cincinnati

CASSELS, ANDREW
91/2 Bowman 340
92/3 Bowman 387
95/6 Bowman 4
93/4 Donruss 142
94/5 Donruss 178
95/6 Donruss 148
96/7 Donruss 162
97/8 Donruss 146
97/8 DonrussCanadianIce 66
97/8 DonrussElite 48
97/8 DonrussPreferred 94
97/8 DonrussPriority 64
93/4 EASports 57
94/5 Flair 71
96/7 Flair 41
94/5 Fleer 86
96/7 Fleer 46
95/6 FleerMetal 64
96/7 FleerNHLPicks 104
92/3 FleerUltra 70
93/4 FleerUltra 33
94/5 FleerUltra 300
95/6 FleerUltra 66
97/8 KatchMedallion 19
95/6 Kraft
93/4 Leaf 50
94/5 Leaf 276
95/6 Leaf 147
96/7 Leaf 78
97/8 Leaf 106
97/8 Omega 28
91/2 OPC/Topps 176
92/3 O-Pee-Chee 222
91/2 opcPremier 72
98/9 Pacific 115
97/8 PacificCrown 166
97/8 PcfcDynag! 21,-Tandem 39
97/8 PacificInvincible 23
97/8 PacificParamount 26
98/9 PacificParamount 26
90/1 Panini(MTL) 3
93/4 PaniniSticker 123
95/6 PaniniSticker 25
96/7 PaniniSticker 28
97/8 PaniniSticker 21
91/2 Parkhurst 285
92/3 Parkhurst 298
93/4 Parkhurst 359
94/5 Parkhurst 97, V58
95/6 Parkhurst 364
93/4 Pinnacle 103
94/5 Pinnacle 319
96/7 Pinnacle 82
97/8 Pinnacle 178
97/8 PinnacleBeAPlayer 169
97/8 PinnacleCertified 130
97/8 PinnacleInside 106
95/6 Playoff 46
95/6 POG 124
93/4 PowerPlay 104
93/4 Premier 65
94/5 Premier 227
89/90 ProCards(AHL) 191
95/6 ProMagnet 127
90/1 ProSet 615
91/2 ProSet 395
90/1 Score 422
91/2 Score(CDN) 238, 607
91/2 Score(U.S) 57T
92/3 Score 323
93/4 Score 164
94/5 Score 34
95/6 Score 136
96/7 Score 146
97/8 Score 134
94/5 Select 141
95/6 SkyBoxEmotion 74
95/6 SkyBoxImpact 72
96/7 SkyBoxImpact 53
94/5 SP 50
95/6 SP 61
96/7 SP 72
95/6 Summit 158
96/7 Summit 44
92/3 Topps 23
95/6 Topps 30
95/6 ToppsFinest 74
91/2 ToppsStadiumClub 329
92/3 ToppsStadiumClub 39
93/4 ToppsStadiumClub 74
95/6 ToppsStadiumClub 61
95/6 ToppsSuperSkills 4
90/1 UpperDeck 265
91/2 UpperDeck 379, 551
92/3 UpperDeck 288
93/4 UpperDeck 346
94/5 UpperDeck 317, SP32
95/6 UpperDeck 492, SE36
96/7 UpperDeck 74
95/6 UDBeAPlayer 30
96/7 UDBlackDiamond 123
95/6 UDCollChoice 52
96/7 UDCollChoice 115
97/8 UDCollChoice 113
91/2 HFD/JuniorWhalers
92/3 HFD/DairyMart
93/4 HFD/Coke
90/1 MTL

CASSELSTAHL, DANIEL
94/5 ElitSet 178

CASSIDY, BRUCE
88/9 ProCards(Saginaw)
89/90 ProCards(IHL) 51
88/9 CHI/Coke
93/4 Indianapolis
82/3 Ottawa67s
83/4 Ottawa67s
84/5 Ottawa67s

CASTELLA, REUBEN
91/2 SketchOHL 174

CASTELLAN, JASON
90/1 SketchOHL 280

CATELLIER, CHRIS
90/1 SketchWHL 238
91/2 SketchWHL 53
89/90 Victoria

CATENACCI, MAURIZIO
96/7 DEL 100

CATON, MURRAY
91/2 AvantGardeBCJHL 8

CATTARINCH, JOE
83&87 HallOfFame 168
83 HHOF Postcard (M)
1910-11 Imperial (C56) 16
27-32 LaPresse 27/8
95/6 MTL/Forum 03APR96

CAUFIELD, JAY
90/1 ProSet 504
89/90 PGH/Foodland 12
91/2 PGH/Elbys
92/3 PGH/Coke

CAUSEY, CAREY
91/2 AvantGardeBCJHL 113

CAVA, PETER
98 BowmanCHL 18
95/6 Slapshot 365
96/7 SSMarie

CAVALIERE, DAVE
93/4 Birmingham 21
89/90 Nashville

CAVALLINI, GINO
91/2 Bowman 368, 415
96/7 DEL 152
95/6 EdgeIce 159
87/8 OPC/Topps 146
88/9 OPC/Topps 149
89/90 OPC/Topps 176
90/1 OPC/Topps 36
91/2 OPC/Topps 281
87/8 PaniniSticker 415
88/9 PaniniSticker 103
89/90 PaniniSticker 123
90/1 PaniniSticker 265
91/2 PaniniSticker 24
91/2 Pinnacle 216
93/4 Premier 232
90/1 ProSet 261
91/2 ProSet 218
90/1 Score 63, -HotCards 27
91/2 Score(CDN) 338, 478
91/2 Score(U.S) 258, 308
92/3 Score 42
93/4 Score 414
92/3 Topps 234
91/2 ToppsStadiumClub 34
92/3 ToppsStadiumClub 480
93/4 ToppsStadiumClub 152
90/1 UpperDeck 38
91/2 UpperDeck 187, 646
85/6 CGY/RedRooster
92/3 QUE/PetroCanada
87/8 STL
87/8 STL/Kodak
88/9 STL
88/9 STL/Kodak
89/90 STL/Kodak
90/1 STL/Kodak
91/2 STL
94/5 Milwaukee
84/5 Moncton 26

CAVALLINI, PAUL
90/1 Bowman 22
91/2 Bowman 378
92/3 Bowman 193
93/4 Donruss 88
94/5 Donruss 135
92/3 FleerUltra 185, 432
94/5 FleerUltra 49
93/4 Leaf 397
94/5 Leaf 79
89/90 O-Pee-Chee 269
92/3 O-Pee-Chee 379
90/1 OPC/Topps 57
91/2 OPC/Topps 328
89/90 opcSticker 19 /159
89/90 PaniniSticker 127
90/1 PaniniSticker 276
91/2 PaniniSticker 35
92/3 PaniniSticker 23
91/2 Parkhurst 154
93/4 Parkhurst 50
94/5 Parkhurst V12
94/5 ParkieSE 42
91/2 Pinnacle 182, 411
92/3 Pinnacle 319
93/4 Pinnacle 370
94/5 Pinnacle 81
94/5 POG 82
93/4 PowerPlay 321
94/5 Premier 246
90/1 ProSet 262, 353
91/2 ProSet 214, -Promo 2of4
92/3 ProSet 159
91/2 PSPlatinum 224
90/1 Score 185, 349
91/2 Score(CDN) 107, 338
91/2 Score(U.S) 107, 308
92/3 Score 22
93/4 Score 172, 538
94/5 Score 94
91 SemicSticker 59
92/3 Topps 233
91/2 ToppsStadiumClub 48
92/3 ToppsStadiumClub 447
90/1 UpperDeck 281
91/2 UpperDeck 184, 646
92/3 UpperDeck 212
93/4 UpperDeck 441, SP-35
94/5 UpperDeck 311, SP108
94/5 DAL
94/5 DAL/Southwest
87/8 STL
87/8 STL/Kodak
88/9 STL
88/9 STL/Kodak
89/90 STL/Kodak
90/1 STL/Kodak
91/2 STL
92/3 WSH/Kodak

CAVANAGH, CHAD
95/6 Slapshot 164

CAVANAGH, MIKE
90/1 SketchOHL 29

CECH, ROMAN
94/5 APS 165
95/6 APS 181

CECH, VRATISLAV
97/8 Bowman 155

CECH, ZDENEK
94/5 APS 294
95/6 APS 28

CECHMANEK, ROMAN
94/5 APS 228
95/6 APS 3, 353, 388

CEGLARSKI, LEN
90/1 ProSet 385

CEJ, JEFF
91/2 SketchWHL 305

CELIO, MANUELE
91 SemicSticker 192
92 SemicSticker 211
93 SemicSticker 124

CELIO, NICOLAI
91/2 UD 665, 'CzechWJC 26

CELLA, TONY
80/1 SSMarie
81/2 SSMarie
82/3 SSMarie

CELY, ZDENEK
94/5 APS 180
95/6 APS 213

CENTRONE, MARC
81/2 Regina 5
82/3 Regina 18
83/4 Regina 18

CERESINO, RAY
45-64 BeeHives(TOR)
51/2 ClevelandBarons

CERMAK, DAVE
94/5 APS 61
95/6 APS 89

CERNICH, KORD
90/1 ProCards 6
91/2 ProCards 211, 330

CERNIK, FRANK
79 PaniniSticker 91
82 SemicSticker 91
84/5 DET/Caesars

CERNY, FRANTISEK
82 SemicSticker 88

CERNY, JOSEF
70/1 Kuvajulkaisut 42
72 Panda
72 SemicSticker 34
74 SemicSticker 70
71/2 WilliamsFIN 23

CERNY, MICHAL
994/5 APS 126
92/3 UpperDeck 603

CERNY, MILAN
94/5 APS 150

CERNY, OTAKAR
94/5 APS 54

CERVEN, MARTIN
97/8 Bowman 90
95/6 Spokane 10

CHABOT, FRÉDÉRIC
90/1 ProCards 66
95/6 FutureLegends 17
97/8 PinnacleBeAPlayer 169
89/90 ProCards'IHL 135
92/3 Fredericton

CHABOT, JOHN
90/1 Bowman 236
94/5 DEL 67
95/6 DEL 67
96/7 DEL 263
84/5 O-Pee-Chee 258
85/6 O-Pee-Chee 244
87/8 OPC/Topps 32
88/9 OPC/Topps 39
89/90 O-Pee-Chee 225
90/1 OPC/Topps 163
85/6 opcSticker 101/233
86/7 opcSticker 230/101
87/8 opcSticker 169/29
87/8 PaniniSticker 151
88/9 PaniniSticker 42
90/1 PaniniSticker 216
90/1 ProCards 488
90/1 ProSet 68
90/1 Score 277
90/1 UpperDeck 113
91/2 UpperDeck 393
87/8 DET/Caesars
88/9 DET
88/9 DET/Caesars
89/90 DET/Caesars
90/1 DET/Caesars
83/4 MTL
86/7 PGH/Kodak

CHABOT, LORNE
33/4 Anonymous (V129) 45
34-43 BeeHives(CHI)
33/4 CndGum (V252)
33-35 DiamondMatch
36-39 DiamondMatch (1), (2), (3)
33/4 Hamilton (V288) 30
33/4 OPC (V304A) 18
55/6 Parkhurst 21
23/4 PaulinsCandy 15
34/5 SweetCaporal
33/4 WWGum (V357) 71
32/3 TOR/OKeefe 1

CHABOT, NICOLAS
96/7 Rimouski

CHADNEY, RANDY
91/2 SketchWHL 55

CHADWICK, BILL (THE BIG WHISTLE)
83&87 HallOfFame 65
83 HHOF Postcard (E)
77-9 Sportscaster 67-21

CHADWICK, ED
52/3 AnonymousOHL 157
45-64 BeeHives(TOR)
58/9 Parkhurst 12
59/60 Parkhurst 5
57/8 Parkhurst(MTL) 24, 25
57/8 Parkhurst(TOR) 2
93/4 Parkie(56/7) 128
61/2 ShirriffCoin 20
56-66 TorontoStar '57
84/5 NovaScotia 25

CHAGNON, PAUL
94/5 Fredericton
95/6 Fredericton
96/7 Fredericton

CHAINEY, ALAIN
91/2 SketchQMJHL 182
87/8 QUE/GeneralFoods
88/9 QUE
88/9 QUE/GeneralFoods
89/90 QUE

CHALANEK, MIROSLAV
94/5 APS 15

CHALIFOUX, DENIS
91/2 ProCards 106
89/90 SketchMEM 70
90/1 SketchQMJHL 51

CHALK, DAVE
78/9 SM-Liiga 119

CHALMERS, WILLIAM
52/3 AnonymousOHL 52

CHALONER, KANE
91/2 SketchWHL 58

CHALUPA, MILAN
79 PaniniSticker 79
82 SemicSticker 80
84/5 DET/Caesars

CHAMBERLAIN, CURTIS
83/4 Saskatoon 17
84/5 Saskatoon

CHAMBERLAIN, ERWIN GROVES (MURPH)
34-43 BeeHives(MTL.C), (TOR)
45-64 BeeHives(MTL)
37/8 OPC (V304E) 147
39/40 OPC (V301-1) 12
43-47 ParadeSportive
38/9 QuakerOats
45-54 QuakerOats

CHAMBERS, DAVE
90/1 ProSet 675
90/1 QUE/PetroCanada

CHAMBERS, RICK
89/90 SketchMEM 27
93/4 Slapshot(Kitchener) 29
94/5 Slapshot(Kitchener) 29

CHAMBERS, SHAWN
90/1 Bowman 180
93/4 Donruss 325
94/5 Donruss 72
95/6 Donruss 126
94/5 Flair 171
94/5 Fleer 204
93/4 FleerUltra 75
94/5 FleerUltra 203
95/6 FleerUltra 259
93/4 Leaf 40
94/5 Leaf 332
95/6 Leaf 234
89/90 OPC/Topps 142
90/1 OPC/Topps 192
98/9 Pacific 174
89/90 PaniniSticker 111
90/1 PaniniSticker 252
93/4 PaniniSticker 219
94/5 PaniniSticker 187
95/6 PaniniSticker 86
95 PaniniWorlds 213
92/3 Parkhurst 406
94/5 Parkhurst 223
95/6 Parkhurst 392
93/4 Pinnacle 87
94/5 Pinnacle 97
96/7 PinnacleBeAPlayer 75
94/5 POG 227
93/4 PowerPlay 229
93/4 Premier 101
94/5 Premier 174
90/1 ProSet 134
90/1 Score 57
91/2 Score(CDN) 572
92/3 Score 508
93/4 Score 391
94/5 Score 153
95/6 Score 86
95 Semic 109
95/6 SkyBoxEmotion 96
95/6 SkyBoxImpact 92
93/4 ToppsStadiumClub 412
90/1 UpperDeck 106
92/3 UpperDeck 104
93/4 UpperDeck 68
95/6 UpperDeck 148
96/7 UpperDeck 287
88/9 MIN/American
96/7 N.J/Sharp
92/3 T.B/Sheraton
93/4 T.B/KashNKarry
94/5 T.B/SkyBoxSportsCafe
91/2 WSH
91/2 WSH/Kodak

CHAD, JOHN
34-43 BeeHives(CHI)

CHANG SHUN, WEI
79 PaniniSticker 358

CHANNEL, CRAIG
89/90 ProCards(IHL) 134

CHAPDELAINE, RENÉ
89/90 ProCards(AHL) 21
90/1 ProCards 429
93/4 Peoria
92/3 Phoenix

CHAPMAN, ARTHUR
34-43 BeeHives(NYA)
33-35 DiamondMatch
36-39 DiamondMatch (1),(2),(3)
35/6 OPC (V304C) 94
39/40 OPC (V301-1) 18
33/4 WWGum (V357) 32
36/7 WWGum (V356) 42

CHAPMAN, BLAIR
77/8 OPC/Topps 174
78/9 OPC/Topps 33
79/80 OPC/Topps 21
80/1 OPC/Topps 48
81/2 OPC 291, Topps(W) 115
77/8 PGH/PuckBuck

CHAPMAN, BRIAN
88/9 ProCards(Binghampton)
89/90 ProCards(AHL) 299
90/1 ProCards 190
91/2 ProCards 109
93/4 Phoenix
95/6 Phoenix

CHAPMAN, CRAIG
90/1 SketchWHL 2
91/2 SketchWHL 122

CHAPMAN, PHIL
52/3 AnonymousOHL 89

CHAPPOT, ROGER
72 SemicSticker 149

CHAPUT, DANIEL
93/4 Hampton

CHAPUT, MARTIN
90/1 SketchQMJHL 46
91/2 SketchQMJHL 233

CHARA, ZDENO
98/9 Pacific 276
97/8 SPAuthentic 186
98/9 SPx"Finite" 52
98/9 UDChoice 124

CHARBONNEAU, JOSÉ
90/1 CanadaNats
95/6 DEL 257
96/7 DEL 145
93/4 FleerUltra 438
93/4 Parkhurst 484
93/4 PowerPlay 457
88/9 ProCards(Sherbrooke)
89/90 ProCards(IHL) 181
93/4 Score 638
93/4 UpperDeck 503
87/8 MTL
88/9 MTL
93/4 VAN/Coins

CHARBONNEAU, L.P.
94/5 Slapshot(MEM) 72

CHARBONNEAU, PATRICK
93/4 Slapshot(Drum.) 17
91/2 SketchQMJHL 251

CHARBONNEAU, STÉPHANE
90/1 SketchMEM 43
90/1 SketchQMJHL 40, 116
91/2 ProCards 536
94/5 Erie
93/4 Phoenix

CHARLAMOV, VALERI
see Valeri Kharlamov

CHARLAND, CARL
94/5 Slapshot(MEM) 63

CHARLEBOIS, BOB
72/3 OPC 309
73/4 QuakerOats 23
72/3 OttawaNationals

CHARLESWORTH, TODD
88/9 ProCards(Mus)
89/90 ProCards'AHL 139
90/1 ProCards 2

CHARROIS, MARTIN
90/1 SketchMEM 52
90/1 SketchQMJHL 9

CHARROIS, YVAN
90/1 SketchQMJHL 105

CHARRON, CRAIG
91/2 Cincinnati
92/3 Cincinnati
94/5 Dayton 5

CHARRON, ERIC
94/5 Fleer 205
94/5 FleerUltra 371
94/5 Premier 343
90/1 ProCards 56
91/2 ProCards 89
94/5 UpperDeck 489
95/6 T.B/SkyBoxSportsCafe
93/4 AtlantaKnights
92/3 Fredericton

CHARRON, ERIC
84/5 Richelieu

CHARRON, GUY
72-84 Dernière 79/80
71/2 EddieSargent 60
72/3 EddieSargent 80
82? JDMcCarthy
74/5 Loblaws, -Update
72/3 OPC 223

73/4 OPC 220
74/5 OPC/Topps 57
75/6 OPC/Topps 32, 319
76/7 OPC/Topps 186, OPC 384
77/8 OPC/Topps 145
78/9 OPC/Topps 18, 22
79/80 OPC/Topps 152
80/1 O-Pee-Chee 352
79 PaniniSticker 62
71/2 TheTorontoSun
90/1 CGY/McGavins
91/2 CGY/IGA
92/3 CGY/IGA 27
69/70 MTL/ProStar
70/1 MTL
78/9 WSH
79/80 WSH
80/1 WSH

CHARRON, YVES
91/2 SketchQMJHL 31

CHARTIER, CHRISTIAN
97/8 UpperDeck 402

CHARTIER, DAVE
81/2 Saskatoon 6
83/4 Saskatoon 10

CHARTIER, SCOTT
91/2 AvantGardeBCJHL 35, 158
93/4 Classic 61
94/5 Classic-Autograph
92/3 WestMich.

CHARTRAIN, ANDRÉ
82/3 Fredericton 16
83/4 Fredericton 17

CHARTRAND, JACQUES
52/3 StLawrence 27

CHARTRAND, RICK
89/90 Rayside

CHARTRAND, SIMON
89/90 Rayside

CHARTRAW, RICK
75/6 O-Pee-Chee 388
76/7 OPC/Topps 244
77/8 O-Pee-Chee 363
78/9 OPC/Topps 238
79/80 OPC/Topps 243
80/1 O-Pee-Chee 364
83/4 EDM
83/4 EDM/McDonald
88/9 EDM/ActionMagazine 96
74/5 MTL
76/7 MTL
77/8 MTL
78/9 MTL
79/80 MTL
80/1 MTL

CHASE, KELLY
90/1 Bowman 14
93/4 Donruss 483
94/5 Donruss 157
94/5 Leaf 396
90/1 O-Pee-Chee 432
91/2 OPC/Topps 23
98/9 Pacific 363
97/8 PacificParamount 156
98/9 PacificParamount 199
96/7 PinnacleBeAPlayer 60
88/9 ProCards(Peoria)
90/1 ProCards 87
96/7 UDCollChoice 122
89/90 STL/Kodak
91/2 STL
86/7 Saskatoon

CHASE, TIM
93/4 Knoxville

CHASLE, YVON
52/3 AnonymousOHL 134

CHASSÉ, DENIS
92/3 ClassicProspects 79
95/6 Donruss 164
94/5 Fleer 184
95/6 FleerUltra 137
95/6 Leaf 132
91/2 ProCards 535
90/1 SketchMEM 54
90/1 SketchQMJHL 13
95/6 SkyBxImpact-Fox 5
94/5 TFinest-BBest(Red) 15
94/5 UpperDeck 414
95/6 UpperDeck 416

CHATTINGTON, TERRANCE
52/3 AnonymousOHL 57

CHAULK, COLIN
95/6 Slapshot 123

CHEBATURKIN, VLADIMIR
93/4 Classic 37
93/4 ClassicFourSport 212
98/9 Pacific 277

CHEECHOO, JONATHAN
98 BowmanCHL 142, 164
98 BowmanCHL A25, SC18
98/9 Topps 230

CHEEVERS, GERRY
65/6 CocaCola
70/1 Colgate Stamp 71
70/1 DadsCookies
70/1 EddieSargent 15
71/2 EddieSargent 16
70/1 Esso Stamp
87 HallOfFame 250
94 HockeyWit 81
72/3 Letraset 8
68/9 O-Pee-Chee 140
69/70 OPC/T. 22, OPC-Sticker
70/1 OPC/Topps 1
71/2 OPC/Topps 54, Topps 4
72/3 OPC 340
73/4 OPC-Posters 6
76/7 OPC/Topps 120
77/8 OPC/Topps 260, -Glossy 2
78/9 OPC/Topps 140, 263
79/80 OPC/Topps 85
80/1 OPC/Topps 168
92/3 OPC 343, -25Years 5
74/5 opcWHA 30
75/6 opcWHA 20, 67
94/5 Parkie(64/5) FS2
95/6 Parkie(66/7) 16, 134
73/4 QuakerOats 8
72 SemicSticker 188
72/3 7ElevenCups
68/9 ShirriffCoin Bo4
77-9 Sportscstr 44-20, 49-1174
91/2 StarPics 61
71/2 TheTorontoSun
65/6 Topps 31
67/8 Topps 99
68/9 Topps 1
71/2 Topps 4
70/1 BOS
71/2 BOS
91/2 BOS/Legends
72/3 Cleveland
94/5 Zellers

CHELIOS, CHRIS
95/6 Aces 9 (Spades)
96/7 Aces 5 (Clubs)
97/8 Aces 3 (Diamonds)
90/1 Bowman 42, 46
91/2 Bowman 398
92/3 Bowman 43, 201
95/6 Bowman 12
93/4 Classic 118, -Aut.
96/7 CorinthianHeadliners
97/8 Corinthian Headliners
93/4 Donruss 65, -IceKing 5
94/5 Donruss 118, -Dominator 6
95/6 Donruss 91, -Dom 7,-Pro 4
96/7 Donruss 71, -Dom 3, -Hit 6
97/8 Donruss 37, -Line2Line 13
96/7 DonrussCanadianIce 56
97/8 D.CdnIce 120,-Scrapbook 4
95/6 DonrussElite 61
96/7 D.Elite 20, -Perspectives
97/8 DonrussElite 31
97/8 DonrussPreferred 127, 171
97/8 D.Priority 99,-OpDay 24
97/8 D.Prio-Postcd 23,-Stamp 23
97/8 D.Studio 30,-Portraits 28
96/7 Duracell DC8
93/4 EASports 25, 186
97/8 EssoOlympic 30
94/5 Flair 32
96/7 Flair 15
94/5 Fleer 39
96/7 Fleer 16, 140, -Norris 2
95/6 FleerMetal 24, -Int.Steel 3
96/7 F.Picks-Dream 2, -Fab 7
92/3 FleerUltra 34, -AS 7
93/4 FleerUltra 40, AS 14, -AW 2
94/5 FleerUltra 40, -AS 8
95/6 FleerUltra 31, 380
96/7 FU 30, -Blue 2, -Power 2
91/2 Gillette 16
95 Globe 107
96/7 GotUmHockeyGreatsCoin
93/4 HockeyWit 12
95/6 Hoyle'WEST 8 (Hearts)
92/3 HumptyDumpty(1)
97/8 KatchMedallion 32
95/6 KennerSLU
97/8 KennerSLU
86/7 Kraft Sports 22
89/90 Kraft 20
90/1 Kraft 6, 81
91/2 Kraft 18
92/3 Kraft'AllStar
93/4 KraftGold
94/5 Kraft-HockeyHeroes
95/6 Kraft'Disk
96/7 Kraft-Rivals, -Trophy
97/8 Kraft-World Pros
93/4 Leaf 51, 290, -GoldAS 2
94/5 Leaf 7
95/6 Leaf 142, -Gold 2, -Road 6
96/7 Leaf 46, 49, 54
97/8 Leaf 64
94/5 LeafLimited 83
95/6 LeafLimited 40
96/7 LeafLimited 1
96/7 LeafPreferred 19, -Steel 7
97/8 Limited 16, 87, 166, 17
97/8 Limited -fabric 58
96/7 Maggers 27
91/2 McDonalds McD22, McH-1
92/3 McDonalds McD-03
93/4 McDonalds McH5
94/5 McDonalds McD16
95/6 McDonalds McD23
96/7 McDonalds McD8
96/7 MetalUniverse 26, -Cool 1
97/8 Omega 48, 245, -StickHa 4
84/5 O-Pee-Chee 259
85/6 OPC/Topps 51, D
86/7 OPC/Topps 171
87/8 OPC/Topps 106
88/9 OPC/Topps 49
89/90 OPC/T. 174, OPC 307,323
90/1 OPC/Topps 29
91/2 OPC/Topps 233, 268
92/3 O-Pee-Chee 13
90/1 opcPremier 13
91/2 opcPremier 17, 150
85/6 opcSticker 125
86/7 opcSticker 6/151
87/8 opcSticker 9
88/9 opcSticker 51
89/90 opcStick. 56,156/14,212/73
89/90 opcStickFS 26
97/8 Pacific-FeaturePer 6
98/9 Pacific 7,-GldC 7,-TmCL 6
97/8 PacificCrown 7
97/8 PacificCC-Gold 6, -TmCL 6
97/8 PacificCrownRoyale 28
97/8 PCR -BladesofSteel 4
97/8 PacificDynagon! 25
97/8 PcfcD-BstKpt 20,-Tandm 35
97/8 PcfcInvincible 28,-Feat 6
97/8 PacificParamount 41
98/9 PcfcParamount 44,-TmCL 6
97/8 PacificRegime 42
97/8 PcfcRevolution 28,-TmCL 6
97/8 PcfcRev -AllStarGame 5
87/8 PaniniSticker 58
88/9 PaniniSticker 253
89/90 PaniniSticker 237, 379
90/1 PaniniSticker 49
91/2 PaniniSticker 10, 329
92/3 PaniniSticker 11, 286
93/4 PaniniSticker 153
94/5 PaniniSticker 134
95/6 PaniniSticker 164
96/7 PaniniSticker 151, 157
97/8 PaniniSticker 129
91/2 Parkhurst 32
92/3 Parkhurst 29, 457, CP13
93/4 Parkhurst 45
94/5 Parkhurst 45
95/6 Parkhurst 38, PP20
95/6 PH-AS 4, -Crown(2) 13
91/2 Pinnacle 58, B9
92/3 Pinnacle 109, -Team 2
93/4 Pinn. 181,223,233, -TP 3
94/5 Pinnacle 94, BR4, TP3
95/6 Pinnacle 50, -First 9, -Full 6
96/7 Pinnacle 34
97/8 Pinnacle 65, -TeamPin 3
97/8 PinnacleBeAPlayer 11
97/8 PinnacleBeeHive 25
97/8 Pinn.Certified 74, -Team 5
96/7 PinnacleFANtasy 11
97/8 PinnacleInside 18
95/6 PinnacleZenith 37
96/7 PinnZenith 68, ZTeam 12
95/6 Playoff 22
96/7 Playoff 370
96/7 PinnacleMint 22
94/5 POG 73
95/6 POG 70, 012
94/5 Post
96/7 Post, -StickUm 3
97/8 Post
93/4 PowerPlay 47
93/4 Premier 94, 237
94/5 Premier 475, 486
95/6 ProMagnet 2
90/1 ProSet 147. 368, 427
91/2 ProSet 48, 278
92/3 ProSet 34
91/2 PSPlatinum 25
87/8 ProSportWatch CW3
90/1 Score 15, 4T, -HotCards 9
91/2 Score(CDN) 455, (U.S) 235
92/3 Score 2, 497, -USA 2
93/4 Score 101, -P.AS 26, -DT 3
94/5 Score 189, CI17, DT8
95/6 Score 3, -Promo 3
96/7 Score 36,-Check 15,-Sup 8
97/8 Score 90, -Checkit 9
92/3 SeasonsPatch 4
94/5 Select 31, FL9
95/6 SelectCertified 2, -Double 4
96/7 SelectCertif 27
94 Semic 111, 338
95 Semic 104
89 SemicSticker 157
91 SemicSticker 130
92 SemicSticker 153
93 SemicSticker 172
95/6 SkBxEmotion 28,-Xcited 20
95/6 SkyBoxImpact 28
96/7 SkBxImpact 18, -Fox 5,
96/7 SkBxImpact-Bladerunner 2
92/3 SourPuckCaps 3
94/5 SP 23
95/6 SP 23, FX3
96/7 SP 27, CW18, HC6
97/8 SPAuthentic 30, I3, S9
96/7 SPx 6
97/8 SPx 9, SPX10
98/9 SPx"Finite" 120
96/7 SportFX MiniStix
97/8 SportFX MiniStix
95/6 Summit 39, -GM 3
96/7 Summit 43
95/6 SuperSticker 22, -DieCut 10
96/7 TeamOut
89/90 Topps-AllStar 1
92/3 Topps 98
95/6 Topps 3, 230, HGA 6
95/6 Topps M18, 9RL
98/9 Topps 166, B2, M17
94/5 ToppsFinest 34
95/6 ToppsFinest 19, 121
96/7 T.Picks 19, ID3, FT6
91/2 ToppsStadiumClub 6
92/3 ToppsStadiumClub 87
93/4 TSC 147, 420, 459, -AS
94/5 TSC 70, -Dynasty 5
95/6 ToppsStadiumClub 10, F2
95/6 ToppsSuperSkills 50
93/4 TSC-Members 2
94/5 TSC-Members 38
95/6 TSC-Members 4
97/8 ToppsSticker 5
90/1 UpperDeck 174, 422, 491
91/2 UpperDeck 37, 354
92/3 UpperDeck 159, 629, WG3
92/3 UD-LockerAS 22
93/4 UD 129, SP-28, AW5, GG2
94/5 UD 26, C29, H7, SP16
95/6 UD 170,238,AS2,H34,SE17
95/6 UD-AllStarPredict MVP9
96/7 UD 31, P15, SS27A, X11
97/8 UD 36, 394, SG7, T4C
93/4 UDBeAPlayer 2
94/5 UDBeAPlayer R97, R109
95/6 UDBeAPlayer 211
96/7 UDBlackDiamond 145
97/8 UDBlackDiamond 29
98/9 UDChoice 46, 223, BH23
95/6 UDCollChoice 37, 380
96/7 UDCC 47, 301, 313, UD31
97/8 UDCC 46, S7, SQ11
96/7 UpperDeck "Ice" 10
97/8 UpperDeckIce 67
96 Wien 159
97/8 Zenith 14, Z39
90/1 CHI/Coke
91/2 CHI/Coke
93/4 CHI/Coke
83/4 MTL
84/5 MTL
85/6 MTL
85/6 MTL/Pennant
85/6 MTL/PepsiPlacemats
85/6? MTL/ProvPlacemats
85/6 MTL/ProvStickers
86/7 MTL
87/8 MTL/Stickers 78-79, 82-83
88/9 MTL
89/90 MTL
89/90 MTL/Figurine
89/90 MTL/Kraft

CHELODI, ARMONDO
95 PaniniWorlds 92
94 Semic 309

CHENG HSIN, LI
79 PaniniSticker 359

CHEBAYEV, ALEXANDER
92/3 Classic 49
93/4 Classic 38
92/3 ClassicFourSport
93/4 ClassicProspects 194
94/5 Leaf 465
93 SemicSticker 137
94/5 ToppsFinest 14
91/2 UD 657, 'CzechWJC 18
93/4 UpperDeck 279
94/5 UpperDeck 263, C12

CHEREDARYK, STEVE
94/5 SigRookies 43

CHERNESKI, STEFAN
97/8 Bowman 117, BB10
98 BowmanCHL 76
97/8 PinnacleBeeHive 63

CHERNIK, ALEXANDER
89/90 SovietStars

CHERNOFF, MIKE
73/4 VancouverBlazers

CHERNOMAZ, RICH
95/6 DEL 403
96/7 DEL 311
89/90 ProCards(IHL) 198
90/1 ProCards 607
91/2 ProCards 586
83/4 N.J.
84/5 N.J.
81/2 Victoria
82/3 Victoria

CHERREY, SCOTT
94/5 SigRookies 5
93/4 Slapshot(NorthBay) 15
94/5 Slapshot(NorthBay) 18
95/6 Slapshot 371

CHERRY, DICK
69/70 O-Pee-Chee 173

CHERRY, DON
52/3 AnonymousOHL 100
96/7 Duracell DC21, DC22
92 NationalGame 22
74/5 OPC/Topps 161
92/3 Parkhurst [x2], -Aut.
93/4 PH-CherryPick D20
97/8 Pinnacle -CBC Sports 2

CHERVIAKOV, ALEXEI
93 SemicSticker 130

CHERVYAKOV, DENIS
92/3 ClassicProspects 69

CHEVALIER, ROB
52/3 AnonymousOHL 68

CHEVELDAE, TIM
91/2 Bowman 47
92/3 Bowman 202, 420
94/5 ClassicImages PL8
93/4 Donruss 96, 507
95/6 Donruss 325
93/4 EASports 42, 217
94/5 Flair 205
92/3 FleerUltra 46
93/4 FleerUltra 14
94/5 FleerUltra 240
95/6 Hoyle'WEST 9 (Hearts)
92/3 Kraft'-Diskk
94/5 Kraft
95/6 Kraft-Crease
93/4 Leaf 195
94/5 Leaf 81
90/1 O-Pee-Chee 430
91/2 OPC/Topps 35
92/3 O-Pee-Chee 128
91/2 opcPremier 175
90/1 PaniniSticker 212
91/2 PaniniSticker 136
92/3 PaniniSticker 111
93/4 PaniniSticker 254
94/5 PaniniSticker 171
91/2 Parkhurst 39, 441
92/3 Parkhurst 37
93/4 Parkhurst 59
95/6 Parkhurst 234
94/5 ParkieSE 203
91/2 Pinnacle 21
92/3 Pinn. 37,269,-Tm2000 20
93/4 Pinnacle 282
94/5 Pinnacle 130
95/6 Pinnacle 136
95/6 Playoff 325
96/7 Playoff 406
94/5 POG 297
95/6 POG 296
93/4 PowerPlay 67
93/4 Premier 66
94/5 Premier 502
88/9 ProCards(Adirondack)
89/90 ProCards(AHL) 326
95/6 ProMagnet 56
90/1 ProSet 602
91/2 ProSet 57, -The Puck 7
92/3 ProSet 43, 251
91/2 PSPlatinum 31
90/1 Score 87
91/2 Score(CDN) 492, (U.S) 272
91/2 Score-YoungStar 25
92/3 Score 275, 417, -Young 21
93/4 Score 68
95/6 Score 212
92/3 SeasonsPatches 7
94/5 Select 102
92/3 Topps 225, 310
95/6 Topps 291
91/2 ToppsStadiumClub 224
92/3 ToppsStadiumClub 199
93/4 ToppsStadiumClub 166
94/5 ToppsStadiumClub 217
90/1 UpperDeck 393
91/2 UpperDeck 129
92/3 UpperDeck 5, 197
93/4 UpperDeck 9
94/5 UpperDeck 75, SP178
95/6 UpperDeck 452, SE179
95/6 UDBeAPlayer 76
95/6 UDCollChoice 319
90/1 DET/Caesars
95/6 WPG
86/7 Saskatoon

CHEVELDAYOFF, KEVIN
90/1 ProCards 507
91/2 ProCards 459

CHEVREFILS, REAL
45-64 BeeHives(BOS)
52/3 Parkhurst 80
53/4 Parkhurst 89
54/5 Parkhurst 63
93/4 Parkie(56/7) 8
54/5 Topps 6
57/8 Topps 1
56-66 TorontoStar 57/8
57/8 BOS

CHEVRIER, ALAIN
86/7 O-Pee-Chee 225
87/8 OPC/Topps 58
89/90 OPC/Topps 132
90/1 O-Pee-Chee 436
87/8 opcSticker 72, 63/204
88/9 opcSticker 162
87/8 PaniniSticker 73
89/90 PaniniSticker 54
90/1 ProSet 230
89/90 CHI/Coke
85/6 N.J
86/7 N.J/SOBER
88/9 WPG/Police

CHEYNE, TRAVIS
92/3 MPSPhotoSJHL 25

CHIASSON, DAN
84/5 Sudbury 6

CHIASSON, PASCAL
91/2 SketchQMJHL 253

CHIASSON, STEVE
90/1 Bowman 234
92/3 Bowman 91
93/4 Donruss 97
95/6 Donruss 69
96/7 Donruss 120
93/4 EASports 38
94/5 Fleer 28
92/3 FleerUltra 282
93/4 FleerUltra 305
94/5 FleerUltra 268
95/6 FleerUltra 23
93/4 Leaf 111
94/5 Leaf 487
95/6 Leaf 193
96/7 Maggers 22
89/90 OPC/Topps 164
90/1 OPC/Topps 94
91/2 OPC/Topps 60, 508
92/3 O-Pee-Chee 160
98/9 Pacific 129
89/90 PaniniSticker 62
90/1 PaniniSticker 207
91/2 PaniniSticker 143
92/3 PaniniSticker 120
93/4 PaniniSticker 251
95/6 PaniniSticker 239
91/2 Parkhurst 268
92/3 Parkhurst 282
93/4 Parkhurst 55
94/5 Parkhurst 68
95/6 Parkhurst 298
91/2 Pinnacle 298
92/3 Pinnacle 339
93/4 Pinnacle 194
94/5 Pinnacle 376
95/6 Pinnacle 189
97/8 PinnacleBeAPlayer 202
95/6 Playoff 15
95/6 POG 57
93/4 PowerPlay 68
93/4 Premier 196
94/5 Premier 327, 348
90/1 ProSet 69
90/1 Score 214
91/2 Score(CDN) 513, (U.S) 293
92/3 Score 185
93/4 Score 221, -PinnacleAS 23
94/5 Score 45
95/6 Score 146
96/7 Score 235
95/6 SkyBoxEmotion 20
95/6 SkyBoxImpact 20
96/7 SP 22
92/3 Topps 37
95/6 Topps 129
96/7 ToppsNHLPicks 125
92/3 ToppsStadiumClub 105
93/4 TSC 247, -AllStar
90/1 UpperDeck 96
91/2 UpperDeck 283
92/3 UpperDeck 546
93/4 UpperDeck 345
94/5 UpperDeck 197, SP101
95/6 UpperDeck 10
96/7 UpperDeck 26
94/5 UDBAP R83, -Aut. 130
95/6 UDCollChoice 43
96/7 UDCollChoice 44
86/7 DET/Caesars
87/8 DET/Caesars
88/9 DET/Caesars
89/90 DET/Caesars
91/2 DET/Caesars

CHIBIREV, IGOR
92/3 ClassicProspects 98
93/4 ClassicProspects 61
93/4 Donruss 436
90/1 O-Pee-Chee 8R
91/2 O-Pee-Chee 14R
94/5 Parkhurst 98
93/4 PowerPlay 350

CHIN, COLIN
93/4 ClassicProspects 81
90/1 ProCards 540
91/2 ProCards 250
89/90 ProCards'IHL 123

CHINN, NICKEY
94 Semic 318
95/6 SheffieldSteelers
97/8 SheffieldSteelers

CHIPMAN, JASON
92/3 BCJHL 208
90/1 SketchOHL 53

CHIPPERFIELD, RON
80/1 O-Pee-Chee 280
74/5 opcWHA 42
75/6 opcWHA 4
76/7 opcWHA 32
77/8 opcWHA 10
79/80 EDM
88/9 EDM/ActionMagazine 74
80/1 QUE

CHISHOLM, ALEXANDER (LEX)
34-43 BeeHives(TOR)
40/1 OPC (V301-2) 148

CHITARONI, MARIO
96/8 DEL 44
88/9 ProCards(NewHaven)
94 Semic 307
93 SemicSticker 224
96 Wien 181
87/8 Flint
84/5 Sudbury 5
85/6 Sudbury 13
89/90 Sudbury 8

CHITARONI, TERRY
92/3 C'Prospects 92
90/1 SketchMEM 121
90/1 SketchOHL 380
91/2 SketchOHL 250
94/5 Slapshot(Brantford) 11
91/2 StarPics 15
91/2 UltimateDP 49, Aut 49
88/9 Sudbury 15
89/90 Sudbury 24
90/1 Sudbury 15
91/2 Sudbury 15

CHLAD, MARTIN
94/5 APS 47
95/6 APS 77

CHLUBNA, TOMAS
94/5 APS 132
95/6 APS 310

CHOKAN, DALE
90/1 SketchOHL 205
91/2 SketchOHL 116

CHOLETTE, JULES
36/7 WWGum (V356) 127

CHOLEWA, MAREK
89 SemicSticker 132
92 SemicSticker 272

CHOQUETTE, DARIN
84/5 Victoria

CHORNEY, MARC
82/3 Post
83/4 SouhaitsRen.KeyChain
83/4 PGH/Heinz

CHORNEY, GRANT
86/7 Regina

CHORSKE, TOM
91/2 Bowman 345
92/3 FleerUltra 112
94/5 Leaf 262
90/1 O-Pee-Chee 490
91/2 OPC/Topps 287
91/2 opcPremier 91
98/9 Pacific 278opc
97/8 PacificRegime 132
90/1 Panini(MTL) 4
91/2 Parkhurst 95
93/4 Parkhurst 384
91/2 Pinnacle 295
92/3 Pinnacle 293
94/5 Pinnacle 182
96/7 Pinnacle 26
97/8 PinnacleBeAPlayer 207
94/5 POG 349
93/4 PowerPlay 375
93/4 Premier 524
94/5 Premier 131
90/1 ProSet 616
92/3 Score 184
95/6 Score 284
91/2 Score(CDN) 613, (U.S) 63T
92/3 Topps 313
91/2 ToppsStadiumClub 276
92/3 ToppsStadiumClub 351
91/2 UpperDeck 427
93/4 UpperDeck 416
94/5 UpperDeck 191
95/6 UDBeAPlayer 43
95/6 CollChoice 237
89/90 MTL
90/1 MTL
95/6 OTT
96/7 OTT/PizzaHut

CHOTOWETZ, KELLY
90/1 SketchWHL 172
89/90 Regina

CHOUINARD, DAVE
90/1 SketchOHL 240
91/2 SketchQMJHL 134

CHOUINARD, ERIC
98 BowmanCHL 104, 143, A15
97/8 UpperDeck 408

CHOUINARD, GUY
72-84 Dernière 79/80
76/7 OPC 316
78/9 O-Pee-Chee 340
81/2 O-Pee-Chee 33, Topps 6
82/3 O-Pee-Chee 41
83/4 O-Pee-Chee 78
77/8 OPC/Topps 237
79/80 OPC/Topps 60
80/1 OPC/Topps 45
81/2 opcSticker 219
82/3 opcSticker 215
80/1 Pepsi Cap
82/3 Post
83/4 SouhaitsRen.KeyChain
77/8 ATL
78/9 ATL/Coke
79/80 ATL
79/80 ATL/B&W
80/1 CGY
81/2 CGY
82/3 CGY

CHOUINARD, JACQUES
80/1 Québec Ramparts

CHOUINARD, MARC
95/6 Classic 29, AS18
95/6 ClassicFiveSport 153

CHOUINARD, MATHIEU
98 BowmanCHL 82, 159, A9
97/8 UpperDeck 399

CHOWANIEC, STEFAN
74 Hellas 93
79 PaniniSticker 127
73/4 WilliamsFIN 87

CHREST, BLAINE
86/7 Saskatoon

CHRETIEN, CLAUDE
51/2 LacStJean 19

CHRISTENSEN, TED
95/6 UDCollChoice 349

CHRISTIAN, BRANDON
94/5 Johnstown 3

CHRISTIAN, DAVE
90/1 Bowman 40
91/2 Bowman 358
92/3 Bowman 6
94/5 ClassicImages 26
95/6 EdgeIce 164
92/3 FleerUltra 273
94/5 MiracleOnIce 5, 6
80/1 OPC/Topps 176
81/2 OPC 359-60, 378, T 7, 66
82/3 O-Pee-Chee 377
83/4 O-Pee-Chee 367
84/5 OPC 1,195,248, Topps 142
85/6 OPC/Topps 99
86/7 OPC/Topps 21, C
87/8 OPC/Topps 88
88/9 OPC/Topps 14
89/90 OPC/Topps 159
90/1 OPC/Topps 263
91/2 OPC/Topps 276
92/3 O-Pee-Chee 289
91/2 opcPremier 53
92/3 opcPremier 1
81/2 opcSticker 136
82/3 opcSticker 206
84/5 opcSticker 133
85/6 opcSticker 110 /243
86/7 opcSticker 248
87/8 opcSticker 235/102
88/9 opcSticker 70/199
89/90 opcSticker 78/219
87/8 PaniniSticker 184
88/9 PaniniSticker 369
89/90 PaniniSticker 345
90/1 PaniniSticker 18
91/2 PaniniSticker 173
91/2 Parkhurst 159
80/1 Pepsi Cap
91/2 Pinnacle 244
92/3 Pinnacle 193
82/3 Post
93/4 Premier 118
90/1 ProSet 6
91/2 ProSet 11, 297, 471
91/2 PSPlatinum 110
90/1 Score 295, 368
91/2 Score(CDN) 589
91/2 Score(U.S) 292, 39T
92/3 Score 198
93/4 Score 440
94 Semic 127
89 SemicSticker 166
91 SemicSticker 142
92 SemicSticker 164
83/4 SouhaitsRen.KeyChain
91/2 ToppsStadiumClub 95
92/3 ToppsStadiumClub 216
90/1 UpperDeck 61
91/2 UpperDeck 541
92/3 UpperDeck 194
79/80 USAOlympicTeam 14
89/90 BOS/SportsAction
90/1 BOS/SportsAction
93/4 CHI/Coke
91/2 STL
80/1 WPG
81/2 WPG
82/3 WPG
84/5 WSH/PizzaHut
85/6 WSH/PizzaHut
86/7 WSH/Kodak
86/7 WSH/Police
87/8 WSH
87/8 WSH/Kodak
88/9 WSH
88/9 WSH/Smokey
89/90 WSH

CHRISTIAN, GORD
93/4 Johnstown 7
94/5 Johnstown 4

CHRISTIAN, JEFF
90/1 ProCards 572
91/2 ProCards 415
95/6 Cleveland

CHRISTIAN, LOU
83/4 NovaScotia 18
84/5 NovaScotia 26

CHRISTIAN, MIKE
96/7 Guelph 13

CHRISTIANSEN, HAL
90/1 SketchWHL 164
91/2 SketchWHL 225
89/90 Regina

CHRISTIANSEN, KEITH
72 SemicSticker 124
72/3 Minnesota

CHRISTIE, FRANK
73/4 BUF

CHRISTIE, JASON
96/7 Portland
89/90 Saskatoon 21

CHRISTIE, MIKE
74/5 Loblaws
74/5 OPC 278
75/6 OPC 366
76/7 OPC 333
77/8 OPC 357
78/9 O-Pee-Chee 291
79/80 O-Pee-Chee 345
80/1 O-Pee-Chee 358
79/80 COL.R

CHRISTIE, RYAN
95/6 Slapshot 293

CHRISTISON, SCOTT
91/2 AirCanadaSJHL B18, 16

CHRISTOFF, STEVE
94/5 MiracleOnIce 7, 8
80/1 OPC/Topps 103
81/2 O-Pee-Chee 160, T(W) 104
82/3 O-Pee-Chee 42
83/4 O-Pee-Chee 169
84/5 O-Pee-Chee 81
82/3 opcSticker 194
79/80 USAOlympicTeam 13
82/3 CGY
80/1 MIN
81/2 MIN

CHRISTOFFER, JUSTIN
91/2 AirCanadaSJHL C37

CHRISTOPHER, DES
90/1 SketchWHL 207

CHRUN, MIKE
90/1 SketchWHL 188
91/2 SketchWHL 203
89/90 Spokane

CHRYSTAL, BOB
45-64 BeeHives(NYR)
54/5 Parkhurst 69
54/5 Topps 2
51/2 ClevelandBarons

CHUBAROV, ARTEM
97/8 UDBlackDiamond 69
98/9 UDChoice 284

CHURCH, BRAD
95/6 Classic 17
95/6 ClassicFiveSport 134
94/5 ClassicImages 82, PD5
95/6 Tetrad 68
95/6 TetradAutobilia 97
96/7 Portland
93/4 PrinceAlbert
95/6 PrinceAlbert

CHURCH, JACK
34-43 BeeHives(TOR)
39/40 OPC (V301-1) 52

CHURLA, SHANE
92/3 FleerUltra 315
94/5 FleerUltra 278
94/5 Leaf 364
97/8 PacificRegime 123
92/3 Parkhurst 316
93/4 Parkhurst 316
95/6 Parkhurst 81
94/5 ParkieSE 41
94/5 Pinnacle 516
96/7 Pinnacle 191
97/8 PinnacleBeAPlayer 182
95/6 Playoff 246
96/7 Playoff 365
93/4 Premier 368
95/6 ProMagnet 121
90/1 ProSet 135
91/2 Score(CDN) 542
93/4 Score 425
94/5 StadiumClub 21
94/5 UpperDeck 186
95/6 UpperDeck 458
97/8 UpperDeck 317
94/5 UDBeAPlayer-Aut. 169
87/8 CGY/RedRooster
94/5 DAL
94/5 DAL/Southwest
83/4 MedicineHat

CHYCHRUN, JEFF
92/3 Bowman 257
92/3 Durivage 33
89/90 O-Pee-Chee 311
90/1 O-Pee-Chee 465
90/1 ProSet 213
90/1 Score 138
91/2 Score(CDN) 626
92/3 Score 364
92/3 Topps 196
92/3 ToppsStadiumClub 298
90/1 UpperDeck 446
89/90 PHA
90/1 PHA

CHYNOWETH, DEAN
97/8 PacificCrown 340
97/8 PinnacleBeAPlayer 246
94/5 Premier 45
90/1 ProCards 511
91/2 ProCards 463
97/8 UpperDeck 222
89/90 NYI

CHYNOWETH, ED
90/1 SketchMEM 71
91/2 SketchWHL 120

CHYZOWSKI, BARRY
89/90 ProCards(IHL) 42

CHYZOWSKI, DAVID
91/2 Bowman 229
90/1 OPC/Topps 146
91/2 OPC/Topps 435
91/2 PaniniSticker 253
90/1 ProCards 509
91/2 ProCards 471
90/1 ProSet 483
90/1 Score 372, -YoungStar 12
91/2 Score(CDN)443
89/90 SketchMEM 3
91/2 ToppsStadiumClub 250
90/1 UpperDeck 228
91/2 UpperDeck 281
89/90 NYI
95/6 Adirondack

CHYZOWSKI, RON
88/9 ProCards(Sherbrooke)

CIARCIA, JERRY
82 SemicSticker 142

CIAVAGLIA, PETER
92/3 Classic 103
92/3 ClassicFiveSport 215
95/6 EdgeIce 121
95 PaniniWorlds 222
91/2 ProCards 12
93/4 Score 474

CICCARELLI, DINO
90/1 Bowman 69, -HatTrick 15
91/2 Bowman 302
92/3 Bowman 176
93/4 Donruss 98
94/5 Donruss 86
95/6 Donruss 30
96/7 Donruss 150
97/8 Donruss 177
97/8 DonrussElite 43
97/8 DonrussPreferred 51
97/8 DonrussPriority 66
97/8 DonrussCanadianIce 77
97/8 DonrussStudio 65
93/4 EASports 41
94/5 Flair 46
96/7 Flair 86
94/5 Fleer 57
92/3 FleerUltra 47, 283
93/4 FleerUltra 32
94/5 FleerUltra 58
95/6 FleerUltra 232
96/7 FleerUltra 156
97/8 KatchMedallion 134
84/5 Kelloggs Disk
90/1 Kraft 7
91/2 Kraft 14
93/4 Leaf 18
94/5 Leaf 44
95/6 Leaf 100
96/7 Leaf 16
97/8 Leaf 83
97/8 Limited 25
96/7 Maggers 57
82/3 McDonalds 7
96/7 MetalUniverse 143
97/8 Omega 97
81/2 O-Pee-Chee 161, T(W) 105
82/3 O-Pee-Chee 162, 165
83/4 O-Pee-Chee 164, 170
84/5 O-Pee-Chee 97
85/6 OPC/Topps 13
86/7 OPC/Topps 138
87/8 OPC/Topps 81
88/9 OPC/Topps 175
89/90 OPC/Topps 41
90/1 OPC/Topps 100
91/2 OPC/Topps 429
92/3 O-Pee-Chee 249
90/1 opcPremier 14
92/3 opcPremier 44
82/3 opcSticker 189
83/4 opcSticker 118, 119
84/5 opcSticker 47
85/6 opcSticker 39 /168
86/7 opcSticker 169
87/8 opcSticker 57, 118/130
88/9 opcSticker 202
89/90 opcSticker 75/214
98/9 Pacific 22
97/8 PacificCrown 15, TmCL 23
97/8 PacificCrownRoyale 124
97/8 PacificDynagon! 115
97/8 PcfcD-BstKpt 88,-Tandm 57
97/8 PacificInvin. 129, -Attack 22
97/8 PacificParamount 171
98/9 PcfcParamnt 94,-TmCL 11
97/8 PacificRegime 183
97/8 PacificRevolution 58
87/8 PaniniSticker 293
88/9 PaniniSticker 93
89/90 PaniniSticker 342
90/1 PaniniSticker 161
91/2 PaniniSticker 207
92/3 PaniniSticker 160
93/4 PaniniSticker 245
95/6 PaniniSticker 182
97/8 PaniniSticker 100
91/2 Parkhurst 193
92/3 Parkhurst 45
93/4 Parkhurst 60, D5
94/5 Parkhurst 65
95/6 Parkhurst 339
94/5 ParkieSE seV2
91/2 Pinnacle 128
92/3 Pinnacle 311
93/4 Pinnacle 127, 239
94/5 Pinnacle 241
95/6 Pinnacle 74
96/7 Pinnacle 31
97/8 Pinnacle 68
97/8 PinnacleBeeHive 29
97/8 PinnacleCertified 105
97/8 PinnacleInside 134
95/6 PinnZenith 51, -Gifted 16
96/7 PinnacleZenith 87
95/6 Playoff 251
94/5 POG 86
95/6 POG 99
93/4 PowerPlay 69
93/4 Premier 49
94/5 Premier 541
90/1 ProSet 308
91/2 ProSet 258
91/2 PSPlatinum 131
83/4 PuffySticker 15
90/1 Score 230, -HotCards 94
91/2 Score(CDN) 128, (U.S) 128
92/3 Score 395
93/4 Score 214
94/5 Score 19, 243, 246
95/6 Score 247
96/7 Score 101
97/8 Score 119, -Checkit 15
94/5 Select 118
95/6 SelectCertified 102
84/5 7ElevenDisk
85/6 7Eleven 9
95/6 SkyBoxEmotion 51
95/6 SkyBoxImpact 50
94/5 Slapshot(Sarnia) 29
83/4 SouhaitsRen.KeyChain
96/7 SP 147
97/8 SPAuthentic 148, I27
95/6 Summit 65
84/5 Topps 73
90/1 Topps TeamLdr 6
92/3 Topps 318
95/6 Topps 77
98/9 Topps
96/7 ToppsNHLPicks FC3
91/2 ToppsStadiumClub 118
92/3 ToppsStadiumClub 399
93/4 ToppsStadiumClub 294
94/5 ToppsStadiumClub 191
95/6 T.StadiumClub 150, PS7
90/1 UpperDeck 76
91/2 UpperDeck 276
92/3 UpperDeck 461
93/4 UpperDeck 136, SP-41
94/5 UpperDeck 5, SP112
95/6 UpperDeck 431, SE28
96/7 UpperDeck 196, 336, P22
96/7 UD-AllStarYCTG AR17
97/8 UpperDeck 154, 199
94/5 UDBeAPlayer R39, R129
95/6 UDBeAPlayer 49
96/7 UDBlackDiamond 148
97/8 UDBlackDiamond 21
98/9 UDChoice 93
95/6 UDCollChoice 89
96/7 UDCollChoice 65
97/8 UDCC 237, S22, SQ22, C2
97/8 UpperDeck"Ice" 22, 66
97/8 Zenith 47
97/8 FLA/WinnDixie
81/2 MIN
82/3 MIN (x2)
83/4 MIN
84/5 MIN
84/5 MIN/7Eleven 12
85/6 MIN
85/6 MIN/7Eleven 1
86/7 MIN/7Eleven 6
87/8 MIN
88/9 MIN/American
89/90 WSH
89/90 WSH/Kodak
90/1 WSH/Kodak
90/1 WSH/Smokey
91/2 WSH
91/2 WSH/Kodak

CICCONE, ENRICO
93/4 Leaf 375
92/3 opcPremier 122
98/9 Pacific 397
97/8 PacificRegime 43
93/4 Parkhurst 219
96/7 PinnacleBeAPlayer 129
95/6 POG 254
90/1 ProCards 120
91/2 UpperDeck 51
92/3 UpperDeck 90
93/4 UpperDeck 528
94/5 UpperDeck 460
95/6 UpperDeck 382
96/7 UpperDeck 238
94/5 UDBAP R16, -Aut. 132
95/6 UDCollChoice 152
94/5 T.B./SkyBoxSportsCafe
95/6 T.B.
95/6 T.B./SkyBoxSportsCafe

CICHOCKI, CHRIS
86/7 OPC/Topps 41
86/7 opcSticker 124/184
88/9 ProCards(Utica)
90/1 ProCards 14
91/2 ProCards 206
85/6 DET/Caesars
92/3 Binghampton
96/7 Cincinnati

CIERNY, JOZEF
92/3 Classic 35
93/4 Classic 127
92/3 ClassicFourSport 182
93/4 ClassicProspects 86
94/5 Score 217
93/4 EDM 11MAR94
94/5 CapeBreton

CIESLA, HANK
52/3 AnonymousOHL 32
45-64 BeeHives(CHI)
63/4 Parkhurst 51
93/4 Parkie(56/7) 29
58/9 Topps 49

CIGER, ZDENO
91/2 Bowman 280, 408
93/4 Donruss 113
94/5 Donruss 274
95/6 Donruss 360

96/7 Donruss 203
95/6 DonrussElite 24
95/6 FleerMetal 53
96/7 FleerNHLPicks 96
92/3 FleerUltra 113
93/4 FleerUltra 315
94/5 FleerUltra 71
95/6 FleerUltra 237
93/4 Leaf 197
94/5 Leaf 65
96/7 Leaf 76
96/7 Maggers 65
91/2 OPC/Topps 352
92/3 O-Pee-Chee 88
90/1 opcPremier 15
92/3 PaniniSticker 175
93/4 PaniniSticker 239
94/5 PaniniSticker 200
96/7 PaniniSticker 259
92/3 Parkhurst 286
93/4 Parkhurst 336
94/5 Parkhurst 76
95/6 Parkhurst 79
92/3 Pinnacle 302
94/5 Pinnacle 70
96/7 Pinnacle 148
93/4 PowerPlay 78
93/4 Premier 456
90/1 ProSet 619
90/1 ScoreTraded 82T
91/2 Score(CDN) 405
92/3 Score 534
93/4 Score 388
94/5 Score 122
96/7 Score 20
94 Semic 198
92 SemicSticker 144
95/6 SP 53
96/7 Summit 19
92/3 Topps 496
95/6 ToppsFinest 107
91/2 ToppsStadiumClub 379
92/3 ToppsStadiumClub 228
93/4 ToppsStadiumClub 73
94/5 ToppsStadiumClub 229
95/6 ToppsStadiumClub 127
90/1 UpperDeck 429
91/2 UpperDeck 385
92/3 UpperDeck 457
93/4 UpperDeck 330
94/5 UpperDeck 28
95/6 UDBeAPlayer 137
96/7 UDCollChoice 95
96 Wien 229
92/3 EDM
90/1 N.J.

CIHAL, MIROSLAV
95/6 APS 230

CIHLAR, JIRI
94/5 APS 177
95/6 APS 189

CIKL, IGOR
95/6 APS 113, 344

CIMELLARO, TONY
96/7 DEL 109
90/1 SketchOHL 54
91/2 SketchOHL 109

CIMETTA, ROBERT
91/2 Bowman 160
94/5 DEL 280
95/6 DEL 276
96/7 DEL 181
90/1 O-Pee-Chee 288
91/2 OPC/Topps 256
91/2 opcPremier 160
92/3 Topps 181
91/2 ToppsStadiumClub 9
92/3 ToppsStadiumClub 83
89/90 BOS/SportsAction
90/1 TOR/P.L.A.Y. 25

CIPRIANO, MARK
90/1 SketchWHL 242
89/90 Victoria

CIRCELLI, ANTHONY
95 Globe 229
95 PaniniWorlds 82
95 Semic 173
92 SemicSticker 248
93 SemicSticker 215

CIRELLA, JOE
83 CanadaJuniors
96/7 DEL 346
93/4 EASports 49
93/4 Leaf 269
82/3 O-Pee-Chee 137
84/5 O-Pee-Chee 110, Topps 85
85/6 OPC/Topps 98
86/7 OPC/Topps 163
87/8 OPC/Topps 170
88/9 OPC/Topps 188
89/90 OPC/Topps 130
90/1 OPC/Topps 107
91/2 OPC/Topps 502
84/5 opcSticker 74
86/7 opcSticker 63, 198/67
87/8 opcSticker 61/203
88/9 opcSticker 79/208
89/90 opcSticker 126
90/1 Panini(QUE) 1
87/8 PaniniSticker 75
88/9 PaniniSticker 268
90/1 PaniniSticker 141
92/3 PaniniSticker 43
91/2 Parkhurst 340
93/4 Parkhurst 347
93/4 Pinnacle 346, -Expansion 3
94/5 Pinnacle 308
82/3 Post
93/4 PowerPlay 91
93/4 Premier 41, 414
90/1 ProSet 243
90/1 Score 305
91/2 Score(CDN) 441
92/3 Score 369
93/4 Score 515
92/3 Topps 163
92/3 ToppsStadiumClub 479
93/4 ToppsStadiumClub 2
90/1 UpperDeck 293
93/4 UpperDeck 65
81/2 COL.R
93/4 FLA
97/8 FLA/WinnDixie
83/4 N.J
84/5 N.J
86/7 N.J/SOBER
88/9 N.J/Caretta
95/6 OTT
89/90 QUE
89/90 QUE/GeneralFoods
89/90 QUE/Police
90/1 QUE
90/1 QUE/PetroCan

CIRELLI, ANTHONY
96/7 DEL 223

CIRILLO, RYAN
95/6 Slapshot 191

CIRJAK, JOHN
97/8 Bowman 95
95/6 Spokane 16

CIRONE, JASON
91/2 ProCards 183
90/1 SketchOHL 30, 178
91/2 UpperDeck 605
91/2 Moncton

CISAR, MARIAN
98 BowmanCHL 58
97/8 PinnacleBeeHive 67

CLACKSON, KIM
81/2 O-Pee-Chee 271
80/1 Pepsi Cap
80/1 QUE
77/8 Winnipeg

CLAESSON, STEFAN
89/90 SemicElitserien 9
90/1 SemicElitserien 82
91/2 SemicElitserien 234

CLAGHORN, SPRAGUE
83&87 HallOfFame 66
83 HHOF Postcard (E)

CLAGUE, JASON
93/4 RedDeer

CLANCY, CHRIS
90/1 SketchOHL 31
91/2 SketchOHL 16

CLANCY, FRANCIS (KING)
25-27 Anonymous 17, 18
33/4 Anonymous (V129) 8
34-43 BeeHives(TOR)
35/6 Champion
24/5 Champs (C144)
33/4 CndGum (V252)
35-40 CrownBrand 111
83&87 HallOfFame 33
33/4 Hamilton V288 17
83 HHOF Postcard (C)
92/3 HHOFLegends 8
27-32 LaPresse 29/30
33/4 OPC (V304A) 31
36/7 OPC (V304D) 125
55/6 Parkhurst 33
59/60 Parkhurst 50
63/4 Parkhurst 20
93/4 Parkie(56/7) P4
94/5 Parkie(64/5) 132
34/5 SweetCaporal
60/1 Topps 47
61/2 Topps-Stamp
23/4 (V145-1) 3
24/5 (V145-2) 3
33/4 WWGum(V357) 13,-Prem.
36/7 WWGum (V356) 29
61/2 York 39
32/3 TOR/OKeefe 7
69/70 TOR
78/9 TOR
80/1 TOR

CLANCY, GREG
89/90 SketchOHL 59
90/1 SketchOHL 81

CLANCY, TERRY
69/70 TOR
72/3 TOR

CLANTARA, ROLAND
51/2 LacStJean 52

CLAPPER, AUBREY (DIT)
33/4 Anonymous (V129) 36
34-43 BeeHives(BOS)
33/4 CndGum (V252)
33-35 DiamondMatch
83&87 HallOfFame 79
83 HHOF Postcard (F)
33/4 OPC (V304A) 8
39/40 OPC (V301-1) 95
94/5 Parkie(64/5)-Greats 8
60/1 Topps 26
61/2 Topps-Stamp
33/4 WWGum (V357) 1
36/7 WWGum (V356) 36
91/2 BOS/Legends

CLARK, ANDREW
96/7 DEL 307
93/4 Slapshot(SSSMarie) 18
94/5 Slapshot(Guelph) 10
95/6 Slapshot 90
95/6 Guelph 2

CLARK, BRETT
97/8 MTL

CLARK, DEAN
88/9 EDM/ActionMagazine 100
84/5 Kamloops

CLARK, DON
91/2 SketchWHL 149
81/2 Saskatoon 4
92/3 Tacoma

CLARK, GARY
95/6 DEL 359
96/7 DEL 182

CLARK, GEORGE
23/4 CrescentSelk. 5
26 Dominion 26

CLARK, KERRY
94/5 C-Enforcers E7
95/6 EdgeIce 171
88/9 ProCards(Springfield)
89/90 ProCards(AHL) 248
90/1 ProCards 620
91/2 ProCards 584
86/7 Saskatoon

CLARK, NORBERT
51/2 LacStJean 20

CLARK, RON
89/90 Rayside

CLARK, WENDEL
90/1 Bowman 159
91/2 Bowman 156
92/3 Bowman 325
95/6 Bowman 45
93/4 Donruss 337
95/6 Donruss 193, 389
96/7 Donruss 98, -Hit 2, -Dom 6
97/8 Donruss 57
96/7 DonrussCanadianIce 29
97/8 DonrussCanadianIce 80
95/6 DonrussElite 27
96/7 DonrussElite 98
97/8 DonrussPriority 150
94/5 Flair 142
96/7 Flair 89
94/5 Fleer 173, -Slapshot 1
95/6 FleerMetal 89
96/7 FleerNHLPicks 130
92/3 FleerUltra 208
93/4 FleerUltra 146
94/5 FleerUltra 172, 354
95/6 FleerUltra 136, 265
96/7 FleerUltra 162
88/9 FritoLay
91/2 Gillette 11
95/6 Hoyle'EAST 8 (Hearts)
92/3 HumptyDumpty (1)
97/8 KatchMedallion 139
91/2 Kelloggs 3
86/7 Kraft Sports 52
89/90 Kraft 34
91/2 Kraft 42
93/4 Kraft-Captain
94/5 Kraft'HockeyHeroes
95/6 Kraft-Ticket
93/4 Leaf 166
94/5 Leaf 542
95/6 Leaf 207
96/7 Leaf 166
94/5 LeafLimited 31
95/6 LeafLimited 70
96/7 LeafLimited 12, -Stubble 20
96/7 LeafPreferred 87, -Steel 48
97/8 Limited 40
96/7 Maggers 153
94/5 McDonalds McD24
96/7 MetalUniverse 148
97/8 Omega 218
86/7 OPC/Topps 149
87/8 OPC/Topps 12
90/1 OPC/Topps 179
91/2 OPC/Topps 464
92/3 O-Pee-Chee 96
91/2 opcPremier 116, 177
86/7 opcSticker 141, 125/185
87/8 opcSticker 152
88/9 opcSticker 172/41
98/9 Pacific 411
97/8 PacificCrown 17, -Slap 10A
97/8 PacificCrownRoyale 129
97/8 PcfcDynag! 121,-Tandm 27
97/8 PacificInvincible 136
97/8 PacificParamount 179
97/8 PacificRevolution 133
90/1 Panini(TOR) 3
87/8 PaniniSticker 320, 330
88/9 PaniniSticker 121
89/90 PaniniSticker 144
90/1 PaniniSticker 286
91/2 PaniniSticker 102
92/3 PaniniSticker 79
93/4 PaniniSticker 227
94/5 PaniniSticker 195
95/6 PaniniSticker 247
96/7 PaniniSticker 213
97/8 PaniniSticker 174
91/2 Parkhurst 170
92/3 Parkhurst 179, CP11
93/4 Parkhurst 475, F9
95/6 Parkhurst 399
94/5 ParkieSE 146
91/2 Pinnacle 250
92/3 Pinnacle 276
93/4 Pinnacle 157, CA23
94/5 Pinnacle 385, GR13. NL5
96/7 Pinn. 196, -Full 9, -First 8
97/8 Pinnacle 185
97/8 PinnacleCertified 71
95/6 PinnacleFANtasy 21
97/8 PinnacleInside 89
95/6 PinnacleZenith 94, -Gifted 3
96/7 PinnacleZenith 24
95/6 Playoff 279
96/7 Playoff 411
94/5 POG 194
95/6 POG 174
93/4 PowerPlay 241
93/4 Premier 359, -Finest 9
94/5 Premier 55, 297, 345
94/5 Prmr-Finest(Topps) 10
95/6 ProMagnet 54
90/1 ProSet 276
91/2 ProSet 225, 585
92/3 ProSet 189
91/2 PSPlatinum 120
87/8 ProSportWatch CW10
90/1 Score 171
91/2 Score(CDN) 116, (U.S) 116
92/3 Score 110
93/4 Score 137
94/5 Score 3, -Promo 3, CI13
95/6 Score 57
96/7 Score 42, -CheckIt 7
97/8 Score 128
97/8 Score(TOR) 5
92/3 SeasonsPatch 70
94/5 Select 20
95/6 SelectCertified 82
96/7 SelectCert. 65, -Promo 65
95/6 SkyBoxImpact 99
96/7 SkyBoxImpact 125
94/5 SP 97
96/7 SP 150
97/8 SPAuthentic 152
95/6 Summit 131, -MadHat 8
96/7 Summit 140
95/6 SuperSticker 77
92/3 Topps 325
95/6 Topps 269, HGC2
98/9 Topps 142
94/5 ToppsFinest 103
95/6 ToppsFinestS 87
91/2 ToppsStadiumClub 124
92/3 ToppsStadiumClub 204
93/4 ToppsStadiumClub 192
95/6 TSC 155, F8, PS8
94/5 TSC-MembersOnly 18
97/8 ToppsSticker 2
95/6 ToppsSuperSkills 45
90/1 UpperDeck 3
91/2 UpperDeck 386
92/3 UpperDeck 89
93/4 UpperDeck 340
94/5 UpperDeck 115, SP145
95/6 UpperDeck 325, SE139
96/7 UpperDeck 342, X15
97/8 UpperDeck 164
93/4 UDBeAPlayer 'Roots 6
94/5 UDBeAPlayer R72, R142
95/6 UDBeAPlayer 55
96/7 UDBlackDiamond 107
98/9 UDChoice 202
95/6 UDCollChoice 103
96/7 UDCollChoice 258
97/8 UDCollChoice 246
94/5 QUE/BurgerKing
85/6 TOR
86/7 TOR
87/8 TOR
87/8 TOR/P.L.A.Y. 6
88/9 TOR/P.L.A.Y. 2
90/1 TOR/P.L.A.Y. 14
92/3 TOR/Kodak
93/4 TOR/Albalene
93/4 TOR/Blacks 1
83/4 Saskatoon 8
84/5 Saskatoon

CLARKE, BOBBY
77/8 Coke Mini
70/1 DadsCookies
72-84 Dernière 79/80, 82/3
70/1 EddieSargent 148
71/2 EddieSargent 152
72/3 EddieSargent 162
70/1 Esso Stamp
88/9 EssoAllStar
87 HallOfFame 258
92/3 HHOFLegends 16
93/4 HockeyWit 80
84/5 KelownaWings 41
91/2 Kraft 54, 67
74/5 LiptonSoup 21
74/5 Loblaws
73/4 MacsMilk Disk
70/1 O-Pee-Chee 195
71/2 OPC/T. 114, -Booklet 10
72/3 OPC 14, -TeamCanada
73/4 OPC/Topps 50
73/4 OPC 134-35, Topps 2, 3
74/5 OPC/T. 3, 135, 154, 260
75/6 OPC/T. 209, 250, 286, 325
76/7 OPC/Topps 2, 3, 70, 215
76/7 OPC 391, T-Glossy 1
77/8 OPC/Topps 115, -Glossy 3
78/9 OPC/Topps 215
79/80 OPC/Topps 125
80/1 OPC/Topps 55
81/2 OPC 240, T(E) 103
82/3 O-Pee-Chee 248
83/4 O-Pee-Chee 258, 262
92/3 OPC 43, -25Years 3
81/2 opcSticker 178
82/3 opcSticker 115
83/4 opcSticker 12, 198, 302
80/1 opcSuperCard 16
92/3 Parkhurst 468
91/2 Pinnacle 386
82/3 Post
81/2 Post PopUp 7
90/1 ProSet 651, 657
83/4 PuffySticker 7
83/4 SouhaitsRen.KeyChain
77-79 Sportscaster 31-03, 60/12
77-79 Sprtscstr 38-891, 69-1649
72/3 Topps 90
71/2 TheTorontoSun
91/2 Trends(72) 57, -Aut.
92/3 Trends(76) 177, -Aut.
90/1 UpperDeck 509
72/3 PHA/MightyMilk
75/6 PHA/GingerAle
83/4 PHA
89/90 PHA
92/3 PHA/UD 12APR93

CLARKE, CHRIS
95/6 DEL 363
91/2 ProCards 560

CLARKE, HERB
1910-11 Imperial(C56) 11

CLARKE, JASON
91/2 SketchOHL 202

CLARKE, JIM
75/6 Phoenix
81/2 Regina 10

CLARKE, JOE
93/4 SSMarie 8
75/6 Hamilton

CLARKE, TODD
83/4 Ottawa67s

CLAUSE, GREG
75/6 Hamilton

CLAUSS, KARL
91/2 Knoxville

CLAYTON, MIKE
84/5 Moncton 12

CLEARWATER, RAY
72/3 Cleveland

CLEARY, DANIEL
96/7 AllSportPPF 178
94/5 AutoPhonex 15, P3
97/8 Bowman 2, 121, BB7
95/6 Classic 83, AS11
97/8 DonrussElite 37, 123
97/8 DE-Craftsmn 10,-BackTo 4
97/8 D.onrussreferred 152, 199
97/8 D.Pref -LineOfTimes 6C
97/8 DonrussPriority 166, 217
97/8 KatchMedallion 33
97/8 Leaf 159, 200
97/8 Limited-fabric 68
97/8 McDonalds McD36
97/8 PacificDynagon! Rookies
97/8 PacificParamount 42
97/8 Pinnacle 10
97/8 PinnacleBeAPlayer 224
97/8 PinnacleCertified E
98/9 SPx"Finite" 20, 128
96/7 SB'AutColl 46, -Aut
97/8 VisionsSig 42
97/8 Score 61
95/6 Slapshot 39
97/8 SPAuthentic 177
95/6 TetradAutobilia 41
95/6 UpperDeck 507
97/8 UpperDeck 247
98/9 UDChoice 44
97/8 UDCollChoice 307
97/8 UpperDeckIce 38

CLEARY, JOE
92/3 Indianapolis

CLEGHORN, ODIE
25-27 Anonymous 46 [x2], 57
91 C55Reprint 25
24/5 Champs(C144)
25 Dominion 117
1911-12 Imperial(C55) 25
1912-13 Imperial(C57) 50
1910-11 Imperial Post 25
23/4 (V145-1) 18
24/5 (V145-2) 45

CLEGHORN, SPRAGUE
25-27 Anonymous 31, 41
91 C55 Reprint 24
24/5 Champs (C144)
1911-12 Imperial C55 24
1912-13 Imperial C57 15
1910-11 Imperial Post 24
24/5 MapleCrispette (V130) 15
61/2 Topps-Stamp
23/4 (V145-1) 11
24/5 (V145-2) 49
95/6 MTL/Forum 21-Oct

CLEMENS, KEVIN
87/8 Regina

CLEMENT, BILL
72/3 EddieSargent 168
74/5 Loblaws
74/5 O-Pee-Chee 357
75/6 OPC/Topps 189
76/7 OPC/Topps 82
77/8 O-Pee-Chee 292
78/9 O-Pee-Chee 364
79/80 O-Pee-Chee 295
80/1 O-Pee-Chee 376
81/2 O-Pee-Chee 39
82/3 O-Pee-Chee 44
92/3 Parkhurst 478
80/1 Pepsi Cap
77/8 ATL
78/9 ATL/Coke
79/80 ATL
79/80 ATL/B&W
80/1 CGY
81/2 CGY

CLEMENT, PATRICK
90/1 SketchMEM 31
91/2 SketchQMJHL 85

CLEMENT, SEAN
88/9 ProCards(Moncton)

CLEMENTS, SCOTT
88/9 ProCards(Indianapolis)

CLIFFORD, CHRIS
88/9 ProCards(Saginaw)
89/90 ProCards'IHL 144
90/1 ProCards 372

CLIMIE, RON
72/3 O-Pee-Chee 318
73/4 OPC-Posters 12
74/5 opcWHA 15
75/6 opcWHA 52
72/3 OttawaNationals

CLINE, BRUCE
52/3 LavalDairy 70
52/3 StLawrence 23
93/4 Parkie(56/7) 106

CLOCH, IVANO
92 SemicSticker 263

CLOUSTON, SHAUN
89/90 ProCards'IHL 166
90/1 ProCards 333
86/7 Portland
87/8 Portland
88/9 Portland

CLOUTIER, COLIN
94/5 SigRookies 4
94/5 Slapshot(MEM) 45

CLOUTIER, DAN
94/5 Classic 22
95/6 Classic 95
94/5 ClassicFourtSport 139
94/5 ClassicImages 49
94/5 C4'Images 113
95/6 Donruss-CdnJr. 2
98/9 Pacific 291
98/9 PacificParamount 150
97/8 PacificRevolution 85
94/5 ParkieSE 210
94/5 Pinnacle 522
93/4 Slapshot(SSMarie) 3
95/6 Slapshot 95, 357
94/5 SP 146
98/9 SPx"Finite" 125
94/5 SRGoldStandard 80
94/5 SRTetrad CV
95/6 Topps 18CJ
94/5 ToppsFinest 145
94/5 UpperDeck 498
97/8 UDBlackDiamond 78
98/9 UDChoice 131
96/7 Binghampton
93/4 SSMarie 27
95/6 Guelph 22

CLOUTIER, DENIS
90/1 SketchQMJHL 111

CLOUTIER, ERIC
95/6 Louisiana-Playoffs

CLOUTIER, FRANÇOIS
94/5 Slapshot(MEM) 65

CLOUTIER, JACQUES
90/1 Bowman 11
91/2 Bowman 146
92/3 Bowman 332
92/3 Durivage 46
93/4 Durivage 18
90/1 OPC/Topps 378
91/2 OPC/Topps 286
92/3 O-Pee-Chee 113
87/8 PaniniSticker 21
90/1 PaniniSticker 197
91/2 Parkhurst 368
88/9 ProCards(Rochester)
90/1 ProSet 428
91/2 PSPlatinum 219
91/2 Score(CDN) 236
92/3 Score 378
97/8 SouhaitsRen.KeyChain
92/3 Topps 66
91/2 ToppsStadiumClub 166
92/3 ToppsStadiumClub 118
90/1 UpperDeck 114
92/3 UpperDeck 324
82/3 BUF/Wendt 9
86/7 BUF
87/8 BUF/BlueShield
87/8 BUF/WonderBread
88/9 BUF/BlueShield
88/9 BUF/WonderBread
89/90 CHI/Coke
90/1 CHI/Coke
91/2 QUE/PetroCanada
92/3 QUE/PetroCanada

CLOUTIER, NICHOL
90/1 SketchQMJHL 243

CLOUTIER, PATRICK
90/1 SketchQMJHL 216

CLOUTIER, RÉAL
72-84 Dernière 77/8, 78/9, 81/2
79/80 OPC/Topps 239
80/1 OPC/Topps 178, 238
82/3 O-Pee-Chee 279, 280
83/4 O-Pee-Chee 62
84/5 O-Pee-Chee 19, Topps 15
81/2 opcSticker 25
82/3 opcSticker 23
83/4 opcSticker 246
74/5 opcWHA 63
75/6 opcWHA 16
76/7 opcWHA 1, 3, 76
77/8 opcWHA 8
80/1 Pepsi Cap
81/2 Post PopUp 17
82/3 Post
83/4 PuffySticker 10
83/4 SouhaitsRen.KeyChain
77-9 Sprtscster 78-04, 90-2139
80/1 QUE
81/2 QUE
82/3 QUE
83/4 QUE
76/7 QuébecNordiques
76 QuébecNordiques/MA

CLOUTIER, RÉJEAN
80/1 DET
84/5 NovaScotia 5

CLOUTIER, SYLVAIN
92/3 Classic 22
92/3 ClassicFourSport
91/2 SketchOHL 350
93/4 Slapshot(Guelph) 9
95/6 Adirondack

CLOWES, LUKE
93/4 Slapshot(Windsor) 22
94/5 Slapshot(Windsor) 24
92/3 Windsor 3

CLUNE, ART
52/3 AnonymousOHL 152

CLUNE, WALTER
51/2 LavalDairy 96
52/3 LavalDairy 96
52/3 StLawrence 12

CLYMER, BEN
95/6 D.Elite-WorldJrs 27

COALTER, BRANDON
95/6 Slapshot 237

COALTER, GARY
74/5 Loblaws
74/5 OPC/Topps 17
75/6 O-Pee-Chee 334

COATES, BRANDON
91/2 SketchWHL 35

COCCIOLO, VINCE
89/90 Portland

COCHRANE, GLEN
86/7 Kraft Sports 63
82/3 Post
83/4 SouhaitsRen.KeyChain
87/8 CHI/Coke
88/9 EDM/ActionMagazine 101
83/4 PHA
85/6 VAN
86/7 VAN

COCKBURN, BILL
24/5 Crescent Falcons 1
27-32 LaPresse 31/2

COCUZ, SASHA
94/5 Slapshot(Sarnia) 26

CODE, CHRIS
90/1 SketchOHL 206

CODE, TONY
93/4 WestMich.

COFFEY, PAUL
95/6 Aces A (Clubs)
90/1 Bowman 211
91/2 Bowman 81
92/3 Bowman 181, 226
95/6 Bowman 41
97/8 Corinthian Headliners
93/4 Donruss 99
94/5 Donruss 54, -Dom. 6
95/6 Donruss 119, -Dom. 7
96/7 Donruss 140, 238, -Dom. 3
96/7 Donruss -Igniter 2, -Elite 5
97/8 Donruss 63, -Line2Line 15
96/7 D.CanadianIce 9, 149
97/8 DCI 64, -Scrap 30,-Nat'l 23
95/6 Don.Elite 85, -Cutting 13
96/7 Don.Elite 72, -Perspective 5
97/8 DonrussElite 63
97/8 DonrussPreferred 12
97/8 DonrussPriority 110
97/8 DonrussStudio 85
96/7 Duracell DC1, JB1
93/4 EASports 37
83/4 Esso
88/9 Esso Sticker
94/5 Flair 47
96/7 Flair 66, -HotNumber 2
94/5 Fleer 58
96/7 Fleer 29, 140, -Norris 3
95/6 FleerMetal 44
96/7 FleerNHLPicks 20
96/7 F.Picks-Fav 8, -Jagged 18
92/3 FleerUltra 80, -AS 1,5
93/4 FleerUltra 71
94/5 FleerUltra 59, -AS 9
95/6 FleerUltra 44
96/7 FU 122, -Blue 3, -Power 3
88/9 FritoLay
91/2 Gillette 37
95 Globe 76
93/4 HockeyWit 46
95/6 Hoyle'WEST 10 (Hearts)
97/8 KatchMedallion 103
84/5 Kelloggs Disk
96/7 KennerSLU (U.S)
97/8 KennerSLU
86/7 Kraft Sports 12
89/90 Kraft 54, -Stickers 3
90/1 Kraft 8, 82
91/2 Kraft 74
92/3 Kraft'AllStar
93/4 Kraft
95/6 Kraft, -Disk
93/4 Leaf 67, -AS 7
94/5 Leaf 168, -FireOnIce 8
95/6 Leaf 144, -RoadTo 5
95/6 L-Gold 2, -FireOnIce 8
96/7 Leaf 164, -Leather 4
97/8 Leaf 21
94/5 LeafLimited 75
95/6 LeafLimited 24
96/7 LeafLimited 18, -Stubble 4
96/7 LeafPreferred 101
97/8 Limited 6,100,108,-fabric 12
96/7 Maggers 62
91/2 McDonalds McD11
92/3 McDonalds Mc D-17
93/4 McDonalds M cD04
94/5 McDonalds McD19
95/6 McDonalds McD4
96/7 McDonalds McD1
96/7 MetalUniv. 67, -IceCarv. 4
97/8 Omega 161
81/2 O-Pee-Chee 111
82/3 O-Pee-Chee 101, 102
83/4 O-Pee-Chee 25
84/5 OPC 217, 239, T. 50, 163
85/6 OPC/Topps 85, T-AS 4
86/7 OPC/Topps 137, T-AS 5
87/8 OPC/Topps 99
88/9 OPC/Topps 179
89/90 OPC/Topps 95
90/1 OPC/Topps 116, 202, C
91/2 OPC/Topps 183, 504
92/3 O-Pee-Chee 5, 187, 318
92/3 OPC-25Years 14
90/1 opcPremier 16
91/2 opcPremier 79
92/3 opcPremier-Star 4
87/8 opcStars 8
88/9 opcStars 6
82/3 opcSticker 104, 105, 160
83/4 opcSticker 94-95
84/5 opcSticker 134, 251-52
85/6 opcSticker 124, 217,
85/6 opcSticker 191/67, 56/204
86/7 opcStkr. 68,188/47,112/126
87/8 opcSticker 89
88/9 opcSticker 233/101
89/90 opcSticker 237
98/9 Pacific 322
97/8 PacificCrown 77
97/8 PacificInvincible 99
98/9 PacificParamount 45
97/8 PacificRegime 140
97/8 PacificRevolution 98
87/8 PaniniSticker 256
88/9 PaniniSticker 333
89/90 PaniniSticker 183, 311
90/1 PaniniSticker 135, 324
91/2 PaniniSticker 276, 336
92/3 PaniniSticker 72, 278
93/4 PaniniSticker 134, 252
94/5 PaniniSticker 215
95/6 PaniniSticker 147, 184
97/8 PaniniSticker 179
95 PaniniWorld 10
91/2 Parkie 140, 212, 225, 297
92/3 Parkhurst 63, 276, 458
93/4 Parkhurst 56, D8
94/5 Parkhurst 63
95/6 Parkhurst 66, PP19, -AS 5,
95/6 PH-Crown(1) 8, -Trophy 4
94/5 ParkieSE seV15
80/1 Pepsi Cap
91/2 Pinnacle 186, 377
92/3 Pinnacle 50, -TeamP 3
93/4 Pinnacle 80, -TeamP 8
94/5 Pinnacle 429, TP 5
95/6 Pinnacle 14
96/7 Pinnacle 14, -TeamP 7
97/8 Pinnacle 153
97/8 P.BAP 12,-TakeANumbr 11
97/8 PinnacleCertified 102
96/7 PinnacleFANtasy 2
97/8 PinnacleInside 160
95/6 Playoff 33, 143, 252
96/7 PinnacleMint 20
95/6 PinnacleZenith 2
96/7 PinnZenith 48, -Champion 4
94/5 POG 93
95/6 POG 102, 013
82/3 Post
96/7 Post
93/4 PowerPlay 70
93/4 Premier 145, -BlackG(T) 6
94/5 Premier 15, 489
95/6 ProMagnet 101
90/1 ProSet 231, 361
91/2 ProSet 190, 312
91/2 PS-ThePuck 21
92/3 ProSet 71
91/2 PSPlatinum 94, PC12
87/8 ProSportWatch CW14
83/4 PuffySticker 3
90/1 Score 6, 319, 332, -Hot 65
91/2 Score(CDN) 115, 262
91/2 Score(U.S) 115, 372
92/3 Score 265, 441
93/4 Score 106, -P.AS 43, -DT 8
94/5 Score DT6
95/6 Score 24, -Golden 5
96/7 Score 142, -Superstition 6
97/8 Score 166
97/8 Score(PHA) 11
93/4 SeasonsPatch 3
94/5 Select 72
95/6 SelectCertified 21
96/7 SelectCertified 89
95 Semic 82
89 SemicSticker 59
91 SemicSticker 58
92 SemicSticker 81
93 SemicSticker 197
94 Semic 86, 337
84/5 7ElevenDisk
85/6 7Eleven 6
95/6 SkyBoxEmotion 52
95/6 SkyBoxImpact 51
96/7 SkyBoxImpact 33, -Fox 6
83/4 SouhaitsRen.KeyChain
94/5 SP 36
95/6 SP 45, E13, FX6
96/7 SP CW13, GF19
97/8 SPAuthentic 113
96/7 SPx 15, HH4
95/6 Summit 16, 198, -GM 9
96/7 Summit 3
95/6 SuperSticker 39, -DieCut 5
91 TeamCanada
96/7 TeamOut
92/3 Topps 5, 182
95/6 Topps 4,265, PF12, HGC11
98/9 Topps 10
94/5 ToppsFinest 56, 68, -Ring 6
95/6 ToppsFinest 137
96/7 ToppsNHLPicks FT7
91/2 ToppsStadiumClub 212
92/3 ToppsStadiumClub 169
93/4 TSC 450, -AllStar, -Finest 4
95/6 T.StdmClub 34, M11, PS4
91/2 TSC-MembersOnly [x2]
93/4 TSC-MembersOnly 3
94/5 TSC-MembersOnly 30
95/6 TSC-MembersOnly 5
95/6 ToppsSuperSkills 29
90/1 UpperDeck 124, 498
91/2 UD 11, 177, 501, 615
92/3 UD 116, -LockerAS 23
93/4 UD 315, SP-42, GG6
94/5 UpperDeck 24, SP22, C31
95/6 UD 226, 248, 396, AS1,F17
95/6 UD H3, H31, R12, SE118
95/6 UD-AllStarPredict MVP8
96/7 UD 268, SS20A, X9, LS10
97/8 UpperDeck 329
94/5 UDBeAPlayer R91, G2
96/7 UDBlackDiamond 151
98/9 UDChoice 151
96/7 UDCC 18, 379, 390, C29
96/7 UDCC 85, 316, UD28
97/8 UDCollChoice 189
83/4 Vachon 22
96 Wien 79
81/2 EDM/RedRooster
82/3 EDM/RedRooster
83/4 EDM
83/4 EDM/Buttons
83/4 EDM/McDonald
84/5 EDM
84/5 EDM/RedRooster
85/6 EDM/RedRooster
86/7 EDM
86/7 EDM/RedRooster
88/9 EDM/ActionMag. 54, 64
96/7 PHA/OceanSpray
87/8 PGH/Kodak
89/90 PGH/Foodland 4
90/1 PGH/Foodland 2
91/2 PGH/Topps

COGHILL, TRENT
90/1 SketchWHL 81
90/1 Saskatoon 15

COHEN, PAUL
90/1 ProCards 505

COLAGIACOMO, ADAM
96/7 AllSportPPF 74
97/8 Bowman 145, BB12
95/6 Classic 88
97 SB'AutColl 49, -Aut.
95/6 Slapshot 170, -Promo
96/7 UpperDeck 369
96/7 UDBlackDiamond 24

COLBORNE, BRETT
92/3 MPSPhotoSJHL 105

COLBOURNE, DARREN
93/4 ClassicProspects 243
92/3 Dayton

COLDWELL, DARYL
81/2 Victoria

COLE, BOB
97/8 Pinnacle -CBC Sports 3

COLE, DANTON
91/2 Bowman 202
96/7 DEL 88
93/4 Donruss 491
94/5 Donruss 172
94/5 FleerUltra 204
94/5 Leaf 259
91/2 OPC/Topps 27
90/1 opcPremier 17
90/1 Panini(WPG) 5
91/2 PaniniSticker 72
92/3 PaniniSticker 56
94/5 PaniniSticker 184
92/3 Parkhurst 408
93/4 Parkhurst 464
94/5 ParkieSE 169
94/5 Pinnacle 45
94/5 POG 222
93/4 PowerPlay 441
94/5 Premier 11
89/90 ProCards'AHL 30
91/2 ProSet 263
91/2 Score(CDN) 240
93/4 Score 655
94/5 Score 131
91/2 ToppsStadiumClub 342
93/4 ToppsStadiumClub 239
90/1 UpperDeck 517
91/2 UpperDeck 210
94/5 UpperDeck 126
92/3 T.B/Sheraton
94/5 T.B/SkyBoxSportsCafe
90/1 WPG/IGA
91/2 WPG/IGA

COLE, JEFF
91/2 AirCanadaSJHL 5, C36

COLE, LES
95/6 Slapshot 373

COLE, MIKE
92/3 BCJHL 217

COLEMAN, JON
93/4 Donruss USA4
93/4 Pinnacle 481
93/4 UpperDeck 563

COLES, BRUCE
94/5 Johnstown 5

COLES, JASON
90/1 SketchOHL 257
91/2 SketchOHL 209

COLLETT, E.J.
25 Dominion 55
25 Willards 45

COLEY, TOM
89/90 NewHaven

COLLEY, KEVIN
98 BowmanCHL 37

COLLIN, ERYC
96/7 Rimouski

COLLINS
91/2 AvantGardeBCJ 163

COLLINS, BILL
69/70 O-Pee-Chee 126
70/1 EddieSargent 104
71/2 EddieSargent 49
72/3 EddieSargent 71
70/1 Esso Stamp
82? JDMcCarthy
74/5 Loblaws
71/2 OPC/Topps 139
72/3 O-Pee-Chee 265
73/4 OPC 163, Topps 158
74/5 O-Pee-Chee 364
68/9 ShirriffCoin MIN7
71/2 TheTorontoSun
69/70 MTL/ProStar
70/1 MTL

COLLINS, GARY
52/3 AnonymousOHL 121
57/8 Parkhurst(TOR) 23

COLLINS, KEN
52/3 AnonymousOHL 115

COLLINS, KEN
95/6 DEL 7

COLLINS, KEVIN
90/1 ProCards 683

COLLINS, MAURICE
52/3 AnonymousOHL 65

COLLINS, SHAWN
93/4 Portland

COLLYARD, BOB
74/5 Loblaws
79 PaniniSticker 216
81/2 Milwaukee 14

COLMAN, MIKE
90/1 ProCards 599
91/2 ProCards 510
90/1 KansasCity 14

COLOMBI, CARLO
91/2 SketchQMJHL 4

COLUMBUS, JEFF
87/8 SSMarie 24

COLVILLE, MAC
34-43 BeeHives(NYR)
39/40 OPC (V301-1) 90
36/7 WWGum (V356) 89

COLVILLE, NEIL
34-43 BeeHives(NYR)
83&87 HallOfFame 5
83 HHOF Postcard (A)
36/7 OPC (V304D) 105
39/40 OPC (V301-1) 39
36/7 WWGum (V356) 91

COLWILL, LES
58/9 Topps 19

COMBE, BERNARD
79 PaniniSticker 380

COMEAU, MARCEL
90/1 ProCards 440
91/2 SketchWHL 148
89/90 Saskatoon 3
92/3 Tacoma
93/4 Tacoma

COMEAU, REY
74/5 Loblaws
72/3 O-Pee-Chee 239
73/4 OPC/Topps 29
74/5 O-Pee-Chee 296
75/6 OPC/Topps 248
76/7 O-Pee-Chee 343
77/8 O-Pee-Chee 346
78/9 O-Pee-Chee 293
79/80 O-Pee-Chee 385
72/3 ATL
74/5 ATL
77/8 ATL

COMFORT, FRED
24/5 Crescent Selkirks 9
23/4 PaulinsCandy 8

COMPLOI, GEORG
95 PaniniWorld 79
94 Semic 296
92 SemicSticker 252
93 SemicSticker 216

CONACHER, BRIAN
64-67 BeeHives(TOR)
71/2 OPC/Topps 138
68/9 ShirriffCoin DET14
71/2 TheTorontoSun
67/8 Topps 17
67/8 York [x2]
68/9 TOR
69/70 TOR
72/3 OttawaNationals

CONACHER, CHARLIE
33/4 Anonymous (V129) 5
34-43 BeeHives(TOR)
35/6 Champion
33/4 CndGum (V252)
83&87 HallOfFame 6
33/4 Hamilton (V288) 49
83 HHOF Postcard (A)
92/3 HHOFLegends 14
27-32 LaPresse 30/1
33/4 OPC (V304A) 34
36/7 OPC (V304D) 123
37/8 OPC (V304E) 138
39/40 OPC (V301-1) 59
55/6 Parkhurst 26
91/2 ProSet 338
34/5 SweetCaporal
36/7 WWGum (V356) 1
32/3 TOR/OKeefe 9

CONACHER, JIM
45-64 BeeHives(CHI), (DET)
51/2 Parkhurst 105
52/3 Parkhurst 103

CONACHER, LIONEL
33/4 CndGum (V252)
33-35 DiamondMatch
25 Dominion 118
27-32 LaPresse 27/8
36/7 OPC (V304D) 102
94/5 Parkie(64/5)-Greats 12
34/5 SweetCaporal
35/6 Triumph
36/7 WWGum (V356) 10

CONACHER, PAT
93/4 Donruss 153
93/4 FleerUltra 342
93/4 Leaf 380
92/3 opcPremier 49
94/5 Parkhurst 107
95/6 Playoff 268
94/5 POG 122
95/6 POG 136
93/4 PowerPlay 358
93/4 Premier 252
89/90 ProCards(AHL) 219
90/1 ProSet 477
91/2 ProSet 427
91/2 Score(CDN) 654
92/3 Score 544
91/2 ToppsStadiumClub 387
93/4 ToppsStadiumClub 179
94/5 ToppsStadiumClub 237
95/6 UDBeAPlayer 92, G4
83/4 EDM/Buttons
83/4 EDM/McDonald
88/9 EDM/ActionMagazine 139
88/9 N.J./Caretta
89/90 N.J
90/1 N.J.
83/4 Moncton 14
84/5 NovaScotia 7

CONACHER, PETE
45-64 BeeHives(CHI, TOR)
52/3 Parkhurst 33
53/4 Parkhurst 70

54/5 Parkhurst 86
57/8 Parkhurst(TOR) 14
93/4 Parkhurst 363

CONACHER, ROY
34-43 BeeHives(BOS)
45-64 BeeHives(CHI)
48-52 Exhibits
39/40 OPC (V301-1) 91
51/2 Parkhurst 50
54/5 Topps 33
91/2 BOS/Legends

CONCANNON, BRENDAN
96/7 Penascola 20

CONN, JOE
45-64 BeeHives(CHI)

CONN, RED
33-35 DiamondMatch
36-39 DiamondMatch (1)

CONN, ROB
91/2 ProCards 494
92/3 Indianapolis
93/4 Indianapolis

CONNELL, ALEX
25-27 Anonymous 16, 28
34-43 BeeHives(MTL.M)
24/5 Champs (C144)
33/4 CndGum (V252)
34/5 SweetCaporal
61/2 Topps-Stamp
83&87 HallOfFame 169
83 HHOF Postcard (M)
24/5 (V145-2) 10

CONNELLY, JACK
23/4 Crescent Selkirks 8

CONNELLY, JIM
52/3 AnonymousOHL 51

CONNELLY, WAYNE
45-64 BeeHives(BOSx2)
64-67 BeeHives(BOS)
62 CeramicTiles
70/1 DadsCookies
70/1 EddieSargent 54
71/2 EddieSargent 186
70/1 Esso Stamp
68/9 OPC/Topps 50
69/70 OPC/Topps 60
70/1 OPC 159
71/2 OPC 237, T. 127
72/3 OPC 296
74/5 opcWHA 54
76/7 opcWHA 122
61/2 Parkhurst 44
95/6 Parkie(66/7) 20
73/4 QuakerOats 35
68/9 ShirriffCoinMIN1
72/3 7ElevenCups
71/2 TheTorontoSun
62/3 Topps 18
66/7 Topps 40
70/1 DET/Marathon
72/3 Minnesota
74/5 Minnesota

CONNOLLY, BERT
36-39 DiamondMatch (1), (2), (3)

CONNOR, CAM
79/80 OPC/Topps 138
80/1 O-Pee-Chee 387
75/6 opcWHA 48
76/7 opcWHA 89
79/80 EDM
88/9 EDM/ActionMagazine 134
78/9 MTL

CONNORS, BOB
23/4 PaulinsCandy 12

CONNORS, CAM
75/6 Phoenix

CONROY, AL
93/4 Premier 352
89/90 ProCards'AHL 314
90/1 ProCards 473
91/2 ProCards 267
92/3 ToppsGold 525
93/4 PHA 26NOV93
93/4 PHA/JCPenney

CONROY, CRAIG
94/5 Classic 51, AA1
94/5 ClassicImages 64, -Aut.

95/6 Donruss 169
95/6 EdgeIce 41
95/6 Leaf 85
98/9 Pacific 364
98/9 PacificParamount 200
97/8 PacificRegime 168
95/6 Pinnacle 218
97/8 PinnacleBeAPlayer 59
95/6 Score 297
95/6 Topps 187
98/9 Topps 47
94/5 Fredericton
95/6 Fredericton

CONSTANT, CHRIS
90/1 SketchWHL 229
91/2 SketchWHL 209

CONSTANTIN, CHARLES
76 QuébecNordiques/MA
76/7 QuébecNordiques

CONSTANTINE, KEVIN
90/1 ProCards 121
92/3 S.J/PacificBell

CONTE, DAVID
78/9 SM-Liiga 74

CONTI, LEONARDO
96/7 DEL 3

CONTE, GIOVANNI
79 PaniniSticker 261

CONTINI, JOE
75/6 Hamilton

CONVERY, BRANDON
92/3 CSC 10
94/5 Classic 82, T67
93/4 ClassicProspects 59
93/4 Donruss CAN8
97/8 Donruss 85
96/7 CanadianIce 144
95/6 EdgeIce 78
96/7 FleerPicks 146
94/5 Leaf 483
96/7 Leaf-GoldL.Rookie 7
96/7 LeafPreferred 132
97/8 Limited 167
97/8 PacificRegime 192
93/4 Pinnacle 470
96/7 Pinnacle 241
97/8 PinnacleInside 152
96/7 PinnacleZenith 132
94/5 Premier 386
97/8 Score 164
97/8 Score(TOR) 14
90/1 SketchOHL 381
91/2 SketchOHL 258
93/4 Slapshot(NiagaraF.) 11, 28
96/7 Summit 174
93/4 UpperDeck 548
94/5 UpperDeck 259
96/7 UpperDeck 186
90/1 Sudbury 12
91/2 Sudbury 16

CONWAY, KEVIN
94 Semic 324
81/2 SSMarie
82/3 SSMarie

COOK, BEN
95/6 Birmingham

COOK, BILL
33/4 Anonymous (V129) 31
34-43 BeeHives(NYR)
35/6 Champion
33-35 DiamondMatch
36-39 DiamondMatch (2)x2, (3)
83&87 HallOfFame 126
83 HHOF Postcard (I)
33/4 OPC (V304A) 38
93/4 Parkie(56/7) P8
23/4 PaulinsCandy 35
34/5 SweetCaporal
60/1 Topps 10
61/2 Topps-Stamp
24/5 (V145-2) 24
33/4 WWGum (V357) 30

COOK, BRAD
93/4 Slapshot(Detroit) 13

COOK, CAM
92/3 MPSPhotoSJHL 150

COOK, DEAN
89/90 ProCards(IHL) 187

COOK, FRED (BUN)
33/4 Anonymous (V129) 46
34-43 BeeHives(BOS)
35/6 Champion
33/4 CndGum (V252)
33-35 DiamondMatch
36-39 DiamondMatch (1),(2),(3)
27-32 LaPresse 28/9
34/5 OPC (V304B) 72
94/5 Parkie(64/5)-Greats10
34/5 SweetCaporal
33/4 WWGum (V357) 66
36/7 WWGum (V356) 68
51/2 Cleveland

COOK, JOE
93/4 ClassicProspects 231
91/2 SketchOHL 163

COOK, LLOYD
25-27 Anonymous 41
24/5 MapleCrispettes (V130) 6
19 Millionaires [x2]

COOK, MICHEL
91/2 AirCanadaSJHL B42
91/2 AirCanadaSJHL 32
92/3 MPSPhotoSJHL 156

COOK, TOM
34-43 BeeHives(MTL.M)
33-35 DiamondMatch
36-39 DiamondMatch (1),(2),(3)
36-39 DiamondMatch (4),(5),(6)
27-32 LaPresse 31/2
37/8 OPC (V304E) 180
36/7 WWGum (V356) 43

COOKE, JAMIE
91/2 ProCards 282

COOKE, MATT
97/8 Bowman 22
98 BowmanCHL 11
95/6 Slapshot 415
98/9 UDChoice 268

COOL, ERIC
90/1 SketchQMJHL 128
91/2 SketchQMJHL 192

COOLEN, TOM
96/7 DEL 112

COOMBS, JOE
95/6 Slapshot 49

COOPER, CARSON
25-27 Anonymous 32
24/25 Champs (C144)
24/5 MapleCrispettes (V130) 9
24/5 (V145-2) 21

COOPER, DAVID
94/5 Classic T7
94/5 ClassicFourSport 151
93/4 ClassicProspects 210
90/1 SketchWHL 38
91/2 SketchWHL 319
97/8 UpperDeck 193

COOPER, IAN
94 Semic 330

COOPER, JEFF
88/9 ProCards(Muskegon)

COOPER, JOE
34-43 BeeHives(NYR)

COOPER, JOHN
93/4 Slapshot(Windsor) 23
94/5 Slapshot(Windsor) 25

COOPER, KORY
97/8 Bowman 20
95/6 Slapshot 31

COOPER, STEPHEN
94 Semic 314

COOPMAN, TODD
89/90 SketchOHL 128
90/1 SketchOHL 258

COPELAND, TODD
90/1 ProCards 573
91/2 ProCards 418
92/3 Cincinnati

COPIJA, MILOSLAW
89 SemicSticker 141
92 SemicSticker 278

COPLEY, JOHN
90/1 ProCards 179
89/90 SketchMEM 42
91/2 SketchOHL 178

COPLEY, RANDY
98 BowmanCHL 114, 125, A34

COPP, ROBERT
34-43 BeeHives(TOR)

CORAM, GREG
82/3 Ottawa67s
83/4 Ottawa67s
84/5 Ottawa67s

CORBEAU, BERT
24/5 Champs (C144)
23/4 (V145-1) 25
24/5 (V145-2) 58

CORBEIL, JUSTIN
87/8 Sudbury 5
89/90 Sudbury 4

CORBET, RENÉ
91/2 Arena 18
94/5 C'Images 78
91/2 Classic 21, -Aut.
94/5 Classic 98, T55
91/2 ClassicFourSport 21
94/5 ClassicImages 78
93/4 ClassicProspects 130
95/6 Donruss 371
95/6 EdgeIce 27
94/5 Flair 143
98/9 Pacific 158
97/8 PacificRegime 50
93/4 Parkhurst 433
94/5 Parkhurst 193
93/4 Pinnacle 448
94/5 Pinnacle 460, RTP6
97/8 PinnacleBeAPlayer 205
94/5 Score 236
97/8 Score(COL) 14
94/5 Select 197
90/1 SketchMEM 63, 105
91/2 SketchQMJHL 287
95/6 SkyBoxEmotion 35
91/2 StarPics 31
94/5 ToppsFinest 97
91/2 UltimateDP 20, 89, -Aut. 20
93/4 UpperDeck 339
94/5 UpperDeck 179
95/6 UpperDeck 100
95/6 UDBeAPlayer 78

CORBETT, PETER
91/2 ProCards 443

CORBETT, SCOTT
95/6 Slapshot 350

CORBIN, VICTOR
51/2 LacStJean 36
52/3 BasDuFleuve 14

CORBIN, YVAN
90/1 SketchQMJHL 179
91/2 SketchOHL 81

COREY, RONALD
88/9 MTL
89/90 MTL
90/1 MTL
91/2 MTL

CORKUM, BOB
93/4 Donruss 10
94/5 Donruss 96
95/6 Donruss 112
94/5 Flair 1
94/5 Fleer 2
94/5 FleerUltra 1
95/6 KennerSLU (U.S)
94/5 Leaf 299
95/6 Leaf 300
98/9 Pacific 334
97/8 PacificCrown 226
91/2 Parkhurst 238
93/4 Parkhurst 6
94/5 ParkieSE 2
94/5 Pinnacle 144
95/6 Pinnacle 121
97/8 PinnacleBeAPlayer 117
95/6 Playoff 221
96/7 Playoff 415
94/5 POG 28
93/4 PowerPlay 282
94/5 Premier 31

89/90 ProCards(AHL) 278
90/1 ProCards 280
91/2 ProCards 8
93/4 Score 637
94/5 Score 158
95/6 Score 42
94/5 SP 4
92/3 Topps 74
95/6 Topps 59
94/5 ToppsFinest 72
92/3 ToppsStadiumClub 179
93/4 ToppsStadiumClub 284
90/1 UpperDeck 35
94/5 UpperDeck 413
95/6 UpperDeck 149
95/6 UDBeAPlayer 112
95/6 UDCollChoice 14
93/4 ANA/Caps 5
94/5 ANA/Carl'sJr
90/1 BUF/Campbell
92/3 BUF/BlueShield
92/3 BUF/Jubilee
96/7 PHO
97/8 PHO

CORMIER, DAN
84/5 Moncton 18

CORMIER, MICHEL
75/6 opcWHA 74
75/6 Phoenix
76/7 Phoenix

CORMIER, SYLVAIN
90/1 SketchQMJHL 197

CORNACCHIA, RICK
89/90 SketchMEM 75
90/1 SketchOHL 349
91/2 SketchOHL 171
93/4 Slapshot(Oshawa) 26

CORNISH, CLAIR
89/90 SketchMEM 98
89/90 SketchOHL 5
90/1 SketchOHL 330

CORPSE, KELI
90/1 SketchOHL 11, 55
91/2 SketchOHL 224
93/4 Slapshot(Kingston) 22
95/6 Fredericton

CORRIGAN, JASON
89/90 SketchOHL 153

CORRIGAN, MIKE
71/2 EddieSargent 224
72/3 EddieSargent 94
70/1 Esso Stamp
74/5 Loblaws
70/1 OPC 227
71/2 OPC/Topps 157
72/3 OPC 74, Topps 89
73/4 OPC/Topps 48
74/5 OPC/Topps 37
75/6 OPC 361
76/7 OPC 268, 386
77/8 OPC/Topps 236
77/8 PGH/PuckBuck
70/1 VAN/RoyalBank
71/2 VAN/RoyalBank 2

CORRIVEAU, ANDRÉ
51-54 LaPatrie 23-Mar52
51/2 LavalDairy 74
52/3 StLawrence 24

CORRIVEAU, RICK
90/1 Score 396
89/90 SketchOHL 40
90/1 SketchOHL 129
91/2 SketchOHL 200

CORRIVEAU, YVON
90/1 OPC/Topps 364
92/3 opcPremier 74
92/3 PaniniSticker 259
92/3 Parkhurst 295
93/4 Premier 208
90/1 ProSet 100
90/1 Score(U.S) 302
92/3 Score 541
92/3 Topps 474
92/3 ToppsStadiumClub 476
93/4 ToppsStadiumClub 9
91/2 UpperDeck 407
92/3 UpperDeck 460
90/1 HFD/JuniorWhalers

86/7 WSH/Police
88/9 WSH
88/9 WSH/Smokey
89/90 WSH

CORSI, JIM
72-84 Dernière 78/9
82 SemicSticker 122
88/9 EDM/ActionMagazine 115

CORSO, DANIEL
95/6 Bowman P7
97/8 Bowman 71
98 BowmanCHL 89
95/6 UpperDeck 510
98/9 UDChoice 269

CORSON, SHAYNE
90/1 Bowman 41
91/2 Bowman 328
92/3 Bowman 82
95/6 Bowman 11
93/4 Donruss 114
94/5 Donruss 221
95/6 Donruss 376
96/7 Donruss 55
97/8 Donruss 42
96/7 DonrussCanadianIce 43
96/7 DonrussElite 58
93/4 EASports 46
94/5 Flair 57
94/5 Fleer 69
96/7 Fleer 95
95/6 FleerMetal 122
92/3 FleerUltra 57, 292
93/4 FleerUltra 51
94/5 FleerUltra 291
95/6 FleerUltra 53, 296
96/7 FleerUltra 85
95/6 Hoyle'WEST J (Hearts)
92/3 HumptyDumpty (2)
89/90 Kraft 21
91/2 Kraft 29
97/8 Kraft -RoadToNagano
93/4 Leaf 46
94/5 Leaf 164
95/6 Leaf 123
96/7 Leaf 163
96/7 LeafLimited 66
96/7 LeafPreferred 26
97/8 Limited 172
97/8 McDonalds -Medallions
96/7 Maggers 143
96/7 MetalUniverse 130
97/8 Omega 116, 248
89/90 O-Pee-Chee 248
90/1 OPC/Topps 58
91/2 OPC/Topps 157, 298
92/3 O-Pee-Chee 231
91/2 opcPremier 161
87/8 opcticker 127/115
89/90 opcSticker 49/195
98/9 Pacific 249
97/8 PacificCrown 246
97/8 PacificCrownRoyale 67
97/8 PacificParamount 93
98/9 PacificParamount 111
97/8 PacificRevolution 69
90/1 Panini(MTL) 5
89/90 PaniniSticker 242
90/1 PaniniSticker 54
91/2 PaniniSticker 196
92/3 PaniniSticker 150
93/4 PaniniSticker 236
94/5 PaniniSticker 202
95/6 PaniniSticker 260
96/7 PaniniSticker 204
95 PaniniWorld 13
91/2 Parkhurst 86
92/3 Parkhurst 53
93/4 Parkhurst 338
94/5 Parkhurst 75, V3
95/6 Parkhurst 174
91/2 Pinnacle 102
92/3 Pinnacle 323
93/4 Pinnacle 249
94/5 Pinnacle 44
96/7 Pinnacle 104, 176
96/7 PinnacleBeAPlayer 62
95/6 PinnacleZenith 98
96/7 PinnacleZenith 107
95/6 Playoff 86
94/5 POG 99
95/6 POG 241

93/4 PowerPlay 79
93/4 Premier 38
94/5 Premier 210
90/1 ProSet 148, 369
91/2 ProSet 413
92/3 ProSet 89
90/1 Score 213, -HotCards 91
91/2 Score(CDN) 65, (U.S) 65
92/3 Score 158
93/4 Score 108, (CDN) DD7
94/5 Score 174
95/6 Score 245
96/7 Score 78
97/8 Score(MTL) 12
94/5 Select 47
95/6 SelectCertified 101
96/7 SelectCertified 73
92 SemicSticker 93
94 Semic 93
95 Semic 91
95/6 SkyBoxEmotion 145
95/6 SkyBoxImpact 138
96/7 SkyBoxImpact 110
94/5 SP 42
95/6 SP 122, FX19
96/7 SP 84
97/8 SPAuthentic 84
95/6 Summit 151
96/7 Summit 137
91 TeamCanada
96/7 TeamOut
92/3 Topps 201
95/6 Topps 55, 229
94/5 ToppsFinest 74
95/6 ToppsFinest 18
96/7 ToppsNHLPicks 139
91/2 ToppsStadiumClub 5
92/3 ToppsStadiumClub 221
93/4 ToppsStadiumClub 40
95/6 ToppsStadiumClub 7
93/4 TSCMembers 12
90/1 UpperDeck 280
91/2 UpperDeck 282, 505
92/3 UpperDeck 330, 541
93/4 UpperDeck 132, SP-49
94/5 UpperDeck 351, SP116
95/6 UpperDeck 101, SE159
96/7 UpperDeck 139
97/8 UpperDeck 298
93/4 UDBAP'Roots 13
94/5 UDBeAPlayer-Aut. 172
96/7 UDBlackDiamond 119
97/8 UDBlackDiamond 107
98/9 UDChoice 103
95/6 UDCollChoice 146
96/7 UDCollChoice 225
97/8 UDCollChoice 137
97/8 ValuNet
97/8 Zenith 67, Z34
92/3 EDM
92/3 EDM/IGA 4
93/4 EDM 29DEC93
86/7 MTL
87/8 MTL
87/8 MTL/Stickers 49-50
88/9 MTL
89/90 MTL
89/90 MTL/Figurine
89/90 MTL/Kraft
90/1 MTL
91/2 MTL
96-98 MTL

CORT, JOE
94/5 Slapshot(Guelph) 6
95/6 Slapshot 86
95/6 Guelph 12
96/7 Guelph 6

CORVO, JOE
96/7 UpperDeck"Ice" 145

COSSETTE, BRYAN
91/2 AirCanadaSJHL D44
92/3 MPSPhotoSJHL 9

COSSETTE, J.M.
52/3 AnonymousOHL 39

COSTEA, MARIAN
79 PaniniSticker 317

COSTELLO, LES
45-64 BeeHives(TOR)
45-54 QuakerOats

COSTELLO, MURRAY
52/3 AnonymousOHL 156
45-64 BeeHives(BOS, CHI)
93/4 Parkie(56/7) 60

COSTELLO, RICK
84/5 O-Pee-Chee 298

CÔTÉ, ALAIN G.
93/4 Durivage 19
91/2 opcPremier 188
89/90 ProCards(AHL) 102
90/1 ProCards 54
91/2 ProSet 417
91/2 MTL
92/3 Fredericton

CÔTÉ, ALAIN
90/1 SketchQMJHL 89
91/2 SketchQMJHL 25

CÔTÉ, ALAIN
90/1 SketchQMJHL 190
91/2 SketchQMJHL 54

CÔTÉ, ALAIN
72-84 Dernière 78/9
72-84 Dernière 81/2
86/7 Kraft Sports 43
79/80 O-Pee-Chee 324
81/2 O-Pee-Chee 272
82/3 O-Pee-Chee 281
83/4 O-Pee-Chee 291
84/5 O-Pee-Chee 278
85/6 O-Pee-Chee 205
86/7 O-Pee-Chee 233
87/8 O-Pee-Chee 254
88/9 O-Pee-Chee 205
85/6 opcSticker 149/18
86/7 opcSticker 20/161
88/9 opcSticker 186/55
87/8 PaniniSticker 169
88/9 PaniniSticker 352
82/3 Post
83/4 Vachon 63
80/1 QUE
81/2 QUE
82/3 QUE
83/4 QUE
84/5 QUE
85/6 QUE
85/6 QUE/GeneralFoods
85/6 QUE/McDonald
85/6 QUE/Pennant
85/6 QUE/Placemat
85/6 QUE/Provigo
86/7 QUE
86/7 QUE/GeneralFoods
86/7 QUE/McDonald
86/7 QUE/YumYum
87/8 QUE/GeneralFoods
87/8 QUE/YumYum
88/9 QUE
88/9 QUE/GeneralFoods

CÔTÉ, ANDRÉ
82/3 Fredericton 24
83/4 Fredericton 20

COTE, BART
90/1 SketchMEM 94
90/1 SketchWHL 219

CÔTÉ, BENOÎT
97/8 Bowman 128

CÔTÉ, FRANK
51/2 BasDuFleuve 51
52/3 BasDuFleuve 36

CÔTÉ, MARTIN
84/5 Richelieu

COTE, MIKE
90/1 SketchOHL 325, 331
91/2 SketchOHL 344

CÔTÉ, PATRICK
95/6 Classic 33
97/8 PinnacleBeAPlayer 235
90/1 SketchQMJHL 252

COTE, RAY
88/9 EDM/ActionMagazine 140
83/4 Moncton 23
84/5 NovaScotia 6

CÔTÉ, ROGER
80/1 Québec

CÔTÉ, SYLVAIN
91/2 Bowman 17, 410
92/3 Bowman 115
93/4 Donruss 367
94/5 Donruss 153
92/3 Durivage 34
93/4 Durivage 35
94/5 Flair 198
94/5 Fleer 234
95/6 FleerMetal 158
92/3 FleerUltra 433
93/4 FleerUltra 445
94/5 FleerUltra 232
95/6 FleerUltra 321
93/4 Leaf 52
94/5 Leaf 140
95/6 Leaf 218
92/3 O-Pee-Chee 277
89/90 OPC/Topps 162
91/2 OPC/Topps 249
98/9 Pacific 412
97/8 PacificCrown 207
88/9 PaniniSticker 237
89/90 PaniniSticker 229
94/5 PaniniSticker 25
96/7 PaniniSticker 137
92/3 Parkhurst 431
93/4 Parkhurst 489
95/6 Parkhurst 222
94/5 ParkieSE 193
91/2 Pinnacle 221
92/3 Pinnacle 182
93/4 Pinnacle 258
94/5 Pinnacle 33
95/6 Pinnacle 65
95/6 Playoff 321
94/5 POG 249
93/4 PowerPlay 259
93/4 Premier 138
94/5 Premier 208
90/1 ProSet 448
91/2 ProSet 82, 512
90/1 Score 83
91/2 Score(CDN) 129, 596
91/2 Score(U.S) 129, 46T
92/3 Score 78
93/4 Score 92, 450
95/6 Score 183
94/5 Select 128
96/7 SkyBoxImpact 138
92/3 Topps 428
95/6 Topps 151
95/6 ToppsFinest 37
96/7 ToppsNHLPicks 153
91/2 ToppsStadiumClub 183
92/3 ToppsStadiumClub 145
93/4 ToppsStadiumClub 66
95/6 ToppsStadiumClub 23
94/5 UpperDeck 354
95/6 UpperDeck 133, SE176
94/5 UDBeAPlayer-Aut. 166
95/6 UDCollChoice 284
96/7 UDCollChoice 287
84/5 HFD/JuniorWhalers
85/6 HFD/JuniorWhalers
86/7 HFD/JuniorWhalers
87/8 HFD/JuniorWhalers
88/9 HFD/JuniorWhalers
89/90 HFD/JuniorWhalers
90/1 HFD/JuniorWhalers
91/2 WSH
91/2 WSH/Kodak
92/3 WSH/Kodak
95/6 WSH
82/3 Fredericton 3

COTTON, HAROLD (BALDY)
33/4 Anonymous V129
34-43 BeeHives(TOR)
33/4 Hamilton V288 39
33/4 OPC (V304A) 35
55/6 Parkhurst 32
33/4 WWGum (V357) 33
36/7 WWGum (V356) 35
32/3 TOR/OKeefe 8

COULIS, TIM
85/6 MIN

COULOMBE, SERGE
90/1 Rayside

COULTER, ART
34-43 BeeHives(NYR)
36-39 DiamondMatch (1), (2), (3)
83&87 HallOfFame 185
83 HHOF Postcard (J)
35/6 OPC (V304C) 93
39/40 OPC (V301-1) 34

COULTER, M.
95/6 Birmingham

COUPAL, GARY
93/4 Slapshot(Sudbury) 17
92/3 Sudbury 21
93/4 Sudbury 16

COURNOYER, B.
88/9 Richelieu

COURNOYER, YVAN
71/2 Bazooka Panel 15
64-67 BeeHives(MTL)
64/5 CokeCap MTL-12
65/6 CocaCola
77/8 Coke Mini
70/1 Colgate Stamp 60
71/2 Colgate Heads
70/1 DadsCookies
72-84 Dernière 72/3, 73/4
70/1 EddieSargent 109
71/2 EddieSargent 102
72/3 EddieSargent 117
70/1 Esso Stamp
88/9 EssoAllStar
71/2 FritoLay
83&87 HallOfFame 136
83 HHOF Postcard (K)
91/2 Kraft 79
72/3 Letraset 15
74/5 LiptonSoup 13
74/5 Loblaws
73/4 MacsMilk Disk
72/3 OPC-TmCanada
68/9 OPC/Topps 62
69/70 O-Pee-Chee 221
69/70 OPC-Stamp, -Sticker
69/70 OPC/Topps 6
70/1 OPC/Topps 50, -Deckle 23
71/2 OPC/Topps 15, 260
71/2 OPC Poster 4
72/3 OPC 29,44,250, T. 10, 131
72/3 OPC-TmCanada
73/4 OPC 157, Topps 115
74/5 OPC/Topps 124, 140
75/6 OPC/Topps 70
76/7 OPC/Topps 30
77/8 OPC/Topps 230
78/9 OPC/Topps 60
94/5 Parkie(64/5) 75, A2
95/6 Parkie(66/7) 60
68/9 Post Marble
72/3 Post Transfers 12
72 SemicSticker 204
68/9 ShirriffCoin MTL13
77-79 Sportscaster 02-13, 15-13
77-79 Sportscaster 58-1392
71/2 TheTorontoSun
65/6 Topps 76
66/7 Topps 72, -USATest 13
67/8 Topps 70
91/2 Trends(72) 82, -Aut.
67/8 York 28-30
93/4 Zellers
67/8 MTL
67/8 MTL/IGA
68/9 MTL
69/70 MTL/ProStar
70/1 MTL
71 MTL/Pins
71/2 MTL [x2]
72/3 MTL
73/4 MTL
74/5 MTL
75/6 MTL
76/7 MTL
77/8 MTL
78/9 MTL
92/3 MTL/OPC 23
95/6 MTL/Forum 12FEB96
88/9 Richelieu

COURTEAU, MAURICE
51/2 LacStJean 59

COURTEAU, YVES
84/5 Moncton 17
85/6 Moncton 24

COURTENAY, ED
93/4 FleerUltra 8
92/3 opcPremier 8
93/4 PaniniSticker 261
93/4 PowerPlay 217
89/90 ProCards(AHL) 80
90/1 ProCards 116
91/2 ProCards 507
93/4 ToppsStadiumClub 72
91/2 UpperDeck 517
92/3 UpperDeck 507
97/8 SheffieldSteelers

COURTNALL, GEOFF
90/1 Bowman 73
91/2 Bowman 318
92/3 Bowman 345
93/4 Donruss 352
94/5 Donruss 50
95/6 Donruss 238
96/7 Donruss 54
97/8 Donruss 47
96/7 DonrussElite 43
93/4 EASports 142
94/5 Fleer 224
92/3 FleerUltra 220
93/4 FleerUltra 76
94/5 FleerUltra 382
95/6 FleerUltra 167, 297
95/6 Hoyle'WEST Q (Hearts)
90/1 Kraft 9
91/2 Kraft 15
93/4 Leaf 72
94/5 Leaf 53
95/6 Leaf 233
96/7 Leaf 158
94/5 LeafLimited 69
95/6 LeafLimited 3
97/8 Limited 24
97/8 Omega 190
92/3 O-Pee-Chee 176
89/90 OPC/Topps 111, T-AS 9
90/1 OPC/Topps 273
91/2 OPC/Topps 305
90/1 opcPremier 18
91/2 opcPremier 101
88/9 opcSticker 222/98
89/90 opcSticker 80
89/90 opcStickFS 29
98/9 Pacific 265
97/8 PacificCrown 62, -Slap 9A
97/8 PacificParamount 157
98/9 PacificParamount 201
97/8 PacificInvincible 118
97/8 PacificRevolution 118
89/90 PaniniSticker 340
90/1 PaniniSticker 159
91/2 PaniniSticker 38
92/3 PaniniSticker 29
93/4 PaniniSticker 170
94/5 PaniniSticker 149
95/6 PaniniSticker 193
96/7 PaniniSticker 205
97/8 PaniniSticker 167
91/2 Parkhurst 186
92/3 Parkhurst 189
93/4 Parkhurst 216
94/5 Parkhurst 240
95/6 Parkhurst 448
91/2 Pinnacle 263
92/3 Pinnacle 187
93/4 Pinnacle 132
94/5 Pinnacle 276
96/7 Pinnacle 146
95/6 PinnacleZenith 58
95/6 Playoff 87, 305
94/5 POG 329
95/6 POG 240
94/5 Post
93/4 PowerPlay 249
93/4 Premier 337
94/5 Premier 186, 525
95/6 ProMagnet 10
90/1 ProSet 309, 521
91/2 ProSet 245
92/3 ProSet 198
91/2 PSPlatinum 123
90/1 Score 124, 5T
91/2 Score(CDN) 150, 270
91/2 Score(U.S.) 150, 380
92/3 Score 234
93/4 Score 78
94/5 Score 161
95/6 Score 255
96/7 Score 32
97/8 Score 184
97/8 Score(STL) 15
92/3 SeasonsPatch 33
94/5 Select 137
95/6 SkyBoxEmotion 146
95/6 SkyBoxImpact 139
96/7 SkyBoxImpact 111
94/5 SP 125
95/6 SP 128
95/6 Summit 119
92/3 Topps 472
95/6 Topps 276
98/9 Topps 139
94/5 ToppsFinest 83
95/6 ToppsFinest 49
96/7 ToppsNHLPicks 149
91/2 ToppsStadiumClub 149
92/3 ToppsStadiumClub 265
93/4 ToppsStadiumClub 413
90/1 UpperDeck 238, 438
91/2 UpperDeck 467
92/3 UpperDeck 39, 240
93/4 UpperDeck 114, SP-163
94/5 UpperDeck 286, SP82
95/6 UpperDeck 120
96/7 UpperDeck 327
94/5 UDBeAPlayer R6, -Aut. 135
98/9 UDChoice 190
95/6 UDCollChoice 31
96/7 UDCollChoice 229
97/8 UDCollChoice 227
84/5 BOS
88/9 EDM/ActionMagazine 88
90/1 STL/Kodak
91/2 VAN
92/3 VAN/RoadTrip
93/4 VAN/Coins
94/5 VAN
95/6 VAN/Building 14
88/9 WSH
88/9 WSH/Smokey
89/90 WSH
89/90 WSH/Kodak
85/6 Moncton 11
81/2 Victoria
82/3 Victoria
84/5 Victoria

COURTNALL, RUSS
90/1 Bowman 47
91/2 Bowman 346, 414
92/3 Bowman 45
93/4 Donruss 80
94/5 Donruss 167
95/6 Donruss 199
96/7 Donruss 194
93/4 EASports 35
94/5 Flair 40, 48
95/6 FleerMetal 150
92/3 FleerUltra 91, 316
93/4 FleerUltra 50, -Speed 2
94/5 FleerUltra 279, -Speed 2
95/6 FleerUltra 168
95/6 Hoyle'WEST K (Hearts)
92/3 HumptyDumpty(2)
86/7 Kraft Sports 53
89/90 Kraft 22
91/2 Kraft 49
93/4 Kraft
93/4 Leaf 65
94/5 Leaf 126
95/6 Leaf 51
96/7 Leaf 29
94/5 LeafLimited 35
96/7 MetalUniverse 156
86/7 OPC/Topps 174
87/8 OPC/Topps 62, P
88/9 OPC/Topps 183
89/90 O-Pee-Chee 239
90/1 OPC/Topps 124
91/2 OPC/Topps 119, T-TL 18
92/3 O-Pee-Chee 284
91/2 opcPremier 58, 194
92/3 opcPremier 20
85/6 opcSticker 20 /151
86/7 opcSticker 149
87/8 opcSticker 156
88/9 opcSticker 175
89/90 opcSticker 53 /197
98/9 Pacific 233
97/8 PacificCrown 275
98/9 PacificParamount 103
97/8 PacificRevolution 64
90/1 Panini(MTL) 6
87/8 PaniniSticker 327
88/9 PaniniSticker 122
90/1 PaniniSticker 56
91/2 PaniniSticker 186
92/3 PaniniSticker 154
93/4 PaniniSticker 268
94/5 PaniniSticker 230
95/6 PaniniSticker 296
96/7 PaniniSticker 292
91/2 Parkhurst 308
92/3 Parkhurst 78
93/4 Parkhurst 53
94/5 Parkhurst 52
95/6 Parkhurst 210
94/5 ParkhurstSE seV30
91/2 Pinnacle 254
92/3 Pinnacle 337
93/4 Pinnacle 268
94/5 Pinnacle 133
96/7 Pinnacle 75, 111
95/6 PinnacleZenith 115
94/5 POG 77
95/6 POG 275
94/5 Post
93/4 PowerPlay 58
93/4 Premier 153
94/5 Premier 395
90/1 ProSet 149
91/2 ProSet 126
91/2 PSPlatinum 62
90/1 Score 148
91/2 Score(CDN) 42, 270
91/2 Score(U.S.) 42, 380
92/3 Score 4
93/4 Score 130
94/5 Score 43
95/6 Score 242
96/7 Score 109
94/5 Select 70
94 Semic 98
95 Semic 95
92 SemicSticker 95
95/6 SkyBoxEmotion 179
95/6 SkyBoxImpact 168
96/7 SkyBoxImpact 132
96/7 SP 161
95/6 Summit 128
96/7 Summit 22
91 TeamCanada
92/3 Topps 276
95/6 Topps 194
98/9 Topps 188
94/5 ToppsFinest 54
96/7 ToppsNHLPicks 107
91/2 ToppsStadiumClub 43
92/3 ToppsStadiumClub 152
93/4 ToppsStadiumClub 55
94/5 ToppsStadiumClub 170
95/6 ToppsStadiumClub 9
93/4 TSC-MembersOnly 19
95/6 ToppsSuperSkills 11
90/1 UpperDeck 259
91/2 UpperDeck 87, 168
92/3 UpperDeck 39, 94, 441
93/4 UpperDeck 32, SP-36
94/5 UpperDeck 31, SP19
95/6 UpperDeck 317
96/7 UpperDeck 350
94/5 UDBeAPlayer R27, G5
95/6 UDBeAPlayer 65
95/6 UDCollChoice 267
96/7 UDCollChoice 276
97/8 UDCollChoice 166
93/4 DAL/Southwest
94/5 DAL
88/9 MTL
89/90 MTL
89/90 MTL/Figurine
89/90 MTL/Kraft
90/1 MTL
91/2 MTL
84/5 TOR
85/6 TOR
86/7 TOR
87/8 TOR
87/8 TOR/3.5" x 5.5"
87/8 TOR/P.L.A.Y. 30
88/9 TOR/P.L.A.Y. 30
96/7 VAN
96/7 VAN/IGA
84/5 KelownaWings 37
82/3 Victoria
83/4 Victoria
84/5 Victoria

COURTNEY, KEN
52/3 AnonymousOHL 93

COURVILLE, LARRY
95/6 Classic 50
95/6 Donruss-CdnJr. 11
95/6 EdgeIce 88
94/5 Pinnacle 540
96/7 Pinnacle 235
97/8 Score 57
97/8 Score(VAN) 13
91/2 SketchOHL 15
94/5 SP 150
95/6 Topps 3CJ
94/5 ToppsFinest 156

COUSINEAU, BRYAN
90/1 Newmarket

COUSINEAU, MARCEL
91/2 Classic 50
91/2 ClassicFourSport 50, -Aut.
93/4 ClassicProspects 111
97/8 Donruss 198, -Rated 7
97/8 D.Cdn.Ice 147,-Gardiens 10
97/8 DonrussPreferred 158
97/8 Leaf 114
97/8 Limited 86, 116, 160
97/8 Limited-fabric 39
97/8 Omega 219
97/8 PinnacleInside 69, -Stop 22
97/8 PinnacleInside -StandUp 4
96/7 PinnacleBeAPlayer 213
97/8 Score 23
97/8 Score(TOR) 3
90/1 SketchQMJHL 122,133,165
91/2 StarPics 47
91/2 UltimateDP 45, 57, -Aut. 45
96/7 UDBlackDiamond 63

COUTOURIER, SYLVAIN
84/5 Richelieu

COUTU, BILLY
25-27 Anonymous 2, 42
24/5 Champs (C144)
25 Dominion 89
23/4 (V145-1) 17
24/5 (V145-2) 44

COUTURE, ALEXANDRE
97/8 Halifax (1), (2)

COUTURE, GERALD (DOC)
45-64 BeeHives(CHI, DET, MTL)
51/2 Parkhurst 17
52/3 Parkhurst 41
53/4 Parkhurst 84
45-54 QuakerOats

COUTURE, ROSARIO (LOLO)
33-35 DiamondMatch
36-39 DiamondMatch (1), (2), (3)
27-32 LaPresse 31/2

COUTURIER, FRANCIS
90/1 SketchQMJHL 95

COUTURIER, SYLVAIN
88/9 ProCards(NewHaven)
89/90 ProCards(AHL) 7
90/1 ProCards 360
91/2 UpperDeck 491
94/5 Milwaukee
92/3 Phoenix

COVENY, CHRIS
92/3 Ottawa67s
91/2 SketchOHL 302

COVENY, MICHAEL
94/5 Slapshot(MEM) 51

COWAN, JEFF
95/6 Classic 82
93/4 Slapshot(Guelph) 20
94/5 Slapshot(Guelph) 23
95/6 Slapshot 23

COWHERD, COLIN
93/4 LasVegas

COWICK, BRUCE
74/5 O-Pee-Chee 386
74/5 WSH

COWIE, ROB
94/5 ClassicImages 57
95/6 EdgeIce 183
91/2 ProCards 174
91/2 Moncton
95/6 Phoenix

COWLEY, BILL
34-43 BeeHives(BOS)
36-39 DiamondMatch (1)
83&87 HallOfFame 170
83 HHOF Postcard (M)
39/40 OPC (V301-1) 98
43-47 ParadeSportive
91/2 BOS/Legends [x3]

COWLEY, JOE
92/3 Indianapolis

COWLEY, WAYNE
96/7 DEL 204
89/90 ProCards(IHL) 206
90/1 ProCards 609
93/4 EDM 12FEB94

COX, ALLAN
90/1 SketchOHL 306
91/2 SketchOHL 56

COX, DAN
33/4 Anonymous (V129) 48
33/4 CndGum (V252)
33/4 OPC (V304A) 1
23/4 PaulinsCandy 18
33/4 WWGum (V357) 69

COX, PETER
90/1 SketchWHL 158
91/2 SketchWHL 45

COX, TIM
90/1 SketchWHL 91
90/1 Saskatoon 20

COXE, CRAIG
90/1 OPC/Topps 339
91/2 OPC/Topps 447
90/1 Panini(VAN) 7
91/2 ProCards 520
90/1 ProSet 544
91/2 ProSet 329
91/2 Score(CDN) 646, (U.S) 96T
91/2 UpperDeck 60
87/8 STL
88/9 STL
88/9 STL/Kodak
85/6 VAN
86/7 VAN
87/8 VAN/Shell
89/90 VAN
90/1 VAN/Mohawk
84/5 Fredericton 27

COYNE, COLLEEN
94/5 Classic W26

CRABB, KEN
94/5 Slapshot(Btf) 21

CRAIEVICH, DAVID
91/2 ProCards 422
89/90 SketchMEM 84
89/90 SketchOHL 13
90/1 SketchOHL 332
93/4 Birmingham 8
94/5 Birmingham
91/2 Cincinnati

CRAIG, GLEN
90/1 SketchOHL 102
91/2 SketchOHL 30
89/90 Windsor

CRAIG, JIM
94/5 MiracleOnIce 9-10
80/1 OPC/Topps 22
79/80 USAOlympicTeam 1
79/80 ATL

CRAIG, MIKE
91/2 Bowman 130
92/3 Bowman 334
93/4 Donruss 81
92/3 FleerUltra 317
93/4 FleerUltra 297
93/4 Leaf 88
94/5 Leaf 510
91/2 OPC/Topps 187
92/3 O-Pee-Chee 103
90/1 opcPremier 19
97/8 PacificCrown 309
92/3 PaniniSticker 95
93/4 PaniniSticker 271
94/5 PaniniSticker 228
91/2 Parkhurst 301
92/3 Parkhurst 314
93/4 Parkhurst 323
94/5 Parkhurst 54
91/2 Pinnacle 219
92/3 Pinnacle 99
93/4 Pinnacle 314
94/5 Pinnacle 399
94/5 POG 231
93/4 PowerPlay 322
93/4 Premier 309
94/5 Premier 538
90/1 ProSet 613
91/2 ProSet 405
91/2 PSPlatinum 189
90/1 ScoreTraded 59T
91/2 Score(CDN) 181, (U.S) 181
92/3 Score 271
93/4 Score 156
97/8 Score(TOR) 11
89/90 SketchMEM 90
89/90 SketchOHL 9
92/3 Topps 238
91/2 ToppsStadiumClub 344
92/3 ToppsStadiumClub 268
93/4 ToppsStadiumClub 355
90/1 UpperDeck 472
91/2 UpperDeck 125
92/3 UpperDeck 65
93/4 UpperDeck 191
94/5 UpperDeck 213
95/6 UDBeAPlayer 17
94/5 DAL

CRAIGDALLIE, MARTY
92/3 BCJHL 66

CRAIGHEAD, JOHN
91/2 AvantGardeBCJHL 165

CRAIGWELL, DALE
92/3 Bowman 198
95/6 EdgeIce 189
92/3 FleerUltra 192
92/3 O-Pee-Chee 271
92/3 PaniniSticker 133
91/2 Parkhurst 389
92/3 Parkhurst 168
93/4 Premier 348
91/2 ProCards 516
92/3 Score 466
91/2 SketchAwards 2
89/90 SketchMEM 85
89/90 SketchOHL 4
90/1 SketchOHL 333
92/3 Topps 60
92/3 ToppsStadiumClub 464
90/1 UpperDeck 464
92/3 UpperDeck 40
93/4 UpperDeck 56
94/5 UpperDeck 380
93/4 S.J./Gameline

CRAMERI, GIAN-MARCO
95 PaniniWorld 126

CRANE, COREY
92/3 Sudbury 13

CRANE, DERRICK
90/1 SketchOHL 130
91/2 SketchOHL 375

CRANE, TODD
95/6 Slapshot 163

CRANSTON, TIM
94 Semic 320
95/6 SheffieldSteelers
97/8 SheffieldSteelers

CRASHLEY, BARRY
72/3 O-Pee-Chee 295
67/8 Topps 105
72/3 LosAngelesSharks

CRAVEN, MURRAY
90/1 Bowman 109
91/2 Bowman 239
92/3 Bowman 280
93/4 Donruss 353
94/5 Donruss 131
95/6 Donruss 46
92/3 FleerUltra 71
93/4 FleerUltra 439
94/5 FleerUltra 223
93/4 Leaf 5
94/5 Leaf 121
95/6 Leaf 6
83/4 O-Pee-Chee 120
85/6 OPC/Topps 53
86/7 OPC/Topps 167
87/8 OPC/Topps 22
88/9 OPC/Topps 79, J
89/90 OPC/Topps 44
90/1 OPC/Topps 318
91/2 OPC/Topps 254
92/3 O-Pee-Chee 127
92/3 opcPremier-Star 3
85/6 opcSticker 95 /228
86/7 opcSticker 244 /136
87/8 opcSticker 69
88/9 opcSticker 98 /222
98/9 Pacific 378
97/8 PacificCrown 238
87/8 PaniniSticker 133
88/9 PaniniSticker 320
90/1 PaniniSticker 116
91/2 PaniniSticker 234
92/3 PaniniSticker 262
93/4 PaniniSticker 169
91/2 Parkhurst 288
92/3 Parkhurst 55, 495
93/4 Parkhurst 208
94/5 Parkhurst 242
95/6 Parkhurst 313
91/2 Pinnacle 177
92/3 Pinnacle 281
93/4 Pinnacle 88
94/5 Pinnacle 291
95/6 Pinnacle 179
96/7 Pinnacle 162
93/4 PowerPlay 458
93/4 Premier 400
94/5 Premier 47
90/1 ProSet 214
91/2 ProSet 175, 393
92/3 ProSet 60
91/2 PSPlatinum 179
90/1 Score 56
91/2 Score(CDN) 482, (U.S) 262
92/3 Score 18
93/4 Score 49
94/5 Score 109
95/6 Score 214
96/7 TeamOut
92/3 Topps 248
95/6 Topps 52
91/2 ToppsStadiumClub 176
92/3 ToppsStadiumClub 442
93/4 ToppsStadiumClub 264
94/5 ToppsStadiumClub 255
90/1 UpperDeck 6
91/2 UpperDeck 306
92/3 UpperDeck 49
93/4 UpperDeck 410
94/5 UpperDeck 45
95/6 UpperDeck 151
95/6 UDBeAPlayer 46
95/6 UDCollChoice 120
91/2 HFD/JuniorWhalers
92/3 HFD/DairyMart
86/7 PHA
89/90 PHA
90/1 PHA
97/8 S.J/PacificBellSheet
93/4 VAN/Coins
84/5 KelownaWingsWHL 44
83/4 MedicineHat

CRAWFORD, BOB
84/5 O-Pee-Chee 68
85/6 OPC/Topps 162
84/5 opcSticker 197
85/6 opcSticker 167/36
84/5 Topps 53
83/4 HFD/JuniorWhalers
84/5 HFD/JuniorWhalers
85/6 HFD/JuniorWhalers
86/7 WSH/Kodak

CRAWFORD, DEREK
92/3 Dayton

CRAWFORD, FLOYD
52/3 BasDuFleuve 45
51/2 LavalDairy 25

CRAWFORD, GLENN
95/6 Classic 98
94/5 Slapshot(Windsor) 8
95/6 Slapshot 411, 438
95/6 UpperDeck 520

CRAWFORD, JEFF
83/4 Moncton 18
81/2 Regina 9
82/3 Regina 22
83/4 Regina 22

CRAWFORD, JOHN
34-43 BeeHives(BOS)
45-64 BeeHives(BOS)
40/1 OPC (V301-2) 134

CRAWFORD, KEN
52/3 AnonymousOHL 181

CRAWFORD, LOU
88/9 ProCards(Adirondack)
89/90 ProCard(AHL) 56
90/1 ProCards 138
91/2 ProCards 62
85/6 NovaScotia 10

CRAWFORD, MARC
96/7 Kraft-Trophy
97/8 Kraft -RoadToNagano
82/3 O-Pee-Chee 342
82/3 Post
91/2 ProCards 357
90/1 SketchOHL 50
97/8 ValuNet
97/8 COL/DenverPostPins
81/2 VAN/Silverwood
83/4 VAN
82/3 Fredericton 17
84/5 Fredericton 23
85/6 Fredericton 4
86/7 Fredericton

CRAWFORD, RUSTY
83&87 HallOfFame 67
83 HHOF Postcard (E)
23/4 PaulinsCandy 70

CREAGH, BRENDAN
95/6 Birmingham
93/4 Greensboro
94/5 Greensboro

CREAMER, PIERRE
89/90 Sketch MEM 50

CREIGTHNEY, NIGEL
92/3 BCJHL 239

CREIGHTON, ADAM
90/1 Bowman 9
91/2 Bowman 394
92/3 Bowman 88
93/4 Donruss 326
95/6 Donruss 336
94/5 Fleer 185
92/3 FleerUltra 409
91/2 Kraft 47
93/4 Leaf 85
89/90 O-Pee-Chee 218
92/3 O-Pee-Chee 85
90/1 OPC/Topps 83
91/2 OPC/Topps 314, 430
91/2 opcPremier 171
92/3 opcPremier 61
87/8 PaniniSticker 31
88/9 PaniniSticker 225
89/90 PaniniSticker 51
90/1 PaniniSticker 193
91/2 PaniniSticker 13
92/3 PaniniSticker 204
93/4 PaniniSticker 215
97/8 PaniniSticker 209
91/2 Parkhurst 113
92/3 Parkhurst 172
94/5 Parkhurst 222
95/6 Parkhurst 444
91/2 Pinnacle 82
92/3 Pinnacle 199
93/4 Pinnacle 272
96/7 Pinnacle 80
95/6 POG 234
90/1 ProSet 50
91/2 ProSet 42,437,-ThePuck 17
92/3 ProSet 103
90/1 Score 82
91/2 Score(CDN) 485
91/2 Score(U.S) 265, 21T
92/3 Score 144
93/4 Score 86
95/6 Score 283
92/3 Topps 451
91/2 ToppsStadiumClub 89
92/3 ToppsStadiumClub 45
93/4 ToppsStadiumClub 5
94/5 ToppsStadiumClub 23
90/1 UpperDeck 4
91/2 UpperDeck 254
92/3 UpperDeck 311
94/5 UpperDeck 348
95/6 UpperDeck 375
95/6 UDBeAPlayer 142
95/6 UDCollChoice 229
84/5 BUF/BlueShield
85/6 BUF
86/7 BUF
87/8 BUF/BlueShield
87/8 BUF/WonderBread
88/9 BUF/WonderBread
89/90 CHI/Coke
90/1 CHI/Coke
92/3 T.B./Sheraton
93/4 T.B./KashNKary
94/5 T.B./SkyBoxSportsCafe
81/2 Ottawa67s
82/3 Ottawa67s
83/4 Ottawa67s

CREIGHTON, DAVE
45-64 BeeHives(BOS), (TOR)
52/3 Parkhurst 76
53/4 Parkhurst 85
54/5 Parkhurst 58
60/1 Parkhurst 10
93/4 Parkie(56/7) 99
57/8 Topps 66

CRESSMAN, GLENN
52/3 AnonymousOHL 127

CRESSMAN, MATT
93/4 WestMich.

CRETTENAUD, YVES
92 SemicSticker 232
93 SemicSticker 260

CRHA, JIRI
81/2 O-Pee-Chee 315
81/2 opcSticker 106
79 PaniniSticker 75
80/1 Pepsi Cap
73/4 WilliamsFIN 45
79/80 TOR
80/1 TOR

CRIMIN, DEREK
91/2 AirCanadaSJHL B45, 27
92/3 MPSPhotoSJHL 65

CRISP, TERRY
91/2 CanadaNats
70/1 EddieSargent 182
71/2 EddieSargent 179
72/3 EddieSargent 128
70/1 Esso Stamp
74/5 Loblaws
71/2 OPC 127
72/3 OPC 88, Topps 103
74/5 OPC 352
75/6 OPC 337
68/9 ShirriffCoin STL10
71/2 TheTorontoSun
87/8 CGY/RedRooster
75/6 PHA/GingerAle
71/2 STL
92/3 T.B./Sheraton
94/5 T.B./SkyBoxSportsCafe
95/6 T.B./SkyBoxSportsCafe
85/6 Moncton 1, 3
86/7 Moncton 1
80/1 SSMarie
81/2 SSMarie
82/3 SSMarie
84/5 SSMarie

CRISTOFOLI, ED
89/90 ProCards(AHL) 194
90/1 ProCards 72

CROCE, PAT
86/7 PHA

CROCKER, COREY
95/6 Slapshot 312

CROCKETT, KEN
91/2 AvantGardeBCJHL 31

CROGHAN, MAURICE
36/7 WWGum (V356) 103

CROMBEEN, MIKE
83/4 O-Pee-Chee 312
83/4 opcSticker 126
82/3 Post
83/4 HFD/JuniorWhalers
84/5 HFD/JuniorWhalers
78/9 STL

CROMBIE, CHRIS
89/90 SketchOHL 30
90/1 SketchOHL 131
91/2 SketchOHL 374

CRONAN, EARL
96/7 Fredericton

CRONIN, SHAWN
90/1 Bowman 128
92/3 OPCPremier 42
90/1 Panini(WPG) 6
91/2 Parkhurst 423
88/9 ProCards(Baltimore)
90/1 ProSet 559
91/2 ProSet 268
91/2 Score(CDN) 423
92/3 Score 366
92/3 Topps 489
92/3 ToppsStadiumClub 471
91/2 UpperDeck 478
92/3 PHA/JCPenney
92/3 PHA/UD 06D EV92
92/3 S.J/Pacific Bell
89/90 WPG/Safeway
90/1 WPG/IGA
91/2 WPG/IGA

CROOP, JEFF
88/9 ProCards(Utica)

CROSS, CORY
94/5 ClassicImages 88
95/6 Leaf 275
97/8 PacificRegime 184
96/7 PinnacleBeAPlayer 143
95/6 Topps 44
94/5 UpperDeck 340
97/8 UpperDeck 365
95/6 T.B.
95/6 T.B./SkyBoxSportsCafe
93/4 AtlantaKnights

CROSSMAN, DOUG
90/1 Bowman 115
92/3 FleerUltra 410
90/1 Kraft 10
82/3 O-Pee-Chee 63
83/4 O-Pee-Chee 263
84/5 O-Pee-Chee 157
87/8 OPC/Topps 182
88/9 OPC/Topps 197
90/1 OPC/Topps 72
91/2 OPC/Topps 341
92/3 OPCPremier 59
86/7 opcSticker237 /107
88/9 opcSticker100 /226
87/8 PaniniSticker 125
90/1 PaniniSticker 91
92/3 Parkhurst 388
82/3 Post
93/4 Premier 159
90/1 ProSet 179
92/3 ProSet 180
90/1 Score 59, 52T
91/2 Score(CDN) 38, (U.S) 38
93/4 Score 25
83/4 SouhaitsRen.KeyChain
90/1 UpperDeck 7, 419
81/2 CHI
82/3 CHI
83/4 CHI
90/1 HFD/JuniorWhalers
88/9 L.A/Smokeys
89/90 NYI
83/4 PHA
86/7 PHA
93/4 Peoria

CROTEAU, GARY
70/1 EddieSargent 141
71/2 EddieSargent 133
72/3 EddieSargent 48
70/1 Esso Stamp
72/3 Letraset 12
74/5 Loblaws
70/1 OPC 189
71/2 OPC/Topps 17
72/3 OPC 3, Topps 83
73/4 OPC 228
74/5 OPC/Topps 36
76/7 OPC 283
77/8 OPC/Topps 52
78/9 O-Pee-Chee 362
79/80 OPC/Topps 158
72 SemicSticker 180
71/2 TheTorontoSun
76/7 COL.R
76/7 COL.R/CokeCans
77/8 COL.R/CokeCans
79/80 COL.R

CROUSE, DUANE
92/3 Tacoma

CROWDER, BRUCE
82/3 O-Pee-Chee 9
83/4 O-Pee-Chee 46
82/3 Post
83/4 SouhaitsRen.KeyChain
83/4 BOS

CROWDER, KEITH
82/3 O-Pee-Chee 10
83/4 O-Pee-Chee 47
84/5 O-Pee-Chee 2
85/6 OPC/Topps 159
86/7 OPC/Topps 130
87/8 OPC/Topps 194
88/9 O-Pee-Chee 206
89/90 O-Pee-Chee 199
90/1 O-Pee-Chee 476
82/3 opcSticker 80
83/4 opcSticker 56
85/6 opcSticker 163/33
86/7 opcSticker 37
87/8 opcSticker 136/245
88/9 opcSticker 30
87/8 PaniniSticker 14
88/9 PaniniSticker 209
84/5 Topps 2
83/4 BOS
84/5 BOS
88/9 BOS/SportsAction
89/90 L.A./Smokeys 10

CROWDER, TROY
91/2 OPC/Topps 374
91/2 opcPremier 169
97/8 PacificD-BestKept 96
90/1 ProSet 620
90/1 ScoreTraded 43T
91/2 Score(CDN) 602, (U.S) 52T
90/1 UpperDeck 441
91/2 UpperDeck 342
90/1 N.J.
96/7 VAN
96/7 VAN/IGA

CROWE, PHIL
93/4 Donruss 446
97/8 PacificD-BestKept 65
92/3 Phoenix

CROWE, RICK
91/2 AvantGardeBCJHL 3

CROWLEY, JOE
91/2 SketchQMJHL 203

CROWLEY, MIKE
98/9 Pacific 378

CROWLEY, TED
92/3 ClassicProspects 112
93/4 FleerUltra 480
94/5 Parkhurst 93
93/4 PowerPlay 500
93/4 Premier-TeamUSA 12
94/5 Score 233
93/4 TSC-TeamUSA 3
94/5 UpperDeck 442
96/7 Cincinnati

CROWTHER, CORY
92/3 BCJHL 103

CROZIER, ROGER
71/2 Bazooka Panel 32
64-67 BeeHives(DET)
64/5 CokeCap DET-1
65/6 CocaCola
70/1 Colgate Stamp 83
70/1 DadsCookies
70/1 EddieSargent 26
71/2 EddieSargent 27
72/3 EddieSargent 32
70/1 Esso Stamp

51/2 LavalDairy 3
72/3 Letraset 3
74/5 Loblaws
71/2 OPC/T-Booklet 5
68/9 OPC/T. 23, OPC-Puck 10
69/70 OPC/T. 55, OPC-Sticker
70/1 OPC 145,OPC/T-Deckle 11
71/2 OPC/Topps 36
72/3 OPC 50, Topps 31
73/4 OPC 153, Topps 108
75/6 O-Pee-Chee 350
94/5 Parkie(64/5) 53, AS1, TW5
95/6 Parkie(66/7) 56, 136
72/3 Post Transfers 10
72 SemicSticker 165
68/9 ShirriffCoin DET2
52/3 StLawrence 43
71/2 TheTorontoSun
64/5 Topps 47
65/6 Topps 42
66/7 Topps 43, -USATest 43
67/8 Topps 48
54-67 TorontoStar 66/7
72/3 BUF
73/4 BUF [x2]
73/4 BUF/BellsMarket
74/5 BUF
75/6 BUF/Linnett
93/4 BUF/NOCO
80/1 TOR

CRUICKSHANK, CURTIS
97/8 Bowman 62, 139, BB19

CRUIKSHANK, GORD
89/90 ProCards'AHL 62

CRUMLEY, CHAD
92/3 MPSPhotoSJHL 66

CRUTCHFIELD, NELSON
34/5 SweetCaporal

CUCKSEY, DON
91/2 Rayside

CUCUZ, SASHA
95/6 Slapshot 179

CUDE, WILFRED
34-43 BeeHives(MTL.C)
34/5 SweetCaporal
35-40 CrownBrand 59
36-39 DiamondMatch (1), (2), (3)
35/6 OPC (V304C) 73
36/7 OPC (V304D) 120
37/8 OPC (V304E) 149
38/9 QuakerOats
36/7 WWGum (V356) 9

CULHANE, JIM
88/9 ProCards(Binghampton)
89/90 ProCards(AHL) 298
90/1 ProCards 504
91/2 ProCards 454
93/4 WestMich.

CULL, DEAN
90/1 SketchOHL 389
91/2 Rayside

CULL, TRENT
90/1 SketchOHL 281
91/2 SketchOHL 177
93/4 Slapshot(Kingston) 19

CULLEN, BARRY
45-64 BeeHives(TOR)
82? JDMcCarthy
58/9 Parkhurst 31, 36
60/1 Parkhurst 32
57/8 Parkhurst(MTL) 22
57/8 Parkhurst(TOR) 21
93/4 Parkie(56/7) 120
91/2 Pinnacle 391
60/1 ShirriffCoin 47
59/60 Topps 25
56-66 TorontoStar 57/8

CULLEN, BRIAN
52/3 AnonymousOHL 25
45-64 BeeHives(NYR, TORx2)
55/6 Parkhurst 13
57/8 Parkhurst(TOR) 9
58/9 Parkhurst 50
93/4 Parkie(56/7) 118
60/1 ShirriffCoin 99
59/60 Topps 55

CULLEN, JOHN
90/1 Bowman 210
91/2 Bowman 1
92/3 Bowman 194, 227
93/4 Donruss 334
95/6 Donruss 156
96/7 Flair 87
92/3 FleerUltra 72, 419
93/4 FleerUltra 20
94/5 FleerUltra 348
95/6 FleerUltra 309
91/2 Kraft 24
93/4 Leaf 245
94/5 Leaf 412
95/6 Leaf 181
92/3 McDonalds McD-18
92/3 O-Pee-Chee 104
89/90 OPC/Topps 145
90/1 OPC/Topps 208
91/2 OPC/Topps 226
90/1 opcPremier 20
91/2 opcPremier 127
89/90 opcSticker 213/92
89/90 opcStickFS 13
97/8 PacificCrown 282
97/8 PcfcDynag! 116,-Tandm 53
97/8 PacificInvincible 130
89/90 PaniniSticker 316
90/1 PaniniSticker 125
91/2 PaniniSticker 314
92/3 PaniniSticker 257
93/4 PaniniSticker 226
97/8 PaniniSticker 107
91/2 Parkhurst 59
92/3 Parkhurst 180
93/4 Parkhurst 473
95/6 Parkhurst 463
94/5 ParkieSE 140
91/2 Pinnacle 125, 391
92/3 Pinnacle 285
93/4 Pinnacle 388
94/5 Pinnacle 397
95/6 POG 248
93/4 PowerPlay 242
93/4 Premier 479
94/5 Premier 423
90/1 ProSet 232
91/2 ProSet 85, 302, CC9
92/3 ProSet 57
91/2 PSPlatinum 175
90/1 Score 164, -HotCards 73
91/2 Score(CDN) 7, 311
91/2 Score(U.S) 7,421, -Young 5
92/3 Score 150, 425
93/4 Score 189
95/6 Score 105
97/8 Score 155
92/3 SeasonsPatches 45
91 SemicSticker 72
94/5 SP 91
92/3 Topps 132
95/6 Topps 74
93/4 TOR/Abalene
91/2 ToppsStadiumClub 289
92/3 ToppsStadiumClub 160
93/4 ToppsStadiumClub 209
90/1 UpperDeck 12, 492
91/2 UpperDeck 84, 235
92/3 UpperDeck 304, 465
93/4 UpperDeck 395
94/5 UpperDeck 281
95/6 UpperDeck 358
94/5 UDBeAPlayer-Aut. 105
95/6 UDCollChoice 181
91/2 HFD/JuniorWhalers
89/90 PGH/Foodland 9
90/1 PGH/Foodland 10
94/5 PGH 7
95/6 T.B
92/3 TOR/Kodak
93/4 TOR/Blacks 16
87/8 Flint

CULLEN, JUSTIN
90/1 SketchOHL 229
91/2 SketchOHL 95

CULLEN, MATT
95/6 DonrussElite-WorldJrs 33
97/8 Omega 1
98/9 Pacific 45
97/8 Score(ANA) 5
98/9 UDChoice 7

CULLEN, RAY
68/9 Bauer
70/1 Colgate Stamp 15
70/1 DadsCookies
70/1 EddieSargent 216
70/1 Esso Stamp
68/9 OPC/Topps 54
69/70 OPC/Topps 130
69/70 OPC-Sticker, -Stamp
70/1 OPC 228,OPC/T-Deckle 31
68/9 ShirriffCoin MIN-9
70/1 VAN/RoyalBank

CULLIMORE, JASSEN
91/2 Arena 22
91/2 Classic 26
91/2 ClassicFourSport 26, -Aut.
94/5 ClassicImages 53
95/6 Donruss 175
95/6 EdgeIce 89
94/5 Leaf 488
95/6 Leaf 25
97/8 PacificRegime 101
94/5 ParkieSE 191
94/5 Premier 477
89/90 SketchOHL 116
90/1 SketchOHL 356
91/2 SketchOHL 146
91/2 StarPics 71
95/6 Topps 101
91/2 UltimateDP 23, -Aut. 23
91/2 UD 72, 690, 'CzechWJC 64
94/5 UpperDeck 247
94/5 UDBeAPlayer 80
96/7 MTL
96/7 MTL/MolsonExport
92/3 Hamilton
91/2 Peterborough 21

CUMMINGS, BURTON
91/2 WPG/IGA
91/2 PSPlatinum 290

CUMMINGS, DON
28/9 PaulinsCandy 52

CUMMINS, JIM
92/3 Classic 94
92/3 ClassicFourSport 209
94/5 Leaf 434
98/9 Pacific 335
97/8 PacificRegime 44
97/8 PinnacleBeAPlayer 80
93/4 ToppsStadiumClub 448
94/5 T.B/SkyBoxSportsCafe

CUNNEYWORTH, RANDY
93/4 Donruss 413
92/3 FleerUltra 73
94/5 FleerUltra 336
89/90 Kraft 48
96/7 Kraft'Disk
87/8 OPC/Topps 150
88/9 OPC/Topps 19
89/90 OPC/Topps 63
90/1 OPC/Topps 67
88/9 opcSticker 231
97/8 PacificCrown 198
87/8 PaniniSticker 148
88/9 PaniniSticker 337
91/2 PaniniSticker 320
92/3 PaniniSticker 260
96/7 PaniniSticker 55
91/2 Parkhurst 284
95/6 Parkhurst 421
94/5 Pinnacle 406
97/8 PinnacleBeAPlayer 175
93/4 Premier 423
95/6 ProMagnet 115
90/1 ProSet 101
91/2 ProSet 392
90/1 Score 276
91/2 Score(CDN) 424
97/8 Score 161
93/4 ToppsStadiumClub 341
94/5 ToppsStadiumClub 38
90/1 UpperDeck 268
96/7 UpperDeck 111
95/6 UDBeAPlayer 81
96/7 UDCollChoice 178
89/90 HFD/JuniorWhalers
90/1 HFD/JuniorWhalers
91/2 HFD/JuniorWhalers
92/3 HFD/DairyMart
93/4 HFD/Coke

94/5 OTT/Bell
95/6 OTT
96/7 OTT/PizzaHut
97/8 OTT
86/7 PGH/Kodak
87/8 PGH/Kodak
89/90 WPG/Safeway

CUNNIFF, JOHN
90/1 ProSet 670
89/90 N.J.
90/1 N.J.
72/3 NewEnglandWhalers

CUNNINGHAM, BOB
61/2 ShirriffCoin 96

CUNNINGHAM, LES
34-43 BeeHives(CHI)
39/40 OPC (V301-1) 78

CUNNINGHAM, RCK
72/3 OttawaNationals

CURLEY, BRENDAN
93/4 Hampton
94/5 Hampton 16

CURLEY, CINDY
94/5 Classic W31

CURRAN, BRIAN
87/8 OPC/Topps 90
90/1 Panini(TOR) 4
87/8 PaniniSticker 95
91/2 ProCards 2
90/1 ProSet 277
90/1 BUF/BlueShield
88/9 TOR/P.L.A.Y. 26

CURRAN, MIKE
69/70 MästarSerien 15
72 SemicSticker 118
72/3 Minnesota
74/5 Minnesota

CURRIE, ALEX
91 C55 Reprint 13
1910-11 Imperial Post 13
1911-12 Imperial (C55) 13
1912-13 Imperial (C57) 32

CURRIE, DAN
92/3 ClassicProspects 150
95/6 EdgeIce 105
88/9 ProCards(Cape Breton)
89/90 ProCard('AHL) 136
90/1 ProCards 222
91/2 ProCards 228
91/2 UpperDeck 347
92/3 EDM/IGA 5
93/4 Phoenix
87/8 SSMarie 2

CURRIE, GLEN
82/3 Post
83/4 SouhaitsRen.KeyChain
81/2 WSH
82/3 WSH
84/5 WSH/PizzaHut

CURRIE, SHELDON
81/2 Milwaukee 11

CURRIE, TONY
80/1 O-Pee-Chee 384
81/2 OPC 292, Topps(W) 116
82/3 O-Pee-Chee 341
78/9 STL
84/5 HFD/JuniorWhalers
82/3 Fredericton 7
83/4 Fredericton 11
85/6 Fredericton 9
84/5 NovaScotia 22

CURRY, FLOYD
45-64 BeeHives(MTL)
72-84 Dernière 77/8
48-52 Exhibits
51-54 LaPatrie 17FEB52
43-47 ParadeSportive
51/2 Parkhurst 12
52/3 Parkhurst 7
53/4 Parkhurst 35
54/5 Parkhurst 15, 89
55/6 Parkhurst 40, 76
57/8 Parkhurst(MTL) 20
93/4 Parkie(56/7) 78
45-54 QuakerOats [x2]
63/4 Québec

CURTH, CHRISTIAN
94/5 DEL 15
95/6 DEL 130
96/7 DEL 320

CURTIN, LUKE
95/6 Bowman P8
94/5 Select 153

CURTIS, PAUL
71/2 EddieSargent 77
72/3 EddieSargent 85
70/1 Esso Stamp
71/2 O-Pee-Chee 4
72/3 O-Pee-Chee 266
71/2 TheTorontoSun

CUSHENAN, IAN
45-64 BeeHives(MTL, NYR)
58/9 Parkhurst 24
63/4 Parkhurst 49

CUTHBERT, CHRIS
97/8 Pinnacle -CBC Sports 4

CUTTS, DON
88/9 EDM/ActionMagazine 152

CUVELIER, CHRIS
79 PaniniSticker 341

CYR, DENNIS
82/3 O-Pee-Chee 43
82/3 Post
80/1 CGY
81/2 CGY
82/3 CHI
83/4 CHI

CYR, PAUL
91/2 Bowman 20
83 CanadaJuniors
86/7 O-Pee-Chee 200
91/2 OPC/Topps 73
85/6 opcSticker 183/552
87/8 PaniniSticker 33
91/2 PaniniSticker 321
91/2 ProCards 100
90/1 ProSet 449
91/2 ProSet 88
90/1 ScoreTraded 72T
91/2 Score(CDN) 413
91/2 ToppsStadiumClub 279
84/5 BUF/BlueShield
85/6 BUF
86/7 BUF
90/1 HFD/JuniorWhalers
91/2 HFD/JuniorWhalers
84/5 KelownaWings 31
81/2 Victoria
82/3 Victoria

CYR, RAY
52/3 AnonymousOHL 81

CYRENNE, CORY
98 BowmanCHL 74

CYRWUS, STANISLAW
92 SemicSticker 276

CZACHOVSKI, LUDVIK
74 Hellas 94
73/4 WilliamsFIN 88

CZAPKA, LUDVIK
89 SemicSticker 137
92 SemicSticker 281

CZOZEPANIEC, ANDRZEJ
74 Hellas 95
73/4 WilliamsFIN 89

CZEPNISHEV, A.
69/70 Soviet Stars
70/1 Soviet Stars
71/2 Soviet Stars

CZERKAWSKI, MARIUSZ
94/5 Donruss 138
95/6 Donruss 21
96/7 DonrussCanadianIce 96
94/5 Flair 9
94/5 Fleer 10
94/5 FleerUltra 11
95/6 FleerUltra 9, -AllRookie 2
94/5 Leaf 82
95/6 Leaf 55, -StudioRookie 17
94/5 LeafLimited 29
95/6 McDonalds 37
98/9 Pacific 279
97/8 PacificCrown 216
98/9 PacificParamount 141

95/6 PaniniSticker 5
96/7 PaniniSticker 261
97/8 PaniniSticker 211
94/5 Parkhurst 20, V55
95/6 Parkhurst 18, 345
94/5 ParkieSE ES5
94/5 Pinnacle 246, 467, RTP12
95/6 Pinnacle 185
96/7 Pinnacle 167
97/8 Pinnacle 122
96/7 PinnacleBeAPlayer 166
95/6 PinnacleFANtasy 4
97/8 PinnacleInside 158
95/6 Playoff 117
96/7 Playoff 368
95/6 POG 34
94/5 Premier 293
94/5 Score 227
95/6 Score 143
97/8 Score 208
94/5 Select 190, YE11
91/2 SemicElitserien 73
92 SemicSticker 288
95/6 SisuLimited 63
95/6 SkyBxImpact-Fox 1
94/5 SP 10
96/7 SP 59
95/6 Topps 153, 7PL, 19NG
94/5 T.Finest-BBest(Red) 20
94/5 UD 239, 534, 543, C5, SP5
95/6 UpperDeck 189, SE6
96/7 UDBlackDiamond 122
95/6 UDCollChoice 50
96/7 UDCollChoice 93
97/8 UDCollChoice 93

CZERLINSKI, JAN
95/6 APS 345

DABANOVICH, JAMIE
91/2 Knoxville

DACHYSHYN, DEAN
83/4 Moncton 22
84/5 NovaScotia 13
85/6 NovaScotia 4

DACKELL, ANDREAS
97/8 Donruss 113
96/7 DonrussCanadianIce 134
94/5 ElitSet 49, -Gold 2
95/6 ElitSet 18, -Champs 10
95 Globe
96/7 Flair 117
96/7 FleerUltra 115
97/8 Limited 137
96/7 MetalUniverse 174
97/8 Omega 154
98/9 Pacific 308
97/8 PacificCrown 278
98/9 PacificParamount 162
95 PaniniWorld 147
96/7 PinnacleBeAPlayer 109
96/7 PinnacleZenith 121
97/8 Score 203
96/7 SelectCertified 118
95 Semic 70
91/2 SemicElitserien 51
92/3 SemicElitserien 64
93/4 SemicElitserien 37
96/7 SP 109
97/8 SPAuthentic 109
96/7 UpperDeck 303
97/8 UpperDeck 323
98/9 UDChoice 146
97/8 UDCollChoice 175
95/6 udElite 36, NA3
96 Wien 68
96/7 OTT/PizzaHut
97/8 OTT

DACORTE, LUIGI
94 Semic 293

DACOSTA, JEFF
93/4 Slapshot(Kingston) 6
95/6 Slapshot 111

DADSWELL, DOUG
90/1 CanadaNats
87/8 CGY/RedRooster
91/2 Cincinnati

92/3 Cincinnati
86/7 Moncton 3

DAFOE, BYRON
95/6 Bowman 97, BB23
92/3 ClassicProspects 73
94/5 Donruss 175
95/6 Donruss 362
96/7 Donruss 221
97/8 Donruss 20
97/8 DonrussElite 60
97/9 DonrussPreferred 71
97/8 D.Priority 104,-PostGen 14
95/6 FleerMetal 173
95/6 FleerUltra 334
94/5 Leaf 283
96/7 Leaf 211
97/8 Limited 63
97/8 Omega 14
98/9 Pacific 74
97/8 PacificCrown 141
97/8 PacificCrownRoyale 9
97/9 PCR -FreezeOut 2
98/9 PcfcParamount 12,-Glove 2
97/8 PcfcRevolution 8,-Return 2
95 PaniniWorld 245
95/6 Parkhurst 375
96/7 PinnacleBeAPlayer 30
97/8 P. BAP-Stacking/Pads 15
95/6 PinnacleZenith 133
94/5 Premier 42
91/2 ProCards 548
96/7 Score 260
97/8 Score 47
97/8 Score(BOS) 13
95/6 SelectCertified 120
96/7 SkyBoxImpact 56
95/6 SP 70
98/9 SPx"Finite" 7
95/6 Summit 192
95/6 Topps 293
98/9 Topps 3
96/7 ToppsNHLPicks RS14
94/5 UpperDeck 447
95/6 UpperDeck 460
96/7 UDBlackDiamond 65
98/9 UDChoice 10
97/8 UDCollChoice 127
96/7 UpperDeck "Ice" 31
97/8 Zenith 40
87/8 Portland
88/9 Portland
89/90 Portland
93/4 Portland

DAGENAIS, EMILE
52/3 LavalDairy 106
52/3 StLawrence 67

DAGENAIS, MIKE
90/1 ProCards 407
91/2 ProCards 528
89/90 SketchOHL 102
92/3 Cincinnati
93/4 Cleveland

DAGENAIS, PIERRE
98 BowmanCHL 100
97/8 PinnacleBeeHive 74

DAHL, BJØRN ANDERS
95 PaniniWorld 245

DAHL, KEVIN
91/2 CanadaNats
92 CanadaWinterOlympics 174
92/3 FleerUltra 266
93/4 FleerUltra 23
92/3 opcPremier 22
92/3 Parkhurst 261
93/4 Parkhurst 298
93/4 Premier 362
93/4 Score 423
93/4 ToppsStadiumClub 432
92/3 UpperDeck 493
92/3 CGY/IGA 23
96/7 LasVegas

DAHLEN, ULF
90/1 Bowman 176
91/2 Bowman 127, 422, 423
92/3 Bowman 143
93/4 Donruss 78, 488
94/5 Donruss 57
95/6 Donruss 92

96/7 Donruss 115
94/5 Flair 161
94/5 Fleer 194
95/6 FleerMetal 128
92/3 FleerUltra 92
93/4 FleerUltra 81
94/5 FleerUltra 192
95/6 FleerUltra 144
95 Globe 48
95/6 Hoyle'WEST 2 (Spades)
95/6 KraftDinner
93/4 Leaf 198
94/5 Leaf 25
95/6 Leaf 157
96/7 Leaf 55
94/5 LeafLimited 76
92/3 O-Pee-Chee 129
88/9 OPC/Topps 47
89/90 OPC/Topps 2
90/1 OPC/Topps 12
91/2 OPC/Topps 177
88/9 opcMini 7
88/9 opcSticker 128/260
88/9 opcStickFS 5
97/8 PacificCrown 74
88/9 PaniniSticker 305
89/90 PaniniSticker 288
91/2 PaniniSticker 110
92/3 PaniniSticker 92
93/4 PaniniSticker 270
94/5 PaniniSticker 221
95/6 PaniniSticker 281
96/7 PaniniSticker 283
97/8 PaniniSticker 130
95 PaniniWorlds 286
91/2 Parkhurst 76
92/3 Parkhurst 310
93/4 Parkhurst 322
94/5 Parkhurst 215
95/6 Parkhurst 245, 452
94/5 ParkieSE ES6
91/2 Pinnacle 152
92/3 Pinnacle 68
93/4 Pinnacle 248
94/5 Pinnacle 48, WE4
95/6 Pinnacle 13
96/7 PinnacleBeAPlayer 35
95/6 PinnacleZenith 7
95/6 Playoff 190
94/5 POG 63
95/6 POG 228
93/4 PowerPlay 59
93/4 Premier 75
94/5 Premier 299
95/6 ProMagnet 118
90/1 ProSet 136
91/2 ProSet 106, 607
92/3 ProSet 80
90/1 Score 22
92/3 Score 330
93/4 Score 107, -International 13
95/6 Score 137
96/7 Score 234
97/8 Score 252
94/5 Select 123
95/6 SelectCertified 25
93 SemicSticker 34
95/6 SkyBoxEmotion 154
95/6 SkyBoxImpact 146
95/6 Summit 15
95/6 SuperSticker 109
92/3 Topps 28
95/6 Topps 227
91/2 ToppsStadiumClub 55
92/3 ToppsStadiumClub 207
93/4 T.StadiumClub 238, 428
94/5 TSC-MembersOnly 42
90/1 UpperDeck 283
92/3 UpperDeck 250
93/4 UpperDeck 360
94/5 UpperDeck 16, SP70
95/6 UpperDeck 381, SE72
95/6 UDCollChoice 297
96/7 UDCollChoice 243
97/8 UDCollChoice 48
96 Wien 60
94/5 DAL
89/90 NYR/MarineMidland
96/7 S.J/PacificBellSheet

DAHLIN, KJELL
86/7 Kraft Sports 23
86/7 O-Pee-Chee 262
86/7 OPC/Topps 15
86/7 opcSticker 18, 126/112
87/8 opcSticker 14/153
85/6 MTL
85/6 MTL/ProvigoStickers
85/6? MTL/ProvigoPlacemats
86/7 MTL
87/8 MTL
87/8 MTL/Stickers 39, 40

DAHLQUIST, CHRIS
91/2 Bowman 128, 415
92/3 Bowman 359
92/3 FleerUltra 267
94/5 Leaf 386
90/1 O-Pee-Chee 528
92/3 O-Pee-Chee 22
91/2 OPC/Topps 142
92/3 opcPremier 38
92/3 Pinnacle 167
93/4 Pinnacle 414
94/5 Pinnacle 402
95/6 POG 197
90/1 ProSet 464
91/2 ProSet 408
91/2 Score (US) 365
92/3 Score 294
93/4 Score 314
92/3 Topps 231
91/2 ToppsStadiumClub 314
92/3 ToppsStadiumClub 57
93/4 ToppsStadiumClub 266
91/2 UpperDeck 307
92/3 CGY/IGA 24
94/5 OTT/Bell
87/8 PGH/Kodak
96/7 LasVegas

DAHLSTROM, CULLY
34-43 BeeHives(CHI)
36-39 DiamondMatch (5), (6)
39/40 OPC (V301-1) 46
40/1 OPC (V301-2) 137

DAHLSTROM, LARS
94/5 ElitSet 94
97/8 udSwedish 178

DAHLSTROM, O.E.
94 Semic 259
92 SemicSticker 41
93 SemicSticker 240

DAIGLE, ALAIN
75/6 OPC 394
76/7 OPC/Topps 156
77/8 OPC/Topps 208
78/9 OPC/Topps 117
79/80 OPC/Topps 227
79/80 CHI

DAIGLE, ALEXANDRE
95/6 Aces 4 (Diamonds)
94/5 CanadaJuniorAlumni 4
93/4 Classic 1, 34, 50-54, 114
93/4 Classic DP1, N1, PR1
93/4 C'Prospects 13
93/4 C'FourSport 185, S11,DS58
93/4 C'4Sport LP22, PP18, TC4
93/4 C4'Images 4, CC14
93/4 Donruss 237, 393, P
93/4 D-RatedRook 1, -Elite 2
94/5 Donruss 211
95/6 Donruss 160, -CanadaJr 16
96/7 Donruss 204
97/8 Donruss 78
96/7 D.CanadianIce 104
97/8 D.CdnIce 122, -National 15
96/7 DonrussElite 84
97/8 DonrussElite 24
97/8 DonrussPreferred 48
97/8 DonrussPriority 22
97/8 DonrussStudio 92
93/4 Durivage 1
94/5 Flair 120, -ScoringPower 2
94/5 Fleer 143
95/6 FleerMetal 104
93/4 FleerUltra 380, -Wave 3
94/5 FleerUltra 146, -AllRookie 3
95/6 FU 111, -High 6, -Rising 2
96/7 FleerUltra 116
93/4 HockeyWit 91
95/6 Hoyle'EAST 9 (Hearts)
97/8 KatchMedallion 98
93/4 KraftDinner
95/6 KraftDinner,'Ticket
93/4 Leaf 311, -Freshman 1
93/4 L-StudioSignature 9
94/5 Leaf 119, -GoldL.Rookie 5
95/6 Leaf 179
96/7 Leaf 80
97/8 Leaf 26
94/5 LeafLimited 87
95/6 LeafLimited 38
97/8 Limited 161
96/7 Maggers 110
94/5 McDonalds 36
95/6 McDonalds 38
96/7 MetalUniverse 105
98/9 Pacific 323
97/8 PacificCrown 250, -T.CL 17
97/8 PacificCrownRoyale 90
97/8 PcfcDynag! 84,-Tandm 54
97/8 PcfcInvincible 93,-Feat 23
97/8 PacificParamount 124
98/9 PacificParamount 170
97/8 PacificRevolution 99
94/5 PaniniSticker 101
95/6 PaniniSticker 47
96/7 PaniniSticker 45
97/8 PaniniSticker 38
93/4 PH 244, C1, D11, E3,F1,G6
94/5 Parkhurst 285, V42
95/6 Parkhurst 150
94/5 ParkieSE 119
93/4 Pinnacle 236, SR1, -Promo
94/5 Pinn. 2, 461, 531, GR6,NL6
95/6 Pinnacle 7
96/7 Pinnacle 133
97/8 Pinnacle 159
97/8 PinnacleCertified 98
95/6 PinnacleFANtasy 3
97/8 PinnacleInside 109
95/6 PinnacleZenith 22
95/6 Playoff 73, 178
94/5 POG 353
95/6 POG 190
93/4 PowerPlay 396, -Rookie 3
93/4 Premier 405, Finest 1
94/5 Prmr 140,195,-Fin.(OPC) 7
95/6 ProMagnet 112
93/4 Score 496, 587, (CDN) DD3
94/5 Score 248, DT21, TF16
95/6 Score 18
96/7 Score 66
97/8 Score 101
94/5 Select 3
95/6 SelectCertified 22
91/2 SketchQMJHL 270
95/6 SkyBoxEmotion 123
95/6 SkyBoxImpact 118
96/7 SkyBoxImpact 88
94/5 SP 81, 136
95/6 SP 103
96/7 SP 106
97/8 SPAuthentic 107
95/6 Summit 21
96/7 Summit 106
95/6 SuperSticker 86
95/6 Topps 342, 5CJ, HGC14
94/5 ToppsFinest 88, 155
93/4 ToppsStadiumClub 300
94/5 ToppsStadiumClub 110
95/6 ToppsStadiumClub 97
93/4 TSCMembersOnly 50
97/8 ToppsSticker 1
95/6 ToppsSuperSkills 24
92/3 UpperDeck 587
93/4 UD 170,250,E15,R3,SP-10
94/5 UpperDeck 87, IG10, SP54
95/6 UpperDeck 271, SE60
96/7 UpperDeck 302
97/8 UpperDeck 117
93/4 UDBeAPlayer 3
94/5 UDBeAPlayer R30
95/6 UDBeAPlayer 188
96/7 UDBlackDiamond 91
98/9 UDChoice 148
95/6 UDCollChoice 208
96/7 UDCollChoice 180, 324
97/8 UDCollChoice 174, SQ25
93/4 OTT/Kraft
94/5 OTT/Bell
95/6 OTT
96/7 OTT/PizzaHut
97/8 OTT
97/8 PHA/Comcast

DAIGLE, CHRISTIAN
97/8 Bowman 79

DAIGNEAULT, J.J.
92/3 Bowman 371
92/3 Durivage 35
93/4 Durivage 10
92/3 FleerUltra 326
93/4 FleerUltra 351
93/4 Leaf 437
94/5 Leaf 407
92/3 O-Pee-Chee 304
91/2 OPC/Topps 456
97/8 PacificD-BestKept 1
90/1 Panini(MTL) 7
91/2 PaniniSticker 192
91/2 Parkhurst 312
92/3 Parkhurst 324
93/4 Parkhurst 377
95/6 Parkhurst 442
93/4 Pinnacle 311
94/5 Pinnacle 224
96/7 PinnacleBeAPlayer 34
95/6 Playoff 163
96/7 Playoff 377
95/6 POG 153
93/4 PowerPlay 367
93/4 Premier 372
88/9 ProCards(Hershey)
88/9 ProCards(Sherbrooke)
90/1 ProSet 466
91/2 ProSet 124
92/3 Score 311
93/4 Score 299
97/8 Score 254
97/8 Score(ANA) 8
92/3 Topps 334
92/3 ToppsStadiumClub 308
93/4 ToppsStadiumClub 475
94/5 ToppsStadiumClub 52
92/3 UpperDeck 331
94/5 UpperDeck 341
97/8 UpperDeck 212
89/90 MTL
89/90 MTL/Kraft
90/1 MTL
91/2 MTL
92/3 MT
92/3 MTL/OPC 25
93/4 MTL
93/4 MTL/Molson
94/5 MTL
86/7 PHA
84/5 VAN
85/6 VAN

DAIGNEAULT, PAUL
90/1 SketchQMJHL 171

DAILEY, BOB
74/5 Loblaws
74/5 OPC/Topps 240
75/6 OPC/Topps 231
76/7 OPC 350
77/8 OPC/Topps 98
78/9 OPC/Topps 131
79/80 OPC/Topps 226
80/1 OPC/Topps 131
81/2 OPC 241, Topps(E) 104
73/4 VAN/RoyalBank
74/5 VAN/RoyalBank
75/6 VAN/RoyalBank
76/7 VAN/RoyalBank

DAINVILLE, BOB
52/3 StLawrence 89

DAIRON, MICHAEL
92/3 BCJHL 123

DALE, ANDREW
93/4 Slapshot(Sudbury) 12
94/5 Slapshot(Sudbury) 11
95/6 Slapshot 142, 394

D'ALESSIO, CORRIE
91/2 ProCards 616

DALEY, JOE
70/1 EddieSargent 17
71/2 EddieSargent 62
68/9 O-Pee-Chee 188
69/70 O-Pee-Chee 152
71/2 OPC/Topps 137
74/5 opcWHA 38
75/6 opcWHA 101
76/7 opcWHA 6, 20, 61
77/8 opcWHA 9
71/2 TheTorontoSun
77/8 Winnipeg

DALEY, JOHN
93/4 Johnstown 21

DALGARNO, BRAD
93/4 Donruss 197
93/4 FleerUltra 364
93/4 Leaf 320
89/90 O-Pee-Chee 246
92/3 Parkhurst 336
93/4 Parkhurst 393
93/4 Pinnacle 333
94/5 Pinnacle 238
94/5 POG 153
93/4 Premier 223
90/1 ProSet 482
93/4 Score 374
91/2 ToppsStadiumClub 371
93/4 ToppsStadiumClub 167
94/5 ToppsStadiumClub 259
93/4 UpperDeck 219
95/6 UDBeAPlayer 10

DALLAIR, STACY
90/1 SketchQMJHL 172
91/2 SketchQMJHL 147

DALLMAN, MARTY
95 Globe 187
88/9 ProCards(Newmarket)
94 Semic 250

DALLMAN, ROD
88/9 ProCards(Springfield)
89/90 ProCards'AHL 245
91/2 ProCards 278
84/5 PrinceAlbert

DALMAD, DUNCAN
95/6 Slapshot 159

DALMAN, DADDY
23/4 PaulinsCandy 13

DALPIAZ, KLAUS
96/7 DEL 184
95 Globe 181
95 PaniniWorlds 257
94 Semic 231
93 SemicSticker 270
96 Wien 210

DAM, TREVOR
90/1 ProCards 403
91/2 ProCards 483
89/90 SketchOHL 25
92/3 Indianapolis
86/7 London 21

DAME, AURELLA "BUNNY"
34-43 BeeHives(MTL.C)

DAME, GEORGE
28/9 PaulinsCandy 83

DAMGAARDR, JASPAR
97/8 udSwedish 138

D'AMICO, JOHN
93/4 ActionPacked 5

D'AMOUR, CLAUDE
89/90 Sudbury 28

D'AMOUR, MARC
88/9 ProCards(Hershey)
89/90 ProCards(AHL) 352
91/2 ProCards 264
85/6 CGY/RedRooster
86/7 Moncton 14
81/2 SSMarie
80/1 SSMarie

DAMPHOUSSE, J.F.
97/8 Bowman 160

DAMPHOUSSE, VINCENT
96/7 Aces 9 (Hearts)
97/8 Aces 8 (Diamonds)
90/1 Bowman 163, -HatTrick 6
91/2 Bowman 170
92/3 Bowman 203, 329
95/6 DEL 443
93/4 Donruss 172
94/5 Donruss 226
95/6 Donruss 202
96/7 Donruss 35
97/8 Donruss 173
96/7 D.CanadianIce 53
97/8 D.CdnIce 115, -National 29
95/6 DonrussElite 96
97/8 DonrussElite 81
97/8 DonrussPreferred 140
97/8 DonrussPriority 164
97/8 DonrussStudio 76
96/7 Duracell JB15
92/3 Durivage 20
93/4 Durivage 11
93/4 EASports 70
94/5 Flair 87
96/7 Flair 47
94/5 Fleer 103
96/7 Fleer 53
95/6 FleerMetal 76
96/7 FleerNHLPicks 36
92/3 FleerUltra 103
93/4 FleerUltra 79
94/5 FleerUltra 107
95/6 FleerUltra 80
96/7 FleerUltra 86
96/7 Got-UmHockeyGreatsCoin
93/4 HockeyWit 72
95/6 Hoyle'EAST 10 (Hearts)
97/8 KatchMedallion 74
89/90 Kraft 35
91/2 Kraft 84
93/4 Kraft-Recipe
94/5 Kraft-Sharpsh
96/7 Kraft'Disk
97/8 Kraft-CaseSerie,-WorldBest
93/4 Leaf 4
94/5 Leaf 69
95/6 Leaf 302
96/7 Leaf 79
97/8 Leaf 109
94/5 LeafLimited 90
95/6 LeafLimited 4
96/7 LeafLimited 84
96/7 LeafPreferred 25
97/8 Limited 137
96/7 Maggers 88
91/2 McDonalds McD16
92/3 McDonalds McD04
94/5 McDonalds McD29
97/8 McDonalds McD21
96/7 MetalUniverse 79
97/8 Omega 117
87/8 O-Pee-Chee 243
88/9 O-Pee-Chee 207
89/90 O-Pee-Chee 272
90/1 OPC/Topps 121, 241
91/2 OPC/Topps 299, T-TL 9
92/3 O-Pee-Chee 192
90/1 opcPremier 21
91/2 opcPremier 104
92/3 opcPremier 3
87/8 opcSticker 128/116
88/9 opcSticker 171/40
89/90 opcSticker 179
98/9 Pacific 250
97/8 PacificCrown 25, -Slap 4B
97/8 PacificCrownRoyale 68
97/8 PacificDynagon! 62
97/8 PcfcD-BstKpt 48,-Tandm 46
97/8 PacificInvincible 70
97/8 PacificParamount 94
98/9 PacificParamount 112
97/8 PacificRegime 102
97/8 PacificRevolution 70
87/8 PaniniSticker 333
88/9 PaniniSticker 123
89/90 PaniniSticker 134
90/1 PaniniSticker 291
91/2 PaniniSticker 92
92/3 PaniniSticker 104
93/4 PaniniSticker 13
94/5 PaniniSticker 14
95/6 PaniniSticker 38
96/7 PaniniSticker 35
97/8 PaniniSticker 29
91/2 Parkhurst 48
92/3 Parkhurst 86, 496
93/4 Parkhurst 104
94/5 Parkhurst 115, V23
95/6 Parkhurst 110
91/2 Pinnacle 91
92/3 Pinnacle 261, 349
93/4 Pinnacle 85, 232, -TmP 10
94/5 Pinnacle 4, NL3, Promo 4
95/6 Pinnacle 84
96/7 Pinnacle 72
97/8 Pinnacle 85
97/8 PinnacleBeAPlayer 157
97/8 PinnacleCertified 72
97/8 PinnacleInside 36
95/6 PinnacleZenith 77
96/7 PinnacleZenith 100
95/6 Playoff 53
94/5 POG 133
95/6 POG 148
96/7 Post, -StickUm
97/8 Post
93/4 PowerPlay 127
93/4 Premier 233, -BlackOPC 2
94/5 Premier 65, -Finest(T) 22
95/6 ProMagnet 16
90/1 ProSet 278
91/2 ProSet 224, 293, 381
92/3 PS-TeamLeader 5
91/2 PSPlatinum 35
96/7 SB-7Eleven
90/1 Score 95, -HotCards 47
91/2 Score(CDN) 268, 609
91/2 Score(U.S.) 300, 338, 59T
92/3 Score 170
93/4 Score 244
94/5 Score 165, NP20
95/6 Score 36
96/7 Score 50
97/8 Score 112, -Checkit 11
97/8 Score(MTL) 4
94/5 Select 59
95/6 SelectCertified 75
96/7 SelectCertified 37
95/6 SkyBoxEmotion 87
95/6 SkyBoxImpact 84
96/7 SkyBoxImpact 61
94/5 SP 58
95/6 SP 75
97/8 SPAuthentic 82
95/6 Summit 64
96/7 Summit 136
95/6 SuperSticker 62, 67
92/3 Topps 55
95/6 Topps 270, 9PL
98/9 Topps 118
94/5 ToppsFinest 98
95/6 ToppsFinest 52
91/2 ToppsStadiumClub 146
92/3 ToppsStadiumClub 191
93/4 ToppsStadiumClub 240
95/6 ToppsStadiumClub 159
97/8 ToppsSticker 2
90/1 UpperDeck 224, 484
91/2 UpperDeck 136, 535
92/3 UpperDeck 6, 307, 476
93/4 UD 295, 380, HT8, SP-77
94/5 UpperDeck 280, SP39
95/6 UpperDeck 66, SE133
96/7 UpperDeck 86
93/4 UDBAP'Roots 25
94/5 UDBAP 120, R112, R102
96/7 UDBlackDiamond 25
98/9 UDChoice 110
95/6 UDCollChoice 320
96/7 UDCollChoice 138
97/8 UDCollChoice 130, SQ32
96/7 UpperDeck"Ice" 32
97/8 Zenith 39, Z57
91/2 EDM/IGA
92/3 MTL
92/3 MTL/OPC 38
93/4 MTL
93/4 MTL/Molson
94/5 MTL
95/6 MTL, MTL/Molson
96-98 MTL
86/7 TOR
87/8 TOR
87/8 TOR/P.L.A.Y. 17
88/9 TOR/P.L.A.Y. 17
90/1 TOR

DAMPIER, ALEX
95/6 SheffieldSteelers
97/8 SheffieldSteelers

DANBY, JOHN
72/3 NewEnglandWhalers

DANDENAULT, ERIC
91/2 ProCards 277
90/1 SketchMEM 53
90/1 SketchQMJHL 10
96/7 Cincinnati

DANDENAULT, MATHIEU
95/6 Bowman 114
95/6 Donruss 234
95/6 LeafLimited 37
95/6 Parkhurst 335
96/7 PinnacleBeAPlayer 95
95/6 SP 43
95/6 ToppsStadiumClub 213
95/6 UpperDeck 497

DANDURAND, LÉO
25-27 Anonymous 15
83&87 HallOfFame 96
83 HHOF Postcard (G)
27-32 LaPresse 27/8
28/9 MTL/LaPatrie 16
95/6 MTL/Forum 1-Apr 96

DANEYKO, KEN
91/2 Bowman 284
92/3 FleerUltra 335
93/4 FleerUltra 358
94/5 FleerUltra 318
95/6 FleerUltra 189
94/5 Leaf 336
89/90 O-Pee-Chee 243
91/2 OPC/Topps 118
97/8 PacificCC 325
87/8 PaniniSticker 76
89/90 PaniniSticker 258
91/2 PaniniSticker 218
91/2 Parkhurst 317
92/3 Parkhurst 332
93/4 Parkhurst 387
94/5 Parkhurst 131
91/2 Pinnacle 142
92/3 Pinnacle 354
93/4 Pinnacle 134
94/5 Pinnacle 330
95/6 Pinnacle 177
93/4 Premier 236
94/5 Premier 79
90/1 ProSet 165
91/2 ProSet 139
90/1 Score 178
92/3 Score 53
93/4 Score 286
94/5 Score 142
97/8 Score(N.J.) 20
92/3 Topps 357
95/6 Topps 188
98/9 Topps 101
91/2 ToppsStadiumClub 103
93/4 ToppsStadiumClub 206
90/1 UpperDeck 427
92/3 UpperDeck 259
97/8 UpperDeck 305
95/6 UDBeAPlayer 48
83/4 N.J.
86/7 N.J./SOBER
88/9 N.J./Caretta
89/90 N.J.
90/1 N.J.
96/7 N.J/Sharp

DANIEL, JARROD
91/2 SketchWHL 184

DANIELS, BETH
92/3 Toledo (1)

DANIELS, BOB
91/2 FerrisState

DANIELS, JEFF
92/3 FleerUltra 377
93/4 Leaf 251
92/3 opcPremier 58
92/3 Parkhurst 492
93/4 Parkhurst 429
93/4 Premier 343
88/9 ProCards(Muskegon)
89/90 ProCards(IHL) 146
91/2 ProCards 298
91/2 Score (CDN) 290, (US) 400
93/4 ToppsStadiumClub 483
91/2 UpperDeck 564
92/3 UpperDeck 508
93/4 UpperDeck 87
91/2 PGH/Elbys
92/3 PGH/Coke
93/4 PGH/Foodland 11

DANIELS, KIMBI
91/2 Parkhurst 346
91/2 Pinnacle 336
91/2 Score (CDN) 289, (US) 399
90/1 SketchWHL 46, 72
92/3 ToppsStadiumClub 453
91/2 UD 492, 'CzechWJC 61
92/3 UpperDeck 75
91/2 PHA/JCPenney

DANIELS, MARK
91/2 AirCanadaSJHL D21

DANIELS, SCOTT
96/7 PinnacleBeAPlayer 170
97/8 PinnacleBeAPlayer 116
90/1 ProCards 192
91/2 ProCards 112
95/6 UpperDeck 328
96/7 PHA/OceanSpray
86/7 Kamloops
88/9 Regina
89/90 Regina

DANIELS, WAYNE
93/4 Slapshot(Oshawa) 26
91/2 Oshawa Dominos 22

DANIELSSON, BJORN
95/6 UDCollChoice 342

DANO, JOZEF
96 Wien 236

DANYLUK, CAM
90/1 SketchMEM 84
90/1 SketchWHL 210, 320
91/2 SketchWHL 335
89/90 Portland

DAOUST, ANDRÉ
69 ColumbusCheckers

DAOUST, DAN
72-84 Dernière 82/3
86/7 Kraft Sports 54
83/4 O-Pee-Chee 328
84/5 O-Pee-Chee 299
85/6 OPC/Topps 164
86/7 O-Pee-Chee 241
89/90 O-Pee-Chee 277
83/4 opcSticker 28, 29
84/5 opcSticker 9-10
85/6 opcSticker 11/139
86/7 opcSticker 146/254
88/9 opcSticker 169/29
89/90 opcSticker 171/37
88/9 PaniniSticker 124
83/4 SouhaitsRen.KeyChain
84/5 Topps 137
83/4 Vachon 83
82/3 MTL
82/3 TOR
83/4 TOR
84/5 TOR
85/6 TOR
86/7 TOR
87/8 TOR
87/8 TOR/P.L.A.Y. 20
88/9 TOR/P.L.A.Y. 20

DAOUST, EDDY
51/2 LacStJean 1

DAPUZZO, PAT
90/1 ProSet 684

DARBY, CRAIG
93/4 Classic 62
94/5 Classic 86, -Aut.
93/4 ClassicProspects 110
95/6 EdgeIce 92
95/6 Pinnacle 213
95/6 Score 305
94/5 UpperDeck 452
93/4 Fredericton
94/5 Fredericton

DARBY, KEVIN
93/4 Fredericton

D'ARCY, RYAN
92/3 WestMich.
93/4 WestMich.

DARK, MICHAIL
87/8 STL/Kodak
88/9 SaltLake 2

DARLING, DION
94/5 Fredericton
95/6 Fredericton
96/7 Fredericton

DARRAGH, HARRY
32/3 TOR/OKeefe 16

DARRAGH, JACK
91 C55 Reprint 17
83&87 HallOfFame 199
83 HHOF Postcard (N)
1910-11 Imperial Post 17
1911-12 Imperial (C55) 17
1912-13 Imperial (C57) 29
23/4 (V145-1) 4

DARVEAU, GUY
89/90 ProCards'AHL 193

DARWIN, HOWARD
92/3 Ottawa67s

DASKELAKIS, CLEON
86/7 Moncton 18
85/6 Moncton 14

DAUGHERTY, BRENT
84/5 Sudbury 4
85/6 Sudbury 11
89/90 Sudbury 6

DAUM, RON
90/1 SketchOHL 262

DAUN, ROB
93/4 Lethbridge

DAVEY, NEIL
84/5 PrinceAlbert

DAVID, RICHARD
72-84 Dernière 78/9

DAVIDSON, BOB
34-43 BeeHives(TOR)
36/7 OPC (V304D) 100
37/8 OPC (V304E) 136
39/40 OPC (V301-1) 5
38/9 QuakerOats
45-54 QuakerOats
91/2 Ultimate06 33, -Aut 33
36/7 WWGum (V356) 48

DAVIDSON, GORDON
34-43 BeeHives(NYR)

DAVIDSON, JOHN
77/8 Coke Mini
74/5 Loblaws
74/5 OPC/Topps 11
75/6 OPC/Topps 183
76/7 OPC/Topps 204
77/8 OPC/Topps 28
78/9 OPC/Topps 211
79/80 OPC/Topps 110
80/1 OPC/Topps 190
81/2 OPC 222, Topps(E) 95
77-9 Sportscaster 80-18
73/4 STL

DAVIDSON, LEE
91/2 AvantGardeBCJHL 159
90/1 ProCards 256
91/2 ProCards 166
90/1 Moncton
91/2 Moncton

DAVIDSON, MATT
93/4 Portland

DAVIDSON, RICK
84/5 Victoria

DAVIDSON, SCOTT
83&87 HallOfFame 137
83 HHOF Postcard (K)

DAVIDSON, SHAWNA
94/5 Classic W25

DAVIDSON, TY
92/3 BCJHL 126

DAVIDSSON, JOHAN
94/5 ElitSet 242, -NHLDraft 2
95/6 ElitSet 53
95 Globe 62
93/4 Parkhurst 538
94/5 ParkieSE 236
94/5 SRGoldStandard 81
95/6 udElite 86, NA10

DAVIE, BOB
33-35 DiamondMatch

DAVIES, CURLY
52/3 AnonymousOHL 128

DAVIES, DAN
92/3 BCJHL 29

DAVIES, DAVE
74/5 SiouxCity

DAVIES, GREG
88/9 ProCards(Muskegon)
87/8 Kamloops
83/4 Victoria

DAVIES, MARK
92/3 BCJHL 194

DAVIS, ANDY
94/5 Knoxville 4
95/6 Richmond

DAVIS, BOB
23/4 PaulinsCandy 54

DAVIS, DON
92/3 Toledo (1)

DAVIS, J.P.
89/90 SketchMEM 80
89/90 SketchOHL 6
90/1 SketchOHL 334
91/2 SketchOHL 164
89/90 Oshawa 20
90/1 Oshawa 28
91/2 Oshawa
91/2 Oshawa/Dominos 27

DAVIS, JUSTIN
95/6 Slapshot 115
96/7 SSMarie

DAVIS, KELLY
81/2 Indianapolis 16
82/3 Indianapolis

DAVIS, LEE
95/6 Birmingham

DAVIS, LORNE
45-64 BeeHives(MTL)

DAVIS, MAL
85/6 opcSticker 186/60
84/5 BUF/BlueShield
85/6 BUF

DAVIS, RYAN
95/6 Slapshot 290

DAVIS, SCOTT
90/1 SketchWHL 16

DAVISON, DWAYNE
81/2 Ottawa67s

DAVYDOV, EVGENY (GENE)
93/4 Donruss 127
92/3 FleerUltra 441
93/4 FleerUltra 58, 323
94/5 FleerUltra 147
93/4 Leaf 24
90/1 O-Pee-Chee 18R
92/3 opcPremier 66
93/4 PaniniSticker 194
91/2 Parkhurst 422
92/3 Parkhurst 211, 226
93/4 Parkhurst 78
94/5 Parkhurst 161
92/3 Pinnacle 226
93/4 Pinnacle 109
94/5 Pinnacle 202
93/4 PowerPlay 269, 397
93/4 Premier 200, 444
94/5 Premier 518
92/3 ProSet 244
91/2 RedAce
92/3 Score 456
93/4 Score 114, 499
91 SemicSticker 92
92/3 Topps 115
93/4 ToppsStadiumClub 34, 487
94/5 ToppsStadiumClub 66
92/3 UD 420, CC19, E8, ER17
93/4 UpperDeck 443, SP-55
94/5 UpperDeck 49
97/8 udSwedish 29, C17

DAVYDOV, MORAT
95 PaniniWorlds 30

DAVYDOV, OLEG
95 PaniniWorlds 32

DAVYDOV, VITALY
70/1 Kuvajulkaisut 1
72 Panda
72 SemicSticker 2
74 SemicSticker 43
69/70 Soviet Stars
70/1 Soviet Stars
71/2 Soviet Stars
71/2 WilliamsFIN 1

DAWE, JASON
91/2 Arena 26
91/2 Classic 31
93/4 Classic 19
91/2 ClassicFourSport 31, -Aut
93/4 ClassicProspects 88
93/4 Donruss 404
94/5 Donruss 245
95/6 Donruss 315
96/7 Donruss 165
95/6 EdgeIce C20
96/7 Fleer 9
95/6 FleerMetal 14
96/7 FleerNHLPicks 122
94/5 FleerUltra 21
95/6 FleerUltra 211
96/7 FleerUltra 15
97/8 KatchMedallion 14
94/5 Leaf 48
96/7 Leaf 93
96/7 MetalUniverse 13
97/8 Omega 20
98/9 Pacific 280
97/8 PacificCrown 314
97/8 PacificInvincible 11
97/8 PacificParamount 18
98/9 PacificParamount 142
97/8 PacificRevolution 13
95/6 PaniniSticker 18
96/7 PaniniSticker 16
95/6 Parkhurst 24
94/5 ParkieSE 20
94/5 Pinnacle 366
95/6 Pinnacle 123
96/7 Pinnacle 10
95/6 Playoff 230
96/7 Playoff 421
95/6 POG 43
94/5 Premier 149
96/7 Score 59
97/8 Score 204
97/8 Score(BUF) 7
90/1 SketchMEM 113
89/90 SketchOHL 106
90/1 SketchOHL 357
91/2 SketchOHL 145
93/4 Slapshot(Peterborough) 27
97/8 SPAuthentic 13
91/2 StarPics 59
95/6 Topps 128, 6PL
98/9 Topps 202
95/6 ToppsFinest 158
95/6 ToppsStadiumClub 147
91/2 UltimateDP 27, 86, -Aut 27
91/2 UpperDeck 75
93/4 UpperDeck 254
94/5 UpperDeck 167
95/6 UpperDeck 61, SE100
96/7 UpperDeck 19
95/6 UDBeAPlayer 50
96/7 UDBlackDiamond 139
97/8 UDBlackDiamond 30
96/7 UDCollChoice 31
97/8 UDCollChoice 32
91/2 Peterborough 1

DAWE, WADE
95/6 Slapshot 317

DAWES, BOB
45-64 BeeHives(TOR)

DAWKINS, MARK
91/2 SketchWHL 310

DAWSON, MIKE
90/1 SketchOHL 56
91/2 SketchOHL 233

DAWSON, WADE
91/2 ProCards 159

DAY, HAP
33/4 Anonymous (V129) 2
34-43 BeeHives(TOR)
24/5 Champs (C144)
33/4 CndGum (V252)
83&87 HallOfFame 80
33/4 Hamilton (V288) 33
83 HHOF Postcard (F)
27-32 LaPresse 28/9
33/4 OPC (V304A) 32
55/6 Parkhurst 34
93/4 Parkie(56/7) 134
33/4 WWGum(V357)10, Prmium
36/7 WWGum (V356) 52
32/3 TOR/OKeefe 4

DAY, JOE
94/5 Parkhurst 138
90/1 ProCards 181
91/2 ProCards 103
91/2 UpperDeck 516
91/2 HFD/JuniorWhalers

DAYLEY, CORY
92/3 BCJHL 112

DAYLEY, WADE
91/2 AvantGardeBCJ 47
92/3 BCJHL 116
91/2 Nainamo

DAYMAN, RYAN
92/3 BCJHL 31

DAZÉ, ERIC
96/7 Aces 7 (Spades)
95/6 Bowman 125, BB18
94/5 C'Images 14
95/6 Donruss 345, -CanadaJr 15
95/6 Donruss-RatedRookie 6
96/7 D-Dom 10,-HitL 12,-RtdR 1
97/8 Donruss 192
96/7 D.CdnIce 20, -OCanada 14
97/8 DonrussCanadianIce 21
95/6 DonrussElite 63
96/7 Don.Elite 71, -Aspirations 1
97/8 DonrussPreferred 116
97/8 DonrussPriority 26
96/7 Duracell JB4
96/7 Flair 16, -HotNumber 3
96/7 Fleer 17, 136, -Rookie 4
95/6 FleerMetal 174
96/7 F.Picks-Fab 9, -Jagged 19
96/7 F.Picks-FantasyForce 4
95/6 F.Ultra 32, 335,-ExtAttckr 2
96/7 FleerUltra 31
95/6 Leaf 226, -StudioRookie 11
96/7 Leaf 202,-Best 2,-Sweater 7
97/8 Leaf 97
94/5 LeafLimited-CanadaJrs 2
95/6 LeafLimited 65, -Rookie 6
96/7 LeafLimited 37, -Bash 10
96/7 L.Prefer. 61,149,-Steel 25
97/8 Limited 65
96/7 Maggers 32
96/7 McDonalds McD3
96/7 MetalUniverse 27
97/8 Omega 49
98/9 Pacific 143
97/8 PacificCrown 108
97/8 PacificCrownRoyale 29
97/8 PcfcDynag! 26,-Tandem 31
97/8 PacificInvincible 29
97/8 PacificParamount 43
98/9 PacificParamount 46
97/8 PacificRevolution 29
95/6 PaniniSticker 159
96/7 PaniniSticker 159
97/8 PaniniSticker 136
95/6 Parkhurst 45, 540, PP40
95/6 Parkhurst-Crown(2) 16
94/5 Pinnacle 529
95/6 Pinnacle 203
96/7 Pinnacle 212, -TeamP 10
96/7 Pinn.-ByTheNumbers 11
97/8 Pinnacle 121
97/8 Pinn. BAP-TakeANumber 2
97/8 PinnacleCertified 122
97/8 PinnacleInside 88
95/6 P.Zenith 122,-RookiRoll 13
96/7 P.Zenith 99, -Team 14
95/6 Playoff 234
95/6 Score 312
96/7 Score 236, -CheckIt 16
97/8 Score 193
95/6 SelectCertified 132
96/7 SelectCertified 79
95/6 SkyBoxImpact 193
96/7 SkyBoxImpact 19, 168
96/7 SkyBx-Fox 7
95/6 SP 22
96/7 SP 26, HC2, CW20
97/8 SPAuthentic 31
96/7 SPx 50, GF1
95/6 Summit 190
96/7 Summit 151, -HiVoltage 7
96/7 TeamOut
95/6 Topps 26, 19CJ
98/9 Topps 195
94/5 ToppsFinest 157
95/6 ToppsFinest 3
96/7 ToppsNHLPicks 77, RS4
95/6 ToppsStadiumClub 195
95/6 TSC-MembersOnly 50
94/5 UpperDeck 497
95/6 UpperDeck 268, H29
96/7 UpperDeck SS18B, X19
96/7 UD 29, 359, LS15
97/8 UpperDeck 41
95/6 UDBeAPlayer 170
97/8 UDBlackDiamond 63
98/9 UDChoice 45
95/6 UDCollChoice 411, 411
96/7 UDCC 45, 313, C20, UD37
97/8 UDCollChoice 53, SQ15
96/7 UpperDeck "Ice" 79
97/8 Zenith 55, Z54

DEA, BILL
45-64 BeeHives(DET), (NYR)
70/1 EddieSargent 53
70/1 Esso Stamp
69/70 O-Pee-Chee 190
70/1 OPC/Topps 30
93/4 Parkie(56/7) 47
57/8 Topps 39

DEACON, DON
39/40 OPC (V301-1) 70

DEADMARSH, ADAM
93/4 Classic 20
94/5 Classic T56, -Aut.
93/4 ClassicFourSport 197, -Aut
94/5 ClassicImages 60
93/4 Donruss USA5
95/6 Donruss 145
96/7 Donruss 145
97/8 Donruss 161, -RedAlert 1
97/8 DonrussCanadianIce 126
97/8 DonrussElite 75
97/8 DonrussPreferred 53
97/8 DonrussPriority 163
97/8 DonrussStudio 70
94/5 Flair 144
94/5 Fleer 174
95/6 FleerMetal 30
94/5 FleerUltra 355
95/6 FleerUltra 129
96/7 FleerUltra 34
97/8 KatchMedallion 37
94/5 Leaf 442
95/6 Leaf 72
97/8 Leaf 57
94/5 LeafLimited-USAJrs 4
97/8 Limited 95, 132, 161
96/7 MetalUniverse 30
97/8 Omega 55
98/9 Pacific 18
97/8 PacificCrown 47
97/8 PacificCrownRoyale 32
97/8 PacificInvincible 33
97/8 PacificParamount 48
98/9 PacificParamount 53
95/6 Parkhurst 54
94/5 ParkieSE 144, 246
93/4 Pinnacle 491
94/5 Pinnacle 253
95/6 Pinnacle 72
96/7 Pinnacle 43
97/8 Pinnacle 114
97/8 PinnacleBeAPlayer 52
97/8 PinnacleCertified 112
97/8 PinnacleInside 170
95/6 Playoff 136
95/6 POG 81
94/5 Premier 449
95/6 Score 168, -CheckIt 6
96/7 Score 93
97/8 Score 146
97/8 Score(COL) 8
94/5 Select 179
91/2 SketchWHL 32
95/6 SkyBxImpact-Fox 4
94/5 SP-Premier 15
95/6 SP 33
96/7 SP 36, CW17
97/8 SPAuthentic 40
95/6 Topps 288, 6NG
94/5 ToppsFinest 31, 118
94/5 TF-BBest(Red) 13
96/7 ToppsNHLPicks 103
92/3 UpperDeck 609
93/4 UpperDeck 562
94/5 UD 261, 562, SP155

95/6 UpperDeck 65,SE22
96/7 UpperDeck 41, P23, X25
97/8 UpperDeck 46, T13A
94/5 UDBeAPlayer R165
95/6 UDBeAPlayer 186
96/7 UDBlackDiamond 81
97/8 UDBlackDiamond 75
98/9 UDChoice 57
95/6 UDCollChoice 294, 360
96/7 UDCollChoice 58
97/8 UDCollChoice 57, SQ45
97/8 UpperDeckIce 18
96/7 COL/PhotoPucks
94/5 QUE/BurgerKing
93/4 Portland

DEADMARSH, BUTCH
74/5 OPC/Topps 73
75/6 opcWHA 59
76/7 opcWHA 53
72/3 BUF

DEADMARSH, JAKE
94/5 AutoPhonex 12
93/4 Portland

DEAN, BARRY
77/8 OPC/Topps 183
78/9 OPC/Topps 142
79/80 O-Pee-Chee 318
76/7 COL.R/CokeCans
75/6 Phoenix

DEAN, KEVIN
97/8 PinnacleBeAPlayer 57
91/2 ProCards 417
95/6 Topps 208
96/7 N.J/Sharp
92/3 Cincinnati

DE ANGELIS, MICHAEL
95 PaniniWorlds 85
95 Semic 172
92 SemicSticker 249
93 SemicSticker 214
85/6 Minn-Duluth 3

DEASLEY, BRYAN
90/1 ProCards 619
91/2 ProCards 580

DEAZELEY, MARK
89/90 SketchMEM 97
90/1 SketchOHL 335
91/2 SketchOHL 153
89/90 Oshawa 19
90/1 Oshawa 22
91/2 Oshawa
91/2 Oshawa/Dominos 26
95/6 Tallahassee 6
92/3 Toledo (1), (2)
93/4 Toledo 14

DEAZELEY, MIKE
89/90 SketchOHL 10

DEBENEDET, NELSON
74/5 Loblaws
74/5 OPC 293
74/5 PGH

DEBLOIS, LUCIEN
72-84 Dernière 77/8
92/3 Durivage 2
78/9 OPC/Topps 136
80/1 OPC/Topps 146
81/2 OPC 74, Topps(W) 79
82/3 O-Pee-Chee 379
83/4 O-Pee-Chee 378, 383
84/5 O-Pee-Chee 260
90/1 O-Pee-Chee 441
91/2 OPC/Topps 96, 102
81/2 opcSticker 232
82/3 opcSticker 212
83/4 opcSticker 284
84/5 opcSticker 290
90/1 PaniniSticker 140
91/2 PaniniSticker 100
82/3 Post
90/1 ProSet 244, 531
91/2 ProSet 491
92/3 Score 371
83/4 SouhaitsRen.KeyChain
90/1 UpperDeck 363
83/4 Vachon 125
79/80 COL.R
84/5 MTL
85/6? MTL/ProvPlacemats
85/6 MTL/ProvStickers

89/90 QUE
89/90 QUE/GeneralFoods
89/90 QUE/Police
90/1 QUE
90/1 QUE/PetroCanada
90/1 TOR/P.L.A.Y. 21
81/2 WPG
82/3 WPG
83/4 WPG

DEBOAR, PETER
95/6 Slapshot 80
89/90 ProCards'IHL 169
90/1 ProCards 326
93/4 Slapshot(Detroit) 24
94/5 Slapshot(MEM) 100

DEBOL, DAVE
79/80 O-Pee-Chee 363
80/1 O-Pee-Chee 381
79 PaniniSticker 215

DEBRIS, DARREN
95/6 Slapshot 270

DEBRUSK, LOUIE
92/3 Bowman 318
93/4 Donruss 108
93/4 Leaf 225
94/5 Leaf 532
98/9 Pacific 398
97/8 PacificDynagon-BestKpt 37
91/2 Parkhurst 281
93/4 Parkhurst 337
95/6 Parkhurst 81
91/2 Pinnacle 347
93/4 Premier 319
91/2 ProSet 535
89/90 SketchOHL 28
90/1 SketchOHL 132
92/3 Topps 392
92/3 ToppsStadiumClub 290
91/2 UpperDeck 249, 526
92/3 UpperDeck 467
93/4 UpperDeck 79
94/5 UpperDeck 485
94/5 UDBeAPlayer R89, -Aut. 29
95/6 UDCollChoice 87
96/7 UDCollChoice 100
91/2 EDM/IGA
92/3 EDM, EDM/IGA 6
93/4 EDM 22DEC93
96/7 EDM

DEBUS, STEVE
94/5 Minnesota

DEBUSSCHERE, DAVE
91/2 AirCanadaSJHL D46
92/3 MPSPhotoSJHL 8

DECAEN, STEVE
91/2 SketchQMJHL 153

DECARIE, ED
1910-11 Imperial C56 13

DECARLE, MIKE
89/90 ProCards(IHL) 104

DECECCO, BRETT
98 BowmanCHL 59
97/8 UpperDeck 409

DECELLES, LUC
93/4 Slapshot(Drum.) 20

DECHAINE, CHRIS
92/3 MPSPhotoSJHL 107

DECIANTIS, ROB
95/6 Classic 86
94/5 Slapshot(Kitchener) 21
95/6 Slapshot 141

DECK, KIM
90/1 SketchWHL 156, 323
87/8 Kamloops
88/9 Kamloops
89/90 Portland

DECKER, TODD
87/8 Kamloops

DECOFF, MIKE
90/1 SketchMEM 15
90/1 SketchOHL 155
89/90 Oshawa 4

DECORBY, IAN
94/5 Erie

DECORTE, LUIGI
95 PaniniWorlds 80

DECOSTY, DEREK
92/3 Wheeling 4
93/4 Wheeling 4
94/5 Wheeling 6

DEEKS, ALAIN
92/3 Hamilton
94/5 Knoxville 16

DEFAZIO, DAN
82/3 Oshawa 14

DEFAZIO, JARRETT
89/90 SketchOHL 57
90/1 SketchOHL 82

DEFELICE, NORMAN
52/3 AnonymousOHL 18
45-64 BeeHives(BOS)

DEFERENZA, FRAN
90/1 SketchWHL 98
91/2 SketchWHL 54

DEGAETANO, PHIL
88/9 ProCards(Maine)

DEGAGNE, ROB
82/3 NorthBay
83/4 NorthBay

DEGIACOMO, DWIGHT
90/1 Mich.Tech

DEGNER, TERRY
90/1 SketchWHL 99
91/2 SketchWHL 290

DEGRACE, YANICK
90/1 SketchQMJHL 170
91/2 SketchQMJHL 208

DEGRAY, DALE
95/6 EdgeIce 111
89/90 OPC/Topps 18
90/1 ProCards 279
88/9 L.A/Smokeys
87/8 TOR
87/8 TOR/P.L.A.Y. 25
96/7 Cincinnati
84/5 Moncton 11
85/6 Moncton 20
80/1 Oshawa 11
81/2 Oshawa 14
82/3 Oshawa 4
92/3 SanDiego

DEGUISE, MICHEL
73/4 Québec
88/9 Richelieu

DEHART, JOHN
91/2 AvantGardeBC 99,159,164

DEHEER, JACK
79 PaniniSticker 282

DEIS, TYLER
92/3 MPSPhotoSJHL 52

DEITER, THOMAS
94/5 DEL 432

DEJORDY, DENIS
71/2 Bazooka Panel 8
64-67 BeeHives(CHI)
64/5 CokeCap CHI30
70/1 Colgate Stamp 84
70/1 DadsCookies
70/1 EddieSargent 73
72/3 EddieSargent 130
70/1 Esso Stamp
68/9 OPC/Topps 12
69/70 OPC/T. 66, -opcSticker
70/1 OPC/Topps 31
71/2 OPC/Topps 63
72/3 OPC 184, Topps 144
94/5 Parkie(64/5) 28
95/6 Parkie(66/7) 39, 139, TW6
68/9 ShirriffCoin CHI 4
71/2 TheTorontoSun
61/2 Topps 37
62/3 Topps 25
63/4 Topps 24
64/5 Topps 22
65/6 Topps 113
66/7 Topps 115, -USATest 50
67/8 Topps 65, 115
71/2 MTL

DELARNDS, SHANE
95/6 Slapshot 10

DELAROSBIL, RAYMOND
90/1 SketchQMJHL 178
91/2 SketchQMJHL 155
93/4 Slapshot(Drum.) 18

DELCOURT, GRANT
83/4 Kelowna
84/5 KelownaWings 18

DELESOY, JASON
92/3 BCJHL 16

DELEURME, JASON
98 BowmanCHL 49
93/4 Tacoma

DELFINO, DAVID
94 Semic 291
92 SemicSticker 243
93 SemicSticker 209

DELGUIDICE, MATT
91/2 opcPremier 96
91/2 Parkhurst 1
90/1 ProCards 125
91/2 ProSet 521
91/2 UpperDeck 463
93/4 Raleigh
95/6 Roanoke

DELIANEDLS, DAN
88/9 ProCards(Utica)

DELISLE, GUY
51/2 BasDuFleuve 12

DELISLE, JOHN
85/6 Minn-Duluth 29

DELISLE, JONATHAN
97/8 Bowman 55
94/5 Slapshot(MEM) 70

DELISLE, XAVIER
94/5 ParkieSE 255
94/5 SP 178

DELIVA, JOEY
91/2 SketchQMJHL 204

DELL, FRANK
89/90 Johnstown 34

DELLAIRE, HENRI
91 C55 Reprint 39
1911-12 Imperial (C55) 39
1912-13 Imperial (C57) 7
1910-11 Imperial Post 39

DELLJANNONE, PATRICK
82 SemicSticker 133

DELLSPERGER, ROLAND
79 PaniniSticker 262

DELMONACO, PASCAL
79 PaniniSticker 379

DELMONTE, DAN
93/4 Slapshot(Peterborough) 24
94/5 Slapshot(Sarnia) 17

DELMONTE, DION
96/7 DEL 331
97/8 SheffieldSteelers

DELMORE, ANDY
94/5 AutoPhonex 13
97/8 Bowman 34
93/4 Slapshot(NorthBay) 5
95/6 Slapshot 336

DELORIMIÈRE, BOB
94/5 Slapshot(Brantford) 2

DELORME, GILBERT
83/4 O-Pee-Chee 186
86/7 O-Pee-Chee 234
90/1 O-Pee-Chee 517
83/4 opcSticker 70
86/7 opcSticker 28/167
91/2 ProCards 300
83/4 SouhaitsRen.KeyChain
83/4 Vachon 43
86/7 DET/Caesars
87/8 DET/Caesars
88/9 DET/Caesars
81/2 MTL
82/3 MTL
82/3 MTL/Steinberg
83/4 MTL
89/90 PGH/Foodland 6
85/6 QUE
85/6 QUE/GeneralFoods
85/6 QUE/McDonald
85/6 QUE/Provigo

86/7 QUE/GeneralFoods
86/7 QUE/McDonald
86/7 QUE/YumYum
92/3 Cleveland 6
93/4 Cleveland

DELORME, MARC
94/5 Slapshot(Brantford) 19

DELORME, RON
78/9 O-Pee-Chee 323
79/80 O-Pee-Chee 284
80/1 O-Pee-Chee 321
81/2 O-Pee-Chee 82
82/3 O-Pee-Chee 347
83/4 O-Pee-Chee 348
84/5 O-Pee-Chee 316
81/2 opcSticker 231
82/3 Post
83/4 Vachon 104
77/8 COL.R/CokeCans
79/80 COL.R
82/3 VAN
83/4 VAN
84/5 VAN
84/5 KelownaWings 39

DELPARTE, GUY
76/7 COL.R
76/7 COL.R/CokeCans

DELVECCHIO, ALEX
71/2 Bazooka Panel 7
45-64 BeeHives(DET)
64-67 BeeHives(DETx2)
62 CeramicTiles
63-5 ChexPhoto
64/5 CokeCap DET-9, DET-10
65/6 CocaCola
70/1 Colgate Stamp 4
70/1 DadsCookies
70/1 EddieSargent 59
71/2 EddieSargent 55
72/3 EddieSargent 76
70/1 Esso Stamp
83&87 HallOfFame 230
83 HHOF Postcard (E)
82? JDMcCarthy
68/9 OPC/Topps 28
69/70 OPC 157, 206, -Sticker
70/1 OPC 157
71/2 OPC/Topps 37, -Booklet 12
72/3 OPC 26, Topps 141
73/4 OPC 1, Topps 141
74/5 OPC/Topps 222
51/2 Parkhurst 63
52/3 Parkhurst 53
53/4 Parkhurst 47
54/5 Parkhurst 36, 90
60/1 Parkhurst 36
61/2 Parkhurst 25
62/3 Parkhurst 32
63/4 Parkhurst 50
91/2 Parkhurst PHC2
92/3 Parkhurst PR19
93/4 Parkie(56/7) 59
94/5 Parkie(64/5) 56
95/6 Parkie(66/7) 53, 127, 148
90/1 ProSet 652, 658
72 SemicSticker 193
60/1 ShirriffCoin 44
61/2 ShirriffCoin 70
68/9 ShirriffCoin DET4
91/2 StarPics 10
54-67 TorontoStar V6, V10
56-66 TorontoStar 57/8, 58/9
63/4 TheTorontoStar
64/5 TheTorontoStar
71/2 TheTorontoSun
54/5 Topps 39
57/8 Topps 34
58/9 Topps 52
59/60 Topps 8
64/5 Topps 95
65/6 Topps 47
66/7 Topps 102, -USATest 63
67/8 Topps 51
69/70 Topps 64
91/2 Ultimate06 68, -Aut 68
63/4 York 50
60/1 YorkGlasses
62/3 YorkTransfer 21
70/1 DET/Marathon
76 DET
96/7 DET/HockeytownPuck

DELVECCHIO, BILL
45-64 BeeHives(DET)

DEMARCHI, PAT
79 PaniniSticker 392

DEMARCO, AB (SR.)
39/40 OPC (V301-1) 82

DEMARCO, AB T. (JR.)
74/5 Loblaws, -Update
69/70 Mästar Serien
71/2 OPC 90
73/4 OPC/Topps 118
74/5 OPC/Topps 89
75/6 OPC/Topps 78
76/7 OPC 374
77/8 OPC 283
71/2 TheTorontoSun
73/4 STL
74/5 VAN/RoyalBank
75/6 VAN/RoyalBank

DEMERES, TONY
40/1 OPC (V301-2) 144

DEMERS, JACQUES
72-84 Dernière 78/9
93/4 Kraft-Coach
86/7 DET/Caesars
87/8 DET/Caesars
88/9 DET
88/9 DET/Caesars
89/90 DET/Caesars
92/3 MTL
92/3 MTL/OPC 10
93/4 MTL
94/5 MTL
82/3 Fredericton 12

DEMERS, NORMAND
89/90 SketchMEM 73
90/1 SketchQMJHL 83

DEMERS, TONY
34-43 BeeHives(MTL.C)
43-47 ParadeSportive

DEMIN, VASSILI
94/5 Erie

DEMITRA, PAVOL
93/4 Donruss 240
94/5 Donruss 133
95/6 EdgeIce 48
94/5 Fleer 144
94/5 FleerUltra 337
93/4 Leaf 366
94/5 Leaf 115
97/8 Omega 191
98/9 Pacific 38
97/8 PacificCrownRoyale 114
98/9 PacificParamount 202
95/6 PaniniSticker 53
96/7 PaniniSticker 52
93/4 Parkhurst 140
95/6 Parkhurst 149
94/5 ParkieSE 121
93/4 Pinnacle 446
97/8 PinnacleBeAPlayer 146
95/6 POG 195
94/5 Premier 336
93/4 Score 624
97/8 Score(STL) 18
94/5 Select 185
97/8 SPAuthentic 142
98/9 SPx"Finite" 76
94/5 ToppsFinest 111
92/3 UpperDeck 602
93/4 UpperDeck 372, SP-108
94/5 UpperDeck 216, SP145
97/8 UpperDeck 146
98/9 UDChoice 186
97/8 UDCollChoice 232
93/4 OTT/Kraft
96/7 LasVegas

DEMMANS, T.
92/3 MPSPhotoSJHL 118

DEMMEL, FRANZ
94/5 DEL 220
95/6 DEL 216
96/7 DEL 360

DEMPSEY, NATHAN
91/2 SketchWHL 221
94/5 StJohns
95/6 StJohns

DENHAM, JEFF
91/2 AvantGardeBCJHL 37

DENIS, LOUIS (LULU)
51/2 LavalDairy 97
52/3 LavalDairy 97
52/3 StLawrence 13
36/7 WWGum (V356) 125

DENIS, MARC
97/8 Bowman 61
97/8 Donruss 202, -RatedRook 4
97/8 D.CdnIce 145, -Gardiens 12
95/6 DonrussElite-WorldJrs 1
97/8 DonrussElite - BackTo 2
97/8 DonrussPreferred 145, 187
97/8 D.Pref -ColourGuard 10
97/8 DonrussPriority-PostGen 18
97/8 D.Studio 25, -Portraits 26
97/8 Leaf 105, 148
97/8 Limited 47, 127, -fabric 47
97/8 PinnacleInside 64
97/8 Score(COL) 3
95/6 UpperDeck 529
97/8 UpperDeck T12B
96/7 UDBlackDiamond 130
96/7 UDCollChoice 363
97/8 UDCollChoice 302
96/7 UpperDeck"Ice" 117
97/8 UpperDeckIce 31

DENISOV, DMITRI
95 PaniniWorlds 38
96 Wien 155

DENNENY, CORBETT
23/4 (V145-1) 40

DENNENY, CYRIL (CY)
25-27 Anonymous 17
24/5 Champs (C144)
83&87 HallOfFame 138
83 HHOF Postcard (K)
60/1 Topps 8
61/2 Topps-Stamp
23/4 (V145-1) 10
24/5 (V145-2) 7

DENNIS, DAN
92/3 MPSPhotoSJHL 20

DENNIS, DUANE
94/5 CapeBreton

DENNISON, HEATH
92/3 BCJHL 158

DENNISON, JOE
1912-13 Imperial (C57) 42

DENOMME, JASON
90/1 SketchMEM 9
90/1 SketchOHL 156
91/2 SketchOHL 328
89/90 Oshawa 8

DENOMME, JAY
91/2 SketchOHL 74

DENT, TED
93/4 Johnstown 5
94/5 Johnstown 6

DEOBALD, LONNY
92/3 MPSPhotoSJHL 56

DEPALMA, LARRY
89/90 ProCards(IHL) 79
90/1 ProCards 111
91/2 ProCards 524
87/8 MIN
88/9 MIN/American

DEPIERO, BOB
82 SemicSticker 140

DEPOURCQ, JOHN
95/6 Louisiana, -Playoffs

DERAAF, HELMUT
94/5 DEL 78
95/6 DEL 76
91 SemicSticker 152
93 SemicSticker 149

DERASPE, PATRICK
91/2 SketchQMJHL 185

DERKATCH, DALE
83 CanadaJuniors
94/5 DEL 305
95/6 DEL 191
81/2 Regina 8
82/3 Regina 13
83/4 Regina 13

DERKSEN, DEVIN
90/1 SketchWHL 100
93/4 Richmond 8

DERKSEN, DUANE
92/3 Classic 91
92/3 ClassicFourSport 208

DERLAGO, BILL
83/4 Esso
86/7 Kraft Sports 74
80/1 OPC/Topps 11
81/2 O-Pee-Chee 305
82/3 O-Pee-Chee 319-20
83/4 O-Pee-Chee 327
84/5 O-Pee-Chee 300
85/6 OPC/Topps 71
86/7 O-Pee-Chee 254
81/2 opcSticker 99, 108
82/3 opcSticker 67, 68
83/4 opcSticker 35
84/5 opcSticker 14
85/6 opcSticker 7
86/7 opcSticker 105/234
87/8 opcSticker 224/91
80/1 Pepsi Cap
82/3 Post
83/4 PuffySticker 1
83/4 7ElevenCokeCup
84/5 7ElevenDisk
83/4 SouhaitsRen.KeyChain
81/2 Topps 9
83/4 Vachon 84
86/7 QUE
80/1 TOR
81/2 TOR
82/3 TOR
83/4 TOR
84/5 TOR
78/9 VAN/RoyalBank
79/80 VAN
86/7 WPG
84/5 KelownaWings 27

DEROUVILLE, PHILIPPE
95/6 Donruss 206
97/8 Donruss 197
97/8 D.Cdn.Ice-Gardiens 11
95/6 EdgeIce 116
95/6 Leaf 111
95/6 Pinnacle 214
95/6 Score 291
91/2 SketchQMJHL 131
93/4 UpperDeck 260
95/6 Cleveland

DERRAUGH, DOUD
96/7 DEL 196

DERUITER, CHRIS
92/3 Clarkson

DESANTIS, MARK
94/5 Classic E10
94/5 ClassicFourSport 150
93/4 ClassicProspects 77
90/1 SketchOHL 32
91/2 SketchOHL 3
91/2 Cornwall 2
94/5 Greensboro

DESAULNIERS, GERRY
51/2 LavalDairy 93
52/3 LavalDairy 93
52/3 StLawrence 4

DESBIENS, ROBERT
51/2 LacStJean 4

DESCHAMPS, MARC
92/3 Wheeling 5

DESCHAMPS, ROB
89/90 SketchOHL 158
90/1 SketchOHL 282

DESCHAUME, LAURENT
95 PaniniWorlds 108
93 SemicSticker 261

DESCHESNE, DONAT
51/2 LavalDairy 20
52/3 BasDuFleuve 41

DESCOTEAUX, MATTHIEU
95/6 Bowman P9

DESGAGNE, MARC
91/2 SketchQMJHL 7

DESILETS, JOFFRE
34-43 BeeHives(MTL.C)
35-40 CrownBrand 109
36/7 OPC (V304D) 114
37/8 OPC (V304E) 156
39/40 OPC (V301-1) 44

DESILETS, MIKE
52/3 AnonymousOHL 158

DESJARDINS, ERIC
91/2 Bowman 329
92/3 Bowman 228, 311
93/4 Donruss 173
94/5 Donruss 177
95/6 Donruss 151
96/7 Donruss 25
97/8 Donruss 141
92/3 Durivage 36
93/4 Durivage 12
93/4 EASports 67
97/8 EssoOlympic 13
94/5 Flair 88
94/5 Fleer 151
96/7 Fleer 79, -Norris 4
95/6 FleerMetal 109
92/3 FleerUltra 104
93/4 FleerUltra 94
94/5 FleerUltra 108
95/6 FleerUltra 116
96/7 FleerUltra 123
97/8 GeneralMills
91/2 Gillette 27
97/8 Kraft-RoadToNagano
93/4 Leaf 203
94/5 Leaf 433
95/6 Leaf 70
96/7 Leaf 27
96/7 LeafPreferred 32
97/8 Limited 80
97/8 McDonalds -Medallions
96/7 MetalUniverse 110
97/8 Omega 162
90/1 O-Pee-Chee 425
91/2 OPC/Topps 14
92/3 O-Pee-Chee 360
91/2 opcPremier 157
98/9 Pacific 324
97/8 PacificCrown 121
98/9 PacificParamount 171
90/1 Panini(MTL) 8
91/2 PaniniSticker 189
92/3 PaniniSticker 156
93/4 PaniniSticker 21
94/5 PaniniSticker 17
95/6 PaniniSticker 119
96/7 PaniniSticker 115
91/2 Parkhurst 85
92/3 Parkhurst 80
93/4 Parkhurst 102
94/5 Parkhurst 118
95/6 Parkhurst 428
91/2 Pinnacle 73
92/3 Pinnacle 16, -Tm2000 9
93/4 Pinnacle 59
94/5 Pinnacle 106
95/6 Pinnacle 110
96/7 Pinnacle 169
96/7 PinnacleBeAPlayer 40
95/6 Playoff 75
94/5 POG 139
95/6 POG 209
93/4 PowerPlay 128
93/4 Premier 32
90/1 ProSet 467
91/2 ProSet 118
92/3 ProSet 86
90/1 ScoreTraded 58T
92/3 Score 23, -YoungStar 28
93/4 Score 128
94/5 Score 110
95/6 Score 207
96/7 Score 159
97/8 Score196
97/8 Score(PHA) 7
94/5 Select 113
94 Semic 87
93 SemicSticker 195
95/6 SkyBoxEmotion 130
95/6 SkyBoxImpact 124
96/7 SkyBoxImpact 93, -Fox 8
95/6 SP 112
96/7 SP 113
95/6 SuperSticker 93
91 TeamCanada
96/7 TeamOut
92/3 Topps 192
95/6 Topps 290
98/9 Topps 35
95/6 ToppsFinest 174
96/7 ToppsNHLPicks 93
91/2 ToppsStadiumClub 214
92/3 ToppsStadiumClub 326
93/4 ToppsStadiumClub 170
94/5 ToppsStadiumClub 263
95/6 ToppsStadiumClub 125
95/6 TSC-MembersOnly 41
90/1 UpperDeck 428
92/3 UpperDeck 268
93/4 UpperDeck 184
94/5 UpperDeck 279
95/6 UD 186, AS9, SE150
96/7 UpperDeck 123
97/8 UpperDeck 332
94/5 UDBAP R105, -Aut 111
96/7 UDBlackDiamond 37
95/6 UDCollChoice 105
96/7 UDCollChoice 195
96/7 UpperDeck"Ice" 47
97/8 ValuNet
96 Wien 83
88/9 MTL
89/90 MTL
89/90 MTL/Kraft
90/1 MTL
91/2 MTL
92/3 MTL
92/3 MTL/OPC 20
93/4 MTL
94/5 MTL
94/5 PHA
96/7 PHA/OceanSpray

DESJARDINS, GERRY
70/1 Colgate Stamp 67
70/1 EddieSargent 45
72/3 EddieSargent 129
70/1 Esso Stamp
69/70 OPC/Topps 99
69/70 OPC-Stamp, -Sticker
70/1 OPC 152
72/3 OPC 119, Topps 38
73/4 OPC 178, Topps 114
75/6 OPC/Topps 125
76/7 OPC/Topps 230
77/8 OPC/Topps 150
75/6 BUF/Linnett

DESJARDINS, KEN
73/4 Québec

DESJARDINS, MARTIN
88/9 ProCards(Sherbrooke)
90/1 ProCards 410
91/2 ProCards 484
89/90 MTL
86/7 Kamloops

DESJARDINS, NORMAN
89/90 ProCards(AHL) 189
90/1 ProCards 69
91/2 ProCards 75

DESJARDINS, STÉPHANE
90/1 SketchMEM 5
90/1 SketchQMJHL 5
91/2 SketchQMJHL 286
94/5 Roanoke

DESLAURIERS, JACQUES
51/2 LavalDairy 82
52/3 StLawrence 25

DESLOGES, STEVE
74/5 SiouxCity

DESMARAIS, MATT
92/3 MPSPhotoSJHL 46

DESNOYERS, DAVID
91/2 SketchQMJHL 3

DESPATIS, CHRIS
95/6 Slapshot 276

DESROCHERS, ERIC
90/1 SketchQMJHL 191

DESROCHERS, PATRICK
97 BowmanCHL 40
98 BowmanCHL 139, A20, SC5
95/6 Slapshot 332
96/7 UpperDeck 371

DESROSIERS, DENNIS
91/2 Cincinnati
92/3 Cincinnati
78/9 Saginaw

DESROSIERS, GILLES
52/3 BasDuFleuve 53
51/2 LacStJean 3

DESROSIERS, JOE
89/90 SketchOHL 95
89/90 Sudbury 30

DESROSIERS, LOUIS
52/3 AnonymousOHL 47
52/3 BasDuFleuve 65

DESSUREAULT, GAETAN
53/4 LaPatrie 20DEC

DESYATKOV, PAVEL
93/4 Pinnacle 505

DETONI, LINO
94 Semic 306
93 SemicSticker 223

DETONI, RENATO
79 PaniniSticker 390

DEULING, JARRET
93/4 Kamloops

DEUTSCHER, TORSTEN
94/5 DEL 36
95/6 DEL 29

DEVELLANO, JIM
85/6 DET/Caesars

DEVEREAUX, BOYD
96/7 AllSportPPF 79
95/6 Bowman P10
97/8 Bowman 23
95/6 Classic 86
97/8 DonrussElite 90
97/8 DonrussPriority 184
95/6 FutureLegends-HotPicks 2
97/8 KatchMedallion 56
97/8 Leaf 149
97/8 PacificParamount 73
97/8 Pinnacle 13
97/8 PinnacleBeAPlayer 237
97/8 PinnacleCertified J
97/8 Score 73
95/6 Slapshot 149, 432
97/8 SPAuthentic 181
98/9 Topps 21
96/7 UDBlackDiamond 86
97/8 UDBlackDiamond 146
97/8 UDCollChoice 311
96/7 UpperDeck"Ice" 122
97/8 Zenith 93
96/7 EDM
97/8 EDM

DEVEREAUX, JOHN
88/9 Flint
91/2 Greensboro

DEVINE, KEVIN
81/2 Indianapolis 10
82/3 Indianapolis
76/7 SanDiegoMariners

DEVLIN, VINCE
92/3 BCJHL 216, 227

DEVRIES, GREG
97/8 PacificRegime 76
97/8 PinnacleBeAPlayer 78
93/4 Slapshot(NiagaraFalls) 5
96/7 UpperDeck 191
96/7 EDM
97/8 EDM
94/5 CapeBreton

DEVUONO, LEN
90/1 SketchOHL 93, 230
90/1 Kitchener 7

DEWALLE, KIRK
93/4 Lethbridge

DEWAR, JEFF
93/4 Seattle

DEWILTZ, DIETER
74 Hellas 109
70/1 Kuvajulkaisut 83

DEWOLF, JOSH
95/6 Classic 59

DEWSBURY, AL
45-64 BeeHives(CHI)
51/2 Parkhurst 38
52/3 Parkhurst 17
53/4 Parkhurst 78
54/5 Parkhurst 78
93/4 Parkie(56/7) 22

DEWSBURY, BILL
83/4 Kingston 28

DEXTER, JASON
95/6 Birmingham

DEY, EDGAR
1910-11 Imperial (C56) 6

DEYELL, MARK
93/4 Saskatoon

DEZAINDE, JOE
95/6 Slapshot 158

DEZAINDE, NORMAN
94/5 SigRookies 24
90/1 SketchOHL 231
91/2 SketchOHL 82
93/4 Slapshot(Kitchener) 8
90/1 Kitchener 15
94/5 Toledo
95/6 Toledo

DIBLEY, GORD
67/8 ColumbusCheckers

DICKENS, ERNEST
34-43 BeeHives(TOR)
45-64 BeeHives(CHI)

DICKSENSON, HERB
52/3 Parkhurst 57

DICKIE, GARY
86/7 Regina
87/8 Regina
88/9 Regina

DICKIE, GORD
91/2 SketchOHL 289
93/4 Slapshot(Kitchener) 6

DICKIE, J.J.
96/7 SSMarie

DICKIE, KEVIN
91/2 AirCanadaSJHL 3

DICKISON, BRIAN
89/90 Rayside

DICKSON, DARRYL
91/2 AirCanadaSJHL D47
92/3 MPSPhotoSJHL 24

DIDMON
91/2 AvantGardeBCJ 160

DIDUCK, GERALD
92/3 Bowman 65
93/4 Donruss 360
92/3 FleerUltra 424
93/4 FleerUltra 440
95/6 FleerUltra 245
93/4 Leaf 387
94/5 Leaf 402
95/6 Leaf 313
89/90 OPC/Topps 182
90/1 O-Pee-Chee 421
91/2 OPC/Topps 280
92/3 O-Pee-Chee 309
90/1 opcPremier 22
89/90 opcSticker 117/256
90/1 Panini(MTL) 9
89/90 PaniniSticker 274
90/1 PaniniSticker 85
91/2 Parkhurst 407
92/3 Parkhurst 419
95/6 Parkhurst 368
91/2 Pinnacle 211
92/3 Pinnacle 81
93/4 Pinnacle 291
94/5 Pinnacle 359
96/7 PinnacleBeAPlayer 167
97/8 PinnacleBeAPlayer 55
93/4 PowerPlay 250
90/1 ProSet 180, 468
91/2 ProSet 502
90/1 Score 139, 23T
92/3 Score 34
93/4 Score 356
92/3 Topps 44
95/6 Topps 247
92/3 ToppsStadiumClub 97
94/5 ToppsStadiumClub 91
90/1 UpperDeck 390
90/1 MTL
84/5 NYI 18
89/90 NYI
97/8 PHO
90/1 VAN/Mohawk
91/2 VAN
92/3 VAN/RoadTrip
93/4 VAN/Coins
94/5 VAN

DIDUCK, JUDY
94/5 Classic W12
97/8 UDCollChoice 283

DIENER, DEREK
93/4 Lethbridge

DIETRICH, DON
83/4 Springfield 21

DIETRICH, LOU
52/3 AnonymousOHL 13

DIETRICH, SHAWN
90/1 SketchWHL 198
91/2 SketchWHL 200
89/90 Spokane

DIETSCH, ANDRE
94/5 DEL 34
97/8 DEL 26

DIFAZIO, ALBERTO
82 SemicSticker 136

DIFAZIO, RALPH
94 Semic 295

DIFRONZO, MICHELE
94/5 Classic W32

DILIO, FRANK
83&87 HallOfFame 81
83 HHOF Postcard (F)

DILLABOUGH, BOB
64-67 BeeHives(BOS)
65/6 CocaCola
70/1 DadsCookies
70/1 EddieSargent 217
68/9 O-Pee-Chee 191
69/70 O-Pee-Chee 150
63/4 Parkhurst 47
65/6 Topps 39
66/7 Topps 98
72/3 Cleveland
72/3 Cleveland/Linnet

DILLON, CECIL
33/4 Anonymous (V129) 32
34-43 BeeHives(NYR)
33/4 CndGum (V252)
33-35 DiamondMatch
36-39 DiamondMatch (2), (3)
34/5 OPC (V304B) 71
33/4 WWGum (V357) 15

DILLON, WAYNE
79/80 O-Pee-Chee 359
75/6 OPC 363
76/7 OPC/Topps 9
77/8 OPC/Topps 166
78/9 OPC/Topps 73
74/5 opcWHA 3
79/80 WPG

DIMAIO, ROB
92/3 Bowman 403
94/5 Leaf 549
90/1 opcPremier 27
92/3 opcPremier 62
98/9 Pacific 75
97/8 PacificCrown 287
93/4 PaniniSticker 218
97/8 PaniniSticker 1
91/2 Parkhurst 325
92/3 Parkhurst 402
93/4 Parkhurst 196
95/6 Parkhurst 431
94/5 Pinnacle 360
97/8 PinnacleBeAPlayer 6
93/4 Premier 242
94/5 Premier 114
88/9 ProCards(Springfield)
89/90 ProCards(AHL) 234
90/1 ProCards 512
90/1 ProSet 625
91/2 ProSet 430
97/8 Score(BOS) 9
92/3 Topps 488
95/6 Topps 92
92/3 ToppsStadiumClub 33
93/4 ToppsStadiumClub 182
90/1 UpperDeck 225
92/3 UpperDeck 529
93/4 UpperDeck 176
95/6 UpperDeck 336
95/6 UDBeAPlayer 105
84/5 Kamloops
94/5 PHA
92/3 T.B/Sheraton
93/4 T.B/KashNKarry
85/6 MedicineHat 5

DIMBAT, ANDREAS
95/6 DEL 68
97/8 DEL 264

DIMITRI, DAVE
93/4 Huntington

DIMITRIEV, IGOR
89/90 SovietNats

DIMME, BIRLEY
52/3 AnonymousOHL 55

DIMUZIO, FRANK
88/9 ProCards(Baltimore)
94 Semic 300
93 SemicSticker 217

DINEEN, BILL
52/3 AnonymousOHL 147
45-64 BeeHives(DET)
53/4 Parkhurst 38
54/5 Parkhurst 15
93/4 Parkhurst PR62
93/4 Parkie(56/7) 50
88/9 ProCards(Adirondack)
92/3 Score 518
54/5 Topps 57
57/8 Topps 49
92/3 PHA/UD 23DEC92
92/3 PHA/UD 27FEB93
63/4 Québec
60/1 Cleveland

DINEEN, GORD
92/3 Durivage 37
95/6 EdgeIce 192
89/90 O-Pee-Chee 256
90/1 O-Pee-Chee 470
94/5 PaniniSticker 106
91/2 ProCards 306
90/1 ProSet 233
94/5 ToppsStadiumClub 219
90/1 UpperDeck 369
84/5 NYI 19
93/4 OTT/Kraft
82/3 Indianapolis
92/3 SanDiego
80/1 SSMarie
81/2 SSMarie

DINEEN, KEVIN
90/1 Bowman 261, -HatTrick 7
91/2 Bowman 6
92/3 Bowman 121
94/5 ClassicImages 21, PL3
93/4 Donruss 249
94/5 Donruss 36
95/6 Donruss 212
92/3 Durivage 12
93/4 Durivage 37
95/6 EdgeIce 130, C3
92/3 FleerUltra 154
93/4 FleerUltra 107
94/5 FleerUltra 156
88/9 FritoLay
97/8 KatchMedallion 26
90/1 Kraft 11
91/2 Kraft 86
93/4 Kraft-Captain
96/7 Kraft-Disk
93/4 Leaf 156, -HatTrick 6
94/5 Leaf 167
95/6 Leaf 205
85/6 OPC/Topps 34
86/7 OPC/Topps 88
87/8 OPC/Topps 124
88/9 OPC/Topps 36
89/90 OPC/T. 20, M, OPC 304
90/1 OPC/Topps 213
91/2 OPC/Topps 285
92/3 O-Pee-Chee 200
90/1 opcPremier 23
85/6 opcSticker 168/39
86/7 opcSticker 56/194
87/8 opcSticker 202/60

88/9 opcSticker 269/133
89/90 opcSticker 270
98/9 Pacific 130
97/8 PacificCrown 218
97/8 PacificCrownRoyale 22
97/8 PacificParamount 33
98/9 PacificParamount 34
94/5 PaniniSticker 41
87/8 PaniniSticker 44
88/9 PaniniSticker 240
89/90 PaniniSticker 219
90/1 PaniniSticker 43
91/2 PaniniSticker 323
92/3 PaniniSticker 186
93/4 PaniniSticker 49
91/2 Parkhurst 348
92/3 Parkhurst 127
93/4 Parkhurst 421
94/5 Parkhurst 172
95/6 Parkhurst 366
91/2 Pinnacle 246, 366
92/3 Pinnacle 14
93/4 Pinnacle 276, CA17
94/5 Pinnacle 426
95/6 Pinnacle 150
94/5 POG 357
95/6 POG 207
93/4 PowerPlay 179
93/4 Premier 167
94/5 Premier 207
90/1 ProSet 102
91/2 ProSet 89, 451
92/3 ProSet 134
91/2 PSPlatinum 46
90/1 Score 212, -HotCards 90
92/3 Score 284, 517
93/4 Score 122
94/5 Score 197
95/6 Score 277
94/5 Select 142
91 SemicSticker 71
96/7 SP 71
92/3 Topps 131
95/6 Topps 143
98/9 Topps 173
91/2 ToppsStadiumClub 162
92/3 ToppsStadiumClub 365
93/4 ToppsStadiumClub 43
90/1 UpperDeck 266
92/3 UpperDeck 256
93/4 UpperDeck 212
94/5 UpperDeck 431
96/7 UpperDeck 270
97/8 UpperDeck 241
96/7 UDBlackDiamond 72
97/8 UDCollChoice109
85/6 HFD/JuniorWhalers
86/7 HFD/JuniorWhalers
87/8 HFD/JuniorWhalers
88/9 HFD/JuniorWhalers
89/90 HFD/JuniorWhalers
90/1 HFD/JuniorWhalers
91/2 PHA/JCPenney
92/3 PHA/JCPenney
92/3 PHA/UD 17JAN93
92/3 PHA/UD 19SEP92
92/3 PHA/UD 23DEC92
93/4 PHA/JCPenney
93/4 PHA 10MAR94
93/4 PHA 16OCT93
94/5 PHA

DINEEN, PETER
88/9 ProCards(Adirondack)
89/90 ProCards(AHL) 327
90/1 ProCards 306
83/4 Moncton 8

DINEEN, SHAWN
89/90 ProCards(IHL) 120
83/4 Moncton 25

DINGMAN, CHRIS
94/5 Classic 17, T10
94/5 ClassicFourSport 133
94/5 C4'Images 110
97/8 Leaf 158
97/8 PacificCrownRoyale 17
97/8 PacificParamount 27
97/8 Pinnacle 7
97/8 PinnacleBeAPlayer 216
97/8 Score 55
94/5 SigRookies 20
94/5 Slapshot(MEM) 43
97/8 UpperDeck 234
92/3 Brandon 3

DINSMORE, CHUCK
24/5 Champs (C144)
24/5 MapleCrispette (V130) 17
24/5 (V145-2) 40

DION, CONNIE
43-47 ParadeSportive

DION, MICHEL
79/80 O-Pee-Chee 316
80/1 OPC/Topps 223
82/3 O-Pee-Chee 267
83/4 O-Pee-Chee 279
84/5 O-Pee-Chee 173
82/3 opcSticker 146, 168
83/4 opcSticker 234
76/7 opcWHA 6, 114
77/8 opcWHA 62
82/3 Post
83/4 PuffySticker 11
83/4 SouhaitsRen.KeyChain
83/4 PGH
83/4 PGH/Heinz
84/5 PGH/Heinz
80/1 QUE

DION, STEVE
90/1 SketchQMJHL 141
91/2 SketchQMJHL 221

DION, TOM
92/3 Wheeling 6

DIONNE, GILBERT
92/3 Bowman 439
92/3 ClassicProspects 87
93/4 Donruss 174
92/3 Durivage 21
93/4 Durivage 13
94/5 Fleer 152
92/3 FleerUltra 105, -Rookie 4
93/4 FleerUltra 141
94/5 FleerUltra 109
92/3 HumptyDumpty (1)
93/4 Leaf 117
92/3 O-Pee-Chee 307
92/3 PaniniSticker 272, M
93/4 PaniniSticker 18
94/5 PaniniSticker 15
91/2 Parkhurst 313, 447
92/3 Parkhurst 81, 237
93/4 Parkhurst 101
94/5 Parkhurst V14
94/5 ParkieSE 91
92/3 Pinnacle 5, -Tm2000 29
93/4 Pinnacle 199
94/5 Pinnacle 422
94/5 POG 134
93/4 PowerPlay 368
93/4 Premier 480
94/5 Premier 366
90/1 ProCards 62
91/2 ProCards 73
92/3 ProSet 92, -PV3, -Rookie 6
92/3 Score 331,-Sharp 7,-Yng 6
93/4 Score 178
92/3 SeasonsPatch 24
89/90 SketchMEM 39
92/3 Topps 13, 19
92/3 ToppsStadiumClub 403
93/4 ToppsStadiumClub 115
91/2 UpperDeck 448
92/3 UD 356, 427, 625,AR2,AR7
93/4 UpperDeck 117
94/5 UpperDeck 57, 384
94/5 UDBeAPlayer R22
92/3 MTL
93/4 MTL
94/5 MTL
94/5 PHA
88/9 Kitchener 18
89/90 Kitchener 19

DIONNE, MARCEL
77/8 Coke Mini
71/2 Colgate Heads
72-84 Dernière 79/80
72-84 Dernière 83/4
88/9 Esso Sticker
88/9 FritoLay
94/5 HHOFLegends 54
82? JDMcCarthy
84/5 Kelloggs Disk
91/2 Kraft 85
74/5 Loblaws
71/2 OPC/Topps 133
72/3 OPC 8, Topps 18
73/4 OPC/Topps 17
74/5 OPC/Topps 72, 84
75/6 OPC/Topps 140, 210, 318
76/7 OPC/Topps 91
76/7 OPC 386, T-Glossy 4
77/8 OPC/T. 1-3, 240, -Glossy 4
78/9 OPC/Topps 120
79/80 OPC/Topps 1, 2, 3, 5, 160
80/1 OPC/T. 20, 81, 162-63, 165
81/2 OPC 141, 150, 156, 391
81/2 Topps 10, 54, (West) 125
82/3 O-Pee-Chee 149, 152, 153
83/4 OPC 150, 151, 152, 211
84/5 O-Pee-Chee 82, Topps 64
85/6 OPC/Topps 90, E
86/7 OPC/Topps 30
87/8 OPC/Topps 129
88/9 OPC/Topps 13
92/3 OPC 294, -25Years 4
88/9 opcStars 8
81/2 opcSticker 147, 235, 267
82/3 opcSticker 230
83/4 opcStick. 1, 294-95, 323-24
84/5 opcSticker 264, 265
85/6 opcSticker 235
86/7 opcSticker 88
87/8 opcSticker 34/179
88/9 opcSticker 244/114
80/1 opcSuperCard 8
79 PaniniSticker 61
87/8 PaniniSticker 113
88/9 PaniniSticker 190
91/2 Pinnacle 385
81/2 Post PopUp 12
90/1 ProSet 653
83/4 PuffySticker 11
83/4 7ElevenCokeCup
84/5 7ElevenDisk
85/6 7Eleven 8
83/4 SouhaitsRen.KeyChain
71/2 TheTorontoSun
91/2 Trends (72) 91, -Aut
92/3 Trends76 179
93/4 Zellers
80/1 L.A.
84/5 L.A./Smokeys
87/8 NYR.

DIOTTE, ROLAND
79/80 Montréal, -B&W

DIPAOLO, MAURO
97/8 Halifax (2)

DIPIETRO, PAUL
93/4 ClassicProspects 104
93/4 FleerUltra 159
93/4 Leaf 248
92/3 Parkhurst 489
93/4 Parkhurst 108
91/2 Pinnacle 350
93/4 Pinnacle 114
94/5 Pinnacle 443
93/4 PowerPlay 369
93/4 Premier 288
94/5 Premier 252
90/1 ProCards 68
91/2 ProCards 70
91/2 ProSet 546
93/4 Score 494
93/4 Slapshot(Sudbury) 24
92/3 Topps 361
92/3 ToppsStadiumClub 98
93/4 ToppsStadiumClub 194
93/4 UpperDeck 108
93/4 MTL
94/5 MTL
92/3 Fredericton
87/8 Sudbury 22
88/9 Sudbury 22
89/90 Sudbury 15, 21

DIRK, ROBERT
92/3 FleerUltra 425
91/2 OPC/Topps 493
91/2 Parkhurst 403
92/3 Parkhurst 425
93/4 Pinnacle 327
94/5 Pinnacle 405
93/4 Premier 284
89/90 ProCards(IHL) 8
90/1 ProSet 522, 603
92/3 Score 279
93/4 Score 288
92/3 Topps 437
95/6 UpperDeck 432
95/6 UDBeAPlayer 159
94/5 ANA/Carl'sJr 3
87/8 STL
88/9 STL
90/1 STL/Kodak
91/2 VAN
92/3 VAN/RoadTrip
93/4 VAN/Coins
94/5 VAN

DISHER, JASON
93/4 Slapshot(Kingston) 9
95/6 ThunderBay

DISIEWICH, JASON
92/3 BCJHL 94
91/2 AvantGardeBCJHL 55, 153
92/3 BCJHL 111
93/4 Dayton 8
91/2 Nainamo

DIVITA, DAVID
91/2 ProCards 17
91/2 Rochester/Genny
91/2 Rochester/Kodak
91/2 Rochestr/Dunkin'Donuts
92/3 Rochester/Kodak
92/3 Rochester/Dunkin'Donuts

DIVJAK, DAN
85/6 Arizona

DIJIAN, J.M.
92 SemicSticker 219

DJELLOUL, SERGE
95 PaniniWorlds 98

DJOOS, PER
94/5 ElitSet 164
95/6 ElitSet 140
90/1 opcPremier 24
90/1 ProSet 603
90/1 ScoreTraded 107T
92/3 Score 372
93 SemicSticker 30
92/3 Topps 93
92/3 ToppsStadiumClub 492
95/6 udElite 203
97/8 udSwedish 18
90/1 DET/Caesars
92/3 Binghampton

DLOUHY, JAN
94/5 APS 53
95/6 APS 79

DOAK, GARY
70/1 DadsCookies
70/1 EddieSargent 218
71/2 EddieSargent 214
71/2 Esso Stamp
68/9 O-Pee-Chee 138
69/70 O-Pee-Chee 202
70/1 OPC/Topps 114
71/2 OPC/Topps 87
72/3 OPC 73, Topps 81
74/5 O-Pee-Chee 361
75/6 O-Pee-Chee 358
76/7 OPC/Topps 7
77/8 OPC/Topps 181
78/9 O-Pee-Chee 305
80/1 O-Pee-Chee 374
68/9 ShirriffCoin BOS14
67/8 Topps 97
70/1 BOS
70/1 VAN/RoyalBank
71/2 VAN/RoyalBank 21

DOAN, SHANE
94/5 AutoPhonex 14
95/6 Bowman 149, BB24
95/6 Classic 7, -AS5
94/5 ClassicImages 85
95/6 Donruss 210, -RatedRook 8
95/6 DonrussElite 109, -Rook 13
95/6 FleerMetal 175
95/6 FleerUltra 336, -High 7
95/6 LeafLimited 7
98/9 Pacific 336
97/8 PacificCrown 330
97/8 PacificRegime 149
95/6 Parkhurst 267
95/6 P.Zenith 132,-RookRoll 15
96/7 Score 262
95/6 SelectCertified 114
95/6 SkyBoxImpact 226
94/5 Slapshot(MEM) 15
95/6 Summit 188
95/6 Topps 314
95/6 ToppsFinest 22
95/6 ToppsStadiumClub 207
95/6 ToppsSuperSkills SR8
95/6 TetradAutobilia 97
95/6 Tetrad 67, 'Promo 4
95/6 UpperDeck 269, H27
96/7 UpperDeck 314
97/8 UpperDeck 131
95/6 UDBeAPlayer 172
95/6 UDCollChoice 403
96/7 UDCollChoice 205
96/7 PHO
97/8 PHO
95/6 WPG
93/4 Kamloops

DOBBIN, BRIAN
89/90 ProCards(AHL) 341
90/1 ProCards 33
91/2 ProCards 375
82/3 Kingston 11
85/6 London 10
94/5 Milwaukee

DOBEK, BOB
76/7 SanDiegoMariners

DOBNI, EVAN
81/2 Regina 7

DOBRESCU, JAY
92/3 MPSPhotoSJHL 7

DOBROTA, ANDREI
91/2 SketchQMJHL 132

DOBRZYNSKI, RALF
94/5 DEL 209

DOBSON, JIM
83/4 Fredericton 6
84/5 Fredericton 17

DODUNSKI, COLIN
91/2 FerrisState

DOERS, MIKE
94/5 Dayton 10

DOHERTY, KEVIN
88/9 Brockville 6

DOHERTY, PAUL
90/1 SketchOHL 103
93/4 Slapshot(Oshawa) 20

DOHLER, UDO
94/5 DEL 111
95/6 DEL 27
96/7 DEL 25

DOIG, JASON
95/6 Bowman 120
97/8 Bowman 48
94/5 Classic CP4
95/6 Classic 31, AS15
95/6 ClassicFiveSport 154, -Aut.
94/5 C'Images 12, CE18, PD9
95/6 Donruss 253
96/7 Fleer 125, -Calder 2
95/6 FleerUltra 337
98/9 Pacific 336
95/6 Parkhurst 529
94/5 ParkieSE 254
94/5 Select 161
96/7 SkyBoxImpact 148
94/5 SP 177
95/6 Topps 355
95/6 ToppsStadiumClub 222
95/6 UpperDeck 499
95/6 UDCollChoice 407
96/7 UpperDeck"Ice" 119
97/8 PHO
95/6 WPG

DOIRON, SHANE
90/1 SketchQMJHL 130
91/2 SketchQMJHL 201

DOLAN, MICK
91/2 FerrisState

DOLANA, LIBOR
94/5 APS 174
95/6 APS 186
91 SemicSticker 120

DOLE, ANDREW
93/4 Sudbury 12

DOLEZAL, JIRI
94/5 DEL 334
95/6 DEL 304
91/2 Jyvas-Hyva 28
95 PaniniWorlds 206
95 Semic 153
89 SemicSticker 193

DOLLARD, DAVID
92/3 BCJHL 52

DOLLAS, BOBBY
94/5 Flair 2
94/5 Leaf 383
97/8 PacificCrown 41
95/6 PaniniSticker 228
96/7 PaniniSticker 227
94/5 Pinnacle 41
96/7 Pinnacle 157
96/7 PinnacleBeAPlayer 96
95/6 Playoff 112
94/5 POG 366
95/6 POG 25
93/4 PowerPlay 283
93/4 Premier 491
94/5 Premier 264
88/9 ProCards(Halifax)
95/6 SkyBoxEmotion 1
95/6 SkyBoxImpact 1
93/4 ToppsStadiumClub 463
94/5 UpperDeck 13
95/6 UpperDeck 395
95/6 UDCollChoice 289
93/4 ANA/Caps 2
94/5 ANA/Carl'sJr 4
96/7 ANA/UpFrontSports 2
90/1 DET/Caesars
87/8 Moncton

DOMBKIEWICZ, MIKE
96/7 Guelph 9

DOME, ROBERT
96/7 AllSportPPF 175
97/8 DonrussPreferred 163
97/8 DonrussPriority 169
98/9 Pacific 350
97/8 Pinnacle 21
97 SB'AutColl 47, -Aut
97/8 Score(PGH) 16
98/9 SPx"Finite" 67
97/8 SPAuthentic 128
97/8 UpperDeck 346
97/8 UDBlackDiamond 88
98/9 UDChoice 171

DOMENICHELLI, HNAT
97/8 Donruss 196
96/7 DonrussCanadianIce 122
97/8 DonrussCanadianIce 131
95/6 DonrussElite-WorldJrs 12
96/7 FleerUltra 74
97/8 Leaf 79
96/7 LeafPreferred 121
96/7 LeafLimited -Rookies 4
97/8 Limited 45
96/7 MetalUniverse 175
98/9 Pacific 116
97/8 PacificCrown 237
97/8 PinnacleInside 93
97/8 Score 68
94/5 Slapshot(MEM) 13
95/6 UpperDeck 539
96/7 UpperDeck 272
97/8 UpperDeck 22
97/8 UDCollChoice 33
93/4 Kamloops

DOMI, TIE
93/4 Donruss 381
94/5 Donruss 60
95/6 Donruss 225
96/7 Duracell DC13
94/5 FleerUltra 392
95/6 FleerUltra 159
97/8 KatchMedallion 140
93/4 Leaf 216
94/5 Leaf 318
96/7 Maggers 152
97/8 Omega 220
90/1 opcPremier 25
98/9 Pacific 28
97/8 PacificCrown 65
98/9 PacificParamount 225
97/8 PacificRevolution 134
94/5 PaniniSticker 167
96/7 PaniniSticker 221
97/8 PaniniSticker 176
91/2 Parkhurst 333
92/3 Parkhurst 434
93/4 Parkhurst 230
95/6 Parkhurst 205
94/5 ParkieSE 202
93/4 Pinnacle 295
94/5 Pinnacle 344
95/6 Pinnacle 159
96/7 PinnacleBeAPlayer 47
95/6 Playoff 94
94/5 POG 250, 344
95/6 POG 263
93/4 Premier 513
94/5 Premier 444
89/90 ProCards'AHL 128
90/1 ProCards 22
91/2 ProSet 440
92/3 Score 408
93/4 Score 312
94/5 Score 123
95/6 Score 275
97/8 Score 219
97/8 Score(TOR) 8
92/3 Topps 395
97/8 ToppsSticker 1
92/3 UpperDeck 99
94/5 UpperDeck 409
96/7 UpperDeck 201
97/8 UpperDeck 196, 368
94/5 UDBAP R65, R168,-Aut. 143
98/9 UDChoice 204
95/6 UDCollChoice 242
96/7 UDCollChoice 261
97/8 UDCollChoice 253
96/7 UpperDeck"Ice" 68
93/4 WPG/Ruffles

DOMKEY, H.
95/6 DEL 348

DOMONSKY, BRAD
95/6 Slapshot 402
96/7 Sudbury 8

DONAHUE, MARK
90/1 SketchOHL 104
93/4 Slapshot(Kitchener) 16

DONALD, DEREK
92/3 Dayton
93/4 Dayton 15

DONALDSON, CRAIG
89/90 SketchMEM 79
89/90 SketchOHL 7
89/90 Oshawa 7

DONALDSON, DALE
93/4 RedDeer

DONATELLI, CLARK
90/1 Bowman 181
90/1 O-Pee-Chee 458
90/1 ProCards 316

DONATO, TED
93/4 Donruss 25
94/5 Donruss 155
95/6 Donruss 263
96/7 Donruss 211
97/8 Donruss 108
92/3 FleerUltra 251
93/4 FleerUltra 267
94/5 FleerUltra 12
95/6 FleerUltra 204
97/8 KatchMedallion 10
93/4 Leaf 54
94/5 Leaf 49
95/6 Leaf 326
97/8 Limited 118
97/8 Omega 15
92/3 opcPremier 30
98/9 Pacific 76
97/8 PacificCrown 209
97/8 PacificCrownRoyale 10
97/8 PacificInvincible 9
97/8 PacificParamount 12
98/9 PacificParamount 13
97/8 PacificRevolution 9
93/4 PaniniSticker 8
94/5 PaniniSticker 2
95/6 PaniniSticker 4
96/7 PaniniSticker 10

97/8 PaniniSticker 4
91/2 Parkhurst 230
92/3 Parkhurst 8
93/4 Parkhurst 283
95/6 Parkhurst 17
94/5 ParkieSE 14
93/4 Pinnacle 102
94/5 Pinnacle 146
96/7 PinnacleBeAPlayer 37
97/8 PinnacleCertified 87
97/8 PinnacleInside 101
94/5 POG 43
95/6 POG 30
93/4 PowerPlay 18
93/4 Premier 146
94/5 Premier 88
92/3 ProSet 221
92/3 Score 479
93/4 Score 262
94/5 Score 27
95/6 Score 28
96/7 Score 30
97/8 Score 171
97/8 Score(BOS) 6
94/5 Sisu-GuestSpecial 1
95/6 SisuLimited 97
96/7 SP 13
97/8 SPAuthentic 7
95/6 Topps 324
92/3 ToppsStadiumClub 271
93/4 ToppsStadiumClub 83
92/3 UpperDeck 202, 393, G20
93/4 UpperDeck 143
94/5 UpperDeck 61
95/6 UpperDeck 80, SE97
96/7 UpperDeck 189, 221
97/8 UpperDeck 221
94/5 UDBeAPlayer-Aut. 141
98/9 UDChoice 11
95/6 UDCollChoice 76
96/7 UDCollChoice 19
97/8 UDCollChoice 14
92/3 BOS

DONNELY, DAVE
90/1 ProCards 131
86/7 CHI/Coke
88/9 EDM/ActionMagazine 150

DONNELLY, GORD
92/3 Durivage 13
92/3 FleerUltra 259
90/1 Panini(WPG) 7
90/1 ProSet 560
91/2 ProSet 357
92/3 Score 111
93/4 ToppsStadiumClub 396
92/3 BUF/Jubillee
94/5 DAL/Southwest
84/5 QUE
85/6 QUE
85/6 QUE/McDonald
86/7 QUE
86/7 QUE/GeneralFoods
87/8 QUE/GeneralFoods
88/9 QUE/GeneralFoods
88/9 QUE
89/90 WPG/Safeway
90/1 WPG/IGA
84/5 Fredericton 6
85/6 Fredericton 20

DONNELLY, JOHN
72/3 Ottawa

DONNELLY, MIKE
92/3 Bowman 342
93/4 Donruss 155
94/5 Donruss 282
95/6 Donruss 232
94/5 Flair 78
92/3 FleerUltra 81
94/5 FleerUltra 97
93/4 Leaf 282
94/5 Leaf 106
95/6 Leaf 217
92/3 O-Pee-Chee 151
95/6 PaniniSticker 170
91/2 Parkhurst 294
93/4 Parkhurst 369
95/6 Parkhurst 57
91/2 Pinnacle 299
92/3 Pinnacle 98
93/4 Pinnacle 172
94/5 Pinnacle 223
95/6 Pinnacle 156
94/5 POG 123
95/6 POG 87
93/4 PowerPlay 359
93/4 Premier 33
94/5 Premier 308
88/9 ProCards(Rochester)
89/90 ProCards(AHL) 274
90/1 ProCards 428
91/2 ProSet 399
92/3 Score 67
93/4 Score 176
95/6 Score 147
92/3 Topps 121
92/3 ToppsStadiumClub 411
93/4 ToppsStadiumClub 374
94/5 ToppsStadiumClub 14
94/5 UpperDeck 199
95/6 UpperDeck 87
95/6 UDBeAPlayer 80
95/6 UDCollChoice 263
87/8 BUF/BlueShield
88/9 BUF/BlueShield
91/2 BUF/BlueShield
91/2 BUF/Campbell
92/3 BUF/BlueShield
94/5 DAL/Southwest

DONNELLY, PETE
73/4 QuakerOats 29
73/4 Vancouver

DONNELLY, TRUMAN
36/7 WWGum (V356) 134

DONOVAN, ROB
94/5 Birmingham
95/6 Birmingham

DONOVAN, RYAN
91/2 AvantGardeBCJHL 109
92/3 BCJHL 171

DONOVAN, SHEAN
95/6 Bowman 140
94/5 C'Images 46, -Aut.
95/6 Classic 92
95/6 Donruss 77, -CanadaJr 19
95/6 Leaf 47
98/9 Pacific 159
97/8 PacificRegime 176
96/7 PaniniSticker 287
95/6 Parkhurst 458
94/5 Pinnacle 539
95/6 Pinnacle 211
97/8 PinnacleBeAPlayer 142
95/6 Score 307
94/5 SP 149
95/6 Summit 177
95/6 Topps 42, CJ 13
94/5 ToppsFinest 158
95/6 ToppsFinest 163
95/6 ToppsStadiumClub 114
94/5 UpperDeck 366
95/6 UpperDeck 131
96/7 UpperDeck 149
97/8 UpperDeck 152
95/6 UDBeAPlayer 3
96/7 UDCollChoice 234
96/7 S.J/PacificBellSheet
97/8 S.J/PacificBellSheet
92/3 Ottawa67s

DONTIGNY, STEVE
90/1 SketchQMJHL 193
91/2 SketchQMJHL 60

DOPITA, JIRI
95/6 APS 20, 369
94/5 DEL 43
96 Wien 122

DOPITA, LUBOS
94/5 APS 267

DOPSON, ROB
95/6 EdgeIce 131
90/1 ProCards 370
91/2 ProCards 301
92/3 Cleveland 15
93/4 Cleveland

DORATY, KEN
33/4 Anonymous (V129) 14
26 Dominion 28
33/4 OPC (V304A) 4
33/4 WWGum (V357) 49
32/3 TOR/OKeefe 15

DORCHUK, DEAN
90/1 SketchWHL 321
89/90 Portland

DORÉ, ANDRÉ
83/4 O-Pee-Chee 313
84/5 O-Pee-Chee 279
82/3 Post
83/4 QUE

DORÉ, DANIEL
90/1 Panini(QUE) 2
91/2 ProCards 539
90/1 UpperDeck 255
88/9 QUE
88/9 QUE/GeneralFoods
89/90 QUE
89/90 QUE/GeneralFoods
89/90 QUE/Police
90/1 QUE
90/1 Halifax

DORÉ, MIKE
90/1 Rayside
91/2 Rayside

DOREY, JIM
70/1 Colgate Stamp 79
72-84 Dernière 78/9
70/1 EddieSargent 197
71/2 EddieSargent 201
70/1 Esso Stamp
69/70 O-Pee-Chee 45
70/1 OPC/Topps 106
71/2 OPC/Topps 57
72/3 OPC 339
75/6 opcWHA 94
76/7 opcWHA 24
73/4 QuakerOats 47
72 SemicSticker 168
71/2 TheTorontoSun
68/9 TOR
70/1 TOR
71/2 TOR
72/3 NewEnglandWhalers
76/7 QuébecNordiques

DORION, DAN
88/9 ProCards(Utica)

DORNHOEFER, GARY
68/9 Bauer
64-67 BeeHives(BOS)
64/5 CokeCap BOS-8
70/1 Colgate Stamp 40
70/1 DadsCookies
70/1 EddieSargent 149
71/2 EddieSargent 151
72/3 EddieSargent 161
70/1 Esso Stamp
72/3 Letraset 3
74/5 Loblaws
68/9 OPC/Topps 94
69/70 OPC/Topps 94
70/1 OPC/Topps 85, -Deckle 33
71/2 OPC 202, Topps 89
72/3 OPC 146, 268, Topps 41,65
73/4 OPC 182, Topps 167
74/5 OPC/Topps 44
75/6 OPC/Topps 129
76/7 OPC/Topps 256
77/8 OPC/Topps 202
94/5 Parkie(64/5) 20
72/3 Post Transfers 3
72 SemicSticker 179
68/9 ShirriffCoin PHA4
71/2 TheTorontoSun
64/5 Topps 72
65/6 Topps 38
70/1 PHA
72/3 PHA/MightyMilk
75/6 PHA/GingerAle

DOROCHIN, I.
95/6 DEL 46

DOROFEYEV, IGOR
92/3 UpperDeck 352

DOROHOY, EDWARD
45-64 BeeHives(MTL)
45-54 QuakerOats

DOROSH, DAVID
90/1 Oshawa 11

D'ORSONNENS, MARTIN
92/3 Clarkson
94/5 Johnstown 7
93/4 Raleigh

DOSDALL, CORY
90/1 SketchWHL 169
91/2 SketchWHL 308

DOUCET, BENOÎT
94/5 DEL 86
95/6 DEL 279, 431
95 PaniniWorlds 66
94 Semic 281
96 Wien 196
85/6 Moncton 26

DOUCET, DAVID
91/2 AirCanadaSJHL C6
92/3 MPSPhotoSJHL 81

DOUCET, WAYNE
90/1 ProCards 497
91/2 ProCards 461
90/1 Score 397
89/90 Sudbury 20

DOUCETTE, DAVE
89/90 SSMarie 27

DOUGLAS, JORDY
79/80 O-Pee-Chee 335
80/1 OPC/Topps 97
84/5 O-Pee-Chee 338
81/2 opcSticker 65
82/3 Post
83/4 SouhaitsRen.KeyChain
82/3 MIN
83/4 MIN

DOUGLAS, KENT
68/9 Bauer
45-64 BeeHives(TOR)
64-67 BeeHives(TOR)
63-5 ChexPhoto
64/5 CokeCap TOR-19
65/6 CocaCola
68/9 OPC/Topps 26
63/4 Parkhurst 7, 67
94/5 Parkie(64/5) 109
95/6 Parkie(66/7) 105
68/9 ShirriffCoin DET6
56-66 TorontoStar 62/3
63/4 TheTorontoStar
65/6 Topps 14
66/7 Topps 82
62/3 YorkTransfer 13
63/4 York 13
64/5 TOR

DOUGLAS, LAYNE
91/2 AirCanadaSJHL 19, A22

DOUGLAS, LESTER (LES)
34-43 BeeHives(DET)
51/2 LavalDairy 100
52/3 LavalDairy 100
40/1 OPC (V301-2) 129
52/3 StLawrence 5

DOUGLAS, RYAN
92/3 BCJHL 157
93/4 Slapshot(Peterborough) 21
93/4 Slapshot(SSMarie) 2

DOULL, DOUG
91/2 SketchOHL 114

DOURIAN, GEORGE
89/90 SketchOHL 71
90/1 SketchOHL 207
91/2 SketchOHL 266
91/2 Sudbury 12

DOURIS, PETER
94/5 Leaf 397
90/1 opcPremier 26
91/2 opcPremier 141
92/3 PaniniSticker 141
95/6 PaniniSticker 225
95/6 Parkhurst 278
95/6 Playoff 222
94/5 POG 30
95/6 POG 18
93/4 PowerPlay 284
93/4 Premier 265
94/5 Premier 184
88/9 ProCards(Peoria)
91/2 ProCards 64
90/1 ProSet 407
91/2 ProSet 347
92/3 Score 384
92/3 Topps 190
92/3 ToppsStadiumClub 402
95/6 UDBeAPlayer 25
94/5 ANA/Carl'sJr 5
89/90 BOS/SportsAction
90/1 BOS/SportsAction
91/2 BOS/SportsAction
87/8 Moncton

DOWD, BILL
81/2 Ottawa67s
82/3 Ottawa67s

DOWD, JIM
92/3 ClassicProspects 22
93/4 ClassicProspects 44
94/5 Donruss 47
94/5 FleerUltra 116
95/6 FleerUltra 260
94/5 Leaf 307
94/5 Parkhurst 279
95/6 Parkhurst 485
94/5 ParkieSE 98
94/5 Pinnacle 439
97/8 PinnacleBeAPlayer 111
93/4 PowerPlay 376
94/5 Premier 321
91/2 ProCards 423
95/6 Topps 316
94/5 ToppsStadiumClub 194
95/6 ToppsStadiumClub 91
94/5 UpperDeck 410
94/5 UDBeAPlayer-Aut. 91

DOWNEY, AARON
95/6 Hampton HRA -20

DOWNEY, BRIAN
93/4 ThunderBay

DOWNEY, JASON
90/1 SketchQMJHL 176
91/2 SketchQMJHL 154
93/4 Dayton 4
94/5 Dayton 4
95/6 Dayton

DOYLE, JASON
95/6 Bowman P11
95/6 Classic 88
95/6 Slapshot 375, 434

DOYLE, JOE
94/5 Slapshot(Sarnia) 5

DOYLE, PAUL
95/6 Slapshot 144

DOYLE, PERRY
95/6 SheffieldSteelers

DOYLE, ROB
88/9 ProCards(Adirondack)
94 Semic 233
93 SemicSticker 272
96 Wien 212

DOYLE, SHANE
88/9 ProCards(Indianapolis)
84/5 Belleville 13

DOYLE, TREVOR
93/4 Slapshot(Kingston) 5

DOYON, MARIO
88/9 ProCards(Saginaw)
89/90 ProCards'IHL 66
90/1 ProCards 443
91/2 ProCards 364
91/2 UpperDeck 441
93/4 Fredericton
90/1 Halifax

DRAG, MILAN
89/90 Victoria

DRAGON, JAROMIR
96 Wien 220

DRAGICEVIC, MILAN
86/7 Regina
87/8 Regina
89/90 Spokane

DRAGON, JOE
93/4 ClassicProspects 237

DRAINVILLE, ROBERT
52/3 LavalDairy 39

DRAISATL, PETER
94/5 DEL 208
95/6 DEL 209, 437
96/7 DEL 353
89 SemicSticker 124
91 SemicSticker 166
92 SemicSticker 182

DRAKE, CLARE
89/90 WPG/Safeway
90/1 WPG/IGA

DRAKE, DALLAS
92/3 Classic 86
94/5 Classic-Aut.
92/3 ClassicFourSport 206, BC9
92/3 C'Prospects 15, BC19, LP5
93/4 Donruss 100, 508
94/5 Flair 206
93/4 FleerUltra 104
94/5 FleerUltra 241
95/6 FleerUltra 326
93/4 Leaf 148
94/5 Leaf 380
95/6 Leaf 268
97/8 Omega 172
98/9 Pacific 337
98/9 PacificParamount 180
97/8 PacificRegime 150
95/6 PaniniSticker 211
93/4 Parkhurst 61
94/5 Parkhurst 261, V90
95/6 Parkhurst 503
93/4 Pinnacle 28
94/5 Pinnacle 225
95/6 Pinnacle 25
95/6 Playoff 326
96/7 Playoff 405
94/5 POG 251
95/6 POG 288
93/4 PowerPlay 71
93/4 Premier 365
94/5 Premier 64
95/6 ProMagnet 57
93/4 Score 246
95/6 Topps 328
98/9 Topps 107
93/4 ToppsStadiumClub 484
93/4 UD 50, HB4, SP-43
94/5 UpperDeck 360
95/6 UpperDeck 17, SE178
97/8 UpperDeck 338
95/6 UDBeAPlayer 83
95/6 UDCollChoice 269
97/8 UDCollChoice 197
96/7 PHO
97/8 PHO
95/6 WPG

DRAPEAU, ÉTIENNE
95/6 Bowman P12
95/6 Classic AS16
95/6 UpperDeck 514
95/6 Halifax

DRAPEAU, GASTON
90/1 SketchQMJHL 180
91/2 SketchQMJHL 124
80/1 QuébecRamparts

DRAPER, DAVE
83/4 Brantford 13

DRAPER, KRIS
93/4 Donruss 423
94/5 Donruss 182
96/7 Donruss 169
96/7 DonrussCanadianIce 92
94/5 Leaf 28
96/7 Leaf 119
92/3 O-Pee-Chee 374
92/3 opcPremier 27
98/9 Pacific 188
97/8 PacificRegime 68
90/1 Panini(WPG) 8
97/8 PinnacleBeAPlayer 20
95/6 POG 94
91/2 ProCards 177
90/1 Score 404
96/7 Score 192
97/8 Score(DET) 12
90/1 SketchOHL 83
92/3 Topps 249
98/9 Topps 168
94/5 ToppsStadiumClub 72
90/1 UpperDeck 466, 473
94/5 UpperDeck 492
95/6 UpperDeck 459
97/8 UpperDeck 62
94/5 UDBeAPlayer-Aut. 25
96/7 UDBlackDiamond 33
90/1 WPG/IGA
91/2 Moncton

DRAPER, TOM
92/3 Bowman 56
95/6 EdgeIce 160
92/3 FleerUltra 14
92/3 O-Pee-Chee 376
92/3 PaniniSticker 243
91/2 Parkhurst 240, 448
91/2 Pinnacle 341
88/9 ProCards(Moncton)
90/1 ProCards 554
91/2 ProCards 20
92/3 ProSet 14
92/3 Score 530
92/3 Topps 278
92/3 ToppsStadiumClub 395
91/2 UpperDeck 552
92/3 UpperDeck 201, 361
91/2 BUF/BlueShield
91/2 BUF/Campbell
89/90 WPG/Safeway
91/2 Rochester/Dunkin'Donuts
91/2 Rochester/Genny

DRAXLER, M.
95/6 DEL 377

DREGER, BARRY
88/9 Brandon 10

DREGER, RON
81/2 Saskatoon 12
83/4 Saskatoon 19
84/5 Saskatoon

DREVENY, GREG
89/90 SketchOHL 92
90/1 SketchOHL 2
91/2 SketchOHL 112
92/3 Sudbury 25

DREVITCH, SCOTT
88/9 ProCards(Maine)
89/90 ProCards(AHL) 76
91/2 Richmond 4
92/3 Richmond

DREVITCH, TODD
91/2 Richmond 6

DRILLON, GORDON
34-43 BeeHives(MTL.C), (TOR)
83&87 HallOfFame 109
83 HHOF Postcard (H)
37/8 OPC (V304E) 142
39/40 OPC (V301-1) 4
40/1 OPC (V301-2) 110
55/6 Parkhurst 25
38/9 QuakerOats

DRINKWATER, GRAHAM
96/7 HHOFLegends 85
83&87 HallOfFame 186
83 HHOF Postcard (J)

DRISCOLL, CHRIS
90/1 SketchOHL 283

DRISCOLL, PETER
76/7 opcWHA 45
79/80 EDM
88/9 EDM/ActionMagazine 7

DRISCOLL, STEVE
84/5 Fredericton 15

DRIVER, BRUCE
90/1 Bowman 87
91/2 Bowman 281
93/4 Donruss 185
96/7 FleerNHLPicks 156
92/3 FleerUltra 336
93/4 FleerUltra 214
95/6 FleerUltra 190
93/4 Leaf 56
94/5 Leaf 377
85/6 OPC/Topps 127
86/7 OPC/Topps 19
87/8 OPC/Topps 79
88/9 OPC/Topps 157
90/1 OPC/Topps 172
91/2 OPC/Topps 294
87/8 opcSticker 60/202
88/9 opcSticker 77/206
98/9 Pacific 292
97/8 PacificRegime 124
87/8 PaniniSticker 74
88/9 PaniniSticker 269
90/1 PaniniSticker 69
91/2 PaniniSticker 225
92/3 PaniniSticker 178

93/4 PaniniSticker 44
91/2 Parkhurst 322
92/3 Parkhurst 333
95/6 Parkhurst 413
91/2 Pinnacle 63
92/3 Pinnacle 278
93/4 Pinnacle 277
94/5 Pinnacle 126
97/8 PinnacleBeAPlayer 87
94/5 POG 150
93/4 PowerPlay 135
93/4 Premier 377
94/5 Premier 292
90/1 ProSet 166
91/2 ProSet 140, 577
92/3 ProSet 99
90/1 Score 109
92/3 Score 251
93/4 Score 263
94/5 Score 115
95/6 Score 257
97/8 Score(NYR) 11
92/3 Topps 384
98/9 Topps 41
91/2 ToppsStadiumClub 122
92/3 ToppsStadiumClub 376
93/4 ToppsStadiumClub 126
94/5 ToppsStadiumClub 35
90/1 UpperDeck 373
92/3 UpperDeck 200
97/8 UpperDeck 110
95/6 UDBeAPlayer 147
84/5 N.J.
86/7 N.J./SOBER
88/9 N.J./Caretta
89/90 N.J.
90/1 N.J.

DROLET, JIM
96/7 Fredericton

DROLET, NANCY
94/5 Classic W18
97/8 EssoOlympic 56
97/8 GeneralMills
97/8 UDCollChoice 277

DROPPA, IVAN
92/3 ClassicProspects 149
93/4 Classic 128
93/4 Donruss 414
93/4 FleerUltra 288
94/5 Leaf 112
93/4 Parkhurst 42
94/5 Parkhurst 49
94/5 ToppsStadiumClub 252
91/2 UpperDeck 'CzechWJC 98
94/5 UpperDeck 435
92/3 Indianapolis
93/4 Indianapolis

DROUILLARD, PHIL
82/3 NorthBay

DROUIN, CLAUDE
80/1 QuébecRamparts

DROUIN, ERIC
97/8 Bowman 67
98 BowmanCHL 111
96/7 Rimouski

DROUIN, JUDE
70/1 Colgate Stamp 18
70/1 EddieSargent 88
71/2 EddieSargent 82
72/3 EddieSargent 100
72/3 Letraset 21
74/5 Loblaws, -Update
70/1 OPC 171
71/2 OPC/Topps 68, -Booklet 21
72/3 OPC 47, Topps 153
73/4 OPC/Topps 125
74/5 OPC/Topps 255
75/6 OPC/Topps 223
76/7 OPC/Topps 106
77/8 OPC/Topps 182
78/9 OPC/Topps 93
79/80 O-Pee-Chee 329
80/1 O-Pee-Chee 285
80/1 Pepsi Cap
71/2 TheTorontoSun
73/4 MIN
79/80 WPG
80/1 WPG

DROUIN, PAUL (POLLY)
34-43 BeeHives(MTL.C)
35-40 CrownBrand 118
37/8 OPC (V304E) 158
39/40 OPC (V301-1) 24
38/9 QuakerOats
36/7 WWGum (V356) 50

DROZDETSKI, NIKOLAI
82 SemicSticker 63

DROZDIAK, DEAN
83/4 Victoria

DRUCE, JOHN
90/1 Bowman-HatTrick 16
91/2 Bowman 293, 413
92/3 Bowman 180
94/5 Donruss 223
92/3 FleerUltra 442
94/5 FleerUltra 98
94/5 Leaf 131
95/6 Leaf 107
92/3 O-Pee-Chee 105
90/1 OPC/Topps 298
91/2 OPC/Topps 206
92/3 opcPremier 80
97/8 PacificD-BestKept 69
91/2 PaniniSticker 200
95/6 PaniniSticker 269
91/2 Parkhurst 415
92/3 Parkhurst 437
91/2 Pinnacle 395
92/3 Pinnacle 185
94/5 Pinnacle 304
95/6 Pinnacle 113
94/5 POG 124
95/6 POG 135
93/4 PowerPlay 360
94/5 Premier(SpcFX) 549
89/90 ProCards'AHL 100
90/1 ProSet 310
91/2 ProSet 251
90/1 Score 246, -YoungStar 25
92/3 Score 121
97/8 Score(PHA) 19
92/3 Topps 188
95/6 Topps 111
91/2 ToppsStadiumClub 331
92/3 ToppsStadiumClub 405
94/5 ToppsStadiumClub 71
90/1 UpperDeck 371
92/3 UpperDeck 205
95/6 UDCollChoice 135
96/7 PHA/OceanSpray
89/90 WSH/Kodak
90/1 WSH/Kodak
90/1 WSH/Smokey
91/2 WSH
91/2 WSH/Kodak

DRUET, M.
85/6 Moncton 18

DRUKEN, HAROLD
97/8 Bowman 146
96/7 UpperDeck 380

DRULIA, STAN
95/6 EdgeIce 100, -Quantum 6
92/3 opcPremier 105
92/3 Parkhurst 177
93/4 Parkhurst 191
89/90 ProCards(AHL) 138
91/2 ProCards 379
92/3 UpperDeck 487
93/4 AtlantaKnights
84/5 Belleville 9
88/9 NiagaraFalls 16

DRUMM, BRIAN
93/4 Slapshot(Oshawa) 26

DRUMMOND, KURT
95/6 SwiftCurrent

DRURY, BRYAN
90/1 SketchOHL 284

DRURY, CHRIS
93/4 Classic 101
95/6 DonrussElite-WorldJrs 34
95/6 UpperDeck 569

DRURY, TED
93/4 Classic 63
94/5 Classic-Autograph
93/4 C4'Images 38
93/4 ClassicProspects 14, LP2
93/4 Donruss 58,437,-RtdRoo 14
94/5 Donruss 183
93/4 FleerUltra 280, -Wave 4
94/5 FleerUltra 88
93/4 Leaf 424
94/5 Leaf 22
97/8 PacificCrown 312
93/4 Parkhurst 35
94/5 Parkhurst 96
95/6 Parkhurst 422
93/4 Pinnacle 447
94/5 Pinnacle 187
97/8 PinnacleBeAPlayer 84
93/4 PowerPlay 303
94/5 Premier 157
93/4 Score 608
97/8 Score(ANA) 11
98/9 Topps 212
93/4 ToppsStadiumClub 443
92/3 UpperDeck 396
93/4 UpperDeck 466, SP20
94/5 UpperDeck 205
95/6 UpperDeck 298
96/7 UpperDeck 115
94/5 UDBeAPlayer-Aut. 34
96/7 UDCollChoice183
97/8 UDCollChoice 6
96/7 ANA/UpFrontSports 5
95/6 OTT

DRYDEN, DAVE
64-67 BeeHives(CHI)
65/6 CocaCola
70/1 Colgate Stamp 80
71/2 EddieSargent 32
72/3 EddieSargent 34
68/9 O-Pee-Chee 150
71/2 OPC/Topps 159
72/3 OPC 241
73/4 OPC 63, Topps 187
79/80 OPC/Topps 71
74/5 opcWHA 20
75/6 opcWHA 104
76/7 opcWHA 85
77/8 opcWHA 28
68/9 ShirriffCoin CHI 13
77-9 Sportscaster 82-23,85-2024
71/2 TheTorontoSun
67/8 Topps 57
72/3 BUF
73/4 BUF
75/6 BUF/Linnett
79/80 EDM
88/9 EDM/ActionMagazine 90

DRYDEN, KEN
71/2 Colgate Heads
72-84 Dernière 72/3
72/3 EddieSargent 124
88/9 Esso Sticker
71/2 FritoLay
83&87 HallOfFame 196
83 HHOF Postcard (N)
72/3 Letraset 2, 22
74/5 LiptonSoup 19
74/5 Loblaws
69/70 MästarSerien 26
71/2 OPC/Topps 45, Booklet 17
71/2 OPC-Poster 22
72/3 OPC 134, 145, 247
72/3 OPC-Crests 12,-TmCanada
72/3 Topps 127, 160, 174
73/4 OPC 136, Topps 4, 10
74/5 OPC/Topps 155
75/6 OPC/Topps 35, 213
76/7 OPC/. 6, 200, T-Glossy 5
77/8 OPC/T. 6, 8, 100,-Glossy 5
78/9 OPC/Topps 50, 68, 70, 262
79/80 OPC/Topps 6, 8, 83, 150
91 SemicSticker 236
77-9 Sportscaster 14-23,48-1145
71/2 TheTorontoSun
91/2 Trends (72) 31, 85, -Aut
96 Wien HL1
71 MTL/Pins
71/2 MTL (x2)
72/3 MTL
74/5 MTL
75/6 MTL
76/7 MTL
77/8 MTL
78/9 MTL
92/3 MTL/OPC 51
95/6 MTL/Forum 16Mar96

DUBÉ, CHRISTIAN
95/6 Classic 34
96/7 DonrussCanadianIce 146
95/6 DonrussElite-WorldJrs 13
96/7 D.Elite 137, -Aspirations 25
96/7 FleerUltra 104, -Rookies 5
96/7 LeafPreferred 135
97/8 Limited 46
96/7 MetalUniverse 176
97/8 PacificParamount 113
94/5 ParkieSE 258
96/7 PinnacleZenith 135
97/8 Score(NYR) 14
94/5 Select 166
96/7 SelectCertified 95
94/5 SP 179
95/6 SP 171
96/7 SP 183
96/7 UpperDeck 296
97/8 UpperDeck 105
96/7 UDBlackDiamond 79
96/7 UDCollChoice357
96/7 UpperDeck"Ice" 136

DUBÉ, DANY
92/3 CanadaNats
93/4 CanadaNats

DUBÉ, DANIELLE
97/8 UDCollChoice 288

DUBÉ, GILLES
45-64 BeeHives(MTL)
52/3 LavalDairy 50
52/3 StLawrence 75

DUBÉ, NORM
72-84 Dernière 78/9
77/8 opcWHA 54

DUBÉ, ROGER
93 Semic 262

DUBÉ, YANICK
94/5 Classsic C2
93/4 Donruss CAN9
93/4 Parkhurst 512
93/4 Pinnacle 471
94/5 SigRookies 3, -Promo 4
94/5 SRGoldStandard 82
91/2 SketchQMJHL 227
93/4 UpperDeck 533

DUBERMAN, JUSTIN
92/3 ClassicProspects 116
93/4 Donruss 471
92/3 Cleveland 18
93/4 Cleveland

DUBINSKY, MIKE
94/5 SigRookies 42
94/5 Slapshot(MEM) 37
92/3 Brandon 4

DUBINSKY, STEVE
93/4 Classic 64
93/4 ClassicProspects 7
93/4 Donruss 70
94/5 Donruss 26
94/5 Leaf 426
97/8 PacificDynag-BestKept 21
93/4 Parkhurst 40
97/8 PinnacleBeAPlayer 166
94/5 Premier 233
93/4 UpperDeck 477
92/3 Clarkson
93/4 Indianapolis

DUBOIS, ERIC
89/90 SketchMEM 68
90/1 SketchQMJHL 55
93/4 AtlantaKnights
91/2 Greensboro

DUBOIS, GUY
72 SemicSticker 152

DUBOIS, PIERRE
79/80 Montréal, -B&W

DUBOIS, ROB
93/4 Slapshot(Oshawa) 16
95/6 Slapshot 30

DUBUKOV, ILJA
93/4 Roanoke
94/5 Roanoke
95/6 Roanoke

DUCE, BRYAN
95/6 Slapshot 145

DUCHARME, BRUNO
90/1 SketchQMJHL 202
91/2 SketchQMJHL 250

DUCHARME, SYLVAIN
91/2 SketchQMJHL 278
93/4 Slapshot(Drum.) 7

DUCHESNE, ALEXANDRE
91/2 SketchQMJHL 290
93/4 Slapshot(Drum.) 24

DUCHESNE, ERIC
90/1 SketchQMJHL 37
91/2 SketchQMJHL 84

DUCHESNE, GAETAN
91/2 Bowman 120, 405
92/3 Bowman 266
93/4 Donruss 301
92/3 Durivage 22
93/4 Durivage 40
92/3 FleerUltra 318
93/4 Leaf 339
94/5 Leaf 547
88/9 O-Pee-Chee 208
90/1 OPC/Topps 319
91/2 OPC/Topps 433
92/3 O-Pee-Chee 143
88/9 opcSticker 187/56
89/90 opcSticker 194/48
87/8 PaniniSticker 183
88/9 PaniniSticker 353
90/1 PaniniSticker 256
91/2 PaniniSticker 117
93/4 PaniniSticker 273
91/2 Parkhurst 305
93/4 Parkhurst 456
92/3 Pinnacle 198
93/4 Pinnacle 377
94/5 Pinnacle 219
94/5 POG 211
95/6 POG 119
82/3 Post
93/4 PowerPlay 433
94/5 Premier 232
90/1 ProSet 137
91/2 ProSet 110
90/1 Score 375
92/3 Score 338
93/4 Score 226, 545
94/5 Score 196
92/3 Topps 406
91/2 ToppsStadiumClub 153
92/3 ToppsStadiumClub 307
90/1 UpperDeck 108
92/3 UpperDeck 469
87/8 QUE/GeneralFoods
88/9 QUE
88/9 QUE/GeneralFoods
93/4 S.J./Gameline
81/2 WSH
84/5 WSH/PizzaHut
85/6 WSH/PizzaHut
86/7 WSH/Kodak
86/7 WSH/Police
80/1 QuébecRamparts

DUCHESNE, PAUL
52/3 BasDuFleuve 46
51/2 LacStJean 45

DUCHESNE, STEVE
90/1 Bowman 146
91/2 Bowman 191, 421
92/3 Bowman 31
93/4 Donruss 276, 484
94/5 Donruss 304
95/6 Donruss 278
96/7 Donruss 182
92/3 Durivage 38
93/4 EASports 109
94/5 Flair 152
94/5 Fleer 186
96/7 Fleer 75
95/6 FleerMetal 105
92/3 FleerUltra 384
93/4 FleerUltra 7
94/5 FleerUltra 182
95/6 FleerUltra 138, 279
96/7 FleerUltra 117
93/4 HockeyWit 8
89/90 Kraft 58
90/1 Kraft 65
93/4 Leaf 176
94/5 Leaf 3
95/6 Leaf 143
94/5 LeafLimited 93
93/4 McDonalds M cD14
96/7 MetalUniverse 106
97/8 Omega 192
88/9 OPC/Topps 182
89/90 OPC/Topps 123, T-AS 10
90/1 OPC/Topps 86
91/2 OPC/Topps 31
92/3 O-Pee-Chee 296
91/2 opcPremier 13
92/3 opcPremier 130
88/9 opcSticker 152/19
89/90 opcSticker 150/10, 165/27
89/90 opcStickFS 32
98/9 Pacific 366
97/8 PacificCrown 302
97/8 PacificCrownRoyale 115
97/8 PacificInvincible 95
97/8 PacificRevolution 119
88/9 PaniniSticker 70
89/90 PaniniSticker 93, 176
90/1 PaniniSticker 241
91/2 PaniniSticker 80
92/3 PaniniSticker 192
93/4 PaniniSticker 76
94/5 PaniniSticker 143
95/6 PaniniSticker 195
96/7 PaniniSticker 50
97/8 PaniniSticker 45
95 PaniniWorlds 3
91/2 Parkhurst 125
92/3 Parkhurst 143
93/4 Parkhurst 168
94/5 Parkhurst 205, V26
95/6 Parkhurst 153
91/2 Pinnacle 42
92/3 Pinnacle 320
93/4 Pinnacle 78
94/5 Pinnacle 108
97/8 Pinnacle 142
96/7 PinnacleBeAPlayer 141
97/8 PinnacleInside 136
95/6 PinnacleZenith 111
95/6 Playoff 88
96/7 Playoff 347
94/5 POG 210
95/6 POG 196
94/5 Post
96/7 Post
93/4 PowerPlay 197
93/4 Prmr 151, -Black(Topps) 2
94/5 Premier 401
90/1 ProSet 115, 350
91/2 ProSet 96, 448
92/3 ProSet 137
90/1 Score 26, -HotCards 15
92/3 Score 151
93/4 Score 190, -PinnacleAS 16
94/5 Score 52
95/6 Score 99
96/7 Score 62
97/8 Score 230
97/8 Score(STL) 16
94/5 Select 145
91 SemicSticker 61
93 SemicSticker 194
95/6 SkyBoxEmotion 124
95/6 SkyBoxImpact 119
96/7 SkyBoxImpact 89
97/8 SPAuthentic 144
95/6 Summit 145
95/6 SuperSticker 87, -DieCut15
96/7 TeamOut
92/3 Topps 271
95/6 Topps 102, 337
98/9 Topps 44
95/6 ToppsFinest 17
96/7 ToppsNHLPicks 73
91/2 ToppsStadiumClub 58
92/3 ToppsStadiumClub 313
93/4 ToppsStadiumClub-AllStar
94/5 ToppsStadiumClub 81
95/6 ToppsStadiumClub 126
90/1 UpperDeck 136
92/3 UD 513, -LockerAS 2
93/4 UpperDeck 217
94/5 UpperDeck 108, SP158
95/6 UpperDeck 49, SE147
96/7 UpperDeck 304
97/8 UpperDeck 114
94/5 UDBAP R64, -Aut. 137
98/9 UDChoice 182
95/6 UDCollChoice 279
96/7 UDCollChoice 182
97/8 UDCollChoice 179
96 Wien 84
88/9 L.A.
88/9 L.A./Smokeys
89/90 L.A./Smokeys 14
90/1 L.A./Smokeys 15
95/6 OTT
96/7 OTT/PizzaHut
91/2 PHA/JCPenney
92/3 QUE/PetroCanada

DUCOLON, TONY
88/9 ProCards(Peoria)
89/90 ProCards(IHL) 12

DUDA, JASON
93/4 Saskatoon

DUDLEY, GEORGE
83&87 HallOfFame 68
83 HHOF Postcard (E)

DUDLEY, RICK
74/5 Loblaws
74/5 OPC 268
79/80 OPC/Topps 37
80/1 O-Pee-Chee 355
81/2 O-Pee-Chee 362
75/6 opcWHA 58
76/7 opcWHA 17
88/9 ProCards(NewHaven)
90/1 ProSet 662
73/4 BUF
74/5 BUF
80/1 BUF/Wendt
89/90 BUF/Campbell
90/1 BUF/Campbell
93/4 BUF/NOCO
75/6 Cincinnati
89/90 NewHaven
93/4 Phoenix
92/3 SanDiego

DUE-BOJE, CHRISTIAN
94/5 ElitSet 109, -GoldCard 4
95/6 ElitSet 28
94 Semic 55
95/6 udElite 39
97/8 udSwedish 169

DUELING, JARRETT
90/1 SketchWHL 308
91/2 SketchWHL 93

DUERDEN, DAVE
97/8 Bowman 3
95/6 Classic 94
95/6 Slapshot 321

DUFAULT, PASCAL
90/1 SketchQMJHL 76

DUFF, RICHARD (DICK)
45-64 BeeHives(TOR)
64-67 BeeHives(MTL)
63-5 ChexPhoto
64/5 CokeCap NYR-9
65/6 CocaCola
70/1 DadsCookies
70/1 EddieSargent 65
71/2 EddieSargent 24
68/9 O-Pee-Chee 161
69/70 O-Pee-Chee 11
71/2 OPC/Topps 164
55/6 Parkhurst 18
57/8 Parkhurst (TOR) 3
58/9 Parkhurst 29
59/60 Parkhurst 38
60/1 Parkhurst 12
61/2 Parkhurst 12
62/3 Parkhurst 2
63/4 Parkhurst 4, 64
92/3 Parkhurst 58 PR24
93/4 Parkie(56/7) 126
94/5 Parkie(64/5) 106
95/6 Parkie(66/7) 78
67 Post FlipBook
60/1 ShirriffCoin 2
61/2 ShirriffCoin 53
62/3 ShirriffCoin 12
68/9 ShirriffCoin MTL11
54-67 TorontoStar V7
56-66 TorontoStar 57/8, 58/9
63/4 TheTorontoStar
71/2 TheTorontoSun

64/5 Topps 46
65/6 Topps 7
66/7 Topps 71
67/8 Topps 2
60/1 York
60/1 YorkGlasses
61/2 York 2
62/3 YorkTransfer 7
63/4 York 9
67/8 York 26
67/8 MTL
67/8 MTL/IGA
68/9 MTL
64/5 TOR
80/1 TOR

DUFF, JOHN
91/2 FerrisState

DUFF, LES
52/3 AnonymousOHL 155

DUFFUS, PARRIS
91/2 AirCanadaSJHL D49
93/4 ClassicProspects 68
97/8 PinnacleInside 75
96/7 LasVegas
92/3 Peoria
93/4 Peoria

DUFFY, BEN
85/6 Minn-Duluth 31

DUFOUR, CLAUDE
51-54 LaPatrie 31Jan54

DUFOUR, GUY
72/3 O-Pee-Chee 328
73/4 OPC-Posters 3
73/4 QuébecNordiques

DUFOUR, LUC
83/4 O-Pee-Chee 48
84/5 O-Pee-Chee 3
83/4 opcSticker 172, 182
83/4 SouhaitsRen.KeyChain
83/4 BOS
84/5 QUE
84/5 Chicoutimi
83/4 Fredericton 3

DUFOUR, MARCEL
51/2 LacStJean 8

DUFRESNE, DAN
91/2 AirCanadaSJHL A36

DUFRESNE, DONALD
92/3 Durivage 39
93/4 FleerUltra 422
93/4 Leaf 355
90/1 Panini(MTL) 10
93/4 Parkhurst 467
88/9 ProCards(Sherbrooke)
90/1 ProSet 469
91/2 ProSet 418
90/1 ScoreTraded 35T
90/1 UpperDeck 332
94/5 UDBeAPlayer-Aut. 45
96/7 EDM
89/90 MTL
90/1 MTL
91/2 MTL
92/3 MTL

DUGGEN, BRAD
81/2 Saskatoon 5

DUGRÉ, YVAN
51/2 LavalDairy 49

DUGUAY, KEVIN
85/6 Kitchener 30

DUGUAY, RON
72-84 Dernière 82/3
78/9 OPC/Topps 177
79/80 OPC/Topps 208
80/1 OPC/Topps 37
81/2 OPC 223, Topps(E) 96
82/3 O-Pee-Chee 217, 221
83/4 O-Pee-Chee 121
84/5 OPC 52, Topps 40
85/6 OPC/Topps 116
87/8 OPC/Topps 110
81/2 opcSticker 171
82/3 opcSticker 134
84/5 opcSticker 42
85/6 opcSticker 32/162
87/8 PaniniSticker 119
89/90 PaniniSticker 96
82/3 Post
91/2 ProCards 317
83/4 PuffySticker 13
85/6 7Eleven 5
83/4 SouhaitsRen.KeyChain
84/5 DET/Caesars
85/6 DET/Caesars
88/9 L.A./Smokeys
86/7 PGH/Kodak

DUGUID, LORNE
33/4 CndGum (V252)
34/5 OPC (V304B) 58
33/4 WWGum (V357) 52

DUHAIME, TREVOR
90/1 SketchQMJHL 210
91/2 SketchQMJHL 165
92/3 Hampton

DUMART, WOODY (PORKY)
34-43 BeeHives(BOS)
45-64 BeeHives(BOS)
94/5 HHOFLegends 45
39/40 OPC (V301-1) 94
43-47 ParadeSportive
51/2 Parkhurst 28
52/3 Parkhurst 72
53/4 Parkhurst 96
93/4 Parkie(56/7) P9
91/2 BOS/Legends

DUMAS, MARK
88/9 ProCards(Binghampton)

DUMAS, ROGER
52/3 BasDuFleuve 22

DUMONSKI, STEVE
95/6 Slapshot 67

DUMONT, JEAN PIERRE
95/6 Bowman P13
97/8 Bowman 60
97/8 PinnacleBeeHive 68
98/9 UDChoice 271

DUMONT, LOUIS
90/1 SketchWHL 168
91/2 SketchWHL 222

DUMOULIN, MARIO
90/1 SketchQMJHL 120
91/2 SketchQMJHL 260

DUNBAR, DALE
85/6 Fredericton 24

DUNCAN, ART
19 Millionaires

DUNCAN, BRETT
94/5 Raleigh
95/6 SaintJohn
93/4 Seattle

DUNCAN, GLEN
81/2 Indianapolis 17
82/3 Indianapolis

DUNCAN, IAIN
88/9 O-Pee-Chee 209
89/90 O-Pee-Chee 293
88/9 opcSticker 32/268, 140/11
89/90 opcSticker136 /257
88/9 opcStickFS 6
88/9 PaniniSticker 154
89/90 PaniniSticker 170
90/1 ProCards 249
87/8 WPG
88/9 WPG/Police
89/90 WPG/Safeway
90/1 WPG/IGA
87/8 Moncton
89/90 Moncton
90/1 Moncton
92/3 Toledo (1), (2)

DUNCAN, TREVOR
89/90 Rayside

DUNCANSON, CRAIG
90/1 ProCards 248
91/2 ProCards 566
89/90 L.A/Smokeys 19
91/2 Baltimore 13
92/3 Binghampton
94/5 Binghampton
90/1 Moncton
85/6 Sudbury 19

DUNCON, IAIN
94/5 Toledo

DUNDAS, ROCKY
88/9 ProCards(Sherbrooke)
83/4 Kelowna
84/5 KelownaWings 17
82/3 Regina 7
83/4 Regina 7

DUNDERDALE, TOM
91 C55 Reprint 6
83&87 HallOfFame 127
83 HHOF Postcard (I)
1911-12 Imperial (C55) 6
1910-11 Imperial (C56) 14
1912-13 Imperial (C57) 5
1910-11 Imperial Post 6

DUNHAM, MIKE
93/4 Classic 56
94/5 Classic-Aut.
94/5 C'FourSport 148
94/5 ClassicImages 61
93/4 C4'Images 20
93/4 ClassicProspects LP3
97/8 Donruss 93
97/8 DonrussCanadianIce 87
97/8 DonrussElite 59
97/8 D.Preferred 40,-ColGurd 17
97/8 DonrussPriority 86
97/8 DonrussStudio 56
95/6 EdgeIce 6, TW10
93/4 FleerUltra 481
95/6 FutureLegends 3, -Pltnm 1
97/8 Leaf 104, -PipeDreams 16
97/8 Limited 78, 194, -fabric 41
98/9 Pacific 262
97/8 PacificDynag-BestKept 106
98/9 PcfcParamnt 122,-Glove 9
97/8 PacificRegime 110
97/8 Pinnacle 79
96/7 PinnacleBeAPlayer 212
97/8 PinnacleBeAPlayer 110
93/4 PowerPlay 501
93/4 Premier-TeamUSA 1
97/8 Score 45, 269
97/8 Score(N.J.) 13
94 Semic 108
93/4 T.StadiumClub-TeamUSA 4
91/2 UD 693, 'CzechWJC 80
96/7 UDBlackDiamond 3
92/3 Maine (1) 2, (2) 18

DUNK, BRETT
87/8 Brockville 21

DUNLOP, BLAKE
74/5 Loblaws
74/5 OPC 308
75/6 OPC/Topps 16
76/7 OPC/Topps 263
79/80 OPC/Topps 174
80/1 O-Pee-Chee 370
81/2 OPC 293, Topps(W) 117
82/3 O-Pee-Chee 301
83/4 O-Pee-Chee 314
81/2 opcSticker 131
82/3 opcSticker 199
83/4 opcSticker 131
82/3 Post
83/4 PuffySticker 13
92/3 STL/UpperDeck 5

DUNN, DAVE
74/5 Loblaws, -Update
74/5 OPC/Topps 152
75/6 OPC/Topps 187
74/5 TOR
75/6 TOR
73/4 VAN/RoyalBank

DUNN, JAMIE
83&87 HallOfFame 217
83 HHOF Postcard (O)
92/3 MPSPhotoSJHL 161

DUNN, JAY
91/2 AirCanadaSJHL 2, A28

DUNN, PAT
95 PaniniWorlds 110
92 SemicSticker 233
93 SemicSticker 263

DUNN, RICHIE
80/1 OPC/Topps 109
81/2 O-Pee-Chee 29
82/3 O-Pee-Chee 45
83/4 O-Pee-Chee 137
84/5 O-Pee-Chee 69
82/3 Post
88/9 ProCards(Rochester)
89/90 ProCards(AHL) 259
83/4 SouhaitsRen.KeyChain
80/1 BUF/Wendt
81/2 BUF 7
82/3 CGY
83/4 HFD/JuniorWhalers

DUNNIGAN, DAVE
91/2 AvantGardeBCJHL 65, 157

DUNPHY, SERGE
95/6 Slapshot 404
92/3 Oshawa

DUNSTAN, GEORDIE
92/3 BCJHL 102

DUPAUL, COSMO
93/4 ClassicFourSport 215

DUPÈRE, DENIS
72/3 EddieSargent 210
71/2 OPC 200
72/3 OPC 167
73/4 OPC 210
74/5 OPC/Topps 105, 219
75/6 OPC/Topps 159
76/7 OPC 334
77/8 OPC 388
78/9 O-Pee-Chee 283
71/2 TheTorontoSun
76/7 COL.R/CokeCans
77/8 COL.R/CokeCans
71/2 TOR
72/3 TOR
73/4 TOR
74/5 WSH

DUPERRON, CHRISTIAN
84/5 Chicoutimi

DUPONT, ANDRÉ
72-84 Dernière 79/80, 81/2
72/3 EddieSargent 194
74/5 Loblaws
72/3 OPC 16, Topps 19
73/4 OPC 113, Topps 183
74/5 OPC/Topps 67
75/6 OPC/Topps 56, 211
76/7 OPC/Topps 131
77/8 OPC/Topps 164
78/9 OPC/Topps 98
79/80 OPC/Topps 178
81/2 O-Pee-Chee 273
82/3 O-Pee-Chee 282
80/1 Pepsi Cap
82/3 Post
75/6 PHA/GingerAle
80/1 QUE
81/2 QUE
82/3 QUE
83/4 QUE
71/2 STL
72/3 STL/8"x10"

DUPONT, JEROME
81/2 CHI
86/7 TOR

DUPONT, NORMAND
81/2 O-Pee-Chee 363
82/3 O-Pee-Chee 378
81/2 opcSticker 139
80/1 Pepsi Cap
82/3 Post
83/4 SouhaitsRen.KeyChain
83/4 HFD/JuniorWhalers
79/80 MTL
80/1 WPG
81/2 WPG
82/3 WPG
77/8 NovaScotia

DUPONT, YAN
96/7 Rimouski

DUPRÉ, YANICK
91/2 Classic 41
91/2 ClassicFourSport 41, -Aut.
91/2 opcPremier 16
90/1 SketchMEM 59, 126
90/1 SketchQMJHL 200
91/2 SketchQMJHL 284
91/2 StarPics 44
92/3 Topps 515
92/3 ToppsStadiumClub 137
91/2 UltimateDP 36, 88, -Aut. 36
92/3 UpperDeck 421
94/5 PHA

DUPUIS, BOB
88/9 EDM/ActionMagazine 118

DUPUIS, GUY
90/1 ProCards 478
91/2 ProCards 137
87/8 Hull

DUPUIS, LORI
97/8 UDCollChoice 291

DUPUIS, MARC
95/6 Slapshot 38

DUPUIS, YVON
77/8 Kalamazoo

DURAND, BRIAN
85/6 Minn-Duluth 25

DURAND, ERIC
93 SemicSticker 253

DURBANO, STEVE
74/5 Loblaws
73/4 OPC 124, Topps 168
74/5 OPC/Topps 106
76/7 OPC/Topps 4, 19, T. 384
76/7 COL.R
74/5 PGH
72/3 STL
72/3 STL/8"x10"
73/4 STL

DURDLE, DARREN
96/7 DEL 27

DURIS, M.
95/6 DEL 108

DURIS, VITEZSLAV
81/2 O-Pee-Chee 316
80/1 Pepsi Cap
80/1 TOR

DURNAN, BILL
45-64 BeeHives(MTL)
51 BerkRoss 17-Jan
83&87 HallOfFame 139
83 HHOF Postcard (K)
93/4 HighLiner 12
91/2 Kraft 37
43-47 ParadeSportive (x3)
55/6 Parkhurst 63
94/5 Parkie(64/5)-Greats 6
45-54 QuakerOats
92/3 MTL/OPC 47
95/6 MTL/Forum 16Dec95

DUROCHER, ANDRÉ
90/1 SketchQMJHL 257

DUSBALON, BEN
96/7 Halifax (1), (2)

DUSSAULT, NORMAND
45-64 BeeHives(MTL)
51/2 LavalDairy 22
43-47 ParadeSportive
45-54 QuakerOats
52/3 StLawrence 96

DUSTIN, BOB
92/3 Minnesota
93/4 Minnesota
94/5 Minnesota

DUTHIE, RYAN
91/2 SketchWHL 17
95/6 Adirondack
94/5 SaintJohn

DUTIAUME, MARK
95/6 Classic 37
94/5 Slapshot(MEM) 41

DUTIAUME, TODD
91/2 SketchWHL 198
92/3 Brandon 5

DUTIL, CHRIS
91/2 AirCanadaSJHL A33
92/3 MPSPhotoSJHL 158

DUTKOWSKI, DUKE
33/4 CndGum (V252)
33-35 DiamondMatch
23/4 PaulinsCandy 26
33/4 WWGum (V357) 56

DUTTON, RED
33/4 Anonymous (V129) 23
34-43 BeeHives(NYA)
33/4 CndGum (V252)
33-35 DiamondMatch
36-39 DiamondMatch (1), (2), (3)
83&87 HallOfFame 7
83 HHOF Postcard (A)
27-32 LaPresse 28/9
23/4 PaulinsCandy 62
60/1 Topps 16
33/4 WWGum (V357) 25
36/7 WWGum (V356) 14

DUUS, JESPER
97/8 DEL 185
94/5 ElitSet 122
95/6 ElitSet 217
95/6 udElite 57

DUVAL, JON
90/1 SketchWHL 39
91/2 SketchWHL 315
94/5 Birmingham

DUVAL, LUC
84/5 Chicoutimi

DUVAL, MURRAY
91/2 ProCards 312
89/90 SketchMEM 21
90/1 SketchWHL 302
89/90 Kamloops

DVORAK, MIROSLAV
79 PaniniSticker 78
82 SemicSticker 83
83/4 SouhaitsRen.Key Chain
83/4 PHA

DVORAK, RADEK
96/7 AllSportPPF 99, 173
95/6 Bowman 130, BB22
95/6 Classic 10, -Aut.
95/6 ClassicFiveSport 156
95/6 Donruss 277, -Rated 10
96/7 Donruss 213
95/6 DonrussElite 19, -Rookie 10
96/7 DonrussElite 105
95/6 FleerMetal 176
95/6 FleerUltra 338, -Extra 3
96/7 FleerUltra 64
96/7 Leaf 160
95/6 LeafLimited 10, -Rookie 7
96/7 MetalUniverse 57
98/9 Pacific 220
97/8 PacificCrown 50
97/8 PaniniSticker 71
97/8 PaniniSticker 56
95/6 Parkhurst 260, 508, PP45
95/6 P.Zenith 147, -RookieRoll 2
96/7 Score 247
97/8 Score 221
95/6 SelectCertified 133
94/5 SigRookies 39
95/6 SkyBoxImpact 200
96/7 SkyBoxImpact 44
95/6 SP 59
95/6 Summit 169
96/7 Summit 169
95/6 Tetrad 62
95/6 TetradAutobilia 42
95/6 Topps 319
95/6 ToppsFinest 125
95/6 ToppsStadiumClub 200
95/6 ToppsSuperSkills SR10
95/6 UpperDeck 260, H26
97/8 UpperDeck 71
95/6 UDBeAPlayer 163
95/6 UDCollChoice 398
96/7 UDCollChoice 348
97/8 UDCollChoice 103
96/7 FLA/WinnDixie
97/8 FLA/WinnDixie

DWYER, GORDIE
97/8 Bowman 53
94/5 Slapshot(MEM) 61

DYCK, ED
72/3 VAN/RoyalBank

DYCK, JOEL
90/1 SketchWHL 57
91/2 SketchWHL 138

DYCK, LARRY
88/9 ProCards(Kalamazoo)
89/90 ProCards(IHL) 93
90/1 ProCards 104
91/2 ProCards 143

DYCK, MIKE
86/7 Regina
87/8 Regina
88/9 Regina

DYCK, PAUL
90/1 SketchWHL 160
92/3 Cleveland 25
93/4 Cleveland
91/2 ProCards 304

DYE, CECIL (BABE)
24/5 Champs (C144)
83 HHOF Postcard (C)
83&87 HallOfFame 34
94/5 HHOFLegends 51
23/4 (V145-1) 23
24/5 (V145-2) 54

DYER, DEAN
89/90 Victoria

DYER, KELLY
94/5 Classic W22

DYHR, NICK
92/3 MPSPhotoSJHL 70

DYKEMAN, ROB
90/1 SketchMEM 36
90/1 SketchOHL 33
91/2 SketchOHL 20
91/2 Cornwall 26

DYKHUIS, KARL
90/1 CanadaNats
91/2 CanadaNats
92 CanadaWinterOlympics 199
92/3 FleerUltra 274
95/6 FleerUltra 283
95/6 Leaf 264
97/8 Omega 209
91/2 OPC/Topps 172
98/9 Pacific 399
97/8 PacificParamount 172
98/9 PacificParamount 217
97/8 PacificRegime 141
95/6 PaniniSticker 122
96/7 PaniniSticker 121
91/2 Parkhurst 262
94/5 ParkieSE 34
93/4 PowerPlay 48
90/1 Score 437
92/3 Score 462
90/1 SketchQMJHL 229
95/6 Topps 118
90/1 UpperDeck 471
91/2 UD 688, 'CzechWJC 62
92/3 UpperDeck 404
93/4 UpperDeck 106
96/7 UpperDeck 311
95/6 UDBeAPlayer 75
91/2 CHI/Coke
94/5 PHA
96/7 PHA/OceanSpray
93/4 Indianapolis

DYKSTRA, STEVE
87/8 opcSticker 146/7
90/1 ProCards 317
85/6 BUF
86/7 BUF
87/8 BUF/WonderBread
88/9 EDM/ActionMagazine 38

DYLLA, E.
95/6 DEL 22

DYNES, BILL
83/4 Brantford 30

DZIEDZIC, JOE
94/5 Classic 37
95/6 Donruss 235
95/6 FleerUltra 339
97/8 PacificCrown 305
96/7 PinnacleBeAPlayer 149
94/5 SigRookies 67
95/6 Topps 336
95/6 UpperDeck 429
96/7 UpperDeck 136
96/7 UDCollChoice 216
97/8 UDCollChoice 213
95/6 PGH/Foodland 13
91/2 Minnesota
92/3 Minnesota
93/4 Minnesota

DZIKOWSKI, JOHN
83/4 Brandon 4
84/5 Brandon 7
85/6 Brandon 7

DZURILLA, VLADIMIR
72 Hellas 80
70/1 Kuvajulkaisut 43
69/70 MästarSerien
92/3 Trends(76) 152
72/3 WilliamsFIN 3

E

EAGLES, MIKE
83 CanadaJuniors
87/8 O-Pee-Chee 253
88/9 opcSticker 191/58
97/8 PacificD-BestKept 101
87/8 PaniniSticker 170
88/9 PaniniSticker 354
91/2 Parkhurst 420
93/4 Parkhurst 229
97/8 PinnacleBeAPlayer 149
93/4 Premier 116
89/90 ProCards(IHL) 68
90/1 ProCards 395
91/2 ProSet 518
92/3 Score 345
93/4 Score 429
93/4 ToppsStadiumClub 14
94/5 UDBeAPlayer-Aut. 157
88/9 CHI/Coke
85/6 QUE
85/6 QUE/GeneralFoods
85/6 QUE/McDonald
85/6 QUE/Provigo
86/7 QUE
86/7 QUE/GeneralFoods
86/7 QUE/McDonald
87/8 QUE/GeneralFoods
95/6 WSH
91/2 WPG/IGA
93/4 WPG/Ruffles
83/4 Fredericton 24
84/5 Fredericton 20
82/3 Kitchener 19

EAKIN, BRUCE
94/5 DEL 91
95/6 DEL 93
96/7 DEL 234
84/5 Moncton 22
85/6 NovaScotia 27
81/2 Saskatoon 9

EAKINS, DALLAS
97/8 PinnacleBeAPlayer 86
88/9 ProCards(Baltimore)
89/90 ProCards(AHL) 41
90/1 ProCards 253
91/2 ProCards 170
97/8 FLA/WinnDixie
96/7 PHO
90/1 Moncton
91/2 Moncton

EARHART, BARRY
86/7 London 9

EARL, TOM
72/3 NewEngland

EAST, JOHN
89/90 SketchOHL 62

EASTWOOD, MIKE
95/6 Donruss 207
94/5 Leaf 378
95/6 Leaf 299
97/8 PacificRegime 125
95/6 PaniniSticker 213
92/3 Parkhurst 494
94/5 ParkieSE 183
95/6 Playoff 216
96/7 Playoff 399
94/5 POG 232
95/6 POG 290
91/2 ProCards 358
94/5 ToppsStadiumClub 167
93/4 UpperDeck 57
95/6 UpperDeck 292
95/6 UDBeAPlayer 102
97/8 PHO
92/3 TOR/Kodak
93/4 TOR/Abalene
93/4 TOR/Blacks 19
94/5 TOR
95/6 WPG
92/3 StJohns

EATON, J.D.
90/1 SketchOHL 382
91/2 SketchOHL 42
90/1 Sudbury 20

EATOUGH, JEFF
82/3 NorthBay

EAVES, MIKE
80/1 OPC/Topps 206
81/2 O-Pee-Chee 171
83/4 O-Pee-Chee 79
84/5 O-Pee-Chee 221
85/6 O-Pee-Chee 213
84/5 opcSticker 244
79 PaniniSticker 222
90/1 ProCards 26
91/2 ProCards 286
83/4 Vachon 4
80/1 MIN
81/2 MIN
82/3 MIN
89/90 PHA

EAVES, MURRAY
83/4 O-Pee-Chee 384
88/9 ProCards(Adirondack)
89/90 ProCards(AHL) 324

EBERLE, DEREK
90/1 SketchWHL 184
91/2 SketchWHL 229

EBERLE, GREG
88/9 ProCards(Peoria)
92/3 Peoria
93/4 Peoria

EBERLE, JÖRG
95 Globe 210
95 PaniniWorlds 127
95 Semic 192
91 SemicSticker 188
92 SemicSticker 208
93 SemicSticker 122
92/3 UpperDeck 384

EBERMANN, BOHUSLAV
79 PaniniSticker 89

ECCLESTONE, TIM
68/9 Bauer
71/2 Bazooka Panel 27
70/1 Colgate Stamp 58
70/1 DadsCookies
70/1 EddieSargent 188
71/2 EddieSargent 56
72/3 EddieSargent 78
70/1 Esso Stamp
72/3 Letraset 9
74/5 Loblaws
68/9 O-Pee-Chee 178
69/70 O-Pee-Chee 179
70/1 OPC/Topps 102, -Sticker
71/2 OPC/Topps 52
72/3 OPC 55, Topps 33
73/4 OPC 144, Topps 124
74/5 OPC 323
76/7 OPC 351
77/8 OPC 364
71/2 TheTorontoSun
74/5 ATL
77/8 ATL

ECKMAIER, J.
95/6 DEL 382

EDBERG, ROLF
80/1 OPC/Topps 65
79 PaniniSticker 194
82 SemicSticker 21
78/9 WSH
79/80 WSH
80/1 WSH

EDDOLLS, FRANK
45-64 BeeHives(NYR)
43-47 ParadeSportive
51/2 Parkhurst 89
45-54 QuakerOats

EDER, STEPHAN
94/5 DEL 332

EDESTRAND, DARRYL
72/3 EddieSargent 181
74/5 Loblaws
71/2 OPC/Topps 187
72/3 OPC 195
73/4 OPC 216
74/5 OPC 313
75/6 OPC/Topps 11
76/7 OPC/Topps 179
77/8 OPC 321
78/9 OPC 377
79/80 OPC 280
71/2 TheTorontoSun
71/2 PGH

EDGER, TREVOR
95/6 Slapshot 241

EDGERTON, DEVIN
93/4 AtlantaKnights
95/6 Phoenix
92/3 Wheeling 7

EDGGINSTON
91/2 AvantGardeBCJHL 161

EDLUND, PAR
94/5 ElitSet 106
95/6 ElitSet 142
95/6 udElite 216
97/8 udSwedish 75

EDMOND, DOMINIC
84/5 Richelieu

EDMONDS, RANDY
94/5 ElitSet 305

EDMUNDSON, GARRY
45-64 BeeHives(TOR)
59/60 Parkhurst 48
60/1 Parkhurst 5
60/1 ShirriffCoin 14

EDMUNDSON, MARK
92/3 Ottawa67s

EDSTROM, LARRY
94/5 ElitSet 176
95/6 ElitSet 202
95/6 udElite 214

EDUR, TOM
77/8 OPC/Topps 169
78/9 OPC/Topps 119
76/7 COL.R
76/7 COL.R/CokeCans
77/8 COL.R/CokeCans

EDWARDS, DAN
83/4 SouhaitsRen.KeyChain
89/90 Oshawa 14
90/1 Oshawa 8

EDWARDS, DON
77/8 OPC/Topps 201
78/9 O-Pee-Chee 336
78/9 OPC/Topps 70, 150
79/80 OPC/Topps 105
80/1 OPC/Topps 92, 166, 215
81/2 OPC 21, 389, Topps(E) 75
82/3 O-Pee-Chee 46
83/4 O-Pee-Chee 80
84/5 O-Pee-Chee 222, 223, 229
85/6 O-Pee-Chee 183
81/2 opcSticker 55
82/3 opcSticker 124
86/7 opcSticker 139/249
82/3 Post
83/4 PuffySticker 2
82/3 StaterMint
83/4 Vachon 5
79/80 BUF/BellsMarket
80/1 BUF/Wendt
81/2 BUF 3
82/3 CGY
85/6 TOR

EDWARDS, GARY
72/3 Letraset 23
74/5 Loblaws
71/2 OPC/Topps 155
72/3 OPC 113, -Crests 9, T. 151
73/4 OPC 199
75/6 OPC/Topps 105
76/7 OPC 365
77/8 OPC 345
78/9 OPC/Topps 6
80/1 OPC 335
71/2 TheTorontoSun
88/9 EDM/ActionMagazine 78
78/9 MIN/Cloverleaf 5
79/80 MIN
80/1 MIN

EDWARDS, MARVEN
52/3 AnonymousOHL 17

EDWARDS, MARV
72/3 EddieSargent 49
69/70 O-Pee-Chee 185
69/70 TOR

EDWARDS, PAUL
80/1 Oshawa 10
81/2 Oshawa 8

EDWARDS, RAY
92/3 Dayton
93/4 Dayton 13
94/5 Huntington 7

EDWARDS, ROY
71/2 Bazooka Panel 21
70/1 DadsCookies
70/1 EddieSargent 62
71/2 EddieSargent 167
72/3 EddieSargent 174
70/1 Esso Stamp
68/9 O-Pee-Chee 144
69/70 OPC/Topps 56
70/1 OPC/Topps 21
71/2 OPC/Topps 99
73/4 OPC/Topps 82
72 SemicSticker 192
68/9 ShirriffCoin DET7
71/2 TheTorontoSun
67/8 Topps 106
70/1 DET/Marathon
71/2 PGH

EDWARDS, TROY
91/2 AirCanadaSJHL A44
92/3 MPSPhotoSJHL 1

EDWARDS, WALTER
95/6 Tallahassee 25

EGAN, MARTIN (PAT)
34-43 BeeHives(NYA)
45-64 BeeHives(BOS), (NYR)

EGELAND, ALLAN
90/1 SketchWHL 126
91/2 SketchWHL 169
92/3 Tacoma
93/4 Tacoma

EGELAND, TRACEY
90/1 ProCards 404
91/2 ProCards 481
92/3 Indianapolis

EGEN, ULRICH
82 SemicSticker 109

EGERS, JACK
72/3 EddieSargent 196
70/1 Esso Stamp
74/5 Loblaws
72/3 OPC 107, Topps 147
73/4 OPC/Topps 79
74/5 OPC/Topps 93
75/6 OPC/Topps 134
71/2 TheTorontoSun
71/2 STL
72/3 STL
72/3 STL/8"x10"
74/5 WSH

EGGER, HEINZ
72 SemicSticker 101

EGGER, K.H.
72 Hellas 50

EGO, KLAUS
72 SemicSticker 103

EHMAN, GERRY
45-64 BeeHives(TOR)
70/1 DadsCookies
70/1 EddieSargent 144
70/1 Esso Stamp
68/9 OPC/Topps 84
69/70 OPC/Topps 83
70/1 OPC 187
59/60 Parkhurst 19
60/1 Parkhurst 8
60/1 ShirriffCoin 19
68/9 ShirriffCoin OAK1

EHRMANTRAUT, LYLE
92/3 MPSPhotoSJHL 57

EIBL, MICHAEL
72 Hellas 58

EICHENMANN, ZDENEK
94/5 APS 14
95/6 APS 114

EICHSTADT, SCOTT
91/2 ProCards 99

EIGNER, TRENT
94/5 Huntington 8

EIMANSBERGER, JOHANN
72 Hellas 56
72 SemicSticker 100

EIRICKSON, SHANE
85/6 Brandon 23

EISEBITT, TORSTEN
94/5 DEL 398
95/6 DEL 418

EISELT, VACLAV
94/5 APS 273
95/6 APS 144

EISENHUT, NEIL
93/4 ClassicProspects 199
95/6 EdgeIce 172
93/4 PowerPlay 459
91/2 ProCards 599
92/3 Hamilton
94/5 SaintJohn

EISKONEN, MARKKU
66/7 Champion 89
65/6 Hellas 95

EK, MAARKO
92/3 Jyvas-Hyva 165
93/4 Jyvas-Hyva 149
93/4 Sisu 151
94/5 Sisu 131
96/7 Sisu 117

EKELUND, PETER
94/5 ElitSet 293
95/6 ElitSet 58
95/6 udElite 87
97/8 udSwedish 93

EKLUND, PER-ERIK (PELLE)
90/1 Bowman 107
91/2 Bowman 241
92/3 Bowman 179
93/4 Donruss 250
94/5 ElitSet 243
95/6 ElitSet 71, -Champs 13
95/6 Elit-Mega 11, -Super
92/3 FleerUltra 155
93/4 FleerUltra 386
93/4 Leaf 177
87/8 OPC/Topps 98
88/9 O-Pee-Chee 211
89/90 O-Pee-Chee 317
90/1 OPC/Topps 254
91/2 OPC/Topps 111
92/3 O-Pee-Chee 242
87/8 OPCStars 9
86/7 opcSticker 127/113
89/90 opcSticker 105/242
87/8 PaniniSticker 132
89/90 PaniniSticker 296
90/1 PaniniSticker 113
91/2 PaniniSticker 228
92/3 PaniniSticker 189
93/4 PaniniSticker 51
95 PaniniWorlds 156
91/2 Parkhurst 128
93/4 Parkhurst 147
94/5 Parkhurst 56
91/2 Pinnacle 134
92/3 Pinnacle 149
93/4 Pinnacle 256
93/4 PowerPlay 180
93/4 Premier 449
90/1 ProSet 215
91/2 ProSet 179
90/1 Score(U.S) 308
92/3 Score 173
93/4 Score 181
89 SemicSticker 19
91 SemicSticker 210
92 SemicSticker 71
93 SemicSticker 39
92/3 Topps 117
91/2 ToppsStadiumClub 182
92/3 ToppsStadiumClub 154
93/4 ToppsStadiumClub 289
90/1 UpperDeck 138
93/4 UpperDeck 120
95/6 udElite 101, 228, 254
97/8 udSwedish 108, 213, S6
96 Wien 66, AS5
86/7 PHA
89/90 PHA
90/1 PHA
91/2 PHA/JCPenney
92/3 PHA/JCPenney
92/3 PHA/UD 28JAN93
93/4 PHA 21OCT93
93/4 PHA/JCPenney
94/5 PHA

EKLUND, PER
94/5 ElitSet 194, -Rookie 5
95/6 ElitSet 34
95/6 udElite 50, 222, NA5
96 Wien 69

EKLUND, THOM
89 SemicSticker 13

EKMAN, KEN
72 SemicSticker 64

EKRT, MARTIN
96/7 DEL 329

ELCOMBE, KELLY
82/3 Fredericton 11

ELDEBRINK, ANDERS
89 SemicSticker 9
93 SemicSticker 20
95/6 udElite DS6
97/8 udSwedish 167, 208, C27
81/2 VAN
81/2 VAN/Silverwood
82/3 Fredericton 9

ELDER, BRIAN
97/8 Bowman 102
94/5 Slapshot(MEM) 27

ELDERS, JASON
92/3 BCJHL 241

ELIAS, PATRIK
94/5 APS 64
97/8 DonrussElite 65
97/8 D.Priority 170,-DirDep 24
97/8 KatchMedallion 80
97/8 Omega 128
98/9 Pacific 26,-GoldCrown 19
97/8 PacificCrownRoyale 74
98/9 PacificParamount 133
97/8 PacificRegime 111
97/8 PacificRevolution 76
97/8 P.BAP 228, -OneTimers 16
97/8 P.BeeHive 53,-TeamBH 20
96/7 SP 180
98/9 SPx"Finite" 49, 123
97/8 SPAuthentic 185, I16
98/9 Topps 62, A7, SB9
97/8 UpperDeck 189
97/8 UDBlackDiamond 44, PC8
98/9 UDChoice 114, SQ12
97/8 UpperDeckIce 60, L7A
97/8 Zenith 81,Z69,-RookRgn 14
97/8 Zenith - RookieZTeam 16
96/7 N.J/Sharp

ELIASSON, MAGNUS
95/6 udElite 91

ELICH, MATT
97/8 Bowman 124
95/6 Slapshot 418

ELIGH, JARRETT
88/9 Brockville 16

ELIK, TODD
90/1 Bowman 151
91/2 Bowman 185
92/3 Bowman 317
93/4 Donruss 489
94/5 Donruss 163
95/6 Donruss 388
94/5 Flair 162
92/3 FleerUltra 93
94/5 FleerUltra 193
94/5 Leaf 226
95/6 Leaf 165
92/3 O-Pee-Chee 20
90/1 OPC/Topps 352
91/2 OPC/Topps 251
91/2 opcPremier 74
91/2 PaniniSticker 85
93/4 PaniniSticker 238
94/5 PaniniSticker 218
91/2 Parkhurst 300
92/3 Parkhurst 77, 292
93/4 Parkhurst 71
94/5 Parkhurst 210
91/2 Pinnacle 264
92/3 Pinnacle 207
93/4 Pinnacle 202
94/5 Pinnacle 275
95/6 Playoff 118
94/5 POG 212
93/4 PowerPlay 80, 434
94/5 Premier 76
89/90 ProCards(AHL) 10
90/1 ProSet 116
91/2 ProSet 94, 410
90/1 Score 297
92/3 Score 307
93/4 Score 185, 581
94/5 Score 125
95/6 Score 58
92/3 Topps 97
91/2 ToppsStadiumClub 310
92/3 ToppsStadiumClub 226
93/4 ToppsStadiumClub 363
90/1 UpperDeck 233
92/3 UpperDeck 210
94/5 UpperDeck 363
95/6 UpperDeck 479
95/6 UDBeAPlayer 89
92/3 EDM
93/4 EDM 06OCT93
90/1 L.A./Smokeys 5
93/4 S.J./Gameline
83/4 Kingston 15
84/5 Kingston 8

ELIOT, DAREN
87/8 PaniniSticker 272
84/5 L.A./Smokeys
88/9 L.A.

ELLACOTT, KEN
82/3 VAN

ELLETT, BOB
84/5 Ottawa67s

ELLETT, DAVE
90/1 Bowman 132
91/2 Bowman 163
92/3 Bowman 204, 291
93/4 Donruss 344
94/5 Donruss 230
95/6 Donruss 340
93/4 EASports 134
94/5 Flair 178
94/5 Fleer 213
92/3 FleerUltra 209
93/4 FleerUltra 38
94/5 FleerUltra 213
91/2 Gillette 17
92/3 HumptyDumpty (2)
89/90 Kraft 49
93/4 Leaf 86
94/5 Leaf 35
92/3 McDonalds McD-05
85/6 O-Pee-Chee 185
86/7 OPC/Topps 144
87/8 OPC/Topps 35
88/9 OPC/Topps 167
89/90 OPC/Topps 69
90/1 OPC/Topps 104
91/2 OPC/Topps 381
92/3 O-Pee-Chee 9
91/2 opcPremier 180
87/8 opcSticker 251/142
88/9 opcSticker 150
89/90 opcSticker 139
98/9 Pacific 78
97/8 PacificParamount 13
98/9 PacificParamount 14
97/8 PacificRegime 112
90/1 Panini(WPG) 9
87/8 PaniniSticker 358
88/9 PaniniSticker 150
89/90 PaniniSticker 167
90/1 PaniniSticker 310
91/2 PaniniSticker 94
92/3 PaniniSticker 83
93/4 PaniniSticker 231
94/5 PaniniSticker 197
95/6 PaniniSticker 205

91/2 Parkhurst 172
92/3 Parkhurst 181
93/4 Parkhurst 205
94/5 Parkhurst 227, V8
95/6 Parkhurst 475
91/2 Pinnacle 111
92/3 Pinnacle 273
93/4 Pinnacle 262
94/5 Pinnacle 209
96/7 PinnacleBeAPlayer 177
94/5 POG 238
95/6 POG 264
93/4 PowerPlay 243
93/4 Premier 297
90/1 ProSet 326, 532
91/2 ProSet 230
92/3 ProSet 186
90/1 Score 65, 67T, -HotCard 29
92/3 Score 152
93/4 Score 119
94/5 Score 83
95/6 Score 129
97/8 Score(BOS) 16
91 SemicSticker 62
92/3 Topps 30
95/6 Topps 207
98/9 Topps 6
91/2 ToppsStadiumClub 274
92/3 ToppsStadiumClub 283
93/4 ToppsStadiumClub 469
94/5 ToppsStadiumClub 42
90/1 UpperDeck 71, 413
92/3 UpperDeck 214
93/4 UpperDeck 215, SP157
94/5 UpperDeck 67
95/6 UpperDeck 144
96/7 UpperDeck 344
93/4 UDBeAPlayer 4
94/5 UDBeAPlayer R50, -Aut. 65
95/6 UDCollChoice 162
90/1 TOR
90/1 TOR/P.L.A.Y. 7
92/3 TOR/Kodak
93/4 TOR/Abalene
93/4 TOR/Blacks 20
94/5 TOR
84/5 WPG/Police
85/6 WPG
85/6 WPG/Police
85/6 WPG/Silverwood
86/7 WPG
87/8 WPG
88/9 WPG/Police
89/90 WPG/Safeway

ELLFOLK, LARS
73/4 WilliamsFIN 278

ELLINGEN, ÅGE
92 SemicSticker 30

ELLIOTT, CHAUCER
83&87 HallOfFame 171
83 HHOF Postcard (M)

ELLIS, AARON
93/4 Donruss USA6
93/4 Pinnacle 479
93/4 Slapshot(Detroit) 3
93/4 UpperDeck 554

ELLIS, RON
71/2 Bazooka Panel 34
64-67 BeeHives(TOR)
64/5 CokeCap TOR-11
65/6 CocaCola
70/1 Colgate Stamp 54
70/1 DadsCookies
70/1 EddieSargent 200
71/2 EddieSargent 203
72/3 EddieSargent 201
70/1 Esso Stamp
71/2 FritoLay
71 Kelloggs
72/3 Letraset 22
74/5 LiptonSoup 6
74/5 Loblaws
73/4 MacsMilk Disk
68/9 OPC/Topps 126
69/70 OPC/Topps 46
70/1 OPC 221
70/1 OPC/T-Deckle 46, -Sticker
71/2 OPC/Topps 113
72/3 OPC 36, -Canada, T. 152
73/4 OPC/Topps 55
74/5 OPC/Topps 12
75/6 OPC/Topps 59
77/8 OPC 311
78/9 OPC/Topps 92
79/80 O-Pee-Chee 373
80/1 O-Pee-Chee 329
94/5 Parkie(64/5) 125
95/6 Parkie(66/7) 106, 136
80/1 Pepsi Cap
67/8 PostFlipBook
68/9 Post Marble
70/1 PostShooters
72 SemicSticker 166
68/9 ShirriffCoin TOR7
71/2 TheTorontoSun
65/6 Topps 82
66/7 Topps 81
67/8 Topps 14
56-66 TorontoStar 64/5
91/2 Trends(72) 76, -Aut
91/2 Ultimate(O6) 34, -Aut 34
67/8 York 16, 17, 22
64/5 TOR
66/7 TOR/Coaster
68/9 TOR
69/70 TOR
70/1 TOR
71/2 TOR
72/3 TOR
73/4 TOR
74/5 TOR
77/8 TOR
78/9 TOR
79/80 TOR

ELMER, W.D.
23/4 PaulinsCandy 34

ELO, HANNU
65/6 Hellas 158

ELOMO, MIIKKA
95/6 Classic 22
95/6 Sisu 336, -NHLDraft 3
96/7 Sisu 148, -Energy 5
94/5 ToppsFinest 143
95/6 UpperDeck 546
95/6 UDCollChoice 333
96/7 Portland

ELOMO, TEEMU
97/8 UDBlackDiamond 15
98/9 UDChoice 276

ELORANTA, KARI
94/5 ElitSet 10
83/4 O-Pee-Chee 81
84/5 O-Pee-Chee 223
83/4 opcSticker 270
89 Pelimiehen
89 SemicSticker 31
83/4 SouhaitsRen.KeyChain
83/4 Vachon 6
82 Valio
82/3 CGY

ELORANTA, MIKA
95/6 Sisu 243
96/7 Sisu-Energy 2

ELSNER, ALEXANDR
95/6 APS 206

ELTERS, HELMUT
94/5 DEL 360

ELVENES, ROGER
94/5 ElitSet 33, -StudioSig 10
95/6 ElitSet 121
95/6 udElite 179

ELVENES, STEFAN
94/5 ElitSet 81, -TopGun 4
95/6 ElitSet 264, -FaceTo 9
94 Semic 76
95/6 udElite 150

ELYNUIK, PAT
90/1 Bowman 137
91/2 Bowman 198
92/3 Bowman 270
93/4 Donruss 368
94/5 Fleer 145
92/3 FleerUltra 434
93/4 FleerUltra 67
94/5 FleerUltra 338
90/1 Kraft 12
93/4 Leaf 6
94/5 Leaf 535
89/90 OPC/Topps 94
90/1 OPC/Topps 71
91/2 OPC/Topps 326
92/3 O-Pee-Chee 201
90/1 opcPremier 28
92/3 opcPremier 119
89/90 opcStickr 35/175, 142/263
89/90 opcStickFS 20
90/1 Panini(WPG) 10
89/90 PaniniSticker 165
90/1 PaniniSticker 312
91/2 PaniniSticker 66
92/3 PaniniSticker 54
93/4 PaniniSticker 29
91/2 Parkhurst 202
92/3 Parkhurst 205
93/4 Parkhurst 224
91/2 Pinnacle 117, 416
92/3 Pinnacle 53
93/4 Pinnacle 382
94/5 Pinnacle 381
93/4 PowerPlay 260, 442
93/4 Premier 51
94/5 Premier 107
90/1 ProSet 327
91/2 ProSet 262
92/3 ProSet 214
90/1 Score 205, -HotCards 86
90/1 Score 'YoungStar 28
92/3 Score 233, -Sharpshootr 23
93/4 Score 223, 580
92/3 Topps 56
91/2 ToppsStadiumClub 132
92/3 ToppsStadiumClub 410
93/4 ToppsStadiumClub 49, 447
90/1 UpperDeck 74
92/3 UpperDeck 312, 537
93/4 UpperDeck 75
94/5 UpperDeck 421
94/5 UDBeAPlayer-Aut. 164
95/6 UDCollChoice 39
94/5 OTT/Bell
94/5 T.B./SkyBoxSportsCafe
87/8 WPG
88/9 WPG
89/90 WPG/Safeway
90/1 WPG/IGA
91/2 WPG/IGA
92/3 WSH/Kodak
84/5 PrinceAlbert

EMBERG, EDDIE
51/2 LavalDairy 108

EMERSON, NELSON
92/3 Bowman 40
93/4 Donruss 383
94/5 Donruss 297
95/6 Donruss 7, 365
96/7 Donruss 73
97/8 DonrussPriority 135
94/5 Fleer 240
95/6 FleerMetal 65
92/3 FleerUltra 393, -Rookies 5
93/4 FleerUltra 45, 453
94/5 FleerUltra 242
95/6 FleerUltra 179, 246
93/4 Leaf 75
94/5 Leaf 80
95/6 Leaf 163
96/7 MetalUniverse 68
97/8 Omega 39
92/3 O-Pee-Chee 181
91/2 opcPremier 138
98/9 Pacific 131
97/8 PacificCrown 349
97/8 PacificCrownRoyale 23
97/8 PacificParamount 34
98/9 PacificParamount 35
97/8 PacificRegime 35
92/3 PaniniSticker B
93/4 PaniniSticker 159
94/5 PaniniSticker 164
95/6 PaniniSticker 216
96/7 PaniniSticker 25
95 PaniniWorlds 18
91/2 Parkhurst 151
92/3 Parkhurst 152, 232
93/4 Parkhurst 497
94/5 Parkhurst 267
95/6 Parkhurst 367
94/5 ParkieSE seV33
91/2 Pinnacle 314
92/3 Pinnacle 36,-Promo(US) 36
93/4 Pinnacle 245
94/5 Pinnacle 325
96/7 Pinnacle 60
95/6 PinnacleZenith 43
95/6 Playoff 217
96/7 Playoff 400
94/5 POG 252
93/4 PowerPlay 209, 472
93/4 Premier 35
94/5 Premier 352
90/1 ProCards 88
91/2 ProSet 557
92/3 ProSet 161, -Rookie 5,-TL 9
90/1 Score 383
92/3 Score 376, 505,-Young 13
93/4 Score 28, 506
94/5 Score 41
95/6 Score 259
96/7 Score 37
92/3 SeasonsPatch 16
94/5 Select 125
95/6 SkyBoxEmotion 192
95/6 SkyBoxImpact 73
94/5 SP 135
95/6 SP 63
95/6 Summit 132
92/3 Topps 11, 480
95/6 Topps 311
98/9 Topps 218
95/6 ToppsFinest 102
96/7 ToppsNHLPicks 135
92/3 ToppsStadiumClub 306
93/4 ToppsStadiumClub 223
94/5 ToppsStadiumClub 240
95/6 ToppsStadiumClub 38
92/3 UpperDeck 18, 166
93/4 UpperDeck 342, SP-175
94/5 UpperDeck 47, SP179
95/6 UD 178, 311, SE126
96/7 UpperDeck 159, 269
97/8 UpperDeck 243
95/6 UDBeAPlayer 38
98/9 UDChoice 43
95/6 UDCollChoice 196
96/7 UDCollChoice 116
97/8 UDCollChoice 115
97/8 UpperDeckIce 1
91/2 STL
93/4 WPG/Ruffles

EMMA, DAVE
93/4 ClassicProspects 98
94/5 Flair 93
94/5 FleerUltra 319
93/4 PowerPlay 377
93/4 Premier 448
91/2 Score (US) 330
93/4 Score 468
92/3 UpperDeck 462
95/6 UpperDeck 155

EMMETT, RICK
93/4 Slapshot(Peterborough) 14
94/5 Slapshot(Kitchener) 13
94/5 Slapshot(Windsor) 21

EMMONS, GARY
89/90 ProCards(IHL) 83
91/2 ProCards 506

EMMONS, JOHN
93/4 Donruss USA7
93/4 Pinnacle 492
92/3 UpperDeck 608
93/4 UpperDeck 557

EMMS, LEIGHTON (HAPPY)
34-43 BeeHives(NYA)
33/4 CndGum (V252)
36-39 DiamondMatch (2), (3)
33/4 OPC (V304A) 40
33/4 WWGum (V357) 55
36/7 WWGum (V356) 59

EMOND, PATRICK
84/5 Chicoutimi

EMPEY, LARRY
92/3 MPSPhotoSJHL 39
94/5 Erie

ENANDER, MICHAEL
94/5 ElitSet 182

ENCINAS, EZEQUIEL
79 PaniniSticker 374

ENDEAN, CRAIG
89/90 ProCards(IHL) 131
86/7 Regina
87/8 Regina

ENGBERG, GARY
72 Panda

ENGBLOM, BRIAN
72-84 Dernière 80/1, 82/3
82/3 McDonalds 29
78/9 OPC/Topps 262
79/80 O-Pee-Chee 361
80/1 O-Pee-Chee 304
81/2 O-Pee-Chee 175
82/3 O-Pee-Chee 362
83/4 O-Pee-Chee 368
84/5 O-Pee-Chee 83, Topps 65
85/6 OPC/Topps 5
86/7 OPC/Topps 40
81/2 opcSticker 33
83/4 opcSticker 203
84/5 opcSticker 118, 271
85/6 opcSticker 233/101
86/7 opcSticker 46/187
80/1 Pepsi Cap
82/3 Post
83/4 PuffySticker 20
86/7 CGY/RedRooster
84/5 L.A./Smokeys
77/8 MTL
78/9 MTL
79/80 MTL
80/1 MTL
81/2 MTL
82/3 WSH

ENGBLOM, DAVE
95/6 udElite 11
97/8 udSwedish 11

ENGEL, ALEXANDER
94/5 DEL 154
95/6 DEL 151
96/7 DEL 228

ENGELBRECHT, BERNHARD
94/5 DEL 337
79 PaniniSticker 97
82 SemicSticker 102

ENGEVIK, GLEN
89/90 Nashville

ENGFER, JON
95/6 Tallahassee 2
88/9 ProCards(NewHaven)
83/4 SSMarie

ENGLUND, PATRIC
94/5 ElitSet 96
95/6 ElitSet 164
95/6 udElite 17
97/8 udSwedish 99

ENGMAN, PETRI
92/3 Jyvas-Hyva 138
95/6 Sisu 17

ENGSTROM, MIKAEL
94/5 ElitSet 114

ENGVIST, KNUT
92/3 BCJHL 25

ENIO, JIM
45-64 BeeHives(DET)

ENNIS, JIM
88/9 ProCards(CapeBreton)
89/90 ProCards(AHL) 300
88/9 EDM/ActionMagazine 92

ENQVIST, OLLI
71/2 WilliamsFIN 298

ENS, KELLY
90/1 ProCards 193
91/2 ProCards 113
88/9 Lethbridge
89/90 Lethbridge

ENSOM, JIM
93/4 Slapshot(NorthBay) 8
94/5 Slapshot(Kitchener) 33
95/6 Slapshot 285

ENVOY, SEAN
84/5 Sudbury 2
85/6 Sudbury 6

EPANTCHISEV, VADIM
94/5 ParkieSE 231
94/5 SigRookies 50
94/5 SRGoldStandard 100
94/5 SP 164
94/5 UpperDeck 514

EPOCH, PAUL
86/7 Kitchener 14

EPPERS, HENRIK
93/4 Slapshot(Peterborough) 13

ERASMAS, RYAN
91/2 AvantGardeBCJHL 98

ERB, JAMIE
93/4 Raleigh

ERDMAN, JOSH
90/1 SketchWHL 330

ERDMANN, ALEXANDER
96/7 DEL 164

EREMENKO, RICK
91/2 AvantGardeBCJHL 17, 155

EREVIK, JONE
79 PaniniSticker 296

ERHOLM, MIKKO
65/6 Hellas 32
70/1 Kuvajulkaisut 226
71/2 WilliamsFIN 242
73/4 WilliamsFIN 305

ERICKSON, AUTRY
60/1 ShirriffCoin 112
61/2 ShirriffCoin 18

ERICKSON, BRYAN
85/6 OPC/Topps 80
86/7 OPC/Topps 101
87/8 OPC/Topps 130
86/7 opcSticker 93/224
87/8 PaniniSticker 282
93/4 Premier 294
91/2 ProSet 516
88/9 L.A.
91/2 WPG/IGA
93/4 WPG/Ruffles

ERICKSON, CHAD
91/2 ProCards 421
95/6 Birmingham
92/3 Cincinnati
93/4 Raleigh

ERICKSON, GRANT
72/3 Cleveland

ERICKSON, KYLE
93/4 Minn-Duluth

ERICKSON, PATRIK
94/5 ElitSet 98
95/6 ElitSet 36, -FaceTo 13
95 Globe 54
91 SemicSticker 47
95/6 udElite 54
97/8 udSwedish 47

ERICSSON, BO
82 SemicSticker 11

ERIEL, BOB
94/5 Slapshot(Kitchener) 28

ERIKSEN, P.E.
79 PaniniSticker 298

ERIKSON, THOMMIE
95 PaniniWorlds 242

ERIKSON, TOMMIE
90/1 ProCards 185

ERIKSSON, ANDERS
93/4 Classic 129
93/4 ClassicFourSport 203
97/8 Donruss 174
96/7 DonrussCanadianIce 145
96/7 DonrussElite 129
95/6 EdgeIce 2
94/5 ElitSet 32
96/7 FleerNHLPicks 180
96/7 FleerUltra 49, -Rookies 6
95/6 FutureLegends 4
95 Globe 58
96/7 Leaf 214
96/7 LeafPreferred 125
97/8 Limited 54
96/7 MetalUniverse 177
98/9 Pacific 189
97/8 PacificParamount 64
98/9 PacificParamount 73
93/4 Parkhurst 540
94/5 ParkieSE 233
96/7 Pinnacle 219
97/8 PinnacleBeAPlayer 180
96/7 PinnacleZenith 137
96/7 SelectCertified 92
94/5 SP 170
96/7 SP 176, -SPXForce 4
98/9 SPx"Finite" 129
97/8 SPAuthentic 56
96/7 Summit 190
98/9 Topps 25
94/5 UpperDeck 518
96/7 UpperDeck 183, X22
96/7 UDCollChoice 356
96/7 UpperDeck"Ice" 83
96 Wien 55
95/6 Adirondack

ERIKSSON, BJORN
95/6 ElitSet 212

ERIKSSON, CLAS
94/5 ElitSet 87
95/6 ElitSet 45
95/6 udElite 71
97/8 udSwedish 63

ERIKSSON, ESKO
70/1 Kuvajulkaisut 120
72 Panda
71/2 WilliamsFIN 170
72/3 WilliamsFIN 121
73/4 WilliamsFIN 175

ERIKSSON, FREDRIK
97/8 udSwedish 191

ERIKSSON, JAN
82 SemicSticker 7

ERIKSSON, JOAKIM
97/8 udSwedish 175, C26

ERIKSSON, JONAS
96/7 DEL 227
94/5 ElitSet 113 -CleanSweep 4
95/6 udElite DS11

ERIKSSON, MARKUS
94/5 ElitSet 289
95/6 ElitSet 66
95/6 udElite 111

ERIKSSON, NIKLAS
94/5 ElitSet 41 -GoldCard 16
95/6 ElitSet 70 -Goldies 7
94 Semic 72
95/6 udElite 103
97/8 udSwedish 112

ERIKSSON, PETER
90/1 UpperDeck 145
95/6 udElite DS16

ERIKSSON, ROLIE
77/8 OPC/Topps 123
78/9 OPC/Topps 241
79/80 O-Pee-Chee 350
79 PaniniSticker 193
78/9 VAN/RoyalBank

ERIKSSON, THOMAS
94/5 ElitSet 262
84/5 O-Pee-Chee 158
82 SemicSticker 5
89 SemicSticker 12
91 SemicSticker 30
92 SemicSticker 53
83/4 PHA

ERIXON, JAN
91/2 Bowman 77
92/3 Bowman 253
88/9 O-Pee-Chee 212
89/90 OPC/Topps 96
90/1 OPC/Topps 187
91/2 OPC/Topps 152, 215
92/3 O-Pee-Chee 207
87/8 PaniniSticker 120
88/9 PaniniSticker 306
90/1 PaniniSticker 104
91/2 PaniniSticker 283
92/3 PaniniSticker 241
91/2 Pinnacle 187
92/3 Pinnacle 191
90/1 ProSet 195
90/1 Score 272, 343
92/3 Score 362
93/4 Score 287

82 SemicSticker 24
93 SemicSticker 35
92/3 Topps 153
91/2 ToppsStadiumClub 151
92/3 ToppsStadiumClub 161
90/1 UpperDeck 366
89/90 NYR/MarineMidland

ERNST, BINGO
51/2 LavalDairy 83
52/3 StLawrence 26

ERONEN, ANSSI
71/2 WilliamsFIN 317

ERREY, BOB
90/1 Bowman 212
91/2 Bowman 85, 413
92/3 Bowman 304
92/3 Durivage 23
93/4 Leaf 377
94/5 Leaf 398
95/6 Leaf 315
89/90 OPC/Topps 50, OPC 315
90/1 OPC/Topps 230
91/2 OPC/Topps 94
92/3 O-Pee-Chee 323
89/90 opcSticker 234/96
97/8 PacificRegime 177
87/8 PaniniSticker 152
89/90 PaniniSticker 315
90/1 PaniniSticker 133
91/2 PaniniSticker 279
91/2 Parkhurst 138
92/3 Parkhurst 374
93/4 Parkhurst 453
94/5 ParkieSE 161
91/2 Pinnacle 257
92/3 Pinnacle 310
93/4 Pinnacle 410, CA21
94/5 Pinnacle 192
96/7 PinnacleBeAPlayer 197
94/5 POG 361
93/4 PowerPlay 435
94/5 Premier 331
90/1 ProSet 234
91/2 ProSet 187
90/1 Score 255
92/3 Score 287
93/4 Score 208, 566
94/5 Score 87
95/6 Score 174
92/3 Topps 95
91/2 ToppsStadiumClub 191
92/3 ToppsStadiumClub 170
93/4 ToppsStadiumClub 404
94/5 ToppsStadiumClub 37
94/5 UpperDeck 401
83/4 PGH
84/5 PGH/Heinz
86/7 PGH/Kodak
87/8 PGH/Kodak
89/90 PGH/Foodland 8
92/3 PGH/Coke
92/3 PGH/Foodland 2
92/3 S.J/PacificBell
96/7 S.J/PacificBellSheet

ERSKINE, JOHN
98 BowmanCHL 134, A24

ERSKINE, WAYNE
84/5 Kingston 19
85/6 Kingston 19
86/7 Kingston 17

ERTEL, TYLER
89/90 SketchOHL 151
90/1 SketchOHL 180
87/8 Kitchener 14

ERUZIONE, MIKE
79/80 USAOlympicTeam 2
94/5 MiracleOnIce 11, 12, 47

ESAU, LEN
90/1 ProCards 150
91/2 ProCards 352
94/5 SaintJohn

ESBJORS, JOACIM
94/5 ElitSet 195
95/6 ElitSet 144
94 Semic 61
95/6 udElite 205
97/8 udSwedish 70

ESBJORS, JONAS
94/5 ElitSet 206
95/6 ElitSet 146
97/8 udSwedish 82

ESCHE, ROBERT
97/8 Bowman 41
98 BowmanCHL 1
95/6 Slapshot 57

ESMANTOVICH, IGOR
90/1 O-Pee-Chee 479
89 SemicSticker 97

ESPE, DAVID
89/90 ProCards(AHL) 161
90/1 ProCards 442
91/2 ProCards 531
89/90 Halifax
90/1 Halifax

ESPOSITO, PHIL
71/2 Bazooka Panel 1
64-67 BeeHives(CHIx2)
63-5 ChexPhoto
64/5 CokeCap CHI-7
65/6 CocaCola
70/1 DadsCookies
70/1 EddieSargent 14
71/2 EddieSargent 7
72/3 EddieSargent 21
70/1 Esso Stamp
88/9 Esso Sticker
95/6 Fanfest 1-5
87 HallOfFame 244
92/3 HHOFLegends 7
71 Kelloggs
95/6 KennerLegend
74/5 Loblaws
73/4 Nabisco
74/5 Nabisco
68/9 OPC/Topps 7
68/9 OPC 208, -PuckSticker 5
69/70 OPC/T. 30, OPC 205, 214
69/70 OPC-Stamp, -Sticker
70/1 OPC/T. 11, OPC 233, 237
70/1 OPC/T-Deckle 6, -Sticker
71/2 OPC/Topps 20, -Booklet 2
71/2 OPC 247, 253, Topps 1-3
72/3 OPC 76, 111, 148, 230
72/3 OPC 272, 280, 283
72/3 opc-Crests 2, -TmCanada
72/3 Topps 61-63, 124, 150, 170
73/4 OPC 133-135, 138
73/4 OPC/Topps 120, T. 1-3, 6
74/5 OPC/Topps 1, 3, 28, 129
74/5 OPC/Topps 200, 244, 246
75/6 OPC/Topps 200, 208, 210
75/6 OPC/Topps 212, 292, 314
76/7 OPC/Topps 5, 245
76/7 OPC 390, T-Glossy 7
77/8 OPC/Topps 5, 55
78/9 OPC/Topps 2, 67, 100
79/80 OPC/Topps 31, 220
80/1 OPC/Topps 100, 149
92/3 OPC 283, -25Years 10
71/2 opcPoster 21
80/1 opcSuperCard 14
4/5 Parkie(64/5) 29, A4
95/6 Parkie(66/7) 33, 138
90/1 ProSet 404
91/2 ProSet 594
72 SemicSticker 184
91 SemicSticker 240
68/9 ShirriffCoin BOS8
77-9 Sportscaster 03-19, 29-08
77-9 Sportscaster 37-869
71/2 TheTorontoSun
65/6 Topps 116
66/7 Topps 63
67/8 Topps 32
98/9 Topps-RookieReprint 10
91/2 Trends(72)30,40,70,84,-Aut
92/3 Trends(76) 102, 153
90/1 UpperDeck 510
71/2 WilliamsFIN 380
70/1 BOS
71/2 BOS
91/2 BOS/Legends
92/3 T.B./Sheraton
94/5 T.B./SkyBoxSportsCafe
95/6 T.B./SkyBoxSportsCafe
87/8 SSMarie 15

ESPOSITO, TONY
71/2 Bazooka Panel 29
70/1 DadsCookies
70/1 EddieSargent 33
71/2 EddieSargent 44
72/3 EddieSargent 66
70/1 Esso Stamp
88/9 Esso Sticker
94/5 HHOFLegends 39
93/4 HighLiner 8
96 KennerLegend
97/8 KennerSLU
72/3 Letraset 13
74/5 LiptonSoup 45
74/5 Loblaws
69/70 O-Pee-Chee 138
70/1 OPC 153, 234, 247, 250
70/1 opc/t-Deckle 32, -Sticker
71/2 OPC/Topps 110, T. 4-6
71/2 opc/t-Booklet 13
72/3 OPC 137, 155, 226, 286
72/3 OPC-TeamCanada
72/3 Topps 20, 64, 121, 173
73/4 OPC/Topps 90
73/4 OPC 136, Topps 4
74/5 OPC/Topps 170
75/6 OPC/Topps 240
76/7 OPC/T. 100, T-Glossy 3
77/8 OPC/Topps 170
78/9 OPC/Topps 70, 89, 250
79/80 OPC/Topps 8, 80
80/1 OPC/Topps 86, 150, 168
81/2 O-Pee-Chee 54, 67
81/2 Topps 11, (West) 126
82/3 O-Pee-Chee 64
83/4 O-Pee-Chee 99
92/3 OPC 194, -25Years 2
71/2 opcPoster 8
81/2 opcSticker 113
80/1 opcSuperCard 4
91/2 Pinnacle 388
82/3 Post
90/1 ProSet 659
83/4 PuffySticker 13
72 SemicSticker 231
83/4 7ElevenCokeCup
95/6 SLU LegendCND
83/4 SouhaitsRen.KeyChain
77-9 Sportscaster 03-19, 5-105
94/5 SRGoldStandard HOF7
71/2 TheTorontoSun
91/2 Trends(72) 30, 31, 96, -Aut
96 Wien-HLegend HL7
71/2 WilliamsFIN 381
79/80 CHI
80/1 CHI/4x6
80/1 CHI/5.5x8.5
81/2 CHI
82/3 CHI
83/4 CHI
92/3 T.B./Sheraton
94/5 T.B/SkyBoxSportsCafe
95/6 T.B/SkyBoxSportsCafe

ESSELMONT, RYAN
92/3 BCJHL 49

ESSELMONT, SHEA
89/90 SketchMEM 4
90/1 SketchWHL 297
89/90 Kamloops
91/2 SketchWHL 62

ESSELMONT, TODD
89/90 SketchMEM 5
90/1 SketchWHL 65
89/90 Kamloops

ESSENSA, BOB
90/1 Bowman 131
91/2 Bowman 193
92/3 Bowman 306
93/4 Donruss 382
93/4 EASports 150
95/6 EdgeIce 126
92/3 FleerUltra 240
93/4 FleerUltra 89
91/2 Gillette 8
92/3 Kraft-Disk
93/4 Kraft-Recipe
93/4 Leaf 38
94/5 Leaf 93
90/1 OPC/Topps 119
91/2 OPC/Topps 307
92/3 O-Pee-Chee 226
90/1 opcPremier 29
89/90 opcStickFS 21
98/9 Pacific 206
97/8 PacificRegime 77
89/90 PaniniSticker 173
90/1 PaniniSticker 311
91/2 PaniniSticker 75
92/3 PaniniSticker 51
93/4 PaniniSticker 199
91/2 Parkhurst 199
92/3 Parkhurst 207
93/4 Parkhurst 234
94/5 Parkhurst 64
91/2 Pinnacle 66
92/3 Pinnacle 190
93/4 Pinnacle 133
94/5 Pinnacle 428
97/8 PinnacleBeAPlayer 185
93/4 PowerPlay 270
93/4 Premier 161
89/90 ProCards(AHL) 34
90/1 ProSet 328
91/2 ProSet 266, 602
92/3 ProSet 211, 267
91/2 PSPlatinum 285
90/1 Score 112, 324
92/3 Score 123
93/4 Score 26
94/5 Score 191
92/3 Topps 183
91/2 ToppsStadiumClub 152
92/3 ToppsStadiumClub 210
93/4 ToppsStadiumClub 254
90/1 UpperDeck 122, 337
92/3 UpperDeck 217
93/4 UpperDeck 144
96/7 EDM
97/8 EDM
89/90 WPG/Safeway
90/1 WPG/IGA
91/2 WPG/IGA
93/4 WPG/Ruffles
87/8 Moncton

ESTOLA, MATTI
72/3 WilliamsFIN 300

ESTRADA, SERGIO
79 PaniniSticker 371

ETCHER, FRED
52/3 AnonymousOHL 96

ETCHES, DEREK
90/1 SketchOHL 383
91/2 SketchOHL 43
89/90 Sudbury 11
90/1 Sudbury 11

ETHIER, MARTIN
97/8 Bowman 47

ETHIER, NEIL
89/90 Sudbury 16

ETHIER, TREVOR
93/4 Saskatoon

ETTNER, M.
95/6 DEL 177

EUSTACHE, EDDIE
52/3 AnonymousOHL 167

EVANS, CHRIS
72/3 EddieSargent 192
74/5 Loblaws, -Update
72/3 OPC 236
73/4 OPC 208
74/5 OPC/Topps 59
76/7 opcWHA 22
72/3 STL
72/3 STL/8"x10"
73/4 STL

EVANS, CORY
91/2 SketchOHL 372
93/4 Slapshot(Windsor) 16
94/5 Slapshot(Windsor) 18

EVANS, DARYL
83/4 O-Pee-Chee 153
83/4 opcSticker 144
88/9 ProCards(Newmarket)
83/4 SouhaitsRen.KeyChain
84/5 L.A./Smokeys
89/90 NewHaven

EVANS, DOUG
91/2 Bowman 203
95/6 EdgeIce 177
90/1 O-Pee-Chee 413
91/2 OPC/Topps 438
92/3 opcPremier 45
90/1 Panini(WPG) 11
93/4 Premier 203
90/1 ProSet 561
91/2 ToppsStadiumClub 321
92/3 PHA/JCPenney
92/3 PHA/UD 14JAN93
87/8 STL
87/8 STL/Kodak
88/9 STL
88/9 STL/Kodak
90/1 WPG/IGA
91/2 WPG/IGA
92/3 Dayton
94/5 Greensboro
93/4 Peoria

EVANS, FRANK
90/1 SketchMEM 76
90/1 SketchWHL 196
91/2 SketchAwards 18
91/2 SketchWHL 8
94/5 LasVegas
89/90 Spokane

EVANS, JACK
45-64 BeeHives(CHI), (NYRx2)
62 CeramicTiles
51/2 Parkhurst 90
53/4 Parkhurst 54
54/5 Parkhurst 72
93/4 Parkie(56/7) 101
60/1 ShirriffCoin 76
61/2 ShirriffCoin 39
54/5 Topps 14
57/8 Topps 55
58/9 Topps 31
59/60 Topps 30, 48
60/1 Topps 30
61/2 Topps-Stamp
62/3 Topps 26

EVANS, JIM
28/9 PaulinsCandy 60

EVANS, KEVIN
89/90 ProCards'IHL 76
90/1 ProCards 100
91/2 ProCards 511
91/2 Score (CDN) 650
93/4 Peoria

EVANS, MIKE
91/2 AirCanadaSJHL C3
92/3 MPSPhotoSJHL 100

EVANS, SHAWN
88/9 ProCards(Springfield)
89/90 ProCards(AHL) 244
91/2 ProCards 96
94/5 Milwaukee

EVANS, STAN
23/4 PaulinsCandy 60

EVANS, STEWART
34-43 BeeHives(MTL.M)
35-40 CrownBrand 77, 155
37/8 OPC (V304E) 164
38/9 QuakerOats
34/5 SweetCaporal
36/7 WWGum (V356) 67

EVASON, DEAN
90/1 Bowman 262
91/2 Bowman 10
92/3 Bowman 133
93/4 Donruss 86
92/3 FleerUltra 193
93/4 FleerUltra 298
94/5 FleerUltra 50
94/5 Leaf 45
87/8 OPC/Topps 166
90/1 OPC/Topps 376
91/2 OPC/Topps 325
92/3 O-Pee-Chee 381
91/2 opcPremier 36
87/8 PaniniSticker 47
90/1 PaniniSticker 44
91/2 PaniniSticker 312
92/3 PaniniSticker 131
93/4 PaniniSticker 259
91/2 Parkhurst 388
92/3 Parkhurst 392
93/4 Parkhurst 319
95/6 Parkhurst 36
94/5 ParkieSE 46
91/2 Pinnacle 153
92/3 Pinnacle 169
93/4 Pinnacle 384
94/5 Pinnacle 346
94/5 POG 78
93/4 PowerPlay 323
94/5 Premier 361
90/1 ProSet 103
91/2 ProSet 84
90/1 Score 259
92/3 Score 103
93/4 Score 353, 550
92/3 Topps 304
91/2 ToppsStadiumClub 145
92/3 ToppsStadiumClub 11
94/5 ToppsStadiumClub 82
90/1 UpperDeck 192
92/3 UpperDeck 281
94/5 UpperDeck 48
95/6 UpperDeck 22
94/5 UDBeAPlayer-Aut. 138
95/6 UDCollChoice 307
94/5 DAL
94/5 DAL/Southwest
86/7 HFD/JuniorWhalers
87/8 HFD/JuniorWhalers
88/9 HFD/JuniorWhalers
89/90 HFD/JuniorWhalers
90/1 HFD/JuniorWhalers
91/2 S.J.

EVASON, HEAVY
88/9 NiagaraFalls 25

EVENSSON, CONNIE
94/5 ElitSet 298
92 SemicSticker 50

EVERBERG, P.A.
97/8 udSwedish 198

EVTUSCHEVSKI, GREG
94/5 DEL 229
95/6 DEL 165
96/7 DEL 240
84/5 Kamloops

EWACHA, ROD
90/1 Mich.Tech
91/2 Mich.Tech

EWEN, DEAN
89/90 ProCards(AHL) 242
91/2 ProCards 452

EWEN, TODD
93/4 Donruss 9
93/4 FleerUltra 252
94/5 FleerUltra 2
93/4 Leaf 427
97/8 PacificRegime 178
90/1 Panini(MTL) 11
94/5 PaniniSticker 123
93/4 Parkhurst 5
92/3 Pinnacle 250
93/4 Pinnacle 409
94/5 Pinnacle 503
93/4 PowerPlay 285
93/4 Premier 369
94/5 Premier 119
90/1 ProSet 470
91/2 ProSet 419
93/4 Score 565
91/2 ToppsStadiumClub 340
93/4 ToppsStadiumClub 309
92/3 UpperDeck 549
93/4 UpperDeck 449
94/5 UpperDeck 427
95/6 UpperDeck 340
95/6 UDBeAPlayer 155
96/7 UDCollChoice 11
94/5 ANA/Carl'sJr 6
89/90 MTL/Kraft
90/1 MTL
91/2 MTL
92/3 MTL
87/8 STL
87/8 STL/Kodak
88/9 STL
88/9 STL/Kodak
96/7 S.J/PacificBellSheet (x2)

EWING, STEVE
86/7 Kitchener 29

EXANTUS, PAUL-EMILE
90/1 SketchQMJHL 265

EXANTUS, PAUL-EMILE
91/2 SketchQMJHL 296

EXELBY, RANDY
88/9 ProCards(Sherbrooke)
89/90 ProCards(IHL) 115
90/1 ProCards 589
90/1 KansasCity 7

EYSSELT, JAN
95/6 DEL 287

EZNICKI, BILL
45-64 BeeHives(TOR)
45-54 QuakerOats

F

FAASEN, DAN
90/1 SketchWHL 205
91/2 SketchWHL 19

FABIAN, PETR
94/5 APS 13
95/6 APS 313

FABIAN, SEAN
91/2 Minnesota

FACHRUTDINOV, MISJAT
see Mishat Fahrutdinov

FACKLER, AARON
94/5 Knoxville 3

FADEJEV, MICHAIL
95/6 APS 166

FADER, DUNCAN
93/4 Slapshot(Kingston) 15
95/6 Slapshot 135

FAFARD, PERRY
84/5 Brandon 12
84/5 Brandon 12

FAGAN, ANDREW
95/6 Slapshot 165

FAGERLI, JAN ROAR
95 PaniniWorlds 238
92 SemicSticker 32

FAGERSTROM, KRISTIAN
95/6 Sisu 7

FAGINKRANTZ, JOHN
92/3 Peoria
93/4 Peoria

FAGIOLI, LUCIANO
87/8 Sudbury 12

FAHEY, REBECCA
97/8 UDCollChoice 292

FAHRUTDINOV, MISHAT
94/5 ElitSet 47
95/6 ElitSet 129
90/1 SemicElitserien 162
91/2 SemicElitserien 264
92/3 SemicElitserien 287
95/6 udElite 195

FAIR, KEITH
93 SemicSticker 119

FAIR, QUINN
91/2 AirCanadaSJHL C9

FAIRBARIN, BILL
77/8 OPC 303
70/1 EddieSargent 123
71/2 EddieSargent 123
72/3 EddieSargent 150
70/1 Esso Stamp
74/5 Loblaws
71/2 OPC/Topps 215
72/3 O-Pee-Chee 87
73/4 OPC/Topps 41
74/5 OPC/Topps 231
75/6 OPC/Topps 109
76/7 OPC/Topps 57
78/9 O-Pee-Chee 267
77/8 Topps 255
71/2 TheTorontoSun

FAIRCHILD, KELLY
94 Classic 71
95/6 FutureLegends 5
94/5 SigRookies 23
94/5 StJohns
95/6 StJohns

FALESY, KEVIN
87/8 Kingston 17
89/90 Kitchener 27

FALK, LARS
91/2 SemicElitserien 304
92/3 SemicElitserien 326

FALK, NIKLAS
95/6 ElitSet 186, -Rookie 3
95/6 udElite 48
97/8 udSwedish 44, UDS3

FALK, STEFAN
94/5 ElitSet 52
95/6 ElitSet 54
89/90 SemicElisterien 117
91/2 SemicElitserien 126
92/3 SemicElitserien 147
95/6 udElite 84
97/8 udSwedish 93

FALKENBERG, BOB
68/9 O-Pee-Chee 141
72/3 O-Pee-Chee 310

FALKMAN, CRAIG
72 SemicSticker 127
72/3 Minnesota

FALLOON, PAT
91/2 Arena 1, 32, -Hologram
92/3 Bowman 361
91/2 Classic 2
91/2 ClassicFourSport 2, -Promo
93/4 Donruss 308, T
94/5 Donruss 83
95/6 Donruss 213
96/7 Donruss 208
93/4 EASports 119
94/5 Flair 163
94/5 Fleer 195
96/7 FleerNHLPicks 102
92/3 FleerUltra 194,-Rookie 6
93/4 FleerUltra 56
94/5 FleerUltra 364
95/6 FleerUltra 284
91/2 Gillette 3
93/4 HockeyWit 98
95/6 Hoyle'WEST 3 (Spades)
92/3 HumptyDumpty (1)
91/2 Kraft 8
93/4 KraftDinner
93/4 Leaf 49, -StudioSignature 2
94/5 Leaf 95
95/6 Leaf 241
96/7 Leaf 102
94/5 LeafLimited 14
92/3 O-Pee-Chee 227
91/2 opcPremier 56
92/3 opcPremier-Star 12
97/8 PacificCrown 199
92/3 PaniniSticker 273, K
93/4 PaniniSticker W
94/5 PaniniSticker 219
91/2 Parkhurst 160
92/3 Parkhurst 161, 233
93/4 Parkhurst 183
94/5 Parkhurst V70
95/6 Parkhurst 424
94/5 ParkieSE 165
91/2 Pinnacle 329
92/3 Pinnacle 9,238,-Tm2000 26
93/4 Pinnacle 20, -Tm 2001 26
94/5 Pinnacle 173
96/7 Pinnacle 115
91/2 Platinum 271
95/6 Playoff 82
96/7 Playoff 361
94/5 POG 214
95/6 POG 227
93/4 PowerPlay 218
93/4 Premier 259
94/5 Premier 521
95/6 ProMagnet 116
91/2 ProSet 558, CC3
92/3 ProSet 166, -Rook 4,-TL 10
91/2 Score(CDN) 640, (U.S) 90T
92/3 Score 125, 436,-Young 14
93/4 Score 133, -Franchise 19
94/5 Score 152
95/6 Score 184
96/7 Score 21
97/8 Score(PHA) 16
92/3 SeasonsPatch 62
94/5 Select 116
91/2 SketchAwards 12
90/1 SketchMEM 87, 100
90/1 SketchWHL 189, 345
91/2 StarPics 2, 36
92/3 Topps 7, 418
95/6 Topps 147
98/9 Topps 182
94/5 ToppsFinest 32
92/3 ToppsStadiumClub 56, 259
93/4 ToppsStadiumClub 224
94/5 ToppsStadiumClub 62
91/2 UltimateDP 2, 56, 58
91/2 UltimateDP 78, 80, -Aut. 58
90/1 UpperDeck 469
91/2 UpperDeck 593
92/3 UD 19, 286, 355,386,WG13
92/3 UD'LockerAS 52
93/4 UD 39, SP-141, -Hero 29
94/5 UpperDeck 307
95/6 UpperDeck 483
96/7 UpperDeck 122
95/6 UDBeAPlayer 95
95/6 UDCollChoice 188
96/7 UDCollChoice 194
96/7 PHA/OceanSpray
91/2 S.J.
93/4 S.J/PacificBell
89/90 Spokane

FANCY, JEFF
90/1 SketchWHL 106
91/2 SketchWHL 66

FANDUL, VJATSESLAV
92/3 Jyvas-Hyva 197
93/4 Jyvas-Hyva 353
93/4 Sisu 220
94/5 Sisu-FireOnIce 3
95/6 Sisu 127, 370

FARDA, RICHARD
95/6 APS 123
72 Hellas 90
74 Hellas 68
70/1 Kuvajulkaisut 44
72 Panda
72 SemicSticker 31
74 SemicSticker 63
71/2 WilliamsFIN 24
72/3 WilliamsFIN 4
73/4 WilliamsFIN 46

FARELLI, CARY
82 SemicSticker 137

FARKAS, ANRAS
79 PaniniSticker 267

FARKAS, JEFF
95/6 DonrussElite-WorldJrs 35
97/8 UDBlackDiamond 125
98/9 UDChoice 306

FARMER, SEAN
94/5 Slapshot(MEM) 59

FARR, ROCKY
74/5 BUF

FARRELL, ARTHUR
83&87 HallOfFame 153
83 HHOF Postcard (L)

FARRELL, BRIAN
94/5 Classic 33

FARRIS, KEVIN
84/5 NovaScotia 26
85/6 NovaScotia 23

FARRISH, DAVE
77/8 OPC/Topps 179
78/9 OPC/Topps 41
79/80 O-Pee-Chee 299
80/1 O-Pee-Chee 311
81/2 O-Pee-Chee 317
83/4 O-Pee-Chee 329
84/5 O-Pee-Chee 301
80/1 Pepsi Cap
88/9 ProCards(Baltimore)
89/90 ProCards(AHL) 49
90/1 ProCards 263
91/2 ProCards 187
83/4 Vachon 85
80/1 TOR
83/4 TOR
90/1 Moncton
91/2 Moncton

FATA, RICO
96/7 AllSportPPF 76
97/8 Bowman 24
98 BowmanCHL 131, A40, SC16
95/6 Slapshot 369
98/9 Topps 225
97/8 UpperDeck 410

FATROLA, RICHARD
89/90 SketchOHL 73
90/1 SketchOHL 4

FAUBERT, MARIO
78/9 O-Pee-Chee 296
81/2 O-Pee-Chee 261
81/2 opcSticker 189

FAULKNER, ANDY
91/2 AvantGardeBCJHL 52, 153
91/2 Nainamo

FAULKNER, ALEX
45-64 BeeHives(DET)
64-67 BeeHives(DET)
62 CeramicTiles
63/4 Parkhurst 42
63/4 York 49

FAUSS, TED
83/4 NovaScotia 21

FAUST, ANDRÉ
92/3 ClassicProspects 47
96/7 DEL 20
94/5 Donruss 184
92/3 Parkhurst 365
93/4 Parkhurst 419
93/4 Pinnacle 209
93/4 ToppsStadiumClub 462
93/4 UpperDeck 63
93/4 PHA 24MAR94

FAUST, ELLIOTT
95/6 Slapshot 206

FAVARO, RANDY
95/6 Spokane 11

FAVELL, DOUG
77/8 Coke Mini
70/1 Colgate Stamp 91
70/1 DadsCookies
70/1 EddieSargent 152
71/2 EddieSargent 156
72/3 EddieSargent 157
70/1 Esso Stamp
72/3 Letraset 11, 21
74/5 Loblaws
69/70 OPC/Topps 88
70/1 OPC 199,OPC/T-Deckle 35
71/2 OPC/Topps 72
72/3 OPC 89, -Crests 16, T. 74
73/4 OPC 158, Topps 119
74/5 OPC/Topps 4, 46
75/6 O-Pee-Chee 381
76/7 O-Pee-Chee 292
77/8 O-Pee-Chee 370
78/9 OPC/Topps 54
79/80 O-Pee-Chee 274
68/9 ShirriffCoin PHA5
71/2 TheTorontoSun
76/7 COL.R
76/7 COL.R/CokeCans
77/8 COL.R/CokeCans
70/1 PHA
72/3 PHA/MightyMilk
73/4 TOR
75/6 TOR

FAVOL, TIM
89/90 SketchOHL 166
90/1 SketchOHL 307
91/2 SketchOHL 262
91/2 Sudbury 17

FAWCETT, LEN
86/7 Kitchener 9

FEAMSTER, DAVE
83/4 O-Pee-Chee 100
82/3 CHI
83/4 CHI

FEARNS, KEN
95/6 Classic 72, -Aut.
95/6 ClassicFiveSport 151, -Aut

FEASBY, SCOTT
89/90 SketchOHL 88

FEATHERSTONE, GLEN
91/2 Bowman 371
90/1 OPC/Topps 387
91/2 OPC/Topps 436
91/2 opcPremier 66
95/6 Parkhurst 363
93/4 PowerPlay 288
93/4 Premier 14
88/9 ProCards(Peoria)
90/1 ProSet 523
90/1 ScoreTraded 25T
91/2 Score(CDN) 587, (U.S) 39T
91/2 ToppsStadiumClub 319
93/4 ToppsStadiumClub 372
94/5 UDBeAPlayer-Aut. 81
91/2 BOS/SportsAction
90/1 STL/Kodak

FEATHERSTONE, TONY
70/1 Esso Stamp
75/6 opcWHA 122
71/2 Topps 106
73/4 MIN

FEDERENKO, BRAD
91/2 AirCanadaSJHL 12
93/4 Minn-Duluth

FEDERKO, BERNIE
90/1 Bowman 238
88/9 FritoLay
94 HockeyWit 47
84/5 Kelloggs Disk
78/9 OPC/Topps 143
79/80 OPC/Topps 215
80/1 OPC/Topps 71, 136
81/2 O-Pee-Chee 288, 300, 304
81/2 Topps 12, 62, (West) 127
82/3 O-Pee-Chee 302, 303
83/4 O-Pee-Chee 315
84/5 OPC 184, 367, Topps 131
85/6 OPC/Topps 104
86/7 OPC/Topps 105
87/8 OPC/Topps 83
88/9 OPC/Topps 81, E
89/90 OPC/Topps 107
90/1 OPC/Topps 191
81/2 opcSticker 128
82/3 opcSticker 197
83/4 opcSticker 125
84/5 opcSticker 54-55
85/6 opcSticker 53
86/7 opcSticker 174
87/8 opcSticker 24
89/90 opcSticker 247/108
80/1 opcSuperCard 18
87/8 PaniniSticker 312
88/9 PaniniSticker 104
90/1 PaniniSticker 209
82/3 Post
90/1 ProSet 70
91/2 ProSet 597
83/4 PuffySticker 18
90/1 Score 252
84/5 7ElevenDisk
90/1 UpperDeck 58
89/90 DET/Caesars
78/9 STL
87/8 STL
87/8 STL/Kodak
88/9 STL
88/9 STL/Kodak
92/3 STL/UpperDeck 14

FEDORCHUK, DEAN
94/5 Classic 52
94/5 Dayton 14

FEDORKO, MIKE
91/2 SketchWHL 262
91/2 PrinceAlbert

FEDOROV, ANTON
94/5 Raleigh

FEDOROV, SERGEI
91/2 AceNoveltyMVP Pin
95/6 Aces J (Hearts)
96/7 Aces Q (Hearts)
91/2 Bowman 50
92/3 Bowman 205, 416
95/6 Bowman 80, BB12
97/8 Corinthian Headliners
93/4 Donruss 101,-Elite U2
94/5 Donruss 173, -Dominator 5
94/5 D-Elite 4, -IceMaster 2
95/6 Don. 285, -Dom 5, -Elite 4
96/7 Donruss 50, -Dom 9, Elite 8
97/8 Donruss 82, -RedAlert 3
96/7 DonrussCanadianIce 55
97/8 D.CdnIce 72,-Scrapbook 26
95/6 DonrussElite 53, -Cutting 9
96/7 DonrussElite 9, -Status 3
97/8 D.Elite 96,-BckTo 5,-Craft 9
97/8 D.Preferred 122,165,-Ln 1B
97/8 D.Priority 12, 214,-DirDp 12
97/8 D.Prio-Postcd 15,-Stamp 15
97/8 D.Studio 21,-HardHats 21
97/8 D.Studio-Portr 21,-Sil 14
93/4 EASports 40
97/8 EssoOlympic 35, 36
94/5 Flair 48, 213-222
94/5 Flair-Centre 2, -Scoring 3
96/7 Flair 26, -CentreIce 2
94/5 Fleer 59, -Headliner 2
96/7 Fleer 30, 142-43
96/7 Fleer-ArtRoss 2,-Pearson 2
95/6 F.Metal 45,-Heav 2,-IntSt 4
96/7 F.Picks-Fab 10, -Fantasy 9
92/3 FleerUltra 48,-Import 3
93/4 FleerUltra 121,-Speed 3
94/5 FleerUltra 60, -AW 3
94/5 FU-Fed 1-12,-Piv 2,-Scor 2
94/5 FU-Speed 3,-Powr 2,-Glbl 1
95/6 FleerUltra 45, 381, -Extra 4
95/6 FU-Pivot 1, -Ultraview 1
96/7 FU 50, -RedLine 1,-Power 4
96/7 Got-UmHockeyGreatsCoin
95 Globe 175
93/4 HockeyWit 69
95/6 Hoyle'WEST A (Spades)
92/3 HumptyDumpty (2)
91 IvanFiodorovSportUnites
97/8 KatchMedallion 49
94/5 KennerSLU
95/6 KennerSLU (U)
96/7 KennerSLU
94 Koululainen
94/5 Kraft-AS, -AW
95/6 Kraft-Ticket
96/7 Kraft, -Trophy
97/8 Kraft-WorldPros,-WorldBest
93/4 Leaf 129
94/5 Leaf 155, -FireOnIce 1
94/5 L-GoldLeafStar 1,-Limited 7
95/6 Leaf 34, -FireOnIce 7
96/7 L. 1,-Leather16,-Sweater 11
97/8 Leaf 135, -BannrSeason 16
94/5 LeafLimited 81, -Gold 9
95/6 LeafLimited 49, -StarsOf 11
96/7 LeafLimited 61
96/7 L.Preferd 65,-Stl 1,-StlP 7
97/8 Limited 98,126,197,-fabric 6
96/7 Maggers 51
92/3 McDonalds McD-06
94/5 McDonalds McD-12
95/6 McDonalds McD-17
96/7 McDonalds McD26
96/7 MetalUni 45,-IceC 5,-Leth 3
90/1 O-Pee-Chee 19R
91/2 OPC/Topps 8, 401
92/3 O-Pee-Chee 195
90/1 opcPremier 30
91/2 opcPremier 68, 173
92/3 opcPremier-Star 20
98/9 Pacific 91,-D.Ice 9,-GldC 13
97/8 PacificCrown 91
97/8 PCC-Supials6,-Slapshot 3B
97/8 PacificCrownRoyale 45
97/8 PCR-BladesOfSteel 8
97/8 PcfcD.! 41,-BestKept 32
97/8 PcfcD.-Dyna 7A, -Tandm 8
97/8 PacificInvin. 46, -Feature 12
97/8 PacificInv.-Attack 9,-Off 7
97/8 PcfcParamount 65,-BigN 8
98/9 PcfcParamnt 74,-SpecD 7
97/8 PacificRegime 69
91/2 PaniniSticker 145, 340
92/3 PaniniSticker 113, 291
93/4 PaniniSticker 246
94/5 PaniniSticker 210, 236a, BB
95/6 PaniniSticker 178
96/7 PaniniSticker 178
95 PaniniWorlds 282
91/2 Parkhurst 38, PHC5
92/3 Parkhurst 39, 219
93/4 Parkhurst 58, W10
94/5 Parkie 305, V39, -YCTG 7
95/6 Parkie 238, 337, PP3, PP52
95/6 PH-Crown(1) 14, -Int.AS 4
94/5 ParkieSE 50, ES16
91/2 Pinnacle 157
92/3 Pinnacle 20, -Team2000 30
93/4 Pinnacle 54, -Team2001 24
94/5 Pinn.150, GR3, TP8, WE5
95/6 Pinn. 44,-ClearS 7,-Roar 6
96/7 Pinnacle 21, -Numbers 3
97/8 Pinnacle 77
96/7 Pinn.BeAPlayer-Biscuit 7
97/8 P. BAP -TakeANumber 5
97/8 PinnacleBeeHive 46
97/8 PinnacleCertified 56
97/8 PinnacleEPIX 5
95/6 PinnacleFANtasy 30
96/7 PinnacleFANtasy 13
97/8 PinnInside 42, -Track 13
96/7 PinnacleMint 8
97/8 PinnacleMint 14
95/6 PinnacleZenith 30, -Team 9
96/7 PinnacleZenith 80, -Team 5
97/8 PlaymateProZone
95/6 Playoff 34, 144, 253
96/7 Playoff 437
94/5 POG 87, 267, 360
95/6 POG 95
94/5 Post
97/8 Post
93/4 PowerPlay 72,-Global 2
93/4 PP-Game 1, -Slapshot 3
93/4 Premier 318, 441
94/5 Premier 40, 276, 520, -Go
94/5 Prmr-Finest(T.) 3, -GoTo 9
95/6 ProMagnet 102
90/1 ProSet 604
91/2 ProSet 53. AC10
92/3 ProSet 40
91/2 PSPlatinum 30, 277, PC7
91/2 RedAce
90/1 Score 20T, -YoungStar 9
91/2 Score(CDN) 298, 382, 470
91/2 Score(U.S) 250, 352, 408
91/2 Score-YoungStar 1, -Hot 4
92/3 Score 252, -YoungStar 5
93/4 Score 250, -International 3
93/4 S-Dynami(U.S) DD9
94/5 Score DT12, NP2, TF7
95/6 Score 100, -BorderBat 13
95/6 S-Dream 2, -Lamplight 5
96/7 Score 77, -Promo 77
96/7 S-Dream 11,-Sudden 14
97/8 Score 91, 264
97/8 Score(DET) 3
92/3 SeasonsPatch 5
94/5 Select 10
95/6 SelectCert. 29,-Double 14
96/7 SelectCert. 55, -Corner.13
94 Semic 146, 348
91 SemicSticker 219
92 SemicSticker 109
95/6 SkyBoxEmotion 53
95/6 SkBxE-Xcel 3, -Xcited 4
95/6 SkyBoxImpact 52
95/6 SkBxI-Count 6, -IceQuake 9
96/7 SBI 34,-Count 2,-Versa 2
89/90 SovietStars
94/5 SP 33, -Premier 24
95/6 SP 44, E12, FX5
96/7 SP 48, CW4, HC5
96/7 SPx 13
97/8 SPx 15, SPX11
97/8 SportFX MiniStix
91/2 StarPics 30
95/6 Summit 31,-GM15,-Mad 9
96/7 Smmt 105,-High 13,-Unt 10
96/7 TeamOut
92/3 Topps 252
95/6 T. 185, 373, M5, PF5, 8PL
98/9 Topps 67, L13
94/5 ToppsFinest 65
94/5 TF-BBest(B) 7, -Division 13
95/6 ToppsFinest 95, 186
95 ToppsFinestBronze 7
96/7 T.Picks 17, FT17, TS11
91/2 ToppsStadiumClub 316
92/3 T.StadiumClub 244, 300
93/4 ToppsStadiumClub 45
94/5 TSC 250, 268, -Finest 6
95/6 T.StadiumClub 169, N7
93/4 TSC-MembersOnly 15
94/5 TSC-MembersOnly 36
95/6 TSC-MembersOnly 15
97/8 ToppsSticker 4
95/6 ToppsSuperSkills 34
91/2 TriGlobeMag.Five 1-5
90/1 UpperDeck 521, 525
91/2 UD 6, 40, 82, 144, 631, E9
92/3 UD 157, 632, E1, WG16
93/4 UpperDeck 171, SP-44
94/5 UD 37, C21, H6, H18, R4
94/5 UD R23, R36, R52, SP113
95/6 UD 215, 279, AS15, F8, H6
95/6 UD R24, R34, R44, SE115
95/6 UD-AllStarPredict MVP2
96/7 UpperDeck 206, 250, HH4
96/7 UD LS14, SS8B, X10
97/8 UD 266,S11,SS3,T7A,GJ5
93/4 UDBeAPlayer 5, -Roots 12
94/5 UDBAP G6, R194, UC7
96/7 UDBlckDiamond 155, RC12
97/8 UDBlackDiamond 82
98/9 UDChoice 75
95/6 UDCollChoice 148, 365, C2
96/7 UDCC 80, 316, S23, UD13
97/8 UDCollChoice 79, SQ19
97/8 udDiamondVision 23
96/7 UpperDeck"Ice" 84
97/8 UpperDeckIce 69, L6C
96 Wien 141
97/8 Zenith 22, Z44
90/1 DET/Caesars
91/2 DET/Caesars

FEDOROV, YURI
80 Soviet MiniPics
79/80 SovietStars
79 PaniniSticker 146

FEDOSOV, VLADIMIR
95/6 DEL 338
96/7 DEL 313
91 SemicSticker 87

FEDOTOV, ANATOLI
93/4 Classic 130
92/3 ClassicProspects 97
93/4 ClassicProspects 62
93/4 UpperDeck 38
97/8 udSwedish 90
94/5 Raleigh

FEDOTOV, SERGEI
96/7 UpperDeck"Ice" 140

FEDULOV, IGOR
95 Semic 132

FEDYK, BRENT
91/2 Bowman 51
96/7 Donruss 163
92/3 FleerUltra 371
93/4 FleerUltra 387
93/4 Leaf 58
94/5 Leaf 517
95/6 Leaf 290
96/7 Leaf 82
91/2 OPC/Topps 376
90/1 opcPremier 31
92/3 opcPremier 26
91/2 PaniniSticker 140
93/4 PaniniSticker 48
94/5 PaniniSticker 42
91/2 Parkhurst 270
92/3 Parkhurst 131
93/4 Parkhurst 148
94/5 Parkhurst 170
95/6 Parkhurst 325
93/4 Pinnacle 119
94/5 Pinnacle 326
96/7 Pinnacle 116
94/5 POG 177
95/6 POG 204
93/4 PowerPlay 181
93/4 Premier 211
94/5 Premier 509
88/9 ProCards(Adirondack)
90/1 ProSet 435
91/2 ProSet 379
91/2 Score(CDN) 412
92/3 Score 337
93/4 Score 14
96/7 Score 191
92/3 Topps 401
91/2 ToppsStadiumClub 238
92/3 ToppsStadiumClub 390
93/4 ToppsStadiumClub 181
94/5 ToppsStadiumClub 169
91/2 UpperDeck 373

92/3 UpperDeck 443
93/4 UpperDeck 373
94/5 UpperDeck 9
95/6 UpperDeck 116
96/7 UpperDeck 46
95/6 UDBeAPlayer 100
95/6 UDCollChoice 324
90/1 DET/Caesars
92/3 PHA/JCPenney
92/3 PHA/UD 4APR93
92/3 PHA/UD 2DEC92
93/4 PHA 21SEP93
93/4 PHA 29MAR94
93/4 PHA/JCPenney
94/5 PHA

FEHER, ARTIE
84/5 Brandon 8
85/6 Brandon 8

FEIFFER, JASON
91/2 AirCanadaSJHL 31, A21

FEISSNER, B.
85/6 Minn-Duluth 34

FELBER, HARALD
74 Hellas 110

FELICETTI, DINO
96/7 DEL 124

FELIX, CHRIS
88/9 ProCards(Baltimore)
89/90 ProCards(AHL) 83
90/1 ProCards 213
81/2 SSMarie
82/3 SSMarie
83/4 SSMarie
84/5 SSMarie
87/8 SSMarie 11

FELLER, J.
95/6 DEL 347

FELSKI, SVEN
94/5 DEL 39
95/6 DEL 37
96/7 DEL 36

FELSNER, BRIAN
97/8 Omega 50

FELSNER, DENNY
92/3 Classic 64
92/3 ClassicFourSport 194
93/4 ClassicProspects 189
92/3 Parkhurst 493
93/4 Parkhurst 267
94/5 ParkieSE 151
92/3 Pinnacle 413
94/5 Premier 436
92/3 Score 481
92/3 Topps 514
92/3 UpperDeck 413
94/5 UpperDeck 114
92/3 Peoria
93/4 Peoria

FENDT, TORSTEN
95/6 DEL 9
96/7 DEL 7

FENNIG, WADE
89/90 Regina

FENTON, ERIC
94/5 ClassicAutograph
92/3 Maine(1) 11
93/4 Portland

FENTON, PAUL
90/1 Bowman 139
91/2 Bowman 256
88/9 O-Pee-Chee 213
92/3 O-Pee-Chee 380
90/1 OPC/Topps 313
91/2 OPC/Topps 331
91/2 opcPremier 187
90/1 Panini(WPG) 12, G
90/1 PaniniSticker 313
90/1 ProSet 329, 533
90/1 Score 156, 57T
91/2 Score(CDN) 14, 593
91/2 Score(U.S) 14
92/3 Score 257
92/3 Topps 173
91/2 ToppsStadiumClub 327
92/3 ToppsStadiumClub 224
90/1 UpperDeck 92
85/6 HFD/JuniorWhalers
91/2 S.J
90/1 TOR
89/90 WPG/Safeway

FENYVES, DAVE
88/9 ProCards(Hershey)
89/90 ProCards(AHL) 335
90/1 ProCards 32
91/2 ProCards 283
85/6 BUF
86/7 BUF

FERA, RICK
94 Semic 325
84/5 Kingston 13
83/4 SSMarie

FERENCE, ANDREW
97/8 Bowman 100
98 BowmanCHL 48
96/7 UpperDeck 374

FERENCE, BRAD
97/8 Bowman 133, BB9
98 BowmanCHL 43, SC6
98/9 UDChoice 261

FERGUS, TOM
90/1 Bowman 157
92/3 Bowman 273
92/3 FleerUltra 426
86/7 Kraft Sports 55
82/3 O-Pee-Chee 11
83/4 O-Pee-Chee 49
84/5 O-Pee-Chee 4, Topps 3
85/6 OPC/Topps 113
86/7 OPC/Topps 84
87/8 OPC/Topps 120
89/90 OPC/Topps 103
90/1 OPC/Topps 63
88/9 O-Pee-Chee 214
92/3 O-Pee-Chee 356
82/3 opcSticker 88
83/4 opcSticker 55
84/5 opcSticker 189
85/6 opcSticker 164/34
86/7 opcSticker 143
87/8 opcSticker 159
88/9 opcSticker 170/39
89/90 opcSticker 173
87/8 PaniniSticker 332
89/90 PaniniSticker 135
90/1 PaniniSticker 282
91/2 Parkhurst 400
82/3 Post
90/1 ProSet 279
91/2 ProSet 234
91/2 PSPlatinum 238
90/1 Score 285
91/2 Score(CDN) 234
92/3 Score 190
83/4 SouhaitsRen.KeyChain
92/3 Topps 311
92/3 ToppsStadiumClub 278
90/1 UpperDeck 83
91/2 UpperDeck 384
83/4 BOS
84/5 BOS
85/6 TOR
86/7 TOR
87/8 TOR
87/8 TOR/P.L.A.Y. 7
88/9 TOR/P.L.A.Y. 3
90/1 TOR
90/1 TOR/P.L.A.Y. 15
92/3 VAN/RoadTrip

FERGUSON, CRAIG
93/4 ClassicProspects 45
94/5 Leaf 525
92/3 Fredericton
93/4 Fredericton
94/5 Fredericton

FERGUSON, DAN
90/1 SketchOHL 358
89/90 SSMarie 24

FERGUSON, GEORGE
74/5 Loblaws, -Updat e
74/5 O-Pee-Chee 302
75/6 OPC/Topps 77
76/7 O-Pee-Chee 286
77/8 O-Pee-Chee 266
78/9 O-Pee-Chee 395
79/80 OPC/Topps 139
80/1 OPC/Topps 44
81/2 O-Pee-Chee 262
82/3 O-Pee-Chee 268
83/4 O-Pee-Chee 171
81/2 opcSticker 184
82/3 opcSticker 150
82/3 Post
82/3 MIN
83/4 MIN
72/3 TOR
74/5 TOR
75/6 TOR
76/7 TOR
77/8 TOR

FERGUSON, IAN
83/4 Oshawa 4

FERGUSON, JEFF
88/9 Lethbridge
89/90 Spokane

FERGUSON, JOHN B.(SR.)
45-64 BeeHives(MTL)
64-67 BeeHives(MTL)
63-5 ChexPhoto
64/5 CokeCap MTL-22
65/6 CocaCola
70/1 DadsCookies
70/1 Esso Stamp
68/9 O-Pee-Chee 20
69/70 OPC/Topps 7, OPC 146
70/1 O-Pee-Chee 264
63/4 Parkhurst 33, 92
94/5 Parkie(64/5) 66
95/6 Parkie(66/7) 59
68/9 Post Marble
68/9 ShirriffCoin MTL10
64/5 Topps 4
65/6 Topps 10
66/7 Topps 70, -USATest 65
67/8 Topps 69
54-67 TorontoStar V11
91/ UltimateO6 9
63/4 York 35
67/8 York 16, 21
67/8 MTL
67/8 MTL/IGA
68/9 MTL
69/70 MTL/ProStar
70/1 MTL
71 MTL/Pins
79/80 WPG
83/4 WPG
84/5 WPG/Police
85/6 WPG
85/6 WPG/Police
86/7 WPG
60/1 Cleveland

FERGUSON, JOHN (JR.)
89/90 ProCards'AHL 198
90/1 ProCards 60
91/2 ProCards 74

FERGUSON, LORNE
45-64 BeeHives(BOS)
51/2 Parkhurst 35
93/4 Parkie(56/7) 54
54/5 Topps 31
57/8 Topps 40
58/9 Topps 55
56-66 TorontoStar 58/9

FERGUSON, NORM
70/1 Colgate Stamp 56
70/1 DadsCookies
70/1 EddieSargent 142
71/2 EddieSargent 136
69/70 OPC 146
71/2 OPC/Topps 179
75/6 opcWHA 92
77/8 opcWHA 52
90/1 ProCards 241
91/2 ProCards 236
72 SemicSticker 173
71/2 TheTorontoSun
76/7 SanDiegoMariners

FERGUSON, SCOTT
91/2 SketchWHL 77
93/4 Kamloops

FERGUSON, TIM
94/5 DEL 23
95/6 DEL 20
96/7 DEL 17

FERLAND, JEANNOT
90/1 SketchQMJHL 259
91/2 SketchQMJHL 189

FERNANDEZ, EMMANUEL (MANNY)
94/5 C-Images 24, CE12, PR9
93/4 Donruss CAN10
95/6 Donruss 10
96/7 DonrussCdn.Ice-Gardien 8
95/6 EdgeIce 139, TW2,-Quant 1
95/6 Leaf 169
97/8 Omega 68
98/9 Pacific 175
95/6 Parkhurst 63
93/4 Pinnacle 457
95/6 Pinnacle 216
95/6 Score 299
91/2 SketchQMJHL 242
95/6 SkyBoxImpact -Fox 14
93/4 UpperDeck 536

FERNER, MARK
93/4 Parkhurst 275
93/4 Premier 478
88/9 ProCards(Rochester)
89/90 ProCards(AHL) 89
90/1 ProCards 208
91/2 ProCards 568
93/4 ToppsStadiumClub 342
91/2 Baltimore 10

FERRANTI, STEVE
93/4 Mich.State

FERRARO, CHRIS
94/5 Classic 39, -Aut.
93/4 ClassicProspects LP4
95/6 EdgeIce 18
93/4 FleerUltra 482
95/6 FutureLegends 6
96/7 Leaf 229
97/8 PacificDynagn-BestKept 60
96/7 Pinnacle 233
93/4 PowerPlay 502
93/4 Premier-TeamUSA 9
94 Semic 129
93/4 T.StadiumClub-TeamUSA 5
91/2 UD 648, 'CzechWJC 74
95/6 Binghampton
96/7 Binghampton
92/3 Maine (2) 25

FERRARO, PETER
95/6 Bowman 134
94/5 Classic 38, -Aut.
93/4 C4'Images 35
93/4 ClassicProspects LP5
95/6 EdgeIce 17
96/7 Fleer 126,-Cald 3,-Prom S3
93/4 FleerUltra 483
95/6 FutureLegends 7
96/7 Leaf -Rookie 4
92/3 Maine (2) 26
96/7 MetalUniverse 178
96/7 PaniniSticker 300
95 PaniniWorlds 235
95/6 Parkhurst 532
96/7 Pinnacle 218
93/4 PowerPlay 503
93/4 Premier-TeamUSA 15
94 Semic 132
95/6 SkyBoxImpact 211
96/7 SkyBoxImpact 149
96/7 Summit 181
93/4 T.StadiumClub-TeamUSA 6
91/2 UD 648, 696,
91/2 UD'CzechWJC 83
95/6 Binghampton
96/7 Binghampton

FERRARO, RAY
96/7 Aces 3 (Clubs)
90/1 Bowman 258
91/2 Bowman 212
92/3 Bowman 128, 229
93/4 Donruss 198
94/5 Donruss 162
95/6 Donruss 144, 297
96/7 Donruss 183
94/5 Fleer 120
96/7 Fleer 49
95/6 FleerMetal 94
96/7 fleerPicks 140
92/3 FleerUltra 123
93/4 FleerUltra 16
94/5 FleerUltra 324
95/6 FleerUltra 93, 273
93/4 HockeyWit 84
95/6 Hoyle'EAST J (Hearts)
92/3 HumptyDumpty (1)
95/6 KraftDinner
93/4 Leaf 121
94/5 Leaf 334
95/6 Leaf 284
96/7 LeafPreferred 16
86/7 OPC/Topps 160
87/8 OPC/Topps 109
88/9 OPC/Topps 114
89/90 OPC/Topps 70
90/1 OPC/Topps 336
91/2 OPC/Topps 304
92/3 O-Pee-Chee 42
86/7 opcSticker 57/195
88/9 opcSticker 268/132
89/90 opcSticker 263/142
92/3 opcPremier-Star 1
97/8 PacificCrown 53
97/8 PacificDynagon! 59
97/8 PcfcD-BstKpt 45,-Tandm 40
97/8 PacificInvincible 66
87/8 PaniniSticker 46
88/9 PaniniSticker 241
89/90 PaniniSticker 222
90/1 PaniniSticker 45
91/2 PaniniSticker 250
92/3 PaniniSticker 198
94/5 PaninStickeri 46
95/6 PaniniSticker 103
96/7 PaniniSticker 269
97/8 PaniniSticker 224
91/2 Parkhurst 110
92/3 Parkhurst 98, 499
93/4 Parkhurst 123
94/5 Parkhurst 134, V86
95/6 Parkhurst 409
91/2 Pinnacle 123
92/3 Pinnacle 154
93/4 Pinnacle 48
94/5 Pinnacle 314
96/7 Pinnacle 29
97/8 Pinnacle 146
96/7 PinnacleBeAPlayer 139
97/8 PinnacleCertified 82
97/8 PinnacleInside 180
95/6 Playoff 173
96/7 Playoff 380
94/5 POG 154
95/6 POG 178
93/4 PowerPlay 382
93/4 Premier 349
94/5 Premier 335
90/1 ProSet 104
91/2 ProSet 156
92/3 ProSet 105
91/2 PSPlatinum 76
90/1 Score 134, 15T
91/2 Score(CDN) 48, (U.S) 48
92/3 Score 298, -Sharpshooter 3
93/4 Score 60
95/6 Score 66
96/7 Score 107
97/8 Score 169
94/5 Select 41
95/6 SkyBoxEmotion 111
95/6 SkyBoxImpact 107
96/7 SkyBoxImpact 57
94/5 SP 69
95/6 Summit 108
92/3 Topps 324
95/6 Topps 245
95/6 ToppsFinest 36
96/7 ToppsNHLPicks 119
91/2 ToppsStadiumClub 3
92/3 ToppsStadiumClub 123
93/4 TSC 50, -Master(1) 6
94/5 ToppsStadiumClub 20
95/6 ToppsStadiumClub 120
95/6 ToppsSuperSkills 23
90/1 UpperDeck 289
91/2 UpperDeck 311
92/3 UpperDeck 12, 193
93/4 UpperDeck 153, SP-90
94/5 UpperDeck 14
95/6 UpperDeck 90, SE143
96/7 UpperDeck 273
94/5 UDBeAPlayer-Aut. 92
96/7 UDBlackDiamond 74
95/6 UDCollChoice 33
96/7 UDCollChoice 131, 320
85/6 HFD/JuniorWhalers
86/7 HFD/JuniorWhalers
87/8 HFD/JuniorWhalers
88/9 HFD/JuniorWhalers
89/90 HFD/JuniorWhalers
83/4 Brandon 20

FERRAS, JOE
88/9 ProCards(Adirondack)

FERSCHWEILER, PAT
92/3 West.Mich
93/4 Roanoke
94/5 Roanoke

FESER, COLLIN
84/5 PrinceAlbert

FESER, TILL
94/5 DEL 283
95/6 DEL 278
96/7 DEL 175

FESS, CHRIS
94/5 Knoxville 18

FETISOV, VYACHESLAV (SLAVA)
90/1 Bowman 80
91/2 Bowman 273
92/3 Bowman 145
95/6 Donruss 272
96/7 Donruss 28
96/7 DonrussElite 99
93/4 EASports 74, 208
96/7 Flair 27
96/7 Fleer 143
92/3 FleerUltra 337
93/4 FleerUltra 174
95 Globe 236
91 IvanFiodorovSportUnites
95/6 Leaf 280
96/7 Leaf 42
96/7 LeafLimited 26
96/7 LeafPreferred 34
97/8 Omega 78
90/1 OPC/Topps 27
91/2 OPC/Topps 175
92/3 O-Pee-Chee 162
97/8 Post
98/9 Pacific 190
97/8 PacificCrown 111
97/8 PacificRevolution 46
79 PaniniSticker 141
90/1 PaniniSticker 75, 339
96/7 PaniniSticker 187
91/2 Parkhurst 96
92/3 Parkhurst 334
95/6 Parkhurst 68, 249
91/2 Pinnacle 101
92/3 Pinnacle 247, 299
93/4 Pinnacle 397
95/6 POG 100
93/4 PowerPlay 136
90/1 ProSet 167
91/2 ProSet 142
92/3 ProSet 96
91/2 PSPlatinum 199
91/2 RedAce
90/1 Score 62
91/2 Score(CDN) 184, (U.S) 184
92/3 Score 97
93/4 Score 229
96/7 Score 73
97/8 Score(DET) 11
82 SemicSticker 53
89 SemicSticker 87
91 SemicSticker 213
79/80 SovietStars
83/4 SovietStars
87/8 SovietStars
89/90 SovietStars
96/7 Summit 128
92/3 Topps 458
91/2 ToppsStadiumClub 24
92/3 ToppsStadiumClub 392
93/4 ToppsStadiumClub 265
90/1 UpperDeck 176
91/2 UpperDeck 410
92/3 UpperDeck 278
94/5 UpperDeck 434
96/7 UDBlackDiamond 2
89/90 N.J.
90/1 N.J.

FEUERSTEIN, H.
95/6 Richmond

FEWSTER, NEIL
91/2 SketchOHL 208
93/4 Slapshot(NiagaraFalls) 15
94/5 Slapshot(Guelph) 11

FICENEC, JAKUB
95/6 APS 129

FICHAUD, ERIC
94/5 Assets 62, 87, DC24, -Fon
95/6 Bowman 155
94/5 Classic 14, C3, CP2, T68
94/5 ClassicFourSport 130
94/5 C4'Images 107, CP20
94/5 ClassicImages 13
96/7 Donruss-RatedRook 8
97/8 Donruss 183
96/7 D.CdnIce 120, -Gardien 6
97/8 D.CdnIce-Gardiens 8
95/6 DonrussElite-Rookie 6
96/7 D.Elite 132, -Aspiration 14
97/8 DonrussElite 87
97/8 D.Preferred 49,-ColGuard 8
97/8 D.Priority 40,-PostGen 12
97/8 DonrussStudio 91
95/6 EdgeIce 93, TW11
94/5 Flair 179
96/7 Flair 115
96/7 Fleer 127, -Calder 4
94/5 FleerUltra 376
96/7 FleerUltra 100, -Rookies 7
95/6 FutureLegends 8, -Pltnm 2
97/8 KatchMedallion 86
94/5 Leaf 443, -Phenoms 7
96/7 Leaf-GoldL.Rookie 9
97/8 Leaf 20, -PipeDreams 15
94/5 LeafLimited 45
96/7 LeafLimited 69
96/7 L.Preferred 119, -L.Steel 53
97/8 Limited 59, 124, 174
97/8 Limited -fabric 56
96/7 Maggers 97
96/7 MetalUniverse 179
97/8 PacificCrown 274
96/7 PaniniSticker 90, 303
95/6 Parkhurst 537
94/5 ParkieSE 174
94/5 Pinnacle 493
96/7 Pinnacle 228
97/8 Pinnacle 66
96/7 PinnacleBeAPlayer 214
97/8 PinnacleInside 31, -Stand 5
96/7 PinnacleZenith 116
95/6 POG 177
94/5 Premier 533
96/7 Score 256
97/8 Score 26
94/5 Select 188
96/7 SelectCertified 103
96/7 SkyBoxImpact 150
95/6 SP 90
96/7 SP 92
94/5 SRGoldStandard 83
96/7 Summit 178
94/5 ToppsFinest 77
96/7 ToppsNHLPicks RS15
94/5 UpperDeck 255
96/7 UpperDeck 96, 12B, X27
97/8 UpperDeck 102
96/7 UDBlackDiamond 105
96/7 UDCollChoice 155, 323
97/8 UDCollChoice 153

FICHUK, PETE
72 SemicSticker 131

FICORELLI, TERRY
91/2 Cincinnati

FIDLER, MIKE
77/8 OPC 290
78/9 OPC/Topps 84
79/80 OPC/Topps 219
81/2 O-Pee-Chee 136
79 PaniniSticker 217
79/80 MIN

FIEBELKORN, JED
91/2 Minnesota
92/3 Minnesota
93/4 Minnesota
94/5 Minnesota

FIELD, WILF
34-43 BeeHives(NYA)
39/40 OPC (V301-1) 64

FIELDER, GUYLE
57/8 Topps 36

FIFE, JEFF
89/90 SketchOHL 93, 197

FIGLIUZZI, STEFAN
96/7 DEL 120
95 Globe 233
95 PaniniWorlds 89
94 Semic 302
93 SemicSticker 227
96 Wien 178

FILATOV, ANATOLI
93/4 Slapshot(NiagaraFalls) 22

FILIMONOV, DIMITRI
93/4 Donruss 239
94/5 Donruss 97
93/4 FleerUltra 381
93/4 Leaf 400
93/4 Parkhurst 139
94/5 Parkhurst 162
93/4 Pinnacle 450
93/4 PowerPlay 398
93/4 Premier 496
92/3 RedAce(Blue) 6, (Violet) 6
93/4 Score 598
92 SemicSticker 106
93 SemicSticker 132
91/2 StarPics 19
93/4 ToppsStadiumClub 468
91/2 UpperDeck 3
93/4 UpperDeck 405, SP-109
94/5 UpperDeck 178
93/4 OTT/Kraft

FILION, MAURICE
72/3 Québec
73/4 Québec

FILIP, JAN
94/5 APS 27

FILIPEK, DARYL
91/2 FerrisState

FILIPENKO, MARK
92/3 BCJHL 132

FILIPENKO, WAYNE
91/2 AirCanadaSJHL A20

FILIPI, MILAN
94/5 APS 39

FILLION, BOB
45-64 BeeHives(MTL)
48-52 Exhibits
43-47 ParadeSportive
45-54 QuakerOats

FILLION, CLAUDE
95/6 Hampton HR A-11

FILLION, DENIS
51/2 BasDuFleuve 57
52/3 BasDuFleuve 44

FILLION, JEAN-MARIE
51/2 BasDuFleuve 48

FILLION, MARCEL
51/2 BasDuFleuve 58
52/3 BasDuFleuve 34

FILLION, PIERRE
90/1 SketchQMJHL 169

FINDLAY, TIM
94/5 Signature 61
94/5 Slapshot(Windsor) 26
95/6 Slapshot 429

FINK, PATRIK
94/5 APS 178
95/6 APS 194

FINKBEINER, LLOYD
51/2 LavalDairy 90

FINLEY, BRIAN
98 BowmanCHL 21, 161, SC17
98/9 Topps 240

FINLEY, JEFF
97/8 PacificRegime 151
96/7 PinnacleBeAPlayer 156
93/4 PowerPlay 405
88/9 ProCards(Springfield)
89/90 ProCards'AHL 252
90/1 ProCards 503
91/2 ProCards 470
92/3 ToppsStadiumClub 426
93/4 PHA 13FEB94
93/4 PHA/JCPenney
96/7 PHO
86/7 Portland

FINN, RON
90/1 ProSet 685

FINN, SEAN
89/90 Johnstown 35

FINN, STEVE
91/2 Bowman 140
92/3 Bowman 185
92/3 Durivage 40
93/4 Durivage 20
93/4 Leaf 422
91/2 OPC/Topps 139
92/3 O-Pee-Chee 7
89/90 opcSticker 191/45
97/8 PacificRegime 93
90/1 Panini(QUE) 3
88/9 PaniniSticker 350
91/2 PaniniSticker 261
92/3 PaniniSticker 216
93/4 PaniniSticker 75
94/5 PaniniSticker 61
92/3 Parkhurst 379
91/2 Pinnacle 138
93/4 Pinnacle 307
94/5 Pinnacle 312
96/7 PinnacleBeAPlayer 188
93/4 Premier 326
94/5 Premier 398
90/1 ProSet 514
91/2 ProSet 204
91/2 Score(CDN) 498, (U.S) 278
92/3 Score 44
93/4 Score 322
92/3 Topps 449
91/2 ToppsStadiumClub 56
92/3 ToppsStadiumClub 384
93/4 TSC 464, -Master (2) 9
94/5 ToppsStadiumClub 192
91/2 UpperDeck 340
96/7 UDCollChoice 132
85/6 QUE/GeneralFoods
85/6 QUE/Provigo
86/7 QUE
86/7 QUE/McDonald
87/8 QUE/GeneralFoods
88/9 QUE
88/9 QUE/GeneralFoods
89/90 QUE
89/90 QUE/GeneralFoods
89/90 QUE/Police
90/1 QUE
90/1 QUE/PetroCanada
91/2 QUE/PetroCanada
92/3 QUE/PetroCanada
94/5 QUE/BurgerKing
86/7 Fredericton

FINN, TYSON
95/6 Slapshot 385

FINNIE, JOHN
89/90 SketchMEM 28

FINNIGAN, FRANK
33/4 Anonymous (V129) 26
34-43 BeeHives(TOR)
24/5 Champs (C144)
33/4 CndGum (V252)
36-39 DiamondMatch (1)
27-32 LaPresse 31/2
33/4 OPC (V304A) 25
24/5 (V145-2) 9
32/3 TOR/OKeefe 12

FINNSTROM, JOHAN
94/5 ElitSet 202, -NHLDraft 4
95/6 ElitSet 115
94/5 SigRookies 6
94/5 SRGoldStandard 84
95/6 udElite 173
97/8 udSwedish 118

FINSTED, MORTAN
94 Semic 260
95 Semic 180
93 SemicSticker 248

FIORENTINO, PETER
89/90 ProCards(IHL) 46
90/1 ProCards 5
91/2 ProCards 190
92/3 Binghampton
94/5 Binghampton
96/7 Binghampton
95/6 LasVegas
87/8 SSMarie 23

FIRSOV, ANATOLI
70/1 Kuvajulkaisut 2
72 Panda
72 SemicSticker 11
74 SemicSticker 42
91 SemicSticker 243
69/70 Soviet Stars
70/1 Soviet Stars
71/2 Soviet Stars
71/2 WilliamsFIN 2

FIRTH, JASON
89/90 SketchMEM 33
89/90 SketchOHL 184
90/1 SketchOHL 232
91/2 SketchOHL 59
88/9 Kitchener 13
89/90 Kitchener 14
90/1 Kitchener 12
94/5 ThunderBay
95/6 ThunderBay

FISCHER, JIRI
98 BowmanCHL 155, A19
98/9 Topps 242

FISCHER, KAI
95/6 DEL 77
96/7 DEL 271

FISCHER, LUBOMIR
94/5 APS 277
95/6 APS 99

FISCHER, PATRICK
95 PaniniWorlds 58

FISCHER, RON
94/5 DEL 379
95/6 DEL 366
95 PaniniWorlds 58
89 SemicSticker 112

FISCHER, WOLFGANG
74 Hellas 112

FISET, MIKE
85/6 Kingston 24
86/7 Kingston 24
87/8 Kingston 24

FISET, STÉPHANE
92/3 Bowman 398
93/4 Donruss 274
94/5 Donruss 225
95/6 Donruss 390
96/7 Donruss 186
97/8 Donruss 179
96/7 D.CdnIce 17, -Gardiens 5
97/8 D.CdnIce 30, -Gardiens 5
96/7 D.Elite 13, -Painted 10
97/8 DonrussElite 54
97/8 DonrussPreferred 136
97/8 DonrussPriority 96
97/8 DonrussStudio 52
92/3 Durivage 47
93/4 Durivage 21
94/5 Flair 145
94/5 Fleer 175
95/6 FleerMetal 31
93/4 FleerUltra 55
94/5 FleerUltra 173
95/6 FleerUltra 131, 220, 369
96/7 FleerUltra 78
95/6 Hoyle'EAST Q (Hearts)
97/8 KatchMedallion 69
93/4 Kraft-Cutout
94/5 Kraft
95/6 Kraft-Crease
93/4 Leaf 301
94/5 Leaf 329
96/7 Leaf 188
97/8 Leaf 93
96/7 LeafLimited 72
96/7 LeafPreferred 57, -Steel 15
97/8 Limited 150, 180
96/7 MetalUniverse 74
97/8 Omega 107
90/1 OPC/Topps 312
92/3 O-Pee-Chee 75
98/9 Pacific 234
97/8 PacificCrown 245
97/8 PacificInvincible 67
97/8 PacificParamount 88
98/9 PacificParamount 104
91/2 PaniniSticker 258
92/3 PaniniSticker 207
94/5 PaniniSticker 63
95 PaniniWorlds 2
91/2 Parkhurst 363
92/3 Parkhurst 378
93/4 Parkhurst 164
95/6 Parkhurst 317, PP35
93/4 Pinnacle 115, -Masks 6
94/5 Pinnacle 102
97/8 Pinnacle 52
97/8 PinnacleCertified 14
97/8 PinnacleInside 23
95/6 PinnacleZenith 119
96/7 PinnacleZenith 20
94/5 POG 292
95/6 POG 82
93/4 PowerPlay 198
93/4 Premier 165
94/5 Premier 333
90/1 ProCards 466
91/2 ProCards 530
95/6 ProMagnet 80
92/3 ProSet 152
90/1 Score 415, -YoungStar 22
92/3 Score 354
93/4 Score 379
94/5 Score 126
95/6 Score 205
96/7 Score 17, -NetWorth 10
97/8 Score 35
96/7 SelectCertified 8
94/5 SP 99
95/6 SP 34
96/7 SP 77
97/8 SPAuthentic 76
95/6 Summit 160, -InTheCr 8
96/7 Summit 98
92/3 Topps 285
95/6 Topps 284
92/3 ToppsStadiumClub 196
93/4 ToppsStadiumClub 315
94/5 ToppsStadiumClub 246
95/6 ToppsStadiumClub 53
91/2 UpperDeck 452
93/4 UpperDeck 203
94/5 UpperDeck 450
95/6 UpperDeck 397, SE23
96/7 UpperDeck 274
95/6 UDBeAPlayer 121
96/7 UDBlackDiamond 85
98/9 UDChoice 97
95/6 UDCollChoice 150
96/7 UDCollChoice 59
89/90 QUE
89/90 QUE/GeneralFoods
89/90 QUE/Police
90/1 QUE
91/2 QUE/PetroCanada
92/3 QUE/PetroCanada
94/5 QUE/BurgerKing
90/1 Halifax

FISHBACK, BRUCE
85/6 Minn-Duluth 16

FISHER, BUD
26 Dominion 29

FISHER, CRAIG
94/5 ClassicImages 22
95/6 EdgeIce 173
95/6 FutureLegends 18
90/1 OPC/Topps 126
90/1 ProCards 30
91/2 ProCards 233
90/1 Score 412
90/1 UpperDeck 155
93/4 Indianapolis

FISHER, DUNCAN
45-64 BeeHives(NYR)

FISHER, ROBERT
51/2 Parkhurst 24

FITCHNER, BOB
72-84 Dernière 78/9
76 QuébecNordiques/MA
76/7 QuébecNordiques

FITZGERALD, BRIAN
89/90 ProCards(AHL) 223

FITZGERALD, ROB
95/6 Slapshot 48

FITZGERALD, RUSTY
95/6 Leaf 316
95/6 Topps 209
95/6 UpperDeck 142
93/4 Minn-Duluth

FITZGERALD, TOM
90/1 Bowman 116
92/3 Bowman 369
93/4 Donruss 121
92/3 FleerUltra 342
93/4 FleerUltra 324
93/4 Leaf 221
94/5 Leaf 516
91/2 OPC/Topps 279
92/3 O-Pee-Chee 394
97/8 PacificCrown 113
98/9 PcfcParamnt 123,-TmCL 14
93/4 Parkhurst 348
95/6 Parkhurst 352
94/5 ParkieSE 64
93/4 Pinnacle 390
94/5 Pinnacle 207
96/7 Pinnacle 57
96/7 PinnacleBeAPlayer 4
93/4 Premier 338
94/5 Premier 53
88/9 ProCards(Springfield)
89/90 ProCards(AHL) 239
91/2 ProSet 431
93/4 Score 493, 554
94/5 Score 163
92/3 Topps 31
95/6 Topps 294
92/3 ToppsStadiumClub 102
93/4 ToppsStadiumClub 392
91/2 UpperDeck 389
92/3 UpperDeck 52
94/5 UpperDeck 320
95/6 UpperDeck 436
96/7 UpperDeck 69
97/8 UpperDeck 286
93/4 FLA
96/7 FLA/WinnDixie
97/8 FLA/WinnDixie
89/90 NYI

FITZPATRICK, BLAINE
95/6 Slapshot 377

FITZPATRICK, DAVE
91/2 AvantGardeBCJ 163
92/3 BCJHL 5

FITZPATRICK, MARK
90/1 Bowman 119
91/2 Bowman 213
92/3 Bowman 394
93/4 Donruss 133
94/5 Donruss 235
95/6 Donruss 301
93/4 EASports 202
92/3 FleerUltra 124, -AW 7
94/5 FleerUltra 296
92/3 Kraft'Disk
93/4 Leaf 335
94/5 Leaf 308
95/6 Leaf 120
90/1 OPC/Topps 395
91/2 OPC/Topps 47
92/3 O-Pee-Chee 204
89/90 PaniniSticker 265
90/1 PaniniSticker 86
92/3 PaniniSticker 195
93/4 PaniniSticker 66
92/3 Parkhurst 99
93/4 Parkhurst 344
94/5 Parkhurst 87
95/6 Parkhurst 88
92/3 Pinnacle 24
93/4 Pinnacle 369
94/5 Pinnacle 236
95/6 Pinnacle 175, -Masks 7
96/7 PinnacleBeAPlayer 10
93/4 PowerPlay 92
94/5 Premier 82
88/9 ProCards(NewHaven)
91/2 ProCards 472
90/1 ProSet 181
92/3 ProSet 107
90/1 Score 102, -HotCards 50
90/1 Score -YoungStar 32
91/2 Score(CDN) 486, (U.S) 266
92/3 Score 210, 526
93/4 Score 171, 537
95/6 Score 173
97/8 Score 234
92/3 Topps 216
95/6 Topps 183
98/9 Topps 194
91/2 ToppsStadiumClub 345
92/3 ToppsStadiumClub 12
93/4 ToppsStadiumClub 307
90/1 UpperDeck 37
91/2 UpperDeck 602
92/3 UpperDeck 332
94/5 UpperDeck 457, SP120
95/6 UpperDeck 423
96/7 FLA/WinnDixie
89/90 NYI
85/6 MedicineHat 23

FITZPATRICK, RORY
93/4 ClassicFourSport 209
94/5 LeafLimited-USAJrs 5
95/6 Parkhurst 535
93/4 Slapshot(Sudbury) 5
94/5 Slapshot(Sud) 3, -Promo
94/5 SP 192
94/5 ToppsFinest 115
95/6 Fredericton
92/3 Sudbury 5

FITZPATRICK, ROSS
89/90 ProCards(AHL) 340
90/1 ProCards 23
91/2 ProCards 207
83/4 Springfield 15

FITZSIMMONS, JASON
90/1 SketchWHL 162
91/2 SketchWHL 242, 280

FIXTER, P
91/2 Cornwall 27

FIZZELL, B.
67/8 ColumbusCheckers
69 ColumbusCheckers

FIZZELL, BRETT
93/4 Portland

FIZZELL, KRIS
95/6 PrinceAlbert

FJELDSTAD, RUNE
95 PaniniWorlds 253

FLAHERTY, JOE
88/9 ProCards(Maine)

FLAHERTY, RAY
80/1 Oshawa 2

FLAHERTY, WADE
95/6 Donruss 280
98/9 Pacific 281
97/8 PacificRegime 179
95/6 Parkhurst 189
95/6 Pinnacle 173
90/1 ProCards 601
91/2 ProCards 517
95/6 Topps 249
95/6 UpperDeck 57
95/6 UDCollChoice 97
92/3 S.J/PacificBell
90/1 KansasCity 3

FLAMAN, DALLAS
95/6 PrinceAlbert

FLAMAN, FERN
45-64 BeeHives(BOSx2), (TOR)
51/2 Parkhurst 80
52/3 Parkhurst 47
53/4 Parkhurst 14
54/5 Parkhurst 20
93/4 Parkhurst PR45
93/4 Parkie(56/7) 2
45-54 QuakerOats
90/1 Score 357
60/1 ShirriffCoin 102
54/5 Topps 25
57/8 Topps 4
58/9 Topps 56
59/60 Topps 29
60/1 Topps 57
61/2 Topps 21
54-67 TorontoStar V6
56-66 Tor.Star 57/8, 58/9, 60/1
91/2 Ultimate(O6) 48,76,-Aut. 48
91/2 BOS/Legends (x2)

FLANAGAN, DAVE
91/2 ProCards 128

FLANAGAN, JOE
93/4 Birmingham 4

FLANDER, CRAIG
93/4 Fredericton

FLASAR, ALES
94/5 APS 3
95/6 APS 338

FLATLEY, PATRICK
90/1 Bowman 124
91/2 Bowman 218
92/3 Bowman 134
83 CanadaJuniors
93/4 Donruss 199
95/6 Donruss 227
94/5 Flair 102
94/5 Fleer 121
92/3 FleerUltra 125
93/4 FleerUltra 34
94/5 FleerUltra 125
93/4 Kraft 'Captain
93/4 Leaf 43
94/5 Leaf 381
95/6 Leaf 151
84/5 O-Pee-Chee 124
85/6 OPC/Topps 83
86/7 OPC/Topps 162
87/8 OPC/Topps 136
88/9 OPC/Topps 191
89/90 O-Pee-Chee 250, 302
90/1 OPC/Topps 350
91/2 OPC/Topps 343
92/3 O-Pee-Chee 342
85/6 opcSticker 73/200
86/7 opcSticker 207/81
87/8 opcSticker 245/136
97/8 PacificRegime 126
87/8 PaniniSticker 101
88/9 PaniniSticker 286
89/90 PaniniSticker 272
90/1 PaniniSticker 82
91/2 PaniniSticker 245
92/3 PaniniSticker 201
93/4 PaniniSticker 60
94/5 PaniniSticker 50
95/6 PaniniSticker 93
91/2 Parkhurst 67, 405
92/3 Parkhurst 342
93/4 Parkhurst 391
95/6 Parkhurst 403
94/5 ParkieSE 103
92/3 Pinnacle 44
93/4 Pinnacle 203, CA14
94/5 Pinnacle 176
95/6 Playoff 62
94/5 POG 155
95/6 POG 173
93/4 PowerPlay 146
93/4 Premier 28
94/5 Premier 178
95/6 ProMagnet 51
90/1 ProSet 182
91/2 ProSet 152, 578
92/3 ProSet 102
91/2 PSPlatinum 77
90/1 Score 174
91/2 Score(CDN) 29, (U.S) 29
92/3 Score 99
93/4 Score 220
94/5 Score 116
95/6 Score 196
97/8 Score(NYR) 12
95/6 SkyBoxEmotion 104
95/6 SkyBoxImpact 100
92/3 Topps 135
95/6 Topps 139
91/2 ToppsStadiumClub 20
92/3 ToppsStadiumClub 477
93/4 ToppsStadiumClub 24
90/1 UpperDeck 118
91/2 UpperDeck 226
93/4 UpperDeck 210
94/5 UpperDeck 371
95/6 UpperDeck 106
95/6 UDBeAPlayer 13
95/6 UDCollChoice 202
84/5 NYI 4
89/90 NYI

FLEETWOOD, BRENT
87/8 Portland
88/9 Portland
89/90 Portland

FLEMING, ADAN
95/6 Slapshot 128

FLEMING, BOB
87/8 Flint

FLEMING, GERRY
92/3 ClassicProspects 37
94/5 MTL
92/3 Fredericton
93/4 Fredericton
96/7 Fredericton

FLEMING, REG (REGGIE)
45-64 BeeHives(CHI)
64-67 BeeHives(BOS), (NYR)
62 CeramicTiles
64/5 CokeCap BOS-19
65/6 CocaCola
70/1 DadsCookies
70/1 EddieSargent 21
70/1 Esso Stamp
73/4 Nabisco
68/9 O-Pee-Chee 167
69/70 OPC/T. 95, OPC-Sticker
70/1 OPC/T. 128, -Deckle 12
72/3 O-Pee-Chee 316
94/5 Parkie(64/5) 8
95/6 Parkie(66/7) 83
73/4 QuakerOats 45
60/1 ShirriffCoin 78
61/2 ShirriffCoin 24
68/9 ShirriffCoin NYR4
61/2 Topps 26
62/3 Topps 42, -Buck
63/4 Topps 31
64/5 Topps 35
65/6 Topps 104
66/7 Topps 93, -USATest 54
67/8 Topps 30

FLEMING, RYAN
93/4 Mich.State

FLEMING, WAYNE
90/1 CanadaNats
91/2 CanadaNats
94/5 ElitSet 300
92/3 SemicElitserien 329

FLEMMING, JONAS
96/7 Sisu 120

FLEMMING, MARKUS
94/5 DEL 288
95/6 DEL 265

FLEMMING, MICHAEL
94/5 DEL 412

FLEMMING, WAYNE
88/9 ProCards(Moncton)
87/8 Moncton
90/1 Moncton
91/2 Moncton

FLESCH, JOHN
74/5 Loblaws Update
75/6 OPC 353
81/2 Milwaukee 5

FLETCHER, CLIFF
90/1 TOR/P.L.A.Y. 4

FLETCHER, CRAIG
91/2 SketchWHL 57
92/3 BCJHL 125

FLETCHER, SCOTT
95/6 Spokane 2

FLETCHER, STEVEN
88/9 ProCards(Moncton)
89/90 ProCards(AHL) 347
90/1 ProCards 537
91/2 ProCards 256

FLETT, BILL
68/9 Bauer
70/1 DadsCookies
70/1 EddieSargent 75
71/2 EddieSargent 67
72/3 EddieSargent 164
70/1 Esso Stamp
74/5 Loblaws
68/9 O-Pee-Chee 159
69/70 OPC/Topps 102
70/1 OPC 161, OPC/T-Sticker
71/2 OPC/Topps 47
72/3 OPC 187
73/4 OPC/Topps 20
74/5 OPC/Topps 64
75/6 OPC 349
76/7 OPC 332
79/80 OPC 266
72 SemicSticker 226
68/9 ShirriffCoin LA8
71/2 TheTorontoSun
72/3 Topps 139
79/80 EDM
88/9 EDM/ActionMagazine 71
74/5 TOR

FLETT, JOSH
92/3 BCJHL 6

FLEURY, CARL
91/2 SketchQMJHL 104
94/5 Roanoke

FLEURY, CHRIS
95/6 UpperDeck 518

FLEURY, SYLVAIN
92/3 Oklahoma

FLEURY, THEOREN
95/6 Aces K (Spades)
96/7 Aces J (Diamonds)
97/8 Aces 7 (Diamonds)
90/1 Bowman 102
91/2 Bowman 249, 270
92/3 Bowman 206, 355
95/6 Bowman 52
93/4 Donruss 46, D
94/5 Donruss 99
95/6 Don. 289,-Marks 6,-ProP 12
96/7 Donruss 159, -HitList 20
97/8 Donruss 160
96/7 D.CdnIce 78, -OCanada 5
97/8 D.CdnIce 23, -National 19
95/6 DonrussElite 106
96/7 DonrussElite 54
97/8 DonrussElite 74
97/8 Donruss Preferred 138
97/8 DonrussPriority 141
97/8 DonrussStudio 81
93/4 EASports 23
95/6 EdgeIce L9
97/8 EssoOlympic 12
94/5 Flair 24
96/7 Flair 11
94/5 Fleer 29
96/7 Fleer 12, -ArtRoss 3
95/6 F.Metal 18,-Heavy 3,-Iron 3
96/7 FleerNHLPicks 24
96/7 FP-FabFifty 11, -Jagged 2
92/3 FleerUltra 21
93/4 FleerUltra 41
94/5 FleerUltra 29
95/6 FU 24, 382,-Creas 3,-Red 2
96/7 FleerUltra 21
91/2 Gillette 4
95 Globe 83
96/7 Got-UmHockeyGreatsCoin
93/4 HockeyWit 94
95/6 Hoyle'WEST 4 (Spades)
92/3 HumptyDumpty (1)
97/8 KatchMedallion 20
95/6 KennerSLU
89/90 Kraft 2
91/2 Kraft 13
93/4 KraftDinner
94/5 Kraft'HockeyH
95/6 KraftDinner, -Disk
96/7 KraftDinner, -Disk, -Flex
97/8 Kraft -CaseSeries, -Stickers
97/8 Kraft -RoadToNagano
97/8 Kraft -WorldsBest
93/4 Leaf 154
94/5 Leaf 55
95/6 Leaf 115,-FireOn 5,-Gold 5
96/7 Leaf 61
97/8 Leaf 136
94/5 LeafLimited 99
95/6 LeafLimited 6
96/7 LeafLimited 67
96/7 LeafPreferd 67, -L.Steel 47
97/8 Limited 24, 157, 177
96/7 Maggers 19
91/2 McDonalds Mc-18
92/3 McDonalds McD07
96/7 McDonalds McD15
97/8 McDonalds McD2, F9
97/8 McDonalds -Medallions
96/7 MetalUniverse 18
97/8 Omega 29, -StickHandle 3
89/90 O-Pee-Chee 232
90/1 OPC/Topps 386
91/2 OPC/T. 282, 322, T-TL 14
92/3 O-Pee-Chee 99
91/2 opcPremier 92
98/9 Pacific 117,-Gld 6,-TmCL 4
97/8 PacificCrown 45
97/8 PacificCrownRoyale 18
97/8 PacificDynagon! 15, 137
97/8 PcfcD-Dyn 4A,-Tand 23, 35
97/8 PacificInvincible 16
97/8 PacificParamount 28
98/9 PcfcParamount 27,-TmCL 4
97/8 PacificRevolution 17
97/8 PcfcRev -ASGm 4,-TmCL 4
90/1 Panini(CGY) 1
90/1 PaniniSticker 176
91/2 PaniniSticker 51
92/3 PaniniSticker 46
93/4 PaniniSticker 179
94/5 PaniniSticker 159
95/6 PaniniSticker 237
96/7 PaniniSticker 234
97/8 PaniniSticker 199
95 PaniniWorlds 24
91/2 Parkhurst 22
92/3 Parkhurst 19
93/4 Parkhurst 28
94/5 Parkhurst V20
95/6 Parkhurst 29
94/5 ParkieSE 28
91/2 Pinnacle 190, 358
92/3 Pinnacle 125
93/4 Pinnacle 79
94/5 Pinnacle 38, NL15
95/6 Pinnacle 6, -FirstStrike 15
96/7 Pinnacle 6
97/8 Pinnacle 103
96/7 PinnacleBAP 159, -Biscuit 4
97/8 PinnacleBeeHive 18
97/8 PinnacleCertified 42
95/6 PinnacleFANtasy 9
97/8 PinnacleInside 40
95/6 PinnacleZenith 11
96/7 P.Zenith 55, -Assailant 11
95/6 Playoff 16
94/5 POG 54
95/6 POG 52, 017
94/5 Post
96/7 Post, -StickUm 2
93/4 PowerPlay 36
93/4 Premier 100, -BlackOPC 13
94/5 Premier 295, -GoToGuy 7
94/5 Premier-Finest(Topps) 19
95/6 ProMagnet 41
90/1 ProSet 33
91/2 ProSet 28, 274, AC20
91/2 ProSet -ThePuck 4
92/3 ProSet 23
91/2 PSPlatinum 16
90/1 Score 226, -YoungStar 6
91/2 Score(CDN) 226, 297
91/2 Score(U.S) 226, 407
91/2 Score-YoungStar 4. -Hot 4
92/3 Score 280
93/4 Score 191, 441
94/5 Score 69, CI15, TF4
95/6 Score 121,-Gld 13,-Lmp 13
96/7 Score 12, -CheckIt 13
97/8 Score 97
94/5 Select 109
95/6 SelectCertified 5,-Double13
96/7 SelectCertified 75
94 Semic 96, 357
95 Semic 96
92 SemicSticker 90
95/6 SisuLimited 81, S&S 9
95/6 SkBxEmotion 21, -Xcited 1
95/6 SkyBoxImpact 21, -Ice 13
96/7 SkyBoxImpact 13
96/7 SB'7Eleven
93 SourPuckCaps 1
94/5 SP 17
95/6 SP 16, E6
96/7 SP 20, CW14, GF15
97/8 SPAuthentic 18, I20
96/7 SPx 5
97/8 SPx 6, SPX14
98/9 SPx"Finite" 12, 107, 167
96/7 SportFX MiniStix
95/6 Summit 8
96/7 Summit 91
91 TeamCanada
96/7 TeamOut
92/3 Topps 208, 220
95/6 Topps 25, 382
95/6 Topps 1HG, 6CG, HGC5
98/9 Topps 27
94/5 ToppsFinest 28
94/5 TF-B.Best(Red) 4, BBest 1
95/6 ToppsFinest 30, 181
96/7 ToppsNHLPicks TS14
91/2 ToppsStadiumClub 355
92/3 ToppsStadiumClub 2
93/4 TSC 390, -Master (2) 5
94/5 T.StadiumClub 25
95/6 T.StadiumClub 165, EN5
94/5 TSC'Members 33
95/6 TSC'Members 7
97/8 ToppsSticker 2
95/6 ToppsSuperSkills 35
90/1 UpperDeck 47, 478
91/2 UD 80, 245, 506, 630
92/3 UpperDeck 285
93/4 UD 3,229,288,GG7,SP-21
94/5 UpperDeck 315, 566, R41
94/5 UpperDeck R58, SP11
95/6 UD 179, 235, AS11, F12,R8
95/6 UD SE101,-ASPrediMVP13
96/7 UpperDeck 22, 208, 4A
96/7 UD GJ12, LS09, P14, X30
97/8 UpperDeck 232
93/4 UDBeAPlayer 21, -Roots 28
94/5 UDBAP R23, -Aut. 123
96/7 UDBlackDiamond 70
97/8 UDBlackDiamond 143
98/9 UDChoice 34, BH25, SQ13
95/6 UDCC 201, 384, C11
96/7 UDCC 35, 200, S20, UD11
96/7 UDCC'Oversize 2of8, 35
97/8 UDCC 40, C14, SQ64
97/8 udDiamondVision 9
96/7 UpperDeck"Ice " 9
97/8 UpperDeckIce 64
97/8 ValuNet
96 Wien 87
97/8 Zenith 12, Z46
90/1 CGY/McGavins
91/2 CGY/IGA
92/3 CGY/IGA 20
88/9 SaltLake 8

FLICHEL, MARTY
92/3 Tacoma
93/4 Tacoma

FLICHEL, TODD
88/9 ProCards(Moncton)
89/90 ProCards(AHL) 37
90/1 ProCards 247
91/2 ProCards 246
92/3 Cincinnati
87/8 Moncton
90/1 Moncton
93/4 Rochester
93/4 Rochester

FLIEGAUF, CHARLY
94/5 DEL 26

FLINCK, TAPIO
70/1 Kuvajulkaisut 189
80/1 Mallasjuoma 201
72 Panda
78/9 SM-Liiga 222
71/2 WilliamsFIN 81
72/3 WilliamsFIN 244
73/4 WilliamsFIN 241

FLINN, TYSON
96/7 Sudbury 9

FLINT, CALVIN
90/1 SketchWHL 232
89/90 Brandon 13
90/1 Brandon 21

FLINTOFT, ROB
87/8 Portland
88/9 Portland

FLINTON, ERIC
95/6 Classic 73
95/6 ClassicFiveSport 160, -Aut.
96/7 Binghampton

FLOCKHART, RON
82/3 O-Pee-Chee 249
83/4 O-Pee-Chee 264
84/5 O-Pee-Chee 174
85/6 O-Pee-Chee 171
86/7 OPC/Topps 146
87/8 OPC/Topps 103
82/3 opcSticker 113
83/4 opcSticker 192
84/5 opcSticker 115-16
85/6 opcSticker 128/246
86/7 opcSticker 177/39
87/8 opcSticker 25/166
87/8 PaniniSticker 317
83/4 SouhaitsRen.KeyChain
84/5 Topps 124
84/5 MTL
83/4 PGH
84/5 PGH/Heinz
87/8 STL/Kodak
77/8 VAN/RoyalBan
92/3 Dallas
93/4 Dallas
84/5 Springfield 13

FLOMENHOFT, STEVEN
93/4 Knoxville
94/5 Knoxville 12

FLORA, PETER
79 PaniniSticker 269

FLORIO, PERRY
93/4 Johnstown 18
94/5 Johnstown 8

FLOYD, LARRY
88/9 ProCards(CapreBreton)
89/90 ProCards(IHL) 113
90/1 ProCards 319
91/2 ProCards 314
83/4 N.J
92/3 SanDiego

FLUGGE, CHRISTIAN
94/5 DEL 327

FLYNN, BILLY
94/5 DEL 53
95/6 DEL 25

FLYNN, BRENT
91/2 Richmond 3
92/3 Richmond
93/4 Richmond 14
95/6 Richmond

FLYNN, DAN
89/90 SketchOHL 96
93/4 Slapshot(SSMaire) 30
93/4 SSMarie 30

FLYNN, MARTY
82/3 Fredericton 26
83/4 Fredericton 26
85/6 Fredericton 25
86/7 Fredericton

FLYNN, N.
90/1 SketchQMJHL 238

FLYNN, PADDY
93/4 OwenSound

FOCHT, DAN
95/6 Bowman P20

FOERSTER, DOUG
88/9 ProCards(Maine)

FOGARTY, BRYAN
90/1 Bowman 173
91/2 Bowman 149
95/6 EdgeIce 165
91/2 OPC/Topps 500
90/1 Panini(QUE) 4
90/1 PaniniSticker 144
91/2 PaniniSticker 259
91/ Parkhurst 146
91/2 Pinnacle 59
89/90 ProCards'AHL 168
90/1 ProSet 515
91/2 ProSet 200
91/2 PSPlatinum 103
90/1 Score 54
91/2 Score(CDN) 457, (U.S) 237
90/1 UpperDeck 548
91/2 UpperDeck 337
94/5 MTL
94/5 MTL/MolsonExport
92/3 PGH/Coke
89/90 QUE
90/1 QUE
90/1 QUE/PetroCanada
91/2 QUE/PetroCanada
89/90 Halifax
85/6 Kingston 13
86/7 Kingston 12
87/8 Kingston 21
88/9 NiagaraFalls 14
86/7 Portland

FOGLIETTA, JOE
94 Semic 301
92 SemicSticker 258
93 SemicSticker 220

FOGOLIN, JOHN LIDIO (LEE)
45-64 BeeHives(CHI), (DET)
51/2 Parkhurst 46
52/3 Parkhurst 55
53/4 Parkhurst 72
54/5 Parkhurst 84

FOGOLIN, LEE (JR.)
74/5 Loblaws
75/6 OPC/Topps 306
76/7 OPC/Topps 253
77/8 OPC/Topps 94
78/9 OPC/Topps 27
79/80 OPC/Topps 183
80/1 OPC/Topps 63
81/2 O-Pee-Chee 112
82/3 O-Pee-Chee 104
83/4 O-Pee-Chee 26
84/5 O-Pee-Chee 240
85/6 O-Pee-Chee 235
86/7 O-Pee-Chee 210
81/2 opcSticker 215
82/3 opcSticker 106
83/4 opcSticker 17, 100
84/5 opcSticker 254
85/6 opcSticker 218/85
86/7 opcSticker 71
80/1 Pepsi Cap
82/3 Post
83/4 SouhaitsRen.KeyChain
83/4 StaterMint H18
83/4 Vachon 23
74/5 BUF
79/80 EDM
81/2 EDM/RedRooster
81/2 EDM/WestEdmonton
82/3 EDM/RedRooster
83/4 EDM/McDonalds
84/5 EDM
84/5 EDM/RedRooster
85/6 EDM/RedRooster
86/7 EDM
86/7 EDM/RedRooster
88/9 EDM/ActionMagazine 42

FOIS, JORDAN
87/8 Sudbury 6
88/9 Sudbury 6

FOKIN, SERGEI
94/5 ElitSet 185
95/6 ElitSet 40
92/3 SemicElitserien 279
95/6 udElite 58
97/8 udSwedish 53

FOLDEN, B.
93/4 Waterloo

FOLEY, COLIN
90/1 SketchWHL 319
91/2 SketchWHL 37
93/4 Portland

FOLEY, GERRY
93/4 Parkie(56/7) 94
57/8 Topps 57

FOLEY, RICK
72/3 EddieSargent 165
72/3 OPC 80
72/3 Topps 98

FOLIGNO, MIKE
90/1 Bowman 247
91/2 Bowman 169
93/4 Donruss 433
92/3 FleerUltra 420
88/9 FritoLay
80/1 OPC/Topps 16, 187
81/2 OPC 87, Topps(W) 87
82/3 O-Pee-Chee 26
83/4 O-Pee-Chee 63
84/5 O-Pee-Chee 20, Topps 16
85/6 OPC/Topps 17
86/7 OPC/Topps 127, D
87/8 OPC/Topps 40
88/9 OPC/Topps 184
89/90 OPC/Topps 78
90/1 OPC/Topps 123, 262
91/2 OPC/Topps 18
81/2 opcSticker 122
82/3 opcSticker 120
83/4 opcSticker 237
84/5 opcSticker 212
85/6 opcSticker 174
86/7 opcSticker 42
87/8 opcSticker 150/12
88/9 opcSticker 257/125
89/90 opcSticker 260/141
87/8 PaniniSticker 29
88/9 PaniniSticker 226
89/90 PaniniSticker 210
90/1 PaniniSticker 25
92/3 PaniniSticker 84
93/4 PaniniSticker 228
92/3 Parkhurst 415
91/2 Pinnacle 292
82/3 Post
93/4 PowerPlay 346
93/4 Premier 262
90/1 ProSet 20
83/4 PuffySticker 7
90/1 Score 133
91/2 Score(CDN) 248
93/4 Score 387, 647
83/4 SouhaitsRen.KeyChain
91/2 ToppsStadiumClub 29
90/1 UpperDeck 378
91/2 UpperDeck 212
93/4 UpperDeck 155
82/3 BUF/Wendt 12
84/5 BUF/BlueShield
85/6 BUF
86/7 BUF
87/8 BUF/BlueShield
87/8 BUF/WonderBread
88/9 BUF/BlueShield
88/9 BUF/WonderBread
89/90 BUF/BlueShield
89/90 BUF/Campbell
93/4 BUF/NOCO
79/80 DET
80/1 DET
93/4 FLA
90/1 TOR/P.L.A.Y. 29
93/4 TOR/Blacks 21
95/6 StJohns

FOLKETT, CURTIS
91/2 AirCanadaSJHL C15
88/9 Brandon 16

FOLTA, PAVEL
94/5 APS 163

FOLTA, PETR
94/5 APS 134
95/6 APS 304

FOMIN, KAUKO
70/1 Kuvajulkaisut 293
71/2 WilliamsFIN 224

FOMRADADS, BLAINE
91/2 AirCanadaSJHL D34

FONSO, ANTONIO
94/5 DEL 408

FONTAINE, LEN
72/3 OPC 244

FONTAS, JON
78/9 Saginaw

FONTEYNE, VALERE (VAL)
45-64 BeeHives(DET)
64-67 BeeHives(DET)
62 CeramicTiles
64/5 CokeCap NYR-14
65/6 CocaCola
70/1 EddieSargent 176
71/2 EddieSargent 163
82? JDMcCarthy
68/9 OPC/Topps 109
69/70 OPC/Topps 119
70/1 OPC 208
71/2 OPC/Topps 189
72/3 OPC 319

60/1 Parkhurst 21
61/2 Parkhurst 21
62/3 Parkhurst 27
94/5 Parkie(64/5) 95
95/6 Parkie(66/7) 57
60/1 ShirriffCoin 48
61/2 ShirriffCoin 67
68/9 ShirriffCoin PGH3
63/4 Topps 61
66/7 Topps 108
71/2 PGH

FONTINATO, LOU
45-64 BeeHives(MTL), (NYR)
62 CeramicTiles
62/3 Parkhurst 52
93/4 Parkhurst PR61
93/4 Parkie(56/7) 93
60/1 ShirriffCoin 97
61/2 ShirriffCoin 111
62/3 ShirriffCoin 23
57/8 Topps 64
58/9 Topps 41
59/60 Topps 5
81/2 TCMA 4
61/2 York 40
60/1 Topps 61
54-67 TorontoStar V8
56-66 TorontoStar 62/3
91/2 UltimateO6 19, -Aut. 19

FOOTE, ADAM
93/4 Donruss 272
97/8 EssoOlympic 21
97/8 Kraft -RoadToNagano
93/4 Leaf 229
94/5 Leaf 529
97/8 McDonalds -Medallions
96/7 MetalUniverse 31
98/9 Pacific 52
97/8 PacificCrown 135
98/9 PacificParamount 54
97/8 PaniniSticker 202
91/2 Parkhurst 371
91/2 Pinnacle 337
93/4 Pinnacle 26
94/5 Pinnacle 432
95/6 Pinnacle 195
96/7 PinnacleBeAPlayer 196
93/4 PowerPlay 418
91/2 PSPlatinum 268
92/3 Score 131
93/4 Score 149
94/5 Score 151
97/8 Score 257
97/8 Score(COL) 12
90/1 SketchMEM 5
90/1 SketchOHL 157
96/7 SP 38
98/9 Topps 189
92/3 ToppsGold 528
92/3 ToppsStadiumClub 468
93/4 ToppsStadiumClub 496
91/2 UpperDeck 529
95/6 UpperDeck 204
97/8 UpperDeck 255
94/5 UDBeAPlayer R42, -Aut. 2
96/7 UDBlackDiamond 52
98/9 UDChoice 228
97/8 UDCollChoice 64
97/8 ValuNet
96/7 COL/PhotoPuck
91/2 QUE/PetroCanada
92/3 QUE/PetroCanada
94/5 QUE/BurgerKing
89/90 SSMarie 15

FORBES, COLIN
97/8 Omega 163
98/9 Pacific 325
98/9 PacificParamount 172
98/9 Topps 49
97/8 UpperDeck 191

FORBES, DAVE
74/5 Loblaws
74/5 OPC 266
75/6 OPC/Topps 173
76/7 OPC/Topps 246
77/8 OPC/Topps 143
78/9 OPC/Topps 167

FORBES, JAKE
25-27 Anonymous 77

FORBES, MIKE
81/2 EDM/RedRooster
88/9 EDM/ActionMagazine 72

FORBES, VERNON
24/5 Champs (C144)
25 Dominion 82
24/5 MapleCrispette (V130) 25
23/4 (V145-1) 29
24/5 (V145-2) 11

FORCH, LIBOR
94/5 APS 241
95/6 APS 14

FORD, BRIAN
89/90 ProCards(AHL) 268
83/4 Vachon 64
83/4 Fredericton 4

FORD, COLIN
87/8 SSMarie 18

FORD, GEORGE
52/3 StLawrence 59

FORD, JOHN
52/3 AnonymousOHL 114

FORD, MIKE
76/7 opcWHA 75

FORESTELL, BRIAN
90/1 SketchOHL 181
89/90 Windsor

FORSANDER, JOHAN
97/8 UDBlackDiamond 99
98/9 UDChoice 293
97/8 udSwedish 85

FORSBERG, JONAS
94/5 ElitSet 170
95/6 ElitSet 27, -Spidermen 9
95 Globe 55
94/5 ParkieSE 245
92/3 SemicElitserien 349

FORSBERG, KENT
92/3 SemicElitserien 332

FORSBERG, PASI
92/3 Jyvas-Hyva 168
93/4 Jyvas-Hyva 298
93/4 Sisu 74

FORSBERG, PETER
95/6 Aces 9 (Hearts)
96/7 Aces K (Hearts)
97/8 Aces Q (Spades)
91/2 Arena 4
95/6 Bowman 85, BB1
91/2 Classic 5
91/2 ClassicFourSport 5
97/8 Corinthian Headliners
95/6 Donruss 65, -Dominator 1
95/6 Donruss-Rookie 2
96/7 Donruss 139,-Hit 14,Top 10
97/8 Donruss 1, -Elite 7, Line 4
96/7 DonrussCanadianIce 6
97/8 D.CdnIce 6, -Scrapbook 18
95/6 DonrussElite 39, -Cutting 4
96/7 DonrussElite 12, -Status 7
97/8 DonrussElite 1, -BackTo 5
97/8 D.Elite -Crafts 23,-PrmNu 1
97/8 DonrussPreferred 2, 173
97/8 D.Pref -WideTins 4, -Tins 9
97/8 D.Pref -Line 7B,-PrecM 12
97/8 DonrussPriority 8, 185
97/8 D.Prio -DirDep 10,-OpDay 8
97/8 D.Prio-Pstcrd 10,-Stamp 10
97/8 D.Studio 15,-HardHats 16
97/8 D.Studio-Portr 15,-Silou 13
96/7 Duracell JB8
94/5 EliteSet 189,-Gld 19,-Gst 3
97/8 EssoOlympic 43
94/5 Flair 146
96/7 Flair 18, -Centre 3, -Now&T
94/5 Fleer 176, -RookieSensat 2
96/7 Fleer 20, 139
96/7 F-ArtRoss 4, -Pearson 3
95/6 F.Metal 32, -IntStl 5,-Win 1
96/7 F.Pick-Dream 3, -Fab 12
94/5 FUltra 356, -Prospect 1
95/6 FleerUltra 131, 383, -High 8
95/6 FU-AllRookie 3, -Extra 5
96/7 FleerUltra 35, -ClearThe 2
95 Globe 21, 253-55, 270
95/6 Hoyle'EAST K (Hearts)
97/8 KatchMedallion 38
97/8 KennerSLU
95/6 Kraft-Ticket
96/7 Kraft-Trophy
97/8 Kraft -WorldsBest
94/5 Leaf 475,-Ltd 28,-Phenom 3
95/6 Leaf 20, -Fire 6, -StudioR 2
96/7 Leaf 159,-Best 8,-Leather 6
97/8 Leaf 3, 170,-Bnr 13,-Fire 12
94/5 LeafLimited 116
95/6 LeafLimited 2, -StarsOf 4
96/7 LeafLimited 29, -Bash 8
96/7 LeafPreferred 110
96/7 LP-Steel 60, -SteelPower 6
97/8 Limited 2,48,109, -fabric 72
96/7 Maggers 36
94/5 McDonalds 31
95/6 McDonalds 7
96/7 McDonalds McD28
97/8 McDonalds McD15
96/7 MetalUniverse 32
96/7 MU-CoolSteel 2, -Lethal 4
97/8 Omega 56, -GameFace 3
97/8 Omega-Silk 3,-StickHand 5
98/9 Pacific 21,-Cramer 3
98/9 Pacific-DynIce 5,-GoldC 8
97/8 PacificCrown 21
97/8 Pac.CC-Supial 4, -Cramer 4
97/8 Pac.CC-Gold 7, -Slap 2A
97/8 PacificCrownRoyale 33
97/8 PCR -Blades 5, Cramer 4
97/8 PCR -Hat 4, -Lamplight 5
97/8 PacificDynagon! 29, 138
97/8 PcfcD-BstKpt 24, -Dyna 5A
97/8 PcfcD-King 2,-Tandm 5, 25
97/8 PcfcInvincible 34,-Attack 5
97/8 PacificInv.-Off 5, -Feature 7
97/8 PcfcParamount 49, -BigN 5
97/8 PacificP-Photoengravings 5
98/9 PcfcP 55,-HOF 3,-SpecD 4
97/8 PacificRegime 51, 216
97/8 PacificRevolution 32
97/8 PcfcRev -ASGme 6,-Icon 3
95/6 PaniniSticker 148, 244, 299
96/7 PaniniSticker 244
97/8 PaniniSticker 201
95 PaniniWorlds 287
95/6 Parkie 237, 316, PP4, PP13
95/6 PH-Crown(1)14, (2) 6
95/6 PH-InterAS 4, -Trophy 3
94/5 ParkieSE 149, ES1
94/5 Pinnacle 266, 479, RTP9
95/6 Pinnacle-ClearShot 8
95/6 P-Roaring20s 15, -First 11
96/7 Pinn. 78, 84, 249, -TmP 2
97/8 Pinnacle 73, 191, -TeamP 7
96/7 P.BAP LTH2B, -Biscuit 5
97/8 P.BeAPlayer -OneTimer 11
97/8 P.BeeHive 9, -TeamBH 9
97/8 PinnCertified 32, -Team 10
97/8 Pinnacle-EPIX 14
95/6 PinnacleFANtasy 25
96/7 PinnacleFANtasy 15
97/8 P.Inside 11,-Can 8,-Track 5
96/7 PinnacleMint 6
97/8 PinnacleMint 3, -Minterntl 2
95/6 PinnacleZenith 70, -Team 8
96/7 P.Zenith 76, -Champion 9
95/6 Playoff 25, 137, 239
96/7 Playoff 357
95/6 POG 77, 029
97/8 Post
94/5 Premier 385, 425
95/6 ProMagnet 77
96/7 SB'7Eleven
94/5 Score TR2
95/6 Score 31, -CheckIt 7
95/6 Score -Dream 5,-Golden 10
96/7 Score 99,-Check 2,-Dream4
97/8 Score 83
97/8 Score(COL) 4
94/5 Select 175, YE7
95/6 SelectCert. 68, -Future 1
96/7 SelectCert.-Cornerstone 15
94 Semic 75, 355
95 Semic 64
92/3 SemicElitserien 242, 347
93 SemicSticker 13
95/6 SkBxEmotion 36, -Xcited 14
95/6 SkBxImpact 35, 229, -Ice 8
96/7 SkyBoxImpact 22
96/7 SkyBx-Blade 3, -VersaTm 3
94/5 SP 96, -Premier 2
95/6 SP 29, FX4, E10
96/7 SP 33, GF2, -SPxForce 1
97/8 SPAuthentic 36, I12
96/7 SPx 8
97/8 SPx 11, SPX16
98/9 SPx"Finite" 95, 178, 166
96/7 SportFX MiniStix
97/8 SportFX MiniStix
91/2 StarPics 35
95/6 Summit 117
96/7 Sumt 142,-High 6,-Untch 5
96/7 TeamOut
95/6 Topps 359, 380, 10NG,YS4
98/9 Topps 1, I8, L1, M8, SB21
94/5 ToppsFinest 1
94/5 TF-BBest(Red) 12,-BBest 2
95/6 ToppsFinest 26, 100
96 ToppsFinestBronze 17
96/7 T.NHLPicks 5, FT16, TS7
95/6 T.StadiumClub 105, G4, N9
94/5 TSC-MembersOnly 47
95/6 TSC-MembersOnly 20
97/8 ToppsSticker 1
95/6 ToppsSuperSkills 18
91/2 UltimateDP 5, 61, 76,-Aut. 5
91/2 UpperDeck 64
92/3 UD 235, 369, 375, 595
94/5 UD 245, 528, 555
94/5 UD C1, H10, SP156
95/6 UD 430, AS17, F1, H8
95/6 UD R25, R37, R54, SE21
95/6 UD-AllStarPredict MVP11
96/7 UpperDeck 239, HH7, LS08
96/7 UpperDeck SS8A, X2
97/8 UD 252, S21, SG21, SS21
97/8 UD T1C, -Blow Up 9
94/5 UDBeAPlayer R152
96/7 UDBlackDiamond 171, RC7
97/8 UDBlckDiamond 106, PC11
98/9 UDChoice 56, 229, 241
98/9 UDChoice BH14, SQ20
95/6 UDCC 26, 371, 391, C20
96/7 UDCC 63,298,314,S3,UD3
97/8 UDCC 54, C21, S21, SQ71
97/8 udDiamondVision 14
95/6 udElite 234
96/7 UpperDeck"Ice" 81
97/8 UpperDeckIce 61,IC12,L4B
97/8 udSwedish UDS1
96 Wien 57, 74
97/8 Zenith 2, -ChasingCup 12
97/8 Zenith -Z19, ZTeam 5
96/7 COL/PhotoPuck
97/8 COL/Postcard
94/5 QUE/BurgerKing

FORSEY, JACK
34-43 BeeHives(TOR)

FORSLUND, TOMAS
92/3 Bowman 384
92/3 C'Prospects 139, BC15
96/7 DEL 357
94/5 ElitSet 65
95/6 ElitSet 242, -FaceTo 7
95 Globe 46
92/3 O-Pee-Chee 70
91/2 opcPremier 31
92/3 PaniniSticker D
95 PaniniWorlds 157
91/2 Parkhurst 20
91/2 Pinnacle 333
91/2 ProSet 527
91/2 Score(CDN) 629, (U.S) 79T
94 Semic 79
95 Semic 69
89/90 SemicElitserien 134
90/1 SemicElitserien 209
93 SemicSticker 41
92/3 Topps 186
92/3 ToppsStadiumClub 280
91/2 UpperDeck 27, 586
92/3 UpperDeck 3, 429, ERT6
95/6 udElite 112
96 Wien 67
91/2 CGY/IGA

FORSMAN, JOHNNY
89/90 SemicElitserien 207

FORSS, MATTI
92/3 Jyvas-Hyva 133
80/1 Mallasjuoma 7
93/4 Sisu 200, 387
95/6 SisuLimited 36
78/9 SM-Liiga 35
73/4 WilliamsFIN 306

FORSS, RISTO
66/7 Champion 57
70/1 Kuvajulkaisut 294

FORSS, T.D.
95/6 Spokane 27

FORSYTHE, TREVOR
91/2 Knoxville

FORTIER, DAVE
74/5 Loblaws-Updat e
74/5 OPC 382
75/6 OPC 336
76/7 OPC 328
76/7 VAN/RoyalBank

FORTIER, FRANÇOIS
98 BowmanCHL 90

FORTIER, MARK
90/1 Bowman 167
89/90 O-Pee-Chee 262
89/90 opcSticker 189/43
90/1 OPC/Topps 176
90/1 Panini(QUE) 5
89/90 PaniniSticker 335
90/1 PaniniSticker 153
88/9 ProCards(Halifax)
90/1 ProSet 245
92/3 ProSet 128
90/1 Score 78
92/3 Topps 226
92/3 ToppsStadiumClub 173
88/9 QUE
88/9 QUE/GeneralFoods
89/90 QUE
89/90 QUE/GeneralFoods
89/90 QUE/Police
90/1 QUE
90/1 QUE/PetroCanada
91/2 QUE/PetroCanada
84/5 Chicoutimi
93/4 Phoenix

FORTIER, SÉBASTIEN
90/1 SketchQMJHL 81
91/2 SketchQMJHL 18
93/4 Wheeling 10

FORTIN, EMILE
36/7 WWGum (V356) 122

FORTIN, JEAN-FRANÇOIS
97/8 Bowman 46, 157, BB7
96/7 UpperDeck 375
96/7 UDBlackDiamond 4

FORTIN, YVES
51/2 LacStJean 55

FOSTER, COREY
91/2 Parkhurst 344
91/2 Pinnacle 332
89/90 ProCards(AHL) 146
90/1 ProCards 231
91/2 ProSet 551
91/2 PSPlatinum 265
91/2 UpperDeck 591
92/3 UpperDeck 53
91/2 PHA/JCPenney
95/6 Cleveland

FOSTER, DARRYL
95/6 Classic 89
93/4 Slapshot(NiagaraFalls) 3
94/5 Slapshot(Detroit) 2
94/5 Slapshot(MEM) 76

FOSTER, DAVE
91/2 AirCanadaSJHL D9
92/3 MPSPhotoSJHL 33

FOSTER, DWIGHT
78/9 O-Pee-Chee 271
81/2 OPC 3, Topps(E) 67
82/3 O-Pee-Chee 138
83/4 O-Pee-Chee 122
84/5 OPC 53, Topps 41
85/6 OPC/Topps 14
81/2 opcSticker 52
83/4 opcSticker 133
87/8 PaniniSticker 17
82/3 Post
83/4 SouhaitsRen.KeyChain
81/2 COL.R
84/5 DET/Caesars
85/6 DET/Caesars

FOSTER, JERRY
89/90 ProCards(AHL) 74

FOSTER, NORM
88/9 ProCards(Maine)
89/90 ProCards(AHL) 60
90/1 ProCards 135
91/2 ProCards 225
91/2 UpperDeck 465

FOTHERINGHAM, SHAWN
92/3 Clarkson

FOTIU, NICK
77/8 OPC/Topps 11
78/9 O-Pee-Chee 367
79/80 O-Pee-Chee 286
80/1 OPC/Topps 184
82/3 O-Pee-Chee 222
83/4 O-Pee-Chee 243
85/6 OPC/Topps 22
75/6 opcWHA 108
82/3 Post
89/90 ProCards(AHL) 20
86/7 CGY/RedRooster
88/9 EDM/ActionMagazine 143

FOUNTAIN, MIKE
94/5 Classic T40
94/5 ClassicFourSport 159
92/3 ClassicProspects 106
93/4 ClassicProspects 175
92/3 CanadaNats
97/8 Donruss 218
97/8 DonrussCanadianIce 136
97/8 PinnacleInside 76
90/1 SketchOHL 336
91/2 SketchOHL 170
96/7 SP 162
91/2 UpperDeck'CzechWJC 52
96/7 VAN
96/7 VAN/IGA
92/3 Hamilton
90/1 Oshawa 6
91/2 Oshawa
91/2 Oshawa Dominos 1

FOURNEL, DAN
91/2 ProCards 32
94/5 Huntington 9

FOURNIER, JACK
1912-13 Imperial (C57) 36

FOURNIER, MARC
83/4 SSMarie

FOURNIER, ROB
89/90 SketchOHL 171
88/9 NiagaraFalls 10

FOURNIER, WADE
95/6 Louisiana, -Playoffs

FOWLER, BOB
89/90 ProCards(IHL) 129

FOWLER, HEC
24/5 Champs (C144)
24/5 MapleCrispette (V130) 3
28/9 PaulinsCandy 87
24/5 (V145-2) 30

FOWLER, JIM
34-43 BeeHives(TOR)
36/7 OPC (V304D) 103
37/8 OPC (V304E) 135
39/40 OPC (V301-1) 55
28/9 PaulinsCandy 74
38/9 QuakerOats

FOWLER, ROB
87/8 Moncton

FOX, GREG
79/80 OPC/Topps 116
80/1 O-Pee-Chee 268
81/2 O-Pee-Chee 65
82/3 O-Pee-Chee 65
83/4 O-Pee-Chee 101
84/5 O-Pee-Chee 175
82/3 opcSticker 235
82/3 Post
83/4 SouhaitsRen.KeyChain
78/9 ATL/Coke
79/80 CHI
80/1 CHI/4x6
80/1 CHI/5.5x8.5
81/2 CHI
82/3 CHI
84/5 PGH/Heinz
77/8 NovaScotia

FOX, HUGHIE
25 Dominion 56

FOX, JIM
81/2 O-Pee-Chee 153
82/3 O-Pee-Chee 154
83/4 O-Pee-Chee 154
84/5 O-Pee-Chee 84, Topps 66
85/6 OPC/Topps 61
86/7 O-Pee-Chee 215
87/8 OPC/Topps 75
88/9 OPC/Topps 139
83/4 opcSticker 293
84/5 opcSticker 268
85/6 opcSticker 236/103
86/7 opcSticker 89/219
87/8 opcSticker 216/84
88/9 opcSticker 154/25
87/8 PaniniSticker 281
88/9 PaniniSticker 76
83/4 PuffySticker 7
83/4 SouhaitsRen.KeyChain
84/5 L.A./Smokeys
88/9 L.A.

FOY, CHRIS
93/4 Richmond 18
94/5 Richmond

FOYN, STEPHAN
92 SemicSticker 46

FOYSTON, FRANK
83&87 HallOfFame 20
83 HHOF Postcard (B)

FRANCELLA, GIULIO
82 SemicSticker 130

FRANCESHETTI, LOU
90/1 Bowman 164
90/1 OPC/Topps 303
91/2 OPC/Topps 354
90/1 Panini(TOR) 6
87/8 PaniniSticker 188
90/1 PaniniSticker 289
88/9 ProCards(Baltimore)
91/2 ProCards 360
90/1 ProSet 280
90/1 Score 266, 368
91/2 Score(CDN) 388
90/1 UpperDeck 396
91/2 UpperDeck 399
90/1 BUF/BlueShield
90/1 TOR
86/7 WSH/Kodak
86/7 WSH/Police
87/8 WSH
87/8 WSH/Kodak
88/9 WSH
88/9 WSH/Smokey
91/2 Rochester/Genny
91/2 Rochester/Kodak

FRANCHE, DELPHIS
51/2 LavalDairy 27
52/3 StLawrence 91

FRANCIS, BOB
89/90 ProCards(IHL) 200
90/1 ProCards 611
94/5 SaintJohn

FRANCIS, EMILE (CAT)
83&87 HallOfFame 231
83 HHOF Postcard (I)
92/3 HHOFLegends 10
74/5 OPC/Topps 9
66/7 Topps 21

FRANCIS, RON
95/6 Aces 7 (Clubs)
96/7 Aces 9 (Spades)
90/1 Bowman 254
91/2 Bowman 90, 421
92/3 Bowman 123
95/6 Bowman 31
93/4 Donruss 261
94/5 Donruss 122
95/6 Donruss 94, -Igniters 10
96/7 Donruss 149, -Dom. 4
97/8 Donruss 137
96/7 DonrussCanadianIce 93
97/8 D.CdnIce 44, -National 20
95/6 DonrussElite 40
96/7 DonrussElite 40
97/8 DonrussElite 113
97/8 DonrussPreferred 142
97/8 DonrussPriority 77

97/8 DonrussStudio 74
94/5 Flair 134
96/7 Flair 75, -ArtRoss 5
94/5 Fleer 162
96/7 Fleer 85, 137, 139
95/6 FleerMetal 116, -IronWar 4
96/7 FleerNHLPicks 16, -Fab 13
96/7 FP-Fantasy 7, -Jagged 16
92/3 FleerUltra 163
93/4 FleerUltra 44
94/5 FleerUltra 163
95/6 FleerUltra 122, 384
95/6 FU-Extra 6, -PrmrPivot 2
96/7 FU 139, -MrMomentum 3
88/9 FritoLay
93/4 HockeyWit 53
97/8 KatchMedallion 116
84/5 Kelloggs Disk
96/7 KennerSLU
90/1 Kraft 13, 83
96/7 Kraft'Prospects
97/8 Kraft-WorldsBest
93/4 Leaf 161
94/5 Leaf 235
95/6 Leaf 45
96/7 Leaf 11
97/8 Leaf 44
94/5 LeafLimited 30
95/6 LeafLimited 23
96/7 LeafLimited 52
96/7 LeafPreferred 62, -Steel 6
97/8 Limited 199
96/7 Maggers 126
96/7 MetalUniverse 125
96/7 MU-CoolSteel 3, -Lethal 5
97/8 Omega 184
82/3 O-Pee-Chee 123
83/4 O-Pee-Chee 138
84/5 O-Pee-Chee 70
85/6 OPC/Topps 140, F
86/7 OPC/Topps 43
87/8 OPC/Topps 187, J
88/9 OPC/Topps 52, A
89/90 OPC/Topps 175
90/1 OPC/Topps 311, T-TL 21
91/2 OPC/Topps 130
92/3 O-Pee-Chee 188, -Promo
90/1 opcPremier 32
91/2 opcPremier 120
87/8 opc Stars 10
82/3 opcSticker 129
83/4 opcSticker 255
84/5 opcSticker 196
85/6 opcSticker 172
86/7 opcSticker 51/190
87/8 opcSticker 206
88/9 opcSticker 264
89/90 opcSticker 269
98/9 Pacific 351
97/8 PacificCrown 123, -Slap 8B
97/8 PacificCrownRoyale 109
97/8 PcfcDynag! 110,-Tandm 60
97/8 PacificInv. 111, -Attack 19
97/8 PacificParamount 164
97/8 PacificRevolution 112
87/8 PaniniSticker 43
88/9 PaniniSticker 242
89/90 PaniniSticker 221
90/1 PaniniSticker 39
91/2 PaniniSticker 281
92/3 PaniniSticker 224
93/4 PaniniSticker 81
94/5 PaniniSticker 73
95/6 PaniniSticker 58, 152
96/7 PaniniSticker 57, 145
97/8 PaniniSticker 50
91/2 Parkhurst 353
92/3 Parkhurst 141
93/4 Parkhurst 160
94/5 Parkhurst 176
95/6 PH 164, PP47, -Trophy 6
91/2 Pinnacle 167
92/3 Pinnacle 303
93/4 Pinnacle 74
94/5 Pinnacle 72
95/6 Pinnacle 39
96/7 Pinnacle 143
97/8 Pinnacle 78
97/8 PinnacleBeeHive 49
97/8 PinnacleCertified 121
97/8 PinnacleInside 52
95/6 PinnacleZenith 35
96/7 P.Zenith 10, -ChampSalu 7
95/6 Playoff 77
96/7 Playoff 360
94/5 POG 183
95/6 POG 215
82/3 Post
93/4 PowerPlay 188
93/4 Premier 424
94/5 Premier 139
95/6 ProMagnet 95
90/1 ProSet 105, 367
91/2 ProSet 188
92/3 ProSet 144
91/2 PSPlatinum 214
83/4 PuffySticker 18
90/1 Score 70, -HotCards 37
91/2 Score(CDN) 487, (U.S) 267
92/3 Score 267
93/4 Score 151
94/5 Score 244, NP18
95/6 Score 187
96/7 Score 56
97/8 Score 132
97/8 Score(PGH) 5
94/5 Select 84
95/6 SelectCertif. 52, -Double 2
96/7 SelectCertif. 12
84/5 7ElevenDisk
85/6 7Eleven 7
95/6 SkyBoxEmotion 136
95/6 SkBxE-Xcel 7, -Xcited 11
95/6 SkyBoxImpact 130
96/7 SkBxImpact 100, -Blade 4
83/4 SouhaitsRen.KeyChain
94/5 SP 92
95/6 SP 115
96/7 SP 127
97/8 SP Authentic 126
97/8 SPx 41
95/6 Summit 42
96/7 Summit 10, -Untouchable 4
95/6 SuperSticker 98
84/5 Topps 54
92/3 Topps 322
95/6 Topps 244, 5PL
98/9 Topps 4, SB22
94/5 ToppsFinest-Ring 16
95/6 ToppsFinest 127
91/2 ToppsStadiumClub 73
92/3 ToppsStadiumClub 352
93/4 ToppsStadiumClub 385
94/5 ToppsStadiumClub 96
95/6 ToppsStadiumClub 22, PS3
94/5 TSC-MembersOnly 22
95/6 TSC-MembersOnly 45
90/1 UpperDeck 67, 314
91/2 UpperDeck 299
92/3 UpperDeck 291
93/4 UpperDeck 351
94/5 UpperDeck 12, SP150
95/6 UD 46, 255,AS18,R11,R59
95/6 UD SE66,-ASPredicMVP23
96/7 UpperDeck 133
97/8 UpperDeck 135, SS25
95/6 UDBeAPlayer 8
96/7 UDBlackDiamond 101
97/8 UDBlackDiamond 11
98/9 UDChoice 169
95/6 UDCollChoice 200, 393
96/7 UDCC 212, 328, UD2
97/8 UDCollChoice 204, SQ54
96/7 UpperDeck"Ice" 55
97/8 UpperDeckIce 65
97/8 Zenith 50, Z53
82/3 HFD/JuniorWhalers
83/4 HFD/JuniorWhalers
84/5 HFD/JuniorWhalers
85/6 HFD/JuniorWhalers
86/7 HFD/JuniorWhalers
87/8 HFD/JuniorWhalers
88/9 HFD/JuniorWhalers
89/90 HFD/JuniorWhalers
90/1 HFD/JuniorWhalers
92/3 PGH/Coke
91/2 PGH/Elbys
91/2 PGH/Foodland 3
91/2 PGH/Topps
92/3 PGH/Foodland 7
92/3 PGH/FoodStickers
93/4 PGH/Foodland 14
94/5 PGH 9
95/6 PGH/Foodland
96/7 PGH/FotoPucks
96/7 PGH/Tribune
80/1 SSMarie
81/2 SSMarie
87/8 SSMarie 8
89/90 SSMarie 13

FRANCIS, TODD
94/5 Slapshot(Brantford) 3
83/4 Brantford 27

FRANCZ, R.
95/6 DEL 19

FRANEK, PETR
94/5 APS 204
95/6 APS 151

FRANK, JEFF
82/3 Regina 17
83/4 Regina 17

FRANK, MARK
82/3 MedicineHat

FRANKE, PETER
94/5 DEL 410
95/6 DEL 408
96/7 DEL 70

FRANKS, JIM
34-43 BeeHives(NYR)

FRANKS, MARK
90/1 SketchWHL 74
91/2 SketchWHL 116
92/3 Brandon 6
93/4 Huntington
94/5 Huntington 10
90/1 Saskatoon 18
91/2 Saskatoon 17

FRANTTI, GORD
91/2 ProCards 515
94/5 Huntington 11

FRANZ, GEORGE
94/5 DEL 254
94/5 DEL 252
95/6 DEL 252
96/7 DEL 141
95 PaniniWorlds 68
94 Semic 283
89 SemicSticker 117
91 SemicSticker 175
93 SemicSticker 165

FRANZEN, RIKARD
94/5 ElitSet 108, -Studio 1
95/6 ElitSet 165, -Mega 13
89/90 SemicElitserien 8
91/2 SemicElitserien 7
92/3 SemicElitserien 33
95/6 udElite 4, 219, 249
96 Wien 51

FRAPPIER, SHAWN
93/4 Slapshot(Sudbury) 7
94/5 Slapshot(Sudbury) 6
95/6 Slapshot 12
92/3 Sudbury 7

FRASER, BARRY
88/9 EDM/ActionMagazine 158

FRASER, CHARLES
23/4 (V145-1) 39

FRASER, CHRIS
89/90 Windsor

FRASER, CRAIG
89/90 SketchOHL 74
90/1 SketchOHL 5
91/2 SketchOHL 34

FRASER, CURT
79/80 OPC/Topps 117
80/1 O-Pee-Chee 287
81/2 O-Pee-Chee 334
82/3 O-Pee-Chee 343
83/4 O-Pee-Chee 102
84/5 O-Pee-Chee 34
85/6 OPC/Topps 3, 139
86/7 OPC/Topps 31
82/3 opcSticker 244
85/6 opcSticker 24/153
87/8 PaniniSticker 231
80/1 Pepsi Cap
82/3 Post
90/1 ProCards 327
91/2 ProCards 619
84/5 Topps 29
86/7 CHI/Coke
87/8 CHI/Coke
88/9 MIN/American
78/9 VAN/RoyalBank
79/80 VAN
80/1 VAN
80/1 VAN/Silverwood
81/2 VAN
81/2 VAN/Silverwood
82/3 VAN
82/3 Victoria

FRASER, GORD
25-27 Anonymous 136
27-32 LaPresse 29/30

FRASER, IAIN
92/3 ClassicProspects 49
93/4 ClassicProspects 15
93/4 Donruss 478
94/5 Donruss 270
93/4 FleerUltra 73, 400, -Prosp 1
94/5 FleerUltra 174
94/5 Leaf 105
94/5 PaniniSticker G
93/4 Parkhurst 434, C19
94/5 Parkhurst 187, 280
94/5 Pinnacle 513
93/4 PowerPlay 419, -RookStd 4
93/4 Premier 525
94/5 Premier 7, -Finest(OPC) 6
91/2 ProCards 468
93/4 Score 625
89/90 SketchMEM 89
89/90 SketchOHL 19, 186, 198
93/4 ToppsStadiumClub 485
94/5 ToppsStadiumClub 32
93/4 UpperDeck 337
94/5 UpperDeck 162
89/90 Oshawa 25

FRASER, KERRY
90/1 ProSet 686

FRASER, LEGS
51/2 LavalDairy 104

FRASER, SCOTTY
23/4 PaulinsCandy 53

FRASER, SCOTT
98/9 Pacific 207
94/5 Fredericton
95/6 Fredericton
96/7 Fredericton

FRASER, SCOTT
80/1 QuébecRamparts

FRASER, TREVER
91/2 SketchWHL 171
92/3 Tacoma
93/4 Tacoma

FRASER, WILLIAM
25 Dominion 81

FRASZKO, ADAM
89 SemicSticker 146

FRAWLEY, DAN
87/8 PaniniSticker 153
88/9 PaniniSticker 338
89/90 ProCards(IHL) 160
90/1 ProCards 274
91/2 ProCards 3
86/7 PGH/Kodak
87/8 PGH/Kodak
91/2 Rochester/Genny
91/2 Rochester/Kodak
92/3 Rochester/Kodak
95/6 Rochester
91/2 Rochestr/Dunkin'Donuts
92/3 Rochestr/Dunkin'Donuts
83/4 Springfield 9

FRAYN, ROBERT
89/90 SketchOHL 175
90/1 SketchOHL 6
91/2 SketchOHL 184

FRAZER, FRITZ
51/2 LavalDairy 106

FRECHETTE, YANNICK
90/1 SketchQMJHL 60
91/2 SketchQMJHL 237

FREDERICK, JOE
93/4 Classic 65
94/5 ClassicFourSport 149
93/4 ClassicProspects 131

FREDERICK, TROY
90/1 ProCards 596
91/2 ProCards 512
88/9 Brandon 8
89/90 Brandon 2

FREDERICKS, RAY
52/3 LavalDairy 104
52/3 StLawrence 70

FREDERICKSON, FRANKIE
83&87 HallOfFame 49
83 HHOF Postcard (D)
24/5 Holland 5
60/1 Topps 34
61/2 Topps-Stamp

FREER, MARK
95/6 EdgeIce 132
93/4 PaniniSticker 118
91/2 Parkhurst 343
92/3 Parkhurst 354
93/4 Premier 142
88/9 ProCards(Hershey)
89/90 ProCards(AHL) 337
90/1 ProCards 47
91/2 ProCards 279
92/3 ProSet 127
93/4 ToppsStadiumClub 29
92/3 UpperDeck 445

FRENCH, JOHN
74/5 opcWHA 33
76/7 opcWHA 105
73/4 QuakerOats 33
72/3 NewEngland

FRENETTE, DEREK
91/2 ProCards 27
92/3 Peoria
93/4 Peoria

FRENGLER, REINHARD
79 PaniniSticker 252

FRENZEL, DIETER
79 PaniniSticker 251

FRESTADIUS, ROBERT
89/90 SemicElitserien 173

FREW, IRVINE
36-39 DiamondMatch (1), (2), (3)

FRIDAY, BILL
91/2 Ultimate(O6) 85

FRIDAY, BOB
51/2 LavalDairy 87

FRIDAY, TIM
85/6 DET/Caesars

FRIDFINNSON, WALLY
24/5 Holland 1
24/5 Crescent Falcons 3

FRIDGEN, DAN
82/3 HFD/JuniorWhalers

FRIEDMAN, DOUG
97/8 EDM

FRIESEN, CURTIS
90/1 SketchWHL 47

FRIESEN, JEFF
95/6 Bowman 84
94/5 CanadaJr.Alumni 13
93/4 Classic 102, CL3, PR2
94/5 Classic 10,C4,R5,T61,-Aut.
94/5 ClassicFourSport 125
94/5 C4'Images 103
94/5 ClassicImages 2, CE2
93/4 C'Prospects 202, 209, -Aut
93/4 Donruss CAN11
95/6 Donruss 162, -CanadaJr 21
95/6 D-ProPointer 11, -Rookie 7
96/7 Donruss 79
97/8 Donruss 55
97/8 DonrussCanadianIce 81
96/7 DonrussElite 53
97/8 DonrussElite 93
97/8 DonrussPreferred 14
97/8 DonrussPriority 70
97/8 DonrussStudio 98
94/5 Flair 164
94/5 Fleer 196, -Rookie 3
95/6 FleerMetal 129
94/5 FleerUltra 365
95/6 FleerUltra 145, -AllRook 4
94/5 Leaf 482, -Phenoms 9
95/6 Leaf 21, -StudioRookies 7
96/7 Leaf 87
97/8 Leaf 102
94/5 LeafLimited -CanadaJrs 3
95/6 LeafLimited 62
96/7 LeafLimited 83
96/7 LeafPreferred 97
97/8 Limited 72, 196
95/6 McDonalds 31
97/8 Omega 200
98/9 Pacific 379
97/8 PacificCrown 63
97/8 PacificCrownRoyale 119
97/8 PcfcDynag! 110,-Tandm 60
97/8 PacificInvincible 124
97/8 PacificParamount 164
98/9 PacificParamount 209
97/8 PacificRevolution 123
95/6 PaniniSticker 278, 304
96/7 PaniniSticker 278
97/8 PaniniSticker 233
93/4 Parkhurst 505
95/6 Parkhurst 182
94/5 ParkieSE 166
93/4 Pinnacle 472
94/5 Pinnacle 252, 532, RTP7
95/6 Pinnacle 55
96/7 Pinnacle 18
97/8 Pinnacle 119
96/7 PinnacleBeAPlayer 190
97/8 PinnacleCertified 81
97/8 PinnacleInside 121
95/6 PinnacleZenith 65
96/7 PinnacleZenith 89
95/6 Playoff 83
96/7 Playoff 362
95/6 POG 223, 030
94/5 Premier 547
95/6 ProMagnet 120
94/5 Score 203, TR8
95/6 Score 91,-Check 10,-Gld 11
96/7 Score 4
97/8 Score 170
94/5 Select 176, YE9
95/6 SelectCertified 56
96/7 SelectCertified 61
95/6 SkyBoxEmotion 155
95/6 SkyBoxImpact 147, 235
96/7 SkyBoxImpact 116
94/5 SP 145
95/6 SP 133
96/7 SP 143
97/8 SPAuthentic 134
95/6 Summit 68
96/7 Summit 144
95/6 Topps 360,15CJ,18NG,YS6
98/9 Topps 128
94/5 ToppsFinest 11, 159
94/5 TF-BowmansBest(Red) 14
95/6 ToppsFinest 27
95/6 ToppsStadiumClub 106
95/6 ToppsSuperSkills 69
93/4 UpperDeck 532, E8
94/5 UD 237, 526, SP161
95/6 UpperDeck 134, SE74
96/7 UpperDeck 332
97/8 UpperDeck 358
94/5 UDBeAPlayer R164
98/9 UDChoice 174
95/6 UDCollChoice 309, 372
96/7 UDCollChoice 238
97/8 UDCollChoice 215, SQ10
96/7 UpperDeck"Ice" 58
97/8 Zenith 33
96/7 S.J/PacificBellSheet (x2)
97/8 S.J/PacificBellSheet (x2)

FRIESEN, KARL
94/5 DEL 314
95/6 DEL 360
89 SemicSticker 103
91 SemicSticker 154

FRIESEN, TERRY
98 BowmanCHL 62
95/6 SwiftCurrent

FRIEST, RON
82/3 MIN

FRIG, LEN
74/5 Loblaws
74/5 OPC/Topps 242
75/6 OPC/Topps 174
76/7 OPC 353
77/8 OPC 384

FRIMAN, JERRY
92/3 SemicElitserien 96

FRIMAN, K.P.
92/3 Jyvas-Hyva 127
93/4 Jyvas-Hyva 225
93/4 Sisu 190
94/5 Sisu 104
95/6 Sisu 175, 340

FRITZ, GEORGE
94/5 DEL 430
95/6 DEL 397

FRITZ, TOMMY
89/90 SemicElitserien 105
90/1 SemicElitserien 108
91/2 SemicElitserien 112
92/3 SemicElitserien 129

FROESE, BOB
83/4 O-Pee-Chee 265
84/5 O-Pee-Chee 159
86/7 OPC/Topps 55
86/7 OPC 263-64, T-AS 7
87/8 OPC/Topps 195
83/4 opcSticker 183
84/5 opcSticker 113
86/7 opcSticker 182/122, 186/45
86/7 opcSticker 236, 193/55
88/9 PaniniSticker 299
89/90 PaniniSticker 284
83/4 SouhaitsRen.KeyChain
84/5 Topps 117
89/90 NYR/MarineMidland
83/4 PHA
86/7 PHA
78/9 Saginaw

FROESE, COLIN
92/3 MPSPhotoSJHL 37

FROH, DAVE
93/4 Slapshot(Oshawa) 5
95/6 Slapshot 192

FROLIKOV, ALEXEI
90/1 O-Pee-Chee 502

FROLOV, DMITRI
96/7 DEL 210
90/1 O-Pee-Chee 523
94 Semic 151
95 Semic 130
92/3 UpperDeck 348

FROSCH, FRANTISEK
94/5 DEL 428
95/6 DEL 391
96/7 DEL 76

FRUTEL, CHRISTIAN
94/5 DEL 315

FRY, CURTIS
92/3 BCJHL 51

FRY, RICK
89/90 Portland

FRYCER, MIROSLAV
72-84 Dernière 81/2
82/3 O-Pee-Chee 321
83/4 O-Pee-Chee 330
85/6 O-Pee-Chee 198
86/7 OPC/Topps 68
82/3 opcSticker 65
83/4 opcSticker 38
85/6 opcSticker 21
86/7 opcSticker 142
87/8 opcSticker 158/18
82/3 Post
83/4 SouhaitsRen.KeyChain
83/4 Vachon 86
88/9 DET/Caesars
88/9 EDM
88/9 EDM/ActionMagazine 153
81/2 QUE
82/3 TOR
83/4 TOR
84/5 TOR
85/6 TOR
86/7 TOR
87/8 TOR
87/8 TOR/P.L.A.Y. 15

FRYKBO, ANDERS
89/90 SemicElitserien 233
91/2 SemicElitserien 245

FRYLEN, EDVIN
94/5 EliteSet 105, -NHLDraft 5
95/6 EliteSet 299
93/4 Parkhurst 536
94/5 SigRookies 17
94/5 SRGoldStandard 85
92/3 SemicElitserien 280, 351
93/4 UpperDeck 572
95/6 udElite 188
97/8 udSwedish 184, UDS15

FRYZLEWICZ, STANISLAV
73/4 WilliamsFIN 90

FTOREK, ROBBIE
72-84 Dernière 81/2
79/80 O-Pee-Chee 267
80/1 OPC/Topps 35
81/2 O-Pee-Chee 274
82/3 O-Pee-Chee 223
83/4 O-Pee-Chee 244
81/2 opcSticker 72
75/6 opcWHA 19
76/7 opcWHA 13
77/8 opcWHA 35
80/1 Pepsi Cap
81/2 PostPopUp 24
82/3 Post
89/90 ProCards'AHL 157
92/3 Trends(76) 189
96/7 N.J/Sharp
80/1 QUE
90/1 QUE/PetroCan
89/90 Halifax
75/6 Phoenix
76/7 Phoenix

FUCHS, ANDREJ
94/5 DEL 351
95/6 DEL 323
96/7 DEL 101

FUCHS, BORIS
94/5 DEL 356
95/6 DEL 326
96/7 DEL 103

FUCHS, LOTHAR
70/1 Kuvajulkaisut 84

FUHR, GRANT
96/7 Aces 8 (Hearts)
90/1 Bowman 189
91/2 Bowman 111, 407
92/3 Bowman 114
95/6 Bowman 25
97/8 Corinthian Headliners
93/4 Donruss 34
94/5 Donruss 212
95/6 Donruss 310
96/7 Donruss 117
97/8 Donruss 153
96/7 D.CanadianIce 109, 148
97/8 DonrussCanadianIce 95
95/6 D.Elite 42, -Painted 9
96/7 D.Elite 29, -Perspective 12
97/8 DonrussElite 110
97/8 DonrussPreferred 60
97/8 D.Priority 82,-PostGen 19
97/8 DonrussStudio 102
93/4 EASports 18
88/9 Esso Sticker
96/7 Flair 80
96/7 Fleer 96
95/6 FleerMetal 123
92/3 FleerUltra 210
93/4 FleerUltra 103
94/5 FleerUltra 262
95/6 FleerUltra 298
96/7 FleerUltra 145
91/2 Gillette 19
93/4 HighLiner 3
93/4 HockeyWit 40
92/3 HumptyDumpty(1)
97/8 KatchMedallion 128
93/4 KennerSLU (U.S)
94/5 KennerSLU (CDN)
86/7 Kraft Sports 13
89/90 Kraft 11
91/2 Kraft 9
92/3 Kraft-Disk
95/6 Kraft-Crease
93/4 Leaf 66, -PaintedWar 5
94/5 Leaf 78
96/7 Leaf 64
97/8 Leaf 123
96/7 LeafLimited 48
97/8 Limited 32, -fabric 45
96/7 Maggers 139
96/7 MetalUniverse 131
97/8 Omega 193
82/3 O-Pee-Chee 105
83/4 O-Pee-Chee 27
84/5 O-Pee-Chee 241
85/6 O-Pee-Chee 207
86/7 OPC/Topps 56
87/8 OPC/Topps 178
88/9 OPC/Topps 59, T-AS 6
89/90 OPC/Topps 192
90/1 OPC/Topps 321
91/2 OPC/Topps 84
92/3 OPC 31, 119, -25Years 15
88/9 opcStars 9
82/3 opcSticker 95, 161
84/5 opcSticker 259
85/6 opcSticker 221/88
86/7 opcSticker 67/198, 121/135
87/8 opcSticker 85
88/9 opcSticker 223, 122/252
88/9 opcSticker 212/83
89/90 opcSticker 228
91/2 opcPremier 100, 191
98/9 Pacific 31
97/8 PacificCrown-InTheCrs 18
97/8 PacificCrownRoyale 116
97/8 PCR-FreezeOut 17
97/8 PacificDynagon! 106
97/8 PcfcD-Stone 19,-Tandm 18
97/8 PacificInvincible 119
97/8 PcfcParamnt 158,-Glove 18
98/9 PcfcP 203,-Glv 12,-T.CL 22
97/8 PcfcRevolutn 120,-Rtrn 17
87/8 PaniniAlbum
87/8 PaniniSticker 254
88/9 PaniniSticker 52, 188, 403
90/1 PaniniSticker 230
92/3 PaniniSticker 75
93/4 PaniniSticker 108
96/7 PaniniSticker 203
97/8 PaniniSticker 172
95 PaniniWorlds 25
91/2 Parkhurst 175
92/3 Parkhurst 182, 250, 497
93/4 Parkhurst 22, D7
95/6 Parkhurst 443, PP9, PP34
91/2 Pinnacle 168
92/3 Pinnacle 267, 301
93/4 Pinnacle 65, -Masks 1
94/5 Pinnacle 421
96/7 Pinnacle 181
97/8 Pinnacle 156, -Masks 10
97/8 Pinnacle -GoalieTin 2
96/7 PinnacleBAP-Stacking 9
97/8 PinnacleBeeHive 44
97/8 PinnacleCertified 10
97/8 P.Inside 51, -Stopper 20
97/8 P.Inside -StandUp 6
95/6 PinnacleZenith 107
96/7 P.Zenith 82, -Champion 3
94/5 POG 273
95/6 POG 8, 245
82/3 Post
93/4 PowerPlay 27, -Netmindr 3
93/4 Premier 218
94/5 Premier 80
90/1 ProSet 82
91/2 ProSet 78,494,-ThePuck 27
92/3 ProSet 183, PV5
91/2 PSPlatinum 117
90/1 Score 275
91/2 Score(CDN) 114, 608
91/2 Score(U.S) 114, 58T
92/3 Score 20, 437
93/4 Score 75
95/6 Score 228
96/7 Score 91
92/3 SeasonsPatch 54
94/5 Select 93
96/7 SelectCertified 35
89 SemicSticker 53
92? 7Elven Cup
96/7 SkyBoxImpact 112
95/6 SP 126
96/7 SP 133
97/8 SPAuthentic 143, S13
96/7 SPx HH10
98/9 SPx"Finite" 77
96/7 Summit 14
96/7 TeamOut
92/3 Topps 350
95/6 Topps 242
98/9 Topps 114, -RookieRprt 5
94/5 ToppsFinest-Ring 4
95/6 ToppsFinest 113
96/7 ToppsNHLPicks ID15
91/2 ToppStadiumClub 258
92/3 ToppsStadiumClub 412
93/4 TSC 260, Master (2) 3
95/6 ToppsStadiumClub 24
95/6 ToppsSuperSkills 88
90/1 UpperDeck 264
91/2 UpperDeck 264, 553
92/3 UpperDeck 271
93/4 UD 163, GG10, SP-15
95/6 UpperDeck 484, SE158
96/7 UpperDeck 140, X33
97/8 UpperDeck 145
94/5 UDBeAPlayer G7
95/6 UDBeAPlayer 196
96/7 UDBlackDiamond 128
97/8 UDBlackDiamond 128
96/7 UDCollChoice 224
97/8 UDCollChoice 225
96/7 UpperDeck"Ice" 62
83/4 Vachon 24
97/8 Zenith 60, Z14
93/4 BUF/NOCO
81/2 EDM/RedRooster
81/2 EDM/WestEdmonton
82/3 EDM/RedRooster
83/4 EDM/McDonalds
84/5 EDM
84/5 EDM/RedRooster
85/6 EDM/RedRooster
86/7 EDM
86/7 EDM/RedRooster
87/8 EDM
88/9 EDM
88/9 EDM/ActionMag. 65, 130
90/1 TOR/P.L.A.Y. 23
82/3 Victoria

FUJITA, RYAN
90/1 SketchWHL 105
91/2 SketchWHL 110
91/2 Saskatoon 19

FUKAMI, SCOTT
90/1 SketchWHL 105
91/2 SketchWHL 69
88/9 Lethbridge

FUKUSHIMA, S.
95/6 Northlowa

FULLAN, LAWRENCE
74/5 Loblaws

FULLUM, RIVAL
89/90 SketchMEM 46
90/1 SketchOHL 24, 182
91/2 SketchOHL 21
91/2 Cornwall 16
87/8 Kitchener 12
88/9 Kitchener 12
89/90 Kitchener 13
94/5 ThunderBay
95/6 ThunderBay

FUNK, FLORIAN
94/5 DEL 136
95/6 DEL 138
96/7 DEL 35

FUNK, FRANZ
72 Hellas 43

FUNK, LORENZ
94/5 DEL 81
95/6 DEL 87
96/7 DEL 34

FUNK, LORNE
72 SemicSticker 102
92 SemicSticker 187
72 Hellas 51
79 PaniniSticker 105

FUREY, KIRK
93/4 OwenSound

FURRER, GASTON
72 SemicSticker 140

FUSCO, MARK
85/6 OPC/Topps 74
84/5 HFD/JuniorWhalers

FUSELLI, JOHN
89/90 SSMarie 30

FUSTER, MARCO
91/2 Richmond 17

GABLER, MICHAEL
94/5 DEL 293

GABRIEL, JEFF
94/5 Greensboro

GADOWSKI, GUY
91/2 Richmond 18
92/3 Richmond

GADSBY, BILL
45-64 BeeHives(CHI), (DETx2)
45-64 BeeHives(NYR)
64-67 BeeHives(DET)
62 CeramicTiles
63-5 ChexPhoto
64/5 CokeCap DET-4
65/6 CocaCola
83&87 HallOfFame 110
83 HHOF Postcard (H)
95/6 HHOFLegends 70
91/2 Kraft 74
51/2 Parkhurst 37
52/3 Parkhurst 56
53/4 Parkhurst 76
54/5 Parkhurst 87
61/2 Parkhurst 27
62/3 Parkhurst 25
63/4 Parkhurst 59
92/3 Parkhurst 53 PR9
93/4 Parkie(56/7) 89, 137
94/5 Parkie(64/5) 54
60/1 ShirriffCoin 90
61/2 ShirriffCoin 79
54/5 Topps 20
57/8 Topps 65
58/9 Topps 34
59/60 Topps 62
60/1 Topps 22
64/5 Topps 96
65/6 Topps 44
56-66 Tor.Star 57/8, 59/60, 61/2
54-67 TorontoStar V5 ,n10
63/4 TheTorontoStar
91/2 UltimateDP 69, -Aut 69
62/3 YorkTransfer 31
63/4 York 39
76 DET

GAETANO, PHIL
94 Semic 294

GAETZ, LINK
91/2 O-Pee-Chee 1S
90/1 opcPremier 33
91/2 Pinnacle 339, 412
88/9 ProCards(Rochester)
89/90 ProCards(IHL) 88
90/1 ProCards 110
90/1 ProSet 411
91/2 ProSet 561
88/9 MIN/American
91/2 S.J

GAFFAR, SHAYNE
90/1 SketchOHL 34
91/2 SketchOHL 12
91/2 Cornwall 15

GAGE, JOAQUIN
95/6 Bowman 154
95/6 Donruss 237
95/6 Leaf 255
95/6 Parkhurst 343
91/2 SketchWHL 46
94/5 CapeBreton
93/4 PrinceAlbert

GAGE, JODY
93/4 ClassicProspects 82
95/6 EdgeIce 63
88/9 ProCards(Rochester)
89/90 ProCards(AHL) 276
90/1 ProCards 285
91/2 ProCards 21
80/1 DET
91/2 Rochester/Dunkin'Donuts
91/2 Rochester/Kodak
92/3 Rochester/Dunkin'Donuts
92/3 Rochester/Kodak
93/4 Rochester
95/6 Rochester

GAGGI, JASON
95/6 Slapshot 32
96/7 Sudbury 10

GAGNÉ, ART
25-27 Anonymous 12
27-32 LaPresse 27/8
23/4 PaulinsCandy 31
28/9 MTL/LaPatrie 2

GAGNÉ, LUC
94/5 Slapshot(Sudbury) 13
95/6 Slapshot 398
96/7 Sudbury 11

GAGNÉ, MARTIN
90/1 SketchMEM 42
90/1 SketchQMJHL 39

GAGNÉ, MAXIME
90/1 SketchQMJHL 124

GAGNÉ, PAUL
81/2 OPC 75, Topps(W) 80
82/3 O-Pee-Chee 139
85/6 OPC/Topps 163
81/2 opcSticker 233
85/6 opcSticker 60/186
88/9 ProCards(Newmarket)
89/90 ProCards(AHL) 122
83/4 SouhaitsRen.KeyChain
81/2 COL.R
83/4 N.J.
84/5 N.J.
85/6 N.J.

GAGNÉ, RÉMI
83/4 NovaScotia 14

GAGNÉ, SIMON
98 BowmanCHL 107, 126, A36
97/8 UpperDeck 411

GAGNÉ, SYLVAIN
79/80 Montréal, -B&W

GAGNÉ, WAYNE
88/9 ProCards(Peoria)

GAGNER, DAVE
90/1 Bowman 186
91/2 Bowman 131, 419, 424
92/3 Bowman 171
95/6 Bowman 33
93/4 Donruss 83
94/5 Donruss 164
95/6 Donruss 58
96/7 Donruss 170
97/8 Donruss 80
97/8 DonrussPriority 103
93/4 EASports 34
96/7 Flair 12
94/5 Fleer 49
95/6 FleerMetal 38
92/3 FleerUltra 94
93/4 FleerUltra 92
94/5 FleerUltra 51
95/6 FleerUltra 229
96/7 FleerUltra 22
92/3 HumptyDumpty (2)
95/6 KraftDinner
93/4 Leaf 128
94/5 Leaf 319
95/6 Leaf 222
96/7 MetalUniverse 19
97/8 Omega 98
88/9 O-Pee-Chee 215
89/90 OPC/Topps 109, N
90/1 OPC/Topps 168
91/2 OPC/Topps 74, T-TL 7
92/3 O-Pee-Chee 80
91/2 opcPremier 128
89/90 opcSticker 203
98/9 Pacific 221
97/8 PacificCrown 159
97/8 PacificCrownRoyale 56
97/8 PacificInvincible 17
97/8 PacificParamount 79
98/9 PacificParamount 95
97/8 PacificRevolution 59
89/90 PaniniSticker 103
90/1 PaniniSticker 248
91/2 PaniniSticker 112
92/3 PaniniSticker 90
93/4 PaniniSticker 269
94/5 PaniniSticker 227
95/6 PaniniSticker 167
96/7 PaniniSticker 219
97/8 PaniniSticker 191
95 PaniniWorlds 25
91/2 Parkhurst 78
92/3 Parkhurst 311
93/4 Parkhurst 317
94/5 Parkhurst 58
95/6 Parkhurst 471
91/2 Pinnacle 71
92/3 Pinnacle 85
93/4 Pinnacle 77
94/5 Pinnacle 334
95/6 Pinnacle 125
96/7 Pinnacle 39
97/8 Pinnacle 156
97/8 PinnacleBeAPlayer 174
97/8 PinnacleCertified 47
97/8 PinnacleInside 181
95/6 Pinn.Zenith 56, -Gifted 11
95/6 Playoff 30
96/7 Playoff 337
94/5 POG 79
95/6 POG 86
93/4 PowerPlay 60
93/4 Premier 183
94/5 Premier 298
90/1 ProSet 138
91/2 ProSet 108, 288
92/3 ProSet 77
91/2 PSPlatinum 60
90/1 Score 108, -Hot 52
91/2 Score(CND) 72, (U.S) 72
92/3 Score 227
93/4 Score 98
95/6 Score 93
96/7 Score 14
97/8 Score 79
94/5 Select 6
95/6 SkyBoxEmotion 45
95/6 SkyBoxImpact 44
94/5 SP 30
95/6 Summit 53
96/7 Summit 80
92/3 Topps 254
95/6 Topps 254
95/6 ToppsFinest 31
91/2 ToppsStadiumClub 117
92/3 ToppsStadiumClub 121
93/4 ToppsStadiumClub 436
94/5 ToppsStadiumClub 45
95/6 ToppsStadiumClub 31
90/1 UpperDeck 248
91/2 UpperDeck 86, 180
92/3 UpperDeck 174
93/4 UpperDeck 145
94/5 UpperDeck 382
95/6 UpperDeck 370, SE24
94/5 UDBeAPlayer R5, -Aut. 77
97/8 UDBlackDiamond 58
98/9 UDChoice 92
95/6 UDCollChoice 7
96/7 UDCollChoice 260
97/8 UDCollChoice 38
97/8 Zenith 75, Z35
94/5 DAL
94/5 DAL/Southwest
97/8 FLA/WinnDixie
87/8 MIN
88/9 MIN/American

GAGNER, KEN
83/4 Brantford 25

GAGNER, ROGER
51/2 BasDuFleuve 44
52/3 BasDuFleuve 1

GAGNON, DAVID
90/1 ProCards 491
91/2 Score(CDN) 277, (U.S) 387
94/5 Roanoke

GAGNON, FRANÇOIS
91/2 SketchQMJHL 15

GAGNON, GERRY
72/3 EddieSargent 133
51/2 LacStJean 11
74/5 Loblaws
72/3 OPC 200
73/4 OPC 161, Topps 178
74/5 OPC 344
75/6 OPC/Topps 101

GAGNON, H.P.
52/3 BasDuFleuve 27

GAGNON, JACK
52/3 BasDuFleuve 40
51/2 LavalDairy 21

GAGNON, J.F.
90/1 SketchQMJHL 161, 263
91/2 SketchQMJHL 169

GAGNON, JOE
93/4 Slapshot(Oshawa) 2
94/5 Slapshot(NorthBay) 1
92/3 Oshawa

GAGNON, JOHN (BLACK CAT)
33/4 Anonymous V129 43
34-43 BeeHives (MTL.C)
35-40 CrownBrand 58
33-35 DiamondMatch
36-39 DiamondMatch (2), (3)
27-32 LaPresse 30/1
33/4 OPC (V304A)19
37/8 OPC (V304E) 154
39/40 OPC (V301-1) 25
43-47 ParadeSportive (x2)
55/6 Parkhurst 65
38/9 QuakerOats
33/4 WWGum (V357) 21
36/7 WWGum (V356) 83

GAGNON, MARC
91/2 AvantGarde 140,146,156

GAGNON, OVILA
52/3 AnonymousOHL 162

GAGNON, PASCAL
91/2 SketchQMJHL 46

GAGNON, PAUL
51/2 BasDuFleuve 47
51/2 LacStJean 6

GAGNON, PIERRE
90/1 SketchMEM 50
90/1 SketchQMJHL 3
88/9 Kitchener 21
87/8 Sudbury 16
91/2 SketchQMJHL 292
89/90 Sudbury 16

GAGNON, SEAN
91/2 SketchOHL 264
93/4 Slapshot(SSMarie) 7
94/5 Dayton 11
95/6 Dayton
93/4 SSMarie 7
91/2 Sudbury 5

GAGNON, YANNICK
93/4 Slapshot(Drum.) 3

GAHN, KRISTIAN
94/5 EliteSet 118
95/6 EliteSet 279
90/1 SemicElitserien 95
91/2 SemicElitserien 24
92/3 SemicElitserien 48
92/3 UpperDeck 232
95/6 udElite 159
97/8 udSwedish 156

GAILBRAITH, WALTER
38/9 BruinsMagazine

GAILER, PETER
82 SemicSticker 104

GAILLOUX, KRIS
92/3 BCJHL 224

GAINER, CLAYTON
93/4 Wheeling 16

GAINEY, BOB
72-84 Dernière 73/4, 80/1
83/4 Esso
86/7 Kraft Sports 24
91/2 Kraft 39
82/3 McDonalds 12
74/5 O-Pee-Chee 388
75/6 OPC/Topps 278
76/7 OPC/Topps 44, 217
77/8 OPC/Topps 129
78/9 OPC/Topps 76
79/80 OPC/Topps 170
80/1 OPC/Topps 58
81/2 OPC 176, 194, Topps 13
82/3 O-Pee-Chee 181, 367
83/4 O-Pee-Chee 187

84/5 O-Pee-Chee 261
85/6 O-Pee-Chee 169
86/7 OPC/Topps 96
87/8 O-Pee-Chee 228
88/9 O-Pee-Chee 216
89/90 O-Pee-Chee 329
81/2 opcSticker 30, 43, 269
82/3 opcSticker 36
83/4 opcSticker 66
84/5 opcSticker 153
85/6 opcSticker 138/10
86/7 opcSticker 12
87/8 opcSticker 12/150
88/9 opcSticker 42/173
89/90 opcSticker 58/200
80/1 opcSuperCard 9
87/8 PaniniSticker 53, 69
80/1 Pepsi Cap
82/3 Post
90/1 ProSet 668
84/5 7ElevenDisk
83/4 SouhaitsRen.KeyChain
92/3 Trends(76) 140
92/3 UpperDeck 'LockerAS 41
83/4 Vachon 44
94/5 DAL/Caps
94/5 DAL/Southwest
73/4 MTL
74/5 MTL
75/6 MTL
76/7 MTL
77/8 MTL
78/9 MTL
79/80 MTL
80/1 MTL
81/2 MTL
82/3 MTL
82/3 MTL/Steinberg
83/4 MTL
84/5 MTL
85/6 MTL
85/6 MTL/Pennant
85/6 MTL/PepsiPlacemats
85/6? MTL/ProvigoPlacemats
85/6 MTL/ProvigoStickers
86/7 MTL
87/8 MTL
87/8 MTL/Kodak
87/8 MTL/Stickers 12, 13, 18
87/8 MTL/Stickers 53, 88
88/9 MTL
89/90 MTL/Figurine
92/3 MTL/OPC 16
95/6 MTL/Forum 23Mar96

GAINOR, DUTCH
27-32 LaPresse 29/30
34/5 SweetCaporal
36/7 WWGum (V356) 98

GALANOV, MAXIM
95/6 Binghampton

GALARNEAU, DAN
91/2 AirCanadaSJHL B39
92/3 MPSPhotoSJHL 160

GALARNEAU, MICHEL
82/3 HFD/JuniorWhalers

GALATI, MIKE
95/6 Slapshot 300
95/6 Guelph 29

GALBRAITH, WALTER
33/4 OPC (V304A) 7

GALCHENYUK, ALEXANDER
92/3 ClassicProspects 96
91/2 O-Pee-Chee 33R
92/3 UpperDeck 353

GALIAY, GUY
79 PaniniSticker 383

GALKIN, ANDREJ
94/5 APS 239
95/6 APS 15

GALL, SANDOR
79 PaniniSticker 313

GALLACE, R.
91/2 SketchOHL 119

GALLACE, STEVE
95/6 Slapshot 295

GALLAGHER, JOHN
34-43 BeeHives(NYA)
27-32 LaPresse 30/1
36/7 OPC (V304D) 108
36/7 WWGum (V356) 41

GALLAGHER, MATT
89/90 Nashville

GALLAGHER, RAY
87/8 Brockville 12
88/9 Brockville 1
93/4 Huntington

GALLANT, CHESTER
95/6 Slapshot 201

GALLANT, GERARD
90/1 Bowman 237
91/2 Bowman 56
92/3 Bowman 169
93/4 Donruss 320
92/3 FleerUltra 284
90/1 Kraft 14
91/2 Kraft 58
93/4 Leaf 310
87/8 OPC/Topps 67
88/9 OPC/Topps 12
89/90 OPC/Topps 172
89/90 OPC 302, Topps-AS 2
90/1 OPC/Topps 133, 322
91/2 OPC/Topps 443
92/3 O-Pee-Chee 163
87/8 opcSticker 106/240
88/9 opcSticker 254
89/90 opcSticker 253, 157/15
89/90 opcStickFS 25
87/8 PaniniSticker 245
88/9 PaniniSticker 43
89/90 PaniniSticker 58
90/1 PaniniSticker 205
91/2 PaniniSticker 142
92/3 PaniniSticker 116
91/2 Parkhurst 269
91/2 Pinnacle 205
92/3 Pinnacle 135
93/4 Pinnacle 404
93/4 PowerPlay 230
93/4 Premier 511
90/1 ProSet 71
91/2 ProSet 63
90/1 Score 180, -Hot 78
91/2 Score(CDN) 34, (U.S) 34
92/3 Score 119
93/4 Score 402, 560
91/2 ToppsStadiumClub 165
92/3 ToppsStadiumClub 218
93/4 ToppsStadiumClub 16, 346
92/3 Topps 92
90/1 UpperDeck 134
92/3 UpperDeck 246
85/6 DET/Caesars
86/7 DET/Caesars
87/8 DET/Caesars
88/9 DET
88/9 DET/Caesars
89/90 DET/Caesars
91/2 DET/Caesars
94/5 T.B./SkyBoxSportsCafe

GALLANT, GORD
75/6 opcWHA 96
76/7 opcWHA 4
74/5 Minnesota

GALLANT, KEVIN
87/8 Regina

GALLANT, SHAUN
95/6 Slapshot 282

GALLANT, TREVOR
95/6 Slapshot 217
93/4 Slapshot(Kitchener) 10
94/5 Slapshot(Kitchener) 11
94/5 Slapshot(NorthBay) 10
91/2 SketchOHL 80

GALLENTINE, BRIAN
95/6 Roanoke
92/3 WestMich.
93/4 WestMich.

GALLEY, GARRY
91/2 Bowman 360
92/3 Bowman 11
93/4 Donruss 251
94/5 Donruss 166
95/6 Donruss 116
96/7 Donruss 106
92/3 Durivage 41
93/4 Durivage 38
93/4 EASports 97
94/5 Fleer 153
92/3 FleerUltra 156
93/4 FleerUltra 124
94/5 FleerUltra 157
95/6 FleerUltra 16
93/4 Leaf 120
94/5 Leaf 264
95/6 Leaf 30
96/7 Leaf 8
94/5 LeafLimited 5
97/8 Omega 108
90/1 OPC/Topps 331
91/2 OPC/Topps 86
92/3 O-Pee-Chee 317
98/9 Pacific 235
97/8 PacificCrown 288
97/8 PacificParamount 89
91/2 PaniniSticker 175
93/4 PaniniSticker 53
94/5 PaniniSticker 43
95/6 PaniniSticker 23
96/7 PaniniSticker 13
91/2 Parkhurst 7, 350
92/3 Parkhurst 364
93/4 Parkhurst 423
94/5 Parkhurst V87
95/6 Parkhurst 21
94/5 ParkieSE 128
91/2 Pinnacle 171
92/3 Pinnacle 103
93/4 Pinnacle 72
94/5 Pinnacle 27
95/6 Pinnacle 4
96/7 Pinnacle 136
95/6 Playoff 124
94/5 POG 182
95/6 POG 46
93/4 PowerPlay 182
93/4 Premier 255
94/5 Premier 535
90/1 ProSet 7
91/2 ProSet 7, 298
91/2 PSPlatinum 211
90/1 Score 253
91/2 Score(CDN) 71, (U.S) 71
92/3 Score 19
93/4 Score 143
94/5 Score 26
95/6 Score 112
96/7 Score 131
94/5 Select 117
95/6 SkyBoxEmotion 15
95/6 SkyBoxImpact 15
97/8 SPAuthentic 73
92/3 Topps 360
95/6 Topps 155
96/7 ToppsNHLPicks 95
91/2 ToppsStadiumClub 175
92/3 ToppsStadiumClub 424
93/4 ToppsStadiumClub 381
95/6 ToppsStadiumClub 3
93/4 TSC-MembersOnly 29
95/6 ToppsSuperSkills 37
90/1 UpperDeck 379
91/2 UpperDeck 439, 607
92/3 UpperDeck 319
93/4 UpperDeck 90
94/5 UpperDeck 19
95/6 UpperDeck 198
96/7 UpperDeck 15
94/5 UDBeAPlayer-Aut. 62
95/6 UDCollChoice 73
97/8 UDCollChoice 30
89/90 BOS/SportsAction
90/1 BOS/SportsAction
84/5 L.A./Smokeys
88/9 L.A.
92/3 PHA/JCPenney
92/3 PHA/UD 13MAR93
92/3 PHA/UD 17DEC92
93/4 PHA 11NOV93
93/4 PHA/JCPenney
94/5 PHA
87/8 WSH
87/8 WSH/Kodak

GALLINGER, DON
34-43 BeeHives(BOS)

GALLOWAY, KYLE
93/4 Roanoke

GALLSTEDT, NIKLAS
89/90 SemicElitserien 32
90/1 SemicElitserien 179
91/2 SemicElitserien 33
92/3 SemicElitserien 59

GALUPPO, SANDY
94/5 Birmingham
92/3 Dayton

GAMACHE, J.G.
52/3 AnonymousOHL 35

GAMBLE, BRUCE
45-64 BeeHives(BOS)
64-67 BeeHives(TOR)
70/1 Colgate Stamp 82
70/1 DadsCookies
70/1 EddieSargent 193
71/2 EddieSargent 160
70/1 Esso Stamp
68/9 O-Pee-Chee 197
69/70 OPC/T. 44, OPC-Sticker
70/1 OPC/Topps 105,-Deckle 44
71/2 OPC/Topps 201, Topps 104
71/2 opcPoster 16
95/6 Parkie(66/7) 118
68/9 Post Marble
60/1 ShirriffCoin 119
68/9 ShirriffCoin TOR15
71/2 TheTorontoSun
62/3 Topps 3
67/8 Topps 18
68/9 TOR
69/70 TOR
70/1 TOR

GAMBLE, RICHARD (DICK)
45-64 BeeHives(MTL)
48-52 Exhibits
51-54 LaPatrie 27Jan52
51/2 Parkhurst 16
52/3 Parkhurst 5
53/4 Parkhurst 18
45-54 QuakerOats
54/5 Topps 1

GAMBLE, TROY
92/3 Bowman 410
91/2 Bowman 315
95/6 EdgeIce 133, TW4
91/2 OPC/Topps 446
90/1 opcPremier 34
90/1 Panini(VAN) 8
91/2 PaniniSticker 37
91/2 Parkhurst 402
89/90 ProCards(IHL) 178
90/1 ProSet 32
91/2 ProSet 238
91/2 PSPlatinum 121
90/1 ScoreTraded 32T
91/2 Score(CDN) 502
91/2 Score(U.S) 282, -Young 29
92/3 Topps 412
91/2 ToppsStadiumClub 218
90/1 UpperDeck 434
91/2 UpperDeck 120
90/1 VAN/Mohawk
90/1 VAN/Molson
91/2 VAN
92/3 Hamilton
85/6 MedicineHat 15

GAMBUCCI, ARY
74/5 Minnesota

GAMBUCCI, GARY
69/70 MåstarSerien 19
72 SemicSticker 123

GANCHAR, PERRY
89/90 ProCards(IHL) 148
90/1 ProCards 379
91/2 ProCards 292
92/3 ClevelandLumberjacks 10
93/4 ClevelandLumberjacks
95/6 ClevelandLumberjacks
81/2 Saskatoon 22

GANI, DARREN
83/4 Belleville 25
84/5 Belleville 22

GANS, DAVE
81/2 Oshawa 11
82/3 Oshawa 19
83/4 Oshawa 27

GANSTER, FRIEDRICH
93 SemicSticker 277

GARATTI, JASON
93/4 Minn-Duluth

GARBER, BRUCE
93/4 Birmingham 19

GARBOCZ, DARIUSZ
92 SemicSticker 275

GARBUTT, MURRAY
90/1 SketchMEM 90
90/1 SketchWHL 25

GARBUTT, MURRAY
91/2 ProCards 514
93/4 Huntington

GARDINER, BRUCE
98/9 Pacific 309
97/8 PacificCrown 172
97/8 PinnacleBeAPlayer 51
97/8 UpperDeck 115
96/7 OTT/PizzaHut
97/8 OTT

GARDINER, CHARLIE (CHUCK)
33/4 CndGum (V252)
23/4 Crescent Selkirks 9
33-35 DiamondMatch
83&87 HallOfFame 128
83 HHOF Postcard (I)
27-32 LaPresse 31/2
28/9 PaulinsCandy 89
60/1 Topps 32
61/2 Topps-Stamp

GARDINER, HERBERT
60/1 Topps 44
61/2 Topps-Stamp
83&87 HallOfFame 154
83 HHOF Postcard (L)
27-32 LaPresse 27/8
23/4 PaulinsCandy 63
28/9 MTL/LaPatrie 9
95/6 MTL/Forum 4Nov95

GARDINER, JAMES
91 C55 Reprint 36
1911-12 Imperial (C55) 36
1912-13 Imperial (C57) 24
1910-11 Imperial Post 36

GARDINER, JEFF
89/90 SketchOHL 159
90/1 SketchOHL 105
91/2 SketchOHL 44

GARDINER, SCOTT
83/4 Belleville 5

GARDINER, WILBERT (BERT)
34-43 BeeHives(MTL.C)

GARDNER, BILL
83/4 O-Pee-Chee 103
84/5 O-Pee-Chee 35
82/3 Post
88/9 ProCards(Saginaw)
83/4 SouhaitsRen.KeyChain
81/2 CHI
82/3 CHI
86/7 HFD/JuniorWhalers
83/4 PGH/Heinz

GARDNER, CALVIN
45-64 BeeHives(BOS), (TOR)
48-52 Exhibits
51/2 Parkhurst 85
52/3 Parkhurst 30
53/4 Parkhurst 99
54/5 Parkhurst 53
93/4 Parkhurst 53 PR57
93/4 Parkie(56/7) 10
45-54 QuakerOats (x4)
54/5 Topps 47
60/1 ClevelandBarons

GARDNER, DAVE
91/2 AirCanadaSJHL A23

GARDNER, DAVE
74/5 Loblaws, -Update
74/5 OPC/Topps 47
75/6 OPC/Topps 119
76/7 OPC 274
77/8 OPC/Topps 258
78/9 O-Pee-Chee 278
73/4 MTL

GARDNER, GEORGE
70/1 EddieSargent 222
71/2 EddieSargent 213
72/3 Letraset 16
70/1 OPC 224
71/2 OPC/Topps 235
71/2 TheTorontoSun
70/1 VAN/RoyalBank
71/2 VAN/RoyalBank 18
72/3 VAN/Nalleys
72/3 LosAngelesSharks
73/4 VancouverBlazers

GARDNER, JIM
83&87 HallOfFame 172
83 HHOF Postcard (M)

GARDNER, JOE
90/1 ProCards 381
91/2 Knoxville

GARDNER, PAUL
77/8 OPC/Topps 24
78/9 OPC/Topps 88
79/80 OPC/Topps 5
81/2 OPC 257, Topps(E) 113
82/3 O-Pee-Chee 236, 269
83/4 O-Pee-Chee 219, 275, 280
81/2 opcSticker 187
82/3 opcSticker 145
83/4 opcSticker 230
82/3 Post
89/90 ProCards(AHL) 113
83/4 PuffySticker 10
83/4 SouhaitsRen.KeyChain
76/7 COL.R/CokeCans
77/8 COL. R/CokeCans
79/80 TOR
93/4 Portland
96/7 Portland

GARDNER, RYAN
95/6 Slapshot 166

GARE, DANNY
76/7 OPC 380
75/6 OPC/Topps 64
76/7 OPC/Topps 222
77/8 OPC/Topps 42
78/9 OPC/Topps 209
79/80 OPC/Topps 61
80/1 OPC/Topps 38, 80, 88, 161
80/1 OPC/Topps 165, 167, 260
81/2 OPC 20, 27-28
81/2 O-Pee-Chee 27-28
81/2 Topps 14, 47, (East) 127
82/3 O-Pee-Chee 83
83/4 O-Pee-Chee 123
84/5 OPC 54, Topps 42
85/6 OPC/Topps 37
86/7 OPC/Topps 69
81/2 opcSticker 53
82/3 opcSticker 184
83/4 opcSticker 135
85/6 opcSticker 35/166
86/7 opcSticker 159/16
82/3 Post
83/4 PuffySticker 17
83/4 SouhaitsRen.KeyChain
74/5 BUF
79/80 BUF/BellsMarket
80/1 BUF/Wendt
93/4 BUF/NOCO
84/5 DET/Caesars
85/6 DET/Caesars
86/7 EDM/RedRooster
88/9 EDM/ActionMagazine 20
94/5 T.B./SkyBoxSportsCafe
95/6 T.B./SkyBoxSportsCafe
84/5 KelownaWings&WHL 23

GAREAU, GUY
51/2 LacStJean 2

GARIEPY, RAYMOND
30s? ABC ChewingGu m 39
45-54 BeeHives(BOS)

GARLAND, SCOTT
76/7 O-Pee-Chee 243
77/8 OPC 302
78/9 OPC 274
76/7 TOR

GARNER, TYRONE
95/6 Slapshot 232

GARNETT, KEVIN
86/7 Kitchener 8

GARON, MATHIEU
95/6 Bowman P14
98 BowmanCHL 81, SC21
97/8 PinnacleBeeHive 71
95/6 UpperDeck 525
98/9 UDChoice 260

GARPENLOV, JOHAN
91/2 Bowman 45
92/3 Bowman 400
93/4 Donruss 309
94/5 Donruss 301
95/6 Donruss 322
93/4 EASports 118
94/5 Flair 165
92/3 FleerUltra 400
93/4 FleerUltra 83
94/5 FleerUltra 194
95 Globe 36
93/4 Leaf 133
94/5 Leaf 234
95/6 Leaf 282
91/2 OPC/Topps 278
90/1 opcPremier 35
97/8 PacificCrown 348
91/2 PaniniSticker 144
93/4 PaniniSticker 257
96/7 PaniniSticker 75
97/8 PaniniSticker 62
91/2 Parkhurst 385
92/3 Parkhurst 397
94/5 Parkhurst 209
95/6 Parkhurst 90
92/3 Pinnacle 122
93/4 Pinnacle 63
94/5 Pinnacle 296
96/7 PinnacleBeAPlayer 67
94/5 POG 215
95/6 POG 120
93/4 PowerPlay 219
93/4 Premier 53
94/5 Premier 201
90/1 ProSet 605
91/2 ProSet 56
91/2 PSPlatinum 29
90/1 ScoreTraded 17T
91/2 Score(CDN) 204, (U.S) 204
92/3 Score 406
93/4 Score 183
94/5 Score 176
89/90 SemicElitserien 67
91/2 SemicElitserien 353
91 SemicSticker 212
93 SemicSticker 38
94/5 SP 45
92/3 Topps 359
95/6 Topps 56
91/2 ToppsStadiumClub 268
92/3 ToppsStadiumClub 212
93/4 ToppsStadiumClub 44
95/6 ToppsStadiumClub 62
90/1 UpperDeck 521, 523
91/2 UpperDeck 28, 167, E15
92/3 UpperDeck 59
93/4 UpperDeck SP-142
94/5 UpperDeck 64
95/6 UpperDeck 129
94/5 UDBeAPlayer R38, -Aut. 61
95/6 UDCollChoice 240
96/7 UDCollChoice 106
95/6 udElite 242
90/1 DET/Caesars
91/2 DET/Caesars
96/7 FLA/WinnDixie
97/8 FLA/WinnDixie
92/3 S.J/PacificBell

GARRETT, DUDLEY (RED)
34-43 BeeHives(NYR)

GARRETT, GUNNER
78/9 Saginaw

GARRETT, JOHN
79/80 O-Pee-Chee 293
80/1 OPC/Topps 77
81/2 O-Pee-Chee 137
82/3 O-Pee-Chee 283
83/4 O-Pee-Chee 349, 354
84/5 O-Pee-Chee 317

85/6 O-Pee-Chee 220
81/2 opcSticker 68
83/4 opcSticker 275
75/6 opcWHA 12
76/7 opcWHA 55
77/8 opcWHA 23
97/8 Pinnacle -CBC Sports 5
82/3 Post
83/4 Vachon 105
82/3 QUE
83/4 QUE
83/4 VAN
84/5 VAN
74/5 Minnesota

GARTHE, M.
95/6 DEL 45

GARTNER, MIKE
96/7 Aces 4 (Diamonds)
90/1 Bowman 220, -HT 8, 17
91/2 Bowman 74
92/3 Bowman 146
93/4 Donruss 218, 494
94/5 Donruss 111
95/6 Donruss 293
96/7 Donruss 206
97/8 Donruss 110
96/7 DonrussCanadianIce 18
97/8 D.CanadianIce 54, 149
96/7 DonrussElite 123
97/8 DonrussElite 147
97/8 DonrussPreferred 47
97/8 DonrussPriority 93
97/8 DonrussStudio 89
96/7 Duracell JB9
93/4 EASports 89
94/5 Flair 180
96/7 Flair-Now&Then 1
94/5 Fleer 214
95/6 FleerMetal 142
96/7 FleerNHLPicks 170
92/3 FleerUltra 135
93/4 F.Ultra 25, -Red 3 -Speed 4
94/5 FleerUltra 214, -Red 3
95/6 FleerUltra 311
96/7 FleerUltra 130
88/9 FritoLay
95 Globe 85
97/8 KatchMedallion 109
84/5 Kelloggs Disk
90/1 Kraft 69
91/2 Kraft 27
93/4 Leaf 213
94/5 Leaf 135, -FireOnIce 11
95/6 Leaf 37
96/7 Leaf 91
95/6 LeafLimited 109
97/8 Limited 40
93/4 McDonalds McD15
96/7 MetalUniverse 116
97/8 Omega 173
80/1 OPC/Topps 49, 195
81/2 OPC 347, Topps(E) 117
82/3 O-Pee-Chee 363
83/4 O-Pee-Chee 364, 369
84/5 OPC 197, 370, Topps 143
85/6 OPC/Topps 46
86/7 OPC/Topps 59
87/8 OPC/Topps 168
88/9 OPC/Topps 50, N
89/90 OPC/Topps 30
90/1 OPC/Topps 373
91/2 OPC/Topps 46
92/3 O-Pee-Chee 245, 300
90/1 opcPremier 36
91/2 opcPremier 147, 164
81/2 opcSticker 190
82/3 opcSticker 153
83/4 opcSticker 207, 240/41
84/5 opcSticker 131, 178, 282
85/6 opcSticker 111/244
86/7 opcSticker 251
87/8 opcSticker 239
88/9 opcSticker 67
89/90 opcSticker 196/52
98/9 Pacific 338
97/8 PacificCrown 22, -Slap 7C
97/8 PacificCrownRoyale 102
97/8 PacificDynagon! 95
97/8 PcfcD-BstKpt 74,-Tandm 65
97/8 PacificInvincible 106
97/8 PacificParamount 139
97/8 PacificRegime 152
97/8 PacificRevolution 105
87/8 PaniniSticker 180
88/9 PaniniSticker 370
89/90 PaniniSticker 104
90/1 PaniniSticker 103
91/2 PaniniSticker 292
92/3 PaniniSticker 237
93/4 PaniniSticker 91
94/5 PaniniSticker 191
95/6 PaniniSticker 204
96/7 PaniniSticker 215
97/8 PaniniSticker 158
91/2 Parkhurst 122, 430, PHC8
92/3 Parkhurst 108
93/4 Parkhurst 400
94/5 Parkhurst 228
95/6 Parkhurst 206
94/5 ParkieSE seV29
91/2 Pinnacle 202
92/3 Pinnacle 94
93/4 Pinnacle 27, 241
94/5 Pinnacle 31
95/6 Pinnacle 75
96/7 Pinnacle 35
97/8 Pinnacle 137
96/7 PinnacleBeAPlayer 25
97/8 PinnacleCertified 85
97/8 PinnacleInside 97
95/6 PinnacleZenith 62
95/6 Playoff 95
96/7 Playoff 349
94/5 POG 233
95/6 POG 261
82/3 Post
93/4 PowerPlay 157
93/4 Premier 375, 384
94/5 Premier 253
90/1 ProSet 196, 351
91/2 ProSet 167, 604
92/3 ProSet 113, 256
91/2 PSPlatinum 84, PC11
83/4 PuffySticker 21
90/1 Score 130, 333, -Hot 60
91/2 Score(CDN) 135, (U.S) 135
92/3 Score 50, 443, 445
93/4 Score 2, 447, -P.AS 8, 46
94/5 Score 112, 242
95/6 Score 204
96/7 Score 154
97/8 Score 139
94/5 Select 95
95/6 SelectCertified 54
89 SemicSticker 75
84/5 7ElevenDisk
85/6 7Eleven 20
95/6 SkyBoxEmotion 169
95/6 SkyBoxImpact 159
96/7 SkyBoxImpact-Blade 5
83/4 SouhaitsRen.KeyChain
96/7 SP 123
97/8 SPAuthentic
95/6 Summit 143
96/7 Summit 28
96/7 TeamOut
92/3 Topps 264, 404
95/6 Topps 98
94/5 ToppsFinest 96
95/6 ToppsFinest 8
96/7 ToppsNHLPicks FC2
91/2 ToppsStadiumClub 51
92/3 ToppsStadiumClub 311
93/4 TSC 110, -AllStar, -Finest 6
95/6 ToppsStadiumClub 162
91/2 TSC-MembersOnly (x2)
95/6 TSC-MembersOnly 22
95/6 ToppsSuperSkills 28
90/1 UpperDeck 277
91/2 UpperDeck 247
92/3 UD 126, -LockerAS 38
93/4 UpperDeck 205, SP-98
94/5 UpperDeck 32, 230, SP78
95/6 UpperDeck 110
96/7 UpperDeck 316
97/8 UpperDeck 128
93/4 UDBeAPlayer 22, -Roots 26
94/5 UDBeAPlayer R127
96/7 UDBlackDiamond 42
95/6 UDCollChoice 149
97/8 UDCollChoice 196
96/7 UpperDeck"Ice" 52
96/7 PHO
97/8 PHO
93/4 TOR/Abalene
94/5 TOR
79/80 WSH
80/1 WSH
81/2 WSH
82/3 WSH
84/5 WSH/PizzaHut
85/6 WSH/PizzaHut
86/7 WSH/Kodak
86/7 WSH/Police
87/8 WSH
87/8 WSH/Kodak
88/9 WSH
88/9 WSH/Smokey

GARTSHORE, DAVID
91/2 LakeSuperior

GARVER, J.
93/4 Waterloo

GARVEY, BRENDAN
92/3 Oklahoma

GARVEY, L.
91/2 Mich.Tech

GARVIN, SCOTT
92/3 BCJHL 231

GASSER, NORBERT
79 PaniniSticker 387

GASSOFF, BOB
74/5 Loblaws
75/6 OPC/Topps 58
76/7 OPC 301, 393
77/8 OPC/Topps 4
92/3 STL/UpperDeck 13

GASSOFF, BRAD
78/9 O-Pee-Chee 388
79/80 O-Pee-Chee 353
76/7 VAN/RoyalBank
77/8 VAN/GingerAle
77/8 VAN/RoyalBank

GATENBY, DAN
87/8 Sudbury 3

GATHERCOLE, PHILIP
91/2 SketchQMJHL 235

GATHERUM, DAVE
52/3 LavalDairy 66
52/3 StLawrence 107

GATTO, GREG
90/1 SketchWHL 315
91/2 SketchWHL 10

GATZOS, STEVE
83/4 PGH
84/5 PGH/Heinz
80/1 SSMarie

GAUCHER, YVES
84/5 Richelieu

GAUDET, DENIS
93/4 Slapshot(NorthBay) 17

GAUDET, KEVIN
96/7 DEL 203

GAUDET, MARC-ANDRÉ
97/8 Bowman 66
98 BowmanCHL 91

GAUDET, PIUS
51/2 BasDuFleuve 32

GAUDETTE, ANDRÉ
74/5 opcWHA 46
73/4 QuakerOats 22
73/4 Quebec

GAUDETTE, PETE
52/3 BasDuFleuve 10

GAUDREAU, ROB
92/3 Classic 82
92 ClassicFourSport 204
92/3 ClassicProspects 16, 140
92/3 ClassicProspects LP3, PR3
93/4 Donruss 310
94/5 Fleer 146
93/4 FleerUltra 98, -Prospects 2
93/4 Leaf 9
94/5 Leaf 39
93/4 PaniniSticker 258
93/4 Parkhurst 189
94/5 Parkhurst 207
93/4 Pinnacle 41
94/5 Pinnacle 349
93/4 PowerPlay 220, -Second 1
93/4 Premier 199
94/5 Premier 4
93/4 Score 247
95/6 Score 141
95/6 Topps 117
93/4 ToppsStadiumClub 174
93/4 UD 149, HB2, HT9, SP-143
94/5 UpperDeck 182, 277
95/6 UpperDeck 165
94/5 UDBeAPlayer-Aut. 85
95/6 UDCollChoice 158
94/5 OTT/Bell
95/6 OTT
93/4 S.J.

GAUDREAULT, ARMAND
51/2 LavalDairy 14
43-47 ParadeSportive

GAUDREAULT, LEO
51/2 LacStJean 32
27-32 LaPresse 27/8
28/9 MTL/LaPatrie 13

GAUL, HORACE
1910-11 Imperial (C56) 31

GAULE, MICHAEL
91/2 SketchQMJHL 236

GAULIN, J.M.
84/5 QUE
85/6 QUE/GeneralFoods
82/3 Fredericton 22
83/4 Fredericton 21
85/6 Fredericton 26
86/7 Fredericton

GAUME, DALLAS
88/9 ProCards(Binghampton)

GAUMOND, ALEXANDRE
91/2 SketchQMJHL 295

GAUS, THOMAS
94/5 DEL 417
95/6 DEL 388
96/7 DEL 296

GAUTHIER, A.
26 Dominion 24

GAUTHIER, ALAIN
90/1 SketchQMJHL 162, 251
91/2 SketchQMJHL 249

GAUTHIER, DANIEL
92/3 ClassicProspects 23
91/2 ProCards 296
92/3 ClevelandLumberjacks 22
93/4 Indianapolis

GAUTHIER, DENIS
95/6 Classic 19, AS14
95/6 DonrussElite-WorldJrs 5
98/9 Pacific 118
93/4 Slapshot(Drum.) 14
95/6 UpperDeck 533

GAUTHIER, DEREK
90/1 SketchOHL 233
91/2 SketchOHL 84
94/5 Slapshot(Brantford) 8
90/1 Kitchener 17

GAUTHIER, DON
89/90 Rayside

GAUTHIER, FERN
45-64 BeeHives(DETx2)
43-47 ParadeSportive (x2)

GAUTHIER, GÉRARD
90/1 ProSet 687

GAUTHIER, JEAN
62 CeramicTiles
63-5 ChexPhoto
63/4 Parkhurst 28, 87
61/2 ShirriffCoin 120
61/2 York 42
63/4 York 29
63/4 Québec

GAUTHIER, LUC
88/9 ProCards(Sherbrooke)
89/90 ProCards(AHL) 197
90/1 ProCards 55
91/2 ProCards 76
92/3 Fredericton
93/4 Fredericton
94/5 Fredericton
95/6 Fredericton
96/7 Fredericton

GAUTHIER, SEAN
90/1 SketchOHL 57
91/2 Moncton
91/2 ProCards 180
96/7 Penascola 21

GAUTHIER, STEVE
84/5 Chicoutimi

GAUVREAU, BRENT
98 BowmanCHL 144, A37

GAVEY, AARON
95/6 Bowman 121
93/4 Classic 21
94/5 Classic 115, T64, C5, R6
93/4 Donruss CAN12
95/6 Donruss 369
96/7 DonrussElite 64
95/6 EdgeIce 101
94/5 Flair 172
94/5 Leaf 452
96/7 Leaf 167
94/5 LeafLimited 118
97/8 PacificRegime 27
96/7 PaniniSticker 129
95/6 Parkhurst 527
93/4 Pinnacle 473
94/5 Pinnacle 251
94/5 Premier 536
94/5 Score 207
96/7 Score 259
94/5 Select 180
91/2 SketchOHL 316
95/6 SkyBoxImpact 221
93/4 Slapshot(SSMarie) 20
95/6 SP 138
96/7 Summit 158
95/6 ToppsFinest 28
95/6 ToppsStadiumClub 138
93/4 UpperDeck 545
95/6 UpperDeck 417
97/8 UpperDeck 28
94/5 UDBeAPlayer R156
95/6 UDBeAPlayer 165
96/7 UDCollChoice 249
95/6 T.B.
93/4 SSMarie 22

GAVIN, STEWART
83/4 O-Pee-Chee 331
84/5 O-Pee-Chee 302
87/8 OPC/Topps 61
88/9 O-Pee-Chee 217
89/90 O-Pee-Chee 214
90/1 O-Pee-Chee 402
85/6 opcSticker 17/148
87/8 PaniniSticker 49
89/90 PaniniSticker 113
90/1 PaniniSticker 260
80/1 Pepsi Cap
82/3 Post
90/1 ProSet 139
91/2 ProSet 404
90/1 Score 244
91/2 Score(CDN) 433
92/3 Score 117
90/1 UpperDeck 150
83/4 Vachon 87
86/7 HFD/JuniorWhalers
87/8 HFD/JuniorWhalers
88/9 MIN/American
80/1 TOR
81/2 TOR
82/3 TOR
83/4 TOR
84/5 TOR

GAWLEY, SEAN
91/2 SketchOHL 298

GEBAUER, A.
95/6 DEL 350

GEBEL, MARTIN
94/5 DEL 237
95/6 DEL 240
96/7 DEL 73

GEDDES, PAUL
94/5 DEL 323
95/6 DEL 299
96/7 DEL 325

GEE, GEORGE
45-64 BeeHive(CHI), (DET)
51/2 Parkhurst 43
52/3 Parkhurst 36
53/4 Parkhurst 83
54/5 Parkhurst 80

GEEKIE, CRAIG
91/2 SketchWHL 213
92/3 Brandon 7

GEESINK, TONY
84/5 Ottawa67s

GEFFERT, PAVEL
94/5 APS 87
95/6 APS 375

GEGENFURTHER, CHRISTIAN
94/5 DEL 383
95/6 DEL 367
96/7 DEL189

GEHRIG, MARIO
94/5 DEL 276
95/6 DEL 273
96/7 DEL 168

GEISEBRECHT, GUS
34-43 BeeHives(DET)

GELDART, GREG
95/6 Tallahassee 14

GELINAS, MARTIN
90/1 Bowman 190
91/2 Bowman 102
93/4 Donruss 271, 501
95/6 Donruss 223
96/7 Donruss 133
97/8 Donruss 41
97/8 DonrussCanadianIce 61
97/8 DonrussPreferred 83
93/4 Durivage 22
93/4 FleerUltra 401
94/5 FleerUltra 383
93/4 Leaf 396
94/5 Leaf 138
96/7 Leaf 127
97/8 Leaf 37
97/8 Limited 185
97/8 Omega 40
90/1 OPC/Topps 64
91/2 OPC/Topps 244
92/3 O-Pee-Chee 19
98/9 Pacific 132
97/8 PacificCrown 67
97/8 PacificCrownRoyale 134
97/8 PcfcDynag! 126,-Tandm 60
97/8 PacificInvincible 141
97/8 PacificParamount 187
98/9 PacificParamount 36
97/8 PacificRevolution 22
90/1 Panini(EDM) 5
91/2 PaniniSticker 128
92/3 PaniniSticker 106
97/8 PaniniSticker 238
91/2 Parkhurst 283
93/4 Parkhurst 166
94/5 Parkhurst V36
95/6 Parkhurst 480
94/5 ParkieSE 184
91/2 Pinnacle 93
92/3 Pinnacle 166
93/4 Pinnacle 366
94/5 Pinnacle 324
95/6 Pinnacle 161
96/7 Pinnacle 83
97/8 Pinnacle 168
97/8 PinnacleCertified 113
97/8 PinnacleInside 103
94/5 POG 335
95/6 POG 273
94/5 Premier 101
90/1 ProSet 83
91/2 ProSet 66
90/1 Score(CND) 301,-Young 21
91/2 Score(CDN) 159, (U.S) 159
91/2 Score-YoungStar 14
92/3 Score 281
93/4 Score 408, 534
96/7 Score 98
97/8 Score 133
97/8 Score(VAN) 5
96/7 Summit 79
92/3 Topps 292
95/6 Topps 176
91/2 ToppsStadiumClub 11
92/3 ToppsStadiumClub 314
90/1 UpperDeck 23
91/2 UpperDeck 266
92/3 UpperDeck 282
93/4 UpperDeck 322, SP-127
94/5 UpperDeck 54, SP172
95/6 UpperDeck 359
96/7 UpperDeck 171
97/8 UpperDeck 167, 200
95/6 UDBeAPlayer 149
95/6 UDCollChoice 176
97/8 UDCollChoice 257, SQ8
97/8 CAR/Postcard
88/9 EDM/ActionMagazine 73
90/1 EDM/McGavins
91/2 EDM/IGA
92/3 EDM/IGA 7
94/5 VAN
95/6 VAN/Building 9
96/7 VAN
96/7 VAN/IGA
87/8 Hull

GELINAS, RYAN
95/6 Slapshot 406

GELINEAU, JACK
45-64 BeeHives(BOS)
48-52 Exhibits
51/2 LavalDairy 4
52/3 StLawrence 37

GELLARD, SAM
73/4 VancouverBlazers

GENDRON, BRYAN
89/90 SketchOHL 120
90/1 SketchOHL 359
91/2 SketchOHL 141
91/2 Peterborough 11

GENDRON, EDGAR
52/3 BasDuFleuve 54
51/2 LacStJean 50

GENDRON, JEAN-GUY
52/3 AnonymousOHL 40
45-64 BeeHives(BOS), (NYR)
64-67 BeeHives(BOS)
62 CeramicTiles
70/1 DadsCookies
70/1 EddieSargent 157
71/2 EddieSargent 153
70/1 Esso Stamp
51-54 LaPatrie 24Jan54
68/9 O-Pee-Chee 185
69/70 OPC 169, -Sticker, T. 96
70/1 OPC/Topps 86
71/2 OPC/Topps 204
72/3 OPC 302
93/4 Parkie(56/7) 88
72 SemicSticker 170
72/3 7ElevenCups
60/1 ShirriffCoin 109
61/2 ShirriffCoin 93
63/4 TheTorontoStar
71/2 TheTorontoSun
57/8 Topps 52
58/9 Topps 51
59/60 Topps 24
60/1 Topps 31
61/2 Topps 57
62/3 Topps 16
63/4 Topps 16
60/1 York
72/3 PHA/MightyMilk
73/4 QuébecNordiques
65/6 QuébecAces

GENDRON, MARTIN
92/3 Classic 23
93/4 Classic 131
92/3 ClassicFourSport 172
93/4 ClassicProspects LP12
93/4 Donruss CAN13
95/6 Donruss 47
93/4 FleerUltra 460
95/6 FleerUltra 174
95/6 Parkhurst 489
93/4 Pinnacle 474
95/6 Pinnacle 201
93/4 PowerPlay 480
95/6 Score 315
90/1 SketchQMJHL 234
91/2 SketchQMJHL 27
95/6 SkyBoxImpact 224
93/4 UpperDeck 259, 540
95/6 WSH
96/7 LasVegas
94/5 Portland
95/6 Portland

GENDRON, PIERRE
91/2 SketchQMJHL 133

GENDRON, PATRICK
90/1 SketchQMJHL 106
91/2 SketchQMJHL 188

GENIK, JASON
92/3 BCJHL 182

GENOVY, AL
77/8 Kalamazoo

GENTILE, FLAVIO
85/6 Arizona

GENZE, ALEXANDER
94/5 DEL 297
95/6 DEL 197
96/7 DEL 340

GEOFFRION, BERNIE
45-64 BeeHives(MTL)
64-67 BeeHives(NYR), (Misc.)
62 CeramicTiles
63-5 ChexPhoto
72-84 Dernière 77/8
48-52 Exhibits (x2)
83&87 HallOfFame 166
83 HHOF Postcard (M)
92/3 HHOFLegends 5
91/2 Kraft 84
51-54 LaPatrie 31Dec51
74/5 OPC/Topps 147
51/2 Parkhurst 14
52/3 Parkhurst 3
53/4 Parkhurst 29
54/5 Parkhurst 8, 100
55/6 Parkhurst 43, 70
57/8 Parkhurst (MTL) 2, 24
58/9 Parkhurst 28
59/60 Parkhurst 33
60/1 Parkhurst 46, 59
61/2 Parkhurst 35
62/3 Parkhurst 48, 53
63/4 Parkhurst 29, 88
92/3 Parkhurst PR32
93/4 Parkhurst PR46
93/4 Parkie(56/7) 68, (64/5) A3
95/6 Parkie(66/7) 89
45-54 QuakerOats
60/1 ShirriffCoin 28
61/2 ShirriffCoin 104
62/3 ShirriffCoin 34
63/4 TheTorontoStar
66/7 Topps 85, -USATest 36
67/8 Topps 29
54-67 TorontoStar V8, V5,n4
56-66 TorontoStar 57/8
91/2 Ultimate(O6) 10,73,83,-Aut.
60/1 York, -Glasses
61/2 York 28
62/3 York Transfer 12
63/4 York 20
72/3 ATL
79/80 MTL
92/3 MTL/OPC 54
95/6 MTL/Forum 13Jan96
65/6 QuébecAces

GEOFFRION, DAN
72-84 Dernière 78/9
81/2 O-Pee-Chee 364
81/2 opcSticker 141
80/1 Pepsi Cap
79/80 MTL
80/1 WPG

GEORGE, CHRIS
94/5 Slapshot(Sarnia) 10
95/6 Slapshot 7

GEORGE, DARCY
92/3 BCJHL 174

GEORGE, ZAC
92/3 BCJHL 26

GERARD, DEAN
91/2 AirCanadaSJHL 8, A32
92/3 MPSPhotoSJHL 45

GERARD, EDDIE
83&87 HallOfFame 200
83 HHOF Postcard (N)
1912-13 Imperial (C57) 34
61/2 Topps-Stamp

GERBE, JOE
96/7 Guelph 12

GEREBI, NICK
91/2 Minnesota

GERHARDSSON, PETER
94/5 ElitSet 249
95/6 ElitSet 158

GERIS, DAVE
93/4 Slapshot(Windsor) 20
94/5 Slapshot(Windsor) 22
95/6 Slapshot 425

GERLITZ, H.
28/9 PaulinsCandy 58

GERLITZ, J.
28/9 PaulinsCandy 57

GERLITZ, P.
28/9 PaulinsCandy 54

GERMAIN, CLAUDE
51/2 LacStJean 57

GERMAIN, DANIEL
91/2 SketchQMJHL 252

GERMAIN, ERIC
88/9 ProCards(NewHaven)
89/90 ProCards(AHL) 12
90/1 ProCards 19
93/4 Richmond 17

GERNANDER, KEN
91/2 ProCards 178
94/5 Binghampton
95/6 Binghampton
96/7 Binghampton
91/2 Moncton

GERNEMIA, RYAN
95/6 SwiftCurrent

GEROW, ROD
85/6 London 24

GERRAUGH, DOUG
95/6 DEL 375

GERRITS, BRIAN
89/90 Saskatoon 16
86/7 Portland

GERSE, DAVE
88/9 Regina

GERUM, CHRISTIAN
94/5 DEL 322
95/6 DEL 291
96/7 DEL 318

GERVAIS, EDDY
91/2 SketchQMJHL 79

GERVAIS, GASTON
52/3 BasDuFleuve 23
51/2 LavalDairy 84

GERVAIS, GEORGE
91/2 AirCanadaSJHL B34

GERVAIS, GUY
52/3 BasDuFleuve 20
51/2 LacStJean 40

GERVAIS, SHAWN
92/3 BCJHL 168
93/4 Seattle

GERVAIS, VICTOR
90/1 ProCards 201
91/2 ProCards 558
95/6 ClevelandLumberjacks
92/3 Hampton
93/4 Hampton

GESCE, DEREK
91/2 AvantGardeDCJ 101

GESCE, DOREL
91/2 AvantGardeBCJ 72,
92/3 BCJHL 9

GETLIFFE, RAY
34-43 BeeHives(BOS), (MTL.C)
35-40 CrownBrand 197
39/40 OPC (V301-1) 29
40/1 OPC (V301-2) 147

GIACOMIN, ED
68/9 Bauer
64-67 BeeHives(NYR)
65/6 CocaCola
70/1 Colgate Stamp 70
70/1 DadsCookies
70/1 EddieSargent 115
71/2 EddieSargent 128
72/3 EddieSargent 147
70/1 Esso Stamp
87 HallOfFame 259
93/4 HHOFLegends 31
72/3 Letraset 10
74/5 LiptonSoup 26
74/5 Loblaws
68/9 OPC/Topps 67, OPC 205
69/70 OPC/Topps 33, OPC 217
70/1 OPC/Topps 68, OPC 244
70/1 OPC-Deckle 42, -Sticker
71/2 OPC/Topps 220, 248, 250
71/2 OPC-Booklet 7, T. 4-6, 90
72/3 OPC 173, Topps 165
73/4 OPC 160, Topps 140
74/5 OPC/Topps 160
75/6 OPC/Topps 55
76/7 OPC/Topps 160
77/8 OPC/Topps 70
69/70 opcMiniSticker
69/70 opcStamp
95/6 Parkie(66/7) 93, AS1
70/1 PostShooters
72/3 Post Transfers 4
72 SemicSticker 213
68/9 ShirriffCoin NY3
77-9 Sportscastr 61-03, 74-1758
65/6 Topps 21
66/7 Topps 23
67/8 Topps 85, 123
56-66 TorontoStar 65/6
71/2 TheTorontoSun
91/2 Ultimate(O6) 20, -Aut 20
95/6 Zellers

GIAMMARCO, FRANCO
86/7 Kingston 7
87/8 Kingston 7

GIANETTIE, MARK
93/4 Slapshot(Sudbury) 13

GIANINI, TIZIANO
91/2 UpperDeck 670
91/2 UD'CzechWJC 31

GIANNETTI, MARK
93/4 Sudbury 13

GIARD, STÉPHANE
91/2 SketchQMJHL 52

GIBB, MYLES
91/2 AirCanadaSJHL B27

GIBBONS, BRIAN
72/3 OttawaNationals

GIBBONS, JEFF
92/3 Toledo (1), (2)
93/4 Toledo 5
94/5 Toledo

GIBBS, BARRY
70/1 EddieSargent 91
71/2 EddieSargent 95
72/3 EddieSargent 108
70/1 Esso Stamp
74/5 Loblaws, -Update
72/3 OPC 101, Topps 169
73/4 OPC 174, Topps 30
74/5 OPC/Topps 203
75/6 OPC/Topps 214
76/7 OPC 341
77/8 OPC 319
78/9 O-Pee-Chee 390
79/80 O-Pee-Chee 304
80/1 O-Pee-Chee 334
71/2 TheTorontoSun
70/1 MIN
73/4 MIN
78/9 STL

GIBBS, RICHARD
92/3 MPSPhotoSJHL 135

GIBSON, DON
90/1 ProCards 340
91/2 ProCards 610
91/2 UpperDeck 495
90/1 VAN/Mohawk

GIBSON, DOUG
75/6 OPC 375

GIBSON, JACK, DR.
83&87 HallOfFame 201
83 HHOF Postcard (N)

GIBSON, JACK
72/3 OttawaNationals

GIBSON, JOHN
83/4 WPG

GIBSON, MIKE
86/7 Regina

GIBSON, STEVE
90/1 SketchOHL 183
91/2 SketchOHL 176
94/5 Wheeling 7
92/3 Windsor 25

GIBSON, WADE
89/90 SketchOHL 66
90/1 SketchOHL 84
91/2 SketchOHL 73
93/4 Slapshot(SSMarie) 21
93/4 SSMarie 23

GIES, JEFF
93/4 Slapshot(SSMarie) 14
95/6 Slapshot 368

GIESEBRECHT, BERT
52/3 LavalDairy 60

GIESBRECHT, JACK
52/3 StLawrence 62
52/3 LavalDairy 112

GIESEBRECHT, ROY (GUS)
39/40 OPC (V301-1) 69

GIFFIN, BOB
93/4 Slapshot(Peterborough) 4
83/4 Ottawa67s
84/5 Ottawa67s

GIFFIN, LEE
88/9 ProCards(Muskegon)
89/90 ProCards(IHL) 37
90/1 ProCards 584
91/2 ProCards 464
90/1 KansasCity 18
83/4 Oshawa 22

GIFFIN, ROB
95/6 Slapshot 311

GIGNAC, CHRIS
91/2 SketchOHL 307

GIGNAC, J.G.
52/3 AnonymousOHL 74

GIGUÈRE, JEAN-SÉBASTIEN
97/8 Bowman 62
95/6 Classic 13, AS13
97/8 Donruss 200, -Rated 10
97/8 D.CdnIce 146, -Gardiens 4
97/8 DonrussPreferred 160
97/8 DonrussStudio 73
97/8 Limited 29, 102, -fabric 9
94/5 ParkieSE 270
97/8 PinnacleInside 63,-Stop 13
96/7 UpperDeck"Ice" 25
95/6 Halifax
96/7 Halifax (1), (2)

GIGUÈRE, STÉPHANE
88/9 Flint

GILBERT, ED
74/5 Loblaws
75/6 O-Pee-Chee 370
76/7 O-Pee-Chee 329

GILBERT, GILLES
74/5 Loblaws
73/4 OPC/Topps 74
74/5 OPC/Topps 10, 132
75/6 OPC/Topps 45
76/7 OPC/Topps 255
77/8 OPC/Topps 125
78/9 OPC/Topps 68, 95
79/80 OPC/Topps 209
80/1 OPC/Topps 175
81/2 OPC 88, Topps(W) 88
82/3 O-Pee-Chee 84
81/2 opcSticker 123
71/2 TheTorontoSun
80/1 DET

GILBERT, GREG
91/2 Bowman 401
92/3 FleerUltra 275
93/4 Leaf 348
94/5 Leaf 341
84/5 OPC 125, Topps 93
85/6 OPC/Topps 126
88/9 OPC/Topps 83
90/1 OPC/Topps 255
91/2 OPC/Topps 149
84/5 opcSticker 90
85/6 opcSticker 75/202
88/9 PaniniSticker 287
90/1 PaniniSticker 196
93/4 Parkhurst 404
94/5 ParkieSE 111
93/4 Pinnacle 405
94/5 Pinnacle 415
93/4 Premier 216
94/5 Premier 169
90/1 ProSet 429
91/2 ProSet 372
90/1 Score 264
91/2 Score(CDN) 539
92/3 Score 134
93/4 Score 305, 561
92/3 Topps 218
95/6 Topps 96
91/2 ToppsStadiumClub 242
92/3 ToppsStadiumClub 323
93/4 ToppsStadiumClub 37
93/4 UpperDeck 404
89/90 CHI/Coke
90/1 CHI/Coke
91/2 CHI/Coke
83/4 NYI/Islander 5
84/5 NYI 5
82/3 Indianapolis

GILBERT, GREG
74/5 SiouxCity

GILBERT, JEAN
73/4 QuebecNordiques

GILBERT, LUC
51/2 BasDuFleuve 25
52/3 BasDuFleuve 64

GILBERT, ROD
71/2 Bazooka Panel 30
45-64 BeeHives(NYR)
64-67 BeeHives(NYR)
64/5 CokeCap NYR-7
65/6 CocaCola
77/8 Coke Mini
70/1 Colgate Stamp 53
70/1 DadsCookies
70/1 EddieSargent 122
71/2 EddieSargent 113
72/3 EddieSargent 141
70/1 Esso Stamp
95/6 HHOFLegends 61
71 Kelloggs
91/2 Kraft 82
72/3 Letraset 14
74/5 LiptonSoup 40
74/5 Loblaws
73/4 MacsMilk Disk
68/9 OPC/Topps 72, OPC 209
68/9 OPC-PuckSticker 9
69/70 OPC/Topps 37
69/70 OPC-Sticker, -Stamp
70/1 OPC/Topps 63
70/1 OPC/T-Deckle 39, -Sticker
71/2 OPC/T. 123, -Booklet 18
72/3 OPC 153, 229, -TeamCdn
72/3 Topps 80, 1254
73/4 OPC 156, Topps 88
74/5 OPC/Topps 141, 201
75/6 OPC/Topps 225, 324
76/7 OPC/Topps 90
76/7 OPC 390, T-Glossy 18
77/8 OPC/Topps 25
71/2 opcPoster 7
94/5 Parkie(64/5) 104, SL5, A1
95/6 Parkie(66/7) 79, 133, 138
91/2 ProSet 593
68/9 ShirriffCoin NYR10
91/2 StarPics 7
61/2 Topps 62
62/3 Topps 59
63/4 Topps 57
64/5 Topps 24
65/6 Topps 91
66/7 Topps 26, -USATest 26
67/8 Topps 90
56-66 TorontoStar 62/3, 64/5
64/5 TheTorontoStar
71/2 TheTorontoSun
91/2 Trends72 74, -Aut
90/1 UpperDeck 512
92/3 Zellers

GILBERTSON, STAN
72/3 EddieSargent 52
72/3 Letraset 19
74/5 Loblaws
71/2 OPC/Topps 183
72/3 OPC 70
73/4 OPC 212
74/5 OPC/Topps 223
75/6 OPC 382
76/7 OPC/Topps 187
71/2 TheTorontoSun
72/3 Topps 101
77/8 Topps 203

GILBY, ANDREW
96/7 Halifax (1), (2)
97/8 Halifax (1)

GILCHRIST, BRENT
91/2 Bowman 336
92/3 Bowman 322
94/5 Fleer 50
92/3 FleerUltra 293
94/5 Leaf 340
97/8 Omega 79
90/1 O-Pee-Chee 422
91/2 OPC/Topps 90
92/3 O-Pee-Chee 221
92/3 opcPremier 129
98/9 Pacific 191
97/8 PacificCrown 136
90/1 Panini(MTL) 12
92/3 PaniniSticker 153
96/7 PaniniSticker 177
91/2 Parkhurst 315
93/4 Parkhurst 52
94/5 Parkhurst 55, V21
95/6 Parkhurst 326
91/2 Pinnacle 236
92/3 Pinnacle 357
93/4 Pinnacle 415
94/5 Pinnacle 185
97/8 PinnacleBeAPlayer 85
93/4 PowerPlay 324
90/1 ProSet 471
91/2 ProSet 414
92/3 ProSet 90
91/2 PSPlatinum 192
90/1 ScoreTraded 87T
91/2 Score(CDN) 259
92/3 Score 46
93/4 Score 206
95/6 Score 261
96/7 Score 49
97/8 Score(DET) 14
92/3 Topps 386
98/9 Topps 95
92/3 ToppsStadiumClub 449
94/5 ToppsStadiumClub 143
92/3 UpperDeck 459
93/4 UpperDeck 329
94/5 UpperDeck 347
95/6 UpperDeck 326
95/6 UDBeAPlayer 71
94/5 DAL
94/5 DAL/Southwest
96/7 DAL/Southwest
92/3 EDM/IGA 8
88/9 MTL
89/90 MTL
89/90 MTL/Kraft
90/1 MTL
91/2 MTL
83/4 Kelowna
84/5 KelownaWingsWHL 16

GILES, CURT
91/2 CanadaNats
92 CanadaWinterOlympics179
82/3 O-Pee-Chee 166
85/6 OPC/Topps 96
86/7 OPC/Topps 119
89/90 O-Pee-Chee 213
90/1 OPC/Topps 228
91/2 OPC/Topps 17
86/7 opcSticker 172/35
87/8 PaniniSticker 110
89/90 PaniniSticker 112
90/1 PaniniSticker 250
90/1 ProSet 140
91/2 ProSet 114
90/1 Score 94
91/2 Score(CDN) 137, (U.S) 137
83/4 SouhaitsRen.KeyChain
92/3 Topps 200, 202
92/3 ToppsStadiumClub 64
90/1 UpperDeck 9
80/1 MIN
82/3 MIN
83/4 MIN
84/5 MIN
85/6 MIN
85/6 MIN/7Eleven 3
87/8 MIN
88/9 MIN/American
79/80 NYI

GILHEN, RANDY
91/2 Bowman 84
92/3 Bowman 327
90/1 OPC/Topps 250
91/2 OPC/Topps 418
92/3 O-Pee-Chee 26
91/2 opcPremier 123
91/2 Parkhurst 335
91/2 Pinnacle 238
92/3 Pinnacle 126
93/4 PowerPlay 93, 473
90/1 ProSet 506
91/2 ProSet 403
91/2 Score(CDN) 157, 566
91/2 Score(U.S) 157, 16T
92/3 Score 268
93/4 Score 643
92/3 Topps 27
91/2 ToppsStadiumClub 275
92/3 ToppsStadiumClub 318
91/2 UpperDeck 603
92/3 UpperDeck 82
93/4 UpperDeck 481
88/9 WPG/Police
95/6 WPG
87/8 Moncton

GILL, HALL
97/8 Omega 16

GILL, TODD
91/2 Bowman 171
92/3 Bowman 375
94/5 ClassicImages PL10
93/4 Donruss 335
95/6 Donruss 14
96/7 Donruss 15
96/7 DonrussElite 79
93/4 EASports 133
93/4 FleerUltra 77
94/5 FleerUltra 215
93/4 Leaf 22
94/5 Leaf 497
95/6 Leaf 278
91/2 OPC/Topps 361
87/8 opcSticker 163/22
98/9 Pacific 367
97/8 PacificCrown 98
90/1 Panini(TOR) 7
87/8 PaniniSticker 324
89/90 PaniniSticker 143
92/3 PaniniSticker 82
95/6 PaniniSticker 206
91/2 Parkhurst 393
94/5 Parkhurst 233
95/6 Parkhurst 202
91/2 Pinnacle 278
92/3 Pinnacle 290
93/4 Pinnacle 68
94/5 Pinnacle 181
95/6 Pinnacle 171
96/7 Pinnacle 176
96/7 PinnacleBeAPlayer 1
96/7 PinnacleZenith 14
94/5 POG 239
95/6 POG 265
93/4 PowerPlay 449
93/4 Premier 4
94/5 Premier 189
90/1 ProSet 534
91/2 ProSet 226
91/2 Score(CDN) 521
92/3 Score 196
93/4 Score 292
94/5 Score 55
95/6 Score 162
96/7 Score 208
95/6 SkyBoxEmotion 170
95/6 SkyBoxImpact 160
96/7 Summit 4
92/3 Topps 374
95/6 Topps 124
91/2 ToppsStadiumClub 336
92/3 ToppsStadiumClub 261
93/4 ToppsStadiumClub 62

94/5 UpperDeck 440
95/6 UpperDeck 117
97/8 UpperDeck 151
94/5 UDBAP R24, G8, -Aut. 104
95/6 UDCollChoice 101
96/7 S.J/PacificBellSheet (x2)
97/8 S.J/PacificBellSheet (x2)
86/7 TOR
87/8 TOR/P.L.A.Y. 13
88/9 TOR/P.L.A.Y. 12
90/1 TOR/P.L.A.Y. 17
93/4 TOR/Abalene
93/4 TOR/Blacks 22
94/5 TOR

GILLAM, SEAN
95/6 Spokane 19

GILLARD, TONY
82/3 NorthBay

GILLIES, CLARK
88/9 Esso Sticker
74/5 Loblaws
82/3 McDonalds 13
75/6 OPC/Topps 199, 323
76/7 OPC/T. 126, 216, OPC 389
77/8 OPC/Topps 250, -Glossy 6
78/9 OPC/Topps 220, OPC 327
79/80 OPC/Topps 130
80/1 OPC/Topps 75
81/2 OPC 202, Topps(E) 88
82/3 O-Pee-Chee 201
83/4 O-Pee-Chee 6
84/5 OPC 126, Topps 94
85/6 OPC/Topps 81
86/7 OPC/Topps 141
87/8 OPC/Topps 96
88/9 OPC/Topps 80
81/2 opcSticker 164
82/3 opcSticker 54, 55
83/4 opcSticker 84
85/6 opcSticker 68/192
86/7 opcSticker 205/77
87/8 PaniniSticker 34
92/3 Pinnacle 250
82/3 Post
83/4 PuffySticker 20
77-9 Sportscaster 47-16
91/2 UpperDeck 640
86/7 BUF
87/8 BUF/BlueShield
87/8 BUF/WonderBread
83/4 NYI
83/4 NYI/Islander 6
84/5 NYI 6
93/4 NYI/Chemical
84/5 KelownaWingsWHL 45

GILLIES, CURT
83/4 SouhaitsRen.KeyChain

GILLIGAN, WILLIAM
79 PaniniSticker 223

GILLINGHAM, TODD
95/6 EdgeIce 151
91/2 ProCards 351
90/1 SketchQMJHL 174
93/4 StJohns

GILLIS, ERROL
24/5 Crescent Selkirks 7
23/4 PaulinsCandy 4

GILLIS, JERE
72-84 Dernière 77/8
78/9 OPC/Topps 109
79/80 O-Pee-Chee 322
80/1 O-Pee-Chee 283
81/2 O-Pee-Chee 232
84/5 O-Pee-Chee 318
82/3 Post
83/4 Vachon 106
77/8 VAN/GingerAle
77/8 VAN/RoyalBank
78/9 VAN/RoyalBank
79/80 VAN
83/4 VAN
84/5 Fredericton 11
85/6 Fredericton 11

GILLIS, MIKE
81/2 O-Pee-Chee 12
82/3 Post
84/5 BOS
79/80 COL.R

GILLIS, PAUL
90/1 Bowman 165
89/90 Kraft 29
86/7 OPC/Topps 168
87/8 O-Pee-Chee 247
89/90 O-Pee-Chee 265
90/1 OPC/Topps 22, 122
91/2 OPC/Topps 469
85/6 opcSticker 150/19
86/7 opcSticker 24/164
87/8 opcSticker 221
89/90 opcSticker 183
90/1 Panini(QUE) 6
87/8 PaniniSticker 167
89/90 PaniniSticker 330
90/1 PaniniSticker 143
91/2 ProCards 489
90/1 ProSet 246
90/1 Score 141
91/2 Score(CDN) 403, (U.S) 364
90/1 UpperDeck 49
91/2 HFD/JuniorWhalers
92/3 HFD/DairyMart
84/5 QUE
85/6 QUE
85/6 QUE/GeneralFoods
85/6 QUE/McDonald
85/6 QUE/Provigo
86/7 QUE
86/7 QUE/GeneralFoods
86/7 QUE/McDonald
86/7 QUE/YumYum
88/9 QUE
87/8 QUE/GeneralFoods
87/8 QUE/YumYum
88/9 QUE/GeneralFoods
89/90 QUE
89/90 QUE/Police
90/1 QUE
90/1 QUE/PetroCanada
82/3 NorthBay
83/4 QUE

GILLIS, RYAN
93/4 Slapshot(NorthBay) 10
94/5 Slapshot(NorthBay) 12
95/6 Slapshot 218

GILLOW, RUSS
72/3 LosAngeles

GILMORE, DAN
95 Classic 88

GILMORE, DAVE
91/2 SketchOHL 363

GILMORE, TOM
72/3 LosAngelesSharks

GILMOUR, BILLY
83&87 HallOfFame 50
83 HHOF Postcard (D)

GILMOUR, DARRYL
88/9 ProCards(Hershey)
90/1 ProCards 427
91/2 ProCards 403
92/3 Phoenix
86/7 Portland

GILMOUR, DOUG
95/6 Aces 3 (Hearts)
96/7 Aces 3 (Hearts)
97/8 Aces 3 (Hearts)
90/1 Bowman 96
91/2 Bowman 255
92/3 Bowman 83
95/6 Bowman 18
93/4 Classic 119, -Aut.
94/5 Clasic-Aut.
93/4 Donruss 341, -Elite 7
94/5 Donruss 8, -IceMaster 3
95/6 Donruss-Igniters 3, -Dom 5
96/7 Donruss 46, 239, -Dom 6
96/7 Donruss-HitList 15
97/8 Donruss 10, -Line 7
96/7 D.CdnIce 112, -OCanada 9
97/8 DCI 49,-Scrap 13,-Nat'l 9
95/6 DonrussElite 92
96/7 D.Elite 44, -Perspectives 6
97/8 DonrussElite 73
97/8 DonrussPreferred 69
97/8 DonrussPriority 52
97/8 DonrussStudio 93
96/7 Duracell DC7, JB7
93/4 EASports 135
94/5 Flair 181, -Center 3
96/7 Flair 90
94/5 Fleer 215, -Headliner 3
96/7 Fleer 107
95/6 FleerMetal 143
96/7 F.Picks 68, -Captain 8
92/3 FleerUltra 211
93/4 FleerUltra 110, 249, -AW3
93/4 FU-PrmrPivots 1, -AS16
94/5 FleerUltra 216, -Pivots 3
94/5 FU-Scoring 3, -Power 3
95/6 FleerUltra 160
96/7 FleerUltra 163
88/9 FritoLay
95 Globe 93
96/7 Got-UmHockeyGreatsCoin
93/4 HockeyWit 61
95/6 Hoyle'WEST 5 (Spades)
92/3 HumptyDumpty (2)
94/5 Incomnet
97/8 KatchMedallion 81
94/5 KennerSLU
94 Koululainen
89/90 Kraft 1
91/2 Kraft 78
93/4 Kraft, -Cutout, -Recipe
94/5 Kraft-Sharpshooter
95/6 Kraft-Ticket
96/7 Kraft'Disk
93/4 Leaf 93, -Gold 6, -Studio 1
94/5 Leaf 99,-Limited 23,-Gold 2
94/5 Leaf-FireOnIce 5
95/6 Leaf 211
96/7 Leaf 74,-Leather 14,-Fire 10
97/8 Leaf 80
94/5 LeafLimited 8, -Gold 3
95/6 LeafLimited 72
96/7 LeafLimited 70, -Bash 4
96/7 LeafPreferred 104,-Steel 10
97/8 Limited 66,82,155 -fabric 19
96/7 Maggers 149
93/4 McDonalds McD05
94/5 McDonalds McD28
95/6 McDonalds McD9
96/7 McDonalds McD14
96/7 MetalUniverse 149
97/8 Omega 129, -StickHand 11
84/5 O-Pee-Chee 185
85/6 OPC/Topps 76
86/7 OPC/Topps 93
87/8 OPC/Topps 175, E
88/9 OPC/Topps 56
89/90 OPC/Topps 74, OPC 204
90/1 OPC/Topps 136
91/2 OPC/Topps 208
92/3 O-Pee-Chee 177
92/3 opcPremier-Star 8
87/8 opcStars 11
84/5 opcSticker 60
85/6 opcSticker 48/178
86/7 opcSticker 177/40
87/8 opcSticker 27
88/9 opcSticker 20
89/90 opcSticker 103/240
98/9 Pacific 93, -GoldCrown 20
97/8 PacificCrown 93, -Supial 11
97/8 PacificCrownRoyale 75
97/8 PcfcDynagn! 69,-Tandm 41
97/8 PacificInvincible 77
97/8 PcfcParamnt 102,-BigN 13
98/9 PacificParamount 47
97/8 PacificRegime 113
97/8 PacificRevolution 77
90/1 Panini(CGY) 2
87/8 PaniniSticker 311
88/9 PaniniSticker 105
89/90 PaniniSticker 28
90/1 PaniniSticker 172
91/2 PaniniSticker 59
92/3 PaniniSticker 77
93/4 PaniniSticker T
94/5 PaniniSticker 190, FF
95/6 PaniniSticker 200
96/7 PaniniSticker 214
97/8 PaniniSticker 66
91/2 Parkhurst 26, 396, -Promo
92/3 Parkhurst 183, 502
92/3 Parkhurst CP1, CP1993
93/4 PH 469, D9, G10, W4
94/5 Parkhurst 313, V80, C23
95/6 Parkhurst 199,-Crown(1) 12
91/2 Pinnacle 92
92/3 Pinnacle 279
93/4 Pinnacle 100, 226
94/5 Pinnacle 135, GR11, NL8
94/5 Pinnacle TP10, WE2
95/6 Pinnacle 61, -1st 3, -Clear 6
96/7 Pinnacle 127, -Numbers 7
97/8 Pinnacle39, -TeamP. 9
96/7 PinnacleBeAPlayer 22
97/8 PinnacleBAP-TakeANum 7
97/8 PinnacleBeeHive 47
97/8 PinnacleCertified 51
97/8 Pinnacle-EPIX 24
97/8 PinnacleInside 73
95/6 PinnacleZenith 54
96/7 P.Zenith 47, -Champion 13
95/6 Playoff 96, 202, 315
96/7 Playoff 356
94/5 POG 45, 234
95/6 POG 22, 257
94/5 Post
96/7 Post, -StickUm 1
93/4 PowerPlay 244, -Point 2
93/4 PP-Gamebreaker 2
93/4 Prmr 390, -Black(OPC) 11
94/5 Premier 225, 279, -GoTo 14
95/6 ProMagnet 73
90/1 ProSet 34
91/2 ProSet 34
92/3 ProSet 184, -TL 11
91/2 PSPlatinum 234
96/7 SB'7Eleven
90/1 Score 155, -Hot 69
91/2 Score(CDN) 218, (U.S) 218
92/3 Score 40
93/4 Score 66, -Franchise 21
93/4 Score(CDN) DD1, -P.AS 44
94/5 Score 185,DT13,NP4,TF23
95/6 Score 73,-Dream 6,-BrdrB 5
96/7 Score 95, -CheckIt 9
97/8 Score 93, -CheckIt 6
97/8 Score(N.J.) 1
92/3 SeasonsPatch 55
93/4 SeasonsPatch 4
94/5 Select 69
95/6 SelectCert. 48, -Double 1
96/7 SelectCertif 15
95/6 SkyBoxEmotion 171
95/6 SkBxImpact 161, -Count 8
96/7 SkBxImpact 126, -Blade 6
94/5 SP 115, -Premier 21
95/6 SP 144
96/7 SP 152, HC3, GF16
97/8 SPAuthentic 88
96/7 SPx 45, HH9
97/8 SPx 25, -SPX5
98/9 SPx"Finite" 47
96/7 SportFX MiniStix
97/8 SportFX MiniStix
95/6 Summit 62
96/7 Summit 118
95/6 SuperSticker 116, 117
92/3 Topps 122
95/6 Topps 234, 3HG, HGC4
95/6 Topps PF17, 8RL
94/5 ToppsFinest 100
94/5 TF-BBest 2, (Blue) 19
95/6 ToppsFinest 170, G55
94 ToppsFinestBronze 6
91/2 ToppsStadiumClub 96
92/3 ToppsStadiumClub 359
93/4 T.StadiumClub 140, 149
93/4 TSC-AllStar, -Master(1) 2
95/6 TSC 184, EN8, N7
93/4 TSC-MembersOnly 21
94/5 TSC-MembersOnly 44
97/8 ToppsStickers 214
95/6 ToppsSuperSkills 14
90/1 UpperDeck 271
91/2 UpperDeck 188, 558
92/3 UpperDeck 21, 215, 639
92/3 UD-LockerAS 24
93/4 UpperDeck 306, 382, AW6
93/4 UD NL5, R7, SP-158
94/5 UD 138, C18, H3, H21, R11
94/5 UD R27, R49, R56, SP167
95/6 UpperDeck 240, 291, SE80
95/6 UD-AllStarPredict MVP10
96/7 UpperDeck 162, 4B, GJ2
96/7 UpperDeck LS11, P29, X10
97/8 UD 91, 198, SG33
97/8 UD SS16,T18B
93/4 UDBAP 41, 42, 43, 45
93/4 UDBAP-Roots 5,11,21
94/5 UDBeAPlayer R1,R111
94/5 UDBAP R180, UC10, -Aut 1
96/7 UDBlackDiamond 28
97/8 UDBlackDiamond 70
98/9 UDChoice 117
95/6 UDCollChoice 5, 359, C21
96/7 UDCC 256, 332, C2, UD45
97/8 UDCC 139,C13,S24,SQ70
96/7 UpperDeck"Ice" 69
97/8 UpperDeckIce 82
97/8 Zenith 46, Z12
90/1 CGY/McGavins
91/2 CGY/IGA
87/8 STL/Kodak
92/3 STL/UpperDeck 2
92/3 TOR/Kodak
93/4 TOR/Abalene
93/4 TOR/Blacks 2
94/5 TOR

GILMOUR, LARRY
91 C55 Reprint 22
1911-12 Imperial (C55) 22
1910-11 Imperial Post 22

GIMAYEV, IREK
80 SovietMiniPics
83/4 SovietStars

GINGRAS, GASTON
72-84 Dernière 80/1, 82/3
86/7 Kraft Sports 25
80/1 O-Pee-Chee 322
81/2 O-Pee-Chee 182
82/3 O-Pee-Chee 182
83/4 O-Pee-Chee 332
84/5 O-Pee-Chee 303
87/8 O-Pee-Chee 229
88/9 OPC/Topps 35
89/90 O-Pee-Chee 270
83/4 opcSticker 40
87/8 opcSticker 8/147
89/90 opcSticker 21/161
80/1 Pepsi Cap
83/4 SouhaitsRen.KeyChain
83/4 Vachon 88
80/1 MTL
81/2 MTL
82/3 MTL
85/6 MTL
86/7 MTL
87/8 MTL
87/8 STL
87/8 STL/Kodak
88/9 STL
88/9 STL/Kodak
82/3 TOR
83/4 TOR
95/6 Fredericton

GINGRAS, MICHEL
89/90 SketchMEM 62

GINNELL, ERIN
86/7 Regina

GIONTA, BRIAN
98/9 UDChoice 298

GIRARD, BOB
76/7 O-Pee-Chee 362
77/8 O-Pee-Chee 255
78/9 O-Pee-Chee 339

GIRARD, DANY
90/1 SketchQMJHL 21
91/2 SketchQMJHL 78

GIRARD, ED
23/4 (V145-1) 1

GIRARD, FRÉDÉRIC
96/7 Rimouski

GIRARD, JONATHAN JR.
98 BowmanCHL 97, 135
98 BowmanCHL A30, SC13
97/8 UpperDeck 403

GIRARD, KEN
57/8 Parkhurst(TOR) 18
93/4 Parkie(56/7) 132

GIRARD, RICK
94/5 Classic T71
93/4 Donruss CAN14
93/4 Pinnacle 475
91/2 SketchWHL 176
93/4 UpperDeck 539

GIRARD, ROLAND
51/2 LacStJean 43

GIRGAN, KYLE
92/3 MPSPhotoSJHL 128

GIRHINY, RICK
90/1 SketchOHL 259

GIROUARD, GIL
51/2 BasDuFleuve 14

GIROUARD, GUY
92/3 Oklahoma

GIROUX, LARRY
74/5 Loblaws
75/6 OPC/Topps 273
73/4 STL
78/9 STL

GIROUX, RÉJEAN
73/4 Québec

GIUCO, SCOTT
93/4 Lethbridge

GIVEN, JASON
91/2 AvantGardeBCJHL 103
92/3 BCJHL 122

GLAD, JARKKO
92/3 Jyvas-Hyva 48
93/4 Sisu 118
95/6 Sisu 275

GLADNEY, BOB
78/9 Saginaw

GLADNEY, JASON
91/2 SketchOHL 92
93/4 Slapshot(Kitchener) 1, 19
95/6 Toledo

GLADU, FERNAND
52/3 BasDuFleuve 3

GLADU, JEAN
43-47 ParadeSportive (x2)

GLADU, PAUL
51/2 Cleveland

GLADU, PATRICK
95/6 Toledo

GLASS, FRANK
91 C55 Reprint 34
1911-12 Imperial (C55) 34
1910-11 Imperial (C56) 5
1912-13 Imperial (C57) 21
1910-11 Imperial Post 34

GLAUDE, GÉRARD
51/2 LavalDairy 32

GLEASON, TODD
90/1 SketchOHL 208
91/2 SketchOHL 339

GLEASON, TRENT
90/1 SketchOHL 106
89/90 Windsor

GLEASON, TROY
90/1 SketchOHL 107

GLENNIE, BRIAN
77/8 Coke Mini
70/1 EddieSargent 196
72/3 EddieSargent 205
70/1 Esso Stamp
74/5 Loblaws
73/4 MacsMilk Disk
70/1 OPC 216
71/2 OPC/Topps 197
72/3 OPC 216, Topps 37
73/4 OPC 170, Topps 163
74/5 OPC 310
75/6 OPC 365
77/8 OPC 275
78/9 O-Pee-Chee 345
79/80 O-Pee-Chee 341
71/2 TheTorontoSun
91/2 Trends(72) 88, -Aut
69/70 TOR
71/2 TOR
72/3 TOR
73/4 TOR
74/5 TOR
75/6 TOR
76/7 TOR
77/8 TOR

GLENNON, MATT
91/2 ProCards 58

GLICKMAN, JASON
87/8 Hull
89/90 Regina

GLOVER, CHRIS
83/4 Brantford 21

GLOVER, FRED
45-64 BeeHives(DET)
51/2 Parkhurst 60
52/3 Parkhurst 40
60/1 Cleveland

GLOVER, HOWARD
45-64 BeeHives(DET), (NYR)
61/2 Parkhurst 19
62/3 Parkhurst 28
60/1 ShirriffCoin 57
61/2 ShirriffCoin 65

GLOVER, MIKE
88/9 ProCards(CapeBreton)
87/8 SSMarie 3

GLOVER, HOWIE
82/3 Brandon 11

GLYNN, BRIAN
91/2 Bowman 132
92/3 Bowman 379
93/4 Donruss 236
92/3 FleerUltra 58
88/9 O-Pee-Chee 243
91/2 OPC/Topps 506
91/2 PaniniSticker 114
92/3 Parkhurst 287
93/4 Parkhurst 141
92/3 Pinnacle 136
93/4 PowerPlay 399
89/90 ProCards'IHL 191
91/2 ProSet 406
91/2 Score(CDN) 446
92/3 Score 361
92/3 Topps 198
91/2 ToppsStadiumClub 388
92/3 ToppsStadiumClub 472
91/2 UpperDeck 158
92/3 UpperDeck 64
93/4 UpperDeck 458
87/8 CGY/RedRooster
92/3 EDM
92/3 EDM/IGA 9
93/4 OTT/Kraft
94/5 VAN
86/7 Saskatoon

GOBEL, ERIC
84/5 Richelieu

GOBEL, T.
95/6 DEL 337

GOC, SASCHA
96/7 DEL 294

GOBER, MIKE
88/9 ProCards(Adirondack)
89/90 ProCards(AHL) 313
90/1 ProCards 312
91/2 Knoxville

GODARD, CHRIS
92/3 BCJHL 207

GODBOUT, BRENT
93/4 Minnesota
94/5 Minnesota

GODBOUT, DANIEL
91/2 SketchOHL 102
94/5 Slapshot(Kitchener) 4

GODBOUT, JASON
94/5 Minnesota

GODDEN, ERNIE
92/3 Windsor 15

GODFREY, WARREN
45-64 BeeHives(BOSx3), (DET)
64-67 BeeHives(BOS), (DET)
62 CeramicTiles
65/6 CocaCola
52/3 Parkhurst 85
53/4 Parkhurst 95
54/5 Parkhurst 56
60/1 Parkhurst 30
61/2 Parkhurst 30
62/3 Parkhurst 36
93/4 Parkhurst PR54
93/4 Parkie(56/7) 51
94/5 Parkie(64/5) 63
60/1 ShirriffCoin 49

61/2 ShirriffCoin 62
54/5 Topps 50
57/8 Topps 41
58/9 Topps 58
59/60 Topps 27
62/3 Topps 4, -Buck
54-67 TorontoStar V9

GODIN, BERT
92/3 ClevelandLumberjacks 16

GODYNYUK, ALEXANDER
93/4 Donruss 135, 438
94/5 Donruss 202
94/5 Flair 72
93/4 FleerUltra 325
94/5 FleerUltra 89
94/5 Leaf 29
92/3 O-Pee-Chee 10
91/2 OPC/Topps 471
97/8 PaniniSticker 26
91/2 Parkhurst 248
93/4 Parkhurst 74
94/5 Parkhurst 100
91/2 Pinnacle 318
94/5 Pinnacle 286
96/7 PinnacleBeAPlayer 83
93/4 Premier 289
91/2 ProSet 563
91/2 PSPlatinum 251
91/2 Score(CDN) 281, (U.S) 391
92/3 Topps 256
92/3 ToppsStadiumClub 88
93/4 ToppsStadiumClub 268
91/2 UpperDeck 466, 609, E16
93/4 UpperDeck 469
94/5 UpperDeck 188
94/5 UDBeAPlayer-Aut. 67
92/3 CGY/IGA 18
93/4 HFD/Coke
90/1 TOR/P.L.A.Y. 30

GOEBEL, BRYCE
91/2 SketchWHL 104
91/2 Saskatoon 6

GOEGAN, GRANT
82 SemicSticker 141

GOEGAN, PETE
45-64 BeeHives(DET)
64-67 BeeHives(DET)
82? JDMcCarthy
60/1 Parkhurst 34
61/2 Parkhurst 23
63/4 Parkhurst 43
94/5 Parkie(64/5) 61
95/6 Parkie(66/7) 54
60/1 ShirriffCoin 50
61/2 ShirriffCoin 75
58/9 Topps 47
59/60 Topps 4
63/4 York 53

GOELITZ, M.
95/6 DEL 303

GOERTZ, DAVE
88/9 ProCards(Muskegon)
89/90 ProCards(IHL) 147
90/1 ProCards 377
84/5 PrinceAlbert
81/2 Regina 6
82/3 Regina 4
83/4 Regina 4

GOHEEN, MOOSE
83&87 HallOfFame 112
83 HHOF Postcard (H)
96/7 HHOFLegends 86
60/1 Topps 63
61/2 Topps-Stamp

GOICOECHEA, YANNICK
92 SemicSticker 234

GOLANOV, MAXIM
93/4 UpperDeck 273
96/7 Binghampton

GOLDEN, MIKE
89/90 ProCards(IHL) 34
90/1 ProCards 11

GOLDHAM, BOB
34-43 BeeHives(TOR)
45-64 BeeHives(DET)
51/2 Parkhurst 67
52/3 Parkhurst 64
53/4 Parkhurst 49
54/5 Parkhurst 39
45-54 QuakerOats
54/5 Topps 46

GOLDIE, DAN
93/4 ClassicProspects 233

GOLDMANN, ERICH
94/5 DEL 289
95/6 DEL 272
96/7 DEL 117

GOLDSTEIN, JORN
79 PaniniSticker 294

GOLDSWORTHY, BILL
70/1 Colgate Stamp 52
70/1 DadsCookies
70/1 EddieSargent 95
71/2 EddieSargent 86
72/3 EddieSargent 104
70/1 Esso Stamp
74/5 Loblaws
68/9 O-Pee-Chee 148
69/70 O-Pee-Chee 195
70/1 OPC/Topps 46
71/2 OPC/Topps 55
72/3 OPC 159, Topps 115
72/3 opc-Crests 10, -TmCanada
73/4 OPC/Topps 62
74/5 OPC/T. 1, 112, 134, 220
75/6 OPC/Topps 180, 321
76/7 OPC/Topps 169
77/8 OPC/Topps 99
72 SemicSticker 220
68/9 ShirriffCoin MilN4
71/2 TheTorontoSun
91/2 Trends(72) 79, -Aut
70/1 MIN
73/4 MIN

GOLDSWORTHY, LEROY (GOLDY)
34-43 BeeHives(CHI)
36-39 DiamondMatch (1), (2), (3)
35/6 OPC (V304C) 96
36/7 WWGum (V356) 73

GOLDUP, GLENN
74/5 OPC 275
75/6 OPC 391
78/9 O-Pee-Chee 337
79/80 O-Pee-Chee 376
80/1 O-Pee-Chee 382
80/1 L.A.
74/5 MTL

GOLDUP, HENRY (HANK)
34-43 BeeHives(TOR)
39/40 OPC (V301-1) 54

GOLEMBIEWSKI, LEO
85/6 Arizona

GOLEMBROSKY, FRANK
73/4 QuébecNordiques

GOLIKOV, ALEXANDER
79 PaniniSticker 154
80 SovietMiniPics
79/80 SovietStars

GOLIKOV, VLADIMIR
79 PaniniSticker 148
82 SemicSticker 66
78 SovietChamps

GOLONKA, JOSEF
94/5 DEL 321
69/70 MästarSerien 2, 7
91 SemicSticker 248

GOLSJUMOV, SERGEI
89 SemicSticker 80

GOLTZ, FRED
90/1 SketchOHL 58
95/6 Louisiana

GOLTZ, JEREMY
85/6 Arizona

GOLUBOVSKY, YAN
94/5 Classic 19, T20
94/5 ClassicFourSport 136
94/5 ClassicImages 30
95/6 Adirondack

GOMAN, VESA
95/6 Sisu 361
96/7 Sisu 156

GOMEZ, SCOTT
98 BowmanCHL 145, A27, SC19
98/9 Topps 232

GONCHAR, SERGEI
92/3 Classic 41, 43
94/5 Classic 27
92/3 ClassicFourSport 184
94/5 ClassicImages 55
95/6 Donruss 173
95/6 EdgeIce 53
96/7 Fleer 117, -Rookie 5
95/6 FleerMetal 159
96/7 FleerNHLPicks-Fab 14
95/6 FleerUltra 322
96/7 FleerUltra 175
95/6 Leaf 26
96/7 Maggers 166
96/7 MetalUniverse 163
98/9 Pacific 441
97/8 PacificCrown 103
98/9 PacificParamount 244
95/6 PaniniSticker 141
96/7 PaniniSticker 135
97/8 PaniniSticker 112
95/6 Parkhurst 225
94/5 ParkieSE 195
95/6 Pinnacle 71
96/7 Pinnacle 40
96/7 PinnacleBeAPlayer 150
95/6 POG 286
95/6 SkyBoxEmotion 187
95/6 SkyBoxImpact 176
96/7 SkyBoxImpact 139, -Fox 9
96/7 SP 165
97/8 SPAuthentic 166
98/9 SPx"Finite" 90
96/7 TeamOut
95/6 Topps 47
96/7 ToppsNHLPicks 91
93/4 UpperDeck 272
94/5 UpperDeck 264
95/6 UpperDeck 305
96/7 UpperDeck 175
97/8 UpperDeck 180
96/7 UDCollChoice 286
97/8 UDCollChoice 273
96/7 UpperDeck"Ice" 75
95/6 WSH
94/5 Portland

GONEAU, DANIEL
97/8 Donruss 190
96/7 DonrussCanadianIce 126
96/7 D.Elite 143, -Aspirations 18
96/7 Flair 116
96/7 FleerUltra 105, -Rookies 8
96/7 LeafPreferred 145
97/8 Limited 148
96/7 MetalUniverse 180
97/8 PacificCrown 327
96/7 PinnacleBeAPlayer 107
96/7 PinnacleZenith 148
97/8 Score(NYR) 18
96/7 SelectCertified 107
96/7 SP 184
98/9 SPx"Finite" 55, 141
93/4 UpperDeck E5
96/7 UpperDeck 295
98/9 UDChoice 137
96/7 UDCollChoice 353
96/7 UpperDeck"Ice" 42

GONEAU, JASON
97/8 Bowman 63

GONZALEZ, FRANCISCO
79 PaniniSticker 372

GOODALL, GLEN
90/1 ProCards 482
91/2 ProCards 191

GOODALL, RON
85/6 Kitchener 29
86/7 Kitchener 27
87/8 Kitchener 27

GOODENOUGH, LARRY
75/6 OPC 373
76/7 OPC/Topps 96
77/8 OPC 359
79/80 O-Pee-Chee 383
75/6 PHA/GingerAle
77/8 VAN/GingerAle
77/8 VAN/RoyalBank

GOODFELLOW, EBENEZER (EBBIE)
33/4 Anonymous (V129) 20
34-43 BeeHives(DET)
33/4 CndGum (V252)
83&87 HallOfFame 35
33/4 Hamilton (V288) 42
83 HHOF Postcard (C)
27-32 LaPresse 30/1
34/5 OPC (V304B) 52
36/7 OPC (V304D) 117
39/40 OPC (V301-1) 66
34/5 SweetCaporal
36/7 WWGum (V356) 11

GOODMAN, PAUL
34-43 BeeHives(CHI)
40/1 OPC (V301-2) 150

GOODWIN, JOHN
83/4 NovaScotia 7
80/1 SSMarie

GOOLD, BILL
51/2 LavalDairy 89

GOOLEY, PAT
87/8 Brockville 23
88/9 Brockville 17

GORALCZYK, ROB
74 Hellas 96
73/4 WilliamsFIN 91

GORBACHEV, SERGEI
94/5 SigRookies FF4

GORDIOUK, VIKTOR
92/3 ClassicProspects 88
96/7 DEL 277
95/6 EdgeIce 149
93/4 FleerUltra 120, -AllRook 2
94/5 FleerUltra 263
94/5 Leaf 468
91/2 O-Pee-Chee 15R
92/3 opcPremier 60
92/3 Parkhurst 17
94/5 ParkieSE 23
93/4 PowerPlay 28
94/5 Premier 456
91 SemicSticker 97
92/3 UpperDeck 579, ER18
92/3 BUF/Jubille
93/4 Rochester

GORDON, BRUCE
81/2 Saskatoon 21

GORDON, CHRIS
94/5 Huntington 12

GORDON, IAN
94/5 AutoPhonex 16
95/6 SaintJohn

GORDON, JACK
45-64 BeeHives(NYR)
74/5 OPC/Topps 238
51/2 ClevelandBarons
60/1 ClevelandBarons

GORDON, LARRY
92/3 Cleveland 2

GORDON, ROB
92/3 BCJHL 147
95/6 DonrussElite-WorldJrs 14
95/6 UpperDeck 538

GORDON, SCOTT
90/1 Bowman 171
90/1 Panini(QUE) 7
88/9 ProCards(Halifax)
89/90 ProCards(AHL) 153
90/1 ProCards 467
90/1 ProSet 634
90/1 QUE/PetroCanada
86/7 Fredericton
89/90 Halifax
90/1 Halifax
93/4 Knoxville

GORDON, TODD
91/2 Greensboro
92/3 Greensboro 13

GORENCE, TOM
79/80 OPC/Topps 51
80/1 O-Pee-Chee 368
81/2 O-Pee-Chee 250
82/3 O-Pee-Chee 250
88/9 EDM/ActionMagazine 87
83/4 Moncton 17

GOREV, ROMAN
93/4 ClassicProspects 141

GORGENLANDER, RUDI
94/5 DEL 120
95/6 DEL 109
96/7 DEL 54

GORGI, MARK
91/2 AirCanadaSJHL C31

GORING, BUTCH
77/8 Coke Mini
71/2 EddieSargent 73
72/3 EddieSargent 92
74/5 Loblaws
71/2 OPC/Topps 152
72/3 OPC 56, Topps 72
73/4 OPC 155, Topps 138
74/5 OPC/Topps 74, 98
75/6 OPC/Topps 221
76/7 OPC/Topps 239
77/8 OPC/Topps 67
78/9 OPC/Topps 151
79/80 OPC/Topps 98
80/1 OPC/Topps 254
81/2 OPC 203, Topps(E) 89
82/3 O-Pee-Chee 200
83/4 O-Pee-Chee 7
84/5 OPC 127, Topps 95
81/2 opcSticker 20
83/4 opcSticker 13, 177
84/5 opcSticker 84, 88
82/3 Post
83/4 SouhaitsRen.KeyChain
71/2 TheTorontoSun
83/4 NYI/Islander 7, 38
93/4 LasVegas

GORMAN, DAVE
75/6 Phoenix

GORMAN, ED
25-27 Anonymous 25

GORMAN, JEFF
90/1 SketchWHL 274
91/2 SketchWHL 260
90/1 PrinceAlbert
91/2 PrinceAlbert
93/4 PrinceAlbert

GORMAN, MIKE
98 BowmanCHL 12

GORMAN, SEAN
92/3 Oklahoma

GORMAN, TOM
83&87 HallOfFame 113
83 HHOF Postcard (H)
36/7 WWGum (V356) 17
95/6 MTL/Forum 1Apr96

GOROKHOV, ILJA
95/6 SP 181

GORSKI, LEROY
81/2 Saskatoon 3

GOSSELIN, DAVID
98 BowmanCHL 109

GOSSELIN, DENIS
90/1 Rayside
91/2 Rayside

GOSSELIN, GUY
88/9 ProCards(Mon)
89/90 ProCards(AHL) 36
85/6 Minn-Duluth 10

GOSSELIN, MARIO
83 CanadaJuniors
86/7 Kraft Sports 44
85/6 OPC/Topps 18
86/7 O-Pee-Chee 235
87/8 O-Pee-Chee 250
88/9 OPC/Topps 173
89/90 O-Pee-Chee 258
90/1 O-Pee-Chee 442
85/6 opcSticker 147/62
86/7 opcSticker 21/162
87/8 opcSticker 231
88/9 opcSticker 193
87/8 PaniniSticker 157
88/9 PaniniSticker 347
90/1 ProCards 349
91/2 ProCards 115
90/1 UpperDeck 91
89/90 L.A/Smokeys 18
83/4 QUE
84/5 QUE
85/6 QUE
85/6 QUE/GeneralFoods
85/6 QUE/McDonald
85/6 QUE/Pennant
85/6 QUE/Placemats
85/6 QUE/Provigo
86/7 QUE
86/7 QUE/GeneralFoods
86/7 QUE/McDonald
87/8 QUE/GeneralFoods
87/8 QUE/YumYum
88/9 QUE
88/9 QUE/GeneralFoods

GOSSELIN, P.
84/5 Chicoutimi

GOSSELIN, STEVE
90/1 SketchQMJHL 23
91/2 SketchQMJHL 86

GOSSMANN, CARSTEN
94/5 DEL 97
95/6 DEL 78

GOTAAS, STEVE
88/9 ProCards(Muskegon)
90/1 ProCards 112
91/2 ProCards 154
93/4 LasVegas
84/5 PrinceAlbert

GOTTSELIG, JOHN
34-43 BeeHives(CHI)
33/4 CndGum (V252)
33-35 DiamondMatch
36-39 DiamondMatch (1), (2), (3)
36-39 DiamondMatch (4), (5), (6)
27-32 LaPresse 30/1
35/6 OPC (V304C) 80
39/40 OPC (V301-1) 50
36/7 WWGum (V356) 55

GOUDIE, BRIAN
90/1 SketchMEM 7
91/2 SketchOHL 336
93/4 Hampton
94/5 Hampton 9
95/6 Richmond

GOUDREAU, MARCEL
69 ColumbusCheckers

GOULD, BOB
84/5 O-Pee-Chee 196
87/8 OPC/Topps 55
89/90 O-Pee-Chee 289
90/1 O-Pee-Chee 398
87/8 opcSticker 237/105
82/3 Post
90/1 ProCards 144
83/4 SouhaitsRen.KeyChain
89/90 BOS/SportsAction
81/2 WSH
82/3 WSH
84/5 WSH/PizzaHut
85/6 WSH/PizzaHut
86/7 WSH/Kodak
86/7 WSH/Police
87/8 WSH
87/8 WSH/Kodak
88/9 WSH
88/9 WSH/Smokey

GOULD, JOHN
74/5 Loblaws
74/5 OPC 381
75/6 OPC/Topps 266
76/7 OPC/Topps 85
77/8 OPC 382
78/9 O-Pee-Chee 309
79/80 O-Pee-Chee 282
77/8 ATL
73/4 BUF
74/5 VAN/RoyalBank
75/6 VAN/RoyalBank
76/7 VAN/RoyalBank

GOULET, BOB
89/90 Johnstown 20

GOULET, MICHEL
91/2 Bowman 392
92/3 Bowman 310
72-84 Dernière 81/2
92/3 Durivage 24
93/4 Donruss 71
93/4 Durivage 42
93/4 EASports 28
83/4 Esso
88/9 Esso Sticker
92/3 FleerUltra 35
93/4 FleerUltra 289
88/9 FritoLay
93/4 HockeyWit 33
84/5 Kelloggs Disk
89/90 Kraft 30
91/2 Kraft 87
86/7 Kraft Sports 45
93/4 Leaf 373
82/3 McDonalds 14, 19
80/1 OPC/Topps 67
81/2 O-Pee-Chee 275
82/3 O-Pee-Chee 237, 284
83/4 O-Pee-Chee 287, 288, 292
84/5 OPC 207,280,366,384,391
85/6 OPC/Topps 150
86/7 OPC/Topps 92, E, T-AS 2
87/8 OPC/Topps 77, M, T-AS 6
88/9 OPC/Topps 54, T-AS 7
89/90 OPC/Topps 57
90/1 OPC/Topps 329
91/2 OPC/Topps 336
92/3 O-Pee-Chee 358
87/8 opcStars 12
88/9 opcStars 10
81/2 opcSticker 75
82/3 opcSticker 25
83/4 opcSticker 166,167,249,250
84/5 opcStkr 140,168,169,64/63
85/6 opcSticker 141
86/7 opcSticker 22, 113/127
87/8 opcSticker 225, 113/125
88/9 opcSticker 188, 192
89/90 opcSticker 186
87/8 PaniniSticker 163
88/9 PaniniSticker 355
89/90 PaniniSticker 326
91/2 PaniniSticker 11
92/3 PaniniSticker 6
93/4 PaniniSticker 148
94/5 PaniniSticker 131
91/2 Parkhurst 36, 215, 428
92/3 Parkhurst 272
93/4 Parkhurst 313
80/1 Pepsi Cap
91/2 Pinnacle 109
92/3 Pinnacle 22
93/4 Pinnacle 399
82/3 Post
93/4 PowerPlay 49
93/4 Premier 386
90/1 ProSet 430
91/2 ProSet 50
92/3 ProSet 32
87/8 ProSportWatch CW11
91/2 PSPlatinum 166, PC15
83/4 PuffySticker 15
90/1 Score 221
91/2 Score(CDN) 201, 265
91/2 Score(U.S) 201, 375
92/3 Score 222, 444
93/4 Score 153
89 SemicSticker 70
84/5 7ElevenDisk
85/6 7Eleven 16
83/4 SouhaitsRen.KeyChain
84/5 Topps 129, 153
92/3 Topps 255, 347
91/2 ToppsStadiumClub 66
92/3 ToppsStadiumClub 69
93/4 ToppsStadiumClub 12
91/2 TSC-MembersOnly
90/1 UpperDeck 133
91/2 UpperDeck 374
92/3 UpperDeck 113
83/4 Vachon 65
90/1 CHI/Coke
91/2 CHI/Coke
93/4 CHI/Coke
80/1 QUE
81/2 QUE
82/3 QUE
83/4 QUE
84/5 QUE
85/6 QUE
85/6 QUE/GeneralFoods
85/6 QUE/McDonald
85/6 QUE/Pennant
85/6 QUE/Placemats

85/6 QUE/Provigo
86/7 QUE
86/7 QUE/McDonald
86/7 QUE/YumYum
87/8 QUE/GeneralFoods
87/8 QUE/YumYum
88/9 QUE
88/9 QUE/GeneralFoods
89/90 QUE
89/90 QUE/GeneralFoods
89/90 QUE/Police
90/1 QUE

GOUPILLE, CLIFFORD (RED)
34-43 BeeHives(MTL.C)
35-40 CrownBrand 116
37/8 OPC (V304E) 178
39/40 OPC (V301-1) 22
40/1 OPC (V301-2) 120

GOURLIE, BRYAN
90/1 SketchWHL 304
87/8 Portland
88/9 Portland
89/90 Portland

GOVERDARIS, CHRIS
90/1 Bowman 259
92/3 C'Prospects 29
96/7 DEL 45
95/6 EdgeIce 166
94/5 Parkhurst 236
90/1 ProCards 187
91/2 ProCards 102
91/2 Score(CDN) 355, (U.S) 325
90/1 HFD/JuniorWhalers
94/5 Milwaukee
93/4 StJohns

GOVERDE, DAVID
92/3 ClassicProspects 54
90/1 ProCards 352
91/2 ProCards 399
92/3 Phoenix
93/4 Phoenix
88/9 Sudbury 2
89/90 Sudbury 19
95/6 Toledo

GOWAN, MARK
92/3 Sudbury 26

GOYER, GERRY
67/8 Topps 54

GOYETTE, DANIELLE
94/5 Classic W7
97/8 UDCollChoice 285

GOYETTE, PHIL
52/3 AnonymousOHL 141
45-64 BeeHives(MTL), (NYR)
64-67 BeeHives(NYR)
62 CeramicTiles
64/5 CokeCap NYR-20
65/6 CocaCola
70/1 Colgate Stamp 10
70/1 DadsCookies
71/2 EddieSargent 30
70/1 Esso Stamp
68/9 OPC/Topps 73
69/70 OPC/T. 21, OPC-Sticker
70/1 OPC/Topps 127, OPC 251
71/2 OPC/Topps 88
57/8 Parkhurst (MTL) 11
58/9 Parkhurst 47
59/60 Parkhurst 4
60/1 Parkhurst 50, 58
61/2 Parkhurst 46
62/3 Parkhurst 37
93/4 Parkhurst PR59
93/4 Parkie(56/7) 74
94/5 Parkie(64/5) 105, 173
95/6 Parkie(66/7) 99, SL5
72 SemicSticker 196
60/1 ShirriffCoin 27
61/2 ShirriffCoin 116
62/3 ShirriffCoin 28
68/9 ShirriffCoin NY5
63/4 Topps 58
64/5 Topps 87
65/6 Topps 92
66/7 Topps 28, -USATest 28
67/8 Topps 25
54-67 TorontoStar V11
71/2 TheTorontoSun
91/2 Ultimate(O6) 11, -Aut 11
60/1 York
61/2 York 30

GOZZI, ANDERS
94/5 EliSet 223
95/6 EliSet 11
89/90 SemicElitserien 19
90/1 SemicElitserien 190
91/2 SemicElitserien 42, 67
95/6 udElite 10
97/8 udSwedish 9

GRABINSKY, JEFF
92/3 BCJHL 38

GRABOSKI, ANTHONY (TONY)
34-43 BeeHives(MTL.C)

GRACHEV, VLADIMIR
92/3 RedAce(Blue) 24,(Violet) 24

GRACIE, BOB
33/4 Anonymous (V129) 40
34-43 BeeHives(MTL.M)
33/4 CndGum (V252)
35-40 CrownBrand 55, 153
33-35 DiamondMatch
36-39 DiamondMatch (1)
34/5 OPC (V304B) 66
37/8 OPC (V304E) 171
38/9 QuakerOats
36/7 WWGum (V356) 38
33/4 WWGum (V357) 63
32/3 TOR/OKeefe 14

GRADIN, HENRIK
92/3 SemicElitserien 247

GRADIN, PETER
89/90 SemicElitserien 12
90/1 SemicElitserien 86
91/2 SemicElitserien 13

GRADIN, THOMAS
84/5 Kelloggs Disk
79/80 OPC/Topps 53
80/1 OPC/Topps 241
81/2 OPC 327,346, Topps 15,64
82/3 O-Pee-Chee 337, 344, 345
83/4 O-Pee-Chee 350
84/5 O-Pee-Chee 319
85/6 OPC/Topps 16
81/2 opcSticker 243
82/3 opcSticker 240
83/4 opcSticker 273
84/5 opcSticker 282
85/6 opcSticker 240
79 PaniniSticker 201
80/1 Pepsi Cap
82/3 Post
83/4 PuffySticker 3
89/90 SemicElitserien 13
82 SemicSticker 148
83/4 7ElevenCokeCups
83/4 SouhaitsRen.KeyChain
83/4 Vachon 107
78/9 VAN/RoyalBank
79/80 VAN
80/1 VAN
80/1 VAN/Silverwood
81/2 VAN
81/2 VAN/Silverwood
82/3 VAN
83/4 VAN
84/5 VAN
85/6 VAN

GRAESEN, MATS
89/90 SemicElitserien 284

GRAF, KRIS
95/6 Spokane 8

GRAFTON, CHRIS
97/8 DonrussStudio 90

GRAHAM, DIRK
90/1 Bowman 8
91/2 Bowman 397
92/3 Bowman 68
93/4 Donruss 63
94/5 Flair 33
94/5 Fleer 40
92/3 FleerUltra 36
93/4 FleerUltra 61
94/5 FleerUltra 41
93/4 Leaf 270
94/5 Leaf 335
86/7 OPC/Topps 143
87/8 OPC/Topps 184
88/9 OPC/Topps 135
89/90 OPC/Topps 52, OPC 301
90/1 OPC/Topps 179
91/2 OPC/Topps 217, 521
92/3 O-Pee-Chee 210
91/2 opcPremier 131
86/7 opcSticker 171/31
88/9 opcSticker 7/136
89/90 opcSticker 12/152
87/8 PaniniSticker 295
88/9 PaniniSticker 25
89/90 PaniniSticker 44
90/1 PaniniSticker 191
91/2 PaniniSticker 16
92/3 PaniniSticker 7
93/4 PaniniSticker 147
91/2 Parkhurst 33
92/3 Parkhurst 271
91/2 Pinnacle 261
92/3 Pinnacle 173
93/4 Pinnacle 24, CA5
94/5 Pinnacle 317
94/5 POG 66
93/4 PowerPlay 50
93/4 Premier 88
94/5 Premier 67
90/1 ProSet 51
91/2 ProSet 51, 323, 570
92/3 ProSet 38
91/2 PSPlatinum 23
90/1 Score 17
91/2 Score(CDN) 15, 322
91/2 Score(U.S) 15, 432
92/3 Score 27
93/4 Score 12
94/5 Score 56
94 Semic 97
91 TeamCanada
92/3 Topps 376
91/2 ToppsStadiumClub 181
92/3 ToppsStadiumClub 342
93/4 ToppsStadiumClub 90
90/1 UpperDeck 131
91/2 UpperDeck 271, 502, AW8
92/3 UpperDeck 272
93/4 UpperDeck 328
94/5 UDBeAPlayer-Aut. 78
88/9 CHI/Coke
89/90 CHI/Coke
90/1 CHI/Coke
91/2 CHI/Coke
93/4 CHI/Coke
85/6 MIN
85/6 MIN/7Eleven 12
87/8 MIN
84/5 Springfield 21

GRAHAM, JIM
28/9 PaulinsCandy 42

GRAHAM, JIM
69 ColumbusCheckers

GRAHAM, JOHN
91/2 AvantGardeBCJ 77, 157

GRAHAM, PAT
82/3 Post
83/4 PGH/Heinz
83/4 TOR

GRAHAM, ROD
82/3 Kingston 24

GRAHAM, ROSS
52/3 AnonymousOHL 7

GRAHAM, ROBB
87/8 Sudbury 13

GRAHAME, RON
78/9 OPC/Topps 219
75/6 opcWHA 50, 61
76/7 opcWHA 107
75/6 Houston
80/1 QUE

GRANATO, CAMMI
93/4 Classic 66
94/5 Classic W37
93/4 ClassicProspects 248

GRANATO, TONY
97/8 Aces K (Clubs)
90/1 Bowman 140, -HT 18
91/2 Bowman 192, 412
92/3 Bowman 50
94/5 ClassicImages PL2
93/4 Donruss 160
94/5 Donruss 145
95/6 Donruss 111
97/8 Donruss 121
96/7 Flair 84
95/6 FleerMetal 70
92/3 FleerUltra 82
93/4 FleerUltra 63
94/5 FleerUltra 305
95/6 FleerUltra 249
95 Globe120
93/4 HockeyWit 32
91/2 Kraft 35
93/4 Leaf 201
94/5 Leaf 229
95/6 Leaf 174
97/8 Limited 144
96/7 Maggers 80
97/8 Omega 201
89/90 OPC/Topps 161, OPC 310
90/1 OPC/Topps 62
91/2 OPC/Topps 88
92/3 O-Pee-Chee 65
89/90 opcStickr 36/176, 241/104
89/90 opcStickFS 10
98/9 Pacific 380
97/8 PacificCrown 203
97/8 PacificDynagon! 111
97/8 PcfcD-BstKpt 109,-Tand 67
97/8 PacificInvincible 125
97/8 PSPlatinum 165 PacificParamount 165
98/9 PacificParamount 210
89/90 PaniniSticker 285
90/1 PaniniSticker 239
91/2 PaniniSticker 83
92/3 PaniniSticker 68
93/4 PaniniSticker 203
94/5 PaniniSticker 176
95/6 PaniniSticker 267
96/7 PaniniSticker 274
98/9 PaniniSticker 227
91/2 Parkhurst 66
92/3 Parkhurst 301
93/4 Parkhurst 93
94/5 Parkhurst V76
95/6 Parkhurst 376
94/5 ParkieSE 83
91/2 Pinnacle 76
92/3 Pinnacle 69, 262
93/4 Pinnacle 137
94/5 Pinnacle 118
97/8 Pinnacle 187
96/7 PinnacleBeAPlayer 142
97/8 PinnacleInside 142
95/6 Playoff 49
96/7 Playoff 340
94/5 POG 125
95/6 POG 139
93/4 PowerPlay 115
93/4 Premier 144, 504
94/5 Premier 183
90/1 ProSet 117
91/2 ProSet 98
92/3 ProSet 74
91/2 PSPlatinum 49
90/1 Score 48, -Young 33
91/2 Score(CDN) 57, (U.S) 57
92/3 Score 243, -USAGreats 4
93/4 Score 52, 444
94/5 Score 71
95/6 Score 233
97/8 Score 77
92/3 SeasonsPatch 11
94 Semic 126
95 Semic 117
91 SemicSticker 147
92 SemicSticker 162
93 SemicSticker 181
94/5 SP 56
96/7 SP 140
97/8 SPAuthentic 135
95/6 Summit 100
92/3 Topps 242
95/6 Topps 58
98/9 Topps 147
91/2 ToppsStadiumClub 97
92/3 ToppsStadiumClub 281
93/4 ToppsStadiumClub 285
95/6 ToppsStadiumClub 116
90/1 UpperDeck 272
91/2 UpperDeck 172, 508
92/3 UpperDeck 185
93/4 UpperDeck 146, SP-69
94/5 UpperDeck 29, SP126
95/6 UpperDeck 201
97/8 UpperDeck 360
94/5 UDBeAPlayer G9, R97
94/5 UDBAP R110,-Aut.114
96/7 UDBlackDiamond 121
95/6 UDCollChoice 194
97/8 UDCollChoice 218
90/1 L.A./Smokeys 11
96/7 S.J/PacificBellSheet (x3)
97/8 S.J/PacificBellSheet (x2)

GRANDBERG, GEOFF
90/1 SketchMEM 83
90/1 SketchWHL 208
91/2 SketchWHL 21

GRANDLUND, MIKE
93/4 Sisu 84

GRANDMAISON, DOMINIC
90/1 SketchQMJHL 247
91/2 SketchQMJHL 257

GRANDMAÎTRE, SYL
81/2 Kingston 9
82/3 Kingston 9

GRANHOLM, HENRIK
65/6 Hellas 134
70/1 Kuvajulkaisut 102

GRANKVIST, ERIK
95/6 EliSet 247
91/2 SemicElitserien 153
92/3 SemicElitserien 176

GRANSTEDT, MICHAEL
89/90 SemicElitserien 202

GRANT, BEN
32/3 TOR/OKeefe 17

GRANT, DAN
70/1 Colgate Stamp 36
70/1 DadsCookies
70/1 EddieSargent 92
71/2 EddieSargent 85
72/3 EddieSargent 103
70/1 Esso Stamp
82? JDMcCarthy
72/3 Letraset 11
74/5 Loblaws
68/9 OPC/Topps 52
69/70 OPC/Topps 125, OPC 208
70/1 OPC/Topps 47, -Sticker
71/2 OPC/Topps 79, -Booklet 11
72/3 OPC 57, Topps 39
73/4 OPC 214, Topps 161
74/5 OPC/Topps 112, 174
75/6 OPC/T. 49, 212, OPC 318
76/7 OPC/Topps 16
77/8 OPC/Topps 147
78/9 O-Pee-Chee 306
69/70 opcMiniSticker
69/70 opcStamp
71/2 TheTorontoSun
70/1 MIN
73/4 MIN
67/8 MTL
67/8 MTL/IGA

GRANT, DANNY
97/8 Halifax (1), (2)

GRANT, DEREK
93/4 Slapshot(NiagaraFalls) 14

GRANT, DOUG
82? JDMcCarthy
74/5 Loblaws
74/5 O-Pee-Chee 347
77/8 O-Pee-Chee 294
78/9 O-Pee-Chee 373

GRANT, KEVIN
89/90 ProCards(IHL) 197
90/1 ProCards 606
91/2 ProCards 575
85/6 Kitchener 8
87/8 Kitchener 8
93/4 Phoenix
88/9 Sudbury 5

GRANT, LEE
92/3 BCJHL 48

GRANT, MIKE
83&87 HallOfFame 218
83 HHOF Postcard (O)

GRANT, PETER
90/1 Mich.Tech

GRATTON, BENOÎT
96/7 Portland

GRATTON, BRAD
87/8 Kingston 19

GRATTON, CHRIS
97/8 Aces 5 (Spades)
93/4 Classic 3, DP3
94/5 Classic-Autograph
93/4 C'FourSport 187, LP24
93/4 C'4Sport DS60, PP20, TC4
93/4 C4'Images 86, 138
93/4 ClassicProspects 16
93/4 Donruss 330,393,V,-Rated2
94/5 Donruss 189
95/6 Donruss 122
96/7 Donruss 173
97/8 Donruss 56
96/7 D.CdnIce 62, -OCanada 8
97/8 D.CanadianIce 39
97/8 DonrussElite 91
97/8 DonrussPreferred 130
97/8 DonrussPriority 118
94/5 Flair 173
94/5 Fleer 206
95/6 FleerMetal 136
93/4 FleerUltra 423, -Wave 5
94/5 FU 205,-Power 3,-AllRook 4
95/6 FleerUltra 151
95/6 Hoyle'EAST 2 (Spades)
97/8 KatchMedallion 104
93/4 Leaf 331, -Freshman 3
94/5 Leaf 86, -G.Rookie4,-Ltd.22
95/6 Leaf 133
96/7 Leaf 120
97/8 Leaf 27
94/5 LeafLimited 56
95/6 LeafLimited 8
97/8 Limited 148
96/7 MetalUniverse 144
97/8 Omega 164
98/9 Pacific 55
97/8 PacificCrown 308
97/8 PacificCrownRoyale 96
97/8 PcfcDynag! 117,-Tandm 62
97/8 PacificInvincible 131
97/8 PacificParamount 131
98/9 PacificParamount 173
97/8 PacificRevolution 100
94/5 PaniniSticker U
95/6 PaniniSticker 126
96/7 PaniniSticker 124
97/8 PaniniSticker 103
93/4 Parkhurst 250, C3, D12, E6
94/5 Parkhurst 220, 282, C22
95/6 Parkhurst 462
94/5 ParkieSE seV16
93/4 Pinnacle 443, SR3
94/5 Pinnacle 19, 468
95/6 Pinnacle 33
96/7 Pinnacle 141
97/8 Pinnacle 183
97/8 PinnacleBeAPlayer 137
97/8 PinnacleCertified 84
97/8 PinnacleInside 110
95/6 PinnacleZenith 15
95/6 Playoff 92
94/5 POG 223
95/6 POG 247
93/4 PowerPlay 443, -Rookie 5
93/4 Premier 410
94/5 Prmr 439, -Finest(OPC) 20
95/6 ProMagnet 70
93/4 Score 596
95/6 Score 39, -CheckIt 4
96/7 Score 148
97/8 Score 168
97/8 Score(PHA) 6
94/5 Select 77
91/2 SketchOHL 225
95/6 SkyBoxEmotion 163
95/6 SkyBoxImpact 154
96/7 SkyBoxImpact 121
94/5 SP 111
96/7 SP 145, HC12
97/8 SPAuthentic 112
97/8 SPx 45
95/6 Summit 45
95/6 SuperSticker 114
96/7 TeamOut
95/6 Topps 70
94/5 ToppsFinest 58
93/4 ToppsStadiumClub 320
94/5 T.StadiumClub 112, 195
95/6 ToppsStadiumClub 134
92/3 UpperDeck 590
93/4 UpperDeck 78, R4, SP-149
94/5 UpperDeck 345, SP75
95/6 UpperDeck 407, SE75
96/7 UpperDeck 337, P10, X32
97/8 UpperDeck 155, 327
93/4 UDBeAPlayer 6
94/5 UDBeAPlayer-Aut. 116
96/7 UDBlackDiamond 77
98/9 UDChoice 150
95/6 UDCollChoice 140, 357
96/7 UDCollChoice 245, 331
97/8 UDCollChoice 236, SQ61
96/7 UpperDeck"Ice" 65
97/8 Zenith 56
97/8 PHA/Comcast
93/4 T.B./KashNKarry
94/5 T.B./HealthPlan
94/5 T.B./SkyBoxSportsCafe
95/6 T.B.
95/6 T.B./SkyBoxSportsCafe

GRATTON, DAN
88/9 ProCards(NewHaven)
82/3 Oshawa 12
83/4 Oshawa 9

GRATTON, GILLES
76/7 OPC/Topps 28
77/8 OPC/Topps 207
74/5 opcWHA 65
72/3 OttawaNationals

GRATTON, KEN
94/5 Slapshot(Brantford) 22
83/4 Brantford 1

GRATTON, MIKE
90/1 Rayside

GRATTON, NORM
74/5 Loblaws, -Update
74/5 OPC 288
75/6 OPC/Topps 34
74/5 BUF

GRAUL, THOMAS
94/5 DEL 38
95/6 DEL 31

GRAVEL, FLORIAN
51/2 LacStJean 53

GRAVEL, FRANÇOIS
88/9 ProCards(Sherbrooke)
89/90 ProCards(AHL) 184

GRAVEL, GREG
80/1 Oshawa 18
81/2 Oshawa 16

GRAVELLE, DAN
93/4 ClassicProspects 234
93/4 Greensboro

GRAVELLE, LÉO
45-64 BeeHives(MTL)
51/2 LavalDairy 109
43-47 ParadeSportive
45-54 QuakerOats
52/3 StLawrence 61

GRAVES, ADAM
91/2 Bowman 97
92/3 Bowman 373
95/6 Bowman 54
93/4 Classic TC7
93/4 Donruss 219
94/5 Donruss 43
95/6 Donruss 82
96/7 Donruss 66
97/8 Donruss 70
97/8 DonrussCanadianIce 97
95/6 DonrussElite 10
96/7 DonrussElite 107
97/8 DonrussElite 47
97/8 DonrussPreferred 133
97/8 DonrussPriority 83
95/6 EdgeIce L1
94/5 Flair 111
94/5 Fleer 132, -Franchise 3
96/7 Fleer 67
96/7 FleerNHLPicks 90
92/3 FleerUltra 136
93/4 FleerUltra 43

94/5 FU 137,-AW 4,-Pwr 4,-Rd 4
95/6 FleerUltra 274
95 Globe 96
93/4 HockeyWit 86
95/6 Hoyle'EAST 3 (Spades)
97/8 KatchMedallion 91
95/6 KennerSLU
93/4 KraftDinner
94/5 Kraft-AW
96/7 Kraft'Disk
93/4 Leaf 130
94/5 Leaf 255
95/6 Leaf 152
96/7 Leaf 20
97/8 Leaf 89
94/5 LeafLimited 73
95/6 LeafLimited 11
97/8 Limited 18
96/7 Maggers 106
94/5 McDonalds 2
97/8 Omega 144
90/1 OPC/Topps 251, OPC 480
91/2 OPC/Topps 167
92/3 O-Pee-Chee 158
91/2 opcPremier 28
98/9 Pacific 293
97/8 PacificCrown 26
97/8 PacificCrownRoyale 83
97/8 PacificDynagon! 77
97/8 PcfcD-BstKpt 58,-Tandm 69
97/8 PacificInvincible 85
97/8 PacificParamount 114
98/9 PacificParamount 151
97/8 PacificRegime 127
97/8 PacificRevolution 86
90/1 Panini(EDM) 6
91/2 PaniniSticker 122
92/3 PaniniSticker 238
93/4 PaniniSticker 92
94/5 PaniniSticker 87, 238a
95/6 PaniniSticker 105
96/7 PaniniSticker 100
91/2 Parkhurst 339
92/3 Parkhurst 346
93/4 Parkhurst 134
94/5 Parkhurst 157, 307, C15
95/6 Parkhurst 137
94/5 ParkieSe seV41
91/2 Pinnacle 16
92/3 Pinnacle 108
93/4 Pinnacle 99
94/5 Pinnacle 62, GR15, TP6
95/6 Pinnacle 45, -Full 8
96/7 Pinnacle 9
97/8 Pinnacle 174
97/8 PinnacleBeAPlayer 58
97/8 PinnacleCertified 96
97/8 PinnacleInside 104
95/6 Pinn.Zenith 33, -Gifted 17
95/6 Playoff 66
94/5 POG 259, 352
95/6 POG 179
93/4 PowerPlay 158
93/4 Premier 106
94/5 Premier 128, 350, -Fin(T) 7
95/6 ProMagnet 96
90/1 ProSet 84
91/2 ProSet 67, 443
92/3 ProSet 115
91/2 PSPlatinum 207
90/1 Score 163
91/2 Score(CDN) 235, 594
91/2 Score(U.S) 358, 44T
92/3 Score 71
93/4 Score 35,-Dynam(U.S.)DD5
94/5 Score 164, -CheckIt C19
94/5 S-DreamTeam DT9
95/6 Score 2
96/7 Score 81
97/8 Score 142
97/8 Score(NYR) 4
94/5 Select 48
95/6 SelectCertified 47
96/7 SelectCertified 51
95/6 SkyBoxEmotion 112
95/6 SkyBoxImpact 108
96/7 SkyBoxImpact 78
94/5 SP 77
95/6 SP 98
96/7 SP 103
97/8 SPAuthentic 103
95/6 Summit 66
96/7 Summit 120
96/7 TeamOut
92/3 Topps 329
95/6 Topps 295, 3PL, HGC26
98/9 Topps 89
94/5 ToppsFinest 23, -Div. 9
94/5 TF-RingLeaders 20
91/2 ToppsStadiumClub 332
92/3 ToppsStadiumClub 150
93/4 TSC 270, -Master(2) 6
94/5 T.StadiumClub 9, 265
95/6 T.StadiumClub 57
93/4 TSC-MembersOnly 35
90/1 UpperDeck 344
91/2 UpperDeck 268, 574
92/3 UpperDeck 388, 453
93/4 UpperDeck 128, HT1, SP99
94/5 UD 10, IG7, R5, R38,SP10
95/6 UD 224, 229, 239, SE57
96/7 UpperDeck 101, 297, P5
97/8 UpperDeck 108
94/5 UDBeAPlayer R117
95/6 UDBeAPlayer 212
96/7 UDBlackDiamond 9
97/8 UDBlackDiamond 2
98/9 UDChoice 134
95/6 UDCollChoice 277, 358
96/7 UDCollChoice 174, 325
97/8 UDCollChoice 163
96/7 UpperDeck"Ice" 44
87/8 DET/Caesars
88/9 DET/Caesars
90/1 EDM/McGavins
92/3 Windsor 5

GRAVES, HILLARD
73/4 OPC/Topps 110
74/5 OPC 306
75/6 OPC/Topps 62
76/7 OPC 273
77/8 OPC 286
78/9 O-Pee-Chee 357
79/80 O-Pee-Chee 294
77/8 VAN/GingerAle
77/8 VAN/RoyalBank
78/9 VAN/RoyalBank
79/80 WPG
74/5 ATL

GRAVES, STEVE
90/1 ProCards 362
86/7 EDM/RedRooster
88/9 EDM/ActionMagazine 32
84/5 NovaScotia 9
85/6 NovaScotia 17
81/2 SSMarie
82/3 SSMarie
83/4 SSMarie

GRAY, ALEX
26 Dominion 11
23/4 PaulinsCandy 20

GRAY, BRANDON
93/4 Slapshot(Oshawa) 6
96/7 Penascola 10

GRAY, JOHN
76/7 opcWHA 25
75/6 Phoenix
77/8 Winnipeg

GRAY, MIKE
91/2 SketchWHL 5
93/4 Saskatoon

GRAY, ROY
95/6 Slapshot 261

GRAY, TERRY
68/9 OPC/Topps 44
61/2 Topps 16
62/3 Topps 20
63/4 QuébecAces
65/6 QuébecAces

GRAYLING, TED
91/2 AirCanadaSJHL D11
92/3 MPSPhotoSJHL 75

GRECO, GUS
82/3 SSMarie
83/4 SSMarie

GRECO, PIERO
97/8 SheffieldSteelers

GREEDER, MIKE
82/3 Indianapolis

GREEN, CORY
92/3 BCJHL 106

GREEN, DARRYL
95/6 Slapshot 366

GREEN, DAVE
91/2 AvantGardeBCJHL 100
92/3 BCJHL 73
93/4 Slapshot(Windsor) 9
94/5 Slapshot(Windsor) 11
92/3 Clarkson

GREEN, DUSTIN
91/2 AvantGardeBCJHL 26
92/3 BCJHL 55

GREEN, GARY
26 Dominion 17
80/1 WSH

GREEN, JOSH
95/6 Bowman P15
95/6 Classic 60, -Aut.
95/6 FutureLegends-SS&D 4

GREEN, REDVERS (RED)
24/5 Champs (C144)
25 Dominion 84
24/5 MapleCrispettes (V130) 10
23/4 (V145-1) 31
24/5 (V145-2) 15

GREEN, RICK
86/7 Kraft Sports 26
77/8 OPC/Topps 245
78/9 O-Pee-Chee 363
79/80 O-Pee-Chee 309
80/1 OPC/Topps 33
81/2 OPC 348, Topps(E) 118
82/3 O-Pee-Chee 183
83/4 O-Pee-Chee 188
84/5 O-Pee-Chee 262
87/8 O-Pee-Chee 234
90/1 opcPremier 37
81/2 opcSticker 193
82/3 opcSticker 156
87/8 opcSticker 11/149
87/8 PaniniSticker 60
91/2 PaniniSticker 147
82/3 Post
90/1 ProSet 436
90/1 ScoreTraded 84T
83/4 SouhaitsRen.KeyChain
90/1 DET/Caesars
91/2 DET/Caesars
82/3 MTL
82/3 MTL/Steinberg
83/4 MTL
84/5 MTL
85/6 MTL
85/6? MTL/ProvigoPlacemats
85/6 MTL/ProvigoStickers
86/7 MTL
87/8 MTL
87/8 MTL/Kodak
87/8 MTL/Stickers 65-66,68,70
88/9 MTL
78/9 WSH
79/80 WSH
80/1 WSH
81/2 WSH

GREEN, SCOTT
88/9 ProCards(NewHaven)
84/5 SSMarie

GREEN, SHAYNE
90/1 SketchWHL 256
91/2 SketchWHL 89
92/3 Dayton
82/3 Victoria
89/90 Victoria

GREEN, WILF (SHORTY)
24/5 Champs (C144)
25 Dominion 83
83&87 HallOfFame 140
83 HHOF Postcard (K)
24/5 MapleCrispettes (V130) 22
23/4 (V145-1) 30
24/5 (V145-2) 14

GREEN, TED
64-67 BeeHives(BOS)
62 CeramicTiles
64/5 CokeCap BOS-6
65/6 CocaCola
70/1 DadsCookies
70/1 EddieSargent 4
71/2 EddieSargent 6
70/1 Esso Stamp
68/9 OPC/Topps 4
69/70 OPC/Topps 23
69/70 OPC 218, -Sticker
70/1 OPC 134
71/2 OPC/Topps 173
75/6 opcWHA 57
76/7 opcWHA 112
94/5 Parkie(64/5) 3
95/6 Parkie(66/7) 6
72/3 7ElevenCups
61/2 ShirriffCoin 16
68/9 ShirriffCoin BOS12
71/2 TheTorontoSun
61/2 Topps 2
62/3 Topps 7, -Buck
63/4 Topps 7
64/5 Topps 32
65/6 Topps 98
66/7 Topps 37, -USATest 37
67/8 Topps 94
56-66 TorontoStar 65/6
70/1 OPC 134
70/1 BOS/Ashtray
71/2 BOS
81/2 EDM/RedRooster
82/3 EDM/RedRooster
83/4 EDM/Buttons
83/4 EDM/McDonald
84/5 EDM/RedRooster
86/7 EDM/RedRooster
88/9 EDM/ActionMagazine 57
90/1 EDM/McGavins
91/2 EDM/IGA
92/3 EDM/IGA 27
72/3 NewEngland
77/8 Winnipeg

GREEN, TRAVIS
96/7 Aces 2 (Spades)
92/3 C'Prospects 126
93/4 Donruss 200
94/5 Donruss 75
95/6 Donruss 208
96/7 Donruss 175
97/8 Donruss 62
97/8 DonrussCanadianIce 65
97/8 DonrussPriority 102
96/7 Fleer 64
95/6 FleerMetal 90
96/7 FleerNHLPicks 70
92/3 FleerUltra 343
93/4 FleerUltra 365
94/5 FleerUltra 126
95/6 FleerUltra 266, -HighSpd 12
96/7 FleerUltra 101
97/8 KatchMedallion 87
93/4 Leaf 127
94/5 Leaf 288
96/7 Leaf 131
95/6 LeafLimited 100
96/7 LeafPreferred 5
97/8 Limited 59, 110
96/7 MetalUniverse 92
97/8 Omega 137
98/9 Pacific 50
97/8 PacificCrown 170
97/8 PcfcDynag! 73,-Tandem 72
97/8 PacificInvincible 81
97/8 PacificParamount 108
98/9 PacificParamount 1
97/8 PacificRevolution 81
96/7 PaniniSticker 92
97/8 PaniniSticker 79
92/3 Parkhurst 343
93/4 Parkhurst 126
94/5 Parkhurst 137
95/6 Parkhurst 400
94/5 Pinnacle 216
96/7 Pinnacle 70
97/8 Pinnacle 167
97/8 PinnacleBeAPlayer 63
97/8 PinnacleCertified 123
97/8 PinnacleInside 130
96/7 PinnacleZenith 26
95/6 Playoff 280
96/7 Playoff 418
94/5 POG 156
95/6 POG 170
93/4 PowerPlay 383
93/4 Premier 489
90/1 ProCards 510
91/2 ProCards 467
93/4 Score 661
96/7 Score 15
97/8 Score 173
96/7 SkyBoxImpact 75
95/6 SP 87
96/7 SP 94
97/8 SPAuthentic 94
98/9 SPx"Finite" 4
95/6 Summit 60
96/7 Summit 61
95/6 Topps 89
98/9 Topps 162
95/6 ToppsFinest 79
93/4 ToppsStadiumClub 394
94/5 ToppsStadiumClub 236
93/4 UpperDeck 59
94/5 UpperDeck 220
95/6 UpperDeck 473, SE138
96/7 UpperDeck 290
97/8 UpperDeck 307
95/6 UDBeAPlayer 15
98/9 UDChoice 5
96/7 UDCollChoice 157
97/8 UDCollChoice 160, SQ39
89/90 Spokane

GREENAN, ROY
52/3 AnonymousOHL 122

GREENE, MATT
93/4 WestMich.

GREENLAW, JEFF
88/9 ProCards(Baltimore)
89/90 ProCards(AHL) 79
90/1 ProCards 210
91/2 ProCards 547
86/7 WSH/Kodak
91/2 WSH
96/7 Cincinnati

GREENLAY, MIKE
94/5 ClassicFourSport 153
89/90 ProCards(AHL) 133
90/1 ProCards 225
93/4 AtlantaKnights
89/90 Saskatoon 5
91/2 Knoxville

GREENOUGH, GLENN
84/5 Sudbury 10
85/6 Sudbury 12

GREENWAY, DAVE
93/4 RedDeer

GREENWOOD, CHUCK
92/3 Wheeling 20

GREENWOOD, JEFF
91/2 AirCanadaSJHL D20
92/3 MPSPhotoSJHL 119

GREER, SCOTT
89/90 Nashville

GREGG, RANDY
83/4 O-Pee-Chee 28
84/5 O-Pee-Chee 242
85/6 O-Pee-Chee 199
89/90 O-Pee-Chee 229
90/1 OPC/Topps 275
83/4 opcSticker 145
84/5 opcSticker 257
85/6 opcSticker 225/92
87/8 opcSticker 94/227
90/1 PaniniSticker 231
91/2 Pinnacle 415
90/1 Score (CND) 306
91/2 Score(CDN) 598, (U.S) 48T
83/4 Vachon 25
82/3 EDM/RedRooster
83/4 EDM
83/4 EDM/Buttons
83/4 EDM/McDonald
84/5 EDM
84/5 EDM/RedRooster
85/6 EDM/RedRooster
86/7 EDM
86/7 EDM/RedRooster
88/9 EDM
88/9 EDM/ActionMagazine 13
91/2 VAN

GREGG, VIC
52/3 StLawrence 64

GREGGA, SHAMUS
93/4 Hampton

GREGOIR, BILL
84/5 Victoria

GREGOIRE, J.F.
90/1 SketchQMJHL 82, 147
91/2 SketchQMJHL 65

GREGOR, COLIN
90/1 SketchWHL 254
95/6 Birmingham
94/5 Hampton 4
88/9 Lethbridge
93/4 Richmond 6

GREGORY, JIM
73/4 TOR

GREGSON, TERRY
90/1 ProSet 688

GREIG, MARK
93/4 Donruss 137, 495
93/4 FleerUltra 334
93/4 Leaf 412
94/5 Leaf 522
92/3 O-Pee-Chee 186
92/3 opcPremier 99
91/2 Pinnacle 352
93/4 Premier 301
90/1 ProCards 180
91/2 ProSet 537
90/1 Score 431
91/2 Score(CDN) 273, (U.S) 383
92/3 Topps 175
92/3 ToppsStadiumClub 421
93/4 ToppsStadiumClub 386
91/2 UpperDeck 456
91/2 HFD/JuniorWhalers
93/4 HFD/Coke
88/9 Lethbridge
89/90 Lethbridge
94/5 SaintJohn

GREIN, ANDRE
94/5 DEL 228
95/6 DEL 227
96/7 DEL 78

GRENIER, DAVID
95/6 Fredericton

GRENIER, LUC
71/2 EddieSargent 76
72/3 EddieSargent 1
71/2 TheTorontoSun

GRENIER, RICHARD
76/7 opcWHA 59
76 QuébecNordiques/MA
76/7 QuébecNordiques

GRENIER, TONY
84/5 PrinceAlbert

GRENKVIST, ERIK
94/5 ElitSet 27

GRENVILLE, CHRIS
91/2 SketchOHL 315
95/6 Birmingham

GRESCHNER, RON
75/6 OPC/Topps 146
76/7 OPC/Topps 154
77/8 OPC/Topps 256
78/9 OPC/Topps 154
79/80 OPC/Topps 78
80/1 OPC/Topps 248
81/2 OPC 224, Topps(E) 97
82/3 O-Pee-Chee 224
84/5 O-Pee-Chee 141
85/6 O-Pee-Chee 182
86/7 OPC/Topps 18
87/8 OPC/Topps 159
90/1 O-Pee-Chee 447
81/2 opcSticker 167
86/7 opcSticker 222/91
87/8 PaniniSticker 104, 108
82/3 Post
90/1 ProSet 197
89/90 NYR/MarineMidland

GRETZKY, BRENT
94/5 Classic 99, T65
94/5 ClassicFourSport 158
94/5 C4'Images 116
94/5 ClassicImages 17
93/4 Donruss 318
95/6 EdgeIce 82
93/4 FleerUltra 424
93/4 Parkhurst 248, C14
94/5 Parkhurst 218, 295, V62
93/4 Pinnacle 429
94/5 Premier 209
93/4 Score 606
89/90 SketchOHL 75
90/1 SketchOHL 7
91/2 SketchOHL 99
92/3 UpperDeck 37
93/4 UpperDeck 354, SP-150
94/5 UpperDeck 69
94/5 UDBAP R161, -Aut. 154
95/6 UDCollChoice 281
92/3 AtlantaKnights
93/4 AtlantaKnights
96/7 LasVegas
96/7 Penascola 12
95/6 StJohns

GRETZKY, KEITH
92/3 Classic 118
92/3 ClassicProspects 99
89/90 ProCards(IHL) 101
91/2 ProCards 322
92/3 UpperDeck 37
87/8 Flint
92/3 SanDiego

GRETZKY, WAYNE
95/6 Aces A (Diamonds)
96/7 Aces A (Clubs)
97/8 Aces J (Clubs)
89/90 ActionPacked
90/1 Bowman 143
91/2 Bowman 173, 176, -Promo
92/3 Bowman 1, 207
95/6 Bowman 1, BB5
96/7 CorinthianHeadliners
97/8 Corinthian Headliners
72-84 Dernière 81/2
93/4 Donruss 152, 396, K
93/4 D-EliteSeries 10, -IceKing 4
94/5 Donruss 127, -Dominator 5
94/5 Donruss-Elite 5, -Ice 4
95/6 Donruss 13, -Elite 7,-Dom 5
96/7 Donruss 93, -Elite 2,-Dom 5
97/8 Donruss 143,-Line 1,-Elite 1
96/7 D.CanadianIce 5, -OCda 7
97/8 D.CdnIce 5,-Ntl 1,-Scrpb 28
95/6 DonrussElite 58, -Cutting 3
96/7 Don.Elite 10, -Perspective 1
97/8 D.Elite 9, 143,-Craftsmn 19
97/8 D.Preferred 4, 172,-Line 6A
97/8 D.Pref -PrecM 3,-Tins 3, 23
97/8 D.Pref -WideTins 1, 12
97/8 DonrussPriority 10, 199
97/8 D.Prio -DirDep 8,-OpDay 10
97/8 D.Prio -Postcrd 7, -Stamp 7
97/8 D.Studio 1, 109,-HardHat 1
97/8 D.Studio-Portr 1,-Silhouet 1
93/4 EASports 63, 192
88/9 Esso Sticker
93/4 FaxPaxWorldOfSport 25
94/5 Flair 79, -Centre 4, -Hot 2
96/7 Flair 59, -Hot 4, -Now 1
94/5 Fleer 94, -Headliner 4
96/7 Fleer 68, -Art 6, -Pearson 4
95/6 FleerMetal 71
95/6 FM-Heavy 4, -IntSteel 6
96/7 FleerNHLPicks 8, -Fab 15
96/7 F.Picks-Dream 1, -Cap 4
92/3 FleerUltra 83, -AS 10,-AW 6
93/4 FleerUltra 114, -AS 15
93/4 FU-Pivots 2, -Scoring 2
94/5 FU 306, -AS 10, -AW5
94/5 FU-Pivot 4,-Scor 4, -Powr 4
95/6 FleerUltra 74, 385, -Extra 7
95/6 FU-Pivot 3, -Ultraview 2
96/7 FU 106, -Red 2, -Power 5
95 Globe 99, 265-67
96/7 GotUm HockeyGreatsCoin
90/1 GretzkyCup Set
94/5 GretzkyPog 1-18
92/3 HighFive 3
93/4 HockeyWit 99
95/6 Hoyle'WEST A (Clubs)
92/3 HumptyDumpty (1)
82? JDMcCarthy
97/8 KatchMedallion 92, 157
97/8 KennerSLU, -1on1
94 Koululainen
95 Koululainen

86/7 Kraft Sports 14
89/90 Kraft 59, -Sticker 2
90/1 Kraft 15, 66
91/2 Kraft 65
92/3 Kraft'AllStar
93/4 Kraft-Captain, -Cutout
94/5 Kraft-AW, -HockeyHero
95/6 KraftDinner
96/7 Kraft-FlexMagnets
97/8 Kraft-CdnPros,-RoadToNag
97/8 Kraft -Stickers, -WorldsBest
93/4 Leaf 304, -Studio 4, -AS 6
94/5 Leaf 345, -Limited 11
94/5 Leaf-Fire 4, -Gold 1
95/6 Leaf 89, -FireOnIce 10
96/7 Leaf 140, -Leather 8, -Fire 5
97/8 Leaf 8, 175,-BnrS 3, -Fire 1
94/5 LeafLimited 10, -Gold 7
95/6 LeafLimited 87, -Stars 3
96/7 LeafLimited 7, -Stubble 3
96/7 LeafPreferred 112
96/7 LP-Power 5, -Vanity 1
97/8 Limited 4, 97, 200
97/8 Limited -Fabric 1, 34
96/7 Maggers 135
82/3 McDonalds 20, 22
91/2 McDonalds McD17, McH-1
97/8 McDonalds McD1, F1
97/8 McDonalds Medallions
98 McDonalds.Nagano
96/7 MetalUniverse 96, -Lethal 6
82/3 Neilsons Set 1-50
97/8 Omega 145, 250,-GmFa 11
97/8 Omega -Silk 8,-StickHan 13
79/80 OPC/Topps 18
80/1 OPC/Topps 3, 87, 162-63,
80/1 OPC/Topps 182, 250
81/2 OPC 106, 125-26, 383-84
81/2 OPC 392, Topps 16, 52
82/3 OPC 1, 99, 106-07, 235,
82/3 OPC 237, 240, 242-43, 247
83/4 OPC 22-23, 29, 203-04,
83/4 OPC 212, 215-17
84/5 OPC 208, 243, 357, 373-74
84/5 OPC 380-83,388, T. 51,154
85/6 OPC/Topps 120,G, -AS 2
85/6 O-Pee-Chee 257-59
86/7 OPC/Topps 3, F
86/7 OPC 259-60, T-AS 3
87/8 OPC/Topps 53, A, T-AS 5
88/9 OPC/Topps 120, B, T-AS 8
89/90 OPC/T. 156, E
89/90 OPC 320, 325, T-AS 11
90/1 OPC/Topps 1-3,120,199, D
90/1 O-Pee-Chee 522, T-TL 12
91/2 OPC/T. 201, 224, 257-58
91/2 OPC/T. 321, 520, 522, 524
91/2 Topps-TL 10
92/3 OPC 15, 220, -25th 12
87/8 opcStars 13
88/9 opcStars 11
90/1 opcPremier 38
91/2 opcPremier 3
81/2 opcSticker 209, 252, 264
82/3 opcStckr 97-98,162,256-59
83/4 opcSticker 7, 89-90, 161,
83/4 opcSticker 301,307, 325-26
84/5 opcStick. 65/64,138, 255-56
84/5 opcStick. 226/227, 229/228
85/6 opcSticker 5, 120, 198/70,
85/6 opcStkr 202/75,54/197,220
86/7 opcStickr 72, 191/52,195/57
86/7 opcSticker 115/129,183/123
87/8 opcStickr 86, 180/37,181/38
87/8 opcSticker 115/127,174/176
88/9 opcSticker 1, 224, 121/251
89/90 opcSticker 154, 166/28
89/90 opcSticker 209/69, FS30
80/1 opcSuperCard 7
98/9 Pacific 99,-Cram 7,-T.CL 17
98/9 Pcfc-DynIce 13,-Gold 23
97/8 PacificCrown 99, -Supial 12
97/8 PCC-Slap 5A, -Gold 15
97/8 PCC-Cramers 7, -TmCL 16
97/8 PacificCrownRoyale 84
97/8 PCR -Blades 14,-Cramer 7
97/8 PCR-HatTrick 11,-Lamp 11
97/8 PacificDynagon! 78, 140
97/8 PcfcD-BstKpt 59,-Dyn 10A
97/8 PcfcD-Kings 6,-Tand 1, 19
97/8 PacificInv. 86, -Feature 21
97/8 PacificInv.-Off 12,-Attack 14
97/8 PcfcParamnt 115,-CdnG 10
97/8 PcfcP.-BigN 14,-Photo 13
98/9 PcfcParamnt 152,-HOF 7
98/9 PcfcP-SpecD 12,-TmCL 17
97/8 PacificRegime 128, 218
97/8 PcfcRevolutn 87,-ASGm 14
97/8 PcfcRev -Icon 7, -TmCL 16
90/1 Panini Album
87/8 PaniniSticker 192, 197-200
87/8 PaniniS. 261, 371,373,389
88/9 PaniniSticker 58, 87, 179
88/9 PaniniSticker 181, 193, 374
90/1 PaniniSticker 242, 332
91/2 PaniniSticker 78, 327
92/3 PaniniSticker 64, 287
93/4 PaniniSticker R
94/5 PaniniSticker 172, AA
95/6 PaniniSticker 266
96/7 PaniniSticker 200
97/8 PaniniSticker 82
95 PaniniWorlds 276
91/2 Parkhurst 73, 207, 222
91/2 Parkhurst 429, 433, 465
92/3 Parkhurst 65, 509
93/4 Parkhurst 99, D1, G1, W1
94/5 Parkie 103, 306, C11, C28
94/5 Parkhurst 100, 449, -AS 1
95/6 PH-Crown(1) 6, (2) 10
94/5 ParkieSE seV20
91/2 Pinnacle 100, 381, B11
92/3 Pinnacle 200,249,-TeamP 5
93/4 Pinnacle 237, 400, 512
93/4 Pinnacle CA11, -TeamP 5
94/5 Pinnacle 200, TP9
95/6 P. 101,-ClearShot 9, -First 2
96/7 Pinnacle 1
96/7 P-Numbers 9, -TeamP 1
97/8 Pinnacle 67,192,-TeamP 4
96/7 Pinn.BeAPlayer-Biscuit 1
97/8 P.BAP-OneTimer 1,-Take 8
97/8 P.BeeHive 33, -TeamCL 16
97/8 P.Certified 100, -Team 7
97/8 Pinnacle-EPIX 1
95/6 PinnacleFANtasy 13
96/7 PinnacleFANtasy 5
97/8 PinnacleInside 3, 9,-Track 1
97/8 PinnacleMint 18
95/6 Pinn.Zenith 13, -ZTeam 4
96/7 P.Zenith 13, Champion 2
95/6 Playoff 50, 159, 269
96/7 Playoff 430
94/5 POG 126, 268, 331
95/6 POG 132, 01
82/3 Post
94/5 Post
96/7 Post
93/4 PowerPlay 116, -Point 3
93/4 PP-Gamebreaker 3
93/4 Premier 330, 380
93/4 Prmr-Black(OPC) 1, (T) 7
94/5 Prmr 130,150,154,280,375
94/5 Prmr-GoToGuy 1
95/6 ProMagnet 62, MAG1
90/1 ProSet 118, 340, 388
90/1 ProSet 394, 703, P2
91/2 PS 101, 285, 324, 574,CC5
91/2 ProSet 'ThePuck 11
92/3 ProSet 66, 246, -TL 6
91/2 PSPlatinum 52, PC4, PC14
83/4 PuffySticker 1
90/1 Score 1, 321, 336, 338, 347
90/1 Score 352-53, 361, 110T
91/2 Score(CDN) 100, 295, 296
91/2 Score(CDN) 303, 312, 317
91/2 Score(CDN) 324, 376
91/2 Score(U.S) 100, 346, 405
91/2 Score(U.S) 406, 413, 422
91/2 Score(U.S) 427,434,-Hot 2
92/3 Score 1, 412, 426, 525
93/4 Score 300, 662, -P.AS 45
93/4 Score(U.S) DD7,-Dream 11
93/4 Score-Franchise 9
94/5 Score 241,DT14,NP1,TF11
95/6 Score 250, -Lamlighter 1
95/6 Score-Dream 1,-Border 2
96/7 Score 41,-Sddn 12,-DrmT 8
97/8 Score 99
97/8 Score(NYR) 1
92/3 SeasonsPatch 9
93/4 SeasonsPatch 5
94/5 Select 83, FL11
95/6 SelectCertified 23, -Gold 2
96/7 SelectCertified 4, -Corner 4
94 Semic 99, 344
95 Semic 99
89 SemicSticker 65
91 SemicSticker 64
92 SemicSticker 84
93 SemicSticker 199
84/5 7Eleven 4.5
84/5 7ElevenDisk
95/6 SkyBoxEmotion 81
95/6 SkBxE-Xcel 4, -Xcited 5
95/6 SkyBoxImpact 79, -Ice 6
95/6 SkBxImpact-Countdown 4
96/7 SBImp 79,-Versa 4,-Ctdn 3
83/4 SouhaitsRen.KeyChain
94/5 SP 54, -2500Gretzky 1
94/5 SP-Premier 17
95/6 SP 127, GC1, E17, FX10
96/7 SP 99, GF1, HC1, CW1
96/7 SP-Inside, -SPxForce 1,5
97/8 SPAuthentic 99, I26, S1
97/8 SPAuthentic M6, T1
96/7 SPx 39,GF1,GT1,HH7,-Aut.
97/8 SPx 30, SPX1, DuoView
98/9 SPx"Finite" 53, 99, 151, 180
77-9 Sportscastr 77-01, 89-2127
97/8 SI.ForKids-GreatMoments
83/4 StaterMint H14
95/6 Summit 24, -GM 18
96/7 Summit 67,-High 5,-Unt 12
96/7 SuperSticker 57, -DieCut 21
91 TeamCanada
96/7 TeamOut
92/3 Topps 1, 123
95/6 Topps 85, 375, HGC20
95/6 Topps M1, PF1, 10ARL
98/9 Topps 219, L7, M4, SB20
98/9 Topps-RookieReprint 1
94/5 ToppsFinest 41, -Ring 5
94/5 ToppsFinest-Division 18
95/6 ToppsFinest 5, 180
96/7 T.Picks FC1, FT10, TS2
91/2 ToppsStadiumClub 1
92/3 T.StadiumClub 18, 256
93/4 TSC 200, -AllStar, -Finest 1
94/5 TSC 99, 270, -Finest 4
95/6 T.StadiumClub 173, M1, N2
95/6 ToppsSuperSkills 15
91/2 TSC-MembersOnly (x3)
93/4 TSC-MembersOnly 5
94/5 TSC-MembersOnly 32
95/6 TSC-MembersOnly 1
97/8 ToppsSticker 4
90/1 UpperDeck 54, 205, 307
90/1 UD 476, 545, -Hol. (x3)
91/2 UD 13, 38, 45, 437, 501
91/2 UD 621, AW1, AW6
91/2 UD'CzechWJC (x2)
92/3 UD 25,33,37,-LockerAS 25
92/3 UD 423, 435, 621, G5, W1
92/3 UD WG10, -Hero 10-18, 26
93/4 UpperDeck 99, HB9, NL1
93/4 UD R1, SP-70, -Trade
94/5 UD 1,226,228,541,C16,H1
94/5 UD H16,R19,R21,R42,R59
94/5 UD G15, SP36, -Jumbo 1
95/6 UD 99, 222, 252,F2,H7,R13
95/6 UD R23, R31, R41, R51
95/6 UD SE128,-ASPredMVP 1
96/7 UD108,209,210,361,389-90
96/7 UD HH1, LS01, SS5A, X1
96/7 UD-AllStarYCTG AR20
97/8 UD 109, 209, 419
97/8 UD GJ8, SG1, SS1, T1B
93/4 UpperDeckBeAPlayer 7
94/5 UDBAP R99, R147, R176
94/5 UDBAP G1, UC1, -Aut 108
95/6 UpperDeckBeAPlayer 97
96/7 UDBlackDiamond 180, RC1
97/8 UDBlackDiamond 144, PC1
98/9 UDChoice 128, 225, 236
98/9 UDChoice 308, BH1, SQ1
95/6 UDCC 1,361, 395, 396, C3
96/7 UDCollChoice 170, 290,329
96/7 UDCC 336, C1, S1, UD1
96/7 UDCC-Oversize 170, 1of8
97/8 UDCollChoice 167, 312
97/8 UDCollChoice C1,S1,SQ90
97/8 udDiamVision 1, DM1,RT1
96/7 UpperDeck"Ice" 112, S1
97/8 UpperDeckIce 90, IC1, L1B
94 UpperDeckSoccer
83/4 Vachon 26
97/8 ValuNet
96 Wien 99
97/8 Zenith 4, Z1,-ChasingCup 2
97/8 Zenith -ZTeam 2
79/80 EDM
80/1 EDM/Zellers
81/2 EDM/RedRooster (x4)
81/2 EDM/WestEdmonton
82/3 EDM/RedRooster (x4)
83/4 EDM
83/4 EDM/Buttons
83/4 EDM/McDonald
84/5 EDM
84/5 EDM/RedRooster (x4)
85/6 EDM/RedRooster (x3)
86/7 EDM
86/7 EDM/RedRooster (x2)
87/8 EDM
88/9 EDM/ActionMag. 46, 55
88/9 L.A./Smokeys
89/90 L.A./Smokeys 1
90/1 L.A./Smokeys 1
90/1 L.A./Smokeys
91/2 L.A./Forum
96/7 NYR 1
83/4 Belleville 27
87/8 SSMarie 29
87/8 Hull

GREYEYES, MARK
87/8 Portland
88/9 Portland

GRIBKO, EVGENY
95 PaniniWorlds 33

GRIER, MIKE
97/8 Donruss 94
96/7 DonrussCanadianIce 141
97/8 DonrussCanadianIce 121
97/8 DonrussElite 62
97/8 DonrussPreferred 44
97/8 DonrussPriority 59
97/8 D.Studio 51,-HardHats 22
96/7 Flair 110
96/7 FleerUltra 58, -Rookies 9
97/8 Leaf 81, -BannerSeason 23
97/8 Limited 27,50,199,-fabric 22
96/7 MetalUniverse 181
97/8 Omega 90
98/9 Pacific 208
97/8 PacificCrown 164
97/8 PcfcDynag! 48,-Tandem 10
97/8 PacificInvincible 55, -Off 10
97/8 PacificParamount 74
98/9 PacificParamount 85
97/8 Pinnacle 177
96/7 PinnacleBeAPlayer 220
97/8 PinnacleCertified 73
97/8 PinnacleInside 85,-Track 29
97/8 Score 153, -Checkit 10
96/7 SelectCertified 101
96/7 SP 177
97/8 SPAuthentic 63, S28
98/9 Topps 31
96/7 UpperDeck 259, P13
97/8 UD 67, 207, SG25, T16A
96/7 UDBlackDiamond 15
97/8 UDCollChoice 88, SQ24
96/7 UpperDeck"Ice" 86
96/7 EDM
97/8 EDM

GRIEVE, BRENT
92/3 Classic 100
92/3 ClassicFourSport 213
93/4 ClassicProspects 128
94/5 FleerUltra 274
94/5 Leaf 485
94/5 Parkhurst 79
94/5 Premier 99, 431
90/1 ProCards 506
91/2 ProCards 453
89/90 SketchMEM 92
89/90 SketchOHL 22
94/5 ToppsStadiumClub 257
94/5 UpperDeck 396
95/6 UpperDeck 307
94/5 UDBeAPlayer-Aut. 42
93/4 EDM 25MAR94
90/1 Oshawa 21

GRIEVE BRIAN
89/90 SketchMEM 81
89/90 SketchOHL 12
90/1 SketchOHL 337
91/2 SketchOHL 165
89/90 Oshawa 9
91/2 Oshawa
91/2 Oshawa Dominos 2, 28

GRIFFI, S
95/6 Birmingham

GRIFFIS, SI
83&87 HallOfFame 155
83 HHOF Postcard (L)

GRIFFITHS, FRANK
93/4 ActionPacked 8

GRIFFITHS, TUFFY
36/7 WWGum (V356) 132

GRIGG, KODY
94/5 Slapshot(NorthBay) 21

GRIGG, VIC
51/2 LavalDairy 102

GRILLO, DEAN
94 Classic 42

GRILLS, CHAD
91/2 SketchOHL 135
93/4 Slapshot(Peterborough) 11
93/4 Slapshot(SSMarie) 22
91/2 Peterborough 4

GRIMES, JAKE
93/4 ClassicProspects 43
89/90 SketchOHL 76
90/1 SketchOHL 8
91/2 SketchOHL 111
94/5 ThunderBay

GRIMES, KEVIN
97/8 Bowman 136

GRIMSON, STU
93/4 Donruss 15
93/4 FleerUltra 253
97/8 KatchMedallion 27
93/4 KraftDinner
93/4 Leaf 330
98/9 Pacific 133
97/8 PacificCrown 296
93/4 Parkhurst 277
94/5 Parkhurst 3
93/4 Pinnacle 401
94/5 Pinnacle 512
94/5 POG 33
93/4 PowerPlay 1
93/4 Premier 357
89/90 ProCards(IHL) 199
93/4 Score 558
98/9 Topps 96
91/2 UpperDeck 416
97/8 UpperDeck 33
95/6 UDBeAPlayer 224
93/4 ANA/Caps 3
90/1 CHI/Coke
91/2 CHI/Coke
82/3 Regina 8
83/4 Regina 8
88/9 SaltLake 12

GRIMWOOD, SCOTT
93/4 RedDeer

GRISDALE, JOHN
75/6 OPC 339
77/8 OPC 277
78/9 O-Pee-Chee 318
72/3 TOR
74/5 VAN/RoyalBank
75/6 VAN/RoyalBank
76/7 VAN/RoyalBank
77/8 VAN/RoyalBank
78/9 VAN/RoyalBank

GRISÉ, PATRICK
90/1 SketchQMJHL 62
91/2 SketchQMJHL 30
88/9 Richelieu

GRNAK, MARIANNE
94/5 Classic W16, W21

GROGER, THOMAS
94/5 DEL 12
95/6 DEL 322

GROKE, JAMIE
85/6 London 20

GROLEAU, FRANÇOIS
91/2 Arena 29
91/2 Classic 35
91/2 ClassicFourSport 35, -Aut.
93/4 ClassicProspects 47
90/1 SketchQMJHL 225
91/2 SketchQMJHL 55
91/2 StarPics 63
91/2 UltimateDP 30, -Aut 30
96/7 Fredericton
94/5 SaintJohn

GROLEAU, MARIUS
52/3 LavalDairy 36

GROLEAU, SAMUEL
91/2 SketchQMJHL 159
94/5 Slapshot(MEM) 54

GRONAU, MARK
94/5 DEL 72
95/6 DEL 51

GRONBORG, RIKAR
92/3 SemicElitserien 257

GRONDIN, JIMMY
96/7 Rimouski

GRONDIN, PHILIPPE
96/7 Rimouski

GRÖNDSTRAND, JARI
94/5 DEL 400
91/2 SemicElitserien 158
93/4 Sisu 65
88/9 QUE
88/9 QUE/GeneralFoods
89/90 QUE
89/90 QUE/GeneralFoods

GRÖNMAN, TUOMAS
96/7 DonrussCanadianIce 139
93/4 Jyvas-Hyva 231
93/4 Parkhurst 523
96/7 SelectCertif 105
95 Semic 3, 225
93/4 Sisu 188
94/5 Sisu-Horoscope 4
95/6 Sisu 126, -DoubleTrouble 1
96/7 Sisu-Sledgehammer 4
95/6 SisuLimited 4
91/2 SketchWHL 154
91/2 UD 677, 'CzechWJC 40
93/4 UpperDeck 270
96/7 UpperDeck 237

GRONVALL, JANNE
92/3 Classic 32
95/6 EdgeIce 80
92/3 Jyvas-Hyva 162
93/4 Jyvas-Hyva 291
93/4 Sisu 64
94/5 Sisu 159, 175
95/6 SisuLimited 75
91/2 UD 672, 'CzechWJC 35
94/5 StJohns
95/6 StJohns

GROSEK, MICHAL
93/4 C'Prospects 9
95/6 Donruss 125
95/6 EdgeIce 68
94/5 Fleer 241
94/5 FleerUltra 393
95/6 Leaf 53
97/8 Omega 21
98/9 Pacific 105
97/8 PacificCrownRoyale 13
98/9 PacificParamount 18
97/8 PacificRegime 19
97/8 PaniniSticker 17
94/5 Parkhurst 266
95/6 Parkhurst 231
94/5 Pinnacle 482
97/8 PinnacleBeAPlayer 187
94/5 Premier 531
97/8 Score 255
97/8 Score(BUF) 8
98/9 Topps 152
94/5 ToppsFinest 64
94/5 UpperDeck 433
95/6 UpperDeck 111

GROSS, LLOYD
33-35 DiamondMatch

GROSS, PAVEL
94/5 DEL 277
95/6 DEL 274
96/7 DEL 169

GROSSE, ERWIN
51/2 LavalDairy 64
52/3 StLawrence 104

GROSSI, DINO
93/4 C'Prospects 137

GROSSMANN, VITALIJ
94/5 DEL 161
95/6 DEL 161

GROSSO, DON
34-43 BeeHives(DET)
40/1 OPC (V301-2) 128

GROULX, WAYNE
94 Semic 239
93 SemicSticker 278
81/2 SSMarie
82/3 SSMarie
83/4 SSMarie
84/5 SSMarie

GRUBA, TONY
94/5 Dayton 15

GRUBAUER, EDGAR
79 PaniniSticker 258

GRUDEN, JOHN
94/5 Classic 53, AA2
94/5 Donruss 179
94/5 Fleer 11
94/5 FleerUltra 254
94/5 Leaf 192
94/5 Premier 447
95/6 Topps 104
91/2 FerrisState

GRUEN, DAN
75/6 opcWHA 128

GRUHL, SCOTT
92/3 ClassicProspects 122
88/9 ProCards(Muskegon)
89/90 ProCards(IHL)150
90/1 ProCards 382
91/2 ProCards 254
94/5 Richmond
95/6 Richmond

GRUNDMANN, OLAF
94/5 DEL 219
95/6 DEL 196
96/7 DEL 339

GRUTH, HENRYK
79 PaniniSticker 121
89 SemicSticker 133
92 SemicSticker 269

GRYP, BOB
74/5 Loblaws
75/6 OPC 348

GSCHLIESSER, ALEX
95 PaniniWorlds 94

GSCHWILL, TMO
94/5 DEL 191
95/6 DEL 176

GUADAS, LEO
51/2 BasDuFleuve 21
84/5 O-Pee-Chee 160
88/9 ProCards(Mai), (Roc)
89/90 ProCards'AHL 212, 273
90/1 ProCards 291, 513
91/2 ProCards 611
88/9 L.A.

GUAY, FRANÇOIS
96/7 DEL 172

GUDAS, LEO
95/6 APS 202
95 Globe 148
91/2 Jyvas-Hyva 30
94 Semic 166
89 SemicSticker 186
92 SemicSticker 125
96 Wien 112

GUENETTE, LUC
85/6 Fredericton 17

GUENETTE, STEVE
90/1 ProCards 627
91/2 ProCards 147
87/8 PGH/Kodak

GUENNELON, GERALD
95 Globe 206
95 PaniniWorlds 100
94 Semic 219

GUÉRARD, DANIEL
93/4 Classic 132

GUÉRARD, STÉPHANE
90/1 Panini(QUE) 8
87/8 QUE/GeneralFoods
88/9 QUE
88/9 QUE/GeneralFoods
89/90 QUE
89/90 QUE/GeneralFoods
89/90 QUE/Police
90/1 QUE
90/1 Halifax

GUERASIMOV, KIRIL
79 PaniniSticker 352

GUERIN, BILL
92/3 Classic 105
93/4 Donruss 186
94/5 Donruss 62
95/6 Donruss 35
96/7 Donruss 180
96/7 DonrussElite 69
94/5 Flair 94
96/7 Flair 53
94/5 Fleer 112
92/3 FleerUltra 338
93/4 FleerUltra 359
94/5 FleerUltra 117
95/6 FleerUltra 191, 261
97/8 KatchMedallion 82
93/4 Leaf 7
94/5 Leaf 146
95/6 Leaf 201
96/7 LeafPreferred 108
97/8 Omega 91
92/3 O-Pee-Chee 308
92/3 opcPremier 120
98/9 Pacific 209
97/8 PacificCrown 117
98/9 PacificParamount 86
97/8 PacificRevolution 54
95/6 PaniniSticker 81
96/7 PaniniStickers 83
91/2 Parkhurst 453
92/3 Parkhurst 97
93/4 Parkhurst 382
94/5 Parkhurst 127
95/6 Parkhurst 124
93/4 Pinnacle 305
94/5 Pinnacle 23
95/6 Pinnacle 32
96/7 Pinnacle 170
97/8 Pinnacle 136
96/7 PinnacleBeAPlayer 29
97/8 PinnacleInside 131
96/7 PinnacleZenith 106
95/6 Playoff 58
94/5 POG 350
95/6 POG 166
93/4 Premier 421
94/5 Premier 231
92/3 ProSet 230
92/3 Score 470
93/4 Score 395
95/6 Score 106
96/7 Score 197
97/8 Score 199
97/8 Score(N.J.) 5
96/7 SelectCertified 26
96/7 SkyBoxImpact 68
95/6 SP 82
96/7 SP 91
97/8 SPAuthentic 86
98/9 SPx"Finite" 36
95/6 Summit 111
92/3 Topps 516
95/6 Topps 88
95/6 ToppsFinest 82
96/7 ToppsNHLPicks 141
92/3 ToppsStadiumClub 17
93/4 ToppsStadiumClub 467
95/6 ToppsStadiumClub 130
95/6 ToppsSuperSkills 44
92/3 UpperDeck 411
94/5 UpperDeck 359
95/6 UpperDeck 373, SE48
96/7 UpperDeck 90
97/8 UpperDeck T13C
94/5 UDBeAPlayer-Aut. 50
96/7 UDBlackDiamond 112
97/8 UDBlackDiamond 38
98/9 UDChoice 84
95/6 UDCollChoice 60
96/7 UDCollChoice 146
97/8 UDCollChoice 147, SQ21
96/7 UpperDeck"Ice "35
96/7 N.J/Sharp

GUETENS, VERN
94/5 Erie

GUEVREMONT, JOCELYN
72/3 EddieSargent 222
74/5 LiptonSoup 48
74/5 Loblaws, -Update
71/2 OPC/Topps 232
72/3 OPC 37, Topps 75
73/4 OPC 143
74/5 OPC/Topps 122
75/6 OPC/Topps 216
76/7 OPC/Topps 108
77/8 OPC/Topps 242
78/9 OPC/Topps 94
79/80 O-Pee-Chee 381
71/2 TheTorontoSun
91/2 Trends(72) 35, -Aut
74/5 BUF
71/2 VAN/RoyalBank 4
72/3 VAN/RoyalBank
73/4 VAN/RoyalBank

GUIDA, PETER
95 PaniniWorlds 61

GUIDOLIN, ALDO
45-64 BeeHives(NYR)
53/4 Parkhurst 66
52/3 StLawrence 17
60/1 ClevelandBarons

GUIDOLIN, ARMAND (BEP)
34-43 BeeHives(BOS)
45-64 BeeHives(CHI)
52/3 LavalDairy 114
74/5 OPC/Topps 34
51/2 Parkhurst 42
52/3 StLawrence 65

GUILLAUME, OLIVIER
91/2 SketchQMJHL 248

GUILET, ROBERT
90/1 SketchQMJHL 241
91/2 SketchQMJHL 129
92/3 Fredericton
93/4 Fredericton
88/9 Richelieu

GUILMETTE, YVES
77/8 Kalamazoo

GUINDON, BOB
74/5 opcWHA 26
73/4 QuébecNordiques
77/8 WinnipegJets

GUINN, ROB
95 Classic 96
94/5 Slapshot(Sarnia) 20
95/6 Slapshot 47

GUIRESTANTE, JOHN
93/4 Slapshot(NorthBay) 19
94/5 Slapshot(NorthBay) 22

GUITARD, DEAN
87/8 Sudbury 19

GUITE, PIERRE
75/6 opcWHA 17
76/7 opcWHA 123
75/6 Cincinnati
73/4 Québec

GULA, LADISLAV
94/5 APS 94

GULASH, GARRY
92/3 BCJHL 10

GULDA, PETER
94/5 DEL 262
95/6 DEL 247
96/7 DEL 139
95 Semic 166

GULLIKSEN, RUNE
95 PaniniWorlds 249
92 SemicSticker 42

GULUTZAN, GLEN
90/1 SketchWHL 222
91/2 SketchWHL 112
90/1 Brandon 24
91/2 Saskatoon 13

GUMMERUS, JARMO
71/2 WilliamsFIN 278

GUNLER, JOAKIM
92/3 SemicElitserien 183

GUNN, JIM
83/4 Victoria

GUNN, ROY
84/5 PrinceAlbert
83/4 Victoria

GÜNTNER, MICHAEL
95 PaniniWorlds 258
94 Semic 234
93 SemicSticker 276

GUNVILLE, RON
89/90 Lethbridge

GUOLLA, STEPHEN
97/8 PacificCC 281
97/8 PcfcDynag! 112,-Tandm 66
97/8 PacificInvincible 126
97/8 UpperDeck 148
97/8 UDCollChoice 220
96/7 S.J/PacificBellSheet
93/4 Mich.State

GUREN, MIROSLAV
94/5 APS 186
95/6 APS 35
94/5 Signature 56
94/5 SP 154
96/7 Fredericton

GUSAROV, ALEXEI
91/2 Bowman 145
94/5 Donruss 216
92/3 FleerUltra 173
91 IFiodorovSportUnites
95 Globe 168
94/5 Leaf 408
96/7 Maggers 42
92/3 O-Pee-Chee 389
91/2 OPC/Topps 355
97/8 PacificRegime 52
91/2 PaniniSticker 260
92/3 PaniniSticker 215
96/7 PaniniSticker 254
97/8 PaniniSticker 207
91/2 Parkhurst 364
93/4 Parkhurst 441
94/5 ParkieSE 148
91/2 Pinnacle 230
92/3 Pinnacle 161
93/4 Pinnacle 261
94/5 Pinnacle 164
97/8 PinnacleBeAPlayer 196
93/4 PowerPlay 420
93/4 Premier 293
91/2 ProSet 207
92/3 ProSet 147
91/2 PSPlatinum 221
91/2 RedAce
91/2 Score(CDN) 356, (U.S) 326
92/3 Score 264
93/4 Score 260
94 Semic 159
89 SemicSticker 82
92 SemicSticker 105
87/8 SovietStars
89/90 SovietStars
91/2 ToppsStadiumClub 330
92/3 ToppsStadiumClub 451
93/4 ToppsStadiumClub 424
94/5 ToppsStadiumClub 67
91/2 UpperDeck 365
92/3 UpperDeck 127
93/4 UpperDeck 362
91/2 QUE/PetroCanada
92/3 QUE/PetroCanada
94/5 QUE/BurgerKing

GUSEV, ALEKSANDR
72 Hellas 62
74 Hellas 44
74 SemicSticker 30
73/4 Soviet Stars 4
74/5 Soviet Stars 4
91/2 Trends(72) 19
72/3 WilliamsFIN 23
73/4 WilliamsFIN 3

GUSMANOV, RAVIL
94/5 Classic 73, T77
94/5 ParkieSE 205
94/5 Premier 323
94/5 ToppsFinest 107
91/2 UD'CzechWJC 3
94/5 UpperDeck 254

GUSTAFSON, JON
91/2 Richmond 16
92/3 Richmond
93/4 Richmond 20

GUSTAFSSON, BENGT-AKE
80/1 OPC/Topps 222
81/2 O-Pee-Chee 353
82/3 O-Pee-Chee 364
83/4 O-Pee-Chee 370
84/5 OPC 198, Topps 144
86/7 OPC/Topps 59
88/9 OPC/Topps 151
91/2 O-Pee-Chee 2S
82/3 opcSticker 157
84/5 opcSticker 130
88/9 PaniniSticker 371
82/3 Post
89/90 SemicElitserien 89
90/1 SemicElitserien 259
91/2 SemicElitserien 91, 348
92/3 SemicElitserien 116
82 SemicSticker 146
89 SemicSticker 20
91 SemicSticker 45
92 SemicSticker 65
93 SemicSticker 15
83/4 SouhaitsRen.KeyChain
79/80 WSH
80/1 WSH
82/3 WSH
84/5 WSH/PizzaHut
85/6 WSH/PizzaHut
87/8 WSH
87/8 WSH/Kodak
88/9 WSH
88/9 WSH/Smokey

GUSTAFSSON, MAGNUS
90/1 SemicElitserien 220

GUSTAFSSON, PER
94/5 ElitSet 276
95/6 ElitSet 231,-Mga 15,-Face 6
96/7 MetalUniverse 58
97/8 PacificCrown 165
97/8 PaniniSticker 59
97/8 PinnacleBeAPlayer 69
89/90 SemicElitserien 104
90/1 SemicElitserien 106
91/2 SemicElitserien 111
92/3 SemicElitserien 131
96/7 SP 179
96/7 UpperDeck 267
96/7 UDBlackDiamond 40
95/6 udElite 76, 226, 253, NA11
97/8 FLA/WinnDixie

GUSTAFSSON, PETER
89/90 SemicElitserien 46
90/1 SemicElitserien 192
91/2 SemicElitserien 45
92/3 SemicElitserien 70

GUSTAVSON, BEN
95/6 Slapshot 268

GUSTAVSSON, PATRIK
90/1 SemicElitserien 139
91/2 SemicElitserien 195

GUSTAVSSON, PER
95/6 UDCollChoice 343

GUSTAVSSON, PETER
89/90 SemicElitserien 282

GUSTAVSSON, STEFAN
94/5 ElitSet 256
95/6 ElitSet 10
90/1 SemicElitserien 291
95/6 udElite 9
97/8 udSwedish 8

GUSTAVSSON, THOMAS
95/6 ElitSet 225
95/6 udElite 82

GUT, KAREL
95/6 APS 398

GUTTLER, GEORG
94/5 DEL 165
95/6 DEL 155

GUY, KEVAN
90/1 Panini(VAN) 9
89/90 ProCards(IHL) 177
91/2 ProCards 576
90/1 ProSet 545
88/9 VAN/Mohawk
90/1 VAN/Mohawk
82/3 MedicineHat
83/4 MedicineHat 14
85/6 Moncton 16
86/7 Moncton 10

GUY, MARK
89/90 SketchOHL 27
90/1 SketchOHL 133

GUZE, RAY
92/3 BCJHL 120

GYÖRI, ARPAD
94/5 APS 115

GYÖRI, DYLAN
98 BowmanCHL 51
96/7 UpperDeck 381

GYLYWOYCHUK, DWAYNE
90/1 SketchWHL 218
91/2 SketchWHL 210
89/90 Brandon 19
90/1 Brandon 13
92/3 Brandon 8
95/6 Dayton
94/5 Greensboro

H

HAAKANA, KARI
93/4 Sisu 264
94/5 Sisu 121
96/7 Sisu 84

HAAKANA, LEO
65/6 Hellas 84
72/3 WilliamsFIN 172

HAAKE, BERND
94/5 DEL 199
95/6 DEL 194
96/7 DEL 337

HAAKSTAD, JASON
92/3 BCJHL 47

HAANPAA, ARI
91/2 Jyvas-Hyva 27
92/3 Jyvas-Hyva 80
93/4 Jyvas-Hyva 287
91 SemicSticker 13
93/4 Sisu 76
94/5 Sisu 22
95/6 Sisu 320
95/6 SisuLimited 79

HAANPAA, JUKKA
66/7 Champion 36

HAAPAKOSKI, MIKKO
92/3 Jyvas-Hyva 173
94 Semic 6
95 Semic 48
92 SemicSticker 9
93 SemicSticker 49
93/4 Sisu 378

HAAPALA, JUKKA
66/7 Champion 1
70/1 Kuvajulkaisut 227

HAAPALA, MARTTI
71/2 WilliamsFIN 259

HAAPALAINEN, HANNU
74 Hellas 5
70/1 Kuvajulkaisut 241
74 SemicSticker 94
78/9 SM-Liiga 6, 179
77-80 Sportscaster 82-1949
71/2 WilliamsFIN 207
72/3 WilliamsFIN 155
73/4 WilliamsFIN 151

HAAPALAINEN, OLAVI
66/7 Champion 182
72/3 WilliamsFIN 156

HAAPAMAKI, JARI
91/2 Jyvas-Hyva 12
92/3 Jyvas-Hyva 31
93/4 Jyvas-Hyva 51
93/4 Sisu 240
94/5 Sisu 107
95/6 Sisu 19

HAAPANIEMI, HARRI
80/1 Mallasjuoma 80

HAAPANIEMI, MARKKU
80/1 Mallasjuoma 187
78/9 SM-Liiga 215

HAAPANIEMI, MIRO
93/4 Sisu 103
94/5 Sisu 96
95/6 Sisu 210

HAAPSAARI, TOMMI
92/3 Jyvas-Hyva 156
93/4 Jyvas-Hyva 296
93/4 Sisu 67
94/5 Sisu 60
95/6 Sisu 112

HAAS, DAVID
88/9 ProCards(CapeBreton)
89/90 ProCards(AHL) 141
90/1 ProCards 220
91/2 ProCards 224

HAAS, JULIUS
72 Hellas 93
74 Hellas 69
70/1 Kuvajulkaisut 45
72/3 WilliamsFIN 5

HABERT, SIEGFRIED
95 PaniniWorlds 274

HABSCHEID, MARC
90/1 Bowman 228
95/6 DEL 15
89/90 OPC/Topps 151
90/1 OPC/Topps 342
91/2 OPC/Topps 250
89/90 opcSticker 198/54
90/1 PaniniSticker 204
91/2 PaniniSticker 138
90/1 ProSet 437
91/2 ProSet 365
90/1 ScoreTraded 24T
91/2 Score(CDN) 583, (U.S) 33T
92/3 Score 546
90/1 UpperDeck 374
91/2 CGY/IGA
89/90 DET/Caesars
91/2 DET
82/3 EDM/RedRooster
84/5 EDM/RedRooster
88/9 EDM/ActionMagazine 59
88/9 MIN
88/9 MIN/American
93/4 LasVegas
94/5 LasVegas
83/4 Moncton 26
84/5 NovaScotia 14
81/2 Saskatoon 14

HACHBORN, LEN
91/2 ProCards 318
90/1 ProSet 4

HACKETT, JEFF
91/2 Bowman 219
92/3 Bowman 348
93/4 Donruss 61
94/5 Donruss 35
96/7 Donruss 88
97/8 Donruss 116
97/8 DonrussCanadianIce 101
97/8 DonrussPreferred 139
97/8 DonrussPriority 68
96/7 Fleer 147
92/3 FleerUltra 195
97/8 KatchMedallion 34
92/3 Kraft-Disk
93/4 Leaf 319
94/5 Leaf 128
96/7 Leaf 54
97/8 Leaf 32
97/8 Limited 160
97/8 Omega 51
91/2 OPC/Topps 382
92/3 O-Pee-Chee 218
90/1 opcPremier 39
91/2 opcPremier 108
98/9 Pacific 144
97/8 PacificCrown 160,-InThe 4
97/8 PacificCrownRoyale 30
97/8 PacificDynagon! 27
97/8 PcfcD-Stone 5,-Tandem 39
97/8 PacificInvincible 30
97/8 PcfcParamount 44,-Glove 4
98/9 PcfcParamount 48,-Glove 5
97/8 PcfcRevolution 30,-Retm 4
89/90 PaniniSticker 276
91/2 PaniniSticker 240
92/3 PaniniSticker 123
92/3 Parkhurst 162
93/4 Parkhurst 312
95/6 Parkhurst 44
91/2 Pinnacle 119
92/3 Pinnacle 105
93/4 Pinnacle 373
96/7 Pinnacle 110
97/8 Pinnacle 72, -Masks 7
97/8 Pinnacle -GoalieTin 3
96/7 PinnacleBeAPlayer 42
97/8 PinnacleCertified 30
97/8 P.Insid 41,-Stop 8,-Stand 7
93/4 PowerPlay 312
88/9 ProCards(Springfield)
89/90 ProCards(AHL) 236
90/1 ProSet 624
91/2 ProSet 331
92/3 ProSet 171
91/2 PSPlatinum 226
90/1 Score 388
91/2 Score(CDN) 326, 642
91/2 Score(U.S) 367, 92T
92/3 Score 82
93/4 Score 38, 541
96/7 Score 85
97/8 Score 15
98/9 SPx"Finite" 21
92/3 Topps 185
98/9 Topps 93, SB5
92/3 ToppsStadiumClub 108
93/4 ToppsStadiumClub 326
91/2 UpperDeck 58
92/3 UpperDeck 308
95/6 UpperDeck 387
96/7 UpperDeck 30
97/8 UpperDeck 38
98/9 UDChoice 49
96/7 UDCollChoice 54
97/8 UDCollChoice 47
93/4 CHI/Coke
91/2 S.J

HACQUOIL, FRANK
23/4 PaulinsCandy 59

HADAMCZIK, ALOIS
94/5 APS 287
95/6 APS 219

HADFIELD, VICTOR
45-64 BeeHives(NYR)
64-67 BeeHives(NYR)
62 CeramicTiles
64/5 CokeCap NYR-11
65/6 CocaCola
70/1 EddieSargent 126
71/2 EddieSargent 121
72/3 EddieSargent 151
72/3 Letraset 4
74/5 Loblaws
68/9 O-Pee-Chee 171
69/70 OPC/Topps 38
70/1 OPC/Topps 62
71/2 OPC/Topps 9
72/3 OPC 31, 250, 272, -TmCdn
72/3 Topps 61, 110, 132
73/4 OPC 108, Topps 181
74/5 OPC/Topps 65
75/6 OPC/Topps 165
76/7 OPC/Topps 226
94/5 Parkie(64/5) 90
95/6 Parkie(66/7) 98, 133, 138
61/2 ShirriffCoin 97
68/9 ShirriffCoin NYR13
71/2 TheTorontoSun
62/3 Topps 60
63/4 Topps 54
64/5 Topps 62
65/6 Topps 27
66/7 Topps 86, -USATest 19
67/8 Topps 88
68/9 Topps 74
56-66 TorontoStar 63/4, 64/5
91/2 Trends(72) 36, -Aut
91/2 Ultimate(O6) 21, -Aut 21
74/5 PGH

HADRASCHEK, C.
95/6 DEL 36

HAEGGLUND, ROGER
84/5 Fredericton 4

HAELZLE, JASON
92/3 Windsor 4

HAFNER, EDVARD
79 PaniniSticker 398

HAGGERTY, RYAN
95/6 EdgeIce 32

HAGGERTY, SEAN
93/4 Classic 103
95/6 Classic 84
94/5 LeafLimited-USAJrs 6
94/5 SigRookies 51
93/4 Slapshot(Detroit) 21
94/5 Slapshot(Detroit) 23
94/5 Slapshot(MEM) 97
95/6 Slapshot 69, -Promo
94/5 SP 191
94/5 ToppsFinest 119

HAGGROTH, LEN
96 Wien HL10

HAGLSPERGER, J.
95/6 DEL 355

HAGMAN, MATTI
81/2 O-Pee-Chee 113
82/3 O-Pee-Chee 108
81/2 opcSticker 213
82/3 opcSticker 103
79 PaniniSticker 172
80/1 Pepsi Cap
82/3 Post
82 SemicSticker 156
96/7 Sisu 199
78/9 SM-Liiga 39
77-80 Sportscaster 32 -747
92/3 Trends (76) 148, 187
73/4 WilliamsFIN 127
80/1 EDM/Zellers
81/2 EDM/RedRooster (x2)
88/9 EDM/ActionMagazine 58

HAGRENIUS, JONATHAN
92/3 SemicElitserien 309

HAGSTROM, ANDERS
70/1 Kuvajulkaisut 24

HAGSTROM, PETER
92/3 SemicElitserien 122
95/6 udElite DS13

HAIDER, REINHARD
94/5 DEL 29

HAIDY, SAM
82/3 SSMarie
83/4 SSMarie

HAINANEN, JOKKE
95/6 Sisu-Painkillers 1

HAINSWORTH, GEORGE
25-27 Anonymous 1
33/4 Anonymous (V129) 13
34-43 BeeHives(TOR)
33/4 CndGum (V252)
83&87 HallOfFame 187
83 HHOF Postcard (J)
27-32 LaPresse 27/8
33/4 OPC (V304A) 15
55/6 Parkhurst 59
93/4 Parkie(56/7) P2
23/4 PaulinsCandy 39
28/9 MTL/LaPatrie 8
95/6 MTL/Forum 8Nov95

HAISZAN, HERBERT
79 PaniniSticker 309

HAJDU, RICHARD
83/4 Victoria
84/5 Victoria

HAJDUSEK, STANISLAV
82 SemicSticker 81

HAJNOS, JANUSZ
92 SemicSticker 283

HAJT, BILL
75/6 OPC/Topps 233
76/7 OPC/Topps 128
77/8 OPC/Topps 27
78/9 OPC/Topps 109
79/80 OPC/Topps 221
80/1 OPC/Topps 337
83/4 O-Pee-Chee 64
84/5 OPC 21, Topps 17
85/6 OPC/Topps 119
86/7 OPC/Topps 52
84/5 opcSticker 214
85/6 opcSticker 176/45
87/8 PaniniSticker 26
82/3 Post
74/5 BUF
80/1 BUF/Wendt
84/5 BUF/BlueShield
85/6 BUF/BlueShield
86/7 BUF/BlueShield
87/8 BUF/BlueShield
84/5 KelownaWingsWHL 50

HAJT, CHRIS
95/6 Bowman P16
97/8 Bowman 35
98 BowmanCHL 2
95/6 Classic 61, 85
95/6 FutureLegends-SS&D 5
94/5 Slapshot(Guelph) 7
95/6 Slapshot 87, 436
98/9 UDChoice 299
95/6 Guelph 13
96/7 Guelph 7, 35

HAJZER, JANOS
79 PaniniSticker 268

HAKALA, ANTERO
66/7 Champion 212

HAKALA, YRGÖ
66/7 Champion 86
65/6 Hellas 87

HAKAMAKI, PENTTI
72 Panda

HAKANEN, MARKKU
66/7 Champion 193
65/6 Hellas 118
70/1 Kuvajulkaisut 121
72 Panda
71/2 WilliamsFIN 171
72/3 WilliamsFIN 122
73/4 WilliamsFIN 176

HAKANEN, MATTI
70/1 Kuvajulkaisut 122
72 Panda
71/2 WilliamsFIN 172
73/4 WilliamsFIN 242

HAKANEN, REIJO
66/7 Champion 202
65/6 Hellas 128
70/1 Kuvajulkaisut 123
72 Panda
71/2 WilliamsFIN 173
73/4 WilliamsFIN 177

HAKANEN, TIMO
95/6 Sisu 366, -NHLDraft 9
96/7 Sisu 159
95/6 UDCollChoice 327

HAKANSSON, ANDERS
84/5 O-Pee-Chee 85
83/4 PGH/Heinz
84/5 L.A
81/2 MIN

HAKANSSON, JONAS
91/2 SemicElitserien 199
92/3 SemicElitserien 216

HAKANSSON, MIKAEL
94/5 ElitSet 208
95/6 ElitSet 106
93/4 Parkhurst 539
91/2 SemicElitserien 329
92/3 SemicElitserien 94
95/6 udElite 164

HAKKARAINEN, ESA
80/1 Mallasjuoma 112
78/9 SM-Liiga 156
73/4 WilliamsFIN 307

HAKSTOL, DAVE
92/3 Indianapolis

HAKULINEN, MARKKU
82 SemicSticker 47
78/9 SM-Liiga 126
77-80 Sportscaster 82-1955

HAKULINEN, YRGÖ
80/1 Mallasjuoma 83
78/9 SM-Liiga 128
77-80 Sportscaster 82-1955
71/2 WilliamsFIN 260

HALA, JIRI
94/5 APS 96

HALAUCA, ALEXANDRU
79 PaniniSticker 315

HALE, LARRY
70/1 EddieSargent 155
71/2 EddieSargent 154
72/3 OPC 53, Topps 44
71/2 TheTorontoSun
75/6 Houston

HALEY, MIKE
95/6 Spokane 17

HALFNIGHT, ASHLEY
93/4 Donruss-Juniors USA8
93/4 Pinnacle 482

HALIFAX, SEAN
93/4 RedDeer

HALKIDIS, BOB
89/90 ProCards(AHL) 270
92/3 ProSet 190
85/6 BUF/BlueShield
86/7 BUF/BlueShield
88/9 BUF/BlueShield
88/9 BUF/WonderBread
95/6 T.B/SkyBoxSportsCafe
90/1 TOR/P.L.A.Y. 27

HALL, BILL
91/2 SketchOHL 297
92/3 Ottawa67s

HALL, CHRIS
93/4 Slapshot(Oshawa) 23
94/5 Slapshot(MEM) 53

HALL, DEAN
89/90 Johnstown 28

HALL, DEL
76/7 opcWHA 78
75/6 Phoenix
76/7 Phoenix

HALL, GLENN
45-64 BeeHives(CHI), (DET)
64-67 BeeHives(CHI)
62 CeramicTiles
63-5 ChexPhoto
64/5 CokeCap CHI-1
65/6 CocaCola
62/3 EdProductoDisk
83&87 HallOfFame 114
83 HHOF Postcard (H)
96/7 HHOFLegends 88
68/9 OPC/Topps 111
68/9 OPC 215, -Puck 13
69/70 OPC/Topps 12
69/70 OPC 207, 211, -Stamp
70/1 OPC 210,OPC/T-Deckle 27
93/4 Parkie(56/7) 141, 152
94/5 Parkie(64/5) 32, 133
95/6 Parkie(66/7) 121, 147, TW6
66/7 Post-Large, -Small
72 SemicSticker 187
60/1 ShirriffCoin 61
61/2 ShirriffCoin 29
62/3 ShirriffCoin 49
68/9 ShirriffCoin St5
91/2 StarPics 52
57/8 Topps 20
58/9 Topps 13
59/60 Topps 28, 32
60/1 Topps 25
61/2 Topps 22, 32, 44, -Stamp
62/3 Topps 24, -Buck
63/4 Topps 23
64/5 Topps 12, 110
65/6 Topps 55
66/7 Topps 54, 126
67/8 Topps 65, 129
54-67 TorontoStar 65/6, V6, V10
56-66 TorontoStar 59/60, 61/2
56-66 TorontoStar 63/4, 64/5
63/4 TheTorontoStar
64/5 TheTorontoStar
85/6 Arizona
92/3 STL/UpperDeck 1

HALL, JASON
90/1 Rayside
91/2 Rayside

HALL, JOE
91 C55 Reprint 2
83&87 HallOfFame 97
83 HHOF Postcard (G)
1911-12 Imperial (C55) 2
1912-13 Imperial (C57) 16
1910-11 Imperial Post 2
95/6 MTL/Forum 14Oct95

HALL, MURRAY
45-64 BeeHives(CHI)
64-67 BeeHives(CHI), (DET)
70/1 EddieSargent 224
71/2 EddieSargent 211
72/3 EddieSargent 212
70/1 OPC/Topps 118
71/2 OPC/Topps 109
72/3 O-Pee-Chee 294
73/4 QuakerOats 14
71/2 TheTorontoSun
62/3 Topps 43
66/7 Topps 105
75/6 Houston
70/1 VAN/RoyalBank
71/2 VAN/RoyalBank 3

HALL, RANDY
89/90 SketchOHL 132
90/1 SketchOHL 74
91/2 SketchOHL 210
93/4 Slapshot(NiagaraFalls) 26

HALL, SCOTT
92/3 BCJHL 219

HALL, TAYLOR
84/5 VAN
85/6 VAN
86/7 VAN
86/7 Fredericton
81/2 Regina 15
82/3 Regina 19
83/4 Regina 19

HALL, TODD
91/2 UpperDeck, 'CzechWJC 77

HALL, TAYLOR
90/1 ProCards 303

HALLBACK, MATHIAS
94/5 ElitSet 241
92/3 SemicElitserien 98

HALLER, KEVIN
91/2 Bowman 28
92/3 Bowman 301
93/4 Donruss 168
92/3 FleerUltra 327
93/4 FleerUltra 352
93/4 Leaf 223
94/5 Leaf 371
91/2 OPC/Topps 473
92/3 O-Pee-Chee 290
97/8 PacificRegime 36
93/4 Parkhurst 376
94/5 Parkhurst 120
95/6 Parkhurst 430
94/5 ParkieSE 126
91/2 Pinnacle 307
92/3 Pinnacle 211
93/4 Pinnacle 193
94/5 Pinnacle 373
97/8 PinnacleBeAPlayer 98
95/6 Playoff 292
93/4 PowerPlay 370
93/4 Premier 339
94/5 Premier 351
90/1 ProCards 265
91/2 ProSet 525
91/2 PSPlatinum 250
91/2 Score(CDN) 276, (U.S) 386
92/3 Score 159
93/4 Score 268
95/6 Topps 178
92/3 Topps 445
91/2 ToppsStadiumClub 382
92/3 ToppsStadiumClub 38
93/4 ToppsStadiumClub 53
91/2 UpperDeck 192
92/3 UpperDeck 479
93/4 UpperDeck 333
94/5 UpperDeck 144
95/6 UpperDeck 357
97/8 UpperDeck 242
93/4 UDBeAPlayer 23
94/5 UDBeAPlayer R56, -Aut. 56
95/6 UDCollChoice 295
91/2 BUF/BlueShield
91/2 BUF/Campbell
92/3 MTL
92/3 MTL/OPC 8
93/4 MTL
93/4 MTL/Molson
94/5 PHA
88/9 Regina

HALLILA, JARI
72/3 WilliamsFIN 342

HALLIN, MATS
83/4 O-Pee-Chee 8
83/4 opcSticker 184
90/1 SemicElitserien 137
91/2 SemicElitserien 187
85/6 MIN
83/4 NYI
83/4 NYI/Islander 8
84/5 NYI 7
81/2 Indianapolis 8
82/3 Indianapolis

HALLOWAY, BRUCE
83/4 Fredericton 13
84/5 Fredericton 3

HALME, ILKKA
65/6 Hellas 119

HALME, JARI
91/2 Jyvas-Hyva 55
94/5 Sisu 37

HALONEN, MARKO
93/4 Jyvas-Hyva 205
93/4 Sisu 262

HALONEN, MIKKO
93/4 Jyvas-Hyva 208
93/4 Sisu 275
94/5 Sisu 172

HALTIA, PATRIK
94/5 ElitSet 215, -NHLDraft 7
94/5 ElitSet-RookieRockets 8
95/6 ElitSet 39, -Spidermen 5
90/1 SemicElitserien 250
91/2 SemicElitserien 81
92/3 SemicElitserien 103

HALTTUNEN, NIKO
94/5 ParkieSE 220
95/6 Sisu 51
94/5 ToppsFinest 132

HALVERSON, CHRIS
95/6 Halifax

HALVERSON, DON
95/6 PrinceAlbert

HALVERSON, TREVOR
91/2 Arena 16
91/2 Classic 18
91/2 ClassicFourSport 18, -Aut
91/2 ProCards 555
89/90 SketchOHL 157
90/1 SketchOHL 308
91/2 StarPics 14
91/2 UltimateDP 17, 73, -Aut 73
91/2 Baltimore 3
94/5 Hampton 7
95/6 Hampton HRA -16
96/7 Portland

HALWARD, DOUG
86/7 Kraft Sports 64
76/7 O-Pee-Chee 306
78/9 O-Pee-Chee 392
80/1 OPC/Topps 207
81/2 O-Pee-Chee 335
83/4 O-Pee-Chee 351
84/5 O-Pee-Chee 320
85/6 O-Pee-Chee 189
86/7 O-Pee-Chee 248
88/9 OPC/Topps 113
83/4 opcSticker 278
84/5 opcSticker 278
85/6 opcSticker 243 /110
86/7 opcSticker 97 /227
82/3 Post
83/4 SouhaitsRen.KeyChain
83/4 Vachon 108
86/7 DET/Caesars
87/8 DET
88/9 DET/Caesars
88/9 EDM
88/9 EDM/ActionMagazine 157
80/1 L.A.
81/2 VAN
81/2 VAN/Silverwood
82/3 VAN
83/4 VAN
84/5 VAN
85/6 VAN

HAMAL, DENNIS
97/8 Bowman 70

HÄMÄLÄINEN, ERIK
95/6 ElitSet 163
95 Hartwall
91/2 Jyvas-Hyva 36
92/3 Jyvas-Hyva 60
93/4 Jyvas-Hyva 106
95 PaniniWorlds 164
95 Semic 4
93/4 Sisu 12, 362, 374
94/5 Sisu 98
95/6 Sisu 178, -GoldCards 5
95/6 udElite 2
97/8 udSwedish 3
96 Wien 4
95 SuomenBeckett 4

HAMALAINEN, JARKKO
92/3 Jyvas-Hyva 95, 149
93/4 Jyvas-Hyva 265
93/4 Sisu 287

HAMALAINEN, J.H.
71/2 WilliamsFIN 319

HAMALAINEN, J.P.
71/2 WilliamsFIN 320

HAMALAINEN, TERO
95/6 Sisu 209

HAMALAINEN, TOMMI
93/4 Sisu 90
95/6 Sisu 218
96/7 Sisu 14, -Energy 4
94/5 ToppsFinest 140

HAMAN, RADEK
95/6 APS 215

HAMEL, GILLES
84/5 O-Pee-Chee 22
87/8 O-Pee-Chee 218
85/6 opcSticker 185/59
87/8 opcSticker253/144
87/8 PaniniSticker 366
88/9 ProCards(Moncton)
84/5 BUF/BlueShield
85/6 BUF/BlueShield
88/9 L.A.
88/9 L.A./Smokeys
86/7 WPG
87/8 WPG

HAMEL, JEAN
82? JDMcCarthy
74/5 Loblaws
74/5 O-Pee-Chee 383
75/6 OPC/Topps 257
76/7 O-Pee-Chee 340
77/8 O-Pee-Chee 348
78/9 O-Pee-Chee 281
79/80 OPC/Topps 262
81/2 O-Pee-Chee 97
84/5 O-Pee-Chee 263
81/2 opcSticker 143
84/5 opcSticker 158
88/9 ProCards(Sherbrooke)
89/90 ProCards(AHL) 201
91/2 SketchQMJHL 294
93/4 Slapshot(Drum.) 25
83/4 Vachon 45
79/80 DET
80/1 DET
82/3 QUE
83/4 QUE
72/3 STL
73/4 STL
83/4 MTL
84/5 MTL

HAMEL, PIERRE
80/1 OPC/Topps 205
81/2 O-Pee-Chee 365
80/1 Pepsi Cap
79/80 WPG
80/1 WPG

HAMELIN, HUGO
91/2 SketchQMJHL 101

HAMELIN, RICHARD
90/1 SketchQMJHL 187
91/2 SketchQMJHL 56

HAMILL, RED
34-43 BeeHives(BOS)
45-64 BeeHives(CHI)

HAMILTON, AL
70/1 EddieSargent 22
71/2 EddieSargent 23
68/9 O-Pee-Chee 70
69/70 O-Pee-Chee 192
79/80 O-Pee-Chee 355
71/2 OPC/Topps 49
74/5 opcWHA 29
75/6 opcWHA 49
76/7 opcWHA 97
77/8 opcWHA 40
73/4 QuakerOats 16
72/3 7ElevenCups
71/2 TheTorontoSun
79/80 EDM
88/9 EDM/ActionMagazine 63

HAMILTON, DAVE
91/2 SketchWHL 51

HAMILTON, GORD
94/5 Slapshot(Sarnia) 28

HAMILTON, GORD
82/3 Ottawa67s
83/4 Ottawa67s

HAMILTON, HUGH
97/8 Bowman 84
94/5 ParkieSE 253
94/5 SigRookies 16
96/7 UpperDeck"Ice" 124
95/6 Spokane 3

HAMILTON, JACK
52/3 LavalDairy 65
52/3 StLawrence 101

HAMILTON, JIM
77/8 PGH/PuckBuck
83/4 PGH

HAMILTON, REGINALD
34-43 BeeHives(TOR)
37/8 OPC (V304E) 137
39/40 OPC (V301-1) 1
40/1 OPC (V301-2) 119
38/9 QuakerOats

HAMM, TRENT
91/2 AirCanadaSJHL 6, C14

HAMMARSTROM, INGE
72 Hellas 37
74/5 Loblaws
74/5 OPC/Topps 88
75/6 OPC/Topps 168
76/7 O-Pee-Chee 358
77/8 O-Pee-Chee 320
78/9 OPC/Topps 174
72 Panda
72 SemicSticker 61
71/2 WilliamsFIN 44
72/3 WilliamsFIN 44
73/4 WilliamsFIN 26
78/9 STL
73/4 TOR
74/5 TOR
75/6 TOR
76/7 TOR
77/8 TOR

HAMMARSTROM, PETER
94/5 ElitSet 88
95/6 ElitSet 52
89/90 SemicElitserien 18
90/1 SemicElitserien 90
91/2 SemicElitserien 14
92/3 SemicElitserien 38
95/6 udElite 85
97/8 udSwedish 12

HAMMER, ROLF
94/5 DEL 189
95/6 DEL 189
96/7 DEL 128

HAMMOND, KEN
92/3 Parkhurst 358
89/90 ProCards(AHL) 129
90/1 ProCards 141
91/2 ProSet 484
92/3 PS-Parkhurst PV4

91/2 ScoreCDN 647, 97T
88/9 EDM/ActionMagazine 52
91/2 S.J

HAMMOND, SCOTT
82/3 Ottawa67s
83/4 Ottawa67s

HAMPEIS, LADA
93/4 Tacoma

HAMPSON, TED
45-64 BeeHives(NYR), (TOR)
64-67 BeeHives(DET)
62 CeramicTiles
70/1 EddieSargent 137
71/2 EddieSargent 94
74/5 Loblaws
68/9 OPC/Topps 85
69/70 OPC/Topps 86
69/70 OPC-Sticker, -Stamp
70/1 OPC 190
71/2 OPC/Topps 101
59/60 Parkhurst 34
95/6 Parkie(66/7) 47
73/4 QuakerOats 4
72 SemicSticker 176
60/1 ShirriffCoin 98
61/2 ShirriffCoin 92
68/9 ShirriffCoin OAK3
71/2 TheTorontoSun
61/2 Topps 59
62/3 Topps 55
67/8 Topps 108
72/3 Minnesota
74/5 Minnesota
63/4 York 52

HAMPTON, RICK
74/5 O-Pee-Chee 329
75/6 OPC/Topps 65
76/7 OPC/Topps 113, OPC 383
77/8 OPC/Topps 63
78/9 OPC/Topps 174
79/80 O-Pee-Chee 330
79 PaniniSticker 54

HAMR, RADEK
95/6 APS 276
92/3 ClassicProspects 142
93/4 ClassicProspects 87
93/4 Leaf 265
93/4 Parkhurst 143
93/4 Score 476
93/4 UpperDeck 34
92/3 OTT

HAMRLIK, MARTIN
91/2 Classic 27
91/2 ClassicFourSport 27
92/3 ClassicProspects 62
91/2 StarPics 18

HAMRLIK, ROMAN
96/7 Aces 3 (Spades)
95/6 Bowman 82
92/3 Classic 1, 60, LP1, 'Promo
93/4 Classic 120
92/3 C'FourSport 151,BC7,LP22
92/3 C'FourSport-Preview, -Aut.
92/3 ClassicProspects 50, BC3
92/3 CSC 5
93/4 Donruss 327
94/5 Donruss 128
95/6 Donruss 256
96/7 Donruss 84, -HitList 16
97/8 Donruss 112
96/7 DonrussCanadianIce 44
97/8 DonrussCanadianIce 123
95/6 DonrussElite 36
96/7 DonrussElite 23
97/8 DonrussElite 94
97/8 DonrussPreferred 141
97/8 DonrussPriority 120
97/8 DonrussStudio 75
93/4 EASports 128
97/8 EssoOlympic 53
96/7 Flair 88
94/5 Fleer 207
96/7 Fleer 104
95/6 FleerMetal 137, -IntSteel 7
92/3 FleerUltra 201, -Imports 4
93/4 FleerUltra 108
94/5 FleerUltra 206
95/6 FleerUltra 152, -RisingStr 3
96/7 FU-Blue 4, -Power 6
96/7 F.Picks-Dream 6, -Fab 16
95 Globe149
97/8 KatchMedallion 135
93/4 Leaf 151
94/5 Leaf 132
95/6 Leaf 295
96/7 Leaf 118
97/8 Leaf 76
95/6 LeafLimited 33
96/7 LeafLimited 4
97/8 Limited 146
96/7 LeafPreferred 90,-Steel 44
96/7 MetalUniverse 145
97/8 Omega 92
92/3 opcPremier 46, -TopRook 2
98/9 Pacific 219
97/8 PacificCrown 100
97/8 PacificCrownRoyale 125
97/8 PcfcDynag! 118,-Tandm 61
97/8 PacificInvincible 132
97/8 PacificParamount 173
98/9 PacificParamount 87
97/8 PacificRevolution 53
94/5 PaniniSticker 188
95/6 PaniniSticker 133
96/7 PaniniSticker 123
97/8 PaniniSticker 101
95 PaniniWorlds 192
92/3 Parkhurst 173, 443
93/4 Parkhurst 190, F2
94/5 Parkhurst V53
95/6 Parkhurst 198, PP25
94/5 ParkieSE 171
92/3 Pinnacle 408
93/4 Pinnacle 34, -Tm2001 18
94/5 Pinnacle 123
95/6 Pinnacle 59
96/7 Pinnacle 113, 178
97/8 PinnacleBeAPlayer 147
95/6 PinnacleFANtasy 11
97/8 PinnacleInside 162
96/7 PinnacleZenith 92
95/6 Playoff 310
96/7 Playoff 416
95/6 POG 255
93/4 PowerPlay 231
93/4 Premier 281, 323, -Finest 2
94/5 Premier 54
95/6 ProMagnet 67
93/4 Score 131
94/5 Score 48
95/6 Score 185
96/7 Score 127
97/8 Score 214
95/6 SelectCertified 20
96/7 SelectCertified 48
93 SemicSticker 101
95/6 SkyBoxEmotion 164
95/6 SkyBoxImpact 155
96/7 SkyBoxImpact 122
94/5 SP 112
95/6 SP 135, E25
96/7 SP 144, HC22
97/8 SPAuthentic 149
96/7 SPx 42
95/6 Summit 56
96/7 Summit 132
95/6 SuperSticker 112, DC20
96/7 TeamOut
95/6 Topps 193, YS13
95/6 ToppsFinest 93
96/7 ToppsNHLPicks 35, FT9
93/4 ToppsStadiumClub 75
95/6 ToppsStadiumClub 89
95 TSC'Members 11
95/6 TSCMembers 37
97/8 ToppsSticker 2
91/2 UD'CzechWJC 88
92/3 UD555, 631, CC8, ER11
93/4 UpperDeck 158, SP-151
94/5 UpperDeck 174, SP164
95/6 UD 152, AS8, H39, SE76
96/7 UD 153, 367, SS13A, X8
97/8 UpperDeck 157, 363, SG47
94/5 UDBeAPlayer R9
95/6 UDBeAPlayer 133
96/7 UDBlackDiamond 143
97/8 UDBlackDiamond 142
98/9 UDChoice 80
95/6 UDCC 92
96/7 UDCC 244, 331, S18,UD25
96/7 UDCC'Oversize 244
97/8 UDCC 240, SQ44
96/7 UpperDeck"Ice" 102
92/3 T.B./Sheraton
94/5 T.B./SkyBoxSportsCafe
95/6 T.B.
95/6 T.B./SkyBoxSportsCafe

HANAS, TREVOR
91/2 SketchWHL 218
93/4 Saskatoon

HANCOCK, QUINN
98 BowmanCHL 57

HAND, TONY
94 Semic 323
95/6 SheffieldSteelers
97/8 SheffieldSteelers

HANDRIK, JÖRG
95/6 DEL 259
96/7 DEL 147
95 PaniniWorlds 69

HANDY, RON
88/9 ProCards(Indianpolis)
89/90 ProCards(IHL) 140
90/1 ProCards 582
91/2 ProCards 513
90/1 KansasCity 5
95/6 Louisiana, -Playoffs
92/3 Peoria
80/1 SSMarie

HANEY, MERV
91/2 SketchWHL 251
91/2 PrinceAlbert
93/4 PrinceAlbert

HANFT, JÖRG
95/6 DEL 271
89 SemicSticker 111

HANGSLEBEN, ALAN
79/80 O-Pee-Chee 307
81/2 O-Pee-Chee 354
81/2 opcSticker 197
80/1 WSH

HANIG, GUS
72 Hellas 53
72 SemicSticker 108

HANISZ, ANDRZEI
94/5 DEL 361
89 SemicSticker 129
92 SemicSticker 267

HANKELA, TIMO
93/4 Jyvas-Hyva 284
93/4 Sisu 59

HANKINSON, BEN
93/4 Pinnacle 210
91/2 ProCards 413
95/6 T.B/SkyBoxSportsCafe
95/6 Adirondack

HANKINSON, CAREY
95/6 DonrussElite-WorldJrs 36

HANKINSON, PETER
90/1 ProCards 254, 547
91/2 ProCards 239
90/1 Moncton

HANLEY, BILL
87 HallOfFame 251

HANLEY, TIM
89/90 ProCards(AHL) 238

HANLON, GLEN
79/80 O-Pee-Chee 337
80/1 OPC/Topps 141
81/2 O-Pee-Chee 336
84/5 OPC 142, Topps 106
85/6 OPC/Topps 149
87/8 OPC/Topps 89
88/9 OPC/Topps 150
89/90 OPC/Topps 144
90/1 OPC/Topps 266
87/8 opcStars 14
81/2 opcSticker 245
84/5 opcSticker 98
85/6 opcSticker 87/220
87/8 opcSticker 109/242
80/1 opcSuperCard 22
87/8 PaniniSticker 238
88/9 PaniniSticker 36
89/90 PaniniSticker 65
90/1 PaniniSticker 203
90/1 ProCards 305
90/1 ProSet 72
90/1 Score 228
83/4 SouhaitsRen.KeyChain
90/1 UpperDeck 395
86/7 DET/Caesars
87/8 DET
88/9 DET
88/9 DET/Caesars
89/90 DET/Caesars
78/9 VAN/RoyalBank
79/80 VAN
80/1 VAN
80/1 VAN/Silverwood
81/2 VAN
81/2 VAN/Silverwood

HANLON, JAMES
94/5 DEL 244
95/6 DEL 229
96/7 DEL 80

HANNA, JOHN B.
88/9 ProCards(CapeBreton)
83/4 Ottawa67s
84/5 Ottawa67s

HANNA, JOHN
45-64 BeeHives(MTL)
64-67 BeeHives(MTL)
60/1 ShirriffCoin 85
58/9 Topps 7
59/60 Topps 31, 53
72/3 Cleveland
63/4 QuébecAces
65/6 QuébecAces

HANNAN, DAVE
91/2 Bowman 155
83/4 O-Pee-Chee 281
89/90 O-Pee-Chee 257
90/1 O-Pee-Chee 449
91/2 OPC/Topps 360
90/1 Panini(TOR) 8
87/8 PaniniSticker 154
91/2 Pinnacle 413
94/5 Pinnacle 446
94/5 Premier 118
90/1 ProSet 535
91/2 Score(CDN) 241
92/3 Score 538
83/4 SouhaitRen.KeyChain
91/2 ToppsStadiumClub 220
93/4 ToppsStadiumClub 47
91/2 UpperDeck 312
92/3 BUF/BlueShield
87/8 EDM
88/9 EDM/ActionMagazine 83
96/7 OTT/PizzaHut
83/4 PGH
83/4 PGH/Heinz
86/7 PGH/Kodak
90/1 TOR/P.L.A.Y. 8

HANNIGAN, GORD
45-64 BeeHives(TOR)
53/4 Parkhurst 3
54/5 Parkhurst 27
45-54 QuakerOats

HANNIGAN, PAT
61/2 ShirriffCoin 83
68/9 ShirriffCoin PHA12
61/2 Topps 58
62/3 Topps 64

HANNON, BRIAN
94/5 DEL 170
95/6 DEL 120
89/90 ProCards(IHL) 136

HANSCH, RANDY
90/1 ProCards 490
83/4 Victoria
84/5 Victoria

HANSEN, BEN
79 PaniniSticker 363

HANSEN, KEVIN
95/6 Slapshot 388
96/7 Sudbury 12

HANSEN, RICK
91/2 PSPlatinum 296

HANSEN, RONNY
89/90 SemicElitserien 261
90/1 SemicElitserien 169

HANSEN, TAVIS
95/6 EdgeIce 69
95/6 Leaf 214
93/4 Tacoma

HANSIS, RON
94/5 Erie

HANSON, DAVE
82/3 Indianapolis

HANSON, DEVON
93/4 Saskatoon

HANSON, KEITH
84/5 Moncton 16

HANSON, MICHAEL
95/6 Slapshot 342

HANSSON, JOHAN
97/8 udSwedish 21

HANSSON, ROGER
96/7 DEL 236
94/5 ElitSet 207, -Gold 20
95/6 ElitSet 93
95 Globe 32
95 PaniniWorlds 158
95 Semic 65
91/2 SemicElitserien 194
92/3 SemicElitserien 211
93 SemicSticker 18
95/6 udElite 144

HANTSCHKE, RALF
94/5 DEL 263
91 SemicSticker 169

HANUS, TIM
93/4 Johnstown 8

HANUSCH, TORSTEN
94/5 DEL 129
95/6 DEL 127

HANZAWA, TSUTOMU
79 PaniniSticker 291

HANZLIK, JIRI
95/6 APS 248

HARALDSEN, HARRY
79 PaniniSticker 299

HARBARUK, NICK
70/1 EddieSargent 172
71/2 EddieSargent 171
72/3 EddieSargent 171
71/2 OPC/Topps 191
72/3 OPC 105
75/6 opcWHA 11
71/2 TheTorontoSun
71/2 PGH
73/4 STL

HARD, V.P.
92/3 Jyvas-Hyva 82
93/4 Jyvas-Hyva 141
93/4 Sisu 141
94/5 Sisu 36
95/6 Sisu 341

HARDER, GRAHAM
91/2 AvantGardeBCJ 21
92/3 BCJHL 67

HARDER, MIKE
91/2 AirCanadaSJHL C35
92/3 MPSPhotoSJHL 145

HARDING, JEFF
88/9 ProCards(Hershey)

HARDING, MICHAEL
90/1 SketchOHL 360
91/2 SketchOHL 136
93/4 Slapshot(Detroit) 12
93/4 Slapshot(Pet.) 5, 28
91/2 Peterborough 6

HARDY, BRUCE
94/5 DEL 73
95/6 DEL 136

HARDY, DAMON
93/4 Slapshot(Oshawa) 7
94/5 Slapshot(Sarnia) 23

HARDY, JOE
72/3 ClevelandCrusaders

HARDY, MARK
92/3 FleerUltra 354
93/4 FleerUltra 343
82/3 O-Pee-Chee 155
83/4 O-Pee-Chee 155
84/5 O-Pee-Chee 86
89/90 O-Pee-Chee 252
91/2 OPC/Topps 406
84/5 opcSticker 272
85/6 opcSticker 234/102
87/8 PaniniSticker 275
91/2 Pinnacle 420
92/3 Pinnacle 220
90/1 ProSet 489
91/2 ProSet 442
90/1 ScoreTraded 104T
91/2 Score(CDN) 453
92/3 Score 247
93/4 Score 415
83/4 SouhaitsRen.KeyChain
93/4 ToppsStadiumClub 414
90/1 UpperDeck 416
84/5 L.A.
87/8 L.A.
88/9 MIN
88/9 MIN/American
89/90 NYR/MarineMidland
93/4 Phoenix

HARGRAVES, JIM
72/3 VAN/RoyalBank

HARILA, KARI
92/3 Jyvas-Hyva 174
93/4 Jyvas-Hyva 325
94 Semic 9
93 SemicSticker 50
93/4 Sisu 36
95/6 Sisu 125

HARJU, ERKKI
65/6 Hellas 45

HARJU, MATTI
66/7 Champion 24
65/6 Hellas 70
70/1 Kuvajulkaisut 103

HARJU, PENTTI
66/7 Champion 116

HARJUMAKI, JARI
93/4 Sisu 62

HARKANEN, TIMO
80/1 Mallasjuoma 72

HARKINS, BRETT
94/5 Classic-Autograph
93/4 ClassicProspects 221
95/6 Leaf 303
97/8 PacificRegime 12

HARKINS, TODD
92/3 Classic 113
90/1 ProCards 624
91/2 ProCards 589
93/4 UpperDeck 80

HARKINS, TIM
71/2 WilliamsFIN 321

HARLOCK, DAVE
93/4 ClassicProspects LP13
93/4 CanadaNats
93/4 Donruss 496
93/4 FleerUltra 461
93/4 PowerPlay 481
94/5 Score CT15
94 Semic 102
90/1 UpperDeck 470

HARLOW, SCOTT
88/9 ProCards(Peoria)
89/90 ProCards(AHL) 66
90/1 ProCards 421

HARMER, DUANE
91/2 SketchOHL 345
93/4 Slapshot(Detroit) 18
93/4 Slapshot(Guelph) 8
94/5 Slapshot(Detroit) 21
94/5 Slapshot(MEM) 95

HARMON, GLEN
45-64 BeeHives(MTL)
51/2 LavalDairy 86
52/3 LavalDairy 86
43-47 ParadeSportive
45-54 QuakerO. 20A, 20B, 20C
52/3 StLawrence 2

HARPER, DEREK
91/2 AvantGardeBCJHL 76
92/3 BCJHL 87, 90

HARPER, KELLY
94/5 Huntington 13

HARPER, TERRY
45-64 BeeHives(MTL)
64-67 BeeHives(MTLx2)
63-5 ChexPhoto
64/5 CokeCap MTL-19
65/6 CocaCola
70/1 EddieSargent 111
71/2 EddieSargent 107
72/3 EddieSargent 96
74/5 Loblaws
92/3 MPSPhotoSJHL 74
68/9 OPC/Topps 57
69/70 O-Pee-Chee 164
70/1 OPC/Topps 53
71/2 OPC/Topps 59
72/3 OPC 172, Topps 119
73/4 OPC/Topps 80
74/5 OPC/Topps 55
75/6 OPC/Topps 255
76/7 OPC/Topps 262
77/8 OPC/Topps 16
78/9 OPC/Topps 214
63/4 Parkhurst 32, 91
94/5 Parkie(64/5) 83
95/6 Parkie(66/7) 66, 148
68/9 Post Marble
68/9 ShirriffCoin MTL12
71/2 TheTorontoSun
64/5 Topps 3
65/6 Topps 68
66/7 Topps 68
67/8 Topps 6
63/4 York 31
67/8 York 33, no# (x2)
66/7 MTL/IGAStamp
67/8 MTL
67/8 MTL/IGA
68/9 MTL/IGA
69/70 MTL/ProStar
70/1 MTL
71/2 MTL
71 MTL/Pins

HARPER, WARREN
88/9 ProCards(Hershey)

HARRIGAN, JERRY
93/4 OwenSound

HARRINGTON, HUGO
25-27 Anonymous 36

HARRINGTON, JOHN
94/5 MiracleOnIce 13-14
79/80 USAOlympicTeam 3

HARRIS, BILLY E. (HINKY)
45-64 BeeHives(TOR)
64-67 BeeHives(DET), (TORx2)
62 CeramicTiles
63-5 ChexPhoto
68/9 OPC/Topps 80
55/6 Parkhurst 20
57/8 Parkhurst (TOR) 15
58/9 Parkhurst 4
59/60 Parkhurst 9
60/1 Parkhurst 15
61/2 Parkhurst 15
62/3 Parkhurst 1
63/4 Parkhurst 11, 71
93/4 Parkhurst63 PR39
93/4 Parkie(56/7) 129
94/5 Parkie(64/5) 126
60/1 ShirriffCoin 8
61/2 ShirriffCoin 54
62/3 ShirriffCoin 13
68/9 ShirriffCoin OAK4
54-67 TorontoStar V7
56-66 TorontoStar 58/9
64/5 TheTorontoStar
64/5 Topps 27
65/6 Topps 53
91/2 Ultimate(O6) 35, -Aut 35
60/1 York
61/2 York 15
62/3 YorkTransfer 26
63/4 York 10
80/1 EDM/Zellers
81/2 EDM/RedRooster
81/2 EDM/WestEdmonton
88/9 EDM/ActionMagazine 104
64/5 TOR

HARRIS, BILLY H.
72/3 EddieSargent 131
74/5 Loblaws

97/8 Limited 21
96/7 Maggers 47
96/7 MetalUniverse 39
97/8 Omega 69
92/3 O-Pee-Chee 123
91/2 opcPremier 143
98/9 Pacific 176
97/8 PacificCrown 214
97/8 PacificCrownRoyale 40
97/8 PcfcDynagn! 35,-Tandm 38
97/8 PacificParamount 57
98/9 PacificParamount 63
92/3 PaniniSticker H
93/4 PaniniSticker 274
94/5 PaniniSticker 231
95/6 PaniniSticker 173
96/7 PaniniSticker 167
91/2 Parkhurst 75
92/3 Parkhurst 72
93/4 Parkhurst 46
94/5 Parkhurst V30
95/6 Parkhurst 58
94/5 ParkieSE 45
91/2 Pinnacle 328
92/3 Pinnacle 34
93/4 Pinnacle 57
94/5 Pinnacle 55
95/6 Pinnacle 70
97/8 Pinnacle 182
97/8 PinnacleCertified 54
97/8 PinnacleInside 138
96/7 PinnacleZenith 19
95/6 Playoff 140
94/5 POG 83
93/4 PowerPlay 61
93/4 Premier 520
94/5 Premier 332
95/6 ProMagnet 122
91/2 ProSet 543
92/3 ProSet 75
91/2 PSPlatinum 258
90/1 Score 430
91/2 Score(CDN)656, (U.S)106T
92/3 Score 51
93/4 Score 168
94/5 Score 148
95/6 Score 225, -CheckIt 8
97/8 Score 198
94/5 Select 50
89/90 SketchOHL 154
90/1 SketchOHL 309
95/6 SkyBoxEmotion 47
95/6 SkyBoxImpact 46
96/7 SkyBoxImpact 29
95/6 SP 40
96/7 SP 45
97/8 SPAuthentic 45
94 Sportflics
95/6 Summit 72
96/7 TeamOut
92/3 Topps 405
95/6 Topps 197
98/9 Topps 148, B13
92/3 ToppsStadiumClub 414
93/4 ToppsStadiumClub 494
94/5 ToppsStadiumClub 107
95/6 ToppsStadiumClub 78
90/1 UpperDeck 359
91/2 UpperDeck 546
92/3 UpperDeck 287
93/4 UpperDeck 204, SP37
94/5 UpperDeck 127, SP20
95/6 UpperDeck 3, SE112
96/7 UpperDeck 44, P27
97/8 UpperDeck 51, 397, T20A
93/4 UpperDeckBeAPlayer 24
94/5 UDBAP R15,R136,-Sig 125
96/7 UDBlackDiamond 54
97/8 UDBlackDiamond 94
98/9 UDChoice 65
95/6 UDCollChoice 224
96/7 UDCollChoice 70
97/8 UDCollChoice 70
97/8 UpperDeckIce 2
94/5 DAL
94/5 DAL/Southwest
96/7 DAL/Southwest

HATCHER, KEVIN
90/1 Bowman 70
91/2 Bowman 296, 409
92/3 Bowman 230, 271
95/6 Bowman 48
93/4 Donruss 369
94/5 Donruss 199
95/6 Donruss 95
96/7 Donruss 29
97/8 Donruss 26
95/6 DonrussElite 17
96/7 DonrussElite 24
97/8 DonrussPreferred 70
97/8 DonrussPriority 100
93/4 EASports 151
97/8 EssoOlympic 31
96/7 Flair 76
94/5 Fleer 53
95/6 FleerMetal 41
96/7 F.Picks-FabFifty 17
92/3 FleerUltra 231
93/4 FleerUltra 118
94/5 FleerUltra 233
95/6 FleerUltra 230
96/7 FleerUltra 140
91/2 Gillette 36
95 Globe 105
93/4 HockeyWit 17
95/6 Hoyle'WEST 7 (Spades)
92/3 HumptyDumpty (1)
97/8 KatchMedallion 117
91/2 Kelloggs 7
91/2 Kraft 20
93/4 Kraft-Captain
93/4 Leaf 34
94/5 Leaf 369
95/6 Leaf 117
96/7 Leaf 48
97/8 Leaf 129
97/8 Limited 21
92/3 McDonalds McD19
96/7 MetalUniverse 126
97/8 Omega 185
87/8 OPC/Topps 68
88/9 OPC/Topps 86
89/90 OPC/Topps 146
90/1 OPC/Topps 147
91/2 OPC/Topps 310, T-TL 16
92/3 O-Pee-Chee 145
91/2 opcPremier 88
98/9 Pacific 352
97/8 PacificCrown 227
97/8 PcfcDynag! 101,-Tandm 62
97/8 PacificInvincible 112
97/8 PacificParamount 149
98/9 PacificParamount 191
87/8 PaniniSticker 179
88/9 PaniniSticker 365
89/90 PaniniSticker 347
90/1 PaniniSticker 167
91/2 PaniniSticker 198
92/3 PaniniSticker 167
93/4 PaniniSticker C
94/5 PaniniSticker 26
95/6 PaniniSticker 175
96/7 PaniniSticker 170
97/8 PaniniSticker 49
91/2 Parkhurst 191
92/3 Parkhurst 198
93/4 Parkhurst 221
94/5 Parkhurst 259, V54
95/6 Parkhurst 56
91/2 Pinnacle 131
92/3 Pinnacle 11
93/4 Pinnacle 90, CA25
94/5 Pinnacle 345
95/6 Pinnacle 10
96/7 Pinnacle 3
97/8 Pinnacle 171
96/7 PinnacleBeAPlayer 14
97/8 PinnacleCertified 86
97/8 PinnInside 98
95/6 PinnacleZenith 44
95/6 Playoff 248
96/7 Playoff 408
94/5 POG 363
95/6 POG 89
93/4 PowerPlay 261
93/4 Premier 435
90/1 ProSet 311, 376
91/2 PS 249, 316, -ThePuck 29
92/3 ProSet 204
91/2 PSPlatinum 127
90/1 Score 90, -HotCards 42
91/2 Score(CDN) 20, 370
91/2 Score(U.S) 20, 340
92/3 Score 273, 439, -USA 13
93/4 Score 136, 450, -Franch 23
95/6 Score 12
96/7 Score 117
97/8 Score 222
97/8 Score(PGH) 8
92/3 SeasonsPatch 48
94/5 Select 148
95/6 SelectCertified 41
94 Semic 114, 342
95 Semic 106
91 SemicSticker 136
92 SemicSticker 151
93 SemicSticker 175
95/6 SkyBoxEmotion 48
95/6 SkyBoxImpact 47
94/5 SP 31
95/6 SP 37
96/7 SP 130
97/8 SPAuthentic 127
95/6 Summit 41
95/6 SuperSticker 34
92/3 Topps 149
95/6 Topps 273
98/9 Topps 73, B14
94/5 ToppsFinest 17
95/6 ToppsFinest 148
96/7 ToppsNHLPicks 33
91/2 ToppsStadiumClub 140
92/3 ToppsStadiumClub 301
93/4 ToppsStadiumClub 153
94/5 ToppsStadiumClub 220
95/6 ToppsStadiumClub 42
94/5 TSC-MembersOnly 28
95/6 TSC-MembersOnly 11
95/6 ToppsSuperSkills 53
90/1 UpperDeck 109, 486
91/2 UpperDeck 98, 361, 511
92/3 UpperDeck 198
93/4 UpperDeck 140, SP169
94/5 UD 332, SP86,SP110
95/6 UD 256, 309, SE25
96/7 UpperDeck 319, P21
97/8 UpperDeck 343
94/5 UDBAP R131, -Aut. 48
96/7 UDBlackDiamond 54
98/9 UDChoice 172
95/6 UDCollChoice 186
96/7 UDCollChoice 71
97/8 UDCollChoice 207
96 Wien 163
96/7 PGH/FotoPuck
86/7 WSH/Kodak
86/7 WSH/Police
87/8 WSH
87/8 WSH/Kodak
88/9 WSH
88/9 WSH/Smokey
89/90 WSH
89/90 WSH/Kodak
90/1 WSH/Kodak
90/1 WSH/Smokey
91/2 WSH
91/2 WSH/Kodak
92/3 WSH/Kodak

HATCHER, MARK
88/9 ProCards(Baltimore)

HATNELL, BOB
90/1 SketchWHL 124

HATOUM, ED
73/4 VancouverBlazers

HAUER, BRETT
93/4 Classic 67
94/5 Classic-Autograph
94/5 ElitSet 268
93/4 FleerUltra 484
95 PaniniWorlds 221
93/4 PowerPlay 504
93/4 Premier-TeamUSA 20
93/4 TSC-TeamUSA 7
93/4 LasVegas

HAUSLER, OLIVER
94/5 DEL 382

HAUTAMAA, JUHA
93/4 Sisu 130
94/5 Sisu 120
95/6 Sisu 41, -Spotlight 8
95/6 SisuLimited 105

HAVANOV, ALEXANDER
93/4 Birmingham 9

HAVEL, JAN
69/70 MästarSerien 10
72 SemicSticker 29
74 SemicSticker 71
71/2 WilliamsFIN 25

HAVELID, NICLAS
94/5 ElitSet 35
95/6 ElitSet 5
91/2 SemicElitserien 11
92/3 SemicElitserien 35
95/6 udElite 5
97/8 udSwedish 2, 209

HAVRAN, PETER
79 PaniniSticker 271

HAVUKAINEN, ARI
71/2 WilliamsFIN 360

HAWERCHUK, DALE
90/1 Bowman 129
91/2 Bowman 31
92/3 Bowman 308
72-84 Dernière 82/3
93/4 Donruss 35
94/5 Donruss 44
95/6 Donruss 384
96/7 Donruss 90
97/8 Donruss 36
95/6 DonrussElite 100
93/4 EASports 16
83/4 Esso
88/9 Esso Sticker
94/5 Flair 18
96/7 Flair 67
94/5 Fleer 21
95/6 FleerMetal 124
96/7 FleerNHLPicks 120
92/3 FleerUltra 15
93/4 FleerUltra 149
94/5 FleerUltra 23
95/6 FleerUltra 299
88/9 FritoLay
93/4 HockeyWit 22
84/5 Kelloggs Disk
86/7 Kraft Sports 75
89/90 Kraft 50
90/1 Kraft 16
91/2 Kraft 36
93/4 Leaf 71
94/5 Leaf 313
95/6 Leaf 184
96/7 Leaf 124
94/5 LeafLimited 94
96/7 Maggers 114
96/7 MetalUniverse 111
82/3 O-Pee-Chee 3, 374, 380-81
83/4 O-Pee-Chee 377, 385
84/5 OPC 339, 393, Topps 152
85/6 OPC/Topps 102, -AS 8
86/7 OPC/Topps 74
87/8 OPC/Topps 149, I
88/9 OPC/Topps 65, K
89/90 OPC/Topps 122
90/1 OPC/Topps 141, T-TL 11
91/2 OPC/Topps 32, 65, T-TL 2
92/3 O-Pee-Chee 212
90/1 opcPremier 40
91/2 opcPremier 1
88/9 opcStars 12
82/3 opcSticker 204, 249
83/4 opcSticker 282
84/5 opcSticker 284, 285
85/6 opcSticker 248
86/7 opcSticker 104
87/8 opcSticker 255
88/9 opcSticker 143
89/90 opcSticker 134
97/8 PacificCrown 225
87/8 PaniniSticker 363
88/9 PaniniSticker 155
89/90 PaniniSticker 162
90/1 PaniniSticker 317
91/2 PaniniSticker 296
92/3 PaniniSticker 247
93/4 PaniniSticker 102
94/5 PaniniSticker 91
95/6 PaniniSticker 189
96/7 PaniniSticker 116
91/2 Parkhurst 18, 216
92/3 Parkhurst 11
93/4 Parkhurst 23
94/5 Parkhurst 29
95/6 Parkhurst 180
91/2 Pinnacle 80
92/3 Pinnacle 316
93/4 Pinnacle 260
94/5 Pinnacle 43
96/7 Pinnacle 44
96/7 PinnacleBeAPlayer 203
95/6 Playoff 306
96/7 Playoff 409
94/5 POG 46
95/6 POG 238
82/3 Post
93/4 PowerPlay 29
93/4 Premier 7, -Finest 11
94/5 Premier 320
90/1 ProSet 330, 415
91/2 ProSet 24
92/3 ProSet 12
87/8 ProSportWatch CW7
91/2 PSPlatinum 11
83/4 PuffySticker 5
90/1 Score 50, 2T, -HotCards 22
91/2 Score(CDN) 266, 479
91/2 Score(U.S) 259, 376
92/3 Score 272
93/4 Score 159
94/5 Score 192
95/6 Score 222
96/7 Score 51
92/3 SeasonsPatch 68
94/5 Select 42
95/6 SelectCertified 97
94 Semic 89
89 SemicSticker 67
92 SemicSticker 94
83/4 7ElevenCokeCup
84/5 7ElevenDisk
85/6 7Eleven 21
95/6 SkyBoxEmotion 147
95/6 SkyBoxImpact 140
96/7 SkyBoxImpact 94
83/4 SouhaitsRen.KeyChain
94/5 SP 15
95/6 SP 123
83/4 StaterMint H7
95/6 Summit 93
95/6 SuperSticker 103
91 TeamCanada
92/3 Topps 296
95/6 Topps 271
95/6 ToppsFinest 153
91/2 ToppsStadiumClub 312
92/3 ToppsStadiumClub 419
93/4 ToppsStadiumClub 220
94/5 ToppsStadiumClub 248
95/6 ToppsStadiumClub 46
90/1 UpperDeck 53, 443
91/2 UpperDeck 12, 79, 126
92/3 UpperDeck 302
93/4 UpperDeck 411, SP16
94/5 UpperDeck 102, SP9
95/6 UpperDeck 38
96/7 UpperDeck 120
94/5 UDBeAPlayer R7, -Aut. 5
95/6 UDCollChoice 245
96/7 UDCollChoice 196
97/8 UDCollChoice 190
96/7 UpperDeck"Ice" 50
83/4 Vachon 126
90/1 BUF/BlueShield
90/1 BUF/Campbell
91/2 BUF/BlueShield
91/2 BUF/Campbell
92/3 BUF/BlueShield
92/3 BUF/Jubilee
93/4 BUF/NOCO
96/7 PHA/OceanSpray
81/2 WPG
82/3 WPG
83/4 WPG
84/5 WPG/Police
85/6 WPG
85/6 WPG/Police
85/6 WPG/Silverwood
86/7 WPG
87/8 WPG
88/9 WPG/Police
89/90 WPG/Safeway

HAWES, CHRIS
91/2 SketchWHL 70

HAWGOOD, GREG
93/4 Donruss 245
95/6 EdgeIce 152
93/4 FleerUltra 388
95/6 FutureLegends 25
93/4 Leaf 266
94/5 Leaf 534
89/90 OPC/Topps 81
90/1 OPC/Topps 236
89/90 opcStickFS 1
89/90 PaniniSticker 189
90/1 PaniniSticker 10
92/3 Parkhurst 361
94/5 Parkhurst 181
93/4 PowerPlay 347
93/4 Premier 422
88/9 ProCards(Maine)
91/2 ProCards 226
90/1 ProSet 442
90/1 ScoreTraded 79T
93/4 Score 396, 642
92/3 Topps 358
92/3 ToppsStadiumClub 495
90/1 UpperDeck 391
89/90 BOS
92/3 EDM/IGA
92/3 PHA/UD 25MAR93
93/4 PHA 16SEP93
94/5 PGH 2
96/7 S.J/PacificBellSheet
84/5 Kamloops
95/6 LasVegas

HAWKINS, SHAWN
89/90 Rayside

HAWKINS, TODD
89/90 ProCards(IHL) 183
90/1 ProCards 324
91/2 ProCards 342
96/7 Cincinnati
93/4 Cleveland
87/8 Flint

HAWLEY, JOE
91/2 ProCards 44
89/90 SketchOHL 105
90/1 SketchOHL 361
92/3 Peoria

HAWLEY, KEN
88/9 ProCards(Hershey)
89/90 ProCards(AHL) 348
90/1 ProCards 40

HAWORTH, ALAN
84/5 O-Pee-Chee 199
85/6 OPC/Topps 117
86/7 OPC/Topps 107
88/9 OPC/Topps 131
85/6 opcSticker 108/241
86/7 opcSticker 255/147
88/9 opcSticker 195
87/8 PaniniSticker 187
83/4 SouhaitsRen.KeyChain
81/2 BUF/Wendt
87/8 QUE/GeneralFoods
87/8 QUE/YumYum
82/3 WSH
84/5 WSH/PizzaHut
85/6 WSH/PizzaHut
86/7 WSH/Kodak
86/7 WSH/Police

HAWORTH, GORDIE
52/3 LavalDairy 68
52/3 StLawrence 22

HAWRYLIW, NEIL
81/2 Indianapolis 15

HAY, BILL
45-64 BeeHives(CHI)
64-67 BeeHives(CHI)
62 CeramicTiles
63-5 ChexPhoto
64/5 CokeCap CHI-11
65/6 CocaCola
94/5 Parkie(64/5) 42
95/6 Parkie(66/7) 30
60/1 ShirriffCoin 77
61/2 ShirriffCoin 34
60/1 Topps 6
61/2 Topps 35, -Stamp
62/3 Topps 35, -Buck
63/4 Topps 34
64/5 Topps 7
65/6 Topps 62
54-67 TorontoStar V8
56-66 TorontoStar 62/3, 65/6
63/4 TheTorontoStar
64/5 TheTorontoStar

HAY, CHARLES
83&87 HallOfFame 36
83 HHOF Postcard (C)

HAY, DON
94/5 Slapshot(MEM) 25
96/7 PHO

HAY, DWAYNE
97/8 Bowman 25
95/6 Classic 38
94/5 Slapshot(Guelph) 9
95/6 Slapshot 89
96/7 UpperDeck"Ice" 123
95/6 Guelph 3
96/7 Guelph 22
97/8 Guelph 35

HAY, GEORGE
61/2 Topps-Stamp
83&87 HallOfFame 98
83 HHOF Postcard (G)
23/4 PaulinsCandy 28
60/1 Topps 15

HAY, SCOTT
94/5 Slapshot(Sarnia) 3

HAYDEN, BRIAN
95/6 Slapshot 153

HAYDEN, JAMIE
90/1 SketchWHL 171

HARLIN, HAYES
95/6 Halifax

HAYES, JAMES
51/2 LacStJean 5
52/3 BasDuFleuve 29

HAYES, PAUL
51/2 LavalDairy 8

HAYFIELD, ROGER
51/2 BasDuFleuve 39
52/3 BasDuFleuve 12

HAYNES, PAUL
34-43 BeeHives(MTL.C)
35-40 CrownBrand 61
36-39 DiamondMatch (2), (3)
27-32 LaPresse
35/6 OPC (V304C) 95
37/8 OPC (V304E) 155
39/40 OPC (V301-1) 31
40/1 OPC (V301-2) 112
38/9 QuakerOats
34/5 SweetCaporal
33/4 WWGum (V357) 6
36/7 WWGum (V356) 33

HAYWARD, BRIAN
91/2 Bowman 122
92/3 Bowman 60
86/7 Kraft Sports 27
85/6 O-Pee-Chee 226
86/7 O-Pee-Chee 255
87/8 O-Pee-Chee 230
88/9 OPC/Topps 195
89/90 O-Pee-Chee 237
90/1 OPC/Topps 23
91/2 OPC/Topps 178
87/8 opcStars 15
88/9 opcStars 13
87/8 opcSticker 75/177, 184/44
88/9 opcSticker 52, 214
89/90 opcSticker 50, 211
87/8 PaniniSticker 55, 376A
88/9 PaniniSticker 251, 402
89/90 PaniniSticker 246, 376
90/1 PaniniSticker 61
91/2 PaniniSticker 106
93/4 PaniniSticker 265
91/2 Pinnacle 83
92/3 Pinnacle 266
90/1 ProSet 150
91/2 ProSet 327
90/1 Score(CND) 304, (U.S) 78T
91/2 Score(CDN) 211, 554, 4T
91/2 ScoreUS 211
83/4 StaterMint H11
92/3 Topps 436

91/2 ToppsStadiumClub 19
92/3 ToppsStadiumClub 364
90/1 UpperDeck 171, 449
91/2 UpperDeck 59
83/4 Vachon 127
86/7 MTL
87/8 MTL
87/8 MTL/Vachon 61, 67, 84
88/9 MTL
89/90 MTL
89/90 MTL/Kraft
91/2 S.J
83/4 WPG
84/5 WPG/Police
85/6 WPG
85/6 WPG/Police

HAYWARD, RICK
89/90 ProCards(IHL) 207
90/1 ProCards 345
91/2 ProCards 469
95/6 ClevelandLumberjacks

HEAD, BARRY
74/5 SiouxCity

HEAD, DON
45-64 BeeHives(BOS)
61/2 ShirriffCoin 11
61/2 Topps 17

HEAD, GALEN
91/2 Knoxville

HEADLEY, FERN (CURLY)
24/5 Champs (C144)
24/5 MapleCrispettes (V130) 4
23/4 PaulinsCandy 37
24/5 (V145-2) 23

HEALEY, GRANT
90/1 Rayside
91/2 Rayside

HEALEY, PAUL
97/8 Donruss 205
95/6 EdgeIce 44
93/4 PrinceAlbert

HEALY, GLENN
91/2 Bowman 224
92/3 Bowman 434
93/4 Donruss 211
94/5 Donruss 283
95/6 Donruss 54
96/7 Donruss 212
93/4 EASports 84
92/3 FleerUltra 126
93/4 FleerUltra 106, 371
95/6 FleerUltra 101
93/4 Leaf 326
94/5 Leaf 310
90/1 O-Pee-Chee 400
91/2 OPC/Topps 368
92/3 O-Pee-Chee 262
88/9 opcStickFS 7
97/8 PacificDynag-BestKept 61
97/8 PacificParamount 180
88/9 PaniniSticker 68
89/90 PaniniSticker 97
90/1 PaniniSticker 88
91/2 PaniniSticker 249
93/4 PaniniSticker 65
91/2 Parkhurst 107
92/3 Parkhurst 341, 505
93/4 Parkhurst 405
95/6 Parkhurst 406
94/5 ParkieSE 117
91/2 Pinnacle 185
92/3 Pinnacle 121
93/4 Pinnacle 365
94/5 Pinnacle 430
95/6 Pinnacle 91
96/7 PinnacleBeAPlayer 140
94/5 POG 287
93/4 PowerPlay 390
93/4 Premier 486
94/5 Premier 388
90/1 ProSet 183
91/2 ProSet 153, -ThePuck 18
91/2 PSPlatinum 73
90/1 Score 294
91/2 Score(CDN) 68, (U.S) 68
92/3 Score 188
93/4 Score 177, 533
95/6 Score 273
96/7 Score 34
97/8 Score 22
97/8 Score(TOR) 2
92/3 Topps 305
95/6 Topps 292
91/2 ToppsStadiumClub 369
92/3 ToppsStadiumClub 356
93/4 ToppsStadiumClub 453
90/1 UpperDeck 18
91/2 UpperDeck 224
93/4 UpperDeck 321
94/5 UpperDeck 455
95/6 UpperDeck 30
96/7 UpperDeck 202
94/5 UDBeAPlayer-Aut. 128
95/6 UDCollChoice 272
88/9 L.A./Smokeys
89/90 NYI

HEANEY, GERALDINE
94/5 Classic W19, W21
97/8 EssoOlympic 57
97/8 GeneralMills
97/8 UDCollChoice 282

HEANEY, MIKE
95/6 Louisiana, -Playoffs

HEAPHY, SHAWN
92/3 ClassicProspects 141
91/2 ProCards 588
93/4 LasVegas

HEARN, DON
91/2 AvantGardeBCJHL 36
92/3 BCJHL 58

HEARN, JAMIE
92/3 Oklahoma

HEARST, ABE
97/8 UpperDeck 404

HEASLIP, MARK
76/7 O-Pee-Chee 376
79/80 O-Pee-Chee 320

HEATLEY, MURRAY
75/6 opcWHA 53

HEATON, SCOTT
95/6 SheffieldSteelers

HEATHWOOD, STEVE
74/5 SiouxCity

HEATLEY, MURRAY
74/5 Minnesota

HEBENTON, ANDY
45-64 BeeHives(BOS), (NYR)
64-67 BeeHives(BOS)
62 CeramicTiles
82? JDMcCarthy
93/4 Parkie(56/7) 97
60/1 ShirriffCoin 91
61/2 ShirriffCoin 90
57/8 Topps 58
58/9 Topps 46
59/60 Topps 16
60/1 Topps 42
61/2 Topps 55, -Stamp
62/3 Topps 54, -Buck
63/4 Topps 15
54-67 TorontoStar V7
56-66 TorontoStar 57/8

HEBENTON, CLAYTON
76/7 Phoenix

HEBERT, GUY
92/3 Bowman 32
93/4 Donruss 13
94/5 Donruss 81
95/6 Donruss 71
96/7 Donruss 164
97/8 Donruss 167
97/8 D.CanadianIce 37
95/6 DonrussElite-Painted 5
97/8 DonrussElite 45
97/8 DonrussPreferred 129
97/8 D.Priority 124,-PostGen 20
97/8 DonrussStudio 37
93/4 EASports 6
94/5 Flair 3
96/7 Flair 1
96/7 Fleer 1, 147
95/6 FleerMetal 1
92/3 FleerUltra 394
93/4 FleerUltra 254
94/5 FleerUltra 3
95/6 FleerUltra 1
96/7 FleerUltra 1
95/6 Hoyle'WEST 8 (Spades)
97/8 KatchMedallion 1
94/5 KraftDinner, -Masks
95/6 Kraft-Crease
96/7 KraftDinner
93/4 Leaf 356
94/5 Leaf 142, -Limited 1
95/6 Leaf 271
96/7 Leaf 88
97/8 Leaf 72, -PipeDreams 7
97/8 Limited 102
96/7 Maggers 5
96/7 MetalUniverse 1
97/8 Omega 2
92/3 O-Pee-Chee 116
92/3 opcPremier 40
98/9 Pacific 54
97/8 PacificCrown 260, -InThe 1
97/8 PcfcCrwnRoyale 1,-Freez 1
97/8 PacificDynagon! 2
97/8 PcfcD-Stone 1,-Tandem 24
97/8 PacificInvincible 2
97/8 PcfcParamount 1,-Gloves 1
98/9 PcfcParamount 2,-Gloves 1
97/8 PcfcRevolution 1,-RtrnTo 1
94/5 PaniniSticker 126
95/6 PaniniSticker 232
96/7 PaniniSticker 223
95 PaniniWorlds 211
92/3 Parkhurst 386
93/4 Parkhurst 279
95/6 Parkhurst 4
94/5 ParkieSE 1
93/4 Pinnacle 167, -Expansion 1
94/5 Pinnacle 15, MA4
95/6 Pinnacle 143
96/7 Pinnacle 88
97/8 Pinnacle 90, -Masks 6
97/8 Pinnacle - GoalieTin 4
96/7 PinnacleBeAPlayer 61
97/8 P.BAP -Stacking/Pads 1
97/8 PinnacleCertified 19
97/8 P.Inside 70, -Stop 6, -Can 7
97/8 P.Inside -BgCan,-StandUp8
97/8 PinnacleMasks
97/8 PinnacleUncut
95/6 PinnacleZenith 99
95/6 Playoff 1, 113
94/5 POG 269
95/6 POG 27
93/4 PowerPlay 2
93/4 Premier 519
94/5 Premier 338
89/90 ProCards(IHL) 5
90/1 ProCards 89
91/2 ProCards 29
95/6 ProMagnet 38, 03
92/3 Score 460
93/4 Score 426, 489, 502
94/5 Score 42, TF1
95/6 Score 94
96/7 Score 13
97/8 Score 6, -NetWorth 1
97/8 Score(ANA) 14
94/5 Select 79
95 Semic 210
95/6 SkyBoxEmotion 2
95/6 SkyBoxImpact 2
96/7 SkyBoxImpact 1
94/5 SP 5
95/6 SP 3
96/7 SP 5
97/8 SPAuthentic S23
98/9 SPx"Finite" 2
95/6 Summit 58
96/7 Summit 75
96/7 TeamOut
92/3 Topps 112
95/6 Topps 112
98/9 Topps 48
94/5 ToppsFinest 20
95/6 ToppsFinest 122
92/3 ToppsStadiumClub 401
93/4 ToppsStadiumClub 295
94/5 ToppsStadiumClub 6
95/6 ToppsStadiumClub 82
92/3 UpperDeck 501
93/4 UpperDeck 1
94/5 UpperDeck 3
95/6 UpperDeck 467, SE3
96/7 UpperDeck 2
97/8 UpperDeck 6
94/5 UDBeAPlayer R47, -Aut. 99
96/7 UDBlackDiamond 53
97/8 UDBlackDiamond 34
98/9 UDChoice 1
95/6 UDCollChoice 287
96/7 UDCollChoice 5, 309
97/8 UDCollChoice 1, SQ42
97/8 Zenith 66, Z11
94/5 ANA/Carl'sJr 9
96/7 ANA/UpFrontSports 21

HEBERT, IAN
94/5 Birmingham

HEBERT, PAT
90/1 SketchQMJHL 195

HEBERT, ROLAND
51/2 LavalDairy 19

HEBKY, DAVID
92/3 BCJHL 215
91/2 SketchWHL 56

HEBST, MARCO
94/5 DEL 141

HECHT, JOCHEN
94/5 AutoPhonex 17
94/5 DEL 282
96/7 DEL 173
97/8 DEL 277

HEDBERG, ANDERS
72-84 Dernière 79/80
95 Globe 70
72 Hellas 38
74 Hellas 25
70/1 Kuvajulkaisut 25
78/9 OPC/Topps 25
79/80 OPC/Topps 240
80/1 OPC/Topps 73
81/2 OPC 225, 237, T. 58,(E) 98
82/3 O-Pee-Chee 225
83/4 O-Pee-Chee 245
84/5 OPC 143, Topps 107
80/1 opcSuperCard 15
81/2 opcSticker 166
83/4 opcSticker 215
84/5 opcSticker 102
85/6 opcSticker 200/73
74/5 opcWHA 17
75/6 opcWHA 40, 72
76/7 opcWHA 66, 125
77/8 opcWHA 3
83/4 PuffySticker 19
72 SemicSticker 69
74 SemicSticker 12
91 SemicSticker 237
83/4 SouhaitsRen.KeyChain
77-9 Sportscster 71-12, 80-1911
92/3 Trends(76) 141
71/2 WilliamsFIN 45
72/3 WilliamsFIN 45
73/4 WilliamsFIN 27

HEDBERG, JOHAN
94/5 ElitSet 40, -CleanSweep 7
95/6 ElitSet 61, -Spidermen 7
95 Globe 6
92/3 SemicElitserien 152
95/6 udElite 94

HEDE, NIKLAS
96/7 DEL 43
95/6 Sisu 223

HEDICAN, BRET
92/3 Classic 87
93/4 Donruss 291
93/4 FleerUltra 66
94/5 FleerUltra 224
95/6 FleerUltra 316
93/4 Leaf 286
94/5 Leaf 425
98/9 Pacific 426
97/8 PacificCrown 284
92/3 Parkhurst 385
93/4 Parkhurst 177
94/5 Parkhurst 243
95/6 Parkhurst 216
92/3 Pinnacle 228
93/4 Pinnacle 315
94/5 Pinnacle 369
95/6 Playoff 317
93/4 PowerPlay 210
93/4 Premier 224
94/5 Premier 162
92/3 ProSet 240
92/3 Score 471
97/8 SPAuthentic 158
92/3 Topps 517
95/6 Topps 72
98/9 Topps 81
92/3 ToppsStadiumClub 203
93/4 ToppsStadiumClub 81
94/5 ToppsStadiumClub 27
92/3 UpperDeck 414
93/4 UpperDeck 185
94/5 UpperDeck 398
95/6 UpperDeck 95
96/7 UpperDeck 173
95/6 UDBeAPlayer 19
95/6 UDCollChoice 255
95/6 VAN/Building 3
96/7 VAN
96/7 VAN/IGA

HEDICAN, TOM
94/5 Slapshot(NorthBay) 25

HEDIN, PIERRE
97/8 UDBlackDiamond 36
98/9 UDChoice 291
97/8 udSwedish 150

HEDINGTON, STEVE
89/90 Sudbury 14

HEDLUND, TOMMY
95/6 ElitSet 160
89/90 SemicElitserien 10
95/6 udElite 7

HEDMAN, GLENN
89/90 SemicElitserien 200

HEED, JONAS
89/90 SemicElitserien 221
90/1 SemicElitserien 30
91/2 SemicElitserien 280
92/3 SemicElitserien 305
97/8 udSwedish 170

HEED, KLAS
89/90 SemicElitserien 102
90/1 SemicElitserien 105
91/2 SemicElitserien 109
92/3 SemicElitserien 128

HEEREMA, JEFF
98 BowmanCHL 146, A31
98/9 Topps 233

HEFFERNAN, GERRY
34-43 BeeHives(MTL.C)
43-47 ParadeSportive

HEFFERNAN, JIMMY
36/7 WWGum (V356) 130

HEFFORD, JAYNA
97/8 UDCollChoice 289

HEGEN, DIETER
94/5 DEL 311
95/6 DEL 94, 433
96/7 DEL 281
95 Globe 225
95 PaniniWorlds 70
94 Semic 287
89 SemicSticker 114
91 SemicSticker 173
93 SemicSticker 158
92/3 UpperDeck 370
96 Wien 198, 217

HEGEN, GERHARD
94/5 DEL 169
95/6 DEL 148

HEIDT, MICHAEL
94/5 DEL 275
95/6 DEL 246
96/7 DEL 138
89 SemicSticker 113
91 SemicSticker 159
92 SemicSticker 174
93 SemicSticker 151

HEIDT, ROBERT
94/5 DET 24
95/6 DEL 21

HEIKKERI, ESKO
80/1 Mallasjuoma 147

HEIKKERI, PERTTI
80/1 Mallasjuoma 146

HEIKKILA, ANTTI
66/7 Champion 47
65/6 Hellas 36
70/1 Kuvajulkaisut 191
80/1 Mallasjuoma 39, 200
72 Panda
78/9 SM-Liiga 63, 221
71/2 WilliamsFIN 82
72/3 WilliamsFIN 245
73/4 WilliamsFIN 243

HEIKKILA, KARI
80/1 Mallasjuoma 29
82 SemicSticker 28
71/2 WilliamsFIN 339

HEIKKILA, LASSE
65/6 Hellas 37

HEIKKILA, MATTI
80/1 Mallasjuoma 53
78/9 SM-Liiga 77

HEIKKINEN, KARI
91/2 Jyvas-Hyva 56
92/3 Jyvas-Hyva 164
93/4 Jyvas-Hyva 292
93/4 Sisu 70
94/5 Sisu 11

HEIKKINEN, MARKKU
92/3 Jyvas-Hyva 77
93/4 Jyvas-Hyva 136
93/4 Sisu 139
94/5 Sisu 3

HEIKKINEN, PERTTI
66/7 Champion 120

HEIKKONEN, HANNU
66/7 Champion 163

HEIMER, ULI
94/5 DEL 94
93 SemicSticker 153

HEIMO, HEIKKI
65/6 Hellas 15

HEINÄNEN, JOKKE
92/3 Jyvas-Hyva 198
93/4 Jyvas-Hyva 352
95 PaniniWorlds 181
93/4 Sisu 224
94/5 Sisu 116, -Junior 2
95/6 Sisu 356
96/7 Sisu 154
95/6 SisuLimited 24

HEINISTO, PASI
92/3 Jyvas-Hyva 115
93/4 Sisu 269

HEINO, HEIKKI
66/7 Champion 73

HEINO, KIMMO
65/6 Hellas 130
70/1 Kuvajulkaisut 104
72 Panda
71/2 WilliamsFIN 112
72/3 WilliamsFIN 82
73/4 WilliamsFIN 128

HEINO, TIMO
80/1 Mallasjuoma 87
78/9 SM-Liiga 129

HEINOLD, PETER
94/5 DEL 434

HEINONEN, ISMO
71/2 WilliamsFIN 361

HEINONEN, MARKKU
72/3 WilliamsFIN 301

HEINONEN, MAURI
72/3 WilliamsFIN 302

HEINONEN, RAINE
73/4 WilliamsFIN 216

HEINONEN, RAUNO
66/7 Champion 72
65/6 Hellas 9, 99
70/1 Kuvajulkaisut 155

HEINONEN, REIJO
72 Panda
71/2 WilliamsFIN 83
72/3 WilliamsFIN 246
73/4 WilliamsFIN 244

HEINRICHS, MARCO
94/5 DEL 213

HEINS, SHAWN
91/2 SketchOHL 131
91/2 Peterborough 25
92/3 Windsor 27

HEINVIRTA, RISTO
66/7 Champion 94

HEINZE, STEVE
92/3 FleerUltra 3
93/4 Leaf 116
94/5 Leaf 404
92/3 O-Pee-Chee 92
92/3 opcPremier 24
98/9 Pacific 79
97/8 PacificCrown 261
91/2 Parkhurst 232
93/4 Pinnacle 53
94/5 Pinnacle 341
96/7 PinnacleBeAPlayer 154
94/5 POG 348
93/4 PowerPlay 289
93/4 Premier 378
94/5 Premier 387
92/3 ProSet 220
92/3 Score 476
93/4 Score 251
97/8 Score(BOS) 10
95/6 Summit 87
92/3 Topps 519
95/6 Topps 278
92/3 ToppsStadiumClub 166
93/4 ToppsStadiumClub 15
94/5 ToppsStadiumClub 137
92/3 UpperDeck 400, AC3
94/5 UpperDeck 327
95/6 UpperDeck 293
94/5 UDBeAPlayer-Aut. 161
97/8 UDCollChoice 20

HEINZLE, KARL
94 Semic 248

HEISIG, BRANJO
94/5 DEL 394
95/6 DEL 164
96/7 DEL 238

HEISKALA, EARL
70/1 Esso Stamp
69/70 O-Pee-Chee 170
70/1 OPC 193
70/1 PHA
72/3 LosAngelesSharks

HEISKANEN, ARTO
92/3 Jyvas-Hyva 194
93/4 Jyvas-Hyva 347
93/4 Sisu 230
94/5 Sisu 30
95/6 Sisu 176
95/6 SisuLimited 27

HEISS, JOSEF
94/5 DEL 200
95/6 DEL 195, 429
96/7 DEL 338
95 Globe218
95 PaniniWorlds 51
94 Semic 272
95 Semic 165
91 SemicSticker 153
92 SemicSticker 172

HEISTAD, JERMAINE
91/2 SketchWHL 324

HEJDUK, MILAN
94/5 APS 34
95/6 APS 330
94/5 SigRookies 52

HEJNA, TONY
90/1 ProCards 90

HELANDER, HANNU
80/1 Mallasjuoma 157
82 SemicSticker 34
78/9 SM-Liiga 45

HELANDER, PEKKA
82 SemicSticker 9
71/2 WilliamsFIN 340

HELD, DANIEL
94/5 DEL 46
95/6 DEL 16
89 SemicSticker 125

HELENIUS, SAMI
93/4 Jyvas-Hyva 266

HELENIUS, TEUVO
66/7 Champion 37

HELIGER, VIC
36-39 DiamondMatch -5

HELIN, JIM
92/3 Jyvas-Hyva 111
93/4 Jyvas-Hyva 206
93/4 Sisu 263

HELISTEN, MIKKO
94/5 ParkieSE 219
95/6 Sisu 319
94/5 ToppsFinest 131

HELJEMO, CLAES
89/90 SemicElitserien 98

HELLE, JARI
72/3 WilliamsFIN 343

HELLE, MARTTI
71/2 WilliamsFIN 174
73/4 WilliamsFIN 178

HELLENBERG, PAR
89/90 SemicElitserien 241
90/1 SemicElitserien 151
91/2 SemicElitserien 253

HELLER, ERHARDT (OTT)
33/4 Anonymous (V129) 34
34-43 BeeHives(NYR)
33/4 CndGum (V252)
33-35 DiamondMatch
36-39 DiamondMatch (1),(2),(3)
33/4 OPC (V304A) 16
39/40 OPC (V301-1) 33
40/1 OPC (V301-2) 142
36/7 WWGum V356 87

HELLGREN, ARI
80/1 Mallasjuoma 89
82 Skopbank
78/9 SM-Liiga 131

HELLGREN, JENS
89/90 SemicElitserien 164
90/1 SemicElitserien 243
91/2 SemicElitserien 173

HELLKVIST, STEFAN
94/5 ElitSet 71
95/6 ElitSet 239, -FaceToFace 7
97/8 udSwedish 114

HELLKVIST, STEFAN
89/90 SemicElitserien 253
90/1 SemicElitserien 166
91/2 SemicElitserien 271
92/3 SemicElitserien 291
95/6 udElite 107

HELMAN, HARRY
23/4 (V145-1) 5

HELMER, TIM
83/4 Ottawa67s
84/5 Ottawa67s

HELMINEN, RAIMO
94/5 ElitSet 67,-Champ 6,-Play 4
95/6 ElitSet 96, -Mega 10
95 Globe141
95 Hartwall
95 PaniniWorlds 179
94 Semic 31
95 Semic 14
90/1 SemicElitserien 135
91/2 SemicElitserien 186
92/3 SemicElitserien 210
89 SemicSticker 39
91 SemicSticker 242
93 SemicSticker 63
95/6 Sisu-GoldCards 12
95/6 udElite 141, 232
96 Wien 14

HELMUTH, ANDY
84/5 Ottawa67s

HELPPOLAINEN, RAIMO
66/7 Champion 97
65/6 Hellas 81

HEMSTRÖM, JENS
94/5 ElitSet 219
90/1 SemicElitserien 147
95/6 udElite 181

HENCHBERGER, LLOYD
51/2 LavalDairy 66

HENDERSON, ARCHIE
88/9 ProCards(Indianapolis)
82/3 HFD/JuniorWhalers
89/90 Nashville
84/5 NovaScotia 12

HENDERSON, BURT
92/3 BCJHL 70
93/4 Tacoma

HENDERSON, GARFIELD
92/3 MPSPhotoSJHL 55
91/2 SketchWHL

HENDERSON, JAY
98 BowmanCHL 77
95/6 RedDeer

HENDERSON, JOHN
51/2 Parkhurst 23

HENDERSON, MURRAY
45-64 BeeHives(BOS)

HENDERSON, PAUL
68/9 Bauer
64-67 BeeHives(DET)
63-5 ChexPhoto
64/5 CokeCap DET-19
65/6 CocaCola
71/2 Colgate Heads
70/1 DadsCookies
70/1 EddieSargent 195
71/2 EddieSargent 200
72/3 EddieSargent 203
70/1 Esso Stamp
71/2 FritoLay
72/3 Letraset 22
73/4 MacsMilk Disk
68/9 OPC/Topps 127
69/70 OPC/Topps 47
70/1 O-Pee-Chee 217
71/2 OPC/Topps 67
72/3 OPC 126, Topps 73
72/3 OPC-Crest 19, -TmCanada
73/4 OPC/Topps 7
74/5 OPC/Topps 219
74/5 opcWHA 57
75/6 opcWHA 42
76/7 opcWHA 84
77/8 opcWHA 31
94/5 Parkie(64/5) 50
95/6 Parkie(66/7) 40
97/8 P.Certified-Smmt 1-4, -Aut
68/9 Post Marble
70/1 PostShooters
72 SemicSticker 167
68/9 ShirriffCoin TOR3
64/5 TheTorontoStar
71/2 TheTorontoSun
65/6 Topps 51
66/7 Topps 46, -USATest 46
67/8 Topps 103
91/2 Trends(72) 71, 98, -Aut.
92/3 Trends(76) 105
68/9 TOR
70/1 TOR
71/2 TOR
72/3 TOR
73/4 TOR

HENDRIK, JORG
94/5 DEL 266

HENDRICKSON
91/2 AvantGardeBCJ 156

HENDRICKSON, DARBY
95/6 Bowman 129
94/5 Classic 104
94/5 ClassicFourSport 135
93/4 ClassicProspects LP6
95/6 Donruss 184
95/6 EdgeIce 79
93/4 FleerUltra 485
95/6 FleerUltra 340
95/6 Leaf 76
97/8 PacificRegime 193
97/8 PinnacleBeAPlayer 178
93/4 PowerPlay 505
93/4 Premier-TeamUSA 4
97/8 Score(TOR) 12
95/6 SelectCertified 142
95/6 SkyBoxImpact 223
95/6 SP 145
95/6 Summit 178
93/4 T.StadiumClub-TmUSA 8
95/6 UpperDeck 505

96/7 UpperDeck 100
97/8 UpperDeck 166
96/7 UDCollChoice 158
97/8 UDCollChoice 250

HENDY, JAMES C.
83&87 HallOfFame 19
83 HHOF Postcard (B)

HENKELMAN, JEFF
95/6 SwiftCurrent

HENNIGAN, GORDON
52/3 Parkhurst 54

HENNIGER, STAN
83/4 NovaScotia 5

HENNING, LORNE
77/8 Coke Mini
72/3 EddieSargent 135
74/5 Loblaws
73/4 OPC 218
74/5 OPC 367
75/6 OPC 354
76/7 OPC/Topps 193
77/8 OPC/Topps 219
78/9 O-Pee-Chee 313
79/80 OPC/Topps 193
79/80 NYI
83/4 NYI/Islander 27

HENRICH, MICHAEL
98 BowmanCHL 30, 127, A6
98/9 Topps 223

HENRIKSEN, KEN
79 PaniniSticker 365

HENRIKSON, GUNNAR
91/2 AvantGardeBCJ 141

HENRIKSSON, HANNU
91/2 Jyvas-Hyva 11
93/4 Jyvas-Hyva 76
91 SemicSticker 11
93/4 Sisu 114
94/5 Sisu 128
95/6 Sisu 30, 177
96/7 Sisu-Hammer 1
95/6 SisuLimited 102

HENRIKSSON, LENNART
91/2 SemicElitserien 219

HENRY, ALEX
98 BowmanCHL 156, A17

HENRY, CAMILLE
52/3 AnonymousOHL 73
45-64 BeeHives(NYR)
64-67 BeeHives(CHI), (NYR)
64/5 CokeCap NYR-21
51-54 LaPatrie 25Jan53
68/9 OPC/Topps 116
69/70 OPC/Topps 17
54/5 Parkhurst 73
93/4 Parkhurst54 PR50
93/4 Parkie(56/7) 100
94/5 Parkie(64/5) 107
60/1 ShirriffCoin 83
61/2 ShirriffCoin 87
54/5 Topps 32
57/8 Topps 63
58/9 Topps 54
59/60 Topps 28, 46
60/1 Topps 53
61/2 Topps 56, -Stamp
62/3 Topps 62
63/4 Topps 56
64/5 Topps 14
65/6 Topps 58
67/8 Topps 26
54-67 TorontoStar V6
56-66 TorontoStar 57/8, 62/3
63/4 TheTorontoStar
91/2 Ultimate(O6) 22, -Aut. 22

HENRY, BURKE
98 BowmanCHL 67

HENRY, DALE
94/5 Classic E3
90/1 ProCards 529
89/90 ProCards(AHL) 231
88/9 ProCards(Springfield)
83/4 Saskatoon 11

HENRY, FRÉDÉRICK
97/8 Bowman 43

HENRY, JIM (SUGAR)
34-43 BeeHives(NYRx2)
45-64 BeeHives(BOS), (CHI)
43-47 ParadeSportive
51/2 Parkhurst 19
52/3 Parkhurst 74
53/4 Parkhurst 86
54/5 Parkhurst 49
92/3 Parkhurst 52 PR7
54/5 Topps 37

HENTTONEN, JUHA
80/1 Mallasjuoma 154

HENZEN, CHARLY
72 SemicSticker 150

HEON, CORY
92/3 MPSPhotoSJHL 42

HEPPLE, ALAN
90/1 ProCards 157
91/2 ProCards 316
89/90 ProCards(AHL) 117
88/9 ProCards(Newmarket)
92/3 Cincinnati
90/1 Newmarket
81/2 Ottawa67s
82/3 Ottawa67s

HEPPNER, KEN
81/2 Regina 14

HERBERS, IAN
93/4 Leaf 423
93/4 Parkhurst 70
93/4 EDM 21NOV93
84/5 KelownaWings&WHL 10
94/5 CapeBreton

HERBERT, BJORN
71/2 WilliamsFIN 279
73/4 WilliamsFIN 195

HERBERT, IAN
95/6 Birmingham

HERBERT, RICK
82/3 Regina 10
83/4 Regina 10

HERBERTS, JAMES
24/5 Champs (C144)
24/5 MapleCrispettes V130 8
24/5 (V145-2) 25

HERBST, A.
95/6 DEL 179

HERBST, M.
95/6 DEL 125
96/7 DEL 205

HERGESHEIMER, PHIL
34-43 BeeHives(CHI)
40/1 OPC (V301-2) 143

HERGESHEIMER, WALLY
45-64 BeeHives(NYR)
51-54 LaPatrie 22Mar53
51/2 Parkhurst 100
52/3 Parkhurst 20
53/4 Parkhurst 67
54/5 Parkhurst 71
93/4 Parkie(56/7) 26
54/5 Topps 22
57/8 Topps 33
54-67 TorontoStarV4 ,n11

HERGOTT, ORRIN
91/2 AirCanadaSJHL B51

HERLICK, DARCY
91/2 AirCanadaSJHL D1
92/3 MPSPhotoSJHL 147

HERLOFSKY, DEREK
95/6 Dayton

HERMAN
91/2 AvantGardeBCJHL 163

HERMANSON, LENNART
94/5 ElitSet 80
90/1 SemicElitserien 142
92/3 SemicElitserien 238

HERN, RILEY
91 C55 Reprint 32
83&87 HallOfFame 232
83 HHOF Postcard (K)
1910-11 Imperial (C55) 32
1911-12 Imperial (C56) 22
1910-11 Imperial Post 32

HERNIMAN, SCOTT
88/9 Sudbury 25

HERNIMAN, STEVE
91/2 ProCards 146
87/8 SSMarie 19

HERNSKY, PETR
94/5 APS 280

HERON, CHRIS
96/7 UpperDeck 382

HERON, RED
34-43 BeeHives(TOR)
39/40 OPC (V301-1) 53
40/1 OPC (V301-2) 140

HEROUX, YVES
96/7 DEL 18
90/1 ProCards 96, 518
91/2 ProCards 34
88/9 Flint
86/7 Fredericton

HERPERGER, CHRIS
95/6 EdgeIce 45
90/1 SketchWHL 67
91/2 SketchWHL 189
93/4 Seattle

HERR, MATT
95/6 DonrussElite-WorldJrs 37

HERRIMAN, DON
73/4 QuakerOats 46

HERRINGTON, RON
92/3 BCJHL 183

HERRON, DENIS
72-84 Dernière 80/1
74/5 Loblaws, -Update
74/5 OPC/Topps 45
75/6 OPC/Topps 68
76/7 OPC/Topps 55
77/8 OPC/Topps 119
78/9 OPC/Topps 172
79/80 OPC/Topps 94
80/1 OPC/Topps 130, 166
82/3 O-Pee-Chee 239, 241, 270
84/5 O-Pee-Chee 176
85/6 O-Pee-Chee 186
81/2 opcSticker 258
82/3 opcSticker 41, 252
84/5 opcSticker 122
79 PaniniSticker 52
80/1 Pepsi Cap
79/80 MTL
80/1 MTL
81/2 MTL
83/4 PGH
77/8 PGH/PuckBuck
83/4 PGH/Heinz
84/5 PGH/Heinz

HERSH, HAROLD
91/2 SketchQMJHL 219
95/6 Fredericton
96/7 Fredericton

HERSH, JAROLD
94/5 Slapshot(MEM) 57

HERTER, JASON
92/3 ClassicProspects 58
91/2 ProCards 600
90/1 UpperDeck 325
92/3 Hamilton

HERVEY, MATT
88/9 ProCards(Moncton)
89/90 ProCards(AHL) 40
90/1 ProCards 251
91/2 ProCards 63
92/3 AtlantaKnights
87/8 Moncton
89/90 Moncton
90/1 Moncton
83/4 Victoria

HERZIG, FALK
94/5 DEL 402
95/6 DEL 421

HERZIG, ROLAND
79 PaniniSticker 249

HES, JIRI
94/5 APS 257
95/6 APS 130

HESHKA, SCOTT
92/3 MPSPhotoSJHL 159

HESS, BOB
75/6 OPC/Topps 264
76/7 OPC 277
77/8 OPC 394
78/9 O-Pee-Chee 358

HESS, MANUEL
94/5 DEL 190
95/6 DEL 190
96/7 DEL 129

HETTLE, FRED
90/1 SketchWHL 300
91/2 SketchWHL 271

HEVONKORPI, RISTO
72/3 WilliamsFIN 279

HEWARD, JAMIE
92/3 C'Prospects 107
91/2 ProCards 308
90/1 SketchWHL 167
92/3 ClevelandLumberjacks 7
93/4 ClevelandLumberjacks
87/8 Regina
89/90 Regina

HEWER, OAK
96/7 SSMarie

HEWITSON, BOB
83&87 HallOfFame 82
83 HHOF Postcard (F)

HEWITT, FOSTER
34-43 BeeHives(Misc.)
83&87 HallOfFame 8
83 HHOF Postcard (A)
92/3 HHOFLegends 13
38/9 QuakerOats

HEWITT, WILLIAM
83&87 HallOfFame 99
83 HHOF Postcard (G)

HEXTALL, BRYAN (SR.)
34-43 BeeHives(NYR)
93/4 HHOFLegends 28
83&87 HallOfFame 141
83 HHOF Postcard (K)
39/40 OPC (V301-1) 86

HEXTALL, BRYAN
70/1 DadsCookies
71/2 EddieSargent 173
72/3 EddieSargent 173
70/1 Esso Stamp
72/3 Letraset 13
69/70 O-Pee-Chee 154
70/1 OPC/Topps 94
71/2 OPC/Topps 16
72/3 OPC 174, Topps 157
73/4 OPC/Topps 43
75/6 OPC/Topps 26
76/7 OPC/Topps 13
71/2 TheTorontoSun
71/2 PGH

HEXTALL, DENNIS
70/1 EddieSargent 133
70/1 Esso Stamp
74/5 Loblaws
69/70 OPC/Topps 107
70/1 OPC 186
71/2 OPC/Topps 244, Topps 128
72/3 OPC 224
73/4 OPC 115, Topps 136
74/5 OPC/Topps 2, 112, 115
75/6 OPC/Topps 310, 321
76/7 OPC/Topps 32
77/8 OPC/Topps 197
78/9 OPC/Topps 48
79/80 O-Pee-Chee 392
72 SemicSticker 172
73/4 MIN
79/80 WSH

HEXTALL, DONEVAN
91/2 Arena 24
91/2 Classic 29
91/2 ClassicFourSport 29, -Aut
90/1 SketchWHL 277
91/2 SketchAwards 15
91/2 SketchWHL 266
91/2 StarPics 11
91/2 UltimateDP 25, 89, -Aut 25
90/1 PrinceAlbert
91/2 PrinceAlbert

HEXTALL, RON
90/1 Bowman 105
91/2 Bowman 234
92/3 Bowman 195
95/6 Bowman 38
94/5 C'Images PL4
93/4 Donruss 196
94/5 Donruss 147
95/6 Donruss 147
96/7 Donruss 61
97/8 Donruss 114
96/7 D.CanadianIce 51
97/8 D.CdnIce 48, -National 26
95/6 DonrussElite 108,-Painted 8
96/7 DonrussElite 2
97/8 DonrussElite 35
97/8 D.Preferred 96,-ColourG 14
97/8 D.Priority 48,-PostGen 9
97/8 DonrussStudio 43
93/4 EASports 114
88/9 Esso Sticker
94/5 Flair 127
96/7 Flair 68
94/5 Fleer 154
96/7 Fleer 80, 144-45, -Vezina 5
95/6 FleerMetal 110
96/7 FleerNHLPicks 80
96/7 F.Picks-Fab 18, -Fantasy 3
92/3 FleerUltra 174, 385
93/4 FleerUltra 366
94/5 FleerUltra 127, 343
95/6 FleerUltra 117, 371
96/7 FleerUltra 124
88/9 FritoLay
93/4 HighLiner 4
95/6 Hoyle'EAST 5 (Spades)
97/8 KatchMedallion 105
97/8 KennerSLU
90/1 Kraft 17
92/3 Kraft'Disk
94/5 KraftDinner
95/6 Kraft
93/4 Leaf 341
94/5 Leaf 50, 495
95/6 Leaf 192
96/7 Leaf 194, -ShutDown 14
97/8 Leaf 52
95/6 LeafLimited-Stick 7
96/7 LeafLimited 35
96/7 LeafPreferred 77, -Steel 9
97/8 Limited 89, -fabric 52
96/7 Maggers 113
96/7 MetalUniv. 112, -Armour 5
97/8 Omega 165, -NoScorZn 9
87/8 OPC/Topps 169, T-AS 2
88/9 OPC/Topps 34
89/90 OPC/Topps 155, OPC 311
90/1 OPC/Topps 243
91/2 OPC/Topps 470
92/3 O-Pee-Chee 84
90/1 opcPremier 41
91/2 opcPremier 38
92/3 opcPremier 57
87/8 opcStars 16
88/9 opcStars 14
87/8 opcStickr 1, 101/234,181/41
87/8 opcStick. 114/126, 129/117
88/9 opcSticker 103
89/90 opcSticker 111
98/9 Pacific 326
97/8 PacificCrown 27, -InThe 14
97/8 PacificCrownRoyale 97
97/8 PCR -FreezeOut 13
97/8 PacificDynagon! 89
97/8 PcfcD-Stone 15,-Tandm 55
97/8 PacificInvincible 100
97/8 PcfcParamnt 132,-Glove 14
98/9 PcfcParamnt 174,-Glove 14
97/8 PcfcRevolutn 101,-RtrnT 14
87/8 PaniniSticker 123, 191, 378
88/9 PaniniSticker 315
89/90 PaniniSticker 302
90/1 PaniniSticker 118
91/2 PaniniSticker 227
93/4 PaniniSticker 77
94/5 PaniniSticker 54
95/6 PaniniSticker 123
96/7 PaniniSticker 113, 146
97/8 PaniniSticker 91
91/2 Parkhurst 126
92/3 Parkhurst 144, CP20
93/4 Parkhurst 118

94/5 Parkhurst 136
95/6 Parkhurst 159, PP33
94/5 ParkieSE 130
91/2 Pinnacle 118
92/3 Pinnacle 340
93/4 Pinnacle 376, -Masks 8
94/5 Pinnacle 274, MA6
95/6 Pinnacle 95, -Masks 8
96/7 Pinnacle 101, -Masks 8
97/8 Pinnacle 100
96/7 Pinn.BeAPlayer-Stacking 3
97/8 PinnacleInside 22, -Stop 18
95/6 PinnacleZenith 97
96/7 PinnacleZenith 46
95/6 Playoff 181
94/5 POG 372
95/6 POG 210
93/4 PowerPlay 147
93/4 Premier 468
95/6 ProMagnet 49, IC06
90/1 ProSet 216
91/2 ProSet 176
92/3 ProSet 129
91/2 PSPlatinum 87
90/1 Score 25, -Hot 14
91/2 Score(CDN) 459, (U.S) 239
92/3 Score 104
93/4 Score 152, 544
94/5 Score 140
95/6 Score 195, -MailIn
96/7 Score 80, -Superstition 9
96/7 Score-Net 11, -Sudden 14
97/8 Score 27
97/8 Score(PHA) 1
94/5 Select 67
95/6 SelectCertified 78
96/7 SelectCert. 63, -Freezer 13
89 SemicSticker 55
95/6 SkyBoxEmotion 131
95/6 SkyBoxImpact 125
96/7 SkyBoxImpact 95, -Zero 5
94/5 SP 87
95/6 SP 109
96/7 SP 116
97/8 SPAuthentic 116
95/6 Summit 133, -InTheCr 10
96/7 Summit 100, -InTheCr 16
96/7 Summit-Untouchable 18
96/7 TeamOut
92/3 Topps 40
95/6 Topps 167, HG12
95/6 ToppsFinest 86
96/7 ToppsNHLPicks ID11
91/2 ToppsStadiumClub 173
92/3 ToppsStadiumClub 288
93/4 ToppsStadiumClub 433
94/5 T.StadiumClub 51, 182
95/6 ToppsStadiumClub 33
95/6 ToppsSuperSkills 77
90/1 UpperDeck 227
91/2 UpperDeck 327
92/3 UpperDeck 532
93/4 UpperDeck 434
94/5 UpperDeck 170, SP147
95/6 UpperDeck 428, SE65
96/7 UD 119, 197, SS2B
95/6 UDBeAPlayer 198
95/6 UDCollChoice 203
96/7 UDCollChoice 191, 326
97/8 UDCollChoice 188
86/7 PHA
89/90 PHA
90/1 PHA
91/2 PHA/JCPenney
94/5 PHA
96/7 PHA/OceanSpray
92/3 QUE/PetroCanada

HEYLIGER, VICTOR
36-39 DiamondMatch (6)

HIBBERT, JAMES (JIM)
93/4 Slapshot(NiagaraFalls) 2
97/8 SheffieldSteelers

HICKE, BILL
45-64 BeeHives(MTL)
64-67 BeeHives(MTL), (NYR)
62 CeramicTiles
63-5 ChexPhoto
64/5 CokeCap MTL-8
65/6 CocaCola
70/1 DadsCookies
70/1 EddieSargent 143
71/2 EddieSargent 175
70/1 Esso Stamp
68/9 OPC/Topps 86
69/70 OPC 145, -Sticker, T. 84
70/1 OPC/Topps 76, -Sticker
70/1 OPC/T.-Deckle 38
71/2 OPC/Topps 142
72/3 OPC 327
59/60 Parkhurst 31
60/1 Parkhurst 40, 56
61/2 Parkhurst 38
62/3 Parkhurst 40
63/4 Parkhurst 25, 84
94/5 Parkie(64/5) 86
95/6 Parkie(66/7) 91
60/1 ShirriffCoin 38
61/2 ShirriffCoin 108
62/3 ShirriffCoin 38
68/9 ShirriffCoin OAK9
71/2 TheTorontoSun
64/5 Topps 98
65/6 Topps 30
60/1 York
61/2 York 16
63/4 York 30

HICKE, ERNIE
71/2 EddieSargent 139
72/3 EddieSargent 3
70/1 Esso Stamp
74/5 Loblaws, -Update
71/2 OPC/Topps 61
72/3 OPC 72, Topps 154
73/4 OPC/Topps 18
74/5 OPC 387
75/6 OPC/Topps 71
76/7 OPC/Topps 87
77/8 OPC/Topps 132
71/2 TheTorontoSun

HICKEY, GREG
75/6 Hamilton

HICKEY, PAT
75/6 OPC 345
76/7 OPC/Topps 107
77/8 OPC/Topps 221
78/9 OPC/Topps 112
79/80 OPC/Topps 86
80/1 OPC/Topps 28
81/2 O-Pee-Chee 318
82/3 O-Pee-Chee 304
81/2 opcSticker 104
74/5 opcWHA 24
79 PaniniSticker 68
80/1 Pepsi Cap
88/9 ProCards(NewHaven)
79/80 TOR
80/1 TOR
92/3 Hamilton (x2)

HICKS, ALEX
98/9 Pacific 353
97/8 PacificRegime 159
95/6 Parkhurst 271
97/8 PinnacleBeAPlayer 177
97/8 Score(PGH) 15
96/7 UpperDeck 6
96/7 UDCollC hoice 9
94/5 LasVegas

HICKS, DOUG
77/8 OPC 361
78/9 OPC/Topps 228
79/80 O-Pee-Chee 379
80/1 OPC/Topps 221
81/2 O-Pee-Chee 114
82/3 O-Pee-Chee 365
82/3 Post
79/80 EDM
80/1 EDM/Zellers
81/2 EDM/RedRooster
88/9 EDM/ActionMagazine 95
81/2 WSH

HICKS, GLENN
81/2 O-Pee-Chee 98
79/80 DET
80/1 DET
77/8 Winnipeg
78/9 Winnipeg

HICKS, GREG
60/1 ClevelandBarons

HICKS, GRIEG
52/3 AnonymousOHL 124

HICKS, WAYNE
62 CeramicTiles
70/1 OPC/Topps 95
63/4 QuébecAces
65/6 QuébecAces

HIDLEBAUGH, MIKE
91/2 AirCanadaSJHL C50

HIEKKARANTA, AARNO
65/6 Hellas 55

HIEMER, MANUEL
96/7 DEL 186

HIEMER, ULICH
95/6 DEL 84
86/7 O-Pee-Chee 226
95 PaniniWorlds 54
94 Semic 277
89 SemicSticker 108
91 SemicSticker 155
84/5 N.J.
86/7 N.J./SOBER

HIETANEN, JORMA
65/6 Hellas 89

HIETANEN, O.J.
73/4 WilliamsFIN 106

HIETANEN, OLLI
71/2 WilliamsFIN 98
72/3 WilliamsFIN 141

HIETANEN, O.T.
73/4 WilliamsFIN 107

HIGGINS, JACK
52/3 AnonymousOHL 105

HIGGINS, MATT
95/6 Bowman P17
98/9 SPx"Finite" 45
98/9 UDChoice 107

HIGGINS, PAUL
82/3 TOR

HIGGINS, TIM
81/2 OPC 57, Topps(W) 69
82/3 O-Pee-Chee 66
83/4 O-Pee-Chee 104
84/5 O-Pee-Chee 111
86/7 O-Pee-Chee 227
82/3 opcSticker 177
87/8 PaniniSticker 250
82/3 Post
79/80 CHI
80/1 CHI/4x6
80/1 CHI/5.5x8.5
81/2 CHI
82/3 CHI
86/7 DET/Caesars
87/8 DET/Caesars
88/9 DET/Caesars
84/5 N.J.

HIIROS, PENTTI
70/1 Kuvajulkaisut 173
71/2 WilliamsFIN 99
72/3 WilliamsFIN 142
73/4 WilliamsFIN 108

HIITELA, SEPPO
78/9 SM-Liiga 64

HILDEBRAND, IKE
45-64 BeeHives(NYR)
54/5 Parkhurst 83
51/2 ClevelandBarons

HILDEBRANDT, ROY
89/90 Rayside

HILGER, RAIMUND
94/5 DEL 380
95/6 DEL 378
96/7 DEL 199
95 PaniniWorlds 67
94 Semic 288
95 Semic 169
92 SemicSticker 180
93 SemicSticker 163
92/3 UpperDeck 373

HILL, AL
79/80 OPC/Topps 166
80/1 O-Pee-Chee 348
88/9 ProCards(Hershey)
89/90 ProCards(AHL) 359
90/1 ProCards 20
91/2 ProCards 213
96/7 Cincinnati

HILL, JOHN MELVIN
34-43 BeeHives(BOS), (TOR)
39/40 OPC (V301-1) 96
45-54 QuakerOats
91/2 BOS/Legends

HILL, KILEY
93/4 SSMarie 24
91/2 SketchOHL 314

HILL, SEAN
92/3 Classic 101
92/3 ClassicFourSport 214
93/4 Donruss 7
94/5 Flair 121
94/5 Fleer 147
92/3 FleerUltra 328
93/4 FleerUltra 182, 255
94/5 FleerUltra 339
93/4 Leaf 353
94/5 Leaf 476
97/8 PacificRegime 133
94/5 PaniniSticker 125
95/6 PaniniSticker 56
95 PaniniWorlds 214
92/3 Parkhurst 487
93/4 Parkhurst 2
94/5 Parkhurst 6
95/6 Parkhurst 416
94/5 ParkieSE 124
93/4 Pinnacle 147, -Expansion 3
94/5 Pinnacle 395
95/6 Pinnacle 93
95/6 Playoff 287
95/6 POG 198
93/4 PowerPlay 3
93/4 Premier 312
94/5 Premier 545
91/2 ProCards 84
93/4 Score 490, 500
95/6 Topps 329
93/4 ToppsStadiumClub 387
94/5 ToppsStadiumClub 28
92/3 UpperDeck 392, 523
93/4 UpperDeck 16, SP-1
94/5 UpperDeck 161
95/6 UpperDeck 323
96/7 UpperDeck 117
95/6 UDBeAPlayer 74
95/6 UDCollChoice 65
92/3 MTL
92/3 MTL/OPC 19
94/5 OTT/Bell
95/6 OTT
96/7 OTT/PizzaHut

HILL, TIM
93/4 Slapshot(Peterborough) 6

HILLBLOM, NIKLAS
90/1 SemicElitserien 219

HILLEBRANDT, JON
93/4 Classic 68
94/5 Classic-Autograph
93/4 ClassicProspects 162
93/4 Premier-TeamUSA 10
93/4 TSC-TmUSA 9
95/6 Binghampton

HILLER, BERND
70/1 Kuvajulkaisut 85

HILLER, WILBERT "DUTCH"
34-43 BeeHives(NYR)
39/40 OPC (V301-1) 89
43-47 ParadeSportive (x2)
45-54 QuakerOats

HILLER, GUIDO
94/5 DEL 45

HILLER, JIM
93/4 ClassicProspects 117
94/5 DEL 195
92/3 FleerUltra 307
92/3 opcPremier 34
92/3 Parkhurst 70, 281
92/3 Pinnacle 399
92/3 UpperDeck 560
94/5 Binghampton

HILLIER, CRAIG
95/6 Bowman P18
97/8 PinnacleBeeHive 64
95/6 Slapshot 257

HILLIER, RANDY
85/6 O-Pee-Chee 212
88/9 OPC/Topps 158
89/90 OPC/Topps 126
90/1 O-Pee-Chee 408
91/2 opcPremier 122
87/8 PaniniSticker 145
90/1 PaniniSticker 137
91/2 Pinnacle 281
90/1 ProSet 507
91/2 ProSet 360
91/2 PSPlatinum 158
90/1 Score 76
91/2 Score(CDN) 580, (U.S) 30T
83/4 SouhaitsRen.KeyChain
83/4 BOS
91/2 BUF/BlueShield
91/2 BUF/Campbell
86/7 PGH/Kodak
87/8 PGH/Kodak
89/90 PGH/Foodland 11
90/1 PGH/Foodland 3

HILLMAN, FLOYD
52/3 AnonymousOHL 83

HILLMAN, LARRY
52/3 AnonymousOHL 3
45-64 BeeHive(BOS)(CHI)(DET)
64-67 BeeHives(TOR)
70/1 DadsCookies
70/1 EddieSargent 158
71/2 EddieSargent 75
72/3 EddieSargent 39
70/1 Esso Stamp
68/9 OPC/Topps 48
69/70 OPC/T. 90, OPC-Sticker
70/1 OPC/Topps 81
71/2 OPC/Topps 168
72/3 OPC 176
61/2 Parkhurst 14
62/3 Parkhurst 17
93/4 Parkie(56/7) 55
94/5 Parkie(64/5) 118
95/6 Parkie(66/7) 104
67 Post FlipBook
72 SemicSticker 178
61/2 ShirriffCoin 59
62/3 ShirriffCoin 17
68/9 ShirriffCoin MIN12
71/2 TheTorontoSun
57/8 Topps 17
58/9 Topps 25
67/8 Topps 80
91/2 Ultimate(O6) 36, -Aut 36
60/1 York
61/2 York 31
63/4 York 11
67/8 York 29
72/3 BUF
70/1 PHA
68/9 TOR
69/70 TOR
77/8 WinnipegJets
78/9 WinnipegJets

HILLMAN, WAYNE
71/2 Bazooka Panel 26
45-64 BeeHives(TOR)
64-67 BeeHives(CHI), (NYR)
62 CeramicTiles
63-5 ChexPhoto
64/5 CokeCap CHI-20
65/6 CocaCola
70/1 DadsCookies
70/1 EddieSargent 160
71/2 EddieSargent 146
72/3 EddieSargent 156
70/1 Esso Stamp
68/9 OPC/Topps 47
69/70 OPC/Topps 91
70/1 OPC 198
71/2 OPC/Topps 62
72/3 OPC 255
94/5 Parkie(64/5) 41
95/6 Parkie(66/7) 84, 138
61/2 ShirriffCoin 21
64/5 TheTorontoStar
71/2 TheTorontoSun (x2)
61/2 Topps 38
62/3 Topps 31
63/4 Topps 27
64/5 Topps 41
66/7 Topps 87, -USATest 34
67/8 Topps 22

HILLOCK, DON
90/1 Newmarket

HILLOCK, MIKE
91/2 AirCanadaSJHL C12
92/3 MPSPhotoSJHL 67
90/1 ProCards 594

HILTON, KEVIN
93/4 Donruss USA9
93/4 Pinnacle 493
93/4 UpperDeck 567

HILTON, HANNU
80/1 Mallasjuoma 93
71/2 WilliamsFIN 299

HILTUNEN, HARRI
70/1 Kuvajulkaisut 328

HIMES, NORMIE
33/4 Anonymous (V129) 21
33/4 CndGum (V252)
33-35 DiamondMatch
36-39 DiamondMatch (1)
27-32 LaPresse 31/2
33/4 OPC (V304A) 29
33/4 WWGum (V357) 44
36/7 WWGum (V356) 92

HINDMARSH, DAVID
83/4 O-Pee-Chee 82
84/5 O-Pee-Chee 224
83/4 Vachon 7
82/3 CGY

HINKS, ROD
90/1 SketchOHL 384
91/2 SketchOHL 252
94/5 Johnstown 9
93/4 OwenSound
90/1 Sudbury 10
91/2 Sudbury 18
92/3 Sudbury 18

HINSE, ANDRÉ
75/6 opcWHA 35
75/6 Houston
76/7 Phoenix

HINTERSTOCKER, HERMANN
79 PaniniSticker 109

HINTERSTOCKER, MARTIN
79 PaniniSticker 106

HINZ, CHAD
96/7 UpperDeck 383
98 BowmanCHL 80

HIRCHE, KLAUS
70/1 Kuvajulkaisut 86

HIRSCH, COREY
95/6 Bowman 145
93/4 CanadaNats
93/4 Classic 133
94/5 Classic 85, T43
94/5 ClassicImages 62
92/3 C'Prospects 65, 74, BC5
93/4 ClassicProspects LP14
93/4 Donruss 216
96/7 Donruss 179
97/8 Donruss 162
96/7 DonrussCanadianIce 73
97/8 DonrussCanadianIce 109
96/7 DonrussElite 34
95/6 EdgeIce 19
96/7 Flair 94
93/4 F.Ultra 64,462, -AllRookie 3
94/5 FleerUltra 330
93/4 Leaf 313
96/7 Leaf 152, -ShutDown 12
97/8 Leaf 146
96/7 LeafLimited 89
96/7 LeafPreferred 33, -Steel 3
97/8 Limited 17, 89
96/7 Maggers 155
97/8 PacificCrown 180
92/3 Parkhurst 344
94/5 Parkhurst 149
95/6 Parkhurst 483
93/4 Pinnacle 220
94/5 Pinnacle RTP1
96/7 Pinnacle 211, -Mask 4
96/7 PinnacleBeAPlayer 51
97/8 Pinn.Inside 29, -StandUp 9
95/6 PinnacleZenith 134
96/7 PinnacleZenith 75
93/4 PowerPlay 482
93/4 Premier-TmCanada 18
93/4 Score 453
94/5 Score CT4
96/7 Score 149,-Net 16,-Sddn 13
97/8 Score 12
97/8 Score(VAN) 11
95/6 SelectCertified 143
96/7 SelectCertified 71
94 Semic 80
89/90 SketchMEM 25
90/1 SketchWHL 306
91/2 SketchWHL 76
95/6 SP 151
96/7 SP 159
95/6 Summit 184
96/7 Summit 125, -InTheCr 15
96/7 ToppsNHLPicks 16
92/3 UpperDeck 463
94/5 UpperDeck 218
95/6 UpperDeck 405
96/7 UpperDeck 168
97/8 UpperDeck 171
96/7 UDBlackDiamond 131
96/7 UDCollChoice 272
97/8 UDCollChoice 258
96/7 UpperDeck"Ice" 71
96/7 VAN
96/7 VAN/IGA
92/3 Binghampton
94/5 Binghampton

HIRSCH, TOM
84/5 O-Pee-Chee 99
84/5 MIN
85/6 MIN
87/8 MIN

HIRSCHFELD, BERT
45-54 QuakerOats

HIRSIMAKI, JARI
95/6 Sisu 143, -Spotlight 7
95/6 SisuLimited 99

HIRSIMAKI, JARI
71/2 WilliamsFIN 341
72/3 WilliamsFIN 344

HIRSIMAKI, JUKKA
80/1 Mallasjuoma 173
78/9 SM-Liiga 182
72/3 WilliamsFIN 303

HIRSIMAKI, TIMO
66/7 Champion 188
70/1 Kuvajulkaisut 125
72 Panda
71/2 WilliamsFIN 175
72/3 WilliamsFIN 123

HIRVONEN, PENTTI
71/2 WilliamsFIN 261

HIRVONEN, RAIMO
80/1 Mallasjuoma 9
82 SemicSticker 31
82 Skopbank
78/9 SM-Liiga 26

HIRVONEN, SEPPO
71/2 WilliamsFIN 318

HIRVONEN, TIMO
93/4 Jyvas-Hyva 207
93/4 Sisu 268
94/5 Sisu 106
95/6 Sisu 294

HIRVONEN, TOMI
95/6 Sisu 242, -NHLDraft 11
96/7 Sisu 36, 94
95/6 UDCollChoice 338

HISLOP, JAMIE
79/80 O-Pee-Chee 380
80/1 O-Pee-Chee 327
81/2 O-Pee-Chee 40
82/3 O-Pee-Chee 47
83/4 O-Pee-Chee 83
80/1 Pepsi Cap
82/3 Post
89/90 ProCards(IHL) 200
90/1 ProCards 612
83/4 SouhaitsRen.KeyChain
83/4 Vachon 8
81/2 CGY
82/3 CGY
92/3 CGY/IGA 29
80/1 QUE

HITCHCOCK, KEN
96/7 DAL/Southwest
92/3 PHA/UD 27FEB93
84/5 Kamloops

HITCHEN, ALLEN
95/6 Slapshot 306

HITCHMAN, LIONEL
38/9 BruinsMagazine
24/5 Champs (C144)
33-35 DiamondMatch
27-32 LaPresse 29/30
33/4 OPC (V304A) 5
23/4 (V145-1) 8
24/5 (V145-2) 4
33/4 WWGum (V357) 34
91/2 BOS/Legends

HITNER, MIKE
90/1 KansasCity 13

HJALM, MICHAEL
94/5 ElitSet 263
95/6 ElitSet 123, -FaceTo 11
89/90 SemicElitserien 180
92/3 SemicElitserien 263
95/6 udElite 180

HJALMAR, HANS
89/90 SemicElitserien 204
90/1 SemicElitserien 242

HJALMARSSON, MATS
91/2 SemicElitserien 301
92/3 SemicElitserien 316

HJERPE, HAKAN
82 SemicSticker 36
78/9 SM-Liiga 218
80/1 Mallasjuoma 193

HJERTAAS, TROY
90/1 SketchWHL 282
91/2 SketchWHL 252
90/1 PrinceAlbert
91/2 PrinceAlbert

HLAVAC, JAN
94/5 APS 84
95/6 APS 288
95/6 Classic 25
95/6 ClassicFiveSport 136
94/5 ParkieSE 213
94/5 SP 158
94/5 UpperDeck 508

HLINKA, IVAN
95/6 APS 395
72 Hellas 99
74 Hellas 70
70/1 Kuvajulkaisut 46
82/3 O-Pee-Chee 346
72 Panda
79 PaniniSticker 83
82/3 Post
72 SemicSticker 40
74 SemicSticker 66
91 SemicSticker 250
92 SemicSticker 122
83/4 SouhaitsRen.KeyChain
77-80 Sportscaster103-2455
92/3 Trends(76) 128
71/2 WilliamsFIN 26
72/3 WilliamsFIN 6
73/4 WilliamsFIN 47
81/2 VAN/Silverwood
82/3 VAN

HLINKA, JAROSLAV
95/6 APS 287

HLINKA, JIRI
94/5 APS 262
95/6 APS 142

HLINKA, MICHAL
94/5 APS 117
95/6 APS 221

HLINKA, MIROSLAV
94/5 APS 90
95/6 APS 286

HLUSHKO, TODD
92/3 CanadaNats
93/4 CanadaNats
93/4 Donruss 469
93/4 FleerUltra 463
97/8 PacificRegime 28
94/5 ParkieSE 25
93/4 PowerPlay 483
93/4 Premier-TmCanada 12
90/1 ProCards 202
91/2 ProCards 567
94/5 Score CT9
89/90 SketchOHL 41
96/7 Summit 194
91/2 Baltimore 9

HLYNYSKY, BILL
81/2 Saskatoon 18

HNIDY, SHANE
91/2 SketchWHL 177
93/4 PrinceAlbert
95/6 PrinceAlbert

HNILICKA, MILAN
95/6 APS 337
91/2 UD-CzechWJC 87

HOACK, RUEDIGER
74 Hellas 115

HOAD, JEFF
90/1 SketchWHL 221
91/2 SketchWHL 215

HOARD, BRIAN
88/9 ProCards(Newmarket)
89/90 ProCards(AHL) 111

HOBERG, ANDERS
86/7 Sudbury 1

HOBIN, MIKE
77/8 NovaScotia
76/7 Phoenix

HOBSON, DOUG
88/9 ProCards(Muskegon)
84/5 PrinceAlbert

HOCK, ROBERT
94/5 DEL 375
95/6 DEL 356
94 Semic 282

HOCKING, JUSTIN
92/3 Classic 16
92/3 ClassicFourSport 165
94/5 Leaf 479
91/2 SketchWHL 12
94/5 UpperDeck 210

HODEK, PETR
94/5 APS 99

HODGE, CHARLIE
52/3 AnonymousOHL 129
45-64 BeeHives(MTLx2)
64-67 BeeHives(MTL)
63-5 ChexPhoto
64/5 CokeCap MTL-1
65/6 CocaCola
70/1 Colgate Stamp 68
70/1 DadsCookies
70/1 EddieSargent 211
70/1 Esso Stamp
68/9 OPC/Topps 78, -Puck 12
69/70 OPC/T. 77, OPC-Sticker
70/1 OPC 229
55/6 Parkhurst 69
57/8 Parkhurst (MTL) 17
58/9 Parkhurst 17
59/60 Parkhurst 16
93/4 Parkie(56/7) FS6
94/5 Parkie(64/5) 82, 139, 148
95/6 Parkie(66/7) 70, 131
60/1 ShirriffCoin 39
68/9 ShirriffCoin OAK7
56-66 TorontoStar 63/4, 64/5
64/5 TheTorontoStar
64/5 Topps 17
65/6 Topps 67
66/7 Topps 65
60/1 York
67/8 MTL
70/1 VAN/RoyalBank
63/4 QuébecAces

HODGE, CLINT
91/2 AirCanadaSJHL D30
92/3 MPSPhotoSJHL 84

HODGE, KEN
91/2 SketchWHL 44

HODGE, KEN (SR.)
68/9 Bauer
64-67 BeeHives(CHI)
65/6 CocaCola
70/1 Colgate Stamp 62
70/1 DadsCookies
70/1 EddieSargent 10
71/2 EddieSargent 8
72/3 EddieSargent 22
70/1 Esso Stamp
74/5 LiptonSoup 28
74/5 Loblaws
68/9 OPC/Topps 8
69/70 OPC/Topps 27
69/79 OPC-Sticker, -Stamp
70/1 OPC/Topps 8, OPC 233
71/2 OPC/Topps 115, 254
72/3 OPC 49, Topps 166
73/4 OPC 26, Topps 133
74/5 OPC/Topps 128, 230
75/6 OPC/Topps 215
76/7 OPC/Topps 25
77/8 OPC/Topps 192
94/5 Parkie(64/5) FS3
95/6 Parkie(66/7) 23
70/1 PostShooters
68/9 ShirriffCoin BOS10
71/2 TheTorontoSun
65/6 Topps 65
66/7 Topps 114
67/8 Topps 98
91/2 Ultimate(O6) 49, -Aut 49
70/1 BOS
70/1 BOS/Ashtray
71/2 BOS

HODGE, KEN (JR.)
91/2 Bowman 347, 362
96/7 DEL 110
92/3 FleerUltra 411
91/2 Kraft 17
91/2 OPC/Topps 5, 440
91/2 opcPremier 41, 154
91/2 PaniniSticker 178, 341
91/2 Parkhurst 2, PHC3
91/2 Pinnacle 203
92/3 Pinnacle 390
88/9 ProCards(Kalamazoo)
89/90 ProCards(IHL) 89
90/1 ProCards 134
90/1 ProSet 587
91/2 ProSet 3
92/3 ProSet 182
91/2 PSPlatinum 6, PC9
90/1 ScoreTraded 85T
91/2 Score(CDN) 113, 383
91/2 Score(U.S) 113, 353
91/2 Score-YoungStar 9
92/3 Score 274
92/3 Topps 306
91/2 ToppsStadiumClub 357
90/1 UpperDeck 529
91/2 UpperDeck 41, 251
92/3 UpperDeck 254
90/1 BOS/SportsAction
91/2 BOS/SportsAction

HODGE, ROB
93/4 WestMich.

HODGES, BOB
90/1 ProSet 689
77-9 Sportscaster 11-19

HODGSON, DAN
84/5 KelownaWings&WHL 56
84/5 PrinceAlbert

HODGSON, TED
51/2 LavalDairy 62
52/3 StLawrence 106
72/3 ClevelandCrusaders
72/3 ClevelandCrusaders/Linnet

HODSON, JASON
92/3 BCJHL 104

HODSON, KEVIN
94/5 Classic T21
93/4 ClassicProspects 218
96/7 Donruss 230
97/8 Donruss 199
96/7 DonrusCanadianIce 136
97/8 DonrussPriority 65
95/6 EdgeIce 3, TW12
96/7 Flair 108
96/7 Leaf-Rookie 2
96/7 LeafPreferred 137
97/8 Limited 17, 89
97/8 Omega 80
98/9 Pacific 192
98/9 PacificParamount 75
95/6 Parkhurst 525
96/7 Pinnacle 99, 238
97/8 Pinnacle 47
96/7 PinnacleBeAPlayer 218
97/8 PinnacleInside-Stopper 10
96/7 PinnacleZenith 136
97/8 Score 24
97/8 Score(DET) 18
90/1 SketchMEM 2
90/1 SketchOHL 158
91/2 SketchOHL 320
97/8 SPAuthentic 179
96/7 Summit 183
96/7 UpperDeck 253
97/8 UpperDeck 272
97/8 UpperDeckIce 33
95/6 Adirondack
92/3 Indianapolis
93/4 SSMarie 28

HOESKTRA, CECIL
60/1 ShirriffCoin 79

HOEKSTRA, ED
68/9 OPC/Topps 98
68/9 ShirriffCoin Ph3
63/4 QuébecAces
65/6 QuébecAces

HOFBAUER, PATRIK
95/6 ElitSet 184

HOFF, GEIR
95 Globe 193
95 PaniniWorlds 244
94 Semic 263
92 SemicSticker 37
93 SemicSticker 237

HOFFART, RANDY
84/5 Saskatoon

HOFFHER, ANTON
72 Hellas 60

HOFFMAN, AARON
91/2 AvantGardeBCJHL 66
92/3 BCJHL 80

HOFFMAN, L.
95/6 DEL 73

HOFFMAN, MATT
89/90 SketchMEM 94
89/90 SketchOHL 15
90/1 SketchOHL 338
93/4 Johnstown 6
94/5 Johnstown 10
91/2 SketchOHL 154

HOFFMAN, MIKE
87/8 Flint
88/9 Flint

HOFFMAN, OLIVER
91 SemicSticker 119

HOFFMANN, JIM
94/5 DEL 187
95/6 DEL 187
96/7 DEL 126

HOFFMANN, PETER
94/5 DEL 406

HOFFMEYER, BOB
89/90 ProCards(AHL) 208
91/2 ProCards 158
84/5 N.J.
88/9 N.J/Caretta

HOFFORD, JIM
88/9 ProCards(Rochester)
89/90 ProCards(AHL) 281
86/7 BUF

HOFFORT, BRUCE
90/1 OPC/Topps 80
90/1 opcPremier 42
89/90 ProCards(AHL) 350
90/1 ProCards 36
91/2 ProCards 326
90/1 ProSet 413
90/1 UpperDeck 135

HOFHERR, ANTON
72 SemicSticker 104

HOFHERR, F.
72 SemicSticker 112

HOFNER, ERNST
94/5 DEL 368
95/6 DEL 358
82 SemicSticker 114

HOGABOAM, BILL
82? JDMcCarthy
74/5 Loblaws
74/5 OPC/Topps 84, 116
75/6 OPC/Topps 67
76/7 OPC/Topps 73, OPC 387
77/8 OPC/Topps 148
79/80 O-Pee-Chee 362
79/80 DET
80/1 DET

HOGAN, MATT
94/5 Slapshot(Sarnia) 25

HOGAN, PETER
98 BowmanCHL 26
95/6 Slapshot 242

HOGANSON, DALE
72-84 Dernière 72/3, 78/9, 81/2
70/1 EddieSargent 68
70/1 Esso Stamp
71/2 OPC/Topps 149
80/1 OPC/Topps 155
81/2 O-Pee-Chee 276
75/6 opcWHA 2
80/1 Pepsi Cap
71/2 TheTorontoSun
71/2 MTL
80/1 QUE
73/4 QuébecNordiques

HOGANSON, DAN
86/7 TOR

HOGARDH, PETER
95/6 ElitSet 200
95/6 udElite 215

HOGDEN, JEFF
89/90 SketchOHL 46
91/2 Cincinnati

HOGG, MURRAY
93/4 Slapshot(Guelph) 21
95/6 Slapshot 53

HOGG, STEVE
93/4 Slapshot(Peterborough) 17
95/6 Slapshot 319

HOGGARTH, RON
90/1 ProSet 690

HOGLUND, JONAS
97/8 Donruss 169
96/7 DonrussCanadianIce 140
97/8 DonrussCanadianIce 36
96/7 DonrussElite 146, -Aspir 12
94/5 ElitSet 292
95/6 ElitSet 213
96/7 FleerUltra 23
96/7 LeafPreferred 124
96/7 LeafLimited-Rookies 10
97/8 Limited 88
97/8 PacificCrown 185
97/8 PcfcDynagn! 16,-Tandm 36
97/8 PacificInvincible 18
97/8 PacificParamount 29
97/8 PaniniSticker 198
96/7 PinnacleBeAPlayer LTH8A
97/8 PinnacleInside 129
96/7 PinnacleZenith 117
97/8 Score 181
96/7 SelectCertified 102
90/1 SemicElitserien 269
91/2 SemicElitserien 99
92/3 SemicElitserien 115
96/7 SP 172
92/3 UpperDeck 222
96/7 UpperDeck 232, X38
97/8 UpperDeck 27
96/7 UDBlackDiamond 44
96/7 UDCollChoice 355
97/8 UDCollChoice 43
95/6 udElite 68, NA8
97/8 MTL

HOGLUND, PATRIK
94/5 ElitSet 266
91/2 SemicElitserien 160
92/3 SemicElitserien 178
95/6 udElite 115
97/8 udSwedish 187

HOGOSTA, GORAN
79 PaniniSticker 184

HOGSTROM, JERK
91/2 SemicElitserien 285

HOGUE, BENOÎT
91/2 Bowman 38
92/3 Bowman 28
94/5 ClassicImages PL7
93/4 Donruss 201
94/5 Donruss 188
95/6 Donruss 70
96/7 Donruss 135
92/3 Durivage 3
93/4 Durivage 29
93/4 EASports 83
96/7 FleerNHLPicks 136
92/3 FleerUltra 127
93/4 FleerUltra 123
94/5 FleerUltra 128
95/6 FleerUltra 312
93/4 Leaf 155
94/5 Leaf 124
95/6 Leaf 134
96/7 Leaf 137
94/5 LeafLimited 20
89/90 O-Pee-Chee 201
90/1 OPC/Topps 215
91/2 OPC/Topps 32, 292
92/3 O-Pee-Chee 132
91/2 opcPremier 179
89/90 opcSticker 337/177
89/90 opcStickFS 4
98/9 Pacific 177
97/8 PacificCrown 240
91/2 PaniniSticker 300
92/3 PaniniSticker 197
93/4 PaniniSticker 59
94/5 PaniniSticker 47
95/6 PaniniSticker 202
96/7 PaniniSticker 171
97/8 PaniniSticker 143
91/2 Parkhurst 332
92/3 Parkhurst 104
93/4 Parkhurst 396
95/6 Parkhurst 330
94/5 ParkieSE 106
91/2 Pinnacle 146
92/3 Pinnacle 62
93/4 Pinnacle 18
94/5 Pinnacle 129
95/6 Pinnacle 186
96/7 Pinnacle 73
97/8 PinnacleBeAPlayer 152
94/5 POG 374
95/6 POG 258
93/4 PowerPlay 148
93/4 Premier 140
94/5 Premier 26
90/1 ProSet 416
91/2 ProSet 17, 435
92/3 ProSet 108
91/2 PSPlatinum 200
91/2 Score(CDN) 134, (U.S) 134
91/2 Score 108T, -YoungStar 31
92/3 Score 276, -Sharp 21
93/4 Score 16
95/6 Score 262
96/7 Score 141
97/8 Score 217
94/5 Select 130
96/7 Summit 56
92/3 Topps 103
95/6 Topps 71
91/2 ToppsStadiumClub 157
92/3 ToppsStadiumClub 425
93/4 ToppsStadiumClub 76
90/1 UpperDeck 402
91/2 UpperDeck 159
92/3 UpperDeck 325
93/4 UpperDeck 456
94/5 UpperDeck 436
95/6 UpperDeck 351, SE171
96/7 UpperDeck 247
95/6 UDBeAPlayer 126
95/6 UDCollChoice 72
96/7 UDCollChoice 72
88/9 BUF/BlueShield
88/9 BUF/WonderBread
89/90 BUF/BlueShield
89/90 BUF/Campbell
90/1 BUF/BlueShield
90/1 BUF/Campbell
96/7 DAL/Southwest

HOGUE, RUSSELL
93/4 PrinceAlbert
95/6 PrinceAlbert

HOHENBERGER, HERBERT
94/5 AutoPhonex 18
94/5 DEL 216
95/6 DEL 204
96/7 DEL 345
95 Globe 186
95 PaniniWorlds 262
90/1 ProCards 63
96 Wien 214

HOHENADHL, FRANK
94/5 DEL 212
95/6 DEL 340

HOINESS, BRENT
91/2 AirCanadaSJHL A43
92/3 MPSPhotoSJHL 91

HOKANSON, JEFF
91/2 AvantGardeBCJ 139

HOLAN, MILOS
93/4 Classic 134
93/4 ClassicProspects 70
93/4 Donruss 244
94/5 Donruss 10
95/6 Donruss 339
96/7 Donruss 20
93/4 FleerUltra 389, -Wave 6
95/6 FleerUltra 2
94/5 Leaf 289
95/6 Leaf 324
95/6 PaniniSticker 230
95 PaniniWorlds 188
93/4 Parkhurst 268
95/6 Parkhurst 2
93/4 Pinnacle 427
96/7 Score 211
93 SemicSticker 91
95/6 Topps 173
93/4 UpperDeck 523, SP115
95/6 UpperDeck 77
95/6 UDCollChoice 265

HOLDEN, BARNEY
91 C55 Reprint 3
1911-12 Imperial (C55) 3
1910-11 Imperial (C56) 4
1910-11 Imperial Post 3

HOLDEN, CORY
95/6 DEL 315
96/7 DEL 97

HOLDEN, JOSH
95/6 Bowman P19
97/8 Bowman 114
98 BowmanCHL 73
95/6 Classic 62, -Aut.
95/6 FutureLegends-SS&D 6
97/8 PinnacleBeeHive 66
96/7 ScoreboardAllSportPPF 78
95/6 UpperDeck 513
97/8 UDBlackDiamond 45
98/9 UDChoice 253

HOLDEN, MARK
83/4 NovaScotia 1
84/5 NovaScotia 1

HOLDEN, PAUL
90/1 ProCards 431
91/2 ProCards 396
89/90 SketchOHL 24

HOLECEK, JIRI
72 Hellas 81
74 Hellas 71
72 Panda
79 PaniniSticker 74
72 SemicSticker 22
74 SemicSticker 51
91 SemicSticker 246
77-80 Sportscaster 83-1983
96 Wien HL16
71/2 WilliamsFIN 27
72/3 WilliamsFIN 7
73/4 WilliamsFIN 48

HOLICEK, MARK
84/5 Saskatoon
86/7 Saskatoon

HOLIK, BOBBY
91/2 Bowman 18
92/3 Bowman 407
93/4 Donruss 183
94/5 Donruss 90
95/6 Donruss 220
97/8 Donruss 140

97/8 DonrussPriority 158
92/3 FleerUltra 339
93/4 FleerUltra 360
95/6 FleerUltra 262
93/4 Leaf 227
94/5 Leaf 252
97/8 Omega 130
91/2 OPC/Topps 7, 56
92/3 O-Pee-Chee 254
90/1 opcPremier 43
92/3 opcPremier 77
98/9 Pacific 263
97/8 PacificCrown 55
97/8 PacificCrownRoyale 76
97/8 PcfcDynagn! 70,-Tandm 45
97/8 PacificInvincible 78
97/8 PacificParamount 103
98/9 PacificParamount 134
97/8 PacificRevolution 78
91/2 PaniniSticker 316, 342
92/3 PaniniSticker 261, 293
97/8 PaniniSticker 65
95 PaniniWorlds 204
91/2 Parkhurst 290
92/3 Parkhurst 96
93/4 Parkhurst 385
94/5 Parkhurst 128
95/6 Parkhurst 125
91/2 Pinnacle 65
92/3 Pinnacle 277
93/4 Pinnacle 71
94/5 Pinnacle 347
97/8 PinnacleBeAPlayer 201
94/5 POG 144
95/6 POG 159
93/4 PowerPlay 378
93/4 Premier 52, 322
94/5 Premier 315
90/1 ProSet 609
91/2 ProSet 79
92/3 ProSet 61
91/2 PSPlatinum 43
90/1 Score 10T, -Young 34
91/2 ScoreCDN 153, US 153
91/2 Score-YoungStar 36
92/3 Score 128
93/4 Score 198
97/8 Score 183
97/8 Score(N.J.) 2
91 SemicSticker 225
96/7 SP 87
97/8 SPAuthentic 89
92/3 Topps 330
95/6 Topps 303, 10PL
98/9 Topps 131
91/2 ToppsStadiumClub 299
92/3 ToppsStadiumClub 106
93/4 ToppsStadiumClub 159
94/5 ToppsStadiumClub 129
90/1 UpperDeck 534
91/2 UpperDeck 233, E3
92/3 UpperDeck 252, 500
93/4 UpperDeck 218
94/5 UpperDeck 314
95/6 UpperDeck 365
97/8 UpperDeck 304
95/6 UDBeAPlayer 202
98/9 UDChoice 115
95/6 UDCollChoice 185
97/8 UDCollChoice 143
97/8 Zenith 68
90/1 HFD/JuniorWhalers
91/2 HFD/JuniorWhalers
96/7 N.J/Sharp

HOLIK, JAROSLAV
94/5 APS 291
72 Hellas 84
74 Hellas 72
70/1 Kuvajulkaisut 47
69/70 MästarSerien 6
74 SemicSticker 60
77-9 Sportscastr 55-14, 51-1218
72/3 WilliamsFIN 8
73/4 WilliamsFIN 49

HOLIK, JIRI
95/6 APS 196, 393
72 Hellas 98
74 Hellas 73
70/1 Kuvajulkaisut 48
69/70 MästarSerien 3
72 Panda
72 SemicSticker 39
74 SemicSticker 61
77-9 Sportscastr 55-14, 51-1218
71/2 WilliamsFIN 28
72/3 WilliamsFIN 9
73/4 WilliamsFIN 50

HOLK, BRIAN
90/1 SketchOHL 260

HOLLAND, BOB
81/2 Indianapolis 19
77/8 NovaScotia

HOLLAND, DENNIS
89/90 ProCards(AHL) 322
90/1 ProCards 471
91/2 ProCards 593
92/3 Cincinnati
86/7 Portland
87/8 Portland
88/9 Portland

HOLLAND, JASON
97/8 Donruss 214
97/8 DonrussCanadianIce 144
95/6 DonrussElite-WorldJrs 6
94/5 SigRookies 11
94/5 Slapshot(MEM) 3
95/6 UpperDeck 537

HOLLAND, JERRY
75/6 OPC 392
76/7 OPC 315

HOLLAND, ROB
82/3 Indianapolis

HOLLENSTEIN, FELIX
95 Semic 191
91 SemicSticker 194
92 SemicSticker 209
93 SemicSticker 127

HOLLETT, BILL (FLASH)
33/4 BeeHives(TOR)
35/6 OPC (V304C) 83
39/40 OPC (V301-1) 41

HOLLETT, FRANK
36/7 WWGum (V356) 62

HOLLETT, STEVE
89/90 ProCards(AHL) 97
84/5 SSMarie

HOLLEY, PAT
87/8 Sudbury 20

HOLLINGER, TERRY
93/4 ClassicProspects 171
94/5 Parkhurst 204
90/1 SketchWHL 165
91/2 SketchWHL 354
92/3 Peoria
93/4 Peoria
89/90 Regina

HOLLINGER, TODD
91/2 AirCanadaSJHL A27

HOLLINGSHEAD, KELLY
91/2 AirCanadaSJHL B20

HOLLINGWORTH, GORDON (BUCKY)
52/3 AnonymousOHL 131
93/4 Parkie(56/7) 62
54/5 Topps 12

HOLLIS, SCOTT
89/90 SketchMEM 96
89/90 SketchOHL 11
90/1 SketchOHL 339
91/2 SketchOHL 155
95/6 Adirondack
93/4 LasVegas

HOLLOWAY, BRUCE
81/2 Regina 13

HOLMAN, JIM
92/3 WestMich.
93/4 WestMich.

HOLMBERG, ERIK
89/90 SemicElitserien 237
90/1 SemicElitserien 14
91/2 SemicElitserien 212
92/3 SemicElitserien 246

HOLMBERG, JORGEN
89/90 SemicElitserien 260
90/1 SemicElitserien 165
91/2 SemicElitserien 270

HOLMBERG, MIKAEL
94/5 ElitSet 198
95/6 ElitSet 68
89/90 SemicElitserien 92
90/1 SemicElitserien 266
95/6 udElite 109

HOLMES, BILL
25-27 Anonymous 14

HOLMES, DARREN
91/2 AvantGardeBC 46, 153

HOLMES, HARRY
25-27 Anonymous 121
83&87 HallOfFame 156
83 HHOF Postcard (L)
94/5 HHOFLegends 49

HOLMES, JAMES
52/3 AnonymousOHL 54

HOLMES, WES
95/6 Slapshot 243

HOLMGREN, LEIF
79 PaniniSticker 192
82 SemicSticker 23
91/2 SemicElitserien 302
92/3 SemicElitserien 324

HOLMGREN, PAUL
77/8 OPC 307
78/9 OPC/Topps 234
79/80 OPC/Topps 156
80/1 OPC/Topps 164, 172
81/2 OPC 242, Topps(E) 105
82/3 O-Pee-Chee 251
83/4 O-Pee-Chee 266
84/5 OPC 100, Topps 74
81/2 opcSticker 179
82/3 opcSticker 116
82/3 Post
90/1 ProSet 673
83/4 SouhaitsRen.KeyChain
92/3 HFD/DairyMart
84/5 MIN
84/5 MIN/7Eleven 7
81/2 PHA/TIckets 9
86/7 PHA
89/90 PHA

HOLMQVIST, LEIF
95 Globe 64
72 Hellas 23
70/1 Kuvajulkaisut 26
69/70 MästarSerien 38, 44
72 Panda
72 SemicSticker 42
91 SemicSticker 234
71/2 WilliamsFIN 46
72/3 WilliamsFIN 46

HOLMROOS, RAINER
73/4 WilliamsFIN 260

HOLMSTRÖM, TOMAS
94/5 AutoPhonex 19
96/7 DonrussCanadianIce 129
94/5 ElitSet 218, -NHLDraft 9
94/5 Elit-Rookie 3
95/6 ElitSet 84, -FaceToFace 8
96/7 Flair 107
95 Globe 50
96/7 LeafLimited-Rookies 9
98/9 Pacific 193
97/8 PacificCrown 319
97/8 PinnacleBeAPlayer 188
96/7 PinnacleZenith 118
97/8 Score(DET) 16
96/7 SelectCertified 97
96/7 UpperDeck 255
95/6 udElite 123, NA15
96 Wien 70

HOLOIEN, DEAN
89/90 Saskatoon 10

HOLOPAINEN, EERO
66/7 Champion 170
65/6 Hellas 106
70/1 Kuvajulkaisut 174
71/2 WilliamsFIN 100
72/3 WilliamsFIN 143
73/4 WilliamsFIN 109

HOLOPAINEN, MIKKO
65/6 Hellas 159

HOLOPAINEN, PAAVO
71/2 WilliamsFIN 300

HOLSCHER, HENRIK
94/5 DEL 313
95/6 DEL 305
96/7 DEL 333

HOLT, BARRY
92/3 MPSPhotoSJHL 133

HOLT, RANDY
77/8 OPC/Topps 34
78/9 O-Pee-Chee 341
79/80 OPC/Topps 4
81/2 O-Pee-Chee 41
83/4 O-Pee-Chee 220
80/1 Pepsi Cap
82/3 Post
80/1 CGY
83/4 PHA
78/9 VAN/RoyalBank
81/2 WSH
82/3 WSH

HOLT, TODD
90/1 SketchWHL 48
91/2 SketchWHL 192

HOLTARI, JUKKA
80/1 Mallasjuoma 86

HOLTBY, GREG
83/4 Saskatoon 5
84/5 Saskatoon

HOLTEN MÖLLER, P.
79 PaniniSticker 363

HOLUNGA, SHANE
91/2 AirCanadaSJHL 20, C45

HOLWAY, ALBERT
24/5 Champs (C144)
24/5 (V145-2) 56

HOLY, ROBERT
94/5 APS 23

HOLZER, M.
95/6 DEL 346

HOLZER, RENZO
79 PaniniSticker 262

HOLZINGER, BRIAN
95/6 Bowman 165
95/6 Classic 74, -Aut
95/6 ClassicFiveSport 159
95/6 Donruss 298
96/7 Donruss 226
97/8 Donruss 74
97/8 DonrussPreferred 93
97/8 DonrussPriority 69
95/6 FleerMetal 177
95/6 FleerUltra 19, 341
95/6 Leaf 250, -StudioRook 14
96/7 Leaf 212
97/8 Leaf 120
97/8 Limited 58, 184
97/8 Omega 23
98/9 Pacific 106
97/8 PacificCrown 158
97/8 PcfcDynagn! 11,-Tandm 32
97/8 PacificParamount 20
98/9 PacificParamount 20
95/6 PaniniSticker 14
95/6 Parkhurst 27
95/6 Pinnacle 205
97/8 PinnacleBeAPlayer 34
97/8 PinnacleCertified 118
97/8 PinnacleInside 163
95/6 PinZenith 126,-RookieRoll 5
95/6 Playoff 126
95/6 POG 39
95/6 Score 310
96/7 Score 266
97/8 Score 172
97/8 Score(BUF) 9
95/6 SelectCert. 110, -Future 6
95/6 SkyBoxEmotion 17, -Next 1
95/6 SkyBoxImpact 190, -Fox 15
95/6 SP 14
96/7 SP 18, HC19
97/8 SPAuthentic 16, S29
95/6 Summit 168
95/6 Topps 24
95/6 ToppsFinest 67
95/6 ToppsStadiumClub 194
91/2 UpperDeck 'CzechWJC 72
95/6 UpperDeck 88
96/7 UpperDeck 16
97/8 UpperDeck 15, SG49
95/6 UDBeAPlayer 161
96/7 UDBlackDiamond 118
98/9 UDChoice 21
96/7 UDCollChoice 24, 342
97/8 UDCollChoice 25, SQ14
97/8 UpperDeckIce 19

HOLZMANN, GEORGE
94/5 DEL 64
95/6 DEL 63
96/7 DEL 249
95 PaniniWorlds 73
82 SemicSticker 120
89 SemicSticker 118
92 SemicSticker 186
93 SemicSticker 160

HOMQVIST, MIKAEL
98/9 UDChoice 289

HONGISTO, KALEVI
78/9 SM-Liiga 145

HONKANEN, ANTERO
71/2 WilliamsFIN 262

HONKANEN, JAAKKO
66/7 Champion 40
65/6 Hellas 35
70/1 Kuvajulkaisut 190
72 Panda
71/2 WilliamsFIN 84
72/3 WilliamsFIN 247
73/4 WilliamsFIN 245

HONKANEN, JOUNI
70/1 Kuvajulkaisut 366

HONKAVAARA, AARNE
96/7 Sisu 187

HONKONEN, MIKKO
95/6 Sisu 76
96/7 Sisu 76

HONMA, SADAKI
79 PaniniSticker 291

HONNEGER, DOUG
95 Semic 190

HOOD, BRUCE
91/2 UltimateDP 86

HOOEY, TODD
84/5 Moncton 19

HOOPER, TOM
83&87 HallOfFame 173
83 HHOF Postcard (M)

HOOPIA, RYAN
97/8 Bowman 101

HOOSON, BILL
91/2 SketchWHL 270

HOOVER, RON
89/90 ProCards(AHL) 65
90/1 ProCards 126
91/2 UpperDeck 287
92/3 Peoria
93/4 Peoria

HOOVER, TIM
82/3 SSMarie
83/4 SSMarie
84/5 SSMarie

HOPE, JARED
95/6 Spokane 14

HOPIAVUORI, RALPH
72/3 Cleveland

HOPKINS, DEAN
88/9 ProCards(Halifax)
89/90 ProCards(AHL) 164
90/1 ProCards 446
91/2 ProCards 545
88/9 EDM/ActionMagazine 135
89/90 Halifax
90/1 Halifax
84/5 NovaScotia 20
85/6 NovaScotia 1

HOPKINS, LARRY
81/2 WPG

HOPKINS, TOM
89/90 SketchOHL 115

HOPPE, MATTHIAS
94/5 DEL 435
95/6 DEL 386
96/7 DEL 293
89 SemicSticker 105

HOPPER, RICK
90/1 SketchWHL 260
91/2 SketchWHL 50

HOPRAMON, RALPH
72/3 ClevelandCrusaders/Linnet

HORACEK, TONY
90/1 Bowman 104
88/9 ProCards(Hershey)
90/1 ProSet 499
91/2 ProSet 455
90/1 PHA
91/2 PHA/JCPenney
84/5 KelownaWingsWHL 20
96/7 Cincinnati
92/3 Indianapolis
93/4 Indianapolis

HORACHEK, PETER
88/9 Flint

HORAK, ROMAN
94/5 APS 113
95/6 APS 282, 373
95 PaniniWorlds 201
95 Semic 161
93 SemicSticker 96
96 Wien 124

HORAN, BRIAN
91/2 ProCards 438

HORAVA, MIROSLAV
94/5 APS 253
95/6 APS 127
90/1 OPC/Topps 337
90/1 ProSet 198
91/2 SemicElitserien 203
92/3 SemicElitserien 226
82 SemicSticker 79
90/1 UpperDeck 13
89/90 NYR/MarineMidland

HORBUL, DOUG
74/5 Loblaws
74/5 O-Pee-Chee 317

HORDY, MIKE
81/2 Indianapolis 1

HORECK, PETER
45-64 BeeHives(BOS), (DET)

HORESOVSKY, JOSEF
72 Hellas 82
74 Hellas 64
70/1 Kuvajulkaisut 49
72 Panda
72 SemicSticker 23
74 SemicSticker 54
71/2 WilliamsFIN 29
72/3 WilliamsFIN 10
73/4 WilliamsFIN 51

HORI, HIROSHI
79 PaniniSticker 287

HORISBERGER, MICHAEL
79 PaniniSticker 263

HORKKO, KARI
80/1 Mallasjuoma 188
78/9 SM-Liiga 216
72/3 WilliamsFIN 208
73/4 WilliamsFIN 279

HORN, ALEXANDER
94/5 DEL 424

HORN, BILL
92/3 Greensboro 3
94/5 Greensboro

HORNE, BUD
52/3 AnonymousOHL 119

HORNER, GEORGE (RED)
33/4 Anonymous (V129) 1
33-43 BeeHives(TOR)
33/4 CndGum (V252)
83&87 HallOfFame 115
33/4 Hamilton (V288) 21
83 HHOF Postcard (H)
95/6 HHOFLegends 68
27-32 LaPresse 7Mar31
33/4 OPC (V304A) 10
36/7 OPC (V304D) 122
37/8 OPC (V304E) 134
39/40 OPC (V301-1) 10
38/9 QuakerOats
34/5 SweetCaporal
33/4 WWGum (V357) 16
36/7 WWGum (V356) 8
32/3 TOR/OKeefe 2

HORNUNG, BLAIRE
91/2 AirCanadaSJHL A7

HORNUNG, BRAD
86/7 Regina

HORNUNG, LARRY
72/3 O-Pee-Chee 317
73/4 QuakerOats 26
71/2 STL

HORTON, BILL
72/3 ClevelandCrusaders

HORTON, BOB
72/3 ClevelandCrusaders/Linnet

HORTON, TIM
45-64 BeeHives(TOR)
64-67 BeeHives(TORx2)
62 CeramicTiles
63-5 ChexPhoto
64/5 CokeCap TOR-7
65/6 CocaCola
70/1 EddieSargent 125
71/2 EddieSargent 169
72/3 EddieSargent 37
70/1 Esso Stamp
83&87 HallOfFame 188
83 HHOF Postcard (J)
93/4 HHOFLegends 24
91/2 Kraft 86
68/9 OPC/Topps 123
68/9 OPC 201, -Puck 18
69/70 OPC 182, 213, Topps 45
69/70 OPC-Sticker
70/1 OPC/Topps 59
71/2 OPC/Topps 186
72/3 OPC 197
73/4 OPC 189
71/2 opcPoster 18
52/3 Parkhurst 58
53/4 Parkhurst 13
54/5 Parkhurst 31, 90
55/6 Parkhurst 3
57/8 Parkhurst(TO R) 22
58/9 Parkhurst 42
59/60 Parkhurst 23
60/1 Parkhurst 1
61/2 Parkhurst 1
62/3 Parkhurst 7
63/4 Parkhurst 16, 76
92/3 Parkhurst PR16
93/4 Parkhurst PR34, DPR3
93/4 Parkie(56/7) 127
94/5 Parkie(64/5) 131, 135
95/6 Parkie(66/7) 103
68/9 Post Marble
66/7 Post'Large
67 Post FlipBook
45-54 QuakerOats
60/1 ShirriffCoin 5
61/2 ShirriffCoin 44
62/3 ShirriffCoin 4
68/9 ShirriffCoin TOR14
64/5 Topps 102, 105
65/6 Topps 79
66/7 Topps 80
67/8 Topps 16, 127
54-67 TorontoStar V10
56-66 TorontoStar '57, 63/4
56-66 TorontoStar 64/5, 65/6
63/4 TheTorontoStar
64/5 TheTorontoStar
71/2 TheTorontoSun
91/2 UltimateDP 37, 84, 97
60/1 York, -Glasses
61/2 York 7
62/3 York Transfers
63/4 York 1
67/8 York 21, 31, 25, no#
72/3 BUF
73/4 BUF
93/4 BUF/NOCO
64/5 TOR
66/7 TOR/Coaster
68/9 TOR
69/70 TOR

HORVATH, BRONCO
45-64 BeeHives (CHI),(NYR)
45-64 BeeHives (TOR)
64-67 BeeHives(TOR)
62 CeramicTiles

93/4 Parkie(56/7) 105
60/1 ShirriffCoin 105
61/2 ShirriffCoin 31
57/8 Topps 7
58/9 Topps 35
59/60 Topps 56
60/1 Topps 54
61/2 Topps 40, -Stamp
62/3 Topps 63
54-67 TorontoStar V7

HORVATH, JASON
91/2 SketchWHL 187

HORVATH, RUDY
45-64 BeeHives(BOS)

HORYNA, ROBERT
90/1 ProCards 165
90/1 Newmarket

HOSEK, MIROSLAV
94/5 APS 259

HOSHINO, YOSHIO
79 PaniniSticker 289

HOSPODAR, ED
80/1 O-Pee-Chee 366
81/2 O-Pee-Chee 233
87/8 BUF/BlueShield
87/8 BUF/WonderBread
82/3 HFD/JuniorWhalers
83/4 HFD/JuniorWhalers
86/7 PHA

HOSSA, MARIAN
98 BowmanCHL 53, SC7
97/8 DonrussElite 28
97/8 DonrussPreferred 162
97/8 PacificDynagon! Rookies
97/8 PacificParamount 125
97/8 Pinnacle 17
98/9 SPx"Finite" 58, 140
98/9 Topps 104
97/8 UpperDeck 326
98/9 UDChoice 142

HOSTAK, MARTIN
95/6 APS 367
91/2 Bowman 233
94/5 ElitSet 238
95/6 ElitSet 104, -FaceTo 10
90/1 opcPremier 44
95 PaniniWorlds 208
91/2 ProCards 285
90/1 ProSet 629
90/1 ScoreTraded 36T
94 Semic 189
92/3 SemicElitserien 236
91/2 ToppsStadiumClub 337
90/1 UpperDeck 542
91/2 UpperDeck 473
95/6 udElite 162
97/8 udSwedish 177
96 Wien 121
90/1 PHA

HOTHAM, GREG
88/9 ProCards(Newmarket)
89/90 ProCards(AHL) 118
83/4 PGH/Heinz
84/5 PGH/Heinz
79/80 TOR

HOUCK, PAUL
88/9 ProCards(Indianapolis)

HOUCK, ROD
92/3 Dayton
88/9 Regina

HOUDA, DOUG
94/5 Leaf 523
90/1 O-Pee-Chee 410
91/2 OPC/Topps 512
97/8 PacificDynag-BestKept 55
97/8 PinnacleBeAPlayer 193
90/1 ProCards 479
91/2 ProSet 81
90/1 Score 11
91/2 Score(CDN) 442
85/6 DET/Caesars
88/9 DET/Caesars
89/90 DET/Caesars
91/2 HFD/JuniorWhalers
92/3 HFD/DairyMart

HOUDE, ÉRIC
98/9 Pacific 251
96/7 Fredericton
95/6 Halifax

HOUDE, MARCEL
51/2 BasDuFleuve 41

HOUGH, MIKE
90/1 Bowman 174
91/2 Bowman 144
92/3 Bowman 178
93/4 Donruss 122
92/3 Durivage 25
93/4 Durivage 45
92/3 FleerUltra 175
94/5 FleerUltra 297
93/4 Leaf 247
94/5 Leaf 504
89/90 O-Pee-Chee 266
90/1 O-Pee-Chee 427
91/2 OPC/Topps 113
92/3 O-Pee-Chee 392
87/8 opcSticker 220/88
89/90 opcSticker 182
97/8 PacificDyna-BestKept 40
90/1 Panini(QUE) 9
91/2 PaniniSticker 254
92/3 PaniniSticker 211
94/5 PaniniSticker 70
91/2 Parkhurst 150
92/3 Parkhurst 380
91/2 Pinnacle 194
92/3 Pinnacle 113
93/4 Pinnacle 402
94/5 Pinnacle 333
96/7 Pinnacle 76
93/4 PowerPlay 94
93/4 Premier 482
94/5 Premier 116
88/9 ProCards(Halifax)
90/1 ProSet 247, 516
91/2 ProSet 463, 582
92/3 ProSet 154, 266
91/2 PSPlatinum 217
91/2 Score(CDN) 112, (U.S) 112
92/3 Score 64
93/4 Score 393, 559
92/3 Topps 297
91/2 ToppsStadiumClub 80
92/3 ToppsStadiumClub 434
93/4 ToppsStadiumClub 466
91/2 UpperDeck 562
95/6 UDBeAPlayer 122
96/7 FLA/WinnDixie
86/7 QUE
86/7 QUE/GeneralFoods
86/7 QUE/McDonald
87/8 QUE/GeneralFoods
89/90 QUE
89/90 QUE/GeneralFoods
89/90 QUE/Police
90/1 QUE
90/1 QUE/PetroCanada
91/2 QUE/PetroCanada
92/3 QUE/PetroCanada
83/4 Fredericton 7
84/5 Fredericton 12
85/6 Fredericton 8
86/7 Fredericton

HOUGHTON, ART
92/3 MPSPhotoSJHL 68

HOUGHTON, DARREN
91/2 AirCanadaSJHL D13
92/3 MPSPhotoSJHL 79

HOUK, ROD
87/8 Regina

HOULDER, BILL
93/4 Donruss 8
93/4 FleerUltra 256
94/5 FleerUltra 4, 362
93/4 Leaf 315
90/1 O-Pee-Chee 399
98/9 Pacific 381
93/4 Parkhurst 272
95/6 Parkhurst 464
94/5 Pinnacle 206
93/4 PowerPlay 4
93/4 Premier 403
94/5 Premier 92
88/9 ProCards(Baltimore)
90/1 ProCards 273
91/2 ProCards 1
90/1 ProSet 417
93/4 Score 639
98/9 Topps 46
93/4 ToppsStadiumClub 419
93/4 UpperDeck 429
94/5 UpperDeck 183
95/6 UpperDeck 475
96/7 UpperDeck 154
94/5 UDBeAPlayer-Aut. 43
95/6 UDCollChoice 243
97/8 S.J/PacificBellSheet
95/6 T.B.
87/8 WSH/Kodak
89/90 WSH

HOULE, GÉRARD
52/3 AnonymousOHL 66

HOULE, RÉJEAN
72-84 Dernière 72/3, 80/1
72/3 EddieSargent 125
70/1 OPC 174
71/2 OPC/Topps 147
72/3 OPC 210
76/7 OPC 360
77/8 OPC/Topps 241
78/9 OPC/Topps 227
79/80 OPC/Topps 34
80/1 OPC/Topps 261
81/2 O-Pee-Chee 183
82/3 O-Pee-Chee 184
81/2 opcSticker 37
74/5 opcWHA 41
80/1 Pepsi Cap
71/2 TheTorontoSun
69/70 MTL/ProStar
70/1 MTL
71/2 MTL
72/3 MTL
76/7 MTL
77/8 MTL
78/9 MTL
79/80 MTL
80/1 MTL
81/2 MTL
82/3 MTL
82/3 MTL/Steinber
73/4 QuébecNordiques

HOULE, YVES
52/3 AnonymousOHL 46

HOUSE, BOB
93/4 ClassicProspects 219
90/1 SketchWHL 190
91/2 SketchWHL 208
91/2 StarPics 69
91/2 UltimateDP 47, -Aut 47
93/4 Indianapolis
89/90 Spokane

HOUSLEY, PHIL
90/1 Bowman 239
91/2 Bowman 197
92/3 Bowman 20, 208
93/4 Donruss 294
95/6 Donruss 74
96/7 Donruss 201
97/8 Donruss 150
93/4 EASports 145
94/5 Fleer 30
96/7 Fleer 59, -Norris 5
95/6 FleerMetal 19
96/7 FleerNHLPicks 22
92/3 FleerUltra 241
93/4 FleerUltra 100, 409, -AS 18
94/5 FleerUltra 269
95/6 FleerUltra 25
96/7 FleerUltra 176
95 Globe 106
93/4 HockeyWit 101
95/6 Hoyle'WEST 9 (Spades)
92/3 HumptyDumpty (2)
90/1 Kraft 18, 85
91/2 Kraft 33
93/4 Leaf 61
94/5 Leaf 450
95/6 Leaf 141
96/7 Leaf 65
96/7 Maggers 93
92/3 McDonalds McD08
93/4 McDonalds McD06
96/7 MetalUniverse 164
97/8 Omega 238
83/4 O-Pee-Chee 65
84/5 O-Pee-Chee 23
85/6 OPC/Topps 63
86/7 OPC/Topps 154
87/8 OPC/Topps 33
88/9 OPC/Topps 119
89/90 OPC/Topps 59
90/1 OPC/Topps 89
91/2 OPC/Topps 395, T-TL 11
92/3 O-Pee-Chee 298
90/1 opcPremier 45
91/2 opcPremier 50
92/3 opcPremier-Star 16
87/8 opcStars 17
83/4 opcSticker 238
84/5 opcSticker 203, 204
85/6 opcSticker 173
86/7 opcSticker 47/188
87/8 opcSticker 151
88/9 opcSticker 255/123
89/90 opcSticker 261
98/9 Pacific 96
97/8 PacificCrown 259
97/8 PacificRevolution 146
90/1 Panini(WPG) 13, H
87/8 PaniniSticker 24
88/9 PaniniSticker 220
89/90 PaniniSticker 205
90/1 PaniniSticker 21
91/2 PaniniSticker 65
92/3 PaniniSticker 61
93/4 PaniniSticker 133, 196
94/5 PaniniSticker 142
95/6 PaniniSticker 241
96/7 PaniniSticker 85
98/9 UDChoice 220
91/2 Parkhurst 205
92/3 Parkhurst 208
93/4 Parkhurst 174
94/5 Parkhurst 197
95/6 Parkhurst 30
94/5 ParkieSE 30
91/2 Pinnacle 4
92/3 Pinnacle 70
93/4 Pinnacle 351, -TeamP 9
94/5 Pinnacle 410
96/7 Pinnacle 19
95/6 PinnacleZenith 104
95/6 Playoff 17, 129
96/7 Playoff 429
95/6 POG 56
93/4 PowerPlay 271, 427
93/4 Premier 36, 503
93/4 Prmr-Black(OPC) 4, (T) 19
94/5 Premier 347, 353, 492
90/1 ProSet 21, 364, 562
91/2 ProSet 267, 295, -Puck 30
92/3 ProSet 212, -TmLeader 14
91/2 PSPlatinum 137
83/4 PuffySticker 12
90/1 Score 145, 3T, -Hot 63
91/2 Score(CDN) 491, (U.S) 271
92/3 Score 299, 440
93/4 Score232,482,520,-P.AS 25
95/6 Score 45
96/7 Score 153
92/3 SeasonsPatch 59
94/5 Select 146
95/6 SelectCertified 86
89 SemicSticker 156
91 SemicSticker 133
92 SemicSticker 149
93 SemicSticker 174
95/6 SkyBoxEmotion 22
95/6 SkyBoxImpact 22
96/7 Blmp 140, -Fox 10,-Blade 7
83/4 SouhaitsRen.KeyChain
94/5 SP 19
95/6 SP 19
96/7 SP 167
97/8 SPAuthentic 168
95/6 Summit 40
96/7 Summit 121
95/6 SuperSticker 16
84/5 Topps 18
92/3 Topps 268, 456
95/6 Topps 166
94/5 ToppsFinest 91
95/6 ToppsFinest 7
91/2 ToppsStadiumClub 65
92/3 ToppsStadiumClub 14
93/4 T.StadiumClub 104, -AllStar
94/5 TSC-MembersOnly 45
95/6 ToppsSuperSkills 66
90/1 UpperDeck 22, 435
91/2 UpperDeck 106, 624
92/3 UpperDeck 24, 276, 628
92/3 UD'LockerAS 26
93/4 UpperDeck 525, SP136
94/5 UpperDeck 169, SP102
95/6 UpperDeck 294, SE13
96/7 UpperDeck 357
94/5 UDBeAPlayer R78
95/6 UDBeAPlayer 72
96/7 UDBlackDiamond 96
95/6 UDCollChoice 212
96/7 UDCollChoice 150
97/8 UDCollChoice 275
96 Wien 161
82/3 BUF/Wendt 11
84/5 BUF/BlueShield
85/6 BUF
86/7 BUF
87/8 BUF/BlueShield
87/8 BUF/WonderBread
88/9 BUF/BlueShield
88/9 BUF/WonderBread
89/90 BUF/BlueShield
89/90 BUF/Campbell
90/1 WPG/IGA
91/2 WPG/IGA

HOUSTON, KEN
77/8 O-Pee-Chee 274
78/9 O-Pee-Chee 348
79/80 O-Pee-Chee 310
80/1 O-Pee-Chee 303
82/3 O-Pee-Chee 366
83/4 O-Pee-Chee 371
82/3 opcSticker 221
83/4 opcSticker 200
80/1 Pepsi Cap
82/3 Post
83/4 SouhaitsRen.KeyChain
77/8 ATL
78/9 ATL/Coke
79/80 ATL
79/80 ATL/B&W
80/1 CGY
81/2 CGY
82/3 WSH

HOVINHEIMO, JAAKKO
66/7 Champion 142

HOWALD, PATRICK
95 Globe 214
95 PaniniWorlds 129
92 SemicSticker
93 SemicSticker 117

HOWARD, BRIAN
87/8 SSMarie 34

HOWATT, GARRY
74/5 Loblaws
74/5 OPC 375
76/7 OPC/Topps 206, OPC 389
77/8 OPC/Topps 194
78/9 OPC/Topps 29
79/80 OPC/Topps 205
80/1 O-Pee-Chee 386
82/3 O-Pee-Chee 140
83/4 O-Pee-Chee 229
82/3 opcSticker 133
82/3 Post
79/80 NYI

HOWE, GORDON (GORDIE)
56 AdventureGum 63
45-64 BeeHives(DETx2)
64-67 BeeHives(DETx2)
62 CeramicTiles
63-5 ChexPhoto
64/5 CokeCap DET-9, DET-10
65/6 CocaCola
70/1 Colgate Stamp 47
70/1 DadsCookies
97/8 DonrussElite -BackTo 8
64/5 Eatons
65/6 Eatons
66/7 Eatons
70/1 EddieSargent 56
62/3 ElProductoDisk
70/1 Esso Stamp
88/9 EssoAllStar
48-52 Exhibits (x2)
83&87 HallOfFame 16
83 HHOF Postcard (B)
92/3 HHOFLegends 9
93/4 HockeyWit 9
95/6 KennerLegend
68/9 OPC/Topps 29
68/9 OPC 203, 700Goals
69/70 OPC/Topps 61
69/70 O-Pee-Chee 193, 215
69/70 OPC-Sticker, -Stamp
70/1 OPC/Topps 29, OPC 238
70/1 OPC/T.-Sticker, -Deckle 18
71/2 OPC 262,Topps 70
71/2 OPC-Booklet 23
79/80 OPC/Topps 175
73/4 opc-Posters 13, 14
74/5 opcWha 1
75/6 opcWHA 66, 100
76/7 opcWHA 50, 72
77/8 opcWHA 1
51/2 Parkhurst 66
52/3 Parkhurst 88
53/4 Parkhurst 50
54/5 Parkhurst 41, 92
60/1 Parkhurst 20
61/2 Parkhurst 20
62/3 Parkhurst 30, 31
63/4 Parkhurst 55
91/2 Parkhurst PHC1
93/4 PH D17,PR33, PR42, PR51
93/4 PH PR60, DPR1, DPR7
93/4 PH(56/7) 43, 145, 171, A1
94/5 PH(64/5) 46, 144, 171, A5
95/6 Parkie(66/7) 42, 126, 142
95/6 Parkie(66/7) 147, 148
66/7 Post-Large, -Small
67/8 Post
90/1 ProSet 654, 660
91/2 ProSet 344
52 RoyalDesserts 8
72 SemicSticker 190
91 SemicSticker 239
60/1 ShirriffCoin 42
61/2 ShirriffCoin 66
62/3 ShirriffCoin 54
68/9 ShirriffCoin DET11
97/8 SPAuthentic M1, T1
77-9 Sportscaster 02-06, 63-09
77-80 Sprtscastr 07-152, 07-168
54/5 Topps 8
57/8 Topps 42
58/9 Topps 8
59/60 Topps 48, 63
64/5 Topps 89
65/6 Topps 108, 122
66/7 Topps 109,121,-USATest23
67/8 Topps 43, 131
98/9 Topps-RookieReprint 7
54-67 TorontoStar 65/6, V, V11
54-67 TorontoStar V 4,n2
56-66 TorontoStar 57/8, 58/9
56-66 TorontoStar 59/60
56-66 TorontoStar 61/2, 63/4
63/4 TheTorontoStar
64/5 TheTorontoStar
71/2 TheTorontoSun
92/3 UD'LockerAS 42, -Aut
92/3 UD-HHeroes 1 27-Sep
93/4 UDBeAPlayer 25
71/2 WilliamsFIN 382
60/1 WonderBread 1
63/4 York 45
60/1 YorkGlasses
62/3 YorkTransfer 19
95/6 Zellers
70/1 DET/Marathon
90/1 HFD/JuniorWhalers
75/6 Houston (x2)

HOWE, MARK
72-84 Dernière 82/3
88/9 EssoAllStar
92/3 FleerUltra 285
90/1 Kraft 19
93/4 Leaf 259
82/3 McDonalds 31
73/4 opc-Posters 14
79/80 OPC/Topps 216
80/1 OPC/Topps 91, 160
81/2 OPC 128, Topps(E) 82
82/3 O-Pee-Chee 252
83/4 O-Pee-Chee 267
84/5 OPC 161, Topps 118
85/6 OPC/Topps 35, 158
86/7 OPC/Topps 123, T-AS 6
87/8 OPC/Topps 54, T-AS 3
88/9 OPC/Topps 6
89/90 OPC/Topps 191
90/1 OPC/Topps 185
91/2 OPC/Topps 466
87/8 opcStars 18
81/2 opcSticker 62, 145
82/3 opcSticker 131
83/4 opcSticker 171, 195, 196
84/5 opcSticker 109
85/6 opcSticker 93/226
86/7 opcSticker 246, 116/130
86/7 opcSticker 184/124
87/8 opcSticker 100, 112/124
87/8 opcSticker 176/174
88/9 opcSticker 104, 124/256
89/90 opcSticker 109/248
74/5 opcWHA 1
75/6 opcWHA 7
76/7 opcWHA 95
77/8 opcWHA 25
87/8 PaniniSticker 124
88/9 PaniniSticker 316
89/90 PaniniSticker 300
90/1 PaniniSticker 122
92/3 PaniniSticker 191
91/2 Parkhurst 130
92/3 Parkhurst 279
91/2 Pinnacle 297, 418
92/3 Pinnacle 244, 322
93/4 Pinnacle 235, 254
94/5 Pinnacle 295
81/2 Post PopUp 11
82/3 Post
93/4 PowerPlay 329
93/4 Premier 157
90/1 ProSet 217
91/2 ProSet 182
83/4 PuffySticker 8
90/1 Score 220, -HotCards 92
91/2 Score(CDN) 472, (U.S) 252
92/3 Score 217
93/4 Score 91
89 SemicSticker 160
91 SemicSticker 134
85/6 7Eleven 14
83/4 SouhaisRen.KeyChain
77-9 Sportscaster 63-9
93/4 ToppsStadiumClub 112
90/1 UpperDeck 261
92/3 UpperDeck 530
93/4 UpperDeckBeAPlayer 25
75/6 Houston
83/4 PHA
86/7 PHA
89/90 PHA
90/1 PHA
91/2 PHA/JCPenney

HOWE, MARTY
79/80 OPC/Topps 46
83/4 O-Pee-Chee 139
84/5 O-Pee-Chee 71
73/4 opc-Posters 14
83/4 opcSticker 54
74/5 opcWHA 1
75/6 opcWHA 75
76/7 opcWHA 15
77/8 opcWHA 65
77-9 Sportscaster 63 -9
84/5 Topps 55
83/4 HFD/JuniorWhalers
75/6 Houston

HOWE, SYD
33-43 BeeHives(DET)
36-39 DiamondMatch (1)
83&87 HallOfFame 174
83 HHOF Postcard (M)
94/5 HHOFLegends 44
33/4 OPC (V304A) 24
39/40 OPC (V301-1) 72
33/4 WWGum (V357) 72
36/7 WWGum (V356) 75

HOWELL, HARRY
68/9 Bauer
45-64 BeeHives(NYR)
64-67 BeeHives(NYR)
62 CeramicTiles
64/5 CokeCap NYR-3
65/6 CocaCola
70/1 DadsCookies

70/1 EddieSargent 134
71/2 EddieSargent 71
72/3 EddieSargent 90
70/1 Esso Stamp
83&87 HallOfFame 83
83 HHOF Postcard (F)
95/6 HHOFLegends 56
91/2 Kraft 73
68/9 OPC/Topps 69
69/70 OPC/Topps 79
70/1 OPC/Topps 72, -Deckle 37
71/2 OPC/Topps 153
72/3 OPC 193
53/4 Parkhurst 57
54/5 Parkhurst 70
92/3 Parkhurst PR15
93/4 Parkhurst DPR6
93/4 Parkie(56/7) 96
94/5 Parkie(64/5) 92
95/6 Parkie(66/7) 80, AS3, TW4
66/7 Post'Large
67/8 Post
60/1 ShirriffCoin 86
61/2 ShirriffCoin 89
68/9 ShirriffCoin NYR11
81/2 TCMA 6
54/5 Topps 3
57/8 Topps 51
58/9 Topps 60
59/60 Topps 20, 54
60/1 Topps 49
61/2 Topps 51, -Stamp
62/3 Topps 46, -Buck
63/4 Topps 48
64/5 Topps 83
65/6 Topps 22
66/7 Topps 91, -USATest 18
67/8 Topps 84, 119, 121
54-67 TorontoStar 66/7
64/5 TheTorontoStar
71/2 TheTorontoSun
91/2 Ultimate(O6) 23, -Aut 23
90/1 UpperDeck 511

HOWSE, DON
77/8 NovaScotia

HOWSE, JASON
91/2 AvantGardeBCJHL 124

HOWSON, SCOTT
82/3 Indianapolis

HOYDA, DAVE
79/80 O-Pee-Chee 338
80/1 O-Pee-Chee 332
81/2 O-Pee-Chee 366
79/80 WPG

HOYDEN, RIKU
71/2 WilliamsFIN 362

HOYLE, JIM
28/9 PaulinsCandy 88

HRBATY, JAN
94/5 APS 292
95/6 APS 175
70/1 Kuvajulkaisut 50
69/70 MästarSerien 11

HRBEK, PETR
95/6 APS 281
92/3 Classic 39
92/3 ClassicProspects 67
94/5 DEL 381
95 Globe 160
95 Semic 163
92 SemicSticker 132

HRDINA, JIRI
91/2 Bowman 82
90/1 OPC/Topps 234
91/2 OPC/Topps 213
89/90 opcSticker 97/234
89/90 opcStickFS 5
90/1 Panini(CGY) 3
90/1 PaniniSticker 182
90/1 ProSet 421
91/2 ProSet 461
91/2 Score(CDN) 418
82 SemicSticker 97
92/3 Topps 272
91/2 ToppsStadiumClub 36
92/3 ToppsStadiumClub 158
90/1 UpperDeck 292
90/1 CGY/McGavins

HRECHKOSY, DAVE
74/5 Loblaws
75/6 OPC/Topps 156, 316
76/7 O-Pee-Chee 364

HREUSS, MICHAEL
94/5 DEL 304
95/6 DEL 283
96/7 DEL 89

HRISTOV, KROUM
79 PaniniSticker 349

HRIVNAK, JIM
91/2 Bowman 305
92/3 Bowman 372
92/3 FleerUltra 435
93/4 FleerUltra 410
93/4 Leaf 312
90/1 OPC/Topps 9
91/2 OPC/Topps 487
92/3 Parkhurst 430
93/4 Pinnacle 407
93/4 PowerPlay 428
89/90 ProCards(AHL) 93
90/1 ProCards 216
91/2 ProCards 549
90/1 ProSet 646
91/2 ProSet 509
90/1 Score 386
93/4 Score 201, 563
92/3 Topps 18
91/2 ToppsStadiumClub 264
92/3 ToppsStadiumClub 325
93/4 ToppsStadiumClub 421
91/2 UpperDeck 343
92/3 UpperDeck 151
90/1 WSH/Smokey
91/2 WSH/Kodak
92/3 WSH/Kodak
94/5 Milwaukee

HRKAC, TONY
90/1 Bowman 172
91/2 Bowman 141
93/4 Donruss 292
95/6 EdgeIce 161
93/4 FleerUltra 411
93/4 Leaf 329
88/9 OPC/Topps 129
89/90 OPC/Topps 64
91/2 OPC/Topps 241
91/2 opcPremier 40
88/9 opcStars 15
88/9 opcSticker 19/152, 129/265
88/9 opcStickFS 8
89/90 opcSticker 25/163
98/9 Pacific 210
90/1 Panini(QUE) 10
88/9 PaniniSticker 106
89/90 PaniniSticker 119
90/1 PaniniSticker 146
93/4 Parkhurst 448
90/1 ProSet 248
91/2 ProSet 205
91/2 PSPlatinum 105
90/1 Score 256
91/2 Score(CDN) 122, 555
91/2 Score(U.S) 122, 5T
91/2 ToppsStadiumClub 136
92/3 Score 407
92/3 Topps 524
90/1 UpperDeck 184
91/2 UpperDeck 56
89/90 QUE
90/1 QUE
90/1 QUE/PetroCanada
87/8 STL
87/8 STL/Kodak
88/9 STL
88/9 STL/Kodak
91/2 S.J.
92/3 Indianapolis
94/5 Milwaukee

HRSTKA, IVO
94/5 APS 20

HRUDEY, KELLY
90/1 Bowman 144
91/2 Bowman 183
92/3 Bowman 42
93/4 Donruss 161
94/5 Donruss 207
95/6 Donruss 215
96/7 Donruss 209
97/8 Donruss 92
96/7 DonrussCanadianIce 36
96/7 DonrussElite 60
97/8 DonrussPriority 85
93/4 EASports 66
94/5 Flair 80
94/5 Fleer 95
92/3 FleerUltra 84
93/4 FleerUltra 131
94/5 FleerUltra 99
95/6 FleerUltra 75
96/7 FleerUltra 150
93/4 HockeyWit 93
92/3 Kraft-Disk
93/4 Kraft-Cutout
94/5 KraftDinner
95/6 Kraft CreaseKeeper
93/4 Leaf 39
94/5 Leaf 189
96/7 Leaf 109
96/7 LeafPreferred 39
97/8 Limited-fabric 27
96/7 Maggers 76
96/7 MetalUniverse 136
85/6 OPC/Topps 122
86/7 OPC/Topps 27
87/8 OPC/Topps 119
88/9 OPC/Topps 155
89/90 OPC/T. 117,166,OPC 305
90/1 OPC/Topps 103
91/2 OPC/Topps 195
92/3 O-Pee-Chee 44
85/6 opcSticker 79/212
86/7 opcSticker 212/84
87/8 opcSticker 242/109
88/9 opcSticker 109/241
89/90 opcSticker 149/268
98/9 Pacific 382
97/8 PacificCrown 337
87/8 PaniniSticker 90
88/9 PaniniSticker 283
89/90 PaniniSticker 89
90/1 PaniniSticker 246
91/2 PaniniSticker 81
92/3 PaniniSticker 63
93/4 PaniniSticker 210
94/5 PaniniSticker 180
95/6 PaniniSticker 276
91/2 Parkhurst 71
92/3 Parkhurst 66
93/4 Parkhurst 97
95/6 Parkhurst 103
94/5 ParkieSE 81
91/2 Pinnacle 39
92/3 Pinnacle 19
93/4 Pinnacle 252
94/5 Pinnacle 292, MA3
95/6 Pinnacle 122
96/7 Pinnacle 120
96/7 PinnacleBeAPlayer 45
97/8 PinnacleInside -StandUp 10
95/6 PinnacleZenith 55
96/7 PinnacleZenith 57
95/6 Playoff 270
96/7 Playoff 367
94/5 POG 282
95/6 POG 143
93/4 PowerPlay 117
93/4 Premier 471
94/5 Premier 462
90/1 ProSet 119
91/2 ProSet 102
92/3 ProSet 70
91/2 PSPlatinum 54, PC6
90/1 Score 115, -HotCards 55
91/2 Score(CDN) 451, (U.S) 231
92/3 Score 155
93/4 Score 140
94/5 Score 145
95/6 Score 198
96/7 Score 68
97/8 Score 50
92/3 SeasonsPatch 12
94/5 Select 34
95/6 SelectCertified 65
96/7 SelectCertified 87
96/7 SP 141
95/6 Summit 55
96/7 Summit 126
95/6 SuperSticker 61
92/3 Topps 29
91/2 ToppsStadiumClub 120
92/3 ToppsStadiumClub 391
93/4 ToppsStadiumClub 54
94/5 ToppsStadiumClub 208
95/6 ToppsStadiumClub 8
95/6 ToppsSuperSkills 87
90/1 UpperDeck 231
91/2 UpperDeck 262
92/3 UpperDeck 270
93/4 UpperDeck 216, SP-71
94/5 UpperDeck 432
95/6 UpperDeck 145
96/7 UpperDeck 330
94/5 UDBAP G13, R13, -Sig 140
96/7 UDBlackDiamond 62
95/6 UDCollChoice 147
96/7 DAL/Southwest
89/90 L.A./Smokeys 16
90/1 L.A./Smokeys 17
83/4 NYI
84/5 NYI 26
96/7 S.J/PacificBellSheet (x2)
97/8 S.J/PacificBellSheet
81/2 Indianapolis 18
82/3 Indianapolis

HRUSKA, DAVID
95/6 RedDeer

HRYCUIK, JIM
74/5 Loblaws
74/5 WSH

HRYCUIK, TONY
92/3 BCJHL 144

HRYNEWICH, STEVE
83/4 Ottawa67s
84/5 Ottawa67s

HSI KIANG, CHENG
79 PaniniSticker 358

HUARD, BILL
93/4 Parkhurst 414
97/8 PinnacleBeAPlayer 31
90/1 ProCards 566
91/2 ProCards 414
93/4 UpperDeck 485
96/7 DAL/Southwest
97/8 EDM
93/4 OTT/Kraft
94/5 OTT/Bell
89/90 Nashville

HUARD, STÉPHANE
91/2 SketchQMJHL 16

HUB, JAROSLAV
94/5 APS 191
95/6 APS 45

HUBALEK, ROMAN
91/2 Knoxville

HUBER, PHIL
91/2 ProCards 458
94/5 SigRookies 38
89/90 SketchMEM 6

HUBER, WILLIE
79/80 OPC/Topps 17
80/1 OPC/Topps 173
81/2 OPC 89, Topps(W) 89
82/3 O-Pee-Chee 85
83/4 O-Pee-Chee 246
87/8 OPC/Topps 93
81/2 opcSticker 126
82/3 opcSticker 185
83/4 opcSticker 139
87/8 opcSticker 31/172
87/8 PaniniSticker 109
82/3 Post
83/4 PuffySticker 21
83/4 SouhaitsRen.KeyChain
79/80 DET
80/1 DET
87/8 VAN/Shell

HUBICK, GREG
75/6 TOR

HUCK, FRAN
70/1 Esso Stamp
69/70 MästarSerien 25, 34
74/5 opcWHA 28
75/6 opcWHA 121
73/4 Topps 63
72/3 STL
72/3 STL/8"x10"
74/5 Minnesota

HUCKLE, JEFF
91/2 AirCanadaSJHL C24

HUCKO, PATRIK
94/5 APS 189

HUCUL, FRED
45-64 BeeHives(CHI)
51/2 Parkhurst 45
52/3 Parkhurst 26
53/4 Parkhurst 71
95/6 udElite DS4

HUDACEK, VLADIMIR
94/5 APS 252
95/6 APS 294

HUDDY, CHARLIE
91/2 Bowman 103
92/3 FleerUltra 308
93/4 FleerUltra 344
89/90 Kraft 12
83/4 O-Pee-Chee 30
84/5 O-Pee-Chee 244
85/6 O-Pee-Chee 187
86/7 O-Pee-Chee 211
87/8 O-Pee-Chee 207
88/9 O-Pee-Chee 218
89/90 OPC/Topps 158
90/1 OPC/Topps 344
91/2 opcPremier 125
83/4 opcSticker 96
84/5 opcSticker 258
85/6 opcSticker 216
86/7 opcSticker 69/199
87/8 opcSticker 87/219
88/9 opcSticker 221/97
89/90 opcSticker 220/79
90/1 Panini(EDM) 7
87/8 PaniniSticker 260
88/9 PaniniSticker 53
89/90 PaniniSticker 82
90/1 PaniniSticker 221
91/2 PaniniSticker 129
91/2 Parkhurst 298
91/2 Pinnacle 225
92/3 Pinnacle 143
93/4 Pinnacle 296
94/5 Pinnacle 178
93/4 PowerPlay 361
93/4 Premier 219
90/1 ProSet 85
91/2 ProSet 400
90/1 Score 199
91/2 Score(CDN) 247, 570
91/2 Score(U.S) 20T
92/3 Score 92
93/4 Score 90
84/5 7ElevenDisk
83/4 SouhaitsRen.KeyChain
92/3 Topps 279
91/2 ToppsStadiumClub 203
92/3 ToppsStadiumClub 372
93/4 ToppsStadiumClub 308
90/1 UpperDeck 341
91/2 UpperDeck 569
94/5 UDBeAPlayer G11
83/4 Vachon 27
81/2 EDM/WestEdmonton
82/3 EDM/RedRooster
83/4 EDM
83/4 EDM/Buttons
83/4 EDM/McDonald
84/5 EDM
84/5 EDM/RedRooster
85/6 EDM/RedRooster
86/7 EDM
86/7 EDM/RedRooster
87/8 EDM
88/9 EDM
88/9 EDM/ActionMagazine 45
90/1 EDM/McGavins

HUDSON, DAVE
72/3 EddieSargent 134
74/5 Loblaws
72/3 O-Pee-Chee 211
73/4 OPC 234
74/5 OPC 335
75/6 OPC/Topps 122
76/7 OPC 299
77/8 OPC 343
78/9 OPC 299
76/7 COL.R
76/7 COL.R/CokeCans
77/8 COL.R/CokeCans

HUDSON, GORDIE
52/3 LavalDairy 117
52/3 StLawrence 46

HUDSON, MIKE
91/2 Bowman 399
92/3 Bowman 73
92/3 FleerUltra 37
90/1 O-Pee-Chee 424
91/2 OPC/Topps 495
92/3 O-Pee-Chee 331
91/2 Parkhurst 260
91/2 Pinnacle 38
92/3 Pinnacle 134
90/1 ProSet 431
91/2 ProSet 369
91/2 Score(CDN) 389
92/3 Score 156
93/4 Score 659
92/3 Topps 172
91/2 ToppsStadiumClub 22
92/3 ToppsStadiumClub 182
94/5 UDBeAPlayer R31
88/9 CHI/Coke
89/90 CHI/Coke
90/1 CHI/Coke
91/2 CHI/Coke
92/3 EDM
94/5 PGH 8
96/7 PHO
85/6 Sudbury 15
89/90 Sudbury 15

HUDSON, ROB
84/5 Ottawa67s

HUEGUENIN, RENÉ
72 SemicSticker 154

HUFFMAN, KERRY
92/3 FleerUltra 386
93/4 FleerUltra 402
93/4 Leaf 291
90/1 O-Pee-Chee 516
92/3 opcPremier 48
88/9 PaniniSticker 317
91/2 Parkhurst 349
92/3 Parkhurst 382
93/4 Premier 43
92/3 ProSet 136
92/3 Score 239
93/4 Score 182
92/3 Topps 387
95/6 Topps 131
92/3 ToppsStadiumClub 381
93/4 ToppsStadiumClub 33
94/5 ToppsStadiumClub 127
92/3 UpperDeck 444
94/5 UDBeAPlayer-Aut. 83
94/5 OTT/Bell
95/6 OTT
89/90 PHA
90/1 PHA
91/2 PHA/JCPenney
92/3 QUE/PetroCan
96/7 LasVegas

HUGGINS, AL
27-32 LaPresse 30/1

HUGHES, BRENT
70/1 EddieSargent 147
71/2 EddieSargent 147
72/3 EddieSargent 155
82? JDMcCarthy
74/5 Loblaws
69/70 O-Pee-Chee 144
71/2 OPC/Topps 205
72/3 OPC 234
73/4 OPC 184
76/7 opcWHA 34
71/2 TheTorontoSun
72/3 STL
76/7 SanDiegoMariners

HUGHES, BRENT
94/5 FleerUltra 255
94/5 Leaf 218
97/8 PacificDyang-BestKept 56
94/5 PaniniSticker 4
94/5 Pinnacle 510
88/9 ProCards(Moncton)
89/90 ProCards(AHL) 31
90/1 ProCards 244
91/2 ProCards 561
94/5 ToppsStadiumClub 234
90/1 UpperDeck 333
89/90 WPG/Safeway
91/2 Baltimore 2
87/8 Moncton
90/1 Moncton

HUGHES, CHUCK E.
93/4 Birmingham 7

HUGHES, FRANK
76/7 opcWHA 81
75/6 Houston
76/7 Phoenix

HUGHES, HOWIE
70/1 EddieSargent 80
68/9 O-Pee-Chee 158
69/70 O-Pee-Chee 142

HUGHES, JACK
24/5 Crescent Selkirks 2
25 Dominion 92
23/4 PaulinsCandy 3
28/9 PaulinsCandy 66

HUGHES, JASON
91/2 SketchOHL 273
93/4 Slapshot(Kitchener) 5
94/5 Slapshot(Kitchener) 6

HUGHES, JOHN
75/6 opcWHA 45
76/7 opcWHA 106
80/1 Pepsi Cap
80/1 EDM/Zellers
88/9 EDM/ActionMagazine 116
79/80 VAN
75/6 Cincinnati

HUGHES, PAT
79/80 OPC/Topps 65
80/1 O-Pee-Chee 347
82/3 O-Pee-Chee 109
83/4 O-Pee-Chee 31, 213
84/5 O-Pee-Chee 245
83/4 opcSticker 327, 328
85/6 opcSticker 229/98
82/3 Post
84/5 7ElevenDisk
83/4 SouhaitsRen.KeyChain
83/4 Vachon 28
85/6 BUF
81/2 EDM/RedRooster
82/3 EDM/RedRooster
83/4 EDM, EDM/Buttons
83/4 EDM/McDonald
84/5 EDM
84/5 EDM/RedRooster
88/9 EDM/ActionMagazine 24
78/9 MTL
77/8 NovaScotia

HUGHES, PETER
87/8 Sudbury 17
89/90 Sudbury 17

HUGHES, RYAN
93/4 Classic 69
94/5 Classic-Autograph
93/4 ClassicProspects 74
91/2 UpperDeck 'CzechWJC 47

HUHTALA, JARMO
78/9 SM-Liiga 59
72/3 WilliamsFIN 304

HUHTALA, JORMA
80/1 Mallasjuoma 37

HUIKARI, JAHU
80/1 Mallasjuoma 100
82 SemicSticker 33
78/9 SM-Liiga 142
71/2 WilliamsFIN 301

HUKKANEN, VWIJO
72/3 WilliamsFIN 280

HULBIG, JOE
97/8 PacificDynag-BestKept 38
97/8 EDM

HULETT, DEAN
93/4 Classic 70
94/5 Classic-Autograph
93/4 ClassicProspects 142
95/6 Louisiana, -Playoffs
93/4 Phoenix

HULL, BOBBY
93/4 ActionPacked BH1-BH2
71/2 Bazooka Panel 4
45-64 BeeHives(CHIx2)
64-67 BeeHives(CHIx2)

62 CeramicTiles
63-5 ChexPhoto
64/5 CokeCap CHI-9
65/6 CocaCola
70/1 DadsCookies
72-84 Dernière 79/80
97/8 DonrussElite -BackTo 6
70/1 EddieSargent 43
71/2 EddieSargent 34
70/1 Esso Stamp
88/9 EssoAllStar
87 HallOfFame 242
96/7 HHOFLegends 89
82? JDMcCarthy
71 Kelloggs
95/6 KennerLegend
96/7 KennerLegend
68/9 OPC/Topps 16
68/9 OPC 204, -Puck Sticker 3
69/70 OPC/Topps 70
69/70 O-Pee-Chee 216
69/70 OPC-Sticker, -Stamp
70/1 OPC/Topps 15, OPC 235
70/1 OPC/T-Deckle 30, -Sticker
71/2 OPC/Topps 50, 261, T. 1
71/2 OPC/T-Booklet 1
72/3 OPC 228, 272, 336
72/3 Topps 61, 126
79/80 OPC/Topps 185
71/2 opcPoster 9
73/4 opc-Posters 16
74/5 opcWHA 50
75/6 opcWHA 1, 65
76/7 opcWHA 3, 5, 65, 100
77/8 opcWHA 50
94/5 Parkie(64/5) 25, 136, A3
94/5 Parkie(64/5) AS5,TW2,TW6
95/6 Parkie(66/7) 21,124,129
95/6 P.(66/7) 130,135,141,AS4
73/4 QuakerOats 50
72 SemicSticker 228
91 SemicSticker 24
60/1 ShirriffCoin 63
61/2 ShirriffCoin 25
62/3 ShirriffCoin 47, 57
68/9 ShirriffCoin Ch1
93 SourPuckCaps P
97/8 SPAuthentic M5, T5
77-9 Sportscaster 0 -20, 50-3
77-80 Sprtscastr 8-181, 57-1358
77-80 Sprtscaster 58- 1381
94/5 SRTetrad CXXII
58/9 Topps 66
59/60 Topps 47
60/1 Topps 58
61/2 Topps 29, -Stamp
62/3 Topps 33, -Buck
63/4 Topps 33
64/5 Topps 20, 107
65/6 Topps 59
66/7 Topps 64, 112, 125
66/7 Topps-USATest 40
67/8 Topps 113, 124
98/9 Topps-RookieReprint 9
54-67 TorontoStar 65/6, V7, V11
56-66 TorontoStar 60/1, 62/3
56-66 TorontoStar 63/4, 64/5
63/4 TheTorontoStar
64/5 TheTorontoStar
71/2 TheTorontoSun
92/3 Trends(76) 107, 39, 142
92/3 Trends(76) 178, -Aut
91/2 Ultimate06 57, 77, 82, 88
91/2 Ultimate06 89, 90, 91, 92
91/2 Ultimate06 96, 'Promo
91/2 Ultimate06-Aut, -Holo
92/3 UD-LockerAS 43
71/2 WilliamsFIN 383
60/1 WonderBread 2
93/4 Zellers
70/1 CHI
79/80 WPG

HULL, BRETT

95/6 Aces J (Diamonds)
96/7 Aces 9 (Diamonds)
90/1 Bowman 24, -HatTrick 1
91/2 Bowman 367, 375
92/3 Bowman 186, 209
95/6 Bowman 43
97/8 Corinthian Headliners
93/4 Donruss 286, U, -Elite 5
94/5 Donruss -Dominators 8
95/6 Donruss 68, -Marksmen 7
95/6 D-ProPointer 6, -Dom 6
96/7 Donruss 197,-TopS 6,-Elit 4
97/8 Donruss 71,-Line 18,-Red 5
96/7 DonrussCanadianIce 65
97/8 DCdnIce 17, -Scrapbook 6
95/6 DonrussElite 7, -Cutting 12
96/7 D.Elite 4, -Perspcectives 9
97/8 DonrussElite 12,-BackTo 6
97/8 D.Preferd 15, 193,-Line 3C
97/8 D.Pref -Tins 18,-WideTins 2
97/8 DonrussPriority 9
97/8 D.Prio -DirDep23,-OpDay 9
97/8 D.Prio-Pstcrd 28,-Stamp 28
97/8 D.Studio 11,-HardHats 20
97/8 D.Studio-Portr 11,-Silhou 8
96/7 Duracell DC5, JB5
93/4 EASports 125
97/8 EssoOlympic 27
93/4 FaxPaxWorldOfSport 26
94/5 Flair 153, -HotNumber 4
96/7 Flair 81, -Centre 4
94/5 Fleer 187, -Slapshot 2
96/7 Fleer 97, -ArtRoss 7
95/6 FleerMetal 125, -IntSteel 9
95/6 FM-HeavyMet 5
96/7 F.Picks-DreamLine 10
96/7 F.Picks-Fab 19, -Fantasy 6
92/3 FleerUltra 186, -AS 12
93/4 FU 117,-Scorng 3, -RedL 4
94/5 FU 183, -AS 11,-RedLight 5
95/6 FU 139,386,-Red 3,-ExtAt 8
96/7 FleerUltra 146, -MrMom 4
91/2 Gillette 14
95 Globe 115
96/7 Got-UmHockeyGreatsCoin
92/3 HighFive 2
93/4 HockeyWit 97
95/6 Hoyle'WEST 10 (Spades)
92/3 HumptyDumpty (2)
94/5 Incomnet
97/8 KatchMedallion 129, 163
91/2 Kelloggs 21
95/6 Kelloggs (x2)
93/4 KennerSLU
94/5 KennerSLU (U.S)
95/6 KennerSLU (U.S)
90/1 Kraft 20, 67
91/2 Kraft 66
92/3 Kraft-AllStar
93/4 Kraft-Captain
94/5 Kraft-HockeyH
95/6 KraftDinner
96/7 KraftDinner
97/8 Kraft -WorldsBest
93/4 Leaf 255, -GoldLeafAS 3
93/4 Leaf-StudioSignature 8
94/5 Leaf 16, -GoldLeadStar 4
95/6 Leaf 209, FireOIce 9, Gld 6
96/7 Leaf 45,-Leathr 3,-Swtrs 12
97/8 Leaf 11,178,-BannrSeas 11
94/5 LeafLimited 2, -Gold 2
95/6 LeafLimited 28, -StarsOf 10
96/7 LeafLimited 24, -Stubble 15
96/7 LeafPreferred 106
96/7 LP-SteelPower 9, -Vanity 5
97/8 Limited 20, 51, 185
97/8 Limited -fabric 28, 38
96/7 Maggers 137
91/2 McDonalds McD13, McH-4
92/3 McDonalds McH02
93/4 McDonalds McD07
94/5 McDonalds McD13
95/6 McDonalds McD6
96/7 McDonalds McD24
97/8 McDonalds McD16
96/7 MetalUniv. 132, -Lethal 7
97/8 Omega 194,-GameFace 17
88/9 OPC/Topps 66
89/90 OPC/Topps 186, F
90/1 OPC/Topps 4, 77, 195
90/1 OPC 513, Topps-TL 2
91/2 OPC/Topps 190, 259, 303
91/2 OPC/T. 403, 516, T-TL 20
92/3 OPC 87, 124, -25Years 21
90/1 opcPremier 47
91/2 opcPremier 49
92/3 opcPremier-Star 21
88/9 opcStars 16
88/9 opcSticker 16/145, 127/259
89/90 opcSticker 22
88/9 opcStickFS 9
98/9 Pacific 16,-Gld 30,-T.CL 22
97/8 PacificCrown 16, -Supial 18
97/8 PCC-Gold 19, -Slap 9C
97/8 PCC-TeamCL 21
97/8 PacificCrownRoyale 117
97/8 PCR-BladesOfSteel 18
97/8 PCR-HatTrick 16, -Lamp 18
97/8 PacificDynagon! 107, 143
97/8 PcfcD-BstKpt 81,-Dyna 14B
97/8 PacificD-Tandem 8, 18
97/8 PacificInv. 120, -Feature 31
97/8 PacificInv.-Attack 21,-Off 18
97/8 PcfcParamnt 159,-BigN 18
97/8 PacificP-Photoengraving 18
98/9 PacificParamount 64
97/8 PacificRegime 169
97/8 PcfcRevoltn 121,-TmCL 21
90/1 PaniniSticker 262, 333
88/9 PaniniSticker 107
89/90 PaniniSticker 117
90/1 PaniniSticker 262, 333
91/2 PaniniSticker 25, 325
92/3 PaniniSticker 16, 289
93/4 PaniniSticker N
94/5 PaniniSticker 140, 235b
95/6 PaniniSticker 194
96/7 PaniniSticker 202
97/8 PaniniSticker 168
95 PaniniWorlds 299, 300
91/2 Parkhurst 157, 219, 432
91/2 Parkhurst 474, PHC6
92/3 Parkhurst 153, 459
93/4 Parkhurst 180, G4, W7
94/5 Parkhurst 309, V35, C20
95/6 Parkhurst 172, PP54
95/6 PH-AllStar 2, -Crown(2) 10
94/5 ParkieSE 154
91/2 Pinnacle 200, 356, 376,B12
92/3 Pinnacle 100, 257, -TmP 6
93/4 Pinnacle 200, CA20
93/4 P-NiftyFifty 1, 10, -TeamP 6
94/5 Pinnacle 450, BR9, TP11
95/6 Pinnacle 15, -Clr2, -Frst 12
96/7 Pinnacle 118, 128
96/7 P-Numbers 6, -TeamP 6
97/8 Pinnacle 35
96/7 Pinn.BeAPlayer-Biscuit 14
97/8 P.BAP 15,-One 6,-Take 13
97/8 P.BeeHive 6,-TeamBH 14
97/8 PinnCertified 70, -Team 19
97/8 Pinnacle-EPIX 18
95/6 PinnacleFANtasy 24
96/7 PinnacleFANtasy 16
97/8 PinnacleInside 24
97/8 P.Inside-Can12,-Track 19
96/7 PinnacleMint 14
97/8 PinnacleMint 23,-Minterntl 3
95/6 PinnZenith 1, -ZTeam 15
96/7 PinnZenith 67, -ZTeam 7
95/6 Playoff 89, 195, 307
96/7 Playoff 427
94/5 POG 203
95/6 POG 7, 23, 236
97/8 Post
93/4 PowerPlay 211, -Point 4
93/4 PP-Slapshot 4
93/4 Premier 425
93/4 Prmr-Black(OPC) 22, (T) 21
94/5 Premier 417, 465
94/5 Prmr-Finest(T) 2, -GoTo 3
95/6 ProMagnet 8
90/1 ProSet 263, 342, 378, 395
90/1 ProSet P3, -Promo 1
91/2 ProSet 215, 290, 320, 326
91/2 ProSet CC6, Promo 4of4
91/2 PS'ThePuck 24
92/3 ProSet 156, 245, -TmLdr 8
91/2 PSPlatinum 109, 282, PC5
90/1 Score 300, 317, 346, 351
90/1 Score 366,-HotCards 100
91/2 Score(CDN) 1,261,294,302
91/2 Score(CDN) 318, 367, 377
91/2 Score(U.S) 1, 337, 347, 371
91/2 Score(U.S) 404, 412, 428
91/2 Score-HotCards 3
92/3 Score 350,411,442,435,500
93/4 Score 335, -P.AS 32
93/4 Score(U.S) DD4,-Dream 18
93/4 Score-TheFranchise 18
94/5 Score100,DT22,NP11,TF20
95/6 Score 235, -BorderBat 6
95/6 S-Dream 9, -Lamplight 11
96/7 Score 19,-SdnD 4,-Supr 11
97/8 Score 81
97/8 Score(STL) 1
92/3 SeasonsPatch 13
93/4 SeasonsPatch 6
94/5 Select 97, FL12
95/6 SelectCert. 4, -GoldTm 6
96/7 SelectCert. 19, -Corner 6
94 Semic 123, 347
95 Semic 113
89 SemicSticker 167
91 SemicSticker 144
92 SemicSticker 156
93 SemicSticker 185
95/6 SkBxEmotion 148, -Xcited 8
95/6 SkBxImpact 141, -Ice 2
96/7 SkBxImpact 113, -Blade 8
94/5 SP 100, -Premier 29
95/6 SP 121, E24
96/7 SP 136, GF4, -SPxForce 2
97/8 SPAuthentic 138, I2, S5, T5
96/7 SPx 40, HH8
97/8 SPx 43, SPx20
98/9 SPx"Finite" 97
96/7 SportFX MiniStix
97/8 SportFX MiniStix
95/6 Summit 13, -GM 17, -Mad 2
96/7 Summit 35, 199, -HiVolt 16
95/6 SuperSticker 101, DC11
96/7 TeamOut
92/3 Topps 2, 260, 340
95/6 Topps 10, 372, 4RL, 10HG
95/6 Topps M7, PF19
98/9 Topps 30, -RookieReprint 6
94/5 ToppsFinest 42, -Div. 15
94/5 T.Finest-BBest(Blue) 15
95/6 ToppsFinest 10, 184
95 ToppsFinest Bronze 8
96/7 T.Picks 29, FT12, TS10
91/2 ToppsStadiumClub 67
92/3 ToppsStadiumClub 1, 258
93/4 T.StadiumClub 65, -AllStar
93/4 TSC-Finest 3, -Master (1) 9
94/5 T.StadiumClub 100
94/5 TSC-Dynasty 3, -Finest 2
95/6 TStadiumClub 183, -PS 9
91/2 TSC-MembersOnly (x2)
93/4 TSC-MembersOnly 6
95/6 TSC-MembersOnly 3, 37
97/8 ToppsSticker 4
95/6 ToppsSuperSkills 48
90/1 UMDHull Set
90/1 UpperDeck 154, 203, 312
90/1 UD 474, 546, -Holo.
91/2 UpperDeck 7, 33, 45
91/2 UpperDeck 464, 622, AW
92/3 UD 29, 423, 620, G7, W2
92/3 UD-LockerAS 27
93/4 UpperDeck 160, 232, GG3
93/4 UD HB3, NL2, R5, SP-137
94/5 UD 229, 333, 569 , C 17
94/5 UD R2, R32, R57, SP66
95/6 UD 233,251,486,R5,SE157
95/6 UD-AllStarPredict MVP3
96/7 UD 324,GJ5, HH13, SS15B
96/7 UD X6, -AllStarYCTGA3
97/8 UpperDeck 141, S16
97/8 UD SG16, SS4, T9C
93/4 UDBeAPlayer 8
94/5 UDBAP R48, G10
95/6 UDBeAPlayer 1, LL3
96/7 UDBlackDiamond 170
97/8 UDBlackDiamond 19, PC18
98/9 UDChoice 183, BH4, SQ22
95/6 UDCC 214, 364, C5
96/7 UDCC 223, 329, S2, UD29
97/8 UDCC 224, C26, S26,SQ76
97/8 udDiamondVision 25
96/7 UpperDeck"Ice" 115
97/8 UDIce 6, IC16, L8C
96 Wien 164
97/8 Zenith 25,Z48,-ChasgCup 7
87/8 CGY/RedRooster
87/8 CGY/FamousFlames 28
87/8 STL
88/9 STL
88/9 STL/Kodak
89/90 STL/Kodak
90/1 STL/Kodak
91/2 STL
92/3 STL/UpperDeck 12, -Aut.
96/7 STL/Dispatch
86/7 Moncton 20

HULL, DENNIS

64-67 BeeHives(CHI)
65/6 CocaCola
70/1 Colgate Stamp 32
70/1 DadsCookies
70/1 EddieSargent 36
71/2 EddieSargent 46
72/3 EddieSargent 67
70/1 Esso Stamp
82? JDMcCarthy
72/3 Letraset 16
74/5 LiptonSoup 17
68/9 O-Pee-Chee 153
69/70 OPC/Topps 71
70/1 OPC/Topps 14
71/2 OPC/Topps 85
72/3 OPC 52,-TmCanada, T.164
73/4 OPC 171, Topps 60
74/5 OPC/Topps 150
75/6 OPC/Topps 254
76/7 OPC/T. 195, T-Glossy 16
77/8 OPC/Topps 225
94/5 Parkie(64/5) 39
95/6 Parkie(66/7) 37
70/1 PostShooters
72/3 Post Transfers 11
68/9 ShirriffCoin CHI 11
71/2 TheTorontoSun
65/6 Topps 64
66/7 Topps 113, -USATest 1
67/8 Topps 56
91/2 Trends(72) 89, -Aut
68/9 CHI
70/1 CHI

HULL, JODY

95/6 FleerMetal 59
95/6 FleerUltra 241
93/4 Leaf 157
90/1 opcPremier 46
97/8 PacificD-BestKept 41
89/90 PaniniSticker 230
93/4 PaniniSticker 115
94/5 PaniniSticker 66
95/6 PaniniSticker 74
92/3 Parkhurst 119
93/4 Parkhurst 76
94/5 Parkhurst 89
95/6 Parkhurst 353
93/4 Premier 212
94/5 Premier 427
91/2 ProCards 201
95/6 ProMagnet 87
90/1 ProSet 490
91/2 Score(CDN) 524
93/4 Score 320
95/6 SP 57
95/6 Topps 134
95/6 ToppsFinest 109
91/2 ToppsStadiumClub 100
93/4 ToppsStadiumClub 344
94/5 ToppsStadiumClub 199
90/1 UpperDeck 322
92/3 UpperDeck 539
93/4 UpperDeck 112, 510
94/5 UpperDeck 176
95/6 UpperDeck 50, SE123
95/6 UDBeAPlayer 190
96/7 UDCollChoice 107
96/7 FLA/WinnDixie
89/90 HFD/JuniorWhalers
92/3 OTT

HULSE, CALE

92/3 Classic 21
92/3 ClassicFourSport 170, -Aut
93/4 ClassicProspects 222
94/5 Leaf 481
98/9 Pacific 119
97/8 PacificDynag-BestKept 12
96/7 Pinnacle 242
97/8 PinnacleBeAPlayer 60
94/5 Premier 407
91/2 SketchWHL 43
98/9 Topps 32
95/6 UpperDeck 437
96/7 UDCollChoice 36

HULST, KENT

89/90 ProCards(AHL) 109
90/1 ProCards 149
91/2 ProCards 380
90/1 Newmarket
96/7 Portland

HULTBERG, JOHN

95/6 Slapshot 107

HUME, FRED

83&87 HallOfFame 233
83 HHOF Postcard (A)

HUMENIUK, SCOTT

91/2 ProCards 97

HUMENNY, LAYNE

92/3 MPSPhotoSJHL 58

HUML, DUSAN

94/5 APS 152

HUNGLE, CASEY

91/2 AvantGardeBCJ 61, 153
92/3 BCJHL 96

HUNT, BRIAN

89/90 ProCards'AHL 38

HUNT, CURTIS

89/90 ProCards(IHL) 186
90/1 ProCards 516
91/2 ProCards 336
87/8 Flint
84/5 PrinceAlbert

HUNT, GREG

91/2 AvantGardeBCJ 83
92/3 BCJHL 173

HUNTER, ANDRIA

94/5 Classic W17

HUNTER, DALE

90/1 Bowman 71
91/2 Bowman 303
92/3 Bowman 303
72-84 Dernière 81/2
93/4 Donruss 370
94/5 Donruss 149
95/6 Donruss 12
96/7 Donruss 199
97/8 Donruss 195
96/7 Duracell DC20
83/4 Esso
94/5 Flair 199
96/7 Flair 99
94/5 Fleer 235
92/3 FleerUltra 232
93/4 FleerUltra 135
94/5 FleerUltra 234
95/6 FleerUltra 175
84/5 Kelloggs Disk
86/7 Kraft Sports 46
93/4 Leaf 118
94/5 Leaf 183
95/6 Leaf 215
96/7 Leaf 51, 56
97/8 Omega 239
81/2 O-Pee-Chee 277
82/3 O-Pee-Chee 285
83/4 O-Pee-Chee 293
84/5 O-Pee-Chee 281
85/6 O-Pee-Chee 179
86/7 OPC/Topps 192
87/8 O-Pee-Chee 245
88/9 OPC/Topps 70
89/90 OPC/Topps 76, OPC 311
90/1 OPC/Topps 129
91/2 OPC/Topps 229
92/3 O-Pee-Chee 18
82/3 opcSticker 26
84/5 opcSticker 179
85/6 opcSticker 151/20
86/7 opcSticker 32
88/9 opcSticker 73/204
92/3 opcPremier-Star 2
98/9 Pacific 442
97/8 PacificCrown 129
97/8 PacificCrownRoyale 139
97/8 PacificInvincible 146
97/8 PacificParamount 194
97/8 PacificRevolution 147
87/8 PaniniSticker 155, 168
88/9 PaniniSticker 372
89/90 PaniniSticker 346
90/1 PaniniSticker 168
91/2 PaniniSticker 203
92/3 PaniniSticker 165
93/4 PaniniSticker 26
94/5 PaniniSticker 21
95/6 PaniniSticker 135
97/8 PaniniSticker 115
91/2 Parkhurst 195
92/3 Parkhurst CP7
93/4 Parkhurst D6
94/5 Parkhurst 254
95/6 Parkhurst 223
80/1 Pepsi Cap
91/2 Pinnacle 40
92/3 Pinnacle 104, 237
93/4 Pinnacle 13
94/5 Pinnacle 85
95/6 Pinnacle 21
95/6 P.Zenith-GiftedGrinder 12
95/6 Playoff 322
94/5 POG 244
82/3 Post
93/4 PowerPlay 262
94/5 Premier 506
95/6 ProMagnet 30
90/1 ProSet 312
91/2 ProSet 506
92/3 ProSet 202
91/2 PSPlatinum 245
90/1 Score 44
91/2 Score(CDN) 56, 336
91/2 Score(U.S) 56, 306
92/3 Score 231, -Sharpshooter 4
93/4 Score 40
94/5 Score 143
95/6 Score 107
96/7 Score 110
97/8 Score 201
94/5 Select 33
95/6 SkyBoxEmotion 188
95/6 SkyBoxImpact 177
83/4 SouhaitsRen.KeyChain
94/5 SP 127
95/6 SP 159
95/6 Summit 5
92/3 Topps 464
95/6 Topps 177
98/9 Topps 58
91/2 ToppsStadiumClub 164
92/3 ToppsStadiumClub 40
94/5 ToppsStadiumClub 134
90/1 UpperDeck 219
91/2 UpperDeck 209
92/3 UpperDeck 131
94/5 UpperDeck 68
95/6 UpperDeck 442
96/7 UpperDeck 178
97/8 UpperDeck 175
95/6 UDBeAPlayer 213
96/7 UDBlackDiamond 82
95/6 UDCollChoice 155
96/7 UDCollChoice 288
97/8 UDCollChoice 271
83/4 Vachon 66
80/1 QUE
81/2 QUE
82/3 QUE
83/4 QUE
84/5 QUE
85/6 QUE
85/6 QUE/GeneralFoods
85/6 QUE/McDonald
85/6 QUE/Pennant
85/6 QUE/Placemat
85/6 QUE/Provigo
86/7 QUE
86/7 QUE/GeneralFoods
86/7 QUE/McDonald
86/7 QUE/YumYum
87/8 WSH
87/8 WSH/Kodak
88/9 WSH
88/9 WSH/Smokey
89/90 WSH
89/90 WSH/Kodak
90/1 WSH/Kodak
90/1 WSH/Smokey
91/2 WSH
91/2 WSH/Kodak
92/3 WSH/Kodak
95/6 WSH

HUNTER, DAVE
79/80 O-Pee-Chee 387
80/1 O-Pee-Chee 293
81/2 O-Pee-Chee 115
82/3 O-Pee-Chee 110
83/4 O-Pee-Chee 32
84/5 O-Pee-Chee 246
88/9 OPC/Topps 62
82/3 opcSticker 102
83/4 opcSticker 154
88/9 opcSticker 235/105
87/8 PaniniSticker 268
88/9 PaniniSticker 339
80/1 Pepsi Cap
82/3 Post
83/4 StaterMint H16
83/4 Vachon 29
79/80 EDM
80/1 EDM/Zellers
81/2 EDM/RedRooster
82/3 EDM/RedRooster
83/4 EDM
83/4 EDM/Buttons
83/4 EDM/McDonald
84/5 EDM
84/5 EDM/RedRooster
85/6 EDM/RedRooster
86/7 EDM
86/7 EDM/RedRooster
88/9 EDM
88/9 EDM/ActionMagazine 40
87/8 PGH/Kodak
88/9 WPG/Police

HUNTER, MARK
91/2 Bowman 9
82/3 O-Pee-Chee 185
86/7 OPC/Topps 57
87/8 OPC/Topps 50
88/9 OPC/Topps 187
91/2 OPC/Topps 109
85/6 opcSticker 137/9
86/7 opcSticker 181
87/8 opcSticker 21/161
88/9 opcSticker 14/141
90/1 Panini(CGY) 4
87/8 PaniniSticker 313
88/9 PaniniSticker 108
91/2 Pinnacle 253
90/1 ProSet 422
91/2 ProSet 390
90/1 ScoreTraded 77T
91/2 Score(CDN) 156, 336
91/2 Score(U.S) 156, 336
92/3 Score 194
95/6 Slapshot 355
92/3 Topps 36
91/2 ToppsStadiumClub 15
92/3 ToppsStadiumClub 396
91/2 UpperDeck 479
83/4 Vachon 46
90/1 CGY/McGavins
91/2 HFD/JuniorWhalers
81/2 MTL
82/3 MTL
82/3 MTL/Steinberg
83/4 MTL
84/5 MTL
87/8 STL/Kodak
82/3 Post

HUNTER, TIM
90/1 O-Pee-Chee 434
97/8 PacificDynag-BestKept 85
90/1 Panini(CGY) 5
87/8 PaniniSticker 216
91/2 Pinnacle 375
90/1 ProSet 423
91/2 ProSet 366
91/2 Score(CDN) 537
92/3 Score 403
91/2 UpperDeck 221
82/3 CGY
85/6 CGY/RedRooster
86/7 CGY/RedRooster
87/8 CGY/RedRooster
90/1 CGY/McGavins
91/2 CGY/IGA
92/3 QUE/PetroCanada
96/7 S.J/PacificBellSheet
93/4 VAN/Coins
94/5 VAN
95/6 VAN/Building 4

HUNTER, TODD
90/1 SketchOHL 285
91/2 SketchOHL 182

HUOKKO, JAN
94/5 ElitSet 6
95/6 ElitSet 65
92/3 SemicElitserien 160
95/6 udElite 99, NA14

HUOTARI, HARRI
72/3 WilliamsFIN 305

HUOTARI, JARI
71/2 WilliamsFIN 342
72/3 WilliamsFIN 323

HURBANEK, JOACHIM
74 Hellas 111

HURD, KELLY
91/2 ProCards 253

HURIG, LARS
94/5 ElitSet 90

HURLBUT, MIKE
92/3 ClassicProspects 138
95/6 EdgeIce 167
89/90 ProCards(IHL) 35
90/1 ProCards 12
91/2 ProCards 196
92/3 UpperDeck 448
92/3 Binghampton

HURLEY, CRAIG
81/2 Saskatoon 17

HURLEY, DARREN
90/1 SketchOHL 9
91/2 SketchOHL 117

HURLEY, MIKE
98 BowmanCHL 54

HURME, HEIKKI
70/1 Kuvajulkaisut 138
71/2 WilliamsFIN 225

HURME, JANI
96/7 Sisu-Gala 4, -Ener 1,-Grn 2

HURME, MARKKU
96/7 Sisu 9

HURST, RON
45-64 BeeHives(TOR)
52/3 LavalDairy 119

HURTIG, LARS
96/7 DEL 153
94/5 ElitSet -TopGun 3
95/6 ElitSet 251
89/90 SemicElitserien 158
90/1 SemicElitserien 238
91/2 SemicElitserien 168
92/3 SemicElitserien 194
95/6 udElite 131

HUSCFO, DIETER
74 Hellas 114

HUSCROFT, JAMIE
97/8 PacificRegime 185
96/7 PaniniSticker 241
97/8 PinnacleBeAPlayer 88
88/9 ProCards(Utica)
89/90 ProCards'AHL 217
90/1 ProCards 577
91/2 ProCards 424
95/6 UDCollChoice 126
88/9 N.J./Caretta

HUSELIUS, KRISTIAN
97/8 udSwedish 60, C22

HUSGEN, JAMIE
88/9 ProCards(Mon)
87/8 Moncton

HUSS, ANDERS
94/5 ElitSet 61, -StudioSig 2
89/90 SemicElitserien 37
90/1 SemicElitserien 187
91/2 SemicElitserien 39
92/3 SemicElitserien 69
95/6 udElite DS1
97/8 udSwedish 30, 205, C18
97/8 udSwedish C22, S12

HUSSEY, MARC
92/3 Classic 18
92/3 ClassicFourSport 167
90/1 SketchWHL 146
91/2 SketchWHL 278

HUSTON, RON
74/5 Loblaws
76/7 opcWHA 36
75/6 Phoenix
76/7 Phoenix

HUTAN, GHEORGHE
79 PaniniSticker 312

HUTANU, VASILE
79 PaniniSticker 315

HUTCHINGS, GREG
90/1 SketchWHL 228

HUTCHINGS, STEVE
85/6 Arizona

HUTCHINSON, TROY
90/1 SketchOHL 286
91/2 SketchOHL 280

HUTCHISON, DAVE
74/5 Loblaws
75/6 OPC 390
76/7 OPC 346, 386
77/8 OPC 380
78/9 O-Pee-Chee 289
79/80 O-Pee-Chee 302
80/1 OPC/Topps 78
82/3 Post
81/2 CHI
80/1 CHI/4x6
78/9 TOR
79/80 TOR
73/4 VancouverBlazers

HUTSON
91/2 AvantGardeBCJHL 163

HUTTON, DWAINE
84/5 KelownaWingsWHL 13
87/8 Flint
83/4 Saskatoon

HUTTON, J.B.
83&87 HallOfFame 100
83 HHOF Postcard (G)

HUURA, ILKKA
71/2 WilliamsFIN 343
72/3 WilliamsFIN 324

HUURA, PASI
91/2 Jyvas-Hyva 48
92/3 Jyvas-Hyva 132
93/4 Jyvas-Hyva 236
91 SemicSticker 10
93 SemicSticker 51
93/4 Sisu 191
95/6 Sisu 34

HUUSKO, ANDERS
94/5 ElitSet 26
95/6 ElitSet 194, -FaceToFace 3
95 Globe 49
91/2 SemicElitserien 77
92/3 SemicElitserien 88
97/8 udSwedish 96, C24

HUUSKO, ERIK
94/5 ElitSet 14
95/6 ElitSet 32, -FaceToFace 3
95 Globe 45
95 PaniniWorlds 150
91/2 SemicElitserien 76
92/3 SemicElitserien 87
95/6 udElite 44

HUYBER, TODD
93/4 Huntington

HVIID, JESPER
79 PaniniSticker 365

HYATT, BRAD
88/9 ProCards(NewHaven)

HYATT, TROY
90/1 SketchWHL 17
91/2 SketchWHL 130
93/4 Seattle

HYKA, TOM
94/5 APS 272

HYLAND, HARRY
91 C55 Reprint 30
83&87 HallOfFame 157
83 HHOF Postcard (L)
1911-12 Imperial (C55) 30
1910-11 Imperial (C56) 10
1912-13 Imperial (C57) 19
1910-11 Imperial Post 30

HYND, JASON
91/2 AirCanadaSJHL B23

HYNES, GORD
90/1 CanadaNats
91/2 CanadaNats
95/6 DEL 387
96/7 DEL 295
92/3 O-Pee-Chee 8
91/2 Parkhurst 235
92/3 Score483, -Cnd.Olympic 5
92/3 ToppsStadiumClub 49
92/3 PHA/JCPenney
92/3 PHA/UD 24OCT92
86/7 Moncton 22

HYNES, WAYNE
94/5 DEL 387
95/6 DEL 396
96/7 DEL 305

HYNNES, CHRIS
94/5 SigRookies 41

HYOKKI, KARI
73/4 WilliamsFIN 271

HYRSKY, TIMO
70/1 Kuvajulkaisut 346

HYTTI, JARI
80/1 Mallasjuoma 183
72/3 WilliamsFIN 325

HYTTI, TIMO
72/3 WilliamsFIN 281

HYTTINEN, KIMMO
93/4 Sisu 85
94/5 Sisu 115

HYVARI, PAULI
65/6 Hellas 88

HYVARI, PENTTI
65/6 Hellas 93

HYVONEN, HANNES
95/6 Sisu 131
96/7 Sisu 141

HYVONEN, SEPO
72/3 WilliamsFIN 173

HYYTIAINEN, PENTTI
66/7 Champion 164
79 PaniniSticker 304

I

IAFRATE, AL
90/1 Bowman 153
91/2 Bowman 300
92/3 Bowman 251
93/4 Donruss 371, 402, Y
94/5 Donruss 205
93/4 EASports 152, 190
94/5 Flair 10
94/5 Fleer 12, -Slapshot 3
92/3 FleerUltra 233
93/4 F.Ultra 11, -AS 8, -Speed 5
94/5 FleerUltra 256, -Speed 4
96/7 FleerUltra 151
93/4 HockeyWit 74
90/1 Kraft 21
93/4 KraftDinner
94/5 Kraft-'HockeyHeroes
93/4 Leaf 141
94/5 Leaf 212
93/4 McDonalds McD16
96/7 MetalUniverse 137
85/6 OPC 210
86/7 OPC/Topps 26
87/8 OPC 238
88/9 OPC/Topps 71
89/90 OPC/Topps 79
90/1 OPC/Topps 91
91/2 OPC/Topps 148
92/3 O-Pee-Chee 341
90/1 opcPremier 48
85/6 opcSticker 13/143
86/7 opcSticker 148
87/8 opcSticker 160/20
88/9 opcSticker 180
89/90 opcSticker 178
97/8 PacificCrownColl. 177
90/1 Panini(TOR) 9
87/8 PaniniSticker 325
88/9 PaniniSticker 118
89/90 PaniniSticker 140
90/1 PaniniSticker 290
91/2 PaniniSticker 208
92/3 PaniniSticker 168
93/4 PaniniSticker 32
94/5 PaniniSticker 7
95/6 PaniniSticker 12
91/2 Parkhurst 194
92/3 Parkhurst 203
93/4 Parkhurst 217
94/5 Parkhurst 15, seV22
91/2 Pinnacle 207
92/3 Pinn 66, 233,-Promo(Cdn)
93/4 Pinn 189,-AS19, 47,-TmP 9
94/5 Pinnacle 39,-Promo BR1
96/7 PinnacleBeAPlayer 19
94/5 POG 36
93/4 PowerPlay 263, -Slapshot 5
93/4 Premier 45, 174
94/5 Premier 20, 453
90/1 ProSet 281, 354
91/2 ProSet 250
92/3 ProSet 205
91/2 PSPlatinum 130
90/1 Score 195, 334, -Hot 85
91/2 Score(CDN) 209, (U.S) 209
92/3 Score 11
93/4 Score 188, 450, -Dream 9
94/5 Score 168
95/6 Score 237
92/3 SeasonsPatch 67
94/5 Select 80
89 SemicSticker 162
91 SemicSticker 135
93 SemicSticker 173
95/6 SkyBoxEmotion 7
95/6 SkyBoxImpact 8
92/3 Topps 133
96/7 ToppsNHLPicks 117
91/2 ToppsStadiumClub 372
92/3 ToppsStadiumClub 302
93/4 T.StadiumClub 80, 455, -AS
94/5 ToppsStadiumClub 202
93/4 TSCMembersOnly 31
90/1 UpperDeck 157, 539
91/2 UpperDeck 318
92/3 UD 54, -LockerAS 37
93/4 UpperDeck 183, SP-170
94/5 UpperDeck 82, SP94
96/7 UpperDeck 331
97/8 UpperDeck 357
93/4 UDBeAPlayer 26
95/6 UDCollChoice 195
97/8 UDCollChoice 223
96/7 S.J/PacificBellSheet
97/8 S.J/PacificBellSheet
84/5 TOR
85/6 TOR
86/7 TOR
87/8 TOR
87/8 TOR/P.L.A.Y. 19
88/9 TOR/P.L.A.Y. 19
90/1 TOR
90/1 WSH/Kodak
91/2 WSH
91/2 WSH/Kodak
92/3 WSH/Kodak
83/4 Belleville 20

IAKOVENKO, ANDREI
92/3 Greensboro 9
92/3 SanDiego

IGINLA, JAROME
97/8 Aces 4 (Spades)
96/7 AllSportPPF 177
95/6 Classic 11
95/6 ClassicFiveSport 132
97/8 Donruss 14, 226, -Line17
96/7 D.Cdn.Ice 124, -OCanada 4
97/8 D.Cdn.Ice 12, -National 13
95/6 DonrussElite-WorldJrs 15
96/7 D.Elite 131, -Aspirations 19
97/8 D.Elite 13, 121,-Craftmn 17
97/8 D.Preferd 17, 166,-Line 7A
97/8 DonrussPriority 31, 191
97/8 D.Prio -DirDep 9,-OpDay 19
97/8 D.Prio-Pstcrd 20,-Stamp 20
97/8 D.Studio 12,-HardHats 12
97/8 D.Studio-Port 12,-Silhou 24
96/7 Flair 103
96/7 FleerUltra 24, -Rookies 10
96/7 Got-UmHockeyGreatsCoin
97/8 KatchMedallion 21
96/7 Kraft-TrophyProspects
97/8 Leaf 14,180,-BannrSeas 20
96/7 LeafLimited-Rookies 2
96/7 LeafPreferred 118
97/8 Limited 43, 114, 177
97/8 Limited -fabric 61
97/8 McDonalds McD12
96/7 MetalUniverse 182
97/8 Omega 30
98/9 Pacific 120
97/8 PacificCrown 12
97/8 PCC-Cramers 3, -Supial 3
97/8 PCC-Gold 5, -TeamCL 4
97/8 PacificCrownRoyale 19
97/8 PacificDynagon 17, 137
97/8 PcfcD-BstKpt 13,-Dyna 4B
97/8 PacificD-Tandem 3, 23
97/8 PacificInv. 19, -Attack 4
97/8 PacificInv.-Feature 5, -Off 4
97/8 P.Paramount 30, -CdnGrt 3
98/9 PacificParamount 28
97/8 PacificRegime 29
97/8 PacificRevolution 18
97/8 PaniniSticker 194, 251, 252
94/5 ParkieSE 260
97/8 Pinnacle 31
96/7 PinnacleBeAPlayer LTH1A
97/8 PinnacleCertified 55
96/7 PinnacleFANtasy 7
97/8 PinnacleInside 17,-Track 28
96/7 PinnacleMint 29
97/8 PinnacleMint 9
96/7 PinnacleZenith 119
97/8 Score 123, -CheckIt 7
94/5 Select 165
96/7 SelectCertified 93
94/5 Slapshot(MEM) 9
94/5 SP 181
95/6 SP 170
96/7 SP 23, -SPxForce 4, 5
97/8 SPAuthentic 20, S24
97/8 SPx 7, -DuoView
97/8 SportFX MiniStix
98/9 Topps 52, I3
97/8 ToppsSticker 3
96/7 UpperDeck 181, P19, X21
97/8 UD 24, GJ4, S24, SG12
96/7 UDBlckDiamond 164, RC19
97/8 UDBlackDiamond 21
98/9 UDChoice 35
96/7 UDCollChoice 349
97/8 UDCollChoice 34, 315, C29
97/8 UDCollChoice S12, SQ12
96/7 UpperDeck"Ice" 78
97/8 UpperDeckIce 20, L5C
97/8 Zenith 1, Z20
93/4 Kamloops

IGNATIUS, OLLI
80/1 Mallasjuoma 8

IGNATIEV, VICTOR
92/3 ClassicProspects 128

IHALAINEN, VEIKKO
70/1 Kuvajulkaisut 228
71/2 WilliamsFIN 243
73/4 WilliamsFIN 308

IHNACAK, MIROSLAV
87/8 PaniniSticker 336
88/9 ProCards(Adirondack)
89/90 ProCards(AHL) 155
90/1 ProCards 463
86/7 TOR
89/90 Halifax
90/1 Halifax

IHNACAK, PETER
94/5 DEL 240
95/6 DEL 234
96/7 DEL 85
83/4 OPC 334
83/4 opcSticker 32
85/6 opcSticker 19/150
87/8 PaniniSticker 334
89/90 ProCards(AHL) 120
83/4 PuffySticker 3
82 SemicSticker 96
83/4 Vachon 90
82/3 TOR
83/4 TOR
84/5 TOR
85/6 TOR
86/7 TOR
87/8 TOR
87/8 TOR/P.L.A.Y. 24

IHRIG, J.C.
94/5 Huntington 14

IIVONEN, SEPPO
66/7 Champion 139

IKOLA, SEPPO
65/6 Hellas 58

IKONEN, JOUKO
71/2 WilliamsFIN 322

IKONEN, JUHA
93/4 Jyvas-Hyva 203
94/5 Sisu 16
95/6 Sisu 93
96/7 Sisu 89

IKONEN, MARKKU
93/4 Sisu 156
94/5 Sisu 110
95/6 Sisu 62

ILAVSKY, SLAVOMIR
94 Semic 206

ILIEV, ATANAS
79 PaniniSticker 347

ILIEV, GUEORGUI
79 PaniniSticker 348

ILITCH, MIKE
91/2 ProSet-AC22

ILLIKAINEN, DARIN
85/6 Minn-Duluth 8

ILMIVALTA, PEKKA
93/4 Sisu 281

ILVASKY, SLAVOMIR
94 Semic 206

ILYIN, ROMAN
91/2 O-Pee-Chee 34R

IMBEAU, JEAN
90/1 SketchQMJHL 267
91/2 SketchQMJHL 67

IMBER, SHAWN
90/1 SketchMEM 19
90/1 SketchOHL 159
91/2 SketchOHL 323

IMBURGIA, CHUCK
95/6 Toledo

IMDAHL, THOMAS
94/5 DEL 359
95/6 DEL 231

IMES, CHRIS
95/6 EdgeIce 168
93/4 FleerUltra 486
92/3 Maine(2) 19
93/4 PowerPlay 506
93/4 Prmr-TeamUSA 11
93/4 T.StadiumClub-TmUSA 10
91/2 UD'CzechWJC 75
92/3 Maine(1) 5, 19

IMHAUSER, PETER
90/1 SemicElitserien 133

IMLACH, GEORGE (PUNCH)
62 CeramicTiles
63-5 ChexPhoto
87 HallOfFame 243
93/4 HHOFLegends 25
51/2 LavalDairy 37
59/60 Parkhurst 15
63/4 Parkhurst 19, 79
60/1 ShirriffCoin 20
61/2 ShirriffCoin 57
62/3 ShirriffCoin 15
52/3 StLawrence 54
64/5 Topps 45
65/6 Topps 11
66/7 Topps 11, -USATest 11
61/2 York 38
64/5 TOR
66/7 TOR/Coaster
79/80 TOR

IMMONEN, JORMA
80/1 Mallasjuoma 11
78/9 SM-Liiga 27
72/3 WilliamsFIN 101
73/4 WilliamsFIN 129

IMMONEN, MARTTI
80/1 Mallasjuoma 136
71/2 WilliamsFIN 151
72/3 WilliamsFIN 102

IMMONEN, SANTERI
95/6 Sisu 44

IMMONEN, WALTTERI
91/2 Jyvas-Hyva 24
92/3 Jyvas-Hyva 54
93/4 Jyvas-Hyva 110
95 PaniniWorlds 170
94 Semic 19
95 Semic 7
93 SemicSticker 52
93/4 Sisu 8
94/5 Sisu 24
95/6 Sisu 46, -Double 2
96/7 Sisu 45, -AtTheGala 3
95/6 SisuLimited 11

IMOO, DUSTY
90/1 SketchWHL 183
88/9 Lethbridge
89/90 Lethbridge
91/2 ProCards 258

IMPOLA, KALLE
72/3 WilliamsFIN 282

ING, PETER
91/2 Bowman 157
91/2 OPC/Topps 145
90/1 opcPremier 49
91/2 opcPremier 33
90/1 Panini(TOR) 10
91/2 PaniniSticker 99
90/1 ProSet 639
91/2 ProSet 222, 388
91/2 PSPlatinum 41
90/1 Score 414, 11T
91/2 Score(CDN) 55, 612
91/2 Score(U.S) 55, 62T
91/2 Score-YoungStar 12
92/3 Topps 423
91/2 ToppsStadiumClub 352
92/3 ToppStadiumClub 347
90/1 UpperDeck 432
91/2 UpperDeck 118
90/1 TOR
93/4 LasVegas

INGARFIELD, EARL
68/9 Bauer
45-64 BeeHives(NYRx2)
64-67 BeeHives(NYR)
62 CeramicTiles
64/5 CokeCap NYR-10
65/6 CocaCola
70/1 DadsCookies
70/1 EddieSargent 132
70/1 Esso Stamp
68/9 OPC/Topps 102
69/70 OPC/T. 87, OPC-Sticker
70/1 OPC 191, OPC/T-Sticker
94/5 Parkie(64/5) 91
95/6 Parkie(66/7) 87
72 SemicSticker 177
60/1 ShirriffCoin 92
61/2 ShirriffCoin 82
68/9 ShirriffCoin PIT2
58/9 Topps 18
59/60 Topps 10
61/2 Topps 49
62/3 Topps 51, -Buck
63/4 Topps 55
64/5 Topps 65
66/7 Topps 30
54-67 TorontoStar V10

INGLIS, BILL
70/1 EddieSargent 27
70/1 OPC/Topps 130

INGMAN, JAN
89/90 SemicElitserien 87
90/1 SemicElitserien 264

INGRAHAM, CAL
92/3 Maine(1) 16, (2) 34
93/4 Maine 53
95/6 Tallahassee 12

INGRAM, GEOFF
89/90 SketchOHL 117

INGRAM, JIM
91/2 AvantGardeBCJ 56
91/2 Nainamo

INGRAM, RONALD
45-64 BeeHives(DET)
64-67 BeeHives(DET)
63/4 Parkhurst 54
93/4 Parkie(56/7) 33
63/4 York 54

INKINEN, MIKE
95/6 Sisu 270
96/7 Sisu 67

INKPEN, DAVE
79/8 OPC 321
76/7 opcWHA 83

INNANEN, DEREK
92/3 WestMich.
93/4 WestMich.

INNES, JUSON
89/90 PortlandWinterHawks

INNESS, GARY
75/6 OPC/Topps 227
76/7 O-Pee-Chee 331
79/80 OPC 358
77/8 opcWHA 18
74/5 PGH
79/80 WSH

INSAM, ADOLF
79 PaniniSticker 390
82 SemicSticker 132

INTRANUOVO, RALPH
92/3 Classic 27
92/3 ClassicFourSport 176
93/4 ClassicProspects 186
96/7 Donruss 232
95/6 EdgeIce 33
95/6 Leaf 35
96/7 Leaf-GoldLeafRookie 5
96/7 Pinnacle 237
95/6 Score 294
96/7 Score 263
90/1 SketchMEM 20
90/1 SketchOHL 160
91/2 SketchOHL 332
96/7 Summit 175
93/4 UpperDeck 253
96/7 UpperDeck 182
94/5 CapeBreton
93/4 SSMarie 19

INTWERT, DEAN
90/1 SketchWHL 326
91/2 SketchWHL 333
89/90 Portland

IOANNOU, YIANNI
95/6 Classic 82
93/4 Slapshot(NiagaraFalls) 8

IOB, TONY
90/1 SketchMEM 22
90/1 SketchOHL 60
91/2 SketchOHL 325
92/3 Rochester/Kodak

ION, MICKEY
83&87 HallOfFame 9
83 HHOF Postcard (A)

IONITA, ION
79 PaniniSticker 314

IOVIO, EMILIO
96/7 DEL 224
95 PaniniWorlds 86
92 SemicSticker 255

IRBE, ARTURS
92/3 ClassicProspects 117
93/4 Donruss 311
94/5 Donruss 7,-Dom 7,-Mask 4
95/6 Donruss 239
93/4 EASports 120
94/5 Flair 166
94/5 Fleer 197, -Franc 4,-Netm 4
95/6 FleerMetal 130
92/3 FleerUltra 401, -Import 5
93/4 FleerUltra 145
94/5 F.Ultra 195,-Global3,-Pad 2
95/6 FleerUltra 146
95/6 Hoyle'WEST J (Spades)
94/5 KennerSLU (U.S)
95/6 KennerSLU (CDN)
94/5 KraftDinner
95/6 Kraft-CreaseKeeper
93/4 Leaf 199
94/5 Leaf 175, -Limited 21
95/6 Leaf 267
94/5 LeafLimited 74
90/1 O-Pee-Chee 501, 7R
98/9 Pacific 427
97/8 PacificCrown 188
98/9 PacificParamount 235
94/5 PaniniSticker 225
95/6 PaniniSticker 287
92/3 Parkhurst 396
93/4 Parkhurst 451
94/5 Parkhurst V79
95/6 Parkhurst 188, 251
94/5 ParkieSE 162, ES17
95/6 Parkie-Goal 10, -Int.AS 1
94/5 Pinnacle 121, GT9
91/2 Pinnacle 323
93/4 Pinnacle 86
97/8 Pinnacle 74
95/6 PinnacleFANtasy 7
97/8 PinnacleInside 61
95/6 PinnacleZenith 81
96/7 PinnacleZenith 60
95/6 Playoff 84, 191, 302
96/7 Playoff 345
94/5 POG 294
95/6 POG 233
93/4 PowerPlay 221, -Rising 1
93/4 Premier 110, 442
94/5 Premier 260
95/6 ProMagnet 117, IC03, 06
91/2 PSPlatinum 270
92/3 RedAce(Blue) 13,(Violet) 13
92/3 Score 457
93/4 Score 377
94/5 Score 10, TF21
95/6 Score 189
97/8 Score 7
97/8 Score(VAN) 12
94/5 Select 37
95/6 SelectCertified 91
91 SemicSticker 77
95/6 SkyBoxEmotion 156
95/6 SkyBoxImpact 148
89/90 SovietNats
94/5 SP 105
91/2 StarPics 37
95/6 Summit 84
96/7 Summit 110
95/6 SuperSticker 108
92/3 Topps 25
95/6 Topps 296
94/5 ToppsFinest 104, -Div. 16
92/3 ToppsStadiumClub 131
93/4 ToppsStadiumClub 4
94/5 TSC 190, -Dynasty 1
95/6 ToppsStadiumClub 58
93/4 TSC-MembersOnly 17
91/2 TriGlobe 23, 24
91/2 TriGlobeMagFive 16-20
91/2 UpperDeck 532
93/4 UpperDeck 125
94/5 UpperDeck 116, SP71
95/6 UpperDeck 403, SE162
96/7 UpperDeck 248
97/8 UpperDeck 377
95/6 UDBeAPlayer 23
95/6 UDCollChoice 64
96/7 DAL/Southwest
92/3 S.J./PacificBell (x2)
93/4 S.J/PomaioSheet
94/5 S.J/PacificBellSheet

IRCANDIA, LEN
77/8 Kalamazoo

IREDALE, JOHN
94 Semic 328

IRONSTONE, JOE
24/5 (V145-1) 1

IRSAG, JAKE
95/6 Slapshot 44

IRVIN, ALEX
19 Millionaires

IRVIN, J. DICK (SR)
25-27 Anonymous 138
83&87 HallOfFame 101
83 HHOF Postcard (G)
95/6 HHOFLegends 57
60/1 Topps 60
61/2 Topps-Stamp
32/3 TOR/OKeefe 20

IRVIN, DICK (JR.)
97/8 Pinnacle -CBC Sports 6

IRVINE, JACK
51/2 LavalDairy 78
52/3 StLawrence 31

IRVINE, TED
70/1 EddieSargent 114
71/2 EddieSargent 126
72/3 EddieSargent 152
70/1 Esso Stamp
74/5 Loblaws
68/9 OPC/Topps 39
69/70 OPC/Topps 103
70/1 OPC/Topps 65
71/2 OPC 74
72/3 OPC 212
73/4 OPC 248
74/5 OPC/Topps 264
75/6 OPC/Topps 244
76/7 OPC 347
68/9 ShirriffCoin LA2
71/2 TheTorontoSun

IRVING, BERG
28/9 PaulinsCandy 62

IRVING, STU
78/9 Saginaw

IRWING, DOUG
94/5 DEL 326
95/6 DEL 312

IRWIN, GLEN
75/6 HoustonAeros

IRWIN, IVAN
93/4 Parkie(56/7) 107
54/5 Topps 44

IRWIN, JOEL
92/3 BCJHL 62

IRWIN, RICHARD
96/7 Guelph 17

ISAKSSON, ESA
66/7 Champion 10
65/6 Hellas 25
70/1 Kuvajulkaisut 105
72 Panda
72 SemicSticker 78
71/2 WilliamsFIN 61
71/2 WilliamsFIN 113
73/4 WilliamsFIN 309

ISAKSSON, ULF
82 SemicSticker 14

ISBISTER, BRAD
97/8 Bowman 92
95/6 Classic 21
97/8 DonrussElite 46
97/8 DonrussPreferred 154
97/8 DonrussPriority 176
97/8 KatchMedallion 110
97/8 Leaf 162
98/9 Pacific 339
97/8 PacificCrownRoyale 103
97/8 PacificParamount 140
98/9 PacificParamount 181
97/8 Pinnacle 20
97/8 PinnacleBeAPlayer 226
97/8 PinnacleCertified I
97/8 SPAuthentic 189
98/9 SPx"Finite" 65, 146
98/9 Topps 169
97/8 UpperDeck 340
97/8 UDBlackDiamond 24
96/7 UpperDeck"Ice" 125
98/9 UDChoice 161
97/8 UDCollChoice 305
97/8 Zenith 92, -RookieReign 7
97/8 PHO
93/4 Portland

ISEN, COREY
95/6 Slapshot 178

ISERHOFF, NEIL
91/2 SketchOHL 156
91/2 Oshawa
91/2 Oshawa/Dominos 8
92/3 Oshawa

ISKRZYCKI, ANDRZEJ
79 PaniniSticker 123

ISO-ESKELI, JUHANI
66/7 Champion 84
65/6 Hellas 5

ISOMAKI, SAKARI
66/7 Champion 29

ISOTALO, ESA
94/5 Sisu 284

ISRAEL, AARON
94/5 Classic 119
94/5 Johnstown 11

ISRAEL, JAMIE
89/90 SketchMEM 34
90/1 SketchOHL 234
89/90 Kitchener 20
90/1 Kitchener 18

ISRAELSON, LARRY
75/6 opcWHA 46

ISSEL, JASON
93/4 PrinceAlbert
95/6 PrinceAlbert

ISSEL, KIM
88/9 ProCards(CapeBreton)
89/90 ProCards(AHL) 145
90/1 Score 409
84/5 PrinceAlbert

ITAMIES, IRO
95/6 Sisu 82
96/7 Sisu 82

ITO, NORIO
79 PaniniSticker 286

IULIANO, JERRY
83/4 SSMarie

IUSTINIAN, GHEORGHE
79 PaniniSticker 314

IVAN, TOMMY
83&87 HallOfFame 158
83 HHOF Postcard (L)
93/4 HHOFLegends 35
93/4 Parkie(56/7) 42
60/1 ShirriffCoin 80

IVANKOVIC, FRANK
95/6 Slapshot 156

IVANNIKOV, VALERI
95 PaniniWorlds 26
95 Semic 122

IVANOV, DENIS
96/7 Guelph 5

IVARSSON, LARS
94/5 ElitSet 23
95/6 ElitSet 128
89/90 SemicElitserien 99
90/1 SemicElitserien 104
92/3 SemicElitserien 136
95/6 udElite 187

IVARSSON, PIERRE
90/1 SemicElitserien 159
91/2 SemicElitserien 263
92/3 SemicElitserien 277

IWAMOTO, TAKESHI
79 PaniniSticker 285

JAAKKOLA, JARMO
71/2 WilliamsFIN 280

JAAKO, KARI
89/90 SemicElitserien 162
90/1 SemicElitserien 43
91/2 SemicElitserien 291

JÄÄSKELÄINEN, JUHA
91/2 Jyvas-Hyva 37

JÄÄSKELÄINEN, JOONAS
94/5 Sisu 226
95/6 Sisu 290
96/7 Sisu 88

JABLONIC, DON
93/4 Minn-Duluth

JABLONSKI, JEFF
95/6 Roanoke
92/3 Toledo(1), (2)

JABLONSKI, PAT
92/3 Bowman 66
92/3 FleerUltra 202
93/4 FleerUltra 125
94/5 Leaf 446
91/2 OPC/Topps 246
92/3 O-Pee-Chee 311
91/2 opcPremier 29
92/3 opcPremier 95
92/3 Parkhurst 404
93/4 Parkhurst 192
95/6 Parkhurst 386
91/2 Pinnacle 331
93/4 Pinnacle-Masks 5
96/7 PinnacleBeAPlayer 99
93/4 PowerPlay 444
93/4 Premier 186
88/9 ProCards(Peoria)
89/90 ProCards(IHL) 3
90/1 ProCards 97
92/3 ProSet 178
91/2 Score(CDN) 359, (U.S) 329
93/4 Score 349
94/5 SRTetrad CVI
92/3 Topps 396
92/3 ToppsStadiumClub 231
91/2 UpperDeck 107
92/3 UpperDeck 458
96/7 MTL
89/90 STL/Kodak
91/2 STL
92/3 T.B./Sheraton

JACKMAN, JASON
94/5 Slapshot(Guelph) 13
95/6 Slapshot 101
95/6 Guelph 4
96/7 Guelph 20

JACKMAN, RICHARD
97/8 Bowman 36
98 BowmanCHL 5
95/6 FutureLegends-HotPicks 3
95/6 Slapshot 374
96/7 UpperDeck"Ice" 133
96/7 SSMarie [x2]

JACKSON, ART
33-43 BeeHives(TOR)
35/6 OPC (V304C) 88
39/40 OPC (V301-1) 93

JACKSON, DANE
93/4 ClassicProspects 127
94/5 Score 216
92/3 Hamilton
95/6 Rochester

JACKSON, DON
83/4 O-Pee-Chee 33
84/5 O-Pee-Chee 247
79 PaniniSticker 212
83/4 Vachon 30
82/3 EDM/RedRooster
83/4 EDM
83/4 EDM/Buttons
83/4 EDM/McDonald
84/5 EDM
84/5 EDM/RedRooster
85/6 EDM/RedRooster
88/9 EDM/ActionMagazine 76
91/2 QUE/PetroCanada
92/3 QUE/PetroCanada

JACKSON, HAROLD (HAL)
36-39 DiamondMatch (4)
36/7 OPC (V304D) 112
76 DET

JACKSON, HARVEY (BUSHER)
33/4 Anonymous (V129) 6
33-43 BeeHives(TOR)
33/4 CndGum V252
33/4 Hamilton V288 29
83&87 HallOfFame 175
83 HHOF Postcard (M)
27-32 LaPresse 30/1
33/4 OPC (V304A) 33
36/7 OPC (V304D) 124
37/8 OPC (V304E) 139
39/40 OPC (V301-1) 20
55/6 Parkhurst 22
91/2 ProSet 338
38/9 QuakerOats
34/5 SweetCaporal
35/6 Triumph
36/7 WWGum (V356) 51
32/3 TOR/OKeefe 11

JACKSON, JEFF
88/9 O-Pee-Chee 219
90/1 OPC/Topps 249
88/9 opcSticker 190/57
89/90 opcSticker 184/40
90/1 ProCards 459
91/2 ProCards 365
90/1 ProSet 249
90/1 UpperDeck 291
87/8 QUE/GeneralFoods
88/9 QUE
88/9 QUE/GeneralFoods
89/90 QUE
89/90 QUE/GeneralFoods
89/90 QUE/Police
90/1 QUE
84/5 TOR
85/6 TOR
83/4 Brantford 14
90/1 Halifax
91/2 LakeSuperior

JACKSON, JIM
83/4 O-Pee-Chee 84
84/5 O-Pee-Chee 225
83/4 opcSticker 146
88/9 ProCards(Rochester)
89/90 ProCards(AHL) 279
82/3 Ottawa67s
83/4 Ottawa67s
84/5 Ottawa67s

JACKSON, MIKE
90/1 ProCards 169
90/1 Newmarket

JACKSON, PAUL
69 ColumbusCheckers

JACKSON, STAN
33/4 CndGum (V252)
24/5 Champs (C144)
23/4 (V145-1) 27
24/5 (V145-2) 60

JACKSON, WALTER (RED)
33-35 DiamondMatch

JACOB, GUY
88/9 Flint
79/80 Montréal, -B&W
81/2 Oshawa 21

JACOBS, TIM
76/7 O-Pee-Chee 370

JACOBSEN, TOM
96/7 DEL 11
95/6 ElitSet 193
95 Globe 194
94 Semic 256
95 Semic 179
92 SemicSticker 33
93 SemicSticker 233
95/6 udElite 38
96 Wien 203

JACOBSON, GARNET
95/6 PrinceAlbert

JACOBSSON, ORJAN
92/3 SemicElitserien 251

JACOBSSON, PETER
94/5 ElitSet 117
89/90 SemicElitserien 249
90/1 SemicElitserien 158
91/2 SemicElitserien 262
92/3 SemicElitserien 283

JACQUES, ALEXANDRE
97/8 Bowman 80

JACQUES, RÉAL
52/3 BasDuFleuve 7

JACQUES, STEVE
90/1 ProCards 358

JADAMZIK, R.
95/6 DEL 339

JAFFES, IRVING
36-39 DiamondMatch (2)

JAGR, JAROMIR
95/6 Aces Q (Diamonds)
96/7 Aces K (Clubs)
97/8 Aces 10 (Clubs)
94/5 ActionPacked 3
94/5 APS 68

95/6 APS 384
94/5 AutoPhonex JJ1-5
91/2 Bowman 95
92/3 Bowman 231, 302
95/6 Bowman 57, BB7
95/6 CoolTrade 20
96/7 CorinthianHeadliners
97/8 CorinthianHeadliners
93/4 Donruss 270, -IceKings 3
94/5 Donruss 159, -Dominator 4
95/6 Donruss 142, -Dominator 2
95/6 D-Elite 10, -Marksmen 5
96/7 Donruss 43,-Dom 4,-Top 5
97/8 Donruss 188,-Elit 2,-Line 16
96/7 DonrussCanadianIce 1
97/8 D.CdnIce 8, -Scrapbook 9
95/6 DonrussElite 35, -CuttngE 6
96/7 DonrussElite 8, -Perspec 8
97/8 DonrussElite 11, 125
97/8 D.Elite -BackTo 4,-Craft 25
97/8 D.Elite -Primenumbers 6
97/8 D.Preferd 125, 192,-Lin 1C
97/8 D.Pref-Prec 10,-Tin 14, 20
97/8 D.Pref -WideTins 7, 11
97/8 DonrussPriority 18
97/8 D.Prio -DirDep 4,-OpDay 16
97/8 D.Prio-Postcard 4,-Stamp 4
97/8 D.Studio 5,-HardHats 19
97/8 D.Studio-Portr 5,-Silhou 22
93/4 EASports 107
97/8 EssoOlympic 51, 52
96/7 Flair 77, -Centre 5
94/5 Fleer 163, -Slapshot 4
96/7 Fleer 86,137,138,139,141
96/7 Fleer 142,-ArtRos 8,-Pear 5
95/6 FleerMetal 117,-HeavMet 6
95/6 FM-IntSteel 10
96/7 F.Picks-Dream 6, -Fab 20
96/7 F.Picks-FntsyFrce 5
92/3 FleerUltra 164, -AS 6
92/3 FU-UltraImport 6
93/4 FleerUltra 65, -Red 5
94/5 FleerUltra 164, -Global 4
95/6 FleerUltra 123,387, -Extra9
95/6 FU-RedLight 4, -Ultraview 4
96/7 FU 141,-ClearThe 4,-MrM 5
91/2 Gillette 34
95 Globe 157
96/7 Got-UmHockeyGreatsCoin
93/4 HockeyWit 107
95/6 Hoyle'EAST 6 (Spades)
92/3 HumptyDumpty (2)
97/8 KatchMedallion 118, 162
93/4 KennerSLU
94/5 KennerSLU (U)
97/8 KennerSLU, -1on1
91/2 Kraft 3
92/3 Kraft-AllStar
93/4 KraftDinner
94/5 Kraft-HockeyH
95/6 KraftDinner,-Disk
96/7 Kraft-AS, -Trophy
97/8 Kraft -WorldPro,-WorldBest
93/4 Leaf 346
94/5 Leaf 151, -GoldLeafStar 15
95/6 Leaf 71, -Freeze 4
95/6 L-Gold 5, -RoadToThe 3
96/7 Leaf 106, -Best 1,-Leather 5
97/8 Leaf 10,177,-Banr 4,-Fire 3
94/5 LeafLimited 86, -Gold 6
95/6 LeafLimited 73, -StarsOf 8
96/7 LeafLimited 11
96/7 LeafPreferred 22, -Steel 37
96/7 LP-SteelPower 8
97/8 Limited 8, 55, -fabric 14
96/7 Maggers 124
92/3 McDonalds McD-20
93/4 McDonalds McD17
94/5 McDonalds McD10
95/6 McDonalds McD1
96/7 McDonalds McD23
97/8 McDonalds McD20
96/7 MetalUniverse 127
96/7 MU-IceCarv 6, -Lethal 8
97/8 Omega 186,-GameFace 16
97/8 Omega-Silk 10,-StckHan 17
91/2 OPC/Topps 9, 40
92/3 O-Pee-Chee 102
90/1 opcPremier 50
91/2 opcPremier 24
98/9 Pacific 68,-Cram 9,-T.CL 21
98/9 Pcfc-DynIce 16, -GoldC 29
97/8 PacificCrown 68, -Gold 18
97/8 PCC-Cramers 10, -Slap 8C
97/8 PCC-TeamCL 20
97/8 PacificCrownRoyale 110
97/8 PCR-Blades 17, -Cramer 9
97/8 PCR-HatTrick 15, -Lamp 17
97/8 PacificDynagon! 102, 142
97/8 PcfcD-BstKpt 77,-Dyna 13A
97/8 PcfcD-Kings 9,-Tandm 5,22
97/8 PifcInvincible 113,-AttZn 20
97/8 PcfcInv-FeatPer 28,-Off 17
97/8 PcfcParamnt 150,-BigN 17
97/8 PacificP-Photoengraving 17
97/8 PcfcParamnt 192, -HOF 9
98/9 PcfcP-SpecD 16, -TmCL 21
97/8 PacificRegime 160, 220
97/8 PcfcRevoltn 113,-ASGm 17
97/8 PcfcRev -Icon 9, -TmCL 20
91/2 PaniniSticker 275, 344
92/3 PaniniSticker 282, 294, S
93/4 PaniniSticker 82
94/5 PaniniSticker II, 76
95/6 PaniniSticker 63, 150
96/7 PaniniSticker 58
97/8 PaniniSticker 47
95 PaniniWorlds 297
91/2 Parkhurst 132
92/3 Parkhurst 135, 220, 465
93/4 Parkhurst 154
94/5 Parkhurst 174, 314
95/6 PH 165, 244, PP7, PP14
95/6 Parkhurst -AllStar 2
95/6 PH-Crown(2) 1, -InterAS 5
94/5 ParkieSE ES20, seV42
95/6 Parkie-Trophy 2
91/2 Pinnacle 53
92/3 Pinnacle 275, -Tm2000 15
92/3 P-TeamPinnacle 6
93/4 Pinnacle 195, -AllStar 20
93/4 P-TeamP 6, -Tm2001 12
94/5 Pinnacle 98, GR5, TP11
95/6 Pinnacle 11, -ClearShot 11
95/6 Pinnacle-Roaring20s 13
96/7 Pinnacle 102, -Numbers 8
96/7 Pinnacle-TeamP 6
97/8 Pinnacle 30, 130, -TeamP 6
96/7 Pinn.BeAPlayer-Biscuit 9
97/8 P.BAP -OneT. 7,-TakeA 20
97/8 PinBeeHive 7,-TeamBH 10
97/8 P.Certified 35,-Team 14
97/8 Pinnacle-EPIX 20
97/8 P.Inside 6,-Can 13,-Trck 10
96/7 PinnacleMint 4
97/8 PinnacleMint 22
95/6 PinnZenith 3, -ZTeam 11
96/7 P.Zenith 74, -Champion 6
97/8 PlaymateProZone
95/6 Playoff 78, 185, 297
96/7 Playoff 433
94/5 POG 184
95/6 POG 216, 011
97/8 Post
93/4 PowerPlay 189, -Global 3
93/4 PP-PointLeader 5
93/4 Premier 105, 325
93/4 Premier-Black(OPC) 19
94/5 Premier 460
95/6 ProMagnet 93
90/1 ProSet 632
91/2 ProSet 183
92/3 ProSet 141
91/2 PSPlatinum 92
90/1 Score 428, 70T
91/2 Score(CDN) 98, 381
91/2 Score(U.S) 98, 351
91/2 Score-Hot 8, -Young 38
92/3 Score 113, 494, -Young 4
93/4 Score 50, -International 9
94/5 Score 135, NP9
95/6 Score 1, -BorderBattle 14
95/6 S-Dream 8, -Lamplight 12
96/7 Score 29,-DrmT 7,-SddnD 9
97/8 Score 82, -CheckIt 13
97/8 Score(PGH) 4
92/3 SeasonsPatch 35
93/4 SeasonsPatch 7
94/5 Select 60
95/6 SelectCertified 38, -Gold 4
96/7 SelectCert. 43, -Corner 3
94 Semic 183, 351
95 Semic 158
91 SemicSticker 225
92 SemicSticker 135
95/6 SkBxEmotion 137, -Xcited 9
95/6 SkyBoxImpact 131
95/6 SBI-Count 2, -IceQuake 1
96/7 SkyBoxImpact 101
96/7 SkBxI-Count 4, -Versa 5
94/5 SP 89, -Premier 26
95/6 SP 114, E23, FX18
96/7 SP 126, -SPXForce 2, 5
97/8 SPAuthentic 125, I8
96/7 SPx 38
97/8 SPx 42, -Duoview
98/9 SPx"Finite" 94, 165, 174
96/7 SportFX MiniStix
97/8 SportFX MiniStix
91/2 StarPics 70
95/6 Summit 17,-GM 11,-Mad 10
96/7 Summit 85,-Unt. 2,-HVol 15
95/6 SuperSticker 96, -DieCut 23
96/7 TeamOut
95/6 Tetrad F8
92/3 Topps 24
95/6 Topps 200, 374, 5PL
95/6 Topps M8, PF4, YS15
98/9 Topps 111,A5,L4,M6,SB19
94/5 ToppsFinest 33, -Ring 15
94/5 TF-BBest(Blue) 20
95/6 ToppsFinest 70, 185
94 ToppsFinestBronze 1
96/7 T. NHLPicks 1, FT14, TS6
91/2 ToppsStadiumClub 343
92/3 ToppsStadiumClub 498
93/4 T.StadiumClub 98, -AllStar
94/5 ToppsStadiumClub 68
95/6 ToppsStadiumClub 70, G3
93/4 TSC-MembersOnly 44
94/5 TSC-MembersOnly 5
95/6 TSC-MembersOnly 25
97/8 ToppsSticker 5
95/6 ToppsSuperSkills 20
90/1 UpperDeck 356
91/2 UD 20, 42, 256, 617, E6
92/3 UD 16, 28, 622, E14, W3
92/3 UD WG6, -LockerAS 3
93/4 UpperDeck 139, R8
93/4 UD SP-121, -Hero 33
94/5 UD 93, 544, C24, H24
94/5 UD R18, R29, R39, SP60
95/6 UD 465,AS3,F4, R3
95/6 UD R22, R38, R46, SE153
95/6 UD-AllStarPredict MVP17
96/7 UD 320, GJ5, HH18
96/7 UD LS4, SS13B, X17
96/7 UD-AllStarYCTG AR16
97/8 UD 342, S3, SG38, SS2
97/8 UD T5B, -BlowUp 7
94/5 UDBeAPlayer R63
95/6 UDBeAPlayer LL12
96/7 UDBlackDiamond 75, RC5
97/8 UDBlackDiamond 72, PC20
98/9 UDChoice 168, 226
98/9 UDChoice BH5, SQ16
95/6 UDCC 127, 378, 389, C7
96/7 UDCC 211, 294, 328
96/7 UDCC C6, S8, UD43
97/8 UDCC 205, 314, C28
97/8 UDCC S15, SQ89
97/8 udDiamondVision 3, DM4
96/7 UpperDeck"Ice" 101, S7
97/8 UpperDeckIce 68,IC18,L2C
96 Wien 125
97/8 Zenith 31,Z8,-ChasngCup 3
90/1 PGH/Foodland 11
91/2 PGH/Elbys
91/2 PGH/Foodland 11
91/2 PGH/Topps
92/3 PGH/Coke
92/3 PGH/Foodland 3
92/3 PGH/Foodland
93/4 PGH/Foodland 23
94/5 PGH 23
95/6 PGH/Foodland
96/7 PGH/FotoPuck
96/7 PGH/Tribune

JAHMA, TAISTO
66/7 Champion 95

JAKES, TOM
95/6 APS 26

JAKOBSSON, PETER
97/8 udSwedish 51

JAKONEN, MATTI
70/1 Kuvajulkaisut 139
71/2 WilliamsFIN 188

JAVOKENKO, ANDREI
95/6 APS 131
92/3 Rochester/Dunkin'Donuts

JAKS, PAULI
93/4 ClassicProspects 80
94/5 ClassicFourSport 155
91 SemicSticker 197
92 SemicSticker
91/2 UD 663, -CzechWJC 24
94/5 UpperDeck 387
93/4 Phoenix

JALAVA, HARRI
95/6 Sisu 395

JALAVA, PEKKA
66/7 Champion 33

JALAVA, TUOMAS
95/6 Sisu 348

JALBERT, CRAIG
95/6 Slapshot 198

JALBERT, DEAN
89/90 Sudbury 10

JALO, RISTO
91/2 Jyvas-Hyva 14
93/4 Jyvas-Hyva 88
80/1 Mallasjuoma 31
93/4 Sisu 121
94/5 Sisu 213
95/6 Sisu 24, 179, -Spotlight 6
96/7 Sisu 19
95/6 SisuLimited 90
88/9 EDM/ActionMagazine 39

JALONEN, ARI
71/2 WilliamsFIN 302

JALONEN, HANNU
80/1 Mallasjuoma 91
78/9 SM-Liiga 140

JALONEN, JUKKA
93/4 Jyvas-Hyva 73
93/4 Sisu 108

JALONEN, KARI
70/1 Kuvajulkaisut 367
80/1 Mallasjuoma 98
82 SemicSticker 37
89 SemicSticker 42
93/4 Sisu 386
78/9 SM-Liiga 152
71/2 WilliamsFIN 303
82/3 CGY
88/9 EDM/ActionMagazine 148

JAMALAINEN, JARMO
72/3 WilliamsFIN 326

JAMES, ANGELA
94/5 Classic W6
97/8 GameOfHerLife
97/8 UDCollChoice 276

JAMES, BRAD
90/1 ProCards 137

JAMES, DAVID
83/4 Kingston 22

JAMES, GERRY
45-64 BeeHives(TOR)
57/8 Parkhurst(TOR) 8
60/1 Parkhurst 7
93/4 Parkie(56/7) 117
60/1 ShirriffCoin 17

JAMES, GRAHAM
90/1 SketchWHL 66

JAMES, MIKE
81/2 Ottawa67s
82/3 Ottawa67s
83/4 Ottawa67s
92/3 Richmond

JÄMSEN, LASSE
95/6 Sisu 268
96/7 Sisu 64

JAMSEN, LAURI
70/1 Kuvajulkaisut 156
71/2 WilliamsFIN 227
72/3 WilliamsFIN 210
73/4 WilliamsFIN 282

JAN, MILAN
79 PaniniSticker 400

JANASAK, STEVE
94/5 SR-MiracleOnIce 15, 16

JACARIK, PETR
94/5 APS 29
95/6 APS 318

JANECEK, MARTIN
94/5 APS 22

JANECKY, OTAKAR
92/3 Jyvas-Hyva 57
93/4 Jyvas-Hyva 108
95 PaniniWorlds 205
94 Semic 188
89 SemicSticker 191
93/4 Sisu 26, 364
94/5 Sisu 91,373, -FireOnIce 4
95/6 Sisu 53,171,371,-Spotlght 1
96/7 Sisu 185, -Mighty 7
95/6 SisuLimited 14
96 Wien 115

JANECYK, BOB
85/6 O-Pee-Chee 223
86/7 OPC/Topps 131
85/6 opcSticker 239 /107
86/7 opcSticker 91 /222
84/5 L.A./Smokeys
88/9 L.A.

JANELLE, DAN
51/2 BasDuFleuve 42
52/3 BasDuFleuve 9

JANELLEM, ROLAND
91/2 SketchAwards 29

JANIKOWSKI, JANUSZ
94/5 DEL 413
95/6 DEL 419

JANISZEWSKI, HENRYK
79 PaniniSticker 120

JANKOWSKI, LOU
45-64 BeeHives(CHI)
54/5 Parkhurst 79
54/5 Topps 28

JANKU, PAVEL
94/5 APS 193
95/6 APS 40, 380, 387
96 Wien 118

JANNEY, CRAIG
95/6 Aces 2 (Hearts)
90/1 Bomwan 33
91/2 Bowman 355
92/3 Bowman 14
95/6 Bowman 3
93/4 Donruss 295
94/5 Donruss 28
95/6 Donruss 137
96/7 Donruss 154
97/8 Donruss 46
95/6 DonrussElite 33
96/7 DonrussElite 104
97/8 Donruss Priority 154
93/4 EASports 123
94/5 Flair 154
95/6 FleerMetal 131
96/7 FleerNHLPicks 60
92/3 FleerUltra 187
93/4 FleerUltra 134
94/5 FleerUltra 363
95/6 FleerUltra 147
96/7 FleerUltra 131
95 Globe 118
93/4 HockeyWit 4
91/2 Kraft 31
94/5 Kraft-Sharpshooter
93/4 Leaf 181
94/5 Leaf 52
95/6 Leaf 98
96/7 Leaf 36
94/5 LeafLimited 91
95/6 LeafLimited 13
96/7 LeafLimited 51
96/7 LeafPreferred 35
97/8 Limited 67
96/7 MetalUniverse 117
89/90 OPC/Topps 190, OPC 298
90/1 OPC/Topps 212
91/2 OPC/Topps 41
92/3 O-Pee-Chee 325
91/2 opcPremier 93
89/90 opcSticker 29/167, 38/180
88/9 opcStickFS 10
89/90 opcStickFS 2
98/9 Pacific 340
97/8 PacificCrown 148
97/8 PacificRevolution 106
89/90 PaniniSticker 198
90/1 PaniniSticker 14
91/2 PaniniSticker 170
92/3 PaniniSticker 22
93/4 PaniniSticker 157
94/5 PaniniSticker 136
95/6 PaniniSticker 277
96/7 PaniniSticker 198
97/8 PaniniSticker 161
95 PaniniWorlds 228
91/2 Parkhurst 4, 378
92/3 Parkhurst 154
93/4 Parkhurst 443
94/5 Parkhurst 200
95/6 Parkhurst 455
91/2 Pinnacle 57
92/3 Pinnacle 196
93/4 Pinnacle 130
94/5 Pinnacle 84
95/6 Pinnacle 37
96/7 Pinnacle 48
96/7 PinnacleZenith 49
95/6 Playoff 192
96/7 Playoff 384
94/5 POG 204
95/6 POG 226
93/4 PowerPlay 212
93/4 Premier 120
94/5 Premier 60
95/6 ProMagnet 119
90/1 ProSet 8
91/2 ProSet 2
92/3 ProSet 157
91/2 PSPlatinum 3
90/1 Score 118, -HotCards 58
90/1 Score-YoungStar 30
91/2 Score(CDN) 473, (U.S) 253
92/3 Score 285, -USAGreats 11
93/4 Score 186, (U.S) DD4
94/5 Score 127
95/6 Score 15
96/7 Score 57
97/8 Score 154
94/5 Select 139
95/6 SelectCertified 33
96/7 SelectCertified 60
94 Semic 119
95 Semic 107
9 SemicSticker 173
91 SemicSticker 143
92 SemicSticker 160
93 SemicSticker 186
95/6 SkyBoxEmotion 157
95/6 SkyBoxImpact 149
94/5 SP 109
97/8 SPAuthentic 123
95/6 Summit 49
96/7 Summit 64
95/6 SuperSticker 105, 106
92/3 Topps 134
95/6 Topps 95
95/6 ToppsFinestS 4
95/6 ToppsSuperSkills 13
91/2 ToppsStadiumClub 147
92/3 ToppsStadiumClub 41
93/4 TSC 335, -Master(2) 10
95/6 ToppsStadiumClub 179
90/1 UpperDeck 234
91/2 UpperDeck 128, 512
92/3 UpperDeck 125
93/4 UD 225, 303, 323, SP-138
94/5 UpperDeck 18, R16, SP67
95/6 UpperDeck 315, SE73
96/7 UpperDeck 127
97/8 UpperDeck 334
94/5 UDBeAPlayer R52
95/6 UDBeAPlayer 47
96/7 UDBlackDiamond 45
98/9 UDChoice 156
95/6 UDCollChoice 264
96/7 UDCollChoice 207
97/8 UDCollChoice 201
96 Wien 170
88/9 BOS/SportsAction
89/90 BOS/SportsAction
90/1 BOS/SportsAction
96/7 PHO
97/8 PHO

JANOSTIN, PAT
85/6 Minn-Duluth 30

JANOV, MARTEM
94/5 DEL 363

JANSSEN, JAN
79 PaniniSticker 281

JANSSENS, MARK
90/1 Bowman 226
91/2 Bowman 67
94/5 Leaf 361
90/1 OPC/Topps 391
91/2 OPC/Topps 186
92/3 opcPremier 117
97/8 PacificRegime 2
90/1 PaniniSticker 101
93/4 PaniniSticker 127
93/4 Parkhurst 355
94/5 ParkieSE 70
96/7 PinnacleBeAPlayer 199
93/4 Premier 133
90/1 ProSet 199
91/2 ProSet 158
90/1 ScoreTraded 33T
91/2 Score(CDN) 421
93/4 Score 339
91/2 ToppsStadiumClub 113
93/4 ToppsStadiumClub 180
94/5 ToppsStadiumClub 212
90/1 UpperDeck 298
91/2 UpperDeck 228
93/4 UpperDeck 198
94/5 UpperDeck 35
95/6 UpperDeck 312
97/8 UpperDeck 5
92/3 HFD/DairyMart
93/4 HFD/Coke
89/90 NYR/MarineMidland
86/7 Regina
87/8 Regina

JANSSON, CONNY
89/90 SemicElitserien 234
90/1 SemicElitserien 60
91/2 SemicElitserien 239

JANSSON, LARS
94/5 ElitSet 20
95/6 ElitSet 100
89/90 SemicElitserien 174
90/1 SemicElitserien 7
91/2 SemicElitserien 205
92/3 SemicElitserien 228
95/6 udElite 154

JANSSON, MAGNUS
94/5 ElitSet 62
95/6 ElitSet 185
90/1 SemicElitserien 292
91/2 SemicElitserien 70
95/6 udElite 47

JANSSON, MATTI
66/7 Champion 43
65/6 Hellas 43
70/1 Kuvajulkaisut 192

JANSSON, STEFAN
89/90 SemicElitserien 11

JANTOVSKY, JIRI
95/6 APS 332

JANTTI, JYRKI
71/2 WilliamsFIN 365

JANTTI, KIMMO
71/2 WilliamsFIN 366

JANTUNEN, MARKO
94/5 ElitSet 214, -Foreign 3
95/6 ElitSet 147,-Face 4,-Mega 3
91/2 Jyvas-Hyva 50
92/3 Jyvas-Hyva 100
93/4 Jyvas-Hyva 324
95 PaniniWorlds 173
94 Semic 32
93/4 Sisu 54
94/5 Sisu 154, 176, 364, 386
94/5 Sisu -FireOnIce 5
95/6 SisuLimited 69
95/6 udElite 211
97/8 udSwedish 76, UDS4

JAQUES, STEVE
91/2 ProCards 385
93/4 LasVegas

JARDEMYR, DANIEL
90/1 SemicElitserien 84
91/2 SemicElitserien 9
92/3 SemicElitserien 34

JARKKO, ERKKI
66/7 Champion 158

JARKKO, MARTTI
80/1 Mallasjuoma 189
79 PaniniSticker 171
78/9 SM-Liiga 15, 193
72/3 WilliamsFIN 261
73/4 WilliamsFIN 152

JARN, HEIKKI
65/6 Hellas 136
70/1 Kuvajulkaisut 107
72 Panda
72 SemicSticker 77
71/2 WilliamsFIN 62, 115
72/3 WilliamsFIN 103

JAROSLAV, WALTER
94/5 DEL 32

JARRETT, DOUG
64-67 BeeHives(CHI)
65/6 CocaCola
70/1 DadsCookies
70/1 EddieSargent 34
71/2 EddieSargent 41
72/3 EddieSargent 58
70/1 Esso Stamp
74/5 Loblaws
68/9 OPC/Topps 13
69/70 OPC/T. 67, OPC-Sticker
70/1 OPC 150
71/2 OPC/Topps 208
72/3 OPC 97
73/4 OPC 187, Topps 76
74/5 OPC 351
75/6 OPC 333
94/5 Parkie(64/5) 38
95/6 Parkie(66/7) 27
68/9 ShirriffCoin CHI 10
71/2 TheTorontoSun
66/7 Topps 111
67/8 Topps 112
68/9 CHI
70/1 CHI

JARRETT, GARY
70/1 Colgate Stamp 49
70/1 DadsCookies
70/1 EddieSargent 140
71/2 EddieSargent 138
70/1 Esso Stamp
68/9 OPC/Topps 87
69/70 OPC/Topps 85
70/1 OPC/Topps 75
71/2 OPC/Topps 93
74/5 opcWHA 61
75/6 opcWHA 87
73/4 QuakerOats 27
68/9 ShirriffCoin OAK11
71/2 TheTorontoSun
67/8 Topps 44
72/3 Cleveland

JARRY, PIERRE
72/3 EddieSargent 208
82? JDMcCarthy
74/5 Loblaws
72/3 OPC 237
73/4 OPC 186
75/6 OPC 359
74/5 OPC/Topps 171
76/7 OPC/Topps 49
77/8 OPC/Topps 106
72/3 TOR

JARVELA, PEKKA
91/2 Jyvas-Hyva 20
92/3 Jyvas-Hyva 62
89/90 SemicElitserien 203

JÄRVENPÄÄ, HANNU
92/3 Jyvas-Hyva 66
89/90 O-Pee-Chee 292
89/90 opcSticker 145
91/2 SemicElitserien 150
91 SemicSticker 23
93/4 Sisu 273
94/5 Sisu 23, -Horoscope 17
95/6 Sisu 181
86/7 WPG
87/8 WPG
88/9 WPG/Police

JÄRVENPÄÄ, J.P.
78/9 SM-Liiga 100
71/2 WilliamsFIN 208
72/3 WilliamsFIN 157
73/4 WilliamsFIN 218

JÄRVENPÄÄ, JUHA
92/3 Jyvas-Hyva 41
93/4 Jyvas-Hyva 77
93/4 Sisu 122
94/5 Sisu 87, 251
95/6 Sisu 25, 245
96/7 Sisu 39
95/6 SisuLimited 107

JÄRVENPÄÄ, PERTTI
80/1 Mallasjuoma 41
78/9 SM-Liiga 106
72/3 WilliamsFIN 283
73/4 WilliamsFIN 219

JÄRVENPÄÄ, TORSTI
72/3 WilliamsFIN 262

JÄRVENTIE, MARTTI
94/5 Sisu 235
95/6 Sisu 32
96/7 Sisu 98
94/5 ToppsFinest 130

JÄRVI, IIRO
96/7 DEL 60
92/3 Jyvas-Hyva 17
93/4 Jyvas-Hyva 19
89/90 O-Pee-Chee 264
90/1 OPC/Topps 52
89/90 opcSticker 192
89/90 opcStickFS 15
89/90 PaniniSticker 329
90/1 ProCards 451
92 SemicSticker 13
93/4 Sisu 106
94/5 Sisu 31, 379
95/6 Sisu 213, -Spotlight 4
96/7 Sisu-Sledgehammer 8
95/6 SisuLimited 45
88/9 QUE
88/9 QUE/GeneralFoods
89/90 QUE
89/90 QUE/GeneralFoods
89/90 QUE/Police
90/1 QUE

JÄRVINEN, ERKKI
66/7 Champion 192
73/4 WilliamsFIN 179

JÄRVINEN, JARI
92/3 Jyvas-Hyva 88
93/4 Jyvas-Hyva 171
80/1 Mallasjuoma 26
93/4 Sisu 164
78/9 SM-Liiga 52
71/2 WilliamsFIN 345
72/3 WilliamsFIN 329

JÄRVINEN, JOUKO
66/7 Champion 122

JÄRVINEN, J.P.
92/3 Jyvas-Hyva 163

JÄRVINEN, KARI
80/1 Mallasjuoma 34
78/9 SM-Liiga 57
72/3 WilliamsFIN 306, 346

JÄRVINEN, KARI
70/1 Kuvajulkaisut 141
71/2 WilliamsFIN 130
72/3 WilliamsFIN 193
73/4 WilliamsFIN 153

JÄRVINEN, PAULI
92/3 Jyvas-Hyva 160
93/4 Jyvas-Hyva 289
94 Semic 50
90/1 SemicElitserien 237
91/2 SemicElitserien 164
89 SemicSticker 46
91 SemicSticker 14
93 SemicSticker 64
93/4 Sisu 73
94/5 Sisu 75, -FireOnIce 7
95/6 Sisu 318
95/6 SisuLimited 78

JÄRVINEN, RAUNO
72/3 WilliamsFIN 284

JÄRVINEN, TIMO
70/1 Kuvajulkaisut 242
93/4 Sisu 209
71/2 WilliamsFIN 209

JARVIS, DOUG
72-84 Dernière 80/1, 82/3
76/7 OPC/Topps 217, OPC 313
77/8 OPC/Topps 139
78/9 OPC/Topps 13
79/80 OPC/Topps 112
80/1 OPC/Topps 76
81/2 O-Pee-Chee 184
82/3 O-Pee-Chee 367
83/4 O-Pee-Chee 372
84/5 OPC 200, Topps 145
85/6 OPC/Topps 151
86/7 OPC/Topps 28
87/8 OPC/Topps 95
87/8 opcStars 19
81/2 opcSticker 34
82/3 opcSticker 40
83/4 opcSticker 208
84/5 opcSticker 129, 234/235
85/6 opcSticker 109/242
87/8 opcSticker 183/42, 207/74
87/8 PaniniSticker 52, 387
80/1 Pepsi Cap
82/3 Post
83/4 SouhaitsRen.KeyChain
94/5 DAL
86/7 HFD/JuniorWhalers
87/8 HFD/JuniorWhalers
75/6 MTL
76/7 MTL
77/8 MTL
78/9 MTL
79/80 MTL
80/1 MTL
81/2 MTL
82/3 WSH
84/5 WSH/PizzaHut
85/6 WSH/PizzaHut

JARVIS, WES
97/8 Bowman 158

JARVIS, WES H.
88/9 ProCards(Newmarket)
89/90 ProCards(AHL) 106
80/1 WSH
81/2 WSH

JASKARI, JAAKKO
66/7 Champion 48
65/6 Hellas 117

JASKIERSKI, MIECZYSLAW
74 Hellas 97
79 PaniniSticker 131
73/4 WilliamsFIN 92

JASKIN, ALEXEJ
94/5 APS 233
95/6 APS 5

JAUFMANN, ANDREJ
94/5 DEL 114

JAVANAINEN, ARTO
91/2 Jyvas-Hyva 69
92/3 Jyvas-Hyva 192
93/4 Jyvas-Hyva 356
70/1 Kuvajulkaisut 329
80/1 Mallasjuoma 202
82 SemicSticker 38
93/4 Sisu 218, 388
95/6 SisuLimited 25
78/9 SM-Liiga 228

JAVEBLAD, TOMAS
89/90 SemicElitserien 147
90/1 SemicElitserien 225

JAVIN, MIROSLAV
94/5 APS 124
95/6 APS 32

JAX, FREDRIK
93/4 ClassicProspects 133
90/1 SemicElitserien 221
91/2 SemicElitserien 145
92/3 UpperDeck 230

JAY, BOB
93/4 Parkhurst 361
90/1 ProCards 550
91/2 ProCards 252
93/4 UpperDeck 470
93/4 Phoenix

JEAN, MAXIME
91/2 SketchQMJHL 53

JEDAMZIK, RAFAEL
94/5 DEL 83

JEESIMAN, EARL
84/5 Fredericton 25

JEFFREY, LARRY
45-64 BeeHives(DET)
64-67 BeeHives(DETx2),(TOR)
64/5 CokeCap DET-14
68/9 O-Pee-Chee 74
70/1 OPC/Topps 28
63/4 Parkhurst 48
94/5 Parkie(64/5) 59
95/6 Parkie(66/7) 115
68/9 ShirriffCoin NY14
64/5 TheTorontoStar
64/5 Topps 49
65/6 Topps 83
67/8 Topps 21
62/3 YorkTransfer 33
63/4 York 41
68/9 TOR

JEFFREY, MIKE
88/9 ProCards(Maine)
89/90 Johnstown 33
87/8 Moncton

JELINEK, TOMAS
94/5 APS 261
95/6 APS 138, 365
95 Globe 153
94 Semic 179
91 SemicSticker 122
92 SemicSticker 141
93 SemicSticker 103
92/3 UpperDeck 497
93/4 UpperDeck 165
92/3 OTT

JENACEK, LUBOS
94/5 APS 244
95/6 APS 16, 391

JENKINS, CRAIG
89/90 Nashville

JENKINS, JON
94/5 Knoxville 10
83/4 Oshawa 15

JENKINS, ROGER
33-43 BeeHives(MTL.C)
35-40 CrownBrand 80
33-35 DiamondMatch
36-39 DiamondMatch (1)
35/6 OPC (V304C) 92
34/5 SweetCaporal

JENKINS, SCOTT
90/1 SketchOHL 211

JENKINS, TODD
89/90 Nashville

JENNI, MARCEL
95 PaniniWorlds 130

JENNINGS, GRANT
90/1 O-Pee-Chee 510
91/2 OPC/Topps 468
93/4 Parkhurst 427
90/1 ProSet 106
90/1 ScoreTraded 31T
91/2 Score(CDN) 531
92/3 Score 542
94/5 UDBeAPlayer-Aut. 51
89/90 HFD/JuniorWhalers
90/1 HFD/JuniorWhalers
91/2 PGH/Elbys
92/3 PGH/Coke
93/4 PGH/Foodland 2
94/5 PGH 1
83/4 Saskatoon 3
84/5 Saskatoon

JENNINGS, JASON
93/4 ClassicProspects 238
93/4 Johnstown 10
94/5 Johnstown 12
92/3 WestMich.

JENNINGS, WILLIAM (BILL)
33-43 BeeHives(DET)
83&87 HallOfFame 142
83 HHOF Postcard (K)

JENSEN, AL
83/4 O-Pee-Chee 373
84/5 O-Pee-Chee 201
86/7 OPC/Topps 135
83/4 opcSticker 202
84/5 opcSticker 128, 232/233
86/7 opcSticker 252/144
82/3 Post
83/4 SouhaitsRen.KeyChain
84/5 Topps 146
80/1 DET
81/2 WSH
84/5 WSH/PizzaHut
85/6 WSH/PizzaHut
86/7 WSH/Police

JENSEN, CHRIS
88/9 ProCards(Hershey)
89/90 ProCards(AHL) 339
90/1 ProCards 38
91/2 ProCards 275
93/4 Portland
94/5 Portland

JENSEN, DARREN
86/7 opcSticker 187/46

JENSEN, DAVE A.
92/3 UpperDeck 379
84/5 HFD/JuniorWhalers
87/8 WSH
86/7 WSH/Kodak
86/7 WSH/Police

JENSEN, DAVE H.
84/5 Springfield 5

JENSEN, JENS
79 PaniniSticker 368

JENSEN, STEVE
77/8 OPC/Topps 238
78/9 OPC/Topps 45
79/80 O-Pee-Chee 292
80/1 O-Pee-Chee 294
81/2 O-Pee-Chee 154
79 PaniniSticker 220
80/1 L.A

JENSON, WADE
81/2 Victoria

JERABEK, VLADIMIR
95/6 APS 173

JERDING, SÖREN
79 PaniniSticker 368

JEROME, DARCY
90/1 SketchWHL 163

JERRARD, PAUL
89/90 ProCards(IHL) 96
91/2 ProCards 148

JERWA, JOE
33-43 BeeHives(NYA)
36-39 DiamondMatch (2), (3)

JESIOLOWSKI, DAVID
91/2 SketchWHL 274
93/4 Lethbridge

JESSE, SCOTT
78/9 Saginaw

JESSEY, IVAN
88/9 Lethbridge

JESSIMAN, BRENT
82/3 Brandon 16
83/4 Brandon 14

JESSIMAN, EARL
83/4 Fredericton 25

JESTADT, JEFF
91/2 FerrisState
93/4 Roanoke
94/5 Roanoke
95/6 Roanoke

JHALM, MICHAEL
90/1 SemicElitserien 13

JICKLING, MIKE
90/1 SketchMEM 89
90/1 SketchOHL 191
91/2 SketchWHL 7
89/90 Spokane

JINDRICH, ROB
95/6 APS 251

JINMAN, LEE
95/6 Classic 90
93/4 Slapshot(NorthBay) 14
94/5 Slapshot(NorthBay) 17
95/6 Slapshot 58, 223

JIRANEK, MARTIN
92/3 Classic 69
93/4 ClassicProspects 169
96/7 DEL 327
93/4 Portland

JIRIK, JAROSLAV
77-9 Sportscaster 44-3, 45-1069

JOANETTE, KITOUTE
51/2 LavalDairy 75

JOANETTE, ROSAIRO
43-47 ParadeSportive
52/3 StLawrence 20

JOBE, TREVOR
88/9 ProCards(Newmarket)
90/1 ProCards 161
91/2 Richmond 10

JODOIN, CLEMENT
90/1 ProCards 447
91/2 ProCards 544
90/1 Halifax
95/6 Halifax
96/7 Halifax (1), (2)

JODOIN, MARK
93/4 WestMich.

JODOIN, ROGER
51/2 BasDuFleuve 55

JODZIO, RICK
75/6 opcWHA 99
76/7 opcWHA 113
77/8 COL.R/CokeCans

JOFFE, AARON
85/6 Arizona

JOHANNESEN, GLEN
88/9 ProCards(Indinapolis)

JOHANNESON, CONNIE
23/4 Crescent Selkirks 11
28/9 PaulinsCandy 68

JOHANNSON, JIM
90/1 ProCards 396
88/9 SaltLake 17

JOHANNSON, MIKAEL
89/90 SemicElitserien 61

JOHANSEN, ROY
94 Semic 264
93 SemicSticker 243

JOHANSEN, STIG
92 SemicSticker 47

JOHANSEN, TREVOR
78/9 O-Pee-Chee 320
79/80 COL.R
77/8 TOR
78/9 TOR

JOHANSEN, VIDAR
79 PaniniSticker 299

JOHANSSEN, TOM
92 SemicSticker 45
94 Semic 269

JOHANSSON, ANDREAS
97/8 DonrussPriority 134
95/6 EdgeIce 94
94/5 ElitSet 51
97/8 Limited 121, 159
97/8 PaniniSticker 53
96/7 PinnacleBeAPlayer 103
94 Semic 70
91/2 SemicElitserien 101
92/3 SemicElitserien 113
96 Wien 64

JOHANSSON, BJORN
72 Hellas 29
74 Hellas 26
74 SemicSticker 5
72/3 WilliamsFIN 47
73/4 WilliamsFIN 28

JOHANSSON, CALLE
90/1 Bowman 75
91/2 Bowman 294
92/3 Bowman 275
93/4 Donruss 372
94/5 Donruss 243
95/6 Donruss 309
92/3 FleerUltra 234
94/5 FleerUltra 235
95/6 FleerUltra 176
95 Globe 8
93/4 Leaf 153
94/5 Leaf 242
95/6 Leaf 298
96/7 MetalUniverse 165
97/8 Omega 240
89/90 OPC/Topps 16
90/1 OPC/Topps 164
91/2 OPC/Topps 126
92/3 O-Pee-Chee 223
88/9 opcSticker 134/270
88/9 opcStickFS 11
98/9 Pacific 6
98/9 PacificParamount 245
97/8 PacificRegime 208
88/9 PaniniSticker 221
91/2 PaniniSticker 205
93/4 PaniniSticker 31
95/6 PaniniSticker 143
96/7 PaniniSticker 142
97/8 PaniniSticker 113
91/2 Parkhurst 410
92/3 Parkhurst 201
95/6 Parkhurst 218
94/5 ParkieSE 197
91/2 Pinnacle 232
92/3 Pinnacle 30
93/4 Pinnacle 107
94/5 Pinnacle 305
96/7 Pinnacle 85
95/6 POG 285
93/4 PowerPlay 465
93/4 Premier 278
94/5 Premier 59
90/1 ProSet 313
91/2 ProSet 248
92/3 ProSet 203
91/2 PSPlatinum 243
90/1 Score(U.S) 309
91/2 Score(CDN) 155, (U.S) 155
92/3 Score 209
93/4 Score 76
91/2 SemicElitserien 340
92/3 SemicElitserien 341
91 SemicSticker 207
92 SemicSticker 57
93 SemicSticker 25
95/6 SkyBoxEmotion 189
95/6 SkyBoxImpact 178
97/8 SPAuthentic 167
95/6 SuperSticker 132
92/3 Topps 498
95/6 Topps 274
96/7 ToppsNHLPicks 161
91/2 ToppsStadiumClub 188
92/3 ToppsStadiumClub 341
93/4 ToppsStadiumClub 451
90/1 UpperDeck 149
91/2 UpperDeck 316
92/3 UpperDeck 199
97/8 UpperDeck 383
95/6 UDBeAPlayer 54
98/9 UDChoice 219
95/6 UDCollChoice 130
96 Wien 42
87/8 BUF/BlueShield
87/8 BUF/WonderBread
88/9 BUF/BlueShield
88/9 BUF/WonderBread
89/90 WSH
89/90 WSH/Kodak
90/1 WSH/Kodak
90/1 WSH/Smokey
91/2 WSH
91/2 WSH/Kodak
92/3 WSH/Kodak
95/6 WSH

JOHANSSON, DANIEL
94/5 ElitSet 104
95/6 ElitSet 230
95 Globe 56
92/3 SemicElitserien 252
92/3 UpperDeck 599
95/6 udElite 80
97/8 udSwedish 88

JOHANSSON, FREDRIK
94/5 ParkieSE 241
90/1 SemicElitserien 146
95/6 udElite 130
97/8 udSwedish 130

JOHANSSON, JAN
89/90 SemicElitserien 211

JOHANSSON, JIM
89/90 ProCards(IHL) 70

JOHANSSON, JONAS
91/2 SemicElitserien 49
92/3 SemicElitserien 71

JOHANSSON, KARI
66/7 Champion 59
70/1 Kuvajulkaisut 140
71/2 WilliamsFIN 189
72/3 WilliamsFIN 227
73/4 WilliamsFIN 261

JOHANSSON, KENNETH
94/5 ElitSet 161
95/6 ElitSet 224
89/90 SemicElitserien 66, 97
90/1 SemicElitserien 101
92/3 SemicElitserien 249

JOHANSSON, LEIF
89/90 SemicElitserien 213

JOHANSSON, MAGNUS
97/8 udSwedish 73

JOHANSSON, MATHIAS
94/5 ElitSet 234
95/6 ElitSet 44, -Goldies 5
93/4 Parkhurst 537
91/2 SemicElitserien 102, 330
92/3 SemicElitserien 117
95/6 udElite 69
97/8 udSwedish 61
96 Wien 65

JOHANSSON, MIKAEL
94/5 ElitSet 255
95/6 ElitSet 119
95 Globe 30
95 Semic 68
90/1 SemicElitserien 293
91/2 SemicElitserien 65, 350
89 SemicSticker 22
91 SemicSticker 43
92 SemicSticker 64
93 SemicSticker 31
97/8 udSwedish 39, 42, C2

JOHANSSON, NILS
70/1 Kuvajulkaisut 27

JOHANSSON, PETER
89/90 SemicElitserien 24
90/1 SemicElitserien 94

JOHANSSON, PER JOHAN
94/5 ElitSet 251
95/6 ElitSet 174

JOHANSSON, ROGER
91/2 Bowman 257
94/5 ElitSet 259,-Gold 21,-Gst 6
95/6 ElitSt 218,-Face 5,-Chmp 9
92/3 FleerUltra 268
95 Globe 22
90/1 OPC/Topps 96
91/2 OPC/Topps 53
90/1 Panini(CGY) 6
92/3 Parkhurst 263
93/4 Premier 253
90/1 ProSet 424
90/1 ScoreTraded 91T
94 Semic 62
95 Semic 58
91/2 SemicElitserien 139
93 SemicSticker 29
91/2 ToppsStadiumClub 375
93/4 ToppsStadiumClub 133
95/6 udElite 62
97/8 udSwedish 57, 206, 217
97/8 udSwedish C20, UDS7
96 Wien 54
90/1 CGY/McGavins
92/3 CGY/IGA 19

JOHANSSON, STIG-GORAN
72 Hellas 31
70/1 Kuvajulkaisut 28
69/70 MästarSerien 37
72 Panda
72 SemicSticker 47
74 SemicSticker 21
71/2 WilliamsFIN 47
72/3 WilliamsFIN 48

JOHANSSON, SVEN TUMBA
95 Globe 68

JOHANSSON, THOMAS
94/5 ElitSet 121
95/6 ElitSet 30
90/1 SemicElitserien 282
91/2 SemicElitserien 64
92/3 SemicElitserien 81
95/6 udElite 40

JOHANSSON, TORBJORN
95/6 ElitSet 243, -Rookies 5
95/6 udElite 96
97/8 udSwedish 102

JOHN, BERNIE
91/2 SketchOHL 249
91/2 Sudbury 6
92/3 Sudbury 8

JOHNS, DON
64/5 CokeCap NYR-6
94/5 Parkie(64/5) 98
60/1 ShirriffCoin 93
63/4 Topps 64
65/6 Québec

JOHNSON, ALLEN
45-64 BeeHives((DET)
61/2 Parkhurst 22
61/2 ShirriffCoin 72

JOHNSON, ANDERS
94/5 ElitSet 283
89/90 SemicElitserien 69
90/1 SemicElitserien 289
92/3 SemicElitserien 42

JOHNSON, ANDY
95/6 Slapshot 323

JOHNSON, ANTHONY
94 Semic 322

JOHNSON, BILL
52/3 StLawrence 60

JOHNSON, BOB
74/5 Loblaws
90/1 ProSet 674
82/3 CGY
85/6 CGY/RedRooster
86/7 CGY/RedRooster
90/1 PGH/Foodland 7

JOHNSON, BOB G.
74/5 PGH
72/3 STL
72/3 STL/8"x10"

JOHNSON, BRIAN
85/6 Minn-Duluth 18

JOHNSON, CHING
see Ivan Johnson

JOHNSON, CORY
91/2 SketchOHL 227

JOHNSON, CRAIG
93/4 ClassicProspects IA14, LP7
94/5 Flair 155
93/4 FleerUltra 487
95/6 Leaf 273
98/9 Pacific 236
97/8 PacificDynag-BestKept 46
95/6 Pinnacle 208
97/8 PinnacleBeAPlayer 100
93/4 PowerPlay 507
93/4 Premier-TeamUSA 19
94/5 Premier 369
95/6 Score 292
95/6 SP 66
93/4 TSC-TeamUSA 11
94/5 UpperDeck 253
95/6 UpperDeck 139, 308
96/7 UpperDeck 80
97/8 UpperDeck 134
96/7 UDCollChoice 129
94/5 Birmingham
91/2 Minnesota
92/3 Minnesota
92/3 Oklahoma

JOHNSON, CRAIG
92/3 Windsor 19

JOHNSON, DANNY
70/1 EddieSargent 214
71/2 EddieSargent 210
70/1 Esso Stamp
71/2 OPC 95

71/2 TheTorontoSun
70/1 VAN/RoyalBakn

JOHNSON, DION
91/2 AirCanadaSJHL A11
92/3 MPSPhotoSJHL 121

JOHNSON, ERNEST (MOOSE)
91 C55 Reprint 28
83&87 HallOfFame 10
83 HHOF Postcard (A)
1911-12 Imperial (C55) 28
1910-11 Imperial (C56) 30
1912-13 Imperial (C57) 25
1910-11 Imperial Post 28
60/1 Topps 4
61/2 Topps-Stamp

JOHNSON, G.A.
35 JAPattreiouex 89

JOHNSON, GARY
83/4 MedicineHat 4

JOHNSON, GREG
93/4 ClassicProspects 17
93/4 Classic TC1
93/4 Donruss 94
94/5 Donruss 150
96/7 Donruss 111
96/7 FleerNHLPicks 100
93/4 FleerUltra 306, -Wave 7
94/5 FleerUltra 283
95/6 FleerUltra 233
93/4 Leaf 370
94/5 Leaf 355
96/7 Leaf 33
98/9 Pacific 145
93/4 Parkhurst 270
95/6 Parkhurst 338
94/5 ParkieSE 48
93/4 Pinnacle 453
94/5 Pinnacle 511
96/7 Pinnacle 140
93/4 PowerPlay 330
93/4 Premier 457
94/5 Premier 257
93/4 Score 601
94/5 Score CT5
96/7 Score 132
97/8 Score(PGH) 11
96/7 Summit 49
93/4 ToppsStadiumClub 367
90/1 UpperDeck 460
93/4 UpperDeck 452
94/5 UpperDeck 212
95/6 UpperDeck 334
96/7 UpperDeck 254
95/6 UDBeAPlayer 73
96/7 UDCollChoice 78
97/8 UDCollChoice 206

JOHNSON, IVAN (CHING)
33/4 Anonymous (V129) 33
33-43 BeeHives(NYR)
36-39 DiamondMatch (1), (2), (3)
33 GoudeySport 30
83&87 HallOfFame 51
83 HHOF Postcard (D)
94/5 HHOFLegends 41
33/4 OPC (V304A) 39
94/5 Parkie(64/5)-Greats 11
34/5 SweetCaporal
35/6 Triumph
36/7 WWGum (V356) 21

JOHNSON, JASON
93/4 Slapshot(Kitchener) 23

JOHNSON, JAY
91/2 Peterborough 26

JOHNSON, NORMAN JAMES (JIM)
70/1 EddieSargent 153
71/2 EddieSargent 145
70/1 Esso Stamp
68/9 O-Pee-Chee 186
69/70 OPC/Topps 97
71/2 OPC/Topps 48
71/2 TheTorontoSun

JOHNSON, JIM
92/3 Bowman 177
92/3 FleerUltra 95
86/7 O-Pee-Chee 231
87/8 OPC/Topps 196
88/9 OPC/Topps 148
89/90 OPC/Topps 77

90/1 OPC/Topps 98
91/2 OPC/Topps 426
86/7 opcSticker 128/114
87/8 opcSticker 172/31
97/8 PacificCrown 174
87/8 PaniniSticker 143
88/9 PaniniSticker 334
89/90 PaniniSticker 320
92/3 PaniniSticker 94
91/2 Parkhurst 303
91/2 Pinnacle 235
92/3 Pinnacle 137
93/4 Pinnacle 192
94/5 Pinnacle 440
97/8 PinnacleBeAPlayer 104
93/4 Premier 98
90/1 ProSet 235
91/2 ProSet 116
92/3 ProSet 83
90/1 Score 202
91/2 Score(CDN) 52, (U.S) 52
92/3 Score 161
93/4 Score 144
94 Semic 110
92 SemicSticker 155
92/3 Topps 54
92/3 ToppsStadiumClub 75
93/4 ToppStadiumClub 298
94/5 DAL
89/90 PGH/Foodland 2
86/7 PGH/Kodak
87/8 PGH/Kodak
95/6 WSH
96/7 PHO
97/8 PHO

JOHNSON, JOHN
89/90 SketchOHL 144
90/1 SketchOHL 261
89/90 NiagaraFalls
92/3 Toledo 2
93/4 Wheeling 11

JOHNSON, KARL
92/3 MPSPhotoSJHL 17

JOHNSON, LANCE
89/90 SketchMEM 7
90/1 SketchWHL 288
91/2 SketchWHL 83
89/90 Kamloops

JOHNSON, LARRY
72/3 EddieSargent 82

JOHNSON, MARK
80/1 OPC/Topps 69
83/4 O-Pee-Chee 140
84/5 O-Pee-Chee 72
85/6 OPC/Topps 44
86/7 OPC/Topps 112
87/8 OPC/Topps 101
88/9 OPC/Topps 45
89/90 O-Pee-Chee 244
90/1 OPC/Topps 178
83/4 opcSticker 254
84/5 opcSticker 193
85/6 opcSticker 50/181
86/7 opcSticker 200/70
87/8 opcSticker 64/205
79 PaniniSticker 213
87/8 PaniniSticker 83
89/90 PaniniSticker 260
90/1 PaniniSticker 66
90/1 ProSet 168
83/4 PuffySticker 17
89 SemicSticker 174
94/5 SR-MiracleOnIce 17-18
84/5 Topps 56
90/1 UpperDeck 180
79/80 USAOlympicTeam 4
82/3 HFD/JuniorWhalers
83/4 HFD/JuniorWhalers
84/5 HFD/JuniorWhalers
85/6 N.J.
86/7 N.J./SOBER
88/9 N.J./Caretta
89/90 N.J.

JOHNSON, MATT
94/5 Classic 65, T32
95/6 Donruss 217
95/6 FutureLegends 28
95/6 Leaf 64
97/8 PacificCrown 350
94/5 Pinnacle 496

96/7 PinnacleBeAPlayer 215
94/5 Premier 339
93/4 Slapshot(Peterborough) 22
94/5 UpperDeck 203

JOHNSON, MIKE
97/8 KatchMedallion 166
97/8 Omega 221
98/9 Pacific 413
97/8 PacificCrown 335
98/9 PacificParamount 226
97/8 PinnBAP 218,-OneTimer 18
97/8 PinnacleBeeHive54
97/8 SPAuthentic 195
98/9 SPx"Finite" 81, 122
98/9 Topps 42, I14, SB7
97/8 UDBlackDiamond118,PC27
98/9 UDChoice 199, SQ27
97/8 UpperDeckIce 48
97/8 Zenith 82,Z71,-RookRgn 12
97/8 Zenith -RookieZTeam 12

JOHNSON, MIKE
91/2 SketchOHL 300
92/3 Ottawa67s

JOHNSON, MOOSE
see Ernest Johnson

JOHNSON, NORMAN B.
58/9 Topps 17
59/60 Topps 54

JOHNSON, PERRY
98 BowmanCHL 44

JOHNSON, RED
52/3 LavalDairy 110

JOHNSON, SHANE
91/2 AvantGardeBCJ 163
92/3 BCJHL 69
91/2 SketchOHL 342

JOHNSON, TERRY
84/5 O-Pee-Chee 186
86/7 TOR
82/3 Fredericton 14

JOHNSON, TODD
90/1 SketchWHL 148
91/2 SketchWHL 79

JOHNSON, TOM
45-64 BeeHives(BOS), (MTL)
64-67 BeeHives(BOS)
62 CeramicTiles
64/5 CokeCap BOS-10
72-84 Dernière 77/8
48-52 Exhibits
83&87 HallOfFame 52
83 HHOF Postcard (D)
51-54 LaPatrie 8Apr52
51/2 Parkhurst 7
52/3 Parkhurst 9
54/5 Parkhurst 10
55/6 Parkhurst 49, 71
57/8 Parkhurst(MTL) 6
58/9 Parkhurst 7
58/9 Parkhurst 10
59/60 Parkhurst 10
60/1 Parkhurst 44
61/2 Parkhurst 42
62/3 Parkhurst 50
93/4 Parkhurst PR55
93/4 Parkie(56/7) 79, 143
94/5 Parkie(64/5) 12
45-54 QuakerOats
60/1 ShirriffCoin 25
61/2 ShirriffCoin 106
62/3 ShirriffCoin 36
64/5 TheTorontoStar
63/4 Topps 4
64/5 Topps 101
54-67 TorontoStar V7
56-66 TorontoStar 58/9, 59/60
60/1 York, -Glasses
61/2 York 11
95/6 MTL/Forum 8-Jan

JOHNSON, TOM
94/5 Slapshot(Guelph) 15

JOHNSSON, JONAS
96/7 DEL 150
94/5 ElitSet 13
95/6 ElitSet 177
95 PaniniWorlds 148
95/6 udElite 26, 250

JOHNSSON, KIM
95/6 ElitSet 266
95/6 udElite 134
97/8 udSwedish 136

JOHNSSON, PIERRE
94/5 ElitSet 128
95/6 ElitSet 117
95/6 udElite 172

JOHNSTON, B.J.
93/4 Slapshot(Oshawa) 19
94/5 Slapshot(Sarnia) 18
95/6 Slapshot 264
92/3 Oshawa

JOHNSTON BERNHARD
94/5 DEL 247
95/6 DEL 241

JOHNSTON, BRENT
95/6 Slapshot 281

JOHNSTON, CHRIS
91/2 SketchWHL 201
92/3 Brandon 12
95/6 Dayton

JOHNSTON, ED
45-64 BeeHives(BOS)
64-67 BeeHives(BOS)
64/5 CokeCap BOS-1
70/1 DadsCookies
70/1 EddieSargent 5
71/2 EddieSargent 15
72/3 EddieSargent 20
70/1 Esso Stamp
93/4 Kraft-Coach
72/3 Letraset 17
73/4 MacsMilk Disk
68/9 O-Pee-Chee 133
69/70 O-Pee-Chee 200
70/1 OPC 133
71/2 OPC/Topps 172, Topps 4
72/3 OPC 261, Topps 13
73/4 OPC/Topps 23
74/5 OPC 265
75/6 OPC/Topps 185
76/7 OPC 285
77/8 OPC 276
94/5 Parkie(64/5) 15
95/6 Parkie(66/7) 18, 167, 168
71/2 TheTorontoSun
63/4 Topps 2
64/5 Topps 21
65/6 Topps 97
66/7 Topps 99, -USATest 64
67/8 Topps 96
91/2 Trends(72) 93, -Aut.
70/1 BOS
71/2 BOS
79/80 CHI
93/4 PGH/Foodland 19
94/5 PGH 11
95/6 PGH/Foodland
73/4 TOR

JOHNSTON, GREG
94/5 DEL 155
95/6 DEL 156
96/7 DEL 229
87/8 OPC/Topps 102
90/1 ProCards 160
91/2 ProCards 353
92/3 Topps 413
85/6 Moncton 19
90/1 Newmarket
87/8 SSMarie 35

JOHNSTON, JAY
90/1 SketchOHL 225

JOHNSTON, JOEY
71/2 EddieSargent 143
72/3 EddieSargent 45
74/5 Loblaws
71/2 OPC/Topps 182
72/3 OPC 96, Topps 48
73/4 OPC 172, Topps 143
74/5 OPC/Topps 56, 185
75/6 OPC/Topps 193
76/7 OPC 325
71/2 TheTorontoSun

JOHNSTON, KARL
91/2 ProCards 95

JOHNSTON, KURT
95/6 Slapshot 125

JOHNSTON, LARRY
72/3 EddieSargent 82
82? JDMcCarthy
73/4 OPC 251
75/6 OPC 352

JOHNSTON, MARSHALL
71/2 EddieSargent 141
72/3 EddieSargent 44
72/3 OPC 171
73/4 OPC/Topps 21
74/5 OPC/Topps 189
71/2 TheTorontoSun
81/2 COL.R
90/1 Brandon 6

JOHNSTON, MARTY
98 BowmanCHL 86

JOHNSTON, RANDY
81/2 Indianapolis 2
82/3 Indianapolis

JOHNSTON, TYLER
92/3 BCJHL 15

JOHNSTON, GEORGE (WINGY)
33-43 BeeHives(CHI)

JOHNSTONE, ALEX
96/7 Halifax (1), (2)
97/8 Halifax (1), (2)

JOHNSTONE, CHRIS
93/4 Slapshot(NiagaraFalls) 27
95/6 Slapshot 205

JOHNSTONE, EDDIE
79/80 OPC/Topps 179
80/1 O-Pee-Chee 277
81/2 OPC 226, Topps(E) 99
82/3 O-Pee-Chee 226
83/4 O-Pee-Chee 124
84/5 OPC 55, Topps 43
81/2 opcSticker 169
82/3 opcSticker 139
82/3 Post
83/4 SouhaitsRen.KeyChain
93/4 Johnstown 20
94/5 Johnstown 22
89/90 NewHaven

JOHNSTONE, JEFF
95/6 Classic 89
93/4 Slapshot(NiagaraFalls) 10
95/6 Slapshot 193

JOKIHARJU, JUHA
95/6 ElitSet 154
91/2 Jyvas-Hyva 34
92/3 Jyvas-Hyva 68
93/4 Jyvas-Hyva 107
93/4 Sisu 13
94/5 Sisu 169, 320, 383

JOKILAHTI, JARMO
92/3 Jyvas-Hyva 71
93/4 Jyvas-Hyva 140
93/4 Sisu 140

JOKINEN, ARI
80/1 Mallasjuoma 16, 28
78/9 SM-Liiga 103

JOKINEN, JARI
71/2 WilliamsFIN 363
72/3 WilliamsFIN 327

JOKINEN, JORMA
70/1 Kuvajulkaisut 347

JOKINEN, JYRKI
93/4 Jyvas-Hyva 143
93/4 Sisu 157
94/5 Sisu 130

JOKINEN, KARI
70/1 Kuvajulkaisut 310

JOKINEN, OLLI
97/8 DonrussElite 72
97/8 DonrussPreferred 147, 196
97/8 Leaf 155
97/8 PacificDynagon! Rookies
97/8 PacificParamount 90
97/8 Pinnacle 4
97/8 PinnalceCertified F
97/8 Score 65
97/8 UpperDeck 288
98/9 UDChoice 275
97/8 UpperDeckIce 58, L9A

JOKINEN, PENTTI
65/6 Hellas 22

JOKINEN, PETRI
72/3 WilliamsFIN 345

JOLIAT, AURÈLE (AUREL)
25-27 Anonymous 8
33-43 BeeHives(MTL.C)
35/6 Champion
24/5 Champs (C144)
33/4 CndGum (V252)
35-40 CrownBrand 112
33-35 DiamondMatch
36-39 DiamondMatch (1), (2), (3)
25 Dominion 119
83&87 HallOfFame 53
33/4 Hamilton V288 27
83 HHOF Postcard (D)
95/6 HHOFLegends 71
27-32 LaPresse 27/8
24/5 MapleCrispette (V130) 14
34/5 OPC (V304B) 50
37/8 OPC (V304E) 152
43-47 ParadeSportive
55/6 Parkhurst 58
34/5 SweetCaporal
23/4 (V145-1) 14
24/5 (V145-2) 48
33/4 WWGum(V357) 3,Premium
36/7 WWGum (V356) 65
28/9 MTL/LaPatrie 4
92/3 MTL/OPC 21
95/6 MTL/Forum 23Oct96

JOLY, GREG
74/5 Loblaws
74/5 OPC 294
75/6 OPC/Topps 170
76/7 OPC/Topps 52
77/8 OPC 273
78/9 OPC/Topps 148
79/80 O-Pee-Chee 311
80/1 O-Pee-Chee 270
82/3 O-Pee-Chee 86
82/3 Post
79/80 DET
80/1 DET
74/5 WSH

JOMPHE, DAN
84/5 Chicoutimi

JOMPHE, JEAN-FRANÇOIS
93/4 ClassicProspects 123
97/8 PacificRegime 3
90/1 SketchQMJHL 108
96/7 UpperDeck 3
96/7 UDCollChoice 8
96/7 ANA/UpFrontSports 19

JONAK, KIRI
94/5 APS 144

JONATHAN, STAN
81/2 O-Pee-Chee 13
77/8 OPC 270
78/9 OPC/Topps 181
79/80 OPC/Topps 263
80/1 OPC/Topps 113
82/3 Post
83/4 PGH/Heinz

JONES, BOB
90/1 ProCards 301
91/2 ProCards 251
87/8 SSMarie 5
89/90 SSMarie 18
96/7 SSMarie

JONES, BRAD
91/2 Bowman 181
96/7 DEL 67
91/2 OPC/Topps 478
91/2 opcPremier 115
91/2 Parkhurst 127
89/90 ProCards(AHL) 42
91/2 ProSet 456
91/2 Score(CDN) 603, (U.S) 53T
92/3 Topps 299
91/2 ToppsStadiumClub 368
92/3 ToppsStadiumClub 141
91/2 UpperDeck 304
90/1 L.A./Smokeys 21
91/2 PHA/JCPenney
95/6 Binghampton
87/8 SSMarie 7

JONES, CHRIS
91/2 AvantGardeBCJ 62
92/3 BCJHL 105
91/2 Nainamo

JONES, COREY
90/1 SketchWHL 103
91/2 SketchWHL 26
89/90 Victoria

JONES, DARYL
92/3 MPSPhotoSJHL 153

JONES, DOUG
85/6 Kitchener 24
86/7 Kitchener 23
87/8 Kitchener 22

JONES, HARALD
72 SemicSticker 159

JONES, JIMMY
1910-11 Imperial (C56) 19

JONES, JIMMY
78/9 O-Pee-Chee 288
79/80 O-Pee-Chee 288
77/8 TOR
78/9 TOR
79/80 TOR

JONES, KEITH
92/3 Classic 96
92/3 ClassicProspects 43
95/6 Donruss 282
95/6 FleerMetal 160
92/3 FleerUltra 436
93/4 FleerUltra 446
94/5 Leaf 506
95/6 Leaf 105
97/8 Limited 18
92/3 opcPremier 14
97/8 PacificCrown 291
95/6 PaniniSticker 140
92/3 Parkhurst 427
93/4 Parkhurst 495
95/6 Parkhurst 217
94/5 Pinnacle 378
95/6 Pinnacle 27
96/7 Pinnacle 93
96/7 PinnacleBeAPlayer 194
95/6 Playoff 323
96/7 Playoff 423
95/6 POG 282
93/4 PowerPlay 466
93/4 Premier 96
93/4 Score 417
95/6 Score 95
96/7 Score 225
97/8 Score 250
97/8 Score(COL) 9
95/6 Topps 73
93/4 ToppsStadiumClub 234
95/6 ToppsStadiumClub 88
92/3 UpperDeck 533
93/4 UpperDeck 377
94/5 UpperDeck 411
95/6 UpperDeck 451, SE85
94/5 UDBeAPlayer-Aut. 131
96/7 UDBlackDiamond 39
95/6 UDCollChoice 166
96/7 UDCollChoice 285
97/8 UDCollChoice 59
92/3 WSH/Kodak
95/6 WSH

JONES, NICK
95/6 Roanoke

JONES, ROB
95/6 Richmond

JONES, RON
75/6 OPC/Topps 247
89/90 Windsor

JONES, STEVE
95/6 Slapshot 329

JONES, TY
97/8 Bowman 142
97/8 UDBlackDiamond 52
98/9 UDChoice 303
95/6 Spokane 7

JONES, WINSTON
88/9 Brockville 4

JONSSON, FREDRIK
97/8 udSwedish 107

JONSSON, HANS
94/5 ElitSet 44
95/6 ElitSet 102
91/2 SemicElitserien 210
92/3 SemicElitserien 231
95/6 udElite 156
97/8 udSwedish 153

JONSSON, JONAS
96/7 DEL 150
90/1 SemicElitserien 121
91/2 SemicElitserien 124

JÖNSSON, JÖRGEN
94/5 ElitSet 69, -Top 5, -Gold 10
95/6 ElitSet 215
95 Globe 38
95 Semic 66
92/3 SemicElitserien 272
94/5 SigRookies 46
95/6 udElite 72, NA9
97/8 udSwedish 64,C21,S4,UD 6

JÖNSSON, KENNY
95/6 Bowman 86
93/4 Classic 135
94/5 Classic 25, R8, T69
93/4 ClassicFourSport 195
94/5 ClassicImages 59
95/6 Donruss 115
96/7 Donruss 74
95/6 DonrussElite 4
96/7 DonrussElite 117
95/6 EdgeIce C4
94/5 ElitSet-GoldCard 11
97/8 EssoOlympic 46
94/5 Flair 182
94/5 Fleer 216
96/7 Fleer 65
95/6 FleerMetal 144
96/7 FleerPicks 92
94/5 FleerUltra 377
95/6 FleerUltra 161
96/7 FleerUltra 102
95 Globe 15
97/8 KatchMedallion 88
94/5 Leaf 472
95/6 Leaf 24
96/7 Leaf 60
94/5 LeafLimited 115
95/6 LeafLimited 88
96/7 LeafPreferred 28
95/6 McDonalds McD36
96/7 MetalUniverse 93
98/9 Pacific 282
98/9 PacificParamount 143
97/8 PacificRegime 116
95/6 PaniniSticker 208, 306
96/7 PaniniSticker 93
97/8 PaniniSticker 76
93/4 Parkhurst 535
95/6 Parkhurst 203
94/5 ParkieSE 173
94/5 Pinnacle 264, 476, RTP4
95/6 Pinnacle 130
96/7 Pinnacle 91
96/7 Playoff 203
95/6 POG 267, 031
94/5 Premier 329
95/6 ProMagnet 72
94/5 Score TR6
95/6 Score 30
96/7 Score 168
94/5 Select 172, YE4
95 Semic 59
92/3 SemicElitserien 253
95/6 SkyBoxEmotion 172
95/6 SkBxImpact 162, -Fox 13
96/7 SkyBoxImpact 76
94/5 SP-Premier 7
95/6 SP 147
96/7 SP 93
97/8 SPAuthentic 95
95/6 Topps 211, 9NG
94/5 ToppsFinest 5
94/5 ToppsFinest-BBest(Red) 18
95/6 ToppsFinest 29
95/6 ToppStadiumClub 107
92/3 UpperDeck 596
94/5 UpperDeck 238, 530
94/5 UD 560, C11, SP168
95/6 UpperDeck 463, SE81
96/7 UpperDeck 101
97/8 UpperDeck 312
94/5 UDBeAPlayer R154
95/6 UDBeAPlayer 180
96/7 UDBlackDiamond 73
97/8 UDBlackDiamond 10
98/9 UDChoice 125
95/6 UDCollChoice 137, 373
96/7 UDCollChoice 159
97/8 UDCollChoice 159
95/6 udElite 240
96 Wien 53
94/5 StJohns

JONSSON, MIKAEL
83/4 Kelowna

JONSSON, PIERRE
96/7 DEL 94

JONSSON, ROGER
97/8 udSwedish 194

JONSSON, STEFAN
94/5 ElitSet 162
95/6 ElitSet 79
89/90 SemicElitserien 225
90/1 SemicElitserien 54
91/2 SemicElitserien 229
92/3 SemicElitserien 185
95/6 udElite 121
97/8 udSwedish 123

JONSSON, TOMAS
94/5 ElitSet 100, -Gold 23
95/6 ElitSet 62, 303, -Mega 5
95/6 ElitSet-Champs 1, -Face 15
95 Globe 14
82/3 O-Pee-Chee 202
83/4 O-Pee-Chee 9
84/5 O-Pee-Chee 128
85/6 OPC/Topps 154
86/7 OPC/Topps 78
87/8 OPC/Topps 190
88/9 OPC/Topps 108
83/4 opcSticker 87
85/6 opcSticker 78/211
86/7 opcSticker 214/86
87/8 PaniniSticker 92
95 PaniniWorlds 141
82/3 Post
94 Semic 54
89/90 SemicElitserien 124
90/1 SemicElitserien 202
91/2 SemicElitserien 131, 342
92/3 SemicElitserien 153
89 SemicSticker 5
91 SemicSticker 32
93 SemicSticker 5
83/4 SouhaitsRen.KeyChain
95/6 udElite 95, 227, 255
97/8 udSwedish 101,201,UDS11
96 Wien 47
88/9 EDM
88/9 EDM/ActionMagazine 149
83/4 NYI
83/4 NYI/Islander 16
84/5 NYI 20

JOORIS, MARK
95/6 DEL 357
96/7 DEL 217

JORDAN, RIC
72/3 NewEngland (x2)

JORDE, MANFRED
94/5 DEL 185

JORGENSON, KEN
82/3 MedicineHat

JORGENSON, KEVIN
87/8 Portland
88/9 Portland
89/90 Portland

JORGENSON, LEN
88/9 Kamloops

JORGENSON, LYNN
78/9 Saginaw

JORMAKKA, TUOMO
80/1 Mallasjuoma 153
78/9 SM-Liiga 161

JORTIKKA, ARI
78/9 SM-Liiga 99

JORTIKKA, HANNU
94/5 ElitSet 302
92/3 Jyvas-Hyva 18
80/1 Mallasjuoma 177
78/9 SM-Liiga 200
73/4 WilliamsFIN 280

JOSEFSSON, OLA
94/5 Elit Set 74
95/6 ElitSet 187
89/90 SemicElitserien 71
90/1 SemicElitserien 287
91/2 SemicElitserien 68
92/3 SemicElitserien 95
95/6 udElite 49

JOSEPH, ANTHONY
90/1 Moncton

JOSEPH, CHRIS
91/2 Bowman 108
93/4 Donruss 492
94/5 Donruss 253
95/6 Donruss 64
94/5 FleerUltra 207
94/5 Leaf 158
91/2 OPC/Topps 432
92/3 O-Pee-Chee 203
88/9 opcSticker 218/88
89/90 opcSticker 225/84
97/8 PacificRegime 202
90/1 Panini(EDM) 8
95/6 Parkhurst 433
94/5 ParkieSE 168
94/5 Pinnacle 156
94/5 POG 228
93/4 PowerPlay 445
93/4 Premier 87
94/5 Premier 374
89/90 ProCards(AHL) 131
90/1 ProSet 443
93/4 Score 576
91/2 Score(CDN) 415
94/5 Score 98
95/6 Topps 93
91/2 ToppsStadiumClub 362
94/5 ToppsStadiumClub 224
90/1 UpperDeck 323
91/2 UpperDeck 436
94/5 UpperDeck 185
95/6 UpperDeck 449
95/6 UDBeAPlayer 98
88/9 EDM
88/9 EDM/ActionMagazine 2
90/1 EDM/McGavins
92/3 EDM
92/3 EDM/IGA 11
93/4 EDM 03NOV93
94/5 PGH/Foodland 17
95/6 PGH/Foodland
94/5 T.B./SkyBoxSportsCafe
96/7 VAN
96/7 VAN/IGA

JOSEPH, CURTIS
91/2 AirCanadaSJHL A49
92/3 Bowman 368
93/4 Donruss 296
94/5 Donruss 287, -Masked 5
95/6 Donruss 135
96/7 Donruss 110, -Between 8
97/8 Donruss 43, -Between 8
96/7 DonrussCanadianIce 116
97/8 DCI 20, -Nat'l 27,-Scrapbk 2
95/6 DonrussElite 59
96/7 DonrussElite 92
97/8 D.Elite 19, -Craftsmen 29
97/8 D.Preferred 84,-ColourG 3
97/8 D.Priority 123,-PostGen 4
97/8 DonrussStudio 29
96/7 Duracell DC4
94/5 EASports 126
95/6 EdgeIce L6
97/8 EssoOlympic 18
94/5 Flair 156
96/7 Flair 33, -HotGlove 5
94/5 Fleer 188, -Netminders 5
96/7 Fleer 37
92/3 FleerUltra 188
93/4 FleerUltra 172
94/5 FleerUltra 184,-PadMen 3
95/6 FleerUltra 140, -PadMen 6
96/7 FleerUltra 59
95/6 FutureLegend 29
93/4 HockeyWit 35
95/6 Hoyle'WEST Q (Spades)
97/8 KatchMedallion 57
96/7 Kelloggs
92/3 Kraft 31
94/5 Kraft-Mask
97/8 Kraft -RoadToNagano
97/8 Kraft -Stickers
93/4 Leaf 2, -Painted 2
94/5 Leaf 208,-Crease 3, -Gold 7
95/6 Leaf 281
96/7 Leaf 28, -ShutDown 5
97/8 Leaf 16, -PipeDreams 4
94/5 LeafLimited 95
96/7 LeafLimited 90
96/7 LeafPreferred-Masked 10
96/7 LeafPreferred-Vanity 13
97/8 Limited 81, 103, 174
97/8 Limited -fabric 23
96/7 McDonalds McD40,-Masks
97/8 McDonalds McD27
97/8 McDonalds -Medallions
96/7 MetalUniverse 53
97/8 Omega 93
90/1 OPC/Topps 171
91/2 OPC/Topps 417
92/3 O-Pee-Chee 339
90/1 opcPremier 51
91/2 opcPremier 165
97/8 PacificCrown 242, -InThe
97/8 PacificCrown-TeamCL 10
97/8 PacificCrownRoyale 53
97/8 PCR-FreezeOut 8
97/8 PacificDynagon! 49
97/8 PcfcD-Stone 9,-Tandem 11
97/8 PacificInvincible 56
97/8 PcfcParamount 75,-Glove 8
98/9 PcfcParamount 227,-Glove 19
97/8 PacificRegime 202
97/8 PcfcRevolution 55,-Retrn 8
90/1 PaniniSticker 272
91/2 PaniniSticker 22
92/3 PaniniSticker 15
93/4 PaniniSticker 166
94/5 PaniniSticker 144
95/6 PaniniSticker 265
96/7 PaniniSticker 255
91/2 Parkhurst 152
92/3 Parkhurst 155, 503
93/4 Parkhurst 175
94/5 Parkhurst 199, V17
95/6 Parkhurst 350
95 PH'Incomnet
91/2 Pinnacle 105
92/3 Pinnacle 54, 264
93/4 Pinnacle 15
94/5 Pinnacle 6,GT13,MA10,TP2
96/7 Pinnacle 164, -Masks 3
97/8 Pinnacle 93, -Masks 4
97/8 Pinnacle -TmP 2, -BigCan
97/8 Pinnacle-StandUp,-GoalT 5
96/7 P.BAP 206,-Stacking14
97/8 P. BAP -Stacking/Pads 7
97/8 PinnacleBeeHive 12
97/8 PinnacleCertified 18
97/8 Pinnacle-EPIX 17
97/8 PinnacleInside 4, 25
97/8 P.Inside-Stopr 12,-Track 21
97/8 PinnacleMasks
97/8 PinnacleMint 24
97/8 PinnacleUncut
96/7 PinnacleZenith 112
94/5 POG 293
94/5 Post
96/7 Post-StickUm 2
93/4 PowerPlay 213
93/4 PP-Game 4, -Net 4
93/4 Premier 222, 272
93/4 Premier-Black(Topps) 18
94/5 Premier 340
89/90 ProCards(IHL)7
90/1 ProSet 638
91/2 ProSet 473
92/3 ProSet 164
91/2 PSPlatinum 225
90/1 Score 151, -Young 15
91/2 Score(CDN) 516, (U.S) 296
91/2 Score-YoungStar 19
92/3 Score 262, -Young 17
93/4 Score 116
94/5 Score 181
95/6 Score 251
96/7 Score 90, -Net 7, -Sudden 6
97/8 Score 31, -NetWorth 5
92/3 SeasonPatches 14
94/5 Select 121
95/6 SelectCertified 84
96/7 SelectCert. 66, -Freezer 7
95/6 SkyBoxEmotion 62
95/6 SkyBoxImpact 60
96/7 SkyBoxImpact 42
94/5 SP 102
95/6 SP 54
96/7 SP 54
97/8 SPAuthentic 60
97/8 SPx 19, SPX9
96/7 Summit 150, -InThe 5
92/3 Topps 237
95/6 Topps 215
98/9 Topps 186, SB4
94/5 ToppsFinest 29
96/7 ToppsNHLPicks 83
91/2 ToppsStadiumClub 362
92/3 ToppsStadiumClub 327
93/4 ToppsStadiumClub 162
94/5 ToppsStadiumClub 142
94/5 TSC -SuperTeam 20
94/5 TSC-MembersOnly 29
97/8 ToppsSticker 5
90/1 UpperDeck 175
91/2 UpperDeck 139
92/3 UpperDeck 186
93/4 UpperDeck 157, -SP139
94/5 UpperDeck 91, H33, SP68
95/6 UpperDeck 296
96/7 UpperDeck 256, X27
97/8 UD 273,S25,SG31,T10B
94/5 UDBAP R71, R101
94/5 UDBAP R174, -Aut109
96/7 UDBlckDiamond 158, RC17
97/8 UDBlackDiamond 126
98/9 UDChoice 81, 251
95/6 UDCollChoice 291
96/7 UDCollChoice 90, 317
97/8 UDCollChoice89, S6, SQ31
96/7 UpperDeck"Ice" 21
97/8 UpperDeckIce 81
97/8 ValuNet
97/8 Zenith 17, Z38
96/7 EDM
97/8 EDM
91/2 STL
89/90 STL/Kodak
90/1 STL/Kodak
92/3 STL/UpperDeck 9

JOSEPH, FABIAN
91/2 CanadaNats
93/4 CanadaNats
92 CanadaWinterOlympics 196
95/6 EdgeIce 162
93/4 FleerUltra 464
93/4 PowerPlay 484
93/4 Premier-TeamCanada 7
88/9 ProCards(CapeBreton)
89/90 ProCards(AHL) 137
92/3 Score-CdnOlympic 8
94/5 Score CT10
94/5 Milwaukee
82/3 Victoria
83/4 Victoria

JOSEPH, TONY
89/90 ProCards(AHL) 48
90/1 ProCards 243
91/2 ProCards 155

JOSEPHSON, MIKE
91/2 AvantGardeBCJ 75, 166
93/4 Kamloops

JOSS, ED
52/3 LavalDairy 120

JOSS, TERRY
95/6 Slapshot 407

JOTKUS, PETE
36/7 WWGum (V356) 104

JOUTSENVUORI, TIMO
71/2 WilliamsFIN 364

JOVANOVSKI, ED
96/7 Aces Q (Spades)
96/7 AllSportPPF 71
94/5 Assets 8, 33, DC9
95/6 Bowman 100, BB19
94/5 Classic 1,C6,CP11,R9,T26
94/5 Classic-Draft Day (x3)
95/6 Classic 98, AS9, BK19,-Aut.
94/5 C4'Sport 115, BC17, HV4
95/6 ClassicFiveSport 138
94/5 C4'Images 94, CP19

94/5 ClassicImages 15, CE17
93/4 ClassicProspects 203
95/6 Donruss-CdnJr 6
96/7 D-Dom 10,-HitLst 3,-Ratd 7
97/8 Donruss 144
96/7 DonrussCanadianIce 35
97/8 DonrussCanadianIce 14
95/6 DonrussElite 68, -Rookie 11
96/7 D.Elite 82, -Aspirations 6
97/8 DonrussElite 33
97/8 DonrussPreferred 19
97/8 DonrussPriority 27
97/8 DonrussStudio 39
96/7 Flair 37, -HotNumber 5
96/7 Fleer 39, -Rookie 6
95/6 FleerMetal 178
96/7 FleerNHLPicks 98, -Fab 21
96/7 F.Picks-Jagged 13
95/6 FleerUltra 342, -Extra 10
96/7 FU 65, -Power 7, -Blue 5
97/8 KatchMedallion 61
96/7 Kraft-Trophy
96/7 Leaf 208,-Fire13,-Leather19
97/8 Leaf 17
94/5 LeafLimited-CdnJr. 5
96/7 LeafLimited 14, -Bash 7
96/7 LeafPreferred 68, -Vanity 8
97/8 Limited 5, 37
96/7 McDonalds McD6
96/7 MetalUniverse 59, -Cool 5
97/8 Omega 99
98/9 Pacific 222
97/8 PacificCrownRoyale 57
97/8 PcfcDynag! 131,-Tandm 49
97/8 PacificInvincible 60
97/8 PacificParamount 80
98/9 PacificParamount 96
97/8 PacificRegime 85
97/8 PacificRevolution 60
96/7 PaniniSticker 68
95/6 Parkhurst 536, PP42
94/5 ParkieSE 207
94/5 Pinnacle 524
96/7 Pinnacle 204, -TeamP 7
96/7 P-ByTheNumbers 4
97/8 Pinnacle 113
97/8 PinnacleBeAPlayer 21
97/8 PinnacleCertified 48
97/8 PinnacleInside 86
95/6 P.Zenith 121, -RookieRoll 7
96/7 PinnacleZenith 45
96/7 Post
96/7 Score 239, -CheckIt 12
97/8 Score 235
95/6 SelectCert. 137, -Future 10
96/7 SelectCertified 30
96/7 SkBxEmotion-Next 9
95/6 SkyBoxImpact 201
96/7 SkyBoxImpact 45, -Fox 11
96/7 SkyBoxImpact-Count 5
93/4 Slapshot(Windsor) 1
94/5 Slapshot(Windsor) 14
94/5 SP 140
95/6 SP 58
96/7 SP 60, GF14
97/8 SPAuthentic 65
96/7 SportFX MiniStix
97/8 SPx 21
98/9 SPx"Finite" 39
95/6 Summit 171
96/7 Summit 163
96/7 TeamOut
95/6 Topps 354, 22CJ
98/9 Topps 177
94/5 ToppsFinest 149
95/6 ToppsFinest 176
96 ToppsFinestBronze 21
96/7 T.Picks FT8, ID5, RS11
95/6 T.StadiumClub ER196, G9
95/6 ToppsSuperSkills SR1
95/6 TSC-MembersOnly 47
94/5 UpperDeck 496
95/6 UpperDeck 501, H24
96/7 UpperDeck 66, 362, P8
96/7 UD SS3B, X11
97/8 UpperDeck 284, 389, SG15
95/6 UDBeAPlayer 178
96/7 UDBlackDiamond 18, RC15
97/8 UDBlackDiamond 141
98/9 UDChoice 91
95/6 UDCollChoice 399
96/7 UDCC 318, 340, UD34
97/8 UDUDCollChoice 101
96/7 UpperDeck"Ice" 88, S3
97/8 UpperDeckIce 26
96/7 FLA/WinnDixie
97/8 FLA/WinnDixie

JOYAL, EDDIE
64-67 BeeHives(DETx2),(TOR)
64/5 CokeCap DET21
70/1 EddieSargent 67
71/2 EddieSargent 74
70/1 Esso Stamp
68/9 OPC/Topps 40
69/70 OPC/Topps 108
69/70 OPC-Stamp, -Sticker
70/1 OPC/Topps 39, -Deckle 3
70/1 OPC/Topps-Sticker
71/2 OPC/Topps 23
75/6 opcWHA 36
72 SemicSticker 205
68/9 ShirriffCoin LA6
71/2 TheTorontoSun
65/6 Topps 85
63/4 York 48

JOYAL, ERIC
90/1 SketchQMJHL 192
91/2 SketchQMJHL 64

JOYCE, BOB
88/9 OPC/Topps 2
89/90 OPC/Topps 73
89/90 opcSticker 126, 31/171
89/90 opcStickFS 3
89/90 PaniniSticker 199
90/1 ProCards 206
91/2 ProCards 172
90/1 Score 291
88/9 BOS/SportsAction (x2)
89/90 BOS/SportsAction
89/90 WSH/Kodak
93/4 LasVegas
94/5 LasVegas
91/2 Moncton

JOYCE, DUANE
89/90 ProCards(IHL) 126
90/1 ProCards 105
91/2 ProCards 523
96/7 Cincinnati

JOYCE, GRAHAM
52/3 AnonymousOHL 120

JOYCE, JOHN
94/5 Birmingham
95/6 Birmingham

JUBENVILLE, JEFF
90/1 SketchWHL 3
91/2 SketchWHL 123
93/4 Tacoma

JUCKES, WINSTON B. (BING)
45-64 Beehives(NYR)

JUCKES, GORDON W.
83&87 HallOfFame 143
83 HHOF Postcard (K)

JUDSON, RICK
92/3 Toledo (1), (2)
93/4 Toledo 22
94/5 Toledo
95/6 Toledo

JUHLIN, PATRIK
94/5 Classic 80, R10, T49
95/6 Donruss 60
94/5 Flair 128
94/5 Fleer 155
94/5 FleerUltra 344
95 Globe 31
95/6 Leaf 44
95/6 Parkhurst 160
94/5 ParkieSE SE133
94/5 Premier 378
94 Semic 68
95 Semic 76
89/90 SemicElitserien 250
90/1 SemicElitserien 171
91/2 SemicElitserien 266
92/3 SemicElitserien 286
93 SemicSticker 11
94/5 SRGoldStandard 86
95/6 TetAutobilia 43
95/6 TetradAutobilia43
94/5 ToppsFinest 6
94/5 UpperDeck 246,553,SP148
95/6 UDBeAPlayer 119
95/6 UDCollChoice 236
95/6 udElite 244
96 Wien 62
94/5 PHA

JULIAN, JASON
91/2 SketchOHL 335
92/3 Oshawa

JULIEN, CLAUDE
88/9 ProCards(Halifax)
89/90 ProCards(AHL) 165
90/1 ProCards 587
91/2 ProCards 171
83/4 Fredericton 16
84/5 Fredericton 8
85/6 Fredericton 15
89/90 Halifax
90/1 KansasCity 12
91/2 Moncton

JULIEN, STÉPHANE
90/1 SketchQMJHL 93
91/2 SketchQMJHL 112
96/7 Penascola 2

JUNEAU, JOÉ
96/7 Aces 4 (Hearts)
92/3 Bowman 292
95/6 Bowman 39
91/2 CanadaNats
92 CanadaWinterOlympics 192
93/4 ClassicProspect -Aut
93/4 Donruss 26, 394, 504
94/5 Donruss 258
95/6 Donruss 136
96/7 Donruss 151
97/8 Donruss 95
96/7 DonrussCanadianIce 38
95/6 DonrussElite 104
96/7 DonrussElite 90
97/8 DonrussElite 41
97/8 DonrussPreferred 13
97/8 DonrussPriority 137
97/8 DonrussStudio 68
93/4 Durivage 27
93/4 EASports 10
94/5 Flair 200
94/5 Fleer 236, -FranchiseFut 5
96/7 Fleer 118
95/6 FleerMetal 161
96/7 FleerNHLPicks 108
92/3 FleerUltra 4, 448
93/4 FleerUltra 49
94/5 FleerUltra 388
95/6 FleerUltra 323
96/7 FleerUltra 177
95/6 Hoyle'EAST 7 (Spades)
97/8 KatchMedallion 152
93/4 Kraft
95/6 Kraft
93/4 Leaf 218,-GoldRookie 2
94/5 Leaf 62, -FireOnIce 7
94/5 Leaf-Limited 25
95/6 Leaf 188
96/7 Leaf 21
97/8 Leaf 53
94/5 LeafLimited 38
95/6 LeafLimited 98
96/7 LeafPreferred 49
97/8 Limited 63
96/7 Maggers 164
96/7 MetalUniverse 166
97/8 Omega 241
92/3 O-Pee-Chee 189
92/3 opcPremier 101
98/9 Pacific 90
97/8 PacificCrown 155,-Slap 12A
97/8 PacificCrownRoyale 140
97/8 PcfcDynag! 131,-Tandm 57
97/8 PacificInvincible 147
97/8 PacificParamount 195
98/9 PacificParamount 246
97/8 PacificRevolution 148
92/3 PaniniSticker L
93/4 PaniniSticker 143, A
94/5 PaniniSticker 19
95/6 PaniniSticker 138
96/7 PaniniSticker 138
91/2 Parkhurst 234
92/3 Parkhurst 2
93/4 Parkhurst 241, 280
94/5 Parkhurst SeV17, C25
95/6 Parkhurst 221
94/5 ParkieSE 198
92/3 Pinnacle 221,-Tm2000 19
93/4 Pinnacle 5,-Team2001 4
94/5 Pinnacle 7
96/7 Pinnacle 160
97/8 Pinnacle 107
97/8 PinnacleBeAPlayer 184
97/8 PinnacleCertified 63
97/8 PinnacleInside 151
95/6 PinnacleZenith 96
96/7 PinnacleZenith 27
95/6 Playoff 105
94/5 POG 245
95/6 POG 283
93/4 PowerPlay 19
93/4 PP-2ndYrStr 2,-PtLdr 6
93/4 Premier 125, 299
93/4 Premier -BlackGold (T) 12
94/5 Premier 100
95/6 ProMagnet 28
92/3 ProSet 219
92/3 Score 453, -Young 22
92/3 Score-CdnOlympicHero 2
93/4 Score 330
94/5 Score 124, TF25
95/6 Score 256
96/7 Score 144
97/8 Score 140
92/3 SeasonPatches 18
94/5 Select 86
95/6 SelectCertified 80
95/6 SkyBoxEmotion 190
95/6 SkyBoxImpact 179
96/7 SkyBoxImpact 141
94/5 SP 126
95/6 SP 158
96/7 SP 166, HC17
97/8 SPAuthentic 163
97/8 SPx 49
95/6 Summit 139
96/7 Summit 7
95/6 SuperSticker 129, -DieCut 8
96/7 TeamOut
92/3 Topps 365
95/6 Topps 216, HGC25
98/9 Topps 151
94/5 ToppsFinest 93
95/6 ToppsFinest 124
92/3 ToppsStadiumClub 297
93/4 ToppsStadiumClub 202
95/6 ToppsStadiumClub 187
95/6 ToppsSuperSkills 25
92/3 UpperDeck 354, 399, 455
92/3 UD CC9, G11, AC1
92/3 UD-LockerAS 53
93/4 UpperDeck 282, 343, HB10
93/4 UD-FutureHeroes 35, -SP9
94/5 UpperDeck 88, R15, SP175
95/6 UpperDeck 25, R17, SE88
96/7 UpperDeck 176, X40
97/8 UpperDeck 176, T18C
93/4 UDBeAPlayer 27
94/5 UDBeAPlayer R85, R100
95/6 UDBeAPlayer 58
96/7 UDBlackDiamond 90
98/9 UDChoice 214
95/6 UDCollChoice 118
96/7 UDCollChoice 277, 334
97/8 UDCollChoice 268
96 Wien 92
92/3 BOS
95/6 WSH

JUNGWIRTH, THOMAS
94/5 DEL 130
95/6 DEL 128

JUNKER, STEVE
93/4 ClassicProspects 193
93/4 Donruss 202
93/4 FleerUltra 367
93/4 Leaf 402
93/4 Parkhurst 394
90/1 SketchMEM 80
90/1 SketchWHL 193
91/2 SketchWHL 9
91/2 UD'CzechWJC 57
93/4 UpperDeck 241
89/90 Spokane

JUNKIN, DALE
90/1 SketchOHL 62
91/2 SketchOHL 199

JUNKKA, JONAS
97/8 udSwedish, 152

JUNNO, JUHA
92/3 Jyvas-Hyva 86

JUNTUNEN, EERO
71/2 WilliamsFIN 226
72/3 WilliamsFIN 209
73/4 WilliamsFIN 281

JUOJARVI, TERO
71/2 WilliamsFIN 344
72/3 WilliamsFIN 328

JURAK, JURAJ
94/5 APS 197
95/6 APS 121

JURSINOV, VLADIMIR
see Vladimir Yursinov

JUSELIUS, HEIKKI
66/7 Champion 102
65/6 Hellas 92
72/3 WilliamsFIN 174

JUSSILA, TIMO
65/6 Hellas 48, 156

JUTILA, TIMO
95 FinnishAllStar 8
95 Globe 130
95 Hartwall
92/3 Jyvas-Hyva 161
93/4 Jyvas-Hyva 285
80/1 Mallasjuoma 160
95 PaniniWorlds 166
95/6 RadioCity
94 Semic 5
95 Semic 5, 202
89/90 SemicElitserien 152
90/1 SemicElitserien 226
91/2 SemicElitserien 154
91 SemicSticker 5
93 SemicSticker 53
93/4 Sisu 63, 368
94/5 Sisu 59, 162, -Fire 6
95/6 Sisu 180, 312, -Gold 6
95/6 Sisu-DoubleTrouble 8
96/7 Sisu 177
95/6 SisuLimited 73
96 Wien 5, AS2

JUTRAS, CLAUDE
90/1 SketchMEM 65
90/1 SketchQMJHL 11
91/2 SketchQMJHL 213
94/5 CapeBreton

JUZDA, BILL
33-43 BeeHives(NYR)
45-64 BeeHives(TOR)
48-52 Exhibits
51/2 Parkhurst 77
45-54 QuakerOats (x3)

JYLHA, JUHA
65/6 Hellas 26
70/1 Kuvajulkaisut 106
71/2 WilliamsFIN 114
73/4 WilliamsFIN 310

JYLHASAARI, TAPIO
70/1 Kuvajulkaisut 330

JYRKKO, JUHA
80/1 Mallasjuoma 206
78/9 SM-Liiga 75

K

KAARELA, JARI
72/3 WilliamsFIN 307

KAARIO, MATTI
80/1 Mallasjuoma 69
78/9 SM-Liiga 112

KAARNA, ILKKA
80/1 Mallasjuoma 137

KABAT, KURT
92/3 Hampton

KABAYAMA, MATT
82/3 MedicineHat
83/4 MedicineHat 17

KABERLE, FRANTISEK SR.
79 PaniniSticker 80

KABERLE, FRANTISEK
94/5 APS 51
95/6 ElitSet 272
95 PaniniWorlds 190
93/4 Upper Deck 261
95/6 udElite 155, NA18
97/8 udSwedish 152
96 Wien 106

KABERLE, TOMAS
95/6 APS 80

KACHOWSKI, MARK
89/90 Pro Cards 159
90/1 ProCards 378
87/8 PGH/Kodak
84/5 Kamloops
85/6 Kamloops

KACHUR, EDDIE
93/4 Parkie (56/7) 37

KACHUR, TRENT
86/7 Regina
87/8 Regina

KACIK, TADEUSZ
74 Hellas 98
73/4 WilliamsFIN 93

KACIK, MARIAN
93/4 OwenSound 12

KADERA, ROMAN
94/5 APS 135
95/6 APS 234
93/4 UpperDeck 267

KADLEC, ARNOLD
82 SemicStickers 82

KADLEC, DRAHOMIR
94/5 DEL 176
95/6 DEL 172
96/7 DEL 115
92/3 Jyvas-Hyva 9
95 PaniniWorlds 189
94 Semic 170
95 Semic 144
89 SemicStickers 187
93 SemicStickers 92

KADOW, HARALD
72 Hellas 48

KAEBEL, BUTCH
93/4 Birmingham 5
93/4 Peoria

KAESE, TRENT
87/8 Flint

KAHELIN, TIMO
92/3 Jyvas-Hyva 139
93/4 Jyvas-Hyva 255
93/4 Sisu 284

KAHIILUOLO, TOMMI
96/7 Sisu 31

KAHL, EGON
79 PaniniSticker 367

KAHONEN, JURKI
70/1 Kuvajulkaisut 314

KAIKKONEN, ARI
70/1 Kuvajulkaisut 368
71/2 WilliamsFIN 304

KAIPAINEN, MATTI
93/4 Sisu 124
94/5 Sisu 69
95/6 Sisu 236
96/7 Sisu 34

KAIPONEN, LASSE
71/2 WilliamsFIN 323

KAISER, VERN
45-64 BeeHives(MTL)
45-54 QuakerOats

KAISTAKARI, JARMO
80/1 Mallasjuoma 132

KAITALA, RISTO
66/7 Champion 8
65/6 Hellas 17

KAIVOLA, ANTTI
72/3 WilliamsFIN 285

KAJER, MILOS
94/5 APS 69
95/6 APS 90

KAJKL, MILAN
79 PaniniSticker 77

KAJULA, TIMO
70/1 Kuvajulkaisut 369

KAKKO, ERIK
91/2 Jyvas-Hyva 54
92/3 Jyvas-Hyva 144
93/4 Jyvas-Hyva 316
93/4 Sisu 33
94/5 Sisu 269
95/6 Sisu 21
96/7 Sisu 16

KALAWSKY, CRAIG
86/7 Regina
87/8 Regina
83/4 Kingston 20
82/3 NorthBay

KALETA, ALEXANDER
33-43 BeeHives(CHI)
45-64 BeeHives(NYR)

KALLEVA, PETRI
93/4 Sisu 61

KALLIO, JORMA
66/7 Champion 194
70/1 Kuvajulkaisut 126
72 Panda
78/9 SM-Liiga 177
71/2 WilliamsFIN 176
72/3 WilliamsFIN 124
73/4 WilliamsFIN 180

KALLIO, MARKKU
94/5 Sisu 311

KALLIO, TOMI
78/9 SM-Liiga 195
72/3 WilliamsFIN 263

KALLIO, TOMI
95/6 Sisu 335, -Drafted 5
96/7 Sisu 146
95/6 UDCollChoice 334

KALLIOMAKI, TUOMAS
93/4 Jyvas-Hyva 172
93/4 Sisu 171
95/6 Sisu 350

KALLIONIEMI, RIKU
95/6 Sisu 303
96/7 Sisu 97

KALLIONPAA, MARTTI
65/6 Hellas 64

KALLUR, ANDERS
80/1 OPC/Topps 156
81/2 OPC 204, Topps(E) 90
82/3 OPC 203
81/2 opcSticker 162
82/3 opcSticker 57
82/3 Post
79/80 NYI
83/4 NYI/Islander 9
84/5 NYI 8

KALMIKOV, KONSTANTIN
96/7 Sudbury 13

KALMOKOSKI, ARI
71/2 WilliamsFIN 305

KALT, DIETER
96/7 DEL 178
95 PaniniWorlds 267
94 Semic 241
95 Semic 186
93 SemicSticker 279
96 Wien 217

KALTEVA, PETRI
93/4 Jyvas-Hyva 295
93/4 Sisu 61
94/5 Sisu 296
95/6 Sisu 316

KAMARAINEN, JOUKO
80/1 Mallasjuoma 104
78/9 SM-Liiga 147

KAMBEITZ, JIM
83/4 MedicineHat 20

KAMEL, NOEL
92/3 MPSPhotoSJHL 73

KAMENEV, VASILI
95 SR-FF5

KAMENSKY, VALERI
92/3 Bowman 432
93/4 Donruss 277
94/5 Donruss 116
95/6 Donruss 236
96/7 Donruss 14
97/8 Donruss 132
96/7 DonrussCanadianIce 32
97/8 DonrussCanadianIce 82
95/6 DonrussElite 22
96/7 DonrussElite 118
97/8 DonrussElite 44
97/8 DonrussPriority 87
94/5 Flair 147
94/5 Fleer 177
96/7 Fleer 21, -ArtRoss 9
95/6 FleerMetal 33
96/7 FPicks-Dream 9, -Fab 22
93/4 FleerUltra 84
94/5 FleerUltra 357
95/6 FleerUltra 221
96/7 FleerUltra 36
91/2 Gillette 30
95 Globe 179
92/3 HumptyDumpty (1)
93/4 Leaf 207
94/5 Leaf 117
96/7 Leaf 170
96/7 LeafLimited 81
96/7 LeafPreferred 53, -Steel 59
97/8 Limited 47, 111
96/7 Maggers 43
96/7 MetalUniverse 33
97/8 Omega 57
90/1 O-Pee-Chee 4R
92/3 O-Pee-Chee 266
91/2 OPC/Topps 513
98/9 Pacific 160
97/8 PacificCrown 213
97/8 PacificCrownRoyale 34
97/8 PcfcDynagn! 30,-Tandm 42
97/8 PacificInvincible 35
97/8 PacificParamount 50
98/9 PacificParamount 56
97/8 PacificRevolution 33
92/3 PaniniStickers 295, R
93/4 PaniniSticker 72
94/5 PaniniSticker 80
95/6 PaniniSticker 248
96/7 PaniniSticker 248
97/8 PaniniSticker 203
95 PaniniWorlds 36
91/2 Parkhurst 362
92/3 Parkhurst 230, 377
93/4 Parkhurst 438
94/5 Parkhurst 190
95/6 Parkhurst 48
91/2 Pinnacle 340
92/3 Pinnacle 64
93/4 Pinnacle 244
94/5 Pinnacle 343
96/7 Pinnacle 47
97/8 Pinnacle 186
96/7 PinnacleBeAPlayer 33
97/8 PinnacleCertified 67
97/8 PinnacleInside 114
96/7 PinnacleZenith 8
95/6 Playoff 243
96/7 Playoff 420
94/5 POG 195
95/8 POG 74
93/4 PowerPlay 199
93/4 Premier 85
94/5 Premier 32
92/3 Pro Set 148
91/2 RedAce
92/3 Score 360, -YoungStar 24
91/2 ScoreTraded 76T
93/4 Score 326
95/6 Score 268
96/7 Score 157
97/8 Score 186
97/8 Score(COL) 7
94/5 Select 144
95/6 SelectCertified 105
96/7 SelectCertified 67
94 Semic 157
95 Semic 131
89 SemicStickers 91
91 SemicStickers 88
95/6 SkyBoxEmotion 37
95/6 SkyBoxImpact 36
96/7 SkyBoxImpact 23, -Blade 9
87/8 SovietStars
89/90 SovietStars
97/8 SPAuthentic 39
98/9 SPx"Finite" 23
95/6 Summit 6
96/7 Summit 59
95/6 SuperSticker 31
92/3 Topps 53
98/9 Topps 39
95/6 ToppsFinest 164
96/7 ToppsNHLPicks 39
92/3 ToppsStadiumClub 344
93/4 ToppsStadiumClub 237
95/6 ToppsStadiumClub 161
91/2 TriGlobe 11-12
91/2 TriGlobeMagFive 1-5
91/2 UpperDeck 273, SP1
92/3 UpperDeck 27, E20
93/4 UpperDeck 118
94/5 UpperDeck 355
95/6 UpperDeck 489, -Aut 158
96/7 UpperDeck 241, X20
97/8 UpperDeck 254
98/9 UDChoice 58
95/6 UDCollChoice 221
96/7 UDCC 62, -Oversize 62
97/8 UDCollChoice 58
96 Wien 149
96/7 COL/PhotoPucks
91/2 QUE/PetroCanada
92/3 QUE/PetroCanada
94/5 QUE/BurgerKing

KAMES, JAROSLAV
94/5 APS 181
95/6 APS 29

KAMINSKI, B.
95/6 DEL 35

KAMINSKI, DARCY
89/90 Lethbridge

KAMINSKI, KEVIN
93/4 Donruss 505
93/4 Parkhurst 493
96/7 PinnacleBeAPlayer 86
89/90 ProCards 170
90/1 ProCards 448, 544
89/90 QUE
89/90 QUE/GeneralFoods
90/1 QUE
95/6 WSH
89/90 Halifax
93/4 Portland
94/5 Portland
86/7 Saskatoon
89/90 Saskatoon 23

KAMNISKY, MAX
33-43 BeeHives(MTL.M)
36-39 DiamondMatch (1)

KAMINSKY, YAN
93/4 Classic 88
93/4 ClassicProspects 185
93/4 Donruss 456
94/5 Leaf 173
94/5 Pinnacle 263
94/5 Premier 399
92/3 RedAce 33
94/5 Score 221
92/3 UpperDeck 333, 344
93/4 WPG/Ruffles

KAMMERER, AXEL
94/5 DEL 193
95/6 DEL 328
96/7 DEL 106
89 SemicStickers 123

KAMP, CURT
93/4 Seattle

KAMPERSAL, JEFFREY
92/3 Richmond

KAMPMAN, RUDOLPH (BINGO)
33-43 BeeHives(TOR)
39/40 OPC (V301-1) 3
40/1 OPC (V301-2) 109
38/9 QuakerOats

KAMPPURI, HANNU
80/1 Mallasjuoma 168
82 SemicStickers 26
82 Skopbank
78/9 SM-Liiga 1, 65
84/5 N.J.

KAMULA, PETE
52/3 AnonymousOHL 19

KANE, DAN
84/5 Moncton 7

KANE, SHAUN
93/4 Raleigh

KANERVA, PETTERI
80/1 Mallasjuoma 71
78/9 SM-Liiga 109

KANERVO, KARI
92/3 Jyvas-Hyva 175

KANGAS, PASI
95/6 Sisu 266

KANGAS, VESA
89/90 SemicElitserien 161

KANGASALUSIA, PEKA
95/6 Sisu 231
96/7 Sisu 30

KANGASNIEMI, MISKA
95/6 Sisu 60
94/5 ToppsFinest 134

KANKAANPERA, ARI
78/9 SM-Liiga 50

KANKAANPERA, RISTO
78/9 SM-Liiga 56

KANKOVSKY, PETR
94/5 APS 192
95/6 APS 188

KANKOVSKY, ROMAN
94/5 APS 190
95/6 APS 178

KANNEGIESSER, SHELDON
74/5 Loblaws
71/2 OPC/Topps 190
74/5 OPC 338
75/6 OPC/Topps 69
76/7 OPC 335
78/9 OPC 310
71/2 TheTorontoSun

KANNEWURF, FRANK
94/5 DEL 37
95/6 DEL 30

KANNISTO, MIKA
94/5 Sisu 294
95/6 Sisu 221
96/7 Sisu 24

KANTOR, ROBERT
95/6 APS 207

KAONPAA, ESKO
66/7 Champion 149
65/6 Hellas 129
72 Panda
71/2 WilliamsFIN 177
72/3 WilliamsFIN 125

KAPANEN, HANNU
93/4 Jyvas-Hyva 163
93/4 Sisu 160
95/6 Sisu 389
78/9 SM-Liiga 34
71/2 WilliamsFIN 281
73/4 WilliamsFIN 196

KAPANEN, JARI
80/1 Mallasjuoma 14
78/9 SM-Liiga 80
73/4 WilliamsFIN 283

KAPANEN, KIMMO
93/4 Sisu 162
94/5 Sisu 229
95/6 Sisu 2

KAPANEN, SAMI
97/8 DonrussPriority 73
95 Hartwall
92/3 Jyvas-Hyva 102
93/4 Jyvas-Hyva 174
95/6 Kelloggs PopUp 6
97/8 Omega 41
98/9 Pacific 134
97/8 PacificCrown 192
98/9 PacificParamount 37
97/8 PacificRevolution 23
97/8 PaniniSticker 25
95 PaniniWorlds 183
95/6 Parkhurst 516
96/7 PinnacleBeAPlayer 145
94 Semic 39
95 Semic 24, 231
93/4 Sisu 179
94/5 Sisu 163, 209
94/5 Sisu-Magic 5, -FireOnIce 8
95/6 Sisu 12, -Drafted 6,-Gold 13
95/6 SisuLimited 72, -SSD 1
97/8 SPAuthentic 27
98/9 SPx"Finite" 16
95 SuomenBeckett 5
98/9 Topps 178
91/2 UD 674, 'CzechWJC 37
97/8 UpperDeck 239
97/8 UDBlackDiamond 147
98/9 UDChoice 40
96 Wien 19
97/8 Zenith 69

KAPKAIKIN, KONSTANTIN
91/2 O-Pee-Chee 51R

KAPUS, RICHARD
93/4 UpperDeck 265

KAPUSTA, TOMAS
93/4 Jyvas-Hyva 48
95 PaniniWorlds 210
89/90 ProCards 147
90/1 ProCards 235
91/2 ProCards 231
93 SemicStickers 99
93/4 Sisu 250, 361
94/5 Sisu 225, -FireOnIce 9
95/6 Sisu 357, 372
95/6 SisuLimited 87

KAPUSTIN, SERGEI
79 PaniniSticker 153
82 SemicSticker 71
74/5 Soviet Stars 20
78 SovietChamps
80 SovietMiniPics
83/4 SovietStars
92/3 Trends(76) 144

KAPYNEN, TERO
78/9 SM-Liiga 196

KARABIN, LADISLAV
93/4 ClassicProspects 108
93/4 Donruss 472
93/4 Parkhurst 426
93/4 UpperDeck 467
93/4 Cleveland
95/6 Rochester

KARAKAS, KRAIG
93/4 Minn-Duluth

KARAKAS, MIKE
33-43 BeeHives(CHI)
36-39 DiamondMatch (3), (4), (6)
36/7 OPC (V304D) 107
39/40 OPC (V301-1) 47
43-47 ParadeSportive
36/7 WWGum (V356) 123

KARALAHTI, JERE
94/5 ParkieSE 216
95 Semic 237
93/4 Sisu 86, 395
94/5 Sisu 2, -Juniors 4
95/6 Sisu 206
96/7 Sisu 4
94/5 ToppsFinest 126

KARALIS, TOM
89/90 ProCards 117
90/1 ProCards 549
91/2 ProCards 176
87/8 Flint
85/6 Fredericton 21
86/7 Fredericton

KARAMANOS, JON
93/4 Pinnacle 494

KARAMNOV, VITALI
96/7 DEL 259
93/94 Donruss 287
93/4 FleerUltra 412
93/4 Leaf 408
92/3 Parkhurst 387
93/4 Parkhurst 444
92/3 Pinnacle 398
93/4 PowerPlay 429
93/4 Premier 292
93/4 ToppsStadiumClub 478
92/3 UpperDeck 341, 510
93/4 Upper Deck 338

KARAPUU, MIKA
93/4 Sisu 44
96/7 Sisu 121

KARBEL, KARSON
94/5 Dayton 7

KAREL, HELMUT
95 PaniniWorlds 265

KARELIUS, PERTTI
66/7 Champion 80
65/6 Hellas 11

KARGER, REINHARD
70/1 Kuvajulkaisut 87

KARHUNEN, PEKKA
70/1 Kuvajulkaisut 311

KARI, ESA
70/1 Kuvajulkaisut 193

KARI, HARRI
78/9 SM-Liiga 199

KARIYA, PAUL
95/6 Aces 7 (Hearts)
96/7 Aces K (Diamonds)
97/8 Aces A (Spades)
91/2 AvantGardeBC 84, 86, 91
91/2 AvantGardeBC 93, 168
95/6 Bowman 90, BB15
93/4 CanadaNats
93/4 Classic 4, 11, 113
93/4 Classic DP4, N2, TC2
93/4 C'Prospects 18,1A3, LP15
95/6 CoolTrade 8
97/8 Corinthian Headliners
95/6 Donruss 57, -Elite 6,-Dom 6
95/6 D-ProPointer 19, -Rookie 3
96/7 Donruss 142,-Dom 8,-Top 8
97/8 Donruss 7,-Elite 4,-Line 20
96/7 D.CdnIce 3, -OCanada 2
97/8 D.CdnIce 2,-Ntl 3,-Scrap 20
95/6 DonrussElite 31,-CuttingE 5
96/7 DonrussElite 1, -Status 5
97/8 D.Elite 7, 136,-Craftsmn 22
97/8 D.Elite PrimeNumbers 5
97/8 DonrussPreferred 10, 183
97/8 D.Pref -Line 4C,-PrecM 8
97/8 D.Pref-Tin 2,22, -WTin 2,11
97/8 DonrussPriority 13, 204
97/8 D.Prio-DirDep 14,-OpDay12
97/8 D.Prio-Pstcrd 13,-Stamp 13
97/8 D.Studio 4,-HardHats 3
97/8 D.Studio-Portr 4,-Silhouet 5
96/7 Duracell JB20
97/8 EssoOlympic 9
94/5 Flair 4
96/7 Flair 2, -Centre 6
94/5 Fleer 3, -RookieSensation 5
96/7 Fleer 2, 141, -ArtRoss 10
96/7 Fleer-PearsonAward 6
95/6 FleerMetal 2, -HeavyMet 7
96/7 FleerPicks 6, -Dream 5
96/7 FPicks-Fab 23, -Jagged 6
93/4 FleerUltra 465
94/5 FleerUltra -Prospects 3
95/6 FleerUltra 3, 388,-High 11
95/6 FU-Extra 11,-AllRookie 5
96/7 FU 2,-RedLine 3,-Power 8
95 Globe 91
96/7 Got-UmHockeyGreatsCoin
95/6 Hoyle'WEST K (Spades)
94/5 Incomnet
97/8 KatchMedallion 2, 159
96/7 KennerSLU
97/8 KennerSLU -1on1
95/6 KraftDinner
96/7 Kraft'AllStar, -Disk, -Trophy
97/8 Kraft -CaseSeries,-CdnPros
97/8 Kraft -RoadToNagano
97/8 Kraft -Stickers, -WorldsBest
94/5 Leaf 455,-Ltd 27,-Phenom 5
95/6 Leaf 304, -Fire 11, -Studio 3
96/7 Leaf 176.-Fire 4, -Sweatr 5
97/8 Leaf 6,173,-BnrS 1,-Fire 16
94/5 LeafLimited 107, -Gold 5
95/6 LeafLimited 9, -Stars 5
96/7 LeafLimited 17
96/7 LeafPreferd 7,-LeafSteel 34
96/7 LP-SteelPower 11
97/8 Limited 35, 56, 114
97/8 Limited -fabric 19, 40
96/7 Maggers 1
94/5 McDonalds McD32
95/6 McDonalds McD11
96/7 McDonalds McD29
97/8 McDonalds McD9, F6
97/8 McDonalds -Medallions
96/7 MetalUniv. 2, -Lethal 9
96/7 MU-IceCarvings 7
97/8 Omega 3, -GameFace 1
97/8 Omega -Silk 1, -StickHan 1
98/9 Pacific 9, -DynagonIce 1
98/9 Pcfc-GoldCrwn 1,-TmCL 1
97/8 PacificCrown 9, -Supial 1
97/8 PCC-CramersChoice 1
97/8 PCC-Gold 1, -Slapshot 1A
97/8 PacificCrownRoyale 2
97/8 PCR-Blades 1,-Cramers 1
97/8 PCR-HatTrick 1,-Lamp 1
97/8 PacificInvincible 3, -Attack 1
97/8 PacificDynagon! 3, 135
97/8 PacificD-BestKept 2, 103
97/8 PacificD-Dyn 1A, -Kings 1
97/8 PacificD-Tandem 2, 24
97/8 PacificInv.-Feature 1, -Off 1
97/8 P.Paramount 2, -CdnGrt 1
97/8 PcfcP-BigNu 1,-Photoen 1
98/9 PcfcParamnt 3, -SpecDel 1
97/8 PacificRegime 4, 215
97/8 PacificRevolution 2
97/8 PcfcRev -Icon 1,-TeamCL 1
95/6 PaniniSticker 227, 300
96/7 PaniniSticker 153, 222
97/8 PaniniSticker 121, 183
94/5 Parkhurst seV 1
95/6 Parkhurst 3, PP15, PP46
95/6 PH-Crown(1) 4, (2) 4
94/5 ParkieSE 8
94/5 Pinnacle 265, 480, RTP9
95/6 Pinnacle 2,-Clear 3, -Roar 2
96/7 Pinnacle 184, -TeamPin 6
97/8 Pinnacle 53, -TeamP 4
96/7 P.BAP L1H6B, -Biscuit 20
97/8 P.BAP-OneTimers 5
97/8 P.BeeHive 31,-TeamBH 1
97/8 PinnacleCert. 34, -Team 9
97/8 Pinnacle-EPIX 19
95/6 PinnacleFANtasy 26
97/8 PinnInside -Can10,-Track 4
96/7 PinnacleMint 5
97/8 Pinnacle Mint 2
95/6 PinnZenith 17, -Team 14
96/7 PinnacleZenith 90, -Team 2
97/8 PlaymateProZone
95/6 Playoff 2, 114, 223
96/7 Playoff 363
95/6 POG 17, 32
95/6 Post 20
96/7 Post, -StickUm 4
97/8 Post
97/8 Post F6
93/4 PowerPlay 485
93/4 Premier -TeamCanada 17
94/5 Premier 405
95/6 ProMagnet 39
94/5 Score CT1, TR1
95/6 Score 125,-DrmT 7,-GldB 9
96/7 Score 8,-DrmT 2,-SddnD 13
97/8 Score 84, 260, 270
97/8 Score(ANA) 1
94/5 Select 173, YE5
95/6 SelectCertified 13,-Future 3
96/7 SelectCert.14,-Corner 11
95 Semic 86, 206
94 SemicSticker 104
95/6 SkBxEmotion 3, -Xcited 15
95/6 SkBxImp. 3, 230, -Countd 7
96/7 SBI 2,-Countdwn 6,-Versa 6
94/5 SP 1
95/6 SP 1, E1, FX2
96/7 SP 1, CW5, GF9
97/8 SPAuthentic 6, I11
96/7 SPx 1
97/8 SPx 1, SPX19
98/9 SPx"Finite" 116, 153, 179
96/7 SportFX MiniStix
97/8 SportFX MiniStix
95/6 Summit 2, -GM19
96/7 Summit 116,-Volt 3,-Untc 7
95/6 SuperSticker 2, Die-Cut 12
96/7 TeamOut
95/6 Topps 7, 217, 5NG
95/6 Topps HGC7, M13, YS1
98/9 Topps 53 I1
94/5 ToppsFinest 7, -BB(Red) 1
95/6 ToppsFinest 165, 189
95 ToppsFinestBronze 9
96/7 T.NHLPicks FT11, TS4
95/6 TSC EC174, G1, N9
94/5 TSC-MembersOnly 46
95/6 TSCMembersOnly 2
97/8 ToppsSticker 5
95/6 ToppsSuperSkills 16
91/2 UD'CzechWJC 50
92/3 UpperDeck 586
93/4 UpperDeck E10
94/5 UD 235, 527,C2, H14,SP91
95/6 UD 206, 245,AS14, F9, R43
95/6 UD SE1,-ASPredict MVP6
96/7 UD 1,55,HH9,LS12,SS1B
96/7 UD X1,-AllStarYCTG A2
97/8 UD 211, S9, SG9, SS9
97/8 UD T3C, -BlowUp
94/5 UDBAP R103, R126, R151
94/5 UDBAP VC9, -Aut. 151
95/6 UDBeAPlayer LL10
96/7 UDBlackDiamond 175, RC8
97/8 UDBlackDiamond 14, PC26
98/9 UDChoice 4, 224, 240
98/9 UDChoice BH11, SQ25
95/6 UDCC 159, 363, 370, C10
96/7 UDCC1,289,309,C24,UD10
97/8 UDCC 9, 318, C9, S9,SQ85
97/8 udDiamondVision 6
96/7 UpperDeck"Ice" 76, S6
97/8 UpperDeckIce 85, IC9, L1A
96 Wien 94
97/8 Zenith 15, Z45, -ZTeam 6
94/5 ANA/Carl'sJr 10
95/6 ANA
96/7 ANA/UpFrontSports 22
92/3 Maine (2) 20
93/4 Maine 37, 41, 60-61

KARJALA, PEKKA
78/9 SM-Liiga 135

KARJALAINEN, KYOSTI
94/5 ElitSet 261
95/6 ElitSet 105
91/2 Parkhurst 295
90/1 ProCards 350
91/2 ProCards 398
89/90 SemicElitserien 4
92/3 SemicElitserien 193
91/2 UpperDeck 606
92/3 UpperDeck 111, E6
95/6 udElite 163
97/8 udSwedish 173, 219

KARJALAINEN, PETRI
80/1 Mallasjuoma 169
78/9 SM-Liiga 176

KARJALAINEN, SAMI
95/6 Sisu 238

KARJALAINEN, VESA
92/3 Jyvas-Hyva 90
94/5 Sisu 291
95/6 Sisu 145
95/6 SIsuLimited 96

KARKKAINEN, PENTTI
66/7 Champion 133

KARLANDER, AL
70/1 EddieSargent 58
70/1 Esso Stamp
76/7 opcWHA 104
71/2 TheTorontoSun

KARLANDER, KORY
91/2 AirCanadaSJHL 15, D4

KARLBERG, MICAEL
95/6 ElitSet 237
91/2 SemicElitserien 274
92/3 SemicElitserien 293
95/6 udElite 104

KARLIN, MATTIAS
98/9 UDChoice 290

KARLSSON, ANDREAS
94/5 ElitSet 226, -RookRocket 9
95/6 ElitSet 67
95/6 udElite 110
97/8 udSwedish 105

KARLSSON, BENGT-GÖRAN
72 SemicSticker 65

KARLSSON, BERT-OLAV
90/1 SemicElitserien 68

KARLSSON, JACOB
95/6 ElitSet 291
89/90 SemicElitserien 84
90/1 SemicElitserien 257
91/2 SemicElitserien 88
92/3 SemicElitserien 108
92/3 UpperDeck 229
97/8 udSwedish 185

KARLSSON, JAN
89/90 SemicElitserien 248, 266
90/1 SemicElitserien 155
91/2 SemicElitserien 260

KARLSSON, LARS
94/5 ElitSet 231
95/6 ElitSet 168
89/90 SemicElitserien 94
90/1 SemicElitserien 265
91/2 SemicElitserien 30, 93
92/3 SemicElitserien 52, 121

KARLSSON, MARCUS
95/6 DEL 75
95/6 ElitSet 277, -Rookies 8
91/2 SemicElitserien 326
95/6 udElite 158
97/8 udSwedish 155

KARLSSON, MARTIN
96/7 DEL 269

KARLSSON, PENTTI
78/9 SM-Liiga 134
72/3 WilliamsFIN 83
73/4 WilliamsFIN 130

KARLSSON, PETER
92/3 SemicElitserien 282

KARLSSON, RAUNO
70/1 Kuvajulkaisut 295

KARLSSON, ROGER
92/3 SemicElitserien 58

KARLSSON, RONNIE
92/3 SemicElitserien 28

KARLSSON, STEFAN
72 Hellas 32
74 Hellas 27
70/1 Kuvajulkaisut 29
69/70 MästarSerien 45
72 Panda
72 SemicSticker 51
74 SemicSticker 14
71/2 WilliamsFIN 48
72/3 WilliamsFIN 49
73/4 WilliamsFIN 29

KARLSTAD, JON MAGNE
93 SemicSticker 235

KARPA, DAVE
92/3 Classic 68
93/4 FleerUltra 97, -UltraProp 3
98/9 Pacific 57
97/8 PacificDynag-BestKept 3
92/3 Parkhurst 151
93/4 Parkhurst 165
95/6 Parkhurst 273
94/5 ParkieSE 145
96/7 PinnacleBeAPlayer 41
93/4 PowerPlay 421
93/4 Premier 408
94/5 Premier 202
93/4 Score 611
97/8 Score(ANA) 19
93/4 ToppsStadiumClub 296
92/3 UpperDeck 517
93/4 Upper Deck 375
94/5 UpperDeck 41
95/6 UpperDeck 119
97/8 UpperDeck 217
95/6 UDCollChoice 192
95/6 ANA
96/7 ANA/UpFrontSports 17
92/3 QUE/PetroCanada
91/2 FerrisState

KARPEN, MARK
90/1 KansasCity 17

KARPENKO, IGOR
96/7 LasVegas

KARPOV, VALERI
93/4 Classic 90
94/5 Classic 43, R11, T1
93/4 ClassicProspects IA20
95/6 Donruss 191
94/5 Fleer 4
94/5 Leaf 486, -Phenom 10
95/6 Leaf 80
94/5 LeafLimited 51
95/6 Parkhurst 277
94/5 ParkieSE 6
94/5 Pinnacle 486,-RTP11
95/6 POG 19
94/5 Premier 284
95/6 Score 170
94/5 Select 183
94/5 SRGoldStandard 87, GS9
94/5 SRTetrad CVII
95/6 Topps 137
94/5 UD 256, 570, SP92, C6
95/6 UpperDeck 378, SE93
95/6 UDBeAPlayer 205
95/6 UDCollChoice 211
94/5 ANA/Carl'sJr 11

KARPOVTSEV, ALEXANDER
93/4 Classic 89
94/5 Classic AR6
93/4 ClassicProspects 19
93/4 Donruss 212
94/5 Donruss 327
93/4 FleerUltra 372
94/5 Leaf 118
91/2 O-Pee-Chee 35R
97/8 PacificCrown 223
97/8 PaniniSticker 90
93/4 Parkhurst 269
95/6 Parkhurst 142
94/5 ParkieSE 114
93/4 Pinnacle 437
94/5 Pinnacle 364
96/7 PinnacleBeAPlayer 118
95/6 POG 188
93/4 Power Play 391
93/4 Premier 358
94/5 Premier 255
92/3 RedAce(Violet) 10
93/4 Score 591
97/8 Score(NYR) 8
93 SemicSticker 133
94 SemicSticker 138
93/4 ToppsStadiumClub 291
92/3 UpperDeck 351
93/4 UpperDeck 484, -SP 100
94/5 UpperDeck 288
95/6 UpperDeck 288
95/6 UDBeAPlayer 118
97/8 UDCollChoice 169

KARPUK, KENNETH
94/5 DEL 174
95/6 DEL 222

KARRENBAUER, BERND
74 Hellas 105
70/1 Kuvajulkaisut 88

KARSALO, VESA
66/7 Champion 208

KARTIO, DAVE
74/5 SiouxCity

KARTTUNEN, JOHANNES
66/7 Champion 28
65/6 Hellas 66

KARVONEN, JORMA
72/3 WilliamsFIN 286

KARVONEN, PEKKA
72/3 WilliamsFIN 287

KASATONOV, ALEXEI
91/2 Bowman 276
92/3 Bowman 323
93/4 Donruss 5
93/4 EASports 1
92/3 FleerUltra 340
93/4 FleerUltra 257
94/5 FleerUltra 257
95 Globe 237
91 IvanFiodorovSportUnites
93/4 Leaf 381
94/5 Leaf 473
90/1 OPC/Topps 358
91/2 OPC/Topps 439
92/3 O-Pee-Chee 353
90/1 PaniniSticker 335
91/2 PaniniSticker 216
92/3 PaniniSticker 180
91/2 Parkhurst 319
93/4 Parkhurst 2276
94/5 Parkhurst 195
95/6 Parkhurst 15
94/5 ParkieSE 9
91/2 Pinnacle 255
92/3 Pinnacle 289
93/4 Pinnacle 359
94/5 Pinnacle 398
95/6 Playoff 6
94/5 POG 37
95/6 POG 37
93/4 PowerPlay 5
93/4 Premier 492
94/5 Premier 159
90/1 ProSet 169
92/3 ProSet 101
91/2 PSPlatinum 198
91/2 RedAce
90/1 Score 209
91/2 Score(CDN) 194, (U.S) 194
92/3 Score 394
93/4 Score 61, 528
94/5 Score 183
82 SemicSticker 57
89 SemicSticker 81
91 SemicSticker 214
92 SemicSticker 101
94 SemicSticker 143
83/4 SovietStars
87/8 SovietStars
89/90 SovietStars
88 SovietTeam 14
92/3 Topps 152
91/2 ToppsStadiumClub 282
92/3 ToppsStadiumClub 406
93/4 ToppsStadiumClub 332
93/4 Upper Deck 474
90/1 UpperDeck 286
91/2 UpperDeck 185
92/3 UpperDeck 96
94/5 UpperDeck 208
95/6 UpperDeck 69
95/6 UDCollChoice 115
90/1 N.J.

KASKI, JARI
73/4 WilliamsFIN 246

KASKI, MATTI
65/6 Hellas 145

KASKI, OLLI
96/7 DEL 154
94/5 ElitSet 171, -ForeignAffair 8
92/3 Jyvas-Hyva 196
93/4 Jyvas-Hyva 345
95 Semic 32
93/4 Sisu 212
94/5 Sisu 365
95/6 Sisu 353, -DoubleTrouble 3
95/6 SisuLimited 20

KASKI, PEKKA
95/6 APS 81
78/9 SM-Liiga 79

KASLAK, KAMIL
93/4 Sisu 193

KASOWSKI, PETER
92/3 Dayton

KASPARAITIS, DARIUS
92/3 Classic 4, LP4
92/3 CSC 6
93/4 Donruss 203
94/5 Donruss 252
93/4 EASports 80
94/5 Fleer 122
92/3 FleerUltra 344
93/4 FleerUltra 160
94/5 FleerUltra 129
93/4 Leaf 101
94/5 Leaf 27
95/6 Leaf 235
92/3 opcPremier 103
98/9 Pacific 354
97/8 PacificCrown 61
97/8 PacificParamount 151
98/9 PacificParamount 193
94/5 PaniniSticker 52
95/6 PaniniSticker 96
97/8 PaniniSticker 46
92/3 Parkhurst 102, 215
93/4 Parkhurst 122
94/5 Parkhurst 133
95/6 Parkhurst 402
92/3 Pinnacle 407
93/4 Pinnacle 84
94/5 Pinnacle 26
97/8 PinnacleBeAPlayer 159
94/5 POG 161
93/4 PowerPlay 149, -2ndYr 3
93/4 Premier 112, 443
94/5 Premier 211
92/3 RedAce(Blue) 1, (Violet) 11
93/4 Score 124, -Int'lStar 17
94/5 Score 11, -CheckIt 13
95/6 Score 40
97/8 Score 162
97/8 Score(PGH) 10
93 SemicSticker 146
96/7 SP 129
96/7 TeamOut
93/4 ToppsStadiumClub 101
91/2 UD 650, 'CzechWJC 11
92/3 UD 335, 554, 563, 623
93/4 UpperDeck 173, -SP 91
94/5 UpperDeck 298, SP46
95/6 UpperDeck 447
96/7 UpperDeck 293, P11
97/8 UpperDeck 136, 391
94/5 UDBAP R148, -Aut 142
96/7 UDBlackDiamond 61
92/3 UDCollChoice 13, ER7
95/6 UDCollChoice 2
96/7 UDCollChoice 162
97/8 UDCollChoice 211
96/7 PGH/FotoPuck

KASPER, OLIVER
94/5 DEL 352

KASPER, PETER
95 PaniniWorld

KASPER, STEVE
90/1 Bowman 147
91/2 Bowman 187
92/3 Bowman 33
92/3 Durivage 4
81/2 OPC 4, Topps(E) 68
82/3 O-Pee-Chee 12
83/4 O-Pee-Chee 50
85/6 OPC/Topps 79
86/7 OPC/Topps 97
87/8 OPC/Topps 162
88/9 OPC/Topps 176
89/90 OPC/Topps 194
90/1 OPC/Topps 153
91/2 OPC/Topps 302
91/2 opcPremier 85
81/2 opcSticker 51
82/3 opcSticker 81, 253
83/4 opcSticker 53
86/7 opcSticker 40/177
87/8 opcSticker 66B
88/9 opcSticker 27/156
89/90 opcSticker 152/12
87/8 PaniniSticker 15
88/9 PaniniSticker 210
89/90 PaniniSticker 92
90/1 PaniniSticker 238
91/2 PaniniSticker 88
92/3 Parkhurst 403
82/3 Post
93/4 Premier 73
90/1 ProSet 120
91/2 ProSet 449
90/1 Score 247
91/2 Score(CDN) 574
91/2 Score(U.S) 256
91/2 ScoreTraded 24T
92/3 Score 306
92/3 Topps 150
91/2 ToppsStadiumClub 139
92/3 ToppsStadiumClub 71
93/4 ToppsStadiumClub 122
90/1 UpperDeck 140
91/2 UpperDeck 576
83/4 BOS
84/5 BOS
88/9 BOS/SportsAction
89/90 L.A./Smokeys 5
90/1 L.A./Smokeys 7
91/2 PHA/JCPenney
92/3 PHA/UD 19NOV92
92/3 T.B./Sheraton

KASPERCZYK, JEDRZEJ
94/5 DEL 156
95/6 DEL 157
96/7 DEL 212
89 SemicSticker 139
92 SemicSticker 286

KASSLATTER, FABRIZIO
79 PaniniSticker 391

KASTAK, KAMIL
95 Globe 162
95 PaniniWorlds 199
94 Semic 175
92/3 SemicElitserien 143
92 SemicSticker 133
93 SemicSticker 107
93/4 Sisu 193

KASTELIC, ED
90/1 O-Pee-Chee 404
90/1 ProSet 450
89/90 HFD/JuniorWhalers
90/1 HFD/JuniorWhalers
91/2 HFD/JuniorWhalers
87/8 WSH
87/8 WSH/Kodak
84/5 Moncton 24
92/3 Phoenix

KASTELIC, JOE
52/3 AnonymousOHL 31

KASTNER, MILAN
94/5 APS 91

KASZYCKI, MIKE
78/9 OPC/Topps 171
79/80 OPC/Topps 87
80/1 O-Pee-Chee 371
79/80 NYI

KATAINEN, PENTTI
65/6 Hellas 60

KATELNIKOFF, TRACEY
86/7 Saskatoon
89/90 Saskatoon 18

KATHAN, PETER
94/5 DEL 173

KAUFMANN, BEAT
72 SemicSticker 156

KAUHANEN, HEIKKI
71/2 WilliamsFIN 244
73/4 WilliamsFIN 311

KAUHANEN, ILPO
94/5 Sisu 278
95/6 Sisu 108, -Ghost 10
96/7 Sisu 122, -Mighty 3
90/1 SketchOHL 33
91/2 SketchOHL 19
91/2 Cornwall 13

KAUHANEN, TIMO
95/6 Sisu 298

KAUKOKARI, MAURI
70/1 Kuvajulkaisut 108
72 Panda
71/2 WilliamsFIN 116
72/3 WilliamsFIN 84
73/4 WilliamsFIN 131

KAUNONEN, ARTO
78/9 SM-Liiga 206
71/2 WilliamsFIN 190
72/3 WilliamsFIN 228
73/4 WilliamsFIN 262

KAUPINSALO, KARI
80/1 Mallasjuoma 125
78/9 SM-Liiga 154

KAUPPILA, JARI
92/3 Jyvas-Hyva 147
93/4 Jyvas-Hyva 268
94/5 Sisu 230
95/6 Sisu 26
96/7 Sisu 21

KAUPPILA, KARI
80/1 Mallasjuoma 184
78/9 SM-Liiga 210
72/3 WilliamsFIN 211
73/4 WilliamsFIN 284

KAUPPILA, MATTI
73/4 WilliamsFIN 285

KAUTONEN, VELI-PEKKA
96/7 DEL 266
92/3 Jyvas-Hyva 166
93/4 Jyvas-Hyva 299
93/4 Sisu 68
94/5 Sisu 265
95/6 Sisu 198

KAUTTO, MATTI
65/6 Hellas 103

KAVEC, IGNAC
79 PaniniSticker 397

KAWAMURA, KATSUTOSHI
79 PaniniSticker 289

KAY, A.
28/9 PaulinsCandy 55

KAYSER, STEVE
84/5 Ottawa67s

KAZUIK, GARNET
84/5 Brandon 1

KE, CHENG
79 PaniniSticker 356

KEA, ED
75/6 O-Pee-Chee 383
76/7 O-Pee-Chee 361
77/8 O-Pee-Chee 301
78/9 O-Pee-Chee 277
79/80 O-Pee-Chee 390
81/2 OPC 294, Topps(W) 118
82/3 Post
77/8 ATL
78/9 ATL/Coke

KEALTY, JEFF
93/4 Classic 104
95/6 DonrussElite-WorldJrs 28

KEAN, FRED
85/6 London 28
86/7 London 28

KEAN, MITCH
94/5 Huntington 15

KEANE, MIKE
91/2 Bowman 334
92/3 Bowman 290
93/4 Donruss 451
94/5 Donruss 134
92/3 FleerUltra 106
93/4 FleerUltra 196
94/5 FleerUltra 110
93/4 HockeyWit 63
92/3 HumptyDumpty(1)
93/4 Leaf 279
90/1 OPC/Topps 325
91/2 OPC/Topps 434
92/3 O-Pee-Chee 274
98/9 Pacific 178
97/8 PacificCrown 239
91/2 PaniniSticker 190
95/6 PaniniSticker 40
91/2 Parkhurst 311
92/3 Parkhurst 318
91/2 Pinnacle 265
92/3 Pinnacle 164
93/4 Pinnacle 339
94/5 Pinnacle 151
95/6 Pinnacle 83
97/8 PinnacleBeAPlayer 101
94/5 POG 135
95/6 POG 149
93/4 PowerPlay 129
93/4 Premier 139
94/5 Premier 497
90/1 ProSet 151
91/2 ProSet 121
91/2 PSPlatinum 191
90/1 ScoreTraded 102T
91/2 Score(CDN) 251, (U.S) 360
92/3 Score 179
93/4 Score 170
94/5 Score 187
95/6 Score 266
97/8 Score(NYR) 3
98/9 SPx"Finite" 27
92/3 Topps 478
95/6 Topps 281
91/2 ToppsStadiumClub 236
92/3 ToppsStadiumClub 349
93/4 ToppsStadiumClub 92
94/5 ToppsStadiumClub 18
95/6 ToppsStadiumClub 43
90/1 UpperDeck 382
92/3 UpperDeck 164
95/6 UpperDeck 388
97/8 UpperDeck 315
95/6 UDBeAPlayer 103
95/6 UDCollChoice 153
97/8 UDCollChoice 63
88/9 MTL
89/90 MTL
89/90 MTL/Kraft
90/1 MTL
91/2 MTL
92/3 MTL
93/4 MTL
93/4 MTL/Molson
94/5 MTL
95/6 MTL

KEANS, DOUG
84/5 O-Pee-Chee 5, Topps 4
85/6 OPC/Topps 133
86/7 OPC/Topps 22
87/8 OPC/Topps 147
87/8 opcSticker 139/249
87/8 PaniniSticker 4
88/9 ProCards(Baltimore)
84/5 BOS
78/9 Saginaw

KEARNS, DENNIS
72/3 EddieSargent 224
74/5 Loblaws
71/2 OPC/Topps 231
73/4 OPC 162, Topps 173
74/5 OPC 366
75/6 OPC/Topps 188
76/7 OPC 338, 395
77/8 OPC/Topps 175
78/9 OPC/Topps 191
79/80 OPC/Topps 76
80/1 OPC 392
81/2 OPC 337
81/2 opcSticker 249
79 PaniniSticker 58
80/1 Pepsi Cap
71/2 TheTorontoSun
71/2 VAN/RoyalBank 13
72/3 VAN/RoyalBank
73/4 VAN/RoyalBank
74/5 VAN/RoyalBank
75/6 VAN/RoyalBank
76/7 VAN/RoyalBank
77/8 VAN/GingerAle
77/8 VAN/RoyalBank
78/9 VAN/RoyalBank
79/80 VAN
80/1 VAN
80/1 VAN/Silverwood

KEATING, JOHN (JACK)
33-43 BeeHives(DET)
39/40 OPC (V301-1) 67

KEATING, MIKE
75/6 Hamilton

KEATS, GORDON (DUKE)
83&87 HallOfFame 54
83 HHOF Postcard (D)
93/4 HHOFLegends 20
23/4 PaulinsCandy 45

KECZMER, DAN
93/4 Donruss 406
91/2 O-Pee-Chee 3S
93/4 Parkhurst 82
93/4 Pinnacle 218
93/4 PowerPlay 304
93/4 Premier 461
90/1 ProCards 114
94/5 ToppsStadiumClub 262
93/4 UpperDeck 249
95/6 UpperDeck 410
91/2 HFD/JuniorWhalers

KEELING, MELVILLE (BUTCH)
33/4 Anonymous (V129) 30
33-43 BeeHives(NYR)
33-35 DiamondMatch
36-39 DiamondMatch ((1), 2), (3)
33/4 OPC (V304A) 36
33/4 WWGum (V357) 20
36/7 WWGum (V356) 15

KEENAN, CORY
89/90 SketchOHL 179
94/5 AutoPhonex 20
89/90 SketchMEM 40
87/8 Kitchener 11
88/9 Kitchener 11
89/90 Kitchener 12

KEENAN, LARRY
71/2 EddieSargent 31
70/1 Esso Stamp
68/9 OPC/Topps 115
70/1 OPC/Topps 104
61/2 Parkhurst 13
61/2 ShirriffCoin 55
68/9 ShirriffCoin STL9
71/2 TheTorontoSun
61/2 York 32

KEENAN, MIKE
88/9 CHI/Coke
89/90 CHI/Coke
90/1 CHI/Coke
91/2 CHI/Coke
86/7 PHA

KEHLE, MARKUS
94/5 DEL 79
95/6 DEL 298

KEHLE, TONI
72 SemicSticker 93

KEHOE, RICK
72/3 EddieSargent 209
84/5 Kelloggs Disk
74/5 Loblaws
73/4 MacsMilk Disk
72/3 OPC 277
73/4 OPC 60, Topps 179
74/5 OPC/Topps 81
75/6 OPC/Topps 39
76/7 OPC/Topps 124
77/8 OPC/Topps 33
78/9 OPC/Topps 213
79/80 OPC/Topps 109
80/1 OPC/Topps 18, 117
81/2 OPC 254, 260, 267
84/5 7ElevenDisk
83/4 SouhaitsRen.KeyChain
81/2 Topps 17, 60, (East) 128
82/3 O-Pee-Chee 271
83/4 O-Pee-Chee 274, 282
84/5 OPC 177, Topps 125
81/2 opcSticker 182, 261
82/3 opcSticker 143
83/4 opcSticker 11, 231-32
84/5 opcSticker 117
82/3 Post
83/4 PuffySticker 8
74/5 PGH
77/8 PGH/PuckBuck
83/4 PGH/Heinz
84/5 PGH/Heinz
93/4 PGH/Foodland 6
95/6 PGH/Foodland 11
72/3 TOR
73/4 TOR

KEILLER, IAN
91/2 SketchOHL 104

KEILLER, JIM
36/7 WWGum (V356) 120

KEINONEN, HEIKI
66/7 Champion 176
70/1 Kuvajulkaisut 243
71/2 WilliamsFIN 210

KEINONEN, HEIMO
70/1 Kuvajulkaisut 244
71/2 WilliamsFIN 211
72/3 WilliamsFIN 158
73/4 WilliamsFIN 220

KEINONEN, MATTI
66/7 Champion 26
65/6 Hellas 23
92/3 Jyvas-Hyva 120
70/1 Kuvajulkaisut 61, 229
72 SemicSticker 91
77-80 Sportscaster 40-937
71/2 WilliamsFIN 152
72/3 WilliamsFIN 62, 104
73/4 WilliamsFIN 64, 197

KEKALAINEN, JANNE
93/4 Sisu 174
94/5 Sisu 21
94/5 Sisu 278
96/7 Sisu 79
95/6 SisuLimited 71

KEKÄLÄINEN, JARMO
93/4 ClassicProspects 198
94/5 ElitSet 229, -ForeignAff 7
91/2 Jyvas-Hyva 33
92/3 Jyvas-Hyva 158
93/4 Parkhurst 410
94 Semic 26
92 SemicSticker 22
93 SemicSticker 65
91/2 UpperDeck 108, E1
93/4 OTT/Kraft

KELFER, MIKE
89/90 ProCards(AHL) 246
90/1 ProCards 592
90/1 KansasCity 16

KELHAM, A.J.
91/2 SketchWHL 237

KELLAND, CHRIS
94 Semic 316
95/6 SheffieldSteelers
96/7 SheffieldSteelers

KELLER, AARON
95/6 SlapshotMEM 07
93/4 Kamloops

KELLER, FLORIAN
94/5 DEL 386
95/6 DEL 374
96/7 DEL 174

KELLER, HANS
72 SemicSticker 143

KELLER, JOHN
84/5 Kitchener 24

KELLER, RYAN
91/2 AvantGardeBC 57
92/3 BCJHL 213
91/2 Nainamo

KELLETT, KEVIN
95/6 PrinceAlbert

KELLIN, TRAVIS
90/1 SketchWHL 21

KELLOG, ALLAN
52/3 AnonymousOHL 24

KELLOGG, BOB
93/4 ClassicProspects 63
93/4 Indianapolis

KELLY, BOB (HOUND DOG)
71/2 EddieSargent 157
72/3 EddieSargent 163
70/1 Esso Stamp
74/5 Loblaws
71/2 OPC/Topps 203
73/4 O-Pee-Chee 253
74/5 O-Pee-Chee 380
75/6 OPC/Topps 184
76/7 OPC/Topps 219
77/8 OPC/Topps 178
78/9 OPC/Topps 71
79/80 OPC/Topps 14
81/2 OPC 349, Topps(E)
81/2 opcSticker 195
92/3 Parkhurst 477
71/2 TheTorontoSun
75/6 PHA/GingerAle
74/5 PGH
80/1 WSH

KELLY, BROCK
89/90 Nashville

KELLY, CHUCK
67/8 ColumbusCheckers

KELLY, J. BOB (BATTLESHIP)
74/5 OPC/Topps 143
75/6 OPC/Topps 263
76/7 OPC/Topps 261
77/8 OPC/Topps 14
78/9 OPC/Topps 189
79/80 OPC 306
73/4 STL

KELLY, J.P.
82/3 PostCereal
84/5 L.A./Smokeys

KELLY, JIM
91/2 ProSet 293

KELLY, KENDEL
92/3 BCJHL 2

KELLY, LEONARD (RED)
45-64 BeeHives(DET),(TORx2)
64-67 BeeHives(TOR)
62 CeramicTiles
63-5 ChexPhoto
64/5 CokeCap TOR-4
65/6 CocaCola
83&87 HallOfFame 55
83 HHOF Postcard (D)
94/5 HHOFLegends 53
91/2 Kraft 81
74/5 OPC/Topps 76
51/2 Parkhurst 55
52/3 Parkhurst 67
53/4 Parkhurst 40
54/5 Parkhurst 42, 91
60/1 Parkhurst 9
61/2 Parkhurst 9
62/3 Parkhurst 5
63/4 Parkhurst 3, 63
92/3 Parkhurst PR10
93/4 Parkie(56/7) 52, 142, 154
94/5 Parkie(64/65) 127
95/6 Parkie(66/7) 109
52 RoyalDesserts 7
60/1 ShirriffCoin 4
61/2 ShirriffCoin 49
62/3 ShirriffCoin 9
54-67 TorontoStar V8
56-66 TorontoStar 57/8
63/4 TheTorontoStar
54/5 Topps 5
57/8 Topps 48
58/9 Topps 61
59/60 Topps 65
64/5 Topps 44
65/6 Topps 15
66/7 Topps 79, -USATest 42
91/2 Ultimate(O6) 38,79, -Aut 79
90/1 UpperDeck 502
60/1 York, -Glasses
61/2 York 21
62/3 YorkTransfer 20
63/4 York 12
94/5 Zellers
71/2 PGH
64/5 TOR
68/9 TOR
73/4 TOR

KELLY, MARK
95/6 Toledo

KELLY, MIKE
89/90 SketchOHL 47

KELLY, PAT
77/8 COLR./CokeCans
86/7 London 26

KELLY, PAUL
88/9 ProCards(NewHaven)
89/90 ProCards(AHL) 3

KELLY, PETER C.
33-43 BeeHives(DET)
35-40 CrownBrand 63

KELLY, PETER
87/8 Brockville 3
88/9 Brockville 2

KELLY, RED
see Leonard "Red" Kelly

KELLY, REG (PEP)
33/43 BeeHives(TOR)
35/6 Champion
35/6 OPC (V304C) 87
37/8 OPC (V304E) 145
39/40 OPC (V301-1) 9
38/9 QuakerOats
36/7 WWGum 86

KELLY, STEVE
95/6 Classic 6, AS6, BK6
95/6 ClassicFiveSport 128, -Aut
94/5 ClassicImages 39, -PD3
97/8 Donruss 216, -RatedRook 8
97/8 DonrussCanadianIce 130
97/8 Limited 107
96/7 MetalUniverse 183
97/8 PinnacleInside 117
97/8 UpperDeck 188
96/7 EDM
97/8 EDM
93/4 PrinceAlbert
95/6 PrinceAlbert

KELMAN, TODD
92/3 BCJHL 198

KEMP, DYLAN
95/6 PrinceAlbert

KEMP, JOHN
82/3 Kingston 13

KEMPER, ANDREW
91/2 SketchWHL 128
93/4 Saskatoon

KEMPF, MARKUS
94/5 DEL 116
95/6 DEL 117

KEMPPAINEN, HANNU
80/1 Mallasjuoma 120
78/9 SM-Liiga 166

KEMPPAINEN, PASI
94/5 Sisu 310
95/6 Sisu 282

KEMPPI, MIIKKA
94/5 Sisu 271
95/6 Sisu 118

KEMPPINEN, JYRI
71/2 WilliamsFIN 324

KENADY, CHRIS
95/6 Classic 75, -Aut.
95/6 ClassicFiveSport 139

KENDALL, CARL
1912-13 Imperial (C57) 35

KENDALL, WILLIAM
33-43 BeeHives(TOR)
33-35 DiamondMatch
36-39 DiamondMatch (1), (2)

KENNEDY, BOB
88/9 Flint
89/90 Johnstown 24

KENNEDY, DEAN
90/1 Bowman 248
93/4 KraftDisks
94/5 Leaf 500
91/2 OPC/Topps 388
87/8 PaniniSticker 276
92/3 Pinnacle 239
93/4 Pinnacle 178
90/1 ProSet 22
90/1 Score 299
91/2 Score(CDN) 431
92/3 Score 211
93/4 Score 366
83/4 SouhaitsRen.KeyChain
90/1 UpperDeck 380
89/90 BUF/BlueShield
89/90 BUF/Campbell
90/1 BUF/BlueShield
90/1 BUF/Campbell
88/9 L.A.
91/2 WPG/IGA
93/4 WPG/Ruffles
82/3 Brandon 3

KENNEDY, FORBES
45-64 BeeHives(CHI), (DET)
64-67 BeeHives(BOS)
64/5 CokeCap BOS-14
65/6 CocaCola
68/9 OPC/Topps 97
93/4 Parkie(56/7) 35
68/9 ShirriffCoin PHA10
64/5 TheTorontoStar
57/8 Topps 50
58/9 Topps 11
59/60 Topps 52
63/4 Topps 19

KENNEDY, JOE
92/3 BCJHL 89

KENNEDY, MIKE
94/5 ClassicImages 73
93/4 ClassicProspects 79
95/6 Donruss 192
95/6 EdgeIce 140, C14
94/5 Fleer 54
95/6 FleerUltra 39
95//6 Leaf 7
95/6 PaniniSticker 171
91/2 SketchWHL 131
95/6 Topps 27, 7NG
94/5 UpperDeck 326
95/6 UDCollChoice 205
94/5 DAL/Southwest
96/7 DAL/Southwest

KENNEDY, RON
95/6 DEL 123
96/7 DEL 22

KENNEDY, RON
77/8 Kalamazoo

KENNEDY, SHELDON
97/8 Aces 10 (Spades)
93/4 Leaf 246
90/1 O-Pee-Chee 520
91/2 OPC/Topps 317
97/8 PacificRegime 13
93/4 Premier 221
94/5 Premier 408
89/90 ProCards(AHL) 320
91/2 ProCards 134
93/4 Score 361
92/3 Topps 368
91/2 UpperDeck 408
94/5 UpperDeck 437
97/8 UDCollChoice 21
90/1 DET/Caesars
91/2 DET/Caesars

KENNEDY, TED (TEEDER)
45-64 BeeHives(TOR)
64-67 BeeHives(TOR)
48-52 Exhibits
83&87 HallOfFame 69
83 HHOF Postcard (E)
95/6 HHOFLegends 65
51/2 Parkhurst 86
52/3 Parkhurst 44
53/4 Parkhurst 7
54/5 Parkhurst 29, 96, 99
55/6 Parkhurst 29
93/4 Parkie(56/7) 116, 166
45-54 QuakerOats
54-67 TorontoStar V 4,n4

KENNEDY, TROY
88/9 Brandon 9
85/6 Kamloops

KENNEDY, SHANE
94/5 AutoPhonex 21
95/6 Classic 42, 93
95/6 ClassicFiveSport 158
95/6 Slapshot 283
93/4 OwenSound

KENNEY, NICK
96/7 Cincinnati

KENNHOLT, KENNETH
94/5 ElitSet 5
95/6 ElitSet 50, -Champs 14
95/6 ElitSet -FaceToFace 6
89/90 SemicElitserien 56
90/1 SemicElitserien 277
91/2 SemicElitserien 58, 344
92/3 SemicElitserien 79
91 SemicSticker 37
93 SemicSticker 3
95/6 udElite 79
97/8 udSwedish 37

KENNY, BRENDAN
92/3 BCJHL 65
93/4 WestMich.

KENNY, ROB
92/3 Binghampton
94/5 Binghampton

KENT, BRIAN
92/3 Oshawa

KEOGAN, MURRAY
74/5 opcWHA 44
75/6 Phoenix

KEON, DAVE
71/2 Bazooka Panel 11
45-64 BeeHives(TOR)
64-67 BeeHives(TORx2)
62 CeramicTiles
63-5 ChexPhoto
64/5 CokeCap TOR-14
65/6 CocaCola B/X
70/1 DadsCookies
70/1 EddieSargent 208
71/2 EddieSargent 206
72/3 EddieSargent 206
62/3 ElProductoDisk
70/1 Esso Stamp
87 HallOfFame 255
95/6 HHOFLegends 58
72/3 Letraset 1
74/5 LiptonSoup 50
74/5 Loblaws
68/9 OPC 198, -Puck 19
69/70 OPC/Topps 51
69/70 OPC-Stamp, -Sticker
70/1 OPC 219
70/1 OPC/T.-Deckle 47, -Sticker
71/2 OPC/Topps 80, 259
71/2 OPC/Topps-Booklet 16
72/3 OPC 108, Topps 88
73/4 OPC 150, Topps 85
74/5 OPC/Topps 151
79/80 O-Pee-Chee 279
80/1 O-Pee-Chee 272
81/2 OPC 129, Topps(E) 83
71/2 opcPoster 3
75/6 opcWHA 97
76/7 opcWHA 52
61/2 Parkhurst 5
62/3 Parkhurst 15
63/4 Parkhurst 75
92/3 Parkhurst PR21
93/4 Parkie(56/7) FS2, PR67
94/5 Parkie(64/5) 111, A6
95/6 Parkie(66/7) 100, 139, 146
95/6 Parkie (66/7) SL6
66/7 Post'Large, -Small
67 Post FlipBook
68/9 Post Marble
82/3 Post
72 SemicSticker 165
61/2 ShirriffCoin 58
62/3 ShirriffCoin 16, 52, 55
68/9 ShirriffCoin TOR11
63/4 TheTorontoStar
64/5 TheTorontoStar
71/2 TheTorontoSun
64/5 Topps 94
65/6 Topps 17
66/7 Topps 78, -USATest 30
67/8 Topps 11
68/9 Topps 128
54-67 TorontoStar V9
56-66 TorontoStar 61/2, 65/6
91/2 Ultimate(O6) 39, -Aut 39
60/1 WonderBread 3
60/1 York, -Glasses
61/2 York 27
62/3 YorkTransfer 9
63/4 York 6
67/8 York 13, 19, d
94/5 Zellers
64/5 TOR
66/7 TOR/Coaster
68/9 TOR
69/70 TOR
71/2 TOR
72/3 TOR
73/4 TOR
74/5 TOR

KERBER, CHRIS
94/5 Birmingham
95/6 Birmingham

KERCH, ALEXANDER
93/4 ClassicProspects 176
90/1 O-Pee-Chee 474
93/4 EDM 29-Oct-93

KERCH, KERRY
82/3 Kitchener 6

KERESZTY, ADAM
79 PaniniSticker 269

KERESZTES, OTTO
94/5 DEL 347

KERR, ALAN
90/1 Bowman 118
88/9 OPC/Topps 63
90/1 OPC/Topps 50, 315
88/9 opcSticker 106/236
88/9 PaniniSticker 288
89/90 PaniniSticker 275
90/1 PaniniSticker 89
91/2 Parkhurst 273
90/1 ProSet 184
91/2 ProSet 376
90/1 Score (CND) 307
91/2 Score(CDN) 571
90/1 UpperDeck 388
84/5 NYI 9
89/90 NYI
84/5 Springfield 8

KERR, ALBERT
91 C55 Reprint 10
1911-12 Imperial (C55) 10
1912-13 Imperial (C57) 33
1910-11 Imperial Post 10

KERR, ALLEN
89/90 SketchMEM 58

KERR, CHRIS
91/2 AvantGardeBC 81, 128
95/6 Slapshot 421

KERR, DAVID
33-43 BeeHives(NYR)
33/4 CndGum (V252)
35-40 CrownBrand 64
36-39 DiamondMatch (2), (3)
27-32 LaPresse 30/1
34/5 OPC (V304B) 59
39/40 OPC (V301-1) 37
40/1 OPC (V301-2) 139
34/5 SweetCaporal
33/4 WWGum (V357) 19
36/7 WWGum (V356) 53

KERR, KEVIN
88/9 ProCards(Rochester)
90/1 ProCards 282
93/4 Birmingham 15
91/2 Cincinnati
83/4 NorthBay

KERR, RANDY
91/2 AirCanadaSJHL C7

KERR, REG
79/80 OPC/Topps 67
80/1 O-Pee-Chee 377
81/2 OPC 58, Topps(W) 70
82/3 O-Pee-Chee 67
81/2 opcSticker 118
82/3 opcSticker 176
82/3 Post
79/80 CHI
80/1 CHI/4x6
81/2 CHI
88/9 EDM/ActionMagazine 75
83/4 Moncton 11

KERR, SCOTT
83/4 Kitchener 14

KERR, TIM
88/9 Esso Sticker
92/3 FleerUltra 74
81/2 OPC 251
82/3 OPC 253
84/5 OPC 162, 364, Topps 119
85/6 OPC/T. 91, H, OPC 260
86/7 OPC/T. 134, G, OPC 261
87/8 OPC/T. 144, B, T-AS 10
89/90 OPC/Topps 72, G
90/1 OPC/Topps 210
91/2 OPC/Topps 164
91/2 opcPremier 83
92/3 opcPremier 127
87/8 OPC Stars 20
84/5 opcSticker 105, 106
85/6 opcSticker 96
86/7 opcSticker 240
87/8 opcSticker 103
89/90 opcSticker 110, 216
87/8 PaniniSticker 128
88/9 PaniniSticker 321
89/90 PaniniSticker 294, 377
90/1 PaniniSticker 120
91/2 PaniniSticker 226
91/2 Pinnacle 52
92/3 Pinnacle 368
82/3 Post
90/1 ProSet 218
91/2 ProSet 180, 446
91/2 PSPlatinum 80
90/1 Score 177, -HotCards 77
91/2 ScoreCDN 108,565,US 108
91/2 ScoreTraded 15T
92/3 Score 93
84/5 7ElevenDisk

85/6 7Eleven 14
92/3 Topps 351
91/2 ToppsStadiumClub 130
90/1 UpperDeck 247, 304
92/3 HFD/DairyMart
83/4 PHA
86/7 PHA
89/90 PHA
90/1 PHA
93/4 PHA 08MAR94

KERRIGAN, STEVE
92/3 Dayton

KERSEY, JADE
91/2 AvantGardeBCJ 44
92/3 BCJHL 99
91/2 Nainamo

KERTH, WERNER
95 PaniniWorlds 266
94 Semic 243
93 SemicSticker 280
96 Wien 218

KESA, DAN
93/4 ClassicProspects 116
93/4 PowerPlay 460
90/1 SketchWHL 271
91/2 SketchWHL 247
92/3 Hamilton
90/1 PrinceAlbert
91/2 PrinceAlbert

KESALAINEN, ERKKI
73/4 WilliamsFIN 181

KESKINEN, ESA
94/5 ElitSet 177, -ForeignAff 2
95/6 ElitSet 56, 306, -Champs 7
95/6 ElitSet -Mega 6
95 Globe 144
95 Hartwall
91/2 Jyvas-Hyva 62
92/3 Jyvas-Hyva 176
93/4 Jyvas-Hyva 318
95 PaniniWorlds 172
94 Semic 41
95 Semic 9
89 SemicSticker 48
91 SemicSticker 19
92 SemicSticker 24
93/4 Sisu 40, 360, 370, 372
94/5 Sisu 156, 164, 367
94/5 Sisu-Fire 10, -Specials 7
95/6 Sisu-GoldCard 14
95/6 SisuLimited 8
95/6 udElite 89, 225
97/8 udSwedish 94, 222, C25
96 Wien 9

KESKINEN, JERE
93/4 Sisu 18

KESSELL, RICK
72/3 EddieSargent 177

KESSELRING, CASEY
92/3 MPSPhotoSJHL 111

KESSLER, DINO
95 PaniniWorlds 121
92 SemicSticker 204

KETOLA, SIMO
80/1 Mallasjuoma 211

KETOLA, STEFAN
94/5 ElitSet 24
95/6 ElitSet 29
91/2 SemicElitserien 75
92/3 SemicElitserien 320
95/6 udElite 29

KETOLA, TONI
71/2 WilliamsFIN 367

KETOLA, VELI-PEKKA
66/7 Champion 51
72 Hellas 2
74 Hellas 6
65/6 Hellas 38
93/4 Jyvas-Hyva 343
70/1 Kuvajulkaisut 62, 175
80/1 Mallasjuoma 209
75/6 opcWHA 15
76/7 opcWHA 88
72 Panda
72 SemicSticker 79
74 SemicSticker 83
82 SemicSticker 162
91 SemicSticker 230
93/4 Sisu 207
94/5 Sisu 400
95/6 Sisu 387
96/7 Sisu 196
78/9 SM-Liiga 13, 233
77-80 Sportscaster 17-397
96 Wien HL13
71/2 WilliamsFIN 63, 85
72/3 WilliamsFIN 63, 248
73/4 WilliamsFIN 65, 247
81/2 COL.R

KETTER, KERRY
72/3 ATL

KETTERER, MARKUS
93/4 Classic 39
93/4 ClassicProspects 167
95/6 ElitSet 211
95 Globe 127
91/2 Jyvas-Hyva 19
92/3 Jyvas-Hyva 53
94 Semic 4
95 Semic 47
91 SemicSticker 2
92 SemicSticker 3
93 SemicSticker 45
91/2 UpperDeck 23
95/6 udElite 56, 224
96 Wien 32, SG8
93/4 Rochester

KETTUNEN, PERTTI
70/1 Kuvajulkaisut 312

KETTUNEN, SEPPO
72/3 WilliamsFIN 288
73/4 WilliamsFIN 221

KEYES, TIM
95/6 Slapshot 256

KHABIBULIN, NIKOLAI
95/6 Bowman 89
94/5 ClassicImages 42
95/6 Donruss 185
96/7 Don. 172,-Dom 2,-Pipe 9
97/8 Donruss 120
96/7 DonrussCanadianIce 95
97/8 DonrussCanadianIce 75
96/7 DonrussElite 49,-PaintdW 9
97/8 DonrussPreferred 101
97/8 DonrussPriority 36
97/8 DonrussStudio 63
95/6 EdgeIce 70, C12
97/8 EssoOlympic 40
96/7 Flair 71
94/5 Fleer 242
96/7 Fleer 90
95/8 FleerMetal 162
96/7 FleerNHLPicks 86
95/6 FleerUltra 180, 372
96/7 FleerUltra 132
97/8 KatchMedallion 111
95/6 Leaf 27
96/7 Leaf 63,-BestOf 6,-Showd 9
97/8 Leaf 62, -PipeDreams 13
96/7 LeafLimited 60
96/7 LeafPrefered 10
96/7 LP-LeafSteel 30, -Masked 9
97/8 Limited 124, -fabric 30
96/7 MetalUniverse 118
97/8 Omega 174
98/9 Pacific 341
97/8 PacificCrown 6, -InThe 16
97/8 PacificCrownRoyale 104
97/8 PCR -FreezeOut 15
97/8 PacificDynagon! 96
97/8 PcfcD-Stone 17,-Tandm 64
97/8 PacificInvincible 107
97/8 PcfcParamnt 141,-Glove 16
98/9 PcfcPara 182, -Glove 15
97/8 PacificRegime 153
97/8 PcfcRevolutn 107,-Retrn 15
95/6 PaniniSticker 221
96/7 PaniniSticker 189
95/6 Parkhurst 230
95/6 Pinnacle 118
96/7 Pinnacle 161, -Mask 7
97/8 Pinnacle 94, -Masks 9
97/8 Pinnacle -GoalieTin 6
96/7 PinnBeAPlayer-Stacking 7
97/8 P.BAP 13,-Stackg/Pads 13
97/8 PinnacleCertified 16
97/8 P.Inside 44,-Stpr 16,-Stnd 9
96/7 PinnacleZenith 40
95/8 Score 142
96/7 Score 105,-Net 18,-Sddn 15
97/8 Score 10, -NetWorth 9
96/7 SelectCert. 17, -Freezrs 14
94 Semic 135
93 SemicSticker 129
95/6 SkyBoxEmotion 193
95/8 SkyBoxImpact 181
96/7 SkyBoxImpact 105
96/7 SP 120
97/8 SPAuthentic 120, S20
98/9 SPx"Finite" 66
94/5 SRGoldStandard 88
94/5 SRTetrad CVIII
96/7 Summit 41, -Crease 12
96/7 TeamOut
95/6 Topps 48
98/9 Topps 115, I15
95/6 ToppsStadiumClub 157
94/5 ToppsFinest 27
95/6 ToppsFinest 63
91/2 UD 652,-CzechWJC 13
94/5 UpperDeck 420
95/6 UpperDeck 85
96/7 UpperDeck 126
97/8 UpperDeck 129
95/6 UDBeAPlayer 716
96/7 UDBlackDiamond 36
97/8 UDBlackDiamond 53
98/9 UDChoice 162
95/6 UDCollChoice 75
96/7 UDCollChoice 204
97/8 UDCollChoice 193, SQ35
96 Wien 129
97/8 Zenith 76
96/7 PHO (x2)
97/8 PHO
95/6 WPG

KHAIDAROV, RAVIL
91/2 O-Pee-Chee 36R
91/2 RedAce
94 Semic 162
92 SemicSticker 118
92/3 UpperDeck 347

KHALIZOV, SVIATOSLAV
89/90 SovietStars

KHARIN,SERGEI
90/1 ProCards 261
91/2 ProCards 540
91/2 Score(CDN) 284, (U.S) 394
91/2 UpperDeck 381
90/1 WPG/IGA
92/3 Cincinnati
93/4 Dayton 14
95/6 Dayton
89/90 Moncton
90/1 Moncton

KHARLAMOV, ALEXANDER
93/4 Classic 105
94/5 Classic 13, T74
94/5 ClassicFourSport 129
94/5 C4'Images 106
95/8 EdgeIce 56
69/70 MästarSerien 30
93/4 Parkhurst 529
93/4 Pinnacle 504
92/3 RedAce(Blue) 17,(Violet) 12
94/5 Score 213
91/2 Trends 100
95/6 Portland
96/7 Portland

KHARLAMOV, VALERI
95 Globe 241
72 Hellas 76
74 Hellas 45
70/1 Kuvajulkaisut 3
72 Panda
79 PaniniSticker 151
72 SemicSticker 17
74 SemicSticker 34
91 SemicSticker 244
73/4 Soviet Champs 12, 14
79/80 SovietChamps
69/70 Soviet Stars
70/1 Soviet Stars
71/2 Soviet Stars
73/4 Soviet Stars 8, 9
74/5 Soviet Stars 13
88 SovietTeam 13
77-9 Sportscastr 102-14, 26-673
91/2 Trends(72) 58, 100
71/2 WilliamsFIN 3
72/3 WilliamsFIN 24
73/4 WilliamsFIN 4

KHLOPOTNOV, DENIS
96/7 UpperDeck"Ice" 141

KHMYLEV, YURI
93/4 Donruss 36
94/5 Donruss 324
95/6 Donruss 18
96/7 Donruss 185
94/5 Fleer 22
92/3 FleerUltra 260
93/4 FleerUltra 173
94/5 FleerUltra 264
93/4 Leaf 211
94/5 Leaf 297
91/2 O-Pee-Chee 16R
94/5 PaniniSticker 96
95/6 PaniniSticker 17
92/3 Parkhurst 255
94/5 Parkhurst 22
95/8 Parkhurst 23
93/4 Pinnacle 201
94/5 Pinnacle 69
95/6 Playoff 231
96/7 Playoff 414
94/5 POG 53
95/8 POG 45
93/4 PowerPlay 30
93/4 Premier 389
94/5 Premier 14
95/6 ProMagnet 108
92/3 RedAce(Violet) 13
93/4 Score 302
95/6 Score 61
96/7 Score 199
89 SemicSticker 94
87/8 SovietStars
89/90 SovietStars
95/6 Topps 371
93/4 ToppsStadiumClub 241
92/3 UpperDeck 504
94/5 UpperDeck 368
95/6 UpperDeck 27
95/6 UDBeAPlayer 4
95/6 UDCollChoice 23
92/3 BUF/BlueShield
92/3 BUF/Jubilee

KHOMUTOV, ANDREI
95 Globe 178
90/1 O-Pee-Chee 3R
95 PaniniWorlds 50
94 Semic 154
95 Semic 139
82 SemicSticker 68
89 SemicSticker 93
91 SemicSticker 99
93 SemicSticker 148
83/4 SovietStars
87/8 SovietStars
89/90 SovietStars
96 Wien 152

KHRISTICH, DIMITRI
97/8 Aces 4 (Hearts)
91/2 Bowman 307
92/3 Bowman 427
95/6 Bowman 61
93/4 Donruss 373
94/5 Donruss 264
95/6 Donruss 265
96/7 Donruss 56
97/8 Donruss 89
96/7 DonrussCanadianIce 105
97/8 DonrussCanadianIce 58
96/7 DonrussElite 70
97/8 DonrussPreferred 92
97/8 DonrussPriority 39
97/8 DonrussStudio 80
93/4 EASports 154
94/5 Flair 201
96/7 Flair 46
94/5 Fleer 237
96/7 Fleer 50
95/6 FleerMetal 72
96/7 FleerNHLPicks 134
92/3 FleerUltra 235, -Imports 7
93/4 FleerUltra 59
94/5 FleerUltra 236
95/6 FleerUltra 250
96/7 FleerUltra 79
95/6 Hoyle'EAST 8 (Spades)
97/8 KatchMedallion 11
93/4 Leaf 168
94/5 Leaf 190
95/6 Leaf 139
96/7 Leaf 168
97/8 Leaf 29
96/7 LeafPreferred 79
97/8 Limited 73
96/7 MetalUniverse 75
97/8 Omega 17
90/1 O-Pee-Chee 16R
91/2 OPC/Topps 78
92/3 O-Pee-Chee 286
91/2 opcPremier 176
98/9 Pacific 83
97/8 PacificCrown 219
97/8 PcfcDynagn! 60,-Tandm 36
97/8 PacificInvincible 68
97/8 PacificParamount 14
98/9 PacificParamount 15
97/8 PacificRevolution 10
92/3 PaniniSticker N
93/4 PaniniSticker 28
94/5 PaniniSticker 20
95/6 PaniniSticker 266
96/7 PaniniSticker 270
97/8 PaniniSticker 226
91/2 Parkhurst 189
92/3 Parkhurst 428
93/4 Parkhurst 220
94/5 Parkhurst 252
95/6 Parkhurst 108
91/2 Pinnacle 162
92/3 Pinnacle 146, -Tm2000 25
93/4 Pinnacle 44, -Tm2001 23
94/5 Pinnacle 59
96/7 Pinnacle 190
97/8 Pinnacle 179
97/8 PinnacleBeAPlayer 61
97/8 PinnacleCertified 126
97/8 PinnacleInside 124
96/7 PinnacleZenith 88
94/5 POG 246
95/6 POG 133
93/4 PowerPlay 264
93/4 Premier 210
94/5 Premier 534
91/2 ProSet 260
92/3 ProSet 208
91/2 PSPlatinum 242
92/3 RedAce(Blue) 3
91/2 Score(CDN) 175, (U.S) 175
91/2 Score-YoungStar 6
92/3 Score 33,-Sharp 27,-Yng 15
93/4 Score 80
94/5 Score 118
95/6 Score 151
96/7 Score 122
97/8 Score 111
97/8 Score(BOS) 5
94/5 Select 104
96/7 SelectCertified 46
95/6 SkyBoxEmotion 82
95/6 SkyBoxImpact 80
96/7 SkyBoxImpact 58
94/5 SP 130
95/6 SP 67
97/8 SPAuthentic 12
95/6 Summit 153
96/7 Summit 27
95/6 SuperSticker 60
92/3 Topps 470
95/6 Topps 248
98/9 Topps 164
95/6 ToppsFinest 166
91/2 ToppsStadiumClub 359
92/3 ToppsStadiumClub 86
93/4 ToppsStadiumClub 277
94/5 ToppsStadiumClub 12
95/6 ToppsStadiumClub 68
90/1 UpperDeck 537
91/2 UpperDeck 157
92/3 UpperDeck 219
93/4 UpperDeck 135, SP 171
94/5 UpperDeck 76, SP87
95/6 UpperDeck 287
96/7 UpperDeck 76
97/8 UpperDeck 80
95/6 UDBeAPlayer 36
96/7 UDBlackDiamond 108
98/9 UDChoice 12
95/6 UDCollChoice 183
96/7 UDCollChoice 123, 320
97/8 UDCC 119, C17, SQ27
89/90 WSH
90/1 WSH/Kodak
91/2 WSH
91/2 WSH/Kodak
92/3 WSH/Kodak

KIANSTEN, JUSSI
72/3 WilliamsFIN 264

KIBERMANIS, CHRIS
93/4 RedDeer
95/6 RedDeer

KIDD, IAN
89/90 ProCards(IHL) 182
90/1 ProCards 323
91/2 ProCards 601

KIDD, TREVOR
91/2 CanadaNats
94/5 Donruss 4
95/6 Donruss 31, -Between 4
95/6 D-Domin. 8, -ProPointer 16
96/7 Donruss 160
97/8 Donruss 59
96/7 DonrussCanadianIce 37
97/8 DonrussCanadianIce 60
96/7 DonrussElite 45
97/8 DonrussElite 107
97/8 DonrussPreferred 73
97/8 DonrussPriority 98
97/8 DonrussStudio 61
95/6 EdgeIce C21
94/5 Flair 25
96/7 Flair 13
94/5 Fleer 31
96/7 Fleer 13
95/6 FleerMetal 20
93/4 FleerUltra 281
94/5 FleerUltra 30
95/6 FleerUltra 26, -Rising 4
96/7 FleerUltra 25
94/5 Kraft-Dinner
95/6 Kraft-Crease
93/4 Leaf 385
94/5 Leaf 322
95/6 Leaf 83
96/7 Leaf 67
97/8 Leaf 126
95/6 LeafLimited 31
96/7 LeafLimited 25
96/7 LeafPreferred 116
97/8 Limited 10
96/7 Maggers 21
96/7 McDonalds McD34, -Masks
96/7 MetalUniverse 20
97/8 Omega 42
91/2 OPC/Topps 312
98/9 Pacific 135
97/8 PacificCrown 133, -InThe 3
97/8 PacificCrownRoyale 24
97/8 PacificDynagon! 18
97/8 PcfcD-Stone 4,-Tandem 23
97/8 PacificInvincible 20
97/8 PcfcParamount 35,-Glove 3
98/9 PcfcParamount 38, -Glove 4
97/8 PacificRevolution 24
95/6 PaniniSticker 243
96/7 PaniniSticker 233
94/5 Parkhurst 288
95/6 Parkhurst 35, -GoalPatrol 8
94/5 ParkieSE 24
94/5 Pinnacle 365, MA7
95/6 Pinnacle 151
96/7 Pinnacle 174
97/8 Pinnacle 60
96/7 PinnacleBeAPlayer 127
97/8 PinnacleCertified 21
97/8 PinnacleInside 87,-StandUp
95/6 PinnacleZenith 67
96/7 PinnacleZenith 11
95/6 Playoff 233
94/5 POG 275
95/6 POG 60
93/4 PowerPlay 305
94/5 Premier 413,-Finest(OPC) 5
95/6 ProMagnet 45
90/1 Score 438
91/2 Score(CDN) 271, (U.S) 381
92/3 Score-CdnOlympic 12
93/4 Score 660
94/5 Score 259
95/6 Score 19, -Promo 19
96/7 Score 58
97/8 Score 37, -NetWorth 3
95/6 SelectCertified 40
96/7 SelectCertified 21
90/1 SketchMEM 74
90/1 SketchWHL 226, 334
95/6 SkyBoxEmotion 23
95/6 SkBxImpact 23, -Deflect 10
96/7 SkyBoxImpact 14
94/5 SP 21
95/6 SP 21
96/7 SP 21
98/9 SPx"Finite" 15
95/6 Summit 138
96/7 Summit 36
95/6 SuperSticker 17
96/7 TeamOut
92/3 Topps 280
95/6 Topps 154, 4CG, HGC13
98/9 Topps 66
94/5 ToppsStadiumClub 106
95/6 ToppsStadiumClub 72
95/6 SuperSkills 82
90/1 UpperDeck 463
91/2 UpperDeck 449, 684
91/2 UD'CzechWJC 58
92/3 UpperDeck 134, 385
93/4 UpperDeck 399
94/5 UpperDeck 395, SP12
94/5 UD -CdnJr.Alumni 10
95/6 UpperDeck 143, 229, SE15
96/7 UpperDeck 25
97/8 UpperDeck 23
94/5 UDBeAPlayer -Aut 167
98/9 UDChoice 42
95/6 UDCollChoice 69
96/7 UDCollChoice 34, 312
97/8 UDCollChoice 37
88/9 Brandon 21
89/90 Brandon 1
90/1 Brandon 15

KIECA, MARIUSZ
92 SemicSticker 268

KIENASS, TORSTEN
94/5 DEL 84
95/6 DEL 79,436
96/7 DEL 322
95 PaniniWorlds 55
94 Semic 274
92 SemicSticker 179

KIENE, CHRIS
89/90 ProCards(AHL) 221
90/1 ProCards 575
91/2 ProCards 165
91/2 Moncton

KIERECK, MATT
92/3 Sudbury 14

KIESSLING, UDO
94/5 DEL 268
9/6 DEL 248
82 SemicSticker 105
89 SemicSticker 107
91 SemicSticker 157
79 PaniniSticker 100

KIHLSTROM, MATS
89/90 SemicElitserien 220
90/1 SemicElitserien 53
91/2 SemicElitserien 228
89 SemicSticker 7

KIILI, LASSE
66/7 Champion 74
65/6 Hellas 1
70/1 Kuvajulkaisut 157
71/2 WilliamsFIN 228
72/3 WilliamsFIN 212
73/4 WilliamsFIN 198

KIIMALAINEN, MARKKU
80/1 Mallasjuoma 99
82 SemicSticker 40
82 Skopbank
78/9 SM-Liiga 7, 144
77-80 Sportscaster 90-2150

KIISKI, TOMMI
92/3 Jyvas-Hyva 39

KILDUFF, DAVID
91/2 AvantGardeBC 87, 159
92/3 BCJHL 135

KILGER, CHAD
95/6 Bowman 137, BB25
94/5 Classic DP3
95/6 Classic 4, 87, AS10, BK4
95/6 ClassicFiveSport 143
94/5 ClassicImages 84
95/6 Donruss 379, -RatedRook 7
96/7 Donruss 236
97/8 Donruss 175
95/6 DonrussElite 55, -Rookie 9
95/6 FleerMetal 179
95/6 FleerUltra 343
96/7 Leaf 203
97/8 Leaf 137
95/6 LeafLimited 34, -Rookie 3
97/8 Limited 73
98/9 Pacific 146
97/8 PaniniSticker 190
95/6 Parkhurst 255, 500
95/6 P.Zenith 139,-RookRoll 12
96/7 Score 255
95/6 SelectCertified 116
95/6 SkBxEmotion-Next 10
95/6 SkBxImpact 188, -Fox 18
93/4 Slapshot(Kingston) 17
95/6 SP 163
95/6 Summit 179
96/7 Summit 155
95/6 SuperSticker 3
95/6 Topps 301
95/6 ToppsFinest 81
96/7 ToppsNHLPicks 151
95/6 ToppsStadiumClub 202
95/6 ToppsSuperSkills SR5
95/6 UpperDeck 262
96/7 UpperDeck 130
97/8 UpperDeck 130
95/6 UDBeAPlayer 167
96/7 UDCollChoice 200, 337
96/7 PHO
97/8 PHO

KILPATRICK, JOHN
83&87 HallOfFame 116
83 HHOF Postcard (H)

KILPIO, RAIMO
66/7 Champion 15
65/6 Hellas 79
70/1 Kuvajulkaisut 194
72 Panda
96/7 Sisu 189
71/2 WilliamsFIN 86
72/3 WilliamsFIN 249
73/4 WilliamsFIN 248

KILREA, BRIAN
90/1 SketchOHL 100
91/2 SketchOHL 309
84/5 NYI 30
81/2 Ottawa67s
82/3 Ottawa67s
83/4 Ottawa67s
92/3 Ottawa67s

KILREA, HECTOR J. (HEC)
25-27 Anonymous 19, 20
33/4 Anonymous (V129) 17
33-43 BeeHives(DET), (TOR)
27-32 LaPresse 29-30
39/40 OPC (V301-1) 71
35/6 OPC (V304C) 86
33/4 WWGum (V357) 64
36/7 WWGum (V356) 24

KILREA, KEN
33-43 BeeHives(DET)

KILREA, WALTER (WALLY)
33-43 BeeHives(DET)
34/5 OPC (V304B) 63
33/4 WWGum (V357) 53

KIMBLE, DARIN
91/2 Bowman 381
90/1 O-Pee-Chee 437
91/2 OPC/Topps 156
91/2 Parkhurst 377
88/9 ProCards(Halifax)
90/1 ProSet 517
91/2 Score(CDN) 526
92/3 Topps 511
91/2 ToppsStadiumClub 278
92/3 ToppsStadiumClub 486
93/4 CHI/Coke
89/90 QUE
89/90 QUE/GeneralFoods
89/90 QUE/Police
90/1 QUE
90/1 QUE/PetroCanada
91/2 STL

KIMURA, KEVIN
92/3 BCJHL 32

KINASCHUK, BRETT
91/2 AirCanadaSJHL D5
92/3 MPSPhotoSJHL 30

KINCAID, CAMERON
95/6 Slapshot 428

KINCH, ROB
92/3 MPSPhotoSJHL 44

KINDRACHUK, OREST
74/5 Loblaws
74/5 OPC 334
75/6 OPC 389
76/7 OPC/Topps 233
77/8 OPC/Topps 26
78/9 OPC/Topps 114
79/80 OPC/Topps 218
80/1 OPC 292
92/3 Parkhurst 476
75/6 PHA/GingerAle

KING, ARCHIE
75/6 Hamilton

KING, BARRY
87/8 SSMarie 1

KING, DAVE
90/1 CanadaNats
91/2 CanadaNats
89 SemicSticker 52
92 SemicSticker 74
92/3 CGY/IGA 26

KING, DEREK
91/2 Bowman 220
92/3 Bowman 188
93/4 Donruss 204
94/5 Donruss 30
95/6 Donruss 300
97/8 Donruss 69
94/5 Flair 103
94/5 Fleer 123
92/3 FleerUltra 128
93/4 FleerUltra 176
94/5 FleerUltra 325
93/4 HockeyWit 28
96/7 Kraft-Disk
93/4 Leaf 119
94/5 Leaf 188
95/6 Leaf 261
89/90 OPC/Topps 6
90/1 OPC/Topps 128
91/2 OPC/Topps 455
92/3 O-Pee-Chee 79
89/90 opcSticker 116/255
98/9 Pacific 414
97/8 PacificInvincible 24
97/8 PacificParamount 181
98/9 PacificParamount 228
97/8 PacificRegime 37
88/9 PaniniSticker 289
89/90 PaniniSticker 271
91/2 PaniniSticker 247
92/3 PaniniSticker 199
93/4 PaniniSticker 58
95/6 PaniniSticker 92
97/8 PaniniSticker 23
91/2 Parkhurst 108
92/3 Parkhurst 100
93/4 Parkhurst 119
94/5 Parkhurst 132
95/6 Parkhurst 132
91/2 Pinnacle 107
92/3 Pinnacle 17
93/4 Pinnacle 128
94/5 Pinnacle 302
97/8 PinnacleBeAPlayer 40
94/5 POG 157
95/6 POG 172
93/4 PowerPlay 150
93/4 Premier 176
94/5 Premier 304
89/90 ProCards(AHL) 250
90/1 ProSet 185
91/2 ProSet 146
92/3 ProSet 110
91/2 PSPlatinum 201, 286
90/1 ScoreTraded 86T
91/2 Score(CDN) 167, (U.S) 167
92/3 Score 255, -Sharpshootr 15
93/4 Score 48, 362, DD9
95/6 Score 238
97/8 Score(TOR) 18
94/5 Select 9
96/7 SP 95
95/6 SuperSticker 76
92/3 Topps 431
95/6 Topps 202
98/9 Topps 84
91/2 ToppsStadiumClub 82
92/3 ToppsStadiumClub 82
93/4 ToppsStadiumClub 215
94/5 ToppsStadiumClub 108
95/6 ToppsStadiumClub 81
90/1 UpperDeck 407
91/2 UpperDeck 382
92/3 UpperDeck 191
93/4 UpperDeck 417
94/5 UpperDeck 59
96/7 UpperDeck 98
94/5 UDBeAPlayer -Aut 6
97/8 UDCollChoice 112
96/7 UpperDeck"Ice" 40
84/5 SSMarie

KING, ELDRED
90/1 Newmarket

KING, FRANK
45-64 BeeHives(MTL)
51/2 LavalDairy 10

KING, KEVIN
90/1 SketchOHL 70, 161
91/2 SketchOHL 228
89/90 SSMarie 12

KING, KRIS
91/2 Bowman 59
92/3 Bowman 380
92/3 ClassicProspects 74
93/4 Donruss 379
96/7 Kraft'Disk
93/4 Leaf 253
94/5 Leaf 395
90/1 O-Pee-Chee 526
91/2 OPC/Topps 498
92/3 O-Pee-Chee 86
98/9 Pacific 415
97/8 PacificCrown 90
91/2 Parkhurst 337
92/3 Parkhurst 478
93/4 Parkhurst 498
94/5 Parkhurst 269
95/6 Parkhurst 502
91/2 Pinnacle 362
92/3 Pinnacle 168, 253
93/4 Pinnacle 316
96/7 Pinnacle -Trophies 7
97/8 PinnacleBeAPlayer 108
94/5 Premier 220
90/1 ProSet 491
91/2 ProSet 445
90/1 ScoreTraded 76T
91/2 Score(CDN) 402, (U.S) 363
92/3 Score 181
93/4 Score 362
92/3 Topps 509
98/9 Topps 160
91/2 ToppsStadiumClub 26
92/3 ToppsStadiumClub 187
94/5 ToppsStadiumClub 124
90/1 UpperDeck 440
91/2 UpperDeck 330
92/3 UpperDeck 78
93/4 UpperDeck 14
94/5 UpperDeck 308
95/6 UpperDeck 141
94/5 UDBeAPlayer -Aut 15
95/6 UDCollChoice 215
88/9 DET/Caesars
89/90 NYR/MarineMidland
96/7 PHO (x2)
93/4 WPG/Ruffles
95/6 WPG

KING, MIKE
83/4 Kingston 9

KING, SCOTT
90/1 ProCards 492
92/3 ToppsStadiumClub 269
92/3 Toledo 1, 2

KING, STEVEN
93/4 Classic 136
92/3 ClassicProsp. 60, 74, PR1
93/4 Donruss 1
92/3 FleerUltra 355
93/4 FleerUltra 258
93/4 Leaf 410
92/3 Parkhurst 347
93/4 Parkhurst 1
93/4 Pinnacle 345
93/4 PowerPlay 6
93/4 Premier 303
94/5 Premier 220
91/2 ProCards 199
93/4 Score 382, 514
93/4 ToppsStadiumClub 377
92/3 UpperDeck 575
93/4 UpperDeck 24
94/5 ANA/Carl'sJr 12
92/3 Binghampton
83/4 Kingston 19
82/3 Oshawa 13

KING, STEVE
72/3 OttawaNationals

KING, WAYNE
74/5 Loblaws

KINGHAM, ROB
90/1 SketchOHL 36
91/2 SketchOHL 29

KINGHORN, RON
91/2 ProCards 433

KINGSTON, GEORGE
95/6 DEL 428

KINISKY, AL
92/3 BCJHL 178
90/1 SketchWHL 4
91/2 SketchWHL 339

KINNEAR, GEORDIE
90/1 SketchOHL 363
91/2 SketchOHL 132
91/2 Peterborough 24

KINNEY, DONNIE
97/8 Bowman 91

KINNIBURGH, TODD
89/90 Portland

KINNUNEN, JORMA
70/1 Kuvajulkaisut 370

KINNUNEN, KARI
65/6 Hellas 63
70/1 Kuvajulkaisut 176
71/2 WilliamsFIN 101
72/3 WilliamsFIN 144
73/4 WilliamsFIN 110

KINNUNEN, V.P.
80/1 Mallasjuoma 52

KINSACHUK, KENT
92/3 MPSPhotoSJHL 36

KIPRUSOFF, JARMO
70/1 Kuvajulkaisut 296

KIPRUSOFF, MARKO
95/6 Bowman 109
95/6 Donruss 351
95 Globe 131
95 Hartwall
93/4 Jyvas-Hyva 321
95/6 Kelloggs PopUp 2
96/7 Leaf 233
95 PaniniWorlds 169
95/6 Parkhurst 268
96/7 Pinnacle 234
94 Semic 18
95 Semic 2
93/4 Sisu 35
94/5 Sisu 7, 161, -NHLDraft 2
95/6 Sisu 163, 200, -GoldCard 7
95/6 SisuLimited 5
95 SuomenBeckett 6
94/5 ToppsFinest 125
95/6 ToppsStadiumClub 141
91/2 UD 671,-CzechWJC 34
96/7 UpperDeck 188
97/8 udSwedish 135, C13
96 Wien 2, AS3

KIPRUSOFF, MIIKKA
95/6 Sisu 122, -Drafted 8
94/5 ToppsFinest 125
97/8 udSwedish 1, S1

KIRBY, TRAVIS
92/3 MPSPhotoSJHL 141

KIRIAKOU, LOU
84/5 Moncton 9

KIRK, BOB
33-43 BeeHives(NYR)

KIRK, GAVIN
75/6 opcWHA 103
76/7 opcWHA 99
73/4 QuakerOats 5
72/3 OttawaNationals

KIRKPATRICK, ROBERT
33-43 BeeHives(NYR)

KIRTON, MARK
81/2 OPC 90, Topps(W) 90
82/3 OPC 87
83/4 OPC 352
82/3 Post
88/9 ProCards(Newmarket)
83/4 Vachon 109
79/80 TOR
80/1 TOR
83/4 VAN
85/6 Fredericton 19
86/7 Fredericton

KIRTON, SCOTT
92/3 BCJHL 237

KIRVESKOSKI, VEIKKO
73/4 WilliamsFIN 222

KIRWAN, JEFF
95/6 SwiftCurrent

KISH, LARRY
84/5 NovaScotia 25
85/6 NovaScotia 21
92/3 Wheeling 21
93/4 Wheeling 19

KISILIVICH, BRENT
82/3 MedicineHat
83/4 MedicineHat 5

KISIO, KELLY
91/2 Bowman 72
92/3 Bowman 166
93/4 Donruss 55
93/4 EASports 117
92/3 FleerUltra 196
93/4 FleerUltra 155, 282
93/4 Leaf 208
94/5 Leaf 493
84/5 OPC 56
85/6 OPC/Topps 101
86/7 OPC/Topps 116
87/8 OPC/Topps 76
88/9 OPC/Topps 47, 143
89/90 OPC/Topps 171
90/1 OPC/Topps 239
91/2 OPC/Topps 335
92/3 O-Pee-Chee 232
91/2 opcPremier 69
84/5 opcSticker 40
86/7 opcSticker 163/24
87/8 opcSticker 28/168
88/9 opcSticker 239
87/8 PaniniSticker 115
88/9 PaniniSticker 307
89/90 PaniniSticker 287
90/1 PaniniSticker 94
91/2 PaniniSticker 291
92/3 PaniniSticker 124
93/4 PaniniSticker 256
91/2 Parkhurst 165
92/3 Parkhurst 166
93/4 Parkhurst 33
91/2 Pinnacle 231
92/3 Pinnacle 362
93/4 Pinnacle 395
94/5 Pinnacle 306
94/5 POG 55
93/4 Power Play 37
93/4 Premier 455
90/1 ProSet 200
91/2 ProSet 168, 479
91/2 PS-ThePuck 26
92/3 ProSet 167
91/2 PSPlatinum 104
90/1 Score 37
91/2 Score(CDN) 553
91/2 Score(U.S) 288, 3T
92/3 Score 57
93/4 Score 27, 556
92/3 Topps 331
91/2 ToppsStadiumClub 186
92/3 ToppsStadiumClub 454
93/4 ToppsStadium Club 30
90/1 UpperDeck 296
91/2 UpperDeck 515
92/3 UD'LockerAS 28
93/4 UpperDeck 304
95/6 UDCollChoice 193
84/5 DET/Caesars
85/6 DET/Caesars
89/90 NYR/MarineMidland
91/2 S.J

KISTER, ED
86/7 Kitchener 11
85/6 London 11

KITCHEN, BILL
83/4 NovaScotia 2

KITCHEN, MIKE
77/8 OPC 267
78/9 OPC 338
81/2 OPC 83
82/3 Post
83/4 SouhaitsRen.KeyChain
76/7 COL.R/CokeCans
77/8 COL.R/CokeCans
79/80 COL.R
81/2 COL.R
83/4 N.J.

KITCHENER, CRAIG
80/1 Oshawa 3

KITCHING, GARY
91/2 FerrisState

KITTERINGHAM, CRAIG
88/9 ProCards(Hershey)

KIURU, ESKO
66/7 Champion 141

KIURU, JUSSI
93/4 Sisu 201
94/5 Sisu 283
95/6 Sisu 105

KIVELA, ANTERO
80/1 Mallasjuoma 199
79 PaniniSticker 163
78/9 SM-Liiga 19, 219
77-80 Sportscaster 90-2148

KIVELA, KEIJO
78/9 SM-Liiga 54

KIVELA, KIMMO
65/6 Hellas 74

KIVELA, PASI
92/3 Jyvas-Hyva 32

KIVELA, TEPPO
91/2 Jyvas-Hyva 8
92/3 Jyvas-Hyva 6
93/4 Jyvas-Hyva 23
91 SemicSticker 15
93/4 Sisu 95
94/5 Sisu 210, 375, -Horoscp 10
95/6 Sisu 155
96/7 Sisu 155
95/6 SisuLimited 23
97/8 udSwedish 24

KIVELL, ROB
84/5 Victoria

KIVELL, RON
85/6 Moncton 10
83/4 Victoria

KIVI, KARRI
93/4 Jyvas-Hyva 346
95 PaniniWorlds 165
93/4 Sisu 215
94/5 Sisu 134, -Double 3
95/6 Sisu 352
96/7 Sisu 153
97/8 udSwedish 2

KIVIAHO, TOMMY
93/4 Jyvas-Hyva 257
93/4 Sisu 293
94/5 Sisu 338, -Horoscope 16
95/6 Sisu 36
96/7 Sisu 8

KIVILA, PASI
93/4 Jyvas-Hyva 58
93/4 Sisu 248
94/5 Sisu 83

KIVINEN, TEEMU
93/4 Sisu 60

KJELLBERG, PATRIC
94/5 ElitSet 16, -Gold 17, -Top 9
95/6 ElitSet 190, -Champs 2
92/3 opcPremier 29
94 Semic 78
89/90 SemicElitserien 25
90/1 SemicElitserien 91
91/2 SemicElitserien 20
93 SemicSticker 42
92/3 UpperDeck 498
95/6 udElite 53
97/8 udSwedish 46, C1
92/3 MTL
92/3 Fredericton

KJENSTAD, OLAF
91/2 SketchWHL 313
94/5 Birmingham
95/6 Birmingham
93/4 Seattle

KLAPAC, JAN
72 Hellas 88
74 Hellas 74
74 SemicSticker 52
72/3 WilliamsFIN 11
73/4 WilliamsFIN 52

KLAPSTEIN, TERRY
89/90 Victoria

KLASONS, GEORGE
77/8 Kalamazoo

KLASSEN, JASON
91/2 SketchWHL 248
91/2 PrinceAlbert

KLASSEN, MIKE
79/80 Montréal

KLASSEN, RALPH
76/7 O-Pee-Chee 282
77/8 O-Pee-Chee 372
78/9 O-Pee-Chee 346

KLASSEN, TODD
90/1 SketchWHL 111
91/2 SketchWHL 295

KLATT, BILL
72/3 Minnesota

KLATT, TRENT
92/3 Classic 89
93/4 Donruss 82
94/5 Donruss 37
95/6 Donruss 330
93/4 FleerUltra 157,-UltraPros 4
94/5 FleerUltra 53
93/4 Leaf 14
94/5 Leaf 316
95/6 Leaf 57
97/8 Omega 166
98/9 Pacific 327
97/8 PacificCrown 251
98/9 PacificParamount 175
95/6 PaniniSticker 172
91/2 Parkhurst 452
92/3 Parkhurst 317
93/4 Parkhurst 48
94/5 ParkieSE 43
94/5 Pinnacle 442
95/6 Pinnacle 193
96/7 PinnacleBeAPlayer 157
94/5 POG 143
95/6 POG 88
93/4 PowerPlay 62
93/4 Premier 523
94/5 Premier 46
92/3 ProSet 229
92/3 Score 482
97/8 Score(PHA) 8
94/5 SP 29
95/6 Topps 106
92/3 UpperDeck 62
93/4 UpperDeck 152
94/5 UpperDeck 374
95/6 UpperDeck 162
97/8 UpperDeck 120
95/6 UDCollChoice 36

97/8 UDCollChoice 191
94/5 DAL
94/5 DAL/Southwest
96/7 PHA/OceanSpray
91/2 Minnesota

KLEE, KEN
95/6 Bowman 163
92/3 ClassicProspects 82
97/8 PacificRegime 209
97/8 PinnacleBeAPlayer 91
95/6 UpperDeck 128
97/8 UpperDeck 386
95/6 UDBeAPlayer 162
95/6 WSH
93/4 Portland
94/5 Portland

KLEIN, JAMES (DEDE)
33-43 BeeHives(NYA)

KLEIN, LLOYD
33-35 DiamondMatch
36-39 DiamondMatch (1), (2), (3)

KLEINENDORST, KURT
93/4 Raleigh

KLEINENDORST, SCOTT
85/6 HFD/JuniorWhalers
86/7 HFD/JuniorWhalers
87/8 HFD/JuniorWhalers
88/9 HFD/JuniorWhalers
89/90 WSH
89/90 WSH/Kodak

KLEISINGER, CURTIS
91/2 AirCanadaSJHL B16

KLEMENC, PETAR-IGOR
79 PaniniSticker 400

KLEMM, JON
97/8 PacificDynag-BestKept 25
96/7 PinnacleBeAPlayer 144
91/2 ProCards 534
90/1 SketchMEM 71, 77
90/1 SketchWHL 197
95/6 SkyBoxImpact 194
98/9 Topps 113
95/6 UpperDeck 93, SE20
89/90 Spokane

KLENNER, SEBASTIAN
94/5 DEL 405

KLETZEL, DEREK
90/1 SketchWHL 161
91/2 SketchWHL 283

KLEVAKIN, DMITRI
94/5 ParkieSE 232
94/5 SP 166
94/5 UpperDeck 515

KLIEMANN, MATTHIAS
94/5 DEL 392
95/6 DEL 415

KLIMA, PETR
90/1 Bowman 197
91/2 Bowman 96, 104
92/3 Bowman 135
95/6 Bowman 22
93/4 Donruss 317
94/5 Donruss 249
95/6 Donruss 110
96/7 Donruss 196
93/4 EASports 47
94/5 Flair 174
94/5 Fleer 208
95/6 FleerMetal 138
92/3 FleerUltra 59, -Import 8
93/4 FleerUltra 425
94/5 FleerUltra 208
95/6 FleerUltra 153
95/6 Hoyle'EAST 9 (Spades)
91/2 Kelloggs 17
93/4 Leaf 321
94/5 Leaf 171
95/6 Leaf 321
96/7 Leaf 39
96/7 Maggers 145
96/7 MetalUniverse 76
86/7 OPC/Topps 98
87/8 OPC/Topps 26
88/9 OPC/Topps 28
90/1 OPC/Topps 85
91/2 OPC/Topps 193
91/2 opcPremier 61
86/7 opcSticker 129/115, 162/21
87/8 opcSticker 104/237
88/9 opcSticker 251/121
97/8 PacificCrown 347
87/8 PaniniSticker 246
88/9 PaniniSticker 44
90/1 PaniniSticker 228
91/2 PaniniSticker 126
92/3 PaniniSticker 105
93/4 PaniniSticker 234
94/5 PaniniSticker 185
95/6 PaniniSticker 130
96/7 PaniniSticker 126
97/8 PaniniSticker 217
91/2 Parkhurst 280, 458
92/3 Parkhurst 54
93/4 Parkhurst 195
94/5 Parkhurst 219
95/6 Parkhurst 197
91/2 Pinnacle 159
92/3 Pinnacle 344
93/4 Pinnacle 349
94/5 Pinnacle 311
96/7 Pinnacle 79
95/6 Playoff 311
96/7 Playoff 404
94/5 POG 224
95/6 POG 251
93/4 PowerPlay 232
94/5 Premier 318
90/1 ProSet 86
91/2 ProSet 72
91/2 PSPlatinum 37
90/1 Score 232
91/2 Score(CDN) 136, (U.S) 136
92/3 Score 383, -Sharpshootr 24
93/4 Score 242, 518
95/6 Score 65
96/7 Score 202
91 SemicSticker 220
93 SemicSticker 104
95/6 SkyBoxEmotion 165
95/6 SkyBoxImpact 156
94/5 SP 110
95/6 SP 136
95/6 Summit 141
92/3 Topps 26
95/6 Topps 238
95/6 ToppsFinest 112
91/2 ToppsStadiumClub 61
92/3 ToppsStadiumClub 368
94/5 ToppsStadiumClub 136
95/6 ToppsStadiumClub 185
90/1 UpperDeck 282
91/2 UpperDeck 111
92/3 UpperDeck 551
93/4 UpperDeck 291, 526,SP152
94/5 UpperDeck 86
95/6 UpperDeck 118, SE167
96/7 UpperDeck 156
94/5 UDBeAPlayer -Aut 155
95/6 UDCollChoice 134
96/7 UDCollChoice 246
85/6 DET/Caesars
86/7 DET/Caesars
87/8 DET/Caesars
88/9 DET/Caesars
90/1 EDM/McGavins
91/2 EDM/IGA
92/3 EDM/IGA 12
96/7 EDM
94/5 T.B./SkyBoxSportsCafe
95/6 T.B.
95/6 T.B./SkyBoxSportsCafe

KLIMENTIEV, SERGEI
95/6 EdgeIce 64
94/5 SRTetrad CIX
95/6 Rochester

KLIMOVICH, SERGEI
92/3 Classic 46
95/6 EdgeIce 135
92/3 RedAce(Blue) 30,(Violet) 15
92/3 UpperDeck 339
93/4 UpperDeck 275
93/4 Indianapolis

KLIMT, TOMAS
95/6 APS 256
93/4 UpperDeck 263

KLOBOUCEK, JAN
92/3 BCJHL 222

KLOCKARE, STEFAN
94/5 ElitSet 73
95/6 ElitSet 16
90/1 SemicElitserien 183
91/2 SemicElitserien 38
92/3 SemicElitserien 56
92/3 UpperDeck 224
95/6 udElite 24
97/8 udSwedish 20

KLOEPZIG, STEVE
87/8 Kamloops
86/7 Portland

KLOIBER, RALPH
74/5 SiouxCity

KLUCZOWSKI, STEVE
89/90 SketchOHL 54

KLUKAY, JOE
45-64 BeeHives(BOS), (TOR)
48-53 Exhibits
51/2 Parkhurst 74
52/3 Parkhurst 75
53/4 Parkhurst 94
54/5 Parkhurst 54
55/6 Parkhurst 6
45-54 QuakerOats
76 DET

KLUZAK, GORD
83/4 OPC 51
84/5 OPC 6
85/6 OPC 167
86/7 OPC/Topps 54
88/9 OPC/Topps 23
90/1 OPC 495
83/4 opcSticker 185
84/5 opcSticker 186
88/9 opcSticker 25/154
88/9 PaniniSticker 205
90/1 ProSet 383
90/1 Score 367
83/4 SouhaitsRen.KeyChain
84/5 Topps 5
83/4 BOS
84/5 BOS
88/9 BOS/SportsAction
89/90 BOS/SportsAction

KLYN, BRAD
91/2 AvantGardeBC 161
92/3 BCJHL 161

KLYNCK, BERYL
52/3 AnonymousOHL 123

KLYNE, LAWRENCE
92/3 BCJHL 91

KNAPP, JIM
85/6 Minn-Duluth 34

KNESAUREK, ROB
88/9 Sudbury 23
89/90 Sudbury 25

KNIBBS, KALVIN
90/1 SketchWHL 26

KNICKLE, RICK
92/3 C.Prospects 121, BC12
95/6 EdgeIce 122, TW3
89/90 ProCards(IHL) 26
90/1 ProCards 515
91/2 ProCards 320
93/4 Score 466
93/4 Phoenix
92/3 SanDiego

KNIGHT, BRAD
91/2 AvantGardeBCJHL 29

KNIGHT, CURTIS
91/2 AirCanadaSJHL A17
92/3 MPSPhotoSJHL 40

KNIGHT, JASON
91/2 SketchWHL 337
91/2 Saskatoon 9

KNIGHT, JEFF
91/2 AirCanadaSJHL 38, C39
90/1 SketchWHL 44

KNIGHT, KEITH
82/3 Kingston 15

KNIGHT, TERRY
83/4 MedicineHat 7

KNIPSCHEER, FRED
94/5 Classic T4, -Aut
93/4 ClassicProspects 60
94/5 Leaf 331
93/4 Parkhurst 18
94/5 Pinnacle 249
95/6 Pinnacle-FullContact 2
95/6 Playoff 227
94/5 Score 220
94/5 ToppsStadiumClub 17

KNOBLOCH, THOMAS
94/5 DEL 401
95/6 DEL 420

KNOLD, PER CHRISTIAN
92 SemicSticker 48

KNOX, BLAKE
90/1 SketchWHL 49
91/2 SketchWHL 139

KNOX, CAMERON
92/3 BCJHL 145

KNOX, JASON
90/1 KatchWHL 248
91/2 SketchWHL 155
90/1 Saskatoon 7
89/90 Victoria

KNOX, PAUL
52/3 AnonymousOHL 143

KNOX, SEYMOUR
93/4 ActionPacked 7

KNUBLE, MIKE
97/8 Donruss 225
97/8 Limited 2, 17
98/9 Pacific 194
97/8 PinnacleBeAPlayer 43
97/8 PinnacleInside 172
97/8 Score(DET) 20
97/8 SPAuthentic 180
97/8 UpperDeck 187
97/8 UpperDeckIce 39
95/6 Adirondack

KNUTSEN, ESPEN
97/8 DonrussElite 106, 144
97/8 DonrussPreferred 161
97/8 D.Priority 172,-DirDep 26
94/5 ElitSet 264, -ForeignAffair 1
95/6 ElitSet 35, -FaceToFace 13
95 Globe 198, 251
97/8 KatchMedallion 3
97/8 PacificDynagon! Rookies
97/8 PacificParamount 3
95 PaniniWorlds 248
97/8 Pinnacle 1
97/8 PinnacleCertified K
97/8 Score 66
97/8 Score(ANA) 20
94 Semic 261
92 SemicSticker 40
93 SemicSticker 241
97/8 SPAuthentic 169
97/8 UpperDeck 216
97/8 UDBlackDiamond 81
95/6 udElite 51, NA6
97/8 UpperDeckIce 39
96 Wien 206

KNUUDE, MIKE
83/4 Belleville 6
84/5 Belleville 6

KOBERLE, WALTER
79 PaniniSticker 111
72 SemicSticker 115

KOBRC, ROMAN
92/3 BCJHL 233

KOCH, PAUL
95/6 Toledo

KOCHAN, DIETER
92/3 BCJHL 64

KOCHTA, JIRI
94/5 DEL 390
95/6 DEL 406
72 Hellas 87
74 Hellas 75
70/1 Kuvajulkaisut 51
72 SemicSticker 28
74 SemicSticker 58
71/2 WilliamsFIN 30
72/3 WilliamsFIN 12
73/4 WilliamsFIN 53

KOCUR, JOEY
91/2 Bowman 69
92/3 Bowman 80
90/1 OPC/Topps 55
91/2 OPC/Topps 427
92/3 O-Pee-Chee 169
98/9 Pacific 195
97/8 PacificRegime 70
87/8 PaniniSticker 251
89/90 PaniniSticker 67
90/1 PaniniSticker 211
93/4 Parkhurst 401
91/2 Pinnacle 240
92/3 Pinnacle 152
93/4 Pinnacle 184
94/5 Pinnacle 243
97/8 PinnacleBeAPlayer 153
93/4 Premier 512
90/1 ProSet 73
90/1 Score 201
91/2 Score(CDN) 92, (U.S) 92
92/3 Score 24
93/4 Score 270
92/3 Topps 128
91/2 ToppsStadiumClub 365
92/3 ToppsStadiumClub 417
94/5 ToppsStadiumClub 73
90/1 UpperDeck 411
94//5 UpperDeck 479
95/6 UpperDeck 314
85/6 DET/Caesars
86/7 DET/Caesars
87/8 DET/Caesars
88/9 DET/Caesars
89/90 DET/Caesars
83/4 Saskatoon 22

KOCUR, KORY
90/1 ProCards 483
91/2 ProCards 255
90/1 Score 384
89/90 Saskatoon 24
86/7 Saskatoon

KOECK, MATT
93/4 Johnstown 22

KOHARSKI, DON
90/1 ProSet 691

KOHMANN, CHRISTIAN
94/5 DEL 345
95/6 DEL 320

KOHN, LADISLAV
95/6 Bowman 122
96/7 Fleer 128, -Calder 5
94/5 ParkieSE 211
96/7 SkyBoxImpact 151
94/5 UpperDeck 509
95/6 SaintJohn

KOHVAKKA, TEEMU
95 Semic 239
93/4 Sisu 153

KOIKKALAINEN, JAAKKO
66/7 Champion 143
70/1 Kuvajulkaisut 259

KOISTINEN, KEIJO
65/6 Hellas 39
80/1 Mallasjuoma 73

KOIVISTO, RAMI
93/4 Jyvas-Hyva 119
93/4 Sisu 15
94/5 Sisu 102

KOIVISTO, TOM
93/4 Sisu 34
94/5 Sisu 292
95/6 Sisu 217
96/7 Sisu 17

KOIVU, JUKKA
73/4 WilliamsFIN 287

KOIVU, SAKU
97/8 Aces 10 (Diamonds)
95/6 Bowman 148, BB17
93/4 Classic 40
94/5 Classic 95, T35
93/4 ClassicProspect IA15
95/6 CoolTrade 13
95/6 Donruss 283, -RatedRook 1
96/7 Don-Dom 10,-HitL 19,-Rtd 6
97/8 Donruss 53
96/7 DonrussCanadianIce 40
97/8 DonrussCanadianIce 19
95/6 DonrussElite 67, -Rookie 8
96/7 D.Elite 80, -Aspirations 5
97/8 DonrussElite 20
97/8 DonrussPreferred 11
97/8 DonrussPriority 14, 210
97/8 D.Prio-DirDep 21,-OpDay27
97/8 D.Prio-Pstcrd 27,-Stamp 27
97/8 D.Studio 19,-Hrd 15,-Por19
96/7 Duracell JB10
97/8 EssoOlympic 48
95 FinnishAllStar 3
96/7 Flair 48, -HotNumbers 6
96/7 Fleer 54, 136
95/6 FleerMetal 180, -IntSteel 10
95/6 F.Metal -Winner 2
96/7 FleerPicks 76, -Jagged 7
95/6 FleerUltra 344, -ExtraAtt 12
96/7 FleerUltra 87
96/7 Fleer-Rookie 7
95 Globe 139
95 Hartwall
92/3 Jyvas-Hyva 177
93/4 Jyvas-Hyva 323
97/8 KatchMedallion 75
95/6 Kelloggs PopUp 5
95 Koululainen
96/7 Kraft
97/8 Kraft -CaseSeries
97/8 Kraft -WorldPro,-WorldBest
96/7 Leaf 204. -Leathr&Laces 20
97/8 Leaf 19, -BannerSeason 15
95/6 LeafLimited 118,-Rook Ph 9
96/7 LeafLimited 10
96/7 LeafPreferred 45, -Steel 5
97/8 Limited 9, 34, 165, -fabric 8
95/6 McDonalds 39
96/7 McDonalds
97/8 McDonalds McD4, F8
96/7 MetalUniverse 80
97/8 Omega 118, 247
97/8 Omega-Game 10,-Stick 10
98/9 Pacific 252,-DynagonIce 11
98/9 Pcfc-GoldCrn 17,-TmCL 13
97/8 PacificCrown 272
97/8 PacificCrownRoyale 69
97/8 PCR -Blades 12, -Lamp 10
97/8 PcfcDynagn! 63,-Tandm 14
97/8 PacificInvincible 71
97/8 Pac.Inv.-Feature 18, -Off 11
97/8 PcfcParamnt 95,-Photo 12
98/9 PcfcParamount 113
98/9 PcfcP-SpecD 10,-TmCL 13
97/8 PcfcRevolutn 71,-TmCL 13
97/8 PcfcRev -AllStarGame 12
96/7 PaniniSticker 37
97/8 PaniniSticker 28
95 PaniniWorlds 174
93/4 Parkhurst 521
95/6 Parkhurst 263, 505, -Aut
95/6 Parkhurst -CrownColl (2) 15
96/7 Pinnacle 202, -TeamPin 10
97/8 Pinnacle 26, -EPIX 10
97/8 Pinnacle -TeamP 7
96/7 P.BeAPlayer-Biscuit 22
97/8 P.BAP 3, -OneTimers 14
97/8 P.BeeHive 13, -TeamBH 13
97/8 PinnacleCert. 44, -Team 18
97/8 PinnInside 13, 16,-Track 16
96/7 PinnacleMint 9
97/8 PinnacleMint 15
95/6 P.Zenith 144, -RookieRoll 1
96/7 P.Zenith 58, -Assailants 5
95/6 Playoff 164
96/7 Playoff 388
97/8 Post 18
96/7 Score 238, -CheckIt 11
97/8 Score 94
97/8 Score(MTL) 7
96/7 Select 64, -Cornerstone 8
95/6 SelectCertified 117, -Fut 5
94 Semic 27
95 Semic 3, 11, 205, 219-224
93/4 Sisu 41, 389
94/5 Sisu 211, -Junior 1
94/5 Sisu-Special 10,-SupChase
95/6 Sisu 165, 199, 400,-Gold 15
95/6 Sisu-Specl 3,-Hel,-SupBon
95/6 SisuLimited 6
95/6 SkyBoxEmotion-Next 7
95/6 SkyBoxImpact 206
96/7 SkBxImpact 62,169,-Fox 13
97/8 SPAuthentic 80, I31
95/6 SP 73
96/7 SP 79, CW2, HC15
96/7 SPx 21, GF1
97/8 SPx 24
98/9 SPx"Finite" 115
96/7 SportFX MiniStix
97/8 SportFX MiniStix
95/6 Summit 186
96/7 Summit 152, -Voltage 14
95 SuomenBeckett 1
95/6 SuperSticker 65
96/7 TeamOut
95/6 Topps 306
98/9 Topps 76, I9, M18
95/6 ToppsFinest 85
96/7 ToppsNHLPicks RS7
95/6 ToppsStadiumClub 203
95/6 ToppsSuperSkills SR11
95/6 TSC-MembersOnly 46
97/8 ToppsSticker 3
92/3 UpperDeck 617
93/4 UpperDeck 569
95/6 UpperDeck 259, H22
96/7 UD 82, 148, 173, 188
96/7 UD HH5, LS20, X16
97/8 UD 293, GJ9, SG18,SS14B
97/8 UD SS15, T8B
95/6 UDBeAPlayer 174, LL5
96/7 UDBlackDiamond 178, RC2
97/8 UDBlackDiamond 46
98/9 UDChoice 105, BH28, SQ8
95/6 UDCollChoice 397
96/7 UDCC 134, 321, C15,UD38
96/7 UDCC-Oversize 8-Apr
97/8 UDCC 129, C11, S5, SQ47
96/7 UpperDeck"Ice" 89, S4
97/8 UpperDeckIce 78, IC4, L9B
96 Wien 11, 37, AS5, 237-240
96 Wien-Super
97/8 Zenith 26,Z30,-ChsgCup 13
95/6 MTL
95/6 MTL/Molson
96/7 MTL
96/7 MTL/MolsonExport
97/8 MTL

KOIVULAHTI, PERTTI
70/1 Kuvajulkaisut 209
80/1 Mallasjuoma 166
79 PaniniSticker 174
82 Skopbank
78/9 SM-Liiga 17, 190
77-80 Sportscaster 76- 1801
71/2 WilliamsFIN 131
72/3 WilliamsFIN 194
73/4 WilliamsFIN 154

KOIVUNEN, HANNU
66/7 Champion 85
70/1 Kuvajulkaisut 158
71/2 WilliamsFIN 229

KOIVUNEN, JARMO
70/1 Kuvajulkaisut 159
71/2 WilliamsFIN 230
72/3 WilliamsFIN 85
73/4 WilliamsFIN 132

KOIVUNEN, KEIJO
72/3 WilliamsFIN 145

KOIVUNEN, MATTI
65/6 Hellas 24
70/1 Kuvajulkaisut 297

KOIVUNEN, PETRO
92/3 Jyvas-Hyva 119
93/4 Jyvas-Hyva 202
93/4 Sisu 277
94/5 Sisu 66, -Fire 12
95/6 Sisu 89
95/6 SisuLimited 60

KOIVUNEN, TONI
92/3 Jyvas-Hyva 152
93/4 Jyvas-Hyva 263
93/4 Sisu 300
95/6 Sisu 267
96/7 Sisu 68

KOIVUNORO, MIKKO
94/5 Sisu 266
95/6 Sisu 88
96/7 Sisu 92

KOJOLA, HEIKKI
72/3 WilliamsFIN 86

KOKKO, PETRI
94/5 Sisu 19
95/6 Sisu 31
96/7 Sisu 29
94/5 ToppsFinest 127

KOKKO, SAMI
92/3 Jyvas-Hyva 112

KOKKOLA, JARI
70/1 Kuvajulkaisut 338

KOKKONEN, OLLI
72/3 WilliamsFIN 213

KOKKONEN, TIMO
70/1 Kuvajulkaisut 298
71/2 WilliamsFIN 191
72/3 WilliamsFIN 229
73/4 WilliamsFIN 263

KOKRMENT, JINDRICH
82 SemicSticker 90

KOLACEK, KAMIL
94/5 APS 226

KOLEHMAINEN, PASI
95/6 Sisu 273

KOLEHMAINEN, RAINER
65/6 Hellas 133

KOLENDA, MIKE
91/2 FerrisState
95/6 Toledo

KOLESAR, MARK
95/6 Bowman 142
95/6 EdgeIce 86
91/2 SketchWHL 212
96/7 UpperDeck 190
92/3 Brandon 13
94/5 StJohns
95/6 StJohns

KOLIJN, PATRICK
79 PaniniSticker 278

KOLKKA, VAINO
66/7 Champion 195
70/1 Kuvajulkaisut 63, 109
72 Panda
71/2 WilliamsFIN 117
72/3 WilliamsFIN 87
73/4 WilliamsFIN 133

KOLKUNOV, ALEXEI
95/6 SP 182

KOLLIKER, JAKOLO
79 PaniniSticker 260

KOLNIK, LUBOMIR
94 Semic 203
91 SemicSticker 119
92 SemicSticker 143
95/6 Sisu 291, 373
96 Wien 232

KOLSTAD, DEAN
91/2 O-Pee-Chee 4S
89/90 ProCards(IHL) 94
91/2 ProCards 518

KOLZIG, OLAF
95/6 Donruss 254
97/8 DonrussPriority 35
93/4 FleerUltra 447
97/8 Omega 242
91/2 OPC/Topps 290
98/9 Pacific 37, -DynagonIce 20
98/9 Pcfc-GoldCrn 36, -TmCL 27
97/8 PacificCrownRoyale 141
97/8 PCR-FreezeOut 20
97/8 PacificParamount 196
98/9 PcfcP. 20, 247, -Glove 20
97/8 PacificRegime 210
97/8 PcfcRevolutn 149,-Retrn 20
95/6 Parkhurst 220
95/6 Pinnacle 134
97/8 Pinnacle 89
96/7 PinnacleBeAPlayer 78
97/8 PinnacleInside -StandUp 7
93/4 Premier 291
91/2 ProCards 550
90/1 Score 392
97/8 Score 25
98/9 SPx"Finite" 88
96/7 Summit 48
98/9 Topps 193, M2
93/4 ToppsStadiumClub 438
95/6 ToppsStadiumClub 217
93/4 UpperDeck 326
94/5 UpperDeck 486
95/6 UpperDeck 103
96/7 UpperDeck 354
98/9 UDChoice 215
97/8 Zenith 59, Z30
95/6 WSH
91/2 Baltimore 6
93/4 Portland
92/3 Rochester/DunkinDonuts
92/3 Rochester/Kodak

KOMADOSKI, NEIL
74/5 Loblaws
73/4 OPC/Topps 16
74/5 OPC 358
75/6 OPC/Topps 238
76/7 OPC 284
77/8 OPC 344
78/9 OPC 382

KOMARNISKI, ZENITH
97/8 Bowman 86
98 BowmanCHL 46
95/8 UpperDeck 516
98/9 UDChoice 263

KOMAROV, PAVEL
95/6 Binghampton

KOMONOSKY, WARD
84/5 PrinceAlbert

KOMMA, MICHAEL
94/5 DEL 61
95/6 DEL 61

KOMSI, ANTTI
66/7 Champion 209

KONDRASHKIN, SERGEI
93/4 Parkhurst 532
93/4 Pinnacle 511

KONECNY, MICHAL
95/6 APS 210

KÖNIG, RUDY
79 PaniniSticker 307

KONIGER, STEFAN
94/5 DEL 125

KONIK, GEORGE
72 SemicSticker 132
72/3 Minnesota

KONOVALENKO, VIKTOR
70/1 Kuvajulkaisut 5
72 Panda
72 SemicSticker 1
74 SemicSticker 50
70/1 Soviet Stars
71/2 Soviet Stars
71/2 WilliamsFIN 4

KONOWALCHUK, STEVE
91/2 Classic 46
91/2 ClassicFourSport 46, -Aut
92/3 ClassicProspects 102
95/6 Donruss 296
92/3 FleerUltra 437
94/5 FleerUltra 389
95/6 FleerUltra 324
94/5 Leaf 423
95/6 Leaf 323
92/3 opcPremier 15
98/9 Pacific 443
97/8 PacificCrown 69
97/8 PcfcDynag! 132,-Tandm 58
97/8 PacificInvincible 148
97/8 PacificParamount 197
98/9 PacificParamount 248
95/6 PaniniSticker 137
92/3 Parkuhrst 202
93/4 Parkhurst 223
95/6 Parkhurst 493
94/5 ParkieSE 192
94/5 Pinnacle 348
96/7 Pinnacle 131
96/7 PinnacleBeAPlayer 173
95/6 POG 279
94/5 Premier 273
93/4 Score 458
96/7 Score 135
97/8 Score 220
90/1 SketchWHL 312
91/2 SketchWHL 30
95/6 SP 160
91/2 StarPics 9
93/4 ToppsStadiumClub 481
91/2 UltimateDP 41, -Au t 41
91/2 UD'CzechWJC 73
92/3 UpperDeck 418
93/4 UpperDeck 28
94/5 UpperDeck 214
96/7 UpperDeck 179
97/8 UpperDeck 174
95/6 UDBeAPlayer 118
95/6 UDCollChoice 318
96/7 UDCollChoice 281
97/8 UDCollChoice 274
92/3 WSH/Kodak
95/6 WSH

KONROYD, STEVE
92/3 Bowman 18
92/3 FleerUltra 300
82/3 OPC 48
83/4 OPC 85
84/5 OPC 226
87/8 OPC/Topps 153
88/9 OPC/Topps 171
89/90 OPC 220
91/2 OPC/Topps 366
92/3 OPC 238
88/9 opcSticker 110/242
88/9 PaniniSticker 284
91/2 Parkhurst 287
92/3 Parkhurst 299
91/2 Pinnacle 180
92/3 Pinnacle 352
94/5 Pinnacle 339
94/5 Premier 394
90/1 ProSet 52
92/3 ProSet 62
91/2 PSPlatinum 177
90/1 Score 29
91/2 Score(CDN) 189, (U.S) 189
92/3 Score 172
93/4 Score 219
92/3 Topps 411
92/3 ToppsStadiumClub 236
83/4 Vachon 9
81/2 CGY
82/3 CGY
85/6 CGY/RedRooster
89/90 CHI/Coke
90/1 CHI/Coke
91/2 CHI/Coke
91/2 HFD/JuniorWhalers
92/3 HFD/DairyMart
80/1 Oshawa 9

KONSTANTINOV, VLADIMIR
97/8 Aces K (Diamonds)
92/3 Bowman 326
96/7 Donruss 83
97/8 Donruss 65
94/5 Flair 49
94/5 Fleer 60
96/7 Fleer 31, 143, -Norris 6
95/6 FleerMetal 46
92/3 FleerUltra 49
93/4 FleerUltra 150
94/5 FleerUltra 61
95/6 FleerUltra 46
96/7 FU 51, -Blue 6, -Power 9
95 Globe 166
91 IFiodorovSportUnites
93/4 Leaf 237
94/5 Leaf 391
95/6 Leaf 283
96/7 Leaf 110
96/7 MetalUniv. 46, -CoolSleet 6
90/1 O-Pee-Chee 21R
92/3 O-Pee-Chee 267
91/2 opcPremier 118, 155
97/8 PacificCrown 189, -Supial 7
97/8 PacificDynagon! 42
97/8 PcfcD-Dyn 7B,-Tandem 26
97/8 PacificInvin. 47, Feature 13
96/7 PaniniSticker 147, 182
97/8 PaniniSticker 147
91/2 Parkhurst 46
92/3 Parkhurst 283
93/4 Parkhurst 325
95/6 Parkhurst 69
94/5 ParkieSE 53
91/2 Pinnacle 311
92/3 Pinnacle 76
93/4 Pinnacle 264
94/5 Pinnacle 116
95/6 Pinnacle 129
96/7 Pinnacle 65
97/8 PinnacleInside 126
95/6 Playoff 145
94/5 POG 94
93/4 PowerPlay 73
93/4 Premier 108
94/5 Premier 448
91/2 ProSet 533
92/3 ProSet 44
91/2 PSPlatinum 254
91/2 RedAce
91/2 Score(CDN) 659
91/2 Score(U.S) 109T
92/3 Score 31, 503, -YngStar 23
93/4 Score 20
94/5 Score 96
95/6 Score 176
96/7 Score 84
97/8 Score 228
97/8 Score(DET) 9
89 SemicSticker 86
91 SemicSticker 81
92 SemicSticker 108
95/6 SkyBoxEmotion 54
95/6 SkyBoxImpact 53
96/7 SkyBoxImpact 35, -Fox 12
87/8 SovietStars
89/90 SovietStars
96/7 SP 53
96/7 Summit 63
92/3 Topps 14, 165
96/7 ToppsNHLPicks 169
92/3 ToppsStadiumClub 418
93/4 ToppsStadiumClub 333
94/5 ToppsStadiumClub 159
91/2 UpperDeck 594
92/3 UpperDeck 267, 357
92/3 UD AR5, AR7, E10, W5
93/4 Upper Deck 366
94/5 UpperDeck 189
95/6 UpperDeck 190
96/7 UpperDeck 52, P12
97/8 UpperDeck 63, 203
95/6 UDBeAPlayer 216
96/7 UDBlackDiamond 16
96/7 UDCollChoice 82, 302, 316
97/8 UDCollChoice 82, SQ33
96/7 DET/PhotoPucks

KONTIO, ESA
70/1 Kuvajulkaisut 371

KONTNY, JOSEF
94/5 DEL 152
95/6 DEL 147

KONTOS, CHRIS
91/2 CanadaNats
93/4 CanadaNats
93/4 EASports 131
92/3 FleerUltra 412
93/4 FleerUltra 162
93/4 Leaf 160
92/3 opcPremier 123
93/4 PaniniSticker 213
92/3 Parkhurst 176
93/4 Parkhurst 197
93/4 Pinnacle 8
93/4 PowerPlay 233
93/4 Premier 215, -TeamCan 14
89/90 ProCards(AHL) 14
90/1 ProCards 359
93/4 Score 113
94/5 Score CT6
92/3 TSC-MembersOnly
92/3 UpperDeck 502
93/4 UpperDeck 54
87/8 PGH/Kodak
92/3 T.B/Sheraton

KONTSEK, ROMAN
94 Semic 204

KONTTILA, MIKKO
93/4 Sisu 20
94/5 Sisu 111, 350
95/6 Sisu 280

KONTTO, PERTTI
65/6 Hellas 71

KOOPMAN, KEVIN
90/1 SketchWHL 257
91/2 SketchWHL 188

KOOPMANS, BRAD
91/2 AvantGardeBCJHL 70

KOOPMAS, LEO
79 PaniniSticker 282

KOPCZYNSKI, ADAM
74 Hellas 99
73/4 WilliamsFIN 94

KOPEC, DAN
90/1 SketchWHL 227
91/2 SketchWHL 204
90/1 Brandon 12

KÖPF, ERNST
94/5 DEL 98
95/6 DEL 283
95 PaniniWorlds 71
93 Semic 161
94 Semic 284
95 Semic 168
92 SemicSticker 181
92/3 UpperDeck 372

KOPOT, ARTEM
91/2 UD'CzechWJC 9

KOPRIVA, BRETISLAV
94/5 APS 300
95/6 APS 124

KOPTA, PETR
94/5 DEL 425
95/6 DEL 112
96/7 DEL 55

KORAB, JERRY
74/5 Loblaws
72/3 OPC 285
73/4 OPC 203
74/5 OPC 354
75/6 OPC/Topps 192
76/7 OPC/Topps 27
77/8 OPC/Topps 128
78/9 OPC/Topps 231
79/80 OPC/Topps 74
80/1 OPC 300
81/2 OPC 145, Topps(W) 97
81/2 opcSticker 240
83/4 opcSticker 297
83/4 SouhaitsRen.KeyChain
71/2 TheTorontoSun
74/5 BUF
79/80 BUF/BellsMarket
80/1 L.A.
73/4 VAN/RoyalBank

KORBELA, JAROSLAV
82 Semic 95

KORBER, DANIEL
94/5 DEL 279
95/6 DEL 275
96/7 DEL 171

KORCHINSKI, LARRY
83/4 Saskatoon 16

KORDIC, DAN
97/8 PacificRegime 142
91/2 Pinnacle 338
97/8 PinnacleBeAPlayer 158
91/2 ProSet 553
90/1 SketchWHL 40
91/2 PHA/JCPenney
96/7 PHA/OceanSpray

KORDIC, JOHN
90/1 O-Pee-Chee 401
90/1 ProSet 536
91/2 ProSet 468
85/6 MTL
86/7 MTL
87/8 MTL
87/8 MTL/Stickers 57, 58
91/2 QUE/PetroCanada

KORHONEN, ERKKI
80/1 Mallasjuoma 60
78/9 SM-Liiga 84

KORHONEN, JUHA
71/2 WilliamsFIN 368

KORHONEN, MATTI
66/7 Champion 106

KORINEK, PETR
93/4 Jyvas-Hyva 233
93/4 Sisu 205
94/5 Sisu 244, -Fire 13
95/6 Sisu 78, 374
95/6 SisuLimited 68
97/8 udSwedish 181

KORJAKOFF, PEKKA
65/6 Hellas 51

KORKEAMAKI, JORMA
70/1 Kuvajulkaisut 331

KORN, JIM
81/2 OPC 91, Topps(W) 91
82/3 OPC 323
83/4 OPC 335
84/5 OPC 304
90/1 OPC 450
81/2 opcSticker 127
84/5 opcSticker 17
89/90 PaniniSticker 261
83/4 Vachon 91
86/7 BUF
79/80 DET
80/1 DET
88/9 N.J./Caretta
89/90 N.J.
82/3 TOR
83/4 TOR
84/5 TOR
85/6 TOR

KORNEY, MIKE
75/6 OPC 342

KOROL, DAVE
88/9 ProCards(Adirondack)
89/90 ProCards(IHL) 121
90/1 ProCards 309
91/2 ProCards 328

KOROLEV, ANDREI
95/6 ElitSet 295
95/6 udElite 197

KOROLEV, EVGENY
95/6 Slapshot 325

KOROLEV, IGOR
95/6 Bowman 9
93/4 Donruss 297
94/5 Donruss 239
95/6 Donruss 352
95/6 FleerMetal 163
92/3 FleerUltra 395
93/4 FleerUltra 185
95/6 FleerUltra 327
93/4 Leaf 96
94/5 Leaf 90
95/6 Leaf 48
95/6 LeafLimited 32
97/8 Omega 222
91/2 O-Pee-Chee 37R
92/3 opcPremier 53
98/9 Pacific 416
98/9 PacificParamount 229
97/8 PacificRevolution 135
95/6 PaniniSticker 215
96/7 PaniniSticker 199
97/8 PaniniSticker 159
92/3 Parkhurst 158
93/4 Parkhurst 446
95/6 Parkhurst 227
94/5 ParkieSE 156
92/3 Pinnacle 417
95/6 PinnacleZenith 63
95/6 Playoff 327
96/7 Playoff 407
95/6 POG 291
93/4 PowerPlay 214
93/4 Premier 409
92/3 RedAce(Blue) 10,(Violet) 15
93/4 Score 271
94 Semic 161
93 SemicSticker 145
95/6 SP 168
95/6 Summit 28
95/6 Topps 146
95/6 ToppsFinest 84
93/4 ToppsStadiumClub 119
94/5 ToppsStadiumClub 46
95/6 ToppsStadiumClub 131
92/3 UD 338, 581, CC2, ER3
93/4 UpperDeck 353
94/5 UpperDeck 184, 344
95/6 UpperDeck 135, 299, SE90
95/6 UDCollChoice 257
96/7 UDCollChoice 202
96 Wien 145
96/7 PHO
95/6 WPG

KOROLIOUK, ALEXANDER
98/9 Pacific 383
94/5 ParkieSE 228
94/5 SP 165
95/6 SP 179
94/5 UpperDeck 517
97/8 S.J/PacificBellSheet

KOROLL, CLIFF
77/8 Coke Mini
70/1 EddieSargent 37
71/2 EddieSargent 35
72/3 EddieSargent 59
70/1 Esso Stamp
74/5 Loblaws
70/1 OPC 147
71/2 OPC/Topps 209
72/3 OPC 222
73/4 OPC/Topps 28
74/5 OPC/Topps 35
75/6 OPC/Topps 139
76/7 OPC/Topps 242, OPC 382
77/8 OPC/Topps 146
78/9 OPC/Topps 239
79/80 OPC/Topps 102
71/2 TheTorontoSun
79/80 CHI
80/1 CHI/4x6

KOROTKOV, KONSTANTIN
92/3 Classic 56
91/2 UD 654,-CzechWJC 15

KORPELA, KIMMO
72/3 WilliamsFIN 265

KORPISALO, JARI
92/3 Jyvas-Hyva 202
93/4 Jyvas-Hyva 357
95 Latkaliiga 3
94 Semic 42
95 Semic 18
93 SemicSticker 66
93/4 Sisu 223
94/5 Sisu 217, 378, -Fire 14
94/5 Sisu-Magic 8, -Special 2
95/6 Sisu 154, -Spotlight 2
96/7 Sisu 161, 184, -Mighty 8
95/6 SisuLimited 22

KORTELAINEN, MIKA
92/3 Jyvas-Hyva 10
93/4 Sisu 104
94/5 Sisu 105
95/6 Sisu 8
96/7 Sisu 13, -Mighty 4
95/6 SisuLimited 43

KORTESAOJA, JARKKO
95/6 Sisu 69

KORTKO, ROGER
88/9 ProCards(Binghampton)
84/5 NYI 10
81/2 Saskatoon 11
84/5 Springfield 22

KOS, KYLE
97/8 Bowman 156

KOSIR, SASO
79 PaniniSticker 399

KOSIR, TOMAZ
79 PaniniSticker 396

KOSKELA, ILPO
66/7 Champion 109
70/1 Kuvajulkaisut 64, 177
72 Panda
72 SemicSticker 72
74 SemicSticker 100
91 SemicSticker 227
96/7 Sisu 193
77-80 Sportscaster 52-1243
71/2 WilliamsFIN 64, 102
72/3 WilliamsFIN 146
73/4 WilliamsFIN 66, 111

KOSKELA, PEKKA
78/9 SM-Liiga 102

KOSKELA, PENTTI
72 Panda
71/2 WilliamsFIN 178
72/3 WilliamsFIN 126

KOSKELA, TERHO
89/90 SemicElitserien 275
90/1 SemicElitserien 42
91/2 SemicElitserien 292
92/3 SemicElitserien 313

KOSKI, PETRI
92/3 Jyvas-Hyva 150
93/4 Jyvas-Hyva 261
93/4 Sisu 286

KOSKILAHTI, JORMA
78/9 SM-Liiga 214
73/4 WilliamsFIN 286

KOSKIMAKI, TAPANI
66/7 Champion 6
70/1 Kuvajulkaisut 230
78/9 SM-Liiga 160
71/2 WilliamsFIN 245

KOSKIMIES, HEIKKI
65/6 Hellas 155

KOSKINEN, HANNU
80/1 Mallasjuoma 88
82 SemicSticker 44
82 Skopbank
78/9 SM-Liiga 120
77-80 Sportscaster 86- 2064

KOSKINEN, KALLE
93/4 Sisu 6, 142
94/5 Sisu 39, -Junior 5
95/6 Sisu 58
96/7 Sisu 56

KOSKINEN, KARI
70/1 Kuvajulkaisut 332

KOSKINEN, MATTI
66/7 Champion 118
71/2 WilliamsFIN 282
73/4 WilliamsFIN 199

KOSKINEN, TAPIO
74 Hellas 7
70/1 Kuvajulkaisut 195
80/1 Mallasjuoma 205
72 Panda
78/9 SM-Liiga 230
71/2 WilliamsFIN 87
72/3 WilliamsFIN 250
73/4 WilliamsFIN 249

KOSLOWSKI, THORSTEN
94/5 DEL 218

KOSONEN, LAURI
70/1 Kuvajulkaisut 313
72/3 WilliamsFIN 330

KOSTAINY, MILAN
95/6 Slapshot 228

KOSTI, RICK
85/6 Moncton 15

KOSTIAINEN, JOUNI
71/2 WilliamsFIN 325

KOSTICHKIN, PAVEL
92/3 ClassicProspects 137
90/1 O-Pee-Chee 20R
91/2 O-Pee-Chee 17R

KOSTKA, ROBERT
94/5 APS 30
95/6 APS 134

KOSTNER, ERWIN
79 PaniniSticker 388
82 SemicSticker 125

KOSTOLNY, MILAN
94/5 SlapshotMEM 94
95/6 SlapshotOHL 228

KOSTUCH, JEFF
95/6 Classic 93
91/2 SketchOHL 41
95/6 Hampton HRA -18
93/4 OwenSound

KOSTUCH, JIRI
95/6 Classic 93

KOSTUCHENKO, MALCOLM
91/2 AirCanadaSJHL 10

KOSTURIK, MARK
94/5 DEL 65
95/6 DEL 64, 435
96/7 DEL 216

KOSTYNSKI, DOUG
85/6 Moncton 8
86/7 Moncton 4

KOSYL, VALERY
74 Hellas 100
73/4 WilliamsFIN 95

KOTALA, LUMIR
94/5 APS 136

KOTASEK, MARTIN
94/5 APS 200
95/6 APS 48

KOTKANIEMI, MIKAEL
93/4 Jyvas-Hyva 349
93/4 Sisu 231
94/5 Sisu 125
95/6 Sisu 159

KOTKAS, PENTTI
65/6 Hellas 141

KOTNAUER, FRANZ
79 PaniniSticker 306

KOTONSKI, ANDRZEJ
92 SemicSticker 282

KOTRLA, JINDRICH
95/6 APS 163

KOTSOPOULOS, CHRIS
82/3 OPC 124
84/5 OPC 73
87/8 OPC 244
89/90 OPC 279
82/3 opcSticker 132
89/90 opcSticker 180/38
82/3 Post
83/4 SouhaitsRen.KeyChain
89/90 ProCards(IHL) 309
82/3 HFD/JuniorWhalers
83/4 HFD/JuniorWhalers
84/5 HFD/JuniorWhalers
85/6 TOR
86/7 TOR
87/8 TOR
87/8 TOR/P.L.A.Y. 16
88/9 TOR/P.L.A.Y. 16

KOURULA, AARRE
80/1 Mallasjuoma 48

KOUTUANIEMI, JOUNI
80/1 Mallasjuoma 102

KOVACEVIC, JURA
95/6 Slapshot 267

KOVACS, BILL
90/1 SketchOHL 385
91/2 SketchOHL 348
89/90 Sudbury 3
90/1 Sudbury 14

KOVACS, CSABA
79 PaniniSticker 268

KOVACS, FRANK
94/5 DEL 348
90/1 SketchWHL 179
91/2 SketchWHL 232
92/3 Dayton
90/1 Newmarket
87/8 Regina
88/9 Regina
89/90 Regina
95/6 SaintJohn
97/8 SheffieldSteelers

KOVACS, JOHN
90/1 SketchQMJHL 74
91/2 SketchQMJHL 240

KOVALENKO, ANDREI
93/4 Donruss 278
94/5 Donruss 6
95/6 Donruss 374
94/5 Fleer 178
92/3 FleerUltra 387, -Imports 9
93/4 FleerUltra 144
94/5 FleerUltra 175
95 Globe 176
97/8 KatchMedallion 58
93/4 Leaf 122
94/5 Leaf 71
95/6 Leaf 130
96/7 Maggers 83
96/7 MetalUniverse 54
91/2 O-Pee-Chee18R
92/3 opcPremier 93
97/8 PacificCrown 51
97/8 PacificParamount 76
93/4 PaniniSticker 71
96/7 PaniniStickers 42
97/8 PaniniSticker
95 PaniniWorlds 42
92/3 Parkhurst 150, 223
93/4 Parkhurst 167
95/6 Parkhurst 51, 382
92/3 Pinnacle 395
93/4 Pinnacle 171
94/5 Pinnacle 128
96/7 Pinnacle 152
97/8 PinnacleCertified 106
97/8 PinnacleInside 177
95/6 Playoff 138
94/5 POG 196
95/6 POG 75
93/4 PowerPlay 200
93/4 Premier 124, 198
94/5 Premier 97
92/3 RedAce(Blue) 34,(Violet) 16
93/4 Score 174
94/5 Score 39
95/6 Score 253
96/7 Score 196
97/8 Score 178
95 Semic 133
92 SemicSticker 117
96/7 SP 58
93/4 ToppsStadiumClub 77
92/3 UD 567, CC17, ER14, G19
93/4 UpperDeck 85
94/5 UpperDeck 272
95/6 UpperDeck 446
96/7 UDBlackDiamond 51
95/6 UDCollChoice 54
96/7 UDCollChoice 137
97/8 UDCollChoice 90
96 Wien 144
96/7 EDM
97/8 EDM
92/3 QUE/PetroCanada
94/5 QUE/BurgerKing

KOVALEV, ALEXEI
93/4 Classic 137
92/3 C'Prospct 10, 74, BC1, LP2
93/4 ClassicProspects 52, -Aut 5
93/4 Donruss 220
94/5 Donruss 268
95/6 Donruss 216
96/7 Donruss 176
96/7 D.CanadianIce 41
94/5 Flair 112, -ScoringPower 4
94/5 Fleer 133
96/7 Fleer 69
95/6 FleerMetal 95, -Winners 3
92/3 FleerUltra 137, -UltraImp 10
93/4 FleerUltra 115
94/5 FleerUltra 331
95/6 FleerUltra 275
96/7 FleerUltra 107
95 Globe 177
93/4 Leaf 147
94/5 Leaf 92
95/6 Leaf 203
96/7 Leaf 135
94/5 LeafLimited 59
95/6 LeafLimited 48
96/7 LeafPreferred 96
94/5 McDonalds 38
96/7 MetalUniverse 97
92/3 opcPremier 126
98/9 Pacific 294
97/8 PacificCrown 119
97/8 PacificDynagon! 79
97/8 PacificD-Tandem 19, 72
97/8 PacificInvincible 87
97/8 PacificParamount 116
98/9 PacificParamount 153
94/5 PaniniSticker 83
95/6 PaniniSticker 106
96/7 PaniniSticker 104
97/8 PaniniSticker 85
92/3 Parkhurst 109, 225
93/4 Parkhurst 130, 238
94/5 Parkhurst 142
95/6 Parkhurst 139
94/5 Parkie V24, ES-18
92/3 Pinnacle 403
93/4 Pinnacle 76, -Team2001 7
94/5 Pinnacle 107
96/7 Pinnacle 45
97/8 Pinnacle 120
95/6 Playoff 67
94/5 POG 163
95/6 POG 184
93/4 PowerPlay 159
93/4 Premier 187
94/5 Premier 185
92/3 RedAce(Blue) 8, (Violet) 17
93/4 Score 203, -Int'lStars 19
95/6 Score 79
96/7 Score 61
97/8 Score 156
97/8 Score(NYR) 7
94/5 Select 66
95/6 SelectCertified 88
91 SemicSticker 93
95/6 SkyBoxEmotion 113
95/6 SkyBoxImpact 109
96/7 SkyBoxImpact 80
94/5 SP 76
95/6 SP 99
96/7 SP 104, HC7
97/8 SPAuthentic 102
91/2 StarPics 48
95/6 Summit 97
96/7 Summit 82
95/6 SuperSticker 81
95/6 Topps 90, YS9
96/7 ToppsNHLPicks 79
93/4 ToppsStadiumClub 129
95/6 ToppsStadiumClub 218
91/2 UD 655,-CzechWJC 16
92/3 UpperDeck 573, 633
92/3 UD G13,WG9,CC11, ER10
93/4 UD 27, HT7, HB6, SP101
94/5 UpperDeck 207, 567, SP49
95/6 UpperDeck 132, SE56
96/7 UpperDeck 103
97/8 UpperDeck 319
95/6 UDBeAPlayer 182, LL15
96/7 UDBlackDiamond 27
95/6 UDCollChoice 234
96/7 UDCollChoice 176

KOVALEV, ANDREIJ
94/5 DEL 423
95/6 DEL 81

KOVALYOV, ANDREI
91/2 O-Pee-Chee 38R

KOVANEN, TOMMI
96/7 Sisu 70

KOVARIK, MARTIN
94/5 APS 143
95/6 APS 247

KOVIN, V.
80 SovietMiniPics

KOWALCHUK, KEVIN
83/4 Saskatoon 13
84/5 Saskatoon

KOWALCHUK, PETER
52/3 AnonymousOHL 173

KOWALCHUK, SHELDON
88/9 Brandon 13

KOWALCZYK, PAVEL
94/5 APS 185
95/6 APS 34

KOWALSKI, SCOTT
91/2 AvantGardeBCJHL 53
91/2 Nainamo

KOWALSKY, RICK
93/4 C'Prospects 136
90/1 SketchMEM 11
90/1 SketchOHL 162
91/2 SketchOHL 330
94/5 Hampton 13
95/6 Hampton HRA-10
89/90 SSMarie 14
93/4 SSMarie 13

KOZACK, KELLY
83/4 Brandon 5

KOZAK, DAN
74/5 Loblaws
74/5 OPC/Topps 98, 111
75/6 OPC/Topps 276
76/7 OPC/Topps 185
77/8 OPC 316
79/80 OPC 342

KOZAK, GEORGE
96/7 Penascola 23

KOZAK, TODD
91/2 AirCanadaSJHL C23
92/3 MPSPhotoSJHL 90

KOZAKOSKI, JEFF
93/4 Waterloo

KOZJEVNIKOV, ALEXANDER
89/90 SemicElitserien 17
82 SemicSticker 73

KOZLOV, ANDREI
94/5 Erie

KOZLOV, VIKTOR
95/6 Bowman 159
92/3 Classic 61, 62
93/4 Classic 6, DP6
94/5 Classic 113, R12, T61
92/3 C'Prospects 93, BC9, LP4
93/4 ClassicProspects IA18
95/6 Donruss 171
95/6 EdgeIce 145, C10, PR4
94/5 FleerUltra 366, -UltraPros 5
94/5 Leaf 451, -Phenoms 8
95/6 Leaf 73
94/5 LeafLimited 21
95/6 LeafLimited 77
94/5 McDonalds 33
98/9 Pacific 223
97/8 PacificCC 125
97/8 PacificCrownRoyale 58
97/8 PcfcDynag! 113,-Tandm 64
97/8 PacificParamount 166
98/9 PacificParamount 97
95/6 PaniniSticker 279
96/7 PaniniSticker 282
97/8 PaniniSticker 231
95/6 Parkhurst 187, 515
94/5 ParkieSE 159
95/6 ParkieSE seV43
94/5 Pinnacle 477, 481, RTP5
95/6 Pinnacle 99,-GlobalGold 16
95/6 POG 229
94/5 Score TR10
95/6 Score 114
97/8 Score 223
94/5 Select 174, YE6
93 SemicSticker 140
97/8 SPAuthentic 70
95/6 Summit 142
95/6 Topps 357
98/9 Topps 83
94/5 ToppsFinest 46
95/6 ToppsStadiumClub 137
92/3 UpperDeck 613
94/5 UpperDeck 265, C3
95/6 UpperDeck 92
96/7 UpperDeck 152
97/8 UpperDeck 359
94/5 UDBAP R158, -Aut 153
95/6 UDCollChoice 252
96/7 UDCollChoice 237
97/8 UDCollChoice 217
96 Wien 147
97/8 FLA/WinnDixie
92/3 S.J/PacificBell
96/7 S.J/PacificBellSheet
97/8 S.J/PacificBellSheet

KOZLOV, VYACHESLAV (SLAVA)
92/3 Bowman 300
95/6 Bowman 77
93/4 Classic 6
92/3 ClassicProspects 135
93/4 ClassicProspects 214
93/4 Donruss 91
94/5 Donruss 180
95/6 Donruss 134
96/7 Donruss 19
97/8 Donruss 119
96/7 DonrussCanadianIce 71
97/8 D.CdnIce-Scrapbook 25
95/6 DonrussElite 87
96/7 DonrussElite 81
97/8 DonrussElite 25
97/8 DonrussPreferred 134
97/8 DonrussPriority 130
95/6 EdgeIce C17
94/5 Flair 50
94/5 Fleer 61
96/7 Fleer 32
95/6 FleerMetal 47
92/3 FleerUltra 50
93/4 FleerUltra 174
94/5 FleerUltra 284
95/6 FleerUltra 47
96/7 FleerUltra 52
97/8 KatchMedallion 50
93/4 Leaf 303
94/5 Leaf 236
95/6 Leaf 210, -RoadToThe 8
96/7 Leaf 196
97/8 Leaf 31
94/5 LeafLimited 55
96/7 LeafLimited 88
96/7 LeafPreferred-LeafSteel 38
97/8 Limited 91
96/7 Maggers 53
96/7 MetalUniverse 47
97/8 Omega 81
92/3 O-Pee-Chee 235
92/3 opcPremier 71
98/9 Pacific 196
97/8 PacificCrownC 267
97/8 PacificCrownRoyale 46
97/8 PacificInvincible 48
97/8 PacificParamount 66
98/9 PacificParamount 76
94/5 PaniniSticker 208
95/6 PaniniSticker 180
96/7 PaniniSticker 183
97/8 PaniniSticker 153
95 PaniniWorlds 45
91/2 Parkhurst 266
92/3 Parkhurst 40
93/4 Parkhurst 57
94/5 Parkhurst 66, V48
95/6 Parkhurst 65
92/3 Pinnacle 230, -Tm2000 13
94/5 Pinnacle 92
95/6 Pinnacle 128
96/7 Pinnacle 129
97/8 Pinnacle 117
97/8 PinnacleBeAPlayer 97
97/8 PinnacleInside 116
96/7 PinnacleZenith 22
95/6 Playoff 254
94/5 POG 88
95/6 POG 97
93/4 PowerPlay 331,-RisingStr 2
93/4 Premier 494
94/5 Premier 145
92/3 ProSet 225
92/3 RedAce(Blue) 18
92/3 Score 473, -YoungStar 32
93/4 Score 421
94/5 Score 70
95/6 Score 165
96/7 Score 158
97/8 Score 209
97/8 Score(DET) 7
94/5 Select 103
94 Semic 152
95 Semic 137
91 SemicSticker 98
92 SemicSticker 111
95/6 SkyBoxEmotion 55
95/6 SkyBoxImpact 54
96/7 SkyBoxImpact 36
94/5 SP 35
95/6 SP 49
96/7 SP 49
97/8 SPAuthentic 50
95/6 Summit 83
96/7 Summit 84
96/7 TeamOut
92/3 Topps 35
95/6 Topps 322, 8PL
95/6 ToppsFinest 83
96/7 ToppsNHLPicks 67
92/3 ToppsStadiumClub 62
93/4 ToppsStadiumClub 388
94/5 ToppsStadiumClub 97
95/6 ToppsStadiumClub 84
91/2 TriGlobe 13-14
91/2 UpperDeck 5, 462
92/3 UpperDeck 294, WG2
93/4 UpperDeck 495
94/5 UpperDeck 373, SP23
95/6 UpperDeck 154, SE117
96/7 UpperDeck 251
97/8 UpperDeck 271,-BlowUp 5
95/6 UDBeAPlayer 99
96/7 UDBlackDiamond 113
97/8 UDBlackDiamond 129
98/9 UDChoice 78
95/6 UDCollChoice 32
96/7 UDCollChoice 81, C18
97/8 UDCollChoice 85, SQ13
96 Wien 146

KOZUBACK, RICK
91/2 ProCards 406
90/1 SketchWHL 96
92/3 Phoenix

KRAEMER, CHRIS
90/1 SketchOHL 163
91/2 SketchOHL 78

KRAFT, RYAN
94/5 Minnesota

KRAFT, THOMAS
92/3 BCJHL 34

KRAFTCHECK, STEVE
45-64 BeeHives(NYR), (TOR)
51/2 Parkhurst 92
52/3 Parkhurst 23
58/9 Parkhurst 37

KRAIGER, YOGI
51/2 LavalDairy 9
52/3 StLawrence 48
51/2 Laval 9

KRAINZ, MARTIN
95 PaniniWorlds 264
93 SemicSticker 274
94 Semic 235

KRAJICEK, JAN
94/5 APS 188
95/6 APS 37

KRAKE, PAUL
92/3 Oklahoma

KRAKE, PHILIP (SKIP)
70/1 DadsCookies
70/1 EddieSargent 24
70/1 Esso Stamp
68/9 OPC/Topps 3, 43
69/70 OPC 141
70/1 OPC/Topps 126
68/9 ShirriffCoin LA11
67/8 Topps 93
72/3 Cleveland

KRAKIWSKY, SEAN
85/6 Minn-Duluth 32

KRAL, RICHARD
94/5 APS 43
95/6 APS 236

KRALIK, JIRI
82 SemicSticker 76

KRAMER, TED
92/3 Phoenix

KRAMMY, TOMAS
94/5 APS 121
95/6 APS 297

KRANWINKEL, MARKUS
94/5 DEL 226

KRASKE, WOLFGANG
79 PaniniSticker 249

KRASNY, TOMAS
95/6 APS 216

KRASOTKIN, DMITRI
95 PaniniWorlds 29

KRASSNER, MIKE
94/5 Birmingham

KRASTINOV, DIMO
79 PaniniSticker 348

KRATENA, ONDREJ
95/6 APS 119
95/6 UpperDeck 540

KRATKY, PETR
95/6 APS 157

KRATZ, MICHAEL
94/5 DEL 353

KRAUS, RICHARD
92/3 BCJHL 186

KRAUSE, SEAN
91/2 AvantGardeBCJ 60
91/2 Nainamo

KRAUSS, DARYL
91/2 AirCanadaSJHL B43
92/3 MPSPhotoSJHL 144

KRAUSS, ROB
93/4 Birmingham 16

KRAVCHUK, IGOR
92/3 Bowman 408
93/4 Donruss 116
94/5 Donruss 259
93/4 EASports 94
94/5 Flair 58
94/5 Fleer 70
92/3 FleerUltra 38
93/4 FleerUltra 80
94/5 FleerUltra 72
95/6 FleerUltra 54
95 Globe 167
93/4 Leaf 163
94/5 Leaf 244
97/8 Omega 155
90/1 O-Pee-Chee 11R, 12R
91/2 O-Pee-Chee 19R
92/3 O-Pee-Chee 161
98/9 Pacific 310
97/8 PacificParamount 126
98/9 PacificParamount 163
97/8 PacificRegime 170
92/3 PaniniSticker 297, A
94/5 PaniniSticker 205
95/6 PaniniSticker 264
97/8 PaniniSticker 165
91/2 Parkhurst 257, 461
92/3 Parkhurst 35, 291
93/4 Parkhurst 65
95/6 Parkhurst 74
94/5 ParkieSE 58
92/3 Pinnacle 225
93/4 Pinnacle 36
94/5 Pinnacle 96
96/7 PinnacleBeAPlayer 3
95/6 Playoff 148
96/7 Playoff 372
94/5 POG 367
95/6 POG 109
93/4 PowerPlay 81
93/4 Premier 495
94/5 Premier 172
92/3 ProSet 35
91/2 RedAce
92/3 Score 454
93/4 Score 309
94/5 Score 33
92/3 SeasonPatches 69
91 SemicSticker 82
92 SemicSticker 103
95/6 SkyBoxEmotion 63
95/6 SkyBoxImpact 61
92/3 Topps 200
98/9 Topps 36
92/3 ToppsStadiumClub 7
93/4 ToppsStadiumClub 204
91/2 TriGlobe 17-18
92/3 UpperDeck 239, 367, E7
93/4 UpperDeck 174
94/5 UpperDeck 463
95/6 UpperDeck 146
96 Wien 132
92/3 EDM
93/4 EDM 8Oct93
97/8 OTT

KRAVETS, MIKHAIL
92/3 Classic 106
91/2 ProCards 505
92/3 UpperDeck 542

KRAWINKEL, MARKUS
94/5 DEL 226
95/6 DEL 221
96/7 DEL 71

KRAYER, EDDIE
89/90 Nashville

KRECHIN, VLADIMIR
93/4 Classic 41

KREISS, HAROLD
94/5 DEL 274
95/6 DEL 266
96/7 DEL 160
82 SemicSticker 106
89 SemicSticker 109
91 SemicSticker 156
92 SemicSticker 173

KREKULA, FREDRIK
97/8 udSwedish 14

KRENTZ, DALE
94/5 DEL 281
95/6 DEL 372
88/9 ProCards(Binghampton)
89/90 ProCards(AHL) 319

KREPELKA, PAUL
92/3 Hampton

KRESS, JAMIE
92/3 Oshawa

KRETCHINS, VLADIMIR
95/6 Slapshot 422

KRETSCHMER, HORST
79 PaniniSticker 102

KREUTZER, CHRISTOPHER
94/5 DEL 85
95/6 DEL 80

KREUZMANN, JAROSLAV
94/5 APS 160
95/6 APS 261

KRIKKE, HENK
79 PaniniSticker 276

KRINNER, ANTON (TONI)
94/5 DEL 16
95/6 DEL 144
96/7 DEL 244
91 SemicSticker 171

KRISAK, PATRIK
93/4 UpperDeck 266

KRISKO, DAN
90/1 SketchOHL 262
91/2 SketchOHL 216

KRISS, AARON
95/6 Tallahassee 4

KRISTIANSEN, ERIK
94 Semic 262
92 SemicSticker 38
93 SemicSticker 238

KRISTIANSEN, PAL
94 Semic 257

KRITZ, PAVEL
94/5 AutoPhonex 22

KRIVCHENKOV, ALEXEI
95/6 Hampton HRA-13

KRIVOKRASOV, SERGEI
92/3 Classic 42
93/4 Classic 138
92/3 ClassicProspects 38
93/4 ClassicProspects 220
93/4 Donruss 74
94/5 Donruss 91
95/6 Donruss 203
94/5 Fleer 41
92/3 FleerUltra 276
93/4 FleerUltra 112
95/6 FleerUltra 33
93/4 Leaf 434
94/5 Leaf 238
95/6 Leaf 32, -StudioRook 18
92/3 opcPremier 9
98/9 Pacific 147
97/8 PacificCrown 134
97/8 PacificParamount 45
98/9 PacificParamount 124
95/6 PaniniSticker 161
97/8 PaniniSticker 135
92/3 Parkhurst 36
94/5 Parkhurst 50
95/6 Parkhurst 314
94/5 ParkieSE 37, seV19
92/3 Pinnacle 410
93/4 Pinnacle 419
94/5 Pinnacle RTP12
95/6 Pinnacle 154
95/6 POG 65
93/4 PowerPlay 51
94/5 Premier 513
93/4 Score 464
95/6 Score 62
95/6 SkyBoxEmotion 29
95/6 SkyBoxImpact 29, -Fox 6
97/8 SPAuthentic 34
95/6 Topps 16NG
98/9 Topps 211
91/2 TriGlobe 9-10
91/2 UD 658,-CzechWJC 19
92/3 UpperDeck 582, ER5
94/5 UpperDeck 80
95/6 UpperDeck 11
97/8 UpperDeck 37
95/6 UDBeAPlayer 187
95/6 UDCollChoice 96
92/3 Indianapolis
93/4 Indianapolis

KRIZ, ONDREJ
93/4 Dayton 6

KROCAK, JIRI
95/6 APS 277

KROL, JOE
33-43 BeeHives(NYA)

KROMM, RICHARD
84/5 OPC 227
85/6 OPC 222
86/7 OPC 229
87/8 PaniniSticker 103
88/9 ProCards(Springfield)
90/1 ProCards 498
91/2 ProCards 465
89/90 SemicElitserien 136
85/6 CGY/RedRooster

KROMP, WOLFGANG
95 PaniniWorlds 270
94 Semic 249

KRON, ROBERT
91/2 Bowman 320
92/3 Bowman 413
93/4 Donruss 143
94/5 Donruss 114
95/6 Donruss 231
94/5 FleerUltra 90
93/4 Leaf 171
94/5 Leaf 101
95/6 Leaf 257
96/7 Leaf 57
91/2 OPC/Topps 52
92/3 O-Pee-Chee 2
90/1 opcPremier 52
98/9 Pacific 136
97/8 PacificCrown 114
98/9 PacificParamount 39
91/2 PaniniSticker 47
92/3 PaniniSticker 33
96/7 PaniniSticker 31
97/8 PaniniSticker 19
91/2 Parkhurst PHC4
93/4 Parkhurst 90
95/6 Parkhurst 92
94/5 ParkieSE 76
93/4 Pinnacle 421
94/5 Pinnacle 336
95/6 Pinnacle 85
96/7 Pinnacle 132
97/8 PinnacleBeAPlayer 140
94/5 POG 114
93/4 PowerPlay 351
94/5 Premier 296
90/1 ProSet 642
91/2 ProSet 239
91/2 PSPlatinum 122
90/1 ScoreTraded 65T
91/2 Score(CDN) 257
93/4 Score 428
95/6 Score 154
96/7 Score 195
94 Semic 181
89 SemicSticker 199
92 SemicSticker 139
92/3 Topps 80
95/6 Topps 161
91/2 ToppsStadiumClub 240
92/3 ToppsStadiumClub 155
94/5 ToppsStadiumClub 146
90/1 UpperDeck 528
91/2 UpperDeck 225, E8
92/3 UpperDeck 69
93/4 UpperDeck 359, SP61
94/5 UpperDeck 408
95/6 UpperDeck 400
94/5 UDBeAPlayer -Aut 66
95/6 UDCollChoice 298
93/4 HFD/Coke
90/1 VAN/Mohawk
91/2 VAN
92/3 VAN/RoadTrip

KROOPSHOOP, MIKE
93/4 Kamloops

KROPF, BARRET
91/2 AirCanadaSJHL A31

KROPF, M.
95/6 DEL 380

KROSEBERG, GUNNAR
95/6 Madison

KROUPA, VLASTIMIL
93/4 ClassicProspects 4
93/4 Donruss 315
94/5 Donruss 277
93/4 FleerUltra 414
94/5 FleerUltra 196
93/4 Leaf 439
94/5 Leaf 265
94/5 LeafLimited 64
93/4 Parkhurst 266
94/5 ParkieSE 167
94/5 Pinnacle 242
94/5 Premier 113
93/4 UpperDeck 437, SP144
94/5 UpperDeck 453
92/3 S.J./PacificBell
96/7 S.J./PacificBellSheet

KRUCHKOWSKI, CORY
92/3 BCJHL 191

KRUEGER, SHAWN
91/2 SketchOHL 276

KRUG, JASON
92/3 MPSPhotoSJHL 101

KRUGER, RAPHAEL
94/5 DEL 372
95/6 DEL 365

KRULIS, JAN
94/5 APS 74
95/6 APS 82

KRULL, HARALD
82 SemicSticker 108

KRUPP, UWE
91/2 Bowman 26
92/3 Bowman 349
95/6 DEL 444
93/4 Donruss 205
95/6 Donruss 49
96/7 Donruss 114
94/5 Fleer 179
92/3 FleerUltra 129
94/5 FleerUltra 358
97/8 Kraft - WorldsBest
93/4 Leaf 57
94/5 Leaf 422
95/6 Leaf 266
96/7 Leaf 49
96/7 MetalUniverse 34
97/8 Omega 58
88/9 OPC 220
90/1 OPC/Topps 390
91/2 OPC/Topps 155
92/3 OPC 173
91/2 opcPremier 140
98/9 Pacific 161
97/8 PacificCrown 265
97/8 PacificRegime 53
89/90 PaniniSticker 216
90/1 PaniniSticker 22
91/2 PaniniSticker 305
92/3 PaniniSticker 202
95/6 PaniniSticker 252
96/7 PaniniSticker 249
97/8 PaniniSticker 200
91/2 Parkhurst 109
92/3 Parkhurst 101, 453
93/4 Parkhurst 388
95/6 Parkhurst 50
91/2 Pinnacle 19
92/3 Pinnacle 86, 240
93/4 Pinnacle 259
94/5 Pinnacle 382
95/6 Pinnacle 46, -GlobalGold 8
96/7 Pinnacle 24
96/7 PinnacleBeAPlayer 87
94/5 POG 201
95/6 POG 79
93/4 PowerPlay 151
93/4 Premier 3
90/1 ProSet 23
91/2 ProSet 20, 301, 436
92/3 ProSet 109
91/2 PSPlatinum 202
90/1 Score 169
91/2 Score(CDN) 84
91/2 Score(U.S) 84, 104T
92/3 Score 77
93/4 Score 87, -Int'lStars 11
95/6 Score 108
96/7 Score 175
97/8 Score(COL) 15
91 SemicSticker 162
93 SemicSticker 168
95/6 SkyBoxEmotion 38
96/7 SkyBoxImpact 24
96/7 Summit 38
92/3 Topps 158
98/9 Topps 11
96/7 ToppsNHLPicks 163
91/2 ToppsStadiumClub 62
92/3 ToppsStadiumClub 177
93/4 ToppsStadiumClub 138
94/5 ToppsStadiumClub 172
90/1 UpperDeck 187
91/2 UpperDeck 102, 540
92/3 UpperDeck 187
94/5 UpperDeck 310
96/7 UpperDeck 39
94/5 UDBeAPlayer -Aut 163
95/6 UDCollChoice 80
96/7 UDCollChoice 56
86/7 BUF/BlueShield
87/8 BUF/BlueShield
87/8 BUF/WonderBread
88/9 BUF/BlueShield
88/9 BUF/WonderBread
89/90 BUF/BlueShield
89/90 BUF/Campbell
90/1 BUF/BlueShield
90/1 BUF/Campbell
94/5 QUE/BurgerKing

KRUPPKE, GORD
89/90 ProCards(AHL) 312
90/1 ProCards 469
91/2 ProCards 138
93/4 Score 467

KRUSE, ERIC
93/4 Mich.State

KRUSE, PAUL
92/3 Classic 115
94/5 Leaf 352
95/6 Leaf 251
97/8 PacificRegime 117
95/6 PaniniSticker 235
95/6 Pinnacle 66
97/8 PinnacleBeAPlayer 42
95/6 Playoff 130
95/6 POG 53
90/1 ProCards 621
91/2 ProCards 581
89/90 SketchMEM 8
95/6 Topps 51
88/9 Kamloops
89/90 Kamloops

KRUSHEL, ROD
91/2 AirCanadaSJHL 33, A12

KRUSHELNYSKI, MIKE
90/1 Bowman 145
91/2 Bowman 166
92/3 Bowman 2
92/3 Durivage 5
92/3 FleerUltra 421
86/7 Kraft Sports 15
94/5 Leaf 438
83/4 O-Pee-Chee 52
84/5 OPC 248, Topps 6
85/6 OPC/Topps 49
86/7 OPC/Topps 193
87/8 O-Pee-Chee 202
88/9 O-Pee-Chee 221
89/90 OPC/Topps 104
90/1 OPC/Topps 167
91/2 OPC/Topps 324
92/3 O-Pee-Chee 335
91/2 opcPremier 189
83/4 opcSticker 43
84/5 opcSticker 188
85/6 opcSticker 223/90
86/7 opcSticker 74/201
87/8 opcSticker 90/223
88/9 opcSticker 226/100
89/90 opcSticker 153/13
87/8 PaniniSticker 266
89/90 PaniniSticker 94
90/1 PaniniSticker 245
91/2 PaniniSticker 97
92/3 PaniniSticker 78
93/4 PaniniSticker 229
92/3 Parkhurst 411
91/2 Pinnacle 269
93/4 Pinnacle 328
93/4 Premier 169
90/1 ProSet 121, 537
91/2 ProSet 233
91/2 PSPlatinum 119
90/1 Score 227, 47T
91/2 Score(CDN) 33, (U.S) 33
92/3 Score 283
93/4 Score 367
83/4 SouhaitsRen.KeyChain
92/3 Topps 450
91/2 ToppsStadiumClub 54
92/3 ToppsStadiumClub 487
93/4 ToppsStadiumClub 306
90/1 UpperDeck 394
91/2 UpperDeck 320
92/3 UpperDeck 87
94/5 UDBeAPlayer -Aut 177
83/4 BOS
84/5 EDM
84/5 EDM/RedRooster
85/6 EDM/RedRooster
86/7 EDM
86/7 EDM/RedRooster
87/8 EDM
88/9 EDM/ActionMagazine 79
88/9 L.A./Smokeys
89/90 L.A./Smokeys 12
90/1 TOR
90/1 TOR/P.L.A.Y. 20
93/4 TOR/Abalene
93/4 TOR/Blacks 23
79/80 Montréal, -B&W

KRUTOV, VLADIMIR
95 Globe 240
89/90 Kraft 40
90/1 OPC/Topps 380
90/1 PaniniSticker 304, 337
90/1 ProSet 296
90/1 Score 273
89 Semic 89
82 SemicSticker 62
89/90 SovietNats
83/4 SovietStars
87/8 SovietStars
90/1 UpperDeck 77
89/90 VAN

KRUZICH, GARY
88/9 Flint

KRYGIER, TODD
90/1 Bowman 251
91/2 Bowman 2
95/6 Donruss 335
96/7 Donruss 202
95/6 FleerMetal 3
92/3 FleerUltra 438
93/4 FleerUltra 448
95/6 FleerUltra 201
96/7 Leaf 70
90/1 OPC/Topps 260
91/2 OPC/Topps 449
97/8 PacificCrown 318
90/1 PaniniSticker 35
91/2 PaniniSticker 317
95/6 PaniniSticker 226
91/2 Parkhurst 408
94/5 Parkhurst 258
95/6 Parkhurst 276
91/2 Pinnacle 242, 394
92/3 Pinnacle 204
94/5 Pinnacle 455
95/6 Pinnacle 183
96/7 Pinnacle 102
95/6 Playoff 224
96/7 Playoff 363
95/6 POG 20
93/4 PowerPlay 467
93/4 Premier 188
88/9 ProCards(Binghampton)
89/90 ProCards(AHL) 294
90/1 ProSet 107
91/2 ProSet 83
92/3 ProSet 270
90/1 Score 237
91/2 Score(CDN) 97, 637
91/2 Score(U.S) 97, 87T
92/3 Score 98
93/4 Score 357
96/7 Score 203
95/6 SkyBoxImpact 4
92/3 Topps 502
95/6 Topps 163
95/6 ToppsFinest 114
91/2 ToppsStadiumClub 45
92/3 ToppsStadiumClub 474
93/4 ToppsStadiumClub 337
94/5 ToppsStadiumClub 256
95/6 ToppsStadiumClub 19
90/1 UpperDeck 417
91/2 UpperDeck 215, 582
93/4 UpperDeck 207
94/5 UpperDeck 477
95/6 UpperDeck 9
95/6 UDBeAPlayer 93
95/6 UDCollChoice 241
94/5 ANA/Carl'sJr 13
89/90 HFD/JuniorWhalers
90/1 HFD/JuniorWhalers
91/2 WSH
91/2 WSH/Kodak
92/3 WSH/Kodak

KRYKOW, VALERI
92/3 Jyvas-Hyva 16
93/4 Jyvas-Hyva 18
93/4 Sisu 99
94/5 Sisu 260, -Horoscope 11
95/6 Sisu 115
96/7 Sisu 134

KRYS, MARK
93/4 Rochester

KRYSKOW, DAVE
74/5 Loblaws, -Update
74/5 OPC/Topps 62
75/6 OPC/Topps 158
74/5 WSH

KRYWULAK, JASON
90/1 SketchWHL 27
91/2 SketchWHL 178

KRYZNOWSKI, ED
45-64 BeeHives
51/2 Parkhurst 33
52/3 Parkhurst 29

KUBICEK, MICHAL
94/5 APS 101
95/6 APS 62

KUCERA, FRANTISEK
94/5 APS 79
91/2 Bowman 404
92/3 Bowman 7
93/4 Donruss 439
92/3 FleerUltra 277
95/6 FleerUltra 67
94/5 Leaf 392
95/6 Leaf 50
90/1 opcPremier 53
94/5 PaniniSticker 116
95/6 PaniniSticker 34
92/3 Parkhurst 269
94/5 Pinnacle 210
95/6 Playoff 264
95/6 POG 129
90/1 ProCards 411
91/2 ProCards 495
90/1 ProSet 599
91/2 Score(CDN) 390
92/3 Score 346
93/4 Score 372
94 Semic 169
95 Semic 146
89 SemicSticker 184
92 SemicSticker 128
93/4 Sisu 72
95/6 SkyBoxEmotion 75
92/3 Topps 520
95/6 Topps 84
92/3 ToppsStadiumClub 438
93/4 ToppsStadiumClub 442
94/5 ToppsStadiumClub 49
91/2 UpperDeck 468
95/6 UDBeAPlayer 33
95/6 UDCollChoice 304
96 Wien 117
91/2 CHI/Coke
93/4 CHI/Coke

KUCERA, JIRI
94/5 APS 140
94/5 ElitSet 187, -ForeignAff 5
95/6 ElitSet 83
95 Globe 161
91/2 Jyvas-Hyva 57
95 PaniniWorlds 200
94 Semic 190
95 Semic 150
89 SemicSticker 195
93 SemicSticker 98
93/4 Sisu 72
94/5 Sisu 14
95/6 SisuLimited 76
95/6 udElite 126

KUCHARCIK, TOMAS
94/5 APS 153
95/6 APS 253

KUCHERAN, BOB
80/1 Oshawa 5

KUCHMA, BILL
84/5 Ottawa67s

KUCHYNA, PETR
94/5 APS 170
95/6 APS 273
96 Wien 110

KUDA, PETR
94/5 APS 50
95/6 APS 83

KUDASHOV, ALEXEI
93/4 Classic 42
93/4 ClassicProspects 106
96/7 DEL 284
93/4 Donruss 345
94/5 Donruss 84
95/6 EdgeIce 23
94/5 Leaf 181
93/4 Parkhurst 260
94/5 ParkieSE 180
93/4 Pinnacle 445
94/5 Premier 78
93/4 Score 623
95/6 SkyBoxImpact 109
93/4 UpperDeck 427, SP159
93/4 TOR/Abalene
94/5 TOR
93/4 StJohns
94/5 StJohns

KUDELSKI, BOB
91/2 Bowman 189
92/3 Bowman 12
93/4 Donruss 232, 434
94/5 Donruss 227
93/4 EASports 95
94/5 Flair 64
94/5 Fleer 79
93/4 FleerUltra 85
94/5 FleerUltra 80
95/6 Hoyle'East 10 (Spades)
93/4 Leaf 48
94/5 Leaf 314
90/1 OPC/Topps 46
91/2 OPC/Topps 61
92/3 O-Pee-Chee 326
91/2 opcPremier 129
90/1 PaniniSticker 232
91/2 PaniniSticker 87
92/3 PaniniSticker 69
93/4 PaniniSticker 114
94/5 PaniniSticker 65
91/2 Parkhurst 299
92/3 Parkhurst 357
93/4 Parkhurst 408
94/5 Parkhurst 83
94/5 ParkieSE seV35
91/2 Pinnacle 113
92/3 Pinnacle 84
93/4 Pinnacle 38
94/5 Pinnacle 284
95/6 Playoff 260
94/5 POG 105
93/4 PowerPlay 170, 348
93/4 Premier 40
94/5 Premier 245
88/9 ProCards(NewHaven)
95/6 ProMagnet 88
90/1 ProSet 122
91/2 ProSet 99
91/2 PSPlatinum 181
90/1 Score(U.S) 305
91/2 Score(CDN) 154, (U.S) 154
92/3 Score 221
93/4 Score 257, 549
94/5 Score 28
94/5 Select 55
94/5 SP 46
92/3 Topps 145
91/2 ToppsStadiumClub 40
92/3 ToppsStadiumClub 149
93/4 ToppsStadiumClub 120
90/1 UpperDeck 433
91/2 UpperDeck 301
93/4 Upper Deck 17, SP110
94/5 UpperDeck 376, SP29
95/6 UpperDeck 138, SE34
95/6 UDCollChoice 226
89/90 L.A./Smokeys 20
90/1 L.A./Smokeys 20
92/3 OTT
93/4 OTT/Kraft
94/5 Binghampton
95/6 Binghampton

KUDRNA, LADISLAV
95/6 APS 146

KUHL, MARCUS
94/5 DEL 272
95/6 DEL 263
79 PaniniSticker 113
82 SemicSticker 110

KUHN, BERND
72 Hellas 55
82 SemicSticker 110

KUHN, FLORIAN
96/7 DEL 116

KUHN, TYLER
91/2 AirCanadaSJHL 17, D45
92/3 MPSPhotoSJHL 19

KUHNHACKI, ERICH
82 SemicSticker 112
79 PaniniSticker 103

KUHNHAUSER, BERND
94/5 DEL 87
95/6 DEL 92, 428
96/7 DEL 280

KUHNKE, HARALD
94/5 DEL 135
95/6 DEL 137

KUIMALA, ARTO
96/7 Sisu 128

KUIRI, TAPIO
70/1 Kuvajulkaisut 372

KUISMA, ILPO
70/1 Kuvajulkaisut 210
71/2 WilliamsFIN 132
72/3 WilliamsFIN 195
73/4 WilliamsFIN 67, 155

KUISMA, JARMO
72/3 WilliamsFIN 266

KUISMANEN, PERTTI
66/7 Champion 77
70/1 Kuvajulkaisut 160

KUIVALAINEN, PASI
92/3 Jyvas-Hyva 87
93/4 Jyvas-Hyva 164
95 Latkaliiga 9
94 Semic 2
95 Semic 1
93/4 Sisu 161
94/5 Sisu 1, -Magic 1, -NilPhen 9
95/6 Sisu 272, -Ghost 9
96/7 Sisu 69,-AtGala 5,-Mighty 5
95/6 SisuLimited 64

KUJALA, PETRI
93/4 Sisu 144
95/6 Sisu 269

KUKACKA, ZBYNEK
94/5 APS 82
91/2 SketchOHL 306

KUKI, ARTO
94/5 Sisu-Drafted 4
95/6 Sisu 295
96/7 Sisu-Energy 7

KUKKOLA, ILPO
78/9 SM-Liiga 133

KUKUC, PHILIP
94/5 DEL 20

KUKULOWICZ, ADOLPH
52/3 AnonymousOHL 78

KULABUCHOV, VADIM
94/5 APS 270
95/6 DEL 426

KULAGIN, BORIS
73/4 Soviet Stars 23
74/5 SovietStars 23

KULAK, STU
88/9 ProCards(Moncton)
89/90 ProCards(AHL) 33
90/1 ProCards 586
86/7 EDM
86/7 EDM/RedRooster
88/9 EDM/ActionMagazine 44
87/8 QUE/GeneralFoods
86/7 VAN
83/4 Fredericton 23
90/1 KansasCity 9
81/2 Victoria
82/3 Victoria

KULCHISKY, L.
88/9 EDM/ActionMagazine 80
90/1 EDM/McGavins

KULHORANTA, KAI
71/2 WilliamsFIN 326

KULLMAN, ED
45-64 BeeHives(NYR)
51/2 Parkhurst 101
52/3 Parkhurst 18
53/4 Parkhurst 61

KULMALA, ARTO
94/5 Sisu 78
95/6 Sisu 114
96/7 Sisu 128

KULONEN, TIMO
92/3 Jyvas-Hyva 122
93/4 Jyvas-Hyva 226
93/4 Sisu 189
94/5 Sisu 237
95/6 Sisu 139

KULTAKUUSI, MAURI
78/9 SM-Liiga 93

KULTANEN, JARNO
94/5 Sisu 228
95/6 Sisu 73

KULYK, GLENN
85/6 Minn-Duluth 34

KUMAR, BOJAN
79 PaniniSticker 396

KUMMER, WOLFGANG
94/5 DEL 96
95/6 DEL 97
96/7 DEL 131
93 SemicSticker 164

KUMPEL, MARK
90/1 O-Pee-Chee 444
91/2 ProCards 184
97/8 DET/Caesars
85/6 QUE
85/6 QUE/GeneralFoods
85/6 QUE/McDonald
85/6 QUE/Provigo
86/7 QUE/GeneralFoods
86/7 QUE/McDonald
89/90 WPG/Safeway
90/1 WPG/IGA
84/5 Fredericton 19
91/2 Moncton

KUNAST, CHRISTIAN
94/5 DEL 265
95/6 DEL 243
96/7 DEL 114

KUNCE, DANIEL
94/5 DEL 183
95/6 DEL 175
96/7 DEL 133

KUNCE, G.
95/6 DEL 433

KUNGLE, JEFF
91/2 AirCanadaSJHL 1, B41

KUNTAR, LES
92/3 C'Prospects 72
95/6 EdgeIce TH9
94/5 Parkhurst 114
92/3 Fredericton
93/4 Fredericton

KUNTOS, JIRI
94/5 APS 7
95/6 APS 106

KUNTZ, AL
52/3 LavalDairy 108
52/3 StLawrence 66

KUNTZ, DEAN
89/90 Saskatoon 4

KUNTZ, MARK
88/9 Lethbridge
85/6 MedicineHat 3
91/2 Richmond 12
92/3 Richmond

KUOKKANEN, MARTTI
65/6 Hellas 57
71/2 WilliamsFIN 283
73/4 WilliamsFIN 200

KUOPPALA, ISMO
94/5 Sisu 354
95/6 Sisu 87
96/7 Sisu 52

KUOSMANEN, PENTTI
70/1 Kuvajulkaisut 349

KUPACS, ARTUR
94/5 Greensboro

KUPARI, MARKO
93/4 Sisu 155

KUPKA, TOMAS
94/5 APS 266
95/6 APS 143

KURASHOV, KONSTANTIN
90/1 OPC 469
91/2 OPC 52R

KURKINEN, RISTO
93/4 Sisu 158
92/3 Jyvas-Hyva 85
93/4 Jyvas-Hyva 139
90/1 SemicElitserien 111
91/2 SemicElitserien 116
91 SemicSticker 16
94/5 Sisu 325, -Fire 15
95/6 SisuLimited 51

KURRI, JARI
90/1 Bowman 191, -HatTrick 19
92/3 Bowman 94
93/4 Classic 121
96/7 CorinthianHeadliner
97/8 CorinthianHeadliner
93/4 Donruss 151
94/5 Donruss 93
95/6 Donruss 133
96/7 DonrussCanadianIce 49
96/7 DonrussElite 85
88/9 Esso Sticker
95 FinnishAllStar 2
94/5 Flair 81
94/5 Fleer 96
92/3 FleerUltra 85, -Imports 11
93/4 FleerUltra 165
94/5 FleerUltra 100, -Global 5
95/6 FleerUltra 251
96/7 FleerUltra 3
95 Globe 137
93/4 HockeyWit 89
95/6 Hoyle'West 2 (Diamonds)
84/5 Kelloggs Disk
93 Koululainen
95 Koululainen
86/7 Kraft Sports 16
89/90 Kraft 13, -Sticker 5
90/1 Kraft 68
91/2 Kraft 67
93/4 Leaf 240
94/5 Leaf 104
95/6 Leaf 122
94/5 LeafLimited 105
93/4 McDonalds McD8
96/7 MetalUniverse 3
97/8 Omega 59
81/2 OPC 107, Topps 18
82/3 OPC 111
83/4 OPC 34
84/5 OPC 215, 249, T. 52, 161
85/6 OPC/T. 155,-AS 3,OPC 261
86/7 OPC/Topps 108, H
86/7 OPC 258, Topps-AS 10
87/8 OPC/Topps 148, T-AS 4
88/9 OPC/Topps 147
89/90 OPC/Topps 43, I
90/1 OPC/Topps 5, 108
91/2 OPC/Topps 295
92/3 OPC 205
91/2 opcPremier 111
87/8 opcStars 21
81/2 opcSticker 11, 211
82/3 opcSticker 108, 109
83/4 opcSticker 104
84/5 opcSticker 249, 250
85/6 opcSticker 121, 231, 201/74
86/7 opcStic 73,118/132,185/125
87/8 opcSticker 82, 117/129
88/9 opcSticker 227
89/90 opcSticker 221
98/9 Pacific 162
97/8 PCC-SlapShots 1B
97/8 PacificCrownRoyale 35
97/8 PacificParamount 51
97/8 PacificRevolution 34
95/6 PaniniSticker 270
87/8 PaniniSticker 262
88/9 PaniniSticker 59
89/90 PaniniSticker 73, 181
90/1 PaniniSticker 222
92/3 PaniniSticker 66
93/4 PaniniSticker 202
94/5 PaniniSticker 173
96/7 PaniniSticker 109
97/8 PaniniSticker 189
95 PaniniWorlds 293
91/2 Parkhurst 72, 210, 223
92/3 Parkhurst 67, 445
93/4 Parkhurst 365
94/5 Parkhurst 104
95/6 Parkhurst 102, 239
94/5 ParkieSE ES9, seV24
89 Pelimiehen
80/1 Pepsi Cap
91/2 Pinnacle 48
92/3 Pinnacle 60
93/4 Pinnacle 75
94/5 Pinnacle 35, WE7
95/6 Pinnacle 22, -GlobalGold 4
97/8 PinnacleBeAPlayer 7
97/8 PinnacleInside 113
95/6 PinnacleZenith 50
95/6 Playoff 271
96/7 Playoff 412
94/5 POG 127
95/6 POG 134
82/3 Post
94/5 Post
93/4 PowerPlay 118, -GlobalG 4
93/4 Premier 206
94/5 Premier 25
95/6 ProMagnet 63
90/1 ProSet 87, 348
91/2 ProSet 93
92/3 ProSet 68
91/2 PSPlatinum 48
83/4 PuffySticker 5
90/1 Score 158, 348
91/2 ScoreCDN 600
91/2 ScoreTraded 50T
92/3 Score 398
93/4 Score 100, 446, -DD7
93/4 Score -InternationalStars 7
94/5 Score 114
95/6 Score 115
97/8 Score(COL) 5
94/5 Select 71
95/6 SelectCertif 35
96/7 SelectCerti 86
94 Semic 24, 346
95 Semic 17, 204
91 SemicSticker 18
92 SemicSticker 17
93 SemicSticker 67
83/4 7ElevenCokeCup
84/5 7ElevenDisk
85/6 7Eleven 6
94/5 Sisu 207, -Special 2
95/6 Sisu -Specials 4
95/6 SisuLimited 16, -Signed 7
95/6 SkyBoxEmotion 83
95/6 SkyBoxImpact 81
78/9 SM-Liiga 76
83/4 SouhaitsRen.KeyChain
94/5 SP 5, 57
96/7 SP 3
97/8 SPAuthentic 42
77-79 Sportscaster 77- 1848
95/6 Summit 32
96/7 Summit 47
92/3 Topps 51
95/6 Topps 239
94/5 ToppsFinest 81
96/7 ToppsNHLPicks FC4
92/3 ToppsStadiumClub 138
93/4 TSC 400, -MasterPhotos 2
95/6 ToppsStadiumClub 151
92/3 TSC-MembersOnly
90/1 UpperDeck 146
91/2 UpperDeck 24, 366
92/3 UpperDeck 218, WG4
92/3 UD'LockerAS 29
93/4 UpperDeck 332
94/5 UpperDeck 293, 559, SP37
95/6 UpperDeck 372, SE41
96/7 UpperDeck 138, 212, X24
94/5 UDBeAPlayer R25
95/6 UDBeAPlayer 201
95/6 UDCollChoice 16
96/7 UDCollChoice 162, 173
97/8 UDCollChoice 10
83/4 Vachon 31
82 Valio
96 Wien 24, NS4
96/7 ANA/UpFrontSports 23
80/1 EDM/Zellers
81/2 EDM/RedRooster
82/3 EDM/RedRooster
83/4 EDM
83/4 EDM/Buttons
83/4 EDM/McDonald
84/5 EDM
84/5 EDM/RedRooster
85/6 EDM/RedRooster
86/7 EDM
86/7 EDM/RedRooster
87/8 EDM
88/9 EDM
88/9 EDM/ActionMagazine 41

KURT, GARY
71/2 OPC/Topps 181
72/3 OPC 306
75/6 opcWHA 126
76/7 opcWHA 102
75/6 Phoenix
76/7 Phoenix

KURTENBACH, ORLAND
71/2 Bazooka Panel 13
45-64 BeeHives(BOS)
64-67 BeeHives (BOS), (NYR)
64-67 BeeHives (TOR)
64/5 CokeCap BOS-7
65/6 CocaCola
70/1 Colgate Stamp 23
70/1 DadsCookies
70/1 EddieSargent 212
71/2 EddieSargent 216
72/3 EddieSargent 215
70/1 Esso Stamp
72/3 Letraset 7
73/4 MacsMilk Disk
68/9 OPC 170
69/70 OPC 188
70/1 OPC/Topps 117,-Deckle 45
71/2 OPC/Topps 42, -Booklet 20
72/3 OPC 141, -Crests 22
73/4 OPC 4
71/2 opcPoster 12
95/6 Parkie(64/5) 7
95/6 Parkie(66/7) 90, 138
70/1 PostShooters
72/3 Post Transfers 11
72 SemicSticker 209
61/2 ShirriffCoin 14
68/9 ShirriffCoin NY8
64/5 TheTorontoStar
71/2 TheTorontoSun
61/2 Topps 15
63/4 Topps 20
64/5 Topps 18
65/6 Topps 20
66/7 Topps 25, -USATest 25
67/8 Topps 87
72/3 Topps 46
73/4 Topps 157
91/2 Ultimate06 24, -Aut 24
68/9 TOR
70/1 VAN/RoyalBank
71/2 VAN/RoyalBank 6
72/3 VAN/RoyalBank
73/4 VAN/RoyalBank

KURTZ, JUSTIN
94/5 AutoPhonex 23
97/8 Bowman 111
94/5 ParkieSE 262
95/6 SlapshotMEM 32

KURVERS, TOM
91/2 Bowman 319, 412
92/3 Bowman 259
94/5 Fleer 5
93/4 FleerUltra 368
94/5 Leaf 449
85/6 OPC 219
88/9 OPC 222
89/90 OPC/Topps 9
90/1 OPC/Topps 11
92/3 OPC 202
91/2 opcPremier 98
85/6 opcSticker 129/249
86/7 opcSticker 10/155
89/90 opcSticker 84/225
89/90 PaniniSticker 252
90/1 PaniniSticker 287
91/2 PaniniSticker 43
91/2 Parkhurst 112
93/4 Parkhurst 392
94/5 ParkieSE 4
91/2 Pinnacle 7
92/3 Pinnacle 324
94/5 Pinnacle 380
93/4 PowerPlay 384
93/4 Premier 279
90/1 ProSet 282
91/2 ProSet 244, 428
90/1 Score 142
91/2 Score(CDN) 174, 568
91/2 ScoreUS 174
91/2 ScoreTraded 18T
92/3 Score 232
92/3 Topps 118
92/3 ToppsStadiumClub 409
93/4 ToppsStadiumClub 279
95 TSC Members 24
90/1 UpperDeck 160
92/3 UpperDeck 292
93/4 UpperDeck 381
94/5 UpperDeck 123
94/5 ANA/Carl'sJr 14
86/7 BUF
84/5 MTL
85/6 MTL
85/6 MTL/Pennant
85/6 MTL/PepsiPlacemat
85/6 MTL/ProvStickers
85/6? MTL/ProvPlacemats
88/9 N.J./Caretta
90/1 TOR
90/1 VAN/Mohawk

KURZAWSKI, MARK
88/9 ProCards(Saginaw)
89/90 ProCards(IHL) 52

KUSHNER, DALE
91/2 Bowman 247
91/2 OPC/Topps 415
90/1 opcPremier 54
89/90 ProCards(AHL) 243
90/1 ProCards 28
91/2 ProCards 268
91/2 Score(CDN) 512
91/2 ToppsStadiumClub 349
91/2 UpperDeck 429
90/1 PHA
85/6 MedicineHat 12

KUSHNER, DAN
94/5 SaintJohn

KUSTER, HENRY
95/6 Bowman P21
95/6 Classic 63, AS3, -Aut.

KUUKAUPPI, URPO
73/4 WilliamsFIN 201

KUUPPALA, ISMO
96/7 Sisu 52

KUUSINEN, PENTTI
66/7 Champion 181

KUUSISAARI, JUHA
95/6 Sisu 346

KUUSISTO, JARMO
91/2 Jyvas-Hyva 47
92/3 Jyvas-Hyva 128
93/4 Jyvas-Hyva 230
80/1 Mallasjuoma 114
89 SemicSticker 36
93/4 Sisu 186
94/5 Sisu 5, -Magic 3, -Special 5
95/6 Sisu 169, 182
95/6 SisuLimited 30

KUUSISTO, OSMO
70/1 Kuvajulkaisut 178

KUUSISTO, PEKKA
66/7 Champion 20
65/6 Hellas 65
70/1 Kuvajulkaisut 127
72 Panda
71/2 WilliamsFIN 179
72/3 WilliamsFIN 127
73/4 WilliamsFIN 68, 182

KUUSISTO, RIKU
92/3 Jyvas-Hyva 113
93/4 Sisu 274

KUUSITO, VEIKKO
66/7 Champion 113

KUUSKO, ANDERS
95/6 udElite 45

KUWABARA, RYAN
89/90 SketchOHL 55
90/1 SketchOHL 85
91/2 SketchOHL 303
92/3 Fredericton
93/4 Fredericton

KUZELA, MILAN
72 Hellas 96
74 Hellas 76
72 Panda
72/3 WilliamsFIN 13
73/4 WilliamsFIN 54

KUZKIN, VIKTOR
72 Hellas 64
72 Panda
72 SemicSticker 4
74 SemicSticker 45
69/70 Soviet Stars
71/2 Soviet Stars
73/4 Soviet Stars 25
74/5 Soviet Stars 10
91/2 Trends(72) 41
71/2 WilliamsFIN 5
72/3 WilliamsFIN 26

KUZMINSKY, ALEXANDER
91/2 UD 656, -CzechWJC 17

KUZNETSOV, MAXIM
94/5 Select 157
94/5 Sisu 316
95/6 Sisu 3
94/5 SigRookies FF7
95 Tetrad-SR 9
95/6 Tetrad F9

KUZNIK, GREG
98 BowmanCHL 47

KUZNETSOV, YURI
90/1 O-Pee-Chee 489
94/5 Sisu 316
95/6 Sisu 3

KVALEVOG, TOBY
93/4 Donruss USA11
93/4 Pinnacle 480
93/4 UpperDeck 555

KVARTALNOV, ANDREI
91/2 OPC 53R

KVARTALNOV, DMITRI
92/3 CSC 9
92/3 Classic 93, 120, LP6
92/3 C'Prospects 32, BC17, -Aut
93/4 Donruss 27
93/4 EASports 195
92/3 FleerUltra 252, -UltraImp 12
93/4 FleerUltra 82
93/4 Leaf 143
92/3 opcPremier 6
93/4 PaniniSticker 7
92/3 Parkhurst 7, 222
93/4 Parkhurst 287
92/3 Pinnacle 405
93/4 Pinnacle 161
93/4 PowerPlay 20, -2ndYrStar 4
93/4 Premier 197
91/2 ProCards 313
92/3 RedAce(Blue) 9, (Violet) 18
93/4 Score 187
89/90 SovietNats
92/3 UpperDeck 455, 561
92/3 UD'LockerAS 55
93/4 UpperDeck 19
92/3 BOS

KVERKA, JAROMIR
94/5 APS 89
95/6 APS 191

KWASIGROCH, PIOTR (PETER)
94/5 DEL 164
95/6 DEL 163
96/7 DEL 237
89 SemicSticker 148

KWIATKOWSKI, DARREN
87/8 Regina

KWIATKOWSKI, JASON
90/1 SketchWHL 276
91/2 SketchWHL 245
90/1 PrinceAlbert
91/2 PrinceAlbert
92/3 Tacoma

KWIATKOWSKI, JOEL
97/8 Bowman 85
98 BowmanCHL 45

KWONG, LARRY
51/2 LavalDairy 73
52/3 StLawrence 19

KYLE, DOUG
83/4 Saskatoon 20

KYLE, WALTER "GUS"
45-64 BeeHives(NYR)
51/2 Parkhurst 21

KYLE, WALT
93/4 Seattle

KYLE, WILLIAM
51/2 LavalDairy 39

KYLLASTINEN, HANNU
65/6 Hellas 59

KYLLONEN, MARKKU
91/2 Jyvas-Hyva 40

KYLLONEN, PEKKA
70/1 Kuvajulkaisut 373

KYNTOLA, JORMA
65/6 Hellas 53

KYNTOLA, TIMO
70/1 Kuvajulkaisut 179
71/2 WilliamsFIN 103
72/3 WilliamsFIN 147
73/4 WilliamsFIN 112

KYOYA, YOSHIAKI
79 PaniniSticker 288

KYPREOS, NICK
90/1 Bowman 67
91/2 Bowman 301
93/4 Donruss 140
92/3 FleerUltra 301
93/4 Leaf 414
94/5 Leaf 406
90/1 O-Pee-Chee 440
91/2 OPC/Topps 511
91/2 PaniniSticker 204
91/2 Parkhurst 411
92/3 Parkhurst 297
93/4 Pinnacle 83
94/5 Pinnacle 408
97/8 PinnacleBeAPlayer 128
93/4 PowerPlay 105
90/1 ProSet 551
91/2 ProSet 513
93/4 Score 404
91/2 Score(CDN) 432
92/3 Topps 193
91/2 ToppsStadiumClub 307
94/5 ToppsStadiumClub 154
92/3 UpperDeck 447
93/4 UpperDeck 11, -Aut 54
95/6 UpperDeck 493
94/5 UDBeAPlayer R21
92/3 HFD/DairyMart
89/90 WSH
90/1 WSH/Kodak
90/1 WSH/Smokey
91/2 WSH
91/2 WSH/Kodak
83/4 NorthBay

KYRO, ROGER
95/6 ElitSet 173
92/3 UpperDeck 226
95/6 udElite 27

KYSELA, DAN
94/5 APS 118

KYSELA, ROBERT
94/5 APS 220
95/6 APS 170

KYTE, JIM
94/5 Classic E9
87/8 OPC 226
89/90 OPC 295
88/9 opcSticker 145/16
89/90 opcSticker 140/259
87/8 PaniniSticker 362
91/2 Pinnacle 398
90/1 ProCards 374
91/2 ProSet 612
91/2 Score(CDN) 547
83/4 Vachon 128
91/2 CGY/IGA
82/3 WPG
83/4 WPG
84/5 WPG/Police
85/6 WPG
85/6 WPG/Police
86/7 WPG
87/8 WPG
88/9 WPG/Police
93/4 LasVegas
94/5 LasVegas

L

LAAKKIO, SEPPO
70/1 Kuvajulkaisut 280
71/2 WilliamsFIN 153
72/3 WilliamsFIN 105
73/4 WilliamsFIN 202

LAAKSO, AKI
72/3 WilliamsFIN 331

LAAKSONEN, ILKKA
73/4 WilliamsFIN 288

LAAKSONEN, MIKA
94/5 Sisu 137
95/6 Sisu 71, 347
96/7 Sisu 73

LAAKSONEN, TOM
92/3 Jyvas-Hyva 117
95/6 Sisu 208

LAAMANEN, J.P.
95/6 Sisu 263
96/7 Sisu 57

LAAN, JOHN
94/5 Slapshot(Bratford) 15

LAAPAS, JORMA
65/6 Hellas 3

LAAPAS, MANU
95/6 Sisu 327
96/7 Sisu 140

LABADIE, MICHEL
52/3 AnonymousOHL 70

LABARBERA, JASON
98 BowmanCHL 140, A2

LABAYEN, PERICO
79 PaniniSticker 376

LABBÉ, JEAN-FRANÇOIS
90/1 SketchQMJHL 69, 88
91/2 SketchQMJHL 122
93/4 ThunderBay

LABELLE, MARC
91/2 ProCards 87

LABELLE, SERGE
91/2 SketchQMJHL 20

LABENSKI, GREG
98 BowmanCHL 6
95/6 Slapshot 227

LABERGE, GILLES
84/5 Chicoutimi

LABERGE, J.Y.
84/5 Chicoutimi

LABINE, LÉO
45-64 BeeHives(BOS), (DET)
52/3 Parkhurst 81
53/4 Parkhurst 93
54/5 Parkhurst 61
61/2 Parkhurst 33
62/3 Parkhurst 26
93/4 Parkhurst 53, DPR10
93/4 Parkie(56/7) 4
60/1 ShirriffCoin 117
61/2 ShirriffCoin 64
54/5 Topps 19
57/8 Topps 9
58/9 Topps 4
59/60 Topps 7
60/1 Topps 13
91/2 UltimateO6 50, -Aut 50
57/8 BOS

LABOSSIÈRE, GASTON
51/2 LacStJean 51

LABOSSIÈRE, GORDON
45-64 BeeHives(NYR)
64-67 BeeHives(NYR)
70/1 Esso Stamp
68/9 OPC/Topps 38
69/70 OPC/Topps 109
70/1 OPC/Topps 38
72/3 OPC 303
75/6 opcWHA 89
68/9 ShirriffCoin LA5
75/6 Houston
65/6 Québec

LABRAATEN, DAN
79/80 OPC/Topps 92
80/1 OPC/Topps 217
81/2 O-Pee-Chee 42
77/8 opcWHA 57
72 SemicSticker 67
74 SemicSticker 23
81/2 CGY
79/80 DET
80/1 DET

LABRAATEN, JAN
94/5 AutoPhonex 24
95/6 TetradAutobilia 44
95/6 UDCollChoice 353

LABRAATEN, ULF
94/5 ElitSet 306

LABRANCHE, EMMANUEL
93/4 Slapshot(Drum.) 9

LABRE, YVON
73/4 O-Pee-Chee 247
74/5 OPC 345
75/6 OPC/Topps 61
76/7 OPC/Topps 161, OPC 396
77/8 OPC/Topps 31
78/9 OPC 324
79/80 OPC 343
74/5 WSH
79/80 WSH
80/1 WSH

LABRECQUE, PATRICK
96/7 Leaf 224
96/7 Pinnacle 246
91/2 ProCards 532
90/1 SketchQMJHL 215
96/7 Summit 177
95/6 UpperDeck 379
94/5 Fredericton
95/6 Fredericton

LABRIE, GUY
52/3 BasDuFleuve 16
51/2 LavalDairy 47
52/3 StLawrence 74

LABRIER, BOB
84/5 Kamloops
85/6 Kamloops

LACEDELLI, RENATO
79 PaniniSticker 389

LACH, ELMER
33-43 BeeHives(MTL.C)
45-64 BeeHives(MTL)
72-84 Dernière 77/8
48-52 Exhibits (x2)
83&87 HallOfFame 129
83 HHOF Postcard (I)
94/5 HHOFLegends 50
51-54 LaPatrie 16Dec51
40/1 OPC (V301-2) 125
43-47 ParadeSportive
51/2 Parkhurst 1
52/3 Parkhurst 6
53/4 Parkhurst 30, 31
93/4 Parkhurst PR36
94/5 Parkie(64/5)-Greats 4
91/2 ProSet 337
45-54 QuakerOats
54-67 TorontoStar V 4,n6
92/3 MTL/OPC 34
95/6 MTL/Forum 2-Dec

LACHAINE, MARTIN
96/7 Penascola 13

LACHANCE, BOB
93/4 Donruss USA12
93/4 Pinnacle 495
93/4 UpperDeck 564

LACHANCE, GÉRARD
51/2 BasDuFleuve 34
52/3 BasDuFleuve 15

LACHANCE, JIM
88/9 Richelieu

LACHANCE, SCOTT
91/2 Arena 3, 32
92/3 Bowman 438
91/2 Classic 4
91/2 ClassicFourSport 4, -Aut
93/4 Donruss 206
94/5 Donruss 41
95/6 Donruss 353
97/8 Donruss 142
97/8 DonrussPreferred 143
96/7 Flair 55
94/5 Fleer 124
92/3 FleerUltra 130
93/4 FleerUltra 369
94/5 FleerUltra 326
95/6 FleerUltra 94
95/6 Hoyle'EAST J (Spades)
93/4 Leaf 139
94/5 Leaf 372
95/6 Leaf 202
97/8 Leaf 95
97/8 Limited 166
92/3 OPC 390
92/3 opcPremier 79
97/8 PacificCrown 85
92/3 PaniniSticker Q
93/4 PaniniSticker 63
95/6 PaniniSticker 97
96/7 PaniniSticker 99
91/2 Parkhurst 326
92/3 Parkhurst 105
93/4 Parkhurst 120
94/5 Parkhurst 140
92/3 Pinn 223, 244, -Tm2000 6
93/4 Pinnacle 62, -Tm2001 21
94/5 Pinnacle 193
95/6 Pinnacle 167
96/7 PinnacleBeAPlayer 27
95/6 Playoff 281
93/4 PowerPlay 152
93/4 Premier 257, 'Promo 257
94/5 Premier 66
92/3 ProSet 234
92/3 Score 449, -YoungStar 12
93/4 Score 103
94/5 Score 195
95/6 Score 177
97/8 Score 259
92/3 SeasonsPatch 52
95/6 SkyBoxImpact 101
91/2 StarPics 24, 36
92/3 Topps 366
92/3 ToppsStadiumClub 201
93/4 TSC 465, -Master (2) 4
91/2 UltimateDP 4, 56, 60
91/2 UltimateDP 81, -Aut 81
91/2 UD 692,-CzechWJC 79
92/3 UD 360, 398, 409, 571
92/3 UpperDeck AC4, CC16
93/4 UpperDeck 320, SP92
94/5 UpperDeck 412
95/6 UpperDeck 390
94/5 UDBeAPlayer R44, -Aut. 82

LACHER, BLAINE
94/5 Classic 35, R13, T5, -Aut
94/5 C'Images 9, CE9
95/6 Donruss 123,-Btw 1,-Rk 5
94/5 Fleer 13, -RookieSensat 6
95/6 FleerMetal 7
95/6 FleerUltra 10, -AllRookie 6
95/6 FleerUltra-PrmrPadMen 7
95/6 Kraft-Crease
95/6 Leaf 3, -StudioRook 5
95/6 LeafLimited 41
95/6 PaniniSticker 13, 302
95/6 Parkhurst 14
95/6 Pinnacle 147, -Masks 1
95/6 PinnacleZenith 78
95/6 Playoff 7, 119
95/6 POG 38
95/6 ProMagnet 12
95/6 Score 17
95/6 SkyBoxEmotion 8
95/6 SBImpact 9, 232,-Deflect 5
94/5 SP 7, -Premier 8
95/6 Summit 127
95/6 Topps 23, 15NG
94/5 ToppsFinest 95,-BBest(R) 3
95/6 ToppsStadiumClub 104
94/5 TSC-MembersOly 50
94/5 UD 495, 539, SP65
95/6 UD 385, H15, SE7
95/6 UDCollChoice 22
91/2 LakeSuperior

LACKEY, CARL
69/70 MästarSerien 17

LACKY, MIROSLAV
70/1 Kuvajulkaisut 52

LACOMBE, FRANÇOIS
72-84 Dernière 78/9
73/4 QuébecNordiques
76/7 QuébecNordiqes

LACOMBE, MARTIN
90/1 SketchQMJHL 27

LACOMBE, NORMAND
91/2 Bowman 248
91/2 OPC/Topps 357
89/90 PaniniSticker 84
90/1 ProSet 500
90/1 ScoreTraded 99
91/2 Score(CDN) 394
91/2 ToppsStadiumClub 363
85/6 BUF
86/7 BUF
87/8 EDM
88/9 EDM
88/9 EDM/ActionMagazine 81
90/1 PHA

LACOMBE, PATRICK
91/2 SketchQMJHL 87

LACOSTE, YVON
65/6 QuébecAces

LACOUR, ROBIN
93/4 Slapshot(Detroit) 5
94/5 Slapshot(Kitchener) 32
95/6 Slapshot 36
96/7 Sudbury 14

LACOURSIÈRE, JOSEPH
52/3 BasDuFleuve 4
51/2 LacStJean 16

LACOUTURE, DAN
95/6 Classic 64
94/5 Select 154

LACOUTURE, DAVE
92/3 Maine (1) 9, (2) 24

LACROIX, ALPHONSE
25-27 Anonymous 5, 11

LACROIX, ANDRÉ
70/1 Colgate Stamp 29
70/1 DadsCookies
70/1 EddieSargent 154
71/2 EddieSargent 39
70/1 Esso Stamp
68/9 O-Pee-Chee 184
69/70 OPC/Topps 98
69/70 OPC-Sticker, -Stamp
70/1 OPC/Topps 84, -Sticker
71/2 OPC/Topps 33
79/80 OPC/Topps 107
73/4 opc-Posters 10
74/5 opcWHA 60
75/6 opcWHA 10, 64
76/7 opcWHA 70, 80
77/8 opcWHA 30
73/4 QuakerOats 6
72/3 7ElevenCups
68/9 ShirriffCoin PHA6
71/2 TheTorontoSun
70/1 PHA

LACROIX, DANIEL
94/5 Classic E2
93/4 ClassicProspects 69
93/4 Leaf 351
97/8 PacificDynag-BestKept 70
97/8 PacificRegime 143
96/7 PinnacleBeAPlayer 135
89/90 ProCards(IHL) 31
90/1 ProCards 7
91/2 ProCards 194
97/8 Score(PHA) 20
94/5 UpperDeck 283
96/7 PHA/OceanSpray
92/3 Binghampton
95/6 Binghampton

LACROIX, ERIC
92/3 Classic 77
93/4 ClassicProspects 164
94/5 Fleer 97
95/6 FleerUltra 252
98/9 Pacific 163
97/8 PacificCrown 161
94/5 Parkhurst 234
95/6 Parkhurst 107
95/6 Pinnacle 82
95/6 POG 142
97/8 Score(COL) 13
95/6 Topps 32
94/5 UpperDeck 352
95/6 UpperDeck 122
96/7 UpperDeck 244
94/5 UDBeAPlayer-Aut. 13
95/6 UDCollChoice 276
92/3 StJohns
93/4 StJohns

LACROIX, MARTIN
92/3 Classic 78
92/3 ClassicFourSport 200

LACROIX, PIERRE
72-84 Dernière 81/2
81/2 O-Pee-Chee 278
82/3 O-Pee-Chee 286
83/4 opcSticker 261
80/1 Pepsi Cap
83/4 SouhaitsRen.KeyChain
83/4 HFD/JuniorWhalers
80/1 QUE
81/2 QUE

LACROIX, RENÉ
52/3 LavalDairy 116
52/3 StLawrence 29

LADOUCEUR, RANDY
91/2 Bowman 5
92/3 Bowman 107
93/4 EASports 2
84/5 O-Pee-Chee 60
85/6 O-Pee-Chee 216
89/90 O-Pee-Chee 304
90/1 OPC/Topps 162
92/3 O-Pee-Chee 299
90/1 PaniniSticker 41
91/2 Parkhurst 289
95/6 Parkhurst 7
94/5 ParkieSE 3
91/2 Pinnacle 224
92/3 Pinnacle 291
93/4 Pinnacle 389, -Expansion 2
94/5 POG 365
93/4 Premier 469
90/1 ProSet 108
91/2 ProSet 396, 573
91/2 Score(CDN) 407, (U.S) 436
92/3 Score 61
93/4 Score 553
92/3 Topps 344
92/3 ToppsStadiumClub 156

93/4 ToppsStadiumClub 271
94/5 ToppsStadiumClub 69
90/1 UpperDeck 151
95/6 UDBeAPlayer 37
94/5 ANA/Carl'sJr 15
84/5 DET/Caesars
85/6 DET/Caesars
87/8 HFD/JuniorWhalers
88/9 HFD/JuniorWhalers
89/90 HFD/JuniorWhalers
90/1 HFD/JuniorWhalers
91/2 HFD/JuniorWhalers
92/3 HFD/DairyMart

LAFAYETTE, JUSTIN
91/2 ProCards 493

LAFAYETTE, NATHAN
93/4 Classic 22
94/5 ClassicImages 40
93/4 ClassicProspects 195
94/5 Donruss 156
94/5 Flair 190
94/5 FleerUltra 225
94/5 Leaf 216
94/5 PaniniSticker Q
94/5 Parkhurst 247
94/5 ParkieSE seV44
94/5 Pinnacle 453
94/5 POG 340
94/5 Premier 18,-Finest(OPC) 22
91/2 SketchAwards 3
90/1 SketchMEM 114
90/1 SketchOHL 25, 63
91/2 SketchOHL 14
91/2 StarPics 56
91/2 UltimateDP 46, -Aut 46
92/3 UpperDeck 588
94/5 UpperDeck 448
94/5 VAN
91/2 Cornwall 18
93/4 Peoria

LAFERRIÈRE, RICK
81/2 COL.R

LAFLAMME, CHRISTIAN
95/6 Classic 40
95/6 ClassicFiveSport 145
94/5 ClassicImages 87
97/8 Omega 52
98/9 Pacific 148
93/4 UpperDeck E6
97/8 UpperDeck 185

LAFLAMME, DANIEL
90/1 SketchQMJHL 103
91/2 SketchQMJHL 183

LAFLEUR, BRIAN
93/4 Minnesota
94/5 Minnesota

LAFLEUR, GUY
71/2 Colgate Heads
72-84 Dernière 72/3, 73/4
72-84 Dernière 80/1, 83/4
88/9 Esso Sticker
84/5 Kelloggs Disk
89/90 Kraft 31
90/1 Kraft 22
91/2 Kraft 66
74/5 Loblaws
82/3 McDonalds 8
71/2 OPC/Topps 148
72/3 OPC 59, Topps 79
73/4 OPC/Topps 72
74/5 OPC/Topps 232
75/6 OPC/T 126, 208, 290, 322
76/7 OPC/Topps 1-3, 5, 163
76/7 OPC 388, T-Glossy 11
77/8 OPC/Topps 1, 2, 3, 7, 200
77/8 OPC/Topps 214, 216, 218
77/8 OPC/Topps-Glossy 7
78/9 OPC/Topps 3, 63-65,69,90
78/9 O-Pee-Chee 326
79/80 OPC/Topps 1, 2, 3, 7, 200
80/1 OPC/T 10, 82, 162,163,216
81/2 OPC 177, 195, Topps 19
82/3 O-Pee-Chee 186, 187
83/4 O-Pee-Chee 183, 189
84/5 OPC 264, 360, Topps 81
89/90 OPC/Topps 189
90/1 OPC/Topps 142
91/2 OPC/Topps 1-3
71/2 opcPoster 13
80/1 opcSuperCard 10
90/1 opcPremier 55
81/2 opcSticker 29, 41
82/3 opcSticker 28, 29
83/4 opcSticker 2, 58, 59
84/5 opcSticker 149, 150
89/90 opcSticker 245/106
90/1 Panini(QUE) 12, G
90/1 PaniniSticker 145
82/3 Post
90/1 ProSet 250
91/2 ProSet 317
83/4 PuffySticker 4
90/1 Score 290, -HotCards 96
91/2 Score(CDN) 291-93
91/2 Score(U.S) 401, 03
83/4 SouhaitsRen.KeyChain
93 SourPuckCaps 2
77-9 Sportscaster 51-18, 38-07
77-9 Sportscstr 38-895, 57-1356
71/2 TheTorontoSun
90/1 UpperDeck 162
91/2 UpperDeck 219, 638
83/4 Vachon 47
96 Wien HL2
71 MTL/Pins
71/2 MTL
72/3 MTL
73/4 MTL
74/5 MTL
75/6 MTL
76/7 MTL
77/8 MTL
78/9 MTL
79/80 MTL
80/1 MTL
81/2 MTL
82/3 MTL
82/3 MTL/Steinberg
83/4 MTL
84/5 MTL
92/3 MTL/OPC 17, 57
95/6 MTL/Forum 18Mar96
89/90 QUE
89/90 QUE/GeneralFoods
89/90 QUE/Police
90/1 QUE/PetroCanada

LAFLEUR, PATRICK
95/6 Halifax

LAFOLEY, GUY
92/3 Ottawa67s

LAFONTAINE, PAT
95/6 Aces 5 (Spades)
96/7 Aces 7 (Diamonds)
90/1 Bowman 123, -HatTrick 9
91/2 Bowman 222
92/3 Bowman 142
95/6 Bowman 29
97/8 CorinthianHeadliner
72-84 Dernière 82/3
93/4 Donruss 37, -IceKings 2
94/5 Donruss 300
95/6 Donruss 172, -ProPointer 2
96/7 Donruss 113
97/8 Donruss 133
96/7 DonrussCanadianIce 11
97/8 DonrussCanadianIce 69
95/6 DonrussElite 75
96/7 D.Elite 101, -Perspect 10
97/8 DonrussElite 111, 146
97/8 DonrussPreferred 58
97/8 DonrussPriority 160
97/8 DonrussStudio 50
93/4 EASports 15
94/5 Flair 19, -CentreSpotlight 5
96/7 Flair 9
94/5 Fleer 23
96/7 Fleer 11, -ArtRoss 11
95/6 FleerMetal 16, -IntSteel 12
96/7 F.Picks 38, -Dream 10
92/3 FleerUltra 16
93/4 FU 219,-AS 4,-Pivots 3
93/4 FU-Scoring 1, -Speed 6
94/5 FU 24, PremierPivot 5
94/5 FU-Speed 5, -Power 5
95/6 FleerUltra 19, 389
96/7 FU 17, -MrMomentum 6
88/9 FritoLay
91/2 Gillette 23
95 Globe 116
93/4 HockeyWit 105
95/6 Hoyle'EAST Q (Spades)
92/3 HumptyDumpty (2)
97/8 KatchMedallion 93
91/2 Kelloggs 15
93/4 KennerSLU
94/5 KennerSLU (U.S)
96/7 KennerSLU (U.S)
90/1 Kraft 23, 86
91/2 Kraft 25
93/4 Kraft-Captain
94/5 Kraft-HockeyHeroes
96/7 Kraft-Disk
93/4 Leaf 12, -GoldLeafAS 1
93/4 L-StudioSignatures 3
94/5 Leaf 278, -GoldLeafStar 14
95/6 Leaf 140
96/7 Leaf 44
97/8 Leaf 34
94/5 LeafLimited 63
96/7 LeafLimited 59
96/7 LeafPreferred 11, -Steel 22
97/8 Limited 111
91/2 McDonalds McD6
93/4 McDonalds McD18
96/7 MetalUniv.15, -IceCarv 8
97/8 Omega 146, -StickHan 14
84/5 OPC 129, 392, Topps 96
85/6 OPC/Topps 137
86/7 OPC/Topps 2
87/8 OPC/Topps 173
88/9 OPC/Topps 123, C
89/90 OPC/Topps 60
90/1 OPC/T. 184, 315, T-TL 10
91/2 OPC/Topps 80, T-TL 12
92/3 O-Pee-Chee 285
87/8 opcStars 22
90/1 opcPremier 56
91/2 opcPremier 64
92/3 opcPremier-Star 17
85/6 opcSticker 74/201
86/7 opcSticker 206
87/8 opcSticker 243/110
88/9 opcSticker 111
89/90 opcSticker 119
98/9 Pacific 295
97/8 PacificCrownRoyale 85
97/8 PCR -Lamplighter 12
97/8 PacificParamount 117
98/9 PacificParamount 154
97/8 PacificRevolution 88
87/8 PaniniSticker 98
88/9 PaniniSticker 290
89/90 PaniniSticker 264
90/1 PaniniSticker 81
91/2 PaniniSticker 243
92/3 PaniniSticker 246
93/4 PaniniSticker 101, 137
94/5 PaniniSticker 92
96/7 PaniniSticker 15
91/2 Parkhurst 16
92/3 Parkhurst 12
93/4 Parkhurst 289, E8
94/5 Parkhurst 310, V73, C3
95/6 Parkhurst 20, PP49
94/5 ParkieSE 18
91/2 Pinnacle 25
92/3 Pinnacle 7, 254
93/4 Pinn 300, CA3, -Nifty 1, 12
94/5 Pinnacle 350, GR2
95/6 Pinnacle 54
96/7 Pinnacle 27
97/8 Pinnacle 69
96/7 P.BAP LTH8B,-OneTimr 15
97/8 PinnacleBeeHive 43
97/8 PinnacleCertified 80
97/8 PinnacleInside 39
95/6 PinnacleZenith 85
96/7 P.Zenith 83, -Assailant 9
95/6 Playoff 13, 127
94/5 POG 50
95/6 POG 42
93/4 PowerPlay 31, -Point 7
93/4 Premier 171, 490
93/4 Prmr-Black(OPC) 14,(T) 24
94/5 Premier 180, -GoToGuy 6
95/6 ProMagnet 109
90/1 ProSet 186, 372
91/2 ProSet 149, 308, 358, P4
92/3 ProSet 13
91/2 PSPlatinum 157
90/1 Score 250, -HotCards 95
91/2 ScoreCDN 362, 480
91/2 ScoreUS 260, 332, 100T
92/3 Score 6, 420, -ShrpShootr 8
92/3 Score-USAGreats 1
93/4 Score 345, (U.S) DD2
93/4 S-TheFranchise 2,-P.AS 11
93/4 Score-Dream 13
94/5 Score 2, TF3
95/6 Score 201, -BorderBattle 7
95/6 Score-GoldenBlades 8
96/7 Score 139
97/8 Score 104
97/8 Score(NYR) 10
92/3 SeasonsPatch 42
94/5 Select 57
95/6 SelectCertified 18
96/7 SelectCertified 9
94 Semic 120, 359
95 Semic 114
89 SemicSticker 164
91 SemicSticker 138
92 SemicSticker 159
93 SemicSticker 183
95/6 SkyBoxEmotion 18
95/6 SkyBoxImpact 17
96/7 SkyBoxImpact 11,-Blade 10
94/5 SP 12
95/6 SP 12, E5
96/7 SP 15, GF18, HC8
97/8 SPAuthentic 98, I1
96/7 SPx 18
97/8 SPx 5
98/9 SPx"Finite" 56
97/8 SportFX MiniStix
95/6 Summit 34
96/7 Summit 127
95/6 SuperSticker 11, -DieCut 3
92/3 Topps 345
95/6 Topps 13, 250, HGA4
95/6 Topps 6PL, 5RL
94/5 ToppsFinest 70
95/6 ToppsFinest 40, 130
91/2 ToppsStadiumClub 123
92/3 ToppsStadiumClub 95
93/4 ToppsStadiumClub 20, 460
93/4 TSC-AllStar, -Master (1) 1
95/6 ToppsStadiumClub 164
95/6 ToppsSuperSkills 5
90/1 UD 246, 306, 479
91/2 UpperDeck 253, 556
92/3 UpperDeck 165, 456, G3
92/3 UD-LockerAS 4
93/4 UD 137, 221, 287
93/4 UpperDeck HT10, SP-17
94/5 UD 17, IG14, R17, R22
94/5 UD R47, R55, SP99
95/6 UD 386, R19, R29, SE10
96/7 UpperDeck 15, 17B
97/8 UpperDeck 318
93/4 UDBeAPlayer 28
94/5 UDBAP R79, R132,-Aut. 63
97/8 UDBlackDiamnd 133,PC22
98/9 UDChoice 130
95/6 UDCollChoice 157, C27
96/7 UDCC 23, 311, S21, UD40
96/7 UDCC'Oversize 23
97/8 UDCollChoice 31
97/8 UpperDeckIce 72
96 Wien 165
97/8 Zenith 44,Z26,-ChasCup 14
91/2 BUF/BlueShield
91/2 BUF/Campbell
92/3 BUF/BlueShield
92/3 BUF/Jubillee
93/4 BUF/NOCO
84/5 NYI 11
89/90 NYI

LAFORCE, ERNIE
43-47 ParadeSportive

LAFOREST, BOB
82/3 NorthBay

LAFOREST, MAGELLA
51/2 BasDuFleuve 30

LAFOREST, MARK
95/6 EdgeIce 163
89/90 ProCards(AHL) 124
90/1 ProCards 13
91/2 ProCards 208
90/1 UpperDeck 81
94/5 Milwaukee
82/3 NorthBay

LAFORGE, ALAIN
90/1 SketchOHL 386
86/7 Kingston 28
88/9 NiagaraFalls 21
89/90 Sudbury 7
90/1 Sudbury 19

LAFORGE, BILL
88/9 NiagaraFalls 22
80/1 Oshawa 17

LAFORGE, CLAUDE
62/3 Parkhurst 24
68/9 ShirriffCoin PHA11
58/9 Topps 33
59/60 Topps 64

LAFORGE, MARC
88/9 ProCards(Binghampton)
90/1 ProCards 233
91/2 ProCards 216
94/5 CapeBreton
84/5 Kingston 16
85/6 Kingston 16
86/7 Kingston 16

LAFOY, MIKO
82/3 Kingston 20

LAFRAMBOISE, PETE
72/3 EddieSargent 53
74/5 Loblaws
72/3 OPC 263
73/4 OPC 244
74/5 OPC/Topps 166
75/6 OPC 364
74/5 WSH

LAFRANCE, DARRYL
95/6 Classic 91
91/2 SketchOHL 157
93/4 Slapshot(Oshawa) 14
91/2 Oshawa,
91/2 Oshawa/Dominos 14
92/3 Oshawa

LAFRANCE, ERIC
90/1 SketchQMJHL 183
91/2 SketchQMJHL 170

LAFRANCE, LÉO
28/9 MTL/LaPatrie 3

LAFRENIÈRE, CHRIS
90/1 SketchMEM 75
90/1 SketchWHL 195

LAFRENIÈRE, JASON
90/1 CanadaNats
88/9 O-Pee-Chee 223
87/8 opcSticker 130/118, 219/87
88/9 opcSticker 185/54
87/8 PaniniSticker 171
93/4 Parkhurst 466
89/90 ProCards(IHL) 25
85/6 QUE
85/6 QUE/McDonald
86/7 QUE
86/7 QUE/GeneralFoods
87/8 QUE/GeneralFoods
87/8 QUE/YumYum
92/3 AtlantaKnights
83/4 Brantford 6

LAFRENIÈRE, MARC
90/1 Rayside
91/2 Rayside

LAFRENIÈRE, RÉAL
51/2 BasDuFleuve 26
52/3 BasDuFleuve 63

LAGACE, J.G.
74/5 Loblaws-Update
74/5 O-Pee-Chee 299
75/6 OPC/Topps 141
74/5 PGH

LAGANAS, CHRIS
91/2 Greensboro
92/3 Oklahoma

LAGINSKI, AL
89/90 Rayside

LAGRAND, SCOTT
92/3 Classic 79
92/3 ClassicFourSport 201

LAHAYE, LES
52/3 AnonymousOHL 45

LAHDE, KYÖSTI
72/3 WilliamsFIN 176

LAHEY, MATT
95/6 Slapshot 326
96/7 SSMarie

LAHEY, PAT
82/3 SSMarie
83/4 SSMarie

LAHN, STEFAN
95/6 DEL 290
96/7 DEL 317

LAHNALAMPI, D.
94/5 Slapshot(NorthBay) 3

LAHTEENMAKI, ARI
80/1 Mallasjuoma 20
78/9 SM-Liiga 42

LAHTELA, PEKKA
66/7 Champion 65
70/1 Kuvajulkaisut 161
71/2 WilliamsFIN 231
72/3 WilliamsFIN 214

LAHTI, PEKKA
66/7 Champion 27

LAHTINEN, JOUNI
95/6 Sisu 239
96/7 Sisu 37

LAHTINEN, JUHANI
66/7 Champion 201
65/6 Hellas 125
70/1 Kuvajulkaisut 128

LAHTINEN, TIMO
66/7 Champion 200
70/1 Kuvajulkaisut 129
91/2 SemicElitserien 309
71/2 WilliamsFIN 154
72/3 WilliamsFIN 106
73/4 WilliamsFIN 203

LAIDLAW, KEN
69 ColumbusCheckers

LAIDLAW, TOM
81/2 O-Pee-Chee 234
82/3 O-Pee-Chee 227
83/4 O-Pee-Chee 247
84/5 O-Pee-Chee 144
90/1 O-Pee-Chee 524
86/7 OPC/Topps 147
88/9 OPC/Topps 37
89/90 OPC/Topps 34
86/7 opcSticker 223/92
88/9 PaniniSticker 71
82/3 Post
90/1 ProSet 123
90/1 Score 69
90/1 UpperDeck 119
88/9 L.A./Smokeys
89/90 L.A./Smokeys 23
90/1 L.A./Smokeys 12

LAIHO, JARI
80/1 Mallasjuoma 130
78/9 SM-Liiga 172
73/4 WilliamsFIN 312

LAINE, ANTTI
71/2 WilliamsFIN 246

LAINE, ARI
71/2 WilliamsFIN 369

LAINE, ARTO
70/1 Kuvajulkaisut 231
80/1 Mallasjuoma 50
71/2 WilliamsFIN 247
72/3 WilliamsFIN 347
73/4 WilliamsFIN 313

LAINE, ERKKI
91/2 Jyvas-Hyva 51
82 SemicSticker 43
89 SemicSticker 45
93/4 Sisu 291

LAINE, ISMO
72/3 WilliamsFIN 332

LAINE, JUHANI
71/2 WilliamsFIN 284
73/4 WilliamsFIN 204

LAINE, M.IKA
80/1 Mallasjuoma 77
71/2 WilliamsFIN 346

LAINE, PEKKA
80/1 Mallasjuoma 79
78/9 SM-Liiga 125

LAINE, SAMI
95/6 Sisu 212
96/7 Sisu 7

LAINIO, KARI
71/2 WilliamsFIN 370

LAIRD, ROB
90/1 ProCards 217
91/2 ProCards 571
89/90 WSH/Kodak
95/6 Phoenix

LAIRINEN, KARI
89 SemicSticker 43
92/3 Jyvas-Hyva 5

LAITRE, MARTIN
90/1 SketchQMJHL 254

LAJEUNESSE, BRUNO
90/1 SketchQMJHL 132

LAJEUNESSE, MARTIN
90/1 SketchQMJHL 242
91/2 SketchQMJHL 126

LAJEUNESSE, SERGE
70/1 Esso Stamp
71/2 OPC/Topps 136

LAJOIE, CLAUDE
84/5 Chicoutimi

LAJOIE, SERGE
86/7 Kamloops

LAKE, ALLAN
86/7 Kitchener 16
87/8 Kitchener 28

LAKE, FRED
91 C55 Reprint 9
1911-12 Imperial (C55) 9
1910-11 Imperial (C56) 27
1912-13 Imperial (C57) 31
1910-11 Imperial Post 9

LAKOVIC, SASHA
95/6 LasVegas

LAKSO, BOB
88/9 ProCards(Indianapolis)
89/90 ProCards(IHL) 125
90/1 ProCards 542
91/2 ProCards 257

LAKSOLA, PEKKA
96/7 DEL 254
91/2 Jyvas-Hyva 60
92/3 Jyvas-Hyva 167
93/4 Jyvas-Hyva 290
94 Semic 16
95 Semic 33
93/4 Sisu 66
94/5 Sisu 64
95/6 Sisu 111, 183, -DoublTro 8
95/6 SisuLimited 74

LAKSOLA, REIJO
80/1 Mallasjuoma 24
78/9 SM-Liiga 24
73/4 WilliamsFIN 223

LALA, JIRI
94/5 DEL 113
95/6 DEL 115
82 SemicSticker 89
89 SemicSticker 198
91 SemicSticker 114

LALANCETTE, JACQUES
52/3 BasDuFleuve 33
51/2 LacStJean 24

LALANDE, HEC
57/8 Topps 31
93/4 Parkie(56/7) 38

LALIBERTÉ, GAETAN
51/2 BasDuFleuve 18

LALIBERTÉ, HUGUES
90/1 SketchQMJHL 213
91/2 SketchQMJHL 26

LALIBERTÉ, SPIKE
51/2 LavalDairy 59

LALIME, PATRICK
97/8 Donruss 76
97/8 DonrussCdnIce -Gardiens 9
96/7 DonrussElite 133
96/7 Flair 121, -HotGlove 6

96/7 FleerUltra 142
97/8 KennerSLU
97/8 Leaf 111
97/8 Limited 142, 159
97/8 PacificCrown 40, -InThe 17
97/8 PacificDynagon! 103, 142
97/8 PcfcD-BstKpt 78,-Dyn 13B
97/8 PcfcD-Stone 18,-Tand 9, 22
97/8 PacificInv. 114, -Feature 29
97/8 PacificRegime 161
97/8 PaniniSticker 246
96/7 P.BAP-Stacking 1,-LTH10A
97/8 PinnacleCertified 23
97/8 Pinn.Inside 67,-StandUp 6
97/8 Score 40
97/8 Score(PGH) 3
96/7 SelectCert 108
91/2 SketchQMJHL 71
97/8 UD 133, SG40, T12A
96/7 UDBlackDiamond 168
97/8 UDCollChoice 208, SQ40
96/7 UpperDeck"Ice" 54
96/7 PGH/FotoPuck
95/6 Cleveland
94/5 Hampton 3

LALONDE, BOB
72/3 EddieSargent 221
74/5 Loblaws
72/3 OPC 217
73/4 OPC 179, Topps 189
74/5 OPC 392
75/6 OPC/Topps 246
76/7 OPC 278
77/8 OPC 313
78/9 O-Pee-Chee 285
79/80 O-Pee-Chee 326
80/1 O-Pee-Chee 265
71/2 TheTorontoSun
78/9 ATL/Coke
71/2 VAN/RoyalBank 1
72/3 VAN/RoyalBank
73/4 VAN/RoyalBank
74/5 VAN/RoyalBank
75/6 VAN/RoyalBank
76/7 VAN/RoyalBank

LALONDE, EDOUARD (NEWSY)
91 C55 Reprint 42
25 Dominion 95
83&87 HallOfFame 70
83 HHOF Postcard (E)
1911-12 Imperial (C55) 42
1910-11 Imperial (C56) 36
1912-13 Imperial (C57) 44
1910-11 Imperial Post 42
24/5 MapleCrispettes (V130) 27
55/6 Parkhurst 55
23/4 PaulinsCandy 38
60/1 Topps 48
61/2 Topps-Stamp
28/9 MTL/LaPatrie 17
95/6 MTL/Forum 23Sep95

LALONDE, GREGG
95/6 Slapshot 384

LALONDE, GUY
51/2 BasDuFleuve 16

LALONDE, HECTOR
52/3 AnonymousOHL 170

LALONDE, HERVE
52/3 AnonymousOHL 38
51-54 LaPatrie 10Jan54

LALONDE, P.F.
91/2 SketchQMJHL 205

LALONDE, RON
74/5 Loblaws-Update
75/6 OPC/Topps 152
77/8 OPC 378
78/9 O-Pee-Chee 371
74/5 PGH

LALONDE, TODD
94/5 Slapshot(Sudbury) 24
95/6 Slapshot 405
85/6 Sudbury 7
87/8 Sudbury 4
88/9 Sudbury 24
89/90 Sudbury 2

LALOR, MIKE
92/3 Bowman 319
93/4 Donruss 306
86/7 Kraft Sports 28
93/4 Kraft'Captain
93/4 Leaf 399
90/1 OPC/Topps 341
91/2 OPC/Topps 483
90/1 opcPremier 57
87/8 opcSticker 73
90/1 PaniniSticker 267
91/2 Parkhurst 427
92/3 Pinnacle 123
90/1 ProSet 264, 552
91/2 ProSet 255
92/3 ProSet 268
90/1 Score 67, 98T
91/2 Score(CDN) 469, (U.S) 249
92/3 Score 363
92/3 Topps 140
92/3 ToppsStadiumClub 190
90/1 UpperDeck 40
94/5 DAL/Southwest
96/7 DAL/Southwest
85/6 MTL
85/6 MTL/ProvigoStickers
85/6? MTL/ProvigoPlacemats
86/7 MTL
87/8 MTL
87/8 MTL/Stickers 22, 59, 60
88/9 MTL
92/3 S.J/PacificBell
88/9 STL/Kodak
89/90 STL/Kodak
90/1 WSH/Kodak
90/1 WSH/Smokey
91/2 WSH
83/4 NovaScotia 12

LALUK, SCOTT
94/5 Slapshot(MEM) 29
92/3 Brandon 14

LAMARCHE, MARTIN
91/2 SketchQMJHL 90

LAMB, GARTH
89/90 Nashville

LAMB, JEFF
88/9 ProCards(Maine)
89/90 ProCards(IHL) 110

LAMB, JOSEPH
33-43 BeeHives(NYA)
38/9 BruinsMagazine
33-35 DiamondMatch
36-39 DiamondMatch (1)
33/4 OPC (V304A) 2
34/5 SweetCaporal
33/4 WWGum (V357) 41
36/7 WWGum (V356) 37

LAMB, MARK
93/4 Donruss 230
93/4 Leaf 308
94/5 Leaf 337
90/1 OPC/Topps 25
92/3 O-Pee-Chee 322
90/1 Panini(EDM) 10
93/4 PaniniSticker 117
92/3 Parkhurst 116
92/3 Pinnacle 374
93/4 Pinnacle 323, CA16
94/5 Pinnacle 163
94/5 POG 178
93/4 PowerPlay 171
93/4 Premier 271
88/9 ProCards(CapeBreton)
90/1 ProSet 88
90/1 Score (CND) 308
91/2 Score(CDN) 652
92/3 Score 514
93/4 Score 407
92/3 Topps 230
93/4 ToppsStadiumClub 172
94/5 ToppsStadiumClub 206
88/9 EDM
88/9 EDM/ActionMagazine 61
90/1 EDM/McGavins
91/2 EDM/IGA
92/3 OTT
93/4 OTT/Kraft
93/4 PHA 31MAR94
94/5 PHA
82/3 MedicineHat
83/4 MedicineHat 8
84/5 Moncton 6
85/6 Moncton 7

LAMBERT, DAN
92/3 Bowman 356
95/6 FutureLegends 30
93/4 Jyvas-Hyva 26
92/3 O-Pee-Chee 357
91/2 Pinnacle 346
93/4 Sisu 87
92/3 Topps 364
91/2 UpperDeck 592
92/3 UpperDeck 251

LAMBERT, DENNY
95/6 Bowman 98
95/6 FleerUltra 4
98/9 Pacific 311
98/9 PacificParamount 125
97/8 PacificRegime 134
96/7 PinnacleBeAPlayer 68
91/2 ProCards 324
90/1 SketchMEM 17
90/1 SketchOHL 164
95/6 Topps 286
96/7 OTT/PizzaHut
97/8 OTT
92/3 SanDiego
89/90 SSMarie 8

LAMBERT, JUDD
92/3 BCJHL 42

LAMBERT, LANE
84/5 O-Pee-Chee 57
88/9 O-Pee-Chee 224
88/9 opcSticker 183/48
88/9 PaniniSticker 356
84/5 DET/Caesars
85/6 DET/Caesars
87/8 QUE/GeneralFoods
88/9 QUE
88/9 QUE/GeneralFoods
81/2 Saskatoon 19

LAMBERT, ROSS
83/4 Moncton 13
84/5 NovaScotia 23

LAMBERT, SYLVIO
51/2 LacStJean 21

LAMBERT, YVES
91/2 SketchQMJHL 272

LAMBERT, YVON
72-84 Dernière 73/4, 80/1
74/5 Loblaws
74/5 O-Pee-Chee 342
75/6 OPC/Topps 17
76/7 OPC/Topps 232
78/9 OPC/Topps 147
79/80 OPC/Topps 24, 150
80/1 OPC/Topps 246
81/2 O-Pee-Chee 185
82/3 O-Pee-Chee 27
81/2 opcSticker 35
82/3 opcSticker
80/1 Pepsi Cap
82/3 Post
81/2 BUF 16
73/4 MTL
74/5 MTL
75/6 MTL
76/7 MTL
77/8 MTL
78/9 MTL
79/80 MTL
80/1 MTL
81/2 MTL

LAMBY, DICK
79 PaniniSticker 208

LAMING, ANDREW
91/2 SketchWHL 65

LAMIRANDE, CHARLES
51/2 LacStJean 31

LAMIRANDE, GASTON
51/2 LacStJean 39

LAMIRANDE, J.P.
51-54 LaPatrie 1Feb53
51/2 LavalDairy 31
52/3 StLawrence 95

LAMIRANDE, MAURICE
51/2 BasDuFleuve 38
52/3 BasDuFleuve 5

LAMMENS, HANK
92/3 CanadaNats
93/4 Parkhurst 409
88/9 ProCards(Springfield)
89/90 ProCards(AHL) 233

LAMOURIELLO, LOU
88/9 N.J./Caretta
89/90 N.J.
90/1 N.J.
96/7 N.J/Sharp

LAMOTHE, CARL
90/1 SketchQMJHL 255
91/2 SketchQMJHL 148

LAMOTHE, MARC
91/2 SketchOHL 240
93/4 Slapshot(Kingston) 2
94/5 Fredericton
95/6 Fredericton

LAMOUREUX, LÉO
33-43 BeeHives(MTL.C)
43-47 ParadeSportive (x2)
45-54 QuakerOats

LAMOUREUX, MITCH
80/1 Oshawa 15
81/2 Oshawa 6
92/3 SanDiego

LAMOUREUX, PATRICK
91/2 SketchQMJHL 51

LAMOUREUX, ROBERT
72/3 WilliamsFIN 215
73/4 WilliamsFIN 289

LAMPAINEN, MATTI
65/6 Hellas 80

LAMPERT, REINHART
94 Semic 247
93 SemicSticker 287

LAMPINEN, JUHA
96/7 DEL 95
92/3 Jyvas-Hyva 42
93/4 Jyvas-Hyva 85
93/4 Sisu 113
94/5 Sisu 54
95/6 Sisu 232

LAMPMAN, J.
93/4 Waterloo

LAMPMAN, MIKE
76/7 O-Pee-Chee 375
77/8 O-Pee-Chee 396
72/3 STL
72/3 STL/8"x10"
73/4 STL

LAMPMAN, PATRICK
91/2 SketchQMJHL 98

LANDGREN, REINE
89/90 SemicElitserien 232
90/1 SemicElitserien 64
91/2 SemicElitserien 242

LANDON, BRUCE
76/7 opcWHA 48
72/3 NewEngland

LANDON, LARRY
83/4 NovaScotia 23

LANDRY, ERIC
93/4 Slapshot(Guelph) 10
95/6 Slapshot 318

LANDRY, JOHN
82/3 Kingston 17
84/5 Sudbury 11

LANDRY, ROGER
52/3 AnonymousOHL 160

LANDRY, ROLAND
52/3 BasDuFleuve 8

LANE, CHRIS
95/6 Spokane 4

LANE, GORD
77/8 O-Pee-Chee 287
78/9 O-Pee-Chee 284
79/80 O-Pee-Chee 325
80/1 O-Pee-Chee 323
81/2 O-Pee-Chee 212
83/4 O-Pee-Chee 10
85/6 opcSticker 77/210
83/4 NYI/Islander 17
84/5 NYI 21
78/9 WSH

LANG, BILL
90/1 SketchOHL 310
91/2 SketchOHL 60
93/4 Slapshot(N.B) 9

LANG, CHAD
95/6 Classic 94
91/2 SketchOHL 129
93/4 Slapshot(Peterborough) 15
91/2 Peterborough 22

LANG, KAREL
94/5 DEL 225
95/6 DEL 219
96/7 DEL 69
82 SemicSticker 77

LANG, ROBERT
94/5 APS 222
92/3 ClassicProspects 46
93/4 FleerUltra 188
94/5 FleerUltra 101
95 Globe 155
94/5 Leaf 429
92/3 opcPremier 47
98/9 Pacific 355
94/5 PaniniSticker T
92/3 Parkhurst 64, 227
94/5 Parkhurst 286
95/6 Parkhurst 101
94/5 ParkieSE 78
92/3 Pinnacle 411
94/5 Pinnacle 413
97/8 PinnacleBeAPlayer 14
94/5 Premier 218
93/4 Score 456
94 Semic 186
95/6 Topps 186
92/3 UpperDeck 552, ER4
94/5 UpperDeck 175
95/6 UpperDeck 281
94/5 UDBeAPlayer-Aut. 174
95/6 UDCollChoice 175
92/3 Phoenix

LANGAGER, SHANE
89/90 Saskatoon 9

LANGBACKA, JAN
92/3 Jyvas-Hyva 108
93/4 Jyvas-Hyva 198
93/4 Sisu 266
94/5 Sisu 26

LANGDON, DARREN
95/6 Bowman 92
95/6 Donruss 224
95/6 FleerMetal 181
95/6 FleerUltra 102, 345
95/6 Leaf 262
98/9 Pacific 296
95/6 Parkhurst 528
96/7 PinnacleBeAPlayer 9
95/6 SkyBoxImpact 212
95/6 Topps 116
98/9 Topps 172
94/5 Binghampton
92/3 Dayton

LANGE, PATRICK
94/5 DEL 195
95/6 DEL 309

LANGELLE, PETE
33-43 BeeHives(TOR)
39/40 OPC (V301-1) 7
40/1 OPC (V301-2) 117

LANGEN, MIKE
91/2 AirCanadaSJHL A13
90/1 SketchQMJHL 270

LANGENBRUNNER, JAMIE
94/5 Classic 24, T17
94/5 C'Images 48, -Aut.
95/6 Classic 94
93/4 Donruss USA13
96/7 Donruss 218
97/8 Donruss 97
96/7 DonrussCanadianIce 137
97/8 DonrussCanadianIce 103
96/7 D.Elite 144, -Aspirations 21
97/8 DonrussPreferred 20
97/8 DonrussPriority 79
95/6 EdgeIce 141
96/7 Flair 105
96/7 Fleer 129, -Calder 6
95/6 FleerUltra 346
96/7 FleerUltra 43, -Rookies 11
95/6 FutureLegends-Pltnm 6
96/7 Leaf 225
97/8 Leaf 46
94/5 LeafLimited-USAJrs 7
96/7 LeafLimited-Rookies 8
96/7 LeafPreferred 144
97/8 Limited 167
96/7 MetalUniverse 184
97/8 Omega 70
98/9 Pacific 15
97/8 PacificCrown 110
97/8 PcfcDynagn! 36,-Tandm 32
97/8 PacificInvincible 40
97/8 PacificParamount 58
98/9 PacificParamount 65
97/8 PacificRevolution 41
95/6 Parkhurst 60
94/5 ParkieSE 248
93/4 Pinnacle 496
96/7 Pinnacle 247
96/7 Pinn.BeAPlayer LTH6A
97/8 PinnacleInside 100
95/6 PinnacleZenith 129
96/7 PinnacleZenith 139
94/5 Score 211
96/7 Score 254
97/8 Score 211
96/7 SelectCertified 115
96/7 SkyBoxImpact 152
93/4 Slapshot(Peterborough) 20
94/5 SP 194
96/7 SP 46
97/8 SPAuthentic 47, S11
95/6 Summit 170
96/7 Summit 192
95/6 Topps 182
98/9 Topps 7
94/5 ToppsFinest 120
93/4 UpperDeck 566
95/6 UpperDeck 503
96/7 UpperDeck 48
97/8 UpperDeck 260
96/7 UDBlackDiamond 126
98/9 UDChoice 61
96/7 UDCollChoice 74
97/8 UDCollChoice 69
96/7 UpperDeck"Ice" 15
97/8 Zenith 61, Z51
96/7 DAL/Southwest

LANGEVIN, CHRIS
85/6 BUF

LANGEVIN, DAVE
80/1 OPC/Topps 188
81/2 O-Pee-Chee 213
82/3 O-Pee-Chee 204
83/4 O-Pee-Chee 11
84/5 O-Pee-Chee 100
86/7 O-Pee-Chee 218
83/4 opcSticker 83
82/3 Post
83/4 SouhaitsRen.KeyChain
85/6 MIN
85/6 MIN/7Eleven 11
79/80 NYI
83/4 NYI
83/4 NYI/Islander 18
84/5 NYI 22

LANGH, PIERRE
79 PaniniSticker 344

LANGILLE, DEREK
90/1 ProCards 153
91/2 ProCards 173
91/2 Moncton
90/1 Newmarket

LANGKOW, DAYMOND
94/5 AutoPhonex P2
95/6 Classic 5, AS4
95/6 ClassicFiveSport 147
94/5 ClassicImages 83,DP4,PD6
95/6 Donruss 324
97/8 Donruss 18
96/7 DonrussCanadianIce 135
97/8 D.CdnIce 70, -National 21
95/6 DonrussElite-WorldJrs 16
96/7 DonrussElite 134, -Aspir 13
97/8 DonrussElite 36
97/8 DonrussPreferred 23
97/8 DonrussPriority 21
97/8 D.Studio 48,-HardHats 6
96/7 Fleer 130, -Calder 7
95/6 FleerMetal 182
96/7 FleerUltra 157
97/8 KatchMedallion 136
96/7 Leaf 232
97/8 Leaf 103
95/6 LeafLimited 45
96/7 LeafPreferred 140
97/8 Limited 31, 133, 192,
97/8 Limited -fabric 48
96/7 MetalUniverse 185
97/8 Omega 210
98/9 Pacific 400
97/8 PcfcDynag!119,-Tandm 65
97/8 PacificInvincible 133
97/8 PacificParamount 174
95/6 Parkhurst 270
96/7 Pinnacle 240
97/8 Pinnacle 112
97/8 PinnacleBeAPlayer 176
97/8 PinnacleInside 99
95/6 PinnacleZenith 143
96/7 PinnacleZenith 141
97/8 Score 167
95/6 SelectCertified 124
96/7 SelectCertified 117
94/5 SigRookies 22
95/6 SkyBoxImpact 222
96/7 SkyBoxImpact 153
95/6 SP 139
96/7 SP 146
97/8 SPAuthentic 145
96/7 Summit 186
95/6 Tetrad F4
95/6 TetradAutobilia 45
98/9 Topps 72
93/4 UpperDeck E7
95/6 UpperDeck 270, 526
96/7 UpperDeck 340, X30
97/8 UD 158, SG32, T15C
96/7 UDBlackDiamond 46
98/9 UDChoice 192
95/6 UDCollChoice 402
96/7 UDCollChoice 346
97/8 UDCollChoice 243
97/8 UpperDeckIce 15

LANGKOW, SCOTT
95/6 EdgeIce 71
93/4 Portland(WHL)

LANGLOIS, ALBERT
45-64 BeeHives(MTL) (NYR)
64-67 BeeHives(DET)
62 CeramicTiles
64/5 CokeCap DET-2
65/6 CocaCola
58/9 Parkhurst 5
59/60 Parkhurst 45
60/1 Parkhurst 39
61/2 Parkhurst 37
94/5 Parkie(64/5) 52
60/1 ShirriffCoin 24
61/2 ShirriffCoin 94
61/2 Topps-Stamp
62/3 Topps 47, -Buck
63/4 Topps 49
64/5 Topps 13
65/6 Topps 33
60/1 York, -Glasses
89/90 NewHaven

LANGLOIS, CHARLIE
25-27 Anonymous 76
24/5 Champs (C144)
27-32 LaPresse 27/8
24/5 MapleCrispettes V130) 26
24/5 (V145-2) 17
28/9 MTL/LaPatrie 12

LANGLOIS, JOCELYN
90/1 SketchQMJHL 79
91/2 SketchQMJHL 40
61/2 Topps 46

LANGLOIS, PATRICK
92/3 Fredericton
93/4 Fredericton
94/5 Fredericton
95/6 Fredericton
96/7 Fredericton
84/5 Kitchener 9

LANGNER, PAUL
72 Hellas 47
72 SemicSticker 111

LANGSTROM, JUHANI
71/2 WilliamsFIN 286

LANGTRY, DOC
23/4 PaulinsCandy 57

LANGTRY, JACK
25 Dominion 86

LANGWAY, ROD
92/3 Bowman 279
72-84 Dernière 80/1, 82/3
88/9 Esso Sticker
93/4 HockeyWit 26
90/1 Kraft 24
82/3 McDonalds 32
80/1 O-Pee-Chee 344
81/2 O-Pee-Chee 186
82/3 O-Pee-Chee 368
83/4 O-Pee-Chee 365, 374
84/5 O-Pee-Chee 202, 210, 377
85/6 OPC/Topps 8, -AS 10
86/7 OPC/Topps 164
87/8 OPC/Topps 108
88/9 OPC/Topps 180, 192
89/90 OPC/Topps 55
92/3 O-Pee-Chee 347
90/1 OPC/Topps 353
91/2 OPC/Topps 105
81/2 opcSticker 39
82/3 opcSticker 34
83/4 opcSticker 201, 313
84/5 opcSticker 125-26, 230/231
85/6 opcSticker 105, 113
86/7 opcSticker 249/139
87/8 opcSticker 236
88/9 opcSticker 69/198
89/90 opcSticker 77/217
87/8 PaniniSticker 178
88/9 PaniniSticker 366
89/90 PaniniSticker 350
91/2 PaniniSticker 209
92/3 PaniniSticker 169
92/3 Parkhurst 433
80/1 Pepsi Cap
91/2 Pinnacle 195
92/3 Pinnacle 131
82/3 Post
90/1 ProSet 314
91/2 ProSet 259, 587
83/4 PuffySticker 19
90/1 Score 20, -HotCards 11
91/2 Score(CDN) 228, (U.S) 228
92/3 Score 143
93/4 Score 145
89 SemicSticker 159
84/5 7ElevenDisk
85/6 7Eleven 20
83/4 SouhaitsRen.KeyChain
84/5 Topps 147, 156
92/3 Topps 46
91/2 ToppsStadiumClub 225
92/3 ToppsStadiumClub 215
90/1 UpperDeck 57, 309
91/2 UpperDeck 314
96 Wien HL8
78/9 MTL
79/80 MTL
80/1 MTL
81/2 MTL
82/3 WSH
84/5 WSH/PizzaHut
85/6 WSH/PizzaHut
86/7 WSH/Kodak
86/7 WSH/Police
87/8 WSH
87/8 WSH/Kodak
88/9 WSH
88/9 WSH/Smokey
89/90 WSH
89/90 WSH/Kodak
90/1 WSH/Kodak
90/1 WSH/Smokey
91/2 WSH
91/2 WSH/Kodak
92/3 WSH/Kodak

LANIEL, MARC
88/9 ProCards(Utica)
89/90 ProCards(AHL) 227
90/1 ProCards 567
96/7 Cincinnati
93/4 Fredericton

LANIGAN, GERRY
94/5 Slapshot(Detroit) 8
94/5 Slapshot(MEM) 82
95/6 Slapshot 18

LANK, JEFF
91/2 SketchWHL 256
91/2 PrinceAlbert
93/4 PrinceAlbert

LANKSHEAR, MIKE
95/6 Slapshot 102
95/6 Guelph 16
96/7 Guelph 24

LANTEIGNE, ERIC
89/90 Rayside

LANTHIER, J.M.
88/9 ProCards(Maine)
89/90 ProCards(AHL) 220
85/6 VAN
83/4 Fredericton 5
85/6 Fredericton 13
86/7 Fredericton
80/1 Québec

LANTZ, KENT
89/90 SemicElitserien 188
90/1 SemicElitserien 16
91/2 SemicElitserien 217

LANZ, RICK
81/2 O-Pee-Chee 338
82/3 O-Pee-Chee 348
83/4 O-Pee-Chee 353
84/5 O-Pee-Chee 321
85/6 O-Pee-Chee 197
86/7 OPC/Topps 179
87/8 O-Pee-Chee 239
88/9 O-Pee-Chee 225
83/4 opcSticker 280
84/5 opcSticker 276
87/8 opcSticker 157/15
88/9 opcSticker 177/43
80/1 Pepsi Cap
83/4 SouhaitsRen.KeyChain
83/4 Vachon 110
87/8 TOR
87/8 TOR/P.L.A.Y. 11
88/9 TOR/P.L.A.Y. 9
80/1 VAN
80/1 VAN/Silverwood
81/2 VAN
81/2 VAN/Silverwood
82/3 VAN
83/4 VAN
84/5 VAN
85/6 VAN
86/7 VAN
92/3 AtlantaKnights
80/1 Oshawa 24

LANZINGER, GÜNTER
95 PaniniWorlds 271

LAPENSÉE, BRUNO
86/7 Kitchener 25

LAPERRIÈRE, DAN
92/3 Classic 75
92/3 ClassicFourSport 199
93/4 ClassicProspects 184
93/4 Donruss 485
94/5 Donruss 187
94/5 Leaf 156
92/3 opcPremier 39
93/4 Premier 526
94/5 Score 219
94/5 ToppsStadiumClub 243
92/3 UpperDeck 525
92/3 Peoria
93/4 Peoria
96/7 Portland

LAPERRIÈRE, GILLES
52/3 AnonymousOHL 67

LAPERRIÈRE, IAN
94/5 Classic 69, T59
94/5 C'Images 7, CE7, PR3
95/6 Donruss 5
95/6 EdgeIce C2
94/5 Fleer 189
95/6 FleerUltra 141, -AllRookie 7
94/5 Leaf 484
95/6 Leaf 99, -StudioRook 10
95/6 LeafLimited 53
98/9 Pacific 237
97/8 PacificDynag-BestKept 47
95/6 PaniniSticker 155, 190, 305
95/6 Parkhurst 176, 408
95/6 Pinnacle 127
97/8 PinnacleBeAPlayer 189
95/6 Playoff 308
96/7 Playoff 403
95/6 POG 235, 033
94/5 Premier 307
95/6 Score 72
90/1 SketchMEM 14
90/1 SketchQMJHL 14
91/2 SketchQMJHL 281
95/6 SkyBoxEmotion 149
95/6 SkyBoxImpact 142, -Fox 7
93/4 Slapshot(Drum.) 10
94/5 SP-Premier 14
95/6 Topps 347, 20NG
94/5 UpperDeck 306
95/6 UpperDeck 32, SE69
97/8 UpperDeck 83
96/7 UDBlackDiamond 10
95/6 UDCollChoice 19
97/8 UDCollChoice 120
96/7 UpperDeck"Ice" 30

LAPERRIÈRE, JACQUES
45-64 BeeHives(MTL)
64-67 BeeHives(MTL)
63-5 ChexPhoto
64/5 CokeCap MTL-2
65/6 CocaCola, -Booklet C, Y
70/1 DadsCookies
72-84 Dernière 72/3, 73/4
70/1 EddieSargent 97
71/2 EddieSargent 108
72/3 EddieSargent 121
70/1 Esso Stamp
88/9 Esso Sticker
87 HallOfFame 260
72/3 Letraset 2
74/5 Loblaws
68/9 OPC/Topps 58
69/70 OPC/Topps 3, -Sticker
70/1 OPC/Topps 52, OPC 245
70/1 opc/t-Deckle 20, -Sticker
71/2 OPC/Topps 144
72/3 OPC 205, -Crests 11
73/4 OPC 40, Topps 137
74/5 OPC/Topps 202
63/4 Parkhurst 27, 86
94/5 Parkie(64/5) 72, 140, 149
94/5 Parkie(64/5) AS3
95/6 Parkie(66/7) 65, 122, 128
66/7 Post'Large
67/8 Post
67/8 PostFlipBook
68/9 Post Marble
70/1 PostShooters
72 SemicSticker 225
68/9 ShirriffCoin MTL4
64/5 Topps 53
65/6 Topps 3
66/7 Topps 67, 122
67/8 Topps 7
54-67 TorontoStar 65/6
56-66 TorontoStar 64/5, 65/6
64/5 TheTorontoStar
71/2 TheTorontoSun
63/4 York 34
67/8 York 18, no# (x2)
95/6 Zellers
67/8 MTL
67/8 MTL/IGA
68/9 MTL
69/70 MTL/ProStar
70/1 MTL
71 MTL/Pins
71/2 MTL
72/3 MTL
73/4 MTL
74/5 MTL
81/2 MTL
82/3 MTL
83/4 MTL
84/5 MTL
86/7 MTL
87/8 MTL
87/8 MTL/Stickers 8, 11
88/9 MTL
89/90 MTL
90/1 MTL
91/2 MTL
92/3 MTL/OPC 15, 36
95/6 MTL/Forum 10Feb96

LAPIN, MIKE
92/3 Classic 75
92/3 WestMich.
93/4 WestMich.

LAPINKOSKI, MARKO
92/3 Jyvas-Hyva 169

LAPLANTE, DARRYL
95/6 Classic 49

LAPLANTE, ERIC
96/7 Halifax (1), (2)
97/9 Halifax (1)

LAPLANTE, SÉBASTIEN
93/4 Greensboro

LAPLANTE, STEVE
91/2 SketchQMJHL 58

LAPOINTE, CLAUDE
92/3 Bowman 421
93/4 Donruss 285
92/3 Durivage 6
93/4 Durivage 24
92/3 FleerUltra 176
93/4 FleerUltra 403
93/4 Leaf 64
94/5 Leaf 304
91/2 OPC/Topps 431
92/3 O-Pee-Chee 320
97/8 PacificRegime 118
92/3 PaniniSticker 213
94/5 PaniniSticker 58
91/2 Parkhurst 370
93/4 Parkhurst 437
94/5 Pinnacle 231
91/2 Pinnacle 313
92/3 Pinnacle 141
93/4 Pinnacle 294
96/7 PinnacleBeAPlayer 200
93/4 PowerPlay 422
93/4 Premier 251
89/90 ProCards(AHL) 166
90/1 ProCards 445
91/2 ProSet 556
92/3 ProSet 151, -Rookie 12
91/2 PSPlatinum 267
92/3 Score 219
93/4 Score 352
94/5 Score 194
92/3 Topps 94
98/9 Topps 167
92/3 ToppsStadiumClub 93
91/2 UpperDeck 488
92/3 UpperDeck 147
97/8 UpperDeck 311
91/2 QUE/PetroCanada
92/3 QUE/PetroCanada
94/5 QUE/BurgerKing
89/90 Halifax
90/1 Halifax

LAPOINTE, GUY
51/2 BasDuFleuve 11

LAPOINTE, GUY
93/4 ActionPacked 2
77/8 Coke Mini
72-84 Dernière 72/3, 73/4, 80/1
70/1 EddieSargent 105
71/2 EddieSargent 98
72/3 EddieSargent 113
70/1 Esso Stamp
88/9 Esso Sticker
74/5 LiptonSoup 16
74/5 Loblaws
73/4 MacsMilk Disk
70/1 OPC 177
71/2 OPC/Topps 145
72/3 OPC 86, -TmCanada, T. 57
73/4 OPC 114, Topps 170
74/5 OPC/Topps 70
75/6 OPC/Topps 198, 293
76/7 OPC/T. 223, T-Glossy 17
77/8 OPC/Topps 60
78/9 OPC/Topps 260
79/80 OPC/Topps 135, T. 81
80/1 OPC/Topps 201
82/3 O-Pee-Chee 305
80/1 Pepsi Cap
82/3 Post
71/2 TheTorontoSun
91/2 Trends(72) 92, -Aut
92/3 Trends(76) 171
69/70 MTL/ProStar
70/1 MTL
71 MTL/Pins
71/2 MTL
72/3 MTL
73/4 MTL
74/5 MTL
75/6 MTL
76/7 MTL
77/8 MTL
78/9 MTL
79/80 MTL
80/1 MTL
81/2 MTL
95/6 MTL/Forum 9Mar96
84/5 QUE
87/8 QUE/GeneralFoods
88/9 QUE
88/9 QUE/GeneralFoods
89/90 QUE/GeneralFoods

LAPOINTE, HERVÉ
90/1 SketchQMJHL 107
91/2 SketchQMJHL 179

LAPOINTE, MARTIN
91/2 Arena 8
94/5 CanadaJr.Alumni 11
91/2 Classic 9
91/2 ClassicFourSport 9
93/4 ClassicProspects 173
93/4 Durivage 6
95/6 EdgeIce 4, -Quantum 9
94/5 FleerUltra 285
91/2 Gillette 20
93/4 Leaf 336
94/5 Leaf 201
98/9 Pacific 197
97/8 PacificCrown 241
91/2 Parkhurst 267
93/4 Parkhurst 63
94/5 Parkhurst 70
95/6 Parkhurst 340
91/2 Pinnacle 355
92/3 Pinnacle 365
94/5 Pinnacle 449
96/7 PinnacleBeAPlayer 128
93/4 PowerPlay 332
93/4 Premier(Gold) 263
91/2 ProSet 532
92/3 ProSet 226
91/2 Score(CDN) 655,(U.S)105T
92/3 Score 409
97/8 Score(DET) 10
89/90 SketchMEM 61
90/1 SketchMEM 102
90/1 SketchQMJHL 25
91/2 StarPics 5
94/5 ToppsStadiumClub 151
91/2 UltimateDP 9, 65, -Aut
90/1 UpperDeck 467
91/2 UpperDeck 63, 66, 685
91/2 UD'CzechWJC 59
92/3 UpperDeck 405
93/4 UpperDeck 257
94/5 UpperDeck 406
95/6 UpperDeck 200
97/8 UpperDeck 58
94/5 UDBeAPlayer-Aut. 133
96/7 UDBlackDiamond 13
97/8 UDCollChoice 86
91/2 DET/Caesars

LAPOINTE, NORMAND
75/6 opcWHA 85

LAPOINTE, RICK
76/7 OPC/Topps 48
77/8 OPC/Topps 152
78/9 O-Pee-Chee 322
79/80 OPC/Topps 121
81/2 OPC 295, Topps(W) 119
83/4 O-Pee-Chee 294
81/2 opcSticker 134
82/3 Post
84/5 L.A./Smokeys
82/3 QUE
83/4 QUE
83/4 Fredericton 8

LAPOINTE, ROD
87/8 Sudbury 7

LAPOINTE, RON
89/90 ProCards(IHL) 189
88/9 QUE
88/9 QUE/GeneralFoods
79/80 Montréal B&W

LAPOINTE, STEVE
90/1 SketchQMJHL 208

LAPOINTE, SYLVAIN
91/2 SketchQMJHL 216
93/4 Wheeling 17

LAPORTE, BENOIT
95 Semic 198
92 SemicSticker 235

LAPORTE, ROGER
88/9 Richelieu

LAPORTE, YVES
51/2 LacStJean 56

LAPPALAINEN, HARRI
70/1 Kuvajulkaisut 211

LAPPIN, CHRIS
92/3 Greensboro 18

LAPPIN, MIKE
92/3 Classic 76

LAPPIN, PETER
91/2 O-Pee-Chee 5S
89/90 ProCards(IHL) 84
90/1 ProCards 109
91/2 ProCards 522
90/1 Score 403
90/1 UpperDeck 235
88/9 SaltLake 4

LAPRADE, EDGAR
93/4 ActionPacked 1
45-64 BeeHives(NYR)
43-47 ParadeSportive
51/2 Parkhurst 96
52/3 Parkhurst 100
52 RoyalDesserts 3
54/5 Topps 56

LARAQUE, GEORGES
95/6 Classic 28
97/8 EDM

LARCHE, ROGER
90/1 SketchMEM 67
90/1 SketchQMJHL 15
91/2 SketchQMJHL 293
92/3 Greensboro 10
93/4 Roanoke

LARIN, DANIEL
96/7 DEL 242
92/3 Oklahoma

LARIONOV, IGOR
90/1 Bowman 63
91/2 Bowman 326
92/3 Bowman 350
93/4 Donruss 305
94/5 Donruss 106
96/7 Donruss 167
96/7 DonrussCanadianIce 117
96/7 DonrussElite 50
97/8 DonrussPriority 90
96/7 FleerNHLPicks 110
93/4 FleerUltra 415
94/5 FleerUltra 197
95/6 FleerUltra 234
95/6 Hoyle'WEST 3 (Diamonds)
91 IFiodorovSportUnites
95 Globe 239
89/90 Kraft 41
90/1 Kraft 25
93/4 Leaf 391
94/5 Leaf 311
95/6 Leaf 318
96/7 Leaf 104
94/5 LeafLimited 47
96/7 LeafPreferred 75
97/8 Limited 178
96/7 Maggers 61
97/8 Omega 82
90/1 OPC/Topps 359
91/2 OPC/Topps 480
92/3 O-Pee-Chee 159
98/9 Pacific 198
97/8 PacificCrown 49
98/9 PacificParamount 77
90/1 Panini(VAN) 11
90/1 PaniniSticker 294, 336
91/2 PaniniSticker 42
92/3 PaniniSticker 32
94/5 PaniniSticker 217
96/7 PaniniSticker 188
97/8 PaniniSticker 152
95 PaniniWorlds 283
94/5 Parkhurst V88
95/6 Parkhurst 184, 336
91/2 Parkhurst 406
93/4 Parkhurst 185
94/5 ParkieSE 164
91/2 Pinnacle 293
93/4 Pinnacle 367
94/5 Pinnacle 74
95/6 Pinnacle 81
96/7 Pinnacle 74
97/8 Pinnacle 129
97/8 PinnacleInside 146
96/7 PinnacleZenith 96
95/6 Playoff 85
96/7 Playoff 346
94/5 POG 216
95/6 POG 222
93/4 PowerPlay 436
94/5 Premier 170
90/1 ProSet 297
91/2 ProSet 246
91/2 PSPlatinum 126
91/2 RedAce
90/1 Score 123
91/2 Score(CDN) 168, (U.S) 168
92/3 Score 58, -Sharpshooter 13
93/4 Score 535, (U.S) DD8
94/5 Score 61
95/6 Score 254
96/7 Score 178
97/8 Score(DET) 5
94/5 Select 40
96/7 SelectCertified 62
94 Semic 156
89 SemicSticker 90
91 SemicSticker 217
83/4 SovietStars
87/8 SovietStars
89/90 SovietStars
97/8 SPAuthentic 54
95/6 Summit 76
96/7 Summit 40
92/3 Topps 512
95/6 ToppsFinest 57
91/2 ToppsStadiumClub 150
92/3 ToppsStadiumClub 299
91/2 TriGlobe 1-2
90/1 UpperDeck 128, 342
91/2 UpperDeck 298, E18
94/5 UpperDeck 65, 85
95/6 UpperDeck 213, 349
96/7 UpperDeck 51
95/6 UDBeAPlayer 206
98/9 UDChoice 71
95/6 UDCollChoice 239
96/7 UDCollChoice 83
97/8 UpperDeckIce L6B
92/3 S.J./PacificBell
89/90 VAN
90/1 VAN/Mohawk
91/2 VAN
91/2 VAN/Molson

LARIVÉE, FRANÇOIS
95/6 Bowman P22

LARIVÉE, PAUL
51/2 LavalDairy 79
52/3 StLawrence 33

LARIVIÈRE, CHRISTIAN
90/1 SketchQMJHL 221
91/2 SketchAwards 28
93/4 Fredericton

LARIVIÈRE, GARRY
72-84 Dernière 78/9
79/80 O-Pee-Chee 291
81/2 O-Pee-Chee 116
82/3 O-Pee-Chee 116
77/8 opcWHA 26
80/1 Pepsi Cap
82/3 Post
81/2 EDM/RedRooster
81/2 EDM/WestEdmonton
82/3 EDM/RedRooster
88/9 EDM/ActionMagazine 84
75/6 Phoenix
76/7 Phoenix
80/1 QUE

LARIVIÈRE, J.P.
80/1 Québec

LARKIN, BRIAN
86/7 Saskatoon
84/5 Saskatoon

LARKIN, HUEY
80/1 SSMarie
81/2 SSMarie
82/3 SSMarie

LARKIN, JIM
93/4 Birmingham 2
94/5 Birmingham

LARKIN, WAYNE
60/1 Cleveland

LARMER, JEFF
83/4 O-Pee-Chee 230
84/5 O-Pee-Chee 36
83/4 opcSticker 186
91/2 ProCards 613
83/4 SouhaitsRen.KeyChain
83/4 N.J.
85/6 NovaScotia 2

LARMER, STEVE
90/1 Bowman 5
91/2 Bowman 395, 405
92/3 Bowman 61
93/4 Donruss 461
94/5 Donruss 231
95/6 Donruss 2
93/4 EASports 29
94/5 Flair 113
94/5 Fleer 134
92/3 FleerUltra 39
93/4 FleerUltra 129, 373
94/5 FleerUltra 138
95/6 FleerUltra 103
93/4 HockeyWit 43
90/1 Kraft 26
91/2 Kraft 69
94/5 Leaf 270
95/6 Leaf 178
91/2 McDonalds McD15
83/4 O-Pee-Chee 105, 106, 206
84/5 OPC 37, Topps 30
85/6 OPC/Topps 132
86/7 OPC/Topps 139
87/8 OPC/Topps 59
88/9 OPC/Topps 154
89/90 OPC/Topps 179, J
90/1 OPC/Topps 56, T-TL 1
91/2 OPC/Topps 75, T-TL 21
92/3 O-Pee-Chee 32
90/1 opcPremier 58
91/2 opcPremier 60, 135
88/9 opcStars 17
83/4 opcSticker 108, 312
84/5 opcSticker 29
85/6 opcSticker 28/158
86/7 opcSticker 157/15
87/8 opcSticker 81
88/9 opcSticker 12
89/90 opcSticker 17
87/8 PaniniSticker 226
88/9 PaniniSticker 26
89/90 PaniniSticker 43
90/1 PaniniSticker 194
91/2 PaniniSticker 8
92/3 PaniniSticker 5
93/4 PaniniSticker 146
94/5 PaniniSticker 86
95/6 PaniniSticker 107
91/2 Parkhurst 34
92/3 Parkhurst 30
93/4 Parkhurst 404
94/5 Parkhurst 146
91/2 Pinnacle 29, 357
92/3 Pinnacle 74
93/4 Pinnacle 356
94/5 Pinnacle 88
94/5 POG 164
93/4 PowerPlay 52, 392
93/4 Premier 240
94/5 Premier 418, 532
90/1 ProSet 53, 345
91/2 ProSet 49, 279
92/3 ProSet 31
91/2 PSPlatinum 28, 287
83/4 PuffySticker 17
90/1 Score 135, -HotCards 61
91/2 Score(CDN) 140, (U.S) 140
92/3 Score 266
93/4 Score 3, 525, -Dream 22
94/5 Score 40
95/6 Score 211
92/3 SeasonsPatch 2
94/5 Select 112
94 Semic 90
95 Semic 100
91 SemicSticker 73
92 SemicSticker 91
95/6 SkyBoxEmotion 114
83/4 SouhaitsRen.KeyChain
91 TeamCanada
92/3 Topps 497
95/6 Topps 7HG
94/5 ToppsFinest 63
91/2 ToppsStadiumClub 270
92/3 ToppsStadiumClub 54
93/4 T.StadiumClub 236, 398
94/5 ToppsStadiumClub 242
90/1 UpperDeck 242, 499
91/2 UpperDeck 15, 257
92/3 UpperDeck 4, 135, G6
93/4 UpperDeck 172, 471, HT14
94/5 UpperDeck 40
93/4 UDBAP-Roots 22
94/5 UDBAP G12,R169,-Aut 146
95/6 UDCollChoice 154
82/3 CHI
83/4 CHI
86/7 CHI/Coke
87/8 CHI/Coke
88/9 CHI/Coke
89/90 CHI/Coke
90/1 CHI/Coke
91/2 CHI/Coke

LARNER, DON
96/7 LasVegas

LAROCHE, GILLES
51/2 BasDuFleuve 8

LAROCHE, J.F.
91/2 SketchQMJHL 62

LAROCHELLE, CLAUDE
78/9 Saginaw

LAROCHELLE, DANY
91/2 SketchQMJHL 81

LAROCHELLE, MARTIN
91/2 SketchQMJHL 137

LAROCHELLE, WILDOR
25-27 Anonymous 7
33-35 DiamondMatch
36-39 DiamondMatch (1), (2),
36-39 DiamondMatch (3), (4)
33/4 Hamilton (V288) 14
27-32 LaPresse 27/8
33/4 OPC (V304A) 21
34/5 SweetCaporal
33/4 WWGum (V357) 28
36/7 WWGum (V356) 34
28/9 MTL/LaPatrie 7

LAROCQUE, ANDRÉ
80/1 QuébecRamparts

LAROCQUE, DENIS
88/9 ProCards(NewHaven)
89/90 ProCards(IHL) 33
90/1 ProCards 257
92/3 Dayton
89/90 Moncton
90/1 Moncton

LAROCQUE, MARIO
95/6 Bowman P23

LAROCQUE, MICHEL
72-84 Dernière 73/4, 80/1
74/5 Loblaws
74/5 OPC 297
75/6 OPC 362
76/7 OPC/Topps 6, 79
77/8 OPC/Topps 6, 177
78/9 OPC/Topps 158
79/80 O-Pee-Chee 296
81/2 O-Pee-Chee 319
82/3 O-Pee-Chee 324
81/2 opcSticker 105, 259
82/3 opcSticker 77
82/3 Post
73/4 MTL
74/5 MTL
75/6 MTL
76/7 MTL
77/8 MTL
78/9 MTL
79/80 MTL
80/1 MTL
81/2 TOR

LAROCQUE, STÉPHANE
91/2 SketchQMJHL 259

LAROROUK, CAM
84/5 KelownaWings&WHL 19

LAROSE, BENOÎT
90/1 SketchQMJHL 59
91/2 SketchAwards 23
91/2 SketchQMJHL 247

LAROSE, CLAUDE
64-67 BeeHives(MTLx2)
64/5 CokeCap MTL-11
65/6 CocaCola
72-84 Dernière 72/3, 73/4
70/1 EddieSargent 101
71/2 EddieSargent 106
72/3 EddieSargent 122
70/1 Esso Stamp
74/5 Loblaws, -Update
68/9 OPC/Topps 51
69/70 OPC 193, -Sticker, T. 126
70/1 OPC/Topps 56
71/2 OPC/Topps 146
72/3 OPC 231
74/5 OPC/Topps 124
75/6 OPC/Topps 112
76/7 O-Pee-Chee 310
77/8 OPC/Topps 167
77/8 opcWHA 43
94/5 Parkie(64/5) 71
95/6 Parkie(66/7) 69
88/9 ProCards(Binghampton)
88/9 ProCards(Sherbrooke)
72 SemicSticker 199
68/9 ShirriffCoin MIN7
65/6 Topps 75
66/7 Topps 10
67/8 Topps 4
71/2 TheTorontoSun
67/8 MTL
67/8 MTL/IGA
69/70 MTL/ProStar
70/1 MTL
71/2 MTL
72/3 MTL
73/4 MTL
75/6 Cincinnati

LAROSE, GUY
92/3 Bowman 281
92/3 O-Pee-Chee 269
92/3 opcPremier 128
94/5 Parkhurst 37
91/2 Parkhurst 399
88/9 ProCards(Moncton)
89/90 ProCards(AHL) 29
90/1 ProCards 259
91/2 ProCards 195
92/3 Topps 47
92/3 ToppsStadiumClub 237
92/3 UpperDeck 527
90/1 WPG/IGA
87/8 Moncton
90/1 Moncton

LAROSE, PAUL
73/4 QuébecNordiques

LAROUCHE, MIKE
83/4 NorthBay
84/5 Ottawa67s

LAROUCHE, PIERRE
72-84 Dernière 80/1, 82/3, ?
75/6 OPC/Topps 305
76/7 OPC/Topps 1,5,199
76/7 O-Pee-Chee 392
77/8 OPC/Topps 102
78/9 OPC/Topps 35
79/80 OPC/Topps 233
80/1 OPC/Topps 151, 216
81/2 O-Pee-Chee 187
82/3 O-Pee-Chee 125
84/5 OPC 145, 363, Topps 108
85/6 OPC/Topps 54
81/2 opcSticker 38
82/3 opcSticker 127
84/5 opcSticker 103
85/6 opcSticker 85/218
87/8 PaniniSticker 116
80/1 Pepsi Cap
82/3 Post
83/4 PuffySticker 13
83/4 SouhaitsRen.KeyChain
82/3 HFD/JuniorWhalers
77/8 MTL
78/9 MTL
79/80 MTL
80/1 MTL
81/2 MTL
74/5 PGH
77/8 PGH/PuckBuck

LAROUCHE, STEVE
94/5 ClassicImages 31
92/3 ClassicProspects 78
93/4 ClassicProspects 160
95/6 Donruss 39
95/6 FleerUltra 112
95/6 Leaf 94
95/6 PaniniSticker 55
95/6 Pinnacle 209
95/6 Playoff 179
91/2 ProCards 83
95/6 ProMagnet 113
95/6 Score 302
90/1 SketchMEM 29
90/1 SketchQMJHL 30
95/6 SkyBoxEmotion 125
95/6 Topps 38
95/6 UpperDeck 89
93/4 AtlantaKnights
95/6 Binghampton
92/3 Fredericton

LAROUCHELLE, ALLAN
83/4 Saskatoon 23

LARSEN, BRAD
94/5 AutoPhonex 25
97/8 Bowman 116
95/6 Classic 45
95/6 DonrussElite-WorldJrs 17
94/5 ParkieSE 269
94/5 Select 164
94/5 SP 187
95/6 UpperDeck 534
97/8 UDCollChoice 308
96/7 UpperDeck"Ice" 134
95/6 SwiftCurrent

LARSEN, GREG
83/4 NorthBay

LARSON, BRETT
95/6 Madison
93/4 Minn-Duluth

LARSON, DAVE
92/3 Minnesota
93/4 Minnesota
94/5 Minnesota

LARSON, JON
93/4 Knoxville
94/5 Roanoke
95/6 Roanoke

LARSON, NORMAN
33-43 BeeHives(NYA)
40/1 OPC (V301-2) 127

LARSON, REED
84/5 Kelloggs Disk
78/9 OPC/Topps 226
79/80 OPC/Topps 213
80/1 OPC/Topps 43
81/2 OPC 92, Topps(W) 92
82/3 O-Pee-Chee 88, 89
83/4 O-Pee-Chee 125
84/5 OPC 58, Topps 44
85/6 OPC/Topps 55
86/7 OPC/Topps 110
87/8 OPC/Topps 131
88/9 OPC/Topps 145
81/2 opcSticker 124
82/3 opcSticker 180
83/4 opcSticker 134
84/5 opcSticker 36
85/6 opcSticker 33/163
86/7 opcSticker 39/176
87/8 opcSticker 142/251
87/8 PaniniSticker 7
82/3 Post
83/4 PuffySticker 18
83/4 SouhaitsRen.KeyChain
88/9 BOS/SportsAction
79/80 DET
80/1 DET
84/5 DET/Caesars
85/6 DET/Caesars
88/9 EDM/ActionMagazine 56

LARSSON, CARL-ERIK
90/1 SemicElitserien 143

LARSSON, CURT
74 SemicSticker 24
73/4 WilliamsFIN 30

LARSSON, JAN
95/6 ElitSet 274, -Champs 8
95 Semic 73
89/90 SemicElitserien 41
90/1 SemicElitserien 188
91/2 SemicElitserien 41
92/3 SemicElitserien 66
93 SemicSticker 16
95/6 udElite 165
97/8 udSwedish 32, C19

LARSSON, KJELL
92 SemicSticker

LARSSON, KURT
72 Hellas 39

LARSSON, PETER
94/5 ElitSet 193, -Playmaker 5
95/6 ElitSet 23
89/90 SemicElitserien 235
90/1 SemicElitserien 189
91/2 SemicElitserien 43
92/3 SemicElitserien 72
95/6 udElite 34

LARSSON, ROBERT
89/90 SemicElitserien 195

LARSSON, STEFAN
94/5 ElitSet 34
95/6 ElitSet 139, -FaceTo 4
95 Globe 25
95 PaniniWorlds 142
89/90 SemicElitserien 273
90/1 SemicElitserien 34
91/2 SemicElitserien 282
92/3 SemicElitserien 308
95/6 udElite 208
97/8 udSwedish 74

LARSSON, STIG
72 Hellas 34
72/3 WilliamsFIN 50

LARTAMA, MIKA
93/4 Jyvas-Hyva 49
93/4 Sisu 249
95/6 SisuLimited 85

LARTER, TYLER
88/9 ProCards(Baltimore)
89/90 ProCards(AHL) 94
90/1 ProCards 207
91/2 ProCards 181
90/1 Moncton
89/90 Moncton
91/2 Moncton
84/5 SSMarie
87/8 SSMarie 4

LARWAY, DON
77/8 opcWHA 48
75/6 Houston

LASCALA, FRANK
96/7 DEL 220

LASKOSKI, GARY
83/4 O-Pee-Chee 156
83/4 opcSticker 296
83/4 SouhaitsRen.KeyChain

LASSILA, HANNU
82 SemicSticker 27

LATAL, JAROMIR
94/5 APS 5
95/6 APS 103

LATAL, JIRI
95/6 APS 104
91/2 OPC/Topps 444
90/1 opcPremier 59
89/90 ProCards(AHL) 344
90/1 ProSet 501
91/2 ProSet 454
91/2 Score(CDN) 540
90/1 UpperDeck 410
91/2 UpperDeck 404
90/1 PHA
91/2 PHA/JCPenney

LATENDRESSE, MIKE
92/3 Maine (2) 21
93/4 Maine 42
95/6 Birmingham
94/5 Toledo

LATERREUR, YVAN
91/2 SketchQMJHL 261

LATOS, JAMES
84/5 Saskatoon

LATOS, JIM
89/90 ProCards(IHL) 30
90/1 ProCards 585
90/1 KansasCity 20
95/6 Louisiana, -Playoffs
86/7 Portland

LATTA, DAVID
90/1 ProCards 461
91/2 ProCards 376
88/9 QUE
88/9 QUE/GeneralFoods
89/90 QUE
89/90 QUE/GeneralFoods
89/90 QUE/Police
90/1 QUE
92/3 Cincinnati
90/1 Halifax
83/4 Kitchener 19
84/5 Kitchener 23
85/6 Kitchener 22
86/7 Kitchener 22

LATTA, KEN
80/1 SSMarie
81/2 SSMarie

LATTI, PETRI
93/4 Sisu 204
95/6 Sisu 100
96/7 Sisu 104

LATULIPE, MARTIN
93/4 Slapshot(Drum.) 5

LATVALA, JAN
93/4 Sisu 138
94/5 Sisu 29
95/6 Sisu 262
96/7 Sisu 60

LAUER, BRAD
88/9 O-Pee-Chee 226
90/1 OPC/Topps 217
90/1 ProCards 501
91/2 ProCards 490
91/2 ProSet 375
91/2 ToppsStadiumClub 142
91/2 CHI/Coke
95/6 Cleveland
92/3 Indianapolis

LAUFMAN, KEN
52/3 StLawrence 56

LAUGHLIN, CRAIG
83/4 O-Pee-Chee 375
84/5 O-Pee-Chee 203
85/6 O-Pee-Chee 190
86/7 OPC/Topps 35
87/8 OPC/Topps 161
89/90 O-Pee-Chee 275
86/7 opcSticker 253/145
89/90 opcSticker 171/31
87/8 PaniniSticker 182
82/3 Post
81/2 MTL
88/9 TOR/P.L.A.Y. 18
82/3 WSH
84/5 WSH/PizzaHut
85/6 WSH/PizzaHut
86/7 WSH/Kodak
86/7 WSH/Police
87/8 WSH
87/8 WSH/Kodak
95/6 Richmond

LAUGHLIN, PAT
94/5 Erie

LAUGHTON, MIKE
70/1 EddieSargent 136
69/70 O-Pee-Chee 148
70/1 OPC/Topps 74

LAUKKANEN, JANNE
93/4 Classic 43
94/5 Classic 102
94/5 ClassicImages 63
95/6 EdgeIce 28
94/5 Flair 148
94/5 FleerUltra 359
95 Globe 134
92/3 Jyvas-Hyva 21
93/4 Jyvas-Hyva 46
94/5 Leaf 447
95/6 Leaf 46
98/9 Pacific 312
97/8 PacificRegime 135
97/8 PaniniSticker 40
95/6 Parkhurst 52
94/5 ParkieSE 142
94/5 Pinnacle 485, RTP3
97/8 PinnacleBeAPlayer 90
94/5 Premier 411
94/5 Select 181, YE3
94 Semic 17
95 Semic 12
92 SemicSticker 7
93 SemicSticker 54
93/4 Sisu 239, 367
95/6 SisuLimited 83, -Gallery 2
98/9 Topps 153
94/5 ToppsFinest 8
91/2 UpperDeck 22
94/5 UD 251, 565, SP157
96/7 UpperDeck 116
96/7 UDCollChoice 187
96 Wien 29
96/7 OTT/PizzaHut
97/8 OTT
94/5 QUE/BurgerKing

LAUKKANEN, JARI
92/3 Jyvas-Hyva 97
93/4 Jyvas-Hyva 17
70/1 Kuvajulkaisut 281
93/4 Sisu 100
94/5 Sisu 84
95/6 Sisu 9
96/7 Sisu 10

LAUKKANEN, PEKKA
70/1 Kuvajulkaisut 350

LAUKKANNE, TUOMO
80/1 Mallasjuoma 149

LAURENCE, DON
79/80 O-Pee-Chee 369

LAURENCE, RED
78/9 ATL/Coke
81/2 Indianapolis 13
82/3 Indianapolis

LAURIE, ROB
93/4 Johnstown 16
94/5 Johnstown 13
95/6 Toledo

LAURILA, HARRI
91/2 Jyvas-Hyva 29
92/3 Jyvas-Hyva 72
93/4 Jyvas-Hyva 135
94 Semic 13
95 Semic
93 SemicSticker 55
93/4 Sisu 146
94/5 Sisu 170
95/6 Sisu 151, 184
96/7 Sisu 125
95/6 SisuLimited 47

LAURILA, M.
93/4 Waterloo

LAURIN, DON
88/9 Brandon 15

LAURIN, STEVE
90/1 ProCards 555

LAUS, PAUL
94/5 Donruss 201
98/9 Pacific 224
97/8 PacificDynag-DestKept 42
98/9 PacificParamount 98
97/8 PacificRevolution 61
96/7 PaniniSticker 77
95/6 Pinnacle -FullContact 7
96/7 PinnacleBeAPlayer 192
95/6 Playoff 41
95/6 POG 121

93/4 Premier 402
90/1 ProCards 534
91/2 ProCards 293
89/90 Sketch(OHL) 142
93/4 ToppsStadiumClub 292
97/8 UpperDeck 75
93/4 FLA
96/7 FLA/WinnDixie
97/8 FLA/WinnDixie
92/3 ClevelandLumberjacks 3
88/9 NiagaraFalls 17
89/90 NiagaraFalls

LAUWERS, GUY
79 PaniniSticker 339

LAUZON, SERGE
84/5 Chicoutimi

LAVALL, MIKE
95/6 Slapshot 274

LAVALLÉE, KEVIN
94/5 DEL 100
95/6 DEL 142
81/2 O-Pee-Chee 43
82/3 O-Pee-Chee 49, 50
83/4 O-Pee-Chee 157
84/5 O-Pee-Chee 183
82/3 opcSticker 220
80/1 Pepsi Cap
82/3 Post
80/1 CGY
81/2 CGY
82/3 CGY
86/7 PGH/Kodak

LAVALLÉE, MARTIN
90/1 SketchQMJHL 184
91/2 SketchQMJHL 168

LAVALLÉE, MARTIN
90/1 SketchMEM 27
90/1 SketchQMJHL 24

LAVALLÉE, RICHARD
79/80 Montréal, -B&W

LAVALLIÈRE, SÉBASTIEN
90/1 SketchQMJHL 185

LAVARRE, MARK
88/9 ProCards(Binghampton)
87/8 CHI/Coke
83/4 NorthBay
85/6 NovaScotia 8

LAVE, ROB
93/4 Slapshot(NorthBay) 3

LAVENDER, BRIAN
72/3 O-Pee-Chee 270
71/2 STL

LAVIGNE, ERIC
91/2 Arena 19
91/2 Classic 22
91/2 C'FourSport 22, -Aut
93/4 C'Prospects 191
90/1 SketchQMJHL 150
91/2 SketchQMJHL 214
91/2 StarPics 42
91/2 UltimateDP 21, -Aut 21
93/4 Phoenix

LAVIKAINEN, PEKKA
71/2 WilliamsFIN 263

LAVIKAINEN, PENTTI
71/2 WilliamsFIN 264

LAVINSH, ROD
94/5 Raleigh
95/6 Tallahassee 1

LAVIOLETTE, JACK
91 C55 Reprint 45
83&87 HallOfFame 159
83 HHOF Postcard (L)
1910-11 Imperial (C56) 21
1911-12 Imperial (C55) 45
1912-13 Imperial (C57) 46
1910-11 Imperial Post 45
28/9 MTL/LaPatrie 19
95/6 MTL/Forum 20Sep95

LAVIOLETTE, KERRY
83/4 Saskatoon 9

LAVIOLETTE, PETER
93/4 FleerUltra 488
93/4 PowerPlay 508
93/4 Premier-TeamUSA 3
89/90 ProCards(IHL) 43
90/1 ProCards 16
91/2 ProCards 197
93/4 TSC-TeamUSA 12

LAVOIE, DARYL
93/4 Slapshot(Windsor) 5
92/3 Windsor 13

LAVOIE, DOMINIC
90/1 Bowman 26
92/3 FleerUltra 145
93/4 Leaf 415
93/4 Parkhurst 366
88/9 ProCards(Peoria)
89/90 ProCards(IHL) 20
90/1 ProCards 95
90/1 Score 416
93/4 UpperDeck 444
89/90 STL/Kodak
93/4 Phoenix

LAVOIE, ETIENNE
90/1 SketchQMJHL 230
91/2 SketchQMJHL 127

LAVOIE, PAUL
52/3 BasDuFleuve 43

LAVOIE, ROBERTO
80/1 QuébecRamparts

LAW, BRIAN
91/2 AvantGardeBCJ 151

LAW, KIRBY
93/4 Saskatoon

LAWLESS, PAUL
95/6 EdgeIce 112
83/4 O-Pee-Chee 141
89/90 O-Pee-Chee 304
87/8 PaniniSticker 48
85/6 HFD/JuniorWhalers
86/7 HFD/JuniorWhalers
87/8 HFD/JuniorWhalers
96/7 Cincinnati

LAWRENCE, BRETT
91/2 Knoxville

LAWRENCE, DEREK
92/3 BCJHL 220

LAWRENCE, MARK
93/4 ClassicProspects 172
95/6 Leaf 59
89/90 SketchOHL 131
90/1 SketchOHL 108
91/2 SketchOHL 40
94/5 UpperDeck 260
88/9 NiagaraFalls 5
89/90 NiagaraFalls

LAWSON, DAN
70/1 Esso Stamp
74/5 opcWHA 25
75/6 opcWHA 86
76/7 opcWHA 8
73/4 QuakerOats 48
72/3 7ElevenCups
71/2 TheTorontoSun

LAWSON, JEFF
92/3 MPSPhotoSJHL 124

LAWSON, TOM
84/5 Ottawa67s

LAWTON, BRIAN
92/3 Bowman 254
92/3 FleerUltra 197
88/9 opcSticker 198/69
87/8 OPC/Topps 145
88/9 OPC/Topps 20
89/90 OPC/Topps 91
92/3 O-Pee-Chee 276
87/8 PaniniSticker 300
88/9 PaniniSticker 94
92/3 PaniniSticker 132
91/2 Parkhurst 167
92/3 Parkhurst 163
92/3 Pinnacle 71
90/1 ProCards 355
91/2 ProSet 482
92/3 ProSet 173
92/3 Score 343, 375
91/2 Score(CDN) 648, (U.S) 98T
89 SemicSticker 172
92/3 Topps 435
92/3 ToppsStadiumClub 171
91/2 UpperDeck 572
89/90 BOS/SportsAction
83/4 MIN
84/5 MIN
85/6 MIN
87/8 MIN
89/90 QUE
91/2 S.J

LAWTON, DAN
73/4 VancouverBlazers

LAXDAL, DEREK
92/3 CanadaNats
89/90 OPC/Topps 169
89/90 opcSticker 181/39
89/90 ProCards(AHL) 108
90/1 ProCards 494
91/2 ProCards 466
88/9 TOR/P.L.A.Y. 21
83/4 Brandon 19
84/5 Brandon 11
85/6 Brandon 11
94/5 Roanoke

LAXTON, DAN
79/80 Montréal B&W

LAXTON, DOUG
95/6 Birmingham

LAXTON, FRANÇOIS
79/80 Montréal B&W

LAY, MIKE
94/5 DEL 269
95/6 DEL 401
96/7 DEL 309
82/3 MedicineHat
83/4 MedicineHat 21

LAYCOCK, R.
95/6 DEL 18

LAYCOCK, TRAVIS
90/1 SketchWHL 272
91/2 SketchWHL 255
90/1 PrinceAlbert
91/2 PrinceAlbert

LAYCOE, HAL
45-64 BeeHives(BOS), (MTL)
48-52 Exhibits
43-47 ParadeSportive
51/2 Parkhurst 25
52/3 Parkhurst 71
53/4 Parkhurst 87
54/5 Parkhurst 52
45-54 QuakerOats
54/5 Topps 38

LAYLIN, CORY
91/2 Minnesota

LAYTON, IAN
90/1 SketchWHL 154

LAYZELLE, BRAD
94/5 Fredericton

LAZARO, JEFF
91/2 Bowman 352
95/6 DEL 329
96/7 DEL 107
93/4 FleerUltra 489
91/2 OPC/Topps 380
92/3 PaniniSticker 139
95 PaniniWorlds 230
93/4 PowerPlay 509
93/4 Premier-TeamUSA 21
90/1 ProCards 124
91/2 ProCards 65
91/2 ProSet 13
91/2 Score(CDN) 445
94 Semic 131
95 Semic 119
92/3 Topps 224
91/2 ToppsStadiumClub 397
93/4 TSC-TeamUSA 13
91/2 UpperDeck 364
91/2 BOS/SportsAction
92/3 OTT

LAZAROV, DIMITAR
79 PaniniSticker 347

LAZORUK, CAM
83/4 Kelowna

LEACH, BRENN
82/3 Victoria
83/4 Victoria

LEACH, JAMIE
92/3 Bowman 320
90/1 OPC/Topps 377
91/2 OPC/Topps 492
90/1 opcPremier 60
93/4 Premier(Gold) 528
89/90 ProCards(IHL) 143
90/1 Score 420
92/3 Topps 362
91/2 ToppsStadiumClub 296
92/3 ToppsStadiumClub 329
91/2 UpperDeck 447
92/3 UpperDeck 168
91/2 PGH/Elbys
88/9 NiagaraFalls 12
95/6 Rochester

LEACH, JAY
91/2 ProCards 116

LEACH, MARK
90/1 Mich.Tech

LEACH, REGGIE
72/3 EddieSargent 54
74/5 Loblaws
71/2 OPC/Topps 175
72/3 OPC 15, Topps 17
73/4 OPC/Topps 84
74/5 OPC/Topps 95
75/6 OPC/Topps 166, 325
76/7 OPC/Topps 65, 110, 215
76/7 OPC 391, T-Glossy 21
77/8 OPC/Topps 185, -Glossy 8
78/9 OPC/Topps 165
79/80 OPC/Topps 95
80/1 OPC/Topps 70, 249
81/2 OPC 243, Topps(E) 106
82/3 O-Pee-Chee 90
81/2 opcSticker 181
83/4 opcSticker 9
92/3 Parkhurst 471
93/4 Parkhurst D19
82/3 Post
71/2 TheTorontoSun
92/3 Trends(76) 172
70/1 BOS/Ashtray
71/2 BOS
75/6 PHA/GingerAle
81/2 PHA/Tickets 13

LEACH, STEPHEN
91/2 Bowman 306
92/3 Bowman 298
93/4 Donruss 28
92/3 FleerUltra 5
93/4 FleerUltra 268
93/4 Leaf 3
94/5 Leaf 420
89/90 opcSticker 79/220
89/90 OPC/Topps 67
90/1 OPC/Topps 235
91/2 OPC/Topps 100
92/3 O-Pee-Chee 112
91/2 opcPremier 12
97/8 PacificParamount 36
97/8 PacificRegime 171
89/90 PaniniSticker 349
90/1 PaniniSticker 166
91/2 PaniniSticker 211
93/4 PaniniSticker 5
91/2 Parkhurst 6
92/3 Parkhurst 241
93/4 Parkhurst 285
95/6 Parkhurst 284
91/2 Pinnacle 46
92/3 Pinnacle 73
93/4 Pinnacle 73
94/5 Pinnacle 298
93/4 PowerPlay 21
93/4 Premier 507
94/5 Premier 268
90/1 ProSet 315
91/2 ProSet 253, 346
92/3 ProSet 6
91/2 PSPlatinum 151
90/1 Score 279
91/2 ScoreCDN 576, 26T
92/3 Score 54
93/4 Score 88
94/5 Score 79
92/3 Topps 16
98/9 Topps 28
91/2 ToppsStadiumClub 226
92/3 ToppsStadiumClub 68
93/4 ToppsStadiumClub 187
92/3 UpperDeck 61
94/5 UpperDeck 342
95/6 UpperDeck 453
96/7 UpperDeck 142
95/6 UDBeAPlayer 109
91/2 BOS/SportsAction
92/3 BOS
86/7 WSH/Police
88/9 WSH
88/9 WSH/Smokey
89/90 WSH
89/90 WSH/Kodak
90/1 WSH/Kodak
90/1 WSH/Smokey

LEADER, AL
83&87 HallOfFame 176
83 HHOF Postcard (M)

LEAHY, GREG
90/1 SketchWHL 75
87/8 Portland
88/9 Portland
89/90 Portland
90/1 Saskatoon 11

LEASK, ROB
96/7 DEL 31
90/1 SketchOHL 212
91/2 SketchOHL 166
93/4 Johnstown 19
94/5 Johnstown 14
91/2 Oshawa/Dominos 9

LEAVINS, JIM
90/1 SemicElitserien 252

LEBEAU, PATRICK
92/3 ClassicProspects 28
90/1 ProCards 73
91/2 ProCards 72
91/2 Score(CDN) 280, (U.S) 390
91/2 ToppsStadiumClub 373
91/2 UpperDeck 453, 644
93/4 UpperDeck 499

LEBEAU, STÉPHAN
90/1 Bowman 53
91/2 Bowman 333
92/3 Bowman 346
93/4 Donruss 175
94/5 Donruss 234
92/3 Durivage 7
93/4 Durivage 14
93/4 EASports 209
92/3 FleerUltra 329
93/4 FleerUltra 241
94/5 FleerUltra 5
95/6 FleerUltra 5
91/2 Kraft 26
93/4 Leaf 190
94/5 Leaf 162
92/3 O-Pee-Chee 293
90/1 OPC/Topps 388
91/2 OPC/Topps 135
90/1 Panini(MTL) 14
91/2 PaniniSticker 191
92/3 PaniniSticker 151
93/4 PaniniSticker 16
94/5 PaniniSticker 119
91/2 Parkhurst 87
92/3 Parkhurst 82
93/4 Parkhurst 374
94/5 Parkhurst 2, C1
94/5 ParkieSE seV11
91/2 Pinnacle 139
92/3 Pinnacle 341
93/4 Pinnacle 136
94/5 Pinnacle 67
94/5 POG 32
93/4 PowerPlay 130
93/4 Premier 462
94/5 Premier 63
88/9 ProCards(Sherbrooke)
90/1 ProSet 152
91/2 ProSet 120
92/3 ProSet 91
91/2 PSPlatinum 190
90/1 Score 262
91/2 Score(CDN) 494, (U.S) 274
91/2 Score-YoungStar 7
92/3 Score 246
93/4 Score 72
94/5 Score 128
94/5 Select 65
94/5 SP 3
92/3 Topps 69
91/2 ToppsStadiumClub 283
92/3 ToppsStadiumClub 431
93/4 ToppsStadiumClub 343
90/1 UpperDeck 51
91/2 UpperDeck 261, 644
92/3 UpperDeck 213
93/4 UpperDeck 402, SP78
94/5 UpperDeck 53, SP2
94/5 ANA/Carl'sJr 16
89/90 MTL
89/90 MTL/Kraft
90/1 MTL
91/2 MTL
92/3 MTL
92/3 MTL/OPC 7
93/4 MTL

LEBEDEV, GENNADY
90/1 O-Pee-Chee 508

LEBEDEV, YURI
79 PaniniSticker 156
74 SemicSticker 40
82 SemicSticker 74
73/4 Soviet Stars 15
74/5 Soviet Stars 17
79/80 SovietStars
91/2 Trends(72) 37
73/4 WilliamsFIN 6

LEBEL, BOBBY
96/7 Rimouski

LEBEL, LAYNE
90/1 Mich.Tech
91/2 Mich.Tech

LEBEL, ROB
83&87 HallOfFame 117
83 HHOF Postcard (H)

LEBLANC, BILL
51/2 BasDuFleuve 31
52/3 BasDuFleuve 13

LEBLANC, CARL
90/1 SketchQMJHL 66
91/2 SketchQMJHL 29
93/4 Knoxville
94/5 Knoxville 15

LEBLANC, DAN
89/90 SketchOHL 43
90/1 SketchQMJHL 224

LEBLANC, FRANÇOIS
90/1 SketchQMJHL 45

LEBLANC, JACQUES
90/1 SketchQMJHL 211

LEBLANC, JEAN
86/7 Fredericton

LEBLANC, JOHN
91/2 Moncton
92/3 Bowman 419
92/3 O-Pee-Chee 287
89/90 ProCards(AHL) 149
91/2 ProCards 169
92/3 Topps 88
92/3 ToppsStadiumClub 388
88/9 EDM

LEBLANC, J.P.
76/7 O-Pee-Chee 326
77/8 OPC/Topps 133
74/5 opcWHA 36
73/4 QuakerOats 42
72/3 LosAngelesSharks

LEBLANC, MICHEL
95 Semic 197
92 SemicSticker 222

LEBLANC, MIKE
89/90 Rayside

LEBLANC, RAY
95/6 EdgeIce TW1
91/2 Parkhurst 255
89/90 ProCards(IHL) 67
90/1 ProCards 553
91/2 ProCards 502
92/3 Score 486
92/3 UpperDeck 381
87/8 Flint
92/3 Indianapolis
83/4 Kitchener 30

LEBLANC, W.
51/2 LavalDairy 7

LEBLOND, B.
79 PaniniSticker 381

LEBLOND, JEAN
79 PaniniSticker 383

LEBNER, JOSEF
94/5 DEL 58

LEBODA, TED
67/8 ColumbusCheckers

LEBOLD, DAN
94/5 Slapshot(Sudbury) 25

LEBOUTILIER, PAT
93/4 RedDeer

LEBOUTILIER, PETER
97/8 Score(ANA) 17

LEBRASSEUR, PASCAL
90/1 SketchQMJHL 17
91/2 SketchQMJHL 76

LEBRUN, AL
61/2 Topps 61
62/3 Topps 50

LEBRUN, J.C.
52/3 LavalDairy 94

LEBRUN, SEAN
92/3 Richmond
89/90 ProCards(AHL) 247
90/1 ProCards 495
91/2 ProCards 474

LEBSACK, GREG
83/4 Saskatoon 18

LECACHEUR, ROB
90/1 Saskatoon 9

LECAVALIER, VINCENT
97 BowmanCHL 69
98 BowmanCHL 103, 128
98 BowmanCHL A10, SC12
98/9 Topps 224
97/8 UpperDeck 412
97/8 UDBlackDiamond 150
98/9 UDChoice 259
96/7 Rimouski

LECHL, JURGEN
94/5 DEL 329
95/6 DEL 302
96/7 DEL 330

LECHTALER, CHRISTIAN
91/2 SemicElitserien 298

LECKLIN, KIMMO
93/4 Sisu 30
94/5 Sisu 47

LECLAIR, ALAIN
90/1 Rayside

LECLAIR, JACKIE
45-64 BeeHives(MTL)
51/2 LavalDairy 12
52/3 LavalDairy 98
55/6 Parkhurst 36
93/4 Parkie(56/7) 83
52/3 StLawrence 57

LECLAIR, JOHN
95/6 Aces Q (Spades)
97/8 Aces 4 (Clubs)
91/2 Bowman 344
92/3 Bowman 8
95/6 Bowman 63
93/4 ClassicProspects 54
93/4 Donruss 176
94/5 Donruss 98
95/6 Donruss 114, -Dominator 2
96/7 Donruss 36, -HitList 13
97/8 Donruss 29, 229, -Red 7
96/7 DonrussCanadianIce 100
97/8 DCdnIce 93, -Scrapbook 29
95/6 DonrussElite 56
96/7 DonrussElite 57
97/8 DonrussElite 71
97/8 D.Preferred 76,-LineOfT 3A
97/8 DonrussPriority 132, 205
97/8 D.Prio-DirDep 28,-OpDay26
97/8 D.Prio-Pstcrd 21,-Stamp 21
97/8 DonrussStudio 22
97/8 D.Studio-Port 25,-Silhou 15
97/8 EssoOlympic 25
96/7 Flair 69
94/5 Fleer 156

96/7 Fleer 81, 142, S1
96/7 Fleer-ArtRoss 12, S2
95/6 FleerMetal 111, -IronWar 5
96/7 F.Picks 30, -Fantasy 1
96/7 F.Picks-Dream 7, -Fab 24
92/3 FleerUltra 330
93/4 FleerUltra 215
94/5 FleerUltra 111
95/6 FU 118, -Crease 5, -RedL 5
96/7 FleerUltra 125, -Clear 5
95/6 Hoyle'EAST K (Spades)
97/8 KatchMedallion 106
96/7 KennerSLU
95/6 Kraft-Disk
96/7 Kraft-Trophy
97/8 Kraft -WorldsBest
93/4 Leaf 98
94/5 Leaf 5
95/6 Leaf 95
96/7 Leaf 83
97/8 Leaf 100, -BannerSeason 7
95/6 LeafLimited 85
96/7 LeafLimited 15
96/7 LeafPreferred 105,-Steel 39
97/8 Limited 15, 90, 94, 168
97/8 Limited -fabric 63
96/7 Maggers 117
95/6 McDonalds McD20
96/7 McDonalds McD4
96/7 MetalUniv. 113, -Lethal 10
97/8 Omega 167,-GameFace 12
97/8 Omega -StickHandle 15
91/2 OPC/Topps 209
92/3 O-Pee-Chee 386
91/2 opcPremier 105, 186
98/9 Pacific 51,-D.Ice 14,-Gld 24
97/8 PacificCrown 10, -Supial 14
97/8 PCC-SlapShots 6C
97/8 PacificCrownRoyale 98
97/8 PCR-HatTrick 12, -Lamp 13
97/8 PacificDynagon! 90, 141
97/8 PcfcD-BstK 71,-Tand 15, 20
97/8 PcfcInv. 101,-Feature 24
97/8 PacificInv.-AttackZone 17
97/8 PcfcParamnt 133,-Photo 14
98/9 PcfcPara 176, -SpecDel 13
97/8 PacificRegime 144
97/8 PacificRevolution 102
97/8 PcfcRev -AllStarGame 15
95/6 PaniniSticker 116
96/7 PaniniSticker 112
97/8 PaniniSticker 98, 125
91/2 Parkhurst 84
92/3 Parkhurst 326
93/4 Parkhurst 107
94/5 Parkhurst 111
95/6 Parkhurst 157
91/2 Pinnacle 322
93/4 Pinnacle 112
94/5 Pinnacle 272
95/6 Pinnacle 51,-FullContact 10
95/6 Pinnacle-Roaring20s 16
96/7 Pinnacle 49
97/8 Pinnacle 57, 196, -TeamP 8
96/7 P.BeAPlayer-Biscuit 17
97/8 P.BAP 250,-OneTimers 9
97/8 P.BeeHive 5,-TeamBH 12
97/8 P.Certified 119, -Team 20
97/8 Pinnacle-EPIX 23
97/8 P.Inside 58,-Can1,-Track25
97/8 PinnacleMint 20
95/6 PinnacleZenith 59, -Gifted 7
96/7 P.Zenith 17, -Assailant 10
95/6 Playoff 293
94/5 POG 136
95/6 POG 206, 010
93/4 Premier 181
94/5 Premier 117
95/6 ProMagnet 48
91/2 ProSet 545
91/2 PSPlatinum 259
96/7 SB'7Eleven
91/2 Score(CDN) 343, (U.S) 313
93/4 Score 318
95/6 Score 9
96/7 Score 161
97/8 Score 108, -CheckIt 5
97/8 Score(PHA) 4
95/6 SelectCertified 44
96/7 SelectCertified 33
95/6 SkyBoxEmotion 132
95/6 SkyBoxImpact 126, 244
96/7 SkyBoxImpact 96,-Blade 11
94/5 SP 85
95/6 SP 108
96/7 SP 112, GF17
97/8 SPAuthentic 114, I17
96/7 SPx 34
97/8 SPx 38
98/9 SPx"Finite" 60, 102, 164
97/8 SportFX MiniStix
95/6 Summit 75, -MadHatter 3
96/7 Summit 6
95/6 SuperSticker 92
96/7 TeamOut
92/3 Topps 500
95/6 Topps 65, 1PL, HGA9
98/9 Topps 60, A3, M10
98/9 Topps SB16, SB28
95/6 ToppsFinest 60, 179
96/7 ToppsNHLPicks TS1
92/3 ToppsStadiumClub 181
93/4 ToppsStadiumClub 95
95/6 ToppsStadiumClub 77
95/6 TSC-MembersOnly 43
97/8 ToppsSticker 5
95/6 ToppsSuperSkills 42
91/2 UpperDeck 345
92/3 UpperDeck 55
93/4 UpperDeck 167, SP-79
94/5 UpperDeck 330
95/6 UD 7, 247, AS14, SE63
95/6 UD-AllStarPredict MVP24
96/7 UD 118, 368, P3
96/7 UD-AllStarYCTG AR15
97/8 UD 123, S20, SG50, T9B
95/6 UDBeAPlayer 130
96/7 UDBlackDiamond 110
97/8 UDBlackDiamond 65, PC6
98/9 UDChoice 153, 235
98/9 UDChoice BH6, SQ15
95/6 UDCC 261, 376, C23
96/7 UDCC 190, 326, C12, UD8
97/8 UDCollChoice 182, SQ52
96/7 UpperDeck"Ice" 98, S10
97/8 UpperDeckIce 75, L8A
97/8 Zenith 8, Z47,-ChasCup 8
97/8 Zenith -ZTeam 7
91/2 MTL
92/3 MTL
93/4 MTL
94/5 MTL
94/5 PHA/GameSheet
96/7 PHA/OceanSpray
97/8 PHA/Comcast

LECLAIR, NELSON
67/8 ColumbusCheckers

LECLERC, JEAN
52/3 AnonymousOHL 43

LECLERC, MIKE
94/5 Classic 47
94/5 Slapshot(MEM) 38
97/8 UpperDeck 181

LECLERC, PAUL
51/2 LavalDairy 80
52/3 StLawrence 18

LECLERC, RENÉ
76/7 opcWHA 28
73/4 QuébecNordiques

LECLERC, ROLAND
52/3 AnonymousOHL 79

LECOMPTE, ERIC
93/4 Classic 23
94/5 Classic 41, T13
93/4 ClassicFourSport 205
95/6 EdgeIce 136
95/6 FutureLegends 31
91/2 SketchQMJHL 217

LECOMPTE, FRANÇOIS
79/80 Montréal, -B&W

LECOURS, DANNY
81/2 Milwaukee 10

LECUYER, DOUG
81/2 O-Pee-Chee 367
80/1 CHI/4x6
80/1 CHI/5.5x8.5

LEDLIN, FREDERIK
94/5 DEL 291

LEDOCK, RENE
94/5 DEL 140

LEDUC, ALBERT
25-27 Anonymous 6
33/4 Anonymous (V129) 27
27-32 LaPresse 27/8
33/4 OPC (V304A) 46
55/6 Parkhurst 61
28/9 MTL/LaPatrie 10

LEDUC, BOB
72/3 OPC 322
73/4 opc-Posters 9
72/3 OttawaNationals

LEDUC, MIKE
91/2 AvantGardeBCJHL 69

LEDUC, RAYMOND
51/2 BasDuFleuve 5
52/3 BasDuFleuve 60

LEDUC, RICHARD
79/80 O-Pee-Chee 283
80/1 OPC/Topps 122
75/6 opcWHA 113
76/7 opcWHA 41
77/8 opcWHA 13
80/1 Pepsi Cap
80/1 QUE

LEDYARD, GRANT
91/2 Bowman 40
92/3 Bowman 27
93/4 Donruss 89
94/5 Donruss 312
94/5 Flair 42
93/4 FleerUltra 299
94/5 FleerUltra 54
95/6 FleerUltra 40
93/4 Leaf 394
94/5 Leaf 263
90/1 O-Pee-Chee 406
91/2 OPC/Topps 386
92/3 O-Pee-Chee 393
98/9 Pacific 84
97/8 PacificCrown 345
87/8 PaniniSticker 273
92/3 PaniniSticker 244
95/6 PaniniSticker 176
91/2 Parkhurst 241
93/4 Parkhurst 323
92/3 Pinnacle 205
93/4 Pinnacle 413
94/5 Pinnacle 204
95/6 Playoff 141
94/5 POG 84
95/6 POG 90
93/4 PowerPlay 325
94/5 Premier 98
90/1 ProSet 24
90/1 Score 233
91/2 Score(CDN) 401, (U.S) 362
92/3 Score 358
93/4 Score 568
97/8 Score(VAN) 15
92/3 Topps 321
95/6 Topps 157
91/2 ToppsStadiumClub 169
92/3 ToppsStadiumClub 79
95/6 UDBeAPlayer 104
89/90 BUF/BlueShield
89/90 BUF/Campbell
90/1 BUF/BlueShield
90/1 BUF/Campbell
91/2 BUF/BlueShield
91/2 BUF/Campbell
92/3 BUF/BlueShield
94/5 DAL
94/5 DAL/Southwest
96/7 DAL/Southwest
88/9 L.A.
88/9 WSH
88/9 WSH/Smokey

LEE, BILL
52/3 AnonymousOHL 144

LEE, PETER
96/7 DEL 37
78/9 OPC/Topps 244
79/80 OPC/Topps 45
80/1 O-Pee-Chee 278
81/2 OPC 258, Topps(E) 114
81/2 opcSticker 185
82/3 Post
83/4 SouhaitsRen.KeyChain
83/4 PGH/Heinz

LEE, STEVE
77/8 Kalamazoo

LEEB, BRAD
95/6 RedDeer

LEEB, GREG
97/8 Bowman 94
98 BowmanCHL 55
95/6 Spokane 15

LEEMAN, GARY
90/1 Bowman 155, -HatTrick 10
91/2 Bowman 161
92/3 Bowman 192
83 CanadaJuniors
92/3 FleerUltra 22
93/4 FleerUltra 353
86/7 Kraft Sports 56
89/90 Kraft 36
90/1 Kraft 27
91/2 Kraft 10
84/5 O-Pee-Chee 305
87/8 O-Pee-Chee
88/9 OPC/Topps 11
89/90 OPC/Topps 22
90/1 OPC/Topps 135, T-TI 13
91/2 OPC/Topps 188
92/3 O-Pee-Chee 33
91/2 opcPremier 106, 134
87/8 opcSticker 161/21
88/9 opcSticker 178
89/90 opcSticker 168
90/1 Panini(TOR) 12
87/8 PaniniSticker 331
88/9 PaniniSticker 125
89/90 PaniniSticker 133
90/1 PaniniSticker 279
92/3 PaniniSticker 41
91/2 Parkhurst 173, 254
92/3 Parkhurst 323
91/2 Pinnacle 31
92/3 Pinnacle 184
93/4 Premier 397
90/1 ProSet 283
91/2 ProSet 231
91/2 PSPlatinum 115, 162
90/1 Score 40, -HotCards 20
90/1 Score Promo 40
91/2 Score(CDN) 77, (U.S) 77
92/3 Score 171
93/4 Score 147
92/3 Topps 85
91/2 ToppsStadiumClub 158
92/3 ToppsStadiumClub 272
93/4 ToppsStadiumClub 244
90/1 UpperDeck 243, 310
91/2 UpperDeck 272, 528
92/3 UpperDeck 66
94/5 UDBeAPlayer-Aut. 73
92/3 CGY/IGA 3
93/4 MTL
83/4 TOR
84/5 TOR
85/6 TOR
86/7 TOR
87/8 TOR
87/8 TOR/P.L.A.Y. 10
88/9 TOR/P.L.A.Y. 8
90/1 TOR
90/1 TOR/P.L.A.Y. 10
81/2 Regina 12
82/3 Regina 14
83/4 Regina 14

LEEMING, BOB
89/90 Windsor

LEETCH, BRIAN
95/6 Aces 6 (Clubs)
96/7 Aces 8 (Clubs)
97/8 Aces K (Spades)
90/1 Bowman 215
91/2 Bowman 75
92/3 Bowman 149, 232
95/6 Bowman 32, BB14
96/7 CorinthianHeadliners
97/8 CorinthianHeadliners
93/4 Donruss 221
94/5 Donruss 152, -Dominator 2
95/6 Don. 181,-Dom 3,-ProP 5
96/7 Donruss 13
97/8 Donruss 156, 230, -Line 3
96/7 DonrussCanadianIce 108
97/8 DonrussCanadianIce 88
95/6 DonrussElite 98
96/7 DonrussElite 125
97/8 D.Elite 40, 116,-Craftsm 30
97/8 DonrussPreferred 22, 188
97/8 DonrussPriority 74
97/8 D.Prio-Pstcrd 22,-Stamp 22
97/8 DonrussStudio 86
97/8 D.Studio-Portr 35,-Sil 23
93/4 EASports 85, 213
97/8 EssoOlympic 22, 29
94/5 Flair 114, -Scoring P5
96/7 Flair 60
94/5 Fleer 135, -Headliner 5
96/7 Fleer 70, 140, -Norris 7
95/6 FleerMetal 96
95/6 FM-HeavyM 8, -Int.Steel 13
96/7 FleerNHLPicks 12
96/7 F.Picks-Jagged 17, -Fab 25
92/3 FleerUltra 138, -AW 2
93/4 FleerUltra 132
94/5 FleerUltra 139, -AS 2,-AW 7
94/5 FU-SpeedMerchant 7
95/6 FU 104, 390, -Ultraview 5
96/7 FU 108, -Power 10, -Blue 7
95 Globe 103
93/4 HockeyWit 71
95/6 Hoyle'EAST 2 (Diamonds)
92/3 HumptyDumpty (1)
97/8 KatchMedallion 94
91/2 Kelloggs 8
94/5 KennerSLU
96/7 KennerSLU
90/1 Kraft 28
91/2 Kraft 73
94/5 Kraft-AW
96/7 KraftDinner
93/4 Leaf 70
94/5 Leaf 403, -GoldStar 6
95/6 Leaf 93, -GoldStar 3
96/7 Leaf 165
97/8 Leaf 117
94/5 LeafLimited 33
95/6 LeafLimited 90
96/7 LeafLimited 82
96/7 LeafPreferred 42, -Steel 23
97/8 Limited 70, 179, 182
97/8 Limited -fabric 64
96/7 Maggers 102
91/2 McDonalds McD12
92/3 McDonalds McH-04
94/5 McDonalds McD6
96/7 McDonalds McD20
96/7 MetalUniv. 98, -IceCarv 9
97/8 Omega 147
89/90 OPC/T. 136, OPC 321,326
90/1 OPC/Topps 221
91/2 OPC/T. 108,215,269,T-TL 4
92/3 O-Pee-Chee 378, -Box
90/1 opcPremier 61
91/2 opcPremier 57, 183
89/90 opcSticker 39/181, 215/76
89/90 opcSticker 240/103
88/9 opcStickFS 12
89/90 opcStickFS 11
98/9 Pacific 297
97/8 PacificCrown 2, -Slap 5C
97/8 PacificCrownRoyale 86
97/8 PCR-BladesOfSteel 15
97/8 PcfcDynagon! 80,-Dyn 10B
97/8 PcfcD-Bst 62,108,-Tand 19
97/8 PacificInv. 88, -Attack 15
97/8 PacificParamount 118
98/9 PacificParamount 155
97/8 PacificRegime 129
97/8 PacificRevolution 89
88/9 PaniniSticker 301
89/90 PaniniSticker 279, 378
90/1 PaniniSticker 95
91/2 PaniniSticker 284
92/3 PaniniSticker 239
93/4 PaniniSticker 96
94/5 PaniniSticker 88
95/6 PaniniSticker 110
96/7 PaniniSticker 102, 148
97/8 PaniniSticker 84, 120
91/2 Parkhurst 119, 438, 464
91/2 Parkhurst 471, PHC8
92/3 Parkhurst 110, 467
93/4 Parkhurst 131
94/5 Parkhurst 151, V15
95/6 Parkhurst 144, PP21
95/6 Parkie-Crown(2) 14
91/2 Pinnacle 136, B3
92/3 Pinnacle 15, -TeamP 3
93/4 Pinnacle 275, -TeamP 2
94/5 Pinnacle 155, TP4, WE15
95/6 Pinnacle 133, -First 6
96/7 Pinnacle 193
97/8 Pinnacle 92, 195, -TeamP 3
96/7 PinnacleBeAPlayer 55
97/8 PinnacleBeeHive 28
97/8 Pinn.Certified 36, -Team 6
97/8 PinnacleInside 20
97/8 PinnacleMint 19
95/6 PinnacleZenith 32
96/7 PinnacleZenith 85
95/6 Playoff 68, 174, 283
94/5 POG 170, 260, 334
95/6 POG 186
97/8 Post
93/4 PowerPlay 160,-Slap 6
93/4 Premier 25, 505
94/5 Premier 37, 450, 485, 500
95/6 ProMagnet 97
90/1 ProSet 201, 373
91/2 ProSet 159, 309
92/3 ProSet 112, CC4
91/2 PSPlatinum 79, 284
90/1 Score 225,-Hot 93,-Young 2
91/2 Score(CDN) 5, 363, 373
91/2 Score(U.S) 5, 333, 343
92/3 Score 416, 491, 522
92/3 Score-USAGreats 8
93/4 Score 235, -DreamTeam 6
93/4 Score -TheFranchise 13
94/5 Score 184, DT4
95/6 Score 124
96/7 Score 179
97/8 Score 126
97/8 Score(NYR) 2
92/3 SeasonsPatch 28
94/5 Select 24, FL3
95/6 SelectCertified 27
96/7 SelectCertified 76
94 Semic 113, 339
95 Semic 105
89 SemicSticker 161
91 SemicSticker 131
92 SemicSticker 150
93 SemicSticker 171
94/5 SigRookies CF3
95/6 SkBxEmotion 115, -Xcited 6
95/6 SkyBoxImpact 110
96/7 SkyBoxImpact 81, -Fox 14
96/7 SB'7Eleven
94/5 SP 74
95/6 SP 94, E20
96/7 SP 101
97/8 SPAuthentic 100, I39
96/7 SPx 26
97/8 SPx 33
98/9 SPx"Finite" 111
97/8 SportFX MiniStix
94/5 SRGoldStandard L1
95/6 Summit 23, -GM4
96/7 Summit 96
95/6 SuperSticker 79, DC7
96/7 TeamOut
92/3 Topps 261, 293
95/6 Topps 75, HGA1, M16, PF2
98/9 Topps 75, A9, B3
94/5 ToppsFinest 49
95/6 ToppsFinest 115
94/5 TF-BBest 4, (Blue) 12
95 ToppsFinestBronze 14
95/6 ToppsFinest 41
96/7 ToppsNHLPicks FT5, ID1
91/2 ToppsStadiumClub 201
92/3 Topps.StadiumClub 73, 248
93/4 ToppsStadiumClub 88
94/5 TSC 55, 150, -Finest 7
95/6 T.StadiumClub 30, M8, N5
91/2 TSC-MembersOnly
93/4 TSC-MembersOnly 24
94/5 TSC-MembersOnly 3
95/6 TSC-MembersOnly 33
97/8 ToppsSticker 3
95/6 ToppsSuperSkills 19
90/1 UD 253, 315, 485
91/2 UD 35, 153, 610, 612
92/3 UD 284, 434, 640, WG15
92/3 UD-LockerAS 5
93/4 UD 348, NL4, SP-102
94/5 UD 231, 444, C28, H11
94/5 UD R13, R45, R51,SP50
95/6 UD 236, 487, AS7, F18
95/6 UD H33, R18, SE55
95/6 UD-AllStarPredict MVP25
96/7 UpperDeck 300,SS7B,X23
96/7 UD-AllStarYCTG AR19
97/8 UD316,S28,SG22,SS5,T4B
93/4 UDBeAPlayer 9
94/5 UDBAP R46, R149,-Aut. 46
96/7 UDBlackDiamond 12
97/8 UDBlackDiamond 33, PC10
98/9 UDChoice 129, 238
98/9 UDChoice BH29, SQ7
95/6 UDCollChoice 247
96/7 UDCC 169, 303, 325
96/7 UDCC C27, UD30
97/8 UDCollChoice 162, SQ20
97/8 udDiamondVision 12
96/7 UpperDeck"Ice" 43
97/8 UpperDeckIce 76, L10A
96 Wien 160
97/8 Zenith 13, Z65
89/90 NYR/MarineMidland
92/3 NYR

LEFEBVRE, FRÉDÉRIC
88/9 Richelieu
90/1 SketchQMJHL 194

LEFEBVRE, GUY
90/1 SketchQMJHL 96

LEFEBVRE, J.S.
91/2 SketchQMJHL 144

LEFEBVRE, MARTIN
90/1 SketchQMJHL 186

LEFEBVRE, NICOLAS
90/1 SketchQMJHL 84, 248
91/2 SketchQMJHL 266

LEFEBVRE, PATRICE
95/6 EdgeIce 153
90/1 ProCards 337
93/4 LasVegas
94/5 LasVegas
95/6 LasVegas
96/7 LasVegas

LEFEBVRE, STÉPHANE
93/4 Slapshot(Guelph) 19
83/4 NovaScotia 4

LEFEBVRE, SYLVAIN
90/1 Bowman 48
91/2 Bowman 332
92/3 Bowman 307
93/4 Donruss 331
95/6 Donruss 288
96/7 Donruss 81
94/5 Flair 149
94/5 Fleer 180
93/4 FleerUltra 430
94/5 FleerUltra 176, 360
95/6 FleerUltra 222
93/4 Leaf 267
94/5 Leaf 507
95/6 Leaf 292
96/7 Leaf 98
92/3 O-Pee-Chee 303
92/3 opcPremier 108
90/1 OPC/Topps 159
91/2 OPC/Topps 489
97/8 PacificRegime 54
90/1 Panini(MTL) 15
90/1 PaniniSticker 59
94/5 PaniniSticker 196
91/2 Parkhurst 307
92/3 Parkhurst 416
95/6 Parkhurst 321
93/4 Pinnacle 317
94/5 Pinnacle 379
95/6 Pinnacle 131
96/7 PinnacleBeAPlayer 54
95/6 Playoff 26
93/4 PowerPlay 450
93/4 Premier 331
94/5 Premier 364
88/9 ProCards(Sherbrooke)
90/1 ProSet 472
90/1 Score(CND) 307
91/2 Score(CDN) 245

92/3 Score 405
93/4 Score 359
95/6 Score 192
96/7 Score 226
97/8 Score(COL) 16
96/7 Summit 149
92/3 Topps 341
95/6 Topps 279
91/2 ToppsStadiumClub 208
92/3 ToppsStadiumClub 367
93/4 ToppsStadiumClub 48
90/1 UpperDeck 421
91/2 UpperDeck 171
94/5 UpperDeck 335
95/6 UpperDeck 342
94/5 UDBeAPlayer R66, -Aut. 41
89/90 MTL
89/90 MTL/Kraft
90/1 MTL
91/2 MTL
94/5 QUE/BurgerKing
92/3 TOR/Kodak
93/4 TOR/Abalene
93/4 TOR/Blacks 12

LEFLEY, BRYAN
72/3 EddieSargent 139
74/5 Loblaws
72/3 O-Pee-Chee 252
77/8 OPC 297
78/9 OPC 370
76/7 COL.R
76/7 COL.R/CokeCans
77/8 COL.R/CokeCans

LEFLEY, CHUCK
73/4 MTL
72-84 Dernière 72/3, 73/4
74/5 Loblaws, -Update
73/4 OPC 44, Topps 154
74/5 OPC/Topps 178
75/6 OPC/Topps 282
76/7 OPC/Topps 63, OPC 393
77/8 OPC 340
80/1 OPC 395
73/4 Topps 154
72/3 MTL
74/5 MTL

LEGACÉ, MANNY
94/5 CanadaJrAlumni 2
93/4 Classic 24
93/4 ClassicProspects LP16
93/4 CanadaNats
95/6 FutureLegends 9, -Pltnm 3
93/4 Premier-TmCanada 2
94/5 Score CT20
90/1 SketchOHL 263
91/2 SketchOHL 217
93/4 Slapshot(NiagaraFalls) 25
92/3 UpperDeck 585

LEGAULT, ALEXANDRE
90/1 SketchMEM 51
90/1 SketchQMJHL 7
91/2 SketchQMJHL 193

LEGAULT, JAY
97/8 Bowman 148
98 BowmanCHL 20
95/6 Slapshot 239

LEGAULT, MARC
91/2 SketchQMJHL 211

LEGER, BOB
52/3 BasDuFleuve 58
52/3 LavalDairy 95
52/3 StLawrence 102

LEGER, GERMAIN
51/2 LavalDairy 26

LEGER, ROGER
45-64 BeeHives(MTL)
51-54 LaPatrie 11Jan53
43-47 ParadeSportive
45-54 QuakerOats

LEGGE, BARRY
80/1 Pepsi Cap
80/1 WPG

LEGGE, RANDY
76/7 SanDiegoMariners

LEGGETT, ALAN
91/2 ProCards 315
93/4 Raleigh

LEGRIS, HEC
52/3 BasDuFleuve 39

LEGWAND, DAVID
98 BowmanCHL 14, 147, A11
98/9 Topps 234
97/8 UDBlackDiamond 35
98/9 UDChoice 302

LEHIKOINEN, ARI
80/1 Mallasjuoma 139

LEHIKOINEN, TERO
92/3 Jyvas-Hyva 79

LEHKONEN, ISMO
80/1 Mallasjuoma 55

LEHKONEN, TIMO
91/2 Jyvas-Hyva 7
92/3 Jyvas-Hyva 19
93/4 Sisu 375

LEHMAN, HUGHIE
83&87 HallOfFame 202
83 HHOF Postcard (N)
19 Millionaires (x2)
60/1 Topps 38
61/2 Topps-Stamp

LEHMAN, TOMMY
94/5 ElitSet 72
95/6 ElitSet 152, 159
90/1 SemicElitserien 89
91/2 SemicElitserien 18
92/3 SemicElitserien 239
95/6 udElite 15

LEHNER, JOSEF
95/6 DEL 53
96/7 DEL 252
95 PaniniWorlds 57

LEHOUX, GUY
91/2 ProCards 350
90/1 SketchMEM 55
92/3 StJohns
93/4 StJohns
94/5 StJohns
95/6 StJohns

LEHOUX, JASON
96/7 Rimouski

LEHTERA, TERO
94/5 ElitSet 200, -Foreign 10
95 Hartwall
92/3 Jyvas-Hyva 109
93/4 Jyvas-Hyva 197
95 PaniniWorlds 176
95 Semic 27
93/4 Sisu 272
94/5 Sisu 9,-Fire 16,-NHLDraft 6
95/6 Sisu 257, -GoldCards 16
96/7 Sisu 49
95/6 SisuLimited 62
91/2 UD'CzechWJC 32
96 Wien 17

LEHTI, PERTTI
78/9 SM-Liiga 220

LEHTINEN, ARTO
71/2 WilliamsFIN 306

LEHTINEN, JERE
97/8 Aces 2 (Clubs)
95/6 Bowman 150
92/3 Classic 31
94/5 Classic 72, T18
95/6 Donruss 332
96/7 Donruss-RatedRook 4
97/8 Donruss 30
96/7 DonrussCanadianIce 111
96/7 D.Elite 77, -Aspirations 10
97/8 DonrussElite 68
97/8 DonrussPreferred 65
97/8 DonrussPriority 63
95/6 FleerMetal 183, -IntSteel 14
96/7 FleerNHLPicks 144
95/6 FleerUltra 347
95 Hartwall
92/3 Jyvas-Hyva 107
93/4 Jyvas-Hyva 322
97/8 KatchMedallion 45
95 Latkaliiga 1
96/7 Leaf 201
97/8 Leaf 98
95/6 LeafLimited 39
96/7 LeafLimited 77
96/7 LeafPreferred 47, -Steel 63
97/8 Limited 135
97/8 Omega 71
98/9 Pacific 179
97/8 PacificParamount 59
98/9 PacificParamount 66
97/8 PacificRegime 61
97/8 PacificRevolution 42
96/7 PaniniSticker 175
97/8 PaniniSticker 145
95/6 Parkhurst 265, 518
97/8 Pinnacle 118
97/8 PinnacleBeAPlayer 123
97/8 PinnacleInside 187
95/6 PinnacleZenith 145
96/7 PinnacleZenith 51
96/7 Score 246
97/8 Score 188
94 Semic 30
95 Semic 20, 232
93/4 Sisu 47
94/5 Sisu 20, 155, 157
95/6 Sisu 164,397,-Gld 17,-Spl 7
95/6 SisuLimited 9, -Platinum
95/6 SkyBoxImpact 195
95/6 SP 41
97/8 SPAuthentic 48
98/9 SPx"Finite" 28
95/6 Summit 173
96/7 Summit 153
95 SuomenBeckett 2
95/6 ToppsFinest 53
96/7 ToppsNHLPicks RS2
95/6 ToppsStadiumClub 199
92/3 UpperDeck 615
95/6 UpperDeck 398
96/7 UpperDeck 49
97/8 UpperDeck 52, SG26, T8C
95/6 UDBeAPlayer 175
96/7 UDBlackDiamond 87
97/8 UDBlackDiamond 40
98/9 UDChoice 68
96/7 UDCollChoice 75
97/8 UDCollChoice 74
96 Wien 20, 37, AS4
96/7 DAL/Southwest

LEHTINEN, MIKKA
95/6 Sisu 325
96/7 Sisu 136

LEHTIO, RAUNO
66/7 Champion 178
65/6 Hellas 100
70/1 Kuvajulkaisut 245
71/2 WilliamsFIN 212

LEHTIO, RISTO
66/7 Champion 186
65/6 Hellas 101

LEHTO, ANTTI
80/1 Mallasjuoma 58

LEHTO, JONI
96/7 DEL 66
95/6 Sisu 162, 299
95/6 Sisu-Double 4, -Painkill 3
96/7 Sisu 176, -Sledgehammer 9
95/6 SisuLimited 31, -S&S 5
89/90 SketchOHL 53
90/1 SketchOHL 86
96 Wien 33
91/2 ProCards 455

LEHTO, JOUNI
91/2 Richmond 5

LEHTO, KAI
72/3 WilliamsFIN 308

LEHTO, MARKUS
80/1 Oshawa 14

LEHTO, PETTERI
80/1 Mallasjuoma 197

LEHTOLAINEN, PEKKA
66/7 Champion 187
65/6 Hellas 104

LEHTONEN, ANTERO
80/1 Mallasjuoma 176
78/9 SM-Liiga 14, 188
77-80 Sportscaster 54-1273
72/3 WilliamsFIN 267
73/4 WilliamsFIN 156
79/80 WSH

LEHTONEN, ERKKI
80/1 Mallasjuoma 164
78/9 SM-Liiga 187 .

LEHTONEN, LAURI
66/7 Champion 17
65/6 Hellas 69

LEHTONEN, PERTTI
91/2 Jyvas-Hyva 5
92/3 Jyvas-Hyva 4
93/4 Jyvas-Hyva 16
80/1 Mallasjuoma 17
82 SemicSticker 30
93/4 Sisu 91
95/6 Sisu 185, 204, -Double 5
96/7 Sisu 5
95/6 SisuLimited 38
78/9 SM-Liiga 29

LEHTONEN, R.P.
96/7 Sisu 138

LEHTONEN, SAMI
93/4 Sisu 115
94/5 Sisu 168, -Horoscope 19
95/6 Sisu 109
96/7 Sisu 126

LEHTONEN, TIMO
70/1 Kuvajulkaisut 299

LEHTORANTA, VESA
71/2 WilliamsFIN 133
72/3 WilliamsFIN 196

LEHTORINNE, TIMO
71/2 WilliamsFIN 248

LEHVONEN, HENRY
80/1 Mallasjuoma 43

LEIBEL, BRIAN
87/8 Regina
88/9 Regina

LEIDBORG, GUNNAR
94/5 DEL 5
95/6 DEL 384
82 SemicSticker 3

LEIER, DAN
83/4 Saskatoon 6

LEIKKO, SAMU
66/7 Champion 30

LEIME, EIKKE
79/80 Montréal, BW

LEIMU, PEKKA
66/7 Champion 190
70/1 Kuvajulkaisut 65, 130
72 Panda
71/2 WilliamsFIN 180
72/3 WilliamsFIN 128
73/4 WilliamsFIN 183

LEINONEN, ARI
72/3 WilliamsFIN 348

LEINONEN, MARKO
93/4 Sisu 137
95/6 Sisu 261
96/7 Sisu 55

LEINONEN, MIKKO
80/1 Mallasjuoma 107
82/3 O-Pee-Chee 4
83/4 O-Pee-Chee 248
79 PaniniSticker 178
82 SemicSticker 160
82 Skopbank
77-80 Sportscaster 76- 1821
83/4 SouhaitsRen.KeyChain
72/3 WilliamsFIN 268

LEINONEN, SAMI
95/6 Sisu 141

LEINONEN, TUOMAS
72/3 WilliamsFIN 269

LEIRIVAARA, JUHANI
66/7 Champion 130

LEITER, BOB
64-67 BeeHives(BOS)
64/5 CokeCap BOS-24
72/3 EddieSargent 9
74/5 Loblaws
72/3 OPC 218
73/4 OPC/Topps 117
74/5 OPC/Topps 51
75/6 OPC/Topps 191
94/5 Parkie(64/5) 11
71/2 TheTorontoSun
63/4 Topps 14
64/5 Topps 63
72/3 ATL
74/5 ATL
71/2 PGH

LEITER, KEN
87/8 opcSticker 131/119
87/8 PaniniSticker 93
84/5 Springfield 6

LEJCYK, LES
89 SemicSticker 127
92 SemicSticker 266

LEJEUNE, JOZEF
79 PaniniSticker 344

LEKKERIMAKI, SAMI
92/3 Jyvas-Hyva 151
93/4 Jyvas-Hyva 267
93/4 Sisu 292

LEKUM, MIKE
80/1 Oshawa 19
81/2 Oshawa 15

LELACHEUR, ROB
90/1 SketchWHL 82
89/90 Saskatoon 11

LEMAIRE, ED
85/6 Sudbury 17

LEMAIRE, JACQUES
70/1 Colgate Stamp 30
70/1 DadsCookies
72-84 Dernière 72/3, 73/4
70/1 EddieSargent 103
71/2 EddieSargent 105
72/3 EddieSargent 115
70/1 Esso Stamp
87 HallOfFame 245
94/5 Kraft'AwardWinner
72/3 Letraset 15
74/5 LiptonSoup 38
74/5 Loblaws
73/4 MacsMilk Disk
68/9 OPC/Topps 63
69/70 OPC/Topps 8
70/1 OPC/Topps 57
70/1 OPC/T-Deckle 19, -Sticker
71/2 OPC/Topps 71
72/3 O-Pee-Chee 77, Topps 25
73/4 OPC/Topps 56
74/5 OPC/Topps 24
75/6 OPC/Topps 258
76/7 OPC/Topps 129
77/8 OPC/Topps 254
78/9 OPC/Topps 180
94/5 Parkie(64/5) FS1
68/9 Post Marble
70/1 PostShooters
72 SemicSticker 208
68/9 ShirriffCoin MTL14
77-9 Sportscastr 81-19, 85-2035
71/2 TheTorontoSun
67/8 Topps 3
67/8 MTL
67/8 MTL/IGA
68/9 MTL
69/70 MTL/ProStar
70/1 MTL
71 MTL/Pins
71/2 MTL
72/3 MTL
73/4 MTL
74/5 MTL
75/6 MTL
76/7 MTL
77/8 MTL
78/9 MTL
83/4 MTL
84/5 MTL
92/3 MTL/OPC 62
95/6 MTL/Forum 17Feb96
96/7 N.J//Sharp

LEMANDER, HANNU
66/7 Champion 90
65/6 Hellas 85
72/3 WilliamsFIN 175

LEMANOWICZ, DAVID
91/2 AvantGardeBCJHL 18
95/6 Spokane 1

LEMANSKI, CASEY
92/3 BCJHL 163

LEMARQUE, ERIC
91/2 Greensboro

LEMAY, DAVE
90/1 SketchOHL 37
91/2 SketchOHL 5
91/2 Cornwall 5
93/4 OwenSound

LEMAY, J.S.
96/7 Halifax (1), (2)

LEMAY, MARC
80/1 Québec

LEMAY, MOE
96/7 DEL 215
84/5 O-Pee-Chee 322
85/6 O-Pee-Chee 173
86/7 O-Pee-Chee 247, 249
85/6 opcSticker 246/128
88/9 EDM/ActionMagazine 43
82/3 VAN
84/5 VAN
85/6 VAN
86/7 VAN
83/4 Fredericton 12
81/2 Ottawa67s

LEMAY, YANNIK
90/1 SketchQMJHL 223
91/2 SketchQMJHL 17

LEMELIN, RÉJEAN
90/1 Bowman 32
91/2 Bowman 354
92/3 Durivage 48
86/7 Kraft Sports 1
81/2 O-Pee-Chee 44
82/3 O-Pee-Chee 50
83/4 O-Pee-Chee 86
84/5 O-Pee-Chee 228
85/6 OPC/Topps 95
86/7 OPC/Topps 102
88/9 OPC/Topps 186
89/90 OPC/Topps 40
90/1 OPC/Topps 343, 486
91/2 OPC/Topps 497
88/9 opcStars 18
83/4 opcSticker 266
84/5 opcSticker 240
85/6 opcSticker 210/77
86/7 opcSticker 83
88/9 opcSticker 24/153
87/8 PaniniSticker 204
88/9 PaniniSticker 203
89/90 PaniniSticker 195
90/1 PaniniSticker 3
91/2 PaniniSticker 172
90/1 ProSet 9, 382
90/1 Score 159, 365
91/2 Score(CDN) 127, (U.S) 127
84/5 7ElevenDisk
84/5 Topps 25
91/2 ToppsStadiumClub 23
90/1 UpperDeck 209, 215
83/4 Vachon 10
78/9 ATL/Coke
88/9 BOS/SportsAction
89/90 BOS/SportsAction
90/1 BOS/SportsAction
80/1 CGY
81/2 CGY
82/3 CGY
85/6 CGY/RedRooster
86/7 CGY/RedRooster

LEMELIN, ROGER
76/7 COL.R

LEMIEUX, ALAIN
86/7 QUE/McDonald
85/6 Fredericton 7

LEMIEUX, BOB
77/8 Kalamazoo

LEMIEUX, CARL
84/5 Richelieu

LEMIEUX, CLAUDE
95/6 Aces 4 (Hearts)
91/2 Bowman 271, 277
92/3 Bowman 49
95/6 Bowman 13
94/5 ClassicImages PL5
96/7 CorinthianHeadliners
97/8 CorinthianHeadliners
93/4 Donruss 187
94/5 Donruss 82
95/6 Donruss 343
96/7 Donruss 23, -HitList 18
97/8 Donruss 88
96/7 DonrussCanadianIce 115
97/8 D.CdnIce -National 25
96/7 DonrussElite 110
95/6 DonrussElite 44
97/8 DonrussPreferred 126
97/8 DonrussPriority 127
97/8 DonrussStudio 78
92/3 Durivage 14
93/4 Durivage 47
93/4 EASports 77
94/5 Fleer 113
96/7 Fleer 22, 142
95/6 FleerMetal 34, -IronWar 6
92/3 FleerUltra 114
93/4 FleerUltra 5
94/5 FleerUltra 118
95/6 F.Ultra 192, 223, -Crease 6
96/7 FleerUltra 37
97/8 KatchMedallion 39
86/7 KraftSports 29
93/4 Leaf 125
94/5 Leaf 185
95/6 Leaf 311, -Road 10
96/7 Leaf 17
95/6 LeafLimited 27
96/7 LeafLimited 46, -Bash 6
96/7 LeafPreferred 24, -Steel 31
97/8 Limited 15
96/7 Maggers 40
96/7 MetalUniverse 35
97/8 Omega 60
87/8 O-Pee-Chee 227
88/9 O-Pee-Chee 227
89/90 O-Pee-Chee 234
90/1 O-Pee-Chee 451
91/2 OPC/Topps 394
92/3 O-Pee-Chee 67
90/1 opcPremier 62
87/8 opcSticker 19
88/9 opcSticker 43/176
89/90 opcSticker 52/196
98/9 Pacific 164
97/8 PacificCrown 3, -Slap 2C
97/8 PacificCrownRoyale 36
97/8 PacificDynagon! 31
97/8 PcfcD-Dyn 5B,-Tandem 25
97/8 PacificInv. 36,-Feat 8, -Att 6
97/8 PacificParamount 52
98/9 PacificParamount 57
97/8 PacificRevolution 35
87/8 PaniniSticker 63
88/9 PaniniSticker 257
89/90 PaniniSticker 240
91/2 PaniniSticker 224
92/3 PaniniSticker 172
93/4 PaniniSticker 35
95/6 PaniniSticker 1-2, 82
96/7 PaniniSticker 246
91/2 Parkhurst 101
92/3 Parkhurst 89
93/4 Parkhurst 110
94/5 Parkhurst 129, V59
95/6 Parkhurst 319
91/2 Pinnacle 70
92/3 Pinnacle 259, 284
93/4 Pinnacle 251
94/5 Pinnacle 287
95/6 Pinnacle 119,-FirstStrike 10
96/7 Pinnacle 113
97/8 Pinnacle 163
97/8 PinnacleCertified 129
97/8 PinnacleInside 156
95/6 PinnZenith 116, -Gifted 4
96/7 P.Zenith 102,-Champion 10
95/6 Playoff 244
94/5 POG 145
93/4 PowerPlay 137
93/4 Premier 134
94/5 Premier 204
95/6 ProMagnet 76
90/1 ProSet 153, 478
91/2 ProSet 135
92/3 ProSet 98
91/2 PSPlatinum 196
90/1 Score 111, 9
91/2 Score(CDN) 22, (U.S) 22
92/3 Score 8
93/4 Score 160
94/5 Score CI16
95/6 Score 269

96/7 Score 116
97/8 Score 158
97/8 Score(COL) 11
94/5 Select 73
95/6 SelectCert. 99, -Double 19
96/7 SelectCert. 53
95/6 SkyBoxEmotion 97
95/6 SkyBoxImpact 37
96/7 SkyBoxImpact 25,-Blade 12
95/6 SP 35
96/7 SP 39
97/8 SPAuthentic 38
95/6 Summit 129
96/7 Summit 113
96/7 TeamOut
95/6 Topps 114
92/3 Topps 43
98/9 Topps 65
95/6 ToppsFinest 47
96/7 ToppsNHLPicks 89
91/2 ToppsStadiumClub 18
92/3 ToppsStadiumClub 50
93/4 ToppsStadiumClub 39
95/6 T.StadiumClub 189, N3
90/1 UpperDeck 447
91/2 UpperDeck 294
92/3 UpperDeck 163
93/4 UD 296, 391, SP-83
94/5 UpperDeck 303
95/6 UD 44,258,456,E108,SE50
96/7 UD 207, 243, P17
97/8 UpperDeck 47, 202
94/5 UDBeAPlayer-Aut. 27
98/9 UDChoice 55
95/6 UDCC 262, 392, C28
96/7 UDCC 57, 347, UD6
97/8 UDCollChoice 62
96 Wien 91
97/8 Zenith 57, Z36
96/7 COL/PhotoPucks
85/6 MTL
86/7 MTL
87/8 MTL
87/8 MTL/Stickers 31, 33
88/9 MTL
89/90 MTL
89/90 MTL/Kraft
90/1 N.J.

LEMIEUX, JEAN
74/5 Loblaws
75/6 O-Pee-Chee 367
76/7 O-Pee-Chee 272

LEMIEUX, JOCELYN
92/3 Bowman 72
93/4 Donruss 440
92/3 Durivage 15
93/4 Durivage 43
94/5 Leaf 502
90/1 OPC/Topps 237
91/2 OPC/Topps 453
92/3 O-Pee-Chee 153
87/8 PaniniSticker 319
90/1 PaniniSticker 190
91/2 PaniniSticker 20
92/3 PaniniSticker 8
93/4 PaniniSticker 152
94/5 PaniniSticker 114
91/2 Parkhurst 256
92/3 Parkhurst 275
93/4 Parkhurst 93
95/6 Parkhurst 393
93/4 Pinnacle 302
94/5 Pinnacle 89
95/6 Pinnacle 62
94/5 POG 115
93/4 Premier 295
94/5 Premier 122
88/9 ProCards(Sherbrooke)
90/1 ProSet 432
90/1 ScoreTraded 66T
91/2 Score(CDN) 447
92/3 Score 309
93/4 Score 420
92/3 Topps 300
91/2 ToppsStadiumClub 356
92/3 ToppsStadiumClub 446
93/4 ToppsStadiumClub 255
90/1 UpperDeck 544
91/2 UpperDeck 438
94/5 UpperDeck 372
94/5 UDBeAPlayer-Aut. 129
95/6 UDCollChoice 138
96/7 UDCollChoice 42
90/1 CHI/Coke
91/2 CHI/Coke
93/4 CHI/Coke
89/90 MTL
97/8 PHO
87/8 STL/Kodak

LEMIEUX, MARIO
95/6 Aces Q (Hearts)
96/7 Aces A (Spades)
89/90 ActionPacked
90/1 Bowman 204, -HatTrick 2
91/2 Bowman 87
92/3 Bowman 189, 233, 440
95/6 Bowman 40, BB10
92/3 Classic 66, SP, -Aut
83 CanadaJuniors
95/6 CoolTrade 4
96/7 CorinthianHeadliners
97/8 CorinthianHeadliners
93/4 Donruss 262, R, EC, -Ice 7
93/4 Donruss-EliteSeries 1
94/5 Donruss 5, -Dom. 1, -Ice 5
94/5 Donruss-EliteSeries 6
95/6 Don. 270,-Dom1,-ProP 14
96/7 Donruss 131,-Dom.4,-Top 1
96/7 D.CdnIce 31, -OCanada 13
96/7 D.CdnIce-Lemieux 1-25
95/6 DonrussElite 9, 51, 66
95/6 DE-Lemieux 1-7, -Cutting 2
96/7 D.Elite 109, -HartToHart 1
96/7 DE-Lem. 1-6,-Perspective 4
92/3 Durivage 8
93/4 EASports 105, 189
88/9 Esso Sticker
94/5 Flair 135,-CntrSpt 6,-HotN 5
96/7 Flair 78, -Hot 7, -Now 2
96/7 Fleer 87, 137-39,141
96/7 F-ArtRoss 13, -Pearson 7
95/6 FleerMetal 118
95/6 FM-Heavy 9,-IntSteel 15
96/7 F.Picks-Dream1, -Fab 26
96/7 F.Picks-CaptainsChoice 3
92/3 FleerUltra 165,-AS 4,-AW 5
93/4 FleerUltra116,-AW 4,-Red 6
93/4 FU-Pivots 4, -Scoring 4
94/5 FleerUltra 165, -Scoring 5
95/6 FU 288,391,-Ext 13,-Ultra 6
96/7 FU 143, -Power 11, -Red 4
88/9 FritoLay
91/2 Gillette 33
96/7 GreatEagle 1-18
95 Globe 87
96/7 Got-UmHockeyGreatsCoin
92/3 HighFive 5
93/4 HockeyWit 66
92/3 HumptyDumpty (2)
92/3 Kelloggs Poster
95/6 Kelloggs
93/4 KennerSLU
94/5 KennerSLU
93 Koululainen
94 Koululainen
89/90 Kraft 55, -Sticker 5
90/1 Kraft 29, 87
91/2 Kraft 1
92/3 Kraft'AllStar
93/4 Kraft-Captn, -Cutout, -Gold
95/6 Kraft-Ticket
96/7 Kraft'AS, 'Disk, 'Flex
96/7 KraftDinner, -Trophy (x2)
93/4 Leaf 1, 210, -Lemieux 1-10
93/4 L-HatTrick 1, 4,-GoldAS 1
94/5 Leaf 1, -FireOnIce 9
94/5 L-GoldStar 11, -Limited 18
95/6 Leaf 1, -Lemieux 1-10
95/6 Leaf-FreezeFrame 7
96/7 Leaf 84, -Fire 1, -Sweater 1
94/5 LeafLimited 1, -Gold 1
95/6 LeafLimited 1, -StarsOf 1
96/7 LeafLimited 85, -Stubble 7
96/7 LeafPreferred 113,-Vanity 6
96/7 LeafPreferred-SteelPower 2
92 LegendsSports 25
96/7 Maggers 119
92/3 McDonalds McD-21
93/4 McDonalds McH1
95/6 McDonalds McD15
96/7 McDonalds M cD21
96/7 MetalUniv. 128, -IceCarv 10
96/7 MU-LethalWeapons 11
85/6 O-Pee-Chee 262
85/6 OPC/Topps 9, I, OPC 262
86/7 OPC/Topps 122, I, T-AS 9
87/8 OPC/Topps 15, T-AS 11
88/9 OPC/Topps 1, T-AS 2
89/90 OPC/Topps 1, A, T-AS 3
89/90 OPC 312, 319, 327
90/1 OPC/Topps 175,G, T-TL 17
91/2 OPC/Topps 153, 523
92/3 OPC 138, 240, 292
92/3 OPC-25Years 18
90/1 opcPremier 63
91/2 opcPremier 114
92/3 opcPremier-Star 22
87/8 opcStars 23
88/9 opcStars 19
85/6 opcSticker 97, 199/72
86/7 opcSticker 233, 120/134
87/8 opcSticker 170, 120/132
88/9 opcSticker 232, 204/73
88/9 opcSticker 116/246, 210/81
88/9 opcSticker 211/82
89/90 opcSticker 238, 158/18
89/90 opcSticker 208/68, FS 24
87/8 PaniniSticker 146
88/9 PaniniSticker 340, 400-01
89/90 PaniniStickr 184, 309, 375
90/1 PaniniSticker 136, 326
91/2 PaniniSticker 268
92/3 PaniniSticker 220, 280
93/4 PaniniSticker 136, H
94/5 PaniniSticker 74
95/6 PaniniSticker 59
96/7 PaniniSticker 59, 144, 150
95 PaniniWorlds 101, 277
91/2 Parkhurst 137, 467, PHC7
92/3 Parkhurst 136, 462, 498
93/4 PH 425, D2, E2, F10, G2
94/5 Parkhurst 296, V6, C18
95/6 Parkhurst 170, PP2, PP11
95/6 PH-AllStar 1, -Crown(1) 3
91/2 Pinnacle 1, 380, B5
92/3 Pinnacle 300
93/4 Pinnacle 221,230,310,CA18
93/4 P-NiftyFifty 1, 4, -TeamP 5
94/5 Pinnacle 170, TP10, WE8
95/6 P. 192, -Clear 13, -FirstStr 3
96/7 Pinnacle 86,-Trop 1,-TmP 2
96/7 P.BAP-Bisct 2,-Lemieux1-2
95/6 PinnacleFANtasy 8
96/7 PinnacleFANtasy 4
96/7 PinnacleMint 1
95/6 PinnZenith 108, -ZTeam 3
96/7 P.Zenith 114, -Champion 5
95/6 Playoff 79, 186, 298
96/7 Playoff 436
94/5 POG 185
95/6 POG 2, 211
93/4 PowerPlay 190, -Point 8
93/4 PP-Gamebreaker 5
93/4 Premier 37, 91, 185, 220
93/4 Prmr-Black(OPC) 18, (T) 9
93/4 Premier-Finest 10
94/5 Premier 250
95/6 ProMagnet 92
90/1 ProSet 236, 362
91/2 ProSet 194, 318, 581, P3
92/3 ProSet 1, 139
91/2 PSPlatinum 91
87/8 ProSportWatch CW5
90/1 Score 2, 337, -HotCard 34
91/2 Score(CDN) 200, 316, 365
91/2 Score(U.S) 200, 335, 426
91/2 Score-HotCards 5
92/3 Score 390,413,433,448,519
93/4 Score 350, 479, 480
93/4 Score(CND) DD8
93/4 S-Franchise 16, -Dream 10
94/5 Score DT15, TF18
96/7 Score 6, -Dream 6, -Sddn 7
92/3 SeasonsPatch 34
93/4 SeasonsPatch 9
95/6 SelectCertified 1, -Gold 3
96/7 SelectCert. 10, -Corner 2
95 Semic 93
89 SemicSticker 64
92 SemicSticker 86
93 SemicSticker 198
85/6 7Eleven 15
95/6 SkyBoxEmotion 138
95/6 SkBxE-Xcel 8, -Xcited 10
95/6 SkyBoxImpact 132
95/6 SBI -Count 3, -IceQuake 7
96/7 SBI 102, -Count 7, -Versa 7
95/6 SP 113, E22, FX17
96/7 SP 125, CW3
96/7 SPx 37, HH6, SPxForce 1
96/7 SportFX MiniStix
95/6 Summit 118, -GM10
96/7 Smmt 32,-Untch 1,-HighV 8
95/6 SuperSticker 97, DieCut 24
96/7 TeamOut
92/3 Topps 212, 265, 504
95/6 Topps 100, 2RL, HGC30
95/6 Topps M2, PF15
95/6 ToppsFinest 150, 190
96 ToppsFinestBronze 16
96/7 T.NHLPicks 3, FC5, FT15
91/2 ToppsStadiumClub 174
92/3 T.StadiumClub 94, 251
93/4 TSC 143, 146, 148, 310
93/4 TSC-AllStar, -Finest 10
94/5 T.StadiumClub 60, -Finest 1
95/6 T.StadiumClub 180, M2, N2
91/2 TSC-MembersOnly (x3)
95/6 TSC-MembersOnly 24
95/6 ToppsSuperSkills 1
90/1 UpperDeck 59, 144, 305
91/2 UpperDeck 45, 47
91/2 UD 156, 611, AW9
92/3 UD 26, 433, 436, 454, G9
92/3 UD WG11,-LockerAS 6
93/4 UD 301, 407, AW1, E13
93/4 UD GC4, H1, HB7, SP-122
94/5 UpperDeck 22, 200, SP61
95/6 UD 84, 231, AS5, F16, H4
95/6 UD R32, R42, R53, SE152
95/6 UD-AllStarPredict MVP16
96/7 UpperDeck 321, 5B
96/7 UD GJ6, HH16, LS03
94/5 UDBeAPlayer R69
96/7 UDBlckDiamd 75, 166, RC3
95/6 UDCollChoice 256, C25
96/7 UDCC 210,293,335,C5,S7
96/7 UpperDeck"Ice" 114, S7
96 Wien 85
86/7 PGH/Kodak
87/8 PGH/Kodak
89/90 PGH/Elbys
89/90 PGH/Foodland 10
90/1 PGH/Foodland 13
91/2 PGH/Elbys
91/2 PGH/Topps
91/2 PGH/Foodland 4
92/3 PGH/Coke
92/3 PGH/Foodland 1
92/3 PGH/FoodStickers
93/4 PGH/Foodland 1
95/6 PGH/Foodland 23
96/7 PGH/FotoPuck
96/7 PGH/Tribune

LEMIEUX, RÉAL
70/1 EddieSargent 70
71/2 EddieSargent 72
72/3 EddieSargent 91
68/9 OPC/Topps 36
69/70 O-Pee-Chee 190
71/2 OPC/Topps 154
73/4 OPC/Topps 122
68/9 ShirriffCoin LA1
71/2 TheTorontoSun

LEMIEUX, RICHARD
72/3 EddieSargent 218
74/5 Loblaws
72/3 OPC 202
73/4 OPC/Topps 53
74/5 OPC/Topps 114
75/6 OPC/Topps 274
76/7 opcWHA 74
72/3 VAN/RoyalBank
73/4 VAN/RoyalBank

LEMOINE, J.P.
94 Semic 213
92 SemicSticker
93 SemicSticker 254

LEMOINE, PHILIPPE
95 PaniniWorlds 101

LEMOLA, OLLI
71/2 WilliamsFIN 327

LEMONDE, BERNIE
52/3 BasDuFleuve 37
52/3 LavalDairy 90

LEMPIAINEN, MIKO
93/4 Jyvas-Hyva 204
93/4 Sisu 271

LEMPIO, JOACHIM
94/5 DEL 128
79 PaniniSticker 251

LENARDON, TIM
88/9 ProCards(Utica)
91/2 ProCards 146

LENARDUZZI, MIKE
93/4 FleerUltra 72, -Prospects 5
93/4 Parkhurst 87
93/4 Pinnacle 207
90/1 SketchMEM 1
90/1 SketchOHL 165
91/2 SketchOHL 310
89/90 Oshawa 12

LENDZYK, TARAS
91/2 AirCanadaSJHL B13, 37
93/4 Minn-Duluth

LENER, SLAVOMIR
92/3 CGY/IGA 28

LEONHARDT, BJORN
96/7 DEL 183

LEONOV, DMITRI
95/6 Spokane 5

LEONOV, YURI
91/2 O-Pee-Chee 39R

LEOPPKY, MARK
92/3 MPSPhotoSJHL 26

LEPAGE, ANDRÉ
93/4 Slapshot(Drum.)

LEPAGE, BERTRAND
52/3 AnonymousOHL 69
52/3 BasDuFleuve 42

LEPAGE, MARTIN
90/1 SketchQMJHL 138
91/2 SketchQMJHL 207

LEPAUS, MARKO
70/1 Kuvajulkaisut 315
71/2 WilliamsFIN 347

LEPINE, HECTOR
25-27 Anonymous 10

LEPINE, JOS
51/2 LavalDairy 46

LEPINE, ALFRED (PIT)
25-27 Anonymous 13
33/4 Anonymous (V129) 42
33-43 BeeHives(MTL.C)
33/4 CndGum (V252)
35-40 CrownBrand 115
33-35 DiamondMatch
36-39 DiamondMatch (1),(2),(3)
33/4 Hamilton (V288) 23
27-32 LaPresse 27/8
33/4 OPC (V304A) 20
37/8 OPC (V304E) 159
34/5 SweetCaporal
33/4 WWGum (V357) 46
36/7 WWGum (V356) 78
28/9 MTL/LaPatrie 5

LEPISTO, JUSSI
80/1 Mallasjuoma 62
78/9 SM-Liiga 70

LEPPA, HENRY
66/7 Champion 60
72 Hellas 3
74 Hellas 8
70/1 Kuvajulkaisut 180
80/1 Mallasjuoma 65
74 SemicSticker 84
78/9 SM-Liiga 78
77-80 Sportscaster 108- 2573
71/2 WilliamsFIN 104
72/3 WilliamsFIN 148
73/4 WilliamsFIN 69, 113

LEPPANEN, ANTTI
66/7 Champion 152
74 Hellas 9
74 SemicSticker 97
77-80 Sportscaster 16-364
71/2 WilliamsFIN 134
72/3 WilliamsFIN 197
73/4 WilliamsFIN 70, 157

LEPPANEN, JANNE
92/3 Jyvas-Hyva 99

LEPPANEN, JARI
72/3 WilliamsFIN 309

LEPPANEN, KALEVI
66/7 Champion 83
65/6 Hellas 10
70/1 Kuvajulkaisut 300

LEPPANEN, REIJO
74 Hellas 10
70/1 Kuvajulkaisut 142
80/1 Mallasjuoma 185
82 SemicSticker 45
82 Skopbank
78/9 SM-Liiga 212
77-80 Sportscaster 83-1970
71/2 WilliamsFIN 192
72/3 WilliamsFIN 230
73/4 WilliamsFIN 264

LEPPIK, HEIKKI
71/2 WilliamsFIN 285
73/4 WilliamsFIN 205

LEPSA, TOMAZ
79 PaniniSticker 398

LEROUX, FRANÇOIS
97/8 PacificRegime 162
93/4 Parkhurst 412
96/7 PinnacleBeAPlayer 112
95/6 Playoff 81
90/1 ProCards 239
91/2 ProCards 215
90/1 Score 393
88/9 EDM/ActionMagazine 147
92/3 EDM
94/5 PGH 13
95/6 PGH/Foodland 6

LEROUX, FRANÇOIS
92/3 WestMich.

LEROUX, JEAN-YVES
97/8 Donruss 211
97/8 DonrussPreferred 157
97/8 Leaf 161
98/9 PacificParamount 49
97/8 PinnacleBeAPlayer 45
97/8 PinnacleInside 186
97/8 UpperDeck 249
98/9 UDChoice 52

LESCHYSHYN, CURTIS
91/2 Bowman 142
92/3 Bowman 335
93/4 Donruss 273
96/7 Donruss 48
93/4 EASports 110
93/4 FleerUltra 404
95/6 FleerUltra 132
93/4 Leaf 305
94/5 Leaf 548
96/7 Leaf 126
92/3 O-Pee-Chee 306
90/1 OPC/Topps 216
91/2 OPC/Topps 39
97/8 PacificRegime 38
90/1 Panini(QUE) 13
89/90 PaniniSticker 334
90/1 PaniniSticker 150
91/2 PaniniSticker 256
92/3 PaniniSticker 217
95/6 PaniniSticker 253
96/7 PaniniSticker 252
91/2 Parkhurst 367
93/4 Parkhurst 436
91/2 Pinnacle 258
92/3 Pinnacle 46
93/4 Pinnacle 49
94/5 Pinnacle 24
95/6 Playoff 240
94/5 POG 202
95/6 POG 80
93/4 PowerPlay 423
93/4 Premier 487
94/5 Premier 62
90/1 ProSet 251
91/2 ProSet 198
90/1 Score 92, -HotCards 44
91/2 Score(CDN) 58, (U.S) 58
92/3 Score 87
93/4 Score 42
94/5 Score 64
95/6 Score 153
96/7 Score 216
95/6 SkyBoxEmotion 39
95/6 SkyBoxImpact 38
92/3 Topps 124
91/2 ToppsStadiumClub 156
92/3 ToppsStadiumClub 413
93/4 ToppsStadiumClub 336
90/1 UpperDeck 295
91/2 UpperDeck 413
93/4 UpperDeck 133
97/8 UpperDeck 35
95/6 UDBeAPlayer 129
96/7 UDBlackDiamond 7
95/6 UDCollChoice 305
88/9 QUE
88/9 QUE/GeneralFoods
89/90 QUE
89/90 QUE/GeneralFoods
89/90 QUE/Police
90/1 QUE
90/1 QUE/PetroCanada
91/2 QUE/PetroCanada
92/3 QUE/PetroCanada
86/7 Saskatoon

LESIEUR, ARTHUR
35-40 CrownBrand 67
36-39 DiamondMatch (2),(3)

LESKA, PETR
95/6 APS 50

LESLIE, ALEX
52/3 AnonymousOHL 21

LESLIE, GLEN
85/6 London 18

LESLIE, LANCE
94/5 ThunderBay

LESLIE, LAURA
94/5 Classic W11

LESLIE, LEE J.
92/3 Classic 26
92/3 ClassicFourSport 175
90/1 SketchWHL 275
91/2 SketchWHL 243
92/3 Peoria
90/1 PrinceAlbert
91/2 PrinceAlbert

LESSARD, DAVID
91/2 SketchQMJHL 288

LESSARD, JIM
91/2 AvantGardeBC 43, 169
94/5 Dayton 6
91/2 Nainamo

LESSARD, MARIO
79/80 OPC/Topps 8, OPC 389
81/2 OPC 146, Topps(W) 98
82/3 O-Pee-Chee 156
81/2 opcSticker 238
82/3 opcSticker 236
80/1 L.A.

LESSARD, OWEN
90/1 ProCards 405
91/2 ProCards 478
92/3 Indianapolis

LESSARD, PAUL
51/2 BasDuFleuve 24

LESSARD, RICK
89/90 ProCards(IHL) 196
90/1 ProCards 605
91/2 ProCards 519
91/2 ProSet 560
91/2 UpperDeck 520
84/5 Ottawa67s
88/9 SaltLake 18

LESSARD, STÉPHANE
80/1 QuébecRamparts

LESSOR, DOUGLAS
52/3 AnonymousOHL 48

LESTER, DON
94/5 Richmond

LESUEUR, PERCY
91 C55 Reprint 16
83&87 HallOfFame 37
83 HHOF Postcard (C)
1910-11 Imperial (C56) 2
1911-12 Imperial (C55) 16

1912-13 Imperial (C57) 27
1910-11 Imperial Post 16

LESUK, BILL
72/3 OPC 245
73/4 OPC 205
79/80 O-Pee-Chee 312
76/7 opcWHA 121
71/2 TheTorontoSun
72/3 PHA/MightyMilk
77/8 WPG
79/80 WPG
74/5 WSH

LESWICK, JACK
33-35 DiamondMatch

LESWICK, TONY
45-64 BeeHives(DET), (NYR)
51/2 Parkhurst 59
52/3 Parkhurst 65
53/4 Parkhurst 43
54/5 Parkhurst 45
52 RoyalDesserts 1
54/5 Topps 45

LETANG, ALAN
91/2 SketchOHL 26
94/5 Slapshot(Sarnia) 24
91/2 Cornwall 25
95/6 Fredericton
96/7 Fredericton

LETENDRE, LUCE
97/8 GameOfHerLife
97/8 UDCollChoice 290

LETOURNEAU
27-32 LaPresse 27/8

LETOURNEAU, RAY
91/2 ProCards 263

LETOWSKI, TREVOR
97/8 Bowman 26
94/5 Slapshot(Sarnia) 13
95/6 Slapshot 341
96/7 UpperDeck"Ice" 121

LEUENBERGER, MARC
91 SemicSticker 187

LEUENBERGER, SVEN
95 PaniniWorlds 122
91 SemicSticker 180
92 SemicSticker
93 SemicSticker 115

LEVAC, FRÉDÉRIC
96/7 Rimouski

LEVASSEUR, CHRIS
87/8 Moncton

LEVASSEUR, ROB
89/90 Nashville

LÉVEILLE, NORMAND
82/3 O-Pee-Chee 13

LEVEN, JONAS
89/90 SemicElitserien 123
90/1 SemicElitserien 201
91/2 SemicElitserien 130
92/3 SemicElitserien 151

LÉVEQUE, GUY
91/2 Arena 30
91/2 Classic 36
91/2 ClassicFourSport 36, -Aut
92/3 ClassicProspects 124
93/4 ClassicProspects 163
90/1 SketchMEM 116
90/1 SketchOHL 38
91/2 SketchOHL 11
91/2 StarPics 67
91/2 UltimateDP 31, -Aut 31
92/3 UpperDeck 576
93/4 UpperDeck 246
91/2 Cornwall 14
92/3 Phoenix
93/4 Phoenix
94/5 StJohns

LEVER, DON
74/5 Loblaws
72/3 OPC 259
73/4 OPC/Topps 111
74/5 OPC/Topps 94
75/6 OPC/Topps 206, 329
76/7 OPC/Topps 53
77/8 OPC/Topps 111
78/9 OPC/Topps 86
79/80 OPC/Topps 203
80/1 OPC/Topps 124
81/2 O-Pee-Chee 45
82/3 O-Pee-Chee 141
83/4 O-Pee-Chee 224, 231
84/5 O-Pee-Chee 112, Topps 86
85/6 O-Pee-Chee 238
82/3 opcSticker 224
83/4 opcSticker 218
84/5 opcSticker 70
79 PaniniSticker 65
80/1 Pepsi Cap
82/3 Post
90/1 ProCards 293
91/2 ProCards 23
83/4 PuffySticker 7
83/4 SouhaitsRen.KeyChain
79/80 ATL
87/8 BUF/WonderBread
88/9 BUF/WonderBread
80/1 CGY
81/2 COL.R
83/4 N.J.
84/5 N.J.
72/3 VAN/RoyalBank
73/4 VAN/RoyalBank
74/5 VAN/RoyalBank
75/6 VAN/RoyalBank
76/7 VAN/RoyalBank
77/8 VAN/GingerAle
77/8 VAN/RoyalBank
78/9 VAN/RoyalBank
79/80 VAN
91/2 Rochester/Genny
91/2 Rochester/Kodak

LÉVESQUE, BEN
82/3 Kingston 25
83/4 Kingston 3

LÉVESQUE, FRANÇOIS
96/7 Rimouski

LÉVESQUE, GUILDOR
52/3 BasDuFleuve 38
51/2 LacStJean 38
51/2 LavalDairy 29

LÉVESQUE, JONATHAN
96/7 Rimouski

LÉVESQUE, MICHEL
84/5 Richelieu

LEVIE, CRAIG
82/3 O-Pee-Chee 382
83/4 MIN
85/6 MIN
81/2 WPG
82/3 WPG

LEVINS, SCOTT
93/4 Donruss 130, 466
94/5 Donruss 119
93/4 FleerUltra 326
94/5 FleerUltra 148
95/6 PaniniSticker 51
93/4 Parkhurst 80
94/5 Parkhurst 155, 292
95/6 Playoff 180
90/1 ProCards 258
91/2 ProCards 182
93/4 Score 617
93/4 UpperDeck 433, SP-56
94/5 UpperDeck 295
94/5 OTT/Bell
95/6 OTT
90/1 Moncton
91/2 Moncton

LEVINSKY, ALEX
33/4 Anonymous (V129) 9
33-43 BeeHives(CHI)
35-40 CrownBrand 70
36-39 DiamondMatch (2),(3),
36-39 DiamondMatch (4),(5),(6)
33/4 Hamilton (V288) 36
33/4 OPC (V304A) 11
94/5 Parkie(64/5)-Greats 2
33/4 WWGum (V357) 47
36/7 WWGum (V356) 61
32/3 TOR/OKeefe 3

LEVO, TAPIO
91/2 Jyvas-Hyva 71
80/1 Mallasjuoma 208
79 PaniniSticker 168
83/4 PuffySticker 10
82 SemicSticker 154
82 Skopbank
78/9 SM-Liiga 8, 225
83/4 SouhaitsRen.KeyChain
77-80 Sportscaster 78-1849
82 Valio
81/2 COL.R

LEVONEN, JARI
92/3 Jyvas-Hyva 204
93/4 Jyvas-Hyva 359
93/4 Sisu 221
94/5 Sisu 15, -Horoscope 9
95/6 Sisu 156
96/7 Sisu 160
95/6 SisuLimited 26

LEVONEN, JARNO
93/4 Sisu 222
95/6 Sisu 277
96/7 Sisu 80

LEVONEN, JARKKO
72/3 WilliamsFIN 251
73/4 WilliamsFIN 250

LEVONEN, JYRKI
78/9 SM-Liiga 226

LEVONEN, RAULI
80/1 Mallasjuoma 212
78/9 SM-Liiga 235

LEVY, JEFF
92/3 ClassicProspects 52
93/4 Dayton 2
94/5 Huntington 16

LEWICKI, DANNY
45-64 BeeHives(NYR), (TOR)
51/2 Parkhurst 71
93/4 Parkie(56/7) 98
45-54 QuakerOats
54/5 Topps 23
57/8 Topps 61
58/9 Topps 6
54-67 TorontoStar V5,n5
56-66 TorontoStar 58/9

LEWIS, BARRY
96/7 DEL 23

LEWIS, BOB
91/2 AvantGardeBCJHL 94

LEWIS, DAVE
74/5 Loblaws
74/5 OPC 324
75/6 OPC/Topps 108
76/7 OPC/Topps 221
77/8 OPC/Topps 116
78/9 OPC/Topps 162
79/80 OPC/Topps 44
80/1 OPC/Topps 196
82/3 O-Pee-Chee 157
83/4 O-Pee-Chee 158
84/5 OPC 113, Topps 87
85/6 OPC/Topps 66
86/7 OPC/Topps 85
87/8 OPC/Topps 37
85/6 opcSticker 59/185
86/7 opcSticker 197/66
87/8 PaniniSticker 242
83/4 SouhaitsRen.KeyChain
86/7 DET/Caesars
89/90 DET/Caesars
80/1 L.A.
83/4 N.J.
84/5 N.J.
79/80 NYI

LEWIS, HERBERT A.
33-43 BeeHives(DET)
34/5 SweetCaporal
35/6 Triumph
36/7 WWGum (V356) 64

LEWIS, RANDY
90/1 Mich.Tech
91/2 Mich.Tech (x2)

LEY, RICK
70/1 DadsCookies
70/1 EddieSargent 198
71/2 EddieSargent 195
70/1 Esso Stamp
69/70 O-Pee-Chee 183
70/1 OPC/Topps 108
71/2 OPC/Topps 194
79/80 O-Pee-Chee 314
80/1 OPC/Topps 198
81/2 opcSticker 64
75/6 opcWHA 14
76/7 opcWHA 101
90/1 ProSet 666
73/4 QuakerOats 25
71/2 TheTorontoSun
72/3 NewEngland
68/9 TOR
69/70 TOR
70/1 TOR
71/2 TOR

LEYTE, ARTHUR
51/2 BasDuFleuve 29
51/2 LavalDairy 6

LEYTH, COOPER
52/3 StLawrence 52

L'HEUREUX, CONRAD
52/3 BasDuFleuve 59
51/2 LacStJean 28

L'HEUREUX, WILF
23/4 PaulinsCandy 17

LIAPKIN, YURI
74 Hellas 47
72 Panda
72 SemicSticker 14
74 SemicSticker 32
71/2 Soviet Stars
73/4 Soviet Stars 22
74/5 Soviet Stars 7
91/2 Trends(72) 83
71/2 WilliamsFIN 6
73/4 WilliamsFIN 7

LIBA, IGOR
82 SemicSticker 98

LIBETT, NICK
70/1 EddieSargent 60
71/2 EddieSargent 53
72/3 EddieSargent 75
70/1 Esso Stamp
82? JDMcCarthy
74/5 Loblaws
69/70 O-Pee-Chee 162
70/1 OPC 158
71/2 OPC/Topps 140
72/3 OPC 45, Topps 67
73/4 OPC/Topps 49
74/5 OPC/Topps 193
75/6 OPC/Topps 13
76/7 OPC/Topps 171
77/8 OPC/Topps 103
78/9 OPC/Topps 251
79/80 OPC/Topps 198
68/9 ShirriffCoin DET16
71/2 TheTorontoSun

LICARI, TONY
30s? ABC ChewingGum 76

LICHNOVSKY, MARCEL
94/5 DEL 399
95/6 DEL 414

LIDDINGTON, BOB
75/6 opcWHA 105
76/7 Phoenix
70/1 TOR

LIDGREN, JOAKIM
95/6 udElite 100
97/8 udSwedish 106

LIDSTER, DOUG
90/1 Bowman 56
91/2 Bowman 317
92/3 Bowman 267
93/4 EASports 140
92/3 FleerUltra 221
93/4 FleerUltra 374
86/7 Kraft Sports 65
93/4 Leaf 365
94/5 Leaf 353
85/6 O-Pee-Chee 241
86/7 OPC/Topps 32
87/8 O-Pee-Chee 256
88/9 O-Pee-Chee 228
89/90 O-Pee-Chee 284
90/1 OPC/Topps 207
91/2 OPC/Topps 179
92/3 O-Pee-Chee 51
86/7 opcSticker 102/231
87/8 opcSticker 191
88/9 opcSticker 63
89/90 opcSticker 69 /209
97/8 PacificRegime 130
90/1 Panini(VAN) 12
87/8 PaniniSticker 341
88/9 PaniniSticker 135
90/1 PaniniSticker 296
91/2 PaniniSticker 40
92/3 PaniniSticker 37
93/4 PaniniSticker 176
91/2 Parkhurst 184
93/4 Parkhurst 403
95/6 Parkhurst 412
91/2 Pinnacle 189
92/3 Pinnacle 147
93/4 Pinnacle 355
94/5 Pinnacle 409
97/8 PinnacleBeAPlayer 208
93/4 Premier 315
90/1 ProSet 298
91/2 ProSet 247
92/3 ProSet 199
90/1 Score 73
91/2 Score(CDN) 215, (U.S) 215
92/3 Score 124
93/4 Score 65, 524
92/3 Topps 403
91/2 ToppsStadiumClub 72
92/3 ToppsStadiumClub 404
93/4 ToppsStadiumClub 406
94/5 ToppsStadiumClub 122
90/1 UpperDeck 60
91/2 UpperDeck 290
94/5 UpperDeck 400
95/6 UpperDeck 401
94/5 UDBeAPlayer-Aut. 23
84/5 VAN
85/6 VAN
86/7 VAN
87/8 VAN/Shell
88/9 VAN/Mohawk
89/90 VAN
90/1 VAN/Mohawk
90/1 VAN/Molson
91/2 VAN
92/3 VAN/RoadTrip

LIDSTRÖM, NICKLAS
92/3 Bowman 305
93/4 Donruss 102
94/5 Donruss 194
95/6 Donruss 83
96/7 Donruss 119
95/6 DonrussElite 2
97/8 DonrussPriority 43
94/5 ElitSet 285, -GuestSpec 4
97/8 EssoOlympic 45
96/7 Flair 28
94/5 Fleer 62
95/6 FleerMetal 48
96/7 FleerNHLPicks 34
92/3 FleerUltra 51, -Imports 13
92/3 FU-UltraRookie 7
93/4 FleerUltra 220
94/5 FleerUltra 62
96/7 FU 53, -Power 12, -Blue 8
95/6 Hoyle'WEST 4 (Diamonds)
93/4 Leaf 89
94/5 Leaf 141
95/6 Leaf 228
96/7 Leaf 75
97/8 Limited 146
96/7 MetalUniverse 48
97/8 Omega 83, -GameFace 6
92/3 O-Pee-Chee 369
91/2 opcPremier 117, 163
98/9 Pacific 5
97/8 PacificCC 78
97/8 PacificCrownRoyale 47
97/8 PacificInvincible 49
97/8 PacificParamount 67
98/9 PacificParamount 78
97/8 PacificRevolution 47
92/3 PaniniSticker 274, 298, J
93/4 PaniniSticker 253
94/5 PaniniSticker 216
95/6 PaniniSticker 186
96/7 PaniniSticker 185
97/8 PaniniSticker 146
91/2 Parkhurst 37, 445
92/3 Parkhurst 42, 239, 451
93/4 Parkhurst 62
94/5 Parkhurst 61
95/6 Parkhurst 64, 252, PP24
94/5 ParkieSE ES4
95/6 Parkie-InterAS 2
91/2 Pinnacle 320
92/3 Pinnacle 8, -Team2000 3
93/4 Pinnacle 98, -Tm2001 6
94/5 Pinnacle 66, WE16
95/6 Pinnacle 180
96/7 Pinnacle 28
97/8 PinnacleCertified 75
96/7 PinnacleFANtasy 12
97/8 PinnacleInside 91
95/6 Playoff 146
94/5 POG 95
95/6 POG 101
97/8 Post
93/4 PowerPlay 74
93/4 Premier 9
94/5 Premier 52
95/6 ProMagnet 103
91/2 ProSet 531, 610
92/3 ProSet 42
91/2 PSPlatinum 253
92/3 ProSet-TeamLeader 4
91/2 Score(CDN) 621, (U.S) 71T
92/3 Score 391, 502, -Young 11
93/4 Score 158
94/5 Score 119
95/6 Score 51
96/7 Score 176
97/8 Score 182
97/8 Score(DET) 4
94/5 Select 134
95 Semic 56
89/90 SemicElitserien 247
90/1 SemicElitserien 152
91/2 SemicElitser. 255, 322, 341
91 SemicSticker 31
92 SemicSticker 56
93 SemicSticker 23
95/6 SkyBoxEmotion 56
95/6 SkyBoxImpact 55
96/7 SkyBoxImpact 37,-Blade 13
95/6 SP 42
96/7 SP 52
97/8 SPAuthentic 53, S18
98/9 SPx"Finite" 33, 112
96/7 Summit 112
95/6 SuperSticker 41
96/7 TeamOut
92/3 Topps 9, 440
95/6 Topps 107
98/9 Topps 203, B6, M15
95/6 ToppsFinest 69
92/3 T.StadiumClub 43, 253
93/4 T.StadiumClub 196, 429
94/5 ToppsStadiumClub 228
95/6 ToppsStadiumClub 129
95/6 TSC-MembersOnly 19
91/2 UpperDeck 26, 584, 587
92/3 UD 178, 363, AR4, AR7
92/3 UD E9, ERT2, W4
93/4 UpperDeck 150
94/5 UpperDeck 112, SP114
95/6 UD 34, AS7, H36, SE29
96/7 UpperDeck 56, X22
97/8 UD 267, SG45, T14C
94/5 UDBeAPlayer-Aut. 162
96/7 UDBlackDiamond 50
97/8 UDBlckDiamond 119,PC19
98/9 UDChoice 77, 233
95/6 UDCollChoice 228
96/7 UDCollChoice 86, UD33
97/8 UDCollChoice 81, SQ5
95/6 udElite 239
97/8 UpperDeckIce 5, L10C
96 Wien 45, NS5
97/8 Zenith 58, Z55
91/2 DET/Caesars
96/7 DET/PhotoPucks

LIEBSCH, ULRICH
95/6 DEL 69
91 SemicSticker 168

LIEN, SVEN
79 PaniniSticker 297

LIEVERS, BRETT
95/6 FutureLegends 32

LIGHTBODY, QUADE
93/4 Slapshot(Peterborough) 25
94/5 Slapshot(Detroit) 3
94/5 Slapshot(MEM) 77
95/6 Slapshot 9

LIIMATAINEN, PETRI
96/7 DEL 77
94/5 ElitSet 19
89/90 SemicElitserien 6
90/1 SemicElitserien 80
91/2 SemicElitserien 5
92/3 SemicElitserien 32

LILIUS, JARMO
80/1 Mallasjuoma 35
72/3 WilliamsFIN 310

LILJA, ANDRES
95/6 ElitSet 259

LILJA, KARL-ERIK
89/90 SemicElitserien 58

LILJA, TOBIAS
97/8 udSwedish 183

LILJA, TOMAS
94/5 ElitSet 227
89/90 SemicElitserien 155
90/1 SemicElitserien 230
91/2 SemicElitserien 155
92/3 SemicElitserien 184

LILJEBJORN, ÅKE
96/7 DEL 270
97/8 udSwedish 100

LILLEY, JOHN
94/5 Classic-Autograph
94/5 Donruss 260
94/5 Fleer 6
93/4 FleerUltra 490
94/5 FleerUltra 251
94/5 Leaf 178
95 PaniniWorlds 225
94/5 Parkhurst 8
93/4 PowerPlay 510
93/4 Premier-TeamUSA 8
94/5 Premier 499
94/5 Score 228
94/5 Select 191
94 Semic 130
95 Semic 111
93/4 TSC-TeamUSA 14
94/5 ToppsStadiumClub 139
91/2 UD'CzechWJC 70
94/5 UpperDeck 165
94/5 ANA/Carl'sJr 17

LILLEY, LES
52/3 AnonymousOHL 140

LILLIE, JEFF
93/4 Slapshot(Kitchener) 25

LILLIE, SHAWN
91/2 Knoxville

LILLJEBJORN, AKE
94/5 ElitSet 102, -CleanSweep 6
89/90 SemicElitserien 2
90/1 SemicElitserien 27
91/2 SemicElitserien 277
92/3 SemicElitserien 150

LILYHOLM, LEONARD
72 SemicSticker 125
72/3 Minnesota

LIMATAINEN, PETRI
95/6 DEL 226

LIMOGES, RÉNALD
51/2 BasDuFleuve 27
52/3 BasDuFleuve 55

LIND, JUHA
97/8 DonrussPreferred 164
97/8 Leaf 160
97/8 Omega 72
98/9 Pacific 180
98/9 PacificParamount 67
97/8 Pinnacle 2
97/8 Score 64
95 Semic 235
93/4 Sisu 24
94/5 Sisu 49, 150, -Horoscope 1
95/6 Sisu 50
96/7 Sisu 186
95/6 SisuLimited-Gallery 8
97/8 UpperDeck 261
98/9 UDChoice 64

LIND, MATS
74 Hellas 28
72/3 WilliamsFIN 51

LIND, MIKAEL
95/6 ElitSet 171

LINDBERG, BOB
72 SemicSticker 136

LINDBERG, CHRIS
90/1 CanadaNats
91/2 CanadaNats
92 CanadaWinterOlympics 190
94/5 DEL 235
95/6 DEL 232
96/7 DEL 83
92/3 FleerUltra 269
93/4 FleerUltra 62, 405
92/3 opcPremier 4
91/2 Parkhurst 251
92/3 Parkhurst 27
93/4 Parkhurst 440
93/4 Premier 76
89/90 ProCards(AHL) 290
92/3 Score 485, -CndOlympic 6
92/3 Topps 320
92/3 ToppsStadiumClub 407
93/4 ToppsStadiumClub 84
92/3 UpperDeck 97
93/4 UpperDeck 196
92/3 CGY/IGA 21

LINDBERG, HANNU
66/7 Champion 111
70/1 Kuvajulkaisut 30, 282
72 Panda
72 SemicSticker 57
71/2 WilliamsFIN 49

LINDBERG, JAN
73/4 WilliamsFIN 114

LINDBERG, JARI
82 SemicSticker 39

LINDBERG, LASSE
80/1 Mallasjuoma 126

LINDBERG, MATS
94/5 ElitSet 60
95/6 ElitSet 157
89/90 SemicElitserien 23
90/1 SemicElitserien 93
91/2 SemicElitserien 19
92/3 SemicElitserien 40
95/6 udElite 14
97/8 udSwedish 13

LINDBERG, PELLE
95 Globe 65
83/4 O-Pee-Chee 268
85/6 OPC/Topps 110, -AS 6
83/4 opcSticker 197
85/6 opcSticker 193/69, 91/224
83/4 PHA

LINDBERG, TORBJORN
94/5 ElitSet 125
95/6 ElitSet 77
89/90 SemicElitserien 151
90/1 SemicElitserien 229
91/2 SemicElitserien 159
92/3 SemicElitserien 180
95/6 udElite 116

LINDBLOM, CLAES
94/5 ElitSet 83
95/6 ElitSet 130
89/90 SemicElitserien 256
90/1 SemicElitserien 164
91/2 SemicElitserien 269
92/3 SemicElitserien 295
95/6 udElite 199

LINDBLOM, GÖRAN
82 SemicSticker 4

LINDBOM, JOHAN
94/5 ElitSet 235
95/6 ElitSet 55
95/6 udElite 88, NA12

LINDEGREN, PENTTI
65/6 Hellas 140

LINDEN, BJORN
95/6 ElitSet 288

LINDEN, JAMIE
93/4 ClassicProspects 134
95/6 Score 313, 'Promo 313
90/1 SketchWHL 283
91/2 SketchWHL 24
92/3 UpperDeck 38
89/90 Portland
90/1 PrinceAlbert

LINDEN, TREVOR
95/6 Aces 5 (Hearts)
96/7 Aces 5 (Spades)
97/8 Aces 3 (Clubs)
90/1 Bowman 61
91/2 Bowman 327
92/3 Bowman 210, 261
95/6 Bowman 46
93/4 Donruss 354
94/5 Donruss 181
95/6 Donruss 385
96/7 Donruss 102,-Dom 7,-Hit 11
97/8 Donruss 86
96/7 DonrussCanadianIce 52
97/8 D.CdnIce 32, -Charity
97/8 D.CdnIce-National 16
95/6 DonrussElite 45
96/7 DonrussElite 68
97/8 DonrussElite 89
97/8 DonrussPreferred 89
97/8 DonrussPriority 111
97/8 DonrussStudio 101
96/7 Duracell DC11, JB11
97/8 EssoOlympic 8
94/5 Flair 191
96/7 Flair 95
94/5 Fleer 225
96/7 Fleer 112
95/6 FleerMetal 151
92/3 FleerUltra 222
93/4 FleerUltra 109
94/5 FleerUltra 226
95/6 FleerUltra 169, -Crease 7
96/7 FleerUltra 168
96/7 F.Picks-Fab 27, -Captain 9
91/2 Gillette 5
93/4 HockeyWit 106
95/6 Hoyle'WEST 5 (Diamond)
92/3 HumptyDumpty (2)
97/8 KatchMedallion 146
91/2 Kelloggs 20
89/90 Kraft 42
90/1 Kraft 30
91/2 Kraft 30
92/3 Kraft-AllStar
93/4 Kraft-Captain, -Recipe
94/5 Kraft-Sharpshooter
95/6 Kraft-Ticket
96/7 Kraft-Disk
97/8 Kraft -RoadToNagano
93/4 Leaf 193
94/5 Leaf 527
95/6 Leaf 161
96/7 Leaf 187, -Leather 12
97/8 Leaf 39, -Dayln 188-197
94/5 LeafLimited 112
95/6 LeafLimited 42
96/7 LeafLimited 74, -Stubble 18
96/7 LeafPreferred 59, -Steel 24
97/8 Limited 19
96/7 Maggers 158
92/3 McDonalds McD-09
97/8 McDonalds McD22
97/8 McDonalds -Medallions
96/7 MetalUniverse 157
97/8 Omega 230
89/90 OPC/Topps 89, OPC 308
90/1 OPC/Topps 225
91/2 OPC/Topps 364, T-TL 17
92/3 O-Pee-Chee 120
91/2 opcPremier 77
89/90 opcSticker 61, 40/184
89/90 opcStickFS 19
98/9 Pacific 32, -GoldCrown 21
97/8 PacificCrown 154,-Slap 11B
97/8 PacificCrownRoyale 135
97/8 PacificDynagon! 127
97/8 PcfcD-BstKpt 110,-Tand 59
97/8 PacificInvincible 142
97/8 PacificParamount 188
98/9 PacificParamount 144
97/8 PacificRevolution 141
90/1 Panini(VAN) 13, H
89/90 PaniniSticker 148
90/1 PaniniSticker 299
91/2 PaniniSticker 36
92/3 PaniniSticker 28
93/4 PaniniSticker 172
94/5 PaniniSticker 147
95/6 PaniniSticker 288
96/7 PaniniSticker 290
97/9 PaniniSticker 242
91/2 Parkhurst 179
92/3 Parkhurst 190
93/4 Parkhurst 215
94/5 Parkhurst 241
95/6 Parkhurst 209, PP48
94/5 ParkieSE seV5
91/2 Pinnacle 2
92/3 Pinnacle 47, -Tm2000 24
93/4 Pinnacle 43, CA24
93/4 Pinnacle-Tm2001 16
94/5 Pinnacle 8, NL18
96/7 Pinnacle 111
97/8 Pinnacle 106
97/8 PinnacleBeAPlayer 9
97/8 PinnacleBeeHive 40
97/8 PinnacleCertified 104
97/8 PinnacleInside 150
95/6 PinnacleZenith 87, -Gifted 6
96/7 PinnacleZenith 95
95/6 Playoff 208
94/5 POG 343
95/6 POG 271
93/4 PowerPlay 251
93/4 Premier 225
94/5 Premier 75
95/6 ProMagnet 23
90/1 ProSet 299
91/2 ProSet 236, 294, 586
92/3 ProSet 197, -TeamLdr 12
91/2 PSPlatinum 124
90/1 Score 32,-Hot 16,-Young 19
91/2 Score(CDN) 8, 369
91/2 Score(U.S) 8, 339
91/2 Score-YoungStar 11
92/3 Score 305, 438,-Young 16
93/4 Score 117
95/6 Score 208
96/7 Score 173, -CheckIt 10
97/8 Score 144
97/8 Score(VAN) 4
92/3 SeasonsPatch 30
94/5 Select 11
95/6 SelectCert. 87, -Double 11
96/7 SelectCertified 42
95/6 SkyBoxEmotion 180
95/6 SkyBoxImpact 169
96/7 SkyBoxImpact 133
96/7 SB'7Eleven
94/5 SP 122
95/6 SP 150
97/8 SPAuthentic 160
98/9 SPx"Finite" 50
95/6 Summit 102
96/7 Summit 134
95/6 SuperSticker 125
92/3 Topps 499
95/6 Topps 12, 125, HGC12
98/9 Topps 117
95/6 ToppsFinest 144
96/7 ToppsNHLPicks 45
91/2 ToppsStadiumClub 84
92/3 ToppsStadiumClub 80
93/4 ToppsStadiumClub 357
95/6 ToppsStadiumClub 160
97/8 ToppsSticker 5
95/6 ToppsSuperSkills 33
90/1 UpperDeck 256, 480
91/2 UpperDeck 97, 174, 628
92/3 UD 38, 158, 383, WG14
93/4 UpperDeck 383, SP-164
94/5 UpperDeck 319, SP83
95/6 UpperDeck 33, SE82
96/7 UpperDeck 169, P16, X2
97/8 UpperDeck 169, T17B
93/4 UDBeAPlayer-Roots 1
94/5 UDBeAPlayer R53, R139
95/6 UDBeAPlayer 41
96/7 UDBlackDiamond 115
98/9 UDChoice 122
95/6 UDCollChoice 122
96/7 UDCollChoice 268, 333
97/8 UDCollChoice 259
96/7 UpperDeck"Ice" 70
97/8 ValuNet
97/8 Zenith 73
88/9 VAN/Mohawk
89/90 VAN
90/1 VAN/Mohawk
90/1 VAN/Molson
91/2 VAN, VAN/Molson
92/3 VAN/RoadTrip
93/4 VAN/Coins
94/5 VAN
95/6 VAN/Building 16
96/7 VAN/IGA

LINDER, ENGELBERT
95 PaniniWorlds 261

LINDFORS, FREDDY
91/2 SemicElitserien 309
92/3 SemicElitserien 330

LINDFORS, SAKARI
91/2 Jyvas-Hyva 1
92/3 Jyvas-Hyva 2
93/4 Jyvas-Hyva 14
89 SemicSticker 29
91 SemicSticker 3
92 SemicSticker 4
93 SemicSticker 46
93/4 Sisu 83
94/5 Sisu 35, -Nolla 10
95/6 Sisu 202, -GhostGoal 1
96/7 Sisu 2, -Mighty 8
95/6 SisuLimited 37, -Gallery 9
96 Wien 35

LINDGREN, JARI
80/1 Mallasjuoma 171
78/9 SM-Liiga 194

LINDGREN, JOAKIM
95/6 ElitSet 241

LINDGREN, LARS
80/1 OPC/Topps 177
82/3 O-Pee-Chee 349
83/4 O-Pee-Chee 354
79 PaniniSticker 191
80/1 Pepsi Cap
82/3 Post
82 SemicSticker 144
83/4 MIN
79/80 VAN
79/80 VAN/RoyalBank
80/1 VAN
80/1 VAN/Silverwood
81/2 VAN/Silverwood
82/3 VAN

LINDGREN, MATS
93/4 Classic 139
94/5 Classic 108, T23
93/4 ClassicFourSport 198
94/5 ElitSet 63, -Chase
96/7 Flair 109
95 Globe 63
98/9 Pacific 212
97/8 PacificCrown 190
97/8 PaniniSticker 213
95 PaniniWorlds 153
93/4 Parkhurst 511, 534
97/8 PinnacleBeAPlayer 154
91/2 SemicElitserien 328
93/4 UpperDeck 570
97/8 UpperDeck 68
96/7 EDM
97/8 EDM

LINDGREN, TERRY
93/4 RedDeer
95/6 RedDeer

LINDGREN, TORY
89/90 SemicElitserien 244
90/1 SemicElitserien 157
91/2 SemicElitserien 261

LINDH, FREDRIK
94/5 ElitSet 201
92/3 SemicElitserien 355

LINDH, MATS
72 Hellas 35
74 SemicSticker 25

LINDH, PATRIK
89/90 SemicElitserien 238

LINDHOLM, MIKAEL
95/6 ElitSet 248
90/1 ProCards 351
91/2 SemicElitserien 40
92/3 SemicElitserien 73
95/6 udElite 124
89/90 L.A./Smokeys 3

LINDHOLM, ULF
65/6 Hellas 139

LINDMAN, MIKAEL
94/5 ElitSet 37
95/6 ElitSet 178
89/90 SemicElitserien 33
90/1 SemicElitserien 180
91/2 SemicElitserien 34
92/3 SemicElitserien 54
95/6 udElite 21

LINDMARK, ORJAN
94/5 ElitSet 124
95/6 ElitSet 64
89/90 SemicElitserien 130
90/1 SemicElitserien 208
91/2 SemicElitserien 136
92/3 SemicElitserien 159
95/6 udElite 98

LINDMARK, PETER
94/5 ElitSet 75, -CleanSweep 1
95/6 ElitSet 257, -Champs 4
90/1 SemicElitserien 125
91/2 SemicElitserien 176, 337
92/3 SemicElitserien 199
82 SemicSticker 1
89 SemicSticker 3
91 SemicSticker 27

LINDQVIST, FREDRIK
91/2 SemicElitserien 72
91/2 Classic 44
91/2 ClassicFourSport 44, -Aut
94/5 ElitSet 86
95/6 ElitSet 189, -Goldies 3
92/3 SemicElitserien 97
91/2 UltimateDP 39, -Aut 39
95/6 udElite NA7
97/8 udSwedish 45

LINDROOS, JARI
91/2 Jyvas-Hyva 26
92/3 Jyvas-Hyva 74
93/4 Jyvas-Hyva 137
93/4 Sisu 154
94/5 Sisu 25
95/6 Sisu 186, 252
96/7 Sisu 51, -Mighty 9
95/6 SisuLimited 50

LINDROS, BRETT
93/4 CanadaNats
93/4 ClassicProspects 204,LP17
95/6 Donruss 174
94/5 Flair 104
94/5 Fleer 125, -Rookie 7
93/4 FleerUltra 466
94/5 FleerUltra 327, -Prospect 5
95/6 FleerUltra 95, 267
94/5 Leaf 445, -Phenoms 2
95/6 Leaf 15
94/5 LeafLimited 50
95/6 LeafLimited 86
94/5 McDonalds McD34
95/6 McDonalds McD33
95/6 PaniniSticker 94
95/6 Parkhurst 133
94/5 ParkieSE 109, seV36
94/5 Pinnacle 257, 478, RTP11
95/6 Pinnacle -FullContact 7
95/6 PinnacleZenith 84
95/6 Playoff 63, 171
95/6 POG 171
93/4 PowerPlay 486
93/4 Premier-TeamCanada 1
94/5 Premier 384, 514
95/6 ProMagnet 55
94/5 Score CT24, TR3
95/6 Score 14, -CheckIt 3
94/5 Select 178, YE12
95/6 SelectCertified 61
94 Semic 106
95 Semic 101
95/6 SkyBoxEmotion 105
95/6 SkyBoxImpact 102, -Fox 12
93/4 Slapshot(Kingston) 23
94/5 SP 70, -Premier 10
95/6 Summit 104
95/6 Topps 41
94/5 ToppsFinest 9,-BBest(R) 10
95/6 ToppsStadiumClub 108
94/5 UD 240,537,551,C1,SP136
95/6 UD 82, 257, SE54
94/5 UDBeAPlayer R153
95/6 UDCollChoice 129

LINDROS, ERIC
95/6 Aces A (Hearts)
96/7 Aces K (Spades)
97/8 Aces 7 (Hearts)
92/3 Bowman 442
95/6 Bowman 71, BB3
91/2 Classic 1, -Promo
91/2 ClasicFourSport 1
95/6 CoolTrade 9
96/7 CorinthianHeadliners
97/8 CorinthianHeadliners
93/4 Donruss 242, Q, -IceKing 9
93/4 D-EliteSeries 4
94/5 Donruss 137, -Dominator 1
94/5 D-Elite 7, -IceMasters 6
95/6 Donruss 1, -Dominators 1
95/6 D-Marksmen 3, -Pointer 13
96/7 Donruss 137, -Dominator 5
96/7 D-HitList P1, -TopShelf 9
97/8 Donruss 3,-Line 8,-Elite 3
96/7 D.CdnIce 7, -OCanada 11
97/8 D.CdnIce 3,-Ntl 8,-Scrap 32
95/6 DonrussElite 88, 110
95/6 DE-Cutting 1, -Lindros 1-7
96/7 D.Elite 7, 149, -Status 8
96/7 DE-Hart 1, -Lindros 1-6
97/8 DE 10, 119, -BackToFut 1
97/8 D.Elite-Crafts 2,-Primnum 4
97/8 DonrussPreferred 5, 180
97/8 D.Pref-LineOf 2A,-PreMet 7
97/8 D.Pref-Tins 1,21,-WTin 3,10
97/8 DonrussPriority 2, 188
97/8 D.Prio -DirDep 15,-OpDay 2
97/8 D.Prio-Postcard 8,-Stamp 8
97/8 D.Studio 3, 108,-HardHat 2
97/8 D.Studio-Portr 3,-Silhout 2
96/7 Duracell DC6
93/4 EASports 99
97/8 EssoOlympic 6
97/8 FaxPaxWorldOfSport
94/5 Flair 129,-Cntre 7,-ScorP 6
96/7 Flair 70,-Hot 8,-Now 3
94/5 Fleer 157, -Headliner 6
96/7 Fleer 82, -ArtRoss 14
96/7 Fleer-PearsonAward 8
95/6 FleerMetal 112, -Warrior 7
95/6 FM-MetalWinners 4
96/7 FleerNHLPicks 4, -Fab 28
96/7 F.Picks-Captain 1,-Dream 1
92/3 FleerUltra 157
93/4 FleerUltra 161,249,-Pivots 5
94/5 F.Ultra 345, -AS 3,-Pivot 6
94/5 FU--Scoring 6,-UltraPowr 5
95/6 FU 119, 392,-Red 6,-Pivt 4
95/6 FU-Crease 8,-Ultraview 7
96/7 FU 126,-Clear 6,-MrMom 7
95 Globe 88, 262-64
96/7 Got-UmHockeyGreatsCoin
93/4 HockeyWit 88
95/6 Hoyle'EAST A (Hearts)
94/5 Incomnet
97/8 KatchMedallion 107, 158
93/4 KennerSLU
94/5 KennerSLU
96/7 KennerSLU
97/8 KennerSLU, -1on1
94 Koululainen
93/4 KraftDinner, -Cutout
94/5 Kraft-Sharpshooter
95/6 KraftDinner, -Disk, -Trophy
96/7 KraftDinner, -Disk, -Flex
97/8 Kraft -CdnPro,-Rd toNagan
97/8 Kraft -Sticker, -WorldBest
93/4 Leaf 233, -GoldRook 3
93/4 L-HatTrick 7, -StudioSig 10
94/5 Leaf 415, -GoldStar 11
94/5 L-Limited 17, -FireOnIce 6
95/6 Leaf 82, -FireOnIce 2
95/6 L-Gold 4, -RoadToThe 4
96/7 Leaf 148, 240
96/7 L-FireOnIce 8, -Leather 10
96/7 L-Sweaters 3, -BestOf 3
97/8 Leaf 1, 168, -BannerSeas 2
97/8 Leaf -Fire 2, -Lindros 5-Jan
94/5 LeafLimited 58, -Gold 4
95/6 LeafLimited 99, -Stars 2
96/7 LL 47, -Stubble 2,-Bash 1
96/7 LeafPreferred 117,-Steel 18
96/7 LeafPreferred-Promo 77
96/7 LP-SteelPower 12,-Vanity 7
97/8 Limited 30, 50, 183
97/8 Limited -fabric 37, 55
96/7 Maggers 111
94/5 McDonalds McD9
95/6 McDonalds McD2
96/7 McDonalds McD25
97/8 McDonalds McD8, F4
97/8 McDonalds -Medallions
96/7 MetalUniv. 114, -Cool 7
96/7 MU-LethalWeapons 12
92 NationalGame 21
97/8 Omega 168,248,-GmFa 13
97/8 Omega -Silk 9,-StickHan 16
92/3 opcPrmr 102, -TopRook 1
98/9 Pacific 88,-Cram 8,-DynI 15
98/9 Pacific-GoldC 25,-TmCL 19
97/8 PacificCrown 88, -Supial 15
97/8 PCC-Cramers 9, -Gold 17
97/8 PCC-Slap 6B, -TeamCL 18
97/8 PacificCrownRoyale 99
97/8 PCR -Blades 16, -Cramer 8
97/8 PCR -HatTrck 13, -Lamp 14
97/8 PacificDynagon! 91, 141
97/8 PcfcD-BstKpt 72,-Dyn 11A
97/8 PcfcD-Kings 8,-Tandm 1,20
97/8 PacificInv. 102, -Feature 25
97/8 PcfcInv.-Attack 18, -Off 14
97/8 PcfcParamnt 134,-CdnG 11
97/8 PcfcP-BigN 15,-Photoen 15
98/9 PcfcP 177, -HOFBound 8
98/9 PcfcP-SpecD 14, -TmCL 19
97/8 PacificRegime 145, 219
97/8 PcfcRevolutn 103,-ASG 16
97/8 PcfcRev -Icon 8, -TmCL 18
92/3 PaniniSticker P
93/4 PaniniSticker 144, E
94/5 PaniniSticker 38
95/6 PaniniSticker 113, 146
96/7 PaniniSticker 114
97/8 PaniniSticker 92
95 PaniniWorlds 278
92/3 Parkhurst 128, CP6
93/4 PH 236,416,D15,E1,F3,G3
94/5 Parkhurst 301, V69, C17
95/6 Parkie 154, PP1, PP10
95/6 Parkie-Crown(1) 1, (2) 11
95/6 Parkie-Trophy 1
94/5 ParkieSE 131
91/2 Pinnacle 365
92/3 Pinnacle 88, 236,-TeamP 5
92/3 Pinnacle-Team2000 1
93/4 Pinnacle 1, -TeamP 11
93/4 Pinnacle-Team2001 1
94/5 Pinnacle 1, BR16, GR16
94/5 Pinnacle TP8, WE14
95/6 Pinnacle 9,-Clear 4,-Roar 1
96/7 Pinnacle 107, -TeamP 3
96/7 Pinn-ByTheNumbers 14
97/8 Pinnacle 48, -TeamP 5
96/7 PinnacleBeAPlayer LTH7B
96/7 P.BAP-Bisct 3,-Lindros 1,2
97/8 P.BAP 1,-OneT 3,-Take 10
97/8 P.BeeHive 1,-TeamBH 8
97/8 P.Certified 31, -Team 8
97/8 Pinnacle-EPIX 13
97/8 P.Inside 4,-Can 12,-Track 3
95/6 PinnacleFANtasy 27
96/7 PinnacleFANtasy 3
92/3 PinnacleLindros Set 1-30
96/7 PinnacleMint 3
97/8 PinnacleMint 1, -Minterntl 1
95/6 PinnacleZenith 6, -ZTeam 7
96/7 PinnZenith 61, -ZTeam 1
96/7 PinnZenith-Assailants 8
97/8 PlaymateProZone
95/6 Playoff 76, 182, 294
96/7 Playoff 439
94/5 POG 358
95/6 POG 201, 09
94/5 Post
96/7 Post
97/8 Post 1, F1
93/4 PowerPlay 183, -Second 5
93/4 PP-Gamebreaker 6
93/4 Premier 121, 310, -Finest 3
93/4 Prmr-Black(OPC) 12,(T) 13
94/5 Premier 241, 400, -GoTo 10
94/5 Prmr-Finest(Topps) 12
95/6 ProMagnet 47
92/3 ProSet 236
90/1 Score 440, B1-B5, 88T
90/1 Score-YoungStar 40
91/2 Score(CDN) 329-30,384-85
91/2 Score(U.S) 354-56, 88T
91/2 S-HotCard 1, -Young 30
92/3 Score 432, 550
92/3 S-Young 1,-CndOlympic 1
93/4 Score 1, -DreamTeam 12

93/4 S-Franch.15, (CDN) DD1
94/5 Score 1, DT19, NP12
94/5 Score Cl1, TF17
95/6 Score 150, -DreamTeam 3
95/6 S-CheckIt 1, -Lamplight 15
96/7 Score 7, -Check 1,-Dream 1
97/8 Score 88, 265, -CheckIt 1
97/8 Score(PHA) 3
92/3 SeasonsPatch 38
93/4 SeasonsPatch 10
94/5 Select 100, FL5
95/6 SelectCertified 15, -Gold 1
96/7 SelectCertified 1, -Corner. 1
94 Semic 88, 360
95 Semic 94
92 SemicSticker 88
93 SemicSticker 201
89/90 SketchMEM 88
90/1 SketchMEM 96119
89/90 SketchOHL 1,188,195,196
90/1 SketchOHL 1, -Promo 1
91/2 SketchAwards 1, 8, 10
95/6 SkyBoxEmotion 133
95/6 SkBxE-Ntense 4, -Xcel 6
95/6 SkyBoxImpact 127, -Ice 4
95/6 SkBxImpact-Countdown 1
96/7 SkyBoxImpact 97, -Versa 8
96/7 SkBxImpact-Countdown 8
96/7 SB'7Eleven
94/5 SP 84, -Premier 30
95/6 SP 106, E21, FX16
96/7 SP 114, GF6, SPxForce 1
97/8 SPAuthentic 111, I7
96/7 SPx 33
97/8 SPx 36, SPX4
98/9 SPx"Finite" 100, 152, 172
96/7 SportFX MiniStix
97/8 SportFX MiniStix
95/6 Summt 19, -GM 5, -Mad 1
96/7 Summit 117,-High 16,-Unt 6
95/6 SuperSticker 90, DieCut17
91 TeamCanada
96/7 TeamOut
92/3 Topps 529
95/6 Topps 1, 327, 1PL
95/6 Topps HGC6, M4, PF7
98/8 Topps 18, I10, L9, M9
94/5 ToppsFinest 38, -Div. 8
94/5 TF-BBest(Blue) 16
95/6 ToppsFinest 1, 88
94 ToppsFinestBronze 2
96/7 ToppsNHLPicks FT22, TS3
97/8 ToppsSticker 2
95/6 ToppsSuperSkills 40
92/3 ToppsStadiumClub 501
93/4 TSC 10, -Master(1) 5
94/5 TSC 88, 203, -Dynasty 2
95/6 TSC EC181, N1, PS2
92/3 TSC-MembersOnly
93/4 TSC-MembersOnly 28
94/5 TSC-MembersOnly 15
95/6 TSC-MembersOnly 30
90/1 UpperDeck 473
91/2 UpperDeck 7, 9
92/3 UD 88, 470, CC6, G14,WG12
92/3 UD-LockerAS 56
93/4 UpperDeck 30,280, SP-116
93/4 UD H3, HB8, E12, -Hero 31
94/5 UpperDeck 98, C23, H8
94/5 UD H23, R9, R28, SP149
95/6 UD 374, AS17,F3,H1,R2
95/6 UD R21,R33,R52,SE148
95/6 UD-AllStarPredict MVP18
96/7 UD 66,306,SS3A,GJ8,HH3
96/7 UD LS13,-AS YCTGAR13
97/8 UD 331, S6, SG48, SS17
97/8 UD T1A, -BlowUp 8
93/4 UDBeAPlayer 29, -Roots 23
94/5 UDBAP R106, R178, UC2
96/7 UDBlackDiamnd 157, RC20
97/8 UDBlckDiamond 145, PC13
98/9 UDChoice 152, 237
98/9 UDChoice BH8, SQ28
95/6 UDCC 57, 377, 388, C4
96/7 UDCollChoice 188, 291
96/7 UDCC 335, C28, S9
97/8 UDCC 186, C20, S10,SQ88
96/7 UpperDeck"Ice" 113, S10
97/8 UpperDeckIce 88, IC3, L2B
97/8 ValuNet
96 Wien 88
97/8 Zenith 6, Z2,-ChasingCup 4
97/8 Zenith -ZTeam 4
92/3 PHA/JCPenney
92/3 PHA/UD 11FEB93
92/3 PHA/UD 04APR93
92/3 PHA/UD 15NOV92
93/4 PHA/JCPenney
93/4 PHA 29JAN94
93/4 PHA 10APR94, 23OCT93
94/5 PHA
96/7 PHA/OceanSpray
89/90 Oshawa 31
90/1 Oshawa 13
91/2 Oshawa/Dominos 21

LINDSAY, BILL
91 C55 Reprint 21
1911-12 Imperial (C55) 21
1912-13 Imperial (C57) 13
1910-11 Imperial Post 21

LINDSAY, BILL
92/3 Bowman 404
96/7 Donruss 75
92/3 FleerUltra 388
96/7 Leaf 66
92/3 opcPremier 5
97/8 PacificRegime 86
92/3 Parkhurst 376
93/4 Parkhurst 350
95/6 Parkhurst 356
96/7 Pinnacle 192
96/7 PinnacleBeAPlayer 204
95/6 POG 117
93/4 PowerPlay 95
93/4 Premier 436
94/5 Premier 522
92/3 ProSet 239
92/3 Score 463
96/7 Score 223
90/1 SketchWHL 113
91/2 SketchWHL 304
92/3 Topps 373
95/6 Topps 83
93/4 ToppsStadiumClub 253
94/5 ToppsStadiumClub 222
92/3 UpperDeck 472
95/6 UpperDeck 63
97/8 UpperDeck 74
96/7 UDBlackDiamond 11
95/6 UDCollChoice 12
96/7 UDCollChoice 108
97/8 UDCollChoice 108
96/7 UpperDeck"Ice" 22
93/4 FLA
96/7 FLA/WinnDixie
97/8 FLA/WinnDixie
92/3 QUE/PetroCanada

LINDSAY, BOB
87/8 Brockville 13
88/9 Brockville 10

LINDSAY, EVAN
98 BowmanCHL 61

LINDSAY, RYAN
93/4 Slapshot(Oshawa) 25
95/6 Slapshot 253

LINDSAY, SCOTT
91/2 SketchWHL 322

LINDSAY, TED
45-64 BeeHives(CHI), (DET)
64-67 BeeHives(DET)
64/5 CokeCap DET-15
48-52 Exhibits
83&87 HallOfFame 151
83 HHOF Postcard (L)
93/4 HHOFLegends 19
91/2 Kraft 70
51/2 Parkhurst 56
52/3 Parkhurst 87
53/4 Parkhurst 52
54/5 Parkhurst 46
92/3 Parkhurst PR31
93/4 Parkhurst PR49
93/4 Parkie(56/7) 44, 140
94/5 Parkie(64/5) 64
97/8 PinnacleBeeHive 60
52 RoyalDesserts 5
54/5 Topps 51
57/8 Topps 21
58/9 Topps 63
59/60 Topps 6
64/5 Topps 82
54-67 TorontoStar V 4,n8
56-66 TorontoStar 57/8, 58/9
91/2 Ultimate06 70, -Aut 70, 94
92/3 Zellers
76 DET
80/1 DET

LINDSTAHL, SAM
94/5 ElitSet 11
89/90 SemicElitserien 192
90/1 SemicElitserien 76
91/2 SemicElitserien 3
92/3 SemicElitserien 27
95/6 udElite DS9

LINDSTEDT, JOHAN
91/2 SemicElitserien 74

LINDSTROM, CURT
95 Hartwall

LINDSTROM, SEPPO
70/1 Kuvajulkaisut 66, 143
69/70 MästarSerien 20
72 Panda
72 SemicSticker 73
74 SemicSticker 77
77-80 Sportscsster 83-1982
71/2 WilliamsFIN 65, 193
72/3 WilliamsFIN 231
73/4 WilliamsFIN 71, 265

LINDSTROM, WILLY
79/80 O-Pee-Chee 368
80/1 OPC/Topps 142
81/2 O-Pee-Chee 368
82/3 O-Pee-Chee 384
83/4 O-Pee-Chee 35
84/5 O-Pee-Chee 250
85/6 O-Pee-Chee 217
86/7 O-Pee-Chee 232
82/3 opcSticker 209
83/4 opcSticker 91
84/5 opcSticker 260
85/6 opcSticker 227/93
86/7 opcSticker 227/97
77/8 opcWHA 39
80/1 Pepsi Cap
82/3 Post
89/90 SemicElitserien 39
74 SemicSticker 17
83/4 Vachon 32
83/4 EDM
83/4 EDM/Buttons
83/4 EDM/McDonald
84/5 EDM
84/5 EDM/RedRooster
88/9 EDM/ActionMagazine 23
86/7 PGH/Kodak
77/8 WPG
79/80 WPG
80/1 WPG
81/2 WPG
82/3 WPG

LINDFORD, DAVE
88/9 Kamloops

LINDVIST, MAGNUS
97/8 udSwedish 166

LING, DAVID
95/6 Classic 87
95/6 EdgeIce 77
95/6 FutureLegends 10
97/8 Score(MTL) 16
93/4 Slapshot(Kingston) 16
96/7 Fredericton
95/6 SaintJohn

LING, JAMIE
91/2 AirCanadaSJHL 25, A29

LINGEMANN, BORIS
95/6 DEL 90
96/7 DEL 288

LINGREN, STEVE
91/2 SketchWHL 61
94/5 Dayton 16
95/6 Dayton

LINNA, KAJ
95/6 Classic 76
95/6 ClassicFiveSport 141

LINNELL, DEREK
93/4 Raleigh
94/5 Raleigh

LINNONMAA, HARRI
65/6 Hellas 61
72 Hellas 4
70/1 Kuvajulkaisut 67, 110
80/1 Mallasjuoma 10
72 Panda
72 SemicSticker 80
74 SemicSticker 85
78/9 SM-Liiga 36
71/2 WilliamsFIN 66, 118
72/3 WilliamsFIN 64, 88
73/4 WilliamsFIN 134

LINSEMAN, KEN
91/2 Bowman 105
79/80 OPC/Topps 241
80/1 OPC/Topps 24
81/2 OPC 244, Topps(E) 107
82/3 O-Pee-Chee 115
83/4 O-Pee-Chee 36
84/5 O-Pee-Chee 7
88/9 OPC/Topps 118
89/90 OPC/Topps 62
90/1 OPC/Topps 345
91/2 OPC/Topps 146
81/2 opcSticker 176
82/3 opcSticker 112
83/4 opcSticker 102
89/90 opcSticker 26/164
90/1 Panini(EDM) 11
87/8 PaniniSticker 16
88/9 PaniniSticker 211
89/90 PaniniSticker 190
90/1 PaniniSticker 111
82/3 Post
90/1 ProSet 219, 444
83/4 PuffySticker 6
90/1 Score 380, 95T
91/2 Score(CDN) 239, 622
91/2 Score(U.S) 359
83/4 SouhaitsRen.KeyChain
83/4 StaterMint H17
91/2 ToppsStadiumClub 295
83/4 Vachon 33
84/5 BOS
88/9 BOS/SportsAction
89/90 BOS/SportsAction
82/3 EDM/RedRooster
83/4 EDM
83/4 EDM/Buttons
83/4 EDM/McDonald
88/9 EDM/ActionMagazine 47
90/1 EDM/McGavins
81/2 PHA/TIckets 11

LINSEMAN, MIKE
81/2 Kingston 12

LINSEMAN, STEVE
83/4 Brantford 15
84/5 Belleville 18

LINSEMAN, TED
83/4 Kingston 13
84/5 Kingston 27
85/6 Kingston 27
86/7 Kingston 29

LINTEAU, RICHARD
80/1 QuébecRamparts

LIPSETT
91/2 AvantGardeBCJ 161

LIPSETT, CHRIS
92/3 Clarkson

LIPTROTT, PETER
94/5 Slapshot(Brantford) 4
86/7 Kingston 8
87/8 Kingston 8

LIPUMA, CHRIS
92/3 ClassicProspects 118
93/4 ClassicProspects 20
93/4 Donruss 493
93/4 FleerUltra 178, -AllRk 4
94/5 FleerUltra 372
93/4 Pinnacle 208
93/4 PowerPlay 446
89/90 SketchMEM 44
90/1 SketchOHL 235
91/2 SketchOHL 94
94/5 T.B./SkyBoxSportsCafe
92/3 AtlantaKnights
93/4 AtlantaKnights
88/9 Kitchener 25
89/90 Kitchener 25
90/1 Kitchener 24

LIRETTE, NOEL
69 ColumbusCheckers

LISCOMBE, CARL
33-43 BeeHives(DET)
39/40 OPC (V301-1) 74

LISKA, JAROSLAV
95/6 APS 52

LISKO, CRAIG
91/2 FerrisState

LISKO, MATTI
70/1 Kuvajulkaisut 316
72/3 WilliamsFIN 333

LISY, PETER
85/6 Kitchener 20
86/7 London 18

LITMA, LASSE
80/1 Mallasjuoma 159
79 PaniniSticker 169
82 SemicSticker 35
78/9 SM-Liiga 9, 181
77-80 Sportscaster 84-2016
72/3 WilliamsFIN 270
73/4 WilliamsFIN 158

LITTLE, MIKE
93/4 Portland

LITTLE, NEIL
94/5 Classic 75

LITTMAN, DAVID
92/3 Classic 104
95/6 EdgeIce 150
93/4 FleerUltra 237,-AllRookie 5
89/90 ProCards(IHL) 103
90/1 ProCards 269
91/2 ProCards 19
92/3 AtlantaKnights
91/2 Rochester/Genny
91/2 Rochester/DD
91/2 Rochester/Kodak

LITZENBERGER, ED
45-64 BeeHives(CHI),(DET)
45-64 BeeHives(MTL)
64-67 BeeHives(TOR)
62 CeramicTiles
63-5 ChexPhoto
51-54 LaPatrie 8Feb53
61/2 Parkhurst 28
62/3 Parkhurst 12
63/4 Parkhurst 6, 66
93/4 Parkhurst PR66
93/4 Parkie(56/7) 24
60/1 ShirriffCoin 62
61/2 ShirriffCoin 71
62/3 ShirriffCoin 18
52/3 StLawrence 7
57/8 Topps 26
58/9 Topps 16
59/60 Topps 61
60/1 Topps 21
54-67 TorontoStar V6
56-66 TorontoStar 58/9
91/2 UltimateDP 58

LIUKKA, SIMO
96/7 Sisu 114

LIUS, JONI
92/3 Jyvas-Hyva 84
93/4 Jyvas-Hyva 142
93/4 Sisu 152
94/5 Sisu 17
95/6 Sisu 64
95/6 SisuLimited 49
97/8 udSwedish 77

LIUT, MIKE
90/1 Bowman 66
91/2 Bowman 290
90/1 Kraft 31
80/1 OPC/Topps 31
81/2 O-Pee-Chee 289, 301
81/2 Topps 20, (West) 128
82/3 O-Pee-Chee 306
83/4 O-Pee-Chee 309, 316
84/5 OPC 187, Topps 132
85/6 OPC/Topps 88
86/7 OPC/Topps 133
87/8 OPC/Topps 152, T-AS 8
88/9 OPC/Topps 127
89/90 OPC/Topps 97
90/1 OPC/Topps 44
91/2 OPC/Topps 154
87/8 opcStars 24
88/9 opcStars 20
81/2 opcSticker 129, 153
82/3 opcSticker 196
83/4 opcSticker 129
84/5 opcSticker 57
85/6 opcSticker 169/40
86/7 opcSticker 52/191
87/8 opcSticker 209, 121/133
88/9 opcSticker 263
89/90 opcSticker 267/148
87/8 PaniniSticker 38
88/9 PaniniSticker 235
90/1 PaniniSticker 165
91/2 Parkhurst 196
91/2 Pinnacle 169
81/2 Post PopUp 13
82/3 Post
90/1 ProSet 316
91/2 PSPlatinum PC16
83/4 PuffySticker 14
90/1 Score 68, 354, -HotCard 32
91/2 Score(CDN) 99, (U.S) 99
92/3 Score 368
85/6 7Eleven 7
92/3 Topps 307
91/2 ToppsStadiumClub 10
90/1 UpperDeck 127
91/2 UpperDeck 259
85/6 HFD/JuniorWhalers
86/7 HFD/JuniorWhalers
87/8 HFD/JuniorWhalers
88/9 HFD/JuniorWhalers
89/90 HFD/JuniorWhalers
92/3 STL/UpperDeck 4
89/90 WSH/Kodak
90/1 WSH/Kodak
90/1 WSH/Smokey
91/2 WSH
91/2 WSH/Kodak

LIVERNOCHE, PATRICK
93/4 Slapshot(Drum.) 19

LIZARRAGA, JOSIAN
79 PaniniSticker 371

LJUNGBERG, CHRISTER
91/2 SemicElitserien 248

LJUNGBERG, THOMAS
94/5 ElitSet 64
89/90 SemicElitserien 230
90/1 SemicElitserien 112
91/2 SemicElitserien 119
92/3 SemicElitserien 148

LJUSTERANG, PER
89/90 SemicElitserien 154
90/1 SemicElitserien 227
91/2 SemicElitserien 157
92/3 SemicElitserien 259

LLNDSTEDT, JOHAN
90/1 SemicElitserien 294

LOACH, JAMIE
95/6 EdgeIce 123

LOACH, LONNIE
92/3 Classic 95
92/3 ClassicFourSport 210
92/3 FleerUltra 146, 309
92/3 Parkhurst 305
93/4 PowerPlay 7
88/9 ProCards(Saginaw)
89/90 ProCards(IHL) 60
90/1 ProCards 538
91/2 ProCards 120
92/3 UpperDeck 466
88/9 Flint

LOACH, MIKE
93/4 Slapshot(Windsor) 11
95/6 Slapshot 288

LOCAS, JACQUES
48-52 Exhibits
51/2 LavalDairy 95
52/3 LavalDairy 57
75/6 opcWHA 129
43-47 ParadeSportive
45-54 QuakerOats
52/3 StLawrence 81
75/6 Cincinnati

LOCHEAD, BILL
94/5 DEL 343
95/6 DEL 308
96/7 DEL 91
82? JDMcCarthy
74/5 Loblaws
74/5 OPC 318
75/6 OPC/Topps 103
76/7 OPC/Topps 122
77/8 OPC/Topps 212
78/9 OPC/Topps 122
79/80 OPC 301

LOCHER, J.C.
79 PaniniSticker 260

LOCKE, STEVE
88/9 NiagaraFalls 23

LOCKER, DEREK
93/4 Minn-Duluth

LOCKETT, KEN
74/5 Loblaws
74/5 VAN/RoyalBank
75/6 VAN/RoyalBank
76/7 SanDiegoMariners

LOCKHART, TOM
83&87 HallOfFame 38
83 HHOF Postcard (C)

LOCKING, NORMAN
36-39 DiamondMatch (1), (2), (3)

LOCKRIDGE, TIM
81/2 Indianapolis 4
82/3 Indianapolis

LOCKWOOD, JOE
88/9 ProCards(Kalamazoo)

LOCOCO, MIKE
81/2 SSMarie
82/3 SSMarie
83/4 SSMarie

LODER, GREG
94/5 Wheeling 10

LODIN, HANS
94/5 EliteSet 112
95/6 EliteSet 63
89/90 SemicElitserien 175
90/1 SemicElitserien 8
91/2 SemicElitserien 204
92/3 SemicElitserien 227
95/6 udElite 97
97/8 udSwedish 103

LOEWEN, DARCY
92/3 opcPremier 7
92/3 Parkhurst 355
93/4 Parkhurst 407
93/4 Premier 184
89/90 ProCards(AHL) 269
90/1 ProCards 284
91/2 ProCards 4
93/4 ToppsStadiumClub 318
91/2 UpperDeck 421
90/1 BUF/Campbell
92/3 OTT
93/4 OTT/Kraft
94/5 LasVegas
95/6 LasVegas
96/7 LasVegas
91/2 Rochester/DD
91/2 Rochester/Kodak

LOFQVIST, WILLIAM
74 Hellas 30
74 SemicSticker 2
71/2 WilliamsFIN 51
73/4 WilliamsFIN 32

LOFSTROM, JONAS
95/6 EliteSet 169
95/6 udElite 28
97/8 udSwedish 22

LOFSTROM, P.ER
95/6 EliteSet 176
95/6 udElite 25

LOFTHOUSE, MARK
80/1 O-Pee-Chee 331
88/9 ProCards(Hershey)
78/9 WSH
79/80 WSH
89/90 NewHaven

LOGAN, BOB
88/9 ProCards(NewHaven)
87/8 BUF/WonderBreadf

LOGAN, DAN
86/7 Regina
86/7 Saskatoon

LOGAN, DAVE
78/9 O-Pee-Chee 343
80/1 Pepsi Cap
80/1 VAN
80/1 VAN/Silverwood

LOGAN, JIM
52/3 AnonymousOHL 151

LOGAN, TIM
87/8 Regina

LOHKO, RAIMO
66/7 Champion 88

LOHKO, TIMO
96/7 Sisu 113

LOI, BRAD
84/5 Richelieu

LOICQ, PAUL
83&87 HallOfFame 234
83 HHOF Postcard (F)

LOIKALA, J.M.
95/6 Sisu 249

LOISELLE, CLAUDE
90/1 Bowman 175
90/1 Panini(QUE) 14
87/8 PaniniSticker 85
88/9 PaniniSticker 273
90/1 PaniniSticker 151
91/2 Pinnacle 296
92/3 Pinnacle 219
93/4 Premier 328
90/1 ProSet 252
91/2 ProSet 493
90/1 Score 207
91/2 Score(CDN) 532
92/3 Score 328
92/3 Topps 338
90/1 UpperDeck 338
85/6 DET/Caesars
88/9 N.J/Caretta
89/90 QUE
89/90 QUE/GeneralFoods
89/90 QUE/Police
90/1 QUE
90/1 QUE/PetroCanada
90/1 TOR/P.L.A.Y. 12

LOJKIN, ALEXEI
95/6 Fredericton
96/7 Fredericton

LOMAKIN, ANDREI
92/3 Bowman 286
96/7 DEL 39
93/4 Donruss 128
94/5 Donruss 85
93/4 EASports 52
92/3 FleerUltra 372
93/4 FleerUltra 327
94/5 FleerUltra 81
93/4 Leaf 401
94/5 Leaf 302
90/1 O-Pee-Chee 472
91/2 O-Pee-Chee 40R
92/3 O-Pee-Chee 37
91/2 opcPremier 178
92/3 PaniniSticker 193
93/4 PaniniSticker 52
91/2 Parkhurst 131
93/4 Parkhurst 349
94/5 Parkhurst 84
91/2 Pinnacle 305
92/3 Pinnacle 162
93/4 Pinnacle 360
94/5 Pinnacle 337
94/5 POG 106
93/4 PowerPlay 96
93/4 Premier 82
94/5 Premier 177
91/2 PSPlatinum 208
91/2 RedAce
91/2 Score(CDN)660, (U.S)110T
92/3 Score 129
93/4 Score 529
94 Semic 160
89 SemicSticker 98
92 SemicSticker 115
93 SemicSticker 143
91/2 StarPics 17
92/3 Topps 380
92/3 ToppsStadiumClub 115
93/4 ToppsStadiumClub 57, 402
91/2 TriGlobe 3-4
91/2 UpperDeck 518
92/3 UpperDeck 428, E17
93/4 UpperDeck 102
94/5 UpperDeck 471
93/4 FLA
91/2 PHA/JCPenney
92/3 PHA/JCPenney
92/3 PHA/UD 08APR93
92/3 PHA/UD 19DEC92

LOMBARDI, SAL
88/9 ProCards(NewHaven)
94/5 LasVegas

LOMBARDO, JOE
95/6 Slapshot 389
96/7 Sudbury 15

LOMOW, BOYD
83/4 Brandon 13
84/5 Brandon 21

LOMOW, BRIAN
83/4 Brandon 6
84/5 Brandon 3

LOMOW, BYRON
89/90 ProCards(IHL) 141
90/1 ProCards 526
85/6 Brandon 3

LONEY, BRIAN
93/4 ClassicProspects 217
95/6 Parkhurst 481

LONEY, TROY
93/4 EASports 4
92/3 FleerUltra 378
93/4 FleerUltra 259
93/4 Kraft'Captain
94/5 Leaf 435
87/8 OPC/Topps 107
90/1 OPC/Topps 347
88/9 PaniniSticker 341
89/90 PaniniSticker 319
90/1 PaniniSticker 138
94/5 PaniniSticker 124
91/2 Parkhurst 352
93/4 Parkhurst 9
94/5 Parkhurst 5
93/4 Pinnacle 379, CA1
93/4 Pinnacle-Expansion 4
94/5 Pinnacle 396
93/4 PowerPlay 8
93/4 Premier 340
94/5 Premier 363
90/1 ProSet 237
90/1 Score 371
91/2 Score(CDN) 522
92/3 Score 348
93/4 Score 547
94/5 Score 67
92/3 Topps 397
92/3 ToppsStadiumClub 357
93/4 ToppsStadiumClub 395
90/1 UpperDeck 367
91/2 UpperDeck 489
92/3 UpperDeck 208
93/4 UpperDeck 438, SP2
94/5 UpperDeck 385
94/5 UDBeAPlayer-Aut. 84
83/4 PGH
87/8 PGH/Kodak
89/90 PGH/Foodland 13
91/2 PGH/Elbys
91/2 PGH/Foodland 7
92/3 PGH/Coke
92/3 PGH/Foodland 8
92/3 PGH/FoodStickers

LONG, ANDREW
98 BowmanCHL 17
94/5 Slapshot(Guelph) 26
95/6 Slapshot 103
95/6 Guelph 7
96/7 Guelph 25

LONG, BARRY
72/3 OPC 288
80/1 OPC/Topps 258
81/2 O-Pee-Chee 369
81/2 opcSticker 142
75/6 opcWHA 69, 90
76/7 opcWHA 7
80/1 Pepsi Cap
79/80 DET
77/8 WPG
80/1 WPG
83/4 WPG
84/5 WPG/Police
85/6 WPG
85/6 WPG/Police

LONG, BILL
86/7 London 13

LONG, ERIC
94/5 Raleigh

LONG, TED
75/6 Hamilton

LONGAUER, MICHAL
90/1 SketchQMJHL 139
91/2 SketchQMJHL 202

LONGBREAK, DAVID
92/3 BCJHL 45

LONGE, BANNY
81/2 Ottawa67s

LONGMAN, GARY
69 ColumbusCheckers

LONGO, CHRIS
93/4 ClassicFourSport 214
93/4 ClassicProspects 89
89/90 SketchOHL 114, 178
90/1 SketchOHL 364
91/2 SketchOHL 128
91/2 Peterborough 7
93/4 Portland
94/5 Portland

LONGO, MIKE
90/1 Rayside
91/2 Rayside

LONGSTAFF, SCOTT
91/2 AvantGardeBC 2, 155
97/8 SheffieldSteelers

LONN, ANDERS
95/6 udElite DS12
97/8 udSwedish 116

LONNBERG, HARRI
93/4 Sisu 225
95/6 Sisu 308, -Painkill 4

LONSBERRY, ROSS
70/1 EddieSargent 66
71/2 EddieSargent 69
72/3 EddieSargent 166
70/1 Esso Stamp
74/5 Loblaws
69/70 OPC/Topps 104
70/1 OPC/Topps 37
71/2 OPC/Topps 121
72/3 OPC 166, Topps 112
73/4 OPC/Topps 36
74/5 OPC/Topps 144
75/6 OPC/Topps 110
76/7 OPC/Topps 201
77/8 OPC/Topps 257
78/9 OPC/Topps 186
79/80 OPC/Topps 58
80/1 OPC 388
81/2 OPC 263
72 SemicSticker 206
71/2 TheTorontoSun
67/8 Topps 35
75/6 PHA/GingerAle

LOOB, HAKAN
94/5 ElitSet 39, -GoldCard 8
94/5 Elit-Playmakr 6, -TopGun 2
95/6 ElitSet 1, 305, -Champs 3
95/6 Elit-FaceTo 5, -Mega 9
95 Globe52
86/7 Kraft Sports 2
84/5 O-Pee-Chee 229
85/6 O-Pee-Chee 184
87/8 O-Pee-Chee 208
88/9 OPC/Topps 110, O, T-AS 3
88/9 opcStars 21
84/5 opcSticker 242
87/8 opcSticker 44/184
88/9 opcSticker 94, 118/248
87/8 PaniniSticker 201, 214
88/9 PaniniSticker 9
94 Semic 64
95 Semic 75
89/90 SemicElitserien 91
90/1 SemicElitserien 260
91/2 SemicElitserien 92, 315,318
91/2 SemicElitserien 325, 347
92/3 SemicElitserien 111, 337
92/3 SemicElitserien 340, 346
82 SemicSticker 22
91 SemicSticker 38
92 SemicSticker 61
93 SemicSticker 9
95/6 udElite 64, 223, 252
83/4 Vachon 11
85/6 CGY/RedRooster
86/7 CGY/RedRooster
87/8 CGY/RedRooster (x2)

LOOB, PETER
84/5 Fredericton 14

LOOF, MATTIAS
94/5 ElitSet 247
95/6 ElitSet 293
92/3 SemicElitserien 171
95/6 udElite 198
97/8 udSwedish 188

LOONEY, SHELLEY
94/5 Classic W34

LOOV, MATS
94/5 ElitSet 93, -TopGun 10
95/6 ElitSet 122, -FaceTo 11
89/90 SemicElitserien 108
90/1 SemicElitserien 114
92/3 SemicElitserien 266
95/6 udElite 185

LOPONEN, JOUNI
95/6 Sisu 59
96/7 Sisu 58
95/6 SisuLimited 48
97/8 udSwedish 86

LOPPONEN, JARI
71/2 WilliamsFIN 328

LOPRESTI, PETE
76/7 OPC/Topps 184
77/8 OPC/Topps 13
78/9 OPC/Topps 230
79/80 O-Pee-Chee 364
79 PaniniSticker 206
88/9 EDM/ActionMagazine 122

LOPRESTI, SAM
33-43 BeeHives(CHI)

LORD, ADAM
92/3 BCJHL 160

LORD, LARS-ERIK
90/1 SemicElitserien 200

LORD, PHILIPPE
96/7 Rimouski

LORENTZ, DAVE
89/90 SketchOHL 109

LORENTZ, JIM
70/1 EddieSargent 192
71/2 EddieSargent 192
72/3 EddieSargent 36
70/1 Esso Stamp
74/5 Loblaws
70/1 OPC 209
71/2 OPC 227, Topps 13
72/3 OPC 116, Topps 68
73/4 OPC 75, Topps 171
74/5 OPC/Topps 61
75/6 OPC/Topps 28
76/7 OPC/Topps 162
77/8 OPC/Topps 58
78/9 OPC/Topps 161
71/2 TheTorontoSun
72/3 BUF
73/4 BUF
73/4 BUF/BellsMarket
74/5 BUF
75/6 BUF/Linnett

LORENTZ, TOM
85/6 Minn-Duluth 20

LORENZ, DANNY
92/3 ClassicProspects 132
95/6 EdgeIce 113
92/3 FleerUltra 345
93/4 Leaf 343
91/2 ProCards 457

LORENZI, CARLO
95 PaniniWorlds 84

LORENZO, JOHNNY
90/1 SketchQMJHL 196
91/2 SketchQMJHL 70

LORIMER, BOB
79/80 OPC/Topps 181
80/1 OPC/Topps 138
81/2 O-Pee-Chee 214
82/3 O-Pee-Chee 142
83/4 O-Pee-Chee 232
84/5 O-Pee-Chee 114
82/3 opcSticker 228
82/3 Post
83/4 SouhaitsRen.KeyChain
81/2 COL.R
83/4 N.J.
84/5 N.J.
79/80 NYI

LORING, AL
88/9 ProCards(NewHaven)

LORING, BRAD
91/2 AvantGardeBCJHL 145
92/3 BCJHL 36
90/1 SketchWHL 119

LORRAINE, ROD
33-43 BeeHives(MTL.C)
35-40 CrownBrand 117
37/8 OPC (V304E) 176
39/40 OPC (V301-1) 23
38/9 QuakerOats

LOSCH, MIKE
94/5 DEL 49
95/6 DEL 43

LOTH, ANDREAS
94/5 DEL 257
95/6 DEL 255

LOTILA, TENHO
66/7 Champion 5

LOTJONEN, OSMO
71/2 WilliamsFIN 287
73/4 WilliamsFIN 206

LOTTA, DAVE
87/8 QUE/GeneralFoods

LOTVONEN, KIMMO
95/6 Sisu 301
96/7 Sisu 96

LOUBIER, YVES
91/2 SketchQMJHL 274

LOUCKS, BOB
90/1 SketchWHL 137, 149
91/2 SketchWHL 359
89/90 Lethbridge

LOUCKS, SCOTT
90/1 SketchWHL 296
91/2 SketchWHL 87
93/4 Kamloops

LOUGHLIN, CLEM
25-27 Anonymous 127
36-39 DiamondMatch (4)

LOUSTEL, RON
82/3 Brandon 22
81/2 Saskatoon 23

LOUTTIT, EDDI
52/3 AnonymousOHL 11

LOUTTIT, PAUL
81/2 Ottawa67s
82/3 Ottawa67s

LÖVDAL, ÖRJAN
95 Globe 191
95 PaniniWorlds 247
92 SemicSticker 39

LOVE, BRAD
91/2 SketchOHL 198

LOVEDAY, LOWELL
83/4 Moncton 6
84/5 NovaScotia 4

LOVELL, GREG
93/4 Slapshot(Kingston) 1

LOVELL, JOHN
93/4 Slapshot(Guelph) 28
95/6 Slapshot 305
91/2 SketchOHL 25
91/2 Cornwall 6

LOVELL, TIM
93/4 Maine 52

LOVEN, FREDRIK
95/6 SP 188
95/6 UDCollChoice 351

LOVGREN, MIKAEL
97/8 udSwedish 128

LOVSIN, DAVE
91/2 AirCanadaSJHL D32

LOVSIN, KEN
93/4 CanadaNats
93/4 FleerUltra 467
93/4 PowerPlay 487
93/4 Premier-TmCanada 4
90/1 ProCards 195
91/2 ProCards 557
94/5 Score CT16
91/2 Baltimore 5

LOW, KEN
90/1 EDM/McGavins

LOW, RON
74/5 Loblaws
72/3 OPC 258
74/5 OPC/Topps 39
75/6 OPC/Topps 25
76/7 OPC/Topps 69
77/8 OPC 305
78/9 OPC/Topps 237
79/80 OPC 348
80/1 OPC 333
82/3 OPC 112
83/4 OPC 233
84/5 OPC 115
82/3 opcSticker 107
80/1 Pepsi Cap
80/1 EDM/Zellers
81/2 EDM/RedRooster
82/3 EDM/RedRooster
88/9 EDM/ActionMagazine 36
90/1 EDM/McGavins
91/2 EDM/IGA
92/3 EDM/IGA 28
93/4 EDM 25FEB94
83/4 N.J.
84/5 N.J.
72/3 TOR
74/5 WSH
85/6 NovaScotia 25

LOWE, DARREN
88/9 ProCards(Maine)
89/90 ProCards(IHL) 45
90/1 ProCards 310
87/8 Flint

LOWE, JASON
91/2 AvantGardeBCJ 28, 158

LOWE, KEVIN
90/1 Bowman 198
91/2 Bowman 115
92/3 Bowman 99
92/3 Durivage 42
92/3 FleerUltra 60, 356
93/4 FleerUltra 375
84/5 Kelloggs Disk
89/90 Kraft 14
86/7 Kraft Sports 17
89/90 Kraft Sticker 6
81/2 OPC 117
82/3 OPC 113
83/4 OPC 37
84/5 OPC 251
85/6 OPC 239
86/7 OPC/Topps 197
87/8 OPC 200
88/9 OPC 229
89/90 OPC 227, 303
90/1 OPC/Topps 307
91/2 OPC/Topps 220
92/3 OPC 302
87/8 opcStars 25
82/3 opcSticker 96
83/4 opcSticker 101
84/5 opcSticker 253
85/6 opcSticker 219/86
86/7 opcSticker 70/200
87/8 opcSticker 84/216
88/9 opcSticker 219/91
89/90 opcSticker 224/83
97/8 PacificRegime 78
90/1 Panini(EDM) 12
87/8 PaniniSticker 257
88/9 PaniniSticker 54
89/90 PaniniSticker 79, 180
90/1 PaniniSticker 224, 330
91/2 PaniniSticker 131
92/3 PaniniSticker 107
93/4 PaniniSticker 97
91/2 Parkhurst 51
92/3 Parkhurst 348
80/1 Pepsi Cap
91/2 Pinnacle 188, 371
92/3 Pinnacle 338
93/4 Pinnacle 11, -AllStar 3
94/5 Pinnacle 338
95/6 Pinnacle 89
94/5 POG 171
82/3 Post
93/4 PowerPlay 393
93/4 Premier 464
90/1 ProSet 89, 339, 380
91/2 ProSet 76, 572
91/2 PSPlatinum 38
90/1 Score 170, 369, -HotCrd 75
91/2 Score(CDN) 109, (U.S) 109
92/3 Score 39
93/4 Score 112
95/6 Score 248
89 SemicSticker 62
84/5 7ElevenDisk
83/4 SouhaitsRen.KeyChain
92/3 Topps 290
94/5 ToppsFinest-Ring 2
91/2 ToppsStadiumClub 179
92/3 ToppsStadiumClub 385
93/4 TSC 165, -AllStar
94/5 ToppsStadiumClub 173
90/1 UpperDeck 262
91/2 UpperDeck 186
92/3 UpperDeck-Heroes 13
94/5 UpperDeck 393
95/6 UpperDeck 414
97/8 UpperDeck 279
95/6 UDBeAPlayer 40
83/4 Vachon 34
79/80 EDM
81/2 EDM/RedRooster
82/3 EDM/RedRooster
83/4 EDM
83/4 EDM/Buttons
83/4 EDM/McDonald
84/5 EDM
84/5 EDM/RedRooster
85/6 EDM/RedRooster
86/7 EDM
86/7 EDM/RedRooster
87/8 EDM
88/9 EDM
88/9 EDM/ActionMagazine 5
90/1 EDM/McGavins
91/2 EDM/IGA
96/7 EDM
97/8 EDM

LOWE, ROSS ROBERT
45-64 BeeHives(MTL)
51/2 Parkhurst 18
45-54 QuakerOats

LOWE, STEVE
95/6 Classic 95
95/6 Slapshot 174

LOWES, BOB
94/5 Slapshot(MEM) 50

LOWGREN, TORGNY
95/6 ElitSet 238
92/3 SemicElitserien 271
95/6 udElite 106

LOWREY, FRED
24/5 Champs (C144)
24/5 MapleCrispettes (V130) 28
24/5 (V145-2) 36

LOWRY, DAVE
90/1 Bowman 15
91/2 Bowman 373
92/3 Bowman 370
93/4 Donruss 125
94/5 Donruss 20
95/6 Donruss 222
96/7 Donruss 174
94/5 FleerUltra 82
93/4 Leaf 238
94/5 Leaf 414

95/6 Leaf 256
96/7 Leaf 125
90/1 OPC/Topps 370
91/2 OPC/Topps 180
92/3 O-Pee-Chee 219
97/8 PacificRegime 87
87/8 PaniniSticker 353
91/2 PaniniSticker 32
92/3 PaniniSticker 21
94/5 PaniniSticker 69
95/6 PaniniSticker 73
91/2 Parkhurst 376
93/4 Parkhurst 79
91/2 Pinnacle 276
93/4 Pinnacle 408, -Expansion 4
94/5 Pinnacle 184
95/6 Pinnacle 199
96/7 Pinnacle 81
97/8 PinnacleBeAPlayer 183
95/6 Playoff 261
94/5 POG 107
95/6 POG 118
93/4 PowerPlay 97
93/4 Premier 244
94/5 Premier 89
88/9 ProCards(Peoria)
90/1 ProSet 265
90/1 ScoreTraded 38T
91/2 Score(CDN) 149, (U.S.)149
92/3 Score 109
93/4 Score 564
94/5 Score 81
95/6 Score 218
96/7 Score 194
92/3 Topps 42
91/2 ToppsStadiumClub 303
92/3 ToppsStadiumClub 10
93/4 T.StadiumClub 121, 379
90/1 UpperDeck 349
93/4 UpperDeck 67
94/5 UpperDeck 291
95/6 UpperDeck 175
96/7 UpperDeck 264
94/5 UDBeAPlayer-Aut. 102
95/6 UDCC 299
96/7 FLA/WinnDixie
89/90 STL/Kodak
90/1 STL/Kodak
91/2 STL
97/8 S.J/PacificBellSheet
85/6 VAN
86/7 VAN
87/8 VAN/Shell

LOXAM, RYAN
91/2 AvantGardeBCJ 51
92/3 BCJHL 210
91/2 Nainamo

LOYER, PAT
83/4 Brandon 7
84/5 Brandon 9

LOZINSKI, LARRY
81/2 O-Pee-Chee 99

LUBINA, LADISLAV
94/5 APS 45
95/6 APS 325
91 SemicSticker 121

LUBINIECKI, DARYL
81/2 Saskatoon 13

LUCAK, JOSEF
95/6 APS 222

LUCE, DON
71/2 EddieSargent 26
72/3 EddieSargent 33
70/1 Esso Stamp
74/5 Loblaws
72/3 OPC 95
80/1 OPC 302
81/2 OPC 147
71/2 OPC/Topps 166
73/4 OPC/Topps 38
74/5 OPC/Topps 79
75/6 OPC/Topps 113
76/7 OPC/Topps 94
77/8 OPC/Topps 231
78/9 OPC/Topps 58
79/80 OPC/Topps 194
71/2 TheTorontoSun
72/3 Topps 106
81/2 Topps(West) 99
72/3 BUF
73/4 BUF
74/5 BUF
75/6 BUF/Linnett
80/1 BUF/Wendt
93/4 BUF/NOCO
81/2 TOR

LUCE, SCOTT
87/8 Sudbury 24

LUCHINKIN, SERGEI
94/5 SR'Promo 1, -FutureF FF8
95/6 TetradAutobilia46

LUCKNER, HARALD
82 SemicSticker 25
91/2 SemicElitserien 305
92/3 SemicElitserien 327

LUCYCK, CAREY
89/90 ProCards(IHL) 133
90/1 ProCards 548
91/2 ProCards 242

LUDEMANN, MIRCO
94/5 DEL 205
95/6 DEL 200, 434
96/7 DEL 342
95 PaniniWorlds 53
94 Semic 275
96 Wien 194

LUDVIG, JAN
84/5 OPC 116
84/5 opcSticker 76
84/5 Topps 88
87/8 BUF/BlueShield
87/8 BUF/WonderBread
88/9 BUF/BlueShield
88/9 BUF/WonderBread
83/4 N.J.
84/5 N.J.
86/7 N.J./SOBER

LUDWIG, A.
95/6 DEL 343

LUDWIG, CRAIG
91/2 Bowman 221
92/3 FleerUltra 320
94/5 FleerUltra 280
86/7 Kraft Sports 30
93/4 Leaf 432
94/5 Leaf 424
83/4 OPC 190
84/5 OPC 265
85/6 OPC 192
86/7 OPC 220
88/9 OPC 230
89/90 OPC 236
90/1 OPC 412
91/2 OPC/Topps 150
90/1 opcPremier 64
91/2 opcPremier 80
84/5 opcSticker 154
85/6 opcSticker 130/250
86/7 opcSticker 14/156
88/9 opcSticker 48/183
98/9 Pacific 3
97/8 PacificRegime 62
87/8 PaniniSticker 59
88/9 PaniniSticker 254
91/2 PaniniSticker 242
94/5 PaniniSticker 233
91/2 Pinnacle 248, 404
93/4 Pinnacle 303
94/5 Pinnacle 233
93/4 Premier 191
90/1 ProSet 154, 484
91/2 ProSet 155, 411
92/3 ProSet 79
90/1 Score 165, 8T, -HotCard 74
91/2 ScoreCDN 13, 561, 11T
91/2 ScoreUS 13, 11T
92/3 Score 94
93/4 Score 282
92/3 Topps 154
91/2 ToppsStadiumClub 38
92/3 ToppsStadiumClub 354
93/4 ToppsStadiumClub 173
94/5 ToppsStadiumClub 214
90/1 UpperDeck 186
95/6 UDBeAPlayer 128
96/7 UDCC 76
83/4 Vachon 48
94/5 DAL
94/5 DAL/Southwest
96/7 DAL/Southwest
82/3 MTL
82/3 MTL/Steinberg
83/4 MTL
84/5 MTL
85/6 MTL
85/6 MTL/ProvigoSticker
85/6? MTL/ProvigoPlacemat
86/7 MTL
87/8 MTL
87/8 MTL/Stickers 35, 80, 81, 85
88/9 MTL
89/90 MTL
89/90MTL/Figurine
89/90 MTL/Kraft

LUDZIK, STEVE
83/4 O-Pee-Chee 105, 106
84/5 O-Pee-Chee 38, 200
88/9 ProCards(Sag)
89/90 ProCards(AHL) 271
90/1 ProCards 276
91/2 ProCards 15
82/3 CHI
83/4 CHI
86/7 CHI/Coke
87/8 CHI/Coke
93/4 Muskegon
91/2 Rochester/Kodak

LUDGER, MARK
94/5 Roanoke

LUHNING, WARREN
97/8 Score 69

LUHRMANN, SCOTT
92/3 Toledo 1, 2
93/4 Toledo 6
94/5 Toledo
95/6 Toledo

LUIK, JAAN
91/2 ProCards 37
91/2 Cincinnati

LUIK, SCOTT
89/90 SketchMEM 93
89/90 SketchOHL 21
90/1 SketchOHL 341
91/2 Cincinnati
89/90 Oshawa 34
90/1 Oshawa 4

LUKAC, VINVENT
82 SemicSticker 100

LUKEY, CHRIS
87/8 Kingston 28

LUKES, CHRISTIAN
94/5 DEL 301
95/6 DEL 268
96/7 DEL 162

LUKKO, JOUKO
80/1 Mallasjuoma 141

LUKNOWSKY, JAY
95/6 DEL 233
96/7 DEL 84
90/1 Mich.Tech

LUKOWICH, BRAD
94/5 Slapshot(MEM) 19
93/4 Kamloops

LUKOWICH, MORRIS
83/4 Esso
79/80 OPC/Topps 202
80/1 OPC/Topps 107, 227
81/2 O-Pee-Chee 370
82/3 O-Pee-Chee 383
83/4 O-Pee-Chee 386
84/5 O-Pee-Chee 340
85/6 OPC/Topps 129
81/2 opcSticker 138
82/3 opcSticker 205
83/4 opcSticker 281
80/1 opcSuperCard 24
81/2 Post PopUp 19
82/3 Post
83/4 PuffySticker 3
83/4 SouhaitsRen.KeyChain
83/4 StaterMint H9
83/4 Vachon 129
88/9 L.A.
77/8 WPG
79/80 WPG
80/1 WPG
81/2 WPG
82/3 WPG
83/4 WPG
84/5 WPG/Police

LUKSA, CHUCK
79/80 O-Pee-Chee 370
77/8 NovaScotia

LULIN, ANDREJ
95/6 ElitSet 298

LUMBARD, TODD
82/3 Regina 2
83/4 Regina 2
84/5 Springfield 3

LUMELA, PEKKA
80/1 Mallasjuoma 82

LUMLEY, DAVE
80/1 O-Pee-Chee 271
82/3 O-Pee-Chee 114
83/4 O-Pee-Chee 38
84/5 O-Pee-Chee 252
82/3 opcSticker 101
80/1 Pepsi Cap
82/3 Post
83/4 Vachon 35
79/80 EDM
80/1 EDM/Zellers
81/2 EDM/RedRooster
81/2 EDM/WestEdmontonMall
82/3 EDM/RedRooster
83/4 EDM
83/4 EDM/Buttons
83/4 EDM/McDonald
84/5 EDM
84/5 EDM/RedRooster
85/6 EDM/RedRooster
88/9 EDM/ActionMagazine 35
77/8 NovaScotia

LUMLEY, HARRY
45-64 BeeHives(BOS), (CHI)
45-64 BeeHives(DET), (TOR)
48-52 Exhibits
83&87 HallOfFame 21
83 HHOF Postcard (B)
92/3 HHOFLegends 1
43-47 ParadeSportive
51/2 Parkhurst 47
52/3 Parkhurst 59
53/4 Parkhurst 1
54/5 Parkhurst 16, 91, 92, 93
55/6 Parkhurst 1, 70, 73, 74, 76
92/3 Parkhurst 53 PR5
45-54 QuakerOats
54-67 TorontoStar V 5,n2
56-66 TorontoStar 58/9
91/2 Ultimate(O6) 51, -Aut 51

LUMME, JYRKI
91/2 Bowman 321
92/3 Bowman 170
93/4 Donruss 347
94/5 Donruss 190
95/6 Donruss 109
96/7 Donruss 5
93/4 EASports 139, 205
94/5 Flair 192
94/5 Fleer 226
95 Globe 129
96/7 FleerPicks 94
92/3 FleerUltra 223
93/4 FleerUltra 126
94/5 FleerUltra 227
93 Koululainen
93/4 Leaf 231
94/5 Leaf 287
95/6 Leaf 328
96/7 Leaf 123
91/2 OPC/Topps 419
92/3 O-Pee-Chee 265
98/9 Pacific 428
97/8 PacificCrown 232
90/1 Panini(VAN) 14
92/3 PaniniSticker 36
93/4 PaniniSticker 175
94/5 PaniniSticker 151
96/7 PaniniSticker 293
97/8 PaniniSticker 244
91/2 Parkhurst 180
92/3 Parkhurst 191
93/4 Parkhurst 483
95/6 Parkhurst 215
94/5 ParkieSE 190, ES8
91/2 Pinnacle 237
92/3 Pinnacle 65
93/4 Pinnacle 21
94/5 Pinnacle 86
95/6 Pinnacle 73
96/7 Pinnacle 185
94/5 POG 339
95/6 POG 277
93/4 PowerPlay 252
93/4 Premier 475
94/5 Premier 442
88/9 ProCards(She)
90/1 ProSet 300
91/2 ProSet 240
92/3 ProSet 196
91/2 PSPlatinum 237
90/1 Score 132
91/2 Score(CDN) 462, (U.S) 242
92/3 Score 318, -YoungStar 34
93/4 Score 134
94/5 Score 35
95/6 Score 102
96/7 Score 22
97/8 Score(VAN) 8
94 Semic 8
95 Semic 38
91 SemicSticker 202
92 SemicSticker 6
93 SemicSticker 56
94/5 Sisu-GuestSpecial 3
95/6 SisuLimited 101, -Gallery 1
96/7 SP 160
95/6 Summit 164
96/7 TeamOut
92/3 Topps 510
95/6 Topps 204
91/2 ToppsStadiumClub 154
92/3 ToppsStadiumClub 321
93/4 ToppsStadiumClub 108
94/5 ToppsStadiumClub 132
90/1 UpperDeck 297
91/2 UpperDeck 114
92/3 UpperDeck 137
94/5 UpperDeck 148
95/6 UpperDeck 356
96/7 UpperDeck 172
97/8 UpperDeck 378
95/6 UDBeAPlayer 2
98/9 UDChoice 205
96/7 UDCollChoice 269
97/8 UDCollChoice 262
96 Wien 26, -Aut
89/90 MTL
90/1 VAN/Mohawk
91/2 VAN
92/3 VAN/RoadTrip
93/4 VAN/Coins
94/5 VAN
95/6 VAN/Building 6
96/7 VAN
96/7 VAN/IGA

LUND, JAMIE
91/2 AvantGardeBCJ 142

LUND, JOE
51/2 Cleveland

LUND, LARRY
74/5 opcWHA 22
77/8 opcWHA 19
73/4 QuakerOats 19
75/6 Houston

LUND, PENTTI
45-64 BeeHives(BOS), (NYR)
51/2 Parkhurst 31
52/3 Parkhurst 83

LUND, TOM
70/1 Kuvajulkaisut 351
95/6 NorthIowa

LUNDBACK, PATRIK
97/8 udSwedish 95

LUNDBERG, JOAKIM
94/5 ElitSet 213
95/6 ElitSet 188
92/3 SemicElitserien 82
95/6 udElite 41

LUNDBERG, L.G.
79 PaniniSticker 198
96 Wien HL12

LUNDBERG, NICLAS
91/2 SemicElitserien 275

LUNDBERG, PERTTI
89/90 SemicElitserien 265
71/2 WilliamsFIN 348

LUNDE, DALE
72/3 WilliamsFIN 334

LUNDE, LEN
45-64 BeeHives(CHIx2), (DET)
64-67 BeeHives(CHI)
62 CeramicTiles
70/1 Esso Stamp
70/1 OPC 230
60/1 Parkhurst 35
61/2 Parkhurst 24
62/3 Parkhurst 35
60/1 ShirriffCoin 54
58/9 Topps 15
59/60 Topps 22
72/3 WilliamsFIN 129

LUNDELL, PER
96/7 DEL 191
94/5 ElitSet 4
95/6 ElitSet 220
89/90 SemicElitserien 127
90/1 SemicElitserien 204
91/2 SemicElitserien 83
92/3 SemicElitserien 107
95/6 udElite 59

LUNDEN, HANNU
70/1 Kuvajulkaisut 232
71/2 WilliamsFIN 249
73/4 WilliamsFIN 290

LUNDEN, MARTTI
70/1 Kuvajulkaisut 333

LUNDH, STAFFAN
89/90 SemicElitserien 86
90/1 SemicElitserien 267
91/2 SemicElitserien 96
92/3 SemicElitserien 114
95/6 udElite DS20

LUNDHOLM, BENGT
82/3 O-Pee-Chee 385
83/4 O-Pee-Chee 387
84/5 O-Pee-Chee 341
79 PaniniSticker 197
82/3 Post
82 SemicSticker 151
83/4 Vachon 130
81/2 WPG
82/3 WPG
83/4 WPG
84/5 WPG/Police

LUNDHOLM, JOAKIM
89/90 SemicElitserien 259

LUNDIN, HENRIK
92/3 SemicElitserien 317

LUNDMARK, CURT
95/6 DEL 48
91/2 SemicElitserien 360

LUNDMARK, DAVE
83/4 Kingston 11

LUNDMARK, PETER
94/5 ElitSet 221
95/6 ElitSet 283
89/90 SemicElitserien 138
90/1 SemicElitserien 211
92/3 SemicElitserien 261
95/6 udElite 178

LUNDRIGAN, JOE
74/5 Loblaws
74/5 O-Pee-Chee 277
72/3 TOR
74/5 WSH

LUNDSTROM, LARS-ERIK
91/2 SemicElitserien 306
92/3 SemicElitserien 328

LUNDSTROM, MATS
89/90 SemicElitserien 205
90/1 SemicElitserien 38
91/2 SemicElitserien 289

LUNDSTROM, MIKAEL
91/2 SemicElitserien 312
92/3 SemicElitserien 334

LUNDSTROM, P.A.
95/6 ElitSet 275
95/6 SP 187
95/6 UpperDeck 562
95/6 UDCollChoice 346

LUNDSTRÖM, TORD
72 Hellas 30
74 Hellas 29
70/1 Kuvajulkaisut 31
69/70 MästarSerien 40, 47, 48
72 Panda
72 SemicSticker 58
71/2 WilliamsFIN 50
72/3 WilliamsFIN 52
73/4 WilliamsFIN 31

LUNDY, PAT
45-64 BeeHives(CHI)

LUNE, KEVIN
88/9 Brockville 24

LUOJOLA, HANNU
66/7 Champion 54
70/1 Kuvajulkaisut 144
72 SemicSticker 74
78/9 SM-Liiga 159
71/2 WilliamsFIN 67, 194
72/3 WilliamsFIN 232
73/4 WilliamsFIN 266

LUOM, JARI
89/90 SemicElitserien 218
90/1 SemicElitserien 52

LUONGO, CHRIS
92/3 FleerUltra 362
93/4 FleerUltra 96
92/3 opcPremier 35
89/90 ProCards(IHL) 107
90/1 ProCards 484
91/2 ProCards 125
92/3 UpperDeck 534
92/3 OTT

LUONGO, ROBERTO
97/8 Bowman 42, 159, BB18
97/8 DonrussElite 51, -BackTo 7
97/8 PinnacleBeeHive 69
97/8 UDBlackDiamond 131
98/9 UDChoice 258
97/8 Zenith 97, Z77

LUOSTARINEN, TIMO
66/7 Champion 138

LUOTO, HARRY
70/1 Kuvajulkaisut 162

LUOVI, MIKKO
92/3 Jyvas-Hyva 40
93/4 Jyvas-Hyva 82
93/4 Sisu 120
94/5 Sisu-Horoscope 14
95/6 Sisu 309
96/7 Sisu 99
91/2 UD-CzechWJC 33
93/4 UpperDeck 271
97/8 udSwedish 28

LUPIEN, CAM
51/2 LacStJean 26

LUPIEN, GILLES
80/1 O-Pee-Chee 298
77/8 MTL
78/9 MTL
79/80 MTL

LUPIEN, STEVE
90/1 SketchMEM 49
90/1 SketchQMJHL 2

LUPUL, GARY
82/3 O-Pee-Chee 354
83/4 O-Pee-Chee 355
84/5 O-Pee-Chee 323
82/3 Post
84/5 7ElevenDisk
83/4 Vachon 111
80/1 VAN
80/1 VAN/Silverwood
81/2 VAN
81/2 VAN/Silverwood
83/4 VAN
84/5 VAN
85/6 VAN
82/3 Fredericton 5
85/6 Fredericton 6
84/5 KelownaWings 32
82/3 Victoria

LUPZIG, ANDREAS
94/5 DEL 210
95/6 DEL 210, 429
96/7 DEL 355

95 PaniniWorlds 64
92 SemicSticker 189

LUSTH, MATS
94/5 ElitSet 236
95/6 ElitSet 300
90/1 SemicElitserien 129
91/2 SemicElitserien 181
92/3 SemicElitserien 205
95/6 udElite 192
97/8 udSwedish 140

LUTCHENKO, VLADIMIR
72 Hellas 63
74 Hellas 48
70/1 Kuvajulkaisut 6
72 Panda
79 PaniniSticker 142
72 SemicSticker 3
74 SemicSticker 28
78 SovietChamps
69/70 Soviet Stars
70/1 Soviet Stars
71/2 Soviet Stars
73/4 Soviet Stars 10
74/5 Soviet Stars 6
91/2 Trends72 42
71/2 WilliamsFIN 7
72/3 WilliamsFIN 27
73/4 WilliamsFIN 8

LUTES, CRAIG
90/1 SketchOHL 342
91/2 SketchOHL 353
93/4 Slapshot(Windsor) 6
94/5 Birmingham
95/6 Birmingham
90/1 Oshawa 12
91/2 Oshawa
92/3 Windsor 6

LUTHER, GARY
87/8 SSMarie 30

LUTHI, FREDY
95 Globe 211
91 SemicSticker 189
92 SemicSticker
93 SemicSticker 121

LUTHI, PETER
72 SemicSticker 144

LUTTER, PETER
94/5 DEL 362
95/6 DEL 317
96/7 DEL 98

LUTZ, RAINER
94/5 DEL 309

LUZA, PATRICK
91/2 UD'CzechWJC 90

LYASENKO, ILYA
93/4 Slapshot(Sudbury) 18
93/4 Sudbury 17

LYASHENKO, ROMAN
96/7 UpperDeck"Ice" 144

LYDMAN, TONI
95/6 UpperDeck 551

LYLE, GEORGE
80/1 O-Pee-Chee 379
81/2 O-Pee-Chee 100
82/3 Post
80/1 DET
82/3 HFD/JuniorWhalers

LYLYK, DAVID
94/5 Slapshot(Guelph) 21

LYNCH, BERNIE
88/9 Regina

LYNCH, JACK
82? JDMcCarthy
74/5 Loblaws, -Update
72/3 OPC 160
73/4 OPC 232
74/5 OPC 331
75/6 OPC/Topps 116
76/7 OPC 288
77/8 OPC 369
78/9 WSH

LYNCH, P.J.
97/8 Halifax (1), (2)

LYNK, MARK
95/6 Halifax
96/7 Halifax (1), (2)
97/8 Halifax (1)

LYNN, VICTOR IVAN
45-64 BeeHives(TOR)
51/2 Parkhurst 20
45-54 QuakerOats

LYONS, COREY
90/1 ProCards 615
91/2 ProCards 583
88/9 Lethbridge
89/90 Lethbridge

LYONS, CRAIG
90/1 SketchWHL 301
91/2 SketchWHL 85

LYONS, MARC
84/5 Kingston 11
85/6 Kingston 11
86/7 Kingston 22
93/4 Toledo 21

LYSENKO, ALEXANDER
90/1 O-Pee-Chee 500

LYSIAK, TOM
74/5 Loblaws
74/5 OPC/Topps 14, 68
75/6 OPC/Topps 230, 313
76/7 OPC/T.174, OPC 379
77/8 OPC/Topps 127
78/9 OPC/Topps 97
79/80 OPC/Topps 41
80/1 OPC/Topps 247
81/2 O-Pee-Chee 59, 73
81/2 Topps 49, (W) 71
82/3 O-Pee-Chee 68
83/4 O-Pee-Chee 107
84/5 OPC 39, Topps 31
85/6 OPC/Topps 23
81/2 opcSticker 114
82/3 opcSticker 14, 174
83/4 opcSticker 110
84/5 opcSticker 31
79 PaniniSticker 59
82/3 Post
83/4 PuffySticker 15
83/4 SouhaitsRen.KeyChain
74/5 ATL
77/8 ATL
78/9 ATL/Coke
79/80 CHI
80/1 CHI/4x6
81/2 CHI
82/3 CHI

LYULIN, ANDREI
95/6 udElite 189

M

MAATANEN, PASI
92/3 Jyvas-Hyva 50
93/4 Jyvas-Hyva 84
93/4 Sisu 129
94/5 Sisu 28
95/6 Sisu 240

MAATTANEN, RAIMO
65/6 Hellas 75
70/1 Kuvajulkaisut 284

MACADAM, AL
74/5 Loblaws
74/5 O-Pee-Chee 301
75/6 OPC/Topps 253
76/7 OPC/Topps 237, OPC 393
77/8 OPC/Topps 149
78/9 O-Pee-Chee 381
79/80 OPC/Topps 104
80/1 OPC/Topps 34, 139
81/2 OPC 163, Topps(W) 107
82/3 O-Pee-Chee 171
83/4 O-Pee-Chee 173
84/5 O-Pee-Chee 324, Topps 75
85/6 O-Pee-Chee 209
81/2 opcSticker 90
85/6 opcSticker 242/109
78/9 MIN/Cloverleaf 4
79/80 MIN
80/1 MIN
81/2 MIN
82/3 MIN
83/4 MIN
84/5 VAN
85/6 Fredericton 27

MACADAM, DON
90/1 ProCards 240
91/2 ProCards 235
94/5 Milwaukee

MACADAM, GARY
77/8 OPC/Topps 253
78/9 OPC/Topps 42
79/80 OPC/Topps 72
80/1 O-Pee-Chee 288
81/2 O-Pee-Chee 93
84/5 O-Pee-Chee 117
82/3 Post
81/2 Topps (West) 93
81/2 CGY

MACANDREW, LARRY
83/4 Ottawa67s

MACAULAY, ANTHONY
94/5 Hampton 12

MACAUSLAND, LENNIE
90/1 SketchWHL 58
91/2 SketchWHL 185

MACCHIO, RALPH
91/2 ProSetPlatinum 295

MACDERMID, KEN
87/8 Hull

MACDERMID, PAUL
91/2 Bowman 195
92/3 Bowman 282
92/3 FleerUltra 439
89/90 OPC/Topps 183
90/1 OPC/Topps 338
91/2 OPC/Topps 463
89/90 opcSticker266 /147
90/1 Panini(WPG) 15
88/9 PaniniSticker 243
89/90 PaniniSticker 227
91/2 PaniniSticker 69
91/2 Pinnacle 279
90/1 ProSet 331
91/2 ProSet 269
90/1 Score 296
91/2 Score(CDN) 219, (U.S) 219
92/3 Score 59
92/3 Topps 391
91/2 ToppsStadiumClub 254
92/3 ToppsStadiumClub 178
90/1 UpperDeck 218
85/6 HFD/JuniorWhalers
86/7 HFD/JuniorWhalers
87/8 HFD/JuniorWhalers
88/9 HFD/JuniorWhalers
89/90 HFD/JuniorWhalers
94/5 QUE/BurgerKing
90/1 WPG/IGA
91/2 WPG/IGA
91/2 WSH/Kodak
92/3 WSH/Kodak

MACDONAGH, BILL
51/2 LavalDairy 52

MACDONALD, AARON
95/6 Classic 32
95/6 C'FiveSport 142, -Aut
95/6 SwiftCurrent

MACDONALD, B.J.
82/3 Fredericton 2

MACDONALD, BLAIR
80/1 OPC/Topps 32
81/2 O-Pee-Chee 340
82/3 O-Pee-Chee 350
76/7 opcWHA 93
77/8 opcWHA 16
80/1 Pepsi Cap
89/90 ProCards'IHL 164
90/1 ProCards 390
79/80 EDM
88/9 EDM/ActionMagazine 99
81/2 VAN
81/2 VAN/Silverwood
83/4 MedicineHat 6

MACDONALD, BRETT
91/2 ProCards 430
87/8 Flint
88/9 Flint
86/7 Fredericton
85/6 Kitchener 12
83/4 NorthBay

MACDONALD, BRIAN
83/4 Brantford 12

MACDONALD, BRUCE
92/3 Toledo 1, 2
93/4 Toledo 20

MACDONALD, CHRIS
95/6 Slapshot 129

MACDONALD, CLINT
91/2 AvantGardeBCJ 120
92/3 BCJHL 133

MACDONALD, DAVE
94/5 Slapshot (Sudbury) 2
95/6 Slapshot 381
96/7 Guelph 3
83/4 Kelowna

MACDONALD, DOUG
92/3 Classic 92
93/4 UpperDeck 97
96/7 Cincinnati
92/3 Rochester/Dunkin'Donuts
92/3 Rochester/Kodak
93/4 Rochester

MACDONALD, GARETT
94/5 Richmond
95/6 Richmond

MACDONALD, JASON
94/5 Classic 118
90/1 SketchOHL 311
91/2 SketchOHL 277
95/6 Adirondack
93/4 OwenSound

MACDONALD, JOEY
97/8 Halifax (1), (2)

MACDONALD, JOHN
83/4 Belleville 9

MACDONALD, KEVIN
95/6 EdgeIce 106
88/9 ProCards(Muskegon)
89/90 ProCards(AHL) 24
90/1 ProCards 366
91/2 ProCards 388
89/90 Rayside

MACDONALD, KILBY
34-43 BeeHives(NYR)
39/40 OPC (V301-1) 87

MACDONALD, LEONARD
90/1 SketchOHL 184
91/2 SketchOHL 185
89/90 Sudbury 14

MACDONALD, LOWELL
74/5 Loblaws
68/9 OPC/Topps 42
70/1 OPC 206
72/3 OPC 214
73/4 OPC/Topps 128
74/5 OPC/Topps 30, 133, 183
75/6 OPC/Topps 204
76/7 OPC/Topps 33
77/8 OPC 390
94/5 Parkie(64/5) 60
68/9 ShirriffCoin LA7
74/5 PGH
77/8 PGH/PuckBuck

MACDONALD, PARKER
45-64 BeeHives(DET), (TOR)
64-67 BeeHives(BOS), (DET)
62 CeramicTiles
63-5 ChexPhoto
64/5 CokeCap DET-20
65/6 CocaCola
68/9 OPC/Topps 55
55/6 Parkhurst 9, 77
63/4 Parkhurst 44
93/4 Parkie (56/7) 104
94/5 Parkie (64/5) 44
95/6 Parkie(66/7) 55
60/1 ShirriffCoin 59
61/2 ShirriffCoin 69
68/9 ShirriffCoin MIN8
54-67 TorontoStar V11
56-66 TorontoStar 62/3
63/4 TheTorontoStar
64/5 TheTorontoStar
64/5 Topps 11
65/6 Topps 105
63/4 York 40
62/3 YorkTransfer 27
73/4 MIN

MACDONALD, PAUL
91/2 SketchQMJHL 200

MACDONALD, REID
90/1 Mich.Tech
91/2 Mich.Tech

MACDONALD, RYAN
94/5 Slapshot(Detroit) 4
94/5 Slapshot(MEM) 78
95/6 Slapshot 212

MACDONALD, TODD
95/6 EdgeIce 24
96/7 Cincinnati
92/3 Tacoma
93/4 Tacoma

MACDONALD, TOM
90/1 SketchMEM 14
90/1 SketchOHL 166
91/2 SketchOHL 322
93/4 Slapshot(SSMaire) 15
93/4 SSMarie 17

MACDONALD, WILLIE
87/8 Kamloops

MACEACHERN, AL
97/8 Halifax (1), (2)

MACEACHERN, GREG
89/90 SketchMEM 57
90/1 SketchQMJHL 77

MACEACHERN, LIAM
94/5 Slapshot (Sudbury) 18
95/6 Slapshot 397
88/9 ProCards(Peoria)

MACEK, PETR
94/5 APS 254
95/6 APS 132

MACFARLANE, EON
92/3 BCJHL 200

MACGILVRAY, JOHN
52/3 AnonymousOHL 165

MACGREGOR, BRAD
88/9 ProCards(CapreBreton)

MACGREGOR, BRUCE
45-64 BeeHives(DET)
64-67 BeeHives(DETx2)
62 CeramicTiles
63-5 ChexPhoto
64/5 CokeCap DET-16
65/6 CocaCola
70/1 DadsCookies
70/1 EddieSargent 51
71/2 EddieSargent 124
72/3 EddieSargent 153
70/1 Esso Stamp
68/9 OPC/Topps 30
69/70 OPC/Topps 63
70/1 OPC/Topps 27
71/2 OPC/Topps 216
72/3 O-Pee-Chee 103
73/4 OPC 201
74/5 opcWHA 2
75/6 opcWHA 22
62/3 Parkhurst 23
63/4 Parkhurst 41
94/5 Parkie(64/5) 47
95/6 Parkie(66/7) 49
61/2 ShirriffCoin 73
68/9 ShirriffCoin DET8
71/2 TheToronto Sun
64/5 Topps 76
65/6 Topps 110
66/7 Topps 104, -USATest 56
67/8 Topps 102
63/4 York 51
62/3 YorkTransfer 36
70/1 DET/Marathon
88/9 EDM/ActionMagazine 154

MACGUIGAN, GARTH
81/2 Indianapolis 6
82/3 Indianapolis

MACH, MIROSLAV
94/5 APS 63
95/6 APS 91

MACHAC, OLDRICH
72 Hellas 83
74 Hellas 77
70/1 Kuvajulkaisut 53
72 Panda
72 SemicSticker 24
74 SemicSticker 55
71/2 WilliamsFIN 31
72/3 WilliamsFIN 14
73/4 WilliamsFIN 55

MACHALEK, ROB
95/6 APS 108

MACHALEK, VLADIMIR
94/5 APS 225
95/6 APS 172, 238

MACINNES, JOHN
91/2 Mich.Tech

MACINNIS, AL
95/6 Aces 2 (Diamonds)
90/1 Bowman 93
91/2 Bowman 262
92/3 Bowman 51, 211
95/6 Bowman 16
93/4 Donruss 47
94/5 D-Dominators 6
95/6 Donruss 205, -Dominator 7
96/7 Donruss 12
97/8 Donruss 122
96/7 DonrussCanadianIce 15
97/8 DonrussCanadianIce 55
95/6 DonrussElite 15
96/7 DonrussElite 67
97/8 DonrussPreferred 132
97/8 DonrussPriority 144
93/4 EAsports 20
94/5 Flair 157
96/7 Flair 82
94/5 Fleer 190, -Slapshot 5
96/7 Fleer 98
95/6 FleerMetal 126
92/3 FleerUltra 23, -AllStar 8
93/4 FleerUltra 113
94/5 FleerUltra 185
95/6 FleerUltra 300
96/7 FleerUltra 147
88/9 FritoLay
91/2 Gillette 7
95 Globe 79
94 HockeyWit 90
92/3 HumptyDumpty (2)
97/8 KatchMedallion 130
91/2 Kelloggs 16
96/7 KennerSLU
89/90 Kraft 3
90/1 Kraft 33
91/2 Kraft 32
93/4 Kraft-Recipe
96/7 Kraft-Disk
97/8 Kraft -RoadToNagano
93/4 Leaf 180
94/5 Leaf 461
95/6 Leaf 312
96/7 Leaf 174
94/5 LeafLimited 79
95/6 LeafLimited 95
96/7 Maggers 142
91/2 McDonalds McD23
92/3 McDonalds Mc D10
94/5 McDonalds McD15
97/8 McDonalds -Medallions
96/7 MetalUniverse 133
97/8 Omega 195
85/6 O-Pee-Chee 237
86/7 OPC/Topps 173
87/8 OPC/Topps 72, T-AS 9
88/9 O-Pee-Chee 231
89/90 OPC/Topps 49, T-AS 4
90/1 OPC/Topps 127, 197, H
91/2 OPC/Topps 262, 491
92/3 O-Pee-Chee 330
90/1 opcPremier 65
91/2 opcPremier 81
87/8 opcStars 26
85/6 opcSticker 211/78
86/7 opcSticker 86/214
87/8 opcSticker 40, 123/135
88/9 opcSticker 92/220
89/90 opcSticker 5, 95, 159/19
89/90 opcStickFS 27
98/9 Pacific 368
97/8 PacificCrown 202
98/9 PacificParamount 204
90/1 Panini(CGY) 7
87/8 PaniniSticker 205
88/9 PaniniSticker 5
89/90 PaniniSticker 32
90/1 PaniniSticker 185, 328
91/2 PaniniSticker 50, 330
92/3 PaniniSticker 49, 285
93/4 PaniniSticker P
94/5 PaniniSticker 161
95/6 PaniniSticker 197
96/7 PaniniSticker 207
91/2 Parkhurst 28
92/3 Parkhurst 20
93/4 Parkhurst 36, D3
94/5 Parkhurst 35
95/6 Parkhurst 178
94/5 ParkieSE 152
91/2 Pinnacle 220, 339, B8
92/3 Pinnacle 83
93/4 Pinnacle 155, -TmPinn. 3
94/5 Pinnacle 387, BR3
95/6 Pinnacle 79
96/7 Pinnacle 153
97/8 Pinnacle 116
97/8 PinnacleBeAPlayer 125
97/8 PinnacleCertified 120
97/8 PinnacleInside 161
95/6 PinnacleZenith 40
96/7 PinnacleZenith 18
95/6 Playoff 90
94/5 POG 264
95/6 POG 242
96/7 Post
93/4 PowerPlay 38, -Slapshot 7
93/4 Premier 276
94/5 Premier 110, 127, 347, 488
95/6 ProMagnet 9
90/1 ProSet 35, 337
91/2 ProSet 33, 275
92/3 ProSet 22
91/2 PS-ThePuck 5
91/2 PSPlatinum 19, 276
90/1 Score 5, 314, 335, -Hot 36
91/2 Score(CDN) 2, 299, 333
91/2 Score(U.S) 2, 417
92/3 Score 302, 421, 496
93/4 Score 121,-Drm 4,-Fran 3
94/5 Score 120, DT7
95/6 Score 46
96/7 Score 114
97/8 Score 248
97/8 Score(STL) 6
92/3 SeasonsPatch 60
94/5 Select 28
95/6 SelectCertified 72
89 SemicSticker 56
91 SemicSticker 57
92 SemicSticker 77
93 SemicSticker 193
94 Semic 84, 340
95 Semic 85
95/6 SkyBoxEmotion 150
95/6 SkyBoxImpact 143
96/7 SkyBoxImpact 114
94/5 SP 104
95/6 SP 125
97/8 SPAuthentic 184
95/6 Summit 90, -GM14
95/6 SuperSticker 100, 102
91 TeamCanada
96/7 TeamOut
92/3 Topps 452
95/6 Topps 145, HGC22
98/9 Topps 100
94/5 T.Finest-DivisionsBest 12
95/6 ToppsFinest 48
96/7 ToppsNHLPicks 49
91/2 ToppsStadiumClub 79
92/3 ToppsStadiumClub 128
93/4 ToppsStadiumClub 105
94/5 ToppsStadiumClub 56
95/6 ToppsStadiumClub 13
93/4 TSC-MembersOnly 7
94/5 TSC-MembersOnly 34
95/6 TSC-MembersOnly 9
95/6 ToppsSuperSkills 49
90/1 UpperDeck 143, 319, 497
91/2 UpperDeck 8, 243, 632
92/3 UpperDeck 257
93/4 UpperDeck 412, SP22
94/5 UpperDeck 150, 232
94/5 UD C33, R46, SP159
95/6 UpperDeck 290, AS9, SE71
96/7 UpperDeck 141
97/8 UpperDeck 352
93/4 UDBAP'Roots 19
94/5 UDBeAPlayer G14

95/6 UDBeAPlayer 134
98/9 UDChoice 188
95/6 UDCollChoice 313
96/7 UDCollChoice 228, 329
97/8 UDCollChoice 234
97/8 ValuNet
96 Wien 81
82/3 CGY
85/6 CGY/RedRooster
86/7 CGY/RedRooster
87/8 CGY/RedRooster
90/1 CGY/McGavins (x2)
91/2 CGY/IGA
92/3 CGY/IGA 22
82/3 Kitchener 17

MACINNIS, IAN
81/2 Kingston 7

MACINNIS, ROB
88/9 ProCards(CapeBreton)
90/1 ProCards 532
83/4 Kitchener 4
93/4 Richmond 7

MACINTOSH, ANDY
92/3 BCJHL 153
90/1 SketchWHL 6
91/2 SketchWHL 98
93/4 Indianapolis
93/4 Saskatoon

MACINTYRE, DUNCAN
83/4 Belleville 12
84/5 Belleville 4
85/6 Fredericton 10
86/7 Fredericton

MACINTYRE, JASON
94/5 Hampton 17
95/6 Hampton HRA-8

MACISAAC, AL
92/3 Hampton
93/4 Hampton
95/6 Hampton HRA-3

MACISAAC, BOB
91/2 SketchOHL 263
93/4 Slapshot(Sudbury) 23
91/2 Sudbury 7
92/3 Sudbury 3
93/4 Sudbury 25

MACISAAC, DAVE
92/3 Maine(2) 23
93/4 Maine 45

MACISAAC, TODD
91/2 SketchWHL 348
93/4 Lethbridge

MACIVER, NORM
91/2 Bowman 99
92/3 Bowman 425
93/4 Donruss 233
94/5 Donruss 273
96/7 Donruss 69
93/4 EASports 91
94/5 Flair 122
96/7 FleerNHLPicks 112
92/3 FleerUltra 61, 363
93/4 FleerUltra 143
94/5 FleerUltra 149
95/6 FleerUltra 289
93/4 Leaf 189
94/5 Leaf 68
96/7 Leaf 35
91/2 OPC/Topps 103
92/3 O-Pee-Chee 344
92/3 opcPremier 107
97/8 PacificCrown 60
88/9 PaniniSticker 302
93/4 PaniniSticker 112
91/2 Parkhurst 282
92/3 Parkhurst 117
93/4 Parkhurst 137
94/5 Parkhurst 154
95/6 Parkhurst 171, 499
92/3 Pinnacle 157
93/4 Pinnacle 120
94/5 Pinnacle 80
95/6 Pinnacle 170
96/7 PinnacleBeAPlayer 133
94/5 POG 175
93/4 PowerPlay 172
93/4 Premier 64
94/5 Premier 49

89/90 ProCards(AHL) 140
90/1 ProCards 224
92/3 ProSet 50
91/2 Score(CDN) 434
92/3 Score 349
93/4 Score 123
94/5 Score 24
95/6 Score 267
96/7 Score 167
92/3 Topps 96
92/3 ToppsStadiumClub 46
93/4 ToppsStadiumClub 267
92/3 UpperDeck 511
93/4 UD 299, 335, SP111
94/5 UpperDeck 466
94/5 UDBeAPlayer-Aut. 127
95/6 UDCollChoice 270
96/7 UDCollChoice 208
91/2 EDM/IGA
92/3 OTT
93/4 OTT/Kraft
94/5 OTT/Bell
96/7 PHO
97/8 PHO
95/6 PGH/Foodland 8
85/6 Minn-Duluth 5

MACKAY, BRIAN
52/3 AnonymousOHL 133

MACKAY, CALUM
51/2 Parkhurst 9
54/5 Parkhurst 11
55/6 Parkhurst 41
51-54 LaPatrie 14-FEB54
45-54 QuakerOats

MACKAY, DAVID
34-43 BeeHives(CHI)

MACKAY, KEVIN
90/1 SketchOHL 186
91/2 SketchOHL 190
95/6 RedDeer
89/90 Windsor (x2)

MACKAY, MARK
95/6 DEL 404
96/7 DEL 312

MACKAY, MICKEY
83&87 HallOfFame 203
83 HHOF Postcard (N)
19 Millionaires

MACKAY, MURRAY
45-54 QuakerOats
52/3 StLawrence 45

MACKAY, SCOTT
89/90 SketchOHL 35

MACKEIGAN, JACK
82/3 Victoria
83/4 Victoria

MACKELL, FLEMING
45-64 BeeHives(BOS), (TOR)
48-52 Exhibits
51/2 Parkhurst 83
52/3 Parkhurst 82
53/4 Parkhurst 91
54/5 Parkhurst 50
93/4 Parkie(56/7) 3
45-54 QuakerOats
54/5 Topps 36
57/8 Topps 16
58/9 Topps 29
59/60 Topps 19, 60
54-67 TorontoStar V 5,n3
57/8 BOS
91/2 BOS/Legends

MACKELLAR, PETER
93/4 Slapshot (SSMaire) 9
95/6 Slapshot 289
93/4 SSMarie 5

MACKENZIE, BILL
34-43 BeeHives(MTL.M)
35-40 CrownBrand 114
36/7 OPC (V304D) 111
37/8 OPC (V304E) 151
39/40 OPC (V301-1) 81
33/4 WWGum (V357) 61
36/7 WWGum (V356) 44

MACKENZIE, BRIAN
91/2 SketchOHL 267

MACKENZIE, J.M.
86/7 London 10
83/4 SSMarie
84/5 SSMarie

MACKENZIE, KEN
90/1 SketchOHL 399
91/2 SketchOHL 265

MACKENZIE, ROBERT
91/2 SketchOHL 285

MACKENZIE, ROD
94/5 Slapshot(MEM) 66

MACKENZIE, SHAWN
95/6 Halifax
96/7 Halifax (1), (2)
97/8 Halifax (1), (2)

MACKEY, DAVE
94/5 Leaf 280
94/5 Parkhurst 202
94/5 Premier 48
88/9 ProCards(Saginaw)
91/2 ProCards 31
85/6 MedicineHat 22
94/5 Milwaukee
92/3 Peoria
93/4 Peoria
82/3 Victoria
83/4 Victoria

MACKEY, KEN
90/1 ProCards 328

MACKIE, DUB
23/4 PaulinsCandy 14

MACKINNON, PAUL
78 /9 Winnipeg

MACLAREN, DON
81/2 Ottawa67s
82/3 Ottawa67s
83/4 Ottawa67s

MACLEAN, CAIL
93/4 Slapshot (Kingston) 12
95/6 Slapshot 117

MACLEAN, DAVE
83/4 Belleville 4
84/5 Belleville 11
81/2 Oshawa 17

MACLEAN, DON
94/5 AutoPhonex 26
95/6 Classic 30
95/6 ClassicFiveSport 157
97/8 KatchMedallion 70
97/8 Pacific 63
98/9 Pacific 238
97/8 Pinnacle 14
97/8 PinnacleBeAPlayer 241
97/8 SPAuthentic 184
97/8 UDBlackDiamond 57
98/9 UDChoice 102
97/8 UpperDeckIce 53

MACLEAN, DOUG
96/7 FLA/WinnDixie

MACLEAN, JOHN
90/1 Bowman 83
91/2 Bowman 272, 289
92/3 Bowman 130
95/6 Bowman 27
93/4 Donruss 184
94/5 Donruss 151
95/6 Donruss 88
96/7 Donruss 146
97/8 Donruss 155
95/6 DonrussElite 23
94/5 Flair 95
94/5 Fleer 114
95/6 FleerMetal 83
92/3 FleerUltra 115
93/4 FleerUltra 53
94/5 FleerUltra 119
95/6 FleerUltra 89, 193
91/2 Kelloggs 13
93/4 Leaf 264
94/5 Leaf 204
95/6 Leaf 176
96/7 Leaf 195
94/5 LeafLimited 92
97/8 Limited 60
97/8 Omega 202
86/7 OPC/Topps 37
87/8 OPC/Topps 191

88/9 OPC/Topps 10
89/90 OPC/Topps 102
90/1 OPC/Topps 224
91/2 OPC/Topps 239, T-TL 15
91/2 opcPremier 4
88/9 opcSticker 78 /207
89/90 opcSticker 87
98/9 Pacific 384
97/8 PacificCrown 169
97/8 PacificCrownRoyale 63
97/8 PcfcDynagon! 71,-Tand 48
97/8 PacificParamount 104
97/8 PacificRevolution 124
87/8 PaniniSticker 80
88/9 PaniniSticker 274
89/90 PaniniSticker 249
90/1 PaniniSticker 74
91/2 PaniniSticker 213
93/4 PaniniSticker 40
94/5 PaniniSticker 30
95/6 PaniniSticker 83
96/7 PaniniSticker 88
97/8 PaniniSticker 70
92/3 Parkhurst 90
93/4 Parkhurst 115
94/5 Parkhurst 125
95/6 Parkhurst 123
91/2 Pinnacle 115
92/3 Pinnacle 351
93/4 Pinnacle 183
94/5 Pinnacle 101
95/6 Pinnacle 26
96/7 Pinnacle 149
97/8 Pinnacle 14, 184
97/8 PinnacleCertified 91
97/8 PinnacleInside 145
95/6 PinnacleZenith 69
95/6 Playoff 278
94/5 POG 146
95/6 POG 160
93/4 PowerPlay 138
93/4 Premier 193
94/5 Premier 175
95/6 ProMagnet 32
90/1 ProSet 170
91/2 ProSet 136, 307
91/2 ProSetPlatinum 70
90/1 Score 190, -HotCards 83
91/2 Score(CDN) 210, (U.S) 210
92/3 Score 30
93/4 Score 81
94/5 Score 172
95/6 Score 77
96/7 Score 143
97/8 Score 141
97/8 Score(N.J.) 4
94/5 Select 136
95/6 SelectCertified 92
95/6 SkyBoxEmotion 98
95/6 SkyBoxImpact 93
94/5 SP 65
95/6 SP 78
95/6 Summit 106
96/7 Summit 143
92/3 Topps 273
95/6 Topps 140
94/5 ToppsFinest 90
95/6 ToppsFinest 38
91/2 ToppsStadiumClub 144
92/3 ToppsStadiumClub 28
93/4 ToppsStadiumClub 287
95/6 ToppsStadiumClub 26
95/6 ToppsSuperSkills 62
90/1 UpperDeck 161
91/2 UpperDeck 88, 169
92/3 UpperDeck 521
93/4 UpperDeck 134
94/5 UpperDeck 8, SP133
95/6 UpperDeck 74, SE134
96/7 UpperDeck 95
97/8 UpperDeck 94, 292
94/5 UDBeAPlayer 134
97/8 UDBlackDiamond 69
98/9 UDChoice 176
95/6 UDCollChoice 34
97/8 UDCollChoice 146
83/4 N.J.
84/5 N.J.
86/7 N.J./SOBER
88/9 N.J./Caretta
89/90 N.J.
90/1 N.J.

96/7 N.J/Sharp
97/8 S.J/PacificBellSheet
81/2 Oshawa 19
82/3 Oshawa 15

MACLEAN, MAC
87/8 Brockville 4
88/9 Brockville 5

MACLEAN, PAUL
90/1 Bowman 18
84/5 Kelloggs Disk
86/7 Kraft Sports 76
82/3 O-Pee-Chee 386
83/4 O-Pee-Chee 388
84/5 O-Pee-Chee 342, 371
85/6 OPC/Topps 145
86/7 OPC/Topps 114
87/8 OPC/Topps 91
88/9 OPC/Topps 38
89/90 OPC/Topps 129
90/1 OPC/Topps 110
88/9 opcStars 23
82/3 opcSticker 208
83/4 opcSticker 283
84/5 opcSticker 289
85/6 opcSticker 250/180
86/7 opcSticker 108/238
87/8 opcSticker 252
88/9 opcSticker 144
89/90 opcSticker 18/158
87/8 PaniniSticker 354, 364
88/9 PaniniSticker 156
90/1 PaniniSticker 271
82/3 Post
90/1 ProSet 266
83/4 PuffySticker 6
90/1 Score 203
84/5 7ElevenDisk
85/6 7Eleven 21
83/4 SouhaitsRen.KeyChain
90/1 UpperDeck 330
83/4 Vachon 131
88/9 DET/Caesars
96/7 PHO
89/90 STL/Kodak
90/1 STL/Kodak
81/2 WPG
82/3 WPG
83/4 WPG
84/5 WPG/Police
85/6 WPG
85/6 WPG/Police
85/6 WPG/Silverwood
86/7 WPG
87/8 WPG
87/8 Brockville 6
88/9 Brockville 9
93/4 Peoria

MACLEAN, RON
97/8 Pinnacle -CBC Sports 7

MACLEAN, TERRY
88/9 ProCards(Peoria)

MACLEISH, RICK
72/3 EddieSargent 167
74/5 LiptonSoup 20
74/5 Loblaws
71/2 OPC/Topps 207
72/3 OPC 105
73/4 OPC 133, 138, 146
73/4 Topps 1, 6, 135
74/5 OPC/Topps 6, 163
75/6 OPC/Topps 20
76/7 OPC/Topps 121
77/8 OPC/Topps 7, 15,-Glossy 9
78/9 OPC/Topps 125, 263
79/80 OPC/Topps 75
80/1 OPC/Topps 115, 263
81/2 OPC 133, Topps(E) 108
82/3 O-Pee-Chee 273
82/3 opcSticker 147
92/3 Parkhurst 472
71/2 TheTorontoSun
75/6 PHA/GingerAle

MACLELLAN, BRIAN
91/2 Bowman 269
84/5 O-Pee-Chee 87
85/6 O-Pee-Chee 204
86/7 OPC/Topps 33
87/8 OPC/Topps 31
88/9 OPC/Topps 193

89/90 O-Pee-Chee 208
90/1 OPC/Topps 286
91/2 OPC/Topps 50
88/9 opcSticker 162, 197/62
90/1 Panini(CGY) 8
87/8 PaniniSticker 294
88/9 PaniniSticker 95
90/1 ProSet 36
90/1 ScoreTraded 56T
91/2 Score(CDN) 582, (U.S) 32T
91/2 ToppsStadiumClub 206
90/1 UpperDeck 372
90/1 CGY/McGavins
84/5 L.A./Smokeys
86/7 MIN/7Eleven 2
87/8 MIN
88/9 MIN/American

MACLELLAN, SCOTT
81/2 Kingston 2
82/3 Kingston 21
91/2 Rayside

MACLELLAN, TODD
83/4 Saskatoon 14
86/7 Saskatoon

MACLEOD, PAT
92/3 Bowman 433
92/3 O-Pee-Chee 273
91/2 opcPremier 87
91/2 Parkhurst 161
89/90 ProCards(IHL) 90
90/1 ProCards 108
91/2 ProCards 525
91/2 ProSet 559
91/2 Score(CDN) 645, (U.S) 95T
92/3 Topps 317
92/3 ToppsStadiumClub 336
91/2 UpperDeck 578
92/3 UpperDeck 146
91/2 S.J.
87/8 Kamloops
88/9 Kamloops
94/5 Milwaukee

MACMILLAN, BILL
70/1 EddieSargent 205
71/2 EddieSargent 198
72/3 EddieSargent 5
70/1 Esso Stamp
74/5 Loblaws
72/3 OPC 98, Topps 77
74/5 O-Pee-Chee 339
76/7 O-Pee-Chee 312
71/2 TheTorontoSun
72/3 ATL
81/2 COL.R
71/2 TOR

MACMILLAN, BOB
76/7 OPC/Topps 38
77/8 OPC/Topps 141
78/9 OPC/Topps 82
79/80 OPC/Topps 2, 210
80/1 O-Pee-Chee 267
81/2 O-Pee-Chee 46
82/3 O-Pee-Chee 143
83/4 O-Pee-Chee 234
84/5 O-Pee-Chee 40
85/6 O-Pee-Chee 193
82/3 opcSticker 225
83/4 opcSticker 220
84/5 opcSticker 72
79 PaniniSticker 66
80/1 Pepsi Cap
82/3 Post
83/4 PuffySticker 11
83/4 SouhaitsRen.KeyChain
78/9 ATL/Coke
79/80 ATL
79/80 ATL/B&W
80/1 CGY
81/2 COL.R
83/4 N.J.
72/3 Minnesota

MACMILLAN, GARRY
69 ColumbusCheckers

MACMILLAN, JASON
95/6 Slapshot 315

MACMILLAN, JOHN
45-64 BeeHives(TOR)
62 CeramicTiles
63-5 ChexPhoto

61/2 ShirriffCoin 56
62/3 ShirriffCoin 14

MACMILLAN, TRAVIS
94/5 AutoPhonex 27

MACNAIR, SCOTT
94/5 Raleigh

MACNEIL, AL
45-64 BeeHives(CHIx2),(MTL)
45-64 BeeHives(TOR)
64-67 BeeHives(CHI), (NYR)
62 CeramicTiles
64/5 CokeCap CHI-19
65/6 CocaCola
57/8 Parkhurst (TOR) 19
93/4 Parkie(56/7) 121
94/5 Parkie(64/5) 40
95/6 Parkie(66/7) 94
61/2 ShirriffCoin 119
62/3 ShirriffCoin 40
64/5 TheTorontoStar
62/3 Topps 32
63/4 Topps 28
64/5 Topps 26
65/6 Topps 57
66/7 Topps 89
61/2 York
79/80 ATL/B&W
71/2 MTL
77/8 NovaScotia

MACNEIL, BERNIE
75/6 Cincinnati

MACNEIL, IAN
95/6 Slapshot 247

MACNEVIN, TROY
84/5 Kingston 29
85/6 Kingston 29
86/7 Kingston 15

MACOUN, JAMIE
92/3 Bowman 9
92/3 FleerUltra 212
93/4 FleerUltra 431
94/5 FleerUltra 217
94/5 Leaf 418
96/7 Leaf 170
84/5 O-Pee-Chee 230
85/6 O-Pee-Chee 201
86/7 O-Pee-Chee 203
87/8 O-Pee-Chee 214
89/90 O-Pee-Chee 207
90/1 OPC/Topps 265
91/2 OPC/Topps 168
92/3 O-Pee-Chee 371
85/6 opcSticker 212/79
87/8 opcSticker 48 /187
86/7 opcSticker 85 /213
97/8 PacificCrown 231
90/1 Panini(CGY) 9
87/8 PaniniSticker 208
89/90 PaniniSticker 38
90/1 PaniniSticker 178
91/2 PaniniSticker 61
93/4 PaniniSticker 230
94/5 ParkieSE 179
91/2 Pinnacle 114
92/3 Pinnacle 294
93/4 Pinnacle 131
94/5 Pinnacle 297
94/5 POG 240
93/4 PowerPlay 451
93/4 Premier 517
94/5 Premier 102
90/1 ProSet 37
91/2 ProSet 38
92/3 ProSet 188
91/2 PSPlatinum 235
90/1 Score 216
91/2 Score(CDN) 504, (U.S) 284
92/3 Score 88
93/4 Score 224
94/5 Score 106
92/3 Topps 348
91/2 ToppsStadiumClub 160
92/3 ToppsStadiumClub 309
90/1 UpperDeck 101
91/2 UpperDeck 412
95/6 UpperDeck 331
96/7 UpperDeck 166
95/6 UDBeAPlayer 218
83/4 Vachon 12

85/6 CGY/RedRooster
86/7 CGY/RedRooster
90/1 CGY/McGavins
91/2 CGY/IGA
92/3 TOR/Kodak
93/4 TOR/Abalene
93/4 TOR/Blacks 11
94/5 TOR

MACOUX, HENRI
94/5 DEL 256
95/6 DEL 254

MACPHEE, WAYNE
83/4 NorthBay

MACPHERSON, B.J.
90/1 SketchOHL 343
91/2 SketchOHL 158
93/4 Slapshot(NorthBay) 13
90/1 Oshawa 24
91/2 Oshawa
91/2 Oshawa/Dominos 16
92/3 Oshawa
94/5 Toledo
95/6 Toledo

MACPHERSON, BLAIR
85/6 Kitchener 26

MACPHERSON, BUD
45-64 BeeHives(MTL)
51/2 LaPatrie 13-Apr
51/2 Parkhurst 6
52/3 Parkhurst 11
53/4 Parkhurst 22
55/6 Parkhurst 47

MACPHERSON, DARWIN
89/90 ProCards'IHL 2
84/5 Brandon 19
89/90 Saskatoon 25

MACPHERSON, DON
90/1 SketchOHL 87

MACPHERSON, DUNCAN
88/9 ProCards(Springfield)
83/4 Saskatoon 4
84/5 Saskatoon

MACQUSITEN, DOUG
36/7 WWGum (V356) 105

MACSWEYN, RALPH
69/70 OPC/Topps 96
70/1 EddieSargent 145
72/3 LosAngeles
73/4 Vancouver

MACTAVISH, CRAIG
90/1 Bowman 193
91/2 Bowman 100, 416
92/3 Bowman 118
93/4 Donruss 462
96/7 Donruss 103
92/3 FleerUltra 294
93/4 FleerUltra 316
93/4 Kraft-Captain
94/5 Leaf 514
96/7 Leaf 192
86/7 OPC/Topps 178
87/8 O-Pee-Chee 203
88/9 O-Pee-Chee 232
89/90 O-Pee-Chee 230
90/1 OPC/Topps 189
91/2 OPC/Topps 63
92/3 O-Pee-Chee 118
86/7 opcSticker 76/204
87/8 opcSticker 9 /224
88/9 opcSticker 217/87
89/90 opcSticker 226/85
90/1 Panini(EDM) 13
87/8 PaniniSticker 267
88/9 PaniniSticker 60
89/90 PaniniSticker 78
90/1 PaniniSticker 220
91/2 PaniniSticker 132
92/3 PaniniSticker 101
93/4 PaniniSticker 240
91/2 Parkhurst 276
92/3 Parkhurst 48
93/4 Parkhurst 342
94/5 Parkhurst 145
94/5 ParkieSE 132
91/2 Pinnacle 215
92/3 Pinnacle 78
93/4 Pinnacle 96, CA8
94/5 Pinnacle 392
95/6 Pinnacle 148
93/4 PowerPlay 82
93/4 Premier 23
94/5 Premier 103
90/1 ProSet 90
91/2 ProSet 77
90/1 Score 258
91/2 Score(CDN) 202, (U.S) 202
92/3 Score 303
93/4 Score 8
94/5 Score 85
95/6 Score 249
96/7 Score 230
90/1 SketchOHL 365
92/3 Topps 336
94/5 T.Finest-RingLeaders 8
91/2 ToppsStadiumClub 133
92/3 ToppsStadiumClub 125
93/4 ToppsStadiumClub 410
95/6 TSC-MembersOnly 23
90/1 UpperDeck 169
91/2 UpperDeck 284
92/3 UpperDeck 425
93/4 UpperDeck 111
94/5 UpperDeck 225
94/5 UDBeAPlayer 72
96/7 UDCollChoice 227
85/6 EDM/RedRooster
86/7 EDM
86/7 EDM/RedRooster
87/8 EDM
88/9 EDM
88/9 EDM/ActionMagazine 21
90/1 EDM/McGavins
91/2 EDM/IGA
92/3 EDM
92/3 EDM/IGA 13
93/4 EDM 24OCT93
94/5 PHA

MACTAVISH, GORD
77/8 NovaScotia

MACVICAR, ANDY
89/90 Sudbury 18

MACWILLIAM, MIKE
91/2 ProCards 348
88/9 Flint

MADDEN, CHRIS
96/7 Guelph 21

MADELEY, DARRIN
92/3 Classic 65
92/3 ClassicFourSport 193
92/3 ClassicProspects 17, 40
93/4 Donruss 229
93/4 FleerUltra 382
94/5 FleerUltra 340
93/4 Leaf 299
94/5 Leaf 300
93/4 Parkhurst 142
94/5 ParkieSE 120
93/4 Pinnacle 211
94/5 Pinnacle 459
93/4 PowerPlay 400
93/4 Premier 283
94/5 Premier 109
93/4 Score 462
94/5 Score 51
93/4 ToppsStadiumClub 431
93/4 UpperDeck 61
95/6 UpperDeck 158
93/4 OTT/Kraft
94/5 OTT/Bell
91/2 LakeSuperior

MADER, BOB
52/3 AnonymousOHL 87

MADILL, JEFF
95/6 EdgeIce 191
91/2 OPC 6S
88/9 ProCards(Utica)
89/90 ProCards(AHL) 204
90/1 ProCards 571
91/2 ProCards 521
93/4 AtlantaKnights
92/3 Cincinnati

MADORE, STÉPHANE
91/2 SketchQMJHL 151

MAGARRELL, ADAM
94/5 SigRookies 53
95/6 Spokane 22

MAGGS, DARYL
71/2 TheTorontoSun

MAGLIARDITI, MARK
95/6 DonrussElite-WorldJrs 24

MAGNERTOFT, MARK
94/5 ElitSet 237
95/6 ElitSet 89
95/6 udElite 143

MAGNUSON, KEITH
70/1 DadsCookies
70/1 EddieSargent 35
71/2 EddieSargent 48
72/3 EddieSargent 57
70/1 Esso Stamp
74/5 Loblaws
70/1 OPC 151
71/2 OPC/Topps 69
72/3 OPC 71, 268, Topps 65, 87
73/4 OPC 151, Topps 44
74/5 OPC/Topps 75
75/6 OPC/Topps 176
76/7 OPC/Topps 125
77/8 OPC/Topps 89
78/9 OPC/Topps 34
72/3 Post Transfers 5
72 SemicSticker 230
71/2 TheTorontoSun
70/1 CHI
79/80 CHI
80/1 CHI/4x6

MAGNUSSEN, TROND
95 Globe 196
95 PaniniWorlds 246
94 Semic 265
92/3 SemicElitserien 312
93 SemicSticker 244
97/8 udSwedish 62
96 Wien 207

MANGNUSSON, MIKAEL
94/5 ElitSet 3
95/6 ElitSet 29
95/6 udElite 43
92/3 SemicElitserien 85

MAGNUSSON, STEFAN
91/2 SemicElitserien 106
91/2 Minnesota
92/3 Minnesota
93/4 Minnesota

MAGRUDER, DENNY
92/3 Wheeling 19
93/4 Wheeling 20

MAGUIRE, BILL
82/3 NorthBay

MAGUIRE, DEREK
94/5 Classic 56
94/5 Fredericton

MAGUIRE, E.J.
88/9 CHI/Coke
89/90 CHI/Coke
90/1 CHI/Coke
86/7 PHA

MAGUIRE, KEVIN
91/2 Bowman 172
90/1 Panini(TOR) 13
91/2 ProCards 347
90/1 ProSet 538
87/8 BUF/BlueShield
87/8 BUF/WonderBread
88/9 BUF/BlueShield
88/9 BUF/WonderBread
89/90 BUF/BlueShield
89/90 BUF/Campbell
90/1 TOR

MAHAFFY, JOHN
51/2 LavalDairy 55
36/7 WWGum (V356) 133

MAHER, JIM
92/3 Phoenix
93/4 Phoenix
94/5 Toledo

MAHEUX, NICOLAS
95/6 Halifax

MAHON, DAN
82/3 Kingston 14

MAHON, MARK
96/7 DEL 219

MAHONEY, BILL
83/4 MIN
80/1 WSH

MAHONEY, SCOTT
89/90 Sudbury 5

MAHOVLICH, FRANK
71/2 Bazooka Panel 2
45-64 BeeHives(TOR)
64-67 BeeHives(TORx2)
62 CeramicTiles
63-5 ChexPhoto
64/5 CokeCap TOR
65/6 CocaCola
70/1 DadsCookies
72-84 Dernière 72/3, 73/4
70/1 EddieSargent 63
71/2 EddieSargent 104
72/3 EddieSargent 120
62/3 ElProductoDisk
70/1 Esso Stamp
88/9 Esso Sticker
71/2 FritoLay
83&87 HallOfFame 121
83 HHOF Postcard (I)
94/5 HHOFLegends 43
93/4 HockeyWit 56
71 Kelloggs
91/2 Kraft 87
72/3 Letraset 8
73/4 MacsMilk Disk
68/9 OPC/T. 31, OPC-Puck 2
69/70 OPC/Topps 62, OPC 222
69/70 OPC-Stamp, -Sticker
70/1 OPC/Topps 22, OPC 242
70/1 OPC/T-Deckle 17, -Sticker
71/2 OPC/Topps 105
72/3 OPC 102, -Tm.Canada
72/3 Topps 140
73/4 OPC 145, Topps 40
74/5 OPC/Topps 124
74/5 opcWHA 40
75/6 opcWHA 110
76/7 opcWHA 111
77/8 opcWHA 61
57/8 Parkhurst (TOR) 17
58/9 Parkhurst 33
59/60 Parkhurst 24
60/1 Parkhurst 2
61/2 Parkhurst 2
62/3 Parkhurst 4, 18
63/4 Parkhurst 17, 77
92/3 Parkhurst PR29
93/4 Parkhurst PR44
93/4 Parkhurst 56-Autograph A6
93/4 Parkie(56/7) FS5
94/5 Parkie(64/5) 130, 143, SL6
95/6 Parkie(66/7) 102, 124
95/6 Parkie(66/7) 145, 146
66/7 Post'Large, -'Small
67 Post FlipBook
70/1 PostShooters
72 SemicSticker 195
60/1 ShirriffCoin 12
61/2 ShirriffCoin 43
62/3 ShirriffCoin 3, 53
68/9 ShirriffCoin DET12
91/2 StarPics 27
81/2 TCMA 10
63/4 TheTorontoStar
64/5 TheTorontoStar
54-67 TorontoStar 66/7, V6, V10
56-66 TorontoStar 60/1, 62/3
56-66 TorontoStar 64/5, 65/6
56-66 TorontoStar 57/8, 58/9
71/2 TheTorontoSun
64/5 Topps 85
65/6 Topps 81
66/7 Topps 77,131, -USATest 51
67/8 Topps 79
91/2 Trends(72) 26, 30, -Aut
91/2 Ultimate06 40, -Aut 40
92/3 UD'LockerAS 44
60/1 York
60/1 YorkGlasses
61/2 York 3
62/3 YorkTransfer 11
63/4 York 5
67/8 York 18, 20, 28, 35
92/3 Zellers
70/1 DET/Marathon
69/70 MTL/ProStar
70/1 MTL
71 MTL/Pins
71/2 MTL (x2)
72/3 MTL
73/4 MTL
92/3 MTL/OPC 24, 39
95/6 MTL/Forum 11MAR96
64/5 TOR
66/7 TOR/Coaster
69/70 TOR

MAHOVLICH, PETE
64-67 BeeHives(DET)
72-84 Dernière 72/3, 73/4
70/1 EddieSargent 102
71/2 EddieSargent 99
72/3 EddieSargent 114
70/1 Esso Stamp
74/5 LiptonSoup 39
74/5 Loblaws
73/4 MacsMilk Disk
68/9 O-Pee-Chee 143
70/1 OPC/Topps 58
71/2 OPC/Topps 84
72/3 OPC 124, -TmCanada
72/3 Topps 42
73/4 OPC 164, Topps 186
74/5 OPC/Topps 97
75/6 OPC/Topps 50, 209, 322
76/7 OPC/Topps 2,15, T. 388
77/8 OPC/Topps 205
78/9 OPC/Topps 51
79/80 OPC/Topps 187
80/1 OPC/Topps 72
80/1 opcSuperCard 6
95/6 Parkie(66/7) 46
70/1 PostShooters
68/9 ShirriffCoin DET3
71/2 TheTorontoSun
66/7 Topps 103, -USATest 21
91/2 Trends (72) 27, 30, -Aut
92/3 Trends(76) 180
80/1 DET
69/70 MTL/ProStar
70/1 MTL
71 MTL/Pins
71/2 MTL
72/3 MTL
73/4 MTL
74/5 MTL
75/6 MTL
76/7 MTL

MAIA, PIERRICK
95 Globe 202
95 PaniniWorlds 111
94 Semic 223

MAIDL, ANTON
94/5 DEL 138
95/6 DEL 131

MAIER, ARNO
94 Semic 245
93 SemicSticker 281

MAIER, KIM
91/2 AirCanadaSJHL 24, A42
93/4 Knoxville
92/3 Wheeling 9

MAILHOT, JACQUES
88/9 ProCards (Halifax)
89/90 ProCards(IHL) 119
91/2 ProCards 431

MAILLET, CHRIS
93/4 RedDeer

MAILLET, CLAUDE
92/3 Greensboro 14

MAILLOUX, CHRIS
93/4 Slapshot (Detroit) 4

MAILLOUX, ROBERT
98 BowmanCHL 33
95/6 Slapshot 114

MAINER, PETR
94/5 APS 100
95/6 APS 225

MAIR, ADAM
97/8 Bowman 144
95/6 Slapshot 298

MAIR, JIM
72/3 EddieSargent 140
72/3 OPC 232
82 SemicSticker 135

MAISONNEUVE, ROGER
52/3 AnonymousOHL 88

MAITLAND, SHANE
90/1 SketchMEM 93
90/1 SketchWHL 194
91/2 SketchWHL 15

MAJANIEMI, TAPIO
66/7 Champion 114
65/6 Hellas 97

MAJAPURO, RAIMO
73/4 WilliamsFIN 224

MAJAURY, CRAIG
86/7 London 20

MAJAVA, KYOSTI
78/9 SM-Liiga 22
73/4 WilliamsFIN 207

MAJEAU, FERN
43-47 ParadeSportive

MAJESKY, BORIS
97/8 Halifax (2)

MAJIC, RON
94/5 Hampton 20
93/4 Huntington

MAJIC, XAVIER
94/5 Classic 46, -Preview
95/6 Fredericton
94/5 Wheeling 8

MAJOR, BRUCE
90/1 ProCards 545

MAJOR, MARK
90/1 ProCards 380
91/2 ProCards 294
95/6 Adirondack
92/3 Cleveland 24

MAJOROV, BORIS
92/3 Jyvas-Hyva 52
93/4 Jyvas-Hyva 283
93/4 Sisu 57

MAKAROV, SERGEI
90/1 Bowman 92
91/2 Bowman 250, 264
92/3 Bowman 53
93/4 Donruss 304
94/5 Donruss 103
94/5 Flair 167
94/5 Fleer 198
92/3 FleerUltra 24
93/4 FleerUltra 416
94/5 FleerUltra 198
95/6 FleerUltra 148
95 Globe 238
91 IvanFiodorovSportsUnite
89/90 Kraft 4
93/4 Leaf 384
94/5 Leaf 282
95/6 Leaf 293
90/1 O-Pee-Chee 503
92/3 O-Pee-Chee 90
90/1 OPC/Topps 60, P
91/2 OPC/Topps 482
91/2 opcPremier 45
94/5 PaniniSticker 222
95/6 PaniniSticker 282
90/1 Panini(CGY) 10
79 PaniniSticker 157
90/1 PaniniSticker 184, 334
91/2 PaniniSticker 58
92/3 PaniniSticker 47
93/4 PaniniSticker 183
95 PaniniWorlds 284
91/2 Parkhurst 247
92/3 Parkhurst 25
93/4 Parkhurst 188
94/5 Parkhurst 211
91/2 Pinnacle 271
92/3 Pinnacle 335
93/4 Pinnacle 362
94/5 Pinnacle 152
94/5 POG 217
93/4 PowerPlay 222
94/5 Premier 396
90/1 ProSet 38, 379, 396
91/2 ProSet 39
92/3 ProSet 24
91/2 PSPlatinum 15
91/2 RedAce
90/1 Score 71, 329, 350, -Hot 99
91/2 Score(CDN) 51, (U.S) 51
92/3 Score 382, -Sharpshooter 2
93/4 Score 33, 531, -(U.S) DD8
95/6 Score 159
94/5 Select 8
94 Semic 155
82 SemicSticker 60
89 SemicSticker 96
91 SemicSticker 216
95/6 SkyBoxEmotion 158
79/80 SovietStars
83/4 SovietStars
87/8 SovietStars
89/90 SovietStars
94/5 SP 107
92/3 Topps 467
95/6 Topps 171
91/2 ToppsStadiumClub 31
92/3 ToppsStadiumClub 217
94/5 ToppsStadiumClub 123
90/1 UpperDeck 123, 202, 336
91/2 UpperDeck 321
92/3 UpperDeck 314, -E16
93/4 UpperDeck 446, SP145
94/5 UpperDeck 124, 139, SP72
95/6 UpperDeck 24
95/6 UDCollChoice 207
90/1 CGY/McGavins
91/2 CGY/IGA
92/3 CGY/IGA 15
92/3 S.J./PacificBell

MAKAROV, SERGEI B.
90/1 O-Pee-Chee 485

MAKAROV, NIKOLAI
82 SemicSticker 75

MAKATSCH, RAINER
72 Hellas 57
72 SemicSticker 116

MAKELA, ERKKI
91/2 Jyvas-Hyva 52
92/3 Jyvas-Hyva 148
93/4 Jyvas-Hyva 259
93/4 Sisu 297

MAKELA, JARNO
93/4 Sisu 228
95/6 Sisu 158

MÄKELÄ, MIKKO
91/2 Bowman 36
95/6 DEL 98
96/7 DEL 286
94/5 FleerUltra 258
95 Globe 142
92/3 Jyvas-Hyva 181
94/5 Leaf 515
88/9 OPC/Topps 44
89/90 O-Pee-Chee 247
90/1 OPC/Topps 229
91/2 OPC/Topps 503
90/1 opcPremier 66
88/9 opcSticker 108/238
89/90 opcSticker 112/249
87/8 PaniniSticker 100
88/9 PaniniSticker 291
89/90 PaniniSticker 270
90/1 PaniniSticker 237
91/2 PaniniSticker 302
90/1 ProSet 418
90/1 ScoreTraded 26T
91/2 Score(CDN) 549
94 Semic 29
95 Semic 42
89 SemicSticker 41
92 SemicSticker
93 SemicSticker 68
94/5 Sisu-GuestSpecial 5
95/6 SisuLimited 106
91/2 ToppsStadiumClub 261
97/8 udSwedish 180, C28
90/1 BUF/BlueShield
90/1 BUF/Campbell
89/90 L.A./Smokeys 22
89/90 NYI

MAKELA, PEKKA
78/9 SM-Liiga 229

MAKELA, PERTTI
66/7 Champion 34
70/1 Kuvajulkaisut 198
71/2 WilliamsFIN 89
72/3 WilliamsFIN 253
73/4 WilliamsFIN 252

MAKELA, SEPPO
93/4 Sisu 380

MAKELA, TAUNO
80/1 Mallasjuoma 215
78/9 SM-Liiga 239

MAKELA, TIMO
65/6 Hellas 72
91/2 Greensboro

MAKI, BRENT
83/4 Oshawa 23

MAKI, RON P. (CHICO)
45-64 BeeHives(CHIx2)
64-67 BeeHives(CHIx2)
62 CeramicTiles
63-5 ChexPhoto
64/5 CokeCap CHI-16
65/6 CocaCola
70/1 DadsCookies
70/1 EddieSargent 46
71/2 EddieSargent 36
72/3 EddieSargent 60
70/1 Esso Stamp
72/3 Letraset 2
74/5 Loblaws
68/9 OPC/Topps 17
69/70 O-Pee-Chee 137
70/1 O-Pee-Chee 149
71/2 OPC/Topps 210
72/3 O-Pee-Chee 198
73/4 O-Pee-Chee 227
74/5 O-Pee-Chee 395
94/5 Parkie(64/5) 24
95/6 Parkie(66/7) 32
61/2 ShirriffCoin 28
68/9 ShirriffCoin CHI 7
64/5 TheTorontoStar
71/2 TheTorontoSun
62/3 Topps 37
63/4 Topps 41
64/5 Topps 73
65/6 Topps 117
66/7 Topps 110, -USATest 53
67/8 Topps 111
68/9 CHI

MAKI, TIMO
93/4 Jyvas-Hyva 194
93/4 Sisu 257

MAKI, WAYNE
68/9 ShirriffCoin CHI 3
70/1 EddieSargent 210
71/2 EddieSargent 217
72/3 EddieSargent 216
70/1 Esso Stamp
70/1 OPC/Topps 116
71/2 OPC/Topps 58
72/3 OPC 84, Topps 32
72 SemicSticker 221
71/2 TheTorontoSun
67/8 Topps 55
70/1 VAN/RoyalBank
71/2 VAN/RoyalBank 20
72/3 VAN/Nalleys
72/3 VAN/RoyalBank

MAKI-KOKKILA, KIMO
93/4 Jyvas-Hyva 209
93/4 Sisu 270
95/6 Sisu 207

MAKIA, MARTTI
66/7 Champion 93
72/3 WilliamsFIN 178

MAKIA, VEIKKO
66/7 Champion 96

MAKIAHO, TONI
95/6 Sisu 27
96/7 Sisu 23
94/5 ToppsFinest 139

MAKILA, RAYNER
51/2 LacStJean 41

MAKINEN, ARI
80/1 Mallasjuoma 66
78/9 SM-Liiga 73

MAKINEN, ESKO
70/1 Kuvajulkaisut 132
73/4 WilliamsFIN 185

MAKINEN, JUHA
71/2 WilliamsFIN 371

MAKINEN, KARI
66/7 Champion 153
65/6 Hellas 154
93/4 Jyvas-Hyva 253
70/1 Kuvajulkaisut 214
93/4 Sisu 279

MAKINEN, KEITH
66/7 Champion 217

MAKINEN, MARKO
95/6 Sisu 333, -NHLDraft 4

MAKINEN, PEKKA
70/1 Kuvajulkaisut 215
78/9 SM-Liiga 137
71/2 WilliamsFIN 137
72/3 WilliamsFIN 200
73/4 WilliamsFIN 161

MAKINEN, SEPPO
66/7 Champion 145
65/6 Hellas 151
70/1 Kuvajulkaisut 216
71/2 WilliamsFIN 138
72/3 WilliamsFIN 201
73/4 WilliamsFIN 162

MAKINEN, SEPPO
72/3 WilliamsFIN 271
73/4 WilliamsFIN 163

MAKINEN, TAPIO
66/7 Champion 218
96/7 Sisu 116

MAKITALO, JARMO
94/5 ElitSet 77
89/90 SemicElitserien 137
92/3 SemicElitserien 173
82 SemicSticker 41
78/9 SM-Liiga 122
77-79 Sportscaster 90-2152

MAKITALO, JOUNI
78/9 SM-Liiga 237

MAKITALO, KARI
78/9 SM-Liiga 123

MAKKONEN, KARI
80/1 Mallasjuoma 216
78/9 SM-Liiga 18, 240
79/80 EDM
88/9 EDM/ActionMagazine 144

MAKKONEN, PASI
71/2 WilliamsFIN 329

MALAC, PAVEL
94/5 APS 182
95/6 APS 30

MALAKHOV, VLADIMIR
92/3 ClassicProspects 55, BC4
93/4 Donruss 207
94/5 Donruss 307
95/6 Donruss 4
93/4 EASports 79
94/5 Flair 105
94/5 Fleer 126
96/7 FleerNHLPicks 118
92/3 FleerUltra 346, -Import 14
93/4 FleerUltra 235
94/5 FleerUltra 130
95/6 FleerUltra 81
95 Globe 166
97/8 KatchMedallion 76
93/4 Leaf 32, -GoldL.Rookie 9
94/5 Leaf 194
95/6 Leaf 149
97/8 Omega 119
90/1 O-Pee-Chee 2R
92/3 opcPremier 89
98/9 Pacific 253
98/9 PacificParamount 114
97/8 PacificRegime 103
94/5 PaniniSticker 53
95/6 PaniniSticker 42
96/7 PaniniSticker 44
97/8 PaniniSticker 34
92/3 Parkhurst 339
93/4 Parkhurst 125, 239
94/5 Parkhurst 115, V77
94/5 ParkieSE 108
92/3 Pinnacle 409
93/4 Pinnacle 104
94/5 Pinnacle 104, BR2
97/8 PinnacleBeAPlayer 133
95/6 Playoff 273
94/5 POG 162
95/6 POG 151
93/4 PowerPlay 153, -Second 6
93/4 Premier 129, 445, 515
94/5 Premier 546
92/3 RedAce(Blue) 28,(Violet) 28
93/4 Score 157
94/5 Score 62
95/6 Score 117
97/8 Score 247
97/8 Score(MTL) 11
94 Semic 137, 341
91 SemicSticker 80
92 SemicSticker 104
93 SemicSticker 142
95/6 SkyBoxEmotion 88
95/6 SkyBoxImpact 85
94/5 SP 60
97/8 SPAuthentic 83
95/6 Summit 157
96/7 TeamOut
95/6 Topps 113
93/4 ToppsStadiumClub 248
94/5 ToppsStadiumClub 144
91/2 TriGlobe 19,20
91/2 UpperDeck 1
92/3 UD 577, CC12, ER15, G12
92/3 UD'LockerAS 57
93/4 UpperDeck 29, 283, SP93
94/5 UpperDeck 139, SP47
95/6 UpperDeck 466, SE45
96/7 UpperDeck 84
94/5 UDBAP R125, -Aut. 121
98/9 UDChoice 104
95/6 UDCollChoice 143
96/7 UDCollChoice 139
96 Wien 135
95/6 MTL
95/6 MTL/Molson
96-98 MTL
96/7 MTL/MolsonExport

MALARCHUK, CLINT
91/2 Bowman 23
92/3 Bowman 30
93/4 ClassicProspects 85
86/7 Kraft Sports 47
86/7 OPC/Topps 47
87/8 O-Pee-Chee 246
88/9 OPC/Topps 25
89/90 OPC/Topps 170
90/1 OPC/Topps 371
91/2 OPC/Topps 97
86/7 opcSticker 33
88/9 opcSticker 72 /201
87/8 PaniniSticker 158
88/9 PaniniSticker 363
90/1 PaniniSticker 26
91/2 PaniniSticker 301
91/2 Parkhurst 244
91/2 Pinnacle 103, 397
90/1 ProSet 25
91/2 PSPlatinum 159
90/1 Score 289
91/2 Score(CDN) 419, (U.S) 438
92/3 Score 138
92/3 Topps 363
91/2 ToppsStadiumClub 251
92/3 ToppsStadiumClub 186
90/1 UpperDeck 399
91/2 UpperDeck 368
89/90 BUF/BlueShield
89/90 BUF/Campbell
90/1 BUF/BlueShield
90/1 BUF/Campbell
91/2 BUF/BlueShield
91/2 BUF/Campbell
82/3 QUE
83/4 QUE
85/6 QUE
85/6 QUE/GeneralFoods
85/6 QUE/McDonald
85/6 QUE/Pennant
85/6 QUE/Placemat
85/6 QUE/Provigo
86/7 QUE
86/7 QUE/GeneralFoods
86/7 QUE/McDonald
86/7 QUE/YumYum
87/8 WSH
87/8 WSH/Kodak
88/9 WSH
88/9 WSH/Smokey
82/3 Fredericton 6
84/5 Fredericton 10
93/4 LasVegas
94/5 LasVegas
95/6 LasVegas
96/7 LasVegas
92/3 SanDiego

MALENFANT, DAVID
96/7 Rimouski

MALENFANT, RAY
36/7 WWGum (V356) 108

MALEY, BRENNAN
90/1 ProCards 562

MALEY, DAVID
90/1 O-Pee-Chee 438
91/2 OPC/Topps 476
91/2 Parkhurst 99
91/2 Pinnacle 272
90/1 ProSet 171
91/2 ProSet 421
90/1 Score(U.S) 310
91/2 Score(CDN) 426
92/3 Score 370
93/4 ToppsStadiumClub 259
85/6 MTL
86/7 MTL
87/8 MTL
88/9 N.J./Caretta
89/90 N.J.
90/1 N.J.
92/3 S.J/PacificBell

MALGIN, ALBERT
91/2 O-Pee-Chee 54R

MALGUNAS, KEVIN
90/1 SketchWHL 5
91/2 SketchWHL 156
93/4 Hampton
92/3 Richmond

MALGUNAS, STEWART
93/4 Donruss 470
93/4 FleerUltra 390
94/5 Leaf 170
93/4 Parkhurst 420
93/4 Premier 516
90/1 ProCards 487
91/2 ProCards 123
93/4 Score 612
93/4 ToppsStadiumClub 409
93/4 UpperDeck 425
93/4 PHA 18NOV93
93/4 PHA/JCPenney
94/5 PHA
95/6 WPG
96/7 Portland

MALHOTRA, MANNY
98 BowmanCHL 10,148,A5,SC2
98/9 Topps 235
97/8 UpperDeck 413
97/8 UDBlackDiamond 79
98/9 UDChoice 255
96/7 Guelph 8, 32

MALIK, MAREK
95/6 Donruss 150
96/7 Leaf 227
97/8 PacificCrown 322
97/8 PaniniSticker 22
95/6 Parkhurst 99
94/5 ParkieSE 212
96/7 Pinnacle 225
96/7 PinnacleBeAPlayer 110
95/6 Score 298
95/6 Topps 57
94/5 UpperDeck 482, 506, 558
95/6 UpperDeck 58
96/7 UDCollChoice 118
97/8 udSwedish 139

MALINOWSKI, MERLIN
81/2 OPC 76, Topps(W) 81
82/3 O-Pee-Chee 128
83/4 O-Pee-Chee 142
81/2 opcSticker 228
82/3 opcSticker 229
82/3 Post
81/2 COL.R

MALINSKY, JIRI
94/5 APS 26

MALKIA, HEIKKI
80/1 Mallasjuoma 148

MALKOC, DEAN
97/8 PinnacleBeAPlayer 23
91/2 ProCards 409
89/90 SketchMEM 16
90/1 SketchWHL 69
95/6 ToppsStadiumClub 221
95/6 UpperDeck 330
93/4 Indianapolis
89/90 Kamloops

MALLEN, KEN
91 C55 Reprint 7
1911-12 Imperial(C55) 7
1910-11 Imperial Post 7

MALLETT, KURT
94/5 Richmond
95/6 Richmond

MALLETTE, TROY
90/1 Bowman 219
91/2 Bowman 65
93/4 Donruss 227
94/5 Donruss 329
94/5 FleerUltra 150
93/4 Leaf 228
94/5 Leaf 358
90/1 OPC/Topps 277
91/2 OPC/Topps 474
91/2 opcPremier 39
97/8 PacificRegime 14
90/1 PaniniSticker 100
91/2 PaniniSticker 295
93/4 Parkhurst 413
94/5 Parkhurst 160
96/7 PinnacleBeAPlayer 72
94/5 POG 354
93/4 PowerPlay 401
94/5 Premier 303
90/1 ProSet 492
91/2 ProSet 157
90/1 Score 288
91/2 Score(CDN) 178, 601
91/2 Score(U.S) 178
92/3 Topps 335
91/2 ToppsStadiumClub 134
92/3 ToppsStadiumClub 432
93/4 ToppsStadiumClub 444
94/5 ToppsStadiumClub 94
90/1 UpperDeck 11
91/2 UpperDeck 326
93/4 UpperDeck 418
94/5 UpperDeck 196
95/6 UpperDeck 461
91/2 EDM/IGA
89/90 NYR/MarineMidland
93/4 OTT/Kraft
94/5 OTT/Bell
95/6 OTT
90/1 Rayside
87/8 SSMarie 20

MALLGRAVE, MATT
93/4 ClassicProspects 109
94/5 Hampton 19
93/4 StJohns

MALLON, JASON
95/6 Richmond

MALLOY, MIKE
88/9 Brockville 13

MALLY, MIROSLAV
84/5 Springfield 20

MALMIO, JYRKI
65/6 Hellas 54

MALMIVUORI, OLLI
65/6 Hellas 30

MALO, ANDRE
95/6 SheffieldSteelers
96/7 SheffieldSteelers

MALO, GAETAN
94/5 DEL 60
95/6 DEL 60
96/7 DEL 257

MALONE, CLINT
51/2 LavalDairy 91
52/3 StLawrence 15

MALONE, GREG
78/9 OPC/Topps 233
79/80 OPC/Topps 9
80/1 OPC/Topps 186
81/2 O-Pee-Chee 264
82/3 O-Pee-Chee 272
83/4 O-Pee-Chee 284
84/5 O-Pee-Chee 74
85/6 OPC/Topps 118
83/4 opcSticker 229
84/5 opcSticker 194
85/6 opcSticker 166/35
82/3 Post
83/4 PuffySticker 7
83/4 SouhaitsRen.KeyChain
84/5 Topps 57
83/4 HFD/JuniorWhalers
84/5 HFD/JuniorWhalers
85/6 HFD/JuniorWhalers
77/8 PGH/PuckBuck
83/4 PGH/Heinz
86/7 Fredericton

MALONE, JOE
91 C55 Reprint 4
83&87 HallOfFame 204
83 HHOF Postcard (N)
95/6 HHOFLegends 72
1911-12 Imperial (C55) 4
1912-13 Imperial (C57) 48
1910-11 Imperial Post 4
91/2 ProSet 332
60/1 Topps 3
61/2 Topps-Stamp
23/4 (V145-1) 13
92/3 MTL/OPC 55
95/6 MTL/Forum 7OCT95

MALONE, SCOTT
94/5 Classic 66, T45
94/5 Binghampton
95/6 Binghampton

MALONEY, DAN
72/3 EddieSargent 70
74/5 Loblaws
72/3 OPC 264
73/4 OPC/Topps 32
74/5 OPC/Topps 172
75/6 OPC/Topps 177
76/7 OPC/Topps 101
77/8 OPC/Topps 172
78/9 OPC/Topps 21
79/80 O-Pee-Chee 271
80/1 OPC/Topps 118
81/2 O-Pee-Chee 320
82/3 O-Pee-Chee 326
81/2 opcSticker 102
82/3 opcSticker 72
80/1 Pepsi Cap
71/2 TheTorontoSun
78/9 TOR
79/80 TOR
81/2 TOR
82/3 TOR
83/4 TOR
84/5 TOR
86/7 WPG
88/9 WPG/Police

MALONEY, DARREN
91/2 AirCanadaSJHL 43, B22
92/3 MPSPhotoSJHL 71
93/4 WestMich.

MALONEY, DAVE
77/8 Coke Mini
76/7 OPC/Topps 181
77/8 OPC/Topps 41, -Glossy 10
78/9 OPC/Topps 221
79/80 OPC/Topps 159
80/1 OPC/Topps 6
81/2 OPC 227, Topps(E) 100
82/3 O-Pee-Chee 228
83/4 O-Pee-Chee 249
84/5 O-Pee-Chee 146
85/6 OPC/Topps 89
81/2 opcSticker 170, 173
82/3 opcSticker 140
83/4 opcSticker 211
85/6 opcSticker 177/47
82/3 Post
83/4 SouhaitsRen.KeyChain

MALONEY, DON
90/1 Bowman 117
79/80 OPC/Topps 42, 162
80/1 OPC/Topps 231
81/2 OPC 228, Topps(E) 101
82/3 O-Pee-Chee 229
83/4 O-Pee-Chee 250
84/5 OPC 147, Topps 109
85/6 OPC/Topps 94
86/7 OPC/Topps 81
87/8 OPC/Topps 49
90/1 OPC/Topps 31
82/3 opcSticker 137
83/4 opcSticker 212
84/5 opcSticker 95, 96
87/8 opcSticker 29 /169
87/8 PaniniSticker 117
88/9 PaniniSticker 308
89/90 PaniniSticker 231
90/1 PaniniSticker 84
82/3 Post
90/1 ProSet 187
83/4 PuffySticker 21
90/1 Score(U.S) 303
84/5 7Eleven Disk 35
83/4 SouhaitsRen.KeyChain
81/2 Topps(East) 101
84/5 Topps 109
90/1 UpperDeck 20
89/90 NYI

MALONEY, PHIL
45-64 BeeHives(BOS), (TOR)
74/5 OPC/Topps 104
45-54 QuakerOats

MALTAIS, DOMINIC
90/1 SketchQMJHL 85
91/2 SketchQMJHL 108
95/6 Hampton HRA-7

MALTAIS, FRÉDÉRIC
88/9 Richelieu

MALTAIS, STEVE
95/6 EdgeIce 107
89/90 ProCards(AHL) 85
90/1 ProCards 205
91/2 ProCards 153
90/1 Score 417
92/3 T.B./Sheraton
89/90 WSH/Kodak
92/3 AtlantaKnights

MALTBY, KIRK
92/3 Classic 20
92/3 ClassicFourSport 169
93/4 ClassicProspects 21
93/4 Donruss 428
94/5 Donruss 53
94/5 Leaf 230
98/9 Pacific 199
97/8 PacificDynagn-BestKept 33
97/8 PacificRegime 71
94/5 Pinnacle 441
95/6 Pinnacle 126
95/6 Playoff 149
96/7 Playoff 373
93/4 Premier 290
94/5 Premier 72
93/4 Score 627
97/8 Score(DET) 15
90/1 SketchOHL 287
91/2 SketchOHL 278
95/6 Topps 133
93/4 ToppsStadiumClub 299
93/4 UpperDeck 520
94/5 UpperDeck 472
95/6 UpperDeck 41
97/8 UpperDeck 61
94/5 UDBeAPlayer 38
95/6 UDCollChoice 191
97/8 UDCollChoice 84
93/4 EDM 07JAN94
93/4 OwenSound

MALTSEV, ALEXANDER
72 Hellas 70
74 Hellas 49
70/1 Kuvajulkaisut 7
72 Panda
79 PaniniSticker 155
72 SemicSticker 10
74 SemicSticker 36, -CL 2
82 SemicSticker 67
91 SemicSticker 246
69/70 Soviet Stars
70/1 Soviet Stars
71/2 Soviet Stars
73/4 Soviet Stars 20
74/5 Soviet Stars 14
79/80 SovietStars
83/4 SovietStars
91/2 Trends (72) 20

92/3 Trends (76) 161, 190, 200
96 Wien HL6
71/2 WilliamsFIN 8
72/3 WilliamsFIN 28
73/4 WilliamsFIN 9

MALY, MIROSLAV
94/5 DEL 331
95/6 DEL 293
96/7 DEL 321

MALYKHIN, IGOR
92/3 ClassicProspects 86
90/1 O-Pee-Chee 15R
91/2 O-Pee-Chee 20R

MALYSIAK, ANDRZEJ
79 PaniniSticker 128

MANARA, MARTIN
97/8 Bowman 54

MANCINI, RICK
93/4 OwenSound

MANCUSO, TONY
95/6 Tallahassee 26

MANDERVILLE, KENT
91/2 CanadaNats
92 CanadaWinterOlympics 197
95/6 EdgeIce 83
94/5 Leaf 526
92/3 O-Pee-Chee 14
92/3 opcPremier 23
97/8 PacificCrown 289
91/2 Parkhurst 392
92/3 Parkhurst 184
93/4 Parkhurst 204
94/5 Parkhurst 235
94/5 Pinnacle 454
97/8 PinnacleBeAPlayer 165
94/5 POG 235
94/5 Premier 474
92/3 Score 458, -CndOlympic 10
92/3 Topps 148
92/3 ToppsStadiumClub 339
93/4 ToppsStadiumClub 417
94/5 ToppsStadiumClub 253
90/1 UpperDeck 465
92/3 UpperDeck 32
93/4 UpperDeck 420
94/5 UpperDeck 131
94/5 UDBeAPlayer-Aut. 156
97/8 UDCollChoice 118
92/3 TOR/Kodak
93/4 TOR/Abalene
93/4 TOR/Blacks 10
94/5 TOR
92/3 StJohns
95/6 StJohns

MANDICH, DAN
82/3 MIN
83/4 MIN
84/5 MIN
85/6 MIN

MANDO, DEAN
95/6 Slapshot 420

MANELUK, GEORGE
88/9 ProCards(Springfield)
89/90 ProCards(AHL) 241
90/1 ProCards 500
91/2 ProCards 370
95/6 Louisiana, -Playoffs

MANELUK, MIKE
95/6 EdgeIce 13
91/2 SketchWHL 199
92/3 Brandon 15

MANERY, KRIS
78/9 OPC/Topps 107
79/80 OPC/Topps 151
81/2 O-Pee-Chee 371
80/1 Pepsi Cap
78/9 MIN/Cloverleaf 8
79/80 MIN
80/1 WPG

MANERY, RANDY
72/3 EddieSargent 10
74/5 Loblaws
78/9 O-Pee-Chee 266
79/80 O-Pee-Chee 317
80/1 O-Pee-Chee 342
72/3 OPC 260
73/4 OPC/Topps 131
74/5 OPC/Topps 86
75/6 OPC/Topps 44
76/7 OPC/Topps 24
77/8 OPC 389
72/3 ATL
74/5 ATL

MANGOLD, PAT
84/5 Kamloops

MANIAGO, CÉSARE
45-64 BeeHives(MTL), (TOR)
64-67 BeeHives(NYR)
62 CeramicTiles
70/1 Colgate Stamp 63
70/1 EddieSargent 81
71/2 EddieSargent 92
72/3 EddieSargent 110
70/1 Esso Stamp
72/3 Letraset 24
74/5 LiptonSoup 27
74/5 Loblaws
68/9 OPC/Topps 45
69/70 OPC/T. 121, OPC-Sticker
70/1 OPC 173
71/2 OPC/Topps 117, Topps 5
72/3 OPC 138, Topps 104
73/4 OPC 127, Topps 146
74/5 OPC/Topps 26
75/6 OPC/Topps 261
76/7 OPC/Topps 240
77/8 OPC/Topps 23
63/4 Parkhurst 40, 99
95/6 Parkie(66/7) 97
68/9 ShirriffCoin MIN5
71/2 TheTorontoSun
61/2 York 41
70/1 MIN
73/4 MIN
76/7 VAN/RoyalBank
77/8 VAN/GingerAle
77/8 VAN/RoyalBank

MANLEY, BILL
95/6 Halifax
96/7 Halifax (1), (2)
97/8 Halifax (1), (2)

MANLOW, ERIC
93/4 ClassicFourSport 210
95/6 EdgeIce 137
91/2 SketchOHL 87
93/4 Slapshot(Kitchener) 1, 24
94/5 Slapshot(Det) 11, (Kit) 26
94/5 Slapshot(MEM) 85

MANN, CAMERON
97/8 Bowman 4
98/9 Pacific 85
93/4 Slapshot(Peterborough) 16
95/6 Slapshot 313, -Promo
98/9 SPx"Finite" 126
95/6 TetradAutobilia 47
97/8 UDBlackDiamond 138
98/9 UDChoice 17
97/8 UDCollChoice 306
96/7 UpperDeck"Ice" 130

MANN, JIMMY
80/1 OPC/Topps 164, OPC 353
81/2 O-Pee-Chee 372
80/1 Pepsi Cap
88/9 ProCards(Indianapolis)
83/4 QUE
84/5 QUE
85/6 QUE/GeneralFoods
85/6 QUE/Provigo
86/7 QUE/McDonald
79/80 WPG
80/1 WPG
81/2 WPG
82/3 WPG
83/4 WPG

MANN, NORMAN (NORMIE)
34-43 BeeHives(TORx2)

MANN, PAVEL
94/5 DEL 344
95/6 DEL 318, 430

MANN, STEFAN
94/5 DEL 203
95/6 DEL 206
96/7 DEL 349

MANNBERG, NIKLAS
89/90 SemicElitserien 209

MANNIKKO, ERKKI
66/7 Champion 160

MANNINEN, KEVIN
90/1 Mich.Tech

MANNINEN, MIKA
95 Latkaliiga 11
93/4 Sisu 110
94/5 Sisu 108, -Junior 7, -Nolla 1
95/6 Sisu 29

MANNISTO, KEIJO
66/7 Champion 161
70/1 Kuvajulkaisut 217
78/9 SM-Liiga 191
71/2 WilliamsFIN 139
73/4 WilliamsFIN 164

MANNO, BOB
78/9 O-Pee-Chee 349
79/80 O-Pee-Chee 270
81/2 O-Pee-Chee 396
82/3 O-Pee-Chee 325
83/4 O-Pee-Chee 132
84/5 O-Pee-Chee 59
85/6 OPC/Topps 134
82/3 opcSticker 71
82/3 Post
97/8 DET/Caesars
81/2 TOR
77/8 VAN/RoyalBank
78/9 VAN/RoyalBank
79/80 VAN
80/1 VAN/Silverwood

MANSFIELD, GARY
95/6 Hampton HRA25

MANSI, MAURIZIO
96/7 DEL 121
95 PaniniWorlds 95
94 Semic 304
93 SemicSticker 226
96 Wien 179
88/9 Flint

MANSIKKA, REIJO
78/9 SM-Liiga 91

MANSOFF, JASON
92/3 BCJHL 78
93/4 Maine 40

MANSON, DAVE
91/2 Bowman 389
92/3 Bowman 339
93/4 Donruss 109, 509
94/5 Donruss 242
95/6 Donruss 317
93/4 EASports 43
94/5 Flair 207
94/5 Fleer 243
92/3 FleerUltra 62
93/4 FleerUltra 93
94/5 FleerUltra 243
95/6 FleerUltra 181
96/7 FleerUltra 133
93/4 Leaf 159
94/5 Leaf 239
95/6 Leaf 158
93/4 McDonalds McD09
96/7 MetalUniverse 119
89/90 OPC/Topps 150
90/1 OPC/Topps 363, 397
91/2 OPC/Topps 409
92/3 O-Pee-Chee 56
91/2 opcPremier 137
89/90 opcSticker 13/153
98/9 Pacific 254
97/8 PacificDynag-BestKept 49
98/9 PacificParamount 115
89/90 PaniniSticker 47
90/1 PaniniSticker 199
92/3 PaniniSticker 108
93/4 PaniniSticker 242
96/7 PaniniSticker 197
91/2 Parkhurst 49
92/3 Parkhurst 47, CP15
93/4 Parkhurst 335
94/5 Parkhurst 262, V9
95/6 Parkhurst 233
91/2 Pinnacle 62
92/3 Pinnacle 334
93/4 Pinnacle 363
94/5 Pinnacle 51
95/6 Pinnacle 103
96/7 PinnacleBeAPlayer 57
95/6 Playoff 218
96/7 Playoff 401
94/5 POG 257
95/6 POG 295
93/4 PowerPlay 83
93/4 Premier 71
94/5 Premier 121
90/1 ProSet 54
91/2 ProSet 41, 389
92/3 ProSet 55
91/2 PSPlatinum 172
90/1 Score 193
91/2 Score(CDN) 152, 624
91/2 Score(U.S) 152, 74T
92/3 Score 214
93/4 Score 127, -P.AS 38
95/6 Score 59
97/8 Score(MTL) 17
92/3 SeasonsPatch 56
94/5 Select 13
95/6 SkyBoxEmotion 194
95/6 SkyBoxImpact 182
94/5 SP 134
92/3 Topps 389
95/6 Topps 120
98/9 Topps 165
91/2 ToppsStadiumClub 308
92/3 ToppsStadiumClub 436
93/4 T.StadiumClub 183, -AllStar
94/5 ToppsStadiumClub 61
90/1 UpperDeck 85
91/2 UpperDeck 280, 548
92/3 UD 84, -LockerAS 30
93/4 UpperDeck 358, SP50
94/5 UpperDeck 63, SP180
95/6 UpperDeck 51
96/7 UpperDeck 317
93/4 UDBeAPlayer 30
94/5 UDBeAPlayer R41, -Aut. 95
98/9 UDChoice 108
95/6 UDCollChoice 230
97/8 UDCollChoice 136
86/7 CHI/Coke
87/8 CHI/Coke
88/9 CHI/Coke
89/90 CHI/Coke
90/1 CHI/Coke
91/2 EDM/IGA
92/3 EDM
92/3 EDM/IGA 14
93/4 EDM 16OCT93
96/7 MTL/MolsonExport
97/8 MTL
96/7 PHO
95/6 WPG
84/5 PrinceAlbert

MANSSON, JOHAN
91/2 SemicElitserien 178
92/3 SemicElitserien 201

MANTERE, EERO
80/1 Mallasjuoma 74
78/9 SM-Liiga 114

MANTHA, CARL
89/90 SketchMEM 51
90/1 SketchQMJHL 48

MANTHA, GEORGES
34-43 BeeHives(MTL.C)
33/4 CndGum (V252)
35-40 CrownBrand 60
33-35 DiamondMatch
36-39 DiamondMatch (1), (2), (3)
27-32 LaPresse 28/9
33/4 OPC (V304A) 22
37/8 OPC (V304E) 153
39/40 OPC (V301-1) 26
43-47 ParadeSportive (x2)
38/9 QuakerOats
34/5 SweetCaporal
33/4 WWGum (V357) 26
36/7 WWGum (V356) 45

MANTHA, MAURICE
52/3 AnonymousOHL 169

MANTHA, MOE
91/2 Bowman 205
81/2 O-Pee-Chee 373
85/6 OPC/Topps 125
86/7 OPC/Topps 45
87/8 OPC/Topps 51
88/9 OPC/Topps 30
90/1 OPC/Topps 354
91/2 OPC/Topps 477
85/6 opcSticker 98 /229
86/7 opcSticker231 /102
87/8 opcSticker 171/30
88/9 opcSticker 20 0/71
90/1 Panini(WPG) 16
87/8 PaniniSticker 142
80/1 Pepsi Cap
90/1 ProSet 332
90/1 Score(CND) 310
91/2 Score(CDN) 506
91/2 ToppsStadiumClub 287
83/4 Vachon 132
88/9 EDM/ActionMagazine 34
88/9 MIN/American
86/7 PGH/Kodak
80/1 WPG
83/4 WPG
89/90 WPG/Safeway
90/1 WPG/IGA
91/2 WPG/IGA
60/1 Cleveland

MANTHA, SYLVIO
25-27 Anonymous 3, 4
34-43 BeeHives(MTL.C)
24/5 Champs (C144)
33-35 DiamondMatch
36-39 DiamondMatch (1), (2), (3)
83&87 HallOfFame 84
33/4 Hamilton (V288) 18
83 HHOF Postcard (F)
27-32 LaPresse 27/8
24/5 (V145-2) 50
35/6 OPC (V304C) 82
55/6 Parkhurst 60
34/5 SweetCaporal
35/6 Triumph
23/4 V145-1 12
28/9 MTL/LaPatrie 1
95/6 MTL/Forum 25OCT95

MANTIONE, JOE
83/4 Kitchener 1

MARA, PAUL
97/8 Bowman 16, 137, BB3
98/9 UDChoice 297
96/7 UpperDeck"Ice" 149
96/7 Sudbury 16

MARACLE, NORM
98/9 Pacific 200
91/2 SketchWHL 117
98/9 SPx"Finite" 144
95/6 Adirondack
91/2 Saskatoon 3
93/4 Saskatoon

MARAK, ZBYNEK
94/5 APS 238
95/6 APS 19, 382

MARANDUIK, BILL
93/4 Slapshot(Kingston) 13

MARBLE, EVAN
90/1 SketchWHL 59
91/2 SketchWHL 321

MARC, DAN
79 PaniniSticker 379

MARCEL, BERNARD
87 HallOfFame 246

MARCETTA, MILAN
68/9 ShirriffCoin MIN-6

MARCH, HAROLD "MUSH"
34-43 BeeHives(CHI)
35/6 Champion
35-40 CrownBrand 82
33-35 DiamondMatch
36-39 DiamondMatch (1), (2), (3)
36-39 DiamondMatch (4), (5), (6)
39/40 OPC (V301-1) 45
34/5 SweetCaporal
36/7 WWGum (V356) 13

MARCHANT, EDDY
91/2 AirCanadaSJHL C47
93/4 RedDeer

MARCHANT, G.
71/2 STL

MARCHANT, TODD
94/5 Classic 88
94/5 ClassicFourSport 140
93/4 C4'Images 17
94/5 C4'Images 115
94/5 C'FourSport 140
94/5 ClassicImages 8, CE8, PR5
93/4 ClassicProspects LP8
95/6 Donruss 200, -Rookie 8
96/7 Donruss 53
97/8 Donruss 184
95/6 EdgeIce 34, C6
94/5 Fleer 71
95/6 FleerMetal 54
93/4 FleerUltra 491
95/6 FleerUltra 55, -AllRookie 8
94/5 Leaf 505
95/6 Leaf 61, -StudioRookie 8
96/7 Leaf 153
97/8 Limited 144
98/9 Pacific 213
97/8 PacificCrown 320
95/6 PaniniSticker 257
95/6 Parkhurst 347
94/5 ParkieSE 61
95/6 Pinnacle 76
96/7 Pinnacle 117
97/8 Pinnacle 127
97/8 PinnacleBeAPlayer 72
95/6 POG 107
93/4 PowerPlay 511
93/4 Premier-TeamUSA 14
95/6 ProMagnet 85
94/5 Score 226
95/6 Score 34
96/7 Score 217
97/8 Score 243
95/6 SkyBoxEmotion 64
95/6 SkBxImpact 62,234,-Fox 10
94/5 SP-Premier 4
95/6 Topps 29, 3NG
98/9 Topps 64
94/5 T.Finest-BBest(Red) 19
93/4 TSC-TeamUSA 15
95/6 ToppsStadiumClub 102
94/5 TSC-Members 49
92/3 UpperDeck 606
94/5 UpperDeck 159, 323
95/6 UpperDeck 71, SE121
96/7 UpperDeck 59
97/8 UpperDeck 64
95/6 UDBeAPlayer 190
95/6 UDCollChoice 210
96/7 UDCollChoice 97
96/7 EDM
97/8 EDM
94/5 CapeBreton
92/3 Clarkson

MARCHESSAULT, ALAIN
87/8 Brockville 8

MARCHESSAULT, RICHARD
87/8 Brockville 16

MARCHETTI, GIOVANNI
95 PaniniWorlds 78
94 Semic 298
92 SemicSticker 250

MARCHINKO, BRIAN
72/3 EddieSargent 136
72/3 OPC 179

MARCHMENT, BRYAN
91/2 Bowman 208
92/3 Bowman 418
93/4 Donruss 73
92/3 FleerUltra 278
93/4 FleerUltra 335
95/6 FleerUltra 238
93/4 Leaf 224
94/5 Leaf 127
97/8 Omega 211
91/2 OPC/Topps 116
91/2 opcPremier 99
98/9 Pacific 385
97/8 PacificRegime 79
96/7 PaniniStickers 256
92/3 Parkhurst 267
93/4 Pinnacle 283
94/5 Pinnacle 407
93/4 PowerPlay 352
89/90 ProCards(AHL) 44
90/1 ProCards 250
91/2 Score(CDN) 344, 606
91/2 Score(U.S) 314 56T
92/3 Score 288
93/4 Score 386, 577
94/5 Score 107
95/6 Score 270
92/3 Topps 501
91/2 ToppsStadiumClub 384
92/3 ToppsStadiumClub 148
93/4 ToppsStadiumClub 161
94/5 ToppsStadiumClub 84
95/6 UpperDeck 371
97/8 UpperDeck 69, 392
95/6 UDBeAPlayer 39
97/8 UDBlackDiamond 66
95/6 UDCollChoice 67
96/7 UDCollChoice 99
91/2 CHI/Coke
96/7 EDM
97/8 EDM
93/4 HFD/Coke
97/8 S.J/PacificBellSheet
90/1 WPG/IGA
90/1 Moncton

MARCINCZAK, MAREK
79 PaniniSticker 125

MARCINKO, MIROSLAV
94 Semic 196
96 Wien 226

MARCINYSHYN, DAVE
90/1 opcPremier 67
88/9 ProCards(Utica)
89/90 ProCards(AHL) 215
91/2 ProCards 543
90/1 ProSet 623
92/3 Binghampton
96/7 Cincinnati
85/6 Kamloops
86/7 Kamloops
94/5 Milwaukee

MARCOLINI, STEVE
84/5 Kitchener 8
85/6 Kitchener 7
86/7 London 19

MARCON, LOU
59/60 Topps 49

MARCOTTE, DON
72/3 EddieSargent 27
70/1 Esso Stamp
74/5 Loblaws
70/1 OPC 138
71/2 OPC/Topps 176
72/3 OPC 219
73/4 Topps 89
74/5 OPC/Topps 221
75/6 OPC/Topps 269
76/7 OPC/Topps 234
77/8 OPC/Topps 165
78/9 OPC/Topps 236
79/80 OPC/Topps 99
80/1 O-Pee-Chee 336
81/2 O-Pee-Chee 14
82/3 O-Pee-Chee 14
82/3 opcSticker 91
71/2 TheTorontoSun
70/1 BOS
71/2 BOS
91/2 BOS/Legends

MARCOTTE, GASTON
52/3 AnonymousOHL 14

MARCOTTE, JACQUES
52/3 AnonymousOHL 82
53/4 LaPatrie 7-Feb

MARCOTTE, RÉAL
51/2 LacStJean 13

MARCOUX, CHRISTIAN
93/4 Slapshot(Drum.) 16

MARCOUX, ERIC
90/1 SketchQMJHL 201
91/2 SketchQMJHL 289

MARCOUX, HENRY
96/7 DEL 143

MARECEK, PAVEL
95/6 APS 295

MAREK, PETER
94/5 Wheeling 9

MARENGERE, STEVE
83/4 NovaScotia 6

MARHA, JOSEF
94/5 APS 171
95/6 Classic-Autograph

98/9 Pacific 59
98/9 PacificParamount 4
93/4 Parkhurst 516
97/8 Score(COL) 10
94/5 SP 157
98/9 SPx"Finite" 3, 124
97/8 UpperDeck 256
98/9 UDChoice 3

MARIC, ROB
94/5 Slapshot(Kitchener) 25
95/6 Slapshot 136

MARIETTI, BRETT
90/1 SketchOHL 134
91/2 SketchOHL 371

MARIJARVI, J.M.
93/4 Jyvas-Hyva 81
93/4 Sisu 117

MARIK, MICHAL
95/6 APS 245

MARIN, ALBERTO
79 PaniniSticker 373

MARINI, HECTOR
83/4 O-Pee-Chee 235
83/4 opcSticker 221
83/4 PuffySticker 8
83/4 N.J.

MARINIER, ROCH
84/5 Chicoutimi

MARINUCCI, CHRIS
94/5 Classic 100, T41, AA3
94/5 C.Images 95, CE19, PR7
95/6 Donruss 6
95/6 EdgeIce 193
95/6 Leaf 92
95/6 Parkhurst 401
95/6 Pinnacle 206
95/6 Score 309
95/6 Topps 62
93/4 Minn-Duluth

MARIO, FRANK
52/3 LavalDairy 14
52/3 StLawrence 51

MARIUCCI, JOHN
34-43 BeeHives(CHI)
87 HallOfFame 254

MARJAMAKI, PEKKA
66/7 Champion 155
65/6 Hellas 146
72 Hellas 5
74 Hellas 11
70/1 Kuvajulkaisut 68, 212
72 Panda
79 PaniniSticker 167
78/9 SM-Liiga 178
71/2 WilliamsFIN 68, 135
72/3 WilliamsFIN 65, 198
73/4 WilliamsFIN 159
72 SemicSticker 75
74 SemicSticker 78
96/7 Sisu 195
77-80 Sportscaster 19 -436

MARJIN, ALEKSEJ
91 SemicSticker 78

MARK, GORD
88/9 opcSticker 162
94/5 Parkhurst 80
93/4 EDM 23MAR94
84/5 Kamloops

MARK, LEN
84/5 Kamloops
85/6 Kamloops
86/7 Kamloops

MARKARIAN, RALPH
52/3 AnonymousOHL 178

MARKER, GUS
34-43 BeeHives(MTL.M), (TOR)
35-40 CrownBrand 56
35/6 OPC (V304C) 78
37/8 OPC (V304E) 173
39/40 OPC (V301-1) 16
40/1 OPC (V301-2) 113
34/5 SweetCaporal

MARKKANEN, JUSSI
94/5 ParkieSE 215
95/6 Sisu 311
94/5 ToppsFinest 124

MARKKANEN, MIKKO
95/6 Sisu 334, -NHLDraft 12

MARKLUND, LARS
89/90 SemicElitserien 199

MARKOV, DANELL
98/9 Pacific 417

MARKOV, ANDREI
96/7 UpperDeck"Ice" 142

MARKOVICH, MIKE
93/4 Toledo 11

MARKOVSKY, DMITRI
93/4 Portland

MARKS, JACK
1912-13 Imperial(C57) 38

MARKS, JOHN
74/5 Loblaws
74/5 OPC 282
75/6 OPC/Topps 121
76/7 OPC/Topps 114
77/8 OPC/Topps 47
78/9 OPC/Topps 157
79/80 OPC/Topps 16
80/1 OPC/Topps 194
81/2 O-Pee-Chee 70
90/1 ProCards 121
91/2 ProCards 503
79/80 CHI
80/1 CHI/4x6
80/1 CHI/5.5x8.5
81/2 CHI
81/2 Indianapolis 3
92/3 Indianapolis

MARKUS, TODD
91/2 AirCanadaSJHL B31

MARKWART, KELLY
90/1 SketchWHL 175
88/9 Regina
89/90 Regina
90/1 Saskatoon 17

MARKWART, NEVIN
84/5 O-Pee-Chee 8
91/2 OPC/Topps 238
90/1 ProSet 408
84/5 Topps 7
84/5 BOS
89/90 BOS/SportsAction
90/1 BOS/SportsAction
82/3 Regina 15
83/4 Regina 15

MARLEAU, PATRICK
97/8 Bowman 88, 141, BB2
97/8 DonrussElite 99, 128, 145
97/8 D.Elite -BackTo 3, -Craft 11
97/8 D.Preferd 150,198,-Line 5C
97/8 DonrussPriority175,195,216
97/8 D.Prio-DirDep 18,-OpDay29
97/8 D.Prio-Pstcrd 18,-Stamp 18
97/8 KatchMedallion 121
97/8 Leaf 154
97/8 Limited 200
97/8 McDonalds McD34
97/8 Omega 203
98/9 Pacific 386, -TeamCL 23
97/8 PacificCrownRoyale 120
97/8 PacificDynagon! Rookies
97/8 PacificParamount 167
98/9 PcfcPara 211,-TeamCL 23
97/8 PacificRevolution 125
97/8 Pinnacle 12
97/8 PinnacleBeAPlayer 221
97/8 PinnacleCertified C
97/8 SPAuthentic 191
98/9 SPx"Finite" 73, 130
98/9 Topps 170, SB10
96/7 UpperDeck 384
97/8 UpperDeck 354, SG3
96/7 UDBlackDiamond 103
97/8 UDBlackDiamond 140
98/9 UDChoice 173
97/8 UDCollChoice 304
97/8 UpperDeckIce 41
97/8 Zenith 95, -RookieReign 10
97/8 S.J/PacificBellSheet
97/8 S.J/PacificBellSheet

MAROIS, DANIEL
90/1 Bowman 160
91/2 Bowman 165
92/3 Bowman 245
93/4 Donruss 17
92/3 Durivage 16
89/90 Kraft 37
89/90 O-Pee-Chee 273
90/1 OPC/Topps 267
91/2 OPC/Topps 212
92/3 O-Pee-Chee 58
89/90 opcSticker 176/36
89/90 opcStickFS 18
90/1 Panini(TOR) 14
89/90 PaniniSticker 137
90/1 PaniniSticker 284
91/2 PaniniSticker 95
91/2 Parkhurst 329
93/4 Parkhurst 282
94/5 Parkhurst 18
91/2 Pinnacle 27
92/3 Pinnacle 139
90/1 ProSet 284
91/2 ProSet 223
91/2 PSPlatinum 118
90/1 Score 122, -YoungStar 3
91/2 Score(CDN) 474, (U.S) 254
92/3 Score 63
92/3 Topps 49
91/2 ToppsStadiumClub 197
92/3 ToppsStadiumClub 63
90/1 UpperDeck 179
91/2 UpperDeck 331
92/3 UpperDeck 71
88/9 TOR/P.L.A.Y. 15
90/1 TOR/P.L.A.Y. 24

MAROIS, JEAN
51/2 LavalDairy 2
51-54 LaPatrie 8MAR53
43-47 ParadeSportive
52/3 StLawrence 36

MAROIS, MARIO
91/2 Bowman 380
72-84 DernièreHeure 81/2
86/7 Kraft Sports 77
81/2 O-Pee-Chee 279
82/3 O-Pee-Chee 287
83/4 O-Pee-Chee 295
84/5 O-Pee-Chee 282
85/6 O-Pee-Chee 194
87/8 O-Pee-Chee 220
88/9 O-Pee-Chee 233
89/90 O-Pee-Chee 260
90/1 OPC/Topps 158
91/2 OPC/Topps 82
84/5 opcSticker 166-167
85/6 opcSticker 144/14
87/8 opcSticker250 /141
88/9 opcSticker 142/15
89/90 opcSticker 185/41
87/8 PaniniSticker 359
88/9 PaniniSticker 151
89/90 PaniniSticker 336
80/1 Pepsi Cap
82/3 Post
90/1 ProSet 253, 524
91/2 ProSet 477
90/1 Score 229, 94T
91/2 Score(CDN) 546
91/2 ToppsStadiumClub 12
90/1 UpperDeck 8
83/4 Vachon 67
81/2 QUE
82/3 QUE
83/4 QUE
84/5 QUE
85/6 QUE/GeneralFoods
85/6 QUE/Provigo
89/90 QUE
89/90 QUE/GeneralFoods
89/90 QUE/Police
90/1 QUE
90/1 STL/Kodak
86/7 WPG
87/8 WPG
85/6 WPG/Police
88/9 WPG/Police
92/3 Hamilton

MAROSTE, MARK
94/5 DEL 137
95/6 DEL 40

MAROTTE, GILLES
68/9 Bauer
70/1 Colgate Stamp 65
70/1 DadsCookies
70/1 EddieSargent 78
71/2 EddieSargent 70
72/3 EddieSargent 89
70/1 Esso Stamp
72/3 Letraset 1
74/5 Loblaws
68/9 OPC/Topps 14
69/70 OPC/Topps 68
70/1 OPC/Topps 34
71/2 OPC/Topps 151
72/3 OPC 27, Topps 167
73/4 OPC 5, Topps 188
74/5 OPC 373
75/6 OPC/Topps 164
76/7 OPC/Topps 192
95/6 Parkie(66/7) 17
72 SemicSticker 202
68/9 ShirriffCoin CHI 15
66/7 Topps 36
67/8 Topps 59
91/2 Ultimate06 59, -Aut 59
68/9 CHI

MAROUELLI, DAN
90/1 ProSet 692

MARQUET, SÉBASTIEN
93 SemicSticker 256

MARQUETTE, DALE
88/9 ProCards(Saginaw)
89/90 ProCards(IHL) 64

MARRIN, PETER
76/7 opcWHA 96
77/8 opcWHA 51

MARRIOTT, JAMIE
91/2 AvantGardeBCJHL 38

MARSH, BLAIR
91/2 AvantGardeBCJHL 160
92/3 BCJHL 235
93/4 Maine 56

MARSH, BRAD
90/1 Bowman 158
92/3 FleerUltra 364
80/1 O-Pee-Chee 338
81/2 O-Pee-Chee 47
82/3 O-Pee-Chee 254
83/4 O-Pee-Chee 269
84/5 O-Pee-Chee 163
89/90 O-Pee-Chee 276
85/6 OPC/Topps 72
86/7 OPC/Topps 175
87/8 OPC/Topps 128
88/9 OPC/Topps 64
90/1 OPC/Topps 155
91/2 OPC/Topps 19
81/2 opcSticker 225
86/7 opcSticker 235/106
88/9 opcSticker 101/233
89/90 opcSticker 175/35
90/1 Panini(TOR) 15
87/8 PaniniSticker 127
89/90 PaniniSticker 141
90/1 PaniniSticker 277
92/3 Parkhurst 123
80/1 Pepsi Cap
91/2 Pinnacle 361, 401
92/3 Pinnacle 378
82/3 Post
90/1 ProSet 285
91/2 ProSet 378
92/3 ProSet 126, 264
90/1 Score 219
91/2 Score(CDN) 416
92/3 Score 293
93/4 Score 392, -P.AS 10
92/3 Topps 215
92/3 ToppsStadiumClub 482
93/4 ToppsStadiumClub-AllStar
90/1 UpperDeck 199
78/9 ATL/Coke
79/80 ATL
79/80 ATL/B&W
80/1 CGY
93/4 OTT/Kraft
94/5 OTT/Bell
95/6 OTT
83/4 PHA
86/7 PHA
88/9 TOR/P.L.A.Y. 25
90/1 TOR

MARSH, PETER
79/80 OPC/Topps 147
80/1 O-Pee-Chee 314
81/2 O-Pee-Chee 71
81/2 CHI
82/3 CHI
79/80 WPG

MARSHALL, CHARLES
52/3 AnonymousOHL 20

MARSHALL, BERT
71/2 Bazooka Panel 25
64-67 BeeHives(DET)
65/6 CocaCola
70/1 DadsCookies
70/1 EddieSargent 131
71/2 EddieSargent 134
72/3 EddieSargent 47
74/5 Loblaws
68/9 OPC/Topps 79
69/70 OPC/T. 80, OPC-Sticker
70/1 OPC 188
71/2 OPC/Topps 73
72/3 OPC 130, Topps 162
73/4 OPC/Topps 51
74/5 OPC/Topps 177
75/6 OPC/Topps 72
76/7 OPC/Topps 62
77/8 OPC/Topps 206
78/9 OPC/Topps 49
68/9 ShirriffCoin OAK8
71/2 TheTorontoSun
66/7 Topps 51
67/8 Topps 46
81/2 COL.R

MARSHALL, CHRIS
93/4 Birmingham 12
91/2 Cincinnati

MARSHALL, DON
45-64 BeeHives(MTL), (NYR)
64-67 BeeHives(NYR)
62 CeramicTiles
64/5 CokeCap NYR-22
65/6 CocaCola
70/1 Colgate Stamp 27
70/1 DadsCookies
71/2 EddieSargent 208
70/1 Esso Stamp
68/9 OPC/Topps 75
69/70 OPC/Topps 39
70/1 OPC/Topps 129
71/2 OPC/Topps 199
55/6 Parkhurst 35
57/8 Parkhurst (MTL) 8
58/9 Parkhurst 44
59/60 Parkhurst 37
60/1 Parkhurst 42, 57, 59
61/2 Parkhurst 40
62/3 Parkhurst 43
93/4 Parkie(56/7) 76
94/5 Parkie(64/5) 88
95/6 Parkie(66/7) 82
72 SemicSticker 197
60/1 ShirriffCoin 23
61/2 ShirriffCoin 103
62/3 ShirriffCoin 33
68/9 ShirriffCoin NY7
71/2 TheTorontoSun
63/4 Topps 59
64/5 Topps 97
65/6 Topps 29
66/7 Topps 24, -USATest 24
67/8 Topps 23, 130
54-67 TorontoStar V8
54-67 TorontoStar 66/7
56-66 TorontoStar 60/1
91/2 Ultimate06 13, -Aut 13
60/1 York
61/2 York 6
60/1 YorkGlasses
62/3 YorkTransfer 28
71/2 TOR

MARSHALL, GRANT
95/6 Bowman 162
92/3 Classic 13
93/4 Classic 140
92/3 ClassicFourtSport 162
93/4 ClassicProspects 188
96/7 Donruss 222
95/6 Leaf 327
96/7 Leaf 169
96/7 PaniniSticker 172
95/6 Parkhurst 533
96/7 PinnacleBeAPlayer 146
96/7 Score 261
90/1 SketchOHL 88
91/2 SketchOHL 299
95/6 UpperDeck 362
96/7 UpperDeck 47
96/7 UDCollChoice 77
96/7 DAL/Southwest
92/3 Ottawa67s
93/4 StJohns

MARSHALL, JACK
91 C55 Reprint 29
83&87 HallOfFame 39
83 HHOF Postcard (C)
1911-12 Imperial(C55) 29
1910-11 Imperial(C56) 33
1910-11 Imperial Post 29

MARSHALL, JASON
93/4 CanadaNats
93/4 FleerUltra 468
95/6 Leaf 190
98/9 Pacific 60
97/8 PacificRegime 5
97/8 PinnacleBeAPlayer 54
93/4 PowerPlay 488
91/2 ProCards 25
91/2 Score(CDN) 278, (U.S) 388
94 Semic 105
90/1 SketchWHL 117
90/1 UpperDeck 453
92/3 UpperDeck 68
96/7 ANA/UpFrontSports 15
92/3 Peoria

MARSHALL, PAUL
90/1 ProCards 297
81/2 TOR
93/4 Birmingham 10

MARSHALL, RICK
90/1 SketchOHL 10
91/2 SketchOHL 105
92/3 Windsor 18

MARSHALL, WILLIE
55/6 Parkhurst 17
58/9 Parkhurst 19

MARSON, LARRY
91/2 Oshawa/Domino's 30

MARSON, MIKE
74/5 Loblaws
75/6 OPC/Topps 43
74/5 WSH

MARTAN, JOHN
52/3 AnonymousOHL 109

MARTEL, JAKE
90/1 SketchQMJHL 258
95/6 Slapshot 215

MARTEL, KEN
90/1 Mich.Tech

MARTELL, STEVE
91/2 ProCards 559
89/90 SketchOHL 34
90/1 SketchOHL 135
92/3 Hampton

MARTHINSEN, JIM
95 Globe 190
95 PaniniWorlds 236
94 Semic 251
95 Semic 177
92 SemicSticker 27
93 SemicSticker 229
96 Wien 202

MARTIKAINEN, KARI
92/3 Jyvas-Hyva 59
93/4 Jyvas-Hyva 105
93/4 Sisu 11
94/5 Sisu 95
95/6 Sisu 48

MARTIKAINEN, PERTTI
71/2 WilliamsFIN 265

MARTIN, BLAKE
90/1 SketchOHL 64

MARTIN, BRIAN
83/4 Belleville 7
92/3 Hampton

MARTIN, CHRIS
82/3 Kitchener 29

MARTIN, CLARE
45-64 BeeHives(DET)

MARTIN, CRAIG
94/5 Classic E6
93/4 ClassicProspects 78
95/6 Leaf 189
95/6 Parkhurst 229
91/2 ProCards 241
90/1 SketchQMJHL 228
95/6 Topps 94
87/8 Hull

MARTIN, DON
88/9 ProCards(CapeBreton)
89/90 ProCards(IHL) 102
86/7 London 16

MARTIN, FRANK
45-64 BeeHives(BOS)
53/4 Parkhurst 97
93/4 Parkie(56/7) 34
54/5 Topps 30
63/4 Québec

MARTIN, GEORGE
51/2 Parkhurst 39
82/3 Fredericton 15
83/4 Fredericton 18
84/5 Fredericton 22

MARTIN, GRANT
94/5 DEL 436
95/6 DEL 399
96/7 DEL 308

MARTIN, HANS
70/1 Kuvajulkaisut 301

MARTIN, HUBERT (PIT)
64-67 BeeHives(DET)
63-5 ChexPhoto
64/5 CokeCap DET-8
77/8 Coke Mini
70/1 Colgate Stamp 31
70/1 DadsCookies
70/1 EddieSargent 39
71/2 EddieSargent 42
72/3 EddieSargent 68
70/1 Esso Stamp
74/5 LiptonSoup 37
74/5 Loblaws
68/9 OPC/Topps 18
69/70 OPC/Topps 75
70/1 OPC/Topps 18, OPC 253
71/2 OPC/Topps 39
72/3 OPC 24, Topps 99
73/4 OPC 73, Topps 164
74/5 OPC/Topps 58
75/6 OPC/Topps 48
76/7 OPC/Topps 76, OPC 382
77/8 OPC/Topps 135
78/9 O-Pee-Chee 286
94/5 Parkie(64/5) 51
95/6 Parkie(66/7) 1
72 SemicSticker 224
68/9 ShirriffCoin CHI 6
71/2 TheTorontoSun
64/5 Topps 1
65/6 Topps 52
66/7 Topps 41
67/8 Topps 116
54-67 TorontoStar 66/7
90/1 UpperDeck 513
70/1 CHI
78/9 VAN/RoyalBank

MARTIN, JACK
88/9 CHI/Coke
89/90 CHI/Coke
96/7 OTT/PizzaHut
90/1 QUE/PetroCanada
91/2 QUE/PetroCanada
92/3 QUE/PetroCanada

MARTIN, JACQUES
97/8 OTT

MARTIN, JASON
91/2 AirCanadaSJHL D7

MARTIN, JEFF
95/6 Slapshot 423

MARTIN, MATT
93/4 Classic 57
93/4 C4'Images 28
93/4 ClassicProspects 150, LP9

93/4 Donruss 497
94/5 Donruss 34
93/4 FleerUltra 432
94/5 Leaf 159
97/8 PacificRegime 194
93/4 Parkhurst 471
93/4 Premier-TmUSA 23
94/5 Premier(FX) 550
93/4 Score 635
93/4 T.StadiumClub-TmUSA 16
93/4 UpperDeck 447
92/3 Maine (1) 4
94/5 StJohns

MARTIN, MIKE
94/5 AutoPhonex 28
95/6 Classic 9, 98
93/4 Slapshot(Windsor) 4
94/5 Slapshot(Windsor) 5
95/6 Slapshot 408, -Promo
96/7 Binghampton
92/3 Windsor 2

MARTIN, NEAL
94/5 Slapshot(Sudbury) 5
95/6 Slapshot 387
93/4 SSMarie 10

MARTIN, PETE
36/7 WWGum (V356) 31

MARTIN, PETER
81/2 Victoria

MARTIN, PIERRE
79/80 Montréal, -B&W

MARTIN, PIT
see Hubert "Pit" Martin

MARTIN, RICHARD
71/2 Colgate Heads
72/3 EddieSargent 35
74/5 LiptonSoup 33
74/5 Loblaws
73/4 MacsMilk Disk
71/2 OPC/T. 161, OPC-Poster
72/3 OPC 157, -Crests, T. 145
73/4 OPC 173, Topps 155
74/5 OPC/Topps 42, 127, 190
75/6 OPC/Topps 175, 208, 212
75/6 OPC/Topps 289, 315
76/7 OPC/Topps 5, 210, 214
76/7 OPC 380, T-Glossy 19
77/8 OPC/Topps 180,-Glossy 11
78/9 OPC/Topps 80
79/80 OPC/Topps 149
80/1 OPC/Topps 51
71/2 TheTorontoSun
91/2 Trends (72) 49, -Aut
92/3 Trends (76) 125
72/3 BUF
73/4 BUF
73/4 BUF/BellsMarket
74/5 BUF
75/6 BUF/Linnett
79/80 BUF/BellsMarket
80/1 BUF/Wendt
93/4 BUF/NOCO

MARTIN, RON
33-35 DiamondMatch
33/4 WWGum (V357) 7

MARTIN, RONNY
94/5 DEL 196
95/6 DEL 413

MARTIN, TERRY
74/5 OPC/Topps 126
77/8 O-Pee-Chee 318
78/9 OPC/Topps 118
81/2 O-Pee-Chee 321
82/3 O-Pee-Chee 329
83/4 O-Pee-Chee 336
84/5 O-Pee-Chee 306
82/3 opcSticker 66
80/1 Pepsi Cap
82/3 Post
89/90 ProCards(AHL) 261
90/1 ProCards 292
91/2 ProCards 22
83/4 SouhaitsRen.KeyChain
83/4 Vachon 92
88/9 EDM/ActionMagazine 146
79/80 TOR
80/1 TOR
81/2 TOR
82/3 TOR
83/4 TOR
84/5 NovaScotia 24
91/2 Rochester/Genny
91/2 Rochester/Kodak
92/3 Rochester/Kodak
93/4 Rochester

MARTIN, TOM
90/1 ProCards 419
72/3 Ottawa
83/4 Victoria

MARTIN, TUOMO
80/1 Mallasjuoma 134
78/9 SM-Liiga 90

MARTINEAU, DON
74/5 Loblaws

MARTINEAU, PATRICE
90/1 SketchMEM 38
90/1 SketchQMJHL 28
91/2 SketchQMJHL 88

MARTINEC, PATRIK
94/5 APS 85
95/6 APS 284

MARTINEC, TOMAS
94/5 APS 18
94/5 DEL 181
95/6 DEL 184

MARTINEC, VLADIMIR
95/6 APS 396
72 Hellas 89
74 Hellas 78
70/1 Kuvajulkaisut 54
72 Panda
79 PaniniSticker 86
72 SemicSticker 30
74 SemicSticker 56
92/3 Trends (76) 156
71/2 WilliamsFIN 32
72/3 WilliamsFIN 15
73/4 WilliamsFIN 56

MARTINI, DARCY
94/5 CapeBreton
90/1 Mich.Tech
91/2 Mich.Tech (x3)

MARTINI, MARIO
83/4 Belleville 15
84/5 Sudbury 3

MARTINIUK, ALEXANDER
74 Hellas 50
72 Panda
72 SemicSticker 15
74 SemicSticker 39
71/2 Soviet Stars
73/4 Soviet Stars 17
91/2 Trends (72) 50
71/2 WilliamsFIN 9
73/4 WilliamsFIN 10

MARTINSON, JOE
91/2 AirCanadaSJHL C29

MARTINSON, STEVE
88/9 ProCards(She)
90/1 ProCards 308
91/2 ProCards 319
88/9 MTL
89/90 MTL
92/3 SanDiego

MARTISEN, THOMAS
79 PaniniSticker 295

MARTONE, MIKE
95/6 Slapshot 308

MARTTILA, JUKKA
91/2 Jyvas-Hyva 59
92/3 Jyvas-Hyva 157
91 SemicSticker 8

MARTTILA, NIKO
91/2 Jyvas-Hyva 53
92/3 Jyvas-Hyva 30
93/4 Jyvas-Hyva 50
93/4 Sisu 241
94/5 Sisu 12
95/6 Sisu 18

MARTTINEN, JAAKKO
65/6 Hellas 138
70/1 Kuvajulkaisut 163
72 Panda
78/9 SM-Liiga 30
71/2 WilliamsFIN 119
72/3 WilliamsFIN 89
73/4 WilliamsFIN 135

MARUK, DENNIS
76/7 OPC/Topps 86
77/8 OPC/Topps 21
78/9 OPC/Topps 141
79/80 OPC/Topps 223
80/1 O-Pee-Chee 284
81/2 OPC 17, 313, 350, 357, 383
81/2 Topps 65, (E) 120
82/3 OPC 55, 359, 369, 370
83/4 O-Pee-Chee 174, 292
84/5 O-Pee-Chee 101, Topps 76
85/6 OPC/Topps 111
86/7 OPC/Topps 60
87/8 OPC/Topps 117
81/2 opcSticker 191
82/3 opcSticker 151
83/4 opcSticker 204-05
84/5 opcSticker 48
86/7 opcSticker 170/30
87/8 opcSticker 50/189
79 PaniniSticker 60
87/8 PaniniSticker 298
82/3 Post
83/4 PuffySticker 18
83/4 SouhaitsRen.KeyChain
83/4 MIN
84/5 MIN
84/5 MIN/7Eleven 9
85/6 MIN
86/7 MIN/7Eleven 8
87/8 MIN
78/9 WSH
79/80 WSH
80/1 WSH
81/2 WSH
82/3 WSH

MARUSAK, JIRI
95/6 APS 38

MARUSCHAK, DUANE
90/1 SketchWHL 133
89/90 Lethbridge

MARX, GORD
95/6 LasVegas

MASA, MARTIN
92/3 BCJHL 60

MASAK, MARTIN
95/6 APS 63

MACISAAC, AL
94/5 Hampton 2

MASKARINEC, MARTIN
94/5 APS 183
95/6 APS 128
91 SemicSticker 110

MASLENNIKOV, IGOR
90/1 O-Pee-Chee 14R
91/2 O-Pee-Chee 21R
91 SemicSticker 91

MASLOV, NIKOLAI
91/2 O-Pee-Chee 55R

MASNICK, PAUL
45-64 BeeHives(MTL)
51/2 Parkhurst 8
54/5 Parkhurst 13
45-54 QuakerOats
52/3 StLawrence 11

MASON, BOB
87/8 opcSticker 238/105
89/90 opcSticker 188/42
87/8 PaniniSticker 175
88/9 PaniniSticker 20
89/90 PaniniSticker 344
89/90 ProCards(AHL) 88
91/2 ProCards 617
87/8 CHI/Coke
88/9 QUE
88/9 QUE/GeneralFoods
86/7 WSH/Kodak
89/90 WSH
92/3 Hamilton
94/5 Milwaukee

MASON, CHARLIE
36-39 DiamondMatch (1), (2), (3)

MASON, DOUG
91/2 SketchOHL 256

MASON, RON
93/4 Mich.State

MASON, WES
95/6 Bowman P24
94/5 Slapshot(Sarnia) 19
95/6 Slapshot 349, 435

MASSA, ROB
94/5 Slapshot(Sarnia) 15

MASSÉ, PATRICE
80/1 Québec

MASSE, GERRARD
92/3 Windsor 12

MASSE, MIKE
92/3 MPSPhotoSJHL 87

MASSINEN, VESA
71/2 WilliamsFIN 330

MASSON, DALE
89/90 SketchMEM 24
90/1 SketchWHL 294
91/2 SketchWHL 86
89/90 Kamloops

MASSY, DIDIER
91 SemicSticker 183
92 SemicSticker 199

MASTAD, MILT
91/2 AvantGardeBCJHL 111
93/4 Seattle

MASTERS, KEVIN
90/1 SketchWHL 147
91/2 SketchWHL 267

MASTERTON, MATT
95/6 Slapshot 413

MATALAMAKI, KAJ
66/7 Champion 46
65/6 Hellas 46
70/1 Kuvajulkaisut 196
72 Panda
71/2 WilliamsFIN 88
72/3 WilliamsFIN 252
73/4 WilliamsFIN 251

MATATALL, BRUCE
91/2 AirCanadaSJHL B47
92/3 MPSPhotoSJHL 64

MATATALL, CRAIG
91/2 AirCanadaSJHL 29, C1

MATCZAK, WOJCIECH
92 SemicSticker 285

MATECHUK, ROD
84/5 Saskatoon

MATEKA, EDDIE
52/3 AnonymousOHL 30

MATERI, LEE
92/3 MPSPhotoSJHL 69

MATHERS, FRANK
45-64 BeeHives(TOR)
88/9 ProCards(Hershey)
45-54 QuakerOats

MATHERS, MIKE
90/1 SketchWHL 299
91/2 SketchWHL 81

MATHIAS, TREVOR
91/2 AirCanadaSJHL C42

MATHIASEN, DWIGHT
87/8 PGH/Kodak

MATHIESON, JIM
90/1 ProCards 197
91/2 ProCards 554
91/2 Baltimore 8
93/4 Portland
94/5 Portland
95/6 Portland
86/7 Regina
87/8 Regina
88/9 Regina
89/90 Regina

MATHIEU, ALEXANDRE
97/8 Bowman 123
98 BowmanCHL 115
96/7 Halifax (1), (2)
97/8 Halifax (1), (2)

MATHIEU, GILBERT
72 SemicSticker 160

MATHIEU, MARQUIS
90/1 SketchQMJHL 114
91/2 SketchQMJHL 162
94/5 Toledo
93/4 Wheeling 13

MATHIEU, NANDO
72 SemicSticker 138

MATIER, MARK
90/1 SketchMEM 18
90/1 SketchOHL 167
91/2 SketchOHL 326
93/4 SSMarie 3

MATIKAINEN, PENTTI
96/7 DEL 46
93/4 Jyvas-Hyva 43
80/1 Mallasjuoma 143
89 SemicSticker 27
92 SemicSticker
93 SemicSticker 88
93/4 Sisu 233
95/6 Sisu 70
71/2 WilliamsFIN 266

MATIKAINEN, PETRI
96/7 DEL 255

MATINEC, TOM
95/6 APS 117

MATSOS, DAVID
90/1 SketchMEM 10
90/1 SketchOHL 168
91/2 SketchOHL 329
89/90 SSMarie 23
93/4 SSMarie 12

MATTE, CHRISTIAN
97/8 Donruss 207, -RatedRook 6
97/8 DonrussCanadianIce 137
97/8 UpperDeck 257

MATTE, JOE
34-43 BeeHives(CHI)

MATTEAU, STÉPHANE
91/2 Bowman 258
92/3 Bowman 340
93/4 Donruss 463
94/5 Donruss 15
93/4 Durivage 44
92/3 FleerUltra 279
93/4 FleerUltra 290
94/5 FleerUltra 332
93/4 Leaf 114
94/5 Leaf 32
92/3 O-Pee-Chee 69
91/2 OPC/Topps 383
90/1 opcPremier 68
98/9 Pacific 387
97/8 PacificCrown 280
97/8 PacificParamount 168
98/9 PacificParamount 212
90/1 Panini(CGY) 11
91/2 PaniniSticker 62
93/4 PaniniSticker 150
91/2 Parkhurst 259
92/3 Parkhurst 268
93/4 Parkhurst 41
94/5 Parkhurst 150
95/6 Parkhurst 446
92/3 Pinnacle 180
93/4 Pinnacle 344
94/5 Pinnacle 329
96/7 PinnacleBeAPlayer 169
94/5 POG 165
93/4 PowerPlay 313
93/4 Premier 415
94/5 Premier 317
89/90 ProCards(IHL) 192
90/1 ProSet 593
91/2 ProSet 27
90/1 Score 381
91/2 Score(CDN) 242
92/3 Score 543
93/4 Score 398
95/6 Score 227
92/3 Topps 463
91/2 ToppsStadiumClub 391
92/3 ToppsStadiumClub 363
93/4 ToppsStadiumClub 127
94/5 ToppsStadiumClub 216
90/1 UpperDeck 535
91/2 UpperDeck 121
92/3 UpperDeck 540
93/4 UpperDeck 214
94/5 UpperDeck 136
95/6 UpperDeck 60
96/7 UpperDeck 326
95/6 UDBeAPlayer 5
96/7 UDCollChoice 230
90/1 CGY/McGavins
91/2 CGY/IGA
93/4 CHI/Coke
97/8 S.J/Pacific BellSheet
87/8 Hull

MATTERSDORFER, DARCY
91/2 SketchWHL 70

MATTEUCCI, MIKE
91/2 AirCanadaSJHL 21, D43
91/2 LakeSuperior

MATTHEWS, JAMIE
91/2 Classic 37
91/2 ClassicFourSport 37, -Aut
90/1 SketchMEM 124
90/1 SketchOHL 387
91/2 SketchOHL 261
93/4 Slapshot (Sudbury) 16
91/2 StarPics 6
91/2 UltimateDP 32, -Aut 32
91/2 UpperDeck 76
89/90 Sudbury 8
90/1 Sudbury 9
91/2 Sudbury 19
92/3 Sudbury 10
93/4 Sudbury 9

MATTHEWS, RON
52/3 LavalDairy 40
52/3 StLawrence 86

MATTHIASSON, MARCUS
97/8 udSwedish 34

MATTHIES, JEREMY
91/2 AirCanadaSJHL D33
92/3 MPSPhotoSJHL 155

MATTILA, HANNU
92/3 Jyvas-Hyva 49
93/4 Jyvas-Hyva 78
93/4 Sisu 127
94/5 Sisu 76
95/6 Sisu 38
96/7 Sisu 35

MATTILA, JUKKA
70/1 Kuvajulkaisut 131
71/2 WilliamsFIN 181
72/3 WilliamsFIN 130
73/4 WilliamsFIN 184

MATTINGLY, J.P.
88/9 ProCards(Baltimore)
89/90 ProCards(AHL) 103

MATTIS, MIKE
93/4 Mich.State

MATTIUSSI, RICHARD "DICK"
70/1 EddieSargent 139
70/1 Esso Stamp
69/70 O-Pee-Chee 147
70/1 O-Pee-Chee 192

MATTLI, GEORG
79 PaniniSticker 261

MATTSSON, JESPER
93/4 Classic 141
93/4 C'FourSport 201
95/6 EdgeIce 76
94/5 ElitSet 280
95/6 ElitSet 92
95 Globe 61
94/5 ParkieSE 244
91/2 SemicElitserien 198, 332
92/3 SemicElitserien 217
94/5 SP 171
94/5 UpperDeck 519
95/6 SaintJohn

MATTSSON, MARKUS
80/1 O-Pee-Chee 394
81/2 O-Pee-Chee 374
80/1 Pepsi Cap
82 SemicSticker 159
77-80 Sportscaster 51-1201
82 Valio
72/3 WilliamsFIN 311
80/1 WPG
77/8 Winnipeg

MATTSSON, TEPPO
80/1 Mallasjuoma 111
78/9 SM-Liiga 155

MATTSSON, TORBJORN
90/1 SemicElitserien 83

MATULIK, IVAN
89/90 ProCards(AHL) 150
90/1 ProCards 527
91/2 ProCards 537

MATUSOVICH, SCOTT
93/4 Birmingham 6

MATUSZEK, MIKE
89/90 SketchOHL 170

MATVICHUK, ALEX
94/5 Slapshot (NorthBay) 11
95/6 Slapshot 216
93/4 Seattle

MATVICHUK, RICHARD
91/2 Arena 6
91/2 Classic 7
91/2 ClassicFourSport 7
93/4 ClassicProspects 151
93/4 Donruss 418
94/5 Donruss 303
96/7 Donruss 97
97/8 Donruss 193
92/3 FleerUltra 321
93/4 FleerUltra 180
94/5 Leaf 269
92/3 opcPremier 83
97/8 PacificDynag-BestKept 29
92/3 Parkhurst 74
94/5 Parkhurst 57
95/6 Parkhurst 328
92/3 Pinnacle 391
93/4 Pinnacle 182
96/7 PinnacleBeAPlayer 195
95/6 Playoff 249
94/5 Premier 187
93/4 Score 285
96/7 Score 229
90/1 SketchMEM 108
90/1 SketchWHL 83
91/2 SketchWHL 113
91/2 StarPics 57
98/9 Topps 210
91/2 UltimateDP 7, 63, -Aut 63
91/2 UD'CzechWJC 48
92/3 UpperDeck 505
93/4 UpperDeck 55
94/5 UpperDeck 157
95/6 UpperDeck 37
94/5 DAL/Southwest
96/7 DAL/Southwest
90/1 Saskatoon 14
91/2 Saskatoon 14

MATWIJIW, STAN
91/2 SketchWHL 261
93/4 Lethbridge
91/2 PrinceAlbert

MAUDIE, BOB
94/5 Slapshot(MEM) 22
96/7 Binghampton
93/4 Kamloops

MAURER, A.
95/6 DEL 349

MAURICE, MIKE
93/4 ClassicProspects 64
92/3 Hamilton
85/6 Kingston 22
86/7 Kingston 19

MAURICE, PAUL
93/4 Slapshot (Detroit) 23
94/5 Slapshot (Detroit) 25
94/5 Slapshot (MEM) 99

MAVETY, LARRY
90/1 SketchOHL 23
91/2 SketchOHL 110
83/4 Belleville 29
84/5 Belleville 3

MAXNER, WAYNE
89/90 SketchOHL 48
91/2 SketchOHL 192
86/7 London 4
85/6 Sudbury 5

MAXWELL, BOBBY
94/5 SaintJohn

97/8 Pinnacle 176
96/7 PinnacleBeAPlayer 175
94/5 POG 89
95/6 POG 103
93/4 PowerPlay 333
93/4 Premier 412
94/5 Prmr 203, -Finest(OPC) 19
93/4 Score 631
94/5 Score 258
97/8 Score 190
97/8 Score(DET) 6
89/90 SketchOHL 77
90/1 SketchOHL 12
91/2 SketchOHL 113
97/8 SPAuthentic 57, S22
95/6 Topps 28
98/9 Topps 105
93/4 ToppsStadiumClub 441
93/4 UpperDeck 508
94/5 UpperDeck 365
95/6 UpperDeck 301
96/7 UpperDeck 55
97/8 UpperDeck 59, 390
98/9 UDChoice 72
96/7 UDCollChoice 89
97/8 UDCollChoice 83

MCCASKILL, TED
72/3 LosAngeles

MCCAUGHEY, BRAD
88/9 ProCards(Peoria)
92/3 Phoenix

MCCAULEY, ALEX
96/7 Sudbury 1

MCCAULEY, ALYN
97/8 Bowman 5
94/5 Classic DP5
95/6 Classic 53, 92
95/6 DonrussElite-WorldJrs 18
97/8 DonrussElite 38, 117
97/8 DonrussPreferred 153
97/8 D.Priority 181, 206, 220
97/8 D.Prio -DirectDeposit 20
97/8 KatchMedallion 141
97/8 Leaf 152
98/9 Pacific 418
97/8 PacificCrownRoyale 130
97/8 PacificDynagon! Rookies
97/8 PacificParamount 182
94/5 ParkieSE 264
97/8 Pinnacle 18
97/8 PinnacleBeAPlayer 222
97/8 PinnacleBeeHive 55
97/8 PinnacleCertified G
97/8 PinnacleMint 28
97/8 Score 52
97/8 Score(TOR) 17
94/5 Select 162
94/5 SigRookies 47
95/6 Slapshot 278
94/5 SP 183
95/6 SP 173
97/8 SPAuthentic 195
98/9 SPx"Finite" 83, 132
98/9 Topps 79
97/8 UpperDeck 371
96/7 UDBlackDiamond 78
97/8 UDBlackDiamond 141
98/9 UDChoice 200
97/8 UDCollChoice 299
96/7 UpperDeck"Ice" 129
97/8 Zenith 97,Z77,-RookRgn 11

MCCAULEY, BILL
93/4 ClassicFourSport 213
93/4 Slapshot(Detroit) 10
94/5 Slapshot(Detroit) 12
94/5 Slapshot(MEM) 86

MCCAULEY, WES
93/4 Knoxville
94/5 Muskegon

MCCLANAHAN, ROB
94/5 MiracleOnIce 19, 20
80/1 OPC/Topps 232
83/4 O-Pee-Chee 251
84/5 O-Pee-Chee 325
83/4 PuffySticker 20
83/4 SouhaitsRen.KeyChain
79/80 USAOlympicTeam 5

MCCLEARY, TRENT
95/6 Bowman 135
95/6 FleerUltra 280
95/6 Parkhurst 420
90/1 SketchWHL 50
91/2 SketchWHL 190
95/6 OTT
93/4 ThunderBay

MCCLELLAND, DARWIN
88/9 Kamloops

MCCLELLAND, KEVIN
84/5 O-Pee-Chee 253
87/8 O-Pee-Chee 201
90/1 OPC/Topps 389
85/6 opcSticker 230/99
86/7 opcSticker 77/205
91/2 ProCards 344
90/1 Score 287
89/90 DET/Caesars
90/1 DET/Caesars
83/4 EDM
83/4 EDM/Buttons
83/4 EDM/McDonald
84/5 EDM
84/5 EDM/RedRooster
85/6 EDM/RedRooster
86/7 EDM
86/7 EDM/RedRooster
87/8 EDM
88/9 EDM
88/9 EDM/ActionMagazine 109
83/4 PGH/Heinz
92/3 StJohns

MCCOLGAN, GARY
88/9 ProCards(Kalamazoo)
83/4 Oshawa 21

MCCONNELL, DON
89/90 SketchOHL 146
90/1 SketchOHL 265
89/90 NiagaraFalls
87/8 SSMarie 10

MCCONNELL, RYAN
92/3 MPSPhotoSJHL 113

MCCOOL, FRANK
45-54 QuakerOats

MCCORD, BOB
52/3 AnonymousOHL 130
64-67 BeeHives(BOS)
64/5 CokeCap BOS-4
68/9 O-Pee-Chee 146
69/70 OPC/Topps 123
70/1 OPC/Topps 41
94/5 Parkie(64/5) 10
95/6 Parkie(66/7) 43
68/9 ShirriffCoin MIN11
63/4 Topps 6
64/5 Topps 10
65/6 Topps 46
72/3 STL

MCCORMACK, JOHN
45-64 BeeHives(MTL), (TOR)
51/2 LaPatrie 20APR52
52/3 Parkhurst 15
53/4 Parkhurst 34
54/5 Parkhurst 9
45-54 QuakerOats
23/4 PaulinsCandy 43

MCCOSH, SHAWN
92/3 Classic 111
92/3 ClassicFourtSport 217
90/1 ProCards 436
91/2 ProCards 390
94/5 Binghampton
88/9 NiagaraFalls 8
92/3 Phoenix

MCCOSH, SHAYNE
90/1 SketchOHL 238
91/2 SketchOHL 91
93/4 Slapshot(Detroit) 20
93/4 Slapshot(Windsor) 13
94/5 Slapshot(Windsor) 22
94/5 Slapshot(MEM) 96
90/1 Kitchener 19

MCCOURT, DALE
72-84 Dernière 79/80
78/9 OPC/Topps 132
79/80 OPC/Topps 63
80/1 OPC/Topps 245
81/2 O-Pee-Chee 86, 96, 105
81/2 Topps 21, 51, (W) 129
82/3 O-Pee-Chee 28
83/4 O-Pee-Chee 66
81/2 opcSticker 120
82/3 opcSticker 119
83/4 opcSticker 236
84/5 opcSticker 13
81/2 Post PopUp 4
82/3 Post
83/4 PuffySticker 11
83/4 SouhaitsRen.KeyChain
83/4 Vachon 93
81/2 BUF 17
82/3 BUF/Wendt 14
79/80 DET
80/1 DET
75/6 Hamilton

MCCOURT, DAN
90/1 ProSet 693

MCCOURT, MIKE
87/8 Brockville 5
88/9 Brockville 22
94/5 ThunderBay

MCCOY, MARK
90/1 SketchWHL 68
91/2 SketchWHL 181

MCCRACKEN, JAKE
97/8 UpperDeck 400
96/7 SSMarie

MCCRADY, SCOTT
88/9 ProCards(Kalamazoo)
90/1 ProCards 614
85/6 MedicineHat 10

MCCREARY, BILL
90/1 ProSet 694

MCCREARY, BILL E.
52/3 AnonymousOHL 59
70/1 Esso Stamp
68/9 O-Pee-Chee 182
69/70 O-Pee-Chee 181
73/4 VAN/RoyalBank

MCCREARY, KEITH
70/1 Colgate Stamp 34
70/1 DadsCookies
70/1 EddieSargent 168
71/2 EddieSargent 174
72/3 EddieSargent 4
70/1 Esso Stamp
74/5 Loblaws
68/9 O-Pee-Chee 193
69/70 OPC/Topps 114
69/70 OPC-Stamp, -Sticker
70/1 OPC/Topps 93, -Sticker
71/2 OPC/Topps 188
72/3 OPC 25, Topps 27
73/4 OPC/Topps 13
74/5 OPC/Topps 14, 103
68/9 ShirriffCoin PIT10
71/2 TheTorontoSun
91/2 UltimateO6 98
72/3 ATL
71/2 PGH

MCCREARY, MARK
93/4 Toledo 15

MCCREEDY, JOHN
34-43 BeeHives(TOR)

MCCRIMMON, BRAD
91/2 Bowman 48
92/3 Bowman 67
92/3 FleerUltra 52
93/4 Leaf 395
80/1 O-Pee-Chee 354
81/2 O-Pee-Chee 15
82/3 O-Pee-Chee 255
83/4 O-Pee-Chee 270
84/5 O-Pee-Chee 164
85/6 OPC/Topps 158
86/7 OPC/Topps 5
87/8 OPC/Topps 85
88/9 OPC/Topps 178, T-AS 10
89/90 O-Pee-Chee 203
90/1 OPC/Topps 320
91/2 OPC/Topps 60, 79
90/1 opcPremier 69
87/8 opcStars 27
88/9 opcStars 24
82/3 opcSticker 90
83/4 opcSticker 193
85/6 opcSticker 92/225
86/7 opcSticker 247
87/8 opcSticker 99/233
88/9 opcSticker 96, 20/250
88/9 opcSticker 207/77
89/90 opcSticker 91
97/8 PacificDyang-BestKept 75
87/8 PaniniSticker 121, 126
88/9 PaniniSticker 6, 408
89/90 PaniniSticker 33
90/1 PaniniSticker 173
96/7 PaniniSticker 33
91/2 Parkhurst 271
93/4 Parkhurst 358
91/2 Pinnacle 214
92/3 Pinnacle 124
93/4 Pinnacle 358
94/5 Pinnacle 427
96/7 PinnacleBeAPlayer 168
82/3 Post
93/4 Premier 391
90/1 ProSet 39, 438
91/2 ProSet 377, 609
91/2 PSPlatinum 170
90/1 Score 184, 37T
91/2 Score(CDN) 16, (U.S)16
92/3 Score 141
93/4 Score 54, 527
89 SemicSticker 63
83/4 SouhaitsRen.KeyChain
92/3 Topps 301
91/2 ToppsStadiumClub 14
92/3 ToppsStadiumClub 21
90/1 UpperDeck 294, 430
95/6 UDBeAPlayer 51
87/8 CGY/RedRooster
90/1 DET/Caesars
91/2 DET/Caesars
93/4 HFD/Coke
83/4 PHA
86/7 PHA
96/7 PHO
84/5 KelownaWingsWHL 55

MCCRIMMON, KELLY
90/1 SketchWHL 214
91/2 SketchWHL 216
88/9 Brandon 18
90/1 Brandon 7

MCCRONE, JOHN
94 Semic 313

MCCRORY, SCOTT
88/9 ProCards(Baltimore)
89/90 ProCards(AHL) 282
90/1 ProCards 275

MCCULLOUGH, SCOTT
87/8 Sudbury 18

MCCUSKER, RED
23/4 PaulinsCandy 24

MCCUSKIER, DON
91/2 AvantGardeBCJHL 123

MCCUTCHEON, DARWIN
88/9 ProCards(Indianapolis)
86/7 Moncton 8
88/9 SaltLake 13

MCCUTCHEON, JEFF
92/3 MPSPhotoSJHL 60

MCDONAGH, BILL
45-64 BeeHives(NYR)

MCDONALD, ALVIN (AB)
45-64 BeeHives(CHI), (MTL)
64-67 BeeHives(BOS), (DET)
62 CeramicTiles
64/5 CokeCap BOS-21
65/6 CocaCola
70/1 DadsCookies
70/1 EddieSargent 178
71/2 EddieSargent 59
70/1 Esso Stamp
72/3 Letraset 6
68/9 O-Pee-Chee 180
68/9 OPC/Topps 107
69/70 OPC/Topps 18
70/1 OPC 215
71/2 OPC/Topps 134
72/3 OPC 321
76/7 OPC/Topps 218
58/9 Parkhurst 30
59/60 Parkhurst 20
60/1 Parkhurst 56, 60
94/5 Parkie(64/5) 14
95/6 Parkie(66/7) 50
60/1 ShirriffCoin 72
61/2 ShirriffCoin 33
68/9 ShirriffCoin STL12
54-67 TorontoStar V10
56-66 TorontoStar 58/9
71/2 TheTorontoSun
60/1 Topps 33
61/2 Topps 27
62/3 Topps 38, -Buck
63/4 Topps 37
64/5 Topps 16
65/6 Topps 50
91/2 Ultimate06 60, -Aut 60
92/3 STL/UpperDeck 8

MCDONALD, BRENT
95/6 RedDeer

MCDONALD, BRIAN
91/2 AvantGardeBCJ 131

MCDONALD, BUCKO
see Wilfred "Bucko" McDonald

MCDONALD, DEAN
91/2 Knoxville

MCDONALD, DOUG
93/4 C'Prospects 211

MCDONALD, JACK
91 C55 Reprint 8
1911-12 Imperial (C55) 8
1912-13 Imperial (C57) 17
1910-11 Imperial Post 8

MCDONALD, LANNY
83/4 Esso
88/9 Esso Sticker
88/9 EssoAllStar
93/4 HHOFLegends 34
94 HockeyWit 85
84/5 Kelloggs Disk
86/7 Kraft Sports 3
74/5 Loblaws
76/7 OPC 348
74/5 OPC/Topps 168
75/6 OPC/Topps 23
77/8 OPC/Topps 5, 110
78/9 OPC/Topps 78
79/80 OPC/Topps 5, 153
80/1 OPC/Topps 62
81/2 OPC 77, 85, T 52, (W) 82
82/3 O-Pee-Chee 38, 51, 52
83/4 OPC 74, 75, 87, 208
84/5 OPC 231, Topps 26
85/6 OPC/Topps 1
86/7 OPC/Topps 8, J
87/8 OPC/Topps 20
88/9 O-Pee-Chee 234
89/90 OPC/Topps 7
81/2 opcSticker 227
82/3 opcSticker 214
83/4 opcSticker 8, 162, 263, 303
84/5 opcSticker 237, 238
85/6 opcSticker 215
86/7 opcSticker 80
87/8 opcSticker 43
88/9 opcSticker 94, 85/215
89/90 opcSticker 92/231
80/1 opcSuperCard 5
87/8 PaniniSticker 215
88/9 PaniniSticker 10
89/90 PaniniSticker 39
92/3 Pinnacle 242
82/3 Post
83/4 PuffySticker 6
83/4 7ElevenCokeCup
84/5 7ElevenDisk
85/6 7Eleven 3
83/4 SouhaitsRen.KeyChain
82/3 StaterMint
83/4 StaterMint 1
92/3 Trends(76) 174
90/1 UpperDeck 508
92/3 UD'LockerAS 45
83/4 Vachon 13
94/5 Zellers
81/2 CGY
82/3 CGY
85/6 CGY/RedRooster
86/7 CGY/RedRooster (x2)
87/8 CGY/RedRooster (x2)
79/80 COL.R
73/4 TOR
74/5 TOR
75/6 TOR
76/7 TOR
77/8 TOR
78/9 TOR
79/80 TOR

MCDONALD, PARKER
89/90 NewHaven

MCDONALD, RANDY
74/5 SiouxCity

MCDONALD, RON
83/4 Oshawa 24

MCDONALD, TIM
85/6 Minn-Duluth 34

MCDONALD, WALKER
95/6 Slapshot 46

MCDONALD, WILFRED (BUCKO)
34-43 BeeHives(DETx2), (TOR)
39/40 OPC V301-1 13
36/7 WWGum (V356) 84

MCDONELL, KENT
96/7 Guelph 11

MCDONNELL, JOE
93/4 Slapshot(Kitchener) 28
89/90 SketchMEM 26
90/1 SketchOHL 248
91/2 SketchOHL 97
86/7 Kitchener 30
87/8 Kitchener 4
88/9 Kitchener 4
89/90 Kitchener 4
90/1 Kitchener 3
83/4 Moncton 7

MCDONOUGH, AL
71/2 OPC/Topps 150
72/3 OPC 235
73/4 OPC 89, Topps 176
75/6 opcWHA 33
76/7 opcWHA 77
71/2 TheTorontoSun

MCDONOUGH, HUBIE
90/1 Bowman 120
91/2 Bowman 214
94/5 ClassicImages 29
95/6 EdgeIce-Quantum 5
90/1 OPC/Topps 366
91/2 OPC/Topps 389
90/1 PaniniSticker 92
88/9 ProCards(NewHaven)
91/2 ProCards 473
90/1 ProSet 188
90/1 Score 222
91/2 Score(CDN) 450
91/2 ToppsStadiumClub 260
92/3 ToppsStadiumClub 335
90/1 UpperDeck 226
91/2 UpperDeck 138
89/90 NewHaven
92/3 SanDiego

MCDOUGALL, BILL
93/4 Donruss 323
93/4 FleerUltra 426
93/4 Leaf 379
93/4 Parkhurst 463
90/1 ProCards 481
91/2 ProCards 133
93/4 UpperDeck 324
93/4 AtlantaKnights

MCDOUGALL, KEVIN
90/1 SketchOHL 289
89/90 Windsor

MCDOUGALL, TOM
51/2 BasDuFleuve 20
51/2 LavalDairy 45
52/3 StLawrence 84

MCDOWALL, DAVE
82/3 Brandon 9
90/1 ProCards 413
91/2 CHI/Coke

MCDUFFE, PETE
74/5 Loblaws
71/2 OPC/Topps 225
74/5 OPC/Topps 173
75/6 OPC/Topps 256
71/2 TheTorontoSun

MCEACHERN, SHANE
94/5 Slapshot (Brantford) 16

MCEACHERN, SHAWN
92/3 Bowman 415
93/4 Donruss 154, 473
94/5 Donruss 95
95/6 Donruss 373
96/7 Donruss 190
94/5 Flair 136
94/5 Fleer 164
95/6 FleerMetal 8
92/3 FleerUltra 379
93/4 FleerUltra 133, 345
94/5 FleerUltra 166
95/6 FleerUltra 205
93/4 Leaf 217, -GoldL.Rook 7
94/5 Leaf 232
96/7 Leaf 9
97/8 Omega 156
92/3 O-Pee-Chee 359
92/3 opcPremier 94
98/9 Pacific 313
97/8 PacificCrown 224
97/8 PacificCrownRoyale 91
98/9 PacificParamount 164
97/8 PacificRevolution 93
92/3 PaniniSticker 222
93/4 PaniniSticker 84
96/7 PaniniSticker 7
91/2 Parkhurst 355
92/3 Parkhurst 142
93/4 Parkhurst 242, 364
94/5 Parkhurst 173
95/6 Parkhurst 280
92/3 Pinnacle 420
93/4 Pinnacle 105, -Tm2001 9
94/5 Pinnacle 127
96/7 PinnacleBeAPlayer 119
94/5 POG 186
95/6 POG 28
93/4 PowerPlay 119, -Second 7
93/4 Prmr 123,353, -Black(T) 4
94/5 Premier 354
92/3 ProSet 237
92/3 Score 459
93/4 Score 67, 497
94/5 Score 108
95/6 Score 81
96/7 Score 151
93/4 SeasonsPatch 11
94/5 Sisu-GuestSpecial 4
95/6 SP 10
93/4 SPAuthentic 110
95/6 Summit 155
92/3 Topps 481
95/6 Topps 321
95/6 ToppsFinest 91
92/3 ToppsStadiumClub 205
93/4 ToppsStadiumClub 189
94/5 ToppsStadiumClub 211
95/6 ToppsStadiumClub 83
92/3 UD 368, 412, 565, 634
92/3 UpperDeck CC14, G17
93/4 UpperDeck 454, SP-72
94/5 UpperDeck 163
95/6 UpperDeck 360, SE95
94/5 UDBAP R75, -Aut. 101
98/9 UDChoice 138
95/6 UDCollChoice 145
96/7 UDCollChoice 20
97/8 UDCollChoice 180
96/7 OTT/PizzaHut
97/8 OTT
92/3 PGH/Coke
92/3 PGH/FoodStickers
92/3 PGH/Foodland 9
94/5 PGH 3

MCELMURY, JIM
75/6 OPC/Topps 14
77/8 OPC 352
72 SemicSticker 119

MCELWEE, MATT
95/6 Dayton

MCEWEN, BRAD
91/2 AirCanadaSJHL 23
92/3 MPSPhotoSJHL 95

MCEWEN, DOUG
94 Semic 326

MCEWEN, DENNIS
94/5 Hampton 14
86/7 London 23
93/4 Hampton

MCEWEN, HUGH
90/1 Mich.Tech
91/2 Mich.Tech

MCEWEN, MIKE
77/8 OPC/Topps 232
78/9 OPC/Topps 187
79/80 OPC/Topps 66
80/1 OPC/Topps 185
81/2 O-Pee-Chee 215
82/3 O-Pee-Chee 207
82/3 Post
91/2 ProCards 374
79/80 COL.R
86/7 HFD/JuniorWhalers

MCFADDEN, JIM
51/2 Parkhurst 44
45-64 BeeHives(CHI), (DET)
52/3 Parkhurst 38
53/4 Parkhurst 77

MCFARLANE, MARK
90/1 SketchWHL 51

MCFATRIDGE, SEAN
91/2 SketchWHL 108
92/3 Brandon 16
91/2 Saskatoon 20

MCFAYDEN, DON
36-39 DiamondMatch (1), (2), (3)

MCFEE, DALE
84/5 PrinceAlbert

MCGARVEY, WILLIE
89/90 SketchOHL 111

MCGEE, FRANK
83&87 HallOfFame 56
83 HHOF Postcard (D)

MCGEOUGH, JIM
89/90 ProCards(IHL) 116
90/1 ProCards 315
92/3 Richmond

MCGHAN, MIKE
93/4 PrinceAlbert
95/6 PrinceAlbert

MCGILL, BOB
92/3 Bowman 429
82/3 O-Pee-Chee 327
91/2 OPC/Topps 216
91/2 opcPremier 8
85/6 opcSticker 15/145
91/2 Pinnacle 98
82/3 Post
90/1 ProSet 55
91/2 ProSet 47, 480
92/3 Score 386
90/1 ScoreTraded 49T
91/2 Score(CDN) 327, 560
91/2 Score(U.S) 368, 10T
92/3 Topps 209
92/3 ToppsStadiumClub 483
91/2 UpperDeck 62
87/8 CHI/Coke
88/9 CHI/Coke
89/90 CHI/Coke
90/1 CHI/Coke
91/2 S.J.
81/2 TOR
84/5 TOR
85/6 TOR
86/7 TOR

MCGILL, JACK
35-40 CrownBrand 81
36-39 DiamondMatch(1),(2),(3)
35/6 OPC (V304C) 74
34/5 SweetCaporal
36/7 WWGum (V356) 77

MCGILL, RYAN
92/3 FleerUltra 373
93/4 FleerUltra 177
94/5 PaniniSitcker 44
92/3 Parkhurst 366
93/4 Parkhurst 415
89/90 ProCards(IHL) 56
90/1 ProCards 394
91/2 ProCards 498
93/4 Score 649
92/3 UpperDeck 494
94/5 UpperDeck 160
92/3 PHA/JCPenney
92/3 PHA/UD 10Jan93,11Feb93
93/4 PHA 07NOV93
93/4 PHA/JCPenney

MCGILLIS, DAN
98/9 Pacific 328
97/8 PacificCrown 294
97/8 PinnacleBeAPlayer 131
96/7 EDM
97/8 EDM

MCGILVARY, GLEN
92/3 MPSPhotoSJHL 85

MCGIMSIE, BILL
83&87 HallOfFame 71
83 HHOF Postcard (E)

MCGINN, MARK
92/3 Oklahoma

MCGLYNN, DICK
72 SemicSticker 133

MCGLYNN, PETE
89/90 SketchOHL 70
90/1 SketchOHL 89
91/2 SketchOHL 241

MCGOWAN EVERETT
28/9 PaulinsCandy 81

MCGOWAN, CAL
91/2 ProCards 149
89/90 SketchMEM 9
90/1 SketchWHL 293
95/6 Binghampton
88/9 Kamloops
89/90 Kamloops

MCGRATH, PETER
83/4 NorthBay

MCGREGOR, PERCY
23/4 PaulinsCandy 50

MCGUANE, DANA
93/4 Roanoke
94/5 Roanoke

MCGUFFIN, MATT
90/1 SketchOHL 39
91/2 SketchOHL 6

MCGUIGAN, BILL
94/5 SlapshotPromo
94/5 Slapshot(Kitchener) 18

MCGUIRE, E.J.
91/2 ProCards 67
95/6 Slapshot 105
96/7 Guelph 28

MCGUIRE, MIKE
91/2 AvantGardeBCJHL 54
92/3 BCJHL 136
91/2 Nainamo

MCGUIRE, PIERRE
93/4 HFD/Coke

MCHUGH, MIKE
91/2 OPC 7S
88/9 ProCards(Kalamazoo)
89/90 ProCards(IHL) 86
90/1 ProCards 113
91/2 Score(CDN) 651

MCHUGH, JUSTIN
91/2 Minnesota
92/3 Minnesota
93/4 Minnesota
94/5 Minnesota

MCIANTYRE, IAN
91/2 SketchQMJHL 180

MCILHARGEY, JACK
78/9 O-Pee-Chee 294
79/80 O-Pee-Chee 367
82/3 Post
91/2 ProCards 618
75/6 PHA/GingerAle
77/8 VAN/GingerAle
77/8 VAN/RoyalBank
78/9 VAN/RoyalBank
79/80 VAN
92/3 Hamilton

MCINENLY, BERT
33/4 OPC (V304A) 41

MCINERNEY, EOIN
95/6 Slapshot 157

MCINNES, DARIN
86/7 Regina

MCINNES, PAUL
94/5 Slapshot(Sarnia) 12
95/6 Slapshot 34

MCINNIS, MARTY
92/3 Bowman 352
92/3 ClassicProspects 133
93/4 Donruss 457
94/5 Donruss 311
94/5 Flair 106
92/3 FleerUltra 347
93/4 FleerUltra 370
94/5 FleerUltra 131
94/5 Leaf 157
92/3 O-Pee-Chee 135
92/3 opcPremier 12
98/9 Pacific 121
98/9 PacificParamount 29
97/8 PacificRevolution 19
93/4 PaniniSticker 62
96/7 PaniniSticker 95
97/8 PaniniSticker 193
91/2 Parkhurst 327
92/3 Parkhurst 106
93/4 Parkhurst 390
95/6 Parkhurst 134
94/5 ParkieSE 104
94/5 Pinnacle 153
96/7 Pinnacle 62, 112
94/5 POG 158
93/4 PowerPlay 385
93/4 Premier 57
94/5 Premier 244
92/3 ProSet 233
92/3 Score 465
93/4 Score 405
94/5 Score 88
95/6 Score 217
97/8 Score 210
92/3 Topps 302
95/6 Topps 323
98/9 Topps 103
92/3 ToppsStadiumClub 213
93/4 ToppsStadiumClub 257
92/3 UpperDeck 394, 410
93/4 UpperDeck 392
94/5 UpperDeck 106
95/6 UpperDeck 52
96/7 UpperDeck 102
97/8 UpperDeck 26
94/5 UDBeAPlayer R4, -Aut. 14
95/6 UDCollChoice 59
96/7 UDCollChoice 160
97/8 UDCollChoice 42

MCINTOSH, BOB
91/2 AirCanadaSJHL D31

MCINTOSH, DAN
52/3 AnonymousOHL 90

MCINTOSH, MURRAY
94/5 DEL 162
95/6 DEL 154

MCINTOSH, PAUL
78/9 Saginaw

MCINTYRE, ANDY
91/2 Saskatoon 18

MCINTYRE, JASON
93/4 Hampton

MCINTYRE, JOHN
91/2 Bowman 180
92/3 Bowman 336
94/5 Leaf 365
90/1 OPC/Topps 382
91/2 OPC/Topps 37
90/1 Panini(TOR) 16
91/2 Parkhurst 296
93/4 Parkhurst 482
92/3 Pinnacle 214
89/90 ProCards(AHL) 121
90/1 ProSet 457
91/2 ProSet 401
90/1 ScoreTraded 46T
91/2 Score(CDN) 182, (U.S) 182
92/3 Score 347
92/3 Topps 369
91/2 ToppsStadiumClub 324
92/3 ToppsStadiumClub 117
94/5 ToppsStadiumClub 244
91/2 UpperDeck 218
92/3 UpperDeck 118
93/4 UpperDeck 527
94/5 UpperDeck 478
90/1 L.A./Smokeys 22
93/4 VAN/Coins
95/6 VAN/Building 15

MCINTYRE, JOHN A. (JACK)
45-64 BeeHives(BOS)
70/1 EddieSargent 9
52/3 Parkhurst 77
54/5 Parkhurst 88
60/1 Parkhurst 24
93/4 Parkie(56/7) 27
60/1 ShirriffCoin 46
64/5 TheTorontoStar
54/5 Topps 43
57/8 Topps 28

MCINTYRE, LARY
72/3 TOR

MCINTYRE, LLOYD
28/9 PaulinsCandy 48
36/7 WWGum (V356) 121

MCINTYRE, MANY
51/2 BasDuFleuve 54

MCINTYRE, ROB
91/2 FerrisState
94/5 Knoxville 21
94/5 StJohns

MCIVOR, TREVOR
89/90 SketchMEM 95
89/90 SketchOHL 16
90/1 SketchOHL 109
89/90 Oshawa 22

MCKAVE, TODD
92/3 BCJHL 229

MCKAY, BILL
92/3 MPSPhotoSJHL 14

MCKAY, BRUCE
81/2 Milwaukee 7

MCKAY, CALLUM
45-54 BeeHives(MTL)

MCKAY, DOUG
89/90 ProCardsAHL 287
88/9 N.J/Caretta

MCKAY, MARTIN
94 Semic 311
95/6 Sheffield

MCKAY, MICHAEL
94/5 Slapshot(MEM) 75

MCKAY, MURDO
51/2 LavalDairy 5

MCKAY, RANDY
90/1 Bowman 227
92/3 Bowman 296
93/4 Donruss 454
94/5 Leaf 400
95/6 Leaf 314
97/8 Omega 131
98/9 Pacific 264
98/9 PacificParamount 135
97/8 PacificRegime 114
95/6 PaniniSticker 84
92/3 Parkhurst 331
93/4 Pinnacle 322
94/5 Pinnacle 222
95/6 Pinnacle 92
96/7 Pinnacle 38
97/8 PinnacleBeAPlayer 160
95/6 POG 162
94/5 Premier 271
88/9 ProCards(Adirondack)
89/90 ProCards(AHL) 318
91/2 ProSet 422
91/2 Score(CDN) 604, (U.S) 54T
92/3 Score 339
93/4 Score 319
97/8 Score(N.J.) 12
95/6 SkyBoxEmotion 99
95/6 SkyBoxImpact 94
92/3 Topps 106
95/6 Topps 201, 10PL
98/9 Topps 90, SB29
92/3 ToppsStadiumClub 450
95/6 ToppsStadiumClub 153
91/2 UpperDeck 313
95/6 UpperDeck 444
95/6 UDBeAPlayer 52
96/7 UDCollChoice 154
90/1 DET/LittleCaesars
96/7 N.J/Sharp

MCKAY, RAY
71/2 TheTorontoSun

MCKAY, ROSS
90/1 ProCards 177

MCKAY, SCOTT
93/4 ClassicProspects 216
90/1 SketchOHL 136
91/2 SketchOHL 376
94/5 Greensboro

MCKECHNEY, GARNET
82/3 Kitchener 13
83/4 Kitchener 10
84/5 Kitchener 3

MCKECHNIE, CRAIG
91/2 AirCanadaSJHL A8
92/3 MPSPhotoSJHL 149

MCKECHNIE, DARRIN
86/7 Regina
87/8 Regina

MCKECHNIE, WALT
71/2 Bazooka Panel 28
70/1 Colgate Stamp 1
70/1 EddieSargent 89
71/2 EddieSargent 129
72/3 EddieSargent 43
70/1 Esso Stamp
72/3 Letraset 5
74/5 Loblaws, -Update
70/1 OPC 172
71/2 OPC 124, OPC-Poster
72/3 OPC 192
73/4 OPC 152, Topps 127
74/5 OPC/Topps 56
75/6 OPC/Topps 194
76/7 OPC/Topps 196, OPC 385
77/8 OPC/Topps 32
78/9 O-Pee-Chee 344
79/80 OPC/Topps 68
80/1 O-Pee-Chee 378
82/3 O-Pee-Chee 91
82/3 opcSticker 186
82/3 Post
83/4 PuffySticker 14
83/4 SouhaitsRen.KeyChain
71/2 TheTorontoSun
78/9 TOR
79/80 TOR

MCKEE, COREY
91/2 AirCanadaSJHL A25

MCKEE, BRIAN
90/1 ProCards 552
91/2 ProCards 40
92/3 Peoria

MCKEE, JAY
95/6 ClassicFiveSport 135
96/7 Fleer 131
96/7 FleerUltra 18, -Rookies 12
96/7 MetalUniverse 186
96/7 Pinnacle 222
97/8 PinnacleBeAPlayer 122
96/7 SkyBoxImpact 154
93/4 Slapshot(Sudbury) 3
95/6 Slapshot 183, -Promo
97/8 UpperDeck 231
93/4 Sudbury 3

MCKEE, MIKE
93/4 ClassicProspects 91
93/4 Donruss 479
93/4 PowerPlay 424
93/4 Score 630

MCKEGNEY, TONY
90/1 Bowman 168
91/2 Bowman 387
80/1 OPC/Topps 144
81/2 OPC 22, Topps(E) 76
82/3 O-Pee-Chee 29
83/4 O-Pee-Chee 60, 296
84/5 O-Pee-Chee 283
85/6 OPC/Topps 156
87/8 OPC/Topps 172
88/9 OPC/Topps 4
89/90 OPC/Topps 4
90/1 OPC/Topps 333
91/2 OPC/Topps 484
81/2 opcSticker 57
82/3 opcSticker 122
83/4 opcSticker 239
84/5 opcSticker 171
85/6 opcSticker 45 /176
88/9 opcSticker 17 /146
90/1 Panini(QUE) 15
87/8 PaniniSticker 118
88/9 PaniniSticker 109
90/1 PaniniSticker 149
82/3 Post
90/1 ProSet 254
83/4 PuffySticker 17
90/1 Score(CDN) 311
91/2 Score(CDN) 104, (U.S) 104
83/4 SouhaitsRen.KeyChain
91/2 ToppsStadiumClub 281
90/1 UpperDeck 340
83/4 Vachon 68
79/80 BUF/BellsMarket
80/1 BUF/Wendt
81/2 BUF 11
82/3 BUF/Wendt 13
85/6 MIN
85/6 MIN/7Eleven 5
89/90 QUE
90/1 QUE
90/1 QUE/PetroCanada
87/8 STL
87/8 STL/Kodak
88/9 STL
88/9 STL/Kodak

MCKENNA, PAUL
92/3 BCJHL 7

MCKENNA, SEAN
87/8 PaniniSticker 284
88/9 ProCards(Newmarket)
89/90 ProCards(AHL) 115
84/5 BUF/BlueShield
85/6 BUF
88/9 L.A.
88/9 TOR/P.L.A.Y. 27

MCKENNA, STEVE
92/3 MPSPhotoSJHL 108
97/8 Omega 109
98/9 Pacific 239
97/8 PinnacleBeAPlayer 244

MCKENNEY, DON
52/3 AnonymousOHL 111
45-64 BeeHives(BOS), (NYR)
45-64 BeeHives(TOR)
64-67 BeeHives(TORx2)
62 CeramicTiles
64/5 CokeCap TOR-17
93/4 Parkie(56/7) 6
94/5 Parkie(64/5) 112
60/1 ShirriffCoin 108
61/2 ShirriffCoin 6
64/5 TheTorontoStar
54/5 Topps 35
57/8 Topps 13
58/9 Topps 62
59/60 Topps 9
60/1 Topps 40
61/2 Topps 12, -Stamp
62/3 Topps 10, -Buck
63/4 Topps 53
64/5 Topps 81
65/6 Topps 112
54-67 TorontoStar V9
56-66 TorontoStar 57/8, 61/2
91/2 BOS/Legends
57/8 BOS
64/5 TOR

MCKENNY, JIM
70/1 DadsCookies
70/1 EddieSargent 201
71/2 EddieSargent 194
72/3 EddieSargent 198
70/1 Esso Stamp
74/5 LiptonSoup 23
74/5 Loblaws
73/4 MacsMilk Disk
71/2 OPC/Topps 43
72/3 OPC 83, Topps 54
73/4 OPC/Topps 39
74/5 OPC/Topps 198
75/6 OPC/Topps 311
76/7 OPC 302
77/8 OPC 374
72/3 Post Transfers 4
72 SemicSticker 189
68/9 ShirriffCoin TOR16
71/2 TheTorontoSun
69/70 TOR
70/1 TOR
71/2 TOR
72/3 TOR
73/4 TOR
74/5 TOR
75/6 TOR
76/7 TOR
77/8 TOR

MCKENZIE, BILL
76/7 O-Pee-Chee 267
78/9 O-Pee-Chee 275
79/80 COL.R

MCKENZIE, GORDON
24/5 CrescentFalcons 12

MCKENZIE, JIM
91/2 Bowman 7
91/2 OPC/Topps 24
93/4 Parkhurst 357
94/5 Parkhurst 178
96/7 PinnacleBeAPlayer 69
89/90 ProCards(AHL) 302
90/1 ProCards 175
91/2 ProSet 391
91/2 ToppsStadiumClub 354
91/2 UpperDeck 494
93/4 UpperDeck 23
97/8 UpperDeck 357
90/1 HFD/JuniorWhalers
91/2 HFD/JuniorWhalers
92/3 HFD/DairyMart
94/5 PGH 20
96/7 PHO
97/8 PHO (x2)
95/6 WPG

MCKENZIE, JOHN
64-67 BeeHives(CHI)
64/5 CokeCap CHI-18
65/6 CocaCola
70/1 Colgate Stamp 59
70/1 DadsCookies
71/2 EddieSargent 3
70/1 Esso Stamp
68/9 OPC/Topps 9
69/70 OPC/Topps 28
70/1 OPC/Topps 6, OPC 241
71/2 OPC/Topps 82
72/3 OPC 338
75/6 opcWHA 77
76/7 opcWHA 103
77/8 opcWHA 41
60/1 Parkhurst 37
61/2 Parkhurst 34
94/5 Parkie(64/5) 36
95/6 Parkie(66/7) 10
72 SemicSticker 185
72/3 7ElevenCups
60/1 ShirriffCoin 43
68/9 ShirriffCoin BOS11
71/2 TheTorontoSun
63/4 Topps 42
64/5 Topps 30
65/6 Topps 94
66/7 Topps 97, -USATest 66
67/8 Topps 39
91/2 Ultimate06 52, -Aut 52
70/1 BOS
71/2 BOS

MCKICHAN, STEVE
90/1 ProCards 341

MCKIE, RYAN
95/6 Slapshot 177

MCKILLOP, BOB
90/1 SketchOHL 66

MCKIM, ANDREW
92/3 ClassicProspects 14
96/7 DEL 38
94/5 Parkhurst 16
90/1 ProCards 626
91/2 ProCards 343
96 Wien AS6

MCKINLAY, MIKE
91/2 AvantGardeBCJ 125
92/3 BCJHL 164

MCKINLEY, BARRY
93/4 ThunderBay
94/5 ThunderBay
95/6 ThunderBay

MCKINLEY, ROB
84/5 Kamloops
85/6 Kamloops
86/7 Kamloops
86/7 Regina
87/8 Regina

MCKINNEY, BRYAN
94/5 Slapshot (Guelph) 4
95/6 Slapshot 88
95/6 Guelph 18

MCKINNON, ALEX
24/5 Champs (C144)
24/5 (V145-2) 16

MCKINNON, BRIAN
82/3 Ottawa67s
83/4 Ottawa67s

MCKINNON, KEN
36/7 WWGum (V356) 118

MCKINNON, KEVIN
94/5 Erie

MCKINNON, PAUL
79/80 WSH
80/1 WSH

MCKINIGHT, WES
34-43 BeeHives(Misc.)

MCLANE, MARK
87/8 Hull

MCLAREN, KYLE
95/6 Bowman 151
95/6 Donruss 334
96/7 Donruss 219
95/6 DonrussElite-Rookie 15
97/8 DonrussPreferred 107
96/7 Fleer 5
95/6 FleerMetal 184
95/6 FleerUltra 349
96/7 FleerUltra 9
96/7 Leaf 142
96/7 MetalUniverse 8
98/9 Pacific 86
97/8 PacificCrown 42
96/7 PaniniSticker 5
95/6 Parkhurst 262
95/6 P.Zenith 127, -RookRoll 17
95/6 POG 35
96/7 Score 258
97/8 Score(BOS) 19
95/6 SelectCertified 139
95/6 SkyBoxImpact 189
96/7 SkyBoxImpact 6
95/6 SP 8
96/7 SP 8
97/8 SPAuthentic 11
95/6 Summit 194
96/7 Summit 159
95/6 Topps 309
95/6 ToppsFinest 111
96/7 ToppsNHLPicks RS13
95/6 ToppsStadiumClub 63
95/6 ToppsSuperSkills SR9
95/6 UpperDeck 421
96/7 UpperDeck 9, SS25B, X37
97/8 UpperDeck 13
95/6 UDBeAPlayer 173
97/8 UDBlackDiamond 54
98/9 UDChoice 16
96/7 UDCollectorChoice 15, 341
97/8 UDCollChoice 15
93/4 Tacoma

MCLAREN, STEVE
93/4 Slapshot(NorthBay) 4
94/5 Slapshot(NorthBay) 5

MCLARREN, RICK
92/3 BCJHL 141

MCLARTY, JIM
91/2 AirCanadaSJHL 9, C20

MCLAUGHLIN, FREDERIC
83&87 HallOfFame 189
83 HHOF Postcard (J)

MCLAUGHLIN, MIKE
94/5 Binghampton
92/3 Rochester/Dunkin'Donuts
92/3 Rochester/Kodak

MCLAY, DAVE
83/4 Kelowna
86/7 Portland

MCLEAN, BRETT
95/6 UpperDeck 506
98/9 UDChoice 270

MCLEAN, DARREN
91/2 AirCanadaSJHL C25
92/3 MPSPhotoSJHL 12

MCLEAN, GREG
93/4 Slapshot(Kitchener) 4
94/5 Slapshot(Kitchener) 5

MCLEAN, JACK
34-43 BeeHives(TOR)

MCLEAN, JEFF
92/3 Classic 85
92/3 ClassicFourSport
93/4 C'Prospects 139

MCLEAN, JIM
91/2 AirCanadaSJHL B6

MCLEAN, KIRK
90/1 Bowman 57
91/2 Bowman 310
92/3 Bowman 212, 285
93/4 Donruss 355
94/5 Donruss 22, -Masked 6
95/6 Donruss 16
96/7 Donruss 3
97/8 Donruss 189
97/8 DonrussPriority 162
96/7 DonrussCanadianIce 33
97/8 DonrussCanadianIce 79
96/7 DonrussElite 121
97/8 DonrussStudio 88
93/4 EASports 144
94/5 Flair 193
94/5 Fleer 227, -Netminder 6
96/7 Fleer 113
95/6 FleerMetal 152
92/3 FleerUltra 224
93/4 FleerUltra 29
94/5 FleerUltra 228
95/6 FleerUltra 170, 373
96/7 FleerUltra 169
92/3 HumptyDumpty (1)
97/8 KatchMedallion 147
89/90 Kraft 43
90/1 Kraft 70
92/3 Kraft'Disk
93/4 Kraft'Cutout
94/5 KraftDinner
95/6 Kraft-Crease
93/4 Leaf 55, -PaintedWariorr 3
94/5 Leaf 109, -CreasePatrol 7
95/6 Leaf 102
96/7 Leaf 43
97/8 Leaf 74
94/5 LeafLimited 23
95/6 LeafLimited 67
97/8 Limited 3, 106
95/6 McDonalds McD30
96/7 McD'Masks
96/7 MetalUniverse 158
97/8 Omega 43
89/90 OPC/Topps 61
90/1 OPC/Topps 257
91/2 OPC/Topps 221
92/3 O-Pee-Chee 349
90/1 opcPremier 70
91/2 opcPremier 158
89/90 opcSticker 64
88/9 opcSticker 55/186, 136/7
88/9 opcStickFS 13
98/9 Pacific 225
97/8 PacificCrown 258
97/8 PcfcDynagon! 128,-Tand 56
97/8 PacificInvincible 143
97/8 PacificParamount 189
90/1 Panini(VAN) G
88/9 PaniniSticker 132
89/90 PaniniSticker 155
90/1 PaniniSticker 296
91/2 PaniniSticker 45
92/3 PaniniSticker 27
93/4 PaniniSticker 177
94/5 PaniniSticker 153
95/6 PaniniSticker 298
96/7 PaniniSticker 291
91/2 Parkhurst 181, 440
92/3 Parkhurst 192
93/4 Parkhurst 213
94/5 Parkhurst 238
95 PH'Incomnet
95/6 Parkie 213, -GoalPatrol 11
94/5 ParkieSe seV10
91/2 Pinnacle 158
92/3 Pinnacle 246, 330
93/4 Pinnacle 158, -TeamP. 7
94/5 Pinnacle 60, GT11
95/6 Pinnacle 132
96/7 Pinnacle 90
97/8 Pinnacle 88
97/8 PinnacleBeAPlayer 118
97/8 PinnacleCertified 27
97/8 PinnacleInside 60
95/6 PinnacleZenith 57
95/6 Playoff 101
94/5 POG 270
95/6 POG 278
93/4 PowerPlay 253
93/4 Premier 113
94/5 Premier 85, 397
95/6 ProMagnet 24
90/1 ProSet 302, 355
91/2 ProSet 501, 603, P1, -Aut.
91/2 PS-ThePuck 28, -Promo
92/3 ProSet 193, 250
91/2 PSPlatinum 239
90/1 Score 93, -HotCards 46
91/2 Score(CDN) 481, (U.S) 261
92/3 Score 385, 417
93/4 Score 47
94/5 Score 60
95/6 Score 49
96/7 Score 155
97/8 Score 43
97/8 Score(VAN) 10
92/3 SeasonsPatch 71
94/5 Select 64
96/7 SelectCertified 22
95/6 SelectCertified 63
93 SemicSticker 190
95/6 SkyBoxEmotion 181
95/6 SkyBxImp 170, -Deflect 12
96/7 SkyBoxImpact 134
94/5 SP 124
95/6 SP 152
97/8 SPAuthentic 159
95/6 Smmt 69, -InTheCrease 14
96/7 Summit 68
95/6 SuperSticker 127
96/7 TeamOut
92/3 Topps 130, 225, 270
95/6 Topps 277, 13HG
94/5 ToppsFinest 61
95/6 ToppsFinest 161
91/2 ToppsStadiumClub 105
92/3 ToppsStadiumClub 193
93/4 ToppsStadiumClub 163
94/5 T.StadiumClub 188, 223
95/6 ToppsStadiumClub 41
97/8 ToppsSticker 4
95/6 ToppsSuperSkills 89
90/1 UpperDeck 278
91/2 UpperDeck 191
92/3 UpperDeck 22, 299
93/4 UpperDeck 156, SP-165
94/5 UpperDeck 133, H34, SP84
95/6 UpperDeck 136, SE83
96/7 UpperDeck 348
97/8 UpperDeck 375
93/4 UDBeAPlayer'Roots 7
94/5 UDBeAPlayer R73, R107
95/6 UDBeAPlayer 200
97/8 UDBlackDiamond 31
95/6 UDCollChoice 71
96/7 UDCollChoice 271
87/8 VAN/Shell
88/9 VAN/Mohawk
89/90 VAN
90/1 VAN/Mohawk
90/1 VAN/Molson
91/2 VAN
91/2 VAN/Molson
92/3 VAN/RoadTrip
93/4 VAN/Coins
94/5 VAN
95/6 VAN/Building 1
96/7 VAN
96/7 VAN/IGA
83/4 Oshawa 2

MCLEAN, TERRY
89/90 ProCards(IHL) 10

MCLEARY, MARK
82/3 Victoria

MCLELLAN, BLONDIE
28/9 PaulinsCandy 45

MCLELLAN, CAM
89/90 Regina

MCLELLAN, DUSTY
91/2 AvantGardeBCJHL 25, 155
92/3 BCJHL 204
93/4 Johnstown 11

MCLELLAN, TODD
88/9 ProCards(Springfield)
84/5 Saskatoon

MCLENNAN, JAMIE
91/2 Classic 40
91/2 ClassicFourSport 40, -Aut
93/4 ClassicProspects 112
93/4 Donruss 458
94/5 Donruss 88
94/5 Flair 107
94/5 Fleer 127
94/5 FleerUltra 328
94/5 KraftDinner
94/5 Leaf 74
98/9 Pacific 369
98/9 PacificParamount 205
95/6 Parkhurst 404
94/5 Pinnacle 250
97/8 PinnacleBeAPlayer 107
94/5 POG 286
93/4 PowerPlay 386
94/5 Prmr 143, Finest(OPC) 21
94/5 Score 224
97/8 Score(STL) 20
94/5 Select 189
90/1 SketchMEM 79
90/1 SketchWHL 129
91/2 SketchAwards 16
91/2 StarPics 32
91/2 UltimateDP 35, -Aut 35
91/2 UltimateDP 57, 89
94/5 UpperDeck 252, SP137
98/9 UDChoice 187
89/90 Lethbridge
91/2 Richmond 20

MCLEOD, AL
75/6 opcWHA 88
76/7 opcWHA 47
75/6 Phoenix

MCLEOD, DON
74/5 opcWHA 48
75/6 opcWHA 32
76/7 opcWHA 129
77/8 opcWHA 14

MCLEOD, JACK
45-64 BeeHives(NYR)
51/2 Parkhurst 98
52/3 Parkhurst 102

MCLEOD, JIM
73/4 QuakerOats 17
72/3 7ElevenCups

MCLEOD, PETE
85/6 London 15

MCLLWAIN, DAVE
90/1 Bowman 136
91/2 Bowman 196
94/5 Donruss 315
94/5 Flair 123
94/5 Leaf 260
88/9 OPC/Topps 132
90/1 OPC/Topps 299
91/2 OPC/Topps 95
90/1 Panini(WPG) 17
90/1 PaniniSticker 319
91/2 PaniniSticker 73
94/5 PaniniSticker 100
95/6 PaniniSticker 219
94/5 Parkhurst 157
94/5 Pinnacle 54
94/5 POG 355
93/4 PowerPlay 402
94/5 Premier 446
88/9 ProCards(Muskegon)
90/1 ProSet 333
91/2 ProSet 434
90/1 Score 231
91/2 Score(CDN) 233,(U.S)102T
92/3 Score 122
93/4 Score 418, 583
92/3 Topps 393
91/2 ToppsStadiumClub 202
92/3 ToppsStadiumClub 491
94/5 ToppsStadiumClub 31
90/1 UpperDeck 216
91/2 UpperDeck 222, 527
92/3 UpperDeck 93
93/4 UpperDeck 524
94/5 UpperDeck 423
94/5 UDBeAPlayer-Aut.9
93/4 OTT/Kraft
94/5 OTT/Bell
87/8 PGH/Kodak
92/3 TOR/Kodak
93/4 TOR/Blacks 9
89/90 WPG/Safeway
90/1 WPG/IGA
95/6 Cleveland
84/5 Kitchener 21

MCMAHON, MARK
98 BowmanCHL 3
95/6 Slapshot 137

MCMAHON, MIKE
68/9 Bauer
65/6 CocaCola
70/1 DadsCookies
70/1 EddieSargent 28
68/9 OPC/Topps 46
70/1 OPC 143
72/3 OPC 305
43-47 ParadeSportive
45-54 QuakerOats
68/9 ShirriffCoin MIN10
65/6 Topps 24
72/3 Minnesota
74/5 Minnesota

MCMANUS, SAM
36/7 WWGum V356 79

MCMASTERS, JIM
72/3 Cleveland/Linnet
72/3 Cleveland

MCMEEKIN, KEN
52/3 AnonymousOHL 179

MCMICHAEL, SCOTT
83/4 Belleville 18

MCMILLAN, CASEY
86/7 Kamloops
87/8 Kamloops
88/9 Lethbridge

MCMILLAN, JOHN
63/4 Parkhurst 15

MCMILLAN, PAUL
91/2 AvantGardeBCJ 108

MCMILLAN, TYLER
91/2 AirCanadaSJHL A4
92/3 MPSPhotoSJHL 146

MCMILLEN, DAVE
90/1 SketchWHL 253
91/2 SketchWHL 157
92/3 Tacoma

MCMORRAN, LARRY
93/4 Lethbridge
93/4 Seattle

MCMULKIN, JOHN
91/2 SketchWHL 175

MCMULLIN, BRYAN
95/6 Guelph 23

MCMULLIN, JOHN H.
96/7 N.J/Sharp

MCMUNN, HAROLD
23/4 Crescent Selkirks 13
24/5 Holland 2
28/9 PaulinsCandy 70

MCMURCHY, TOM
88/9 EDM/ActionMagazine 31
82/3 Brandon 12
85/6 NovaScotia 18
83/4 Springfield 10

MCMURRAY, ED
88/9 ProCards(Peoria)

MCMURTRY, CHRIS
91/2 SketchOHL 340
93/4 Slapshot(Sudbury) 4
93/4 Sudbury 4

MCNAB, MAX
45-64 BeeHives(DET)

MCNAB, PETER
75/6 OPC/Topps 252
76/7 OPC/Topps 118
77/8 OPC/Topps 7, 18
78/9 OPC/Topps 212
79/80 OPC/Topps 39
80/1 OPC/Topps 94, 167, 220
81/2 OPC 5, Topps(E) 69
82/3 O-Pee-Chee 16
83/4 O-Pee-Chee 53
84/5 O-Pee-Chee 326
81/2 opcSticker 46
82/3 opcSticker 83, 84
83/4 opcSticker 51
85/6 opcSticker 244 /111
82/3 Post
83/4 BOS
74/5 BUF
75/6 BUF/Linnett
86/7 N.J./SOBER
84/5 VAN

MCNAMARA, GEORGE
83&87 HallOfFame 220
83 HHOF Postcard (O)

MCNAMARA, GERRY
80/1 TOR

MCNAMARA, HAROLD
1910-11 Imperial (C56) 32

MCNAMARA, JERRY
52/3 AnonymousOHL 153

MCNAMARA, LEN
90/1 SketchOHL 299

MCNAMEE, PETER
75/6 Phoenix

MCNEIL, DOUG
51/2 LavalDairy 99

MCNEIL, GERRY
45-64 BeeHives(MTL)
48-52 Exhibits
51-54 LaPatrie 2 Dec51
43-47 ParadeSportive
51/2 Parkhurst 15
52/3 Parkhurst 12
53/4 Parkhurst 25
54/5 Parkhurst 1
55/6 Parkhurst 52
45-54 QuakerOats (x3)

MCNEIL, SHAWN
97/8 Bowman 99
98 BowmanCHL 71
94/5 Slapshot(MEM) 24

MCNEILL
91/2 AvantGardeBCJHL 161

MCNEILL, BILL
63/4 Parkhurst 56
93/4 Parkie(56/7) 48
57/8 Topps 44
59/60 Topps 41

MCNEILL, MIKE
91/2 Bowman 143
92/3 Bowman 424
91/2 OPC/Topps 408
89/90 ProCards(IHL) 72
90/1 ProSet 600
91/2 ProSet 467
92/3 Topps 166
91/2 ToppsStadiumClub 241
92/3 ToppsStadiumClub 294
91/2 UpperDeck 524
90/1 CHI/Coke
91/2 QUE/PetroCanada
94/5 Milwaukee

MCNEILL, STEVE
94/5 DEL 264

MCNELIS, BILL
93/4 Waterloo

MCNUTT, STEVE
90/1 SketchWHL 110

MCPHEE, GEORGE
85/6 O-Pee-Chee 252

MCPHEE, MIKE
90/1 Bowman 43
91/2 Bowman 339
92/3 Bowman 89
92/3 FleerUltra 322
93/4 FleerUltra 300
86/7 Kraft Sports 31
89/90 Kraft Sticker 1
94/5 Leaf 203
85/6 O-Pee-Chee 225
86/7 O-Pee-Chee 221
88/9 O-Pee-Chee 237
89/90 OPC/Topps 84
90/1 OPC/Topps 137
91/2 OPC/Topps 252
92/3 O-Pee-Chee 199
86/7 opcSticker 15/157
88/9 opcSticker 47/182
89/90 opcSticker 59 /201
90/1 Panini(MTL) 16
87/8 PaniniSticker 66
88/9 PaniniSticker 258
89/90 PaniniSticker 243
90/1 PaniniSticker 63
91/2 PaniniSticker 188
91/2 Parkhurst 310
93/4 Parkhurst 51
91/2 Pinnacle 147
92/3 Pinnacle 342
93/4 Pinnacle 163
94/5 Pinnacle 105
94/5 POG 80
93/4 PowerPlay 326
93/4 Premier 135, 214
94/5 Premier 163
90/1 ProSet 155
91/2 ProSet 129
91/2 Score(CDN) 147, (U.S) 147
92/3 Score 91
93/4 Score 85
94/5 Score 17
95/6 Summit-GM 21
92/3 Topps 45
91/2 ToppsStadiumClub 210
92/3 ToppsStadiumClub 452
93/4 ToppsStadiumClub 6
90/1 UpperDeck 384
91/2 UpperDeck 487
92/3 UpperDeck 538
93/4 UpperDeck 43
94/5 DAL
84/5 MTL
85/6 MTL
85/6 MTL/ProvigoStickers
85/6? MTL/ProvigoPlacemats
86/7 MTL
87/8 MTL
87/8 MTL/Kodak
87/8 MTL/Stickers 17, 29, 37, 38
88/9 MTL
89/90 MTL
89/90 MTL/Figurine
89/90 MTL/Kraft
90/1 MTL
91/2 MTL
83/4 NovaScotia 19

MCPHEE, WAYNE
94/5 Slapshot(Brantford) 13

MCPHERSON, A.
71/2 STL

MCPHERSON, BUD
48-52 Exhibits

MCPHERSON, DARWIN
90/1 ProCards 94
92/3 Dayton
93/4 Dayton 16

MCPHERSON, JIM
45-54 QuakerOats

MCPOLIN, JUSTIN
95/6 Slapshot 172

MCQUAID, CHRIS
89/90 ProCards'AHL 158
89/90 Halifax
90/1 Halifax
95/6 Halifax
96/7 Halifax (1), (2)
97/8 Halifax (1), (2)

MCQUAT, JASON
93/4 Slapshot(Oshawa) 24
95/6 Louisiana, -Playoffs
92/3 Oshawa

MCQUAT, ROB
93/4 Slapshot(Oshawa) 18
92/3 Oshawa

MCQUEEN, DAVE
95/6 Slapshot 330

MCRAE, BASIL
90/1 Bowman 187
89/90 O-Pee-Chee 216
90/1 OPC/Topps 151
87/8 opcSticker 227/94
89/90 PaniniSticker 109
90/1 PaniniSticker 249
91/2 PaniniSticker 119
92/3 Parkhurst 391
93/4 PowerPlay 430
90/1 ProSet 141
91/2 ProSet 409
92/3 ProSet 176
90/1 Score 261
91/2 Score(CDN) 391
92/3 Score 356, 509
93/4 Score 436
93/4 ToppsStadiumClub 273
90/1 UpperDeck 30
91/2 UpperDeck 388
95/6 UpperDeckBeAPlayer 6
86/7 DET/Caesars
87/8 MIN
88/9 MIN/American
86/7 QUE
83/4 TOR
82/3 Fredericton 10

MCRAE, CHRIS
89/90 ProCards(AHL) 308
90/1 ProCards 472
91/2 ProCards 240

MCRAE, GORD
75/6 OPC/Topps 203
76/7 OPC 337
74/5 TOR
75/6 TOR
76/7 TOR
77/8 TOR

MCRAE, JIM
82/3 Fredericton 25

MCRAE, KEN
90/1 O-Pee-Chee 411
90/1 Panini(QUE) 16
88/9 ProCards(Halifax)
91/2 ProCards 542
90/1 ProSet 255
89/90 QUE
89/90 QUE/GeneralFoods
89/90 QUE/Police
90/1 QUE
91/2 QUE/PetroCanada
89/90 Sudbury 12
95/6 Phoenix
92/3 StJohns
93/4 StJohns
85/6 Sudbury 14

MCREAVY, PAT
34-43 BeeHives(DET)

MCREYNOLDS, BRIAN
95/6 EliteSet 260
89/90 ProCards(AHL) 47
90/1 ProCards 24
91/2 ProCards 209
95/6 udElite 147
91/2 UpperDeck 434
89/90 WPG/Safeway
92/3 Binghampton
93/4 Phoenix

MCSHEFFREY, BRYAN
74/5 Loblaws, -Update
73/4 O-Pee-Chee 219
72/3 VAN/RoyalBank
73/4 VAN/RoyalBank

MCSORLEY, CHRIS
88/9 ProCards(Indianapolis)
87/8 Flint
94/5 LasVegas
95/6 LasVegas
96/7 LasVegas
92/3 Toledo 1, 2
93/4 Toledo 2

MCSORLEY, MARTY
91/2 Bowman 184
92/3 Bowman 35
93/4 Donruss 256, 447
94/5 Donruss 168
95/6 Donruss 354
96/7 Duracell DC9
93/4 EAsports 62
95/6 Edge-Living L2
94/5 Flair 82
94/5 Fleer 98
96/7 fleerPicks 166
92/3 FleerUltra 310
93/4 FleerUltra 227, 394
94/5 FleerUltra 102
95/6 FleerUltra 76
95/6 Hoyle'WEST 6 (Diamonds)
97/8 KatchMedallion 122
96/7 Kraft-Mascots
93/4 Leaf 352
94/5 Leaf 174
95/6 Leaf 309
97/8 Omega 204
87/8 O-Pee-Chee 205
90/1 OPC/Topps 17, 392
91/2 OPC/Topps 225, 322
92/3 O-Pee-Chee 261
98/9 Pacific 388
97/8 PacificCrown 333
98/9 PacificParamount 213
89/90 PaniniSticker 99
90/1 PaniniSticker 234
91/2 PaniniSticker 84
92/3 PaniniSticker 73
93/4 PaniniSticker 208
94/5 PaniniSticker 178
95/6 PaniniSticker 274
91/2 Parkhurst 69
92/3 Parkhurst 304, CP17
93/4 Parkhurst 161
94/5 Parkhurst 106
95/6 Parkhurst 105
91/2 Pinnacle 35
92/3 Pinnacle 156
93/4 Pinnacle 374
94/5 Pinnacle 61
95/6 Pinnacle 36
96/7 Pinnacle 67
95/6 Playoff 51
94/5 POG 130
95/6 POG 140
94/5 Post
93/4 PowerPlay 191
93/4 Premier 395
94/5 Premier 146
90/1 ProSet 124
91/2 ProSet 100
92/3 ProSet 69
91/2 PSPlatinum 184
90/1 Score 271
91/2 Score(CDN) 217, 297
91/2 Score(U.S) 217, 407
92/3 Score 26
93/4 Score 212, 542
94/5 Score 20
95/6 Score 92
94/5 Select 124
92/3 Topps 171
95/6 Topps 162
98/9 Topps 155
94/5 T.Finest-RingLeader s 11
91/2 ToppsStadiumClub 267
92/3 ToppsStadiumClub 481
93/4 TSC 155, -Finest 8
90/1 UpperDeck 212
91/2 UpperDeck 199
92/3 UpperDeck 322
93/4 UpperDeck 487, GG9
94/5 UpperDeck 33, SP127
95/6 UpperDeck 193, SE129
96/7 UpperDeck 106, 29A
94/5 UDBAP R10, R150, G15
95/6 UDBeAPlayer 225
95/6 UDCollChoice 44
96/7 UDCollChoice 172
97/8 UDCollChoice 221
96/7 UpperDeck"Ice"60
85/6 EDM/RedRooster
86/7 EDM
86/7 EDM/RedRooster
87/8 EDM
88/9 EDM/ActionMagazine 37
88/9 L.A./Smokeys
89/90 L.A./Smokeys 17
90/1 L.A./Smokeys 18
83/4 PGH
84/5 PGH/Heinz
93/4 PGH/Foodland 5
96/7 S.J/PacificBellSheet (x2)
97/8 S.J/PacificBellSheet

MCSWEEN, DON
95 PaniniWorlds 215
94/5 POG 179
88/9 ProCards(Rochester)
89/90 ProCards(AHL) 280
90/1 ProCards 290
91/2 ProCards 16
94/5 UpperDeck 301
94/5 ANA/Carl'sJr 18
91/2 Rochester/Dunkin'Donuts
91/2 Rochester/Genny
91/2 Rochester/Kodak
92/3 SanDiego

MCTAGGART, JIM
93/4 Seattle

MCTAMNEY, JOE
89/90 SketchOHL 63
93/4 Dallas

MCTAVISH, DALE
89/90 SketchOHL 110
91/2 SketchOHL 127
91/2 Peterborough 16

MCTAVISH, GORD
79/80 WPG

MCVEIGH, CHARLIE
33-35 DiamondMatch
36-39 DiamondMatch (1)
33/4 OPC (V304A) 44
23/4 PaulinsCandy 27
33/4 WWGum (V357) 38
36/7 WWGum (V356) 93

MCVEY, WARD
24/5 Crescent Falcons 7

MCVICAR, JACK
27-32 LaPresse 30/1

MCVIE, TOM
88/9 ProCards(Utica)
89/90 ProCards(AHL) 214
90/1 ProCards 564
79/80 WPG

MEAD, SCOTT
92/3 MPSPhotoSJHL 123

MEADMORE, NEIL
88/9 ProCards(Moncton)
89/90 ProCards(AHL) 39

MEAGHER, MAURICE
91/2 SketchWHL 345

MEAGHER, RICK
82/3 O-Pee-Chee 144
88/9 O-Pee-Chee 235
89/90 OPC/Topps 116
90/1 OPC/Topps 125, OPC 488
91/2 OPC/Topps 58
87/8 PaniniSticker 316
89/90 PaniniSticker 125
90/1 PaniniSticker 273
90/1 ProSet 267, 389
91/2 PS'Promo 3of4
90/1 Score 267, 359
83/4 SouhaitsRen.KeyChain
91/2 ToppsStadiumClub 85
90/1 UpperDeck 208, 285
83/4 N.J.
84/5 N.J.
87/8 STL
87/8 STL/Kodak
88/9 STL
88/9 STL/Kodak
89/90 STL/Kodak
90/1 STL/Kodak
92/3 STL/UpperDeck 23
77/8 NovaScotia
92/3 Peoria

MEANS, ERIC
91/2 Minnesota
92/3 Minnesota
93/4 Minnesota

MEARNS, RICK
91/2 SketchWHL 33

MEARS, GLEN
95/6 Toledo

MEASURES, ALLAN
92/3 Jyvas-Hyva 123
93/4 Jyvas-Hyva 86
93/4 Sisu 119
94/5 Sisu 61
95/6 Sisu 33, 376
95/6 SisuLimited 103

MECIAR, STANISLAV
95/6 APS 224
94/5 ElitSet 174
93/4 Jyvas-Hyva 350
93/4 Sisu 216

MECKLING, BRENT
82/3 MedicineHat
83/4 MedicineHat 16

MEDE, ROGER
94/5 DEL 146

MEDEIROS, BRIAN
93/4 OwenSound

MEDICUS, DIETER
94/5 DEL 8
95/6 DEL 169

MEDRIK, STANISLAV
95/6 APS 33
94 Semic 197
91 SemicSticker 112
96 Wien 225

MEEHAN, GERRY
70/1 Colgate Stamp 20
70/1 EddieSargent 20
71/2 EddieSargent 17
72/3 EddieSargent 29
70/1 Esso Stamp
74/5 Loblaws, -Update
70/1 OPC/Topps 125
71/2 OPC/Topps 160, T. 74
72/3 OPC 22, Topps 16
73/4 OPC/Topps 22
74/5 OPC/Topps 99
76/7 OPC 35, 396, Topps 35
77/8 OPC/Topps 53
78/9 OPC/Topps 128
71/2 TheTorontoSun
72/3 BUF
73/4 BUF
75/6 BUF/Linnett
74/5 VAN/RoyalBank

MEEHAN, JEREMY
93/4 Slapshot(Detroit) 11

MEEHAN, PAT
91/2 AvantGardeBCJHL 68
92/3 BCJHL 84

MEEK
91/2 AvantGardeBCJHL 163

MEEKER, HOWIE
45-64 BeeHives(TOR)
48-52 Exhibits
51/2 Parkhurst 72
52/3 Parkhurst 42
93/4 Parkie(56/7) 133
45-54 QuakerOats (x2)

MEGER, PAUL
45-64 BeeHives(MTL)
48-52 Exhibits
51/2 LaPatrie 3-Feb
51/2 Parkhurst 2
52/3 Parkhurst 4
53/4 Parkhurst 21
54/5 Parkhurst 94
55/6 Parkhurst 51
45-54 QuakerOats

MEHALKO, BRAD
94/5 ParkieSE 265
94/5 SP 184
93/4 Lethbridge

MEIGHAN, RON
83/4 PGH/Heinz
82/3 NorthBay

MEIKLE, DEREK
91/2 AirCanadaSJHL D48

MEISNER, KEVIN
88/9 Sudbury 8

MEISSNER, DON
45-64 BeeHives(BOS)
60/1 ShirriffCoin 111
61/2 ShirriffCoin 15
61/2 Topps 6, 64
63/4 Topps 60

MEISTER,RUPERT
94/5 DEL 51
95/6 DEL 2
96/7 DEL 48

MEITINGER, HOLGER
82 SemicSticker 113

MEJZLIK, ROMAN
94/5 APS 196
95/6 APS 212

MELAMETSA, ANSSI
80/1 Mallasjuoma 51
85/6 WPG
85/6 WPG/Police

MELANOVSKY, MAREK
95/6 APS 195
95/6 UpperDeck 543

MELANSON, BRUCE
83/4 Oshawa 19

MELANSON, DEAN
93/4 Classic 143
93/4 ClassicProspects 102
90/1 SketchQMJHL 209
91/2 SketchQMJHL 21
93/4 Rochester
95/6 Rochester

MELANSON, ROB
90/1 SketchQMJHL 153
92/3 Cleveland 23
91/2 Knoxville

MELANSON, ROLLIE
92/3 Bowman 187
83/4 O-Pee-Chee 12
84/5 O-Pee-Chee 130, 387
85/6 O-Pee-Chee 230
87/8 OPC/Topps 19
88/9 OPC/Topps 160
91/2 opcPremier 97
83/4 opcSticker 88, 317
84/5 opcSticker 92
87/8 opcSticker 213/80
88/9 opcSticker 151/18
87/8 PaniniSticker 271
88/9 PaniniSticker 69
89/90 ProCards(AHL) 213
90/1 ProCards 579
92/3 Topps 298
92/3 ToppsStadiumClub 184
91/2 UpperDeck 575
88/9 L.A.
84/5 MIN
85/6 MIN
83/4 NYI
83/4 NYI/Islander 22

MELANSON, STAN
90/1 SketchQMJHL 231
91/2 SketchQMJHL 28

MELENFANT, KEN
91/2 AirCanadaSJHL D27

MELFI, PATRIK
91/2 SketchQMJHL 72

MELICHERCIK, JAN
95/6 Halifax

MELIN, BRAD
84/5 Victoria

MELKERSSON, TOMMY
94/5 ElitSet 119
95/6 ElitSet 180
89/90 SemicElitserien 35
90/1 SemicElitserien 184
91/2 SemicElitserien 35
92/3 SemicElitserien 55
95/6 udElite 23
97/8 udSwedish 19

MELLANBY, SCOTT
91/2 Bowman 236
92/3 Bowman 163
95/6 Bowman 37
93/4 Donruss 126
94/5 Donruss 42
95/6 Donruss 37
96/7 Donruss 49
97/8 Donruss 171
96/7 DonrussCanadianIce 107
95/6 DonrussElite 86
96/7 DonrussElite 32
97/8 DonrussElite 76
97/8 DonrussPreferred 135
97/8 DonrussPriority 129
97/8 DonrussStudio 41
92/3 Durivage 17
93/4 Durivage 46
93/4 EASports 53
94/5 Flair 65
94/5 Fleer 80
96/7 Fleer 40
95/6 FleerMetal 60
92/3 FleerUltra 295
93/4 FleerUltra 328
94/5 FleerUltra 298
95/6 FleerUltra 242, -Crease 10
96/7 FleerUltra 66
97/8 KatchMedallion 62
96/7 KennerSLU
93/4 Leaf 262
94/5 Leaf 182
95/6 Leaf 87
96/7 Leaf 132
97/8 Leaf 110
94/5 LeafLimited 103
96/7 LeafLimited 50, -Stubble 17
96/7 LeafPreferred 111, -Steel 8
97/8 Limited 110
96/7 MetalUniverse 60
97/8 Omega 100
88/9 OPC/Topps 21
89/90 O-Pee-Chee 253
90/1 OPC/Topps 173
91/2 OPC/Topps 200
92/3 O-Pee-Chee 140
91/2 opcPremier 30
98/9 Pacific 226
97/8 PacificCrown 321
97/8 PacificCrownRoyale 59
97/8 PcfcDynagon! 54, -Tand 53
97/8 PacificInvincible 61
97/8 PacificParamount 81
98/9 PacificParamount 99
88/9 PaniniSticker 322
91/2 PaniniSticker 238
93/4 PaniniSticker 243
94/5 PaniniSticker 67
95/6 PaniniSticker 75
96/7 PaniniSticker 67
97/8 PaniniSticker 63
91/2 Parkhurst 50
92/3 Parkhurst 52
93/4 Parkhurst 81
94/5 Parkhurst 85
95/6 Parkhurst 355
91/2 Pinnacle 45
92/3 Pinnacle 346
93/4 Pinnacle 168, -Expansion 6
94/5 Pinnacle 73
95/6 Pinnacle 78
96/7 Pinnacle 126
96/7 PinnacleBeAPlayer 171
97/8 PinnacleCertified 107
97/8 PinnacleInside 165
95/6 PinnacleZenith 25
96/7 PinnacleZenith 16
95/6 Playoff 154
96/7 Playoff 387
94/5 POG 108
95/6 POG 116
93/4 PowerPlay 98
93/4 Premier 249
94/5 Premier 144
95/6 ProMagnet 89
90/1 ProSet 220
91/2 ProSet 172, 383
92/3 ProSet 54
91/2 PSPlatinum 173
90/1 Score 242
91/2 Score(CDN) 575
91/2 Score(U.S) 279, 25T
92/3 Score 148
93/4 Score 63, 503
94/5 Score 102
95/6 Score 134
96/7 Score 31, -Superstition 13
97/8 Score 177
94/5 Select 85
95/6 SelectCertified 3
96/7 SelectCertified 84
96/7 SkyBoxImpact 46
94/5 SP 47
95/6 SP 55
96/7 SP 65
97/8 SPAuthentic 68
95/6 Summit 57
96/7 Summit 8
95/6 SuperSticker 49
96/7 TeamOut
92/3 Topps 444
95/6 Topps 260
98/9 Topps 13
95/6 ToppsFinest 136
96/7 ToppsNHLPicks 101
91/2 ToppsStadiumClub 110
92/3 ToppsStadiumClub 462
93/4 ToppsStadiumClub 31, 369
95/6 ToppsStadiumClub 170
95/6 TSC-MembersOnly 32
91/2 UpperDeck 542
92/3 UpperDeck 119
93/4 UpperDeck 107, SP-57
94/5 UpperDeck 92, SP121
95/6 UpperDeck 399
96/7 UpperDeck 200, 265, X25
97/8 UpperDeck 282
94/5 UDBeAPlayer-Aut. 170
96/7 UDBlackDiamond 127
97/8 UDBlackDiamond 92
98/9 UDChoice 90
95/6 UDCollChoice 171
96/7 UDCollChoice 102
97/8 UDCollChoice 100, SQ37
91/2 EDM/IGA
92/3 EDM/IGA 15
93/4 FLA
94/5 FLA/HealthPlan
96/7 FLA/WinnDixie
97/8 FLA/WinnDixie
86/7 PHA
89/90 PHA
90/1 PHA

MELLIOS, LOUI
91/2 AvantGardeBCJHL 117
92/3 BCJHL 180, 184

MELLOR, TOM
82? JDMcCarthy
72 SemicSticker 121

MELNECHUK, JEFF
93/4 Slapshot(Sudbury) 2
93/4 Sudbury 23

MELNYK, DOUG
91/2 Cincinnati

MELNYK, GERRY
45-64 BeeHives(CHI), (DET)
82? JDMcCarthy
68/9 OPC/Topps 120
60/1 Parkhurst 28
60/1 ShirriffCoin 51
61/2 ShirriffCoin 38

MELNYK, LARRY
86/7 OPC/Topps 95
89/90 O-Pee-Chee 288
90/1 O-Pee-Chee 419
86/7 opcSticker 224/93
88/9 opcSticker 53/184
89/90 opcSticker 73/212
87/8 PaniniSticker 111
82/3 Post
84/5 EDM
84/5 EDM/RedRooster
88/9 EDM/ActionMagazine 14
87/8 VAN/Shell
88/9 VAN/Mohawk
89/90 VAN
84/5 NovaScotia 15

MELNYK, SCOTT
86/7 Portland

MELOCHE, DENIS
73/4 Vancouver

MELOCHE, ERIC
90/1 SketchMEM 69
90/1 SketchQMJHL 18
91/2 SketchQMJHL 280

MELOCHE, GILLES
72/3 EddieSargent 50
72/3 Letraset 18
74/5 Loblaws
82/3 McDonalds 3
72/3 OPC 112, Topps 69
73/4 O-PeeChee 2, Topps 175
74/5 OPC/Topps 205
75/6 OPC/Topps 190
76/7 OPC/Topps 36
77/8 OPC/Topps 109
78/9 OPC/Topps 28
79/80 OPC/Topps 136
80/1 OPC/Topps 47
81/2 OPC 165, Topps(W) 109
82/3 O-Pee-Chee 170
83/4 O-Pee-Chee 177
84/5 OPC 104, Topps 79
87/8 OPC/Topps 107
88/9 OPC/Topps 8
81/2 opcSticker 93
82/3 opcSticker 195
84/5 opcSticker 51
86/7 opcSticker 59
87/8 opcSticker 168/28
88/9 opcSticker 238/108
87/8 PaniniSticker 140
78/9 MIN/Cloverleaf 1
79/80 MIN
80/1 MIN
81/2 MIN
82/3 MIN
83/4 MIN
84/5 MIN
84/5 MIN/7Eleven 8
86/7 PGH/Kodak
87/8 PGH/Kodak

MELOCHE, JASON
91/2 Cornwall 1
91/2 SketchOHL 2

MELOFF, CHRIS
72/3 OttawaNationals

MELROSE, BARRY
93/4 Kraft-Coach
79/80 O-Pee-Chee 386
82/3 O-Pee-Chee 328
80/1 Pepsi Cap
82/3 Post
89/90 ProCards(AHL) 321
90/1 ProCards 476
91/2 ProCards 140
81/2 TOR
79/80 WPG

MELROSE, KEVIN
90/1 ProCards 613
91/2 ProCards 574

MELUZIN, ROMAN
94/5 APS 198
95/6 APS 41, 379
91/2 UD-CzechWJC 94
96 Wien 119

MELYAKOV, IGOR
94/5 Classic DP6

MENARD, CARL
90/1 SketchQMJHL 80
91/2 SketchQMJHL 19

MENARD, HOWARD
69/70 O-Pee-Chee 73
70/1 OPC/Topps 124

MENARD, MARTIN
97/8 Bowman 164
94/5 Slapshot(MEM) 68

MENARD, STÉPHANE
90/1 SketchQMJHL 235
91/2 SketchQMJHL 5
94/5 Knoxville 5

MENARD, TERRY
93/4 ThunderBay
95/6 ThunderBay

MENDE, KARSTEN
94/5 DEL 211
95/6 DEL 203
96/7 DEL 344
94 Semic 278

MENDEL, ROBERT
95/6 DEL 6
96/7 DEL 5
90/1 ProCards 198
91/2 ProCards 335

MENGES, GREG
91/2 Greensboro
92/3 Greensboro 19

MENHART, MARIAN
95/6 PrinceAlbert

MENICCI, TOM
94/5 Hampton 11

MENTIS, JIM
84/5 Victoria

MENYHART, GASPAR
79 PaniniSticker 271

MENZ, R.
85/6 Minn-Duluth 34

MERCALFE, SCOTT
93/4 Knoxville

MERCIER, DON
86/7 Moncton 15

MERCIER, MARTIN
92/3 Maine (2) 32

MEREDITH, GREG
83/4 O-Pee-Chee 88

MERK, KLAUS
94/5 DEL 70
95/6 DEL 50, 440
96/7 DEL 247
95 Globe 217
95 PaniniWorlds 52
94 Semic 271
92 SemicSticker 171
93 SemicSticker 150
96 Wien 192

MERKOSKY, GLENN
88/9 ProCards(Adirondack)
89/90 ProCards(AHL) 323
90/1 ProCards 470
91/2 ProCards 141
94/5 Slapshot(Sudbury) 24

MERRA, MARTTI
92/3 Jyvas-Hyva 103
93/4 Jyvas-Hyva 193
93/4 Sisu 255

MERRICK, WAYNE
74/5 Loblaws
74/5 OPC/Topps 66
75/6 OPC/Topps 228
76/7 OPC/Topps 18, OPC 383
77/8 OPC/Topps 176
78/9 OPC/Topps 258
79/80 OPC/Topps 169
80/1 O-Pee-Chee 345
81/2 O-Pee-Chee 216
82/3 O-Pee-Chee 205
82/3 Post
79/80 NYI
83/4 NYI
83/4 NYI/Islander 10
93/4 NYI/Chemical
72/3 STL
72/3 STL/8"x10"
73/4 STL

MERRITT, RYAN
90/1 SketchOHL 187
91/2 SketchOHL 61
89/90 Windsor

MERSCH, MIKE
89/90 ProCards(IHL) 161
90/1 ProCards 386
87/8 Flint
88/9 Flint

MERTZIG, JAN
95/6 ElitSet 253, -Rookies 6
95/6 udElite 117
97/8 udSwedish 120, C8

MERZ, SUZANNE
94/5 Classic W28

MESICEK, PAVEL
94/5 APS 123

MESICEK, RADEK
94/5 APS 234
95/6 APS 321

MESIKAMMEN, ILKKA
66/7 Champion 75
65/6 Hellas 2
70/1 Kuvajulkaisut 197
78/9 SM-Liiga 203
71/2 WilliamsFIN 232
72/3 WilliamsFIN 216
73/4 WilliamsFIN 291

MESSER, KEVIN
91/2 AirCanadaSJHL D6
92/3 MPSPhotoSJHL 120

MESSIER, DOUG
83/4 Moncton 1

MESSIER, ERIC
97/8 KatchMedallion 167
97/8 Limited 125
97/8 Omega 61
98/9 Pacific 165
98/9 PacificParamount 58
97/8 PacificRegime 55
97/8 PacificRevolution 36
97/8 PinnacleBeAPlayer 204
91/2 SketchQMJHL 111
97/8 SPAuthentic 178
97/8 UpperDeck 45
97/8 UDBlackDiamond 13
98/9 UDChoice 53

MESSIER, JOBY
92/3 Classic 72, LP10
92/3 ClassicFourSport 196, -Aut.
92/3 C'Prospects 76, 127, BC13
93/4 FleerUltra 170, -AllRookie 6
93/4 Leaf 298
94/5 Leaf 375
93/4 Parkhurst 399
94/5 Pinnacle 497
93/4 PowerPlay 161
93/4 Premier 522
94/5 Premier 476
93/4 ToppsStadiumClub 339
93/4 UpperDeck 73
92/3 Binghampton
94/5 Binghampton

MESSIER, MARK
95/6 Aces J (Clubs)
96/7 Aces Q (Diamonds)
97/8 Aces Q (Hearts)
90/1 Bowman 199, -HatTrick 4
91/2 Bowman 114, 'Promo
92/3 Bowman 113, 234
95/6 Bowman 8, BB6
95/6 CoolTrade 5
96/7 CorinthianHeadliners
97/8 CorinthianHeadliners
93/4 Donruss 220, O
94/5 Donruss 9, -Dom 1, -Ice 7
95/6 Donruss 271, -Igniters 5
96/7 Donruss 16,-Elite 5,-Hit 8
97/8 Donruss 4, -Line2Line 23
96/7 D.CdnIce 87, -OCanada 3
97/8 D.CdnIce 50,-Na'l 2,-Scr 23
95/6 DonrussElite 46,-Cutting 8
96/7 D.Elite 22, -Perspectives 2
97/8 DonrussElite 5, 127, 150
97/8 D.Elite-Crafts 4, -Prime 3
97/8 DonrussPreferred 7, 177
97/8 D.Pref -Line 7C, -PrecM 4
97/8 D.Pref -Tins 15, -WideTin 8
97/8 DonrussPriority 16, 189
97/8 D.Prio -DirDep 7,-OpDay 14
97/8 D.Prio -Postcrd 6, -Stamp 6
97/8 D.Studio 9,-Portr 9,-Sil 6
93/4 EASports 87
83/4 Esso
88/9 Esso Sticker
97/8 EssoOlympic 20
94/5 Flair 115, -CentreIce 8
96/7 Flair 61, -Hot 9,-Now 1
94/5 Fleer 136, -Headliner 7
96/7 Fleer 68,71, -ArtRoss 15
95/6 FleerMetal 97, -Iron 8
96/7 F.Picks-Captain 5, -Fab 29
92/3 FleerUltra 139, -AW 1, 10
93/4 FleerUltra 183, -Pivots 6
94/5 FU 140,-AS 4,-Piv 7,-Pwr 7
95/6 FU 105, 393,-CrC 11,-Piv 5
96/7 FU 109,-Clear 7,-MrMom 8
88/9 FritoLay
91/2 Gillette 31
95 Globe 84
96/7 Got-UmHockeyGreatsCoin
92/3 HighFive 4
93/4 HockeyWit 102
95/6 Hoyle'EAST A (Diamond)
92/3 HumptyDumpty (2)
97/8 KatchMedallion 148
92/3 Kelloggs Poster
93/4 KennerSLU
94/5 KennerSLU (U.S)
96/7 KennerSLU
97/8 KennerSLU
94 Koululainen
86/7 Kraft Sports 18
89/90 Kraft 15
90/1 Kraft 32, 71
91/2 Kraft 16
92/3 Kraft-AllStar
93/4 Kraft-Captain
94/5 Kraft-Sharpshooter
95/6 KraftDinner
97/8 Kraft-CaseSeries, -CdnPros
97/8 Kraft -WorldsBest
93/4 Leaf 158
94/5 Leaf 11, -Gold 5,-Limited 15
95/6 Leaf 68
96/7 Leaf 180,-Fire15,-Sweater 8
97/8 Leaf 9, 176, -FireOnIce 11
94/5 LeafLimited 89
95/6 LeafLimited 75
96/7 LeafLimited 65, -Bash 2
96/7 LeafPreferred 66, -Steel 42
96/7 LeafPreferred-SteelPower 4
97/8 Limited 25, 84,187
97/8 Limited -fabric 44, 59
96/7 Maggers 99
82/3 McDonalds 15
92/3 McDonalds McH-01
95/6 McDonalds McD5
96/7 McDonalds McD22
96/7 MetalUniverse 99
96/7 MU-CoolSteel 8, -Lethal 13
97/8 Omega 231,250,-GamF 19
97/8 Omega-Silk 12,-StckHan 20
80/1 O-Pee-Chee 289
81/2 O-Pee-Chee 118
82/3 O-Pee-Chee 108, 117
83/4 O-Pee-Chee 23, 39
84/5 OPC 213, 254, Topps 159
85/6 O-Pee-Chee 177
86/7 OPC/Topps 186
87/8 OPC/Topps 112
88/9 OPC/Topps 93
89/90 OPC/Topps 65
90/1 OPC/Topps 130, 193
90/1 OPC 519, T-TL 16
91/2 OPC/Topps 346
92/3 O-Pee-Chee 208, 258
92/3 OPC-25Years 13, -Box
90/1 opcPremier 71
91/2 opcPremier 51
92/3 opcPremier-Star 15
87/8 opcStars 28
88/9 opcStars 25
81/2 opcSticker 210
82/3 opcSticker 94, 159
83/4 opcSticker 97, 98, 157
84/5 opcSticker 5, 249, 261
85/6 opcSticker 228/95
86/7 opcSticker 79
87/8 opcSticker 92
88/9 opcSticker 230
89/90 opcSticker 227
98/9 Pacific 11,-Dynl 18,-Gld 34
97/8 PacificCC 11, -Supial 13
97/8 PCC-Career 1, -Gold 16
97/8 PCC-Cramers 8, -Slap 5B
97/8 PacificCrownRoyale 136
97/8 PCR-Blades 20,-HatTrck 19
97/8 PCR -Lamplighter 20
97/8 PacificDynagon! 81, 140
97/8 PcfcD-Bst 63,-King 7,-Tan 3
97/8 PacificInv. 89, -Feature 22
97/8 Pac.Inv.-Attack 17, -Off 13
97/8 PacificParamount 190
97/8 PcfcParamount -CdnGrt 12
97/8 PcfcP-BgNum 20,-Photo 20
98/9 PcfcParamnt 236, HOF 10
98/9 PcfcP-SpecD 19,-TmCL 26
97/8 PacificRegime 131
97/8 PacificRevolution 142
97/8 PcfcRev -AllStarGame 19
90/1 Panini(EDM) 14, G
87/8 PaniniSticker 194, 252, 263
87/8 PaniniSticker 195-96
88/9 PaniniSticker 61
89/90 PaniniSticker 74
90/1 PaniniSticker 219
91/2 PaniniSticker 124
92/3 PaniniSticker 233
93/4 PaniniSticker I
94/5 PaniniSticker 82
95/6 PaniniSticker 102
96/7 PaniniSticker 101
97/8 PaniniSticker 83
95 PaniniWorlds 279
91/2 Parkhurst 121, 213, 468
91/2 Parkhurst 475, PHC8
92/3 Parkhurst 111, CP4
93/4 Parkhurst 127, D4
94/5 Parkhurst V33, C27
95/6 Parkhurst 136, PP6, PP12
95/6 PH-Crown(2) 7
94/5 ParkieSE 113
80/1 Pepsi Cap
91/2 Pinnacle 50, 390
92/3 Pinnacle 1
93/4 Pinnacle 125, 238, CA15
94/5 Pinnacle 300, GR9, TP9
95/6 Pinnacle 5,-FirstStrike 1
95/6 Pinnacle-FullContact 12
96/7 Pinnacle 2,-Num 12,-TmP 4
97/8 Pinnacle 27, 194, -TeamP 5
96/7 PinnBAP 111, -Biscuit 19
96/7 PinnBAP-Messier 1, 2
97/8 P.BAP -TakeANumber 17
97/8 P.BeeHive 30, -TeamBH 2
97/8 PinnCertified 43, -Team 12
97/8 Pinnacle-EPIX 12
95/6 PinnacleFANtasy 18
96/7 PinnacleFANtasy 6
97/8 PinnacleInside 50
97/8 P.Inside-Track 18, -Can 22
96/7 PinnacleMint 16
97/8 PinnacleMint 13
95/6 Pinn.Zenith 18, -ZTeam 5
96/7 P.Zenith 94, -Champion 1
95/6 Playoff 175, 284
96/7 Playoff 424
94/5 POG 166
95/6 POG 6, 24, 180
81/2 Post PopUp 15
82/3 Post
97/8 Post, F3
93/4 PowerPlay 162, -Point 9
93/4 Premier 430
94/5 Premier 1, 278, -GoTo 15
95/6 ProMagnet 98, -Pro 4
90/1 ProSet 91, 349, 381, 386
90/1 ProSet 397, 704
91/2 ProSet 74, 282, 439, 579
92/3 ProSet 111, CC1
91/2 PSPlatinum 81, PC20
91/2 PS'ThePuck 19
87/8 ProSportWatch CW13
83/4 PuffySticker 4
90/1 Score 100,315,360, -Hot 33
91/2 Score(CDN) 263, 310
91/2 Score(CDN) 505, 635
91/2 Score(U.S) 285, 373
91/2 Score(U.S) 420, 85T
92/3 Score 300, 431, 493, 521
93/4 Score 200, (U.S) DD5
94/5 Score DT16, TF15
95/6 Score 50,-DrmT 4,-GldB 15
96/7 Score 24,-DrmT 5,-Sddn 10
97/8 Score 85
97/8 Score(VAN) 3
92/3 SeasonsPatch 26
94/5 Select 1
95/6 SelectCert. 14, -Double 15
96/7 SelectCert 36, -Corner 5
94 Semic 94, 350
95 Semic 97
89 SemicSticker 69
91 SemicSticker 63
92 SemicSticker 85
93 SemicSticker 202
95/6 SkBxEmotion 116,-Ntense3
95/6 SkyBoxImpact 111,-Count 5
95/6 SkyBoxImpact-IceQuake 5
96/7 SkBxImpact 82, -Blade 14
83/4 7ElevenCokeCups
84/5 7ElevenDisk
83/4 SouhaitsRen.KeyChain
94/5 SP 73, -Premier 28
95/6 SP 92, E19, FX14
96/7 SP 98, CW11, GF10
97/8 SPAuthentic 157, I16
96/7 SPx 27, HH5
97/8 SPx 32, SPX3
98/9 SPx"Finite" 160
83/4 StaterMint H20
95/6 Summit 1, -GM16
96/7 Summit 111, 198,-Voltage 1
95/6 SuperSticker 78, 80
91 TeamCanada
96/7 TeamOut
92/3 Topps 258, 274
95/6 Topps 5, 240, HGC29
95/6 Topps M3, 3PL, 1RL
98/9 Topps 138, L11, M19
98/9 Topps-RookieReprint 2
94/5 ToppsFinest 16, -Ring 1
94/5 T.Finest-BBest(Blue) 2
95/6 ToppsFinest 50, 99
96 ToppsFinestBronze 15
96/7 T.Picks 25, FC6, TS5
91/2 ToppsStadiumClub 111
92/3 T.StadiumClub 241, 443
93/4 ToppsStadiumClub 35
94/5 TSC 1, -Dynasty 2, -Fin. 3
95/6 TSC EC178, M9, N8
93/4 TSC-MembersOnly 27
94/5 TSC-MembersOnly 19
95/6 TSC-MembersOnly 40
97/8 ToppsSticker 1
95/6 ToppsSuperSkills 60
90/1 UpperDeck 44, 206, 321
90/1 UD 494, Hol (x3)
91/2 UD 14, 246, 545, 610, 620
92/3 UD 242, 432, 437, 453
92/3 UD -Heroes 13,-LockerAS 7
93/4 UD 51, 298, GC5, SP-103
94/5 UD 62, 234, 563, C22
94/5 UD H4, R34, R54, SP51
95/6 UD 169, 217, AS16, SE141
95/6 UD F7, H9, R39, R56
95/6 UD-AllStarPredict MVP19
96/7 UD 108, 135, 299, GJ11
96/7 UD HH2, LS2, SS9A
96/7 UD-AllStarYCTG AR14
97/8 UD 374, S5, SG11
97/8 UD SS11, T11B, -BlowUp 6
96/7 UDBlackDiamnd 100, RC11
97/8 UDBlackDiamond 7, PC23
98/9 UDChoice 211, BH9, SQ29
95/6 UDCollChoice 220, C6
96/7 UDCollChoice 166, 296
96/7 UDCollC 335, C30, S10
97/8 UDCollChoice 168, SQ49
96/7 UpperDeck"Ice" 111, S1
97/8 UpperDeckIce 71, IC11,L3B
83/4 Vachon 36
96 Wien 86
97/8 Zenith 16, Z64
79/80 EDM
80/1 EDM/Zellers
81/2 EDM/RedRooster
82/3 EDM/RedRooster
83/4 EDM
83/4 EDM/Buttons
83/4 EDM/McDonald
84/5 EDM
84/5 EDM/RedRooster
85/6 EDM/RedRooster
86/7 EDM
86/7 EDM/RedRooster
87/8 EDM
88/9 EDM
88/9 EDM/ActionMag. 89,105
90/1 EDM/McGavins (x2)
92/3 NYR

MESSIER, MITCH
92/3 ClassicProspects 76
88/9 ProCards(Kalamazoo)
89/90 ProCards(IHL) 98
90/1 ProCards 102
91/2 ProCards 151

MESSURI, JOHN
91/2 ProCards 439
89/90 Johnstown 21

MESZAROS, DAVE
84/5 Moncton 21
85/6 Moncton 5

MESZOLY, ANDRAS
79 PaniniSticker 270

METCALFE, JASON
95/6 Slapshot 244

METCALFE, SCOTT
88/9 ProCards(Rochester)
89/90 ProCards(AHL) 262
90/1 ProCards 267
88/9 EDM/ActionMagazine 127
83/4 Kingston 10
84/5 Kingston 6
85/6 Kingston 6
86/7 Kingston 10
95/6 Rochester

METHOT, FRANÇOIS
95/6 Bowman P25
97/8 Bowman 57
98 BowmanCHL 95
95/6 UpperDeck 521

MELICKA, PAVEL
95/6 APS 259

METLYUK, DENIS
92/3 Classic 45
94/5 Classic 91, T50
92/3 ClassicFourSport 186
94/5 ClassicFourSport 157
93/4 ClassicProspects 215
91/2 UD 653,-CzechWJC 14

METRO, R.
93/4 Waterloo

METRO, TERRY
91/2 AirCanadaSJHL C22

METROPOLIT, GLEN
96/7 Penascola 7

METTAVAINIO, JAN-OVE
89/90 SemicElitserien 149
90/1 SemicElitserien 232

METTOVAARA, SAMI
93/4 Jyvas-Hyva 177
93/4 Sisu 176
94/5 Sisu 44
95/6 Sisu 337

METZ, DON
34-43 BeeHives(TOR)
45-64 BeeHives(TOR)
39/40 OPC (V301-1) 8
40/1 OPC (V301-2) 111
45-54 QuakerOats

METZ, NICK
34-43 BeeHives(TOR)
45-64 BeeHives(TOR)
35/6 OPC (V304C) 84
37/8 OPC (V304E) 144
39/40 OPC (V301-1) 51
40/1 OPC (V301-2) 133, 141
38/9 QuakerOats
45-54 QuakerOats
35/6 Triumph
36/7 WWGum (V356) 28

MEULENBROEKS, JOHN
83/4 Brantford 28
85/6 Moncton 21

MEUNIER, YVES
90/1 SketchQMJHL 204
91/2 SketchQMJHL 22, 59

MEURER, PETER
24/5 Crescent Selkirks 13

MEWS, HARRY
91/2 ProCards 565
92/3 Hampton

MEYER, ANDREAS
79 PaniniSticker 259

MEYER, D.
95/6 DEL 72, 432

MEYER, FRITZ
94/5 DEL 14
95/6 DEL 5

MEYER, JASON
95 PaniniWorlds 56
94 Semic 276
81/2 Regina 11
82/3 Regina 21

MEYER, JAYSON
95/6 DEL 202
96/7 DEL 343

95 Semic 167
96 Wien 195
83/4 Regina 21

MEYERS, DAN
91/2 AirCanadaSJHL A2

MICALEF, CORRADO
83/4 O-Pee-Chee 116, 126
85/6 O-Pee-Chee 200
83/4 opcSticker 147
83/4 SouhaitsRen.KeyChain
84/5 DET/Caesars

MICHALCHUK, CHAD
91/2 SketchQMJHL 229
91/2 SketchWHL 114
91/2 Saskatoon 15

MICHAUD, MARK
94/5 Birmingham
87/8 Brockville 7
93/4 Hampton

MICHAYLUK, DAVE
92/3 ClassicProspects 123
88/9 ProCards(Muskegon)
89/90 ProCards(IHL) 153
90/1 ProCards 389
91/2 ProCards 288
92/3 ClevelandLumberjacks 13
93/4 ClevelandLumberjacks
95/6 ClevelandLumberjacks
81/2 Regina 20
83/4 Springfield 11

MICHEL, STEFFEN
94/5 DEL 278
95/6 DEL 269

MICHELETTI, JOE
82/3 Post
81/2 COL.R

MICHELIN, LEO
52/3 AnonymousOHL 36

MICHELLER, KLAUS
94/5 DEL 239
95/6 DEL 223
96/7 DEL 74

MICHON, MICHEL
90/1 SketchWHL 332

MICIAK, DARREN
91/2 ProCards 435

MICK, TROY
91/2 Knoxville
86/7 Portland
87/8 Portland
88/9 Portland
89/90 Regina

MICKEY, LARRY
70/1 DadsCookies
70/1 EddieSargent 74
71/2 EddieSargent 149
70/1 Esso Stamp
74/5 Loblaws
68/9 O-Pee-Chee 195
70/1 O-Pee-Chee 162
71/2 OPC/Topps 167
71/2 TheTorontoSun
72/3 BUF
73/4 BUF
74/5 BUF
69/70 TOR

MICKOLAJAK, T.
93/4 Minn-Duluth

MICKOSKI, NICK
45-64 BeeHives(NYR)
51/2 Parkhurst 97
52/3 Parkhurst 101
53/4 Parkhurst 62
54/5 Parkhurst 75
93/4 Parkie(56/7) 25
54/5 Topps 29
57/8 Topps 32
58/9 Topps 27
59/60 Topps 37, 53

MICNEAULT, JOHN
73/4 VancouverBlazers

MICULNIC, JEREMY
95/6 Classic 82
94/5 Slapshot(Sarnia) 7
95/6 Slapshot 28

MIDDENDORF, MAX
88/9 ProCards(Halifax)
89/90 ProCards(AHL) 172
91/2 ProCards 217
87/8 QUE/GeneralFoods
89/90 Halifax
84/5 Sudbury 12
85/6 Sudbury 22
89/90 Sudbury 22

MIDDLEBROOK, LINDSAY
88/9 EDM/ActionMagazine 102

MIDDLETON, MARCUS
90/1 SketchOHL 40
89/90 Sudbury 12

MIDDLETON, MARK
83/4 SouhaitsRen.KeyChain

MIDDLETON, RICK
84/5 Kelloggs Disk
74/5 Loblaws Update
82/3 McDonalds 9
74/5 OPC 304
75/6 OPC/Topps 37
76/7 OPC/Topps 127
77/8 OPC/Topps 246
78/9 OPC/Topps 113
79/80 OPC/Topps 10, T. 81
80/1 OPC/Topps 94, 251
81/2 O-Pee-Chee 2, 18, 19
81/2 Topps 22, 46, (East) 129
82/3 O-Pee-Chee 6, 15
83/4 O-Pee-Chee 43, 54, 214
84/5 OPC 9, 352, Topps 8
85/6 OPC/Topps 64, 159
86/7 OPC/Topps 157
87/8 OPC/Topps 115
88/9 OPC/Topps 87
89/90 O-Pee-Chee 304
81/2 opcSticker 45
82/3 opcSticker 78, 79, 262
83/4 opcSticker 14, 44, 45
83/4 opcSticker 183, 329, 330
84/5 opcSticker 142, 181, 182
85/6 opcSticker 159/29
86/7 opcSticker 35/172
87/8 opcSticker 98/232, 138/248
88/9 opcSticker 229, 26/155
87/8 PaniniSticker 12
82/3 Post
83/4 PuffySticker 10
84/5 7ElevenDisk
85/6 7Eleven 1
83/4 BOS
84/5 BOS
88/9 BOS/SportsAction
91/2 BOS/Legends

MIDGLEY, JIM
95/6 Slapshot 213

MIEHM, KEVIN
92/3 ClassicProspects 63
95/6 EdgeIce 128
93/4 FleerUltra 205,-Prospects 6
93/4 Parkhurst 447
93/4 Premier(Gold) 264
89/90 ProCards(IHL) 11
90/1 ProCards 93
91/2 ProCards 28
92/3 UpperDeck 543
92/3 Peoria

MIELCZAREK, TED
87/8 Sudbury 2
88/9 Sudbury 3
89/90 Sudbury 1

MIELO, B.
91/2 SketchOHL 118

MIETTINEN, TOM
93/4 Jyvas-Hyva 173
93/4 Parkhurst 522
94/5 ParkieSE 221
95 Semic 236
94/5 Sisu 86, -NHLDraft 7
95/6 Sisu 330
96/7 Sisu 144
94/5 ToppsFinest 133

MIGAY, RUDY
45-64 BeeHives(TOR)
52/3 Parkhurst 96
53/4 Parkhurst 17
54/5 Parkhurst 21
55/6 Parkhurst 12
57/8 Parkhurst(TOR) 6
93/4 Parkie(56/7) 111
45-54 QuakerOats
60/1 ShirriffCoin 18

MIGNACCA, SONNY
90/1 SketchWHL 23
91/2 SketchWHL 314

MIGNEAULT, JOHN
75/6 Phoenix

MIKKULAINEN, JARMO
92/3 Jyvas-Hyva 201
93/4 Jyvas-Hyva 351
93/4 Sisu 213
94/5 Sisu 80
95/6 Sisu 152, 300

MIKAELSSON, PAR
89/90 SemicElitserien 214

MIKESCH, S.
93/4 Waterloo

MIKHAILOV, BORIS
95 Globe 243
72 Hellas 72
74 Hellas 51
70/1 Kuvajulkaisut 8
72 Panda
79 PaniniSticker 150
72 SemicSticker 13
74 SemicSticker 33
73/4 Soviet Champs 3, 14, 15
78 SovietChamps
69/70 Soviet Stars
70/1 Soviet Stars
80 SovietMiniPics
71/2 Soviet Stars
73/4 Soviet Stars 6, 9, 24
74/5 Soviet Stars 11, 24
77-9 Sportscaster 102-14,26-673
91/2 Trends(72) 43
71/2 WilliamsFIN 10
72/3 WilliamsFIN 29
73/4 WilliamsFIN 11

MIKHAILOVSKY, MAXIM
90/1 O-Pee-Chee 9R
91/2 OPC 22R, 29R, 30R

MIKITA, STAN
71/2 Bazooka Panel 35
45-64 BeeHives(CHI)
64-67 BeeHives(CHI)
62 CeramicTiles
63-5 ChexPhoto
64/5 CokeCap CHI-21
65/6 CocaCola
70/1 DadsCookies
70/1 EddieSargent 48
71/2 EddieSargent 33
72/3 EddieSargent 63
70/1 Esso Stamp
88/9 Esso Sticker
83&87 HallOfFame 226
83 HHOF Postcard (O)
92/3 HHOFLegends 15
93/4 HockeyWit 39
71 Kelloggs
72/3 Letraset 10
74/5 Loblaws
68/9 OPC 155, 202, 211, T. 20
68/9 O-Pee-Chee-Puck 1
69/70 OPC/Topps 76
69/70 OPC-Sticker, -Stamp
70/1 OPC/Topps 20
70/1 OPC 240, -Sticker
71/2 OPC/Topps 125
72/3 OPC 177, Topps 56n
72/3 OPC-Crests 5, -TmCanada
73/4 OPC 6, Topps 145
74/5 OPC/Topps 20, 69
75/6 OPC/Topps 30, 317
76/7 OPC/Topps 225
77/8 OPC/Topps 195
78/9 OPC/Topps 75
79/80 OPC/Topps 155
93/4 Parkie(56/7) FS3
94/5 Parkie(64/5) 26, 138, 147
94/5 Parkie(64/5) 170, SL2, TW3
95/6Parkie(66/7)24,125,AS5,SL2
95/6 Parkie(66/7)TW1,TW2,TW3
97/8 PinnacleBeeHive 59
66/7 Post'Large
67/8 Post
90/1 ProSet 405, 655
72 SemicSticker 227
60/1 ShirriffCoin 71
61/2 ShirriffCoin 22
62/3 ShirriffCoin 46
68/9 ShirriffCoin CHI 9
93 SourPuckCaps 4
77-9 Sportscastr 12-22, 51-1224
81/2 TCMA 13
98/9 Topps-RookieReprint 8
54-67 TorontoStar 65/6, V9
56-66 TorontoStar 63/4, 64/5
63/4 TheTorontoStar
64/5 TheTorontoStar
71/2 TheTorontoSun
60/1 Topps 14
61/2 Topps 36, -Stamp
62/3 Topps 34, -Buck
63/4 Topps 36
64/5 Topps 31, 106
65/6 Topps 60
66/7 Topps 62, 124,-USATest 62
67/8 Topps 64, 114, 126
91/2 Trends(72) 61, -Aut
92/3 UD'LockerAS 46
92/3 Zellers
68/9 CHI
70/1 CHI
79/80 CHI

MIKKELSON, BILL
74/5 Loblaws
72/3 OPC 79, Topps 118
74/5 OPC/Topps 23
75/6 OPC/Topps 207
74/5 WSH

MIKKOLA, ARI
78/9 SM-Liiga 81
72/3 WilliamsFIN 177

MIKKOLA, HEIKKI
66/7 Champion 104

MIKKOLA, NIKO
95 Semic 240
93/4 Sisu 50
94/5 Sisu 88

MIKKOLAINEN, REIJO
92/3 Jyvas-Hyva 180
89 SemicSticker 38
93/4 Sisu 53
95/6 Sisu 37, 187

MIKLENDA, JAROSLAV
93/4 Parkhurst 519
93/4 UpperDeck 573

MIKOL, JIM
45-64 BeeHives(TOR)
64/5 CokeCap NYR-12
94/5 Parkie(64/5) 99
64/5 Topps 36
60/1 ClevelandBarons

MIKOLASEK, TOMAS
94/5 APS 66
95/6 APS 92

MIKULCHIK, OLEG
95/6 UpperDeck 471

MILANI, TOM
82 SemicSticker 138
77/8 Kalamazoo 9

MILBURY, MIKE
77/8 OPC/Topps 134
78/9 OPC/Topps 59
79/80 OPC/Topps 114
80/1 OPC/Topps 191
81/2 O-Pee-Chee 16
83/4 O-Pee-Chee 55
84/5 O-Pee-Chee 10
87/8 PaniniSticker 8
82/3 Post
90/1 ProSet 661
83/4 SouhaitsRen.KeyChain
83/4 BOS
84/5 BOS

MILFORD, JAKE
87 HallOfFame 253

MILKS, HIBBERT (HIB)
25-27 Anonymous 48, 52

MILL, JIM
93/4 Huntington
93/4 Roanoke

MILLAR, COLIN
88/9 NiagaraFalls 13

MILLAR, CRAIG
98/9 Pacific 215
97/8 PinnacleBeAPlayer 239
97/8 SPAuthentic 182
95/6 SwiftCurrent

MILLAR, MIKE
94/5 DEL 159
95/6 DEL 159
96/7 DEL 235
88/9 ProCards(Baltimore)
89/90 ProCards(AHL) 67
90/1 ProCards 168
89/90 BOS/SportsAction
83/4 Brantford 20
90/1 Newmarket

MILLAR, P.
88/9 EDM/ActionMagazine 80

MILLEN, COREY
91/2 Bowman 60
92/3 Bowman 57
93/4 Donruss 181
94/5 Donruss 148
92/3 FleerUltra 86
93/4 FleerUltra 361
94/5 FleerUltra 120
93/4 Leaf 361
94/5 Leaf 187
91/2 OPC/Topps 461
92/3 O-Pee-Chee 334
97/8 PacificCrown 107
92/3 PaniniSticker 70
93/4 PaniniSticker 207
91/2 Parkhurst 292
92/3 Parkhurst 306
93/4 Parkhurst 381
94/5 Parkhurst 122
95/6 Parkhurst 304
92/3 Pinnacle 138
93/4 Pinnacle 350
94/5 Pinnacle 425
94/5 POG 147
95/6 POG 84
93/4 PowerPlay 379
93/4 Premier 493
89/90 ProCards(IHL) 44
91/2 PSPlatinum 185
91/2 Score(CDN) 348, (U.S) 318
92/3 Score 111,-Sharpshooter26
93/4 Score 62, 519
94/5 Score 99
95/6 Score 172
92/3 Topps 326
91/2 ToppsStadiumClub 71
92/3 ToppsStadiumClub 296
93/4 ToppsStadiumClub 437
91/2 UpperDeck 110, 604
92/3 UpperDeck 48
93/4 UpperDeck 483, SP-84
94/5 UpperDeck 25
95/6 UpperDeck 105
96/7 UpperDeck 231
95/6 UDCollChoice 274
94/5 DAL/Southwest
89/90 NYR/MarineMidland

MILLEN, GREG
90/1 Bowman 3
79/80 O-Pee-Chee 281
80/1 OPC/Topps 158
81/2 OPC 134, Topps(E) 115
82/3 O-Pee-Chee 126
83/4 O-Pee-Chee 143
84/5 OPC 75, Topps 58
85/6 O-Pee-Chee 221
88/9 OPC/Topps 117
89/90 OPC/Topps 137
90/1 OPC/Topps 335
82/3 opcSticker 130
83/4 opcSticker 262
84/5 opcSticker 198
85/6 opcSticker 51/182
88/9 PaniniSticker 100
89/90 PaniniSticker 129
90/1 PaniniSticker 188
97/8 Pinnacle -CBC Sports 9
82/3 Post
90/1 ProSet 56
83/4 PuffySticker 16
90/1 Score 42
83/4 SouhaitsRen.KeyChain
90/1 UpperDeck 213
90/1 CHI/Coke
82/3 HFD/JuniorWhalers
83/4 HFD/JuniorWhalers
84/5 HFD/JuniorWhalers
89/90 QUE
87/8 STL
87/8 STL/Kodak
88/9 STL
88/9 STL/Kodak

MILLEN, JOE
91/2 PGH/Foodland 6

MILLER, AARON
93/4 ClassicProspects 105
95/6 EdgeIce 29
97/8 PacificCrown 317
97/8 PinnacleBeAPlayer 75
97/8 UpperDeck 258

MILLER, AL
51/2 LavalDairy 57
52/3 LavalDairy 7

MILLER, AREN
97/8 PinnacleBeeHive 70
95/6 Spokane 30

MILLER, BOB
79/80 OPC/Topps 196
80/1 OPC/Topps 236
82/3 Post
81/2 COL.R
84/5 L.A./Smokeys

MILLER, BRAD
91/2 Parkhurst 243
93/4 Parkhurst 306
89/90 ProCards(AHL) 264
90/1 ProCards 272
90/1 ProSet 591
91/2 ProSet 354
92/3 ToppsStadiumClub 475
88/9 BUF/WonderBread
90/1 BUF/Campbell
91/2 BUF/BlueShield
91/2 BUF/Campbell
92/3 BUF/BlueShield
86/7 Regina
87/8 Regina
88/9 Regina
91/2 Rochester/Kodak
92/3 StJohns

MILLER, COLIN
90/1 SketchMEM 23
90/1 SketchOHL 169
91/2 SketchOHL 321
92/3 AtlantaKnights
93/4 AtlantaKnights
95/6 Dayton
89/90 SSMarie 11

MILLER, DENNIS
91/2 ProCards 434

MILLER, EARL
27-32 LaPresse 30/1

MILLER, GARY
89/90 SketchOHL 160
90/1 SketchOHL 312
91/2 SketchOHL 89

MILLER, GUS
92/3 BCJHL 228

MILLER, JASON
92/3 ClassicProspects 13
91/2 OPC/Topps 163
91/2 ProCards 420
91/2 Score(CDN) 342, (U.S) 312
95/6 Sisu 222, 377
90/1 SketchWHL 28
90/1 UpperDeck 335

MILLER, JAY
91/2 Bowman 178
91/2 OPC/Topps 467
87/8 PaniniSticker 18
88/9 PaniniSticker 212
91/2 ProSet 402
91/2 Score(CDN) 543
91/2 ToppsStadiumClub 63
90/1 UpperDeck 414
88/9 BOS/SportsAction
89/90 L.A./Smokeys 15
90/1 L.A./Smokeys 16
85/6 Moncton 23

MILLER, KEITH
88/9 ProCards(Halifax)
89/90 ProCards(IHL) 137

MILLER, KELLY
90/1 Bowman 76
91/2 Bowman 292
92/3 Bowman 338
93/4 Donruss 365
94/5 Donruss 52
95/6 Donruss 159
92/3 FleerUltra 236
93/4 FleerUltra 88
94/5 FleerUltra 390
93/4 Leaf 254
94/5 Leaf 519
87/8 OPC/Topps 189
88/9 OPC/Topps 130
89/90 OPC/Topps 131
90/1 OPC/Topps 81
91/2 OPC/Topps 342
92/3 O-Pee-Chee 142
90/1 opcPremier 72
89/90 opcSticker 74/213
98/9 Pacific 444
97/8 PacificRegime 211
87/8 PaniniSticker 186
88/9 PaniniSticker 373
89/90 PaniniSticker 348
90/1 PaniniSticker 156
91/2 PaniniSticker 202
92/3 PaniniSticker 166
93/4 PaniniSticker 30
91/2 Parkhurst 414
93/4 Parkhurst 491
94/5 Parkhurst 256, V72
95/6 Parkhurst 219
91/2 Pinnacle 23, 372
92/3 Pinnacle 160
93/4 Pinnacle 284
94/5 Pinnacle 158
96/7 PinnacleBeAPlayer 46
95/6 Playoff 324
94/5 POG 247
95/6 POG 280
93/4 PowerPlay 468
93/4 Premier 474
94/5 Premier 222
90/1 ProSet 318
91/2 ProSet 256, 611, 615
90/1 Score 168
91/2 Score(CDN) 81, 339
91/2 Score(U.S) 81, 309
92/3 Score 55, -USAGreats 14
93/4 Score 30
94/5 Score 63
95/6 Score 271
92/3 Topps 479
95/6 Topps 126
91/2 ToppsStadiumClub 106
92/3 ToppsStadiumClub 361
93/4 ToppsStadiumClub 17
90/1 UpperDeck 130
91/2 UpperDeck 133
92/3 UpperDeck 35, 179
93/4 UpperDeck 384
94/5 UpperDeck 151
95/6 UpperDeck 346
95/6 UDCollChoice 82
86/7 WSH/Kodak
87/8 WSH
87/8 WSH/Kodak
88/9 WSH
88/9 WSH/Smokey
89/90 WSH
89/90 WSH/Kodak
90/1 WSH/Kodak
90/1 WSH/Smokey
91/2 WSH
91/2 WSH/Kodak
92/3 WSH/Kodak
95/6 WSH

MILLER, KEVIN
91/2 Bowman 57
92/3 Bowman 391
93/4 Donruss 298
94/5 Donruss 11
92/3 FleerUltra 396
93/4 FleerUltra 218
94/5 FleerUltra 186
95 Globe 119
93/4 Leaf 192

94/5 Leaf 129
91/2 OPC/Topps 125
92/3 O-Pee-Chee 291
90/1 opcPremier 73
97/8 PacificCrown 46
92/3 PaniniSticker 115
94/5 PaniniSticker 139
96/7 PaniniSticker 66
91/2 Parkhurst 40
93/4 Parkhurst 178
94/5 ParkieSE 150
91/2 Pinnacle 133
92/3 Pinnacle 313
93/4 Pinnacle 126
94/5 Pinnacle 289
95/6 Pinnacle 146
96/7 Pinnacle 15
96/7 PinnacleBeAPlayer 165
94/5 POG 205
95/6 POG 224
93/4 PowerPlay 215
93/4 Premier 8
94/5 Premier 21
89/90 ProCards(IHL) 29
90/1 ProSet 493
91/2 ProSet 60
91/2 PSPlatinum 168
90/1 ScoreTraded 18T
91/2 Score(CDN) 126, 339
91/2 Score(U.S) 126, 309
91/2 Score-YoungStar 40
92/3 Score 229
93/4 Score 89
94/5 Score 25
94 Semic 116
92 SemicSticker 166
92/3 Topps 129
91/2 ToppsStadiumClub 286
92/3 ToppsStadiumClub 229
93/4 ToppsStadiumClub 193
90/1 UpperDeck 444
91/2 UpperDeck 142
92/3 UpperDeck 35, 482
93/4 UpperDeck 408
94/5 UpperDeck 451
96/7 UpperDeck 236
95/6 UDCollChoice 275
97/8 UDCollChoice 50

MILLER, KIP
91/2 Bowman 139
95/6 EdgeIce 138
91/2 opcPremier 42
91/2 OPC/Topps 387
91/2 Parkhurst 142
91/2 Pinnacle 306
90/1 ProCards 452
91/2 ProSet 555
90/1 Score(U.S) 330
91/2 Score(CDN) 274, (U.S) 384
90/1 UpperDeck 522
91/2 UpperDeck 431
92/3 UpperDeck 35, 247
93/4 UpperDeck 421
91/2 QUE/PetroCanada
90/1 Halifax

MILLER, KRIS
91/2 ProCards 394

MILLER, KURT
95/6 Adirondack
91/2 LakeSuperior

MILLER, LUC
94/5 Slapshot(Kitchener) 23

MILLER, PAUL
83/4 Moncton 15

MILLER, PERRY
78/9 OPC/Topps 16
79/80 OPC/Topps 157
81/2 O-Pee-Chee 101
75/6 opcWHA 6
80/1 DET

MILLER, ROD
93/4 Minn-Duluth

MILLER, SCOTT
92/3 Windsor 23

MILLER, SHANNON
97/8 GameOfHerLife

MILLER, TODD
95/6 Slapshot 343

MILLER, TOM
72/3 EddieSargent 137
72/3 OPC 32, Topps 76
73/4 OPC 249

MILLER, WARREN
81/2 OPC 130, Topps(E) 84
82/3 O-Pee-Chee 127
82/3 Post
82/3 HFD/JuniorWhalers

MILLER, ZDENEK
95/6 APS 76

MILLETTE, ANDRÉ
88/9 Richelieu

MILLEY, NORMAN
98 BowmanCHL 38, 129, A16
97/8 UpperDeck 414
96/7 Sudbury 17

MILLHAM, MIKE
92/3 Wheeling 10

MILLIE, LES
95/6 SheffieldSteelers

MILLIER, PIERRE
84/5 Chicoutimi

MILLIKEN, ROB
92/3 BCJHL 232

MILLS, CRAIG
95/6 Bowman 99
95/6 Donruss 292
95/6 DonrussElite-WorldJrs 19
95/6 Parkhurst 497
95/6 Slapshot 52
97/8 SPAuthentic 176
95/6 UpperDeck 527
97/8 UpperDeck 251

MILLS, MARK
96/7 Cincinnati

MILTON, KJELL-RUNE
70/1 Kuvajulkaisut 32
69/70 MästarSerien 43
72 SemicSticker 62
74 SemicSticker 16
71/2 WilliamsFIN 52

MINARD, MIKE
95/6 Slapshot 56

MINER, JOHN
88/9 EDM/ActionMagazine 30
85/6 NovaScotia 14
82/3 Regina 5
83/4 Regina 5

MINETTI, TINO
71/2 WilliamsFIN 349

MINGE, LESZEK
89 SemicSticker 147

MINKHURST, BILL
95/6 Slapshot 126

MINKKILA, TIMO
71/2 WilliamsFIN 331

MINNIS, MIKE
92/3 BCJHL 83

MINOR, DOUG
90/1 SketchOHL 188
89/90 SSMarie 9

MINOR, GERRY
81/2 O-Pee-Chee 342
82/3 O-Pee-Chee 352
80/1 Pepsi Cap
80/1 VAN
80/1 VAN/Silverwood
81/2 VAN
81/2 VAN/Silverwood
82/3 VAN

MIO, ED
80/1 O-Pee-Chee 341
81/2 O-Pee-Chee 119
82/3 O-Pee-Chee 230
83/4 O-Pee-Chee 127
84/5 OPC 61, Topps 45
81/2 opcSticker 216
82/3 opcSticker 142
83/4 opcSticker 209
80/1 Pepsi Cap
91/2 UpperDeck 639
84/5 DET/Caesars
80/1 EDM/Zellers
88/9 EDM/ActionMagazine 51

MIRABELLO, JIM
93/4 Huntington
94/5 Huntington 26
95/6 Tallahassee 20

MIRABILE, STEVE
92/3 Hampton

MIRAC, SILVERO
91/2 AvantGardeBCJHL 39
92/3 BCJHL 46

MIREAU, BRENT
84/5 Brandon 2
85/6 Brandon 2

MIRONOV, BORIS
92/3 Classic 44
92/3 ClassicFourSport 185, -Aut.
93/4 Donruss 384, 429, -Rated 9
94/5 Donruss 218
96/7 Flair 34
93/4 FleerUltra 454, -Wave 8
94/5 FleerUltra 73, -AllRookie 5
95/6 FleerUltra 239
93/4 Leaf 364
94/5 Leaf 179, -GoldLeafRook 8
97/8 Omega 94
98/9 Pacific 216
98/9 PacificParamount 90
97/8 PacificRegime 81
96/7 PaniniSticker 265
97/8 PaniniSticker 216
93/4 Parkhurst 264
95/6 Parkhurst 75
94/5 ParkieSE 57
94/5 Pinnacle 188
96/7 PinnacleBeAPlayer 88
95/6 Playoff 150
94/5 POG 102
93/4 PowerPlay 474, -Rookie 6
93/4 Premier 394
94/5 Premier 288, -Fin(OPC) 17
92/3 RedAce(Blue) 15,(Violet) 15
93/4 Score 607
94/5 Score 255
93/4 ToppsStadiumClub 338
94/5 ToppsStadiumClub 85
91/2 TriGlobe 21-22
91/2 UD 662,-CzechWJC 23
93/4 UpperDeck 492, SP-176
94/5 UpperDeck 172
97/8 UpperDeck 276
98/9 UDChoice 83
96/7 EDM
97/8 EDM
93/4 WPG/Ruffles

MIRONOV, DMITRI
94/5 Donruss 58
97/8 Donruss 130
94/5 Flair 183
94/5 Fleer 217
92/3 FleerUltra 422, -Imports 15
93/4 FleerUltra 127
94/5 FleerUltra 218
95/6 FleerUltra 290
94/5 Leaf 254
95/6 Leaf 96
97/8 Omega 4
90/1 O-Pee-Chee 514
91/2 OPC/Topps 515, OPC 23R
92/3 OPC 71
98/9 Pacific 202
97/8 PacificCrown 234
97/8 PacificParamount 4
97/8 PacificRevolution 3
95/6 PaniniSticker 67
96/7 PaniniSticker 65
97/9 PaniniSticker 182
91/2 Parkhurst 391
92/3 Parkhurst 417
93/4 Parkhurst 477
94/5 Parkhurst 232
95/6 Parkhurst 437
92/3 Pinnacle 247, 419
94/5 Pinnacle 229
97/8 Pinnacle 125
97/8 PinnacleBeAPlayer 170
95/6 Playoff 189
94/5 POG 241
95/6 POG 219
93/4 PowerPlay 245
93/4 Premier 419
94/5 Premier 165

92/3 RedAce(Blue) 22,(Violet) 22
92/3 Score 468
93/4 Score 209
95/6 Score 180
97/8 Score 240
97/8 Score(ANA) 4
91 SemicSticker 84
92 SemicSticker 107
95/6 SkyBoxEmotion 139
94/5 SP 120
98/9 SPx"Finite" 31
91/2 StarPics 58
92/3 Topps 144
96/7 ToppsNHLPicks 167
92/3 ToppsStadiumClub 5
90/1 UpperDeck 514
92/3 UpperDeck 83
93/4 UpperDeck 513
94/5 UpperDeck 222, SP79
95/6 UpperDeck 322
96/7 UpperDeck 138
97/8 UpperDeck 213
94/5 UDBeAPlayer-Aut. 19
95/6 UDCollChoice 125
96/7 UDCollChoice 221
97/8 UDCollChoice 3
96 Wien 133
96/7 ANA/UpFrontSports
95/6 PGH/Foodland 25
92/3 TOR/Kodak
93/4 TOR/Abalene
93/4 TOR/Blacks 8
94/5 TOR

MISAWA, MINORU
79 PaniniSticker 285

MISAWA, SATORU
79 PaniniSticker 290

MISEK, PETR
82 SemicSticker 85

MISHAKOV, EVGENY
72 Hellas 71
70/1 Kuvajulkaisut 9
72 SemicSticker 12
74 SemicSticker 48
70/1 Soviet Stars
71/2 Soviet Stars
91/2 Trends(72) 75
71/2 WilliamsFIN 11
72/3 WilliamsFIN 30

MISHKIN, VLADIMIR
89/90 SovietNats

MISKOLCZI, TED
89/90 SketchOHL 78
90/1 SketchOHL 290
94/5 Slapshot(Brantford) 18

MISZUK, JOHN
68/9 OPC/Topps 93
69/70 OPC/T. 124, OPC-Sticker
76/7 opcWHA 57
68/9 ShirriffCoin PHA2

MITHCELL, DAN
95/6 Spokane 29

MITCHELL, DAVE
92/3 WestMich.
93/4 WestMich.
92/3 Windsor 30

MITCHELL, GREG
85/6 Arizona

MITCHELL, HERB
25-27 Anonymous 38, 39
24/5 (V145-2) 29

MITCHELL, JEFF
95/6 Classic 84
94/5 LeafLimited-USAJrs 8
93/4 Slapshot(Detroit) 14
94/5 Slapshot(Detroit) 15
94/5 Slapshot(MEM) 89
94/5 SP 195
94/5 ToppsFinest 121

MITCHELL, RED
34-43 BeeHives(CHI)
89/90 ProCards(AHL) 192
90/1 ProCards 65
91/2 ProCards 144
86/7 Portland
87/8 Portland
88/9 Portland

MITCHELL, TOM
88/9 ProCards(Binghampton)

MITCHELL, T.
24/5 Crescent Falcons 8

MITEW, T.
95/6 DEL 47

MITROVIC, SAVO
93/4 Greensboro

MITTELFELLNER, V.
95/6 DEL 370

MITTELSTEADT, JOE
89/90 SketchMEM 17
90/1 SketchWHL 295
89/90 Kamloops
87/8 Portland
88/9 Portland

MITTINEN, TOMMI
94/5 Sisu-Junior 3

MITTON, PAUL
89/90 SketchOHL 107
90/1 SketchOHL 110
94/5 Slapshot(Brantford) 12

MIX, HOLGER
94/5 DEL 42
95/6 DEL 39

MIX, TOM
92/3 BCJHL 74

MOBERG, DAN
82/3 Victoria

MODANO, MIKE
95/6 Aces 3 (Diamonds)
96/7 Aces 6 (Diamonds)
97/8 Aces 7 (Spades)
90/1 Bowman 188
91/2 Bowman 125, 415
92/3 Bowman 151
95/6 Bowman 35
93/4 Donruss 76, F
94/5 Donruss 193, -IceMasters 8
95/6 Donruss 62, -ProPointer 8
96/7 Donruss 22, -Dom 9, -Top 7
97/8 Donruss 104, -Line2Line 14
96/7 DonrussCanadianIce 25
97/8 DonrussCanadianIce 13
95/6 DonrussElite 32
96/7 DonrussElite 116
97/8 D.Elite 2,129,-Craftsmen 18
97/8 D.Preferred 8, 176,-Line 5A
97/8 D.Pref -Tins 7, -WideTins 5
97/8 DonrussPriority 11, 192
97/8 D.Prio-DirDep 13,-OpDay11
97/8 D.Prio-Pstcrd 12,-Stamp 12
97/8 D.Studio 13,-Port 13,-Sil 19
93/4 EASports 33
97/8 EssoOlympic 24
94/5 Flair 43,-Centre 9,-Scoring7
96/7 Flair 23
94/5 Fleer 55, -Slapshot 6
96/7 Fleer 27
95/6 FleerMetal 42, -Heavy 10
96/7 FleerNHLPicks-Dream 7
96/7 F.Picks-Fab 30, -Jagged 11
92/3 FleerUltra 96
93/4 FleerUltra 194
94/5 FleerUltra 55,-Pivots 8
94/5 FU-Speed 7,-UltraPower 8
95/6 FleerUltra 41, 394,-Extra 14
96/7 FleerUltra 44
91/2 Gillette 15
95 Globe 111
93/4 HockeyWit 60
95/6 Hoyle'WEST 7 (Diamonds)
97/8 KatchMedallion 46
91/2 Kelloggs 4
95/6 KennerSLU
96/7 KennerSLU (U)
90/1 Kraft 34
91/2 Kraft 48
94/5 Kraft-Sharpshooter
97/8 Kraft -WorldsBest
93/4 Leaf 202
94/5 Leaf 9, -Gold 10, -Limited 6
95/6 Leaf 227
96/7 Leaf 12,-Fire 14,-Leather 15
97/8 Leaf 15, 181,-Banr 9,-Fire 6
94/5 LeafLimited 60
95/6 LeafLimited 51
96/7 LeafLimited 13, -Stubble 8

96/7 L.Preferred 44,150,-Steel28
97/8 Limited 19, 452, 193
97/8 Limited -fabric 67
96/7 Maggers 49
93/4 McDonalds McD10
96/7 MetalUniverse 40
97/8 Omega 73, 246
97/8 Omega -GameF 5,-StickH 7
90/1 OPC/Topps 348, F
91/2 OPC/Topps 367
92/3 O-Pee-Chee 313
90/1 opcPremier 74
98/9 Pacific 181,-Crmr 5,-D.Ice 8
98/9 Pcfc-GoldCr 12, -TeamCL 8
97/8 PacificCrown 4, -Supial 5
97/8 PCC-TeamCL 8
97/8 PcfcCrwnRoyale 41,-Blad 7
97/8 PCR-HatTrick 6,-Lampl 7
97/8 PacificDynagon! 37
97/8 PcfcD-BstKpt 30,-Tandm 42
97/8 PcfcInv. 41,-Att 8,-Feat 11
97/8 PcfcParamount 60,-Photo 8
98/9 PcfcP 68,-Spec 6,-TmCL 8
97/8 PacificRegime 63
97/8 PcfcRevolution 43,-TmCL 8
97/8 PcfcRev -AllStarGame 10
90/1 PaniniSticker 253, 340
91/2 PaniniSticker 116
92/3 PaniniSticker 91
93/4 PaniniSticker X
94/5 PaniniSticker 226, 239b
95/6 PaniniSticker 168
96/7 PaniniSticker 168
97/8 PaniniSticker 139
91/2 Parkhurst 81
92/3 Parkhurst 75
93/4 Parkhurst 49, F6
94/5 Parkhurst 308, V2, C6
95/6 Parkhurst 55
94/5 ParkieSE 47
91/2 Pinnacle 5
92/3 Pinn 155, 260, -Tm2000 2
93/4 Pinnacle 40, -Tm2001 17
94/5 Pinnacle 3, BR5, GR8,WE9
95/6 Pinnacle 108,-Roaring20s 5
97/8 Pinnalce 91
96/7 Pinn.BeAPlayer-Biscuit 8
97/8 P.BAP -OneTimers 10
97/8 P.BeeHive 26,-TeamBH 3
97/8 PinnacleCertified 33
95/6 PinnacleFANtasy 14
97/8 PinnacleInside 15
95/6 P.Zenith 24, -ZTeam 10
96/7 P.Zenith 1, -Assailant 2
95/6 Playoff 31, 142, 250
96/7 Playoff 352
94/5 POG 81
95/6 POG 85
93/4 PowerPlay 63, -Slapshot 8
93/4 Premier 46, -Finest 6
94/5 Premier 230, -GoToGuy 4
94/5 Premier-Finest(Topps) 9
95/6 ProMagnet 124, MAG3
90/1 ProSet 142
91/2 ProSet 105
92/3 ProSet 76, -TL 7
91/2 PSPlatinum 55
90/1 Score 120, 327
90/1 S-HotCard 97, -Young 20
91/2 Score(CDN) 313, 467
91/2 Score(U.S) 247, 423
91/2 Score-YoungStar 35
92/3 Score 139, 427, -Young 40
92/3 Score-USAGreats 5
93/4 Score 142, -P.AS 28
93/4 Score-TheFranchise 5
94/5 Score 188, DT17,TF6,NP16
95/6 Score 120,-Bordr 9,-Gold 6
96/7 Score 72, -Superstition 4
97/8 Score 92, 262
92/3 SeasonsPatch 65
94/5 Select 38, -Jumbo
95/6 SelectCertified 17
96/7 SelectCertified 2
94 Semic 125
95 Semic 116
91 SemicSticker 141
92 SemicSticker 157
93 SemicSticker 182
95/6 SkBxEmotion 49, -Xcited 3
95/6 SkyBoxImpact 48
96/7 SkyBoxImpact 30

94/5 SP 28
95/6 SP 36, E11
96/7 SP 40, HC25
97/8 SPAuthentic 43, I37
96/7 SPx 11
97/8 SPx 13
98/9 SPx"Finite" 109, 169
97/8 SportFX MiniStix
94 Sportflics
95/6 Summit 14
96/7 Summit 23
95/6 SuperSticker 32, 33
96/7 TeamOut
92/3 Topps 441
95/6 Topps 80, HGA3
98/9 Topps 50, L12, M5
94/5 T.Finest 106, -BBest(B) 6
95/6 ToppsFinest 128
96/7 ToppsNHLPicks 51
91/2 ToppsStadiumClub 187
92/3 ToppsStadiumClub 4
93/4 T.StadiumClub 130, -AllStar
95/6 ToppsStadiumClub 168
94/5 TSC-MembersOnly 25
97/8 ToppsSticker 3
95/6 ToppsSuperSkills 46
90/1 UpperDeck 46, 346
91/2 UpperDeck 32, 160
92/3 UD 9, 305,-LockerAS 31
93/4 UD 294, 397, SP-38
94/5 UD 58, IG8, R37, SP21
95/6 UpperDeck 220, 420, SE26
95/6 UD-AllStarPredict MVP14
96/7 UD 43, 363, 19A, GJ9, X21
97/8 UpperDeck 56, S26, SG29
97/8 UpperDeck SS29, T16B
93/4 UDBeAPlayer 31, -Roots 24
94/5 UDBeAPlayer R8, R114
95/6 UDBeAPlayer 153
96/7 UDBlackDiamond 99, RC16
97/8 UDBlackDiamond 80, PC25
98/9 UDChoice 69, BH16, SQ24
95/6 UDCollChoice 238, C16
96/7 UDCC 69, 315, S15, UD17
96/7 UDCC-Oversize 69
97/8 UDCC 65, C2, S8, SQ82
96/7 UpperDeck"Ice" 82
97/8 UpperDeckIce 62, L8B
96 Wien 166
97/8 Zenith 37, Z58,-ChasCup 5
94/5 DAL/Cap
94/5 DAL/Southwest
96/7 DAL/Southwest

MODES, WERNER
72 SemicSticker 99

MODIG, LARS
94/5 ElitSet 101
95/6 ElitSet 76
89/90 SemicElitserien 148
90/1 SemicElitserien 228
91/2 SemicElitserien 156
92/3 SemicElitserien 177
95/6 udElite 114

MODIN, FREDRIK
96/7 DonrussCanadianIce 130
94/5 ElitSet 273,-NHLDr 3, -Rk 1
95/6 ElitSet 19
95 Globe 59
98/9 Pacific 419
97/8 PacificCrown 127
98/9 PaniniSticker 181
96/7 PinnacleBeAPlayer 216
97/8 Score(TOR) 13
96/7 SelectCertified 112
94/5 SigRookies 7
96/7 UpperDeck 345
97/8 UpperDeck 162
97/8 UDCollChoice 249
95/6 udElite 35, 220, NA4
97/8 udSwedish 190
96 Wien 73

MODRY, JAROSLAV
94/5 APS 97
92/3 ClassicProspects 146
93/4 ClassicProspects 24
93/4 Donruss 455
94/5 Donruss 197
93/4 FleerUltra 362, -Wave 9
94/5 Leaf 496
94/5 PaniniSticker D
96/7 PaniniSticker 275

93/4 Parkhurst 386
94/5 Parkhurst 123, 290
95/6 Parkhurst 418
93/4 PowerPlay 380, -Rookie 7
93/4 Premier 307
94/5 Premier 512
93/4 Score 616
93/4 ToppsStadiumClub 411
93/4 UpperDeck 319
94/5 UpperDeck 473
95/6 OTT

MOE, BILL
45-64 BeeHives(NYR)

MOELLER, DARWEIN
83/4 KelownaWings

MOEN, JEFF
92/3 Minnesota
93/4 Minnesota
94/5 Minnesota

MOES, MIKE
90/1 ProCards 148
90/1 Newmarket

MOESER, DUANNE
94/5 DEL 9
95/6 DEL 12
96/7 DEL 12

MOFFAT, CORRI
91/2 AirCanadaSJHL A10, 18
92/3 MPSPhotoSJHL 77

MOFFAT, LYLE
74/5 O-Pee-Chee 379
79/80 O-Pee-Chee 277
77/8 opcWHA 64
74/5 TOR
77/8 WPG
79/80 WPG

MOFFAT, MIKE
81/2 Kingston 23

MOFFAT, RON
83/4 Brantford 7

MOFFETT, GREG
83/4 NovaScotia 24

MOGER, SANDY
92/3 Classic 67
92/3 ClassicFourSport 192, -Aut.
93/4 ClassicProspects 187
95/6 Donruss 245
95/6 FleerUltra 11
95/6 Leaf 272
98/9 Pacific 240
97/8 PacificRegime 15
95/6 PaniniSticker 6
96/7 PinnacleBeAPlayer 172
95/6 SelectCertified 140
95/6 Summit 185
96/7 Summit 53
98/9 Topps 59
95/6 UpperDeck 332
92/3 Hamilton

MOGILNY, ALEXANDER
96/7 Aces J (Clubs)
90/1 Bowman 240
91/2 Bowman 30
92/3 Bowman 34, 235
95/6 Bowman 5, BB9
93/4 Classic 122, N7, -Aut
95/6 CoolTrade 19
93/4 Donruss 39, C, -Elite 8
94/5 Donruss 92
95/6 Donruss 275
96/7 Donruss 181,-Dom 7,-Top 4
97/8 Donruss 106
96/7 DonrussCanadianIce 91
97/8 DonrussCanadianIce 45
95/6 DonrussElite 18, -Cuttng 7
96/7 DonrussElite 56, -Status 9
97/8 DonrussElite 69
97/8 DonrussPreferred 39, 170
97/8 DonrussPriority 119
93/4 EASports 17, 191
97/8 EssoOlympic 39
94/5 Flair 20, -Scoring 8
96/7 Flair 96
94/5 Fleer 25
96/7 Fleer 114, 138, -ArtRoss 16
95/6 FleerMetal 153, -IntSteel 16
95/6 FM-Winners 5
96/7 F.Picks-Dream 4, -Fab 31
96/7 FleerNHLPicks-Jagged 3
92/3 FleerUltra 18, -Imports 16
93/4 FU 238,-Spd 7,-AS5,-Red 7
94/5 FU 26, AS 5, -Glbl 6, -Spd 8
95/6 FleerUltra 20,317, -Extra 15
96/7 FU 170, -Power 13, -Red 5
96/7 Got-UmHockeyGreatsCoin
93/4 HockeyWit 75
95/6 Hoyle'EAST 3 (Diamonds)
92/3 HumptyDumpty (1)
91 IvanFiodorovSportUnites
97/8 KatchMedallion 149
94/5 KennerSLU
94 Koululainen
91/2 Kraft 60
93/4 KraftDinner
94/5 Kraft-Sharpshooter
95/6 KraftDinner
96/7 KraftDinner, -Flex
93/4 Leaf 91, -GoldAS 8, -HT 2
94/5 Leaf 256, -FireOnIce 10
95/6 Leaf 187, -Freezer 8
96/7 Leaf 162,-Fire 2,-Leather 11
97/8 Leaf 25
94/5 LeafLimited 36
95/6 LeafLimited 83, -StarsOf 6
96/7 LeafLimited 8, -Stubble 13
96/7 LeafPreferred 2, -Steel 51
97/8 Limited 68, 104, 122
97/8 Limited -fabric 51
96/7 Maggers 159
92/3 McDonalds McD22
93/4 McDonalds McD19
94/5 McDonalds McD8
95/6 McDonalds McD21
96/7 McDonalds McD11
97/8 McDonalds F2
96/7 MetalUniv. 159, -Lethal 14
96/7 MetalUniv.-IceCarvings 11
97/8 Omega 232
90/1 OPC/Topps 42, A
91/2 OPC/Topps 32, 171
92/3 O-Pee-Chee 279
90/1 opcPremier 75
98/9 Pacific 89
97/8 PacificCrown 89, -Slap 11C
97/8 PacificCrownRoyale 137
97/8 PacificDynagon! 129
97/8 PcfcD-Dyn 15B,-Tandm 55
97/8 PcfcInv.144,-Att 24,-Feat 35
98/9 PacificParamount 237
97/8 PacificRegime 203
97/8 PacificRevolution 143
90/1 PaniniSticker 338
91/2 PaniniSticker 304
92/3 PaniniSticker 248, 299
93/4 PaniniSticker J
94/5 PaniniSticker 94
95/6 PaniniSticker 294
96/7 PaniniSticker 288
97/8 PaniniSticker 237
95 PaniniWorlds 285
91/2 Parkhurst 12
92/3 Parkhurst 13, 218
93/4 Parkhurst 21
94/5 Parkhurst 21, ES14
95/6 Parkhurst 212, 246, PP18
95/6 Parkie-Crown(2) 3
94/5 ParkieSE seV34
91/2 Pinnacle 163
92/3 Pinnacle 77, -Tm2000 28
93/4 Pinnacle 10, -Nifty 1, 2
93/4 P-TeamP 12, -Tm2001 2
94/5 Pinnacle 125, BR17
96/7 Pinnacle 87, 194
97/8 Pinnacle 58
96/7 P.BeAPlayer-Biscuit 24
97/8 P.BAP 247,-TakeANum 18
97/8 PinnacleCertified 60
97/8 PinnacleInside 34,-Track 27
95/6 PinnacleZenith 31
96/7 PinnZenith 34, -ZTeam 9
95/6 Playoff 102, 209, 318
96/7 Playoff 422
94/5 POG 44
95/6 POG 272
94/5 Post
93/4 PowerPlay 32, -Global 5
93/4 PP-PointLeader 10
93/4 Premier 148, 172, 245
93/4 Premier-Black(OPC) 10
94/5 Premier 50, -GoToGuy 13
95/6 ProMagnet 22
90/1 ProSet 26
91/2 ProSet 16
92/3 ProSet 19
91/2 PSPlatinum 14, 283
91/2 RedAce
90/1 Score 43, -YoungStar 26
91/2 Score(CDN) 456, (U.S) 236
91/2 Score-YoungStar 13
92/3 Score 248, -YoungStar 8
93/4 Score 222, 477, -Dream 20
93/4 Score (U.S) DD2, -P.AS 22
93/4 Score-International 8
94/5 Score 200
95/6 Score 21, -GoldenBlades 3
96/7 Score 16,-Suddn 8,-DrmT 9
97/8 Score 129
97/8 Score(VAN) 2
93/4 SeasonsPatch 12
94/5 Select 22
95/6 SelectCertified 43
96/7 SelectCertified 70
91 SemicSticker 218
95/6 SkyBoxEmotion 182
95/6 SkyBoxImpact 171
96/7 SkBxImpact 135, -Blade 15
94/5 SP 13
95/6 SP 148, E28
96/7 SP 158, GF12
97/8 SPAuthentic 155
96/7 SPx 47
95/6 Summit 48
96/7 Summit 107,-Unt. 9,-HiV 11
95/6 SuperSticker 122, 124
96/7 TeamOut
92/3 Topps 382
95/6 Topps 225, 376, 6PL
98/9 Topps 207
94/5 ToppsFinest 68, 99
95/6 ToppsFinest 140, 160
96 ToppsFinestBronze 19
96/7 T.NHLPicks 9, FT19, TS9
91/2 ToppsStadiumClub 195
92/3 ToppsStadiumClub 320
93/4 T.StadiumClub 91, -AllStar
95/6 ToppsStadiumClub 1, EN9
96/7 TSC-MembersOnly 26
94/5 TSC-MembersOnly 6
95/6 TSC-MembersOnly 10
95/6 ToppsSuperSkills 36
90/1 UpperDeck 24
91/2 UpperDeck 267, 618, SE2
92/3 UpperDeck 167,456,WG18
92/3 UD-LockerAS 8
93/4 UD 234,488,H10,HB1,HT15
93/4 UD SP-18, -HockeyHero 34
94/5 UD 334, 552, H9, SP10
95/6 UD 188, 221, AS10, SE173
95/6 UD R6,R35,-ASPredMVP 4
96/7 UD 167,X12, SS10B, HH12
97/8 UpperDeck T19B
94/5 UDBeAPlayer R68
95/6 UDBeAPlayer 204
96/7 UDBlackDiamond 89
97/8 UDBlackDiamond 97
98/9 UDChoice 210
95/6 UDCollChoice 163
96/7 UDCC 267, 333, C3, UD4
96/7 UDCC-Oversize 8of8
97/8 UDCC 256, SQ69
96/7 UpperDeck"Ice" 104
97/8 Zenith 79
89/90 BUF/BlueShield
89/90 BUF/Campbell
90/1 BUF/BlueShield
90/1 BUF/Campbell
91/2 BUF/BlueShield
91/2 BUF/Campbell
92/3 BUF/BlueShield
92/3 BUF/Jubillee
93/4 BUF/NOCO
96/7 VAN
96/7 VAN/IGA

MOHNINGER, BRET
91/2 AirCanadaSJHL C26

MOHNS, DOUG
52/3 AnonymousOHL 107
68/9 Bauer
45-64 BeeHives(BOS)
64-67 BeeHives(CHI)
62 CeramicTiles
64/5 CokeCap CHI-2
65/6 CocaCola
70/1 DadsCookies
70/1 EddieSargent 47
71/2 EddieSargent 84
72/3 EddieSargent 102
70/1 Esso Stamp
74/5 Loblaws
68/9 OPC/Topps 19
69/70 OPC/T. 72, OPC-Sticker
70/1 OPC/Topps 16, -Deckle 29
71/2 OPC/Topps 242
72/3 OPC 75, Topps 78
73/4 OPC 241
74/5 OPC/Topps 181
54/5 Parkhurst 57
93/4 Parkie(56/7) 18
94/5 Parkie(64/5) 27
95/6 Parkie(66/7) 35
60/1 ShirriffCoin 106
61/2 ShirriffCoin 10
68/9 ShirriffCoin CHI 8
54-67 TorontoStar 66/7, V9
56-66 TorontoStar 65/6
71/2 TheTorontoSun
54/5 Topps 18
57/8 Topps 12
58/9 Topps 50
59/60 Topps 58
60/1 Topps 52
61/2 Topps 10, -Stamp
62/3 Topps 6, -Buck
63/4 Topps 3
64/5 Topps 25
65/6 Topps 118
66/7 Topps 61, -USATest 61
67/8 Topps 63
91/2 Ultimate(O6) 53, -Aut 53
57/8 BOS
91/2 BOS/Legends
74/5 WSH

MOISE, MARTIN
97 BowmanCHL 72
98 BowmanCHL 113

MOISIO, MARKKU
71/2 WilliamsFIN 213
72/3 WilliamsFIN 159
73/4 WilliamsFIN 225

MOISIO, PEKKA
66/7 Champion 92

MOKOSAK, CARL
88/9 ProCards(Maine)
89/90 ProCards(IHL) 132
90/1 ProCards 304, 412
82/3 CGY

MOKOSAK, JOHN
88/9 ProCards(Adirondack)
90/1 ProCards 127
91/2 ProCards 192
92/3 Phoenix
81/2 Victoria
82/3 Victoria

MOKROS, MILAN
94/5 DEL 153
95/6 DEL 149
96/7 DEL 245

MOLANDER, RUBAN
91/2 SemicElitserien 37

MOLANDER, URBAN
90/1 SemicElitserien 181

MOLBERG, RUNE
79 PaniniSticker 295

MOLER, MIKE
84/5 BUF/BlueShield

MOLIN, LARS
82/3 O-Pee-Chee 353
82/3 opcSticker 245
82/3 Post
82 SemicSticker 149
83/4 SouhaitsRen.KeyChain
83/4 Vachon 113
81/2 VAN
81/2 VAN/Silverwood
82/3 VAN
83/4 VAN

MOLIN, OVE
94/5 ElitSet 85
95/6 ElitSet 20, -Goldies 2
91/2 SemicElitserien 48
92/3 SemicElitserien 68
95/6 udElite 33
97/8 udSwedish 27

MOLIN, SACHA
94/5 ElitSet 166

MOLINA, ALFIO
72 SemicSticker 157

MOLLEKEN, LORNE
91/2 SketchWHL 100
91/2 Saskatoon 1
84/5 Springfield 2

MOLLER, MIKE
89/90 ProCards(AHL) 305
88/9 EDM/ActionMagazine 136
85/6 NovaScotia 3
93/4 RedDeer

MOLLER, RANDY
91/2 Bowman 58
86/7 Kraft Sports 48
94/5 Leaf 344
83/4 O-Pee-Chee 297
84/5 O-Pee-Chee 284
85/6 O-Pee-Chee 240
87/8 O-Pee-Chee 251
89/90 O-Pee-Chee 259
90/1 O-Pee-Chee 515
91/2 OPC/Topps 371
83/4 opcSticker 248
84/5 opcSticker 174
85/6 opcSticker 145/15
87/8 opcSticker 229/96
89/90 opcSticker 195/49
87/8 PaniniSticker 162
88/9 PaniniSticker 351
89/90 PaniniSticker 331
91/2 Pinnacle 256
92/3 Pinnacle 176
94/5 Pinnacle 401
90/1 ProSet 202
91/2 ProSet 163
90/1 Score 45
91/2 Score(CDN) 79, (U.S) 79
92/3 Score 289
93/4 Score 422
83/4 SouhaitsRen.KeyChain
92/3 Topps 407
91/2 ToppsStadiumClub 2
92/3 ToppsStadiumClub 484
93/4 ToppsStadiumClub 435
90/1 UpperDeck 418
83/4 Vachon 69
92/3 BUF/BlueShield
92/3 BUF/Jubillee
89/90 NYR/MarineMidland
82/3 QUE
83/4 QUE
84/5 QUE
85/6 QUE
85/6 QUE/GeneralFoods
85/6 QUE/McDonald
85/6 QUE/Pennant
85/6 QUE/Placemats
85/6 QUE/Provigo
86/7 QUE
86/7 QUE/GeneralFoods
86/7 QUE/McDonald
87/8 QUE/GeneralFoods
88/9 QUE
88/9 QUE/GeneralFoods
89/90 QUE

MOLLING, JOCHEN
94/5 DEL 55
95/6 DEL 409
96/7 DEL 251

MOLLOY, MITCH
88/9 ProCards(Maine)
90/1 ProCards 283
89/90 Johnstown 29
92/3 SanDiego

MOLNAR, PETR
94/5 APS 207
95/6 APS 159

MOLSON, HARTLAND
83&87 HallOfFame 221
83 HHOF Postcard (O)
95/6 MTL/Forum 25Mar96

MOLYNEAUX, LARRY
34-43 BeeHives(NYR)

MOMESSO, SERGIO
90/1 Bowman 17
91/2 Bowman 309
92/3 Bowman 316
93/4 Donruss 349
95/6 Donruss 380
92/3 Durivage 26
93/4 Durivage 33
92/3 FleerUltra 225
93/4 FleerUltra 47
94/5 FleerUltra 384
95/6 FleerUltra 313
86/7 Kraft Sports 32
93/4 Leaf 250
94/5 Leaf 499
95/6 Leaf 58
90/1 OPC/Topps 244
91/2 OPC/Topps 462
92/3 O-Pee-Chee 377
91/2 opcPremier 55
97/8 PacificInvincible 121
90/1 PaniniSticker 263
91/2 PaniniSticker 44
91/2 Parkhurst 185
92/3 Parkhurst 421
93/4 Parkhurst 212
94/5 Parkhurst 249
95/6 Parkhurst 473
91/2 Pinnacle 34
92/3 Pinnacle 163
93/4 Pinnacle 393
94/5 Pinnacle 307
94/5 POG 342
94/5 Premier 356
90/1 ProSet 268
91/2 ProSet 242
92/3 ProSet 194
91/2 PSPlatinum 240
90/1 Score 224
91/2 Score(CDN) 121, (U.S) 121
92/3 Score 79
93/4 Score 255
95/6 Score 161
95/6 Summit 163
92/3 Topps 214
91/2 ToppsStadiumClub 17
92/3 ToppsStadiumClub 42
93/4 ToppsStadiumClub 323
94/5 ToppsStadiumClub 65
95/6 ToppsStadiumClub 123
90/1 UpperDeck 19
91/2 UpperDeck 571
92/3 UpperDeck 85
93/4 UpperDeck 104
94/5 UpperDeck 65, 85
95/6 UpperDeck 125
94/5 UDBeAPlayer-Aut. 178
95/6 UDCollChoice 99
85/6 MTL
85/6 MTL/ProvigoSticker
85/6? MTL/ProvigoPlacemats
86/7 MTL
87/8 MTL
87/8 MTL/Stickers 55, 56
87/8 STL
88/9 STL
88/9 STL/Kodak
89/90 STL/Kodak
90/1 STL/Kodak
91/2 VAN
92/3 VAN/RoadTrip
93/4 VAN/Coins
95/6 VAN/Building 12

MONAHAN, GARRY
70/1 Colgate Stamp 13
70/1 EddieSargent 207
71/2 EddieSargent 199
72/3 EddieSargent 202
70/1 Esso Stamp
74/5 Loblaws, -Update
69/70 OPC 160
70/1 OPC/Topps 112
72/3 OPC 207
73/4 OPC 226
75/6 OPC 357
76/7 OPC 295
77/8 OPC/Topps 96, OPC 341
78/9 OPC 268, 393
71/2 TheTorontoSun
67/8 Topps 8
67/8 MTL
67/8 MTL/IGA
68/9 MTL
70/1 TOR
71/2 TOR
72/3 TOR
73/4 TOR
78/9 TOR
74/5 VAN/RoyalBank
75/6 VAN/RoyalBank
76/7 VAN/RoyalBank
77/8 VAN/GingerAle
77/8 VAN/RoyalBank

MONAHAN, HARTLAND
76/7 OPC/Topps 203

MONDOU, ARMAND
33/4 Anonymous (V129) 44
34-43 BeeHives(MTL.C)
35-40 CrownBrand 125
36-39 DiamondMatch (1), (2), (3)
27-32 LaPresse 28/9
33/4 OPC (V304A) 48
37/8 OPC (V304E) 177
39/40 OPC (V301-1) 27
34/5 SweetCaporal
33/4 WWGum (V357) 17

MONDOU, PIERRE
72-84 Dernière 80/1, 83/4
78/9 OPC/Topps 102
79/80 OPC/Topps 211
80/1 OPC/Topps 42
81/2 O-Pee-Chee 188
82/3 O-Pee-Chee 188
83/4 O-Pee-Chee 191
84/5 O-Pee-Chee 266
85/6 O-Pee-Chee 211
82/3 opcSticker 35
83/4 opcSticker 68
84/5 opcSticker 162
85/6 opcSticker 133/253
80/1 Pepsi Cap
82/3 Post
83/4 7ElevenCokeCups
83/4 Vachon 49
77/8 MTL
78/9 MTL
79/80 MTL
80/1 MTL
81/2 MTL
82/3 MTL
82/3 MTL/Steinberg
83/4 MTL
84/5 MTL

MONDT, NIKOLAUS
95/6 DEL 99
96/7 DEL 287

MONETTE, JACQUES
51/2 BasDuFleuve 45
52/3 BasDuFleuve 35

MONGEAU, MICHEL
95/6 EdgeIce 178
92/3 FleerUltra 203
92/3 Pinnacle 388
89/90 ProCards(IHL) 17
90/1 ProCards 91
91/2 ProCards 26
90/1 Score 395
92/3 ToppsStadiumClub 415
90/1 UpperDeck 345
91/2 UpperDeck 213
91/2 STL
88/9 Flint
93/4 Peoria

MONGEON, HUGHES
90/1 SketchQMJHL 189
91/2 SketchQMJHL 32

MONGRAIN, STEVE
95/6 Halifax
97/8 Halifax (1)

MONONEN, ERKKI
66/7 Champion 107
70/1 Kuvajulkaisut 181
72 Panda
72 SemicSticker 81
71/2 WilliamsFIN 69, 105
72/3 WilliamsFIN 149

MONONEN, LAURI
72 Hellas 6
70/1 Kuvajulkaisut 69, 182
72 Panda
72 SemicSticker 82
74 SemicSticker 99
78/9 SM-Liiga 32
71/2 WilliamsFIN 70, 288
72/3 WilliamsFIN 66
73/4 WilliamsFIN 72, 115
75/6 Phoenix
76/7 Phoenix

MONRISSON, SANDY
52/3 AnonymousOHL 164

MONTANARI, MARK
96/7 DEL 102
95 PaniniWorlds 91
89/90 ProCards(AHL) 57
90/1 ProCards 142
89/90 SketchMEM 30
86/7 Kitchener 18
87/8 Kitchener 19
88/9 Kitchener 19

MONTANDON, GIL
95 Globe 215
95 PaniniWorlds 131
95 Semic 193
91 SemicSticker 198
92 SemicSticker
93 SemicSticker 128

MONTIETH, DWAYNE
88/9 Regina

MONTEMURRO, CARLO
52/3 AnonymousOHL 92

MONTGOMERY, JIM
93/4 Classic 55, -Aut
93/4 C4'Images 16
93/4 ClassicProspects 25
96/7 DEL 348
93/4 Donruss 300, -Rated 13
95/6 EdgeIce 46
93/4 FleerUltra 413
94/5 FleerUltra 187, 312
95/6 FutureLegends 11
94/5 Leaf 258, 348
93/4 Parkhurst 176
94/5 Parkhurst 198
94/5 ParkieSE 93
93/4 Pinnacle 438
94/5 Pinnacle 159
93/4 PowerPlay 431
93/4 Premier 488
94/5 Premier 91
93/4 Score 621
93/4 UpperDeck 472
94/5 UpperDeck 132
94/5 MTL
92/3 Maine (1) 12, (2) 27
93/4 Maine 61

MONTGOMERY, SCOTT
86/7 Kitchener 26
87/8 Kitchener 29

MODDY, BILL
92/3 BCJHL 140

MOOG, ANDY
90/1 Bowman 35
91/2 Bowman 361, 418
92/3 Bowman 79
93/4 Donruss 87
94/5 Donruss 108
95/6 Donruss 290
96/7 Donruss 166
97/8 Donruss 40
96/7 DonrussCanadianIce 90
97/8 DonrussCanadianIce 85
96/7 DonrussElite 3
97/8 DonrussElite 66
97/8 DonrussPreferred 113
97/8 DonrussPriority 108
93/4 EASports 12
94/5 Flair 44
96/7 Flair 24
94/5 Fleer 56
95/6 FleerMetal 43
92/3 FleerUltra 6
93/4 FleerUltra 2, 301
94/5 FleerUltra 56
95/6 FleerUltra 42, -PadMen 8
96/7 FleerUltra 45
91/2 Gillette 29
91/2 Kelloggs 10
86/7 Kraft Sports 19
90/1 Kraft 35
91/2 Kraft 59
92/3 Kraft'Disk
94/5 KraftDinner, -Masks
95/6 Kraft-Crease
93/4 Leaf 369
94/5 Leaf 47
96/7 Leaf 99
97/8 Limited 28, -fabric 36
96/7 Maggers 50
91/2 McDonalds McD9
97/8 McDonalds McD28
96/7 MetalUniverse 41
97/8 Omega 120,-NoScorZone 6
81/2 O-Pee-Chee 120
83/4 O-Pee-Chee 40
84/5 O-Pee-Chee 255
85/6 OPC/Topps 12
86/7 O-Pee-Chee 212
87/8 O-Pee-Chee 204
89/90 OPC/Topps 160
90/1 OPC/Topps 294, OPC 486
91/2 OPC/Topps 338
92/3 O-Pee-Chee 184
90/1 opcPremier 76
91/2 opcPremier 133
83/4 opcSticker 99, 155
84/5 opcSticker 262
85/6 opcSticker 123, 220/87
86/7 opcSticker 66/197
87/8 opcSticker 93/226
89/90 opcSticker 30/170
98/9 Pacific 255
97/8 PacificCrown 35, -InThe 6
97/8 PacificCrownRoyale 70
97/8 PCR -FreezeOut 10
97/8 PacificDynag-BestKept 31
97/8 PacificInvincible 42
97/8 PcfcParamnt 96,-Glove 10
97/8 PacificRegime 64
97/8 PcfcRevolutn 72,-Retrn 10
87/8 PaniniSticker 255
89/90 PaniniSticker 191
90/1 PaniniSticker 11
91/2 PaniniSticker 179
92/3 PaniniSticker 135
93/4 PaniniSticker 9
95/6 PaniniSticker 177
97/8 PaniniSticker 173
91/2 Parkhurst 8
92/3 Parkhurst 3
93/4 Parkhurst 47
94/5 Parkhurst 51
95 PH'Incomnet
95/6 Parkhurst 59
91/2 Pinnacle 126, 379
92/3 Pinnacle 91, 263
93/4 Pinnacle 347
94/5 Pinnacle 315, GT14, MA8
95/6 Pinnacle 114, -Masks 5
96/7 Pinnacle 166
97/8 Pinnacle 70
96/7 P.BeAPlayer 7 -Stacking 12
97/8 PinnacleCertified 5
97/8 PinnacleInside 47
95/6 PinnacleZenith 105
96/7 PinnacleZenith 110
95/6 Playoff 32
96/7 Playoff 382
94/5 POG 277
95/6 POG 92
93/4 PowerPlay 64
93/4 Premier 476
94/5 Premier 81, 511
95/6 ProMagnet 125
90/1 ProSet 10, 382
91/2 ProSet 10, 299, P5
91/2 PS -ThePuck 2, 'Promo
92/3 ProSet 7
91/2 PSPlatinum 4
90/1 Score 140, 365, -Hot 62
91/2 Score(CDN) 90, (U.S) 90
92/3 Score 120
93/4 Score 11, 516
94/5 Score 173
95/6 Score 64
96/7 Score 104
97/8 Score 8
97/8 Score(MTL) 1
92/3 SeasonsPatch 19
94/5 Select 94
95/6 SelectCertified 77
96/7 SelectCertified 25
83/4 7ElevenCokeCup
95/6 SkyBoxEmotion 50
95/6 SkyBoxImpact 49
83/4 SouhaitsRen.KeyChain
94/5 SP 32
96/7 SP 44
97/8 SPAuthentic 81
98/9 SPx"Finite" 44
83/4 StaterMint H15
95/6 Summit 96, -InTheCreas 12
96/7 Summit 130
95/6 SuperSticker 35
92/3 Topps 394
95/6 Topps 53, 14HG
91/2 ToppsStadiumClub 211
92/3 ToppsStadiumClub 430
93/4 ToppsStadiumClub 470
94/5 ToppsStadiumClub 231
95/6 ToppsSuperSkills 83
90/1 UpperDeck 209, 232
91/2 UpperDeck 147
92/3 UpperDeck 1, 329
93/4 UpperDeck 478, SP-39
94/5 UpperDeck 81, SP111
95/6 UpperDeck 191
97/8 UpperDeck 294
94/5 UDBeAPlayer-Aut. 30
97/8 UDBlackDiamond 113
98/9 UDChoice 106
95/6 UDCollChoice 62
97/8 UDCollChoice 67, SQ34
83/4 Vachon 37
92/3 BOS
88/9 BOS/SportsAction
89/90 BOS/SportsAction
90/1 BOS/SportsAction (x2)
91/2 BOS/SportsAction (x2)
94/5 DAL
94/5 DAL/Southwest
96/7 DAL/Southwest
81/2 EDM/RedRooster
82/3 EDM/RedRooster
83/4 EDM
83/4 EDM/Buttons
83/4 EDM/McDonald
84/5 EDM
84/5 EDM/RedRooster
85/6 EDM/RedRooster
86/7 EDM
86/7 EDM/RedRooster (x2)
88/9 EDM/ActionMagazine 91
97/8 MTL

MOON, CAM
90/1 SketchWHL 87
90/1 Saskatoon 3

MOON, SCOTT
88/9 ProCards(Utica)

MOONEY, MATTHEW
90/1 Rayside
91/2 Rayside

MOONEY, MIKE
89/90 Rayside

MOORE, BARRIE
95/6 EdgeIce 65
91/2 SketchOHL 259
93/4 Slapshot(Sudbury) 15
94/5 Slapshot(Sudbury) 14
95/6 Rochester
93/4 Sudbury 15
91/2 Sudbury 20
92/3 Sudbury 17

MOORE, BLAINE
92/3 BCJHL 238
95/6 LasVegas
96/7 LasVegas
94/5 Richmond

MOORE, CHARLIE
83/4 Belleville 13
84/5 Belleville 8

MOORE, DAVID
91/2 Cincinnati

MOORE, DEAN
91/2 AirCanadaSJHL A15
92/3 MPSPhotoSJHL 106

MOORE, DICKIE
see Richard "Dickie" Moore

MOORE, GREG
92/3 MPSPhotoSJHL 98

MOORE, JIM
51/2 LavalDairy 36
52/3 StLawrence 3

MOORE, KEVIN
91/2 FerrisState

MOORE, MIKE
87/8 Portland
88/9 Portland

MOORE, RICHARD (DICKIE)
45-64 BeeHives(MTL)
64-67 BeeHives(TOR)
62 CeramicTiles
64/5 CokeCap TOR-16
72-84 Dernière 77/8
48-52 Exhibits
83&87 HallOfFame 190
83 HHOF Postcard (J)
51/2 LaPatrie 9-Mar
52/3 Parkhurst 10
53/4 Parkhurst 28
54/5 Parkhurst 2
55/6 Parkhurst 38
57/8 Parkhurst(MTL) 14
58/9 Parkhurst 8
59/60 Parkhurst 14
60/1 Parkhurst 38, 57
61/2 Parkhurst 36
62/3 Parkhurst 42
92/3 Parkhurst PR26
93/4 Parkhurst DPR12
93/4 Parkie(56/7) 70
94/5 Parkie(64/5) 116
45-54 QuakerOats
60/1 ShirriffCoin 22
61/2 ShirriffCoin 107
62/3 ShirriffCoin 37
63/4 TheTorontoStar
54-67 TorontoStar V6
56-66 TorontoStar 58/9, 62/3
60/1 York, -Glasses
61/2 York 5
62/3 YorkTransfer 22
92/3 MTL/OPC 63
95/6 MTL/Forum 10Jan96
64/5 TOR

MOORE, SCOTT
90/1 SemicElitserien 71
91/2 SemicElitserien 241

MOORE, SKEETER
85/6 Minnesota-Duluth 1

MOORES, TOM
91/2 SketchOHL 214
93/4 Slapshot(NiagaraFalls) 17

MORAAL, ARI
83/4 Kingston 4
84/5 Kingston 3
85/6 Kingston 3
86/7 Kingston 3
87/8 Kingston 1

MORABITO, JOHN
91/2 AvantGardeBCJ 12
92/3 BCJHL 190
95/6 Birmingham

MORAN, ANDY
25-27 Anonymous 11
23/4 PaulinsCandy 29

MORAN, BRAD
98 BowmanCHL 72

MORAN, IAN
94/5 Classic 101
93/4 FleerUltra 492
97/8 PacificDynag-BestKept 79
97/8 PinnacleBeAPlayer 93
93/4 PowerPlay 512
93/4 Premier-TeamUSA 2
95/6 SkyBoxImpact 216
93/4 T.StadiumClub-TmUSA 17
95/6 T.StadiumClub 219
95/6 PGH/Foodland 20, 24

MORAN, PADDY
91 C55 Reprint 1
83&87 HallOfFame 144
83 HHOF Postcard (K)
1910-11 Imperial (C56) 28
1911-12 Imperial (C55) 1
1912-13 Imperial (C57) 18
1910-11 Imperial Post 1
60/1 Topps 2
61/2 Topps-Stamp

MORAVEC, DAVID
95/6 APS 309

MORDOCK, LORIN
92/3 BCJHL 181

MORE, JAYSON
92/3 Bowman 388
94/5 Leaf 509
92/3 O-Pee-Chee 312
98/9 Pacific 98
98/9 PacificParamount 126
91/2 Parkhurst 387
92/3 Parkhurst 394
93/4 Parkhurst 452
91/2 Pinnacle 342
97/8 PinnacleBeAPlayer 70
95/6 Playoff 303
96/7 Playoff 417
93/4 Premier 227
90/1 ProCards 99
92/3 ProSet 169
92/3 Score 147
92/3 Topps 245
92/3 ToppsStadiumClub 60
93/4 ToppsStadiumClub 208
94/5 ToppsStadiumClub 165
92/3 UpperDeck 488
97/8 PHO
92/3 S.J/PacificBell

MORE, PAUL
83/4 Brandon 15
84/5 Brandon 23

MOREAU, ERIC
91/2 SketchQMJHL 191

MOREAU, ETHAN
94/5 Classic 12, T14
95/6 Classic 97, AS12
94/5 C'FourSport 128, BC20
94/5 C'FourSport-Picks 25
94/5 C4'Images 105
94/5 ClassicImages 50
96/7 Donruss 228
97/8 Donruss 50
96/7 DonrussCanadianIce 127
97/8 DonrussCanadianIce 83
96/7 D.Elite 136, -Aspirations 20
97/8 DonrussElite 52
97/8 DonrussPreferred 35
97/8 DonrussPriority 116
97/8 D.Studio 83,-HardHats 23
95/6 EdgeIce 134
96/7 Flair 104
96/7 FleerUltra 32, -Rookies 13
95/6 FutureLegends 34,-Pltnm 7
97/8 KatchMedallion 35
96/7 Leaf -Rookie 1
97/8 Leaf 143
96/7 LeafLimited-Rookies 1
96/7 LeafPreferred 139
97/8 Limited 60, 87, 94
96/7 MetalUniverse 187
97/8 PcfcDynagon! 28,-Tand 40
97/8 PacificInvincible 31
97/8 PacificParamount 46
95/6 Parkhurst 540
96/7 Pinnacle 239
97/8 Pinnacle 189
96/7 PinnacleBeAPlayer LTH4A
97/8 PinnacleInside 184
96/7 PinnacleZenith 133
96/7 Score 268
97/8 Score 151
96/7 SelectCertified 116
91/2 SketchOHL 212
93/4 Slapshot(N.Falls) 13, 28
94/5 Slapshot(Sudbury) 20
96/7 SP 31
96/7 Summit 184
96/7 UpperDeck 187
97/8 UpperDeck 250
96/7 UDBlackDiamond 69
96/7 UDCollChoice 354
97/8 UDCollChoice 51

MOREAU, SÉBASTIEN
92/3 MPSPhotoSJHL 165
91/2 SketchQMJHL 106

MOREL, DENIS
90/1 ProSet 695

MOREN, DARREN
84/5 Saskatoon
83/4 Victoria

MORENZ, HOWIE
25-27 Anonymous 9
33/4 Anonymous (V129) 41
34-43 BeeHives(MTL.C)
24/5 Champs (C144)
33/4 CndGum (V252)
35-40 CrownBrand 57
33-35 DiamondMatch
36-39 DiamondMatch (1), (2), (3)
33 GoudeySport 24
83&87 HallOfFame 106
33/4 Hamilton (V288) 8
83 HHOF Postcard (H)
95/6 HHOFLegends 69
27-32 LaPresse 27/8
24/5 MapleCrispette (V130) 12
33/4 OPC (V304A) 23
36/7 OPC (V304D) 121
43-47 ParadeSportive
55/6 Parkhurst 57
93/4 Parkie(56/7) P1
91/2 ProSet 336
34/5 SweetCaporal
60/1 Topps 59
61/2 Topps-Stamp
23/4 (V145-1) 15
24/5 (V145-2) 47
33/4 WWGum (V357) 36, -Prem.
36/7 WWGum (V356) 18, 100
28/9 MTL/LaPatrie 14
92/3 MTL/OPC 13
95/6 MTL/Forum 28Oct95

MORET, LEO
28/9 PaulinsCandy 44

MORGAN, CHRIS
91/2 AirCanadaSJHL A18

MORGAN, JASON
93/4 Slapshot(Kitchener) 13
94/5 Slapshot(Kitchener) 14
95/6 Slapshot 121

MORGANTI, AL
91/2 StarPics 1

MORIARITY, GERALD
95/6 Slapshot 333

MORIN, DEREK
89/90 SketchOHL 89
90/1 SketchOHL 13

MORIN, ERIC
79/80 Montréal

MORIN, GUILLAUME
91/2 SketchQMJHL 173

MORIN, J.M.
91/2 SketchQMJHL 138

MORIN, JOE
89/90 SketchOHL 165
87/8 Kingston 10

MORIN, MARC
84/5 Chicoutimi

MORIN, MIKE
85/6 Brandon 19
91/2 LakeSuperior
95/6 Richmond
84/5 Saskatoon

MORIN, NATHAN
91/2 SketchQMJHL 158

MORIN, OLIVIER
97/8 Bowman 74

MORIN, PETE
34-43 BeeHives(MTL.C)
43-47 ParadeSportive
52/3 StLawrence 16
36/7 WWGum (V356) 129

MORIN, STÉPHANE
91/2 Bowman 148
92/3 Durivage 9
95/6 EdgeIce 169
91/2 OPC/Topps 159
91/2 PaniniSticker 263
92/3 PaniniSticker 214
91/2 Parkhurst 147
91/2 Pinnacle 245
89/90 ProCards(AHL) 167
90/1 ProCards 455
91/2 ProSet 201
91/2 PSPlatinum 100
91/2 Score(CDN) 254, (U.S) 361
91/2 Score-YoungStar 39
92/3 Topps 316
91/2 ToppsStadiumClub 216
92/3 ToppsStadiumClub 469
90/1 UpperDeck 524
91/2 UpperDeck 433
91/2 QUE/PetroCanada
89/90 Halifax
90/1 Halifax
92/3 Hamilton

MORIN, VIC
80/1 SSMarie

MORISSETTE, ALAIN
91/2 ProCards 303

MORISSETTE, DAVE
90/1 SketchQMJHL 199
91/2 Hampton
93/4 Roanoke

MORK, GARY
69 ColumbusCheckers

MORMINA, BOB
83/4 Springfield 12

MORO, MARC
97/8 Bowman 17
95/6 Classic 24
95/6 C'FiveSport 140, -Aut
93/4 Slapshot(Kingston) 4
95/6 Slapshot 116
96/7 SSMarie

MOROCCO, RICK
92 SemicSticker
82/3 NorthBay
80/1 SSMarie

MORODER, MIRKO
95 PaniniWorlds 93

MOROZOV, ALEXEI
97/8 DonrussElite 108
97/8 DonrussPreferred 155
97/8 DonrussPriority 183
97/8 KatchMedallion 119
97/8 Leaf 164
97/8 McDonalds McD38
97/8 Omega 187
98/9 Pacific 95
97/8 PacificCrownRoyale 111
97/8 PacificParamount 152
98/9 PacificParamount 194
97/8 Pinnacle 6
97/8 PinnacleBeAPlayer 212
97/8 P.BeeHive -TeamBH 24
97/8 PinnacleCertified H
97/8 PinnacleMint 27
97/8 Score 74
97/8 Score(PGH) 18
94/5 Select 158
94/5 SigRookies FF10
95/6 SigRookies 'Promo
97/8 SPAuthentic 190, I15
98/9 SPx"Finite" 68, 149
95/6 Tetrad 61
95/6 TetradAutobilia 48
98/9 Topps 70
95/6 UpperDeck 553
97/8 UpperDeck 233, 341
97/8 UDBlackDiamond 130, PC5
98/9 UDChoice 166
96/7 UpperDeck"Ice" 139
97/8 UpperDeckIce 56, L7B
97/8 Zenith 94, Z67,-RookRgn 8
97/8 Zenith -RookieZTeam 18

MOROZOV, VALENTIN
94/5 SigRookies 68

MORQUE, CHRIS
94/5 Huntington 17

MORRIS, BURNEY
23/4 PaulinsCandy 64
28/9 PaulinsCandy 73

MORRIS, DEREK
97/8 Bowman 109
97/8 DonrussElite 114, 132

97/8 DonrussPriority 182
97/8 Omega 31
98/9 Pacific 53
98/9 PacificParamount 30
97/8 PinnacleBeAPlayer 245
97/8 SPAuthentic 175
98/9 SPx"Finite" 13, 136
98/9 Topps 69
97/8 UpperDeck 233
97/8 UDBlackDiamond 104
98/9 UDChoice 29
97/8 UpperDeckIce 51
97/8 Zenith 88, Z68

MORRIS, ELWYN
45-54 QuakerOats

MORRIS, JON
90/1 Bowman 84
91/2 Bowman 286
90/1 O-Pee-Chee 457
91/2 OPC/Topps 332
89/90 ProCards(AHL) 207
91/2 ProCards 426
90/1 ProSet 621
91/2 ProSet 424
90/1 Score 401
91/2 Score(CDN) 548
91/2 ToppsStadiumClub 360
90/1 UpperDeck 65
91/2 UpperDeck 216
90/1 N.J.
92/3 Cincinnati

MORRIS, KEITH
92/3 CanadaNats

MORRIS, RICK
75/6 opcWHA 91

MORRISON, AARON
90/1 SketchOHL 267
91/2 SketchOHL 106

MORRISON, ADAM
83/4 Victoria
84/5 Victoria

MORRISON, ANDREW
95/6 Slapshot 29

MORRISON, BRENDAN
92/3 BCJHL 117
98/9 Pacific 265
97/8 PinnacleBeeHive 56
97/8 SPAuthentic 193
98/9 SPx"Finite" 48, 145
98/9 UDChoice 120
97/8 Zenith 99, -RookieReign 4

MORRISON, CRAIG
83/4 Oshawa 17

MORRISON, DAVE
94/5 DEL 157
95/6 DEL 158
96/7 DEL 233
84/5 Fredericton 1

MORRISON, DON
45-64 BeeHives(DET)

MORRISON, GEORGE
71/2 EddieSargent 191
70/1 Esso Stamp
71/2 OPC/Topps 223
72/3 O-Pee-Chee 314
71/2 TheTorontoSun
72/3 Minnesota

MORRISON, IKE
28/9 PaulinsCandy 50

MORRISON, JIM
45-64 BeeHives(TOR)
70/1 EddieSargent 169
70/1 Esso Stamp
69/70 O-Pee-Chee 156
70/1 OPC/Topps 90
52/3 Parkhurst 28
53/4 Parkhurst 15
54/5 Parkhurst 18, 94
55/6 Parkhurst 8, 76
57/8 Parkhurst(TOR) 11
60/1 Parkhurst 61
93/4 Parkie(56/7) 115
45-54 QuakerOats
60/1 ShirriffCoin 95
59/60 Topps 36
60/1 Topps 9
56-66 TorontoStar 57/8, 58/9

63/4 QuébecAces
65/6 QuébecAces
81/2 Kingston 24
82/3 Kingston 1

MORRISON, JOHN (CRUTCHY)
23/4 PaulinsCandy 48

MORRISON, JUSTIN
90/1 SketchOHL 67
91/2 SketchOHL 229
91/2 StarPics 45
91/2 Ultimate DP52, -Au t 52

MORRISON, KEVIN
75/6 opcWHA 63, 80
76/7 opcWHA 10, 68
79/80 COL.R
85/6 Kamloops
84/5 PrinceAlbert
76/7 SanDiegoMariners

MORRISON, LEW
72/3 EddieSargent 13
70/1 Esso Stamp
74/5 Loblaws, -Update
70/1 OPC 197
71/2 OPC 89
72/3 OPC 143, Topps 58
74/5 OPC/Topps 125
76/7 OPC 307
77/8 OPC 300
72/3 ATL
70/1 PHA
72/3 PHA/MightyMilk

MORRISON, MARK
83 CanadaJuniors
81/2 Victoria
82/3 Victoria
84/5 Victoria

MORRISON, MIKE
85/6 Kitchener 15

MORRISON, ROD
45-64 BeeHives(DET)

MORRISON, SCOTT
94 Semic 321

MORRISSEY, DAN
91/2 AvantGardeBCJHL 78
92/3 BCJHL 88

MORRONE, MIKE
94/5 Slapshot(Detroit) 9
94/5 Slapshot(MEM) 83
95/6 Slapshot 65
93/4 OwenSound

MORROW, BRENDAN
97/8 Bowman 98, 147, BB16
98 BowmanCHL 60

MORROW, KEN
94/5 MiracleOnIce 21, 22
80/1 OPC/Topps 9
81/2 OPC 205, Topps(E) 91
82/3 O-Pee-Chee 206
83/4 O-Pee-Chee 13
84/5 OPC 131, Topps 97
85/6 OPC/Topps 93
86/7 OPC/Topps 65
87/8 OPC/Topps 66
88/9 OPC/Topps 53
81/2 opcSticker 165
82/3 opcSticker 58
83/4 opcSticker 73
84/5 opcSticker 93
86/7 opcSticker 215/87
87/8 opcSticker 246/137
87/8 PaniniSticker 94
88/9 PaniniSticker 285
82/3 Post
91/2 UpperDeck 637
83/4 NYI
83/4 NYI/Islander 19
84/5 NYI 23

MORROW, SCOTT
96/7 Cincinnati
94/5 SaintJohn

MORROW, STEVE
91/2 ProCards 284

MORSHAUSER, GUS
87/8 Kitchener 6
88/9 Kitchener 10

MORTH, TOM
82 SemicSticker 19

MORTIER, DARREN
94/5 Slapshot(Sarnia) 8
95/6 Slapshot 337

MÖRTL, HERBERT
79 PaniniSticker 308

MORTON, DEAN
88/9 ProCards(Adirondack)
89/90 ProCards(AHL) 328
90/1 ProCards 314
92/3 Cincinnati

MORTON, RICK
90/1 SketchOHL 189
91/2 SketchOHL 272

MORTSON, CLEVELAND
63/4 QuébecAces
65/6 QuébecAces

MORTSON, GUS
45-64 BeeHives(CHI), (TOR)
48-52 Exhibits
51/2 Parkhurst 73
52/3 Parkhurst 39
53/4 Parkhurst 81
54/5 Parkhurst 81
93/4 Parkie(56/7) 30
45-54 QuakerOats
54/5 Topps 17
57/8 Topps 25
58/9 Topps 38
56-66 TorontoStar 57/8
54-67 TorontoStar V 4, n7

MÖRZ, JOHAN
82 SemicSticker 117

MOSCALUK, GARY
88/9 ProCards(Saginaw)
89/90 ProCards(IHL) 65

MOSDELL, KEN
34-43 BeeHives(NYA)
45-64 BeeHives(MTL)
48-52 Exhibits
51-54 LaPatrie 20Jan52
43-47 ParadeSportive
51/2 Parkhurst 11
52/3 Parkhurst 8
53/4 Parkhurst 33
54/5 Parkhurst 12
55/6 Parkhurst 39
93/4 Parkie(56/7) 41
45-54 QuakerOats
54-67 TorontoStar V 5,n7

MOSER, JAY
94/5 Minnesota

MOSEY, SCOTT
84/5 SSMarie

MOSHER, RALPH
85/6 NovaScotia 23

MOSIENKO, BILL
45-64 BeeHives(CHI)
83&87 HallOfFame 11
83 HHOF Postcard (A)
93/4 HHOFLegends 22
43-47 ParadeSportive
51/2 Parkhurst 49
52/3 Parkhurst 27
53/4 Parkhurst 80
92/3 Parkhurst 53 PR20
54/5 Topps 54
91/2 UltimateO6 61, -Aut 61

MOSS, C.J.
93/4 Slapshot(Kingston) 3

MOSS, JOE
90/1 EDM/McGavins

MOSS, TYLER
95/6 Classic 87, AS7
95/6 ClassicFiveSport 144
97/8 DonrussPriority 179
97/8 KatchMedallion 23
97/8 Omega 32
98/9 Pacific 122
97/8 PcfcCrwnRoyale 20,-Frez 4
97/8 PinnacleBeAPlayer 230
97/8 SPAuthentic 174
97/8 UDBlackDiamond 108
97/8 UpperDeckIce 32

MOTKOV, DIMTRI
92/3 ClassicProspects 57
90/1 O-Pee-Chee 5R

MOTT, MORRIS
74/5 Loblaws Update
69/70 MästarSerien 33
74/5 OPC/Topps 48

MOTTAU, MIKE
98 UDChoice 300

MOTTER, ALEX
34-43 BeeHives(BOS)
40/1 OPC (V301-2) 115

MOUGENAL, RYAN
97/8 Bowman 27
95/6 Slapshot 133
93/4 OwenSound

MOUSER, TIM
92/3 Toledo (1), (2)
93/4 Toledo 4

MOUTON, CLAUDE
87/8 MTL

MOVSESSIAN, VIC
94/5 Classic W23

MOWERS, JOHN
34-43 BeeHives(DET)
40/1 OPC (V301-2) 105

MOXAM, DARREN
93/4 Slapshot(Oshawa) 15
93/4 Slapshot(Peterborough) 7
95/6 Slapshot 390
84/5 Belleville 12
86/7 Kitchener 13

MOXEY, JIM
76/7 O-Pee-Chee 349

MOXNESS, ROB
91/2 Rayside

MOYLAN, COREY
93/4 Slapshot(SSMarie) 26

MOYLAN, DAVE
90/1 ProCards 439
91/2 ProCards 156
84/5 Sudbury 13
85/6 Sudbury 10
89/90 Sudbury 5

MOYON, CHRISTOPHE
95 PaniniWorlds 99
94 Semic 214

MRAZEK, RADEK
94/5 APS 210
95/6 APS 160

MRHALEK, ROMAN
91/2 AirCanadaSJHL C28

MROZIK, RICK
93/4 Minn-Duluth

MRUK, JERZY
89 SemicSticker 128

MUCHA, JARO
94/5 DEL 158
95/6 DEL 153

MUHLBAUER, THOMAS
94/5 DEL 115
95/6 DEL 327

MUCKALT, BILL
91/2 AvantGardeBCJ 82
92/3 BCJHL 77

MUCKLER, JOHN
52/3 AnonymousOHL 175
93/4 Kraft'Coach
90/1 ProSet 665
92/3 BUF/BlueShield
82/3 EDM/RedRooster
83/4 EDM/Buttons
83/4 EDM/McDonald
84/5 EDM/RedRooster
85/6 EDM/RedRooster
86/7 EDM/RedRooster
88/9 EDM/ActionMagazine 68
90/1 EDM/McGavins

MUEGGLER, BRIAN
89/90 SketchOHL 127
89/90 NiagaraFalls

MUELLER, BRAD
84/5 Brandon 6

MUELLER, BRIAN
95/6 Classic 77, -Aut
95/6 ClassicFiveSport 146
91/2 UD'CzechWJC 66
92/3 Clarkson

MUELLER, REGAN
93/4 Seattle

MUFTIYEV, RALL
95 PaniniWorlds 39

MUHR, ALBERT
79 PaniniSticker 272

MÜHR, MANFRED
95 PaniniWorlds 272
95 Semic 187

MUIKKU, JORMA
70/1 Kuvajulkaisut 260

MUIR, BRYAN
97/8 EDM

MUIR, JIM
36/7 WWGum (V356) 128

MUIR, WAYNE
94/5 Slapshot(Brantford) 17
92/3 Greensboro 8
87/8 SSMarie 28
89/90 SSMarie 21

MUISE, RANDY
91/2 AirCanadaSJHL B33

MUJCIN, MIRSAD
91/2 SketchWHL 296

MUKHOMETOV, ILDAR
91/2 UD'CzechWJC 10

MULCAHY, BILL
79/80 Montréal, BW

MULHERN, RICK
76/7 O-Pee-Chee 265
77/8 O-Pee-Chee 373
78/9 OPC/Topps 256
79/80 OPC/Topps 133
80/1 O-Pee-Chee 350
77/8 ATL
80/1 WPG

MULICK, ROB
95/6 Slapshot 378
96/7 SSMarie

MULLAHY, BRAD
94/5 Raleigh

MULLEN, BRIAN
90/1 Bowman 217
91/2 Bowman 61
92/3 Bowman 139
92/3 FleerUltra 348
86/7 Kraft Sports 78
94/5 Leaf 419
83/4 O-Pee-Chee 389
84/5 O-Pee-Chee 344
85/6 O-Pee-Chee 195
86/7 OPC/Topps 38
88/9 OPC/Topps 91
89/90 OPC/Topps 24
90/1 OPC/Topps 292
91/2 OPC/Topps 129
92/3 O-Pee-Chee 260
91/2 opcPremier 166
92/3 opcPremier 111
83/4 opcSticker 148
86/7 opcSticker 109/242
89/90 opcSticker 243
89/90 PaniniSticker 286
90/1 PaniniSticker 96
91/2 PaniniSticker 289
92/3 PaniniSticker 125
93/4 PaniniSticker 61
91/2 Parkhurst 166
91/2 Pinnacle 135
92/3 Pinnacle 333
93/4 Pinnacle 122, 324
93/4 Premier 154
90/1 ProSet 203
91/2 ProSet 165
91/2 PSPlatinum 106
83/4 PuffySticker 4
90/1 Score 84
91/2 Score(CDN) 59, 269, 552
91/2 Score(U.S) 59, 379, 2T
92/3 Score 278, -USAGreats 12
93/4 Score 347
94 Semic 128

95 Semic 120
83/4 7ElevenCokeCup
84/5 7ElevenDisk
83/4 StaterMint H10
92/3 Topps 104
91/2 ToppsStadiumClub 222
92/3 ToppsStadiumClub 420
94/5 ToppsStadiumClub 213
90/1 UpperDeck 182
91/2 UpperDeck 57
92/3 UpperDeck 317, 468
83/4 Vachon 134
89/90 NYR/MarineMidland
91/2 S.J.
82/3 WPG
83/4 WPG
84/5 WPG/Police
85/6 WPG
85/6 WPG/Police
85/6 WPG/Silverwood
86/7 WPG

MULLEN, JOE
90/1 Bowman 97
91/2 Bowman 79
92/3 Bowman 58
93/4 Donruss 257
95/6 Donruss 38, 251
96/7 Donruss 191
94/5 Fleer 165
92/3 FleerUltra 166
93/4 FleerUltra 171
94/5 FleerUltra 167
95/6 FleerUltra 124, 206
95 Globe112
93/4 HockeyWit 78
86/7 Kraft Sports 4
89/90 Kraft 60
90/1 Kraft 36, 72
93/4 Leaf 300
94/5 Leaf 385
95/6 Leaf 155
96/7 Leaf 14
82/3 O-Pee-Chee 307
83/4 O-Pee-Chee 317
84/5 O-Pee-Chee 367
84/5 OPC 188, Topps 133
85/6 OPC/Topps 7
86/7 OPC/Topps 44
87/8 OPC/Topps 126, G
88/9 OPC/Topps 76
89/90 OPC/Topps 196, O
89/90 OPC 324, T-AS 5
90/1 OPC/Topps 218
91/2 OPC/Topps 69
92/3 O-Pee-Chee 23
90/1 opcPremier 77
91/2 opcPremier 153
87/8 opcStars 29
82/3 opcSticker 200
84/5 opcSticker 61
85/6 opcSticker 47/177
86/7 opcSticker 82/208
87/8 opcSticker 36, 186/47
88/9 opcSticker 95
89/90 opcSticker 90, 160/20
89/90 opcSticker 214/75
89/90 opcStickFS 23
87/8 PaniniSticker 210, 384
88/9 PaniniSticker 11
89/90 PaniniSticker 27, 380, 384
90/1 PaniniSticker 183
91/2 PaniniSticker 278
92/3 PaniniSticker 223
93/4 PaniniSticker 83
95/6 PaniniSticker 64
91/2 Parkhurst 141
92/3 Parkhurst 368
93/4 Parkhurst 159
94/5 Parkhurst 180
91/2 Pinnacle 176
92/3 Pinnacle 360
93/4 Pinnacle 240
94/5 Pinnacle 149
96/7 Pinnacle 61
94/5 POG 187
95/6 POG 32
93/4 PowerPlay 192
93/4 Premier 498
94/5 Premier 517
90/1 ProSet 40, 343, 508
91/2 ProSet 191
92/3 ProSet 142, 262

87/8 ProSportWatch CW8
90/1 Score 208, 7T, -Hot 88
91/2 Score(CDN) 269, 488
91/2 Score(U.S) 268, 379
92/3 Score 3, -USAGreats 9
93/4 Score 7
94/5 Score 57
95/6 Score 252, -BorderBattle 8
96/7 Score 201
94/5 Select 16
94 Semic 118
89 SemicSticker 170
91 SemicSticker 146
92 SemicSticker 163
93 SemicSticker 178
95/6 SkyBoxEmotion 9
95/6 SkyBoxImpact 10
96/7 SP 131
95/6 Summit 92
92/3 Topps 113
94/5 T.Finest-RingLeaders 10
91/2 ToppsStadiumClub 7
92/3 ToppsStadiumClub 20
93/4 ToppsStadiumClub 19
94/5 ToppsStadiumClub 50
95/6 ToppsStadiumClub M7
93/4 TSC-MembersOnly 33
90/1 UpperDeck 252, 423
91/2 UpperDeck 201
92/3 UpperDeck 144
93/4 UpperDeck 186
94/5 UpperDeck 346
95/6 UpperDeck 16
95/6 UDBeAPlayer 154
95/6 UDCollChoice 25
96/7 UDCollChoice 22
96 Wien 169
86/7 CGY/RedRooster
86/7 CGY/RedRooster
87/8 CGY/RedRooster
90/1 PGH/Foodland 8
91/2 PGH/Topps
91/2 PGH/Elbys(x2)
92/3 PGH/Coke
92/3 PGH/FoodStickers
92/3 PGH/Foodland 6
93/4 PGH/Foodland 25
94/5 PGH 6
96/7 PGH/Tribune
92/3 STL/UpperDeck 16

MULLER, GREG
94/5 DEL 298
95/6 DEL 319

MULLER, JOSEF
96/7 DEL 193

MULLER, KIRK
95/6 Aces 2 (Spades)
90/1 Bowman 82
91/2 Bowman 274
92/3 Bowman 138, 236
93/4 Donruss 177
94/5 Donruss 255
95/6 Donruss 129
96/7 Donruss 161
97/8 Donruss 38
96/7 D.CdnIce 47, -OCanada 10
97/8 D.CanadianIce 47
95/6 DonrussElite 54
97/8 DonrussPreferred 120
96/7 Duracell DC10
93/4 EASports 69
94/5 Flair 89
96/7 Flair-Now&Then 2
94/5 Fleer 104
95/6 FleerMetal 91
96/7 FleerNHLPicks 138
92/3 FleerUltra 107
93/4 FleerUltra 21, -AS 9
94/5 FleerUltra 313
95/6 FleerUltra 268
95/6 FleerUltra 96
88/9 FritoLay
91/2 Gillette 21
93/4 HockeyWit 19
95/6 Hoyle'EAST 4 (Diamonds)
95/6 KennerSLU (U)
90/1 Kraft 37, 88
91/2 Kraft 12
93/4 KraftDinner, -Cutout
94/5 Kraft-HockeyHeroes
93/4 Leaf 182

94/5 Leaf 163
95/6 Leaf 41
96/7 Leaf 72
94/5 LeafLimited 37
97/8 Limited 156
92/3 McDonalds McD23
93/4 McDonalds McD20
96/7 MetalUniverse 150
85/6 OPC/Topps 84
86/7 OPC/Topps 94
87/8 OPC/Topps 157
88/9 OPC/Topps 84, F
89/90 OPC/Topps 117
90/1 OPC/Topps 245, T-TL 7
91/2 OPC/Topps 22, 191
92/3 O-Pee-Chee 327
90/1 opcPremier 78
91/2 opcPremier 86, 145
85/6 opcSticker 64
86/7 opcSticker 201/74
87/8 opcSticker 65
88/9 opcSticker 75
89/90 opcSticker 83/224
98/9 Pacific 227
97/8 PacificCrown 217
97/8 PacificInvincible 62
97/8 PacificParamount 82
87/8 PaniniSticker 70, 79
88/9 PaniniSticker 275
89/90 PaniniSticker 251
90/1 PaniniSticker 73
91/2 PaniniSticker 219
92/3 PaniniSticker 148
93/4 PaniniSticker 14
94/5 PaniniSticker 12
95/6 PaniniSticker 91
96/7 PaniniSticker 212
97/8 PaniniSticker 58
91/2 Parkhurst 89
92/3 Parkhurst 83, 504, CP5
93/4 Parkhurst 378
94/5 Parkhurst V4
95/6 Parkhurst 129, 474
94/5 ParkieSE 88
91/2 Pinnacle 3
92/3 Pinnacle 111
93/4 Pinnacle 180
94/5 Pinnacle 82, GR7, NL2
96/7 Pinnacle 147
97/8 Pinnacle 190
97/8 PinnacleBeAPlayer 121
97/8 PinnacleCertified 117
97/8 PinnacleInside 108
95/6 PinnacleZenith 45
95/6 Playoff 65
96/7 Playoff 344
94/5 POG 137
95/6 POG 168
94/5 Post
93/4 PowerPlay 131
93/4 Prmr 509, -Black(OPC) 24
94/5 Premier 305, -GoToGuy 11
95/6 ProMagnet 52
90/1 ProSet 172, 371
91/2 ProSet 134, 412
92/3 ProSet 87
91/2 PSPlatinum 66
90/1 Score 160, -HotCards 71
91/2 Score(CDN) 110, 361, 614
91/2 Score(U.S) 110, 331, 64T
92/3 Score 225,-Sharpshooter29
93/4 Score 234, DD6, -P.AS 7
94/5 Score 146, CI10
95/6 Score 96
96/7 Score 103
97/8 Score 105
92/3 SeasonsPatch 25
94/5 Select 107
95/6 SelectCertified 103
95/6 SkyBoxEmotion 106
95/6 SkyBoxImpact 103
96/7 SkyBoxImpact 127
94/5 SP 68
95/6 SP 142
96/7 SP 156
95/6 Summit 121
95/6 SuperSticker 74
90/1 Topps TeamLeader 7
92/3 Topps 490
95/6 Topps 115
98/9 Topps 145
94/5 T.Finest 44, -BBest(B) 10
91/2 ToppsStadiumClub 193
92/3 ToppsStadiumClub 387
93/4 T.StadiumClub 67, -AllStar
94/5 ToppsStadiumClub 130
95/6 ToppsStadiumClub 177
90/1 UpperDeck 267, 311
91/2 UpperDeck 149, 519
92/3 UD 180, -LockerAS 9
93/4 UpperDeck 148, SP-80
94/5 UpperDeck 66, IG9, SP40
95/6 UpperDeck SE52
96/7 UpperDeck 165
97/8 UpperDeck 76
94/5 UDBeAPlayer R3, -Aut. 40
95/6 UDCollChoice 142
96/7 UDCollChoice 259
97/8 UDCollChoice 98
97/8 FLA/WinnDixie
91/2 MTL
92/3 MTL
92/3 MTL/OPC 26
93/4 MTL
93/4 MTL/Molson
94/5 MTL
84/5 N.J.
85/6 N.J.
86/7 N.J./SOBER
88/9 N.J./Caretta
89/90 N.J.
90/1 N.J.
81/2 Kingston 15

MULLER, MIKE
93/4 ClassicProspects 71
91/2 Minnesota

MULLER, ZDENEK
94/5 APS 282

MULLIN, KORY
91/2 SketchWHL 301
95/6 StJohns
93/4 Tacoma

MULLIN, MATTHEW
91/2 SketchOHL 181
94/5 Slapshot(Sudbury) 21
92/3 Windsor 29

MULOIN, WAYNE
70/1 DadsCookies
70/1 EddieSargent 135
70/1 Esso Stamp
75/6 opcWHA 102
72/3 Cleveland

MULROY, TERRY
74/5 SiouxCity

MULTANEN, JARI
93/4 Jyvas-Hyva 258
93/4 Sisu 299

MULVENNA, GLENN
92/3 opcPremier 97
88/9 ProCards(Muskegon)
89/90 ProCards(IHL) 162
90/1 ProCards 387
91/2 ProCards 289
92/3 UpperDeck 490
87/8 Kamloops

MULVEY, GRANT
75/6 OPC/Topps 272
76/7 OPC/Topps 167
77/8 OPC/Topps 101
78/9 OPC/Topps 261
79/80 OPC/Topps 88
80/1 OPC/Topps 27, 212
81/2 OPC 60, Topps(W) 72
82/3 O-Pee-Chee 69
82/3 opcSticker 173
82/3 Post
79/80 CHI
80/1 CHI/4x6
80/1 CHI/5.5x8.5
81/2 CHI
82/3 CHI
83/4 N.J.

MULVEY, PAUL
78/9 WSH
79/80 WSH
80/1 WSH

MUNCK, JARI
92/3 Jyvas-Hyva 76
93/4 Jyvas-Hyva 20
93/4 Sisu 92

MUNDAY, TRAVIS
91/2 SketchWHL 355

MUNDY, BUSTER
36/7 WWGum (V356) 101

MUNGER, G.
84/5 Chicoutimi

MUNI, CRAIG
93/4 Donruss 405
94/5 Flair 21
92/3 FleerUltra 296
94/5 FleerUltra 265
94/5 Leaf 373
87/8 O-Pee-Chee 206
88/9 O-Pee-Chee 236
89/90 O-Pee-Chee 231, 303
90/1 O-Pee-Chee 423
91/2 OPC/Topps 479
87/8 opcStars 30
89/90 opcSticker 229/88
90/1 Panini(EDM) 15
87/8 PaniniSticker 258
89/90 PaniniSticker 80
90/1 PaniniSticker 217
91/2 PaniniSticker 133
93/4 Parkhurst 291
94/5 Pinnacle 143
91/2 Pinnacle 262
93/4 Pinnacle 298
97/8 PinnacleBeAPlayer 19
93/4 PowerPlay 299
94/5 Premier 216
90/1 ProSet 92
91/2 ProSet 382
90/1 Score 38
91/2 Score(CDN) 67, (U.S) 67
92/3 Score 81
93/4 Score 266, 579
94/5 Score 29
90/1 UpperDeck 21
91/2 UpperDeck 372
95/6 UDBeAPlayer 14
86/7 EDM
86/7 EDM/RedRooster
87/8 EDM
88/9 EDM
88/9 EDM/ActionMagazine 33
90/1 EDM/McGavins
91/2 EDM/IGA
92/3 EDM/IGA 16

MUNITZ, RAMON
79 PaniniSticker 372

MURANO, ERIC
90/1 ProCards 338
91/2 ProCards 606
91/2 UpperDeck 50
92/3 Hamilton

MURANO, ERIC
90/1 ProCards 338
91/2 ProCards 606
91/2 UpperDeck 50
92/3 Hamilton

MUNRO, BRYAN
92/3 BCJHL 30

MUNRO, DUNCAN
25-27 Anonymous 91
24/5 Champs (C144)
25 Dominion 57
26 Dominion 12
24/5 MapleCrispettes (V130) 1
24/5 (V145-2) 34
25 Willards 52

MUNRO, GERRY
25-27 Anonymous 62
24/5 Champs (C144)
24/5 (V145-2) 33

MURCHESON, BRENT
92/3 BCJHL 97

MURDOCH, BOB J.
94/5 DEL 296
95/6 DEL 193
96/7 DEL 336
72-84 Dernière 72/3
74/5 Loblaws
74/5 OPC/Topps 194
75/6 OPC/Topps 33
76/7 OPC/Topps 74
77/8 O-Pee-Chee 371
78/9 OPC/Topps 91
79/80 OPC 351, 276
81/2 O-Pee-Chee 48
82/3 O-Pee-Chee 53
80/1 Pepsi Cap
82/3 Post
90/1 ProSet 377, 680
78/9 ATL/Coke
79/80 ATL
79/80 ATL/B&W
80/1 CGY
81/2 CGY
85/6 CGY/RedRooster
86/7 CGY/RedRooster
87/8 CHI/Coke
72/3 MTL
89/90 WPG/Safeway
90/1 WPG/IGA

MURDOCH, BOB L.
76/7 OPC/Topps 54, OPC 383
77/8 OPC/Topps 39

MURDOCH, DON
77/8 OPC/Topps 244,-Glossy 12
78/9 OPC/Topps 11
79/80 OPC/Topps 168
80/1 OPC/Topps 203
80/1 Pepsi Cap
80/1 EDM/Zellers
88/9 EDM/ActionMagazine 120

MURDOCH, JOHN MURRAY
33/4 Anonymous (V129) 29
34-43 BeeHives(NYR)
33/4 CndGum (V252)
24/5 Crescent Falcons 4
33-35 DiamondMatch
36-39 DiamondMatch (1), (2), (3)
33/4 OPC (V304A) 37
33/4 WWGum (V357) 68
36/7 WWGum (V356) 88

MURNAGHAN, KEVIN
95/6 Slapshot 359

MURPHY, CORY
95/6 Slapshot 358
92/3 Ottawa67s

MURPHY, DAN
91/2 AvantGardeBCJ 48
92/3 BCJHL 110
92/3 Maine (1) 8, (2) 22
91/2 Nainamo

MURPHY, GORD
90/1 Bowman 106
91/2 Bowman 235
92/3 Bowman 315
93/4 Donruss 131
94/5 Donruss 55
95/6 Donruss 161
93/4 EASports 50, 197, 207
94/5 Flair 66
94/5 Fleer 81
96/7 FleerNHLPicks 162
92/3 FleerUltra 253
93/4 FleerUltra 329
94/5 FleerUltra 83
95/6 FleerUltra 61, 243
93/4 Leaf 284
94/5 Leaf 250
95/6 Leaf 146
90/1 OPC/Topps 302
91/2 OPC/Topps 89
92/3 O-Pee-Chee 101
89/90 opcStickFS 12
97/8 PacificRegime 88
89/90 PaniniSticker 303
90/1 PaniniSticker 115
91/2 PaniniSticker 230
94/5 PaniniSticker 71
95/6 PaniniSticker 77
91/2 Parkhurst 227
93/4 Parkhurst 345
95/6 Parkhurst 357
91/2 Pinnacle 140
92/3 Pinnacle 132
93/4 Pinnacle 380, -Expansion 2
94/5 Pinnacle 141
95/6 Pinnacle 181
96/7 PinnacleBeAPlayer 44
95/6 Playoff 262
94/5 POG 112
95/6 POG 122
93/4 PowerPlay 99
93/4 Premier 465
94/5 Premier 19
90/1 ProSet 221
91/2 ProSet 171
92/3 ProSet 11
91/2 PSPlatinum 156
90/1 Score 117, -HotCards 56
90/1 Score-YoungStar 13
91/2 Score(CDN) 43, (U.S) 43
92/3 Score 29
93/4 Score 95, 548
94/5 Score 117
95/6 Score 104
95/6 SkyBoxEmotion 70
95/6 SkyBoxImpact 68
92/3 Topps 114
91/2 ToppsStadiumClub 248
92/3 ToppsStadiumClub 445
93/4 ToppsStadiumClub 439
94/5 ToppsStadiumClub 128
90/1 UpperDeck 86
91/2 UpperDeck 392
93/4 UpperDeck 521
94/5 UpperDeck 438
95/6 UpperDeck 21
96/7 UpperDeck 68
97/8 UpperDeck 285
95/6 UDCollChoice 190
91/2 BOS/SportsAction
96/7 FLA/WinnDixie
97/8 FLA/WinnDixie
89/90 PHA
90/1 PHA
91/2 PHA/JCPenney

MURPHY, J.
91/2 Sketch 291

MURPHY, JAY
94/5 Richmond
95/6 Richmond

MURPHY, JODIE
93/4 SSMarie 18

MURPHY, JOE
90/1 Bowman 196
91/2 Bowman 109
92/3 Bowman 174
93/4 Donruss 66
94/5 Donruss 38
95/6 Donruss 146
96/7 Donruss 144
96/7 DonrussElite 102
94/5 Flair 34
94/5 Fleer 42
95/6 FleerMetal 25
92/3 FleerUltra 63
93/4 FleerUltra 163
95/6 FleerUltra 217
93/4 Leaf 179
94/5 Leaf 284
95/6 Leaf 109
96/7 Leaf 185
96/7 Maggers 29
96/7 MetalUniverse 134
90/1 OPC/Topps 302
91/2 OPC/Topps 48
92/3 O-Pee-Chee 100
97/8 PacificCrown 150
97/8 PacificParamount 160
90/1 Panini(EDM) 16
92/3 PaniniSticker 100
94/5 PaniniSticker 129
95/6 PaniniSticker 162
97/8 PaniniSticker 171
91/2 Parkhurst 52
92/3 Parkhurst 273
93/4 Parkhurst 38, F8
94/5 Parkhurst 44
95/6 Parkhurst 309
91/2 Pinnacle 206
92/3 Pinnacle 23
93/4 Pinnacle 45
94/5 Pinnacle 68
95/6 Pinnacle 8
96/7 PinnacleBeAPlayer 28
95/6 PinnacleZenith 4
94/5 POG 67
95/6 POG 66
93/4 PowerPlay 53
93/4 Premier 273, -Finest 8
94/5 Premier 34
95/6 ProMagnet 3
90/1 ProSet 93
91/2 ProSet 68
92/3 ProSet 49
91/2 PSPlatinum 171
90/1 Score 293
91/2 Score(CDN) 519, (U.S) 299
92/3 Score 321
93/4 Score 348, (US) DD6
94/5 Score 170
95/6 Score 110
96/7 Score 100
97/8 Score 163
97/8 Score(STL) 3
94/5 Select 44
95/6 SelectCertified 50
95/6 SkyBoxEmotion 30
95/6 SkyBoxImpact 30
94/5 SP 27
96/7 SP 132
95/6 Summit 10
96/7 Summit 86
95/6 SuperSticker 24
92/3 Topps 38
95/6 Topps 280
95/6 ToppsFinestS 58
96/7 ToppsNHLPicks 143
91/2 ToppsStadiumClub 313
92/3 ToppsStadiumClub 34
95/6 ToppsStadiumClub 52
90/1 UpperDeck 190
91/2 UpperDeck 474
92/3 UpperDeck 152
93/4 UpperDeck 47
94/5 UpperDeck 416
95/6 UpperDeck 278
96/7 UpperDeck 325
97/8 UpperDeck 349
95/6 UDCollChoice 156
94/5 UDBeAPlayer-Aut. 87
96/7 UDCollChoice 48
97/8 UDCollChoice 231
93/4 CHI/Coke
87/8 DET/Caesars
88/9 DET/Caesars
90/1 EDM/McGavins
91/2 EDM/IGA
97/8 S.J/PacificBellSheet

MURPHY, JONATHAN
93/4 Slapshot(Peterborough) 2
95/6 Slapshot 309

MURPHY, KEITH
91/2 AirCanadaSJHL 30, B40

MURPHY, KEVIN
92/3 Clarkson

MURPHY, LARRY
90/1 Bowman 177
91/2 Bowman 78
92/3 Bowman 153
95/6 Bowman 34
93/4 Donruss 263
94/5 Donruss 27
95/6 Donruss 366
96/7 Donruss 39
96/7 DonrussCanadianIce 86
95/6 DonrussElite 8
93/4 EASports 103
94/5 Flair 137
94/5 Fleer 166
96/7 Fleer 108, -Norris 9
95/6 FleerMetal 145
96/7 FleerNHLPicks 52
92/3 FleerUltra 167
93/4 FleerUltra 184
94/5 FleerUltra 168
95/6 FleerUltra 125, 314
96/7 FleerUltra 164
93/4 HockeyWit 48
91/2 Kraft 71
95/6 Kraft-Disk
93/4 Leaf 16, -GoldLeafAS 2
94/5 Leaf 249
95/6 Leaf 186
96/7 Leaf 100
94/5 LeafLimited 12
95/6 LeafLimited 97
96/7 MetalUniverse 151
97/8 Omega 85
81/2 OPC 148, 393, T.(W) 100
82/3 O-Pee-Chee 151, 158
83/4 O-Pee-Chee 159
84/5 O-Pee-Chee 204
85/6 O-Pee-Chee 236
86/7 OPC/Topps 185
87/8 OPC/Topps 133, H, T-AS 7
88/9 OPC/Topps 141
89/90 OPC/Topps 128
90/1 OPC/Topps 47
91/2 OPC/Topps 277
92/3 O-Pee-Chee 209
87/8 opcStars 31
81/2 opcSticker 239
82/3 opcSticker 232
83/4 opcSticker 298
84/5 opcSticker 127
87/8 opcSticker 119/131, 232/98
88/9 opcSticker 71/200
89/90 opcSticker 199/55
98/9 Pacific 203
98/9 PacificParamount 80
97/8 PacificRevolution 49
87/8 PaniniSticker 176
88/9 PaniniSticker 367
89/90 PaniniSticker 108
90/1 PaniniSticker 251
91/2 PaniniSticker 270
92/3 PaniniSticker 228
93/4 PaniniSticker 86, 135
94/5 PaniniSticker 80
95/6 PaniniSticker 209
96/7 PaniniSticker 216
91/2 Parkhurst 358
92/3 Parkhurst 137
93/4 Parkhurst 162
94/5 Parkhurst 179
95/6 Parkhurst 207, PP23
91/2 Pinnacle 143
92/3 Pinnacle 292
93/4 Pinnacle 52
94/5 Pinnacle 215
96/7 Pinnacle 189
97/8 PinnacleBeAPlayer 141
95/6 PinnacleZenith 106
96/7 PinnacleZenith 111
95/6 Playoff 97
94/5 POG 191
95/6 POG 266, 019
93/4 PowerPlay 193
93/4 Premier 173, 189
93/4 Premier-Black(Topps) 23
94/5 Premier 10, 492
90/1 ProSet 143
91/2 ProSet 193
92/3 ProSet 146
91/2 PSPlatinum 213
83/4 PuffySticker 9
90/1 Score 206
91/2 Score(CDN) 31, (U.S) 31
92/3 Score 45
93/4 Score 23
94/5 Score 5, -Promo 5
95/6 Score 260
96/7 Score 75
97/8 Score(DET) 8
94/5 Select 143
95/6 SelectCertified 90
94 Semic 81
95 Semic 83
92 SemicSticker 82
93 SemicSticker 191
95/6 SkyBoxEmotion 173
95/6 SkyBoxImpact 163
96/7 SkyBoxImpact 128, -Fox 15
83/4 SouhaitsRen.KeyChain
95/6 SP 143
96/7 SP 154
95/6 Summit 126
96/7 Summit 11
95/6 SuperSticker 121
91 TeamCanada
96/7 TeamOut
92/3 Topps 447
95/6 Topps 255
98/9 Topps 33, B9, SB26
94/5 ToppsFinest-Ring 18
95/6 ToppsFinest 42
91/2 ToppsStadiumClub 112
92/3 ToppsStadiumClub 375
93/4 ToppsStadiumClub 283
95/6 ToppsStadiumClub 144
93/4 TSC-MembersOnly 32
95/6 TSC-MembersOnly 16
90/1 UpperDeck 229
91/2 UpperDeck 302
92/3 UpperDeck 241
93/4 UpperDeck 374

94/5 UpperDeck 99
95/6 UpperDeck 86, H38, SE170
96/7 UpperDeck 161, X39
93/4 UDBAP-Roots 8
94/5 UDBAP R170, -Aut. 148
98/9 UDChoice 70
95/6 UDCollChoice 151, 386
96/7 UDCollChoice 265
96 Wien 82
91/2 PGH/Elbys
91/2 PGH/Topps
91/2 PGH/Foodland 10
92/3 PGH/Coke
92/3 PGH/FoodStickers
92/3 PGH/Foodland 10
93/4 PGH/Foodland 13
94/5 PGH 24
84/5 WSH/PizzaHut
85/6 WSH/PizzaHut
86/7 WSH/Kodak
87/8 WSH
87/8 WSH/Kodak
87/8 WSH/Police
88/9 WSH
88/9 WSH/Smokey

MURPHY, MIKE
72/3 EddieSargent 195
74/5 Loblaws
72/3 OPC 215
74/5 OPC/Topps 224
75/6 OPC/Topps 52
76/7 OPC/Topps 21
77/8 OPC/Topps 22
78/9 OPC/Topps 229
79/80 OPC/Topps 31
80/1 O-Pee-Chee 286
81/2 OPC 149, Topps(W) 101
81/2 opcSticker 241
79 PaniniSticker 69
90/1 ProCards 335
83/4 SouhaitsRen.KeyChain
80/1 L.A.
71/2 STL
72/3 STL
72/3 STL/8"x10"

MURPHY, ROB
90/1 Panini(VAN) 16
90/1 OPC/Topps 37
89/90 ProCards(IHL) 172
91/2 ProCards 607
90/1 ProSet 546
92/3 ProSet 121
91/2 ScoreCDN 397
92/3 UpperDeck 108
90/1 VAN/Mohawk
91/2 VAN
93/4 Phoenix

MURPHY, RON
52/3 AnonymousOHL 61
45-64 BeeHives(CHI), (NYR)
64-67 BeeHives(DET)
62 CeramicTiles
64/5 CokeCap DET-12
65/6 CocaCola
68/9 O-Pee-Chee 139
69/70 O-Pee-Chee 204
54/5 Parkhurst 76
93/4 Parkie(56/7) 102
94/5 Parkie(64/5) 48
95/6 Parkie(66/7) 15
60/1 ShirriffCoin 75
61/2 ShirriffCoin 36
57/8 Topps 29
58/9 Topps 59
59/60 Topps 66
60/1 Topps 41
61/2 Topps 34, -Stamp
62/3 Topps 40
63/4 Topps 40
64/5 Topps 56
65/6 Topps 111
66/7 Topps 96, -USATest 33
67/8 Topps 100

MURPHY, TOD
91/2 AirCanadaSJHL D22
92/3 MPSPhotoSJHL 116

MURRAY, ADAM
91/2 SketchWHL 29

MURRAY, ADRIAN
93/4 Slapshot(Peterborough) 26
95/6 Slapshot 310

MURRAY, AL
34-43 BeeHives(NYA)
36-39 DiamondMatch (1), (2), (3)
36/7 OPC (V304D) 104
36/7 WWGum (V356) 54

MURRAY, ANDY
89/90 PHA
93/4 WPG/Ruffles

MURRAY, BOB F.
76/7 O-Pee-Chee 309
77/8 OPC/Topps 12
78/9 OPC/Topps 89
79/80 OPC/Topps 55
80/1 OPC/Topps 181
81/2 OPC 61, Topps(W) 73
82/3 O-Pee-Chee 70
83/4 O-Pee-Chee 108
84/5 OPC 41, Topps 32
85/6 OPC/Topps 114
86/7 OPC/Topps 64
87/8 OPC/Topps 156
90/1 OPC/Topps 138
81/2 opcSticker 119
83/4 opcSticker 109
84/5 opcSticker 26
87/8 PaniniSticker 223
88/9 PaniniSticker 22
90/1 Score 376
83/4 7ElevenCokeCup
83/4 SouhaitsRen.KeyChain
79/80 CHI
80/1 CHI/4x6
81/2 CHI
82/3 CHI
83/4 CHI
86/7 CHI/Coke
87/8 CHI/Coke
89/90 CHI/Coke

MURRAY, BOB J.
74/5 Loblaws
74/5 O-Pee-Chee 336
75/6 O-Pee-Chee 386
76/7 O-Pee-Chee 363
75/6 VAN/RoyalBank
76/7 VAN/RoyalBank

MURRAY, BRYAN
90/1 ProCards 664
90/1 DET/Caesars
91/2 DET/Caesars
97/8 FLA/WinnDixie
82/3 WSH
86/7 WSH/Kodak
86/7 WSH/Police
87/8 WSH/Kodak
88/9 WSH/Smokey

MURRAY, CHRIS
95/6 FutureLegends 12
97/8 PacificRegime 39
96/7 MTL
94/5 Fredericton
95/6 Fredericton
93/4 Kamloops

MURRAY, GLENN
91/2 Arena 14
91/2 Classic 15
91/2 C'FourSport 15, -Aut
92/3 ClassicProspects 89
93/4 Donruss 22
94/5 Donruss 246
93/4 Leaf 317
94/5 Leaf 4
97/8 Omega 110
92/3 O-Pee-Chee 74
92/3 opcPremier 52
98/9 Pacific 241
98/9 PacificParamount 105
92/3 PaniniSticker 142
91/2 Parkhurst 229
92/3 Parkhurst 9
93/4 Parkhurst 16
95/6 Parkhurst 440
94/5 ParkieSE 11
92/3 Pinnacle 224
94/5 Pinnacle 169
95/6 Playoff 299
94/5 POG 41

93/4 Premier 477
94/5 Premier 173
92/3 ProSet 222
92/3 Score 484
90/1 SketchMEM 111
90/1 SketchOHL 388
91/2 SketchOHL 245
91/2 StarPics 64
92/3 Topps 370
92/3 ToppsStadiumClub 393
93/4 ToppsStadiumClub 59
91/2 UltimateDP 15, -Aut 15
91/2 UltimateDP 71, 84
91/2 UpperDeck 69
92/3 UpperDeck 401
93/4 UpperDeck 189
94/5 UpperDeck 23
95/6 UpperDeck 394
97/8 UpperDeck 81
95/6 UDBeAPlayer 144
98/9 UDChoice 99
95/6 PGH/Foodland 2
89/90 Sudbury 6
90/1 Sudbury 13
91/2 Sudbury 21

MURRAY, HERMAN
36/7 WWGum (V356) 113

MURRAY, KEN
36/7 WWGum (V356) 109

MURRAY, MARTY
95/6 Bowman 152
93/4 Donruss CAN17
95/6 Donruss 284, -CdaJr 10
95/6 Donruss-Rated 11
97/8 Donruss 221
95/6 FleerMetal 185
96/7 FleerNHLPicks 178
95/6 FleerUltra 350
95/6 FutureLegends 35
97/8 Limited 39
95/6 Parkhurst 530
93/4 Pinnacle 477
94/5 Pinnacle 536
97/8 PinnacleBeAPlayer 199
95/6 PinnacleZenith 142
95/6 SelectCertified 141
91/2 SketchWHL 206
95/6 SkyBoxImpact 192
96/7 SkyBoxImpact 155
94/5 Slapshot(MEM) 48
94/5 SP 148
95/6 Summit 191
95/6 ToppsStadiumClub 198
95/6 Topps 338, CJ6
94/5 ToppsFinest 161
93/4 UpperDeck 550
95/6 UpperDeck 500
95/6 UDCollChoice 405
92/3 Brandon 17
95/6 SaintJohn

MURRAY, MIKE
94/5 Classic 114
95/6 Dayton
93/4 Knoxville
94/5 Knoxville 9
94/5 SaintJohn
95/6 SaintJohn

MURRAY, PAT
90/1 opcPremier 79
91/2 ProCards 276
90/1 ProSet 630
91/2 Score(CDN) 351, (U.S) 321
91/2 UpperDeck 451
94/5 Knoxville 20

MURRAY, REM
97/8 Donruss 127
96/7 DonrussCanadianIce 123
96/7 DonrussElite 145, -Aspir 22
97/8 DonrussPreferred 56
96/7 Flair 111
96/7 FleerUltra 60, -Rookies 14
95/6 FutureLegends 14
96/7 Got-UmHockeyGreatsCoin
97/8 Leaf 140
96/7 LeafPreferred 136
97/8 Limited 141, 173
96/7 MetalUniverse 188
97/8 PacificCrown 112
97/8 PcfcDynagon! 50,-Tand 50
97/8 PacificInvincible 57

97/8 Pinnacle 133
96/7 PinnacleBeAPlayer LTH5B
97/8 PinnacleInside 94
96/7 PinnacleZenith 146
97/8 Score 227
96/7 SelectCertified 119
96/7 SP 178
96/7 UpperDeck 261
97/8 UpperDeck 70
96/7 UDBlackDiamond 17
96/7 UDCollChoice 352
97/8 UDCollChoice 91
96/7 UpperDeck"Ice" 19
96/7 EDM
97/8 EDM
93/4 Mich.State

MURRAY, ROB
90/1 Bowman 74
95/6 FutureLegends 15
90/1 O-Pee-Chee 460
79 PaniniSticker 99
88/9 ProCards(Baltimore)
91/2 ProCards 164
90/1 ProSet 553
82 SemicSticker 103
90/1 WSH/Smokey
91/2 WPG/IGA
91/2 Moncton

MURRAY, SCOTT
91/2 AirCanadaSJHL B38

MURRAY, TERRY
73/4 OPC 259
82/3 Post
88/9 ProCards(Baltimore)
89/90 ProCards(AHL) 92
90/1 ProSet 679
81/2 WSH
82/3 WSH
89/90 WSH/Kodak
90/1 WSH/Kodak
94/5 PHA

MURRAY, TIM
92/3 MPSPhotoSJHL 110

MURRAY, TROY
90/1 Bowman 13
91/2 Bowman 388
92/3 Bowman 93
92/3 FleerUltra 242, 443
88/9 FritoLay
92/3 HumptyDumpty (1)
84/5 O-Pee-Chee 42
89/90 O-Pee-Chee 219
85/6 OPC/Topps 146
86/7 OPC/Topps 25
87/8 OPC/Topps 74
88/9 OPC/Topps 106
90/1 OPC/Topps 160
91/2 OPC/Topps 87
92/3 O-Pee-Chee 64
91/2 opcPremier 75
85/6 opcSticker 29/159
86/7 opcSticker 154/7, 189/49
87/8 opcSticker 79/212
88/9 opcSticker 10/139
89/90 opcSticker 11/151
87/8 PaniniSticker 227
88/9 PaniniSticker 27
89/90 PaniniSticker 48
90/1 PaniniSticker 200
91/2 PaniniSticker 17
92/3 PaniniSticker 57
94/5 PaniniSticker 104
91/2 Parkhurst 206
91/2 Pinnacle 33
92/3 Pinnacle 49
93/4 Pinnacle 318
94/5 Pinnacle 139
93/4 Premier 182
94/5 Premier 188
90/1 ProSet 57
91/2 ProSet 46, 514, 588
92/3 ProSet 215
91/2 PSPlatinum 247
90/1 Score 243
91/2 Score(CDN) 53, 585
91/2 Score(U.S) 53, 35T
92/3 Score 189
93/4 Score 272
92/3 SeasonsPatch 58
92/3 Topps 284

91/2 ToppsStadiumClub 167
92/3 ToppsStadiumClub 31
93/4 ToppsStadiumClub 230
90/1 UpperDeck 112
91/2 UpperDeck 565
92/3 UpperDeck 129
94/5 UDBeAPlayer-Aut. 176
82/3 CHI
83/4 CHI
86/7 CHI/Coke
87/8 CHI/Coke
88/9 CHI/Coke
89/90 CHI/Coke
90/1 CHI/Coke
93/4 CHI/Coke
94/5 OTT/Bell
91/2 WPG/IGA

MURTO, MATTI
72 Hellas 7
74 Hellas 12
70/1 Kuvajulkaisut 70, 111
80/1 Mallasjuoma 13
72 Panda
72 SemicSticker 83
74 SemicSticker 86
96/7 Sisu 197
78/9 SM-Liiga 37
77-80 Sportscaster 41-961
71/2 WilliamsFIN 71, 120
72/3 WilliamsFIN 67, 90
73/4 WilliamsFIN 136

MURTOVAARA, PETRI
95/6 Sisu 241

MURZYN, DANA
91/2 Bowman 412
92/3 Bowman 71
93/4 Donruss 348
93/4 FleerUltra 441
93/4 Leaf 292
86/7 OPC/Topps 58
87/8 OPC/Topps 138
90/1 OPC/Topps 304
92/3 O-Pee-Chee 241
97/8 PacificDynag-BestKept 97
90/1 Panini(CGY) 12
87/8 PaniniSticker 42
93/4 Parkhurst 486
91/2 Pinnacle 260
92/3 Pinnacle 172
93/4 Pinnacle 273
94/5 Pinnacle 198
96/7 PinnacleBeAPlayer 160
93/4 Premier 311
90/1 ProSet 41
91/2 ProSet 498
90/1 Score 274
91/2 Score(CDN) 231, (U.S) 357
92/3 Score 168
93/4 Score 298
94/5 Score 134
92/3 Topps 194
92/3 ToppsStadiumClub 353
90/1 UpperDeck 348
87/8 CGY/RedRooster
90/1 CGY/McGavins
85/6 HFD/JuniorWhalers
86/7 HFD/JuniorWhalers
87/8 HFD/JuniorWhalers
91/2 VAN
92/3 VAN/RoadTrip
93/4 VAN/Coins
94/5 VAN
95/6 VAN/Building 5
96/7 VAN
96/7 VAN/IGA

MUSAKKA, JOAKIM
94/5 ElitSet 282
95/6 ElitSet 31

MUSIAL, DAVID
94/5 DEL 292
95/6 DEL 282

MUSIL, FRANTISEK
94/5 APS 75
91/2 Bowman 259
92/3 Bowman 157
92/3 FleerUltra 270
93/4 FleerUltra 283
94/5 FleerUltra 31
93/4 Leaf 236
94/5 Leaf 545

89/90 O-Pee-Chee 217
91/2 OPC/Topps 68
92/3 O-Pee-Chee 66
97/8 PacificRegime 136
87/8 PaniniSticker 292
88/9 PaniniSticker 87
90/1 PaniniSticker 258
97/8 PaniniSticker 44
95 PaniniWorlds 197
91/2 Pinnacle 282
92/3 Pinnacle 51
93/4 Pinnacle 101
94/5 Pinnacle 64
93/4 PowerPlay 307
93/4 Premier 229
94/5 Premier 258
90/1 ProSet 425
91/2 ProSet 368
90/1 Score 223, 19T
91/2 Score(CDN) 142, (U.S) 142
92/3 Score 83
93/4 Score 303
94/5 Score 139
95 Semic 162
92 SemicSticker 126
92/3 Topps 142
91/2 ToppsStadiumClub 235
92/3 ToppsStadiumClub 67
93/4 ToppsStadiumClub 169
90/1 UpperDeck 383
96 Wien 111
90/1 CGY/McGavins
91/2 CGY/IGA
92/3 CGY/IGA 16
87/8 MIN
88/9 MIN/AmericanDairy
95/6 OTT
96/7 OTT/PizzaHut

MUSTANIEMI, ARI
70/1 Kuvajulkaisut 374

MUSTONEN, JOUNI
91/2 Jyvas-Hyva 39

MUSTONEN, PASI
80/1 Mallasjuoma 59

MUTCH, TOM
91/2 ProCards 441

MUTTON, JIM
87/8 Kitchener 20

MUUKKONEN, JARMO
92/3 Jyvas-Hyva 118
93/4 Sisu 267
94/5 Sisu 81
95/6 Sisu 90
96/7 Sisu 85

MUZZATTI, JASON
92/3 Classic 114
92 ClassicFourSport 221
94/5 ClassicImages 52
96/7 Flair 42
93/4 FleerUltra 284
94/5 Leaf 470
97/8 PacificRegime 40
95/6 Parkhurst 362
96/7 PinnacleBeAPlayer 131
94/5 Premier 373
91/2 ProCards 592
97/8 Score(NYR) 17
93/4 UpperDeck 482
95/6 UpperDeck 491
96/7 UpperDeck 71
96/7 UDCollChoice 117
94/5 SaintJohn

MYDAN, SCOTT
90/1 SketchWHL 333
87/8 Portland
88/9 Portland
89/90 Portland

MYERS, JOHNNY
24/5 Crescent Falcons 11

MYERS, MIKE
92/3 CanadaNats

MYERS, MURRAY
73/4 VancouverBlazers

MYHRES, BRANTT
95/6 Donruss 45
95/6 FleerUltra 154
95/6 Leaf 75
97/8 PacificCrown 334

97/8 PinnacleBeAPlayer 203
90/1 SketchWHL 317
91/2 SketchWHL 360
95/6 UpperDeck 23
95/6 T.B/SkyBoxSportsCafe

MYHRES, DAVID
90/1 SketchOHL 111

MYLANDER, KEVIN
93/4 Seattle

MYLES, DAVID
91/2 SketchOHL 191
89/90 Windsor

MYLES, MARK
89/90 SketchOHL 113
90/1 SketchOHL 366

MYLES, VIC
34-43 BeeHives(NYR)

MYLLARI, RON
83/4 Ottawa

MYLLOYKOSKI, MIKKO
93/4 Jyvas-Hyva 45
93/4 Sisu 237
95/6 Sisu 22
96/7 Sisu 110

MYLLYMAKI, ARI
66/7 Champion 117

MYLLYNIEMI, MIKKO
66/7 Champion 50
65/6 Hellas 40

MYLLYS, JARMO
92/3 Bowman 125
94/5 ElitSet 260, -Foreign 4
95/6 ElitSet 74, 302, -Mega 12
95/6 ElitSet-Spidermen 8
95 FinnishAllStar 1
95 Globe 128
95 Hartwall
93/4 Jyvas-Hyva 224
95/6 Kelloggs PopUp 1
91/2 O-Pee-Chee 8S
90/1 opcPremier 80
91/2 opcPremier 15
95 PaniniWorlds 161
91/2 Parkhurst 162
91/2 ProCards 509
88/9 ProCards(Kalamazoo)
89/90 ProCards(IHL) 95
95/6 RadioCity
94 Semic 1, 332
95 Semic 35, 207
93 SemicSticker 47
93/4 Sisu 183
94/5 Sisu 160, -Specials 9
95/6 Sisu-GoldCards 2
95/6 SisuLimited 28
92/3 Topps 251
92/3 ToppsStadiumClub 113
91/2 UpperDeck 537
92/3 UpperDeck E19
95/6 udElite 113, 230
97/8 udSwedish 117, S7
96 Wien 1, AS1, SG3
91/2 S.J.

MYLNIKOV, SERGEI
90/1 O-Pee-Chee 445
89 SemicSticker 79
89/90 SovietNats
87/8 SovietStars
89/90 QUE
89/90 QUE/GeneralFoods
89/90 QUE/Police

MYLNIKOV, JEREMY
91/2 AirCanadaSJHL C5
96/7 Penascola 4

MYNTTINEN, MIKKO
70/1 Kuvajulkaisut 213
71/2 WilliamsFIN 136
72/3 WilliamsFIN 199
73/4 WilliamsFIN 160

MYRE, PHIL
72-84 Dernière 79/80
70/1 EddieSargent 112
71/2 EddieSargent 101
72/3 EddieSargent 2
70/1 Esso Stamp
74/5 Loblaws
72/3 OPC 43, Topps 109

74/5 OPC 270
73/4 OPC/Topps 77
75/6 OPC/Topps 308
76/7 OPC/Topps 17
77/8 OPC/Topps 193
78/9 OPC/Topps 87
79/80 OPC/Topps 189
80/1 OPC/Topps 8
71/2 TheTorontoSun
72/3 ATL
74/5 ATL
93/4 CHI/Coke
81/2 COL.R
89/90 DET/Caesars
69/70 MTL/ProStar
70/1 MTL
71/2 MTL
96/7 OTT/PizzaHut
78/9 STL

MYRRA, JOUKO
95/6 Sisu 147

MYRVOLD, ANDERS
95/6 Donruss 228
96/7 Leaf 220
95/6 Parkhurst 517
94 Semic 254
96/7 Summit 197

MYSHKIN, V.
80 SovietMintPics

MYSJKIN, VLADIMIR
82 SemicSticker 52

MYYRYLAINEN, REIJO
70/1 Kuvajulkaisut 283

N

NABOKOV, DMITRI
94/5 AutoPhonex 30
97/8 Bowman 119
98/9 Pacific 150
97/8 PacificRevolution 31
94/5 Select 159
95/6 SP 177
98/9 SPx"Finite" 19, 139
95/6 Tetrad 70
95/6 UpperDeck 552
97/8 UDBlackDiamond 85
98/9 UDChoice 50

NACHBAUER, DON
81/2 O-Pee-Chee 138
82/3 Post
88/9 ProCards(Hershey)
89/90 ProCards(AHL) 345
88/9 EDM/ActionMagazine 113

NACHTMANN, MARKUS
96/7 DEL 136

NADEAU, PATRICK
90/1 SketchQMJHL 91
91/2 SketchQMJHL 120

NADJIWAN, JAMIE
84/5 Sudbury 14

NADRACHAL, VLADIMIR
72 Panda

NAGIER, PAT
85/6 Kamloops

NAGLER, M.
95/6 DEL 13

NAGURNY, SHAWN
82/3 MedicineHat

NAGY, AARON
89/90 SketchOHL 32
90/1 SketchOHL 137
91/2 SketchOHL 365

NAGY RICHARD
91/2 AirCanadaSJHL 36, A38

NAGY, ZOLTAN
79 PaniniSticker 317

NAIDA, ANATOLI
94/5 APS 271
95/6 APS 263
91/2 O-Pee-Chee 56R

NAKAYAMA, IWAO
79 PaniniSticker 287

NAMESTNIKOV, YEVGENY (JOHN)
93/4 ClassicProspects 153
93/4 Donruss 502
94/5 Parkhurst 246
94/5 Score 218
95/6 Topps 46

NANNE, LOU
77/8 Coke Mini
71/2 EddieSargent 93
72/3 EddieSargent 111
70/1 Esso Stamp
74/5 Loblaws
69/70 O-Pee-Chee 198
71/2 OPC/Topps 240
72/3 OPC 10, Topps 93
73/4 OPC 246
74/5 OPC 325
75/6 OPC/Topps 143
76/7 OPC/Topps 173
77/8 OPC/Topps 36
71/2 TheTorontoSun
73/4 MIN
94/5 Minnesota

NANNE, MARY
88/9 ProCards(Saginaw)
89/90 ProCards(IHL) 54
90/1 ProCards 397

NANSEN, TOMAS
95/6 ElitSet 276

NANTAIS, RICHARD
76/7 O-Pee-Chee 357

NANZEN, TOMAS
94/5 ElitSet 56
90/1 SemicElitserien 12
91/2 SemicElitserien 209
95/6 udElite 157

NAPIER, MARK
72-84 Dernière 80/1
86/7 Kraft Sports 20
79/80 OPC/Topps 222
80/1 OPC/Topps 111
81/2 OPC 178, Topps 23
82/3 O-Pee-Chee 178, 189
83/4 O-Pee-Chee 182, 192
84/5 O-Pee-Chee 105
85/6 O-Pee-Chee 253
86/7 OPC/Topps 183
81/2 opcSticker 36
82/3 opcSticker 38, 39
83/4 opcSticker 64, 65
86/7 opcSticker 75/202
75/6 opcWHA 78
76/7 opcWHA 108
77/8 opcWHA 12
80/1 Pepsi Cap
82/3 Post
83/4 SouhaitsRen.KeyChain
87/8 BUF/BlueShield
87/8 BUF/WonderBread
88/9 BUF/BlueShield
88/9 BUF/WonderBread
89/90 BUF/Campbell
84/5 EDM
84/5 EDM/RedRooster
85/6 EDM/RedRooster
86/7 EDM
86/7 EDM/RedRooster
88/9 EDM/ActionMagazine 28
83/4 MIN
84/5 MIN
78/9 MTL
79/80 MTL
80/1 MTL
81/2 MTL
82/3 MTL
82/3 MTL/Steinberg

NAPOLITANO, JOSEPH
90/1 SketchQMJHL 249
91/2 SketchQMJHL 268
88/9 Richelieu

NARDELLA, ROBERT
96/7 DEL 163
96 Wien 177

NÄRHI, MARKKU
71/2 WilliamsFIN 307
72/3 WilliamsFIN 179

NÄRVÄNEN, REIJO
72/3 WilliamsFIN 273

NARVANMAA, JOUKO
91/2 Jyvas-Hyva 65
92/3 Jyvas-Hyva 178
93/4 Jyvas-Hyva 320
89 SemicSticker 35
93/4 Sisu 31

NASATO, LUC
94/5 Slapshot(Kitchener) 15

NASATO, LUBO
95/6 Slapshot 13

NASH, DON
52/3 AnonymousOHL 28

NASH, SHANE
95/6 Slapshot 194

NASH, TOM
89/90 ProCards(IHL) 18

NASH, TYSON
94/5 Slapshot(MEM) 14
93/4 Kamloops

NASHEIM, RICK
94 Semic 244
93 SemicSticker 282
96 Wien 216

NASIB, ERKAN
66/7 Champion 68
65/6 Hellas 122

NASLUND, MARKUS
91/2 Arena 12
91/2 Classic 13
91/2 ClassicFourSport 13
93/4 ClassicProspects 26
93/4 Donruss 269, -Rated 8
94/5 Donruss 51
93/4 FleerUltra 395, -Wave 10
94/5 FleerUltra 349
95/6 FleerUltra 291
95 Globe 43
93/4 Leaf 289, -Freshman 4
94/5 Leaf 211
97/8 Omega 233
98/9 Pacific 431
97/8 PacificCrown 128
94/5 PaniniSticker I
96/7 PaniniSticker 296
97/8 PaniniSticker 239
93/4 Parkhurst 245, C5
94/5 Parkhurst 287
95/6 Parkhurst 163
94/5 ParkieSE 136, seV4
93/4 Pinnacle 449, -SR8
94/5 Pinnacle 370
96/7 PinnacleBeAPlayer 123
93/4 PowerPlay 412
94/5 Premier 44
93/4 Score 597
97/8 Score 150
97/8 Score(VAN) 7
95/6 SelectCertified 106
90/1 SemicElitserien 23
91/2 SemicElitserien 214
92/3 SemicElitserien 240
92 SemicSticker 67
93 SemicSticker 14
95/6 SP 116
91/2 StarPics 41
95/6 ToppsFinest 154
93/4 ToppsStadiumClub 393
91/2 UltimateDP 13, 69, 76
91/2 UltimateDP 83, -Aut 83
92/3 UpperDeck 234
93/4 UpperDeck 500, SP123
94/5 UpperDeck 190, SP151
95/6 UpperDeck 73, SE67
96/7 UpperDeck 170
97/8 UpperDeck 173
94/5 UDBeAPlayer-Aut. 68
96/7 UDCollChoice 275
97/8 UDCollChoice 261
95/6 udElite 245
93/4 PGH/Foodland 20
94/5 PGH 15
95/6 PGH/Foodland 4
96/7 VAN
96/7 VAN/IGA

NASLUND, MATS
72-84 Dernière 83/4
95/6 Donruss 53
94/5 ElitSet-GoldCard 14
88/9 EssoAllStar
94/5 Fleer 14
88/9 FritoLay
95 Globe 72
86/7 Kraft Sports 33
89/90 Kraft 23
83/4 SouhaitsRen.KeyChain
83/4 O-Pee-Chee 193
84/5 O-Pee-Chee 267
85/6 OPC/Topps 102
86/7 OPC/Topps 161, T-AS 8
87/8 OPC/Topps 16, L
88/9 OPC/Topps 156
89/90 OPC/Topps 118, H
88/9 opcStars 26
83/4 opcSticker 71
84/5 opcSticker 155, 156
85/6 opcSticker 131
86/7 opcSticker 11, 122/182
87/8 opcSticker 6
88/9 opcSticker 50, 215/85
89/90 opcSticker 46
87/8 PaniniSticker 61
88/9 PaniniSticker 259, 406
89/90 PaniniSticker 234
90/1 PaniniSticker 62
91/2 Pinnacle 389
87/8 ProSportWatch CW17
83/4 PuffySticker 1
91/2 SemicElitserien 188, 349
92/3 SemicElitserien 220
82 SemicSticker 13
91 SemicSticker 49
92 SemicSticker 63
95/6 UDCollChoice 321
83/4 Vachon 50
82/3 MTL
82/3 MTL/Steinberg
83/4 MTL
84/5 MTL
85/6 MTL
85/6 MTL/Pennant
85/6 MTL/PepsiPlacemat
85/6? MTL/ProvigoPlacemat
85/6 MTL/ProvigoSticker
86/7 MTL
87/8 MTL
87/8 MTL/Kodak
87/8 MTL/Stickers 27, 45-48, 87
88/9 MTL
89/90 MTL
89/90 MTL/Figurine
89/90 MTL/Kraft

NASREDDINE, ALAIN
91/2 SketchQMJHL 277

NASREDDINE, SAMY
97/8 Bowman 45

NASSTROM, ANDERS
92/3 SemicElitserien 224

NASTER, MARIO
94/5 DEL 167

NATTRASS, RALPH
45-64 BeeHives(CHI)

NATTRESS, RIC
91/2 Bowman 266
92/3 Bowman 63
92/3 FleerUltra 374
88/9 O-Pee-Chee 238
90/1 O-Pee-Chee 459
92/3 O-Pee-Chee 98
88/9 opcSticker 91/219
90/1 Panini(CGY) 13
87/8 PaniniSticker 307
90/1 ProSet 426
91/2 ProSet 363
90/1 Score (CND) 302
91/2 Score(CDN) 249
92/3 Score 344
93/4 Score 381
92/3 Topps 219
91/2 ToppsStadiumClub 217
92/3 ToppsStadiumClub 328
87/8 CGY/RedRooster
90/1 CGY/McGavins
91/2 CGY/IGA
82/3 MTL
82/3 MTL/Steinberg
83/4 MTL
84/5 MTL
92/3 PHA/JCPenney
92/3 PHA/UD 21JAN93

NATYSHASK, MIKE
88/9 ProCards(Halifax)

NAUD, DANIEL
94/5 DEL 10

NAUD, SYLVAIN
89/90 SketchMEM 63
90/1 SketchQMJHL 52

NAUKKARINEN, SEPPO
65/6 Hellas 132

NAUMANN, ANDREAS
95/6 DEL 44
91/2 UD 678,-CzechWJC 41

NAUSS, RYAN
93/4 Slapshot(Peterborough) 19

NAVRATIL, MILAN
94/5 APS 12
95/6 APS 115

NAYLOR, MIKE
95/6 Dayton

NAZAROV, ANDREI
92/3 Classic 7
94/5 Classic 87
92/3 ClassicFourSport 157
94/5 ClassicImages 93
93/4 ClassicProspects 180
93/4 Donruss 490
95/6 Donruss 187
95/6 EdgeIce 146
94/5 Fleer 199
95/6 FleerMetal 132
94/5 FleerUltra 367
95/6 FleerUltra 303
94/5 Leaf 328
95/6 Leaf 131
97/8 PacificCrown 307
97/8 PaniniSticker 235
94/5 Parkhurst 216
95/6 Parkhurst 186
95/6 Pinnacle 190
94/5 Premier 461
92/3 RedAce(Blue) 26,(Violet) 26
94/5 Score 239
95/6 Topps 121
94/5 UpperDeck 270
95/6 UpperDeck S E164
96/7 UDCollChoice 242
92/3 S.J/PacificBell
96/7 S.J/PacificBellSheet
97/8 S.J/PacificBellSheet

NAZEN, TOMAS
92/3 SemicElitserien 232

NCWANA, LLEW
93/4 ThunderBay
94/5 ThunderBay
95/6 ThunderBay

NDUR, RUMUN
94/5 SigRookies 37
93/4 Slapshot(Guelph) 25
94/5 Slapshot(Guelph) 24
97/8 UpperDeck 184
95/6 Rochester

NEAL, FRANK
80/1 Mallasjuoma 3
78/9 SM-Liiga 113

NEAL, JAY
94/5 Toledo

NEALE, HARRY
97/8 Pinnacle -CBC Sports 9

NEATON, PAT
94/5 Classic 107, T53
93/4 ClassicProspects 10
95/6 EdgeIce 174
94/5 Leaf 469
95 PaniniWorlds 216
93/4 PowerPlay 413
94/5 Premier 483
93/4 Score 632
93/4 ClevelandLumberjacks

NECAS, ANTONIN
94/5 APS 164

NECKAR, STANISLAV
93/4 Classic 106
94/5 Classic-Autograph
95/6 Donruss 131
95/6 FleerUltra 113
95/6 Leaf 43
96/7 PaniniSticker 54
95/6 Parkhurst 148
95/6 Pinnacle 49
96/7 PinnacleBeAPlayer 184
95/6 POG 199
95/6 Topps 91
95/6 ToppsStadiumClub 112
94/5 UpperDeck 377
95/6 UpperDeck 68
95/6 UDCollChoice 170
96/7 UDCollChoice 185
94/5 OTT/Bell
95/6 OTT
96/7 OTT/PizzaHut
97/8 OTT

NEDOMA, MILAN
94/5 APS 102
95/6 APS 56
91/2 UD-CzechWJC 89

NEDOMANSKY, VACLAV
72 Hellas 92
74 Hellas 79
70/1 Kuvajulkaisut 55
69/70 MästarSerien 4, 5, 8
79/80 OPC/Topps 132
80/1 OPC/Topps 202
81/2 OPC 94, Topps(W) 94
81/2 opcSticker 125
74/5 opcWHA 49
75/6 opcWHA 27
76/7 opcWHA 1, 64, 120
72 Panda
82/3 Post
72 SemicSticker 33
74 SemicSticker 57, CL3
91 SemicSticker 249
77-9 Sportscaster 74-24, 20-469
71/2 WilliamsFIN 33
72/3 WilliamsFIN 16
73/4 WilliamsFIN 57
79/80 DET
80/1 DET
94/5 Knoxville 22
95/6 LasVegas

NEDVED, JAROSLAV
94/5 APS 76
95/6 APS 278
93/4 ClassicProspects 6

NEDVED, PETR
91/2 Bowman 324
92/3 Bowman 396
93/4 Donruss 356, 486
95/6 Donruss 252
96/7 Donruss 76
97/8 Donruss 152
97/8 DonrussCanadianIce 71
97/8 DonrussPreferred 33
96/7 Flair 79
94/5 Fleer 137
96/7 Fleer 88, 143, -ArtRoss 17
96/7 F.Picks-Jagged 9,-Fab 32
96/7 F.Picks-Fantasy 10
92/3 FleerUltra 226, -Import 17
93/4 FleerUltra 68
94/5 FleerUltra141,333,-Global 7
95/6 FleerUltra 292
95 Globe 97
97/8 KatchMedallion 120
90/1 Kraft 38
91/2 Kraft 11
93/4 Leaf 78
94/5 Leaf 360
95/6 Leaf 301
96/7 Leaf 71
97/8 Leaf 51
94/5 LeafLimited 67
96/7 LeafLimited 39, -Stubble 12
96/7 LeafPreferred 82, -Steel 56
97/8 Limited 156
96/7 Maggers 123
96/7 MetalUniverse 129
92/3 O-Pee-Chee 89
90/1 opcPremier 81
91/2 OPC/Topps 141
97/8 PacificCrown 13, -Slap 8A
97/8 PacificDynagon! 104
97/8 PcfcD-BstKpt 80,-Tandm 22
97/8 PacificInvincible 115
97/8 PacificParamount 153
97/8 PacificRegime 163
90/1 Panini(VAN) 17
91/2 PaniniSticker 49
92/3 PaniniSticker 31, 300
93/4 PaniniSticker 171
94/5 PaniniSticker 137
95/6 PaniniSticker 104
96/7 PaniniSticker 56
97/8 PaniniSticker 52
91/2 Parkhurst 178
92/3 Parkhurst 418, 449
94/5 Parkhurst V44
95/6 Parkhurst 438
94/5 ParkieSE 116
91/2 Pinnacle 192
92/3 Pinnacle 127, 249
93/4 Pinnacle 106
94/5 Pinnacle 58, WE18
96/7 Pinnacle 108
97/8 Pinnacle 124
97/8 PinnacleCertified 95
97/8 PinnacleInside 133
95/6 PinnacleZenith 103
96/7 P.Zenith 54, -Assailant 13
95/6 Playoff 300
94/5 POG 169
95/6 POG 212
93/4 PowerPlay 254, 490
93/4 Premier 6, -TmCanada 15
94/5 Premier 286
90/1 ProSet 402, 643
91/2 ProSet 235
90/1 Score 50T, -YoungStar 37
91/2 Score(CDN) 124, (US) 124
92/3 Score 101
93/4 Score 231, -International 22
94/5 Score CT2
95/6 Score 220
96/7 Score 38
97/8 Score 143
97/8 Score(PGH) 6
94/5 Select 120
95/6 SkyBoxEmotion 140
95/6 SkyBoxImpact 133
96/7 SkBxImpact 103, -Blade 16
96/7 SP 128
95/6 Summit 91
96/7 Summit 148
92/3 Topps 422
95/6 Topps 304
94/5 ToppsFinest 101
96/7 ToppsNHLPicks 37
91/2 ToppsStadiumClub 280
92/3 ToppsStadiumClub 457
93/4 ToppsStadiumClub 18
94/5 ToppsStadiumClub 205
95/6 ToppsStadiumClub 64
90/1 UpperDeck 351, 353
91/2 UpperDeck 227, E5
92/3 UpperDeck 263
94/5 UpperDeck 164, SP141
95/6 UpperDeck 462, SE154
96/7 UpperDeck 134, 26B
97/8 UpperDeck 137
95/6 UDBeAPlayer 156
96/7 UDBlackDiamond 95
95/6 UDCollChoice 323
96/7 UDCollChoice 219, 328
97/8 UDCollChoice 209, SQ3
96/7 UpperDeck"Ice" 56
95/6 PGH/Foodland 17
96/7 PGH/FotoPuck
90/1 VAN/Mohawk
91/2 VAN
92/3 VAN/RoadTrip

NEDVED, ZDENEK
95/6 Bowman 91
95 Classic 97
95/6 Donruss 157, -Rated 5
96/7 Leaf 230
93/4 Parkhurst 518
95/6 Parkhurst 254
96/7 Pinnacle 243
93/4 Slapshot(Sudbury) 9
94/5 Slapshot(Sud.) 8, -Promo
96/7 Summit 193
95/6 ToppsStadiumClub 139
95/6 UpperDeck 441
92/3 Sudbury 11
93/4 Sudbury 10

NEEDHAM, BILL
72/3 CLEV/Linnet
60/1 Cleveland

NEEDHAM, BOB
92/3 BCJHL 54

NEEDHAM, MIKE
92/3 Classic 108
92/3 FleerUltra 380
93/4 Leaf 214
92/3 opcPremier 106
92/3 Parkhurst 370
93/4 Premier 472
90/1 ProCards 375
91/2 ProCards 297
89/90 SketchMEM 10
93/4 ToppsStadiumClub 452
92/3 UpperDeck 489
92/3 PGH/Coke
93/4 PGH/Foodland 15
95/6 Adirondack
87/8 Kamloops
88/9 Kamloops
89/90 Kamloops

NEELY, BOB
74/5 Loblaws
74/5 O-Pee-Chee 272
75/6 OPC/Topps 245
76/7 OPC/Topps 194
77/8 O-Pee-Chee 347
73/4 TOR
74/5 TOR
75/6 TOR
76/7 TOR
77/8 TOR

NEELY, CAM
91/2 AceNoveltyMVP Pin 71002
95/6 Aces 10 (Spades)
90/1 Bowman 29
91/2 Bowman 348, 366
92/3 Bowman 62
95/6 Bowman 17
94/5 Classic-Autograph
95/6 CoolTrade 1
93/4 Donruss 29, -Elite U4
94/5 Donruss 269, -Dominator 4
95/6 Donruss 165
96/7 Donruss 205
95/6 DonrussElite 14
93/4 EASports 11, 212
94/5 Flair 11
94/5 Fleer 15, -Headliner 8
95/6 FleerMetal 9, -Iron 9
92/3 FleerUltra 7
93/4 FleerUltra 138
94/5 FleerUltra 13, -AW 8
94/5 FU-Power 6, -RedLight 6
95/6 FU 12, -Crease 12, -Red 7
88/9 FritoLay
93/4 HockeyWit 36
95/6 Hoyle'EAST 5(Diamonds)
92/3 HumptyDumpty (2)
95/6 KennerSLU
89/90 Kraft 56
90/1 Kraft 39, 84
94/5 Kraft-AwardWinner
95/6 Kraft-Ticket
93/4 Leaf 99
94/5 Leaf 267, -GoldStar 9
95/6 Leaf 113
96/7 Leaf 86
94/5 LeafLimited 49
95/6 LeafLimited 81
96/7 Maggers 15
91/2 McDonalds McD1, McH-1
94/5 McDonalds 22
97 OmniTel.PhoneCard
84/5 O-Pee-Chee 327
85/6 O-Pee-Chee 228
86/7 O-Pee-Chee 250
87/8 OPC/Topps 69
88/9 OPC/Topps 58, T-AS
89/90 OPC/Topps 15, K
90/1 OPC/Topps 69, 201, T-TL 3
91/2 OPC/Topps 170, 192, 266
92/3 O-Pee-Chee 174
90/1 opcPremier 82
91/2 opcPremier 107
88/9 opcStars 27
87/8 opcSticker 143
88/9 opcSticker 22, 167
89/90 opcSticker 33
87/8 PaniniSticker 10
88/9 PaniniSticker 213
89/90 PaniniSticker 182, 192
90/1 PaniniSticker 9, 327
91/2 PaniniSticker 176, 332
92/3 PaniniSticker 143
93/4 PaniniSticker 3
94/5 PaniniSticker 3, 238
95/6 PaniniSticker 8, 153
96/7 PaniniSticker 3
92/3 Parkhurst 248, CP14
93/4 Parkhurst 10
94/5 Parkhurst 11, V64
95/6 Parkhurst 12
91/2 Pinnacle 78, B6
92/3 Pinnacle 25, 232
93/4 Pinnacle 30
94/5 Pinnacle 65, BR12
94/5 Pinnacle GR17, TP12
95/6 Pinn.-Clear 5,-First 5,-Full 1
96/7 Pinnacle 136
95/6 PinnacleFANtasy 1
95/6 PinnacleZenith 61
95/6 Playoff 8, 120, 228
94/5 POG 39, 328, 336
95/6 POG 31, 003, 025
93/4 PowerPlay 22
93/4 Premier 254
94/5 Premier 129, 419, 505
94/5 Premier-Finest(Topps) 8
95/6 ProMagnet 13
90/1 ProSet 11, 358
91/2 ProSet 5, 300
92/3 ProSet 8
91/2 PSPlatinum 1
90/1 Score 4, 323, 340, -Hot 67
91/2 Score(CDN) 6, 305
91/2 Score(U.S) 6, 301
92/3 Score 10
93/4 Score 342
94/5 Score 4, CI8, DT23, TF2
95/6 Score 209,-Brdr 3,-Lamp 3
96/7 Score 111, -CheckIt 4
94/5 Select 39
95/6 SelectCertified 57, -Gold 7
89 SemicSticker 71
91 SemicSticker 68
95/6 SkBxEmotion 10,-Ntense 1
95/6 SkBxImpact 11,238, -Ice 10
94/5 SP 9, -Premier 23
95/6 SP 6, E4
97/8 SPAuthentic M3, T3, T6
96/7 SPx 4
95/6 Summit 81, -GM 12, -Mad 4
96/7 Summit 29
95/6 SuperSticker 7
92/3 Topps 32
95/6 Topps 15, 221, HGC23
95/6 Topps M11, 7PL, PF10
94/5 ToppsFinest 22
94/5 T.Finest -BBest 5, (Blue)3
95/6 ToppsFinest 9, 110
95 ToppsFinestBronze 10
96/7 ToppsNHLPicks 137
91/2 ToppsStadiumClub 64
92/3 ToppsStadiumClub 316
93/4 ToppsStadiumClub 216
94/5 ToppsStadiumClub 8, 266
95/6 ToppsStadiumClub 163, N3
94/5 TSC-MembersOnly 4
95/6 TSC-MembersOnly 36
95/6 ToppsSuperSkills 63
90/1 UpperDeck 156, 493
91/2 UpperDeck 78, 234
92/3 UpperDeck 86
93/4 UpperDeck 356, SP-10
94/5 UpperDeck 364, R33, SP6
95/6 UD 1, 237, AS10, SE94, F5
95/6 UD R1,-ASPredict MVP-22
96/7 UpperDeck 13
94/5 UDBeAPlayer R143
95/6 UDCC 102, 355, C14
96/7 UDCC 16, 310, S5, UD41
88/9 BOS/SportsAction (x2)
89/90 BOS/SportsAction (x2)
90/1 BOS/SportsAction
91/2 BOS/SportsAction (x2)
84/5 VAN
85/6 VAN
84/5 KelownaWingsWHL 43

NEIL, CONNIE
24/5 Holland 9
23/4 Crescent Selkirks 14

NEIL, HARRY
24/5 CrescentFalcons 13
24/5 Holland 7

NEIL, SCOTT
94 Semic 327
95/6 SheffieldSteelers

NEILL, MIKE
88/9 ProCards(Maine)
82/3 SSMarie

NEILSEN, CHRIS
98 BowmanCHL 130, A28

NEILSON, COREY
94/5 SigRookies 48
93/4 Slapshot(NorthBay) 6
94/5 Slapshot(NorthBay) 7
95/6 Slapshot 59

NEILSON, DAVID
90/1 SketchWHL 265
91/2 SketchWHL 250
94/5 Knoxville 13
94/5 LasVegas
95/6 SaintJohn

NEILSON, JIM
64-67 BeeHives(NYR)
64/5 CokeCap NYR-15
65/6 CocaCola
70/1 DadsCookies
70/1 EddieSargent 121
71/2 EddieSargent 122
72/3 EddieSargent 154
70/1 Esso Stamp
74/5 Loblaws
68/9 OPC 172, 207, Topps 70
69/70 OPC/T. 35, OPC-Sticker
70/1 OPC 185
71/2 OPC/Topps 112
72/3 OPC 60, Topps 66
73/4 OPC/Topps 123
74/5 OPC/Topps 109
75/6 OPC/Topps 270
76/7 OPC 344
77/8 OPC 317
94/5 Parkie(64/5) 102
95/6 Parkie(66/7) 81
72 SemicSticker 211
68/9 ShirriffCoin NY12
64/5 TheTorontoStar
71/2 TheTorontoSun
62/3 Topps 49
63/4 Topps 50
64/5 Topps 103
65/6 Topps 89
66/7 Topps 88, -USATest 55
67/8 Topps 91
68/9 Topps 70
72/3 Topps 66
91/2 Ultimate(O6) 25, -Aut 25

NEILSON, ROGER
90/1 ProSet 672
89/90 NYR/MarineMidland
78/9 TOR

NEININGER, TONY
72 SemicSticker 147

NEILBA, JAN
94/5 APS 281
95/6 APS 75
82 SemicSticker 84

NELLIGAN, SAM
74/5 SiouxCity

NELLIS, JIM
91/2 AirCanadaSJHL D39
92/3 MPSPhotoSJHL 89

NELSON, BRIAN
85/6 Minn-Duluth 27

NELSON, CHAD
95/6 Louisiana Playoffs

NELSON, CHRIS
92/3 Cincinnati
93/4 Raleigh

NELSON, CRAIG
95/6 Slapshot 152

NELSON, DAVE
90/1 PrinceAlbert
91/2 PrinceAlbert

NELSON, FRANCIS
83&87 HallOfFame 160
83 HHOF Postcard (L)

NELSON, JEFF
91/2 Arena 27
94/5 CanadaJr.Alumni 3
91/2 Classic 32
94/5 Classic 48
91/2 ClassicFourSport 32, -Aut
94/5 ClassicFourSport 146
94/5 C'Images 66, CE15, PR1
93/4 ClassicProspects 155
95/6 Donruss 128
95/6 EdgeIce 54
95/6 Leaf 246
94/5 ParkieSE 199
90/1 SketchMEM 104
90/1 SketchWHL 281
91/2 SketchWHL 265
91/2 StarPics 43
91/2 UltimateDP 28,75, -Aut 28
91/2 UD 689,-CzechWJC 63
94/5 UpperDeck 250
95/6 WSH
93/4 Portland
94/5 Portland
95/6 Portland

NELSON, KODIE
82/3 MedicineHat
84/5 Victoria

NELSON, TODD
92/3 ClassicProspects 42
94/5 Donruss 238
94/5 Flair 202
94/5 Leaf 273
90/1 ProCards 383
91/2 ProCards 307
92/3 Topps 50
92/3 ClevelandLumberjacks 12
93/4 Portland
94/5 Portland

NEMCHINOV, SERGEI
92/3 Bowman 426
93/4 Donruss 214
94/5 Donruss 125
95/6 Donruss 378
94/5 Flair 116
94/5 Fleer 138
92/3 FleerUltra 140
93/4 FleerUltra 203
94/5 FleerUltra 142
93/4 Leaf 252
94/5 Leaf 153
95/6 Leaf 236
97/8 Omega 139
90/1 O-Pee-Chee 493
91/2 OPC/Topps 514, OPC 24R
92/3 O-Pee-Chee 316
91/2 opcPremier 25
98/9 Pacific 283
97/8 PacificCrown 102
92/3 PaniniSticker 234
93/4 PaniniSticker 93
94/5 PaniniSticker 85
96/7 PaniniSticker 110
91/2 Parkhurst 334
92/3 Parkhurst 114, 236, 447
93/4 Parkhurst 128
95/6 Parkhurst 141
94/5 ParkieSE 115
91/2 Pinnacle 317
92/3 Pinnacle 158
93/4 Pinnacle 51
94/5 Pinnacle 220
95/6 Pinnacle 152
96/7 Pinnacle 11
95/6 Playoff 285
94/5 POG 167
95/6 POG 181
93/4 PowerPlay 163
93/4 Premier 42
94/5 Premier 443
91/2 ProSet 441
92/3 ProSet 117
91/2 PSPlatinum 205
91/2 RedAce
91/2 Score(CDN) 617, (U.S) 67T
92/3 Score 115, -Sharpshooter 5
93/4 Score 218, -International 16
94/5 Score 14
95/6 Score 41
89 SemicSticker 95
91 SemicSticker 96
89/90 SovietNats
92/3 Topps 287
95/6 Topps 141
92/3 ToppsStadiumClub 340
93/4 ToppsStadiumClub 245
94/5 ToppsStadiumClub 41
91/2 UpperDeck 355
92/3 UpperDeck 298, E13
93/4 UpperDeck 371
94/5 UpperDeck 156
95/6 UpperDeck 166
96/7 UpperDeck 298
95/6 UDBeAPlayer 209
95/6 UDCollChoice 283
96/7 UDCollChoice 175

NEMCICKY, TOMAS
95/6 APS 47
93/4 UpperDeck 264

NEMECEK, JAN
94/5 APS 275
94/5 Slapshot(MEM) 52

NEMETH, STEVE
95/6 SheffieldSteelers

NEMETH, THOMAS
90/1 SketchOHL 41
91/2 SketchOHL 17
91/2 Cornwall 21
92/3 Dayton
93/4 Dayton 11

NEMIROVSKY, DAVID
95/6 Bowman 119
97/8 KatchMedallion 63
96/7 Leaf 219
97/8 PacificCrown 191
95/6 Parkhurst 359
96/7 Pinnacle 236
97/8 PinnacleBeAPlayer 167
95/6 Slapshot 272, 346
96/7 Summit 191
95/6 ToppsStadiumClub 223
97/8 UpperDeck 77
97/8 UDCollChoice 106
96/7 FLA/WinnDixie

NENONEN, ESKO
65/6 Hellas 82

NENONEN, MARTTI
80/1 Mallasjuoma 219
78/9 SM-Liiga 236

NENOV, MILCHO
79 PaniniSticker 350

NESICH, JIM
88/9 ProCards(Sherbrooke)
89/90 ProCards(AHL) 182
90/1 ProCards 61
91/2 ProCards 145

NESS, JAY
91/2 LakeSuperior

NESSMAN, RYAN
91/2 AvantGardeBCJHL 22

NESTAK, PAVEL
95/6 APS 201

NESTER, KELLY
87/8 Hull

NESTERENKO, ERIC
45-64 BeeHives(CHI), (TOR)
64-67 BeeHives(CHIx2)
62 CeramicTiles
64/5 CokeCap CHI-15
65/6 CocaCola
70/1 EddieSargent 38
70/1 Esso Stamp
68/9 O-Pee-Chee 154
69/70 O-Pee-Chee 136
70/1 OPC/Topps 19
71/2 OPC/Topps 213
53/4 Parkhurst 10
54/5 Parkhurst 19, 95
55/6 Parkhurst 15, 75
93/4 Parkie(56/7) 39
94/5 Parkie(64/5) 33
95/6 Parkie(66/7) 26
45-54 QuakerOats
60/1 ShirriffCoin 69
61/2 ShirriffCoin 23
68/9 ShirriffCoin CHI 14
63/4 TheTorontoStar
71/2 TheTorontoSun
57/8 Topps 24
58/9 Topps 53
59/60 Topps 1
61/2 Topps 28
62/3 Topps 41
63/4 Topps 39
64/5 Topps 91
65/6 Topps 119
66/7 Topps 60, -USATest 60
67/8 Topps 60
56-66 TorontoStar 57/8
90/1 UpperDeck 503
70/1 CHI

NETEDU, VALERIAN
79 PaniniSticker 312

NETHERY, LANCE
94/5 DEL 271
95/6 DEL 262
96/7 DEL 156
88/9 EDM/ActionMagazine 70

NEUBAUER, R.
95/6 DEL 288

NEUFELD, RAY
83/4 O-Pee-Chee 144
84/5 OPC 76, Topps 59
85/6 OPC/Topps 58
86/7 OPC/Topps 177
88/9 O-Pee-Chee 239
83/4 opcSticker 260
84/5 opcSticker 199
85/6 opcSticker 171/43
86/7 opcSticker 106/235
88/9 opcSticker 141/14
87/8 PaniniSticker 369
89/90 ProCards(AHL) 69
83/4 SouhaitsRen.KeyChain
82/3 HFD/JuniorWhalers
83/4 HFD/JuniorWhalers
84/5 HFD/JuniorWhalers
85/6 HFD/JuniorWhalers
85/6 WPG/Police
86/7 WPG
87/8 WPG
88/9 WPG/Police
84/5 KelownaWingsWHL 33

NEUMEIER, TROY
91/2 ProCards 602
90/1 SketchWHL 269
95/6 Adirondack
92/3 Hamilton
90/1 PrinceAlbert

NEUVONEN, JARI
93/4 Sisu 128

NEVALAINEN, MATTI
96/7 Sisu 118

NEVALAINEN, SEPPO
71/2 WilliamsFIN 267

NEVILLE, DAVID
36/7 WWGum (V356) 111

NEVIN, BOB
71/2 Bazooka Panel 14
45-64 BeeHives(TOR)
64-67 BeeHives(NYR)
62 CeramicTiles
63-5 ChexPhoto
64/5 CokeCap NYR-8
65/6 CocaCola
70/1 Colgate Stamp 38
70/1 DadsCookies
70/1 EddieSargent 127
71/2 EddieSargent 90
72/3 EddieSargent 112
70/1 Esso Stamp
74/5 Loblaws
69/70 opcMiniSticker
68/9 OPC/Topps 76
69/70 OPC/Topps 40
70/1 OPC/Topps 60
71/2 OPC/Topps 44
72/3 OPC 267
74/5 OPC 378
75/6 OPC/Topps 123, 320
76/7 opcWHA 73
58/9 Parkhurst 13
61/2 Parkhurst 10
62/3 Parkhurst 10
63/4 Parkhurst 10, 70
94/5 Parkie(64/5) 103
95/6 Parkie(66/7) 85, 144
66/7 Post'Large, 'Small
61/2 ShirriffCoin 47
62/3 ShirriffCoin 7
68/9 ShirriffCoin NYR9
71/2 TheTorontoSun
64/5 Topps 77
65/6 Topps 93
66/7 Topps 27, -USATest 27
67/8 Topps 28
54-67 TorontoStar 66/7
91/2 Ultimate(O6) 26, -Aut 26
60/1 York
61/2 York 26
63/4 York 8

NEWBERRY, JOHN
83/4 NovaScotia 8

NEWBERRY, SCOTT
92/3 MPSPhotoSJHL 125

NEWHOOK, RON
94/5 Slapshot(Sudbury) 23
95/6 Slapshot 403

NEWMAN, DAN
77/8 O-Pee-Chee 362
78/9 O-Pee-Chee 270
88/9 EDM/ActionMagazine 129

NEWMAN, D.
93/4 Muskegon

NEWMAN, DWAYNE
90/1 SketchWHL 237
91/2 SketchWHL 52
88/9 Brandon 3
89/90 Brandon 12

NEWMAN, MIKE
91/2 AvantGardeBCJHL 89
92/3 BCJHL 124

NEWMAN, TOM
93/4 Greensboro
91/2 Minnesota
92/3 Minnesota

NEWSON, MATT
92/3 Hamilton

NEWTON, CAM
75/6 opcWHA 119

NEZIOL, TOM
91/2 Cincinnati

NIBON, JARET
95/6 Slapshot 324

NICHOL, SCOTT
93/4 PortlandWinterHawks
95/6 Rochester

NICHOLLS, BERNIE
90/1 Bowman 221, -HatTrick 20
91/2 Bowman 76
92/3 Bowman 161
93/4 Donruss 188
95/6 Donruss 24
96/7 Donruss 198
97/8 Donruss 34
96/7 DonrussCanadianIce 106
96/7 DonrussElite 75
94/5 Flair 35
94/5 Fleer 43
95/6 FleerMetal 26
92/3 FleerUltra 64
93/4 FleerUltra 86
94/5 FleerUltra 42, 275
95/6 FleerUltra 34
96/7 FleerUltra 152
88/9 FritoLay
93/4 HockeyWit 64
95/6 Hoyle'WEST 8 (Diamonds)
90/1 Kraft 40, 73
95/6 Kraft
93/4 Leaf 169
94/5 Leaf 462
95/6 Leaf 84
96/7 Leaf 50
96/7 LeafPreferred 60
97/8 Limited 36
96/7 Maggers 34

96/7 MetalUniverse 138
83/4 O-Pee-Chee 160
84/5 OPC 88, Topps 67
85/6 OPC/Topps 148
86/7 OPC/Topps 159, K
87/8 OPC/Topps 183
88/9 OPC/Topps 169
89/90 OPC/Topps 47
90/1 OPC/Topps 13, 17
91/2 OPC/Topps 174
92/3 O-Pee-Chee 52
88/9 opcStars 28
90/1 opcPremier 83
83/4 opcSticker 292
84/5 opcSticker 269
85/6 opcSticker 232
86/7 opcSticker 95
87/8 opcSticker 214
88/9 opcSticker 151/27
89/90 opcSticker 155
98/9 Pacific 389
97/8 PacificCrown 255
97/8 PacificInvincible 127
87/8 PaniniSticker 278
88/9 PaniniSticker 77
89/90 PaniniSticker 88
90/1 PaniniSticker 106
91/2 PaniniSticker 288
92/3 PaniniSticker 109
93/4 PaniniSticker 39
94/5 PaniniSticker 28
95/6 PaniniSticker 156
96/7 PaniniSticker 161
97/8 PaniniSticker 228
91/2 Parkhurst 278
92/3 Parkhurst 49, 328
93/4 Parkhurst 117
95/6 Parkhurst 37
94/5 ParkieSE 38
91/2 Pinnacle 300
92/3 Pinnacle 120
93/4 Pinnacle 165
94/5 Pinnacle 499
96/7 Pinnacle 41
97/8 Pinnacle 165
97/8 PinnacleCertified 109
97/8 PinnacleInside 185
95/6 PinnacleZenith 46
96/7 PinnacleZenith 32
95/6 Playoff 23
96/7 Playoff 355
94/5 POG 68
95/6 POG 64
93/4 PowerPlay 139
93/4 Premier 274
94/5 Premier 403
95/6 ProMagnet 5
90/1 ProSet 204, 352
91/2 ProSet 166, 286
92/3 ProSet 52
91/2 PSPlatinum 174
83/4 PuffySticker 10
90/1 Score 9, -HotCards 5
91/2 Score(CDN) 460, (U.S) 240
92/3 Score 340
93/4 Score 19
94/5 Score 74, 245
95/6 Score 29
96/7 Score 65
97/8 Score 180
94/5 Select 17
89 SemicSticker 73
91 SemicSticker 67
95/6 SkyBoxEmotion 31
95/6 SkyBoxImpact 31
83/4 SouhaitsRen.KeyChain
94/5 SP 25, -Premier 25
95/6 SP 26
96/7 SP 139
97/8 SPAuthentic 132
95/6 Summit 135, -MadHat 1
96/7 Summit 115
92/3 Topps 438
95/6 Topps 122
98/9 Topps 78
94/5 ToppsFinest 87
96/7 ToppsNHLPicks 131
91/2 ToppsStadiumClub 245
92/3 ToppsStadiumClub 448
93/4 ToppsStadiumClub 111
95/6 ToppsStadiumClub 28
95/6 ToppsSuperSkills 72

90/1 UpperDeck 34
91/2 UpperDeck 356, 566
92/3 UpperDeck 290, 624
93/4 UpperDeck 58, SP-85
94/5 UpperDeck 83, SP-106
95/6 UpperDeck 97, SE16
96/7 UpperDeck 334, X31
97/8 UpperDeck 150
96/7 UDBlackDiamond 59
95/6 UDCollChoice 169, C17
96/7 UDCollChoice 50
96/7 UpperDeck"Ice" 57
92/3 EDM/IGA 17
84/5 L.A/Smokeys
88/9 L.A.
88/9 L.A/Smokeys
89/90 NYR/MarineMidland
96/7 S.J/PacificBellSheet
97/8 S.J/PacificBellSheet (x2)

NICHOLLS, DAVE
94/5 Slapshot(Kitchener) 29
82/3 Kitchener 18

NICHOLLS, JAMIE
88/9 ProCards(CapeBreton)

NICHOLS, ROB
88/9 ProCards(Adirondack)
89/90 ProCards(IHL) 111
90/1 ProCards 299
91/2 ProCards 329
83/4 NorthBay
92/3 SanDiego

NICHOLSON, DAN
81/2 Oshawa 9
82/3 Oshawa 18

NICKEL, HARTMUT
94/5 DEL 127
74 Hellas 108
70/1 Kuvajulkaisut 89

NICKEL, STACEY
84/5 KelownaWings&WHL 3
86/7 Regina

NICOL, BRETT
90/1 SketchOHL 138

NICOL, CREGG
86/7 Regina
87/8 Regina

NICOLETTI, MARTIN
88/9 ProCards(Sherbrooke)

NICOLLS, JAMIE
92/3 Greensboro 11
93/4 Greensboro
86/7 Portland

NICOLLS, PAUL
92/3 BCJHL 33

NICOLSON, DEREK
95/6 ThunderBay

NICOLSON, GRAEME
81/2 COL.R

NIECKAR, BARRY
93/4 Raleigh
94/5 SaintJohn

NIEDERBERGER, ANDREAS
94/5 DEL 88
95/6 DEL 82, 438
96/7 DEL 273
95 Globe 222
95 PaniniWorlds 60
94 Semic 279
89 SemicSticker 106
93 SemicSticker 154

NIEDERMAYER, ROB
95/6 Bowman 76
93/4 Classic 5, DP5, -Aut
94/5 Classic-Autograph
93/4 ClassicFourSport 189
93/4 ClassicProspects 27
93 C4'Images 30
93/4 Donruss 134, I, -Rated 4
94/5 Donruss 113
95/6 Donruss 51
96/7 Donruss 24
97/8 Donruss 191
96/7 DonrussCanadianIce 13
95/6 DonrussElite 65
96/7 DonrussElite 15
97/8 DonrussPreferred 61
94/5 Flair 67

94/5 Fleer 82
96/7 Fleer 41
95/6 FleerMetal 61
93/4 FU 330, -Speed 8,-Wave 11
94/5 FleerUltra 84
95/6 FleerUltra 62
96/7 FleerUltra 67
95/6 Hoyle'EAST 6 (Diamonds)
97/8 KatchMedallion 64
93/4 Kraft-Gold
96/7 Kraft-Mascot
93/4 Leaf 293, -Freshman 6
94/5 Leaf 225, -GoldRook 7
95/6 Leaf 197
96/7 Leaf 22
97/8 Leaf 58
94/5 LeafLimited 11
95/6 LeafLimited 35
96/7 LeafLimited 78, -Stubble 19
96/7 LeafPreferred 12, -Steel 61
97/8 Limited 79
96/7 MetalUniverse 61
97/8 PacificCrown 269
97/8 PacificParamount 83
94/5 PaniniSticker H
95/6 PaniniSticker 71
96/7 PaniniSticker 72
93/4 Parkhurst 246, C4, E5, G5
94/5 Parkhurst 294, V22
95/6 Parkhurst 82
94/5 ParkieSE 68
93/4 Pinnacle 439, SR4
94/5 Pinnacle 168, 469
95/6 Pinnacle 100
96/7 Pinnacle 32
97/8 Pinnacle 157
97/8 PinnacleInside 182
95/6 PinnacleZenith 110
96/7 PinnacleZenith 84
95/6 Playoff 42, 263
96/7 Playoff 435
94/5 POG 109
94/5 Post
93/4 PowerPlay 349,-Rookie 8
93/4 Premier 270
94/5 Premier 306,-Finest(OPC) 9
95/6 ProMagnet 86
93/4 Score 592
95/6 Score 48
96/7 Score 3
97/8 Score 253
94/5 Select 25
95/6 SelectCertified 96
96/7 SelectCertified 7
90/1 SketchWHL 29
91/2 SketchWHL 327
96/7 SkyBoxImpact 47
95/6 SP 60
96/7 SP 62
97/8 SPAuthentic 67, S19
95/6 Summit 105
96/7 Summit 147
95/6 SuperSticker 50
95/6 Topps 31
98/9 Topps 37
95/6 ToppsFinest 98
96/7 ToppsNHLPicks 99
93/4 ToppsStadiumClub 449
94/5 ToppsStadiumClub 22, 117
95/6 ToppsStadiumClub 94
95/6 ToppsSuperSkills 22
92/3 UpperDeck 593
93/4 UD 98, E11, H4, SP-58
94/5 UpperDeck 287, SP30
95/6 UpperDeck 310, SE35
96/7 UpperDeck 262, 28B, X3
97/8 UpperDeck 281, SG44
93/4 UDBeAPlayer 10
94/5 UDBeAPlayer R55, R119
95/6 UDBeAPlayer 184
96/7 UDBlackDiamond 140
97/8 UDBlackDiamond 22
98/9 UDChoice 94
95/6 UDCollChoice 40
96/7 UDCollChoice 103, 318
97/8 UDCollChoice 105, SQ18
97/8 UpperDeckIce 14
96/7 FLA/WinnDixie
97/8 FLA/WinnDixie

NIEDERMAYER, SCOTT
91/2 Arena 2
92/3 Bowman 313

95/6 Bowman 64
94/5 CanadaJr.Alumni 12
91/2 Classic 3
91/2 ClassicFourSport 3, -Aut
93/4 Donruss 189, M
94/5 Donruss 161
95/6 Donruss 105
96/7 Donruss 188
97/8 Donruss 72
97/8 DonrussPriority 37
97/8 EssoOlympic 14
94/5 Flair 96
96/7 Flair-Now&Then 3
94/5 Fleer 115
96/7 Fleer 60
95/6 FleerMetal 84
96/7 FleerNHLPicks 116
92/3 FleerUltra 116
93/4 FleerUltra 95
94/5 FleerUltra 121
95/6 FleerUltra 90,194, -Rising 5
96/7 FleerUltra 94
93/4 HockeyWit 54
95/6 Hoyle'EAST 7 (Diamonds)
97/8 KatchMedallion 83
93/4 Leaf 80, -GoldL.Rookie 14
94/5 Leaf 237
95/6 Leaf 150, -RoadToThe 9
96/7 Leaf 198
94/5 LeafLimited 40
95/6 LeafLimited 43
96/7 MetalUniverse 87
97/8 Omega 132
91/2 opcPremier 35
92/3 opcPremier 113
98/9 Pacific 266
97/8 PacificCrown 247
98/9 PacificParamount 136
97/8 PacificRevolution 79
92/3 PaniniSticker 179
93/4 PaniniSticker 42
95/6 PaniniSticker 88
96/7 PaniniSticker 86
97/8 PaniniSticker 72
91/2 Parkhurst 94
92/3 Parkhurst 95
93/4 Parkhurst 111, 240
95/6 Parkhurst 388
94/5 ParkieSE 95, seV12
91/2 Pinnacle 349
92/3 Pinnacle 241, 304
92/3 Pinnacle-Team2000 12
93/4 Pinnacle 111, -Tm2001 14
94/5 Pinnacle 75
97/8 Pinnacle 115
96/7 PinnacleBeAPlayer 59
97/8 PinnacleInside 95
95/6 PinnacleZenith 27
95/6 Playoff 59
94/5 POG 351
95/6 POG 164
93/4 PowerPlay 140
93/4 Premier 470
94/5 Premier 240, 539
95/6 ProMagnet 33
91/2 ProSet 547, CC4
92/3 ProSet 232
91/2 Score(CDN) 577, (U.S) 27T
92/3 Score 401, -YoungStar 33
93/4 Score 217
94/5 Score 22
95/6 Score 52
96/7 Score 108
97/8 Score 229
97/8 Score(N.J.) 7
94/5 Select 101
95/6 SelectCertified 70
89/90 SketchMEM 18
90/1 SketchMEM 97
90/1 SketchOHL 289
91/2 SketchAwards 11, 13
95/6 SkyBoxEmotion 100
95/6 SkyBoxImpact 95
96/7 SkyBoxImpact 69
94/5 SP 67
95/6 SP 84
96/7 SP 90
91/2 StarPics 13
95/6 Summit 50
96/7 Summit 57
95/6 SuperSticker 71

96/7 TeamOut
92/3 Topps 223
95/6 Topps 164, YS14
98/9 Topps 143, B8
95/6 ToppsFinest 103
92/3 ToppsStadiumClub 209
93/4 ToppsStadiumClub 403
94/5 ToppsStadiumClub 93
95/6 ToppsStadiumClub G8
95/6 ToppsSuperSkills 27
91/2 UltimateDP 3, 56, 59, 75
91/2 UltimateDP 79, 80, -Aut. 3
90/1 UpperDeck 461
91/2 UD-CzechWJC 53
92/3 UD 406,562,AC5,CC5,WG1
93/4 UpperDeck 25, 284, SP-86
94/5 UD 324, C34, IG6, SP134
95/6 UpperDeck 383, SE137
96/7 UpperDeck 92, 28A
97/8 UpperDeck 301
93/4 UDBeAPlayer 32
94/5 UDBAP R37, R128,-Aut. 88
96/7 UDlackDiamond 137
98/9 UDChoice 119
95/6 UDCollChoice 3
96/7 UDCollChoice 149
97/8 UDCollChoice 148
96/7 UpperDeck"Ice" 36
96/7 N.J/Sharp
89/90 Kamloops

NIEKAMP, JIM
71/2 TheTorontoSun
72/3 LosAngelesSharks
75/6 Phoenix
76/7 Phoenix

NIELSEN, CARSTEN
79 PaniniSticker 367

NIELSEN, FRITS
79 PaniniSticker 366

NIELSEN, JEFF
98/9 Pacific 61
96/7 Binghampton

NIELSON, JENS
94/5 EliteSet 287
95/6 EliteSet 286
89/90 SemicElitserien 141
90/1 SemicElitserien 214
91/2 SemicElitserien 142
92/3 SemicElitserien 163
95/6 udElite 184
97/8 udSwedish 111

NIELSON, JEFF
94/5 Classic 89
94/5 Binghampton
95/6 Binghampton
91/2 Minnesota
92/3 Minnesota
93/4 Minnesota

NIELSON, LEN
88/9 ProCards(Moncton)
87/8 Moncton
86/7 Regina

NIEMEGEERS, KYLE
91/2 AirCanadaSJHL C10
92/3 MPSPhotoSJHL 11

NIEMELÄ, JOUNI
70/1 Kuvajulkaisut 352

NIEMENRANTA, OLAVI
80/1 Mallasjuoma 78
78/9 SM-Liiga 124

NIEMI, A.J.
95/6 Sisu 250
95/6 UpperDeck 549

NIEMI, ESKO
96/7 Sisu 188

NIEMI, HEIKKI
72/3 WilliamsFIN 272

NIEMI, JAAKKO
78/9 SM-Liiga 224
73/4 WilliamsFIN 253

NIEMI, KARI
72/3 WilliamsFIN 289

NIEMI, MARKO
70/1 Kuvajulkaisut 317

NIEMI, MIKKO
93/4 Sisu 116

NIEMI, TAUNO
65/6 Hellas 121

NIEMINEN, LASSE
92/3 Jyvas-Hyva 78
93/4 Jyvas-Hyva 138
93/4 Sisu 147
94/5 Sisu 57
95/6 Sisu 65

NIEMINEN, MIKA
94/5 EliteSet 22, -Playmaker 3
95 FinnishAllStar 7
95 Globe 135
95 Hartwall
91/2 Jyvas-Hyva 44
95 PaniniWorlds 185
94 Semic 36
95 Semic 40
92/3 SemicElitserien 197
89 SemicSticker 50
91 SemicSticker 17
92 SemicSticker 19
93 SemicSticker 69
95/6 Sisu-GoldCard 18
96 Wien 22

NIEMINEN, PEKKA
72/3 WilliamsFIN 180

NIEMINEN, PERTTI
65/6 Hellas 6

NIEMINEN, VILLE
95/6 Sisu 113

NIENHUIS, KEVAN
86/7 Moncton 11

NIENHUIS, KRAIG
96/7 DEL 42

NIEUWENDYK, JOE
95/6 Aces 10 (Clubs)
90/1 Bowman 91
91/2 Bowman 252
92/3 Bowman 59
93/4 Donruss 48
94/5 Donruss 56
95/6 Donruss 40, -Igniters 9
96/7 Donruss 195
97/8 Donruss 186
96/7 DonrussCanadianIce 63
97/8 DonrussCanadianIce 51
95/6 DonrussElite 50
96/7 DonrussElite 62
97/8 DonrussElite 61
97/8 DonrussPreferred 115
97/8 DonrussPriority 140
97/8 DonrussStudio 55
93/4 EASports 21
94/5 Fleer 32
95/6 FleerMetal 21
96/7 FleerPicks-FabFifty 33
92/3 FleerUltra 25
93/4 FleerUltra 130
96/7 FleerUltra 46
88/9 FritoLay
93/4 HockeyWit 82
95/6 Hoyle'WEST 9 (Diamonds)
97/8 KatchMedallion 47
89/90 Kraft 5
90/1 Kraft 41, 74
93/4 Kraft-Captain, -CutOut
96/7 KraftDinner
97/8 Kraft -RoadToNagano
93/4 Leaf 126
94/5 Leaf 228
95/6 Leaf 305
96/7 Leaf 34
97/8 Leaf 108
94/5 LeafLimited 82
95/6 LeafLimited 56
96/7 LeafLimited 75
96/7 LeafPreferred 27, -Steel 45
97/8 Limited 43
96/7 Maggers 45
94/5 McDonalds 21
95/6 McDonalds 12
97/8 McDonalds -Medallions
96/7 MetalUniverse 42
97/8 Omega 74
88/9 OPC/Topps 16
89/90 OPC/Topps 138
90/1 OPC/Topps 87, T-TL 8

91/2 OPC/Topps 223
92/3 O-Pee-Chee 354
90/1 opcPremier 84
91/2 opcPremier 48
88/9 opcStars 29
88/9 opcSticker 90, 205/74
88/9 opcSticker 216/86, 125/257
89/90 opcSticker 101
88/9 opcStickFS 14
98/9 Pacific 25
97/8 PacificCrown 266
97/8 PacificCrownRoyale 42
97/8 PcfcDynagon! 92,-Tand 43
97/8 PacificInvincible 43
97/8 PacificParamount 61
98/9 PacificParamount 69
97/8 PacificRevolution 44
90/1 Panini(CGY) 14
88/9 PaniniSticker 12, 404
89/90 PaniniSticker 29
90/1 PaniniSticker 174
91/2 PaniniSticker 53
92/3 PaniniSticker 40
93/4 PaniniSticker 182
94/5 PaniniSticker 156
95/6 PaniniSticker 233
96/7 PaniniSticker 169
97/8 PaniniSticker 144
91/2 Parkhurst 23
92/3 Parkhurst 21
93/4 Parkhurst 31
94/5 Parkhurst 33, C4
95/6 Parkhurst 33, 329
91/2 Pinnacle 54
92/3 Pinnacle 31
93/4 Pinnacle 198, CA4
94/5 Pinnacle 90
96/7 Pinnacle 183
97/8 Pinnacle 110
96/7 PinnacleBeAPlayer 53
97/8 PinnacleBeeHive 20
97/8 PinnacleCertified 76
97/8 PinnacleInside 115
95/6 PinnacleZenith 112
96/7 PinnacleZenith 63
95/6 Playoff 18
96/7 Playoff 334
94/5 POG 56
95/6 POG 49
93/4 PowerPlay 39
93/4 Premier 205
94/5 Premier 537
95/6 ProMagnet 43
90/1 ProSet 2, 344
91/2 ProSet 29, 569
92/3 ProSet 26
91/2 PSPlatinum 18
90/1 Score 30, -HotCards 45
91/2 Score(CDN) 170, (U.S) 170
92/3 Score 193
93/4 Score 199, (CDN) DD4
94/5 Score 159
95/6 Score 229
96/7 Score 152
97/8 Score 135
94/5 Select 131
95/6 SelectCert. 32, -Double 10
96/7 SelectCertified 88
89 SemicSticker 74
91 SemicSticker 69
95/6 SkyBoxEmotion 24
95/6 SkyBoxImpact 24
96/7 SkyBoxImpact 31
94/5 SP 20
95/6 SP 38
97/8 SPAuthentic 49
96/7 SPx 12
98/9 SPx"Finite" 26
95/6 Summit 162, -MadHat 13
96/7 Summit 65
95/6 SuperSticker 18
92/3 Topps 105
95/6 Topps 233
98/9 Topps 161
95/6 ToppsFinest 168
96/7 ToppsNHLPicks 61
91/2 ToppsStadiumClub 60
92/3 ToppsStadiumClub 37
93/4 ToppsStadiumClub 96
94/5 ToppsStadiumClub 166
95/6 ToppsStadiumClub 18
93/4 TSC-MembersOnly 18

90/1 UpperDeck 26
91/2 UpperDeck 263
92/3 UpperDeck 128
93/4 UpperDeck 396, SP-23
94/5 UpperDeck 276, SP13
95/6 UpperDeck 285, SE12
96/7 UpperDeck 245, P20
97/8 UpperDeck 50
94/5 UDBeAPlayer-Aut. 96
97/8 UDBlackDiamond 16
98/9 UDChoice 62
95/6 UDCollChoice 133
96/7 UDCollChoice 68, 315
97/8 UDCollChoice 68
97/8 ValuNet
97/8 Zenith 63, Z15
96/7 DAL/Southwest
87/8 CGY/RedRooster
90/1 CGY/McGavins
91/2 CGY/IGA
92/3 CGY/IGA 17

NIGHBOR, FRANK
25-27 Anonymous 16
24/5 Champs (C144)
83&87 HallOfFame 72
83 HHOF Postcard (E)
60/1 Topps 35
61/2 Topps-Stamp
23/4 (V145-1) 2
24/5 (V145-2) 6

NIGRO, FRANK
83/4 O-Pee-Chee 337
83/4 opcSticker 149
92 SemicSticker
82/3 TOR
83/4 TOR

NIINIMAA, JANNE
93/4 Classic 44
94/5 Classic 105, T51
93/4 ClassicFourSport 207
97/8 Donruss 99
96/7 DonrussCanadianIce 128
97/8 D.CdnIce-Scrapbook 21
96/7 D.Elite-Aspirations 16
97/8 DonrussElite 92
97/8 DonrussPreferred 26
97/8 DonrussPriority 84
97/8 DonrussStudio 100
96/7 Flair 120
96/7 FleerUltra 127, -Rookies 15
95 Hartwall
97/8 Leaf 75
96/7 LeafPreferred 127
97/8 Limited 16, 136, 168
97/8 Limited -fabric 69
96/7 MetalUniverse 189
98/9 Pacific 24
97/8 PacificCrown 173
97/8 PcfcDynagon! 92,-Tand 16
97/8 PacificInv. 103, -Feature 26
97/8 PacificParamount 135
98/9 PacificParamount 91
97/8 PaniniSticker 94, 245
93/4 Parkhurst 520
94/5 ParkieSE 217
97/8 PinnacleBeAPlayer 144
97/8 PinnacleInside 179
96/7 PinnacleZenith 124
97/8 Score 165
97/8 Score(PHA) 9
96/7 SelectCertified 104
95 Semic 227
93/4 Sisu 6, 390
94/5 Sisu 58
95/6 Sisu 251, -Gold 8, -Super
95/6 SisuLimited 13
94/5 SP 162
96/7 SP 186
97/8 SPx 37
98/9 SPx"Finite" 35
94/5 ToppsFinest 128
96/7 UpperDeck 310
97/8 UpperDeck 124, SG41, T8A
96/7 UDBlackDiamond 154
98/9 UDChoice 86
96/7 UDCollChoice 361
97/8 UDCollChoice 183, SQ26
96/7 UpperDeck"Ice" 49
97/8 UpperDeckIce 21
96 Wien 6
96/7 PHA/OceanSpray

NIINIMÄKI, JARI
72/3 WilliamsFIN 312

NIINIVIITA, TIMO
72/3 WilliamsFIN 290
78/9 SM-Liiga 104

NIITTOAHO, HANNU
66/7 Champion 58
70/1 Kuvajulkaisut 145
80/1 Mallasjuoma 195
78/9 SM-Liiga 205
71/2 WilliamsFIN 195
72/3 WilliamsFIN 233
73/4 WilliamsFIN 267

NIITTYMÄKI, MIKA
96/7 Sisu 133

NIKANDER, HARRY
91/2 Jyvas-Hyva 72
92/3 Jyvas-Hyva 200
80/1 Mallasjuoma 217
78/9 SM-Liiga 227

NIKANDER, JARKKO
92/3 Jyvas-Hyva 27
93/4 Jyvas-Hyva 47
93/4 Sisu 247
94/5 Sisu 52
95/6 Sisu 317
96/7 Sisu 129

NIKITIN, VALERI
70/1 Kuvajulkaisut 10
70/1 Soviet Stars

NIKKILÄ, SEPPO
66/7 Champion 183
65/6 Hellas 112

NIKKO, JAN
92/3 Jyvas-Hyva 37
93/4 Jyvas-Hyva 75
93/4 Parkhurst 524
95 Semic 226
93/4 Sisu 111
95/6 Sisu 220
96/7 Sisu 18
95/6 SisuLimited 84

NIKOLISHIN, ANDREI
92/3 Classic 48
94/5 Classic 70, R14, T28
92/3 ClassicFourSport 189
95/6 Donruss 124
94/5 Fleer 87
96/7 FleerNHLPicks 172
94/5 FleerUltra 301
95/6 FleerUltra 68
95/6 Leaf 11
97/8 PacificDynag-BestKept 102
95/6 PaniniSticker 29
96/7 PaniniSticker 32
97/8 PaniniSticker 117
95/6 Parkhurst 94
94/5 ParkieSE 72
94/5 Pinnacle 487
95/6 Pinnacle 98
96/7 Pinnacle 179
96/7 PinnacleBeAPlayer 137
94/5 Premier 421
95/6 Score 169
94/5 Select 184
95 Semic 123
95/6 SkyBoxEmotion 76
95/6 SkyBoxImpact 74
95/6 Topps 361, 22NG
94/5 ToppsFinest 10
95/6 ToppsStadiumClub 149
91/2 UpperDeck'CzechWJC 7
92/3 UpperDeck 340
94/5 UpperDeck 241, C9, SP122
95/6 UpperDeck 55, SE38
95/6 UDCollChoice 21
96/7 UDCollChoice 114

NIKOLOV, ANGEL
94/5 APS 206
95/6 APS 153
95/6 Classic-Autograph

NIKULIN, IGOR
95 PaniniWorlds 35

NILAN, CHRIS
91/2 Bowman 351
72-84 Dernière 80/1, 83/4
86/7 Kraft Sports 34
83/4 O-Pee-Chee 194
84/5 O-Pee-Chee 268
86/7 O-Pee-Chee 199
90/1 O-Pee-Chee 454
85/6 opcSticker 127/245
87/8 opcSticker 15/154
88/9 opcSticker 245/115
88/9 OPC/Topps 31
91/2 OPC/Topps 170, 311
87/8 PaniniSticker 68
90/1 PaniniSticker 85
91/2 PaniniSticker 183
80/1 Pepsi Cap
91/2 Pinnacle 289
90/1 ProSet 205, 409
87/8 ProSportWatch CW17
90/1 Score(U.S) 311, 22T
91/2 Score(CDN) 197, (U.S) 197
92/3 Score 76
89 SemicSticker 175
91/2 ToppsStadiumClub 244
90/1 UpperDeck 368, 442
91/2 UpperDeck 237
83/4 Vachon 51
90/1 BOS/SportsAction
80/1 MTL
81/2 MTL
82/3 MTL
82/3 MTL/Steinberg
83/4 MTL
84/5 MTL
85/6 MTL
85/6 MTL/Pennant
85/6 MTL/PepsiPlacemats
85/6? MTL/ProvigoPlacemats
85/6 MTL/ProvigoStickers
86/7 MTL
87/8 MTL
87/8 MTL/Kodak
87/8 MTL/Stickers 19, 20
89/90 NYR/MarineMidland

NILL, JIM
83/4 O-Pee-Chee 357
84/5 O-Pee-Chee 11
89/90 O-Pee-Chee 224
90/1 ProCards 475
83/4 SouhaitsRen.KeyChain
83/4 Vachon 114
88/9 DET/Caesars
82/3 VAN
83/4 VAN
85/6 WPG
85/6 WPG/Police
86/7 WPG

NILSEN, NILS
79 PaniniSticker 296

NILSEN, SJUR ROBERT
95 PaniniWorlds

NILSSON, BILLY
92/3 SemicElitserien 250

NILSSON, FREDRIK
94 Semic 59
89/90 SemicElitserien 252
90/1 SemicElitserien 170
91/2 SemicElitserien 272
92/3 SemicElitserien 290
93 SemicSticker 17
97/8 udSwedish 132

NILSSON, HARDY
95/6 DEL 74
96/7 DEL 268

NILSSON, HENRIK
94/5 ElitSet 59
95/6 ElitSet 205
90/1 SemicElitserien 172
91/2 SemicElitserien 267
92/3 SemicElitserien 288
95/6 udElite 218
97/8 udSwedish 71

NILSSON, KENT
95 Globe 71
80/1 OPC/Topps 106, 197
81/2 OPC 34, 52-53, T. 24, 43
82/3 O-Pee-Chee 54
83/4 O-Pee-Chee 89
84/5 O-Pee-Chee 232
81/2 opcSticker 218
82/3 opcSticker 217
83/4 opcSticker 267, 268
84/5 opcSticker 245
85/6 opcSticker 208
87/8 opcSticker 88/220
80/1 opcSuperCard 3
80/1 Pepsi Cap
81/2 Post PopUp 28
82/3 Post
83/4 PuffySticker 3
82 SemicSticker 147
89 SemicSticker 24
91 SemicSticker 50
83/4 7ElevenCokeCup
83/4 SouhaitsRen.KeyChain
82/3 StaterMint
83/4 Vachon 14
79/80 ATL
79/70 ATL/B&W
80/1 CGY
81/2 CGY
82/3 CGY
88/9 EDM/ActionMagazine 27
77/8 WPG

NILSSON, L.G.
72 Hellas 33
70/1 Kuvajulkaisut 33
69/70 MästarSerien 36
72 Panda
72 SemicSticker 54
74 SemicSticker 19
71/2 WilliamsFIN 53
72/3 WilliamsFIN 53

NILSSON, MAGNUS
98/9 UDChoice 288
97/8 udSwedish 137

NILSSON, MARCUS
95/6 FutureLegends-Hot 4
95/6 SP 185
95/6 UpperDeck 560
97/8 UDBlackDiamond 137
98/9 UDChoice 296
95/6 UDCollChoice 345
97/8 udSwedish 43, S2

NILSSON, MATS
89/90 SemicElitserien 106
90/1 SemicElitserien 109

NILSSON, MIKAEL
95/6 ElitSet 153

NILSSON, O.
89/90 SemicElitserien 22

NILSSON, ORJAN
91/2 SemicElitserien 137
92/3 SemicElitserien 157

NILSSON, PER
89/90 SemicElitserien 186

NILSSON, PETER
94/5 ElitSet 7, 50
95/6 ElitSet 254
89/90 SemicElitserien 64
90/1 SemicElitserien 288
91/2 SemicElitserien 71
92/3 SemicElitserien 91
95/6 udElite 118, DS8

NILSSON, PETTER
96/7 DEL 347
91/2 SemicElitserien 161
92/3 SemicElitserien 182
91/2 SemicElitserien 127

NILSSON, STEFAN
94/5 ElitSet 18, 258, -RookRc 10
94/5 ElitSet-Playmaker 2
95/6 ElitSet 42, 252
94 Semic 63
89/90 SemicElitserien 114, 160
90/1 SemicElitserien 240
91/2 SemicElitserien 167
92/3 SemicElitserien 186, 258
95/6 udElite 65, 122
97/8 udSwedish 58, 124, 200
97/8 udSwedish 212, C7, UDS12

NILSSON, THOMAS
91/2 SemicElitserien 10

NILSSON, ULF
74 Hellas 31
78/9 OPC/Topps 255
79/80 OPC/Topps 30, Topps 163
80/1 OPC/Topps 116
81/2 OPC 229, Topps(E) 102
81/2 opcSticker 172
74/5 opcWHA 4
75/6 opcWHA 83
76/7 opcWHA 2, 3, 5, 9
77/8 opcWHA 15
74 SemicSticker 8, -CL 4
82 SemicSticker 145
77-9 Sportscastr 71-12, 80-1911
92/3 Trends(76) 143
91/2 UpperDeck 643
96 Wien HL11
73/4 WilliamsFIN 33

NIMIGON, STEVE
93/4 Slapshot(NiagaraFalls) 9
95/6 Slapshot 188

NISKANEN, PETRI
70/1 Kuvajulkaisut 334

NISKAVAARA, JAAKO
95/6 UDCollChoice 332

NISSINEN, PEKKA
78/9 SM-Liiga 127

NISSINEN, TERO
96/7 Sisu 86

NISTICO, LOU
75/6 opcWHA 13

NISTOR, CONSTANTIN
79 PaniniSticker 318

NITTEL, ADAM
95/6 Slapshot 203

NIUKKANEN, PETRI
80/1 Mallasjuoma 174

NIXON, DAN
52/3 LavalDairy 15
52/3 StLawrence 38

NIXON, JULIAN
74/5 SiouxCity

NOACK, RUDIGER
70/1 Kuvajulkaisut 90

NOBILI, MARIO
90/1 SketchQMJHL 233
91/2 SketchQMJHL 146
91/2 StarPics 34
91/2 UltimateDP 51, -Au t 51

NOBLE, JEFF
85/6 Kitchener 18
86/7 Kitchener 17
87/8 Kitchener 18

NOBLE, REG
25-27 Anonymous 96
24/5 Champs (C144)
83&87 HallOfFame 22
83 HHOF Postcard (B)
23/4 (V145-1) 26
24/5 (V145-2) 51

NOEL, CLAUDE
89/90 SketchOHL 176
92/3 Dayton

NOEL, MIKE
74/5 SiouxCity

NOHEL, PAVEL
94/5 APS 16
95/6 APS 112

NOKELAINEN, ESKO
92/3 Jyvas-Hyva 137

NOKIKURU, KIMMO
66/7 Champion 39

NOKKOSMÄKI, NEMO
93/4 Sisu 217

NOLAN, JEFF
90/1 SketchOHL 112

NOLAN, OWEN
96/7 Aces 4 (Clubs)
97/8 Aces 5 (Clubs)
91/2 Bowman 134
92/3 Bowman 237, 328
95/6 Bowman 58
93/4 Donruss 279
94/5 Donruss 45
95/6 Donruss 153, 268, -Marks 2
96/7 Donruss 6, -HitList 17
97/8 Donruss 84
96/7 DonrussCanadianIce 54
97/8 D.CdnIce 108, -National 30
95/6 DonrussElite 26
96/7 DonrussElite 14, -Status 6
97/8 DonrussPreferred 108
97/8 DonrussPriority 46
96/7 Duracell DC19
93/4 EASports 113
96/7 Flair 85, -HotNumber 10
94/5 Fleer 181
96/7 Fleer 100
95/6 FleerMetal 133
96/7 F.Picks-FabFifty 34
92/3 FleerUltra 177
93/4 FleerUltra 154
94/5 FleerUltra 177
95/6 FU 133, 304,-Crs 13,-Red 8
96/7 FleerUltra 153
91/2 Gillette 25
93/4 HockeyWit 57
95/6 Hoyle'EAST 8 (Diamonds)
92/3 HumptyDumpty (2)
97/8 KatchMedallion 124
97/8 KennerSLU -1on1
91/2 Kraft 55
96/7 KraftDinner, -Disks
93/4 Leaf 42
94/5 Leaf 144
95/6 Leaf 240
96/7 Leaf 128
97/8 Leaf 23
94/5 LeafLimited 41
95/6 LeafLimited 93
96/7 LeafLimited 20, -Bash 3
97/8 Limited 117, 196
96/7 LeafPreferred 6, -Steel 62
96/7 Maggers 131
92/3 McDonalds McD24
95/6 McDonalds McD10
96/7 MetalUniverse 139
97/8 Omega 205
91/2 OPC/Topps 64
92/3 O-Pee-Chee 382
90/1 opcPremier 86
91/2 opcPremier 193
98/9 Pacific 390
97/8 PacificCrown 151,-TmCL22
97/8 PacificCrownRoyale 121
97/8 PcfcDynagon! 114,-Tand 50
97/8 PacificInvincible 128
97/8 PacificParamount 169
98/9 PacificParamount 214
97/8 PacificRevolution 126
90/1 Panini(QUE) 17
91/2 PaniniSticker 266
92/3 PaniniSticker 210
93/4 PaniniSticker 70
95/6 PaniniSticker 249
96/7 PaniniSticker 277
97/8 PaniniSticker 230
91/2 Parkhurst 143
92/3 Parkhurst 145, 455, CP13
93/4 Parkhurst 163, F4
94/5 Parkhurst V43
95/6 Parkhurst 49, 453
94/5 ParkieSE 143
91/2 Pinnacle 156
92/3 Pinnacle 6, -Team2000 10
93/4 Pinnacle 151, -Tm2001 28
94/5 Pinnacle 76
95/6 Pinnacle 12, -FullContact 3
96/7 Pinnacle 186
97/8 Pinnacle 49
96/7 Pinn.BeAPlayer-Biscuit 25
97/8 PinnacleBeeHive 22
97/8 PinnacleCertified 59
96/7 PinnacleFANtasy 18
97/8 PinnacleInside 27
95/6 PinnacleZenith 16, -Gifted 9
96/7 P.Zenith 37, -Assailant 14
95/6 Playoff 27, 241
96/7 Playoff 335
94/5 POG 197
95/6 POG 76
93/4 PowerPlay 201
93/4 Premier 267, -Finest 4
94/5 Premier 457
90/1 ProSet 401, 635
91/2 ProSet 196
92/3 ProSet 153
91/2 PSPlatinum 101
90/1 Score 435, 80T,-Young 36
91/2 Score(CDN) 143, (U.S) 143
92/3 Score 286,-YoungStar 37
92/3 Score-Sharpshooter 12
93/4 Score 32
95/6 Score 83,-ChckIt 2,-Lamp 4
96/7 Score 69, -CheckIt 8
97/8 Score 102, -CheckIt 17
92/3 SeasonsPatch 46
94/5 Select 4
95/6 SelectCertified 19
96/7 SelectCertified 56
93 SemicSticker 207
89/90 SketchOHL 180
95/6 SkBxEmotion 40, -Ntense 6
95/6 SkBxImpact 150,240,-Ice11
96/7 SkyBoxImpact 117
94/5 SP 95
95/6 SP 129
96/7 SP 138
97/8 SPAuthentic 131
96/7 SPx 41
97/8 SPx 44
98/9 SPx"Finite" 71
97/8 SportFX MiniStix
95/6 Summit 12, -MadHat. 1
96/7 Summit 45
95/6 SuperSticker 110
96/7 TeamOut
92/3 Topps 349
95/6 Topps 305
98/9 Topps 156
95/6 ToppsFinestS 142
96/7 ToppsNHLPicks 57
91/2 ToppsStadiumClub 259
92/3 ToppsStadiumClub 78
93/4 ToppsStadiumClub 397
94/5 ToppsStadiumClub 102
95/6 ToppsStadiumClub 65
95/6 TSC-MembersOnly 8
97/8 ToppsSticker 2
90/1 UpperDeck 351, 352
91/2 UpperDeck 367, 619
92/3 UpperDeck 17, 321
93/4 UD 175, HT16, SP-128
94/5 UpperDeck 103, SP63
95/6 UD 176, 225, 246, 495
95/6 UD AS13, R7, SE163
96/7 UpperDeck 146, P18, X19
96/7 UD-AllStarYCTG A6
97/8 UD 147, SG24, T6A
93/4 UDBeAPlayer 33
94/5 UDBeAPlayer R51, -Aut. 59
96/7 UDBlackDiamond 111
97/8 UDBlackDiamond 9
98/9 UDChoice 175
95/6 UDCollChoice 259, C12
96/7 UDCC 233, 330, S25,UD42
97/8 UDCC 214, C30, SQ78
97/8 udDiamondVision 13
96/7 UpperDeck"Ice" 59
97/8 UpperDeckIce 10, L3C
97/8 Zenith 27, Z60
90/1 QUE/PetroCanada
91/2 QUE/PetroCanada
92/3 QUE/PetroCanada
94/5 QUE/BurgerKing
96/7 S.J/PacificBellSheet (x4)
97/8 S.J/PacificBellSheet (x3)

NOLAN, TED
90/1 SketchMEM 24
90/1 SketchOHL 176
91/2 SketchOHL 318
93/4 Slapshot(SSMarie) 29
89/90 SSMarie
93/4 SSMarie 30

NOLET, D.
90/1 SketchQMJHL 266

NOLET, SIMON
70/1 Colgate Stamp 51
70/1 EddieSargent 150
71/2 EddieSargent 148
72/3 EddieSargent 158
74/5 Loblaws
68/9 O-Pee-Chee 187
70/1 OPC 194
71/2 OPC/Topps 206
72/3 OPC 125, Topps 26
73/4 OPC 222
74/5 OPC/Topps 187
75/6 OPC/Topps 220, 319
76/7 OPC/Topps 64
72 SemicSticker 174
71/2 TheTorontoSun
76/7 COL.R
76/7 COL.R/CokeCans
70/1 PHA

84/5 QUE
85/6 QUE
85/6 QUE/GeneralFoods
86/7 QUE
86/7 QUE/GeneralFoods
65/6 Québec Aces

NOONAN, BRIAN
92/3 Bowman 98
93/4 Donruss 464
94/5 Donruss 140
95/6 Donruss 242
92/3 FleerUltra 280
93/4 FleerUltra 291
95/6 FleerUltra 301
93/4 Leaf 398
94/5 Leaf 217
88/9 OPC/Topps 165
92/3 O-Pee-Chee 234
90/1 opcPremier 87
88/9 opcSticker 11/140
88/9 opcStickFS 15
98/9 Pacific 432
97/8 PacificCrown 339
88/9 PaniniSticker 28
92/3 PaniniSticker 9
93/4 PaniniSticker 149
91/2 Parkhurst 264
94/5 Parkhurst 143
95/6 Parkhurst 445
92/3 Pinnacle 194
93/4 Pinnacle 162
94/5 Pinnacle 131
96/7 Pinnacle 30
96/7 PinnacleBeAPlayer 201
94/5 POG 168
95/6 POG 237
93/4 PowerPlay 314
93/4 Premier 13
94/5 Premier 28
88/9 ProCards(Saginaw)
90/1 ProSet 433
91/2 PSPlatinum 165
92/3 Score 89
93/4 Score 411
95/6 Score 156
97/8 Score(VAN) 18
92/3 Topps 159
92/3 ToppsStadiumClub 400
95/6 ToppsStadiumClub 121
91/2 UpperDeck 380
92/3 UpperDeck 117
94/5 UpperDeck 302
95/6 UpperDeck 272
95/6 UDCollChoice 116
96/7 UDCollChoice 232
87/8 CHI/Coke
88/9 CHI/Coke
91/2 CHI/Coke
93/4 CHI/Coke

NORBERG, KENT
89/90 SemicElitserien 189

NORD, BJÖRN
94/5 ElitSet 133
95/6 ElitSet 192
95 Globe 24
92/3 SemicElitserien 84
92/3 UpperDeck 231
95/6 udElite 42
97/8 udSwedish 38

NORD, TOMAS
89/90 SemicElitserien 128
90/1 SemicElitserien 205

NORDBERG, ROBERT
94/5 ElitSet 42
95/6 ElitSet 82
90/1 SemicElitserien 245
91/2 SemicElitserien 170
92/3 SemicElitserien 188
95/6 udElite 128
97/8 udSwedish 127

NORDBLAD, CHRISTER
71/2 WilliamsFIN 289

NORDFELDT, HENRIK
94/5 ElitSet 281
95/6 ElitSet 132
97/8 udSwedish 192

NORDGREN, JOHAN
97/8 udSwedish 168

NORDIN, ANDERS
70/1 Kuvajulkaisut 34

NORDIN, HAKAN
89/90 SemicElitserien 272
90/1 SemicElitserien 31
91/2 SemicElitserien 279

NORDIN, URBAN
89/90 SemicElitserien 181
90/1 SemicElitserien 15

NORDLANDER, B.O.
72 Panda
72 SemicSticker 48
71/2 WilliamsFIN 54

NORDMARK, ROBERT
94/5 ElitSet 131
90/1 O-Pee-Chee 433
89/90 opcSticker 66/206
90/1 Panini(VAN) 18
90/1 ProSet 547
91/2 SemicElitserien 256
92/3 SemicElitserien 285
95/6 Sisu 302, 378, -DbleTro 4
96/7 Sisu-Sledgehammer 2
95/6 SisuLimited 32
87/8 STL/Kodak
88/9 VAN/Mohawk
89/90 VAN
90/1 VAN/Mohawk

NORDQVIST, NICKLAS
94/5 ElitSet 277
95/6 ElitSet 244

NORDSTROM, CARLIN
91/2 AirCanadaSJHL A46

NORDSTRÖM, PETER
94/5 ElitSet 180
95/6 ElitSet 214
95/6 udElite 73
97/8 udSwedish 52

NORDSTRÖM, ROGER
94/5 ElitSet 188, -StudioSig 8
95/6 ElitS. 258,-Mega 7,-Spdr 14
95 Globe 2
95 PaniniWorlds 136
95 Semic 52, 209
90/1 SemicElitserien 126
91/2 SemicElitserien 177
92/3 SemicElitserien 200
95/6 udElite 133
97/8 udSwedish 133

NOREN, DARRYL
90/1 ProCards 525
91/2 Greensboro
92/3 Greensboro 12

NORGREN, JOHAN
94/5 ElitSet 8
90/1 SemicElitserien 134
91/2 SemicElitserien 185
92/3 SemicElitserien 204
92/3 UpperDeck 225

NORIS, JOE
76/7 opcWHA 46
77/8 opcWHA 5
71/2 TheTorontoSun
73/4 BUF
71/2 PGH
76/7 SanDiegoMariners

NORMAN, TODD
94/5 AutoPhonex 31
97/8 Bowman 28
95/6 Classic 85
94/5 ParkieSE 267
94/5 Select 168
93/4 Slapshot(Guelph) 12
94/5 Slapshot(Gue.) 19, -Promo
95/6 Slapshot 99
94/5 SP 185
95/6 Guelph 8
96/7 Guelph 15, 32

NORMAND, DEAN
91/2 AirCanadaSJHL A1
92/3 MPSPhotoSJHL 29

NORMANDIN, ERIC
97/8 Bowman 77
96/7 Rimouski

NORMANDIN, MATHIEU
96/7 Rimouski

NORONEN, MIKA
97/8 UDBlackDiamond 26
98/9 UDChoice 278

NORPPA, TIMO
92/3 Jyvas-Hyva 61
93/4 Jyvas-Hyva 117
94 Semic 48
93 SemicSticker 70
93/4 Sisu 14
95/6 Sisu 296
96/7 Sisu 90

NORRENA, FREDRIK
94/5 Sisu 97
95/6 Sisu 324, -Ghost 5
96/7 Sisu 135, -Mighty 7
95/6 SisuLimited 1

NORRIS, BRUCE
83&87 HallOfFame 205
83 HHOF Postcard (N)

NORRIS, CLAYTON
90/1 SketchWHL 30
91/2 SketchWHL 318

NORRIS, DAVE
75/6 Hamilton

NORRIS, DWAYNE
93/4 CanadaNats
92/3 Classic 70
92/3 ClassicFourSport 195, -Aut.
94/5 ClassicImages 34
92/3 ClassicProspects 66
96/7 DEL 351
93/4 Donruss 480
93/4 FleerUltra 470
94/5 Leaf 494
94/5 Parkhurst 192
93/4 PowerPlay 491
93/4 Premier-TmCanada 13
94/5 Score 238, CT7

NORRIS, JACK
70/1 Esso Stamp
70/1 O-Pee-Chee 165
75/6 opcWHA 114
72/3 7ElevenCups
75/6 Phoenix

NORRIS, JAMES D.
83&87 HallOfFame 57
83 HHOF Postcard (D)

NORRIS, JAMES
83&87 HallOfFame 145
83 HHOF Postcard (K)

NORRISH, ROD
73/4 MIN

NØRSTEBØ, SVEIN ENOK
95 PaniniWorlds 241
94 Semic 255
93 SemicSticker 234
96 Wien 205

NORSTROM, MATTIAS
94/5 Classic 96
93/4 ClassicProspects 5
93/4 Donruss 465
95/6 Donruss 248
95/6 EdgeIce 20
93/4 FleerUltra 376
94/5 FleerUltra 334
95/6 FleerUltra 106
96/7 FleerUltra 80
93/4 Leaf 426
94/5 Leaf 57
95/6 Leaf 288
97/8 PacificRegime 94
97/8 PaniniSticker 276
98/9 PaniniSticker 219
93/4 Parkhurst 256
94/5 Parkhurst 152
95/6 Parkhurst 143
94/5 Pinnacle 489, RTP2
97/8 PinnacleBeAPlayer 38
93/4 Premier 418
94/5 Select 194
91/2 SemicElitserien 12
92/3 SemicElitserien 30
96/7 SP 76
98/9 Topps 136
96/7 ToppsNHLPicks 171
93/4 ToppsStadiumClub 371
93/4 UpperDeck 522
94/5 UpperDeck 418
96/7 UpperDeck 277
97/8 UpperDeck 82
96/7 UDCollChoice 130
94/5 Binghampton

NORTHARD, JASON
91/2 AvantGardeBCJ 80
92/3 BCJHL 114
91/2 Nainamo

NORTHCOTT, LAURENCE (BALDY)
33/4 Anonymous (V129) 49
34-43 BeeHives(MTL.M)
33/4 CndGum (V252)
35-40 CrownBrand 51
34/5 OPC (V304B) 60
36/7 OPC (V304D) 130
37/8 OPC (V304E) 166
34/5 SweetCaporal
35/6 Triumph
33/4 WWGum (V357) 48
36/7 WWGum (V356) 22

NORTHEY, WILLIAM
83&87 HallOfFame 161
83 HHOF Postcard (L)
95/6 MTL/Forum 3Apr96

NORTON, CHRIS
88/9 ProCards(Moncton)
89/90 ProCards(AHL) 43
90/1 ProCards 252
91/2 ProCards 386
89/90 Moncton
90/1 Moncton

NORTON, DARCY
88/9 ProCards(Kalamazoo)
89/90 ProCards(IHL) 77
90/1 ProCards 320
91/2 ProCards 321
92/3 Cincinnati
86/7 Kamloops
87/8 Kamloops

NORTON, JEFF
90/1 Bowman 122
91/2 Bowman 225
93/4 Donruss 303
94/5 Donruss 132
95/6 Donruss 117
94/5 Flair 168
92/3 FleerUltra 349
93/4 FleerUltra 417
94/5 FleerUltra 199
96/7 FleerUltra 61
93/4 Leaf 390
94/5 Leaf 98
95/6 Leaf 74
89/90 OPC/Topps 120
90/1 OPC/Topps 166
91/2 OPC/Topps 243
89/90 PaniniSticker 273
90/1 PaniniSticker 93
91/2 PaniniSticker 248
92/3 PaniniSticker 205
93/4 PaniniSticker 64
94/5 PaniniSticker 224
96/7 PaniniSticker 264
91/2 Parkhurst 331
92/3 Parkhurst 337
93/4 Parkhurst 455
95/6 Parkhurst 349
91/2 Pinnacle 172
92/3 Pinnacle 102
93/4 Pinnacle 353
94/5 Pinnacle 99
95/6 Pinnacle 188
96/7 PinnacleBeAPlayer 187
94/5 POG 218
95/6 POG 244
93/4 PowerPlay 223
93/4 Premier 447
90/1 ProSet 189
91/2 ProSet 148
91/2 PSPlatinum 78
90/1 Score 157, -Hot 70
91/2 Score(CDN) 222, (U.S) 222
91/2 Score-YoungStar 16
92/3 Score 56
93/4 Score 69, 522
95/6 Score 178
92/3 ToppsGold 526
95/6 Topps 69
96/7 ToppsNHLPicks 157
91/2 ToppsStadiumClub 98
92/3 ToppsStadiumClub 324
93/4 ToppsStadiumClub 495
94/5 ToppsStadiumClub 86
90/1 UpperDeck 386
91/2 UpperDeck 357
93/4 UpperDeck 512
95/6 UpperDeck 160
94/5 UDBeAPlayer R57, -Aut. 90
95/6 UDCollChoice 112
96/7 EDM
97/8 FLA/WinnDixie
89/90 NYI
92/3 S.J/PacificBell

NORTON, STEVE
93/4 Mich.State

NORWICH, CRAIG
80/1 OPC/Topps 53
79 PaniniSticker 209
79/80 WPG

NORWOOD, LEE
88/9 O-Pee-Chee 240
89/90 OPC/Topps 75
90/1 OPC/Topps 285
89/90 opcSticker 251/114
87/8 PaniniSticker 235
89/90 PaniniSticker 68
90/1 PaniniSticker 202
91/2 PaniniSticker 214
91/2 Parkhurst 373
90/1 ProSet 74
90/1 ScoreTraded 74T
91/2 Score(CDN) 528
91/2 ToppsStadiumClub 317
90/1 UpperDeck 78
86/7 DET/Caesars
87/8 DET/Caesars
88/9 DET/Caesars
88/9 DET
89/90 DET/Caesars
90/1 N.J.
80/1 QUE
81/2 WSH
82/3 WSH

NOSE, VIRGIL
90/1 Rayside
91/2 Rayside

NOSEWORTHY, DAVE
89/90 SketchOHL 44

NOTTINGHAM, MIKE
84/5 Kamloops
85/6 Kamloops

NOVA, MILAN
79 PaniniSticker 85

NOVAK, AARON
93/4 Minn-Duluth

NOVAK, EDVARD
72 SemicSticker 37
74 SemicSticker 75
71/2 WilliamsFIN 34

NOVAK, JACK
52/3 AnonymousOHL 125

NOVAK, JIRI
79 PaniniSticker 82
74 SemicSticker 65
73/4 WilliamsFIN 58

NOVAK, RICHARD
89/90 ProCards(IHL) 106

NOVOSJOLOV, WALDEMAR
94/5 DEL 358

NOVOTNY, JIRI
95/6 APS 241

NOVOTNY, MAREK
94/5 APS 162
95/6 APS 176

NOVY, HELMUT
70/1 Kuvajulkaisut 91

NOVY, MILAN
83/4 opcSticker 187
83/4 PuffySticker 19
74 SemicSticker 59
82 SemicSticker 87
83/4 SouhaitsRen.KeyChain
92/3 Trends(76) 155, 186, 198
82/3 WSH

NOWAK, DANIEL
94/5 DEL 433
95/6 DEL 392, 431
96/7 DEL 299

NOWAK, HANK
82? JDMcCarthy
74/5 Loblaws, -Update
76/7 OPC/Topps 224

NOWICKI, ANDY
93/4 RedDeer

NUMMELA, TAPIO
70/1 Kuvajulkaisut 246

NUMMELIN, PETTERI
95/6 ElitSet 206
95 Hartwall
95 PaniniWorlds 167
95/6 RadioCity
94 Semic 12
95 Semic 39
93/4 Sisu 32
94/5 Sisu 62, 153,
94/5 Sisu-Special 3, -Magic 2
95/6 Sisu-GoldCards 9
95/6 SisuLimited 3
95/6 udElite 209
96 Wien 3

NUMMELIN, TIMO
66/7 Champion 76
72 Hellas 8
70/1 Kuvajulkaisut 164
80/1 Mallasjuoma 178
82 Mallasjuoma
79 PaniniSticker 165
82 SemicSticker 29
82 Skopbank
78/9 SM-Liiga 3, 201
77-80 Sportscaster 48-1152
71/2 WilliamsFIN 233
72/3 WilliamsFIN 68, 217
73/4 WilliamsFIN 73, 292

NUMMINEN, KALEVI
66/7 Champion 148
65/6 Hellas 160
74 SemicSticker 98
77-80 Sportscaster 75-1800

NUMMINEN, REIMA
71/2 WilliamsFIN 372

NUMMINEN, TEEMU
93/4 Jyvas-Hyva 297
93/4 Sisu 71
95/6 Sisu 329

NUMMINEN, TEPPO
90/1 Bowman 138
91/2 Bowman 201
92/3 Bowman 299
93/4 Donruss 385
94/5 Donruss 267
95/6 Donruss 261
96/7 Donruss 126
93/4 EASports 146
94/5 Flair 208
96/7 Fleer 91, -Norris 8
95/6 FleerMetal 164
96/7 FleerNHLPicks 72
92/3 FleerUltra 243
93/4 FleerUltra 455
94/5 FleerUltra 244
95/6 FleerUltra 182
96/7 FleerUltra 134
95 Globe 133
93 Koululainen
93/4 Leaf 135
94/5 Leaf 233
95/6 Leaf 247
96/7 Leaf 113
96/7 MetalUniverse 120
97/8 Omega 175
90/1 OPC/Topps 385
91/2 OPC/Topps 274
92/3 O-Pee-Chee 4
98/9 Pacific 342
97/8 PacificCrown 122
98/9 PacificParamount 183
90/1 Panini(WPG) 18
89/90 PaniniSticker 172
90/1 PaniniSticker 307
91/2 PaniniSticker 71
92/3 PaniniSticker 52
93/4 PaniniSticker 197
94/5 PaniniSticker 169
95/6 PaniniSticker 220
96/7 PaniniSticker 194
97/8 PaniniSticker 156
91/2 Parkhurst 200
92/3 Parkhurst 438
93/4 Parkhurst 231
94/5 Parkhurst 270
95/6 Parkhurst 228
94/5 ParkieSE ES10
91/2 Pinnacle 166
92/3 Pinnacle 215
93/4 Pinnacle 92
94/5 Pinnacle 77
95/6 Pinnacle 67
96/7 Pinnacle 8
95/6 Playoff 107, 328
96/7 Playoff 350
94/5 POG 346
95/6 POG 294
93/4 PowerPlay 272
93/4 Premier 269
94/5 Premier 376
90/1 ProSet 334
91/2 ProSet 261
92/3 ProSet 210
91/2 PSPlatinum 248
90/1 Score 176
91/2 Score(CDN) 101, (U.S) 101
92/3 Score 102
93/4 Score 132
94/5 Score 91
95/6 Score 139
96/7 Score 5
94 Semic 10, 335
95 Semic 37
91 SemicSticker 201
92 SemicSticker 5
93 SemicSticker 57
94/5 Sisu-GuestSpecial 6
95/6 SisuLimited 93, -S&S 6
95/6 SkyBoxEmotion 195
95/6 SkyBoxImpact 183
96/7 SkyBoxImpact 106, -Fox 16
96/7 SP 122
97/8 SPAuthentic 122
95/6 Summit 113
96/7 Summit 55
92/3 Topps 339
95/6 Topps 67
98/9 Topps 57
95/6 ToppsFinest 167
91/2 ToppsStadiumClub 302
92/3 ToppsStadiumClub 77
93/4 ToppsStadiumClub 164
94/5 ToppsStadiumClub 152
91/2 UpperDeck 240
92/3 UpperDeck 326
93/4 UpperDeck 53
94/5 UpperDeck 113
95/6 UpperDeck 275
96/7 UpperDeck 131
97/8 UpperDeck 336
95/6 UDBeAPlayer 68
98/9 UDChoice 157
95/6 UDCollChoice 292
96/7 UDCollChoice 209
97/8 UDCollChoice 200
96 Wien 27
96/7 PHO
97/8 PHO
88/9 WPG/Police
89/90 WPG/Safeway
90/1 WPG/IGA
91/2 WPG/IGA
93/4 WPG/Ruffles
95/6 WPG

NURMBERG, TIMO
95/6 Sisu 116
96/7 Sisu 130

NURMI, HEIKKI
72/3 WilliamsFIN 160
73/4 WilliamsFIN 226

NURMI, JUHA
80/1 Mallasjuoma 167
89/90 SemicElitserien 163

NURMI, PER
70/1 Kuvajulkaisut 183
71/2 WilliamsFIN 106
72/3 WilliamsFIN 150
73/4 WilliamsFIN 117

NURMI, SEPPO
66/7 Champion 166
70/1 Kuvajulkaisut 247
71/2 WilliamsFIN 214
72/3 WilliamsFIN 161
73/4 WilliamsFIN 227

NURMINEN, AARO
65/6 Hellas 107

NURMINEN, JAAKKO
70/1 Kuvajulkaisut 199

NURMINEN, JARI
72/3 WilliamsFIN 291

NURMINEN, JUHA
93/4 Sisu 290
94/5 Sisu-FireOnIce 17
95/6 Sisu 10

NURMINEN, KAI
95/6 ElitSet 228
93/4 Jyvas-Hyva 329
97/8 PacificRegime 95
98/9 PaniniSticker 221
96/7 SelectCertified 91
93/4 Sisu 48
94/5 Sisu 101,-Fire 18,-Horos 13
95/6 Sisu 166, 197
95/6 SisuLimited 86
96/7 SP 181
96/7 UpperDeck 275
93 Wien 36
95/6 udElite 90
97/8 udSwedish 81, 211, C6

NURMINEN, TIMO
70/1 Kuvajulkaisut 302
73/4 WilliamsFIN 293

NUTIKKA, V.P.
94/5 ParkieSE 222
95/6 Sisu 279
96/7 Sisu 77
94/5 SP 159
94/5 ToppsFinest 135

NUUTINEN, SAMI
92/3 Jyvas-Hyva 106
93/4 Jyvas-Hyva 195
93 SemicSticker 58
93/4 Sisu 260
94/5 Sisu 122
95/6 Sisu 85, -DoubleTrouble 6
95/6 SisuLimited 56

NYBERG, PATRIK
91/2 SemicElitserien 249

NYGARDS, PER
90/1 SemicElitserien 280
91/2 SemicElitserien 63

NYGREN, HÅKAN
69/70 MästarSerien 39
72 Panda
72 SemicSticker 53
71/2 WilliamsFIN 55

NYKOLUK, MIKE
45-64 BeeHives(TOR)
57/8 Parkhurst(TOR) 16
93/4 Parkie(56/7) 130
81/2 TOR
82/3 TOR
83/4 TOR

NYKOPP, TIMO
92/3 Jyvas-Hyva 20
95/6 Sisu 150

NYKVIST, HANNU
80/1 Mallasjuoma 63

NYKYFORUK, CURTIS
88/9 Regina
89/90 Victoria

NYLANDER, MICHAEL
91/2 Classic 47
91/2 ClassicFourSport 47, -Aut.
93/4 Donruss 144, 407
94/5 Donruss 74
95/6 FleerMetal 22
93/4 FleerUltra 105, -UltraPros 7
94/5 FleerUltra 32
95/6 FleerUltra 213
95 Globe 35
93/4 Leaf 94
94/5 Leaf 149
96/7 Leaf 115
97/8 Omega 33
92/3 opcPremier 19
98/9 Pacific 123
98/9 PacificParamount 31
93/4 PaniniSticker 128
96/7 PaniniSticker 237
92/3 Parkhurst 294
93/4 Parkhurst 83
94/5 Parkhurst 32
95/6 Parkhurst 34
92/3 Pinnacle 400
93/4 Pinnacle 166
94/5 Pinnacle 142
96/7 Pinnacle 151
94/5 POG 57
95/6 POG 54
93/4 PowerPlay 106
93/4 Premier 99
94/5 Premier 237
93/4 Score 383
94/5 Score 59
95/6 Score 289
96/7 Score 79
91/2 SemicElitserien 21
92/3 SemicElitserien 338, 339
93 SemicSticker 40
94/5 Sisu-GuestSpecial 7
95/6 Sisu-Specials 10
95/6 SisuLimited 54, -Gallery 3
95/6 SP 20
91/2 StarPics 23
95/6 ToppsFinest 172
93/4 ToppsStadiumClub 186
95/6 ToppsStadiumClub 154
91/2 UltimateDP 42, -Aut 42
91/2 UltimateDP 76, 88
92/3 UD 236, 378, 520, ER2
93/4 UD 70, HT13, NL1, SP-62
94/5 UpperDeck 79, 556, SP103
95/6 UpperDeck 454, SE102
96/7 UpperDeck 27
95/6 UDBeAPlayer 148
98/9 UDChoice 32
95/6 UDCollChoice 311
96/7 UDCollChoice 38, 312
95/6 udElite 237
96 Wien 61
92/3 HFD/DairyMart
93/4 HFD/Coke

NYLANDER, PETER
92/3 SemicElitserien 356
94/5 SigRookies 21
95/6 UpperDeck 559
97/8 udSwedish 31

NYLUND, GARY
91/2 Bowman 228
84/5 O-Pee-Chee 307
85/6 O-Pee-Chee 172
86/7 O-Pee-Chee 243
87/8 OPC/Topps 82
88/9 OPC/Topps 15
89/90 OPC/Topps 105
90/1 OPC/Topps 233
91/2 OPC/Topps 101
84/5 opcSticker 15, 16
85/6 opcSticker 14/144
86/7 opcSticker 137/245
87/8 opcSticker 80/213
89/90 opcSticker 114/251
87/8 PaniniSticker 224
88/9 PaniniSticker 23
90/1 PaniniSticker 80
91/2 PaniniSticker 251
91/2 Pinnacle 406
90/1 ProSet 190
91/2 ProSet 150
90/1 Score 86
91/2 Score(CDN) 192, (U.S) 192
92/3 Score 381
84/5 7ElevenDisk
83/4 SouhaitsRen.KeyChain
91/2 ToppsStadiumClub 163
90/1 UpperDeck 139
91/2 UpperDeck 406
83/4 Vachon 94
86/7 CHI/Coke
87/8 CHI/Coke
89/90 NYI
82/3 TOR
83/4 TOR
84/5 TOR
85/6 TOR

NYMAN, HARRI
80/1 Mallasjuoma 75
78/9 SM-Liiga 115

NYMAN, STEFAN
90/1 SemicElitserien 59
91/2 SemicElitserien 232

NYMAN, TERO
96/7 Sisu 11

NYROP, BILL
76/7 OPC/Topps 188
77/8 OPC/Topps 91
78/9 OPC/Topps 134
92/3 Trends(76) 158
81/2 MIN
76/7 MTL
77/8 MTL
91/2 Knoxville

NYSTROM, BOB
74/5 Loblaws
73/4 O-Pee-Chee 202
74/5 OPC/Topps 123
75/6 OPC/Topps 259, 323
76/7 OPC/Topps 153
77/8 OPC/Topps 62
78/9 OPC/Topps 153
79/80 OPC/Topps 217
80/1 OPC/Topps 102
81/2 O-Pee-Chee 217
82/3 O-Pee-Chee 208
83/4 O-Pee-Chee 14
84/5 OPC 132, Topps 98
85/6 OPC/Topps 11
86/7 OPC/Topps 104
82/3 opcSticker 59
83/4 opcSticker 85
84/5 opcSticker 85
85/6 opcSticker 69/193
86/7 opcSticker 204/76
82/3 Post
91/2 UpperDeck 641
79/80 NYI
83/4 NYI
83/4 NYI/Islander 11
84/5 NYI 12
93/4 NYI/Chemical
84/5 KelownaWingsWHL 35

NYSTRÖM, JARI
70/1 Kuvajulkaisut 335
80/1 Mallasjuoma 213

NYSTROM, KAREN
94/5 Classic W20
97/8 UDCollChoice 295

NYSTROM, MURRAY
85/6 London 6
86/7 London 14

NYSTRÖM, SEPP
66/7 Champion 41
65/6 Hellas 47

NYYSSÖNEN, TOMMI
95/6 Sisu 83
96/7 Sisu 83

O

OAKE, SCOTT
97/8 Pinnacle - CBC Sports 10

OAKLEY, ERNIE
51/2 LavalDairy 60

OATES, ADAM
95/6 Aces 10 (Hearts)
96/7 Aces 4 (Spades)
97/8 Aces 5 (Diamonds)
90/1 Bowman 16
91/2 Bowman 384, 406
92/3 Bowman 213, 258
95/6 Bowman 44
92/3 ClassicProspects 35, BC18
93/4 Donruss 18, B
95/6 Donruss 386, -Igniters 1
96/7 Donruss 41
97/8 Donruss 25, 228
96/7 DonrussCanadianIce 8
97/8 D.CdnIce 78, -National 7
95/6 DonrussElite 80
96/7 DonrussElite 31
97/8 DonrussPreferred 100
97/8 DonrussPriority 149
97/8 DonrussStudio 32
93/4 EASports 9, 188
95/6 EdgeIce L3
94/5 Flair 12, -HotNumber 6
96/7 Flair 5
94/5 Fleer 16
96/7 Fleer 6, -ArtRoss 18
95/6 FleerMetal 10,-HeavyMt 11
96/7 FleerNHLPicks 28, -Fab 35
96/7 FleerNHLPicks-Jagged 15
92/3 FleerUltra 8
93/4 FleerUltra 156, -AS 7
93/4 FU-Oates 1-12, -Pivots 7
94/5 FleerUltra 14, -Pivots 9
95/6 FU 13, 395,-Pivot 6,-Ext 16
96/7 FU 10, -Red 6, -Power 14
95 Globe 90
93/4 HockeyWit 5
95/6 Hoyle'EAST 9 (Diamonds)
97/8 KatchMedallion 153
94/5 KennerSLU
96/7 KennerSLU (U.S)
91/2 Kraft 5
94/5 Kraft-Sharpshooter
95/6 Kraft
96/7 KraftDinner, -Trophy
97/8 Kraft -WorldsBest
93/4 Leaf 235, -HatTricks 8
94/5 Leaf 305, -Gold 14, -Ltd. 2
95/6 Leaf 81
96/7 Leaf 112
97/8 Leaf 130
94/5 LeafLimited 104
95/6 LeafLimited 108
96/7 LeafLimited 5
96/7 LeafPreferred 40, -Steel 54
97/8 Limited 33, 112, 162
96/7 Maggers 13
92/3 McDonalds McD11
93/4 McDonalds McD21
96/7 MetalUniverse 9, -Lethal 15
97/8 Omega 243
87/8 OPC/Topps 123
88/9 OPC/Topps 161
89/90 OPC/Topps 185
90/1 OPC/Topps 149
91/2 OPC/Topps 265, 347, 448
92/3 OPC 172, 272, -25Years 20
90/1 opcPremier 88
91/2 opcPremier 7
92/3 opcPremier-Star 13
87/8 opcSticker 105 /238
98/9 Pacific 445
97/8 PacificCrown 37, -Slap 12B
97/8 PacificCrownRoyale 142
97/8 PcfcDynagon! 133,-Tand 56
97/8 PacificInvincible 149
97/8 PacificParamount 198
98/9 PacificParamount 349
97/8 PacificRevolution 150
87/8 PaniniSticker 248
88/9 PaniniSticker 45
90/1 PaniniSticker 275
91/2 PaniniSticker 31
92/3 PaniniSticker 136
93/4 PaniniSticker 2, 138
94/5 PaniniSticker 1, CC
95/6 PaniniSticker 3
96/7 PaniniSticker 4
97/8 PaniniSticker 116
91/2 Parkhurst 155, 233
92/3 Parkhurst 4
93/4 Parkhurst 11
94/5 Parkhurst 311, V46
95/6 Parkhurst 16, PP53
94/5 ParkieSE 13
91/2 Pinnacle 6, 378
92/3 Pinnacle 40
93/4 Pinnacle 185
94/5 Pinnacle 120
95/6 Pinnacle 3
96/7 Pinnacle 130
97/8 Pinnacle 62
97/8 PinnacleBeeAPlayer 5
97/8 PinnacleBeeHive 38
97/8 PinnacleCertified 49
95/6 PinnacleFANtasy 5
97/8 PinnacleInside 28
95/6 PinnacleZenith 10
96/7 PinnacleZenith 41
95/6 Playoff 9, 121, 229
94/5 POG 35
95/6 POG 29
93/4 PowerPlay 23, -Point 11
93/4 Premier 50, 74
93/4 Prmr-Black(OPC) 3, (T) 5
94/5 Premier 135, 277
95/6 ProMagnet 14, 01
90/1 ProSet 269
91/2 ProSet 219, 291, CC7
91/2 PS-Promo 1 -ThePuck 25
92/3 ProSet 3
91/2 PSPlatinum 113
90/1 Score 85, -HotCards 41
91/2 Score(CDN) 458, (U.S) 238
91/2 Score-HotCards 6
92/3 Score 250
93/4 Score 125, 478, (U.S) DD3
93/4 S-Dream 17, -P.AS 9
94/5 Score 141, NP3
95/6 Score 119
96/7 Score 162
97/8 Score 117
92/3 SeasonsPatch 20
93/4 SeasonsPatch 13
94/5 Select 58
95/6 SelectCert. 11, -Double 5
96/7 SelectCert. 68
95/6 SkBxEmotion 11, -Xcel 1
95/6 SkyBoxImpact 12
96/7 SkyBoxImpact 7, -Blade 17
94/5 SP 8
95/6 SP 7
96/7 SP 11, HC29
97/8 SPAuthentic 162
97/8 SPx 48, SPX12
91/2 StarPics 40
95/6 Summit 4
96/7 Summit 15
95/6 SuperSticker 5, 8
96/7 TeamOut
92/3 Topps 475
95/6 Topps 180, 381, 7PL
98/9 Topps 179, SB23
94/5 ToppsFinest 67, -Div. 3
95/6 ToppsFinest 43
91/2 ToppsStadiumClub 108
92/3 T.StadiumClub 188, 245
93/4 T.StadiumClub 93, -AllStar
93/4 TSC-Master(1) 11
95/6 T.StadiumClub 40
93/4 TSC-MembersOnly 37
94/5 TSC-MembersOnly 16
97/8 ToppsSticker 4
95/6 ToppsSuperSkills 2
90/1 UpperDeck 173, 483
91/2 UpperDeck 94, 252, 627
92/3 UpperDeck 133, 455, 637
92/3 UD-LockerAS 10
93/4 UpperDeck 226, 286, 327
93/4 UpperDeck H6, HT5, SP-11
94/5 UpperDeck 11, H20, R12
94/5 UpperDeck R26, R44, SP7
95/6 UpperDeck 197, SE5, R16
95/6 UD-AllStarPredict MVPR28
96/7 UpperDeck 216, X40
97/8 UD 177, SG56, SS12, T18A
94/5 UDBeAPlayer R45
96/7 UDBlackDiamond 152
97/8 UDBlackDiamond 109
98/9 UDChoice 217
95/6 UDCollChoice 197
96/7 UDCC 12, 310, C21, UD15
97/8 UDCC 266, S28, SQ23
96/7 UpperDeck"Ice" 2
97/8 UpperDeckIce 17
96 Wien 100
97/8 Zenith 32, Z41
91/2 BOS/SportsAction
92/3 BOS
85/6 DET/Caesars
86/7 DET/Caesars
87/8 DET/Caesars
88/9 DET/Caesars
89/90 STL/Kodak
90/1 STL/Kodak
91/2 STL
92/3 STL/UpperDeck 17

OATES, MATT
93/4 Indianapolis

OATMAN, ED
91 C55 Reprint 5
1911-12 Imperial (C55) 5
1912-13 Imperial (C57) 47
1910-11 Imperial Post 5
23/4 PaulinsCandy 61

OBERG, FREDRIK
95/6 ElitSet 301, -FaceTo 12
95/6 udElite 193
92/3 SemicElitserien 195
97/8 udSwedish 147

OBERLIN, RICH
88/9 ProCards(Indianapolis)

OBERRAUCH, ROBERTO
95 Globe 228
95 PaniniWorlds 81
92 SemicSticker
93 SemicSticker 211
96 Wien 176

OBLOJ, TADEUSZ
74 Hellas 101
79 PaniniSticker 133
73/4 WilliamsFIN 96

OBRESA, PETER
94/5 DEL 104
95/6 DEL 101
89 SemicSticker 119

O'BRIEN, ANDY
82/3 Kitchener 26

O'BRIEN, DAN
89/90 Nashville

O'BRIEN, DAVE
88/9 ProCards(Binghampton)
89/90 ProCards(IHL) 19
90/1 ProCards 92

O'BRIEN, DENNIS
74/5 Loblaws
73/4 OPC 88
76/7 OPC 387
79/80 OPC 375
74/5 OPC/Topps 96
75/6 OPC/Topps 53
76/7 OPC/Topps 34
77/8 OPC/Topps 173
78/9 OPC/Topps 104
71/2 TheTorontoSun
73/4 Topps 177
73/4 MIN
92/3 Toledo 1

O'BRIEN, J.A.
83&87 HallOfFame 206
83 HHOF Postcard (N)
95/6 MTL/Forum 27Mar96

O'BRIEN, MAURICE
90/1 SketchOHL 90

O'BRIEN, SEAN
94/5 Richmond
95/6 Tallahassee 7

OBSUT, JAROSLAV
95/6 SwiftCurrent

O'CALLAHAN, JACK
36/7 WWGum (V356) 107

O'CALLAHAN, JACK
94/5 MiracleOnIce 23, 24
84/5 O-Pee-Chee 43
86/7 O-Pee-Chee 207
84/5 Topps 33
79/80 USAOlympicTeam 6
86/7 CHI/Coke
88/9 N.J/Caretta

OCHOA, ALEX
92/3 Cincinnati

O'CONNELL, JOHN
91/2 Minnesota

O'CONNELL, MIKE
80/1 OPC/Topps 61
81/2 OPC 6, Topps(E) 70
82/3 O-Pee-Chee 17
83/4 O-Pee-Chee 56
84/5 O-Pee-Chee 12, Topps 9
85/6 OPC/Topps 2
86/7 OPC/Topps 140
87/8 OPC/Topps 141
88/9 OPC/Topps 92
89/90 O-Pee-Chee 223
90/1 OPC/Topps 114
82/3 opcSticker 89
84/5 opcSticker 185
83/4 opcSticker 52
85/6 opcSticker 161/31
86/7 opcSticker 160/17
87/8 opcSticker 107/241
88/9 opcSticker 248/118
89/90 opcSticker 249/112
87/8 PaniniSticker 240
89/90 PaniniSticker 69
90/1 PaniniSticker 215
82/3 Post
90/1 ProCards 296
90/1 ProSet 114
83/4 SouhaitsRen.KeyChain
83/4 BOS
84/5 BOS
79/80 CHI
80/1 CHI/4x6
86/7 DET/Caesars
87/8 DET/Caesars
88/9 DET
88/9 DET/Caesars
89/90 DET/Caesars

O'CONNOR, ERIC
91/2 SketchQMJHL 166

O'CONNOR, HERBERT (BUDDY)
34-43 BeeHives(MTL.C)
45-64 BeeHives(NYR)
43-47 ParadeSportive (x2)
45-54 QuakerOats
36/7 WWGum V356 114
95/6 MTL/Forum 6Dec96

O'CONNOR, MIKE
94 Semic 315
95/6 SheffieldSteelers

O'CONNOR, MYLES
91/2 OPC/Topps 509
93/4 Parkhurst 274
93/4 Premier(Gold) 527
89/90 ProCards(AHL) 206
90/1 ProCards 576
91/2 ProCards 425
91/2 Score(CDN) 352, (U.S) 322
91/2 UpperDeck 485
90/1 N.J.
96/7 Cincinnati

O'CONNOR, SCOTT
94 Semic 312

O'CONNOR, TERRY
52/3 AnonymousOHL 161

O'CONNOR, TOM
93/4 Classic 107, CL7

ODDLEIFSON, CHRIS
74/5 Loblaws
74/5 OPC/Topps 108
75/6 OPC/Topps 169
76/7 OPC/Topps 112, OPC 395
77/8 OPC/Topps 209
78/9 OPC/Topps 183
79/80 O-Pee-Chee 305
80/1 O-Pee-Chee 295
81/2 opcSticker 246
74/5 VAN/RoyalBank
75/6 VAN/RoyalBank
76/7 VAN/RoyalBank
77/8 VAN/GingerAle
77/8 VAN/RoyalBank
78/9 VAN/RoyalBank
79/80 VAN

ODELEIN, LEE
91/2 ProCards 447

ODELEIN, LYLE
93/4 Donruss 167
94/5 Donruss 272
95/6 Donruss 281
96/7 Duracell DC2, JB2
94/5 Fleer 105
92/3 FleerUltra 331
93/4 FleerUltra 354
94/5 FleerUltra 112
93/4 Leaf 283
94/5 Leaf 137
95/6 Leaf 195
91/2 OPC/Topps 350
98/9 Pacific 267
97/8 PacificCrown 143
92/3 Parkhurst 325
93/4 Parkhurst 370
95/6 Parkhurst 381
94/5 ParkieSE 89
93/4 Pinnacle 301

94/5 Pinnacle 132
95/6 Pinnacle 196
95/6 Playoff 165
96/7 PinnacleBeAPlayer 148
97/8 PinnacleBeAPlayer 17
94/5 POG 140
93/4 PowerPlay 132
94/5 Premier 43
88/9 ProCards(Peoria)
89/90 ProCards(AHL) 185
90/1 ProSet 617
93/4 Score 283
96/7 Score 224
97/8 Score(N.J.) 15
94/5 ToppsStadiumClub 104
91/2 UpperDeck 482
93/4 UpperDeck 7
95/6 UpperDeck 153
96/7 UpperDeck 289
97/8 UpperDeck 306
95/6 UDBeAPlayer 111
95/6 UDCollChoice 6
90/1 MTL
91/2 MTL
92/3 MTL
93/4 MTL
94/5 MTL
94/5 MTL/MolsonExport
95/6 MTL
95/6 MTL/MolsonExport
96/7 N.J/Sharp

ODELEIN, SELMAR
88/9 ProCards(CapeBreton)
87/8 EDM
88/9 EDM/ActionMagazine 26

O'DETTE, MATT
93/4 Slapshot(Kitchener) 21
95/6 Slapshot 154

ODGERS, JEFF
92/3 Bowman 397
94/5 FleerUltra 368
94/5 Leaf 439
96/7 Maggers
97/8 Omega 62
92/3 O-Pee-Chee 190
98/9 Pacific 166
97/8 PacificCrown 157
92/3 PaniniSticker 130
93/4 PaniniSticker 260
97/8 PaniniSticker 2
91/2 Parkhurst 386
92/3 Parkhurst 398
96/7 PinnacleBeAPlayer 193
93/4 PowerPlay 224
93/4 Premier 497
90/1 ProCards 600
97/8 Score(BOS) 18
92/3 Topps 483
92/3 ToppsStadiumClub 142
93/4 ToppsStadiumClub 114
94/5 ToppsStadiumClub 11
91/2 UpperDeck 597
92/3 S.J/PacificBell
88/9 Brandon 12
89/90 Brandon 20
90/1 KansasCity 2

ODJICK, GINO
91/2 Bowman 316
93/4 Donruss 346
94/5 Donruss 241
94/5 Fleer 228
92/3 FleerUltra 427
93/4 FleerUltra 442
94/5 FleerUltra 229
93/4 Leaf 418
94/5 Leaf 200
91/2 OPC/Topps 203
97/8 PacificDynag-BestKept 98
94/5 PaniniSticker 150
92/3 Parkhurst 422
93/4 Parkhurst 485
94/5 ParkieSE 186
93/4 Pinnacle 308
94/5 Pinnacle 177
94/5 POG 151
93/4 PowerPlay 461
90/1 ProCards 334
91/2 ProSet 505
91/2 Score(CDN) 237
92/3 Score 540
93/4 Score 385
94/5 Score 9
97/8 Score(VAN) 16
89/90 SketchMEM 54
91/2 ToppsStadiumClub 338
90/1 UpperDeck 518
91/2 UpperDeck 195
94/5 UpperDeck 465
95/6 UpperDeck 338
97/8 UpperDeck 206, 379
95/6 UDBeAPlayer 222
95/6 UDCollChoice 290
96/7 UDCollChoice 274
97/8 UDCollChoice 263
90/1 VAN/Mohawk
91/2 VAN
92/3 VAN/RoadTrip
93/4 VAN/Coins
94/5 VAN
95/6 VAN/Building 13
96/7 VAN
96/7 VAN/IGA

ODMARK, ULF
89/90 SemicElitserien 184
90/1 SemicElitserien 19
91/2 SemicElitserien 221
92/3 SemicElitserien 241

ODNOKON, MARK
91/2 SketchWHL 263
85/6 Minn-Duluth 17
91/2 PrinceAlbert

ODNOKON, PAT
90/1 PrinceAlbert

O'DONNELL, FRED
73/4 O-Pee-Chee 223
85/6 Kingston 4
86/7 Kingston 2

O'DONNELL, MARK
91/2 SketchOHL 292

O'DONNELL, SEAN
92/3 ClassicProspects 109
98/9 Pacific
97/8 PacificRegime 96
96/7 PinnacleBeAPlayer 152
91/2 ProCards 10
90/1 SketchOHL 390
91/2 Rochester/Genny
91/2 Rochester/Kodak
92/3 Rochester/Dunkin'Donuts
92/3 Rochester/Kodak
93/4 Rochester
88/9 Sudbury 7
89/90 Sudbury 17
90/1 Sudbury 6

O'DONOGHUE, DON
71/2 OPC/Topps 180
71/2 TheTorontoSun
71/2 EddieSargent 142

ODROWSKI, GERRY
45-64 BeeHives(DET)
72/3 O-Pee-Chee 304
74/5 opcWHA 14
62/3 Parkhurst 20
60/1 ShirriffCoin 58
61/2 ShirriffCoin 78
72/3 LosAngelesSharks
63/4 QuébecAces
71/2 STL

O'DWYER, BILL
89/90 ProCards(AHL) 71
90/1 ProCards 420

O'FLAHERTY, GERRY
74/5 Loblaws
72/3 OPC 278
73/4 OPC 250
74/5 OPC/Topps 71
75/6 OPC/Topps 307
76/7 OPC 287
77/8 OPC 377
78/9 OPC 365
72/3 VAN/RoyalBank
73/4 VAN/RoyalBank
74/5 VAN/RoyalBank
75/6 VAN/RoyalBank
76/7 VAN/RoyalBank
77/8 VAN/RoyalBank

O'FLAHERTY, JAMES
52/3 StLawrence 71

O'FLAHERTY, JOHN (PEANUTS)
34-43 BeeHives(NYA)
52/3 LavalDairy 111

O'FLAHERTY, PAT
91/2 AvantGardeBCJ 114
92/3 BCJHL 179

OGLIVIE, BRIAN
74/5 Loblaws 262

O'GRADY, MIKE
95 Classic 51

OGRODNICK, JOHN
91/2 Bowman 71, 409
90/1 Bowman 223
80/1 O-Pee-Chee 359
81/2 OPC 95, Topps(W) 95
82/3 O-Pee-Chee 79, 92
83/4 O-Pee-Chee 115, 128
84/5 OPC 62, 356, Topps 46
85/6 OPC/Topps 70, J, -AS 1
86/7 OPC/Topps 87
87/8 OPC/Topps 134
88/9 OPC/Topps 153
90/1 OPC/Topps 174, T-TL 18
91/2 OPC/Topps 365
92/3 O-Pee-Chee 351
81/2 opcSticker 121
82/3 opcSticker 179
83/4 opcSticker 137, 138
84/5 opcSticker 34, 35
84/5 opcSticker 137
85/6 opcSticker 37, 119
86/7 opcSticker 158
87/8 opcSticker 218
87/8 PaniniSticker 165
89/90 PaniniSticker 290
90/1 PaniniSticker 99
91/2 PaniniSticker 293
91/2 Parkhurst 115
91/2 Pinnacle 145
82/3 Post
90/1 ProSet 206
91/2 ProSet 169
91/2 PSPlatinum 204
83/4 PuffySticker 16
90/1 Score 113
91/2 Score(CDN) 36, (U.S) 36
92/3 Score 329
83/4 SouhaitsRen.KeyChain
91/2 ToppsStadiumClub 273
92/3 ToppsStadiumClub 222
90/1 UpperDeck 258
91/2 UpperDeck 476
80/1 DET
84/5 DET/Caesars
85/6 DET/Caesars
86/7 DET/Caesars
89/90 NYR/MarineMidland
86/7 QUE

O'HAGAN, PAUL
89/90 SketchMEM 78
89/90 SketchOHL 14, 194
90/1 SketchOHL 344
89/90 Oshawa 24
90/1 Oshawa 20

O'HAGAN, SEAN
90/1 SketchOHL 344
89/90 Windsor

O'HARA, COLIN
95/6 SwiftCurrent

OHLING, JENS
94/5 ElitSet 38, -StudioSig 3
95/6 ElitSet 33
89/90 SemicElitserien 62
90/1 SemicElitserien 286
91/2 SemicElitserien 69
92/3 SemicElitserien 90
95/6 udElite 52
97/8 udSwedish 176

OHLSSON, BENGT
92 SemicSticker 26

OHLUND, MATTIAS
97/8 DonrussElite 98, 139
97/8 DonrussPriority 171
94/5 ElitSet 288,-NHLDr 1,-Rk 4
95/6 ElitSet 75, -Mega 8
95 Globe 57
97/8 KatchMedallion 150
97/8 Omega 234
98/9 Pacific 2
97/8 PacificParamount 192
98/9 PacificParamount 238
97/8 PacificRevolution 144
94/5 ParkieSE 243
97/8 PinnacleBeAPlayer 215
97/8 Score 63
97/8 Score(VAN) 6
94/5 SigRookies 14
94/5 SP 172
95/6 SP 184
97/8 SPAuthentic 196
98/9 SPx"Finite" 127
94/5 SRGoldStandard 89
98/9 Topps 54, A4, B5, I12,SB11
94/5 UpperDeck 520
97/8 UpperDeck 380
97/8 UDBlackDiamond 120
95/6 udElite 119, 229,256,NA16
97/8 UpperDeckIce 42
96 Wien 52
97/8 Zenith 85,Z73,-RookRgn 13
97/8 Zenith -RookieZTeam 11

OHMAN, JENS
89/90 SemicElitserien 183
90/1 SemicElitserien 18
91/2 SemicElitserien 222

OHMAN, ROGER
96/7 DEL 232
94/5 ElitSet 272
95/6 ElitSet 88, -Goldies 9
89/90 SemicElitserien 7
90/1 SemicElitserien 131
91/2 SemicElitserien 182
92/3 SemicElitserien 209
95/6 udElite 139
87/8 Moncton

OHMAN, STEFAN
94/5 ElitSet 228

OHRLUND, TORBJORN
92/3 SemicElitserien 44

O'HUNTER, PAT
28/9 PaulinsCandy 43

OIJENNUS, MARKUS
93/4 Sisu 79
94/5 Sisu 114
95/6 Sisu 321

OIJENNUS, OIVA
80/1 Mallasjuoma 161
78/9 SM-Liiga 183
72/3 WilliamsFIN 162
73/4 WilliamsFIN 228

OJANEN, JANNE
95 Globe 136
95 Hartwall
93 Koululainen
95 Latkaliiga 12
90/1 OPC/Topps 30
92/3 opcPremier 17
90/1 PaniniSticker 78
95 PaniniWorlds 171
93/4 Premier 16
88/9 ProCards(Utica)
90/1 ProSet 173
94 Semic 35
95 Semic 8
92 SemicSticker
93 SemicSticker 71
94/5 Sisu-Mag 4,-Spel 4,-Fire 19
95/6 Sisu 322, -GoldCards 19
96/7 Sisu-Mighty 6, -Specials 6
95/6 SisuLimited 77, -Gallery 4
93/4 ToppsStadiumClub 184
90/1 UpperDeck 290
91/2 UpperDeck 25
97/8 udSwedish 141, 214
97/8 udSwedish C12, UDS13
96 Wien 8
89/90 N.J.

OJANEN, MARK
93/4 Sisu 105
94/5 Sisu 132
95/6 Sisu 14

OJANEN, REIJO
65/6 Hellas 149

OJANSUU, JOURKO
66/7 Champion 49

OKAL, MIROSLAV
94/5 APS 194
95/6 APS 42

OKAL, ZDENEK
94/5 APS 195
95/6 APS 43

OKKONEN, ILKKA
71/2 WilliamsFIN 308

OKSALA, JORMA
66/7 Champion 154
70/1 Kuvajulkaisut 218

OKSALA, OSSI
70/1 Kuvajulkaisut 261

OKSANEN, HANNU
78/9 SM-Liiga 60
72/3 WilliamsFIN 313

OKSANEN, JUKKA
72/3 WilliamsFIN 349

OKSANEN, LASSE
66/7 Champion 203
72 Hellas 9
65/6 Hellas 114
70/1 Kuvajulkaisut 71, 133
80/1 Mallasjuoma 32
69/70 MästarSerien 13
72 Panda
72 SemicSticker 84
74 SemicSticker 87
91 SemicSticker 23
78/9 SM-Liiga 55
77-80 Sportscaster 45-1057
71/2 WilliamsFIN 72, 182
72/3 WilliamsFIN 69, 131
73/4 WilliamsFIN 186

OKSIUTA, ROMAN
94/5 ClassicImages 35
92/3 ClassicProspects 11
93/4 Donruss 111, -Ratedk 15
95/6 Donruss 66
96/7 Donruss 44
94/5 Fleer 72
95/6 FleerMetal 154
95/6 FleerUltra 171, -AllRook 9
96/7 FleerUltra 4
93/4 Leaf 411
95/6 Leaf 77, -StudioRookie 16
96/7 MetalUniverse 4
91/2 O-Pee-Chee 57R
97/8 PacificRegime 164
95/6 PaniniSticker 292
96/7 PaniniSticker 224
97/8 PaniniSticker 48
93/4 Parkhurst 258
95/6 Parkhurst 211
93/4 Pinnacle 451
95/6 Pinnacle 63
96/7 Pinnacle 139
95/6 Playoff 210
96/7 Playoff 397
92/3 RedAce(Blue) 20,(Violet) 20
95/6 Score 285
96/7 Score 76
97/8 Score(PGH) 13
93 SemicSticker 141
95/6 SkyBoxEmotion 183
95/6 SkyBoxImpact 172, -Fox 2
96/7 SkyBoxImpact 3
95/6 Topps 317, 8NG
94/5 T.Finest-BBest(Red) 5
95/6 ToppsFinestS 94
95/6 ToppsStadiumClub 132
93/4 UpperDeck 509
95/6 UpperDeck 476
96/7 UDCollChoice 10
96/7 ANA/UpFrontSports 3
93/4 EDM 04FEB94
94/5 CapeBreton

OKTJABREV, ARTUR
92/3 RedAce(Blue) 31,(Violet) 25

OLASKI, MIKE
92/3 BCJHL 72

OLAUSSON, FREDRIK
90/1 Bowman 135
91/2 Bowman 210
92/3 Bowman 295
93/4 Donruss 386, 430
94/5 Fleer 73
92/3 FleerUltra 244, -Imports 18
93/4 FleerUltra 147
94/5 FleerUltra 74
95 Globe 26
89/90 Kraft 51
93/4 Leaf 124
94/5 Leaf 327
87/8 O-Pee-Chee 225
90/1 OPC/Topps 242
91/2 OPC/Topps 45
92/3 O-Pee-Chee 121
98/9 Pacific 356
97/8 PacificCrown 149
98/9 PacificParamount 195
90/1 Panini(WPG) 19
87/8 PaniniSticker 361
90/1 PaniniSticker 318
91/2 PaniniSticker 67
92/3 PaniniSticker 60
93/4 PaniniSticker 198
96/7 PaniniSticker 230
97/8 PaniniSticker 54
91/2 Parkhurst 203
92/3 Parkhurst 212
93/4 Parkhurst 227
91/2 Pinnacle 74
92/3 Pinnacle 202
93/4 Pinnacle 392
94/5 Pinnacle 303
96/7 PinnacleBeAPlayer 134
94/5 POG 103
93/4 PowerPlay 273, 342
93/4 Premier 63
94/5 Premier 319
90/1 ProSet 335
91/2 ProSet 264
91/2 PSPlatinum 133
90/1 Score 81
91/2 Score(CDN) 18, (U.S) 18
92/3 Score 13
93/4 Score 79, 645
94/5 Score 147
89/90 SemicElitserien 77
89 SemicSticker 10
92 SemicSticker 59
93 SemicSticker 26
92/3 Topps 120
98/9 Topps 150
91/2 ToppsStadiumClub 185
92/3 ToppsStadiumClub 346
94/5 ToppsStadiumClub 198
90/1 UpperDeck 237
91/2 UpperDeck 383
92/3 UpperDeck 136
93/4 UpperDeck 209
94/5 UpperDeck 394
97/8 UpperDeck 139
94/5 UDBeAPlayer-Aut. 8
95/6 UDCollChoice 98
95/6 udElite 247
93/4 EDM 09FEB94
86/7 WPG
87/8 WPG
88/9 WPG/Police
89/90 WPG/Safeway
90/1 WPG/IGA
91/2 WPG/IGA
93/4 WPG/Ruffles

OLBRICH, MICHAEL
94/5 DEL 175
95/6 DEL 170

OLCZYK, ED
90/1 Bowman 161
91/2 Bowman 204
92/3 Bowman 278
92/3 FleerUltra 245, 357
96/7 FleerUltra 81
88/9 FritoLay
91/2 Kelloggs 18
89/90 Kraft 38
91/2 Kraft 62
93/4 Leaf 90
96/7 Leaf 117
96/7 MetalUniverse 77
97/8 Omega 188
85/6 OPC/Topps 86
86/7 OPC/Topps 82
87/8 OPC/Topps 104
88/9 OPC/Topps 125, G
89/90 OPC/Topps 133
90/1 OPC/Topps 206
91/2 OPC/Topps 182
92/3 O-Pee-Chee 375
91/2 opcPremier 196
85/6 opcSticker 26/154
86/7 opcSticker 156/14
87/8 opcSticker 76/210
88/9 opcSticker 181
89/90 opcSticker 172
98/9 Pacific 357
97/8 PacificCrown 92
97/8 PacificCrownRoyale 112
97/8 PacificInvincible 116
97/8 PacificParamount 154
90/1 Panini(TOR) 17
87/8 PaniniSticker 230
88/9 PaniniSticker 126
89/90 PaniniSticker 132
90/1 PaniniSticker 283
91/2 PaniniSticker 64
92/3 PaniniSticker 55
96/7 PaniniSticker 193
91/2 Parkhurst 204
92/3 Parkhurst 213, 350
93/4 Parkhurst 402
91/2 Pinnacle 193, 386
92/3 Pinnacle 145
93/4 Pinnacle 154
94/5 Pinnacle 420
97/8 PinnacleInside 169
93/4 PowerPlay 394
93/4 Premier 398
90/1 ProSet 286, 563
91/2 ProSet 265
92/3 ProSet 213
91/2 PSPlatinum 134
90/1 Score 210, -HotCards 89
90/1 ScoreTraded 51T
91/2 Score(CDN) 60, (U.S) 60
92/3 Score 145, -USAGreats 15
93/4 Score 37
95/6 Score 282
96/7 Score 198
97/8 Score 206
97/8 Score(PGH) 7
94 Semic 115
89 SemicSticker 169
91 SemicSticker 148
92 SemicSticker 161
93 SemicSticker 184
96/7 SP 75
92/3 Topps 17
91/2 ToppsStadiumClub 57
92/3 ToppsStadiumClub 157
93/4 ToppsStadiumClub 197
90/1 UpperDeck 222, 431
91/2 UpperDeck 99, 387
92/3 UpperDeck 211
93/4 UpperDeck 115
94/5 UpperDeck 274
95/6 UDBeAPlayer 141
95/6 UDCollChoice 106
86/7 CHI/Coke
87/8 TOR
87/8 TOR/P.L.A.Y. 9
88/9 TOR/P.L.A.Y. 6
90/1 WPG/IGA
91/2 WPG/IGA
95/6 WPG

OLDENBORGER, JEFF
94/5 Slapshot(MEM) 2

O'LEARY, B.
91/2 Cornwall 27

O'LEARY, KELLY
94/5 Classic W39

O'LEARY, MICKEY
24/5 Champs (C144)

OLENICI, ADRIAN
79 PaniniSticker 318

OLENIUK, DEVON
87/8 Kamloops
84/5 Saskatoon
86/7 Saskatoon

OLENYN, JERRY
94/5 LasVegas

OLSEHUK, BILL
79/80 COL.R

OLSEVICH, DAN
80/1 DET

OLSEON, CORY
85/6 Arizona

OLIMB, LARRY
92/3 Classic 90
91/2 Minnesota

OLIVEIRA, MIKE
95/6 Slapshot 122

OLIVEIRA, SAM
91/2 SketchOHL 7
91/2 Cornwall 9

OLIVER, DAVID
94/5 Classic 57, AA6, R16, T24
94/5 ClassicImages 79
95/6 Donruss 8, -Rookie 4
95/6 EdgeIce 35, C7
94/5 Flair 60
94/5 Fleer 74
95/6 FleerMetal 55
95/6 FleerUltra 56, -AllRook 10
95/6 Hoyle'WEST 10 (Diamond)
95/6 Leaf 9, -StudioRook 4
95/6 LeafLimited 89
95/6 PaniniSticker 263
95/6 Parkhurst 76
94/5 ParkieSE 60
94/5 Pinnacle 490
95/6 Pinnacle 42
96/7 Pinnacle 51
95/6 Playoff 38
96/7 Playoff 358
95/6 POG 34, 108
95/6 Score 60
96/7 Score 193
95/6 SkyBoxEmotion 65
95/6 SkBxImpact 63, 231, -Fox 3
94/5 SP-Premier 13
95/6 Summit 98
95/6 Topps 366, 8HG, 14HG
94/5 T.Finest-BBest(Red) 6
95/6 ToppsFinest 62
95/6 ToppsStadiumClub 109
95/6 ToppsSuperSkills 71
94/5 UpperDeck 269, SP117
95/6 UpperDeck 167, SE120
96/7 UpperDeck 60
95/6 UDBeAPlayer 64
95/6 UDCollChoice 13
96/7 UDCollChoice 96
94/5 CapeBreton

OLIVER, HARRY
33/4 Anonymous (V129) 39
38/9 BruinsMagazine
33-35 DiamondMatch
36-39 DiamondMatch (1), (2), (3)
83&87 HallOfFame 146
83 HHOF Postcard (K)
94/5 HHOFLegends 38
33/4 O-Pee-Chee (V304A) 9
23/4 PaulinsCandy 69
33/4 WWGum (V357) 23

OLIVER, LAWRENCE
92/3 BCJHL 230

OLIVER, MURRAY
45-64 BeeHives(BOS), (DET)
64-67 BeeHives(BOS)
62 CeramicTiles
64/5 CokeCap BOS-16
65/6 CocaCola
70/1 DadsCookies
70/1 EddieSargent 86
71/2 EddieSargent 88
72/3 EddieSargent 107
70/1 Esso Stamp
74/5 Loblaws
68/9 O-Pee-Chee 194
69/70 OPC/Topps 52
70/1 OPC 167
71/2 OPC/Topps 239
74/5 OPC 291
75/6 OPC 335
60/1 Parkhurst 22
94/5 Parkie(64/5) 2, 169
95/6 Parkie(66/7) 9, 140
66/7 Post'Large
68/9 Post Marble
60/1 ShirriffCoin 55
61/2 ShirriffCoin 8
68/9 ShirriffCoin TOR9
71/2 TheTorontoSun
60/1 Topps-Stamp
61/2 Topps 14
62/3 Topps 12, -Buck
63/4 Topps 10
64/5 Topps 79
65/6 Topps 34
66/7 Topps 95
67/8 Topps 82
54-67 TorontoStar V10
73/4 MIN
80/1 MIN
81/2 MIN
68/9 TOR
69/70 TOR

OLIVER, SIMON
92/3 MPSPhotoSJHL 2

OLIVERIO, MIKE
83/4 SSMarie
84/5 SSMarie
87/8 SSMarie 17

OLIWA, KRZYSZTOF
93/4 ClassicProspects 73
97/8 Omega 133
98/9 Pacific 268
98/9 PacificParamount 137
97/8 PinnacleBeAPlayer 229
94/5 SRTetrad CX
97/8 UpperDeck 302

OLKKONEN, PEKKA
66/7 Champion 206
65/6 Hellas 12

OLLILA, JUKKA
92/3 Jyvas-Hyva 38
93/4 Jyvas-Hyva 80
93/4 Sisu 112
95/6 Sisu 313
93/4 UpperDeck 269

OLLSON, JOHN
85/6 NovaScotia 9
81/2 Ottawa67s
82/3 Ottawa67s

OLMSTEAD, BERT
45-64 BeeHives(CHI),(MTL)
45-64 BeeHives(TOR)
48-52 Exhibits
87 HallOfFame 248
51-54 LaPatrie 16Mar52
51/2 Parkhurst 5
52/3 Parkhurst 93
53/4 Parkhurst 19
54/5 Parkhurst 5
55/6 Parkhurst 42
57/8 Parkhurst(MTL) 19, 25
58/9 Parkhurst 27
59/60 Parkhurst 40
60/1 Parkhurst 4
61/2 Parkhurst 4
93/4 Parkhurst 60 PR56
93/4 Parkie(56/7) 71, 146
45-54 QuakerOats
60/1 ShirriffCoin 11
61/2 ShirriffCoin 52
62/3 ShirriffCoin 11
62/3 Topps 57
56-66 TorontoStar 58/9
60/1 York, -Glasses
61/2 York 19
92/3 MTL/OPC 58
95/6 MTL/Forum 6Jan96

OLOFSSON, TONY
89/90 SemicElitserien 177
90/1 SemicElitserien 11

OLSON, ATLE
97/8 udSwedish 65

OLSEN, DARRYL
89/90 ProCards(IHL) 195
90/1 ProCards 604
91/2 ProCards 577

OLSEN, ERIC
95/6 Slapshot 108

OLSEN, OYSTEIN
92 SemicSticker 36
93 SemicSticker 242

OLSEN, TOM ERIK
95 PaniniWorlds 243
93 SemicSticker 247

OLSON, BOB
91/2 Mich.Tech

OLSON, BOYD
96/7 Fredericton

OLSON, EDDIE
51/2 Cleveland

OLSSON, ANDREAS
94/5 ElitSet 253

OLSSON, CHRISTER
94/5 ElitSet 97
95/6 ElitSet-Mega 14
97/8 PacificBestKept 66
96/7 PaniniSticker 208
95 PaniniWorlds 145
92/3 SemicElitserien 60
97/8 udSwedish 69, 203, 223
97/8 udSwedish C4, S3
96 Wien 50, AS2
96/7 OTT/PizzaHut

OLSSON, FREDRIK
90/1 SemicElitserien 218

OLSSON, JOHN
83/4 Springfield 5

OLSSON, JONAS
97/8 udSwedish 193

OLSSON, MATTIAS
94/5 ElitSet 225
95/6 ElitSet 296
89/90 SemicElitserien 82
90/1 SemicElitserien 255
91/2 SemicElitserien 86
92/3 SemicElitserien 110
95/6 udElite 191

OLSSON, N.O.
79 PaniniSticker 199

OLSSON, OVE
82 SemicSticker 20

OLSSON, PETER
95/6 udElite DS19

OLSSON, ROGER
70/1 Kuvajulkaisut 35

OLSSON, STEFAN
89/90 SemicElitserien 231
90/1 SemicElitserien 70
91/2 SemicElitserien 244

OLUND, TOMAS
89/90 SemicElitserien 47
90/1 SemicElitserien 195

OLYMPIEV, SERGEI
93/4 Slapshot(Kit) 26
94/5 Slapshot(Kit) 24

O'MALLEY, TERRY
69/70 MästarSerien 18

O'MEARA, CLIFF
23/4 Crescent Selkirks 1
24/5 Crescent Selkirks 10
23/4 PaulinsCandy 9
28/9 PaulinsCandy 78

OMSKOV, STEFAN
95 Globe 39

ONDREJKA, MARTIN
94/5 DEL 215
95/6 DEL 214

O'NEILL, DON
89/90 SketchOHL 112
90/1 SketchOHL 367
91/2 SketchOHL 138
91/2 Peterborough 14

O'NEILL, JAMES (PEGGY)
34-43 BeeHives(BOS)
36/7 WWGum (V356) 63

O'NEILL, JEFF
94/5 Assets 57, 82, -FonCard
95/6 Bowman 118, BB26
93/4 Classic 108, 115, CL1, N3
93/4 Classic PR2, -Aut
94/5 Classic 5, C7, R15, T29
94/5 C'FourSport 119, BC19,
94/5 C'4Sport HV19, TC4, -Fon
94/5 C4'Images 98
94/5 ClassicImages 44, CE16
93/4 C'Prospects 205, 209
95/6 Donruss 244, -CanadaJr 14
95/6 Donruss-RatedRook 4
96/7 Donruss-RatedRookie 5
97/8 Donruss 16
96/7 DonrussCanadianIce 82
95/6 DonrussElite 21, -Rookie 12
96/7 D.Elite 39, -Aspirations 9
97/8 DonrussPreferred 100
97/8 DonrussPriority 125
95/6 FleerMetal 186
96/7 FleerNHLPicks 158
95/6 FleerUltra 351
96/7 Leaf 209
94/5 LeafLimited-CanadaJrs 6
95/6 LeafLimited 63, -Rookie 8
96/7 LeafLimited 68
96/7 LeafPreferred 9
97/8 Limited 61
96/7 MetalUniverse 69
98/9 Pacific 137
98/9 PacificParamount 40
97/8 PacificCrown 140
96/7 PaniniSticker 30
95/6 Parkhurst 259
94/5 Pinnacle 534
96/7 Pinnacle 210
97/8 Pinnacle 154
97/8 PinnacleBeAPlayer 130
97/8 PinnacleCertified 128
97/8 PinnacleInside 149
95/6 P.Zenith 130, -RookRoll 18
96/7 PinnacleZenith 29
96/7 Score 250
97/8 Score 147
95/6 SelectCert. 118, -Future 8
96/7 SelectCertified 90
95/6 SkyBoxImpact 202, -Fox 11
93/4 Slapshot(Guelph) 2, 26
94/5 Slapshot(Guelph) 25
94/5 SP 152
95/6 SP 64
96/7 SP 67
97/8 SPAuthentic 28
95/6 Summit 183
96/7 Summit 168
95/6 SuperSticker 55
95/6 Topps 285, 20CJ
94/5 ToppsFinest 162
95/6 ToppsFinest 96
96/7 ToppsNHLPicks RS17
95/6 ToppsStadiumClub 192
95/6 ToppsSuperSkills SR3
93/4 UpperDeck E4
95/6 UpperDeck 264
96/7 UpperDeck 70
97/8 UpperDeck 34
95/6 UDBeAPlayer 166
96/7 UDBlackDiamond 92
98/9 UDChoice 37
95/6 UDCollChoice 401
96/7 UDCollChoice 121, 343
97/8 UDCollChoice 117

O'NEILL, MIKE
92/3 ClassicProspects 39
92/3 Parkhurst 441
94/5 Parkhurst 268
90/1 ProCards 344
91/2 ProCards 259
90/1 Moncton

O'NEILL, PEGGY
see James "Peggy" O'Neill

O'NEILL, RYAN
91/2 SketchOHL 180
92/3 Windsor 10

ONDOFRYCHUK, DARRYL
91/2 SketchWHL 158

OPP, DARREN
91/2 AirCanadaSJHL 39, D19

OPRANDI, ROBERT
79 PaniniSticker 380

OPULSKIS, JURIS
94/5 APS 127

ORBAN, BILL
67/8 Topps 109

ORCT, ZDENEK
94/5 APS 203
95/6 APS 150

ORDMAN, ROB
83/4 Brandon 8

O'REAR, HAYDEN
93/4 Knoxville
94/5 Knoxville 7

O'REE, WILLIE
45-64 BeeHives(BOS)
82? JDMcCarthy
97/8 PinnacleBeeHive 75
97/8 UpperDeck -Promo 22

O'REGAN, TOM
94/5 DEL 59
95/6 DEL 54
96/7 DEL 250
84/5 PGH/Heinz

O'REILLY, SEAN
89/90 SketchOHL 90
90/1 SketchOHL 14
91/2 SketchOHL 382

O'REILLY, TERRY
74/5 Loblaws
73/4 OPC 254
74/5 OPC 295
75/6 OPC/Topps 301
76/7 OPC/Topps 130, OPC 381
77/8 OPC/Topps 220
78/9 OPC/Topps 40, OPC 382
79/80 OPC/Topps 238
80/1 OPC/Topps 56
81/2 OPC 7, Topps(E) 71
82/3 O-Pee-Chee 18
84/5 OPC 13, Topps 10
81/2 opcSticker 50
82/3 opcSticker 85
85/6 opcSticker 161/32
82/3 Post
91/2 PSPlatinum 289
83/4 PuffySticker 12
84/5 Topps 10
83/4 BOS
84/5 BOS
88/9 BOS/SportsAction
91/2 BOS/Legends

OREKHOVSKI, OLEG
95/6 Classic 65, -Aut
95/6 TetradAutobilia 49
94/5 SigRookies FF6

ORIMUS, PEKKA
78/9 SM-Liiga 58

ORLANDO, GAETANO
95 Globe 232
95 PaniniWorlds 87
94 Semic 299
95 Semic 174
92 SemicSticker 253
93 SemicSticker 218
96 Wien 180
85/6 BUF
86/7 BUF
79/80 Montréal, -B&W

ORLANDO, JIM
34-43 BeeHives(DET)
39/40 OPC (V301-1) 65
76 DET

ORLANDO, STEFAN
94/5 ElitSet 28, -GoldCard 22
95/6 ElitSet 57,-Chmp 11,-Gld 6
94 Semic 71
95 Semic 71
89/90 SemicElitserien 115
90/1 SemicElitserien 116
91/2 SemicElitserien 118
92/3 SemicElitserien 140
95/6 udElite 83

ÖRNSKOG, STEFAN
95 PaniniWorlds 155
97/8 udSwedish 91, 207, 218
97/8 udSwedish C23, UDS8

ORO, JAN
71/2 WilliamsFIN 316

O'ROURKE, DAN
91/2 SketchWHL 311
95/6 Louisiana-Playoffs

ORR, BOBBY
68/9 Bauer
92/3 BayBank
71/2 Bazooka Panel 36
77/8 Coke Mini
71/2 Colgate Heads
70/1 Colgate Stamp 87
70/1 DadsCookies
70/1 EddieSargent 1
71/2 EddieSargent 10
72/3 EddieSargent 17
70/1 Esso Stamp
88/9 Esso Sticker
83&87 HallOfFame 61
83 HHOF Postcard (E)
92/3 HHOFLegends 4
97/8 KennerSLU -12
92 LegendsPostcards 7
72/3 Letraset 5, 17
74/5 LiptonSoup 8
74/5 Loblaws
73/4 MacsMilk Disk
68/9 OPC/Topps 2
68/9 OPC 200, 214, -Puck 4
69/70 OPC/Topps 24, OPC 209
69/70 OPC 212, -Sticker, -Stamp
69/70 O-Pee-Chee 209, 212
70/1 OPC/Topps 3, -Deckle 4
70/1 OPC/Topps-Sticker
70/1 OPC 236,246,248,249,252
71/2 OPC/T. 100, -Booklet 24
71/2 OPC 245, 251, Topps 2, 3
71/2 OPC-Poster 1
72/3 OPC 58, 127, 129, 142
72/3 OPC 175, 227, 280, 283
72/3 OPC-Crest, Topps 62-63
72/3 T. 100, 122, 171-72, 176
73/4 OPC 30, Topps 150
74/5 OPC/Topps 2, 28, 100
74/5 OPC/Topps 130, 248
75/6 OPC/Topps 100, 209, 210
75/6 OPC/Topps 288, 314
76/7 OPC/T. 213, T-Glossy 20
77/8 OPC/Topps 251
78/9 O-Pee-Chee 300
95/6 Parkie(66/7) 7, 134
95/6 Parkie(66/7) SR1, TW5
91/2 Pinnacle 392
95/6 PinnacleFANtasy 31
67/8 Post
70/1 PostShooters
72/3 Post Transfers 1
72 SemicSticker 223
91 SemicSticker 238
68/9 ShirriffCoin Bo5
77-9 Sportscaster 01-02, 04-83
97/8 SI.ForKids-GreatMoments
81/2 TCMA 9
71/2 TheTorontoSun
66/7 Topps 35, -USATest 35
67/8 Topps 92, 118, 128
92/3 Trends(76) 104, 126, -Aut
92/3 Trends(76) 184, 196
71/2 WilliamsFIN 384
70/1 BOS
71/2 BOS
91/2 BOS/Legends
80/1 Oshawa 25

ORRGREN, KENT
89/90 SemicElitserien 285

ORSOLINI, LIONEL
94 Semic 227

ORTIZ, SEAN
95/6 Dayton

OSBORNE, BRAD
88/9 Brockville 20

OSBORNE, DON
90/1 Mich.Tech
91/2 Mich.Tech
93/4 ThunderBay
94/5 ThunderBay

OSBORNE, KEITH
92/3 ClassicProspects 85
89/90 ProCards(IHL) 21
90/1 ProCards 76
91/2 ProCards 341
93/4 UpperDeck 76
92/3 AtlantaKnights
88/9 NiagaraFalls 15

OSBORNE, MARK
90/1 Bowman 156
91/2 Bowman 209
93/4 FleerUltra 433
94/5 FleerUltra 335
94/5 Leaf 503
82/3 O-Pee-Chee 93
83/4 O-Pee-Chee 252
84/5 O-Pee-Chee 148
88/9 O-Pee-Chee 241
89/90 O-Pee-Chee 274
90/1 OPC/Topps 227
91/2 OPC/Topps 345
82/3 opcSticker 182
88/9 opcSticker 168/28
89/90 opcSticker 174/34
90/1 Panini(TOR) 18
88/9 PaniniSticker 127
89/90 PaniniSticker 138
90/1 PaniniSticker 278
91/2 PaniniSticker 77
93/4 Parkhurst 476
91/2 Pinnacle 96
92/3 Pinnacle 305
94/5 Pinnacle 500
82/3 Post
93/4 PowerPlay 452
93/4 Premier 268
90/1 ProSet 287, 564
91/2 ProSet 270
90/1 Score 104, 28T
91/2 Score(CDN) 39, (U.S) 39
92/3 Score 277
93/4 Score 316
83/4 SouhaitsRen.KeyChain
84/5 Topps 110
92/3 Topps 77
91/2 ToppsStadiumClub 21
92/3 ToppsStadiumClub 379
94/5 ToppsStadiumClub 76
90/1 UpperDeck 5
91/2 UpperDeck 296
92/3 UpperDeck 72
94/5 UpperDeck 316
94/5 UDBAP R113, -Aut. 18
87/8 TOR
87/8 TOR/P.L.A.Y. 23
88/9 TOR/P.L.A.Y. 23
92/3 TOR/Kodak
93/4 TOR/Abalene
93/4 TOR/Blacks 7
94/5 TOR
90/1 WPG/IGA
91/2 WPG/IGA
95/6 Cleveland

OSBORNE, MATT
95 Classic 93
95/6 Slapshot 299
95/6 UpperDeck 515

OSBURN, RANDY
72/3 TOR

OSGOOD, CHRIS
96/7 Aces 10 (Spades)
95/6 Bowman 66
91/2 Classic 43
91/2 ClassicFourSport 43, -Aut
93/4 C4'Images 56
94/5 ClassicImages 71, PR4
92/3 ClassicProspects 26
93/4 ClassicProspects 28
93/4 Donruss 424
94/5 Donruss 251
95/6 Donruss 23
96/7 Donruss 95,-Dom 2,-Betw 5
97/8 Donruss 13, -Between 5
96/7 DonrussCanadianIce 10
97/8 DCI 28, -Nt'l 6, -Scrapbk 5
96/7 DonrussElite 21, 148
97/8 DonrussElite 53,-Craftsm 7
97/8 D.Preferred 81,-ColourG 7
97/8 DonrussPriority 81, 203
97/8 D.Prio-OpDay 23,-PstGen 8
97/8 D.Prio-Pstcrd 30,-Stamp 30
97/8 D.Studio 87, -Portraits 36
95/6 EdgeIce C18
96/7 Flair 29, -HotGlove 7
94/5 Fleer 63
96/7 Fleer 33, 144-46, -Vezina 6
95/6 FleerMetal 49
96/7 F.Picks 10,-Fab 36,-FanF 2
93/4 FleerUltra 308, -Wave 12
94/5 FleerUltra 64
95/6 FleerUltra 236,374,-High 13
96/7 FleerUltra 54
97/8 KatchMedallion 52
97/8 KennerSLY, 1on1
96/7 Kraft-AS, -Trophy
94/5 Leaf 315,-GoldLeafRook 10
95/6 Leaf 254
96/7 Leaf 151,-BestOf 4,-Shut 13
97/8 Leaf 47, -PipeDreams 14
94/5 LeafLimited 96

95/6 LeafLimited 61
96/7 LeafLimited 6
96/7 LeafPreferred 50,-Masked 6
96/7 L.Preferred-VanityPlates 3
97/8 Limited 3,115,171,-fabric 25
96/7 Maggers 58
96/7 McDonalds McD7
97/8 McDonalds McD32
96/7 MetalUniv 49, -Armour, 6
97/8 Omega 86,-NoScoring Zn 4
98/9 Pacific 204,-GoldCrown 14
97/8 PacificCrown 137, -InThe 7
97/8 PacificCrownRoyale 49
97/8 PCR-FreezeOut 7
97/8 PacificDynagon! 43
97/8 PcfcD-Stone 7,-Tandm 12
97/8 PacificInvincible 50
97/8 PcfcParamount 69,-Glove 7
98/9 PcfcParamount 81,-Glove 8
97/8 PcfcRevolution 50,-Retrn 7
94/5 PaniniSticker X
95/6 PaniniSticker 187
96/7 PaniniSticker 180
93/4 Parkhurst 329, C17
94/5 Parkhurst 283
95/6 Parkhurst 67, PP30
94/5 ParkieSE 54
93/4 Pinnacle 431
94/5 Pinnacle 199, 471, GT16
95/6 Pinnacle 160
96/7 Pinnacle 99, -TeamP 9
97/8 Pinnacle 34, -TeamP 10
96/7 P.BeAPlayer-Stacking 2
97/8 P.BAP 25,-Stacking/Pads 6
97/8 PinnacleBeeHive 37
97/8 PinnacleCertified 4
97/8 PinnacleInside 9
96/7 PinnacleMint 25
95/6 PinnacleZenith 80
96/7 P.Zenith 105, -ZTeam 18
96/7 Playoff 378
93/4 PowerPlay 334, -Rookie 9
94/5 Premier 87, 199
94/5 Premier-Finest(OPC) 8
93/4 Score 609
94/5 Score 256
95/6 Score 202
96/7 Score 129,-Sudden 5,-Net 6
97/8 Score 2, -NetWorth 4
97/8 Score(DET) 17
96/7 SelectCert. 20,-Freezers 10
90/1 SketchMEM 123
90/1 SketchWHL 24
91/2 SketchWHL 196
95/6 SkyBoxImpact 56
96/7 SkyBoxImpact 38, -Zero 6
95/6 SP 48
96/7 SP 51, HC21, -SPxForce 3
97/8 SPAuthentic 51
96/7 SPx 16
91/2 StarPics 55
95/6 Summit 122, -InThe 9
96/7 Summit 135,-Crs 13,-Unt 13
96/7 TeamOut
95/6 Topps 345, YS12
98/9 Topps 134
95/6 ToppsFinest 159
96/7 ToppsNHLPicks ID8, FT2
93/4 ToppsStadiumClub 350
94/5 ToppsStadiumClub 138
95/6 ToppsStadiumClub 135
95/6 TSC-MembersOnly 21
91/2 UltimateDP 38, -Aut 38, 57
93/4 UpperDeck 519
94/5 UpperDeck 130
95/6 UD 445, AS19, E116
96/7 UpperDeck 53, SS30B, X7
95/6 UDBeAPlayer 193
96/7 UDBlackDiamond 132
97/8 UDBlackDiamond 39
98/9 UDChoice 74, 248
95/6 UDCollChoice 136
96/7 UDCC 84, -Oversize 84
97/8 UDCollChoice 80
96/7 UpperDeck"Ice" 18
97/8 UpperDeckIce 30
97/8 Zenith 35, Z17
96/7 DET/PhotoPucks

O'SHEA, DANNY
70/1 Colgate Stamp 16
70/1 DadsCookies
70/1 EddieSargent 90
71/2 EddieSargent 37
72/3 EddieSargent 189
70/1 Esso Stamp
69/70 OPC/Topps 131
71/2 OPC/Topps 211
72/3 OPC 201
95/6 Slapshot 251
71/2 TheTorontoSun
71/2 STL
72/3 STL
72/3 STL/8"x10"
93/4 Dayton 10

O'SHEA, KEVIN
70/1 EddieSargent 25
71/2 EddieSargent 22
72/3 EddieSargent 190
72/3 O-Pee-Chee 257
71/2 TheTorontoSun
72/3 STL/8"x10"

OSIECKI, MARK
92/3 Pinnacle 376
90/1 ProCards 618
91/2 ProSet 528
91/2 UpperDeck 533
95/6 Tallahassee 13
91/2 CGY/IGA

OSMAK, COREY
93/4 Minn-Duluth

OSSIPOV, SERGEI
92/3 AtlantaKnights

OSTLER, K.
95/6 DEL 344

ÖSTLING, STIG
72 Hellas 26
74 Hellas 41
79 PaniniSticker 186
72/3 WilliamsFIN 60

ÖSTLUND, THOMAS
94/5 ElitSet 66, -CleanSweep 3
95/6 ElitSet 183, -Mega 4
95/6 ElitSet-Spidermen 3
95 Globe 5
95 PaniniWorlds 137
89/90 SemicElitserien 3
90/1 SemicElitserien 75
91/2 SemicElitserien 2
92/3 SemicElitserien 75
95/6 udElite 37, 251
96 Wien 40

O'SULLIVAN, CHRIS
93/4 Donruss USA15
96/7 DonrussCanadianIce 133
97/8 Leaf 141
96/7 LeafPreferred 122
97/8 Limited 54
93/4 Pinnacle 484
96/7 PinnacleZenith 138
96/7 SelectCertified 111
93/4 UpperDeck 565
96/7 UpperDeck 230, X4
97/8 UpperDeck 235
96/7 UDBlackDiamond 19
97/8 UDCollChoice 35

O'SULLIVAN, KEVIN
93/4 Classic 71
93/4 Fredericton
94/5 Fredericton

OSWALD, GÜNTER
94/5 DEL 243
95/6 DEL 351
96/7 DEL 260
95 PaniniWorlds 72

OTEVREL, JAROSLAV
92/3 ClassicProspects 143
93/4 ClassicProspects 126
92/3 Parkhurst 399
95/6 Sisu 358, 379
93/4 ToppsStadiumClub 293

OTT, ANDREAS
94/5 DEL 411
95/6 DEL 225

OTTILA, RAULI
66/7 Champion 79
70/1 Kuvajulkaisut 165
71/2 WilliamsFIN 234
72/3 WilliamsFIN 218
73/4 WilliamsFIN 294

OTTMANN, CHRIS
89/90 SketchOHL 169
90/1 SketchOHL 313

OTTO, JOEL
90/1 Bowman 99
91/2 Bowman 260
92/3 Bowman 69
93/4 Donruss 49
94/5 Donruss 102
95/6 Donruss 355
92/3 FleerUltra 26
93/4 FleerUltra 285
94/5 FleerUltra 270
95/6 FleerUltra 27, 285
95 Globe 113
89/90 Kraft 6
93/4 Leaf 28
94/5 Leaf 272
97/8 Omega 169
86/7 O-Pee-Chee 247, 249
87/8 O-Pee-Chee 212
88/9 O-Pee-Chee 242
89/90 O-Pee-Chee 205
90/1 OPC/Topps 369
91/2 OPC/Topps 428
92/3 O-Pee-Chee 82
91/2 opcPremier 102
86/7 opcSticker 130/116
87/8 opcSticker 42/183
88/9 opcSticker 83/212
89/90 opcSticker 96/233
98/9 Pacific 329
97/8 PacificRegime 146
90/1 Panini(CGY) 15
87/8 PaniniSticker 212
88/9 PaniniSticker 13
91/2 PaniniSticker 60
92/3 PaniniSticker 43
93/4 PaniniSticker 185
94/5 PaniniSticker 155
95/6 PaniniSticker 115
96/7 PaniniSticker 119
91/2 Parkhurst 253
92/3 Parkhurst 259
93/4 Parkhurst 34
94/5 Parkhurst V38
95/6 Parkhurst 162
94/5 ParkieSE 31
91/2 Pinnacle 179
92/3 Pinnacle 328
93/4 Pinnacle 179
94/5 Pinnacle 217
96/7 PinnacleBeAPlayer 76
95/6 Playoff 295
94/5 POG 58
95/6 POG 205
93/4 PowerPlay 40
93/4 Premier 48
94/5 Premier 508
90/1 ProSet 43
91/2 ProSet 37
92/3 ProSet 28
91/2 PSPlatinum 17
90/1 Score 128
91/2 Score(CDN) 96, (U.S) 96
92/3 Score 332
93/4 Score 74
94/5 Score 18
95/6 Score 186
97/8 Score(PHA) 14
94 Semic 124
95 Semic 115
92 SemicSticker 167
95/6 SP 111
92/3 Topps 471
95/6 Topps 236
91/2 ToppsStadiumClub 170
92/3 ToppsStadiumClub 305
93/4 ToppsStadiumClub 128
94/5 ToppsStadiumClub 197
95/6 ToppsStadiumClub 14, N8
90/1 UpperDeck 141
91/2 UpperDeck 165
92/3 UpperDeck 220
93/4 UpperDeck 124, SP-24
94/5 UpperDeck 43
95/6 UpperDeck 366, SE151
96/7 UpperDeck 124
97/8 UpperDeck 333
93/4 UDBeAPlayer 34
94/5 UDBAP R2, R133, -Aut. 69
96/7 UDBlackDiamond 29
95/6 UDCollChoice 88
96/7 UDCollChoice 193
96 Wien 171
85/6 CGY/RedRooster
86/7 CGY/RedRooster
87/8 CGY/RedRooster
90/1 CGY/McGavins
91/2 CGY/IGA
92/3 CGY/IGA 4
96/7 PHA/OceanSpray
84/5 Moncton 10

OTTOSSON, KRISTOFER
95/6 ElitSet 195
95/6 udElite 46

OTTOSSON, PETER
94/5 ElitSet 99
95/6 ElitSet 46
94 Semic 65
89/90 SemicElitserien 95
90/1 SemicElitserien 268
91/2 SemicElitserien 97
92/3 SemicElitserien 119
92 SemicSticker 66
95/6 udElite 74

OUELLET, GEORGES
51/2 LavalDairy 53

OUELLET, STÉPHANE
90/1 SketchQMJHL 125

OUELLETTE, DENIS
93/4 Fredericton

OUELLETTE, ADELARD
36-39 DiamondMatch (2), (3)

OUELLETTE, FRANCIS
91/2 ProCards 432
90/1 SketchQMJHL 157
94/5 Erie

OUIMET, MARK
95/6 Adirondack

OVASKA, NIKO
91/2 SketchWHL 240

OVIATT, STEVE
93/4 Tacoma

OVSTEDAL, ROAR
79 PaniniSticker 298

OWCHAR, DENNIS
75/6 OPC 380
76/7 OPC 314
77/8 OPC 391
78/9 OPC/Topps 19
74/5 PGH
77/8 PGH/PuckBuck

OWEN, GEORGE
27-32 LaPresse 31/2

ÖYSTILÄ, JOUKO
72 Hellas 20
72 Panda
72 SemicSticker 76
74 SemicSticker 82
71/2 WilliamsFIN 80, 110
72/3 WilliamsFIN 80, 154
73/4 WilliamsFIN 84, 125

OYSTRICK, TREVOR
90/1 Rayside
91/2 Rayside

OZELLIS, FALK
94/5 DEL 166
95/6 DEL 166
96/7 DEL 241

OZOLINSH, SANDIS
97/8 Aces J (Hearts)
93/4 Donruss 312
94/5 Donruss 120
95/6 Donruss 34
96/7 Donruss 104
97/8 Donruss 60, -Line 24
97/8 DonrussCanadianIce 119
95/6 DonrussElite 93
97/8 DonrussElite 83
97/8 DonrussPreferred 103
97/8 DonrussPriority 45
97/8 DonrussStudio 82
94/5 Flair 169
96/7 Flair 19
94/5 Fleer 200, -TheFranchise 6
96/7 Fleer 23, -Norris 10
95/6 FleerMetal 35
96/7 F.Picks-Dr 9,-Fab 37,-Jag 8
92/3 FleerUltra 402, -Imports 19
93/4 FleerUltra 169
94/5 FleerUltra 200
95/6 FleerUltra 149, 224
96/7 FleerUltra 38
95/6 FutureLegends 46
97/8 KatchMedallion 40
95/6 KennerSLU (U.S)
97/8 KennerSLU
93/4 Leaf 73
94/5 Leaf 169
95/6 Leaf 183
96/7 Leaf 197
97/8 Leaf 118
94/5 LeafLimited 43
95/6 LeafLimited 52
97/8 Limited 106, 145
96/7 Maggers 44
94/5 McDonalds 11
96/7 MetalUniverse 36
97/8 Omega 63
92/3 opcPremier 104
98/9 Pacific 167
97/8 PacificCrown 75
97/8 PcfcDynagon! 32,-Tand 41
97/8 PacificInvincible 37
97/8 PacificParamount 53
98/9 PacificParamount 59
97/8 PacificRevolution 37
94/5 PaniniSticker 223
95/6 PaniniSticker 283
96/7 PaniniSticker 251
97/8 PaniniSticker 206
92/3 Parkhurst 164
93/4 Parkhurst 187
94/5 Parkhurst 208, V7, C21
95/6 Parkie 185, 320, -IntAS 2
93/4 Pinnacle 142
94/5 Pinnacle 22, WE11
96/7 Pinnacle 159
97/8 Pinnacle 128
97/8 PinnacleBeAPlayer 115
97/8 PinnacleCertified 89
97/8 PinnacleInside 137
95/6 PinnacleZenith 101
95/6 Playoff 193
96/7 Playoff 385
94/5 POG 219
95/6 POG 231
93/4 PowerPlay 225
93/4 Premier 168
94/5 Premier 239, 430
92/3 RedAce(Blue) 21,(Violet) 21
93/4 Score 261, -International 18
94/5 Score 36
95/6 Score 67
96/7 Score 43
97/8 Score 174
97/8 Score(COL) 6
94/5 Select 63
95/6 SkyBoxEmotion 159
95/6 SkyBoxImpact 39
96/7 SkyBoxImpact 26, -Fox 17
94/5 SP 108
95/6 SP 32
97/8 SPAuthentic 41
95/6 Summit 137
96/7 Summit 12
95/6 SuperSticker 29
96/7 TeamOut
98/9 Topps 121, B10
94/5 ToppsFinest 57, -Div. 17
95/6 ToppsFinest 141
96/7 ToppsNHLPicks 21
93/4 ToppsStadiumClub 362
94/5 T.StadiumClub 177, 204
93/4 TSC-MembersOnly 11
91/2 UD 661,-CzechWJC 22
92/3 UpperDeck 568, ER16
93/4 UpperDeck 72, SP-146
94/5 UpperDeck 490, SP73
95/6 UD 168, 470, SE109
96/7 UD 37, SS20B, X9
96/7 UD-AllStarYCTG A10
97/8 UD 44, SG28, T20C
95/6 UDBeAPlayer 183
96/7 UDBlackDiamond 98
97/8 UDBlackDiamond 27
98/9 UDChoice 60
95/6 UDCollChoice 9
96/7 UDCollChoice 60, UC35
97/8 UDCollChoice 60, SQ38
96/7 UpperDeck"Ice" 80
97/8 UpperDeckIce 24
92/3 S.J/PacificBell

P

PAAKKARINEN, JYRKI
80/1 Mallasjuoma 140

PÄÄKKÖNEN, KALEVI
72/3 WilliamsFIN 274

PAANANEN, MIKA
92/3 Jyvas-Hyva 83
93/4 Jyvas-Hyva 147
93/4 Sisu 148
94/5 Sisu 82
95/6 Sisu 61
96/7 Sisu 62

PAATERO, ORVO
66/7 Champion 129

PAAVOLA, JARI
80/1 Mallasjuoma 196

PACAL, TOMAS
94/5 APS 32
95/6 APS 319

PACK, RAY
95/6 Birmingham

PACLIK, ROBERT
94/5 DEL 27

PACULA, IRENEUSZ
94/5 DEL 160
95/6 DEL 160
89 SemicSticker 149

PADDOCK, GORDON
88/9 ProCards(Hershey)
89/90 ProCards(AHL) 351
90/1 ProCards 524
83/4 Brandon 3

PADDOCK, JOHN
80/1 Pepsi Cap
88/9 ProCards(Hershey)
90/1 ProCards 15
80/1 QUE
91/2 WPG/IGA
93/4 WPG/Ruffles

PADELEK, IVAN
95/6 APS 13

PADDEN, KEVIN
94/5 Slapshot(Windsor) 15
95/6 Tallahassee 8

PAEK, JIM
92/3 Bowman 383
90/1 CanadaNats
92/3 FleerUltra 168
94/5 Leaf 512
92/3 O-Pee-Chee 328
91/2 OPC/Topps 437
91/2 Parkhurst 133
92/3 Parkhurst 375
91/2 Pinnacle 344
93/4 Pinnacle 278
94/5 Pinnacle 389
95/6 Playoff 288
93/4 Premier 243
94/5 Premier 422
88/9 ProCards(Muskegon)
89/90 ProCards(IHL) 158
91/2 ProSet 554
91/2 PSPlatinum 266
92/3 Score 537
93/4 Score 334
92/3 Topps 243
92/3 ToppsStadiumClub 437
93/4 ToppsStadiumClub 401
91/2 UpperDeck 308
93/4 UpperDeck 192
94/5 OTT/Bell
92/3 PGH/Coke
91/2 PGH/Elbys
91/2 PGH/Foodland 1
92/3 PGH/Foodland 11
92/3 PGH/FoodStickers
93/4 PGH/Foodland 9

PAGE, FRED
93/4 ActionPacked 9

PAGE, MARGOT
94/5 Classic W10

PAGÉ, PIERRE
93/4 Kraft'Coach
85/6 CGY/RedRooster
86/7 CGY/RedRooster
87/8 CGY/RedRooster
91/2 QUE/PetroCanada
92/3 QUE/PetroCanada
84/5 Moncton 3

PAGE, SCOTT
96/7 Sudbury 18

PAGEAU, CORY
90/1 SketchOHL 268

PÅHLSSON, SAMUEL
95/6 ElitSet 273
95/6 SP 183
95/6 UDCollChoice 350
95/6 udElite 168
97/8 udSwedish 161

PAICE, FRANK
62/3 Topps 61

PAIEMENT, RÉAL
81/2 Milwaukee 2

PAIEMENT, ROSAIRE
70/1 Colgate Stamp 39
70/1 DadsCookies
70/1 EddieSargent 220
71/2 EddieSargent 218
70/1 Esso Stamp
70/1 OPC 226
71/2 OPC 233, Topps 24
72/3 OPC 333
73/4 opc-Posters 5
74/5 opcWHA 7
75/6 opcWHA 106
76/7 opcWHA 37
77/8 opcWHA 36
73/4 QuakerOats 3
71/2 TheTorontoSun
70/1 VAN/RoyalBank
71/2 VAN/RoyalBank 9
72/3 VAN/Nalleys

PAIEMENT, STEVEN
90/1 SketchQMJHL 126

PAIEMENT, WILF
72-84 Dernière 79/80, 82/3
74/5 O-Pee-Chee 292
75/6 OPC/Topps 195, 319
76/7 OPC/Topps 37
77/8 OPC/Topps 130
78/9 OPC/Topps 145
79/80 OPC/Topps 190
80/1 OPC/Topps 225
81/2 OPC 306,311,326, T. 25,63
82/3 O-Pee-Chee 288
83/4 O-Pee-Chee 298
84/5 O-Pee-Chee 285
87/8 OPC/Topps 180
81/2 opcSticker 96, 110
82/3 opcSticker 22
84/5 opcSticker 175
85/6 opcSticker 152/23
79 PaniniSticker 67
87/8 PaniniSticker 32
80/1 Pepsi Cap
81/2 Post PopUp 22
82/3 Post
83/4 SouhaitsRen.KeyChain
83/4 Vachon 70
86/7 BUF
76/7 COL.R
76/7 COL.R/CokeCans
77/8 COL.R/CokeCans
82/3 QUE
83/4 QUE
84/5 QUE
85/6 QUE/Provigo
86/7 QUE/McDonald
79/80 TOR
80/1 TOR
81/2 TOR

PAILLE, MARCEL
52/3 AnonymousOHL 64
52/3 BasDuFleuve 51
45-64 BeeHives(NYR)
64-67 BeeHives(NYR)
64/5 CokeCap NYR-23
94/5 Parkie(64/5) 101
64/5 Topps 92

PAINE, GREG
91/2 FerrisState

PAIVINEN, MATTI
66/7 Champion 23

PAJALA, JUKKA
70/1 Kuvajulkaisut 375

PAJONKOWSKI, FRANK
95 Globe 201
94 Semic 230
93 SemicSticker 264
96 Wien 190

PAKARINEN, STEN
72/3 WilliamsFIN 350

PAKOLA, SEPPO
80/1 Mallasjuoma 2
78/9 SM-Liiga 23

PAKRATZ, JOE
94/5 Minnesota

PAKSAL, REIJO
66/7 Champion 67
70/1 Kuvajulkaisut 146
71/2 WilliamsFIN 196
72/3 WilliamsFIN 234
73/4 WilliamsFIN 268

PALADIEV, EVGENY
74 Hellas 52
70/1 Kuvajulkaisut 12
74 SemicSticker 31
69/70 Soviet Stars
70/1 Soviet Stars
73/4 Soviet Stars 21
71/2 Trends(72) 38
73/4 WilliamsFIN 12

PALAMAR, ED
52/3 AnonymousOHL 9

PALANGIO, PETER
34-43 BeeHives(CHI)

PALAZZARI, DOUG
77/8 O-Pee-Chee 354

PALECEK, JOSEF
95/6 APS 314
72 Hellas 94
74 Hellas 80
72/3 WilliamsFIN 17
73/4 WilliamsFIN 59

PALECZNY, LARRY
97/8 Bowman 29
95/6 Slapshot 303

PALFFY, ZIGMUND
97/8 Aces 9 (Diamonds)
91/2 Classic 23
91/2 ClassicFourSport 23
93/4 ClassicProspects 50
93/4 Donruss 459
95/6 Donruss 316
96/7 Donruss 45
97/8 Donruss 125, -RedAlert 8
96/7 DonrussCanadianIce 58
97/8 DonrussCanadianIce 33
95/6 DonrussElite 13
96/7 DonrussElite 52
97/8 DonrussElite 34, 130
97/8 DonrussPreferred 106
97/8 DonrussPriority 58, 212
97/8 D.Prio -DirectDeposit 22
97/8 D.Prio-Pstcrd 32,-Stamp 32
97/8 D.Studio 46,-Hrd 13,-Prt 31
95/6 Edgelce 195, C24
96/7 Flair 56
94/5 Fleer 128
96/7 Fleer 66
95/6 FleerMetal 92
96/7 FleerNHLPicks 50
96/7 F.Picks-Fab 38,-Jagged 20
94/5 FleerUltra 329
95/6 FleerUltra 100,269,-High 14
96/7 FleerUltra 103
97/8 KatchMedallion 90
97/8 KennerSLU
96/7 KraftDinner, -Disk
97/8 Kraft-WorldPro, -WorldBest
94/5 Leaf 253
96/7 Leaf 23,-Fire 7, -Leather 7
97/8 Leaf 55
96/7 LeafLimited 57
96/7 LeafPreferred 103,-Steel 32
97/8 Limited 12, 163, 181
97/8 Limited -fabric 24
96/7 Maggers 95
96/7 McDonalds M cD18
96/7 MetalUniverse 95
97/8 Omega 140, -StickHand 12
98/9 Pacific 284,-Gld 22,-T.CL16
97/8 PacificCrown 5, -TmCL 15
97/8 PcfcCrwnRoyale 79,-Hat 10
97/8 PcfcDynagn! 74,-BstKpt 57
97/8 PacificD-Dyn 9B,-Tandm 11
97/8 Pcfclnv. 82,-Att 13,-Feat 20
97/8 PacificParamount 109
98/9 PacificParamount 145
98/9 PcfcP-SpecD 11,-TmCL 16
97/8 PacificRegime 119
97/8 PcfcRevolutn 82,-TmCL 15
96/7 PaniniSticker 5
97/8 PaniniSticker 73
93/4 Parkhurst 397
95/6 Parkhurst 131
94/5 ParkieSE 107
94/5 Pinnacle 256, RTP5
95/6 Pinnacle 88
96/7 Pinnacle 100
97/8 Pinnacle 56
96/7 P.BeAPlayer-Biscuit 15
97/8 PinnacleBeAPlayer 135
97/8 PinnacleBeeHive 42
97/8 PinnacleCertified 94
97/8 Pinnaclelnside 14,-Track 22
96/7 P.Zenith 97, -Assailant 7
95/6 Playoff 172
96/7 Playoff 379
95/6 POG 169
94/5 Premier 459
94/5 Score 235
95/6 Score 267
96/7 Score 120
97/8 Score 106
94/5 Select 196
96/7 SelectCertified 23
92 SemicSticker 140
94 Semic 207
96/7 SkyBoxImpact 77,-Blade 18
95/6 SP 86
96/7 SP 97, HC28
97/8 SPAuthentic 91, I38
96/7 SPx 29
97/8 SPx 28, SPX13
98/9 SPx"Finite" 114
97/8 SportFX MiniStix
95/6 Summit 144
96/7 Summit 20
96/7 TeamOut
95/6 Topps 348
98/9 Topps 184, L3, M11, SB17
95/6 ToppsFinest 117
95/6 ToppsStadiumClub 99
97/8 ToppsSticker 5
91/2 UD 16, 71,-CzechWJC 97
94/5 UD 343, 529, SP138
95/6 UpperDeck 140, SE51
96/7 UD 97, SS21A, X17
97/8 UD 99, S22, SG5, SS26
95/6 UDBeAPlayer 24
96/7 UDBlackDiamond 6
97/8 UDBlackDiamond 18
98/9 UDChoice 121, BH13
95/6 UDCollChoice 94
96/7 UDCC 156, 323, UD24
97/8 UDCC150, C16, S16, SQ66
97/8 udDiamondVision 21
96/7 UpperDeck"Ice" 94
97/8 UpperDecklce 16
96 Wien 234
97/8 Zenith 30, Z27

PALICHUK, ED
82/3 Brandon 13
83/4 KelownaWings

PALINEK, MARTIN
95/6 APS 231

PALLA, ANTAL
79 PaniniSticker 270

PALLIN, ROB
85/6 Minn-Duluth 4

PALLO, SAIMANN
77-79 Sportscaster108-2587

PALM, JORGEN
89/90 SemicElitserien 271
90/1 SemicElitserien 35

PALMATEER, MIKE
77/8 OPC/Topps 211
78/9 OPC/Topps 70, 160
79/80 OPC/Topps 8, 197
80/1 OPC/Topps 95
81/2 OPC 338,351,394, T(E) 121
82/3 O-Pee-Chee 66
83/4 O-Pee-Chee 338
84/5 O-Pee-Chee 308
81/2 opcSticker 194
83/4 opcSticker 39
84/5 opcSticker 18, 22
80/1 opcSuperCard 23
81/2 Post PopUp 9
83/4 PuffySticker 5
83/4 7ElevenCokeCups
83/4 SouhaitsRen.KeyChain
83/4 Vachon 95
76/7 TOR
77/8 TOR
78/9 TOR
79/80 TOR
82/3 TOR
83/4 TOR
80/1 WSH
81/2 WSH

PALMER, BRAD
82/3 O-Pee-Chee 21
83/4 BOS
81/2 MIN
82/3 Victoria

PALMER, CHRIS
90/1 ProCards 565

PALMER, DREW
93/4 Seattle

PALMER, JAY
83/4 Brandon 12

PALMER, ROB
78/9 O-Pee-Chee 298
79/80 O-Pee-Chee 352
80/1 OPC/Topps 104
80/1 L.A

PALMER, SAM
91 SemicSticker 185
92 SemicSticker
93 SemicSticker 111

PALMER, STEVE
92/3 Clarkson

PALMQVIST, BJORN
72 Hellas 36
74 Hellas 32
70/1 Kuvajulkaisut 36
72 Panda
72 SemicSticker 60
74 SemicSticker 20
71/2 WilliamsFIN 56
72/3 WilliamsFIN 54

PALMU, HANNU
72/3 WilliamsFIN 132

PALO, MARKO
94/5 ElitSet 197
95/6 ElitSet 268
95 Hartwall
92/3 Jyvas-Hyva 22
93/4 Jyvas-Hyva 54
95 PaniniWorlds 175
94 Semic 37
95 Semic 13
93/4 Sisu 244, 379
95/6 Sisu-GoldCard s 20
95/6 SisuLimited 88
95 SuomenBeckett 8
95/6 udElite 140
96 Wien 13

PALO-OJA, KARI
66/7 Champion 189
65/6 Hellas 127
70/1 Kuvajulkaisut 134
72 Panda
71/2 WilliamsFIN 183
72/3 WilliamsFIN 133
73/4 WilliamsFIN 187

PALSOLA, SAKARI
95/6 Sisu 106
96/7 Sisu 102

PALUCH, SCOTT
88/9 ProCards(Peoria)
89/90 ProCards(IHL) 4

PANCHAREK, FRANTISEK
72 Panda
72 SemicSticker 26
74 SemicSticker 13
71/2 WilliamsFIN 35

PANCOE, DON
89/90 SketchOHL 140
88/9 NiagaraFalls 20
89/90 NiagaraFalls

PANDOLFO, JAY
93/4 Donruss USA16
97/8 PacificDynag-BestKept 53
93/4 Pinnacle 497
96/7 SP 180
93/4 UpperDeck 556
97/8 UpperDeck 93
96/7 UDBlackDiamond 21
97/8 UDCollChoice 145
96/7 N.J/Sharp

PANEK, CHRIS
95/6 DEL 49
88/9 ProCards(NewHaven)
89/90 ProCards(AHL) 19

PANG, DARREN
88/9 OPC/Topps 51
89/90 OPC/Topps 31
88/9 opcSticker 8/137, 135/6
88/9 opcStickFS 16
89/90 opcSticker 10/150
88/9 PaniniSticker 21
89/90 PaniniSticker 42
87/8 CHI/Coke
88/9 CHI/Coke
82/3 Ottawa67s
83/4 Ottawa67s

PANIN, MIKHAIL
90/1 O-Pee-Chee 492

PANKEWICZ, GREG
93/4 ClassicProspects 57
90/1 SketchOHL 180
91/2 Knoxville
89/90 Regina

PANKOV, DMITRI
95/6 Richmond

PANTELEYEV, GRIGORI
92/3 ClassicProspects 130
92/3 FleerUltra 254
93/4 FleerUltra 179
92/3 Parkhurst 243
93/4 Score 337
92/3 UpperDeck 492

PAOLICCO, DAN
90/1 SketchQMJHL 144

PAONE, PAT
93/4 Slapshot(Pet) 8

PAPIKE, JOE
34-43 BeeHives(CHI)

PAPINEAU, JUSTIN
98 BowmanCHL 31, 149, A1
97/8 UpperDeck 415

PAPINEAU, ROB
90/1 SketchOHL 113

PAPISTA, COSTA
89/90 Sudbury 3
85/6 Sudbury 8

PAPPAS, PERRY
90/1 SketchMEM 13
90/1 SketchOHL 170
91/2 SketchOHL 319
93/4 SSMarie 11

PAPPIN, JIM
64-67 BeeHives(TOR)
70/1 Colgate Stamp 43
70/1 EddieSargent 41
71/2 EddieSargent 40
72/3 EddieSargent 64
70/1 Esso Stamp
72/3 Letraset 10
74/5 LiptonSoup 36
74/5 Loblaws
68/9 OPC/Topps 21
69/70 OPC 133, Topps 73
70/1 OPC/Topps 13
71/2 OPC/Topps 98
72/3 OPC 42, Topps 148
73/4 OPC/Topps 112
74/5 OPC/Topps 69, 113
75/6 OPC/Topps 234, 317
94/5 Parkie(64/5) 123
95/6 Parkie(66/7) 107, 134
67 Post FlipBook
68/9 ShirriffCoin CHI 16
64/5 TheTorontoStar
71/2 TheTorontoSun
64/5 Topps 64
65/6 Topps 16
66/7 Topps 76, -USATest 49
67/8 Topps 78
91/2 Ultimate(O6) 62, -Aut 62
67/8 York 32
67/8 York (x2)
68/9 CHI
70/1 CHI
64/5 TOR
68/9 TOR
69/70 TOR

PAQUET, DAVE
90/1 SketchMEM 68
90/1 SketchQMJHL 16
91/2 SketchQMJHL 113

PAQUET, NORMAND
90/1 SketchQMJHL 212
91/2 SketchQMJHL 2

PAQUETTE, ANDY
85/6 Sudbury 16
88/9 Sudbury 20

PAQUETTE, CHARLES
91/2 SketchQMJHL 103

PAQUETTE, DARRYL
95/6 Hampton HRA-4
95/6 Portland
90/1 Sudbury 1

PAQUETTE, FRANÇOIS
90/1 SketchQMJHL 127
91/2 SketchQMJHL 199

PAQUETTE, PHIL
89/90 Sudbury 23

PAQUETTE, R.
67/8 ColumbusCheckers

PAQUIN, GERALD
52/3 BasDuFleuve 18

PAQUIN, PAT
91/2 SketchQMJHL 184

PARA, KELLY
86/7 Kamloops

PARADIS, DAN
90/1 SketchMEM 45
90/1 SketchQMJHL 42
91/2 SketchQMJHL 95

PARADIS, STÉPHANE
91/2 SketchQMJHL 140

PARADISE, BOB
72/3 EddieSargent 11
74/5 Loblaws
74/5 OPC 343
75/6 OPC/Topps 21
76/7 OPC 368
77/8 OPC 203
78/9 O-Pee-Chee 375
72/3 ATL
74/5 PGH

PARADISE, DICK
73/4 QuakerOats 49
72/3 Minnesota

PARÉ, JEAN-PHILIPPE
98 BomwanCHL 94

PARE, PAT
79/80 Montréal
79/80 Montréal BW

PARENT, BERNARD (BERNIE)
64-67 BeeHives(BOS)
65/6 CocaCola
70/1 Colgate Stamp 93
70/1 DadsCookies
72-84 Dernière 77/8
70/1 EddieSargent 146
71/2 EddieSargent 205
70/1 Esso Stamp
93/4 HighLiner 7
74/5 LiptonSoup 18
74/5 Loblaws
74/5 Nabisco 15
68/9 OPC/Topps 89
69/70 OPC/Topps 89
69/70 OPC-Sticker, -Stamp
70/1 OPC/Topps 78
71/2 OPC/Topps 131
73/4 OPC/Topps 66
74/5 OPC/T. 4, 60, 138, 249,251
75/6 OPC/Topps 213, 291, 300
76/7 OPC/Topps 10
77/8 OPC/Topps 8, 65
78/9 OPC/Topps 15, 68, 70
79/80 OPC/Topps 6, 8
92/3 OPC 217, -25Years 1
92/3 Parkhurst 470
94/5 Parkie(64/5) FS4
95/6 Parkie(66/7) 14
91/2 Pinnacle 384
92/3 Pinnacle 246
72 SemicSticker 175
68/9 ShirriffCoin PHA1
71/2 TheTorontoSun
86/7 PHA
92/3 PHA/UD 12APR93
71/2 TOR

PARENT, JACQUES
88/9 ProCards(Sherbrooke)
89/90 ProCards(AHL) 196
90/1 SketchQMJHL 98
92/3 Fredericton
93/4 Fredericton
94/5 Fredericton
95/6 Fredericton
96/7 Fredericton
87/8 Hull

PARENT, SÉBASTIEN
90/1 SketchQMJHL 36, 41
91/2 SketchQMJHL 91

PARIKKA, PEKKA
70/1 Kuvajulkaisut 262

PARIKKA, SEPPO
66/7 Champion 55
70/1 Kuvajulkaisut 147
71/2 WilliamsFIN 197
72/3 WilliamsFIN 235
73/4 WilliamsFIN 269

PARIS, TIM
88/9 ProCards(Adirondack)

PARISE, J.P.
70/1 DadsCookies
70/1 EddieSargent 94
71/2 EddieSargent 83
72/3 EddieSargent 101
70/1 Esso Stamp
74/5 LiptonSoup 4
74/5 Loblaws, -Update
73/4 MacsMilk Disk
68/9 O-Pee-Chee 149
69/70 OPC/Topps 127
70/1 OPC/T.-Sticker, OPC 168
71/2 OPC/Topps 243
72/3 OPC 199, -TmCanada
73/4 OPC/Topps 46
74/5 OPC/Topps 83
75/6 OPC/Topps 127
76/7 OPC/Topps 182
77/8 OPC/Topps 29
78/9 O-Pee-Chee 350
79/80 OPC/Topps 118
72 SemicSticker 219
71/2 TheTorontoSun
91/2 Trends(72) 99, -Aut
70/1 MIN
73/4 MIN
78/9 MIN/Cloverleaf 3
80/1 MIN
81/2 MIN

PARIZEAU, MICHEL
72/3 OPC 335
74/5 opcWHA 52
73/4 QuakerOats 43
71/2 TheTorontoSun
73/4 Québec
71/2 STL

PARK, BRAD
77/8 Coke Mini
71/2 Colgate Heads
70/1 DadsCookies
72-84 Dernière 79/80
70/1 EddieSargent 124
71/2 EddieSargent 116
72/3 EddieSargent 144
70/1 Esso Stamp
88/9 Esso Sticker
94/5 HHOFLegends 42
94 HockeyWit 10
72/3 Letraset 20
74/5 LiptonSoup 10
74/5 Loblaws
73/4 MacsMilk Disk
70/1 OPC/Topps 67, -Deckle 43
70/1 O-Pee-Chee 239
71/2 OPC/Topps 40, 257
72/3 OPC 85,114,227, -Crest 15
72/3 OPC-TmCanada, T. 30,123
73/4 OPC/Topps 165
74/5 OPC/Topps 50, 131, 141
75/6 OPC/Topps 260
76/7 OPC/Topps 60, T-Glossy 2
77/8 OPC/Topps 190, -Glossy13
78/9 OPC/Topps 79, 263
79/80 OPC/Topps 23, 164
80/1 OPC/Topps 74
81/2 OPC 8, Topps(E) 72
82/3 O-Pee-Chee 19
83/4 O-Pee-Chee 129
84/5 OPC 63, 378, 390, T. 47
81/2 opcSticker 48
82/3 opcSticker 82
83/4 opcSticker 48, 178
84/5 opcSticker 38, 231/230
80/1 opcSuperCard 1
82/3 Post
83/4 PuffySticker 15
72 SemicSticker 194
94/5 SigRookies CF2
77-9 Sportscaster 07-17, 29-692
71/2 TheTorontoSun
91/2 Trends(72) 95, -Aut
93/4 Zellers
91/2 BOS/Legends
84/5 DET/Caesars
85/6 DET/Caesars

PARK, JIM
77/8 opcWHA 56

PARK, RICHARD
95/6 Bowman 123
93/4 Donruss USA17
95/6 Donruss 331
95/6 FleerMetal 187
95/6 Leaf 221
94/5 LeafLimited-USAJrs 9
95/6 LeafLimited 36
97/8 PacificRegime 6
95/6 Parkhurst 169
94/5 ParkieSE 249
93/4 Pinnacle 498
95/6 Pinnacle 220
94/5 Score 210
95/6 Score 295
94/5 SigRookies 12
95/6 SkyBoxImpact 217
94/5 SP 175
95/6 SP 120
95/6 Topps 119
94/5 ToppsFinest 112
95/6 ToppsFinest 89
95/6 ToppsStadiumClub 208
93/4 UpperDeck 553
94/5 UpperDeck 525
95/6 UpperDeck 419
97/8 UpperDeck 215
95/6 UDBeAPlayer 185
96/7 UDCollChoice 217
95/6 PGH/Foodland 7

PARKER, JEFF
90/1 O-Pee-Chee 497
88/9 ProCards(Rochester)
88/9 BUF/BlueShield
88/9 BUF/WonderBread
89/90 BUF/BlueShield
89/90 BUF/Campbell

PARKER, SHANE
94/5 Slapshot(NorthBay) 25
95/6 Slapshot 230

PARKER, STAN
52/3 AnonymousOHL 86

PARKS, GREG
95/6 ElitSet 175, -FaceTo 2
90/1 opcPremier 89
92/3 Parkhurst 491

91/2 ProCards 462
94/5 Score CT11
92/3 SemicElitserien 170
95/6 udElite 32

PARNELL, GREG
90/1 Mich.Tech
91/2 Mich.Tech

PARR, MAURICE
51/2 BasDuFleuve 53

PARRISH, DWIGHT
91/2 FerrisState

PARRISH, MARK
95/6 DonrussElite-WorldJrs 38

PARRO, DAVE
82/3 O-Pee-Chee 371
82/3 opcSticker 158
81/2 WSH
82/3 WSH

PARSON, MIKE
90/1 ProCards 129
94/5 Portland

PARSON, STEVE
90/1 SketchOHL 129
91/2 SketchOHL 283
93/4 Slapshot(Kingston) 20
94/5 ThunderBay
95/6 ThunderBay

PARSONS, DARREN
86/7 Regina
88/9 Regina

PARSONS, GEORGE
34-43 BeeHives(TOR)
38/9 QuakerOats

PARTANEN, ERKKI
65/6 Hellas 135

PARTANEN, JARMO
71/2 WilliamsFIN 350

PARTH, ELMAR
94 Semic 292

PARTINEN, LALLI
66/7 Champion 98
65/6 Hellas 83
70/1 Kuvajulkaisut 72, 112
72 Panda
96/7 Sisu 191
77-9 Sportscaster 36-845
71/2 WilliamsFIN 121
72/3 WilliamsFIN 91
73/4 WilliamsFIN 74, 137

PARVIAINEN, JARI
92/3 Jyvas-Hyva 145
93/4 Jyvas-Hyva 260
93/4 Sisu 283

PASANA, JARI
96/7 DEL 221

PASCAL, BRENT
81/2 Regina 19

PASCALL, BRAD
92/3 Rochester/Kodak
93/4 Rochester

PASCO, RON
94/5 Greensboro
95/6 Tallahassee 5

PASCUCCI, RON
93/4 Hampton
94/5 Hampton 5
95/6 Hampton HRA-6
96/7 Portland

PASEK, DUSAN
92/3 Jyvas-Hyva 101
89/90 ProCards(IHL) 82
82 SemicSticker 93
91 SemicSticker 113
88/9 MIN/AmericanDairy

PASHAL, KEVIN
92/3 BCJHL 214

PASHKOV, ALEXANDER
79/80 SovietChamps

PASHULKA, STEVE
92/3 MPSPhotoSJHL 43

PASIN, DAVE
86/7 OPC/Topps 76
88/9 ProCards(NewHaven)
90/1 ProCards 425
86/7 Moncton 7
84/5 PrinceAlbert

PASLAWSKI, GREG STEPHEN
92/3 Bowman 277
95/6 EdgeIce 179
92/3 FleerUltra 375
87/8 OPC/Topps 10
89/90 O-Pee-Chee 268
90/1 OPC/Topps 154
92/3 O-Pee-Chee 193
87/8 opcSticker 23 /164
90/1 Panini(WPG) 20
87/8 PaniniSticker 314
90/1 PaniniSticker 309
91/2 Parkhurst 365
92/3 Parkhurst 132
91/2 Pinnacle 286
92/3 Pinnacle 370
93/4 Pinnacle 337
90/1 ProSet 336
91/2 ProSet 469
92/3 ProSet 155
91/2 PSPlatinum 220
90/1 Score 249
91/2 Score(CDN) 579, (U.S) 29T
92/3 Score 175, -Sharpshootr 16
93/4 Score 290
92/3 Topps 33
92/3 ToppsStadiumClub 275
90/1 UpperDeck 239
92/3 UpperDeck 531
83/4 Vachon 52
92/3 PHA/JCPenney
92/3 PHA/UD 25FEB93
92/3 PHA/UD 27NOV92
91/2 QUE/PetroCanada
87/8 STL
87/8 STL/Kodak
88/9 STL
88/9 STL/Kodak
89/90 WPG/Safeway
90/1 WPG/IGA

PASMA, ROD
90/1 SketchOHL 42
91/2 SketchOHL 234
95/6 Louisiana, -Playoffs

PASQUALOTTO, G.
79 PaniniSticker 388

PASSARELLI, VAL
91/2 FerrisState

PASSERO, DAN
96/7 SSMarie

PASSMORE, STEVE
90/1 SketchQMJHL 255
94/5 CapeBreton
93/4 Kamloops

PASTIKA, MICHAEL
94/5 DEL 421

PASTINSKY, OLIVER
93/4 Slapshot(SSMarie) 4
93/4 SSMarie 4

PATAFIE, BRIAN
84/5 Moncton 1
85/6 Moncton 18
86/7 Moncton 6
83/4 NovaScotia 18
81/2 Ottawa

PATEMAN, JERRY
90/1 ProSet 696

PATENAUDE, RUSTY
74/5 opcWHA 51
75/6 opcWHA 76
76/7 opcWHA 19

PATERA, PAVEL
94/5 APS 58
95/6 APS 93, 371, 385
97/8 udSwedish 10
96 Wien 114

PATERSON, COREY
88/9 Regina
89/90 Regina
92/3 Wheeling 11
93/4 Wheeling 3

PATERSON, JOE
88/9 ProCards(NewHaven)
89/90 ProCards(IHL) 41
90/1 ProCards 8
91/2 ProCards 203
95/6 Slapshot 380
80/1 DET
88/9 L.A.
96/7 SSMarie

PATERSON, MARK
88/9 ProCards(Saginaw)
81/2 Ottawa67s
82/3 Ottawa67s
83/4 Ottawa67s

PATERSON, RICK
83/4 O-Pee-Chee 109
84/5 O-Pee-Chee 44
82/3 Post
80/1 CHI/4x6
81/2 CHI
82/3 CHI
86/7 CHI/Coke
93/4 Cleveland
95/6 Cleveland

PATEY, DOUG
79/80 O-Pee-Chee 298

PATEY, LARRY
74/5 Loblaws
75/6 OPC/Topps 137, 316
76/7 OPC 320
77/8 OPC/Topps 199
78/9 OPC/Topps 8
79/80 OPC/Topps 57
80/1 O-Pee-Chee 310
81/2 O-Pee-Chee 303
82/3 O-Pee-Chee 308
84/5 OPC 149, Topps 111
82/3 Post
78/9 STL

PATOINE, RÉMY
88/9 Richelieu

PATRICK, CRAIG
72/3 EddieSargent 75
74/5 LiptonSoup 46
74/5 Loblaws, -Update
94/5 MiracleOnIce 43, 44
78/9 O-Pee-Chee 387
71/2 OPC/Topps 184
72/3 OPC 221
73/4 OPC/Topps 52
74/5 OPC/Topps 262
75/6 OPC/Topps 178
77/8 OPC 278
72 SemicSticker 130

PATRICK, FRANK
83&87 HallOfFame 23
83 HHOF Postcard (B)
94/5 HHOFLegends 48
1910-11 Imperial (C56) 1

PATRICK, GLEN
79 PaniniSticker 210

PATRICK, JAMES
90/1 Bowman 225
91/2 Bowman 66
92/3 Bowman 127
83 CanadaJuniors
93/4 Donruss 213, 408
94/5 Donruss 185
96/7 Donruss 158
93/4 EASports 86
94/5 Flair 26
94/5 Fleer 33
92/3 FleerUltra 141
93/4 FleerUltra 336
94/5 FleerUltra 33
88/9 FritoLay
93/4 Leaf 232
94/5 Leaf 271
96/7 MetalUniverse 21
84/5 O-Pee-Chee 150
85/6 OPC/Topps 15
86/7 OPC/Topps 113
87/8 OPC/Topps 18
88/9 OPC/Topps 69
89/90 OPC/Topps 90
90/1 OPC/Topps 131
91/2 OPC/Topps 253
92/3 O-Pee-Chee 215
91/2 opcPremier 172
85/6 opcSticker 83/214
86/7 opcSticker 220/90
87/8 opcSticker 30/171
88/9 opcSticker 246/116
89/90 opcSticker242 /105
97/8 PacificDynag-BestKept 14
87/8 PaniniSticker 107
88/9 PaniniSticker 330
89/90 PaniniSticker 289
90/1 PaniniSticker 97
91/2 PaniniSticker 287
92/3 PaniniSticker 240
96/7 PaniniSticker 236
91/2 Parkhurst 120
92/3 Parkhurst 113
93/4 Parkhurst 360
94/5 Parkhurst 40
95/6 Parkhurst 303
91/2 Pinnacle 26
92/3 Pinnacle 140
93/4 Pinnacle 246
94/5 Pinnacle 196
94/5 POG 59
93/4 PowerPlay 164, 353
93/4 Premier 149
94/5 Premier 30
90/1 ProSet 207
91/2 ProSet 164
92/3 ProSet 119
91/2 PSPlatinum 82
90/1 Score 194, -HotCards 84
91/2 Score(CDN) 230, (U.S) 230
92/3 Score 203
93/4 Score 73, 574
94/5 Score 8
96/7 Score 189
89 SemicSticker 61
84/5 Topps 112
92/3 Topps 71
96/7 ToppsNHLPicks 165
91/2 ToppsStadiumClub 277
92/3 ToppsStadiumClub 394
93/4 ToppsStadiumClub 302
90/1 UpperDeck 185
91/2 UpperDeck 275
92/3 UpperDeck 320
94/5 UpperDeck 424
95/6 UpperDeck 53
94/5 UDBeAPlayer-Aut. 98
93/4 HFD/Coke
89/90 NYR/MarineMidland

PATRICK, LESTER
83&87 HallOfFame 40
83 HHOF Postcard (C)
95/6 HHOFLegends 60
1910-11 Imperial (C56) 26
1912-13 Imperial (C57) 41
93/4 Parkie(56/7) P10
77-9 Sportscastr 62-17, 72-1716
60/1 Topps 1
36/7 WWGum (V356) 94

PATRICK, LYNN
34-43 BeeHives(NYR)
36-39 DiamondMatch (2), (3)
83&87 HallOfFame 207
83 HHOF Postcard (N)
35/6 OPC (V304C) 79
36/7 OPC (V304D) 128
39/40 OPC (V301-1) 36
40/1 OPC (V301-2) 136
36/7 WWGum (V356) 57

PATRICK, MURRAY (MUZZ)
34-43 BeeHives(NYR)
62 CeramicTiles
39/40 OPC (V301-1) 38
79/80 Montréal B&W

PATSCHINSKI, RAINER
74 Hellas 107
70/1 Kuvajulkaisut 92
79 PaniniSticker 253

PATTERSON, COLIN
89/90 Kraft 7
89/90 OPC/Topps 71
90/1 O-Pee-Chee 420
89/90 opcSticker 102/239
90/1 Panini(CGY) 16
89/90 PaniniSticker 36
91/2 ProSet 356
91/2 Score(CDN) 525
92/3 Score 312
92/3 Topps 91
83/4 Vachon 15
91/2 BUF/BlueShield
91/2 BUF/Campbell
92/3 BUF/BlueShield
85/6 CGY/RedRooster
86/7 CGY/RedRooster
87/8 CGY/RedRooster
90/1 CGY/McGavins

PATTERSON, DENNIS
74/5 Loblaws
75/6 OPC/Topps 51

PATTERSON, ED
93/4 ClassicProspects 159
93/4 Donruss 474
94/5 Donruss 265
94/5 Leaf 290
90/1 SketchWHL 52, 291
91/2 SketchWHL 94
94/5 ToppsStadiumClub 232
95/6 PGH/Foodland 14
92/3 ClevelandLumberjacks 17
93/4 ClevelandLumberjacks

PATTERSON, GEORGE
33-35 DiamondMatch
27-32 LaPresse 27/8
33/4 OPC (V304A)14
33/4 WWGum (V357) 35
28/9 MTL/LaPatrie 20

PATTERSON, PHIL
81/2 Ottawa67s
82/3 Ottawa67s
83/4 Ottawa67s

PATTERSON, RON
91/2 AirCanadaSJHL C30

PATTERSSON, HAKAN
72 SemicSticker 66

PAUL, JEFF
95/6 Slapshot 185

PAUL, KYLE
92/3 MPSPhotoSJHL 28

PAULHAUS, ROLAND
25-27 Anonymous 4, 5

PAULIN, CHARLES
92/3 Fredericton

PAULSEN, ERIK
95 PaniniWorlds 250

PAUNA, MATTI
90/1 SemicElitserien 138
91/2 SemicElitserien 193

PAVELEC, STANISLAV
94/5 APS 236
95/6 APS 6

PAVELICH, MARK
94/5 MiracleOnIce 25, 26
82/3 O-Pee-Chee 231
83/4 O-Pee-Chee 238, 239, 253
84/5 OPC 151, Topps 113
85/6 OPC/Topps 69
82/3 opcSticker 138
83/4 opcSticker 213, 214
84/5 opcSticker 97
85/6 opcSticker 84
82/3 Post
83/4 SouhaitsRen.KeyChain
79/80 USAOlympicTeam 12
81/2 NYR

PAVELICH, MARTIN (MARTY)
45-64 BeeHives(DET)
51/2 Parkhurst 54
52/3 Parkhurst 66
53/4 Parkhurst 44
54/5 Parkhurst 43
93/4 Parkie(56/7) 53
54/5 Topps 34
76 DET

PAVELICH, MATT
87 HallOfFame 261

PAVESE, JIM
87/8 PaniniSticker 310
82/3 Post
90/1 ProCards 423
88/9 DET/Caesars
80/1 SSMarie
81/2 SSMarie

PAVLAS, PETR
95/6 APS 226
95 Semic 145
91 SemicSticker 108

PAVLIK, KAREL
95/6 APS 223

PAVLIN, FABIAN
79/80 Montréal B&W

PAVLU, MARTIN
95 Semic 176
82 SemicSticker 139
96 Wien 182

PAVONI, RETO
95 Globe 208
95 PaniniWorlds 116
91 SemicSticker 178
92 SemicSticker 196

PAWLACZYK, DAN
93/4 Slapshot(Detroit) 16
94/5 Slapshot(Detroit) 19
94/5 Slapshot(MEM) 93
95/6 Slapshot 63

PAWLUK, JEFF
91/2 SketchOHL 359

PAWLUK, MIKE
92/3 BCJHL 148, 245

PAWLUK, RYAN
93/4 Slapshot(Kitchener) 12
95/6 Slapshot 314, 426

PAWLYSCHYN, WALTER
52/3 StLawrence 35
52/3 LavalDairy 8

PAYAN, EUGENE
91 C55 Reprint 43
1911-12 Imperial (C55) 43
1912-13 Imperial (C57) 9
1910-11 Imperial Post 43

PAYER, SERGE
95/6 Slapshot 138
96/7 UpperDeck 385

PAYETTE, ANDRÉ
95 Classic 95
93/4 Slapshot(SSMarie) 8
95/6 Slapshot 360

PAYETTE, DANIELLE
95/6 Halifax

PAYETTE, JEAN
72/3 O-Pee-Chee 311
73/4 QuébecNordiques

PAYNE, DAVIS
97/8 PacificDynag-BestKept 7
92/3 Greensboro 7
93/4 Greensboro
94/5 Greensboro
90/1 Mich.Tech
91/2 Mich.Tech (x2)

PAYNE, JASON
95/6 Slapshot 14

PAYNE, STEVE
79/80 OPC/Topps 64
80/1 OPC/Topps 139, OPC 274
81/2 OPC 166, Topps(W) 110
82/3 O-Pee-Chee 172
83/4 O-Pee-Chee 178
84/5 O-Pee-Chee 106, Topps 80
86/7 O-Pee-Chee 219
85/6 OPC/Topps 65
81/2 opcSticker 22, 92
82/3 opcSticker 191
83/4 opcSticker 121
84/5 opcSticker 49
85/6 opcSticker 42/170
83/4 SouhaitsRen.KeyChain
79/80 MIN
78/9 MIN/Cloverleaf 7
80/1 MIN
81/2 MIN
82/3 MIN
83/4 MIN
84/5 MIN
84/5 MIN/7Eleven 11
85/6 MIN
87/8 MIN

PAYNTER, KENT
88/9 ProCards(Saginaw)
89/90 ProCards(AHL) 101
90/1 ProCards 196
91/2 ProCards 168
91/2 WPG/IGA
82/3 Kitchener 25
83/4 Kitchener 12
84/5 Kitchener 17
94/5 Milwaukee
91/2 Moncton
85/6 NovaScotia 20

PAZLER, LUBOS
94/5 APS 263

PEACOCK, SHANE
91/2 Classic 48
91/2 ClassicFourSport 48, -Aut
90/1 SketchWHL 123
91/2 SketchWHL 343
91/2 StarPics 33
91/2 UltimateDP 43, -Aut 43
89/90 Lethbridge
93/4 Lethbridge

PEACOSH, GENE
74/5 opcWHA 27
75/6 opcWHA 24
76/7 opcWHA 60, 71
73/4 QuakerOats 24

PEAKE, PAT
91/2 Arena 11
91/2 Classic 12
93/4 Classic 12, 33, -Aut
91/2 ClassicFourSport 12, -Aut
93/4 ClassicProspects 29
93/4 Donruss 361
94/5 Donruss 318
95/6 Donruss 230
94/5 Flair 203
94/5 Fleer 238
93/4 FleerUltra 449
94/5 FleerUltra 237
95/6 FleerUltra 325
94/5 Leaf 83, -GoldLeafRook 12
94/5 PaniniSticker C
94/5 Parkhurst 281, V63
95/6 Parkhurst 488
94/5 ParkieSE 196
93/4 Pinnacle 436, -SR9
94/5 Pinnacle 136
97/8 PinnacleBeAPlayer 171
95/6 Playoff 214
93/4 PowerPlay 469, -Rookie 10
94/5 Premier 12
93/4 Score 590
95/6 Score 181
96/7 Score 67
90/1 SketchMEM 106
90/1 SketchOHL 114, 125
91/2 SketchOHL 35
91/2 StarPics 39
95/6 ToppsStadiumClub 136
91/2 UltimateDP 12, -Aut 12, 68
91/2 UD 697,-CzechWJC 84
93/4 UpperDeck 518, SP-172
94/5 UpperDeck 125, SP176
95/6 UpperDeck 163, SE175
96/7 UpperDeck 353
97/8 UpperDeck 179
96/7 UDCollChoice 282
95/6 WSH

PEAL, ALLEN
52/3 AnonymousOHL 113

PEARCE, FRANK
51/2 BasDuFleuve 9
52/3 BasDuFleuve 25

PEARCE, GARY
90/1 SketchWHL 176
91/2 SketchWHL 223
89/90 Regina

PEARCE, RANDY
89/90 SketchMEM 29
87/8 Kitchener 23
88/9 Kitchener 23
89/90 Kitchener 23
93/4 Portland

PEARCE, PERRY
96/7 OTT/PizzaHut
95/6 WPG

PEARN, PERRY
97/8 OTT
95/6 WPG

PEARSON, ANDY
85/6 Kingston 9

PEARSON, MEL
72/3 Minnesota

PEARSON, ROB
92/3 Bowman 381
93/4 Donruss 339
92/3 FleerUltra 423
93/4 FleerUltra 434
93/4 Leaf 174
92/3 O-Pee-Chee 136
91/2 opcPremier 65
92/3 PaniniSticker 80
91/2 Parkhurst 169
92/3 Parkhurst 414
93/4 Parkhurst 474
91/2 Pinnacle 304
92/3 Pinnacle 245, 287
92/3 Pinnacle-Team2000 23
93/4 Pinnacle 89
94/5 Pinnacle 375
93/4 PowerPlay 453
93/4 Premier 137
94/5 Premier 341
91/2 ProSet 562
92/3 ProSet 191, -Rookie 9
91/2 Score(CDN) 341, 385
91/2 Score(U.S) 311
92/3 Score 333, -YoungStar 18
93/4 Score 96
94/5 Score 137
89/90 SketchOHL 79
90/1 SketchOHL 15
92/3 Topps 168
92/3 ToppsStadiumClub 377
93/4 ToppsStadiumClub 498
91/2 UpperDeck 598
92/3 UpperDeck 318
93/4 UpperDeck 48
94/5 UpperDeck 180
95/6 UpperDeck 212
94/5 UDBeAPlayer-Aut. 76
90/1 TOR/P.L.A.Y. 11
92/3 TOR/Kodak
93/4 TOR/Abalene
93/4 TOR/Blacks 6
90/1 Oshawa 19
95/6 Portland

PEARSON, SCOTT
91/2 Bowman 150
93/4 Donruss 106
94/5 Donruss 196
94/5 FleerUltra 75
93/4 Leaf 297
94/5 Leaf 349
90/1 OPC/Topps 356
91/2 OPC/Topps 297
90/1 Panini(TOR) 19
94/5 PaniniSticker 204
92/3 Parkhurst 381
94/5 Parkhurst 78
95/6 Parkhurst 22
93/4 Pinnacle 375
94/5 Pinnacle 213
94/5 POG 100
94/5 Premier 124
89/90 ProCards(AHL) 119
91/2 ProSet 208
93/4 Score 376, 543
91/2 Score(CDN) 138, (U.S) 138
91/2 ToppsStadiumClub 178
91/2 UpperDeck 336
93/4 UpperDeck 389
94/5 UpperDeck 97
95/6 UpperDeck 135
93/4 EDM 15DEC93
92/3 QUE/PetroCanada
90/1 TOR
85/6 Kingston 15
86/7 Kingston 11
87/8 Kingston 22
88/9 NiagaraFalls 11
95/6 Rochester

PEARSON, TED
84/5 Moncton 14

PEAT, STEPHEN
98 BowmanCHL 136, A4
97/8 UpperDeck 405

PECA, DAVE
95/6 Slapshot 40

PECA, JUSTIN
94/5 Erie
91/2 Mich.Tech

PECA, MICHAEL
97/8 Aces A (Clubs)
94/5 CanadaJr.Alumni 7
92/3 Classic 17
93/4 Classic 25
94/5 Classic 116, T72
92/3 ClassicFourSport 166
93/4 ClassicProspects 154
93/4 Donruss CAN18
94/5 Donruss 266
95/6 Donruss 266
97/8 Donruss 21
97/8 DonrussCanadianIce 89
97/8 DonrussPreferred 34
97/8 DonrussPriority 145
97/8 DonrussStudio 72
94/5 Fleer 229, -Rookie 8
94/5 FleerUltra-UltraProspects 6
95/6 FleerUltra 212
97/8 KatchMedallion 16
94/5 Leaf 193
95/6 Leaf 114
97/8 Limited 39
97/8 Omega 24
98/9 Pacific 27, -GoldCrown 5
97/8 PacificCrown 341, -Gold 4
97/8 PcfcCrwnRoyal 15,-Lamp 4
97/8 PcfcDynag! 12,136,-Dyn 3B
97/8 PcfcD-BstK 105,-Tan 21,33
97/8 PcfcInvi. 13,-Att 3, -Off 3
97/8 PacificParamount 21
98/9 PacificParamount 21
97/8 PcfcRevolution 15,-TmCL 3
97/8 PaniniSticker 13, 122
94/5 Parkhurst 245
95/6 Parkhurst 290
93/4 Pinnacle 478
94/5 Pinnacle 260, RTP8
96/7 Pinnacle 125
97/8 Pinnacle 101
97/8 PinnacleBeAPlayer 44
97/8 PinnacleCertified 99
97/8 PinnacleInside 128
95/6 Playoff 128
95/6 POG 41
94/5 Premier(FX) 275
94/5 Score 237
95/6 Score 157
96/7 Score 209
97/8 Score 187, 268, -CheckIt 14
97/8 Score(BUF) 11
94/5 Select 198
90/1 SketchOHL 391, 392
91/2 SketchOHL 247
96/7 SkyBoxImpact 12
98/9 SPx"Finite" 9
95/6 Topps 350
98/9 Topps 94
94/5 ToppsFinest 59
97/8 ToppsSticker 3
93/4 UpperDeck 542
94/5 UD257,533,547,C10,SP173
95/6 UpperDeck 333
96/7 UpperDeck 21
97/8 UpperDeck 227, T7C
94/5 UDBeAPlayer-Aut. 165
98/9 UDChoice 24
96/7 UDCollChoice 32
97/8 UDCollChoice 26
95/6 VAN/Building 17
92/3 Ottawa67s
90/1 Sudbury 21
91/2 Sudbury 22

PECK, JIM
74/5 SiouxCity

PEDDIGREW, JEFF
93/4 Seattle

PEDERSEN, ALLEN
87/8 OPC/Topps 174
88/9 OPC/Topps 103
90/1 O-Pee-Chee 505
91/2 OPC/Topps 128
87/8 opcSticker 132 /120
92/3 Parkhurst 300
93/4 Premier 439
90/1 ProSet 12
90/1 Score 181
91/2 Score(CDN) 599
93/4 ToppsStadiumClub 366
88/9 BOS/SportsAction
89/90 BOS/SportsAction
90/1 BOS/SportsAction
92/3 HFD/DairyMarket
82/3 MedicineHat
83/4 MedicineHat 9
85/6 Moncton 4
96/7 Penascola 22

PEDERSON, BARRY
83/4 SouhaitsRen.KeyChain

PEDERSEN, KRISTIAN
91/2 SemicElitserien 114
92/3 SemicElitserien 130

PEDERSEN, TOM
79 PaniniSticker 364

PEDERSON, BARRY
92/3 Bowman 48
88/9 FritoLay
86/7 Kraft Sports 66
82/3 O-Pee-Chee 20
83/4 O-Pee-Chee 57
84/5 OPC 14, Topps 11
85/6 OPC/Topps 52
86/7 OPC/Topps 34
87/8 OPC/Topps 177
88/9 OPC/Topps 32
89/90 O-Pee-Chee 281
90/1 OPC/Topps 134
92/3 O-Pee-Chee 295
91/2 opcPremier 124
82/3 opcSticker 92, 93
83/4 opcSticker 49, 50
84/5 opcSticker 187
86/7 opcSticker 38 /175
87/8 opcSticker 188
88/9 opcSticker 65
89/90 opcSticker 60
87/8 PaniniSticker 346
88/9 PaniniSticker 138
89/90 PaniniSticker 153
90/1 ProSet 238
91/2 ProSet 351
83/4 PuffySticker 7
91/2 Score(CDN) 639
92/3 Topps 241
90/1 UpperDeck 329
83/4 BOS
84/5 BOS
90/1 PGH/Foodland 4
86/7 VAN
87/8 VAN/Shell
88/9 VAN/Mohawk
89/90 VAN
82/3 Victoria

PEDERSON, DENIS
95/6 Bowman 138
93/4 Classic 26, -Aut.
94/5 Classic 112, T37
93/4 ClassicFourSport 196
95/6 Donruss 257, -CdnJr 20
95/6 FleerMetal 195
95/6 FleerUltra 359
96/7 Leaf 226
97/8 Limited 154
98/9 Pacific 269
97/8 PacificCrown 221
97/8 PacificInvincible 79
95/6 Parkhurst 395
94/5 Pinnacle 538
96/7 Pinnacle 221
96/7 PinnacleBeAPlayer 217
97/8 Score(N.J.) 11
95/6 SkyBoxImpact 207
94/5 SP 144
95/6 Topps 12CJ
98/9 Topps 214, I4
94/5 ToppsFinest 163
95/6 UpperDeck 354
96/7 UpperDeck 288
97/8 UpperDeck 97
97/8 UDCollChoice 149
96/7 N.J/Sharp
93/4 PrinceAlbert

PEDERSON, MARK
91/2 Bowman 242
92/3 Bowman 390
92/3 O-Pee-Chee 157
90/1 OPC/Topps 82
91/2 OPC/Topps 399
90/1 Panini(MTL) 17
92/3 PaniniSticker 188
91/2 Parkhurst 345
92/3 Pinnacle 213
88/9 ProCards(Sherbrooke)
90/1 ProSet 618
90/1 Score 387
91/2 Score(CDN) 435
92/3 Score 263
92/3 Topps 327
91/2 ToppsStadiumClub 291
92/3 ToppsStadiumClub 168
90/1 UpperDeck 532
91/2 UpperDeck 363
92/3 UpperDeck 209
90/1 MTL
91/2 PHA/JCPenney
85/6 MedicineHat 19

PEDERSON, TODD
82/3 MedicineHat

PEDERSON, TOM
92/3 ClassicProspects 145
92/3 FleerUltra 403
92/3 opcPremier 33
93/4 Parkhurst 184
94/5 Pinnacle 448
93/4 PowerPlay 226
94/5 Premier 142
93/4 UpperDeck 92
95/6 UDCollChoice 38
92/3 S.J/PacificBell

PEER, BRIAN
83/4 SSMarie

PEER, BRIT
84/5 SSMarie

PEERLESS, BLAINE
81/2 Milwaukee 4

PEET, SHAUN
92/3 BCJHL 108

PEETERS, PETE
91/2 Bowman 237
80/1 O-Pee-Chee 279
81/2 OPC 245, Topps(E) 109
82/3 O-Pee-Chee 22
83/4 OPC 44,48,58,209,221,222
84/5 OPC 15, Topps 12
85/6 OPC/Topps 75
86/7 OPC/Topps 77
87/8 OPC/Topps 25, 44
88/9 OPC/Topps 180
89/90 OPC/Topps 195
90/1 OPC/Topps 109
91/2 OPC/Topps 29
88/9 opcStars 30
81/2 opcSticker 177
82/3 opcSticker 117
83/4 opcSticker 41, 42, 170, 318
84/5 opcSticker 144, 184
85/6 opcSticker 160
88/9 opcSticker 207/78
87/8 PaniniSticker 174
88/9 PaniniSticker 364
82/3 Post
90/1 ProSet 502, -POM
91/2 PSPlatinum PC2
83/4 PuffySticker 9
91/2 Score(CDN) 544
83/4 SouhaitsRen.KeyChain
91/2 ToppsStadiumClub 88
90/1 UpperDeck 424
91/2 UpperDeck 642
83/4 BOS
84/5 BOS
89/90 PHA
90/1 PHA
86/7 WSH/Kodak
86/7 WSH/Police
87/8 WSH
87/8 WSH/Kodak
88/9 WSH
88/9 WSH/Smokey

PEGG, JAMIE
89/90 SketchOHL 104
90/1 SketchOHL 368

PEHRSON, JOAKIM
89/90 SemicElitserien 43
90/1 SemicElitserien 191

PEHU, SAKARI
72/3 WilliamsFIN 314

PEIPMANN, JASON
92/3 BCJHL 14

PEIRSON, JOHN
45-64 BeeHives(BOSx2)
51/2 Parkhurst 34
52/3 Parkhurst 78
53/4 Parkhurst 88
54/5 Parkhurst 60
93/4 Parkie(56/7) 5
57/8 BOS
91/2 BOS/Legends

PEITSOMA, JUKKA
80/1 Mallasjuoma 133

PEJCHAR, RUDOLF
94/5 APS 139
95/6 APS 244

PEK, GYORGY
79 PaniniSticker 273

PEKAREK, DAVID
90/1 SketchMEM 66
90/1 SketchQMJHL 12
91/2 SketchQMJHL 239

PEKKA, SAMI
94/5 Sisu 70

PEKKARINEN, V.P.
93/4 Jyvas-Hyva 178
93/4 Sisu 170
94/5 Sisu 127
95/6 Sisu 79

PEKKI, SEMI
95/6 Sisu 237
96/7 Sisu 40
95/6 SisuLimited 108

PELCHAT, PATRICK
98 BowmanCHL 88

PELCHAT, ROD
51/2 LacStJean 27

PELENSKY, PERRY
83/4 Springfield 13

PELKTOLA, PEKKA
95/6 Sisu 362

PELL, GORDON
89/90 SketchOHL 80
90/1 SketchOHL 213
91/2 SketchOHL 23
91/2 Cornwall 4

PELLA, DEAN
87/8 Kingston 18
88/9 Sudbury 12

PELLA, TYLER
87/8 Kingston 23
88/9 Sudbury 11

PELLAERS, RYAN
91/2 SketchWHL 67

PELLEGRIMS, MIKE
96/7 DEL

PELLEGRINO, SANTINO
94 Semic 305
92 SemicSticker 260
93 SemicSticker 228

PELLERIN, BRIAN
91/2 ProCards 45
90/1 SketchWHL 266
92/3 Peoria
93/4 Peoria
90/1 PrinceAlbert

PELLERIN, SCOTT
92/3 Classic 81
92/3 ClassicFourSport 202
92/3 ClassicProspects 18, 90
93/4 FleerUltra 142
93/4 Leaf 167
98/9 Pacific 370
97/8 PacificCrown 95
93/4 Parkhurst 116
97/8 PinnacleBeAPlayer 50
93/4 Score 373
97/8 Score(STL) 12
93/4 ToppsStadiumClub 13
93/4 UpperDeck 52
92/3 Maine (1) 7

PELLETIER, FRANÇOIS
89/90 SketchMEM 66

PELLETIER, GASTON
52/3 AnonymousOHL 77
72 SemicSticker 155

PELLETIER, JEAN-MARC
98/9 UDChoice 301

PELLETIER, LLOYD
90/1 SketchWHL 53
91/2 SketchWHL 235

PELLETIER, MARCEL
51-54 LaPatrie 30Mar52
51/2 LavalDairy 33
52/3 StLawrence 90

PELLINEN, PETRI
71/2 WilliamsFIN 332

PELOFFY, ANDRÉ
74/5 WSH

PELTOLA, ARI
70/1 Kuvajulkaisut 336
80/1 Mallasjuoma 207
78/9 SM-Liiga 232

PELTOLA, JUHANI
66/7 Champion 159

PELTOLA, MIKKO
92/3 Jyvas-Hyva 170
93/4 Jyvas-Hyva 288
95 Semic 29
93/4 Sisu 69
95/6 Sisu 102
96/7 Sisu 178
97/8 udSwedish 142

PELTOLA, PEKKA
91/2 Jyvas-Hyva 10
92/3 Jyvas-Hyva 131
93/4 Jyvas-Hyva 22
93/4 Sisu 97
94/5 Sisu 68

PELTOLA, TEUVO
66/7 Champion 146

PELTOMAA, TIMO
96/7 DEL 63
91/2 Jyvas-Hyva 15
92/3 Jyvas-Hyva 44
93/4 Jyvas-Hyva 79
95 Semic 50
91 SemicSticker 25
92 SemicSticker 18
93 SemicSticker 72
93/4 Sisu 125
94/5 Sisu 43, 158, -Horoscope 8
95/6 Sisu 227
96/7 Sisu-Sledgehammer 7
95/6 SisuLimited 104

PELTONEN, ESA
72 Hellas 10
74 Hellas 13
70/1 Kuvajulkaisut 73, 285
80/1 Mallasjuoma 5
72 Panda
79 PaniniSticker 170
72 SemicSticker 85
74 SemicSticker 88
82 SemicSticker 49
78/9 SM-Liiga 31
77-80 Sportscaster 49-175
71/2 WilliamsFIN 73, 155
72/3 WilliamsFIN 70, 107
73/4 WilliamsFIN 75, 138

PELTONEN, JARI
70/1 Kuvajulkaisut 337

PELTONEN, JARMO-SAKARI
96/7 DEL 267

PELTONEN, JARNO
93/4 Jyvas-Hyva 83
93/4 Sisu 123
95/6 Sisu 235
96/7 Sisu 32

PELTONEN, JONNI
70/1 Kuvajulkaisut 337
80/1 Mallasjuoma 113
78/9 SM-Liiga 157
73/4 WilliamsFIN 314

PELTONEN, JORMA
66/7 Champion 197
65/6 Hellas 126
70/1 Kuvajulkaisut 74, 135
72 Panda
71/2 WilliamsFIN 184
72/3 WilliamsFIN 134
73/4 WilliamsFIN 188

PELTONEN, MATTI
66/7 Champion 162
65/6 Hellas 148
70/1 Kuvajulkaisut 219

PELTONEN, PASI
93/4 Sisu 211
94/5 Sisu 103
95/6 Sisu 153
96/7 Sisu 152

PELTONEN, TIMO
80/1 Mallasjuoma 115
78/9 SM-Liiga 158

PELTONEN, VILLE
95/6 Bowman 133
94/5 Classic 97, T63
96/7 Donruss 224
95 Hartwall
92/3 Jyvas-Hyva 15
93/4 Jyvas-Hyva 28
95/6 Kelloggs PopUp 4
95 Latkaliiga 5
96/7 Leaf 144
95 PaniniWorlds 178
95/6 Parkhurst 456, 521
94 Semic 33
95 Semic 16, 230
93/4 Sisu 101, 365, 391
94/5 Sisu 166, -Horoscope 6
95/6 Sisu 172,-GoldC 21,-Pain 5
95/6 SisuLimited 41, -Platinum
95 SuomenBeckett 3
92/3 UpperDeck 616
95/6 UpperDeck 384
96/7 UpperDeck 335
96/7 UDCollChoice 241
97/8 udSwedish 79, C5, UDS5
96 Wien 16, 37, AS6
96/7 S.J/PacificBellSheet

PELTONIEMI, OSSI
66/7 Champion 219

PELTONIEMI, PEKKA
66/7 Champion 121

PELUSO, MIKE
92/3 FleerUltra 365
93/4 Leaf 407
94/5 Leaf 546
91/2 OPC/Topps 293
97/8 PacificCrown 306
93/4 PaniniSticker 116
92/3 Parkhurst 118
92/3 Pinnacle 379
93/4 Pinnacle 385
94/5 Pinnacle 423
96/7 PinnacleBeAPlayer 136
95/6 POG 161
89/90 ProCards(IHL) 57
91/2 ProCards 496
90/1 ProSet 601
92/3 ProSet 122
91/2 ScoreCDN 529
92/3 Score 536
93/4 Score 265, 551
95/6 Topps 10PL
93/4 ToppsStadiumClub 497
91/2 UpperDeck 414
90/1 CHI/Coke
91/2 CHI/Coke
92/3 OTT

PELYK, MIKE
70/1 DadsCookies
70/1 EddieSargent 203
71/2 EddieSargent 197
72/3 EddieSargent 200
70/1 Esso Stamp
70/1 OPC/Topps 107
71/2 OPC/Topps 92
72/3 OPC 17, Topps 107
73/4 OPC/Topps 71
76/7 OPC 342
74/5 opcWHA 19
68/9 Post Marble
68/9 ShirriffCoin TOR8
71/2 TheTorontoSun
68/9 TOR
69/70 TOR
70/1 TOR

71/2 TOR
72/3 TOR
73/4 TOR
76/7 TOR
75/6 Cincinnati

PELZER, JAMES
91/2 AvantGardeBCJHL 96

PENCHTHALT, TONY
92/3 Tacoma

PENDERGAST, MIKE
91/2 UD'CzechWJC 69

PENELTON, PAUL
85/6 Kitchener 25

PENICKA, LUBOMIR
82 SemicSticker 94

PENK, JAN
94/5 APS 260
95/6 APS 133

PENN, SHAWN
94/5 Toledo
95/6 Toledo

PENNANEN, OLLI
78/9 SM-Liiga 49

PENNANEN, PENTTI
66/7 Champion 136
70/1 Kuvajulkaisut 263

PENNELL, FRED
87/8 Sudbury 10
88/9 Sudbury 10

PENNEY, CHAD
94/5 Classic 68, T48
94/5 ClassicFourSport 145
93/4 ClassicProspects 65
94/5 Leaf 241
94/5 Premier 267
90/1 SketchOHL 314
91/2 SketchOHL 58
93/4 UpperDeck 436
93/4 SSMarie 9

PENNEY, JACKSON
92/3 CanadaNats
95/6 DEL 402
96/7 DEL 310
90/1 ProCards 115

PENNEY, RYAN
95/6 Slapshot 182

PENNEY, STEVE
86/7 Kraft Sports 79
84/5 O-Pee-Chee 269
85/6 OPC/Topps 4
86/7 O-Pee-Chee 222
85/6 opcSticker 126
83/4 MTL
84/5 MTL
85/6 MTL
85/6 MTL/Pennant
85/6 MTL/PepsiPlacemats
85/6? MTL/ProvigoPlacemats
85/6 MTL/ProvigoStickers
86/7 WPG
87/8 Moncton
83/4 NovaScotia 15

PENNINGTON, CLIFF
45-64 BeeHives(BOSx2)
64-67 BeeHives(BOS)
62 CeramicTiles
61/2 ShirriffCoin 1
61/2 Topps 19
62/3 Topps 14

PENNISTON, DON
51/2 LavalDairy 58

PENNOCK, BERKLEY
93/4 RedDeer

PENNOCK, TREVOR
91/2 AvantGardeBCJHL 126
90/1 SketchWHL 18

PENNOYER, ROB
92/3 BCJHL 128

PENSTOCK, BYRON
90/1 SketchWHL 224
91/2 SketchWHL 302
94/5 Slapshot(MEM) 26
90/1 Brandon 18
92/3 Brandon 18

PENTON, SCOTT
93/4 OwenSound

PENTTILA, TIM
80/1 Mallasjuoma 170

PENTTINEN, JUKKA
95/6 Sisu 258
96/7 Sisu 46

PEPEUNIG, GERHARD
79 PaniniSticker 308

PEPIN, BOB
52/3 LavalDairy 52
52/3 StLawrence 83

PEPIN, RENÉ
52/3 BasDuFleuve 52
51/2 LavalDairy 42
52/3 StLawrence 82

PEPIN, ROB
43-47 ParadeSportive

PEPLINSKI, JIM
83/4 Esso
86/7 Kraft Sports 5
81/2 O-Pee-Chee 49
82/3 O-Pee-Chee 55
83/4 O-Pee-Chee 90
84/5 O-Pee-Chee 233
86/7 OPC/Topps 182
87/8 O-Pee-Chee 209
88/9 O-Pee-Chee 243
89/90 O-Pee-Chee 206
90/1 OPC/Topps 38
82/3 opcSticker 216
87/8 opcSticker 46
86/7 opcSticker 84/212
88/9 opcSticker 88/218
89/90 opcSticker 99/236
87/8 PaniniSticker 213
88/9 PaniniSticker 14
89/90 PaniniSticker 37
80/1 Pepsi Cap
82/3 Post
83/4 7ElevenCokeCup
83/4 SouhaitsRen.KeyChain
82/3 StaterMint
83/4 Vachon 16
80/1 CGY
81/2 CGY
82/3 CGY
85/6 CGY/RedRooster
86/7 CGY/RedRooster
87/8 CGY/RedRooster

PEPPERALL, COLIN
97/8 Bowman 30
98 BowmanCHL 19
95/6 Slapshot 197

PEPPERALL, RYAN
95 Classic 46, 86
94/5 Slapshot(Kitchener) 16
95/6 Slapshot 147, -Promo

PERALA, O.P.
71/2 WilliamsFIN 351

PERÄOJA, SEPPO
70/1 Kuvajulkaisut 185

PERCIVAL, ROB
88/9 Brockville 15

PEREIRA, LEN
94/5 Raleigh

PEREZ, DENIS
95 PaniniWorlds 102
94 Semic 215
92 SemicSticker
93 SemicSticker 255
96 Wien 186

PERHOMAA, PENTTI
70/1 Kuvajulkaisut 376
80/1 Mallasjuoma 95

PERHONMAA, MATTI
71/2 WilliamsFIN 309

PERKINS, DARREN
90/1 SketchWHL 279
91/2 SketchWHL 244
93/4 Hampton
90/1 PrinceAlbert
91/2 PrinceAlbert
94/5 ThunderBay
95/6 ThunderBay
93/4 Toledo 12
94/5 Toledo

PERKINS, ROSS
74/5 opcWHA 39

PERKINS, TERRY
86/7 Fredericton
88/9 SaltLake 3

PERKKIÖ, MARKKU
78/9 SM-Liiga 150

PERKOVIC, STEVE
93/4 Hampton

PERNA, DOMINIC
97/8 Bowman 49
98 BowmanCHL 83, 163

PERNA, MIKE
93/4 Slapshot(NiagaraFalls) 24
95/6 Slapshot 202

PERONMAA, PETRI
96/7 Sisu 111

PERPICH, JOHN
90/1 WSH/Kodak

PERREAULT, ALBERT
36/7 WWGum (V356) 115

PERREAULT, BOB
45-64 BeeHives(BOSx2)
64-67 BeeHives(BOS)
62 CeramicTiles
62/3 Topps 2
56-66 TorontoStar 62/3

PERREAULT, FERNAND
51/2 LavalDairy 98
52/3 LavalDairy 38
51/2 Cleveland

PERREAULT, GERRY
51/2 LacStJean 7

PERREAULT, GILBERT
71/2 Bazooka Panel 6
70/1 Colgate Stamp 28
70/1 DadsCookies
72-84 Dernière 82/3
70/1 EddieSargent 23
71/2 EddieSargent 19
72/3 EddieSargent 31
70/1 Esso Stamp
88/9 Esso Sticker
84/5 Kelloggs Disk
91/2 Kraft 80
74/5 LiptonSoup 2
74/5 Loblaws
70/1 OPC/Topps 131
71/2 OPC/T. 60, 246, -Booklet 8
72/3 OPC 136, -TmCnd, T. 120
73/4 OPC/Topps 70
74/5 OPC/Topps 25
75/6 OPC/Topps 10
76/7 OPC/Topps 2-3, 180, 214
76/7 OPC 380, Topps-Glossy 9
77/8 OPC/T. 7, 210, -Glossy 14
78/9 OPC/Topps 130
79/80 OPC/Topps 180
80/1 OPC/Topps 80, 262
81/2 O-Pee-Chee 30
82/3 O-Pee-Chee 25, 30
83/4 O-Pee-Chee 67
84/5 OPC 24, Topps 19
85/6 OPC/Topps 160, K
86/7 OPC/Topps 79
71/2 opcPoster 14
81/2 opcSticker 60
82/3 opcSticker 118
83/4 opcSticker 4, 240-41
84/5 opcSticker 201-02
85/6 opcSticker 188
86/7 opcSticker 43 /179
80/1 opcSuperCard 2
81/2 Post PopUp 2
82/3 Post
91/2 ProSet 596
83/4 PuffySticker 8
90/1 Score 355
84/5 7ElevenDisk
85/6 7Eleven 2
83/4 SouhaitsRen.KeyChain
71/2 TheTorontoSun
91/2 Trends(72) 51, -Aut
92/3 Trends(76) 162
95/6 Zeller's
72/3 BUF
73/4 BUF
73/4 BUF/BellsMarket
74/5 BUF
75/6 BUF/Linnett
80/1 BUF/Wendt
81/2 BUF 4
82/3 BUF/Wendt 7
84/5 BUF/BlueShield
85/6 BUF
86/7 BUF
93/4 BUF/NOCO

PERREAULT, JOCELYN
88/9 ProCards(Hershey)

PERREAULT, KIRBY
90/1 Mich.Tech
91/2 Mich.Tech

PERREAULT, NICOLAS
93/4 Mich.State
94/5 SaintJohn
95/6 Toledo

PERREAULT, YANIC
91/2 Arena 31
91/2 Classic 39
91/2 ClassicFourSport 39, -Aut
93/4 ClassicProspects 113
95/6 Donruss 375
96/7 Donruss 21
96/7 DonrussCanadianIce 76
96/7 DonrussElite 76
97/8 DonrussPriority 142
95/6 EdgeIce 184,C8,-Quantum3
95/6 FleerMetal 73
95/6 FleerUltra 253
97/8 KatchMedallion 71
96/7 KraftDinner
95/6 Leaf 249
96/7 Leaf 7
96/7 LeafPreferred 107
96/7 Maggers 81
97/8 Omega 111
98/9 Pacific 243
97/8 PacificCrownRoyale 64
98/9 PacificParamount 106
97/8 PacificRegime 97
97/8 PacificRevolution 65
96/7 PaniniSticker 272
94/5 Parkhurst 230
95/6 Parkhurst 372
96/7 Pinnacle 42
97/8 PinnacleBeeHive 35
95/6 PinnacleZenith 113
96/7 PinnacleZenith 86
91/2 ProCards 339
92/3 Score 487
96/7 Score 25
91/2 SketchAwards 22, 30
90/1 SketchMEM 115
90/1 SketchQMJHL 100, 146
97/8 SPAuthentic 75, S8
91/2 StarPics 22
95/6 Summit 166
95/6 Topps 223
92/3 UpperDeck 70
95/6 UpperDeck 28, SE130
96/7 UpperDeck 79
95/6 UDBeAPlayer 150
97/8 UDBlackDiamond 127
98/9 UDChoice 96
96/7 UDCollChoice 126
91/2 UltimateDP 34, -Aut 34
91/2 UltimateDP 54, 87, 89
97/8 Zenith 64, Z29
92/3 StJohns
93/4 StJohns

PERRETT, CRAIG
91/2 AirCanadaSJHL C34

PERRIER, BRYANT
89/90 ProCards(IHL) 100

PERRON, JEAN
84/5 MTL
85/6 MTL
85/6 MTL/ProvigoStickers
86/7 MTL
87/8 MTL
87/8 MTL/Stickers 7, 10

PERROT, NATHAN
95 Classic 39
95/6 Slapshot 236
96/7 SSMarie

PERRY, ALAN
88/9 ProCards(Indianapolis)
92/3 Oklahoma

PERRY, BRIAN
69/70 O-Pee-Chee 84

PERRY, DON
78/9 Saginaw

PERRY, JEFF
90/1 SketchWHL 292
94/5 SaintJohn
95/6 SaintJohn

PERRY, RANDY
97/8 Bowman 96
93/4 Lethbridge

PERRY, TOM
91/2 AirCanadaSJHL B10
92/3 MPSPhotoSJHL 35

PERSCHAU, DIRK
94/5 DEL 44
95/6 DEL 32
96/7 DEL 26

PERSIGEHL, DAVE
93/4 Huntington
94/5 Huntington 27

PERSSON, HAKAN
92/3 SemicElitserien 256

PERSSON, JERRY
94/5 ElitSet 257
95/6 ElitSet 199
91/2 SemicElitserien 294
92/3 SemicElitserien 311

PERSSON, JOAKIM
96/7 DEL 92
94/5 ElitSet 192, -Rookie 7
95/6 ElitSet 4, -Spidermen 1
90/1 SemicElitserien 274
91/2 SemicElitserien 46, 55
95/6 udElite 1, NA1
97/8 udSwedish 182

PERSSON, MIKAEL
92/3 SemicElitserien 315

PERSSON, RICARD
95/6 Donruss 304
94/5 ElitSet 55
97/8 PacificRegime 172
96/7 PinnacleBeAPlayer 210
89/90 SemicElitserien 126
90/1 SemicElitserien 203
91/2 SemicElitserien 132
92/3 SemicElitserien 156
95/6 ToppsStadiumClub 225

PERSSON, STEFAN
78/9 OPC/Topps 144
79/80 OPC/Topps 32
80/1 OPC/Topps 219
81/2 OPC 206, Topps(E) 92
82/3 O-Pee-Chee 209
83/4 O-Pee-Chee 15
84/5 O-Pee-Chee 133, Topps 99
82/3 Post
89/90 SemicElitserien 112
90/1 SemicElitserien 118
83/4 SouhaitsRen.KeyChain
79/80 NYI
83/4 NYI/Islander 20
84/5 NYI 24

PERSSON, TORBJORN
94/5 ElitSet 132
90/1 SemicElitserien 122
91/2 SemicElitserien 123
92/3 SemicElitserien 142

PERTHALER, CHRIS
93 SemicSticker 283

PERTTULA, ANTTI
70/1 Kuvajulkaisut 184
71/2 WilliamsFIN 140
72/3 WilliamsFIN 202
73/4 WilliamsFIN 165

PERTTULA, PEKKA
65/6 Hellas 142

PERVUKHIN, VASILI
82 SemicSticker 55
79 PaniniSticker 143
78 SovietChamps
83/4 SovietStars
87/8 SovietStars

PESAT, IVO
94/5 APS 229
95/6 APS 4

PESCHKE, FRANK
94/5 DEL 396
95/6 DEL 417

PESETTI, RON
87/8 Moncton

PEST, TREVOR
91/2 Nainamo

PESUT, GEORGE
75/6 O-Pee-Chee 360

PETÄJÄAHO, SAKARI
80/1 Mallasjuoma 57

PETAWABANO, RODNEY
91/2 SketchQMJHL 83

PETENDRA, KEVIN
82/3 Kitchener 14

PETEREK, JAN
94/5 APS 137
95/6 APS 305

PETERNOUSEK, GEORGE
79 PaniniSticker 277

PETERS, ANDREW
98 BowmanCHL 150, A33

PETERS, DIETMAR
74 Hellas 104
70/1 Kuvajulkaisut 93
79 PaniniSticker 250

PETERS, FRANK
28/9 PaulinsCandy 47

PETERS, GARY
65/6 CocaCola
70/1 EddieSargent 151
70/1 Esso Stamp
68/9 OPC/Topps 99
69/70 O-Pee-Chee 171
70/1 OPC 196
65/6 Topps 28
71/2 BOS
70/1 PHA

PETERS, GEOFF
95/6 Bowman P26
95 Classic 89
95/6 Slapshot 190, 440
95/6 UpperDeck 522

PETERS, JASON
91/2 AvantGardeBCJ 134
90/1 SketchWHL 251
90/1 Saskatoon 25
89/90 Victoria

PETERS, JAMES M. (JIM)
45-64 BeeHives(BOS),(CHI)
45-65 BeeHives(DET)
43-47 ParadeSportive
51/2 Parkhurst 41
52/3 Parkhurst 35
53/4 Parkhurst 69
45-54 QuakerOats

PETERS, JAMES S.
70/1 EddieSargent 77
69/70 O-Pee-Chee 143
72/3 OPC 224
73/4 OPC 231

PETERS, JIM
93/4 Birmingham 11
93/4 Dayton 5

PETERS, ROB
95/6 Dayton

PETERS, ROLAND
74 Hellas 103
79 PaniniSticker 254

PETERS, TONY
92/3 Dayton

PETERSON, BRENT
95 Classic 78
95 ClassicFiveSport 148, -Aut
91/2 Mich.Tech

PETERSON, BRENT
86/7 Kraft Sports 67
83/4 O-Pee-Chee 68
84/5 O-Pee-Chee 25
85/6 OPC/Topps 47
86/7 O-Pee-Chee 251
87/8 O-Pee-Chee 263
85/6 opcSticker 178/48
86/7 opcSticker 100 /229
87/8 opcSticker 199/58
91/2 SketchWHL 47
83/4 SouhaitsRen.KeyChain
82/3 BUF/Wendt 17
84/5 BUF/BlueShield
80/1 DET
88/9 HFD/JuniorWhalers
85/6 VAN
86/7 VAN
86/7 Moncton 17
93/4 Portland

PETERSON, CORY
94/5 AutoPhonex 32

PETERSON, TOBY
97/8 UDBlackDiamond 135
98/9 UDChoice 307

PETHKE, MARC
94/5 DEL 192
95/6 DEL 171
96/7 DEL 113

PETIT, MICHEL
90/1 Bowman 170
91/2 Bowman 158
92/3 Bowman 101
92/3 Durivage 43
94/5 Leaf 444
87/8 O-Pee-Chee 262
89/90 O-Pee-Chee 251
90/1 OPC/Topps 271
91/2 OPC/Topps 166
92/3 O-Pee-Chee 185
87/8 opcSticker 196/55
87/8 PaniniSticker 342
88/9 PaniniSticker 304
89/90 PaniniSticker 291
90/1 PaniniSticker 148
91/2 PaniniSticker 98
91/2 Parkhurst 252
93/4 Parkhurst 304
94/5 Parkhurst 39
91/2 Pinnacle 49
92/3 Pinnacle 206
93/4 PowerPlay 308
93/4 Premier 141
94/5 Premier 406
90/1 ProSet 256, 539
91/2 ProSet 492
90/1 Score 187, 54T
91/2 Score(CDN) 103, (U.S) 103
92/3 Score 38
93/4 Score 275
92/3 Topps 337
91/2 ToppsStadiumClub 311
92/3 ToppsStadiumClub 195
93/4 ToppsStadiumClub 232
90/1 UpperDeck 181
91/2 UpperDeck 359
93/4 UpperDeck 66
92/3 CGY/IGA 13
89/90 QUE
89/90 QUE/GeneralFoods
89/90 QUE/Police
90/1 QUE
90/1 QUE/PetroCanada
90/1 TOR
90/1 TOR/P.L.A.Y. 18
83/4 VAN
84/5 VAN
86/7 VAN
85/6 Fredericton 16

PETITCLERC, MAXIME
91/2 SketchQMJHL 291

PETRASH, KEN
94/5 DEL 231
95/6 DEL 228
96/7 DEL 79

PETRASEK, DAVID
97/8 udSwedish 87

PETRE, HENRIK
97/8 UDBlackDiamond 67
98/9 UDChoice 292

PETRENKO, SERGEI
93/4 Classic 91
93/4 Donruss 43
93/4 FleerUltra 275
93/4 Leaf 425
93/4 Parkhurst 292

93 SemicSticker 139
93/4 ToppsStadiumClub 373
92/3 UpperDeck 346
93/4 UpperDeck 450
93/4 Rochester

PETRIC, JEFF
95/6 Dayton

PETRILAINEN, PASI
95/6 Sisu 110
96/7 Sisu 127
95/6 UpperDeck 550
97/8 UDBlackDiamond 48
98/9 UDChoice 279

PETRONI, PIERRE
91/2 SketchQMJHL 23

PETROV, NIKOLAY
79 PaniniSticker 349

PETROV, OLEG
94/5 Classic AR4
92/3 ClassicProspects 8
93/4 ClassicProspects 177
93/4 Donruss 452
94/5 Donruss 61
94/5 Flair 90
94/5 FleerUltra 314
93/4 Leaf 260
94/5 Leaf 354
92/3 opcPremier 96
94/5 PaniniSticker B
92/3 Parkhurst 486
94/5 Parkhurst 119, 291
94/5 ParkieSE seV40
93/4 Pinnacle 212
94/5 Pinnacle 203
94/5 POG 138
93/4 PowerPlay 371
94/5 Premier 377
94/5 Premier-Finest(OPC) 13
93/4 Score 459
94/5 Score 260
94/5 ToppsStadiumClub 241
93/4 UpperDeck 84
94/5 UpperDeck 137, SP41
95/6 UpperDeck 343
92/3 MTL
92/3 MTL/OPC 56
94/5 MTL
95/6 MTL
92/3 Fredericton
93/4 Fredericton

PETROV, SERGEI
93/4 Minn-Duluth

PETROV, VLADIMIR
95 Globe 242
72 Hellas 75
74 Hellas 53
70/1 Kuvajulkaisut 11
69/70 MästarSerien 28
79 PaniniSticker 147
72 SemicSticker 16
74 SemicSticker 35
73/4 Soviet Champs 11
80 SovietMiniPics
69/70 Soviet Stars
70/1 Soviet Stars
71/2 Soviet Stars
73/4 Soviet Stars 7, 9
74/5 Soviet Stars 12
78 SovietChamps
77-9 Sportscastr 102-14, 26-673
91/2 Trends(72) 52, 54
71/2 WilliamsFIN 12
72/3 WilliamsFIN 31
73/4 WilliamsFIN 13

PETROVICKY, ROBERT
92/3 Classic 6
93/4 Classic 144
92/3 ClassicFourSport 156
93/4 Donruss 145
92/3 FleerUltra 302
93/4 FleerUltra 337
93/4 Leaf 187
94/5 Leaf 387
92/3 opcPremier 36
97/8 PacificBestKept 82
97/8 PaniniSticker 166
92/3 Parkhurst 61
93/4 Parkhurst 89
94/5 Parkhurst 94
92/3 Pinnacle 402
93/4 PowerPlay 107
93/4 Score 277
97/8 Score(STL) 9
94 Semic 210
93 SemicSticker 106
91/2 UD'CzechWJC 93
92/3 UpperDeck 569, ER20
93/4 UpperDeck 37, SP-63
94/5 UpperDeck 361
97/8 UpperDeck 350
94/5 UDBeAPlayer R84
96 Wien 233
92/3 HFD/DairyMart

PETROVICKY, RONALD
98 BowmanCHL 78

PETROVKA, VLADIMIR
91 SemicSticker 124

PETRUIC, JEFF
90/1 SketchWHL 151
91/2 SketchWHL 281

PETRUK, RANDY
95/6 Bowman P27
97/8 Bowman 83
98 BowmanCHL 42, SC10
94/5 Slapshot(MEM) 23
95/6 UpperDeck 524

PETRUNIN, ANDREI
95 Classic 66, -Aut
94/5 SP 190
95/6 SP 178
95/6 UpperDeck 556
96/7 UpperDeck"Ice" 143

PETTERESSON, DANIEL
89/90 SemicElitserien 208

PETTERLE, BRIAN
80/1 SSMarie

PETTERSSON, ANDERS
89/90 SemicElitserien 132

PETTERSSON, HAKAN
72 Hellas 40
74 Hellas 33
71/2 WilliamsFIN 57
72/3 WilliamsFIN 55

PETTERSSON, HANS
89/90 SemicElitserien 222
90/1 SemicElitserien 58

PETTERSSON, HENRIK
92/3 SemicElitserien 292

PETTERSSON, JORGEN
81/2 OPC 296, Topps(W) 121
82/3 O-Pee-Chee 309
83/4 O-Pee-Chee 318
84/5 O-Pee-Chee 189
81/2 opcSticker 135
82/3 opcSticker 202
83/4 opcSticker 123
84/5 opcSticker 59
82/3 Post
83/4 PuffySticker 15
89/90 SemicElitserien 280
82 SemicSticker 152
85/6 HFD/JuniorWhalers
92/3 STL/UpperDeck 18
86/7 WSH/Police

PETTERSSON, LARS-GUNNAR
89/90 SemicElitserien 157
90/1 SemicElitserien 236
91/2 SemicElitserien 166
92/3 SemicElitserien 191
89 SemicSticker 25

PETTERSSON, MARTIN
89/90 SemicElitserien 206

PETTERSSON, MIKAEL
94/5 ElitSet 239
95/6 ElitSet 134
92/3 SemicElitserien 237, 289
95/6 udElite 196
97/8 udSwedish 189

PETTERSSON, OVE
89/90 SemicElitserien 176
90/1 SemicElitserien 9

PETTERSSON, PETER
95/6 udElite DS15

PETTERSSON, RONNIE
90/1 SemicElitserien 283
97/8 udSwedish 36

PETTERSSON, TOMMY
90/1 SemicElitserien 22
91/2 SemicElitserien 223

PETTINGER, GORDON
34-43 BeeHives(DET)
36/7 WWGum (V356) 76

PETZ, RYAN
91/2 SketchWHL 323

PEYTON, CHRIS
95/6 Halifax

PHAIR, LYLE
88/9 ProCards(NewHaven)

PHELPS, CHRIS
90/1 SketchOHL 115
91/2 SketchOHL 27
94/5 Hampton 10
95/6 Hampton HRA17

PHILIP, JOCHEN
74 Hellas 118

PHILIP, MARSHALL
92/3 Dayton

PHILIPP, RAINER
79 PaniniSticker 108
72 SemicSticker 109

PHILLIPOFF, HAROLD
79/80 OPC/Topps 27
78/9 ATL/Coke

PHILLIPS, BILL
27-32 LaPresse 28/9
33/4 OPC (V304A) 43
77/8 ATL

PHILLIPS, CHRIS
96/7 AllSportPPF 72
95/6 Bowman P28
97/8 Bowman 105
95/6 DonrussElite-WorldJrs 7
97/8 DonrussElite 64
97/8 DonrussPreferred 149, 197
97/8 DonrussPriority 180
97/8 DonrussStudio 103
95/6 FutureLegends-HotPicks 1
97/8 KatchMedallion 99
97/8 Leaf 156, 198
97/8 Limited 80, -fabric 42
97/8 McDonalds McD37
98/9 Pacific 314
97/8 PacificCrownRoyale 92
97/8 PacificDynagon! Rookies
97/8 PacificParamount 127
98/9 PacificParamount 165
97/8 Pinnacle 5
97/8 PinnacleBeAPlayer 219
97/8 PinnacleCertified B
97/8 Score 71
95/6 SP 176
97/8 SPAuthentic 187, I22
95/6 UpperDeck 517
97/8 UpperDeck 325
96/7 UDBlackDiamond 57
97/8 UDBlackDiamond 28
98/9 UDChoice 143
97/8 UDCollChoice 301
96/7 UpperDeck"Ice" 137
97/8 UpperDeckIce 47
97/8 Zenith 98, Z79
97/8 OTT
95/6 PrinceAlbert

PHILLIPS, GUY
88/9 ProCards(Saginaw)
90/1 ProCards 42
85/6 MedicineHat 4
93/4 Richmond 2

PHILLIPS, JASON
85/6 Brandon 20

PHILLIPS, ROB
91/2 AirCanadaSJHL B5
92/3 MPSPhotoSJHL 117

PHILLIPS, RYAN
92/3 Tacoma
93/4 Tacoma

PHILLIPS, TOM
83&87 HallOfFame 208
83 HHOF Postcard (N)

PICARD, J.F.
90/1 SketchQMJHL 121

PICARD, MICHEL
92/3 Bowman 437
94/5 ClassicImages 67
95/6 Donruss 328
95/6 EdgeIce 49, -Quantum 7
92/3 FleerUltra 404
95/6 Leaf 289
92/3 O-Pee-Chee 179
91/2 opcPremier 20
91/2 Parkhurst 56
91/2 Pinnacle 327
89/90 ProCards(AHL) 297
90/1 ProCards 172
91/2 ProSet 538
91/2 Score(CDN) 347, (U.S) 317
92/3 Topps 439
92/3 ToppsStadiumClub 119
91/2 UpperDeck 48
91/2 HFD/JuniorWhalers
93/4 Portland

PICARD, NATHALIE
94/5 Classic W14

PICARD, NOEL
70/1 Colgate Stamp 88
70/1 DadsCookies
70/1 EddieSargent 190
71/2 EddieSargent 180
72/3 EddieSargent 185
70/1 Esso Stamp
69/70 O-Pee-Chee 175
70/1 OPC 212
71/2 OPC/Topps 224
72/3 OPC 180
94/5 Parkie(64/5) 69
68/9 ShirriffCoin STL7
71/2 TheTorontoSun
72/3 ATL
71/2 STL
72/3 STL/8"x10"
92/3 STL/UpperDeck 6

PICARD, ROBERT
72-84 Dernière 77/8, 79/80
78/9 OPC/Topps 39
79/80 OPC/Topps 91
80/1 OPC/Topps 255
81/2 O-Pee-Chee 189
82/3 O-Pee-Chee 190, 299
84/5 O-Pee-Chee 345
85/6 O-Pee-Chee 215
87/8 O-Pee-Chee 248
89/90 O-Pee-Chee 261
85/6 opcSticker 252/132
86/7 opcSticker 30/170
87/8 opcSticker 230/97
89/90 opcSticker 190/44
79 PaniniSticker 55
87/8 PaniniSticker 160
89/90 PaniniSticker 333
80/1 Pepsi Cap
82/3 Post
83/4 Vachon 135
81/2 MTL
82/3 MTL
82/3 MTL/Steinber
85/6 QUE
85/6 QUE/McDonald
85/6 QUE/Pennant
85/6 QUE/Placemat
86/7 QUE
86/7 QUE/GeneralFoods
86/7 QUE/YumYum
87/8 QUE/GeneralFoods
87/8 QUE/YumYum
88/9 QUE
88/9 QUE/GeneralFoods
89/90 QUE
89/90 QUE/GeneralFoods
89/90 QUE/Police
80/1 TOR
78/9 WSH
79/80 WSH
83/4 WPG
84/5 WPG/Police

PICCARRETO, BRANDON
91/2 SketchQMJHL 176

PICHETTE, DAVE
72-84 Dernière 81/2
81/2 O-Pee-Chee 280
82/3 O-Pee-Chee 289
83/4 O-Pee-Chee 299
85/6 OPC/Topps 21
85/6 opcSticker 63/190
89/90 ProCards(AHL) 169
84/5 N.J.
80/1 QUE
81/2 QUE
82/3 QUE
83/4 QUE
89/90 Halifax

PICHETTE, J.J.
52/3 AnonymousOHL 72
52/3 BasDuFleuve 28

PICHETTE, J.M.
51/2 LacStJean 10

PICKARD, ALLAN
83&87 HallOfFame 209
83 HHOF Postcard (N)

PICKARD, JIM
83/4 NYI/Islander 30
84/5 NYI 31

PICKARD, PAUL
93/4 Huntington
94/5 Huntington 23

PICKELL, DOUG
89/90 ProCards(IHL) 201
85/6 Kamloops
86/7 Kamloops
87/8 Kamloops
88/9 SaltLake 15

PICKETTS, HAL
33-35 DiamondMatch

PICKFORD, WARREN
91/2 AirCanadaSJHL C16
92/3 MPSPhotoSJHL 115

PIECKO, JAN
79 PaniniSticker 134

PIERCE, RANDY
79/80 OPC/Topps 137
80/1 O-Pee-Chee 340
79/80 COL.R
84/5 HFD/JuniorWhalers

PIERSOL, MIKE
91/2 SketchWHL 159
92/3 Tacoma
93/4 Tacoma

PIERSON, BOB
83/4 Brantford 22

PIETELA, MIKA
95/6 Sisu 216
96/7 Sisu 15, -Energy 6,-Green 4

PIETELA, SAKARI
95/6 Sisu 393
96/7 Sisu-AtTheGala 7

PIETRANGELO, FRANK
91/2 Bowman 89
93/4 EASports 210
92/3 FleerUltra 303
93/4 FleerUltra 338
91/2 OPC/Topps 114
92/3 O-Pee-Chee 115
88/9 PaniniSticker 331
93/4 PaniniSticker 132
92/3 Parkhurst 296
93/4 Parkhurst 352
92/3 Pinnacle 309
93/4 Pinnacle 343
93/4 Premier 287
88/9 ProCards(Muskegon)
90/1 ProSet 509
92/3 ProSet 64
90/1 ScoreTraded 55T
91/2 Score(CDN) 425, (U.S) 440
92/3 Score 535
93/4 Score 419
92/3 Topps 522
91/2 ToppsStadiumClub 364
92/3 ToppsStadiumClub 96
93/4 ToppsStadiumClub 272
90/1 UpperDeck 403
92/3 UpperDeck 273
93/4 UpperDeck 401
92/3 HFD/DairyMart
93/4 HFD/Coke
91/2 PGH/Elbys
91/2 PGH/Topps

PIHLAPURO, PENTTI
66/7 Champion 135

PIIKKILÄ, MARKU
91/2 Jyvas-Hyva 9
92/3 Jyvas-Hyva 34
93/4 Jyvas-Hyva 59
93/4 Sisu 245

PIISINEN, JORMA
78/9 SM-Liiga 71

PIITULAINEN, OSSI
91/2 Jyvas-Hyva 42

PIK, HERBERT
79 PaniniSticker 306

PIKE, ALF (RED)
34-43 BeeHives(NYR)
39/40 OPC (V301-1) 84
60/1 ShirriffCoin 100

PILLION, PIERRE
91/2 SketchQMJHL 271

PILLONI, PATRICK
95 PaniniWorlds 268

PILON, NEIL
84/5 Kamloops

PILON, RICHARD
92/3 Bowman 264
91/2 OPC/Topps 379
98/9 Pacific 285
98/9 PacificParamount 146
97/8 PacificRegime 120
92/3 Parkhurst 490
94/5 ParkieSE 105
97/8 PinnacleBeAPlayer 81
93/4 Premier 417
89/90 ProCards(IHL) 6
90/1 ProSet 486
90/1 ScoreTraded 45T
91/2 Score(CDN) 417
92/3 Topps 492
98/9 Topps 91
92/3 ToppsStadiumClub 230
93/4 ToppsStadiumClub 113
97/8 UpperDeck 101
89/90 NYI

PILON, RON
52/3 AnonymousOHL 132

PILOTE, PIERRE
45-64 BeeHives(CHI)
64-67 BeeHives (CHIx2)
62 CeramicTiles
63-5 ChexPhoto
64/5 CokeCap CHI-3
65/6 CocaCola
83&87 HallOfFame 191
83 HHOF Postcard (J)
68/9 OPC/Topps 124
93/4 Parkie(56/7) 32
94/5 Parkie(64/5) 31, 134, 145
94/5 Parkie(64/5) AS2, TW1
95/6Parkie(66/7)AS2,34,123,147
68/9 Post Marble
66/7 Post'Large
60/1 ShirriffCoin 66
61/2 ShirriffCoin 27
62/3 ShirriffCoin 50
68/9 ShirriffCoin TOR18
54-67 TorontoStar 65/6, V8
64/5 TheTorontoStar
57/8 Topps 22
58/9 Topps 36
59/60 Topps 2, 60
60/1 Topps 65
61/2 Topps 24, -Stamp
62/3 Topps 28, -Buck
63/4 Topps 25
64/5 Topps 59, 109
65/6 Topps 56
66/7 Topps 59, 123,-USATest 59
67/8 Topps 62, 122
91/2 Ultimate06 63, -Aut 63
94/5 Zellers
68/9 TOR

PILOUS, RUDY
87 HallOfFame 247
61/2 ShirriffCoin 40
61/2 Topps 23
62/3 Topps 23

PILUT, LARRY
95/6 udElite DS18

PIMPLE, RICK
72/3 CLEV/Linnet

PINCHES, JOHN
90/1 SketchOHL 116
91/2 SketchOHL 32

PINDER, GERRY
70/1 EddieSargent 42
71/2 EddieSargent 132
70/1 Esso Stamp
69/70 MästarSerien 24
70/1 OPC 148
71/2 OPC/Topps 185
72/3 OPC 341
73/4 opc-Posters 7
74/5 opcWHA 9
76/7 opcWHA 11
73/4 QuakerOats 11
71/2 TheTorontoSun
70/1 CHI
72/3 Cleveland
76/7 SanDiegoMariners

PINEAU, MARCEL
93/4 Maine 57

PINEO, GREGG
91/2 SketchQMJHL 194

PINFOLD, DENNIS
90/1 SketchWHL 108
92/3 Tacoma
93/4 Tacoma

PION, RICHARD
90/1 ProCards 77
91/2 ProCards 43
92/3 Peoria
93/4 Peoria

PIPA, LEOS
94/5 APS 172
95/6 APS 192

PIRILÄ, MIKA
71/2 WilliamsFIN 373

PIRJETA, LASSE
93/4 Sisu 52
94/5 Sisu 123
95/6 Sisu 331
91/2 SketchWHL 160

PIRKKALANIEMI, MARKKO
72/3 WilliamsFIN 335

PIROUTEK, RADIM
94/5 APS 219
95/6 APS 161

PIRRONG, JON
96/7 Penascola 11

PIRSKAINEN, TUOMO
66/7 Champion 42
65/6 Hellas 42

PIRTTIAHO, RISTO
66/7 Champion 151

PIRUS, ALEX
77/8 OPC/Topps 204

PISA, ALES
94/5 APS 33
95/6 APS 335
95/6 UpperDeck 545

PISA, TOMAS
95/6 APS 334

PISIAK, RYAN
91/2 SketchWHL 259
91/2 PrinceAlbert

PISKOR, MICHAL
94/5 APS 133
95/6 APS 233

PISTO, JERRY
93/4 Sisu 166
96/7 Sisu 71

PITIRRI, RICHARD
95/6 Slapshot 169

PITLICK, LANCE
97/8 PacificRegime 137
97/8 PinnacleBeAPlayer 109
90/1 ProCards 27
96/7 OTT/PizzaHut
97/8 OTT

PITRE, DIDIER
91 C55 Reprint 41
83&87 HallOfFame 130
83 HHOF Postcard (I)

1911-12 Imperial (C55) 41
1910-11 Imperial (C56) 23
1912-13 Imperial (C57) 45
1910-11 Imperial Post 41
28/9 MTL/LaPatrie 18
95/6 MTL/Forum 27Sep95

PITTIS, DOMENIC
97/8 Donruss 212, -RatedRook 5
97/8 DonrussCanadianIce 140
97/8 Score(PGH) 20
91/2 SketchWHL 347
95/6 Cleveland
93/4 Lethbridge

PITTMAN, CHRIS
93/4 Slapshot(Kitchener) 11
94/5 Slapshot(Kitchener) 12
95/6 Slapshot 279

PITTMAN, MICHAEL
93/4 Slapshot(Guelph) 13
94/5 Slapshot(Guelph) 17
95/6 Slapshot 97
95/6 Guelph 9

PIUHOLA, JUSSI
66/7 Champion 134
70/1 Kuvajulkaisut 264

PIVETZ, MARK
92/3 MPSPhotoSJHL 140

PIVONKA, MICHAL
90/1 Bowman 68
91/2 Bowman 291, 413
92/3 Bowman 294
93/4 Donruss 374
94/5 Donruss 292
95/6 Donruss 197
96/7 Donruss 60
96/7 DonrussCanadianIce 50
96/7 DonrussElite 35
95/6 EdgeIce 124, C23
96/7 Fleer 119
92/3 FleerUltra 237
93/4 FleerUltra 101
94/5 FleerUltra 238
95/6 FleerUltra 177
96/7 FleerUltra 178
95 Globe 156
95/6 Hoyle'EAST 10 (Diamonds)
96/7 KraftDinner
93/4 Leaf 178
94/5 Leaf 114
95/6 Leaf 162
96/7 LeafLimited 36
96/7 LeafPreferd 100
96/7 Maggers 165
96/7 MetalUniverse 167
90/1 OPC/Topps 68
91/2 OPC/Topps 327
92/3 O-Pee-Chee 30
97/8 PacificCrown 285
90/1 PaniniSticker 154
91/2 PaniniSticker 206
92/3 PaniniSticker 161
93/4 PaniniSticker 27
95/6 PaniniSticker 136
96/7 PaniniSticker 139
97/8 PaniniSticker 111
91/2 Parkhurst 412
92/3 Parkhurst 432
93/4 Parkhurst 487
95/6 Parkhurst 487
91/2 Pinnacle 277
92/3 Pinnacle 151
93/4 Pinnacle 67
94/5 Pinnacle 323
96/7 Pinnacle 173
96/7 PinnacleBeAPlayer 13
96/7 PinnacleZenith 62
94/5 POG 248
93/4 PowerPlay 265
93/4 Premier 321, 360
94/5 Premier 259
90/1 ProSet 319
91/2 ProSet 252
92/3 ProSet 201
91/2 PSPlatinum 132
90/1 Score 268
91/2 Score(CDN) 193, (U.S) 193
92/3 Score 253
93/4 Score 118, -International 15
95/6 Score 258
96/7 Score 33
96/7 SelectCertified 52
94 Semic 178
91 SemicSticker 223
92 SemicSticker 138
95/6 SkyBoxImpact 180
96/7 SkyBoxImpact 142
95/6 SP 157
95/6 Summit 147
96/7 Summit 25
92/3 Topps 107
95/6 Topps 330
95/6 ToppsFinest 147
96/7 ToppsNHLPicks 55
91/2 ToppsStadiumClub 44
92/3 ToppsStadiumClub 382
93/4 ToppsStadiumClub 405
90/1 UpperDeck 80
91/2 UpperDeck 229
92/3 UpperDeck 261
93/4 UpperDeck 154
95/6 UpperDeck 392
96/7 UpperDeck 355
94/5 UDBeAPlayer-Aut. 160
95/6 UDCollChoice 260
96/7 UDCollChoice 280
96 Wien 126
86/7 WSH/Kodak
86/7 WSH/Police
87/8 WSH
87/8 WSH/Kodak
88/9 WSH
88/9 WSH/Smokey
89/90 WSH
89/90 WSH/Kodak
90/1 WSH/Kodak
90/1 WSH/Smokey
91/2 WSH
91/2 WSH/Kodak
92/3 WSH/Kodak
95/6 WSH

PLACATKA, TOMAS
94/5 APS 274

PLACHTA, JACEK
94/5 DEL 253
95/6 DEL 251
96/7 DEL 140

PLAGER, BARCLAY
70/1 DadsCookies
70/1 EddieSargent 184
71/2 EddieSargent 182
72/3 EddieSargent 187
70/1 Esso Stamp
72/3 Letraset 12
74/5 Loblaws
68/9 O-Pee-Chee 177
69/70 O-Pee-Chee 176
70/1 OPC/Topps 99
71/2 OPC/Topps 66
72/3 OPC 35, Topps 136
73/4 OPC/Topps 47
74/5 OPC/Topps 87
75/6 OPC/Topps 205
72 SemicSticker 186
68/9 ShirriffCoin STL8
71/2 TheTorontoSun
71/2 STL
72/3 STL
72/3 STL/8"x10"
73/4 STL
78/9 STL
92/3 STL/UpperDeck 24

PLAGER, BILL
70/1 EddieSargent 187
71/2 EddieSargent 190
72/3 EddieSargent 7
72/3 OPC 122
72/3 Topps 12
72/3 ATL
71/2 STL
89/90 NewHaven

PLAGER, BOB
70/1 EddieSargent 183
71/2 EddieSargent 189
72/3 EddieSargent 186
70/1 Esso Stamp
74/5 Loblaws
68/9 OPC/Topps 112
69/70 OPC/Topps 13
70/1 OPC 211
71/2 OPC/Topps 103
72/3 OPC 161, Topps 96
73/4 OPC 148, Topps 134
74/5 OPC/Topps 107
75/6 OPC/Topps 131
76/7 OPC 369
77/8 OPC 285
90/1 ProCards 98
68/9 ShirriffCoin STL2
71/2 TheTorontoSun
71/2 STL
72/3 STL
72/3 STL/8"x10"
73/4 STL
92/3 STL/UpperDeck 7

PLAMONDON, GERARD (GERRY)
52/3 BasDuFleuve 50
45-64 BeeHives(MTL)
51/2 LavalDairy 85
52/3 LavalDairy 85
43-47 ParadeSportive
45-54 QuakerOats
52/3 StLawrence 14

PLAMONDON, JEAN
88/9 Richelieu

PLAMONDON, RAY
81/2 Regina 18

PLANCHE, JAMES
51/2 LavalDairy 50

PLANDOWSKI, DARRYL
93/4 Seattle

PLANOVSKY, ANTONIN
94/5 APS 120

PLANTE, CAM
90/1 ProCards 583
82/3 Brandon 6
83/4 Brandon 11
90/1 KansasCity 19

PLANTE, DAN
93/4 Classic 72
94/5 Classic 81, T42
93/4 ClassicProspects 95
94/5 Donruss 48
94/5 Leaf 214
97/8 PacificRegime 121
94/5 Pinnacle 488
94/5 Premier 266
95/6 SkyBoxImpact 210
97/8 UpperDeck 309

PLANTE, DEREK
93/4 Classic 73
94/5 Classic-Autograph
93/4 C4'Images 43
93/4 ClassicProspects 30
93/4 Donruss 45
94/5 Donruss 78
95/6 Donruss 190
96/7 Donruss 107
97/8 Donruss 149
97/8 DonrussCanadianIce 35
97/8 DonrussElite 82
97/8 DonrussPreferred 72
97/8 DonrussPriority 25
97/8 DonrussStudio 36
94/5 Fleer 26
93/4 FleerUltra 276, -Wave 13
94/5 FleerUltra 27, -AllRookie 6
96/7 FleerUltra 19
95/6 Hoyle'EAST J (Diamonds)
93/4 Leaf 258
94/5 Leaf 33, -GoldLeafRook 11
95/6 Leaf 166
97/8 Leaf 112
94/5 LeafLimited 44
97/8 Limited 49, 184
96/7 MetalUniverse 16
97/8 Omega 25
98/9 Pacific 107
97/8 PacificCrown 262
97/8 PcfcDynagon! 13,-Tand 28
97/8 PacificInvincible 14
97/8 PacificParamount 22
94/5 PaniniSticker K
95/6 PaniniSticker 16
96/7 PaniniSticker 22
97/8 PaniniSticker 12
93/4 Parkhurst 293, C18
94/5 Parkhurst 277, V82
95/6 Parkhurst 294
94/5 ParkieSE 19, seV39
93/4 Pinnacle 435
94/5 Pinnacle 95, 472
95/6 Pinnacle 149
96/7 Pinnacle 5
97/8 Pinnacle 169
97/8 PinnacleCertified 110
97/8 PinnacleInside 148
94/5 POG 47
95/6 POG 40
93/4 PowerPlay 300, -Rookie 11
93/4 Premier 285
94/5 Premier 194, 501
94/5 Premier-Finest(OPC) 3
93/4 Score 589
94/5 Score 251
95/6 Score 213
96/7 Score 174
97/8 Score 109
97/8 Score(BUF) 12
95/6 SkyBoxImpact 18
96/7 SP 16
95/6 Topps 103
93/4 ToppsStadiumClub 491
94/5 ToppsStadiumClub 30
93/4 TSC-MembersOnly 48
93/4 UpperDeck 475
94/5 UpperDeck 142, SP100
95/6 UpperDeck 409
96/7 UpperDeck 223
95/6 UDBeAPlayer 16
96/7 UDBlackDiamond 83
95/6 UDCollChoice 51
96/7 UDCollChoice 27
97/8 UDCollChoice 24, SQ62
96/7 UpperDeck"Ice" 7

PLANTE, ERIC
90/1 SketchMEM 60
90/1 SketchQMJHL 4
91/2 SketchQMJHL 285
93/4 Slapshot(Drum.) 15

PLANTE, JACQUES
45-64 BeeHives(MTL), (NYR)
64-67 BeeHives(NYR)
62 CeramicTiles
64/5 CokeCap NYR-1
71/2 Colgate Heads
70/1 DadsCookies
72-84 Dernière 77/8
70/1 EddieSargent 199
72/3 EddieSargent 207
70/1 Esso Stamp
71/2 FritoLay
83&87 HallOfFame 76
83 HHOF Postcard (F)
92/3 HHOFLegends 11
93/4 HighLiner 10
91/2 Kraft 6, 76
51/2 LavalDairy 92
52/3 LavalDairy 92
72/3 Letraset 9
73/4 MacsMilk Disk
68/9 O-Pee-Chee 181, -Puck 15
69/70 OPC 180, 207, -Sticker
70/1 OPC 222
71/2 OPC/T. 195, 256, T. 6, 10
71/2 OPC/Topps-Booklet 4
72/3 OPC 92, Topps 24
71/2 OPC-Poster 15
74/5 opcWHA 64
75/6 opcWHA 34
54/5 Parkhurst 97, 98, 99
55/6 Parkhurst 50, 71, 75
57/8 Parkhurst(MTL) 15
58/9 Parkhurst 21, 22, 26, 35, 39
59/60 Parkhurst 41
60/1 Parkhurst 53
61/2 Parkhurst 49
62/3 Parkhurst 49
92/3 Parkhurst PR1
93/4 Parkhurst PR43
93/4 Parkie(56/7) 72, 135, 151
95 PH'Incomnet
94/5 Parkie(64/5) 100
70/1 PostShooters
91/2 ProSet 341
72 SemicSticker 169
60/1 ShirriffCoin 21
61/2 ShirriffCoin 113
62/3 ShirriffCoin 25, 43, 58, 59
52/3 StLawrence 1
81/2 TCMA 12
54-67 TorontoStar V7, V11
56-66 TorontoStar 57/8, 61/2
56-66 TorontoStar 5 Sep-60
64/5 TheTorontoStar
71/2 TheTorontoSun
63/4 Topps 45
64/5 Topps 68
60/1 York, -Glasses
61/2 York 23
62/3 YorkTransfer 2
83/4 MTL
92/3 MTL/OPC 32, 40
95/6 MTL/Forum 27Jan96
92/3 STL/UpperDeck 22
70/1 TOR
71/2 TOR
72/3 TOR

PLANTE, J.M.
52/3 LavalDairy 67
94/5 Birmingham

PLANTE, MICHEL
73/4 VancouverBlazers

PLANTE, PHILIPPE
96/7 Rimouski

PLANTE, PIERRE
74/5 Loblaws
73/4 OPC 255
74/5 OPC/Topps 149, 197
75/6 OPC/Topps 309
76/7 O-Pee-Chee 371
77/8 O-Pee-Chee 385
78/9 OPC/Topps 179
79/80 O-Pee-Chee 275
80/1 O-Pee-Chee 369
71/2 TheTorontoSun
72/3 STL
73/4 STL

PLAQUIN, KEN
90/1 Mich.Tech
91/2 Mich.Tech (x2)

PLASSE, MICHEL
72-84 Dernière 72/3, 73/4, 81/2
74/5 Loblaws, -Update
73/4 O-Pee-Chee 252
74/5 OPC/Topps 257
75/6 OPC/Topps 249
76/7 OPC/Topps 172
77/8 OPC/Topps 92
78/9 OPC/Topps 36
79/80 OPC/Topps 69
81/2 O-Pee-Chee 281
80/1 Pepsi Cap
76/7 COL.R
76/7 COL.R/CokeCans
77/8 COL.R/CokeCans
79/80 COL.R
72/3 MTL
73/4 MTL
80/1 QUE
81/2 QUE

PLASSE, STEVE
88/9 Richelieu

PLATA, ED
52/3 AnonymousOHL 148

PLATNER, TONI
94/5 DEL 285

PLAVSIC, ADRIEN
90/1 Bowman 62
91/2 Bowman 312
92/3 Bowman 363
91/2 CanadaNats
92 CanadaWinterOlympics 189
92/3 FleerUltra 428
92/3 O-Pee-Chee 156
91/2 OPC/Topps 162
90/1 opcPremier 90
90/1 Panini(VAN) 19
93/4 Premier 201
89/90 ProCards'IHL 14
90/1 ProSet 644
90/1 Score 394
92/3 Score 531, -CndOlymic 11
93/4 Score 358
92/3 Topps 323
91/2 ToppsStadiumClub 196
92/3 ToppsStadiumClub 15
93/4 ToppsStadiumClub 201
91/2 UpperDeck 424
92/3 UpperDeck 519
94/5 UpperDeck 381
95/6 UDCollChoice 233
89/90 STL/Kodak
95/6 T.B/SkyBoxSportsCafe
90/1 VAN/Mohawk
91/2 VAN
92/3 VAN/RoadTrip
93/4 VAN/Coins
94/5 VAN

PLAVUCHA, VLASTIMIL
94 Semic 208

PLAYFAIR, JIM
89/90 ProCards(IHL) 62
90/1 ProCards 398
91/2 ProCards 479
88/9 EDM/ActionMagazine 142
94/5 Dayton 20
95/6 Dayton
92/3 Indianapolis
84/5 NovaScotia 17
85/6 NovaScotia 22

PLAYFAIR, LARRY
80/1 O-Pee-Chee 296
84/5 OPC 26, Topps 20
85/6 OPC/Topps 131
86/7 OPC/Topps 195
87/8 OPC/Topps 57
84/5 opcSticker 207
87/8 opcSticker 211/77
82/3 Post
81/2 BUF 10
82/3 BUF/Wendt 10
84/5 BUF/BlueShield
85/6 BUF
88/9 BUF/BlueShield
88/9 BUF/WonderBread
89/90 BUF/BlueShield
89/90 BUF/Campbell
88/9 L.A.
84/5 KelownaWingsWHL 38

PLAZA, ANTONIO
79 PaniniSticker 376

PLEAU, LARRY
70/1 EddieSargent 107
71/2 EddieSargent 100
75/6 opcWHA 56
76/7 opcWHA 26
73/4 QuakerOats 18
72 SemicSticker 229
71/2 TheTorontoSun
69/70 MTL/ProStar
70/1 MTL
71/2 MTL
72/3 NewEngland

PLESH, MIKE
83/4 Kingston 6
84/5 Kingston 10

PLETSCH, FRED
52/3 AnonymousOHL 101

PLETT, WILLI
77/8 OPC/Topps 17
78/9 O-Pee-Chee 317
79/80 O-Pee-Chee 382
80/1 O-Pee-Chee 320
81/2 O-Pee-Chee 35
82/3 O-Pee-Chee 173
83/4 O-Pee-Chee 179
81/2 opcSticker 222
87/8 PaniniSticker 302
80/1 Pepsi Cap
81/2 Post PopUp 27
82/3 Post
83/4 SouhaitsRen.KeyChain
81/2 Topps 26
77/8 ATL
78/9 ATL/Coke
79/80 ATL
79/80 ATL/B&W
88/9 BOS/SportsAction
80/1 CGY
81/2 CGY
82/3 MIN
83/4 MIN
84/5 MIN
84/5 MIN/7Eleven 2
85/6 MIN/7Eleven 7
86/7 MIN/7Eleven 3

PLOMMER, TOM
97/8 SheffieldSteelers

PLOTKA, WOLFGANG
70/1 Kuvajulkaisut 94

PLUCK, DAVE
93/4 Slapshot(Windsor) 7
94/5 Slapshot(Windsor) 9
92/3 Windsor 7

PLUMB, ANDREW
92/3 BCJHL 152

PLUMB, RANDY
81/2 Kingston 25

PLUMB, RON
79/80 O-Pee-Chee 328
75/6 opcWHA 98
76/7 opcWHA 94
77/8 opcWHA 24
73/4 VancouverBlazers
75/6 Cincinnati

PLUMMER, TOM
95/6 Sheffield

POAPST, STEVE HAMPTON
93/4 Portland
94/5 Portland
95/6 Portland
96/7 Portland

POCHIPINSKI, TREVOR
91/2 ProCards 378
92/3 Wheeling 12

PODDUBNY, WALT
83/4 O-Pee-Chee 339
84/5 O-Pee-Chee 309
87/8 OPC/Topps 142, K
88/9 OPC/Topps 170
89/90 OPC/Topps 184
90/1 O-Pee-Chee 426
83/4 opcSticker 150
87/8 opcSticker 32
88/9 opcSticker 240
89/90 opcSticker 85/226
87/8 PaniniSticker 112
88/9 PaniniSticker 309
82/3 Post
90/1 ProSet 479
90/1 Score 278
91/2 Score(CDN) 400
83/4 SouhaitsRen.KeyChain
91/2 ToppsStadiumClub 177
83/4 Vachon 96
88/9 EDM/ActionMagazine 141
89/90 N.J.
90/1 N.J.
88/9 QUE
88/9 QUE/GeneralFoods
82/3 TOR
83/4 TOR
84/5 TOR
85/6 TOR

PODEIN, SHJON
92/3 ClassicProspects 9
93/4 FleerUltra 140
94/5 FleerUltra 346
94/5 Leaf 531
98/9 Pacific 330
97/8 PacificRegime 147
95 PaniniWorlds 224
93/4 Parkhurst 66
94/5 Parkhurst 81
95/6 Parkhurst 426
95/6 POG 203
93/4 PowerPlay 84
90/1 ProCards 229
91/2 ProCards 218
93/4 Score 424
97/8 Score(PHA) 13
93/4 ToppsStadiumClub 474
93/4 UpperDeck 60
94/5 UpperDeck 356
95/6 UpperDeck 150
96/7 UpperDeck 308
97/8 UpperDeck 328
95/6 UDBeAPlayer 77
92/3 EDM
93/4 EDM 26JAN94
94/5 PHA
96/7 PHA/OceanSpray

PODKONICKY, ANDREJ
98 BowmanCHL 56

PODLAHA, JOSEF
94/5 APS 248

PODLOSKI, RAY
88/9 ProCards(Maine)
86/7 Moncton 26

PODLUBNY, DAVID
90/1 SketchWHL 60

PODOLKA, MICHAL
95/6 Slapshot 356
96/7 SSMarie

PODOLLAN, JASON
91/2 AvantGardeBCJHL 104
94/5 Classic T27
95/6 DonrussElite-WorldJrs 20
94/5 SigRookies 13
95/6 SP 172
96/7 SP 173
94/5 SRGoldStandard 90
93/4 UpperDeck E3
97/8 UpperDeck 165
97/8 UDCollChoice 251
96/7 FLA/WinnDixie
95/6 Spokane 12

PODOLSKY, NELSON
52/3 LavalDairy 59

PODSIADLO, KRZYSZTOF
89 SemicSticker 140

PODWYSCOCKI, BOGDAN
74/5 SiouxCity

POESCHEK, RUDY
94/5 Leaf 75
97/8 PacificRegime 186
94/5 Pinnacle 390
94/5 Premier(FX) 274
90/1 ProCards 18
91/2 ProCards 167
93/4 UpperDeck 461
95/6 UDBeAPlayer 53
84/5 Kamloops
89/90 NYR/MarineMidland
94/5 T.B/SkyBoxSportsCafe
95/6 T.B.
95/6 T.B/SkyBoxSportsCafe
85/6 Kamloops
86/7 Kamloops
91/2 Moncton
92/3 StJohns

POETA, TONY
52/3 AnonymousOHL 110

POHJA, HANNU
70/1 Kuvajulkaisut 318

POHJA, TOMMI
92/3 Jyvas-Hyva 159
93/4 Jyvas-Hyva 293
93/4 Sisu 77

POHL, ANTON
72 Hellas 49

POHL, MICHAEL
94/5 DEL 388
95/6 DEL 379
92 SemicSticker 191

POHL, TREVOR
86/7 Portland

POHL, TROY
86/7 Portland

POHLING, J.
95/6 DEL 424

POHORELEC, DUSAN
94 Semic 209

POHTINEN, TAPIO
71/2 WilliamsFIN 268

POIKOLAINEN, JUHA
71/2 WilliamsFIN 290

POIKOLAINEN, JYRKI
93/4 Sisu 294

POIKOLAINEN, PEKKA
95/6 Sisu 264
96/7 Sisu 59

POILE, DAVE
82/3 WSH
86/7 WSH/Police
87/8 WSH/Kodak
88/9 WSH/Smokey
89/90 WSH/Kodak
90/1 WSH/Kodak

POILE, NORMAN (BUD)
34-43 BeeHives(TOR)
45-64 BeeHives(DET), (NYR)
45-54 QuakerOats

POIRIER, CARL
91/2 SketchQMJHL 258

POIRIER, CLAUDE
90/1 SketchQMJHL 92
91/2 SketchQMJHL 102

POIRIER, DAN
89/90 SketchOHL 64
95/6 ThunderBay

POIRIER, GORDON
51/2 BasDuFleuve 1

POIRIER, J.F.
88/9 Richelieu

POIRIER, JOEL
93/4 Slapshot(Sudbury) 21
93/4 Slapshot(Windsor) 15
94/5 Slapshot(Windsor) 17
95/6 Portland
92/3 Sudbury 24
93/4 Sudbury 20

POIRIER, PHILIPPE
95/6 Slapshot 226

POIRIER, S.
90/1 EDM/McGavins

POITRAS, CONRAD
51/2 BasDuFleuve 3

POITRAS, MARTIN
96/7 Rimouski

POITRAS, ROGER
79/80 Montréal B&W

POJAR, CHRIS
94/5 Raleigh

POKORNY, ANDREAS
94/5 DEL 207
95/6 DEL 201
91 SemicSticker 160

POLACIK, RANDY
92/3 BCJHL 137

POLAK, JIRI
95/6 APS 109

POLANO, MIKE
90/1 SketchOHL 191, 250
91/2 SketchOHL 76
84/5 DET/Caesars
89/90 Windsor

POLASEK, LIBOR
95/6 APS 340
92/3 Classic 34
92/3 ClassicFourSport 181, -Aut
93/4 ClassicProspects 161
92/3 Hamilton

POLCAR, ALES
95/6 APS 21
94/5 DEL 19

POLICH, MIKE
79/80 O-Pee-Chee 333
80/1 O-Pee-Chee 363
81/2 O-Pee-Chee 172
78/9 MIN/Cloverleaf 6
79/80 MIN
80/1 MIN
77/8 NovaScotia

POLIKARKIN, VYACHESLAV
94/5 Erie

POLILLO, PAUL
94/5 Slapshot(Brantford) 6

POLIS, GREG
71/2 EddieSargent 172
72/3 EddieSargent 178
74/5 Loblaws
71/2 OPC/Topps 41, -Booklet 9
72/3 OPC 34, Topps 43
73/4 OPC 176, Topps 75
74/5 OPC/Topps 164
75/6 OPC/Topps 201
76/7 OPC/Topps 117
77/8 OPC/Topps 112
78/9 OPC/Topps 246
79/80 O-Pee-Chee 273
71/2 TheTorontoSun
71/2 PGH
79/80 WSH

POLIZIANI, DAN
52/3 AnonymousOHL 23

POLJANSEK, SILVO
79 PaniniSticker 399

POLLA, STEFAN
94/5 ElitSet 205
95/6 ElitSet 170
95/6 udElite 31

POLLACK, CHRIS
95/6 Roanoke

POLLARD, RICK
90/1 SketchOHL 315

POLLOCK, SAM
83&87 HallOfFame 147
83 HHOF Postcard (K)
96/7 HHOFLegends 90
95/6 MTL/Forum 6Apr96

POLLONI, FABIO
79 PaniniSticker 389
82 SemicSticker 131

POLONIC, TOM
69/70 O-Pee-Chee 199

POLONICH, DENNIS
77/8 OPC/Topps 4, 228
78/9 OPC/Topps 66, 106
79/80 OPC/Topps 224
80/1 OPC/Topps 54
79/80 DET
80/1 DET

POLUPANOV, VIKTOR
70/1 Kuvajulkaisut 13
70/1 Soviet Stars

POLYCHRONOPOULOS, NICK
91/2 SketchWHL 249
91/2 PrinceAlbert

POMICHTER, MIKE
94/5 Classic 58, AA7, T15, -Aut.
94/5 ClassicImages 94
92/3 UpperDeck 607
93/4 Indianapolis

PONER, JIM
84/5 Springfield 15

PONTO, VESA
93/4 Jyvas-Hyva 145
93/4 Sisu 143
94/5 Sisu 8
95/6 Sisu 57

POOLE, NICK
95/6 Dayton

POOLEY, PAUL
84/5 WPG/Police

POPE, BRENT
89/90 SketchOHL 101
90/1 SketchOHL 369
91/2 SketchOHL 352
93/4 Wheeling 12

POPE, RICKY
85/6 Arizona

POPEIL, JAN
73/4 QuakerOats 21

POPEIN, LARRY
45-64 BeeHives(NYR)
93/4 Parkie(56/7) 95
60/1 ShirriffCoin 84
54/5 Topps 55
57/8 Topps 54
58/9 Topps 28
59/60 Topps 21
56-66 TorontoStar 58/9

POPIEL, POUL
75/6 Houston
70/1 EddieSargent 213
71/2 EddieSargent 212
70/1 Esso Stamp
69/70 O-Pee-Chee 158
70/1 OPC/Topps 122
71/2 OPC 1
72/3 OPC 67, Topps 142
74/5 opcWHA 59
75/6 opcWHA 68, 120
76/7 opcWHA 27
77/8 opcWHA 63
71/2 TheTorontoSun
65/6 Topps 40
88/9 EDM/ActionMagazine 86
70/1 VAN/RoyalBank
71/2 VAN/RoyalBank 7

POPIESCH, THOMAS
94/5 DEL 330
95/6 DEL 113
96/7 DEL 58

POPIKHIN, EVGENY
91/2 O-Pee-Chee 41R

POPOVIC, PETER (PETR)
93/4 Donruss 180
94/5 Donruss 313
94/5 ElitSet 203,-GuestSpecial 7
94/5 FleerUltra 315
95 Globe 19
93/4 Leaf 417
94/5 Leaf 176
97/8 PacificRegime 104
96/7 PaniniSticker 43
97/8 PaniniSticker 35
93/4 Parkhurst 103
95/6 Parkhurst 111
94/5 ParkieSE 86
94/5 Pinnacle 457
96/7 PinnacleBeAPlayer 6
94/5 POG 141
93/4 PowerPlay 372
93/4 Premier 361
94/5 Premier 158
93/4 Score 626
94 Semic 56
89/90 SemicElitserien 243
90/1 SemicElitserien 154
91/2 SemicElitserien 259
92/3 SemicElitserien 278
93 SemicSticker 8
93/4 UpperDeck 445
94/5 UpperDeck 428
95/6 UpperDeck 192
93/4 MTL
93/4 MTL/Molson
94/5 MTL
95/6 MTL
95/6 MTL/Molson
96-98 MTL
96/7 MTL/MolsonExport

PORCO, JOHN
96/7 DEL 127
89/90 SketchOHL 81
90/1 SketchOHL 16
94/5 Hampton 6

PORKKA, TONI
96/7 DEL 51
91/2 ProCards 269
95/6 Sisu 97
96/7 Sisu-Sledgehammer 6

POROSYSHYN, JEREMY
92/3 MPSPhotoSJHL 88

PORTEOUS, F.
28/9 PaulinsCandy 79

PORTEOUS, KEN
80/1 SSMarie

PORTER, RED
25 Dominion 106
27-32 LaPresse 27/8

PORTLAND, JACK
34-43 BeeHives(MTL.C)
39/40 OPC (V301-1) 40

PORVARI, J.P.
71/2 WilliamsFIN 310

PORVARI, JUKKA
80/1 Mallasjuoma, 163
82 Mallasjuoma
82 SemicSticker 153
82 Skopbank
78/9 SM-Liiga 11, 186
77-80 Sportscaster 72-1705
82 Valio
81/2 COL.R

POSA, VICTOR
87/8 Flint

POSMA, MIKE
90/1 ProCards 563

POSMYK, MAREK
95/6 APS 183
98 BowmanCHL 7
95/6 UpperDeck 542

POSPISIL, DAVE
94/5 APS 40
95/6 APS 326

POSPOSIL, FRANTISEK
95/6 APS 394
72 Hellas 86
74 Hellas 81
70/1 Kuvajulkaisut 56
72 Panda
72 SemicSticker 27
74 SemicSticker 52
71/2 WilliamsFIN 36
72/3 WilliamsFIN 18
73/4 WilliamsFIN 60

POSS, GREG
89/90 ProCards(AHL) 61
90/1 ProCards 136
91/2 ProCards 30

POTAJCUK, ANDREJ
94/5 APS 92
95/6 APS 289

POTH, JAN
79 PaniniSticker 272

POTI, TOM
95 Classic 67
95/6 DonrussElite-WorldJrs 31
95/6 UpperDeck 568

POTOMSKI, BARRY
96/7 PinnacleBeAPlayer 24
90/1 SketchOHL 139
91/2 SketchOHL 366
95/6 Phoenix
92/3 Toledo 2
93/4 Toledo 24

POTTER, CHRIS
93/4 Roanoke
94/5 Roanoke
95/6 Roanoke

POTTINGER, MARKUS
95/6 DEL 364
96/7 DEL 187

POTVIN, DENIS
72-84 Dernière 77/8
88/9 Esso Sticker
91/2 Kraft 61, 72
74/5 Loblaws
82/3 McDonalds 18, 33
74/5 OPC/Topps 195, 233, 252
75/6 OPC/Topps 275, 287, 323
76/7 OPC/Topps 5
76/7 OPC 389, T-Glossy 10
77/8 OPC/Topps 10, -Glossy 15
78/9 OPC/Topps 245, OPC 334
79/80 OPC/Topps 70
80/1 OPC/Topps 120
81/2 OPC 199,209, T.27, (E) 130
82/3 O-Pee-Chee 210
83/4 O-Pee-Chee 2, 16
84/5 O-Pee-Chee 134, 216, 389
83/4 SouhaitsRen.KeyChain
84/5 Topps 100, 162
85/6 OPC/Topps 25
86/7 OPC/Topps 129
87/8 OPC/Topps 1
92/3 O-Pee-Chee 57, -25Yrs 7
81/2 opcSticker 151, 159
82/3 opcSticker 46
83/4 opcSticker 81, 82, 169, 175
84/5 opcSticker 78,79,145,66/65
85/6 opcSticker 70/198
86/7 opcSticker 209
87/8 opcSticker 247
80/1 opcSuperCard 13
87/8 PaniniSticker 91
82/3 Post
90/1 ProSet 656
91/2 ProSet-HOF 2
83/4 PuffySticker 20
77-9 Sportscastr 17-09, 56-1324
92/3 Trends(76) 181
90/1 UpperDeck 515
79/80 NYI
83/4 NYI
83/4 NYI/Islander 21
84/5 NYI 25, 33
93/4 NYI/Chemical

POTVIN, FÉLIX
95/6 Aces 4 (Spades)
97/8 Aces 4 (Diamonds)
94/5 BAP'Magazine
92/3 Bowman 77
95/6 Bowman 79
93/4 Classic 123, N9
93 C4'Images 121
92/3 ClassicProspects 80, BC7
93/4 ClassicProspects 51
97/8 CorinthianHeadliner
93/4 Donruss 343, W,
94/5 Donruss 12, -EliteSeries 8
94/5 D-Domin 7, -MaskMarv 17
95/6 Donruss 9, -Bet 9, -Dom 8
96/7 Donruss 96, -Between 10
97/8 Donruss 154, -Between 9
96/7 D.CdnIce 67, -Gardien 3
97/8 D.CdnIce 56, -Gardien 2
93/4 D-Elite U3, -IceKings 6
95/6 D.Elite 97, -Painted 2
96/7 D.Elite 5, -Painted 6
97/8 D.Elite 100, 131,-Craft 13
97/8 D.Preferred 99,-ColGurd 5
97/8 DonrussPriority 101, 198
97/8 D.Prio-OpDay 25,-PstGen 3
97/8 D.Prio-Pstcrd 29,-Stamp 29
97/8 D.Studio 66,-Port 34,-Sil 20
96/7 Duracell JB12
93/4 Durivage 32
93/4 EASports 138, 215
95/6 EdgeIce L7
94/5 Flair 184
96/7 Flair 91, -HotGlove 8
94/5 Fleer 218, -Netminder 7
96/7 Fleer 109, -Vezina 7
95/6 FleerMetal 146
92/3 FleerUltra 213
93/4 FleerUltra 30
94/5 FleerUltra 219, -AS 12
94/5 FleerUltra-Pad 4, -Power 4
95/6 FleerUltra 162,375, -Pad 9
96/7 FleerUltra 165
93/4 HighLiner 13
93/4 HockeyWit 34
95/6 Hoyle'WEST J (Diamonds)
97/8 KatchMedallion 142
96/7 Kelloggs
95/6 KennerSLU
93/4 Kraft-Cutout
94/5 Kraft, -Masks
95/6 Kraft-Crease
96/7 Kraft-Mascot
93/4 Leaf 409, -Painted 1
93/4 L-AS10, -GoldLeafRook 4
94/5 Leaf 186,-CrsP 14,-GldL 13
95/6 Leaf 160
96/7 Leaf 156, -ShutDown 8
97/8 Leaf 24, -PipeDreams 5
94/5 LeafLimited 16
95/6 LeafLimited 29, -StickSide 3
96/7 LeafLimited 80
96/7 LeafPreferred 36
96/7 LP-Masked 5, -Vanity 10
97/8 Limited 29,57,77, -fabric 15
96/7 Maggers
94/5 McDonalds McD14
95/6 McDonalds McD26
96/7 McDonalds McD38, 'Masks
97/8 McDonalds McD31
96/7 MetalUniv. 152, -Armour 7
97/8 Omega 223, -NoScorZn 10
92/3 O-Pee-Chee 73
92/3 opcPremier 114, -Rookie 4
98/9 Pacifc 29, -GoldCrown 31
97/8 PacificCrown 29, -Supial 19
97/8 PCC-InCage 20, -TmCL 24
97/8 PacificCrownRoyale 131
97/8 PCR-FreezeOut 19
97/8 PcfcDynagon! 122,-Tand 17
97/8 PcfcD-BstKpt 92,-Stone 20
97/8 PacificInv. 137, -Feature 33
97/8 PcfcParamnt 183,-Glove 20
97/8 PacificRegime 195
97/8 PcfcRevolution 136,-Ret 19
92/3 PaniniSticker G
93/4 PaniniSticker 139, 232
94/5 PaniniSticker 198
95/6 PaniniSticker 210
96/7 PaniniSticker 211
91/2 Parkhurst 398
92/3 Parkhurst 187, 507
94/5 Parkhurst 229
93/4 Parkie 202, 237, D14, W9
95/6 Parkhurst 204
95 PH'Incomnet
95/6 PH-Crown(2), -Goal 2
94/5 Parkie seV32
91/2 Pinnacle 345
92/3 Pinnacle 364, -Team2000 5
93/4 Pinnacle 190, -Tm2001 5
94/5 Pinnacle 83, GT8, NL9,TP1
95/6 Pinn 142,-Mask 4,-Roar 10
96/7 Pinnacle 96, 104
97/8 Pinnacle 95
96/7 P.BeAPlayer-Stacking 6
97/8 P.BAP 4,-StackingPads 3
97/8 PinnacleBeeHive 16
97/8 PinnacleCertified 11
97/8 Pinnacle-EPIX 11
95/6 PinnacleFANtasy 29
97/8 P.Inside 46,-Trck 20,-Stp 21
96/7 PinnacleMint 24
95/6 P.Zenith 76, -ZTeam 17
96/7 P.Zenith 31, -ZTeam 16
95/6 Playoff 98, 204
96/7 Playoff 364
94/5 POG 296
95/6 POG 268
94/5 Post
96/7 Post
93/4 PowerPlay 246, -Second 8
93/4 PP-Game 7,-Risng 3,-Net 5
93/4 Premier 30, 111, 126, 385
93/4 Prmr-Black(OPC) 17, (T) 3
94/5 Premier 238, 313, 355
95/6 ProMagnet 74
91/2 ProCards 354
92/3 ProSet 242
92/3 Score 472, 501, -Young 39
93/4 Score 5, 484
94/5 Score 160, DT2
95/6 Score 4, 316
96/7 Score 172,-Sddn 12,-Sup 5
97/8 Score 29, -NetWorth 16
97/8 Score(TOR) 1
93/4 SeasonsPatch 14
94/5 Select 90
95/6 SelectCertified 69
96/7 SelectCert. 31, -Freezer 8
90/1 SketchMEM 26, 72
90/1 SketchQMJHL 35, 159
91/2 SketchAwards 26
95/6 SkyBoxEmotion 174
95/6 SkBxImpact 164, -Deflect 3
96/7 SkyBoxImpact 129, -Zero 7
94/5 SP 117
95/6 SP 146, E27
96/7 SP 153, GF7, -Inside
97/8 SPAuthentic 151
96/7 SPx 44
95/6 Summit 80, -InThe 5
96/7 Summit 72,-Creas 9,-Unt 17
95/6 SuperSkills 85
95/6 SuperSticker 120, DC19
96/7 TeamOut
92/3 Topps 3
95/6 Top. 315,8CG,HGC18,M22
98/9 Topps 29
94/5 ToppsFinest 26
95/6 ToppsFinest 105, 135
96 ToppsFinestBronze 18
96/7 ToppsNHLPicks ID14
92/3 ToppsStadiumClub 338
93/4 ToppsStadiumClub 280
94/5 T.StadiumClub 15, 185
95/6 ToppsStadiumClub 80, EN3
93/4 TSC-Finest 5, -Master(2) 12
93/4 TSC-MembersOnly 1
94/5 TSC-MembersOnly 40
95/6 TSC-MembersOnly 13
97/8 ToppsSticker 1
90/1 UpperDeck 458
91/2 UpperDeck 460
92/3 UD 79, CC3, 'LockerAS 58
93/4 UpperDeck 159, 285
93/4 UD NL6, SP-160, -Hero 28
94/5 UpperDeck 367, H28, SP80
95/6 UpperDeck 48, 228, AS20
95/6 UpperDeck H17, SE168
96/7 UD 341, 360, SS11A, X33
97/8 UpperDeck 367
93/4 UDBAP 11, -Roots 3
94/5 UDBAP R81, R138, R173
95/6 UDBeAPlayer 195
96/7 UDBlackDiamond 129
97/8 UDBlackDiamond 5
95/6 UDCollChoice 114
96/7 UDCC 257, S11, UD20
96/7 UDCC-Oversize 257, 7of8

97/8 UDCC 252, 332, SQ29
96/7 UpperDeck"Ice" 67
97/8 UpperDeckIce 29
97/8 Zenith 38, Z42
92/3 TOR/Kodak
93/4 TOR/Abalene
93/4 TOR/Blacks 24
94/5 TOR

POTVIN, JEAN
74/5 Loblaws
74/5 OPC/Topps 101
75/6 OPC/Topps 36
76/7 OPC/Topps 93, 170
77/8 OPC/Topps 144
78/9 O-Pee-Chee 287
79/80 O-Pee-Chee 334
71/2 TheTorontoSun
79/80 NYI

POTVIN, MARC
94/5 FleerUltra 259
94/5 Leaf 541
90/1 ProCards 486
91/2 UpperDeck 405
93/4 HFD/Coke
96/7 Portland

POTVIN, RICK
89/90 Rayside

POTVIN, STEVE
95 Classic 89
93/4 Slapshot(Sudbury) 20
92/3 Sudbury 23
93/4 Sudbury 19

POTYOK, SHAWN
91/2 AvantGardeBC 11, 155

POTZ, JERZY
74 Hellas 85
79 PaniniSticker 124
89 SemicSticker 135
73/4 WilliamsFIN 97

POUDRIER, DAN
94/5 DEL 75
95/6 DEL 34
87/8 QUE/GeneralFoods
85/6 Fredericton 22
86/7 Fredericton

POUDRIER, SERGE
96/7 DEL 6
95 Globe 204
95 PaniniWorlds 103
94 Semic 220
92 SemicSticker
93 SemicSticker 252
96 Wien 185

POUGET, CHRISTIAN
96/7 DEL 177
95 PaniniWorlds 113
92 SemicSticker
96 Wien 189

POUIOT, MARTIN
96/7 Halifax 2

POUKAR, JIRI
94/5 APS 173
95/6 APS 190

POULIN, CHARLES
92/3 C'Prospects 27
90/1 SketchQMJHL 220
91/2 SketchQMJHL 12
93/4 Fredericton

POULIN, DANIEL
77/8 Kalamazoo

POULIN, DAVE
90/1 Bowman 36
91/2 Bowman 359
92/3 Bowman 19
93/4 Donruss 362
92/3 FleerUltra 9
93/4 FleerUltra 193, 450, -AW 5
94/5 FleerUltra 391
88/9 FritoLay
93/4 Leaf 332
84/5 O-Pee-Chee 165
85/6 OPC/Topps 128
86/7 OPC/Topps 71
87/8 OPC/Topps 39
88/9 OPC/Topps 100
89/90 OPC/Topps 115, OPC 313
90/1 OPC/Topps 362
91/2 OPC/Topps 507
92/3 O-Pee-Chee 367
87/8 opcStars 30, 32
84/5 opcSticker 110
85/6 opcSticker 89
86/7 opcSticker 241
87/8 opcSticker 98/232, 179/34
89/90 opcSticker 129
87/8 PaniniSticker 130, 386
88/9 PaniniSticker 323
89/90 PaniniSticker 305
90/1 PaniniSticker 4
92/3 PaniniSticker 137
93/4 PaniniSticker 4
92/3 Parkhurst 242
93/4 Parkhurst 488
94/5 Parkhurst 253
92/3 Pinnacle 116
93/4 Pinnacle 229, 387
94/5 Pinnacle 179
93/4 PowerPlay 470
93/4 Premier 228
94/5 Premier 236
90/1 ProSet 13
91/2 ProSet 12
92/3 ProSet 9
91/2 PSPlatinum 5
90/1 Score 217
91/2 Score(CDN) 452, (U.S) 232
92/3 Score 359
93/4 Score 228, 552
94/5 Score 38
84/5 Topps 120
92/3 Topps 155
91/2 ToppsStadiumClub 253
92/3 ToppsStadiumClub 13
93/4 T.StadiumClub 142, 301
90/1 UpperDeck 177
93/4 UpperDeck 355, AW8
94/5 UDBeAPlayer-Aut. 124
89/90 BOS/SportsAction
90/1 BOS/SportsAction
91/2 BOS/SportsAction
92/3 BOS
83/4 PHA
86/7 PHA
89/90 PHA

POULIN, GEORGE
91 C55 Reprint 44
1911-12 Imperial (C55) 44
1910-11 Imperial (C56) 24
1912-13 Imperial (C57) 8
1910-11 Imperial Post 44

POULIN, PATRICK
91/2 Arena 7
91/2 Classic 8
91/2 ClassicFourSport 8, -Aut
93/4 Donruss 146
94/5 Donruss 144
95/6 Donruss 269
93/4 Durivage 50
94/5 Fleer 44
95/6 FleerMetal 27
92/3 FleerUltra 304
93/4 FleerUltra 122, 292
94/5 FleerUltra 43
93/4 Leaf 113, -GoldL.Rook 10
94/5 Leaf 390
95/6 Leaf 237
92/3 opcPremier 85
97/8 PacificCrown 230
93/4 PaniniSticker 126
95/6 PaniniSticker 158
92/3 Parkhurst 60
93/4 Parkhurst 307
95/6 Parkhurst 42
94/5 ParkieSE 32
92/3 Pinnacle 418, -Tm2000 14
93/4 Pinnacle 61, -Tm2001 8
94/5 Pinnacle 283
95/6 Pinnacle 135
95/6 Playoff 133
96/7 Playoff 369
94/5 POG 69
95/6 POG 67
93/4 PowerPlay 108, 315,-Sec 9
94/5 Premier 316
92/3 ProSet 227
92/3 Score 478, -YoungStar 31
93/4 Score 202, 571
94/5 Score 6, 'Promo 6
95/6 Score 158
90/1 SketchMEM 98
90/1 SketchQMJHL 1, 152
91/2 SketchQMJHL 10
95/6 SkyBoxEmotion 32
95/6 SkyBoxImpact 32
91/2 StarPics 36, 68
95/6 Summit 99
95/6 SuperSticker 25
92/3 Topps 328
95/6 Topps 326, 4PL
92/3 ToppsStadiumClub 211
93/4 ToppsStadiumClub 157
94/5 ToppsStadiumClub 13
95/6 ToppsStadiumClub 212
91/2 UltimateDP 8, 64, -Aut 8
91/2 UD 65, 'CzechWJC 51
92/3 UD 416, 557, CC18, G16
93/4 UpperDeck 138, NL2, SP30
94/5 UpperDeck 36
95/6 UpperDeck 208, SE106
97/8 UpperDeck 366
94/5 UDBeAPlayer-Aut. 168
95/6 UDCollChoice 187
97/8 UDCollChoice 242
93/4 CHI/Coke
92/3 HFD/DairyMart
97/8 MTL

POULIN, PAT
80/1 Oshawa 6

POULIN, RICK
89/90 Rayside

POULIOT, MARIO
91/2 SketchQMJHL 24

POULSEN, MARCO
93/4 Jyvas-Hyva 27
93/4 Sisu 98
95/6 Sisu 345
95/6 SisuLimited 94

POUND, IAN
84/5 Kitchener 12
85/6 Kitchener 11
86/7 London 17

POUNDER, CHERYL
94/5 Classic W3

POUSAZ, JACQUES
72 SemicSticker 148

POUSSE, PIERRE
95 PaniniWorlds 109
92 SemicSticker 240
93 SemicSticker 265

POUSSU, PENTTI
72/3 WilliamsFIN 292

POUZAR, JAROSLAV
95/6 APS 397
83/4 O-Pee-Chee 41
84/5 O-Pee-Chee 256
83/4 opcSticker 151, 159
79 PaniniSticker 87
83/4 Vachon 38
82/3 EDM/RedRooster
83/4 EDM
83/4 EDM/Buttons
83/4 EDM/McDonald
84/5 EDM
84/5 EDM/RedRooster
86/7 EDM
88/9 EDM/ActionMagazine 18

POWELL, KEVIN
91/2 AirCanadaSJHL D16
92/3 Tacoma

POWER, ANDREW
93/4 Slapshot(Oshawa) 12

POWER, LARRY
81/2 Ottawa67s
82/3 Ottawa67s

POWER, R.
91 C55 Reprint 40
1911-12 Imperial (C55) 40
1910-11 Imperial Post 40

POWER, RYAN
95/6 Slapshot 229
97/8 Halifax (1), (2)

POWIS, JEFF
67/8 Topps 110

POWERS, JIM
93/4 Raleigh
94/5 Raleigh

POWIS, LYNN
74/5 Loblaws
73/4 OPC 209
74/5 OPC/Topps 227
76/7 opcWHA 86

PÕYHIÄ, HARRI
80/1 Mallasjuoma 142

POZZO, KEVIN
94/5 Slapshot(MEM) 30

PRACEY, RICK
88/9 Brockville 12
89/90 SSMarie 10

PRACHAR, KAMIL
94/5 APS 208
95/6 APS 152
94 Semic 167
92 SemicSticker 127

PRAJSLER, PETR
90/1 O-Pee-Chee 481
88/9 ProCards(NewHaven)
90/1 ProCards 347
91/2 ProCards 57
90/1 ProSet 481
89/90 L.A./Smokeys 11

PRATT, BABE
see Walter "Babe" Pratt

PRATT, HARLAN
95/6 RedDeer

PRATT, KELLY
74/5 PGH

PRATT, NOLAN
93/4 Portland

PRATT, STACY
83/4 Brandon

PRATT, STAN
36/7 WWGum (V356) 126

PRATT, TOM
88/9 ProCards(NewHaven)

PRATT, TRACY
70/1 DadsCookies
70/1 EddieSargent 19
71/2 EddieSargent 25
72/3 EddieSargent 30
70/1 Esso Stamp
72/3 Letraset 3
74/5 Loblaws
69/70 OPC/Topps 111
70/1 OPC 146
71/2 OPC/Topps 107
72/3 OPC 69, Topps 84
73/4 OPC/Topps 54
74/5 OPC/Topps 41
75/6 OPC/Topps 133
76/7 OPC 275
68/9 ShirriffCoin OAK10
71/2 TheTorontoSun
72/3 BUF
73/4 BUF
76/7 COL.R
76/7 COL.R/CokeCans
74/5 VAN/RoyalBank
75/6 VAN/RoyalBank

PRATT, WALTER (BABE)
34-43 BeeHives(NYR), (TOR)
83&87 HallOfFame 162
83 HHOF Postcard (L)
93/4 HHOFLegends 29
39/40 OPC (V301-1) 85
55/6 Parkhurst 31
94/5 Parkie(64/5)-Greats 3
45-54 QuakerOats

PRAZAK, KAREL
94/5 APS 285

PRAZMA, MARTY
86/7 Saskatoon

PRAZNIK, JODY
89/90 Saskatoon 6

PRECECHTEL, JAROMIR
94/5 APS 278
95/6 APS 100

PREFONTAINE, BRAD
91/2 AirCanadaSJHL C2
95/6 Birmingham

PREMAK, GARY
92/3 CanadaNats
87/8 Kamloops

PRENTICE, DEAN
45-64 BeeHives(BOS), (NYRx2)
64-67 BeeHives(BOS), (DET)
62 CeramicTiles
64/5 CokeCap BOS-17
65/6 CocaCola
70/1 DadsCookies
70/1 EddieSargent 165
71/2 EddieSargent 89
70/1 Esso Stamp
68/9 OPC/Topps 32
69/70 OPC/Topps 115
70/1 OPC 201
72/3 OPC 289
54/5 Parkhurst 74
93/4 Parkhurst54 DPR9
93/4 Parkie(56/7) 91
94/5 Parkie(64/5) 5
95/6 Parkie(66/7) 51, 147, 148
72 SemicSticker 218
61/2 ShirriffCoin 84
68/9 ShirriffCoin DET5
54-67 TorontoStar V8
56-66 TorontoStar 58/9, 62/3
56-66 TorontoStar 64/5
71/2 TheTorontoSun
57/8 Topps 62
58/9 Topps 32
59/60 Topps 17
60/1 Topps 37
61/2 Topps 54, -Stamp
62/3 Topps 53, -Buck
63/4 Topps 13
64/5 Topps 19
65/6 Topps 102
66/7 Topps 45, -USATest 45
67/8 Topps 45
91/2 Ultimate(O6) 27, -Aut 27
73/4 MIN

PRESLEY, WAYNE
91/2 Bowman 402
92/3 Bowman 76
94/5 Leaf 521
90/1 O-Pee-Chee 456
91/2 opcPremier 89
87/8 OPC/Topps 179
88/9 OPC/Topps 185
89/90 OPC/Topps 98
91/2 OPC/Topps 385
87/8 PaniniSticker 228
89/90 PaniniSticker 52
91/2 PaniniSticker 19
93/4 PaniniSticker 107
91/2 Parkhurst 163
93/4 Parkhurst 294
94/5 Parkhurst 27
91/2 Pinnacle 68
93/4 Pinnacle 425
94/5 Pinnacle 321
93/4 Premier 162
90/1 ProSet 434
91/2 ProSet 44, 488
91/2 PSPlatinum 228
90/1 ScoreTraded 92T
91/2 Score(CDN) 221, 559
91/2 Score(U.S) 221, 9T
92/3 Score 213
93/4 Score 296
95/6 Score 223
92/3 Topps 424
91/2 ToppsStadiumClub 215
92/3 ToppsStadiumClub 24
93/4 ToppsStadiumClub 233
94/5 ToppsStadiumClub 196
90/1 UpperDeck 339
91/2 UpperDeck 371
95/6 UDBeAPlayer 45
95/6 UDCollChoice 179
92/3 BUF/BlueShield
92/3 BUF/Jubillee
86/7 CHI/Coke
87/8 CHI/Coke
88/9 CHI/Coke
89/90 CHI/Coke
90/1 CHI/Coke
91/2 S.J.
82/3 Kitchener 12
83/4 Kitchener 16
84/5 Kitchener 20
85/6 NovaScotia 16
84/5 SSMarie

PREST, TREVOR
91/2 AvantGardeBCJHL 42

PRESTBERG, PELLE
97/8 udSwedish 59

PRESTON, BRIAN
92/3 BCJHL 23

PRESTON, DAN
91/2 SketchOHL 103
95/6 Slapshot 73

PRESTON, RICH
82/3 O-Pee-Chee 71
83/4 O-Pee-Chee 110
84/5 O-Pee-Chee 118
86/7 opcSticker 199/69
80/1 OPC/Topps 41
85/6 OPC/Topps 139
86/7 OPC/Topps 61
76/7 opcWHA 115
82/3 Post
83/4 SouhaitsRen.KeyChain
84/5 Topps 34
79/80 CHI
80/1 CHI/4x6
80/1 CHI/5.5x8.5
81/2 CHI
82/3 CHI
83/4 CHI
86/7 CHI/Coke
91/2 CHI/Coke
93/4 CHI/Coke
75/6 Houston
84/5 N.J.
77/8 Winnipeg
81/2 Milwaukee 6

PRETTY, DAVID
80/1 QuébecRamparts

PREUSS, GUNTHER
94/5 Del 143
95/6 DEL 141

PREVOST, STACY
91/2 AirCanadaSJHL B12
92/3 MPSPhotoSJHL 168

PRIAKIN, SERGEI
90/1 Bowman 103
89/90 Kraft 8
90/1 Panini(CGY) 17
90/1 ProSet 594
95/6 Sisu 91, 380
96/7 Sisu 93
95/6 SisuLimited 61
90/1 CGY/McGavins

PRIBYLA, KAMIL
94/5 APS 125

PRICE, GERRY
52/3 AnonymousOHL 12

PRICE, MATT
95/6 Slapshot 119

PRICE, NOEL
52/3 AnonymousOHL 149
72/3 EddieSargent 8
70/1 Esso Stamp
74/5 Loblaws
68/9 OPC/Topps 110
70/1 OPC 163
72/3 OPC 163
73/4 OPC 256
74/5 OPC 356
75/6 OPC 331
58/9 Parkhurst 6
59/60 Parkhurst 42
93/4 Parkie(56/7) 131
68/9 ShirriffCoin PGH4
72/3 ATL
65/6 QuébecAces

PRICE, PAT
86/7 Kraft Sports 49
76/7 O-Pee-Chee 318
77/8 O-Pee-Chee 308
78/9 O-Pee-Chee 368
79/80 O-Pee-Chee 347
80/1 O-Pee-Chee 299
81/2 O-Pee-Chee 265
82/3 O-Pee-Chee 274
84/5 O-Pee-Chee 286
80/1 Pepsi Cap
82/3 Post
83/4 Vachon 71
79/80 EDM
88/9 EDM/ActionMagazine 82
87/8 MIN
83/4 QUE
84/5 QUE
85/6 QUE
85/6 QUE/GeneralFoods
85/6 QUE/McDonald
85/6 QUE/Pennant
85/6 QUE/Placemats
85/6 QUE/Provigo
86/7 QUE
86/7 QUE/McDonald
87/8 QUE/GeneralFoods
83/4 Brantford 23

PRIEST, MERV
90/1 SketchWHL 220
91/2 SketchWHL 207
89/90 Brandon 22
90/1 Brandon 2

PRIESTLAY, KEN
90/1 CanadaNats
91/2 Parkhurst 359
88/9 ProCards(Rochester)
89/90 ProCards(AHL) 257
91/2 ProSet 460
91/2 ScoreCDN 658
91/2 UpperDeck 525
87/8 BUF/BlueShield
89/90 BUF/BlueShield
91/2 PGH/Elbys
95/6 SheffieldSteelers
97/8 SheffieldSteelers
92/3 ClevelandLumberjacks 21
84/5 Victoria

PRILLO, ERIC
90/1 SketchQMJHL 90

PRIMEAU, ERIC
84/5 Richelieu

PRIMEAU, JOE
33/4 Anonymous (V129) 7
34-43 BeeHives(TOR)
83&87 HallOfFame 131
33/4 Hamilton (V288) 2
83 HHOF Postcard (I)
27-32 LaPresse 29/30
33/4 OPC (V304A) 12
55/6 Parkhurst 24
91/2 ProSet 338
34/5 SweetCaporal
33/4 WWGum (V357) 40
32/3 TOR/OKeefe 10

PRIMEAU, KEITH
91/2 Bowman 46
93/4 Donruss 425
94/5 Donruss 46
95/6 Donruss 42
96/7 Donruss 138
97/8 Donruss 185
96/7 CanadianIce 27
97/8 CanadianIce 22
96/7 DonrussElite 73
97/8 DonrussElite 23
97/8 DonrussPreferred 18
97/8 DonrussPriority 38
97/8 DonrussStudio 42
95/6 EdgeIce L4
97/8 EssoOlympic 19
94/5 Flair 51
96/7 Flair 43
94/5 Fleer 64
96/7 Fleer 34
95/6 FleerMetal 50, -Iron 10
92/3 FleerUltra 286
93/4 FleerUltra 239
94/5 FleerUltra 65
95/6 FleerUltra 48,-Risg 6,-Cr 14
96/7 FleerUltra 75
93/4 HockeyWit 67
97/8 KatchMedallion 29
97/8 Kraft-RoadToNagano
93/4 Leaf 276
94/5 Leaf 266
95/6 Leaf 170
96/7 Leaf 154
97/8 Leaf 119
94/5 LeafLimited 110

95/6 LeafLimited 92
96/7 LeafPreferred 84
97/8 Limited 126
96/7 Maggers 54
97/8 McDonald's, -Medallions
96/7 MetalUniverse 70
97/8 Omega 44
90/1 opcPremier 91
91/2 OPC/Topps 309
98/9 Pacific 138, -TmCL 5
97/8 PacificCrown 52,-TmCL 5
97/8 PacificCrownRoyale 25
97/8 PacificDynagon! 22
97/8 PcfcD-BstKpt 17,-Tandm 30
97/8 PacificInvincible 25
97/8 PacificParamount 37
98/9 PacificP 41, -TmCL 5
97/8 PcfcRevolution 25,-TmCL 5
92/3 PaniniSticker 117
93/4 PaniniSticker 250
94/5 PaniniSticker 214
95/6 PaniniSticker 181
96/7 PaniniSticker 186
97/8 PaniniSticker 27
92/3 Parkhurst 277
93/4 Parkhurst 327
94/5 Parkhurst 67, V66
95/6 Parkhurst 72
93/4 Pinnacle 420
94/5 Pinnacle 40
95/6 Pinnacle 197
96/7 Pinnacle 168
97/8 Pinnalce 109
97/8 P.BAP -TakeANumber 15
97/8 PinnacleCertified 57
97/8 PinnacleInside 189
95/6 PinnacleZenith 83
96/7 PinnacleZenith 101
95/6 Playoff 35
94/5 POG 90
95/6 POG 93
93/4 PowerPlay 75, -RsngStar 4
93/4 Premier 256
94/5 Premier 330
91/2 ProCards 126
90/1 ProSet 606
90/1 Score 436, 90T, -Young 38
91/2 Score(CDN) 144, (U.S.)144
92/3 Score 316
93/4 Score 364
95/6 Score 264
96/7 Score 54
97/8 Score 98
94/5 Select 15
95/6 SelectCert. 71,-Double 16
96/7 SelectCertified 40
89/90 SketchOHL 130, 189
95/6 SkyBoxEmotion 57
95/6 SkBxE-Ntense 2, -Xcited 12
95/6 SkyBoxImpact 57, 241
96/7 SkyBoxImpact 39
94/5 SP 37
95/6 SP 47
96/7 SP 68
97/8 SPAuthentic 24
95/6 Summit 140
96/7 Summit 16
95/6 SuperSticker 40
92/3 Topps 99
95/6 Topps 54, GC21
98/9 Topps 124
96/7 ToppsNHLPicks 109
91/2 ToppsStadiumClub 305
92/3 ToppsStadiumClub 485
93/4 ToppsStadiumClub 217
94/5 ToppsStadiumClub 16
95/6 ToppsStadiumClub 66, F3
97/8 ToppsSticker 4
95/6 ToppsSuperSkills 47
90/1 UpperDeck 351, 354
91/2 UpperDeck 258
93/4 UpperDeck 413, SP-45
94/5 UpperDeck 337, SP24
95/6 UpperDeck 159, 223, SE27
96/7 UD 203, 271,SS9B,P4,X34
97/8 UpperDeck 29, SG55
95/6 UDBeAPlayer 115
96/7 UDBlackDiamond 5
97/8 UDBlackDiamond 3
98/9 UDChoice 39
95/6 UDCollChoice 161
96/7 UDCollChoice 87
97/8 UDCC 110, C6, SQ55
96/7 UpperDeck"Ice" 27
97/8 UpperDeckIce 25
97/8 ValuNet
97/8 Zenith 54, Z13
90/1 DET/Ceasars
91/2 DET/Caesars
88/9 NiagaraFalls 4
89/90 NiagaraFalls

PRIMEAU, KEVIN
91/2 EDM/IGA
92/3 EDM/IGA 29
93/4 EDM 09MAR94
80/1 VAN/Silverwood

PRIMEAU, WAYNE
95/6 Bowman 157
94/5 Classic 15, CP1, T8
95/6 Classic 93
94/5 ClassicFourSport 131
94/5 C4'Images 108
94/5 ClassicImages 47
97/8 Donruss 67
97/8 DonrussPriority 72
96/7 Fleer 132
96/7 FleerUltra 20, -Rookies 16
95/6 FutureLegends 36
96/7 Leaf 231
96/7 LeafPreferred 131
97/8 Limited 101
96/7 MetalUniverse 17
97/8 PacificCrown 43
95/6 Parkhurst 26
96/7 Pinnacle 220
97/8 Score(BUF) 13
95/6 SkyBoxImpact 191
96/7 SkyBoxImpact 156
95/6 Slapshot 240, 301
95/6 Topps 222
98/9 Topps 146
93/4 UpperDeck E9
95/6 UpperDeck 433
96/7 UpperDeck 20
97/8 UpperDeck 17
97/8 UDBlackDiamond 76
96/7 UDCollChoice 25
93/4 OwenSound

PRINCE, GUY
91/2 AvantGardeBC 71
92/3 BCJHL 75
93/4 Dayton 12

PRINDOLO, CONSTANT
79/80 Montréal, B&W

PRIOR, CRAIG
90/1 SketchQMJHL 214

PRIOR, DAVE
91/2 ProCards 188
91/2 WPG/IGA
91/2 Moncton
89/90 Rayside

PRIOR, GARY
94/5 DEL 6
95/6 DEL 1
96/7 DEL 1

PRITCHARD, BRUCE
84/5 Victoria

PRITCHETT, GRANT
91/2 SketchOHL 343
93/4 Slapshot(Guelph) 24

PROBERT, BOB
91/2 Bowman 55
92/3 Bowman 85
93/4 Donruss 104
95/6 Donruss 247
96/7 Donruss 8
92/3 FleerUltra 53
93/4 FleerUltra 309
95/6 FleerUltra 218
88/9 FritoLay
97/8 KatchMedallion 36
93/4 Leaf 186
88/9 OPC/Topps 181
91/2 OPC/Topps 198
92/3 O-Pee-Chee 252
88/9 opcSticker 247/117
97/8 PacificCrown 290
88/9 PaniniSticker 46
91/2 PaniniSticker 146
93/4 PaniniSticker 249
94/5 PaniniSticker 213
91/2 Parkhurst 272
92/3 Parkhurst 41, CP9
93/4 Parkhurst 333
94/5 Parkhurst 71
95/6 Parkhurst 312
91/2 Pinnacle 183
92/3 Pinnacle 56
93/4 Pinnacle 7
94/5 Pinnacle 404
96/7 Pinnacle 84
95/6 Playoff 134
95/6 POG 68
93/4 PowerPlay 335
93/4 Premier 177
90/1 ProSet 76
91/2 ProSet 61
92/3 ProSet 46
91/2 PSPlatinum 34
90/1 Score 143
91/2 Score(CDN) 73, (U.S) 73
92/3 Score 52, -Sharpshooter 17
93/4 Score 59
96/7 Score 156
92/3 SeasonsPatch 8
92/3 Topps 63
95/6 Topps 299
98/9 Topps 97
91/2 ToppsStadiumClub 59
92/3 ToppsStadiumClub 355
93/4 ToppsStadiumClub 137
95/6 ToppsStadiumClub 152
90/1 UpperDeck 448
91/2 UpperDeck 239
92/3 UpperDeck 248
93/4 UpperDeck 200, SP46
95/6 UpperDeck 469, SE105
96/7 UpperDeck 33, SS29B
97/8 UpperDeck 39, 197
95/6 UDBeAPlayer 221
97/8 UDCollChoice 49
85/6 DET/Caesars
86/7 DET/Caesars
87/8 DET/Caesars
88/9 DET/Caesars
90/1 DET/Caesars
91/2 DET/Caesars
83/4 Brantford 3
84/5 SSMarie

PROBST, SKIP
88/9 ProCards(Peoria)
91/2 ProCards 450

PROBST, PAUL
72 SemicSticker 151

PROCEVIAT, DICK
67/8 ColumbusCheckers

PROCEVIAT, STEVE
90/1 Rayside

PROCHAZKA, FRANTISEK
95/6 DEL 410
94 Semic 172
93 SemicSticker 94

PROCHAZKA, LIBOR
94/5 APS 52
95/6 APS 84, 363
97/8 udSwedish 4
96 Wien 109

PROCHAZKA, MARTIN
94/5 APS 57
95/6 APS 94, 370, 386
98/9 Pacific 420
97/8 PacificParamount 184
97/8 Score 62
97/8 Score(TOR) 20
95 Semic 155
91/2 UD'CzechWJC 96
96 Wien 116

PROCHAZKA, STANISLAV
94/5 APS 36
95/6 APS 328

PRODGERS, GEORGE (GOLDIE)
24/5 Champs (C144)
1912-13 Imperial (C57) 37
23/4 (V145-1) 32

PROFT, PARIS
96/7 DEL 202

PROHASKA, F.
79 PaniniSticker 303

PROKHOROV, VITALI
92/3 Classic 51
93/4 ClassicProspects 92
93/4 Donruss 290
94/5 Donruss 126
95/6 EliteSet 221
92/3 FleerUltra 397
94/5 FleerUltra 188
93/4 Leaf 326
94/5 Leaf 295
92/3 opcPremier 64
92/3 Parkhurst 157
93/4 Parkhurst 450
94/5 Parkhurst 206
92/3 Pinnacle 404
94/5 Pinnacle 367
94/5 POG 206
93/4 PowerPlay 432
93/4 Premier 452
92/3 RedAce(Blue) 5, (Violet) 5
92 SemicSticker 120
94/5 ToppsStadiumClub 19
92/3 UpperDeck 486
93/4 UpperDeck 363
94/5 UpperDeck 173
95/6 udElite 66
93/4 Peoria

PROKOPEC, MIKE
95/6 FutureLegends 50
95/6 Parkhurst 308
96/7 PinnacleZenith 149
91/2 SketchOHL 13
93/4 Slapshot(Guelph) 16
91/2 Cornwall 17
93/4 Indianapolis

PROKOPETZ, JASON
92/3 MPSPhotoSJHL 82

PROKOPEV, ALEXANDER
91/2 O-Pee-Chee 25R

PROKUPEK, LADISLAV
94/5 APS 176
95/6 APS 193
93/4 Parkhurst 514

PRONGER, CHRIS
95/6 Bowman 62
93/4 Classic 2, DP2
94/5 Classic AR5
93/4 C'FourSport 12, 186, DS59
93/4 C'4Sport LP23, PP19, TC4
93/4 C4'Images 8, 135
93/4 ClassicProspects 31, -Aut
93/4 Donruss 150, 393, J,-Rtd 3
94/5 Donruss 215
95/6 Donruss 63,319,-Pointer 17
96/7 Donruss 63
97/8 Donruss 100
97/8 DonrussCanadianIce 90
97/8 DonrussPreferred 109
97/8 DonrussPriority 91
97/8 EssoOlympic 15
94/5 Flair 73
94/5 Fleer 88
96/7 Fleer 99
95/6 FleerMetal 127
96/7 FleerNHLPicks 114
93/4 FleerUltra 339, -Wave 14
94/5 FleerUltra 91, -AllRookie 7
95/6 FleerUltra 69, 302
95/6 Hoyle'EAST Q (Diamonds)
93/4 KraftGold
97/8 Kraft- RoadToNagano
93/4 Leaf 257, -Freshman 2
94/5 Leaf 268,-GoldL.R 9,-Ltd 10
95/6 Leaf 242
96/7 Leaf 5
97/8 Leaf 90
94/5 LeafLimited 22
95/6 LeafLimited 107
97/8 Limited 85
96/7 Maggers 141
97/8 McDonald's -Medallions
96/7 MetalUniverse 135
97/8 Omega 196
98/9 Pacific 44
97/8 PacificCrown 124
98/9 PacificParamount 206
94/5 PaniniSticker M
95/6 PaniniSticker 198
96/7 PaniniSticker 201
97/8 PaniniSticker 170
93/4 Parkhurst 249, C2, D13
94/5 Parkhurst 274, V40
95/6 Parkhurst 175
94/5 ParkieSE 73
93/4 Pinnacle 456, SR2
94/5 Pinnacle 11, 466
96/7 Pinnacle 58
97/8 PinnacleInside 175
95/6 PinnacleZenith 28
95/6 Playoff 309
94/5 POG 121
95/6 POG 243
93/4 PowerPlay 354, -Rookie12
93/4 Premier 485
94/5 Premier 198, 381, 484
94/5 Premier-Finest(OPC) 11
95/6 ProMagnet 8
93/4 Score 586
94/5 Score 252
95/6 Score 6, -CheckIt 5
96/7 Score 166
97/8 Score(STL) 7
94/5 Select 111
91/2 SketchOHL 134
95/6 SkyBoxEmotion 151
95/6 SkyBoxImpact 144
96/7 SkyBoxImpact 115
93/4 Slapshot(Peterborough) 29
94/5 SP 48
95/6 SP 124
96/7 SP 135, -Holoview HC20
97/8 SPAuthentic 139
98/9 SPx"Finite"
95/6 Summit 30
95/6 SuperSkills 54
95/6 SuperSticker 104
95/6 Topps 308, HGC15
98/9 Topps 181, B1, I7, SB25
94/5 ToppsFinest 62
93/4 ToppsStadiumClub 290
94/5 TSC 111, 235, D5
95/6 ToppsStadiumClub 69
92/3 UpperDeck 591
93/4 UpperDeck 190, H5, SP-64
94/5 UpperDeck 52, SP33
95/6 UpperDeck 174, SE160
96/7 UpperDeck 144, 155, P24
96/7 UpperDeck SS27B, X36
97/8 UpperDeck 142, 398
93/4 UDBeAPlayer 35
94/5 UDBeAPlayer R43
95/6 UDBeAPlayer 18
96/7 UDBlackDiamond 150
97/8 UDBlackDiamond 83
98/9 UDChoice 185
95/6 UDCollChoice 232
96/7 UDCollChoice 226
97/8 UDCollChoice 233
96/7 UpperDeck"Ice" 63
97/8 ValuNet
93/4 HFD/Coke
91/2 Peterborough 2

PRONGER, SEAN
95/6 Bowman 153
94/5 Classic 93
97/8 Donruss 98
97/8 DonrussPreferred 123
97/8 DonrussPriority 109
97/8 Limited 101
97/8 PacificCrown 156
96/7 Pinnacle 223
97/8 PinnacleBeAPlayer 132
97/8 Score(ANA) 18
97/8 SPAuthentic 2
97/8 UpperDeck 7
97/8 UDCollChoice 2
96/7 ANA/UpFrontSports 20
94/5 Knoxville 11

PRONOVOST, ANDRÉ
45-64 BeeHives(BOS), (DET)
45-64 BeeHives(MTL)
64-67 BeeHives(DET)
62 CeramicTiles
57/8 Parkhurst (MTL) 7
58/9 Parkhurst 3
59/60 Parkhurst 35
60/1 Parkhurst 55, 58
61/2 Parkhurst 51
63/4 Parkhurst 45
93/4 Parkie(56/7) 75
94/5 Parkie(64/5) 62
60/1 ShirriffCoin 32
61/2 ShirriffCoin 3
61/2 Topps 5, -Stamp
62/3 Topps 19
62/3 YorkTransfer 30
63/4 York 43

PRONOVOST, CLAUDE
51-54 LaPatrie 3Jan54
93/4 Parkie(56/7) 15

PRONOVOST, JEAN
70/1 Colgate Stamp 50
70/1 DadsCookies
70/1 EddieSargent 162
71/2 EddieSargent 168
72/3 EddieSargent 176
70/1 Esso Stamp
72/3 Letraset 23
74/5 Loblaws
69/70 OPC 155
70/1 OPC 202
71/2 OPC/Topps 118
72/3 OPC 64
73/4 OPC/Topps 11
74/5 OPC/Topps 110
75/6 OPC/Topps 280, 326
76/7 OPC/Topps 14, 218
77/8 OPC/Topps 261
78/9 OPC/Topps 184
79/80 OPC/Topps 7, 77
81/2 O-Pee-Chee 355
81/2 opcSticker 196
79 PaniniSticker 64
72 SemicSticker 216
71/2 TheTorontoSun
72/3 Topps 143
78/9 ATL/B&W
78/9 ATL/Coke
79/80 ATL
71/2 PGH
74/5 PGH
77/8 PGH/PuckBuck
80/1 WSH

PRONOVOST, MARCEL
45-64 BeeHives(DET)
64-67 BeeHives(TORx2)
62 CeramicTiles
63-5 ChexPhoto
64/5 CokeCap DET-3
65/6 CocaCola
83&87 HallOfFame 148
83 HHOF Postcard (K)
96/7 HHOFLegends 77
82? JDMcCarthy
68/9 OPC/Topps 125
51/2 Parkhurst 68
52/3 Parkhurst 61
53/4 Parkhurst 41
54/5 Parkhurst 34
60/1 Parkhurst 29
61/2 Parkhurst 29
62/3 Parkhurst 33
63/4 Parkhurst 46
93/4 Parkhurst PR65
93/4 Parkie(56/7) 58
94/5 Parkie(64/5) 55
95/6 Parkie(66/7) 108
68/9 Post Marble
70/1 PostFlipBook
60/1 ShirriffCoin 56
61/2 ShirriffCoin 68
68/9 ShirriffCoin TOR13
54-67 TorontoStar V6, V10
56-66 TorontoStar 60/1
56-66 TorontoStar 63/4, 65/6
63/4 TheTorontoStar
64/5 TheTorontoStar
54/5 Topps 27
57/8 Topps 43
58/9 Topps 24
59/60 Topps 44
64/5 Topps 39
65/6 Topps 80
66/7 Topps 20, -USATest 20
67/8 Topps 81
91/2 Ultimate06 71, -Aut 71
62/3 YorkTransfer 23
63/4 York 38
67/8 York 33, 34
76 DET
80/1 DET
68/9 TOR
69/70 TOR

PRONOVOST, REN
52/3 BasDuFleuve 47
51/2 LacStJean 35

PROPP, BRIAN
90/1 Bowman 37
91/2 Bowman 123, 424
92/3 Bowman 272
93/4 Donruss 441
93/4 FleerUltra 340
94/5 FleerUltra 92
80/1 OPC/Topps 1, 39
81/2 OPC 246, Topps(E) 110
82/3 O-Pee-Chee 256
83/4 O-Pee-Chee 218, 271
84/5 O-Pee-Chee 166
85/6 OPC/Topps 141
86/7 OPC/Topps 86
87/8 OPC/Topps 158
88/9 OPC/Topps 168, J
89/90 OPC/Topps 139
90/1 OPC/Topps 8
91/2 OPC/Topps 227
92/3 O-Pee-Chee 350
90/1 opcPremier 92
87/8 opcStars 33
81/2 opcSticker 180
82/3 opcSticker 111
83/4 opcSticker 199
84/5 opcSticker 112
85/6 opcSticker 90/223
86/7 opcSticker 239
87/8 opcSticker 67, 97/230
88/9 opcSticker 97/221
89/90 opcSticker 106/245
87/8 PaniniSticker 131, 193
88/9 PaniniSticker 324
89/90 PaniniSticker 306
90/1 PaniniSticker 5, 325
91/2 PaniniSticker 115
92/3 PaniniSticker 93
93/4 PaniniSticker 267
94/5 PaniniSticker 115
91/2 Parkhurst 82
93/4 Parkhurst 85
91/2 Pinnacle 184
92/3 Pinnacle 178
93/4 Pinnacle 342
82/3 Post
90/1 ProSet 14, 360, 460
91/2 ProSet 113
92/3 ProSet 257
91/2 PSPlatinum 187, PC17
83/4 PuffySticker 11
90/1 Score 269, 34T
91/2 Score(CDN) 223, (U.S) 223
92/3 Score 72
93/4 Score 513
94/5 Score 247
83/4 SouhaitsRen.KeyChain
92/3 Topps 65
91/2 ToppsStadiumClub 237
92/3 ToppsStadiumClub 374
90/1 UpperDeck 2, 409
91/2 UpperDeck 260
92/3 UpperDeck 177
93/4 UpperDeck 368
89/90 BOS/SportsAction
93/4 HFD/Coke
81/2 PHA/Tickets 12
83/4 PHA
86/7 PHA
89/90 PHA
84/5 KelownaWingsWHL 34

PROPROK, IVO
94/5 APS 223
95/6 APS 137

PROSKURNI, ANDREW
95/6 Slapshot 348

PROSOFSKY, GARRETT
97/8 UpperDeck 416

PROSOFSKY, JASON
91/2 ProCards 325
90/1 SketchWHL 31
91/2 UpperDeck 432

PROSOFSKY, TYLER
92/3 Tacoma
93/4 Tacoma

PROSPAL, VACLAV
94/5 Classic 29
93/4 ClassicProspects 174
97/8 Donruss 219, -RatedRook 3
97/8 DonrussCanadianIce 135
97/8 DonrussElite 80
97/8 DonrussPreferred 105
97/8 DonrussPriority 165, 190
97/8 KatchMedallion 165
97/8 Leaf 132, 165
97/8 Limited 38, 91, 100
97/8 McDonalds McD39
97/8 PacificCrownRoyale 100
97/8 PacificParamount 136
97/8 Pinnacle 19
97/8 PinnacleBeAPlayer 213
97/8 P.BeeHive 52,-TeamBH 21
97/8 PinnacleInside 143
97/8 PinnacleMint 30
97/8 Score(PHA) 18
97/8 SPAuthentic 188
97/8 UpperDeck 125, SG27
97/8 UDBlackDiamond PC21
98/9 UDChoice 145
97/8 UDCollChoice 185
97/8 UpperDeckIce 45, L7C
97/8 Zenith91,Z74,-RookReign 6
97/8 Zenith -RookieZTeam 13

PROTSENKO, BORIS
95/6 Bowman P29

PROULX, CHRISTIAN
93/4 ClassicProspects 8
94/5 Parkhurst 121
90/1 SketchQMJHL 218
91/2 SketchQMJHL 167
93/4 Fredericton
94/5 Fredericton

PROULX, HUGO
90/1 SketchMEM 57
91/2 SketchQMJHL 282
94/5 Greensboro

PROVARI, JUKKO
79 PaniniSticker 177

PROVAZNIK, JIRI
94/5 APS 46

PROVENCAL, JACQUES
88/9 Richelieu

PROVEZANO, MARK
95/6 Slapshot 220

PROVOST, CLAUDE
52/3 AnonymousOHL 138
68/9 Bauer
45-64 BeeHives(MTL)
64-67 BeeHives(MTL)
62 CeramicTiles
63-5 ChexPhoto
64/5 CokeCap MTL-14
65/6 CocaCola
72-84 Dernière 77/8
51-54 LaPatrie 13Dec52
68/9 O-Pee-Chee 163, 216
69/70 O-Pee-Chee 167
57/8 Parkhurst (MTL) 12
58/9 Parkhurst 43
59/60 Parkhurst 18
60/1 Parkhurst 54, 58
61/2 Parkhurst 50
62/3 Parkhurst 41
63/4 Parkhurst 36, 95
93/4 Parkie(56/7) 73
94/5 Parkie(64/5) 70, AS6, SL4
95/6 Parkie(66/7) 61, 137, 146
60/1 ShirriffCoin 33
61/2 ShirriffCoin 105
62/3 ShirriffCoin 35
68/9 ShirriffCoin MTL16
54-67 TorontoStar V9
56-66 TorontoStar 61/2, 65/6
63/4 TheTorontoStar
64/5 TheTorontoStar
64/5 Topps 23
65/6 Topps 8
66/7 Topps 9, -USATest 9
67/8 Topps 71
60/1 York
61/2 York 17
62/3 YorkTransfer 14
63/4 York 28
67/8 York (no# x 2), 20, 36
67/8 MTL
67/8 MTL/IGA
68/9 MTL
69/70 MTL/ProStar
71 MTL/Pins
92/3 MTL/OPC 43

PROVOST, PAUL
51/2 BasDuFleuve 37

PRPIC, TONY
96/7 Penascola 17
93/4 Fredericton
96/7 Fredericton

PRPICH, DAVE
91/2 SketchOHL 193

PRUD'HUMME, CARL
94/5 Slapshot(MEM) 58

PRUNEAU, MARTIAL
52/3 BasDuFleuve 2
51/2 LavalDairy 13
52/3 LavalDairy 56
52/3 StLawrence 79

PRUSA, PETER
74 Hellas 106
70/1 Kuvajulkaisut 95

PRUSA, SVEN
94/5 DEL 346

PRUSEK, MARTIN
95/6 APS 293

PRYL, STANISLAV
70/1 Kuvajulkaisut 57

PRYOR, CHRIS
88/9 ProCards(Springfield)
89/90 ProCards(AHL) 254
90/1 ProCards 499
91/2 ProCards 475
87/8 MIN
84/5 Springfield 16

PRYSTAI, METRO
45-64 BeeHives(CHI), (DET)
82? JDMcCarthy
51/2 Parkhurst 65
52/3 Parkhurst 60
53/4 Parkhurst 42
54/5 Parkhurst 35
93/4 Parkie(56/7) 57
54/5 Topps 24

PTACEK, FRANTISEK
94/5 APS 77
95/6 APS 275

PUCHER, RENE
94 Semic 205

PUCHNIAK, ROB
91/2 SketchWHL 197
89/90 Brandon 16
90/1 Brandon 19

PUDAS, ALBERT
23/4 PaulinsCandy 21

PUGA, DUANE
92/3 BCJHL 79

PUGLIESE, MARIO
79 PaniniSticker 392

PUHAKKA, KEITH
70/1 Kuvajulkaisut 286
71/2 WilliamsFIN 156
72/3 WilliamsFIN 108
73/4 WilliamsFIN 208

PUHAKKA, MIKA
95/6 Sisu 226
96/7 Sisu 25

PUHALSKI, GREG
82/3 Kitchener 21
83/4 Kitchener 15
84/5 Kitchener 19
85/6 London 13
92/3 Toledo 1, 2
93/4 Toledo 19
94/5 Toledo
95/6 Toledo

PUISE, JEAN
35/6 OPC (V304C) 91

PUJKOV, VICTOR
69/70 MästarSerien 22

PULENTE, GINO
91/2 LakeSuperior

PULFORD, BOB
45-64 BeeHives(TOR)
64-67 BeeHives(TORx2)
62 CeramicTiles
63-5 ChexPhoto
64/5 CokeCap TOR-20
65/6 CocaCola
70/1 Colgate Stamp 2
70/1 DadsCookies
70/1 EddieSargent 72
71/2 EddieSargent 66
70/1 Esso Stamp
83&87 HallOfFame 24
83 HHOF Postcard (B)
68/9 OPC/Topps 129
69/70 OPC/T. 53, OPC-Sticker
70/1 OPC/Topps 36
71/2 OPC/Topps 94
74/5 OPC/Topps 229
71/2 opcPoster 2
57/8 Parkhurst(TOR) 4
58/9 Parkhurst 1, 45
59/60 Parkhurst 28
60/1 Parkhurst 19
61/2 Parkhurst 8
62/3 Parkhurst 11
63/4 Parkhurst 12, 72
93/4 Parkie(56/7) 113
94/5 Parkie(64/5) 110
95/6 Parkie(66/7) 114, 145
66/7 Post-Large, -Small
67 PostFlipBook
68/9 Post Marble
91/2 PS'HOF 3
72 SemicSticker 203
60/1 ShirriffCoin 13
61/2 ShirriffCoin 46
62/3 ShirriffCoin 6
68/9 ShirriffCoin TOR4
54-67 TorontoStar V6, V11
56-66 TorontoStar 57/8
56-66 TorontoStar 63/4, 64/5
63/4 TheTorontoStar
64/5 TheTorontoStar
71/2 TheTorontoSun
64/5 Topps 60
65/6 Topps 18
66/7 Topps 19
67/8 Topps 19
60/1 York
61/2 York 14
62/3 YorkTransfer 15
63/4 York 18
67/8 York 15, 24, 32, no# (x 4)
79/80 CHI
81/2 CHI
93/4 CHI/Coke
64/5 TOR
66/7 TOR/Coaster
69/70 TOR

PULKKINEN, HANNU
78/9 SM-Liiga 48
72/3 WilliamsFIN 254
73/4 WilliamsFIN 254

PULKKINEN, PETRI
92/3 Jyvas-Hyva 116
93/4 Jyvas-Hyva 200
93/4 Sisu 258

PULKKINEN, REINO
78/9 SM-Liiga 92
72/3 WilliamsFIN 163

PULLI, HEINO
66/7 Champion 185
65/6 Hellas 111

PULLI, KALEVI
71/2 WilliamsFIN 374
65/6 Hellas 108

PULLI, MARKKU
66/7 Champion 174
65/6 Hellas 105
70/1 Kuvajulkaisut 248

PULLIAINEN, JARI
91/2 Jyvas-Hyva 64

PULLINEN, REIMA
80/1 Mallasjuoma 192
78/9 SM-Liiga 107

PULLISHY, GLEN
91/2 AvantGardeBCJHL 33

PULLOLA, TOM
91/2 Jyvas-Hyva 46
92/3 Jyvas-Hyva 135
93/4 Jyvas-Hyva 237
93/4 Sisu 196
95/6 Sisu 349

PUMPLE, RICK
72/3 Cleveland

PUNSCHNIK, GERHARD
93 SemicSticker 285

PUOLANNE, LAURI
95/6 Sisu 203
96/7 Sisu 6

PUPILLO, DANIEL
82 SemicSticker 129

PUPPA, DAREN
96/7 Aces 6 (Spades)
90/1 Bowman 242
91/2 Bowman 37
92/3 Bowman 16
93/4 Donruss 316
94/5 Donruss 100
95/6 Donruss 84
96/7 Donruss 34
97/8 Donruss 123
96/7 DonrussCanadianIce 102
97/8 DonrussCanadianIce 110
96/7 DonrussElite 114
97/8 DonrussElite 79
97/8 DonrussPreferred 110
97/8 DonrussPriority 136
97/8 DonrussStudio 44
94/5 Flair 175
94/5 Fleer 209
96/7 Fleer 105, 146, 147, -Vez 8
95/6 FleerMetal 139
92/3 FleerUltra 261
93/4 FleerUltra 427
94/5 FleerUltra 209
95/6 FleerUltra 155, 376
96/7 FleerUltra 159
97/8 KatchMedallion 137
97/8 KennerSLU
90/1 Kraft 43
94/5 Kraft
95/6 Kraft-CreaseKeeper
96/7 KraftDinner
93/4 Leaf 403
94/5 Leaf 224
95/6 Leaf 243
96/7 Leaf 73, -ShutDown 15
97/8 Leaf 50
94/5 LeafLimited 109
95/6 LeafLimited 58
96/7 LeafLimited 58
96/7 LeafPreferred 69, -Steel 17
97/8 Limited 170, 192
96/7 Maggers 144
96/7 MetalUniv. 146, -Armour 8
97/8 Omega 212
89/90 O-Pee-Chee 200
90/1 OPC/Topps 204, 238
91/2 OPC/Topps 333
92/3 O-Pee-Chee 53
98/9 Pacific 403
97/8 PacificCrownRoyale 126
97/8 PacificRegime 187
97/8 PacificRevolution 129
87/8 PaniniSticker 23
89/90 PaniniSticker 214
90/1 PaniniSticker 31
91/2 PaniniSticker 298
94/5 PaniniSticker 189
95/6 PaniniSticker 134
96/7 PaniniSticker 125
91/2 Parkhurst 14
92/3 Parkhurst 412
93/4 Parkhurst 468
94/5 Parkhurst 225
95/6 Parkhurst 195
91/2 Pinnacle 137
92/3 Pinnacle 327
93/4 Pinnacle 361
94/5 Pinnacle 71, GT15
95/6 Pinnacle 105
96/7 Pinnacle 97
97/8 Pinnacle 84
97/8 P.BAP 76,-TakeANum 16
97/8 PinnacleCertified 22
97/8 PinnacleInside 45
95/6 PinnacleZenith 120
96/7 PinnacleZenith 43
95/6 Playoff 198
94/5 POG 295
95/6 POG 256
93/4 PowerPlay 234
93/4 Premier 364
94/5 Premier 410
90/1 ProSet 27, 365
91/2 ProSet 21
91/2 PSPlatinum 9
90/1 Score 60, 318, -Hot 26
91/2 Score(CDN) 106, (U.S) 106
92/3 Score 47
93/4 Score 273, 530
94/5 Score 72, TF22
95/6 Score 210
96/7 Score 118,-Net 13,-Sddn 11
97/8 Score 18
94/5 Select 45
95/6 SelectCertified 58
96/7 SelectCert. 69, -Freezers 9
95/6 SkyBoxEmotion 166
95/6 SkyBoxImpact 157
96/7 SkyBoxImpact 123, -Zero 8
95/6 SP 137
97/8 SPAuthentic 147
95/6 Summit 85
96/7 Summit 77, -IntheCrease 4
92/3 Topps 457
95/6 Topps 226
94/5 ToppsFinest 53
95/6 ToppsFinestS 11
91/2 ToppsStadiumClub 231
92/3 ToppsStadiumClub 370
93/4 ToppsStadiumClub 275
94/5 T.StadiumClub 162, 183
95/6 ToppsStadiumClub 6
90/1 UpperDeck 166
91/2 UpperDeck 248
93/4 UpperDeck 473
94/5 UpperDeck 204
95/6 UpperDeck 205, SE78
96/7 UpperDeck 338
97/8 UpperDeck 362
95/6 UDBeAPlayer 85
97/8 UDBlackDiamond 74
98/9 UDChoice 191
95/6 UDCollChoice 117
96/7 UDCollChoice 247, 331
97/8 UDCollChoice 235
85/6 BUF
86/7 BUF
87/8 BUF/BlueShield
87/8 BUF/WonderBread
88/9 BUF/BlueShield
88/9 BUF/WonderBread
89/90 BUF/BlueShield
89/90 BUF/Campbell
90/1 BUF/BlueShield
90/1 BUF/Campbell
91/2 BUF/BlueShield
91/2 BUF/Campbell
92/3 BUF/BlueShield
92/3 BUF/Jubillee
94/5 T.B./HealthPlan
94/5 T.B./SkyBoxSportsCafe
95/6 T.B.
95/6 T.B./SkyBoxSportsCafe

PURCELL, BILL
90/1 Newmarket

PURCELL, TOM
89/90 SketchOHL 164

PURDIE, BRAD
91/2 AirCanadaSJHL D36
92/3 Maine (2) 28
93/4 Maine 47

PURDIE, DENNIS
89/90 SketchOHL 36
90/1 SketchMEM 120
90/1 SketchOHL 140
91/2 SketchOHL 362
93/4 Johnstown 12
94/5 Johnstown 15
95/6 Toledo
92/3 Windsor 24

PURDON, NEAL
94/5 ThunderBay
95/6 ThunderBay

PURDY, BRIAN
90/1 SketchWHL 216
91/2 SketchWHL 202
89/90 Brandon 21
90/1 Brandon 14

PUROLA, LAVI
52/3 AnonymousOHL 62

PURPUR, CLIFFORD (FIDO)
34-43 BeeHives(CHI)

PURSCHEL, DIETER
70/1 Kuvajulkaisut 96

PURVES, JOHN
95/6 EdgeIce 190
95/6 FutureLegends 37
89/90 ProCards(AHL) 78
90/1 ProCards 212
91/2 ProCards 551
91/2 Baltimore 11
84/5 Belleville 7

PUSCHACHER, MICHAEL
95 Globe 182
95 PaniniWorlds 256
95 Semic 183
96 Wien 211

PUSCHNIAK, ROB
90/1 SketchWHL 231

PUSHNIG, ANDREAS
95 Globe 185
94 Semic 240
95 Semic 188
93 SemicSticker 284
96 Wien 215

PUSCHNIK, GERHARD
94 Semic 242

PUSEY, CHRIS
83/4 Brantford 19

PUSHKOV, SERGEI
94/5 ElitSet 291
94 Semic 153

PUSHKOV, VICTOR
69/70 Soviet Stars

PUSHOR, JAMIE
91/2 Arena 23
95/6 Bowman 103
91/2 Classic 28
91/2 ClassicFourSport 28, -Aut
95/6 Donruss 337
97/8 Donruss 52
96/7 DonrussCanadianIce 118
94/5 Leaf 459
97/8 Limited 136
97/8 PacificCrown 215
96/7 PinnacleBeAPlayer 102
96/7 PinnacleZenith 147
94/5 Premier 478
97/8 Score(DET) 19
90/1 SketchMEM 122
90/1 SketchWHL 128
91/2 SketchWHL 342
96/7 SkyBoxImpact 157
91/2 StarPics 3
96/7 Summit 196
98/9 Topps 51
95/6 ToppsStadiumClub 224
91/2 UltimateDP 24,-Au t 24
91/2 UpperDeck 63, 73
96/7 UpperDeck 54
95/6 Adirondack

PUSIE, JEAN
36-39 DiamondMatch (1)

PUSKAS, CHRIS
90/1 Rayside

PUTNIK, WALTER
93 SemicSticker 286

PUUSTINEN, KARI
71/2 WilliamsFIN 269

PYATT, NELSON
74/5 Loblaws
76/7 OPC 98, 396, Topps 98
77/8 OPC/Topps 252
78/9 O-Pee-Chee 354
76/7 COL.R
76/7 COL.R/CokeCans
77/8 COL.R/CokeCans

PYCHA, PAVEL
94/5 APS 114
95/6 APS 66
91 SemicSticker 118

PYE, BILL
92/3 Rochester/Dunkin'Donuts
92/3 Rochester/Kodak

PYKA, REEMPT
94/5 DEL 233
95/6 DEL 230, 432
96/7 DEL 82
94 Semic 285

PYKE, DERRICK
95/6 Halifax

PYLYPOW, KEVIN
82/3 Brandon 2
81/2 Regina 17

PYLYPUIK, PAT
90/1 SketchWHL 139
88/9 Lethbridge
89/90 Lethbridge
92/3 Toledo 1, 2
93/4 Toledo 9

PYNNÖNEN, PENTTI
66/7 Champion 198
65/6 Hellas 113

PYSZ, PATRICK
94/5 DEL 17
95/6 DEL 280

PYTEL, HENRYK
79 PaniniSticker 130

PYYHTIÄ, JUHANI
65/6 Hellas 90

PYYKKÖ, PAULI
78/9 SM-Liiga 98

QUACKENBUSH, HUBERT (BILL)
45-64 BeeHives(BOS), (DET)
82? JDMcCarthy
51/2 Parkhurst 26
52/3 Parkhurst 68
53/4 Parkhurst 100
54/5 Parkhurst 51
54/5 Topps 49
91/2 BOS/Legends [x2]

QUAPP, VLADIMIR
94/5 DEL 105

QUENNEVILLE, CHAD
95/6 Classic 79, -Aut.
95/6 ClassicFiveSport 149, -Aut.

QUENNEVILLE, JOEL
79/80 O-Pee-Chee 336
80/1 OPC/Topps 19
81/2 O-Pee-Chee 78, T(W) 83
83/4 O-Pee-Chee 145
84/5 O-Pee-Chee 77, Topps 60
85/6 OPC/Topps 103
86/7 OPC/Topps 118
88/9 OPC/Topps 3
89/90 O-Pee-Chee 211
90/1 O-Pee-Chee 418
83/4 opcSticker 225
85/6 opcSticker 170
86/7 opcSticker 55
91/2 ProCards 356
83/4 SouhaitsRen.KeyChain
79/80 COL.R
81/2 COL.R
83/4 HFD/JuniorWhalers
84/5 HFD/JuniorWhalers
85/6 HFD/JuniorWhalers
86/7 HFD/JuniorWhalers
87/8 HFD/JuniorWhalers
88/9 HFD/JuniorWhalers
89/90 HFD/JuniorWhalers
92/3 StJohns

QUENNEVILLE, YVON
90/1 Rayside

QUILTY, JOHN
34-43 BeeHives(MTL.C)
40/1 OPC (V301-2) 106
45-54 QuakerOats 46

QUINN, DAN
90/1 Bowman 65
91/2 Bowman 376
92/3 Bowman 289
95/6 Donruss 240
96/7 Donruss 92
95/6 FleerMetal 106
94/5 FleerUltra 307
95/6 FleerUltra 281
94/5 Leaf 61, 413
95/6 Leaf 258
84/5 O-Pee-Chee 234
85/6 O-Pee-Chee 176
86/7 O-Pee-Chee 204
87/8 OPC/Topps 171
88/9 OPC/Topps 41
89/90 OPC/Topps 152
90/1 OPC/Topps 272
91/2 OPC/Topps 393
92/3 O-Pee-Chee 264
90/1 opcPremier 93
86/7 opcSticker 87
87/8 opcSticker 173
88/9 opcSticker 236
89/90 opcSticker 234/97
90/1 Panini(VAN) 20
87/8 PaniniSticker 147
88/9 PaniniSticker 342
89/90 PaniniSticker 314
90/1 PaniniSticker 305
91/2 PaniniSticker 27
95/6 PaniniSticker 49
91/2 Parkhurst 351
94/5 Pinnacle 504
91/2 Pinnacle 84, 408
95/6 POG 192
91/2 Premier 27
90/1 ProSet 303
91/2 ProSet 209
90/1 Score 55, -HotCards 24
91/2 Score (CDN) 615, (US) 62
91/2 Score Traded 65T
92/3 Score 43
95/6 Score 175
96/7 Score 228
97/8 Score(PGH) 14
95/6 SkyBoxEmotion 126
95/6 SkyBoxImpact 120
95/6 Summit 116
95/6 SuperSticker 85
92/3 Topps 143
95/6 Topps 261
91/2 ToppsStadiumClub 243
92/3 ToppsStadiumClub 22
95/6 ToppsStadiumClub 142
90/1 UpperDeck 260
91/2 UpperDeck 358, 563
95/6 UpperDeck 483, SE145
94/5 UDBeAPlayer-Aut. 89
95/6 UDCollChoice 70
96/7 UDCollChoice 198
85/6 CGY/RedRooster
86/7 PGH/Kodak
87/8 PGH/Kodak
89/90 PGH/Foodland
90/1 VAN/Mohawk
83/4 Belleville 3

QUINN, JIM
82/3 Kitchener 16
83/4 Kitchener 2

QUINN, PAT
70/1 Colgate Stamp 72
70/1 DadsCookies
70/1 EddieSargent 209
71/2 EddieSargent 219
72/3 EddieSargent 6
70/1 Esso Stamp
74/5 Loblaws
69/70 O-Pee-Chee 186, -Sticker
70/1 OPC/Topps 120, -Deckle 1
71/2 OPC/Topps 122
72/3 OPC 183, -Crest 1
73/4 OPC/Topps 61
74/5 OPC 286
75/6 OPC 172
76/7 OPC 289, 379
71/2 TheTorontoSun
72/3 ATL
74/5 ATL
84/5 L.A/Smokeys
69/70 TOR
70/1 VAN
71/2 VAN 5
72/3 VAN/Nalley's

QUINNELL, BOB
91/2 AvantGardeBCJHL 132
92/3 BCJHL 101

QUINNEY, KEN
88/9 ProCards(Halifax)
89/90 ProCards(AHL) 162
90/1 ProCards 458
91/2 ProCards 127
91/2 UpperDeck 419
85/6 QUE
86/7 QUE/GeneralFoods
87/8 QUE/GeneralFoods
85/6 Fredericton 14
89/90 Halifax
90/1 Halifax
93/4 LasVegas
94/5 LasVegas
95/6 LasVegas
96/7 LasVegas

QUINT, DERON
95/6 Bowman 107
93/4 Classic 109, CL5
94/5 Classic T78
94/5 ClassicImages 74, -Aut.
93/4 ClassicProspects 206
93/4 Donruss USA18
95/6 Donruss 364
96/7 Donruss 225
95/6 DonrussElite 89
95/6 FleerMetal 188
95/6 FleerUltra 352
96/7 Leaf 143
94/5 LeafLimited-USAJrs 10
97/8 PacificCrown 304
95/6 Parkhurst 269
94/5 ParkieSE 247
93/4 Pinnacle 485
94/5 Score 208
95/6 SelectCertified 129
94/5 SigRookies 26
95/6 SkyBoxImpact 227
94/5 SP 193
95/6 SP 165
95/6 Summit 181
95/6 Topps 258
94/5 ToppsFinest 116
95/6 ToppsFinest 101
95/6 ToppsStadiumClub 197
93/4 UpperDeck 561
94/5 UpperDeck 524
95/6 UpperDeck 498
96/7 UpperDeck 128
96/7 UDCollChoice 206
97/8 UDCollChoice 202
96/7 PHO
97/8 PHO
95/6 WPG
93/4 Seattle

QUINTAL, STÉPHANE
92/3 Bowman 337
95/6 Donruss 314
94/5 Fleer 244
93/4 FleerUltra 456
94/5 FleerUltra 245
95/6 FleerUltra 257
94/5 Leaf 293
97/8 PacificCrown 324
94/5 PaniniSticker 170
95/6 PaniniSticker 45
92/3 Parkhurst 384
93/4 Parkhurst 500
95/6 Parkhurst 117
93/4 Pinnacle 326
94/5 Pinnacle 501
97/8 PinnacleBeAPlayer 94
94/5 POG 258
93/4 PowerPlay 475
94/5 Premier 6
88/9 ProCards(Maine)
90/1 ProSet 410
91/2 ProSet 350
91/2 Score(CDN) 437
92/3 Score 242
93/4 Score 412, 509
95/6 SkyBoxEmotion 89
96/7 TeamOut
92/3 Topps 484
92/3 ToppsStadiumClub 350
93/4 ToppsStadiumClub 242
93/4 UpperDeck 529
95/6 UDCollChoice 280
89/90 BOS/SportsAction
90/1 BOS/SportsAction
95/6 MTL
95/6 MTL/Molson
96/7 MTL
96/7 MTL/MolsonExport
97/8 MTL
93/4 WPG/Ruffles
84/5 Richelieu

QUINTIN, JEAN-FRANÇOIS
92/3 Classic 107
93/4 FleerUltra 192, -Prospect 8
92/3 opcPremier 37
94/5 Parkhurst 212
89/90 ProCards(IHL) 97
90/1 ProCards 117
92/3 Score 488
92/3 UpperDeck 483
93/4 UpperDeck 21

QUIRING, TYLER
91/2 AvantGardeBCJHL 116
93/4 RedDeer

QUIRK, STEPHEN
97/8 Halifax (2)

R

RAATESALMI, REIJO
70/1 Kuvajulkaisut 377

RABBITT, PAT
81/2 Milwaukee 1

RACETTE, JULES
51/2 LacStJean 12

RACICOT, ANDRÉ
91/2 Bowman 337, 411
92/3 Durivage 49
93/4 Durivage 15
92/3 FleerUltra 332
93/4 FleerUltra 355
93/4 Leaf 294
91/2 OPC/Topps 450
92/3 opcPremier 11
92/3 Parkhurst 321
93/4 Pinnacle 332
93/4 Premier 313
89/90 ProCards(AHL) 180
90/1 ProCards 67
91/2 ProCards 78
91/2 Score(CDN) 285, (U.S) 395
93/4 Score 437
91/2 ToppsStadiumClub 377
93/4 ToppsStadiumClub 26
91/2 UpperDeck 377
92/3 UpperDeck 430
91/2 MTL
92/3 MTL
93/4 MTL
94/5 Portland

RACICOT, PAOLO
91/2 SketchQMJHL 105

RACINE, BRUCE
88/9 ProCards(Muskegon)
89/90 ProCards(AHL) 180
89/90 ProCards(IHL) 152
90/1 ProCards 517
91/2 ProCards 295
92/3 Cleveland 14
93/4 St.John's
94/5 St.John's

RACINE, YVES
90/1 Bowman 230
91/2 Bowman 44
92/3 Bowman 331
93/4 Donruss 246
93/4 Durivage 34
92/3 FleerUltra 287
94/5 FleerUltra 316
93/4 Leaf 115
94/5 Leaf 388
92/3 O-Pee-Chee 297
90/1 OPC/Topps 361
91/2 OPC/Topps 228
97/8 PacificRegime 30
91/2 PaniniSticker 141
92/3 PaniniSticker 119
95 PaniniWorlds 7
91/2 Parkhurst 265
93/4 Parkhurst 422
94/5 Parkhurst 168
91/2 Pinnacle 233
92/3 Pinnacle 332
93/4 Pinnacle 372
94/5 Pinnacle 391
95/6 Pinnacle 178
97/8 PinnacleBeAPlayer 27
95/6 POG 154
93/4 PowerPlay 406
94/5 Premier 176, 426
89/90 ProCards(AHL) 317
90/1 ProCards 474
91/2 ProSet 54
91/2 Score(CDN) 158, (U.S) 158
91/2 Score-YoungStar 37
92/3 Score 74
93/4 Score 264, 540
94/5 Score 162
95/6 Score 221
95 Semic 80
92/3 Topps 277
95/6 Topps 138
91/2 ToppsStadiumClub 198
92/3 ToppsStadiumClub 6
93/4 ToppsStadiumClub 304
94/5 ToppsStadiumClub 239
91/2 UpperDeck 498
92/3 UpperDeck 142
93/4 UpperDeck 194
94/5 UpperDeck 171
94/5 MTL
94/5 MTL/MolsonExport
95/6 MTL
93/4 PHA 13NOV93
93/4 PHA/JCPenney

RADEVIC, RADIM
94/5 APS 17

RADKE, AL
91/2 AvantGardeBCJHL 152

RADLEIN, PETER
87/8 Brockville 25

RAEDAR, CAP
88/9 L.A/Smokeys

RAFALSKI, BRIAN
95/6 ElitSet 172
91/2 UD'CzechWJC 78

RAGLAN, CLARENCE
45-64 BeeHives (CHI)
51/2 Parkhurst 36
53/4 Parkhurst 79

RAGLAN, HERB
90/1 ProSet 525
91/2 ProSet 470
91/2 Score(CDN) 536
91/2 QUE/PetroCanada
92/3 QUE/PetroCanada
87/8 STL
88/9 STL
87/8 STL/Kodak
88/9 STL/Kodak
89/90 STL/Kodak
84/5 Kingston 24

RAGNARSSON, MARCUS
95/6 Bowman 111, BB29
95/6 Donruss 264, -Rated 13
96/7 Donruss 234
96/7 DonrussCanadianIce 83
95/6 DonrussElite 38, -Rookie 7
94/5 ElitSet 224
96/7 Fleer 101, -Rookie 8
95/6 FleerMetal 189
96/7 FleerNHLPicks 126
95/6 FleerUltra 353, -High 15
95 Globe 18
96/7 Leaf 183
95/6 LeafLimited 78
96/7 LeafLimited 42, -Rookie 1
96/7 LeafPreferred 52, -Steel 13
96/7 MetalUniverse 140
97/8 Pacific-BestKept 86
96/7 PaniniSticker 279
97/8 PaniniSticker 234
95 PaniniWorlds 144
95/6 Parkhurst 519, 531, PP41
96/7 Pinnacle 207
95/6 P.Zenith 141, -Rookie 8
96/7 PinnacleZenith 79
96/7 Score 242
95/6 SelectCertified 138
89/90 SemicElitserien 59
90/1 SemicElitserien 281
91/2 SemicElitserien 62
92/3 SemicElitserien 80
95/6 SkyBoxImpact 220
96/7 SkyBoxImpact 118, -Fox 18
95/6 SP 132
95/6 Summit 195
96/7 Summit 165
96/7 TeamOut
95/6 Topps 287
95/6 ToppsFinest 76
96/7 ToppsNHLPicks RS7
95/6 ToppsStadiumClub 148
95/6 UpperDeck 439
96/7 UpperDeck 148
97/8 UpperDeck 149
95/6 UDBeAPlayer 164
98/9 UDChoice 178
96/7 UDCollChoice 236
97/8 UDCollChoice 222
96 Wien 49
96/7 S.J/PacificBellSheet
97/8 S.J/PacificBellSheet (x2)

RAGOT, MIKE
85/6 Kamloops

RAGULIN, ALEXANDER
72 Hellas 65
74 Hellas 54
70/1 Kuvajulkaisut 14
69/70 MästarSerien 23, 31
72 Panda
72 SemicSticker 5
74 SemicSticker 27
91 SemicSticker 245
73/4 Soviet Champs 8, 10
69/70 Soviet Stars
70/1 Soviet Stars
71/2 Soviet Stars
73/4 Soviet Stars 12
91/2 Trends 65
71/2 WilliamsFIN 13
72/3 WilliamsFIN 32
73/4 WilliamsFIN 14

RAHKONEN, ANTTI
95/6 Sisu 314
96/7 Sisu 124

RAHM, NIKLAS
95/6 ElitSet 232
92/3 SemicElitserien 133
95/6 udElite 77

RAIKKONEN, MIKKO
66/7 Champion 168
70/1 Kuvajulkaisut 251
71/2 WilliamsFIN 217
72/3 WilliamsFIN 166
73/4 WilliamsFIN 232

RAILIO, SEPPO
72/3 WilliamsFIN 109

RÄISÄNEN, PERTTI
71/2 WilliamsFIN 314

RAITAINEN, RAULI
95/6 Sisu 363
92/3 Jyvas-Hyva 203
93/4 Jyvas-Hyva 358
94 Semic 38
95 Semic 51
93 SemicSticker 73
93/4 Sisu 229
94/5 Sisu 48
95/6 SisuLimited 21

RAITER, MARK
90/1 SketchWHL 84
91/2 SketchWHL 103
95/6 Birmingham
90/1 Saskatoon 5
91/2 Saskatoon 5

RAJALA, KARI
65/6 Hellas 76

RAJALA, MIKA
78/9 SM-Liiga 162
72/3 WilliamsFIN 315
73/4 WilliamsFIN 116

RAJALA, OLLI-PEKKA
80/1 Mallasjuoma 127

RAJAMAKI, TOMMI
94/5 ParkieSE 226
94/5 Sisu-NHLDraft 5
95/6 Sisu 355
96/7 Sisu 151
94/5 ToppsFinest 123
94/5 UpperDeck 512

RAJANIEMI, VESA
78/9 SM-Liiga 82

RAJNOHA, PAVEL
94/5 APS 184
95/6 APS 184

RALEIGH, DON
45-64 BeeHives(NYR)
51-54 LaPatrie 15Mar53
51/2 Parkhurst 93
52/3 Parkhurst 99
53/4 Parkhurst 68
54/5 Parkhurst 68
54/5 Topps 53

RALPH, JIM
88/9 ProCards(Newmarket)
85/6 NovaScotia 15
81/2 Ottawa67s
83/4 Springfield 2

RAM, JAMIE
94/5 Classic 59, AA8
95/6 EdgeIce 21
96/7 Leaf 235
94/5 Binghampton
95/6 Binghampton
90/1 Mich.Tech
91/2 Mich.Tech

RAMAGE, ROB
90/1 Bowman 162
91/2 Bowman 154
92/3 FleerUltra 413
89/90 Kraft 39
90/1 Kraft 44
80/1 OPC/Topps 213
81/2 OPC 79, Topps(W) 84
82/3 O-Pee-Chee 310
83/4 O-Pee-Chee 319
84/5 OPC 190, Topps 134
85/6 O-Pee-Chee 196
86/7 OPC/Topps 17
87/8 OPC/Topps 160
88/9 O-Pee-Chee 244
89/90 O-Pee-Chee 329
90/1 OPC/Topps 317
91/2 OPC/Topps 55
91/2 opcPremier 76
81/2 opcSticker 154, 229
82/3 opcSticker 223
83/4 opcSticker 130
84/5 opcSticker 62, 136
86/7 opcSticker 180/44
87/8 opcSticker 20/160
88/9 opcSticker 84/213
90/1 Panini(TOR) 20
87/8 PaniniSticker 306
90/1 PaniniSticker 280
91/2 PaniniSticker 96
92/3 Parkhurst 175
91/2 Pinnacle 228
92/3 Pinnacle 389
81/2 PostPopUp 21
82/3 Post
93/4 PowerPlay 407
93/4 Premier-Finest 12
90/1 ProSet 288
91/2 ProSet 232, 407
92/3 ProSet 177
83/4 PuffySticker 16
90/1 Score 36
91/2 Score(CDN) 573
91/2 Score(US) 233, 23T
92/3 Score 351
93/4 Score 36, 653
84/5 7ElevenDisk
85/6 7Eleven 17
91/2 ToppsStadiumClub 239
90/1 UpperDeck 62
92/3 UpperDeck 105
79/80 COL.R
81/2 COL.R
93/4 MTL
93/4 PHA 21FEB94
93/4 PHA/JCPenney
87/8 STL/Kodak
92/3 STL/UpperDeck 21
90/1 TOR

RAMBO, DEAN
90/1 SketchWHL 76
90/1 Saskatoon 8

RAMEN, MARCUS
94/5 ElitSet 167

RAMOSER, ROLAND
91/2 AvantGardeBCJ 24, 155

RAMPA, PEKKA
73/4 WilliamsFIN 189

RAMPTON, JOE
83/4 SSMarie

RAMSAY, BEATTIE
25 Dominion 59

RAMSAY, BRUCE
93/4 ThunderBay
94/5 ThunderBay
95/6 ThunderBay

RAMSAY, CRAIG
77/8 Coke Mini
72/3 EddieSargent 38
74/5 Loblaws
72/3 OPC 262
73/4 OPC 213
74/5 OPC 305
75/6 OPC/Topps 271
76/7 OPC/Topps 78
77/8 OPC/Topps 191
78/9 OPC/Topps 9
79/80 OPC/Topps 207
80/1 OPC/Topps 13
81/2 O-Pee-Chee 31
83/4 O-Pee-Chee 69
84/5 OPC 27, Topps 21
85/6 OPC/Topps 32
84/5 opcSticker 215
85/6 opcSticker 175/44, 192/68
82/3 Post
83/4 SouhaitsRen.KeyChain
72/3 BUF
73/4 BUF
74/5 BUF
79/80 BUF/BellsMarket
80/1 BUF/Wendt
81/2 BUF 1, 3
84/5 BUF/BlueShield
85/6 BUF
93/4 BUF/NOCO
96/7 OTT/PizzaHut
97/8 OTT

RAMSEY, MIKE
91/2 Bowman 32
92/3 FleerUltra 19
93/4 FleerUltra 396
94/5 Leaf 536
94/5 MiracleOnIce 27, 28
80/1 OPC/Topps 127
82/3 O-Pee-Chee 32
83/4 O-Pee-Chee 70
84/5 O-Pee-Chee 28, Topps 22
85/6 OPC/Topps 77
86/7 OPC/Topps 115
87/8 OPC/Topps 63
88/9 OPC/Topps 133
89/90 OPC/Topps 140
90/1 OPC/Topps 192
91/2 OPC/Topps 236
83/4 opcSticker 243
84/5 opcSticker 211
85/6 opcSticker 180/49
86/7 opcSticker 44/180
87/8 opcSticker 149/11
88/9 opcSticker 260/128
87/8 PaniniSticker 25
88/9 PaniniSticker 222
90/1 PaniniSticker 24
91/2 PaniniSticker 299
92/3 PaniniSticker 253
91/2 Parkhurst 19
92/3 Parkhurst 256
91/2 Pinnacle 64
92/3 Pinnacle 21
93/4 Pinnacle 394
94/5 Pinnacle 412
82/3 Post
90/1 ProSet 28
91/2 ProSet 25, 568
91/2 PSPlatinum 13

90/1 Score 23, -HotCards 13
91/2 Score(CDN) 61, (U.S) 61
92/3 Score 28
93/4 Score 179
89 SemicSticker 158
83/4 SouhaitsRen.KeyChain
84/5 Topps 22
92/3 Topps 473
91/2 ToppsStadiumClub 135
92/3 ToppsStadiumClub 386
90/1 UpperDeck 168
79/80 USAOlympicTeam 11
81/2 BUF 12
82/3 BUF/Wendt 15
84/5 BUF/BlueShield
85/6 BUF
86/7 BUF
87/8 BUF/BlueShield
87/8 BUF/WonderBread
88/9 BUF/BlueShield
88/9 BUF/WonderBread
89/90 BUF/BlueShield
89/90 BUF/Campbell
90/1 BUF/BlueShield
90/1 BUF/Campbell
91/2 BUF/BlueShield
91/2 BUF/Campbell
92/3 BUF/BlueShield
92/3 BUF/Jubille
93/4 BUF/NOCO
93/4 PGH/Foodland 16

RAMSTEDT, JOHAN
94/5 SRAutoPhonex 33
95/6 SRTetradAutobilia 50
95/6 UDCollChoice 341
95/6 udElite DS5

RANCOURT, ALAIN
88/9 Richelieu

RANCOURT, FERNAND
52/3 BasDuFleuve 30

RANDALL, BRUCE
88/9 ProCards(Hershey)

RANDALL, KEN
24/5 Champs(C144) 17
24/5 MapleCrescents(V130) 24
23/4 (V145-1) 34
24/5 (V145-2) 12

RANFORD, BILL
95/6 Aces 3 (Clubs)
91/2 Bowman 101
92/3 Bowman 106
95/6 Bowman 24
93/4 Classic TC4
93/4 Donruss 117
94/5 Donruss 171
95/6 Donruss 323
96/7 Donruss 87
97/8 Donruss 172
96/7 DonrussCanadianIce 75
97/8 DonrussCanadianIce 46
95/6 DonrussElite 12
96/7 DonrussElite 97
97/8 DonrussPreferred 52
97/8 DonrussPriority 55
93/4 EASports 48, 221
95/6 EdgeIce L5
94/5 Flair 61
96/7 Flair 6
94/5 Fleer 75
96/7 Fleer 7
95/6 FleerMetal 56
92/3 FleerUltra 65
93/4 FleerUltra 158
94/5 FleerUltra 76
95/6 FleerUltra 57
96/7 FleerUltra 11
91/2 Gillette 9
95 Globe 75
93/4 HockeyWit 76
95/6 Hoyle'WEST Q (Diamonds)
92/3 HumptyDumpty (2)
97/8 KatchMedallion 154
90/1 Kraft 45
91/2 Kraft 44
92/3 Kraft'Disk
93/4 Kraft, 'Recipe
94/5 Kraft
95/6 Kraft-Crease
93/4 Leaf 68, -Painted 10
94/5 Leaf 60, -CreasePatrol 10
95/6 Leaf 86
96/7 Leaf 2
97/8 Leaf 33
94/5 LeafLimited 9
95/6 LeafLimited 103
96/7 LeafLimited 22
96/7 LeafPreferred 3, -Steel 40
97/8 Limited 14
96/7 Maggers 12
91/2 McDonalds McD21
96/7 McD'Masks
96/7 MetalUniverse 10
87/8 OPC/Topps 13
89/90 O-Pee-Chee 233
90/1 OPC/Topps 226, OPC 467
91/2 OPC/Topps 356
92/3 O-Pee-Chee 137
90/1 opcPremier 94
91/2 opcPremier 18
92/3 opcPremier-Star 19
89/90 opcSticker 23 0/89
98/9 Pacific 446
97/8 PacificCrown 233
97/8 PcfcDynagon! 134,-Tand 51
97/8 PacificInvincible 150
97/8 PacificParamount 199
90/1 Panini(EDM) 17
87/8 PaniniSticker 5
89/90 PaniniSticker 81
90/1 PaniniSticker 218
91/2 PaniniSticker 125
92/3 PaniniSticker 99
93/4 PaniniSticker U
94/5 PaniniSticker 207
96/7 PaniniSticker 2
97/8 PaniniSticker 110
95 PaniniWorlds 1
91/2 Parkhurst 53
92/3 Parkhurst 50
93/4 Parkhurst 67
94/5 Parkhurst 72, V75
95/6 Parkhurst 78, 282, -Goal 9
91/2 Pinnacle 170, B7
92/3 Pinnacle 4
93/4 Pinnacle 81
94/5 Pinnacle 285, GT6, NL13
96/7 Pinnacle 89
97/8 Pinnacle 46
96/7 PinnacleBeAPlayer 16
97/8 PinnacleCertified 12
97/8 PinnacleInside 35,-Stop 23
95/6 PinnacleZenith 47
96/7 PinnacleZenith 72
95/6 Playoff 151, 258
96/7 Playoff 374
94/5 POG 279
95/6 POG 113
93/4 PowerPlay 85, -Net. 6
93/4 Premier 258
94/5 Premier 435
95/6 ProMagnet 84
90/1 ProSet 94, 390
91/2 ProSet 70, 283
91/2 PSPlatinum 36
92/3 ProSet 51
90/1 Score 79, 331, 245
90/1 Score 358, 369
91/2 Score(CDN) 30, (U.S) 30
92/3 Score 236, 424, 495
93/4 Score 155, -Franchise 7
95/6 Score 239
96/7 Score 40, -NetWorth 15
97/8 Score 13
92/3 SeasonsPatch 57
94/5 Select 5
95/6 SelectCertified 55
94 Semic 79, 331
95 Semic 77, 201, 208
92 SemicSticker 75
95/6 SkyBoxEmotion 66
95/6 SkyBoxImpact 64
96/7 SkyBoxImpact 8
94/5 SP 41
95/6 SP 9
96/7 SP 9
97/8 SPAuthentic 165
95/6 Summit 71
95/6 SuperSticker 42, 45
91 TeamCanada
92/3 Topps 126
95/6 Topps 241, HGC8
94/5 ToppsFinest -Ring 17
95/6 ToppsFinest 51
96/7 ToppsNHLPicks 85
91/2 ToppsStadiumClub 249
92/3 ToppsStadiumClub 66
93/4 ToppsStadiumClub 131
94/5 ToppsStadiumClub 29
95/6 T.StadiumClub 2, EN6
95/6 ToppsSuperSkills 86
90/1 UpperDeck 42, 201
91/2 UpperDeck 10, 117
92/3 UpperDeck 262
93/4 UpperDeck 180, SP52
94/5 UpperDeck 21, SP27
95/6 UpperDeck SE32
96/7 UpperDeck 8, SS30A
97/8 UpperDeck 178
94/5 UDBeAPlayer R28, -Aut 16
96/7 UDBlackDiamond 80
95/6 UDCollChoice 246
96/7 UDCollChoice 17
97/8 UDCollChoice 267
96/7 UpperDeck"Ice" 3
96 Wien 76
88/9 EDM
88/9 EDM/ActionMagazine 60
90/1 EDM/McGavins
91/2 EDM/IGA
92/3 EDM
92/3 EDM/IGA 18
93/4 EDM 22OCT93
86/7 Moncton 5

RANGER, JOE
87/8 Kitchener 25
85/6 London 2

RANHEIM, PAUL
90/1 Bowman 100
91/2 Bowman 251
92/3 Bowman 96
93/4 Donruss 50, 442
92/3 FleerUltra 27
93/4 FleerUltra 286
89/90 Kraft 9
93/4 Leaf 170
94/5 Leaf 370
90/1 OPC/Topps 20
91/2 OPC/Topps 15
92/3 O-Pee-Chee 36
98/9 Pacific 139
90/1 Panini(CGY) 18
90/1 PaniniSticker 181, 342
91/2 PaniniSticker 54
92/3 PaniniSticker 44
93/4 PaniniSticker 184
91/2 Parkhurst 249
92/3 Parkhurst 260
93/4 Parkhurst 32
95/6 Parkhurst 361
91/2 Pinnacle 252
92/3 Pinnacle 67
93/4 Pinnacle 265
94/5 Pinnacle 138
95/6 Playoff 265
94/5 POG 116
95/6 POG 127
93/4 PowerPlay 309
93/4 Premier 481
94/5 Premier 96
90/1 ProSet 44
91/2 ProSet 31
92/3 ProSet 29
90/1 Score 248
91/2 Score(CDN) 21, (U.S) 21
92/3 Score 149
93/4 Score 165
92/3 Topps 486
95/6 Topps 232
98/9 Topps 102
91/2 ToppsStadiumClub 50
92/3 ToppsStadiumClub 144
93/4 ToppsStadiumClub 151
90/1 UpperDeck 104
91/2 UpperDeck 472
92/3 UpperDeck 328
93/4 UpperDeck 131
94/5 UpperDeck 430
95/6 UpperDeck 13
95/6 UDBeAPlayer 87
95/6 UDCollChoice 78
90/1 CGY/McGavins
91/2 CGY/IGA
92/3 CGY/IGA 14

RANKIN, FRANK
83&87 HallOfFame 132
83 HHOF Postcard (I)

RANTALA, TIMO
66/7 Champion 103

RANTANEN, ESKO
66/7 Champion 169
70/1 Kuvajulkaisut 249
71/2 WilliamsFIN 215
72/3 WilliamsFIN 164
73/4 WilliamsFIN 229

RANTANEN, JARMO
66/7 Champion 61
65/6 Hellas 14
92/3 Jyvas-Hyva 81
93/4 Jyvas-Hyva 146
70/1 Kuvajulkaisut 148
93/4 Sisu 145
71/2 WilliamsFIN 198
72/3 WilliamsFIN 236
73/4 WilliamsFIN 270

RANTANEN, KALEVI
78/9 SM-Liiga 110

RANTANEN, KARI
70/1 Kuvajulkaisut 353

RANTANEN, KIMMO
71/2 WilliamsFIN 291

RANTANEN, MARKO
93/4 Sisu 4
95/6 Sisu 247

RANTASILA, JUHA
66/7 Champion 35
65/6 Hellas 34
70/1 Kuvajulkaisut 75, 113
72 Panda
72 SemicSticker 92
71/2 WilliamsFIN 122
72/3 WilliamsFIN 71, 92
73/4 WilliamsFIN 139

RASANEN, ERKKI
66/7 Champion 125
70/1 Kuvajulkaisut 266

RASANEN, JUHA
71/2 WilliamsFIN 333

RÄSÄNEN, PEKKA
80/1 Mallasjuoma 47

RÄSÄNEN, TEIJO
72/3 WilliamsFIN 181

RASMUSSEN, ERIK
94/5 Classic DP7
95/6 DonrussElite-WorldJrs 39
97/8 Leaf 153
97/8 PacificDynagon! Rookies
97/8 PacificParamount 23
97/8 Pinnacle 3
97/8 PinnacleBeAPlayer 217
97/8 Score 58
97/8 Score(BUF) 16
94/5 Select 152
97/8 SPAuthentic 173
98/9 SPx"Finite" 10, 142
97/8 UpperDeck 226
98/9 UDChoice 25
96/7 UpperDeck"Ice" 146
97/8 UpperDeckIce 57
97/8 Zenith 87, Z72,-RookRgn 3

RASTIO, JARMO
80/1 Mallasjuoma 124
78/9 SM-Liiga 170

RASTIO, TEPPO
66/7 Champion 13
65/6 Hellas 20
77-80 Sportscaster 50- 1199
71/2 WilliamsFIN 250

RATCHFORD, MIKE
52/3 AnonymousOHL 150

RATCHUK, PETER
98 BowmanCHL 99, SC14
95/6 Classic 68

RATELLE, JEAN
45-64 BeeHives(NYRx2)
64-67 BeeHives(NYR)
62 CeramicTiles
65/6 CocaCola
70/1 Colgate Stamp 25
71/2 Colgate Heads
70/1 DadsCookies
72-84 Dernière 79/80
70/1 EddieSargent 118
71/2 EddieSargent 114
72/3 EddieSargent 142
70/1 Esso Stamp
87 HallOfFame 249
72/3 Letraset 14
74/5 Loblaws
73/4 MacsMilk Disk
68/9 OPC/Topps 77
69/70 OPC/Topps 42, -Sticker
69/70 OPC-Stamp
70/1 OPC 181
70/1 OPC /T-Deckle 40, -Sticker
71/2 OPC/Topps 97
71/2 opcPoster 19
72/3 OPC 12, 48, 168, 250
72/3 OPC 280, 283, -TmCanada
72/3 Topps 62, 63, 50, 130, 175
73/4 OPC 141, Topps 73
74/5 OPC/Topps 145
75/6 OPC/Topps 243, 324
76/7 OPC/Topps 2, 80
76/7 OPC 381, T-Glossy 22
77/8 OPC/Topps 40, -Glossy 16
78/9 OPC/Topps 155
79/80 OPC/Topps 225
80/1 OPC/Topps 6
61/2 ShirriffCoin 98
68/9 ShirriffCoin NYR2
94/5 Parkie(64/5) 89
95/6 Parkie(66/7) 88
70/1 PostShooters
72 SemicSticker 214
71/2 TheTorontoSun
61/2 Topps 60
62/3 Topps 58
63/4 Topps 63
65/6 Topps 25
66/7 Topps 29, -USATest 29
67/8 Topps 31
91/2 Trends(72) 66, -Aut
93/4 Zellers
91/2 BOS/Legends

RATH, MARIUS
95 Globe 195
94 Semic 266
95 Semic 182
92 SemicSticker 43
93 SemicSticker 246
96 Wien 209

RATHBONE, JASON
92/3 Hampton

RATHJE, MIKE
92/3 Classic 3, LP3, -Aut.
93/4 Classic 145
92/3 ClassicFourSport 153,LP23
93/4 C4'Images 92
93/4 ClassicProspects 32
92/3 CSC 8
93/4 Donruss 314
94/5 Donruss 170
95/6 Donruss 305
93/4 FleerUltra 418, -Wave 15
94/5 FleerUltra 201
93/4 Leaf 419
94/5 Leaf 139
97/8 PacificRegime 180
94/5 PaniniSticker Y
95/6 PaniniSticker 285
93/4 Parkhurst 458
94/5 ParkieSE 160
93/4 Pinnacle 442
94/5 Pinnacle 363
95/6 Pinnacle 155
93/4 PowerPlay 437
93/4 Premier 427
93/4 Score 595
94/5 Score 261
90/1 SketchWHL 41
91/2 SketchWHL 330
95/6 SkyBoxEmotion 160
95/6 SkyBoxImpact 151
93/4 StadiumClub 322
94/5 StadiumClub 215
95/6 Topps 191
92/3 UpperDeck 589
93/4 UpperDeck 460, SP147
94/5 UpperDeck 168
92/3 S.J/PacificBell
96/7 S.J/PacificBellSheet
97/8 S.J/PacificBellSheet

RATUSHNY, DAN
91/2 CanadaNats
92 CanadaWinterOlympics 195
93/4 UpperDeck 245

RÄTY, TERO
72/3 WilliamsFIN 151

RAU, TORSTEN
94/5 DEL 180

RAUBAL, A.
95/6 DEL 110, 341

RAUBAL, MICHAEL
94/5 DEL

RAUBEL, TONI
94/5 DEL 124

RAUCH, MARTIN
91 SemicSticker 186
92 SemicSticker 203

RAUHALA, REINE
91/2 SemicElitserien 146
92/3 SemicElitserien 161
92/3 UpperDeck 598

RAUNIO, MATTI
95/6 Sisu 304

RAUNIO, TAPIO
65/6 Hellas 50

RAUSSE, ERROL
79/80 WSH

RAUTAKALLIO, PEKKA
72 Hellas 11
74 Hellas 14
70/1 Kuvajulkaisut 200
80/1 Mallasjuoma 218
80/1 O-Pee-Chee 356
81/2 O-Pee-Chee 50
81/2 opcSticker 223
82/3 opcSticker 218
76/7 opcWHA 116
72 Panda
79 PaniniSticker 164
80/1 Pepsi Cap
82/3 Post
74 SemicSticker 79
82 SemicSticker 161
91 SemicSticker 229
78/9 SM-Liiga 2, 223
77-80 Sportscaster 47- 1106
82 Valio
71/2 WilliamsFIN 90
72/3 WilliamsFIN 72, 255
73/4 WilliamsFIN 76, 255
79/80 ATL
79/80 ATL/B&W
80/1 CGY
81/2 CGY
75/6 Phoenix
76/7 Phoenix

RAUTAKORPI, JUKKA
95/6 Sisu 394

RAUTALAMMI, TAPIO
66/7 Champion 21
65/6 Hellas 73
70/1 Kuvajulkaisut 201

RAUTALIN, PENTTI
66/7 Champion 11
65/6 Hellas 27
70/1 Kuvajulkaisut 233
71/2 WilliamsFIN 251

RAUTEE, MATTI
70/1 Kuvajulkaisut 166
71/2 WilliamsFIN 235
72/3 WilliamsFIN 219
73/4 WilliamsFIN 295

RAUTEE, PEKKA
70/1 Kuvajulkaisut 167
78/9 SM-Liiga 207
71/2 WilliamsFIN 236
72/3 WilliamsFIN 220
73/4 WilliamsFIN 296

RAUTIAINEN, MATTI
80/1 Mallasjuoma 40
79 PaniniSticker 179
78/9 SM-Liiga 12, 105
72/3 WilliamsFIN 293
73/4 WilliamsFIN 230

RAUTIAINEN, TUOMO
70/1 Kuvajulkaisut 220
71/2 WilliamsFIN 141
72/3 WilliamsFIN 203
73/4 WilliamsFIN 166

RAUTIO, JANI
93/4 Jyvas-Hyva 167
93/4 Sisu 173

RAUTIO, KAI
96/7 DEL 53
92/3 Jyvas-Hyva 8
95/6 Sisu 72, 219

RAUTIO, MIKA
91/2 Jyvas-Hyva 31
95 Latkaliiga 6
94/5 Sisu 118, -Nolla 6
95/6 Sisu 284
95/6 SisuLimited 55

RAUTIO, SAMULI
93/4 Jyvas-Hyva 286
93/4 Sisu 78
94/5 Sisu 126

RAVENTOS, TONI
79 PaniniSticker 374

RANTI, ANTTI
66/7 Champion 100
65/6 Hellas 94
70/1 Kuvajulkaisut 287
71/2 WilliamsFIN 157
72/3 WilliamsFIN 110
73/4 WilliamsFIN 209

RAVLICH, MATT
64-67 BeeHives(CHI)
65/6 CocaCola
70/1 Colgate Stamp 69
70/1 DadsCookies
70/1 EddieSargent 71
70/1 Esso Stamp
68/9 O-Pee-Chee 152
69/70 O-Pee-Chee 161
70/1 OPC/Topps 32
94/5 Parkie(64/5) 35
95/6 Parkie(66/7) 22
68/9 ShirriffCoin CHI 12
65/6 Topps 115
66/7 Topps 58, -USATest 58

RAWSON, GEOFF
89/90 SketchOHL 129
90/1 SketchOHL 269
91/2 SketchOHL 215
89/90 NiagaraFalls

RAY, J.M.
84/5 Richelieu

RAY, ROB
97/8 KatchMedallion 17
98/9 Pacific 108
97/8 PacificRegime 21
92/3 Parkhurst 252
94/5 Parkhurst 30
94/5 Pinnacle 514
88/9 ProCards(Rochester)
89/90 ProCards(AHL) 256
90/1 ProCards 277
90/1 ProSet 419
91/2 ProSet 355
91/2 Score(CDN) 610
93/4 Score 433
96/7 Score 200
97/8 Score 242
97/8 Score(BUF) 14
90/1 UpperDeck 516
91/2 UpperDeck 349
97/8 UpperDeck 228
95/6 UDBeAPlayer 56
96/7 UDBlackDiamond 32
95/6 UDCollChoice 198
97/8 UDCollChoice 23
89/90 BUF/Campbell
90/1 BUF/BlueShield
90/1 BUF/Campbell
91/2 BUF/BlueShield
91/2 BUF/Campbell
92/3 BUF/BlueShield
92/3 BUF/Jubillee

RAY, VERN
93/4 ThunderBay

RAYMOND, ALAIN
90/1 ProCards 78
91/2 ProCards 38
82/3 NorthBay

RAYMOND, DONAT
83&87 HallOfFame 73
83 HHOF Postcard (E)
95/6 MTL/Forum 25Mar96

RAYMOND, ERIC
89/90 SketchMEM 55
90/1 SketchQMJHL 73
91/2 SketchQMJHL 241
93/4 Wheeling 8

RAYMOND, JACQUES
92/3 MTL/OPC 18

RAYMOND, PAUL
36-39 DiamondMatch (1)
43-47 ParadeSportive
34/5 SweetCaporal
33/4 WWGum (V357) 18

RAYMOND, RICHARD
90/1 SketchOHL 43
91/2 SketchOHL 4
91/2 Cornwall 3

RAYNER, CLAUDE (CHUCK / CHARLIE)
34-43 BeeHives(NYA)
45-64 BeeHives(NYR)
48-52 Exhibits (x2)
83&87 HallOfFame 163
83 HHOF Postcard (L)
96/7 HHOFLegends 80
51/2 Parkhurst 104
52/3 Parkhurst 22
53/4 Parkhurst 59
52 RoyalDesserts 2

READ, MEL
51/2 LavalDairy 65

READE, MARK
81/2 Kingston 4
82/3 Kingston 12

READY, RYAN
95/6 Slapshot 45

REARDON, KEN
34-43 BeeHives(MTL.C)
45-64 BeeHives(MTL)
48-52 Exhibits
83&87 HallOfFame 25
83 HHOF Postcard (B)
40/1 OPC (V301-2) 116
43-47 ParadeSportive
55/6 Parkhurst 64
59/60 Parkhurst 22
45-54 QuakerOats
92/3 MTL/OPC 42
95/6 MTL/Forum 25Nov95

REARDON, TERRY
34-43 BeeHives(MTL.C)

REASONER, MARTY
94/5 Classic DP8
95/6 DonrussElite-WorldJrs 40
94/5 Select 150
95/6 UpperDeck 566
96/7 UpperDeck"Ice" 150

REAUGH, DARYL
91/2 Bowman 19
91/2 OPC/Topps 391
88/9 ProCards(CapeBreton)
89/90 ProCards(AHL) 291
90/1 ProCards 184
91/2 ProCards 93
91/2 StadiumClub 326
90/1 UpperDeck 541
87/8 EDM
88/9 EDM/ActionMagazine 62
90/1 HFD/JuniorWhalers
84/5 Kamloops
85/6 NovaScotia 13

RÉAUME, MARC
52/3 AnonymousOHL 146
45-64 BeeHives(TOR)
63-5 ChexPhoto
70/1 Esso Stamp
70/1 OPC/Topps 119
55/6 Parkhurst 7
57/8 Parkhurst(TOR) 12
58/9 Parkhurst 20
59/60 Parkhurst 11
60/1 Parkhurst 25
63/4 Parkhurst 37, 96
93/4 Parkie(56/7) 114
60/1 ShirriffCoin 52
63/4 York 32
76 DET
70/1 VAN/RoyalBank

REAY, BILL
45-64 BeeHives(MTL)
48-52 Exhibits
51-54 LaPatrie 10FEB52
74/5 OPC/Topps 204
43-47 ParadeSportive
51/2 Parkhurst 13
52/3 Parkhurst 2
55/6 Parkhurst 66
57/8 Parkhurst (TOR) 25
58/9 Parkhurst 25
94/5 Parkie(64/5) 43
45-54 QuakerOats
63/4 Topps 22
64/5 Topps 38
65/6 Topps 54
66/7 Topps 53
70/1 CHI

REBEK, JEREMY
95/6 Slapshot 297
93/4 OwenSound

RECCHI, MARK
97/8 Aces 5 (Hearts)
90/1 Bowman 206
91/2 Bowman 83
92/3 Bowman 314
95/6 Bowman 51
93/4 Classic TC5, -Aut.
92/3 ClassicProspects 34, BC20
93/4 ClassicProspects LP24
94/5 ClassicImages PL6
93/4 Donruss 252
94/5 Donruss 121
95/6 Donruss 48
96/7 Donruss 27
97/8 Donruss 136
96/7 DonrussCanadianIce 23
97/8 D.Cdn.Ice 53, -National 18
95/6 DonrussElite 103
96/7 DonrussElite 26
97/8 DonrussPreferred 46
97/8 DonrussPriority 61
97/8 DonrussStudio 57
93/4 EASports 101
94/5 Flair 130
96/7 Flair 49
94/5 Fleer 106, -Headliner 9
96/7 Fleer 55
95/6 FleerMetal 77
92/3 FleerUltra 158, 250
93/4 FleerUltra 236, -RedLight 8
94/5 FleerUltra 158
95/6 FleerUltra 82
96/7 FleerUltra 88
95 Globe 98
93/4 HockeyWit 104
95/6 Hoyle'EAST K (Diamonds)
97/8 KatchMedallion 77
91/2 Kelloggs 9
97/8 KennerSLU
91/2 Kraft 2
94/5 Kraft-HockeyH
95/6 Kraft
93/4 Leaf 205
94/5 Leaf 89, -GoldL.Star 15
95/6 Leaf 65
96/7 Leaf 37
97/8 Leaf 127
94/5 LeafLimited 71
95/6 LeafLimited 54
96/7 LeafPreferd 115
97/8 Limited 52, 152
91/2 McDonalds McD4
93/4 McDonalds M cD22
95/6 McDonalds McD24
96/7 MetalUniverse 81
97/8 Omega 121
90/1 OPC/Topps 280
91/2 OPC/Topps 196, T-TL 5
92/3 O-Pee-Chee 373
98/9 Pacific 256
97/8 PacificCrown 298, -Slap 4A
97/8 PacificCrownRoyale 71
97/8 PacificDynagon 64-Tand 47
97/8 PacificInvincible 72
97/8 PacificParamount 97
98/9 PacificParamount 116
97/8 PacificRevolution 73
90/1 PaniniSticker 130, 341
91/2 PaniniSticker 280
92/3 PaniniSticker 185
93/4 PaniniSticker 46
94/5 PaniniSticker 39, DD
95/6 PaniniSticker 41
96/7 PaniniSticker 38
97/8 PaniniSticker 32
91/2 Parkhurst 134, 347
92/3 Parkhurst 130
93/4 Parkhurst 149
94/5 Parkhurst 165, 315
95/6 Parkhurst 383
94/5 Parkie seV28
91/2 Pinnacle 151, 360
92/3 Pinnacle 80
93/4 Pinnacle 50, Tm2001 30
93/4 Pinnacle-NiftyFifty 1, 13
94/5 Pinnacle 53
95/6 Pinnacle 24
96/7 Pinnacle 64
97/8 Pinnacle 104
96/7 PinnacleBeAPlayer 20
97/8 PinnacleBeeHive 23
97/8 PinnacleCertified 58
97/8 PinnacleInside 112
95/6 P.Zenith 8, -Gifted 14
95/6 Playoff 54
94/5 POG 180
95/6 POG 150
96/7 Post
93/4 PowerPlay 184,-PointLdr 12
93/4 Premier 230
94/5 Premier 90, -Finest(T) 21
88/9 ProCards(Muskegon)
95/6 ProMagnet 17
90/1 ProSet 239
91/2 ProSet 184, 313, CC8
92/3 ProSet 131
91/2 PSPlatinum 97
90/1 Score 186, -Hot 81
90/1 Score-YoungStar 35
91/2 Score(CDN) 145, (U.S) 145
91/2 Score -YoungStar 22
92/3 Score 180,-YgStr 7,-Shar18
93/4 Score 150, 442, (U.S) DD1
93/4 Score-Pinnacle AS 6
94/5 Score 50, NP7
95/6 Score 10, -Golden 18
96/7 Score 26
97/8 Score 130, -CheckIt 2
97/8 Score(MTL) 5
92/3 SeasonsPatch 41
94/5 Select 30
95/6 SelectCertified 10
94 Semic 101
91 SemicSticker 74
93 SemicSticker 205
95/6 SkyBoxEmotion 90
95/6 SkyBoxImpact 86
96/7 SkyBoxImpact 63
94/5 SP 62
95/6 SP 72
96/7 SP 85
97/8 SPAuthentic 79, I25
98/9 SPx"Finite" 43
95/6 Summit 26
96/7 Summit 17
95/6 SuperSticker 64
92/3 Topps 267, 410
95/6 Topps 165, HGC27, 9PL
94/5 T.Finest 109, -Division 5
95/6 ToppsFinest 119
96/7 ToppsNHLPicks 63
91/2 ToppsStadiumClub 256
92/3 ToppsStadiumClub 183
93/4 T.StadiumClub 136, -AllStar
95/6 ToppsStadiumClub 48
93/4 TSC-MembersOnly 34
94/5 TSC-MembersOnly 9
97/8 ToppsSticker 4
95/6 ToppsSuperSkills 58
90/1 UpperDeck 178, 487
91/2 UpperDeck 92, 346
92/3 UD 327,-Locker AS 11
93/4 UD 222, 300, 350, SP-117
94/5 UpperDeck 94, 441, SP58
95/6 UpperDeck 490, SE43
96/7 UpperDeck 87
97/8 UpperDeck 84
94/5 UDBeAPlayer R18, -Aut. 7
96/7 UDBlackDiamond 149
97/8 UDBlackDiamond 23
98/9 UDChoice 109, 231
95/6 UDCollChoice 108
96/7 UDCollChoice 135
97/8 UDCollChoice 133, SQ75
97/8 UpperDeckIce 23
96 Wien 96
97/8 Zenith 36, Z24
95/6 MTL
95/6 MTL/Molson
96-8 MTL
96/7 MTL/MolsonExport
90/1 PGH/Foodland 6
91/2 PGH/Elbys
91/2 PGH/Topps
92/3 PHA/JCPenney
92/3 PHA/UD 03OCT92
92/3 PHA/UD 04APR93
92/3 PHA/UD 09JAN93
92/3 PHA/UD 11MAR93
93/4 PHA 05OCT93
93/4 PHA 18DEC93
93/4 PHA/JCPenney
86/7 Kamloops
87/8 Kamloops

REDDEN, WADE
95 Autobilia 51
94/5 AutoPhonex 34, P5
94/5 Classic CP3
95/6 Classic 2, 100, AS2
95/6 ClassicFiveSport 124
94/5 C.Images 5, CE5, PD2
95/6 Donruss-CanadaJr 5
97/8 Donruss 48, -Line2 19
96/7 DonrussCanadianIce 121
97/8 DonrussCanadianIce 31
95/6 DonrussElite-WorldJrs 8
96/7 D.Elite 140, -Aspiration 24
97/8 DonrussElite 86
97/8 DonrussPreferred 97
97/8 DonrussPriority 131
97/8 DonrussStudio 97
96/7 Flair 118
96/7 FleerUltra 118, -Rookies 17
97/8 KatchMedallion 100
97/8 Leaf 113
96/7 LeafPreferred 130
94/5 LeafLimited-CanadaJrs 7
96/7 LeafLimited-Rookies 5
97/8 Limited 176, 189
97/8 McDonalds McD 6
96/7 MetalUniverse 190
98/9 Pacific 315
97/8 PacificCrown 276
97/8 PcfcDynagon! 85,-Tand 68
97/8 PacificInvincible 95
94/5 ParkieSE 256
94/5 Pinnacle 527
96/7 PinnacleBeAPlayer LTH9B
96/7 PinnacleZenith 128
94/5 Select 160
96/7 SelectCertified 100
94/5 Slapshot(MEM) 31
94/5 SP 139
95/6 SP 169
96/7 SP 185
97/8 SPAuthentic 108
98/9 SPx"Finite" 59
95 Tetrad-SR 5
95/6 Tetrad F5
95/6 TetradAutobilia51
95/6 Topps 1CJ
98/9 Topps 61, I5, B15
94/5 ToppsFinest 151
94/5 UpperDeck 504
96/7 UpperDeck 305, X35
97/8 UD 118, SG36, T20B
96/7 UDBlackDiamond 179
97/8 UDBlackDiamond 50
98/9 UDChoice 140
96/7 UDCollChoice 362
97/8 UDCollChoice 176, SQ6
96/7 UpperDeck"Ice" 97
97/8 UpperDeckIce 50
96/7 OTT/PizzaHut
97/8 OTT

REDDICK, ELDON
95/6 EdgeIce 154, TW5,-Quantm
90/1 O-Pee-Chee 452
88/9 opcSticker 146/17
89/90 opcSticker137/258
90/1 Panini(EDM) 18
87/8 PaniniSticker 357
89/90 ProCards(AHL) 143
91/2 ProCards 222
90/1 ProSet 445
86/7 WPG
87/8 WPG
88/9 WPG/Police
84/5 Brandon 20
94/5 LasVegas
95/6 LasVegas

REDDICK, STAN
93/4 Raleigh

REDDING, GEORGE
24/5 Champs (C144)
24/5 (V145-2) 28

REDDO, RONNY
95/6 DEL 416

REDDO, TONY
94/5 DEL 204

REDDON, LESLIE
94/5 Classic W15
97/8 UDCollChoice 278

REDMOND, CRAIG
85/6 OPC/Topps 121
88/9 EDM
88/9 EDM/ActionMagazine 161
84/5 L.A/Smokeys

REDMOND, DAN
89/90 ProCards(AHL) 82

REDMOND, DICK
71/2 EddieSargent 144
72/3 EddieSargent 46
72/3 Letraset 18
74/5 Loblaws
71/2 OPC 106
72/3 OPC 151, Topps 113
73/4 OPC/Topps 12
74/5 OPC/Topps 186
75/6 OPC/Topps 218
76/7 OPC/Topps 12
77/8 OPC/Topps 213
78/9 OPC/Topps 23
79/80 OPC/Topps 129
80/1 OPC/Topps 36
81/2 OPC 9, Topps(E) 73
71/2 TheTorontoSun

REDMOND, EDDIE
51/2 LavalDairy 72

REDMOND, KEITH
92/3 ClassicProspects 144
93/4 ClassicProspects 76
93/4 Donruss 448
94/5 Leaf 15
94/5 Parkhurst 110
91/2 SketchOHL 122
92/3 Phoenix
93/4 Phoenix

REDMOND, MICKEY
70/1 Colgate Stamp 44
70/1 DadsCookies
70/1 EddieSargent 106
71/2 EddieSargent 52
72/3 EddieSargent 74
70/1 Esso Stamp
74/5 Loblaws
73/4 MacsMilkDisk
73/4 Nabisco 22
74/5 Nabisco 16
68/9 O-Pee-Chee 64
70/1 OPC 175
71/2 OPC/Topps 102
72/3 OPC 99, Topps 155
72/3 OPC-TeamCanada
73/4 OPC 180, Topps 190
74/5 OPC/Topps 6, 84, 120
75/6 OPC/Topps 120
76/7 OPC/Topps 243
72 SemicSticker 233
68/9 ShirriffCoin MTL18
71/2 TheTorontoSun
91/2 Trends(72) 18, -Aut
90/1 DET/Caesars
96/7 DET/HockeytownPuck
67/8 MTL
67/8 MTL/IGA
68/9 MTL
69/70 MTL/ProStar
70/1 MTL
71 MTL/Pins

REDNICEK, JOSEF
94/5 DEL 393

REDPATH, OLIVER
24/5 Crescent Falcons 5

REDQUEST, GREG
75/6 Hamilton

REED, KELLY
90/1 SketchOHL 141
91/2 SketchOHL 368

REEDS, MARK
88/9 ProCards(Binghampton)
92/3 Peoria
93/4 Peoria

REEKIE, JOE
90/1 Bowman 125
91/2 Bowman 215
92/3 Bowman 137
93/4 Donruss 321
93/4 Leaf 234
94/5 Leaf 437
91/2 OPC/Topps 144
92/3 O-Pee-Chee 224
92/3 opcPremier 70
97/8 PacificRegime 212
91/2 PaniniSticker 252
91/2 Parkhurst 328
93/4 Parkhurst 460
91/2 Pinnacle 285
92/3 Pinnacle 382
93/4 Pinnacle 288
94/5 Pinnacle 351
97/8 PinnacleBeAPlayer 136
93/4 Premier 433
94/5 Premier 167
90/1 ProSet 487
91/2 ProSet 429
92/3 ProSet 179
91/2 Score(CDN) 123, (U.S) 123
92/3 Score 397, 510
93/4 Score 167
95/6 SkyBoxEmotion 191
92/3 Topps 184
91/2 ToppsStadiumClub 304
92/3 ToppsStadiumClub 264
93/4 ToppsStadiumClub 486
91/2 UpperDeck 483
92/3 UpperDeck 106
95/6 UpperDeckBeAPlayer 66
87/8 BUF/BlueShield
87/8 BUF/WonderBread
88/9 BUF/BlueShield
88/9 BUF/WonderBread
92/3 T.B./Sheraton
82/3 NorthBay

REESE, JEFF
92/3 Bowman 412
93/4 Donruss 443
96/7 Donruss 31
94/5 Leaf 59
90/1 OPC/Topps 349
91/2 OPC/Topps 81
92/3 O-Pee-Chee 77
90/1 Panini(TOR) 21
90/1 PaniniSticker 281
93/4 PaniniSticker 187
91/2 Parkhurst 250
92/3 Parkhurst 264
95/6 Parkhurst 460
94/5 ParkieSE 74
93/4 PowerPlay 355
93/4 Premier 302
94/5 Premier 27
88/9 ProCards(Newmarket)
90/1 ProSet 540
91/2 Score(CDN) 410
93/4 Score 394, 650
96/7 Score 213
92/3 Topps 385
92/3 ToppsStadiumClub 322
93/4 ToppsStadiumClub 22
92/3 UpperDeck 442
94/5 UpperDeck 476
92/3 CGY/IGA 9
93/4 HFD/Coke
90/1 TOR/P.L.A.Y. 26
95/6 WSH
85/6 London 27

REESOR, JASON
93/4 Slapshot(NiagaraFalls) 16

REEVE, JAMIE
82/3 Regina 3
83/4 Regina 3
93/4 Tacoma

REEVES, KYLE
90/1 SketchWHL 109
91/2 ProCards 39
92/3 Peoria
93/4 Toledo 26

REEVES, R.
24/5 Champs (C144)

REEVES, SHELLEY
88/9 ProCards(Peoria)

REGAN, LARRY
45-64 BeeHives(BOS), (TOR)
59/60 Parkhurst 17
60/1 Parkhurst 13
93/4 Parkie(56/7) 16
60/1 ShirriffCoin 16
52/3 StLawrence 103
57/8 Topps 6
58/9 Topps 10
60/1 York
57/8 BOS

REGEHR, ROBYN
98 BowmanCHL 137, A14
97/8 UpperDeck 406

REGIER, DARCY
81/2 Indianapolis 5
82/3 Indianapolis

REGNIER, CURT
90/1 SketchWHL 264
91/2 SketchWHL 253
90/1 PrinceAlbert
91/2 PrinceAlbert

REGNIER, RICHARD
80/1 Mallasjuoma 85

REGNIER, TOM
80/1 Mallasjuoma 84

REHNBERG, HENRIK
95/6 UDCollChoice 347
95/6 udElite 61

REIBEL, EARL
45-64 BeeHives(BOS)
53/4 Parkhurst 36
54/5 Parkhurst 37, 97
93/4 Parkie(56/7) 49, 147
54/5 Topps 52
57/8 Topps 45
58/9 Topps 57
54-67 TorontoStar V 5,n8

REICH, JEREMY
97/8 Bowman 143
96/7 UpperDeck 386

REICHAL, MARTIN
92/3 Classic 28
92/3 ClassicFourSport 177
94/5 DEL 378
95/6 DEL 439, 376
96/7 DEL 198
96 Wien 199

REICHEL, ROBERT
91/2 Bowman 267
92/3 Bowman 401
95/6 DEL 116
96/7 DEL 445
93/4 Donruss 51
94/5 Donruss 169
94/5 Flair 27
94/5 Fleer 34
92/3 FleerUltra 28
93/4 FleerUltra 164
94/5 FleerUltra 34
95/6 FleerUltra 28
96/7 FleerUltra 26
95 Globe 59
94/5 Kraft-Sharpshooter
93/4 Leaf 59
94/5 Leaf 243
94/5 LeafLimited 39
96/7 MetalUniverse 22

97/8 Omega 141
92/3 O-Pee-Chee 93
91/2 OPC/Topps 411
90/1 opcPremier 95
98/9 Pacific 286
97/8 PacificCrown 326
97/8 PacificCrownRoyale 80
97/8 PacificParamount 110
98/9 PacificParamount 147
97/8 PacificRevolution 83
91/2 PaniniSticker 63, 343
92/3 PaniniSticker 42, 301
93/4 PaniniSticker 180
94/5 PaniniSticker 154
97/8 PaniniSticker 77
95 PaniniWorlds 298
91/2 Parkhurst 21, -Promo
92/3 Parkhurst 26
93/4 Parkhurst 300
94/5 Parkhurst 34, V47
91/2 Pinnacle 56
92/3 Pinnacle 101
93/4 Pinnacle 35
94/5 Pinnacle 12, WE13
96/7 PinnacleBeAPlayer 81
94/5 POG 60
93/4 PowerPlay 41, -Rising 5
93/4 Premier 404
94/5 Premier 213, -Finest (T) 20
90/1 ProSet 595
91/2 ProSet 361
91/2 PSPlatinum 163
90/1 Score 30T, -Young 29
91/2 ScoreCDN 483, US 263
91/2 S-YoungStar 24
92/3 Score 106
93/4 Score 204, -International 6
94/5 Score NP17
97/8 Score 218
94/5 Select 138
91 SemicSticker 224
92 SemicSticker 142
93 SourPuckCaps 5
94 Semic 184
97/8 SPAuthentic 97
92/3 Topps 157
91/2 ToppsStadiumClub 393
92/3 ToppsStadiumClub 180
93/4 ToppsStadiumClub 198
90/1 UpperDeck 533
91/2 UpperDeck 223
92/3 UpperDeck 42
93/4 UpperDeck 313, HT4
94/5 UpperDeck 357, SP104
96/7 UpperDeck 228
97/8 UpperDeck 104
97/8 UDBlackDiamond 49
98/9 UDChoice 126
97/8 UDCollChoice 151
96 Wien 128
97/8 Zenith 70
90/1 CGY/McGavins
91/2 CGY/IGA
92/3 CGY/IGA 5

REICHENBERG, RONNY
89/90 SemicElitserien 139
90/1 SemicElitserien 217

REICHERT, CRAIG
91/2 SketchWHL 18
93/4 RedDeer

REID, BILL
92/3 MPSPhotoSJHL 126

REID, BRANDON
97/8 Halifax (1), (2)

REID, CHARLIE
23/4 PaulinsCandy 68

REID, DAVE
45-64 BeeHives(TOR)

REID, DAVE
91/2 Bowman 153
93/4 Donruss 403
96/7 FleerNHLPicks 176
93/4 FleerUltra 269
94/5 Leaf 501
90/1 OPC/Topps 290
91/2 OPC/Topps 423
89/90 opcSticker 170/30
97/8 PacificRegime 65
90/1 Panini(TOR) 22
91/2 PaniniSticker 104
96/7 PaniniSticker 11
97/8 PaniniSticker 99
92/3 Parkhurst 249
95/6 Parkhurst 281
94/5 ParkieSE 12
93/4 Pinnacle 191
94/5 Pinnacle 234
96/7 Pinnacle 182
96/7 PinnacleBeAPlayer 121
95/6 Playoff 122
96/7 Playoff 386
93/4 PowerPlay 290
93/4 Premier 67
94/5 Premier 51
90/1 ProSet 541
91/2 ProSet 229, 348
91/2 ProCards 66
90/1 ScoreTraded 109T
91/2 Score(CDN) 173, (U.S) 173
92/3 Score 380
93/4 Score 371
94/5 Score 80
96/7 Score 220
96/7 Summit 146
92/3 Topps 521
95/6 Topps 76
91/2 ToppsStadiumClub 78
93/4 ToppsStadiumClub 100
90/1 UpperDeck 364
91/2 UpperDeck 217, 531
97/8 UpperDeck 264
94/5 UDBAP R88, -Aut. 103
97/8 UDCollChoice 73
91/2 BOS/SportsAction
96/7 DAL/Southwest
88/9 TOR/P.L.A.Y. 24
90/1 TOR
85/6 Moncton 22
86/7 Moncton 24

REID, EDWARD
52/3 AnonymousOHL 4

REID, GRAYDEN
90/1 SketchOHL 293
91/2 SketchOHL 294
91/2 UltimateDP 53, -Aut 53

REID, JARRET
90/1 SketchMEM 12
90/1 SketchOHL 150, 171
91/2 SketchOHL 324
93/4 SSMarie 15

REID, JAY
82/3 MedicineHat

REID, JEFF
90/1 SketchOHL 44
91/2 SketchOHL 18
92/3 Cornwall 22
93/4 Knoxville
94/5 LasVegas

REID, JEREMY
51/2 Cleveland

REID, JOHN
88/9 ProCards(Saginaw)
91/2 ProCards 449
84/5 Belleville 20
89/90 Nashville

REID, KEVIN
90/1 SketchOHL 172
91/2 SketchOHL 355

REID, REG
24/5 (V145-2) 55

REID, SHAWN
94/5 Classic 60, AA9
95/6 Binghampton

REID, TOM
70/1 EddieSargent 85
71/2 EddieSargent 81
72/3 EddieSargent 99
70/1 Esso Stamp
74/5 Loblaws
70/1 OPC/Topps 43
71/2 O-Pee-Chee 21
73/4 OPC/Topps 109
74/5 OPC/Topps 52
75/6 OPC/Topps 277
76/7 OPC/Topps 123
77/8 O-Pee-Chee 306
71/2 TheTorontoSun
70/1 MIN
73/4 MIN

REIER, MIKE
90/1 SketchOHL 214
92/3 Dayton

REIERSON, DAVE
94/5 DEL 131
95/6 DEL 129
88/9 SaltLake 9

REIGLE, ED
51/2 Cleveland

REIJONEN, ESKO
66/7 Champion 124
65/6 Hellas 4

REIJONEN, TUOMAS
96/7 Sisu 131
95/6 UDCollChoice 336

REIL, JOACHIM
94/5 DEL 376
82 SemicSticker 107

REILLY, GARY
89/90 Lethbridge

REIMER, ANDREW
91/2 SketchWHL 142

REIMER, MARK
88/9 ProCards(Adirondack)
89/90 ProCards(AHL) 325
90/1 ProCards 311
91/2 ProCards 121
86/7 Saskatoon

REIMER, ROB
90/1 SketchWHL 150

REIMOLA, PEKKA
70/1 Kuvajulkaisut 354

REINDL, FRANZ
79 PaniniSticker 110
82 SemicSticker 118

REINER, PHIL
72 Hellas 54

REINHARD, FRANCIS
72 SemicSticker 139

REINHART, PAUL
90/1 Bowman 60
83/4 Esso
84/5 Kelloggs Disk
86/7 Kraft Sports 6
89/90 Kraft 44, -Sticker 1
80/1 OPC/Topps 157
81/2 O-Pee-Chee 36
82/3 O-Pee-Chee 56
83/4 O-Pee-Chee 91
84/5 O-Pee-Chee 235
85/6 OPC/Topps 48
86/7 O-Pee-Chee 205
87/8 OPC/Topps 143
89/90 OPC/Topps 148
90/1 OPC/Topps 293, T-TL 5
87/8 opcStars 34
81/2 opcSticker 224
82/3 opcSticker 219
83/4 opcSticker 264
85/6 opcSticker 209/76
87/8 opcSticker 39
89/90 opcSticker 65
87/8 PaniniSticker 206
90/1 PaniniSticker 293
80/1 Pepsi Cap
82/3 Post
90/1 ProSet 304
83/4 PuffySticker 5
90/1 Score 173
84/5 7ElevenDisk
85/6 7Eleven 3
83/4 SouhaitsRen.KeyChain
82/3 StaterMint
81/2 Topps 28
90/1 UpperDeck 110
83/4 Vachon 17
79/80 ATL
79/80 ATL/B&W
80/1 CGY
81/2 CGY
82/3 CGY
85/6 CGY/RedRooster
86/7 CGY/RedRooster
86/7 CGY/RedRooster
87/8 CGY/RedRooster
88/9 VAN/Mohawk
89/90 VAN

REIRDON, TODD
94/5 Raleigh

REIS, SHAWN
91/2 AirCanadaSJHL B14

REISE, LEO
45-64 BeeHives(DET)
45-64 BeeHives(NYR)
51/2 Parkhurst 69
52/3 Parkhurst 49
53/4 Parkhurst 65
54/5 Parkhurst 67
23/4 PaulinsCandy 36
52 RoyalDesserts 6
91/2 Ultimate(06) 28, -Aut 28
23/4 (V145-1) 33
76 DET

REISINGER, RALF
94/5 DEL 312
95/6 DEL 211

REITER, JODY
91/2 AirCanadaSJHL C4
92/3 MPSPhotoSJHL 97

REJA, DAN
95/6 Slapshot 50

REKOMAA, ESKO
65/6 Hellas 143

RELAS, TIMO
70/1 Kuvajulkaisut 186
71/2 WilliamsFIN 107

RENARD, JASON
91/2 SketchWHL 246
91/2 PrinceAlbert

RENARD, JOHN
93/4 Richmond 9

RENAUD, MARK
83/4 SouhaitsRen.KeyChain
82/3 HFD/JuniorWhalers

RENAUD, PHIL
51/2 LavalDairy 18
52/3 StLawrence 40

RENBERG, MIKAEL
95/6 Aces Q (Clubs)
95/6 Bowman 83
93/4 ClassicProspects 33
93/4 Donruss 255, -Elite U1
93/4 Donruss-RatedRookie 5
94/5 Donruss 236, -Dom. 4
95/6 Donruss 80,-Elite 3, -Dom 2
96/7 Donruss 125
97/8 Donruss 151
96/7 DonrussCanadianIce 77
97/8 DonrussCanadianIce 96
95/6 DonrussElite 94
96/7 DonrussElite 33
97/8 DonrussPreferred 68
97/8 DonrussPriority 75
97/8 DonrussStudio 49
94/5 ElitSet 199,-GuestSpecial 5
94/5 Flair 131
94/5 Fleer 158, -Franchise 7
96/7 Fleer 83
95/6 FleerMetal 113,-Int.Steel 17
96/7 FleerNHLPicks 46
93/4 FleerUltra 391, -Wave 16
94/5 FleerUltra 159, -AllRookie 8
94/5 FU-Global 8, -Power 7
95/6 FU 120, -Rsng 7,-HiSpd 16
96/7 FleerUltra 128
95 Globe 29, 259-61, 268
95/6 Hoyle'EAST 2 (Clubs)
97/8 KatchMedallion 138
96/7 KennerSLU
97/8 Kraft-WorldsBest
93/4 Leaf 323, -Freshamn 5
94/5 Leaf 54, -GoldL.Rookie 6
94/5 Leaf-GoldLeafStar 9
95/6 Leaf 128, -Gold 6
95/6 Leaf-Fire 12, -Freeze 3
96/7 Leaf 108
97/8 Leaf 38
94/5 LeafLimited 48
96/7 LeafLimited 79
97/8 Limited 64
96/7 LeafPreferred 58, -Steel 58
96/7 Maggers 115
94/5 McDonalds McD39
95/6 McDonalds McD22
96/7 MetalUniverse 115
97/8 Omega 213
98/9 Pacific 404
97/8 PacificCrown 59
97/8 PacificInvincible 104
97/8 PacificParamount 175
98/9 PacificParamount 219
97/8 PacificRevolution 130
94/5 PaniniSticker E
95/6 PaniniSticker 117
96/7 PaniniSticker 118
97/8 PaniniSticker 99
95 PaniniWorlds 288
93/4 Parkhurst 251, C12
94/5 Parkhurst 272, V78
95/6 Parkhurst 161, 243, -Aut.
95/6 PH-Crown(1) 7, -Int.AS 6
94/5 ParkieSE 129, ES3
93/4 Pinnacle 454, SR6
94/5 Pinnacle 79, 464, WE10
95/6 Pinnacle 41,-Roaring20s 12
96/7 Pinnacle 55
97/8 Pinnacle 144
96/7 PinnacleBeAPlayer 91
97/8 PinnacleInside 119
95/6 P.Zenith 42, -Gifted 8
96/7 P.Zenith 109, -Assailant 4
95/6 Playoff 183
94/5 POG 181
93/4 PowerPlay 408, -Global 6
93/4 PP-RookieStandouts 13
94/5 Premier 191, 294, 383
94/5 Premier-Finest(OPC) 16
95/6 ProMagnet 50
93/4 Score 602
94/5 Score 249
95/6 Score 35, -Lamplighter 8
96/7 Score 177
97/8 Score 138
94/5 Select 61
95/6 SelectCert. 31, -Double 12
94 Semic 67
90/1 SemicElitserien 241
91/2 SemicElitserien 171
92/3 SemicElitserien 190
93 SemicSticker 12
95/6 SkyBoxEmotion 134,-Ntn 5
95/6 SkyBoxImpact 128, 245
96/7 SkyBoxImpact 98
94/5 SP 83
95/6 SP 107
96/7 SP 115
95/6 Summit 44
96/7 Summit 73
95/6 SuperSkills 8
95/6 SuperSticker 91, DC18
96/7 TeamOut
95/6 Topps18,353,M12,YS3,1PL
98/9 Topps 16
95/6 ToppsFinest 120
96 ToppsFinestBronze 22
93/4 ToppsStadiumClub 269
94/5 TSC 145, -Dynasty 4
95/6 T.StadiumClub 110,G7,PS5
93/4 TSC-MembersOnly 47
92/3 UpperDeck 233
93/4 UpperDeck 486, SP118
94/5 UpperDeck 271, 561, SP59
95/6 UpperDeck 194, SE149
96/7 UpperDeck 307, P2, SS23B
97/8 UpperDeck 119, 361
94/5 UDBeAPlayer R74, -Aut. 24
96/7 UDBlackDiamond 49
98/9 UDChoice 197
95/6 UDCollChoice 222
96/7 UDCC 189, 326, C25
97/8 UDCollChoice 184, SQ9
95/6 udElite 235
96/7 UpperDeck"Ice" 46
96 Wien 58, 237, 240,-Aut,-Supr
97/8 Zenith 45, Z31
93/4 PHA 04NOV93
93/4 PHA/JCPenney
94/5 PHA
96/7 PHA/OceanSpray

RENÉ, PATRICE
90/1 SketchQMJHL 94

RENFREW, BRIAN
95/6 Dayton
92/3 WestMich.
93/4 WestMich.

RENNETTE, TYLER
97/8 Bowman 6, 131

RENNEY, TOM
92/3 CanadaNats
93/4 CanadaNats
90/1 SketchWHL 287
91/2 SketchAwards 17
91/2 SketchWHL 75

RENTZSCH, MARCO
94/5 DEL 63
95/6 DEL 56
96/7 DEL 253
92 SemicSticker 176

RENZ, ANDREAS
94/5 DEL 438
95/6 DEL 393
96/7 DEL 300

REPNEV, VLADIMIR
74/5 SovietStars 21

REPO, SEPPO
72 Hellas 12
70/1 Kuvajulkaisut 265
72 Panda
79 PaniniSticker 173
72 SemicSticker 86
74 SemicSticker 89
77-80 Sportscaster 74-1760
71/2 WilliamsFIN 74, 292
72/3 WilliamsFIN 73
73/4 WilliamsFIN 77, 210
76/7 Phoenix

REPP, CARL
89/90 ProCards(AHL) 8

RESCH, GLENN (CHICO)
84/5 Kelloggs Disk
74/5 Loblaws
74/5 OPC 353
75/6 OPC/Topps 145
76/7 OPC/T. 6, 250, T-Glossy 6
77/8 OPC/T. 6, 50, -Glossy 17
78/9 OPC/Topps105
79/80 OPC/Topps 6, 20
80/1 OPC/Topps 235
81/2 OPC 80, 83, 389, T.(W) 85
82/3 O-Pee-Chee 145, 146
83/4 O-Pee-Chee 236
84/5 OPC 119, Topps 89
85/6 OPC/T 36, L
86/7 OPC/Topps 105, 158
81/2 opcSticker 230
82/3 opcSticker 222
83/4 opcSticker 222, 223
84/5 opcSticker 68, 69
85/6 opcSticker 61/187
86/7 opcSticker234 /105
91/2 Pinnacle 393
82/3 Post
83/4 PuffySticker 12
84/5 7ElevenDisk
85/6 7Eleven 11
83/4 SouhaitsRen.KeyChain
90/1 UpperDeck 507
81/2 COL.R
83/4 N.J.
84/5 N.J.
85/6 N.J.
79/80 NYI
86/7 PHA

RESSMANN, GERALD
95 PaniniWorlds 273

RETTEW, SCOTT
84/5 Chicoutimi

RETTSCHLAG, ADAM
91/2 SketchWHL 299

RETTSCHLAG, GUS
92/3 BCJHL 3

RETZER, STEPHAN
94/5 DEL 255
95/6 DEL 253
96/7 DEL 142

REUNAMÄKI, MATTI
66/7 Champion 167
65/6 Hellas 98

REUSSE, WES
92/3 BCJHL 13

REUTA, VICTOR
93/4 Slapshot(Guelph) 15

REUTER, RENE
94/5 DEL 139
95/6 DEL 139

REVELL, DAN
82/3 Indianapolis
80/1 Oshawa 4
81/2 Oshawa 5

REVENBERG, JIM
89/90 ProCards(IHL) 180
90/1 ProCards 339

REY, PHIL
79 PaniniSticker 382

REYNOLDS, BOBBY
95/6 DEL 331
96/7 DEL 411
89/90 ProCards(AHL) 126
90/1 ProCards 152
91/2 ProCards 552
91/2 Baltimore 4
90/1 Newmarket

REYNOLDS, TODD
88/9 Brockville 21

REZANSOFF, JESSIE
96/7 Fredericton
95/6 SwiftCurrent

REZNICEK, JOSEF
96/7 DEL 411
91 SemicSticker 107

RHÉAUME, HERB
25-27 Anonymous 12

RHÉAUME, DOMINIC
90/1 SketchQMJHL 232
91/2 SketchQMJHL 128

RHÉAUME, MANON
92/3 Classic 59
93/4 Classic 112,146,149-50,N8
93/4 Classic MR1,-Promo,-Aut
94/5 Classic 120, W1,W21,CP15
94/5 Classic-Aut., -Preview
94/5 C'Assets 21,46,72,97,DC10
94/5 C'Asset-FonCard
92/3 C'FourSport 224, BC11
93/4 C4'Images 111, 147, -Aut.
93/4 C4'Images IP4, CC15
94/5 C4'Images 118, E5
92/3 C'Prospects 1-7, 100, -Aut.
92/3 C'Prospects BC10,LP1,PR2
93/4 C'Prosp 129, 239, 250,-Aut
94/5 C'Images 72, CE20
95/6 EdgeIce 155, -Promo [x3]
95/6 FutureLegends 38
97/8 GameOfHerLife
92/3 AtlantaKnights
93/4 AtlantaKnights
93/4 Knoxville
94/5 LasVegas

RHÉAUME, PASCAL
93/4 ClassicProspects 129, 145
97/8 Donruss 215
97/8 Limited 53, 66
97/8 Omega 197
98/9 Pacific 371
97/8 PinnacleBeAPlayer 227
91/2 SketchQMJHL 115

RHINEHART, DWAYNE
91/2 AirCanadaSJHL 40, C46

RHINES, BRAD
76/7 SanDiegoMariners

RHLICEK, JEFF
84/5 KelownaWings 15

RHODES, DAMIAN
92/3 ClassicProspects 111
93/4 ClassicProspects 34
95/6 Donruss 274
96/7 Donruss 156
97/8 Donruss 166
96/7 DonrussCanadianIce 16
97/8 DonrussCanadianIce 125
96/7 DonrussElite 113
97/8 DonrussElite 42
97/8 D.Preferred 37,-ColGurd 18
97/8 DonrussPriority 57
97/8 DonrussStudio 71
96/7 Flair 64
96/7 Fleer 76
93/4 FleerUltra 435
96/7 FleerUltra 119

97/8 KatchMedallion 101
93/4 Leaf 367
96/7 Leaf 47, -ShutDown 7
97/8 Leaf 45, -PipeDreams 11
96/7 LeafLimited 55
96/7 LeafPreferred 109,-Steel 50
97/8 Limited 57, 186, -fabric 60
96/7 McDonalds McD39, 'Masks
97/8 McDonalds McD30
96/7 MetalUniv. 107, -Armour19
97/8 Omega 157
98/9 Pacific 1
97/8 PacificCrown 146
97/8 PcfcDynagon! 86,-Tand 69
97/8 PacificParamount 128
98/9 PacificP 166, -GloveSide 13
97/8 PacificRevolution 94
96/7 PaniniSticker 47
93/4 Parkhurst 470
95/6 Parkhurst 200, 417
96/7 Pinnacle 150
97/8 Pinnacle 44
96/7 PinnacleBeAPlayer 202
97/8 PinnacleCertified 20
97/8 PinnacleInside 65
96/7 PinnacleZenith 53
93/4 PowerPlay 454
94/5 Premr 269,-Finest(OPC) 18
90/1 ProCards 167
91/2 ProCards 355
93/4 Score 604
96/7 Score 136, -NetWorth 17
97/8 Score 16, -NetWorth 7
96/7 SelectCert 28, -Freezers 15
96/7 SkyBoxImpact 90
95/6 SP 104
96/7 SP 110
96/7 Summit 21, -Crease 7
98/9 Topps 74
97/8 ToppsSticker 3
93/4 UpperDeck 364
94/5 UpperDeck 154
95/6 UpperDeck 337
96/7 UpperDeck 112
97/8 UpperDeck 322
96/7 UDBlackDiamond 71
98/9 UDChoice 139
96/7 UDCollChoice 186, 324
97/8 UDCollChoice 178
96/7 UpperDeck"Ice" 45
96/7 OTT/PizzaHut
97/8 OTT
93/4 TOR/Abalene
93/4 TOR/Kodak
94/5 TOR
90/1 MichiganTech
90/1 Newmarket
92/3 StJohns
93/4 StJohns

RHODIN, THOMAS
94/5 ElitSet 15
95/6 ElitSet 41
90/1 SemicElitserien 258
91/2 SemicElitserien 87
92/3 SemicElitserien 109
95/6 udElite 60

RIBBLE, JERRY
90/1 SketchOHL 45

RIBBLE, PAT
79/80 OPC/Topps 199
80/1 O-Pee-Chee 393
81/2 O-Pee-Chee 339
83/4 O-Pee-Chee 54
77/8 ATL
78/9 ATL/Coke
82/3 CGY
80/1 WSH

RIBEIRO, MIKE
98 BowmanCHL 85, 132, A38
97/8 UpperDeck 417

RICARD, ERIC
89/90 ProCards(AHL) 16
90/1 ProCards 434
91/2 ProCards 371

RICCI, MIKE
91/2 Bowman 246
92/3 Bowman 406
93/4 Donruss 280
94/5 Donruss 104
95/6 Donruss 120
96/7 Donruss 177
97/8 Donruss 180
96/7 DonrussCanadianIce 99
97/8 DonrussPriority 107
94/5 Flair 150
94/5 Fleer 182
92/3 FleerUltra 178, 389
93/4 FleerUltra 168
94/5 FleerUltra 178
95/6 FleerUltra 134
91/2 Gillette 32
94 HockeyWit 79
91/2 Kraft 52
93/4 Kraft'Recipe
93/4 KraftDinner
93/4 Leaf 23
94/5 Leaf 240
95/6 Leaf 156
96/7 Leaf 141
97/8 Leaf 65
96/7 LeafPreferred 78
97/8 Limited 58
96/7 Maggers 39
91/2 OPC/Topps 13, 194
92/3 O-Pee-Chee 329
90/1 opcPremier 96
91/2 opcPremier 23
92/3 opcPremier 91
98/9 Pacific 391
97/8 PacificCrown 109
91/2 PaniniSticker 231, 338
92/3 PaniniSticker 184
93/4 PaniniSticker 69
95/6 PaniniSticker 245
95 PaniniWorlds 14
91/2 Parkhurst 123
92/3 Parkhurst 146
93/4 Parkhurst 439
94/5 Parkhurst 186, V52
95/6 Parkhurst 318
91/2 Pinnacle 32
92/3 Pinnacle 314
93/4 Pinnacle 110, -Tm2000 20
94/5 Pinnacle 280
96/7 PinnacleBeAPlayer 116
95/6 PinnacleZenith 91
94/5 POG 198
95/6 POG 73
93/4 PowerPlay 202
93/4 Premier 62
94/5 Premier 548
95/6 ProMagnet 78
90/1 ProSet 631
91/2 ProSet 170
92/3 ProSet 133
91/2 PSPlatinum 85
90/1 Score 433, 60T
90/1 Score-YoungStar 39
91/2 Score(CDN) 28, (U.S) 28
91/2 Score-YoungStar 10
92/3 Score 84
93/4 Score 120
95/6 Score 234, -CheckIt 12
96/7 Score 106
97/8 Score(COL) 17
94/5 Select 114
95/6 SelectCert.-Double 6
95 Semic 92
89/90 SketchOHL 100, 183, 190
95/6 SkyBoxEmotion 41
95/6 SkyBoxImpact 40
94/5 SP 98
96/7 SP 37
97/8 SPAuthentic 136
91/2 StarPics 60
95/6 Summit 109
96/7 Summit 70
95/6 SuperSticker 30
92/3 Topps 86
91/2 ToppsStadiumClub 386
92/3 ToppsStadiumClub 408
93/4 ToppsStadiumClub 176
94/5 ToppsStadiumClub 3
95/6 ToppsStadiumClub 71
90/1 UpperDeck 351, 355
91/2 UpperDeck 143
92/3 UpperDeck 477, 627
93/4 UpperDeck 352, SP129
94/5 UpperDeck 284, SP64
95/6 UpperDeck 457
96/7 UD 36, 205, 295, P25
97/8 UpperDeck 48
93/4 UDBAP'Roots 10
94/5 UDBAP R49, R108,-Aut. 37
96/7 UDBlackDiamond 109
97/8 UDBlackDiamond 64
98/9 UDChoice 180
95/6 UDCollChoice 282
97/8 UDCollChoice 61
96/7 COL/PhotoPucks
90/1 PHA
91/2 PHA/JCPenney
94/5 QUE/BurgerKing
92/3 QUE/PetroCanada
97/8 S.J/PacificBellSheet (x2)

RICCIARDI, JEFF
89/90 SketchOHL 61
91/2 SketchOHL 304
93/4 Indianapolis

RICCIARDI, MIKE
90/1 SketchOHL 91

RICE, MURRAY
84/5 Brandon 10
85/6 Brandon 10

RICE, STEVEN
26 Dominion 27

RICE, STEVEN
92/3 ClassicProspects 150
93/4 Donruss 107
95/6 Donruss 81
95/6 EdgeIce C13
93/4 FleerUltra 181
94/5 FleerUltra 302
97/8 KatchMedallion 28
94/5 Leaf 324, 477
95/6 Leaf 198
90/1 opcPremier 97
97/8 Pacific-BestKept 18
97/8 PacificParamount 38
95/6 PaniniSticker 33
93/4 Parkhurst 72
95/6 Parkhurst 95
91/2 Pinnacle 334
94/5 Pinnacle 154
95/6 Pinnacle 166
96/7 PinnacleBeAPlayer 8
95/6 Playoff 156
95/6 POG 128
93/4 PowerPlay 86
91/2 ProCards 227
90/1 ProSet 626
90/1 Score 390
91/2 Score(CDN) 420
92/3 Score 545
95/6 Score167
97/8 Score 76
89/90 SketchMEM 38
89/90 SketchOHL 181, 187
90/1 SketchOHL 249
94/5 Slapshot-Promo
95/6 Topps 109
93/4 ToppsStadiumClub 446
94/5 ToppsStadiumClub 54
90/1 UpperDeck 462, 473
91/2 UpperDeck 440, 441
92/3 UpperDeck 98
93/4 UpperDeck 367
94/5 UpperDeck 294
95/6 UpperDeck 210
97/8 UpperDeck 32
94/5 UDBeAPlayer-Aut. 49
95/6 UDCollChoice 218
91/2 EDM/IGA
92/3 EDM
93/4 EDM 02JAN94
87/8 Kitchener 16
88/9 Kitchener 16
89/90 Kitchener 17
90/1 Kitchener 29

RICE, TYLER
91/2 AirCanadaSJHL 34

RICH, D.
95/6 DEL 325

RICHARD, HENRI
52/3 AnonymousOHL 139
71/2 Bazooka Panel 5
45-64 BeeHives(MTL)
64-67 BeeHives(MTL)
62 CeramicTiles
63-5 ChexPhoto
64/5 CokeCap MTL-16
65/6 CocaCola
65/6 CocaCola D/Z
70/1 Colgate Stamp 14
70/1 DadsCookies
72-84 Dernière 72/3, 73/4, 77/8
70/1 EddieSargent 98
71/2 EddieSargent 103
72/3 EddieSargent 119
62/3 ElProductoDisk
70/1 Esso Stamp
71/2 FritoLay
83&87 HallOfFame 91
83 HHOF Postcard (G)
93/4 HockeyWit 52
95/6 KennerSLU-Legends(CDN)
91/2 Kraft 88
51-54 LaPatrie 18Jan53
72/3 Letraset 15
74/5 Loblaws
68/9 O-Pee-Chee 165, Topps 64
68/9 OPC-Puck 21
69/70 OPC 163, Topps 11
69/70 OPC-Sticker
70/1 OPC 176,OPC/T-Deckle 24
71/2 OPC/Topps 120
71/2 OPC/Topps-Booklet 6
72/3 OPC 251
73/4 OPC/Topps 87
74/5 OPC/Topps 243, OPC 321
57/8 Parkhurst (MTL) 4
58/9 Parkhurst 2
59/60 Parkhurst 39
60/1 Parkhurst 47, 57
61/2 Parkhurst 43
62/3 Parkhurst 38
63/4 Parkhurst 23, 82
92/3 Parkhurst PR28
93/4 Parkhurst D18
93/4 Parkie(56/7) 66
94/5 Parkie(64/5) 67
95/6 Parkie(66/7) 58, 133
66/7 Post'Large
67 Post FlipBook
67/8 Post
68/9 Post Marble
72 SemicSticker 198
60/1 ShirriffCoin 34
61/2 ShirriffCoin 110
62/3 ShirriffCoin 41
68/9 ShirriffCoin MTL15
94/5 SigRookies CF5
81/2 TCMA 7
63/4 TheTorontoStar
64/5 TheTorontoStar
71/2 TheTorontoSun
54-67 TorontoStar V6, V10
56-66 TorontoStar 578, 58/9
56-66 TorontoStar 62/3, 63/4
56-66 TorontoStar 65/6, 5Sep-60
64/5 Topps 48
65/6 Topps 71
66/7 Topps 8, -USATest 8
67/8 Topps 72
91/2 Ultimate(O6) 14,81,95,-Aut.
92/3 UpperDeck-LockerAS 47
60/1 York
60/1 YorkGlasses
61/2 York 18
62/3 YorkTransfer 10
63/4 York 19
94/5 Zellers
67/8 MTL
67/8 MTL/IGA
68/9 MTL
69/70 MTL/ProStar
70/1 MTL
71 MTL/Pins
71/2 MTL
72/3 MTL
73/4 MTL
74/5 MTL
82/3 MTL
92/3 MTL/OPC 3, 61
95/6 MTL/Forum 28Jan96

RICHARD, JACQUES
72-84 Dernière 81/2
74/5 Loblaws
72/3 OPC 279
73/4 OPC/Topps 169
74/5 OPC/Topps 14, 139
75/6 OPC/Topps 117
76/7 OPC/Topps 8
77/8 OPC 366
81/2 OPC 268, 285, Topps 29
82/3 O-Pee-Chee 290
81/2 opcSticker 71
80/1 Pepsi Cap
82/3 Post
72/3 ATL
80/1 QUE
81/2 QUE
82/3 QUE
83/4 QUE

RICHARD, JASON
93/4 Johnstown 17

RICHARD, J.M.
88/9 ProCards(Halifax)
89/90 ProCards(AHL) 173
90/1 ProCards 457
91/2 ProCards 243
84/5 Chicoutimi
89/90 Halifax
90/1 Halifax
93/4 LasVegas
94/5 LasVegas
95/6 LasVegas

RICHARD, MAURICE (ROCKET)
34-43 BeeHives(MTL.C)
45-64 BeeHives(MTL)
64-67 BeeHives(MTL)
72-84 Dernière 77/8, 80/1
48-52 Exhibits (x5)
83&87 HallOfFame 1
83 HHOF Postcard (A)
92/3 HHOFLegends 3
93/4 HockeyWit 16
96/7 KennerLegend
97/8 KennerSLU-Legends
91/2 Kraft 6, 65
51/2 LaPatrie 2-Dec
27-32 LaPresse 16Feb46
43-47 ParadeSportive
51/2 Parkhurst 4
52/3 Parkhurst 1
53/4 Parkhurst 24, 30
54/5 Parkhurst 7
55/6 Parkhurst 37, 72, 73
57/8 Parkhurst (MTL) 5
58/9 Parkhurst 38
59/60 Parkhurst 2
60/1 Parkhurst 45
93/4 Parkhurst DPR5, PR36
93/4 Parkie PR48, PR63, D16
93/4 Parkie(56/7) 65, 139, A2
94/5 Parkie(64/5)-Great 5
91/2 ProSet 337
97/8 PinnacleBeeHive 61
45-54 QuakerOats
92/3 S-Autograph, -Rocket
92/3 Score(CND) 548, 549
94/5 SR-CoolFive CF4
56-66 TorontoStar 57/8, 58/9
60/1 WonderBread 4
92/3 Zellers
92/3 MTL/OPC 6, 29
95/6 MTL/Forum 16Dec95

RICHARD, MIKE
88/9 ProCards(Baltimore)
89/90 ProCards(AHL) 86

RICHARD, RODNEY
98 BowmanCHL 13

RICHARD, SERGE
84/5 Richelieu

RICHARDS, BRAD
98 BowmanCHL 116
97/8 UpperDeck 418

RICHARDS, MARK
95/6 Tallahassee 17, 21

RICHARDS, STEVE
95/6 Hampton HRA-15

RICHARDS, TODD
95/6 EdgeIce 175
89/90 ProCards(AHL) 183
92/3 Topps 79
91/2 UpperDeck 430
93/4 LasVegas
94/5 LasVegas

RICHARDS, TRAVIS
93/4 Classic 74
94/5 Classic-Autograph
94/5 ClassicImages 92
93/4 FleerUltra 493
93/4 PowerPlay 513
93/4 Premier-TeamUSA 7
93/4 T.StadiumClub-TmUSA 18
91/2 Minnesota
92/3 Minnesota

RICHARDSON, BILL
52/3 LavalDairy 113
52/3 StLawrence 68

RICHARDSON, DAVE
94/5 Parkie(64/5) 94

RICHARDSON, GEORGE
83&87 HallOfFame 85
83 HHOF Postcard (F)

RICHARDSON, GLENN
75/6 Hamilton

RICHARDSON, KEN
91/2 SketchWHL 230
93/4 RedDeer

RICHARDSON, LUKE
91/2 Bowman 167
92/3 Bowman 255
93/4 Donruss 115
92/3 FleerUltra 297
93/4 FleerUltra 318
88/9 O-Pee-Chee 245
90/1 O-Pee-Chee 428
91/2 OPC/Topps 123, 351
92/3 O-Pee-Chee 171
91/2 opcPremier 46
88/9 opcSticker 173/42
97/8 PacificRegime 82
90/1 Panini(TOR) 23
88/9 PaniniSticker 119
89/90 PaniniSticker 142
94/5 PaniniSticker 206
95 PaniniWorlds 5
91/2 Parkhurst 274
91/2 Pinnacle 212
92/3 Pinnacle 41, 235
93/4 Pinnacle 139
94/5 Pinnacle 431
95/6 P.Zenith-GiftedGrinder 1
94/5 POG 338
94/5 Premier 466
90/1 ProSet 289
91/2 ProSet 387
90/1 Score 236
91/2 Score(CDN) 139, 620
91/2 Score(U.S) 139, 70T
92/3 Score 62
93/4 Score 252
97/8 Score(PHA) 10
92/3 Topps 409
95/6 Topps 108
98/9 Topps 159
91/2 ToppsStadiumClub 172
92/3 ToppsStadiumClub 456
90/1 UpperDeck 362
91/2 UpperDeck 418, 522
94/5 UpperDeck 215
96/7 UpperDeck 61
97/8 UpperDeck 330
95/6 UDBeAPlayer 70
97/8 UDCollChoice 96
91/2 EDM/IGA
92/3 EDM
92/3 EDM/IGA 19
93/4 EDM 01DEC93
96/7 EDM
87/8 TOR
87/8 TOR/P.L.A.Y. 27
90/1 TOR

RICHARDSON, TERRY
79/80 O-Pee-Chee 377

RICHER, ANTOINE
95 Globe 207
95 PaniniWorlds 114
94 Semic 224
95 Semic 200
92 SemicSticker 237
93 SemicSticker 266
96 Wien 187

RICHER, STÉPHANE J.G.
95/6 DEL 270
96/7 DEL 165
93/4 Premier 327
88/9 ProCards(Sherbrooke)
89/90 ProCards'AHL 195
90/1 ProCards 354
91/2 ProCards 86
93/4 ToppsStadiumClub 347

RICHER, STÉPHANE J.J.
90/1 Bowman 45, HT11
91/2 Bowman 330
92/3 Bowman 46
93/4 Donruss 190
94/5 Donruss 79
95/6 Donruss 178
96/7 Donruss 108
96/7 DonrussCanadianIce 98
97/8 DonrussCanadianIce 104
96/7 DonrussElite 36
92/3 Durivage 18
93/4 Durivage 48
93/4 EASports 76
94/5 Flair 97
94/5 Fleer 116, -Slapshot 7
95/6 FleerMetal 86
96/7 FleerNHLPicks 128
92/3 FleerUltra 117
93/4 FleerUltra 152
94/5 FleerUltra 122
95/6 FleerUltra 92, 195
96/7 FleerUltra 89
88/9 FritoLay
95/6 Hoyle'EAST 3 (Clubs)
96 KennerSLU (U.S)
86/7 Kraft Sports 35
89/90 Kraft 24
90/1 Kraft 46, 89
91/2 Kraft 21
95/6 Kraft
93/4 Leaf 138
94/5 Leaf 24
95/6 Leaf 91
96/7 Leaf 18
95/6 LeafLimited 68
96/7 LeafPreferred 76
96/7 MetalUniverse 82
87/8 O-Pee-Chee 233
88/9 OPC/Topps 5
89/90 OPC/Topps 153
90/1 OPC/Topps 186
91/2 OPC/Topps 298, 369
92/3 O-Pee-Chee 76
90/1 opcPremier 98
91/2 opcPremier 113
92/3 opcPremier-Star 18
88/9 opcStars 31
88/9 opcSticker 40
89/90 opcSticker 51
98/9 Pacific 405
97/8 PacificCrown 44
97/8 PCC-Slap 4C, -TeamCL 13
97/8 PacificCrownRoyale 72
97/8 PacificDynagon! 65
97/8 PcfcD-BstKpt 18,-Tand 48
97/8 PacificInvincible 73
97/8 PacificParamount 98
98/9 PacificParamount 220
97/8 PacificRegime 105
90/1 Panini(MTL) 18
87/8 PaniniSticker 65
88/9 PaniniSticker 260
89/90 PaniniSticker 239
90/1 PaniniSticker 53
91/2 PaniniSticker 193
92/3 PaniniSticker 173
93/4 PaniniSticker 37
94/5 PaniniSticker 32
95/6 PaniniSticker 85
91/2 Parkhurst 100
92/3 Parkhurst 91
93/4 Parkhurst 113
94/5 Parkhurst V50
95/6 Parkhurst 118
94/5 ParkieSE 100
91/2 Pinnacle 14
92/3 Pinnacle 361
93/4 Pinnacle 143
94/5 Pinnacle 166, BR14
95/6 Pinnacle 35
96/7 Pinnacle 33
97/8 Pinnacle 160

96/7 PinnacleBeAPlayer 50
95/6 PinnacleZenith 39
96/7 PinnacleZenith 42
95/6 Playoff 60
96/7 Playoff 342
94/5 POG 148
95/6 POG 163
93/4 PowerPlay 141
93/4 Premier 158
94/5 Premier 105
95/6 ProMagnet 34
90/1 ProSet 156, 370
91/2 ProSet 122, 420
92/3 ProSet 93
91/2 PSPlatinum 67
90/1 Score 75, -HotCards 38
91/2 Score(CDN) 581
91/2 Score(U.S) 234, 31T
92/3 Score 140
93/4 Score 34
95/6 Score 130, -Golden 14
96/7 Score 232
97/8 Score 213
97/8 Score(MTL) 8
94/5 Select 108
95/6 SelectCertified 39
95/6 SkyBoxEmotion 101
95/6 SkyBoxImpact 96
94/5 SP 64
95/6 SP 85
96/7 SP 83
98/9 SPx"Finite" 78
95/6 Summit 52
96/7 Summit 99
95/6 SuperSticker 69
96/7 TeamOut
90/1 Topps TeamLeader 4
92/3 Topps 160
95/6 Topps 231, HGC28
94/5 T.Finest 94, -Division 10
91/2 ToppsStadiumClub 86
92/3 ToppsStadiumClub 9
93/4 ToppsStadiumClub 61
95/6 T.StadiumClub 176, PS10
95/6 ToppsSuperSkills 41
90/1 UpperDeck 276
91/2 UpperDeck 244, 536
92/3 UpperDeck 56
93/4 UpperDeck 403, SP87
94/5 UpperDeck 388, SP44
95/6 UpperDeck 426, SE47
96/7 UpperDeck 94
98/9 UDChoice 193
95/6 UDCollChoice 250
97/8 UDCollChoice 138
85/6 MTL
85/6? MTL/ProvigoPlacemats
85/6 MTL/ProvigoStickers
86/7 MTL
87/8 MTL
87/8 MTL/Stickers 51, 52, 54
88/9 MTL
89/90 MTL
89/90 MTL/Figurine
89/90 MTL/Kraft
90/1 MTL
96/7 MTL
84/5 Chicoutimi

RICHEY, STEVE
81/2 Kingston 22
82/3 Kingston 23

RICHISON, GRANT
89/90 ProCards(AHL) 46
90/1 ProCards 255
91/2 ProCards 244
90/1 Moncton

RICHMOND, STEVE
86/7 O-Pee-Chee 208
88/9 ProCards(NewHaven)

RICHTER, BARRY
93/4 Classic 75
94/5 Classic-Autograph
93/4 C4'Images 24
93/4 FleerUltra 494
95/6 FutureLegends 39
95 PaniniWorlds 217
93/4 PowerPlay 514
93/4 Premier-TeamUSA 18
96/7 ToppsNHLPicks 177
93/4 T.StadiumClub-TmUSA 19
96/7 UpperDeck 219
94/5 Binghampton
95/6 Binghampton

RICHTER, DAVE
87/8 O-Pee-Chee 261
87/8 opcSticker 19 0/51
87/8 PaniniSticker 344
90/1 ProCards 522
83/4 MIN
84/5 MIN
87/8 STL
88/9 STL
88/9 STL/Kodak
86/7 VAN
87/8 VAN/Shell

RICHTER, MIKE
90/1 Bowman 218
91/2 Bowman 70
92/3 Bowman 238, 354
95/6 Bowman 14
97/8 CorinthianHeadliner
93/4 Donruss 223
94/5 Donruss 165, -Masked 8
95/6 Donruss 59
96/7 Donruss 184
97/8 Donruss 124
96/7 DonrussCanadianIce 26
97/8 D.Cdn.Ice 107,-Scrap 15
96/7 DonrussElite 96, -Painted 2
97/8 DonrussElite 56
97/8 D.Preferred 124,-ColGrd 15
97/8 D.Priority 143,-PostGen 5
97/8 DonrussStudio 59,-Portr 33
93/4 EASports 90
97/8 EssoOlympic 33
94/5 Flair 117
96/7 Flair 62, -HotGloves 9
94/5 Fleer 139, -Netminder 8
95/6 FleerMetal 98
96/7 fleerPicks 84, -DreamLine 2
92/3 FleerUltra 142
93/4 FleerUltra 228
94/5 FleerUltra 143, -PadMen 5
95/6 FleerUltra 276
96/7 FleerUltra 110
91/2 Gillette 39
95 Globe 100
93/4 HockeyWit 1
95/6 Hoyle'EAST 4 (Clubs)
97/8 KatchMedallion 95
94 KennerSLU
97/8 KennerSLU -1on1
91/2 Kraft 88
94/5 Kraft
95/6 Kraft-Crease
96/7 Kraft-TrophyProspects
93/4 Leaf 185
94/5 Leaf 18, -Crease 8, -Star 3
95/6 Leaf 42
96/7 Leaf 178, -ShutDown 11
97/8 Leaf 70, -PipeDreams 8
94/5 LeafLimited 17
96/7 LeafLimited 41
96/7 LeafPreferred 55, -Steel 46
96/7 LP-MaskedMarauder 11
97/8 Limited 32, 134, -fabric 11
96/7 Maggers 101
92/3 McDonalds McD-25
94/5 McDonalds
96/7 McD'Masks
97/8 McDonalds McD29
96/7 MetalUniv. 100, -Armour 10
97/8 Omega 148, -NoScorZn 8
90/1 OPC/Topps 330
91/2 OPC/Topps 11, 91
92/3 O-Pee-Chee 259
91/2 opcPremier 78
98/9 Pacific 298
97/8 PacificCrown 197,-InThe 13
97/8 PacificCrownRoyale 87
97/8 PCR-FreezeOut 12
97/8 PacificDynagon! 82
97/8 PcfcD-Stone 14,-Tandm 70
97/8 PacificInvincible 90
97/8 PcfcParamnt 119,-Glove 13
98/9 PcfcParamnt 156,-Glove 12
97/8 PcfcRevolution 90,-Retr 13
90/1 PaniniSticker 98, 345
91/2 PaniniSticker 290
92/3 PaniniSticker 231
93/4 PaniniSticker 99
94/5 PaniniSticker 90
95/6 PaniniSticker 112
96/7 PaniniSticker 103
95 PaniniWorlds 212
91/2 Parkhurst 117
92/3 Parkhurst 112
93/4 Parkhurst 129
94/5 Parkhurst V5
95/6 Parkie 138, PP31, -Goal 12
94/5 ParkieSE 110
91/2 Pinnacle 164, 384
92/3 Pinnacle 75, 270, -TeamP 1
93/4 Pinnacle 242
94/5 Pinnacle 10, GT2, TP2
95/6 Pinnacle 47
96/7 Pinnacle 112, -Mask 2
97/8 Pinnacle 55, -BigCans
97/8 Pinnacle-GoalTin 7,-Mask 2
96/7 P.BeAPlayer-Stacking 10
97/8 P.BAP 37,-Stackng/Pad 10
97/8 PinnacleBeeHive 41
97/8 PinnacleCertified 13
96/7 PinnacleFANtasy 10
97/8 PinnacleInside 81, -Can 5
97/8 P.Inside-Stop 5, -Track 26
97/8 PinnacleMask
97/8 PinnacleUncut
95/6 PinnacleZenith 53
96/7 P.Zenith 66, -Champion 14
95/6 Playoff 69
94/5 POG 288, 337
95/6 POG 189
93/4 PowerPlay 165
93/4 Premier 135
94/5 Premier 70, 155, 314
89/90 ProCards(IHL) 48
95/6 ProMagnet 99, IC04
90/1 ProSet 398, 627
91/2 ProSet 161
92/3 ProSet 116
91/2 PSPlatinum 83, 279
96/7 SB'7Eleven
90/1 Score 74, -YoungStar 27
91/2 Score(CDN) 120, (U.S) 120
91/2 Score-YoungStar 2
92/3 Score 5, -Youngr 9, -USA 6
93/4 Score 99
94/5 Score 130
95/6 Score 140, 321
96/7 Score 150,-Sddn 9,-Supr 12
97/8 Score 11, -NetWorth 6
97/8 Score(NYR) 16
92/3 SeasonsPatch 29
94/5 Select 133, FL7
95/6 SelectCertified 73
96/7 SelectCert. 39,-Freezers 11
94 Semic 107
95 Semic 218
91 SemicSticker 128
92 SemicSticker 148
93 SemicSticker 170
95/6 SkyBoEmotion 117
95/6 SkyBoxImpact 112
96/7 SkyBoxImpact 83
94/5 SP 75
95/6 SP 95
96/7 SP 100, HC27,-SPxForce 3
97/8 SPAuthentic 101
96/7 SPx 28
97/8 SPx 31
95/6 Summit 115, -InThe 11
96/7 Summit 145, -InThe 2
95/6 SuperSticker 83
96/7 TeamOut
92/3 Topps 367
95/6 Topps 212, HGA10
98/9 Topps 200
94/5 ToppsFinest 86, -Division 6
94/5 TF-BowmansBest(Blue) 13
95/6 ToppsFinest 169
96/7 ToppsNHLPicks ID13
91/2 ToppsStadiumClub 92
92/3 T.StadiumClub 242, 266
93/4 ToppsStadiumClub 64
94/5 ToppsStadiumClub 181
95/6 ToppsStadiumClub 49, N4
94 TSC-MembersOnly 45
97/8 ToppsSticker 5
95/6 ToppsSuperSkills 74
90/1 UpperDeck 32
91/2 UD 34, 175, 610, 634
92/3 UpperDeck 145
93/4 UpperDeck 42
94/5 UpperDeck 78, H30, SP52
95/6 UpperDeck 438, H12, SE58
96/7 UpperDeck 109
97/8 UD 107, GJ11, SG53, T10C
95/6 UDBeAPlayer 191
96/7 UDBlackDiamond 35
97/8 UDBlackDiamond 4
98/9 UDChoice 135, 246
95/6 UDCollChoice 306
96/7 UDCollChoice 167, 325
97/8 UDCollChoice 161, SQ30
96/7 UpperDeck"Ice" 41
97/8 UpperDeckIce 3
96 Wien 158
97/8 Zenith 18, Z63
89/90 NYR/MarineMidland

RICHTER, PAVEL
94/5 APS 299
79 PaniniSticker 88

RIDDERWALL, ROLF
94 Semic 53
89/90 SemicElitserien 50
91/2 SemicElitserien 320, 336
92/3 SemicElitserien 26
89 SemicSticker 4
91 SemicSticker 28

RIDEOUT, SCOTT
93/4 Portland

RIDLEY, CURT
76/7 OPC/Topps 197
77/8 OPC 395
78/9 O-Pee-Chee 302
80/1 TOR
76/7 VAN/RoyalBank
77/8 VAN/GingerAle
77/8 VAN/RoyalBank
79/80 VAN

RIDLEY, MIKE
90/1 Bowman 77
91/2 Bowman 308
92/3 Bowman 360
93/4 Donruss 375
95/6 Donruss 250
96/7 Donruss 141
93/4 EASports 153
94/5 Flair 185
94/5 Fleer 219
95/6 FleerMetal 155
92/3 FleerUltra 238
93/4 FleerUltra 148
94/5 FleerUltra 378
95/6 FleerUltra 163, 318
93/4 Leaf 102
94/5 Leaf 374
95/6 Leaf 212
86/7 OPC/Topps 66, L
87/8 OPC/Topps 8
88/9 OPC/Topps 104
89/90 OPC/Topps 165, B
90/1 OPC/Topps 327
91/2 OPC/Topps 245
92/3 O-Pee-Chee 305
86/7 opcSticker 221, 131/117
87/8 opcSticker234/101
88/9 opcSticker 74/205
89/90 opcSticker 81, 164/26
97/8 PacificCrown 206
87/8 PaniniSticker 181
88/9 PaniniSticker 374
89/90 PaniniSticker 339
90/1 PaniniSticker 163
91/2 PaniniSticker 199
92/3 PaniniSticker 162
93/4 PaniniSticker 25
94/5 PaniniSticker 23
95/6 PaniniSticker 289
97/8 PaniniSticker 243
91/2 Parkhurst 192
92/3 Parkhurst 200
93/4 Parkhurst 218
94/5 Parkhurst 250
95/6 Parkhurst 214
94/5 ParkieSE 178
91/2 Pinnacle 94
92/3 Pinnacle 170
93/4 Pinnacle 135
94/5 Pinnacle 384
96/7 Pinnacle 172
95/6 Playoff 319
94/5 POG 236
95/6 POG 270
93/4 PowerPlay 266
93/4 Premier 78
94/5 Premier 301
90/1 ProSet 320
91/2 ProSet 254
91/2 PSPlatinum 128
90/1 Score 33
91/2 ScoreCDN 503, US 283
92/3 Score 187,-Sharpshooter 6
93/4 Score 197
94/5 Score 199
95/6 Score 236
96/7 Score 184
94/5 Select 19
95/6 SkyBoxEmotion 184
95/6 SkyBoxImpact 173
94/5 SP 118
92/3 Topps 236
91/2 ToppsStadiumClub 68
92/3 ToppsStadiumClub 200
93/4 ToppsStadiumClub 123
94/5 ToppsStadiumClub 105
95/6 ToppsStadiumClub 51
90/1 UpperDeck 97
91/2 UpperDeck 112
92/3 UpperDeck 173
93/4 UpperDeck 341, SP173
94/5 UpperDeck 177, SP169
95/6 UpperDeck 75
95/6 UDBeAPlayer 63
96/7 UDBlackDiamond 125
95/6 UDCollChoice 48
97/8 UDCollChoice 264
96/7 VAN
96/7 VAN/IGA
86/7 WSH/Kodak
87/8 WSH
87/8 WSH/Kodak
88/9 WSH
88/9 WSH/Smokey
89/90 WSH
89/90 WSH/Kodak
90/1 WSH/Kodak
90/1 WSH/Smokey
91/2 WSH
91/2 WSH/Kodak
92/3 WSH/Kodak

RIDPATH, BRUCE
91 C55 Reprint 14
1911-12 Imperial (C55) 14
1910-11 Imperial (C56) 34
1912-13 Imperial (C57) 28
1910-11 Imperial Post 14

RIEDER, DANA
90/1 SketchWHL 32
91/2 SketchWHL 317

RIEDMEIER, ERWIN
72 SemicSticker 98

RIEHL, JEREMY
91/2 SketchWHL 179

RIEHL, KEVIN
94/5 AutoPhonex 35
90/1 SketchWHL 33
91/2 SketchWHL 329
93/4 Raleigh
94/5 Raleigh

RIEKKINEN, PAAVO
70/1 Kuvajulkaisut 234

RIEL, GUY
80/1 QuébecRemparts

RIENDEAU, VINCENT
90/1 Bowman 20
91/2 Bowman 372
92/3 Bowman 262
95/6 DEL 335
94/5 Flair 13
92/3 FleerUltra 288
94/5 FleerUltra 15
94/5 Kraft, -Masks
89/90 OPC/Topps 186
90/1 OPC/Topps 177
91/2 OPC/Topps 370
89/90 opcStickFS 17
89/90 PaniniSticker 120
90/1 PaniniSticker 268
92/3 Parkhurst 278
94/5 Parkhurst 14
92/3 Pinnacle 177
93/4 Pinnacle 312
94/5 Pinnacle 212
94/5 POG 272
93/4 Premier 411
94/5 Premier 324
90/1 ProSet 270
91/2 ProSet 213
91/2 PSPlatinum 112
90/1 Score 107
91/2 Score(CDN) 23
91/2 Score(U.S) 23, 43T
92/3 Score 396
93/4 Score 276
92/3 Topps 466
91/2 ToppsStadiumClub 128
92/3 ToppsStadiumClub 172
94/5 ToppsStadiumClub 43
90/1 UpperDeck 152
91/2 UpperDeck 220
87/8 STL
88/9 STL
88/9 STL/Kodak
89/90 STL/Kodak
90/1 STL/Kodak

RIFFEL, KEVIN
91/2 AirCanadaSJHL B9

RIGGIN, DENNIS
52/3 AnonymousOHL 1
62 CeramicTiles

RIGGIN, PAT
81/2 O-Pee-Chee 37
82/3 O-Pee-Chee 372
84/5 O-Pee-Chee 205, 218, 386
85/6 OPC/Topps 136
81/2 opcSticker 12, 221
84/5 opcSticker 65/66, 233/232
85/6 opcSticker 106/238
86/7 opcSticker 41/178
80/1 Pepsi Cap
82/3 Post
83/4 PuffySticker 21
81/2 Topps 30
84/5 Topps 148, 164
79/80 ATL
80/1 CGY
81/2 CGY
87/8 PGH/Kodak
82/3 WSH
84/5 WSH/PizzaHut
85/6 WSH/PizzaHut

RIGGIN, TRAVIS
95/6 Slapshot 173
93/4 Slapshot(Kitchener) 7, 27
94/5 Slapshot(Kitchener) 9

RIGOLET, GERALD
72 SemicSticker 158

RIIHIJÄRVI, HEIKKI
92/3 Jyvas-Hyva 64
93/4 Jyvas-Hyva 116
93/4 Sisu 10

RIIHIJARVI, JUHA
93/4 Classic 45
93/4 ClassicProspects 48
92/3 Jyvas-Hyva 73
95 Latkaliiga 7
94 Semic 40
95 Semic 46
93 SemicSticker 74
93/4 Sisu 369, 384
94/5 Sisu-Horoscope 12
95/6 Sisu 99, 179, -Spotlight 3
96/7 Sisu-AtGala 2, -Helmet
95/6 SisuLimited 35
97/8 udSwedish 146, C14
96 Wien 34

RIIHIJARVI, TEEMU
95 Classic 12
95/6 Sisu 92, -NHLDraft 2
96/7 Sisu 91
95/6 UpperDeck 548
95/6 UDCollChoice 331

RIIHIMÄKI, HANNU
80/1 Mallasjuoma 21

RIIHIMÄKI, MARKKU
70/1 Kuvajulkaisut 202
71/2 WilliamsFIN 91
72/3 WilliamsFIN 256
73/4 WilliamsFIN 256

RIIHINEN, JANI
95/6 UDCollChoice 330

RIIHIRANTA, HEIKKI
72 Hellas 13
70/1 Kuvajulkaisut 76, 114
80/1 Mallasjuoma 4
74/5 opcWHA 31
75/6 opcWHA 125
76/7 opcWHA 58
72 Panda
78/9 SM-Liiga 25
74 SemicSticker 80
71/2 WilliamsFIN 123
72/3 WilliamsFIN 74, 93
73/4 WilliamsFIN 78, 140

RIITAHAARA, PENTTI
66/7 Champion 19
65/6 Hellas 68

RIKALA, JORMA
65/6 Hellas 49
70/1 Kuvajulkaisut 115
72 Panda
71/2 WilliamsFIN 124
72/3 WilliamsFIN 94
73/4 WilliamsFIN 141

RILAY, BILL
83/4 NovaScotia 9

RILCOF, KEVIN
91/2 AvantGardeBCJHL 5
92/3 BCJHL 22

RILEY, BILL
77/8 OPC 360
78/9 O-Pee-Chee 292
79/80 O-Pee-Chee 303
78/9 WSH

RILEY, JACK
36-39 DiamondMatch (1)
34/5 SweetCaporal

RILEY, RON
72/3 OttawaNationals

RIMMEL, PAT
94/5 APS 10
95/6 APS 107

RINDELL, HARRY
92/3 Jyvas-Hyva 1
93/4 Jyvas-Hyva 13
93/4 Sisu 82
95/6 Sisu 391

RING, TOMAS
91/2 SemicElitserien 138

RINGLER, TIM
81/2 Milwaukee 15

RINKINEN, J.P.
96/7 Sisu 115

RINNE, JOUNI
78/9 SM-Liiga 169
77-80 Sprtscaster 87- 2072
73/4 WilliamsFIN 315

RINTANEN, KIMMO
93/4 Jyvas-Hyva 229
95 Semic 19, 229
93/4 Sisu 203
95/6 Sisu 130
96/7 Sisu 145, -Mighty 1
92/3 UpperDeck 618

RIOPELLE, HOWARD (RIP)
45-64 BeeHives(MTL)
51/2 LavalDairy 101
43-47 ParadeSportive
45-54 QuakerOats
52/3 StLawrence 55

RIOUX, DANIEL
80/1 Québec
84/5 Moncton 25

RIOUX, PIERRE
94/5 DEL 92

RIPLEY, VICTOR
33-35 DiamondMatch
36-39 DiamondMatch (1)
34/5 OPC (V304B) 67
33/4 WWGum (V357) 54

RISDALE, MIKE
90/1 SketchWHL 166
91/2 SketchWHL 238
89/90 Regina

RISEBROUGH, DOUG
72-84 Dernière 80/1, 82/3
84/5 Kelloggs Disk
86/7 Kraft Sports 7
75/6 OPC/Topps 107
76/7 OPC/Topps 109, OPC 388
77/8 OPC/Topps 189
78/9 OPC/Topps 249
79/80 OPC/Topps 13
80/1 O-Pee-Chee 275
81/2 O-Pee-Chee 190
82/3 O-Pee-Chee 57
83/4 O-Pee-Chee 92
84/5 O-Pee-Chee 236
85/6 O-Pee-Chee 243
86/7 OPC/Topps 196
83/4 opcSticker 269
84/5 opcSticker 241
80/1 Pepsi Cap
82/3 Post
90/1 ProSet 663
83/4 PuffySticker 1
83/4 7ElevenCokeCup
84/5 7ElevenDisk
83/4 SouhaitsRen.KeyChain
83/4 Vachon 18
82/3 CGY
85/6 CGY/RedRooster
86/7 CGY/RedRooster
87/8 CGY/RedRooster
90/1 CGY/McGavins
91/2 CGY/IGA
74/5 MTL
75/6 MTL
76/7 MTL
77/8 MTL
78/9 MTL
79/80 MTL
80/1 MTL
81/2 MTL

RISIDORE, RYAN
93/4 Slapshot(Guelph) 5
94/5 Slapshot(Guelph) 5
95/6 Slapshot 85
94/5 SRTetrad CXII
95/6 Guelph 20

RISKU, RAINER
80/1 Mallasjuoma 19
78/9 SM-Liiga 85

RISSLING, GARY
84/5 PGH/Heinz

RITCHIE, BYRON
97/8 Bowman 108
93/4 Lethbridge

RITCHIE, DARREN
94/5 Slapshot(MEM) 40
92/3 Brandon 19
95/6 SaintJohn

RITCHIE, JIM
89/90 SSMarie 6

RIUTTA, BRUCE
72 SemicSticker 120

RIVARD, FERNARD
74/5 Loblaws

RIVARD, FRANÇOIS
91/2 SketchQMJHL 130

RIVARD, JEAN-FRANÇOIS
90/1 SketchQMJHL 102
91/2 SketchQMJHL 181

RIVARD, STEFAN
93/4 Slapshot(NorthBay) 12
94/5 Slapshot(NorthBay) 14

RIVERAIN, R.
84/5 Chicoutimi

RIVERS, A.J.
97/8 Halifax (2)

RIVERS, ANDY
84/5 Kingston 15
86/7 Kingston 14

RIVERS, DARYL
95/6 Slapshot 280

RIVERS, GUS
27-32 LaPresse 29/30

RIVERS, JAMIE
94/5 AutoPhonex B1
95/6 Bowman 132
95 Classic 97
95/6 Donruss 342, -CanadaJr.
95/6 EdgeIce 95
95/6 FutureLegends 40
96/7 Leaf 236
94/5 LeafLimited-CanadaJrs 8
97/8 Omega 198
98/9 Pacific 372
94/5 Pinnacle 526
97/8 PinnacleBeAPlayer 231
97/8 Score(STL) 13
94/5 SigRookies 36
91/2 SketchOHL 257
95/6 SkyBoxImpact 218
96/7 SkyBoxImpact 158
93/4 Slapshot(Sudbury) 8
94/5 Slapshot(Sud.) 7, -Promo
94/5 SP 141
95/6 Topps 21CJ
94/5 ToppsFinest 152
94/5 UpperDeck 501
95/6 UpperDeck 477
96/7 UpperDeck 145
91/2 Sudbury 8
92/3 Sudbury 9
93/4 Sudbury 8

RIVERS, SHAWN
93/4 ClassicProspects 107
96/7 DEL 8
95/6 EdgeIce 108
93/4 Score 470
90/1 SketchOHL 393
91/2 SketchOHL 260
94/5 SRTetrad CXIII
92/3 AtlantaKnights
93/4 AtlantaKnights
90/1 Sudbury 18
91/2 Sudbury 9

RIVERS, WAYNE
72/3 O-Pee-Chee 315
74/5 opcWHA 13
75/6 opcWHA 38
73/4 QuakerOats 44
64/5 TheTorontoStar
63/4 Topps 17
76/7 SanDiegoMariners

RIVET, CRAIG
95/6 Leaf 310
97/8 Pacific-BestKept 51
97/8 PinnacleBeAPlayer 102
91/2 SketchOHL 235
93/4 Slapshot(Kingston) 21
94/5 Fredericton
95/6 Fredericton
96/7 Fredericton
97/8 MTL

RJYABYKIN, DIMITRI
94/5 SRTetrad CXI
95/6 UpperDeck 557

ROACH, DAVE
88/9 ProCards(CapeBreton)

ROACH, GARY
91/2 SketchOHL 337
93/4 Slapshot (SSMaire) 13
94/5 Slapshot (NorthBay) 23
93/4 SSMarie 14

ROACH, JOHN
33/4 Anonymous (V129) 18
24/5 Champs (C144)
33/4 CndGum (V252)
27-32 LaPresse 29/30
34/5 OPC (V304B) 53
23/4 (V145-1) 28
24/5 (V145-2) 52
33/4 WWGum (V357) 67

ROACH, MICKEY
24/5 Champs (C144)
24/5 MapleCrispette (V130) 23
23/4 (V145-1) 38
24/5 (V145-2) 18

ROB, LUBOS
94/5 APS 106
95/6 APS 67
93 SemicSticker 97

ROBAZZA, RINO
61/2 Topps 39
63/4 QuébecAces
65/6 QuébecAces

ROBB, DOUG
81/2 Milwaukee 12

ROBBINS, ADAM
95/6 Slapshot 41

ROBBINS, MATT
93/4 ClassicProspects 230

ROBBINS, TREVOR
90/1 SketchWHL 88

ROBERGE, JEAN
90/1 SketchQMJHL 53
91/2 SketchQMJHL 234

ROBERGE, MARIO
92/3 Durivage 27
93/4 Durivage 16
92/3 Parkhurst 322
88/9 ProCards(Sherbrooke)
89/90 ProCards(AHL) 187
90/1 ProCards 57
91/2 ProSet 415
91/2 MTL
92/3 MTL
93/4 MTL
93/4 MTL/MolsonExport
95/6 Fredericton

ROBERGE, ROGER
52/3 LavalDairy 44
52/3 StLawrence 73

ROBERGE, SERGE
88/9 ProCards(Sherbrooke)
89/90 ProCards(AHL) 200
90/1 ProCards 454
91/2 ProCards 538
90/1 Halifax
95/6 Rochester

ROBERT, CLAUDE
51/2 LavalDairy 17
52/3 StLawrence 47

ROBERT, RENÉ
72-84 Dernière 79/80
72/3 EddieSargent 42
74/5 LiptonSoup 24
74/5 Loblaws
72/3 O-Pee-Chee 2, Topps 161
73/4 OPC/Topps 139
74/5 OPC/Topps 42, 142
75/6 OPC/Topps 46, 296, 315
76/7 OPC/Topps 42, 214
77/8 OPC/Topps 222
78/9 OPC/Topps 188
79/80 OPC/Topps 12
80/1 OPC/Topps 239, 259
81/2 O-Pee-Chee 322
82/3 O-Pee-Chee 330
71/2 TheTorontoSun
72/3 BUF
73/4 BUF
74/5 BUF
75/6 BUF/Linnett
93/4 BUF/NOCO
79/80 COL.R
71/2 PGH
81/2 TOR

ROBERTO, PHIL
71/2 EddieSargent 109
74/5 Loblaws, -Upadate
71/2 OPC/Topps 228
72/3 OPC 82, Topps 52
73/4 OPC 3, Topps 151
74/5 OPC/Topps 208
75/6 OPC/Topps 80
76/7 OPC 345
71/2 TheTorontoSun
72/3 Topps 52
73/4 Topps 151
76/7 COL.R
69/70 MTL/ProStar
71/2 MTL (x2)
71/2 STL
72/3 STL
72/3 STL/8"x10"
73/4 STL
93/4 Birmingham 20
94/5 Birmingham
95/6 Birmingham

ROBERTS, ALEX
90/1 ProCards 408
92/3 Toledo (1), (2)

ROBERTS, BOB
51/2 LavalDairy 103

ROBERTS, DAVE
94/5 AutoPhonex 36
93/4 Classic 76
94/5 Classic 106, T58, -Aut
94/5 ClassicFourSport 141
95/6 EdgeIce C1
93/4 FleerUltra 495
94/5 Leaf 478
95/6 Leaf 13
97/8 Limited 31
97/8 PacificRegime 204
95/6 PaniniSticker 191
97/8 PaniniSticker 240
94/5 Parkhurst 201
95/6 Parkhurst 179
95/6 Pinnacle 157
96/7 PinnacleBeAPlayer 93
93/4 PowerPlay 515
93/4 Premier-TeamUSA 16
94/5 Score 222
95/6 Score 286
97/8 Score(VAN) 19
94 Semic 134
95/6 SkyBoxEmotion 152
95/6 Topps 43
93/4 T.StadiumClub-TmUSA 20
97/8 UDCollChoice 265
96/7 VAN
96/7 VAN/IGA

ROBERTS, DOUG
70/1 EddieSargent 138
72/3 EddieSargent 26
70/1 Esso Stamp
82? JDMcCarthy
74/5 Loblaws
68/9 OPC/Topps 88
69/70 OPC/Topps 81
70/1 OPC/Topps 71
71/2 Topps 83
73/4 OPC 207
74/5 OPC 312
67/8 Topps 50

ROBERTS, GARY
96/7 Aces 2 (Clubs)
90/1 Bowman 95
91/2 Bowman 263
92/3 Bowman 109, 214
93/4 Donruss 52
94/5 Donruss 143
95/6 Donruss 372
97/8 DonrussPreferred 63
97/8 DonrussPriority 106
93/4 EASports 22
94/5 Flair 28
94/5 Fleer 35
92/3 FleerUltra 29
93/4 FleerUltra 187
94/5 FleerUltra 35, -RedLight 7
95/6 FleerUltra 29
95/6 Hoyle'WEST K (Diamonds)
94/5 Kraft'HockeyHeroes
93/4 Leaf 36
94/5 Leaf 326
95/6 Leaf 277
94/5 LeafLimited 114
96/7 Maggers 25
93/4 McDonalds M cD11
97/8 Omega 45
89/90 O-Pee-Chee 202
90/1 OPC/Topps 161
91/2 OPC/Topps 320
92/3 O-Pee-Chee 72
91/2 opcPremier 126
92/3 opcPremier-Star 14
89/90 opcSticker 98 /235
98/9 Pacific 140
97/8 PacificParamount 39
98/9 PacificParamount 42
97/8 PacificRevolution 26
90/1 Panini(CGY) 19
87/8 PaniniSticker 217
88/9 PaniniSticker 15
89/90 PaniniSticker 35
90/1 PaniniSticker 179
91/2 PaniniSticker 52
92/3 PaniniSticker 45
93/4 PaniniSticker 181
94/5 PaniniSticker 160
95/6 PaniniSticker 236
96/7 PaniniSticker 149, 240
91/2 Parkhurst 24, 436
92/3 Parkhurst 22, CP8
93/4 Parkhurst 302
94/5 Parkhurst V29
95/6 Parkhurst 301
94/5 ParkieSE 27
91/2 Pinnacle 37
92/3 Pinnacle 3, 242
93/4 Pinnacle 55
94/5 Pinnacle 115, -NL16
95/6 Pinnacle 137
97/8 Pinnacle 170
97/8 PinnacleBeAPlayer 73
95/6 Playoff 19
94/5 POG 61
95/6 POG 55
93/4 PowerPlay 42
93/4 Premier 382, 510
94/5 Premier 445, -Finest(T) 16
95/6 ProMagnet 44
90/1 ProSet 45
91/2 ProSet 30
92/3 ProSet 21, -TeamLdr 1
91/2 PSPlatinum 161
90/1 Score 106
91/2 Score(CDN) 199, (U.S) 199
92/3 Score 322, -Sharpshooter 1
93/4 Score 241, (CDN) DD4
93/4 Score-PinnacleAS 29
94/5 Score 186, CI12
95/6 Score 97
94/5 Select 147
93 SemicSticker 208
95/6 SkyBoxEmotion 25
97/8 SPAuthentic 26
95/6 Summit 150
92/3 Topps 116
95/6 Topps 78
94/5 ToppsFinest 82, -Div. 19
91/2 ToppsStadiumClub 126
92/3 ToppsStadiumClub 48
93/4 TSC 235, -Finest 9, -AS
94/5 ToppsStadiumClub 230
90/1 UpperDeck 29
91/2 UpperDeck 190
92/3 UD 289,-LockerAS 32
93/4 UD 151, HT3, SP25
94/5 UpperDeck 20, SP14
95/6 UpperDeck 19
97/8 UpperDeck 240
94/5 UDBeAPlayer-Aut. 17
97/8 UDBlackDiamond 86
98/9 UDChoice 36
95/6 UDCC 174
86/7 CGY/RedRooster
87/8 CGY/RedRooster
90/1 CGY/McGavins
91/2 CGY/IGA
92/3 CGY/IGA 6
86/7 Moncton 12
82/3 Ottawa67s
83/4 Ottawa67s
84/5 Ottawa67s

ROBERTS, GORDIE
91 C55 Reprint 33
1911-12 Imperial (C55) 33
1910-11 Imperial (C56) 3
1912-13 Imperial (C57) 23
1910-11 Imperial Post 33

ROBERTS, GORD
92/3 Bowman 197
92/3 FleerUltra 255
83&87 HallOfFame 222
83 HHOF Postcard (O)
79/80 O-Pee-Chee 265
80/1 OPC/Topps 112
81/2 OPC 167, Topps(W) 111
82/3 O-Pee-Chee 174
83/4 O-Pee-Chee 180
84/5 O-Pee-Chee 107
85/6 OPC/Topps 28
86/7 OPC/Topps 42
87/8 OPC/Topps 41
90/1 OPC/Topps 256
91/2 OPC/Topps 494
92/3 O-Pee-Chee 233
92/3 opcPremier 86
83/4 opcSticker 114
85/6 opcSticker 43 /171
87/8 opcSticker 55 /196
88/9 PaniniSticker 102
90/1 PaniniSticker 269
91/2 Pinnacle 274
92/3 Pinnacle 312
93/4 Pinnacle 319
93/4 Premier 275
90/1 ProSet 271, 510
91/2 ProSet 458
90/1 Score 245, 83T
91/2 Score(CDN) 422, (U.S) 439
92/3 Score 201
93/4 Score 274
92/3 Topps 176
92/3 ToppsStadiumClub 185
93/4 ToppsStadiumClub 41
92/3 BOS
81/2 MIN
82/3 MIN
83/4 MIN
84/5 MIN
84/5 MIN/7Eleven 5
85/6 MIN
86/7 MIN/7Eleven 10
87/8 MIN
91/2 PGH/Elbys
97/8 PHO
87/8 STL
88/9 STL
88/9 STL/Kodak
89/90 STL/Kodak
83/4 Victoria
83/4 Victoria

ROBERTS, JAMES M.
72/3 Letraset 14
77/8 OPC 281, 392
78/9 O-Pee-Chee 342

ROBERTS, JIM W.
64-67 BeeHives(MTL)
64/5 CokeCap MTL-26
65/6 CocaCola
70/1 DadsCookies
72-84 Dernière 72/3
72-84 Dernière 73/4
70/1 EddieSargent 179
71/2 EddieSargent 181
72/3 EddieSargent 126
70/1 Esso Stamp
74/5 Loblaws
68/9 OPC/Topps 113
69/70 OPC 174, -Sticker, -T. 14
70/1 OPC 213
71/2 OPC/Topps 116
72/3 OPC 269
73/4 OPC 181
74/5 OPC/Topps 78
75/6 OPC 378
76/7 OPC/Topps 119, 217
77/8 OPC 281
94/5 Parkie(64/5) 79
95/6 Parkie(66/7) 72, 135
88/9 ProCards(Springfield)
89/90 ProCards(AHL) 253
90/1 ProCards 182
72 SemicSticker 182
68/9 ShirriffCoin STL6
71/2 TheTorontoSun
65/6 Topps 74
66/7 Topps 6
67/8 MTL
69/70 MTL/ProStar
71/2 MTL (x2)
72/3 MTL
73/4 MTL
74/5 MTL
75/6 MTL
76/7 MTL
86/7 PGH/Kodak

ROBERTS, MINPY
52/3 AnonymousOHL 22

ROBERTS, SCOTT
93/4 Huntington

ROBERTS, STEVE
91/2 AvantGardeBCJHL 27
92/3 BCJHL 50
95/6 Dayton

ROBERTS, TIM
92/3 Wheeling 13
93/4 Wheeling 7
94/5 Wheeling 5

ROBERTS, W.
24/5 CrescentSelkirks 5
23/4 PaulinsCandy 6

ROBERTSON, BOB
52/3 LavalDairy 103
52/3 StLawrence 69

ROBERTSON, CHRIS
88/9 Brandon 14

ROBERTSON, EARL
33-34 BeeHives(NYA)
39/40 OPC (V301-1) 63

ROBERTSON, FRED
33/4 Anonymous (V129) 15
32/3 TOR/OKeefe 18

ROBERTSON, GEORGE
45-64 BeeHives(MTL)
45-54 QuakerOats

ROBERTSON, GRANT
83/4 Belleville 23
84/5 Belleville 19

ROBERTSON, IAIN
94 Semic 329

ROBERTSON, JIM
52/3 AnonymousOHL 103

ROBERTSON, J.R.
83&87 HallOfFame 102
83 HHOF Postcard (G)

ROBERTSON, KEN
52/3 AnonymousOHL 99

ROBERTSON, KEVIN
91/2 AvantGardeBCJ 110
92/3 BCJHL 170
90/1 SketchWHL 215
89/90 Brandon 11
90/1 Brandon 9

ROBERTSON, ROGER
84/5 Belleville 23

ROBERTSON, TORRIE
85/6 O-Pee-Chee 218
86/7 O-Pee-Chee 214
90/1 ProCards 520
90/1 ProSet 77
83/4 HFD/JuniorWhalers
84/5 HFD/JuniorWhalers
85/6 HFD/JuniorWhalers
86/7 HFD/JuniorWhalers
87/8 HFD/JuniorWhalers
88/9 HFD/JuniorWhalers
81/2 WSH
84/5 Victoria

ROBICHAUD, ANDRÉ
92/3 BCJHL 85

ROBICHAUD, RYAN
95/6 Slapshot 91
95/6 Guelph 25
96/7 Guelph 10

ROBIDAS, STÉPHANE
97/8 Bowman 65

ROBIDOUX, FLORENT
83/4 Springfield 16

ROBILLARD, MARC
91/2 SketchOHL 83

ROBBINS, TREVOR
91/2 SketchWHL 101
92/3 Brandon 20
90/1 Saskatoon 2
91/2 Saskatoon 2

ROBINSON, BILL
51/2 LavalDairy 107
90/1 SketchQMJHL 68
52/3 StLawrence 58

ROBINSON, CLAUDE
83&87 HallOfFame 192
83 HHOF Postcard (J)

ROBINSON, DEREK
92/3 BCJHL 165

ROBINSON, DOUG
64/5 CokeCap CHI-14
65/6 CocaCola
70/1 Esso Stamp
68/9 O-Pee-Chee 160
94/5 Parkie(64/5) 34
95/6 Parkie(66/7) 96
68/9 ShirriffCoin LA12
64/5 Topps 84
65/6 Topps 26

ROBINSON, EARLE
34-43 BeeHives(MTL.Can, Mar)
35-40 CrownBrand 54, 196
34/5 OPC (V304B) 55
36/7 OPC (V304D) 115
37/8 OPC (V304E) 165
34/5 SweetCaporal
36/7 WWGum (V356) 85
33/4 WWGum (V357) 5

ROBINSON, JANE
94/5 Classic W8

ROBINSON, JASON
95/6 Slapshot 195

ROBINSON, JUSTIN
94/5 Slapshot(NorthBay) 20
95/6 Slapshot 11

ROBINSON, LARRY
90/1 Bowman 150
91/2 Bowman 177
92/3 Bowman 215
93/4 ClassicProspects 53
77/8 Coke Mini
72-84 Dernière 72/3, 73/4
72-84 Dernière 80/1, 83/4
83/4 Esso
88/9 Esso Sticker
94 HockeyWit 92
84/5 Kelloggs Disk
86/7 Kraft Sports 36
90/1 Kraft 47
91/2 Kraft 80
74/5 Loblaws
82/3 McDonalds 17, 34
73/4 OPC 237
74/5 OPC 280
75/6 OPC/Topps 241
76/7 OPC/Topps 151
77/8 OPC/T. 2, 30, T-Glossy 18
78/9 OPC/Topps 180, 210, 264
78/9 O-Pee-Chee 326, 329
79/80 OPC/Topps 50
80/1 OPC/Topps 84, 230
81/2 OPC 179, 196, Topps 31
82/3 O-Pee-Chee 191
83/4 O-Pee-Chee 195
84/5 OPC 270, Topps 82
85/6 OPC/Topps 147
86/7 OPC/Topps 62, M, T-AS 12
87/8 OPC/Topps 192
88/9 O-Pee-Chee 246
89/90 O-Pee-Chee 235
90/1 OPC/Topps 261
91/2 OPC/Topps 458
92/3 OPC 167, -25Years 6
81/2 opcSticker 31, 42, 148
82/3 opcSticker 31, 169
83/4 opcSticker 60, 61
84/5 opcSticker 147-148
85/6 opcSticker 140
86/7 opcSticker 8, 23/183
87/8 opcSticker 16
88/9 opcSticker 39/170
89/90 opcSticker 55/199
80/1 opcSuperCard 11
87/8 PaniniSticker 57
89/90 PaniniSticker 245
90/1 PaniniSticker 244
91/2 PaniniSticker 82
91/2 Parkhurst 74
80/1 Pepsi Cap
91/2 Pinnacle 208, 382, 403
82/3 Post
81/2 Post PopUp 16
90/1 ProSet 125
91/2 ProSet 104
87/8 ProSportWatch CW1
83/4 PuffySticker 2
90/1 Score 260
91/2 Score(CDN) 511, (U.S) 291
83/4 7ElevenCokeCup
84/5 7ElevenDisk
85/6 7Eleven 10
83/4 SouhaitsRen.KeyChain
91/2 ToppsStadiumClub 252
92/3 Trends(76) 182
90/1 UpperDeck 52
91/2 UpperDeck 499
92/3 UpperDeck'LockerAS 48
83/4 Vachon 53
89/90 L.A./Smokeys 7
90/1 L.A./Smokeys 9
73/4 MTL
74/5 MTL
75/6 MTL
76/7 MTL
77/8 MTL
78/9 MTL
79/80 MTL
80/1 MTL
81/2 MTL
82/3 MTL
82/3 MTL/Steinberg
83/4 MTL
84/5 MTL
85/6 MTL
85/6 MTL/Pennant
85/6 MTL/PepsiPlacemats
85/6 MTL/ProvigoStickers
85/6? MTL/ProvigoPlacemats
86/7 MTL
87/8 MTL
87/8 MTL/Kodak
87/8 MTL/Stickers 72, 73
88/9 MTL

ROBINSON, MOE
77/8 NovaScotia

ROBINSON, NICK
96/7 SSMarie

ROBINSON, ROB
89/90 ProCards(IHL) 22
90/1 ProCards 79
92/3 ToppsGold 527
91/2 STL
92/3 Peoria

ROBINSON, SCOTT
89/90 ProCards(IH)L 78
90/1 ProCards 118
91/2 ProCards 150

ROBINSON, STÉPHANE
84/5 Richelieu

ROBINSON, TODD
97/8 Bowman 93
98 BowmanCHL 52
95/6 UpperDeck 508

ROBINSON, JEFF
93/4 Raleigh

ROBITAILLE, LUC
90/1 Bowman 152, -HatTrick 12
91/2 Bowman 188
92/3 Bowman 70, 216
95/6 Bowman 23
93/4 Donruss 162, 396, WC
94/5 Donruss-IceMasters 9
95/6 Donruss 104, 348
96/7 Donruss 7
97/8 Donruss 90
96/7 DonrussCanadianIce 64
97/8 DonrussCanadianIce 68
95/6 DonrussElite 105
96/7 DonrussElite 78
97/8 DonrussElite 85
97/8 DonrussPreferred 121
97/8 DonrussPriority 32
97/8 DonrussStudio 53
92/3 Durivage 28
93/4 Durivage 41
93/4 EASports 64, 200
88/9 Esso Sticker
94/5 Flair 138, -HotNumber 7
94/5 Fleer 167
95/6 FleerMetal 99
92/3 FleerUltra 87, -AllStar 11
93/4 F.Ultra 208, -AS 13, -Red 9
94/5 FleerUltra 103, 350
95/6 FleerUltra 277
96/7 FleerUltra 111
88/9 FritoLay
91/2 Gillette 1
95 Globe 94
93/4 HockeyWit 96
95/6 Hoyle'EAST 5 (Clubs)
92/3 HumptyDumpty (2)
94/5 Incomnet
97/8 KatchMedallion 72
92/3 Kelloggs Poster
94/5 KennerSLU
95/6 KennerSLU (U.S)
90/1 Kraft 48, 75
91/2 Kraft 70
93/4 KraftDinner
93/4 Leaf 20, -GoldLeafAS 9
94/5 Leaf 20, 463
95/6 Leaf 129
96/7 Leaf 134
97/8 Leaf 121
94/5 LeafLimited 88
95/6 LeafLimited 91
96/7 LeafLimited 27
96/7 LeafPreferred 13
97/8 Limited 75
96/7 Maggers 104
91/2 McDonalds McD14
92/3 McDonalds Mc D-12
93/4 McDonalds McH3
96/7 MetalUniverse 101
97/8 Omega 112
87/8 OPC/Topps 42, D, T-AS 12
88/9 OPC/Topps 124, P, T-AS 1
89/90 OPC/Topps 88
90/1 OPC/Topps 194, 209
91/2 OPC/Topps 260, 405
92/3 O-Pee-Chee 6
90/1 opcPremier 99
91/2 opcPremier 34
87/8 opsStars 35
88/9 opcStars 32
87/8 opcSticker 187/48, 114/244
87/8 opcStick. 122 /134, 133/121
87/8 opcStick. 148/267, 177/175
88/9 opcSticker 157
98/9 Pacific 244
97/8 PacificCrown 145
97/8 PacificCrownRoyale 65
97/8 PacificInvincible 91
97/8 PacificParamount 91
98/9 PacificParamount 107
97/8 PacificRevolution 66
87/8 PaniniSticker 277, 379
88/9 PaniniSticker 78
89/90 PaniniSticker 95, 177
90/1 PaniniSticker 233, 331
91/2 PaniniSticker 91, 324
92/3 PaniniSticker 65, 288
93/4 PaniniSticker 201
94/5 PaniniSticker 174
95/6 PaniniSticker 61
96/7 PaniniSticker 105
95 PaniniWorlds 21
91/2 Parkhurst 68, 224
92/3 Parkhurst 68, 501
93/4 Parkhurst 91
94/5 Parkhurst V67
95/6 Parkhurst 140
94/5 ParkieSE 137
91/2 Pinnacle 17, 385, B10
92/3 Pinnacle 175, 251
93/4 Pinnacle 145,-TeamP 4
93/4 Pinnacle-NiftyFifty 1, 5
94/5 Pinnacle 400, TP7
97/8 Pinnacle 149
96/7 PinnacleBeAPlayer 12
97/8 PinnacleBeeHive 36
97/8 PinnacleCertified 92
97/8 PinnacleInside 168
95/6 PinnacleZenith 48
96/7 PinnacleZenith 36
95/6 Playoff 71, 286
95/6 POG 183
94/5 Post
96/7 Post
93/4 PowerPlay 120, -PtLdr 13
93/4 Premier 90, 180
94/5 Premier 346, 526, 540
94/5 Premier-Finest (T) 13
95/6 ProMagnet 100
90/1 ProSet 126, 341
91/2 ProSet 95, 286, P6
91/2 PS-ThePuck 12
92/3 ProSet 72
91/2 PSPlatinum 50
90/1 Score 150, 315, -Hot 66
91/2 Score(CDN) 3, 375
91/2 Score(U.S) 3, 345
92/3 Score 290, 498
93/4 Score 245, 451, -P.AS 37
93/4 S-DreamTeam 24
94/5 Score DT10
95/6 Score 54, -Lamplight 9
96/7 Score 113
97/8 Score 149
92/3 SeasonsPatch 10
94/5 Select 32, FL10
95/6 SelectCertified 53
96/7 SelectCertified 13
94 Semic 92, 353
95 Semic 89
89 SemicSticker 68
91 SemicSticker 70
92 SemicSticker 89
93 SemicSticker 204
95/6 SkyBoxEmotion 118
95/6 SkyBoxImpact 113, -Ice 14
94/5 SP 93
95/6 SP 97
96/7 SP 102
97/8 SPAuthentic 77, I18
95/6 Summit 89, -MadHatter 14
96/7 Summit 13
95/6 SuperSticker 82
91 TeamCanada
96/7 TeamOut
92/3 Topps 101, 266
95/6 Topps 40, 352, 379
95/6 Topps HG2, HGC19
98/9 Topps 174
94/5 ToppsFinest 89, -Div. B4
95/6 ToppsFinest 24
96/7 ToppsNHLPicks 87
91/2 ToppsStadiumClub 159
92/3 ToppsStadiumClub 44, 247
93/4 TSC 87, -Finest 7, -AllStar
94/5 T.SC 57, -Dynasty 4
95/6 ToppsStadiumClub 100
95/6 ToppsSuperSkills 56
90/1 UpperDeck 73
91/2 UpperDeck 145, 507, 623
92/3 UD 8, 216, G2, WG20
92/3 UD'LockerAS 33
93/4 UpperDeck 231, 293, 414
93/4 UD GG8, HT17, SP 73
94/5 UpperDeck 194, SP152
95/6 UpperDeck 8, 244, SE144
97/8 UpperDeck 290
93/4 UDBeAPlayer 12
94/5 UDBAP R95, -Aut. 113
97/8 UDBlackDiamond 76
98/9 UDChoice 98, BH12
95/6 UDCollChoice 164
96/7 UDCollChoice 171
97/8 UDCollChoice 170
96 Wien 93
97/8 Zenith 41, Z56
88/9 L.A.
88/9 L.A./Smokeys
89/90 L.A./Smokeys 8
90/1 L.A./Smokeys 10
94/5 PGH 14

ROBITAILLE, MIKE
71/2 EddieSargent 29
74/5 Loblaws, -Update
71/2 OPC/Topps 8
73/4 OPC/Topps 121
74/5 OPC/Topps 159
75/6 OPC/Topps 24
76/7 OPC 359
71/2 TheTorontoSun
72/3 BUF
73/4 BUF
74/5 VAN/RoyalBank
75/6 VAN/RoyalBank
76/7 VAN/RoyalBank

ROBITAILLE, PAT
92/3 Clarkson

ROBITAILLE, RANDY
97/8 Score(BOS) 12
97/8 UpperDeck 182

ROBSON, BOB
91/2 AirCanadaSJHL 50

ROBSON, RYAN
94/5 Slapshot(MEM) 42

ROCCA, TONY
84/5 Kingston 22

ROCCOARDO, JEFF
95/6 LasVegas

ROCHE, DAVE
95/6 Bowman 144
93/4 ClassicFourSport 211
95/6 Donruss 287
97/8 PacificCrown 253
97/8 Score(PGH) 17
91/2 SketchOHL 139
93/4 Slapshot(Peterborough) 3
93/4 Slapshot(Windsor) 18
94/5 Slapshot(Windsor) 20
95/6 PGH/Foodland 16
91/2 Peterborough 19

ROCHE, DESSE
36-39 DiamondMatch (1)
27-32 LaPresse 30/1
33/4 WWGum (V357) 70

ROCHE, EARL
36-39 DiamondMatch (1)
27-32 LaPresse 30/1
33/4 WWGum (V357) 62

ROCHE, SCOTT
94/5 Classic DP9
95 Classic 54, 90
94/5 SigRookies FF9
93/4 Slapshot(NorthBay) 21
94/5 Slapshot(NorthBay) 2
95/6 Slapshot 207, -Promo

ROCHEFORT, DAN
84/5 Richelieu

ROCHEFORT, LÉON
71/2 EddieSargent 63
72/3 EddieSargent 81
68/9 OPC/Topps 95
69/70 OPC/T. 105, OPC-Sticker
71/2 OPC/Topps 135
72/3 OPC 204
75/6 OPC 374
68/9 ShirriffCoin PHA9
71/2 TheTorontoSun
67/8 York
72/3 ATL
67/8 MTL
71/2 MTL
74/5 VAN/RoyalBank
63/4 QuébecAces

ROCHEFORT, NORMAND
91/2 Bowman 73
72-84 Dernière 81/2
92/3 Durivage 44
82/3 McDonalds 35
82/3 O-Pee-Chee 291
83/4 O-Pee-Chee 300
84/5 O-Pee-Chee 287
84/5 opcSticker 176
85/6 opcSticker 148/17
88/9 opcSticker 182/47
87/8 PaniniSticker 161
91/2 Pinnacle 273
82/3 Post
90/1 ProSet 494
90/1 Score 149
91/2 Score(CDN) 171, (U.S) 171
92/3 Score 377
83/4 SouhaitsRen.KeyChain
90/1 UpperDeck 437
83/4 Vachon 72
89/90 NYR/MarineMidland
80/1 QUE
81/2 QUE
82/3 QUE
83/4 QUE
84/5 QUE
85/6 QUE
85/6 QUE/GeneralFoods
85/6 QUE/McDonald
86/7 QUE
86/7 QUE/McDonald
86/7 QUE/YumYum
86/7 QUE/GeneralFoods
87/8 QUE/GeneralFoods
87/8 QUE/Yum Yum
93/4 AtlantaKnights

ROCHEFORT, RICHARD
97/8 Bowman 21
95/6 Slapshot 399
94/5 Slapshot(Sudbury) 15
96/7 Sudbury 19

ROCHETTE, ERIC
90/1 SketchMEM 35
90/1 SketchQMJHL 22

ROCHETTE, GAETAN
77/8 NovaScotia

ROCHON, FRANK
75/6 opcWHA 51

RODDON, MIKE
83&87 HallOfFame 164
83 HHOF Postcard (L)

RODEK, STAN
52/3 AnonymousOHL 168

RODERICK, JOHN
93/4 Peoria

RODGERS, MARC
91/2 SketchQMJHL 45
93/4 Knoxville
93/4 LasVegas
94/5 LasVegas
95/6 LasVegas
92/3 Wheeling 14

RODMAN, ANDY
87/8 Brockville 24

RODRIGUE, ALEX
94/5 Slapshot(MEM) 55

RODRIGUE, GUILLAUME
96/7 Rimouski

RODRIGUE, SYLVAIN
90/1 SketchMEM 25
90/1 SketchQMJHL 20
91/2 SketchQMJHL 96

ROEDGER, ROY
82 SemicSticker 121
89 SemicSticker 122

ROENICK, JEREMY
95/6 Aces 5 (Diamonds)
96/7 Aces 5 (Diamonds)
97/8 Aces 6 (Spades)
94/5 ActionPacked 1
90/1 Bowman 1
91/2 Bowman 386, 403
92/3 Bowman 78, 217
95/6 Bowman 20
95/6 CoolTrade 3
96/7 CorinthianHeadliner
97/8 CorinthianHeadliner
95/6 DEL 446
93/4 Donruss 67, E, -Elite 6
94/5 Donruss 222,-Dom 5,-Elite9
95/6 Donruss 27,-ProP 1,-Ignit 7
96/7 Donruss 2, -Dom 9, -Hit 4
97/8 Donruss 6
96/7 DonrussCanadianIce 57
97/8 D.CdnIce 100,-Scrapbook 7
95/6 DonrussElite 47,-Cutting 14
96/7 DonrussElite 27, -Status 12
97/8 DonrussElite 77
97/8 DonrussPreferred 88
97/8 DonrussPriority 133
97/8 D.Prio-Pstcrd 33,-Stamp 33
97/8 D.Studio 40,-Portraits 30
93/4 EASports 27
97/8 EssoOlympic 28
94/5 Flair 36, -Scoring 9,-Cntr 10
96/7 Flair 72
94/5 Fleer 45, -Slapshot 8
96/7 Fleer 18, -ArtRoss 19
95/6 FleerMetal 28, -IntSteel 17
96/7 FleerNHLPicks-Dream 2
96/7 FPicks-Fab 39, -Jagged 10
92/3 FleerUltra 41,-Roenick 1-12
93/4 FleerUltra, 186-Pivots 8
94/5 FU 44,-UltraP 8,-Speed 9
95/6 FleerUltra 35, 396, -Pivot 7
95/6 FU-Ultraview 8, -Crease 15
96/7 FleerUltra 135
91/2 Gillette 13
95 Globe 117
96/7 Got-UmHockeyGreatsCoin
93/4 HockeyWit 103
95/6 Hoyle'WEST A (Hearts)
92/3 HumptyDumpty (2)
94/5 Incomnet
97/8 KatchMedallion 112
91/2 Kelloggs 5
93/4 KennerSLU
94/5 KennerSLU (U.S)
96/7 KennerSLU (U.S)
97/8 KennerSLU 1on1
91/2 Kraft 56
92/3 Kraft'AllStar
93/4 Kraft'Captain
94/5 Kraft'Sharpshooter
93/4 Leaf 27, -StudioSignat 7
94/5 Leaf 63,-Gld 2,-Ltd 5,-Fire 2
95/6 Leaf 116
96/7 Leaf 191, -Leath 13,-Fire 11
97/8 Leaf 22
94/5 LeafLimited 61, -Gold 8
95/6 LeafLimited 80, -StarsOf 12
96/7 LeafLimited 86
96/7 LeafPreferred 4
97/8 Limited 105, 120, 140
97/8 Limited -fabric 35
96/7 Maggers 30
92/3 McDonalds McD-13
93/4 McDonalds M cD12
94/5 McDonalds McD20
95/6 McDonalds McD16
96/7 McDonalds M cD12
96/7 MetalUniverse 121
97/8 Omega 176
90/1 OPC/Topps 7
91/2 OPC/Topps 106
92/3 OPC 345, 383, -25Years 23
90/1 opcPremier 100
91/2 opcPremier 52, 174
92/3 opcPremier-Star 5
97/8 Pacific-FeaturePer 27
98/9 Pacific 97
97/8 PacificCrown 97, -Slap 7B
97/8 PCC-Supial 16, -TmCL 19
97/8 PacificCrownRoyale 105
97/8 PacificDynagon! 97
97/8 PcfcD-Dyn 12A, -Tandm 63
97/8 PacificInvincible 108
97/8 PacificParamount 142
98/9 PacificParamount 184
97/8 PacificRevolution 108
90/1 PaniniSticker 201
91/2 PaniniSticker 12
92/3 PaniniSticker 4
93/4 PaniniSticker M
94/5 PaniniSticker 127, HH
95/6 PaniniSticker 157
96/7 PaniniSticker 158
97/8 PaniniSticker 157
91/2 Parkhurst 29, 439
92/3 Parkhurst 31, CP2
93/4 Parkhurst 309, W6
94/5 Parkhurst 302, V65, C5
95/6 Parkhurst 307
94/5 ParkieSE 35
91/2 Pinnacle 120, 359
92/3 Pinn. 10, 256, -Tm2000 27
93/4 Pinnacle 140,-TeamP 11
93/4 P-NiftyF 1, 15,-Tm2001 20
94/5 Pinnacle 165, GR14, WE3
95/6 Pinn. 106, -FullC 4, -Roar 4
96/7 Pinnacle 98, TeamP 3
97/8 Pinnacle 33, 197
96/7 PinnacleBeAPlayer 5
97/8 P.BAP -TakeANumber 12
97/8 PinnacleCertified 65
95/6 PinnacleFANtasy 23
97/8 PinnacleInside 59
95/6 Playoff 24, 135, 236
96/7 PinnacleMint 15
95/6 PinnacleZenith 72, -Team 6
96/7 P.Zenith 30, -Team 10
94/5 POG 70
95/6 POG 6, 0261
96/7 Post
93/4 PowerPlay 54, -PointLdr 14
93/4 PP-Gamebreaker 8
93/4 Premier 450, 500
94/5 Premier 200, -Finest(T) 11
94/5 Premier-GoToGuy 8
95/6 ProMagnet 4
90/1 ProSet 58
91/2 ProSet 40, 280, 605
91/2 ProSet-ThePuck 6
92/3 ProSet 30, 252, -TL 2
91/2 PSPlatinum 24
90/1 Score 179, 369, Promo 179
90/1 S'HotCards 31, -Young 24
91/2 Score(CDN) 220, 309, 334
91/2 Score(U.S) 220, 305, 418
91/2 S-HotCard 10, -Young 21
92/3 Score 200,422,499, -USA 3
92/3 S-Shrpshtr 10, -Young 10
93/4 Score 240, (U.S.)DD6
93/4 S-Franchise 4, -AS 39, 50
94/5 Score CI6,DT18,NP6,TF5
95/6 Score 55,-Bordr 10,-Gld 19
96/7 Score 137,-Check 5,-Sud 5
97/8 Score 107
92/3 SeasonsPatch 1

93/4 SeasonsPatch 15
94/5 Select 29
95/6 SelectCertif. 60, -Double 7
96/7 SelectCertified 77
94 Semic 122, 352
95 Semic 118
91 SemicSticker 149
92 SemicSticker 158
93 SemicSticker 180
95/6 SkyBoxEmotion 33, Promo
95/6 SkBxE-Xcel 2, -Xcited 2
95/6 SkyBoxImpact 33, 243
96/7 SkyBoxImpact 108,-Blade 9
95/6 SkyMotion
94/5 SP 22, -Premier 18
95/6 SP 24, E7
96/7 SP 119, CW7
97/8 SPAuthentic 118
96/7 SPx 7
97/8 SPx 39, SPX2
96/7 SportFX MiniStix
97/8 SportFX MiniStix
95/6 Summit 82
96/7 Summit 138, -Voltage 10
95/6 SuperSticker 21, DieCut9
92/3 Topps 400
95/6 Topps 3, 235
95/6 Topps HGA2, PF8, 4PL
98/9 Topps 171
94/5 ToppsFinest 73, -Best(B) 5
95/6 ToppsFinest 175, G25
95 ToppsFinestBronze 13
96/7 ToppsNHLPicks 47, FT18
91/2 ToppsStadiumClub 46
92/3 T.StadiumClub 167, 255
93/4 T.StadiumClub 190, -AS
94/5 ToppsStadiumClub 59
95/6 ToppsStadiumClub 166
93/4 TSC-MembersOnly 20
94/5 TSC-MembersOnly 27
97/8 ToppsSticker 1
95/6 ToppsSuperSkills 65
90/1 UpperDeck 63, 316, 481
91/2 UpperDeck 36, 166, 629
92/3 UpperDeck 274, G8, WG19
92/3 UD'LockerAS 34
93/4 UpperDeck 235, 289, 314
93/4 UD HT18, R10, SP31
94/5 UpperDeck 322, SP17
94/5 UD C19, H13, IG3, R8
95/6 UD 227,241,422,SE104, F6
95/6 UD R47,-ASPredict MVP12
96/7 UpperDeck 35, 205, 312
96/7 UD HH17, SS15A, X12
97/8 UD 127, S17, SG57, T16C
93/4 UDBeAPlayer 13,-Roots 30
94/5 UDBAP UC6, -Aut. 12
94/5 UDBAP R12, R144
96/7 UDBlackDiamond 167
97/8 UDBlackDiamond 59
98/9 UDChoice 158
95/6 UDCollChoice 85
96/7 UDCollChoice 46, 297, 313
96/7 UDCC UD18, S6
97/8 UDCC 195, S13, SQ79
96/7 UpperDeck"Ice" 51, S8
97/8 UpperDeckIce 27
96 Wien 167
97/8 Zenith 19, Z22
89/90 CHI/Coke
90/1 CHI/Coke
91/2 CHI/Coke
93/4 CHI/Coke
96/7 PHO (3)
97/8 PHO (x3)

ROENICK, TREVOR
93/4 Maine 58

ROEST, STACY
91/2 SketchWHL 326
95/6 Adirondack

ROFF, PAUL
85/6 Minn-Duluth 11

ROGANO, BEN
88/9 NiagaraFalls 24

ROGER, SÉBASTIEN
98 BowmanCHL 106

ROGERS, KEN
91/2 AirCanadaSJHL 7, B17
92/3 MPSPhotoSJHL 134

ROGERS, MIKE
72-84 Dernière 82/3
79/80 OPC/Topps 43
80/1 OPC/Topps 143
81/2 O-Pee-Chee 127, 135, 140
81/2 Topps 32, 53, (E) 131
82/3 O-Pee-Chee 232
83/4 O-Pee-Chee 254
84/5 OPC 152, Topps 114
85/6 OPC/Topps 39
81/2 opcSticker 61
82/3 opcSticker 136
83/4 opcSticker 217
84/5 opcSticker 99
85/6 opcSticker 86 /219
75/6 opcWHA 8
77/8 opcWHA 17
82/3 Post
83/4 SouhaitsRen.KeyChain
85/6 EDM/RedRooster
88/9 EDM/ActionMagazine 128

ROGERS, SCOTT
91/2 AirCanadaSJHL C44
93/4 ClasicProspects 241

ROGGER, BRIAN
90/1 SketchQMJHL 154

ROGLES, CHRIS
93/4 Classic 77
94/5 Classic-Autograph
93/4 ClassicProspects 213
92/3 Clarkson
93/4 Indianapolis

RÖHL, DIETER
70/1 Kuvajulkaisut 98

ROHLICEK, JEFF
89/90 ProCards(IHL) 175
90/1 ProCards 357
91/2 ProCards 397
86/7 Fredericton
92/3 Toledo 2
93/4 Toledo 16

ROKLIK, PAVEL
94/5 APS 249

ROHLIN, LEIF
95/6 Donruss 344
94/5 EltSet 175,-Gld 12,-Stud 11
95 Globe 23
95 PaniniWorlds 143
89/90 SemicElitserien 245
90/1 SemicElitserien 153
91/2 SemicElitserien 257
92/3 SemicElitserien 281
96/7 VAN
96/7 VAN/IGA

ROHLOFF, JON
93/4 Classic 78
94/5 Classic-Autograph
93/4 ClassicProspects 224
95/6 Donruss 86
94/5 FleerUltra 260
95/6 Leaf 322
97/8 PacificRegime 16
96/7 PinnacleBeAPlayer 207
94/5 Premier 516
95/6 Topps 196
94/5 UpperDeck 378
95/6 UpperDeck 127
96/7 UpperDeck 11
96/7 UDCollChoice 21

ROHRBACK, DIRK
94/5 DEI 134
95/6 DEL 135

ROHRBACH, WILFRED
70/1 Kuvajulkaisut 97

ROKAMA, JOUNI
91/2 Jyvas-Hyva 61
92/3 Jyvas-Hyva 172
93/4 Jyvas-Hyva 314
93/4 Sisu 29
94/5 Sisu-Nolla. 4

ROLAND, LAYNE
91/2 SketchWHL 42
93/4 Portland

ROLFE, DALE
70/1 DadsCookies
70/1 EddieSargent 55
71/2 EddieSargent 118
72/3 EddieSargent 146
70/1 Esso Stamp
74/5 Loblaws
68/9 OPC/Topps 41
69/70 OPC/T. 100, OPC-Sticker
70/1 OPC 156
71/2 OPC/Topps 219
72/3 OPC 271
73/4 OPC 177
74/5 OPC 341
71/2 TheTorontoSun
70/1 DET/Marathon

ROLLINS, AL
45-64 BeeHives(CHIx2), (TOR)
48-52 Exhibits
51/2 Parkhurst 76
52/3 Parkhurst 31
53/4 Parkhurst 82
54/5 Parkhurst 77
92/3 Parkhurst 54 PR8
93/4 Parkhurst 51 DPR4
93/4 Parkie(56/7) 28
45-54 QuakerOats (x2)
54/5 Topps 26

ROLLINS, JERRY
76/7 opcWHA 43
76/7 Phoenix

ROLOSON, DWAYNE
94/5 Classic 61, AA10, -Aut
94/5 ClassicImages 41
97/8 Donruss 148
95/6 EdgeIce 73, TW8
95/6 FutureLegends 19
97/8 Omega 34
98/9 Pacific 124
97/8 PacificRegime 31
97/8 Pinnacle 87
96/7 PinnacleBeAPlayer 211
97/8 Score 38
97/8 UDCollChoice 41
94/5 SaintJohn
95/6 SaintJohn

ROLSTON, BRIAN
93/4 Classic 79
94/5 Classic 76, T38, -Aut.
94/5 ClassicFourSport 142
94/5 ClassicImages 97
93/4 ClassicProspects 90, LP10
95/6 Donruss 286, -ProPointer 9
95/6 EdgeIce 8
94/5 Flair 98
94/5 Fleer 117
93/4 FleerUltra 496
94/5 FleerUltra 320, -Prospect 7
94/5 Leaf 441
95/6 Leaf 294
94/5 LeafLimited 4
98/9 Pacific 270
97/8 Pacific-BestKept 54
97/8 PacificParamount 105
95/6 Parkhurst 394
94/5 ParkieSE 99
94/5 Pinnacle 255, 473, RTP8
95/6 Pinnacle 172
96/7 Pinnacle 7
93/4 PowerPlay 516
93/4 Premier-TeamUSA 5
94/5 Premier 438
94/5 Score TR7
95/6 Score 80
97/8 Score 205
97/8 Score(N.J.) 6
94/5 Select 177, YE10
94 Semic 133
94/5 SP-Premier 12
95/6 Topps 362, 13NG
94/5 T.Finest 4, -Best(R) 9
93/4 TSC-TeamUSA 21
91/2 UD 699, 'CzechWJC 86
94/5 UD 258, SP135, C13
95/6 UpperDeck 14
96/7 UpperDeck 285
97/8 UpperDeck 92, SG17
94/5 UDBeAPlayer-Aut. 33
95/6 UDCollChoice 273, 366
96/7 UDCollChoice 151
97/8 UDCollChoice 144
96/7 N.J/Sharp
91/2 LakeSuperior

ROMAINE, MARK
90/1 ProCards 578
93/4 Birmingham 18
91/2 Cincinnati

ROMAN, TOM
87/8 Brockville 9

ROMANCHUCK, TYLER
90/1 SketchWHL 34
91/2 SketchWHL 23

ROMANCHYCH, LARRY
72/3 EddieSargent 12
74/5 Loblaws
73/4 OPC/Topps 185
74/5 OPC/Topps 157
75/6 OPC/Topps 153
76/7 OPC 281
72/3 ATL
74/5 ATL

ROMANIUK, RUSS
92/3 Bowman 276
93/4 CanadaNats
93/4 FleerUltra 471
94/5 FleerUltra 394
92/3 O-Pee-Chee 263
91/2 opcPremier 162
92/3 PaniniSticker 59
91/2 Parkhurst 198
94/5 Parkhurst 265
91/2 Pinnacle 324
93/4 PowerPlay 492
91/2 ProSet 565
91/2 PSPlatinum 274
91/2 Score(CDN) 627, (U.S) 77T
92/3 Topps 390
92/3 ToppsStadiumClub 164
94/5 ToppsStadiumClub 260
91/2 UpperDeck 46
91/2 WPG/IGA

ROMANO, ROBERTO
86/7 OPC/Topps 152
86/7 opcSticker229 /100
84/5 PGH/Heinz
86/7 PGH/Kodak
80/1 QuébecRemparts

ROMANOV, STANISLAV
95 PaniniWorlds 48
96 Wien 150

ROMBOUGH, DOUG
74/5 Loblaws, -Update
74/5 OPC 279
75/6 OPC/Topps 161
73/4 BUF

ROME, BRIAN
82/3 Ottawa67s
84/5 SSMarie

ROMER, ANDY
94/5 DEL 11

ROMER, HEINRICH
94/5 DEL 11
95/6 DEL 17

ROMFO, JEFF
93/4 Minn-Duluth

ROMISHEVSKY, IGOR
72 Hellas 66
70/1 Kuvajulkaisut 15
69/70 MästarSerien 29
72 Panda
72 SemicSticker 6
74 SemicSticker 46
69/70 Soviet Stars
70/1 Soviet Stars
71/2 Soviet Stars
71/2 WilliamsFIN 14
72/3 WilliamsFIN 33

ROMMEL, WES
91/2 AirCanadaSJHL B3

ROMNES, DOC
34-43 BeeHives(CHI), (TOR)
33-35 DiamondMatch
36-39 DiamondMatch (1)

RONAN, ED
92/3 ClassicProspects 134
92/3 FleerUltra 333
92/3 opcPremier 41
92/3 Parkhurst 88
91/2 ProCards 90
93/4 ToppsStadiumClub 262
92/3 UpperDeck 491
92/3 MTL
92/3 MTL/OPC 45
93/4 MTL
94/5 MTL
95/6 WPG (x2)

RONAN, SKENE (SKEIN)
91 C55 Reprint 26
1911-12 Imperial (C55) 26
1912-13 Imperial (C57) 14
1910-11 Imperial Post 26

RONDEAU, JEREMY
95/6 SwiftCurrent

RONKAINEN, JARMO
70/1 Kuvajulkaisut 319

RONKAINEN, VESA
72/3 WilliamsFIN 294

RONNING, CLIFF
91/2 Bowman 313
92/3 Bowman 411
93/4 Donruss 357
94/5 Donruss 278
95/6 Donruss 79
96/7 Donruss 47
93/4 EASports 141
94/5 Flair 194
94/5 Fleer 230
92/3 FleerUltra 227
93/4 FleerUltra 119
94/5 FleerUltra 230
93/4 Leaf 183
94/5 Leaf 66
96/7 Leaf 173
89/90 OPC/Topps 45
91/2 OPC/Topps 59
92/3 O-Pee-Chee 94
89/90 opcSticker 20 /160
98/9 Pacific 343
97/8 PacificCrown 200
97/8 PacificCrownRoyale 106
97/8 PacificParamount 143
98/9 PacificParamount 185
89/90 PaniniSticker 122
91/2 PaniniSticker 46
92/3 PaniniSticker 30
93/4 PaniniSticker 168
94/5 PaniniSticker 145
95/6 PaniniSticker 290
96/7 PaniniSticker 295
91/2 Parkhurst 182
92/3 Parkhurst 193
93/4 Parkhurst 210
95/6 Parkhurst 479
94/5 ParkieSE 188
91/2 Pinnacle 106
92/3 Pinnacle 12
93/4 Pinnacle 69, 234
94/5 Pinnacle 113
95/6 Pinnacle 184
96/7 Pinnacle 163
97/8 PinnacleInside 173
95/6 Playoff 211
96/7 Playoff 398
94/5 POG 27
95/6 POG 269
93/4 PowerPlay 255
93/4 Premier 81
94/5 Premier 291
88/9 ProCards(Peoria)
95/6 ProMagnet 25
90/1 ProSet 526
91/2 ProSet 241
92/3 ProSet 195
91/2 PSPlatinum 236
90/1 ScoreTraded 81T
91/2 Score(CDN) 212, (U.S) 212
92/3 Score 254
93/4 Score 17, 443
94/5 Score 86
95/6 Score 75
96/7 Score 163
97/8 Score 244
92/3 SeasonsPatch 32
94/5 Select 122
95/6 SP 154
96/7 SP 124
92/3 Topps 81
95/6 Topps 99
96/7 ToppsNHLPicks105
91/2 ToppsStadiumClub 298
92/3 ToppsStadiumClub 373
93/4 ToppsStadiumClub 125
94/5 ToppsStadiumClub 200
95/6 ToppsStadiumClub 128
91/2 UpperDeck 208
92/3 UpperDeck 160
93/4 UpperDeck 211
94/5 UpperDeck 358
95/6 UpperDeck 102, SE174
96/7 UpperDeck 315
97/8 UpperDeck 132
95/6 UDBeAPlayer 91
95/6 UDCollChoice 17
96/7 UDCollChoice 270
97/8 UDCollChoice 199
96/7 UpperDeck"Ice"53
96/7 PHO
97/8 PHO
87/8 STL/Kodak
88/9 STL/Kodak
90/1 STL/Kodak
94/5 VAN
91/2 VAN
91/2 VAN/Molson
92/3 VAN/RoadTrip
93/4 VAN/Coins
95/6 VAN/BuildingADream 7

RONNQVIST, JONAS
97/8 udSwedish

RONNQVIST, PETTER
94/5 ElitSet 271
95/6 ElitSet 99, -Spidermen 10
91/2 SemicElitserien 56
92/3 SemicElitserien 76
95/6 udElite 152
97/8 udSwedish 149

RONTY, PAUL
45-64 BeeHives(BOS), (NYR)
48-52 Exhibits
51/2 Parkhurst 95
52/3 Parkhurst 24
53/4 Parkhurst 63
54/5 Parkhurst 66
54/5 Topps 15

ROODBOL, KEES
91/2 AvantGardeBCJ 112
92/3 BCJHL 166, 212

ROONEY, LARRY
91/2 Richmond 2

ROONEY, STEVE
87/8 O-Pee-Chee 223
89/90 ProCards'AHL 210
90/1 ProCards 364
85/6 MTL
85/6 MTL/ProvigoStickers
85/6? MTL/ProvigoPlacemats
86/7 MTL
87/8 MTL
88/9 N.J./Caretta
87/8 WPG

ROOT, BILL
72-84 Dernière 83/4
83/4 O-Pee-Chee 196
84/5 O-Pee-Chee 271
88/9 ProCards(Newmarket)
89/90 ProCards(AHL) 112
90/1 ProCards 162
82/3 MTL
82/3 MTL/Steinberg
83/4 MTL
84/5 TOR
86/7 TOR
90/1 Newmarket

ROSA, PAVEL
97/8 Bowman 51

ROSA, STANISLAV
94/5 APS 215

ROSANDER, OLA
89/90 SemicElitserien 227
90/1 SemicElitserien 69
91/2 SemicElitserien 243

ROSATI, MICHAEL
96/7 DEL 159
95 Globe 226
95 PaniniWorlds 77
95 Semic 171
93 SemicSticker 210
96 Wien 174
88/9 NiagaraFalls 6

ROSBERG, JARI
70/1 Kuvajulkaisut 303
71/2 WilliamsFIN 237
72/3 WilliamsFIN 221
73/4 WilliamsFIN 297

ROSCOE, RON
75/6 Hamilton

ROSE, ARTHUR
51/2 LavalDairy 94

ROSE, JARRETT
95/6 Slapshot 132

ROSE, JAY
91/2 Cincinnati

ROSEN, JOHN
94/5 ElitSet 12
95/6 ElitSet 80, -Goldies 8
95/6 udElite 132, NA17

ROSEN, ROGER
95/6 ElitSet 297, -Rookies 9
95/6 udElite 201
97/8 udSwedish 195, 220, C30

ROSENBERG, KARI
93/4 Jyvas-Hyva 44
95 Latkaliiga 10
93/4 Sisu 234
94/5 Sisu 34, -Junior 6, -Nolla 5
95/6 Sisu 16, -GhostGoal 6
95/6 SisuLimited 82

ROSENBLATT, HOWIE
92/3 ClassicProspects 44
91/2 ProCards 60
92/3 Cincinnati
94/5 Greensboro

ROSENHECK, JERRY
92/3 Clarkson

ROSENQVIST, PER
92/3 SemicElitserien 212

ROSOL, PETR
94 Semic 187
89 SemicSticker 200

ROSS, ART
38/9 BruinsMagazine
91 C55 Reprint 31
83&87 HallOfFame 74
83 HHOF Postcard (E)
96/7 HHOFLegends 82
1911-12 Imperial (C55) 31
1910-11 Imperial (C56) 8, 12
1912-13 Imperial (C57) 20
1910-11 Imperial Post 31
60/1 Topps 27
61/2 Topps Stamp
36/7 WWGum V356 96
91/2 BOS/Legends

ROSS, BRIAN
83/4 Kitchener 25

ROSS, DON
72 SemicSticker 122

ROSS, GORD
91/2 SketchOHL 361

ROSS, PATRIK
89/90 SemicElitserien 116
90/1 SemicElitserien 117
91/2 SemicElitserien 120
92/3 SemicElitserien 141

ROSS, PHIL
83&87 HallOfFame 58
83 HHOF Postcard (D)

ROSS, TOM
93/4 Mich.State

ROSSITER, KYLE
98 BowmanCHL 157, A7

ROSSETTI, LUC
79 PaniniSticker 263

ROSSETTI, MIKE
91/2 ProCards 56
89/90 Johnstown 25

ROSSI, REIJO
72/3 WilliamsFIN 275

ROSSIGNOL, ROLAND
51/2 BasDuFleuve 43

ROST, SONNY
30s? ABC ChewingGum 37

ROSVALL, KAI
70/1 Kuvajulkaisut 235
71/2 WilliamsFIN 252
73/4 WilliamsFIN 316

ROTA, DARCY
74/5 Loblaws
74/5 OPC 269
75/6 OPC/Topps 66
76/7 OPC/Topps 47
77/8 OPC/Topps 117
78/9 OPC/Topps 47
79/80 O-Pee-Chee 360
80/1 O-Pee-Chee 301
81/2 O-Pee-Chee 343
82/3 O-Pee-Chee 355
83/4 O-Pee-Chee 358
84/5 O-Pee-Chee 328
83/4 opcSticker 272
84/5 opcSticker 280
80/1 Pepsi Cap
82/3 Post
83/4 PuffySticker 5
84/5 7ElevenDisk
83/4 SouhaitsRen.KeyChain
84/5 Topps 139
83/4 Vachon 115
79/80 ATL/B&W
80/1 VAN
80/1 VAN/Silverwood
81/2 VAN
81/2 VAN/Silverwood
82/3 VAN
83/4 VAN
84/5 VAN

ROTA, RANDY
74/5 Loblaws
74/5 OPC 362
75/6 OPC/Topps 237
76/7 O-Pee-Chee 353

RÖTHELI, ANDRE
91 SemicSticker 195
92 SemicSticker 213

ROTHSCHILD, SAM
25-27 Anonymous 100
24/5 Champs (C144)
24/5 MapleCrispette (V130) 19
24/5 (V145-2) 37

ROTKIRCH, JOHANN
72 SemicSticker 114

ROUHIAINEN, MARKKU
71/2 WilliamsFIN 270

ROULEAU, MICHEL
73/4 QuébecNordiques

ROULSTON, TOM
82/3 O-Pee-Chee 118
83/4 O-Pee-Chee 42
84/5 O-Pee-Chee 179
83/4 opcSticker 103
84/5 opcSticker 123
83/4 Vachon 39
88/9 EDM/ActionMagazine 15
82/3 EDM/RedRooster
84/5 PGH/Heinz

ROUPE, CLAES
89/90 SemicElitserien 118

ROUPE, MAGNUS
89/90 SemicElitserien 90
90/1 SemicElitserien 263
91/2 SemicElitserien 94
95/6 udElite DS14

ROUSE, BOB
93/4 Donruss 333
92/3 FleerUltra 214
93/4 Leaf 230
89/90 OPC/Topps 26
91/2 opcPremier 151
97/8 PacificRegime 72
89/90 PaniniSticker 351
90/1 PaniniSticker 164
91/2 PaniniSticker 101
91/2 Parkhurst 176
94/5 ParkieSE 51
92/3 Pinnacle 358
93/4 Pinnacle 289
94/5 Pinnacle 374
95/6 Pinnacle 163
94/5 POG 359
93/4 Premier 207
94/5 Premier 393
90/1 ProSet 554
91/2 ProSet 228
90/1 Score 147
91/2 Score(CDN) 246
92/3 Score 130
93/4 Score 304
96/7 Score 125
95/6 Topps 206
93/4 ToppsStadiumClub 353
94/5 ToppsStadiumClub 238
90/1 UpperDeck 89
94/5 UpperDeck 55
95/6 UDBeAPlayer 88
84/5 MIN
85/6 MIN
86/7 MIN/7Eleven 9
87/8 MIN
88/9 MIN/American
90/1 TOR/P.L.A.Y. 6
93/4 TOR/Abalene
92/3 TOR/Kodak
93/4 TOR/Blacks 5
89/90 WSH
89/90 WSH/Kodak

ROUSEK, MARTIN
94/5 APS 217
95/6 APS 168

ROUSSEAU, BOBBY
45-64 BeeHives(MTL)
64-67 BeeHives(MTL)
62 CeramicTiles
63-5 ChexPhoto
64/5 CokeCap MTL-15
65/6 CocaCola
70/1 Colgate Stamp 35
70/1 DadsCookies
70/1 EddieSargent 96
71/2 EddieSargent 117
72/3 EddieSargent 145
70/1 Esso Stamp
74/5 Loblaws
68/9 OPC/Topps 65
69/70 OPC/Topps 9
70/1 OPC 170,OPC/T-Deckle 14
71/2 OPC/Topps 218
72/3 OPC 233
73/4 OPC 233
74/5 OPC 326
62/3 Parkhurst 47
63/4 Parkhurst 35, 94
94/5 Parkie(64/5) 84
95/6 Parkie(66/7) 77, 126
95/6 Parkie(66/7) 143, 148, SL4
67 Post FlipBook
66/7 Post'Large, 'Small
68/9 Post Marble
72 SemicSticker 200
61/2 ShirriffCoin 117
62/3 ShirriffCoin 29, 56
68/9 ShirriffCoin MTL9
71/2 TheTorontoSun
64/5 Topps 80
65/6 Topps 70
66/7 Topps 7, 132, -USATest 7
67/8 Topps 68
54-67 TorontoStar 66/7, V11
56-66 TorontoStar 63/4
61/2 York 35
63/4 York 25
67/8 York 33
62/3 YorkTransfer 18
70/1 MIN
67/8 MTL
67/8 MTL/IGA
68/9 MTL
69/70 MTL/ProStar
71 MTL/Pins

ROUSSEAU, GUY
52/3 AnonymousOHL 142
51-54 LaPatrie 5Apr53
51-54 LaPatrie 17Jan54

ROUSSEAU, ROLLAND
51/2 LavalDairy 88
52/3 StLawrence 8

ROUSSEL, DOMINIC
92/3 Bowman 92
93/4 ClassicProspects 55
93/4 Donruss 243
94/5 Donruss 263
95/6 Donruss 267
96/7 DonrussCdnIce-Gardien 7
93/4 Durivage 39
92/3 FleerUltra 159
93/4 FleerUltra 392
92/3 Kraft-Disk
93/4 Kraft-Cutout
93/4 Leaf 244
94/5 Leaf 223
92/3 O-Pee-Chee 198
92/3 opcPremier 51, -TopRook 3
92/3 PaniniSticker 183
94/5 PaniniSticker 45
91/2 Parkhurst 450
92/3 Parkhurst 129
93/4 Parkhurst 417
94/5 Parkhurst 169
91/2 Pinnacle 343
92/3 Pinnacle 96, -Team2000 11
93/4 Pinnacle 97, -Masks 4
94/5 Pinnacle 208
94/5 POG 290
93/4 PowerPlay 409
93/4 Premier 335
94/5 Premier 56
90/1 ProCards 31
91/2 ProCards 265
91/2 ProSet 552
92/3 ProSet 235
92/3 Score 464, -YoungStar 36
93/4 Score 82
94/5 Score 105
95/6 Score 182
92/3 SeasonsPatch 40
96/7 Summit 50
92/3 Topps 10, 213
92/3 ToppsStadiumClub 315
93/4 ToppsStadiumClub 109
91/2 UpperDeck 583
92/3 UpperDeck 31, AC6
93/4 UpperDeck 336
94/5 UpperDeck 397
95/6 UDBeAPlayer 157
92/3 PHA/UD 11FEB93
92/3 PHA/UD 21MAR93
92/3 PHA/UD 22OCT92
92/3 PHA/JCPenney
93/4 PHA 09DEC93
93/4 PHA 19MAR94
93/4 PHA/JCPenney
94/5 PHA

ROUSSON, BORIS
93/4 ClassicProspects 183
91/2 ProCards 200
95/6 Sisu 95, 161, 381
95/6 Sisu-Ghost 2, -Special 2
96/7 Sisu 95,181,-Gm 3,-Might 2
95/6 SisuLimited 29
90/1 SketchQMJHL 64
97/8 udSwedish 50
92/3 Binghampton

ROUSU, MIUIKA
95/6 Sisu 332
96/7 Sisu 142, -Energy 9

ROUTANEN, ARTO
89/90 SemicElitserien 100
95/6 udElite 174

ROUTHIER, J.M.
88/9 ProCards(Halifax)
89/90 ProCards(AHL) 160
89/90 QUE/Police
89/90 Halifax

ROUTHIER, STÉPHANE
93/4 Slapshot(Drum.) 2

ROUVALI, SIMO
95/6 Sisu 132
96/7 Sisu 143

ROW, TODD
96/7 Halifax (1),(2)
97/8 Halifax (1)

ROWLAND, DEAN
91/2 AvantGardeBCJ 85

ROWBOTHAM, DAVE
88/9 ProCards(Binghampton)

ROWBOTHAM, KEN
89/90 SketchOHL 82
90/1 SketchOHL 17

ROWE, BOBBY
91 C55 Reprint 23
1911-12 Imperial (C55) 23
1912-13 Imperial (C57) 11
1910-11 Imperial Post 23

ROWE, JON
92/3 MPSPhotoSJHL 99

ROWE, SEAN
95/6 Louisiana

ROWE, TOM
79/80 OPC/Topps 99, 113
80/1 OPC/Topps 214
81/2 O-Pee-Chee 139
78/9 WSH
79/80 WSH
83/4 Moncton 12

ROWELL, RYAN
96/7 Halifax (1),(2)

ROWLAND, CHRIS
90/1 SketchWHL 310
91/2 SketchWHL 34
89/90 Spokane
94/5 ThunderBay

ROWORTH, KIRK
89/90 Saskatoon 17

ROY, ADAM
93/4 Minn-Duluth

ROY, ALLAIN
92/3 CanadaNats
94/5 Sisu-Nolla. 8

ROY, ANDRÉ
95/6 Edgelce 60

ROY, CLAUDE
52/3 AnonymousOHL 34

ROY, DARCY
81/2 Ottawa67s
82/3 Ottawa67s
83/4 Ottawa67s

ROY, GEORGES
51/2 LavalDairy 30
52/3 StLawrence 92

ROY, JEAN-YVES
92/3 Classic 80
92 ClassicFourSport 203
94/5 ClassicImages 96
93/4 ClassicProspects 182
97/8 PacificCrown 313
94/5 Score CT12
97/8 Score(BOS) 11
94/5 UpperDeck 407
97/8 UpperDeck 12
97/8 UDCollChoice 19
92/3 Binghampton
94/5 Binghampton
92/3 Maine (1) 14

ROY, LUC
51/2 LacStJean 22

ROY, MARTIN
90/1 SketchQMJHL 118, 136
91/2 SketchQMJHL 186
95/6 Richmond

ROY, MARC-OLIVIER
97/8 Bowman 44

ROY, PATRICK
95/6 Aces A (Spades)
96/7 Aces A (Hearts)
97/8 Aces K (Hearts)
90/1 Bowman 50
91/2 Bowman 335
92/3 Bowman 74, 239
95/6 Bowman 15
92/3 ClassicProspects 33
95/6 CoolTrade 16
96/7 CorinthianHeadliners
97/8 CorinthianHeadliners
93/4 Donruss 178, L,-Elit 9,-Ice 1
94/5 Donruss 328, -Elite 10
94/5 Donruss-Masked 9, -Dom 3
95/6 Donruss 338, -Between 7
96/7 Donruss 112,-Elit 10,-Bet 1
97/8 Donruss 5, -Elite 5,-Betwn 1
96/7 D.CdnIce 19, -Gardiens 1
97/8 D.CdnIce 1,-Gard 1,-Scp 27
95/6 DonrussElite 64, -Painted 1
96/7 DonrussElite 66, -Painted 1
97/8 DonrussElite 14,142
97/8 D.Elite-Craft 14,-PrmNum 2
97/8 DonrussPreferred 86, 168
97/8 D.Pref -ColGrd 1,-PrecM 5
97/8 D.Pref-Tin 5,24,-WTin 9,12
97/8 DonrussPriority 1, 197
97/8 D.Prio-OpDay 1,-PostGen 1
97/8 D.Prio-Postcard 1,-Stamp 1
97/8 DonrussStudio 7, 110
97/8 D.Studio-Portr 7,-Sil 3
96/7 Duracell DC17, JB17
92/3 Durivage 50, -Aut
93/4 Durivage 17, -Aut
93/4 EASports 72
97/8 EssoOlympic 17
94/5 Flair 91, -HotNumbers 8
96/7 Flair 20,-N&T 2, -HotG 10
94/5 Fleer 107, -Netminder 9
96/7 Fleer 24,-Pears 9, -Vez 9
95/6 FleerMetal 78
92/3 FleerUltra 108, -AS 3,-AW 4
93/4 FleerUltra 39, -AS 1
94/5 FleerUltra 113,-AS 6,-Pre 6
95/6 FU 83, 225, 377, -Prem 10
96/7 FleerUltra 39, -Clear 8
96/7 F.Picks-Dream 8, -Fab 40
91/2 Gillette 28
95 Globe 73
93/4 HighLiner 1
93/4 HockeyWit 3
95/6 Hoyle'EAST As
92/3 HumptyDumpty (1)
94/5 Incomnet
97/8 KatchMedallion 41, 160
91/2 Kelloggs 1
92/3 Kelloggs Post er
93/4 KennerSLU
96/7 KennerSLU
97/8 KennerSLU -1on1
94 Koululainen
86/7 Kraft Sports 37
89/90 Kraft 25
90/1 Kraft 49, 90
91/2 Kraft 76
92/3 Kraft-AllStar, -Disk
93/4 Kraft'Cutout, -Gold
94/5 Kraft , 'Masks
95/6 Kraft'Crease
96/7 KraftDinner
97/8 Kraft-CdnPro, -RoadToNag
97/8 Kraft -Sticker
93/4 Leaf 33, 100, -Painted 4
93/4 Leaf-GoldAS 5, -Studio
94/5 Leaf 41,-Gld 3,-Ltd 12,-Cr 1
95/6 Leaf 200
96/7 Leaf 38, -Shut 1,-Sweater 2
97/8 Leaf 128, 187, -PipeDrm 3
94/5 LeafLimited 28
95/6 LeafLimited 66, -Stick 4
96/7 LeafLimited 9, -Stubble 1
96/7 LeafPrefrd 1,-Stl 36,-Msk 4
97/8 Limited 44, 151, 198,-fab 20
96/7 Maggers 35
96/7 McD'Masks
91/2 McDonalds McD8, McH-6
92/3 McDonalds Mc H-06
93/4 McDonalds M cD23
94/5 McDonalds 4
95/6 McDonalds 25
96/7 McDonalds M cD30
97/8 McDonalds McD23, F5
97/8 McDonalds -Medallions
96/7 MetalUniverse 37
96/7 MU-Armour 11, -Cool 9
97/8 Omega 64, 249, -Silks 4
97/8 Omega -NoScoringZone 2
86/7 OPC/Topps 53
87/8 OPC/Topps 163
88/9 OPC/Topps 116, T-AS 12
89/90 OPC/Topps 17, T-AS 6
89/90 OPC 298, 307, 322
90/1 OPC/Topps 198, 219, E
90/1 OPC 512
91/2 OPC/Topps 270, 413
92/3 O-Pee-Chee 111, 164
92/3 OPC -25Years 19, -Box
90/1 opcPremier 101
91/2 opcPremier 14, 170
87/8 opcStars 36
88/9 opcStars 33
86/7 opcSticker 5, 19, 132/118
87/8 opcSticker 13, 73
88/9 opcSticker 38, 45, 159, 167
88/9 opcSticker 214, 115/245
89/90 opcSticker 57, 128, 211
89/90 opcSticker 161/21, 210/72
89/90 opcStickFS 28
98/9 Pacific 33, -Cram 4,-D.Ice 6
98/9 Pcfc-GoldCrown 9,-TmCL 7
97/8 PacificCrown 33
97/8 PCC-Cramer 5, -Gold 8
97/8 PCC-InThe 5, -TeamCL 7
97/8 PacificCrownRoyale 37
97/8 PCR-Bla 6,-Cramr 5,-Frz 5
97/8 PacificDynagon! 33, 138
97/8 PacificD-BestKept 26
97/8 PcfcD-Dynamic 6A, -King 3
97/8 PcfcD-Stone 6,-Tand 4, 25
97/8 PacificInvincible 38, -Feat 9
97/8 PcfcParamount 54,-BigN 6
97/8 PcfcP-CdnGrt 4,-Glove 5
97/8 PacificP-Photoengraving 6
98/9 PcfcParamount 60,-Glove 6
98/9 PcfcP. HOF 4, -TmCL 7
97/8 PacificRegime 56, 217
97/8 PcfcRevolution 38,-TmCL 7
97/8 PcfcRev -AllStarGame 7
97/8 PcfcRev-Icons 4,-RetrnTo 5
90/1 Panini(MTL) 19, G
87/8 PaniniSticker 56, 376B
88/9 PaniniSticker 252, 402
89/90 PaniniStick. 235, 376, 383
90/1 PaniniSticker 51, 323
91/2 PaniniSticker 184, 333
92/3 PaniniSticker 147, 277
93/4 PaniniSticker B
94/5 PaniniSticker 18
95/6 PaniniSticker 46
96/7 PaniniSticker 247
97/8 PaniniSticker 127, 208
91/2 PH 90, 220, 442, 463, 470
92/3 Parkhurst 84, 463, 510
93/4 PH 100, D10, E4, G9
94/5 PH 113, 312, -Crash 12
95/6 Parkhurst 113, 323
95/6 PH-Crown(2) 2, -Goal 3
94/5 ParkieSE seV3
91/2 Pinnacle 175, 387, B1
92/3 Pinnacle 130
93/4 Pinnacle 150, 228, -Team 1
94/5 Pinn. 30,GT5,MA1,NL1,TP1
95/6 Pinnacle 169,-Clr 10,-Frst 4
96/7 Pinnacle 138,-Tm 8,-Msk 1
97/8 Pinnacle 29, -GoalieTin 8
97/8 Pinnacle -Masks 5,-TmP 1
96/7 P.BeAPlayer-Stacking 13
97/8 P.BAP-Stack/Pad 4,-Take 4
97/8 P.BeeHive 19,-TeamBH 15
97/8 Pinn.Certified 2, -Team 2
97/8 Pinnacle-EPIX 7
95/6 PinnacleFANtasy 10
96/7 PinnacleFANtasy 19
97/8 P.Inside 37,-Can 1,-BigCan
97/8 PinnInside -Stop 1, -Track 2
97/8 PinnacleMasks
96/7 PinnacleMint 21
97/8 PinnacleMint 11
97/8 PinnacleUncut
95/6 P.Zenith 117, -ZTeam 1
96/7 P.Zenith 35, -Champion 11
97/8 PlaymateProZone
95/6 Playoff 55, 166, 274
96/7 Playoff 431
94/5 POG 283
95/6 POG 155, 005, 027
96/7 Post
97/8 Post, F2
93/4 PowerPlay 133
93/4 PP-Game 9, -Net 7
93/4 Premier 1, -Promo 1
93/4 Prmr-Black(OPC) 8, (T) 22
94/5 Premier 125, 310, 455
95/6 ProMagnet 19
90/1 ProSet 157, 359, 391, 399
91/2 PS 125, 304, 599, 613,CC2
91/2 PS-ThePuck 14
92/3 ProSet 2, 85, CC2
91/2 PSPlatinum 61
90/1 Score 10,312,344,354,364
90/1 S-Promo 10, -HotCards 25
91/2 Score(CDN) 75, 314, 372
91/2 Score(U.S) 75, 342, 424
92/3 Score 295,418,428,489,527
93/4 Score 315, -AS 18
93/4 S-Dream 2, -Franchise 10
94/5 Score DT1, TF12
95/6 Score 145, 324, -Dream 11
96/7 Score 1, -Dream 12, -Net 1
97/8 Score 33, -NetWorth 13
97/8 Score(COL) 1
92/3 SeasonsPatch 21
93/4 SeasonsPatch 16
94/5 Select 96, FL1
95/6 SelectCertified 81, -Gold 10
96/7 SelectCertified 81, -Freez 2
89 SemicSticker 54
91 SemicSticker 52
93 SemicSticker 189
95/6 SkyBoxEmotion 91
95/6 SkBxImpact 87, -Deflect 8
96/7 SkyBoxImpact 27, -Zero 9
96/7 SkBxI-Countdown 9
94/5 SP 59
95/6 SP 30, E9
96/7 SP 35, CW6, GF3
97/8 SPAuthentic 37, I24, S2, T2
96/7 SPx 10, HH2
97/8 SPx 10, -DuoView
98/9 SPx"Finite" 24,119,154,171
95/6 Summit 149,-GM 1,-InThe 3
96/7 Summit 87, -In 1, -Untou 15
95/6 SuperSticker 66, -DieCut 2
96/7 TeamOut
92/3 Topps 110, 263, 491, 508
95/6 Topps 60, 377, PF3
95/6 Topps HGC1, 1CG, M20
98/9 Topps 190, L8, M16
98/9 Topps -RookieReprint 4
94/5 ToppsFinest 30
94/5 TF-Division 1, -Ring 14
95/6 ToppsFinest 13, 145
94 ToppsFinestBronze 3
96/7 T.Picks 11, ID7, FT1
91/2 ToppsStadiumClub 107
92/3 T.StadiumClub 133, 252
93/4 T.StadiumClub 231, -AS
93/4 TSC-Finest 11, -Master(1) 7
94/5 TSC 33, 178, -Finest 9
95/6 T.StadiumClub 15, EN4, M3
91/2 TSC-MembersOnly
93/4 TSC-MembersOnly 23
94/5 TSC-MembersOnly 1
97/8 ToppsSticker 247
95/6 ToppsSuperSkills 81
90/1 UD 153, 207, 317, 496
90/1 UpperDeck-Promo 241
91/2 UpperDeck 137, 614
92/3 UD 149, 438, 440, W6
92/3 UpperDeck'LockerAS 12
93/4 UD 49, SP-81, AW4, NL6
94/5 UD 121, SP42, H5, H26
95/6 UD 39,297,SE110,H15,R55
96/7 UD 38, 196, 199, 365
96/7 UD HH11, LS6, X5, SS2A
97/8 UD 210, 420, SG2, S2
97/8 UD SS30, T2B, GJ2
93/4 UDBAP'Roots 2
94/5 UDBAP R121, R179, UC8
95/6 UDBeAPlayer 197
96/7 UDBlackDiamond 174, RC4
97/8 UDBlackDiamond 41, PC2
98/9 UDChoice 54, 232, 243
98/9 UDChoice 309, BH21, SQ3
95/6 UDCollChoice 95
96/7 UDCollChoice 65, 307, 314
96/7 UDCC 346, S4, UD19
97/8 UDCC 56, 316, S23, SQ86
97/8 udDiamondVision 2, DM2
96/7 UpperDeck"Ice" 107, S5
97/8 UpperDeckIce 83,IC2,L10B
97/8 ValuNet
96 Wien SG7
97/8 Zenith 10,Z3,-ChasngCup 1
97/8 Zenith -ZTeam 3
96/7 COL/PhotoPucks
97/8 COL/DenverPostPins 3
97/8 COL/Postcard
85/6 MTL
85/6? MTL/ProvigoPlacemats
85/6 MTL/ProvigoStickers
86/7 MTL
87/8 MTL
87/8 MTL/Stickers 23, 42-43,
87/8 MTL/Stickers 69,71,74, 76
88/9 MTL
89/90 MTL
89/90 MTL/Figurine

89/90 MTL/Kraft
90/1 MTL
91/2 MTL
92/3 MTL
92/3 MTL/OPC 30
93/4 MTL
94/5 MTL
95/6 MTL

ROY, PIERRE
75/6 opcWHA 25
73/4 QuébecNordiques
76/7 QuébecNordiques
77/8 NovaScotia

ROY, SERGE
90/1 ProCards 426

ROY, SIMON
91/2 SketchQMJHL 61

ROY, STÉPHANE
90/1 CanadaNats
91/2 CanadaNats
92/3 CanadaNats
92 CanadaWinterOlympics 175
88/9 ProCards(Kalamazoo)
94/5 SigRookies 8

ROY, TRAVIS
95/6 PinnacleFANtasy 31

ROYER, REMI
95/6 Bowman P30
98 BowmanCHL 87

ROYLAND, LAYNE
90/1 SketchWHL 331

ROYMARK, TOM
79 PaniniSticker 297

ROZON, MARTI
91/2 SketchQMJHL 175

ROZSIVAL, MICHAL
98 BowmanCHL 64, SC20

RUARK, MARK
90/1 SketchWHL 203

RUARK, MIKE
91/2 ProCards 393
90/1 SketchWHL 311
92/3 Phoenix
89/90 Portland

RUBACHUK, BRAD
91/2 ProCards 11
90/1 SketchWHL 127
94/5 Binghampton
88/9 Lethbridge
89/90 Lethbridge
91/2 Rochester/Dunkin'Donuts
91/2 Rochester/Kodak
92/3 Rochester/Dunkin'Donuts
92/3 Rochester/Kodak
93/4 Rochester

RUBIC, ROB
84/5 Kitchener 16
85/6 Sudbury 9

RUCCHIN, STEVE
94/5 ClassicImages 56
95/6 Donruss 140
97/8 Donruss 49
97/8 DonrussPreferred 45
95/6 FleerMetal 4
95/6 FleerUltra 202
95/6 Leaf 54
97/8 Leaf 101
97/8 Limited
96/7 MetalUniverse 5
97/8 Omega 5
98/9 Pacific 62
97/8 PacificCrown 104
97/8 PacificCrownRoyale 3
97/8 PcfcDynagon! 4,-Tandm 30
97/8 PacificParamount 5
98/9 PacificParamount 5
95/6 PaniniSticker 222
96/7 PaniniSticker 226
97/8 PaniniSticker 184
95/6 Parkhurst 272
95/6 Pinnacle 58
96/7 Pinnacle 137
97/8 Pinnacle 151
96/7 PinnacleBeAPlayer 186
97/8 PinnacleCertified 64
97/8 PinnacleInside 188
95/6 POG 26
96/7 Score 186
97/8 Score 176
97/8 Score(ANA) 3
95/6 SP 4
96/7 SP 6
97/8 SPAuthentic 5
95/6 Topps 33
95/6 ToppsFinest 64
95/6 ToppsStadiumClub 214
94/5 UpperDeck 480
95/6 UpperDeck 425, SE92
96/7 UpperDeck 214
97/8 UpperDeck 2
96/7 UDBlackDiamond 20
98/9 UDChoice 6
96/7 UDCollChoice3
97/8 UDCollChoice 7
94/5 ANA/Carl'sJr 19
95/6 ANA
96/7 ANA/UpFrontSports 11

RUCHAR, MILAN
94/5 APS 67

RUCHTY, MATT
91/2 ProCards 410

RUCINSKI, MIKE
98/9 Pacific 46
93/4 Slapshot(Detroit) 6
94/5 Slapshot(Detroit) 5
94/5 Slapshot(MEM) 79
95/6 Slapshot 61

RUCINSKI, MIKE
88/9 ProCards(Saginaw)
89/90 ProCards(IHL) 61
86/7 Moncton 25

RUCINSKY, MARTIN
94/5 APS 221
91/2 Classic 17
91/2 ClassicFourSport 17, -Aut.
93/4 Donruss 281
96/7 Donruss 123
96/7 DonrussCanadianIce 81
96/7 Flair 50
92/3 FleerUltra 390
93/4 FleerUltra 191
94/5 FleerUltra 179
93/4 Leaf 152
96/7 Leaf 96
97/8 Omega 122
92/3 opcPremier 124
98/9 Pacific 257
97/8 PacificCrown 220
98/9 PacificParamount 117
93/4 PaniniSticker 74
96/7 PaniniSticker 39
97/8 PaniniSticker 36
95 PaniniWorlds 202
91/2 Parkhurst 366
92/3 Parkhurst 149
93/4 Parkhurst 170
94/5 Parkhurst 191
95/6 Parkhurst 379
93/4 Pinnacle 196
94/5 Pinnacle 416
96/7 Pinnacle 63
97/8 Pinnacle 172
96/7 PinnacleBeAPlayer 124
97/8 PinnacleInside 96
93/4 PowerPlay 203
93/4 Premier 67
91/2 ProCards 230
92/3 ProSet 238
92/3 Score 474
93/4 Score 254
96/7 Score 134
97/8 Score 152
97/8 Score(MTL) 9
94 Semic 177
95 Semic 152
92 SemicSticker 136
96/7 SkyBoxImpact 64
92/3 Topps 523
98/9 Topps 15
96/7 ToppsNHLPicks 59
93/4 ToppsStadiumClub 11
94/5 ToppsStadiumClub 126
91/2 UpperDeck 19, 70
92/3 UpperDeck 556
93/4 UpperDeck 6
94/5 UpperDeck 201
95/6 UpperDeck 485
96/7 UpperDeck 280
97/8 UpperDeck 89
96/7 UDCollChoice 143
96-98 MTL
92/3 QUE/PetroCanada
94/5 QUE/BurgerKing

RUCK, COLIN
90/1 SketchWHL 181
89/90 Regina

RUDBERG, JONAS
91/2 SketchOHL 333

RUDDICK, KEN
92/3 MPSPhotoSJHL 51
89/90 SketchOHL 134
90/1 SketchOHL 18
89/90 NiagaraFalls

RUDENKO, BOGDAN
95/6 Slapshot 140

RUDY, WES
92/3 BCJHL 20

RUEL, CLAUDE
72-84 Dernière 80/1
69/70 MTL/ProStar
71 MTL/Pins
76/7 MTL
77/8 MTL
78/9 MTL
79/80 MTL
80/1 MTL

RUETER, DIRK
80/1 SSMarie
81/2 SSMarie

RUFF, JASON
92/3 Classic 109
92/3 ClassicFourSport 216
92/3 ClassicProspects 45
91/2 ProCards 46
90/1 SketchWHL 138
92/3 UpperDeck 522
93/4 AtlantaKnights
88/9 Lethbridge
89/90 Lethbridge
92/3 Peoria

RUFF, LINDY
80/1 O-Pee-Chee 319
82/3 O-Pee-Chee 31
84/5 O-Pee-Chee 29, Topps 23
86/7 OPC/Topps 4
88/9 OPC/Topps 40
90/1 OPC/Topps 143
84/5 opcSticker 213
87/8 PaniniSticker 35
82/3 Post
91/2 ProCards 6
82/3 BUF/Wendt 5
84/5 BUF/BlueShield
85/6 BUF
86/7 BUF
88/9 BUF/BlueShield
87/8 BUF/BlueShield
87/8 BUF/WonderBread
88/9 BUF/WonderBread
96/7 FLA/WinnDixie
89/90 NYR/MarineMidland
91/2 Rochester/Dunkin'Donuts
91/2 Rochester/Genny
91/2 Rochester/Kodak
92/3 SanDiego

RUISMA, MATTI
80/1 Mallasjuoma 214

RUISMA, V.M.
78/9 SM-Liiga 20, 238

RULLIER, JOÉ
96/7 Rimouski

RUMBLE, DARREN
92/3 FleerUltra 148
93/4 FleerUltra 153
94/5 PaniniSticker 107
92/3 Parkhurst 356
93/4 Parkhurst 411
93/4 PowerPlay 173
93/4 Premier 356
89/90 ProCards(AHL) 342
90/1 ProCards 34
91/2 ProCards 271
93/4 ToppsStadiumClub 418
92/3 UpperDeck 110
93/4 OTT/Kraft
86/7 Kitchener 7
87/8 Kitchener 24
88/9 Kitchener 28

RUMRICH, JÜRGEN
94/5 DEL 66
95/6 DEL 66
96/7 DEL 262
95 PaniniWorlds 74
94 Semic 286
92 SemicSticker 185

RUMRICH, MICHAEL
94/5 DEL 214
95/6 DEL 213
95 Globe 220
95 PaniniWorlds 65
92 SemicSticker 184
93 SemicSticker 167

RUNDQVIST, THOMAS
94 Semic 69
89/90 SemicElitserien 85
90/1 SemicElitserien 261
91/2 S.Elitserien 90,314,324,346
92/3 SemicElitserien 112
82 SemicSticker 17
89 SemicSticker 18
91 SemicSticker 39
92 SemicSticker 62
93 SemicSticker 10

RUNGE, PAUL
34-43 BeeHives(MTL.M)
36-39 DiamondMatch (2), (3)
36/7 OPC (V304D) 106
37/8 OPC (V304E) 167
28/9 PaulinsCandy 56
36/7 WWGum (V356) 81

RUOHONEN, JUHANI
66/7 Champion 171
70/1 Kuvajulkaisut 250
78/9 SM-Liiga 89
71/2 WilliamsFIN 216
72/3 WilliamsFIN 165
73/4 WilliamsFIN 231

RUOKONEN, MIIKKA
93/4 Jyvas-Hyva 56
95/6 Sisu 74
96/7 Sisu 74

RUOKOSALMI, ILPO
71/2 WilliamsFIN 293

RUONTIMO, KARI
66/7 Champion 87

RUOTANEN, ARTO
94/5 ElitSet 190
95/6 ElitSet 114
80/1 Mallasjuoma 90
90/1 SemicElitserien 102
91/2 SemicElitserien 110
91 SemicSticker 12
71/2 WilliamsFIN 311

RUOTSALAINEN, MARKKU
70/1 Kuvajulkaisut 378

RUOTSALAINEN, REIJO
70/1 Kuvajulkaisut 379
80/1 Mallasjuoma 96
82 Mallasjuoma
82/3 O-Pee-Chee 233
83/4 O-Pee-Chee 255
84/5 OPC 153, Topps 115
85/6 OPC/Topps 112, M
86/7 OPC/Topps 128
83/4 opcSticker 216
84/5 opcSticker 101
85/6 opcSticker 81
86/7 opcSticker 60, 225/94
89 Pelimiehen
82/3 Post
83/4 PuffySticker 19
82 SemicSticker 155
89 SemicSticker 30
85/6 7Eleven 13
95/6 Sisu 274, -Double 7
95/6 SisuLimited 66
82 Skopbank
78/9 SM-Liiga 10, 138
83/4 SouhaitsRen.KeyChain
77-80 Sportscaster 86- 2041
71/2 WilliamsFIN 312
88/9 EDM/ActionMagazine 22
89/90 N.J.

RUOTSALAINEN, VESA
92/3 Jyvas-Hyva 93
93/4 Jyvas-Hyva 175
93/4 Sisu 168
96/7 Sisu 112

RUPONEN, PASI
92/3 Jyvas-Hyva 140
93/4 Jyvas-Hyva 256
93/4 Sisu 288

RUPP, DUANE
70/1 EddieSargent 166
72/3 EddieSargent 180
70/1 Esso Stamp
69/70 OPC 153, -Sticker 20
70/1 OPC/Topps 89
72/3 OPC 154, Topps 28
69/70 opcMiniSticker
75/6 opcWHA 18
67/8 Topps 20
71/2 TheTorontoSun

RUPP, MICHAEL
98 BowmanCHL 151, A3
98/9 Topps 236

RUPRECHT, TOMAS
95/6 APS 264

RUPRECHT, VACLAV
94/5 APS 146
95/6 APS 252

RUSHFORTH, PAUL
91/2 SketchOHL 67

RUSHTON, JASON
92/3 BCJHL 195

RUSK, MIKE
93/4 Slapshot(Guelph) 6
94/5 Slapshot(Guelph) 20

RUSKA, RYAN
94/5 Slapshot(MEM) 10

RUSKOWSKI, TERRY
79/80 OPC/Topps 141
80/1 OPC/Topps 119
81/2 OPC 62, Topps(W) 74
82/3 O-Pee-Chee 72
83/4 O-Pee-Chee 161
84/5 O-Pee-Chee 89, Topps 68
85/6 OPC/Topps 33
86/7 OPC/Topps 111
87/8 OPC/Topps 73
81/2 opcSticker 117
82/3 opcSticker 178
83/4 opcSticker 291
84/5 opcSticker 270
85/6 opcSticker237 /104
86/7 opcSticker 226
87/8 opcSticker 167/26
76/7 opcWHA 38
77/8 opcWHA 37
87/8 PaniniSticker 138, 150
82/3 Post
90/1 SketchWHL 92
79/80 CHI
81/2 CHI
80/1 CHI/4x6
80/1 CHI/5.5x8.5
84/5 L.A/Smokeys
87/8 MIN
88/9 MIN/American
86/7 PGH/Kodak
75/6 HoustonAeros
77/8 WinnipegJets
90/1 Saskatoon 1

RUSNAK, CHAD
92/3 MPSPhotoSJHL 47
91/2 SketchWHL 107
91/2 Saskatoon 8

RUSNAK, DARIUS
92/3 Jyvas-Hyva 91
82 SemicSticker 92
91 SemicSticker 115

RUSS, OTHMAR
79 PaniniSticker 304

RUSSELL, BLAIR
83&87 HallOfFame 178
83 HHOF Postcard (M)

RUSSELL, BLAINE
95/6 PrinceAlbert

RUSSELL, CAM
94/5 Leaf 382
97/8 PacificRegime 45
89/90 ProCards(IHL) 71
90/1 ProCards 400
91/2 ProCards 486
90/1 Score 408
93/4 ToppsStadiumClub 286
91/2 UpperDeck 352
95/6 UDBeAPlayer 84
93/4 CHI/Coke

RUSSELL, ERNEST
91 C55 Reprint 35
83&87 HallOfFame 133
83 HHOF Postcard (I)
1911-12 Imperial (C55) 35
1910-11 Imperial (C56) 20
1912-13 Imperial (C57) 26
1910-11 Imperial Post 35

RUSSELL, KERRY
91/2 ProCards 105

RUSSELL, PHIL
74/5 Loblaws
73/4 OPC 243
74/5 OPC/Topps 226
75/6 OPC/Topps 102, 211
76/7 OPC/Topps 31, OPC 382
77/8 OPC/Topps 235
78/9 OPC/Topps 12
79/80 OPC/Topps 143
80/1 OPC/Topps 226
81/2 O-Pee-Chee 51
82/3 O-Pee-Chee 58
83/4 O-Pee-Chee 237
84/5 O-Pee-Chee 120
85/6 OPC/Topps 30
86/7 OPC/Topps 142
81/2 opcSticker 226
83/4 opcSticker 271
84/5 opcSticker 75
85/6 opcSticker 58/184
80/1 Pepsi Cap
82/3 Post
89/90 ProCards(IHL) 163
90/1 ProCards 391
91/2 ProCards 309
83/4 PuffySticker 9
83/4 SouhaitsRen.KeyChain
79/80 ATL
79/80 ATL/B&W
80/1 CGY
81/2 CGY
82/3 CGY
83/4 N.J.
84/5 N.J.
84/5 KelownaWings 54
92/3 Cleveland 5

RUSSELL, SCOTT
97/8 Pinnacle -CBC Sports 11

RUSSELL, TED
95/6 Dayton

RUSSO, MATT
92/3 MPSPhotoSJHL 63

RUTHERFORD, JIM
77/8 Coke Mini
71/2 EddieSargent 176
72/3 EddieSargent 175
70/1 Esso Stamp
82? JDMcCarthy
72/3 Letraset 7
74/5 Loblaws
72/3 OPC 15, Topps 97
73/4 OPC/Topps 59
74/5 OPC/Topps 225
75/6 OPC/Topps 219
76/7 OPC/Topps 88
77/8 OPC/Topps 239
78/9 OPC/Topps 74
79/80 OPC/Topps 122
80/1 OPC/Topps 125
80/1 Pepsi Cap
91/2 SketchOHL 47
70/1 DET/Marathon
79/80 DET
80/1 DET
71/2 PGH

RUTHERFORD, M.
25 Dominion 58

RUTHERFORD, PAUL
91/2 Richmond 7

RUTLAND, ART
82/3 Fredericton 21

RUTLEDGE, CHRIS
84/5 Belleville 28

RUTLEDGE, WAYNE
68/9 ShirriffCoin LA-9
72/3 O-Pee-Chee 329
76/7 opcWHA 6
77/8 opcWHA 11
75/6 HoustonAeros

RUTTAN, JACK
83&87 HallOfFame 149
83 HHOF Postcard (K)

RUUSKA, ARI
71/2 WilliamsFIN 352

RUUTTI, MATTI
71/2 WilliamsFIN 313

RUUTTU, CHRISTIAN
90/1 Bowman 244
91/2 Bowman 25, 411
92/3 Bowman 341
93/4 Donruss 72
95/6 ElitSet 207, 307
95 FinnishAllStar 6
92/3 FleerUltra 281
95 Globe 143
93 Koululainen
93/4 Leaf 334
87/8 OPC/Topps 121
88/9 OPC/Topps 18
89/90 OPC/Topps 68
90/1 OPC/Topps 182
91/2 OPC/Topps 115
92/3 opcPremier 2
87/8 opc Stars 37
87/8 opcSticker 134/122,144/253
88/9 opcSticker 256/124
89/90 opcSticker 255/116
87/8 PaniniSticker 28
88/9 PaniniSticker 227
89/90 PaniniSticker 207
90/1 PaniniSticker 20
91/2 PaniniSticker 306
92/3 PaniniSticker 250
91/2 Parkhurst 242
92/3 Parkhurst 34
93/4 Parkhurst 39
94/5 Parkhurst 42
94/5 ParkieSE ES12
89 Pelimiehen
94/5 Pinnacle 434
91/2 Pinnacle 60
92/3 Pinnacle 317
93/4 Pinnacle 116
95/6 Playoff 103
94/5 POG 71
93/4 Premier 355
90/1 ProSet 29
91/2 ProSet 22
95/6 RadioCity
90/1 Score 77
91/2 Score(CDN) 45, (U.S) 45
92/3 Score 334
93/4 Score 84
94 Semic 43
95 Semic 22
91 SemicSticker 205
92 SemicSticker 15
93 SemicSticker 75
94/5 Sisu-GuestSpecial 8
95/6 SisuLimited 42, -S&S 2
92/3 Topps 485
91/2 ToppsStadiumClub 33
92/3 ToppsStadiumClub 330
93/4 ToppsStadiumClub 103
94/5 ToppsStadiumClub 131
90/1 UpperDeck 170
91/2 UpperDeck 104, E11
92/3 UpperDeck 446
93/4 UpperDeck 141
94/5 UpperDeck 56
95/6 UDCollChoice 278
95/6 udElite 210, 258, 233
96 Wien 25
86/7 BUF
87/8 BUF/BlueShield
87/8 BUF/WonderBread
88/9 BUF/BlueShield

88/9 BUF/WonderBread
89/90 BUF/BlueShield
89/90 BUF/Campbell
90/1 BUF/BlueShield
90/1 BUF/Campbell
91/2 BUF/BlueShield
91/2 BUF/Campbell
93/4 CHI/Coke

RUZICKA, VLADIMIR
94/5 APS 265
95/6 APS 135
92/3 Bowman 431
93/4 Donruss 228
92/3 FleerUltra 10
93/4 FleerUltra 383
93/4 Leaf 438
90/1 OPC/Topps 393
92/3 O-Pee-Chee 228
91/2 opcPremier 144
92/3 PaniniSticker 138
91/2 Parkhurst 3
92/3 Parkhurst 5
91/2 Pinnacle 181
92/3 Pinnacle 59
93/4 Pinnacle 406
93/4 PowerPlay 174
90/1 ProSet 588
91/2 ProSet 353
92/3 ProSet 5
91/2 PSPlatinum 152
90/1 ScoreTraded 44T
91/2 Score(CDN) 411, (U.S) 83T
92/3 Score 208
93/4 Score 154, 562
89 SemicSticker 190
92/3 Topps 333
91/2 ToppsStadiumClub 383
92/3 ToppsStadiumClub 358
90/1 UpperDeck 538
91/2 UpperDeck 288
92/3 UpperDeck 258, E4
91/2 BOS/SportsAction
92/3 BOS
93/4 OTT/Kraft

RYABCHIKOV, EVGENIY
94/5 Classic 18, T6
94/5 ClassicFourSport 123
94/5 ClassicImages 70
95/6 EdgeIce 61
93/4 Parkhurst 533
93/4 Pinnacle 508
94/5 SigRookies 9

RYAN, GREGORY
89/90 SketchOHL 33
90/1 SketchOHL 142
91/2 SketchOHL 377
92/3 Ottawa67s

RYAN, TERRY
77/8 Kalamazoo 7
72/3 Minnesota

RYAN, TERRY
94/5 AutoPhonex 37, B2
92/3 BCJHL 201
95/6 Classic 8
95/6 ClassicFiveSports 130
94/5 ClassicImages 18, PD8
97/8 Donruss 24
96/7 D.CdnIce 142,-OCanada 16
97/8 CanadianIce 128
96/7 DonrussElite-Aspirations 11
96/7 LeafPreferred 141
97/8 Limited 123
97/8 Pinnacle 11
97/8 PinnacleInside 167
96/7 PinnacleZenith 144
97/8 Score(MTL) 15
95/6 Tetrad 66, F10
95/6 TetradAutobilia 98

RYBAR, JOSEF
94/5 APS 159
95/6 APS 260
92/3 BCJHL 76

RYBOVIC, LUBOMIR
94 Semic 195

RYCHEL, WARREN
93/4 Donruss 156
94/5 Donruss 240
93/4 FleerUltra 346
93/4 Leaf 263
94/5 Leaf 323
98/9 Pacific 168
97/8 PacificCrown 130
92/3 Parkhurst 309
93/4 Parkhurst 98
94/5 ParkieSE 84
94/5 Pinnacle 509
97/8 PinnacleBeAPlayer 32
94/5 POG 128
93/4 PowerPlay 362
93/4 Premier 266
88/9 ProCards(Saginaw)
89/90 ProCards(IHL) 69
90/1 ProCards 399
91/2 ProCards 175
93/4 Score 640
97/8 Score(ANA) 13
93/4 ToppsStadiumClub 258
92/3 UpperDeck 547
93/4 UpperDeck 93
96/7 ANA/UpFrontSports 8
91/2 Moncton
84/5 Sudbury 15

RYDEN, JORGEN
89/90 SemicElitserien 75
90/1 SemicElitserien 249
91/2 SemicElitserien 80

RYDER, COLIN
92/3 BCJHL 134

RYDER, DAN
90/1 SketchOHL 394
91/2 SketchOHL 255
93/4 Roanoke
94/5 Roanoke
90/1 Sudbury 7
91/2 Sudbury 13

RYDING, STEVE
91/2 Knoxville

RYDMAN, BLAINE
72/3 Minnesota

RYMSHA, ANDY
96/7 DEL 130

RYDMARK, DANIEL
94/5 ElitSet 91, -Top 7, -Gold 5
95 Globe 33
95 PaniniWorlds 151
94 Semic 66
89/90 SemicElitserien 93
90/1 SemicElitserien 141
91/2 SemicElitserien 192
92/3 SemicElitserien 214
92 SemicSticker 68
97/87 udSwedish 144, S8
95/6 Phoenix

RYHÄNEN, LEEVI
65/6 Hellas 86

RYNYCH, ANDY
89/90 ProCards(AHL) 144
90/1 ProCards 80

RYSANEK, ROMAN
94/5 APS 138
95/6 APS 302
93 SemicSticker 100

S

SAADETIN, ALI
66/7 Champion 191
70/1 Kuvajulkaisut 136

SAAL, JASON
95 Classic 84
95/6 EdgeIce 81
93/4 Slapshot(Detroit) 2
94/5 Slapshot(Detroit) 16
94/5 Slapshot(MEM) 90
95/6 StJohns

SAARELA, JARI
78/9 SM-Liiga 117

SAARELA, PASI
93/4 Jyvas-Hyva 227
93/4 Sisu 199
95/6 Sisu 253
96/7 Sisu 54, -Mighty 2

SAARELAINEN, JUHANI
71/2 WilliamsFIN 142

SAARI, TIMO
66/7 Champion 196
72 Hellas 21
70/1 Kuvajulkaisut 137
80/1 Mallasjuoma 49
71/2 WilliamsFIN 158
72/3 WilliamsFIN 111
73/4 WilliamsFIN 211

SAARIKKO, ILKKA
71/2 WilliamsFIN 253

SAARIKKO, KARI
80/1 Mallasjuoma 152
78/9 SM-Liiga 94

SAARIKORPI, JORMA
66/7 Champion 177
70/1 Kuvajulkaisut 252
71/2 WilliamsFIN 143
72/3 WilliamsFIN 204
73/4 WilliamsFIN 167

SAARIKOSKI, TIMO
92/3 Jyvas-Hyva 125
93/4 Jyvas-Hyva 113
96 PaniniWorlds 182
94 Semic 47
93 SemicSticker 76
93/4 Sisu 25
94/5 Sisu 135, -Horoscope 7
95/6 Sisu 54

SAARINEN, ARI
93/4 Jyvas-Hyva 354
93/4 Sisu 226
94/5 Sisu 94
95/6 Sisu 160

SAARINEN, OLLI
80/1 Mallasjuoma 68
78/9 SM-Liiga 116

SAARINEN, PASI
95/6 Sisu 233

SAARINEN, ROD
90/1 SketchOHL 239
90/1 Kitchener 27

SAARINEN, SAMI
92/3 Jyvas-Hyva 190

SAARINEN, SIMO
91/2 Jyvas-Hyva 6
92/3 Jyvas-Hyva 3
93/4 Jyvas-Hyva 15
89 SemicSticker 33
91 SemicSticker 7
92 SemicSticker 10
92 SemicSticker 10
93/4 Sisu 88
94/5 Sisu 99
95/6 Sisu 4
95/6 SisuLimited 39

SAARINEN, TONI
95/6 Sisu 228
96/7 Sisu 26

SAARINEN, VEIJO
66/7 Champion 64
70/1 Kuvajulkaisut 304
71/2 WilliamsFIN 199

SAARIO, KAI
71/2 WilliamsFIN 353

SAARNI, TARMO
73/4 WilliamsFIN 298

SAARNIO, RAUMO
72/3 WilliamsFIN 336

SABLIK, LUKAS
95/6 APS 177

SABO, ED
92/3 Richmond

SABO, STEVE
92/3 MPSPhotoSJHL 163

SABOL, SHAUN
88/9 ProCards(Hershey)
89/90 ProCards(AHL) 333
90/1 ProCards 46
91/2 ProCards 202

SABOURIN, GARY
68/9 Bauer
70/1 Colgate Stamp 57
70/1 DadsCookies
70/1 EddieSargent 186
71/2 EddieSargent 177
72/3 EddieSargent 183
70/1 Esso Stamp
72/3 Letraset 6
74/5 Loblaws
68/9 OPC/Topps 117
69/70 OPC/Topps 19
70/1 OPC/Topps 96, -Deckle 28
71/2 OPC 13
72/3 OPC 91, Topps 163
73/4 OPC 168, Topps 184
74/5 OPC 368
76/7 OPC 266
75/6 OPC/Topps 299
69/70 opcMiniSticker
68/9 ShirriffCoin STL11
71/2 TheTorontoSun
71/2 STL
72/3 STL
72/3 STL/8"x10"
73/4 STL
92/3 STL/UpperDeck 15
74/5 TOR

SABOURIN, KEN
91/2 OPC/Topps 43
9/01 Panini(CGY) 20
89/90 ProCards(IHL) 204
90/1 ProCards 610
90/1 ProSet 596
91/2 Score(CDN) 398
91/2 ToppsStadiumClub 396
91/2 UpperDeck 417
90/1 WSH/Kodak
91/2 WSH
94/5 Milwaukee
86/7 Moncton 13
88/9 SaltLake 19
82/3 SSMarie
83/4 SSMarie
84/5 SSMarie

SACCO, DAVE
93/4 Classic 80
94/5 Classic-Autograph
94/5 Donruss 309
95/6 EdgeIce 14
93/4 FleerUltra 497
94/5 Leaf 58
96/7 Leaf 218
96/7 Pinnacle 213
93/4 PowerPlay 517
93/4 Premier-TeamUSA 13
94/5 Score 240
93/4 T.StadiumClub-TmUSA 22
94/5 UpperDeck 328
94/5 ANA/Carl'sJr 20

SACCO, JOE
92/3 Bowman 417
93/4 Donruss 2
94/5 Donruss 64
95/6 Donruss 302
92/3 FleerUltra 215
93/4 FleerUltra 260
94/5 FleerUltra 6
95/6 Hoyle'WEST 2 (Clubs)
94/5 Leaf 274
95/6 Leaf 164
92/3 O-Pee-Chee 355
98/9 Pacific 287
97/8 PacificCrown 208
94/5 PaniniSticker 122
96/7 PaniniSticker 232
97/8 PaniniSticker 186
95 PaniniWorlds 229
91/2 Parkhurst 395
92/3 Parkhurst 185
93/4 Parkhurst 273
94/5 ParkieSE 5
94/5 Pinnacle 232
97/8 PinnacleBeAPlayer 39
94/5 POG 29
95/6 POG 21
93/4 PowerPlay 9
93/4 Premier 329
94/5 Premier 309
90/1 ProCards 156
92/3 Score 532
95/6 Score 68
91/2 Score(CDN) 349, (US) 319
97/8 Score(ANA) 7
95 Semic 112
97/8 SPAuthentic 3
95/6 Topps 86
92/3 ToppsStadiumClub 398
93/4 ToppsStadiumClub 256
94/5 ToppsStadiumClub 161
92/3 UpperDeck 266, 382
93/4 UpperDeck 36, SP-3
94/5 UpperDeck 166
95/6 UpperDeck 43
96/7 UpperDeck 4
97/8 UpperDeck 214
94/5 UDBeAPlayer R87, -Aut. 79
95/6 UDCollChoice 68
97/8 UDCollChoice 5
94/5 ANA/Carl'sJr 21
90/1 TOR
90/1 Newmarket
92/3 StJohns

SACHARUK, LARRY
74/5 Loblaws
75/6 OPC/Topps 76, 327

SADJINA, ALEXANDER
79 PaniniSticker 307

SAGANIUK, ROCKY
80/1 OPC/Topps 64
81/2 O-Pee-Chee 323
82/3 O-Pee-Chee 331
82/3 opcSticker 69
80/1 Pepsi Cap
82/3 Post
84/5 PGH/Heinz
80/1 TOR
81/2 TOR
79/80 TOR

SAGISSOR, TOM
90/1 ProCards 58
91/2 ProCards 81

SAGLO, ROSTISLAV
96/7 Penascola 6

SAHARCHUK, DENNIS
90/1 SketchWHL 199, 327
91/2 SketchWHL 38
89/90 Spokane

SAHLMAN, JARMO
71/2 WilliamsFIN 271

SAHLSTEDT, KALLE
92/3 Jyvas-Hyva 134
93/4 Jyvas-Hyva 228
95 Semic 21
93/4 Sisu 195
94/5 Sisu 55, -Junior 10
95/6 Sisu 103
96/7 Sisu 101

SAHLSTEN, PETTER
91/2 SemicElitserien 8

SAIKKONEN, MATTI
78/9 SM-Liiga 132

SAILER, PETR
95/6 APS 72

SÄILYNOJA, KEIJO
91/2 Jyvas-Hyva 22
92/3 Jyvas-Hyva 56
93/4 Jyvas-Hyva 112
92 SemicSticker 23
93/4 Sisu 17
94/5 Sisu 124
95/6 Sisu 52
96/7 Sisu 48

SAIMO, SIMO
66/7 Champion 2

SAINDON, PAUL
51/2 LavalDairy 70

SAINE, ERKKI
65/6 Hellas 44

SAINIO, SIMO
65/6 Hellas 28

SAINT AMOUR, MARTIN
90/1 ProCards 70
91/2 Cincinnati

SAINT AMOUR, STÉPHANE
91/2 SketchQMJHL 161
93/4 Slapshot(Drum.) 12

SAINT AUBIN, JOE
89/90 SketchMEM 47
90/1 SketchOHL 241
88/9 Kitchener 14
89/90 Kitchener 15
90/1 Kitchener 13

SAINT CROIX, RICK
81/2 O-Pee-Chee 252
82/3 O-Pee-Chee 258
83/4 O-Pee-Chee 340
84/5 O-Pee-Chee 310
83/4 opcSticker 36
85/6 opcSticker 8 /136
83/4 Vachon 98
82/3 TOR
83/4 TOR
88/9 WPG/Police

SAINT CYR, GERRY
90/1 SketchWHL 249
91/2 SketchWHL 64
93/4 ThunderBay
94/5 Toledo

SAINT CYR, RAY
52/3 AnonymousOHL 44

SAINT GERMAIN, FRANÇOIS
88/9 Richelieu

SAINT GERMAIN, MATT
91/2 SketchOHL 137
93/4 Slapshot(Peterborough) 12
91/2 Peterborough 18

SAINT GERMAIN, RALPH
27-32 LaPresse 30/1

SAINT HILAIRE, IRENE
52/3 BasDuFleuve 19
52/3 LavalDairy 55
52/3 StLawrence 87

SAINT JACQUES, KEVIN
92/3 ClassicProspects 136
90/1 SketchWHL 134
91/2 SketchWHL 352
92/3 Indianapolis
89/90 Lethbridge

SAINT JACQUES, MICHEL
90/1 SketchMEM 30
90/1 SketchQMJHL 33
91/2 SketchQMJHL 82

SAINT JAMES, TOM
82/3 Kitchener 7

SAINT JEAN, JACQUES
79/80 Montréal

SAINT JEAN, MAURICE
52/3 BasDuFleuve 24
51/2 LacStJean 25

SAINT JOHN, MIKE
89/90 SketchOHL 143

SAINT LAURENT, ANDRÉ
75/6 OPC 387
76/7 OPC/Topps 29
77/8 OPC/Topps 171
78/9 OPC/Topps 32
79/80 OPC/Topps 73
80/1 O-Pee-Chee 316
83/4 O-Pee-Chee 286
83/4 SouhaitsRen.KeyChain
83/4 PGH/Heinz

SAINT LAURENT, DOLLARD
45-64 BeeHives(CHI), (MTL)
48-52 Exhibits
51/2 LaPatrie 24Feb
52/3 Parkhurst 52
53/4 Parkhurst 23
55/6 Parkhurst 48
57/8 Parkhurst (MTL) 10
93/4 Parkhurst PR68
93/4 Parkie(56/7) 69
45-54 QuakerOats
60/1 ShirriffCoin 74
61/2 ShirriffCoin 35
58/9 Topps 5
59/60 Topps 43
61/2 Topps 31, 44
62/3 Topps 30
91/2 Ultimate06 15, -Aut 15

SAINT LAURENT, SAM
88/9 ProCards(Adirondack)
89/90 ProCards(AHL) 315
90/1 ProCards 9
91/2 ProCards 193
86/7 DET/Caesars

SAINT LOUIS, FRANCE
94/5 Classic W2
97/8 GameOfHerLife
97/8 UDCollChoice 284

SAINT LOUIS, JOSH
95/6 SwiftCurrent

SAINT LOUIS, TODD
95/6 Slapshot 175

SAINT MARIE, ROGER
51/2 BasDuFleuve 28
52/3 BasDuFleuve 62

SAINT MARSEILLE, DEREK
77/8 NovaScotia

SAINT MARSEILLE, FRANK
71/2 Bazooka Panel 17
70/1 Colgate Stamp 22
70/1 DadsCookies
70/2 EddieSargent
71/2 EddieSargent 184
72/3 EddieSargent 188
70/1 Esso Stamp
74/5 Loblaws
69/70 O-Pee-Chee 177
70/1 O-Pee-Chee 214
70/1 OPC/T-Deckle 26, -Sticker
71/2 OPC/Topps 38, -Booklet 15
72/3 OPC 65, Topps 71
73/4 OPC 262
74/5 OPC/Topps 98, OPC 374
75/6 OPC/Topps 15
76/7 OPC 276
71/2 TheTorontoSun
71/2 STL
72/3 STL/8"x10"
92/3 STL/UpperDeck 19
77/8 NovaScotia

SAINT ONGE, DAVID
96/7 Rimouski

SAINT PIERRE, DAVID
92/3 ClassicProspects 108
90/1 SketchQMJHL 236
91/2 SketchQMJHL 145
91/2 UD'CzechWJC 49
95/6 Hampton HRA -14

SAINT PIERRE, MARCEL
51/2 BasDuFleuve 35

SAINT PIERRE, YAN
91/2 SketchQMJHL 243
93/4 Slapshot(Drum.) 8

SAINT SAUVEUR, CLAUDE
76/7 OPC 379
73/4 opc-Posters 18
74/5 opcWHA 62
75/6 opcWHA 124
76/7 opcWHA 90
77/8 opcWHA 7
73/4 Vancouver

SAKAC, MARCEL
92/3 BCJHL 118

SAKAC, MARCEL
72 Panda
72 SemicSticker 21
74 SemicSticker 72
71/2 WilliamsFIN 37

SAKIC, BRIAN
90/1 SketchWHL 114, 344
91/2 SketchWHL 292
91/2 UpperDeck 461
92/3 UpperDeck 36

SAKIC, JOE
95/6 Aces K (Clubs)
96/7 Aces A (Diamonds)
94/5 BAP'Magazine 4
90/1 Bowman 169
91/2 Bowman 133
92/3 Bowman 240, 244
95/6 Bowman 42, BB11
96/7 CorinthianHeadliner
97/8 CorinthianHeadliner
93/4 Donruss 282
94/5 Donruss 141
95/6 Donruss 167, -Elite 2
96/7 Donruss 1, -Elite 7, -Top 3
97/8 Donruss 117, -Line 12
96/7 D.CdnIce 74, -OCanada 1
97/8 DCI 102,-Scrap 3, -Nt'l 17
95/6 DonrussElite 16
96/7 DonrussElite 120,-Status 11
97/8 DonrussElite 49, 115
97/8 D.Elite-Crafts 3,-PrNum 11
97/8 DonrussPreferred 128, 175
97/8 D.Pref -Line 8A, -PrecM 11

97/8 D.Pref -Tins 8, -WideTins 3
97/8 DonrussPriority 17, 208
97/8 D.Prio-DirDep 11,-OpDay15
97/8 D.Prio -Postcrd 9, -Stamp 9
97/8 D.Studio 23,-HardHats 17
97/8 D.Studio-Portrait 23,-Sil 12
96/7 Duracell DC3, JB3
93/4 EASports 112
97/8 EssoOlympic 7
94/5 Flair 151
96/7 Flair 21, -Centre 7
94/5 Fleer 183
96/7 Fleer 25, 137, -ArtRoss 20
96/7 Fleer-Peason 10
95/6 FleerMetal 36, -Heavy 12
95/6 FleerMetal-Int.Steel 19
96/7 FleerNHLPicks 2, -Dream 9
96/7 F.Picks-Captain 6, -Fab 41
92/3 FleerUltra 179, 250
93/4 FleerUltra 242
94/5 FleerUltra 180
95/6 F.Ultra 135, 397, -Pivots 8
95/6 FU-Extra 17, -Ultraview 9
96/7 FU 40, -Red 7, -Power 15
91/2 Gillette 22
96/7 Got-UmHockeyGreatsCoin
93/4 HockeyWit 100
95/6 Hoyle'EAST A (Clubs)
92/3 HumptyDumpty (1)
97/8 KatchMedallion 42
91/2 Kelloggs 12
96/7 KennerSLU
97/8 KennerSLU- 1on1
89/90 Kraft 32
90/1 Kraft 50, 79
91/2 Kraft 41
93/4 Kraft-Captain, -Cutout
94/5 Kraft'Sharpshooter
95/6 Kraft
96/7 Kraft-Captain, -Trophy
97/8 Kraft-CdnPros,-RoadToNag
97/8 Kraft -Sticker
93/4 Leaf 87
94/5 Leaf 165, -Limited 19
95/6 Leaf 182
96/7 Leaf 139, -Fire 3, -Leather 1
97/8 Leaf 35,-Banner 24, -Fire 7
94/5 LeafLimited 106
95/6 LeafLimited 64
96/7 LeafLimited 56, -Stubble 16
96/7 LeafPreferred 37, -Steel 11
96/7 LeafPreferred-SteelPower 1
97/8 Limited 36, 132, 190
97/8 Limited -fabric 4, 5
96/7 Maggers 37
91/2 McDonalds McD5
92/3 McDonalds McD26
93/4 McDonalds McD24
94/5 McDonalds McD1
95/6 McDonalds
96/7 McDonalds McD10
97/8 McDonalds McD5
97/8 McDonalds -Medallions
96/7 MetalUni 38,-Let 16,-Ice 12
97/8 Omega 65, -GameFace 4
97/8 Omega -Silk 5, -StickHan 6
89/90 OPC/Topps 113, OPC 313
90/1 OPC/Topps 384, T-TL 14
91/2 OPC/Topps 16, 96, T-TL 8
92/3 OPC 54, 55, -25Years 22
90/1 opcPremier 102
91/2 opcPremier 70
92/3 opcPremier-Star 11
89/90 opcSticker 187, 41/185
98/9 Pacific 169,-D.Ice 7,-Gld 10
97/8 PacificCrown 38, -Gold 9
97/8 PacificCC-SlapShots 2B
97/8 PacificCrownRoyale 38
97/8 PCR-HatTrick 5, -Lamp 6
97/8 PacificDynagon! 34
97/8 PcfcD-BstKpt 27,-Dyna 6B
97/8 PacificD-Kings 4, -Tandm 2
97/8 PacificInv. 39, -Feature 10
97/8 PacificInv.-Attack 7, -Off 6
97/8 PcfcParamount 55,-BigN 7
97/8 PcfcP-CdnGreat 5,-Photo 7
98/9 PcfcParamnt 61,-SpecDel 5
97/8 PacificRegime 57
97/8 PcfcRevolution 39,-ASGm 8
90/1 Panini(QUE) 18
89/90 PaniniSticker 327
90/1 PaniniSticker 139
91/2 PaniniSticker 257, 334
92/3 PaniniSticker 209
93/4 PaniniSticker G
94/5 PaniniSticker 56
95/6 PaniniSticker 246
96/7 PaniniSticker 155, 245
97/8 PaniniSticker 204
95 PaniniWorlds 20
91/2 Parkhurst 148
92/3 Parkhurst 147
93/4 Parkhurst 169, E9
94/5 Parkhurst V34, -YCTG 19
95/6 Parkhurst 46, PP8, PP16
94/5 ParkieSE 147
91/2 Pinnacle 150, 381
92/3 Pinnacle 150, -Tm2000 21
93/4 Pinnacle 290, CA19
93/4 Pinnacle-Tm2001 25
94/5 Pinnacle 50, NL4
95/6 Pinnacle-Roaring20s 17
96/7 Pinnacle 201, -TeamP 1
97/8 Pinnacle 32
96/7 Pinn.BeAPlayer-Biscuit 16
97/8 P.BAP 83,-TakeANum 19
97/8 P.BeeHive 4, -TeamBH 19
97/8 PinnacleCertified 50
97/8 Pinnacle-EPIX 3
96/7 PinnacleFANtasy 17
97/8 P.Inside 54,-Can 15,-Trck 8
96/7 PinnacleMint 11
95/6 Pinn.Zenith 64, -Team 13
96/7 P.Zenith 44, -Champion 8
95/6 Playoff 28, 139, 242
96/7 Playoff 432
94/5 POG 199
95/6 POG 72
94/5 Post
96/7 Post, -StickUm 4
97/8 Post, F5
93/4 PowerPlay 204, -Ldr. 15
93/4 Premier 10, -BlackOPC 15
94/5 Premier 480, -GoToGuy 2
95/6 ProMagnet 79
90/1 ProSet 257, 375
91/2 ProSet 199,315,-ThePck 23
92/3 ProSet 150
91/2 PSPlatinum 102
96/7 SB'7Eleven
90/1 Score 8, -Hot 7, -Young 8
91/2 Score(CDN) 25, 366
91/2 S(U.S) 25, 336, -Young 20
92/3 Score 240, 434, -Young 20
93/4 Score 135, (CDN) DD5
93/4 Score-Dream 14, -P.AS 13
93/4 Score-TheFranchise 17
94/5 Score NP19, TF 19
95/6 Score 5,-Golden1,-Border 4
96/7 Score 9,-Dream 3,-Sddn 11
97/8 Score 125
97/8 Score(COL) 18
92/3 SeasonsPatch 47
93/4 SeasonsPatch 17
94/5 Select 62
95/6 SelectCertified 45, -Gold 8
96/7 SelectCertified 16,-Corner 9
95 Semic 87
91 SemicSticker 75
93 SemicSticker 206
95/6 SkyBoxEmotion 42
95/6 SkBxE-Xcel 9, -Xcited 13
95/6 SkyBoxImpact 41
96/7 SkyBoxImpact 28, -Versa 9
96/7 SkyBx-Countdown 10
95/6 SkyMint
94/5 SP 94, -Premier 27
95/6 SP 31, E8
96/7 SP 34, CW19, -InsideInfo
97/8 SPAuthentic 35, I4
96/7 SPx 9
97/8 SPx 12, -DuoView
98/9 SPx"Finite" 22, 92, 163
96/7 SportFX MiniStix
97/8 SportFX MiniStix
95/6 Summit 61
96/7 Sumt 1, -Untchb 3, Voltge 2
95/6 SuperSkills 17
95/6 SuperSticker 27, DC 4
96/7 TeamOut
92/3 Topps 495
95/6 Topps 266, M6, PF20
98/9 Topps 68, L10, M20
94/5 ToppsFinest 69
94/5 TF-BBest 3, (Blue) 18
95/6 ToppsFinest 15, 80
96/7 T.Picks FT20, TS12
91/2 ToppsStadiumClub 389
92/3 T.oppsStadiumClub 3
93/4 ToppsStadiumClub 32, -AS
95/6 ToppsStadiumClub EC167
93/4 TSC-MembersOnly 39
94/5 TSC-MembersOnly 13
95/6 TSC-MembersOnly 17
97/8 ToppsSticker 2
90/1 UpperDeck 164, 301, 490
91/2 UpperDeck 333, 616
92/3 UpperDeck 36, 255, WG8
92/3 UD-LockerAS 13
93/4 UD 69,223,H9,NL3,SP-130
94/5 UD 404, H17, SP65
95/6 UD 54, 242, R14, R27
95/6 UD R36, R45, SE111
95/6 UD-AllStarPredict MVP5
96/7 UpperDeck 204, 240, X3
96/7 UD HH20, LS07, SS16A
97/8 UD 253, GJ7, S4, SG35
97/8 UD SS19, T3A, -BlowUp 3
93/4 UDBeAPlayer 14, -Roots 16
94/5 UDBeAPlayer R96
96/7 UDBlackDiamnd 169, RC10
97/8 UDBlackDiamond 96, PC29
98/9 UDChoice 59, 230
98/9 UDChoice BH19, SQ11
95/6 UDCollChoice 288, 362, C9
96/7 UDCCollChoice 64, 299
96/7 UDCC 314, 336, C7, UD5
97/8 UDCC 55, C18, S19, SQ63
97/8 udDiamondVision 20, DM5
96/7 UpperDeck"Ice" 108, S5
97/8 UpperDeckIce 79, IC10
97/8 ValuNet
96 Wien 95
97/8 Zenith 29, Z7
96/7 COL/PhotoPucks
88/9 QUE
88/9 QUE/GeneralFoods
89/90 QUE
89/90 QUE/GeneralFoods
89/90 QUE/Police
90/1 QUE/PetroCanada
91/2 QUE/PetroCanada
92/3 QUE/PetroCanada
94/5 QUE/BurgerKing

SAKURAI, TERUO
79 PaniniSticker 290

SALAJKO, JEFF
95/6 Slapshot 331
92/3 Ottawa67s

SALEI, RUSLAN
96/7 FleerUltra 5
96/7 MetalUniverse 191
97/8 PacificRevolution 4
97/8 PinnacleBeAPlayer 124
96/7 SelectCertified 109
96/7 SP 169
98/9 Topps 99
96/7 UpperDeck 215
95/6 LasVegas

SALESKI, DON
77/8 Coke Mini
74/5 Loblaws
72/3 OPC 213
74/5 OPC 283
75/6 OPC/Topps 262
76/7 OPC/Topps 81
77/8 OPC/Topps 233
78/9 OPC/Topps 257
79/80 COL.R
75/6 PHA/GingerAle

SALEVA, HENRY
80/1 Mallasjuoma 182
78/9 SM-Liiga 86
72/3 WilliamsFIN 95
73/4 WilliamsFIN 143

SALFI, KENT
92/3 Maine (1) 13

SALFICKY, DUSAN
94/5 APS 25
95/6 APS 317

SALLAMAA, ASKO
66/7 Champion 210

SALLE, JOHAN
94/5 ElitSet 244
95/6 ElitSet 265
90/1 SemicElitserien 130
91/2 SemicElitserien 183
92/3 SemicElitserien 208
95/6 udElite 137

SALLINEN, PASI
71/2 WilliamsFIN 334

SALMELAINEN, TOMMI
72 Hellas 14
80/1 Mallasjuoma 6
72 Panda (x2)
72 SemicSticker 87
78/9 SM-Liiga 33
71/2 WilliamsFIN 75, 125
72/3 WilliamsFIN 96
73/4 WilliamsFIN 142

SALMI, MATTI
66/7 Champion 52
65/6 Hellas 41
70/1 Kuvajulkaisut 203
72 Panda
71/2 WilliamsFIN 92
72/3 WilliamsFIN 257

SALMINEN, ASKO
73/4 WilliamsFIN 299

SALMINEN, HEIKKI
73/4 WilliamsFIN 190

SALMINEN, JUSSI
95/6 UDCollChoice 339

SALMINEN, KIMMO
94/5 Sisu 73, -Magic 9
95/6 Sisu 63
96/7 Sisu 63

SALMINEN, MAURI
72/3 WilliamsFIN 295

SALMINEN, PETRI
70/1 Kuvajulkaisut 338

SALMINEN, TEIJO
70/1 Kuvajulkaisut 355

SALMING, BORJE
72-84 Dernière 79/80
88/9 Esso Sticker
95 Globe 67
72 Hellas 42
94 HockeyWit 37
84/5 Kelloggs Disk
86/7 Kraft Sports 57
74/5 LiptonSoup 41
74/5 Loblaws
74/5 OPC/Topps 180
75/6 OPC/Topps 283, 294
76/7 OPC/Topps 22
77/8 OPC/Topps 2, 140
78/9 OPC/Topps 240, OPC 330
79/80 OPC/Topps 40
80/1 OPC/Topps 85, 210
81/2 OPC 307, 315, Topps 33
82/3 O-Pee-Chee 332
83/4 O-Pee-Chee 341
84/5 O-Pee-Chee 311
85/6 O-Pee-Chee 248
86/7 OPC/Topps 169
87/8 O-Pee-Chee 237
88/9 O-Pee-Chee 247
89/90 O-Pee-Chee 278
81/2 opcSticker 98, 111
82/3 opcSticker 75, 76
83/4 opcSticker 33, 34
84/5 opcSticker 7, 8
85/6 opcSticker 12
86/7 opcSticker 136/244
87/8 opcSticker 165
88/9 opcSticker 174
80/1 opcSuperCard 19
87/8 PaniniSticker 326
88/9 PaniniSticker 120
80/1 Pepsi Cap
82/3 Post
81/2 Post PopUp 18
87/8 ProSportWatch CW16
83/4 PuffySticker 6
90/1 SemicElitserien 77
91/2 SemicElitserien 4
92/3 SemicElitserien 36
82 SemicSticker 143
92 SemicSticker 60
83/4 7ElevenCokeCups
85/6 7Eleven 18
83/4 SouhaitsRen.KeyChain
77-79 Sportscaster 70-1663
92/3 Trends(76) 145, 188, 197
83/4 Vachon 97
72/3 WilliamsFIN 56
73/4 WilliamsFIN 34
89/90 DET/Caesars
73/4 TOR
74/5 TOR
75/6 TOR
76/7 TOR
77/8 TOR
78/9 TOR
79/80 TOR
80/1 TOR
81/2 TOR
82/3 TOR
83/4 TOR
84/5 TOR
85/6 TOR
86/7 TOR
87/8 TOR
87/8 TOR/P.L.A.Y. 8
88/9 TOR/P.L.A.Y. 5

SALMING, STIG
79 PaniniSticker 189

SALMON, TIM
83/4 Kingston 12

SALMOND, SCOTT
91/2 AvantGardeBCJHL 73

SALO, ARI
92/3 Jyvas-Hyva 65
93/4 Jyvas-Hyva 115
90/1 SemicElitserien 5
93/4 Sisu 5
94/5 Sisu 119

SALO, JUHA
92/3 Jyvas-Hyva 63
70/1 Kuvajulkaisut 339

SALO, KALEVI
65/6 Hellas 56

SALO, ROBERT
92/3 Jyvas-Hyva 110
93/4 Jyvas-Hyva 201
93/4 Sisu 259
94/5 Sisu 93
95/6 Sisu 84

SALO, SAMI
95/6 Sisu 124
96/7 Sisu 137, -RookieEnergy 3

SALO, TAPANI
66/7 Champion 207

SALO, TOMMY
94/5 ClassicImages 3, CE3, PR8
95/6 Donruss 196
97/8 Donruss 33
97/8 DonrussCanadianIce 106
97/8 DonrussElite 101
97/8 DonrussPreferred 32
97/8 D.Priority 121,-PostGen 15
95/6 EdgeIce 196, C22
94/5 ElitSet-GoldCard 24
96/7 Flair 57
95/6 FleerMetal 191, -Winners 6
95/6 FleerUltra 97, 354
95/6 FutureLegends 41
95 Globe 3
95/6 Leaf 177
96/7 Leaf 221
97/8 Limited 130
97/8 Omega 142
98/9 Pacific 288
97/8 PacificCrown 56
97/8 PacificCrownRoyale 81
97/8 PacificDynagon! 75
97/8 PcfcD-Stone 13,-Tandm 67
97/8 PacificInvincible 83
97/8 PacificParamount 111
98/9 PcfcParamnt 148,-Glove 11
97/8 PcfcRevolution 84,-Retn 12
95/6 PaniniSticker 101
97/8 PaniniSticker 74
95/6 Parkhurst 128
95/6 Pinnacle 202
96/7 Pinnacle 244
97/8 Pinnacle 59
96/7 PinnacleBeAPlayer 77
97/8 P.BAP -Stacking/Pads 14
97/8 PinnacleCertified 24
97/8 PinnacleInside 49
95/6 Playoff 282
95/6 Score 314
97/8 Score 9, -NetWorth 12
95/6 SelectCertified 112
95 Semic 53
91/2 SemicElitserien 254
92/3 SemicElitserien 275
95/6 SkBxEmotion 107, -Next 5
95/6 SkyBoxImpact 104
97/8 SPAuthentic 93
96/7 Summit 189
98/9 Topps 88
95/6 ToppsStadiumClub 211
95/6 UpperDeck 413
96/7 UDBlackDiamond 31
95/6 UDCollChoice 235
97/8 UDCollChoice 158
95/6 udElite 246
96 Wien 39, SG9

SALO, VESA
96/7 DEL 151
95/6 ElitSet 227
92/3 Jyvas-Hyva 89
93/4 Jyvas-Hyva 166
93/4 Sisu 169
95/6 Sisu 96
95/6 SisuLimited 67
95/6 udElite 81

SALOMAA, LAURI
66/7 Champion 150
70/1 Kuvajulkaisut 221
71/2 WilliamsFIN 218
72/3 WilliamsFIN 167
73/4 WilliamsFIN 233

SALOMAA, S.V.
96/7 Sisu 123
95/6 TetradAutobilia 52

SALOMATIN, ALEXEI
95/6 ElitSet 133,-FaceToFace 12
95/6 udElite 194
97/8 udSwedish 98

SALOMONSSON, ANDREAS
96/7 DEL 104
94/5 ElitSet 265
95/6 ElitSet 108
91/2 SemicElitserien 224
92/3 SemicElitserien 243
95/6 udElite 167
97/8 udSwedish 163

SALOMONSSON, STIG
93/4 Greensboro

SALON, IVAN
93/4 Saskatoon

SALONEN, KARI
72/3 WilliamsFIN 237
73/4 WilliamsFIN 272

SALONEN, MARTTI
66/7 Champion 56
70/1 Kuvajulkaisut 149
71/2 WilliamsFIN 200

SALONEN, SAMI
94/5 ParkieSE 223
95/6 Sisu 359
96/7 Sisu 162
94/5 ToppsFinest 137
95/6 UpperDeck 547
95/6 UDCollChoice 328

SALOSENSAARI, ESA
70/1 Kuvajulkaisut 340

SALOVAARA, BARRY
82? JDMcCarthy
78/9 SM-Liiga 96

SALSTEN, PETTER
95 PaniniWorlds 239
94 Semic 258
95 Semic 178
90/1 SemicElitserien 79
92 SemicSticker 29
93 SemicSticker 231
96 Wien 204

SALVADOR, BRYAN
93/4 Lethbridge

SALVO, LINO
91/2 SketchQMJHL 156

SALZBRUNN, JEFF
89/90 Nashville

SAMEC, JIM
83/4 SSMarie

SAMIS, PHIL
52/3 StLawrence 9
51/2 Cleveland

SAMPSON, GARY
86/7 WSH/Kodak

SAMSONOV, SERGEI
96/7 AllSportPPF 176
97/8 DonElite 16, 134,-Craft 12
97/8 DonrussPreferred 148,195
97/8 D.Pref -Line 4B,-PrecM 15
97/8 D.Pref -Tins 11, -WideTin 6
97/8 D.Priority 178, 200, 218
97/8 D.Prio -DirDep 6,-OpDay 30
97/8 D.Prio-Pstcrd 17,-Stamp 17
97/8 KatchMedallion 12
97/8 Leaf 151,199,-FireOnIce 15
97/8 Limited 131, -fabric 21
97/8 McDonalds McD40
97/8 Omega 18
98/9 Pacific 87,-Cram 1, -D.Ice 3
98/9 Pacific-GoldCrn 2,-TmCL 2
97/8 PacificDynagon! Rookies
97/8 PacificParamount 15
98/9 PcfcP 16,-SpcD 3,-TmCL 2
97/8 Pinnacle 9
97/8 PinnacleBeAPlayer 220
97/8 PinnacleBeeHive -TmBH 23
97/8 PinnacleCertified D
97/8 PinnacleMint 26
97/8 Score 59
97/8 Score(BOS) 14
97 SB'AutColl-Au t.
97/8 SB'VisionsSig 43
94/5 SP 189
95/6 SP 180, GC2
97/8 SPAuthentic 172, S4
98/9 SPx"Finite" 5, 101, 121, 155
98/9 Topps 108, A2, I11, SB8
95/6 UpperDeck 554
97/8 UD 219, SG30, -BlowUp 10
97/8 UDBlackDiamond 37, PC28
98/9 UDChoice 13, BH22, SQ6
96/7 UpperDeck"Ice "138
97/8 UpperDeckIce 43, IC20,L6A
97/8 Zenith 86, Z66, -RookRgn 1
97/8 Zenith -RookieZTeam 14

SAMUELSSON, KJELL
90/1 Bowman 111
91/2 Bowman 240
92/3 Bowman 165
93/4 Donruss 259
95/6 Donruss 368
92/3 FleerUltra 169
94/5 FleerUltra 351
95/6 FleerUltra 286
95 Globe 27
93/4 Leaf 274
89/90 OPC/Topps 100
90/1 OPC/Topps 61
91/2 OPC/Topps 211, 329
92/3 O-Pee-Chee 230
97/8 PacificCrown 329
88/9 PaniniSticker 318
90/1 PaniniSticker 110
91/2 PaniniSticker 239
91/2 Parkhurst 356
92/3 Parkhurst 373
93/4 Parkhurst 432
95/6 Parkhurst 155
94/5 ParkieSE 138, ES7
91/2 Pinnacle 149, 407
92/3 Pinnacle 306
93/4 Pinnacle 293
94/5 Pinnacle 277
96/7 PinnacleBeAPlayer 189
95/6 Playoff 184
94/5 POG 192
93/4 PowerPlay 414
93/4 Premier 34
94/5 Premier 73
90/1 ProSet 222
91/2 ProSet 181
90/1 Score 197
91/2 Score(CDN) 207, (U.S) 207
92/3 Score 195
93/4 Score 184

91/2 SemicElitserien 339
93 SemicSticker 22
92/3 Topps 352
95/6 Topps 259
98/9 Topps 205
91/2 ToppsStadiumClub 70
92/3 ToppsStadiumClub 466
93/4 T.StadiumClub 251, 426
90/1 UpperDeck 116
91/2 UpperDeck 396
94/5 UpperDeck 128
95/6 UpperDeck 350
94/5 PGH 21
92/3 PGH/Coke
92/3 PGH/Foodland 14
93/4 PGH/Foodland 18
89/90 PHA
90/1 PHA
91/2 PHA/JCPenney
96/7 PHA/OceanSpray

SAMUELSSON, MORGAN
94/5 ElitSet 172
95/6 ElitSet 12,-Face 1,-Goldie 1
95 PaniniWorlds 146
89/90 SemicElitserien 159
90/1 SemicElitserien 63
91/2 SemicElitserien 236
92/3 SemicElitserien 49
95/6 udElite 18

SAMUELSSON, TOMMY
94/5 ElitSet 110, -Studio 4
90/1 SemicElitserien 251
91/2 SemicElitserien 82
92/3 SemicElitserien 104
89/90 SemicElitserien 76
82 SemicSticker 10
89 SemicSticker 8
91 SemicSticker 33

SAMUELSSON, ULF
91/2 Bowman 88, 408, 419
92/3 Bowman 351
93/4 Donruss 264
94/5 Donruss 296
95/6 Donruss 89, 243
93/4 EASports 104
94/5 Flair 139
94/5 Fleer 168
95/6 FleerMetal 100
92/3 FleerUltra 170, -Imports 20
93/4 FleerUltra 204
94/5 FleerUltra 169
95/6 FleerUltra 126, 278
95 Globe 7
93/4 Leaf 92
94/5 Leaf 205
95/6 Leaf 206
87/8 OPC/Topps 23
88/9 OPC/Topps 136
89/90 O-Pee-Chee 210
90/1 O-Pee-Chee 511
91/2 OPC/Topps 323
92/3 O-Pee-Chee 270
87/8 opcSticker 205/64
88/9 opcSticker 265/129
98/9 Pacific 299
97/8 PacificCrown 171
98/9 PacificParamount 157
87/8 PaniniSticker 41
88/9 PaniniSticker 238
89/90 PaniniSticker 228
91/2 PaniniSticker 277
92/3 PaniniSticker 229
93/4 PaniniSticker 87
94/5 PaniniSticker 79
95/6 PaniniSticker 66
96/7 PaniniSticker 107
97/8 PaniniSticker 88
95 PaniniWorlds 289
91/2 Parkhurst 361
92/3 Parkhurst 369, 446
93/4 Parkhurst 155
94/5 Parkhurst 183
95/6 Parkhurst 411
91/2 Pinnacle 267
92/3 Pinnacle 296
93/4 Pinnacle 29
94/5 Pinnacle 46
97/8 PinnacleBeAPlayer 126
95/6 Playoff 176
94/5 POG 193
95/6 POG 187
93/4 PowerPlay 194
93/4 Premier 132
94/5 Premier 391
90/1 ProSet 109
91/2 ProSet 459
92/3 ProSet 143
91/2 PSPlatinum 95
90/1 Score 152, -Hot 64
91/2 Score(CDN) 82, 308
91/2 Score(U.S) 82, 304
92/3 Score 90
93/4 Score 161
94/5 Score 156, CI7
95/6 Score 203
97/8 Score 239
97/8 Score(NYR) 15
92 SemicSticker 58
93 SemicSticker 21
95/6 SkyBoxEmotion 119
95/6 SkyBoxImpact 114
96/7 SkyBoxImpact 84
95/6 Summit 78
92/3 Topps 127
95/6 Topps 144
98/9 Topps 127
91/2 ToppsStadiumClub 328
92/3 ToppsStadiumClub 440
93/4 ToppsStadiumClub 356
95/6 ToppsStadiumClub 11, F7
94/5 TSC-MembersOnly 17
90/1 UpperDeck 287
91/2 UpperDeck 230, E17
92/3 UpperDeck 189
93/4 UpperDeck 142
94/5 UpperDeck 209
95/6 UpperDeck 448, SE142
96/7 UpperDeck 104
97/8 UpperDeck 204, 313, 395
95/6 UDBeAPlayer 223
95/6 UDCollChoice 79
97/8 UDCollChoice 171
96 Wien 44
84/5 HFD/JuniorWhalers
85/6 HFD/JuniorWhalers
86/7 HFD/JuniorWhalers
87/8 HFD/JuniorWhalers
88/9 HFD/JuniorWhalers
89/90 HFD/JuniorWhalers
90/1 HFD/JuniorWhalers
91/2 PGH/Elbys
91/2 PGH/Foodland 2
91/2 PGH/Topps
92/3 PGH/Clark
92/3 PGH/Foodland 12
92/3 PGH/FoodSticker
93/4 PGH/Foodland 3
94/5 PGH 5
96/7 PGH/Tribune

SAMULI, JOUNI
70/1 Kuvajulkaisut 168
71/2 WilliamsFIN 238
72/3 WilliamsFIN 222
73/4 WilliamsFIN 300

SANDA, DALIBOR
95/6 APS 265

SANDALAX, ALEX
51/2 LavalDairy 38

SANDBACK, DARRELL
93/4 Seattle

SANDBERG, MIKAEL
94/5 ElitSet 290
95/6 ElitSet 198, -Spidermen 13
92/3 SemicElitserien 301
95/6 udElite 204
97/8 udSwedish 68

SANDELIN, SCOTT
88/9 ProCards(Sherbrooke)
89/90 ProCards(AHL) 332
90/1 ProCards 41
87/8 MTL

SANDERS, FRANK
72/3 Minnesota

SANDERS, GRANT
84/5 Kitchener 28

SANDERS, REGGIE
95/6 EdgeIce 102

SANDERSON, DEREK
71/2 Bazooka Panel 12
71/2 Colgate Heads
70/1 Colgate Stamp 6
70/1 DadsCookies
70/1 EddieSargent 3
71/2 EddieSargent 4
70/1 Esso Stamp
74/5 Loblaws
73/4 Nabisco
68/9 OPC/Topps 6, OPC 213
69/70 OPC 201, -Sticker, T. 31
70/1 O-Pee-Chee 136
70/1 OPC/T-Deckle 5, -Sticker
71/2 OPC/Topps 65
73/4 OPC 183, Topps 182
74/5 OPC 290
75/6 OPC/Topps 73
76/7 OPC/Topps 20
77/8 OPC/Topps 46
94/5 Parkie(64/5) FS6
95/6 Parkie(66/7) 19
68/9 ShirriffCoin BOS7
71/2 TheTorontoSun
67/8 Topps 33
70/1 BOS
70/1 BOS/Ashtray
71/2 BOS
77/8 VAN/GingerAle

SANDERSON, GEOFF
95/6 Aces 6 (Hearts)
97/8 Aces 2 (Diamonds)
92/3 Bowman 136
95/6 Bowman 67
93/4 Classic-Canada TC6, -Aut
93/4 ClassicProspects 56
93/4 Donruss 147
94/5 Donruss 77
95/6 Donruss 201
96/7 Donruss 40
97/8 Donruss 79
96/7 D.CdnIce 114,-OCanada 15
97/8 D.CdnIce 41, -National 14
96/7 DonrussElite 127
97/8 DonrussElite 67
97/8 DonrussPreferred 85
97/8 DonrussPriority 49
97/8 DonrussStudio 84
93/4 EASports 58
94/5 Flair 74
96/7 Flair 44
94/5 Fleer 89, -Slapshot 9
96/7 Fleer 47
95/6 FleerMetal 66
92/3 FleerUltra 75
93/4 FleerUltra 151, -Speed 9
94/5 FleerUltra 93, -Speed 10
95/6 FleerUltra 70
96/7 FleerUltra 76
93/4 HockeyWit 6
95/6 Hoyle'EAST 6 (Clubs)
97/8 KatchMedallion 30
93/4 KraftDinner
96/7 KraftDinner
93/4 Leaf 77
94/5 Leaf 219
95/6 Leaf 88
96/7 Leaf 105
97/8 Leaf 28
94/5 LeafLimited 54
96/7 LeafPreferred 86
97/8 Limited 119, 135
96/7 MetalUniverse 71
92/3 O-Pee-Chee 122
98/9 Pacific 80
97/8 PacificCrown 270
97/8 PacificCrownRoyale 26
97/8 PcfcDynagon! 23,-Tand 38
97/8 PacificInvincible 26
92/3 PaniniSticker V
93/4 PaniniSticker L
94/5 PaniniSticker 109
95/6 PaniniSticker 28
96/7 PaniniSticker 23
97/8 PaniniSticker 20
95 PaniniWorlds 12
91/2 Parkhurst 57
92/3 Parkhurst 62
93/4 Parkhurst 86
94/5 Parkhurst 95, V49, C10
95/6 Parkhurst 91
91/2 Pinnacle 309
92/3 Pinnacle 307
93/4 Pinnacle 9
94/5 Pinnacle 63, BR8
95/6 Pinnacle 38
96/7 Pinnacle 187
97/8 Pinnacle 45
97/8 PinnacleBeAPlayer 112
97/8 PinnacleBeeHive 50
97/8 PinnacleCertified 125
97/8 PinnacleInside 78
95/6 PinnacleZenith 14
95/6 Playoff 266
94/5 POG 117
95/6 POG 125
93/4 PowerPlay 109, -Rising 6
93/4 Premier 156
94/5 Prmr 205, 527, -Fin.(T) 15
95/6 ProMagnet 129
91/2 ProSet 536
92/3 ProSet 63, -Rookie 11
91/2 PSPlatinum 256
91/2 Score(CDN) 354, (U.S) 324
92/3 Score 108
93/4 Score 213
94/5 Score 144, TF10
95/6 Score 111
96/7 Score 119
97/8 Score 110
94/5 Select 68
95/6 SelectCertified 26
90/1 SketchWHL 54, 336
95/6 SkyBoxEmotion 77
95/6 SkyBoxImpact 75
96/7 SkyBoxImpact 54
94/5 SP 52
96/7 SP 69
97/8 SPAuthentic 25
97/8 SPx 22
97/8 SportFX MiniStix
95/6 Summit 38
96/7 Summit 24
95/6 SuperSticker 51, 53
92/3 Topps 402
95/6 Topps 14, 318
94/5 ToppsFinest 108
95/6 ToppsFinest 173
96/7 ToppsNHLPicks 65
92/3 ToppsStadiumClub 111
93/4 ToppsStadiumClub 408
95/6 ToppsStadiumClub 172
93/4 TSC-MembersOnly 36
94/5 TSC-MembersOnly 8
95/6 ToppsSuperSkills 21
91/2 UpperDeck 588
92/3 UpperDeck 293
93/4 UD 292, 316, HT2, SP-65
94/5 UpperDeck 6, SP34
95/6 UpperDeck 20, SE127
96/7 UpperDeck 75
97/8 UpperDeck 30, SS22
95/6 UDBeAPlayer 62
96/7 UDBlackDiamond 138
98/9 UDChoice 27
95/6 UDCollChoice 293, C22
96/7 UDCollChoice 113, 319
97/8 UDCollChoice 116, SQ73
96/7 UpperDeck"Ice" 28
97/8 UpperDeckIce 8
91/2 HFD/JuniorWhalers
92/3 HFD/DairyMart
93/4 HFD/Coke

SANDERSON, GUY
92/3 Clarkson

SANDFORD, ED
45-64 BeeHives(BOS)
51/2 Parkhurst 22
52/3 Parkhurst 69
53/4 Parkhurst 90
54/5 Parkhurst 64
54/5 Topps 48
54-67 TorontoStarV4 ,n10
91/2 BOS/Legends

SANDHOLM, RYAN
91/2 AirCanadaSJHL A24
92/3 MPSPhotoSJHL 103

SANDIE, JOEL
90/1 SketchOHL 69
91/2 SketchOHL 244
91/2 Sudbury 10
92/3 Sudbury 4

SANDILANDS, NEIL
83/4 Kitchener 6

SANDIS, MIKE
84/5 Springfield 1

SANDKE, PETER
90/1 SketchQMJHL 58
91/2 SketchQMJHL 275

SANDLAK, JIM
90/1 Bowman 55
93/4 Donruss 138
92/3 FleerUltra 228
87/8 O-Pee-Chee 264
89/90 O-Pee-Chee 267, 316
90/1 OPC/Topps 18
92/3 O-Pee-Chee 168
87/8 opcSticker 66A, 194/53
87/8 opcSticker 135/123
90/1 Panini(VAN) 21
87/8 PaniniSticker 352
88/9 PaniniSticker 139
89/90 PaniniSticker 156
90/1 PaniniSticker 297, 306
92/3 PaniniSticker 34
94/5 PaniniSticker 113
91/2 Parkhurst 405
93/4 Parkhurst 84
94/5 Parkhurst 91
91/2 Pinnacle 294
92/3 Pinnacle 210
93/4 Pinnacle 364
94/5 POG 118
90/1 ProSet 301, 305
91/2 ProSet 497
90/1 Score (CND) 303
91/2 Score(CDN) 260
92/3 Score 379
93/4 Score 397, 532
92/3 Topps 41
92/3 ToppsStadiumClub 175
91/2 UpperDeck 577
92/3 UpperDeck 120
93/4 UpperDeck 393
93/4 HFD/Coke
85/6 VAN
86/7 VAN
87/8 VAN/Shell
88/9 VAN/Mohawk
89/90 VAN
90/1 VAN/Mohawk
91/2 VAN
92/3 VAN/RoadTrip

SANDLES, DALE
85/6 Kingston 2
86/7 Kingston 4

SANDLIN, TOMMY
94/5 ElitSet 296
91/2 SemicElitserien 303
92/3 SemicElitserien 325, 342
89 SemicSticker 2

SANDNER, CHRISTOPHER
94/5 DEL 317
95/6 DEL 354

SANDS, CHARLIE
33/4 Anonymous (V129) 16
34-43 BeeHives(BOS), (MTL.C)
35-40 CrownBrand 198
39/40 OPC (V301-1) 56
40/1 OPC (V301-2) 120
36/7 WWGum (V356) 27
33/4 WWGum (V357) 58

SANDS, JASON
95/6 Slapshot 118

SANDS, MIKE
83 CanadaJuniors

SANDSTRÖM, TOMAS
90/1 Bowman 141,-HatTrick 21
91/2 Bowman 174, 179
92/3 Bowman 22
95/6 Bowman 10
93/4 Donruss 163, 475
94/5 Donruss 271
95/6 Donruss 118
96/7 Donruss 78
95/6 DonrussElite 74
97/8 DonrussPriority 117
93/4 EASports 65
94/5 ElitSet 286, -Guest 2
94/5 Fleer 169
95/6 FleerMetal 119
96/7 FleerPicks 66
92/3 FleerUltra 88
93/4 FleerUltra 246
94/5 FleerUltra 352
95/6 FleerUltra 293, -Crease 16
95 Globe 28
93/4 HockeyWit 87
97/8 KatchMedallion 4
91/2 Kraft 63
93/4 Leaf 106
94/5 Leaf 207
95/6 Leaf 265
96/7 Leaf 81
95/6 LeafLimited 60
96/7 Maggers 127
97/8 Omega 6
85/6 OPC/Topps 123
86/7 O-Pee-Chee 230
87/8 OPC/Topps 28
88/9 OPC/Topps 121
89/90 OPC/Topps 54, C
90/1 OPC/Topps 301
91/2 OPC/Topps 173
92/3 O-Pee-Chee 91
91/2 opcPremier 82
87/8 opcStars 38
87/8 opcSticker 35
88/9 opcSticker 242/110
89/90 opcSticker 244
98/9 Pacific 63
97/8 PacificCrown 293
97/8 PacificCrownRoyale 4
97/8 PacificParamount 6
98/9 PacificParamount 6
87/8 PaniniSticker 114
88/9 PaniniSticker 310
89/90 PaniniSticker 281
90/1 PaniniSticker 243
91/2 PaniniSticker 79
92/3 PaniniSticker 67
93/4 PaniniSticker 205
95/6 PaniniSticker 62
96/7 PaniniSticker 61
97/8 PaniniSticker 150
95 PaniniWorlds 290
91/2 Parkhurst 70
93/4 Parkhurst 362
94/5 Parkhurst 175
95/6 Parkhurst 166
91/2 Pinnacle 178
92/3 Pinnacle 345
93/4 Pinnacle 263
94/5 Pinnacle 313
96/7 Pinnacle 156
97/8 Pinnacle 180
95/6 PinnacleZenith 79
94/5 POG 188
95/6 POG 214
93/4 PowerPlay 121
93/4 Premier 434
94/5 Premier 108
90/1 ProSet 127
91/2 ProSet 97
92/3 ProSet 287
91/2 PSPlatinum 53
90/1 Score 183, -Hot 79
91/2 Score(CDN) 490, (U.S) 270
92/3 Score 199
93/4 Score 129, -International 21
95/6 Score 279
96/7 Score 126
97/8 Score 258
97/8 Score(ANA) 12
95/6 SelectCertified 107
94 Semic 354
91/2 SemicElitserien 319
91 SemicSticker 208
92 SemicSticker 69
93 SemicSticker 32
95/6 SkyBoxEmotion 141
95/6 SkyBoxImpact 134
94/5 SP 90
95/6 SP 118
97/8 SPAuthentic 4
95/6 Summit 94
96/7 Summit 81
92/3 Topps 421
95/6 Topps 228
98/9 Topps 12
95/6 ToppsFinest 12
91/2 ToppsStadiumClub 209
92/3 ToppsStadiumClub 220
93/4 ToppsStadiumClub 25
95/6 ToppsStadiumClub 118
90/1 UpperDeck 251
91/2 UpperDeck 30, 85, 141, E7
92/3 UpperDeck 424
93/4 UpperDeck 188
94/5 UpperDeck 461
95/6 UpperDeck 185, SE156
96/7 UpperDeck 137
95/6 UDBeAPlayer 160
95/6 UDCollChoice 139
96/7 UDCollChoice 215
96 Wien 59
90/1 L.A./Smokeys 6
94/5 PGH 10
95/6 PGH/Foodland 15

SANDSTROM, ULF
89/90 SemicElitserien 179
90/1 SemicElitserien 235
91/2 SemicElitserien 172
89 SemicSticker 16
95/6 udElite DS3

SANDWITH, TERRAN
92/3 ClassicProspects 114
91/2 SketchWHL 214

SANFORD, JASON
91/2 AvantGardeBCJ 138
92/3 BCJHL 95

SANGSTER, DARRYL
92/3 MPSPhotoSJHL 104

SANGSTER, JACK
83/4 Brandon 18
84/5 Brandon 18
85/6 Brandon 18

SANGSTER, ROB
89/90 SketchOHL 58
87/8 Kitchener 17
88/9 Kitchener 17
89/90 Kitchener 18

SANIPASS, EVERETT
91/2 Bowman 135
91/2 OPC/Topps 315
90/1 Panini(QUE) 19
91/2 PaniniSticker 262
88/9 ProCards(Saginaw)
89/90 ProCard(IHL) 63
90/1 Score 28
91/2 ToppsStadiumClub 284
87/8 CHI/Coke
88/9 CHI/Coke
89/90 CHI/Coke
90/1 QUE/PetroCanada

SANKO, RON
82/3 Kingston 16
85/6 Kitchener 23
83/4 NorthBay

SANSCARTIER, ALAIN
90/1 SketchQMJHL 113
91/2 SketchQMJHL 75

SANTALA, SEPPO
73/4 WilliamsFIN 317

SANTANEN, ARI
96/7 Sisu 119

SANTANEN, PEKKA
78/9 SM-Liiga 163

SANTURIAN, OLEG
93/4 Richmond 13

SANZA, NICK
82 SemicSticker 123

SAPARIK, RICHARD
94/5 Slapshot(MEM) 62

SAPERGIA, BRENT
88/9 ProCards(Indianapolis)
89/90 ProCards(IHL) 114
90/1 ProCards 318
91/2 ProCards 331
92/3 Toledo 1

SAPOSHNIKOV, ANDREJ
96/7 DEL 211

SAPOZHNIKOV, ANDREI
93/4 Classic 92
93 SemicSticker 135

SARAULT, YVES
91/2 Classic 49
91/2 ClassicFourSport 49, -Aut.
97/8 Score(COL) 20
90/1 SketchMEM 125
90/1 SketchQMJHL 175

91/2 SketchQMJHL 163
91/2 UltimateDP 44, -Aut 44
92/3 Fredericton
93/4 Fredericton
94/5 Fredericton

SARAZBAR, JOSE
79 PaniniSticker 375

SARAZIN, PIERRE
79 PaniniSticker 341

SARDA, ROGER
51/2 LacStJean 49

SARGANT, SHANE
87/8 SSMarie 27

SARGENT, GARY
77/8 OPC/Topps 113
78/9 OPC/Topps 37
79/80 OPC/Topps 52
80/1 OPC/Topps 237
78/9 MIN/Cloverleaf 1
79/80 MIN
80/1 MIN
81/2 MIN
82/3 MIN

SARICH, CORY
95/6 Bowman P31
97/8 Bowman 115
98 BowmanCHL 68
95/6 UpperDeck 519
98/9 UDChoice 265
96/7 UpperDeck"Ice" 132

SARJEANT, GEOFF
94/5 ClassicFourSport 154
92/3 ClassicProspects 71
95/6 EdgeIce 147
96/7 Leaf 228
94/5 UpperDeck 375
96/7 Cincinnati
90/1 Mich.Tech
91/2 Mich.Tech (x3)
92/3 Peoria
93/4 Peoria

SÄRKILAHTI, OLLI
72/3 WilliamsFIN 353

SARNO, PETER
98 BowmanCHL 16

SAROS, SEPPO
71/2 WilliamsFIN 272

SARRONLAHTI, JARI
71/2 WilliamsFIN 254
73/4 WilliamsFIN 318

SARTIALA, TIMO
72/3 WilliamsFIN 182

SARTJÄRVI, PEKKA
72/3 WilliamsFIN 183

SASKAMOOSE, FRED
54/5 Parkhurst 82

SASS, PAUL
91/2 LakeSuperior

SASSEVILLE, FRANÇOIS
93/4 Slapshot(Drum.) 21
96/7 Halifax 1, 2

SASSO, TOM
91/2 ProCards 436

SATAN, MIROSLAV
95/6 Bowman 112
95/6 Classic-Aut.
94/5 ClassicImages 58
96/7 Donruss 215
95/6 FleerMetal 190
95/6 FleerUltra 355
96/7 FleerUltra 62
96/7 Leaf 189
96/7 MetalUniverse 55
97/8 Omega 26
98/9 Pacific 81
97/8 PacificCrown 132
97/8 PacificCrownRoyale 16
97/8 PcfcDynagon! 14,-Tand 21
97/8 PacificInvinsible 15
97/8 PacificParamount 24
98/9 PacificParamount 22
97/8 PacificRevolution 16
96/7 PaniniSticker 260
97/8 PaniniSticker 18, 126
95/6 Parkhurst 348, 509
97/8 Pinnacle 135
96/7 PinnacleBeAPlayer 39
95/6 PinnacleZenith 150
96/7 Score 249
97/8 Score 232
97/8 Score(BUF) 15
95/6 SelectCertified 125
95/6 SkyBoxImpact 197
96/7 SkyBoxImpact 170
95/6 SP 52
97/8 SPAuthentic 15
96/7 Summit 166
95/6 Topps 283
96/7 ToppNHLPicks SR12
95/6 ToppsStadiumClub 122
95/6 UpperDeck 302
96/7 UpperDeck 260
97/8 UDBlackDiamond 62
98/9 UDChoice 22
96/7 UDCollChoice 98
96 Wien 231
97/8 Zenith 51
96/7 EDM

SATERDALEN, JEFF
92/3 Richmond

SATERI, ESA
93/4 Sisu 242
94/5 Sisu 65

SATHER, GLEN
70/1 DadsCookies
70/1 EddieSargent 167
70/1 Esso Stamp
68/9 O-Pee-Chee 134
69/70 OPC/Topps 116
70/1 O-Pee-Chee 205
71/2 OPC/Topps 221
75/6 OPC/Topps 222
76/7 opcWHA 56
68/9 ShirriffCoin BOS14
71/2 TheTorontoSun
67/8 Topps 38
92/3 UD'LockerAS 49
81/2 EDM/RedRooster
82/3 EDM/RedRooster
83/4 EDM/Buttons
83/4 EDM/McDonald
84/5 EDM/RedRooster
85/6 EDM/RedRooster
86/7 EDM/RedRooster
88/9 EDM/ActionMag. 49, 117
92/3 EDM/IGA 26
93/4 EDM 10A PR94
74/5 MTL
73/4 STL

SATOR, TED
87/8 BUF/WonderBread
88/9 BUF/WonderBread

SAUER, E.J.
91/2 ProCards 440

SAUMIER, MARC
88/9 ProCards(Sherbrooke)
89/90 ProCards(AHL) 188
91/2 ProCards 392
87/8 Hull
94/5 Muskegon

SAUMIER, RAY
89/90 ProCards(AHL) 284

SAUNDERCOOK, PAUL
90/1 ProCards 415

SAUNDERS, DAVE
88/9 O-Pee-Chee 248
88/9 opcSticker 61/196
87/8 VAN/Shell

SAUNDERS, LEE
92/3 Maine(2) 29
93/4 Maine 49

SAUNIER, BRUNO
94 Semic 216
92 SemicSticker 225

SAURDIFF, CORWIN
94/5 Hampton 21
95/6 Hampton HRA -23

SAURIO, MATTI
66/7 Champion 7
65/6 Hellas 31
70/1 Kuvajulkaisut 236
71/2 WilliamsFIN 255
73/4 WilliamsFIN 319

SAURIOL, CLAUDE-CHARLES
90/1 SketchQMJHL 134
87/8 Hull

SAUTER, DOUG
88/9 Brandon 19
89/90 Brandon 23
85/6 MedicineHat 8
86/7 Regina
87/8 Regina
83/4 Springfield 24
92/3 Wheeling 22
93/4 Wheeling 18

SAUTER, HARDY
90/1 SketchWHL 217
91/2 SketchWHL 2
89/90 Brandon 7
90/1 Brandon 5

SAUVÉ, BOB
76/7 O-Pee-Chee 308
78/9 O-Pee-Chee 265
79/80 OPC/Topps 49
80/1 OPC/T. 166, 168, OPC 266
81/2 OPC 23, Topps(E) 77
82/3 O-Pee-Chee 34
83/4 O-Pee-Chee 61, 71
84/5 O-Pee-Chee 30
85/6 O-Pee-Chee 174
86/7 OPC/Topps 124
87/8 OPC/Topps 140
81/2 opcSticker 56
82/3 opcSticker 181
83/4 opcSticker 242
84/5 opcSticker 208
85/6 opcSticker 181/50, 190/63
86/7 opcSticker 152/7
87/8 opcSticker 75/208
87/8 PaniniSticker 220
82/3 Post
79/80 BUF/BellsMarket
80/1 BUF/Wendt
81/2 BUF 8
82/3 BUF/Wendt 6
84/5 BUF/BlueShield
86/7 CHI/Coke
87/8 N.J.
88/9 N.J/Caretta

SAUVÉ, J.F.
82/3 O-Pee-Chee 33
85/6 opcSticker 155/27
86/7 opcSticker 23/163
82/3 Post
83/4 QUE
84/5 QUE
85/6 QUE/GeneralFoods
86/7 QUE/McDonald
85/6 QUE/Provigo

SAUVÉ, PHILIPPE
98 BowmanCHL 101, 160, A23
98/9 Topps 241
96/7 Rimouski

SAVAGE, ALAIN
91/2 SketchQMJHL 69

SAVAGE, BRIAN
95/6 Bowman 87
93/4 CanadaNats
93/4 Classic 81, TC3
94/5 Classic 34, T36, -Aut.
93/4 ClassicProspects LP18
94/5 Donruss 276
95/6 Donruss 20
96/7 Donruss 168
97/8 Donruss 109
95/6 DonrussElite 28
97/8 DonrussPreferred 62
97/8 DonrussPriority 128
94/5 Fleer 108
95/6 FleerMetal 79, -Winners 7
93/4 FleerUltra 472
95/6 FleerUltra 84, -High 17
94/5 Leaf 292
95/6 Leaf 175, -Studio 15
96/7 Leaf 111
97/8 Leaf 68
95/6 LeafLimited 82
97/8 Limited 71
97/8 Omega 123
98/9 Pacific 49
97/8 PacificCrown 142
97/8 PacificParamount 99
98/9 PacificParamount 118
95/6 PaniniSticker 36
97/8 PaniniSticker 30
95/6 Parkhurst 112
94/5 ParkieSE 90
94/5 Pinnacle 248, RTP10
95/6 Pinnacle 94
96/7 Pinnacle 134
97/8 Pinnacle 152
97/8 PinnacleInside 135
95/6 PinnacleZenith 20
95/6 POG 144
93/4 PowerPlay 493
93/4 Premier-TmCanada 16
94/5 Premier 16
94/5 Score 230, CT8
95/6 Score 76
96/7 Score 147
97/8 Score 191
97/8 Score(MTL) 6
94/5 Select 192
95/6 SkyBoxEmotion 92
95/6 SkyBoxImpact 88, -Fox 9
95/6 Summit 167
95/6 Topps 349, 21NG
94/5 ToppsFinest-BBest(Red) 8
95/6 ToppsFinest 23
95/6 ToppsStadiumClub 37
94/5 UpperDeck 244
95/6 UpperDeck 36, SE132
97/8 UpperDeck 299
95/6 UDBeAPlayer 138
98/9 UDChoice 111
96/7 UDCollChoice 140
97/8 UDCollChoice 131
96/7 UpperDeck"Ice" 34
94/5 MTL
95/6 MTL/Molson
95/6 MTL
96-8 MTL

SAVAGE, JOEL
95/6 DEL 381
96/7 DEL 192
89/90 ProCards(AHL) 263
90/1 ProCards 266
91/2 ProCards 13
91/2 UpperDeck 423
91/2 Rochester/Dunkin'Donuts
91/2 Rochester/Genny
91/2 Rochester/Kodak
92/3 Rochester/Kodak

SAVAGE, MIKE
83/4 Belleville 11

SAVAGE, NICOLAS
93/4 Slapshot(Drum.) 6

SAVAGE, REGGIE
93/4 Durivage 23
92/3 opcPremier 121
92/3 Parkhurst 426
94/5 Parkhurst 194
90/1 ProCards 199
91/2 ProCards 570
91/2 Score(CDN) 350, (U.S) 320
92/3 TSC-MembersOnly
92/3 UpperDeck 474
92/3 WSH/Kodak
91/2 Baltimore 7

SAVARD, ANDRÉ
74/5 Loblaws
74/5 OPC 285
75/6 OPC/Topps 155
76/7 OPC/Topps 43
77/8 OPC/Topps 118
78/9 OPC/Topps 253
79/80 OPC/Topps 25
80/1 O-Pee-Chee 375
81/2 OPC 24, Topps(E) 78
84/5 O-Pee-Chee 288
81/2 opcSticker 54
84/5 opcSticker 170
82/3 Post
83/4 SouhaitsRen.KeyChain
83/4 Vachon 73
80/1 BUF/Wendt
81/2 BUF 13
83/4 QUE
84/5 QUE
87/8 QUE/GeneralFoods
92/3 QUE/PetroCanada
85/6 Fredericton 28
86/7 Fredericton

SAVARD, DENIS
90/1 Bowman 6
91/2 Bowman 342
92/3 Bowman 64
72-84 Dernière 82/3
93/4 Donruss 319
94/5 Donruss 284
95/6 Donruss 233
96/7 Donruss 34, 51, 114
92/3 Durivage 10
93/4 Durivage 25
88/9 Esso Sticker
92/3 FleerUltra 109
93/4 FleerUltra 428
94/5 FleerUltra 373
95/6 FleerUltra 219
88/9 FritoLay
93/4 HockeyWit 38
95/6 Hoyle'WEST 3 (Clubs)
90/1 Kraft 51
91/2 Kraft 77
93/4 Kraft-Captain
93/4 Leaf 372
94/5 Leaf 166
95/6 Leaf 127
96/7 Maggers 28
82/3 McDonalds 23
81/2 OPC 63, Topps(W) 75
82/3 O-Pee-Chee 73
83/4 O-Pee-Chee 96, 111
84/5 OPC 45, 355, Topps 35
85/6 OPC/Topps 73
86/7 OPC/Topps 7, N
87/8 OPC/Topps 127
88/9 OPC/Topps 26, H
89/90 OPC/Topps 5
90/1 OPC/Topps 28
91/2 OPC/Topps 330
92/3 O-Pee-Chee 35
87/8 opcStars 39
88/9 opcStars 34
90/1 opcPremier 103
91/2 opcPremier 71
92/3 opcPremier-Star 6
81/2 opcSticker 112
82/3 opcSticker 171
83/4 opcSticker 106, 107, 153
84/5 opcSticker 24, 25
85/6 opcSticker 22
86/7 opcSticker 150
87/8 opcSticker 78
88/9 opcSticker 13
89/90 opcSticker 16
97/8 PacificCrown 343
90/1 Panini(MTL) 20
87/8 PaniniSticker 225
88/9 PaniniSticker 29
89/90 PaniniSticker 49
90/1 PaniniSticker 198
91/2 PaniniSticker 187
92/3 PaniniSticker 152
93/4 PaniniSticker 17
94/5 PaniniSticker 181
96/7 PaniniSticker 164
91/2 Parkhurst 93, 211
92/3 Parkhurst 85
93/4 Parkhurst 193
94/5 Parkhurst 217
95/6 Parkhurst 40
91/2 Pinnacle 28
92/3 Pinnacle 61, -Promo 61
93/4 Pinnacle 391, CA22
94/5 Pinnacle 340
95/6 Playoff 237
94/5 POG 225
95/6 POG 62
82/3 Post
81/2 Post PopUp 3
93/4 PowerPlay 447
93/4 Premier 305
94/5 Premier 69
90/1 ProSet 59, 473
91/2 ProSet 128, 305
92/3 ProSet 64, 260
91/2 PSPlatinum 64, PC18
83/4 PuffySticker 18
90/1 Score 125, 1T, -Hot 59
91/2 Score(CDN) 165, (U.S) 165
92/3 Score 202
93/4 Score 105, 555
95/6 Score 281
96/7 Score 121
92/3 SeasonsPatch 23
89 SemicSticker 66
85/6 7Eleven 4
84/5 7ElevenDisk
83/4 SouhaitsRen.KeyChain
92/3 Topps 414
91/2 ToppsStadiumClub 213
92/3 ToppsStadiumClub 467
93/4 ToppsStadiumClub 297
95/6 TSCMembers 23
90/1 UpperDeck 44, 426
91/2 UpperDeck 242
92/3 UpperDeck 10, 162, 638
93/4 UD 502, SP-153, GG1
94/5 UpperDeck 415, SP76
95/6 UpperDeck 434
94/5 UDBeAPlayer-Aut. 94
96/7 UDBlackDiamond 58
95/6 UDCollChoice 132
80/1 CHI/4x6
80/1 CHI/5.5x8.5
81/2 CHI
82/3 CHI
83/4 CHI
86/7 CHI/Coke
87/8 CHI/Coke
88/9 CHI/Coke
89/90 CHI/Coke
90/1 MTL
91/2 MTL
92/3 MTL
92/3 MTL/OPC 50
94/5 T.B/SkyBoxSportsCafe
79/80 Montréal, -B&W

SAVARD, FRÉDÉRIC
88/9 Richelieu

SAVARD, JEAN
72-84 Dernière 77/8

SAVARD, MARC
90/1 SketchMEM 64, 130
90/1 SketchQMJHL 250
91/2 SketchQMJHL 74
93/4 Dayton 9

SAVARD, MARC
97/8 Bowman 7
95/6 Classic 91
98/9 Pacific 300
94/5 ParkieSE 263
97/8 Pinnacle 15
97/8 PinnacleCertified L
97/8 Score 67
97/8 Score(NYR) 19
93/4 Slapshot(Oshawa) 22
95/6 Slapshot 250
94/5 SP 182
98/9 SPx"Finite" 54
98/9 UDChoice 133

SAVARD, MIKE
91/2 AirCanadaSJHL B21
92/3 MPSPhotoSJHL 154

SAVARD, RAY
86/7 Regina

SAVARD, SERGE
70/1 Colgate Stamp 74
70/1 DadsCookies
72-84 Dernière 72/3, 73/4
72-84 Dernière 80/1, 82/3
70/1 EddieSargent 110
71/2 EddieSargent 110
72/3 EddieSargent 123
70/1 Esso Stamp
88/9 Esso Sticker
87 HallOfFame 256
934 HockeyWit 42
91/2 Kraft 77
74/5 LiptonSoup 11
74/5 Loblaws
73/4 MacsMilkDisk
69/70 OPC/Topps 4
69/70 OPC 210, -Sticker
70/1 OPC/Topps 51
71/2 OPC/Topps 143
72/3 OPC 185, -TmCanada
73/4 OPC/Topps 24
74/5 OPC/Topps 53
75/6 OPC/Topps 144
76/7 OPC/Topps 205
77/8 OPC/Topps 45
78/9 OPC/Topps 190, OPC 335
79/80 OPC/Topps 101
80/1 OPC/Topps 26
82/3 O-Pee-Chee 390
95/6 Parkie(66/7) 74
80/1 Pepsi Cap
82/3 Post
68/9 Post Marble
72/3 Post Transfers 8
68/9 ShirriffCoin MTL17
83/4 SouhaitsRen.KeyChain
71/2 TheTorontoSun
91/2 Trends(72) 53, -Aut
90/1 UpperDeck 506
95/6 Zellers
67/8 MTL/IGA
68/9 MTL
69/70 MTL/ProStar
70/1 MTL
71 MTL/Pins
71/2 MTL
72/3 MTL
73/4 MTL
74/5 MTL
75/6 MTL
76/7 MTL
77/8 MTL
78/9 MTL
79/80 MTL
80/1 MTL
81/2 MTL
87/8 MTL
88/9 MTL
89/90 MTL
90/1 MTL
91/2 MTL
92/3 MTL/OPC 4, 11
95/6 MTL/Forum 24Feb96
81/2 WPG
82/3 WPG

SAVARIA, MARTIN
84/5 Richelieu

SAVARY, NEIL
94/5 Slapshot(MEM) 74

SAVCHENKOV, ALEXANDER
95/6 Tallahassee 15

SAVENKO, BODGAN
93/4 Slapshot(NiagaraFalls) 19
94/5 Indianapolis

SAVICKIJ, ALEXANDER
94/5 APS 145

SAVIJCKI, JARKKO
96/7 Sisu 22

SAVILLE, JOHN
74/5 SiouxCity

SAVOIA, RYAN
95/6 EdgeIce 117
95/6 Cleveland

SAVOIE, CLAUDE
93/4 Classic 147
93/4 ClassicProspects 121
90/1 SketchQMJHL 260
91/2 SketchQMJHL 262

SAVOIE, MICHEL
91/2 SketchQMJHL 49

SAVOLAINEN, HANNU
78/9 SM-Liiga 130

SAVOLAINEN, KARI
93/4 Jyvas-Hyva 133
93/4 Sisu 135
95/6 Sisu 390

SAVOLAINEN, MATIAS
66/7 Champion 215

SAVOLAINEN, PERTTI
78/9 SM-Liiga 69

SAVOLAINEN, REIMO
66/7 Champion 214

SAVOLAINEN, RISTO
66/7 Champion 216

SAVOLAINEN, VEIKKO
66/7 Champion 172
70/1 Kuvajulkaisut 253
71/2 WilliamsFIN 219
73/4 WilliamsFIN 234

SAVUNEN, JUKKA
66/7 Champion 4
70/1 Kuvajulkaisut 237

SAWCHUK, TERRY
45-64 BeeHives(BOS), (DETx2)
64-67 BeeHives(TOR)
62 CeramicTiles
64/5 CokeCap TOR-24
65/6 CocaCola
48-52 Exhibits
83&87 HallOfFame 46
83 HHOF Postcard (D)
96/7 HHOFLegends 73
93/4 HighLiner 11
93/4 HockeyWit 83
82? JDMcCarthy
91/2 Kraft 75
68/9 OPC/T. 34, OPC-Puck 20
69/70 O-Pee-Chee 189
70/1 OPC 231
51/2 Parkhurst 61
52/3 Parkhurst 86
53/4 Parkhurst 46
54/5 Parkhurst 33, 96, 100
60/1 Parkhurst 31
61/2 Parkhurst 31
63/4 Parkhurst 53
91/2 Parkhurst PHC9
92/3 Parkhurst PR2
93/4 Parkhurst PR37, PR53
93/4 Parkie(56/7) 17
94/5 Parkie(64/5) 119, TW4
95/6 Parkie(66/7) 120
91/2 ProSet 343
60/1 ShirriffCoin 41
61/2 ShirriffCoin 77
63/4 TheTorontoStar
54/5 Topps 58
57/8 Topps 35
58/9 Topps 2
59/60 Topps 42
64/5 Topps 6
65/6 Topps 12
66/7 Topps 13
54-67 TorontoStar V7, V11, 66/7
56-66 TorontoStar 60/1, 62/3
56-66 TorontoStar 57/8, 64/5
60/1 YorkGlasses
62/3 YorkTransfer 25
63/4 York 37
91/2 BOS/Legends (x2)
64/5 TOR

SAWTELL, DREW
89/90 Saskatoon 15

SAWYER, DAN
94/5 Johnstown 18

SBROCCA, CHRISTIAN
96/7 Penascola 16

SCAMURRA, PETER
79/80 WSH

SCANLAN, DEREK
94/5 ThunderBay

SCANLAN, FRED
83&87 HallOfFame 118
83 HHOF Postcard (H)

SCANTLEBURY, STU
90/1 SketchWHL 233
91/2 SketchWHL 211
90/1 Brandon 17
92/3 Tacoma

SCANZANO, JASON
92/3 MPSPhotoSJHL 142

SCAP, IVAN
79 PaniniSticker 395

SCAPNIELLO, MARCO
92 SemicSticker 257

SCAPINELLO, RAY
90/1 ProSet 697

SCARDOCCHIO, ENRICO
91/2 SketchQMJHL 171

SCARLATA, CHRIS
92/3 Hampton

SCATCHARD, DAVE
97/8 Omega 235
98/9 Pacific 433
98/9 PacificParamount 239
97/8 PinnacleBeAPlayer 234
94/5 SigRookies 54
97/8 SPAuthentic 161
98/9 UDChoice 209
93/4 Portland

SCERBAN, BEDRICK
95/6 APS 358
94/5 ElitSet 25
95/6 ElitSet 17, -FaceToFace 2
95 PaniniWorlds 191
94 Semic 174
92/3 SemicElitserien 53
89 SemicSticker 182
91 SemicSticker 105
93 SemicSticker 93
95/6 udElite 20

SCEVIOUR, DARIN
85/6 NovaScotia 19

SCHALL, JURGEN
94/5 DEL 121
95/6 DEL 121
96/7 DEL 61

SCHADEN, MARIO
95 PaniniWorlds 269
94 Semic 246
93 SemicSticker 268, 288

SCHADLER, THOMAS
94/5 DEL 422

SCHAEFER, PETER
97/8 Bowman 118
95 Classic 14
94/5 Slapshot(MEM) 47
96/7 UDBlackDiamond 88
97/8 UDCollChoice 297
96/7 UpperDeck"Ice" 135

SCHAEFFER, JEFF
95/6 SwiftCurrent

SCHAFFLER, JAMES
91/2 AirCanadaSJHL B2

SCHAFER, MIKE
92/3 WestMich.
93/4 WestMich.

SCHAFER, PAXTON
95/6 Classic 41
97/8 Donruss 201, -Rated 2
97/8 DonrussCanadianIce 133
97/8 Limited 142
97/8 PacificDynag-BestKept 8
97/8 UpperDeck 183

SCHAFER, JERRY
79 PaniniSticker 280

SCHAFFER, RYAN
92/3 BCJHL 169

SCHALLER, PASCAL
95 PaniniWorlds 132

SCHAMEHORN, KEVIN
89/90 ProCards(IHL) 75
87/8 Flint

SCHARF, CHRIS
91/2 SketchOHL 231

SCHEIDT, TYLER
91/2 AirCanadaSJHL A34

SCHEIFELE, STEVE
90/1 ProCards 44
91/2 Richmond 15

SCHELLA, JOHN
75/6 opcWHA 21
76/7 opcWHA 128
73/4 QuakerOats 7
72/3 7ElevenCups
71/2 TheTorontoSun
75/6 Houston
71/2 VAN/RoyalBank 19

SCHENDELEV, SERGEJ
94/5 DEL 306
95/6 DEL 107
96/7 DEL 52

SCHERTZ, JAN
94/5 DEL 48
95/6 DEL 42
96/7 DEL 41

SCHEUER, TYSON
92/3 BCJHL 225

SCHICHTL, HANS
72 Hellas 59
72 SemicSticker 97

SCHIEBEL, BRIAN
91/2 AvantGardeBCJHL 58
92/3 BCJHL 43
91/2 Nainamo

SCHIFFEL, HEINRICH
94/5 DEL 387
95/6 DEL 368
96/7 DEL 190
92 SemicSticker 177

SCHILCHER, F.
79 PaniniSticker 303

SCHILCHER, WERNER
79 PaniniSticker 309

SCHILL, DAVE
89/90 Kitchener 10

SCHILL, LEE
91/2 AvantGardeBCJHL 137

SCHILLER, PETER
82 SemicSticker 111

SCHILLGARD, JOHAN
91/2 SemicElitserien 50

SCHILLING, PAUL
72 SemicSticker 135

SCHINKEL, CHRIS
91/2 AirCanadaSJHL C43
92/3 MPSPhotoSJHL 32

SCHINKEL, KEN
52/3 AnonymousOHL 26
71/2 Bazooka Panel 33
45-64 BeeHives(NYR)
70/1 Colgate Stamp 61
70/1 DadsCookies
70/1 EddieSargent 174
71/2 EddieSargent 162
72/3 EddieSargent 170
70/1 Esso Stamp
68/9 OPC/Topps 106
69/70 OPC/T. 117, OPC-Sticker
70/1 OPC/Topps 92
71/2 OPC/Topps 64
72/3 O-Pee-Chee 256
60/1 ShirriffCoin 96
61/2 ShirriffCoin 99
68/9 ShirriffCoin Pi1
71/2 TheTorontoSun
60/1 Topps 50
63/4 Topps 62
71/2 PGH

SCHINKO, MARCO
94/5 DEL 62

SCHINKO, THOMAS
95/6 DEL 62
96/7 DEL 258
94 Semic 289
91 SemicSticker 170
92 SemicSticker 188

SCHISTAD, ROBERT
95 PaniniWorlds 237
94 Semic 252
93 SemicSticker 230
96 Wien 201

SCHLEGEL, BRAD
90/1 CanadaNats
91/2 CanadaNats
92 CanadaWinterOlympics 198
95/6 DEL 133
92/3 opcPremier 28
95 PaniniWorlds 4
91/2 Parkhurst 413
92/3 Parkhurst 199
92/3 Score 477, -CdnOlympic 9
94/5 Score CT18
92/3 Topps 377
92/3 ToppsStadiumClub 29
92/3 UpperDeck 101
91/2 WSH/Kodak
85/6 London 21
86/7 London 8

SCHLICKENRIEDER, JOSEF
94/5 DEL 148
95/6 DEL 126
89 SemicSticker 104

SCHLIEBENER, ANDY
84/5 O-Pee-Chee 329
82/3 Fredericton 19
83/4 Fredericton 22
84/5 Fredericton 24
85/6 Fredericton 18

SCHLODER, ALOIS
72 Hellas 52
79 PaniniSticker 107
72 SemicSticker 107

SCHMALZ, KEVIN
90/1 SketchWHL 236
89/90 Brandon 18

SCHMAUTZ, BOBBY
72/3 EddieSargent 219
74/5 Loblaws
72/3 OPC 181
73/4 OPC/Topps 35
74/5 OPC/Topps 27, 117
75/6 OPC/Topps 251
76/7 OPC/Topps 189
77/8 OPC/Topps 59
78/9 OPC/Topps 248
79/80 OPC/Topps 144
80/1 Pepsi Cap
71/2 TheTorontoSun
79/80 EDM
88/9 EDM/ActionMagazine 16
71/2 VAN/RoyalBank 12
72/3 VAN/RoyalBank
73/4 VAN/RoyalBank
80/1 VAN
80/1 VAN/Silverwood

SCHMAUTZ, CLIFF
70/1 EddieSargent 29
70/1 Esso Stamp
70/1 O-Pee-Chee 142

SCHMID, LORENZ
79 PaniniSticker 264

SCHMID, UDO
94/5 DEL 365

SCHMIDT, CHRIS
90/1 SketchWHL 152
91/2 SketchWHL 268
93/4 Seattle

SCHMIDT, DARREN
92/3 MPSPhotoSJHL 31
93/4 Slapshot(Kitchener) 22
82/3 Brandon 5

SCHMIDT, DON
85/6 Kamloops
86/7 Kamloops
87/8 Kamloops
88/9 Kamloops
84/5 PrinceAlbert

SCHMIDT, GREG
95/6 RedDeer

SCHMIDT, JACK
34-43 BeeHives(BOS)
51/2 LavalDairy 69
52/3 StLawrence 17

SCHMIDT, JOE
51/2 BasDuFleuve 7

SCHMIDT, MICHAEL
94/5 DEL 299
95/6 DEL 336
91 SemicSticker 158
93 SemicSticker 152

SCHMIDT, MILT
34-43 BeeHives(BOS)
83&87 HallOfFame 165
83 HHOF Postcard (L)
94/5 HHOFLegends 40
40/1 OPC (V301-2) 132
43-47 ParadeSportive
51/2 Parkhurst 29
52/3 Parkhurst 70
53/4 Parkhurst 92
54/5 Parkhurst 59
92/3 Parkhurst PR23
93/4 Parkhurst DPR2
93/4 Parkie(56/7) 21
94/5 Parkie(64/5) 22
60/1 ShirriffCoin 120
54/5 Topps 60
63/4 Topps 1
64/5 Topps 70
65/6 Topps 96
54-67 TorontoStar V 4,n9
57/8 BOS
91/2 BOS/Legends (x3)
74/5 WSH

SCHMIDT, MORITZ
94/5 DEL 40

SCHMIDT, NORM
83/4 PGH
86/7 PGH/Kodak
80/1 Oshawa 13
81/2 Oshawa 7
82/3 Oshawa 21

SCHMIDT, RYAN
95/6 Slapshot 327

SCHMIESS, TREVOR
91/2 AirCanadaSJHL A26

SCHMITZ, CHRISTIAN
94/5 DEL 80
95/6 DEL 313
96/7 DEL 96

SCHMYR, DEAN
91/2 AvantGardeBCJ 127

SCHNARR, WERNER
24/5 Champs (C144)
24/5 (V145-2) 26

SCHNEIDAWIND, MICHAEL
96/7 DEL 200

SCHNEIDER, ANDY
93/4 ClassicProspects 170
94/5 DEL 371
95/6 DEL 369
93/4 Donruss 468
94/5 ElitSet 217
90/1 SketchWHL 55
91/2 SketchWHL 174
91/2 UpperDeck 'CzechWJC 56

SCHNEIDER, BUZZ
94/5 MiracleOnIce 29, 30

SCHNEIDER, GEOFF
87/8 Kingston 27

SCHNEIDER, J.A.
90/1 SketchOHL 46
91/2 SketchOHL 10
93/4 Birmingham 14
91/2 Cornwall 12

SCHNEIDER, MATHIEU
90/1 Bowman 52
91/2 Bowman 343
92/3 Bowman 190
95/6 Bowman 81
93/4 Donruss 179
94/5 Donruss 233
95/6 Donruss 55
96/7 Donruss 18
96/7 DonrussCanadianIce 97
97/8 DonrussCanadianIce 116
96/7 DonrussElite 88
97/8 DonrussPriority 34
93/4 EASports 68
94/5 Fleer 109
95/6 FleerMetal 93
92/3 FleerUltra 110
94/5 FleerUltra 114
95/6 FleerUltra 88, 270
97/8 KatchMedallion 143
93/4 Leaf 53
94/5 Leaf 195
95/6 Leaf 67
96/7 Leaf 190
94/5 LeafLimited 101
96/7 MetalUniverse 153
97/8 Omega 224
92/3 O-Pee-Chee 166
90/1 OPC/Topps 372
91/2 OPC/Topps 392
91/2 opcPremier 181
98/9 Pacific 72
97/8 PacificCrown 179
98/9 PacificParamount 230
90/1 Panini(MTL) 21
90/1 PaniniSticker 60
91/2 PaniniSticker 195
92/3 PaniniSticker 157
93/4 PaniniSticker 22
94/5 PaniniSticker 16
95/6 PaniniSticker 99
96/7 PaniniSticker 220
91/2 Parkhurst 88
92/3 Parkhurst 319
93/4 Parkhurst 373
94/5 Parkhurst V32
95/6 Parkhurst 130
94/5 ParkieSE 92
91/2 Pinnacle 209
92/3 Pinnacle 79
93/4 Pinnacle 37, Tm2001 27
94/5 Pinnacle 56
95/6 Pinnacle 28
96/7 Pinnacle 124
97/8 Pinnacle 150
97/8 PinnacleBeAPlayer 206
95/6 PinnacleZenith 21
95/6 Playoff 64
96/7 Playoff 343
94/5 POG 142
95/6 POG 176
96/7 Post
93/4 PowerPlay 134
93/4 Premier 163
94/5 Premier 181
89/90 ProCards(AHL) 199
95/6 ProMagnet 53
90/1 ProSet 158
91/2 ProSet 119
92/3 ProSet 91
90/1 Score 127, -YoungStar 18
91/2 Score(CDN) 105, (U.S) 105
92/3 Score 69
93/4 Score 18
94/5 Score 103
95/6 Score 206
96/7 Score 115
97/8 Score 160
97/8 Score(TOR) 10
94/5 Select 23
95/6 SelectCertified 8
91 SemicSticker 137
93 SemicSticker 177
95/6 SkyBoxEmotion 108
95/6 SkyBoxImpact 105
95/6 SP 89
96/7 SP 155
95/6 Summit 25
96/7 Summit 30
95/6 SuperSticker 73, 75
96/7 TeamOut
92/3 Topps 253
95/6 Topps 36
95/6 ToppsFinestS 56
96/7 ToppsNHLPicks 53
91/2 ToppsStadiumClub 262
92/3 ToppsStadiumClub 70
93/4 TSC 391, -Master(2) 11
95/6 ToppsStadiumClub 59
95/6 TSC-MembersOnly 44
95/6 ToppsSuperSkills 6
90/1 UpperDeck 334
91/2 UpperDeck 328
92/3 UpperDeck 545
93/4 UpperDeck 31
94/5 UpperDeck 101
95/6 UpperDeck 161
96/7 UpperDeck 343
97/8 UpperDeck 372, 399
95/6 UDBeAPlayer 20
98/9 UDChoice 198
95/6 UDCollChoice 322
96/7 UDCollChoice 262
89/90 MTL/Kraft
90/1 MTL
91/2 MTL
92/3 MTL
93/4 MTL
93/4 MTL/Molson
94/5 MTL

SCHNEIDER, ROCHUS
94/5 DEL 123
95/6 DEL 24
96/7 DEL 21

SCHNEIDER, SCOTT
88/9 ProCards(Moncton)
89/90 ProCards(AHL) 52
90/1 ProCards 260
91/2 ProCards 362
87/8 Moncton
90/1 Moncton

SCHNEIDER, WALTER
79 PaniniSticker 305

SCHNEITBERGER, OTTO
72 Hellas 44
72 SemicSticker 105

SCHNOBRICH, TIM
94/5 DEL 22
95/6 DEL 182

SCHOCK, RON
64-67 BeeHives(BOS)
64/5 CokeCap BOS-23
70/1 Colgate Stamp 42
70/1 EddieSargent 170
71/2 EddieSargent 170
72/3 EddieSargent 179
70/1 Esso Stamp
72/3 Letraset 23
74/5 LiptonSoup 43
74/5 Loblaws
68/9 OPC/Topps 118
69/70 OPC/Topps 120, -Sticker
70/1 OPC/Topps 91,-Dkl 9,-Stckr
71/2 OPC/Topps 56
72/3 OPC 81, Topps 59
73/4 OPC 200, Topps 113
74/5 OPC/Topps 167
75/6 OPC/Topps 75, 326
76/7 OPC/Topps 248, OPC 392
77/8 OPC/Topps 51
78/9 O-Pee-Chee 384
94/5 Parkie(64/5) 21
95/6 Parkie(66/7) 13
68/9 ShirriffCoin STL1
71/2 TheTorontoSun
65/6 Topps 36
66/7 Topps 100
71/2 PGH
74/5 PGH

SCHOEN, BRYAN
95/6 Louisiana
93/4 Toledo 28

SCHOENFELD, JIM
72/3 EddieSargent 41
74/5 Loblaws
72/3 OPC 220
73/4 OPC/T. 86, OPC 137, T. 5
74/5 OPC/Topps 121
75/6 OPC/Topps 138
76/7 OPC/Topps 241
77/8 OPC/Topps 108
78/9 OPC/Topps 178, 234
79/80 OPC/Topps 171
80/1 OPC/Topps 96
82/3 O-Pee-Chee 94
83/4 O-Pee-Chee 59
82/3 opcSticker 183
83/4 opcSticker 136
82/3 Post
83/4 PuffySticker 8
83/4 SouhaitsRen.KeyChain
90/1 UpperDeck 505
72/3 BUF
73/4 BUF
74/5 BUF
75/6 BUF/Linnett
79/80 BUF/BellsMarket
80/1 BUF/Wendt
81/2 BUF 6
85/6 BUF
93/4 BUF/NOCO
88/9 N.J/Caretta
97/8 PHO
95/6 WSH

SCHOFIELD, DAVE
88/9 ProCards(Kalamazoo)

SCHOFIELD, DWIGHT
84/5 O-Pee-Chee 191

SCHOLZ, ECKHARD
79 PaniniSticker 254

SCHOLZ, OLAF
94/5 DEL 108
95/6 DEL 330
96/7 DEL 108

SCHOENECK, DREW
91/2 SketchWHL 161
92/3 Tacoma

SCHONMOSER, C.
95/6 DEL 342

SCHOOLEY, DEREK
94/5 Huntington 18
92/3 WestMich.
93/4 WestMich.

SCHOPF, PAT
93 SemicSticker 110

SCHOTT, TED
95/6 Spokane 28

SCHRAEDER, CHAD
91/2 AvantGardeBCJ 14
92/3 BCJHL 203

SCHRAMM, JOSEF
72 SemicSticker 94

SCHRAPP, DENNIS
94/5 DEL 30
95/6 DEL 3

SCHRAVEN, T.
95/6 DEL 373

SCHREIBER, WALLY
94/5 DEL 261
95/6 DEL 258
96/7 DEL 146
94/5 Score CT22
81/2 Regina 16

SCHRIEFER, R.J.
95/6 NorthIowa

SCHRINER, DAVE (SWEENEY)
34-43 BeeHives(NYA), (TOR)
35/6 Champion
36-39 DiamondMatch (1), (2), (3)
83&87 HallOfFame 236
83 HHOF Postcard (J)
36/7 OPC (V304D) 98
39/40 OPC (V301-1) 14
40/1 OPC (V301-2) 122
55/6 Parkhurst 27
45-54 QuakerOats
36/7 WWGum (V356) 58

SCHRINER, MARTY
91/2 UD'CzechWJC 68
94/5 Roanoke
95/6 Roanoke

SCHRODER, KLAUS
94/5 DEL 33

SCHUBERT, ANDREAS
94/5 DEL 56
95/6 DEL 58
96/7 DEL 206

SCHUBERT, THOMAS
94/5 DEL 397
95/6 DEL 412
91/2 UD 681,'CzechWJC 44

SCHUCASK, C.
91/2 SketchOHL 98

SCHULER, ALAN
92/3 Richmond
93/4 Richmond 4

SCHULER, LAURA
97/8 UDCollChoice 294

SCHULMISTRA, RICHARD
94/5 Classic 31

SCHULTE, PAXTON
93/4 ClassicProspects 124
91/2 SketchWHL 13

SCHULTZ, ANDREAS
94/5 EliteSet 165

SCHULTZ, DAVE
74/5 LiptonSoup 30
74/5 Loblaws
73/4 OPC 137, 166, T. 5, 149
74/5 OPC/Topps 5, 154, 196
75/6 OPC/Topps 147, 211
76/7 OPC/T. 4, 150, OPC 391
77/8 OPC 353
78/9 OPC/Topps 66, 225
79/80 OPC/Topps 4, 134
92/3 Parkhurst 473
75/6 PHA/GingerAle

SCHULTZ, DEREK
97/8 Bowman 97, 127
95/6 Spokane 20

SCHULTZ, IGOR
94/5 DEL 117
95/6 DEL 118
96/7 DEL 64

SCHULTZ, KEN
51/2 Cleveland

SCHULTZ, LASSE
80/1 Mallasjuoma 155

SCHULTZ, MARTIN
94/5 DEL 118
95/6 DEL 119

SCHULZ, KARSTEN
94/5 DEL 439
95/6 DEL 400

SCHUMPERLI, BERNARD
91/2 UD 667,'CzechWJC 28

SCHUR, HARTWIG
74 Hellas 117

SCHURE, PETER
91/2 Cincinnati

SCHUST, BEN
95/6 Slapshot 364
96/7 SSMarie

SCHUSTER, ALEXANDER
94/5 DEL 286

SCHUSTER, MANFRED
89 SemicSticker 110

SCHUTT, ROD
79/80 OPC/Topps 234
80/1 O-Pee-Chee 307
81/2 OPC 259, Topps(E) 116
81/2 opcSticker 186
77/8 NovaScotia

SCHWAB, COREY
95/6 Bowman 164
94/5 Classic E5
97/8 Donruss 77
96/7 DonrElite 128
95/6 EdgeIce 9, -Quantum 12
97/8 Leaf 96
96/7 LeafPreferred 126
97/8 Limited 130
97/8 PacificCrown 126
95/6 Parkhurst 389
96/7 PinnacleBeAPlayer 104
91/2 ProCards 416
90/1 SketchWHL 19
97/8 UpperDeck 153
97/8 UDCollChoice 244

SCHWABE, JENS
94/5 DEL 395
91/2 UD 680,'CzechWJC 43

SCHWARK, BOB
91/2 AirCanadaSJHL D10

SCHWARTZ, DARREN
93/4 ClassicProspects 247
89/90 Johnstown 30
95/6 Tallahassee 9
92/3 Wheeling 15
93/4 Wheeling 2

SCHWARTZ, OLIVER
94/5 DEL 355

SCHWELE, S.
95/6 DEL 192

SCHWEYER, ROB
93/4 OwenSound

SCISSONS, SCOTT
91/2 CanadaNats
93/4 Donruss 210
93/4 Leaf 243
93/4 Parkhurst 121
90/1 Score 432
90/1 SketchWHL 77
90/1 UpperDeck 357
91/2 UpperDeck 428
93/4 UpperDeck 511, SP-94
89/90 Saskatoon 19
90/1 Saskatoon 19

SCLISIL, ENIO
52/3 Parkhurst 32

SCOLLAN, MARK
91/2 AirCanadaSJHL 11

SCOTT, BLAIR
89/90 Victoria
91/2 SketchOHL 101

SCOTT, BRAD
90/1 SketchWHL 173

SCOTT, BRIAN
94/5 AutoPhonex 38
93/4 ClassicProspects 148
94/5 ParkieSE 268
95/6 Slapshot 396
93/4 Slapshot(Kingston) 8
94/5 Slapshot(Kitchener) 31
94/5 SP 186
96/7 Sudbury 20

SCOTT, CHUBBY
23/4 PaulinsCandy 52

SCOTT, DENNIS
89/90 SketchOHL 137
89/90 NiagaraFalls

SCOTT, GANTON
24/5 Champs (C144)
24/5 MapleCrispette (V130) 29
24/5 (V145-2) 38

SCOTT, GREG
91/2 SketchOHL 206
93/4 Huntington

SCOTT, IRVIN
52/3 AnonymousOHL 49

SCOTT, JERRY
84/5 Ottawa67s

SCOTT, KEVIN
91/2 Cincinnati

SCOTT, LAURIE
23/4 PaulinsCandy 40

SCOTT, RON
89/90 ProCards(AHL) 5
90/1 ProCards 424
89/90 NewHaven

SCOTT, TRAVIS
93/4 Slapshot(Windsor) 3
94/5 Slapshot(Windsor) 3
95/6 Slapshot 231

SCREMIN, CLAUDIO
90/1 ProCards 597
91/2 ProCards 508
90/1 KansasCity 1

SCRUTON, HOWIE
81/2 Kingston 19

SCULLION, BERT
51/2 BasDuFleuve 49

SEALE, T.
91/2 Mich.Tech

SEARBROOKE, GLEN
88/9 ProCards(Hershey)
89/90 ProCards(AHL) 336

SEARLE, DOUG
89/90 SketchOHL 119
90/1 SketchOHL 371
91/2 SketchOHL 140
93/4 Knoxville
94/5 Knoxville 6
91/2 Peterborough 9

SEARLES, STEVE
90/1 SketchQMJHL 173
91/2 SketchQMJHL 119

SEARS, SVERRE
93/4 Greensboro
94/5 Greensboro

SEATON, BRYANT
81/2 Victoria

SEATON, MIKE
90/1 SketchWHL 8
89/90 Victoria

SEBASTIEN, JEFF
90/1 SketchWHL 313
91/2 SketchWHL 136
89/90 Portland
88/9 Regina

SEBEK, VENCI
94/5 DEL 385
95/6 DEL 150

SEBESTA, PAVEL
95/6 APS 308

SEBESTU, RICHARD
95/6 APS 211

SECA, DYLAN
94/5 Slapshot(Kitchener) 34

SECEMSKI, KRYSTOF
94/5 Slapshot(Sudbury) 16

SECORD, AL
90/1 Bowman 12
94/5 ClassicImages 89
80/1 OPC/Topps 129
81/2 O-Pee-Chee 72
82/3 O-Pee-Chee 60, 74, 96
83/4 O-Pee-Chee 95, 112, 219
84/5 O-Pee-Chee 46
86/7 OPC/Topps 100
87/8 OPC/Topps 111
88/9 O-Pee-Chee 249
82/3 opcSticker 175
83/4 opcSticker 111, 156, 160
86/7 opcSticker 155/10
87/8 opcSticker 74/207
88/9 opcSticker 179
87/8 PaniniSticker 229
82/3 Post
90/1 ProSet 60
83/4 PuffySticker 16
84/5 7ElevenDisk
83/4 SouhaitsRen.KeyChain
91/2 UpperDeck 635
81/2 CHI
82/3 CHI
83/4 CHI
86/7 CHI/Coke
89/90 CHI/Coke
87/8 TOR
87/8 TOR/P.L.A.Y. 14
88/9 TOR/P.L.A.Y. 14

SECORD, BRIAN
95 Classic 83
95/6 Slapshot 370
96/7 Penascola 14

SEDIN, DANIEL
97/8 UDBlackDiamond 114
98/9 UDChoice 294
97/8 udSwedish 159, C15
97/8 udSwedish S11, UDS2

SEDIN HENRIK
97/8 UDBlackDiamond 136
98/9 UDChoice 295
97/8 udSwedish 160, C16
97/8 udSwedish S10, UDS9

SEDLAK, ZDENEK
94/5 APS 201
95/6 APS 49

SEDLBAUER, RON
76/7 OPC 271
77/8 OPC 368
78/9 OPC/Topps 139
79/80 OPC/Topps 19
80/1 OPC/Topps 134
81/2 O-Pee-Chee 324
80/1 CHI/4x6
75/6 VAN/RoyalBank
76/7 VAN/RoyalBank
77/8 VAN/RoyalBank
78/9 VAN/RoyalBank
79/80 VAN

SEDY, PETR
94/5 APS 98
95/6 APS 59

SEEBERGER, CHRISTIAN
94/5 DEL 177
95/6 DEL 173

SEESVUORI, RISTO
70/1 Kuvajulkaisut 222
71/2 WilliamsFIN 144

SEFTEL, STEVE
88/9 ProCards(Baltimore)
89/90 ProCards(AHL) 90
90/1 ProCards 203
91/2 ProCards 556
91/2 Baltimore 12
85/6 Kingston 8
86/7 Kingston 20
87/8 Kingston 20

SEGUIN, BRETT
89/90 SketchOHL 49
90/1 SketchOHL 92
91/2 SketchOHL 301
93/4 Muskegon
94/5 Muskegon
95/6 Muskegon
84/5 L.A./Smokeys

SEGUIN, STEVE
81/2 Kingston 13
82/3 Kingston 10

SEHER, KURT
90/1 SketchWHL 61
91/2 SketchWHL 133

SEIBEL, CHAD
90/1 SketchWHL 280
91/2 SketchWHL 40
94/5 Greensboro
88/9 Lethbridge
90/1 PrinceAlbert

SEIBERT, EARL
34-43 BeeHives(CHI)
36-39 DiamondMatch (1), (4)
36-39 DiamondMatch (5), (6)
83&87 HallOfFame 150
83 HHOF Postcard (K)
93/4 HHOFLegends 27
39/40 OPC (V301-1) 76
93/4 Parkie(56/7) P12

SEIBERT, OLIVER
83&87 HallOfFame 193
83 HHOF Postcard (J)

SEIKER, SHANE
90/1 SketchWHL 328

SEILING, RIC
78/9 OPC/Topps 242
79/80 OPC/Topps 119
80/1 OPC/Topps 159
81/2 O-Pee-Chee 32
82/3 O-Pee-Chee 35
83/4 O-Pee-Chee 72
84/5 O-Pee-Chee 31
86/7 O-Pee-Chee 201
82/3 opcSticker 123
84/5 opcSticker 216
85/6 opcSticker 182/51
82/3 Post
83/4 SouhaitsRen.KeyChain
80/1 BUF/Wendt
81/2 BUF 15
82/3 BUF/Wendt 8
84/5 BUF/BlueShield
85/6 BUF
86/7 DET/Caeasars
75/6 Hamilton

SEILING, ROD
64-67 BeeHives(NYR)
64/5 CokeCap NYR-16
70/1 DadsCookies
70/1 EddieSargent 128
71/2 EddieSargent 119
72/3 EddieSargent 148
70/1 Esso Stamp
74/5 Loblaws , -Update
68/9 OPC/Topps 71
69/70 OPC/T. 36, OPC-Sticker
70/1 OPC 184
71/2 OPC/Topps 53
72/3 OPC 194, -TmCnd, T. 149
73/4 OPC/Topps 9
74/5 OPC/Topps 102
75/6 OPC/Topps 229
76/7 OPC 280
77/8 OPC/Topps 226
78/9 O-Pee-Chee 394
94/5 Parkie(64/5) 93
95/6 Parkie(66/7) 95
72/3 Post Transfers 6
68/9 ShirriffCoin NYR1
71/2 TheTorontoSun
64/5 Topps 67
65/6 Topps 23
66/7 Topps 22, -USATest 22
67/8 Topps 27
91/2 Trends(72) 21, -Aut.
78/9 ATL/Coke
74/5 TOR
75/6 TOR

SEILING, SCOTT
95/6 Slapshot 254, 296

SEILS, JASON
94/5 Minnesota

SEISTAMO, JOUNI
66/7 Champion 156
65/6 Hellas 152

SEITZ, DAVE
92/3 Clarkson

SEIVO, JYRKI
73/4 WilliamsFIN 118

SEJBA, JIRI
94/5 APS 37
92/3 Jyvas-Hyva 58
90/1 ProCards 286
91/2 ProCards 5
89 SemicSticker 196
91/2 UpperDeck 362
90/1 BUF/BlueShield
90/1 BUF/Campbell
91/2 Rochester/Dunkin'Donuts
91/2 Rochester/Genny
91/2 Rochester/Kodak

SEJEJS, NORMUNDS
95/6 APS 156

SEKERA, MARTIN
94/5 APS 44

SEKERAS, LUBOMIR
95/6 APS 227
94 Semic 192
96 Wien 222

SELÄNNE, TEEMU
95/6 Aces 8 (Clubs)
96/7 Aces J (Hearts)
97/8 Aces J (Diamonds)
94/5 BAP'Magazine
95/6 Bowman 75, BB2
93/4 Classic 124, N5
93/4 ClassicProspects LP23
96/7 CorinthianHeadliner
97/8 CorinthianHeadliner
93/4 Donruss 387, 395, Z
93/4 Donruss-Elite 3, -Ice 10
94/5 Donruss 210, -Dominator 8
95/6 Donruss 100
96/7 Donruss 157,-Top 2,-Dom 8
97/8 Donruss 159,-Line 2,-Elit 12
96/7 DonrussCanadianIce 85
97/8 D.CdnIce 74, -Scrapbook 8
95/6 D.Elite 73, -Cutting 15
96/7 DonrussElite 59, -Status 10
97/8 D.Elite 17, 120, 149,-Back 3
97/8 D.Elite-Craft 15,-PrmNum 7
97/8 DonrussPreferred 95, 178
97/8 D.Pref -Line 5B,-PrecM 9
97/8 D.Pref -Tins 4, -WideTins 4
97/8 DonrussPriority 6, 187
97/8 D.Prio -DirDep 15,-OpDay 6
97/8 D.Prio-Pstcrd 14,-Stamp 14
97/8 D.Studio 18, 107,-HardH 11
97/8 D.Studio-Portraits 18,-Sil 17
93/4 EASports 149
97/8 EssoOlympic 50
95 FinnishAllStar 4
94/5 Flair 209
96/7 Flair 3, -Centre 8
94/5 Fleer 245
96/7 Fleer 3, -ArtRoss 21
95/6 FleerMetal 165, -IntSteel 20
96/7 F.Picks-Dream 5, -Fab 42
92/3 FleerUltra 444, -Import 21
93/4 FleerUltra 48, -AS 11,-AW 6
93/4 FU-Red 10, -Speed 10
94/5 F.Ultra 246,-Global 9,-Red8
95/6 FleerUltra 183
96/7 FU 6, -Red 8, -Power 16
95 Globe 140
93/4 HockeyWit 55
95/6 Hoyle'WEST 4 (Club)
91/2 Jyvas-Hyva 21
97/8 KatchMedallion 5
94/5 KennerSLU
97/8 KennerSLU
93 Koululainen
93/4 KraftDinner
95/6 Kraft-Ticket
96/7 Kraft-Mascot
97/8 Kraft-WorldsBest
93/4 Leaf 13, 110, -GoldAS 3
93/4 L-GoldRook 1, -HT 3
94/5 Leaf 362, -Ltd 26, -Fire 12
95/6 Leaf 137
96/7 Leaf 52, 238, -Fire 9
97/8 Leaf 18,182,-BannerSeas 8
94/5 LeafLimited 68
95/6 LeafLimited 44, -Stars 7
96/7 LeafLimited 64
96/7 LeafPreferred 56,-Vanity 11
96/7 LP-SteelPower 10
97/8 Limited 11,56,143,-fabric 43
96/7 Maggers 2
93/4 McDonalds McH2
94/5 McDonalds McD25
95/6 McDonalds McD19
96/7 McDonalds McD2
97/8 McDonalds McD11
96/7 MetalUniverse 6, -Lethal 17
97/8 Omega7,247,-GameFace 2
97/8 Omega -Silk 2, -StckHan 2
92/3 opcPremier 68
98/9 Pacific 8,-D.Ice 2,-GoldC 2
97/8 PacificCrown 8
97/8 PCC-Gold 2, -Slapshot 1C
97/8 PCC-Supial 2, -TeamCL 1
97/8 PacificCrownRoyale 5
97/8 PCR-Blades 2, -Cramer 2
97/8 PCR-HatTrick 2, -Lamp 2
97/8 PacificDynagon! 5, 135
97/8 PcfcD-BstKpt 4,-Dynam 1B
97/8 PacificD-Tandem 7, 24
97/8 PacificInvincible 4, -Attack 2
97/8 PacificInv.-Feature 2, -Off 2
97/8 PacificParamount 7
97/8 PcfcP-BigNum 2,-Photo 2
98/9 PcfcParamount 7,-HOF 1
98/9 PcfcP-SpecDel 2, -TmCL 1
97/8 PacificRegime 7
97/8 PacificRevolution 5
97/8 PcfcRev-ASGame 1,-Icon 2
93/4 PaniniSticker 142, Q
94/5 PaniniSticker 166
95/6 PaniniSticker 217
96/7 PaniniSticker 225
97/8 PaniniSticker 188
95 PaniniWorlds 294
92/3 Parkhurst 209, 217, 500
93/4 Parkhurst 233, 235, G8, W3
94/5 Parkhurst 300, V81, C26
95/6 Parkhurst 232, 250, 275
95/6 Parkie PP17, PP51, -AS 5
95/6 Parkie-Crown(1) 9, -Aut.
94/5 ParkieSE 201, ES13
92/3 Pinnacle 406
93/4 Pinnacle 4, 222, -TeamP 12
93/4 P-Team2001 10, -Nifty 1,3
94/5 Pinnacle 25 BR15, GR1
94/5 Pinnacle NL11, WE1
95/6 Pinnacle-Roaring20s 19
96/7 Pinnacle 155,250, -ByThe 1
97/8 Pinnacle 86
96/7 P.BAP LTH1B, -Biscuit 11
97/8 P.BAP -OneTimers 8
97/8 P.BeeHive 2, -TeamBH 11
97/8 P.Certified 39, -Team 16
97/8 Pinnacle-EPIX 15
95/6 PinnacleFANtasy 15
97/8 P.Inside 38,-Can 19,-Trk 11
96/7 PinnacleMint 13
97/8 PinnacleMint 7, -Minterntl 4
95/6 PinnacleZenith 102
96/7 P.Zenith 28, -ZTeam 3
95/6 Playoff 108, 219, 329
96/7 Playoff 428
94/5 POG 253
95/6 POG 292
94/5 Post
97/8 Post
93/4 PowerPlay 274, -Global 7
93/4 PP-Sec 10,-PtLdr 16,-Slp 9
93/4 Premier 92, 130, 148, 483
93/4 Prmr-Black(OPC) 20, (T) 1
94/5 Premier 95, 243, 416
95/6 ProMagnet 58
93/4 Score 331, 477,-P.AS 32,50
93/4 S-Dream 21, -Franchise 24
93/4 S-IntAS 2, (CDN) DD2
94/5 Score 176, TF26
95/6 Score 7,-Golden2,-Lamp 14
96/7 Score 145,-Sddn 15,-Supr 1
97/8 Score 113
97/8 Score(ANA) 2
93/4 SeasonsPatch 18
94/5 Select 74
95/6 SelectCertif 76
96/7 SelectCert 32, -Cornerst 12
94 Semic 20, 345
95 Semic 41
91 SemicSticker 21
92 SemicSticker 11
93 SemicSticker 77
94/5 Sisu-GuestSpecial 9

95/6 SisuLimited 15, -S&S 3
95/6 SkyBoxEmotion 196
95/6 SkyBoxImpact 184, -Ice 15
96/7 SkyBoxImpact 4, -Blade 20
96/7 SkyBoxImpact-VersaTm 10
94/5 SP 131, -Premier 22
95/6 SP 2, E2, FX1
96/7 SP 2, -Inside, -SPxForce 2
97/8 SPAuthentic 1, I19
96/7 SPx 2
97/8 SPx 2, SPX18
98/9 SPx"Finite" 1, 104, 157
96/7 SportFX MiniStix
95/6 Summit 54
96/7 Summit 133,-Unt 8,-HiV 12
95/6 SuperSticker 133, 134
96/7 TeamOut
95/6 Topps 195, YS11, 9CG
95/6 Topps M9, PF18, 2PL
98/9 Topps 109, L15, M1, SB13
94/5 T.Finest 76, -BBest(B) 14
94 ToppsFinestBronze 5
95/6 ToppsFinest 35, 155
96/7 T.Picks 7, FT21, TS8
93/4 T.StadiumClub 141, 210
93/4 TSC-Master(1) 4, -AS
95/6 T.StdmClub 188, EN2, G2
93/4 TSC-MembersOnly 10
94/5 TSC-MembersOnly 43
95/6 TSC-MembersOnly 14
97/8 ToppsSticker 4
95/6 ToppsSuperSkills 31
91/2 UpperDeck 21
92/3 UD 574, CC10, ER6, G15
92/3 UD'LockerAS 35
93/4 UD 281, 309, 448, AW2, R2
93/4 UD SP4, SP-177,-Hero 32
94/5 UD 90, 557, IG13,R3, SP88
95/6 UD 171, 253, AS12, R49
95/6 UD SE89,-ASPredict MVP7
96/7 UD 211,HH15,LS16,SS10A
96/7 UD X16, -AllStarYCTG A4
97/8 UD 1, S8, SG8, SS8, T5A
93/4 UDBeAPlayer 15,-Roots 17
94/5 UDBAP R11, UC4, -Aut. 11
96/7 UDBlackDiamnd 146, RC18
97/8 UDBlackDiamond 95, PC15
98/9 UDChoice 8,242,BH15,SQ5
95/6 UDCollChoice 244
96/7 UDCollChoice 2, 309, 336
96/7 UDCC C19, S13, UD7
97/8 UDCC 8, C8, S18, SQ80
97/8 udDiamondVision 16
96/7 UpperDeck"Ice" 77, S6
97/8 UD"Ice" 80, IC8, L9C
96 Wien 31
97/8 Zenith 24, Z6, -ZTeam 1
96/7 ANA/UpFrontSports 24
93/4 WPG/Ruffles
94/5 WPG/Bookmark
95/6 WPG (x2)

SELBY, BRITON
64-67 BeeHives(TOR)
65/6 CocaCola
70/1 Colgate Stamp 37
70/1 DadsCookies
70/1 EddieSargent 202
71/2 EddieSargent 183
70/1 Esso Stamp
68/9 OPC/Topps 96
69/70 OPC/Topps 48
70/1 OPC/Topps 111
71/2 OPC/Topps 226
94/5 Parkie(64/5) 121
95/6 Parkie(66/7) 111
95/6 Parkie(66/7) 132
73/4 QuakerOats 39
68/9 ShirriffCoin PHA7
66/7 Topps 18
66/7 TOR/Coaster
69/70 TOR

SELIGER, MARC
94/5 DEL 384
95/6 DEL 103
94/5 SigRookies 30
91/2 UD 683, 'CzechWJC 46
96 Wien 193

SELIVANOV, ALEXANDER
94/5 AutoPhonex 39
95/6 Bowman 73
94/5 ClassicImages 16
95/6 Donruss 90
96/7 Donruss 32
95/6 DonrussElite 84
96/7 DonrussElite 95
94/5 Fleer 210
96/7 Fleer 106
95/6 FleerMetal 140
95/6 FleerUltra 310
96/7 FleerUltra 160
95/6 Leaf 49
96/7 Leaf 62
96/7 LeafLimited 45
96/7 LeafPreferred 43
96/7 MetalUniverse 147
97/8 Omega 214
98/9 Pacific 406
97/8 PacificDynag-BestKept 89
97/8 PacificParamount 176
98/9 PacificParamount 221
95/6 PaniniSticker 132
97/8 PaniniSticker 102
95/6 Parkhurst 194
95/6 Pinnacle 116
96/7 Pinnacle 77
96/7 PinnacleZenith 21
95/6 Playoff 199
96/7 Playoff 390
95/6 POG 252
96/7 Score 27, -Superstition 10
97/8 Score 245
96/7 SkyBoxImpact 124
94/5 SP 113
95/6 SP 140
96/7 SP 148
97/8 SPAuthentic 146
98/9 SPx"Finite" 80
96/7 Summit 58
95/6 Topps 367, 11NG
98/9 Topps 85
94/5 ToppsFinest 79
95/6 ToppsFinest 32
96/7 ToppsNHLPicks 123
95/6 ToppsStadiumClub 111
94/5 UpperDeck 425, 532,SP165
95/6 UpperDeck 316, SE77
96/7 UpperDeck 339
97/8 UpperDeck 156
95/6 UDBeAPlayer 145
97/8 UDBlackDiamond 121
98/9 UDChoice 195
95/6 UDCollChoice 165
96/7 UDCollChoice 253
97/8 UDCollChoice 241
95/6 T.B.
95/6 T.B./SkyBoxSportsCafe

SELJANIN, SERGEI
94 Semic 141

SELKE, FRANK
83&87 HallOfFame 41
83 HHOF Postcard (C)
55/6 Parkhurst 68
59/60 Parkhurst 47
93/4 Parkie(56/7) 85
95/6 MTL/Forum 27Mar96

SELKE, FRANK (JR.)
81/2 TOR

SELKIRK, JASON
91/2 AirCanadaSJHL A5

SELMSER, SEAN
95/6 Hampton HRA -19
93/4 RedDeer

SELWOOD, BRAD
71/2 EddieSargent 207
75/6 opcWHA 82
71/2 TheTorontoSun
72/3 NewEngland
70/1 TOR
71/2 TOR

SELYANIN, SERGEI
91/2 O-Pee-Chee 58R

SEMAK, ALEXANDER
92/3 Bowman 164
93/4 Donruss 191
96/7 Donruss 26
93/4 EASports 75
94/5 Flair 99
94/5 Fleer 118
92/3 FleerUltra 341
93/4 FleerUltra 166
94/5 FleerUltra 321
95/6 FleerUltra 271
93/4 Leaf 35
94/5 Leaf 543
91/2 O-Pee-Chee 42R
92/3 PaniniSticker 176, 296
93/4 PaniniSticker 36
94/5 PaniniSticker 29
95/6 PaniniSticker 127
96/7 PaniniSticker 97, 127
91/2 Parkhurst 323
92/3 Parkhurst 329
93/4 Parkhurst 109
95/6 Parkhurst 135
93/4 Pinnacle 47
94/5 Pinnacle 362
96/7 Pinnacle 188
93/4 PowerPlay 142
93/4 Premier 102
92/3 Score 451
93/4 Score 284, -Int.AS 14
96/7 Score 212
94 Semic 158
91 SemicSticker 94
92 SemicSticker 113
95/6 SkyBoxEmotion 109
92/3 Topps 419
95/6 Topps 97
92/3 ToppsStadiumClub 444
93/4 ToppsStadiumClub 365
94/5 ToppsStadiumClub 245
91/2 UpperDeck 4
92/3 UpperDeck 45, ERT5
93/4 UpperDeck 178, SP-88
94/5 UpperDeck 219
95/6 UpperDeck 40
96/7 UpperDeck 98
94/5 UDBeAPlayer-Aut. 4
95/6 UDCollChoice 56
96/7 UDCollChoice 163
95/6 T.B/SkyBoxSportsCafe
96/7 VAN
96/7 VAN/IGA

SEMANDEL, KURT
90/1 ProCards 598
90/1 KansasCity 15

SEMCHUK, BRAD
90/1 ProCards 430
92/3 Phoenix

SEMENIUK, TREVOR
83/4 MedicineHat 10
84/5 Victoria

SEMENKO, DAVE
79/80 O-Pee-Chee 371
80/1 O-Pee-Chee 360
81/2 O-Pee-Chee 121
82/3 O-Pee-Chee 119
80/1 Pepsi Cap
82/3 Post
83/4 SouhaitsRen.KeyChain
83/4 StaterMint H19
83/4 Vachon 40
79/80 EDM
80/1 EDM/Zellers
81/2 EDM/RedRooster
82/3 EDM/RedRooster
83/4 EDM
83/4 EDM/Buttons
83/4 EDM/McDonald
84/5 EDM
84/5 EDM/RedRooster
85/6 EDM/RedRooster
88/9 EDM/ActionMagazine 6
87/8 TOR
87/8 TOR/P.L.A.Y. 26

SEMENOV, ANATOLI
91/2 Bowman 113
92/3 Bowman 423
93/4 Donruss 3
94/5 Donruss 326
95/6 Donruss 312
93/4 EASports 5
94/5 Flair 5
92/3 FleerUltra 429
93/4 FleerUltra 261
94/5 FleerUltra 7
93/4 Leaf 338
94/5 Leaf 303
95/6 Leaf 238
90/1 O-Pee-Chee 468
91/2 OPC/Topps 390
92/3 O-Pee-Chee 83
90/1 opcPremier 104
97/8 PacificCrown 106
90/1 Panini(EDM) 19
91/2 PaniniSticker 127
93/4 PaniniSticker 174
94/5 PaniniSticker 118
91/2 Parkhurst 279
92/3 Parkhurst 420
93/4 Parkhurst 3
94/5 Parkhurst 1
95/6 Parkhurst 429
92/3 Pinnacle 386
93/4 Pinnacle 368
94/5 Pinnacle 322
94/5 POG 347
93/4 PowerPlay 10
93/4 Premier 506
94/5 Premier 524
90/1 ProSet 608
91/2 RedAce
90/1 ScoreTraded 39T
91/2 Score(CDN) 258
92/3 Score 336,-Sharpshooter28
93/4 Score 93, 536
94/5 Score 16
89 SemicSticker 99
92/3 Topps 68
91/2 ToppsStadiumClub 366
92/3 ToppsStadiumClub 143
93/4 ToppsStadiumClub 368
91/2 TriGlobeMagFive 11-15
90/1 UpperDeck 405
91/2 UpperDeck 269, E4
92/3 UpperDeck 20, 535
93/4 UpperDeck 46, SP-4
94/5 UpperDeck 105
96/7 UDCollChoice 7
90/1 EDM/McGavins
91/2 EDM/IGA
94/5 PHA

SEMIN, NIKOLAI
92/3 UpperDeck 610

SENDT, THORSTEN
94/5 DEL 217

SENECAL, MARIO
51/2 BasDuFleuve 56
52/3 BasDuFleuve 49

SENECAL, SYLVAIN
84/5 Richelieu

SENN, TREVOR
95/6 Richmond
92/3 Wheeling 16

SENTES, RICK
72/3 OttawaNationals

SENTNER, PETER
90/1 ProCards 361
91/2 Greensboro

SEPKOWSKI, TODD
84/5 Sudbury 8

SEPOVALOV, VLADIMIR
72 Hellas 61
74 Hellas 63

SEPPÄ, JYRKI
80/1 Mallasjuoma 36
72/3 WilliamsFIN 351

SEPP"ÄNEN, LEO
72 Hellas 15
74 Hellas 15
70/1 Kuvajulkaisut 254
74 SemicSticker 93
78/9 SM-Liiga 87
71/2 WilliamsFIN 220
72/3 WilliamsFIN 168
73/4 WilliamsFIN 235

SEPPÄNEN, VEIKKO
73/4 WilliamsFIN 236

SEPPO, JUKKA
96/7 DEL 239
91/2 Jyvas-Hyva 2
92/3 Jyvas-Hyva 11
95 Latkaliiga 8
93 SemicSticker 78
93/4 Sisu 253
94/5 Sisu-Horoscope 2
95/6 Sisu 343, -Specials 9
95/6 SisuLimited 95

SERAFINI, RON
75/6 Phoenix

SERGOTT, KEITH
91/2 FerrisState

SERIKOW, ALEXANDER
95/6 DEL 279
96/7 DEL 176

SEROSKI, JOE
95/6 Slapshot 362
96/7 SSMarie

SEROWIK, JEFF
90/1 ProCards 154
91/2 ProCards 337
96/7 LasVegas
92/3 StJohns

SERTICH, MIKE
85/6 Minn-Duluth 33
93/4 Minn-Duluth

SERVATIUS, DARREN
89/90 Johnstown 22

SERVATIUS, RON
89/90 Nashville

SERVISS, TOM
72/3 LosAngelesSharks

SETHERENG, MORTEN
79 PaniniSticker 300

SETIKOVSKY, JINDRICH
94/5 APS 290
95/6 APS 243

SEVA, JAN
92/3 Jyvas-Hyva 43
93/4 Jyvas-Hyva 87
93/4 Sisu 131
95/6 Sisu 35

SEVCIK, FRANTIÇEK
94/5 APS 111
95/6 APS 209
70/1 Kuvajulkaisut 58

SEVCIK, JAROSLAV
95/6 DEL 332
88/9 ProCards(Halifax)
89/90 ProCards'AHL 176
90/1 ProCards 460
89/90 Halifax
90/1 Halifax

SEVECEK, RENE
95/6 APS 299

SEVERYN, BRENT
93/4 FleerUltra 331
94/5 Leaf 342
97/8 PacificRegime 58
93/4 Parkhurst 77
94/5 Parkhurst 90
96/7 PinnacleBeAPlayer 185
93/4 Premier 392
94/5 Premier 334
88/9 ProCards(Halifax)
89/90 ProCards(AHL) 171
90/1 ProCards 456
91/2 ProCards 408
93/4 Score 652
95/6 Topps 243
93/4 UpperDeck 453
93/4 FLA
84/5 Brandon 24
89/90 Halifax
90/1 Halifax

SÉVIGNY, L.P.
94/5 ParkieSE 259
94/5 SP 180

SÉVIGNY, PIERRE
92/3 ClassicProspects 51
93/4 Donruss 169
94/5 Donruss 195
93/4 Durivage 2
93/4 Leaf 392
94/5 Leaf 309
94/5 PaniniSticker 11
93/4 Parkhurst 106, C7
94/5 Parkhurst 117
91/2 ProCards 88
93/4 Score 634
90/1 SketchQMJHL 226
94/5 ToppsStadiumClub 193
90/1 UpperDeck 456
93/4 UpperDeck 455, SP-82
94/5 UpperDeck 402
93/4 MTL
94/5 MTL
94/5 MTL/MolsonExport
92/3 Fredericton
95/6 Fredericton
96/7 Fredericton

SÉVIGNY, PIERRE
84/5 Chicoutimi

SÉVIGNY, RICHARD
72-84 Dernière 80/1
80/1 O-Pee-Chee 385
81/2 O-Pee-Chee 191, 387
83/4 O-Pee-Chee 189, 197
84/5 O-Pee-Chee 289
81/2 opcSticker 40, 256
82/3 Post
83/4 7ElevenCokeCup
83/4 SouhaitsRen.KeyChain
83/4 Vachon 54
79/80 MTL
80/1 MTL
81/2 MTL
82/3 MTL
82/3 MTL/Steinberg
83/4 MTL
84/5 QUE
85/6 QUE
85/6 QUE/GeneralFoods
85/6 QUE/McDonald
85/6 QUE/Provigo
86/7 QUE
86/7 QUE/GeneralFoods
86/7 QUE/McDonald
87/8 QUE/GeneralFoods

SEVON, JORMA
82 SemicSticker 42
78/9 SM-Liiga 192

SEVON, SEPPO
80/1 Mallasjuoma 42
78/9 SM-Liiga 101
72/3 WilliamsFIN 276

SEXSMITH, DEAN
84/5 Brandon 5
85/6 Brandon 5

SEXTON, DAN
87/8 Regina
83/4 Victoria
84/5 Victoria

SEXTON, WILLIAM
52/3 AnonymousOHL 108

SEYMOUR, DEAN
91/2 AirCanadaSJHL 26, A47

SEYMOUR, GLEN
86/7 Portland

SGUALDO, RENÉ
72 SemicSticker 153

SHACK, EDDIE
45-64 BeeHives(NYR), (TORx2)
64-67 BeeHives(TOR)
62 CeramicTiles
63-5 ChexPhoto
64/5 CokeCap TOR-23
65/6 CocaCola
70/1 Colgate Stamp 41
70/1 DadsCookies
70/1 EddieSargent 69
71/2 EddieSargent 20
70/1 Esso Stamp
68/9 O-Pee-Chee 137
69/70 OPC 139, -Sticker, T. 106
70/1 OPC/T 35, -Deckle 2
71/2 OPC/Topps 96
72/3 OPC 274, -Crests 17
73/4 OPC 242
61/2 Parkhurst 7
62/3 Parkhurst 14
63/4 Parkhurst 9, 69
93/4 Parkie(56/7) FS4
94/5 Parkie(64/5) 117
95/6 Parkie(66/7) 113
60/1 ShirriffCoin 87
61/2 ShirriffCoin 48
62/3 ShirriffCoin 8
68/9 ShirriffCoin BOS1
63/4 TheTorontoStar
71/2 TheTorontoSun
58/9 Topps 30
59/60 Topps 57
60/1 Topps 7
64/5 Topps 71
66/7 Topps 17
67/8 Topps 34
56-66 TorontoStar 61/2, 65/6
91/2 Ultimate(O6) 41, -Aut 41
60/1 York
61/2 York 25
62/3 YorkTransfer 32
63/4 York 4
64/5 TOR
66/7 TOR/Coaster
68/9 TOR
73/4 TOR
74/5 TOR

SHADRIN, VLADIMIR
74 Hellas 55
72 Hellas 78
70/1 Kuvajulkaisut 16
72 Panda
72 SemicSticker 19
74 SemicSticker 37
70/1 Soviet Stars
71/2 Soviet Stars
73/4 Soviet Stars 18
74/5 Soviet Stars 15
71/2 WilliamsFIN 15
72/3 WilliamsFIN 34
73/4 WilliamsFIN 15

SHANAHAN, BRENDAN
97/8 Aces 10 (Hearts)
90/1 Bowman 85
91/2 Bowman 288
92/3 Bowman 183
95/6 Bowman 28
96/7 CorinthianHeadliner
97/8 CorinthianHeadliner
95/6 DEL 447
96/7 D.CdnIce 101,-OCanada 12
97/8 DCdnIce 67,-Scrp 33,-Nt'l 5
93/4 Donruss 299
94/5 Donruss 174
95/6 Donruss 180, 377, -Mark 8
96/7 Donruss 178, -Elite 6, -Hit 7
97/8 Donruss 181,-Elite9,-Line10
95/6 DonrussElite 3
96/7 D.Elite 126, -Perspectives 7
97/8 DonrussElite 18, 133
97/8 D.Elite -Craft27 -PrmNum 9
97/8 .Preferred 3, 184,-Line 2C
97/8 D.Pref-PrecM 1,-Tins 12, 19
97/8 D.Pref -WideTins 7, 10
97/8 DonrussPriority 19, 186
97/8 D.Prio -DirDep 1,-OpDay 17
97/8 D.Prio-Postcard 2,-Stamp 2
97/8 D.Studio 6, 105,-HardHat 9
97/8 D.Studio-Portraits 6, -Sil 11
96/7 Duracell DC12
93/4 EASports 124
97/8 EssoOlympic 10
94/5 Flair 158, -HotNumber 9
96/7 Flair 30
94/5 Fleer 191, -Headliner 10
96/7 Fleer 48
95/6 FleerMetal 67, -Iron 13
96/7 FleerNHLPicks 40, -Fab 43
96/7 F.Picks-Dream 7, -Cptn 10
92/3 FleerUltra 189
93/4 FleerUltra 245
94/5 FU 189, -Red 9, -Power 9
95/6 FU 142, 247, -Crease 17
96/7 FleerUltra 55, -Clear 9
97/8 GeneralMills
95 Globe 86
93/4 HockeyWit 29
95/6 Hoyle'WEST 5 (Club)
92/3 HumptyDumpty -1
97/8 KatchMedallion 53
95/6 KennerSLU
96/7 KennerSLU (U.S)
97/8 KennerSLU
91/2 Kraft 7
93/4 KraftDinner
94/5 Kraft'AllStar
96/7 Kraft'Trophy
97/8 Kraft-RoadToNagano
93/4 Leaf 30, -GoldAS 9
94/5 Leaf 113, -Limited 20
95/6 Leaf 121
96/7 Leaf 146,-Swtr 10,-Leatr 17

97/8 Leaf 12, 179,-BnrS 6,-Fire 5
94/5 LeafLimited 97
95/6 LeafLimited 94
96/7 LeafLimited 2, -Bash 9
96/7 LeafPreferred 31, -Steel 29
97/8 Limited 1, 38, 169
97/8 Limited -fabric 13, 53
96/7 Maggers 74
94/5 McDonalds 30
97/8 McDonalds McD14
97/8 McDonalds -Medallions
96/7 MetalUniverse 50
96/7 MU-Lethal 18, -Cool 10
97/8 Omega 87, -GameFace 7
97/8 Omega -StickHandle 8
88/9 OPC/Topps 122
89/90 OPC/Topps 147
90/1 OPC/Topps 259
91/2 OPC/Topps 140, 191
92/3 O-Pee-Chee 244
90/1 opcPremier 105
91/2 opcPremier 130
89/90 opcSticker 89/230
98/9 Pacific 14, -GoldCrown 15
97/8 PacificCrown 14, -Slap 3A
97/8 PCC-GoldCrown 10
97/8 PcfcCrownRoy 50,-Blade 9
97/8 PCR-HatTrick 7,-Lamp 8
97/8 PacificDynagon! 44, 139
97/8 PcfcD-BstKpt 34,-Dyna 8A
97/8 PacificD-Tandem 6, 26
97/8 PacificInvin. 51, -Attack 10
97/8 PacificInv-Feature 14,-Off 8
97/8 PcfcParamount 70,-BigN 9
97/8 PcfcP-CdnGrts 6, -Photo 9
98/9 PcfcParamnt 82, -SpecD 8
97/8 PacificRegime 73
97/8 PcfcRevolutn 51,-ASGm 11
88/9 PaniniSticker 276
89/90 PaniniSticker 255
90/1 PaniniSticker 64
91/2 PaniniSticker 222
92/3 PaniniSticker 17
93/4 PaniniSticker 158
94/5 PaniniSticker 141, 237A,EE
95/6 PaniniSticker 31
96/7 PaniniSticker 26
97/8 PaniniSticker 154
95 PaniniWorlds 16
91/2 Parkhurst 153
92/3 Parkhurst 156, CP10
93/4 Parkhurst 172
94/5 Parkhurst 196, 298
95/6 Parkhurst 97, -AS 3
95 PH'Incomnet
91/2 Pinnacle 41
92/3 Pinnacle 114, 248
93/4 Pinnacle 205, -Tm2001 29
93/4 Pinnacle-NiftyFifty 1, 14
94/5 Pinnacle 32,BR6,GR10,TP6
95/6 Pinnacle-Full 5, -Roaring 18
96/7 Pinnacle 56,-TmP 5,-ByN 2
97/8 Pinnacle 80, -TeamP 8
96/7 P.BAP LTH3B, -Biscuit 10
97/8 P.BAP -OneTimers 4
97/8 PinnacleBeeHive 3
97/8 P.Certified 61, -Team 17
97/8 Pinnacle-EPIX 16
95/6 PinnacleFANtasy 6
96/7 PinnacleFANtasy 8
97/8 P.Inside 1,-Can 21,-Trck 14
96/7 PinnacleMint 18
97/8 PinnacleMint 6
95/6 P.Zenith 86, -ZTeam 16
96/7 P.Zenith 77, -ZTeam 4
95/6 Playoff 47, 157
94/5 POG 207, 265
95/6 POG 126
96/7 Post, -StickUm 3
93/4 PowerPlay 216, -Slap 10
93/4 Premier 247
94/5 Premier 215, 529
94/5 Premier-Finest(Topps) 5
95/6 ProMagnet 130
90/1 ProSet 174
91/2 ProSet 131, 475
92/3 ProSet 163
91/2 PSPlatinum 111
96/7 SB-7Eleven
90/1 Score 146, -Young 23
91/2 Score(CDN) 588
91/2 Score(U.S) 286, 38T
92/3 Score 392
93/4 Score 238
94/5 Score 155, CI5, NP8
95/6 Score 20, -Golden 17
96/7 Score 2, -Check 6, -Sddn 3
97/8 Score 80, -CheckIt 3
97/8 Score(DET) 1
92/3 SeasonsPatch 15
94/5 Select 129, FL4
95/6 SelectCert. 64, -Double 9
96/7 SelectCertified 72
94 Semic 100
95 Semic 88
95/6 SkBxEmotion 78, -Ntense 7
95/6 SkyBoxImpact 76
96/7 SkBxImpact 55, -Blade 21
94/5 SP 101
95/6 SP 62, E16
96/7 SP 50, CW8, -Inside
97/8 SPAuthentic 55, I10
96/7 SPx 19
97/8 SPx 7, 16
98/9 SPx"Finite" 32, 96, 158
97/8 SportFX MiniStix
95/6 Summit 124, -GM 20
96/7 Summit 139
95/6 SuperSticker 52, DC22
91 TeamCanada
92/3 Topps 295
95/6 Topps 16, 370, GC10, M10
98/9 Topps 216
94/5 ToppsFinest 92, -Div. 14
95/6 ToppsFinest 39, 65
91/2 ToppsStadiumClub 199
92/3 ToppsStadiumClub 371
93/4 ToppsStadiumClub 389
95/6 ToppsStadiumClub 25, F1
93/4 TSC-MembersOnly 16
95/6 TSC-MembersOnly 26
97/8 ToppsSticker 1
95/6 ToppsSuperSkills 55
90/1 UpperDeck 269
91/2 UpperDeck 561
92/3 UpperDeck 122
93/4 UpperDeck 140
94/5 UD 292, IG4, R7, SP69
95/6 UD 184, AS4, SE125, R4
95/6 UD-AllStarPredict MVP20
96/7 UD 252, P1, SS6B, X14
96/7 UD-AllStarYCTG A9
97/8 UD 268, GJ13, S14
97/8 UD SG14, SS14, T6B
93/4 UDBeAPlayer 16
94/5 UDBAP R86, R104, R137
94/5 UDBeAPlayer-Aut. 86
96/7 UDBlackDiamond 114
97/8 UDBlackDiamond 149, PC3
98/9 UDChoice 76, BH24, SQ9
95/6 UDCollChoice 4
96/7 UDCC 112, 319, C14,UD26
97/8 UDCC 76, C4, S14, SQ74
97/8 udDiamondVision 11, DM6
96/7 UpperDeck"Ice" 85, S2
97/8 UpperDeckIce 84, IC14,L2A
97/8 ValuNet
96 Wien 90
97/8 Zenith 3,Z9,-ZTm 9,-Chas 6
96/7 DET/HockeytownPuck
96/7 DET/PhotoPucks
88/9 N.J/Caretta
89/90 N.J.
90/1 N.J.
91/2 STL
85/6 London 9
86/7 London 6

SHANAHAN, CHRIS
96/7 Sudbury 21

SHANAHAN, RYAN
93/4 Slapshot(Sudbury) 10
94/5 Slapshot(Sudbury) 9
95/6 Slapshot 392
92/3 Sudbury 12
93/4 Sudbury 11

SHANAHAN, SEAN
76/7 COL.R
76/7 COL.R/CokeCans

SHAND, DAVE
77/8 OPC 355
78/9 O-Pee-Chee 356
79/80 O-Pee-Chee 394
80/1 O-Pee-Chee 282
79 PaniniSticker 57
80/1 Pepsi Cap
77/8 ATL
78/9 ATL/Coke
79/80 ATL
79/80 ATL/B&W
80/1 TOR

SHANK, DANIEL
90/1 Bowman 235
90/1 OPC/Topps 34
88/9 ProCards(Adirondack)
90/1 ProCards 489
91/2 ProCards 119
90/1 ProSet 78
90/1 Score 377
90/1 UpperDeck 99
95/6 LasVegas
92/3 SanDiego

SHANNON, DARRIN
91/2 Bowman 24
92/3 Bowman 385
93/4 Donruss 388
94/5 Donruss 139
94/5 Flair 210
92/3 FleerUltra 246
94/5 FleerUltra 395
93/4 Leaf 194
94/5 Leaf 251
90/1 OPC/Topps 310
91/2 OPC/Topps 214
92/3 O-Pee-Chee 332
91/2 opcPremier 146
97/8 PacificRegime 154
92/3 PaniniSticker 58
93/4 PaniniSticker 192
91/2 Parkhurst 201
92/3 Parkhurst 436
93/4 Parkhurst 499
94/5 ParkieSE 204
91/2 Pinnacle 243
92/3 Pinnacle 106
93/4 Pinnacle 266
94/5 Pinnacle 279
95/6 Pinnacle 69
96/7 PinnacleBeAPlayer 183
94/5 POG 254
93/4 Premier 261
94/5 Premier 254
89/90 ProCards(AHL) 275
90/1 ProCards 278
90/1 ProSet 592
91/2 ProSet 14, 515
92/3 ProSet 218
91/2 PSPlatinum 246
90/1 Score 410
91/2 Score(CDN)438, (U.S)107T
92/3 Score 36
93/4 Score 280
95/6 Score 103
92/3 Topps 167
91/2 ToppsStadiumClub 361
92/3 ToppsStadiumClub 55
93/4 ToppsStadiumClub 191
91/2 UpperDeck 322, 581
92/3 UpperDeck 132
90/1 BUF/Campbell
96/7 PHO
97/8 PHO
91/2 WPG/IGA
93/4 WPG/Ruffles
95/6 WPG

SHANNON, DARRYL
97/8 Pacific72
98/9 Pacific 109
96/7 PaniniSticker 21
97/8 PaniniSticker 14
91/2 Parkhurst 390
96/7 PinnacleBeAPlayer 90
88/9 ProCards(Newmarket)
90/1 ProCards 151
91/2 ProSet 490
97/8 Score(BUF) 19
91/2 UpperDeck 493
94/5 UpperDeck 483
95/6 UpperDeck 282
90/1 TOR/P.L.A.Y. 22
95/6 WPG
90/1 Newmarket

SHANNON, GERALD
35-40 CrownBrand 123
36-39 DiamondMatch (1)
37/8 OPC (V304E) 179

SHANNON, JERRY
34-43 BeeHives(MTL.M)

SHANNON, JOHN
97/8 Pinnacle -CBC Sports 12

SHANNON, RYAN
98 BowmanCHL 63

SHANTZ, BRIAN
89/90 SketchMEM 11
88/9 Kamloops
89/90 Kamloops

SHANTZ, JEFF
92/3 Classic 15
93/4 Classic 27
92/3 ClassicFourSport 164
93/4 Donruss 75
94/5 Donruss 247
95/6 Donruss 209
93/4 Leaf 405
94/5 Leaf 196
95/6 Leaf 252
98/9 Pacific 151
97/8 PacificRegime 46
94/5 PaniniSticker O
93/4 Parkhurst 314
94/5 Parkhurst 46, 289
93/4 Pinnacle 428
94/5 Pinnacle 458
97/8 PinnacleBeAPlayer 173
94/5 Premier 342
94/5 Premier-Finest(OPC) 23
93/4 Score 605
90/1 SketchWHL 174
91/2 SketchWHL 219
95/6 Topps 179
93/4 ToppsStadiumClub 348
94/5 ToppsStadiumClub 92
93/4 UD 258, 451, SP-32
94/5 UpperDeck 379
95/6 UpperDeck 182
97/8 UpperDeck 248
95/6 UDCollChoice 124
96/7 UDCollChoice 53
93/4 CHI/Coke
93/4 Indianapolis

SHAO TANG, PIEN
79 PaniniSticker 356

SHARIFJANOV, VADIM
93/4 Classic 110, CL6
94/5 Classic 21, T39
94/5 ClassicFourSport 138
94/5 C4'Images 112
93/4 ClassicProspects 207
97/8 Donruss 204
97/8 DonrussCanadianIce 134
97/8 Leaf 163
97/8 Limited 78
93/4 Parkhurst 527
93/4 Pinnacle 503
97/8 PinnacleInside 183
94/5 Score 212
97/8 Score 56
97/8 Score(N.J.) 17
94/5 SRGoldStandard 91
94/5 SRTetrad CXIV
92/3 UpperDeck 612
93/4 UpperDeck 574

SHARPLES, JEFF
95/6 EdgeIce 156
88/9 OPC/Topps 48
89/90 OPC/Topps 42
88/9 opcSticker249 /119
88/9 opcStickFS 17
88/9 PaniniSticker 38
89/90 PaniniSticker 66
90/1 ProCards 559
87/8 DET/Caesars
88/9 DET
88/9 DET/Caesars
83/4 Kelowna
84/5 KelownaWings 4
93/4 LasVegas
94/5 LasVegas
95/6 LasVegas
86/7 Portland

SHARPLES, SCOTT
92/3 StJohns

SHARPLES, WARREN
90/1 ProCards 625
91/2 ProCards 591

SHARPLEY, GLEN
77/8 OPC/Topps 158
78/9 OPC/Topps 175
79/80 OPC/Topps 93
80/1 OPC/Topps 218
81/2 OPC 64, Topps(W) 76
82/3 O-Pee-Chee 75
81/2 opcSticker 116
79 PaniniSticker 63
81/2 CHI
78/9 MIN/Cloverleaf 7
80/1 MIN

SHARRERS, MATT
92/3 BCJHL 155

SHASHOV, VLADIMIR
90/1 O-Pee-Chee 506

SHASTIN, EVGENY
90/1 O-Pee-Chee 6R

SHATALOV, YURI
74/5 Soviet Stars 9
91/2 Trends72 29

SHAUNESSY, SCOTT
88/9 ProCards(Halifax)
89/90 ProCards(IHL) 124
90/1 ProCards 385
91/2 ProCards 247
92/3 Cincinnati

SHAUNESSY, STEVE
91/2 Cincinnati

SHAVER, AL
93/4 ActionPacked 6

SHAVER, CLAUDE
91/2 Cornwall 28

SHAVER, RYAN
95/6 Slapshot 427

SHAW, BOB
83/4 KelownaWings

SHAW, BRAD
90/1 Bowman 260
91/2 Bowman 8
92/3 Bowman 111
93/4 Donruss 234
93/4 EASports 92, 203
92/3 FleerUltra 366
93/4 FleerUltra 167
94/5 FleerUltra 151
93/4 Kraft-Captain, -Recipe
93/4 Leaf 11
90/1 OPC/Topps 144, 279
91/2 OPC/Topps 442
90/1 PaniniSticker 48, 344
91/2 PaniniSticker 311
92/3 PaniniSticker 265
93/4 PaniniSticker 120
91/2 Parkhurst 62
92/3 Parkhurst 352
94/5 ParkieSE 122
91/2 Pinnacle 88
92/3 Pinnacle 371
93/4 Pinnacle 271, CA16
94/5 Pinnacle 162
94/5 POG 176
93/4 PowerPlay 175
94/5 Premier 161
90/1 ProSet 110
91/2 ProSet 87
92/3 ProSet 124
91/2 PSPlatinum 45
90/1 Score 99, 325
91/2 Score(CDN) 509, (U.S) 289
92/3 Score 85
93/4 Score 15
94/5 Score 76
92/3 Topps 89
91/2 ToppsStadiumClub 83
92/3 ToppsStadiumClub 65
90/1 UpperDeck 90, 327
91/2 UpperDeck 297
92/3 UpperDeck 109
89/90 HFD/JuniorWhalers
90/1 HFD/JuniorWhalers
91/2 HFD/JuniorWhalers
92/3 OTT
93/4 OTT/Kraft
81/2 Ottawa67s
82/3 Ottawa67s
83/4 Ottawa67s

SHAW, DEAN
84/5 Brandon 4

SHAW, DAVID
91/2 Bowman 64
92/3 Bowman 141
92/3 FleerUltra 256
93/4 Leaf 249
86/7 O-Pee-Chee 236
87/8 O-Pee-Chee 252
88/9 OPC/Topps 57
89/90 OPC/Topps 39, OPC 326
90/1 O-Pee-Chee 403
91/2 OPC/Topps 306
86/7 opcSticker 31 /171, 133/119
87/8 opcSticker 223/90
88/9 opcSticker243 /110
97/8 PacificRegime 188
91/2 PaniniSticker 294
91/2 Pinnacle 251
92/3 Pinnacle 343
93/4 Pinnacle 124
94/5 Pinnacle 435
93/4 Premier 179
94/5 Premier 358
90/1 ProSet 495
90/1 Score 98
91/2 Score(CDN) 161, (U.S) 161
92/3 Score 183
93/4 Score 205
92/3 Topps 420
91/2 ToppsStadiumClub 306
92/3 ToppsStadiumClub 162
93/4 ToppsStadiumClub 229
90/1 UpperDeck 15
91/2 UpperDeck 409
94/5 UDBeAPlayer-Aut. 136
91/2 EDM/IGA
89/90 NYR/MarineMidland
85/6 QUE
85/6 QUE/GeneralFoods
85/6 QUE/McDonald
85/6 QUE/Provigo
86/7 QUE
86/7 QUE/GeneralFoods
86/7 QUE/McDonald
95/6 T.B.
84/5 Fredericton 2
82/3 Kitchener 9
83/4 Kitchener 27

SHAW, JIM
75/6 opcWHA 55

SHAW, LLOYD
93/4 Seattle

SHAWARA, MITCH
93/4 PrinceAlbert
95/6 PrinceAlbert

SHEA, JAMES
90/1 SketchOHL 117
91/2 SketchOHL 45

SHEA, MICHAEL
95 Globe 189
94 Semic 236
95 Semic 185
93 SemicSticker 271

SHEARER, DAN
75/6 Hamilton

SHEARER, ROB
93/4 Slapshot(Windsor) 14
94/5 Slapshot(Windsor) 16
95/6 Slapshot 419

SHEDDEN, DARRYL
95/6 Louisiana, -Playoffs

SHEDDEN, DOUG
83/4 O-Pee-Chee 285
85/6 O-Pee-Chee 247
86/7 OPC/Topps 153
87/8 O-Pee-Chee 249
83/4 opcSticker 228
84/5 opcSticker 120
85/6 opcSticker 102/234
86/7 opcSticker 164/24
87/8 opcSticker 226/93
82/3 Post
88/9 ProCards(Newmarket)
89/90 ProCards(AHL) 125
90/1 ProCards 158
90/1 ProSet 542
83/4 SouhaitsRen.KeyChain
86/7 DET/Caesars
83/4 PGH/Heinz
84/5 PGH/Heinz
86/7 QUE
90/1 TOR
95/6 Louisiana, -Playoffs
90/1 Newmarket
80/1 SSMarie

SHEEHAN, BOB
71/2 OPC/Topps 177
72/3 OPC 297
76/7 OPC/Topps 183
78/9 O-Pee-Chee 311
77/8 opcWHA 47
73/4 QuakerOats 20
71/2 TheTorontoSun
71/2 MTL
89/90 NewHaven

SHEEHAN, JAMES
90/1 SketchOHL 118
91/2 SketchOHL 65

SHEEHAN, MURRAY
94/5 Slapshot(Detroit) 6
94/5 Slapshot(MEM) 80
95/6 Slapshot 68

SHEEHY, NEIL
87/8 O-Pee-Chee 213
90/1 OPC/Topps 188
91/2 OPC/Topps 407
87/8 opcSticker 38 /181
87/8 PaniniSticker 209
91/2 Score(CDN) 636, (U.S) 86T
85/6 CGY/RedRooster
86/7 CGY/RedRooster
91/2 CGY/IGA
88/9 WSH
88/9 WSH/Smokey
89/90 WSH
89/90 WSH/Kodak
90/1 WSH/Smokey
84/5 Moncton 4

SHEEHY, TIM
76/7 opcWHA 33
72 SemicSticker 128
72/3 NewEngland

SHEFLO, ALEC
87/8 Kamloops

SHELLEY, JODY
97/8 Bowman 76
95/6 Halifax
96/7 Halifax (1), (2)

SHELTON, DOUG
67/8 Topps 53

SHEMKO, MIKE
90/1 SketchWHL 240

SHENDELEV, SERGEI
94 Semic 142
95 Semic 127

SHENG WEN, CHEN
79 PaniniSticker 360

SHEPARD, BRAD
90/1 SketchOHL 316
91/2 SketchOHL 55

SHEPARD, KEN
93/4 Slapshot(Oshawa) 3
96/7 Binghampton

SHEPELEV, SERGEI
83/4 SovietStars

SHEPOVALOV, VLADIMIR
72/3 WilliamsFIN 35

SHEPPARD, BRENT
91/2 AirCanadaSJHL D40

SHEPPARD, GREGG
74/5 LiptonSoup 29
74/5 Loblaws
72/3 OPC 240
73/4 OPC/Topps 8
74/5 OPC/Topps 184
75/6 OPC/Topps 235
76/7 OPC/Topps 155
77/8 OPC/Topps 95
78/9 OPC/Topps 18

79/80 OPC/Topps 172
80/1 O-Pee-Chee 325
82/3 Post

SHEPPARD, JOHN
25-27 Anonymous 129
33/4 CndGum (V252)
33-35 DiamondMatch
33/4 OPC (V304A)30
23/4 PaulinsCandy 47

SHEPPARD, JOHN
84/5 Ottawa67s

SHEPPARD, KEN
91/2 Oshawa Dominos 5

SHEPPARD, RAY
91/2 Bowman 63
92/3 Bowman 25
93/4 Donruss 105
94/5 Donruss 293
95/6 Donruss 198, 276, -Marks 4
96/7 Donruss 210
97/8 Donruss 101
97/8 DonrussCanadianIce 29
95/6 DonrussElite 102
97/8 DonrussPreferred 36
97/8 DonrussPriority 114
94/5 Flair 52
96/7 Flair 38
94/5 Fleer 65
96/7 Fleer 42
95/6 FleerMetal 134
92/3 FleerUltra 289
93/4 FleerUltra 310
94/5 FleerUltra 66
95/6 FleerUltra 49, 305, -Red 9
96/7 FleerUltra 68
95/6 Hoyle'WEST 6 (Clubs)
97/8 KatchMedallion 65
93/4 Leaf 44
94/5 Leaf 107
95/6 Leaf 118
96/7 Leaf 114
97/8 Leaf 115
94/5 LeafLimited 26
95/6 LeafLimited 106
96/7 LeafPreferred 92
97/8 Limited 141
96/7 MetalUniverse 62
88/9 OPC/Topps 55
89/90 OPC/Topps 119
90/1 O-Pee-Chee 446
91/2 OPC/Topps 289
92/3 O-Pee-Chee 154
90/1 opcPremier 106
91/2 opcPremier 2
88/9 opcStars 35
88/9 opcSticker 262, 126/258
89/90 opcStickr 257/136,259/140
88/9 opcStickFS 18
97/8 PacificCrown 80
97/8 PcfcDynagon! 55,-Tand 52
97/8 PacificInvincible 63
97/8 PacificParamount 84
88/9 PaniniSticker 228
89/90 PaniniSticker 211
91/2 PaniniSticker 286
92/3 PaniniSticker 121
93/4 PaniniSticker 247
94/5 PaniniSticker 211, 237b
95/6 PaniniSticker 183
96/7 PaniniSticker 69
97/8 PaniniSticker 61
91/2 Parkhurst 41
92/3 Parkhurst 280
93/4 Parkhurst 330
95/6 Parkhurst 457
94/5 ParkieSE 49
91/2 Pinnacle 155
92/3 Pinnacle 119
93/4 Pinnacle 153
94/5 Pinnacle 14
96/7 Pinnacle 91, 233
97/8 Pinnacle 164
97/8 PinnacleBeAPlayer 46
97/8 PinnacleCertified 90
97/8 PinnacleInside 139
95/6 PinnacleZenith 92
95/6 Playoff 36
96/7 Playoff 338
94/5 POG 91
95/6 POG 98
93/4 PowerPlay 76
94/5 Premier 429, -Finest(T) 6
95/6 ProMagnet 104
90/1 ProSet 496
91/2 ProSet 162, 380
92/3 ProSet 47
91/2 PSPlatinum 169
90/1 ScoreTraded 97T
91/2 Score(CDN) 213, 586
91/2 Score(U.S) 213, 36T
92/3 Score 163, -Sharp. 20
93/4 Score 83
94/5 Score 175, NP15
95/6 Score 127
96/7 Score 112
97/8 Score 121
94/5 Select 56
95/6 SkyBoxEmotion 58
95/6 SkyBoxImpact 152
96/7 SkyBoxImpact 48
94/5 SP 38
95/6 SP 130
96/7 SP 66
95/6 Summit 77
96/7 Summit 88
92/3 Topps 257
94/5 ToppsFinest 50
95/6 ToppsFinestS 16
96/7 ToppsNHLPicks 129
91/2 ToppsStadiumClub 381
92/3 ToppsStadiumClub 85
94/5 ToppsStadiumClub 40
95/6 ToppsStadiumClub 215
90/1 UpperDeck 420
91/2 UpperDeck 390, 573
92/3 UpperDeck 296
93/4 UpperDeck 398
94/5 UpperDeck 152
95/6 UD 254, 348, SE161
96/7 UpperDeck 122, 263
97/8 UpperDeck 280
94/5 UDBeAPlayer R54
95/6 UDBeAPlayer 60
96/7 UDBlackDiamond 66
95/6 UDCollChoice 177
96/7 UDCollChoice 111
97/8 UDCC 99, C5, SQ60
96/7 UpperDeck"Ice" 23
87/8 BUF/BlueShield
87/8 BUF/WonderBread
88/9 BUF/BlueShield
88/9 BUF/WonderBread
89/90 BUF/BlueShield
89/90 BUF/Campbell
96/7 FLA/WinnDixie
97/8 FLA/WinnDixie

SHERBAN, TREVOR
90/1 SketchWHL 85
91/2 SketchWHL 297
90/1 Saskatoon 6

SHERF, JOHNNY
34-43 BeeHives(DET)

SHERIDAN, JOHN
75/6 opcWHA 107

SHERIDAN, RHONDA
87/8 Kingston 5

SHERMERHORN, DAN
92/3 BCJHL 193, 206
93/4 Maine 48

SHERO, FRED
45-64 BeeHives(NYR)
74/5 OPC/Topps 21
92/3 Parkhurst 480
51/2 Cleveland

SHERRID, DAVE
88/9 ProCards(Baltimore)

SHERRY, SIMON
93/4 Slapshot(Sudbury) 19
94/5 Slapshot(Sudbury) 19
95/6 Slapshot 401
93/4 Sudbury 18

SHERSTENKA, DAN
90/1 SketchWHL 115
91/2 SketchWHL 183

SHERVEN, GORD
94/5 DEL 302
95/6 DEL 89
96/7 DEL 278
83 CanadaJuniors
85/6 EDM/RedRooster
88/9 EDM/ActionMagazine 12
85/6 MIN

SHEVALIER, JEFF
97/8 PacificRegime 98
91/2 SketchOHL 68
93/4 Slapshot(NorthBay) 20
97/8 UDCollChoice 128
95/6 Phoenix

SHEWCHUK, JACK
34-43 BeeHives(BOS)
40/1 OPC (V301-2) 126

SHIBICKY, ALEX
34-43 BeeHives(NYR)
36/7 OPC (V304D) 109
39/40 OPC (V301-1) 88
36/7 WWGum (V356) 90

SHIBICKY, ALEX JR.
74/5 SiouxCity

SHICK, ROB
90/1 ProSet 698

SHIELDS, ALLEN
34-43 BeeHives(NYA)
35-40 CrownBrand 120
35/6 OPC (V304C) 89
37/8 OPC (V304E) 162
33/4 WWGum Premium
36/7 WWGum (V356) 60

SHIELDS, STEVE
94/5 Classic 62, T9
97/8 Donruss 51
97/8 D.CdnIce 132,-Scrapbk12
97/8 DonrussPreferred 80
97/8 DonrussPriority 115
97/8 DonrussStudio 79
97/8 Leaf 86
97/8 Limited 23, 63
97/8 Omega 27
98/9 Pacific 110
97/8 PacificRegime 22
96/7 Pinnacle 216
97/8 Pinnacle 97
97/8 PinnacleBeAPlayer
97/8 PinnacleCertified 7
97/8 PinnacleInside 77, -Stop 19
97/8 Score 44
97/8 Score(BUF) 2
97/8 UpperDeck 18
95/6 Rochester

SHIER, ANDREW
94/5 Classic 44
94/5 Richmond

SHILL, JACK
34-43 BeeHives(TOR)
36/7 OPC (V304D) 99
36/7 WWGum (V356) 39

SHINES, JIM
71/2 TheTorontoSun

SHINSKI, RICK
78/9 STL

SHIPLEY, BLAKE
92/3 MPSPhotoSJHL 41

SHIRJAEV, VALERI
90/1 O-Pee-Chee 13R
91/2 O-Pee-Chee 59R
89 Semic 84
89/90 SovietNats

SHMYR, PAUL
71/2 EddieSargent 140
71/2 OPC 6
80/1 OPC/Topps 66
75/6 opcWHA 5
76/7 opcWHA 69
77/8 opcWHA 59
82/3 Post
72/3 Post Transfers 6
71/2 TheTorontoSun
72/3 Cleveland
76/7 SanDiegoMariners
70/1 CHI
79/80 MIN
80/1 MIN

SHMYRKO, GORD
82/3 MedicineHat
83/4 MedicineHat 22

SHOCK, BECKY
92/3 Toledo (1)

SHOCKEY, JOHN
95/6 Spokane 24

SHOCKEY, PARRY
95/6 Spokane 26

SHOEBOTTOM, BRUCE
88/9 ProCards(Maine)
89/90 ProCards(AHL) 63
90/1 ProCards 130
91/2 ProCards 36
90/1 ProSet 411
92/3 Rochester/Dunkin'Donuts
92/3 Rochester/Kodak

SHOLD, TERRY
85/6 Minn-Duluth 2

SHORE, EDDIE
33/4 Anonymous (V129) 37
34-43 BeeHives(BOS)
38/8 BruinsMagazine
33-35 DiamondMatch
33 GoudeySport 19
83&87 HallOfFame 223
83 HHOF Postcard (O)
95/6 HHOFLegends 63
27-32 LaPresse 27/8
33/4 OPC (V304A) 3
36/7 OPC (V304D) 118
39/40 OPC (V301-1) 100
93/4 Parkie(56/7) P7
34/5 SweetCaporal
60/1 Topps 20
35/6 Triumph
36/7 WWGum (V356) 5
91/2 BOS/Legends

SHORE, HAMBY
91 C55 Reprint 12
1911-12 Imperial (C55) 12
1912-13 Imperial (C57) 30
1910-11 Imperial Post 12

SHORT, KAYLE
90/1 SketchOHL 215
91/2 SketchOHL 349
93/4 Slapshot(Guelph) 4
92/3 Sudbury 19

SHORT, STEVE
83/4 Brantford 16

SHTALENKOV, MIKHAIL
93/4 Classic 148
92/3 ClassicProspects 94
93/4 ClassicProspects 49
94/5 Donruss 314
94/5 Fleer 7
94/5 FleerUltra 252
95 Globe 164
94/5 Leaf 209
97/8 Omega 8
91/2 O-Pee-Chee 43R
98/9 PacificParamount 127
97/8 PacificRegime 8
95 PaniniWorlds 27
94/5 Parkhurst 4
95/6 Parkhurst 6
94/5 Pinnacle 331
95/6 Pinnacle 145
97/8 PinnacleBeAPlayer
94/5 Premier 3
92/3 RedAce(Blue) 19,(Violet) 19
97/8 Score 21
97/8 Score(ANA) 16
95 Semic 121, 211
91 SemicSticker 79
92 SemicSticker 100
95/6 Topps 344
94/5 UpperDeck 462
95/6 UpperDeck 91
96/7 UpperDeck 7
95/6 UDBeAPlayer 69
98/9 UDChoice 2
95/6 UDCollChoice 227
96/7 UDCollChoice 4
94/5 ANA/Carl'sJr 22
95/6 ANA
96/7 ANA/UpFrontSports 1

SHU CHING, HSIANG
79 PaniniSticker 360

SHUCHUK, GARY
93/4 Donruss 157
93/4 FleerUltra 12, -Prospects 9
93/4 Leaf 222
92/3 Parkhurst 484
93/4 Parkhurst 95
94/5 ParkieSE 85
93/4 Premier 499
91/2 ProCards 132
91/2 Score(CDN) 345, (U.S) 315
93/4 ToppsStadiumClub 351
94/5 ToppsStadiumClub 47
91/2 UpperDeck 376
93/4 UpperDeck 13
94/5 UDBeAPlayer-Aut. 36
95/6 Phoenix

SHUDRA, RON
88/9 ProCards(CapeBreton)
89/90 ProCards(IHL) 128
88/9 EDM/ActionMagazine 11
95/6 SheffieldSteelers
97/8 SheffieldSteelers
85/6 Kamloops
86/7 Kamloops

SHUMAN, MIKE
90/1 Halifax

SHUPE, JACK
81/2 Victoria

SHURUPOV, ANDREI
95/6 Slapshot 54

SHUTE, DAVE
90/1 SketchWHL 35
91/2 Knoxville
93/4 Raleigh

SHUTT, STEVE
93/4 ActionPacked 4
77/8 Coke Mini
72-84 Dernière 72/3, 73/4
72-84 Dernière 80/1, 83/4
88/9 Esso Sticker
74/5 Loblaws
74/5 OPC 316
75/6 OPC/Topps 181
76/7 OPC/Topps 59
77/8 OPC/Topps 1, 3, 7
77/8 OPC/T. 120,217,-Glossy 19
78/9 OPC/T. 63,67,170,OPC 333
79/80 OPC/Topps 90
80/1 OPC/Topps 89, 165, 180
81/2 OPC 180, 197, T. 34, 56
82/3 O-Pee-Chee 192
83/4 O-Pee-Chee 198
84/5 O-Pee-Chee 272
81/2 opcSticker 32, 44
82/3 opcSticker 32, 33
83/4 opcSticker 6, 57
80/1 Pepsi Cap
82/3 Post
83/4 PuffySticker 6
83/4 7ElevenCokeCup
83/4 SouhaitsRen.KeyChain
77-9 Sportscastr 43-13, 50-1178
92/3 Trends(76) 183
95/6 Zellers
83/4 Vachon 55
72/3 MTL
73/4 MTL
74/5 MTL
75/6 MTL
76/7 MTL
77/8 MTL
78/9 MTL
79/80 MTL
80/1 MTL
81/2 MTL
82/3 MTL
82/3 MTL/Steinberg
83/4 MTL
95/6 MTL/Forum 20Mar96

SHUTTER, WALTER
86/7 Saskatoon

SHVIDKY, DENIS
97/8 UDBlackDiamond 116
98/9 UDChoice 286

SIALIMOV, VIKTOR
82 SemicSticker 65
85/6 Arizona

SICARD, M.
93/4 SSMarie 32

SICINSKI, BOB
73/4 QuakerOats 12

SIDELNIKOV, ALEKSANDR
74 Hellas 56
73/4 Soviet Stars 3
74/5 Soviet Stars 3
91/2 Trends72 28
73/4 WilliamsFIN 16

SIDEROFF, DEAN
91/2 AirCanadaSJHL A35

SIDORKIEWICZ, PETER
90/1 Bowman 255
91/2 Bowman 13
92/3 Bowman 162
93/4 EASports 96, 206
92/3 FleerUltra 150, 367
92/3 Kraft'Disk
89/90 OPC/Topps 11
90/1 OPC/Topps 14
91/2 OPC/Topps 296
92/3 O-Pee-Chee 175
92/3 opcPremier 112
89/90 opcSticker 42/188, FS6
89/90 PaniniSticker 220
90/1 PaniniSticker 38
91/2 PaniniSticker 310
93/4 PaniniSticker 121
91/2 Parkhurst 286
92/3 Parkhurst 120, 450
91/2 Pinnacle 234
92/3 Pinnacle 371
93/4 Pinnacle 381, -Masks 10
90/1 ProSet 451
91/2 ProSet 90
92/3 ProSet 125
90/1 Score 46, -Young 4
91/2 Score(CDN) 203, (U.S) 203
92/3 Score 41, 515
93/4 Score 102, -P.AS 17
93/4 Score-Franchise 14
92/3 Topps 332
91/2 ToppsStadiumClub 125
92/3 ToppsStadiumClub 27
93/4 ToppsStadiumClub-AllStar
90/1 UpperDeck 69
91/2 UpperDeck 325
92/3 UpperDeck 14, 480
89/90 HFD/JuniorWhalers
90/1 HFD/JuniorWhalers
91/2 HFD/JuniorWhalers
80/1 Oshawa 21
81/2 Oshawa 3
82/3 Oshawa 3
83/4 Oshawa 1

SIEBERT, ALBERT (BABE)
33/4 Anonymous (V129) 28
34-43 BeeHives(MTL.C)
33/4 CndGum (V252)
35-40 CrownBrand 110
83&87 HallOfFame 59
83 HHOF Postcard (D)
27-32 LaPresse 28/9
34/5 OPC (V304B) 49
37/8 OPC (V304E) 150
55/6 Parkhurst 62
38/9 QuakerOats
34/5 SweetCaporal
33/4 WWGum (V357) 8
36/7 WWGum (V356) 3
95/6 MTL/Forum 20Nov96

SIEKKINEN, A.P.
91/2 Jyvas-Hyva 25
92/3 Jyvas-Hyva 70
93/4 Jyvas-Hyva 134
95 Latkaliiga 4
93/4 Sisu 136
94/5 Sisu 50, -Nolla. 7
95/6 Sisu 56, -GhostGoalie 7
96/7 Sisu-Mighty 9
95/6 SisuLimited 46

SIGOUIN, MICHAEL
92/3 BCJHL 21

SIHVONEN, PERTTI
70/1 Kuvajulkaisut 255

SIHVONEN, PETTERI
92/3 Jyvas-Hyva 141

SIHVONEN, TONI
92/3 Jyvas-Hyva 142
93/4 Jyvas-Hyva 327
93/4 Sisu 45
94/5 Sisu 136
95/6 Sisu 211
96/7 Sisu 12

SIIMES, RAULI
70/1 Kuvajulkaisut 341

SIISSALA, ARTO
71/2 WilliamsFIN 294
73/4 WilliamsFIN 212

SIITARINEN, JORMA
70/1 Kuvajulkaisut 223
71/2 WilliamsFIN 145
72/3 WilliamsFIN 205
73/4 WilliamsFIN 119

SIIVONEN, HANNU
70/1 Kuvajulkaisut 238
78/9 SM-Liiga 153
71/2 WilliamsFIN 256

SILANDER, JUKKA
72/3 WilliamsFIN 337

SILIUS, KARI
72/3 WilliamsFIN 296

SILK, DAVE
94/5 MiracleOnIce 31, 32
84/5 O-Pee-Chee 16
79/80 USAOlympicTeam 10
85/6 WPG
85/6 WPG/Police

SILLANPÄÄ, KARI
66/7 Champion 25
65/6 Hellas 13

SILLANPÄÄ TEEMU
92/3 Jyvas-Hyva 105
93/4 Jyvas-Hyva 196
93/4 Sisu 261
94/5 Sisu 56
95/6 Sisu 285

SILLGREN, HARRI
93/4 Jyvas-Hyva 328
93/4 Sisu 49
94/5 Sisu 112
95/6 Sisu 133, -Painkiller 6
97/8 udSwedish 197

SILLINGER, MIKE
93/4 Donruss 92
95/6 Donruss 219
92/3 FleerUltra 290
93/4 FleerUltra 311
95/6 FleerUltra 203
93/4 Leaf 306
94/5 Leaf 394
91/2 OPC/Topps 337
90/1 opcPremier 107
98/9 Pacific 331
97/8 PacificCrown 336
92/3 Parkhurst 38
93/4 Parkhurst 331
95/6 Parkhurst 274
97/8 PinnacleBeAPlayer 16
95/6 Playoff 3, 225
96/7 Playoff 331
95/6 POG 22
93/4 PowerPlay 336
94/5 Premier 171
91/2 ProCards 130
91/2 Score(CDN) 357, (U.S) 327
93/4 Score 651
90/1 SketchWHL 186
90/1 UpperDeck 452
91/2 UpperDeck 457
92/3 UpperDeck 524
94/5 UpperDeck 22, 200
95/6 UpperDeck 72, SE91
96/7 UpperDeck 349
97/8 UpperDeck 170
94/5 UDBeAPlayer 171
97/8 UDCollChoice 260
96/7 VAN
96/7 VAN/IGA
87/8 Regina
88/9 Regina
89/90 Regina

SILLMAN, TUOMO
71/2 WilliamsFIN 185
72/3 WilliamsFIN 135
73/4 WilliamsFIN 191

SILLS, FRANÇOIS
94/5 DEL 238
95/6 DEL 114
96/7 DEL 59

SILTALA, MIKE
81/2 Kingston 18
82/3 Kingston 8

SILTANEN, RISTO
91/2 Jyvas-Hyva 18
80/1 O-Pee-Chee 315
81/2 O-Pee-Chee 118, 122
82/3 O-Pee-Chee 129
83/4 O-Pee-Chee 146
84/5 O-Pee-Chee 78
86/7 OPC/Topps 187
81/2 opcSticker 214
83/4 opcSticker 257
86/7 opcSticker 29 /168
79 PaniniSticker 166
87/8 PaniniSticker 159
80/1 Pepsi Cap
82/3 Post
83/4 PuffySticker 14
82 SemicSticker 157
95/6 Sisu 140
95/6 SisuLimited 92
78/9 SM-Liiga 5, 51
83/4 SouhaitsRen.KeyChain
77-80 Sportscaster 75-1796
84/5 Topps 61
72/3 WilliamsFIN 316
79/80 EDM
80/1 EDM/Zellers
81/2 EDM/RedRooster
81/2 EDM/WestEdmonton
88/9 EDM/ActionMagazine 48
82/3 HFD/JuniorWhalers
83/4 HFD/JuniorWhalers
84/5 HFD/JuniorWhalers
85/6 HFD/JuniorWhalers
85/6 QUE
85/6 QUE/McDonald
86/7 QUE
86/7 QUE/GeneralFoods

SILVASTI, MIKKO
70/1 Kuvajulkaisut 320

SILVCHENKO, VADIM
93/4 Wheeling 15
94/5 Wheeling 4

SILVENNOINEN, JUHA
74 Hellas 16
80/1 Mallasjuoma 81
78/9 SM-Liiga 189
71/2 WilliamsFIN 273
73/4 WilliamsFIN 168

SILVER, CHAD
88/9 Regina

SILVER, HARRY
71/2 WilliamsFIN 239
72/3 WilliamsFIN 223

SILVER, SHAWN
93/4 Slapshot(Sudbury) 1
93/4 Slapshot(Windsor) 2
93/4 Sudbury 21

SILVERMAN, ANDY
95/6 Binghampton
96/7 Binghampton
92/3 Maine 13
93/4 Maine 38

SIM, JONATHAN
97/8 Bowman 31
98 BowmanCHL 15
95/6 Slapshot 263, 340

SIM, TREVOR
92/3 CanadaNats
93/4 CanadaNats
93/4 FleerUltra 473
93/4 PowerPlay 494
93/4 Premier-TmCanada 11
90/1 ProCards 230
89/90 SketchMEM 20
89/90 Kamloops
94/5 Milwaukee

SIMARD, MARTIN
90/1 ProCards 616
91/2 ProSet 526
91/2 CGY/IGA
94/5 Milwaukee
88/9 SaltLake 11

SIMARD, SÉBASTIEN
96/7 Rimouski

SIMCIK, JAN
91/2 SketchQMJHL 141

SIMEK, MARTIN
94/5 APS 81

SIMICEK, ROBERT
94/5 APS 130

SIMICEK, ROMAN
95/6 APS 306

SIMIONI, MARIO
92 SemicSticker 262
84/5 Moncton 15

SIMMER, CHARLIE
79/80 OPC/Topps 191
80/1 OPC/Topps 4, 83, 161
80/1 OPC/Topps 165, 171, 240
81/2 OPC 142, 151, 391
81/2 Topps 35, (W) 130
82/3 O-Pee-Chee 159
83/4 O-Pee-Chee 162
84/5 OPC 90, 358, Topps 69
85/6 OPC/Topps 87
86/7 OPC/Topps 145
87/8 OPC/Topps 52
88/9 O-Pee-Chee 250
81/2 opcSticker 144, 236, 266
82/3 opcSticker 237
83/4 opcSticker 290
84/5 opcSticker 266
85/6 opcSticker 158/28
86/7 opcSticker 36/173
87/8 opcSticker 137/246
87/8 PaniniSticker 2, 11
90/1 ProCards 300
91/2 ProCards 333
83/4 PuffySticker 8
83/4 7ElevenCokeCup
83/4 SouhaitsRen.KeyChain
84/5 Topps 69
84/5 BOS
80/1 L.A.
87/8 PGH/Kodak

SIMMONS, DON
45-64 BeeHives(BOSx2)
64-67 BeeHives(TOR)
63-5 ChexPhoto
65/6 CocaCola
63/4 Parkhurst 2, 62
60/1 ShirriffCoin 101
62/3 ShirriffCoin 22
57/8 Topps 14
58/9 Topps 44
59/60 Topps 11
60/1 Topps 43
65/6 Topps 88
56-66 TorontoStar 57/8, 58/9
63/4 York 15
64/5 TOR

SIMMONS, GARY
74/5 Loblaws-Update
74/5 OPC 371
75/6 OPC/Topps 29
76/7 OPC/Topps 176
78/9 OPC 385

SIMMS, BRAD
95/6 Slapshot 345

SIMOES, STEFAN
90/1 SketchQMJHL 148
91/2 SketchQMJHL 197

SIMOLA, JARI
72/3 WilliamsFIN 352

SIMON
95/6 DEL 437

SIMON, CHRIS
96/7 Flair 100
93/4 FleerUltra 224, -AllRookie 7
93/4 Leaf 416
94/5 Leaf 339
97/8 PacificRegime 213
93/4 Parkhurst 171, C13
93/4 Pinnacle 219
94/5 Pinnacle 506
97/8 PinnacleBeAPlayer 65
93/4 Score 473
96/7 Score 190
89/90 SketchOHL 56
91/2 SketchOHL 313
93/4 UpperDeck 243, SP-131
94/5 UpperDeck 299
97/8 UpperDeck 205, 387
94/5 UDBeAPlayer-Aut. 58
96/7 UDBlackDiamond 67
96/7 UDCollChoice 66
97/8 UDCollChoice 269
96/7 UpperDeck"Ice" 73
94/5 QUE/BurgerKing
92/3 QUE/PetroCanada

SIMON, DARCY
91/2 ProCards 71
92/3 Fredericton

SIMON, DIETER
74 Hellas 116
79 PaniniSticker 250

SIMON, JASON
89/90 ProCards(AHL) 203
90/1 ProCards 569
91/2 ProCards 442
96/7 LasVegas
86/7 London 11
89/90 Nashville

SIMON, JOE
94/5 Slapshot(Brantford) 9
93/4 Muskegon
87/8 Sudbury 11

SIMON, JURGEN
94/5 DEL 194
95/6 DEL 178
96/7 DEL 118

SIMON, TODD
93/4 ClassicProspects 228
94/5 Donruss 16
95/6 EdgeIce 157
94/5 Pinnacle 491
94/5 Premier 469
94/5 Score 234
94/5 Select 195
90/1 SketchOHL 270
91/2 SketchOHL 211
94/5 ToppsStadiumClub 221
94/5 UpperDeck 456
95/6 LasVegas
92/3 Rochester/Dunkin'Donuts
92/3 Rochester/Kodak
93/4 Rochester

SIMONEN, SAMI
93/4 Sisu 177
94/5 Sisu 33
95/6 Sisu 77
96/7 Sisu 75

SIMONI, STEVE
83/4 Ottawa67s
84/5 Ottawa67s

SIMONSON, DEREK
92/3 MPSPhotoSJHL 50

SIMPSON, BOB
77/8 O-Pee-Chee 310
78/9 O-Pee-Chee 372

SIMPSON, CRAIG
90/1 Bowman 201
91/2 Bowman 107
92/3 Bowman 150
93/4 Donruss 31
94/5 Donruss 112
92/3 FleerUltra 66
93/4 FleerUltra 277
94/5 FleerUltra 266
89/90 Kraft 16
90/1 Kraft 52
91/2 Kraft 81
93/4 Leaf 344
94/5 Leaf 198
86/7 OPC/Topps 122
87/8 OPC/Topps 80
88/9 OPC/Topps 27
89/90 OPC/Topps 99
90/1 OPC/Topps 240
91/2 OPC/Topps 460
92/3 O-Pee-Chee 225
88/9 opcStars 36
87/8 opcSticker 166/25
88/9 opcSticker 228
89/90 opcSticker 217/77
88/9 opcSticker 123 /255
90/1 Panini(EDM) 20
87/8 PaniniSticker 149
88/9 PaniniSticker 62
89/90 PaniniSticker 75
90/1 PaniniSticker 229
91/2 PaniniSticker 130
92/3 PaniniSticker 102
93/4 PaniniSticker 237
91/2 Parkhurst 54
92/3 Parkhurst 51
93/4 Parkhurst 19
94/5 Parkhurst V11
94/5 ParkieSE 22
91/2 Pinnacle 196
92/3 Pinnacle 321
93/4 Pinnacle 396
94/5 Pinnacle 294
93/4 PowerPlay 301
93/4 Premier 231, 333
94/5 Premier 349
90/1 ProSet 95
91/2 ProSet 69,-ThePuck 9
92/3 ProSet 56
91/2 PSPlatinum 40
90/1 Score 58, -Hot 2
91/2 Score(CDN) 475, (U.S) 255
92/3 Score 260, -Sharp. 30
93/4 Score 139, 557
94/5 Score 54
92/3 Topps 356
94/5 T.Finest-RingLdrs 7
91/2 ToppsStadiumClub 137
92/3 ToppsStadiumClub 473
93/4 ToppsStadiumClub 305
90/1 UpperDeck 129
91/2 UpperDeck 286
92/3 UpperDeck 309
93/4 UpperDeck 430, SP-19
94/5 UpperDeck 50
94/5 UDBAP R77, R120
94/5 UDBeAPlayer -Aut 122
95/6 UDCollChoice 231
87/8 EDM
88/9 EDM
88/9 EDM/ActionMagazine 93
90/1 EDM/McGavins
91/2 EDM/IGA
92/3 EDM
92/3 EDM/IGA 20
86/7 PGH/Kodak
82/3 Indianapolis

SIMPSON, GEORGE
93/4 Huntington

SIMPSON, JOE
25-27 Anonymous 82
83&87 HallOfFame 26
83 HHOF Postcard (B)
23/4 PaulinsCandy 41

SIMPSON, REGAN
92/3 MPSPhotoSJHL 86

SIMPSON, REID
97/8 PinnacleBeAPlayer 47
89/90 ProCards'AHL 354
90/1 ProCards 29
91/2 ProCards 272
96/7 N.J/Sharp

SIMPSON, SHAWN
88/9 ProCards(Baltimore)
89/90 ProCards(AHL) 98
90/1 ProCards 215
87/8 SSMarie 13

SIMOSON, TERRY
90/1 WPG/IGA
91/2 WPG/IGA
95/6 WPG (x2)

SIMPSON, TODD
97/8 PacificCrown 73
96/7 PinnacleBeAPlayer 105
97/8 UpperDeck 238
97/8 UDCollChoice 36
94/5 SaintJohn
95/6 SaintJohn
93/4 Saskatoon

SIMPSON, TOM
74/5 opcWHA 16
75/6 opcWHA 81
72/3 OttawaNationals

SIMPSON, WADE
89/90 SketchMEM 83
89/90 SketchOHL 8
90/1 SketchOHL 345
91/2 SketchOHL 167
89/90 Oshawa 10
90/1 Oshawa 15
91/2 Oshawa
91/2 Oshawa/Dominos 4
92/3 Oshawa

SIMS, AL
74/5 Loblaws
74/5 OPC 333
75/6 OPC/Topps 136
79/80 O-Pee-Chee 272
80/1 OPC/Topps 233
81/2 OPC 131, Topps(E) 85
81/2 opcSticker 66
89/90 ProCards(IHL) 138
90/1 ProCards 539
91/2 ProCards 261
96/7 S.J/PacificBellSheet

SIMURDA, DAVE
82/3 Kingston 19
83/4 Kingston 23

SINCLAIR, DARREN
95/6 Spokane 6

SINCLAIR, REG
45-64 BeeHives(NYR)
51/2 Parkhurst 103
52/3 Parkhurst 104

SINDEL, JAROMIR
94/5 APS 70
91/2 Jyvas-Hyva 49
92/3 Jyvas-Hyva 155
82 SemicSticker 78
89 SemicSticker 179
93/4 Sisu 58

SINDEL, ROMAN
95/6 APS 228

SINDELAR, ROMAN
85/6 Minn-Duluth 21

SINDEN, HARRY
52/3 AnonymousOHL 85
87 HallOfFame 241
93/4 HHOFLegends 33
66/7 Topps 31
91/2 Trends(72) 94, -Aut
91/2 BOS/Legends

SINGBUSH, ALEX
34-43 BeeHives(MTL.C)
40/1 OPC (V301-2) 114

SINISALO, ILKKA
90/1 Bowman 112
80/1 Mallasjuoma 15
82 Mallasjuoma
84/5 O-Pee-Chee 167
85/6 O-Pee-Chee 188
86/7 OPC/Topps 36
88/9 OPC/Topps 111
90/1 OPC/Topps 152
91/2 OPC/Topps 510
90/1 opcPremier 108
86/7 opcSticker 238/108
87/8 PaniniSticker 136
88/9 PaniniSticker 325
90/1 PaniniSticker 123
82/3 Post
90/1 ProSet 223, 461
90/1 Score 286
90/1 ScoreTraded 93T
82 SemicSticker 158
91 SemicSticker 206
94/5 Sisu 90
95/6 Sisu 293
95/6 SisuLimited 59
78/9 SM-Liiga 40
83/4 SouhaitsRen.KeyChain
90/1 UpperDeck 120
83/4 PHA
86/7 PHA
89/90 PHA

SINKKONEN, KEIJO
66/7 Champion 99
72/3 WilliamsFIN 184

SINKKONEN, MARTTI
66/7 Champion 101
65/6 Hellas 96
72/3 WilliamsFIN 185

SINNER, STEPHAN
94/5 DEL 71
95/6 DEL 57
96/7 DEL 207

SIP, RADEK
94/5 APS 216
95/6 APS 167
90/1 SketchWHL 141
91/2 SketchWHL 341

SIREN, ESA
71/2 WilliamsFIN 159
72/3 WilliamsFIN 112

SIREN, JAAKKO
66/7 Champion 105
65/6 Hellas 131
71/2 WilliamsFIN 186

SIREN, JORMA
72/3 WilliamsFIN 277
73/4 WilliamsFIN 169

SIREN, VILLE
94/5 ElitSet 246
91/2 Jyvas-Hyva 17
90/1 OPC/Topps 383
88/9 PaniniSticker 335
90/1 ProSet 144
94 Semic 15
92/3 SemicElitserien 181
91 SemicSticker 9
92 SemicSticker 8
93 SemicSticker 59
86/7 PGH/Kodak
87/8 PGH/Kodak

SIRKKA, JEFF
89/90 ProCards(AHL) 59
90/1 ProCards 406
91/2 ProCards 477
85/6 Kingston 14
86/7 Kingston 23
87/8 Kingston 12
93/4 Portland
92/3 Rochester/Dunkin'Donuts
92/3 Rochester/Kodak

SIRKKOLA, RISTO
72/3 WilliamsFIN 278

SIRO, JARMO
72/3 WilliamsFIN 317

SIRO, JUKKA
72/3 WilliamsFIN 318

SIROIS, BOB
76/7 OPC 323
77/8 OPC 351
78/9 OPC/Topps 96, 131
79/80 OPC/Topps 29
80/1 O-Pee-Chee 313
78/9 WSH
79/80 WSH

SIROTA, JASON
91/2 AvantGardeBCJ 64

SIRVIÖ, ARTO
92/3 Jyvas-Hyva 92
93/4 Jyvas-Hyva 179
80/1 Mallasjuoma 12
93/4 Sisu 175
94/5 Sisu 92
95/6 Sisu 292
96/7 Sisu 78
89/90 SemicElitserien 278
90/1 SemicElitserien 41

SISKA, RANDY
85/6 MedicineHat 21
83/4 Victoria
84/5 Victoria

SISTONEN, TEEMU
70/1 Kuvajulkaisut 224

SITTLER, DARRYL
77/8 Coke Mini
72-84 Dernière 82/3
71/2 EddieSargent 204
72/3 EddieSargent 204
70/1 Esso Stamp
88/9 Esso Sticker
95/6 HHOFLegends 67
93/4 HockeyWit 73
84/5 Kelloggs Disk
91/2 Kraft 40
74/5 LiptonSoup 3
74/5 Loblaws
73/4 MacsMilkDisk
70/1 OPC 218
71/2 OPC/Topps 193
72/3 OPC 188
73/4 OPC/Topps 132
74/5 OPC/Topps 40, 219
75/6 OPC/Topps 150, 328
76/7 OPC/Topps 66, 207
76/7 OPC 394, T-Glossy 8
77/8 OPC/Topps 38, -Glossy 20
78/9 OPC/T. 4, 30, 64, OPC 331
78/9 OPC/Topps 65, 69
79/80 OPC/Topps 120
80/1 OPC/Topps 50, 165, 193
81/2 OPC 308,311-12, T. 36
82/3 O-Pee-Chee 257
83/4 O-Pee-Chee 257, 258, 272
84/5 OPC 168, Topps 121
92/3 OPC 191, -25Years 8
81/2 opcSticker 97, 109
82/3 opcSticker 114
83/4 opcSticker 3, 191
84/5 opcSticker 108
85/6 opcSticker 36 /167
80/1 opcSuperCard 20
92/3 Pinnacle 248
82/3 Post
90/1 ProSet 403
83/4 PuffySticker 10
84/5 7ElevenDisk
83/4 SouhaitsRen.KeyChain
77-9 Sportscstr 47-18, 53-1265
71/2 TheTorontoSun
92/3 Trends 173, 175, 199, -Aut
90/1 UpperDeck 504
95/6 Zellers
84/5 DET/Caesars
83/4 PHA
70/1 TOR
71/2 TOR
72/3 TOR
73/4 TOR
74/5 TOR
75/6 TOR
76/7 TOR
77/8 TOR
78/9 TOR
79/80 TOR
80/1 TOR
81/2 TOR

SITTLER, RYAN
94/5 ClassicImages 65
93/4 Donruss USA19
93/4 Pinnacle 499
91/2 UD 695, 'CzechWJC 82
93/4 UpperDeck 551

SITTLOW, CHRIS
93/4 Minn-Duluth

SIVERTSON, DARYN
84/5 KelownaWingsWHL 6
85/6 Arizona

SIVONEN, HEIKKI
66/7 Champion 173

SJEPELEV, SERGEI
82 SemicSticker 61

SJERVIN, GRANT
94/5 Richmond
95/6 Richmond

SJOBERG, LARS-ERIK
69/70 MästarSerien 42
89/90 SemicElitserien 251
90/1 SemicElitserien 161

SJOBERG, LARS-ERIK
72 Hellas 27
74 Hellas 34
70/1 Kuvajulkaisut 37
79/80 O-Pee-Chee 396
74/5 opcWHA 66
75/6 opcWHA 109
76/7 opcWHA30, 63
77/8 opcWHA 21
72 SemicSticker 45
74 SemicSticker 4
72/3 WilliamsFIN 57
73/4 WilliamsFIN 35
77/8 WPG
79/80 WPG

SJÖDIN, TOMMY
93/4 EASports 32
92/3 FleerUltra 323
93/4 FleerUltra 233
95 Globe 16
92/3 opcPremier 109

95 PaniniWorlds 139
92/3 Parkhurst 79, 224
92/3 Pinnacle 401
93/4 PowerPlay 65
93/4 Score 248
95 Semic 61
89/90 SemicElitserien 30
90/1 SemicElitserien 177
91/2 SemicElitserien 31
92/3 SemicElitserien 336, 344
93 SemicSticker 24
93/4 ToppsStadiumClub 106
92/3 UpperDeck 528
96 Wien 48, AS3

SJOGREN, THOMAS
94/5 ElitSet 46
90/1 ProCards 204
89/90 SemicElitserien 229
91/2 SemicElitserien 296
92/3 SemicElitserien 323
95/6 Sisu 265, 382, -Spotlight 5
96/7 Sisu 65, -Mighty 5
95/6 SisuLimited 52

SJOKVIST, NIKLAS
97/8 udSwedish 54

SJOLUND, ANDREAS
95/6 UDCollChoice 340

SJÖMAN, ARI
73/4 WilliamsFIN 320

SJOO, HASSE
89/90 SemicElitserien 107

SJÖROOS, RAUNO
80/1 Mallasjuoma 194

SJÖSTEDT, BO
71/2 WilliamsFIN 295

SKALDE, JARROD
93/4 ClassicProspects 192
95/6 Edgelce 15
93/4 Leaf 333
97/8 PinnacleBeAPlayer 198
93/4 PowerPlay 11
91/2 ProCards 411
92/3 ProSet 231
91/2 Score(CDN) 282, (U.S) 392
89/90 SketchMEM 91
89/90 SketchOHL 2, 193
90/1 SketchOHL 346
92/3 Topps 84
92/3 ToppsStadiumClub 189
91/2 UpperDeck 446
92/3 UpperDeck 91
93/4 UpperDeck 12
94/5 LasVegas
89/90 Oshawa 18
95/6 SaintJohn

SKARDA, RANDY
90/1 ProCards 81

SKELLETT, JASON
89/90 SketchOHL 91
90/1 SketchOHL 216

SKENE, DAN
92/3 BCJHL 234

SKILLGARD, JOHN
90/1 SketchWHL 223
90/1 Brandon 16

SKILLITER, WILLIE
91/2 SketchOHL 275
93/4 OwenSound

SKINNARI, VILLE
93/4 Sisu 285

SKINNER, ALFRED
24/5 Champs (C144)
24/5 MapleCrispettes (V130) 5
24/5 (V145-2) 27

SKINNER, JIM
82? JDMcCarthy
93/4 Parkie(56/7) 63
80/1 DET

SKINNER, LARRY
76/7 COL.R

SKLOPINTSEV, ANDREI
95 PaniniWorlds 31

SKOJDT, CHARLIE
81/2 Indianapolis 7

SKOGLUND, EMIL
92/3 SemicElitserien 162

SKOLD, JOAKIM
91/2 SemicElitserien 250

SKOOG, ROBERT
89/90 SemicElitserien 146
90/1 SemicElitserien 224
91/2 SemicElitserien 152
92/3 SemicElitserien 175

SKOPAC, TONY
94/5 ElitSet 230
92/3 SemicElitserien 89
95/6 udElite DS10

SKOPINTSEV, ANDREI
95/6 DEL 10
96 Wien 140

SKOREPA, ZDENEK
94/5 APS 214
95/6 Slapshot 120

SKORODENSKI, WARREN
85/6 O-Pee-Chee 255, 264
87/8 EDM
88/9 EDM/ActionMagazine 131
85/6 NovaScotia 11

SKORYNA, CHRIS
91/2 SketchOHL 36
93/4 Slapshot(Guelph) 18

SKOSKYREV, SERGEI
90/1 O-Pee-Chee 496

SKOULA, MARTIN
98 BowmanCHL 22, 158, A39

SKOV, ELMER
52/3 AnonymousOHL 10

SKOV, GLEN
45-64 BeeHives(DET)
51/2 Parkhurst 57
52/3 Parkhurst 63
53/4 Parkhurst 48
54/5 Parkhurst 40
93/4 Parkie(56/7) 23
54/5 Topps 16
57/8 Topps 30
58/9 Topps 3
59/60 Topps 12
76 DET

SKOVIRA, MIROSLAV
95/6 APS 237

SKRASTINS, KARLIS
95/6 Sisu 326, 383

SKRBEK, PAVEL
95/6 APS 348

SKRIKO, PETRI
90/1 Bowman 54
91/2 Bowman 364
86/7 Kraft Sports 68
86/7 O-Pee-Chee 252
87/8 O-Pee-Chee 255
88/9 OPC/Topps 137
89/90 OPC/Topps 33, D
90/1 OPC/Topps 316
91/2 OPC/Topps 30
87/8 opcStars 40
86/7 opcSticker103 /232
87/8 opcSticker 192
88/9 opcSticker 64
89/90 opcSticker 70
90/1 Panini(VAN) 22
87/8 PaniniSticker 347
88/9 PaniniSticker 140
89/90 PaniniSticker 147
90/1 PaniniSticker 298
90/1 ProSet 306
91/2 ProSet 8, 517
90/1 Score 154
91/2 Score(CDN) 188
91/2 Score(U.S) 188, 72T
89 SemicSticker 44
91 SemicSticker 204
92 SemicSticker 12
93 SemicSticker 79
91/2 ToppsStadiumClub 315
90/1 UpperDeck 147, 302
91/2 UpperDeck 334
84/5 VAN
85/6 VAN
86/7 VAN
87/8 VAN/Shell
88/9 VAN/Mohawk
89/90 VAN

SKRUDLAND, BRIAN
90/1 Bowman 49
91/2 Bowman 331
93/4 Donruss 124
94/5 Donruss 130
96/7 Donruss 118
93/4 EASports 51
94/5 Flair 68
92/3 FleerUltra 111
93/4 FleerUltra 332
94/5 FleerUltra 85
95/6 FleerUltra 63
86/7 Kraft Sports 38
93/4 Kraft-Captain
96/7 Kraft'Disk
93/4 Leaf 325
94/5 Leaf 177
96/7 Leaf 69
87/8 O-Pee-Chee 235
90/1 OPC/Topps 270
91/2 OPC/Topps 298, 349
92/3 O-Pee-Chee 45
98/9 Pacific 182
97/8 PacificCrown 295
97/8 PacificParamount 120
90/1 Panini(MTL) 22
87/8 PaniniSticker 67
90/1 PaniniSticker 55
91/2 PaniniSticker 194
94/5 PaniniSticker 64
95/6 PaniniSticker 72
91/2 Parkhurst 314
92/3 Parkhurst 266
93/4 Parkhurst 75
95/6 Parkhurst 358
94/5 ParkieSE 63
91/2 Pinnacle 160
92/3 Pinnacle 347
93/4 Pinnacle 188, CA9, -Exp. 5
94/5 Pinnacle 21
96/7 PinnacleBeAPlayer 205
95/6 Playoff 43
94/5 POG 110
93/4 PowerPlay 100
93/4 Premier 26, 508
94/5 Premier 265
90/1 ProSet 159
91/2 ProSet 127, 306
90/1 Score 238
91/2 Score(CDN) 514, (U.S) 294
92/3 Score 136
93/4 Score 258, 505
94/5 Score 53
95/6 Score 74
96/7 Score 133
94/5 Select 126
96/7 SP 64
95/6 Summit 136
96/7 Summit 39
92/3 Topps 408
91/2 ToppsStadiumClub 129
92/3 ToppsStadiumClub 114
93/4 T.StadiumClub 177, 349
94/5 ToppsStadiumClub 36
90/1 UpperDeck 93
91/2 UpperDeck 422
93/4 UpperDeck 96, SP-59
94/5 UpperDeck 331
95/6 UpperDeck 276
96/7 UDBlackDiamond 64
94/5 FLA/HealthPlan
96/7 FLA/WinnDixie
85/6 MTL
85/6? MTL/ProvigoPlacemats
85/6 MTL/ProvigoStickers
86/7 MTL
87/8 MTL
87/8 MTL/Stickers 34, 36
88/9 MTL
89/90 MTL
89/90 MTL/Figurine
89/90 MTL/Kraft
90/1 MTL
91/2 MTL
92/3 MTL
97/8 NYR/GameSheet 27
83/4 NovaScotia 11
81/2 Saskatoon 10

SKRYPEC, GERRY
90/1 SketchOHL 94
91/2 SketchOHL 296
93/4 Slapshot(Detroit) 19
93/4 Slapshot(NiagaraFalls) 4
92/3 Ottawa67s

SKUDRA, PETER
98/9 Pacific 358
97/8 PacificRevolution 114
97/8 SPAuthentic 130
98/9 UDChoice 170
94/5 Greensboro

SKUTA, VITEZSLAV
94/5 APS 122
95/6 APS 341

SKVORSTSOV, ALEXANDER
83/4 SovietStars

SLABY, VACLAV
95/6 APS 229

SLANEY, JOHN
94/5 Donruss 298
96/7 FleerNHLPicks 154
94/5 Leaf 96
93/4 Parkhurst 494
94/5 Parkhurst 257
95/6 Parkhurst 47
94/5 Pinnacle 214
96/7 PinnacleBeAPlayer 100
94/5 Premier 402
93/4 Score 636
94/5 Score 262
89/90 SketchOHL 185
90/1 SketchOHL 47
91/2 SketchOHL 1
94/5 ToppsStadiumClub 39, 113
90/1 UpperDeck 360, 457
91/2 UD'CzechWJC 54
94/5 UpperDeck 39
96/7 UpperDeck 81
97/8 PHO
91/2 Cornwall 24
93/4 PortlandPirates

SLANINA, PETER
82 SemicSticker 99
89 SemicSticker 183
91 SemicSticker 109

SLANSKY, VACLAV
93/4 RedDeer

SLAPKE, PETER
74 Hellas 120
70/1 Kuvajulkaisut 99
79 PaniniSticker 252

SLATER, CHRIS
93/4 Mich.State

SLATER, KEN
83/4 Kingston 27
84/5 Kingston 4

SLATER, PETER
72/3 LosAngelesSharks

SLAVIK, MICHAL
94/5 APS 11
95/6 APS 111

SLAVIK, ROBERT
94/5 APS 95
95/6 APS 54

SLAWSON, RANDY
82/3 Brandon 17

SLEAVER, JOHN
52/3 AnonymousOHL 177

SLEGR, JIRI
94/5 APS 209
93/4 Donruss 358
94/5 Donruss 294
92/3 FleerUltra 430
93/4 FleerUltra 136
94/5 FleerUltra 385
95 Globe 151
93/4 Leaf 31
94/5 Leaf 520
92/3 opcPremier 54
98/9 Pacific 71
98/9 PacificParamount 196
96/7 PaniniSticker 263
92/3 Parkhurst 196
93/4 Parkhurst 214
94/5 Parkhurst V27
95/6 Parkhurst 344
94/5 ParkieSE 189
93/4 Pinnacle 417
95/6 POG 110
93/4 PowerPlay 256
93/4 Premier 164
94/5 Premier 543
93/4 Score 378
94 Semic 182, 343
91 SemicSticker 106
92 SemicSticker 131
91/2 StarPics 29
93/4 ToppsStadiumClub 42
91/2 UpperDeck 18
92/3 UpperDeck 515, ER9
93/4 UpperDeck 18, SP-166
94/5 UpperDeck 95
95/6 UpperDeck 42
94/5 UDBAP R123, -Aut. 119
95/6 UDCollChoice 144
96 Wien 113
92/3 VAN/RoadTrip
93/4 VAN/Coins
94/5 VAN
95/6 VAN/Building 11

SLEIGHER, LOUIS
83/4 O-Pee-Chee 301
84/5 O-Pee-Chee 290
83/4 Vachon 74
84/5 BOS
82/3 QUE
83/4 QUE

SLEMKO, RYAN
90/1 SketchWHL 322

SLEWIDGE, LYNDON
87/8 SSMarie 6

SLIZ, GREG
84/5 Ottawa67s

SLIZEK, LADISLAV
94/5 APS 268

SLOAN, TOD
45-64 BeeHives(CHI)
64-67 BeeHives(TOR)
48-52 Exhibits
51/2 Parkhurst 87
52/3 Parkhurst 48
53/4 Parkhurst 5
54/5 Parkhurst 30, 98
55/6 Parkhurst 10, 77
57/8 Parkhurst(TOR) 5
93/4 Parkie(56/7) 112, 144, 174
45-54 QuakerOats
60/1 ShirriffCoin 64
58/9 Topps 42
59/60 Topps 13
60/1 Topps 51
54-67 TorontoStar V7
56-66 TorontoStar 58/9
56-66 TorontoStar 5 Sep-60
91/2 Ultimate(O6) 42, -Aut 42

SLOANE, BLAKE
93/4 Donruss USA20
93/4 Pinnacle 486

SLOBODIAN, PETE
34-43 BeeHives(NYA)

SLOTA, KEVIN
95/6 Slapshot 176

SLOTTE, ULF
66/7 Champion 213

SLOWAKIEWICZ, ANDRZEJ
74 Hellas 20
79 PaniniSticker 122
73/4 WilliamsFIN 98

SLOWAKIEWICZ, JOSEF
74 Hellas 87
73/4 WilliamsFIN 99

SLOWAKIEWICZ, TADEUSZ
79 PaniniSticker 119

SLOWINSKI, ED
45-64 BeeHives(NYR)
51/2 Parkhurst 102
52/3 Parkhurst 19

SLUKYNSKY, TIM
91/2 AirCanadaSJHL C27
92/3 MPSPhotoSJHL 166

SLY, DARRYL
70/1 EddieSargent 221
70/1 Esso Stamp
70/1 OPC/Topps 115
68/9 TOR
70/1 VAN/RoyalBank

SLY, RYAN
95/6 Slapshot 386
96/7 Sudbury 22

SMAIL, DOUG
90/1 Bowman 134
91/2 Bowman 118
92/3 Bowman 362
82/3 O-Pee-Chee 388
83/4 O-Pee-Chee 390
84/5 O-Pee-Chee 346
85/6 O-Pee-Chee 175
86/7 O-Pee-Chee 256, 257
87/8 OPC/Topps 181
88/9 O-Pee-Chee 251
89/90 O-Pee-Chee 294
90/1 OPC/Topps 268
91/2 OPC/Topps 334
92/3 O-Pee-Chee 196
83/4 opcSticker 287
85/6 opcSticker 255/135
87/8 opcSticker 254/145
88/9 opcSticker 137/8
89/90 opcSticker 141/260
90/1 Panini(WPG) 21
87/8 PaniniSticker 367
88/9 PaniniSticker 158
89/90 PaniniSticker 171
90/1 PaniniSticker 308
91/2 PaniniSticker 111
80/1 Pepsi Cap
92/3 Pinnacle 377
90/1 ProSet 462
91/2 ProSet 117, 466
90/1 Score 196
91/2 Score(CDN) 12, 592
91/2 Score(U.S) 12, 69T
92/3 Score 197
92/3 Topps 459
91/2 ToppsStadiumClub 255
92/3 ToppsStadiumClub 334
90/1 UpperDeck 105
92/3 UpperDeck 124
83/4 Vachon 136
92/3 OTT
91/2 QUE/PetroCanada
80/1 WPG
81/2 WPG
82/3 WPG
83/4 WPG
84/5 WPG/Police
85/6 WPG
85/6 WPG/Police
86/7 WPG
87/8 WPG
88/9 WPG/Police
89/90 WPG/Safeway

SMAILL, WALTER
91 C55 Reprint 27
1911-12 Imperial (C55) 27
1912-13 Imperial (C57) 22
1910-11 Imperial Post 27

SMALL, BRIAN
83/4 Belleville 10
81/2 Ottawa67s

SMALL, TODD
91/2 AirCanadaSJHL A30

SMANIOTTO, LOUIS
79 PaniniSticker 384

SMART, CADRIN
91/2 SketchWHL 344

SMART, JASON
91/2 ProCards 305
89/90 Saskatoon 20
92/3 Cleveland 20
95/6 Toledo

SMART, KELLY
97/8 Bowman 106
94/5 Slapshot(MEM) 35

SMAZAL, HEIKO
95/6 DEL 292
96/7 DEL 319

SMAZAL, MIKE
94/5 DEL 252

SMEATON, COOPER
83&87 HallOfFame 42
83 HHOF Postcard (C)

SMEDSO, DALE
75/6 Cincinnati

SMEETS, PIERRE
79 PaniniSticker 339

SMEHLIK, RICHARD
94/5 APS 128
92/3 Classic 40
93/4 Donruss 40
94/5 Donruss 136
95/6 Donruss 76
94/5 Flair 22
94/5 Fleer 27
92/3 FleerUltra 262, -Import 22
93/4 FleerUltra 200
94/5 FleerUltra 28
95 Globe 147
93/4 Leaf 188
94/5 Leaf 306
95/6 Leaf 276
92/3 opcPremier 90
98/9 Pacific 42
97/8 PacificRegime 23
93/4 PaniniSticker 110
94/5 PaniniSticker 98
95/6 PaniniSticker 22
92/3 Parkhurst 14
93/4 Parkhurst 20
94/5 Parkhurst 28
92/3 Pinnacle 393
94/5 Pinnacle 17
95/6 Pinnacle 187
97/8 PinnacleBeAPlayer 74
94/5 POG 52
93/4 PowerPlay 33
93/4 Premier 521
94/5 Premier 93
93/4 Score 249
94/5 Score 129
94 Semic 168
92 SemicSticker 129
95/6 Topps 168
93/4 ToppsStadiumClub 107
92/3 UpperDeck 564, ER1
93/4 UpperDeck 169
94/5 UpperDeck 181
96/7 UpperDeck"Ice" 6
92/3 BUF/BlueShield
92/3 BUF/Jubillee

SMELLE, CARL
52/3 LavalDairy 81
52/3 StLawrence 34

SMELLE, TOM
52/3 LavalDairy 84
52/3 StLawrence 21

SMERICAK, MARIAN
94 Semic 193
96 Wien 223

SMETAK, MARTIN
94/5 APS 9
95/6 APS 339

SMICEK, JIRI
94/5 DEL 349

SMID, KAREL
94/5 APS 142
95/6 APS 246

SMILIE, ROB
92/3 BCJHL 176

SMILLIE, STEVE
91/2 SketchOHL 367

SMIRNOV, ALEXANDER
95 Globe170
92/3 Jyvas-Hyva 179
93/4 Jyvas-Hyva 326
90/1 O-Pee-Chee 499
91/2 O-Pee-Chee 60R
94 Semic 139
95 Semic 125
89 SemicSticker 83
93/4 Sisu 39
94/5 Sisu 77
96 Wien 139

SMITH, ADAM
91/2 AvantGardeBCJ 32
93/4 UpperDeck E1
96/7 Binghampton

92/3 Tacoma
93/4 Tacoma

SMITH, AL
70/1 EddieSargent 161
71/2 EddieSargent 61
70/1 Esso Stamp
72/3 Letraset 19
70/1 OPC/Topps 87
71/2 OPC/Topps 27
76/7 OPC/Topps 152
79/80 O-Pee-Chee 300
80/1 OPC/Topps 252
73/4 opc-Posters 1
77/8 opcWHA 49
73/4 QuakerOats 2
71/2 TheTorontoSun
72/3 NewEngland
69/70 TOR

SMITH, ALEX
25-27 Anonymous 22
33/4 Anonymous (V129) 47
33/4 CndGum (V252)
36-39 DiamondMatch (1)

SMITH, ALF
83&87 HallOfFame 194
83 HHOF Postcard (J)

SMITH, BARRY
87/8 BUF/WonderBread
88/9 BUF/WonderBread
79/80 COL.R

SMITH, BARRY
94/5 Erie 3
93/4 Knoxville
94/5 Knoxville 2

SMITH, BILLY
93/4 ActionPacked 3
77/8 Coke Mini
88/9 Esso Sticker
93/4 HockeyWit 95
74/5 Loblaws
82/3 McDonalds 4, 16
73/4 OPC 142, Topps 162
74/5 OPC/Topps 82
75/6 OPC 372
76/7 OPC/Topps 46
77/8 OPC/Topps 229
78/9 OPC/Topps 62
79/80 OPC/Topps 242
80/1 OPC/Topps 5, 60, 264
81/2 OPC 207, 209, Topps(E) 93
82/3 O-Pee-Chee 206, 211
83/4 O-Pee-Chee 17
84/5 OPC 135, Topps 101
86/7 O-Pee-Chee 228
88/9 OPC/Topps 17
81/2 opcSticker 161
82/3 opcSticker 60, 61, 251
83/4 opcSticker 16, 86, 316
84/5 opcSticker 91
85/6 opcSticker 76/209
86/7 opcSticker 213/85
87/8 PaniniSticker 89
82/3 Post
83/4 PuffySticker 19
83/4 SouhaitsRen.KeyChain
97/8 SPAuthentic M2, T2
96/7 FLA/WinnDixie
97/8 FLA/WinnDixie
79/80 NYI
83/4 NYI
83/4 NYI/Islander 23, 36
84/5 NYI 27, 34
93/4 NYI/Chemical

SMITH, BILL
91/2 SketchOHL 96

SMITH, BOBBY
90/1 Bowman 51
91/2 Bowman 117
92/3 Bowman 54
92/3 FleerUltra 97
86/7 Kraft Sports 39
89/90 Kraft 26
90/1 Kraft 53
91/2 Kraft 82
79/80 OPC/Topps 206
80/1 OPC/Topps 17
81/2 OPC 157, 170, 174
82/3 O-Pee-Chee 175, 176
83/4 O-Pee-Chee 181
84/5 O-Pee-Chee 273
85/6 O-Pee-Chee 181, Topps 83
86/7 OPC/Topps 188
87/8 OPC/Topps 48
88/9 OPC/Topps 88, D
89/90 OPC/Topps 188, OPC 396
90/1 OPC/Topps 287
91/2 OPC/Topps 398
92/3 O-Pee-Chee 396
90/1 opcPremier 109
81/2 opcSticker 88
82/3 opcSticker 188
83/4 opcSticker 116
84/5 opcSticker 151-52
85/6 opcSticker 132/252
86/7 opcSticker 13
87/8 opcSticker 10
88/9 opcSticker 46
89/90 opcSticker 47
87/8 PaniniSticker 62
88/9 PaniniSticker 261
89/90 PaniniSticker 236
90/1 PaniniSticker 52
91/2 PaniniSticker 113
92/3 PaniniSticker 96
91/2 Parkhurst 83, 217
91/2 Pinnacle 210
92/3 Pinnacle 142
81/2 PostPopUp 5
90/1 ProSet 160, 463
91/2 ProSet 115, 289
92/3 ProSet 81, 259
91/2 PSPlatinum PC13
83/4 PuffySticker 14
90/1 Score 61, 75T
91/2 Score(CDN) 32, (U.S) 32
92/3 Score 205, 446
83/4 SouhaitsRen.KeyChain
81/2 Topps 37, 55, (W) 131
92/3 Topps 388
91/2 ToppsStadiumClub 25
92/3 ToppsStadiumClub 427
90/1 UpperDeck 72, 406
91/2 UpperDeck 293
83/4 Vachon 56
78/9 MIN/Cloverleaf 5
79/80 MIN
80/1 MIN
81/2 MIN
82/3 MIN
83/4 MTL
84/5 MTL
85/6 MTL
85/6 MTL/Pennant
85/6 MTL/PepsiPlacemat
85/6? MTL/ProvigoPlacemat
85/6 MTL/ProvigoSticker
86/7 MTL
87/8 MTL
87/8 MTL/Kodak
87/8 MTL/Stickers 26, 28, 30, 32
87/8 MTL/Stickers 41, 86
88/9 MTL
89/90 MTL
89/90 MTL/Figurine
89/90 MTL/Kraft

SMITH, BRAD
81/2 O-Pee-Chee 103
87/8 PaniniSticker 335
80/1 Pepsi Cap
90/1 SketchOHL 200
90/1 SketchWHL 314
91/2 SketchWHL 27
80/1 CGY
86/7 TOR
87/8 TOR
87/8 TOR/P.L.A.Y. 22
95/6 Adirondack
94/5 Dayton 17
89/90 Portland
93/4 Portland
89/90 Windsor

SMITH, BREBT
89/90 ProCards(AHL) 158
89/90 Halifax

SMITH, BRIAN STUART
60/1 Parkhurst 27

SMITH, BRIAN
68/9 Bauer

SMITH, CHRIS
93/4 Mich.State
83/4 Moncton 2
80/1 Oshawa 20
81/2 Oshawa 2

SMITH, CLINT (SNUFFY)
34-43 BeeHives(NYR)
95/6 HHOFLegends 59
39/40 OPC (V301-1) 35
91/2 ProSet-HOF 6

SMITH, DALLAS
70/1 EddieSargent 16
71/2 EddieSargent 11
72/3 EddieSargent 19
70/1 Esso Stamp
72/3 Letraset 5
74/5 Loblaws
68/9 O-Pee-Chee 136
69/70 OPC/Topps 25
70/1 OPC 137
71/2 OPC/Topps 170
72/3 OPC 21, Topps 45
73/4 OPC 167, Topps 42
74/5 OPC/Topps 146
75/6 OPC/Topps 118
76/7 OPC/Topps 105
60/1 ShirriffCoin 116
61/2 ShirriffCoin 2
68/9 ShirriffCoin BOS13
71/2 TheTorontoSun
60/1 Topps-Stamp
61/2 Topps 4
62/3 Topps 9
66/7 Topps 101, -USATest 3
67/8 Topps 41
70/1 BOS
71/2 BOS

SMITH, DAMIEN
94 Semic 319

SMITH, DARIN
88/9 ProCards(Peoria)
89/90 ProCards(IHL) 9
90/1 ProCards 591
91/2 ProCards 248
90/1 KansasCity 8
85/6 London 12
93/4 Seattle

SMITH, DAVE
94/5 Binghampton

SMITH, DENIS
52/3 BasDuFleuve 6
52/3 LavalDairy 12
52/3 StLawrence 42

SMITH, D.J.
97/8 Bowman 37
95/6 Classic 36, 98
95/6 ClassicFiveSport 155
97/8 Donruss 206
97/8 DonrussCanadianIce 142
97/8 Limited 37
94/5 Slapshot(Windsor) 7
95/6 Slapshot 410
97/8 UpperDeck 194

SMITH, DENNIS
88/9 ProCards(Adirondack)
89/90 ProCards(AHL) 96
91/2 ProCards 54
81/2 Kingston 21
82/3 Kingston 2
83/4 Kingston 2

SMITH, DEREK
78/9 OPC/Topps 222
79/80 OPC/Topps 89
80/1 OPC/Topps 199
81/2 OPC 25, Topps(E) 79
82/3 O-Pee-Chee 95
81/2 opcSticker 59
82/3 Post

SMITH, DERRICK
91/2 Bowman 245
95/6 EdgeIce 142
90/1 O-Pee-Chee 463
92/3 O-Pee-Chee 363
91/2 OPC/Topps 486
87/8 PaniniSticker 135
89/90 PaniniSticker 304
91/2 PaniniSticker 232
90/1 ProSet 503
91/2 ProSet 174
91/2 Score(CDN) 444
80/1 BUF/Wendt
86/7 PHA
89/90 PHA
90/1 PHA

SMITH, DESMOND
34-43 BeeHives(MTL.M)
35-40 CrownBrand 124
37/8 OPC (V304E) 148
39/40 OPC (V301-1) 77

SMITH, DON
91 C55 Reprint 19
1911-12 Imperial (C55) 19
1912-13 Imperial (C57) 12
1910-11 Imperial Post 19

SMITH, DOUG
82/3 O-Pee-Chee 160
84/5 O-Pee-Chee 91
86/7 O-Pee-Chee 202
90/1 OPC/Topps 326
86/7 BUF
87/8 BUF/BlueShield
87/8 BUF/WonderBread
88/9 EDM/ActionMagazine 69
84/5 L.A/Smokeys
89/90 VAN
91/2 FerrisState

SMITH, ED
84/5 Sudbury 16

SMITH, FIONA
97/8 UDCollChoice 293

SMITH, FLOYD
45-64 BeeHives(DET)
64-67 BeeHives(DETx3)
62 CeramicTiles
64/5 CokeCap DET-17
65/6 CocaCola
70/1 DadsCookies
70/1 EddieSargent 30
70/1 Esso Stamp
68/9 OPC/Topps 130
69/70 OPC/Topps 49
70/1 OPC 140
71/2 OPC/Topps 158
74/5 OPC/Topps 176
63/4 Parkhurst 57
94/5 Parkie(64/5) 45
95/6 Parkie(66/7) 52
68/9 Post Marble
68/9 ShirriffCoin TOR12
64/5 TheTorontoStar
64/5 Topps 42
65/6 Topps 109
66/7 Topps 106
67/8 Topps 52
63/4 York 42
68/9 TOR
69/70 TOR
79/80 TOR

SMITH, FRANK D.
83&87 HallOfFame 103
83 HHOF Postcard (G)

SMITH, GALRIN
89/90 SketchOHL 65
90/1 SketchOHL 217
91/2 SketchOHL 100
93/4 Roanoke
94/5 Wheeling 11

SMITH, GARY
70/1 Colgate Stamp 90
70/1 EddieSargent 129
71/2 EddieSargent 43
72/3 EddieSargent 61
70/1 Esso Stamp
74/5 LiptonSoup 15
74/5 Loblaws
68/9 O-Pee-Chee 176
69/70 OPC/Topps 78
70/1 OPC/Topps 69
71/2 T. 124, OPC/T-Booklet 22
72/3 OPC 117, 155, Topps 114
73/4 OPC/Topps 126
74/5 OPC/Topps 22
75/6 OPC/Topps 115
76/7 OPC 317
77/8 OPC/Topps 184
79/80 OPC/Topps 103
72 SemicSticker 171
68/9 ShirriffCoin OAK6
71/2 TheTorontoSun
73/4 VAN/RoyalBank
74/5 VAN/RoyalBank
75/6 VAN/RoyalBank
79/80 WPG

SMITH, GEOFF
90/1 Bowman 192
91/2 Bowman 112
92/3 Bowman 95
93/4 Donruss 112, 435
93/4 Leaf 302
94/5 Leaf 366
92/3 O-Pee-Chee 338
90/1 OPC/Topps 33
91/2 OPC/Topps 301
90/1 Panini(EDM) 21
94/5 Parkhurst 82
91/2 Pinnacle 283
92/3 Pinnacle 192
93/4 Pinnacle 416
94/5 Pinnacle 354
90/1 ProSet 446
91/2 ProSet 384
90/1 Score 326, 373
91/2 Score(CDN) 87, (U.S) 87
92/3 Score 192
93/4 Score 306, 646
92/3 Topps 275
91/2 ToppsStadiumClub 42
92/3 ToppsStadiumClub 84
90/1 UpperDeck 326
94/5 UpperDeck 109
90/1 EDM/McGavins
91/2 EDM/IGA
92/3 EDM
92/3 EDM/IGA 21
93/4 EDM 20NOV93

SMITH, GORD
76/7 OPC 303
77/8 OPC 387
78/9 O-Pee-Chee 347
79/80 O-Pee-Chee 285
79/80 WPG
74/5 WSH
78/9 WSH
82/3 Brandon 18

SMITH, GREG
77/8 OPC 269
78/9 O-Pee-Chee 303
79/80 OPC/Topps 11
81/2 OPC 168, Topps(W) 112
82/3 O-Pee-Chee 96
83/4 O-Pee-Chee 130
84/5 O-Pee-Chee 64
83/4 opcSticker 140
87/8 PaniniSticker 172
82/3 Post
83/4 SouhaitsRen.KeyChain
84/5 DET/Caesars
85/6 DET/Caesars
78/9 MIN/Cloverleaf 3
79/80 MIN
80/1 MIN
86/7 WSH/Kodak
86/7 WSH/Police
87/8 WSH
87/8 WSH/Kodak

SMITH, HOOLEY
see Reginald J. Smith

SMITH, JAMES STEVE
90/1 Bowman 200
91/2 Bowman 106, 417
92/3 Bowman 24
93/4 Donruss 68
94/5 Donruss 183
95/6 Donruss 179
93/4 EASports 26
94/5 Flair 37
94/5 Fleer 46
92/3 FleerUltra 42
93/4 FleerUltra 231
94/5 FleerUltra 45
95 Globe 78
89/90 Kraft 17
91/2 Kraft 85
93/4 Leaf 95
94/5 Leaf 257
95/6 Leaf 194
88/9 O-Pee-Chee 252
89/90 O-Pee-Chee 228
90/1 OPC/Topps 368
91/2 OPC/Topps 21
92/3 O-Pee-Chee 108
91/2 opcPremier 136
88/9 opcSticker 225/99
89/90 opcSticker 223/82
97/8 PacificDynag-BestKept 22
90/1 Panini(EDM) 22
87/8 PaniniSticker 259
88/9 PaniniSticker 55
89/90 PaniniSticker 83
90/1 PaniniSticker 226
91/2 PaniniSticker 121
92/3 PaniniSticker 12
93/4 PaniniSticker 154
91/2 Parkhurst 31
92/3 Parkhurst 32, 444
93/4 Parkhurst 310
95/6 Parkhurst 43
91/2 Pinnacle 18
92/3 Pinnacle 57
93/4 Pinnacle 70
94/5 Pinnacle 211
95/6 Pinnacle 191
96/7 Pinnacle 81
94/5 POG 74
93/4 PowerPlay 55
93/4 Premier 39
94/5 Premier 133
90/1 ProSet 96, 704
91/2 ProSet 73, 284, 370
92/3 ProSet 37
91/2 PSPlatinum 27
90/1 Score 129
91/2 Score(CDN) 11, 623
91/2 Score(U.S) 11, 73T
92/3 Score 48
93/4 Score 192
94/5 Score 121
95/6 Score 27
94 Semic 85
95 Semic 81
92 SemicSticker 79
91 TeamCanada
92/3 Topps 315
95/6 Topps 205
94/5 ToppsFinest-Ring 12
91/2 ToppsStadiumClub 230
92/3 ToppsStadiumClub 383
93/4 ToppsStadiumClub 218
90/1 UpperDeck 148
91/2 UpperDeck 350
94/5 UDBeAPlayer R62
95/6 UDBeAPlayer 123
91/2 CHI/Coke
93/4 CHI/Coke
85/6 EDM/RedRooster
86/7 EDM
86/7 EDM/RedRooster
87/8 EDM
88/9 EDM
88/9 EDM/ActionMagazine 121
90/1 EDM/McGavins
83/4 Moncton 10
84/5 NovaScotia 11

SMITH, JARETT
97/8 Bowman 122, BB15

SMITH, JASON
92/3 Classic 10
92/3 ClassicFourSport 159, -Aut.
93/4 ClassicProspects 135
93/4 Donruss 182
94/5 Donruss 256
95/6 Donruss 279
93/4 FleeUltra 363, -Wave 17
94/5 FleerUltra 322
93/4 Leaf 389
94/5 Leaf 245
98/9 Pacific 421
97/8 PacificRegime 196
93/4 Parkhurst 379
94/5 Parkhurst 130
93/4 Pinnacle 433
94/5 Pinnacle 417
97/8 PinnacleBeAPlayer 191
93/4 PowerPlay 381
94/5 Premier 344
93/4 Score 613
90/1 SketchWHL 62
91/2 SketchWHL 226
94/5 ToppsStadiumClub 83
93/4 UpperDeck 252
96/7 N.J/Sharp

SMITH, JASON
91/2 SketchWHL 309
94/5 Erie

SMITH, JEFF
90/1 SketchOHL 218
91/2 SketchOHL 290
83/4 Springfield 17

SMITH, JIM
87/8 Sudbury 9
88/9 Sudbury 9
92/3 Wheeling 20

SMITH, JOE
82/3 NorthBay

SMITH, JOHN
51/2 LavalDairy 44

SMITH, JON
88/9 ProCards(Binghampton)
89/90 ProCards(AHL) 296

SMITH, KEN
45-64 BeeHives(BOS)

SMITH, MARK
98 BowmanCHL 70

SMITH, MARTIN
91/2 AirCanadaSJHL 4, B29
92/3 Richmond

SMITH, MATT
91/2 SketchWHL 63

SMITH, MICHAEL
93/4 Classic 82
93/4 ClassicProspects 244
91/2 LakeSuperior
93/4 Roanoke
94/5 Roanoke
95/6 Roanoke

SMITH, NEIL
92/3 WestMich.

SMITH, NORMAN
34-43 BeeHives(DET)
36/7 WWGum (V356) 74

SMITH, RANDY
90/1 CanadaNats
91/2 CanadaNats
92 CanadaWinterOlympics 193
88/9 ProCards(Kalamazoo)
89/90 ProCards(IHL) 87
92/3 Score-CndOlympic 4
93/4 LasVegas
83/4 Saskatoon 12

SMITH, REGINALD (HOOLEY)
25-27 Anonymous 21
34-43 BeeHives(MTL.M)
35/6 Champion
24/5 Champs (C144)
25 Dominion 69
83&87 HallOfFame 43
83 HHOF Postcard (C)
95/6 HHOFLegends 62
27-32 LaPresse 29/30
34/5 OPC (V304B) 69
35/6 OPC (V304C) 76
36/7 OPC (V304D) 132
39/40 OPC (V301-1) 17
34/5 SweetCaporal
24/5 (V145-2) 5
25 Willards 47
33/4 WWGum(V357) 31,-Prem
36/7 WWGum (V356) 20

SMITH, RICK
70/1 EddieSargent 11
71/2 EddieSargent 5
70/1 Esso Stamp
70/1 OPC 135
71/2 OPC/Topps 174
72/3 OPC 23, 284, Topps 34
76/7 OPC 269
77/8 OPC/Topps 104
78/9 OPC/Topps 164
79/80 OPC/Topps 59
75/6 opcWHA 41
71/2 TheTorontoSun
70/1 BOS
71/2 BOS
80/1 WSH
74/5 Minnesota
83/4 Saskatoon 21

SMITH, RON
91/2 ProCards 212
96/7 Cincinnati

SMITH, RUSSELL
96/7 Rimouski (2)

SMITH, RYAN
91/2 AirCanadaSJHL C11
90/1 SketchWHL 131
91/2 SketchWHL 205
92/3 Brandon 21
93/4 Lethbridge

SMITH, SANDY
90/1 ProCards 373
91/2 ProCards 299
92/3 Cleveland 19

SMITH, SID
45-64 BeeHives(TOR)
48-52 Exhibits
51/2 Parkhurst 84
52/3 Parkhurst 45
53/4 Parkhurst 2
54/5 Parkhurst 22
55/6 Parkhurst 2, 75
57/8 Parkhurst(TOR) 10
93/4 Parkie (56/7) 109
45-54 QuakerOats
56-66 TorontoStar '57
91/2 Ultimate06 43, -Aut 43

SMITH, STEVE
see James Steve Smith

SMITH, STEVE
88/9 ProCards(Rochester)
89/90 ProCards(AHL) 272
90/1 ProCards 287
83/4 Springfield 22
80/1 SSMarie
81/2 SSMarie
82/3 SSMarie

SMITH, STEVE
89/90 SketchMEM 37
90/1 SketchOHL 240
89/90 Kitchener 28
90/1 Kitchener 8

SMITH, STEVE
90/1 SketchOHL 199
91/2 SketchOHL 187

SMITH, STEVE
88/9 SaltLake 7

SMITH, STUART
82/3 HFD/JuniorWhalers

SMITH, TOD
82/3 Oshawa 6

SMITH, TOM
83&87 HallOfFame 237
83 HHOF Postcard (H)
85/6 Arizona

SMITH, TRAVIS
91/2 AirCanadaSJHL C48
92/3 MPSPhotoSJHL 152

SMITH, TREVOR
87/8 Kingston 29

SMITH, TROY
95/6 Slapshot 60

SMITH, VERN
88/9 ProCards(Springfield)
89/90 ProCards(AHL) 293
90/1 ProCards 533
91/2 ProCards 387
84/5 Springfield 7

SMITH, WAYNE
85/6 Minn-Duluth 6

SMITH, WYATT
95/6 DonrussElite-WorldJrs 41
94/5 Select 156

SMOLEJ, ROMAN
79 PaniniSticker 397

SMOLIK, JAROSLAV
95/6 APS 218, 343

SMOLINSKI, BRYAN
93/4 Donruss 30
94/5 Donruss 21
95/6 Donruss 138, 327
96/7 Donruss 99
96/7 Flair 58
94/5 Fleer 17
96/7 Fleer 89
95/6 FleerMetal 120
96/7 FleerNHLPicks 132
93/4 FleerUltra 232, -AllRookie 8
94/5 FleerUltra 16, -AllRookie 9
95/6 FleerUltra 14, 294
95/6 Hoyle'EAST 7 (Clubs)
93/4 Leaf 204
94/5 Leaf 130, -GoldL.Rook 14
95/6 Leaf 239
94/5 LeafLimited 57
97/8 Omega 143
98/9 Pacific 289
97/8 PacificCrown 196
97/8 PacificCrownRoyale 82
97/8 PcfcDynagon! 76,-Tand 68
97/8 PacificInvincible 84
97/8 PacificParamount 112
98/9 PacificParamount 149
94/5 PaniniSticker A
95/6 PaniniSticker 60
96/7 PaniniSticker 62
97/8 PaniniSticker 81
92/3 Parkhurst 481
93/4 Parkhurst 259
94/5 Parkhurst 12, 276
95/6 Parkhurst 168
94/5 Parkie seV26
93/4 Pinnacle 217
94/5 Pinnacle 13, 470
96/7 Pinnacle 125
96/7 PinnacleBeAPlayer 132,
97/8 PinnacleCertified 108
97/8 PinnacleInside 178
95/6 Playoff 188
96/7 Playoff 389
94/5 POG 38
95/6 POG 213
93/4 PowerPlay 291, -Rookie 14
93/4 Premier 466
94/5 Premier 196, 479
94/5 Premier-Finest(OPC) 2
95/6 ProMagnet 91
93/4 Score 472
95/6 Score 43
96/7 Score 88
97/8 Score 241
94/5 Select 132
95/6 SkyBoxEmotion 142
95/6 SkyBoxImpact 135
96/7 SkyBoxImpact 104
94/5 SP 11
95/6 Summit 156
98/9 Topps 38
93/4 ToppsStadiumClub 274
94/5 ToppsStadiumClub 103
95/6 ToppsStadiumClub 210
93/4 UpperDeck 242, SP12
94/5 UpperDeck 399, SP96
95/6 UpperDeck 494
96/7 UpperDeck 322
97/8 UpperDeck 310
94/5 UDBeAPlayer-Aut. 47
96/7 UDBlackDiamond 120
95/6 UDCollChoice 178
96/7 UDCollChoice 218
97/8 UDCollChoice 152
96/7 UpperDeck"Ice" 39
95/6 PGH/Foodland 24
93/4 Mich.State

SMRKE, JOHN
79/80 O-Pee-Chee 340
78/9 STL

SMRKE, LOUIS
51/2 LavalDairy 24
52/3 StLawrence 94

SMRKE, STAN
51/2 LavalDairy 23
52/3 StLawrence 97

SMYL, STAN
83/4 Esso
84/5 Kelloggs Disk
86/7 Kraft Sports 69
80/1 OPC/Topps 128, 208
81/2 OPC 328, Topps 38
82/3 O-Pee-Chee 356
83/4 O-Pee-Chee 359
84/5 OPC 330, Topps 140
85/6 OPC/Topps 68
86/7 OPC/Topps 50
87/8 OPC/Topps 4
88/9 O-Pee-Chee 253
89/90 O-Pee-Chee 283
82/3 opcSticker 242
83/4 opcSticker 274
84/5 opcSticker 281
85/6 opcSticker 247
86/7 opcSticker 96
87/8 opcSticker 198
88/9 opcSticker 60
89/90 opcSticker 68/208
90/1 Panini(VAN) 23
87/8 PaniniSticker 337, 349
88/9 PaniniSticker 141
89/90 PaniniSticker 159
90/1 PaniniSticker 292
80/1 Pepsi Cap
82/3 Post
81/2 Post PopUp 25
90/1 ProSet 548
83/4 PuffySticker 2
90/1 Score 374
85/6 7Eleven 19
84/5 7ElevenDisk
83/4 SouhaitsRen.KeyChain
90/1 UpperDeck 299
83/4 Vachon 116
79/80 VAN
79/80 VAN/RoyalBank
80/1 VAN
80/1 VAN/Silverwood
81/2 VAN
81/2 VAN/Silverwood
82/3 VAN
83/4 VAN
84/5 VAN
85/6 VAN
86/7 VAN
87/8 VAN/Shell
88/9 VAN/Mohawk
89/90 VAN
90/1 VAN/Mohawk
84/5 KelownaWingsWHL 28

SMYTH, BRAD
95/6 FutureLegends 20
97/8 PacificRegime 99
96/7 PinnacleZenith 150
96/7 SelectCertified 113
90/1 SketchOHL 143
94/5 Birmingham

SMYTH, GREG
93/4 Premier 306
89/90 ProCards(AHL) 177
90/1 ProCards 453
91/2 ProSet 465
92/3 CGY/IGA 7
88/9 QUE
88/9 QUE/GeneralFoods
91/2 QUE/PetroCanada
89/90 Halifax
90/1 Halifax

SMYTH, KEVIN
92/3 Classic 24
94/5 Classic 47, T30
92/3 ClassicFourtSport 173
93/4 ClassicProspects 225
93/4 Donruss 444
94/5 Donruss 59
95/6 FleerUltra 71
94/5 Leaf 320
95/6 PaniniSticker 30
94/5 Parkhurst 99
94/5 Premier 68
94/5 Score 225
90/1 SketchWHL 155
91/2 SketchWHL 279
95/6 UpperDeck 181

SMYTH, MATT
85/6 London 17

SMYTH, RYAN
97/8 Aces 3 (Spades)
94/5 AutoPhonex B3
94/5 Classic 6, C8
94/5 ClassicFourSport 120
94/5 C4'Images 99
95/6 Donruss 321, -CanadaJr 22
96/7 Donruss 223
97/8 Donruss 158,-Ln 22,-Red 2
96/7 D.CanadianIce 89
97/8 D.CdnIce 52,-Nt'l 10,-Scr 17
96/7 DonrussElite 124
97/8 D.Elite 70, 140,-Craftsm 21
97/8 D.Preferd 119, 189,-Line 1A
97/8 DonrussPriority 24, 201
97/8 D.Prio -DirDep 5,-OpDay 18
97/8 D.Prio-Pstcrd 19,-Stamp 19
97/8 D.Studio 16,-HardHats 8
97/8 D.Studio-Portraits 16,-Sil 21
96/7 Flair 35
97/8 KatchMedallion 59
95/6 Leaf 196
96/7 Leaf 171
97/8 Leaf 49,184,-BnS 10,-Fire 9
94/5 LeafLimited-CanadaJrs 9
96/7 LeafPreferrd 72
97/8 Limited 26, -fabric 50
97/8 Omega 95, -GameFace 9
98/9 Pacific 94, -TeamCL 10
97/8 PacificCrown 94, -Gold 12
97/8 PacificCrownRoyale 54
97/8 PCR-Blades 11, -HatTrick 9
97/8 PacificDynagon! 51
97/8 PcfcD-BstKpt 39,-Tandm 47
97/8 PacificInvincible 58
97/8 PcfcParamnt 77,-CdnGrt 8
98/9 PacificParamount 92
97/8 PacificRegime 83
97/8 PcfcRevolutn 56,-TmCL 10
97/8 PaniniSticker 212
94/5 Pinnacle 535
95/6 Pinnacle 204
96/7 PinnacleBeAPlayer 198
97/8 PinnacleCertified 79
95/6 PinnacleZenith 137
96/7 PinnacleZenith 104
95/6 Score 304
97/8 Score 120, -CheckIt 8
95/6 SelectCertified 121
94/5 SigRookies 31
95/6 SkyBoxImpact 198
94/5 SP 142
96/7 SP 56
97/8 SPAuthentic 61
94/5 SRGoldStandard 92, GS18
95/6 Summit 176
96/7 TeamOut
95/6 TetradAutobilia 99
95/6 Topps 8CJ
98/9 Topps 40
94/5 ToppsFinest 165
97/8 ToppsSticker 4
94/5 UpperDeck 443, SP118
96/7 UpperDeck 258
97/8 UpperDeck 274
98/9 UDChoice 82
97/8 UDCollChoice 92
97/8 UpperDeckIce 6, L5A
97/8 Zenith 71, Z16
96/7 EDM
97/8 EDM

SMYTHE, CONN
83&87 HallOfFame 27
83 HHOF Postcard (B)
92/3 HHOFLegends 2
36/7 WWGum (V356) 95
32/3 TOR/OKeefe 19

SMYTHE, STAFFORD
59/60 Parkhurst 36

SNEDDEN, DENNIS
91/2 ProCards 615
93/4 Toledo 13

SNEDDON, BOB
70/1 Esso Stamp

SNELL, CHRIS
93/4 C'Prospects 93
95/6 EdgeIce 185
91/2 ProCards 7
89/90 SketchOHL 51
90/1 SketchOHL 95
91/2 SketchAwards 4
90/1 UpperDeck 468
93/4 Minn-Duluth
95/6 Phoenix
91/2 Rochestr/Dunkin'Donuts
91/2 Rochester/Genny
91/2 Rochester/Kodak
92/3 Rochester/Dunkin'Donuts
92/3 Rochester/Kodak
93/4 StJohns

SNELL, TED
74/5 Loblaws, -Update

SNEPSTS, HAROLD
83/4 Esso
75/6 OPC 396
76/7 OPC 366, 395
77/8 OPC 295
78/9 O-Pee-Chee 380
79/80 OPC/Topps 186
80/1 O-Pee-Chee 312
81/2 O-Pee-Chee 344
82/3 O-Pee-Chee 357
83/4 O-Pee-Chee 360
84/5 O-Pee-Chee 108
85/6 O-Pee-Chee 232
89/90 O-Pee-Chee 286
81/2 opcSticker 250
82/3 opcSticker 243
85/6 opcSticker 44/175
87/8 opcSticker 110/243
87/8 PaniniSticker 241
80/1 Pepsi Cap
82/3 Post
91/2 ProCards 35
90/1 ProSet 527
90/1 ScoreTraded 61T
83/4 7ElevenCokeCup
84/5 7ElevenDisk
83/4 SouhaitsRen.KeyChain
83/4 Vachon 117
85/6 DET/Caesars
86/7 DET/Caesars
84/5 MIN
90/1 STL/Kodak
75/6 VAN/RoyalBank
76/7 VAN/RoyalBank
77/8 VAN/GingerAle
77/8 VAN/RoyalBank
78/9 VAN/RoyalBank
79/80 VAN
80/1 VAN
80/1 VAN/Silverwood
81/2 VAN/Silverwood
82/3 VAN
83/4 VAN
88/9 VAN/Mohawk
89/90 VAN
84/5 KelownaWingsWHL 47

SNESAR, SHAWN
89/90 Saskatoon 8
92/3 Hampton
93/4 Hampton
94/5 Richmond

SNIDER, ED
92/3 PHA/UD 12APR93

SNITA, MARCIN
95/6 Slapshot 353

SNITZER, ROB
88/9 ProCards(Moncton)
89/90 ProCards(AHL) 50
90/1 Moncton
91/2 Moncton

SNOPEK, JAN
93/4 Slapshot(Oshawa) 4
95/6 Slapshot 248

SNOW, GARTH
93/4 Classic 58
94/5 Classic 84, T57, R17
94/5 ClassicFourSport 143
93/4 C4'Images 21
93/4 ClassicProspects 35
93/4 Donruss 481
96/7 Donruss 257
97/8 Donruss 11, -Between 7
97/8 DCndIce 38, -Scrapbook 10
97/8 DonrussPreferred 111
97/8 D.Priority 138,-PostGen 16
95/6 FleerUltra 287
94/5 Leaf 180
96/7 Leaf 97
97/8 Limited 170
97/8 Omega 170
98/9 Pacific 434
97/8 PacificCrown 147,-InThe 15
97/8 PacificCR-FreezeOut 14
97/8 PacificDynagon! 93
97/8 PcfcD-Stone 16,-Tandm 54
97/8 PcfcParamnt 137,-Glov 15
98/9 PacificParamount 240
95/6 Parkhurst 425
97/8 Pinnacle 63, -Masks 8
97/8 Pinnacle -GoalieTin 9
97/8 P.BAP 77,-Stacking/Pad 12
97/8 PinnacleCertified 28
97/8 PinnacleInside 68, -BigCan
97/8 P.Inside-Stand 4, -Stop 17
97/8 PinnacleUncut
93/4 PowerPlay 425
96/7 Score 204
93/4 Score 628
97/8 Score 3, -NetWorth 8
97/8 Score(PHA) 2
95/6 SkyBoxImpact 215
98/9 SPx"Finite" 86
98/9 Topps 122
95/6 UpperDeck 289
95/6 UDBeAPlayer 57
98/9 UDChoice 207
98/9 PHA/OceanSpray
92/3 Maine(1) 15, (2) 33

SNOW, JASON
90/1 SketchOHL 96
89/90 Windsor

SNUGGERUD, DAVE
90/1 Bowman 249
91/2 Bowman 29
92/3 Bowman 309
90/1 OPC/Topps 340
91/2 OPC/Topps 441
90/1 PaniniSticker 19
91/2 PaniniSticker 308
91/2 Pinnacle 223
92/3 Pinnacle 183
90/1 ProSet 30
91/2 ProSet 18
90/1 ScoreTraded 48T
91/2 Score(CDN) 206, (U.S) 206
92/3 Score 182
91/2 ToppsStadiumClub 320
90/1 UpperDeck 189
91/2 UpperDeck 194
89/90 BUF/BlueShield
89/90 BUF/Campbell
90/1 BUF/BlueShield
90/1 BUF/Campbell
91/2 BUF/BlueShield
91/2 BUF/Campbell

SNYDER, DAN
95/6 Slapshot 294

SOBCHUK, DENNIS
74/5 opcWHA 56
75/6 opcWHA 115
76/7 opcWHA 29
77/8 opcWHA 53
86/7 Regina
87/8 Regina
75/6 Cincinnati

SOBCHUK, GENE
75/6 Cincinnati

SOBEK, JEANINE
94/5 Classic W35

SOBERLAK, PETER
89/90 ProCards'AHL 134
90/1 ProCards 226
91/2 ProCards 229
85/6 Kamloops

SOCCIO, LEN
96/7 DEL 218

SÖDERBERG, AKI
72 SemicSticker 70

SODERBERG, ANDERS
94/5 ElitSet 220
95/6 ElitSet 103, -Goldies 10
94/5 ParkieSE 234
91/2 SemicElitserien 333
94/5 SP 169
94/5 UpperDeck 521
95/6 udElite 161, 221
97/8 udSwedish 158

SODERGREN, HAKAN
89/90 SemicElitserien 60
90/1 SemicElitserien 290
89 SemicSticker 23

SODERHOLM, PATRIK
89/90 SemicElitserien 190

SODERLUND, CENNETH
89/90 SemicElitserien 140
90/1 SemicElitserien 215
91/2 SemicElitserien 143
92/3 SemicElitserien 172

SODERSTROM, DAN
72 SemicSticker 68
74 SemicSticker 10
73/4 WilliamsFIN 38

SÖDERSTRÖM, TOMMY
93/4 Classic 125
92/3 ClassicProspects 91, BC8
93/4 Donruss 253
96/7 Donruss 72
93/4 EASports 102
92/3 FleerUltra 160, -Imports 23
93/4 FleerUltra 217
94/5 FleerUltra 160
95/6 FleerUltra 99
95 Globe 1
95/6 Kraft-Crease
93/4 Leaf 37, -GoldLeafRook 12
94/5 Leaf 184
96/7 Leaf 51
93/4 PaniniSticker 55
92/3 Parkhurst 367, 448
93/4 Parkhurst 150
95/6 Parkhurst 127, 240
93/4 Pinnacle 19
94/5 Pinnacle 309
95/6 Pinnacle 90
93/4 PowerPlay 185
93/4 PP-Second 11, -Net 8
93/4 Premier 55, 122
93/4 Score 336, -International 5
95/6 Score 215
96/7 Score 82
94 Semic 52, 334
95 Semic 54, 212
89/90 SemicElitserien 51
90/1 SemicElitserien 273
91/2 SemElitserien 54, 316, 338
92/3 SemicElitserien 343
91 SemicSticker 29
92 SemicSticker 51
93 SemicSticker 19
95/6 Summit 46
95/6 Topps 334
93/4 T.StadiumClub 340, 430
94/5 ToppsStadiumClub 24
92/3 UpperDeck 377, 475
93/4 UpperDeck 182
94/5 UpperDeck 474
95/6 UpperDeck 313, SE140
95/6 UDCollChoice 28
95/6 udElite 238
97/8 udSwedish 33, 199
96 Wien 38, SG4
92/3 PHA/UD 11FEB93
92/3 PHA/UD 26JAN93
93/4 PHA 19JAN94
93/4 PHA/JCPenney

SÖDERVIK, JUHANI
66/7 Champion 144
70/1 Kuvajulkaisut 267

SODKE, SONNY
82/3 Brandon 4

SOETAERT, DOUG
80/1 O-Pee-Chee 324
82/3 O-Pee-Chee 389
83/4 O-Pee-Chee 391
84/5 O-Pee-Chee 347
82/3 opcSticker 211
83/4 opcSticker 288
85/6 opcSticker 136/8
86/7 opcSticker 16/159
83/4 Vachon 137
84/5 MTL
85/6 MTL
85/6? MTL/ProvigoPlacemats
85/6 MTL/ProvigoStickers
81/2 WPG
82/3 WPG
83/4 WPG
89/90 NewHaven
81/2 Ottawa67s

SOFIKITAS
91/2 AvantGardeBCJHL 163

SOGAARD, KLM
92 SemicSticker 31
93 SemicSticker 236

SOHLMAN, RAULI
80/1 Mallasjuoma 45
78/9 SM-Liiga 88

SOINI, VOITTO
66/7 Champion 70
70/1 Kuvajulkaisut 150
71/2 WilliamsFIN 201

SOKKA, MIKKO
96/7 Sisu 139

SOKKANEN, JUHA
80/1 Mallasjuoma 144

SOKOLSKY, JAMIE
97/8 Bowman 38
95/6 Slapshot 37

SOLARI, KELVIN
93/4 Slapshot(Peterborough) 23

SOLBACH, CARSTEN
94/5 DEL 429
95/6 DEL 385
96/7 DEL 292

SOLDERER, ERICH
94 Semic 238
93 SemicSticker 274

SOLEWAY, JAY
80/1 CGY

SOLF, PATRICK
94/5 DEL 50
95/6 DEL 33

SOLHEIM, KEN
83/4 O-Pee-Chee 131
88/9 EDM/ActionMagazine 8
82/3 MIN
84/5 MIN
85/6 NovaScotia 6

SOLING, JONAS
96/7 Sudbury 23

SOLINGER, BOB
45-64 BeeHives(TOR)
51/2 Parkhurst 88
52/3 Parkhurst 50
53/4 Parkhurst 16
45-54 QuakerOats

SOLINSKI, JASEK
89 SemicSticker 144

SOLLY, JIM
94/5 Huntington 19
92/3 Oklahoma

SOLODUKHIN, VJATSJESLAV
72/3 WilliamsFIN 36
91/2 Trends72 28

SOMERS, ART
33-35 DiamondMatch
36-39 DiamondMatch (2)
24/5 Holland 3
27-32 LaPresse 30/1
33/4 OPC (V304A) 17
28/9 PaulinsCandy 49

SOMERS, CHRIS
86/7 London 29

SOMERVILLE, ROSS
25 Dominion 113

SOMERVUORI, EERO
95/6 Sisu 256
97/8 UDBlackDiamond 139
98/9 UDChoice 281

SOMMER, ROY
88/9 EDM/ActionMagazine 110
96/7 S.J/PacificBellSheet
92/3 Richmond
93/4 Richmond 11
94/5 Richmond
95/6 Richmond

SOMMERS, DARB
23/4 PaulinsCandy 58

SOMNEZ, JIM
90/1 SketchOHL 19
88/9 Sudbury 18
89/90 Sudbury 13

SOMNER, GLEN
79/80 MIN
80/1 MIN
81/2 MIN

SONMOR, GLEN
72/3 Minnesota

SONNENBERG, MARTIN
98 BowmanCHL 69

SOPEL, BRENT
95/6 SwiftCurrent

SORACREPPA, MARTINO
92 SemicSticker 264

SORENSON, KELLY
92/3 Hampton
93/4 Hampton
94/5 Hampton 15

SORMUNEN, PASI
92/3 Jyvas-Hyva 13
93/4 Jyvas-Hyva 21
94 Semic 11
95 Semic 6
93 SemicSticker 60
93/4 Sisu 89
95/6 Sisu 45
96/7 Sisu 44, -Hammer 3

SOROCHAN, JASON
90/1 SketchWHL 135
91/2 SketchWHL 350

SOROCHAN, LEE
95/6 Donruss-CanadaJr 9
94/5 Pinnacle 528
91/2 SketchWHL 338
94/5 SP 147
95/6 Topps 9CJ
94/5 ToppsFinest 153
95/6 Binghampton
96/7 Binghampton
93/4 Lethbridge

SOROKIN, SERGEI
93/4 Classic 93
95/6 DEL 85
96/7 DEL 274
91/2 OPC 44R
94 Semic 144
93 SemicSticker 134
92/3 UpperDeck 343

SORRELL, JOHN
34-43 BeeHives(DET)
33/4 CndGum (V252)
33/4 OPC (V304A) 42
39/40 OPC (V301-1) 60
36/7 WWGum (V356) 25

SOSKIN, BARRY
92/3 Toledo (1), (2)
93/4 Toledo 3
94/5 Toledo
95/6 Toledo
93/4 Waterloo

SOTROPA, J.
91/2 AirCanadaSJHL D37
92/3 MPSPhotoSJHL 139

SOUCHOTTE, KURTISE
91/2 AirCanadaSJHL B49
92/3 MPSPhotoSJHL 72

SOUCY, ALFRED
52/3 AnonymousOHL 42

SOUCY, CHRISTIAN
93/4 ClassicProspects 75
94/5 FleerUltra 276
94/5 ParkieSE 33
94/5 UpperDeck 223
93/4 Indianapolis

SOUDEK, KAREL
95/6 APS 58

SOUKOROFF, PHIL
93/4 Johnstown 9

SOULE, RUSS
83/4 Belleville 28

SOULES, JASON
91/2 ProCards 219
90/1 SketchOHL 219
90/1 UpperDeck 75
88/9 NiagaraFalls 9

SOULES, NATE
85/6 Arizona

SOULLIÈRE, STÉPHANE
93/4 Slapshot(Oshawa) 11
94/5 Slapshot(Sarnia) 11
92/3 Oshawa

SOURAY, SHELDON
98/9 Pacific 271
98/9 PacificParamount 138
94/5 SigRookies 27

SOUTHERN, BRUCE
88/9 WPG/Police

SOUTOKORVA, OSMO
89/90 SemicElitserien 150
90/1 SemicElitserien 231
91/2 SemicElitserien 208
97/8 udSwedish 121

SOVA, TOMMI
94/5 ParkieSE 224
95/6 Sisu 49
94/5 ToppsFinest 138

SPACEK, JAROSLAV
94/5 APS 148
95/6 APS 249

SPANGLER, KEN
89/90 ProCards(IHL) 118
91/2 ProCards 446
88/9 Flint

SPARKES, BRAD
85/6 Kitchener 28

SPARKS, TODD
90/1 SketchQMJHL 131
91/2 SketchQMJHL 215
96/7 Fredericton
95/6 Richmond

SPARLING, H.E.
85/6 London 5
86/7 London 5

SPARROW, SPUNK
23/4 PaulinsCandy 49

SPECK, FRED
71/2 EddieSargent 220
72/3 OPC 331
71/2 TheTorontoSun
72/3 Minnesota

SPEER, MIKE
93/4 ClassicProspects 168
91/2 ProCards 487
90/1 SketchOHL 185, 294
94/5 Slapshot(Brantford) 20
92/3 Indianapolis

SPEIRS, PETE
23/4 Crescent Selkirks 3
24/5 Crescent Selkirks12
23/4 PaulinsCandy 2
28/9 PaulinsCandy 76

SPELDA, JAROSLAV
94/5 APS 28

SPENCE, WALLY
92/3 MPSPhotoSJHL 21

SPENCER, BRIAN
72/3 EddieSargent 132
74/5 Loblaws
71/2 OPC/Topps 198
72/3 OPC 61, Topps 53
73/4 OPC/Topps 83
74/5 OPC 328
75/6 OPC 384
76/7 OPC/Topps 191
77/8 OPC/Topps 9
78/9 OPC/Topps 137
71/2 TheTorontoSun
74/5 BUF
71/2 TOR

SPENCER, IRV
62 CeramicTiles
60/1 ShirriffCoin 88
61/2 ShirriffCoin 86
61/2 Topps 47
62/3 Topps 17
73/4 VancouverBlazers

SPENCER, SEAN
90/1 SketchOHL 97
91/2 SketchOHL 295
92/3 Ottawa

SPENRATH, GREG
91/2 ProCards 145
93/4 LasVegas

SPERGER, ZDENEK
94/5 APS 107
95/6 APS 74

SPERO, KEVIN
91/2 SketchOHL 168
91/2 Oshawa
91/2 Oshawa/Dominos 10
92/3 Oshawa

SPEYERS, CHRIS
24/5 Champs (C144)
33-35 DiamondMatch

SPINA, STEVE
93/4 Slapshot(SSMaire) 27

SPINK, LONNIE
85/6 Kamloops

SPITIZ, TIM
91/2 SketchOHL 79
93/4 Slapshot(Kitchener) 1, 9
94/5 Slapshot(Kitchener) 10

SPLETT, JAMIE
90/1 SketchWHL 178
88/9 Regina
89/90 Regina

SPOLTORE, JOHN
89/90 SketchOHL 149
90/1 SketchOHL 317
91/2 SketchOHL 66
95/6 Louisiana, -Playoffs

SPRACHEK, JAROSLAV
97/7 udSwedish 55

SPRATT, LEN
84/5 Kingston 9

SPREGNER, JIM
85/6 Minn-Duluth 22

SPRING, DON
81/2 O-Pee-Chee 375
82/3 O-Pee-Chee 392
83/4 O-Pee-Chee 392
80/1 Pepsi Cap
82/3 Post
83/4 SouhaitsRen.KeyChain
80/1 WPG
81/2 WPG
82/3 WPG

SPRING, FRANK
75/6 OPC 341

SPRING, JESSE
24/5 Champs (C144)
23/4 (V145-1) 36
24/5 (V145-2) 20

SPROTT, JIM
90/1 ProCards 464
91/2 ProCards 377
90/1 Halifax
86/7 London 12

SPROXTON, DENNIS
90/1 SketchWHL 70

SPRUCE, ANDY
78/9 O-Pee-Chee 378
77/8 COL.R/CokeCans
76/7 VAN/RoyalBank
84/5 Sudbury 1

SPRY, BRAD
90/1 SketchOHL 98

SPRY, EARL
94/5 DEL 227
95/6 DEL 224
96/7 DEL 75

SPURR, CHAD
96/7 SSMarie

SRDINKO, JAN
94/5 APS 237
95/6 APS 7

SREK, PAVEL
94/5 APS 80
95/6 APS 274

SRSEN, TOMAS
95/6 APS 17, 368
94/5 ElitSet 45, -TopGun 1
90/1 ProCards 237
91/2 ProCards 234
95 Semic 156
92/3 SemicElitserien 166

STACCHI, MIKE
95/6 Roanoke

STACEY, BRIAN
91/2 SketchOHL 373
95/6 Slapshot 372

STACKHOUSE, RON
71/2 EddieSargent 64
72/3 EddieSargent 77
70/1 Esso Stamp
82? JDMcCarthy
74/5 Loblaws
71/2 OPC 83
72/3 OPC 287
73/4 OPC 236
74/5 OPC/Topps 188
75/6 OPC/Topps 111
76/7 OPC/Topps 72
77/8 OPC/Topps 157
78/9 OPC/Topps 72
79/80 OPC/Topps 154
80/1 OPC/Topps 228
81/2 O-Pee-Chee 266
82/3 O-Pee-Chee 275
81/2 opcSticker 188
82/3 Post
71/2 TheTorontoSun
74/5 PGH
77/8 PGH/PuckBuck

STADEY, BEN
93/4 Waterloo

STADLER, WAITER
72 SemicSticker 95

STAFFORD, B.
88/9 EDM/ActionMagazine 80
90/1 EDM/McGavins

STAGG, BRIAN
91/2 SketchOHL 232

STAHAN, BUTCH
51/2 LavalDairy 105
52/3 StLawrence 72

STAHL, MIKAEL
89/90 SemicElitserien 185
90/1 SemicElitserien 20

STAIOS, STEVE
91/2 Arena 20
91/2 Classic 24
91/2 ClassicFourSport 24, -Aut.
93/4 ClassicProspects 149
96/7 Leaf 223
97/8 PinnacleBeAPlayer 161
90/1 SketchMEM 107
90/1 SketchOHL 266, 271
91/2 SketchOHL 219
91/2 StarPics 51
91/2 UltimateDP 22, -Aut 22
96/7 UpperDeck 218
93/4 Peoria
92/3 Sudbury 27

STAIT, BILL
92/3 MPSPhotoSJHL 54

STAJDUHAR, NICK
93/4 Classic 28
94/5 Classic 83
93/4 ClassicFourSport 199
93/4 Donruss CAN19
93/4 Parkhurst 507
93/4 Pinnacle 463
90/1 SketchOHL 144
91/2 SketchOHL 380
93/4 UpperDeck 543
96/7 UpperDeck 194
96/7 Penascola 19
94/5 CapeBreton

STAKOWSKI, HARTLEY
67/8 ColumbusCheckers

STAMBERT, ORVAR
89/90 SemicElitserien 54
90/1 SemicElitserien 279
91/2 SemicElitserien 60

STAMBLER, LORNE
78/9 O-Pee-Chee 301
78/9 TOR
79/80 WPG
81/2 Indianapolis 12
82/3 Indianapolis

STAMP, ERIC
91/2 SketchOHL 195

STANDISH, BOB
91/2 AirCanadaSJHL D3

STANEK, ED
93/4 Waterloo

STANFIELD, FRED
64-67 BeeHives(CHIx2)
64/5 CokeCap CHI-6
65/6 CocaCola
70/1 DadsCookies
70/1 EddieSargent 12
71/2 EddieSargent 1
72/3 EddieSargent 15
70/1 Esso Stamp
74/5 Loblaws, -Update
68/9 OPC/Topps 10
69/70 OPC/Topps 32
70/1 OPC/Topps 5, -Deckle 7
71/2 OPC/Topps 7
72/3 OPC 150, Topps 135
74/5 OPC/Topps 31
75/6 O-Pee-Chee 332
76/7 OPC/Topps 58
77/8 OPC/Topps 161
78/9 O-Pee-Chee 352
94/5 Parkie(64/5) 37
95/6 Parkie(66/7) 25
68/9 ShirriffCoin BOS9
71/2 TheTorontoSun
65/6 Topps 63
66/7 Topps 56
67/8 Topps 36
91/2 Ultimate(O6) 54, -Aut 54
70/1 BOS
71/2 BOS
75/6 BUF/Linnett
73/4 MIN

STANFIELD, JIM
71/2 EddieSargent 78
72/3 EddieSargent 86

STANFIELD, ROB
95/6 Slapshot 134

STANGBY, SHANE
90/1 SketchWHL 252

STANGLE, FRANK
36/7 WWGum (V356) 110

STANIFORTH, KENT
90/1 SketchWHL 144
91/2 SketchWHL 272

STANIOWSKI, ED
76/7 OPC/Topps 104
77/8 OPC/Topps 54
79/80 O-Pee-Chee 327
80/1 O-Pee-Chee 328
82/3 O-Pee-Chee 393
82/3 opcSticker 210
82/3 Post
78/9 STL
81/2 WPG
82/3 WPG

STANKIEWICZ, BRIAN
94 Semic 232
93 SemicSticker 269

STANLEY, ALLAN
45-64 BeeHives(NYR), (TORx2)
64-67 BeeHives(TOR)
62 CeramicTiles
63-5 ChexPhoto
64/5 CokeCap TOR-26
65/6 CocaCola
83&87 HallOfFame 238
83 HHOF Postcard (G)
95/6 HHOFLegends 66
68/9 O-Pee-Chee 183, -Puck 16
51/2 Parkhurst 94
52/3 Parkhurst 21
53/4 Parkhurst 64
58/9 Parkhurst 23
59/60 Parkhurst 44
60/1 Parkhurst 16
61/2 Parkhurst 16
62/3 Parkhurst 9
63/4 Parkhurst 1, 61
92/3 Parkhurst52 PR11
93/4 Parkie(56/7) 20
94/5 Parkie(64/5) 115
95/6 Parkie(66/7) 110, 122
60/1 ShirriffCoin 6
61/2 ShirriffCoin 42
62/3 ShirriffCoin 2
68/9 ShirriffCoin PHA3
63/4 TheTorontoStar
64/5 TheTorontoStar
54/5 Topps 41
57/8 Topps 15
64/5 Topps 104
66/7 Topps 16,128, -USATest 16
67/8 Topps 13
54-67 TorontoStar 66/7, V9
56-66 TorontoStar 60/1, 63/4
91/2 Ultimate(O6) 44,75, -Aut 44
60/1 York
60/1 YorkGlasses
61/2 York 9
63/4 York 14
67/8 York no#, 26
64/5 TOR
68/9 TOR
69/70 TOR

STANLEY, BARNEY
83&87 HallOfFame 12
83 HHOF Postcard (A)
23/4 PaulinsCandy 30
19 Millionaires [x2]

STANLEY, DARRYL
86/7 PHA
87/8 VAN/Shell
89/90 VAN
81/2 Saskatoon 2
83/4 Springfield 23

STANLEY, GRAHAM
89/90 ProCards(AHL) 18
90/1 ProCards 353

STANLEY, LORD
83&87 HallOfFame 13
83 HHOF Postcard (A)
92/3 HHOFLegends 18

STANOWSKI, ED
83/4 SouhaitsRen.KeyChain

STANOWSKI, WALTER (WALLY)
34-43 BeeHives(TOR)
45-64 BeeHives(NYR), (TOR)
39/40 OPC (V301-1) 11
40/1 OPC (V301-2) 103
45-54 QuakerOats

STANSFIELD, SEAN
88/9 Sudbury 16

STANTIEN, ROMAN
94/5 APS 242
95/6 APS 22

STANTON, PAUL
91/2 Bowman 91
92/3 Bowman 284
95/6 DEL 267
96/7 DEL 161
92/3 FleerUltra 381
92/3 O-Pee-Chee 361
91/2 OPC/Topps 339
90/1 opcPremier 110
91/2 PaniniSticker 274
93/4 Parkhurst 288
92/3 Pinnacle 308
93/4 Pinnacle 330
93/4 Premier 5
89/90 ProCards(IHL) 156
90/1 ProSet 633
91/2 ProSet 457
90/1 ScoreTraded 27T
91/2 Score(CDN) 406, (U.S) 366
92/3 Score 135
93/4 Score 321, 510
92/3 Topps 460
91/2 ToppsStadiumClub 380
92/3 ToppsStadiumClub 52
93/4 ToppsStadiumClub 52
90/1 UpperDeck 404
91/2 UpperDeck 203
92/3 UpperDeck 100
91/2 PGH/Elbys
91/2 PGH/Foodland 13
92/3 PGH/Coke
92/3 PGH/Foodland 13

STAPLES, JEFF
94/5 Slapshot(MEM) 28
92/3 Brandon 22

STAPLETON, MIKE
94/5 Leaf 147
97/8 PacificRegime 155
94/5 Pinnacle 228
96/7 PinnacleBeAPlayer 92
88/9 ProCards(Saginaw)
90/1 ProCards 402
93/4 Score 638
86/7 CHI/Coke

87/8 CHI/Coke
91/2 CHI/Coke
93/4 EDM 08APR94
92/3 PGH/Coke
93/4 PGH/Foodland 21
96/7 PHO
97/8 PHO
95/6 WPG

STAPLETON, PAT
45-64 BeeHives(BOSx2)
64-67 BeeHives(BOS), (CHI)
62 CeramicTiles
70/1 Colgate Stamp 77
70/1 DadsCookies
70/1 EddieSargent 44
71/2 EddieSargent 45
72/3 EddieSargent 69
70/1 Esso Stamp
91/2 Kraft 69
72/3 Letraset 13
73/4 MacsMilkDisk
68/9 OPC/Topps 15
69/70 OPC/T. 69, OPC-Sticker
70/1 OPC/Topps 17
71/2 OPC/Topps 25, 258
72/3 OPC 4, 249, T. 70, 129
72/3 OPC-TeamCanada
73/4 OPC-Posters 4
74/5 opcWHA 35
95/6 Parkie(66/7) 38, 123, 139
95/6 Playoff 39
61/2 ShirriffCoin 13
68/9 ShirriffCoin CHI 2
71/2 TheTorontoSun
61/2 Topps 18
62/3 Topps 8
65/6 Topps 120
66/7 Topps 57,129, USATest 57
67/8 Topps 61
54-67 TorontoStar 66/7
91/2 Trends(72) 9, -Aut
68/9 CHI

STARIBACHER, SYLVESTER
79 PaniniSticker 305

STARIKOV, SERGEI
90/1 ProCards 557
91/2 ProCards 327
82 SemicSticker 59
83/4 SovietStars
87/8 SovietStars
89/90 N.J.
92/3 SanDiego

STARK, JAY
86/7 Portland

STARKE, JOE
36-39 DiamondMatch (1)

STARNYSKI, AARON
94/5 Slapshot(Sud) 22

STAROSTENKO, D.
93/4 ClassicProspects 118
92/3 RedAce(Blue) 25,(Violet) 25
94/5 Binghampton
95/6 Binghampton

STARR, HAROLD
36-39 DiamondMatch (2), (3)

STARSHINOV, VYACHESLAV
70/1 Kuvajulkaisut 17
69/70 MästarSerien 35
72 Panda
72 SemicSticker 8
74 SemicSticker 44
69/70 Soviet Stars
70/1 Soviet Stars
71/2 Soviet Stars
91/2 Trends72 38
71/2 WilliamsFIN 16

STARTUP, JAMES
91/2 SketchWHL 106
91/2 Saskatoon 23

STAS, SERGEI
94/5 Erie

STASCHE, JOACHIM
74 Hellas 102
79 PaniniSticker 255

STASIUK, JEREMY
95/6 Dayton

STASIUK, VIC
45-64 BeeHives(BOS), (DETx3)
62 CeramicTiles
82? JDMcCarthy
51/2 Parkhurst 62
52/3 Parkhurst 90
53/4 Parkhurst 39
61/2 Parkhurst 32
62/3 Parkhurst 22
63/4 Parkhurst 58
93/4 Parkhurst PR64
93/4 Parkie(56/7) 9, 169
60/1 ShirriffCoin 103
61/2 ShirriffCoin 63
57/8 Topps 11
58/9 Topps 9
59/60 Topps 14
60/1 Topps 66
54-67 TorontoStar V6
62/3 YorkTransfer 30
57/8 BOS
70/1 PHA

STASTNY, ANTON
72-84 Dernière 81/2
86/7 Kraft Sports 50
81/2 O-Pee-Chee 282
82/3 O-Pee-Chee 292, 294
83/4 O-Pee-Chee 302
84/5 O-Pee-Chee 291
85/6 OPC/Topps 78
86/7 OPC/Topps 125
87/8 OPC/Topps 185
88/9 OPC/Topps 98
81/2 opcSticker 70
82/3 opcSticker 24
83/4 opcSticker 252
84/5 opcSticker 178
85/6 opcSticker 147
86/7 opcSticker 27
87/8 opcSticker 228
88/9 opcSticker 194
87/8 PaniniSticker 166
88/9 PaniniSticker 357
80/1 Pepsi Cap
82/3 Post
83/4 PuffySticker 14
94 Semic 202
83/4 SouhaitsRen.KeyChain
83/4 Vachon 75
80/1 QUE
81/2 QUE
82/3 QUE
83/4 QUE
84/5 QUE
85/6 QUE
85/6 QUE/GeneralFoods
85/6 QUE/McDonald
85/6 QUE/Pennant
85/6 QUE/Placemats
85/6 QUE/Provigo
86/7 QUE
86/7 QUE/GeneralFoods
86/7 QUE/McDonald
86/7 QUE/YumYum
87/8 QUE/GeneralFoods
87/8 QUE/YumYum
88/9 QUE
88/9 QUE/GeneralFoods

STASTNY, BOHUSLAV
72 Hellas 91
74 Hellas 82
72 Panda
72 SemicSticker 32
74 SemicSticker 64
71/2 WilliamsFIN 38
72/3 WilliamsFIN 19
73/4 WilliamsFIN 61

STASTNY, MARIAN
72-84 Dernière 81/2
82/3 McDonalds 10
82/3 O-Pee-Chee 295
83/4 O-Pee-Chee 303
84/5 O-Pee-Chee 292
82/3 opcSticker 20
83/4 opcSticker 168, 251
84/5 opcSticker 177
86/7 opcSticker 144/252
79 PaniniSticker 90
82/3 Post
83/4 PuffySticker 16
83/4 SouhaitsRen.KeyChain
83/4 Vachon 76
81/2 QUE
82/3 QUE
83/4 QUE
84/5 QUE
85/6 TOR

STASTNY, PETER
90/1 Bowman 86
91/2 Bowman 287
92/3 Bowman 249
72-84 Dernière 81/2
93/4 Donruss 487
94/5 Donruss 191
94/5 Flair 159
92/3 FleerUltra 118, -Imports 24
94/5 FleerUltra 190
88/9 FritoLay
93/4 HockeyWit 70
84/5 Kelloggs Disk
86/7 Kraft Sports 51
89/90 Kraft 33
90/1 Kraft 54
91/2 Kraft 83
82/3 McDonalds 24
81/2 OPC 269, 286, 287, 395
82/3 O-Pee-Chee 276, 292, 293
83/4 O-Pee-Chee 304
84/5 O-Pee-Chee 277, 293
85/6 OPC/Topps 31
86/7 OPC/Topps 20
87/8 OPC/Topps 21
88/9 OPC/Topps 22
89/90 OPC/Topps 143
90/1 OPC/Topps 334
91/2 OPC/Topps 191, 275
92/3 O-Pee-Chee 216
88/9 opcStars 37
81/2 opcSticker 69, 263
82/3 opcSticker 15, 19, 167
83/4 opcSticker 167, 253
84/5 opcSticker 141, 164-65
85/6 opcSticker 156
86/7 opcSticker 26
87/8 opcSticker 222
88/9 opcSticker 189
89/90 opcSticker 182
79 PaniniSticker 84
87/8 PaniniSticker 164
88/9 PaniniSticker 358
89/90 PaniniSticker 324
90/1 PaniniSticker 70
91/2 PaniniSticker 220
92/3 PaniniSticker 174
93/4 PaniniSticker 41
91/2 Parkhurst 103, 209
94/5 Parkhurst 203
80/1 Pepsi Cap
91/2 Pinnacle 266
92/3 Pinnacle 359
94/5 Pinnacle 134
94/5 POG 208
82/3 Post
94/5 Premier 182
90/1 ProSet 175, 176
91/2 ProSet 143, -ThePuck 16
92/3 ProSet 100
87/8 ProSportWatch CW12
91/2 PSPlatinum 194
83/4 PuffySticker 13
90/1 Score 96, -HotCards 48
91/2 Score(CDN) 66, (U.S) 66
92/3 Score 291
93/4 Score 22
94 Semic 200
84/5 7ElevenDisk
85/6 7Eleven 16
83/4 SouhaitsRen.KeyChain
91/2 ToppsStadiumClub 263
92/3 ToppsStadiumClub 140
81/2 Topps 39, 61
84/5 Topps 130
92/3 Topps 469
92/3 Trends(76) 131
90/1 UpperDeck 163
91/2 UpperDeck 113
94/5 UpperDeck 60
83/4 Vachon 77
96 Wien 227
90/1 N.J.
80/1 QUE
81/2 QUE
82/3 QUE
83/4 QUE
84/5 QUE
85/6 QUE
85/6 QUE/GeneralFoods
85/6 QUE/McDonald
85/6 QUE/Pennant
85/6 QUE/Placemats
85/6 QUE/Provigo
86/7 QUE
86/7 QUE/GeneralFoods
86/7 QUE/McDonalds
86/7 QUE/YumYum
87/8 QUE/GeneralFoods
87/8 QUE/YumYum
88/9 QUE
88/9 QUE/GeneralFoods
89/90 QUE
89/90 QUE/GeneralFoods
89/90 QUE/Police
90/1 QUE

STASZAK, RAY
85/6 DET/Caesars

STAUBER, PETE
91/2 ProCards 129

STAUBER, ROBB
92/3 FleerUltra 311
93/4 FleerUltra 347
90/1 OPC/Topps 181
92/3 opcPremier 115
92/3 Parkhurst 303
94/5 Parkhurst 109
95/6 Parkhurst 25
93/4 Pinnacle 338, -Masks 3
93/4 PowerPlay 363
93/4 Premier 109
94/5 Premier 248
90/1 ProCards 418
93/4 Score 346
93/4 ToppsStadiumClub 327
90/1 UpperDeck 165
92/3 UpperDeck 495
94/5 UDBeAPlayer R59
96/7 Portland
95/6 Rochester

STAVJANA, ANTONIN
94/5 APS 230
95/6 APS 8, 357, 389
95 Globe 150
91/2 Jyvas-Hyva 41
95 PaniniWorlds 194
94 Semic 173
92/3 SemicElitserien 127
89 SemicSticker 181
91 SemicSticker 111
96 Wien 105

STAVJANA, MIROSLAV
94/5 APS 240

STEARNS, CAL
60/1 Cleveland

STEBLECKI, ROMAN
89 SemicSticker 145

STEBLYK, BRENT
82/3 MedicineHat
83/4 MedicineHat 12

STECHER, DINO
91 SemicSticker 179

STEEGE, BRANDON
91/2 Minnesota
92/3 Minnesota
93/4 Minnesota
94/5 Minnesota

STEEL, GREG
78/9 Saginaw

STEEN, ANDERS
80/1 Pepsi Cap
80/1 WPG

STEEN, THOMAS
90/1 Bowman 133
91/2 Bowman 200
92/3 Bowman 312
96/7 DEL 33
93/4 Donruss 389
94/5 Donruss 154
93/4 EASports 148
92/3 FleerUltra 247
93/4 FleerUltra 69
94/5 FleerUltra 396
95 Globe 40
86/7 Kraft Sports 80
90/1 Kraft 55
93/4 Leaf 165
94/5 Leaf 376
82/3 O-Pee-Chee 391
83/4 O-Pee-Chee 393
84/5 O-Pee-Chee 348
85/6 O-Pee-Chee 206
86/7 O-Pee-Chee 257
87/8 O-Pee-Chee 221
88/9 O-Pee-Chee 254
89/90 O-Pee-Chee 290
90/1 OPC/Topps 283
91/2 OPC/Topps 218
92/3 O-Pee-Chee 385
83/4 opcSticker 289
84/5 opcSticker 292
85/6 opcSticker 253/133
86/7 opcSticker 110/243
88/9 opcSticker 138/9
89/90 opcSticker 144
90/1 Panini(WPG) 22
87/8 PaniniSticker 365
88/9 PaniniSticker 159
89/90 PaniniSticker 163
90/1 PaniniSticker 316
91/2 PaniniSticker 68
92/3 PaniniSticker 53
93/4 PaniniSticker 191
95 PaniniWorlds 291
92/3 Parkhurst 214
93/4 Parkhurst 502
94/5 Parkhurst 263
91/2 Pinnacle 275
92/3 Pinnacle 29
93/4 Pinnacle 159
94/5 Pinnacle 171
94/5 POG 255
93/4 PowerPlay 275, 476
93/4 Premier 11
94/5 Premier 471
90/1 ProSet 356, 565
91/2 ProSet 271
92/3 ProSet 217
91/2 PSPlatinum 138
90/1 Score 14, -HotCards 8
91/2 Score(CDN) 198, (U.S) 198
92/3 Score 80
93/4 Score 71
94/5 Score 65
82 SemicSticker 150
89 SemicSticker 15
91 SemicSticker 209
92 SemicSticker 70
93 SemicSticker 36
92/3 Topps 141
91/2 ToppsStadiumClub 207
93/4 ToppsStadiumClub 282
94/5 ToppsStadiumClub 176
90/1 UpperDeck 94, 313
91/2 UpperDeck 181
92/3 UpperDeck 154
93/4 UpperDeck 166
94/5 UpperDeck 192
94/5 UDBeAPlayer-Aut. 159
83/4 Vachon 138
81/2 WPG
82/3 WPG
83/4 WPG
84/5 WPG/Police
85/6 WPG
85/6 WPG/Police
86/7 WPG
87/8 WPG
88/9 WPG/Police
89/90 WPG/Safeway
90/1 WPG/IGA
91/2 WPG/IGA
93/4 WPG/Ruffles

STEER, JAMIE
93/4 ClassicProspects 240
94/5 Dayton 22
92/3 Greensboro 16
90/1 Mich.Tech
91/2 Mich.Tech (x3)

STEFAN, GREG
82? JDMcCarthy
84/5 OPC 65, Topps 48
85/6 OPC/Topps 157
86/7 OPC/Topps 51
87/8 OPC/Topps 186
88/9 OPC/Topps 68
89/90 OPC/Topps 23
88/9 opcStars 38
84/5 opcSticker 41
85/6 opcSticker 31/161
86/7 opcSticker 165
88/9 opcSticker 252/122
89/90 opcSticker 248/109
87/8 PaniniSticker 237
88/9 PaniniSticker 37
89/90 PaniniSticker 59
85/6 DET/Caesars
86/7 DET/Caesars
87/8 DET/Caesars
88/9 DET/Caesars
89/90 DET/Caesars
80/1 Oshawa 22

STEFAN, JOE
90/1 ProCards 519

STEFAN, LEO
94/5 DEL 206
95/6 DEL 208
96/7 DEL 290
95 Globe 223
95 PaniniWorlds 75
94 Semic 290
96 Wien 200

STEFFAN, JEFF
81/2 Oshawa 22
82/3 Oshawa 8
83/4 Oshawa 25

STEFFAN, TODD
82/3 Kitchener 23

STEIGER, EWALD
94/5 DEL 310

STEIGER, HELMUT
94/5 DEL 267
96/7 DEL 148
82 SemicSticker 119
89 SemicSticker 116
91 SemicSticker 174

STEIGER, HOLGER
95/6 DEL 260

STEIN, PHILIP
34-43 BeeHives(TOR)

STEINBOCK, STEFAN
94/5 DEL 325
95/6 DEL 301
96/7 DEL 328

STEINECKER, STEFAN
94/5 DEL 57
95/6 DEL 52
92 SemicSticker 178

STEINEGGER, MARTIN
95 PaniniWorlds 123

STEINER, ONDREJ
94/5 APS 158
95/6 APS 255
92/3 Classic 37
92/3 UpperDeck 604

STEINMETZ, T.
93/4 Waterloo

STELCICH, MARTIN
94/5 APS 213

STELLJES, MATT
92/3 Minnesota

STELMAK, JAMIE
91/2 AirCanadaSJHL B36
92/3 MPSPhotoSJHL 137

STELNOV, IGOR
91/2 O-Pee-Chee 26R
92/3 SemicElitserien 260
89 SemicSticker 85
87/8 SovietStars

STEMKOWSKI, PETER
64-67 BeeHives(TOR)
65/6 CocaCola
70/1 EddieSargent 50
71/2 EddieSargent 115
72/3 EddieSargent 143
70/1 Esso Stamp
74/5 LiptonSoup 42
74/5 Loblaws
68/9 OPC/Topps 33
69/70 OPC/Topps 65
70/1 OPC/Topps 25, OPC 182
71/2 OPC/Topps 217
72/3 O-Pee-Chee 78
73/4 O-Pee-Chee 217
74/5 OPC/Topps 77
75/6 OPC/Topps 303
76/7 OPC/Topps 166
77/8 O-Pee-Chee 272
78/9 O-Pee-Chee 290
94/5 Parkie(64/5) 113
95/6 Parkie(66/7) 112
67 Post FlipBook
68/9 ShirriffCoin DET10
77-9 Sportscastr 64-16, 68-1623
71/2 TheTorontoSun
65/6 Topps 84
66/7 Topps 15, -USATest 15
67/8 Topps 12
67/8 York no# (x3), 14
92/3 S.J/PacificBell

STEN, MARKO
92/3 Jyvas-Hyva 191
93/4 Sisu 210

STENFORS, PEKKA
78/9 SM-Liiga 231

STENLUND, OLA
89/90 SemicElitserien 197

STENVALL, HELKKO
66/7 Champion 12
65/6 Hellas 19
70/1 Kuvajulkaisut 239

STEPAN, BRAD
87/8 SSMarie 25

STEPANEK, MARTIN
94/5 APS 65
95/6 APS 85

STEPHAN, GREG
95/6 Slapshot 79

STEPHAN, JOE
89/90 ProCards(IHL) 127

STEPHENS, CHARLIE
97/8 PinnacleBeeHive 72

STEPHENS, TROY
89/90 SketchOHL 98
90/1 SketchOHL 372

STEPHENSON, BOB
79/80 O-Pee-Chee 391
79/80 TOR

STEPHENSON, KEN
72/3 OttawaNationals

STEPHENSON, SLADE
91/2 SketchWHL 356

STEPHENSON, WAYNE
51/2 BasDuFleuve 10

STEPHENSON, WAYNE
72/3 EddieSargent 191
72/3 OPC 275
73/4 OPC/Topps 31
74/5 OPC/Topps 218
75/6 OPC 355
76/7 OPC/Topps 190
77/8 OPC/Topps 142
78/9 OPC/Topps 223
79/80 OPC/Topps 38
80/1 OPC/Topps 121
75/6 PHA/GingerAle
72/3 STL
72/3 STL/8"x10"
73/4 STL
79/80 WSH
80/1 WSH

STERFLINGER, ROBERT
94/5 DEL 99
95/6 DEL 86
96/7 DEL 275

STERFLINGER, THOMAS
94/5 DEL 336
95/6 DEL 294
96/7 DEL 323

STERN, MIKE
81/2 Oshawa 13
82/3 Oshawa 17
83/4 Oshawa 20

STERN, RONNIE
93/4 Durivage 28
92/3 FleerUltra 271
93/4 Leaf 261

94/5 Leaf 399
95/6 Leaf 204
97/8 PacificCrown 346
90/1 Panini(VAN) 24
95/6 PaniniSticker 238
92/3 Parkhurst 265
93/4 Parkhurst 303
92/3 Pinnacle 217
95/6 Playoff 131
95/6 POG 59
93/4 PowerPlay 43
93/4 Premier 341
94/5 Premier 71
89/90 ProCards(IHL) 179
90/1 ProSet 549
91/2 ProSet 362
91/2 Score(CDN) 408
92/3 Score 237
93/4 Score 409
95/6 Topps 181
93/4 ToppsStadiumClub 68
94/5 UpperDeck 27
95/6 UpperDeck 368
96/7 UpperDeck 28
94/5 UDBeAPlayer R122
95/6 UDBeAPlayer 79
91/2 CGY/IGA
92/3 CGY/IGA 25
88/9 VAN/Mohawk
90/1 VAN/Mohawk
87/8 Flint

STERNER, ULF
95 Globe 69
74 Hellas 35
70/1 Kuvajulkaisut 38
69/70 MästarSerien 41, 48
72 Panda
72 SemicSticker 56
91 SemicSticker 235
71/2 WilliamsFIN 58
73/4 WilliamsFIN 36

STEVENS, JOHN
88/9 ProCards(Hershey)
89/90 ProCards(AHL) 346
90/1 ProCards 189
91/2 ProCards 108
83/4 Oshawa 26

STEVENS, KEVIN
90/1 Bowman 208
91/2 Bowman 92, 418, 421, 422
92/3 Bowman 241, 366
95/6 Bowman 59
92/3 ClassicProspects 31
93/4 Donruss 265
94/5 Donruss 229
95/6 Donruss 221
95/6 DonrussElite 95
97/8 DonrussPriority 42
93/4 EASports 106
95/6 EdgeIce L10
94/5 Flair 140
94/5 Fleer 170
95/6 FleerMetal 11, -Iron 11
92/3 FleerUltra 171, -AS 1, 5
93/4 FleerUltra 229, -AS 6
94/5 FleerUlra 170, -Red 10
95/6 FU 127, 207, -Crease 18
95 Globe 122
93/4 HockeyWit 20
95/6 Hoyle'EAST 8 (Clubs)
92/3 HumptyDumpty (1)
97/8 KatchMedallion 96
93/4 Leaf 69, -Gold 4, -HTAS 9
94/5 Leaf 356
95/6 Leaf 216
94/5 LeafLimited 46
95/6 LeafLimited 96
96/7 Maggers 78
91/2 McDonalds McD3
92/3 McDonalds McH03
93/4 McDonalds McD25
97/8 Omega 149
90/1 OPC/Topps 360
91/2 OPC/Topps 267, 421
92/3 O-Pee-Chee 29
90/1 opcPremier 111
91/2 opcPremier 26
98/9 Pacific 301
97/8 PacificCrown 115
97/8 PacificParamount 121
98/9 PacificParamount 158
97/8 PacificRevolution 91
89/90 PaniniSticker 321
90/1 PaniniSticker 131
91/2 PaniniSticker 269
92/3 PaniniSticker 221, 281
93/4 PaniniSticker 79
94/5 PaniniSticker 78
95/6 PaniniSticker 7
97/8 PaniniSticker 225
91/2 Parkhurst 135, 473
92/3 Parkhurst 138, 466
93/4 Parkhurst 158
94/5 Parkhurst 177
95/6 Parkhurst 10, 370
94/5 Parkie seV9
91/2 Pinnacle 191, B4
92/3 Pinnacle 288, -TeamP 4
93/4 Pinnacle 149, -TeamP 4
93/4 Pinnacle-NiftyFifty 1, 9
94/5 Pinnacle 299, TP7
97/8 Pinnacle 143
95/6 PinnacleFANtasy 28
97/8 PinnacleInside 153
95/6 Playoff 10, 123
96/7 Playoff 333
94/5 POG 189
95/6 POG 33
93/4 PowerPlay 195, -Point 17
93/4 Premier 170, 370
94/5 Premier 290, -Finest(T) 17
95/6 ProMagnet 15
90/1 ProSet 240
91/2 ProSet 185, 314, P2
92/3 ProSet 140
91/2 PSPlatinum 93
90/1 Score 53, -YoungStar 17
91/2 Score(CDN) 468, (U.S) 248
92/3 Score 25, 492, -USA 10
93/4 Score 325, -Dream 23
93/4 Score(CDN) DD8, -P.AS 15
94/5 Score 182, CI4
95/6 Score 44
97/8 Score 159
97/8 Score(NYR) 6
92/3 SeasonsPatch 66
93/4 SeasonsPatch 19
94/5 Select 106
91 SemicSticker 145
93 SemicSticker 179
95/6 SkBxEmotion 12, -Ntense 8
95/6 SkyBoxImpact 13
96/7 SP 73
95/6 Summit 67
95/6 SuperSticker 9
96/7 TeamOut
92/3 Topps 259, 343, 429
95/6 Topps282, 5PL, 11HG
94/5 ToppsFinest 80, -Ring 13
96/7 ToppsNHLPicks 81
91/2 ToppsStadiumClub 234
92/3 T.StadiumClub 110, 257
93/4 TSC 158, 457, -AllStar
95/6 T.StadiumClub 50, F6
95/6 ToppsSuperSkills 61
90/1 UpperDeck 14
91/2 UpperDeck 154, 613
92/3 UD 275, 454, 630, G4
92/3 UD-LockerAS 14
93/4 UD124, 126, 230, HT19
94/5 UpperDeck 390, SP62
95/6 UpperDeck 96, SE96
96/7 UpperDeck 78, X34
95/6 UDCollChoice 219
96/7 UDCollChoice 124
95/6 Zenith 52, -GiftedGrinder 2
89/90 PGH/Elbys
89/90 PGH/Foodland 7
90/1 PGH/Foodland 9
91/2 PGH/Elbys
91/2 PGH/Topps
91/2 PGH/Foodland 8
92/3 PGH/Foodland 15
92/3 PGH/Coke
92/3 PGH/FoodSticker
93/4 PGH/Foodland 17
94/5 PGH 19
96/7 PGH/Tribune

STEVENS, MIKE
95/6 EdgeIce 118
88/9 ProCards(Springfield)
89/90 ProCards'AHL 240
90/1 ProCards 146
91/2 ProCards 345
92/3 Binghampton
95/6 Cleveland
85/6 Fredericton 5
86/7 Fredericton
83/4 Kitchener 21
84/5 Kitchener 25
90/1 Newmarket

STEVENS, P.C.
23/4 PaulinsCandy 33

STEVENS, RANDY
95/6 Classic 80, -Aut.
91/2 SketchWHL 82
93/4 Kamloops
91/2 Mich.Tech

STEVENS, SCOTT
95/6 Aces 2 (Clubs)
91/2 Bowman 369
92/3 Bowman 160, 242
95/6 Bowman 50, BB4
93/4 Donruss 192
94/5 Donruss 262, -Dominator 2
95/6 Donruss 163
96/7 Donruss 57, -HitList 9
97/8 Donruss 194
96/7 DonrussCanadianIce 103
97/8 DonrussCanadianIce 114
95/6 DonrussElite 70
96/7 DonrussElite 30
96/7 Duracell DC16, JB16
93/4 EASports 73
94/5 Flair 100
96/7 Flair 54
94/5 Fleer 119
96/7 Fleer 61
95/6 FleerMetal 85, -IronWar 12
92/3 FleerUltra 119
93/4 FleerUltra 189
94/5 FleerUltra 123, 196
95/6 FleerUltra 91, 197
96/7 FleerUltra 95
88/9 FritoLay
95 Globe 81
93/4 HockeyWit 65
95/6 Hoyle'EAST 9 (Clubs)
92/3 HumptyDumpty (1)
97/8 KatchMedallion 84
95/6 KennerSLU
90/1 Kraft 56
91/2 Kraft 53
93/4 Kraft-Captain
94/5 Kraft-AllStar
95/6 Kraft-Ticket
96/7 Kraft-Disk
97/8 Kraft-RoadToNagano
93/4 Leaf 60
94/5 Leaf 363, -GoldLeafStar 12
95/6 Leaf 124
96/7 Leaf 175
94/5 LeafLimited 85
96/7 LeafLimited 23
96/7 LeafPreferred 38
97/8 Limited 176
96/7 Maggers 92
91/2 McDonalds McD24
92/3 McDonalds McD27
93/4 McDonalds McD26
94/5 McDonalds 7
97/8 McDonalds -Medallions
96/7 MetalUniverse 88
97/8 Omega 134
83/4 O-Pee-Chee 376
84/5 OPC 206, Topps 149
85/6 OPC/Topps 62
86/7 OPC/Topps 126
87/8 OPC/Topps 25
88/9 OPC/Topps 60, T-AS 4
89/90 OPC/Topps 93
90/1 OPC/Topps 211, 394
91/2 OPC/Topps 481
92/3 OPC 251, 336, -25Years 16
88/9 opcStars 39
90/1 opcPremier 112
91/2 opcPremier 84
83/4 opcSticker 188
85/6 opcSticker 107/239
86/7 opcSticker 254/146
87/8 opcSticker 233/99
88/9 opcSticker 68
89/90 opcSticker 76/215
98/9 Pacific 272
97/8 PacificCrown 273
97/8 PacificCrownRoyale 77
98/9 PacificParamount 139
87/8 PaniniSticker 177
88/9 PaniniSticker 368
89/90 PaniniSticker 341
90/1 PaniniSticker 155
91/2 PaniniSticker 26
92/3 PaniniSticker 181
93/4 PaniniSticker 43
94/5 PaniniSticker 34
95/6 PaniniSticker 89
96/7 PaniniSticker 80
91/2 Parkhurst 102
92/3 Parkhurst 92, CP18
93/4 Parkhurst 114
94/5 Parkhurst V41, C13
95/6 Parkhurst 121, -AS 4
94/5 ParkieSE 97
91/2 Pinnacle 81
92/3 Pinnacle 280
93/4 Pinnacle25,CA13,-TeamP 3
94/5 Pinnacle 310, TP5
95/6 Pinnacle 86, -FullContact 2
96/7 Pinnacle 4
97/8 Pinnacle 158
97/8 PinnacleCertified 115
97/8 PinnacleInside 154
95/6 PinnacleZenith 89
96/7 PinnacleZenith 73
95/6 Playoff 61, 167
94/5 POG 152, 262, 345
95/6 POG 165
96/7 Post
93/4 PowerPlay 143
93/4 Premier 80
94/5 Premier 126, 153, 370
94/5 Premier 451, 494
95/6 ProMagnet 35
90/1 ProSet 321, 528
91/2 ProSet 216, 292, 423
92/3 ProSet 95
91/2 PSPlatinum 72
90/1 Score 188,341,40T, -Hot 82
91/2 Score(CDN) 40, 307, 595
91/2 Score(U.S) 40, 303, 45T
93/4 Score 111, -P.AS 4
93/4 S-Franchise 11, -Dream 5
92/3 Score 75, 429
94/5 Score 193, CI2, DT5, TF13
95/6 Score 160
96/7 Score 138
97/8 Score 224
97/8 Score(N.J.) 8
92/3 SeasonsPatch 50
94/5 Select 82, FL8
95/6 SelectCert. 66, -Double 18
96/7 SelectCertified 54
94 Semic 83
89 SemicSticker 58
91 SemicSticker 56
92 SemicSticker 78
93 SemicSticker 196
95/6 SkyBoxEmotion 102
95/6 SkyBoxImpact 97
96/7 SkyBoxImpact 70
94/5 SP 66
95/6 SP 81, FX13
96/7 SP 89
97/8 SPAuthentic 85, I35
96/7 SPx 24
97/8 SPx 26
95/6 Summit 134, -GM8
96/7 Summit 9
95/6 SuperSticker 68, 72
91 TeamCanada
96/7 TeamOut
92/3 Topps 156, 269
95/6 Topps 275,6RL,M17,PF13
98/9 Topps 23, B12
94/5 ToppsFinest 18, -Div. 7
95/6 ToppsFinest 33, S152
96/7 ToppsNHLPicks 115, ID4
91/2 ToppsStadiumClub 265
92/3 ToppsStadiumClub 151
93/4 T.StadiumClub 383, -AllStar
94/5 ToppsStadiumClub 4
95/6 T.StadiumClub 45, F4, N1
93/4 TSC-MembersOnly 30
94/5 TSC-MembersOnly 10
95/6 TSC-MembersOnly 27
95/6 ToppsSuperSkills 7
90/1 UpperDeck 236, 436, 482
91/2 UpperDeck 132, 539
92/3 UD 297, 'LockerAS 15
93/4 UpperDeck 119, SP89
94/5 UD 73,C30,IG5, R48, SP45
95/6 UD 482, AS2, H35, SE49
95/6 UD-AllStarPredict MVP27
96/7 UpperDeck 286, P9, X36
97/8 UpperDeck 95, 396, T11C
93/4 UDBeAPlayer 36
94/5 UDBeAPlayer 219, R146
96/7 UDBlackDiamond 124
97/8 UDBlackDiamond 17
98/9 UDChoice 113, 239
95/6 UDCollChoice 223
96/7 UDCC 148, 305, 322, UD36
97/8 UDCollChoice 140
97/8 ValuNet
96 Wien 80
96/7 N.J/Sharp
90/1 STL/Kodak
92/3 STL/UpperDeck 20
82/3 WSH
84/5 WSH/PizzaHut
85/6 WSH/PizzaHut
86/7 WSH/Police
86/7 WSH/Kodak
87/8 WSH
87/8 WSH/Kodak
88/9 WSH
88/9 WSH/Smokey
89/90 WSH
89/90 WSH/Kodak

STEVENSON, JASON
91/2 SketchOHL 90

STEVENSON, JEREMY
90/1 SketchOHL 48
91/2 SketchOHL 8
93/4 Slapshot(SSMarie) 25
91/2 Cornwall 10
94/5 Greensboro

STEVENSON, SHAYNE
91/2 OPC/Topps 121
90/1 Score 405
89/90 SketchMEM 49
89/90 SketchOHL 182
90/1 SketchOHL 123
91/2 UpperDeck 332
92/3 AtlantaKnights
88/9 Kitchener 20
89/90 Kitchener 21
86/7 London 15

STEVENSON, TURNER
94/5 CanadaJr.Alumni 6
95/6 Donruss 218
94/5 Fleer 110
94/5 FleerUltra 317
94/5 Leaf 492
95/6 Leaf 285
97/8 PacificRegime 106
95/6 Parkhurst 385
95/6 Pinnacle 115
97/8 PinnacleBeAPlayer 181
94/5 Premier 392
90/1 Score 426
90/1 SketchWHL 9
91/2 SketchWHL 125
95/6 Topps 34
91/2 UD 691, -CzechWJC 65
93/4 UpperDeck 248
94/5 UpperDeck 221, SP162
95/6 UpperDeck 202
96/7 UpperDeck 85
97/8 UpperDeck 297
95/6 UDCollChoice 167
94/5 MTL
95/6 MTL
95/6 MTL/Molson
96/7 MTL
96/7 MTL/MolsonExport
97/8 MTL
92/3 Fredericton
93/4 Fredericton
94/5 Fredericton

STEVENSON, T.
91/2 SketchWHL 273

STEWART, ALAN
90/1 opcPremier 113
88/9 ProCards(Utica)
90/1 ProSet 480
90/1 N.J

STEWART, BILL
52/3 AnonymousOHL 94

STEWART, BILL
36-39 DiamondMatch (5), (6)
36/7 WWGum (V356) 135

STEWART, BILL
95/6 DEL 353
95 Globe 23
79/80 O-Pee-Chee 313
93 SemicSticker 213
83/4 TOR

STEWART, BLAIR
82? JDMcCarthy
78/9 O-Pee-Chee 355
79/80 O-Pee-Chee 332

STEWART, BOB
77/8 Coke Mini
72/3 EddieSargent 56
74/5 Loblaws
73/4 OPC 188, Topps 159
74/5 OPC/Topps 92
75/6 OPC/Topps 47
76/7 OPC 291
77/8 OPC 299
78/9 OPC/Topps 46
79/80 O-Pee-Chee 297
78/9 STL

STEWART, BRIAN
95/6 Slapshot 376
96/7 SSMarie

STEWART, CAM
94/5 Classic-Autograph
93/4 ClassicProspects 36
93/4 Donruss 20
94/5 Donruss 316
93/4 FleerUltra 270
93/4 Leaf 337
94/5 Leaf 281
93/4 Parkhurst 284
93/4 Pinnacle 434
93/4 PowerPlay 292
94/5 Premier 111
93/4 Score 588
93/4 ToppsStadiumClub 440
93/4 UpperDeck 464
94/5 UpperDeck 487

STEWART, CHARLES
25-27 Anonymous 39

STEWART, DAVE
90/1 SketchOHL 71
91/2 SketchOHL 236
92/3 Phoenix
93/4 Phoenix
94/5 Roanoke
95/6 Roanoke

STEWART, DOUG
91/2 AvantGardeBCJHL 63
83/4 Brantford 11
82/3 Ottawa67s

STEWART, GARY
88/9 ProCards(Indianapolis)

STEWART, GAYE
34-43 BeeHives(TORx2)
45-64 BeeHives(CHI), (DET)
43-47 ParadeSportive
51/2 Parkhurst 99
52/3 Parkhurst 25
45-54 QuakerOats
91/2 Ultimate(O6) 54, -Aut 45

STEWART, GLENN
94/5 Greensboro

STEWART, JACK
34-43 BeeHives(DET)
45-64 BeeHives(CHI), (DET)
51 BerkRoss
83&87 HallOfFame 210
83 HHOF Postcard (N)
40/1 OPC (V301-2) 124
51/2 Parkhurst 53
76 DET

STEWART, JOHN
74/5 OPC/Topps 175
72/3 ATL
91/2 Rayside

STEWART, MICHAEL
92/3 Classic 71
92/3 ClassicFourSport 197
94/5 ClassicFourSport 147
92/3 Binghampton
94/5 Binghampton

STEWART, NELSON (NELS)
25-27 Anonymous 92, 97
34-43 BeeHives(NYA)
38/9 BruinsMagazine
33/4 CndGum (V252)
33-35 DiamondMatch
36-39 DiamondMatch (1), (2), (3)
83&87 HallOfFame 86
83 HHOF Postcard (F)
27-32 LaPresse 28/9
33/4 OPC (V304A) 6
34/5 SweetCaporal
60/1 Topps 5
61/2 Topps-Stamp
33/4 WWGum (V357) 12

STEWART, PAUL
90/1 ProSet 699

STEWART, RALPH
74/5 Loblaws
74/5 OPC/Topps 158
75/6 OPC/Topps 182
76/7 OPC/Topps 229
77/8 OPC 386
76/7 VAN/RoyalBan

STEWART, RED
25-27 Anonymous 40

STEWART, RON
45-64 BeeHives(TOR)
64-67 BeeHives(BOS), (TORx2)
62 CeramicTiles
63-5 ChexPhoto
64/5 CokeCap TOR-12
65/6 CocaCola
70/1 EddieSargent 120
70/1 Esso Stamp
68/9 O-Pee-Chee 168
69/70 OPC/Topps 41
70/1 OPC/Topps 64
71/2 OPC/Topps 236
74/5 OPC/Topps 233
52/3 Parkhurst 94
53/4 Parkhurst 9
54/5 Parkhurst 23
55/6 Parkhurst 5
57/8 Parkhurst (TOR) 7
58/9 Parkhurst 14
59/60 Parkhurst 26
60/1 Parkhurst 6
61/2 Parkhurst 6
62/3 Parkhurst 6
63/4 Parkhurst 14, 74
93/4 Parkie(56/7) 110
94/5 Parkie(64/5) 128
95/6 Parkie(66/7) 2
45-54 QuakerOats
60/1 ShirriffCoin 10
62/3 ShirriffCoin 21
68/9 ShirriffCoin NYR16
63/4 TheTorontoStar
64/5 TheTorontoStar
64/5 Topps 99
65/6 Topps 103
66/7 Topps 94
54-67 TorontoStar V8
56-66 TorontoStar 57/8, 58/9
56-66 TorontoStar 62/3
60/1 York
61/2 York 20
63/4 York 3
64/5 TOR

STEWART, RYAN
93/4 Slapshot(Windsor) 19

STEWART, RYAN
84/5 Kamloops
87/8 Moncton

STEWART, SCOTT
91/2 AirCanadaSJHL B24

STICKLE, LEON
90/1 ProSet 700

STIENBURG, TREVOR
89/90 ProCards(AHL) 154
90/1 ProCards 462
91/2 ProCards 372
85/6 QUE/GeneralFoods
88/9 QUE
88/9 QUE/GeneralFoods
86/7 Fredericton
89/90 Halifax
90/1 Halifax

STILES, TONY
84/5 Moncton 23
85/6 Moncton 12

STILL, ALASTAIR
90/1 SketchOHL 395
91/2 SketchOHL 230
88/9 Sudbury 17
89/90 Sudbury 2
90/1 Sudbury 17

STILLMAN, CORY
95/6 Bowman 131, BB27
92/3 Classic 5, 8, LP5
93/4 Classic 29
94/5 Classic 49, T11
92/3 ClassicFourSport 155, -Aut.
94/5 ClassicFourSport 144
94/5 ClassicImages 38
93/4 ClassicProspects 190
92/3 CSC 7
95/6 Donruss 152, -Rated 12
96/7 Donruss 231
96/7 DonrussElite 106
97/8 DonrussPriority 88
95/6 EdgeIce 74
95/6 FleerUltra 214
97/8 KatchMedallion 24
95/6 Leaf 5
96/7 Leaf 138
96/7 LeafPreferred 15
97/8 Omega 35
98/9 Pacific 125
97/8 PacificCrown 211
97/8 PacificCrownRoyale 21
98/9 PacificParamount 32
97/8 PacificRevolution 20
96/7 PaniniSticker 238
95/6 Parkhurst 299
94/5 ParkieSE 29
94/5 Pinnacle 494
95/6 Pinnacle 212
97/8 Pinnacle BeAPlayer 24
97/8 PinnacleInside 164
95/6 P.Zenith 123, -RookRoll 16
96/7 P.Zenith 113
95/6 POG 51
94/5 Premier 515
95/6 Score 300
96/7 Score 243
97/8 Score 225
95/6 SelectCertified 128
96/7 SelectCertified 58
90/1 SketchOHL 192
91/2 SketchAwards 5
91/2 SketchOHL 175
96/7 SkyBoxImpact 172
95/6 SP 17
97/8 SPAuthentic 19
95/6 Topps 332
98/9 Topps 191
95/6 ToppsFinest 61
96/7 ToppsNHLPicks 145, RS9
95/6 ToppsSuperSkills SR4
94/5 UpperDeck 268
95/6 UpperDeck 283
96/7 UpperDeck 229
95/6 UDBeAPlayer 132
98/9 UDChoice 33
95/6 UDCollChoice 111
96/7 UDCollChoice 40
97/8 Zenith 52
94/5 SaintJohn
92/3 Windsor 31

STILLMAN, FREDRIK
95/6 DEL 55
94/5 ElitSet 216,-Gld 6,-Studio 5
95 Globe 17
95 PaniniWorlds 140
94 Semic 57
95 Semic 56
89/90 SemicElitserien 101
90/1 SemicElitserien 103
91/2 SemicElitserien 108, 345
92/3 SemicElitserien 135
91 SemicSticker 34
93 SemicSticker 7
97/8 udSwedish 89, S5

STITT, MARK
95/6 Toledo

STIVER, DAN
93/4 ClassicProspects 99
93/4 StJohns

STOCCO, REGAN
93/4 Slapshot(Guelph) 7
94/5 Slapshot(Guelph) 8
95/6 Slapshot 81
95/6 Guelph

STOCK, COREY
90/1 SketchWHL 309
91/2 SketchWHL 162
92/3 Tacoma
93/4 Tacoma

STOCK, DEAN
97/8 Halifax (1), (2)

STOCKHAM, DARRYL
94/5 Slapshot(MEM) 46

STODDARD, JACK
52/3 Parkhurst 97
53/4 Parkhurst 60

STOGH, HARKIE
95/6 Slapshot 35

STOILOV, LUBOMIR
79 PaniniSticker 351

STOJANOV, ALEK
91/2 Arena 5
95/6 Bowman 141
91/2 Classic 6
91/2 ClassicFourSport 6, -Aut.
95/6 Donruss 329
95/6 Leaf 297
96/7 PinnacleBeAPlayer 80
90/1 SketchMEM 110
90/1 SketchOHL 220
91/2 StarPics 46
95/6 Topps 368
91/2 UltimateDP 6, 62, -Aut 62
91/2 UltimateDP-Promo
95/6 UpperDeck 195

STOLK, DARREN
89/90 ProCards'IHL 157
90/1 ProCards 384
91/2 ProCards 579

STOLP, JEFF
93/4 Dayton 17
94/5 Dayton 18, 24
91/2 Minnesota

STRÖMBERG, MIKA
95 Hartwall
91/2 Jyvas-Hyva 23
92/3 Jyvas-Hyva 55
93/4 Jyvas-Hyva 111
94 Semic 14
95 Semic 26
93 SemicSticker 61
93/4 Sisu 9
94/5 Sisu-Junior 9
95/6 Sisu 47,168,-Dble 2,-Gld 10
96/7 Sisu 42, 183, -AtGala 6
95/6 SisuLimited 12
94/5 SRTetrad CXV
95 SuomenBeckett 7
96 Wien 18

STOMPF, LADISLAV
94/5 DEL 110
95/6 DEL 105

STONE, MATT
90/1 SketchOHL 99
91/2 SketchOHL 311

STONE, MIKE
94/5 Huntington 20

STONE, SHAWN
91/2 SketchWHL 31

STONIER, TROY
95/6 Slapshot 271

STOPAR, ROB
89/90 SketchOHL 94
90/1 SketchOHL 242
90/1 Kitchener 9

STOREY, RED
83&87 HallOfFame 28
83 HHOF Postcard (B)
94/5 HHOFLegends 37

STORF, FLORIAN
94/5 DEL 106
95/6 DEL 104
96/7 DEL 49

STORK, DEAN
92/3 BCJHL 12

STORM, JIM
94/5 Classic-Autograph
93/4 ClassicProspects 37
93/4 Donruss 445
94/5 Donruss 280
94/5 Leaf 213
93/4 Parkhurst 354
94/5 Pinnacle 237
93/4 PowerPlay 356
93/4 Premierr-TeamUSA 22
93/4 Score 610
93/4 T.StadiumClub-TmUSA 23
94/5 ToppsStadiumClub 26
93/4 HFD/Coke
90/1 Mich.Tech
91/2 Mich.Tech

STORMQVIST, JAN-ERIK
89/90 SemicElitserien 34
90/1 SemicElitserien 182

STORR, JAMIE
95/6 Bowman 128
94/5 CanadaJr.Alumni 15
94/5 Classic 7, C9, R18, T33
94/5 ClassicFourSport 121
94/5 C4'Images 100
94/5 ClassicImages 75
93/4 Donruss CAN20
95/6 Donruss 67,-Ptr 15,-CaJr. 1
97/8 Donruss 31
97/8 DonrussPreferred 27
97/8 DonrussPriority 153
94/5 Fleer 99, -Rookie 9
96/7 Fleer 133, -Calder 8
95/6 FleerMetal 192
94/5 FleerUltra-Prospects 8
95/6 FleerUltra 77, 356
96/7 FleerUltra 82, -Rookies 18
95/6 FutureLegends 42, -Pltnm 8
94/5 Leaf-Phenoms 1
95/6 Leaf 12, -StudioRookie 13
97/8 Leaf 138
94/5 LeafLimited-CanadaJrs 10
95/6 LeafLimited 101
97/8 Limited 76
96/7 MetalUniverse 192
97/8 Omega 113
98/9 Pacific 245
98/9 PacificParamount 108
96/7 PaniniSticker 302
93/4 Parkhurst 508
95/6 Parkhurst 104
94/5 ParkieSE 80
93/4 Pinnacle 458
94/5 Pinnacle254,475,521,RTP1
97/8 Pinnacle 82
95/6 Playoff 52
94/5 Premier 437
95/6 ProMagnet 64
94/5 Score 201, TR5
97/8 Score 46
95/6 SelectCertified 136
91/2 SketchOHL 270
95/6 SkBxEmotion 84, -Next 4
95/6 SkyBoxImpact 204
96/7 SkyBoxImpact 159
94/5 Slapshot(Windsor) 2
94/5 SP 137
95/6 Topps 363, 2CJ
98/9 Topps 24
94/5 ToppsFinest 12, 146
94/5 T.Finest-BBest (Red) 7
93/4 UpperDeck 538
94/5 UD 236, 531, 568, SP128
95/6 UpperDeck 47
97/8 UpperDeck 287
94/5 UDBeAPlayer R157
95/6 UDCollChoice 213
97/8 UpperDeckIce 34
93/4 OwenSound (x4)
95/6 Phoenix

STOS, JASON
90/1 SketchOHL 193
91/2 SketchOHL 183
92/3 Toledo 1
89/90 Windsor

STOS, JOHN
90/1 SketchOHL 119
91/2 Rayside
89/90 Windsor

STOTHERS, MIKE
88/9 ProCards(Hershey)
89/90 ProCards(AHL) 343
90/1 ProCards 39
91/2 ProCards 270
81/2 Kingston 20

STOUGHTON, BLAINE
74/5 OPC 348
75/6 OPC/Topps 265
79/80 O-Pee-Chee 356
80/1 OPC/Topps 30, 59, 161,167
81/2 OPC 132, Topps(E) 86
82/3 O-Pee-Chee 122, 130, 131
83/4 O-Pee-Chee 135, 136, 147
84/5 O-Pee-Chee 154
81/2 opcSticker 63
82/3 opcSticker 126
83/4 opcSticker 258, 259
77/8 opcWHA 6
82/3 Post
83/4 PuffySticker 15
83/4 SouhaitsRen.KeyChain
82/3 HFD/JuniorWhalers
83/4 HFD/JuniorWhalers
74/5 TOR
75/6 TOR
91/2 Cincinnati
92/3 Cincinnati

STOWE, MARK
90/1 SketchWHL 263
90/1 PrinceAlbert

SOYANOVICH, DAVE
83/4 NovaScotia 17

STOYANOVICH, STEVE
83/4 HFD/JuniorWhalers
81/2 Indianapolis 11
82/3 Indianapolis

STRACHAN, AL
93/4 ActionPacked 10

STRACHAN, WAYNE
91/2 LakeSuperior

STRAIN, RYAN
90/1 SketchWHL 90
91/2 SketchWHL 163
90/1 Saskatoon 24

STRAKA, JOSEF
95/6 APS 165

STRAKA, MARTIN
94/5 APS 155
95/6 Bowman 72
92/3 Classic 33
92/3 ClassicFourSport 180
93/4 Donruss 266
94/5 Donruss 224
94/5 Flair 141
94/5 Fleer 171
95/6 FleerMetal 107
92/3 FleerUltra 382
93/4 FleerUltra 244
94/5 FleerUltra 171
95/6 FleerUltra 282
93/4 Leaf 220
94/5 Leaf 36
95/6 Leaf 253
94/5 LeafLimited 62
92/3 opcPremier 21
98/9 Pacific 82
97/8 PacificCrown 139
98/9 PacificParamount 197
97/8 PacificRevolution 115
96/7 PaniniSticker 76
97/8 PaniniSticker 57
95 PaniniWorlds 207
92/3 Parkhurst 140
93/4 Parkhurst 156
94/5 Parkhurst V16
95/6 Parkhurst 145, 397
94/5 ParkieSE 134
92/3 Pinnacle 402
93/4 Pinnacle 204
94/5 Pinnacle 352
95/6 Playoff 289
96/7 Playoff 410
94/5 POG 190
95/6 POG 193
93/4 PowerPlay 415, -Rising 7
93/4 Premier 155
94/5 Premier 164
95/6 ProMagnet 114
93/4 Score 375
94/5 Score 82
95/6 Score 132
94/5 Select 36
95 Semic 160
95/6 SkyBoxEmotion 127
95/6 SkyBoxImpact 121
97/8 SPAuthentic 129
95/6 Topps 246
98/9 Topps 45
95/6 ToppsFinestS 92
93/4 ToppsStadiumClub 415
94/5 ToppsStadiumClub 34
95/6 ToppsStadiumClub 87
91/2 UD'CzechWJC 99
92/3 UpperDeck 559, ER19
93/4 UpperDeck 40, SP-125
94/5 UpperDeck 289, SP153
95/6 UpperDeck 427, SE146
96/7 UpperDeck 65
95/6 UDBeAPlayer 106
96/7 UpperDeck"Ice" 24
96/7 FLA/WinnDixie
95/6 OTT
92/3 PGH/Coke
92/3 PGH/Foodland 17
93/4 PGH/Foodland 8
94/5 PGH 25

STRAKA, MICHAL
94/5 APS 156
95/6 APS 254

STRAKHOV, YURI
90/1 O-Pee-Chee 484

STRANDBERG, TOMAS
94/5 ElitSet 48
95/6 ElitSet 156, -FaceTo 1
89/90 SemicElitserien 254
90/1 SemicElitserien 167
91/2 SemicElitserien 17
92/3 SemicElitserien 39
95/6 udElite 13
97/8 udSwedish 7

STRANDER, A.P.
80/1 Mallasjuoma 116

STRANDER, PEKKA
78/9 SM-Liiga 174

STRANKA, G.
95/6 DEL 334

STRANSKY, VLADIMIR
95/6 APS 291

STRATTON, ART
63/4 York 44

STRAUB, JOSEF
94/5 APS 199
95/6 APS 39

STRAUB, BRIAN
91/2 ProCards 323

STRAUSSE, CHRIS
94/5 DEL 319
95/6 DEL 284

STRBA, MARTIN
95/6 APS 73

STREBNICKI, MAREK
94/5 DEL 241
95/6 DEL 235
96/7 DEL 86

STREET, KEITH
89/90 ProCards(IHL) 171

STRELOW, WARREN
90/1 N.J.

STREU, CRAIG
96/7 DEL 15

STRIDA, FLORIAN
95/6 APS 315

STRIEMITZER, KLAUS
94/5 DEL 354

STRINGER, REJEAN
91/2 AirCanadaSJHL A9
92/3 MPSPhotoSJHL 122

STROBEL, ERIC
94/5 MiracleOnIce 35, 36
79/80 USAOlympicTeam 9

STROHACK, MARK
90/1 SketchOHL 295

STROHMAIER, HERBERT
79 PaniniSticker 391

STROKA, RAFAL
92 SemicSticker 274

STROM, DENNIS
90/1 SemicElitserien 119
91/2 SemicElitserien 122
92/3 SemicElitserien 144

STROM, INGEMAR
89/90 SemicElitserien 187
90/1 SemicElitserien 21
91/2 SemicElitserien 220

STROM, PETER
94/5 ElitSet 233, -NHLDraft 8
95/6 ElitSet 148, -Goldies 4
94/5 ParkieSE 242
95/6 udElite 212
97/8 udSwedish 83

STROMBACK, DOUG
93/4 Huntington
84/5 Kitchener 13

STRÖMBERG, MIKA
95 PaniniWorlds 163

STROMQVIST, HAKAN
89/90 SemicElitserien 172

STROMVALL, JOHAN
94/5 ElitSet 30, -Studio 7
95/6 ElitSet 249
89/90 SemicElitserien 156
90/1 SemicElitserien 234
91/2 SemicElitserien 163
92/3 SemicElitserien 187
95/6 udElite 125

STRONG, KEN
95 Globe 183

STRUCH, DAVID
90/1 SketchWHL 78
94/5 SaintJohn
95/6 SaintJohn
89/90 Saskatoon 12
90/1 Saskatoon 10
91/2 Saskatoon 10

STRUDWICK, JASON
95/6 EdgeIce 96
94/5 Slapshot(MEM) 21
93/4 Kamloops

STRUEBY, TODD
90/1 CanadaNats
91/2 ProCards 585
88/9 EDM/ActionMagazine 132
83/4 Moncton 20
84/5 NovaScotia 10
81/2 Saskatoon 16

STRUMM, BOB
93/4 LasVegas
94/5 LasVegas
95/6 LasVegas
96/7 LasVegas

STUART, BILL
23/4 V145-1 22
24/5 V145-2 31

STUART, BRAD
98 BowmanCHL 66, 138
98 BowmanCHL A22, SC8

STUART, BRUCE
91 C55 Reprint 15
83&87 HallOfFame 224
83 HHOF Postcard (O)
1911-12 Imperial (C55) 15
1910-11 Imperial (C56) 17
1910-11 Imperial Post 15

STUART, HOD
83&87 HallOfFame 87
83 HHOF Postcard (F)

STUART, IRA
28/9 PaulinsCandy 61

STUCK, DAN
88/9 ProCards(Hershey)
89/90 ProCards(AHL) 358

STUCKEY, MARK
94/5 DEL 248

STUMPEL, JOZEF
91/2 Classic 34
91/2 ClassicFourSport 34
92/3 ClassicProspects 83, BC16
95/6 DEL 448
93/4 Donruss 23
94/5 Donruss 322
95/6 Donruss 195
97/8 Donruss 134
97/8 DonrussCanadianIce 43
97/8 DonrussElite 26
97/8 DonrussPreferred 55
97/8 DonrussPriority 60
96/7 Flair 7
93/4 FleerUltra 212, -AllRookie 9
94/5 FleerUltra 261
97/8 Kraft-WorldsBest
93/4 Leaf 404
94/5 Leaf 143
95/6 Leaf 223
96/7 Leaf 116
97/8 Leaf 40
97/8 Limited 96
97/8 Omega 114
98/9 Pacific 246, -TeamCL 12
97/8 PacificCrown 71
97/8 PacificCrownRoyale 66
97/8 PcfcDynagon! 9,-Tandm 31
97/8 PacificInvincible 10
97/8 PacificParamount 92
98/9 PacificParamount 109
97/8 PcfcRevolutn 67,-TmCL 12
96/7 PaniniSticker 9
97/8 PaniniSticker 3
91/2 Parkhurst 231
92/3 Pinnacle 412
97/8 Pinnacle 138
93/4 Parkhurst 15
94/5 Parkhurst 19, 293
95/6 Parkhurst 13
94/5 Pinnacle 418
97/8 PinnacleCertified 97
97/8 PinnacleInside 127
93/4 PowerPlay 293
93/4 Premier 416
94/5 Premier 214
96/7 Score 187
97/8 Score 122
97/8 SPAuthentic 71
98/9 SPx"Finite" 41
98/9 Topps 132, SB24
93/4 ToppsStadiumClub 488
92/3 UpperDeck 485
93/4 UpperDeck 379
94/5 UpperDeck 155
95/6 UpperDeck 157
96/7 UpperDeck 12
95/6 UDBeAPlayer 208
96/7 UDBlackDiamond 60
98/9 UDChoice 100
95/6 UDCollChoice 308
97/8 UDCollChoice 18, SQ17
96 Wien 230
97/8 Zenith 28, Z23

STURGEON, MIKE
82/3 Brandon 19

STURGEON, PETER
75/6 O-Pee-Chee 393

STURM, MARCO
95/6 DEL 261
96/7 DEL 149
97/8 DonrussPriority 168
97/8 KatchMedallion 125
97/8 Omega 206
98/9 Pacific 392
97/8 PacificCrownRoyale 122
98/9 PacificParamount 215
97/8 PacificRevolution 127
97/8 P.BAP 243, -OneTimers 19
97/8 Pinn.BeeHive -TeamBH 25
97/8 SPAuthentic 192, I40
98/9 SPx"Finite" 72, 150
98/9 Topps 17, I2, SB12
97/8 UpperDeck 355
97/8 UDBlackDiamond 71, PC12

98/9 UDChoice 181
97/8 UpperDeckIce 52
97/8 Zenith96,Z76,-RookReign 9
97/8 Zenith -RookieZTeam 15
97/8 S.J/PacificBellSheet (x3)

SUCHAN, GREG
89/90 SketchOHL 133
89/90 NiagaraFalls

SUCHANEK, KAREL
95/6 APS 220

SUCHANEK, PAVEL
91/2 AvantGardeBCJHL 30
92/3 BCJHL 68

SUCHANEK, RUDOLF
94/5 APS 103
95/6 APS 55

SUCHY, JAN
70/1 Kuvajulkaisut 59
69/70 MästarSerien 12
72 SemicSticker 36
74 SemicSticker 67
91 SemicSticker 247
71/2 WilliamsFIN 39

SUCHY, RADOSLAV
97/8 Bowman 64

SUGDEN, BRANDON
95/6 Slapshot 160

SUHONEN, ALPO
66/7 Champion 44
93/4 Jyvas-Hyva 103
70/1 Kuvajulkaisut 187
93/4 Sisu 2
89/90 WPG/Safeway

SUHRADA, JIRI
95/6 APS 217

SUHY, ANDY
93/4 Toledo 8
92/3 Toledo (1), (2)

SUIKKANEN, KAI
80/1 Mallasjuoma 105
78/9 SM-Liiga 148

SUK, JOE
87/8 Hull

SUK, STEVE
93/4 Mich.State

SUKOVIC, MIL
91/2 SketchQMJHL 8

SULANDER, ARI
95 Hartwall
93/4 Jyvas-Hyva 104
93/4 Sisu 3
94/5 Sisu 41, -Nolla 3, -Special 8
95/6 Sisu 43,167,-Ghost 3,-Gld 3
96/7 Sisu 41, 175, -AtGala 8
96/7 Sisu-Green 1, -Mighty 4
95/6 SisuLimited 10
96 Wien 10

SULKU, SEBASTIEN
93/4 Sisu 7
95/6 Sisu 137

SULLAMAA, PETRI
92/3 Jyvas-Hyva 51

SULLIMAN, DOUG
90/1 Bowman 110
80/1 O-Pee-Chee 306
82/3 O-Pee-Chee 132
83/4 O-Pee-Chee 148
85/6 O-Pee-Chee 234
86/7 OPC/Topps 121
87/8 OPC/Topps 116
88/9 OPC/Topps 172
90/1 O-pee-Chee 473
82/3 opcSticker 128
83/4 opcSticker 256
87/8 opcSticker 59/200
87/8 PaniniSticker 82
82/3 Post
83/4 SouhaitsRen.KeyChain
82/3 HFD/JuniorWhalers
83/4 HFD/JuniorWhalers
84/5 N.J.
86/7 N.J/SOBER
90/1 N.J.
89/90 PHA

SULLIVAN, ANDY
93/4 StJohns

SULLIVAN, BOB
83/4 O-Pee-Chee 149
83/4 opcSticker 189
83/4 SouhaitsRen.KeyChain
82/3 HFD/JuniorWhalers

SULLIVAN, BRIAN
92/3 ClassicProspects 77
91/2 ProCards 412

SULLIVAN, CHRIS
93/4 Mich.State

SULLIVAN, GEORGE (RED)
45-64 BeeHives(BOS), (NYR)
51/2 Parkhurst 27
52/3 Parkhurst 79
93/4 Parkie(56/7) 86, 170
94/5 Parkie(64/5) 108
60/1 ShirriffCoin 82
61/2 ShirriffCoin 91
54/5 Topps 42
57/8 Topps 56
58/9 Topps 48
59/60 Topps 59
60/1 Topps 18
61/2 Topps 48
63/4 Topps 44
64/5 Topps 29
65/6 Topps 87
54-67 TorontoStar V7
56-66 TorontoStar 59/60
91/2 Ultimate(O6) 29, -Aut 29

SULLIVAN, JEFF
96/7 Halifax (1), (2)
97/8 Halifax (1), (2)

SULLIVAN, JERRY
65/6 Hellas 137

SULLIVAN, KEVIN
90/1 ProCards 595
90/1 KansasCity 6

SULLIVAN, MIKE
92/3 Bowman 116
95/6 Donruss 211
95/6 Leaf 167
92/3 O-Pee-Chee 144
97/8 PacificRegime 32
93/4 PaniniSticker 262
91/2 Parkhurst 383
92/3 Parkhurst 395
93/4 Parkhurst 454
95/6 Parkhurst 300
93/4 Pinnacle 287
97/8 PinnacleBeAPlayer 179
93/4 Premier 21
90/1 ProCards 307
92/3 Score 533
93/4 Score 390
92/3 Topps 282
92/3 ToppsStadiumClub 262
93/4 ToppsStadiumClub 139
92/3 UpperDeck 46
94/5 UDBeAPlayer-Aut. 75
92/3 S.J/PacificBell

SULLIVAN, MICHAEL
90/1 Rayside

SULLIVAN, PETER
79/80 O-Pee-Chee 378
80/1 OPC/Topps 29
76/7 opcWHA 42
77/8 opcWHA 27
80/1 Pepsi Cap
77/8 WPG
79/80 WPG
80/1 WPG

SULLIVAN, RED
see George Sullivan

SULLIVAN, STEVE
96/7 Donruss 229
97/8 Donruss 39
97/8 DonrussCanadianIce 94
97/8 DonrussPreferred 131
97/8 DonrussPriority 92
95/6 EdgeIce 10
95/6 FutureLegends 21, -Pltnm 4
96/7 Leaf-Rookie 10
97/8 Leaf 84
96/7 LeafPreferred 143
97/8 Limited 46, 116
98/9 Pacific 422
97/8 PacificCrown 283
97/8 PcfcDynagon! 123,-Tand 52
97/8 PacificInvincible 138
97/8 PaniniSticker 175
96/7 Pinnacle 226
97/8 Pinnacle 134
96/7 PinnacleBeAPlayer 209
97/8 PinnacleCertified 83
97/8 PinnacleInside 102
96/7 PinnacleZenith 140
97/8 Score 185
97/8 Score(TOR) 7
96/7 SkyBoxImpact 160
93/4 Slapshot(SSMaire) 24
97/8 SPAuthentic 154
96/7 Summit 180
96/7 UpperDeck 185
97/8 UpperDeck 160
97/8 UDCollChoice 248, SQ4
96/7 N.J/Sharp
93/4 SSMarie 16

SULLIVAN, STEVE
91/2 ProCards 443

SULLIVAN, TOM
90/1 SketchOHL 120
91/2 SketchOHL 186

SUMMANEN, ARTO
72/3 WilliamsFIN 186

SUMMANEN, RAIMO
95 Hartwall
91/2 Jyvas-Hyva 16
92/3 Jyvas-Hyva 182
89 SemicSticker 40
91 SemicSticker 20
92 SemicSticker 16
93/4 Sisu 377
94/5 Sisu-Horoscope 15
95/6 Sisu-GoldCards 22
95/6 SisuLimited 7
96 Wien 7
83/4 EDM/McDonald
85/6 EDM/RedRooster
86/7 EDM
86/7 EDM/RedRooster
88/9 EDM/ActionMagazine 3
84/5 NovaScotia 16

SUMMER, STEVE
89/90 ProCards(AHL) 310

SUMMERHILL, BILL
34-43 BeeHives(MTL.C)

SUMMERS, JOHN
95/6 Tallahassee 27

SUMNER, ROB
89/90 Victoria

SUNDBERG, REINO
89/90 SemicElitserien 217
90/1 SemicElitserien 51
91/2 SemicElitserien 226

SUNDBLAD, NIKLAS
91/2 Arena 15
91/2 Classic 16
91/2 C.FourSport 16, -Autograph
93/4 ClassicProspects 143
96/7 Leaf 234
96/7 Pinnacle 230
90/1 SemicElitserien 96
91/2 SemicElitserien 23
92/3 SemicElitserien 46
91/2 StarPics 8
96/7 Summit 176
91/2 UltimateDP 16, -Aut 16
91/2 UltimateDP 72, 85
92/3 UpperDeck 227
94/5 SaintJohn
95/6 SaintJohn

SUNDELIN, ERKKI
71/2 WilliamsFIN 257
73/4 WilliamsFIN 321

SUNDERLAND, MATHIEU
95 Classic 23
93/4 Slapshot(Drum.) 23
96/7 Rimouski

SUNDIN, MATS
95/6 Aces 10 (Diamonds)
96/7 Aces 8 (Diamonds)
97/8 Aces 9 (Clubs)
91/2 Bowman 137
92/3 Bowman 344
95/6 Bowman 49
96/7 CorinthianHeadliners
97/8 CorinthianHeadliners
93/4 Donruss 283, S
95/6 Donruss 176
96/7 Donruss 30
97/8 Donruss 139, -RedAlert 9
96/7 DonrussCanadianIce 12
97/8 DonrussCanadianIce 40
95/6 DonrussElite 72,-Cutting 11
96/7 DonrussElite 55
97/8 DonrussElite 58
97/8 DonrussPreferred 38
97/8 DonrussPriority 56
97/8 D.Studio 67,-HardHats 24
96/7 Duracell JB13
93/4 EASports 111
94/5 ElitSet 24, 232, -Guest 1
95/6 ElitSet 141
97/8 EssoOlympic 41, 42
94/5 Flair 186
96/7 Flair 92, -Centre 9
94/5 Fleer 220
96/7 Fleer 110
95/6 FleerMetal 147, -IntSteel 21
92/3 FleerUltra 180, -Imports 25
93/4 FleerUltra 137
94/5 FleerUltra 220, 379
95/6 FU 164,-Extra 19,-PremP 9
96/7 FleerUltra 166, -MrMom 9
95 Globe 13, 252, 256-58, 269
93/4 HockeyWit 51
95/6 Hoyle'WEST 7 (Clubs)
92/3 HumptyDumpty -2
97/8 KatchMedallion 144
96/7 KennerSLU
97/8 KennerSLU -1on1
90/1 Kraft 42
91/2 Kraft 4
94/5 Kraft'HockeyHeroes
95/6 Kraft
96/7 Kraft'FlexMagnets
96/7 KraftTeamMVPs
97/8 Kraft-CaseSer, -WorldPro
97/8 Kraft-WorldsBest
93/4 Leaf 136
94/5 Leaf 530
95/6 Leaf 244, -FireOnIce 8
96/7 Leaf 53
97/8 Leaf 142, -BannerSeasn 19
94/5 LeafLimited 42
95/6 LeafLimied 120, -StarsOf 9
96/7 LeafLimited 28
96/7 LeafPreferred 14, -Steel 33
97/8 Limited 9, 13, 128
97/8 Limited -fabric 16, 26
96/7 Maggers
95/6 McDonalds 18
97/8 McDonalds McD13, F10
96/7 MetalUniverse 154
97/8 Omega 225, -StickHand 18
91/2 OPC/Topps 12, 219
92/3 O-Pee-Chee 110
90/1 opcPremier 114
98/9 Pacific 13,-Gld 32,-T.CL 25
97/8 PacificCrown 205,-Slap 10B
97/8 PacificCrownRoyale 132
97/8 PCR-HatTrick 17
97/8 PacificDynagon! 124, 144
97/8 PcfcD-BstKt 93,-Tand 16,27
97/8 PacificInv. 139, -Feature 34
97/8 PacificParamount 185
98/9 PacificParamount 231
98/9 PcfcP-SpecD 17,-TmCL 25
97/8 PcfcRevolutn 137,-TmCL24
90/1 Panini(QUE) 20, H
91/2 PaniniSticker 255
92/3 PaniniSticker 212, 302
93/4 PaniniSticker 68
94/5 PaniniSticker 55
95/6 PaniniSticker 201
96/7 PaniniSticker 218
97/8 PaniniSticker 179
95 PaniniWorlds 292
91/2 Parkhurst 144
92/3 Parkhurst 148, 221
93/4 Parkhurst 435, F5
94/5 Parkhurst 185
95/6 Parkhurst 201, 247, C28
95/6 Parkhurst -InterAS 6
94/5 ParkieSE 175, ES2, seV37
91/2 Pinnacle 10, 389
92/3 Pinnacle 90, Tm2000 7
93/4 Pinnacle 2, Tm2001 15
94/5 Pinnacle 386, NL10
95/6 Pinnacle 19, -Roaring20s 7
96/7 Pinnacle 144
97/8 Pinnacle 50
96/7 P.BeAPlayer-Biscuit 12
97/8 PinnacleBeeHive 39
97/8 P.Certified 53, -Team 15
97/8 PinnacleInside 21
97/8 P.Inside-Can 23, -Track 23
96/7 PinnacleMint 17
97/8 PinnacleMint 10
95/6 PinnacleZenith 19
96/7 PinnacleZenith 64
95/6 Playoff 99
94/5 POG 237
95/6 POG 259
93/4 PowerPlay 205
93/4 PP-Global 8, -Point 18
93/4 Premier-BlackOPC 6
93/4 Premier 460, -Finest 5
94/5 Premier 160, 345, 412
95/6 ProMagnet 75
90/1 ProSet 636
91/2 ProSet 197
92/3 ProSet 149
91/2 PSPlatinum 99
90/1 Score 398, 100T, -Young 7
91/2 Score(CDN) 130, (U.S) 130
91/2 Score-YoungStar 3
92/3 Score 153, -YoungStar 3
93/4 Score 9,-(CND) DD5, Intl 10
94/5 Score 89
95/6 Score 56,-Bordr 15,-Gld 16
96/7 Score 160, -Superstition 3
97/8 Score 95
97/8 Score(TOR) 4
94/5 Select 21
95/6 SelectCertified 7
96/7 SelectCertified 85
94 Semic 74
95 Semic 62
89/90 SemicElitserien 72
91/2 SemicElitserien 323, 357
92/3 SemicElitserien 348
91 SemicSticker 211
92 SemicSticker 72
93 SemicSticker 33
95/6 SkyBoxEmotion 175
95/6 SkyBoxImpact 165
96/7 SkyBoxImpact 130
94/5 SP 116
95/6 SP 141, E26
96/7 SP 151, CW12, HC20
97/8 SPAuthentic 150, 133, S12
96/7 SPx 43
97/8 SPx 46, SPX17
98/9 SPx"Finite" 82, 118, 162
96/7 SportFX MiniStix
97/8 SportFX MiniStix
91/2 StarPics 50
95/6 Summit 9
96/7 Summit 51
95/6 SuperSticker 118
96/7 TeamOut
92/3 Topps 125
95/6 Topps 19, 150, 10CG
98/9 Topps 71, L2
94/5 ToppsFinest 110
95/6 ToppsFinest 177
95 ToppsFinestBronze 11
96/7 ToppsNHLPicks 43, TS13
91/2 ToppsStadiumClub 300
92/3 ToppsStadiumClub 478
93/4 T.StadiumClub 370, 425
94/5 ToppsStadiumClub 90
95/6 ToppsStadiumClub 75
94/5 TSC-MembersOnly 26
95/6 TSC-MembersOnly 18
97/8 ToppsSticker 5
95/6 ToppsSuperSkills 32
90/1 UpperDeck 365
91/2 UD 31, 93, 134, E13
92/3 UD 121, 374, E18, WG17
92/3 UD'LockerAS 59
93/4 UpperDeck 220, 228, 302
93/4 UD 419, HT20, SP-132
94/5 UD 51, 548, SP170
95/6 UD 147, 219, AS18, E169
96/7 UD 160, GJ13, LS19
96/7 UD P28, SS23A, X38
96/7 UD-AllStarYCTG A7
97/8 UD 369, S13, SG13
97/8 UD SS13, T14B
94/5 UDBeAPlayer R76
95/6 UDBeAPlayer 203
96/7 UDBlackDiamnd 163, RC13
97/8 UDBlackDiamond 77, PC30
98/9 UDChoice 203, BH17,SQ19
95/6 UDCollChoice 90, C30
96/7 UDCC 255, 332, C29,UD44
97/8 UDCC 245, 320, C23
97/8 UDCC S17, SQ83
97/8 udDiamondVision 17
95/6 udElite 236
97/8 UpperDeckIce 73,IC13,L4C
96 Wien 56, NS3, -Aut
97/8 Zenith 48, Z52
90/1 QUE/PetroCanada
91/2 QUE/PetroCanada
92/3 QUE/PetroCanada

SUNDIN, RONNIE
92/3 SemicElitserien 308
95/6 udElite 207

SUNDLOV, MICHAEL
94/5 ElitSet 126,-Gold15,-Cln 2
95/6 ElitSet 15, -Spidermen 2
95/6 ElitSet-Champs 12,-Mega 1
89/90 SemicElitserien 28
90/1 SemicElitserien 175
91/2 SemicElitserien 28
92/3 SemicElitserien 51
95/6 udElite 19
97/8 udSwedish 17, 216

SUNDQVIST, CARL
72 Hellas 28
72/3 WilliamsFIN 58

SUNDQVIST, K.J.
74 Hellas 36
74 SemicSticker 7
73/4 WilliamsFIN 37

SUNDSTROM, NIKLAS
95/6 Bowman 113, BB21
93/4 Classic 8, DP8
94/5 Classic 79, T44
93/4 ClassicFourSport 192
95/6 Donruss 82, -Rated 3
96/7 Donruss 237
97/8 Donruss 178
95/6 DonrussElite 60, -Rookie 14
96/7 DonrussElite 47
97/8 DonrussPriority 67
94/5 ElitSet 284
96/7 Fleer 72
95/6 FleerMetal 193, -IntSteel 22
95/6 FleerUltra 357, -Extra 18
96/7 FleerUltra 112
95 Globe 60
96/7 Leaf 172
97/8 Leaf 36
95/6 LeafLimited 104, -Rookie 4
97/8 Limited 64
96/7 MetalUniverse 102
97/8 Omega 150
98/9 Pacific 302
97/8 PacificCrown 86
97/8 PacificCrownRoyale 88
98/9 PacificParamount 159
96/7 PaniniSticker 108
97/8 PaniniSticker 89
93/4 Parkhurst 506
95/6 Parkhurst 261, 514
94/5 ParkieSE 237
97/8 PinnacleInside 155
95/6 P.Zenith 128, -RookRoll 14
96/7 Score 269
97/8 Score 194
97/8 Score(NYR) 5
95/6 SelectCertified 135
91/2 SemicElitserien 331
92/3 SemicElitserien 244
95/6 SkyBoxImpact 213, -Fox 16
96/7 SkyBoxImpact 85
94/5 SP 168
95/6 SP 96
96/7 SP HC26
97/8 SPAuthentic 104
95/6 Summit 187
95/6 Topps 341
98/9 Topps 197
95/6 ToppsFinest 59
96/7 ToppsNHLPicks RS18
95/6 T.StadiumClub ER205
95/6 ToppsSuperSkills SR14
92/3 UpperDeck 597
95/6 UpperDeck 261, H28
96/7 UpperDeck 107, X24
97/8 UpperDeck 106, T7B
95/6 UDBeAPlayer 177
98/9 UDChoice 132
95/6 UDCollChoice 408
96/7 UDCollChoice 168
97/8 UDCollChoice 165, SQ41

SUNDSTROM, OLIE
93/4 Cleveland
89/90 SemicElitserien 122
90/1 SemicElitserien 199
91/2 SemicElitserien 129

SUNDSTROM, PATRIK
90/1 Bowman 89
91/2 Bowman 279
86/7 Kraft Sports 70
83/4 O-Pee-Chee 361
84/5 OPC 331
85/6 OPC/Topps 115
86/7 OPC/Topps 156
87/8 OPC/Topps 34
88/9 OPC/Topps 67
89/90 OPC/Topps 56, 77
90/1 OPC/Topps 306
91/2 OPC/Topps 191, 451
83/4 opcSticker 152
84/5 opcSticker 279
85/6 opcSticker 241/108
86/7 opcSticker 101/230
87/8 opcSticker 201
89/90 opcSticker 82/223
87/8 PaniniSticker 348
88/9 PaniniSticker 277
89/90 PaniniSticker 250
90/1 PaniniSticker 65
91/2 PaniniSticker 217
91/2 Pinnacle 290
90/1 ProSet 175, 176
91/2 ProSet 141
91/2 PSPlatinum 71
90/1 Score 19
91/2 Score(CDN) 117, (U.S) 117
82 SemicSticker 15
89 SemicSticker 21
85/6 7Eleven 19
91/2 ToppsStadiumClub 229
90/1 UpperDeck 288
91/2 UpperDeck 369
83/4 Vachon 118
88/9 N.J./Caretta
89/90 N.J.
90/1 N.J.
82/3 VAN
83/4 VAN
84/5 VAN
85/6 VAN
86/7 VAN

SUNDSTROM, PETER
94/5 ElitSet 127
84/5 OPC 155, Topps 116
90/1 SemicElitserien 136
91/2 SemicElitserien 191
92/3 SemicElitserien 219
82 SemicSticker 16
89/90 N.J.
87/8 WSH
87/8 WSH/Kodak
88/9 WSH
88/9 WSH/Smokey

SUNI, ERKKI
70/1 Kuvajulkaisut 288
71/2 WilliamsFIN 160
72/3 WilliamsFIN 187

SUNOHARA, VICKY
97/8 GameOfHerLife
97/8 GeneralMills
97/8 UDCollChoice 280

SUOKAS, JARI
70/1 Kuvajulkaisut 321

SUOKKO, ERKKI
65/6 Hellas 110

SUOKKO, JORMA
66/7 Champion 184
65/6 Hellas 109

SUOKNUUTI, SIMO
70/1 Kuvajulkaisut 305
71/2 WilliamsFIN 258

SUOMALAINEN, JUKKA
95/6 Sisu 138

SUOMINEN, TAPANI
66/7 Champion 31
65/6 Hellas 77

SUOMINEN, VEIKKO
70/1 Kuvajulkaisut 306
72 Panda
78/9 SM-Liiga 62
71/2 WilliamsFIN 187
72/3 WilliamsFIN 136
73/4 WilliamsFIN 192

SUONIEMI, RAIMO
74 Hellas 17
74 SemicSticker 90
71/2 WilliamsFIN 146
72/3 WilliamsFIN 206
73/4 WilliamsFIN 170

SUORANIEMI, KARI
94/5 ElitSet 116
80/1 Mallasjuoma 92
89/90 SemicElitserien 194
92/3 SemicElitserien 255
89 SemicSticker 37

SUORANIEMI, SEPPO
72 Hellas 22
74 Hellas 18
80/1 Mallasjuoma 179
74 SemicSticker 81
82 SemicSticker 32
82 Skopbank
78/9 SM-Liiga 202
77-80 Sportscaster 85-2017
71/2 WilliamsFIN 161
72/3 WilliamsFIN 113
73/4 WilliamsFIN 120

SUORSA, JARI
96/7 Sisu 38

SUP, MICHAEL
94/5 APS 88
95/6 APS 139
91/2 AvantGardeBCJHL 16
91/2 SketchWHL 90

SURA, TAPANI
72/3 WilliamsFIN 238
73/4 WilliamsFIN 273

SURETTE, BRIAN
95/6 Halifax

SUSHINSKI, MAXIM
93/4 Pinnacle 510

SUSI, TIMO
80/1 Mallasjuoma 162
82 SemicSticker 48
82 Skopbank
78/9 SM-Liiga 185
77-80 Sportscaster 91-2169

SUTER, BOB
94/5 MiracleOnIce 33, 34
79/80 USAOlympicTeam 8

SUTER, GARY
90/1 Bowman 101
91/2 Bowman 254
92/3 Bowman 55
93/4 Donruss 53, 415
94/5 Donruss 217
95/6 Donruss 99
96/7 Donruss 130
95/6 DonrussElite 11
93/4 EASports 19
94/5 Flair 38
94/5 Fleer 47
96/7 Fleer 19
95/6 FleerMetal 29
92/3 FleerUltra 30
93/4 FleerUltra 226
94/5 FleerUltra 46
95/6 FleerUltra 36
96/7 FleerUltra 33
95 Globe 104
93/4 HockeyWit 41
89/90 Kraft 61
91/2 Kraft 72
86/7 Kraft Sports 8
93/4 Leaf 140
94/5 Leaf 317
95/6 Leaf 219
96/7 Leaf 32
96/7 Maggers 31
96/7 MetalUniverse 28
86/7 OPC/Topps 189
87/8 OPC/Topps 176
88/9 OPC/Topps 43, T-AS 11
89/90 OPC/Topps 108
90/1 OPC/Topps 205
91/2 OPC/Topps 151
92/3 O-Pee-Chee 278
88/9 opcStars 40
86/7 opcSticker 134/120, 192/54
87/8 opcSticker 49
88/9 opcSticker 89, 113/243
89/90 opcSticker 100
98/9 Pacific 152
97/8 PacificCrown 212
90/1 Panini(CGY) 21, H
87/8 PaniniSticker 207
88/9 PaniniSticker 7
89/90 PaniniSticker 30
90/1 PaniniSticker 177
91/2 PaniniSticker 57
92/3 PaniniSticker 48
93/4 PaniniSticker 186
94/5 PaniniSticker 133
95/6 PaniniSticker 165
96/7 PaniniSticker 163
95 PaniniWorlds 219
91/2 Parkhurst 25
92/3 Parkhurst 23
93/4 Parkhurst 299
94/5 Parkhurst 47, V74
95/6 Parkhurst 39, PP26
91/2 Pinnacle 11, 392
92/3 Pinnacle 195
93/4 Pinnacle 14
94/5 Pinnacle 137
95/6 Pinnacle 68
96/7 Pinnacle 195
96/7 PinnacleBeAPlayer 180
95/6 PinnacleZenith 73
95/6 Playoff 238
94/5 POG 75
95/6 POG 69
93/4 PowerPlay 44
93/4 Premier 178, -BlckTopps 10
94/5 Premier 168
90/1 ProSet 46
91/2 ProSet 32, 276
92/3 ProSet 27
91/2 PSPlatinum 20
90/1 Score 88
91/2 Score(CDN) 464, (U.S) 244
92/3 Score 17
93/4 Score 13
94/5 Score 44
95/6 Score 82
96/7 Score 182
94 Semic 121
89 SemicSticker 155
91 SemicSticker 132
92 SemicSticker 152
93 SemicSticker 176
95/6 SkyBoxEmotion 34
95/6 SkyBoxImpact 34
96/7 SkyBoxImpact 20
95/6 SP 25
96/7 SP 29
95/6 Summit 59
96/7 TeamOut
92/3 Topps 308
95/6 Topps 156, 9HG
98/9 Topps 26
95/6 ToppsFinest 126
96/7 ToppsNHLPicks 41
91/2 ToppsStadiumClub 143
92/3 ToppsStadiumClub 423
93/4 ToppsStadiumClub 228
95/6 ToppsStadiumClub 124
90/1 UpperDeck 273
91/2 UpperDeck 341, 510
92/3 UpperDeck 249
93/4 UpperDeck 357
94/5 UpperDeck 74, SP107
95/6 UD 284, AS8, SE107
96/7 UpperDeck 235, X37
94/5 UDBAP R94, -Aut. 112
98/9 UDChoice 47
95/6 UDCollChoice 8
96/7 UDCollChoice 52
97/8 UDCollChoice 45
96 Wien 162
85/6 CGY/RedRooster
86/7 CGY/RedRooster
87/8 CGY/RedRooster
90/1 CGY/McGavins
91/2 CGY/IGA
92/3 CGY/IGA 8

SUTHERLAND, BILL
71/2 EddieSargent 188
68/9 O-Pee-Chee 196
69/70 O-Pee-Chee 172
70/1 OPC/Topps 83
71/2 OPC/Topps 141
89/90 ProCards(AHL) 75
71/2 TheTorontoSun
68/9 TOR
79/80 WPG
81/2 WPG
82/3 WPG
84/5 WPG/Police
85/6 WPG
85/6 WPG/Police
86/7 WPG
88/9 WPG/Police
60/1 Cleveland
63/4 QuébecAces
65/6 QuébecAces

SUTHERLAND, J.T.
83&87 HallOfFame 44
83 HHOF Postcard (C)

SUTHERLAND, STEVE
76/7 opcWHA 127
72/3 LosAngeles
76/7 QuébecNordiques
76 QuébecNordiques/MA

SUTINEN, TIMO
96/7 DEL 134
74 Hellas 19
74 SemicSticker 91, -CL1
71/2 WilliamsFIN 108
72/3 WilliamsFIN 152
73/4 WilliamsFIN 79, 121

SUTTER, BRENT
90/1 Bowman 126
91/2 Bowman 226
92/3 Bowman 147
93/4 Donruss 69
94/5 Donruss 290
92/3 FleerUltra 43
93/4 FleerUltra 206
94/5 FleerUltra 47
90/1 Kraft 57
91/2 Kraft 43
93/4 Leaf 142
94/5 Leaf 30
82/3 O-Pee-Chee 216
83/4 O-Pee-Chee 18
84/5 O-Pee-Chee 80, 136
85/6 OPC/Topps 107
86/7 OPC/Topps 117
87/8 OPC/Topps 27
88/9 OPC/Topps 7
89/90 OPC/Topps 14
90/1 OPC/Topps 258
91/2 OPC/Topps 165
92/3 O-Pee-Chee 60
90/1 opcPremier 115
91/2 opcPremier 156
82/3 opcSticker 56
84/5 opcSticker 88
85/6 opcSticker 71, 117
86/7 opcSticker 211
87/8 opcSticker 241/107
88/9 opcSticker 105/235
89/90 opcSticker 115/252
97/8 PacificCrown 186
87/8 PaniniSticker 99
88/9 PaniniSticker 292
89/90 PaniniSticker 266
90/1 PaniniSticker 90
91/2 PaniniSticker 246
93/4 PaniniSticker 151
96/7 PaniniSticker 165
91/2 Parkhurst 35
92/3 Parkhurst 33, CP3
93/4 Parkhurst 308
91/2 Pinnacle 79
92/3 Pinnacle 39
93/4 Pinnacle 91
94/5 Pinnacle 117
94/5 POG 72
93/4 PowerPlay 56
93/4 Premier 147
90/1 ProSet 191
91/2 ProSet 154, 374
92/3 ProSet 36
91/2 PSPlatinum 74, 164
90/1 Score 39, -HotCards 19
91/2 Score(CDN) 463
91/2 Score(U.S) 243, 103T
92/3 Score 112
93/4 Score 44
94/5 Score 32
95/6 Score 272
94 Semic 91
92 SemicSticker 92
83/4 SouhaitsRen.KeyChain
91 TeamCanada
84/5 Topps 102
92/3 Topps 75
91/2 ToppsStadiumClub 180
92/3 ToppsStadiumClub 428
93/4 ToppsStadiumClub 211
94/5 ToppsStadiumClub 218
90/1 UpperDeck 249
91/2 UpperDeck 140, 645
92/3 UpperDeck 199
95/6 UDBeAPlayer 140
91/2 CHI/Coke
93/4 CHI/Coke
83/4 NYI
83/4 NYI/Islander 12
84/5 NYI 13
89/90 NYI
84/5 KelownaWings&WHL 29

SUTTER, BRIAN
78/9 O-Pee-Chee 319
79/80 OPC/Topps 84
80/1 OPC/Topps 244
81/2 OPC 297, Topps(W) 122
82/3 O-Pee-Chee 298, 311
83/4 O-Pee-Chee 308, 320
84/5 OPC 192, Topps 135
85/6 OPC/Topps 135, N
86/7 OPC/Topps 72, O
81/2 opcSticker 133
82/3 opcSticker 198
83/4 opcSticker 127, 128
84/5 opcSticker 56
85/6 opcSticker 46
86/7 opcSticker 175/38
88/9 opcSticker 15/142
87/8 PaniniSticker 303
88/9 PaniniSticker 110
82/3 Post
90/1 ProSet 676
83/4 PuffySticker 17
91/2 Score(CDN) 268, (U.S) 378
85/6 7Eleven 17
91/2 UpperDeck 645
87/8 STL
87/8 STL/Kodak
88/9 STL
89/90 STL/Kodak
90/1 STL/Kodak
92/3 STL/UpperDeck 25

SUTTER, DARRYL
81/2 OPC 65, Topps(W) 77
82/3 O-Pee-Chee 76
83/4 O-Pee-Chee 113
84/5 O-Pee-Chee 47, Topps 36
85/6 OPC/Topps 100
86/7 OPC/Topps 49
83/4 opcSticker 105
84/5 opcSticker 30
85/6 opcSticker 23/152
86/7 opcSticker 151/6
87/8 PaniniSticker 234
88/9 ProCards(Saginaw)
89/90 ProCards(IHL) 58
83/4 SouhaitsRen.KeyChain
91/2 UpperDeck 645
80/1 CHI/4x6
80/1 CHI/5.5x8.5
81/2 CHI
82/3 CHI
86/7 CHI/Coke
87/8 CHI/Coke
90/1 CHI/Coke
91/2 CHI/Coke
93/4 CHI/Coke
97/8 S.J/PacificBellSheet

SUTTER, DUANE
90/1 Bowman 12
81/2 O-Pee-Chee 211
82/3 O-Pee-Chee 212
83/4 O-Pee-Chee 19
84/5 O-Pee-Chee 137
85/6 O-Pee-Chee 227
86/7 OPC/Topps 39
87/8 OPC/Topps 43
89/90 O-Pee-Chee 221
90/1 O-Pee-Chee 466
82/3 opcSticker 52
85/6 opcSticker 72/199
86/7 opcSticker 210
87/8 PaniniSticker 102
90/1 ProSet 61
91/2 UpperDeck 645
87/8 CHI/Coke
88/9 CHI/Coke
89/90 CHI/Coke
96/7 FLA/WinnDixie
97/8 FLA/WinnDixie
83/4 NYI
83/4 NYI/Islander 13
84/5 NYI 14
96/7 S.J/PacificBellSheet
97/8 S.J/PacificBellSheet
84/5 KelownaWingsWHL 48
93/4 Indianapolis

SUTTER, RICH
91/2 Bowman 370
92/3 Bowman 256
92/3 FleerUltra 398
93/4 FleerUltra 293
84/5 O-Pee-Chee 169
85/6 O-Pee-Chee 208
86/7 OPC/Topps 29
87/8 O-Pee-Chee 258
88/9 O-Pee-Chee 255
89/90 O-Pee-Chee 282
90/1 O-Pee-Chee 405
91/2 OPC/Topps 143
84/5 opcSticker 111
86/7 opcSticker 242/109
87/8 opcSticker 193/52
88/9 opcSticker 57/190
89/90 opcSticker 62/204
87/8 PaniniSticker 350
88/9 PaniniSticker 142
89/90 PaniniSticker 157
91/2 PaniniSticker 33
92/3 PaniniSticker 19
93/4 PaniniSticker 160
91/2 Parkhurst 372
91/2 Pinnacle 268
93/4 Pinnacle 108
94/5 Pinnacle 235
93/4 PowerPlay 317
90/1 ProSet 272
91/2 ProSet 217
91/2 PSPlatinum 108
90/1 Score 281
91/2 Score(CDN) 63, 268
91/2 Score(U.S) 63, 378
92/3 Score 327
93/4 Score 323, 498
92/3 Topps 434
91/2 ToppsStadiumClub 192
92/3 T.StadiumClub 389, 488
93/4 ToppsStadiumClub 46
90/1 UpperDeck 328
91/2 UpperDeck 317, 645
92/3 UpperDeck 143, 184
93/4 CHI/Coke
83/4 PGH/Heinz
83/4 PHA
90/1 STL/Kodak
91/2 STL
86/7 VAN
87/8 VAN/Shell
88/9 VAN/Mohawk
89/90 VAN
84/5 KelownaWingsWHL 24

SUTTER, RON
91/2 Bowman 238
92/3 Bowman 175
93/4 Donruss 288, 482
92/3 FleerUltra 190
93/4 Leaf 275
94/5 Leaf 351
84/5 OPC 170, Topps 122
85/6 OPC/Topps 6
86/7 OPC/Topps 109
87/8 OPC/Topps 113
88/9 OPC/Topps 126
89/90 OPC/Topps 173
90/1 OPC/Topps 45
91/2 OPC/Topps 232, 329
92/3 O-Pee-Chee 362
91/2 opcPremier 95
84/5 opcSticker 107
86/7 opcSticker 243/110
87/8 opcSticker 102/235
89/90 opcSticker 107/246
97/8 PacificRegime 181
87/8 PaniniSticker 137
89/90 PaniniSticker 299
90/1 PaniniSticker 109
91/2 PaniniSticker 233
92/3 PaniniSticker 20
93/4 PaniniSticker 161
91/2 Parkhurst 158
92/3 Parkhurst 389
91/2 Pinnacle 95
93/4 Pinnacle 95
94/5 Pinnacle 383
97/8 PinnacleBeAPlayer 106
93/4 Premier 103
94/5 Premier 428
90/1 ProSet 224
91/2 ProSet 178, 476
92/3 ProSet 162
91/2 PSPlatinum 222
90/1 Score 153
91/2 Score(CDN) 268, 619
91/2 Score(U.S) 298, 378, 69T
92/3 Score 86
93/4 Score 39
94/5 Score 177
95/6 Score 113
92/3 Topps 371
91/2 ToppsStadiumClub 49
92/3 ToppsStadiumClub 36, 488
93/4 ToppsStadiumClub 86
90/1 UpperDeck 68
91/2 UpperDeck 309, 645
93/4 UpperDeck 33
83/4 PHA
86/7 PHA
89/90 PHA
90/1 PHA
91/2 STL
96/7 S.J/PacificBellSheet
97/8 S.J/PacificBellSheet
84/5 KelownaWings&WHL 40

SUTTON, BOYD
91/2 Greensboro
92/3 Oklahoma

SUTTON, DAVE
91/2 Rayside

SUTTON, KEN
92/3 Bowman 422
92/3 FleerUltra 20
93/4 Leaf 295
94/5 Leaf 498
92/3 O-Pee-Chee 165
91/2 Parkhurst 239
92/3 Parkhurst 254
91/2 Pinnacle 325
92/3 Pinnacle 216
93/4 Pinnacle 336
94/5 Pinnacle 437
93/4 Premier 89
89/90 ProCards(AHL) 260
90/1 ProCards 271
91/2 Score(CDN) 283, (U.S) 393
92/3 Score 292
93/4 Score 410
92/3 Topps 59
92/3 ToppsStadiumClub 292
93/4 ToppsStadiumClub 219
91/2 UpperDeck 458
91/2 BUF/BlueShield
91/2 BUF/Campbell
92/3 BUF/BlueShield
92/3 BUF/Jubillee
89/90 Saskatoon 7

SUTTON, SCOTT
89/90 Rayside
91/2 Rayside

SUTVLA, KEN
67/8 ColumbusCheckers

SUVANTO, ESA
70/1 Kuvajulkaisut 342

SUVANTO, HARRI
92/3 Jyvas-Hyva 124
93/4 Sisu 192
94/5 Sisu 100
95/6 Sisu 134

SUZOR, MARK
78/9 O-Pee-Chee 307
77/8 COL.R/CokeCans
78/9 Saginaw

SVABERG, BO
94/5 ElitSet 79
95/6 ElitSet 95
90/1 SemicElitserien 145
91/2 SemicElitserien 197
92/3 SemicElitserien 213
95/6 udElite 145

SVARTVADET, PER
94/5 ElitSet 245
95/6 ElitSet 107
94/5 ParkieSE 235
95/6 udElite 166
97/8 udSwedish 162, 204, 215

SVEDBERG, LENNART
95 Globe 66
70/1 Kuvajulkaisut 39
69/70 MästarSerien 46, 50
72 Panda
72 SemicSticker 46
91 SemicSticker 232
71/2 WilliamsFIN 59

SVEDBERG, MATHIAS
94/5 ElitSet 111
90/1 SemicElitserien 107
91/2 SemicElitserien 113
92/3 SemicElitserien 132

SVEHLA, ROBERT
95/6 Donruss 370
96/7 Donruss 77
94/5 ElitSet 43, -TopGun 6
96/7 Flair 39
96/7 Fleer 43
95/6 FleerMetal 194
96/7 FleerNHLPicks 42
95/6 FleerUltra 358, -High 18
96/7 FleerUltra 69
95/6 Leaf 230
96/7 Leaf 77
96/7 MetalUniverse 63
97/8 Omega 101
98/9 Pacific 228
97/8 PacificCrown 243
97/8 PcfcDynagon! 56,-Tand 51
98/9 PacificParamount 100
96/7 PaniniSticker 74
97/8 PaniniSticker 55
95/6 Parkhurst 84
96/7 Pinnacle 38
97/8 Pinnacle 25, 141
97/8 PinnacleInside 159
95/6 PinnacleZenith 148
96/7 Score 83
97/8 Score 189
95/6 SelectCertified 115
92/3 SemicElitserien 207
93 SemicSticker 102
96/7 SkyBoxImpact 49
96/7 SP 63
98/9 SPx"Finite" 38
95/6 Summit 196
96/7 Summit 52
96/7 TeamOut
95/6 Topps 257
95/6 ToppsFinest 183
95/6 ToppsStadiumClub 216
95/6 UpperDeck 172
96/7 UpperDeck 67
97/8 UpperDeck 73
95/6 UDBeAPlayer 169
98/9 UDChoice 88

96/7 UDCollChoice 104
97/8 UDCollChoice 104, SQ2
96 Wien 221
96/7 FLA/WinnDixie
97/8 FLA/WinnDixie

SVEJKOVSKY, JAROSLAV
95/6 Bowman P32
97/8 Donruss 220, -Rated 9
97/8 DonrussCanadianIce 143
97/8 D.Elite 22, 141,-Craftsm 5
97/8 D.Preferd 146, 167,-Line 8B
97/8 D.Priority 167,219,-DirD 19
97/8 D.Studio 47, -Portraits 32
96/7 Flair 125
97/8 KatchMedallion 48
97/8 Leaf 67, 167
97/8 Limited 33,96,143,-fabric 32
97/8 McDonalds McD35
98/9 Pacific 447
97/8 PacificCrown 277
97/8 PacificCrownRoyale 143
97/8 PacificParamount 200
97/8 Pinnacle 25
97/8 PinnacleBeAPlayer 242
97/8 PinnacleInside 125
97/8 PinnacleMint 25
97/8 Score 53
97/8 SPAuthentic S26
97/8 UpperDeck 195, SG52
97/8 UDCollChoice 272
97/8 UpperDeckIce 40
96/7 Portland

SVENSSON, ANDERS
90/1 SemicElitserien 132
91/2 SemicElitserien 184
92/3 SemicElitserien 202

SVENSSON, LEIF
79/80 O-Pee-Chee 374
78/9 WSH
79/80 WSH

SVENSSON, MAGNUS
95/6 Donruss 166
94/5 ElitSet-GoldCard 13
95 Globe 12
95/6 Leaf 10
95/6 PaniniSticker 78
95 PaniniWorlds 138
95/6 Parkhurst 83
94 Semic 58
95 Semic 55, 203
89/90 SemicElitserien 125
91/2 SemicElitserien 133
92/3 SemicElitserien 158
95/6 SkyBoxEmotion 71
95/6 SkyBoxImpact 69
95/6 udElite 243
97/8 udSwedish 97, 104, C11
96 Wien 46

SVENSSON, NILS-GUNNAR
89/90 SemicElitserien 103

SVENSSON, PER-JOHAN (PELLE)
96/7 DEL 40
94/5 ElitSet 57
95/6 ElitSet 120
92/3 SemicElitserien 265
95/6 udElite 182

SVERZTOV, ALEXANDER
91/2 UD-CzechWJC 8

SVETLIK, MARTIN
90/1 SketchWHL 101

SVETLOV, SERGEI
82 SemicSticker 69

SVOBODA, LADISLAV
95/6 APS 146

SVOBODA, OLDRICH
95/6 APS 53
93/4 Jyvas-Hyva 254
94 Semic 164
92 SemicSticker 123
93/4 Sisu 280

SVOBODA, PETR
94/5 APS 205
90/1 Bowman 46
91/2 Bowman 341
92/3 Bowman 47
93/4 Donruss 41
95/6 Donruss 306
93/4 EASports 14
92/3 FleerUltra 263
89/90 Kraft 27
86/7 KraftSports 40
93/4 Leaf 131
94/5 Leaf 393
95/6 Leaf 180
88/9 O-Pee-Chee 256
89/90 O-Pee-Chee 238
90/1 OPC/Topps 246
91/2 OPC/Topps 76
92/3 O-Pee-Chee 109
91/2 opcPremier 168
88/9 opcStars 41
85/6 opcSticker 139/11
86/7 opcSticker 17/160
87/8 opcSticker 18/158
88/9 opcSticker 44/177
89/90 opcSticker 54/198
97/8 PacificCrown 277
90/1 Panini(MTL) 23
88/9 PaniniSticker 255
89/90 PaniniSticker 244
90/1 PaniniSticker 50
91/2 PaniniSticker 185
96/7 PaniniSticker 120
97/8 PaniniSticker 97
91/2 Parkhurst 237
95/6 Parkhurst 427
94/5 ParkieSE 21
91/2 Pinnacle 197
92/3 Pinnacle 117
93/4 Pinnacle 32
94/5 Pinnacle 424
95/6 Pinnacle 168
96/7 PinnacleBeAPlayer 56
95/6 POG 208
93/4 Premier 308, 324
90/1 ProSet 161
91/2 ProSet 123
92/3 ProSet 16
91/2 PSPlatinum 65
90/1 Score 191
91/2 Score(CDN) 95, (U.S) 95
92/3 Score 114
93/4 Score 110
95/6 Score 287
97/8 Score(PHA) 17
96/7 SP 111
92/3 Topps 312
91/2 ToppsStadiumClub 127
92/3 ToppsStadiumClub 227
93/4 ToppsStadiumClub 132
90/1 UpperDeck 193
91/2 UpperDeck 285
93/4 UpperDeck 465
95/6 UpperDeck 76
95/6 UDCollChoice 93
92/3 BUF/BlueShield
92/3 BUF/Jubillee
84/5 MTL
85/6 MTL
85/6 MTL/Pennant
85/6 MTL/PepsiPlacemats
85/6? MTL/ProvigoPlacemats
85/6 MTL/ProvStickers
86/7 MTL
87/8 MTL
87/8 MTL/Stickers 75. 77
88/9 MTL
89/90 MTL
89/90 MTL/Figurine
89/90 MTL/Kraft
90/1 MTL
91/2 MTL
94/5 PHA
96/7 PHA/OceanSpray

SVOBODA, VALERY
95/6 Slapshot 424

SVOZIL, LADISLAV
95/6 APS 292

SWAIN, BRAD
92/3 BCJHL 19

SWAIN, GARRY
76/7 opcWHA 91

SWAN, JIM
86/7 Portland

SWANJORD, S.
93/4 Waterloo

SWANSON, BRAD
93/4 Portland

SWANSON, BRIAN
95/6 DonrussElite-WorldJrs 42

SWARBRICK, GEORGE
68/9 O-Pee-Chee 174
70/1 OPC/Topps 82
68/9 ShirriffCoin OAK5
70/1 PHA

SWARD, MARTIN
94/5 ElitSet 89
95/6 ElitSet 113, -Spidermen 11
95/6 udElite 170

SWARTZ, TIM
95/6 Slapshot 383
96/7 Sudbury 24

SWEENEY, BOB
90/1 Bowman 28
91/2 Bowman 357
92/3 Bowman 5, 402
92/3 FleerUltra 264
93/4 FleerUltra 278
94/5 Leaf 417
88/9 OPC/Topps 134
89/90 OPC/Topps 135, OPC 304
90/1 OPC/Topps 99
91/2 OPC/Topps 99
92/3 O-Pee-Chee 21
92/3 opcPremier 110
88/9 opcSticker 38, 28/168
88/9 opcSticker 130/266, FS 19
88/9 PaniniSticker 214
90/1 PaniniSticker 15
91/2 PaniniSticker 177
93/4 PaniniSticker 104
92/3 Parkhurst 251
93/4 Parkhurst 290
94/5 ParkieSE 17
91/2 Pinnacle 222
93/4 Pinnacle 118
94/5 Pinnacle 411
95/6 Playoff 232
93/4 PowerPlay 34
93/4 Premier 431
90/1 ProSet 15
91/2 ProSet 6
90/1 Score 235
91/2 Score(CDN) 176, (U.S) 176
92/3 Score 317
93/4 Score 146
92/3 Topps 111
91/2 ToppsStadiumClub 75
92/3 ToppsStadiumClub 455
93/4 ToppsStadiumClub 63
90/1 UpperDeck 198
91/2 UpperDeck 391
92/3 UpperDeck 47, 449
93/4 UpperDeck 312
94/5 UpperDeck 445
95/6 UpperDeck 443
95/6 UDBeAPlayer 26
96/7 UDCollChoice 37
88/9 BOS/SportsAction
89/90 BOS/SportsAction
90/1 BOS/SportsAction
91/2 BOS/SportsAction
92/3 BUF/BlueShield
92/3 BUF/Jubillee
86/7 Moncton 21

SWEENEY, DON
91/2 Bowman 365
92/3 Bowman 5, 402
93/4 Donruss 21
94/5 Donruss 281
95/6 Donruss 101
93/4 EASports 8
94/5 Flair 14
94/5 Fleer 18
92/3 FleerUltra 257
93/4 FleerUltra 271
94/5 FleerUltra 17
95/6 FleerUltra 208
93/4 Leaf 281
94/5 Leaf 518
95/6 Leaf 191
91/2 OPC/Topps 319
92/3 O-Pee-Chee 40
97/8 PacificRegime 17
91/2 PaniniSticker 180
93/4 PaniniSticker 11
95/6 PaniniSticker 11
97/8 PaniniSticker 7
91/2 Parkhurst 228
92/3 Parkhurst 244
93/4 Parkhurst 13
95/6 Parkhurst 283
94/5 ParkieSE 15
91/2 Pinnacle 419
92/3 Pinnacle 179
93/4 Pinnacle 269
94/5 Pinnacle 91
95/6 Pinnacle 141
96/7 PinnacleBeAPlayer 97
94/5 POG 40
95/6 POG 35
93/4 PowerPlay 24
93/4 Premier 334
94/5 Premier 262
89/90 ProCards(AHL) 58
90/1 ProSet 412
91/2 PSPlatinum 153
90/1 Score 51
91/2 Score(CDN) 146, (U.S) 146
92/3 Score 186
93/4 Score 169
94/5 Score 101
95/6 Score 163
97/8 Score(BOS) 20
95/6 SkyBoxEmotion 13
95/6 SP 11
96/7 SP 10
92/3 Topps 417
95/6 Topps 127
98/9 Topps 141
91/2 ToppsStadiumClub 370
92/3 ToppsStadiumClub 337
93/4 ToppsStadiumClub 117
95/6 ToppsStadiumClub 146
95/6 ToppsSuperSkills 26
91/2 UpperDeck 338
92/3 UpperDeck 391
93/4 UpperDeck 101
94/5 UpperDeck 446
95/6 UpperDeck 35
96/7 UpperDeck 136, 217
97/8 UpperDeck 14
94/5 UDBeAPlayer-Aut. 60
95/6 UDCollChoice 91
96/7 UDCollChoice 14
89/90 BOS/SportsAction
90/1 BOS/SportsAction
91/2 BOS/SportsAction
92/3 BOS

SWEENEY, TIM
91/2 Bowman 261
93/4 Donruss 11
94/5 Donruss 214
94/5 Flair 6
93/4 FleerUltra 262
94/5 FleerUltra 8
94/5 Leaf 21
97/8 Omega 151
90/1 opcPremier 116
98/9 Pacific 303
97/8 PacificCrown 183
90/1 Panini(CGY) 22
95 PaniniWorlds 226
93/4 Parkhurst 7
94/5 Parkhurst 9
94/5 Pinnacle 93
97/8 PinnacleBeAPlayer 156
94/5 POG 34
93/4 PowerPlay 12
93/4 Premier 426
94/5 Premier 147
89/90 ProCards(IHL) 203
90/1 ProSet 597
91/2 ProSet 364
90/1 ScoreTraded 13T
95 Semic 108
91/2 ToppsStadiumClub 394
93/4 ToppsStadiumClub 473
90/1 UpperDeck 531
91/2 UpperDeck 375
92/3 UpperDeck 95
93/4 UpperDeck 385
94/5 UpperDeck 38
93/4 ANA/Caps 1
90/1 CGY/McGavins
91/2 CGY/IGA

SWEET, TROY
90/1 SketchOHL 347
91/2 SketchOHL 159
90/1 Oshawa 9
91/2 Oshawa

SWEITZER, JASON
95/6 Slapshot 252

SWENSON, BARKLEY
91/2 SketchWHL 257
91/2 PrinceAlbert
92/3 Tacoma

SWIATEK, ANDRZEJ
89 SemicSticker 136

SWIBENKO, MARCO
94/5 DEL 41
95/6 DEL 38

SWINSON, WES
93/4 Slapshot(Kitchener) 20
94/5 Slapshot(Kitchener) 22
95/6 Slapshot 127

SWITZER, DEREK
89/90 SketchOHL 150
90/1 SketchOHL 318

SWITZER, JASON
91/2 AvantGardeBCJHL 23
92/3 BCJHL 199

SYCHRA, MARTIN
93/4 Slapshot(Kingston) 14
94/5 Fredericton

SYDOR, DARRYL
92/3 Bowman 321
93/4 Donruss 164
94/5 Donruss 70
95/6 Donruss 73
92/3 FleerUltra 312
93/4 FleerUltra 60
94/5 FleerUltra 308
95/6 FleerUltra 78
97/8 KatchMedallion 48
93/4 Leaf 206, -GoldL.Rook 15
94/5 Leaf 136
95/6 Leaf 199
97/8 Limited 6
97/8 Omega 75
92/3 O-Pee-Chee 11
91/2 opcPremier 90
92/3 opcPremier 16
98/9 Pacific 183
97/8 PacificCC 48
97/8 PcfcDynagon! 39,-Tand 34
97/8 PacificDParamount 62
98/9 PacificParamount 70
92/3 PaniniSticker F
95/6 PaniniSticker 275
97/8 PaniniSticker 140
95 PaniniWorlds 6
92/3 Parkhurst 69
93/4 Parkhurst 96
95/6 Parkhurst 371
94/5 ParkieSE 82
91/2 Pinnacle 321
93/4 Pinnacle 113
94/5 Pinnacle 328
95/6 Pinnacle 96
97/8 Pinnacle 139
96/7 PinnacleBeAPlayer 176
95/6 Playoff 160
96/7 Playoff 375
95/6 POG 141
93/4 PowerPlay 122
93/4 Premier 226
94/5 Premier 86
91/2 ProSet 542
92/3 ProSet 228
90/1 Score 425
91/2 Score(CDN) 631, (U.S) 81T
92/3 Score 410
93/4 Score 311
94/5 Score 97
95/6 Score 26
97/8 Score 238
89/90 SketchMEM 12
90/1 SketchOHL 307
91/2 SketchAwards 14
95/6 SkyBoxEmotion 85
95/6 SkyBoxImpact 82
96/7 Summit 33
92/3 Topps 39
92/3 ToppsStadiumClub 72
93/4 ToppsStadiumClub 225
94/5 ToppsStadiumClub 164
90/1 UpperDeck 358
91/2 UpperDeck 549
92/3 UpperDeck 63
93/4 UpperDeck 83, SP-74
94/5 UpperDeck 104
95/6 UpperDeck 5
97/8 UpperDeck 54
94/5 UDBeAPlayer R90, -Aut. 26
98/9 UDChoice 67
95/6 UDCollChoice 83
97/8 UDCollChoice 72
96/7 DAL/Southwest
88/9 Kamloops
89/90 Kamloops

SYKES, PHIL
91/2 Bowman 194
86/7 O-Pee-Chee 216
91/2 OPC/Topps 189
90/1 Panini(WPG) 23
87/8 PaniniSticker 285
88/9 ProCards(NewHaven)
89/90 ProCards(AHL) 4
91/2 Score(CDN) 534
91/2 ToppsStadiumClub 271
84/5 L.A/Smokeys
88/9 L.A.
90/1 WPG/IGA
91/2 WPG/IGA

SYKORA, MAREK
94/5 APS 279

SYKORA, MICHAL
93/4 Classic 30
93/4 ClassicProspect 38
93/4 Donruss 307
94/5 Donruss 204
94/5 Fleer 201
94/5 FleerUltra 369
93/4 Leaf 431
94/5 Leaf 122
97/8 PacificRegime 47
95/6 PaniniSticker 286
96/7 PaniniSticker 285
97/8 PaniniSticker 132
93/4 Parkhurst 257
95/6 Parkhurst 181
93/4 Pinnacle 452
96/7 PinnacleBeAPlayer 113
95/6 POG 230
94/5 Premier 362
93/4 Score 600
91/2 SketchWHL 164
95/6 Topps 105
93/4 UpperDeck 489
94/5 UpperDeck 195
96/7 UpperDeck 151
92/3 S.J/PacificBell
96/7 S.J/PacificBellSheet
92/3 Tacoma
93/4 Tacoma

SYKORA, OTTO
94/5 DEL 341
95/6 DEL 307
96/7 DEL 334

SYKORA, PETR
94/5 Assets 60, 85, -FonCard
95/6 Bowman 116
94/5 Classic DP10
95/6 Classic 18, -Aut.
95/6 ClassicFiveSport 137
94/5 C4'Images 117
94/5 C'Images 81, CE11, PD4
95/6 Donruss-RatedRook 2, 16
96/7 DonrussCanadianIce 72
96/7 DonrussElite 122, -Aspirt 3
95/6 EdgeIce 11
96/7 Fleer-Rookie 9
96/7 FleerNHLPicks 74
96/7 FleerUltra 96
95/6 FutureLegends 22
96/7 Leaf 206
96/7 LeafLimited 54
96/7 LeafPreferred 21, -Steel 12
96/7 MetalUniverse 89
97/8 Omega 135
98/9 Pacific 273
96/7 PaniniSticker 81
97/8 PaniniSticker 68
95/6 Parkhurst 512, 523, PP43
96/7 Pinnacle 200
97/8 PinnacleBeAPlayer 134
96/7 PinnacleZenith 56
96/7 Score 237
97/8 Score(N.J.) 14
95/6 SelectCertified 144
96/7 SkBxImpact 71,171,-Fox 19
95/6 SP 83
96/7 SP 88
97/8 SPAuthentic 90
96/7 SPx 23
96/7 Summit 170
98/9 Topps 2
95/6 ToppsFinest 134
96/7 ToppsNHLPicks 6
95/6 TSC-MembersOnly 49
95/6 UpperDeck 318
96/7 UD 93, SS21B, X26
98/9 UDChoice 112
96/7 UDCollChoice 147, 339
96/7 N.J/Sharp

SYKORA, VACLAV
93/4 Jyvas-Hyva 223
93/4 Sisu 182
95/6 Sisu 388

SYLVEGARD, PATRIK
94/5 ElitSet 103
95/6 ElitSet 90
92/3 SemicElitserien 215
95/6 udElite 146
97/8 udSwedish 145

SYLVESTER, DEREK
93/4 Slapshot(NiagaraFalls) 21

SYLVIA, MIKE
95/6 DonrussElite-WorldJrs 43
95/6 UpperDeck 565

SYMES, BRAD
94/5 SigRookies 64
93/4 Portland

SYNOWIETZ, HEINRICH
96/7 DEL 208

SYNOWIETZ, PAUL
96/7 DEL 209

SYNYSHIN, DOUG
89/90 SketchOHL 42

SYPOSZ, JANUSZ
92 SemicSticker 270

SYVASALMI, KARI
93/4 Sisu 227
95/6 Sisu 365

SZABO, DAVE
91/2 SketchOHL 64

SZABO, TONY
93/4 Roanoke

SZATMARY, ROB
92/3 BCJHL 82

SZEJA, JAN
73/4 WilliamsFIN 100

SZERYK, JEFF
90/1 Kitchener 16
89/90 SSMarie 25

SZOKE, MARK
90/1 SketchMEM 81
90/1 SketchWHL 213
91/2 SketchWHL 6
93/4 Lethbridge

SZOPINSKI, ROBERT
89 SemicSticker 134
92 SemicSticker 271

SZTURM, PAT
94/5 ThunderBay
95/6 ThunderBay

SZUMLAK, STANLEY
87/8 Regina

SZURA, JOE
68/9 O-Pee-Chee 175
70/1 OPC/Topps 73
72/3 OPC 313
72/3 LosAngelesSharks

SZYSKY, CHRIS
95/6 SwiftCurrent

T

TA CHUN, WA
79 PaniniSticker 357

TABARA, ZDISLAV
94/5 APS 298
95/6 APS 2

TABARACCI, RICK
91/2 Bowman 207
92/3 Bowman 324
93/4 Donruss 363
94/5 Donruss 49
95/6 Donruss 214
96/7 Donruss 10
97/8 DonrussPriority 105
94/5 Flair 204
92/3 FleerUltra 445
94/5 FleerUltra 239
93/4 Leaf 241
96/7 Leaf 149
97/8 Omega 36
91/2 OPC/Topps 375
98/9 Pacific 126
97/8 PacificCrown 256
97/8 PacificParamount 31
98/9 PacificParamount 33
97/8 PacificRevolution 21
90/1 Panini(WPG) 24
94/5 Parkhurst 255
95/6 Parkhurst 32
93/4 Pinnacle 299
94/5 Pinnacle 444, MA5
96/7 Pinnacle 66
96/7 PinnacleBeAPlayer 164
94/5 POG 299
93/4 PowerPlay 267
93/4 Premier 239
94/5 Premier 367
89/90 ProCards(AHL) 45
90/1 ProCards 343
91/2 ProCards 185
90/1 ProSet 649
91/2 Score(CDN) 244
92/3 Score 529
93/4 Score 403
96/7 Score 23
97/8 Score 28
92/3 Topps 453
98/9 Topps 77
91/2 ToppsStadiumClub 395
92/3 ToppsStadiumClub 135
93/4 TSC 378, -Master (2) 7
94/5 ToppsStadiumClub 74
95/6 ToppsStadiumClub 119
97/8 ToppsSticker 4
90/1 UpperDeck 520
91/2 UpperDeck 339
92/3 UpperDeck 58, 358
94/5 UpperDeck 187
95/6 UpperDeck 196, SE103
97/8 UpperDeck 236
90/1 WPG/IGA
91/2 WPG/IGA
90/1 Moncton
91/2 Moncton

TABARIN, DIMITRI
94/5 SigRookies 32
94/5 SRGoldStandard 93

TABOBONDUNG, BARRY
80/1 Oshawa 8

TABOR, JAN
94/5 DEL 404
95/6 DEL 423

TABORSKY, PAVEL
94/5 APS 78
95/6 APS 9

TAGLIANETTI, PETER
94/5 Donruss 89
92/3 FleerUltra 204
93/4 FleerUltra 397
88/9 O-Pee-Chee 257
89/90 O-Pee-Chee 297
90/1 O-Pee-Chee 435
90/1 opcPremier 117
89/90 opcSticker 146/265
88/9 PaniniSticker 152
89/90 PaniniSticker 174
93/4 Parkhurst 430
94/5 ParkieSE 141
92/3 Pinnacle 383
94/5 Pinnacle 505
93/4 Premier 248
90/1 ProSet 505
90/1 ScoreTraded 16T
91/2 Score(CDN) 448
93/4 Score 295
93/4 ToppsStadiumClub 243
93/4 UpperDeck 100
91/2 PGH/Elbys
91/2 PGH/Foodland 14
93/4 PGH/Foodland 22
94/5 PGH 18
87/8 WPG
88/9 WPG/Police
89/90 WPG/Safeway

TAILLEFER, PETE
52/3 LavalDairy 26

TAILLEFER, TERRY
88/9 ProCards(Maine)

TAILLENS, RETO
72 SemicSticker 162

TAIMIO, TOMI
78/9 SM-Liiga 41

TAIT, TERRY
84/5 Springfield 11
80/1 SSMarie
81/2 SSMarie
82/3 SSMarie
87/8 SSMarie 33

TAJCNAR, RUDOLF
72 Hellas 85
74 Hellas 83
72 Panda
72 SemicSticker 25
74 SemicSticker 69
72/3 WilliamsFIN 20

TAKALA, MARKKU
93/4 Sisu 276

TAKHAR, DALJIT
92/3 BCJHL 218

TAKKO, KARI
91/2 Jyvas-Hyva 67
92/3 Jyvas-Hyva 189
93/4 Jyvas-Hyva 344
80/1 Mallasjuoma 220
87/8 PaniniSticker 288
88/9 PaniniSticker 85
89/90 PaniniSticker 102
89 Pelimiehen
90/1 ProCards 106
93/4 Sisu 208
94/5 Sisu 27,151,-Nolla 2,-Spe 6
95/6 Sisu 149, -GhostGoalie 4
96/7 Sisu 149, -Mighty 1, -Super
95/6 SisuLimited 19, -Gallery 6
90/1 UpperDeck 543
97/8 udSwedish 84
90/1 EDM/McGavins
87/8 MIN
88/9 MIN/AmericanDairy

TALAFOUS, DEAN
75/6 OPC/Topps 197
76/7 OPC/Topps 103
77/8 OPC/Topps 49
78/9 OPC/Topps 149
79/80 OPC/Topps 54
80/1 OPC/Topps 132
81/2 O-Pee-Chee 235

TALAKOWSKI, RON
93/4 ThunderBay

TALBOT, JEAN-GUY
45-64 BeeHives(MTL)
64-67 BeeHives(MTL)
62 CeramicTiles
63-5 ChexPhoto
64/5 CokeCap MTL-17
65/6 CocaCola
72-84 Dernière 77/8
70/1 EddieSargent 189
51-54 LaPatrie 2Mar52
68/9 O-Pee-Chee 179
69/70 OPC/Topps 15
70/1 OPC/Topps 100
55/6 Parkhurst 53
57/8 Parkhurst(MTL) 9
58/9 Parkhurst 41
59/60 Parkhurst 49
60/1 Parkhurst 52
61/2 Parkhurst 48
62/3 Parkhurst 51
63/4 Parkhurst 22, 81
93/4 Parkhurst PR52
93/4 Parkie(56/7) 80
94/5 Parkie(64/5) 76
95/6 Parkie(66/7) 68
60/1 ShirriffCoin 35
61/2 ShirriffCoin 109
62/3 ShirriffCoin 39, 44
63/4 TheTorontoStar
64/5 Topps 52
65/6 Topps 4
66/7 Topps 3
67/8 Topps 104
54-67 TorontoStar V9
56-66 TorontoStar 58/9
91/2 Ultimate(O6) 16
60/1 York
61/2 York 12
62/3 YorkTransfer 4
63/4 York 23
67/8 MTL
92/3 MTL/OPC 53
72/3 STL
73/4 STL

TALLAIRE, GERALD
91/2 AirCanadaSJHL 35, B19
92/3 MPSPhotoSJHL 3

TALLAIRE, SEAN
91/2 AirCanadaSJHL C18
97/8 Score(BOS) 3
91/2 LakeSuperior

TALLAS, ROB
91/2 AvantGardeBCJ 106, 119
98/9 Pacific 100
91/2 SketchWHL 126
97/8 UpperDeck 223
93/4 Seattle

TALLBERG, THOMAS
94/5 ElitSet 1
95/6 ElitSet 22
91/2 SemicElitserien 44
92/3 SemicElitserien 62

TALLON, DALE
71/2 Colgate Heads
70/1 Colgate Stamp 81
70/1 DadsCookies
70/1 EddieSargent 215
71/2 EddieSargent 209
72/3 EddieSargent 211
70/1 Esso Stamp
72/3 Letraset 20
74/5 LiptonSoup 22
74/5 Loblaws
73/4 MacsMilk Disk
70/1 OPC 225
71/2 OPC 234, -Booklet 3, T. 95
71/2 opcPoster 5
72/3 OPC 121, -Crests 21, T. 15
73/4 OPC 211, Topps 129
74/5 OPC 360
75/6 OPC 351
76/7 OPC/Topps 89, OPC 382
77/8 OPC/Topps 124
78/9 OPC/Topps 146
70/1 PostShooters
72/3 Post Transfers 2
91/2 ProSet 595
72 SemicSticker 222
71/2 TheTorontoSun
91/2 Trends(72) 22, -Aut
70/1 VAN/RoyalBank
71/2 VAN/RoyalBank 11
72/3 VAN/RoyalBank

TAMBELLINI, STEVE
80/1 O-Pee-Chee 365
81/2 OPC 81, Topps(W) 86
82/3 O-Pee-Chee 134, 147
83/4 O-Pee-Chee 93, 223
84/5 O-Pee-Chee 237
87/8 O-Pee-Chee 259
88/9 O-Pee-Chee 258
82/3 opcSticker 226
83/4 opcSticker 219
84/5 opcSticker 239
88/9 opcSticker 62/197
87/8 PaniniSticker 351
82/3 Post
83/4 PuffySticker 4
83/4 SouhaitsRen.KeyChain
83/4 Vachon 19
81/2 COL.R
79/80 NYI
85/6 VAN
86/7 VAN
87/8 VAN/Shell

TAMER, CHRIS
93/4 Classic 83
94/5 Classic 94, -Aut
93/4 ClassicProspects 119
95/6 EdgeIce 119
94/5 Leaf 513
98/9 Pacific 359
97/8 PacificRegime 165
95/6 Parkhurst 436
94/5 Pinnacle 259, RTP4
96/7 PinnacleBeAPlayer 182
94/5 Premier 224
95/6 Topps 169
94/5 UpperDeck 318
97/8 UpperDeck 345
94/5 PGH 12
95/6 PGH/Foodland 18
93/4 ClevelandLumberjacks

TAMER, JOHN
84/5 Belleville 25

TAMMELIN, RAULI
70/1 Kuvajulkaisut 169
80/1 Mallasjuoma 186
78/9 SM-Liiga 213
71/2 WilliamsFIN 240
72/3 WilliamsFIN 224
73/4 WilliamsFIN 301

TAMMI, JUHANI
65/6 Hellas 102

TAMMI, JUKKA
96/7 DEL 47
95 Hartwall
91/2 Jyvas-Hyva 13
92/3 Jyvas-Hyva 36
93/4 Jyvas-Hyva 74
95 PaniniWorlds 162F
94 Semic 3
95 Semic 30, 216
89 SemicSticker 28
91 SemicSticker 4
93/4 Sisu 109
94/5 Sisu 38, -Magic 10
95/6 Sisu 339,-Ghost 8,-GoldC 4
95/6 SisuLimited 91
96 Wien 12

TAMMI, V.M.
70/1 Kuvajulkaisut 356

TAMMINEN, JOE
93/4 Minn-Duluth

TAMMINEN, JUHANI
72 Hellas 16
74 Hellas 20
70/1 Kuvajulkaisut 77, 170, 357
80/1 Mallasjuoma 190
79 PaniniSticker 176
72 SemicSticker 88
74 SemicSticker 92
82 SemicSticker 50
92 SemicSticker 194
96/7 Sisu 198
82 Skopbank
78/9 SM-Liiga 16, 208
77-80 Sportscaster 46-1084
71/2 WilliamsFIN 76, 162
72/3 WilliamsFIN 75, 114
73/4 WilliamsFIN 80, 144
76/7 Phoenix

TAMMINEN, KAUKO
71/2 WilliamsFIN 335

TAMMINEN, TEEMU
93/4 Sisu 252

TAMMINEN, TINY
51/2 LacStJean 37

TANAKA, YASUSHIN
79 PaniniSticker 288

TANCILL, CHRIS
92/3 ClassicProspects 20
93/4 Donruss 84
93/4 Parkhurst 318
96/7 Pinnacle 71
93/4 Premier 429
90/1 ProCards 179
91/2 ProCards 104
91/2 ProSet 539
91/2 UpperDeck 455
96/7 S.J/PacificBellSheet

TANEVSKI, DAN
90/1 SketchOHL 221
93/4 SSMarie 2

TANGUAY, ALEX
98 BowmanCHL 108, 152
98 BowmanCHL A35, SC15
98/9 Topps 237
97/8 UDBlackDiamond 105
98/9 UDChoice 257
96/7 Halifax (1), (2)
97/8 Halifax (1), (2 x2)

TANGUAY, CHRIS
82/3 Fredericton 20
83/4 Fredericton 10

TANGUAY, MARTIN
93/4 ClassicProspects 132
91/2 SketchQMJHL 135
93/4 AtlantaKnights
93/4 Knoxville
88/9 Richelieu

TANNAHILL, DON
72/3 OPC 238
73/4 OPC/Topps 69
74/5 OPC/Topps 117
72/3 VAN/RoyalBank
73/4 VAN/RoyalBank

TANNER, JOHN
90/1 opcPremier 118
90/1 Panini(QUE) 21
91/2 ProCards 366
90/1 ProSet 637
92/3 Score 452
89/90 SketchOHL 38
90/1 SketchOHL 145, 377
91/2 UpperDeck 119
90/1 QUE/PetroCanada
92/3 QUE/PetroCanada

TANSOWNY, STEVE
92/3 MPSPhotoSJHL 53

TANTI, TONY
90/1 Bowman 213
91/2 Bowman 34
92/3 Bowman 172
83 CanadaJuniors
94/5 DEL 54
95/6 DEL 59
96/7 DEL 256
88/9 FritoLay
86/7 Kraft Sports 71
89/90 Kraft 45
83/4 O-Pee-Chee 362
84/5 OPC 332, 369, Topps 141
85/6 OPC/Topps 153
86/7 OPC/Topps 120
87/8 OPC/Topps 97
88/9 OPC/Topps 82
89/90 O-Pee-Chee 280
90/1 OPC/Topps 157
91/2 OPC/Topps 133
92/3 O-Pee-Chee 34
84/5 opcSticker 274-75
85/6 opcSticker 245/127
86/7 opcSticker 99
87/8 opcSticker 195
88/9 opcSticker 59
89/90 opcSticker 71
87/8 PaniniSticker 345
88/9 PaniniSticker 143
89/90 PaniniSticker 149
90/1 PaniniSticker 124
91/2 Parkhurst 236
90/1 ProSet 241
87/8 ProSportWatch CW15
90/1 Score 137
91/2 Score(CDN) 49, (U.S) 49
92/3 Score 116
84/5 7ElevenDisk
92/3 Topps 235
91/2 ToppsStadiumClub 285
92/3 ToppsStadiumClub 312
90/1 UpperDeck 197
92/3 UpperDeck 182
83/4 Vachon 119
91/2 BUF/BlueShield
91/2 BUF/Campbell
81/2 CHI
90/1 PGH/Foodland 14
83/4 VAN
84/5 VAN
85/6 VAN
86/7 VAN
87/8 VAN/Shell
88/9 VAN/Mohawk
89/90 VAN
80/1 Oshawa 16
81/2 Oshawa 18
82/3 Oshawa 11

TAPASOV, ANATOLI
69/70 Soviet Stars
70/1 Soviet Stars
71/2 Soviet Stars
83&87 HallOfFame 239
83 HHOF Postcard (D)

TARASOV, YEVGENY
96 Wien 131

TARASUK, ALLAN
82/3 Brandon 15
83/4 Brandon 21

TARASUK, RICK
91/2 SketchOHL 269

TARASYENKO, ANDREI
95 PaniniWorlds 40

TARDIF, CHRISTIAN
90/1 SketchQMJHL 71
91/2 SketchQMJHL 33

TARDIF, MARC
70/1 Colgate Stamp 17
72-84 Dernière 72/3, 78/9, 81/2
71/2 EddieSargent 112
72/3 EddieSargent 118
83/4 Esso
70/1 Esso Stamp
70/1 OPC 179
71/2 OPC/Topps 29
72/3 OPC 11, Topps 105
79/80 OPC/Topps 108
80/1 OPC/Topps 256
81/2 OPC 283
82/3 OPC 296
83/4 OPC 305
81/2 opcSticker 76
82/3 opcSticker 21
83/4 opcSticker 247
73/4 opc-Posters 20
80/1 opcSuperCard 17
74/5 opcWHA 43,
75/6 opcWHA 30, 71
76/7 opcWHA 1, 2, 5, 118
77/8 opcWHA 20
80/1 Pepsi Cap
82/3 Post
90/1 SketchOHL 109
91/2 SketchQMJHL 73
71/2 TheTorontoSun
69/70 MTL/ProStar
70/1 MTL
71/2 MTL
72/3 MTL
80/1 QUE
81/2 QUE
82/3 QUE
83/4 QUE
76 QuébecNordiques/MA
76/7 QuébecNordiques

TARDIF, MARC
93/4 ClassicProspects 223
92/3 AtlantaKnights

TARDIF, PATRICE
95/6 Classic T60
94/5 C'Images 27, CE14
95/6 Donruss 87
95/6 EdgeIce 97
94/5 Fleer 192
95/6 Leaf 22
95/6 Score 88
95/6 Topps 172
94/5 UpperDeck 470
92/3 Maine (1) 10
93/4 Maine 46

TARDIF, STEVE
93/4 Slapshot(Drum.) 22

TARKIAINEN, JUHA
66/7 Champion 211

TARKO, K.P.
72/3 WilliamsFIN 354

TARNOWSKI, CHRISTIAN
85/6 Kamloops
86/7 Kamloops
86/7 Regina
84/5 Victoria

TARNSTROM, DICK
94/5 ElitSet 211, -NHLDraft 10
95/6 ElitSet 9
94/5 ParkieSE 239
92/3 SemicElitserien 31
95/6 udElite 3, NA2

TARRANT, JERRY
89/90 ProCards(IHL) 27
91/2 ProCards 373

TARTARI, STÉPHANE
90/1 SketchQMJHL 115

TARVAINEN, JUSSI
94/5 ParkieSE 225
93/4 Sisu 180
94/5 Sisu 71, -Junior 8, -Draft 3
95/6 Sisu 75
96/7 Sisu 81
94/5 ToppsFinest 142

TASALA, LASSE
80/1 Mallasjuoma 33

TASKULA, KEITH
80/1 Mallasjuoma 135

TATARINOV, MIKHAIL
91/2 Bowman 298
92/3 Bowman 395
92/3 FleerUltra 181
91 IvanFiodorovSportUnites
93/4 Leaf 342
91/2 OPC/Topps 465
92/3 O-Pee-Chee 253
91/2 opcPremier 62
91/2 PaniniSticker 210
92/3 PaniniSticker 208
91/2 Parkhurst 145
91/2 Pinnacle 97
92/3 Pinnacle 35
90/1 ProSet 647
91/2 ProSet 462
91/2 PSPlatinum 218
91/2 RedAce
90/1 ScoreTraded 53T
91/2 Score(CDN) 37, 562
91/2 Score(U.S) 37, 12T
92/3 Score 107
93/4 Score 328
94 Semic 336
91 SemicSticker 215
92 SemicSticker 102
92/3 Topps 180
91/2 ToppsStadiumClub 390
92/3 ToppsStadiumClub 47
90/1 UpperDeck 401
92/3 UpperDeck 183
93/4 UpperDeck 386
91/2 QUE/PetroCanada
92/3 QUE/PetroCanada
90/1 WSH/Kodak
90/1 WSH/Smokey

TATTNER, MICHAEL
94/5 DEL 373

TAUBERT, KRISTIAN
92/3 Jyvas-Hyva 47

TAUGHER, JOHNNY
36/7 WWGum (V356) 116

TAURIAINEN, JARMO
70/1 Kuvajulkaisut 380
80/1 Mallasjuoma 109

TAVI, MIKKO
93/4 Jyvas-Hyva 176
93/4 Sisu 165
94/5 Sisu 113
92/3 Clarkson

TAYLOR, ANDREW
94/5 SigRookies 65
93/4 Slapshot(Kitchener) 18, 27
94/5 Slapshot(Kitchener) 20

94/5 Slapshot(Detroit) 13
94/5 Slapshot(MEM) 87
95/6 Slapshot 70

TAYLOR, BART
91/2 AvantGardeBCJ 121
92/3 BCJHL 172

TAYLOR, BILL
34-43 BeeHives(TOR)
39/40 OPC (V301-1) 15
40/1 OPC (V301-2) 107

TAYLOR, BOBBY
73/4 O-Pee-Chee 238
92/3 Parkhurst 475
75/6 PHA/GingerAle

TAYLOR, CHRIS
92/3 ClassicProspects 113
95/6 Score 303
89/90 SketchOHL 26
90/1 SketchOHL 146
91/2 SketchOHL 370
91/2 UpperDeck 454

TAYLOR, FRED (CYCLONE)
91 C55 Reprint 20
83&87 HallOfFame 14
83 HHOF Postcard (A)
1911-12 Imperial (C55) 20
1910-11 Imperial (C56) 15
1912-13 Imperial (C57) 43
1910-11 Imperial Post 20
19 Millionaires (x2)
60/1 Topps 46
61/2 Topps-Stamp

TAYLOR, DAVE
90/1 Bowman 149, -HatTrick 22
91/2 Bowman 186, 416
92/3 Bowman 37
92/3 FleerUltra 313
93/4 FleerUltra 348
93/4 HockeyWit 21
93/4 Leaf 374
78/9 OPC/Topps 353
79/80 OPC/Topps 232
80/1 OPC/Topps 137
81/2 OPC 143, 152, 353, 391
81/2 Topps 40, (West) 132
82/3 O-Pee-Chee 161
83/4 O-Pee-Chee 163
84/5 O-Pee-Chee 92
85/6 O-Pee-Chee 214
86/7 OPC/Topps 63
87/8 OPC/Topps 118
88/9 OPC/Topps 46
89/90 OPC/Topps 58
90/1 OPC/Topps 314
91/2 OPC/Topps 138
81/2 opcSticker 149, 237, 268
82/3 opcSticker 164, 231
84/5 opcSticker 267
85/6 opcSticker 238/106
86/7 opcSticker 90/220
87/8 opcSticker 215/83
88/9 opcSticker 155/26
89/90 opcSticker 151/11
87/8 PaniniSticker 280
88/9 PaniniSticker 79
89/90 PaniniSticker 98
90/1 PaniniSticker 236
91/2 PaniniSticker 89
93/4 PaniniSticker 206
91/2 Parkhurst 67, 214
92/3 Parkhurst 307
93/4 Parkhurst 367
91/2 Pinnacle 249, 373
92/3 Pinnacle 367
93/4 Pinnacle 412
93/4 PowerPlay 364
90/1 ProSet 128
91/2 ProSet 103, 325
92/3 ProSet 258
83/4 PuffySticker 12
90/1 Score 166
91/2 Score(CDN) 214, 264, 325
91/2 Score(U.S) 214, 374, 435
92/3 Score 49
93/4 Score 389
84/5 7ElevenDisk
85/6 7Eleven 8
92/3 Topps 446
91/2 ToppsStadiumClub 232
92/3 ToppsStadiumClub 234
93/4 TSC-MembersOnly 14
90/1 UpperDeck 214
91/2 UpperDeck 270
80/1 L.A.
84/5 L.A/Smokeys
88/9 L.A.
88/9 L.A/Smokeys
89/90 L.A/Smokeys 6
90/1 L.A/Smokeys 8

TAYLOR, DYLAN
95/6 Slapshot 124

TAYLOR, ERIC
79/80 Montréal B&W

TAYLOR, GARY
90/1 SketchOHL 222

TAYLOR, GREG
91/2 AirCanadaSJHL D28

TAYLOR, HARRY
45-64 BeeHives(TOR)
45-54 QuakerOats

TAYLOR, JACK
51/2 LavalDairy 67

TAYLOR, KARL
89/90 SketchOHL 45
90/1 SketchOHL 319

TAYLOR, MARK
83/4 O-Pee-Chee 273
84/5 OPC 180, Topps 127
83/4 opcSticker 190
84/5 opcSticker 121
83/4 PGH
84/5 PGH/Heinz

TAYLOR, MATT
84/5 Belleville 29

TAYLOR, MIKE
94/5 Richmond
95/6 Richmond

TAYLOR, PAUL
91/2 AvantGardeBCJ 49, 158
94/5 Dayton 2

TAYLOR, RANDY
88/9 ProCards(Indianapolis)
89/90 ProCards(IHL) 151

TAYLOR, ROD
92/3 Hampton
93/4 Hampton
94/5 Hampton 8
95/6 Hampton HRA-12

TAYLOR, RYAN
95/6 Slapshot 184

TAYLOR, SCOTT
85/6 Kitchener 13
86/7 Kitchener 12

TAYLOR, TED
71/2 EddieSargent 223
72/3 OPC 312
73/4 QuakerOats 28
65/6 Topps 95
75/6 Houston
70/1 VAN/RoyalBank
71/2 VAN/RoyalBank 17

TAYLOR, TIM
95/6 Donruss 349
94/5 FleerUltra 286
98/9 Pacific 101
97/8 PacificDynag-BestKept 35
97/8 PinnacleBeAPlayer 114
89/90 ProCards(AHL) 80
90/1 ProCards 211
91/2 ProCards 563
97/8 SPAuthentic 9
94/5 SRTetrad CXVI
95/6 Topps 132
94/5 UpperDeck 325
95/6 UpperDeck 295
95/6 UDBeAPlayer 101
91/2 Baltimore 1

TAYLOR, TIM
92 SemicSticker 146

TAYLOR, W.J.
45-54 QuakerOats

TEAL, GORDON
28/9 PaulinsCandy 65

TEAL, JEFF
83/4 NovaScotia 22

TEBBUTT, GREG
83/4 PGH

TEEVENS, MARK
94/5 DEL 69
95/6 DEL 70
96/7 DEL 265
88/9 ProCards(Indianapolis)

TE HSI, LIU
79 PaniniSticker 359

TEICHMANN, BRAD
90/1 SketchOHL 20
91/2 SketchOHL 46

TEIJONMAA, OLLI
71/2 WilliamsFIN 336

TEIMONEN, MIIKKA
95/6 Sisu 288

TEJKL, PETER
94/5 APS 4
95/6 APS 105

TEMPLETON, BERT
89/90 SketchOHL 173
90/1 SketchOHL 323
91/2 SketchOHL 72
93/4 Slapshot(NorthBay) 23
95/6 Slapshot 6
82/3 NorthBay
83/4 NorthBay

TENHUNEN, SEPPO
80/1 Mallasjuoma 97
78/9 SM-Liiga 139

TENISI, GUIDO
82 SemicSticker 124

TENNANT, KEN
52/3 AnonymousOHL 126

TEPPER, STEPHEN
93/4 Roanoke

TERBENCHE, PAUL
70/1 OPC/Topps 123
73/4 O-Pee-Chee 229
75/6 opcWHA 112
67/8 Topps 58
72/3 BUF
73/4 BUF
77/8 WinnipegJets

TERECHOV, ALEXANDER
95/6 APS 323

TERNSTROM, DICK
97/8 udSwedish 5

TERRERI, CHRIS
91/2 Bowman 283
92/3 Bowman 386
93/4 Donruss 194
94/5 Donruss 285
96/7 Donruss 38
93/4 EASports 78
96/7 Fleer 102
92/3 FleerUltra 120
93/4 FleerUltra 209, 250
94/5 FleerUltra 323
95/6 FleerUltra 306
91/2 Gillette 38
93/4 HockeyWit 31
92/3 HumptyDumpty (2)
92/3 Kraft'Disk
93/4 Leaf 430
94/5 Leaf 134
96/7 Leaf 94
96/7 Maggers 129
90/1 OPC/Topps 239, 284
91/2 OPC/Topps 422
92/3 O-Pee-Chee 282
91/2 opcPremier 197
98/9 Pacific 40
97/8 PacificCrownRoyale 31
97/8 PacificRegime 48
90/1 PaniniSticker 68
91/2 PaniniSticker 221
92/3 PaniniSticker 171
93/4 PaniniSticker D
94/5 PaniniSticker 36
96/7 PaniniSticker 280
91/2 Parkhurst 98
92/3 Parkhurst 93
93/4 Parkhurst 112
95/6 Parkhurst 451
94/5 ParkieSE 94
91/2 Pinnacle 247
92/3 Pinnacle 274
93/4 Pinnacle 267
94/5 Pinnacle 335
96/7 Pinnacle 103
97/8 PinnacleBeAPlayer 30
94/5 POG 285
93/4 PowerPlay 144
93/4 Premier 213
94/5 Premier 13, 83
88/9 ProCards(Utica)
90/1 ProSet 481
91/2 ProSet 137
92/3 ProSet 97
91/2 PSPlatinum 68, 197, 288
90/1 Score 239
91/2 Score(CDN) 151, (U.S) 151
91/2 Score-YoungStar 15
92/3 Score 270
93/4 Score 237
95/6 Score 243
96/7 Score 28
97/8 Score 48
92/3 SeasonsPatch 51
91 SemicSticker 129
96/7 SkyBoxImpact 119
95/6 SP 131
97/8 SPAuthentic 33
96/7 Summit 89
92/3 Topps 303
95/6 ToppsFinest 149
91/2 ToppsStadiumClub 297
92/3 ToppsStadiumClub 74
93/4 ToppsStadiumClub 328
90/1 UpperDeck 183
91/2 UpperDeck 115
92/3 UpperDeck 43
93/4 UpperDeck 110
95/6 UpperDeck 450
96/7 UpperDeck 147
97/8 UpperDeck 40
95/6 UDBeAPlayer 27
96/7 UDCollChoice 239, 330
89/90 N.J.
90/1 N.J.
96/7 S.J/PacificBellSheet

TERRION, GREG
86/7 Kraft Sports 58
81/2 O-Pee-Chee 155
82/3 O-Pee-Chee 333
83/4 O-Pee-Chee 342
84/5 O-Pee-Chee 312
86/7 O-Pee-Chee 244
87/8 O-Pee-Chee 241
82/3 opcSticker 234
83/4 opcSticker 37
84/5 opcSticker 19
85/6 opcSticker 18/149
86/7 opcSticker 147/255
87/8 opcSticker 153/14
88/9 ProCards(Newmarket)
83/4 SouhaitsRen.KeyChain
83/4 Vachon 99
82/3 TOR
83/4 TOR
84/5 TOR
85/6 TOR
86/7 TOR
87/8 TOR
87/8 TOR/P.L.A.Y. 21

TERTYSHNY, SERGEI
94/5 Portland
95/6 Portland

TERVO, HEIMO
65/6 Hellas 78

TERVONEN, KAI
92/3 Jyvas-Hyva 14
93/4 Jyvas-Hyva 25
93/4 Sisu 93

TESARIK, RADIM
94/5 APS 187
95/6 APS 36

TESSIER, BRIAN
86/7 Kingston 6

TESSIER, ORVAL
52/3 AnonymousOHL 104
60/1 ShirriffCoin 114
82/3 CHI
83/4 CHI

TESSIER, PATRICK
91/2 SketchQMJHL 34

TETARENKO, JOEY
95/6 UpperDeck 523

TETRAULT, DANIEL
97/8 Bowman 134
96/7 UpperDeck 376

TETZLAFF, JEFF
95/6 Slapshot 25

TEXEIRA, CHUCK
92/3 Maine (2) 31
93/4 Maine 51

TEZIKOV, ALEXEI
98 BowmanCHL 118

THACKER, ROD
87/8 SSMarie 32

THALER, ALEXANDER
95 PaniniWorlds 83
94 Semic 297

THANNER, RUDOLPH
72 Hellas 46

THEBERGE, EDOUARD
51/2 BasDuFleuve 23

THEBERGE, GERRY
51/2 LacStJean 14

THEBERGE, GREG
82/3 Post
81/2 WSH

THELIN, MATS
89/90 SemicElitserien 4
90/1 SemicElitserien 78
91/2 SemicElitserien 6
92/3 SemicElitserien 29
82 SemicSticker 8
84/5 BOS

THELVIN, MICHAEL
87/8 OPC/Topps 24
87/8 PaniniSticker 9
88/9 PaniniSticker 206
88/9 BOS/SportsAction
89/90 BOS/SportsAction

THÉODORE, JOSÉ
94/5 AutoPhonex B5
96/7 Donruss 227
97/8 Donruss 81, -BetweenThe 6
96/7 D.CndIce-Gardiens 10
97/8 D.CdnIce-Gard 6,-Scrap 14
95/6 DonrussElite -WorldJrs 2
96/7 DonrussElite 139
97/8 D.Preferred 102,-ColGrd 11
97/8 DonrussStudio 24
96/7 Flair 112
96/7 Fleer 134, -Calder 9
96/7 Leaf-Rookie 3
97/8 Leaf 122, -PipeDreams 9
97/8 Limited 81,151,152, -fab 71
97/8 PacificRegime 107
96/7 Pinnacle 217
97/8 PinnInside 56, -Stopper 14
96/7 Score 267
97/8 Score 42
97/8 Score(MTL) 3
94/5 SigRookies 10
96/7 SkyBoxImpact 161
94/5 Slapshot(MEM) 73
96/7 SP 174
97/8 SPAuthentic S21
96/7 Summit 182
95/6 UpperDeck 530
96/7 UpperDeck 279
97/8 UD 85, SG60, T12C
96/7 UDBlackDiamond 116
96/7 UDCollChoice 351
97/8 UDCollChoice 135
96/7 UpperDeck"Ice" 90
97/8 UpperDeckIce 36
96/7 Fredericton

THÉORET, LUC
98 BowmanCHL 65
96/7 UpperDeck 377

THERIAULT, JOEL
95/6 Halifax

THERIAULT, PATRICK
92/3 Clarkson

THERIAULT, PAUL
81/2 Oshawa 23
82/3 Oshawa 23
83/4 Oshawa 14

THERIEN, CHRIS
93/4 CanadaNats
93/4 Classic 84
94/5 ClassicImages 32
93/4 ClassicProspects LP19
95/6 Donruss 72
95/6 EdgeIce 47, C9
94/5 Flair 132
94/5 Fleer 159
95/6 FleerMetal 114
93/4 FleerUltra 474
94/5 FleerUltra 347
95/6 FleerUltra 121
94/5 Leaf 480
95/6 Leaf 18
98/9 Pacific 332
97/8 PacificRegime 148
95/6 PaniniSticker 118, 301
95/6 Parkhurst 156
94/5 ParkieSE 127
94/5 Pinnacle 495
95/6 Pinnacle 165
95/6 Playoff 296
93/4 PowerPlay 495
93/4 Premier-TmCanada 9
94/5 Premier 322
94/5 Score CT19
95/6 Score 98
97/8 Score 256
97/8 Score(PHA) 15
95/6 SkyBoxEmotion 135
95/6 SkyBoxImpact 129, -Fox 8
98/9 SPx"Finite" 63
95/6 Topps 364, 12NG
98/9 Topps 144
94/5 ToppsFinest 13
94/5 UpperDeck 248
95/6 UpperDeck 107
95/6 UDBeAPlayer 21
95/6 UDCollChoice 184, 374
96/7 UDCollChoice 197
94/5 PHA
96/7 PHA/OceanSpray

THÉRIEN, GASTON
96/7 Rimouski

THERRIEN, BENOÎT
90/1 SketchQMJHL 68
91/2 SketchQMJHL 47

THERRIEN, GASTON
82/3 Fredericton 18

THERRIEN, MARIO
90/1 SketchQMJHL 86
91/2 SketchQMJHL 36

THERRIEN, MICHEL
83/4 NovaScotia 16
80/1 QuébecRamparts

THERRIEN, PIERRE-LUC
97/8 Bowman 140, BB20
96/7 UpperDeck 372

THIBAUDEAU, GILLES
90/1 PaniniSticker 288
90/1 ProSet 290
87/8 MTL
88/9 MTL
89/90 NYI

THIBAULT, DANIEL
90/1 SketchQMJHL 87
91/2 SketchQMJHL 110

THIBAULT, DAVID
97/8 Bowman 78

THIBAULT, ETIENNE
91/2 SketchQMJHL 13

THIBAULT, GILLES
52/3 AnonymousOHL 76

THIBAULT, JOCELYN
96/7 Aces 6 (Hearts)
93/4 Classic 10, DP10
93/4 ClassicFourSport 194
93/4 C4'Images 74
94/5 ClassicImages 6, CE6
93/4 ClassicProspects 39
93/4 Donruss 275, -Rated 11
94/5 Donruss 71
95/6 Donruss 97
96/7 Donruss 101,-Dom 2,-Bet 7
97/8 Donruss 35, -Between 10
96/7 D.CdnIce 2, -Gardiens 2
97/8 D.CdnIce 15, -Gardiens 7
95/6 DonrussElite 1, -Painted 7
96/7 DonrussElite 6, -Painted 5
97/8 D.Elite 88,-BackToTheFut 2
97/8 D.Preferred 87,-ColGrd 9
97/8 DonrussPriority 78
97/8 D.Prio-OpDay 21,-PstGen 6
97/8 D.Prio-Pstcrd 36,-Stamp 36
97/8 DonrussStudio 77
93/4 Durivage 3, -Aut
96/7 Flair 51, -HotGlove 11
96/7 Fleer 56
96/7 FleerNHLPicks 82
93/4 FleerUltra 406, -Wave 18
94/5 FleerUltra 361
95/6 FU 258,-High 19, -Rising 8
96/7 FleerUltra 90
97/8 KatchMedallion 78
96/7 Kraft'Trophy
93/4 Leaf 428, -Freshman 10
94/5 Leaf 231, -GoldL.Rook 15
95/6 Leaf 97
96/7 Leaf 182, -BestOf 9, -Shut 3
97/8 Leaf 42, -PipeDreams 12
94/5 LeafLimited 15
95/6 LeafLimited 79
96/7 LeafLimited 44
96/7 LeafPreferred 73, -Steel 55
96/7 LP-MaskedMarauder 8
97/8 Limited 44, 123, -fabric 62
96/7 Maggers 82
96/7 McDonalds McD36, 'Masks
96/7 MetalUniverse 83
97/8 Omega 124
98/9 Pacific 258
97/8 PacificCrown 168,-InThe 11
97/8 PacificDynagon! 66
97/8 PcfcD-Stone 11,-Tandm 13
97/8 PacificInvincible 74
98/9 PacificParamount 119
97/8 PacificRevolution 74
94/5 PaniniSticker 62
95/6 PaniniSticker 254
96/7 PaniniSticker 36
93/4 Parkhurst 247, C16
94/5 Parkhurst 189, 275, V61
95/6 Parkhurst 53, 384
93/4 Pinnacle 440
94/5 Pinnacle 205, GT18
95/6 Pinnacle 158, -Masks 10
96/7 Pinnacle 142, -Masks 9
96/7 Pinnacle-ByTheNumbers13
97/8 Pinnacle 98
96/7 P.BeAPlayer-Stacking 15
97/8 P.BAP 10,-Stacking/Pads 9
97/8 PinnacleBeeHive 32
97/8 PinnacleCertified 26
97/8 P.Inside 43, -Track 17
97/8 P.Inside-StandUp 3, -Can 6
97/8 P.Inside-Stoppr 15 -BigCan
96/7 PinnacleMint 27
95/6 PinnacleZenith 34
96/7 P.Zenith 69, -ZTeam 11
95/6 Playoff 29
96/7 Playoff 336
93/4 PowerPlay 426,-Rookie 15
93/4 Premier 393
94/5 Premier 123
93/4 Score 593
94/5 Score 250
95/6 Score 131
96/7 Score 96,-NetW 9,-SddnD 8
97/8 Score 41, -NetWorth 11
97/8 Score(MTL) 2
95/6 SelectCert. 30, -Future 4
96/7 SelectCert. 3, -Freezers 12
91/2 SketchQMJHL 123
95/6 SkyBoxEmotion 43
95/6 SkBxImpact 42, -Deflect 7
96/7 SkyBoxImpact 65
95/6 SP 76
96/7 SP 81, HC11
95/6 Summit 29, -InTheCrease 7
96/7 Summit 102, -Crease 11
95/6 Topps 343
98/9 Topps 217
93/4 ToppsStadiumClub 479
94/5 ToppsStadiumClub 114

95/6 ToppsStadiumClub 98
97/8 ToppsSticker 2
93/4 UpperDeck 394, SP-133
94/5 UpperDeck 147
95/6 UpperDeck 369, SE131
96/7 UpperDeck 83, SS11B, X5
97/8 UpperDeck 90
95/6 UDBeAPlayer 199
96/7 UDBlackDiamond 41
95/6 UDCollChoice 316
96/7 UDCollChoice 136, 321
97/8 UDCollChoice 134
96/7 UpperDeck"Ice" 91, S4
97/8 Zenith 65, Z33
96-98 MTL
94/5 QUE/BurgerKing

THIBAULT, LARRY
52/3 AnonymousOHL 102

THIBEAULT, DAVID
98 BowmanCHL 96

THIBEAULT, MARC
91/2 SketchQMJHL 254

THIEL, ROB
87/8 Kitchener 9
88/9 Kitchener 9

THIESSEN, KELLY
90/1 SketchWHL 64
89/90 Brandon 3

THIESSEN, TRAVIS
90/1 SketchWHL 145
91/2 SketchWHL 277
92/3 ClevelandLumberjacks 4
93/4 ClevelandLumberjacks
93/4 Indianapolis

THIETKE, MARK
84/5 Kamloops
83/4 Saskatoon 24

THIFFAULT, CHARLES
90/1 MTL
91/2 MTL
81/2 QUE
82/3 QUE
85/6 QUE
86/7 QUE
86/7 QUE/GeneralFoods

THIFFAULT, MAURICE
51/2 LacStJean 33

THIVIERGE, SÉBASTIEN
95/6 DEL 286

THOLSON, STAFFAN
91/2 SemicElitserien 307

THOMAS, BILL
35/6 OPC (V304C) 85
32/3 TOR/OKeefe 13

THOMAS, CY
45-54 QuakerOats

THOMAS, D.
92/3 S.J/PacificBell

THOMAS, GORD
84/5 Ottawa67s

THOMAS, REG
76/7 opcWHA 82
77/8 opcWHA 29

THOMAS, SCOTT
92/3 Classic 74
92/3 ClasssicFourSport 198
92/3 ClassicProspects 19, 125
93/4 Leaf 360
93/4 Parkhurst 25
93/4 PowerPlay 302
93/4 Premier 336
93/4 Score 469
90/1 SketchWHL 143
91/2 SketchWHL 165
93/4 ToppsStadiumClub 471
93/4 UpperDeck 247
96/7 Cincinnati
92/3 Rochester/Dunkin'Donuts
92/3 Rochester/Kodak
93/4 Rochester

THOMAS, STEVE
90/1 Bowman 4, -HatTrick 13
91/2 Bowman 391
92/3 Bowman 117
95/6 Bowman 19
93/4 Donruss 208
94/5 Donruss 142
95/6 Donruss 32, 363
96/7 Donruss 193
95/6 DonrussElite 71
93/4 EASports 82
94/5 Flair 108
94/5 Fleer 129, -Slapshot 10
96/7 Fleer 62
95/6 FleerMetal 88
92/3 FleerUltra 131
93/4 FleerUltra 216
94/5 FleerUltra 132
95/6 FleerUltra 263
96/7 FleerUltra 97
95/6 Hoyle'EAST 10 (Clubs)
92/3 HumptyDumpty (2)
86/7 Kraft Sports 59
93/4 Leaf 81
94/5 Leaf 67
95/6 Leaf 125
96/7 Leaf 25
94/5 LeafLimited 6
95/6 LeafLimited 84
96/7 MetalUniverse 90
86/7 O-Pee-Chee 245
87/8 OPC/Topps 188
88/9 O-Pee-Chee 259
89/90 OPC/Topps 82
90/1 OPC/Topps 92
91/2 OPC/Topps 210
92/3 O-Pee-Chee 395
91/2 opcPremier 195
86/7 opcSticker 135/121,140/250
87/8 opcSticker 154/15
89/90 opcSticker 15/157
98/9 Pacific 274
97/8 PacificCrown 195
87/8 PaniniSticker 329
88/9 PaniniSticker 30
89/90 PaniniSticker 50
91/2 PaniniSticker 14
92/3 PaniniSticker 203
93/4 PaniniSticker 57
94/5 PaniniSticker 51
95/6 PaniniSticker 95
96/7 PaniniSticker 78
95 PaniniWorlds 22
91/2 Parkhurst 105
92/3 Parkhurst 338, 454
93/4 Parkhurst 124
94/5 Parkhurst V68
95/6 Parkhurst 390
94/5 ParkieSE 102
91/2 Pinnacle 116
92/3 Pinnacle 128
93/4 Pinnacle 173
94/5 Pinnacle 52, BR11
95/6 Pinnacle-FullContact 6
96/7 Pinnacle 53
97/8 PinnacleBeAPlayer 71
95/6 P.Zenith 114, -Gifted 18
96/7 PinnacleZenith 33
95/6 Playoff 169
94/5 POG 159
95/6 POG 158
93/4 PowerPlay 154
93/4 Premier 300
94/5 Premier 495
94/5 Permier-Finest(Topps) 14
90/1 ProSet 62
91/2 ProSet 45, 438
92/3 ProSet 106
91/2 PSPlatinum 203
90/1 Score 66, -HotCards 30
91/2 Score(CDN) 94
91/2 Score(U.S) 94, 51T
92/3 Score 12
93/4 Score 141
94/5 Score 37
95/6 Score 226
96/7 Score 64
97/8 Score(N.J.) 10
94/5 Select 105
95/6 SkyBoxImpact 98
96/7 SkyBoxImpact 72
93 SourPuckCaps 6
94/5 SP 71
95/6 SP 80
95/6 Summit 161
96/7 Summit 31
92/3 Topps 222
95/6 Topps 256
94/5 ToppsFinest 37
95/6 ToppsFinest 14
96/7 ToppsNHLPicks 75
91/2 ToppsStadiumClub 109
92/3 ToppsStadiumClub 369
93/4 ToppsStadiumClub 195
94/5 ToppsStadiumClub 80
95/6 ToppsStadiumClub 16
90/1 UpperDeck 221
91/2 UpperDeck 162, 534
92/3 UpperDeck 171
93/4 UpperDeck 122, SP-95
94/5 UpperDeck 275, SP139
95/6 UpperDeck 472, SE136
96/7 UpperDeck 284
94/5 UDBAP R171, -Aut. 145
95/6 UDCollChoice 248
96/7 UDCC 145, 322, C16
96/7 UpperDeck"Ice" 37
87/8 CHI/Coke
88/9 CHI/Coke
89/90 CHI/Coke
90/1 CHI/Coke
96/7 N.J/Sharp
85/6 TOR
86/7 TOR

THOMAS, WAYNE
72-84 Dernière 72/3, 73/4
74/5 Loblaws-Update
73/4 OPC 221
75/6 OPC 347
76/7 OPC/Topps 84
77/8 OPC/Topps 19
78/9 OPC/Topps 166
79/80 OPC/Topps 126
88/9 ProCards(Peoria)
89/90 ProCards(IHL) 23
87/8 CHI/Coke
73/4 MTL
74/5 MTL
75/6 TOR
76/7 TOR

THOMERSON, BOB
74/5 SiouxCity

THOMLINSON, DAVE
90/1 Bowman 21
88/9 ProCards(Peoria)
89/90 ProCards(IHL) 15
90/1 ProCards 82
91/2 ProCards 53
91/2 UpperDeck 557
89/90 STL/Kodak
92/3 Binghampton
83/4 Brandon 10
84/5 Brandon 22
85/6 Brandon 22
95/6 Phoenix

THOMPSON, ADAM
91/2 LakeSuperior
81/2 Saskatoon 8

THOMPSON, BLAINE
93/4 SSMarie 21

THOMPSON, BRENT
93/4 Premier 46
91/2 ProCards 402
92/3 Score 455
90/1 SketchWHL 43
95/6 Slapshot 83
92/3 Topps 161
92/3 ToppsStadiumClub 92
93/4 ToppsStadiumClub 489
91/2 UpperDeck 608

THOMPSON, BRETT
95/6 Guelph 24
96/7 Guelph 2

THOMPSON, BRIAN
91/2 SketchOHL 317
93/4 Slapshot(SSMarie) 19

THOMPSON, CECIL (TINY)
34-43 BeeHives(BOS)
33-35 DiamondMatch
83&87 HallOfFame 15
83 HHOF Postcard (A)
27-32 LaPresse 29/30
34/5 OPC (V304B) 68
39/40 OPC (V301-1) 75
94/5 Parkie(64/5)-Greats 9
34/5 SweetCaporal
60/1 Topps 55
33/4 WWGum (V357) 57
36/7 WWGum (V356) 12
91/2 BOS/Legends

THOMPSON, CHAD
88/9 ProCards(Peoria)
91/2 Knoxville

THOMPSON, CHRIS
95/6 Slapshot 8

THOMPSON, COREY
91/2 AirCanadaSJHL B4

THOMPSON, DALLAS
92/3 Tacoma
93/4 Tacoma

THOMPSON, DEREK
87/8 Sudbury 23
88/9 Sudbury 14

THOMPSON, DEWAR
52/3 LavalDairy 53
52/3 StLawrence 88

THOMPSON, ERROL
74/5 Loblaws
75/6 OPC/Topps 114
76/7 OPC/Topps 259, OPC 394
77/8 OPC 293
78/9 OPC/Topps 57
79/80 OPC/Topps 106
80/1 OPC/Topps 234
79/80 DET
80/1 DET
72/3 TOR
73/4 TOR
74/5 TOR
76/7 TOR
77/8 TOR

THOMPSON, JAMIE
92/3 Maine (2) 36

THOMPSON, J.G.
51/2 LacStJean 54

THOMPSON, JIM
48-52 Exhibits
56-66 TorontoStar 57/8

THOMPSON, JIM
94/5 ANA/Carl'sJr 23

THOMPSON, PAUL
33/4 Anonymous (V129) 50
34-43 BeeHives(CHI)
36-39 DiamondMatch (1), (2), (3)
36-39 DiamondMatch (4), (5)
35/6 Triumph
36/7 WWGum (V356) 6

THOMPSON, RHYS
34-43 BeeHives(TOR)

THOMPSON, SHAWN
91/2 AirCanadaSJHL B15

THOMPSON, TIM
93/4 Slapshot(NiagaraFalls) 6

THOMPSON, TINY
see Cecil Thompson

THOMPSON, TOM
92/3 MPSPhotoSJHL 131

THOMPSON, WAYNE
83/4 NovaScotia 20

THOMS, BILL
33/4 Anonymous (V129) 10
33-43 BeeHives(TOR)
33/4 Hamilton (V288) 7
37/8 OPC (V304E) 143
39/40 OPC (V301-1) 48
38/9 QuakerOats
33/4 WWGum (V357) 50

THOMSEN, STEEN
79 PaniniSticker 366

THOMSON, BRUE
82/3 Brandon 8

THOMSON, FLOYD
74/5 Loblaws
74/5 OPC 298
75/6 OPC/Topps 149
76/7 OPC 356
77/8 OPC 358
71/2 STL
72/3 STL
72/3 STL/8"x10"
73/4 STL

THOMSON, GREG
94/5 DEL 232
95/6 DEL 106
96/7 DEL 50

THOMSON, JIM
89/90 ProCards(AHL) 225
90/1 ProCards 422
92/3 Topps 67

THOMSON, JIM R.
45-64 BeeHives(TOR)
51/2 Parkhurst 82
52/3 Parkhurst 43
53/4 Parkhurst 8
54/5 Parkhurst 32
55/6 Parkhurst 11
93/4 Parkie(56/7) 119
45-54 QuakerOats
57/8 Topps 23
54-67 TorontoStarV5 ,n11

THOMSON, TOM
91/2 AirCanadaSJHL C32

THÖNY, ROGER
93 SemicSticker 126

THORESEN, PETTER
95 PaniniWorlds 252
94 Semic 270
92 SemicSticker 44
93 SemicSticker 239

THORKILDSEN, KJELL
79 PaniniSticker 300

THORN, H.
95/6 DEL 311

THORNBERG, OVE
94/5 ElitSet 76, -TopGun 8
89/90 SemicElitserien 109
90/1 SemicElitserien 113
91/2 SemicElitserien 117
92/3 SemicElitserien 137

THORNBURY, TOM
84/5 Fredericton 21

THORNTON, BOB
93/4 Slapshot(NorthBay) 18

THORNTON, ERIN
91/2 AvantGardeBCJHL 129
92/3 BCJHL 35
90/1 SketchWHL 187

THORNTON, JOE
96/7 AllSportPPF 171
97/8 AutColl 4, -Athletic 2, -Aut
97/8 Bowman 32, 125, BB1
95 Classic 95
97/8 DonrussElite 6, 138, 148
97/8 D.Elite -BackTo 1,-Crafts 24
97/8 DonrussPreferred 151, 200
97/8 D.Pref -Line 2B, -PrecM 2
97/8 D.Pref -Tin 16, -WideTin 1
97/8 DonrussPriority173,207,215
97/8 D.Prio -DirDep25,-OpDay28
97/8 D.Prio-Pstcrd 16,-Stamp 16
97/8 D.Studio 54,-Portraits 22
97/8 Leaf 41, 150, -FireOnIce 14
97/8 Limited 92, 187
97/8 McDonalds McD33
97/8 Omega 19
98/9 Pacific 102
97/8 PacificCrownRoyale 11
97/8 PCR-Blades 3, -Cramer 3
97/8 PCR-HatTrick 3, -Lamp 3
97/8 PacificDynagon! Rookies
97/8 PcfcParamount 16,-BigN 3
97/8 PcfcP-CdnGrts 2,-Photo 3
97/8 PcfcRevolution 11,-TmCL 2
97/8 Pinnacle 23
97/8 P.BAP 232, -OneTimer 20
97/8 P.BeeHive 51, -TeamBH 22
97/8 PinnacleCertified A
97/8 PinnacleMint 29
97 SB'AutColl 45, GB29, -Aut
97/8 Score 54
97/8 Score(BOS) 17
95/6 Slapshot 363
97/8 SPAuthentic 171,I9,S7,T3
98/9 SPx"Finite" 133
98/9 Topps 112, I13
97/8 ToppsSticker 5
96/7 UpperDeck 370
97/8 UD 218,SG6,SS6,-BlwUp 2
96/7 UDBlackDiamond 160
97/8 UDBlckDiamond 112,PC17
98/9 UDChoice 19
97/8 UDCollChoice 296
96/7 UpperDeck"Ice" 116
97/8 UpperDeckIce 46, IC6, L1C
97/8 VisionsSig 41
97/8 Zenith 100,Z74,-RookRgn 2
97/8 Zenith -RookieZTeam
96/7 SSMarie (x2)

THORNTON, SCOTT
91/2 Bowman 168
95/6 Donruss 262
94/5 Leaf 431
95/6 PaniniSticker 258
94/5 Parkhurst 73
95/6 Pinnacle 162
96/7 PinnacleBeAPlayer 153
95/6 POG 112
90/1 ProSet 640
91/2 Score(CDN) 605, (U.S) 55T
89/90 SketchOHL 83
95/6 Topps 82
91/2 ToppsStadiumClub 378
90/1 UpperDeck 459
91/2 UpperDeck 353, 521
94/5 UpperDeck 426
91/2 EDM/IGA
93/4 EDM 02FEB94
96-98 MTL
96/7 MTL/MolsonExport
90/1 TOR

THORNTON, SHAWN
95/6 Slapshot 316

THORNTON, STEVEN
96/7 DEL 180

THORP, MATT
69 ColumbusCheckers

THORPE, ROBERT
90/1 SketchOHL 122
91/2 SketchOHL 69

THUDIUM, CALVIN
90/1 SketchMEM 91
90/1 SketchWHL 212
87/8 Portland
88/9 Portland

THUN, CHRISTER
65/6 Hellas 144

THURESSON, MARCUS
94/5 ElitSet 29
95/6 ElitSet 226
89/90 SemicElitserien 142
90/1 SemicElitserien 213
91/2 SemicElitserien 140
92/3 SemicElitserien 164
95/6 udElite 92

THURIER, ALFRED (FRED)
34-43 BeeHives(NYA)
51/2 ClevelandBarons

THURSTON, BRENT
90/1 SketchMEM 78
90/1 SketchWHL 204

THURSTON, ERIC
81/2 Victoria
82/3 Victoria
83/4 Victoria

THURSTON, TREVOR
91/2 AirCanadaSJHL A19

THUSBERG, JORMA
70/1 Kuvajulkaisut 116
72 Panda
71/2 WilliamsFIN 126
72/3 WilliamsFIN 97
73/4 WilliamsFIN 145

THUSS, CHUCK
95/6 Louisiana Playoffs

THYER, MARIO
89/90 ProCards(IHL) 85
90/1 ProCards 119
91/2 ProCards 157
90/1 Score 382
92/3 Cincinnati

TIAINEN, RAIMO
66/7 Champion 9

TIAINEN, TERO
95/6 Sisu 289
96/7 Sisu 87

TIBBATTS, DEREK
90/1 SketchWHL 79
91/2 SketchWHL 111
90/1 Saskatoon 12
91/2 Saskatoon 12
93/4 Saskatoon

TIBBATTS, DEREK
93/4 Saskatoon

TIBBATTS, TRENT
92/3 MPSPhotoSJHL 96

TICHY, MAREK
94/5 APS 235

TICHY, MILAN
92/3 ClassicProspects 25
93/4 FleerUltra 247, -AllRook 10
93/4 PowerPlay 101
91/2 ProCards 485
93/4 Score 461
92/3 Indianapolis

TIDEY, ALEX
88/9 EDM/ActionMagazine 163

TIDSBURY, SHANE
92/3 BCJHL 175

TIE, JUSSI
95/6 UDCollChoice 325

TIGLIANI, GIORGIO
79 PaniniSticker 387

TIILIKAINEN, JUKKA
93/4 Jyvas-Hyva 199
95 Semic 228
93/4 Sisu 265
95/6 Sisu 129

TIINUS, MARKKU
92/3 Jyvas-Hyva 114

TIKHONOV, VASILI
92/3 Jyvas-Hyva 188
92/3 S.J/PacificBell

TIKHONOV, VIKTOR
90/1 O-Pee-Chee 17R
89 SemicSticker 77
92 SemicSticker 98
89/90 SovietNats
79/80 SovietChamps
83/4 SovietStars
87/8 SovietStars

TIKKANEN, ESA
90/1 Bowman 194
91/2 Bowman 98
92/3 Bowman 144
93/4 Donruss 215
95/6 Donruss 17
97/8 EssoOlympic 49
95 FinnishAllStar 5
94/5 Flair 160
94/5 Fleer 193
95/6 FleerMetal 87
92/3 FleerUltra 67
93/4 FleerUltra 377
94/5 FleerUltra 191
95/6 FleerUltra 143, 264
96/7 FleerUltra 171
91/2 Gillette 2
95 Globe 138
95/6 Hoyle'WEST 8 (Clubs)
93 Koululainen
95 Koululainen
89/90 Kraft 18
93/4 Leaf 288
95/6 Leaf 319
96/7 Maggers 161
96/7 MetalUniverse 160
87/8 OPC/Topps 7
88/9 O-Pee-Chee 260
89/90 OPC/Topps 12, OPC 328
90/1 OPC/Topps 156
91/2 OPC/Topps 378, T-TL 6
92/3 O-Pee-Chee 319
91/2 opcPremier 121
87/8 opcSticker 83/215
88/9 opcSticker 220/92
89/90 opcSticker 219/78
98/9 Pacific 448
97/8 PacificCrown 249
97/8 PacificParamount 85
90/1 Panini(EDM) 23
87/8 PaniniSticker 264
88/9 PaniniSticker 63
90/1 PaniniSticker 223

91/2 PaniniSticker 123
92/3 PaniniSticker 103
93/4 PaniniSticker 95
95/6 PaniniSticker 192
96/7 PaniniSticker 297
97/8 PaniniSticker 86
95 PaniniWorlds 295
91/2 Parkhurst 55
92/3 Parkhurst 46
93/4 Parkhurst 135
95/6 Parkhurst 173, 235, 478
94/5 ParkieSE 157, ES11
89 Pelimiehen
91/2 Pinnacle 24
92/3 Pinnacle 336
93/4 Pinnacle 279
94/5 Pinnacle 174
95/6 Pinnacle 57
96/7 Pinnacle 46
96/7 PinnacleBeAPlayer 31
95/6 Playoff 196
96/7 Playoff 392
94/5 POG 209
95/6 POG 239
93/4 PowerPlay 395, -Global 9
93/4 Premier 282
94/5 Premier 504, 528
95/6 ProMagnet 7
90/1 ProSet 97
91/2 ProSet 71
92/3 ProSet 53
91/2 PSPlatinum 39
90/1 Score 13, 342, -HotCard 6
91/2 Score(CDN) 461, (U.S) 241
92/3 Score 16,-Promo(CND2) 16
93/4 Score 97
94/5 Score 136
95/6 Score 123
97/8 Score 236
94 Semic 34, 349
95 Semic 43
91 SemicSticker 203
92 SemicSticker 14
93 SemicSticker 80
94/5 Sisu-GuestSpecial 10
95/6 SisuLimited 40, -S&S 8
95/6 SkyBoxEmotion 153
95/6 SkyBoxImpact 145
94/5 SP 103
95/6 SP 153
96/7 TeamOut
92/3 Topps 476
91/2 ToppsStadiumClub 69
92/3 ToppsStadiumClub 104
93/4 TSC 477, -Master (2) 1
94/5 ToppsStadiumClub 258
90/1 UpperDeck 167
91/2 UpperDeck 83, 182, E10
92/3 UpperDeck 188
93/4 UpperDeck 457, SP-104
94/5 UpperDeck 42, SP160
95/6 UpperDeck 126, SE70
96/7 UpperDeck 352
97/8 UpperDeck 111
95/6 UDCollChoice 268
96/7 UDCollChoice 273
96 Wien 28
85/6 EDM/RedRooster
86/7 EDM
86/7 EDM/RedRooster
87/8 EDM
88/9 EDM
88/9 EDM/ActionMagazine 29
90/1 EDM/McGavins
91/2 EDM/IGA
92/3 EDM/IGA 23
97/8 FLA/WinnDixie
96/7 VAN
96/7 VAN/IGA

TIKKONEN, PEKKA
93/4 Sisu 178

TILEY, BRAD
92/3 ClassicProspects 129
91/2 ProCards 61
90/1 SketchMEM 6
90/1 SketchOHL 173
92/3 Phoenix
93/4 Phoenix

TILLEY, TOM
91/2 Bowman 377
95/6 FutureLegends 43
90/1 O-Pee-Chee 498
89/90 PaniniSticker 128
93/4 Parkhurst 442
90/1 ProCards 83
93/4 UpperDeck 491
87/8 STL
88/9 STL
88/9 STL/Kodak
89/90 STL/Kodak

TILLIDY, ROB
45-54 QuakerOats

TILSON, MICHAEL
95/6 Slapshot 110

TILTGEN, DEAN
90/1 SketchWHL 104
91/2 SketchWHL 289

TIMANDER, MATTIAS
96/7 DonrussCanadianIce 138
96/7 DonrussElite 135
94/5 ElitSet 179
95/6 ElitSet 101, -FaceTo 10
96/7 Flair 101
96/7 LeafPreferred 120
97/8 PacificCrown 235
97/8 PaniniSticker 5
97/8 PinnacleBeAPlayer 151
96/7 PinnacleZenith 134
96/7 SelectCertified 99
92/3 SemicElitserien 233
96/7 SP 170
95/6 udElite 153, NA19
96/7 UpperDeck 220
97/8 UpperDeck 224
96/7 UDBlackDiamond 47

TIMCHENKO, OLEG
98 BowmanCHL 105

TIMEWELL, JASON
91/2 AvantGardeBCJHL 67

TIMGREN, RAY
45-64 BeeHives(TOR)
48-52 Exhibits
51/2 Parkhurst 78
45-54 QuakerOats
54/5 Topps 13

TIMMINS, SEAN
91/2 AirCanadaSJHL D26

TIMOSCHUK, ROLAND
94/5 DEL 186
95/6 DEL 186
96/7 DEL 197

TIMONEN, KIMMO
93/4 Jyvas-Hyva 165
94/5 ParkieSE 218
95 Semic 10
95 Semic 233
93/4 Sisu 163, 396
95/6 Sisu 123, -Double 1
96/7 Sisu 182
95/6 SisuLimited 65
94/5 SP 160
94/5 ToppsFinest 129
93/4 UpperDeck 268
94/5 UpperDeck 510

TIMORFEYEV, BORIS
95 PaniniWorlds 37

TIMOSAARI, ARI
70/1 Kuvajulkaisut 381
80/1 Mallasjuoma 108
71/2 WilliamsFIN 315

TING WEN, TSUI
79 PaniniSticker 355

TINORDI, MARK
91/2 Bowman 124
92/3 Bowman 218, 399
93/4 Donruss 79
94/5 Donruss 206
95/6 Donruss 255
96/7 Donruss 153
93/4 EASports 31
94/5 Flair 45
94/5 Fleer 239
92/3 FleerUltra 98
93/4 FleerUltra 213
94/5 FleerUltra 57
95/6 FleerUltra 178
95 Globe 80
92/3 HumptyDumpty (1)
91/2 Kraft 22
93/4 Kraft-Captain
94/5 Leaf 91
96/7 Leaf 31
91/2 OPC/Topps 308
92/3 O-Pee-Chee 17
98/9 Pacific 449
97/8 PacificCrown 181
91/2 PaniniSticker 109
92/3 PaniniSticker 97
93/4 PaniniSticker 275
94/5 PaniniSticker 232
95/6 PaniniSticker 144
91/2 Parkhurst 304
92/3 Parkhurst 76
93/4 Parkhurst 320
94/5 Parkhurst 59
95/6 Parkhurst 224
91/2 Pinnacle 199
92/3 Pinnacle 18, 252
93/4 Pinnacle 16, CA6
94/5 Pinnacle 29
95/6 Pinnacle -FullContact 10
95/6 Playoff 215
94/5 POG 85
95/6 POG 284
93/4 PowerPlay 66
93/4 Premier 24
94/5 Premier 24, 452
90/1 ProSet 145
91/2 ProSet 107, 575
92/3 ProSet 78
91/2 PSPlatinum 58
90/1 Score(U.S) 304
91/2 Score(CDN) 93, (U.S) 93
91/2 Score-YoungStar 18
92/3 Score 7
93/4 Score 53
94/5 Score 68
95/6 Score 144
96/7 Score 11
94 Semic 82
95 Semic 84
92 SemicSticker 83
95/6 Summit 93
91 TeamCanada
92/3 Topps 4
95/6 Topps 198
98/9 Topps 157
94/5 ToppsFinest 25
91/2 ToppsStadiumClub 392
92/3 ToppsStadiumClub 435
93/4 ToppsStadiumClub 384
95/6 ToppsStadiumClub 67
94/5 TSC-MembersOnly 21
91/2 UpperDeck 295
92/3 UpperDeck 73
93/4 UpperDeck 89
94/5 UpperDeck 369, SP177
95/6 UpperDeck 94
97/8 UpperDeck 385
95/6 UDBeAPlayer 220
95/6 UDCollChoice 141
96/7 UpperDeck"Ice" 74
94/5 DAL
95/6 WSH

TIPLER, CURTIS
95/6 Bowman P33

TIPPETT, BRAD
90/1 SketchWHL 182
91/2 SketchWHL 241

TIPPETT, DAVE
93/4 Leaf 349
86/7 OPC/Topps 148
87/8 OPC/Topps 86
88/9 OPC/Topps 85
89/90 OPC/Topps 134
90/1 OPC/Topps 183
91/2 OPC/Topps 384
90/1 opcPremier 119
89/90 opcSticker 268/149
87/8 PaniniSticker 51
88/9 PaniniSticker 244
89/90 PaniniSticker 226
90/1 PaniniSticker 37
93/4 PaniniSticker 85
92/3 Parkhurst 372
93/4 PowerPlay 410
93/4 Premier 387
90/1 ProSet 111, 555
90/1 Score 192, 29T
91/2 Score(CDN) 409, (U.S) 437
93/4 Score 584
93/4 ToppsStadiumClub 124
90/1 UpperDeck 270
91/2 UpperDeck 480
84/5 HFD/JuniorWhalers
85/6 HFD/JuniorWhalers
86/7 HFD/JuniorWhalers
87/8 HFD/JuniorWhalers
88/9 HFD/JuniorWhalers
89/90 HFD/JuniorWhalers
92/3 PGH/Coke
92/3 PGH/Foodland 16
93/4 PHA 6JAN94
93/4 PHA/JCPenney
90/1 WSH/Kodak
90/1 WSH/Smokey
91/2 WSH
91/2 WSH/Kodak

TIRKKONEN, ANTTI
95/6 Sisu 342

TIRKKONEN, HEIKKI
70/1 Kuvajulkaisut 268

TIRKKONEN, PAAVO
66/7 Champion 128
70/1 Kuvajulkaisut 269

TIRKKONEN, PEKKA
96/7 DEL 197
91/2 Jyvas-Hyva 32
92/3 Jyvas-Hyva 96
93/4 Jyvas-Hyva 168
94 Semic 25
94/5 Sisu 40, 171
95/6 Sisu 80
95/6 SisuLimited 70

TISDALE, TIM
89/90 ProCards(AHL) 142
90/1 ProCards 227
94/5 Fredericton
92/3 Wheeling 17
94/5 Wheeling 2

TITOV, GERMAN
93/4 Classic 94
93/4 Donruss 56
94/5 Donruss 228
95/6 Donruss 229
96/7 Donruss 58
95/6 DonrussElite 41
94/5 Flair 29
94/5 Fleer 36
96/7 Fleer 14
96/7 FleerNHLPicks 106
94/5 FleerUltra 36
96/7 FleerUltra 27
95/6 Hoyle'WEST 9 (Clubs)
92/3 Jyvas-Hyva 185
93/4 Leaf 309
94/5 Leaf 261
95/6 Leaf 31
96/7 Maggers 24
96/7 MetalUniverse 23
97/8 Omega 37
98/9 Pacific 127
97/8 PacificCrown 263
97/8 PcfcDynagon! 19,-Tand 34
97/8 PacificInvincible 21
97/8 PacificParamount 32
94/5 PaniniSticker 158
95/6 PaniniSticker 234
96/7 PaniniSticker 235
97/8 PaniniSticker 192
93/4 Parkhurst 255
95/6 Parkhurst 28
94/5 ParkieSE 26
94/5 Pinnacle 167
95/6 Pinnacle 52
96/7 Pinnacle 36
96/7 PinnacleBeAPlayer 49
97/8 PinnacleCertified 88
95/6 Playoff 20
96/7 Playoff 354
95/6 POG 50
93/4 PowerPlay 310
94/5 Premier 9
95/6 ProMagnet 42
93/4 Score 614
94/5 Score 95
95/6 Score 71
96/7 Score 165
97/8 Score 197
93/4 Sisu 352, 376
94/5 Sisu 361 -GuestSpecial 11
95/6 SkyBoxImpact 25
96/7 SkyBoxImpact 15
94/5 SP 18
95/6 SP 18
96/7 SP 24
97/8 SPAuthentic 22
96/7 Summit 108
94/5 ToppsFinest 75
93/4 ToppsStadiumClub 364
93/4 UpperDeck 476
94/5 UpperDeck 2
95/6 UpperDeck 207, SE14
96/7 UpperDeck 227
98/8 UDChoice 30
95/6 UDCollChoice 15
96/7 UDCollChoice 39
97/8 UDCollChoice 39
96 Wien 154

TITUS, STEPHEN
86/7 London 27

TIURIKOV, VLADIMIR
91 SemicSticker 85

TJALLDEN, MIKAEL
92/3 SemicElitserien 352

TJARNQVIST, DANIEL
94/5 ElitSet 209, -Rookie 6
95/6 ElitSet 116
94/5 SigRookies 49
95/6 SP 186
95/6 udElite 175
97/8 udSwedish 40, C3, S14

TJERNYCH, ALEXANDER
89 SemicSticker 100

TJUMENEV, VIKTOR
87/8 SovietStars

TKACHUK, GRANT
88/9 ProCards(Rochester)
89/90 ProCards(IHL) 105
90/1 ProCards 281
84/5 Saskatoon
86/7 Saskatoon

TKACHUK, KEITH
95/6 Aces J (Spades)
96/7 Aces 10 (Hearts)
97/8 Aces 8 (Hearts)
95/6 Bowman 69
96/7 CorinthianHeadliners
97/8 CorinthianHeadliners
93/4 Donruss 390
94/5 Donruss 192
95/6 Donruss 78, -ProPointer 7
96/7 Donruss 134,-Dom 8,-Hit 10
97/8 Donruss 83, 227, -Red 4
96/7 DonrussCanadianIce 22
97/8 DonrussCanadianIce 16
95/6 DonrussElite 81
96/7 DonrussElite 61, -Status 2
97/8 D.Elite 112, -Craftsmen 28
97/8 D.Preferred 6, 191,-Line 3B
97/8 DonrussPriority 3, 202
97/8 D.Prio -DirDep 17,-OpDay 3
97/8 D.Prio-Pstcrd 26,-Stamp 26
97/8 D.Studio 8, -HardHats 7
97/8 D.Studio-Portraits 8, -Sil 18
96/7 Duracell DC18, JB18
97/8 EssoOlympic 23
94/5 Flair 211
96/7 Flair 73
94/5 Fleer 246, -Franchise 8
96/7 Fleer 92, 141, -ArtRoss 22
95/6 FleerMetal 166,-IronWar 14
96/7 FleerNHLPicks 18, -Fab 44
96/7 F.Picks-Captain 7,-Dream 5
92/3 FleerUltra 446
93/4 FleerUltra 111
94/5 FleerUltra 247, -Power 10
95/6 FleerUltra 184, -Crease 20
96/7 FleerUltra 136,-Clear 10
95/6 Hoyle'WEST 10 (Clubs)
97/8 KatchMedallion 113
97/8 KennerSLU
94/5 Kraft-Sharpshooter
95/6 Kraft-Disk
96/7 Kraft-TeamMVP
97/8 Kraft -WorldsBest
93/4 Leaf 105, -GoldL.Rook 11
94/5 Leaf 94
95/6 Leaf 79
96/7 Leaf 133,-Best 5,-Leather 2
97/8 Leaf 73, 185
94/5 LeafLimited 108
95/6 LeafLimited 57
96/7 LeafLimited 3, -Bash 5
96/7 LeafPreferd 89,148,-Van 12
97/8 Limited 83, 133, 138, 140
97/8 Limited -fabric 18
96/7 McDonalds McD13
97/8 McDonalds McD7
96/7 MetalUniverse 122
96/7 MU-CoolStee 11, -Lethal 19
97/8 Omega 177,245,-G.Face 15
92/3 O-Pee-Chee 346
92/3 opcPremier 43
98/9 Pacific 344,-Gld 27,-T.CL20
97/8 PacificCrown 28, -Supial 17
97/8 PacificCrown-Slapshot 7A
97/8 PacificCrownRoyale 107
97/8 PCR-HatTrick 14, -Lamp 16
97/8 PcfcDynagon! 98,-BstKt 76
97/8 PcfcD-Dyna 12B,-Tandm 6
97/8 PacificInvincible 109,-Off 16
97/8 PacificParamount 144
97/8 PcfcP-BigNm 16,-Photo 16
98/9 PacificParamount 186
98/9 PcfcP-SpecD 15, -TmCL 20
97/8 PacificRegime 156
97/8 PcfcRevoltn 109,-TmCL 19
93/4 PaniniSticker 193
94/5 PaniniSticker 168
95/6 PaniniSticker 214
96/7 PaniniSticker 191
97/8 PaniniSticker 123, 162
91/2 Parkhurst 424
92/3 Parkhurst 206
93/4 Parkhurst 228
94/5 Parkhurst 264
95/6 Parkhurst 501
94/5 ParkieSE seV38
92/3 Pinnacle 222
93/4 Pinnacle 33, CA26
94/5 Pinnacle 103, GR18, NL12
95/6 Pinnacle -FullContact 11
96/7 Pinnacle 114
97/8 Pinnacle 40, -TeamP 6
96/7 Pinn.BeAPlayer-Biscuit 6
97/8 P.BeAPlayer 22,-OneTimr 2
97/8 P.BeeHive 14, -TeamBH 17
97/8 PinnCertified 37, -Team 11
97/8 Pinnacle-EPIX 6
97/8 PinnInside 5, 18, -Track 24
96/7 PinnacleMint 19
97/8 PinnacleMint 21
95/6 P.Zenith 74, -GiftedGrndr 1
96/7 P.Zenith 6, -ZTeam 12
95/6 Playoff 109, 220
96/7 Playoff 351
94/5 POG 256
95/6 POG 16, 293
93/4 PowerPlay 276, -Rising 8
93/4 Premier 27, 502
94/5 Prmr 242, 300, -Fin.(T) 18
95/6 ProMagnet 59
92/3 ProSet 243
92/3 Score 450, -YoungStar 29
93/4 Score 195
94/5 Score CI14
95/6 Score 33, -CheckIt 11
96/7 Score 47, -CheckIt 3
97/8 Score 87, -CheckIt 4
94/5 Select 75
95/6 SelectCert. 37, -Double 17
96/7 SelectCert. 24, -Corner 10
95/6 SkBxEmotion 197,-Ntense9
95/6 SkyBoxImpact 185, 239
96/7 SkBxImpact 107, -Blade 22
94/5 SP 132
95/6 SP 164, E30
96/7 SP 118, GF5, -Inside
97/8 SPAuthentic 119, I23
96/7 SPx 35
97/8 SPx 40, SPX15
98/9 SPx"Finite" 64
95/6 Summit 152, -GM6
96/7 Summit 104
95/6 SuperSticker 136
96/7 TeamOut
92/3 Topps 102
95/6 Topps 152, 2PL, 7RL
95/6 Topps HGA5, M14
98/9 Topps 154, A6, M13, SB18
94/5 T.Finest 19, -BBest(B) 17
95/6 ToppsFinest 123
92/3 ToppsStadiumClub 116
93/4 ToppsStadiumClub 135
94/5 ToppsStadiumClub 5
95/6 ToppsStadiumClub 90, F9
94/5 TSC-MembersOnly 39
97/8 ToppsSticker 3
95/6 ToppsSuperSkills 51
91/2 UD 698, -CzechWJC 85
92/3 UpperDeck 364, 398, 419
92/3 UD AC2, CC15, G18
93/4 UD 195, NL5, SP-178
94/5 UpperDeck 145, SP89
95/6 UpperDeck 243, 464, SE88
96/7 UD 313, HH8, LS17, SS6A
96/7 UD X15, -AllStarYCTG A11
97/8 UD 126, S15, SG37
97/8 UD SS23, T6C
94/5 UDBeAPlayer R36
95/6 UDBeAPlayer 215, LL1
96/7 UDBlackDiamond 153
97/8 UDBlckDiamond 110,PC14
98/9 UDChoice 160, BH2, SQ30
95/6 UDCollChoice 168,356,382
96/7 UDCollChoice 201, 295,327
96/7 UDCollChoice C26, UD16
97/8 UDCC 194, C27, SQ87
97/8 udDiamondVision 18
96/7 UpperDeck"Ice" 100, S8
97/8 UpperDeckIce 70, IC15,L3A
96 Wien 168
97/8 Zenith 7, Z18
96/7 PHO (x2)
97/8 PHO
93/4 WPG/Ruffles
95/6 WPG

TKACHUK, PETE
51/2 LavalDairy 34

TKACS, WOJCIECH
92 SemicSticker 287

TKACZUK, DANIEL
97/8 Bowman 8, 152, BB4
98 BowmanCHL 34, SC3
97/8 PinnacleBeeHive 65
95/6 Slapshot 17
98/9 Topps 227
96/7 UpperDeck 387
96/7 UDBlackDiamond 38
97/8 UDBlackDiamond 55
98/9 UDChoice 254
97/8 UDCollChoice 298

TKACZUK, WALT
71/2 Bazooka Panel 31
71/2 Colgate Heads
70/1 DadsCookies
70/1 EddieSargent 117
71/2 EddieSargent 120
72/3 EddieSargent 149
70/1 Esso Stamp
72/3 Letraset 4
74/5 LiptonSoup 12
74/5 Loblaws
69/70 OPC/Topps 43
70/1 O-Pee-Chee 180
70/1 OPC/T-Deckle 41
71/2 OPC/Topps 75
72/3 OPC 110, -Crests 14, T. 14
73/4 OPC/Topps 25
74/5 OPC/Topps 119
75/6 OPC/Topps 128
76/7 OPC/Topps 220
77/8 OPC/Topps 90
78/9 OPC/Topps 235
79/80 OPC/Topps 15
80/1 OPC/Topps 211
72 SemicSticker 212
71/2 TheTorontoSun

TOAL, MIKE
88/9 EDM/ActionMagazine 111

TOCCHET, RICK
90/1 Bowman 108, -HatTrick 14
91/2 Bowman 230
92/3 Bowman 159
95/6 Bowman 36
93/4 Donruss 267

95/6 Donruss 41
96/7 Donruss 122
97/8 Donruss 45
97/8 DonrussPriority 148
96/7 Duracell DC14
94/5 Flair 83
94/5 Fleer 100
96/7 Fleer 8
95/6 FleerMetal 74, -IronWar 15
92/3 FleerUltra 172
93/4 FleerUltra 225
94/5 FleerUltra 309
95/6 FleerUltra 79, -Crease 19
96/7 FleerUltra 12
95 Globe 92
93/4 HockeyWit 58
95/6 Hoyle'WEST J (Clubs)
91/2 Kelloggs 2
89/90 Kraft 57, -Sticker 2
90/1 Kraft 58
91/2 Kraft 45
93/4 Leaf 109
94/5 Leaf 100, 474
95/6 Leaf 29
96/7 Leaf 90
94/5 LeafLimited 117
97/8 Limited 83
96/7 Maggers 14
91/2 McDonalds McD2
96/7 MetalUniverse 11
97/8 Omega 178
87/8 OPC/Topps 2
88/9 OPC/Topps 177
89/90 OPC/Topps 80
90/1 OPC/Topps 26, T-TL 9
91/2 OPC/Topps 160, T-TL 13
92/3 O-Pee-Chee 148
90/1 opcPremier 120
91/2 opcPremier 63
88/9 opcSticker 99/225
89/90 opcSticker 108/247
98/9 Pacific 92
97/8 PacificCrown 311
97/8 PacificParamount 145
98/9 PacificParamount 187
87/8 PaniniSticker 134
88/9 PaniniSticker 326
89/90 PaniniSticker 295
90/1 PaniniSticker 121
91/2 PaniniSticker 229, 331
92/3 PaniniSticker 226
93/4 PaniniSticker 80
94/5 PaniniSticker 77
95/6 PaniniSticker 271
96/7 PaniniSticker 6
91/2 Parkhurst 129, 354
92/3 Parkhurst 139, CP12
93/4 Parkhurst 428
94/5 Parkhurst V25
95/6 Parkhurst 287
94/5 ParkieSE 79
91/2 Pinnacle 20
92/3 Pinnacle 282
93/4 Pinnacle 174
94/5 Pinnacle 371, BR18, GR12
96/7 Pinnacle 23
97/8 PinnacleBeAPlayer 127
97/8 PinnacleInside 174
95/6 Pinn.Zenith 118, -Gifted 5
95/6 Playoff 161
96/7 Playoff 376
95/6 POG 137
93/4 PowerPlay 196
93/4 Premier 72
94/5 Premier 281, 346
95/6 ProMagnet 65
90/1 ProSet 225, 374
91/2 ProSet 177, 311, 580
92/3 ProSet 138
91/2 PSPlatinum 88
90/1 Score 80, -HotCards 40
91/2 Score(CDN) 9, 306, 364
91/2 Score(U.S) 9, 302, 334
92/3 Score 245
93/4 Score 340, -P.AS 14
94/5 Score CI11
95/6 Score 37
96/7 Score 92
97/8 Score 246
92/3 SeasonsPatch 37
94/5 Select 2
95/6 SelectCertified 98

94 Semic 95, 358
95 Semic 98
92 SemicSticker 98
93 SemicSticker 200
95/6 SkyBxEmotion 86,-Nten 10
95/6 SkyBoxImpact 83, 247
96/7 SkyBoxImpact 9
94/5 SP 55
96/7 SP 12
97/8 SPAuthentic 121
95/6 Summit 103
95/6 SuperSticker 59
91 TeamCanada
96/7 TeamOut
92/3 Topps 70
95/6 Topps 264, -HiddenGem 15
98/9 Topps 34
94/5 ToppsFinest 52
95/6 ToppsFinest 133
96/7 ToppsNHLPicks 111
91/2 ToppsStadiumClub 35
92/3 ToppsStadiumClub 76
93/4 T.StadiumClub 329, -AllStar
94/5 ToppsStadiumClub 160
95/6 ToppsStadiumClub 32, F5
95/6 ToppsSuperSkills 64
90/1 UpperDeck 263, 488
91/2 UpperDeck 91, 122, 503
92/3 UD 239, 454, 'LockerAS 16
93/4 UD 179, 233, HT12,SP-126
94/5 UpperDeck 224, SP129
95/6 UpperDeck 274, SE40
96/7 UpperDeck 10, X32
97/8 UpperDeck 339
94/5 UDBeAPlayer G17
95/6 UDBeAPlayer 82
96/7 UDBlackDiamond 55
95/6 UDCollChoice 254
96/7 UDCollChoice 18
96/7 UpperDeck"Ice" 4
96 Wien 89
91/2 PGH/Elbys
91/2 PGH/Foodland 5
92/3 PGH/Coke
92/3 PGH/Foodland 4
92/3 PGH/FoodSticker
93/4 PGH/Foodland 4
86/7 PHA
89/90 PHA
90/1 PHA
91/2 PHA/JCPenney
97/8 PHO
81/2 SSMarie
82/3 SSMarie
83/4 SSMarie
87/8 SSMarie 26

TOCHER, RYAN
91/2 SketchOHL 204
95/6 Slapshot 235

TODD, DICK
89/90 SketchOHL 123
90/1 SketchOHL 376
91/2 SketchOHL 123
91/2 Peterborough 23

TODD, KEVIN
92/3 Bowman 21
92/3 FleerUltra 121,-Rookie 8
93/4 FleerUltra 294
91/2 Gillette 40
93/4 Leaf 15
94/5 Leaf 350
91/2 OPC/Topps 400
92/3 O-Pee-Chee 1
91/2 opcPremier 22
97/8 PacificCrown 182
92/3 PaniniSticker 275, O
96/7 PaniniSticker 271
91/2 Parkhurst 97, 444
92/3 Parkhurst 94, 238, 285
93/4 Parkhurst 37
94/5 Parkhurst 108
95/6 Parkhurst 374
91/2 Pinnacle 308
92/3 Pinnacle 272, -Tm2000 22
93/4 Pinnacle 270
96/7 PinnacleBeAPlayer 101
93/4 PowerPlay 318
88/9 ProCards(Utica)
89/90 ProCards(AHL) 205
90/1 ProCards 570
91/2 ProSet 548

92/3 ProSet 94, -Rookie 7
91/2 PSPlatinum 260
91/2 Score(CDN) 287, (U.S) 397
92/3 Score 162, -YoungStar 19
93/4 Score 338, 507
97/8 Score(ANA) 6
92/3 Topps 15, 228
92/3 ToppsStadiumClub 465
93/4 ToppsStadiumClub 8
91/2 UpperDeck 401
92/3 UD 11, 303, 365, AR3, AR7
93/4 UpperDeck 88, 440, SP33
94/5 UpperDeck 120
95/6 UpperDeck 364
97/8 UpperDeck 3
94/5 UDBeAPlayer-Aut. 74
96/7 UDCollChoice 127
97/8 UDCollChoice 11
96/7 UpperDeck"Ice" 1
96/7 ANA/UpFrontSports
93/4 CHI/Coke
92/3 EDM

TODOROV, ATANAS
79 PaniniSticker 351

TOEWS, LORNE
90/1 SketchWHL 36
91/2 SketchWHL 316

TOFFOLO, MARK
78/9 Saginaw

TOIVANEN, HARRI
80/1 Mallasjuoma 76

TOIVOLA, MARKO
95/6 Sisu 119

TOIVOLA, TERO
93/4 Sisu 75

TOIVONEN, HARRI
78/9 SM-Liiga 121

TOIVONEN, KALEVI
66/7 Champion 179

TOIVONEN, K.P.
70/1 Kuvajulkaisut 204
72 Panda

TOIVIONEN, TIMO
72/3 WilliamsFIN 355

TOKARCZYK, TREVOR
95/6 Slapshot 367
96/7 SSMarie

TOKARZ, LES
74 Hellas 88
79 PaniniSticker 135
73/4 WilliamsFIN 101

TOKARZ, WIESLAV
74 Hellas 89
73/4 WilliamsFIN 102

TOLJANICH, MARK
91/2 SketchWHL 300
93/4 RedDeer

TOLKUNOV, DMITRI
98 BowmanCHL 117

TOLVANEN, ISMO
71/2 WilliamsFIN 337

TOLVANEN, J.
95/6 DEL 168

TOMAJKO, JAN
95/6 APS 122
95/6 UpperDeck 544

TOMAN, ILMAR
94/5 DEL 419

TOMASEK, ALEX
94/5 APS 6
95/6 APS 301

TOMASONI, DICK
72 SemicSticker 137

TOMASSONI, DAVE
82 SemicSticker 128

TOMBERLIN, JUSTIN
92/3 Maine (2) 30
93/4 Maine 50

TOMEK, MICHAL
94/5 APS 245
95/6 APS 23

TOMILIN, VITALI
92/3 Classic 53
92/3 ClassicFourSport 191
93/4 UpperDeck 278

TOMLINSON, D.
96/7 DEL 170

TOMLAK, MIKE
91/2 Bowman 14
90/1 OPC/Topps 95
91/2 OPC/Topps 410
90/1 PaniniSticker 46
91/2 PaniniSticker 319
90/1 ProCards 176
91/2 ProCards 114
90/1 ProSet 452
91/2 Score(CDN) 538
91/2 ToppsStadiumClub 266
90/1 UpperDeck 343
91/2 UpperDeck 310
89/90 HFD/JuniorWhalers
90/1 HFD/JuniorWhalers
94/5 Milwaukee

TOMLINSON, DAVE
92/3 ClassicProspects 12
95/6 EdgeIce 114
94/5 PaniniSticker S
91/2 ProCards 346
93/4 Phoenix
92/3 StJohns

TOMLINSON, JUSTIN
94/5 Raleigh

TOMLINSON, KIRK
88/9 ProCards(Kalamazoo)
91/2 ProCards 122
88/9 Kitchener 22
93/4 LasVegas

TOMLINSON, MIKE
89/90 SketchOHL 108
90/1 SketchOHL 373
91/2 SketchOHL 126
91/2 Peterborough 10

TOMMILA, ESA
92/3 Jyvas-Hyva 46
93/4 Jyvas-Hyva 89
93/4 Sisu 126
95/6 Sisu 188

TOMMILA, TERO
71/2 WilliamsFIN 375

TOMS, C.
1910-11 Imperial (C56) 29

TOMS, JEFF
97/8 PacificCrown 342
91/2 SketchOHL 334
93/4 Slapshot(SSMarie) 23
93/4 SSMarie 25

TON, ANDY
95 PaniniWorlds 133
91 SemicSticker 190
92 SemicSticker 207
93 SemicSticker 118

TON, PETR
94/5 APS 62
95/6 APS 95

TONELLI, JOHN
90/1 Bowman 148
91/2 Bowman 175
88/9 Esso Sticker
79/80 OPC/Topps 146
80/1 O-Pee-Chee 305
81/2 O-Pee-Chee 218
82/3 O-Pee-Chee 213
83/4 O-Pee-Chee 20
84/5 OPC 138, Topps 103
85/6 OPC/Topps 41, O, T-AS 7
86/7 OPC/Topps 132
87/8 OPC/Topps 84
89/90 OPC/Topps 8
90/1 OPC/Topps 281
91/2 OPC/Topps 161
91/2 opcPremier 37, 159
82/3 opcSticker 49
83/4 opcSticker 74, 75
84/5 opcSticker 80, 81
85/6 opcSticker 80, 116
86/7 opcSticker 81/207
87/8 opcSticker 47/186
88/9 opcSticker 87/217
89/90 PaniniSticker 90

90/1 PaniniSticker 235
91/2 PaniniSticker 90
91/2 Pinnacle 284
82/3 Post
90/1 ProSet 129
91/2 ProSet 373
92/3 ProSet 263
91/2 PSPlatinum 22
83/4 PuffySticker 21
90/1 Score 89
91/2 Score(CDN) 172, 567
91/2 Score(U.S) 172, 17T
92/3 Score 342
92/3 Topps 119
83/4 SouhaitsRen.KeyChain
91/2 ToppsStadiumClub 189
92/3 ToppsStadiumClub 159
90/1 UpperDeck 95
86/7 CGY/RedRooster
87/8 CGY/RedRooster
91/2 CHI/Coke
75/6 Houston
88/9 L.A./Smokeys
89/90 L.A./Smokeys 13
90/1 L.A./Smokeys 14
79/80 NYI
83/4 NYI
83/4 NYI/Islander 14
84/5 NYI 15
93/4 NYI/Chemical

TONINATO, JIM
85/6 Minn-Duluth 12

TONOZAKI, KAZUMA
79 PaniniSticker 286

TOOKEY, TIM
93/4 ClassicProspects 84
88/9 ProCards(NewHaven)
89/90 ProCards(AHL) 353
90/1 ProCards 51
91/2 ProCards 281
82/3 Fredericton 8

TOOMEY, DICK
72 SemicSticker 134

TOOMEY, SEAN
85/6 Minn-Duluth 24

TOPATIGH, LUCIO
95 PaniniWorlds 88
95 Semic 175
92 SemicSticker 261
93 SemicSticker 221

TOPPAZZINI, JERRY
45-64 BeeHives(BOS)
62 CeramicTiles
82? JDMcCarthy
53/4 Parkhurst 98
92/3 Parkhurst 27
93/4 Parkie(56/7) 1
60/1 ShirriffCoin 110
61/2 ShirriffCoin 9
54/5 Topps 21
57/8 Topps 5
58/9 Topps 45
59/60 Topps 38
60/1 Topps 28
61/2 Topps 9
62/3 Topps 13, -Buck
63/4 Topps 18
54-67 TorontoStar V8
91/2 Ultimate(O6) 55
57/8 BOS

TOPPAZZINI, TED
52/3 AnonymousOHL 145

TOPPAZZINI, ZELLIO
45-64 BeeHives(BOS)
52/3 Parkhurst 73

TOPOLINSKY, CRAIG
94/5 DEL 147

TOPOLL, DEL
51-54 LaPatrie 27Dec53

TOPOROWSKI, BRAD
91/2 SketchWHL 14

TOPOROWSKI, KERRY
91/2 ProCards 499
90/1 SketchMEM 85
90/1 SketchWHL 206
91/2 UltimateDP 89, -Au t 48
95/6 Adirondack
92/3 Indianapolis

93/4 LasVegas
94/5 LasVegas
89/90 Spokane

TOPORWOSKI, SHANE
97/8 Donruss 224
95/6 EdgeIce 84
93/4 PrinceAlbert
95/6 StJohns

TOPOROWSKI, TERRY
91/2 UltimateDP 48

TORCHIA, MIKE
92/3 ClassicProspects 119
95/6 Donruss 143
95/6 FleerUltra 43
95/6 Leaf 213
95/6 Score 311
91/2 SketchAwards 6
89/90 SketchMEM 31
89/90 SketchOHL 191, 192
90/1 SketchOHL 244
91/2 SketchOHL 75
91/2 StarPics 26
91/2 UltimateDP 50,57,89, -Aut.
88/9 Kitchener 6
89/90 Kitchener 6
90/1 Kitchener 6

TOREN, JOHAN
79 PaniniSticker 279

TORGAJEV, PAVEL
95/6 FleerUltra 215
95/6 Parkhurst 302
93/4 Sisu 46

TORKKEL, KARI
66/7 Champion 62
70/1 Kuvajulkaisut 151
71/2 WilliamsFIN 202
72/3 WilliamsFIN 239
73/4 WilliamsFIN 274

TORKKELI, JORMA
80/1 Mallasjuoma 106
78/9 SM-Liiga 151

TORKKELI, VEIKKO
80/1 Mallasjuoma 103
78/9 SM-Liiga 143
91/2 Jyvas-Hyva 45
92/3 Jyvas-Hyva 130
93/4 Jyvas-Hyva 239
88/9 ProCards(Saginaw)
89/90 ProCards(IHL) 55
91 SemicSticker 22
93/4 Sisu 194
94/5 Sisu 13, -FireOnIce 20
95/6 Sisu 104, 189
96/7 Sisu 107
95/6 SisuLimited 34

TORKKI, JARI
96/7 DEL 194

TÖRMÄ, HANNU
66/7 Champion 3
65/6 Hellas 29

TÖRMÄNEN, ANTTI
95/6 Bowman 117
95/6 Donruss 347, -Rated 15
95/6 FleerMetal 196
95/6 FleerUltra 360
95 Hartwall
95 Latkaliiga 2
96/7 PaniniStickers 53
95/6 Parkhurst 415, 522
95/6 P.Zenith 135, -RookieRoll 4
96/7 PinnacleZenith 78
96/7 Score 265
95/6 SelectCertified 111
94 Semic 28
95 Semic 49
93/4 Sisu 16
94/5 Sisu 63, -Magic 7, -Draft 8
95/6 Sisu-GoldCards 23
95/6 SisuLimited 17
95/6 SP 105
95/6 Summit 174
96/7 Summit 161
95/6 ToppsFinest 118
95/6 ToppsStadiumClub 156
95/6 ToppsSuperSkills SR13
95/6 UpperDeck 347
96/7 UpperDeck 114
96/7 UDCollChoice 184

96 Wien 15
95/6 OTT

TORNBORG, JOHAN
94/5 ElitSet 212
95/6 ElitSet 294
95/6 udElite 190
97/8 udSwedish 186

TOROPCHENKO, LEONID
92/3 ClassicProspects 95
93/4 ClassicProspects 212
93/4 ClevelandLumberjacks

TORREL, DOUG
92/3 Hamilton

TORREY, BILL
83/4 NYI/Islander 28
84/5 NYI 28

TORREY, JEFF
92/3 Richmond

TORTI, SLOAN
86/7 Kingston 27

TORTORELLA, JOHN
88/9 ProCards(NewHaven)
89/90 BUF/Campbell
90/1 BUF/Campbell
97/8 PHO
95/6 Rochester

TORY, JEFF
91/2 AvantGardeBC 88, 159
92/3 BCJHL 138

TOSIO, RENATO
95 Globe 209
95 PaniniWorlds 117
95 Semic 189
91 SemicSticker 177
92 SemicSticker 195
93 SemicSticker 109

TOSKALA, VESA
95/6 Sisu 230, -NHLDraft 7
96/7 Sisu 27,-Energy 8,-Mighty 6
95/6 SisuLimited 100
95/6 UDCollChoice 335

TOTH, RADEK
94/5 APS 251
95/6 APS 126

TOTH, TONY
92/3 MPSPhotoSJHL 164

TOTTLE, SCOTT
85/6 Fredericton 1

TOUHEY, BILL
33/4 CndGum (V252)
33/4 OPC (V304A) 26

TOUJIKOV, ROUSLAN
94/5 Roanoke

TOUPAL, KAMIL
94/5 APS 31
95/6 APS 61

TOUPAL, RADEK
95/6 APS 65
94/5 DEL 377
92/3 Jyvas-Hyva 28
95 PaniniWorlds 209
95 Semic 149
91 SemicSticker 117

TOUPIN, SIMON
90/1 SketchQMJHL 129
91/2 SketchQMJHL 177

TOUSIGANT, DAN
85/6 Minn-Duluth 23

TOUZIMSKY, ZDENEK
94/5 APS 73
95/6 APS 182

TOVELL, TREVOR
90/1 SketchMEM 86
90/1 SketchWHL 192
89/90 Spokane

TOWNSEND, SCOTT
90/1 SketchWHL 37
91/2 SketchWHL 325
93/4 Lethbridge

TOWNSHEND, GRAEME
89/90 ProCards(AHL) 70
90/1 ProCards 133
91/2 ProCards 456
89/90 BOS/SportsAction
93/4 OTT/Kraft

TOYE, RANDY
91/2 SketchWHL 20

TRACHTA, DAVID
94/5 APS 161
95/6 APS 262

TRACHTA, KAREL
94/5 APS 289
95/6 APS 242

TRACY, JOE
91/2 SemicElitserien 247

TRACZE, STEVE
95/6 Slapshot 42

TRADER, LARRY
83 CanadaJuniors
88/9 ProCards(Binghampton)
84/5 DET/Caesars
87/8 MTL
87/8 MTL/Stickers 44

TRAINER, CHRIS
83/4 Kitchener 28

TRAMPUH, ROBBIE
92/3 BCJHL 131

TRAPP, BARRY
82/3 Regina 24
83/4 Regina 24

TRAPP, BOB
23/4 PaulinsCandy 42

TRAPP, DOUG
82/3 Regina 6
83/4 Regina 6

TRAUB, PUSS
23/4 PaulinsCandy 23

TRAVERSE, PATRICK
91/2 SketchQMJHL 63
89/90 ProCards'IHL 174

TRAVNICEK, ZDENEK
94/5 DEL 300
95/6 DEL 389
96/7 DEL 72

TRAYNOR, PAUL
97/8 Bowman 39
94/5 Slapshot(Kitchener) 8
95/6 Slapshot 139

TREBIL, DAN
97/8 Donruss 105
92/3 Minnesota
93/4 Minnesota
94/5 Minnesota

TREFILOV, ANDREI
93/4 Classic 95
92/3 ClassicProspects 30, BC2
93/4 ClassicProspects 181
93/4 Donruss 409
94/5 Donruss 244
95/6 Donruss 273
94/5 FleerUltra 271
95 Globe 163
94/5 Leaf 87
91/2 O-Pee-Chee 45R
93/4 Parkhurst 29
95/6 Parkhurst 296
93/4 PowerPlay 311
94/5 Premier 166
92/3 RedAce(Blue) 4, (Violet) 4
93/4 Score 599
94 Semic 136
92 SemicSticker 99
91/2 StarPics 49
92/3 UpperDeck 345, 514
95/6 UpperDeck 277
96/7 UpperDeck 225
94/5 SaintJohn

TREMBLAY, CLÉMENT
51/2 BasDuFleuve 4
52/3 BasDuFleuve 32

TREMBLAY, DAVE
90/1 SketchQMJHL 29
91/2 SketchQMJHL 80

TREMBLAY, DENIS
79/80 Montréal B&W

TREMBLAY, DIDIER
98 BowmanCHL 84
95/6 Halifax
96/7 Halifax (1), (2)
97/8 Halifax (1)

TREMBLAY, FRANK
85/6 London 16

TREMBLAY, GILLES
45-64 BeeHives(MTLx2)
64-67 BeeHives(MTLx2)
62 CeramicTiles
64/5 CokeCap MTL-21
65/6 CocaCola
68/9 OPC/Topps 66
69/70 O-Pee-Chee 168
62/3 Parkhurst 46
63/4 Parkhurst 21, 80
94/5 Parkie(64/5) 77
95/6 Parkie(66/7) 71
68/9 Post Marble
66/7 Post'Large
67 Post FlipBook
67/8 PostFlipBook
61/2 ShirriffCoin 112
62/3 ShirriffCoin 24
68/9 ShirriffCoin MTL7
63/4 TheTorontoStar
64/5 Topps 2
66/7 Topps 4, -USATest 4
67/8 Topps 5
54-67 TorontoStar V10
60/1 York, -Glasses
61/2 York 4
62/3 YorkTransfer 34
63/4 York 21
67/8 MTL
67/8 MTL/IGA
68/9 MTL
69/70 MTL/ProStar
80/1 Québec

TREMBLAY, JACQUES
87/8 Kingston 4

TREMBLAY, JEAN-CLAUDE
64-67 BeeHives(MTL)
45-64 BeeHives(MTLx2)
62 CeramicTiles
63-5 ChexPhoto
64/5 CokeCap MTL-3
65/6 CocaCola
70/1 Colgate Stamp 64
70/1 DadsCookies
72-84 Dernière 77/8, 78/9
70/1 EddieSargent 99
71/2 EddieSargent 97
70/1 Esso Stamp
71/2 FritoLay
68/9 OPC/Topps 59, OPC 206
69/70 OPC/Topps 5
70/1 OPC 178
71/2 OPC/Topps 130, 252
72/3 OPC 293
73/4 opc-Posters 2
74/5 opcWHA 18
75/6 opcWHA 62, 130
76/7 opcWHA 2, 40, 62
77/8 opcWHA 44
62/3 Parkhurst 54
63/4 Parkhurst 31, 90
94/5 Parkie(64/5) 74
95/6 Parkie(66/7) 67, 137
66/7 Post'Large, 'Small
67 Post FlipBook
68/9 Post Marble
70/1 PostShooters
73/4 QuakerOats 30
72/3 7ElevenCups
60/1 ShirriffCoin 36
61/2 ShirriffCoin 118
62/3 ShirriffCoin 30
68/9 ShirriffCoin MTL5
81/2 TCMA 3
63/4 TheTorontoStar
64/5 TheTorontoStar
71/2 TheTorontoSun
64/5 Topps 88
65/6 Topps 69
66/7 Topps 5, -USATest 5
67/8 Topps 73
56-66 TorontoStar 65/6
61/2 York 34
62/3 YorkTransfer 6
63/4 York 24
67/8 York 13, 19, 24
67/8 York
67/8 MTL
67/8 MTL/IGA
68/9 MTL
69/70 MTL/ProStar
70/1 MTL
71/2 MTL
71 MTL/Pins
73/4 QuébecNordiques
76/7 QuébecNordiques
76 QuébecNordiques/MA

TREMBLAY, JEROME
97/8 Bowman 75

TREMBLAY, JULES
51/2 LacStJean 42

TREMBLAY, LUDGER
51/2 LavalDairy 11
52/3 StLawrence 49

TREMBLAY, M.A.
51/2 LacStJean 34

TREMBLAY, MARIO
72-84 Dernière 80/1, 83/4
83/4 Esso
84/5 Kelloggs Disk
75/6 OPC/Topps 223
76/7 OPC/Topps 97
77/8 OPC/Topps 163
78/9 O-Pee-Chee 376
79/80 OPC/Topps 123
80/1 O-Pee-Chee 297
81/2 O-Pee-Chee 192
82/3 O-Pee-Chee 57, 193
83/4 O-Pee-Chee 199
84/5 O-Pee-Chee 274
85/6 O-Pee-Chee 245
86/7 O-Pee-Chee 223
82/3 opcSticker 30
83/4 opcSticker 69
84/5 opcSticker 161
85/6 opcSticker 134/254
86/7 opcSticker 9/154
80/1 Pepsi Cap
81/2 Post PopUp 23
82/3 Post
83/4 PuffySticker 5
83/4 SouhaitsRen.KeyChain
83/4 Vachon 57
74/5 MTL
75/6 MTL
76/7 MTL
77/8 MTL
78/9 MTL
79/80 MTL
80/1 MTL
81/2 MTL
82/3 MTL
82/3 MTL/Steinberg
83/4 MTL
84/5 MTL
85/6 MTL
85/6 MTL/Pennant
85/6 MTL/PepsiPlacemats
85/6? MTL/ProvigoPlacemats
85/6 MTL/ProvigoStickers
95/6 MTL
96/7 MTL

TREMBLAY, MICHEL
98 BowmanCHL 93

TREMBLAY, NELSON
67/8 ColumbusCheckers

TREMBLAY, NILS
52/3 BasDuFleuve 31
51/2 LavalDairy 51
52/3 StLawrence 80
51/2 Laval 51

TREMBLAY, PAUL
51/2 LacStJean 29

TREMBLAY, REGIS
89/90 SketchMEM 65

TREMBLAY, SÉBASTIEN
90/1 SketchQMJHL 246
91/2 SketchQMJHL 269

TREMBLAY, TREVOR
90/1 Rayside
91/2 Rayside

TREMBLAY, VINCENT
82/3 O-Pee-Chee 334
82/3 opcSticker 70
93/4 Slapshot(Drum.) 13
81/2 TOR
82/3 TOR

TREMBLAY, YANNICK
97/8 Omega 226
98/9 Pacific 423

TRÉPANIER, PASCAL
91/2 SketchQMJHL 107

TRESL, LADISLAV
95/6 APS 208
88/9 ProCards(Halifax)
89/90 ProCards(AHL) 175
90/1 ProCards 433
91/2 ProCards 614
89/90 Halifax

TRETIAK, DOUG
92/3 Hamilton

TRETIAK, VLADISLAV
90/1 CanadaNats
92/3 CanadaNats
72-84 Dernière 82/3
95 Globe 235
72 Hellas 79
74 Hellas 57
91 IvanFiodorovUnitesHeart
70/1 Kuvajulkaisut 18
72 Panda
79 PaniniSticker 140
72 SemicSticker 20
74 SemicSticker 26
82 SemicSticker 51
91 SemicSticker 241
73/4 SovietChamps 6, 11, 13
73/4 Soviet Champs 15, 16
80 SovietMiniPics
70/1 Soviet Stars
71/2 Soviet Stars
73/4 Soviet Stars 2
74/5 Soviet Stars 2
79/80 SovietStars
83/4 SovietStars
77-79 Sportscaster 78- 1861
91/2 Trends(72) 11, 31, 71, -Aut
92/3 Trends(76) 103, 108, 163
71/2 WilliamsFIN 17
72/3 WilliamsFIN 37
73/4 WilliamsFIN 17
90/1 CHI/Coke

TRETOWICZ, DAVE
92/3 Classic 112
92/3 ClassicFourSport 218
92/3 Phoenix

TRIHEY, HARRY
83&87 HallOfFame 88
83 HHOF Postcard (F)

TRIM, LEE
84/5 Brandon 13
85/6 Brandon 13

TRIMPER, TIM
80/1 O-Pee-Chee 357
81/2 O-Pee-Chee 376
82/3 O-Pee-Chee 394
82/3 Post
80/1 CHI/4x6
80/1 CHI/5.5x8.5
80/1 WPG
81/2 WPG
84/5 Springfield 12

TRINEER, NEAIL
81/2 Kingston 8

TRIPP, JOHN
95 Classic 55, 91
95/6 Slapshot 238
97/8 Bowman 9

TRIULZI, ROBERTO
95 PaniniWorlds 134
95 Semic 194

TRNKA, PAVEL
94/5 APS 49
97/8 Omega 9
97/8 SPAuthentic 170

TROFIMENKOFF, DAVID
91/2 SketchWHL 353
93/4 Lethbridge

TROINI, JASON
96/7 Halifax (1), (2)
97/8 Halifax (1), (2)

TROJAN, RICHARD
94/5 DEL 418
95/6 DEL 390
96/7 DEL 298

TROMBLEY, RHETT
91/2 SketchWHL 99
93/4 Slapshot(SSMarie) 16
95/6 LasVegas
96/7 LasVegas
91/2 Saskatoon 7
94/5 Toledo

TROSCHINSKY, ALEXEI
91/2 UD'CzechWJC 6

TROTTIER, BRYAN
91/2 Bowman 93
92/3 Bowman 152, 243
72-84 Dernière 82/3
93/4 Donruss 268
88/9 Esso Sticker
93/4 FleerUltra 398
88/9 FritoLay
94 HockeyWit 44
84/5 IslanderNews Set
93/4 Leaf 318
82/3 McDonalds 25
76/7 OPC/Topps 67, 115, 216
77/8 OPC/Topps 105
78/9 OPC/T. 10,64-65, OPC 325
79/80 OPC/Topps 2,3,7,100,165
80/1 OPC/Topps 40
81/2 OPC 200,210, T. 41,(E) 132
82/3 O-Pee-Chee 5, 214, 215
83/4 O-Pee-Chee 21
84/5 OPC 139, 214, T. 104, 160
85/6 OPC/Topps 60
86/7 OPC/Topps 155, P
87/8 OPC/Topps 60, O
88/9 OPC/Topps 97
89/90 OPC/Topps 149
90/1 OPC/Topps 6, 291
91/2 OPC/Topps 472
92/3 OPC 107,130, -25Years 9
87/8 OPCStars 41
90/1 opcPremier 121
81/2 opcSticker 152, 160
82/3 opcSticker 47, 48
83/4 opcSticker 76, 77
84/5 opcSticker 86, 87
85/6 opcSticker 65
86/7 opcSticker 216
87/8 opcSticker 240/106
88/9 opcSticker 112
89/90 opcSticker 118
87/8 PaniniSticker 96
88/9 PaniniSticker 293
89/90 PaniniSticker 269, 382
90/1 PaniniSticker 83
92/3 PaniniSticker 227
91/2 Parkhurst 208, 360, 431
93/4 Parkhurst 431
91/2 Pinnacle 241
93/4 Pinnacle 411
82/3 Post
93/4 PowerPlay 416
93/4 Premier 296
90/1 ProSet 192, 511
91/2 ProSet 192
91/2 PSPlatinum 216, PC19
83/4 PuffySticker 21
90/1 Score 270, 106T
91/2 Score(CDN) 229, (U.S) 229
92/3 Score 157
93/4 Score 567
84/5 7ElevenDisk
85/6 7Eleven 12
83/4 SouhaitsRen.KeyChain
97/8 SPAuthentic M4, T4
77-9 Sportscaster 46-21, 47-16
77-9 Sportscasterr 49-1197
76/7 Topps-Glossy 15
92/3 Topps 416
91/2 ToppsStadiumClub 91
92/3 ToppsStadiumClub 26
90/1 UpperDeck 137, 425
91/2 UpperDeck 329
92/3 UD'LockerAS 50
96 Wien HL9
79/80 NYI
83/4 NYI
83/4 NYI/Islander 15, 37
84/5 NYI 16, 35
89/90 NYI
90/1 PGH/Foodland 15
91/2 PGH/Elbys
91/2 PGH/Foodland 12
91/2 PGH/Topps
93/4 PGH/Foodland 12
96/7 PGH/Tribune
84/5 KelownaWings 26

TROTTIER, DAVE
34-43 BeeHives(MTL.M)
33/4 CndGum (V252)
35-40 CrownBrand 52
34/5 OPC (V304B) 62
36/7 OPC (V304D) 126
37/8 OPC (V304E) 168
34/5 SweetCaporal
36/7 WWGum (V356) 70

TROTTIER, GUY
71/2 Bazooka Panel 23
70/1 Esso Stamp
71/2 OPC 5
72/3 OPC 326
73/4 QuakerOats 40
71/2 TheTorontoSun
72/3 OttawaNationals
70/1 TOR
71/2 TOR

TROTTIER, JOEL
97/8 Bowman 10
98 BowmanCHL 40
95/6 Slapshot 273

TROTTIER, MONTY
81/2 Indianapolis 14
82/3 Indianapolis
84/5 Springfield 19

TROTTIER, ROCKY
89/90 ProCards(AHL) 356
82/3 MedicineHat
83/4 MedicineHat 13

TROTZ, BARRY
90/1 ProCards 218
91/2 ProCards 572
93/4 Portland
95/6 Portland
96/7 Portand
81/2 Regina 21

TRUCKWELL, HARRY
23/4 PaulinsCandy 51

TRUDEL, J.G.
91/2 SketchQMJHL 190
94/5 Slapshot(MEM) 64

TRUDEL, LOUIS
34-43 BeeHives(CHI), (MTL.C)
35-40 CrownBrand 156
33-35 DiamondMatch
36-39 DiamondMatch (1), (2), (3)
36-39 DiamondMatch (4), (5), (6)
36/7 WWGum (V356) 71

TRUDEL, MARTIN
90/1 SketchQMJHL 65
91/2 SketchQMJHL 11

TRUE, MADS
92/3 MPSPhotoSJHL 5

TRUE, SOREN
89/90 ProCardS(IHL) 47
90/1 ProCards 530
91/2 ProCards 311

TRUKHNO, LEONID
91/2 O-Pee-Chee 61R

TRUNTSCHKA, BERND
94/5 DEL 95
95/6 DEL 96
96/7 DEL 285
89 SemicSticker 120
91 SemicSticker 164
93 SemicSticker 162

TRUNTSCHKA, GERD
89 SemicSticker 115
91 SemicSticker 163
93 SemicSticker 157

TRZCINSKI, JASON
91/2 LakeSuperior

TSCHUMI, RICK
95 Globe 216
91 SemicSticker 181
92 SemicSticker 197
93 SemicSticker 114

TSCHUPP, CHRIS
94/5 Erie

TSELIOS, NIKOS
97/8 Bowman 138
97/8 UDBlackDiamond 91
98/9 UDChoice 304

TSUJIRA, STEVE
88/9 ProCards(Maine)
83/4 Springfield 6

TSULYGIN, NIKOLAI
93/4 Classic 46
94/5 Classic T2
93/4 ClassicFourSport 206
95/6 EdgeIce 16
95 PaniniWorlds 28
93/4 Parkhurst 526
93/4 Pinnacle 507
94/5 SigRookies 33
94/5 SRGoldStandard 94
92/3 UpperDeck 614
96/7 ANA/UpFrontSports

TSIGANKOV, GENNADI
72 Hellas 67
74 Hellas 58
79 PaniniSticker 145
72 SemicSticker 7
74 SemicSticker 29
73/4 Soviet Champs 10
71/2 Soviet Stars
73/4 Soviet Stars 11
74/5 Soviet Stars 8
79/80 SovietStars
91/2 Trends(72) 67
71/2 WilliamsFIN 18
72/3 WilliamsFIN 38
73/4 WilliamsFIN 18

TSYGRUOV, DENIS
94/5 Classic 78
94/5 Donruss 200
94/5 Flair 23
94/5 FleerUltra 267
94/5 Leaf 161
94/5 Pinnacle 258, RTP3
94/5 Premier 29

TSYPLAKOV, VLADIMIR
93/4 ClassicProspects 103
97/8 Omega 115
98/9 Pacific 247
97/8 PacificCrown 82
97/8 PcfcDynagon! 61,-Tand 43
97/8 PacificInvincible 69
98/9 PacificParamount 110
97/8 PaniniSticker 218
95/6 Parkhurst 377
97/8 PinnacleBeAPlayer 197
97/8 SPAuthentic 74
98/9 SPx"Finite" 40
98/9 Topps 14
97/8 UpperDeck 289
96/7 UDBlackDiamond 8
98/9 UDChoice 101
97/8 UDCollChoice 122
95/6 LasVegas

TSYPLAKOV, YURI
97/8 UpperDeck 47

TSYRKUNOV, OLEG
95/6 Slapshot 287

TUCKER, CHRIS
91/2 UD'CzechWJC 67
94/5 Richmond

TUCKER, DARCY
95/6 Donruss-CanadaJr 13
97/8 Donruss 182
96/7 DonrussCanadianIce 143
97/8 DonrussCanadianIce 111
97/8 DonrussPreferred 28
95/6 EdgeIce 42
96/7 FleerNHLPicks 148
95/6 FutureLegends 23, -Pltnm 5
96/7 Leaf-Rookie 8
97/8 Leaf 77
96/7 LeafPreferred 134
97/8 Limited 34, 53
98/9 Pacific 407
97/8 PacificCrown 83
94/5 Pinnacle 537
96/7 Pinnacle 223
97/8 Pinnacle 140
97/8 PinnacleBeAPlayer 119

96/7 PinnacleZenith 130
97/8 Score 202
97/8 Score(MTL) 13
91/2 SketchWHL 88
94/5 Slapshot(MEM) 12
95/6 Topps 16CJ
98/9 Topps 183
94/5 ToppsFinest 164
94/5 UpperDeck 503
96/7 UpperDeck 281
97/8 UpperDeck 88
96/7 UpperDeck"Ice" 33
96/7 MTL
95/6 Fredericton
93/4 Kamloops

TUCKER, GIB
89/90 SketchMEM 43
90/1 SketchOHL 245
91/2 SketchOHL 85
89/90 Kitchener 22
90/1 Kitchener 20

TUCKER, JOHN
93/4 Donruss 328
94/5 Donruss 87
95/6 Donruss 311
92/3 FleerUltra 414
93/4 FleerUltra 211
94/5 FleerUltra 210
93/4 Leaf 21
94/5 Leaf 38
95/6 Leaf 269
86/7 OPC/Topps 67
87/8 OPC/Topps 154
88/9 OPC/Topps 74
89/90 OPC/Topps 37
90/1 OPC/Topps 374
90/1 opcPremier 122
85/6 opcSticker 184/58
86/7 opcSticker 48/189
87/8 opcSticker 145/254
87/8 PaniniSticker 30
88/9 PaniniSticker 229
89/90 PaniniSticker 212
90/1 PaniniSticker 157
93/4 PaniniSticker 212
95/6 PaniniSticker 125
92/3 Parkhurst 405
93/4 Parkhurst 462
95/6 Parkhurst 192
94/5 ParkieSE 170
93/4 Pinnacle 144, CA22
94/5 Pinnacle 226
95/6 Playoff 312
94/5 POG 226
95/6 POG 249
93/4 PowerPlay 235
93/4 Premier 473
94/5 Premier 132
90/1 ProSet 322, 420
93/4 Score 354
94/5 Score 23
95/6 Score 191
91/2 ToppsStadiumClub 335
93/4 ToppsStadiumClub 38
90/1 UpperDeck 387
92/3 UpperDeck 548
93/4 UpperDeck 409
95/6 UpperDeck 78
95/6 UDBeAPlayer 120
95/6 UDCollChoice 104
84/5 BUF/BlueShield
85/6 BUF
86/7 BUF
87/8 BUF/BlueShield
87/8 BUF/WonderBread
88/9 BUF/BlueShield
88/9 BUF/WonderBread
90/1 BUF/BlueShield
90/1 BUF/Campbell
95/6 T.B.
92/3 T.B/Sheraton
94/5 T.B/SkyBoxSportsCafe
95/6 T.B/SkyBoxSportsCafe
89/90 WSH/Kodak
82/3 Kitchener 24
83/4 Kitchener 20

TUCKER, MICHEL
72 SemicSticker 161

TUDIN, DAN
95/6 Slapshot 266

TUER, AL
88/9 ProCards(Binghampton)
89/90 ProCards(AHL) 289
90/1 ProCards 313
91/2 ProCards 367
92/3 Cincinnati
81/2 Regina 22
82/3 Regina 9
83/4 Regina 9

TUGNUTT, RON
91/2 Bowman 151
93/4 Donruss 12, A, 453
94/5 Donruss 69
97/8 Donruss 103
97/8 DonrussCanadianIce 6
97/8 DonrussPriority 76
95/6 EdgeIce 57
92/3 FleerUltra 298
93/4 FleerUltra 263
93/4 Leaf 277
94/5 Leaf 46
97/8 Omega 158
89/90 O-Pee-Chee 263
90/1 OPC/Topps 367
91/2 OPC/Topps 181
92/3 O-Pee-Chee 211
98/9 Pacific 316
97/8 PacificCrown 87
97/8 PacificCrownRoyale 93
97/8 PacificInvincible 96
98/9 PacificParamount 167
97/8 PacificRevolution 95
90/1 Panini(QUE) 22
89/90 PaniniSticker 332
90/1 PaniniSticker 142
91/2 PaniniSticker 267
91/2 Parkhurst 149, 277
92/3 Parkhurst 290
91/2 Pinnacle 124
92/3 Pinnacle 366
93/4 Pinnacle 187
94/5 Pinnacle 172
97/8 Pinnacle 99
97/8 PinnacleBeAPlayer 36
97/8 PinnacleCertified 29
97/8 PinnacleInside 82
93/4 PowerPlay 13
93/4 Premier 286
94/5 Premier 523
88/9 ProCards(Halifax)
90/1 ProSet 258
91/2 ProSet 202
91/2 PSPlatinum 98
90/1 Score 126
91/2 Score(CDN) 41, (U.S) 41
91/2 Score-YoungStar 33
92/3 Score 387
93/4 Score 368, 504
94/5 Score 21
95/6 Score 70
97/8 Score 49
91/2 ToppsStadiumClub 115
93/4 ToppsStadiumClub 325
90/1 UpperDeck 27
91/2 UpperDeck 277
93/4 UpperDeck 426, SP5
94/5 UpperDeck 321
97/8 UpperDeck 113
97/8 UDCollChoice 181
92/3 EDM/IGA 24
94/5 MTL
94/5 MTL/MolsonExport
96/7 OTT/PizzaHut
97/8 OTT
87/8 QUE/GeneralFoods
89/90 QUE
89/90 QUE/GeneralFoods
89/90 QUE/Police
90/1 QUE
90/1 QUE/PetroCanada
91/2 QUE/PetroCanada
95/6 Portland

TUIN, R.P.
81/2 Milwaukee 13

TULEY, BRAD
89/90 SSMarie 20

TULI, JUKKA
70/1 Kuvajulkaisut 343

TULI, RAIMO
66/7 Champion 22

TULLY, BRENT
94/5 CanadaJr.Alumni 9
93/4 Classic 31
93/4 Donruss CAN21
93/4 Pinnacle 464
90/1 SketchOHL 374
91/2 SketchOHL 130
93/4 Slapshot(Peterborough) 9
92/3 UpperDeck 592
93/4 UpperDeck 530
91/2 Peterborough 5

TUMBA, SVEN
91 SemicSticker 233

TUMBACH, TROY
94/5 DEL 144
95/6 DEL 41

TUOHIMAA, HARRI
91/2 Jyvas-Hyva 4
80/1 Mallasjuoma 128
78/9 SM-Liiga 171
71/2 WilliamsFIN 376

TUOHIMAA, JUHA
91/2 Jyvas-Hyva 35
92/3 Jyvas-Hyva 94
80/1 Mallasjuoma 94
78/9 SM-Liiga 136

TUOHIMAA, PASI
80/1 Mallasjuoma 118
71/2 WilliamsFIN 377

TUOMAINEN, MARKO
95/6 Donruss 56
95/6 EdgeIce 36
95/6 Leaf 171
95/6 Topps 189
91/2 UD 675, -CzechWJC 38
95/6 UpperDeck 12
95/6 UDCollChoice 121
92/3 Clarkson

TUOMAINEN, TIMO
66/7 Champion 132
70/1 Kuvajulkaisut 270

TUOMENOKSA, ANTTI
92/3 Jyvas-Hyva 98
93/4 Jyvas-Hyva 170
93/4 Sisu 167
94/5 Sisu 89, -Horoscope 3
95/6 Sisu 190

TUOMI, RISTO
80/1 Mallasjuoma 204

TUOMINEN, JOUNI
95/6 Sisu 144

TUOMINEN, OLLI
80/1 Mallasjuoma 119
78/9 SM-Liiga 165

TUOMINEN, PASI
95/6 Sisu 364
96/7 Sisu 158

TUOMISTO, MARTTI
80/1 Mallasjuoma 46

TUOMISTO, PEKKA
91/2 Jyvas-Hyva 3
92/3 Jyvas-Hyva 12
93/4 Jyvas-Hyva 24
70/1 Kuvajulkaisut 382
80/1 Mallasjuoma 101
93 SemicSticker 81
93/4 Sisu 102
94/5 Sisu 18
95/6 Sisu 214

TUPA, MARTIN
95/6 APS 185

TURCOTTE, ALFIE
94/5 DEL 440
89/90 ProCards(AHL) 81
90/1 ProCards 200
83/4 MTL
84/5 MTL
84/5 KelownaWings 25

TURCOTTE, DARREN
90/1 Bowman 216
91/2 Bowman 62
92/3 Bowman 156
93/4 Donruss 224
94/5 Donruss 286
95/6 Donruss 43, 295, -ProP 10
96/7 Donruss 59
97/8 Donruss 176
94/5 Flair 75
94/5 Fleer 90
95/6 FleerMetal 167
92/3 FleerUltra 143
93/4 FleerUltra 341
94/5 FleerUltra 94
95/6 FleerUltra 72, 328
96/7 FleerUltra 154
95 Globe 123
93/4 HockeyWit 30
95/6 Hoyle'EAST J (Clubs)
93/4 Leaf 45
94/5 Leaf 210
95/6 Leaf 173
96/7 Leaf 184
97/8 Limited 191
91/2 McDonalds McD7
96/7 MetalUniverse 141
90/1 OPC/Topps 48, K
91/2 OPC/Topps 71
92/3 O-Pee-Chee 387, -Promo
90/1 opcPremier 123
98/9 Pacific 373
97/8 PacificCrown 229
98/9 PacificParamount 128
90/1 PaniniSticker 107
91/2 PaniniSticker 285
92/3 PaniniSticker 235
93/4 PaniniSticker 94
95/6 PaniniSticker 27
96/7 PaniniSticker 281
91/2 Parkhurst 118
92/3 Parkhurst 345
93/4 Parkhurst 356
95/6 Parkhurst 93, 498
94/5 ParkieSE 75
91/2 Pinnacle 47
92/3 Pinnacle 33
93/4 Pinnacle 386
94/5 Pinnacle 161
95/6 Pinnacle 20
96/7 Pinnacle 165
96/7 PinnacleBeAPlayer 70
95/6 Playoff 267
96/7 Playoff 413
94/5 POG 119
93/4 PowerPlay 166, 357
93/4 Premier 246
94/5 Premier 2
95/6 ProMagnet 128
90/1 ProSet 208, 400
91/2 ProSet 160, 310
92/3 ProSet 114
90/1 Score 241, -YoungStar 16
91/2 Score(CDN) 196, (US) 196
91/2 Score-YoungStar 28
92/3 Score 224
93/4 Score 24, 570
94/5 Score 169
95/6 Score 224
96/7 Score 219
97/8 Score 251
97/8 Score(STL) 8
91 SemicSticker 139
95/6 SkyBoxEmotion 79
95/6 SkyBoxImpact 186
94/5 SP 49
96/7 SP 142
95/6 Summit 22
96/7 Summit 54
92/3 Topps 203
95/6 Topps 251, HGA7
91/2 ToppsStadiumClub 346
92/3 ToppsStadiumClub 360
93/4 ToppsStadiumClub 476
94/5 ToppsStadiumClub 201
95/6 ToppsStadiumClub 27
90/1 UpperDeck 274, 475
91/2 UpperDeck 90, 155, 513
92/3 UpperDeck 169
93/4 UpperDeck SP-66
94/5 UpperDeck 84, SP123
95/6 UD 481, SE180, SE37
96/7 UpperDeck 333
94/5 UDBAP R14, R124,-Aut. 35
95/6 UDCollChoice 24
96/7 UDCollChoice 235, 330
97/8 UDCollChoice 219
93/4 HFD/Coke
89/90 NYR/MarineMidland
96/7 S.J/PacificBellSheet (x2)
95/6 WPG

TUREANU, DORU
79 PaniniSticker 316

TUREK, FILIP
94/5 APS 109
95/6 APS 68

TUREK, MATT
91/2 SketchOHL 341

TUREK, ROMAN
94/5 APS 93
95/6 APS 354
95/6 DEL 289
97/8 Donruss 64
97/8 DonrussPriority 29
96/7 Flair 106
97/8 Leaf 56
97/8 Limited 42, 113
98/9 Pacific 184
98/9 PacificParamount 71
97/8 PacificRegime 66
95 PaniniWorlds 187
97/8 PinnacleBeAPlayer 35
97/8 PinnInside 79, -Stopper 9
97/8 Score 36
95 Semic 142
93 SemicSticker 90
96/7 SP 175
96/7 UpperDeck X28
97/8 UpperDeck 53
96/7 UDBlackDiamond 1
96/7 UDCollChoice 358
97/8 UpperDeckIce 35
96 Wien 102, AS1, SG6

TURGEON, PIERRE
95/6 Aces 8 (Hearts)
96/7 Aces 10 (Clubs)
97/8 Aces 6 (Clubs)
90/1 Bowman 241
91/2 Bowman 27
92/3 Bowman 23
95/6 Bowman 6
97/8 CorinthianHeadliner
93/4 Donruss 209, N
94/5 Donruss 23
95/6 Donruss 61, -Igniters 4
96/7 Donruss 17, -Dominators 6
97/8 Donruss 28
96/7 DonrussCanadianIce 110
97/8 D.CdnIce 24, -National 24
95/6 DonrussElite 90,-Cutting 10
96/7 DonrussElite 112
97/8 DonrussElite 105
97/8 DonrussPreferred 117
97/8 DonrussPriority 41
97/8 DonrussStudio 64
96/7 Duracell JB14
92/3 Durivage 11
93/4 Durivage 30
93/4 EASports 81, 222
94/5 Flair 109
94/5 Fleer 130
96/7 Fleer 57, -ArtRoss 23
95/6 FleerMetal 80
96/7 FleerNHLPicks 32, -Fab 45
92/3 FleerUltra 132
93/4 FU 197,-AS 3,-Piv 9,-Scor 5
94/5 FleerUltra 133
95/6 FleerUltra 85
96/7 FleerUltra 148
91/2 Gillette 35
93/4 HockeyWit 27
97/8 KatchMedallion 131
91/2 Kelloggs 6
95/6 KennerSLU (U.S)
90/1 Kraft 59, 91
93/4 KraftDinner
95/6 Kraft-Ticket
93/4 Leaf 25, 340, -HatTrick 5
94/5 Leaf 367, -Limited 14
95/6 Leaf 90, -Freeze 2
96/7 Leaf 186, -Leather 18
97/8 Leaf 43
94/5 LeafLimited 52
95/6 LeafLimited 102
96/7 LeafLimited 38
96/7 LeafPreferred 70, -Steel 26
97/8 Limited 158, 172
96/7 Maggers 85
93/4 McDonalds McD27
94/5 McDonalds McD26
95/6 McDonalds McD13
96/7 McDonalds McD19
96/7 MetalUniverse 84
97/8 Omega 199
88/9 OPC/Topps 194
89/90 OPC/Topps 25, P
90/1 OPC/Topps 66, M, T-TL 20
91/2 OPC/Topps 416
92/3 O-Pee-Chee 47
90/1 opcPremier 24
91/2 opcPremier 59
88/9 opcSticker 133/269, FS 20
89/90 opcSticker 262
98/9 Pacific 374
97/8 PacificCrown 32, -Slap 9B
97/8 PacificCrownRoyale 118
97/8 PacificDynagon! 108
97/8 PcfcD-BstKpt 83,-Tandm 59
97/8 PacificInvincible 122
97/8 PacificParamount 161
98/9 PacificParamount 207
97/8 PacificRegime 173
97/8 PacificRevolution 122
88/9 PaniniSticker 230
89/90 PaniniSticker 204
90/1 PaniniSticker 28
91/2 PaniniSticker 303
92/3 PaniniSticker 196
93/4 PaniniSticker F
94/5 PaniniSticker 48
95/6 PaniniSticker 37
96/7 PaniniSticker 40
97/8 PaniniSticker 164
91/2 Parkhurst 106
92/3 Parkhurst 103
93/4 Parkhurst 389, E10, F7
94/5 Parkhurst 135, C14
95/6 Parkhurst 109, PP50
94/5 ParkieSE seV31
91/2 Pinnacle 30
92/3 Pinnacle 165, -Tm2000 17
93/4 Pinnacle 160, 225,-Nifty 1,7
93/4 Pinnacle-Tm2001 13
94/5 Pinnacle 78
95/6 Pinn. 34,-Clear 14,-Roar 20
96/7 Pinnacle 22
97/8 Pinnacle 75
97/8 P.BAP -TakeANumber 14
97/8 PinnacleCertified 62
97/8 PinnacleInside 122
95/6 PinnacleZenith 38
96/7 P.Zenith 39, -Assailant 12
95/6 Playoff 56
94/5 POG 160
95/6 POG 145
93/4 PowerPlay 155, -Point 19
93/4 Premier 190, -Black(T) 20
93/4 Premier-Finest 7
94/5 Premier 115
95/6 ProMagnet 18
90/1 ProSet 31, 366
91/2 ProSet 15, 433
92/3 ProSet 104
91/2 PSPlatinum 10
96/7 SB'7Eleven
90/1 Score 110,-Hot 53,-Young 1
91/2 Score(CDN) 4, 257, 332
91/2 Score(U.S) 4,377,416,101T
92/3 Score 325, 430, -Young 27
92/3 Score-Sharpshooter 25
93/4 Score 6, (CDN) DD9
93/4 Score-Dream 15, -P.AS 5
93/4 Score-Franchise 12
94/5 Score 166, NP14, TF14
95/6 Score 90,-Border 1,-Lamp 6
96/7 Score 71, -SuddenDeath 1
97/8 Score 118
97/8 Score(STL) 2
92/3 SeasonsPatch 53
94/5 Select 46
95/6 SelectCertified 49
96/7 SelectCertified 82
91 SemicSticker 66
95/6 SkyBoxEmotion 93
95/6 SkyBoxImpact 89
96/7 SkyBoxImpact 66,-Blade 23
94/5 SP 91
95/6 SP 71, E15
96/7 SP 137
97/8 SPAuthentic 141
96/7 SPx 22
98/9 SPx"Finite" 74
95/6 Summit 43
96/7 Summit 90
95/6 SuperSticker 63, DC1
96/7 TeamOut
92/3 Topps 289
95/6 Topps 21, 224, 7CG
95/6 Topps 9PL, HGC3
98/9 Topps 208
94/5 T.Finest 78, -BBest(B) 9
95/6 ToppsFinest 46, 182
91/2 ToppsStadiumClub 77
92/3 ToppsStadiumClub 276
93/4 T.StadiumClub 145, 380
93/4 TSC-AllStar, -Master(2) 8
95/6 TSC 175, EN7, PS1
93/4 TSC-MembersOnly 38
94/5 TSC-MembersOnly 20
95/6 TSC-MembersOnly 39
97/8 ToppsSticker 1
95/6 ToppsSuperSkills 9
90/1 UpperDeck 43, 318
91/2 UpperDeck 176, 554
92/3 UD 175, 'LockerAS 17
93/4 UD 224, 297, 347, AW7
93/4 UD H7, HT11, SP-96
94/5 UpperDeck 77, SP48
95/6 UD 389, AS15, SE44
97/8 UpperDeck 353
93/4 UDBeAPlayer 37
94/5 UDBeAPlayer R80
95/6 UDBeAPlayer 152
96/7 UDBlackDiamond 135
97/8 UDBlackDiamond 100
98/9 UDChoice 184
95/6 UDCollChoice 131, C15
96/7 UDCC 133, 321, S19
96/7 UDCC'Oversize 133, 5of8
97/8 UDCollChoice 226, SQ56
96/7 UpperDeck"Ice" 61
97/8 Zenith 23, Z61
87/8 BUF/BlueShield
87/8 BUF/WonderBread
88/9 BUF/BlueShield
88/9 BUF/WonderBread
89/90 BUF/BlueShield
89/90 BUF/Campbell
90/1 BUF/BlueShield
90/1 BUF/Campbell
95/6 MTL
95/6 MTL/Molson

TURGEON, SYLVAIN
90/1 Bowman 81
92/3 Bowman 167
83 CanadaJuniors
93/4 Donruss 235
94/5 Donruss 105
92/3 Durivage 29
93/4 Durivage 36
93/4 EASports 94
94/5 Fleer 148
92/3 FleerUltra 149
93/4 FleerUltra 190
94/5 FleerUltra 341
93/4 Leaf 74
94/5 Leaf 191
95/6 Leaf 33
84/5 OPC 79, 372, Topps 62
85/6 OPC/Topps 43
86/7 OPC/Topps 103
87/8 OPC/Topps 70
88/9 OPC/Topps 24
90/1 OPC/Topps 73
91/2 OPC/Topps 231
92/3 O-Pee-Chee 315
91/2 opcPremier 184
92/3 opcPremier 116
84/5 opcSticker 191, 192
85/6 opcSticker 165
86/7 opcSticker 53
87/8 opcSticker 205/61
87/8 PaniniSticker 36, 50
88/9 PaniniSticker 245
90/1 PaniniSticker 71
93/4 PaniniSticker K
94/5 PaniniSticker 105
95/6 PaniniSticker 52
91/2 Parkhurst 91
92/3 Parkhurst 121
93/4 Parkhurst 136
94/5 Parkhurst 153, V51
95/6 Parkhurst 146
91/2 Pinnacle 226
92/3 Pinnacle 373
93/4 Pinnacle 64

94/5 Pinnacle 288
95/6 Playoff 290
94/5 POG 173
93/4 PowerPlay 176
93/4 Premier 97
94/5 Premier 23
90/1 ProSet 177, 474
91/2 ProSet 416
92/3 ProSet 123
90/1 Score 116, 108T
91/2 Score(CDN) 208, 267
91/2 Score(U.S) 208, 377
92/3 Score 367, 516
93/4 Score 46
84/5 7ElevenDisk
92/3 Topps 375
92/3 ToppsStadiumClub 59
93/4 ToppsStadiumClub 482
90/1 UpperDeck 70
91/2 UpperDeck 579
92/3 UpperDeck 107
93/4 UpperDeck 44
94/5 UpperDeck 336, SP146
95/6 UpperDeck 177
94/5 UDBeAPlayer R60
83/4 HFD/JuniorWhalers
84/5 HFD/JuniorWhalers
85/6 HFD/JuniorWhalers
86/7 HFD/JuniorWhalers
87/8 HFD/JuniorWhalers
88/9 HFD/JuniorWhalers
90/1 MTL
91/2 MTL
89/90 N.J.
92/3 OTT
93/4 OTT/Kraft
94/5 OTT/Bell

TURKIEWICZ, JIM
76/7 opcWHA 18

TURKULAINEN, RAIMO
66/7 Champion 127
70/1 Kuvajulkaisut 271

TURMEL, NICOLAS
91/2 SketchQMJHL 114

TURMEL, RICHARD
83/4 Fredericton 15

TURNBULL, DALE
87/8 SSMarie 9
89/90 SSMarie 17

TURNBULL, IAN
74/5 Loblaws
74/5 O-Pee-Chee 289
75/6 OPC/Topps 41
76/7 OPC/Topps 39
77/8 OPC/Topps 186, 215
78/9 OPC/Topps 127
79/80 OPC/Topps 228
80/1 OPC/Topps 133
81/2 OPC 309, Topps 42
81/2 opcSticker 100
80/1 opcSuperCard 21
80/1 Pepsi Cap
73/4 TOR
74/5 TOR
75/6 TOR
76/7 TOR
77/8 TOR
78/9 TOR
79/80 TOR
80/1 TOR

TURNBULL, PERRY
86/7 Kraft Sports 81
80/1 OPC/Topps 169
81/2 OPC 298, Topps(W) 123
82/3 O-Pee-Chee 312
83/4 O-Pee-Chee 321
84/5 O-Pee-Chee 349
85/6 O-Pee-Chee 254
86/7 OPC/Topps 170
82/3 opcSticker 203
83/4 opcSticker 124
82/3 Post
83/4 MTL
87/8 STL/Kodak
92/3 STL/UpperDeck 26
84/5 WPG/Police
85/6 WPG
85/6 WPG/Police
86/7 WPG

TURNER, BART
93/4 Mich.State

TURNER, BOB
45-64 BeeHives(CHIx2), (MTL)
64-67 BeeHives(CHI)
62 CeramicTiles
55/6 Parkhurst 54
57/8 Parkhurst(MTL) 13
58/9 Parkhurst 40
59/60 Parkhurst 43
60/1 Parkhurst 43
61/2 Parkhurst 41
93/4 Parkie(56/7) 81
60/1 ShirriffCoin 37
61/2 ShirriffCoin 37
61/2 Topps 41
62/3 Topps 29
63/4 Topps 32
56-66 TorontoStar 58/9
60/1 York

TURNER, BRAD
93/4 FleerUltra 475
93/4 Premier-TmCanada 10
91/2 ProCards 381

TURNER, DAN
82/3 MedicineHat
83/4 MedicineHat 11

TURNER, JACK
67/8 ColumbusCheckers
69 ColumbusCheckers

TURNER, LLOYD
83&87 HallOfFame 29
83 HHOF Postcard (B)

TURNER, MARK
91/2 ProCards 245
87/8 Kingston 11
85/6 Sudbury 18
88/9 Sudbury 21
89/90 Sudbury 18

TURNER, SCOTT
91/2 SketchOHL 124
91/2 Peterborough 3

TURPEINEN, UNTO
71/2 WilliamsFIN 274

TURTIAINEN, KIMMO
72/3 WilliamsFIN 297

TURUNEN, JYRKI
66/7 Champion 131
70/1 Kuvajulkaisut 272

TURUNEN, KIMMO
70/1 Kuvajulkaisut 322

TURUNEN, MARTTI
70/1 Kuvajulkaisut 273

TURUNEN, O.P.
71/2 WilliamsFIN 354
72/3 WilliamsFIN 338

TURUNEN, TIMO
72 Hellas 17
70/1 Kuvajulkaisut 188
71/2 WilliamsFIN 109
72/3 WilliamsFIN 76, 153
73/4 WilliamsFIN 81, 122

TURUNEN, TOMMI
95/6 Sisu 305
96/7 Sisu 103

TURVEY, WARD
23/4 Crescent Selkirks 10

TUSTIAN, ROB
91/2 ProCards 42
90/1 Mich.Tech

TUSTIN, NORMAN
34-43 BeeHives(NYR)

TUTEN, AUDLEY
34-43 BeeHives(CHI)

TUTT, BRIAN
96/7 DEL 297
89/90 ProCards(AHL) 91
93/4 Sisu 363

TUTT, W. THAYER
83&87 HallOfFame 134
83 HHOF Postcard (I)

TUTTLE, STEVE
92/3 FleerUltra 205
89/90 OPC/Topps 157
90/1 OPC/Topps 273
89/90 PaniniSticker 126
90/1 ProCards 84
91/2 ProCards 41
90/1 ProSet 278
90/1 UpperDeck 195
87/8 STL
88/9 STL
88/9 STL/Kodak
89/90 STL/Kodak
90/1 STL/Kodak
94/5 Milwaukee

TUULOLA, MARKO
92/3 Jyvas-Hyva 26
93/4 Jyvas-Hyva 235
94 Semic 7
95 Semic 25
93/4 Sisu 187
94/5 Sisu 6
95/6 Sisu 248
96/7 Sisu 43

TUYL, CLYDE
95/6 SheffieldSteelers
97/8 SheffieldSteelers

TUZZOLINO, TONY
93/4 Mich.State

TVERDOVSKY, OLEG
95/6 Bowman 88
93/4 Classic 111
94/5 Classic 2, CP12, R19, T3
94/5 Classic-Preview
94/5 ClassicFourSport 116, HV8
94/5 C4'Images 95
93/4 ClassicProspects 208
95/6 Donruss 3, -Rookie 6
96/7 Donruss 105
97/8 Donruss 54, -Line2Line 6
97/8 DonrussCanadianIce 62
95/6 DonrussElite 6
97/8 DonrussElite 109
97/8 DonrussPreferred 137
97/8 DonrussPriority 53
97/8 DonrussStudio 38
96/7 Flair 74
94/5 Fleer 8, -Rookie Sen. 10
96/7 Fleer 93
95/6 FleerMetal 5
94/5 FleerUltra -Prospects 9
95/6 FleerUltra 6
96/7 FleerUltra 137
97/8 KatchMedallion 114
94/5 Leaf -Phenoms 6
95/6 Leaf 28, -StudioRookie 6
96/7 Leaf 3
97/8 Leaf 92
94/5 LeafLimited 24
95/6 LeafLimited 46
96/7 LeafPreferred 71
97/8 Limited 93
95/6 McDonalds 35
96/7 MetalUniverse 123
97/8 Omega 179
98/9 Pacific 345
97/8 PacificCrown 252
97/8 PcfcDynagon! 99,-Tand 66
97/8 PacificInvincible 110
97/8 PacificParamount 146
98/9 PacificParamount 188
95/6 PaniniSticker 231
96/7 PaniniSticker 192
97/8 PaniniSticker 163
93/4 Parkhurst 531
95/6 Parkhurst 9, 496
93/4 Pinnacle 506
94/5 Pinnacle261, RTP2
95/6 Pinnacle 60
96/7 Pinnacle 145
97/8 Pinnacle 166
97/8 PinnacleCertified 103
97/8 PinnacleInside 132
95/6 PinnacleZenith 71
96/7 PinnacleZenith 70
95/6 Playoff 4
96/7 Playoff 332
95/6 POG 24
94/5 Premier 464
95/6 ProMagnet 37
94/5 Score 214, TR4
95/6 Score 16
96/7 Score 89
97/8 Score 195
94/5 Select 169, YE2
95/6 SelectCertified 79,-Future 9
95/6 SkyBoxEmotion 4
95/6 SkyBoxImpact 5, 236
96/7 SkyBoxImpact 109
94/5 SP 2, -Premier 5
95/6 SP 166
96/7 SP 121
95/6 Summit 37
96/7 Summit 129
95/6 SuperSticker 1, 4
95/6 Topps 365, 4NG, YS7
94/5 ToppsFinest 2
94/5 TF-BBest 4, (Red) 2
96/7 ToppsNHLPicks 97
95/6 ToppsStadiumClub 113
97/8 ToppsSticker 1
95/6 ToppsSuperSkills 12
94/5 UD 243, 540, C14, SP93
95/6 UpperDeck 408, SE2
96/7 UpperDeck 129, 25A
97/8 UpperDeck 335, SG42
94/5 UDBeAPlayer R160
95/6 UDBeAPlayer 61
96/7 UDBlackDiamond 102
98/9 UDChoice 159
95/6 UDCollChoice 81
96/7 UDCollChoice 199, 327
97/8 UDCollChoice 198, SQ28
96/7 UpperDeck"Ice" 99
94/5 ANA/Carl'sJr 24
96/7 PHO

TVETEN, ERIK
95 PaniniWorlds 254

TWIST, TONY
97/8 KatchMedallion 132
94/5 Leaf 13, 454
98/9 Pacific 375
97/8 PacificCrown 254
97/8 PacificParamount 162
98/9 PacificParamount 208
96/7 PaniniSticker 210
88/9 ProCards(Peoria)
90/1 ProCards 85
91/2 Score(CDN) 396
93/4 Score 400
96/7 Score 207
97/8 Score 157
97/8 Score(STL) 10
95/6 Topps 203
97/8 UpperDeck 201
95/6 UDBeAPlayer 214
96/7 UDCollChoice 231
97/8 UDCollChoice 230
91/2 QUE/PetroCanada
92/3 QUE/PetroCanada
89/90 STL/Kodak
86/7 Saskatoon

TWOHEY, JEFF
89/90 SketchOHL 118
91/2 Peterborough 15

TWOMEY, CHRISTIAN
92/3 BCJHL 209

TYBURSKI, ED
88/9 ProCards(Springfield)
89/90 ProCards(AHL) 249

TYERS, SHAWN
85/6 Kitchener 19

TYJNYCH, ALEXANDER
89/90 ProCards 144
90/1 ProCards 236

TYMCHUK, GREG
95/6 Slapshot 200

TYMCHYSHYN, DARREN
91/2 AvantGardeBCJHL 40
92/3 BCJHL 56

TYNKKYNEN, MATTI
80/1 Mallasjuoma 123
78/9 SM-Liiga 168

UBRIACO, GENE
69/70 O-Pee-Chee 149
92 SemicSticker
92/3 AtlantaKnights
93/4 AtlantaKnights

UDLE, CLARK
96/7 Halifax(1)

UDVARI, FRANK
83&87 HallOfFame 240
83 HHOF Postcard (N)

UDVARI, STEVE
89/90 SketchOHL 138
89/90 NiagaraFalls
87/8 SSMarie 12

UENS, JIM
81/2 Oshawa 20

UHER, ZDENEK
95/6 APS 352

UITUS, PEKKA
66/7 Champion 175
70/1 Kuvajulkaisut 256
71/2 WilliamsFIN 221
72/3 WilliamsFIN 169
73/4 WilliamsFIN 237

UJCIK, VIKTOR
94/5 APS 175
95/6 APS 136, 378
91/2 UD'CzechWJC 92

UJVARI, LUBOMIR
70/1 Kuvajulkaisut 60

UKKOLA, TIMO
80/1 Mallasjuoma 18

UKKONEN, VEIKKO
66/7 Champion 16
65/6 Hellas 123

UKSILA, C.
19 Millionaires

ULANDER, MATS
82 SemicSticker 18

ULANOV, IGOR
92/3 Bowman 392
94/5 FleerUltra 397
94/5 Leaf 416
91/2 O-Pee-Chee 62R
92/3 O-Pee-Chee 229
97/8 PaniniSticker 106
91/2 Parkhurst 421
92/3 Parkhurst 440
97/8 PinnacleBeAPlayer 209
93/4 PowerPlay 477
94/5 Premier 179
92/3 ProSet 216
92/3 Score 467
95 Semic 129
92/3 Topps 468
92/3 ToppsStadiumClub 366
91/2 UpperDeck 590
92/3 UpperDeck 300, E15
94/5 UDBeAPlayer-Aut.70
96/7 UDCollChoice 252
97/8 UDCollChoice 239
97/8 MTL
93/4 WPG/Ruffles

ULIN, PATRIK
92/3 SemicElitserien 297

ULION, GRETZHEN
94/5 Classic W29

ULLMAN, NORM
71/2 Bazooka Panel 18
45-64 BeeHives(DET)
64-67 BeeHives(DET)
62 CeramicTiles
63-5 ChexPhoto
64/5 CokeCap DET-7
65/6 CocaCola
71/2 Colgate Head
70/1 Colgate Stamp 12
70/1 DadsCookies
70/1 EddieSargent 204
71/2 EddieSargent 193
72/3 EddieSargent 197
70/1 Esso Stamp
88/9 Esso Sticker
71/2 FritoLay
83&87 HallOfFame 104
83 HHOF Postcard (G)
92/3 HHOFLegends 17
82? JDMcCarthy
72/3 Letraset 17
74/5 LiptonSoup 1
74/5 Loblaws
73/4 MacsMilkDisk
68/9 OPC/Topps 131
69/70 OPC/Topps 54, -Stamp
70/1 OPC/Topps 110,-Deckle 48
71/2 OPC/Topps 30
72/3 OPC 147, Topps 168
73/4 OPC 27, Topps 148
74/5 OPC/Topps 219, 236
71/2 opcPoster 11
76/7 opcWHA 126
60/1 Parkhurst 26
61/2 Parkhurst 26
62/3 Parkhurst 21
63/4 Parkhurst 52
92/3 Parkhurst PR25
93/4 Parkie(56/7) 45
94/5 Parkie(64/5) 58, AS4, SL3
95/6 Parkie(66/7) 45, 136, SL3
66/7 Post'Large
68/9 Post Marble
72 SemicSticker 163
60/1 ShirriffCoin 45
61/2 ShirriffCoin 76
68/9 ShirriffCoin TOR10
81/2 TCMA 1
57/8 Topps 46
58/9 Topps 65
59/60 Topps 45
64/5 Topps 15
65/6 Topps 49
66/7 Topps 52, -USATest 52
67/8 Topps 101, 132
54-67 TorontoStar V7
56-66 Tor.Star 58/9,64/5,65/6
63/4 TheTorontoStar
64/5 TheTorontoStar
71/2 TheTorontoSun
91/2 UltimateDP 72, 78, -Aut 72
63/4 York 47
62/3 YorkTransfer 29
94/5 Zellers
69/70 TOR
71/2 TOR
72/3 TOR
73/4 TOR
74/5 TOR

ULRICH, MARTIN
96/7 DEL 166
95 Globe 184
95 PaniniWorlds 259
94 Semic 237
93 SemicSticker 273

ULVIRA, EDOUARD
82 SemicSticker 86

UNDERHILL, J.
90/1 SketchQMJHL 206

UNGER, GARY
71/2 Bazooka Panel 19
71/2 Colgate Heads
70/1 Colgate Stamp 7
70/1 DadsCookies
70/1 EddieSargent 61
71/2 EddieSargent 178
72/3 EddieSargent 184
70/1 Esso Stamp
72/3 Letraset 6
74/5 LiptonSoup 5
74/5 Loblaws
74/5 Nabisco
68/9 O-Pee-Chee 142
69/70 O-Pee-Chee 159
70/1 OPC/Topps 26, -Deckle 16
70/1 OPC/Topps-Sticker
71/2 OPC/Topps 26, -Booklet 14
72/3 OPC 120, Topps 35
73/4 OPC/Topps 15
74/5 OPC/Topps 197, 237
75/6 OPC/Topps 40, 327
76/7 OPC 68, 260, 393/T 68,260
77/8 OPC/Topps 35
78/9 OPC/Topps 5, 110
79/80 OPC/Topps 33
80/1 O-Pee-Chee 273
81/2 O-Pee-Chee 123
82/3 O-Pee-Chee 120
71/2 opcPoster 20
72/3 Post Transfers 1
90/1 ProCards 368
89/90 ProCards(IHL) 112
72 SemicSticker 191
68/9 ShirriffCoin DET9
77-9 Sportscastr 18-23, 52-1232
71/2 TheTorontoSun
79/80 ATL
79/80 ATL/B&W
70/1 DET/Marathon
81/2 EDM/RedRooster
82/3 EDM/RedRooster
88/9 EDM/ActionMagazine 1
80/1 L.A.
71/2 STL
72/3 STL
72/3 STL/8"x10"
73/4 STL (x2)
78/9 STL
92/3 STL/UpperDeck 27

UNIAC, JOHN
89/90 SketchMEM 36
90/1 SketchOHL 246
90/1 Kitchener
88/9 Kitchener 8
89/90 Kitchener 8
87/8 Sudbury 14
95/6 Tallahassee 11
92/3 Wheeling 18

UNIACKE, RICK
93/4 Slapshot(SSMarie) 10
95/6 Slapshot 361
96/7 SSMarie

UNKILA, MAURI
72/3 WilliamsFIN 339

UNSINN, XAVIER
89 SemicSticker 102

UNTERLUGGAUER, GERHARD
95 PaniniWorlds 263

UOTILA, ILMO
80/1 Mallasjuoma 61
78/9 SM-Liiga 68

UOTILA, PENTTI
66/7 Champion 199
65/6 Hellas 116

URPALAINEN, SEPPO
80/1 Mallasjuoma 151
72/3 WilliamsFIN 188

URVIKKO, JOUKO
80/1 Mallasjuoma 27
78/9 SM-Liiga 47

USKI, JANI
92/3 Jyvas-Hyva 153
93/4 Jyvas-Hyva 269
93/4 Sisu 298

USTORF, PETER
96/7 DEL 246

USTORF, STEFAN
95/6 Bowman 147
92/3 Classic 29
92/3 ClassicFourSport 178
95/6 Donruss 294
96/7 Donruss 25
95/6 EdgeIce 55
95 Globe 224
96/7 PaniniSticker 143
95/6 Parkhurst 520, 538
93 SemicSticker 159
94/5 SigRookies 28
95/6 SP 161
94/5 SRGoldStandard 95
92/3 UpperDeck 371
95/6 UpperDeck 502
96/7 UDCollChoice 284
95/6 WSH
94/5 Portland
95/6 Portland

UUSIKARTANO, JARI
72/3 WilliamsFIN 319

UUSIMAA, V.M.
71/2 WilliamsFIN 355
72/3 WilliamsFIN 356

UVAJEV, VYACHESLAV
91 SemicSticker 86

UVRIA, EDUARD
94/5 DEL 251
95/6 DEL 245

VAAHTOLUOTO, TIMO
71/2 WilliamsFIN 338

VÄÄNÄNEN, AUVO
80/1 Mallasjuoma 30
78/9 SM-Liiga 97

VAATAMOINEN, ANTERO
70/1 Kuvajulkaisut 275
80/1 Mallasjuoma 145

VÄÄTAMÖINEN, MATTI
72/3 WilliamsFIN 189

VÄÄTAMÖINEN, TIMO
66/7 Champion 91
65/6 Hellas 91
72/3 WilliamsFIN 190

VACATKO, VLADIMIR
82 SemicSticker 115

VACHON, ROGATIEN
77/8 Coke Mini
70/1 Colgate Stamp 85
70/1 DadsCookies
72-84 Dernière 77/8
70/1 EddieSargent 100
71/2 EddieSargent 68
72/3 EddieSargent 87
70/1 Esso Stamp
94 HockeyWit 24
72/3 Letraset 1
74/5 LiptonSoup 7
74/5 Loblaws
68/9 O-Pee-Chee 164, 212
69/70 O-Pee-Chee 165
70/1 OPC/Topps 49, -Deckle 22
71/2 OPC/Topps 156
72/3 OPC 100, Topps 51
73/4 OPC/Topps 64
74/5 OPC/Topps 235
75/6 OPC/Topps 160, 213, 297
76/7 OPC/Topps 40
77/8 OPC/Topps 8,160,-Glos 21
78/9 OPC/Topps 20
79/80 OPC/Topps 235
80/1 OPC/Topps 110, 168
81/2 OPC 10, Topps(E) 74
82/3 OPC 23
81/2 opcSticker 47
94/5 Parkie(64/5) FS5
95/6 Parkie(66/7) 75, 137
91/2 Pinnacle 387
68/9 Post Marble
72/3 Post Transfers 12
82/3 Post
72 SemicSticker 232
68/9 ShirriffCoin MTL2
77-9 Sportscastr 43-06, 50-1197
71/2 TheTorontoSun
67/8 Topps 75
92/3 Trends 154, 185, 195, -Aut.
67/8 York (x4), 15, 31, 32
79/80 DET
67/8 MTL
67/8 MTL/IGA
68/9 MTL
69/70 MTL/ProStar
70/1 MTL
71 MTL/Pins
71/2 MTL (x2)

VACHON, MARC
89/90 Johnstown 32

VACHON, NICHOLAS
93/4 Knoxville
95/6 Phoenix

VACHON, PAT
85/6 London 25
86/7 London 7

VADNAIS, CAROL
70/1 Colgate Stamp 86
70/1 DadsCookies
72-84 Dernière 79/80, 82/3
70/1 EddieSargent 130
71/2 EddieSargent 137
72/3 EddieSargent 25
70/1 Esso Stamp
74/5 Loblaws
68/9 OPC/Topps 81
69/70 OPC/Topps 82
69/70 opc-MiniSticker, -Stamp
70/1 OPC/Topps 70, -Deckle 36
70/1 OPC/Topps-Sticker
71/2 OPC/Topps 46
72/3 OPC 39, Topps 85
73/4 OPC/Topps 58
74/5 OPC/Topps 165
75/6 OPC/Topps 27
76/7 OPC/Topps 257, OPC 390
77/8 OPC/Topps 154
78/9 OPC/Topps 85
79/80 OPC/Topps 145
80/1 OPC/Topps 57
81/2 O-Pee-Chee 236
82/3 O-Pee-Chee 148
83/4 opcSticker 224
72 SemicSticker 181
68/9 ShirriffCoin OAK5
71/2 TheTorontoSun
67/8 Topps 9
67/8 MTL
67/8 MTL/IGA

VÄHÄNEN, KIM
93/4 Sisu 238

VAHANEN, TIMO
70/1 Kuvajulkaisut 383

VAIC, LUBOMIR
98/9 Pacific 435
97/8 PacificParamount 191

VAIHINEN, KARI
80/1 Mallasjuoma 181

VAIHINEN, RISTO
70/1 Kuvajulkaisut 358

VAIL, ERIC
74/5 Loblaws
74/5 OPC 391
75/6 OPC/Topps 135, 313
76/7 OPC/Topps 51
77/8 OPC/Topps 168
78/9 OPC/Topps 129
79/80 OPC/Topps 188
80/1 OPC/Topps 15
81/2 O-Pee-Chee 38
82/3 O-Pee-Chee 97
81/2 opcSticker 220
80/1 Pepsi Cap
81/2 Topps 43
74/5 ATL
77/8 ATL
78/9 ATL/Coke
79/80 ATL
79/80 ATL/B&W
80/1 CGY

VAINIO, RISTO
66/7 Champion 66
70/1 Kuvajulkaisut 152
71/2 WilliamsFIN 203
72/3 WilliamsFIN 240
73/4 WilliamsFIN 275

VAINIO, SEPPO
65/6 Hellas 21

VAIR, STEVE
91 C55 Reprint 18
1910-11 Imperial (C55) 18
1912-13 Imperial (C57) 10
1910-11 Imperial Post 18

VÄISÄNEN, MATTI
70/1 Kuvajulkaisut 117
72 Panda
71/2 WilliamsFIN 127
72/3 WilliamsFIN 99
73/4 WilliamsFIN 147

VAISANEN, PERTTI
70/1 Kuvajulkaisut 345

VAIVE, JEFF
81/2 Ottawa67s
82/3 Ottawa67s

VAIVE, RICK
90/1 Bowman 250
91/2 Bowman 39
83/4 Esso
84/5 Kelloggs Disk
86/7 Kraft Sports 60
80/1 OPC/Topps 242
81/2 OPC 310, Topps 44
82/3 O-Pee-Chee 314, 335, 336
83/4 O-Pee-Chee 323, 324, 343
84/5 OPC 313, 368, Topps 138
85/6 OPC/Topps 106
86/7 OPC/Topps 191
87/8 OPC/Topps 155
88/9 OPC/Topps 77
89/90 OPC/Topps 82, 125
90/1 OPC/Topps 148
91/2 OPC/Topps 457
81/2 opcSticker 101
82/3 opcSticker 62, 63
83/4 opcSticker 25, 26
84/5 opcSticker 11, 12, 139
85/6 opcSticker 6
86/7 opcSticker 138
87/8 opcSticker 155
88/9 opcSticker 9-138
89/90 opcSticker 256/117
87/8 PaniniSticker 328
88/9 PaniniSticker 31
89/90 PaniniSticker 206
90/1 PaniniSticker 23
91/2 PaniniSticker 297
80/1 Pepsi Cap
82/3 Post
90/1 ProSet 32
91/2 ProSet 26
87/8 ProSportWatch CW9
83/4 PuffySticker 2
90/1 Score 103
91/2 Score(CDN) 26, (U.S) 26
83/4 7ElevenCokeCup
84/5 7ElevenDisk
85/6 7Eleven 18
83/4 SouhaitsRen.KeyChain
91/2 ToppsStadiumClub 13
90/1 UpperDeck 376
91/2 UpperDeck 179
83/4 Vachon 100
88/9 BUF/BlueShield
89/90 BUF/BlueShield
89/90 BUF/Campbell
90/1 BUF/BlueShield
90/1 BUF/Campbell
91/2 BUF/BlueShield
91/2 BUF/Campbell
87/8 CHI/Coke
88/9 CHI/Coke
80/1 TOR
81/2 TOR
82/3 TOR
83/4 TOR
84/5 TOR
86/7 TOR
85/6 TOR
79/80 VAN
92/3 Hamilton

VAKIPARTA, ERKKI
70/1 Kuvajulkaisut 207
80/1 Mallasjuoma 210
72 Panda
78/9 SM-Liiga 234
71/2 WilliamsFIN 95
72/3 WilliamsFIN 260
73/4 WilliamsFIN 258

VALASEK, HORST
94/5 APS 297
95/6 APS 1

VALEK, OLDRICH
94/5 APS 179
89 SemicSticker 197
93/4 Sisu 289

VALENTA, PETR
90/1 SketchQMJHL 6
91/2 SketchQMJHL 224

VALENTI, SVEN
94/5 DEL 294
95/6 DEL 285

VALENTINE, CHRIS
94/5 DEL 82
95/6 DEL 88
82/3 O-Pee-Chee 373
82/3 opcSticker 155
82/3 Post
81/2 WSH
82/3 WSH

VALESANO, MIKE
85/6 Minn-Duluth 34

VALICEVIC, CHRIS
93/4 Greensboro
95/6 Louisiana, -Playoff

VALICEVIC, ROB
91/2 LakeSuperior
95/6 Louisiana, -Playoffs

VALIHARJU, SAKARI
70/1 Kuvajulkaisut 384

VÄLIKANGAS, MATTI
66/7 Champion 220

VÄLILÄ, MIKA
92/3 Jyvas-Hyva 129
93/4 Jyvas-Hyva 238
95 Semic 34
93/4 Sisu 197

VALIMAKI, JYRKI
70/1 Kuvajulkaisut 364

VÄLIMÄKI, TEPPO
72/3 WilliamsFIN 359

VALIMONT, CARL
89/90 ProCards(IHL) 184
90/1 ProCards 325
91/2 ProCards 603

VALIOJA, ESA
80/1 Mallasjuoma 165

VALIOTS, JAAK
91/2 Rayside

VALIQUETTE, JACK
76/7 OPC 294
77/8 OPC/Topps 64
78/9 O-Pee-Chee 391
79/80 OPC/Topps 229
80/1 OPC/Topps 108
79/80 COL.R
76/7 TOR
77/8 TOR

VALIQUETTE, STÉPHAN
95/6 Slapshot 382
96/7 Sudbury 25

VALK, GARRY
91/2 Bowman 314
93/4 Donruss 401
94/5 Donruss 198
94/5 Flair 7
94/5 FleerUltra 253
94/5 Leaf 206
91/2 OPC/Topps 117
93/4 Parkhurst 4
94/5 Parkhurst V19
95/6 Parkhurst 5
94/5 ParkieSE 7
91/2 Pinnacle 291
92/3 Pinnacle! 181
94/5 Pinnacle 119
96/7 PinnacleBeAPlayer 155
94/5 POG 370
93/4 PowerPlay 286
93/4 Premier 354
94/5 Premier 372
90/1 ProCards 322
95/6 ProMagnet 40
91/2 ProSet 499
91/2 Score(CDN) 195, (U.S) 195
92/3 Score 355
93/4 Score 641
97/8 Score(PGH) 12
92/3 Topps 383
91/2 ToppsStadiumClub 318
92/3 ToppsStadiumClub 493
93/4 ToppsStadiumClub 407
94/5 ToppsStadiumClub 89
90/1 UpperDeck 530
91/2 UpperDeck 152
92/3 UpperDeck 114
93/4 UpperDeck 515
94/5 UpperDeck 282, IG12, SP3
94/5 UDBAP R116, -Aut 118
94/5 ANA/Carl'sJr 8
95/6 ANA
90/1 VAN/Mohawk

VALK, PHIL
91/2 AvantGardeBCJHL 92
92/3 BCJHL 115

VALKEAPÄÄ, PERTTI
72 Hellas 18
74 Hellas 21
80/1 Mallasjuoma 158
74 SemicSticker 95
78/9 SM-Liiga 4, 180
72/3 WilliamsFIN 77, 207
73/4 WilliamsFIN 171

VALKONEN, PERTTI
66/7 Champion 108

VALLÉE, SÉBASTIEN
94/5 SigRookies 55

VALLIÈRE, MICHEL
96/7 DEL 316
95 Globe 200
95 PaniniWorlds 97
94 Semic 211
93 SemicSticker 250
96 Wien 184

VALLINGA, MIKE
95/6 Slapshot 92

VALLIS, LINDSAY
92/3 C'Prospects 41
91/2 ProCards 82
90/1 SketchWHL 10
92/3 Fredericton
93/4 Fredericton

VALOIS, RICHARD
88/9 Richelieu

VALOIS, STÉPHANE
88/9 Richelieu

VALTONEN, JORMA
72 Hellas 19
65/6 Hellas 16
70/1 Kuvajulkaisut 78, 205
72 Panda [x2]
72 SemicSticker 90
74 SemicSticker 76
78/9 SM-Liiga 198
77-9 Sprtscstr 16-364, 107-2559
71/2 WilliamsFIN 77, 93
72/3 WilliamsFIN 78, 258
73/4 WilliamsFIN 82, 123

VAN ALLEN, SHAUN
92/3 C'Prospects 64, 150
93/4 Donruss 14
95/6 Donruss 26
96/7 Donruss 86
92/3 FleerUltra 299
93/4 FleerUltra 264
95/6 FleerUltra 7
94/5 Leaf 338
95/6 Leaf 248
91/2 OPC/Topps 414
98/9 Pacific 317
97/8 PacificRegime 138
95/6 PaniniSticker 223
96/7 PaniniSticker 231
92/3 Parkhurst! 288
93/4 Parkhurst 278
95/6 Parkhurst 8
95/6 Pinnacle 102
96/7 PinnacleBeAPlayer 163
95/6 Playoff 115
94/5 POG 31
95/6 POG 23
93/4 PowerPlay 15
93/4 Premier 396
94/5 Premier 432
88/9 ProCards(CapeBreton)
89/90 ProCards(AHL) 151
90/1 ProCards 223
91/2 ProCards 221
95/6 Score 166
96/7 Score 227
95/6 SkyBoxEmotion 5
95/6 SkyBoxImpact 6
95/6 Topps 297
93/4 ToppsStadiumClub 361
94/5 ToppsStadiumClub 207
91/2 UpperDeck 52
93/4 UpperDeck 506
94/5 UpperDeck 312
95/6 UpperDeck 488
95/6 UDCollChoice 173
96/7 UDCollChoice 6
94/5 ANA/Carl'sJr
92/3 EDM/IGA 25
96/7 OTT/PizzaHut
97/8 OTT
86/7 Saskatoon

VAN AMBURG, SEAN
90/1 Rayside
91/2 Rayside

VAN BOXMEER, JOHN
83/4 SouhaitsRen.KeyChain

VANBIESBROUCK, JOHN
95/6 Aces 7(Spades)
96/7 Aces Q(Clubs)
97/8 Aces Q (Diamonds)
94/5 ActionPacked 2
91/2 Bowman 68
92/3 Bowman 132
95/6 Bowman 30
90/1 Bowman 222
96/7 CorinthianHeadliners
97/8 CorinthianHeadliners
93/4 Donruss 132
94/5 Donruss 176, -IceMaster 10
94/5 D-Masked 10, Dominat 3
95/6 Donruss 106
96/7 Donruss 187,-Bet 4, -Dom 1
97/8 Donruss 58,-Bet 3, -ElitS 8
96/7 DonrussCanadianIce 84
97/8 D.CdnIce 7, -Scrapbook 16
95/6 DonrussElite 83, -Painted 6
96/7 DonrussElite 74, -Painted 4
97/8 DonrussElite 3, 126
97/8 D.Elite -Craft 1, -PrmNum 8
97/8 DonrussPreferred 9, 182
97/8 D.Pref -ColGrd 4,-PrecM 13
97/8 D.Pref -Tin 6, -WideTin 8
97/8 DonrussPriority 5, 193
97/8 D.Prio -OpDay 5, -PstGen 2
97/8 D.Prio-Pstcrd 11,-Stamp 11
97/8 DonrussStudio 17
97/8 D.Studio-Portraits 17,-Sil 16
93/4 EASports 54
97/8 EssoOlympic 34
94/5 Flair 69
96/7 Flair 40, -HotGlove 12
94/5 Fleer 83, -Netminder 10
96/7 Fleer 44, -Vezina 10
95/6 FleerMetal 62
96/7 FPicks 88,-Dream8,-Fab 46
92/3 FleerUltra 144
93/4 FleerUltra 333
94/5 FleerUltra 86
95/6 FleerUltra 64, 378, -Pad 11
96/7 FleerUltra 70
95 Globe 101
93/4 HighLiner 5
95/6 Hoyle'EAST Q (Clubs)
94/5 Incomnet
97/8 KatchMedallion 66
97/8 KennerSLU
90/1 Kraft 60
92/3 Kraft'Disk
93/4 KraftDinner
94/5 KraftDinner, -Masks
95/6 Kraft-Crease
96/7 KraftDinner
93/4 Leaf 371, -Painted 8
94/5 Leaf 70,-Cr 5,-Ltd 9,-Gld 13
95/6 Leaf 172
96/7 Leaf 193,-ShutD 2,-Sweat 4
97/8 Leaf 5, 172, -PipeDream 2
94/5 LeafLimited 72
95/6 LeafLimited 47, -Stick 6
96/7 LeafLimited 30
96/7 LeafPreferred 41
96/7 LP-Masked 3, -Vanity 2
97/8 Limited 5, 62, 113, -fabric 7
96/7 Maggers 68
96/7 McDonalds M cD35, 'Masks
97/8 McDonalds, McD24
96/7 MetalUniverse 64
96/7 MU-Armour 12, -Cool 12
97/8 Omega 102, -NoScorZn 5
86/7 OPC/Topps 9, T-AS 1
87/8 OPC/Topps 36
88/9 OPC/Topps 102
89/90 OPC/Topps 114
90/1 OPC/Topps 75
91/2 OPC/Topps 353
92/3 OPC 275
88/9 opcStars 42
85/6 opcSticker 88 /221
86/7 opcStic 218,114/128,190/51
87/8 opcSticker 33/178
88/9 opcSticker 241/109
89/90 opcSticker 246/107
98/9 Pacific 34, -TeamCL 11
97/8 PacificCrown 34
97/8 PCC-Supial 9, -TeamCL 11
97/8 PCC-Gold 13, -InThe 10
97/8 PacificCrownRoyale 60
97/8 PCR-FreezeOut 9
97/8 PacificDynagon! 57
97/8 PacificD-BstKpt 43,-King 5
97/8 PacificD-Stone 10,-Tand 13
97/8 PcfcInvincible 64,-Feat 17
97/8 PcfcParamount 86,-BigN 11
97/8 PcfcP-Glovesid 9,-Photo 11
98/9 PacificParamount 178
97/8 PacificRegime 89
97/8 PacificRevolution 62
97/8 PcfcRev-Retrn 9,-TmCL 11
87/8 PaniniSticker 106
88/9 PaniniSticker 300
89/90 PaniniSticker 282
90/1 PaniniSticker 108
91/2 PaniniSticker 282
92/3 PaniniSticker 232
93/4 PaniniSticker 98
94/5 PaniniSticker 72
95/6 PaniniSticker 79
96/7 PaniniSticker 70
91/2 Parkhurst 338
92/3 Parkhurst 349
93/4 Parkhurst 73
94/5 Parkhurst V13, C9
95/6 Parkhurst 85, PP5, PP29
95/6 PH-Crown(2) 12, -Goal 7
94/5 ParkieSE 67
91/2 Pinnacle 121, 367
92/3 Pinnacle 186
93/4 Pinn.148,-Mask 9,-Exp 1
94/5 Pinnacle 100, GT3, MA2
96/7 Pinn. 203,-Mask 6,-TmP 8
97/8 Pinn. 37, -Masks 1,-TmP 10
97/8 Pinnacle -BigCan, -Stand 2
96/7 P.BAP LT H10B,-Stacking 4
97/8 P.BAP-Stack/Pad 8,-Take 6
97/8 P.BeeHive 27,-TeamBH 5
97/8 P.Certified 6, -Team 3
97/8 Pinnacle-EPIX 2
95/6 PinnacleFANtasy 16
96/7 PinnacleFANtasy 9
97/8 PinnacleInside 19, -Can 3
97/8 Pinn.In-Stopper 2, -Track 7
97/8 PinnacleMasks
96/7 PinnacleMint 26
97/8 PinnacleMint 4
97/8 PinnacleUncut
95/6 PinnacleZenith 36
96/7 P.Zenith 91, -ZTeam 17
97/8 PlaymateProZone
95/6 Playoff 44
96/7 Playoff 425
94/5 POG 261, 280
95/6 POG 123
96/7 Post
93/4 PowerPlay 102
93/4 Premier 160, 314
94/5 Premier 82, 360
95/6 ProMagnet 90
90/1 ProSet 209
91/2 ProSet 447
91/2 PSPlatinum PC1
90/1 Score 175, -HotCards 76
91/2 Score(CND) 10, (U.S) 10
92/3 Score 160, -USAGreats 7
93/4 Score 162, 445, 492, 501
94/5 Score TF9
95/6 Score 241, 322
96/7 Score 63, -Promo 63
96/7 S-NetWorth 8, -Sudden 7
97/8 Score 34, -NetWorth 15
94/5 Select 7
95/6 SelectCertified 85
96/7 SelectCertified 59, -Freez 4
95 Semic 102, 217
89 SemicSticker 154
91 SemicSticker 127
92 SemicSticker 147
95/6 SkyBoxEmotion 72
95/6 SkBxImpact 70, -Deflect 6
96/7 SkyBoxImpact 50, -Zero 10
94/5 SP 44
95/6 SP 56
96/7 SP 61, CW9, GF8
97/8 SPAuthentic 69, I5
97/8 SPx 20, -DuoView
95/6 Summit 130, -InThe 15
96/7 Summit 66, -Crease 10
95/6 SuperSticker 46, 47
96/7 TeamOut
92/3 Topps 169
95/6 Topps 252, HGA8, PF9
98/9 Topps 215
94/5 ToppsFinest 40, -Best(B) 8
95/6 ToppsFinest 20, 188
96/7 ToppsNHLPicks ID12
91/2 ToppsStadiumClub 323

92/3 ToppsStadiumClub 58
93/4 TSC 85, 330, -Master(1) 10
94/5 ToppsStadiumClub 95
95/6 ToppsStadiumClub 35
93/4 TSC-MembersOnly 40
94/5 TSC-MembersOnly 7
95/6 TSC-MembersOnly 34
97/8 ToppsSticker 2
95/6 ToppsSuperSkills 78
90/1 UpperDeck 279
91/2 UpperDeck 324
92/3 UpperDeck 44
93/4 UpperDeck 8, SP-60
94/5 UD 46, SP31, C20, H32
95/6 UD 321, AS19, H19, SE122
96/7 UD 63, GJ7, HH6, SS2B,X7
97/8 UD 72, S7, SG54, T2C
93/4 UDBAP'Roots 27
94/5 UDBAP R20, R135,-Aut. 20
96/7 UDBlackDiamond 165, RC6
97/8 UDBlackDiamond 42
98/9 UDChoice 89, 247, BH10
95/6 UDCollChoice 253, 368
96/7 UDCC 101, 318, 348, UD12
97/8 UDCC 102, 317, S2, SQ84
97/8 udDiamondVision 7
96/7 UpperDeck"Ice" 110, S3
97/8 UpperDeckIce 74, IC17
96 Wien 156
97/8 Zenith 9, Z4
94/5 FLA/HealthPlan
96/7 FLA/WinnDixie
97/8 FLA/WinnDixie
89/90 NYR/MarineMidland
80/1 SSMarie
81/2 SSMarie
82/3 SSMarie
87/8 SSMarie 16

VAN BLISEN, HARRY
79 PaniniSticker 276

VAN BOXMEER, JOHN
76/7 OPC 330
77/8 OPC 315
78/9 OPC/Topps 224
79/80 OPC/Topps 96
80/1 OPC/Topps 183
81/2 OPC 26, Topps(E) 80
82/3 O-Pee-Chee 36, 37
83/4 O-Pee-Chee 73
81/2 opcSticker 58
82/3 opcSticker 121
83/4 opcSticker 244
82/3 Post
88/9 ProCards(Rochester)
89/90 ProCards(AHL) 266
83/4 PuffySticker 9
83/4 SouhaitsRen.KeyChain
83/4 Vachon 78
76/7 COL.R/CokeCans
77/8 COL.R/CokeCans
79/80 BUF/BellsMarket
80/1 BUF/Wendt
81/2 BUF 2
82/3 BUF/Wendt 4
90/1 BUF/Campbell
74/5 MTL
92/3 Rochester/Kodak
93/4 Rochester

VANCLIEF, CHRIS
89/90 Oshawa 33

VANDAL, J.P.
51/2 BasDuFleuve 15

VANDALE, DUANE
92/3 MPSPhotoSJHL 94

VANDENBERGHE, M.
91/2 SketchWHL 334
88/9 Brandon 4
89/90 Brandon 5
90/1 Brandon 3
94/5 Dayton 19

VAN DEN BROEK, KLASS
79 PaniniSticker 278

VANDENBUSSCHE, RYAN
97/8 PinnacleBeAPlayer 223
90/1 SketchOHL 49
91/2 SketchOHL 22
95/6 Binghampton
96/7 Binghampton
91/2 Cornwall 7
93/4 StJohns
94/5 StJohns

VAN DER HORST, JAMIE
97/8 SheffieldSteelers

VANDERKRACHT, BRAM
90/1 SketchMEM 88
90/1 SketchWHL 211
91/2 SketchWHL 194
89/90 Spokane

VANDERKRACHT, MIKE
90/1 SketchWHL 225

VANDERMEER, PETE
93/4 RedDeer

VANDERSLOT, ADRIAN
88/9 NiagaraFalls 18

VANDERWAL, WES
95/6 Slapshot 148

VANDERYDT, R.
94/5 Raleigh 1

VAN DORP, WAYNE
90/1 O-Pee-Chee 527
88/9 ProCards(Rochester)
89/90 CHI/Coke
88/9 EDM/ActionMagazine 164
87/8 PGH/Kodak
91/2 QUE/PetroCanada
92/3 QUE/PetroCanada

VAN DRUNEN, DAVE
95/6 PrinceAlbert

VAN DYK, CHRIS
95/6 ClassicFiveSport 150
94/5 Slapshot(Windsor) 6
95/6 Slapshot 409

VAN HELLEMOND, ANDY
90/1 ProSet 701

VAN HERZELE, LARRY
84/5 Belleville 14
83/4 Brantford 10

VANI, CARMINE
94 Semic 310
93 SemicSticker 222
81/2 Kingston 10
82/3 Kingston 6
83/4 Kitchener 17

VANIK, MILOS
94/5 DEL 142
95/6 DEL 140
96/7 DEL 335

VAN IMPE, DARREN
95/6 EdgeIce 12
96/7 FleerUltra 7
95/6 Leaf 138
96/7 MetalUniverse 193
97/8 PacificCrown 286
97/8 PacificInvincible 5
96/7 PaniniSticker 229
97/8 PaniniSticker 185
97/8 Score(ANA) 9
90/1 SketchMEM 117
90/1 SketchWHL 268
91/2 SketchWHL 258
96/7 SP 4
96/7 UpperDeck 213
97/8 UpperDeck 4
97/8 UDCollChoice 4
96/7 ANA/UpFrontSports 16
90/1 PrinceAlbert
91/2 PrinceAlbert
93/4 RedDeer

VAN IMPE, ED
71/2 Bazooka Panel 3
64-67 BeeHives(CHI)
70/1 Colgate Stamp 78
70/1 DadsCookies
70/1 EddieSargent 159
71/2 EddieSargent 150
72/3 EddieSargent 160
70/1 Esso Stamp
72/3 Letraset 11
74/5 Loblaws
68/9 OPC/Topps 91
69/70 OPC/T. 92, OPC-Sticker
70/1 OPC/Topps 80
70/1 OPC/T-Deckle 34, -Sticker
71/2 OPC/Topps 126
72/3 OPC 33, Topps 9
73/4 O-Pee-Chee 206
74/5 OPC/Topps 85
75/6 OPC/Topps 38
76/7 OPC/Topps 157
92/3 Parkhurst 479
95/6 Parkie(66/7) 36, 139
71/2 TheTorontoSun
63/4 Topps 30
72/3 PHA/MightyMilk
75/6 PHA/GingerAle

VAN KESSEL, JOHN
89/90 ProCards(AHL) 26
90/1 ProCards 348
91/2 ProCards 400
89/90 SketchOHL 162
94/5 CapeBreton

VANKKA, LEO
66/7 Champion 115

VANLEYEN, THORSTEN
94/5 DEL 90

VANNE, ANTTI
70/1 Kuvajulkaisut 359

VANNE, ARI
70/1 Kuvajulkaisut 360

VAN OENE, DARREN
95/6 Bowman P34
94/5 Slapshot(MEM) 44
95/6 UpperDeck 511

VAN ONLANGS, ROBERT
79 PaniniSticker 280

VAN ROOYEN, KEITH
85/6 Sudbury 23

VAN RYAN, MIKE
96/7 UpperDeck 378
98/9 UDChoice 266

VAN SLOOTEN, MIKE
86/7 Regina
87/8 Regina

VAN SOLDT, FRANK
79 PaniniSticker 277

VANSTAALDUINEN, BART
91/2 AirCanadaSJHL 22, B37
93/4 Mich.State

VAN TASSEL, M.
93/4 Waterloo

VANTIGHEM, TRAVIS
91/2 AirCanadaSJHL D12
92/3 MPSPhotoSJHL 78

VAN VOLSEN, JOE
93/4 Slapshot(SSMarie) 17
95/6 Slapshot 51
93/4 SSMarie 26

VAN VOLSEN, MIKE
95/6 Slapshot 33

VAN WIEREN, LARRY
79 PaniniSticker 279

VARADA, VACLAV
97/8 Donruss 217
97/8 DonrussCanadianIce 141
97/8 DonrussPreferred 159
96/7 Flair 102
97/8 Leaf 48, 166
97/8 Limited 23, 178
98/9 Pacific 111
98/9 PacificParamount 23
94/5 SigRookies 1
96/7 SP 171
96/7 UpperDeck 224
97/8 UpperDeck 229
98/9 UDChoice 20

VARCOE, F.
93/4 SSMarie 32

VARDALE, DUANE
91/2 AirCanadaSJHL D38

VARGA, CHRIS
90/1 SketchOHL 21
91/2 SketchOHL 38

VARGA, JOHN
93/4 Donruss USA21
93/4 Pinnacle 500
93/4 UpperDeck 559
92/3 Tacoma
93/4 Tacoma
91/2 SketchWHL 150

VARGAS, ERNIE
89/90 ProCards(IHL) 170

VARGO, JAMIE
89/90 Windsor

VARHOLIK, JAN
94 Semic 194

VARIS, PETRI
92/3 Jyvas-Hyva 199
93/4 Jyvas-Hyva 109
95 PaniniWorlds 180
94 Semic 46
95 Semic 28
93 SemicSticker 82
93/4 Sisu 23, 393
95/6 Sisu 259, -Spec 1,-Paink 7
96/7 Sisu 47, 180, -AtTheGala 1
95/6 SisuLimited 18

VARITSKI, IGOR
95/6 DEL 162
95 PaniniWorld 43

VARJANEN, KARI
66/7 Champion 82
70/1 Kuvajulkaisut 171

VARJANOV, NIKOLAI
90/1 O-Pee-Chee 504

VARJONEN, TOMMI
92/3 Jyvas-Hyva 29
93/4 Jyvas-Hyva 52
93/4 Sisu 251
94/5 Sisu 74

VARLAMOV, SERGEI
97/8 Bowman 120
98 BowmanCHL 79, SC9
98/9 Pacific 58
97/8 PinnacleBeeHive 73
98/9 Topps 231
95/6 SwiftCurrent

VARNAKOV, MICHAEL
87/8 SovietStars

VARPELA, MATTI
66/7 Champion 45

VARTIAINEN, EERO
78/9 SM-Liiga 146

VARTIAINEN, MATTI
66/7 Champion 123

VARTIAINEN, SEPPO
72/3 WilliamsFIN 320
73/4 WilliamsFIN 124

VARVIO, JARKKO
92/3 Classic 30
92/3 ClassicFourSport 179
93/4 ClassicProspects 125
93/4 Donruss 90, -RatedRook 6
94/5 Donruss 129
93/4 FleerUltra 302, -Wave 19
94/5 FleerUltra 281
92/3 Jyvas-Hyva 24
93/4 Leaf 383, -Freshman 8
94/5 Leaf 199
94/5 PaniniSticker Z
93/4 Parkhurst 252, C8
94/5 ParkieSE 40
93/4 Pinnacle 430
93/4 Score 620
94 Semic 44
95 Semic 44
93 SemicSticker 83
93/4 Sisu 371
94/5 Sisu-Guest 12
95/6 Sisu 306
96/7 Sisu 108
95/6 SisuLimited 89
91/2 UD 676, 'CzechWJC 39
93/4 UpperDeck 422, SP-40
94/5 UpperDeck 429

VARY, JOHN
89/90 SketchOHL 155
90/1 SketchOHL 75, 320
91/2 SketchOHL 237
95/6 Louisiana, -Playoffs

VASICEK, TOMAS
94/5 APS 116

VASIJEVA, HERBERT
95/6 Slapshot 94

VASILEVSKI, ALEX
94/5 ClassicImages 11
95/6 EdgeIce 98
94/5 Slapshot(MEM) 49

VASILIEV, ALEXEI
95/6 TetradAutobilia 53
95/6 UpperDeck 555

VASILIEV, ANDREI
95/6 Parkhurst 513
95/6 UpperDeck 412

VASILIEV, IVAN
95/6 APS 336

VASILIEV, MIKHAIL
83/4 SovietStars

VASILIEV, VALERI
72 Hellas 68
74 Hellas 59
70/1 Kuvajulkaisut 19
79 PaniniSticker 144
82 SemicSticker 56
73/4 Soviet Champs 13
80 SovietMiniPics
70/1 Soviet Stars
73/4 Soviet Stars 5
74/5 Soviet Stars 5
79/80 SovietStars
91/2 Trends 68
92/3 Trends 132
96 Wien HL4
72/3 WilliamsFIN 39
73/4 WilliamsFIN 19

VASILIEV, VLADIMIR
94/5 DEL 198

VASILJEVS, HERBERT
94/5 DEL 230
95/6 Guelph 10

VASKE, DENNIS
92/3 Bowman 28
94/5 FleerUltra 134
95/6 FleerUltra 272
91/2 OPC/Topps 230
97/8 PacificRegime 122
95/6 PaniniSticker 100
92/3 Parkhurst 335
94/5 Parkhurst 141
94/5 Pinnacle 456
97/8 PinnacleBeAPlayer 120
95/6 Playoff 170
93/4 PowerPlay 387
93/4 Premier 438
90/1 ProCards 508
91/2 ProCards 460
91/2 Score(CDN) 340, (U.S) 310
95/6 SkyBoxEmotion 110
95/6 SkyBoxImpact 106
92/3 Topps 87
92/3 ToppsStadiumClub 362
93/4 ToppsStadiumClub 358
91/2 UpperDeck 49
92/3 UpperDeck 50, 383
96/7 UpperDeck 107

VASKO, ELMER
45-64 BeeHives(CHI)
64-67 BeeHives(HCI)
62 CeramicTiles
63-5 ChexPhoto
64/5 CokeCap CHI-4
65/6 CocaCola
68/9 O-Pee-Chee 147, -Sticker 8
93/4 Parkie(56/7) 31
94/5 Parkie(64/5) 30, 141
60/1 ShirriffCoin 73
61/2 ShirriffCoin 26
63/4 TheTorontoStar
64/5 TheTorontoStar
57/8 Topps 27
58/9 Topps 12
59/60 Topps 3
60/1 Topps 23
61/2 Topps 25, -Stamp
62/3 Topps 27, -Buck
63/4 Topps 26
64/5 Topps 5
65/6 Topps 114
54-67 TorontoStar V9
56-66 TorontoStar 60/1, 61/2
91/2 UltimateDP 64, -Aut 64

VASKO, RICK
80/1 DET

VASSIEUX, JEAN
79 PaniniSticker 382

VAUGHAN, DOUG
52/3 AnonymousOHL 117

VAUGHAN, KEVIN
93/4 Slapshot(Oshawa) 17

VAUGHAN, LYLE
91/2 AirCanadaSJHL C40

VAUGHN, DR. R.L.
89/90 SketchOHL 97
83/4 Belleville 8
84/5 Belleville 2

VAUHKONEN, JONNI
92/3 Jyvas-Hyva 146
93/4 Jyvas-Hyva 262
93/4 Parkhurst 525
95 Semic 234
93/4 Sisu 296, 392
94/5 Sisu 174
96/7 Sisu 105
92/3 UpperDeck 619

VAUTOUR, YVON
81/2 O-Pee-Chee 84
81/2 COL.R
84/5 Fredericton 26

VAVRECKA, JAN
94/5 APS 8
95/6 APS 31

VEALE, BRIAN
91/2 AvantGardeBC 105, 147
92/3 BCJHL 113

VEBER, JIRI
95/6 APS 10
95 PaniniWorlds 196
95 Semic 147

VECCHIARELLI, JOHN
94 Semic 303
93 SemicSticker 219

VECCIA, RON
84/5 SSMarie

VEHMANEN, HANNU
70/1 Kuvajulkaisut 361

VEHMANEN, JORMA
66/7 Champion 14
70/1 Kuvajulkaisut 79, 240
80/1 Mallasjuoma 117
72 SemicSticker 89
96/7 Sisu 194
78/9 SM-Liiga 164
71/2 WilliamsFIN 78, 163
72/3 WilliamsFIN 115
73/4 WilliamsFIN 83, 213

VEIJALAINEN, ARI
71/2 WilliamsFIN 378

VEILLEUX, ERIC
93/4 ClassicProspects 67
91/2 SketchQMJHL 245

VEILLEUX, STEVE
89/90 ProCards(IHL) 167
90/1 ProCards 332
91/2 ProCards 79
92/3 Fredericton

VEISOR, MIKE
75/6 OPC 385
77/8 OPC 393
80/1 O-Pee-Chee 361
79/80 CHI
82/3 HFD/JuniorWhalers
83/4 HFD/JuniorWhalers

VEITCH, DARREN
95/6 EdgeIce 180
87/8 OPC/Topps 114
87/8 PaniniSticker 239
88/9 PaniniSticker 39
82/3 Post
89/90 ProCards(AHL) 123
90/1 ProCards 155
86/7 DET/Caesars
87/8 DET/Caesars
88/9 TOR/P.L.A.Y. 22
80/1 WSH
81/2 WSH
82/3 WSH
85/6 WSH/PizzaHut
91/2 Moncton
90/1 Newmarket
92/3 Peoria
93/4 Peoria

VEJVODA, OTAKAR
94/5 APS 59
95/6 APS 96, 372
97/8 udSwedish 15

VELISCHEK, RANDY
91/2 Bowman 152
92/3 Bowman 131
92/3 Durivage 45
89/90 O-Pee-Chee 245
90/1 O-Pee-Chee 453
91/2 OPC/Topps 377
92/3 O-Pee-Chee 288
90/1 opcPremier 125
90/1 Panini(QUE) 23
89/90 PaniniSticker 259
91/2 PaniniSticker 265
90/1 ProSet 518
91/2 ProSet 206
91/2 Score(CDN) 477
91/2 Score(U.S) 257, 64T
92/3 Topps 430
91/2 ToppsStadiumClub 27
92/3 ToppsStadiumClub 460
90/1 UpperDeck 392
91/2 UpperDeck 484
83/4 MIN
85/6 N.J.
86/7 N.J/SOBER
88/9 N.J/Caretta
89/90 N.J.
91/2 QUE/PetroCanada
94/5 Milwaukee
84/5 Springfield 4
vellinga, mike
95/6 Guelph 21
96/7 Guelph 19

VELLUCCI, MIKE
88/9 ProCards(Binghampton)
83/4 Belleville 17

VENASKY, VIC
74/5 OPC 389
75/6 OPC/Topps 312
76/7 OPC/Topps 211
77/8 OPC/Topps 187
78/9 O-Pee-Chee 321
79/80 O-Pee-Chee 269
80/1 O-Pee-Chee 290

VENDERMEER, PETE
95/6 RedDeer

VENEDAM, SEAN
97/8 Bowman 11
93/4 Slapshot(Sudbury) 11
94/5 Slapshot(Sudbury) 10
95/6 Slapshot 393
93/4 Sudbury 24

VENERUZZO, GARY
68/9 OPC/Topps 119
70/1 OPC/Topps 101
72/3 OPC 330
74/5 opcWHA 55
76/7 opcWHA 21
73/4 QuakerOats 32
72/3 LosAngelesSharks
75/6 Cincinnati
76/7 SanDiegoMariners

VENTO, JOUNI
96/7 DEL 231
92/3 Jyvas-Hyva 195
93/4 Jyvas-Hyva 355
93/4 Sisu 214
94/5 Sisu 53, 177
95/6 Sisu 354

VERÄVÄINEN, HEIKKI
66/7 Champion 18
65/6 Hellas 67

VERBEEK, PAT
90/1 Bowman 257
91/2 Bowman 12
92/3 Bowman 112
83 CanadaJuniors
93/4 Donruss 148
94/5 Donruss 299
95/6 Donruss 29
96/7 Donruss 200
97/8 Donruss 23
96/7 DonrussCanadianIce 48
97/8 DonrussCanadianIce 27
95/6 DonrussElite 76
96/7 DonrussElite 42
97/8 DonrussPreferred 57
93/4 EASports 59
94/5 Flair 76
96/7 Flair 25
94/5 Fleer 91
95/6 FleerMetal 101

96/7 FleerNHLPicks-Dream 10
92/3 FleerUltra 305
93/4 FleerUltra 175
94/5 FleerUltra 95
95/6 FleerUltra 107
96/7 FleerUltra 47
91/2 Gillette 24
91/2 Kraft 23
93/4 Kraft-Captain
93/4 Leaf 144
94/5 Leaf 172
95/6 Leaf 16
96/7 Leaf 59
97/8 Leaf 78
94/5 LeafLimited 27
96/7 LeafLimited 33
96/7 LeafPreferred 8, -Steel 14
97/8 Limited 75
96/7 Maggers 105
96/7 MetalUniverse 43
97/8 Omega 76
84/5 OPC 121, Topps 90
85/6 OPC/Topps 56
86/7 OPC/Topps 46
87/8 OPC/Topps 6, 146
88/9 OPC/Topps 29
89/90 OPC/Topps 32, 293
90/1 OPC/Topps 112
91/2 OPC/Topps 499, T-TL 1
92/3 O-Pee-Chee 197
91/2 opcPremier 5
88/9 opcStars 43
84/5 opcSticker 73
86/7 opcSticker 202/75
87/8 opcSticker 58 /199
88/9 opcSticker 81/210
98/9 Pacific 185
97/8 PacificCrown 162
97/8 PacificCrownRoyale 43
97/8 PacificInvincible 44
97/8 PacificParamount 63
87/8 PaniniSticker 81
88/9 PaniniSticker 278
90/1 PaniniSticker 36
91/2 PaniniSticker 313
92/3 PaniniSticker 256
93/4 PaniniSticker 124
94/5 PaniniSticker 112
95/6 PaniniSticker 108
97/8 PaniniSticker 137
95 PaniniWorlds 17
91/2 Parkhurst 64
93/4 Parkhurst 353
92/3 Parkhurst 58
94/5 Parkhurst 92
95/6 Parkhurst 407
94/5 Parkie seV7
91/2 Pinnacle 43
93/4 Pinnacle 243, CA10
92/3 Pinnacle 348
94/5 Pinnacle 37
95/6 Pinnacle 111
96/7 Pinnacle 68
97/8 Pinnacle 173
96/7 PinnacleBeAPlayer 38
97/8 PinnacleCertified 111
97/8 PinnacleInside 157
95/6 PinnacleZenith 82
96/7 PinnacleZenith 93
95/6 Playoff 70
96/7 Playoff 359
94/5 POG 120
95/6 POG 182
93/4 PowerPlay 110
93/4 Premier 47
94/5 Premier 390
90/1 ProSet 112
91/2 ProSet 86, 303
91/2 PS'ThePuck 10, -Promo
92/3 ProSet 58
91/2 PSPlatinum 44
90/1 Score 35, -HotCards 18
91/2 Score(CDN) 70, (U.S) 70
92/3 Score 282
93/4 Score 10
94/5 Score CI18
95/6 Score 122
96/7 Score 94
97/8 Score 124, -CheckIt 18
92/3 SeasonsPatch 44
94/5 Select 76
96/7 SelectCertified 49
95/6 SelectCertified 108
95/6 SkyBoxEmotion 120
95/6 SkyBoxImpact 115
94/5 SP 72
95/6 SP 93
96/7 SP 41
95/6 Summit 107
96/7 Summit 5
84/5 Topps 90
92/3 Topps 493
95/6 Topps 37, PL3
98/9 Topps 120
95/6 ToppsFinest 131
96/7 ToppsNHLPicks 69
91/2 ToppsStadiumClub 102
92/3 ToppsStadiumClub 197
93/4 ToppsStadiumClub 36
94/5 ToppsStadiumClub 120
95/6 ToppsStadiumClub 17
95/6 TSC-MembersOnly 35
95/6 ToppsSuperSkills 43
90/1 UpperDeck 172
91/2 UpperDeck 193
92/3 UpperDeck 7, 204
93/4 UpperDeck 331, SP-67
94/5 UpperDeck 278, SP124
95/6 UpperDeck 98, AS13
96/7 UpperDeck 249
97/8 UpperDeck 262
93/4 UDBeAPlayer 38
94/5 UDBeAPlayer R61. -Aut. 71
96/7 UDBlackDiamond 136
95/6 UDCollChoice 55
97/8 UDCollChoice 66, SQ16
96/7 UpperDeck"Ice" 17
96/7 DAL/Southwest
89/90 HFD/JuniorWhalers
90/1 HFD/JuniorWhalers
91/2 HFD/JuniorWhalers
92/3 HFD/DairyMart
93/4 HFD/Coke
83/4 N.J.
84/5 N.J.
86/7 N.J/SOBER
88/9 N.J/Caretta

VERBEEK, BRIAN
84/5 Kingston 23
85/6 Kingston 23

VERCHOTA, PHIL
94/5 SR'MiracleOnIce 37, 38
79/80 USAOlympicTeam 7

VERMETTE, MARK
89/90 ProCards(AHL) 163
90/1 ProCards 450
91/2 UpperDeck 470
88/9 QUE
88/9 QUE/GeneralFoods
91/2 QUE/PetroCanada
92/3 QUE/PetroCanada
89/90 Halifax
90/1 Halifax
93/4 LasVegas

VERMEULEN, PHIL
79 PaniniSticker 342

VERNER, ANDREW
91/2 Arena 25
91/2 Classic 30
91/2 ClassicFourSport 30, -Aut.
92/3 ClassicProspects 84
89/90 SketchOHL 121
90/1 SketchOHL 375
91/2 SketchOHL 143
91/2 StarPics 21, 36
91/2 UltimateDP 26, 57, -Aut. 26
91/2 UpperDeck 74
97/8 udSwedish 134
91/2 Peterborough 12

VERNON, MIKE
97/8 Aces 2 (Hearts)
90/1 Bowman 94
91/2 Bowman 253
92/3 Bowman 86
83 CanadaJuniors
93/4 Donruss 54
95/6 Donruss-Between 3
96/7 Donruss 52
97/8 Donruss 73
96/7 DonrussCanadianIce 94
97/8 DCI 118, -Nat'l 28, -Scap 31
96/7 DonrussElite 86
97/8 D.Preferred 82,-ColGrd 12
97/8 D.Priority -PostGeneral 11
97/8 DonrussStudio 69
93/4 EASports 24
95/6 EdgeIce L8
94/5 Flair 53
94/5 Fleer 66
96/7 Fleer 144
92/3 FleerUltra 31
93/4 FleerUltra 207
94/5 FleerUltra 287
95/6 FleerUltra 50, -PadMen 12
93/4 HockeyWit 45
97/8 KatchMedallion 126
86/7 Kraft Sports 9
89/90 Kraft 62, -Sticker 4
90/1 Kraft 61, 76
91/2 Kraft 19
92/3 Kraft-Disk
93/4 Kraft-Cutout
94/5 Kraft
95/6 Kraft-Crease
96/7 Kraft Trophy
93/4 Leaf 83, -Painted 7
94/5 Leaf 464
95/6 Leaf 8
96/7 Leaf 147
97/8 Leaf 94
96/7 LeafPreferred-Steel 57
97/8 Limited 188, -fabric 17
96/7 Maggers 60
91/2 McDonalds McD20
97/8 Omega 207
87/8 O-Pee-Chee 215
88/9 O-Pee-Chee 261
89/90 OPC/Topps 163
89/90 OPC 300, T-AS 12
90/1 OPC Topps 351, L
91/2 OPC/Topps 107, 247
92/3 O-Pee-Chee 247
88/9 opcStars 44
90/1 opcPremier 126
91/2 opcPremier 9
87/8 opcSticker 41/182
88/9 opcSticker 86 /216
89/90 opcStick 94, 167/29, FS34
98/9 Pacific 393
97/8 PacificCrown 24, -InThe 8
97/8 PacificCrownRoyale 123
97/8 PCR-FreezeOut 18
97/8 PacificDynagon! 45
97/8 PcfcD-Stone 8, -Tandem 44
97/8 PacificInv. 52, -Feature 15
97/8 PcfcParamnt 170,-Glove 19
98/9 PacificParamount 18, 216
97/8 PacificRevolution 128
97/8 PcfcRev-Rtrn 18,-TmCL 22
90/1 Panini(CGY) 23
87/8 PaniniSticker 203
88/9 PaniniSticker 4
89/90 PaniniSticker 6,7, 34, 178
90/1 PaniniSticker 175, 329
91/2 PaniniSticker 55, 328
92/3 PaniniSticker 39
93/4 PaniniSticker 188
94/5 PaniniSticker 162
95/6 PaniniSticker 188
91/2 Parkhurst 27
92/3 Parkhurst 24
93/4 Parkhurst 301
95/6 Parkhurst 334
94/5 ParkieSE 52
91/2 Pinnacle 132
92/3 Pinnacle 318
93/4 Pinnacle 231, -Masks 2
94/5 Pinnacle 377, GT10
95/6 Pinnacle-Masks 6
96/7 Pinnacle 16
97/8 Pinnacle 36
97/8 PinnacleCertified 8
97/8 PinnacleInside 84, -Cans 8
97/8 P.Inside-Stoppr 11,-Stand 1
95/6 PinnacleZenith 60
95/6 Playoff 255
94/5 POG 278
95/6 POG 104
93/4 PowerPlay 45
93/4 Premier 15, -Promo 15
93/4 Premier-Black(OPC) 15
94/5 Premier 302, 348
95/6 ProMagnet IC05
90/1 ProSet 47, 338
91/2 ProSet 35, 277
92/3 ProSet 25
91/2 PSPlatinum 21
90/1 Score 52, -HotCards 23
91/2 Score(CDN) 80, (U.S) 80
92/3 Score 60
93/4 Score 43, -P.AllStar 40
95/6 Score 219, 319
96/7 Score 164, -NetWorth 14
97/8 Score 4
92/3 SeasonsPatch 61
94/5 Select 54
95/6 SelectCertified 42
95/6 SkyBoxEmotion 59
97/8 SPAuthentic 133
95/6 Summit 114
96/7 Summit 101
92/3 Topps 20
95/6 Topps 11, 160
98/9 Topps 86
94/5 ToppsFinest 36
91/2 ToppsStadiumClub 269
92/3 ToppsStadiumClub 345
93/4 T.StadiumClub 319, -AllStar
94/5 ToppsStadiumClub 79, 189
95/6 ToppsStadiumClub 12
95/6 ToppsSuperSkills 84
90/1 UpperDeck 254, 495
91/2 UpperDeck 163
92/3 UpperDeck 112
93/4 UpperDeck 177
94/5 UpperDeck 141, SP115
95/6 UpperDeck 4
97/8 UpperDeck 60, 356
98/9 UDChoice 177
95/6 UDCollChoice 100
97/8 UDCollChoice 77, SQ53
85/6 CGY/RedRooster
86/7 CGY/RedRooster
87/8 CGY/RedRooster
90/1 CGY/McGavins
91/2 CGY/IGA
92/3 CGY/IGA 10
97/8 S.J/PacificBellSheet (x3)
84/5 Moncton 20

VERTALA, TIMO
97/8 UDBlackDiamond 25
98/9 UDChoice 277

VERVERGAERT, DENNIS
74/5 Loblaws
74/5 OPC/Topps 117, 207
75/6 OPC/Topps 42
76/7 OPC/Topps 175, OPC 395
77/8 OPC/Topps 56
78/9 OPC/Topps 52
79/80 OPC/Topps 214
80/1 OPC/Topps 99
81/2 O-Pee-Chee 356
73/4 VAN/RoyalBank
74/5 VAN/RoyalBank
75/6 VAN/RoyalBank
76/7 VAN/RoyalBank
77/8 VAN/GingerAle
77/8 VAN/RoyalBank
78/9 VAN/RoyalBank
80/1 WSH

VESA, KIMMO
93/4 Sisu 184

VESCHRAEGAN, BOB
79 PaniniSticker 343

VESCIO, KEVIN
82/3 NorthBay
83/4 NorthBay

VESELOVSKY, PETER
94/5 APS 149

VESEY, JIM
94 Semic 201
88/9 ProCards(Peoria)
89/90 ProCards(IHL) 16
91/2 BOS/SportsAction
93/4 Phoenix

VESSLIN, ESA
66/7 Champion 32

VESTERGAARD, CHAD
91/2 AvantGardeBCJHL 115
92/3 BCJHL 177

VETTERAINO, SCOTT
90/1 Mich.Tech
91/2 Mich.Tech

VÉZINA, GEORGES
25-27 Anonymous 3
91 C55 Reprint 38
24/5 Champs (C144)
25 Dominion 120
83&87 HallOfFame 30
83 HHOF Postcard (B)
93/4 HHOFLegends 26
1911-12 Imperial (C55) 38
1912-13 Imperial (C57) 1
1910-11 Imperial Post 38
27-32 LaPresse 27/8
24/5 MapleCrispette (V130) 13
55/6 Parkhurst 56
93/4 Parkie(56/7) P3
91/2 ProSet 333
60/1 Topps 19
61/2 Topps-Stamp
23/4 (V145-1) 19
24/5 (V145-2) 43
28/9 MTL/LaPatrie 21
92/3 MTL/OPC 28
95/6 MTL/Forum 30Sep95

VÉZINA, J.J.
79/80 Montréal, -B&W

VIAL, DENNIS
93/4 Parkhurst 406
89/90 ProCards(IHL) 32
90/1 ProSet 628
91/2 Score(CDN) 428
95/6 UDBeAPlayer 131
91/2 DET/Caesars
93/4 OTT/Kraft
94/5 OTT/Bell
95/6 OTT
96/7 OTT/PizzaHut
97/8 OTT
88/9 NiagaraFalls 7

VICHOREK, MARK
90/1 ProCards 590
88/9 Flint

VICKERS, CHRIS
84/5 Ottawa

VICKERS, STEVE
74/5 LiptonSoup 34
74/5 Loblaws
72/3 OPC 254
73/4 OPC/Topps 57
74/5 OPC/Topps 29
75/6 OPC/Topps 19, 295, 324
76/7 OPC/Topps 75, OPC 390
77/8 OPC/Topps 136
78/9 OPC/Topps 55
79/80 OPC/Topps 195
80/1 OPC/Topps 23
82/3 Post

VIENONEN, JUSSI
93/4 Sisu 22

VIENS, STÉPHAN
91/2 SketchQMJHL 121

VIERIMAA, HANNU
80/1 Mallasjuoma 129

VIGLASI, RON
84/5 KelownaWingsWHL 9
82/3 Victoria

VIGNEAULT, ALAIN
91/2 SketchQMJHL 222
97/8 MTL
87/8 Hull

VIGNOLA, RÉJEAN
83/4 Fredericton 19

VIHANTO, PENTTI
66/7 Champion 53
70/1 Kuvajulkaisut 153
71/2 WilliamsFIN 204
72/3 WilliamsFIN 241
73/4 WilliamsFIN 276

VIILMA, OLLI
70/1 Kuvajulkaisut 291
71/2 WilliamsFIN 165

VIINIKAINEN, JUHA
96/7 Sisu 66
95/6 UDCollChoice 329

VIITA, MAURI
71/2 WilliamsFIN 356

VIITAKOSKI, MATTI
96/7 Sisu 109

VIITAKOSKI, VESA
93/4 Classic 48
94/5 Classic 45, T12
93/4 ClassicProspects 42
93/4 Donruss 60
94/5 Donruss 295
94/5 FleerUltra 272
91/2 Jyvas-Hyva 58
93/4 Leaf 433
94/5 Leaf 34
93/4 Parkhurst 263, C20
93/4 Pinnacle 444
94/5 Premier 472
93/4 Score 622
94 Semic 22
95 Semic 45
93 SemicSticker 84
93/4 UpperDeck 344, SP-26
94/5 SaintJohn
95/6 SaintJohn

VIITALA, JARI
70/1 Kuvajulkaisut 323
80/1 Mallasjuoma 38
78/9 SM-Liiga 61

VIITALAHTI, KARI
78/9 SM-Liiga 95
71/2 WilliamsFIN 275
73/4 WilliamsFIN 238

VIITANEN, PENTTI
71/2 WilliamsFIN 296
73/4 WilliamsFIN 214

VIKSTRÖM, SEPPO
66/7 Champion 63

VIKTORSSON, JAN
95/6 ElitSet 191, -Champs 15
89/90 SemicElitserien 63
90/1 SemicElitserien 285
91/2 SemicElitserien 67, 352
92/3 SemicElitserien 99
91 SemicSticker 41
95/6 udElite 55
97/8 udSwedish 48

VIKULOV, VLADIMIR
72 Hellas 77
74 Hellas 60
70/1 Kuvajulkaisut 20
72 SemicSticker 18
74 SemicSticker 49
69/70 Soviet Stars
70/1 Soviet Stars
71/2 Soviet Stars
91/2 Trends(72) 47
92/3 Trends(76) 164
71/2 WilliamsFIN 19
72/3 WilliamsFIN 40
73/4 WilliamsFIN 20

VILANDER, JUKKA
91/2 Jyvas-Hyva 63
92/3 Jyvas-Hyva 186
93/4 Jyvas-Hyva 317
89 SemicSticker 47
93/4 Sisu 42

VILEN, JORMA
66/7 Champion 180
70/1 Kuvajulkaisut 257
71/2 WilliamsFIN 222
72/3 WilliamsFIN 170
73/4 WilliamsFIN 239

VILEN, PETRI
93/4 Sisu 235

VILGRAIN, CLAUDE
92/3 Bowman 191
92/3 O-Pee-Chee 133
91/2 Parkhurst 321
89/90 ProCards(AHL) 211
90/1 ProCards 558
91/2 ProSet 425
91/2 PSPlatinum 195
92/3 Score 326, -Sharp 14
92/3 Topps 187
92/3 ToppsStadiumClub 422
90/1 UpperDeck 250

VILJANEN, RISTO
72/3 WilliamsFIN 357

VILJANEN, TIMO
78/9 SM-Liiga 209

VILLA, ISMO
80/1 Mallasjuoma 121
78/9 SM-Liiga 167
77-80 Sportscaster 91-2165
73/4 WilliamsFIN 322

VILLE, CHRISTOPHE
95 Globe 203
94 Semic 225
95 Semic 199
92 SemicSticker 238
93 SemicSticker 267

VILLEMURE, GILLES
71/2 Bazooka Panel 10
70/1 Colgate Stamp 89
71/2 EddieSargent 127
70/1 Esso Stamp
74/5 Loblaws
70/1 OPC 183
71/2 OPC/Topps 18, 248
72/3 OPC 132, 286, T 64, 137
73/4 OPC 119, Topps 153
74/5 OPC/Topps 179
75/6 OPC 379
76/7 OPC/Topps 61
71/2 TheTorontoSun
63/4 Topps 46
64/5 Topps 74
67/8 Topps 86

VILLENEUVE, BRUNO
90/1 SketchQMJHL 145
91/2 Knoxville
93/4 Knoxville

VILNEFF, MARK
90/1 SketchOHL 296

VILONEN, MIKKO
70/1 Kuvajulkaisut 324
80/1 Mallasjuoma 156

VINARD, ALAIN
79 PaniniSticker 384

VINCE, BILL
82/3 Brandon 10

VINCELLETTE, DAN
89/90 ProCards(IHL) 59
91/2 ProCards 480
87/8 CHI/Coke
88/9 CHI/Coke
90/1 QUE/PetroCanada
92/3 AtlantaKnights

VINCENT, PASCAL
90/1 SketchQMJHL 70
91/2 SketchQMJHL 246

VINCENT, PAUL
95/6 EdgeIce 85
94/5 SigRookies 34
94/5 SRGoldStandard 96
93/4 Seattle
95/6 StJohn's

VINCENT, ROB
51/2 LacStJean 30

VINCENT, SHAWN
83/4 Kelowna

VINES, MARK
90/1 ProSet 702

VINET, CLAUDE
52/3 AnonymousOHL 137

VINOGRADOV, ALEXANDER
95 PaniniWorlds 46

VINOUKUROV, DENIS
91/2 UD'CzechWJC 4

VIPOND, KELLY
91/2 SketchOHL 142
91/2 Peterborough 27
92/3 Windsor 20

VIRAG, DUSTY
94/5 Slapshot(NorthBay) 16
95/6 Slapshot 222

VIRHIMO, TAPIO
70/1 Kuvajulkaisut 258
80/1 Mallasjuoma 44
78/9 SM-Liiga 43
71/2 WilliamsFIN 223
72/3 WilliamsFIN 171
73/4 WilliamsFIN 193

VIRKGUNEN, TOMMY
91/2 AvantGardeBCJHL 170

VIRKKU, KALEVI
65/6 Hellas 18

VIRMANEN, MATTI
80/1 Mallasjuoma 56

VIROLAINEN, MIKKO
93/4 Sisu 55

VIRTA, HANNU
95 Globe 132
95 Hartwall
91/2 Jyvas-Hyva 66
92/3 Jyvas-Hyva 183
93/4 Jyvas-Hyva 315
95/6 Kelloggs PopU p 3
95 PaniniWorlds 168
95 Semic 23
89 SemicSticker 34
91 SemicSticker 6
93/4 Sisu 37
95/6 Sisu-GoldCards 11
95/6 SisuLimited 2, -Gallery 7
96 Wien 23
82/3 BUF/Wendt 16
84/5 BUF/BlueShield
85/6 BUF

VIRTA, HEIKKI
70/1 Kuvajulkaisut 362

VIRTA, PASI
80/1 Mallasjuoma 180
78/9 SM-Liiga 118

VIRTA, PEKKA
94/5 Sisu-MagicNumbers 6
95/6 Sisu 146, 360
96/7 Sisu 157

VIRTA, SEPPO
80/1 Mallasjuoma 172

VIRTA, TONY
96/7 DEL 56
92/3 Jyvas-Hyva 33
93/4 Jyvas-Hyva 53
93/4 Sisu 243
94/5 Sisu 46
95/6 Sisu 224

VIRTANEN, ANTO
66/7 Champion 38
65/6 Hellas 33
70/1 Kuvajulkaisut 206
72 Panda
71/2 WilliamsFIN 94
72/3 WilliamsFIN 259
73/4 WilliamsFIN 257

VIRTANEN, ANTTI
66/7 Champion 165
65/6 Hellas 147

VIRTANEN, HANNU
70/1 Kuvajulkaisut 363

VIRTANEN, JAAKKO
70/1 Kuvajulkaisut 325

VIRTANEN, JANNE
91/2 Jyvas-Hyva 68
92/3 Jyvas-Hyva 193
93/4 Jyvas-Hyva 348
93/4 Sisu 219
94/5 Sisu 67, 157, 281

VIRTANEN, JARI
93/4 Sisu 133
94/5 Sisu 72
95/6 Sisu 39
78/9 SM-Liiga 141

VIRTANEN, JORMA
72 Panda
78/9 SM-Liiga 111
72/3 WilliamsFIN 98
73/4 WilliamsFIN 146

VIRTANEN, JUHA
95/6 Sisu 142
95/6 SisuLimited 98

VIRTANEN, JUKKA
92/3 Jyvas-Hyva 184
70/1 Kuvajulkaisut 344
80/1 Mallasjuoma 203
93/4 Sisu 385

VIRTANEN, MARKO
92/3 Jyvas-Hyva 75
93/4 Jyvas-Hyva 148
94 Semic 49
93 SemicSticker 85
93/4 Sisu 150
94/5 Sisu-Horoscope 18
95/6 Sisu 67, -Painkiller 8
95/6 SisuLimited 53
97/8 udSwedish 172

VIRTANEN, TIMO
71/2 WilliamsFIN 357
72/3 WilliamsFIN 358

VIRTUE, TERRY
90/1 SketchOHL 329
90/1 SketchWHL 107
93/4 Wheeling 14

VISCOVICH, PETER
84/5 Kingston 17
85/6 Kingston 17
86/7 Kingston 18

VISHEAU, MARK
93/4 ClassicProspects 101
90/1 SketchOHL 147
91/2 SketchOHL 378

VISHNEVSKY, VITALI
97/8 UDBlackDiamond 93
98/9 UDChoice 285

VISKARI, ESA
66/7 Champion 137

VISKARI, TIMO
66/7 Champion 126
70/1 Kuvajulkaisut 274

VIT, PAVEL
95/6 DEL 425
96/7 DEL 62

VITALE, PHIL
52/3 LavalDairy 72
52/3 StLawrence 28

VITEK, JIRI
95/6 APS 214

VITELI, JARMO
70/1 Kuvajulkaisut 326
71/2 WilliamsFIN 358
72/3 WilliamsFIN 340

VITELI, PETRI
71/2 WilliamsFIN 359

VITOLINSH, HARIJS
93/4 ClassicProspects 197
95/6 ElitSet 285
90/1 O-Pee-Chee 521
93/4 Parkhurst 496
93/4 UpperDeck 428
95/6 udElite 183

VITUCCI, NICK
91/2 Greensboro
92/3 Hampton
93/4 Peoria
93/4 Toledo 7
94/5 Toledo

VIVEIROS, EMANUEL
96/7 DEL 314
88/9 ProCards(Kalamazoo)
90/1 ProCards 183
84/5 PrinceAlbert

VIZZUTTI, CHAD
92/3 BCJHL 159

VLACH, ROSTISLAV
94/5 APS 246
95/6 APS 18, 390
91/2 Jyvas-Hyva 38
89 SemicSticker 194

VLASAK, TOMAS
94/5 APS 218
95/6 APS 169
93/4 Parkhurst 515

VLASOV, IGOR
95/6 UpperDeckElite DS2

VLASSENKOV, DMITRI
97/8 UDBlackDiamond 124
98/9 UDChoice 287

VLK, PETR
95/6 APS 187
89 SemicSticker 189
91 SemicSticker 123

VLZEK, IVAN
94/5 APS 147
95/6 Sisu 276, 384, -Double 7
96/7 Sisu 72

VODILA, JAN
89 SemicSticker 192

VODRAZKA, JAN
95/6 Slapshot 72

VOGEL, TONY
94/5 DEL 303
95/6 DEL 183, 250
92 SemicSticker 192
81/2 Regina 23
82/3 Regina 11
83/4 Regina 11

VOHRALIK, KAREL
74 Hellas 84
73/4 WilliamsFIN 62

VOISARD, GAETAN
91/2 UD 664, 'CzechWJC 25

VOJTYNEK, HENRYK
74 Hellas 90
73/4 WilliamsFIN 103

VOKOUN, TOMAS
94/5 APS 48
97/8 Donruss 209, -Rated 1
97/8 DonrussCanadianIce 138
97/8 Leaf 157
97/8 PinnacleInside 72
96/7 Fredericton

VOLAK, MILAN
94/5 APS 151
95/6 APS 258

VOLCAN, MICKEY
83/4 O-Pee-Chee 94
90/1 ProCards 365
83/4 SouhaitsRen.KeyChain
83/4 Vachon 20
82/3 HFD/JuniorWhalers
84/5 Moncton 13
85/6 NovaScotia 24

VOLCHKOV, ALEXANDRE
96/7 AllSportPPF 73
97/8 Bowman 12
95/6 FutureLegends-SS&D 1
97 SB'AutColl 48, GB30
95/6 Slapshot 16, 431

VOLCHKOV, ALEXANDER (SR.)
74 Hellas 61
73/4 Soviet Stars 13
91/2 Trends 59
73/4 WilliamsFIN 21

VOLEK, DAVID
95/6 APS 270
90/1 Bowman 127
91/2 Bowman 223
92/3 Bowman 196
92/3 FleerUltra 350
89/90 OPC/Topps 85, OPC 309
90/1 OPC/Topps 300
91/2 OPC/Topps 488
92/3 O-Pee-Chee 3
89/90 opcSticker 43/189,113/250
89/90 opcStickFS 9
89/90 PaniniSticker 267
91/2 PaniniSticker 241
92/3 PaniniSticker 200
91/2 Parkhurst 104
92/3 Parkhurst 340
93/4 Parkhurst 395
94/5 Parkhurst 139
91/2 Pinnacle 198
92/3 Pinnacle 188
93/4 Pinnacle 423
93/4 PowerPlay 388
93/4 Premier 371
90/1 ProSet 193
91/2 ProSet 147
91/2 PSPlatinum 75
90/1 Score 12
91/2 Score(CDN) 88, (U.S) 88
92/3 Score 166
93/4 Score 495
91 SemicSticker 222
93 SemicSticker 108
92/3 Topps 204
91/2 ToppsStadiumClub 204
92/3 ToppsStadiumClub 319
93/4 ToppsStadiumClub 324
90/1 UpperDeck 1
91/2 UpperDeck 89, 173
92/3 UpperDeck 313
93/4 UpperDeck 370
89/90 NYI

VÖLK, JOSEF
72 Hellas 45
72 SemicSticker 96

VOLKOV, MIKHAIL
93/4 ClassicProspects 104
91/2 UD'CzechWJC 5
93/4 Rochester
95/6 Rochester

VOLLAND, ANDREAS
94/5 DEL 188
95/6 DEL 188

VOLLHOFFER, TROY
88/9 ProCards(Muskegon)
88/9 Flint
84/5 Saskatoon

VOLMAR, DOUG
73/4 O-Pee-Chee 215

VOLOGIAMINOV, IVAN
94/5 Slapshot(MEM) 6
93/4 Lethbridge

VOLPE, MIKE
85/6 Kitchener 10

VOLSTAD, CRAIG
91/2 AirCanadaSJHL C17

VOLTSHKOV, A.
see Alexander Volchkov

VON STEFENELLI, PHIL
92/3 Hamilton
91/2 ProCards 604

VONTRZCINSKI, A.
95/6 DEL 198

VOPAT, JAN
94/5 APS 211
95/6 APS 362
92/3 Classic 36
92/3 ClasicFourSport-Autograph
96/7 Donruss 216
95/6 EdgeIce 186
96/7 FleerUltra 83
96/7 Leaf 222
97/8 PacificCrown 271
95 PaniniWorlds 193
96/7 Pinnacle 214
94 Semic 171
95 Semic 143
91/2 UD 'CzechWJC 95
92/3 UpperDeck 601
97/8 UpperDeck 79
97/8 UDCollChoice 126
96 Wien 108
95/6 Phoenix

VOPAT, ROMAN
95/6 Bowman 139
95/6 Donruss 307
96/7 Donruss 216
97/8 Donruss 147
96/7 Fleer 135, -Calder 10
97/8 Leaf 69
97/8 Limited 129, 180
96/7 MetalUniverse 194
95/6 Parkhurst 447
96/7 Pinnacle 231
97/8 PinnacleBeAPlayer 103
96/7 Score 252
94/5 SigRookies 2
95/6 SkyBoxImpact 219
96/7 SkyBoxImpact 162
94/5 SRGoldStandard 97
95/6 UpperDeck 440
97/8 UpperDeck 78
97/8 UDCollChoice 124
95/6 PrinceAlbert

VORDERBRUGGEN, REINER
94/5 DEL 335

VOREL, MAREK
95/6 APS 346

VORLICEK, FRANTISEK
94/5 APS 295
95/6 APS 174

VOROBIEV, ILYA
94/5 DEL 109
96/7 DEL 57

VOROBIEV, PIOTR
94/5 DEL 103
95/6 DEL 100

VOROBIEV, VLADIMIR
97/8 Donruss 210
97/8 DonrussCanadianIce 139
97/8 Limited 97, 121, 197
98/9 Pacific 304
97/8 Pinnacle 188
97/8 PinnacleInside 123
97/8 Score 75
97/8 Score(NYR) 13
97/8 UDCollChoice 164
96/7 Binghampton

VORONOV, SERGEI
95/6 Hampton HRA22

VOS, RALPH
96/7 DEL 222

VOSHELL, TOD
83/4 Kelowna

VOSKERTIAN, CHRISTIAN
79 PaniniSticker 342

VOSS, CARL
34-43 BeeHives(DET)
35-40 CrownBrand 79
36-39 DiamondMatch (1), (2), (3)
83&87 HallOfFame 225
83 HHOF Postcard (O)
37/8 OPC (V304E) 175
36/7 WWGum (V356) 66

VOSSEN, DALE
91/2 SketchWHL 236

VOSSEN, JAMIE
95/6 Slapshot 211

VOSTA, ONDREJ
94/5 APS 108
95/6 APS 69

VOSTRIKOV, SERGEI
91/2 O-Pee-Chee 27R

VOZAR, PATRICK
94/5 DEL 122
95/6 DEL 122

VRABEC, THOMAS
91 SemicSticker 200
92 SemicSticker 215

VRATARIC, RICH
95/6 Slapshot 196

VRLA, DAN
94/5 APS 232
95/6 APS 11

VUJTEK, VLADIMIR
94/5 APS 131
95/6 APS 303
93/4 FleerUltra 319
94/5 FleerUltra 293
93/4 Parkhurst 339
92/3 Pinnacle 396
97/8 PinnacleBeAPlayer 113
93/4 PowerPlay 343
93/4 Premier 459
94/5 Premier 503
93/4 Score 465
91/2 SketchWHL 303
93/4 StadiumClub 278
92/3 UpperDeck 417, 496
93/4 UpperDeck 168
92/3 EDM
92/3 EDM/IGA 22
93/4 EDM 29JAN94

VUJTEK, VLADIMIR (SR.)
94/5 APS 293
95/6 APS 27

VUKONICH, MIKE
92/3 Classic 110
92/3 ClassicFourSport 219
91/2 ProCards 391
92/3 Phoenix

VUKOTA, MICK
90/1 OPC/Topps 10
91/2 OPC/Topps 25
98/9 Pacific 259
94/5 ParkieSE 101
97/8 PinnacleBeAPlayer 56
90/1 ProSet 488
91/2 Score(CDN) 387
92/3 Score(U.S) 549
91/2 ToppsStadiumClub 309
90/1 UpperDeck 39
91/2 UpperDeck 135
95/6 UpperDeck 380
97/8 MTL
89/90 NYI
84/5 KelownaWings&WHL 22

VUORI, ARI
92/3 Jyvas-Hyva 187
93/4 Jyvas-Hyva 319
89 SemicSticker 49
93/4 Sisu 51, 109
95/6 Sisu 191

VUORINEN, JARMO
80/1 Mallasjuoma 22

VUORINEN, J.P.
78/9 SM-Liiga 108

VUORINEN, TEEMU
95/6 Sisu 234
96/7 Sisu 28

VUORIO, JARI
80/1 Mallasjuoma 67

VUORIO, MATTI
93/4 Sisu 282

VUORIVIRTA, JUHA
94/5 SigRookies 29
95/6 Sisu 120, -NHLDraft 10
94/5 ToppsFinest 141

VYBORNY, DAVID
95/6 APS 280
94/5 Classic 77
94 Semic 185
95 Semic 148
92/3 UpperDeck 600
97/8 udSwedish 165
94/5 CapeBreton

VYBORNY, FRANTISEK
94/5 APS 283
95/6 APS 267

VYHLIDAL, MICHAEL
94/5 APS 169
95/6 APS 179

VYKOUKAL, JIRI
95/6 APS 271, 360
94/5 ElitSet 279, -Foreign 6
95 Globe 152
95 PaniniWorlds 195
90/1 ProCards 214
91/2 ProCards 562
96 Wien 107

WADDELL, DON
91/2 ProCards 332
87/8 Flint
88/9 Flint

WADEL, JASON
91/2 SketchOHL 238

WAGAR, BLAIR
91/2 AirCanadaSJHL A41

WÄGER, ROMAN
91 SemicSticker 193
93 SemicSticker 123

WAGHORN, GRAHAM
94 Semic 317

WAGHORNE, FRED
83&87 HallOfFame 119
83 HHOF Postcard (H)

WAGNER, BERND
94/5 DEL 250
91 SemicSticker 161

WAGNER, THOMAS
94/5 DEL 403
95/6 DEL 422

WAHL, GREG
91/2 AirCanadaSJHL C33
92/3 MPSPhotoSJHL 138

WAHL, HENRIK
70/1 Kuvajulkaisut 289

WAHLBERG, MIKAEL
94/5 ElitSet 163
95/6 ElitSet 21
92/3 SemicElitserien 65
95/6 udElite 30

WAHLSTEN, JALI
92/3 Jyvas-Hyva 67
93/4 Jyvas-Hyva 118
93 SemicSticker 86

WAHLSTEN, JUHANI
66/7 Champion 78
65/6 Hellas 8

WAHLSTEN, SAMI
94 Semic 45
93 SemicSticker 87
93/4 Sisu 19

WAHLSTEN, VEIJO
73/4 WilliamsFIN 302

WAIBEL, HARALD
94/5 DEL 308
95/6 DEL 145

WAINIO, PATRICK
78/9 SM-Liiga 66

WAISER, DERRICK
97/8 Bowman 68

WAITE, JIMMY
91/2 Bowman 396
92/3 Bowman 120
93/4 Donruss 302
93/4 Durivage 49
93/4 FleerUltra 419
93/4 Leaf 324
94/5 Leaf 405
90/1 OPC/Topps 214
91/2 OPC/Topps 127
98/9 Pacific 346
92/3 Parkhurst 270
93/4 Parkhurst 181
94/5 Parkhurst 214
91/2 Pinnacle 316
93/4 Pinnacle 371
94/5 Pinnacle MA9
93/4 PowerPlay 438
93/4 Premier 388
94/5 Premier 496
89/90 ProCards(IHL) 73
90/1 ProCards 401
91/2 ProSet 530
90/1 Score 407
91/2 ScoreCDN 632
91/2 ScoreTraded 82T
93/4 Score 365, 539
92/3 Topps 100
92/3 ToppsStadiumClub 35
91/2 UpperDeck 443
92/3 UpperDeck 67
93/4 UpperDeck 501
94/5 UDBeAPlayer-Aut. 126
88/9 CHI/Coke
91/2 CHI/Coke
97/8 PHO
92/3 S.J/PacificBell

WAKALUK, DARCY
91/2 Bowman 33
92/3 Bowman 148
94/5 ClassicImages PL9
93/4 Donruss 420
94/5 Donruss 17
92/3 FleerUltra 99
94/5 FleerUltra 282
95/6 FleerUltra 231
94/5 Leaf 152
92/3 O-Pee-Chee 63
94/5 PaniniSticker 234
91/2 Parkhurst 306
92/3 Parkhurst 315
95/6 Parkhurst 331
94/5 ParkieSE 44
94/5 Pinnacle 157
93/4 PowerPlay 327
93/4 Premier 399
94/5 Premier 81, 424
88/9 ProCards(Rochester)
89/90 ProCards(AHL) 258
90/1 ProCards 288
91/2 ScoreCDN 653
92/3 Score 313
93/4 Score 432
95/6 Score 197
96/7 Score 210
92/3 Topps 108
95/6 Topps 313
95/6 ToppsFinest 156
92/3 ToppsStadiumClub 153
93/4 ToppsStadiumClub 276
94/5 ToppsStadiumClub 187

94/5 UpperDeck 459
95/6 UDBeAPlayer 90
94/5 DAL
94/5 DAL/Southwest
96/7 PHO
97/8 PHO
83/4 KelownaWings
84/5 KelownaWingsWHL 2

WAKEFIELD, LANCE
91/2 AirCanadaSJHL D50

WAKELY, ERNIE
70/1 Colgate Stamp 92
70/1 EddieSargent 181
71/2 EddieSargent 185
70/1 Esso Stamp
72/3 Letraset 12
70/1 OPC/Topps 97
71/2 OPC/Topps 81
75/6 opcWHA 132
76/7 opcWHA 92
73/4 QuakerOats 41
71/2 TheTorontoSun
71/2 STL
76/7 SanDiegoMariners

WALBERT, TORE
79 PaniniSticker 294

WALBY, STEFFAN
92/3 BCJHL 61, 246
93/4 ClassicProspects 97
93/4 StJohns
94/5 StJohns
95/6 StJohns

WALCOT, BRAD
82/3 Kingston 22
83/4 Oshawa 13
85/6 Sudbury 24

WALCOTT, RICHIE
91/2 ProCards 564
93/4 Hampton

WALDER, RAYMOND
91 SemicSticker 191
92 SemicSticker 205

WÄLITALO, GÖTE
82 SemicSticker 2

WALKER, CHAD
83/4 Kelowna

WALKER, DARBY
91/2 SketchWHL 312

WALKER, GORD
88/9 ProCards(NewHaven)
89/90 ProCards(AHL) 22
84/5 Kamloops

WALKER, HOWARD
82/3 O-Pee-Chee 59
80/1 WSH
81/2 WSH

WALKER, JACK
83&87 HallOfFame 75
83 HHOF Postcard (E)
94/5 HHOFLegends 47

WALKER, JEFF
89/90 SketchOHL 148
90/1 SketchOHL 272
91/2 SketchOHL 133
89/90 NiagaraFalls
91/2 Peterborough 17

WALKER, JOHN
94/5 DEL 242
95/6 DEL 236
96/7 DEL 87
88/9 ProCards(Utica)

WALKER, KELLY
85/6 Arizona

WALKER, KURT
78/9 O-Pee-Chee 282
76/7 TOR
77/8 TOR

WALKER, SCOTT
95/6 Bowman 143
93/4 ClassicProspects 165
95/6 Donruss 303
95/6 EdgeIce 90
95/6 Leaf 108
98/9 PacificParamount 129
97/8 PacificRegime 205
95/6 Parkhurst 484
97/8 PinnacleBeAPlayer 33
91/2 SketchOHL 274
95/6 UpperDeck 418
96/7 UpperDeck 351
96/7 VAN
96/7 VAN/IGA
93/4 OwenSound

WALKER, TODD
91/2 SketchOHL 9
91/2 Cornwall 11

WALL, BOB
64-67 BeeHives(DET)
70/1 DadsCookies
70/1 EddieSargent 191
71/2 EddieSargent 50
70/1 Esso Stamp
68/9 O-Pee-Chee 156
69/70 OPC 140, -Sticker
70/1 OPC/Topps 98
72/3 OPC 323
68/9 ShirriffCoin LA3
66/7 Topps 49

WALL, KYÖSTI
65/6 Hellas 62

WALLACE, BRUCE
52/3 AnonymousOHL 58

WALLACE, GREG
85/6 Kamloops

WALLENBERG, PATRIK
95/6 UpperDeck 563
95/6 UDCollChoice 352
95/6 udElite 70
97/8 udSwedish 66

WALLENIUS, JUHANI
80/1 Mallasjuoma 131
78/9 SM-Liiga 173

WALLIN, CLAES-GORAN
91/2 SemicElitserien 311

WALLIN, ESA
80/1 Mallasjuoma 122

WALLIN, JESSE
95/6 Bowman P35
97/8 Bowman 104
98/9 UDChoice 262
96/7 UpperDeck"Ice" 128
95/6 RedDeer

WALLIN, MAGNUS
89/90 SemicElitserien 257

WALLIN, MATS
79 PaniniSticker 188

WALLIN, NICLAS
97/8 udSwedish 25

WALLIN, PER
94/5 ElitSet 21
95/6 ElitSet 118
90/1 SemicElitserien 24
91/2 SemicElitserien 218
92/3 SemicElitserien 270

WALLIN, PETER
94/5 AutoPhonex 40
95/6 ElitSet 161, -Rookies 1
89/90 SemicElitserien 129
95/6 TetradAutobilia 54
95/6 UDCollChoice 354
95/6 udElite 177

WALLWORK, BOB
91/2 Cincinnati

WALSER, DERRICK
98 BowmanCHL 119
98/9 Topps 229
96/7 Rimouski

WALSH
91/2 AvantGardeBCJHL 160

WALSH, FLAT
27-32 LaPresse 29/30

WALSH, GORD
95/6 Classic 87
93/4 Slapshot(Kingston) 7
95/6 Slapshot 112

WALSH, KURT
95/6 Bowman P36
95/6 Slapshot 249, 304, 437

WALSH, MARTY
91 C55 Reprint 11
83&87 HallOfFame 89
83 HHOF Postcard (F)
1910-11 Imperial (C56) 7
1911-12 Imperial (C55) 11
1912-13 Imperial (C57) 49
1910-11 Imperial Post 11

WALSH, MIKE
88/9 ProCards(Springfield)
89/90 ProCards(AHL) 230
91/2 ProCards 52

WALSH, SHAWN
93/4 Classic 59

WALSH, TREVOR
90/1 SketchOHL 194
89/90 Windsor

WALTER, JAROSLAV
95/6 APS 198

WALTER, RYAN
86/7 Kraft Sports 41
79/80 OPC/Topps 236
80/1 OPC/Topps 154
81/2 OPC 352, Topps(E) 122
82/3 O-Pee-Chee 194
83/4 O-Pee-Chee 200
84/5 O-Pee-Chee 275
86/7 O-Pee-Chee 224
87/8 O-Pee-Chee 231
88/9 O-Pee-Chee 262
89/90 O-Pee-Chee 240
90/1 OPC/Topps 296
81/2 opcSticker 192
82/3 opcSticker 152
83/4 opcSticker 62, 63
84/5 opcSticker 159
87/8 opcSticker 17/157
88/9 opcSticker 40/171
90/1 Panini(MTL) 24
88/9 PaniniSticker 262
91/2 Parkhurst 401
92/3 Pinnacle 255
82/3 Post
90/1 ProSet 475
91/2 ProSet 504
83/4 PuffySticker 3
91/2 Score(CDN) 591, (U.S) 41T
93/4 ToppsStadiumClub 185
83/4 Vachon 58
82/3 MTL
82/3 MTL/Steinberg
83/4 MTL
84/5 MTL
85/6 MTL
85/6 MTL/ProvigoStickers
85/6? MTL/ProvigoPlacemats
86/7 MTL
87/8 MTL
87/8 MTL/Stickers 24, 25
88/9 MTL
89/90 MTL
89/90 MTL/Kraft
90/1 MTL
91/2 VAN
78/9 WSH
79/80 WSH
80/1 WSH
81/2 WSH
84/5 KelownaWings 36

WALTERS, GREG
90/1 ProCards 147
91/2 ProCards 349
89/90 SketchOHL 50
90/1 Newmarket

WALTERS, RON
72/3 O-Pee-Chee 301

WALTERS, S.
28/9 PaulinsCandy 69

WALTIN, MATS
89/90 SemicElitserien 57
90/1 SemicElitserien 56
74 SemicSticker 18
82 SemicSticker 6

WALTON, JIM
82/3 Post
71/2 TheTorontoSun

WALTON, MIKE
64-67 BeeHives(TOR)
65/6 CocaCola
70/1 Colgate Stamp 3
70/1 DadsCookies
70/1 EddieSargent 206
71/2 EddieSargent 12
72/3 EddieSargent 24
70/1 Esso Stamp
68/9 OPC/Topps 132
69/70 OPC/T. 50, OPC-Sticker
70/1 OPC/Topps 109
71/2 OPC/Topps 171
72/3 OPC 94
73/4 opc-Posters 15
76/7 OPC/Topps 23
77/8 OPC 350
78/9 OPC/Topps 38
74/5 opcWHA 10
75/6 opcWHA 26
95/6 Parkie(66/7) 101
68/9 Post Marble
68/9 ShirriffCoin TOR5
71/2 TheTorontoSun
65/6 Topps 86
66/7 Topps 14, -USATest 14
67/8 Topps 15
67/8 York 13, 23, [3x no#]
71/2 BOS
69/70 TOR
70/1 TOR
76/7 VAN/RoyalBank
77/8 VAN/GingerAle
77/8 VAN/RoyalBank
74/5 Minnesota

WALZ, WES
91/2 Bowman 353
93/4 Donruss 57
94/5 Donruss 319
93/4 FleerUltra 287
94/5 FleerUltra 37
93/4 Leaf 393
94/5 Leaf 154
91/2 OPC/Topps 134
90/1 opcPremier 127
93/4 Parkhurst 305
94/5 Parkhurst 38
94/5 POG 62
94/5 Premier 137
91/2 ProCards 48
90/1 ProSet 589
90/1 Score 418
91/2 Score(CDN) 430
91/2 ToppsStadiumClub 325
90/1 UpperDeck 527
91/2 UpperDeck 123
93/4 UpperDeck 431
94/5 UpperDeck 350
90/1 BOS/SportsAction
95/6 Adirondack
88/9 Lethbridge
89/90 Lethbridge

WAMSLEY, RICK
90/1 Bowman 98
91/2 Bowman 268
92/3 Bowman 97
72-84 Dernière 83/4
82/3 McDonalds 5
82/3 O-Pee-Chee 195
83/4 O-Pee-Chee 201
86/7 O-Pee-Chee 240
87/8 OPC/Topps 65
89/90 O-Pee-Chee 204
90/1 O-Pee-Chee 409
91/2 OPC/Topps 459
92/3 O-Pee-Chee 310
82/3 opcSticker 37, 252
83/4 opcSticker 72
84/5 opcSticker 157
86/7 opcSticker 179/43
87/8 opcSticker 22/163
89/90 opcSticker 93 /232
90/1 Panini(CGY) 24
87/8 PaniniSticker 305
90/1 PaniniSticker 186
91/2 Parkhurst 394
90/1 ProSet 48
91/2 ProSet 367
90/1 Score 309
91/2 Score(CDN) 232
92/3 Topps 425
91/2 ToppsStadiumClub 294
92/3 ToppsStadiumClub 53
90/1 UpperDeck 10
91/2 UpperDeck 130
83/4 Vachon 59
90/1 CGY/McGavins
91/2 CGY/IGA
81/2 MTL
82/3 MTL
82/3 MTL/Steinberg
83/4 MTL
87/8 STL/Kodak

WANCHUK, MIKE
77/8 Kalamazoo

WANHAINEN, ROLF
92/3 UpperDeck 223

WANNSTROM, JORGEN
89/90 SemicElitserien 212

WARD, AARON
93/4 Classic 85
93/4 ClassicProspects 120
94/5 ClassicAutograph
94/5 ClassicImages 98
93/4 Donruss 93
95/6 EdgeIce 5
93/4 Leaf 359
94/5 Leaf 312
97/8 PacificRegime 74
93/4 Parkhurst 262
95/6 Parkhurst 71
93/4 Pinnacle 432
97/8 PinnacleBeAPlayer 200
93/4 Premier 484
94/5 Score 229
93/4 ToppsStadiumClub 423
93/4 UpperDeck 479
94/5 UpperDeck 153
97/8 UpperDeck 270
95/6 Adirondack

WARD, CALEB
94/5 Slapshot(Windsor) 23
95/6 Slapshot 26

WARD, COLIN
92/3 WestMich.
93/4 WestMich.

WARD, DIXON
92/3 Classic 84
93/4 Donruss 449
92/3 FleerUltra 431
93/4 FleerUltra 102
93/4 Leaf 97
92/3 opcPremier 67
98/9 Pacific 112
98/9 PacificParamount 24
97/8 PacificRegime 24
92/3 Parkhurst 194
93/4 Parkhurst 209
94/5 Parkhurst 102
93/4 Pinnacle 176
94/5 Pinnacle 239
96/7 PinnacleBeAPlayer 130
93/4 PowerPlay 257, 365
93/4 Premier 58, 127
94/5 Premier 112
93/4 Score 210, 654
97/8 Score(BUF) 3
93/4 ToppsStadiumClub 454
92/3 UpperDeck 580, CC1
93/4 UpperDeck 62, SP-167
97/8 UpperDeck 21
93/4 VAN/Coins
95/6 Rochester

WARD, ED
95/6 Bowman 105
93/4 ClassicProspects 196
97/8 PacificRegime 33
95/6 Parkhurst 305
97/8 PinnacleBeAPlayer 172

WARD, GEORGE
94/5 Slapshot(Kitchener) 27
95/6 Slapshot 155

WARD, JASON
97/8 Bowman 129, BB5
98 BowmanCHL 9
95/6 Slapshot 186
96/7 UpperDeck 388
98/9 UDChoice 272
97/8 UDCollChoice 303

WARD, JIM
34-43 BeeHives(MTL.M)
33/4 CndGum (V252)
35-40 CrownBrand 121, 154
27-32 LaPresse 28/9
34/5 OPC (V304B) 56
37/8 OPC (V304E) 170
38/9 QuakerOats
34/5 SweetCaporal
33/4 WWGum (V357) 37
36/7 WWGum (V356) 2

WARD, LANCE
95/6 Bowman P37
95/6 RedDeer

WARD, RON
72/3 O-Pee-Chee 332
74/5 opcWHA 21
75/6 opcWHA 73
76/7 opcWHA 35
73/4 QuakerOats 34
72/3 7ElevenCups
71/2 TheTorontoSun
69/70 TOR
71/2 VAN/RoyalBank 8

WARD, SPENCER
92/3 BCJHL 192

WARD, WES
94/5 Slapshot(Windsor) 13
95/6 Slapshot 417

WARDEN, JIM
79 PaniniSticker 207

WARDEN, TOM
93/4 ThunderBay

WARE, JEFF
95/6 Classic 15, 91
94/5 ClassicImages 86
97/8 DonrussCanadianIce 129
94/5 ParkieSE 257
94/5 Select 163
95/6 Slapshot 246
94/5 SP 188
97/8 UpperDeck 370
96/7 UpperDeck"Ice" 131

WARE, MIKE
88/9 ProCards(CapeBreton)
90/1 ProCards 232
88/9 EDM/ActionMagazine 151
97/8 SheffieldSteelers
93/4 Mich.State
95/6 StJohns

WARES, EDDIE
34-43 BeeHives(DET)
39/40 OPC (V301-1) 73

WARNER, JIM
79/80 O-Pee-Chee 384
79 PaniniSticker 221

WARR, ANDREW
97/8 Halifax (2)

WARR, STEVE
72/3 Ottawa

WARRENER, RHETT
95/6 Bowman 108
95/6 Donruss 358
95/6 DonrussElite-WorldJrs 9
96/7 PinnacleBeAPlayer 138
94/5 SigRookies 35,-GoldStd 98
95/6 Topps 272
95/6 ToppsStadiumClub 140
95/6 UpperDeck 528
96/7 UpperDeck 266
96/7 FLA/WinnDixie
97/8 FLA/WinnDixie (x2)
93/4 Saskatoon

WARRENER, TREVOR
91/2 AirCanadaSJHL B7
92/3 MPSPhotoSJHL 129

WARRINER, MIKE
92/3 BCJHL 146

WARRINER, TODD
95/6 Bowman 106
93/4 ClassicProspects LP20
93/4 CanadaNats
94/5 Classic 108
95/6 Donruss 85
97/8 Donruss 91
93/4 FleerUltra 476
95/6 Leaf 101
97/8 Limited 162
97/8 PacificCrown 257
97/8 PaniniSticker 177
95/6 Parkhurst 472
95/6 Pinnacle 219
96/7 PinnacleBeAPlayer 122
97/8 PinnacleInside 166
93/4 PowerPlay 496
93/4 Premier-TeamCanada 19
94/5 Score CT3
95/6 Score 296
97/8 Score 207
97/8 Score(TOR) 9
90/1 SketchOHL 195
91/2 SketchOHL 173
93/4 Slapshot(Kitchener) 15
95/6 Topps 45
96/7 UpperDeck 163
97/8 UpperDeck 163
94/5 UDBeAPlayer R163
96/7 UDBlackDiamond 93
97/8 UDCollChoice 254
94/5 StJohns
95/6 StJohns
92/3 Windsor 17, 31

WARRING, JEREMY
90/1 SketchWHL 102
91/2 SketchWHL 22

WARUS, MIKE
88/9 ProCards(Moncton)

WARWICK, GRANT
34-43 BeeHives(NYR)
45-64 BeeHives(BOS), (MTL)
48-52 Exhibits
45-54 QuakerOats

WASAMA, JARMO
65/6 Hellas 124
96/7 Sisu 190

WASHBURN, STEVE
95/6 Classic 92
94/5 ClassicImages 36, -Aut.
97/8 Donruss 115
95/6 EdgeIce 25
96/7 FleerUltra 71
96/7 Leaf 237
96/7 LeafPreferred 138
97/8 Omega 103
98/9 Pacific 229
97/8 PacificRegime 90
96/7 Pinnacle 232
97/8 PinnacleBeAPlayer 139
91/2 SketchOHL 308
98/9 Topps 158
97/8 UDCollChoice 107
97/8 FLA/WinnDixie
92/3 Ottawa

WASHKURAK, JOEL
90/1 SketchOHL 72

WASKE, RON
83/4 NYI/Islander 30

WASLEY, CHARLIE
92/3 Minnesota
93/4 Minnesota
94/5 Minnesota

WASNIE, NICK
33/4 CndGum V252
33/4 Hamilton (V288) 1
33/4 OPC (V304A) 47
28/9 PaulinsCandy 64

WASSERMANN, SEPP
94/5 DEL 339
95/6 DEL 306

WASYLKO, STEVE
95/6 Bowman P38
95/6 Slapshot 71

WASYLUK, TREVOR
95/6 Bowman P39
95/6 UpperDeck 512

WATCHORN, JEFF
89/90 SketchMEM 13
90/1 SketchWHL 292
91/2 SketchWHL 92
89/90 Kamloops

WATHEM , TREVOR
91/2 AirCanadaSJHL A16
92/3 MPSPhotoSJHL 61

WATKINS, LANNY
90/1 SketchWHL 258
91/2 SketchWHL 320

WATSON, BILL
86/7 OPC/Topps 151
87/8 PaniniSticker 232
88/9 ProCards(Saginaw)
86/7 CHI/Coke
87/8 CHI/Coke

WATSON, BLAKE
24/5 Crescent Falcons 14

WATSON, BRENT
90/1 SketchOHL 223
91/2 SketchOHL 351

WATSON, BRYAN
70/1 DadsCookies
70/1 EddieSargent 164
71/2 EddieSargent 164
72/3 EddieSargent 172
70/1 Esso Stamp
82? JDMcCarthy
74/5 Loblaws
68/9 OPC 173
70/1 OPC 204
71/2 OPC 132
72/3 OPC 90, 268
73/4 OPC 14
76/7 OPC 385
77/8 OPC 342
78/9 OPC 316
69/70 OPC/Topps 112
74/5 OPC/Topps 5, 259
75/6 OPC/Topps 31
76/7 OPC/Topps 4, 228
72 SemicSticker 217
71/2 TheTorontoSun
65/6 Topps 45
66/7 Topps 48
72/3 Topps 65, 116
73/4 Topps 144
80/1 EDM/Zellers
88/9 EDM/ActionMagazine 124
67/8 MTL
71/2 PGH

WATSON, HARRY
34-43 BeeHives(NYA)
45-64 BeeHives(TOR)
25 Dominion 114
83&87 HallOfFame 105
83 HHOF Postcard (G)
96/7 HHOFLegends 79
51/2 Parkhurst 70
52/3 Parkhurst 46
53/4 Parkhurst 12
54/5 Parkhurst 17
93/4 Parkhurst DPR11
93/4 Parkie(56/7) 36
45-54 QuakerOats (x2)
54-67 TorontoStar V5, n6
91/2 Ultimate06 46, -Aut 46
25 Willards 43

WATSON, JIM
77/8 Coke Mini
70/1 EddieSargent 32
71/2 EddieSargent 21
70/1 Esso Stamp
74/5 Loblaws
74/5 OPC 303
82/3 OPC 259
68/9 OPC/Topps 90
69/70 OPC/Topps 93
71/2 OPC/Topps 165
75/6 OPC/Topps 202
76/7 OPC/Topps 247
77/8 OPC/Topps 43
78/9 OPC/Topps 247
79/80 OPC/Topps 26
80/1 OPC/Topps 224
72/3 7ElevenCups
68/9 ShirriffCoin DET15
67/8 Topps 107
90/1 UpperDeck 514
75/6 PHA/GingerAle
72/3 LosAngelesSharks

WATSON, JOE
77/8 Coke Mini
70/1 DadsCookies
70/1 EddieSargent 156
71/2 EddieSargent 158
72/3 EddieSargent 159
70/1 Esso Stamp
74/5 Loblaws
70/1 OPC/Topps 79, OPC 144
72/3 OPC 62, Topps 156
73/4 OPC/Topps 91
74/5 OPC/Topps 217
75/6 OPC/Topps 281
76/7 OPC/Topps 45
77/8 OPC/Topps 247
78/9 OPC/Topps 43
92/3 Parkhurst 474
95/6 Parkie(66/7) 3
71/2 TheTorontoSun
66/7 Topps 33
75/6 PHA/GingerAle

WATSON, PHIL
52/3 AnonymousOHL 80
34-43 BeeHives(NYR)
39/40 OPC (V301-1) 83
43-47 ParadeSportive
93/4 Parkie(56/7) 108
61/2 ShirriffCoin 19
61/2 Topps 1
62/3 Topps 1
36/7 WWGum (V356) 80

WATSON, ROSS
52/3 AnonymousOHL 159

WATT, MIKE
95/6 DonrussElite-WorldJrs 21
98/9 SPx"Finite" 138
95/6 UpperDeck 536
97/8 EDM

WATT, TOM
90/1 ProSet 677
90/1 TOR/P.L.A.Y. 5
81/2 WPG
82/3 WPG
95/6 StJohns

WATTERS, TIM
82/3 O-Pee-Chee 395
83/4 O-Pee-Chee 394
84/5 O-Pee-Chee 350
87/8 O-Pee-Chee 219
89/90 O-Pee-Chee 212
90/1 O-Pee-Chee 461
82/3 Post
93/4 Premier 298
90/1 ProSet 458
90/1 Score 204
91/2 ScoreCDN 523
83/4 StaterMint H12
90/1 UpperDeck 117
91/2 UpperDeck 471
83/4 Vachon 139
88/9 L.A/Smokeys
89/90 L.A/Smokeys 2
90/1 L.A/Smokeys 4
81/2 WPG
82/3 WPG
83/4 WPG
84/5 WPG/Police
85/6 WPG
85/6 WPG/Police
86/7 WPG
87/8 WPG
90/1 Mich.Tech
92/3 Phoenix

WATTS, MORGAN
85/6 London 8

WAVER, JEFF
88/9 ProCards(Muskegon)
90/1 ProCards 523
84/5 Brandon 16
85/6 Brandon 16

WAY, JIM
89/90 Sudbury 9

WAY, SHAWN
89/90 SketchOHL 84

WEAVER, DAVE
92/3 WestMich.

WEAVER, JASON
90/1 SketchOHL 348
91/2 SketchOHL 160
90/1 Oshawa 25
91/2 Oshawa
91/2 Oshawa/Dominos 18

WEAVER, SCOTT
91/2 AirCanadaSJHL D23

WEBB, STEPHEN
97/8 PacificCrown 248
97/8 UpperDeck 308
92/3 Windsor 22

WEBBER, MIKE
83/4 NorthBay

WEBER, CHRISTIAN
95 Globe 212
91 SemicSticker 196
92 SemicSticker
93 SemicSticker 125

WEBER, MARC
91/2 UD 666, 'CzechWJC 27

WEBER, PATRIK
94/5 APS 42
95/6 APS 329

WEBSTER, CHRIS
87/8 Brockville 19
88/9 Brockville 23

WEBSTER, DAVE
82/3 Kitchener 30

WEBSTER, GLEN
90/1 SketchWHL 230
89/90 Brandon 14
90/1 Brandon 10

WEBSTER, TOM
70/1 DadsCookies
70/1 EddieSargent 57
71/2 EddieSargent 135
70/1 Esso Stamp
70/1 OPC 155
71/2 OPC/Topps 78
74/5 opcWHA 8
75/6 opcWHA 95
76/7 opcWHA 14
77/8 opcWHA 55
90/1 ProSet 667
70/1 DET/Marathon
94/5 PHA
72/3 NewEngland

WECKSTRÖM, KARI
80/1 Mallasjuoma 150

WEDL, ALEXANDER
94/5 DEL 107
95/6 DEL 152
96/7 DEL 230

WEEKES, KEVIN
97/8 DonrussPriority 177
95/6 EdgeIce 26
97/8 Omega 104
98/9 Pacific 230
97/8 PacificCrownRoyale 61
97/8 SPAuthentic
97/8 FLA/WinnDixie
93/4 OwenSound

WEEKLEY, DAVE
93/4 Huntington

WEEKS, STEVE
92/3 Bowman 274
82/3 O-Pee-Chee 234
89/90 O-Pee-Chee 285
90/1 O-Pee-Chee 407
82/3 opcSticker 141
87/8 PaniniSticker 39
89/90 PaniniSticker 150
92/3 Pinnacle 380
82/3 Post
90/1 ProCards 331
92/3 Score 547
92/3 Topps 461
92/3 TopspsStadiumClub 273
90/1 UpperDeck 107
84/5 HFD/JuniorWhalers
85/6 HFD/JuniorWhalers
86/7 HFD/JuniorWhalers
87/8 HFD/JuniorWhalers
92/3 OTT
88/9 VAN/Mohawk
89/90 VAN

WEENK, HEATH
90/1 SketchWHL 185
91/2 SketchWHL 220

WEGLEITNER, MIKE
84/5 KelownaWings 11

WEIDENBACH, ANDY
90/1 SketchOHL 124

WEIDENBACH, JOHN
93/4 Mich.State

WEIGHT, DOUG
96/7 Aces 10 (Diamonds)
97/8 Aces 8 (Spades)
92/3 Bowman 36
95/6 Bowman 68
97/8 DEL 449
93/4 Donruss 118
94/5 Donruss 3
95/6 Donruss 25
96/7 Donruss 85, -Elite 3, -Hit 5
97/8 Donruss 32
96/7 DonrussCanadianIce 14
97/8 DonrussCanadianIce 86
95/6 DonrussElite 5
96/7 DonrussElite 25, -Status 4
97/8 DonrussElite 103
97/8 DonrussPreferred 74, 181
97/8 DonrussPriority 161
97/8 DonrussStudio 95
93/4 EASports 45
97/8 EssoOlympic 26
94/5 Flair 62
96/7 Flair 36
96/7 Fleer 38, -ArtRoss 24
95/6 FleerMetal 57
96/7 F.Picks-Fab 47, -Jagged 4
92/3 FleerUltra 358
93/4 FleerUltra 195
94/5 FleerUltra 77
95/6 FleerUltra 58
96/7 FleerUltra 63
95 Globe 125
95/6 Hoyle'WEST Q (Clubs)
97/8 KatchMedallion 60
95/6 Kraft
96/7 KraftDinner, -Flex
97/8 Kraft-CaseSerie,-WorldBest
93/4 Leaf 184
94/5 Leaf 40
95/6 Leaf 145
96/7 Leaf 136, -BestOf 7, -Fire 6
97/8 Leaf 131
94/5 LeafLimited 53
95/6 LeafLimited 110
96/7 LeafLimited 71
96/7 LeafPreferred 54, -Steel 49
97/8 Limited 173, 191
96/7 McDonalds McD16
97/8 McDonalds McD18
96/7 MetalUniv. 56, -Lethal 20
97/8 Omega 96
92/3 O-Pee-Chee 114
91/2 opcPremier 32, 139
98/9 Pacific 217
97/8 PacificCrown 138
97/8 PacificCrownRoyale 55
97/8 PcfcDynagon! 52,-Tand 46
97/8 PacificInvincible 59
97/8 PacificParamount 78
98/9 PacificParamount 93
97/8 PacificRevolution 57
92/3 PaniniSticker 236
93/4 PaniniSticker 235
94/5 PaniniSticker 199
95/6 PaniniSticker 259
96/7 PaniniSticker 257
97/8 PaniniSticker 215
95 PaniniWorlds 231
91/2 Parkhurst 116
92/3 Parkhurst 115, 229
93/4 Parkhurst 69
94/5 Parkhurst 74
95/6 Parkhurst 346
94/5 ParkieSE seV23
91/2 Pinnacle 310, 383
92/3 Pinnacle 189
93/4 Pinnacle 17
94/5 Pinnacle 18
96/7 Pinn. 158,-Numbr 5,-TmP 4
97/8 Pinnacle 54
96/7 PinnacleBeAPlayer 174
97/8 PinnacleBeeHive 34
97/8 PinnacleCertified 66
97/8 PinnacleInside 48
96/7 PinnacleZenith 12
95/6 Playoff 259
96/7 Playoff 434
94/5 POG 101
95/6 POG 105
93/4 PowerPlay 87
93/4 Premier 136
94/5 Premier 8
95/6 ProMagnet 83
91/2 ProSet 549
91/2 PSPlatinum 263
96/7 SB'7Eleven
91/2 Score(CDN) 286, (U.S) 396
92/3 Score 314
93/4 Score 253
94/5 Score 58
95/6 Score 263
96/7 Score 170,-Chek 14,-Sup 2
97/8 Score 100
94/5 Select 27
95/6 SelectCertified 109
96/7 SelectCertified 50
95/6 SkyBoxEmotion 67
95/6 SkyBoxImpact 65
96/7 SkyBoxImpact 43,-Blade 24
94/5 SP 39
95/6 SP 50, FX9
96/7 SP 57, CW10, HC24
97/8 SPAuthentic 58, I32, S14
96/7 SPx 17
97/8 SPx 17, -Duoview
98/9 SPx"Finite" 34, 113
95/6 Summit 110
96/7 Summit 92,-Untouchable 11
95/6 SuperSticker 43
92/3 Topps 477
95/6 Topps 158
98/9 Topps 8
95/6 ToppsFinest 104
96/7 ToppsNHLPicks 23
92/3 ToppsStadiumClub 380
93/4 ToppsStadiumClub 382
95/6 ToppsStadiumClub 74
95/6 TSC-MembersOnly 12
97/8 ToppsSticker 4
91/2 UpperDeck 440, 444
92/3 UpperDeck 279
93/4 UD 291, 442, SP-53
94/5 UD 44, 549, SP28
95/6 UD 280, AS16, SE31
96/7 UD 58, SS17A, X13
97/8 UD 65, GJ12, SG20
97/8 UD SS10, T13B
93/4 UDBeAPlayer 39
94/5 UDBAP R118, -Aut. 117
96/7 UDBlackDiamond 172
97/8 UDBlackDiamond 84
98/9 UDChoice 85
95/6 UDCollChoice 172
96/7 UDCC 91, 317 C9, UD9
97/8 UDCC 87, 319, C3, SQ68
97/8 udDiamondVision 15
96/7 UpperDeck"Ice" 87, S9
97/8 UpperDeckIce 9
96 Wien 172
97/8 Zenith 62, Z50
92/3 EDM
93/4 EDM 27NOV93
96/7 EDM
97/8 EDM

WEILAND, COONEY
33/4 Anonymous (V129) 24
34-43 BeeHives(BOS)
83&87 HallOfFame 120
83 HHOF Postcard (H)
33/4 OPC (V304A) 27
39/40 OPC (V301-1) 92
33/4 WWGum (V357) 65
36/7 WWGum (V356) 69
91/2 BOS/Legends

WEILAND, RALPH
34/5 SweetCaporal

WEINFURTHER, MICHAEL
94/5 DEL 338
95/6 DEL 295

WEINRICH, ERIC
90/1 Bowman 90
91/2 Bowman 278
92/3 Bowman 343
93/4 Donruss 136, 416
94/5 Donruss 302
93/4 EASports 56
92/3 FleerUltra 76, 306
93/4 FleerUltra 295
95 Globe 108
93/4 Leaf 271
94/5 Leaf 221
92/3 O-Pee-Chee 95
92/3 opcPremier 63
90/1 OPC/Topps 416
91/2 OPC/Topps 10, 92
98/9 Pacific 153
98/9 PacificParamount 50
97/8 PacificRegime 49
91/2 PaniniSticker 223
93/4 PaniniSticker 130
98/9 PaniniSticker 134
91/2 Parkhurst 318
92/3 Parkhurst 56
93/4 Parkhurst 311
94/5 Parkhurst 43, V83
95/6 Parkhurst 310
91/2 Pinnacle 89
92/3 Pinnacle 297
93/4 Pinnacle 281
94/5 Pinnacle 186
95/6 Pinnacle 182
96/7 PinnacleBeAPlayer 71
93/4 PowerPlay 111, 319
93/4 Premier 195
94/5 Premier 106
88/9 ProCards(Utica)
89/90 ProCards(AHL) 222
90/1 ProSet 622
91/2 ProSet 133
91/2 PSPlatinum PC10
90/1 Score 389
91/2 Score(CDN) 131, 380
91/2 Score(U.S) 131, 350
91/2 Score-YoungStar 26
92/3 Score 308
93/4 Score 227, 573
94 Semic 112
92 SemicSticker 154
92/3 Topps 399
95/6 Topps 289
91/2 ToppsStadiumClub 339
92/3 ToppsStadiumClub 165
90/1 UpperDeck 245
91/2 UpperDeck 44, 344, 509
92/3 UpperDeck 195, 553
93/4 UpperDeck 497
94/5 UpperDeck 119
95/6 UpperDeck 45
96/7 UpperDeck 34, X4
97/8 UpperDeck 246
94/5 UDBAP R19, -Aut. 139
95/6 UDCollChoice 63
96/7 UDCollChoice 51
97/8 UDCollChoice 52
96/7 UpperDeck"Ice" 12
93/4 CHI/Coke
92/3 HFD/DairyMart
89/90 N.J.
90/1 N.J.

WEINRICH, JASON
94/5 Huntington 21
92/3 Maine (1) 6
93/4 Maine 39

WEINSTOCK, ULF
79 PaniniSticker 187

WEIR, BERT
84/5 Ottawa

WEIR, JOHN
83/4 Brantford 18

WEIR, NOLAN
91/2 AirCanadaSJHL C38
92/3 MPSPhotoSJHL 16

WEIR, STAN
74/5 Loblaws
74/5 OPC 355
75/6 OPC/Topps 132, 316
76/7 OPC 270
77/8 OPC 356
79/80 OPC 331
80/1 OPC/Topps 153
81/2 OPC 124
80/1 Pepsi Cap
79/80 EDM
80/1 EDM/Zellers
81/2 EDM/RedRooster
81/2 EDM/WestEdmontonMall
88/9 EDM/ActionMagazine 66
75/6 TOR
76/7 TOR

WEIR, WALLY
72-84 Dernière 78/9, 81/2
79/80 O-Pee-Chee 388
81/2 O-Pee-Chee 284
82/3 O-Pee-Chee 297
83/4 O-Pee-Chee 306
80/1 Pepsi Cap
82/3 Post
83/4 Vachon 79
80/1 QUE
81/2 QUE
82/3 QUE
83/4 QUE
76 QuébecNordiques/MA
76/7 QuébecNordiques

WEISENBACH, HEINZ
72 SemicSticker 106

WEISHAAR, TOBY
91/2 SketchWHL 166
92/3 Tacoma

WEISHAUPT, ERICH
79 PaniniSticker 96
82 SemicSticker 101

WEISS, DAVE
87/8 Kingston 9
84/5 Kitchener 10
85/6 Kitchener 6
86/7 Kitchener 6

WEISS, DOUG
88/9 ProCards(Springfield)
89/90 Johnstown 31

WEISS, KEN
93/4 Richmond 1

WEISSMAN, MIKE
72/3 WilliamsFIN 321

WEISSMANN, ONDREJ
94/5 APS 296

WELCH, JASON
91/2 LakeSuperior

WELKER
91/2 AvantGardeBCJHL 163

WELLS, BRAD
83/4 Brandon 9

WELLS, BRIAN
83/4 Brandon 1

WELLS, BRYAN
93/4 ThunderBay

WELLS, CHRIS
95/6 Bowman 136
94/5 Classic 20, T54
94/5 ClassicFourSport 137, TC4
94/5 C4'Images 111
94/5 ClassicImages 19
97/8 PacificRegime 91
97/8 PinnacleBeAPlayer 62
94/5 SigRookies 15
91/2 SketchWHL 141
96/7 FLA/WinnDixie
97/8 FLA/WinnDixie
95/6 PGH/Foodland 3
93/4 Seattle

WELLS, JAY
91/2 Bowman 35
85/6 O-Pee-Chee 178
86/7 O-Pee-Chee 217
87/8 OPC/Topps 151
86/7 opcSticker 92/223
87/8 opcSticker 212/79
97/8 PacificRegime 189
87/8 PaniniSticker 274
88/9 PaniniSticker 72
94/5 Pinnacle 507
94/5 Premier 249
92/3 Score(U.S) 548
93/4 Score 416
95/6 UDBeAPlayer 29
90/1 BUF/BlueShield
90/1 BUF/Campbell
91/2 BUF/BlueShield
91/2 BUF/Campbell
80/1 L.A.
84/5 L.A/Smokeys
88/9 L.A.
89/90 PHA

WELLS, JEFF
95/6 Birmingham
96/7 Cincinnati

WELLS, MARC
94/5 MiracleOnIce 39, 40

WELSH, KEITH
94/5 Slapshot(Kitchener) 17
95/6 Slapshot 150

WELTE, WADE
91/2 AirCanadaSJHL D14
92/3 MPSPhotoSJHL 80

WELTER, JASON
92/3 MPSPhotoSJHL 92

WELTER, JOSH
92/3 MPSPhotoSJHL 92

WELZ, MARKUS
96/7 DEL 332

WENAAS, JEFF
89/90 ProCards(IHL) 194
85/6 MedicineHat 13
88/9 SaltLake 21

WENAAS, STUART
83/4 Kelowna

WENNBERG, PETER
92/3 SemicElitserien 269

WENSINK, JOHN
80/1 O-Pee-Chee 390
78/9 OPC/Topps 133
79/80 OPC/Topps 182
80/1 Pepsi Cap
82/3 Post
81/2 COL.R
80/1 QUE

WENTWORTH, MARVIN (CY)
36/7 WWGum (V356) 19
34-43 BeeHives(MTL.C&M)
35-40 CrownBrand 119, 157
34/5 OPC (V304B) 61
36/7 OPC (V304D) 116
37/8 OPC (V304E) 163
39/40 OPC (V301-1) 30
38/9 QuakerOats
34/5 SweetCaporal
33/4 WWGum V357 43

WENTZELL, JAMIE
95/6 Slapshot 161

WERENKA, BRAD
92/3 Classic 99
92/3 ClassicFourSport 212
92/3 Parkhurst 289
93/4 Parkhurst 68
97/8 PinnacleBeAPlayer 41
93/4 Score 438
94/5 Score CT21
93/4 UpperDeck 41, SP-54
92/3 EDM
93/4 EDM 27DEC93
94/5 Milwaukee

WERENKA, DARCY
91/2 Arena 28
91/2 Classic 33
91/2 ClassicFourSport 33, -Aut
93/4 ClassicProspects 96
90/1 SketchMEM 101
90/1 SketchWHL 122
91/2 SketchWHL 351
91/2 StarPics 54
91/2 UltimateDP 29, -Au t 29
92/3 UpperDeck 594
94/5 Binghampton
92/3 Brandon 23
89/90 Lethbridge

WERENKA, NIGEL
91/2 AirCanadaSJHL D25
92/3 MPSPhotoSJHL 162

WERNBLOM, MAGNUS
94/5 ElitSet 68
95/6 ElitSet 110
91/2 SemicElitserien 215
92/3 SemicElitserien 235
95/6 udElite 160, NA20
97/8 udSwedish 157, UDS14

WENER, THOMAS
91 SemicSticker 172

WERNER, THOMAS
94/5 DEL 133
95/6 DEL 134

WESENBERG, BRIAN
97/8 Bowman 33
95 Classic 26, 85
94/5 Slapshot(Guelph) 16
95/6 Slapshot 96
95/6 Guelph 15
96/7 Guelph 14

WESLEY, BLAKE
82/3 O-Pee-Chee 133
83/4 O-Pee-Chee 307
84/5 O-Pee-Chee 294
82/3 Post
83/4 SouhaitsRen.KeyChain
83/4 Vachon 80
82/3 HFD/JuniorWhalers
83/4 QUE
85/6 TOR
84/5 Fredericton 28

WESLEY, GLEN
91/2 Bowman 350
92/3 Bowman 15
93/4 Donruss 19
94/5 Donruss 232
95/6 Donruss 186
94/5 Fleer 92
95/6 FleerMetal 68
92/3 FleerUltra 11
93/4 FleerUltra 272
94/5 FleerUltra 18, 303
95/6 FleerUltra 248
93/4 Leaf 268
94/5 Leaf 6, 460
95/6 Leaf 231
94/5 LeafLimited 13
88/9 OPC/Topps 166
89/90 OPC/Topps 51
90/1 OPC/Topps 379
91/2 OPC/Topps 452
92/3 O-Pee-Chee 150
88/9 opcStickFS 21
89/90 opcSticker 27/165
98/9 Pacific 141
97/8 PacificCrown 244
88/9 PaniniSticker 207
89/90 PaniniSticker 200
90/1 PaniniSticker 6
91/2 PaniniSticker 182
92/3 PaniniSticker 145
93/4 PaniniSticker 6
94/5 PaniniSticker 6
91/2 Parkhurst 5
92/3 Parkhurst 6
93/4 Parkhurst 17
94/5 Parkhurst 17
95/6 Parkhurst 98
91/2 Pinnacle 112
92/3 Pinnacle 326
93/4 Pinnacle 383
94/5 Pinnacle 388
95/6 Pinnacle 80
97/8 Pinnacle 132
95/6 Playoff 158
95/6 POG 130
93/4 PowerPlay 25
93/4 Premier 114
94/5 Premier 357
90/1 ProSet 16
91/2 ProSet 1
92/3 ProSet 10
91/2 PSPlatinum 7
90/1 Score 97,-HotC 57,-YngS 8
91/2 Score(CDN) 493, (U.S) 273
92/3 Score 230
93/4 Score 243
95/6 Score 194
94/5 Select 81
95/6 SkyBoxImpact 77
97/8 SPAuthentic 23
95/6 Summit 73
96/7 TeamOut
92/3 Topps 346
95/6 Topps 213
94/5 ToppsFinest 60
96/7 ToppsNHLPicks 155
91/2 ToppsStadiumClub 190
92/3 ToppsStadiumClub 279
93/4 ToppsStadiumClub 222
94/5 ToppsStadiumClub 210
95/6 ToppsStadiumClub 4
95/6 ToppsSuperSkills 39
90/1 UpperDeck 377
91/2 UpperDeck 370
92/3 UpperDeck 244
93/4 UpperDeck 208
94/5 UpperDeck 89, SP125
95/6 UpperDeck 137
97/8 UpperDeck 244
95/6 UDBeAPlayer 116
98/9 UDChoice 41
95/6 UDCollChoice 315
97/8 UDCollChoice 114
88/9 BOS/SportsAction
89/90 BOS/SportsAction
90/1 BOS/SportsAction
91/2 BOS/SportsAction
92/3 BOS
86/7 Portland

WEST, DAN
93/4 Slapshot(Windsor) 21

WEST, JOSEPH
96/7 DEL 213

WEST, MARK
83/4 Brantford 9

WEST, RUSS
90/1 SketchOHL 142
91/2 SketchWHL 282

WEST, STEVE
77/8 Winnipeg

WESTERBY, BOB
94/5 Slapshot(MEM) 20
93/4 Kamloops
95/6 Rochester

WESTFALL, ED
64-67 BeeHives(BOS)
65/6 CocaCola
77/8 Coke Mini
64/5 CokeCap BOS-18
70/1 EddieSargent 7
71/2 EddieSargent 2
72/3 EddieSargent 127
70/1 Esso Stamp
74/5 LiptonSoup 47
74/5 Loblaws
68/9 O-Pee-Chee 135
69/70 OPC/Topps 29
70/1 OPC 139
71/2 OPC/Topps 169
72/3 OPC 104,-Crests 13, T. 159
73/4 OPC/Topps 67
74/5 OPC/Topps 32
75/6 OPC/Topps 302
76/7 OPC/Topps 11
77/8 OPC/Topps 153
78/9 OPC/Topps 232
94/5 Parkie(64/5) 6
95/6 Parkie(66/7) 4
72/3 Post Transfers 10
68/9 ShirriffCoin BOS2
71/2 TheTorontoSun
63/4 Topps 8
64/5 Topps 51
65/6 Topps 37
66/7 Topps 32, -USATest 32
67/8 Topps 95
91/2 Ultimate(06) 56, -Aut 56
70/1 BOS
71/2 BOS
91/2 BOS/Legends
93/4 NYI/Chemical

WESTLUND, TODD
91/2 Minnesota
92/3 Minnesota

WESTLUND, TOMMY
97/8 udSwedish 23

WESTNER, DAVE
78/9 Saginaw

WESTRUM, PAT
79 PaniniSticker 211

WESTWICK, HARRY
83&87 HallOfFame 135
83 HHOF Postcard (I)

WETHERILL, DARREN
91/2 LakeSuperior
94/5 Richmond
95/6 Richmond

WETZEL, CARL
72 SemicSticker 117
72/3 Minnesota

WETZE, TODD
91/2 SketchOHL 213
95/6 Toledo

WETZELL, STIG
70/1 Kuvajulkaisut 290
80/1 Mallasjuoma 1
78/9 SM-Liiga 21
71/2 WilliamsFIN 164
72/3 WilliamsFIN 79, 116
73/4 WilliamsFIN 148

WEVERS, MIKE
92/3 MPSPhotoSJHL 132

WHARRAM, KEN
52/3 AnonymousOHL 176
45-64 BeeHives(CHI)
64-67 BeeHives(CHI)
62 CeramicTiles
63-5 ChexPhoto
64/5 CokeCap CHI-17
65/6 CocaCola
68/9 OPC/Topps 22
69/70 OPC/Topps 74
94/5 Parkie(64/5) 23, 137, 150
95/6 Parkie(66/7) 29, AS6
60/1 ShirriffCoin 70
61/2 ShirriffCoin 32
68/9 ShirriffCoin CHI 5
54-67 TorontoStar V11
56-66 TorontoStar 58/9, 62/3
56-66 TorontoStar 63/4, 64/5
63/4 TheTorontoStar
58/9 Topps 14
61/2 Topps 30, 43
62/3 Topps 39
63/4 Topps 38
64/5 Topps 28, 108
65/6 Topps 61
66/7 Topps 117, -USATest 44
67/8 Topps 117, 125
68/9 CHI

WHEATCROFT, JIM
88/9 Lethbridge

WHEELDON, SIMON
89/90 ProCards(IHL) 39
90/1 ProCards 246
91/2 ProCards 553
90/1 WPG/IGA
91/2 Baltimore 14
90/1 Moncton
83/4 Victoria

WHEELER, SHAWN
93/4 ClassicProspects 235
91/2 Greensboro
93/4 Hampton
92/3 Peoria

WHELAN, SHANE
86/7 London 24

WHIDDEN, BOB
72/3 Cleveland

WHISTLE, BILL
88/9 Brandon 11

WHISTLE, ROB
88/9 ProCards(Baltimore)

WHITAKER, GORD
87/8 Moncton

WHITCROFT, FRED
83&87 HallOfFame 45
83 HHOF Postcard (C)

WHITE, ALTON
67/8 ColumbusCheckers
69 ColumbusCheckers
72/3 LosAngelesSharks

WHITE, ALVIN
77/8 Kalamazoo

WHITE, BILL
71/2 EddieSargent 47
72/3 EddieSargent 62
70/1 Esso Stamp
74/5 Loblaws
73/4 MacsMilkDisk
68/9 OPC/Topps 37
69/70 OPC/Topps 101
71/2 OPC/Topps 11
72/3 OPC 158, 248, T. 40, 128
72/3 opc-Crests 6, -TmCanada
73/4 OPC 78, Topps 180
74/5 OPC/Topps 90, 136
75/6 OPC/Topps 157
76/7 OPC/Topps 235
68/9 ShirriffCoin LA4
71/2 TheTorontoSun
91/2 Trends(72) 15, -Aut.
70/1 CHI

WHITE, BILL
85/6 Sudbury 26
89/90 Sudbury 33

WHITE, CLUCKER
23/4 PaulinsCandy 55

WHITE, COLIN
94/5 Slapshot(MEM) 67

WHITE, GEORGE
92/3 BCJHL 187
84/5 Moncton 5
85/6 Moncton 6

WHITE, JASON
91/2 AvantGardeBCJ 143, 156
90/1 SketchWHL 157, 234
90/1 Brandon 22

WHITE, JIM
74/5 SiouxCity

WHITE, KAM
94/5 Slapshot(NorthBay) 6
94/5 Slapshot(Sarnia) 4
95/6 Slapshot 208

WHITE, KEVIN
90/1 SketchOHL 321

WHITE, K.J.
89/90 Windsor

WHITE, MIKE
95/6 Slapshot 27

WHITE, PETER
93/4 Donruss 431
95/6 EdgeIce 37
95/6 FleerUltra 240
93/4 PowerPlay 344
93/4 Score 629
93/4 EDM 28JAN94
94/5 CapeBreton

WHITE, ROB
52/3 AnonymousOHL 106

WHITE, SCOTT
92/3 ClassicProspects 56
91/2 Greensboro
90/1 KansasCity 11

WHITE, SHERMAN
51-54 LaPatrie 29Nov53
51/2 LavalDairy 35

WHITE, TODD
98/9 Pacific 154

WHITE, TONY
76/7 O-Pee-Chee 279, 396
77/8 O-Pee-Chee 314

WHITE, TRENT
97/8 Bowman 89
96/7 UpperDeck"Ice" 127
95/6 Spokane 9

WHITFIELD, TRENT
98 BowmanCHL 50

WHITLEY, BRIAN
94/5 Slapshot(NorthBay) 15
95/6 Slapshot 221

WHITLOCK, BOB
74/5 opcWHA 12
75/6 opcWHA 93

WHITMORE, KAY
91/2 Bowman 3
92/3 Bowman 155
93/4 Donruss 359
93/4 FleerUltra 443
94/5 Leaf 524
90/1 OPC/Topps 232
91/2 opcPremier 182
92/3 opcPremier 87
92/3 PaniniSticker 255
91/2 Parkhurst 58
92/3 Parkhurst 423
93/4 Parkhurst 478
91/2 Pinnacle 22
93/4 Pinnacle 138
94/5 Pinnacle 438
93/4 PowerPlay 462
93/4 Premier 514
94/5 Premier 85, 134
88/9 ProCards(Binghampton)
89/90 ProCards'AHL 303
90/1 ProSet 610
91/2 PSPlatinum 178
90/1 Score 402
91/2 Score(CDN) 625, (U.S) 75T
92/3 Score 304
93/4 Score 360
92/3 Topps 381
92/3 ToppsStadiumClub 459
93/4 ToppsStadiumClub 60
91/2 UpperDeck 291
92/3 UpperDeck 76
91/2 HFD/JuniorWhalers
92/3 VAN/RoadTrip
93/4 VAN/Coins
94/5 VAN
95/6 VAN/Building 2

WHITMORE, KEITH
90/1 SketchOHL 297

WHITNEY, DEAN
93/4 PrinceAlbert

WHITNEY, MIKE
95/6 RedDeer

WHITNEY, RAY
91/2 Classic 20
92/3 Classic 119, -Promo
91/2 ClassicFourSport 20, -Aut
92/3 ClassicFourSport 223
94/5 Donruss 117
95/6 Donruss 308
94/5 Fleer 202
93/4 FleerUltra 420
95/6 FleerUltra 150
94/5 Leaf 448
95/6 Leaf 208, -RoadToThe 1
97/8 Omega 105
98/9 Pacific 231
98/9 PacificParamount 101
97/8 PacificRevolution 63
95/6 PaniniSticker 280
96/7 PaniniSticker 286
91/2 Parkhurst 454
92/3 Parkhurst 160
93/4 Parkhurst 182
95/6 Parkhurst 183
94/5 ParkieSE 163
92/3 Pinnacle 227
94/5 Pinnacle 316
96/7 Pinnacle 20
97/8 PinnacleBeAPlayer 105
95/6 Playoff 304
95/6 POG 225
93/4 PowerPlay 439
94/5 Premier 33
92/3 ProSet 241
92/3 Score 475
93/4 Score 324
95/6 Score 84
91/2 SketchAwards 20
90/1 SketchMEM 82
90/1 SketchWHL 201
95/6 SkyBoxEmotion 161
94/5 SP 106
97/8 SPAuthentic 66
98/9 SPx"Finite" 37
96/7 Summit 83
92/3 Topps 205
95/6 Topps 68
92/3 ToppsStadiumClub 490
94/5 ToppsStadiumClub 149
95/6 ToppsStadiumClub 86
92/3 UpperDeck 407
93/4 UpperDeck 4
94/5 UpperDeck 149, SP163
95/6 UpperDeck 62
96/7 UpperDeck 150
95/6 UDBeAPlayer 125
98/9 UDChoice 87
95/6 UDCollChoice 225
96/7 UDCollChoice 240
97/8 FLA/WinnDixie
92/3 S.J/PacificBell
95/6 S.J/PacificBellSheet
89/90 Spokane

WHITTEN, ERIN
93/4 ClassicProspects 249, -Aut
94/5 Classic W40
93/4 Toledo 27

WHITTEN, WADE
90/1 SketchMEM 8
90/1 SketchOHL 175
91/2 SketchOHL 347
89/90 SSMarie 16

WHITTLE, JEFF
91/2 SketchWHL 167

WHITTOM, DAVE
90/1 SketchMEM 58
91/2 SketchQMJHL 283

WHITTON, MIKE
95/6 Toledo
92/3 WestMich.
93/4 WestMich.

WHITWORTH, DAVE
92/3 BCJHL 129

WHYNOT, CRAIG
95/6 Slapshot 258

WHYTE, DARRYL
93/4 Slapshot(Kitchener) 3
94/5 Slapshot(Kitchener) 3

WHYTE, DEAN
84/5 Belleville 21

WHYTE, GEORGE
52/3 AnonymousOHL 63

WHYTE, SEAN
92/3 ClassicProspects 101
94/5 Classic W30
90/1 ProCards 346
91/2 ProCards 401
92/3 Phoenix

WICKBERG, HÅKAN
72 Hellas 41
74 Hellas 37
70/1 Kuvajulkaisut 40
72 Panda
72 SemicSticker 52
74 SemicSticker 9
71/2 WilliamsFIN 60
72/3 WilliamsFIN 59
73/4 WilliamsFIN 39

WICKENHEISER, CHRIS
93/4 RedDeer
95/6 RedDeer

WICKENHEISER, DOUG
82/3 McDonalds 26
81/2 O-Pee-Chee 193
82/3 O-Pee-Chee 196
83/4 O-Pee-Chee 202
84/5 O-Pee-Chee 193
85/6 O-Pee-Chee 229
87/8 OPC/Topps 193
88/9 O-Pee-Chee 263
83/4 opcSticker 67
84/5 opcSticker 58
85/6 opcSticker 52/183
88/9 opcSticker 56/187
87/8 PaniniSticker 318
80/1 Pepsi Cap
83/4 SouhaitsRen.KeyChain
83/4 Vachon 60
80/1 MTL
81/2 MTL
82/3 MTL
82/3 MTL/Steinberg
83/4 MTL
87/8 VAN/Shell
89/90 WSH
92/3 Peoria

WICKENHEISER, HAYLEY
94/5 Classic W13
97/8 EssoOlympic 58
97/8 GameOfHerLife
97/8 UDCollChoice 279

WICKENHEISER, KURT
82/3 Regina 16
83/4 Regina 16

WICKS, RON
91/2 UltimateO6 87

WICKSTROM, K.A.
74 Hellas 38
73/4 WilliamsFIN 40

WICKWARE, RANDY
81/2 Victoria

WIDING, JUHA
70/1 Colgate Stamp 11
70/1 DadsCookies
70/1 EddieSargent 76
71/2 EddieSargent 65
72/3 EddieSargent 93
70/1 Esso Stamp
74/5 Loblaws
71/2 OPC/Topps 86, -Booklet 19
72/3 OPC 46
73/4 OPC 159
74/5 OPC/Topps 258
75/6 OPC/Topps 142, 320
76/7 OPC 354
77/8 opcWHA 33
71/2 TheTorontoSun
72/3 Topps 108
73/4 Topps 156

WIDMER, JASON
95/6 Leaf 287
90/1 SketchMEM 129
90/1 SketchWHL 136
91/2 SketchWHL 357
93/4 Lethbridge

WIEBE, ART
34-43 BeeHives(CHI)
36-39 DiamondMatch (1), (2), (3)
36-39 DiamondMatch (4), (5), (6)
36/7 OPC (V304D) 113
39/40 OPC (V301-1) 49
36/7 WWGum (V356) 124

WIEBE, DAN
92/3 Toledo 2

WIECZOREK, DARIUSZ
89 SemicSticker 130

WIEGAND, CHUCK
93/4 Johnstown 13

WIEGAND, JOHN
93/4 Mich.State

WIELAND, MARKUS
96/7 DEL 137

WIELOCH, SLAWOMIR
92 SemicSticker 284

WIEMER, JASON
94/5 Classic 8, T66
94/5 ClassicFourSport 122
94/5 C4'Images 101
95/6 Donruss 11
94/5 Flair 176
94/5 Fleer 211
94/5 FleerUltra 374,-Prospect 10
95/6 FleerUltra 156
94/5 Leaf 489, -Phenoms 4
95/6 Leaf 23, -StudioRookie 19
94/5 LeafLimited 119
98/9 Pacific 128
97/8 PacificDynag-BestKept 90
95/6 Parkhurst 193
94/5 ParkieSE 172
94/5 Pinnacle 484
95/6 Pinnacle 77
96/7 PinnacleBeAPlayer 26
94/5 Premier 463
95/6 Score 149
94/5 Select 171
94/5 T.Finest-BBest(Red) 16
94/5 TF-BowmansBest 5
93/4 UpperDeck E3
94/5 UpperDeck 262, SP166
95/6 UpperDeck 391
96/7 UpperDeck 157
95/6 T.B.
95/6 T.B/SkyBoxSportsCafe
93/4 Portland

WIEMER, JIM
91/2 Bowman 363
90/1 O-Pee-Chee 439
91/2 OPC/Topps 475
88/9 ProCards(CapeBreton)
90/1 ProSet 413
91/2 Score(CDN) 535
91/2 ToppsStadiumClub 16
89/90 BOS/SportsAction
91/2 BOS/SportsAction
88/9 EDM/ActionMagazine 25
89/90 NewHaven

WIENKE, STEVE
86/7 Kamloops

WIESEL, ADAM
95/6 Classic 81, -Aut.
95/6 C'FiveSport 152
95/6 Fredericton
96/7 Fredericton

WIEST, RICK
86/7 Kamloops

WIGHT, DAVE
96/7 SSMarie

WIGLE, DENNIS
84/5 Ottawa67s

WIITA, MARTIN
91/2 SemicElitserien 148

WIKLANDER, LARS GORAN
95/6 ElitSet 203, -Rookies 4
95/6 udElite 217
97/8 udSwedish 67

WIKLANDER, MIKAEL
94/5 ElitSet 191
95/6 ElitSet 179
95/6 udElite 22

WIKMAN, JUHA
72/3 WilliamsFIN 298

WIKSTRÖM, SAMI
92/3 Jyvas-Hyva 143
93/4 Jyvas-Hyva 264
93/4 Sisu 295

WIKSTRÖM, SEPPO
70/1 Kuvajulkaisut 307
71/2 WilliamsFIN 205
72/3 WilliamsFIN 242

WIKULOW, SERGEI
94/5 DEL 168

WILCOX, ARCHIE
34/5 OPC (V304B) 57
33/4 WWGum (V357) 9

WILCOX, GEORGE
87/8 Hull

WILD, MARTIN
79 PaniniSticker 104

WILDER, ARCHIE
34-43 BeeHives(DET)
40/1 OPC (V301-2) 145

WILDGOOSE, LYLE
93/4 ClassicProspects 242
93/4 Raleigh
94/5 Raleigh

WILENIUS, BEN
66/7 Champion 110
78/9 SM-Liiga 211
71/2 WilliamsFIN 241
72/3 WilliamsFIN 225
73/4 WilliamsFIN 303

WILEY, JIM
74/5 Loblaws
74/5 VAN/RoyalBank
76/7 VAN/RoyalBank

WILFORD, MARTY
97/8 Bowman 18
95/6 Slapshot 233

WILKIE, BOB
95/6 DEL 11
94/5 Parkhurst 171
89/90 ProCards(AHL) 307
90/1 ProCards 477
91/2 Score(CDN) 358, (U.S) 328

WILKIE, BRIAN
86/7 Regina

WILKIE, DAVID
92/3 C'FourSport 160
92/3 Classic 11, LP7
93/4 Donruss USA22
95/6 EdgeIce 43
96/7 Flair 113
96/7 FleerUltra 91, -Rookies 19
96/7 Got-UmHockeyGreatsCoin
94/5 Leaf 458
95/6 Leaf 259
96/7 MetalUniverse 195
97/8 PacificCrown 54
93/4 Pinnacle 487
96/7 PinnacleBeAPlayer 108
94/5 Premier 481
90/1 SketchWHL 11
91/2 SketchWHL 95
96/7 SP 82
96/7 ToppsNHLPicks 173
93/4 UpperDeck 558
96/7 UpperDeck 282
96/7 MTL
96/7 MTL/MolsonExport
94/5 Fredericton
93/4 Kamloops

WILKINS, BARRY
71/2 EddieSargent 221
72/3 EddieSargent 217
70/1 Esso Stamp
74/5 Loblaws, -Update
72/3 OPC 109, Topps 102
71/2 OPC/Topps 230
74/5 OPC/Topps 182
75/6 OPC/Topps 148
76/7 OPC/Topps 102
71/2 TheTorontoSun
70/1 VAN/RoyalBank
71/2 VAN/RoyalBank 14
72/3 VAN/Nalleys
72/3 VAN/RoyalBank
73/4 VAN/RoyalBank

WILKINSON, BILL
92/3 WestMich.
93/4 WestMich.

WILKINSON, DEREK
97/8 Donruss 213
95/6 EdgeIce 103
95/6 FutureLegends 44
91/2 SketchOHL 48

WILKINSON, NEIL
90/1 Bowman 184
93/4 Donruss 62
93/4 EASports 116, 219
92/3 FleerUltra 198
92/3 HumptyDumpty (2)
93/4 Leaf 357
90/1 OPC/Topps 305, OPC 443
91/2 OPC/Topps 348
91/2 opcPremier 110
92/3 PaniniSticker 128
91/2 Parkhurst 382
92/3 Parkhurst 165
93/4 Parkhurst 315
95/6 Parkhurst 439
91/2 Pinnacle 108
92/3 Pinnacle 27
93/4 Pinnacle 354
88/9 ProCards(Kalamazoo)
89/90 ProCards(IHL) 91
90/1 ProSet 465
91/2 ProSet 328, 483
92/3 ProSet 168
91/2 PSPlatinum 229
91/2 Score(CDN) 328, 558
91/2 Score(U.S) 369, 8T
92/3 Score 235
93/4 Score 138, 523
92/3 Topps 76
91/2 ToppsStadiumClub 293
92/3 ToppsStadiumClub 219
90/1 UpperDeck 547
91/2 UpperDeck 55, 95
92/3 UpperDeck 30
93/4 UpperDeck 378
94/5 UpperDeck 392
97/8 UpperDeck 347
94/5 UDBeAPlayer R70, -Aut. 44
93/4 CHI/Coke
91/2 S.J.

WILKINSON, PETER
92/3 WestMich.
93/4 WestMich.

WILKS, BRIAN
88/9 ProCards(NewHaven)
89/90 ProCards(AHL) 148
82/3 Kitchener 15
83/4 Kitchener 9
84/5 Kitchener 15

WILLARD, ROD
83/4 Springfield 18

WILLBERG, ESA
70/1 Kuvajulkaisut 292

WILLETT, PAUL
91/2 ProCards 368

WILLIAMS, ANDREW
95/6 Slapshot 55

WILLIAMS, BARRY
74/5 PGH

WILLIAMS, DAN
89/90 Johnstown 26

WILLIAMS, DARRYL
88/9 ProCards(NewHaven)
89/90 ProCards(AHL) 25
90/1 ProCards 416
91/2 ProCards 369
92/3 Phoenix
93/4 Phoenix

WILLIAMS, DAVE
92/3 Bowman 377
94/5 Leaf 538
92/3 O-Pee-Chee 250
92/3 ProSet 172
92/3 Score 539
92/3 Topps 372
92/3 ToppsStadiumClub 461
92/3 UpperDeck 51
94/5 ANA/Carl'sJr 25

WILLIAMS, DAVE (TIGER)
76/7 O-Pee-C hee373
77/8 O-Pee-Chee 383, 394
77/8 OPC/Topps 4, OPC 383
78/9 OPC/Topps 66, OPC 359
79/80 OPC/Topps 4, 97
80/1 OPC/Topps 105, 164
81/2 O-Pee-Chee 345, 385
82/3 O-Pee-Chee 358
83/4 O-Pee-Chee 363
86/7 OPC/Topps 6
81/2 opcSticker 247
86/7 opcSticker 94/225
87/8 PaniniSticker 283
80/1 Pepsi Cap
81/2 Post PopUp 10
82/3 Post
83/4 PuffySticker 4
83/4 7ElevenCokeCups
84/5 7ElevenDisk
83/4 SouhaitsRen.KeyChain
83/4 Vachon 120
84/5 DET/Caesars
88/9 L.A.
74/5 TOR
75/6 TOR
76/7 TOR
77/8 TOR
78/9 TOR
80/1 VAN
80/1 VAN/Silverwood
81/2 VAN
81/2 VAN/Silverwood
82/3 VAN
83/4 VAN

WILLIAMS, ERNIE
26 Dominion 18

WILLIAMS, GORDIE
83/4 Springfield 7

WILLIAMS, JACK
89/90 SketchMEM 48
90/1 SketchOHL 247
91/2 SketchOHL 57
89/90 Kitchener 9
90/1 Kitchener 28

WILLIAMS, JEFF
93/4 Slapshot(Guelph) 17
94/5 Slapshot(Guelph) 18
95/6 Slapshot 98
95/6 Guelph 11

WILLIAMS, JOHN
85/6 London 30

WILLIAMS, MIKE
93/4 Slapshot(Peterborough) 18
95/6 Slapshot 322
92/3 Toledo 1

WILLIAMS, ROD
84/5 KelownaWings 14
85/6 Brandon 21
86/7 Regina

WILLIAMS, SEAN
88/9 ProCards(Saginaw)
89/90 ProCards'IHL 50
90/1 ProCards 393
91/2 ProCards 488
92/3 Indianapolis

WILLIAMS, STEVE
91/2 AvantGardeBCJ 95
92/3 BCJHL 130

WILLIAMS, TOM C.
74/5 Loblaws
74/5 O-Pee-Chee 394
76/7 O-Pee-Chee 319
78/9 O-Pee-Chee 314
75/6 OPC/Topps 179
77/8 OPC/Topps 5, 44
72/3 NewEngland

WILLIAMS, THOMAS MARK
45-64 BeeHives(BOS)
64-67 BeeHives(BOS)
62 CeramicTiles
64/5 CokeCap BOS-11
65/6 CocaCola
70/1 Colgate Stamp 5
70/1 DadsCookies
70/1 EddieSargent 83
71/2 EddieSargent 130
70/1 Esso Stamp
68/9 OPC/Topps 11
69/70 OPC/Topps 128
70/1 OPC 169
71/2 OPC/Topps 31
75/6 OPC/Topps 79, 330
94/5 Parkie(64/5) 4
95/6 Parkie(66/7) 11
61/2 ShirriffCoin 17
68/9 ShirriffCoin BOS16
71/2 TheTorontoSun
62/3 Topps 21
63/4 Topps 12
64/5 Topps 58
65/6 Topps 35
66/7 Topps 38, -USATest 38
67/8 Topps 40
54-67 TorontoStar V11
70/1 MIN
51/2 Cleveland
60/1 Cleveland

WILLIAMS, WARREN
75/6 OPC/Topps 217

WILLIAMSON, ANDREW
95/6 Slapshot 199

WILLIAMSON, GLEN
91/2 WPG/IGA

WILLIAMSON, MIKE
91/2 SketchWHL 28
93/4 Portland

WILLIS, JORDAN
95/6 EdgeIce 143

WILLIS, RALPH
52/3 AnonymousOHL 98

WILLIS, RICK
95/6 Binghampton
96/7 Binghampton

WILLIS, SHANE
97/8 Bowman 113
98 BowmanCHL 75
95 Classic 48
96/7 UDBlackDiamond 26
97/8 UDCollChoice 300
96/7 UpperDeck"Ice" 126
95/6 PrinceAlbert

WILLIS, TYLER
92/3 BCJHL 71
97/8 Bowman 87, 162
95/6 SwiftCurrent

WILLMANN, DIETER
94/5 DEL 287

WILLNER, BRAD
91/2 LakeSuperior

WILLSIE, BRIAN
98 BowmanCHL 8
95/6 Slapshot 100
98/9 UDChoice 273
95/6 Guelph 14
96/7 Guelph 18

WILM, CLARK
93/4 Saskatoon

WILMOT, LEFTY
30s? ABC ChewingGum 41

WILSON, BEHN
79/80 OPC/Topps 111
80/1 OPC/Topps 145
81/2 OPC 239, Topps 45
82/3 O-Pee-Chee 260
81/2 opcSticker 175
82/3 Post
83/4 PuffySticker 12
86/7 CHI/Coke
87/8 CHI/Coke
81/2 PHA/Tickets 10

WILSON, BERT
74/5 OPC 384
75/6 OPC 338
76/7 OPC 378
78/9 OPC 369
80/1 Pepsi Cap
80/1 CGY

WILSON, BOB
52/3 AnonymousOHL 171

WILSON, CAREY
90/1 Bowman 214
91/2 Bowman 265
92/3 FleerUltra 272
86/7 Kraft Sports 10
85/6 O-Pee-Chee 191
86/7 OPC/Topps 166
87/8 O-Pee-Chee 211
88/9 OPC/Topps 75
89/90 OPC/Topps 66
90/1 OPC/Topps 54, 101
91/2 OPC/Topps 85
88/9 opcMini 45
90/1 opcPremier 128
85/6 opcSticker 213/82
88/9 opcSticker 266/130
89/90 opcSticker 239/102
87/8 PaniniSticker 211
88/9 PaniniSticker 246
89/90 PaniniSticker 280
90/1 PaniniSticker 105
91/2 PaniniSticker 56
91/2 Pinnacle 364
92/3 Pinnacle 369
90/1 ProSet 210, 453
91/2 ProSet 36
90/1 Score 254, 42T
91/2 Score(CDN) 227, (U.S) 227
92/3 Score 127
91/2 ToppsStadiumClub 301
91/2 UpperDeck 538
85/6 CGY/RedRooster
86/7 CGY/RedRooster
91/2 CGY/IGA
92/3 CGY/IGA 11
88/9 HFD/JuniorWhalers
90/1 HFD/JuniorWhalers
89/90 NYR/MarineMidland

WILSON, CHAD
92/3 BCJHL 151

WILSON, COLIN
91/2 SketchOHL 125
91/2 Peterborough 20
92/3 Windsor 8

WILSON, CRAIG
89/90 SketchOHL 69

WILSON, CULLY
23/4 PaulinsCandy 67

WILSON, DOUG
90/1 Bowman 2
91/2 Bowman 400
92/3 Bowman 75, 219
93/4 EASports 115
92/3 FleerUltra 199
93/4 FleerUltra 230
91/2 Kelloggs 19
84/5 Kelloggs Disk
90/1 Kraft 62, 77
91/2 Kraft 34
82/3 McDonalds 36
78/9 OPC/Topps 168
80/1 OPC/Topps 12
81/2 OPC 66, Topps(W) 78
82/3 O-Pee-Chee 77, 78
83/4 O-Pee-Chee 114
84/5 OPC 48, Topps 37
85/6 OPC/Topps 45, P, T-AS 11
86/7 OPC/Topps 106
87/8 OPC/Topps 14
88/9 OPC/Topps 89
89/90 OPC/Topps 112
90/1 OPC/Topps 111, 203, N
91/2 OPC/Topps 49
92/3 O-Pee-Chee 281
90/1 opcPremier 129
91/2 opcPremier 6
82/3 opcSticker 163, 172, 254
83/4 opcSticker 112, 165
84/5 opcSticker 27
85/6 opcSticker 25, 122
86/7 opcSticker 153
87/8 opcSticker 76/211
88/9 opcSticker 6/135
89/90 opcSticker 14/156
87/8 PaniniSticker 222
88/9 PaniniSticker 24
89/90 PaniniSticker 45
90/1 PaniniSticker 189
91/2 PaniniSticker 18
92/3 PaniniSticker 129
93/4 PaniniSticker 264
91/2 Parkhurst 168
92/3 Parkhurst 167
91/2 Pinnacle 13, 369
92/3 Pinnacle 52
82/3 Post
93/4 Premier 77
90/1 ProSet 63, 346
91/2 ProSet 52, 478, 584
92/3 ProSet 165
91/2 PSPlatinum 107
83/4 PuffySticker 14
90/1 Score 280, 320, -Hot 68
91/2 Score(CDN) 35, 551
91/2 Score(U.S) 35, 1T
92/3 Score 15
93/4 Score 115
92/3 SeasonsPatch 63
85/6 7Eleven 4
83/4 SouhaitsRen.KeyChain
92/3 Topps 482
91/2 ToppsStadiumClub 131
92/3 ToppsStadiumClub 470
90/1 UpperDeck 223
92/3 UpperDeck 150
79/80 CHI
80/1 CHI/4x6
81/2 CHI
82/3 CHI
86/7 CHI/Coke
87/8 CHI/Coke
88/9 CHI/Coke
89/90 CHI/Coke
90/1 CHI/Coke
91/2 S.J.

WILSON, DUNC
71/2 EddieSargent 222
72/3 EddieSargent 213
70/1 Esso Stamp
72/3 Letraset 20
74/5 Loblaws
71/2 OPC 24
72/3 OPC 18
73/4 OPC 257
74/5 OPC 327
77/8 OPC/Topps 8, 224
71/2 TheTorontoSun
72/3 Topps 91
77/8 PGH/PuckBuck
73/4 TOR
74/5 TOR
70/1 VAN/RoyalBank
71/2 VAN/RoyalBank 15
72/3 VAN/RoyalBank

WILSON, GORD (PHAT)
83&87 HallOfFame 195
83 HHOF Postcard (J)
23/4 PaulinsCandy 16

WILSON, JEFF
90/1 SketchOHL 196
87/8 Kingston 6

WILSON, JESSE
90/1 SketchWHL 12
91/2 SketchWHL 132

WILSON, JOHN
45-64 BeeHives(DET), (TOR)
52/3 Parkhurst 89
53/4 Parkhurst 51
54/5 Parkhurst 44
59/60 Parkhurst 13
60/1 Parkhurst 14
60/1 ShirriffCoin 15
61/2 ShirriffCoin 100
54/5 Topps 4
57/8 Topps 47
58/9 Topps 22
91/2 Ultimate06 65, -Aut 65
76/7 COL.R/CokeCans
77/8 PGH/PuckBuck

WILSON, LANDON
95/6 Bowman 95
97/8 Donruss 87
95/6 EdgeIce 30
96/7 FleerUltra 41, -Rookies 20
95/6 FutureLegends 24
96/7 Leaf 215
97/8 Leaf 147
97/8 Limited 52
96/7 MetalUniverse 196
97/8 PacificCrown 105
95/6 Parkhurst 526
96/7 PinnacleBeAPlayer 106
96/7 PinnacleZenith 142
96/7 Score 257
95/6 SelectCertified 134
96/7 Summit 188
95/6 UpperDeck 424
96/7 UpperDeck 242
97/8 UpperDeck 10

WILSON, LARRY
45-64 BeeHives(CHI)
52/3 Parkhurst 92
53/4 Parkhurst 74
54/5 Parkhurst 85
54/5 Topps 40

WILSON, MIKE
95/6 Bowman 94
93/4 Classic 32
95/6 EdgeIce 66
95/6 FutureLegends 45
97/8 PacificRegime 25
95/6 Parkhurst 534
96/7 PinnacleBeAPlayer 23
97/8 Score(BUF) 20
93/4 Slapshot(Sudbury) 6
94/5 Slapshot(Sudbury) 4
92/3 Sudbury 6
93/4 Sudbury 6
95/6 Rochester

WILSON, MITCH
88/9 ProCards(Muskegon)
89/90 ProCards(IHL) 149
90/1 ProCards 376

WILSON, MURRAY
72-84 Dernière 72/3, 73/4
74/5 Loblaws
74/5 OPC 359
75/6 OPC/Topps 162
76/7 OPC/Topps 254
77/8 OPC/Topps 69
72/3 MTL
73/4 MTL
74/5 MTL
75/6 MTL
76/7 MTL
77/8 MTL

WILSON, RICK
74/5 Loblaws
74/5 OPC 284
75/6 OPC 356
76/7 OPC 293
77/8 OPC/Topps 57
94/5 DAL
81/2 Kingston 17

WILSON, ROB
85/6 Sudbury 25
87/8 Sudbury 25
89/90 Sudbury 25
97/8 SheffieldSteelers

WILSON, RON
87/8 PaniniSticker 291
93/4 PowerPlay 373
93/4 Premier 194
89/90 ProCards(IHL) 188
87/8 MIN
78/9 TOR
79/80 TOR
77/8 Kalamazoo 2

WILSON, RON LEE
91/2 Bowman 382
92/3 Bowman 364
93/4 FleerUltra 356
93/4 Leaf 316
80/1 OPC/Topps 243
81/2 O-Pee-Chee 377
87/8 O-Pee-Chee 224
91/2 OPC/Topps 120
81/2 opcSticker 140
91/2 PaniniSticker 34
92/3 PaniniSticker 18
93/4 PaniniSticker 162
80/1 Pepsi Cap
88/9 ProCards(Moncton)
89/90 ProCards(AHL) 51
90/1 ProSet 529
91/2 ProSet 220
91/2 Score(CDN) 533
92/3 Score 365
93/4 Score 431, 657
92/3 Topps 78
91/2 ToppsStadiumClub 347
92/3 ToppsStadiumClub 429
93/4 MTL
90/1 STL/Kodak
91/2 STL
79/80 WPG
80/1 WPG
83/4 WPG
84/5 WPG/Police
85/6 WPG
85/6 WPG/Police
86/7 WPG
87/8 WPG
77/8 NovaScotia

WILSON, ROSS
89/90 ProCards(AHL) 17
90/1 ProCards 437
91/2 ProCards 389

WILSON, RUSS
80/1 DET

WILSON, STACY
94/5 Classic W9
97/8 EssoOlympic 60
97/8 UDCollChoice 287

WILSON, STEVE
92/3 Dayton
93/4 Dayton 3
94/5 Dayton 3, 23
95/6 Phoenix

WINCH, JASON
91/2 ProCards 14
89/90 SketchOHL 135
90/1 SketchOHL 274
89/90 NiagaraFalls
91/2 Rochester/Kodak
92/3 Rochester/Kodak

WINCHES, HERB
95/6 Birmingham

WINDLER, HARALD
94/5 DEL 68

WING, JOHNNY
36/7 WWGum (V356) 102

WINGERTER, MARK
84/5 KelownaWings 21

WINGFIELD, BRAD
92/3 BCJHL 8

WINKLER, CHRIS
92/3 MPSPhotoSJHL 127

WINKLER, HAL
23/4 PaulinsCandy 46

WINNES, CHRIS
91/2 Pinnacle 351
91/2 ProSet 522
91/2 UpperDeck 514
92/3 UpperDeck 380
91/2 BOS/SportsAction

WINSTANLEY, JEFF
96/7 DEL 119

WIRTZ, ARTHUR
83&87 HallOfFame 90
83 HHOF Postcard (F)

WIRTZ, BILL
83&87 HallOfFame 179
83 HHOF Postcard (M)
70/1 CHI

WIRZENIUS, OLLI
65/6 Hellas 115

WISE, TONY
24/5 Crescent Falcons 10

WISEMAN, BRIAN
94/5 Classic 63

WISEMAN, CARL
91/2 SketchQMJHL 100

WISEMAN, EDDIE
34-43 BeeHives(NYA)
40/1 OPC (V301-2) 149

WISEMAN, LYALL
51/2 LavalDairy 63
52/3 LavalDairy 121
52/3 StLawrence 100

WISKE, RON
84/5 NYI 31

WISMER, CHRIS
95/6 Slapshot 302

WISSMAN, STEVE
93/4 LasVegas

WISTE, JIM
70/1 DadsCookies
70/1 EddieSargent 223
74/5 opcWHA 34
73/4 QuakerOats 1
70/1 VAN/RoyalBank
72/3 CLEV/Linnet

WITEHALL, JOHAN
90/1 SemicElitserien 48
97/8 udSwedish 110

WITKOWSKI, BYRON
92/3 WestMich.

WITT, BRENDAN
95/6 Bowman 127
94/5 Classic 90, C10, T75
93/4 Donruss CAN22
95/6 Donruss 361, -Pointer 18
96/7 DonrussElite 83
96/7 Fleer 120
95/6 FleerMetal 197
95/6 FleerUltra 361, -HighS 20
96/7 LeafPreferred 74
96/7 MetalUniverse 168
98/9 Pacific 450
97/8 PacificRegime 214
96/7 PaniniSticker 136
95/6 Parkhurst 258
93/4 Pinnacle 465
97/8 PinnacleBeAPlayer
95/6 P.Zenith 124, -RookieRoll 3
96/7 PinnacleZenith 50
95/6 ProMagnet 27
94/5 Score 205
96/7 Score 270
95/6 SelectCertified 119
91/2 SketchWHL 129
95/6 SkBxEmotion-Next 6
95/6 SkyBoxImpact 225
96/7 SkyBoxImpact 143
95/6 SP 162
95/6 Summit 189
96/7 Summit 162
95/6 Topps 346
95/6 ToppsFinest 106
95/6 ToppsStadiumClub 193
93/4 UpperDeck 544
95/6 UpperDeck 265
96/7 UpperDeck 177
97/8 UpperDeck 384
95/6 UDCollChoice 400
96/7 UDCollChoice 283, 345
95/6 WSH
93/4 Seattle

WITT, JARED
92/3 MPSPhotoSJHL 136

WITTBROCK, MARC
94/5 DEL 145
95/6 DEL 132

WITTENBERG, TOM
92/3 BCJHL 1

WITTLIFF, PHIL
94/5 Milwaukee

WITTMAN, DON
97/8 Pinnacle -CBC Sports 13

WITTMAN, THEO
95 PaniniWorlds

WITTWER, BRUNO
72 SemicSticker 141

WLASOW, LEO
93/4 Maine 37, 54

WOCHY, STEVE
51/2 Cleveland

WOHL, PAVEL
89 SemicSticker 177

WOHLERS, NICK
92/3 StJohns

WOIT, BENNY
45-64 BeeHives(DET)
82? JDMcCarthy
51/2 Parkhurst 58
52/3 Parkhurst 62
53/4 Parkhurst 45
54/5 Parkhurst 38
93/4 Parkie(56/7) 40
54/5 Topps 9

WOJTYNEK, HENRYK
79 PaniniSticker 118

WOLAK, MIKE
89/90 ProCards'IHL 13
85/6 Kitchener 16

WOLANIN, CHRIS
91/2 Greensboro
92/3 Greensboro 2

WOLANIN, CRAIG
90/1 Bowman 166
91/2 Bowman 138
92/3 Bowman 41
95 Globe 110
90/1 OPC/Topps 40
91/2 OPC/Topps 199
86/7 opcSticker 58
97/8 PacificDynag-BestKept 94
97/8 PacificRegime 197
90/1 Panini(QUE) 24
87/8 PaniniSticker 77
88/9 PaniniSticker 270
91/2 PaniniSticker 264
95 PaniniWorlds 218
91/2 Parkhurst 369
91/2 Pinnacle 217
92/3 Pinnacle 107
94/5 Pinnacle 445
94/5 Premier 228
90/1 ProSet 519
91/2 ProSet 203
90/1 Score 187
91/2 Score(CDN) 74, (U.S) 74
92/3 Score 21
93/4 Score 406
94 Semic 109
95 Semic 103
92/3 Topps 487
91/2 ToppsStadiumClub 4
92/3 ToppsStadiumClub 317
91/2 UpperDeck 486
97/8 UpperDeck 373
95/6 UDBeAPlayer 59
85/6 N.J.
86/7 N.J/SOBER
88/9 N.J/Caretta
89/90 N.J.
90/1 QUE/PetroCanada
91/2 QUE/PetroCanada
92/3 QUE/PetroCanada
94/5 QUE/BurgerKing
84/5 Kitchener 7

WOLANSKI, PAUL
89/90 SketchOHL 136
90/1 SketchOHL 275
91/2 SketchOHL 383
88/9 NiagaraFalls 3
89/90 NiagaraFalls

WOLF, MANFRED
82 SemicSticker 116
89 SemicSticker 121

WOLF, RUDOLF
94/5 APS 119
95/6 APS 296

WOLFE, BERNIE
76/7 OPC/Topps 227
77/8 OPC/Topps 138
78/9 OPC/Topps 81
78/9 WSH

WOLFE, DWIGHT
97/8 Halifax (1), (2)

WOLFE, HARRY
81/2 SSMarie
82/3 SSMarie
83/4 SSMarie
84/5 SSMarie
87/8 SSMarie 31

WOLITSKI, SHELDON
91/2 AvantGardeBCJ 4, 155

WOO, LARRY
90/1 SketchWHL 250
89/90 Victoria

WOOD, DAN
84/5 Fredericton 9
81/2 Kingston 14

WOOD, DEREK
93/4 Lethbridge

WOOD, DODY
95/6 Bowman 161
91/2 Classic 38
91/2 ClassicFourSport 38, -Aut.
97/8 PacificDynag-BestKept 87
93/4 Parkhurst 186
90/1 SketchWHL 13
91/2 SketchWHL 134
91/2 StarPics 12
91/2 UltimateDP 33, -Aut. 33
93/4 UpperDeck 238
95/6 UpperDeck 415
92/3 S.J/PacificBell
96/7 S.J/PacificBellSheet

WOOD, FRASER
81/2 Ottawa67s

WOOD, GORD
87/8 Kingston 2

WOOD, IAN
95/6 DEL 310
96/7 DEL 93
84/5 NovaScotia 19

WOOD, JASON
92/3 BCJHL 109

WOOD, MARTY
81/2 Regina 24

WOOD, PRYCE
88/9 Brandon 22
89/90 Brandon 4

WOOD, RANDY
90/1 Bowman 121
91/2 Bowman 227
92/3 Bowman 246
95/6 Donruss 154
93/4 EASports 196
92/3 FleerUltra 265
93/4 FleerUltra 279
93/4 Leaf 226
94/5 Leaf 544
95/6 Leaf 168
88/9 OPC/Topps 140
89/90 OPC/Topps 35
90/1 OPC/Topps 97
91/2 OPC/Topps 205
88/9 opcSticker 107/237
88/9 opcStickFS 22
88/9 PaniniSticker 294
90/1 PaniniSticker 79
91/2 PaniniSticker 244
92/3 PaniniSticker 251
93/4 PaniniSticker 105
91/2 Parkhurst 13
93/4 Parkhurst 297
94/5 Parkhurst 25
91/2 Pinnacle 104
92/3 Pinnacle 133, 234
93/4 Pinnacle 177
94/5 Pinnacle 218
95/6 Pinnacle 164
95/6 Playoff 205
96/7 Playoff 395
94/5 POG 51
95/6 POG 262
93/4 PowerPlay 35
93/4 Premier 119
94/5 Premier 61
90/1 ProSet 194
91/2 ProSet 151, 359
92/3 ProSet 20
91/2 PSPlatinum 160
90/1 Score 119
91/2 Score(CDN) 501
91/2 Score(U.S) 281, 42T
92/3 Score 73
93/4 Score 55
95/6 Score 63
92 SemicSticker 168
92/3 Topps 170
91/2 ToppsStadiumClub 221
92/3 ToppsStadiumClub 206
93/4 ToppsStadiumClub 89
90/1 UpperDeck 16
91/2 UpperDeck 289
92/3 UpperDeck 245
93/4 UpperDeck 22
95/6 UDBeAPlayer 35
95/6 UDCollChoice 74
91/2 BUF/Campbell
91/2 BUF/BlueShield
92/3 BUF/BlueShield
92/3 BUF/Jubillee
89/90 NYI

WOOD, WAYNE
76/7 opcWHA 31
77/8 opcWHA 42

WOODALL, FRANK
24/5 Holland 4
23/4 Crescent Selkirks 12

WOODBURN, STEVEN
95 PaniniWorlds 104
92 SemicSticker 226

WOODBURN, TIM
93/4 Birmingham 22

WOODBURN, TOM
71/2 STL

WOODCROFT, CRAIG
93/4 CanadaNats
93/4 FleerUltra 477
93/4 Premier-TmCanada 5
93/4 PowerPlay 497
91/2 ProCards 492
94 Semic 103
92/3 Indianapolis

WOODGATE, PETE
82/3 NorthBay
83/4 NorthBay

WOODLEY, DAN
89/90 ProCards(AHL) 190
90/1 ProCards 64
95/6 Slapshot 19
87/8 Flint
86/7 Portland

WOODLEY, DAVE
90/1 ProCards 528

WOODS, BOB
89/90 ProCards(AHL) 218
90/1 ProCards 560
88/9 Brandon 2
95/6 Hampton HRA-21
93/4 Johnstown 4

WOODS, BRAD
88/9 Brandon 5

WOODS, BROCK
90/1 SketchOHL 73
91/2 SketchOHL 279
92/3 Greensboro 4
93/4 Wheeling 6
94/5 Wheeling 3

WOODS, MARTIN
91/2 SketchQMJHL 255

WOODS, PAUL
78/9 OPC/Topps 159
79/80 OPC/Topps 48
80/1 OPC/Topps 148
81/2 O-Pee-Chee 104
82/3 O-Pee-Chee 98
83/4 O-Pee-Chee 133
84/5 O-Pee-Chee 66
82/3 opcSticker 187
82/3 Post
79/80 DET
80/1 DET

WOODS, STEVE
90/1 SketchOHL 224

WOOG, DAN
92/3 Minnesota
93/4 Minnesota
94/5 Minnesota

WOOG, DOUG
92/3 Minnesota
93/4 Minnesota
94/5 Minnesota

WOOLF, MARK
90/1 SketchMEM 92
90/1 SketchWHL 200
94/5 Huntington 22

WOOLLARD, CHAD
96/7 SSMarie

WOOLLEY, JASON
91/2 CanadaNats
92 CanadaWinterOlympics 194
92/3 Classic 97
94/5 ClassicImages 90
93/4 Donruss 364
95/6 Donruss 260
96/7 FleerNHLPicks 62
95/6 FleerUltra 244
93/4 Leaf 273
95/6 Leaf 307
92/3 opcPremier 98
98/9 Pacific 113
97/8 PacificCrown 279
92/3 Parkhurst 429
93/4 Parkhurst 490
95/6 Parkhurst 89
92/3 Pinnacle 415
96/7 PinnacleBeAPlayer 58
92/3 Score -CndOlympic 7
93/4 Score 435
97/8 Score(BUF) 17
92/3 UpperDeck 422
93/4 UpperDeck 462
95/6 UpperDeck 335, SE124
97/8 UpperDeck 138
97/8 UDCollChoice 203
98/9 Topps 9
92/3 WSH/Kodak
93/4 Portland

WORDEN, SCOTT
93/4 Mich.State

WORMALD, BRENT
92/3 BCJHL 226

WORRELL, PETER
97/8 Bowman 56
98/9 Pacific 232
94/5 Slapshot(MEM) 71

WORSLEY, LORNE (GUMP)
45-64 BeeHives(MTL), (NYR)
64-67 BeeHives(MTL)
62 CeramicTiles
63-5 ChexPhoto
65/6 CocaCola
70/1 DadsCookies
70/1 EddieSargent 84
71/2 EddieSargent 96
72/3 EddieSargent 105
70/1 Esso Stamp
88/9 Esso Sticker
83&87 HallOfFame 180
83 HHOF Postcard (M)
93/4 HHOFLegends 30
94 HockeyWit 14
72/3 Letraset 4
68/9 OPC/Topps 56
68/9 OPC 199, 212, -Puck 6
69/70 OPC/T. 1, OPC-Sticker
70/1 OPC/Topps 40
71/2 OPC/Topps 241
71/2 opcPoster 23
72/3 OPC 28, 286, T. 55, 64
73/4 OPC 230
53/4 Parkhurst 53
63/4 Parkhurst 39, 98
92/3 Parkhurst53 PR4
93/4 Parkhurst63 PR41
93/4 Parkie(56/7) 92, A4
94/5 Parkie(64/5) 81
95/6 Parkie(66/7)76,121,131,135
66/7 Post-Large, -Small
67 Post FlipBook
67/8 PostFlipBook
68/9 Post Marble
72/3 Post Transfers 9
72 SemicSticker 201
61/2 ShirriffCoin 85
68/9 ShirriffCoin MTL1
77-9 Sportscaster 06-07
81/2 TCMA 2
54-67 TorontoStar V9
56-66 TorontoStar 57/8
56-66 TorontoStar 60/1, 61/2
71/2 TheTorontoSun
54/5 Topps 10
57/8 Topps 53
58/9 Topps 39
59/60 Topps 15, 54
60/1 Topps 36
61/2 Topps 50, 64, 65, -Stamp
62/3 Topps 45, -Buck
65/6 Topps 2
66/7 Topps 2, 65, 130
66/7 Topps'USATest 2
67/8 Topps 1
91/2 Ultimate06 17, -Aut. 17
63/4 York 22
67/8 York 17,18,22,24,35, (no#)
93/4 Zellers
70/1 MIN
73/4 MIN
67/8 MTL
67/8 MTL/IGA
68/9 MTL
71 MTL/Pins
92/3 MTL/OPC 64
95/6 MTL/Forum 31Jan96
63/4 QuébecAces

WORSTER, WIL
92/3 Toledo 1

WORTERS, ROY
25-27 Anonymous 47
34-43 BeeHives(NYA)
35-40 CrownBrand 65
33-35 DiamondMatch
36-39 DiamondMatch (1), (2), (3)
83&87 HallOfFame 60

83 HHOF Postcard (D)
33/4 OPC (V304A) 45
35/6 Triumph
33/4 WWGum (V357) 11
36/7 WWGum (V356) 7

WORTMAN, KEVIN
92/3 Classic 116
92/3 ClassicFourSport 220
91/2 ProCards 578

WOTTON, MARK
95/6 Leaf 296
90/1 SketchWHL 86
91/2 SketchWHL 115
96/7 VAN
96/7 VAN/IGA
90/1 Saskatoon 16
91/2 Saskatoon 16
93/4 Saskatoon

WOTTON, SCOTT
91/2 AirCanadaSJHL A48

WOYTOWICH, BOB
68/9 Bauer
65/6 CocaCola
70/1 DadsCookies
70/1 EddieSargent 163
71/2 EddieSargent 165
70/1 Esso Stamp
72/3 Letraset 7
68/9 OPC/Topps 49, OPC 192
69/70 OPC 151, -Sticker
70/1 OPC/T. 88,-Deck 8, -Sticker
71/2 OPC/Topps 28
72/3 O-Pee-Chee 325
75/6 opcWHA 123
94/5 Parkie(64/5) 13
95/6 Parkie(66/7) 8
68/9 ShirriffCoin MIN2
71/2 TheTorontoSun
65/6 Topps 100
66/7 Topps 34
69/70 Topps 113
71/2 PGH

WRAY, DICK
51/2 LavalDairy 28
52/3 LavalDairy 118

WREGGET, KEN
91/2 Bowman 231
92/3 Bowman 182
95/6 Donruss 182
96/7 Donruss 136
97/8 Donruss 27
97/8 DonrussCanadianIce 76
97/8 DonrussPreferred 118
94/5 Fleer 172
92/3 FleerUltra 383
93/4 FleerUltra 399
94/5 FleerUltra 353
95/6 FleerUltra 128
86/7 Kraft Sports 61
94/5 Leaf 76
95/6 Leaf 19
96/7 Leaf 40
97/8 Leaf 82
97/8 Limited 188
87/8 O-Pee-Chee 242
88/9 O-Pee-Chee 264
89/90 O-Pee-Chee 22, 255
90/1 O-Pee-Chee 415
91/2 OPC/Topps 136
87/8 opcSticker 164/23
88/9 opcSticker 177/44
98/9 Pacific 360
97/8 PacificCrown 201
87/8 PaniniSticker 322
88/9 PaniniSticker 117
90/1 PaniniSticker 112
91/2 PaniniSticker 236
95/6 PaniniSticker 68
91/2 Parkhurst 357
92/3 Parkhurst 371
95/6 Parkhurst 167
94/5 ParkieSE 139
92/3 Pinnacle 356
93/4 Pinnacle 325
94/5 Pinnacle 230
95/6 Pinnacle 107
97/8 Pinnacle 96
97/8 PinnacleCertified 17
97/8 PinnacleInside 32
95/6 Playoff 80
95/6 POG 220
93/4 PowerPlay 417
93/4 Premier 277
94/5 Premier 328
94/5 Premier 84
90/1 ProSet 226
91/2 ProSet 450
91/2 PSPlatinum 210
90/1 Score 263
91/2 Score(CDN) 141, (U.S) 141
92/3 Score 399
93/4 Score 329
95/6 Score 126
96/7 Score 183
97/8 Score 32
97/8 Score(PGH) 2
95/6 SkyBoxEmotion 143
95/6 SkyBoxImpact 136
94/5 SP 88
95/6 Summit 112
96/7 Summit 60
92/3 Topps 494
95/6 Topps 190
91/2 ToppsStadiumClub 8
92/3 ToppsStadiumClub 130
94/5 ToppsStadiumClub 133
95/6 ToppsSuperSkills 79
90/1 UpperDeck 89
91/2 UpperDeck 206
94/5 UpperDeck 362
95/6 UpperDeck 108
96/7 UpperDeck 135
97/8 UpperDeck 344
95/6 UDBeAPlayer 67
95/6 UDCollChoice 314
96/7 UDCollChoice 220
97/8 UDCollChoice 210
92/3 PGH/Coke
93/4 PGH/Foodland 10
94/5 PGH 16
95/6 PGH/Foodland 9
96/7 PGH/FotoPuck
89/90 PHA
90/1 PHA
91/2 PHA/JCPenney
84/5 TOR
85/6 TOR
86/7 TOR
87/8 TOR
87/8 TOR/P.L.A.Y. 29
88/9 TOR/P.L.A.Y. 29
84/5 KelownaWingsWHL 53

WREN, BOB
93/4 Classic 33
93/4 ClassicFourSport 216
91/2 SketchOHL 37
93/4 Slapshot(Detroit) 25

WRIGHT, BILLY
90/1 SketchOHL 322
91/2 SketchOHL 63

WRIGHT, DARREN
82/3 Kitchener 22
83/4 Kitchener 7
84/5 Kingston 21
85/6 Kingston 21
93/4 PrinceAlbert
95/6 PrinceAlbert

WRIGHT, JAMIE
95/6 DonrussElite-WorldJrs 22
98/9 Pacific 186
93/4 Slapshot(Guelph) 11
94/5 Slapshot(Guelph) 12
95/6 Slapshot 93
95/6 UpperDeck 535
95/6 Guelph 27

WRIGHT, JOHN
74/5 Loblaws
74/5 OPC/Topps 156
72/3 VAN/RoyalBank
73/4 VAN/RoyalBank

WRIGHT, LARRY
74/5 Loblaws
78/9 O-Pee-Chee 360

WRIGHT, MARK
95/6 Sheffield

WRIGHT, PETER
51/2 LavalDairy 41
52/3 StLawrence 85

WRIGHT, SHAYNE
95/6 EdgeIce 67
93/4 OwenSound
95/6 Rochester

WRIGHT, TYLER
91/2 Arena 9
94/5 CanadaJr.Alumni 8
91/2 Classic 10
91/2 ClassicFourSport 10, -Aut
93/4 ClassicProspects 140
93/4 FleerUltra 240,-Prospect 10
93/4 Leaf 347
92/3 opcPremier 32
93/4 Parkhurst 340
93/4 Pinnacle 214
97/8 PinnacleBeAPlayer 64
93/4 Score 463
90/1 SketchMEM 112
90/1 SketchWHL 56
91/2 SketchWHL 191
95/6 SkyBoxImpact 199
91/2 StarPics 16, 36
91/2 UltimateDP 10, 66, -Aut. 10
91/2 UD 67, 686, 'CzechWJC 60
92/3 UpperDeck 558
93/4 UpperDeck 256
95/6 UpperDeck 327
93/4 EDM 27FEB94
94/5 CapeBreton

WTZEL, TODD
90/1 SketchOHL 273

WUNSCH, ALEXANDER
94/5 DEL 112
95/6 DEL 314

WYCHERLY, RALPH
34-43 BeeHives(NYAx2)

WYKOFF, SCOTT
88/9 ProCards(Maine)

WYNIA, SJON
91/2 AvantGardeBCJHL 50
92/3 BCJHL 93
91/2 Nanaimo

WYNNE, DEREK
91/2 AirCanadaSJHL B44
92/3 MPSPhotoSJHL 62

WYNNE, JOHN
90/1 SketchOHL 121
91/2 SketchOHL 28

WYROZUB, RANDY
70/1 EddieSargent 31
70/1 O-Pee-Chee 141
72/3 BUF

WYWROT, PETE
52/3 LavalDairy 46
52/3 StLawrence 76

WYZANSKY, BEN
94/5 Johnstown 19
92/3 Richmond

YACHIMEL, BERT
83/4 Moncton 16

YACHMENEV, VITALI
95/6 Bowman 115, BB20
94/5 Classic CP5
95/6 Classic 90
95/6 Donruss 318, -Rated 9
96/7 Donruss 233
96/7 DonrussCanadianIce 80
95/6 DonrussElite 52, -Rookie 2
96/7 DonrussElite 94
96/7 Fleer 51, -Rookie 10
95/6 FleerMetal 198, -IntSteel 23
96/7 FleerNHLPicks 142
95/6 FleerUltra 362
96/7 FleerUltra 84
96/7 Leaf 157
95/6 LeafLimited-Rookie 5
96/7 LeafLimited 34
96/7 LeafPreferred 99, -Steel 4
96/7 MetalUniverse 78
97/8 PacificCrown 167
96/7 PaniniSticker 266
97/8 PaniniSticker 222
95/6 Parkhurst 266, 506, PP37
94/5 ParkieSE 229
96/7 Pinnacle 206
97/8 PinnacleInside 144
95/6 P.Zenith 131, -RookRoll 11
96/7 PinnacleZenith 52
96/7 Score 241
97/8 Score 212
95/6 SelectCertified 130
94/5 SigRookie-Promo 5
94/5 SRGoldStandard 99
94/5 SRTetrad C XVII
95/6 SkyBoxImpact 205
96/7 SkBxImpact 59,173,-Fox 20
93/4 Slapshot(NorthBay) 22, 25
94/5 Slapshot(NorthBay) 24
94/5 SP 167
95/6 SP 68, FX11
96/7 SP 78
96/7 SPx 20, GF1
95/6 Summit 180
96/7 Summit 171
95/6 Topps 351
95/6 ToppsFinest 157
96/7 ToppsNHLPicks RS3
95/6 ToppsStadiumClub ER190
95/6 TSC-MembersOnly 48
95/6 ToppsSuperSkills SR15
94/5 UpperDeck 513
95/6 UpperDeck 263, H21
96/7 UpperDeck 77, SS24A, X20
97/8 UpperDeck 291, SG43
95/6 UDBeAPlayer 181
96/7 UDBlackDiamond 43
95/6 UDCollChoice 409
96/7 UDCC 125, 320, C8, UD32
97/8 UDCollChoice 123, SQ43

YAGANISKI, JASON
91/2 AirCanadaSJHL C19

YAGER, CAM
91/2 AirCanadaSJHL A37

YAKABUSKI, MARK
92/3 Ottawa67s

YAKE, TERRY
91/2 Bowman 4
92/3 ClassicProspects 148
93/4 Donruss 4
94/5 Donruss 124
93/4 EASports 3, 201
93/4 FleerUltra 221, 265
94/5 FleerUltra 9
95/6 FutureLegends 49
93/4 Leaf 406
94/5 Leaf 88
91/2 OPC/Topps 169
98/9 Pacific 376
93/4 PaniniSticker 125
94/5 PaniniSticker 121
92/3 Parkhurst 293
93/4 Parkhurst 271
94/5 Parkhurst V10
93/4 Pinnacle 340, -Expansion 5
94/5 Pinnacle 282
97/8 PinnacleBeAPlayer 190
93/4 PowerPlay 14
93/4 Premier 432
88/9 ProCards(Binghampton)
89/90 ProCards(AHL) 304
90/1 ProCards 186
90/1 Score 419
93/4 Score 259, 511
94/5 Score 93
92/3 Topps 432
91/2 ToppsStadiumClub 374
92/3 ToppsStadiumClub 496
93/4 ToppsStadiumClub 490
94/5 ToppsStadiumClub 226
91/2 UpperDeck 323
92/3 UpperDeck 512
93/4 UpperDeck 311, SP6
93/4 UDBeAPlayer 40
93/4 ANA/Caps 4
92/3 HFD/DairyMart
85/6 Brandon 14

YAKHANOV, ANDREI
95 PaniniWorlds 34

YAKIMISHYN, SHAWN
90/1 SketchWHL 80
91/2 SketchWHL 119
90/1 Saskatoon 23
91/2 Saskatoon 22

YAKIWCHUK, DALE
81/2 Milwaukee 8

YAKOVENKO, ANDREI
91/2 OPC 63R

YAKUBOV, RAVIL
91/2 OPC 46R
95 PaniniWorlds 34
92/3 RedAce(Blue) 29,(Violet) 29
92/3 UpperDeck 349
97/8 udSwedish 164

YAKUSHEV, ALEXEI
72 Hellas 74
74 Hellas 46
70/1 Kuvajulkaisut 4
74 SemicSticker 38
73/4 Soviet Champs 7, 9, 10
69/70 Soviet Stars
70/1 Soviet Stars
73/4 Soviet Stars 19
74/5 Soviet Stars 16
77-9 Sportscaster 103-08
77-9 Sprtscstr 71-1686, 84-2015
91/2 Trends(72) 70, 97
92/3 Trends(76) 106
72/3 WilliamsFIN 25
73/4 WilliamsFIN 5

YAREMA, BRENDAN
94/5 Slapshot(Sarnia) 16
95/6 Slapshot 344

YAREMCHUK, GARY
81/2 TOR

YAREMCHUK, KEN
88/9 ProCards(Newmarket)

YARI, J.D.
81/2 SSMarie

YASHIN, ALEXEI
95/6 Aces 8 (Spades)
96/7 Aces 2 (Diamonds)
97/8 Aces 8 (Clubs)
92/3 Classic 2, 61, LP2
93/4 Classic 34, 96
94/5 Classic AR3
92/3 ClassicFourSport 40, LP25
93/4 C4'Images 125, 130, CC13
93/4 ClassicProspects 40, LP25
93/4 C'Prospects-ROY 1, -Aut.
93/4 Donruss 238,-Rtd 7,-Elit U5
94/5 Donruss 63
95/6 Donruss 107
96/7 Donruss 124
97/8 Donruss 19
96/7 DonrussCanadianIce 61
97/8 DCdnIce 127,-Scrapbook11
95/6 DonrussElite 79
96/7 DonrussElite 41
97/8 DonrussElite 27
97/8 DonrussPreferred 42
97/8 DonrussPriority 147, 213
97/8 DonrussStudio 31
97/8 EssoOlympic 37
94/5 Flair 124, -ScoringPower 10
96/7 Flair 65
94/5 Fleer 149, -Franchise 9
96/7 Fleer 77
96/7 FleerNHLPicks 48
96/7 F.Picks-Fab 48, -Jagged 5
93/4 FleerUltra 384, -Wave 20
94/5 FU 152,-Globl 10,-AllRo 10
95/6 FleerUltra 114, -Rising 9
96/7 FleerUltra 120
95 Globe 172
97/8 KatchMedallion 102
94/5 Kraft-Sharpshooter
96/7 KraftDinner, -FlexMagnet
97/8 Kraft-CaseSerie,-WorldBest
93/4 Leaf 386, -Freshman 9
94/5 Leaf 19, -GoldLeafStar 5
94/5 Leaf-Limtd. 16,-GoldRook 3
95/6 Leaf 153
96/7 Leaf 101
97/8 Leaf 59
94/5 LeafLimited 80
95/6 LeafLimited 50
96/7 LeafLimited 31
96/7 LeafPreferred 17, -Steel 16
97/8 Limited 69, 71, 189
96/7 Maggers 109
94/5 McDonalds McD3
96/7 MetalUniverse 108
97/8 Omega 159
98/9 Pacific 318, -TeamCL 18
97/8 PacificCrown 120
97/8 PacificCrownRoyale 94
97/8 PcfcDynagon! 87,-Tand 70
97/8 PacificInvincible 97
97/8 PacificParamount 129
98/9 PcfcParamnt 168,-T.CL 18
97/8 PacificRevolution 96
94/5 PaniniSticker L
95/6 PaniniSticker 48
96/7 PaniniSticker 48
98/9 PaniniSticker 43
93/4 Parkhurst 254, C10, E7
94/5 Parkhurst 273, C16
95/6 Parkhurst 151, 242
94/5 ParkieSE 123, seV21
93/4 Pinnacle 455, SR5
94/5 Pinn. 28, 465, NL7, WE17
96/7 Pinnacle 121
97/8 Pinnacle 126
96/7 PinnacleBeAPlayer 48
97/8 PinnacleBeeHive 21
97/8 PinnacleCertified 78
97/8 Pinnacle-EPIX 4
97/8 PinnacleInside 57
96/7 Pinn.Zenith 23, -Assailant 1
95/6 Playoff 74
94/5 POG 174
95/6 POG 191
94/5 Post
96/7 Post
97/8 Post
93/4 PowerPlay 403
93/4 PP-Global 10, -Rookie 16
93/4 Premier 317
94/5 Premier 192, 365
94/5 Premier-Finest(OPC) 15
92/3 RedAce(Blue) 27,(Violet) 27
93/4 Score 603, (CDN) DD3
94/5 Score 253
95/6 Score 230, -Golden 7
96/7 Score 181
97/8 Score 116
94/5 Select 135
96/7 SelectCertified 83
95/6 SelectCertified 36
93 SemicSticker 136
94 Semic 147
95 Semic 136
95/6 SkyBoxEmotion 128
95/6 SkBxE-Xcel 5, -Xcited 7
95/6 SkyBoxImpact 122
96/7 SkyBoxImpact 91
94/5 SP 79
95/6 SP 101
96/7 SP 108, HC13
97/8 SPAuthentic 105
96/7 SPx 31
97/8 SPx 35
98/9 SPx"Finite" 57, 98
97/8 SportFX MiniStix
95/6 Summit 101, -MadHatter 12
96/7 Summit 34
96/7 TeamOut
95/6 Topps 170, 2CG, YS5
98/9 Topps 5
94/5 ToppsFinest 5, 56
95/6 ToppsFinest 151
93/4 ToppsStadiumClub 359
94/5 T.StadiumClub 116, 175
95/6 ToppsStadiumClub 182
93/4 TSC-MembersOnly 42
94/5 TSC-MembersOnly 14
97/8 ToppsSticker 5
91/2 UD 651, 'CzechWJC 12
92/3 UpperDeck 334, 349
93/4 UD 277, 349, H8, SP-112
94/5 UpperDeck 129, 554, SP55
95/6 UpperDeck 15, SE59
96/7 UpperDeck 110
97/8 UpperDeck 321, SG23
93/4 UDBeAPlayer 17, -Roots 14
94/5 UDBAP R92,R172,-Aut.150
96/7 UDBlackDiamond 159
97/8 UDBlackDiamond 111
98/9 UDChoice 141, SQ10
95/6 UDCollChoice 189, C18
96/7 UDCollChoice 179, 324
97/8 UDCC 173, C15, SQ72
96/7 UpperDeck"Ice" 96
97/8 UpperDeckIce 28
96 Wien 148
97/8 Zenith 72
93/4 OTT/Kraft
94/5 OTT/Bell
95/6 OTT
96/7 OTT/PizzaHut
97/8 OTT

YASHIN, OLEG
91/2 O-Pee-Chee 64R
93/4 Roanoke
94/5 Roanoke

YASHIN, SERGEI
90/1 O-Pee-Chee 482
89 SemicSticker 88
89/90 SovietNats
87/8 SovietStars

YATES, JOE
91/2 SketchOHL 239
93/4 Slapshot(NiagaraFalls) 7

YATES, ROSS
94/5 DEL 151
96/7 DEL 157

YAWNEY, TRENT
91/2 Bowman 393
89/90 O-Pee-Chee 222
90/1 OPC/Topps 297
91/2 OPC/Topps 255
97/8 PacificDynagon-BestKept 84
89/90 PaniniSticker 53
90/1 PaniniSticker 187
91/2 Parkhurst 245
92/3 Parkhurst 262
92/3 Pinnacle 174
93/4 Pinnacle 123
94/5 Pinnacle 245
91/2 ProCards 491
90/1 ProSet 64
90/1 Score 292
91/2 Score(CDN) 439
92/3 Score 216
93/4 Score 332
91/2 ToppsStadiumClub 205
93/4 ToppsStadiumClub 472
94/5 ToppsStadiumClub 44
90/1 UpperDeck 82
95/6 UDBeAPlayer 146
92/3 CGY/IGA 12
88/9 CHI/Coke
89/90 CHI/Coke
90/1 CHI/Coke
83/4 Saskatoon 2
84/5 Saskatoon

YDERSTROM, DICK
74 Hellas 39
74 SemicSticker 13
73/4 WilliamsFIN 41

YEATMAN, D.
28/9 PaulinsCandy 67

YEGOROV, ALEXEI
96/7 FleerNHLPicks 174
96/7 Leaf 216
96/7 SkyBoxImpact 163
96/7 Summit 195
96/7 UpperDeck 192

YELLE, STÉPHANE
95/6 Bowman 124
95/6 Donruss 350
96/7 Donruss 220
96/7 DonrussCanadianIce 45
95/6 FleerUltra 363
96/7 Leaf 150
98/9 Pacific 170
97/8 PacificCrown 344
95/6 Parkhurst 539
96/7 PinnacleBeAPlayer 15
97/8 Score(COL) 19
91/2 SketchOHL 161
93/4 Slapshot(Oshawa) 10
96/7 Summit 156
96/7 UpperDeck 40
97/8 UpperDeck 49
96/7 UDCollChoice 61
91/2 Oshawa
91/2 Oshawa/Dominos 6
92/3 Oshawa

YELLOWAGA, KEVIN
89/90 Saskatoon 14

YEO, MICHAEL
90/1 SketchOHL 396
91/2 SketchOHL 253
93/4 Slapshot(Sudbury) 22
90/1 Sudbury 23
91/2 Sudbury 23
92/3 Sudbury 20
93/4 Sudbury 22

YEPANTCHINSEV, VADIM
see Vadim Epantchinsev

YERKOWICH, SERGEI
96/7 LasVegas

YEWCHUK, MARTY
95/6 Louisiana

YINGST, DOUGH
88/9 ProCards(Hershey)

YINGST, MATT
94/5 Johnstown 20

YLÄJÄ, MIKKO
73/4 WilliamsFIN 323

YLI-MAENPAA, KARI
89/90 SemicElitserien 196

YLI-MAENPAA, MIKE
93/4 Sisu 185
94/5 Sisu 45
95/6 Sisu 98

YLÖNEN, JUHA
95 Hartwall
92/3 Jyvas-Hyva 23
93/4 Jyvas-Hyva 114
97/8 Omega 180
98/9 Pacific 347
97/8 PinnacleBeAPlayer 240
93/4 Sisu 21
95/6 Sisu 254, -GoldCards 24
96/7 Sisu 53
96 Wien 21
91/2 UD 673, 'CzechWJC 36
97/8 UpperDeck 192
98/9 UDChoice 164
97/8 PHO

YLÖNEN, PETRI
95 Globe 199
95 PaniniWorlds 96
94 Semic 212
95 Semic 195
92 SemicSticker 220
93 SemicSticker 249
96 Wien 183

YLÖNEN, URPO
66/7 Champion 71
70/1 Kuvajulkaisut 80, 154
69/70 MästarSerien 14
72 Panda
79 PaniniSticker 162
72 SemicSticker 71
91 SemicSticker 226
96/7 Sisu 192
78/9 SM-Liiga 197
71/2 WilliamsFIN 79, 206
72/3 WilliamsFIN 243
73/4 WilliamsFIN 277

YLÖNEN, VEIJO
73/4 WilliamsFIN 324

YORK, HARRY
97/8 Donruss 138
96/7 DonrussElite 130
97/8 DonrussPreferred 50
97/8 DonrussPriority 156
96/7 Flair 122
96/7 FleerUltra 149
97/8 Leaf 73
97/8 Limited 1, 158
97/8 PacificCrown 176
97/8 PcfcDynagon! 109,-Tand 61
97/8 Pinnacle 161
96/7 PinnacleBeAPlayer LTH2A
96/7 PinnacleZenith 131
97/8 Score 192
97/8 Score(STL) 5
96/7 SelectCertified 96
96/7 SP 134
96/7 UpperDeck 329
97/8 UpperDeck 140
97/8 UDCollChoice 229

YORK, JASON
94/5 Donruss 115
94/5 Flair 54
94/5 FleerUltra 288
94/5 Leaf 275
98/9 Pacific 319
97/8 PacificDynag-BestKept 67
94/5 ParkieSE 56
97/8 PinnacleBeAPlayer 95
91/2 ProCards 139
89/90 SketchMEM 32
90/1 SketchOHL 197
95/6 UpperDeck 306
96/7 UpperDeck 5
96/7 OTT/PizzaHut
97/8 OTT

YORK, MICHAEL
95/6 DonrussElite-WorldJrs 44
96/7 UpperDeck"Ice" 147

YORK, SHAWN
91/2 AvantGardeBCJHL 59
92/3 BCJHL 100
91/2 Nainamo

YOUNG, ADAM
92/3 BCJHL 162
93/4 Slapshot(Windsor) 10
94/5 Slapshot(Windsor) 12
95/6 Slapshot 414
92/3 Windsor 11

YOUNG, ALAN
94/5 DEL 420
95/6 DEL 394
96/7 DEL 302

YOUNG, B.J.
95/6 RedDeer
97/8 Bowman 112

YOUNG, BARRY
90/1 SketchOHL 397
91/2 SketchOHL 248
89/90 Sudbury 22
90/1 Sudbury 3
91/2 Sudbury 11

YOUNG, BILL
72/3 LosAngelesSharks
72/3 Minnesota

YOUNG, C.J.
93/4 FleerUltra 248
92/3 Parkhurst 246
93/4 Premier 347
90/1 ProCards 617
93/4 ToppsStadiumClub 316
92/3 UpperDeck 395

YOUNG, CLAYTON
89/90 SketchMEM 19
89/90 Kamloops

YOUNG, DON
82/3 NorthBay

YOUNG, DOUG
34-43 BeeHives(DET), (MTL.C)
35-40 CrownBrand 200
26 Dominion 23
39/40 OPC (V301-1) 58
36/7 WWGum (V356) 49

YOUNG, GEORGE
91/2 AvantGardeBCJHL 45
91/2 Nainamo

YOUNG, HOWIE
45-64 BeeHives(CHI), (DET)
62 CeramicTiles
68/9 O-Pee-Chee 151
68/9 OPC/Topps 82
61/2 ShirriffCoin 74
68/9 ShirriffCoin OAK12
63/4 Topps 29
67/8 Topps 49
62/3 YorkTransfer 35

YOUNG, IAN
94/5 DEL 324
95/6 DEL 300
91/2 Oshawa/Dominos 30

YOUNG, JASON
91/2 Classic 45
91/2 ClassicFourSport 45, -Aut.
93/4 ClassicProspects 226
90/1 SketchOHL 398
91/2 SketchOHL 251
91/2 StarPics 65
91/2 UltimateDP 40, -Aut 40
91/2 Rayside
92/3 Rochester/Dunkin'Donuts
92/3 Rochester/Kodak
93/4 Rochester
89/90 Sudbury 20
90/1 Sudbury 16
91/2 Sudbury 24

YOUNG, JOEY
91/2 SketchWHL 151

YOUNG, JOHN
93/4 Greensboro
90/1 Mich.Tech
91/2 Mich.Tech

YOUNG, MATT
91/2 SketchWHL 182

YOUNG, SCOTT
89/90 ProCards(AHL) 13
90/1 ProCards 438

YOUNG, SCOTT A.
90/1 Bowman 253
91/2 Bowman 86
95/6 DEL 450
93/4 Donruss 284
94/5 Donruss 310
95/6 Donruss 36
96/7 Donruss 129
96/7 DonrussCanadianIce 30
92/3 FleerUltra 391
94/5 FleerUltra 181
95/6 FleerUltra 226
95 Globe 124
97/8 KatchMedallion 6
93/4 Leaf 108
94/5 Leaf 108
95/6 Leaf 317
96/7 Leaf 181
96/7 LeafPreferred 98
89/90 O-Pee-Chee 209
90/1 OPC/Topps 84
91/2 OPC/Topps 235
89/90 opcSticker 44/190
89/90 opcSticker 264/143, FS7
98/9 Pacific 48
97/8 PacificCrown 187
97/8 PacificParamount 8
89/90 PaniniSticker 224
90/1 PaniniSticker 34
91/2 PaniniSticker 273
93/4 PaniniSticker 73
94/5 PaniniSticker 59
95/6 PaniniSticker 250
96/7 PaniniSticker 253
95 PaniniWorlds 227
92/3 Parkhurst 383
95/6 Parkhurst 322
93/4 Pinnacle 129
94/5 Pinnacle 361
96/7 Pinnacle 197
97/8 PinnacleBeAPlayer 143
96/7 PinnacleZenith 115
94/5 POG 200
95/6 POG 78
93/4 PowerPlay 206
94/5 Premier 519
90/1 ProSet 113
91/2 ProSet 195
90/1 Score 21,-Hot 12,-Young 14
91/2 Score(CDN) 507, (U.S) 287
93/4 Score 56
95/6 Score 278
96/7 Score 140
97/8 Score(ANA) 10
95 Semic 110
96/7 Summit 78
96/7 ToppsNHLPicks 113
91/2 ToppsStadiumClub 74
93/4 ToppsStadiumClub 261
94/5 ToppsStadiumClub 153
95/6 ToppsStadiumClub 47
90/1 UpperDeck 87
92/3 UpperDeck 397
96/7 UpperDeck 42
95/6 UDBeAPlayer 107
96/7 UDBlackDiamond 48
95/6 UDCollChoice 271
96 Wien 173
89/90 HFD/JuniorWhalers
90/1 HFD/JuniorWhalers
92/3 QUE/PetroCanada
94/5 QUE/BurgerKing

YOUNG, STEVE
89/90 Portland

YOUNG, TIM
76/7 OPC/Topps 158, OPC 387
77/8 OPC/T. 2, 223, -Glossy 22
78/9 OPC/Topps 138
79/80 OPC/Topps 36
80/1 OPC/Topps 174
81/2 OPC 169, Topps(W) 113
82/3 O-Pee-Chee 177
83/4 O-Pee-Chee 395
84/5 O-Pee-Chee 351
81/2 opcSticker 94
83/4 Vachon 140
78/9 MIN/Cloverleaf 8
79/80 MIN
80/1 MIN
81/2 MIN
82/3 MIN
83/4 WPG

YOUNG, WARREN
86/7 O-Pee-Chee 209
85/6 OPC/Topps 152
85/6 opcSticker 100
85/6 DET/Caesars
86/7 PGH/Kodak

YOUNG, WENDELL
90/1 Bowman 203
93/4 EASports 132
95/6 EdgeIce 109, TW6
92/3 FleerUltra 206
92/3 Kraft-Disk
90/1 OPC/Topps 309
92/3 opcPremier 76
90/1 PaniniSticker 127
93/4 PaniniSticker 221
92/3 Parkhurst 170
92/3 Pinnacle 381
93/4 Premier 166, -Masks 7
90/1 ProSet 512
90/1 Score 298
92/3 Score 511
93/4 Score 341
94/5 SR-Tetrad CXVIII
90/1 UpperDeck 102
89/90 PGH/Foodland 14
91/2 PGH/Elbys
92/3 T.B/Sheraton
93/4 T.B/KashNKarry
94/5 T.B/SkyBoxSportsCafe
86/7 VAN
84/5 Fredericton 18
85/6 Fredericton 12
82/3 Kitchener 8

YOUNGHAMS, TOM
78/9 O-Pee-Chee 295
79/80 OPC/Topps 177
80/1 O-Pee-Chee 343
81/2 O-Pee-Chee 173
79 PaniniSticker 218
78/9 MIN/Cloverleaf 9
79/80 MIN
80/1 MIN

YRJÖLÄ, JUHA
72/3 WilliamsFIN 360

YSEBAERT, PAUL
91/2 Bowman 53
92/3 Bowman 376
93/4 Donruss 376, 417
94/5 Donruss 2
95/6 Donruss 258
92/3 FleerUltra 54
93/4 FleerUltra 457
94/5 FleerUltra 277
95/6 FleerUltra 157
91/2 Kraft 46
96/7 Kraft-Disk
93/4 Leaf 388
94/5 Leaf 202
95/6 Leaf 185
97/8 Omega 215
90/1 OPC/Topps 49
91/2 OPC/Topps 248
92/3 O-Pee-Chee 46
98/9 Pacific 408
97/8 PacificCrown 178
97/8 PacificCrownRoyale 127
97/8 PacificInvincible 134
97/8 PacificParamount 177
98/9 PacificParamount 222
97/8 PacificRevolution 131
92/3 PaniniSticker 118
93/4 PaniniSticker 248
94/5 PaniniSticker 132
95/6 PaniniSticker 129
91/2 Parkhurst 42, 435
92/3 Parkhurst 43
93/4 Parkhurst 504
94/5 Parkhurst 48
95/6 Parkhurst 191
91/2 Pinnacle 36
92/3 Pinnacle 93
93/4 Pinnacle 348
94/5 Pinnacle 301
95/6 Pinnacle 17
97/8 PinnacleBeAPlayer 163
95/6 Playoff 313
95/6 POG 250
93/4 PowerPlay 277
94/5 Premier 368
88/9 ProCards(Utica)
89/90 ProCards'AHL 209
95/6 ProMagnet 69
90/1 ProSet 607
91/2 ProSet 59, 608
92/3 ProSet 41, 248, PV1
91/2 PSPlatinum 167
90/1 Score 406
91/2 Score(CDN) 166, (U.S) 166
92/3 Score 95, 414, -Young 35
93/4 Score 239, 517
95/6 Score 116
95/6 SkyBoxEmotion 167
92/3 Topps 58, 314
95/6 Topps 320
91/2 ToppsStadiumClub 171
92/3 ToppsStadiumClub 378
93/4 ToppsStadiumClub 360
90/1 UpperDeck 375
91/2 UpperDeck 278
92/3 UpperDeck 176
93/4 UpperDeck 365, SP-179
94/5 UpperDeck 491
95/6 UpperDeck 109, SE165
96/7 UpperDeck 159
97/8 UpperDeck 159
95/6 UDBeAPlayer 139
98/9 UDChoice 194
95/6 UDCollChoice 27
96/7 UDCollChoice 251
91/2 DET/Caesars
95/6 T.B.
95/6 T.B/SkyBoxSportsCafe
93/4 WPG/Ruffles

YTTER, MATS
94/5 ElitSet 134
95/6 ElitSet 126, -Spidermen 12
89/90 SemicElitserien 240
90/1 SemicElitserien 150
91/2 SemicElitserien 252
92/3 SemicElitserien 274
95/6 udElite 186

YUDIN, ALEXANDER
91/2 O-Pee-Chee 47R
92/3 UpperDeck 333, 336

YULE, STEVE
89/90 SketchMEM 22
90/1 SketchWHL 286
91/2 SketchWHL 78
88/9 Kamloops
89/90 Kamloops

YUNG KE, YANG
79 PaniniSticker 355

YUNG SHENG, CHANG
79 PaniniSticker 357

YURSINOV, VLADIMIR
92/3 JyvasHyva 171
93/4 Jyvas-Hyva 313
90/1 O-Pee-Chee 494
93/4 Sisu 28, 373
94/5 Sisu 152
69/70 Soviet Stars
79/80 SovietStars
83/4 SovietStars
87/8 SovietStars
73/4 WilliamsFIN 217

YUSHKEVICH, DIMTRI
93/4 Classic 97
93/4 Donruss 254
94/5 Donruss 308
95/6 Donruss 387
93/4 EASports 98, 225
94/5 Fleer 160
92/3 FleerUltra 161
93/4 FleerUltra 198
94/5 FleerUltra 161
95 Globe171
93/4 Leaf 82
94/5 Leaf 37
95/6 Leaf 291
92/3 opcPremier 65
97/8 PacificCrown 153
95/6 PaniniSticker 121
97/8 PaniniSticker 173
92/3 Parkhurst 133
93/4 Parkhurst 145
94/5 Parkhurst 163
95/6 Parkhurst 469
92/3 Pinnacle 394
93/4 Pinnacle 146
94/5 Pinnacle 227
93/4 PowerPlay 186
93/4 Premier 18
94/5 Premier 468
92/3 RedAce(Blue) 35,(Violet) 35
93/4 Score 216
97/8 Score(TOR) 16
95 Semic 126
93 SemicSticker 144
95/6 Topps 192
93/4 ToppsStadiumClub 492
94/5 ToppsStadiumClub 78
92/3 UpperDeck 333, 350, 570
92/3 UpperDeck CC20, ER12
93/4 UpperDeck 127, SP-119
94/5 UpperDeck 349
95/6 UpperDeck 81, 376
95/6 UDBeAPlayer 7
95/6 UDCollChoice 249
96/7 UDCollChoice 164, 263
96 Wien 137
92/3 PHA/JCPenney
92/3 PHA/UD 08APR93
92/3 PHA/UD 11FEB93
92/3 PHA/UD 12NOV92
93/4 PHA 10FEB94
93/4 PHA 12DEC93
93/4 PHA/JCPenney
94/5 PHA

YZERMAN, STEVE
95/6 Aces 3 (Spades)
96/7 Aces 7 (Hearts)
89/90 ActionPacked
94/5 ActionPacked 4
90/1 Bowman 233, -Hat Trick 5
91/2 Bowman 41, 42, -Promo
92/3 Bowman 103, 220
95/6 Bowman 21
83 CanadaJuniors
97/8 CorinthianHeadliners
93/4 Donruss 95, G
94/5 Donruss 1
95/6 Donruss 96, -Igniters 8
96/7 Donruss 171, 240
97/8 Donruss 2, -Elite 6, -Line 5
96/7 DonrussCanadianIce 39
97/8 D.CdnIce 4,-Nt'l 4,-Scrap 19
95/6 DonrussElite 99
96/7 D.Elite 38, -Perspectives 3
97/8 D.Elite 15, 122,-BackTo 8
97/8 D.Elite -Crafts 16,-PrmN 10
97/8 DonrussPreferred 41, 179
97/8 D.Pref -Line 6B,-PrecM 14
97/8 D.Pref -Tins 13,-WideTins 6
97/8 DonrussPriority 4, 209
97/8 D.Prio -DirDep 2, -OpDay 4
97/8 D.Prio-Postcard 3,-Stamp 3
97/8 D.Studio 10, 106,-HardH 10
97/8 D.Studio-Portraits 10,-Sil 10
96/7 Duracell DC15
93/4 EASports 39
94/5 Flair 55, -HotNumber 10
96/7 Flair 31, -Centre 10
94/5 Fleer 67
96/7 Fleer 35, -ArtRoss 25
95/6 FleerMetal 51
96/7 F.Picks-Fab 49, -Captn 2
92/3 FleerUltra 55
93/4 FleerUltra 201, -AS 12 6
93/4 FU-Pivots 10, -Scoring 6
94/5 FleerUltra 67, -Pivots 10
94/5 FU-Scoring 7, -Power 10
95/6 FleerUltra 51, -Extra 20
96/7 FleerUltra 56, -MrMom. 10
88/9 FritoLay
95 Globe 89
96/7 Got-UmHockeyGreatsCoin
93/4 HockeyWit 108
92/3 HumptyDumpty (1)
97/8 KatchMedallion 54, 161
91/2 Kelloggs 14
93/4 KennerSLU
94/5 KennerSLU
97/8 KennerSLU- 1on1
89/90 Kraft 63, -Sticker 3
90/1 Kraft 63, 78
91/2 Kraft 68
92/3 Kraft-AllStar
93/4 Kraft-Captain
94/5 Kraft-HockeyHero
96/7 Kraft'Disk
97/8 Kraft -RoadToN,-WorldBest
93/4 Leaf 162, -HT 10, -Studio 5
94/5 Leaf 148
95/6 Leaf 60
96/7 Leaf 13, 239, -Fire 12
97/8 Leaf 4, 171,-BnnrS 5,-Fire 4
94/5 LeafLimited 120
95/6 LeafLimited 105
96/7 LeafLimited 40, -Stubble 14
96/7 LeafPreferred 102,-Vanity 4
97/8 Limited 41, 115, 165
97/8 Limited -fabric 49, 70
96/7 Maggers 55
91/2 McDonalds McD19
92/3 McDonalds McD14
93/4 McDonalds McD13
96/7 McDonalds McD17
97/8 McDonalds McD19, F3
97/8 McDonalds -Medallions
96/7 MetalUniverse 51
97/8 Omega 88, -GameFace 8
97/8 Omega -Silk 6,-StickHand 9
84/5 OPC 67, 385, Topps 49
85/6 OPC/Topps 29
86/7 OPC/Topps 11
87/8 OPC/Topps 56, C
88/9 OPC/Topps 196, L
89/90 OPC/Topps 83, L
90/1 OPC/T. 133,222,J, T-TL 19
91/2 OPC/Topps 60,424, T-TL 3
92/3 OPC 61,321, -25Years 17
90/1 opcPremier 130
91/2 opcPremier 73, 142
84/5 opcSticker 37
85/6 opcSticker 30
86/7 opcSticker 161/20
87/8 opcSticker 111
88/9 opcSticker 253
89/90 opcSticker 254
98/9 Pacific 19, -DynIce 10
98/9 Pacific -GoldC 16, -TmCL 9
97/8 PacificCrown 19, -Supial 8
97/8 PCC-Cramer 6, -Gold 11
97/8 PCC-Slap 3C, -TeamCL 9
97/8 PacificCrownRoyale 51
97/8 PCR-Blades 10, -Cramer 6
97/8 PCR-HatTrick 8, -Lamp 9
97/8 PacificDynagon! 46, 139
97/8 PcfcD-BstKpt 36, -Dyn 8B
97/8 PacificD-Tandem 7, 26
97/8 PacificInv. 53, -Attack 11
97/8 PacificInv-Feature 16,-Off 9
97/8 PcfcParamount 71,-BigN 10
97/8 PcfcP-CdnGrts 7,-Photo 10
98/9 PacificParamnt 83, -HOF 5
98/9 PcfcP-SpecDel 9,-Tm CL 9
97/8 PacificRegime 75
97/8 PacificRevolution 52
97/8 PcfcRev -Icon 5,-TeamCL 9
87/8 PaniniSticker 243
88/9 PaniniSticker 47
89/90 PaniniSticker 57
90/1 PaniniSticker 208
91/2 PaniniSticker 134
92/3 PaniniSticker 112
93/4 PaniniSticker V
94/5 PaniniSticker 209
95/6 PaniniSticker 179
96/7 PaniniSticker 181
97/8 PaniniSticker 149
95 PaniniWorlds 280

91/2 Parkhurst 44, 434
92/3 Parkhurst 44, 456
93/4 Parkhurst 326, W5
94/5 Parkhurst 299, V57
95/6 Parkhurst 70
94/5 ParkieSE 55
91/2 Pinnacle 75, 383
92/3 Pinnacle 241, 258, 350
93/4 Pinn. 175, CA7, -Nifty 1,8
94/5 Pinnacle 271
96/7 Pinnacle 25
97/8 Pinnacle 71, -TeamP 9
96/7 P.BAP LTH9A, -Biscuit 13
97/8 PinnBeeHive 11, -TmBH 16
97/8 Pinn.Certified 38, -Team 13
97/8 Pinnacle-EPIX 9
97/8 P.Inside 24,-Can 14,-Trck 9
96/7 PinnacleMint 12
97/8 PinnacleMint 5
95/6 PinnacleZenith 93
96/7 Pinn.Zenith 5, -ZTeam 6
95/6 Playoff 147
96/7 Playoff 366
94/5 POG 92
95/6 POG 96
97/8 Post
93/4 PowerPlay 77, -PointLdr 20
93/4 PP-Gamebreaker 10
93/4 Premier 280
93/4 Prmr-Black(OPC) 23, (T) 16
94/5 Premier 235, -GoToGuy 12
95/6 ProMagnet 105
90/1 ProSet 79, 347
91/2 ProSet 62, 281, 571
91/2 PS-ThePuck 8
92/3 ProSet 39, 247, -TL 3
91/2 PSPlatinum 32
96/7 SB'7Eleven
90/1 Score 3, 339, -Hot 4
91/2 Score(CDN) 190, 335
91/2 Score(U.S) 190, 419
92/3 Score 400, 423
93/4 Score 310, 448, -P.AS 36
93/4 Score(U.S) DD9,-Dream 16
93/4 Score-TheFranchise 6
94/5 Score 150, DT20
95/6 Score 240, -Golden 12
96/7 Score 60, -Sudden 2
97/8 Score 86, 263
97/8 Score(DET) 2
92/3 SeasonsPatch 6
93/4 SeasonsPatch 20
94/5 Select 35
95/6 SelectCertified 94
96/7 SelectCert. 41, -Corner 14
89 SemicSticker 72
91 SemicSticker 65
92 SemicSticker 87
93 SemicSticker 203
85/6 7Eleven 5
84/5 7ElevenDisk
95/6 SkyBoxEmotion 60
95/6 SkyBoxImpact 58
96/7 SkyBoxImpact 40,-Blade 25
94/5 SP 34
95/6 SP 46, E14, FX7
96/7 SP 47, CW15, -Inside
97/8 SPAuthentic 52, I21, S3
96/7 SPx 14, HH3
97/8 SPx 14, -DuoView
98/9 SPx"Finite" 30, 93, 156, 175
96/7 SportFX MiniStix
95/6 Summit 154
96/7 Summit 76
95/6 SuperSkills 10
95/6 SuperSticker 37, DC25
96/7 TeamOut
92/3 Topps 207
95/6 Topps 237, HGC16
98/9 Topps 175
94/5 ToppsFinest 84
95/6 ToppsFinest 162
96/7 T.Picks 31, FC7, TS15
91/2 ToppsStadiumClub 81
92/3 T.StadiumClub 19, 254
93/4 T.StadiumClub 70, -AllStar
95/6 ToppsStadiumClub 20
97/8 ToppsSticker 5
90/1 UD 56, 303, 477,-Holo. (x2)
91/2 UpperDeck 146, 626
92/3 UpperDeck 155, G10, WG7
92/3 UD-LockerAS 36
93/4 UD 227, 290, 388, E14
93/4 UD HT6, NL3, R6, SP-47
94/5 UpperDeck 300, 550, H22
94/5 UD IG1, R24, R43, SP25
95/6 UD 113,218,R15,R58,SE30
95/6 UD-AllStarPredict MVP15
96/7 UD 50, GJ1, HH19, SS16B
96/7 UD X13, -AllStarYCTG AR5
97/8 UD 57, S19, SG19
97/8 UD SS20,T3B
93/4 UDBeAPlayer 18, -Roots 4
94/5 UDBAP R29, R115, UC5
94/5 UDBAP G18, -Aut. 115
96/7 UDBlackDiamond 162, RC9
97/8 UDBlackDiamond 123, PC7
98/9 UDChoice 73, 310
98/9 UDChoice BH27, SQ18
95/6 UDCollChoice 266, C26
96/7 UDCollC hoice79, 292, C10
96/7 UDCollChoice S22, UD14
97/8 UDCollChoice 78, 313, C19
97/8 UDCollChoice S29, SQ67
97/8 udDiamondVision 4, DM3
96/7 UpperDeck"Ice" 109, S2
97/8 UpperDeckIce 89, IC19,L5B
97/8 ValuNet
96 Wien 101
97/8 Zenith 5, Z21,-ChasCup 15
85/6 DET/Caesars
86/7 DET/Caesars
87/8 DET/Caesars
88/9 DET
88/9 DET/Caesars
89/90 DET/Caesars
90/1 DET/Caesars
91/2 DET/Caesars
96/7 DET/HockeytownPuck
96/7 DET/PhotoPuck

Z

ZABAWA, ANDRZEJ
79 PaniniSticker 132

ZABEL, NORBERT
94/5 DEL 182

ZABRANSKY, LIBOR
94/5 APS 104
95/6 APS 60
97/8 Score(STL) 17
97/8 UpperDeck 144

ZACH, HANS
94/5 DEL 77
95/6 DEL 146

ZACH, JOHANN
79 PaniniSticker 112

ZADINA, MAREK
94/5 APS 38
95/6 APS 235

ZADRAZIL, JIRI
95/6 APS 24

ZAICHKOWSKI, JASON
92/3 BCJHL 143

ZAINE, ROD
71/2 TheTorontoSun

ZAITSEV, SERGEI
90/1 O-Pee-Chee 487

ZAJANKALA, GEORGE
91/2 SketchWHL 124
92/3 Cleveland 11
95/6 Dayton
94/5 Knoxville 17

ZAJIC, JOSEF
94/5 APS 35
95/6 APS 97

ZAJICEK, JAN
79 PaniniSticker 81

ZAJONC, PETR
95/6 APS 232

ZAKALL, BRIAN
91/2 AvantGardeBCJ 74

ZALAPSKI, ZARLEY
90/1 Bowman 207
91/2 Bowman 15
92/3 Bowman 173
93/4 Donruss 149, 410
94/5 Donruss 248
95/6 Donruss 177
96/7 Donruss 4
93/4 EASports 55
94/5 Flair 30
92/3 FleerUltra 77
93/4 FleerUltra 234
94/5 FleerUltra 38
92/3 HumptyDumpty (1)
93/4 Leaf 8
94/5 Leaf 294
95/6 Leaf 225
96/7 Leaf 95
89/90 OPC/Topps 168
90/1 OPC/Topps 78
91/2 OPC/Topps 344
92/3 O-Pee-Chee 248
89/90 opcSticker 45/191, 232/93
89/90 opcStickFS 14
97/8 PacificDynag-BestKept 15
89/90 PaniniSticker 318
90/1 PaniniSticker 126
91/2 PaniniSticker 322
92/3 PaniniSticker 263
93/4 PaniniSticker 129
95/6 PaniniSticker 242
91/2 Parkhurst 61
92/3 Parkhurst 59
93/4 Parkhurst 88
94/5 Parkhurst 31
95/6 Parkhurst 31
91/2 Pinnacle 110
92/3 Pinnacle 271
93/4 Pinnacle 257
94/5 Pinnacle 342
96/7 Pinnacle 119
97/8 PinnacleBeAPlayer 68
95/6 Playoff 132
94/5 POG 64
95/6 POG 58
93/4 PowerPlay 112
93/4 Premier 20
94/5 Premier 379
90/1 ProSet 242
91/2 ProSet 91
92/3 ProSet 59
91/2 PSPlatinum 47
90/1 Score 218
91/2 Score(CDN) 111, (U.S) 111
92/3 Score 238
93/4 Score 104, -PinnacleAS 2
95/6 Score 69
96/7 Score 205
94/5 Select 140
89 SemicSticker 60
91 SemicSticker 60
95/6 SkyBoxEmotion 26
95/6 SkyBoxImpact 26
96/7 SP 25
95/6 SuperSticker 19
96/7 TeamOut
92/3 Topps 82
95/6 Topps 263
98/9 Topps 196
91/2 ToppsStadiumClub 228
92/3 ToppsStadiumClub 25
93/4 T.StadiumClub 102, -AllStar
94/5 ToppsStadiumClub 141
95/6 ToppsStadiumClub 96
90/1 UpperDeck 33
91/2 UpperDeck 231
92/3 UD 316, -LockerAS 18
93/4 UpperDeck 213
94/5 UpperDeck 110
95/6 UpperDeck 480
96/7 UpperDeck 24
95/6 UDBeAPlayer 108
95/6 UDCollChoice 123
96/7 UDCollChoice 41
91/2 HFD/JuniorWhalers
92/3 HFD/DairyMart
93/4 HFD/Coke
97/8 MTL
89/90 PGH/Elbys
89/90 PGH/Foodland 3
90/1 PGH/Foodland 12

ZAMBITO, MISTY
93/4 Huntington

ZAMBON, M.
91/2 AvantGardeBCJHL 158

ZAMOJSKI, JACEK
89 SemicSticker 131
92 SemicSticker 273

ZAMUNER, ROB
92/3 Classic 98
92/3 ClassicFourSport 211
93/4 Donruss 329
97/8 DonrussPriority 112
92/3 FleerUltra 415
93/4 FleerUltra 199
97/8 Kraft -RoadToNagano
93/4 Leaf 173
94/5 Leaf 427
97/8 Limited 88
97/8 McDonalds -Medallions
97/8 Omega 216
92/3 opcPremier 69
98/9 Pacific 409, -TeamCL 24
97/8 PacificCrown 204
98/9 PcfcParamnt 233,-TmCL 24
97/8 PcfcRevolut 132,-TmCL 23
93/4 PaniniSticker 214
96/7 PaniniSticker 131
97/8 PaniniSticker 108
92/3 Parkhurst 171
93/4 Parkhurst 194
94/5 Parkhurst 224
92/3 Pinnacle 414
93/4 Pinnacle 121
96/7 PinnacleBeAPlayer 114
95/6 Playoff 200
93/4 PowerPlay 236
93/4 Premier 19
89/90 ProCards(IHL) 40
90/1 ProCards 1
91/2 ProCards 204
95/6 ProMagnet 68
93/4 Score 291
97/8 Score 200
92/3 Topps 426
98/9 Topps 43
92/3 ToppsStadiumClub 439
93/4 ToppsStadiumClub 376
94/5 ToppsStadiumClub 48
92/3 UpperDeck 583, CC4
93/4 UpperDeck 202, SP-154
94/5 UpperDeck 468
96/7 UpperDeck 158
97/8 UpperDeck 364
94/5 UDBAP R175, -Aut. 147
98/9 UDChoice 196
96/7 UDCollChoice 248
97/8 UDCollChoice 238
97/8 ValuNet
92/3 T.B/Sheraton
94/5 T.B/SkyBoxSportsCafe
95/6 T.B.
95/6 T.B/SkyBoxSportsCafe

ZANIBBI, ROB
85/6 Sudbury 4
87/8 Sudbury 26
88/9 Sudbury 26
89/90 Sudbury 23
90/1 Sudbury 25
91/2 Sudbury 1
92/3 Sudbury 2

ZANIER, MARK
83/4 Moncton 4

ZANIER, MIKE
92 SemicSticker 244
88/9 EDM/ActionMagazine 4
84/5 NovaScotia 18

ZANUSSI, JOE
76/7 OPC 324

ZANUSSI, RON
78/9 OPC/Topps
79/80 OPC/Topps
80/1 OPC/Topps 192
81/2 O-Pee-Chee 325
78/9 MIN/Cloverleaf 9
79/80 MIN
80/1 MIN
81/2 TOR

ZANUTTO, MIKE
95/6 Slapshot 245

ZAPORKAN, TERRY
84/5 KelownaWings&WHL 12
83/4 KelownaWings

ZAPT, BILL
92/3 BCJHL 240

ZARILLO, BRUCE
94 Semic 308

ZARILLO, BRUNO
96/7 DEL 352

ZAROWNY, AARON
93/4 Lethbridge

ZARRILLO, BRUNO
95 Globe 231
95 PaniniWorlds 90
92 SemicSticker 254
93 SemicSticker 225

ZATOPEK, LIBOR
95/6 APS 239

ZAVAROUKINE, NIKOLAI
93/4 Classic 49
93/4 Parkhurst 530
94/5 ParkieSE 230
94/5 SP 163
94/5 UpperDeck 516

ZAVISH, BRAD
90/1 SketchWHL 14
91/2 SketchWHL 358
93/4 EDM 27MAR94
94/5 CapeBreton

ZAWATSKY, ED
91/2 Rochester/Genny

ZAYONCE, DEAN
90/1 SketchWHL 118
91/2 Greensboro
93/4 Greensboro
94/5 Greensboro

ZBONTAR, MARJAN
79 PaniniSticker 395

ZDRAHAL, PAVEL
95/6 APS 307

ZDUNEK, PIOTR
89 SemicSticker 138
92 SemicSticker 279

ZEDNIK, RICHARD
96/7 DonrussCanadianIce 125
97/8 KatchMedallion 156
96/7 LeafPreferred 133
96/7 MetalUniverse 197
97/8 Omega 244
98/9 Pacific 451
97/8 PacificCrownRoyale 144
98/9 PacificParamount 250
97/8 P.BAP -OneTimers 17
96/7 PinnacleZenith 120
96/7 SelectCertified 110
97/8 SPAuthentic 197
98/9 SPx"Finite" 135
98/9 Topps 92
96/7 UpperDeck 356
97/8 UpperDeck 388
97/8 UDBlackDiamond 51
98/9 UDChoice 218
97/8 UpperDeckIce 55
97/8 Zenith 83,Z78,-RookRgn 15
97/8 Zenith -RookieZTeam 17
96/7 Portland

ZEHNDER, ANDREAS
95 PaniniWorlds

ZEHR, JEFF
95/6 Slapshot 416
97/8 Bowman 149

ZEIDEL, LARRY
45-64 BeeHives(DET)
68/9 OPC/Topps 92
52/3 Parkhurst 91
53/4 Parkhurst 73

ZELENKA, JIRI
94/5 APS 83
95/6 APS 279

ZELEPUKIN, VALERI
92/3 Bowman 430
93/4 Donruss 193
94/5 Donruss 291
95/6 Donruss 320
94/5 Flair 101
92/3 FleerUltra 122
93/4 FleerUltra 222
94/5 FleerUltra 124
93/4 KraftDinner
93/4 Leaf 104
94/5 Leaf 17
95/6 Leaf 260
91/2 O-Pee-Chee 65R
98/9 Pacific 218
97/8 PacificCrown 299
92/3 PaniniSticker 177
93/4 PaniniSticker 38
94/5 PaniniSticker 33
96/7 PaniniSticker 87
97/8 PaniniSticker 67
91/2 Parkhurst 324
92/3 Parkhurst 228, 327
93/4 Parkhurst 383
94/5 Parkhurst 124
95/6 Parkhurst 391
91/2 Pinnacle 354
92/3 Pinnacle 286
93/4 Pinnacle 94
94/5 Pinnacle 49
95/6 Pinnacle 194
95/6 Playoff 168
94/5 POG 149
93/4 PowerPlay 145
94/5 Premier 58
91/2 ProCards 427
92/3 ProSet -RookieG.Ldr 10
91/2 PSPlatinum 261
92/3 RedAce(Blue) 7, (Violet) 7
92/3 Score 206
93/4 Score 278
94/5 Score 49
95/6 Score 179
97/8 Score(N.J.)
92/3 Topps 462
98/9 Topps 187
92/3 ToppsStadiumClub 99
93/4 ToppsStadiumClub 314
94/5 ToppsStadiumClub 225
91/2 TriGlobe 15-16
91/2 UpperDeck 589
92/3 UpperDeck 295, E12
93/4 UpperDeck 369
94/5 UpperDeck 143
97/8 UpperDeck 303
95/6 UDBeAPlayer 207
96/7 UpperDeck"Ice" 38
96/7 N.J/Sharp

ZELEZNY, OTTO
95/6 APS 199

ZEMLAK, RICHARD
94/5 C'Promo PR1
89/90 ProCards(IHL) 154
90/1 ProCards 623
91/2 ProCards 590
87/8 MIN
85/6 QUE
86/7 QUE
86/7 QUE/GeneralFoods

ZEMLICKA, RICHARD
95/6 APS 290, 366
94/5 DEL 47
95 Globe 154
95 PaniniWorlds 198
94 Semic 180
95 Semic 151
91 SemicSticker 125
92 SemicSticker 134
93 SemicSticker 95
96 Wien 120

ZENHAUSERN, ALDO
79 PaniniSticker 259

ZENT, JASON
94/5 Classic 117
94/5 C'Images 54, -Aut
95/6 EdgeIce 50
96/7 OTT/PizzaHut

ZERWESZ, RAINER
94/5 DEL 101
95/6 DEL 212
96/7 DEL 356

ZETEK, ONDREJ
94/5 APS 212
95/6 APS 154

ZETTEL, MICHAEL
94/5 DEL 223

ZETTERBERG, PATRIK
94/5 EliteSet 254
95/6 EliteSet 292

ZETTERSTROM, LARS
79 PaniniSticker 190
78/9 VAN/RoyalBank

ZETTLER, ROB
92/3 Bowman 84
90/1 OPC/Topps 289
91/2 OPC/Topps 272
92/3 O-Pee-Chee 366
91/2 opcPremier 21
97/8 PacificCrown 101
92/3 PaniniSticker 127
94/5 Parkhurst 164
91/2 Pinnacle 213
92/3 Pinnacle 89
96/7 PinnacleBeAPlayer 64
88/9 ProCards(Kalamazoo)
89/90 ProCards(IHL) 81
91/2 ProSet 330
91/2 Score(CDN) 643
91/2 Score(U.S) 370, 93T
92/3 Score 191
93/4 Score 413
92/3 Topps 227
91/2 ToppsStadiumClub 194
92/3 ToppsStadiumClub 225
94/5 ToppsStadiumClub 109
91/2 UpperDeck 61
94/5 UpperDeck 454
93/4 PHA 24FEB94
94/5 PHA
91/2 S.J.
92/3 S.J/PacificBell
87/8 SSMarie 14

ZEZEL, PETER
90/1 Bowman 19
91/2 Bowman 164
92/3 Bowman 263
93/4 Donruss 338
92/3 FleerUltra 216
93/4 FleerUltra 436
93/4 Leaf 107
94/5 Leaf 533
85/6 OPC/Topps 24
86/7 OPC/Topps 190
87/8 OPC/Topps 71
88/9 OPC/Topps 146
89/90 OPC/Topps 27
90/1 OPC/Topps 15
91/2 OPC/Topps 445
92/3 O-Pee-Chee 337
90/1 opcPremier 131
85/6 opcSticker 94/227
86/7 opcSticker 245/137
87/8 opcSticker 96/229
88/9 opcSticker 102/234
89/90 opcSticker 23
98/9 Pacific 436
87/8 PaniniSticker 129
89/90 PaniniSticker 118
90/1 PaniniSticker 264
91/2 PaniniSticker 103
92/3 PaniniSticker 81
91/2 Parkhurst 174
92/3 Parkhurst 410
93/4 Parkhurst 206
91/2 Pinnacle 174, 414
92/3 Pinnacle 283
93/4 Pinnacle 297
94/5 Pinnacle 109
96/7 PinnacleBeAPlayer 94
93/4 PowerPlay 455
93/4 Premier 454
94/5 Premier 22
90/1 ProSet 274, 556
91/2 ProSet 227
92/3 ProSet 187
91/2 PSPlatinum 232
90/1 Score 24, 6T
91/2 Score(CDN) 489, (U.S) 269
92/3 Score 174
93/4 Score 31
92/3 Topps 319
98/9 Topps 56
91/2 ToppsStadiumClub 104
92/3 ToppsStadiumClub 433
93/4 ToppsStadiumClub 116
90/1 UpperDeck 17
91/2 UpperDeck 241
92/3 UpperDeck 389
93/4 UpperDeck 199
94/5 UpperDeck 140

95/6 UpperDeck 377
94/5 UDBeAPlayer -Aut. 100
96/7 UDCollChoice 222
94/5 DAL/Southwest
86/7 PHA
88/9 STL/Kodak
89/90 STL/Kodak
90/1 TOR/P.L.A.Y. 19
92/3 TOR/Kodak
93/4 TOR/Abalene
93/4 TOR/Blacks 4

ZHAMNOV, ALEXEI
95/6 Aces K (Hearts)
95/6 Bowman 60
93/4 Donruss 380
94/5 Donruss 73
95/6 Donruss 155,-Elite 1,-Ignt 6
96/7 Donruss 89
97/8 Donruss 96
96/7 DonrussCanadianIce 88
97/8 DonrussCanadianIce 91
95/6 DonrussElite 29
96/7 DonrussElite 65
97/8 DonrussPriority 62
93/4 EASports 147
94/5 Flair 212
96/7 Flair 17
94/5 Fleer 247
96/7 Fleer 94
95/6 FleerMetal 168, -Winners 9
96/7 FleerNHLPicks 56
96/7 FPicks-Fab 50, -Jagged 14
92/3 FleerUltra 447
93/4 FleerUltra 128
94/5 FleerUltra 398
95/6 FU 185, 398, -Pivots 10
95/6 FU-Red10,-Ultraview 10
95 Globe 173
95/6 Kraft, -Disk
93/4 Leaf 84, -GoldLeafRook 5
94/5 Leaf 97
95/6 Leaf 104,-Fir 3,-Fra 5,-Gld 4
96/7 Leaf 107
94/5 LeafLimited 113
96/7 LeafPreferred 95
94/5 McDonalds 27
95/6 McDonalds 3
96/7 MetalUniverse 29
97/8 Omega 53
91/2 O-Pee-Chee 48R
92/3 opcPremier 13
98/9 Pacific 155
97/8 PacificCrown 316
97/8 PacificInvincible 32
97/8 PacificParamount 47
98/9 PacificParamount 51
93/4 PaniniSticker 190
94/5 PaniniSticker 163
95/6 PaniniSticker 212
96/7 PaniniSticker 196
98/9 PaniniSticker 128
92/3 Parkhurst 210
93/4 Parkhurst 243, 503
94/5 Parkhurst 260
95/6 Parkhurst 226, 241
94/5 Parkie seV45
92/3 Pinnacle 416
93/4 Pinnacle 56
94/5 Pinnacle 147
95/6 Pinnacle 23,-Roaring20s 11
96/7 Pinnacle 13
97/8 Pinnacle 123
96/7 PinnacleBeAPlayer 11
97/8 PinnacleBeAPlayer 99
97/8 PinnacleCertified 101
97/8 PinnacleInside 107
95/6 PinnacleZenith 26
96/7 PinnacleZenith 108
95/6 Playoff 110, 330
94/5 POG 375
95/6 POG 15, 289
93/4 PowerPlay 278,-Second 12
93/4 PP-RisingStars 9
93/4 Prmr 128, 420, -Black(T) 8
94/5 Premier 217
95/6 ProMagnet 60
92/3 RedAce(Blue) 2, (Violet) 2
93/4 Score 256, (CND) DD2
94/5 Score 154
95/6 Score 85,-Brdr 12,-Lamp 10
96/7 Score 128
97/8 Score 175
94/5 Select 51
95/6 SelectCert. 6, -Double 20
94 Semic 150, 356
91 SemicSticker 95
92 SemicSticker 110
95/6 SkyBoxEmotion 198
95/6 SkBxE-Xcel 10, -Xcited 17
95/6 SkBxImpact 187,-Ice 12
96/7 SkyBoxImpact 21
94/5 SP 133
95/6 SP 167
96/7 SP 30
97/8 SPAuthentic 32
96/7 SPx 36
95/6 Summit 3, -MadHatter 5
96/7 Summit 37
95/6 SuperSticker 135
95/6 Topps 22, 331, 2PL
98/9 Topps 135
94/5 ToppsFinest 102
95/6 ToppsFinest 78
93/4 ToppsStadiumClub 56
95/6 ToppsStadiumClub 95
95/6 ToppsSuperSkills 70
91/2 TriGlobe 7-8
91/2 UpperDeck 2
92/3 UD 578, ER8,-LockerAS 60
93/4 UpperDeck 162, SP-180
94/5 UpperDeck 7, SP90
95/6 UD 64, 234, F13, R28
96/7 UpperDeck 125, 233, 24B
97/8 UpperDeck 42, T19C
94/5 UDBeAPlayer-Aut. 21
96/7 UDBlackDiamond 106
97/8 UDBlackDiamond 56
98/9 UDChoice 48
95/6 UDCollChoice 49, 383, C8
96/7 UDCC 203, 327, C11
97/8 UDCollChoice SQ46
96 Wien 143
93/4 WPG/Ruffles
95/6 WPG

ZHDAN, ALEXANDER
93/4 Richmond 3

ZHITNIK, ALEXEI
93/4 Donruss 165
94/5 Donruss 279
95/6 Donruss 50
96/7 Donruss 11
96/7 DonrussElite 115
96/7 Flair 10
95/6 FleerMetal 17
96/7 FleerNHLPicks 152
92/3 FleerUltra 314
93/4 FleerUltra 87
94/5 FleerUltra 104
95/6 FleerUltra 22, -Rising 10
95 Globe 169
97/8 KatchMedallion 18
93/4 Leaf 123, -GoldLeafRook 8
94/5 Leaf 8
95/6 Leaf 4
96/7 Leaf 155
94/5 LeafLimited 111
92/3 opcPremier 125
98/9 Pacific 114
97/8 PacificCrown 236
98/9 PacificParamount 25
94/5 PaniniSticker 179
95/6 PaniniSticker 20
96/7 PaniniSticker 17
97/8 PaniniSticker 11
92/3 Parkhurst 71
93/4 Parkhurst 92
94/5 Parkhurst 101
95/6 Parkhurst 19, -InterAS 3
92/3 Pinnacle 392
93/4 Pinnacle 23
94/5 Pinnacle 87
95/6 Pinnacle 64
96/7 Pinnacle 180
95/6 Playoff 14
94/5 POG 131
95/6 POG 47
93/4 PowerPlay 123
93/4 Premier 2
94/5 Premier 57
95/6 ProMagnet 107
93/4 Score 148
94/5 Score 171
95/6 Score 47
96/7 Score 70
97/8 Score(BUF) 18
96/7 SelectCertified 45
95 Semic 128
95/6 SkyBoxEmotion 19
95/6 SkyBoxImpact 19
94/5 SP 16
95/6 SP 15
96/7 SP 19
97/8 SPAuthentic 17
91/2 StarPics 38
96/7 Summit 69
95/6 SuperSticker 13
96/7 TeamOut
95/6 Topps 49
98/9 Topps 192
93/4 ToppsStadiumClub 221
95/6 ToppsStadiumClub 143
91/2 UD 660, 'CzechWJC 21
92/3 UD 566, CC7, ER13
93/4 UpperDeck 161, SP-75
94/5 UpperDeck SP38
95/6 UpperDeck 187, SE11
96/7 UpperDeck 17
97/8 UDBlackDiamond 1
98/9 UDChoice 26
95/6 UDCollChoice 303
96/7 UDCollChoice 26, 311
97/8 UDCollChoice 29
96 Wien 134

ZHLUKTOV, VICTOR
79 PaniniSticker 149
82 SemicSticker 64
79/80 SovietStars
83/4 SovietStars
92/3 Trends(76) 138

ZHOLTOK, SERGEI
92/3 Classic 50
93/4 C'Prospects 227
93/4 Leaf 376
94/5 Leaf 508
98/9 Pacific 320
97/8 PacificCrown 328
97/8 PaniniSticker 39
92/3 Parkhurst 482
93/4 Parkhurst 281
94/5 ParkieSE 10
97/8 PinnacleBeAPlayer 192
93/4 PowerPlay 294
93/4 Score 475
94/5 ToppsStadiumClub 254
91/2 UD 659, 'CZechWJC 20
93/4 UpperDeck 244
94/5 UpperDeck 419
97/8 UpperDeck 116
97/8 UDCollChoice 177
96/7 OTT/PizzaHut
97/8 OTT
95/6 LasVegas
96/7 LasVegas

ZHURIN, ALEXANDER
93/4 Slapshot(Kingston) 10

ZIB, LUKAS
95/6 APS 57

ZIDLICKY, MARKE
94/5 APS 56
95/6 APS 86

ZIEGLER, JOHN
87 HallOfFame 257

ZIESCHE, JOACHIM
70/1 Kuvajulkaisut 100

ZIESCHE, STEFFAN
95/6 DEL 111
91/2 UD 679, 'CzechWJC 42

ZIETARA, WALENTI
74 Hellas 91
79 PaniniSticker 129
73/4 WilliamsFIN 104

ZILIOTTO, MARK
89/90 ProCards'AHL 64

ZILKA, KEN
91/2 SketchWHL 195

ZIMA, ALEX
94/5 APS 19
95/6 APS 116, 383

ZIMAKOV, SERGEI
95/6 UpperDeck 558

ZIMIN, EVGENY
72 Panda
72 SemicSticker 9
74 SemicSticker 47
69/70 Soviet Stars
71/2 Soviet Stars
91/2 Trends(72) 14
71/2 WilliamsFIN 20

ZIMMER, BRAD
90/1 SketchMEM 127
90/1 SketchWHL 125
91/2 SketchWHL 349
89/90 Lethbridge
93/4 RedDeer

ZIMMER, DEVIN
91/2 AirCanadaSJHL D8

ZIMMERMAN, JASON
92/3 MPSPhotoSJHL 34

ZIMMERMAN, SHAWN
92/3 MPSPhotoSJHL 38
93/4 WestMich.

ZINGER, VIKTOR
69/70 MästarSerien 27, 29
69/70 Soviet Stars

ZININE, DIMITRI
93/4 Jyvas-Hyva 169
93/4 Sisu 172

ZINOVJEV, DIMITRI
90/1 O-Pee-Chee 478

ZIVNY, MARTIN
94/5 APS 154
95/6 APS 257

ZMOLEK, DOUG
92/3 Classic 88
92/3 ClassicFourSport 207, -Aut
93/4 Donruss 313
92/3 FleerUltra 405
93/4 Leaf 112
94/5 Leaf 453
91/2 OPC 9S
92/3 opcPremier 18
97/8 PacificCrown 297
93/4 PaniniSticker 263
92/3 Parkhurst 393
93/4 Parkhurst 457
93/4 Pinnacle 117
96/7 PinnacleBeAPlayer 151
93/4 Premier 143
93/4 Score 327
93/4 ToppsStadiumClub 171
92/3 UpperDeck 509
93/4 UpperDeck 193
94/5 DAL/Southwest
92/3 S.J/PacificBell
91/2 Minnesota

ZMRHAL, PAVEL
94/5 APS 166

ZNAROK, OLEG
91/2 Jyvas-Hyva 70
90/1 O-Pee-Chee 477

ZOHIL, JASON
90/1 SketchOHL 198, 243
91/2 SketchOHL 268
91/2 Sudbury 25
89/90 Windsor

ZOL, DIANO
92/3 BCJHL 53

ZOLOTOV, ROMAN
92/3 Classic 55

ZOMBO, MIKE
85/6 London 19

ZOMBO, RICK
91/2 Bowman 54
92/3 Bowman 87
92/3 O-Pee-Chee 97
90/1 OPC/Topps 21
91/2 OPC/Topps 454
89/90 PaniniSticker 64
90/1 PaniniSticker 206
91/2 PaniniSticker 137
91/2 Parkhurst 380
91/2 Pinnacle 259, 393, 410
92/3 Pinnacle 129
93/4 Pinnacle 306
94/5 Pinnacle 447
90/1 ProSet 80
91/2 ProSet 64, 474
90/1 Score 101, -HotCards 49
91/2 Score(CDN) 177
91/2 Score(U.S) 177, 60T
92/3 Score 154
93/4 Score 211
94/5 Score 75
92/3 Topps 288
91/2 ToppsStadiumClub 32
92/3 ToppsStadiumClub 100
90/1 UpperDeck 115
91/2 UpperDeck 395
95/6 UpperDeck 319
95/6 UDBeAPlayer 136
86/7 DET/Caesars
87/8 DET/Caesars
88/9 DET/Caesars
88/9 DET
89/90 DET/Caesars
90/1 DET/Caesars
91/2 STL

ZOMBON, MIKE
91/2 AvantGardeBCJ 34

ZORICA, JOE
52/3 AnonymousOHL 2

ZORYK, STEVE
93/4 Slapshot(SSMarie) 11
95/6 Slapshot 269

ZUBICEK, PAVEL
95/6 APS 205

ZUBKOV, VLADIMIR
82 SemicSticker 72
83/4 SovietStars

ZUBOV, SERGEI
92/3 C.Prospects 70, 74, BC6
93/4 ClassicProspects 115
93/4 Donruss 225
94/5 Donruss 219
95/6 Donruss 130, 357, -Domn 3
96/7 Donruss 91
95/6 DonrussElite 37
96/7 DonrussElite 111
97/8 DonrussPreferred 91
97/8 DonrussPriority 51
95/6 EdgeIce C16
94/5 Flair 118
94/5 Fleer 140, -Franchise 10
96/7 Fleer 28
95/6 FleerMetal 121, -IntSteel 24
95/6 FM-MetalWinners 8
96/7 FleerNHLPicks 26
92/3 FleerUltra 359
93/4 FleerUltra 243
94/5 FleerUltra 144
95/6 FleerUltra 108, 295
96/7 FleerUltra 48
95 Globe 165
93/4 Leaf 164
94/5 Leaf 111
95/6 Leaf 126
96/7 Leaf 130
94/5 LeafLimited 65
95/6 LeafLimited 74
96/7 LeafPreferred 63
97/8 Limited 93
97/8 Omega 77
91/2 O-Pee-Chee 28R, 30R
98/9 Pacific 56
97/8 PacificCrown 76
97/8 PacificCrownRoyale 44
97/8 PcfcDynagon! 40,-Tand 44
97/8 PacificInvincible 45
98/9 PacificParamount 72
97/8 PacificRevolution 45
94/5 PaniniSticker 89
95/6 PaniniSticker 111
96/7 PaniniSticker 64
97/8 PaniniSticker 138
92/3 Parkhurst 351
93/4 Parkhurst 133
94/5 Parkhurst 144
95/6 Parkie 434, PP27, -IntAS 3
93/4 Pinnacle 156
94/5 Pinnacle 36
96/7 Pinnacle 122
95/6 PinnacleZenith 66
96/7 PinnacleZenith 38
95/6 Playoff 187
96/7 Playoff 383
94/5 POG 172
95/6 POG 217
93/4 PowerPlay 167, -Rising 10
93/4 Premier 217
94/5 Premier 221, 382, 493
95/6 ProMagnet 94
93/4 Score 313
95/6 Score 188
96/7 Score 171
94/5 Select 14
95/6 SelectCertified 67
94 Semic 140
95/6 SkyBoxEmotion 144
95/6 SkyBoxImpact 137
96/7 SkyBoxImpact 32
94/5 SP 78
95/6 SP 117
96/7 SP 43
97/8 SPAuthentic 46
95/6 Summit 74
96/7 Summit 119
95/6 SuperSticker 99
95/6 Topps 333
98/9 Topps 176, B7
95/6 ToppsFinest 171
93/4 ToppsStadiumClub 312
95/6 ToppsStadiumClub 92
92/3 UpperDeck 516
93/4 UpperDeck 181
94/5 UpperDeck 100, SP142
95/6 UD 474, H37, SE155
96/7 UpperDeck 246, X39
97/8 UpperDeck 263
96/7 UDBlackDiamond 56
98/9 UDChoice 66
95/6 UDCollChoice 10
96/7 UDCollChoice 214
96/7 UpperDeck"Ice" 16
96 Wien 136
96/7 DAL/Southwest
95/6 PGH/Foodland 12
92/3 Binghampton

ZUBRUS, DAINIUS
96/7 AllSportPPF 98, 170
97/8 Donruss 75
96/7 DonrussCanadianIce 147
96/7 D.Elite 141, -Aspirations 15
97/8 DonrussElite 50, 135
97/8 D.Preferd 59, 190,-Line 8C
97/8 D.Priority 23, -DirDep 29
97/8 D.Prio-Pstcrd 34,-Stamp 34
97/8 D.Studio 26,-Hrd 5,-Port 27
96/7 Flair 119
96/7 FleerUltra 129
97/8 KatchMedallion 108
97/8 Leaf 124, 186, -BanrSea 22
97/8 Leaf-FireOnIce 13
96/7 LeafLimited-Rookies 6
96/7 LeafPreferred 128
97/8 Limited 109, 195, -fabric 3
96/7 MetalUniverse 198
97/8 Omega 171,-GameFace 14
98/9 Pacific 333, -GoldC 26
97/8 Pacific-OffTheGlass 15
97/8 PacificCrown 303
97/8 PcfcCrRoyal 101,-Lamp 15
97/8 PacificDynagon! 94
97/8 PcfcD-Dyn 11B, -Tandem 9
97/8 PacificInvincible 105
97/8 PacificParamount 138
98/9 PacificParamount 179
97/8 PacificRevolution 104
98/9 PaniniSticker 95, 249
97/8 Pinnacle 105
97/8 PinnacleBeAPlayer 26
97/8 PinnacleCertified 116
97/8 Pinn.Inside 33, -Track 30
96/7 PinnacleZenith 123
96/7 SB'AutColl-Aut.
97/8 Score 249
97/8 Score(PHA) 12
96/7 SelectCertified 120
96/7 SP 117
97/8 SPAuthentic 117, S25
98/9 Topps SB30
96/7 UpperDeck 309
97/8 UD 122, SG59, T15B
96/7 UDBlackDiamond 68
97/8 UDBlackDiamond 8
97/8 UDCollChoice 187
97/8 UpperDeckIce 49
97/8 VisionsSig 40, A20, -Aut.
96/7 PHA/OceanSpray

ZUBYCK, JOHN
96/7 Guelph 4

ZUK, GREG
84/5 KelownaWings&WHL 5
83/4 KelownaWings

ZUKE, MIKE
80/1 OPC/Topps 209
81/2 OPC 299, Topps(W) 124
82/3 O-Pee-Chee 313
83/4 O-Pee-Chee 322
84/5 O-Pee-Chee 80, Topps 63
85/6 OPC/Topps 19
81/2 opcSticker 132
84/5 opcSticker 195
82/3 Post
83/4 HFD/JuniorWhalers
84/5 HFD/JuniorWhalers
85/6 HFD/JuniorWhalers

ZUKE, MIKE
93/4 Slapshot(SSMarie
89/90 SSMarie 26
93/4 SSMarie 32
96/7 SSMarie

ZUKIWSKY, JARRETT
90/1 SketchWHL 247
91/2 SketchWHL 284
89/90 Victoria

ZUKIWSKY, JON
95/6 Bowman P40
93/4 RedDeer
95/6 RedDeer

ZULTEK, MATT
97/8 Bowman 132

ZULYNIAK, SHANE
90/1 SketchWHL 278
91/2 SketchWHL 264
90/1 PrinceAlbert
91/2 PrinceAlbert
93/4 PrinceAlbert

ZURBA, PETER
91/2 AvantGardeBCJ 13
92/3 BCJHL 189

ZWAKMAN, GREG
92/3 Minnesota
93/4 Minnesota
94/5 Minnesota

ZWIJACK, TIM
80/1 SSMarie

ZWIKEL, ALAIN
79 PaniniSticker 340

ZWYER, DAVE
92/3 MPSPhotoSJHL 148

ZYTYNSKY, TARAS
83/4 Springfield 24
79/80 Montréal, -B&W

ZYUZIN, ANDREI
96/7 AllSportPPF 77, 197
95/6 Classic 69, -Aut
95/6 FutureLegends-SSD 8
97/8 Omega 208
98/9 Pacific 394
96/7 SB'AutColl 50, -Aut
98/9 SPx"Finite" 134
98/9 UDChoice 179
97/8 S.J/PacificBellSheet (x2)

ZYWITZA, SVEN
94/5 DEL 13
95/6 DEL 14
96/7 DEL 14

GLOSSARY OF TERMS AND ABBREVIATIONS

ACC	American Card Catalogue coding system. Candy and gum card sets are noted with a "V" (ie. V304A O-Pee-Chee) while cigarette cards are noted with a "C" (ie. C55 Imperial Tobacco).
AHL	American Hockey League
Ana.	Mighty Ducks of Anaheim
AS	All-Star
ATG	All-Time Great
Atl.	Atlanta Flames
Aut.	Austria
AW	Award Winners
BCJHL	British Columbia Junior Hockey League
Bos.	Boston Bruins
Brand Name	A card set's name. The name is most often found on the face of the card.
Buf.	Buffalo Sabres
Cal.	California Golden Seals
Car.	Carolina Hurricanes
Cdn.	Canada
Cgy.	Calgary Flames
Chi.	Chicago Blackhawks
CL	Checklist
Cle.	Cleveland Barons
CIS.	Commonwealth of Independent States
Col.	Colorado Rockies
Col.	Colorado Avalanche
CSR	Czechoslovakia
Cze.	Czech Republic
Dal.	Dallas Stars
Det.	Detroit Red Wings
DT	Dream Team
ECHL	East Coast Hockey League
Edm.	Edmonton Oilers
Error (Err.)	Error cards include misspellings, mistaken photos and wrong bios. Each card's error is listed in brackets after the card.
Fin.	Finland
Fla.	Florida Panthers
Fra.	France
G	Goalie
Ger.	Germany
GM	General Manager
G.B.	Great Britain
Hfd.	Hartford Whalers
HL	Highlight
HOF	Hall of Fame
IHL	International Hockey League
Ita.	Italy
K.C.	Kansas City Scouts
L.A.	Los Angeles Kings
LC	Last Card
LL	League Leader(s)
Min.	Minnesota North Stars
Mtl.	Montréal Canadiens
MVP	Most Valuable Player
NHL	National Hockey League
NHLPA	National Hockey League Players' Association
N.J.	New Jersey Devils
No #	No number on card
Nor.	Norway
NYI.	New York Islanders
NYR.	New York Rangers
Oak.	Oakland Seals
Ott.	Ottawa Senators
P.E.I.	Prince Edward Island
Pha.	Philadelphia Flyers
Pho.	Phoenix Roadrunners
PHPA	Professional Hockey Players' Association
Pgh.	Pittsburgh Penguins
OHL	Ontario Hockey League
QMJHL	Québec Major Junior Hockey League
Que.	Québec Nordiques
RC	Rookie Card. As outlined in *The Rookie Card Checklist*, a Rookie Card is a player's first appearance in a regular issued NHL licensed card set. A player's rookie card can be from one year only and must be in a set featuring current NHL players. Retrospective, minor league, major junior, European league, draft pick and tournament sets do not have rookie cards. Insert/chase cards (including parallel sets), regional, food and other oddball sets are also not recognized as rookie cards, European issued NHL sets (specifically, Parkhurst) do have rookie cards, as do WHA sets (specifically, O-Pee-Chee) from the 1970's. A player can have only one rookie card from each brand set. The player's regular card in a set is considered his rookie card. Draft pick and tournament subset cards (such as World Juniors) may be classified as rookie cards. A player's rookie card may not be from the same year as their actual NHL rookie season. Rookie cards do not necessarily feature a player in an NHL uniform. A player does not have rookie cards in every set from his given rookie card year. Cards identified with "Rookie" or "Rookie Card" by the company are not necessarily true rookie cards. Not every player has a rookie card; some players have only one rookie card while others may have as many as ten or more.
RB	Record Breaker
Rus.	Russia
S.J.	San Jose Sharks
SJHL	Saskatchewan Junior Hockey League
Slo.	Slovakia
Stl.	St. Louis Blues
Sui.	Switzerland
Swe.	Sweden
T.B.	Tampa Bay Lightning
TC	Team Card or Checklist
TL	Team Leader(s)
Tor.	Toronto Maple Leafs
USCL	United States College League
USA.	United States of America
Van.	Vancouver Canucks
w/	with
WHA	World Hockey Association
WHL	Western Hockey League
Wpg.	Winnipeg Jets
Wsh.	Washington Capitals
USSR	Union of Soviet Socialist Republics
xcx	Cameo appearance. Another player is shown visibly on some-one else's card.
/b	Card Back

Alphabetical Directory of Card Issuers

Books on Numismatics and Collectables

The Charlton Standard Catalogue of Canadian Coins - 53rd edition
No other coin catalogue offers so much! The obverse and reverse of each coin is fully illustrated. Canadian commercial and commemorative coins from the 1600s to the 1990s are presented, including specimen sets, collector coins and test tokens. Details are given about the designer, modeller, die axis, composition and size. A general introduction to Canadian numismatics, grading tips and information on the production of coins are also provided.
344 pages; 5-1/2" x 8-1/2"; softcover;
B204 - $12.95 Cdn. ($9.95 U.S.)

The Charlton Standard Catalogue of Canadian Government Paper Money - 11th edition
Over 300 years of Canadian paper money. This new edition illustrates and prices all Canadian government paper money from the French colonial issues of 1685 to the current Bank of Canada notes. Army bills, provincial issues, municipal notes, Province of Canada bills, Dominion of Canada issues, special serial numbers and paper money errors are all included. The introduction gives a history of paper money in Canada, useful terminology, and tips on grading notes.
328 pages; 5-1/2" x 8-1/2"; softcover;
B205 - $19.95 Cdn. ($17.95 U.S.)

The 1999 Charlton Coin Guide - 38th edition
An essential guide for pricing your collection. This catalogue lists, illustrates and prices all Canadian, Newfoundland and Maritime coinage, as well as Canadian medals, tokens and paper money. Also included are collector issues, Olympic coins and U.S. and world gold coins.
120 pages; 5-1/2" x 8-1/2"; softcover;
B209 - $4.95 Cdn. ($3.95 U.S.)

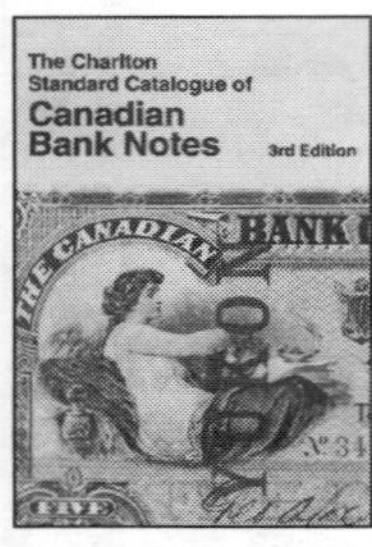

The Charlton Standard Catalogue of Canadian Bank Notes - 3rd edition
More information than in any other book on Canadian bank notes. All the bank notes produced in Canada since the 1800s, from the Bank of Acadia to The Zimmerman Bank are in this one easy-to-use, illustrated reference. A brief history of each of the banks is also included with detailed explanations of face and back designs. For this edition a team of numismatic experts has expanded the data and updated the prices.
550 pages; 8-1/2" x 11"; softcover;
B206 - $59.95 Cdn. ($45.95 U.S.)

The Charlton Canadian Numismatic Library
Features of this CD-ROM include a zoom-in function for bank notes which allows the viewer to closely examine the notes; a Full Text Retrieval search engine allows you to look for specific coins, bank notes, topics and values using key words or search variables; a "cut and paste" feature allows you to update the spreadsheet you currently use to manage your collection; a Master Coin Collection spreadsheet is included in Excel and Lotus 123. Contains the complete text and illustrations of the Canadian Coin 52nd edition and the Government Paper Money 10th edition.
CD205 - $24.95 Cdn. ($19.95 U.S.)

The Charlton Standard Catalogue of Royal Doulton Beswick Figurines - 6th edition, Jean Dale
The most authoritative source for all Royal Doulton figurines. Over 3,500 models are listed, priced and illustrated, along with details of their sizes, colour, designers, issue dates and varieties. Vellum and stoneware figurines produced at the Lambeth Studio, HN and M series models are all included in this edition. Also featured are tips on building a collection, backstamps and dating and an informative history of the factory by renowned Doulton historian Louise Irvine.
478 pages; 7" x 9"; softcover;
B105 - $29.95 Cdn. ($24.95 U.S.)

The Charlton Standard Catalogue of Royal Doulton Animals - 2nd edition, Jean Dale
Complete and comprehensive listings of all the animal models issued by Royal Doulton. New additions are the early stoneware animal figures of George Tinworth, Mark Marshall, Leslie Harradine and John Broad. There are more than 1,200 illustrations, complete with detailed listings of each model.
544 pages; 7" x 9"; softcover;
B104 - $29.95 Cdn. ($24.95 U.S.)

The Charlton Standard Catalogue of Royal Doulton Beswick Jugs - 4th edition, Jean Dale
The most comprehensive guide to Royal Doulton and Beswick jugs. This catalogue features over 550 up-to-date listings and prices for all toby and character jugs, liquor containers and loving cups produced by Royal Doulton, plus a chapter on the toby and character jugs produced by the John Beswick Studio. Tips on how to start and build your own collection, sections on backstamps, handle variations, special commissions, prototypes and promotional items are also included.
672 pages; 7" x 9"; softcover;
B114 - $29.95 Cdn. ($24.95 U.S.)

The Charlton Standard Catalogue of Royal Doulton Beswick Storybook Figurines - 4th edition, Jean Dale
This illustrated catalogue covers figurines from Alice in Wonderland, Beatrix Potter and Bunnykins to Little Likeables, The Pig Prom and Walt Disney. More than 375 photographs complete with name, number, designer, dates of issue, discontinued dates and varieties, as well as a complete alphabetical and model number indices for easy cross-referencing.
344 pages; 7" x 9"; softcover;
B103 - $24.95 Cdn. ($19.95 U.S.)

The Charlton Standard Catalogue of Royal Doulton Beswick Storybook Figurines CD-ROM - 4th edition, Jean Dale
This medium provides a simple new way to price and catalogue all storybook figurines. Each piece is illustrated in COLOUR with an accompanying backstamp and all the data that is found in the book. A full text retrieval search engine makes it easy to quickly locate any figurine. A built-in spreadsheet conversion program allows the collector to record the pricing and colourway details in Lotus 123 and Excel spreadsheet programs.
CD126 - $24.95 Cdn. ($19.95 U.S.)

FOR COMPLETE ORDERING INFORMATION CONTACT US

✦ www.charltonpress.com ✦ e-mail: chpress@charltonpress.com
✦ Tel.: 1-800-442-6042 ✦ Fax: 1-800-442-1542

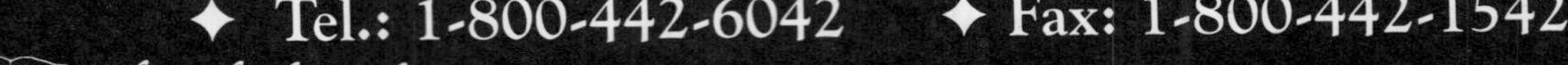

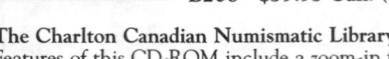